The

EUROPA WORLD OF LEARNING

2008

58th Edition

VOLUME II

NAMIBIA–ZIMBABWE
INDEX

Routledge
Taylor & Francis Group

LONDON AND NEW YORK

First published 1947
Fifty-eighth Edition 2007
© **Routledge 2007**

Albert House, 1–4 Singer Street, London, EC2A 4BQ, United Kingdom
(Routledge is an imprint of the Taylor & Francis Group, an Informa business)

ISBN13: 978-1-85743-436-1 (The Set)
ISBN13: 978-1-85743-459-0 (Vol. II)

ISSN 0084-2117

Library of Congress Catalog Card Number 47-30172

Editor: Anthony Gladman

Freelance editorial team: Rebecca Bomford, Karina Holly, Eric Smith,
Nicholas Walmsley, Kristina Wischenkämper, Gareth Wyn Jones

Associate Editor, Directory Research: James Middleton

Editorial Clerical Assistant: Charley McCartney

Editorial Director: Paul Kelly

Typeset in New Century Schoolbook

Typeset by Data Standards Limited, Frome, Somerset
Printed and bound in Great Britain by Polestar Wheatons, Exeter

FOREWORD

THE EUROPA WORLD OF LEARNING first appeared in 1947, and has since become established as an authoritative reference work on academic institutions all over the world. This is the fifty-eighth edition, and appears in two-volume format. Volume I contains introductory essays on academic subjects, information on more than 550 international organizations, and individual chapters on academic institutions in countries from Afghanistan to Myanmar. Volume II contains chapters on countries from Namibia to Zimbabwe, and a comprehensive index of institutions in both volumes.

In this edition, for the first time, introductory surveys feature in every chapter. Information on regulatory and representative bodies in the higher education sector has been included in selected chapters. The section covers ministries, government agencies and departments, funding and accrediting bodies and other organizations of national importance.

We have once again tried to ensure that we provide the latest possible information about institutions included in THE EUROPA WORLD OF LEARNING. Every year, a revision form showing current entry details is sent to each institution; research on the internet and in the world's press, as well as contact with official sources all over the world, supplements this method of revision.

We are always grateful to those individuals and organizations who help us to bring our information up to date with their prompt replies. We particularly emphasize the necessity for revised entries to be returned to us without delay, since important material may otherwise be held over until a later edition. Only by maintaining a strict timetable can the regular production of such a large work as THE EUROPA WORLD OF LEARNING be assured.

We should like to point out that, in the sections on Universities and Colleges, our classification usually follows the practice of the country concerned. This in no way implies any official evaluation on our part. We suggest that readers who are interested in the matter of the equivalence of institutions, degrees or diplomas, should correspond directly with the institutions concerned, or with the national or international bodies set up for this purpose. For selected countries, these organizations now appear in the regulatory and representative bodies section under the heading Accreditation.

An online version of THE EUROPA WORLD OF LEARNING complements the print edition, providing a full range of sophisticated search and browse functions, and regular updates of content. The site offers an unprecedented level of access to institutions of higher education and learning world-wide, and to the people who work within them. For further details of the online version, please see page vi.

August 2007

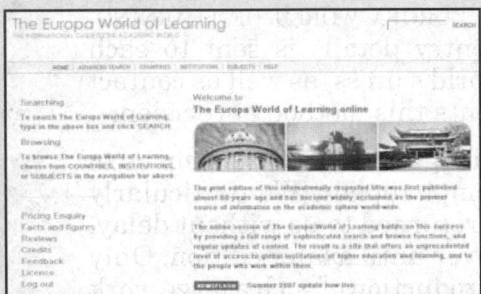

CONTENTS

SPECIAL NOTE

Entries within the sections Learned Societies and Research Institutes
are grouped under the following headings

GENERAL

AGRICULTURE, FISHERIES AND VETERINARY
    SCIENCE

ARCHITECTURE AND TOWN PLANNING

BIBLIOGRAPHY, LIBRARY SCIENCE AND
    MUSEOLOGY

ECONOMICS, LAW AND POLITICS

EDUCATION

FINE AND PERFORMING ARTS

HISTORY, GEOGRAPHY AND ARCHAEOLOGY

LANGUAGE AND LITERATURE

MEDICINE

NATURAL SCIENCES
    General
    Biological Sciences
    Mathematical Sciences
    Physical Sciences

PHILOSOPHY AND PSYCHOLOGY

RELIGION, SOCIOLOGY AND ANTHROPOLOGY

TECHNOLOGY

ABBREVIATIONS

AB — Alberta
Abog. — Abogado (lawyer)
Acad. — Academy; Academician
ACT — Australian Capital Territory
Admin. — Administrative, Administration
AFRC — Agricultural and Food Research Council
AIDS — acquired immunodeficiency syndrome
AK — Alaska
AL — Alabama
ALECSO — Arab League Educational, Cultural and Scientific Organization
Apdo — Apartado (Post Box)
approx. — approximately
AR. — Arkansas
Arq. — Arquiteto (Portuguese), Arquitecto (Spanish)
ASCE — American Society of Civil Engineers
Asscn — Association
Assoc. — Associate
Asst — Assistant
ATC — Art Teacher's Certificate
Atty — Attorney
AUPELF — Association des Universités Partiellement ou Entièrement de Langue Française
Avda — Avenida
Ave — Avenue
Avv. — Avvocato (Advocate)
AZ — Arizona

BA — Bachelor of Arts
BC — British Columbia
Bd, Bld, Blv., Blvd — Boulevard
Bdul — Bulevardul
BILD — Bureau International de Liaison et de Documentation
Bldg — Building
Blvr — Bulevar
BP — Boîte postale
Br.(s) — Branch(es)
Brig. — Brigadier
BRGM — Bureau de Recherches Géologiques et Minières
Bro. — Brother
BSc — Bachelor of Science
B/TEC — Bachelor of Technology
Bul. — Bulvar (boulevard)
bulv. — bulvarỹs (boulevard)

c. — circa (approximately)
CA — California
CAE — College of Advanced Education
CAR — Central African Republic
Ccl — Council
CD-ROM — compact disk read only memory
CEA — Commissariat à l'Energie Atomique
CEO — Chief Executive Officer
CERN — European Organization for Nuclear Research
CGIAR — Consultative Group on International Agricultural Research
Chair. — Chairman, Chairwoman, Chairperson
CIRAD — Centre de Coopération Internationale en Recherche Agronomique pour le Développement

Cmdr — Commander
CNAA — Council for National Academic Awards
CNR — Consiglio Nazionale delle Ricerche
cnr — corner
CNRS — Centre National de la Recherche Scientifique
Co — Company; County
CO — Colorado
c/o — care of
Col — Colonel
colln — Collection
Comm. — Commission
Commr — Commissioner
Conf. — Conference
Corpn — Corporation
Corresp. — Correspondent, Corresponding
CP — Case postale; Casella postale; Caixa postal (Post Box)
Cr — Contador
CSIRO — Commonwealth Scientific and Industrial Research Organization
CT — Connecticut
CTFT — Centre Technique Forestier Tropical
Cttee — Committee
DC — District of Colombia
DE — Delaware
Del. — Delegate, delegation
Dept — Department
Deptl — Departmental
DES — Department of Education and Science
devt — development
DF — Distrito Federal
Dipl. — Diploma
Dir — Director
Dist. — District
Div.(s) — Division(s)
Doc. — Docent
Dott. — Dottore
Dott.ssa — Dottoressa
Doz. — Dozent (lecturer)
Dr — Doctor
Dr. — Drive
Dra — Doctora
Dr Hab. — Doktor Habilitowany (Assistant Professor)
Drs — Doctorandus (Dutch or Indonesian higher degree)
DSIR — Department of Scientific and Industrial Research

E — East; Eastern
EC — European Community
Econ. — Economics
ECOSOC — Economic and Social Council (UN)
ECSC — European Coal and Steel Community
Edif. — Edificio (Building)
edn — edition
EEC — European Economic Community
e.g. — exempli gratia
Eng. — Engineer; Engineering
EngD — Doctor of Engineering
ESA — European Space Agency
ESCAP — Economic and Social Commission for Asia and the Pacific

esp. — especially
ESRC — Economic and Social Research Council
Est. — Established
etc. — et cetera
ETH — Eidgenössische Technische Hochschule
EU — European Union
Exec. — Executive

f. — founded
FAO — Food and Agriculture Organization
Fed. — Federation, Federal
FL — Florida
fmr(ly) — former(ly)
Fr — Father
F.t.e. — Full-time equivalent (staff)
F.U.T. — Federal University of Technology

GA — Georgia
Gdns — Gardens
Gen. — General
Gov. — Governor
Govt — Government

HQ — Headquarters
HE — His Eminence; His (Her) Excellency
HI — Hawaii
HIV — human immunodeficiency virus
HM — His (Her) Majesty
HND — Higher National Diploma
Hon. — Honourable; Honorary
HRH — His (Her) Royal Highness

IA — Iowa
IAEA — International Atomic Energy Agency
IAU — International Astronomical Union
IBE — International Bureau of Education
ICPHS — International Council for Philosophy and Humanistic Studies
ICSU — International Council of Scientific Unions
ID — Idaho
IEC — International Electrotechnical Commission
IEMVT — Institut d'Elevage et de Médecine Vétérinaire des Pays Tropicaux
IFAN — Institut Fondamental d'Afrique Noire
IFLA — International Federation of Library Associations and Institutions
IGU — International Geographical Union
IICA — Instituto Interamericano de Cooperación para la Agricultura
IL — Illinois
ILO — International Labour Organisation
IMU — International Mathematical Union
IN — Indiana
Inc. — Incorporated
incl. — include(s), including
Ind. — Independent

Ing.	Engineer
INRA	Institut National de la Recherche Agronomique
Instn	Institution
Int.	International
Ir	Ingénieur (Engineer)
IRAT	Institut de Recherches Agronomiques Tropicales et des Cultures Vivrières
IRC	Institut de Recherches sur le Caoutchouc
IRCC	Institut de Recherches du Café, du Cacao et autres plantes stimulantes
IRCT	Institut de Recherches du Coton et des Textiles Exotiques
IRFA	Institut de Recherches sur les Fruits et Agrumes
IRHO	Institut de Recherches pour les Huiles et Oléagineux
irreg.	irregular
ISME	International Society for Music Education
ISO	International Organization for Standardization
IUB	International Union of Biochemistry
IUBS	International Union of Biological Sciences
IUCr	International Union of Crystallography
IUGG	International Union of Geodesy and Geophysics
IUGS	International Union of Geological Sciences
IUHPS	International Union of the History and Philosophy of Science
IUIS	International Union of Immunological Societies
IUMS	International Union of Microbiological Societies
IUNS	International Union of Nutritional Sciences
IUPAB	International Union of Pure and Applied Biophysics
IUPAC	International Union of Pure and Applied Chemistry
IUPAP	International Union of Pure and Applied Physics
IUPHAR	International Union of Pharmacology
IUPS	International Union of Physiological Sciences
IUTAM	International Union of Theoretical and Applied Mechanics
Jl	Jalan
Jr	Junior
JSC	Joint Stock Company
jt(ly)	joint(ly)
km	kilometre(s)
KS	Kansas
küç.	küçasi (street)
kv.	kvartal (apartment block), kvartira (apartment)
KY	Kentucky
LA	Louisiana
Lic.	Licenciado
Licda	Licenciada
Lt	Lieutenant
Ltd	Limited
m	metre(s)
m.	million
MA	Master of Arts; Massachusetts
Mag.	Magister (master)
Man.	Manager, Managing

MB	Manitoba
MD	Maryland
ME	Maine
Mem.(s)	Member(s)
Mgr	Monseigneur; Monsignor;
Magister	(Master's degree)
MI	Michigan
Min.	Minister; Ministry
misc.	miscellaneous
MIT	Massachusetts Institute of Technology
mm	millimetre(s)
MN	Minnesota
MO	Missouri
MRC	Medical Research Council
MS	Master of Science; Mississippi
MSc	Master of Science
MSS	Manuscripts
MT	Montana
N	North; Northern
nám	náměstí (square)
NASA	National Aeronautics and Space Administration
Nat.	National
NB	New Brunswick
NC	North Carolina
ND	North Dakota; National Diploma
NE	Nebraska
NERC	Natural Environment Research Council
NGO	Non-Governmental Organization
NH	New Hampshire
NJ	New Jersey
NL	Newfoundland and Labrador
NM	New Mexico
NS	Nova Scotia
NSW	New South Wales
NT	Northwest Territories
NU	Nunavut Territory
NV	Nevada
NY	New York
NZ	New Zealand
OAS	Organization of American States
obl.	oblast
ODA	Overseas Development Administration
OECD	Organisation for Economic Co-operation and Development
Of.	Oficina
OFS	Orange Free State
OH	Ohio
OIC	Organization of the Islamic Conference
OK	Oklahoma
On.	Onorevole (Italian)
ON	Ontario
ONERA	Office National d'Etudes et de Recherches Aérospatiales
opp.	opposite
OR	Oregon
Org.	Organization
OU	Open University
PA	Pennsylvania
PE	Prince Edward Island
PEN	Poets, Playwrights, Essayists, Editors and Novelists (Club)
PhD	Doctor of Philosophy
pl.	place; platz; ploshchad (square)
PMB	Private Mail Bag
POB	Post Office Box
pr.	prospekt (avenue)
Pres.	President
Prin.	Principal
Prof.	Professor
Publ.(s)	Publication(s)

QC	Québec
q.v.	quod vide (to which refer)
rd	road
Rep.	Representative; Represented
retd	retired
Rev.	Reverend
RI	Rhode Island
RP	Révérend Père
Rr.	Rruga
Rt Hon.	Right Honourable
Rt Rev.	Right Reverend
S	South; Southern
SA	South Africa(n); South Australia
SAR	Special Administrative Region
SC	South Carolina
SD	South Dakota
SDI	Selective Dissemination of Information
Sec.	Secretary
SERC	Science and Engineering Research Council
SK	Saskatchewan
s/n	sin número (without number)
Soc.	Society
spec.	special
Sq.	Square
Sr	Senior
St	Saint, Sint; Street
Sta	Santa
Ste	Sainte
str.	strada, stradă, Strasse (street)
tel.	telephone
TN	Tennessee
Treas.	Treasurer
TX	Texas
u.	utca (street)
UK	United Kingdom
ul.	ulica, ulitsa (street)
UN	United Nations
UNDP	United Nations Development Programme
UNESCO	United Nations Educational, Scientific and Cultural Organization
UNICEF	United Nations International Children's Emergency Fund
Univ.	University
UNRWA	United Nations Relief and Works Agency
UNU	United Nations University
URSI	Union Radio-Scientifique Internationale
USA	United States of America
USIS	United States Information Service
UT	Utah
VA	Virginia
Vols	Volumes
VT	Vermont
vul.	vulitsa, vulytsa (sreet)
W	West; Western
WA	Western Australia; Washington (State)
WHO	World Health Organization
WI	Wisconsin
WTO	World Trade Organization
WV	West Virginia
WY	Wyoming
YT	Yukon Territory

INTERNATIONAL TELEPHONE CODES

To make international calls to telephone and fax numbers listed in *The Europa World of Learning*, dial the international code of the country from which you are calling, followed by the appropriate country code for the institution you wish to call (listed below), followed by the area code (if applicable) and telephone or fax number listed in the entry.

	Country code	+ or – GMT*
Afghanistan	93	+4½
Albania	355	+1
Algeria	213	+1
Andorra	376	+1
Angola	244	+1
Antigua and Barbuda	1 268	–4
Argentina	54	–3
Armenia	374	+4
Australia	61	+8 to +10
Australian External Territories:		
Australian Antarctic Territory	672	+3 to +10
Christmas Island	61	+7
Cocos (Keeling) Islands	61	+6½
Norfolk Island	672	+11½
Austria	43	+1
Azerbaijan	994	+5
Bahamas	1 242	–5
Bahrain	973	+3
Bangladesh	880	+6
Barbados	1 246	–4
Belarus	375	+2
Belgium	32	+1
Belize	501	–6
Benin	229	+1
Bhutan	975	+6
Bolivia	591	–4
Bosnia and Herzegovina	387	+1
Botswana	267	+2
Brazil	55	–3 to –4
Brunei	673	+8
Bulgaria	359	+2
Burkina Faso	226	0
Burundi	257	+2
Cambodia	855	+7
Cameroon	237	+1
Canada	1	–3 to –8
Cape Verde	238	–1
Central African Republic	236	+1
Chad	235	+1
Chile	56	–4
China, People's Republic	86	+8
Special Administrative Regions:		
Hong Kong	852	+8
Macao	853	+8
China (Taiwan)	886	+8
Colombia	57	–5
Comoros	269	+3
Congo, Democratic Republic	243	+1
Congo, Republic	242	+1
Costa Rica	506	–6
Côte d'Ivoire	225	0
Croatia	385	+1

	Country code	+ or – GMT*
Cuba	53	–5
Cyprus	357	+2
	90 3-	
'Turkish Republic of Northern Cyprus'	92	+2
Czech Republic	420	+1
Denmark	45	+1
Danish External Territories:		
Faroe Islands	298	0
Greenland	299	–1 to –4
Djibouti	253	+3
Dominica	1 767	–4
Dominican Republic	1 809	–4
Ecuador	593	–5
Egypt	20	+2
El Salvador	503	–6
Equatorial Guinea	240	+1
Eritrea	291	+3
Estonia	372	+2
Ethiopia	251	+3
Fiji	679	+12
Finland	358	+2
Finnish External Territory:		
Åland Islands	358	+2
France	33	+1
French Overseas Regions and Departments:		
French Guiana	594	–3
Guadeloupe	590	–4
Martinique	596	–4
Réunion	262	+4
French Overseas Collectivities:		
French Polynesia	689	–9 to –10
Mayotte	262	+3
Saint Pierre and Miquelon	508	–3
Wallis and Futuna Islands	681	+12
Other French Overseas Territory:		
New Caledonia	687	+11
Gabon	241	+1
Gambia	220	0
Georgia	995	+4
Germany	49	+1
Ghana	233	0
Greece	30	+2
Grenada	1 473	–4
Guatemala	502	–6
Guinea	224	0
Guinea-Bissau	245	0
Guyana	592	–4
Haiti	509	–5
Honduras	504	–6
Hungary	36	+1
Iceland	354	0

	Country code	+ or – GMT*
India	91	+5½
Indonesia	62	+7 to +9
Iran	98	+3½
Iraq	964	+3
Ireland	353	0
Israel	972	+2
Italy	39	+1
Jamaica	1 876	–5
Japan	81	+9
Jordan	962	+2
Kazakhstan	7	+6
Kenya	254	+3
Kiribati	686	+12 to +13
Korea, Democratic People's Republic (North Korea)	850	+9
Korea, Republic (South Korea)	82	+9
Kuwait	965	+3
Kyrgyzstan	996	+5
Laos	856	+7
Latvia	371	+2
Lebanon	961	+2
Lesotho	266	+2
Liberia	231	0
Libya	218	+1
Liechtenstein	423	+1
Lithuania	370	+2
Luxembourg	352	+1
Macedonia, former Yugoslav republic	389	+1
Madagascar	261	+3
Malawi	265	+2
Malaysia	60	+8
Maldives	960	+5
Mali	223	0
Malta	356	+1
Marshall Islands	692	+12
Mauritania	222	0
Mauritius	230	+4
Mexico	52	–6 to –7
Micronesia, Federated States	691	+10 to +11
Moldova	373	+2
Monaco	377	+1
Mongolia	976	+7 to +9
Montenegro	382	+1
Morocco	212	0
Mozambique	258	+2
Myanmar	95	+6½
Namibia	264	+2
Nauru	674	+12
Nepal	977	+5¾
Netherlands	31	+1
Netherlands Dependencies:		
Aruba	297	–4
Netherlands Antilles	599	–4
New Zealand	64	+12
New Zealand's Dependent and Associated Territories:		
Tokelau	690	–10
Cook Islands	682	–10
Niue	683	–11
Nicaragua	505	–6
Niger	227	+1
Nigeria	234	+1
Norway	47	+1

	Country code	+ or – GMT*
Norwegian External Territory:		
Svalbard	47	+1
Oman	968	+4
Pakistan	92	+5
Palau	680	+9
Palestinian Autonomous Areas	970 or 97-	
	2	+2
Panama	507	–5
Papua New Guinea	675	+10
Paraguay	595	–4
Peru	51	–5
Philippines	63	+8
Poland	48	+1
Portugal	351	0
Qatar	974	+3
Romania	40	+2
Russian Federation	7	+2 to +12
Rwanda	250	+2
Saint Christopher and Nevis	1 869	–4
Saint Lucia	1 758	–4
Saint Vincent and the Grenadines	1 784	–4
Samoa	685	–11
San Marino	378	+1
São Tomé and Príncipe	239	0
Saudi Arabia	966	+3
Senegal	221	0
Serbia	381	+1
Seychelles	248	+4
Sierra Leone	232	0
Singapore	65	+8
Slovakia	421	+1
Slovenia	386	+1
Solomon Islands	677	+11
Somalia	252	+3
South Africa	27	+2
Spain	34	+1
Sri Lanka	94	+5½
Sudan	249	+2
Suriname	597	–3
Swaziland	268	+2
Sweden	46	+1
Switzerland	41	+1
Syria	963	+2
Tajikistan	992	+5
Tanzania	255	+3
Thailand	66	+7
Timor-Leste	670	+9
Togo	228	0
Tonga	676	+13
Trinidad and Tobago	1 868	–4
Tunisia	216	+1
Turkey	90	+2
Turkmenistan	993	+5
Tuvalu	688	+12
Uganda	256	+3
Ukraine	380	+2
United Arab Emirates	971	+4
United Kingdom	44	0
United Kingdom Crown Dependencies	44	0
United Kingdom Overseas Territories:		

	Country code	+ or − GMT*
Anguilla	1 264	−4
Ascension Island	247	0
Bermuda	1 441	−4
British Virgin Islands	1 284	−4
Cayman Islands	1 345	−5
Diego Garcia (British Indian Ocean Territory)	246	+5
Falkland Islands	500	−4
Gibraltar	350	+1
Montserrat	1 664	−4
Pitcairn Islands	872	−8
Saint Helena	290	0
Tristan da Cunha	290	0
Turks and Caicos Islands	1 649	−5
United States of America	1	−5 to −10
United States Commonwealth Territories:		
Northern Mariana Islands	1 670	+10
Puerto Rico	1 787	−4
United States External Territories:		
American Samoa	1 684	−11
Guam	1 671	+10
United States Virgin Islands	1 340	−4
Uruguay	598	−3
Uzbekistan	998	+5
Vanuatu	678	+11
Vatican City	39	+1
Venezuela	58	−4
Viet Nam	84	+7
Yemen	967	+3
Zambia	260	+2
Zimbabwe	263	+2

* Time difference in hours + or − Greenwich Mean Time (GMT). The times listed compare the standard (winter) times. Some countries adopt Summer (Daylight Saving) Time — i.e. +1 hour — for part of the year.

NAMIBIA

The Higher Education System

From 1925 Namibia was under South African control, first as a League of Nations protectorate and then as a *de facto* province. Independence was finally achieved in 1990. The University of Namibia was founded in 1992, based on the former Windhoek College of Education, following a report by a Presidential commission into the state of higher education in Namibia. In 2002/03 13,536 students were enrolled in tertiary education.

Admission to the University is based upon results in the International General Certificate of Secondary Education examinations; however, Higher International General Certificate of Secondary Education passes are given more weight when applicants are being evaluated. Non-degree university-level qualifications include two- or three-year Certificate courses and three- or four-year Diploma courses. Undergraduate Bachelors degree programmes last four years and are offered in most subjects fields. The two foremost postgraduate degrees are the Masters and the Doctorate; the former is a one-year (full-time) or three-year (part-time) course, and the latter requires at least two years of study following the Masters.

Post-secondary technical and vocational education is offered by the Polytechnic of Namibia (founded 1980), and qualifications include Certificate (one year), Diploma (three years) and Bachelors of Technology.

Learned Societies

GENERAL

Namibia Scientific Society: POB 67, Windhoek 9000; tel. (61) 225372; fax (61) 226846; e-mail nwg@iafrica.com.na; f. 1925; ornithology, spelaeology, botany, archaeology, herpetology, astronomy, ethnology; 1,100 mems (900 ordinary, 200 exchange); library of 8,000 vols; Pres. B. GUHRING; publs *Journal* (annually), *Mitteilungen/Newsletter/Nuusbrief, Mitteilungen der Ornithologischen Arbeitsgruppe.*

UNESCO Office Windhoek: Windhoek 9000, POB 24519, Windhoek; Located at: Oppenheimer House, 5 Brahms St, Windhoek West, Windhoek; tel. (61) 2917220; fax (61) 2917000; e-mail windhoek@unesco.org; designated Cluster Office for Angola, Lesotho, Namibia, South Africa and Swaziland; Dir JOHNNY MCCLAIN.

ARCHITECTURE AND TOWN PLANNING

Namibia Institute of Architects: Love St, POB 1478, Windhoek; tel. (61) 231559; fax (61) 232007; e-mail nia@mweb.com.na; f. 1952; 98 mems; Pres. DEON PRETORIUS.

LANGUAGE AND LITERATURE

British Council: 1–5 Fidel Castro St, Windhoek; tel. (61) 226776; fax (61) 227530; e-mail general.enquiries@britishcouncil.org.na; internet www.britishcouncil.org/namibia; the office in Pretoria, South Africa, is responsible for all British Council work in Namibia (see chapter on South Africa); Officer in Charge PATIENCE MAHLALELA.

Goethe-Zentrum/Namibisch-Deutsche Stiftung für kulturelle Zusammenarbeit (Goethe-Centre/Namibian-German Institute for Cultural Co-operation): 1–5 Fidel Castro St, POB 1208, 9000 Windhoek; tel. (61) 225700; fax (01) 221256; e-mail ll@nads.org.na; internet www.goethe.de/af/win/deindex.htm; f. 1988; affiliated to Goethe-Institut (see chapter on Germany); promotes use of the German language in Namibia and cultural exchange between Namibia and Germany; Dir SABINE ERLENWEIN.

Research Institutes

NATURAL SCIENCES

Biological Sciences

Desert Ecological Research Unit of Namibia: POB 953, Walvis Bay; fax (64) 205197; e-mail gmk@mweb.com.na; internet www.drfn.com.na; f. 1963; research in Namib Desert and semi-arid Namibia, emphasizing basic and applied research, conservation biology, community applications, training and environmental education; library of 1,600 vols, 15,000 documents; Dir M. K. SEELY.

National Botanical Research Institute: c/o Ministry of Agriculture, Water and Rural Development, Private Bag 13184, Windhoek; tel. (61) 2029111; fax (61) 258153; e-mail info@nbri.org.na; f. 1953; herbarium colln of 74,000 plant specimens; gene bank colln of 2,500 seed accessions; botanical reference library; incorporates National Botanic Garden; library of 3,053 books, 320 periodicals; Head Dr GILLIAN L. MAGGS-KÖLLING.

Libraries and Archives

Swakopmund

Sam Cohen Library: POB 361, Swakopmund; tel. (64) 402695; fax (64) 400763; e-mail info@swakopmund-museum.org.na; internet www.swakopmund-museum.org.na; f. 1977; 10,000 vols on south-west Africa and Africana; attached to Museum Swakopmund (see below).

Windhoek

Namibian Agriculture and Water Information Centre: Private Bag 13184, Windhoek 9000; tel. (61) 2087763; fax (61) 2087776; e-mail hoffmannm@mawrd.gov.na; f. 1966; 30,555 books, 600 periodical titles; 284 theses, 69 videos, 4,200 pamphlets, 1,960 govt reports, 3,065 audiovisual items; depository for FAO publs; Librarian M. HOFFMANN.

National Archives of Namibia: Private Bag 13250, 1–9 Eugene Marais St, Windhoek 9000; tel. (61) 2935211; fax (61) 2935217; e-mail natarch@mec.gov.na; f. 1939; houses 7 km of govt records, private collns, 6,000 maps, 20,000 photographs, microforms, films, sound recordings, posters; 1,000 periodical titles and 9,000 other publs; Chief Archivist WERNER HILLEBRECHT.

National Library of Namibia: Eugene Marais St, Private Bag 13349, Windhoek; tel. (61) 2935111; fax (61) 2935308; e-mail jloubser@mec.gov.na; internet www.nln.gov.na; f. 1994; legal deposit and general reference library; deposit library for UN, WTO and World Bank publications; Head JOHAN LOUBSER; publ. *National Bibliography of Namibia* (every 3 years).

Windhoek Public Library: Private Bag 13183, Windhoek 9000; tel. (61) 224899; f. 1924; 75,000 vols; Librarian L. HANSMANN.

Museums and Art Galleries

Lüderitz

Lüderitz Museum: POB 512, Lüderitz 9000; tel. (63) 202346; fax (63) 2346; f. 1966; incorporates finds of Friedrich Eberlanz of archaeological, herpetological, botanical and mineralogical interest, incl. Bushman Stone Age tools; Supervisor G. SCHEELE-SCHMIDT.

Swakopmund

Museum Swakopmund: POB 361, Strand St, Swakopmund; tel. and fax (64) 402046; e-mail info@swakopmund-museum.org.na; internet www.swakopmund-museum.org.na; f. 1951; natural history, mineralogy, marine life, history, archaeology, ethnology, technology; Chair. M. WEBER; publ. newsletter (in three languages).

Windhoek

National Art Gallery of Namibia: POB 994, Windhoek 9000; tel. (61) 231160; fax (61) 240930; e-mail nagn@mweb.com.na; internet www.nagn.org.na; f. 1947; exhibitions, lectures, educational programmes; Dir A. H. EINS; publ. *Newsletter* (4 a year).

National Museum of Namibia: POB 1203, Windhoek; tel. (61) 276800; fax (61) 228636; e-mail library@natmus.cul.na; internet www.natmus.cul.na; f. 1907; natural history, history, anthropology, archaeology, education; library of 6,000 vols, 600 journal titles; Deputy Dir E. MOOMBOLAH GOAGOSES; publ. *Cimbebasia.*

University

UNIVERSITY OF NAMIBIA

Private Bag 13301, 340 Mandume Ndemu-
fayo Ave, Pioneerspark, Windhoek
Telephone: (61) 2063111
Fax: (61) 2063866
E-mail: registrar@unam.na
Internet: www.unam.na

Founded 1992 upon the dissolution of the
Academy, Windhoek
State control
Language of instruction: English
Academic year: January to November
Chancellor: HE Dr Sam S. Nujoma
Vice-Chancellor: Prof. Lazarus Hangula

Pro Vice-Chancellor (Academic Affairs and
Research): Zach J. N. Kazapua
Pro Vice-Chancellor (Administration and
Finance) (vacant): Geofrey Kiangi
Registrar (vacant)
Librarian: M. M. Viljoen
Library of 132,334 vols, 40,000 UNIN books
and documents, 498 periodicals
Number of teachers: 343
Number of students: 6,444 (4,017 full-time,
2,427 distance-learning)

DEANS

Faculty of Agriculture and Natural
Resources: Prof. I. Lupanga (acting)
Faculty of Economics and Management
Science: Prof. Andre du Pisani

Faculty of Education: Prof. P. K. Wainaina
Faculty of Humanities and Social Science:
Prof. A. G. Behrens
Faculty of Law: Prof. M. O. Hinz
Faculty of Medical and Health Sciences: Prof.
A. Van Dyk
Faculty of Science: Prof. E. M. R. Kiremire

ATTACHED RESEARCH INSTITUTES

Centre for External Studies: Dir Haa-
veshe Nekongo-Nielsen.
Human Rights Documentation Centre:
Dir Dr J. N. Horn.
Justice Training Centre: Dir Justice A. M.
Silungwe.
Language Centre: Dir R. K. Ndjoze-Ojo.

NAURU

The Higher Education System

During 1947–68 Nauru was a UN Trusteeship, administered by Australia on behalf of Australia, New Zealand and the United Kingdom. Independence was declared in 1968. There is a branch campus of the University of the South Pacific on the island but most Nauruans receive tertiary level education overseas.

Museums and Galleries

Aiwo

Arts and Crafts Centre: Aiwo, Nauru; tel. 444-3292; f. 1993; baskets, stone tools, fishing nets, a pandanus grater, *ingurig* (grass skirts made from hibiscus), paintings, photographs; spec. collns shells, written materials; organizes craft classes; access by arrangement with Ministry of Internal Affairs.

Nauru Phosphate Corporation Museum: Aiwo, Nauru; tel. 444-3382; fax 444-3791; f. 1995 by the Nauru Phosphate foundation; photographs and items from 20th century, paeticularly the Second World War, incl. Japanese weapons and ammunition, colonial-era cannons, Japanese pottery; access by arrangement with Ministry of Internal Affairs; reported to be closed pending settlement of island-wide land disputes.

University

UNIVERSITY OF THE SOUTH PACIFIC, NAURU CAMPUS

Private Bag, Nauru Post Office, Aiwo, Nauru 00674

Telephone: and fax 444-3774

E-mail: lauti_a@usp.ac.fj

Internet: www.usp.ac.fj/index.php?id=usp_nauru_home

Founded 1987

Campus Dir: ALAMANDA LAUTI

Library Officer: DALYS DANNANG

Library: periodicals, video cassettes and reference books; all documents in English.

NEPAL

The Higher Education System

There are five state universities in Nepal, the oldest of which is Tribhuvan University (founded in 1959). The main Beljhundi campus of the state-run Mahendra Sanskrit University (founded in 1986) was badly damaged during an arson attack in 2002, during which buildings, administrative records and library holdings were destroyed. There is one private university in Banepa. In 1999/2000 the universities had a total enrolment of more than 120,000 students. While the Ministry of Education and Sports administers the education system at the primary and the secondary levels, Tribhuvan University is responsible for developing curricula at college and Bachelors degree level.

Admission to higher education is on the basis of successful completion of the School Leaving Certificate or the Higher Secondary Certificate. Students with the Higher Secondary Certificate may enter directly onto Bachelors degree courses, whereas students with the School Leaving Certificate must obtain the Proficiency Certificate, a university-level course lasting two years which is regarded as the first cycle of university education. The second cycle of university-level education is the Bachelors degree, which lasts four years in most disciplines but slightly longer (five-and-a-half-years) in disciplines such as medicine, veterinary medicine and animal husbandry. Following the Bachelors degree the first postgraduate degree is the Masters, which is a two- to three-year course. Students seeking the Masters must undertake one year of National Development Service. The highest university-level degree is the Doctor of Philosophy, awarded after a final three-year period of study following the Masters.

The Directorate of Technical and Vocational education is the government agency with overall responsibility for provision of technical and vocational education, which is offered at various secondary levels.

Learned Societies

GENERAL

Royal Nepal Academy: Kamaladi, Kathmandu; tel. (1) 4221283; f. 1957; promotes Nepalese drama, music and literature; awards prizes annually; 178 mems; library of 10,562 vols, 4,697 periodicals; Vice-Chancellor MOHAN KOIRALA; publs *Kabita* (on Nepalese poetry, quarterly), *Prajna* (quarterly).

Royal Nepal Academy of Science and Technology (RONAST): POB 3323, Khumaltar, Lalitpur; tel. (1) 5547715; fax (1) 5547713; e-mail info@ronast.org.np; internet www.ronast.org.np; f. 1982; 157 mems; library of 10,000 vols, 150 periodicals; Chancellor THE PRIME MINISTER OF NEPAL; Vice-Chancellor Prof. Dr DAYANANDA BAJRACHARYA; Sec. Prof. Dr KRISHNA MARANDHAR; publs *RONAST Communicator* (4 a year), *SAT Journal* (annually).

UNESCO Office Kathmandu: Jawalakhel, POB 14391, Kathmandu; Located at: Ring Rd, Bansbari, Kathmandu; tel. (1) 5554769; fax (1) 5554450; e-mail kathmandu@unesco .org; internet www.unesco.org.np; Dir KOTO KANNO.

LANGUAGE AND LITERATURE

Alliance Française: Ganeshman Singh Path, Tripureshwor, POB 452 Kathmandu; tel. (1) 4242832; fax (1) 4242621; e-mail dafk@afk.wlink.com.np; internet www .france-in-nepal.org/frenchalliance/; offers courses and exams in French language and culture and promotes cultural exchange with France; Dir CHANTAL LAMA.

British Council: POB 640, Lainchaur, Kathmandu; tel. (1) 4410798; fax (1) 4410545; e-mail library@britishcouncil.org .np; internet www.britishcouncil.org/nepal; f. 1959; teaching centre; offers courses and exams in English language and British culture and promotes cultural exchange with the UK; 6,774 mems; library of 15,036 vols, 30 periodicals, 54 video cassettes, 219 audio items, DVDs and CD-ROMs; Dir JOHN FRY; Information Services Man. RAJU SHAKYA; publ. *E-Newsletter*.

Research Institutes

GENERAL

International Centre for Integrated Mountain Development (ICIMOD): Khumaltar, Lalitpur, POB 3226, Kathmandu; tel. (1) 5003222; fax (1) 5003299; e-mail icimod@ icimod.org; internet www.icimod.org; f. 1983; autonomous org. sponsored by govts of the regional mem. countries, Austria, Denmark, Germany, the Netherlands, Norway and Switzerland, to help promote an economically and environmentally sound ecosystem, and to improve the living standards of the mountain people in the Hindu Kush-Himalayan region; aims to serve as a focal point for multi-disciplinary documentation, training and applied research, and as a consultative centre in scientific and practical matters pertaining to mountain devt; mem. countries: Afghanistan, Bangladesh, Bhutan, China, India, Myanmar, Nepal, Pakistan; Dir-Gen. ANDREAS SCHILD.

Libraries and Archives

Kathmandu

National Archives: Ram Shah Path, Kathmandu; tel. (1) 4251315; f. 1967; 35,000 MSS, 60,000 microfilm copies of MSS in private collections, 16,000 historical documents, 10,000 vols; facilities for researchers; Archivist SANI MAIYA; publ. *Abhilekh*.

Nepal-India Cultural Centre and Library: Embassy of India, RNAC Bldg, New Rd, Kathmandu; tel. (1) 4243497; fax (1) 4255414; e-mail nbsk@mos.com.np; f. 1952; 60,000 vols; Librarian SANJAY K. BIHANI.

Tribhuvan University Central Library: Kirtipur, Kathmandu 2; tel. (1) 4212834; fax (1) 4226964; e-mail tucl@healthnet.org.np; internet www.tucl.org.np; f. 1959; 200,000 vols; depository for the UN; Librarian KRISHNA MANI BHANDARI (acting); publs *Bulletin* (quarterly), *Education Quarterly*, *Journal of Tribhuvan University*, *Nepalese National Bibliography*.

Lalitpur

Madan Puraskar Pustakalaya: Lalitpur; tel. (1) 5521014; fax (1) 5536390; e-mail info@ mpp.org.np; internet www.mpp.org.np; f. 1941; 19,000 vols, 3,900 periodical titles, posters in Nepali language; Librarian KAMAL MANI DIXIT.

Nepal National Library: Harihar Bhawan, Pulchowk, POB 182, Lalitpur; tel. (1) 5521132; fax (1) 5536461; e-mail nnl@nnl .wlink.com.np; internet www.natlib.gov.np; f. 1957; 75,000 vols, 96 periodicals, 1,000 rare books and manuscripts, 1,500 children's books, 400 other items; Librarian DASHARATH THAPA.

Museums and Art Galleries

Kathmandu

National Museum of Nepal: Museum Rd, Chhauni, Kathmandu; tel. (1) 4211504; f. 1928; art, history, culture, ethnology, philately, natural history; art gallery; illustrates the art history of Nepal; library of 10,000 vols; Chief SANU NANI KANSAKAR; publ. *Nepal Museum*.

Patan Museum: Patan Darbar, Kathmandu; tel. and fax (1) 5521492; e-mail ptmuseum@mos.com.np; internet www .patanmuseum.gov.np; f. 1997; 18th c. royal palace housing Hindu and Buddhist sacred art of Nepal, Nepalese metalwork, photographs of Nepal taken in 1899, and a Hindu Tantric MS; Dir BHIM PRASAD NEPAL.

Universities

KATHMANDU UNIVERSITY

POB 6250, Dhulikhel, Kavre, Kathmandu

Telephone: (11) 661399
Fax: (11) 661443
E-mail: kuweb@ku.edu.np
Internet: www.ku.edu.np

Founded 1991
State-funded, autonomous control
Academic year: August to June

Language of instruction: English
Chancellor: Rt Hon. PRIME MINISTER OF NEPAL
Pro-Chancellor: Hon. MINISTER FOR EDUCATION
Vice-Chancellor: Dr SURESH RAJ SHARMA
Registrar: Dr SITARAM ADHIKARY
Library of 25,000 vols and 150 periodicals
Number of students: 4,890 (incl. 3,107 enrolled in affiliated colleges)

DEANS

School of Arts: Dr BHADRA MAN TULADHAR
School of Education: Dr KEDAR NATH SHRESTHA
School of Engineering: Dr DINESH CHAPAGAIN
School of Management: Dr BIJAY K. C.
School of Medical Sciences: Dr NARENDRA RANA
School of Science: Dr PUSHPA RAJ ADHIKARY
There are 11 affiliated colleges

MAHENDRA SANSKRIT UNIVERSITY

POB 5003, Kathmandu
Telephone: (1) 4221510
Fax: (1) 4221510
Founded 1986
State control
Languages of instruction: Sanskrit, Nepali, English
Academic year: July to May
Chancellor (vacant)
Vice-Chancellor: MADHAV RAJ GAUTAM
Rector: Dr BABU RAM POKHAREL
Registrar: Dr BHAJ RAJ PANT
Librarian: KHEM RAJ GYNAWALI
Number of teachers: 315
Number of students: 2,400
Publications: *Maryada* (annual), *Ritumbara* (quaterly)
Depts of Ayurveda, Buddhist Philosophy and Tantra, Darshna, Dernashast, Economics, English, Hindi and Maithali, Itihasa Purana, Karmakanda, Mathematics, Nepali, Nyaya, Political Science, Purva Mamamsa, Veda, Vedanta, Vyakarana, Yoga.

POKHARA UNIVERSITY

Naya Bazaar 9, Pokhara
Telephone: (61) 21867
Fax: (61) 28408

E-mail: uofp@cnet.wlink.com.np
Founded 1996
State-funded, autonomous control
Academic year: August to June
Chancellor: Rt Hon. PRIME MINISTER OF NEPAL
Pro-Chancellor: Hon. MINISTER FOR EDUCATION
Vice-Chancellor: Dr KESHAR JUNG BARAL
Number of students: 4,133
Faculties of Eng., Humanities, Management, Science; 26 affiliated colleges.

PURBANCHAL UNIVERSITY

POB 142, Biratnagar, Eastern Region
Telephone: (21) 22165
Fax: (21) 21204
E-mail: info@puniv.edu.np
Internet: www.puniv.edu.np
Founded 1995
State-funded, autonomous control
Academic year: August to June
Languages of instruction: English, Nepalese
Chancellor: Rt Hon. PRIME MINISTER OF NEPAL
Pro-Chancellor: Hon. MINISTER FOR EDUCATION
Publications: *Bulletin* (monthly), *Business Horizon*, *Expressions*
Faculties of Arts, Education, Management and Science and Technology
There are 65 affiliated colleges.

TRIBHUVAN UNIVERSITY

POB 8212, Kirtipur, Kathmandu
Telephone: (1) 4330433
Fax: (1) 4331964
E-mail: vcofficc@hcalthnet.org.np
Internet: www.tribhuvan-university.edu.np
Founded 1959
Autonomous control
Languages of instruction: Nepali, English
Academic year: July to June
60 Constituent campuses under the Univ., and 278 private campuses throughout the country affiliated to Tribhuvan Univ.
Chancellor: HM THE KING OF NEPAL
Vice-Chancellor: Prof. Dr GOVIND PRASAD SHARMA
Rector: Prof. Dr MAHENDRA PRASAD SINGH

Registrar: GEETA BHAKA JOSHI
Library: see Libraries and Archives
Number of teachers: 5,957
Number of students: 123,566
Publications: *Contributions to Nepalese Studies*, *Economic Journal of Development Issues* (2 a year), *Education and Development* (CERID, annual), *Journal of Development and Administrative Studies* (CEDA, annual), *Nepalese Journal of Development and Rural Studies* (Central Department of Rural Development (Kirtipur), 2 a year), *Tribhuvan University Today* (annual), *TU Journal* (Research Division, 2 a year)

DEANS

Faculty of Education: Prof. Dr NARENDRA BAHADUR MAHARJAN
Faculty of Humanities and Social Science: Prof. Dr TRI RATNA MANANDHAR
Faculty of Law: Prof. KANAK BIKRAM THAPA
Faculty of Management: Prof. Dr PARASÂR KOIRALA
Institute of Agriculture and Animal Science: Prof. Dr DURGA DUTTA DHAKAL
Institute of Eng.: Prof. Dr RAM KRISHNA POKHANEL
Institute of Forestry: Assoc. Prof. ASHOK KUMAR MALLIK
Institute of Medicine: Prof. Dr RAMESH KANT ADHIKANI
Institute of Science and Technology: Prof. Dr GOVINDA PRASAD SHARMA ZHIMISE

ATTACHED RESEARCH INSTITUTES

Centre for International Relations: Exec. Dir Dr CHANDRA LAL SHRESTHA.

Research Centre for Applied Science and Technology (RECAST): Exec. Dir Prof. Dr MOHAN BIKRAM GEWALI.

Research Centre for Economic Development and Administration (CEDA): Exec. Dir Mr ABULLIASH.

Research Centre for Educational Innovation and Development (CERID): Exec. Dir Dr HRIDAYA RATNA BAJRACHARYA.

Research Centre for Nepal and Asian Studies (CNAS): Exec. Dir NIRMAL MAN TULADHAR.

NETHERLANDS

The Higher Education System

Universitet Leiden (Leiden University—founded in 1575) is the oldest existing university in the Netherlands. It was founded when the Low Countries or Netherlands were under Spanish rule. In 1579 the seven northernmost provinces of the Netherlands formed the Treaty of Utrecht, declared their independence from Spain in 1581 and in 1648 were recognized as the independent United Provinces or Dutch Republic under the terms of the Treaty of Westphalia. Institutions established in the period 1579–48 include Rijksuniversiteit Groningen (the University of Groningen—founded in 1614), Universiteit van Amsterdam (the University of Amsterdam—founded in 1632) and Universiteit Utrecht (Utrecht University—founded in 1636).

The modern higher education system is subject to a number of different legislative acts, including the Higher Professional Education Act, the University Education Act (both 1986) and the Higher Education and Research Act (1993). The last of these granted greater autonomy to institutions and introduced a 'credit'-based system for the award of degrees. The Netherlands participates in the Bologna Process to establish a European Higher Education Area, the first phase of which is to adopt a credit-based system of comparable degrees with two main cycles (undergraduate and graduate). The new system of Bachelors and Masters degrees is expected to be fully implemented by 2010. Higher education institutions are either universities (Universiteiten) or universities of professional education (Hogescholen). The Minister of Education, Culture and Science, advised by an Education Council, is responsible for educational legislation and its enforcement. In 2004/05 199,350 students were enrolled at the Netherlands' 13 universities, while some 346,210 students were enrolled at the 54 institutes of higher vocational education.

There are also public and private universities in the Dutch Dependencies of Aruba and Netherlands Antilles; the public universities are the Universiteit van Aruba (founded in 1988) and University of the Netherlands Antilles (founded in 1970; current status since 1979). In Aruba there were an estimated 1,704 students in higher education in 2003/04, and in Netherlands Antilles there were 795 students enrolled in university-level institutions in 2000/01.

The two-tier system of undergraduate Bachelors and postgraduate Masters degrees was first introduced in 2002 and is expected to be adopted by all university-level institutions by 2010. The undergraduate Bachelors degree is a three-year programme of study, starting with one year of general studies. The first postgraduate degree is the Masters, a one- to three-year course of study involving research, a written thesis or final test. A Masters in medicine lasts three years and students are required to study for a further three to six years to qualify for independent practice. Following completion of the Masters, the Doctorate is awarded after a minimum of four years of research and public defence of a thesis.

Other than the universities, undergraduate Bachelors degrees are also offered by the Hogescholen, which have mostly been founded since 1986. The main focus of the hogescholen is on professional degrees and titles in several subject areas, including economics and management, engineering and technology, healthcare, behavioural science and social studies, agriculture and the environment, fine arts, performing arts and education. The Association of Hogescholen is responsible for quality assurance and accreditation.

Post-secondary technical and vocational education (middelbaar beroepsonderwijs—MBO) is administered according to the Adult and Vocational Education Act (1996). The MBO is divided into four levels of qualifications (in ascending order): assistant training (six months to one year), basic vocational training (two to three years), vocational training (two to four years) and management training (three to four years). Alternatively, school-leavers with 10 years of primary and secondary education may undertake apprenticeships based in the workplace.

Regulatory and Representative Bodies

GOVERNMENT

Ministry of Education, Culture and Science: Rijnstraat 50, POB 16375, 2500 BJ The Hague; tel. (70) 4123456; fax (70) 4123450; e-mail webmaster@minocw.nl; internet www.minocw.nl; Minister Dr RONALD HANS ANTON PLASTERK.

ACCREDITATION

ENIC/NARIC Netherlands: Centre for Int. Recognition and Certification (CIRC), Kortenaerkade 11, Postbus 29777, 2502 LT The Hague; tel. (70) 4260270; fax (70) 4260395; e-mail circ@nuffic.nl; internet www.nuffic.nl; Contact LUCIE DE BRUIN.

Nederlands-Vlaamse Accreditatieorganisatie (Accreditation Organisation of the Netherlands and Flanders): POB 85498, 2508 CD The Hague; Parkstraat 28, 2514 JK The Hague; tel. (70) 3122300; fax (70) 3122301; e-mail info@nvao.net; internet www.nvao.net; independently ensures the quality of higher education in the Netherlands and Flanders by assessing and accrediting programmes; Chair. K. L. L. M. (KARL) DITTRICH.

NATIONAL BODIES

HBO-raad (Netherlands Association of Universities of Applied Sciences): Postbus 123, 2501 CC The Hague; Prinsessegracht 21, The Hague; tel. (70) 3122121; fax (70) 3122100; e-mail post@hbo-raad.nl; internet www.hbo-raad.nl; 44 govt-funded univs of applied sciences; works to strengthen the social position of the univs of applied sciences; Dirs AD DE GRAAF, ARIAN VAN STAA.

Nederlandse Organisatie voor Internationale Samenwerking in het Hoger Onderwijs (Netherlands Organization for International Co-operation in Higher Education): Kortenaerkade 11, 2518 AX The Hague; POB 29777, 2502 LT The Hague; tel. (70) 4260260; fax (70) 4260399; e-mail nuffic@nuffic.nl; internet www.nuffic.nl; f. 1952 by the Netherlands univs to promote int. co-operation in the academic and scientific fields; provides information on postgraduate int. courses; advises various educational and govt bodies on matters of academic equivalence and the recognition of professional credentials; promotes int. co-operation in several European and nat. exchange programmes; offers educational and scientific help to developing countries; Gen. Dir Drs S. P. VAN DEN EIJNDEN; Communications Dir H. TEEKENS; publs *Study in the Netherlands:* *your Gateway to Europe* (annual), *Nieuwsbrief* (quarterly).

Nederlandse Vereniging van Pedagogen en Onderwijskundigen (NVO) (Dutch Society of Educational Psychologists): Korte Elisabethstraat 11, 3511 JG Utrecht; tel. (30) 2322407; e-mail info@nvo.nl; internet www.nvo.nl; f. 1962; maintenance of standards in univ. education; 2,800 mems; publs *Nederlands Tijdschrift voor Opvoeding, Vorming en Onderwijs* (6 a year).

Rectoren College (Netherlands Rectors' Conference): POB 19270, 3501 DG Utrecht; tel. (31) (30) 334441; fax (31) (30) 333540; Chair. Prof. Dr TH. J. M. VAN ELS; Sec. H. J. GRAAFLAND.

Vereniging van Samenwerkende Nederlandse Universiteiten (Association of Universities in the Netherlands): POB 13739, 2501 ES The Hague; tel. (70) 3021400; fax (70) 3021495; e-mail post@vsnu.nl; internet www.vsnu.nl; f. 1985; Chair. (vacant).

Learned Societies

GENERAL

Hollandsche Maatschapij der Wetenschappen (Dutch Society of Sciences): Spaarne 17, POB 9698, 2003 LR

Haarlem; f. 1752; furthering contact between scientists and laymen by arranging lectures on scientific subjects and awarding annual prizes and subsidies for research and publication of scientific work; 550 mems; Pres. M. C. VAN VEEN; Secs Prof. Dr A. A. VERRIJN STUART (Natural Sciences), Prof. Dr D. M. SCHENKEVELD (Humanities and Social Sciences).

Koninklijke Nederlandse Akademie van Wetenschappen (Royal Netherlands Academy of Arts and Sciences): POB 19121, 1000 GC Amsterdam; tel. (20) 5510700; fax (20) 6204941; e-mail knaw@bureau.knaw.nl; internet www.knaw.nl; f. 1808; 300 mems (200 ordinary, 40 corresp., 60 foreign); divisions of Humanities and Social Sciences (Chair. Prof. Dr M. A. SCHENKEVELD-VAN DER DUSSEN), Science (Chair. Prof. Dr P. C. VAN DER VLIET); attached learned socs: see Learned Societies; attached research institutes: see Research Institutes; attached libraries and archives: see Libraries and Archives; Pres. Prof. WILLEM J. M. LEVELT; Sec.-Gen. Prof. Dr R. KAPTEIN; Chair C. H. MOEN; publs *Jaarboek, Akademienieuws, Verslag van de Gewone Vergaderingen der Afdeling Natuurkunde, Verhandelingen Eerste en Tweede Reeks der Afdeling Natuurkunde, Mededelingen der Afdeling Letterkunde, Verhandelingen der Afdeling Letterkunde.*

Suid-Afrikaanse Instituut: Keizersgracht 141, 1015 CK Amsterdam; tel. (20) 624-9318; fax (20) 638-2596; f. 1939; study of Afrikaans language and literature, history and culture of South Africa; library of 30,000 vols.

AGRICULTURE, FISHERIES AND VETERINARY SCIENCE

Koninklijke Landbouwkundige Vereniging (Royal Society for Agricultural Science): POB 79, 6700 AB Wageningen; Located at: 'Gebouw Achter de Aula', Gen. Foulkesweg 1A, 6703 BG Wageningen; tel. (317) 485191; fax (317) 483976; e-mail office@klv.nl; internet www.klv.nl; f. 1886; agricultural and environmental research, debates, seminars, workshops on career development; 6,000 mems; Dir PAUL DEN BESTEN; publs *KLV Update* (newsletter, in Dutch, quarterly), *Netherlands Journal of Agricultural Science (NJAS)* (in English, quarterly).

Koninklijke Maatschappij Tuinbouw en Plantkunde (Royal Dutch Horticultural Society): POB 87910, 2508 DH The Hague; tel. (70) 4161410; fax (70) 4161429; e-mail postmaster@groei.nl; internet www.groei.nl; f. 1872; 60,000 mems; Gen. Sec. J. P. VAN LEEUWEN; publ. *Groei & Bloei* (11 a year).

Koninklijke Nederlandse Bosbouw Vereniging (Royal Netherlands Forestry Society): Colijnplein 20, 2555 HA Den Haag; tel. (70) 3688222; internet www.knbv.nl; f. 1910; 620 mems; Chair. Ir W. H. J. DE BEAUFORT; Sec. Ir T. WINKELMAN; publ. *Nederlands Bosbouw Tijdschrift* (every 2 months).

Nederlandse Tuinbouwraad (Netherlands Horticultural Council): POB 175, 2180 AD Hillegom; tel. 252515254; fax 252519714; f. 1908; represents the common technical and economic interests of the mem. organizations; mems: 10 national organizations of co-operatives and producers of edible and non-edible horticultural products; Chairman Dr SJAAK LANGESLAG.

ARCHITECTURE AND TOWN PLANNING

Bond Heemschut: 'Korenmetershuis', NZ Kolk 28, 1012 PV Amsterdam; tel. (20) 6225292; fax (20) 6240571; e-mail info@heemschut.nl; internet www.heemschut.nl; f. 1911; asscn for safeguarding the architec-

tural heritage of the Netherlands; 12,000 mems; Chair. Ir E. H. Baron VAN TUYLL VAN SEROOSKERKEN; 11 Provincial sub-cttees.

College van Toezicht (Architects' Supervisory Commission): Keizersgracht 321, 1016 EE, POB 19606, 1000 GP Amsterdam; tel. (20) 5553666; fax (20) 5553699; e-mail bna@bna.nl; internet www.bna.nl; f. 1988 to supervise Code of Conduct; 9 mems; Chair. H. B. A. VERHAGEN; Secs A. M. GUNCKEL, J. J. ROOS.

Genootschap Architectura et Amicitia (A. et A.): Waterlooplein 211, 1011 PG Amsterdam; tel. (20) 6220188; e-mail mail@aeta.nl; internet www.aeta.nl; f. 1855; 225 mems; Chair. H. VAN HEESWIJK; Sec. F. BROEKSMA; publ. *FORUM* (quarterly).

Koninklijke Maatschappij tot Bevordering der Bouwkunst Bond van Nederlandse Architekten (BNA) (Royal Institute of Dutch Architects): POB 19606, 1000 GP Amsterdam; premises at: Keizersgracht 321, 1016 EE Amsterdam; tel. (20) 5553666; fax (20) 5553699; e-mail bna@bna.nl; internet www.bna.nl; f. 1842; 3,000 mems; publ. *BladNA* (monthly).

Netherlands Architecture Institute: Museum Park 25, 3015 CB Rotterdam; POB 237, 3000 AE Rotterdam; tel. (10) 4401200; fax (10) 4366975; e-mail info@nai.nl; internet www.nai.nl; f. 1988; museum, archives, collections; library of 35,000 vols; Dir AARON BETSKY; publ. *Archis* (monthly).

Raad voor Cultuur (Council for Culture): POB 61243, 2506 AE Den Haag; tel. (70) 3106686; fax (70) 3614727; e-mail cultuur@cultuur.nl; internet www.cultuur.nl; f. 1995; 25 mems; Sec. Dr J. A. BRANDENBARG; publs *Annual Report, Newsletter.*

Rijksdienst voor de Monumentenzorg (Department for Conservation): POB 1001, 3700 BA Zeist; premises at: Broederplein 41, 3703 CD Zeist; tel. (30) 6983456; fax (30) 6916189; e-mail info@monumentenzorg.nl; internet www.monumentenzorg.nl; f. 1918; re-formed 1947; library of 50,000 vols, 500 periodicals; publs *Annual Report, Newsletter.*

BIBLIOGRAPHY, LIBRARY SCIENCE AND MUSEOLOGY

FOBID Netherlands Library Forum: POB 16146, 2500 BC Den Haag; tel. (70) 3090115; fax (70) 3090200; e-mail info@fobid.nl; internet www.fobid.nl; f. 1974; library umbrella org. for advocacy and development in the field of legal matters, professional education, classification standards, int. affairs; promotion of co-operation and integration among public, research and special libraries in the Netherlands; mems: Netherlands Public Library Asscn (VOB), Netherlands Asscn for Library, Information and Knowledge Professionals (NVB), Nat. Library of the Netherlands (KB) and UKB, the co-operative Association of 13 University Libraries, the Nat. Library and the Library of the Royal Dutch Academy of Science; Sec. Dr MARIAN KOREN.

Nederlandse Museumvereniging (Netherlands Museums Association): POB 2975, 1000 CZ Amsterdam; premises at: Rapenburgerstraat 123, 1011 VL Amsterdam; tel. (20) 5512900; fax (20) 5512901; e-mail info@museumvereniging.nl; internet www.museumvereniging.nl; f. 1926; 400 museum mems; Chair. Drs D. LOKIN; Dir Drs M. C. VAN DER SMAN; Sec. R. KERVEZEE; publ. *Museumvisie* (quarterly).

Nederlandse Vereniging voor Beroepsbeoefenaren in de bibliotheek-, informatie- en kennissector (NVB) (Netherlands Association for Library, Information and Knowledge Professionals): Nieuwegracht 15,

3512 LC Utrecht; tel. (30) 2311263; fax (30) 2311830; e-mail nvbinfo@wxs.nl; internet www.nvb-online.nl; f. 1912; 2,500 individual, 700 institutional mems; maintenance of lawful regulation of library system, arrangement of meetings and international co-operation, professional education; Pres. Drs J. S. M. SAVENIJE; Sec. M. P. VAN BUIJTENEN; publs *NVB—Nieuwsbrief, Informatie Professional.*

Vereniging van Openbare Bibliotheken (Netherlands Public Library Association): POB 16146, 2500 BC The Hague; premises at: Grote Marktstraat 43, 2511 BH The Hague; tel. (70) 3090100; fax (70) 3090200; e-mail infolijn@debibliotheken.nl; internet www.debibliotheken.nl; f. 1972; 500 mem. instns; Chair Prof. E. JURGENS; publ. *Bibliotheek Blad* (every 2 weeks).

ECONOMICS, LAW AND POLITICS

Internationaal Juridisch Instituut (International Legal Institute): Spui 186, 2511 BW The Hague; tel. (70) 3460974; fax (70) 3625235; e-mail iji@worldonline.nl; internet www.iji.nl; f. 1918; supplies legal opinions regarding private international law and foreign (also mostly private) law to the Netherlands judiciary, the Netherlands bar and to other mems of the legal profession, such as civil law notaries; also gives information to judges and lawyers outside the Netherlands; Pres. A. V. M. STRUYCKEN; Dir Prof. A. L. G. A. STILLE; Sec. T. HEUKELS.

Koninklijke Vereniging voor de Staathuishoudkunde (Royal Netherlands Economic Association): c/o De Nederlandsche Bank NV, POB 98, 1000 AP Amsterdam; tel. (20) 5242280; fax (20) 5242500; e-mail kvs@dnb.nl; internet www.dnb.nl/kvs; f. 1849; 2,100 mems; Chair. Prof. Dr H. A. KEUZENKAMP; Sec. Drs H. J. BROUWER; publs *De Economist* (4 a year), *Preadviezen* (annually), *Jaarboek* (annually).

Nederlandse Vereniging voor Internationaal Recht (Netherlands Branch of International Law Association): POB 9520, 2300 RA Leiden; Steenschuur 25, 2311 ES Leiden; tel. (71) 5277748; fax (71) 5277383; e-mail info@nvir.org; internet www.nvir.org; f. 1910; 560 mems; Pres. Prof. Dr N. J. SCHRIJVER; Hon. Sec. Dr M. M. T. A. BRUS; publ. *Mededelingen* (2 a year).

Vereniging voor Agrarisch Recht (Agrarian Law Society): 'de Leeuwenborch' Hollandseweg 1, 6706 KN Wageningen; tel. (317) 484486; Sec. H. C. A. WALDA.

Vereniging voor Arbeidsrecht (Labour Law Society): POB 132, 3440 AC Woerden; tel. (6) 51108682; fax (348) 434701; f. 1946; 940 mems; Sec. G. J. J. RENSINK; publ. publs monographs.

Volkenrechtelijk Instituut (Institute of Public International Law): Utrecht University, Achter Sint Pieter 200, 3512 HT Utrecht; tel. (30) 2537060; fax (30) 2537073; f. 1955; library of 21,000 vols; publ. *Nova et Vetera Iuris Gentium.*

FINE AND PERFORMING ARTS

Koninklijke Nederlandse Toonkunstenaars-vereniging (Royal Netherlands Association of Musicians): Haarlemmerstraat 116, 1013 EX Amsterdam; tel. (20) 5221020; fax (20) 6200229; e-mail office@kntv.nl; internet www.kntv.nl; f. 1875; 3,400 mems; Chair. H. VAN DER HEIJDEN; Sec. DICK VISSER; publ. *KNTV-Magazine* (6 a year).

Maatschappij 'Arti et Amicitiae': Rokin 112, 1012 LB Amsterdam; tel. (20) 6233508; fax (20) 6225206; e-mail arti@arti.nl; internet www.arti.nl; f. 1839; a national society of painters, sculptors and graphic artists; 1,500 mems (incl. 500 artist mems); exhibition gallery; Pres. THOMAS MOHR; Secs VERA DE GROOT, HENDRIK KAPTEIN; publ. *De Nieuwe* (6 a year).

Maatschappij tot Bevordering der Toonkunst (Society for the Advancement of Music): 1e Jacob Van Campenstraat 59, 1072 BD Amsterdam; tel. (20) 6713091; fax (20) 6716576; e-mail info@toonkunst.org; internet www.toonkunst.org; f. 1829; 6,500 mems; library of 18,000 vols; Chair. H. HIERCK; publ. *Toonkunst-Nieuws*.

Nederlandse Toonkunstenaarsraad (Council of Organizations of Musicians in the Netherlands): Valeriusplein 20, Amsterdam; f. 1948 to protect professional interests; 3,000 mems; Chair. Dr N. J. C. M. KAPPEYNE VAN DE COPPELLO; Man. Dir Ir. R. C. BROEK; publ. *A Musical Guide for Holland* (every 2 years).

Rijksbureau voor Kunsthistorische Documentatie (Netherlands Institute for Art History): POB 90418, 2509 LK The Hague; Located at: Prins Willem-Alexanderhof 5, 2595 BE The Hague; tel. (70) 3339777; fax (70) 3339789; e-mail info@rkd.nl; internet www.rkd.nl; f. 1932; library of 450,000 vols, periodicals and catalogues, and press-cuttings, archives, 3,500,000 photos and reproductions; Dir Prof. Dr RUDOLF E. EKKART; publs *Oud-Holland* (quarterly), *RKD Bulletin* (2 a year).

Stichting Nederlands Filminstituut (Netherlands Film Institute): POB 515, Hilversum, Steynlaan 8; f. 1948; film and television academy; lecture and information service, and a film and group media distribution service; Man. Dir Dr J. A. HES.

Theater Instituut Nederland (Netherlands Theatre Institute): Herengracht 168, 1016 BP Amsterdam; POB 19304, 1000 GH ; tel. (20) 5513300; fax (20) 5513303; e-mail info@tin.nl; internet www.tin.nl; f. 1993; service organization and research institute for the professional theatre; theatre museum; library of 100,000 vols and sound archives and 6,000 video cassettes of the Dutch theatre; Netherlands centre of the International Theatre Institute; Dir KEES VUYK; publs *Carnet* (in French and English), *Nederlands Theaterjaarboek* (annually).

Vereniging 'Sint Lucas' (St Luke Association): Zomerdijk-straat 20, Amsterdam; f. 1880; Chair. BART PEIZEL; Sec. THEO SWAGEMAKERS.

Wagner Genootschap Nederland (Netherlands Wagner Fellowship): Savornin Lohmanlaan 4, 1181 XM Amsterdam; tel. (20) 6417364; fax (20) 6409575; e-mail bestuur@wagnergenootschap.nl; internet www.wagnergenootschap.nl; f. 1961; Dir HANK NEUGARTEN; Sec. HILKE DE MUNNIK.

HISTORY, GEOGRAPHY AND ARCHAEOLOGY

Centraal Bureau voor Genealogie (Central Bureau for Genealogy): POB 11755, 2502 AT The Hague; tel. (70) 3150570; fax (70) 3478394; e-mail algemeen@cbg.nl; internet www.cbg.nl; f. 1945; large genealogical and heraldic collections; 14,350 mems; library of 100,000 vols; Dir Dr A. J. LEVER; publs *Genealogie* (4 a year), *Jaarboek* (annually).

Internationaal Instituut voor Sociale Geschiedenis (International Institute of Social History): Cruquiusweg 31, 1019 AT Amsterdam; tel. (20) 6685866; fax (20) 6654181; e-mail info@iisg.nl; internet www.iisg.nl; f. 1935; attached to Royal Netherlands Acad. of Arts and Sciences; library of 1,000,000 vols, archives, especially on the labour movement, 60,000 periodicals; Dir J. KLOOSTERMAN; publs *Annual Report, Inter-*national Review of Social History* (3 a year, plus supplement).

Koninklijk Fries Genootschap voor Geschiedenis en Cultuur/Keninklik Frysk Genoatskip foar Skiednis en Kultuer (Royal Frisian Society for History and Culture): Turfmarkt 11, 8911 KS Leeuwarden; tel. (58) 2555500; e-mail fries .genootschap@friesmuseum.nl; internet www .friesgenootschap.nl; f. 1827; 1,800 mems; Pres. A. E. DUURSMA-OLTHUIS; Sec. Drs E. MAKKES VAN DER DEIJL; publs *De Vrije Fries* (annually), *Fryslân* (4 a year).

Koninklijk Nederlands Aardrijkskundig Genootschap (Royal Dutch Geographical Society): POB 80123, 3508 TC Utrecht; tel. (30) 2534056; fax (30) 2535523; e-mail info@ knag.nl; internet www.knag.nl; f. 1873; 3,800 mems; Dir EELKO POSTMA; publs *Geografie* (9 a year), *Journal of Economic and Social Geography (TESG)* (5 a year), *Netherlands Geographical Studies* (irregular).

Koninklijk Nederlands Historisch Genootschap (Royal Dutch Historical Society): POB 90406, 2509 LK The Hague; tel. (70) 3140363; fax (70) 3140637; e-mail kngb@ inghist.nl; internet www.knhg.nl; f. 1845; 1,700 mems; Chief Officer Dr G. N. VAN DER PLAAT; publs *Bijdragen en Mededelingen betreffende de Geschiedenis der Nederlanden* (quarterly), *HG-Nieuws* (quarterly).

Koninklijk Oudheidkundig Genootschap (Royal Antiquarian Society): POB 74888, 1070 DN Amsterdam; tel. (20) 6747380; e-mail kog@rijksmuseum.nl; f. 1858; colln of applied art (furniture, silver, sculpture, etc.), paintings, objects of historical value, prints and drawings concerning the topography of Amsterdam, manners and customs of the Netherlands; coins, medals, books; 500 mems; library of 6,100 vols; Pres. Drs R. E. KISTEMAKER; Sec. Drs E. M. DONNER.

Nederlandsch Economisch-Historisch Archief (NEHA) (Netherlands Economic-Historical Archives Society): Cruquiusweg 31, 1019 AT Amsterdam; tel. (20) 6685866; fax (20) 6654181; e-mail info@neha.nl; internet www.neha.nl; f. 1914; attached to Royal Netherlands Acad. of Arts and Sciences (KNAW); specializes in economic history and business studies; 400 mems; library of 100,000 vols on economic history; Dirs J. KLOOSTERMAN, L. HEERMA VAN VOSS; publ. *Tijdschrift voor Sociale en Economische Geschiedenis* (quarterly).

Vereniging Gelre: Markt 1, 6811 CG Arnhem; internet www.vereniginggelre.nl; f. 1897; historical society of the province of Gelderland; Pres. Dr KEVERLING BUISMAN; publs *Bijdragen en Mededelingen* (annually), *Werken*.

LANGUAGE AND LITERATURE

Alliance Française: Adresse : Kaap Hoorndreef 30, 3563 AT Utrecht; tel. (30) 265-09-92; fax (30) 265 09 24; e-mail bd@ alliance-francaise.nl; internet www .alliance-francaise.nl; offers courses and exams in French language and culture and promotes cultural exchange with France; attached offices in Alkmaar, Amersfoort, Apeldoorn, Arnhem, Baarland, Bergen-op-Zoom, Betuwe, Boskoop, Brakel, Breda, Den Haag, Den Helder, Deventer, Dordrecht, Eindhoven, Enschede, Friesland, Hart van Zeeland, Hoorn, Kennemerland, Maastricht, Meppel, Nijmegen, Ommen, Roermond, Roosendaal, Rotterdam, Twente, Utrecht, Vorden, Walcheren, Zutphen and Zwolle; Pres. V. O. VAN DER SPEK-CHOUZENOUX.

British Council: Weteringschans 85A, 1017 RZ Amsterdam; tel. (20) 5506060; fax (20) 6207389; e-mail information@britishcouncil .nl; internet www.britishcouncil.org/ netherlands; offers exams in English language and British culture and promotes cultural exchange with the UK; Dir DAVID ALDERDICE.

Goethe-Institut: Herengracht 470, 1017 CA Amsterdam; tel. (20) 5312900; fax (20) 6384631; e-mail info@amsterdam.goethe .org; internet www.goethe.de/be/ams/ deindex.htm; offers courses and exams in German language and culture and promotes cultural exchange with Germany; attached centre in Rotterdam; Dir Dr CHRISTIAN LÜFFE.

Instituto Cervantes: Domplein 3, 3512 JC Utrecht; tel. (30) 2334261; fax (30) 2332970; e-mail cenutr@cervantes.es; internet utrecht .cervantes.es; offers courses and exams in Spanish language and culture and promotes cultural exchange with Spain and Spanish-speaking Latin and Central America; library: library of 13,000 vols; Dir JAIME OTERO ROTH.

Maatschappij der Nederlandse Letterkunde (Society of Netherlands Literature): POB 9501, Witte Singel 27, 2300 RA Leiden; tel. (71) 5144962; fax (71) 5272836; e-mail mnl@library.leidenuniv.nl; internet www .maatschappijdernederlandseletterkunde.nl; f. 1766; 1,400 mems; Chair. Dr ERNESTINE VAN DER WALL; Sec. Dr LEO VAN MARIS; publs *Tijdschrift voor Nederlandse Taal- en Letterkunde* (4 a year), *Jaarboek der Maatschappij* (annual).

Nederlandsche Vereeniging voor Druk-en Boekkunst (Netherlands Society for the Art of Printing and Book-production): J. van Banning str. 2C, 2381 AV Zoeterwoude; f. 1938; 300 mems; Chair. Drs G. J. KEYSER; Sec. Drs K. THOMASSEN; publs *Mededelingen* (irregular), books.

Netherlands Centre of the International PEN: Graaftsweg 3, 6512 BM Nijmegen; f. 1923; 350 mems; Sec. DAAN CARTENS; publ. *PEN Nieuwsbrief* (2 a year).

MEDICINE

Genootschap ter bevordering van Natuur-, Genees- en Heelkunde (Association for Advancement of Natural, Medical and Surgical Sciences): Plantage Muidergracht 12, Amsterdam; tel. (20) 525-5125; fax (20) 525-5124; e-mail secr.ecsi@chem.uva.nl; f. 1790; Pres. Dr G. N. BOUMAN; Sec. Dr F. M. M. GRIFFOEN.

Koninklijke Nederlandsche Maatschappij tot bevordering der Geneeskunst (Royal Dutch Medical Association): Lomanlaan 103, 3526 XD Utrecht; POB 20051, 3502 LB Utrecht; tel. (30) 2823911; fax (30) 2823326; e-mail communicatie@fed.knmg.nl; internet www.knmg.nl; f. 1849; library on history of medicine in the Netherlands; 33,000 mems; Dir W. P. RIJKSEN; publs *Arts in Spe* (quarterly), *Medisch Contact* (weekly).

Koninklijke Nederlandse Maatschappij ter Bevordering der Pharmacie (Royal Dutch Association for the Advancement of Pharmacy): Alexanderstraat 11, POB 30460, 2500 GL The Hague; tel. (70) 3737373; fax (70) 3106530; e-mail communicatie@knmp .nl; internet www.knmp.nl; f. 1842; c. 3,500 mems; Pres. MARTIN FAVIÉ; Sec. Drs L. H. A. J. ARTS; publ. *Pharmaceutisch Weekblad*.

Nederlandse Vereniging van Specialisten in de Dento-Maxillaire Orthopaedie: J. M. de Muinck Keizerlaan 27, 3555 JT Utrecht; tel. (30) 2430684; fax (30) 2432061; e-mail gaelema@orthodontist.nl; internet www.orthodontist.nl; f. 1953; Pres. Dr J. J. G. M. PILON; Sec. Drs G. A. ELEMA.

Nederlandse Vereniging voor Heelkunde (Association of Surgeons of the Netherlands): POB 20061, Lomanlaan 103, 3502 LB Utrecht; tel. (30) 2823327; fax (30) 2823329; f. 1902; 1,400 mems; Hon. Sec. Dr A. B. BIJNEN; publ. *The European Journal of Surgery* (monthly, in English).

Nederlandse Vereniging voor Microbiologie (Netherlands Society for Microbiology): C/o National Institute for Public Health and the Environment (RIVM), POB 1, 3720 BA Bilthoven; tel. (30) 2743924; fax (30) 2744434; e-mail nvvm@fems-microbiology .org; internet www.fems-microbiology.org/ nvvm; f. 1911; microbiology, bacteriology, virology; 1,300 mems; Pres. Prof. Dr. B. OUDEGA; Sec. Dr E. SMIT; publ. *Bionieuws*.

Nederlandse Vereniging voor Neurologie: POB 20050, 3502 LB Utrecht; tel. (30) 2823343; e-mail nvneuro@knmg.nl; internet www.neurologie.nl; f. 1871, reorganized 1974; 800 mems; Pres. Prof. Dr M. DE VISSER; Sec. Prof. Dr C. H. POLMAN; publ. *Clinical Neurology and Neurosurgery*.

Nederlandse Vereniging voor Orthodontische Studie (Netherlands Orthodontics Society): Mahatma Gadhistraat 10, 3066 VA Rotterdam; tel. (10) 2020006; f. 1946; 700 mems; Sec. M. LEUNISSE.

Nederlandse Vereniging voor Psychiatrie (Netherlands Association for Psychiatry): POB 20062, 3502 LB, Utrecht; tel. (30) 2823303; fax (30) 2888400; e-mail info@nvvp .net; internet www.nvvp.net; f. 1871, reorganized 1973; 3,090 mems; Pres. Prof. Dr R. J. VAN DEN BOSCH; Sec. P. NIESINK; publ. *Tijdschrift voor Psychiatrie*.

Nederlandse Vereniging voor Tropische Geneeskunde en Internationale Gezondheidszorg (Netherlands Society of Tropical Medicine and International Health): POB 83, 6700 AD Wageningen; tel. (317) 428622; fax (317) 428622; e-mail nvtg@xs4all .nl; internet www.nvtg.org; f. 1907; 950 mems; Pres. C. VAN DER DOES; Sec. J. J. A. DEKKER.

Vereniging voor Volksgezondheid en Wetenschap (Netherlands Society of Public Health and Science): Admiraal Helfrichlaan 1, 3527 KV Utrecht; tel. (70) 3030045; fax (70) 3030045; e-mail venw@wanadoo.nl; internet www.verenigingvenw.nl; f. 1985 (formerly Algemene Nederlandse Vereniging voor Sociale Gezondheidszorg); scientific approach to health and health care questions; 800 mems; Pres. Prof. Dr H. F. L. GARRETSEN; Sec. Dr KARIEN STRONKS; publs *Tijdschrift voor Gezondheidswetenschappen* (8 a year), *European Journal of Public Health* (4 a year).

NATURAL SCIENCES
General
Koninklijke Nederlandse Natuurhistorische Vereniging (Royal Dutch Society for Natural History): Oudegracht 237, 3511 NK Utrecht; tel. (30) 2314797; fax (30) 2368907; e-mail bureau@knnv.nl; internet www.knnv .nl; f. 1901; 8,300 mems; Chair. A. VAN WEELDEREN; publ. *Natura* (6 a year).

Stichting Natuur en Milieu (Society for Nature and Environment): Donkerstraat 17, 3511 KB Utrecht; tel. (30) 2331328; fax (30) 2331311; internet www.snm.nl; f. 1972; nature conservation and environmental protection; Dir A. J. M. VAN DEN BIGGELAAR; publ. *Natuur en milieu* (monthly).

Thijmgenootschap (Society of Christian Scholars in the Netherlands): Kerkhofweg 23A, 5912 GN Venlo; tel. (77) 3520010; e-mail info@thijmgenootschap.nl; internet www .thijmgenootschap.nl; f. 1904; 1,500 mems; Pres. Prof. Dr FONS PLASSCHAERT; Sec. Drs MATHIJS NOTERMANS; publ. *Annalen van het Thijmgenootschap* (quarterly).

Vereniging tot Behoud van Natuurmonumenten in Nederland (Society for the Preservation of Nature Reserves in the Netherlands): Postbus 9955, 1243 ZS 's-Graveland; tel. (35) 6559933; fax (35) 6563174; internet www.natuurmonumenten .nl; f. 1905; 860,000 mems; the society controls 300 nature reserves; Pres. Dhr H. H. F. WIJFFELS; Dir C. N. DE BOER; publ. *Natuurbehoud* (quarterly).

Biological Sciences
Koninklijke Nederlandse Botanische Vereniging (Royal Dutch Botanical Society): c/o Dr A. M. Wagner, Biologisch Laboratorium, Vrije Universiteit, De Boelelaan 1087, 1081 HV Amsterdam; tel. (20) 5485538; f. 1845; 635 mems; Pres. Prof. Dr H. VAN DEN ENDE; First Sec. Dr A. M. WAGNER; publ. *Acta Botanica Neerlandica*.

Koninklijke Nederlandse Dierkundige Vereniging (Royal Dutch Zoological Society): Gedragsbiologie, Universiteit Utrecht, Padualaan 8, 3584 CH Utrecht; internet www.kndv.nl; f. 1872; 610 mems; Pres. Prof. Dr J. J. BOLHUIS; Sec. Dr M. A. ZANDBERGEN; publ. *Animal Biology* (online).

Nederlandse Entomologische Vereniging (Netherlands Entomological Society): Plantage Middenlaan 64, 1018 DH Amsterdam; tel. (20) 5256246; fax (20) 5256528; e-mail admnev@bio.uva.nl; internet www .nev.nl; f. 1845; library of 80,000 vols; 650 mems; Pres. Drs J. VAN TOL; Sec. SJ. TIEMERSMA; publs *Tijdschrift voor Entomologie, Entomologische Berichten*; publ. *Entomologia Experimentalis et Applicata* (annually).

Nederlandse Mycologische Vereniging (Netherlands Mycological Society): Centraalbureau voor Schimmelcultures, POB 85167, 3508 AD Utrecht; tel. (30) 2122600; e-mail nmv@cbs.knaw.nl; internet www.mlf.sci.kun .nl/nmv; f. 1908; 650 mems; study of fungi; Pres. L. JALINK; Sec.-Gen. STALPERS DEN BRINKER; publ. *Coolia* (4 a year).

Nederlandse Ornithologische Unie (Netherlands Ornithological Union): Couwenhoven 56 12, 3703 EW Amsterdam; internet nioz.nl/en/deps/mee/ardea/nou.htm; f. 1901; study of ornithology; 1,067 mems; library of c. 120 periodicals; Pres. Dr R. H. DRENT; publs *Ardea* (2 a year), *Limosa* (quarterly).

Nederlandse Vereniging voor Parasitologie (Netherlands Society for Parasitology): Afd. Biomedisch Onderzoek, Meibergdreef 39, 1105 AZ Amsterdam; tel. (10) 463-6746; fax (10) 463-6152; e-mail h.schallig@kit.nl; f. 1961; 175 mems; Pres. Prof. Dr A. G. M. TIELENS; Sec. Dr H. D. F. H. SCHALLIG.

Nederlandse Zoötechnische Vereniging (Netherlands Association for Animal Production): POB 332, 6700 AH Wageningen; internet www.zod.wau.nl/nzv; f. 1930; 850 mems; Pres. Dr Ir L. A. DEN HARTOG; Sec. Dr Ir H. BOVENHUIS.

Stichting Koninklijk Zoölogisch Genootschap 'Natura Artis Magistra' (Royal Zoological Society): Plantage Kerklaan 38–40, 1018 CZ Amsterdam; tel. (20) 5233400; fax (20) 5233481; e-mail info@artis.nl; internet www.artis.nl; f. 1838; Dirs Dr M. T. FRANKENHUIS, Drs H. R. HOFSTEE; publs *Bijdragen tot de Dierkunde* (4 a year), *Artis* (6 a year).

Mathematical Sciences
Koninklijk Wiskundig Genootschap (Royal Dutch Mathematical Society): CWI, POB 94079, 1090 GB Amsterdam; tel. (20) 5924226; fax (20) 5924199; e-mail wiskgenoot@wiskgenoot.nl; internet www .wiskgenoot.nl; f. 1778; 1,270 mems; library

of 16,400 vols and journals of mathematics and its applications; Pres. Prof. Dr J. VAN MILL; Sec. Dr Ir H. J. J. TE RIELE; publs *Nieuw Archief voor Wiskunde* (4 a year), *Pythagoras* (6 a year).

Vereniging voor Statistiek en Operationele Research (Netherlands Society for Statistics and Operations Research): POB 2095, 2990 DB Barendrecht; tel. (180) 623796; fax (180) 623670; e-mail admin@ vvs-or.nl; internet www.vvs-or.nl; f. 1945; 1,000 mems; Chair Prof. Dr A. W. VAN DER VAART; Treasurer Prof Dr S. J. KOOPMAN; publs *Stator* (4 a year), *Statistica Neerlandica* (4 a year).

Physical Sciences
Koninklijk Nederlands Geologisch Mijnbouwkundig Genootschap (Royal Geological and Mining Society of the Netherlands): POB 80123 3508 TC Utrecht; tel. (30) 2532412; fax (30) 2535523; e-mail kngmg@ knag.nl; internet www.kngmg.nl; f. 1912; 1,500 mems; Pres. Drs P. A. C. DE RUITER; Sec. Drs L. VAN DE VATE; publs *Geologie en Mijnbouw* (Journal of Geosciences, quarterly), *Geo.brief* (8 a year).

Koninklijk Nederlands Meteorologisch Instituut (Royal Netherlands Meteorological Institute): Wilhelminalaan 10, 3732 GK De Bilt; POB 201, 3730 AE De Bilt; tel. (30) 2206911; fax (30) 2210407; e-mail prv@knmi .nl; internet www.knmi.nl; f. 1854; meteorology, climatology, oceanography, seismology; library of 140,000 vols; spec. collns incl. Polar expeditions; Dir-in-Chief Prof. Dr J. DE JONG; publs *Maandoverzicht van het weer*, *Seismological Bulletin*, scientific reports and technical reports, daily weather maps, rain observations.

Koninklijke Nederlandse Chemische Vereniging (Royal Netherlands Chemical Society): Vlietweg 16, 2266 KA Leidschendam; POB 249, 2260 AE Leidschendam; tel. (70) 3378790; fax (70) 3378799; e-mail kncv@ kncv.nl; internet www.kncv.nl; f. 1903; 11,500 mems; Pres. Prof. Dr E. VELTKAMP; Sec. Dr Ir. I. P. THONUS; publs *Chemisch 2 Weekblad* (26 a year), *European Journal of Inorganic Chemistry* (monthly), *European Journal of Organic Chemistry* (monthly).

Nederlandse Natuurkundige Vereniging (Netherlands Physical Society): POB 3140, 3502 GC Utrecht; tel. (30) 2844586; fax (30) 2844501; e-mail a.jelles@nnv.nl; internet www.nnv.nl; f. 1921 to improve the study of physics and safeguard the interests of physicists; 3,800 mems; Chair. Prof. Dr Ir H. E. A. VAN DER AKKER; Sec. Dr E. W. A. LINGEMAN; publ. *Nederlands Tijdschrift voor Natuurkunde* (12 a year).

Nederlandse Vereniging voor Weer- en Sterrenkunde (Netherlands Society for Meteorology and Astronomy); e-mail j.a.de .boer@fwn.rug.nl Stichting De Koepel, Sterrenwacht 'Sonnenborgh', Zonnenburg 2, 3512 NL Utrecht; tel. (30) 2311360; fax (30) 2342852; e-mail dekoepel@knoware.nl; internet www.dekoepel.nl; f. 1901; 6,000 mems; publs *Zenit* (monthly), *Sterrengids* (annually), *Gids voor Sterren en Planeten* (annually).

PHILOSOPHY AND PSYCHOLOGY
Algemene Nederlandse Vereniging voor Wijsbegeerte (General Netherlands Philosophical Society): c/o Erasmus Universiteit, Faculteit der Wijsbegeerte, POB 90153, 5000 DR Rotterdam; e-mail anvw@fwb.eur.nl; internet www.eur.nl/fw/anvw/; f. 1933; 150 mems; Pres. Dr J. A. VAN RULER; Sec. Dr H. A. KROP; publ. *Algemeen Tijdschrift voor Wijsbegeerte*.

Affiliated societies:

Internationale School voor Wijsbegeerte (International School of Philosophy): Dodeweg 8, 3832 RD Leusden; tel. (33) 4227200; fax (33) 4227208; e-mail info@isvw.nl; internet www.isvw.nl; f. 1916; courses and conferences in philosophy; 1,800 mems; library of 3,000 vols; Pres. Prof. FRANS JACOBS; Man. Dir RENÉ GUDE.

KIVI Aftdeling Filosofie en Techniek: 23 Prinsessegracht, POB 30424, 2500 GK The Hague; f. 1847; Chair R. E. C. H. TIEPEL; Sec. J. GROENHOEF.

Nederlands Genootschap voor Esthetica (Dutch Society for Aesthetics): Utrecht; internet www.nge.nl; f. 1997; publ. *Jaarboek voor Esthetica*.

Nederlandse Vereniging voor Godsdienstwijsbegeerte: Groningen; f. 1995.

Nederlandse Vereniging voor Logica en Wijsbegeerte der Exacte Wetenschappen: POB 80103, 3508 TC Utrecht; f. 1947; organizes scientific symposia; 150 mems; Chair. Prof. Dr J.-J. CH. MEYER; Sec. Dr R. VERBRUGGE.

Nederlandse Vereniging voor Wetenschapsfilosofie (Netherlands Society for Philosophy of Science): Faculty of Philosophy, Vrije Universiteit, De Boelelaan 1105, Amsterdam; tel. (20) 5986681; fax (20) 5986635; e-mail h.w.de.regt@ph.vu.nl; f. 1979; organization of conferences and lectures; 125 mems; Pres. Prof. T. A. F. KUIPERS; Sec. Dr H. W. DE REGT.

Vereniging voor Filosofie en Geneeskunde: POB 616, 6200 MD Maastricht; tel. (43) 881144; f. 1981; Sec. G. A. M. WIDDERSHOVEN.

Vereniging 'Het Spinozahuis': Paganinidreef 66, 2253 SK Voorschoten; tel. and fax (71) 5612759; e-mail vspinoza@xs4all.nl; internet www.spinozahuis.nl; f. 1897; Sec. TH. VAN DER WERF.

Vereniging voor Reformatorische Wijsbegeerte: POB 3206, 3760 DE Soest; tel. (35) 5880205; fax (35) 5880981; e-mail reform.philos@planet.nl; internet www.aspecten.org; f. 1935; 600 mems; Dir H. A. C. WEIGAND-TIMMER; publs *Beweging* (4 a year), *Philosophia Reformata* (in Dutch and English, 2 a year).

Vereniging voor Wijsbegeerte des Rechts: Amsterdam; f. 1918.

Vereniging voor Wijsbegeerte te 's-Gravenhage: Spreeuwenlaan 10, 2566 ZN 's-Gravenhage; f. 1907; Sec. M. ZUIDGEEST.

Wijsgerige Vereniging Thomas van Aquino: POB 37, 5260 AA Vught; tel. (73) 6579017; f. 1933; philosophical conferences; 160 mems; Pres. Prof. Dr A. LEIJEN; Sec. Prof. Dr R. A. TE VELDE.

Bataafsch Genootschap der Proefondervindelijke Wijsbegeerte (Experimental Natural Philosophy Society): POB 597, 3000 AN Rotterdam; tel. (10) 411-7947; fax (10) 213-1208; f. 1769; 380 mems; organizes 6 lectures for mems each year; awards biannual prizes and an int. Steven Hoogendijk Award, every 3 years; Pres. Prof. Dr G. J. OLSAER; Sec. Ir G. H. G. LAGERS.

Nederlands Psychoanalytisch Genootschap (Netherlands Psychoanalytical Association): Maliestraat 1A, 3581 SH Utrecht; tel. (30) 2307080; fax (30) 2343883; e-mail npg@npsai-utrecht.nl; internet www.npg-utrecht.nl; f. 1947; 155 mems; Sec. Dr J. N. SCHREUDER.

RELIGION, SOCIOLOGY AND ANTHROPOLOGY

Fryske Akademy: POB 54, 8900 AB Leeuwarden; premises at: Doelestraat 8, 8911 DX Leeuwarden; tel. (58) 2131414; fax (58) 2131409; e-mail fa@fa.knaw.nl; internet www.fryske-akademy.nl; f. 1938; attached to Royal Netherlands Acad. of Arts and Sciences; devoted to the scientific study of Friesland, the Frisians and their language, history and culture; 500 mems; 3,000 donors; library of 20,000 vols; Man. Dir J. H. C. M. BIEMANS; Scientific Dir Dr L. G. JANSMA; publs *It Beaken* (scientific, 4 a year), *Ut de Smidte fan de Fryske Akademy* (information, 4 a year), *De Vrije Fries* (history, annually).

Koninklijk Instituut voor Taal-, Land- en Volkenkunde (Royal Netherlands Institute of Southeast Asian and Caribbean Studies): Reuvensplaats 2, 2311 BE Leiden; POB 9515, 2300 RA Leiden; tel. (71) 5272295; fax (71) 5272638; e-mail kitlv@kitlv.nl; internet www.kitlv.nl; f. 1851; attached to Royal Netherlands Acad. of Arts and Sciences; advances the study of the social sciences and humanities of south-east Asia and the Caribbean, particularly the former Dutch colonies of Indonesia and Suriname, and the Netherlands Antilles and Aruba; 1,670 mems; library of 500,000 vols; spec. collns incl. Indonesia; Dir Prof. Dr G. J. OOSTINDIE; publs *Bijdragen* (3 a year), *Bibliotheca Indonesica* (monograph series), *Excerpta Indonesica* (online), *Caribbean Abstracts* (online), *Nieuwe West-Indische Gids* (2 a year).

TECHNOLOGY

Koninklijk Instituut van Ingenieurs (Royal Institute of Engineers in the Netherlands): 23 Prinsessegracht, POB 30424, 2500 GK The Hague; tel. (70) 3919940; fax (70) 3919840; e-mail kivi@kivibur.nl; internet www.kivi.nl; f. 1847; 15,000 mems; Pres. Ir. J. A. DEKKER; Managing Dir Ir P. L. M. GILISSEN; Sec. Ir. A. MOS; publ. *De Ingenieur* (every 2 weeks); publ. *Kivi-nieuws* (every 2 weeks).

Stichting Economisch Instituut voor de Bouwnijverheid (Economic Institute for the Building Industry): De Cuserstraat 89, 1081 CN Amsterdam; tel. (20) 6429342; fax (20) 6449089; e-mail eib@eib.nl; internet www.eib.nl; f. 1956; Dir. Prof. Drs A. P. BUUR; Chair Drs B. G. A. KEMPEN; publ. *Bouw/Werk* (4 vols a year).

Technologiestichting STW (Technology Foundation): POB 3021, 3502 GA Utrecht; Van Vollenhovenlaan 661, 3527 JP Utrecht; tel. (30) 6001211; fax (30) 6014408; e-mail info@stw.nl; internet www.stw.nl; f. 1981; improves and stimulates applied sciences and engineering by sponsoring research at (technical) univs in the Netherlands and promotes co-operation between those institutes and industry; also assists in implementing special governmental research programmes; Dir Dr A. A. J. M. FRANKEN.

Research Institutes

GENERAL

Rathenau Instituut (Rathenau Institute): Koninginnegracht 56, 2514 AE The Hague; Postbus 85525, 2508 CE The Hague; tel. (70) 3421542; fax (70) 3633488; e-mail info@rathenau.nl; internet www.rathenau.nl; f. 1986; attached to Royal Netherlands Acad. of Arts and Sciences; supports social and political opinion-forming on issues arising from scientific and technological development; Dir J. STAMAN.

AGRICULTURE, FISHERIES AND VETERINARY SCIENCE

Agrotechnology and Food Innovations: POB 17, 6700 AA Wageningen; tel. (317) 475029; fax (317) 475347; e-mail info.agrotechnologyandfood@wur.nl; internet www.agrotechnologyandfood.wur.nl; f. 1989 by merger of Sprenger Inst. and Inst. for Storage and Processing of Agricultural Produce; 320 staff; research on post-harvest physiology and quality parameters, storage and container systems, processing and cell and molecular biology, product development, logistics expert systems and computer image analyses; Dir Dr Ir A. H. EENINK.

Alterra, Research Instituut voor de Groene Ruimte (Alterra, Institute for Green World Research): POB 47, 6700 AA Wageningen; premises at: Droevendaalsesteeg 3, 6708 PB Wageningen; tel. (317) 474700; fax (317) 419000; e-mail info@alterra.nl; internet www.alterra.wur.nl; f. 2000 through merger of DLO Winand Staring Centre for Integrated Land, Soil and Water Research, Instuut voor Bos- en Natuuronderzoek and part of DLO-Instituut voor Agrobiologisch Onderzoek; research in fields of ecology, land use and the environment; Dirs Prof. Dr W. VAN VIERSSEN, Prof. Dr H. J. P. EIJSACKERS, Drs W. J. M. HOOGENDOORN-BEKS.

DLO-Instituut voor Agrobiologisch Onderzoek (Research Institute for Agrobiology and Soil Fertility): Postbus 17, 6700 AA Wageningen; Centrum de Born, Bornsesteeg 59, 6708 PD Wageningen; tel. (317) 475000; fax (317) 475347; e-mail info.agrotechnologyandfood@wur.nl; internet www.agrotechnologyandfood.wur.nl; f. 1976; Dir Dr C. D. DE GOOIJER.

DLO-Rijksinstituut voor Visserij Onderzoek (Netherlands Institute for Fisheries Research): Haringkade 1, 1976 UP IJmuiden; POB 68, 1970 AB IJmuiden; tel. (255) 564646; fax (255) 564644; e-mail postmaster@rivo.dlo.nl; internet www.rivo.dlo.nl; f. 1912; biological, chemical, hydrographical, technical and technological fisheries research; annexe of the Shellfish Department at Yerseke; Dir Dr JAN W. D. M. HENFLING.

Internationaal Agrarisch Centrum/International Agricultural Centre: POB 88, 6700 AB Wageningen; Lawickse Allee 11, 6701 AN Wageningen; tel. (317) 495495; fax (317) 495395; e-mail info.iac@wur.nl; internet www.iac.wur.nl; f. 1951 by the Ministry of Agriculture, Nature Management and Fisheries; IAC supports professionals and organisations in developing and improving the livelihoods of people, ensures safe access to food and the conservation of natural resources, develops and provides professional development training programmes, consultancy services, action learning initiatives and topical seminars, knowledge and expertise brokering and online course programmes; Dir Dr Ir. A. HUIJSMAN.

International Institute for Land Reclamation and Improvement (Alterra–ILRI): Lawickse Allee 11, POB 47, 6700 AA Wageningen; tel. (317) 495549; fax (317) 495590; e-mail ilri@ilri.nl; internet www.ilri.nl; f. 1955; collects and disseminates information on land reclamation and improvement and undertakes supplementary research work; postgraduate courses; 30 staff; Dir Ir C.B. DE ZEEUW; publ. publs series: *Publications, Bibliographies, Annual Report*.

Koninklijk Instituut voor de Tropen (KIT) (Royal Tropical Institute): POB 95001, 1090 HA Amsterdam; Mauritskade

63, 1092 AD Amsterdam; tel. (20) 5688711; fax (20) 6684579; e-mail communication@kit .nl; internet www.kit.nl; f. 1910; int. research and training org. that focuses on improving communication between the Western and non-Western world; collects and disseminates information on the developing world; 850 mems; library: see Libraries; Tropical Museum: see Museums and Art Galleries; Chair. Prof. Dr R. RABBINGE; Pres. Dr J. DONNER; publ. *Survey of Activities* (annual report).

Landbouw-Economisch Instituut (Agricultural Economics Research Institute): POB 29703, 2502 LS The Hague; premises at: Burgemeester Patijnlaan 19, 2585 BE The Hague; tel. (70) 3358330; fax (70) 3615624; e-mail informatie.lei@wur.nl; internet www .lei.dlo.nl; f. 1940 to further the knowledge of business and social economics and related problems concerning Dutch agriculture and fisheries in the widest sense; library of 20,000 vols; Dir Prof. Dr L. C. ZACHARIASSE; publ. *Leidraad* (every 2 months).

Nederlands Agronomisch-Historisch Instituut (Institute of Agricultural History): Oude Kijk in 't Jatstraat 26, Groningen; tel. (50) 3635949; f. 1949 to advance the study of and to facilitate scientific research in agricultural history by maintaining an Institute at Groningen University and an international library of 12,000 vols; Dir (vacant); publ. *Historia Agriculturae* (1 or 2 a year).

Plantenziektenkundige Dienst (Plant Protection Service): Geertjesweg 15, POB 9102, 6700 HC Wageningen; tel. (317) 496911; fax (317) 421701; e-mail pd.info@pd .agro.nl; internet www.minlnv.nl/pd; f. 1899; activities include phytosanitary inspection of plants, issue of plant health certificates and design of laws for disease and pest prevention and control, integrated plant protection, diagnostics of diseases and pests, location offices, three per district; Dir Prof. Dr. L. VAN VLOTEN-DOTING; publs *Verslagen en Mededelingen Plantenziektenkundige Dienst* (Reports and Communications of the Plant Protection Service), *Annual Report*, *Newsletter* (in Dutch, 8 a year).

ECONOMICS, LAW AND POLITICS

Centraal Bureau voor de Statistiek (Central Bureau of Statistics): POB 4000, 2270 JM Voorburg; Located at: Prinses Beatrixlaan 428, 2273 XZ Voorburg; tel. (70) 3373800; fax (70) 3877429; e-mail infoserv@cbs.nl; internet www.cbs.nl; f. 1899; Dir-Gen. Prof. Dr J. VAN SINDEREN; economic and social statistical research; library of 410,000 vols, 100,000 microfiche; publs *Statistical Yearbook of the Netherlands*, *Statistisch Bulletin* (weekly), *Historical Statistics of the Netherlands*.

Centre for Peace and Conflict Research of the University of Groningen: Oude Kijk in 't Jatstraat 5/9, 9712 EA Groningen; tel. (50) 635655; fax (50) 635635; f. 1961 as Polemical Institute of the University of Groningen; peace research centre for multidisciplinary research on war, conflict and security, and university teaching; library of 10,000 vols, 150 periodicals; Research Coordinator Prof. Dr HERMAN DE LANGE; publs *Transaktie*, *Peace and Security Yearbook* (in Dutch).

ECORYS Nederland BV: POB 4175, 3006 AD Rotterdam; Located at: Watermanweg 44, 3067 GG Rotterdam; tel. (10) 4538800; fax (10) 4530768; e-mail netherlands@ecorys .com; internet www.ecorys.nl; f. 1929 as Netherlands Economic Institute (NEI); economic research and policy advice; consulting and training; programme management and implementation; monitoring and evaluation;

areas covered incl. economics and competitiveness, regions, cities and real estate, transport, mobility and infrastructure, social policy and govt; Chair. MAX VAN DER SLEEN.

Institute of Social Studies: see under Colleges.

International Institute for Asian Studies: POB 9515, 2300 RA Leiden; Located at: Nonnensteeg 1–3, 2311 VJ Leiden; tel. (71) 5272227; fax (71) 5274162; e-mail iias@let .leidenuniv.nl; internet www.iias.nl; f. 1993 by Royal Netherlands Acad. of Arts and Sciences and three Dutch univs; post-doctoral research in humanities and social sciences; Chair. Prof. P. VAN DER VEER; Dir Prof. W. A. L. STOKHOF; publs *Newsletter* (3 a year), *Annual Report*.

Nederlands Instituut voor Internationale Betrekkingen 'Clingendael' (Netherlands Institute of International Relations 'Clingendael'): POB 93080, 2509 AB The Hague; Located at: 7 Clingendael, 2597 VH The Hague; tel. (70) 3245384; fax (70) 3282002; e-mail info@clingendael.nl; internet www.clingendael.nl; f. 1983; research on int. issues; lectures; postgraduate courses, training in int. negotiation; information and documentation; library of 26,000 vols, 300 periodicals; Dir Prof. Dr J. W. DE ZWAAN; publ. *Internationale Spectator* (monthly).

Nederlands Interdisciplinair Demografisch Instituut (Netherlands Interdisciplinary Demographic Institute): Lange Houtstraat 19, 2511 CV The Hague; POB 11650, 2502 AR The Hague; tel. (70) 3565200; fax (70) 3647187; e-mail info@nidi .nl; internet www.nidi.nl; f. 1970; research, training, information and documentation in the field of population studies; 60 mems; library of 6,000 vols, 2,500 reprints, 15,000 articles, etc.; Dir Prof. Dr ir. F. J. WILLEKENS; publs *Bevolking en Gezin* (Population and Family, 3 a year), *Demos* (10 a year, also online), *NIDI Reports*.

Nederlands Studiecentrum Criminaliteit en Rechtshandhaving (NCSR) (Netherlands Institute for the Study of Criminal Behaviour and Law Enforcement): Postbus 792, 2300 AT Leiden; Wassenaarsewag 72, 2333 AL Leiden; tel. (71) 5278527; fax (71) 5278537; e-mail nscr@nscr.nl; internet www .nscr.nl; f. 1992; Dir Prof. G. J. N. BRUINSMA.

HISTORY, GEOGRAPHY AND ARCHAEOLOGY

Roosevelt Study Center: Postbus 6001, 4330 LA Middelburg; Abdij 8, 4331 BK Middelburg; tel. (118) 631590; fax (118) 631593; e-mail rsc@zeeland.nl; internet www.roosevelt.nl; attached to Royal Netherlands Acad. of Arts and Sciences; research institute, conference centre and library on modern US history and Dutch–US relations; Dir Prof. Dr C. A. VAN MINNEN; publ. *The Roosevelt Review* (annual).

MEDICINE

Interuniversitair Cardiologisch Instituut Netherlands (Interuniversity Cardiology Institute of the Netherlands): Located at: Catharijnesingel 52, 3511 GC Utrecht; Postbus 19258, 3501 DG Utrecht; tel. (30) 2333600; fax (30) 2315940; e-mail info@icin .knaw.nl; internet www.icin.nl; attached to Royal Netherlands Acad. of Arts and Sciences; Dirs W. H. VAN GILST, C. A. VISSER.

Interuniversitair Oogheelkundig Instituut (Netherlands Ophthalmic Research Institute): AMC, Meibergdreef 47, 1105 BA Amsterdam Zuidoost; tel. (20) 5666101; fax (20) 5666121; e-mail receptie@ioi.knaw.nl; internet www.ioi.knaw.nl; attached to Royal

Netherlands Acad. of Arts and Sciences; Dir P. VAN 'T KLOOSTER.

Kahn, W., Institute of Theoretical Psychiatry and Neuroscience: Het Nateland 1, 3911 XZ Rhenen (Achterberg); tel. and fax (317) 618708; e-mail wimkahn1@hotmail .com; f. 1997; 24 mems; develops theoretical models in the fields of psychiatry, psychology, neuroscience and philosophy, for the diagnosis and treatment of mental health disorders; 10 depts; Dir Dr WILLEM H. J. MARTENS; publ. *WKITPN–Publication* (4 a year).

MEG Centrum VUMC: De Boelelaan 1117, Postbus 7057, 1007 MB Amsterdam; tel. (20) 4440729; fax (20) 4444816; e-mail bw.dijk@ vumc.nl; internet www.vumc.nl/meg; attached to Vrije Universiteit Medical Centre; research into magnetoencephalography; Co-ordinator B. W. VAN DIJK.

Nederlands Instituut voor Hersenonderzoek (Netherlands Institute for Brain Research): Meibergdreef 33, 1105 AZ Amsterdam Zuidoost; tel. (20) 5665500; fax (20) 6961006; e-mail secretariaat@nih.knaw .nl; internet www.nih.knaw.nl; f. 1909; attached to Royal Netherlands Acad. of Arts and Sciences; research into maturation, adaptation and ageing of the nervous system; 90 mems; library of 5,000 vols; Dir Prof. D. F. SWAAB; publ. *Yearly Progress Report* with list of publications.

TNO Preventie en Gezondheid (TNO Prevention and Health): POB 2215, 2301 CE Leiden; tel. (71) 5181818; fax (71) 5181910; e-mail info@pg.tno.nl; internet www.health.tno.nl; f. 1994; scientific research in the fields of public health and prevention of illness; postgraduate courses in occupational health; library of 20,000 vols; Dir Dr W. R. F. NOTTEN; publ. *Annual Report*.

Vereniging Het Nederlands Kanker Instituut—Antoni van Leeuwenhoek Ziekenhuis (Netherlands Cancer Institute–Antoni van Leeuwenhoek Hospital): Plesmanlaan 121, 1066 CX Amsterdam; tel. (20) 5129111; fax (20) 6172625; e-mail nkilib@nki.nl; internet www.nki.nl; f. 1913; library of 14,600 vols; basic and translational cancer research, clinical cancer research diagnostic, surgical and medical oncology, radiotherapy; Patron HKH QUEEN BEATRIX; Pres. Prof. Dr A. J. M. BERNS; Sec. P. BELTMAN; publ. *Scientific Report* (annual).

NATURAL SCIENCES

General

Nederlandse Organisatie voor Toegepast – Natuurwetenschappelijk Onderzoek (TNO) (Netherlands Organization for Applied Scientific Research): Schoemakerstraat 97, POB 6050, 2600 JA Delft; tel. (15) 2696900; fax (15) 2612403; e-mail infodesk@tno.nl; internet www.tno.nl; f. 1930; strategic policy and innovation consultancy; building, materials and information technology, mechanical and production engineering, product design and development, telecommunications, quality control, health and safety, nutrition, environment and energy; library of 16,000 vols; Pres. J. A. DEKKER; publs *TNO Magazine* (English), *Toegepaste Wetenschap* (Dutch), *Annual Report* (in Dutch and English).

Nederlandse Organisatie voor Wetenschappelijk Onderzoek (NWO) (Netherlands Organization for Scientific Research): Laan van Nieuw Oost Indië 300, 2593 CE The Hague; POB 93138, 2509 AC The Hague; tel. (70) 3440640; fax (70) 3850971; e-mail nwo@nwo.nl; internet www .nwo.nl; f. 1988; stimulates and co-ordinates pure and applied research in all fields of learning; Pres. Prof. Dr P. NIJKAMP; Dir-Gen. LEO COOLEN; publs *Jaarboek*, *Newsletter* (research reports in the Netherlands).

Stichting voor Wetenschappelijk Onderzoek van de Tropen (WOTRO) (Netherlands Foundation for the Advancement of Tropical Research): Laan van Nieuw Oost Indië 131, 2593 CE The Hague; POB 93120, 2509 AC The Hague; tel. (70) 3440763; fax (70) 3819873; e-mail wotro@nwo.nl; f. 1964; advancement of tropical research both pure and applied by awarding grants; Chair. Prof. Dr B. J. M. ZEGERS; Sec. Dr R. R. VAN KESSEL-HAGESTEIJN; publ. *Annual Report*.

Biological Sciences

Afdeling Biologisch Rijksuniversiteit Groningen: (Department of Biology, University of Groningen): Kerklaan 30, POB 14, 9750 AA Haren; tel. (50) 3632021; fax (50) 3635205; f. 1969; ecology, genetics, microbiology, plant and animal physiology, biotechnology, marine biology, environmental biology; library of 50,000 vols; Dir Prof. Dr J. M. KOOLHAAS.

Centraalbureau voor Schimmelcultures (Fungal Biodiversity Centre): POB 85167, 3508 AD Utrecht; Located at Uppsalalaan 8, 3584 CT Utrecht; tel. (30) 2122600; fax (30) 2512097; e-mail info@cbs.knaw.nl; internet www.cbs.knaw.nl; attached to Royal Netherlands Acad. of Arts and Sciences; research on biosystematics of the fungal kingdom; maintains collns of living moulds and yeasts; Dir Prof. Dr P. W. CROUS; publs *Studies in Mycology*, *CBS Biodiversity Series*.

Hortus Botanicus Leiden: Postbus 9516, 2300 RA Leiden; Located at: Rapenburg 73, Leiden; tel. (71) 5277249; fax (71) 5275199; e-mail hortus@hortus.leidenuniv.nl; internet www.hortus.leidenuniv.nl; Dir Dhr dr ir JAN DE KONIG.

Hortus Haren: POB 179, 9750 AD Haren (Gr); tel. (50) 5370053; f. 1642, renewed 1929; 8,000 species; Dir (vacant).

Instituut voor Plantenziektenkundig Onderzoek (IPO–DLO) (DLO–Research Institute for Plant Protection): Binnenhaven 5, POB 9060, 6700 GW Wageningen; tel. (317) 476000; fax (317) 410113; e-mail info@ipo.dlo.nl; f. 1949; prevention, management and control of plant diseases and pests; library of 24,000 vols; Dir Dr Ir N. G. HOGENBOOM; publ. *Annual Report*.

Nationaal Herbarium Nederland (National Herbarium of the Netherlands): Einsteinweg 2, 2333 CC Leiden; POB 9514, 2300 RA Leiden; tel. (71) 5273515; fax (71) 5273511; internet www.nationaalherbarium.nl; f. 1829; investigation of flora (taxonomy, geography), particularly of the Netherlands and the Tropics; library of 35,000 vols, 1,000 periodicals; Dir Prof. Dr P. BAAS; publs *Blumea* (general), *Persoonia* (Mycology), *Gorteria* (Netherlands flora), *Flora Malesiana* (Phanerog., ferns), *Flora Malesiana Bulletin*, *Internat. Ass. Wood Anatomists Journal*.

Nederlands Instituut voor Oecologisch Onderzoek (Nederlands Institute of Ecology): Postbus 1299, 3600 BG Maarssen; Located at Rijksstraatweg 6, 3631 AC Nieuwersluis; tel. (294) 239312; fax (294) 232078; e-mail webredactie@nioo.knaw.nl; internet www.nioo.knaw.nl; f. 1992; attached to Royal Netherlands Acad. of Arts and Sciences; incorporates Centre for Estuarine and Coastal Ecology (in Yerseke), Centre for Limnology (in Nieuwersluis) and Centre for Terrestrial Ecology (in Heteren); Dir L. E. M. VET.

Nederlands Instituut voor Ontwikkelingsbiologie (Netherlands Institute for Developmental Biology): Universiteitscentrum De Uithof, Uppsalalaan 8, 3584 CT Utrecht; Universiteitscentrum De Uithof, POB 85164, 3508 CT Utrecht; tel. (30) 2121800; fax (30) 2516464; e-mail nimwegen@niob.knaw.nl; internet www.niob.knaw.nl; attached to Royal Netherlands Acad. of Arts and Sciences; research on animal development (esp. the early development of vertebrates); Dirs Prof. R. H. A. PLASTERK, Prof. J. C. CLEVERS.

Mathematical Sciences

Stichting Centrum voor Wiskunde en Informatica (CWI) (Foundation Centre for Mathematics and Computer Science): Kruislaan 413, 1098 SJ Amsterdam; POB 94079, 1098 GB Amsterdam; tel. (20) 5929333; fax (20) 5924199; e-mail info@cwi.nl; internet www.cwi.nl; f. 1946; carries out research in mathematics and computer science through its institute, CWI; Dir Prof. Dr J. K. LENSTRA.

Attached centre:

CWI – Centrum voor Wiskunde en Informatica (Centre for Mathematics and Computer Science): Kruislaan 413, 1098 SJ Amsterdam; POB 94079, 1098 GB Amsterdam; tel. 5929333; fax 5924199; e-mail info@cwi.nl; internet www.cwi.nl; f. 1946; 220 mems; four sections: (1) Modelling, Analysis and Simulation (Head Prof. Dr J. G. VERWER); (2) Information Systems (Head Prof. Dr M. L. KERSTEN); (3) Software Engineering (Head Prof. Dr P. KLINT); (4) Probability, Networks and Algorithms (Head Prof. Dr A. SCHRIJVER); library: see Libraries; Dir Prof. Dr J. K. LENSTRA; publs *CWI Quarterly*, *CWI Tracts*, *CWI Syllabi*, *Annual Report* (incl. Overview of Research Activities, in English).

Physical Sciences

Astronomical Institute: University of Utrecht, POB 80000, 3508 TA Utrecht; tel. (30) 2535200; fax (30) 2535201; e-mail astronomy@phys.uu.nl; internet www.astro.uu.nl; f. 1643 (formerly Sonnenborgh Observatory); studies in solar physics, stellar atmospheres, plasma and high energy astrophysics, space research, astrophysical instrumentation, astroparticle physics, massive stars, nucleosynthesis; library of 30,000 vols; Scientific Dir Prof. Dr NORBERT LANGER.

Koninklijk Nederlands Instituut voor Onderzoek der Zee (Royal Netherlands Institute for Sea Research): POB 59, 1790 AB Den Burg, Texel; Landsdiep 4, 1797 SZ Den Hoorn; tel. (222) 369300; fax (222) 319674; e-mail texel@nioz.nl; internet www.nioz.nl; f. 1876; scientific marine research; ships; Dir Prof. Dr C. H. R. HEIP; publ. *Journal of Sea Research* (quarterly).

Nationaal Instituut voor Kernfysica en Hoge Energie Fysica (NIKHEF) (National Institute for Nuclear Physics and High Energy Physics): Kruislaan 409, 1098 SJ Amsterdam; POB 41882, 1009 DB Amsterdam; tel. (20) 5922000; fax (20) 5925155; e-mail t60@nikhef.nl; internet www.nikhef.nl; has a 900 MeV pulse stretcher and storage ring (AmPs) and auxiliary instrumentation for basic research in hadronic structure physics; Dirs Prof. Dr J. J. ENGELEN, Prof. Dr J. W. VAN HOLTEN, Drs A. J. VAN RIJN.

Netherlands Institute of Applied Geoscience TNO—National Geological Survey: POB 80015, 3508 TA Utrecht; Located at: Princetonlaan 6, 3584 CB Utrecht; tel. (30) 2564256; fax (30) 2564475; e-mail info@nitg.tno.nl; internet www.nitg.tno.nl; f. 1903; Dir Dr M. J. VAN BRACHT; publs *Netherlands Journal of Geosciences* (quarterly), *Information, Edition Geo-Energy* (newsletter, 2 a year), *Information, Edition*

Geohydrology, Geochemistry and Geomechanics (newsletter, annually), *Geological Maps*.

Stichting Ruimteonderzoek Nederland (SRON) (Space Research Organization Netherlands): Sorbonnelaan 2, 3584 CA Utrecht; tel. (30) 2535600; fax (30) 2540860; e-mail info@sron.nl; internet www.sron.nl; f. 1983 to continue the activities of the Cttee for Geophysics and Space Research; develops and exploits equipment for space research and for terrestrial research from space; Gen. Dir Prof. Dr J. A. M. BLEEKER.

Stichting voor Fundamenteel Onderzoek der Materie (FOM) (Foundation for Fundamental Research on Matter): POB 3021, 3502 GA Utrecht; tel. (30) 6001211; fax (30) 6014406; e-mail info@fom.nl; internet www.fom.nl; f. 1946; carries out physics research through 200 university teams in 3 institutes of its own, and 1 used in jtly with universities; Man. Dir Dr K. H. CHANG.

Attached institutes:

FOM-Instituut voor Atoom- en Molecuulfysica (FOM Institute of Atomic and Molecular Physics): Located at: Kruislaan 407, 1098 SJ Amsterdam; POB 41883, 1009 DB Amsterdam; tel. (20) 6081234; fax (20) 6684106; e-mail secr@amolf.nl; internet www.amolf.nl; f. 1949; 150 mems; facilities include mass-spectrometers, spectrographs, molecular beam apparatus, microwave interferometers, laser equipment, beam plasma experiments, a PDP 11 computer and a nanocentre; library of 2,200 vols; Gen. Dir Prof. Dr L. D. NOORDAM; publ. *Annual Report*.

FOM-Instituut voor Plasmafysica (FOM Institute of Plasma Physics): Located at: Edisonbaan 14, 3439 NM Nieuwegein; POB 1207, 3430 BE Nieuwegein; tel. (30) 6096999; fax (30) 6031204; internet www.rijnh.nl; f. 1959; research in plasma physics, plasma containment, heating; free electron laser; molecular cooling; plasma surface interaction; EUV mirrors; 120 mems; library of 7,000 vols, 13,000 reports; Dir Prof. Dr A. W. KLEYN.

KVI (Nuclear Accelerator Facility): Zernikelaan 25, 9747 AA Groningen; tel. (50) 3633600; fax (50) 3634003; internet www.kvi.nl; f. 1975; AVF cyclotron, ion sources, traps for short-living isotopes; Dir Prof. Dr M. N. HARAKEH.

FOM-Instituut voor Subatomaire Fysica (FOM-Institute for Subatomic Physics): Located at: Kruislaan 409, 1098 SJ Amsterdam; POB 41882, 1009 DB Amsterdam; tel. (20) 5925075; fax (20) 5925054; internet www.nikhef.nl; f. 1981; Dir Prof. Dr F. L. LINDE.

RELIGION, SOCIOLOGY AND ANTHROPOLOGY

Meertens Instituut (Meertens Institute): Postbus 94264, 1090 GG Amsterdam; Joan Muyskenweg 25, 1096 CJ Amsterdam; tel. (20) 4628500; fax (20) 4628555; e-mail info@meertens.knaw.nl; internet www.meertens.knaw.nl; f. 1926; attached to Royal Netherlands Acad. of Arts and Sciences; research into and documentation of Dutch language and culture; Dir Prof. H. J. BENNIS.

Netherlands Institute for Advanced Study in the Humanities and Social Sciences (NIAS): Meijboomlaan 1, 2242 PR Wassenaar; tel. (70) 5122700; fax (70) 5117162; e-mail nias@nias.knaw.nl; internet www.nias.knaw.nl; f. 1970; attached to Royal Netherlands Acad. of Arts and Sciences; aims to encourage research in the humanities and social sciences; fellowships awarded annually (20 to foreign scholars, 20 to Dutch scholars);

Rector Prof. Dr W. P. BLOCKMANS; Exec. Dir Dr W. R. HUGENHOLTZ; publs *NIAS Newsletter* (2 a year), *Uhlenbeck Lecture* (annual), *Ortelius Lecture* (annual), *Jelle Zijlstra Lecture* (annual).

TECHNOLOGY

Instituut voor Milieu en Agritechniek (IMAG-DLO) (Institute of Agricultural and Environmental Engineering): POB 43, 6700 AA Wageningen; tel. (317) 476300; fax (317) 425670; e-mail postkamer@imag.dlo.nl; internet www.imag.dlo.nl; f. 1974; 180 mems; Dir Ir. A. A. JONGEBREUR.

Nationaal Lucht- en Ruimtevaartlaboratorium (NLR) (National Aerospace Laboratory): Anthony Fokkerweg 2, 1059 CM Amsterdam; POB 90502, 1006 BM Amsterdam; tel. (20) 5113113; fax (20) 5113210; e-mail info@nlr.nl; internet www .nlr.nl/public; f. 1919; fluid dynamics, flight mechanics, flight testing and operations, structures and materials, space technology, remote sensing, information technology, electronics and instrumentation; library of 7,000 vols, 4,800 conference proceedings, 2,500 theses, 112,000 reports, etc.; Chair. of Board J. VAN HOUWELINGEN; Dir Ir. F. HOLWERDA; publs technical reports, miscellaneous.

Netherlands Energy Research Foundation (ECN): Located at: Westerduinweg 3, Petten (NH); POB 1, 1755 ZG Petten (NH); tel. (224) 564949; fax (224) 564480; e-mail info@ecn.nl; internet www.ecn.nl; f. 1955 as *Reactor Centrum Nederland — RCN*; carries out energy research; under contract from the govt, nat. and int. orgs and industry; Dir Dr A. B. M. HOFF.

Libraries and Archives

Alkmaar

Regionaal Archief (Regional Record Office): Hertog Aalbrechtweg 5, POB 9232, 1800 GE Alkmaar; tel. (72) 5662626; fax (72) 5622633; e-mail regionaal@archiefalkmaar .nl; internet www.archiefalkmaar.nl; f. 1990; municipal archives, books about Alkmaar and North Holland, etc.; also regional archives for the area; pictures, prints, maps, relating to Alkmaar and surroundings; 50,000 vols; Municipal Archivist (vacant); publs *Annual Report, Inventories of Archives.*

Amersfoort

Bibliotheek van het Oud Katholiek Seminarie (Library of the Old Catholic Seminary): Koningin Wilhelminalaan 3, 3818 HN Amersfoort; tel. (33) 4617569; fax (33) 4619340; e-mail l.nieuwenhuiz@freeler .nl; f. 1725; 10,000 vols; Librarian L. NIEUWENHUIZEN.

Openbare Leeszaal en Bibliotheek (Public Library): Zonnehof 12, 3811 ND Amersfoort; tel. (33) 631914; f. 1913; 190,000 vols; Librarian E. A. MURRIS.

Amsterdam

Bibliotheca Philosophica Hermetica: Bloemgracht 31–35, 1016 KC Amsterdam; tel. (20) 6258079; fax (20) 6200973; e-mail bph@ritmanlibrary.nl; internet www .ritmanlibrary.nl; f. 1957; private library, open to researchers by appt; 5,000 vols printed before 1800, 600 MSS, 15,000 modern titles; specialises in early printed books and MSS in the field of the Christian-hermetic tradition (alchemy, hermetism, mysticism and rosicrucianism); also modern biographical and bibliographical reference works, text-editions, scholarly works, books on the modern esoteric tradition; Archivist CARLOS GILLY.

Bibliotheek Centrum voor Wiskunde en Informatica (Library of the Centre for Mathematics and Computer Science): Kruislaan 413, POB 94079, 1090 GB Amsterdam; tel. (20) 5924027; fax (20) 5924026; e-mail bibl@cwi.nl; internet www.cwi.nl/library; f. 1946; special scientific library on non-elementary mathematics and its applications and computer science; 47,000 vols, 1,000 current periodicals, 155,000 reports; Librarian AY-LING ONG.

Bibliotheek van de Vrije Universiteit (Library of the Free University): De Boelelaan 1103, 1081 HV Amsterdam; tel. (20) 4445200; fax (20) 4445259; e-mail www@ ubvu.vu.nl; internet www.ubvu.vu.nl; f. 1880; 1,000,000 vols on sciences, medicine and social sciences, 50,000 maps; Librarian Drs J. G. DE ROOS.

Bibliotheek van het Koninklijk Instituut voor de Tropen (Library of the Royal Tropical Institute): Mauritskade 63, 1092 AD Amsterdam; tel. (20) 5688298; fax (20) 6654423; e-mail library@kit.nl; internet www.kit.nl; f. 1910; 230,000 vols, 11,000 periodicals, 25,000 maps; Head of Information, Library and Documentation Drs J. H. W. VAN HARTEVELT.

Boekmanstichtings Bibliotheek (Library of the Boekman Foundation): Herengracht 415, 1017 BP Amsterdam; tel. (20) 6243739; fax (20) 6385239; e-mail secretariaat@ boekman.nl; internet www.boekman.nl; f. 1963; all fields of art and culture, and related policy; 53,000 vols, 150 current periodicals; Librarian S. LEEFSMA; publ. *Boekman.*

Economisch-Historische Bibliotheek Amsterdam: Cruquiusweg 31, 1019 AT Amsterdam; tel. (20) 6685866; fax (20) 6654181; e-mail cse@iisg.nl; internet www .neha.nl; f. 1932; a dept of Netherlands Economic-Historical Archives Foundation, 120,000 vols; special collection of 16th–18th-century books on commerce and bookkeeping, and on Dutch business history and companies; Librarian J. J. SEEGERS; publ. *Tijdschrift voor Sociale en Economische Geschiedenis.*

KB, Bureau Nederlands Centrum voor Rechtshistorische Documentatie en Rechtsiconografie (Netherlands Centre for Documentation of History of Law, National Library of the Netherlands): O. Z. Achterburgwal 217, 1012 DL Amsterdam; tel. (20) 5253412; f. 1967; documentation system of catchword data from 33,000 articles, brochures and books on the history of law in the Netherlands; juridical iconography (c. 5,000 pictures and 3,000 slides); Dir Mrs M. A. BECKER-MOELANDS; publ. *Rechtshistorisch Nieuws* (3 a year).

Nederlands Instituut voor Oorlogsdocumentatie (Netherlands Institute for War Documentation): Herengracht 380, 1016 CJ Amsterdam; tel. (20) 5233800; fax (20) 5233888; e-mail info@niod.knaw.nl; internet www.niod.knaw.nl; f. 1945; attached to Royal Netherlands Acad. of Arts and Sciences; Dutch, German and Allied collections on the history of World War II; 50,000 vols; Dir Dr J. C. H. BLOM.

Rijksakademie van Beeldende Kunsten Bibliotheek (Library of the State Academy of Fine Arts): Sarphatistraat 470, 1018 GW Amsterdam; tel. (20) 5270300; fax (20) 5270301; e-mail info@rijksakademie.nl; internet www.rijksakademie.nl; f. 1870; 30,000 vols, 6,000 prints and drawings and 1,000 sculptures and plaster casts.

Stadhuis Bibliotheek: Stadhuis Amsterdam, kamer 1131, Amstel 1, 1011 PN Amsterdam; f. 1892; 75,000 vols on law, administration and statistics; Librarian N. E. MOKKUM.

Universiteitsbibliotheek Amsterdam (Amsterdam University Library): POB 19185, 1000 GD Amsterdam; Singel 421–425, 1012 WP Amsterdam; tel. (20) 5252301; fax (20) 5252311; e-mail secr-uba@uva.nl; internet www.uba.uva.nl; f. 1578; 4,000,000 vols, 145,000 maps, 160 medieval and 70,000 modern MSS, 500,000 letters; incl. Bibliotheca Rosenthaliana (f. 1880, 100,000 vols, 850 MSS), Réveil-Archives, Vondel, Frederik van Eeden and Albert Verwey collns; Tetterode colln; several historical Church collns; libraries of Royal Dutch Book Trade Asscn, Royal Geographical Soc., Royal Netherlands Soc. of Medicine, etc.; Chief Librarian A. J. H. A. VERHAGEN; Chief Curator J. C. E. BELINFANTE; publ. *Studia Rosenthaliana* (every 6 months).

Arnhem

Rijksarchief in Gelderland: Markt 1, 6811 CG Arnhem; tel. (26) 4420148; fax (26) 4459792; e-mail gelderland@rad.archief.nl; f. 1878; contains the archives of the Dukes of Guelders and succeeding provincial administrations, and of other regional and local authorities; of private persons, families, enterprises, religious bodies, etc. (since 12th century); archive material for northern Limburg before 1580; Archivist Dr F. KEVERLING BUISMAN.

Stichting Arnhemse Openbare en Gelderse Wetenschappelijke Bibliotheek (Arnhem Public and Learned Library): Koningstraat 26, 6811 DG, Arnhem; POB 1168, 6801 ML Arnhem; tel. (26) 3543111; fax (26) 4458616; e-mail bibliotheekarnhem@ biblioarnhem.nl; internet www.biblioarnhem .nl; f. 1856; 750,000 vols, 130 MSS; Librarian A. J. HOVY.

Assen

Rijksarchief in Drenthe te Assen (State Archives of Drenthe): Brink 4, 9401 HS Assen; POB 595, 9400 AN Assen; tel. (592) 313523; f. 1879; public records of the Province of Drenthe; archives of private persons, institutions and enterprises; 7,500 vols; Dir Dr P. BROOD.

De Bilt

Bibliotheek van het Koninklijk Nederlands Meteorologisch Instituut (Library of the Royal Netherlands Meteorological Institute): Wilhelminalaan 10, De Bilt; POB 201, 3730 AE De Bilt; tel. (30) 2206855; fax (30) 2210407; e-mail biblioth@knmi.nl; internet www.knmi.nl/voorl/bibliothek; f. 1854; 140,000 vols on meteorology, physical oceanography and geophysics (especially seismology); Librarian W. J. JANSEN.

Delft

Gemeentearchief Delft Bibliotheek (Library of the Municipal Archives of Delft): Oude Delft 169, 2611 HB Delft; tel. (15) 2602341; fax (15) 2602355; e-mail archief@ delft.nl; internet www.delft.nl/archief; f. 1859; 30,000 vols mainly on history of Delft, genealogy and heraldry; special collections: Delft early printed books, House of Orange-Nassau, Naundorff; Librarian J. A. METER HAGG.

TU Delft Library (Library of the Delft University of Technology): Prometheusplein 1, POB 98, 2600 MG Delft; tel. (15) 2785678; fax (15) 2785706; e-mail library@tudelft.nl; internet www.library.tudelft.nl; f. 1842; the largest technical and scientific library in the Netherlands; 637,500 vols, 4,242 periodicals (3,567 electronic), 3,880 e-books; Librarian Drs M. A. M. HEIJNE.

Deventer

Stadsarchief en Athenaeumbibliotheek (Municipal Library): POB 351, 7400 AJ Deventer; Klooster 12, 7411 NH Deventer; tel. (570) 693887; fax (570) 693747; e-mail info@sab.hsij.nl; internet www.hsij.nl/www/sab; f. 1560; 250,000 vols, 550 MSS, 380 incunabula, 400 post-incunabula; Librarian Dr H. PEETERS.

Stadsarchief Deventer (Record Office): Klooster 12, 7411 NH Deventer; tel. (570) 693713; fax (570) 693437; e-mail info.sab@saxion.nl; internet www.sabdeventer.nl; f. 1853; 10,000 vols; municipal archives 1241–1950, judicial archives 1423–1811, archives of chapter 1123–1591, church registers 1542–1811, notarial archives 1811–1905; Dir J. B. L. M. PEETERS.

Dordrecht

Stadsarchief Dordrecht (Dordrecht Record Office): Stek 13, 3311 XS Dordrecht; tel. (78) 6492311; fax (78) 6492388; e-mail stadsarchief@dordrecht.nl; internet www.dordrecht.nl/stadsarchief; f. 1885; archives of the City of Dordrecht and of nearby towns; books and prints of Dordrecht and its environs; 35,000 vols, 250 periodicals; Archivist CH. JEURGENS; Librarian J. ALLEBLAS.

Echt

Bibliotheca Lilboschensis (Lilbosch Abbey Library): Pepinusbrug 6, 6102 RJ Echt; f. 1885; 40,000 vols; theology, monastica, cisterciensia; Librarian (vacant).

Eindhoven

Bibliotheek der Technische Universiteit Eindhoven (Library of the Eindhoven University of Technology): POB 90159, 5600 RM Eindhoven; tel. (40) 2472381; fax (40) 2447015; e-mail helpdesk.bib@tue.nl; internet www.tue.nl/bib; f. 1956; 600,000 vols, 5,000 current periodicals; Head Librarian Drs J. C. M. FIGDOR.

Openbare Bibliotheek Eindhoven (Eindhoven Public Library): Gebouw de Witte Dame Emmasingel 22, 5611 AZ Eindhoven; tel. (40) 2604260; fax (40) 2461225; e-mail info@obeindhoven.nl; internet www.obeindhoven.nl; f. 1916; 800,000 vols; Librarian H. VEEN.

Enschede

Dinkel University Library, University of Twente: POB 217, 7500 AE Enschede; tel. (53) 4892777; fax (53) 4893599; e-mail info@dinkel.utwente.nl; internet www.dinkel.utwente.nl/scinfo; f. 1964; 375,000 vols, 2,700 periodicals; Librarian P. DAALMANS.

Groningen

Bibliotheek der Rijksuniversiteit te Groningen (Library of the State University): POB 559, 9700 AN Groningen; Located at: Broerstraat 4, 9712 CP Groningen; tel. (50) 3635000; fax (50) 3634996; e-mail info@ub.rug.nl; internet www.rug.nl/bibliotheek; f. 1615; 3,000,000 vols, 1,100 MSS, 210 incunabula; Librarian A. C. KLUGKIST.

Groninger Archieven (Archives of Groningen): Cascadeplein 4, 9726 AD Groningen; Postbus 30040, 9700 RM Groningen; tel. (50) 5992000; fax (50) 5992050; e-mail info@groningerarchieven.nl; internet www.groningerarchieven.nl; f. 1824; 20,000 vols; Archivist (vacant).

Haarlem

Bibliotheek van Teylers Museum (Teyler Museum Library): Spaarne 16, 2011 CH Haarlem; tel. (23) 5319010; fax (23) 5342004; e-mail info@teylersmuseum.nl; internet www.teylersmuseum.nl; f. 1778; 125,000 vols (natural sciences); Librarian Drs M. A. M. VAN HOORN.

Rijksarchief in Noord-Holland te Haarlem (State Archives of North Holland): Kleine Houtweg 18, 2012 CH Haarlem; tel. (23) 5172700; fax (23) 5172720; e-mail info@noordhollandsarchief.org; internet www.noordhollandsarchief.org; Dir Drs R. C. HOL.

Stadsbibliotheek (Municipal and Public Library): Doelenplein 1, 2011 XR Haarlem; tel. (23) 5157600; fax (23) 5157669; e-mail stadsbibliotheek@haarlem.nl; internet www.bibliotheeksite.nl/haarlem; f. 1596; 552,000 vols, 280 MSS, 192 incunabula; Dir A. F. SKOLNIK-KOOIMAN.

Kampen

Gemeente-Archief (Record Office): Molenstraat 28, 8261 JW Kampen; tel. (38) 3370770; fax (38) 3370779; e-mail gemeentearchief@kampen.nl; internet www.gemeentearchiefkampen.nl; archives of the town 1251–1955; Archivist D. HARE; publ. *De Archieven der gemeente Kampen, I, II and III*.

Leeuwarden

Buma Bibliotheek (Buma Library): POB 2637, 8901 AC Leeuwarden; tel. (58) 7890789 Located at: Boterhoek 1, 8911 DH Leeuwarden; e-mail info@tresoar.nl; internet www.tresoar.nl; f. 1876; books on Greek and Roman antiquities; 50,000 vols; Librarian D. P. DE VRIES.

Historisch Centrum Leeuwarden (Leeuwarden History Centre): Grote Kerkstraat 29, 8911 DZ Leeuwarden; tel. (58) 2338399; fax (58) 2332315; e-mail historischcentrum@leeuwarden.nl; internet www.historischcentrumleeuwarden.nl; f. 1838; works (incl. MSS) about Leeuwarden; topographical collection, mainly historical; 18,000 vols; Archivist and Librarian J. FOLKERTS.

Provinsjale Biblioteek fan Fryslân (Frisian Provincial Library): POB 464, Boteroek 1, 8901 BG Leeuwarden; tel. (58) 2945020; fax (58) 2945043; e-mail info@pbf.nl; internet www.pbf.nl; f. 1852; 450,000 vols; Dir-Librarian Dr G. J. VAN DEN BROEK.

TRESOAR Frysk Histoarysk en Letterkundich Sintrum (TRESOAR Frisian Historical and Literary Centre): POB 2367, 8901 AC Leeuwarden; Located at: Boterhoek 1-3, 8911 DH Leeuwarden; tel. (58) 7890789; fax (58) 7890777; e-mail info@tresoar.nl; internet www.tresoar.nl; f. 2002; Dir D. P. DE VRIES.

Leiden

Bibliotheek der Universiteit Leiden (Leiden University Library): Witte Singel 27, 2311 BG Leiden; POB 9501, 2300 RA Leiden; tel. (71) 5272800; fax (71) 5272836; e-mail secretariaat@library.leidenuniv.nl; internet ub.leidenuniv.nl; f. 1575; 2,300,000 vols, 50,000 MSS, 70,000 maps; Librarian KURT DE BELDER.

Bibliotheek van de Maatschappij der Nederlandse Letterkunde (Library of the Society of Dutch Literature): Witte Singel 27, POB 9501, 2300 RA Leiden; tel. (71) 5272832; fax (71) 5272836; e-mail mnl@library.leidenuniv.nl; internet www.leidenuniv.nl/host/mnl/biblio.html; f. 1766; 110,000 vols, 3,300 MSS; Librarian Drs R. BREUGELMANS.

Maastricht

Kunst, Cultuur en Onderwijs afdeling, Gemeentearchief Maastricht (Art, Culture and Education Department, Municipal Record Office of Maastricht): POB 882, 6200 AW Maastricht; Located at: Avenue Céramique, 6221 KV Maastricht; tel. (43) 292222; f. 1849; municipal and family archives, church records, MSS, topographical collections relating to Maastricht and the Province of Limburg; Archivist Drs P. A. W. DINGEMANS.

Rijksarchief in Limburg (State Archives of Limburg): St Pieterstraat 5–7, 6211 JM Maastricht; tel. (43) 3217051; fax (43) 3255640; e-mail info@rijksarchieflimburg.nl; internet www.rijksarchieflimburg.nl; Pres. P. D. WESTERVELD (acting).

Stadsbibliotheek Maastricht, Centre Céramique (Municipal Library): POB 1992, 6201 BZ Maastricht; Located at: Avenue Céramique 50, 6221 KV Maastricht; tel. (43) 3505600; fax (43) 3505599; internet www.centreceramique.nl; f. 1662; 500,000 vols, including 107 incunabula, 297 post-incunabula, 1,600 periodicals, special collections and documentation relating to the Province of Limburg, devotional material and chess literature; Dir Dr W. KUIPER; publ. *Limburgensia*.

Middelburg

Zeeuws Archief (Zeeland Archives): Postbus 70, 4330 AB Middelburg; tel. (118) 678800; fax (118) 628094; e-mail info@zeeuwsarchief.nl; internet www.zeeuwsarchief.nl; f. 1843; Archivist Drs R. L. KOOPS.

Zeeuwse Bibliotheek (Zeeland Library): Kousteensedijk 7, 4331 JE Middelburg; Postbus 8004 4330 EA Middelburg; tel. (118) 654000; fax (118) 654001; e-mail info@zeeuwsebibliotheek.nl; internet www.zeeuwsebibliotheek.nl; f. 1985; 777,168 vols, 6,500 MSS, 5,000 periodicals; Dir G. E. HUISMAN.

Nijmegen

Universiteitsbibliotheek Nijmegen (Library of the University of Nijmegen): Erasmuslaan 36, POB 9100, 6500 HA Nijmegen; tel. (24) 3612440; fax (24) 3615944; e-mail secretariaat@ubn.kun.nl; internet www.kun.nl/ubn; f. 1923; 2,000,000 vols; Librarian Drs H. P. A. SMIT.

Rotterdam

Gemeentebibliotheek (Municipal Library): Hoogstraat 110, 3011 PV Rotterdam; tel. (10) 2816100; fax (10) 2816181; e-mail communicatie@bibliotheek.rotterdam.nl; internet www.bibliotheek.rotterdam.nl; f. 1604; 1,550,000 vols, 200 MSS, Erasmus collection 5,000 vols; Dir Ir F. H. MEIJER.

Gemeentelijke Archiefdienst (Municipal Record Office): Hofdijk 651, 3032 CG Rotterdam; POB 71, 3000 AB Rotterdam; tel. (10) 2434567; fax (10) 2434666; e-mail info@gar.rotterdam.nl; internet www.gar.rotterdam.nl; f. 1857; city archives, church records, notarial archives, Chamber of Commerce records 1797–1922, family archives, topographical collection, sound archives, historical library; Archivist Drs E. A. G. VAN DEN BENT.

Rotterdamsch Leeskabinet (Rotterdam Library): Burg. Oudlaan 50, POB 1738, 3000 DR Rotterdam; tel. (10) 4081195; e-mail kabinet@ubib.eur.nl; internet www.eur.nl/ub/rlk.html; f. 1859; history, art, art history, language and literature, biography, theology, philosophy, social sciences, geography; 235,000 vols; Librarian Drs J. W. DE JONG; publs *Kwartaalbericht, Jaarverslag*.

Universiteitsbibliotheek Erasmus Universiteit Rotterdam (Library of the Erasmus University of Rotterdam): POB 1738, 3000 DR Rotterdam; Located at: Burgemeester Oudlaan 50, 3062 PA Rotterdam; tel. (10) 4081198; fax (10) 4089050; e-mail balie@ubib.eur.nl; internet www.eur.nl/ub; f. 1913; 1,000,000 vols; economics and management, medicine and health, law, culture and society; University Librarian Dr PAUL E. L. J. SOETAERT.

's-Hertogenbosch

Brabants Historisch Informatie Centrum (Historical Information Centre for North Brabant): POB 81, 5201 AB 's-Hertogenbosch; tel. (73) 6818500; fax (73) 6146439; e-mail info@bhic.nl; internet www .brabantarchieven.nl; f. 1860 as Rijksarchief in de Provincie Noord Brabant; records since 13th century; Record Office contains c. 200,000 vols; 30,000 vols, 8,000 charters; Archivist Drs R. BASTIAANSE; publ. *Inventarisreeks*.

Stadsbibliotheek 's-Hertogenbosch: Hinthamerstraat 72, 5211 MR 's-Hertogenbosch; tel. (73) 6123033; fax (73) 6144925; e-mail stadsbibliotheek@sbdenbosch.nl; internet www.sbdenbosch.nl; f. 1915; 270,000 vols, 18,000 compact discs; Librarian G. DE ROOIJ.

The Hague

Bibliotheek van het Centraal Bureau voor de Statistiek (Library of Statistics Netherlands): Prinses Beatrixlaan 428, POB 4000, 2270 JM Voorburg; tel. (70) 3375151; fax (70) 3375984; e-mail bibliotheek@cbs.nl; internet www.cbs.nl/nl/service/bibliotheek; f. 1899; 380,000 vols; Librarian M. WIJNGAARDEN.

Bibliotheek van het Vredespaleis (Peace Palace Library): 2 Carnegieplein, 2517 KJ The Hague; tel. (70) 3024242; fax (70) 3024166; internet www.ppl.nl; f. 1913; int. public and municipal law, diplomatic history, int. relations; Grotius Collection; 700,000 vols; Dir J. VERVLIET; publs acquisitions list (quarterly), *Bibliography for the Centre for Studies and Research of the Hague Academy of International Law* (annually).

Koninklijke Bibliotheek (Royal Library): Located at: Prins Willem-Alexanderhof 5, 2595 BE The Hague; POB 90407, 2509 LK The Hague; tel. (70) 3140911; fax (70) 3140450; e-mail info@kb.nl; internet www .kb.nl; f. 1798; National Library, responsible for the development, documentation and management of the nat. cultural heritage; depository for all Dutch publs and the nat. bibliography; research library for the humanities and social sciences; centre of expertise in preservation and restoration; focal point of inter-library co-operation; 2,200,000 books, 15,000 current periodicals, newspapers, MSS; spec. collns incl. chess, cookery, children's books; Dir Gen. Dr W. VAN DRIMMELEN; publs *Jaarverslag, Nederlandse Bibliografie*, special bibliographies, exhibition catalogues.

Nationaal Archief (National Archives): POB 90520, 2509 LM The Hague; Prins Willem Alexanderhof 20, 2595 BE The Hague; tel. (70) 3315400; fax (70) 3315540; e-mail info@nationaalarchief.nl; internet www.nationaalarchief.nl; f. 1802; 90 km of archives; 80,000 vols, 700 journals; Dir Dr M.W. VAN BOVEN; publ. *Inventories of Archives*.

Openbare Bibliotheek (Public Library): POB 12653, 2500 DP The Hague; Spui 68, 2511 BT The Hague; tel. (70) 3534401; fax (70) 3534504; e-mail secr@dobdenhaag.nl; internet www.dobdenhaag.nl; f. 1906; 980,000 vols, 190,000 children's books, music library of 55,000 vols and 60,000 compact discs, 21,000 audio-visual items; 16 branch libraries, 2 mobile libraries; Dir A. E. H. L. BURGERS VAN DEN BOGAERT.

Tweede Kamer der Staten-Generaal; Dienst Bibliotheek en Dienst Documentatie (Second Chamber of the States-General; Library Department and Documentation Department): Plein 2, POB 20018, 2500 EA The Hague; tel. (70) 3182315; fax (70) 3182307; e-mail bibliotheek@tk.parlement.nl; f. 1815; 100,000 vols; Librarian J. C. KEUKENS; Head of Documentation P. VAN RIJN.

Tilburg

Universiteit van Tilburg Bibliotheek (Tilburg University Library): Warandelaan 2, POB 90153, 5000 LE Tilburg; tel. (13) 662124; fax (13) 662996; e-mail library@uvt .nl; internet www.uvt.nl/bibliotheek; f. 1927; economics, applied computer sciences, social sciences, law, history, philosophy, linguistics; 900,000 vols; Librarian H. GELEIJNSE.

Utrecht

Gemeentebibliotheek Utrecht (Municipal Library): Oude Gracht 167, POB 80, 3500 AB Utrecht; tel. (30) 2861800; fax (30) 2861990; e-mail info@gbu.nl; internet www.utrecht.nl/ bibliotheek; f. 1892; 795,000 vols, 10 brs, music library; Dir A. G. J. VAN VLIMMEREN.

Universiteitsbibliotheek Utrecht (Library of Utrecht University): POB 80124, 3508 TC Utrecht; premises at: Heidelberglaan 3, 3584 CS Utrecht; tel. (30) 2536600; fax (30) 2538398; e-mail info@library.uu.nl; internet www.library.uu.nl; f. 1584; 4,500,000 vols, 2,500 MSS, 900 incunabula, 110,000 vols printed before 1800, MSS and printed books of the medieval libraries of the Utrecht churches and religious houses, two 16th century private libraries; special collections in the fields of literature, theology, history, botany, medicine, 18th and 19th century science libraries, and on the province and city of Utrecht; Librarian Drs J. S. M. SAVENIJE.

Utrechts Archief (Utrecht Archives): Alexander Numankade 199–201, 3572 KW Utrecht; tel. (30) 2866611; fax (30) 2866600; e-mail info@hetutrechtsarchief.nl; internet www.hetutrechtsarchief.nl; f. 1805; records of the City and Province of Utrecht, church history, political pamphlets, regional newspapers, national railway history; 70,000 vols; Archivist Drs J. T. J. JAMAR.

Wageningen

Bibliotheek Wageningen Universiteit (Wageningen University Library): Gen. Foulkesweg 19, POB 9100, 6700 HA Wageningen; tel. (317) 484440; fax (317) 484761; e-mail helpdesk.library@wur.nl; internet library.wur.nl; f. 1873; 1,500,000 vols, 15,000 current periodicals; Chief Librarian D. VAN ZAANE; publs *Wageningen Agricultural University Papers*, Theses.

Zwolle

Historisch Centrum Overijssel (Overijssel Historical Centre): Eikenstraat 20, 8021 WX Zwolle; tel. (38) 4266300; fax (38) 4266333; e-mail info@hcov.nl; internet www .historischcentrumoverijssel.nl; f. 2000; library of 60,000 vols; collns incl. provincial archives 1528–1948, judicial archives 1333–1979, notarial archives 1811–1915, old church registers and civil registers 1592–1942, archives of monasteries 1225–1811, industrial archives 1850–1980, Zwolle municipal archives 1265–1970, notarial archives 1811–1925, cadastral archives 1811–1980, family archives since 13th century; 9,500 m of archives, 9,500 charters; 12,220 maps and drawings; 100,000 photographs and negatives, 1,000 historical films; Dir Drs B. LOOPER.

Museums and Art Galleries

Alkmaar

Stedelijk Museum Alkmaar: Canadaplein 1, 1811 KE Alkmaar; tel. (72) 5110737; fax (72) 5151476; e-mail museum@alkmaar.nl; internet www.stedelijkmuseumalkmaar.nl; f. c.1550; municipal museum; antiquarian and art collection from Alkmaar and its environs, paintings by van Heemskerck, van de Velde the Elder, Allart and Caesar B. van Everdingen, Honthorst; objects include old silver, glass, pottery, porcelain, tiles and modern art; collection of antique toys and dolls; Dir S. DE VRIES.

Amsterdam

Allard Pierson Museum Amsterdam: Oude Turfmarkt 127, 1012 GC Amsterdam; tel. (20) 5252556; fax (20) 5252561; e-mail allard.pierson.museum@uva.nl; internet www.uba.uva.nl/apm; f. 1934; the archaeological museum of the University of Amsterdam; scientific research centre for students of archaeology and history of art, and public museum; archaeology of ancient Egypt, Near East, Greece, Etruria, Roman Empire; Chief Curator Prof. Dr R. A. LUNSINGH SCHEURLEER; publs *Mededelingenblad van de Vereniging van Vrienden*, Allard Pierson series.

Amstelkring Museum: (Our Lord in the Attic): Oudezijds Voorburgwal 40, 1012 GE Amsterdam; tel. (20) 6246604; fax (20) 6381822; e-mail info@opsolder.nl; internet www.opsolder.nl; f. 1888; merchant's house of 1661 with a clandestine Catholic church in the attic; exhibits of ecclesiastical art since 16th century; library of 1,500 vols; Dir J. KIERS.

Amsterdams Historisch Museum (Amsterdam Historical Museum): POB 3302, 1001 AC Amsterdam; tel. (20) 5231822; fax (20) 6207789; e-mail info@ahm .amsterdam.nl; internet www.ahm.nl; f. 1926; exhibits of the city's history over 700 years including archaeological finds, artefacts, paintings, prints and models; library of 22,000 vols on history of Amsterdam, Dutch art history and applied industrial arts; special collection: Jan and Casper Luyken collection.

Nederlands Scheepvaartmuseum (Netherlands Maritime Museum): Kattenburgerplein 1, 1018 KK Amsterdam; tel. (20) 5232222; fax (20) 5232213; e-mail info@ scheepvaartmuseum.nl; internet www .scheepvaartmuseum.nl; f. 1916; closed until 2009 for reconstruction; models, paintings, charts, globes, technical drawings, nautical instruments, arms and relics, full-size replica East-Indiaman; library of 60,000 vols, spec. collns: early navigation textbooks, voyages and travel, navigation, Dutch sea atlases; Dir W. BIJLEVELD; publ. *Zee Magazijn* (quarterly).

Rembrandthuis Museum: Jodenbreestr. 4–6, 1011 NK Amsterdam; tel. (20) 6249486; fax (20) 6232246; internet www .rembrandthuis.nl; f. 1907; Rembrandt etchings and drawings, and paintings by his teacher and pupils; the artist lived here 1639–58; Dir A. R. E. DE HEER; publs catalogues, *Bulletin* (2 a year).

Rijksmuseum (State Museum): Stadhouderskade 42, 1071 ZD Amsterdam; POB 74888, 1070 DN Amsterdam; tel. (20) 6747000; fax (20) 6747001; e-mail info@ rijksmuseum.nl; internet www.rijksmuseum .nl; f. 1800; paintings, sculpture, drawings, history, porcelain, glass, costumes, silver, furniture, Asiatic art (main museum closed while major renovation work is undertaken;

Masterpieces Collection of 400 of the most important works on display in the Philips Wing during this period); library of 80,000 vols; Dir-Gen. Prof. Drs R. DE LEEUW; Man. Dir J. W. SIEBURGH; Dir of Collections Dr J. P. SIGMOND; Curator (Paintings) Dr J. P. FILEDT KOK; Curator (Sculpture and Applied Art) Dr R. J. BAARSEN; Curator (National Historical Collection) Dr C. J. ZANDVLIET; Curator (Prints) Drs G. LUIJTEN; Curator (Asiatic Art) Drs P. C. M. LUNSINGH SCHEURLEER; Librarian Drs G. J. M. KOOT; publs *Bulletin* (4 a year), annual reports.

Stedelijk Museum: POB 75082, 1070 AB Amsterdam; tel. (20) 5732911; fax (20) 6752716; e-mail info@stedelijk.nl; internet www.stedelijk.nl; f. 1895; modern paintings and sculpture, especially American and European trends since 1950; graphics and drawings; applied arts and industrial design; temporary exhibitions on contemporary art; library of 23,000 vols, 95,000 catalogues; Dir HANS VAN BEERS; publs *Bulletin* (in Dutch and English), Catalogues.

Tropenmuseum (Museum of the Royal Tropical Institute): POB 95001, 1090 HA Amsterdam; Linnaeusstraat 2, Amsterdam; tel. (20) 5688200; fax (20) 5688331; internet www.tropenmuseum.nl; f. 1916; presents a picture of life and work in the tropics and sub-tropics; children's museum; library of 18,000 vols; Dir R. SCHENK.

Van Gogh Museum: Paulus Potterstraat 7, POB 75366, 1070 AJ Amsterdam; tel. (20) 5705200; fax (20) 5705222; e-mail info@vangoghmuseum.nl; internet www.vangoghmuseum.nl; f. 1973 to house collections of the Vincent van Gogh Foundation; paintings and drawings by van Gogh and his contemporaries; van Gogh's personal collection including English and French prints and graphics, Japanese wood-cuts, documents and personal correspondence with his brother, Theo van Gogh; Theo's personal collection; library of 12,500 vols; archives of the art historian M. E. TRALBAUT; special collection: 19th century literature (mainly French) read by van Gogh; Dir JOHN LEIGHTON; publs *Van Gogh Bulletin* (quarterly), *Cahier Vincent* (Scientific research, annually).

Apeldoorn

Paleis Het Loo: Koninklijk Park 1, 7315 JA Apeldoorn; tel. (55) 5772448; fax (55) 5219983; e-mail info@paleishetloo.nl; internet www.paleishetloo.nl; f. 1971; collection of portraits, furniture, documents, etc., relating to the Dutch royal family, the House of Orange-Nassau; library of 20,000 vols; Dir Dr J. R. TER MOLEN.

Arnhem

Historisch Museum het Burgerweeshuis: Bovenbeekstraat 21, 6811 CV Arnhem; tel. (26) 4426900; fax (26) 4436315; f. 1995; pre-1900 applied art, history, archaeology, glass and silver, Delftware, topographic collection of Gelderland.

Museum voor Moderne Kunst (Museum for Modern Art): Utrechtseweg 87, 6812 AA Arnhem; tel. (26) 34512431; fax (26) 4435148; e-mail petra.versluis@arnhem.nl; internet www.mmkarnhem.nl; f. 1920; post-1900 sculpture, Dutch realistic paintings, design, jewellery, contemporary art; Dir M. MEYER.

Nederlands Openluchtmuseum (Netherlands Open Air Museum): Postbus 649, 6800 AP Arnhem; Located at: Schelmseweg 89, 6816 SJ Arnhem; tel. (26) 3576111; fax (26) 3576147; e-mail directie@openluchtmuseum.nl; internet www.openluchtmuseum.nl; f. 1912; history of daily life; information retrie-

val; library of 40,000 vols, 278 periodicals; Dir Dr J. A. M. F. VAESSEN.

Delft

Koninklijk Nederlands Leger- en Wapenmuseum 'Generaal Hoefer' (Royal Netherlands Army and Arms Museum 'General Hoefer'): Korte Geer 1, 2611 CA Delft; tel. (15) 2150500; fax (15) 2150544; f. 1913; exhibition covering 2,000 years of Netherlands' military history; weapons from prehistory to the present; uniforms, equipment, medals, paintings; library of 225,000 vols and collection of prints; Dir J. A. BUYSE; publs *Annual Report*, *Armamentaria* (annually).

Museum Lambert van Meerten: Oude Delft 199, 2611 HD Delft; tel. (15) 2602358; fax (15) 2138744; e-mail gemeentemusea@delft.nl; internet www.lambertvanmeerten-delft.nl; f. 1909; 19th c. art collector's house; 16th–19th c. Dutch Titels, Delft faience, paintings, furniture; Curators Drs MARJOLEINE GROEN, Drs RONALD E. BROUWER.

Museum Nusantara: Sint Agathaplein 4–5, 2611 HR, Delft; tel. (15) 2602358; fax (15) 2138744; e-mail gemeentemusea@delft.nl; internet www.nusantra-delft.nl; f. as Ethnographic Museum of Delft; history and culture of the Indonesian archipelago; colln incl. exhibitions of Dutch involvement in Indonesia since the 17th century, incl. the Dutch East India Co. (1602–1799) and the Colonial Period (1800–1949); Indonesian art, culture, religion, musical instruments, puppets, jewellery, wooden carvings, masks, textiles; maquettes of 19th century, Indonesian houses and ships; Dir DANIËLLE H. A. C. LOKIN.

Museum 'Het Prinsenhof': St Agathaplein 1, 2611 HR Delft; tel. (15) 2602358; fax (15) 2138744; e-mail gemeentemusea@delft.nl; internet www.prinsenhof-delft.nl; f. 1948; historical colln of City of Delft, paintings of the Delft School, Eighty Years' War, William the Silent; Dir Drs D. H. A. C. LOKIN.

Den Helder

Marinemuseum: Hoofdgracht 3, 1781 AA Den Helder; tel. (223) 657534; fax (223) 657282; e-mail info@marinemuseum.nl; internet www.marinemuseum.nl; f. 1962; history of the Royal Netherlands Navy since 1813, collections of models, navigational instruments, paintings, photographs, etc.; three-cylinder submarine 'Tonijn' (1966), minesweeper 'Abraham Crynssen' (1937), ironclad ram ship 'Schorpioen' (1868), and other craft; library: small specialized library; Dir Cmdr HARRY DE BLES.

Deventer

Gemeentemusea Deventer (Municipal Museums of Deventer): POB 5000, 7400 GC Deventer; tel. (570) 693783; fax (570) 693788; e-mail info@deventermusea.nl; internet www.deventermusea.nl; f. 1963; Dir C. F. C. G. BOISSEVAIN.

Associated museums:

Historisch Museum Deventer: Brink 56, 7411 BV Deventer; tel. (570) 693780; fax (570) 693788; e-mail info@deventermusea.nl; internet www.deventermusea.nl; f. 1915; local history, paintings, drawings, applied arts, bicycles; Dir C. F. C. G. BOISSEVAIN.

Speelgoedmuseum Deventer: Brink 47, Deventer; tel. (570) 693786; fax (570) 693788; e-mail info@deventermusea.nl; internet www.deventermusea.nl; f. 1982; toys, mechanical toys, trains, dolls; Dir C. F. C. G. BOISSEVAIN.

Eindhoven

Van Abbemuseum: Bilderdijklaan 10, POB 235, 5600 AE Eindhoven; tel. (40) 2381000; fax (40) 2460680; e-mail info@vanabbemuseum.nl; internet www.vanabbemuseum.nl; f. 1936; large collection of modern and contemporary art including Lissitzky collection and conceptual collection; library of 120,000 vols; Dir CHARLES ESCHE.

Enschede

Rijksmuseum Twenthe, Enschede: Lasondersingel 129, 7514 BP Enschede; tel. (53) 4358675; fax (53) 4359002; e-mail info@rijksmuseum-twenthe.nl; internet www.rijksmuseum-twenthe.nl; f. 1930; fine and applied art from Middle Ages to the present; library of 15,000 vols; Dir Drs D. A. S. CANNEGIETER; publ. *Bulletin* (quarterly).

Gouda

Stedelijk Museum 'de Moriaan' ('The Blackamoor' Municipal Museum): 29 Westhaven, Gouda; tel. (182) 588444; fax (182) 588671; Dutch Merchants' house containing authentic 18th-century tobacco shop; collection of Dutch clay pipes and Gouda pottery; Dir Dr N. C. SLUIJTER-SEIJFFERT.

Stedelijk Museum 'Het Catharina Gasthuis' (St Catherine Hospital, Municipal Museum): Oosthaven 9, Gouda; tel. (182) 588440; fax (182) 588671; e-mail infomuseum@gouda.nl; 18th c. town dispensary; antique toys, surgeons' Guild Room, decorative art since late 16th c., Gasthuis kitchen and chapel, important collection of art since 15th c.; Dir Dr N. C. SLUIJTER-SEIJFFERT.

Groningen

Groninger Museum: Located at: Museumeiland 1, 9711 ME Groningen; Museumeiland 1, 9711 ME Groningen; tel. (50) 3666555; fax (50) 3120815; e-mail info@groningermuseum.nl; internet www.groningermuseum.nl; f. 1894; prehistory and history; paintings of local school; Dutch and Flemish of 16th and 17th c.: Fabritius, Jordaens, Rubens, Sweerts, Teniers; drawings: Rembrandt, Averkamp, Van Goyen, Cuyp, Lievens; painting since 19th c.; extensive collection of Far-Eastern ceramics; collection of applied art; photography, design and fashion collections; library of 38,000 vols incl. book collection on modern art and artists and collection of modern art since 1979; Dir KEES VAN TWIST.

Haarlem

Frans Halsmuseum: Groot Heiligland 62, POB 3365, 2001 DJ Haarlem; tel. (23) 5115775; fax (23) 5115776; e-mail franshalsmuseum@haarlem.nl; internet www.franshalsmuseum.com; f. 1913; pictures since 15th century, focusing on the Haarlem school and Frans Hals; applied arts, contemporary art; Dir KAREL SCHAMPERS.

Teylers Museum: Spaarne 16, 2011 CH Haarlem; tel. (23) 5319010; fax (23) 5342004; e-mail info@teylersmuseum.nl; internet www.teylersmuseum.nl; f. 1778; paintings, drawings, palaeontology, geology, mineralogy, natural history, physics, numismatics; library of 125,000 vols (natural science); Dir M. SCHARLOO; publs *Verhandelingen van Teylers Godgeleerd Genootschap*, *Verhandelingen van Teylers Tweede Genootschap*, *Archives du Musée Teyler*.

Heerlen

Thermenmuseum Heerlen: Coriovallumstraat 9, POB 1, 6400 AA Heerlen; tel. (45) 5605100; fax (45) 5603915; e-mail info@thermenmuseum.nl; internet www.thermenmuseum.nl; f. 1977; collection includes Roman bath house excavated in 1940–41 and other objects from Roman period; Curator (vacant).

Hoorn

Westfries Museum: Rode Steen 1, 1621 CV Hoorn; tel. (229) 280022; fax (229) 280029; e-mail info@wfm.nl; internet www.wfm.nl; the baroque building dates from 1632, museum f. 1879; 17th and 18th c. painting, prints, oak panelling, glass, pottery, silver, furniture, costumes, interiors, objects of trade, navigation and business, folk art, historical objects from Hoorn and West Friesland, prehistoric finds; Dir R. J. SPRUIT; publ. publs annual reports.

Leerdam

Stichting Nationaal Glasmuseum (National Glass Museum): Lingedijk 28, 4142 LD Leerdam; tel. (345) 612714; e-mail info@nationaalglasmuseum.nl; internet nationaalglasmuseum.nl; f. 1953; art glass, industrial glass and bottles, contemporary Dutch colln and works from other European countries and America; small library; Curator Drs J. MEIHUIZEN.

Leeuwarden

Fries Museum: Turfmarkt 11, 8911 KS Leeuwarden; tel. (58) 2123001; fax (58) 2132271; e-mail info@friesmuseum.nl; internet www.friesmuseum.nl; f. 1827; painting, local history, archaeology, decorative arts, prints and drawings, Second World War, Mata Hari gallery, modern art; Dir CEES VAN 'T VEEN; publs *Visitor's Guide* (English, French and German), exhibition catalogues.

Princessehof Leeuwarden, Nationaal Keramiekmuseum (Princessehof Leeuwarden, National Museum of Ceramics): Grote Kerkstraat 11, 8911 DZ Leeuwarden; tel. (58) 2948958; fax (58) 2948968; e-mail museum@princessehof.nl; internet www.princessehof.nl; f. 1917; Asian and European ceramics and tiles, contemporary ceramics; library of 20,000 vols; Dir CEES VAN 'T VEEN; publ. *Keramika* (quarterly).

Leiden

Naturalis (National Museum of Natural History): Located at: Darwinweg 2, 2300 RA Leiden; POB 9517, 2333 CR Leiden; tel. (71) 5687600; fax (71) 5687666; e-mail naturalis@naturalis.nnm.nl; internet www.naturalis.nl; f. 1820; library of 108,000 vols, 8,000 periodical (zoology library 78,000 vols, 5,000 periodicals; geology library 30,000 vols, 3,000 periodicals), palaeontology; Dir Drs R. J. M. VAN HENGSTUM; publs *Zoölogische Mededelingen, Zoölogische Verhandelingen, Scripta Geologica, Technical Bulletin NNM, Nederlandse Faunistische Mededelingen.*

Rijksmuseum van Oudheden (National Museum of Antiquities): POB 11114, 2301 EC Leiden; Rapenburg 28, 2311 EW Leiden; tel. (71) 5163163; fax (71) 5149941; e-mail info@rmo.nl; internet www.rmo.nl; f. 1818; prehistoric, Roman and Medieval periods in the Netherlands; Egyptian, Mesopotamian, Greco-Roman and ancient European collns; library of 30,000 vols, 25 periodicals; Dir Drs W. WEIJLAND.

Rijksmuseum voor de Geschiedenis van de Natuurwetenschappen en van de Geneeskunde 'Museum Boerhaave' (National Museum of the History of Science and Medicine): Lange St. Agnietenstraat 10, 2312 WC Leiden; POB 11280, 2301 EG Leiden; tel. (71) 5662605; fax (71) 5120344; e-mail informatie@museumboerhaave.nl; internet www.museumboerhaave.nl; f. 1928; historical scientific and medical instruments and documents, anatomical preparations,

portraits; library of 25,000 vols, MSS; Dir Dr G. A. C. VEENEMAN.

Rijksmuseum voor Volkenkunde (National Museum of Ethnology): Steenstraat 1, Postbus 212, 2300 AE Leiden; tel. (71) 5168800; fax (71) 5128437; e-mail info@rmv.nl; internet www.rmv.nl; f. 1837; collections from Africa, the Middle East, the Islamic and Indian cultural areas, the Far East, Pacific, South-East Asia, the Americas and the circumpolar regions; library of 50,000 vols; Dir Dr S. B. ENGELSMAN; publs *Annual Report, Mededelingen.*

Stedelijk Museum 'de Lakenhal' Leiden: Oude Singel 28–32, POB 2044, 2301 CA Leiden; tel. (71) 5165360; fax (71) 5134489; e-mail postbus@lakenhal.nl; internet www.lakenhal.nl; f. 1872; pictures of Leiden school; memorial table (triptych) and altar pieces by Lucas van Leyden and C. Engebrechtsz; Rembrandt, Jan Steen, Jan van Goyen, van Mieris, Dou, modern Leiden school: Verster, Kamerlingh Onnes and contemporary Dutch art; furniture, silver, glass, tapestry, etc.; period rooms; history of the town; library of 4,604 vols, 10,500 catalogues; Dir Drs H. BOLTEN-REMPT.

Stichting Geld- en Bankmuseum (Money and Banking Museum): Located at: Rapenburg 26, 2301 EA Leiden; POB 2407, 3500 GK Utrecht; tel. (30) 2910492; fax (30) 2910467; e-mail info@sgbm.nl; internet www.penningkabinet.nl; f. 1816 as Rijksmuseum Het Koninklijk Penningkabinet; merged with Nederlands Muntmuseum 2004; coins from Greek and Roman times to the present, medals, paper money, engraved gems; library of 12,000 vols on numismatics and glyptics; Dir T. KUIPERS; Curator Drs A. POL; publs *Jaarboek voor Munt- en Penningkunde, De Beeldenaar* (every 2 months).

Maastricht

Bonnefantenmuseum — Provinciaal Museum Limburg (Limburg Provincial Museum): Postbus 1735, 6201 BS Maastricht; Located at: Avenue Céramique 250, Maastricht; tel. (43) 3290190; fax (43) 3290199; e-mail info@bonnefanten.nl; internet www.bonnefanten.nl; f. 1863, refounded 1968; early Italian painting (1300–1550); Neutelings collection (medieval sculpture and applied arts; Maasland sculpture (incl. works by Jan van Steffeswert); contemporary art (incl. works by René Daniëls, Peter Duig, Gary Hume, Sol LeWitt and Roman Signer); Dir A. M. U. VAN GREVENSTEIN.

Natuurhistorisch Museum Maastricht (Maastricht Natural History Museum): Located at: De Bosquetplein 6, 6211 KJ Maastricht; tel. (43) 3505490; fax (43) 3505475; e-mail mail@nhmmaastricht.nl; internet www.nhmmaastricht.nl; f. 1912; flora, fauna and soils of the Limburg area, late Cretaceous fossils; library of 30,000 vols; Chief Officer Drs D. TH. DE GRAAF; publ. *Natuurhistorisch Maandblad* (monthly).

Muiden

Muiderslot: Stichting Rijksmuseum Muiderslot, Herengracht 1, Postbus 33, 1398 ZG Muiden; tel. (294) 256262; fax (294) 261056; e-mail kasteel@muiderslot.nl; internet www.muiderslot.com; 13th c. castle furnished in early 17th c. style: paintings, tapestries, furniture and armoury; Dir W. 'T HOOFT.

Naarden

Comenius Museum: Kloosterstraat 33, 1411 RS Naarden; tel. (35) 6943045; fax (35) 6941949; e-mail info@comeniusmuseum.nl; internet www.comeniusmuseum.nl; f. 1924; J. A. Comenius mausoleum and

museum; library of 2,500 vols; Man. INGRID KACZMAREK.

Nijmegen

Museum Het Valkhof: Kelfkensbos 59, 6511 TB Nijmegen; tel. (24) 3608805; fax (24) 3608656; e-mail mhv@museumhetvalkhof.nl; internet www.museumhetvalkhof.nl; f. 1998; archaeology, cultural history, and fine art, mainly related to Nijmegen and the province of Gelderland; modern art, mainly related to the Netherlands; Dir Drs M. BROUWER.

Otterlo

Kröller-Müller Museum: Nationale Park de Hoge Veluwe, Houtkampweg 6, 6731 AW Otterlo; POB 1, 6730 AA Otterlo; tel. (318) 591241; fax (318) 591515; e-mail information@kmm.nl; internet www.kmm.nl; f. 1938; large collection of paintings by Van Gogh, paintings and sculpture since 19th c., old masters, open-air modern sculpture collection (Moore, Serra, Volten), ceramics, drawings, graphic art; library of 40,000 vols; Dir Dr E. J. VAN STRAATEN.

Nederlands Tegelmuseum (Netherlands Tile Museum): Eikenzoom 12, 6731 BH Otterlo; tel. (318) 591519; fax (318) 592000; e-mail info@nederlandstegelmuseum.nl; internet www.nederlandstegelmuseum.nl; f. 1961; extensive collection of Netherlands tiles, since 1500; library of 930 vols; Dir M. H. VAN MEURS.

Roermond

Stedelijk Museum Roermond (Roermond Municipal Museum): Andersonweg 4, 6041 JE Roermond; tel. (475) 333496; fax (475) 336299; e-mail museum@roermond.nl; internet museum.roermond.nl; f. 1932; archaeology, historical and contemporary art and design, architecture and art of Dr P. J. H. Cuypers (1827–1921); Curator Drs R. HOEKSTRA.

Rotterdam

Historisch Museum der Stad Rotterdam: Korte Hoogstraat 31, 3011 GK Rotterdam; tel. (10) 2176767; fax (10) 4334499; history, archaeology, domestic life, technology, art; Dir C. O. A. Baron SCHIMMELPENNINCK VAN DER OIJE.

Maritiem Museum Rotterdam: Leuvehaven 1, 3011 EA Rotterdam; POB 988, 3000 AZ Rotterdam; tel. (10) 4132680; fax (10) 4137342, e-mail info@maritiemmuseum.nl; internet www.maritiemmuseum.nl; f. 1874, new building 1986; models of ships since 15th c., globes, atlases, 20,000 books; ironclad warship 'Buffel'; special children's exhibition; Dir C. O. A. Baron SCHIMMELPENNINCK VAN DER OIJE; publs *MM Journaal* (2 a year), *Jaarverslag* (annually).

Museum Boijmans Van Benningen: Museumpark 18–20, 3015 CX Rotterdam; tel. (10) 4419400; fax (10) 4360500; e-mail info@boijmans.rotterdam.nl; internet www.boijmans.nl; f. 1849; Dutch School including paintings by Van Eyck, Bosch, Pieter Brueghel, Hals, Rembrandt, van Ruysdael, Hobbema, Jan Steen; Baroque School, French School, Impressionists; old, modern and contemporary paintings and sculpture; drawings since 15th c. from Dutch, Flemish, French, German, Italian and Spanish schools, old and modern prints; glass, Dutch silver, old pewter, laces and ceramics, among which an important collection of Persian, Spanish, Italian and Dutch pottery and tiles; furniture, industrial design; library of 125,000 vols and catalogues, 200 periodical titles; Gen. Man. SJAREL EX; publ. publs catalogues.

Wereldmuseum Rotterdam: Willemskade 25, 3016 DM Rotterdam; tel. (10) 2702100;

fax (10) 2707182; e-mail secr@
wereldmuseum.rotterdam.nl; internet www
.wereldmuseum.rotterdam.nl; f. 1885; exhibitions on regional collections, festivities,
music, arts and crafts, modern non-western
art; ethnological and archaeological collections from Indonesia, realm of Islam, Asia,
Africa, America and Oceania; Dir S. BREMER;
publ. *Jaarverslag* (annual report).

's-Hertogenbosch

Noordbrabants Museum: Verwersstraat
41, 5211 HT 's-Hertogenbosch; POB 1004,
5200 BA 's-Hertogenbosch; tel. (73) 6877877;
fax (73) 6877899; e-mail info@
noordbrabantsmuseum.nl; internet www
.noordbrabantsmuseum.nl; f. 1837; North
Brabant prehistorical, historical and folklore
collections, paintings, sculpture, metalwork,
prints, coins, etc.; Dir Drs M. M. A. VAN
BOVEN; publ. *Noordbrabants Museum
Nieuws* (quarterly).

The Hague

Haags Fotomuseum: Stadhouderslaan 43,
2517 HV The Hague; tel. (70) 3381144;
internet www.fotomuseumdenhaag.nl; f.
2003; contemporary photography as well as
photos from the collection of the Gemeentemuseum.

Haags Gemeentemuseum: Stadhouderslaan 41, 2517 HV The Hague; POB 72,
2501 CB The Hague; tel. (70) 3381111; fax
(70) 3381112; e-mail info@gemeentemuseum
.nl; internet www.gemeentemuseum.nl; f.
1862; Modern Art (since 19th c.); Decorative
Arts (ceramics, glass, silver, furniture) and
design since early 20th c.; costumes and
fashion from 1750 to the present; musical
instruments from 15th c. to the present; art
and music library; Dir Dr J. L. LOCHER
(acting).

**Koninklijk Kabinet van Schilderijen
Mauritshuis** (Royal Picture Gallery): Korte
Vijverberg 8, 2513 AB The Hague; tel. (70)
3023456; fax (70) 3653819; e-mail
communicatie@mauritshuis.nl; internet
www.mauritshuis.nl; f. 1822; 15th, 16th and
17th c. Dutch and Flemish masters
(Rembrandt, Vermeer, Hals, Rubens, Ruis-
dael, Ter Borch, Van Dyck, Holbein, R. v.d.
Weyden); Dir F. J. DUPARC; publ. *Annual
Report*.

Museon: Stadhouderslaan 37, 2517 HV The
Hague; tel. (70) 3381338; fax (70) 3381339;
e-mail info@museon.nl; internet www
.museon.nl; f. 1904; astronomy and geology,
biology and ecology, history and archaeology,
geography and ethnology, science and technology; library; Dir B. MOLSBERGEN.

Museum Meermanno: Prinsessegracht 30,
2514 AP The Hague; tel. (70) 3462700; fax
(70) 3630350; e-mail info@meermanno.nl;
internet www.meermanno.nl; f. 1848; medieval MSS, incunabula; modern typography,
book plates, private press books; Dir LEO
VOOGT; publ. *Leeslint* (2 a year).

Museum Mesdag te 's-Gravenhage: Laan
van Meerdervoort 7F, The Hague; tel. (70)
3621434; fax (70) 3614026; internet www
.museummesdag.nl; f. 1903; Dutch pictures
1860–1920; French pictures of the Barbizon
school; Oriental objects; Dir J. LEIGHTON;
publs *Annual Report, Museum Mesdag
Nederlandse 19e eeuwse Schilderijen, Catalogue de l'école française XIX siècle*.

Museum voor Communicatie (Museum of
Communication): Zeestraat 82, The Hague;
tel. (70) 330-7500; fax (70) 360-8926; e-mail
info@muscom.nl; internet www.muscom.nl; f.
1929; objects and documents, etc., concerning
the history and working of the services of
posts, telegraphs and telephones in the
Netherlands; international stamp gallery;

library of 20,000 vols; Dir Drs B. KOEVOETS;
publs annual reports, illustrated guide.

Utrecht

Centraal Museum Utrecht: Nicolaasher-
khof 10, 3512 XC Utrecht; tel. (30) 2362362;
fax (30) 2332006; e-mail info@
centraalmuseum.nl; internet www
.centraalmuseum.nl; f. 1921; paintings and
sculpture of Utrecht School, Utrecht Cara-
vaggisti; doll's house, 12th c. Utrecht ship,
applied art and design; Rietveld Collection,
brick Bruna collection; Chair E. J. VERLOOP.

Veere

Museum 'De Schotse Huizen': Kaai 25–27,
4351 AA Veere; tel. (118) 501744; e-mail
info@schotsehuizen.nl; internet www
.schotsehuizen.nl; f. 1950; Chinese and Japanese ceramics; prints, nat. costumes, furniture, statues, exhibitions of paintings; sited
in 16th-century merchants' houses; Dir J.
VAN DEN BROEKE.

Museum 'De Vierschaar': Markt 5, 4351
AG Veere; tel. (118) 506064; f. 1881; tribunal,
council-chamber and exhibition rooms; old
standards and flags; pictures; golden cup of
Maximilian from Burgundy (1546); memorabilia from the house of Oranje-Nassau; Dir
P. BLOM.

Venlo

Limburgs Museum: Keulsepoort 5, 5911
BX Venlo; POB 1203, 5900 BE Venlo; tel. (77)
3522112; fax (77) 3548396; e-mail info@
limburgsmuseum.nl; internet www
.limburgsmuseum.nl; f. 2000; prehistory,
Roman and medieval collection, history of
Limburg, art and applied art; coins and
medals; Dir J. SCHATORJÉ.

Vlissingen

Zeeuws maritiem muZEEum Vlissingen:
Nieuwendijk 11, 4381 BV Vlissingen; tel.
(118) 412498; fax (118) 430307; e-mail info@
muzeeum.nl; internet www.muzeeum.nl; f.
2002; maritime collection (pilotage, light-
houses, marine archaeology, fishery); local
history (souvenirs of Admiral de Ruyter,
paintings, ceramics, wood carvings, engravings, tiles, coins and medals); library of 700
vols; Curator W. WEBER.

Wageningen

**Museum Historische Landbouwtech-
niek** (Museum for the History of Agricultural Engineering): Droevendaalsesteeg 50,
6708 PB Wageningen; tel. (317) 415774; fax
(317) 417613; e-mail museum.landbouw@
wur.nl; internet www.aenf.wau.nl/mhl; f.
1980; library of 500,000 vols; Dir J. W. VAN
BRAKEL.

Universities

UNIVERSITEIT VAN AMSTERDAM
(University of Amsterdam)

POB 19268, 1000 GG Amsterdam
Located at: Spui 21, 1012 WX Amsterdam

Telephone: (20) 525-9111
Fax: (20) 525-2136
E-mail: info@uva.nl
Internet: www.uva.nl

Founded 1632
State university
Language of instruction: Dutch
Academic year: September to July

President: Dr KAREL VAN DER TOORN
Rector Magnificus: Prof. P. F. VAN DER
  HEIJDEN
Dirs: Dr R. SCHEERENS, Drs J. W. A. VERLAAN
Librarian: Drs A. J. H. A. VERHAGEN

Library: see Libraries and Archives
Number of teachers: 550
Number of students: 24,000
Publications: *Athenaeum Illustre* (4 a year),
  Gids van de Universiteit van Amsterdam
  (annually)

DEANS

Faculty of Dentistry: Prof. Dr W. BEERTSEN
Faculty of Economics and Econometrics:
  Prof. Dr J. VAN DER GAAG
Faculty of Humanities: Prof. Dr A. C. J. HULK
Faculty of Law: Prof. J. A. PETERS
Faculty of Medicine: Prof. Dr L. J. GUNNING-
  SCHEPERS
Faculty of Science: Prof. Dr W. HOOGLAND
Faculty of Social and Behavioural Sciences:
  Prof. Dr D. C. VAN DEN BOOM

ATTACHED INSTITUTES

**Amsterdam Centre for International
Law:** POB 19123, 1000 GC Amsterdam; Located at: Turfdraagsterpad 9, 1012 XT
Amsterdam; tel. (20) 5252961; fax (20)
5252900; e-mail M.A.vanTrigt@uva.nl;
internet www.jur.uva.nl/aciluk/home.cfm;
Dir Prof. P. A. NOLLKAEMPER.

**Amsterdam Centre for Language and
Communication (ACLC):** Spuistraat 210,
1012 VT Amsterdam; tel. (20) 5252543; fax
(20) 5253052; e-mail aclc-fgw@uva.nl;
internet www.hum.uva.nl/aclc; Dir Prof. Dr
A. BAKER.

Amsterdam Graduate Business School:
Roetersstraat 11, 1018 WB Amsterdam; tel.
(20) 5254286; fax (20) 5255092; e-mail
agbs-fee@uva.nl; internet www.agbs.nl; Dir
Prof. B. REES.

**Amsterdam Institute for Private Law
(AIP):** e-mail aip@jur.uva.nl.

**Amsterdam Research Institute for Glo-
bal Issues and Development Studies
(AGIDS):** Nieuwe Prinsengracht 130, 1018
VZ Amsterdam; tel. (20) 5254062; fax (20)
5254051; internet www2.fmg.uva.nl/agids;
Dir Prof. Dr I. BAUD.

**Amsterdam School for Cultural Analy-
sis:** Spuistraat 210, 1012 VT Amsterdam; tel.
(20) 5253874; fax (20) 5253052; e-mail asca@
hum.uva.nl; internet www.hum.uva.nl/asca;
Dir Prof. W. WESTSTEIJN.

**Amsterdam School for Social Science
Research (ASSR):** Kloveniersburgwal 48,
1012 CX Amsterdam; tel. (20) 5252262; fax
(20) 5252446; e-mail assr@pscw.uva.nl;
internet www.assr.nl; Dir Prof. Dr A.
HARDON.

**Amsterdam Study Centre for the Metro-
politan Environment (AME):** Nieuwe
Prinsengracht 130, 1018 VZ Amsterdam;
tel. (20) 5254062; fax (20) 5254051; internet
www2.fmg.uva.nl/ame; Dir Prof. Dr R.
KLOOSTERMAN.

**Anton Pannekoek Astronomical Insti-
tute:** Kruislaan 403, 1098 SJ Amsterdam;
tel. (20) 5257491; fax (20) 5257484; e-mail
secr-astro@science.uva.nl; internet www
.astro.uva.nl/home2.html; Dir Prof. B. REES.

Centre for Environmental Law (CEL):
Postbus 1030, 1000 BA Amsterdam; tel. (20)
5253075; fax (20) 5254742; internet www.jur
.uva.nl/cvm.

Hugo Sinzheimer Institute: Rokin 84,
1012 KX Amsterdam; tel. (20) 5253560; fax
(20) 5253648; e-mail hsi@jur.uva.nl; internet
www.sinzheimer.com; Dir Dr R. KNEGT.

Informatics Institute: e-mail agbs-fee@uva
.nl; internet www.science.uva.nl/research/cs.

**Institute for Biodiversity and Ecosys-
tem Dynamics (IBED):** internet www
.science.uva.nl/ibed.

Institute of Culture and History (ICH): internet www.hum.uva.nl/ich.

Institute for Information Law: Rokin 84, 1012 KX Amsterdam; tel. (20) 5253406; fax (20) 5253033; e-mail ivir@ivir.nl; internet www.ivir.nl/index-english.html.

Institute for Logic, Language and Computation (ILLC): Plantage Muidergracht 24, 1018 TV Amsterdam; tel. (20) 5256051; fax (20) 5252506; e-mail illc@science.uva.nl; internet www.illc.uva.nl.

Institute for Migration and Ethnic Studies: Oudezijds Achterburgwal 237, 1012 DL Amsterdam; tel. (20) 5253627; fax (20) 5253628; e-mail imes@fmg.uva.nl; internet www2.fmg.uva.nl/imes; Dir Prof. M. J. A. PENNINX.

Institute of Molecular Chemistry: Nieuwe Achtergracht 166, 1018 WV Amsterdam; tel. (20) 5256421; fax (20) 5256422; e-mail secr-imc@science.uva.nl; internet www.science.uva.nl/imc.

Institute for Theoretical Physics (ITFA): Valckenierstraat 65, 1018 XE Amsterdam; tel. (20) 5255773; fax (20) 5255778; e-mail itf@science.uva.nl; internet www.science.uva.nl/research/itf; Dir Prof. Dr F. A. BAIS.

Korteweg-de Vries Institute for Mathematics: Plantage Muidergracht 24, 1018 TV Amsterdam; tel. (20) 5255217; fax (20) 5255101; internet www.science.uva.nl/research/math; Dir Prof. Dr C. A. J. KLAASSEN.

National Institute for Nuclear Physics and High Energy Physics (NIKHEF): Kruislaan 409, 1098 SJ Amsterdam; tel. (20) 5922000; internet www.nikhef.nl; Dir Prof. Dr K. J. F. GAEMERS.

Psychology Research Institute: Roetersstraat 15, 1018 WB Amsterdam; tel. (20) 5256891; fax (20) 6391896; internet www.fmg.uva.nl/psy_research; Dir Prof. Dr J. VAN DER PLIGT.

RESAM: Roetersstraat 11, 1018 WB Amsterdam; tel. (20) 5255261; fax (20) 5254036; e-mail resam-fee@uva.nl; internet www.fee.uva.nl/resam.

SCO-Kohnstamm Institute: Wibautstraat 4, 1091 GM Amsterdam; tel. (20) 5251201; fax (20) 5251200; e-mail receptie@educ.uva.nl; internet www.sco-kohnstamminstituut.uva.nl.

Swammerdam Institute for Life Sciences: tel. (20) 5255187; fax (20) 5257934; e-mail lutz@science.uva.nl; internet www.science.uva.nl/sils; Dir Prof. Dr A. J. VAN TUNEN.

Van der Waals-Zeeman Institute for Experimental Physics: Valckenierstraat 65, 1018 XE Amsterdam; tel. (20) 5255663; fax (20) 5255788; e-mail wzi@science.uva.nl; internet www.science.uva.nl/wz; Dir Prof. Dr M. S. GOLDEN.

ERASMUS UNIVERSITEIT ROTTERDAM

Burgemeester Oudlaan 50, POB 1738, 3000 DR Rotterdam

Telephone: (10) 4081111
E-mail: erasmusweb@daz.eur.nl
Internet: www.eur.nl

Founded 1973 by amalgamation of the Nederlandse Economische Hogeschool (f. 1913) and the Medische Faculteit Rotterdam (f. 1966).
Academic year: September to July
Chairman of Supervisory Board: C. A. J. HERKSTRÖTER
Chairman of Executive Board: Dr J. C. M. VAN EIJNDHOVEN
Rector: Prof. Dr S. W. J. LAMBERTS

Secretary: P. J. JASPAR
Librarian: Dr P. E. L. J. SOETAERT
Number of students: 18,000
Publication: *Annual Report*

DEANS

Faculty of Business Administration: Prof. Dr H. G. VAN DISSEL
Faculty of History and Arts: Prof. Dr M. SPARREBOOM
Faculty of Medicine and Health Sciences: Prof. Dr P. J. VAN DER MAAS
Faculty of Philosophy: Prof. Dr T. VAN WILLIGENBURG
Faculty of Social Sciences: Prof. Dr W. A. HAFKAMP
School of Economics: Prof. Dr H. R. COMMANDEUR
School of Law: Prof. J. W. DE ZWAAN
Graduate School of Business: M. J. PAGE

ASSOCIATED INSTITUTIONS

Cardiovascular Research School.

Erasmus Research Institute of Management (ERIM).

Netherlands Institute for Health Sciences (NIHES).

Postgraduate School of Molecular Medicine.

Research School for Safety and Security in Society (OMV).

UNIVERSITEIT VOOR HUMANISTIEK
(University for Humanist Studies)

Postbus 797, 3500 AT Utrecht

Telephone: (30) 2390100
Fax: (30) 2340738
E-mail: bureau.ieb@uvh.nl
Internet: www.uvh.nl

Founded 1989
State control
Academic year: September to June
Chancellors: Prof. Dr P. M. DERKX, Prof. Dr H. LETICHE, Prof. H. A. M. MANSCHOT
Rector: H. KUNNEMAN
Librarian: Drs A. GASENBEEK

Library of 22,000 vols
Number of teachers: 31
Number of students: 260

PROFESSORS

COENEN, H. L. M., Sciences of Man, Society and Culture
ELDERS, A. D. M., Theories of World Views
HOUTEN, D. J. VAN, Social Policy, Planning and Organization
KUNNEMAN, H. P., Practical Humanist Studies
MANSCHOT, H. A. M., Philosophy and Ethics
MASO, I., Philosophy of Science, Methodology and the Theory of Research
VRIES, T. DE, Regional Health Care

ATTACHED INSTITUTE

Research Institute: Van Asch van Wijckskade 28, 3512 VS Utrecht; Dir Prof. D. J. VAN HOUTEN.

UNIVERSITEIT LEIDEN
(Leiden University)

POB 9500, Rapenburg 70, 2300 RA Leiden

Telephone: (71) 5272727
Fax: (71) 5273118
E-mail: study@lo.leidenuniv.nl
Internet: www.leidenuniv.nl

Founded 1575
State control
Language of instruction: Dutch
Academic year: September to July
President: A. W. KIST
Vice-President: J. E. J. VAN BERGEN

Rector: Prof. D. D. BREIMER
Librarian: Drs P. W. J. L. GERRETSEN
Number of teachers: 1,625
Number of students: 15,262

DEANS

Faculty of Archaeology: Prof. Dr L. P. LOUWE KOOIJMANS
Faculty of Arts: Prof. Dr B. WESTERWEEL
Faculty of Law: Prof. H. FRANKEN
Faculty of Medicine: Prof. Dr B. J. VERMEER
Faculty of Philosophy: Prof. Dr D. T. RUNIA
Faculty of Science: Prof. Dr K. R. LIBBENGA
Faculty of Social Science: Prof. Dr R. B. ANDEWEG
Faculty of Theology: Prof. Dr E. G. E. VAN DER WALL

AFFILIATED INSTITUTE

Instituut voor Internationale Studien: POB 9555, 2333 AK Leiden; tel. 5273411; fax 5273619; f. 1970; promotes co-operation between university depts in teaching and research on contemporary intl affairs; Dir Dr PH. P. EVERTS.

UNIVERSITEIT MAASTRICHT
(University of Maastricht)

POB 616, 6200 MD Maastricht

Telephone: (43) 3882222
Fax: (43) 3884898
E-mail: communicatie@bu.unimaas.nl
Internet: www.unimaas.nl

Founded 1976; the University of Limburg (www.tul.edu) was established in 2001, in partnership with Hasselt Universiteit (see chapter on Belgium)
State control
Languages of instruction: Dutch, English
Academic year: September to June
Chairman of Board of Trustees: Dr J. KREMERS
Rector: Prof. Dr G. P. M. F. MOLS
Chairman of the University Board: J. P. W. M. BEURSGENS
Librarian: J. D. GILBERT

Publication: *Doc UM cnt* (research and developments in problem-based learning, 2 a year)
Library of 410,000 vols, 2,400 current periodicals
Number of teachers: 1,100
Number of students: 10,688

DEANS

Faculty of Cultural Studies: Prof. Dr Ir W. E. BIJKER, Prof. Dr P. TUMMEC
Faculty of Economics: Prof. Dr A. VAN WITTELOOSTUIJN, Prof. Dr F. PALM
Faculty of General Sciences: Prof. Dr. K. L. BOON
Faculty of Health Sciences: Prof Dr J. A. M. MAARSE
Faculty of Law: Prof. G. MOLS
Faculty of Medicine: Prof. Dr G. KOUTSTRA
Faculty of Psychology: Prof. Dr G. J. KOK

OPEN UNIVERSITEIT NEDERLAND

Postbus 2960, 6401 DL Heerlen

Telephone: (45) 5762222
Fax: (45) 5711486
E-mail: info@ou.nl
Internet: www.ou.nl

Founded 1984; university level courses or higher vocational training in six fields of study; distance education courses consist of one or two modules/units of 100 hours of study; 12 study centres, 3 regional information points
State control
Language of instruction: Dutch

Chair of Executive Board: Drs M. A. M. WÖLTGENS
Director: Drs T. J. F. M. BOVENS
Rector: Prof. Dr Ir. F. MULDER
Pro-Rector: Prof. Dr W. M. G. JOCHEMS
Registrar: Y. SMEETS-BERKERS
Librarian: Y. SMEETS-BERKERS

Library of 30,000 vols
Number of teachers: 228
Number of students: 24,000
Publications: *Modulair, OnderwijsInnovatie* (4 a year)

DEANS

School of Cultural Studies: Prof. Dr J. VAN MARLE
School of Education: Prof. Dr H. P. A. BOSHUIZEN
School of Informatics: Prof. Dr Ir R. R. BAKKER
School of Law: Prof. Dr H. C. G. SPOORMANS
School of Management: Prof. Dr H. M. J. VAN DEN BOSCH
School of Psychology: Prof. Dr R. W. J. VAN HEZEWIJK
School of Science: Prof. Dr F. PEREZ SALGADO
Educational Technology Expertise Centre: Prof. Dr W. M. G. JOCHEMS

PROFESSORS

School of Cultural Studies:
VAN DER DUSSEN, W. J.
MARLE, J. VAN
WESSEL, L. H. M.
School of Education:
BOSHUIZEN, H. P. A.
School of Informatics:
BAKKER, R. R.
VAN DE CRAATS, J.
JEURING, J. T.
JOOSTEN, S. M. M.
UDINK TEN CATE, A.
School of Law:
BOON, P. J.
RINKES, J. G. J.
SLOOT, B. P.
SPOORMANS, H. C. G.
School of Management:
VAN DEN AARDEMA, H. M. J.
VAN DEN BOSCH, H. M. J.
VAN DEN HEIJDEN, B. I. J. M.
HEEMSTRA, F. J.
HERST, A. C. C.
HOMAN, T.
JEPMA, C. J.
KORSTEN, A. F. A.
KUSTERS, R. J.
PEER, H. W. G. M.
SEMEIJN, J. J. S.
STORM, P. M.
VERSTEGEN, B. H. J.
School of Psychology:
CLAESSEN, J. F. M.
VON GRUMBKOW, J.
VAN HEZEWIJK, R. W. J.
VAN KEMENADE, J. A.
VAN DER MOLEN, H. T.
School of Science:
VAN DAM-MIERAS, M. C. E.
GLASBERGEN, P.
MARTENS, P.
PEREZ SALGADO, F.
REIJNDERS, L.
Educational Technology Expertise Centre:
JOCHEMS, W. M. G.
KIRSCHNER, P. A.
KOPER, E. J. R.
VAN MERRIENBOER, J. J. G.
Rude de Moor Centre:
COONEN, H. W. A. M.
STIJNEN, P. J. J.

VERMEULEN, M. J. M.
ZWANEVELD, G.

RADBOUD UNIVERSITEIT NIJMEGEN

Comeniuslaan 4, POB 9102, 6500 HC Nijmegen
Telephone: (24) 3616161
Fax: (24) 3564606
E-mail: int.relations@dcm.kun.nl
Internet: www.kun.nl

Founded 1923 as Katholieke Universiteit Nijmegen; present name 2004
Private control
Languages of instruction: Dutch, English
Academic year: September to July
Trustees: STICHTING KATHOLIEKE UNIVERSITEIT
Chairman of the University Board: Ir R. J. DE WIJKERSLOOTH DE WEERDESTEYN
Rector Magnificus: Prof. Dr C. W. P. M. BLOM
Secretary-General: Dr P. SARS
Librarian: Dr A. H. LAEVEN
Number of teachers: 3,825
Number of students: 12,677
Publications: *K. U. Nieuws* (weekly), *K. U. Zien* (quarterly)

DEANS

Faculty of Arts: Prof. Dr J. A. H. G. M. BOTS
Faculty of Law: Prof. mr C. J. H. JANSEN
Faculty of Medical Sciences: Prof. Dr G. P. VOOIJS
Faculty of Policy Sciences: Prof. Dr B. DANKBAAR
Faculty of Philosophy: Prof. Dr M. L. J. KARSKENS
Faculty of Science, Mathematics and Computing Science: Prof. Dr S. E. WENDELAAR BONGA
Faculty of Social Sciences: Prof. Dr J. R. M. GERRIS
Faculty of Theology: P. NISSEN

ATTACHED INSTITUTES

Dienst Instituut voor Toegepaste sociale wetenschappen: Toernooiveld 5, 6525 ED Nijmegen; applied social sciences; Dir (vacant).
F. C. Donders Centrum voor Cognitieve Neuro-Imaging: Dir Prof. Dr P. HAGOORT.
Institute for Cellular Signalling: Toernooiveld 1, POB 9010, 6500 GL Nijmegen; Dir Prof. Dr J. J. H. H. M. DE PONT.
Instituut voor Leraar en School: Erasmusplein 1, 6525 HT Nijmegen; university teacher training; Dirs Dr E. V. SCHALKWIJK, Drs A. J. FRIK.
Instituut voor Onderwijskundige Dienstverlening: Toernooiveld 212, POB 6540, 6503 GA Nijmegen; research and development in higher education; Dir Dr J. M. H. M. WILLEMS.
Katholiek Documentatiecentrum: Erasmuslaan 36, POB 9100, 6500 HA Nijmegen; documentation of Dutch Catholicism; Dir Dr J. H. ROES.
Katholiek Studiecentrum: Erasmusplein 1, POB 9103, 6500 HD Nijmegen; study of topics relating to the Christian inspiration; Dir Drs G. P. A. DIERICK.
Max Planck Institut für Psycholinguistik: Wundtlaan 1, 6525 XD Nijmegen; Dir Prof. Dr W. J. M. LEVELT.
Nijmeegs Instituut voor Cognitie en Informatie: Montessorilaan 3, POB 9104, 6500 HE Nijmegen; institute for cognition and information; Dir Prof. Dr CH. M. M. DE WEERT.
Nijmegen SON Research Instituut: Toernooiveld 1, POB 9010, 6500 GL Nijmegen; Dir Prof. Dr C. W. HILBERS.

Research Instituut voor Materialen: Toernooiveld 1, POB 9010, 6500GL Nijmegen; materials research; Dir Prof. Dr Ir J. C. MAAN.
Thomas More Academie: Erasmusplein 1, POB 9103, 6500 KD Nijmegen; Dir Drs C. R. J. GOVAART.
Titus Brandsma Institute: Erasmusplein 1, 6525 HT Nijmegen; bibliography and documentation of the study of religious experience and spiritual life; Dir Prof. Dr H. H. BLOMMESTIJN.

RIJKSUNIVERSITEIT GRONINGEN
(University of Groningen)

Broerstraat 5, POB 72, 9700 AB Groningen
Telephone: (50) 3639111
Fax: (50) 3635380
E-mail: communications@rug.nl
Internet: www.rug.nl

Founded 1614
State control
Languages of instruction: Dutch, English
Academic year: September to September
Pres.: Dr S. K. KUIPERS
Rector Magnificus: Prof. Dr F. ZWARTS
Dir: Dr K. DUPPEN
Registrars: Drs L. VERVELD, Drs F. S. M. HOOGMA
Librarian: Dr A. C. KLUGKIST
Number of teachers: 2,300
Number of students: 25,000
Publication: *Broerstraat 5* (quarterly)

DEANS

Faculty of Arts: Prof. Dr G. DE HAAN
Faculty of Law: Prof. Dr L. C. A. VERSTAPPEN
Faculty of Medicine: Prof. Dr S. POPPEMA
Faculty of Management and Econ.: Prof. Dr H. G. SOL
Faculty of Philosophy: Prof. Dr M.R. TER HARK
Faculty of Science: Prof. Dr S. DAAN
Faculty of Social Sciences: Prof. Dr H. A. L. KIERS
Faculty of Spatial Sciences: Prof. Dr G. J. J. LINDEN
Faculty of Theology: Prof. Dr E. NOORD

ATTACHED INSTITUTES

Graduate School for Astronomy: POB 800, 9700 AV Groningen; tel. (50) 3634073; fax (50) 3636100; e-mail secr@astro.rug.nl; internet www.rug.nl/sterrenkunde/ informatievoor/buitenlandsestudiekiezers.
Graduate School for Atomic and Nuclear Physics: Zernikelaan 25, 9747 AA Groningen; tel. (50) 3637437; fax (50) 3634003; e-mail fantom@kvi.nl; internet www.fantom.kvi.nl.
Graduate School for Behavioural and Cognitive Neurosciences: POB 196, 9700 AD Groningen; tel. (50) 3634734; fax (50) 3638875; e-mail c.m.alma@med.umcg.nl; internet www.rug.nl/bcn.
Graduate School for Behavioural and Social Sciences: Grote Kruisstraat 2/1, 9712 TS Groningen; tel. (50) 3636480; fax (50) 3636521; internet www.rug.nl/gmw/ onderzoek/graduate_school.
Graduate School for Biomolecular Science and Biotechnology: POB 14, 9750 AA Haren; tel. (50) 3634203; fax (50) 3632154; e-mail t.hummel@rug.nl; internet www.rug.nl/gbb.
Graduate School for Chemical Engineering: Nijenborgh 4, 9747 AG Groningen; tel. (50) 3634233; fax (50) 3634296; e-mail stratingh@rug.nl; internet www.rug.nl/ scheikunde/onderzoek/scholen/stratingh.

Graduate School for Drug Exploration and Biomedical Engineering: POB 196, 9700 AD Groningen; tel. (50) 3633163; fax (50) 3632612; e-mail guideoffice@med.umcg.nl; internet www.graduateschoolguide.nl.

Graduate School for Ecological and Evolutionary Studies: POB 14, 9750 AA Haren; tel. (50) 3632311; fax (50) 3635205; e-mail j.h.m.nunnink@rug.nl; internet www.rug.nl/biologie/onderzoek/onderzoekinstitu ten/cees.

Graduate School for Economics and Business: POB 800, 9700 AV Groningen; tel. (50) 3633749; fax (50) 3633720; e-mail a.c.koning@eco.rug.nl; internet som.rug.nl.

Graduate School for Health Research: POB 196, 9700 AD Groningen; tel. (50) 3632868; fax (50) 3632406; e-mail ncg@med.umcg.nl; internet www.rug.nl/nch.

Graduate School for the Humanities: POB 716, 9700 AS Groningen; tel. (50) 3633723; fax (50) 3634900; e-mail letterern@let.rug.nl; internet www.rug.nl/let/onderzoek/graduateschoolforthehuma nities.

Graduate School for Materials Science: Nijenborgh 4, 9747 AG Groningen; tel. (50) 3637361; fax (50) 3634500; e-mail e.t.van.dijken@rug.nl; internet www.rug.nl/zernike/education.

Graduate School for Mathematics and Computing Science: POB 800, 9700 AV Groningen; tel. (50) 3633973; fax (50) 3633800; e-mail secretariaat@math.rug.nl; internet www.rug.nl/informatica/organisatie/overorganisatie/iwi.

Graduate School for Theology and Religion Studies: Oude Boteringestraat 38, 9712 GK Groningen; tel. (50) 3638017; fax (50) 3636200; e-mail m.c.buigel-de-witte@rug.nl; internet www.rug.nl/corporate/onderzoek/gradschoolthrs.

Graduate School of Philosophy: Oude Boteringestraat 52, 9712 GL Groningen; tel. (50) 3636161; fax (50) 3636160; e-mail k.e.gardiner@rug.nl; internet www.rug.nl/gradschoolphilosophy.

Graduate School of Spatial Sciences: POB 800, 9700 AV Groningen; tel. (50) 3633898; fax (50) 3633901; e-mail s.e.tiggelaar@rug.nl; internet www.rug.nl/frw/onderzoek/graduateschool.

Groningen Graduate School of Law: POB 716, 9700 AS Groningen; tel. (50) 3636145; fax (50) 3636735; e-mail ggsl@rug.nl; internet www.rug.nl/ggsl; Dir Prof. Dr HERMAN E. BRÖRING.

TECHNISCHE UNIVERSITEIT DELFT
(Delft University of Technology)

POB 5, 2600 AA Delft
Located at: Julianalaan 134, 2628 BL Delft

Telephone: (15) 2789111
Fax: (15) 2786522
E-mail: info@tudelft.nl
Internet: www.tudelft.nl
Founded 1842
State control
Language of instruction: Dutch
Academic year: September to July
President: Ir G.J. VAN LUIJK
Rector Magnificus: Prof. Dr Ir J.T. FOKKEMA
Librarian: M.A.M. HEIJNE

Library: c. 1,000,000 vols
Number of teachers: 190 full-time professors
Number of students: 13,000

Publications: *Delft Integraal, Delft Outlook, Delta, Jaarverslag, Quarterly Progress Report, Statistisch Jaarboek, Studiegids, Wetenschappelijk Verslag*

DEANS

Faculty of Aerospace Engineering: Prof. Dr Ir TH. DE JONG
Faculty of Applied Sciences: Prof. Ir K. C. A. M. LUYBEN
Faculty of Architecture: Ir H. BEUNDERMAN
Faculty of Civil Engineering and Geosciences: Prof. Ir L. DE QUELERIJ
Faculty of Design, Engineering and Production: Prof. Ir W.L. DALMIJN
Faculty of Information Technology and Systems: Prof. Dr Ir J. VAN KATWIJK
Faculty of Technology, Policy and Management: Prof. Dr H. PRIEMUS

ASSOCIATED INSTITUTES

Adhesion Institute: Kluijverweg 3, 2629 HS Delft; tel. (15) 2785353; fax (15) 2787151; e-mail hi@lr.tudelft.nl; internet www.hi.tudelft.nl.

Batch Knowledge Centre (BKC): POB 5015, 2600 GA Delft; tel. (15) 2781147; fax (15) 2783422; e-mail z.verwater-lukszo@tbm.tudelft.nl; internet www.batchcentre.tudelft.nl; Dir Dr Z. VERWATER-LUKSO.

CIM Centre Delft (CCD): Landbergstraat 3, 2628 CE Delft; tel. (15) 2786876; fax (15) 2783910.

Delft Institute for Earth-Oriented Space Research (DEOS): Thijsseweg 11, 2600 GA Delft; tel. (15) 2783289; fax (15) 2783711; e-mail DEOS@geo.tudelft.nl; internet www.deos.tudelft.nl.

Delft Institute for Information Technology in Service Engineering (DITSE): Jaffalaan 5, 2628 BX Delft; tel. (15) 2788509; fax (15) 2783429; e-mail sol@ditse.tudelft.nl; internet www.ditse.tudelft.nl; Dir Prof. Dr H. G. SOL.

Delft Institute for Sustainable Energy (DISE): Julianalaan 136, 2628 BL Delft; tel. (15) 2782647; fax (15) 2788047.

Delft University Research Center of Intelligent Sensor Microsystems (DISens): Mekelweg 4, 2628 CD Delft; tel. (15) 2785745; fax (15) 2785755; e-mail DISens@tudelft.nl; internet www.disens.tudelft.nl; Dir Prof. Dr P.M. SARRO.

Delft University Wind Energy Research Institute (Duwind): Stevinweg 1, 2628 CN Delft; tel. (15) 2785170; fax (15) 2785347; e-mail duwind@tudelft.nl; internet www.duwind.tudelft.nl.

ICTO Expertise Centre: Kanaalweg 2B, 2628 EB Delft; tel. (15) 2784686; e-mail ICTO@TUDelft.nl; internet www.icto.tudelft.nl.

Interduct: Rotterdamseweg 145, 2628 AL Delft; tel. (15) 2787233; fax (15) 2786682; e-mail Mail@Interduct.TUDelft.NL; internet www.interduct.tudelft.nl.

Interfaculty Reactor Institute (IRI): Mekelweg 15, 2629 JB Delft; tel. (15) 2786744; fax (15) 2786422; e-mail secretary@iri.tudelft.nl; internet www.iri.tudelft.nl; Dir Prof. Dr I. H. M. VERKOOIJEN.

International Centre for Research in Simulation, Motion and Navigation Technologies (SIMONA): Kluyverweg 1, 2629 HS Delft; tel. (15) 2785315; fax (15) 2786480; e-mail H.Lindenburg@LR.TUDelft.NL; internet www.simona.tudelft.nl; Man. Dir M. P. OOSTEN.

International Research Centre for Telecommunications-transmission and Radar (IRCTR): Mekelweg 4, 2628 CD Delft; tel. (15) 2781034; fax (15) 2784046; e-mail irctr@et.tudelft.nl; internet irctr.et.tudelft.nl; Dir Prof. Dr L. P. LIGTHART.

Koiter Institute: Kluyverweg 1, 2629 HS Delft; tel. (15) 2785460; fax (15) 2611465; e-mail R.deBorst@LR.tudelft.nl.

Power Electronics and Electromagnetic Power Conversion Centre (VEMC): Mekelweg 4, 2628 CD Delft; tel. (15) 2786259; fax (15) 2782968; internet ee.its.tudelft.nl/epp/Bu_VEMC.htm.

Research Institute for Housing, Urban and Mobility Studies (OTB): Jaffalaan 9, 2628 BX Delft; tel. (15) 2787951; fax (15) 2784422; e-mail mailbox@otb.tudelft.nl; internet www.otb.tudelft.nl; Dir Prof. Dr P. J. BOELHOUWER.

Technology Institute for Embedded Systems (TIES): Mekelweg 4, 2628 CD Delft; internet www.ties.tudelft.nl.

Workgroup Offshore Technology (WOT): POB 5048, 2600 GA Delft; tel. (15) 2787951; fax (15) 2784422; e-mail an@offshore.tudelft.nl; internet www.offshore.tudelft.nl.

TECHNISCHE UNIVERSITEIT EINDHOVEN
(Eindhoven University of Technology)

Den Dolech 2, Postbus 513, 5600 MB Eindhoven

Telephone: (40) 2479111
Fax: (40) 2475187
E-mail: csc@tue.nl
Internet: www.tue.nl
Founded 1956
State control
Languages of instruction: Dutch, English
Academic year: September to August
Chairman of the Executive Board: A. H. LUNDQVIST
Secretary of the University: Ir H. P. J. M. ROUMEN
Rector Magnificus: C. J. VAN DUIJN
Chairman of the University Council: Dr L. N. J. H. NELISSEN
Librarian: Drs C. T. J. KLIJS

Number of teachers: 220 professors
Number of students: 7,200

Publications: *Annual Report, Matrix* (4 a year)

DEANS

Faculty of Applied Physics: Prof. Dr Ir K. KOPINGA
Faculty of Biomedical Engineering: Prof. Dr Ir F. P. T. BAAIJENS
Faculty of Building and Architecture: Prof. Ir J. WESTRA
Faculty of Chemical Engineering and Chemistry: Prof. Dr J. W. NIEMANTSVERDRIET
Faculty of Electrical Engineering: Prof. Dr Ir J. H. BLOM
Faculty of Industrial Design: Prof. Dr Ir M. J. W. SCHOUTEN
Faculty of Mathematics and Computing Science: Prof. Dr K. M. VAN HEE
Faculty of Mechanical Engineering: Prof. Dr Ir D. H. VAN CAMPEN
Faculty of Technology Management: Prof. Dr S. W. DOUMA

ATTACHED INSTITUTES

Centre for Plasma Physics and Radiation Technology (CPS): tel. (40) 2474048; fax (40) 2438060; e-mail office.cps@tue.nl; internet www.cps.tue.nl; Dir Prof. Dr M. G. VAN DER WIEL.

Communication Technology – Basic Research and its Applications (COBRA): tel. (40) 2474884; fax (40) 2452277; e-mail office@cobra.tue.nl; internet www.cobra.tue.nl; Dirs Prof. Dr H. H. BRONGERSMA, Prof. Dr R. A. J. JANSSEN, Prof. Ir G. D. KHOE, Drs P. MAIJ, Ing. F. SNIJDERS.

Engineering Mechanics Institute: tel. (40) 2474696; fax (40) 2437175; e-mail EMschool@tue.nl; internet www.em.tue.nl; Dir Prof. Dr Ir R. DE BORST.

Euler Institute for Discrete Mathematics and its Applications: tel. (40) 2473121; fax (40) 2435810; e-mail eidma@tue.nl; internet www.win.tue.nl/math/eidma; Man. Prof. Dr Ir H. C. A. VAN TILBORG.

Eurandom: tel. (40) 2478100; fax (40) 2478190; e-mail office@eurandom.tue.nl; internet www.eurandom.tue.nl; Dir F. DEN HOLLANDER.

European Institute of Retailing and Services Studies (EIRASS): tel. (40) 2475994; fax (40) 2438488; e-mail eirass@bwk.tue.nl; internet www.bwk.tue.nl/urb/eirass/eirass.htm; Dir Prof. H. TIMMERMANS.

Institute for Business Engineering and Technology Application (BETA): tel. (40)2474733; fax (40) 2472607; e-mail beta@tm.tue.nl; internet www.tm.tue.nl/beta; Dir Prof. Dr A. G. DE KOK.

Institute for Programming Research and Algorithmics (IPA): tel. (40) 2474124; fax (40) 2475361; e-mail ipa@tue.nl; internet www.win.tue.nl/ipa; Man. Prof. Dr M. T. DE BERG.

J. F. Schouten Institute for User–System Interaction Research: tel. (40) 2472264; fax (40) 2472607; e-mail jfs@tue.nl; internet www.tm.tue.nl/jfschouten; Dir Prof. Dr D. G. BOUWHUIS.

Materials Analysis, Testing, Technology and Research (MATTeR): tel. (40) 2474950; Dir Prof. Dr G. DE WITH.

NRSC-Catalysis: tel. (40) 2473071; fax (40) 2475054; e-mail eirass@bwk.tue.nl; internet www.nrsc-catalysis.nl; Dir Prof. Dr P. W. N. M. VAN LEEUWEN.

Polymers PTN: tel. (40) 2473090; fax (40) 2436999; e-mail zsptn@chem.tue.nl; Dir Prof. Dr E. W. MEIJER (acting).

TILBURG UNIVERSITY

Warandelaan 2, POB 90153, 5000 LE Tilburg
Telephone: (13) 4669111
Fax: (13) 4663019
E-mail: tilburguniversity@uvt.nl
Internet: www.tilburguniversity.nl
Founded 1927
State control
Academic year: September to August
Chancellor and Rector: Prof. Dr F. VAN DER DUYN SCHOUTEN
Chief Administrative Officer: Drs J. J. A. VAN DE RIET
Chief Information Officer: H. GELEIJNSE
Number of teachers: 450
Number of students: 10,000
Publication: *UNIVERS* (weekly)

DEANS

Faculty of Arts: Prof. Dr J. G. G. GOEDEGE-BUURE
Faculty of Economics and Business Administration: Prof. Dr TH. M. M. VERHALLEN
Faculty of Law: Prof. PH. EIJLANDER
Faculty of Philosophy: Prof. Dr B. C. G. J. VAN ROERMUND
Faculty of Social and Behavioural Sciences: Prof. Dr A. DE RUIJTER
Faculty of Theology: Prof. Dr W. J. C. WEREN

RESEARCH CENTRES

Babylon, Centre for Studies of Multicultural Society: tel. (13) 4662668; fax (13) 4663110; internet www.uvt.nl/babylon; Dirs Prof. Dr G. EXTRA, Prof. Dr F. VAN DE VIJVER.

Center-AR, Center for Applied Research: tel. (13) 4663261; fax (13) 4668780; internet www.center-ar.nl; Dirs Prof. Dr H. FLEUREN, Drs J. DE RANITZ.

CentERdata: tel. (13) 4668325; fax (13) 4662764; e-mail centerdata@uvt.nl; internet www.uvt.nl/centerdata/nl; Dir Dr M. DAS.

CentER for Economic Research: tel. (13) 4663050; fax (13) 4663066; e-mail center@uvt.nl; internet center.kub.nl; Dir Prof. Dr TH. M. M. VERHALLEN.

Center for Social Enterprise: tel. (13) 4663018; fax (13) 4662892; e-mail cmo@uvt.nl; Dir Prof. Dr J. J. GRAAFLAND.

CIE, Cente for Intercultural Ethics: tel. (13) 4662595; fax (13) 4663134; Dir Prof. Dr K. W. MERKS.

CLS, Center for Language Studies: tel. (13) 4662614; fax (13) 4663110; e-mail r.v.harl@let.kun.nl; Dir Prof. Dr R. VAN HOUT.

FIT, Tilburg Institute of Fiscal Law: tel. (13) 4662412; fax (13) 4663073; e-mail fit@uvt.nl; internet www.uvt.nl/fit.

Globus, Institute for Globalization and Sustainable Development: tel. (13) 4669111; e-mail viv.mestdagh@uvt.nl; internet www.tilburguniversity.nl/Globus; Chair Prof. Dr K. ZOETEMAN.

Infolab, Research Group on Information Technology and Communication Technology: tel. (13) 4663020; fax (13) 4663069; e-mail infolab@uvt.nl.

IVA, Institute for Applied Social Research: tel. (13) 4668466; fax (13) 4668477; e-mail iva@uvt.nl; internet www.iva.nl.

IVO, Development Research Institute: tel. (13) 4662264; fax (13) 4663015; e-mail secr.ivo@uvt.nl; internet ivo.uvt.nl; Dir G. DE GROOT.

Liturgical Institute: tel. (13) 4662056; fax (13) 4663134; e-mail liturgischinstituut@uvt.nl; Chair G. ROUWHORST.

Netspar, Network for Studies on Pensions, Aging and Retirement: tel. (13) 4662109; fax (13) 4663066; e-mail secretariaat@netspar.nl.

Nexus Institute: tel. (13) 4663450; fax (13) 4663434; e-mail nexus@nexus-instituut.nl; Chair R. RIEMAN.

Oldendorff Research Institute: tel. (13) 4663140; fax (13) 4668183; e-mail a.j.schults@uvt.nl; Dir Prof. ARTS.

OSA, Institute for Labour Studies: tel. (13) 4663350; fax (13) 4663349; e-mail osa@uvt.nl; Chair Prof. Dr P. ESTER.

School for Research into Legislative Problems.

Schoordijk Institute: tel. (13) 4662739; fax (13) 4662537; e-mail schoordijk.instituut@uvt.nl; internet www.tilburguniversity.nl/schoordijk; Comparative Law and Jurisprudence; Prof. P. EIJLANDER.

TELOS, Brabant Centre for Problems of Durability: tel. (13) 4668712; fax (13) 4663499; e-mail telos@uvt.nl; Chair Prof. Dr Ir. J. T. MOMMAAS.

Tias Business School: tel. (13) 4668600; fax (13) 4668699; e-mail tiasinfo@tias.edu; internet www.tias.edu; Chair A. BAAN.

TICER, Tilburg Innovation Centre for Electronic Resources: tel. (13) 4668310; fax (13) 4668383; e-mail ticer@uvt.nl.

Tilburg Center of Finance: tel. (13) 4668367; fax (13) 4662875; e-mail tfc@uvt.nl.

TILEC, Tilburg Law and Economics Centre: tel. (13) 4668789; e-mail TILEC@uvt.nl; internet www.tilburguniversity.nl/tilec; Dirs E. VAN DAMME, P. LAROUCHE.

TISSER, Tilburg Institute for Social and Socio-Economic Research: tel. (13) 4662454; fax (13) 4668068; e-mail o.a.nadolinskaia@uvt.nl.

UNIVERSITEIT TWENTE
(University of Twente)

POB 217, 7500 AE Enschede
Telephone: (53) 4899111
Fax: (53) 4892000
E-mail: info@utwente.nl
Internet: www.utwente.nl
Founded 1961
Rector: Prof. Dr TH. F. A. VAN VUGHT
Dirs: Dr H. W. TE BEEST, Prof. Dr H. M. DE JONG
Librarian: Dr G. A. J. S. VAN MARLE
Number of students: 7,000

CHAIRMEN OF DEPARTMENTS

Applied Educational Science: Prof. Dr J. M. PIETERS
Applied Mathematics: Prof. Dr A. BAGCHI
Business Administration: Prof. Dr Ir J. J. KRABBENDAM
Chemical Technology: Prof. Dr W. E. VAN DER LINDEN
Electrical Engineering: Prof. Dr Ir J. VAN AMERONGEN
Informatics: Prof. Dr H. BRINKSMA
Mechanical Engineering: Prof. Ir H. GROO-TENBOER
Public Administration: Prof. H. M. DE JONG
Social Sciences and Philosophy: Prof. Dr E. SEYDEL
Technical Physics: Prof. Dr J. GREVE

ATTACHED CENTRE

Centre for Clean Technology and Environmental Policy (CSTM): tel. (53) 4893203; fax (53) 4894850; e-mail secr@cstm.utwente.nl; internet www.utwente.nl/cstm; Dir Prof. Dr H. TH. A. BRESSERS.

Centre for Higher Education Policy Studies (CHEPS): tel. (53) 4893263; fax (53) 4340392; e-mail secr@cheps.utwente.nl; internet www.utwente.nl/cheps; Dir Prof. J. ENDERS.

Centre for Integrated Manufacturing and Development (CIPV): internet www.cipv.utwente.nl; Dir Prof. Dr F. J. A. M. VAN HOUTEN.

Centre for Production, Logistics and Operations Management (CPLOM): internet www.cplom.utwente.nl; Dir Prof. Dr A. VAN HARTEN.

Centre for Telematics and Information Technology (CTIT): internet www.ctit.utwente.nl; Dir P. M. G. APERS.

Drebbel Institute for Mechatronics: internet www.drebbel.utwente.nl; Dir Prof. J. VAN AMERONGEN.

Institute for Biomedical Technology (BMTI): tel. (53) 4893367; fax (53) 4892319; internet www.utwente.nl/bmti.

Institute for Governance Studies (IGS): tel. (53) 4893280; fax (53) 4894734; e-mail info@igs.utwente.nl; internet www.igs.utwente.nl; Dir Prof. Dr W. VAN ROSSUM.

Institute of Mechanics, Processes and Control – Twente (Impact): tel. (53) 4892489; fax (53) 4893471; internet www.impact.utwente.nl; Dir Prof. Dr H. TIJDE-MAN.

Interuniversity Centre for Educational Research (ICO): tel. (53) 4893613; fax (53) 4892849; e-mail ico@edte.utwente.nl; internet www.utwente.nl/ico; Dir Prof. Dr A. J. M. DE JONG.

MESA+: tel. (53) 4892715; fax (53) 4892575; e-mail info@mesaplus.utwente.nl; internet www.mesaplus.utwente.nl; Dir Prof. Dr D. REINHOUDT.

Netherlands Graduate School of Science, Technology and Modern Culture (WTMC): internet www.wmw.utwente.nl/wtmc; Dir Prof. Dr A. RIP.

Research School for Process Technology (OSPT): fax (53) 4894738; internet ospt .ct.utwente.nl; Dir Prof. Dr H. E. A. VAN DEN AKKER.

Twente Institute for Communication Research (TwiCoR): tel. (53) 4894996; fax (53) 4342895; internet www.tcw.utwente.nl.

Twente Institute of Mechanics (TIM): e-mail tim@tim.utwente.nl; internet www .tim.utwente.nl; Dir Prof. Dr H. TIJDEMAN.

UNIVERSITEIT UTRECHT
(Utrecht University)

POB 80125, 3508 TC Utrecht
Telephone: (30) 2539111
Fax: (30) 2533388
E-mail: info.oo@uu.nl
Internet: www.uu.nl
Founded 1636
Languages of instruction: Dutch, English
Academic year: September to July
Chair. of the University Board: YVONNE C. M. T. VAN ROOY
Rector Magnificus: Prof. WILLEM-HENDRIK GISPEN
Library of 4,000,000 vols
Number of teachers: 3,000
Number of students: 28,000
Publications: *Ublad* (university magazine, weekly), *Annual Report*

DEANS

Faculty of Arts and the Humanities: Prof. J. W. BERTENS
Faculty of Social and Behavioural Sciences: Prof. W. KOOPS
Faculty of Geosciences: Prof. G. J. VAN DER ZWAAN
Faculty of Medicine: Prof. J. C. STOOF
Faculty of Veterinary Medicine: Prof. A. W. C. A. CORNELISSEN
Faculty of Law, Economics and Governance: Prof. D. DORRESTEIJN
Faculty of Science: Prof. G. VAN KOTEN

PROFESSORS

Faculty of Arts (Kromme Nieuwegracht 46, 3512 HJ Utrecht):

BRAIDOTTI, R., Comparative Women's Studies
VAN BUUREN, M. B., Modern Literature (French)
EDEL, D. R., Celtic Languages
VAN EIJCK, D. J. N., Logical Aspects of Computational Linguistics
GERRITSEN, W. P., Dutch Medieval Literature
DE GROOT, R., Music of the Low Countries after 1600
HART, P., Utrecht Studies
HECHT, P. A., History of Visual Arts in Renaissance and Modern Times
HERRLITZ, W., German Language
VAN DEN HOVEN, P. J., Linguistics
JANSSEN, H. L., Studies of Medieval Castles
DE JONG, F., Islam Languages and Cultures
Mrs JONG, M. B., Medieval History
KLAMT, J. C. J. A., History of Medieval Art
KLOEK, J. J., Social History of Literature
LANDSBERGEN, S. P. J., Language and Speech Automation
LASARTE, F. J., Latin-American Studies
MEYER, B. W., Visual Arts during the Renaissance in Italy and the Netherlands and their Underlying Relationship
MIJNHARDT, W. W., Post-Middle Ages History
MOORTGAT, J., Linguistics, Language Informatics
NOOTEBOOM, S. G., Linguistics, in particular Phonetics

OP DE COUL, P. M., History of Music after 1600
ORBÁN, A. P., Vulgar and Medieval Latin
OTTENHEYM, K. A., History of Architecture
POLLMANN, M. M. W., Social Functions of Language Disciplines
PRAK, M. R., Post-Medieval History (Social Relationships)
REULAND, E. J., Linguistics, specifically Syntax
RIGHART, J. A., Post-Medieval History, in particular Internal Political Relations
SANCISI-WEERDENBURG, H. W. A. M., Ancient History and Culture
SCHENKEVELD VAN DER DUSSEN, M. A., Dutch Renaissance Literature
SCHOENMAKERS, H., Theatre Science
SCHWEGMAN, M. J., Women's History
SICCAMA, J. G., History of Security Issues
STUMPEL, J. F. H. J., Iconology and Art Theory
URICCHIO, W., History of Film and Television
VELLEKOOP, C., History of Music before 1600
VERKUIJL, H. J., Dutch Language
VOOGD, P. J. DE, Modern Literature
VAN DER VOORT, C. M. M.
WESTHOFF, G. J., Didactics of Modern Languages
VAN ZANDEN, J. L., Post-Medieval History (Social Relationships)
ZONNEVELD, W., Linguistics, in particular Phonology, English Linguistics

Faculty of Biology (Sorbonnelaan 16, 3584 CA Utrecht; tel. (30) 2532276):

VAN DEN BIGGELAAR, J. A. M., Experimental Embryology
BOERSMA, K. TH., Didactics of Biology
VAN DAMME, J. M. M., Ecological Population Genetics
DURSTON, A. J., Organismal Embryology
GOOS, H. J. TH., Comparative Endocrinology
VAN DE GRIND, W. A. P. F. L., Comparative Physiology
HOEKSTRA, W. P. M., Microbiology
HOGEWEG, P., Theoretical Biology
VAN HOOFF, J. A. R. A. M., Comparative Physiology
VAN DER HORST, D. J., Metabolic Physiology
KOLLÖFFEL, CHR., Botany
LAAT, S. W. DE, Developmental Biology
LAMBERS, J. T., Ecophysiology
VAN LEEUWEN, C. J., Biological Toxicology (Ecological Risk Assessment)
VAN LOON, L. C., Phytopathology
VAN DER MAAS, P. J. M., Plant Taxonomy
VAN NOORDWIJK, A. J., Population Ecology of Animals
SAYER, J. A., International Aspects of Nature Protection
SEINEN, W., Biological Toxicology
VERKLEIJ, A. J., Electromicroscopy
VERRIPS, C. T., Applied Molecular Biology
VISSCHER, H., Palaeobotany
VOORMA, H. O., Molecular Biology
WEISBEEK, P. J., Molecular Genetics
WERGER, M. J. A., Botanical Ecology

Faculty of Chemistry (Sorbonnelaan 16, 3584 CA Utrecht; tel. (30) 2533791; fax (30) 2533072):

VAN DEN BOSCH, H., Biochemistry
BRANDSMA, L., Organic Chemistry
VAN DUIJNEVELDT, F. B., Theoretical Chemistry
VAN EERDEN, J. P. J. M., Macroscopic Physical Chemistry
EGMOND, M. R., Applied Enzymology
VAN EIJNDHOVEN, J. C. M., Technological Research of Aspect
FRENKEL, D., Physical Computer Simulation
GEUS, J. W., Inorganic Chemistry
DE HAAS, G. H., Biophysics

HAVERKAMP, J., Analytical Chemistry
HOLLANDER, J. A., In vivo NMR Spectroscopy
JENNESKENS, L. W., Physical Organic Chemistry
KAMERLING, J. P., Organic Chemistry of Natural Substances
KAPTEIN, R., NMR Spectroscopy
KELLY, J. J., Electrochemistry
KONINGSBERGER, D. C., Inorganic Chemistry
VAN KOTEN, G., Organic Chemistry
KROON, J., Chemistry
DE KRUIJF, H. A. M., Toxicology and Society
DE KRUIJFF, B., Molecular Biology of Biomembranes
LEKKERKERKER, H. N. W., Physical Chemistry
VAN DER MAAS, J. H., Spectrochemical Analysis
MEIJERINK, A., Chemistry of Solids
PHILIPSE, A. P., Physical Chemistry
TURKENBURG, W. C., Science and Society
VELDINK, G. A., Organic Aspects of Bio-Catalysis
VAN DE VEN, J., Materials Science
VERHEIJ, H. M., Biochemistry
VLIEGENTHART, J. F. G., Bio-Organic Chemistry
WIRTZ, K. W. A., Biochemistry

Faculty of Earth Sciences (Budapestlaan 4, 3584 CD Utrecht; tel. (30) 2535050; fax (30) 2535030):

DAS, H. A., Radioanalysis in Geochemistry
EISMA, D., Marine Sedimentology
JONG, B. M. W. S. DE, Petrology and Experimental Petrology
LEEUW, J. W. DE, Organic Geochemistry
MEULENKAMP, J. E., Stratigraphy and Palaeontology
MONDT, J. C., Exploratory Geophysics
OONK, H. A. J., Thermodynamics
PRIEM, H. N. A., Isotope Geology
SNIEDER, R. K., Seismology
SPIERS, CH. J., Experimental Rock-Deformation
VAN DER WEIJDEN, C. H., Marine Geochemistry and Hydrochemistry
WHITE, S. H., Structural Geology and Tectonics
WONG, TH. E., Sedimentary Geology of Subsoils in the Netherlands
WORTEL, M. J. R., Tectonophysics

Faculty of Geographical Sciences (Heidelberglaan 2, 3584 CS Utrecht; tel. (30) 2532044; fax (30) 2540604):

VAN DEN AKKER, C., Ground and Surface Water Quality
VAN DEN BERG, M., Urban and Regional Planning
BURROUGH, P. A., Physical Geography of Landscapes
DIELEMAN, F. M. J., Human Geography of Urban Industrialized Countries
VAN GINKEL, J. A., Human Geography
GLASBERGEN, P., Environmental Policies
GROENEWEGEN, P. P., Environmental and Social Aspects of Health and Health Care
HAUER, J., Methods and Techniques in Geographical Research
HOEKVELD, G. A., Education and Regional Geography
HOOIMEIJER, P., Regional Aspects of Population Issues
KOSTER, E. A., Landscape Architecture
KREUKELS, A. M. J., Urban and Regional Planning
LAMBOOY, J. G., Geographical Economics
LUNING, H. A., Town and Country Planning in Developing Countries
NIEUWENHUIS, J. D., Soil Mechanics of Natural Systems
ORMELING, F. J., Cartography
OTTENS, H. F. L., Human Geography

VAN RIJN, L. C., Mechanics of Fluids (Geographical Modelling)
SCHILDER, G. G., History of Cartography
TERWINDT, J. H. J., Physiogeographical Processes
VELLINGA, M. L., Human Geography (Developing Countries)
VONKEMAN, G. H., Environmental Studies
VAN WEESEP, J., Human Geography
WEVER, E., Human Geography (Economic Geography and International Economics)

Faculty of Law (Janskerhof 3, 3512 BK Utrecht; tel. (30) 2537017; fax (30) 2537300):

ANDRIESSEN, F. H. J. J., European Integration
BACKES, CH. W., Environmental Law
BAEHR, P. R., Human Rights
BAHLMAN, J. P., Business Economics
TEN BERGE, J. B. J. M., Administrative Law
VAN DEN BERGH, R., Economics of Law
BOELE-WOELKI, K. S. R. D., International and Comparative Private Law
BOON, D., Animals and Law
BOVENKERK, F., Criminology
BOVENS, M. A. P., Philosophy of Law
BRANTS, C. H., Penal Law and Law of Criminal Procedure
BRINKHOFF, J. J., Industrial Property
BRUINSMA, J. F., Sociology of Law
VAN BUUREN, P. J. J., Governmental Law
CURTIN, D. M., Law of International Organizations
DALHUISEN, J. H., International Commercial Law
GROSHEIDE, F. W., Private Law
VAN HALL, A., Law of Public Water and Water Boards
HARTKAMP, A. S., Private Law, particularly Civil Law
HEYMAN, H. W., Notarial Law
HOL, A. M., Theory of Law
HONDIUS, E. H., Civil Law
VAN HOOF, G. J. H., Social Economic Law
VAN HUIZEN, P. H. J. G., Commercial Traffic Law
IDENBURG, PH. A., Management Sciences
IN 'T VELD, R. I., Management of Public Government
JASPERS, A. PH. C. M., Social Law
KABEL, J. J. C., Mass Media Law
KELK, C., Penitentiary Law
KOERS, A. W., International Law
KUMMELING, H. R. B. M., Constitutional and Administrative Law
KWIATKOWSKA, B., International Maritime Law
MEIJKNECHT, P. A. M., Civil Law
VAN MENS, K. L. H., Fiscal Law
MOOIJ, A. W. M., Forensic Psychiatry
MORTELMANS, K. J. M., Social Economic Law
NIEUWENBURG, C. K. F., Political Economy
VAN REENEN, P., Causes of Violations of Human Rights
ROSCAM ABBING, H. D. C., Health Law
SCHILFGAARDE, P., Business Law
SIEGERS, J. J., Economics
SOONS, A. H. A., International Law
SPRUIT, J. E., History of Roman Law
STILLE, A. L. G. A., Notarial Law
SWART, A. H. J., Penitentiary Law
VERVAELE, J. A. E., Maintenance of Law and Order
VREE, J. K. DE, International and Political Relations

Faculty of Mathematics and Informatics (Budapestlaan 6, 3584 CD Utrecht; tel. (30) 2531515; fax (30) 2518394):

VAN DALEN, D., Logic and Philosophy of Mathematics
DIEKMANN, O., Applied Mathematics
DUISTERMAAT, J. J., Pure and Applied Mathematics
GILL, R. D., Stochastics

HAZEWINKEL, M., Algebraic Chemistry
DE LANGE, J., Didactics of Teaching Mathematics and Computer Science
VAN LEEUWEN, J., Informatics
LOOIJENGA, E. J. N., Pure Mathematics
MARS, J. G. M., Mathematics
MEERTENS, L. T. G., Programming Technology
MEIJER, J. J. CH., Informatics
OORT, F., Mathematics
OVERMARS, M. H., Computer Science
SIERSMA, D., Mathematics
SWIERSTRA, S. D., Informatics
TREFFERS, A., Field-Specific Education
VERHULST, F., Quantitative Analysis of Dynamic Systems
VAN DER VORST, H. A., Mathematics
ZAGIER, D. B., Pure Mathematics

Faculty of Medicine (Universiteitsweg 100, 3584 CG Utrecht; tel. (30) 2538888; fax (30) 2539025):

AKKERMANS, L. M. A., Gastrointestinal Physiology
BÄR, P. R., Experimental Neurology
BATTERMAN, J. J., Radiotherapy
BAX, N. M. A., Paediatric Surgery
BEEMER, F. A., Clinical Genetics
VAN BEL, F., Neonatology
VAN BERGE HENEGOUWEN, G. P., Gastroenterology
BERGER, R., Chemistry of Hereditary Metabolic Diseases
BERNARDS, R. A., Molecular Carcinogenesis
BIJLSMA, J. W. J., Rheumatology
BLIJHAM, G. H., Clinical Medicine
BORST, C., Experimental Cardiology
BOS, J. L., Physiological Chemistry
BOSMAN, F., Dental Physics
BOUMA, B. N., Biochemistry of Haemostasis
BREDEE, J. J., Cardio-pulmonic Surgery
VAN BRONSWIJK, J. E. M. H., Biological Agents in Domestic Hygiene
BRUYNZEEL-KOOMEN, C. A. F. M., Dermatology-Allergology
BUITELAAR, I. K., Biopsychosocial Determinants in Human Behaviour
BURBACH, J. P. H., Molecular Biology of Neuropeptides
CAPEL, P. J. A., Experimental Immunology
CLEVERS, J. C., Clinical Immunology
COHEN-KETTENIS, P. T., Gender Development and Child and Youth Psychopathology
DEJONCKERE, P. H., Speech Therapy and Phoniatrics
VAN DER DONK, J. A. W. M., Cell Biology
DUIJNSTEE, M. S. H., Innovations in Home Care
DUURSMA, S. A., Clinical Medicine
EIKELBOOM, B. C., Vascular and Transplant Surgery
VAN ENGELAND, H., Psychiatry of Children
ERKELENS, D. W., Clinical Medicine
FELDBERG, M. A. M., Radiodiagnostics
GAST, G. C. DE, Haematology
GEUZE, J. J., Cytology
VAN GIJN, J., Neurology
GISPEN, W. H., Molecular Pharmacology and Neuro-Pharmacology
GOOSZEN, H. G., Surgery
GROBBEE, D. E., Clinical Epidemiology
GRYPDONCLE, M. H. F., Nursing Science
HAUER, R. N. W., Clinical Electrophysiology
HEEREN, TH. J., Psychogeriatrics
HEINTZ, A. P. M., Oncological Gynaecology
HELDERS, P. J. M., Physiotherapy
HENGEVELD, M. W., Sexology
HILLEN, B., Functional Anatomy
HORDIJK, G. J., Oto-rhino-laryngology
TEN HORN, G. H. M. M., Psychiatric Care-Management
VAN HUFFELEN, A. C., Clinical Neurophysiology

HUIZING, E. H., Oto-rhino-laryngology
JONGSMA, H. J., Medical Physiology
KAHN, R. S., Clinical and Biological Psychiatry
KATER, L., Clinical Immunopathology
KNAPE, J. TH. A., Anaesthesiology
KOERSELMAN, G. F., Psychotherapy
KON, M., Plastic and Reconstructive Surgery
KOOMANS, H. A., Nephrology
LAMMERS, J. W. J., Pulmonary Diseases
VAN LONDEN, J., General Health Care
MALI, W. P. TH. M., Radiodiagnostics
MARX, J. J. M., General Internal Medicine
MOSTERD, W. L., Clinical Sports Medicine
VAN NIEUWENHUIZEN, O., Paediatric Neurology in relation to Functional Morphology
VAN NORREN, D., Ophthalmological Physics
OKKEN, A., Paediatrics
PEARSON, P. L., Medical Molecular Genetics
PETERS, A. C. B., Paediatric Neurology
PETERS, P. W. J., Teratology
POLL-THE, B. E., Clinical Congenital Metabolic Diseases
DE PUTTER, C., Special Dental Surgery
VAN REE, J. M., Psychopharmacology
ROBLES DE MEDINA, E. O., Clinical Cardiology
SANGSTER, B., Health Protection
SAVELKOUL, T. J. F., Toxicology
SCHRIJVERS, A. J. P., General Health Care
SCHULPEN, T. W. J., Social Paediatrics
SITSEN, J. M. A., Clinical Pharmacology
SIXMA, J. J., Haematology
SLOOTWEG, P. J., Oral Pathology
SMOORENBURG, G. F., Experimental Audiology
SMOUT, A. J. P. M., Pathophysiology
STAAL, G. E. J., Enzymology
STILMA, J. S., Ophthalmology
STROUS, G. J. A. M., Cellular Biology
SUSSENBACH, J. S., Molecular Biology
THIJSSEN, J. T. H., Clinical Chemistry
TREFFERS, W. F., Ophthalmology
TULLEKEN, C. A. F., Neurosurgery
VAN DEN TWEEL, J. G., Pathology
VAN VEELEN, C. W. M., Functional Neurosurgery
TE VELDE, E. R., Desirable Fertility
VELDMAN, J. E., Experimental Otology and Otoimmunology
VERBOUT, A. J., Orthopaedic Aspects of Spinal and Neuromuscular Disorders
VERHEIJ, T. J. M., Family Medicine
VERHOEF, J., Clinical Microbiology
VERSTEEG, D. H. G., Medical Pharmacology
VIERGEVER, M. A., Image-processing in Medicine
VISSER, G. H. A., Obstetrics
VAN DER VLIET, P. C., Physical Chemistry
VAN VLOTEN, W. A., Dermatology
VOORN, TH. B., General Practice
VAN VROONHOVEN, TH. J. M. V., General Surgery
VAN WAES, P. F. G. M., Röntgen Diagnostics
VAN DE WAL, H. J. C. M., Cardiopulmonic Surgery of Infants and Children
VAN DER WERKEN, CHR., Acute Surgery
WESTENBERG, H. G. M., Neurochemical Aspects of Psychiatry
DE WILDT, D. J., Medical Pharmacology
VAN WIMERSMA GREIDANUS, TJ. B., Neuroendocrinology
VAN DER WINKEL, J. G. J., Immunotherapy
WINNUBST, J. A. M., Psychology of Health and Illness
WOKKE, J. H. J., Neurology focusing on Neuromuscular Diseases
WOLTERS, W. H. G., Paediatric Psychology
ZEGERS, B. J. M., Paediatric Immunology
ZONNEVELD, F. W., Medical Representation Techniques

Faculty of Pharmacy (Sorbonnelaan 16, 3584 CA Utrecht; tel. (30) 2532525; fax (30) 2533953):

BAKKER, A., Pharmaceutical Practice
BEIJNEN, J. H., Bio-Analysis (Research in Clinical Medicine)
BULT, A., Pharmaceutical Analysis
CLERCK, F. F. P., Applied Pulmonary and Cardiovascular Pharmacology
CROMMELIN, D. J. A., Biopharmacy
VAN DIJK, H., Immunology of Phytochemicals
GLERUM, J. H., Clinical Pharmacy
HENNINK, W. E., Pharmaceutical Technology
JANSSEN, L. H. M., Pharmaceutical Chemistry
DE JONG, J. G. A. M., Management Aspects of Pharmaceutical Practice
LABADIE, R. P., Pharmacognosy
LISKAMP, R. M. J., Molecular Medicinal Chemistry
MAES, R. A. A., Toxicology
NIJKAMP, F. P., Molecular Pharmacology
OLIVIER, B., Applied Pharmacology of the Central Nervous System
PORSIUS, A. J., Pharmacotherapy
RUITER, A., Food Chemistry and Bromatology
THIJSSEN, J. H. H., Clinical Chemistry
TOLLENAERE, J. P. A. E., Computational Medicinal Chemistry
VERBATEN, M. N., Human Psychophysiology and Psychopharmacology

Faculty of Philosophy (Heidelberglaan 8, 3584 CS Utrecht; tel. (30) 2531831; fax (30) 2532816):

BERGSTRA, J. A., Applied Logic
VAN DALEN, D., Logic and Philosophy
GEERTSEMA, H. P., Calvinist Philosophy
MANSFELD, J., History of Philosophy in the Ancient World and the Middle Ages
MIDDELBURG, C. A., Applied Logic
VAN REIJEN, W. L., Political and Social Philosophy
RUNIA, D. T., The Tradition of Platonism in Relation to Early Christianity
SCHUHMANN, K. J., History of Modern and Renaissance Philosophy
VERBEEK, TH. H. M., 17th-Century Ideology from the Dutch Perspective

Faculty of Physics and Astronomy (Princetonplein 5, 3584 CC Utrecht; tel. (30) 2533284; fax (30) 2539282):

ANDRIESSE, C. D., Electricity Supplies
VAN BEIJEREN, H., Theoretical Physics
BEIJERINCK, H. C. W., Atomic and Interface Physics
BLEEKER, J. A. M., Space Research
BUIJS, A., Experimental Physics
BUILTJES, P. J. H., Chemistry of the Atmosphere
CROWE, A., Medical and Physiological Physics
DIEKS, D. G. B. J., Foundations and Philosophy of the Natural Sciences
DIJKHUIS, J. I., Semiconductor Laser Optics
DRONKERS, J. M., Physics of Coastal Systems
ERKELENS, C. J., Human Physics
ERNÉ, F. C., Current Issues in Physics
ERNST, M. H. J. J., Theoretical Physics
FEINER, L. F., Theory of Condensed Materials
HABRAKEN, F. H. P. M., Physics Education
HEARN, A. G., Astrophysics
HEIDEMAN, H. G. M., Experimental Physics
VAN HIMBERGEN, J. E. J. M., Theoretical Physics
HOLTSLAG, A. A. M., Meteorology (Forecasting) Techniques
T. JANSSEN, G., Theoretical Physics
HOOFT, T. W. J. M., Theory of Solids
KAMERMANS, R., Experimental Physics and Experimental Nuclear Physics

KOENDERINK, J. J., Human Physics
KUPERUS, M., Astrophysics
LAMERS, H. J. G. L. M., Astronomy
LELIEVELD, J., Atmospheric Chemistry
LEVINE, Y. K., Biophysics
LIJNSE, P. L., Development of Physics Concepts and Methods in Education
LOURENS, W., Physics Informatics
NIEHAUS, A., Experimental Physics
OERLEMANS, J., Dynamics of the Climate
POLMAN, A., Advancement of Atomic and Interface Physics
RUIJGROK, TH. W., Theoretical Physics and Mechanics
DE RUIJTER, W. P. M., Physical Oceanography
SARIS, F. W., Atomic and Molecular Physics
SCHÜLLER, F. C., Plasma Physics
SCHUURMANS, C. J. E., Meteorology
SINKE, W. C., Physical and Chemical Properties of Thin Layers
SMIT, J., Theoretical High-Energy Physics
TJON, J. A., Theoretical Physics
VERBUNT, F. W. M., High-Energy Astrophysics
VERLINDE, E. P., Theoretical Physics
VAN DER WEG, W. F., Technical Physics
DE WIT, B. Q. P. J., Theoretical Physics
DE WITT HUBERTS, P. K. A., Reactor Physics
DE WIJN, H. W., Solid State Physics
ZIMMERMAN, J. TH. F., Physical Oceanography

Faculty of Social Sciences (Heidelberglaan 1, 3584 CS Utrecht):

ADRIAANSENS, H. P. M., Social Sciences and Social Processes and Structures
BANCK, G. A., Anthropology of Brazil
BECKER, H. A., Sociology
BENSING, J. M., Clinical Psychology and Health Psychology
BIERMAN, D. J., Parapsychology
VAN DEN BOUT, J., Bereavement Acceptance Process
BRINKGEVE, C. D. A., Primary forms of Cohabitation, Life-course and Identity
Dr COENEN, H. M. H., Labour Issues
DEEN, N., Theory and Practice of Pupil Accompaniment
DERCKSEN, W. J., Social Sciences (Socio-Economic Policy)
DUBBELDAM, L. F. B., Education in Developing Countries
ELBERS, E. P. J. M., Communication, Thought and Culture Issues
ENGBERSEN, G. B. M., Welfare State System
ENTZINGER, H. B., Studies of Multi-Ethnic Societies
GRIENSVEN, G. J. P., Social Epidemiology with respect to HIV/AIDS
GROEBEL, F. J., Social Sciences (Psychology of Mass Communication)
HAAN, E. H. F. DE, Applied Experimental Psychology
HAGENDOORN, A. J. M. W., Social Sciences
HART, H. T, Statistics and Methodology of Pedagogical Research
VAN DER HEIJDEN, P. G. M., Statistics for Social Sciences
HEIJMANS, P. G., Life Psychology
HOKSBERGEN, R. A. C., Adoption
HOX, J. J., Survey Research
IDENBURG, PH. A., Management Sciences
IMELMAN, J. D., Principles of Pedagogics
INGLEBY, J. D., Life Psychology
KANSELAAR, G., Educational Sciences, in particular Educational Psychology
KNULST, W. P., Education in Arts and Cultural Participation
KRUIJT, D. A. N. M., Development Issues
VAN DER LAAN, G., Foundations of Social Work
LAGERWEIJ, N. A. J., Pedagogics and Innovation in Teaching

LEEUW, F. L., Empirical Theoretical Analysis of the Social Effects of Government Policy
MANTE MEIJEE, E. A., Management and Renewal Processes in Large Organizations
OOSTINDIE, G. J., Anthropology of Comparative Sociology (Caribbean)
PILOT, A., Didactics
RAUB, W., Theoretical Sociology
RISPENS, J., Education of Problem Children
ROBBEN, A. C. G. M., Anthropology of Comparative Sociology (Latin America)
RUIJTER, A. DE, Social Anthropology
SCHAUFELI, W. B., Organizational Psychology
SCHETTKAT, R., Social and Institutional Economics
SCHNABEL, P., Mental Health Care
SCHOFFELEERS, J. H., Socio-Economic Changes and Forms of Meaning-Making
SEVENHUYSEN, S. L., Comparative Women's Studies
VAN SON, M. J. M., Clinical and Health Care Psychology
STEVENS, L. M., Orthopedagogics
STROEBE, W., Social and Organizational Psychology
TAZELAAR, F., Sociology
THIJSSEN, J. G. L., Business and Professional Education
TIELMAN, R. A. P., Social and Cultural Aspects of Humanism
TREFFERS, A., Field-Specific Education
VEENHOVEN, R., Humanism
VERMEER, A., Remedial Education
VRIENS, L. J. A., Peace Studies
VROON, P., Theoretical Psychology
VAN WAARDEN, B. F., Intervention, Organization and Policy Issues in Social Sciences
WERTHEIM, A. H., Cognitive Ergonomics
VAN WIJNGAARDEN, P. J., Sociological Aspects of Social Security Issues
WILTERDINK, N. A., Study of Long-term Processes in Social Sciences
WINTER, M. DE, Innovations in Primary Parent and Child Care
WUBBELS, TH., Teacher Behaviour as a factor in the Learning Environment
VAN WYNGAARDEN, P. J., Social Security Issues
VAN ZANTWIJK, R. A. M., Anthropology and Ethno-History of the Indian Peoples of Latin America
VAN DER ZWAN, A., Development of Views on the Adjustment of the Welfare State

Faculty of Theology (Heidelberglaan 2, 3584 CS Utrecht; tel. (30) 2531853; fax (30) 2533241):

ANDREE, T. G. I. M., Ideological Upbringing and Formation in a Multi-religious Context
BECKING, B. E. H. J., Old Testament
VAN BELZEN, J. A., Psychology of Religion
DEN BOEFT, J., Religious History of Hellenism
BRÜMMER, V., Philosophy of Religion
HEEGER, F. R., Ethics
VAN DER HORST, P. W., New Testament
HOUTEPEN, A. W. P., Ecumenics
IMMINK, F. G., Practical Theology
JONGENEEL, J. A. B., Missiology
KLOPPENBORG, M. A. G. T., History of Religions and Comparative Religious Studies
VAN LEEUWEN, TH. M., Science of the Old Testament and History of Israelite Religion
MAAS, T. A., Relationships between Christianity and Modern Culture
MUIS, J., Dogmatics
OTTEN, W., Church History
DE REUVER, A., Education in Calvinist Theology

SCHROTEN, E., Christian Ethics
TIELEMAN, H. J., Sociology of Religions
VRIES, O. H. DE, History and Dogmas of the Baptism

Faculty of Veterinary Medicine (Yalelaan 1, 3584 CL Utrecht; tel. (30) 2534851; fax (30) 2537727):

BARNEVELD, A., General Surgery and Surgery of Large Domestic Animals
BEYNEN, A. C., Experimental Animals
BREUKINK, H. J., Clinical Veterinary Medicine
COLENBRANDER, B., Fertility
CORNELISSEN, A. W. C. A., Parasitology
DIK, K. J., Radiology
VAN DIJK, J. E., Pathology of Rare Animals/ Spontaneous Laboratory Animal Pathology
VAN EDEN, W., Veterinary Immunology
EVERTS, M. F., Veterinary Physiology
FERON, V. J., Biological Toxicology
FINK-GREMMELS-GEHRMANN, J., Pharmacology of Domestic Animals
GIELKENS, A. J. L., Veterinary Medicine for Poultry Farms
VAN GOLDE, L. M. G., Veterinary Biochemistry
GROMMERS, F. J., Relationship between Man and Animal
GRUYS, E., Pathology of Domestic Animals
HELLEBREKERS, L. J., Anaesthesiology of Laboratory Animals
HORZINEK, M. C., Virology
HUIS IN 'T VELD, J. H. J., Microbiology of Food Products of Animal Origin
JANSSEN, J., Knowledge of Veterinary Law
VAN KNAPEN, F., Hygiene of Food of Animal Origin
KROES, R., Biological Toxicology
MELOEN, R. H., Biomedical Identification
VAN MIERT, A. S. J. P. A. M., Veterinary Pharmacology
MOUWEN, J. M. V. M., Pathology
VAN OIRSCHOT, J. T., Veterinarian Vaccinology
VAN OOST, B. A., Clinical and Molecular Genetics of Domestic Animals
OSTERHAUS, A. D. M. E., Environmental Virology
DEN OTTER, W., Cell Biology and Histology
PIJPERS, A., Veterinary Medicine for Poultry Farms
ROTTIER, P. J. M., Molecular Virology
RUITENBERG, E. J., Veterinary Immunology
RIJNBERK, A., Medicine of Small Domestic Animals
SCHALKEN, J. A., Veterinary Oncology
SLUYS, F. J., Medicine of Domestic Animals, Reproduction and Surgery
SPRUIJT, B. M., Good Health of Animals
TIELEN, M. J. M., Lodging and Provision of Animals
VERHEIJDEN, J. H. M., Medicine of Pigs
VOS, J. G., Toxicological Pathology
DE VRIES, H. W., Medicine of Small Domestic Animals
WEIJS, W. A., Veterinary Anatomy and Embryology
VAN DER WEYDEN, G. C., Obstetrics
VAN DER ZEIJST, B. A. M., Veterinary Bacteriology
VAN DER ZUTPHEN, L. F. M., Animals and Experimental Application

ATTACHED RESEARCH INSTITUTES

Bijvoet Research School for Biomolecular Chemistry.

Centre for Resource Studies for Development (CERES).

Debye Research School.

Dutch Postgraduate School for Art History.

Dutch Research School of Theoretical Physics.

Graduate School for Infection and Immunity.

Helmholtz School for Autonomous Systems Research.

Mathematical Research Institute (MRI).

National Graduate School of Linguistics (LOT).

National Research School for the Pathophysiology of the Nervous System.

Netherlands Graduate School of Housing and Urban Research (NETHUR).

Netherlands Research School for Women's Studies (NOV).

Netherlands School for Advanced Studies in Theology and Religion (NOSTER).

Netherlands School for Social and Economic Policy Research (AWSB).

Research School for Atmospheric and Marine Studies (SAMO).

Research School for Biomembranes.

Research School of Developmental Biology.

Research School for Human Rights.

Research School for Psychology and Health (SPH).

VRIJE UNIVERSITEIT, AMSTERDAM (Free University, Amsterdam)

De Boelelaan 1105, 1081 HV Amsterdam
Telephone: (20) 4447777
Fax: (20) 4445300
E-mail: communicatie@dienst.vu.nl
Internet: www.vu.nl
Founded 1880
Language of instruction: Dutch
Academic year: September to September
Rector Magnificus: Prof. Dr T. SMINIA
Vice-Rectors: Prof. J. KLAASSEN, Prof. P. VELLINGA
General Secretary: Prof. P. J. M. BRASIK
Secretary: Prof. P. VLAS
Library: see Libraries and Archives
Number of teachers: 1,400
Number of students: 14,000

DEANS

Faculty of Arts: Prof. W. T. M. FRIJHOFF
Faculty of Dentistry: Prof. Dr J. R. BAUSCH
Faculty of Earth and Life Sciences: Prof. P. VELLINGA
Faculty of Economics and Business Administration: Prof. J. KLAASSEN
Faculty of Human Movement Sciences: Prof. A. P. HOLLANDER
Faculty of Law: Prof. P. VLAS
Faculty of Medicine: Prof. E. A. VAN DER VEEN
Faculty of Philosophy: Prof. A. P. BOS
Faculty of Psychology and Education: Prof. J. F. H. VAN RAPPARD
Faculty of Sciences: Prof. W. HOGERVORST
Faculty of Social-Cultural Sciences: Prof. P. G. KLANDERMANS
Faculty of Theology: Prof. M. E. BRINKMAN

ATTACHED INSTITUTES

Blaise Pascal Institute: e-mail bpi@vu.nl; internet www.bezinningscentrum.nl; Dir A. W. MUSSCHENGA; publ. *In de Marge* (4 a year).

Centre for International Co-operation: tel. (20) 4449090; fax (20) 4449095; e-mail cis@vu.nl; internet www.cis.vu.nl; Dir K. VAN DONGEN.

Centre for Research and Education on Spatial Information: de Boelelaan 1087, 1081 HV Amsterdam; tel. (20) 4449569; fax (20) 4449553; e-mail spinlab@ivm.vu.nl; internet www.spinlab.vu.nl; Man. Dir E. BEINAT.

Graduate School Neurosciences: ; tel. (20) 4449641; e-mail eam.borghols@vumc.nl; internet www.onwa.med.vu.nl; Dir Prof M. P. WITTER.

Institute for Cardiovascular Research: van der Boechorstraat 7, 1081 BT Amsterdam; tel. (20) 4448111; fax (20) 4448255; e-mail icar@physiol.med.vu.nl; Dir Prof. Dr COEN STEHOUWER.

Institute for Environmental Studies: De Boelelaan 1087, 1081 HV Amsterdam; tel. (20) 4449555; fax (20) 4449553; e-mail info@ivm.falw.vu.nl; internet www.ivm.falw.vu.nl; Dir Dr M. W. HOFKES.

Institute for Fundamental and Clinical Human Movement Sciences: van der Boechorststraat 9, 1081 BT Amsterdam; tel. (20) 4448490; e-mail ifkb@fbw.vu.nl; internet www.ifkb.nl; Dirs Dr Ir. L. BLANKEVOORT, Prof. Dr A. DE HAAN, Prof. Dr D. F. STEGEMAN.

Institute for Research in Extramural Medicine: van der Boechorststraat 7, 1081 BT Amsterdam; tel. (20) 4448180; fax (20) 4448181; e-mail info.emgo@med.vu.nl; internet www.emgo.nl; Dir Prof. J. VAN DER MEER.

Oncology Graduate School: de Boelelaan 1117, 1081 HV Amsterdam; tel. (20) 4444054; fax (20) 4442964; e-mail p.keblusek@vumc.nl; internet www.ooa.vu.nl; Chair Prof Dr C. J. L. M. MEIJER.

WAGENINGEN UNIVERSITEIT (Wageningen University)

POB 9101, 6700 HB Wageningen
Costerweg 50, 6701 BH Wageningen
Telephone: (317) 484472
Fax: (317) 484884
E-mail: infodesk.stuvo@wur.nl
Internet: www.wau.nl
Founded 1918
State control
Languages of instruction: Dutch, English
Academic year: September to August
Pres.: Dr A. A. DIJKHUIZEN
Vice-Pres.: Ir K. J. VAN AST
Rector Magnificus: Prof. Dr Ir L. SPEELMAN
Librarian: L. M. F. WAAIJERS
Information Officer: S. VINK
Library: see Libraries and Archives
Number of teachers: 500
Number of students: 4,800
Publication: *Wb*

PROFESSORS

ANTONIDES, G., Econ. of Consumers and Households
VAN ARENDONK, J. A. M, Animal Genetics and Breeding
BAKKER, J., Nematology, Physiology and Molecular Ecology of Nematodes
BEERS, G., Supply Chain Management
BERENDSE, F., Nature Conservation and Plant Ecology
BERG, J. A. VAN DEN, Genomics
BEULENS, A. J. M., Information Technology
BIGMAN, D., Global Food Security and Int. Trade
BINDELS, J., Nutrition during Growth and Devt
BINO, R. J., Metabolomica of Plants
BISSELING, A. H. J., Molecular Biology, Devt Biology of Plants
BLADEREN, P. J. VAN, Toxico-kinetics and Biotransformation
BLANS, G. H. T., Philosophy
BONGERS, F., Forest Ecology and Forest Management Group
BOOM, R. M., Food Process Eng.
BOT, G. P. A., Technical Physics

BOEKEL, M. A. J. S. VAN, Product Design and Quality Management

BREEMEN, N. VAN, Soil Formation and Ecopedology

BRINK, A. VAN DEN, Policy and Management in Land Use Planning

BREGT, A. K., Geo-information Science, Geographical Information Systems

BRUGGEN, A. H. C. VAN, Biological Farming Systems

BRUSSAARD, L., Soil Biology and Biological Soil Quality

CAPELLE, A., Agrification

CLEEF, A. M., Tropical Nature Conservation and Vertebrate Ecology

COHEN STUART, M. A., Physical Chemistry and Colloid Chemistry

CROUS, P. W., Evolutionary Phytopathology

DENNY, P., Aquatic Ecology

DICKE, M., Entomology

DIJK, G. VAN, Theory and Practice of Agricultural Co-operative Organizations

DONS, H. J. M., Entrepreneurship in Life Sciences

ELFRING, T., Innovative Entrepreneurship

EMONS, A. M. C., Plant Cell Biology

FEDDES, R. A., Soil Physics, Ecohydrology and Groundwater Management

FLEER, G. J., Physical and Colloid Chemistry

FOLMER, H., General Econ.

FOLSTAR, P., Knowledge Management of Innovation Processes in Food Production

FRERKS, G. E., Disaster Management

FREWER, L. J., Food Safety and Consumer Behaviour

GIJZEN, H. J., Environmental Biotechnology

GILLER, K. E., Plant Production Systems

GOEWIE, E. A., Social Aspects of Biological Farming

GOLDBACH, R. W., Virology

GORRIS, L. G. M., Food Safety Microbiology

GOVERDE, H. J. M., Political Science in Agriculture and Environment

GRASMAN, J., Mathematical and Statistical Methods

GROENEN, M. A. M., Animal Breeding and Genetics

HAMER, R. J., Technology of Cereal Proteins

HARTOG, L. A. DEN, Developments in Animal Production

HEIDE, D. VAN DER, Human and Animal Physiology

HEIJMAN, W. J. M., Rural Economics, Spatial Aspects of Rural Devt and Transformation

HEYTING, C., Molecular Cell Genetics

HIDDINK, G. J., Nutritional Extension by Intermediary

HOEKSTRA, R. F., Genetics, Populations and Quantitative Genetics

HOLTSLAG, B., Meteorology and Air Quality

HOOG, C. DE, Sociology of the Family

HOWARD-BORJAS, P. L., Gender Studies in Agriculture

HUIRNE, R. B. M., Econ. of Animal Health and Food Safety

IERLAND, E. C. VAN, Environmental Econ. and Natural Resources

JACOBSEN, E., Plant Breeding

JONGEN, W. M. F., Product Design and Quality Management

KATAN, M. B., Nutrition and Epidemiology

KEMP, B., Adaptation Physiology

KOK, F. J., Nutrition and Health

KOOIJ, D. VAN DER, Environmental Microbiology, Drinking Water Supply

KOOIJ, P., Agricultural History

KOORNNEEF, M., Genetics

KOOTEN, O. VAN, Horticultural Production Chains

KORTHALS, M. J. J. A. A., Applied Philosophy

KROEZE, J. H. A., Psychological and Sensorial Aspects of Food and Nutrition

KROMHOUT, D., Public Health Research

KROPFF, M. J., Crop and Weed Ecology

LANKVELD, J. M. G., Dairy Science

LEEMANS, R., Analysis of Environmental Systems

LEENTVAAR, J., Integrated Water Management

LEEUWEN, J. L. VAN, Experimental Zoology

LEEUWIS, C., Communication and Innovation Studies

LEIJNSE, A., Groundwater Quality

LENGKEEK, J., Socio-spatial Analysis of Land Use (Recreation and Tourism)

LEUNISSEN, J. A. M., Bio-informatics

LENTEREN, J. C. VAN, Entomology

LINDEN, E. VAN DER, Food Physics

MAESEN, L. J. G. VAN DER, Plant Taxonomy and Geography

METZ, J. H. M., Technical Design of Farm Systems in Animal Husbandry

MEULEN, B. M. J. VAN DER, Law and Governance

MILITZ, H., Wood Science

MOHREN, G. M. J., Forest Ecology and Forest Management Group

MOL, A. P. J., Environmental Policy

MUISWINKEL, W. B. VAN, Cell Biology and Immunology

MULDER, B. M., Theoretical Cell Physics

MULDER, M., Agricultural Education

MÜLLER, J., Farm Technology

MÜLLER, M., Nutrition, Metabolism and Genomics

NIEHOF, A., Sociology of Consumers and Households

OENEMA, O., Management of Nutrient Fluxes and Soil Fertility

OMTA, S. W. F., Management Studies

OOYEN, A. J. J. VAN, Genetics in Food Technology

OPDAM, P. F. M., Landscape Ecology, Spatial Population Ecology

OSKAM, A. J., Agricultural Econ. and Rural Policy

OUDE LANSINK, A. G. J. M., Business Econ.

PENNINGS, J. M. E., Future Markets

PERDOK, U. D., Soil Technology

PLAS, L. H. W. VAN DER, Plant Physiology

PLOEG, J. D. VAN DER, Rural Sociology

PRINS, H. H. T., Resource Ecology

PUTTEN, W. H. VAN DER, Functional Biodiversity

RAATS, P. A. C., Continuum Mechanics

RABBINGE, R., Sustainable Devt and System Innovation

RICHARDS, P., Technology and Agrarian Devt

RIEMSDIJK, W. H. VAN, Soil Chemistry and Chemical Soil Quality

RIETJENS, I. M. C. M., Toxicology

RULKENS, W. H., Environmental Technology

SANDERS, J. P. M., Valorisation of Plant Production Chains

SAVELKOUL, H. F. J., Cell Biology and Immunology

SCHAAFSMA, G. J., Nutrition and Food

SCHAEPMAN, M. E., Geo-information Science, Remote Sensing

SCHANZ, H., Forest Policy and Forest Management

SCHEFFER, J. J. C., Medicinal and Aromatic Plant Science

SCHEFFER, M., Aquatic Ecology and Water Quality

SCHIPPERS, J. C., Water Supply Technology (IHE)

SCHOUTEN, M. G. C., Ecology of Nature Conservation

SCHULTZ, E., Land and Water Devt (IHE)

SCHUURMAN, E., Philosophy, Reformational

SKIDMORE, A. K., Vegetation and Agricultural Land Use Survey

SLANINA, J., Measuring Methods in Atmospheric Research

SMIT, G., Molecular Flavour Science

SMITS, M. A., Animal Breeding and Genetics

SNOO, G. R. DE, Agri-environment Schemes

SOSEF, M., Biosystematics

SPIERTZ, J. H. J., Crop Ecology, Nutrient and Metabolic Flows

SPRUIJT, B. M., Ethology and Animal Welfare

STAM, P., Plant Breeding, Selection Methods and Sustainable Resistance

STAMS, A. J. M., Microbiology

STAVEREN, W. A. VAN, Nutrition and Gerontology

STEIN, A., Spatial Statistics

STIEKEMA, W. J., Genome Informatics

STRATEN, G. VAN, Systems and Control

STROOSNIJDER, L., Erosion and Soil and Water Conservation

STRUIK, P. C., Crop Physiology

SUDHÖLTER, E. J. R., Organic Chemistry

SYKORA, K. V., Ecological Organisation and Management of Infrastructure

TAMMINGA, S., Animal Nutrition, Ruminants

TERPSTRA, M. J., Consumer Technology and Product Use

TRAMPER, J., Bioprocess Eng.

TRIJP, J. C. M. VAN, Marketing and Consumer Behaviour

TROCH, P. A., Hydrology and Quantitative Water Management

VALK, A. J. J. VAN DER, Land Use Planning

VEER, P. VAN 'T, Human Nutrition and Epidemiology

VELDKAMP, A., Soil and Land Evaluation

VERRETH, J. A. J., Fish Culture and Fisheries

VERSTEGEN, M. W. A., Animal Nutrition, Monogastrics

VERVLOET, J. A. J., Historical Geography of Landscaping in the Netherlands

VET, L. E. M., Evolutionary Ecology

VIERSSEN, W. VAN, Aquatic Ecology

VINCENT, L. F., Irrigation and Water Eng.

VISSER, L. E., Rural Devt Sociology

VISSER, R. G. F., Plant Breeding

VLAK, J. M., Virology

VORAGEN, A. G. J., Food Chemistry

VOS, W. M. DE, Microbiology

VRIES, S. C. DE, Biochemistry

WAGENBERG, A. F. VAN, Facility Management

WIT, P. J. G. M. DE, Phytopathology, Plant-Pathogen Interactions

WOERKUM, C. M. J. VAN, Communication Management

ZACHARIASSE, L. C., Strategic Economics in Agribusiness

ZEE, S. E. A. T. M. VAN DER, Soil Chemistry and Chemical Soil Quality

ZIJPP, A. J. VAN DER, Animal Production Systems

ZWIETERING, M. H., Food Microbiology

ATTACHED CENTRE

Van Hall Larenstein, University of Professional Education: POB 411, 6700 AK Wageningen; tel. (317) 486262; fax (317) 486280; e-mail international@vanhall-larenstein.nl; internet www.vanhall-larenstein.com; languages of instruction: English, Dutch; first degree and masters degree courses in Food, Agriculture and Natural Resource Management; certificate programmes; teaching centres in Leeuwarden, Velp and Deventer/Wageningen; 450 teachers; 4,400 students; Dirs BAS. BESIEGEL, MARTIN JANSEN, ERICA SCHAPER.

Institutes of University Standing

UNIVERSITEIT NYENRODE
(The Netherlands Business School)

Straatweg 25, 3621 BG Breukelen

Telephone: (346) 291211
Fax: (346) 264204
E-mail: info@nyenrode.nl
Internet: www.nyenrode.nl

Founded 1946
Private control
Languages of instruction: English, Dutch

Academic year: September to July
President: Prof. HERMAN BRUGGINK
Dean: Prof. Dr HANS PALM
Registrar: R. GUIJT
Librarian: Dr ONNO MASTENBROEK

Library of 20,000 vols
Number of teachers: 68
Number of students: 350

PROFESSORS
ARNOLD, I., Economics
BAETS, W., Innovation, Knowledge Management and Management Learning
BAKKER, H. J. C., Strategic Management and Performance of Business Integration Issues
BAOURAKIS, G., Entrepreneurship
BERKHOUT, T. M., Real Estate
BLOKDIJK, H. H., Accountancy
BOTS, J. M., Accountancy
BRANDSMA, R. P. C. W. M., Tax Law
BURGGRAAF, P. M. A., Business Excellence and Information Technology
BUURON, G., Entrepreneurship
COMMANDEUR, H. R., Economics for Increasing Returns
VAN DIJK, G., Co-operative Entrepreneurship
DIJKSMA, J., Accountancy
DORSMAN, A., Market Value and Risk Analysis
EBBERS, H. A., International Economics
VAN EENENNAAM, F., Corporate Governance Virtual Network
FLÖREN, GR. H., Entrepreneurship, Family Business
GASPERSZ, J. B. R., Human Resource Management
VAN GOOR, A. R., Logistics
GROENLAND, E. A. G., Consumer Behaviour
HOOGEBOOM, A. B., Real Estate
HUIZER, G. M., Tax Law
HUMMELS, G. J. A., Socially Responsible Investments
JAGERSMA, A. R., International Business
JEURISSEN, R., Business Ethics
KAMERLING, R. N. J.
KAMPSCHÖER, G. W. J. M., Tax Law
KEIZERS, G., Sustainable Entrepreneurship
KEMPERINK, J., Entrepreneurship
KEUNING, D., Accountancy
KLAPWIJK, P. H. P., Supply-Chain Economics
KOELEMEIJER, K., Retailing and Marketing Channels
LACHOTZKI, F. W. I., Business Policy
LANGENDIJK, H. P. A. J., Corporate Governance
MCLAUGHLIN, E. W., Retail Strategy and Marketing
MARISSING, J. P., Competition
VAN MIERT, K., Competition
MOENART, R. K., Strategic Marketing
MOLEVELD, W., Accountancy
VAN MUIJEN, J. J., Organizational Culture
VAN NIEUWKERK, M., International Monetary Environment
OBOLENSKY, N., Leadership
OLIFF, M. D., Strategy Centre
PEELEN, E., Direct Marketing
PHEIJFFER, M., Forensic Accounting
ROBBEN, H., Marketing
ROOBEEK, Economics and Technology
RUIGROK, W., Strategy
SANSOM, K. J., Entrepreneurship
VAN STEENBERGEN, B., Strategy Centre
STEINS BISSCHOP, B. T. M., Law
THIBEAULT, A., Finance
TISSEN, R. J., Human Resources Management
TSÉ, K., Corporate Finance
VAN DER VEEN, J. A. A., Supply-Chain Optimization
VENUGOPAL, V., Operations Management
VIJN, P., Integrated Marketing Communication

VINKE, R. H. W., Human Resource Management
DE VRIES, R. J., Tax Law
WIERDSMA, A. F. M., Management Development
VEN DER ZANDEN, P. M., Financial Accounting and Reporting

ATTACHED RESEARCH CENTRES
Centre for Accounting, Auditing and Control (CAAC): Dir W. G. J. KAPELLE.
Centre for Competence, Personal Development and Leadership: Dir J. J. VAN MUIJEN.
Centre for Human Resources, Organization and Management Effectiveness (CHROME): Dir Prof. Dr R. J. TISSEN.
Centre for Supply Chain Management (CSCM): tel. (346) 291249; fax (346) 291250; internet www.nyenrode.nl/cscm; Dir E. PEELEN.
Centre for Tax Managment (CTM): Dir Prof. Dr R. N. J. KAMMERLING.
European Institute for Business Ethics (EIBE): tel. (346) 291290; fax (346) 291296; e-mail eibe@nyenrode.nl; Dir G. J. W. M. CRIJNS.
Netherlands Institute for Cooperative Entrepreneurship (NICE): tel. (346) 291545; fax (346) 265453; e-mail nice@nyenrode.nl; Dir Prof. Dr G. VAN DIJK.
Nyenrode Centre for Entrepreneurship (NCE): tel. (346) 291545; fax (346) 265453; e-mail nce@nyenrode.nl; Dir G. VAN DIJK.
Nyenrode Centre for Finance (NCF): Dir A. THIBEAULT.
Nyenrode Institute for Competition (NIC): tel. (346) 291614; fax (346) 291250; e-mail nic@nyenrode.nl; Dir D. M. VAN GORP.
Strategy Centre: tel. (346) 291730; fax (346) 291250; internet www.nyenrode.nl/strategycenter; Dir Dr F. VAN EENENNAAM.

KATHOLIEKE THEOLOGISCHE UNIVERSITEIT TE UTRECHT

Located at: Heidelberglaan 2, 3584 TC Utrecht
POB 80101, 3508 TC Utrecht

Telephone: (30) 2532149
Fax: (30) 2533665
E-mail: bureau@ktu.nl
Internet: www.ktu.nl

Founded 1967
Academic year: September to September
Chairman of the Board: Prof. Dr E. M. H. HIRSCH BALLIN
Rector and Chairman of University Council: Prof. Dr P. H. A. I. JONKERS
Registrar: Ir J. J. VAN DE PAS

Number of teachers: 58
Number of students: 300

PROFESSORS
BEENTJES, P. C., Old Testament
FRISHMAN, J., Rabbinic Literature and Judaism
HELLEMANS, G. A. F., Social Sciences
JONKERS, P. H. A. I., Philosophy and History of Philosophy
MENKEN, M. J. J., New Testament
MÜLLER, D., Church History
RIKHOF, H. W. M., Systematic Theology and History of Theology
ROUWHORST, G. A. M., History of Liturgy
VOSMAN, F. J. H., Moral Theology
WISSINK, J. B. M., Practical Theology

ATTACHED INSTITUTE
Franciskaans Studiecentrum: c/o K. T. U., POB 80101, 3508 TC Utrecht; tel. (30) 533875; research in Franciscan spirituality

and the history of the movement in the Netherlands; Dir Dr J. G. J. VAN DEN EIJNDEN.
Thomas Instituut te Utrecht: Dir Prof. Dr H. W. M. RIKHOF.

THEOLOGISCHE UNIVERSITEIT VAN DE CHRISTELIJKE GEREFORMEERDE KERKEN IN NEDERLAND

Wilhelminapark 4, 7316 BT Apeldoorn

Telephone: (55) 5775700
Fax: (55) 5226339
E-mail: theol.tua@planet.nl
Internet: www.tua.nl

Founded 1892

President: Prof. Dr G. C. DEN HERTOG
Librarian: Prof. Dr J. W. MARIS

Library of 40,000 vols
Number of teachers: 11 (6 full-time, 5 part-time)
Number of students: 106 full-time

Publications: *Apeldoornse Studies* (2 a year), *Oikodomē* (4 a year).

THEOLOGISCHE UNIVERSITEIT VAN DE GEREFORMEERDE KERKEN
(Theological University of the Reformed Churches)

Postbus 5026, 8261 GA Kampen

Telephone: (38) 4471710
Fax: (38) 4471711
E-mail: secretariaat@tukampen.nl
Internet: www.tukampen.nl

Founded 1854

Dir: H. HARTOG
Rector: Prof. Dr G. KWAKKEL
Librarian: Drs G. D. HARMANNY

Number of teachers: 14
Number of students: 70

PROFESSORS
VAN HOUWELINGEN, P. H. R., New Testament Exegesis
KAMPHUIS, B., Dogmatics
KWAKKEL, G., Old Testament Exegesis
VAN DER POL, F., Church History and History of Dogma
DE RUIJTER, C. J., Pastoral Theology
TE VELDE, M., Church History and Polity

THEOLOGISCHE UNIVERSITEIT VAN DE GEREFORMEERDE KERKEN IN NEDERLAND
(Theological University of the Reformed Churches in the Netherlands)

Postbus 5021, 8260 GA Kampen

Telephone: (38) 3371600
Fax: (38) 3371613
E-mail: bureau@mail.thuk.nl
Internet: www.thuk.nl

Founded 1854
Languages of instruction: Dutch, English
Academic year: September to August

Rector: Prof. Dr F. DE LANGE
Dean of Students: Drs J. BROEKHUIS
Registrar: Dr H. C. VAN DER SAR
Librarian: J. W. PUTTENSTEIN

Library of 187,500 vols
Number of teachers: 30
Number of students: 172

Publications: *Documentatieblad voor de geschiedenis van de Nederlandse zending en overzeese kerken* (2 a year, in Dutch), *Zeitschrift für Dialektische Theologie* (2 a year, in German)

PROFESSORS
HOLTROP, P. N., Missiology

HOUTMAN, C., Old Testament
JONKER, E. R., Pastoral Theology
KIRN, H.-M., Church History
KOFFEMAN, L. J., Church Polity
DE LANGE, F., Ethics
NEVEN, G. W., Dogmatics
ROUKEMA, R., New Testament

Institutes of International Education

EUROPEAN INSTITUTE OF PUBLIC ADMINISTRATION

POB 1229, 6201 BE Maastricht

Telephone: (43) 3296222
Fax: (43) 3296296
E-mail: eipa@eipa-nl.com
Internet: www.eipa.nl

Founded 1981

Supported by mem. states of the European Union and the Commission of the EU

General Director: Prof. Dr GÉRARD DRUESNE

Library of 19,000 vols, 300 current periodicals; European documentation centre; depositing library of the Council of Europe

Publication: *EIPASCOPE* (quarterly bulletin)

Personal and organizational developments and policy support in European policy-making and implementation; EU institutions and political integration, European public management, community policies and internal markets, legal systems of the EU.

HOGESCHOOL ROTTERDAM (International School in Rotterdam)

Located at: Postbus 25035 3001 HA Rotterdam

Museumpark 40, 3015 CX Rotterdam

Telephone: (10) 2414141
Fax: (10) 2414389
E-mail: studievoorlichting@hro.nl
Internet: www.hogeschool-rotterdam.nl

Founded 1957
State control
Academic year: September to July

President: Drs G. A. EGAS REPÁRAZ
Director: Drs G. M. MOLIER
Registrar: Drs I. J. D. BLAAUW
Librarian: M. BEEKHUIS

Number of teachers: 350
Number of students: 4,000.

INSTITUTE OF SOCIAL STUDIES

POB 29776, 2502 LT The Hague
Located at: Kortenaerkade 12, 2518 AX The Hague

Telephone: (70) 4260460
Fax: (70) 4260799
E-mail: promotions@iss.nl
Internet: www.iss.nl

Founded 1952
Language of instruction: English

Rector: Prof. J. B. OPSCHOOR
Deputy Rector: Dr D. DUNHAM
Dean: Dr D. GASPER
Secretary: E. DE BAEDTS

Library of 100,000 vols
Number of teachers: 82
Number of students: 300

Publication: *Development and Change* (5 a year)

PhD in development studies. MA in development studies with majors in: human resources and employment; local and regional development; politics of alternative development; population and development; public policy and management; rural livelihoods and global change; women, gender development. Diploma programmes in: effective social policies for human development; human rights; international law and sustainable development; managing natural resource conflicts; universalizing socioeconomic security for the poor; children, youth and development; globalization and development; governance, democratization and public policy; modelling and accounting for sustainable development; policy analysis skills for transition economies; feminist development economics; development, law and social justice; MSc in development economics.

PROFESSORS

BJØRKMAN, J. W., Public Policy and Administration
FLINTERMAN, C., Human Rights
HAAR, G. TER, Religion, Human Rights and Social Change
KARSHENAS, M., Development Economics
PRONK, J., Theory and Practice of International Development
ROBISON, R., Political Economy
SAITH, A., Rural Economics
SALIH, M., Politics of Development
SCHRIJVER, N., International Law
SYLVESTER, C., Women and Development Studies
VOS, R., Finance and Development
WUYTS, M., Applied Quantitative Economics

INTERNATIONAL INSTITUTE FOR GEO-INFORMATION SCIENCE AND EARTH OBSERVATION (ITC)

Hengelosestraat 99, POB 6, 7500 AA Enschede

Telephone: (53) 4874444
Fax: (53) 4874400
E-mail: pr@itc.nl
Internet: www.itc.nl

Founded 1950

Develops and transfers knowledge on geoinformation management for sustainable development and the alleviation of poverty in developing countries

Academic year: September to August

Rector: Prof. Dr Ir. MARTIEN MOLENAAR
Director, External Affairs: SJAAK J. J. BEERENS
Head, Educational Affairs: Ir FRED PAATS
Head, Project Services: Ir MARK NOORT
Head, Research: Prof. Dr MARTIN HALE
Librarian: M. T. KOELEN

Library of 26,000 vols
Number of teachers: 100
Number of students: 400

Publications: *Annual Report*, *ITC News* (4 a year), articles in refereed journals, PhD and MSc theses, inaugural addresses, books and book chapters, articles and abstracts, conference proceedings, technical reports etc

CHAIRMEN OF DEPARTMENTS

Earth Observation Science: Prof. Dr A. STEIN
Earth Systems Analysis: Prof. Dr F. VAN DER MEER
Geo-information Processing: Prof. Dr M-J. KRAAK
Natural Resources: Prof. Dr A. SKIDMORE
Urban and Regional Planning and Geo-information Management: C. M. J. PARESI
Water Resources: Dr C. MANNAERTS

LARENSTEIN UNIVERSITY OF PROFESSIONAL EDUCATION

POB 7, 7400 AA Deventer

Telephone: (570) 684600
Fax: (570) 684608
E-mail: ie@larenstein.nl
Internet: www.larenstein.com

Founded 1912; present name 1989
Academic year: August to July

Director: Dhr. YAN WIEBE-WIELING
Librarian: G. H. SLENDEBROEK
Registrar: B. BEISIEGEL

Library of 12,000 vols
Number of teachers: 100
Number of students: 850

First degree courses; Masters degree course.

MAASTRICHT SCHOOL OF MANAGEMENT (MSM)

Located at: Endepolsdomein 150, 6229 EP Maastricht

POB 1203, 6201 BE Maastricht

Telephone: (43) 3870808
Fax: (43) 3870800
E-mail: info@msm.nl
Internet: www.msm.nl

Founded 1952
Language of instruction: English
Academic year: September to August

Chairman of the Board: Prof. P. R. H. M. VAN DER LINDEN
Director: Prof. R. S. J. TUNINGA

Number of teachers: 140 (40 resident; 100 visiting)
Number of students: 600

Publication: *MSM Research Papers: Management & Development* (2 a year)

Management training and research; DBA, PhD and MBA degrees and executive management programmes.

PROFESSORS

FOSTER, S. F., Organizational Behaviour
VAN GEFFEN, L. M. J. H., Organizational Behaviour
VAN DER HEIJDEN, B. I. J. M., Organizational Behaviour
HELING, G. W. J., Organizational Behaviour
SAMSON, R., General and Strategic Management
TUNINGA, R. S. J., International Business and Marketing
DE WIT, B., Strategic Management

UNESCO–IHE

Postbus 3015, 2601 DA Delft
Located at: Westvest 7, 2611 AX Delft

Telephone: (15) 2151715
Fax: (15) 2122921
E-mail: ihe@ihe.nl
Internet: www.unesco-ihe.org

Founded 1957
Language of instruction: English
Academic year: October to September

Dir: Prof. Dr A. MEGANCK

Library of 18,000 vols
Number of teachers: 80
Number of students: 400

Postgraduate MEng, MSc and PhD programmes, and short courses, in Hydraulic Engineering, Hydrology and Water Resources Management, Sanitary Engineering, Water and Environmental Resource Management, Environmental Science and Technology, Urban Infrastructure Management, Hydroinformatics.

HEADS OF DEPARTMENTS

DE RUYTER, E. D., Environmental Resources

LUIJENDIJK, J., Hydroinformatics and Knowledge Management
JASPERS, F. G. W., Management and Institutions
FIGUÈRES, C. M., Municipal Infrastructure
SCHUTTER, J., Water Engineering

Schools of Art, Architecture and Music

Academie van Beeldende Kunsten Rotterdam (Rotterdam Academy of Art): Blaak 10, 3011 TA Rotterdam; POB 1272, 3000 BG Rotterdam; tel. (10) 2414750; fax (10) 2414751; e-mail info@wdka.hro.nl; internet abk.hro.nl; f. 1773 to develop talent in art and design; 120 staff; library: 6,000 vols; Pres. RICHARD E. OUWERKERK.

Academie van Bouwkunst (Academy of Architecture): Waterlooplein 211, 1011 PG Amsterdam; tel. (20) 5318218; fax (20) 6232519; e-mail info@bwk.ahk.nl; internet www.academievanbouwkunst.nl; f. 1908; part of Amsterdam School of the Arts; architecture, urban design and landscape architecture; library: 10,000 vols; 150 teachers; 200 students; Dir Drs A. OXENAAR

HEADS OF DEPARTMENTS
WINGENDER, J. P., Architecture
MARCUSSE, E., City Planning
DOOREN, N. VAN, Landscape Architecture

Academie van Bouwkunst: Onderlangs 9, 6812 CE Arnhem; tel. (26) 3535606; fax (26) 3535604; e-mail bouwkunst@artez.nl; internet www.avb-arnhem.nl; Dir Drs J. JACOBS.

Academie van Bouwkunst (Academy of Architecture): Located at: Tongersestraat 49A, 6211 LM Maastricht; tel. (43) 3219645; e-mail abm@hszuyd.nl; internet www.academievanbouwkunst.com; f. 1947; 45 students; Dean G. BERGERS.

Academie van Bouwkunst Rotterdam (Rotterdam Academy of Architecture): G. J. de Jonghweg 4–6, 3015 GG Rotterdam; tel. (10) 2414855; fax (10) 2414856; internet www.misc.hro.nl/avbr; f. 1965; library: 10,000 vols; 225 students; Dir Z. HEMEL.

Academie voor Architectuur en Stedebouw: Bisschop Zwijsenstraat 5, 5038 VA Tilburg; tel. (877) 875380; fax (877) 873522; e-mail aas@fontys.nl; internet www.fontys.nl/aas; f. 1936; architecture and town planning/design; library: 8,000 vols; 25 teachers; 80 students; Dir M. GLAUDEMANS.

Academie voor Beeldende Kunst en Vormgeving, HVG (School of Visual Arts and Architecture, Academie Minerva HVG): Gedempte Zuiderdiep 158, 9711 HN Groningen; tel. (50) 666700; fax (50) 139352; e-mail p.g.j.leijdekkers@pl.hanze.nl; courses in fine arts, graphic design, textile design, fashion, interior design, architecture, computer graphics, computer animation, illustration; post-graduate courses in computer graphics, computer animation, architecture; 100 teachers; 750 students; Dir Drs P. G. J. LEIJDEKKERS (postgraduate courses).

AKI Akademie voor Beeldende Kunst en Vormgeving (AKI Academy of Visual arts and Design): POB 1440, 7500 BK Enschede; Located at: Campus University of Twente, Hallenweg 5, 7522 NH Enschede; tel. (53) 4824400; fax (53) 4824463; e-mail post@aki.nl; internet www.aki.nl; f. 1949; fine arts, design, fashion, architecture; library: 8,000 vols; Dir S. HUISMANS.

Codarts, Hogeschool voor de Kunsten (Codarts University of Professional Arts Education): Kruisplein 26, 3012 CC Rotterdam; tel. (10) 2171100; fax (10) 2171101; e-mail codarts@codarts.nl; internet www.codarts.nl; consists of the Rotterdams Conservatorium and the Rotterdamse Dansacademie; 200 teachers; 1,000 students; Dir, Rotterdams Conservatorium GEORGE WIEGEL; Artistic Dir, Rotterdamse Dansacademie SAMUEL WUERSTEN.

Conservatorium van Amsterdam: Van Baerlestraat 27, POB 78022, 1070 LP Amsterdam; tel. (20) 5277550; fax (20) 6761506; e-mail info@cva.ahk.nl; internet www.cva.ahk.nl/; f. 1884; library: 30,000 vols; 200 teachers; 800 students; Dean H. DE KAM.

Conservatorium Maastricht (Hogeschool Zuyd): Bonnefantenstraat 15, 6211 KL Maastricht; tel. (43) 3466680; fax (43) 3466689; e-mail info.conservatorium@hszuyd.nl; internet www.hszuyd.nl; f. 1956; Bachelor and Master degrees; library: 30,000 vols; 110 teachers; 450 students; Dir HARRY CUSTERS (acting)

HEADS OF DEPARTMENTS
Classical: Dr J. SLANGEN
Education: Dr J. RADEMAKERS
Jazz: Dr M. RUTTEN.

Attached Institutes:

Conservatorium Gent: Hoogpoort 64, 9000 Ghent, Belgium; Dir JAN RISPENS.

Fontys Conservatorium: Postbus 90907, 5000 GJ Tilburg; Dir JAN WIRKEN.

Design Academy Eindhoven: POB 2125, 5600 CC Eindhoven; tel. (40) 2393939; fax (40) 2393940; e-mail info@designacademy.nl; internet www.designacademy.nl; f. 1950; 200 teachers; 700 students; Dir U. EDELKOORT.

Conservatorium Maastricht (Hogeschool Zuyd): Bonnefantenstraat 15, 6211 KL Maastricht; tel. (43) 3466680; fax (43) 3466689; e-mail info.conservatorium@hszuyd.nl; internet www.hszuyd.nl; f. 1956; Bachelor and Master degrees; library: 30,000 vols; 110 teachers; 450 students; Dir HARRY CUSTERS (acting)

HEADS OF DEPARTMENTS
Classical: Dr J. SLANGEN
Education: Dr J. RADEMAKERS
Jazz: Dr M. RUTTEN.

Attached Institutes:

Conservatorium Gent: Hoogpoort 64, 9000 Ghent, Belgium; Dir JAN RISPENS.

Fontys Conservatorium: Postbus 90907, 5000 GJ Tilburg; Dir JAN WIRKEN.

Hogeschool 's-Hertogenbosch: Onderwijsboulevard 215, 5223 DE ' s-Hertogenbosch; tel. (73) 6295295; fax (73) 6214725; internet www.hsbos.nl; f. 1812; courses in painting, sculpture, graphic art, ceramics, environmental art, illustration, graphic design; library: 10,000 vols; 50 teachers; 350 students; Dir ALEX DE VRIES.

Hogeschool voor de Kunsten Arnhem: Onderlangs 9, 6812 CE Arnhem; tel. (26) 3535635; fax (26) 3535678; e-mail info@hka.nl; internet www.hka.nl; f. 1987; 350 teachers; 1,300 students; Dir W. S. HILLENIUS.

Hogeschool voor de Kunsten Utrecht (Utrecht School of the Arts): Lange Viestraat 2B, POB 1520, 3500 BM Utrecht; tel. (30) 2332256; fax (30) 2332096; e-mail biz@central.hku.nl; internet www.hku.nl; f. 1987 by amalgamation of Utrechts Conservatorium, Academie voor Beeldende Kunsten Utrecht and Academie voor Expressie en door Woord en Gebaar; faculties: visual arts and design; art, media and technology; theatre; music; interfaculty of art and economics; library: 36,000 vols; 350 teachers; 2,900 students; Dir AD WISMAN.

Institute for Housing and Urban Development Studies: Burgemeester Oudlaan 50, 3062 PA Rotterdam; POB 1935, 3000 BX Rotterdam; tel. (10) 4021523; fax (10) 4045671; e-mail ihs@ihs.nl; internet www.ihs.nl; f. 1971; library: 15,000 vols; 33 teachers; 120 students; Dir Prof. Dr NICO VAN DER WINDT.

Koninklijk Conservatorium (Royal Conservatoire): Juliana van Stolberglaan 1, 2595 CA The Hague; tel. (70) 3151515; fax (70) 3151518; e-mail info@koncon.nl; internet www.koncon.nl; f. 1826; library: 50,000 vols; 265 teachers; 1,023 students; Dir FRANS DE RUITER.

Koninklijke Academie van Beeldende Kunsten (Royal Academy of Art): Prinsessegracht 4, 2514 AN The Hague; tel. (70) 3154777; fax (70) 3154778; e-mail post@kabk.nl; internet www.kabk.nl; f. 1682; 140 teachers; 1,000 students; departments of painting, sculpture, monumental and environmental design, graphic and typographic design, textile design, fashion design, interior and furniture design, industrial, photographic and video design, type and media, image and sound; Dir J. VERDUYN LUNEL.

Rijksakademie van Beeldende Kunsten (State Academy of Fine Arts): Sarphatistraat 470, 1018 GM Amsterdam; tel. (20) 5270300; fax (20) 5270301; e-mail info@rijksakademie.nl; internet www.rijksakademie.nl; f. 1870; one- and two-year courses; Chair., Board of Supervisors R. DEN DUNNEN; Librarian M. DIRKER; library: 30,000 vols.

ARUBA

Library
Oranjestad

Biblioteca Nacional Aruba: George Madurostraat 13, Oranjestad, Aruba; tel. 5821580; fax 5825493; e-mail bna@setarnet .aw; internet www.bibliotecanacional.aw; Dir ASTRID J. T. BRITTEN; f. 1949; 200,000 vols; nat. library, with functions of public library and nat. information centre; br. in San Nicolas; 2 bookmobiles.

Universities and Colleges

Aruban School of Music: Vondellaan 2, Oranjestad, Aruba; tel. 5822888; fax 5836529; e-mail arumuziekschool@setarnet .aw; internet www.amsaruba.com; f. 1953; Dir FELIX RAIMOND HOEK; Government support.

UNIVERSIDAD DI ARUBA

San Nicholas, Aruba

Telephone: 5845287

Founded 1970
Private control
Language of instruction: English
Academic year: September to June
President: Dr CARLIN I. BROWNE
Registrar: HILTONIA PETER
Librarian: LISA WEBB
Library of 6,000 vols
Number of teachers: 20
Number of students: 300

DEANS

College of Business Administration: Dr CARLIN I. BROWNE
College of Education: Dr RACHEL JONES
College of Languages: Dr JOSSY MANSUR
College of Liberal Arts: Rev. Fr WILLIAM LAKE

UNIVERSITEIT VAN ARUBA

J. Irausquinplein 4, Postbus 5, Oranjestad
Telephone: 5823901
Fax: 5831770
E-mail: univaruba@setarnet.aw
Founded 1988
State control
Languages of instruction: Dutch, English
Academic year: September to June
President: Dr J. R. FIGAROA-SEMELEER
Rector: Dr J. VAN RIJEN
Secretary (vacant)
Librarian: F. CROES
Library of 20,000 vols
Number of teachers: 30
Number of students: 300
Publication: *Aruba Iuridica* (2 a year)

DEANS

Faculty of Economics: Dr H. M. WENTING
Faculty of Law: Dr J. F. M. JANSSEN

NETHERLANDS ANTILLES

Research Institutes
NATURAL SCIENCES
Biological Sciences

CARMABI Foundation: Piscadera Baai, POB 2090, Curaçao; tel. (9) 4624242; fax (9) 4627680; e-mail info@carmabi.org; internet www.carmabi.org; f. 1956; terrestrial and marine ecology; library of 3,000 vols; Dir Dr WALTER L. BAKHUIS.

Physical Sciences

Meteorologische Dienst van de Nederlandse Antillen (Meteorological Service of the Netherlands Antilles): Seru Mahuma z/n, Curaçao; tel. (9) 8393366; fax (9) 8683999; f. 1950; Dir A. J. DANIA; publ. *Statistics of Meteorological Observations in Netherlands Antilles* (annually).

Libraries and Archives
Willemstad

Biblioteka Públiko Kòrsou/Openbare Bibliotheek Curaçao (Public Library, Curaçao): Abr. M. Chumaceiro Blvd, Willemstad, Curaçao; tel. (9) 4617055; fax (9) 4656247; internet www.curacaopubliclibrary.an; f. 1922; 180,000 vols and small collection of audio-visual material; Antillean and Caribbean collection; adult, children's, mobile and schools' library services, 1 br. library, 2 mobile libraries; Librarian R. M. DE PAULA; publs *Monthly Acquisition List, Quarterly Antillean Caribbean Acquisition List.*

Nationaal Archief: Scharlooweg 77–79, Willemstad, Curaçao; tel. (9) 4614866; fax (9) 4616794; e-mail na@nationalarchives.an; internet www.nationalarchives.an; f. 1969; repository for all non-current government records; 10,000 vols; Dir Drs N.C. ROMER-KENEPA; publ. *Lantèrnu.*

Museums and Art Galleries
Willemstad

Curaçao Museum: Van Leeuwenhockstraat, Willemstad, Curaçao; tel. (9) 4623873; fax (9) 4623777; f. 1946; housed in an old Dutch quarantine station, built 1853; paintings by early 20th c. Dutch masters and contemporary Curaçao artists; 19th c. mahogany furniture; folklore collection; Indian artifacts; library of Antillean books; regular exhibitions of local and international artists; botanical garden and music pavilion; Dir K. DURGUTI; publ. *De Museumbode* (quarterly).

National Archeologisch-Antropologisch Museum van de Netherlandse Antillen: Johan van Walbeeckplein 6B, Willemstad, Curaçao; tel. (9) 4621933; fax (9) 4621936; e-mail naam@curacao.com; internet www .curacao.com/naam; f. 1998; collns from the five islands of the Netherlands Antilles; library of 2,000 vols; Dir L. WITTEVEEN; publ. *Report* (irregular).

Universities and Colleges

Academy of Music: Koninginnelaan z/n, Emmastad, Curaçao; tel. (9) 7373510; f. 1960; run by the Cultural Centre; 534 students; Dir E. PROVENCE.

Saba University School of Medicine: POB 1000, Saba; tel. 4163456; fax 4163458; e-mail info@saba.edu; internet www.saba .edu; f. 1989; private control; library: 8,600 books, 155 periodicals; 79 teachers; 585 students (postgraduate); Chair. of the Board of Trustees Dr PAUL L. DALBEC; President Dr D. L. FREDRICK; Dean Prof. Dr A. MARON; Librarian W. ELLERMEYER

PROFESSORS

DYKSTRA, M. A., Microbiology/Immunology
HOUGH, P. L., Clinical Medicine
KNIGHT, V. A., Physiology
KURTEV, A., Medical Physiology
MARON, A., Healthcare Economics
PATON, D. M., Pharmacology/Medical Ethics
YAKUBOVSKYY, M., Medical Pathology

UNIVERSITY OF THE NETHERLANDS ANTILLES

POB 3059, Willemstad, Curaçao

Telephone: (9) 8684422
Fax: (9) 8685465
E-mail: una@una.an
Internet: www.una.net
Founded 1970 as Institute of Higher Studies, university status 1979
Language of instruction: Dutch
Academic year: September to June
President: Ir H. GEORGE
Rector: G. NARAIN
General Director: R. D. KLEINMOEDIG
Chief Administrative Officer: R. RAVENSTEIN
Librarian: Drs S. R. CRIENS
Library of 100,000 vols
Number of teachers: 93
Number of students: 600

DEANS

Law: Dr J. C. L. B. KOCKEN
Social and Economic Sciences: C. R. T. CAMELIA
Technical Sciences: A. P. ELIZA

NEW ZEALAND

The Higher Education System

New Zealand became a dominion, under the British Crown, in 1907 and achieved full independence in 1947, when it accepted the 1931 Statute of Westminster. Most of the major institutions of higher education were founded during the second half of the 19th century, notably the University of Otago (founded in 1869), the University of Canterbury (founded in 1873), Lincoln University (founded in 1878; current name and status since 1990) and the University of Auckland (founded in 1882; current status since 1962). Higher education consists of universities, polytechnic institutions, colleges of education and schools of art and music. There are eight state universities and in 2004 there were 20 polytechnics. In 2003 there were 138,583 students enrolled at the universities and 117,514 students in the polytechnic system. There is a parallel education system for the indigenous Maori population, who account for 20% of school enrolment. Three Maori institutions (wänanga) in the tertiary sector provide higher learning in ahuatanga Maori (Maori tradition) according to tikanga Maori (Maori custom). In 2004 41,644 students were enrolled in the wänanga. Students from the Dependent Territory of Tokelau and the Associated States of the Cook Islands and Niue may receive higher education either through branches and campuses of the University of the South Pacific or through scholarships to study in New Zealand, Australia, Fiji and other Pacific countries.

Under the Education Act (1989) the Ministry of Education is the supreme body for the provision of education at all levels. The Tertiary Education Commission determines public higher education policy and administers funding, and the New Zealand Qualifications Authority oversees private education providers and government training establishments. The New Zealand Qualifications Authority has established a New Zealand Register of Quality Assured Qualifications ('The Register') which lists all quality assured programmes of study and their international equivalency. The universities are autonomous institutions, each governed by a Council, consisting of elected, appointed or co-opted members, and headed by a Vice-Chancellor. The Senate is an academic board with responsibility for academic affairs. In addition to Government funding dispersed by the Tertiary Education Commission, the universities are also financed by tuition fees, which are subsidized by the State. Following the Education Amendment Act (1990) the polytechnics, colleges of education and wänanga became autonomous institutions and award their own degrees.

Admission to higher education is on the basis of the National Certificate of Educational Achievement. The standard university-level degree system consists of Bachelors, Masters and Doctorate degrees but aspects such as period of study and criteria for award vary among the institutions due to their autonomy. The Bachelors is often a three-year degree, although some disciplines such as medicine require upwards of five years, and is awarded on the basis of 'credits' accrued. An 'Honours' Bachelors degree is a four-year programme of study. The Masters is the first postgraduate degree, and varies in length from one to three years of full-time study. The PhD or DPhil is the highest university-level degree, awarded after a minimum two years of research-based study leading to submission of a thesis. There are also 'higher' doctorates such as the DSc or DLitt awarded after publication of a corpus of work. Institutions of higher education operate a credit-transfer system which allows students to complete their degree in an institution other than the one in which they started.

Post-secondary technical and vocational education is offered by the universities, institutes of technology, polytechnics, colleges of education, professional institutes and the wänanga. The main qualifications are the National Certificate (four levels) and National diploma.

Regulatory and Representative Bodies

GOVERNMENT

Ministry for Culture and Heritage: POB 5364, Wellington; tel. (4) 499-4229; fax (4) 499-4490; e-mail info@mch.govt.nz; internet www.mch.govt.nz; Minister HELEN CLARK.

Ministry of Education: Level 7, St Paul's Sq., 45–47 Pipitea St, Thorndon, Wellington; tel. (4) 463-8000; fax (4) 463-8001; e-mail enquiries.national@minedu.govt.nz; internet www.minedu.govt.nz; Minister STEVE MAHAREY.

Ministry of Research, Science and Technology: POB 5336, Wellington; tel. (4) 917-2900; fax (4) 471-1284; e-mail talk2us@morst.govt.nz; internet www.morst.govt.nz; Minister STEVE MAHAREY.

ACCREDITATION

ENIC/NARIC New Zealand: New Zealand Qualifications Authority, POB 160, Wellington 6015; tel. (4) 804-3413; fax (4) 802-3401; e-mail pamela.hulston@nzqa.govt.nz; internet www.nzqa.govt.nz; Man. PAMELA HULSTON.

New Zealand Qualifications Authority: POB 160, Wellington 6140; Level 13, 125 The Terrace, Wellington 6011; tel. (4) 463-3000; fax (4) 463-3112; e-mail helpdesk@nzqa.govt.nz; internet www.nzqa.govt.nz; co-ordinates the admin. and quality assurance of nat. qualifications in NZ; Chair. SUE SUCKLING; Chief Exec. Dr KAREN POUTASI.

NATIONAL BODIES

Distance Education Association of New Zealand: 61 Heathridge Place, Lincoln, Canterbury 8152; tel. and fax (3) 325-7577; e-mail admin@deanz.org.nz; internet www.deanz.org.nz; promotes growth, devt, research and good practice in distance education; Pres. Dr KINSHUK; Sec. DEREK WINMOTH; publ. *Journal of Distance Learning* (annual).

Institutes of Technology and Polytechnics of New Zealand: POB 10-344, Wellington; Level 12, St John House, 114 The Terrace, Wellington; tel. (4) 471-1162; fax (4) 473-2350; e-mail enquiries@itpnz.ac.nz; internet www.itpnz.ac.nz; 19 mem. institutes of technology and polytechnics; develops and promotes policies, acts as an advocacy body, and promotes academic quality on behalf of its mems; Chair. MARK FLOWERS; Exec. Dir MARTIN EADIE.

New Zealand Vice-Chancellors' Committee: POB 11915, Manners St, Wellington 6142; tel. (4) 381-8500; fax (4) 381-8501; e-mail craigie@nzvcc.ac.nz; internet www.nzvcc.ac.nz; f. 1961; promotes interests of NZ univs; Chair. Prof. ROY SHARP; Exec. Dir LINDSAY TAIAROA.

Tertiary Education Commission: Level 10, 44 The Terrace, POB 27048, Wellington; tel. (4) 462-5200; fax (4) 462-5400; e-mail info@tec.govt.nz; internet www.tec.govt.nz; f. 2003; works with the tertiary-education sector and others to enhance the relevance of, foster excellence in, and enable access to tertiary education and training so that all can meet their full potential and contribute to NZ's ongoing devt and wellbeing; Chair. JIM DONOVAN; Chief Exec. JANICE SHINER.

Learned Societies

GENERAL

Royal Society of New Zealand: POB 598, Wellington; tel. (4) 472-7421; fax (4) 473-1841; e-mail ceo@rsnz.org; internet www.rsnz.org; f. 1867; science, technology; 1,300 mems, 332 fellows, 70 constituent socs; Pres. NEVILLE JORDAN; CEO Dr DIANNE MCCARTHY; publs *Journal of the Royal Society of New Zealand* (quarterly), *Kotuitui: New Zealand Journal of Social Sciences Online* (2 a year), *New Zealand Journal of Agricultural Research* (quarterly), *New Zealand Journal of Botany* (quarterly), *New Zealand Journal of Crop and Horticultural Science* (quarterly), *New Zealand Journal of Geology and Geophysics* (quarterly), *New Zealand Journal of Marine and Freshwater Research* (quarterly), *New Zealand Journal of Zoology* (quarterly).

AGRICULTURE, FISHERIES AND VETERINARY SCIENCE

Agronomy Society of New Zealand: Institute of Natural Resources, Seed Technology Building, Private Bag 11-222, Massey University, Palmerston North; e-mail c.r.mcgill@ massey.ac.nz; internet nzsap.rsnz.org; f. 1970; promotes the advancement of scientific research and the practice of agronomy in New Zealand, and encourages the flow of agronomic information; 150 mems; Pres. Dr BRUCE MCKENZIE; Sec. CRAIG MCGILL; publ. *Agronomy New Zealand* (annually).

New Zealand Institute of Agricultural and Horticultural Science: POB 121063, Henderson, Waitakere City; tel. (9) 812-8506; fax (9) 812-8503; e-mail secretariat@ agscience.org.nz; internet www.agscience.org .nz; f. 1954; 750 mems; Pres. JOHN LANCASHIRE; Sec. and Treasurer Dr WARREN MCNABB; publ. *AgScience* (6 a year).

New Zealand Institute of Forestry: POB 19-840, Christchurch; tel. (3) 318-1056; fax (3) 318-1061; e-mail nzif@paradise.net.nz; internet www.forestry.org.nz; f. 1926 to promote the best use of NZ's resources and to encourage wise use of forest lands; 750 mems; Pres. KET BRADSHAW; Sec. RON O'REILLY; publs *New Zealand Forestry* (quarterly), *NZIF Handbook* (annual).

New Zealand Society of Animal Production Inc.: c/o Dr Jane Kay, Dexcel, Private Bag 3221, Hamilton; tel. (7) 824-0916; fax (7) 824-0916; e-mail nzsap.animal@xtra.co.nz; internet nzsap.org.nz; f. 1940; 530 mems; Exec. Sec. Dr JANE KELLY; publ. *Proceedings* (annually).

New Zealand Society of Soil Science Inc.: c/o Dr Trish Fraser, Crop and Food Research, Private Bag 4704, Christchurch; tel. (3) 325-6400; fax (3) 325-2074; e-mail fraserp@crop.cri.nz; internet nzsss.rsnz.org; f. 1952 to encourage the advancement of soil science; organises annual conferences; 400 mems; Pres. Dr ALEC MACKAY; Sec. Dr TRISH FRASER; publ. *Soil News* (6 a year).

New Zealand Veterinary Association (Inc.): Navigate House, Level 2, 69–71 Boulcott St, POB 11-212, Wellington; tel. (4) 471-0484; fax (4) 471-0494; e-mail nzva@vets .org.nz; internet www.vets.org.nz; f. 1923 to represent, provide services and promote standards for and on behalf of veterinarians; 1,750 mems; Pres. J. MACLACHLAN; Chief Exec. MURRAY GIBB; publs *New Zealand Veterinary Journal* (6 a year, also online), *Vetscript* (monthly).

Royal Agricultural Society of New Zealand (Inc.): POB 54, Woodend, North Canterbury; tel. (3) 313-1004; fax (3) 313-1003; e-mail enquiries@ras.org.nz; internet www .ras.org.nz; f. 1924; promotes the development of agricultural, pastoral, horticultural, stock-raising and forestry resources in New Zealand; 1,000 individual mems, 170 institutional mems; library of 1,000 vols; Pres. MICK LESTER; Exec. Officer CHRIS MASON; publ. *On Show* (2 a year).

ARCHITECTURE AND TOWN PLANNING

New Zealand Institute of Architects: D72 Bldg (Suite 1.5), Dominion Rd, POB 2516, Auckland; tel. (9) 623-6080; fax (9) 623-6081; e-mail info@nzia.co.nz; internet www.nzia.co .nz; f. 1905; supporting the needs of its member architects, and promotes architecture and the living environment of all New Zealanders; 2,889 mems; Chief Exec. BEVERLEY MCRAE.

New Zealand Institute of Surveyors: 5th Fl., St John House, 114 The Terrace, Wellington; tel. (4) 471-1774; fax (4) 471-1907; e-mail nzis@surveyors.org.nz; internet www .surveyors.org.nz; f. 1888; concerned with the professional and ethical conduct of surveyors; 1,300 mems; Pres. Prof. JOHN HANNAH; publ. *NZ Surveyor* (annually); publ. *Survey Quarterly* (4 a year).

BIBLIOGRAPHY, LIBRARY SCIENCE AND MUSEOLOGY

Museums Aotearoa Te Tari Nga whare Taonga o Te Motu The Museums of New Zealand (Inc.): POB 10-928, Wellington; tel. (4) 499-1313; fax (4) 499-6313; e-mail mail@ museums-aotearoa.org.nz; internet www .museums-aotearoa.org.nz; f. 1947 as an ind. professional body representing museums and museum employees in NZ; 327 mems; Exec. Dir PHILLIPA TOCKER; publs *e-museum NEWS* (monthly), *New Zealand Directory of Museums* (annual), *Te Ara – Journal of Museums Aotearoa.*

New Zealand Book Council: Level 7, Navigate House, 69 Boulcott St, Wellington; tel. (4) 499-1569; fax (4) 499-1424; e-mail admin@bookcouncil.org.nz; internet www .bookcouncil.org.nz; f. 1972 to promote a love of books and reading, through a wide range of programmes; 2,500 mems (individuals, schools, libraries, booksellers, publishers); Chair. MAGGIE BARRY; Chief Exec. KAREN ROSS; publ. *Booknotes* (4 a year).

New Zealand Library Association (Inc.): Level 7, Navigate House, 69 Boulcott St, POB 12-212, Wellington; tel. (4) 473-5834; fax (4) 499-1480; e-mail office@lianza.org.nz; internet www.lianza.org.nz; f. 1910; 1,729 (1,268 individual mems, 461 institutional mems); Pres. VYE PERRONE; Sec. ALLI SMITH; publs *Library Life* (11 a year), *The NZ Library & Information Management Journal* (2 a year).

ECONOMICS, LAW AND POLITICS

New Zealand Institute of International Affairs: c/o Victoria University of Wellington, Level 5, Rutherford House, Pipitea Campus, 23 Lambton Quay, POB 600, Wellington 6140; tel. (4) 463-5356; fax (4) 463-6568; e-mail nziia@vuw.ac.nz; internet www .vuw.ac.nz/nziia; f. 1934; to promote understanding of int. questions and problems, particularly those relating to New Zealand, the Pacific, Asia, and the Commonwealth; Pres. Sir KENNETH KEITH; Dir BRIAN LYNCH; Exec. Officer NGAIRE FLYNN; publ. *New Zealand International Review* (6 a year).

New Zealand Law Society: 26 Waring Taylor St, POB 5041, Wellington; tel. (4) 472-7837; fax (4) 473-7909; e-mail inquiries@ lawyers.org.nz; internet www.lawyers.org .nz; f. 1869; 9,057 mems; Exec. Dir A. D. RITCHIE; publ. *LawTalk* (every 2 weeks).

Population Association of New Zealand: POB 225, Wellington; tel. (4) 471-6146; fax (4) 471-4412; internet panz.rsnz.org; f. 1974; to promote population research, understanding and policy development; 132 mems; Pres. WARD FRIESEN; Sec. LESLEY BADDON; publs *Monographs* (irregular), *Newsletter*, *New Zealand Population Review* (2 a year), *Technical Papers.*

FINE AND PERFORMING ARTS

Creative New Zealand (Arts Council of New Zealand Toi Aotearoa): Old Public Trust Bldg, 131–135 Lambton Quay, POB 3806, Wellington; tel. (4) 473-0880; fax (4) 471-2865; e-mail info@creativenz.govt.nz; internet www.creativenz.govt.nz; f. 1994; statutory body formed to encourage and

promote the practice and appreciation of the arts; invests in a wide variety of artists and artistic orgs involved with all areas of the arts; 7 mems; Chair. ALICK SHAW (acting); Chief Exec. STEPHEN WAINWRIGHT.

New Zealand Maori Arts and Crafts Institute: Hemo Rd, POB 334, Rotorua; tel. (7) 348-9047; fax (7) 348-9045; e-mail education@maci.co.nz; internet www .nzmaori.co.nz; f. 1963; aims: the appreciation, promotion, preservation and perpetuation of Maori arts, crafts and culture; 70 mems; Chief Exec. ANDREW TE WHAITI.

HISTORY, GEOGRAPHY AND ARCHAEOLOGY

New Zealand Archaeological Association (Inc.): POB 6337, Dunedin 9059; tel. (3) 474-7474 ext. 819; fax (3) 477-5993; internet www.nzarchaeology.org; f. 1954; 500 mems; Pres. P. BAIN; Sec. M. WHITE; publs *Archaeology in New Zealand* (quarterly), *Monograph series* (irreg.), *New Zealand Journal of Archaeology* (annual).

New Zealand Cartographic Society (Inc.): SGES, University of Auckland, Private Bag 92019, Auckland; tel. (9) 373-7599; fax (9) 373-7434; e-mail info@cartography .org.nz; internet www.cartography.org.nz; f. 1971 promote the development of cartography; Pres. ROB B. PHILLIPS; Sec. PETER WOOD; publ. *Cartogram Newsletter* (irregular).

New Zealand Geographical Society Inc.: School of Geography, Geology and Environmental Science, University of Auckland, Private Bag 92019, Auckland; tel. (9) 373-7599; fax (9) 373 7434; e-mail nzgs@auckland .ac.nz; internet www.nzgs.co.nz; f. 1944 to promote and encourage the study of geography; brs in Auckland, Christchurch, Dunedin, Hamilton, Palmerston North and Wellington; 450 mems (430 in New Zealand, 20 overseas); Pres. Prof. MICHAEL CROZIER; Vice-Pres. JUNE LOGIE; Sec. Prof. RICHARD LE HERON; publ. *New Zealand Geographer* (3 a year).

New Zealand Historic Places Trust: Antrim House, 63 Boulcott St, POB 2629, Wellington 1; tel. (4) 472-4341; fax (4) 499-0669; e-mail information@historic.org.nz; internet www.historic.org.nz; f. 1955; independent trust with statutory responsibilities; identifies, investigates, registers and preserves historic places, including archaeological sites, traditional sites and old European and Maori heritage; 25,000 national mems, Chair. Dame ANNE SALMOND; Chief Exec. BRUCE CHAPMAN; publs *Annual Report*, *Heritage New Zealand* (4 a year).

New Zealand Historical Association: c/o Department of History, University of Auckland, Private Bag 92019, Auckland; internet historians.rsnz.govt.nz; f. 1979; promotes historical study, teaching and research; holds regular national and regional conferences, gives financial or other assistance to the publication of historical research in NZ, expresses opinion on issues of public policy which concern historical study, teaching or research; 300 mems; Pres. Assoc. Prof. LINDA BRYDER; Sec. Dr MALCOLM CAMPBELL.

LANGUAGE AND LITERATURE

Alliance Française: The Dominion Bldg, 78 Victoria St, 3rd Fl., POB 3002, Wellington 6015; tel. (4) 472-1272; fax (4) 472-2936; e-mail alliance@paradise.net.nz; internet www.alliance-francaise.co.nz; offers courses and exams in French language and culture and promotes cultural exchange with France; attached teaching centres in Auckland, Christchurch, Dunedin, Hamilton, Nelson, North Shore, Palmerston North, Rotorua, Timaru and Whangerei; Dir SONIA PLANTEY.

British Council: 44 Hill St, POB 1812, Wellington 1; tel. (4) 924-2880; fax (4) 473-6261; e-mail enquiries@britishcouncil.org.nz; internet www.britishcouncil.org/nz; offers courses and exams in English language and British culture and promotes cultural exchange with the UK; attached office in Auckland; Dir PAULA MIDDLETON.

New Zealand Society of Authors (PEN NZ Inc.): POB 67013, Mt Eden, Auckland 3; tel. and fax (9) 356-8332; e-mail nzsa@clear.net.nz; internet www.authors.org.nz; f. 1934; promotes co-operation and support amongst writers; encourages writing in New Zealand and works to protect the interests of writers; awards annual and bi-annual prizes; has representatives on major literary bodies; 1,000 mems; Pres. CHRIS ELSE; Exec. Dir LIZ ALLEN; publ. *The New Zealand Author* (every 2 months).

MEDICINE

New Zealand Dietetic Association (Inc.): Box 5065, Wellington; tel. (4) 473-3061; e-mail nzda@dietitians.org.nz; internet www.dietitians.org.nz; f. 1943; professional association of registered dietitians and associated nutrition professionals; aims to ensure that members are recognised as the most credible source of food and nutrition knowledge within New Zealand, and to promote good health through appropriate food and nutrition, using evidence-based scientific research; 550 mems; Pres. SANDY CLEMENT; Exec. Dir JAN MILNE; publs *Newsletter* (every 2 years), *Nutrition & Dietetics* (published jtly with Dietitians Association of Australia).

New Zealand Medical Association: POB 156, Wellington; tel. (4) 472-4741; fax (4) 471-0838; e-mail nzma@nzma.org.nz; internet www.nzma.org.nz; f. 1887 to provide advocacy on behalf of doctors and their patients and to provide support and services to members and their practices; 5,000 mems; Chair. Dr ROSS BOSWELL; Chief Exec. Dr CAMERON MCIVER; publ. *New Zealand Medical Journal* (20 a year).

Physiological Society of New Zealand (Inc.): c/o Assoc. Prof. Simon Malpas, Department of Physiology, Faculty of Medical and Health Sciences, University of Auckland, Private Bag 92019, Auckland; e-mail s.malpas@auckland.ac.nz; internet www.bioeng.auckland.ac.nz/psnz/www/index.php; f. 1972; aims to enhance the quality of physiological and related research, and to establish links with similar research societies throughout the world; 180 mems; Pres. Assoc. Prof. BRUCE SMAILL; Sec. Assoc. Prof. SIMON MALPAS; publ. *Proceedings* (annually).

NATURAL SCIENCES

General

New Zealand Association of Scientists: POB 1874, Wellington 6140; fax (4) 473-1841; internet nzas.rsnz.org; f. 1940; promotes and increases public awareness of science; debates scientific issues and influences govt science policy; improves working conditions for scientists and promotes the free exchange of knowledge and int. co-operation; Pres. Dr DAVID LILLIS; Sec. Dr FIONA MCDONALD; publ. *New Zealand Science Review* (quarterly).

Biological Sciences

Entomological Society of New Zealand (Inc.): Bioprotection and Ecology Div., POB 84, Lincoln Univ., Canterbury 7647; tel. (3) 384-0163; e-mail secretary@ento.org.nz; internet www.ento.org.nz; f. 1951; 250 mems; Sec. PAULINE SYRETT; publ. *New Zealand Entomologist* (annual).

New Zealand Ecological Society (Inc.): POB 25178, Christchurch; tel. (3) 318-1056; fax (3) 318-1061; e-mail nzecosoc@paradise.net.nz; internet nzes.org.nz; f. 1951; 594 mems; Sec. SHONA MYERS; publ. *New Zealand Journal of Ecology* (2 a year).

New Zealand Freshwater Sciences Society (Inc.): c/o Dr Brian Sorrell, NIWA, Private Bag 8602, Christchurch; tel. (3) 348-8987; fax (3) 348-5548; internet freshwater.rsnz.org; f. 1968 as New Zealand Limnological Society; present name 2005; aims to promote interest in all aspects of fresh and brackish water research in New Zealand; 320 mems; Pres. NEAL DEANS; Sec. and Treasurer Dr BRIAN SORRELL; publ. *Newsletter* (2 a year).

New Zealand Marine Sciences Society: C/o Vicki Seager, 42 Carlyon Rd, RD 1, Upper Moutere, Nelson 7152; fax (3) 543-2109; e-mail secretary@nzmss.rsnz.org; internet nzmss.rsnz.org; f. 1960; concerned with all aspects of marine science in New Zealand; 400 mems, 47 inst. mems; Sec. VICKI SEAGER; publ. *Marine Sciences Review* (annually).

New Zealand Microbiological Society (Inc.): Dept of Oral Sciences, University of Otago, POB 647, Dunedin 9001; tel. (3) 479-5471; fax (3) 479-7078; e-mail geoffrey.tompkins@stonebow.otago.ac.nz; internet www.nzms.org.nz; f. 1956; 422 mems; Pres. Dr ANDREW HUDSON; Sec. Dr GEOFFREY TOMPKINS; publ. *New Zealand Microbiology* (3 a year).

New Zealand Society for Parasitology: c/o Mason Consulting, Dunns Crossing Rd, RD5, Christchurch; tel. (3) 347-4505; fax (3) 347-4506; e-mail masonp@earthlight.co.nz; internet nzsp.rsnz.org; f. 1972; study of parasites of plants and animals; 100 mems; Pres. Dr W. E. POMROY; Sec. Dr P. MASON; publ. *Proceedings* (annually).

New Zealand Society of Plant Physiologists: HortResearch, Te Puke Research Centre, 412 No. 1 Rd, RD2 Te Puke; tel. (7) 573-3873; fax (7) 573-3871; e-mail mclearwater@hortresearch.co.nz; internet nzspp.hort.cri.nz; f. 1978; 160 mems; Pres. Dr MATTHEW TURNBULL; Sec. and Treasurer Dr MIKE CLEARWATER.

Ornithological Society of New Zealand (Inc.): c/o POB 12397, Wellington; e-mail osnz@xtra.co.nz; internet www.osnz.org.nz; f. 1939 to encourage, organize and promote the study of birds and their habitat; 1,000 mems; Pres. RICHARD HOLDAWAY; Sec. CLAUDIA DUNCAN; publs *Notornis* (quarterly), *Southern Bird* (quarterly).

Mathematical Sciences

New Zealand Mathematical Society: Institute of Information and Mathematical Sciences, Massey University, Private Bag 102 904, Auckland; e-mail w.sweatman@massey.ac.nz; internet www.math.waikato.ac.nz/nzms/nzms.html; f. 1974; 226 mems; Pres. Dr GAVEN MARTIN; Sec. Dr WINSTON SWEATMAN; publ. *NZ Journal of Mathematics* (2 a year).

New Zealand Statistical Association (Inc.): POB 1731, Wellington; internet nzsa.rsnz.org; f. 1950; to promote good statistical practice; 400 mems; small library; Pres. MURRAY JORGENSEN; Sec. Dr JUDI MCWHIRTER; publs *Australian and New Zealand Journal of Statistics* (published jtly with Statistical Society of Australia (Inc.), quarterly), *Newsletter* (quarterly).

Physical Sciences

Geological Society of New Zealand (Inc.): POB 38951, Wellington Mail Centre; e-mail admin@gsnz.org.nz; internet www.gsnz.org.nz; f. 1955 to encourage the advancement of geological sciences in NZ; 7 brs; 722 mems; Pres. KEITH LEWIS; Sec. HELEN NEIL; publ. *Newsletter* (quarterly).

Meteorological Society of New Zealand: c/o POB 6523, Te Aro, Wellington; internet metosc.rsnz.org; f. 1979; 300 mems; Pres. KIM DIRKS; Sec. SIMON KJELLBERG; publ. *Weather and Climate* (annually).

New Zealand Geophysical Society (Inc.): POB 30368, Lower Hutt; tel. (4) 570-1444; fax (4) 570-4603; internet www.nzgs.rsnz.org; f. 1980; 140 mems; Pres. G. LAMARCHE; Sec. V. STAGPOOLE; publ. *Newsletter* (3 a year).

New Zealand Institute of Chemistry (Inc.): c/o Richard Rendle, POB 39-112, Harewood, Christchurch; tel. (3) 359-7275; fax (3) 359-7248; e-mail nzic.office@nzic.org.nz; internet www.nzic.org.nz; f. 1931; 1,000 mems; promotes the study, practice, teaching and management of chemistry; 6 brs; Pres. KEITH GORDON; Hon. Gen. Sec. RICHARD RENDLE; publ. *Chemistry in New Zealand* (4 a year).

New Zealand Institute of Physics: c/o Angela Fraser, Dept of Physics, University of Otago, 730 Cumberland St, Dunedin; e-mail nzip@rsnz.org; internet nzip.rsnz.govt.nz; promotes the study, practice and teaching of physics; 6 brs; 310 mems; Pres. Dr TERRY SCOTT; Sec. ANGELA FRASER.

New Zealand Society for Biochemistry and Molecular Biology (Inc.): Department of Biochemistry, University of Otago, POB 56, Dunedin; 230 full mems, 170 student mems; Pres. Dr SIGURD WILBANK; Sec. JIM MORTON; publ. *NZ BioScience* (4 a year).

Royal Astronomical Society of New Zealand (Inc.): POB 3181, Wellington; e-mail secretary@rasnz.org.nz; internet www.rasnz.org.nz; f. 1920; 200 mems; Pres. B. R. LOADER; Exec. Sec. PAM KILMARTIN; publ. *Southern Stars* (4 a year).

PHILOSOPHY AND PSYCHOLOGY

New Zealand Psychological Society (Inc.): POB 4092, Wellington; tel. (4) 473-4884; fax (4) 473-4889; e-mail office@psychology.org.nz; internet www.psychology.org.nz; f. 1967; promotes the discipline of psychology as a science, high standards of ethical and professional practice, and provides professional support and development to members; 900 full mems, 180 student and subscriber mems; Exec. Dir (vacant) ANGIE FUSSELL; Exec. Sec. LINDEN WILLIAMS; publs *The Bulletin* (2 or 3 a year), *Connections* (newsletter, monthly), *NZ Journal of Psychology* (23 a year).

RELIGION, SOCIOLOGY AND ANTHROPOLOGY

Polynesian Society:; tel. (9) 373-7599 ext. 87463; fax (9) 373-5409; e-mail jps@auckland.ac.nz; internet www.arts.auckland.ac.nz/ant/jps/polysoc.html; f. 1892 to promote studies and publications about the Polynesians and other Pacific peoples past and present; 1,100 mems; library deposited in the Turnbull Library; Pres. Dame JOAN METGE; Sec. RANGIMARIE RAWIRI; publs *Journal* (quarterly), *Memoirs* (irregular).

TECHNOLOGY

Institution of Professional Engineers New Zealand: POB 12241, 101 Molesworth St, Wellington; tel. (4) 473-9444; fax (4) 474-8933; e-mail ipenz@ipenz.org.nz; internet www.ipenz.org.nz; f. 1914; 9,300 mems; 15 brs; Pres. Dr IAN PARTON; Chief Exec. Dr ANDREW CLELAND; publ. *e.nz* (every 2 months).

New Zealand Computer Society (Inc.): Ground Fl., 158 The Terrace, Wellington; tel. (4) 473-1043; fax (4) 473-1025; e-mail nzcs@ nzcs.org.nz; internet www.nzcs.org.nz; f. 1960; develops the professional skills of its members and promotes excellence in information and communication technology; 1,650 mems; Pres. RICHARD DONALDSON; Chief Exec. DOUGLAS WHITE.

New Zealand Hydrological Society: POB 12-300, Wellington 6038; tel. (3) 319-7211; fax (3) 319-7211; e-mail admin@hydrologynz .org.nz; internet www.hydrologynz.org.nz; f. 1961; 500 mems; Pres. PAUL WHITE; Sec. CHRISTINA ROBB; Administrator LINDSAY ROWE; publ. *Journal of Hydrology (New Zealand)* (2 a year).

New Zealand Society for Earthquake Engineering: POB 2193, Wellington; tel. (4) 562-7920; e-mail secretary@nzsee.org.nz; internet www.nzsee.org.nz; f. 1968; promotes the advancement of the science and practice of earthquake engineering, and co-operation among scientists, engineers and other professionals in the field; 700 mems; Pres. MICHAEL PENDER; Sec. DEREK WILSHIRE; publ. *Bulletin* (quarterly).

Operational Research Society of New Zealand (Inc.): POB 6544, Wellesley St, Auckland; e-mail secretary@orsnz.org.nz; internet www.orsnz.org.nz; f. 1964 to promote operational research and management science in New Zealand in both academic and industrial aspects; 150 mems; Pres. DAVID RYAN; Sec. HAMISH WATERER; publ. *Newsletter*.

Research Institutes

AGRICULTURE, FISHERIES AND VETERINARY SCIENCE

AgResearch: 5th Fl., Tower Block, Ruakura Research Centre, East St, Private Bag 3123, Hamilton; tel. (7) 834-6600; fax (7) 834-6640; internet www.agresearch.co.nz; f. 1992 as New Zealand Pastoral Agriculture Research Institute Ltd; groups for Agriculture and Environment, Applied Biotechnologies and for Food and Health; Chief Exec. ANDREW WEST; publs *AgResearch Now* (quarterly), *Annual Report*, *InTouch* (newsletter, monthly).

Forest Research: Private Bag 3020, Rotorua 3201; tel. (7) 343-5899; fax (7) 358-0952; e-mail info@forestresearch.co.nz; internet www.forestresearch.co.nz; f. 1947; a govt-owned Crown Research Institute providing research and technology development for the forestry and wood products industries as well as focusing on the development of biomaterials from plants; library of 300,000 vols (incl. monographs and periodicals); Chief Exec. Dr TOM RICHARDSON; Chief Operating Officer MIKE LEE; publs *NZ Journal of Forestry Science* (3 a year), *Annual Report*.

HortResearch–Horticulture and Food Research Institute of New Zealand, Ltd: Private Bag 92169, 120 Mt Albert Rd, Mt Albert, Auckland; tel. (9) 815-4200; fax (9) 815-4225; e-mail enquiries@hortresearch.co .nz; internet www.hortresearch.co.nz; f. 1992; integrated fruit research using resources in fruit, plants and sustainable production systems to develop technologies and innovative fruit and food products; library of 40,000 vols, 350 periodicals; Chief Exec. PAUL MCGILVARY.

New Zealand Institute for Crop and Food Research Ltd: Private Bag 4704, Christchurch 8020; tel. (3) 325-6400; fax (3) 325-2074; e-mail info@crop.cri.nz; internet www.crop.cri.nz; f. 1992; provides research, technology and services to support the development of high quality, commercially successful products from cereal, vegetable and flower crops and from seafood; expertise in plant breeding and biotechnology, food technology, nutrition, biochemistry, post-harvest technology, agronomy, plant physiology, pest and disease control; Gen. Man. (Research) Dr PRUE WILLIAMS.

New Zealand Institute of Food Science and Technology (Inc.): POB 8031, Palmerston North; tel. (6) 356-1686; fax (6) 356-1687; e-mail rosemary@nzifst.org.nz; internet www.nzifst.org.nz; f. 1965; professional body for the food science and technology industry in NZ; Divisions of Dairy, Food marketing, Food safety, Nutrition and Sensory evaluation; regular branch meetings, technical sessions and an annual conference; education and vocational guidance for young people; 1,000 professional mems; Pres. SALLY HASELL; Exec. Man. ROSEMARY HANCOCK; publs *Food NZ* (every 2 months), *NZIFST Nibbles* (e-mail bulletin, every 2 weeks).

ECONOMICS, LAW AND POLITICS

New Zealand Institute of Economic Research: 8 Halswell St, Thorndon, POB 3479, Wellington; tel. (4) 472-1880; fax (4) 472-1211; e-mail econ@nzier.org.nz; internet www.nzier.org.nz; f. 1958; economic consultation, forecasting and research in New Zealand and overseas; Dir BRENT LAYTON; Chair. MICHAEL WALLS; publs *New Zealand Industry and Regions* (annually), *Quarterly Predictions* (4 a year), *Quarterly Survey of Business Opinion* (4 a year), *Update* (Monthly).

EDUCATION

New Zealand Council for Educational Research: 10th Fl., West Block, Education House, 178–182 Willis St, POB 3237, Wellington; tel. (4) 384-7939; fax (4) 384-7933; internet www.nzcer.org.nz; f. 1934; fosters the study of, and research into, educational matters; prepares and publish reports for teachers and others in the profession; library of 7,900 vols; Chair. Dr MARY HILL; Dir ROBYN BAKER; publs *Annual Report*, *Curriculum Matters* (annually), *New Zealand Annual Review of Education* (2 a year), *New Zealand Journal of Educational Studies* (2 a year), *set—Research Information for Teachers* (2 a year).

MEDICINE

Auckland Medical Research Foundation: Level 8, Bldg 13, Greenlane Clinical Centre, Private Bag 92189, Auckland; tel. (9) 630-9943; fax (9) 630-9796; internet www .adhb.govt.nz/rdo/amrf.htm; f. 1956; financed by public subscription to sponsor and encourage medical research; Chair. WAYNE BROWN; Man. GAIL HUMPHREY; publ. *Annual Report*.

Canterbury Medical Research Foundation: Van der Veer Institute, POB 2682, 16 St Asaph St Christchurch; tel. (3) 378-6052; fax (3) 378-6057; e-mail health@cmrf.org.nz; internet www.cmrf.org.nz; f. 1960; promotion and support of all aspects of medical research; privately financed; Pres. ROBERT JOHNSON; Dir GUY STEWART; publ. *Annual Report*.

Hawke's Bay Medical Research Foundation (Inc.): POB 596, Napier; tel. and fax (6) 879-9199; e-mail jmbax@xtra.co.nz; internet www.hawkesbaymedicalresearch.org.nz; f. 1961 to foster and support medical research and health education in and outside Hawke's Bay; Pres. ANDREW WARES; Sec. J. M. BAXTER.

Health Research Council of New Zealand: POB 5541, Wellesley St, Auckland; tel. (9) 379-8227; fax (9) 377-9988; e-mail info@ hrc.govt.nz; internet www.hrc.govt.nz; f. 1990; initiates, funds and supports health research; advises the govt on issues of health research ethics; Chair. Prof. GRAEME FRASER; Chief. Exec. Dr BRUCE SCOGGINS; publs *Annual Report*, *Ethics Notes* (irregular), *HRC News* (3 a year), *Panui* (Maori health research issues, irregular), *Update* (e-mail bulletin, every 2 weeks).

Palmerston North Medical Research Foundation: c/o POB 648, Palmerston North; tel. (6) 357-0640; fax (6) 358-9105; f. 1959; privately financed; general medical research; Sec. MICHAEL LAWRENCE; publ. *Annual Report*.

Wellington Medical Research Foundation: c/o The Secretary, POB 51-211, Wellington; tel. (4) 232-5475; fax (4) 232-5494; e-mail info@wmrf.co.nz; internet www.wmrf .co.nz; f. 1960; privately financed; supports all forms of medical research; Sec. ROSS MACDONALD.

NATURAL SCIENCES

Biological Sciences

Cawthron Institute: 98 Halifax St East, Private Bag 2, Nelson; tel. (3) 548-2319; fax (3) 546-9464; e-mail info@cawthron.org.nz; internet www.cawthron.org.nz; f. 1919; scientific and technological research into the management and development of New Zealand's coastal and freshwater systems; library of 4,500 vols; Chief Exec. GILLIAN WRATT; publ. *Cawthron Lectures* (annually).

Institute of Environmental Science and Research Ltd (ESR): Kenepuru Science Centre, 34 Kenepuru Drive, POB 50-348, Porirua, Wellington; tel. (4) 914-0700; fax (4) 914-0770; e-mail enquiries@esr.cri.nz; internet www.esr.cri.nz; f. 1992; provides scientific research and consulting services related to public health, environmental health and forensic science to public and private sectors in New Zealand and the Asia-Pacific region; research centres in Auckland, Wellington and Christchurch; Chief Exec. Dr JOHN HAY; publs *Annual Report*, *Briefing Newsletter* (2 a year).

Landcare Research New Zealand Ltd: Canterbury Agriculture and Science Centre, Gerald St, POB 40, Lincoln; tel. (3) 325-6700; fax (3) 325-2127; internet www .landcareresearch.co.nz; f. 1992 as a Crown Research Institute (CRI); research, consultancy services and technology development focused on enhancing natural, productive and urban environments to ensure the future economic prosperity of New Zealand; other activities incl. environmental sciences, remote-sensing and GIS; attached specialist library; Chief Exec. Dr WARREN PARKER; publs *Annual Report*, *Discovery* (quarterly).

Physical Sciences

Carter Observatory: POB 2909, Wellington; tel. (4) 472-8167; fax (4) 472-8230; e-mail astronomy@carterobs.ac.nz; internet www .carterobs.ac.nz; f. 1938; the national observatory; astronomical research and planetarium; national centre for receipt and distribution of astronomical information; co-operation with schools, colleges and universities for education in astronomy; library of 20,000 vols, 434 journals; Chair. RICHARD J. BENTLEY; Senior Astronomer BRIAN CARTER; publs *Annual Report*, *Newsletter*.

GNS Science: 1 Fairway Dr., Avalon, POB 30-368, Lower Hutt; tel. (4) 570-1444; fax (4) 570-4600; e-mail webmaster@gns.cri.nz; internet www.gns.cri.nz; f. 1865 as New Zealand Geological Survey; DSIR Geology &

Geophysics 1990; Institute of Geological and Nuclear Sciences Ltd 1992); a crown research institute; earth and isotope research and consultancy; maintains collections of rocks, minerals and fossils of New Zealand and other countries, including Suter collection of New Zealand Mollusca; responsible for national geological mapping, geophysics and hazard studies, and all applied geology; 300 staff; library of 40,000 vols, 15,000 photos; Chair. CON ANASTASIOU; Chief Exec. Dr ALEX MALAHOFF; publs *Annual Report, Globe Magazine* (annually), *NZ Volcanological Record* (annually).

Mount John University Observatory: POB 56, Lake Tekapo 8770; tel. (3) 680-6000; fax (3) 680-6005; e-mail mjuo@phys .canterbury.ac.nz; internet www.phys .canterbury.ac.nz/research/astronomy; f. 1963; operated by Univ. of Canterbury; research especially into variable stars, stellar spectroscopy and gravitational microlensing; four telescopes in total with apertures of 1.8 m, 1.0 m and two of 0.6 m; Dir Prof. J. B. HEARNSHAW.

National Institute of Water & Atmospheric Research Ltd–NIWA: Private Bag 109695, 269 Khyber Pass Rd, Newmarket, Auckland; tel. (9) 375-2050; fax (9) 375-2051; e-mail exec@niwa.co.nz; internet www.niwa.co.nz; f. 1992; manages and makes use of the natural environment in a sustainable manner; National Climate Centre; National Centre for Fisheries and Aquaculture; National Centre for Climate–Energy Solutions; National Centre for Water Resources; National Centre for Aquatic Biodiversity and Biosecurity; National Centre for Coasts & Oceans; Natural Hazards Centre; Chief Exec. Dr RICK PRIDMORE; publ. *Annual Report*.

New Plymouth Astronomical Society Observatory: POB 818, New Plymouth; e-mail david.hill@clear.net.nz; f. 1920; 60 mems; Sec. DAVID HILL.

TECHNOLOGY

New Zealand Institute for Industrial Research and Development (Industrial Research Ltd): Gracefield Research Centre, 69 Gracefield Rd, POB 31-310, Lower Hutt 5040; tel. (4) 931-3000; fax (4) 566-6004; e-mail info@irl.cri.nz; internet www.irl.cri .nz; f. 1992; a Crown Research Institute; conducts research and devt into science and technology, and advises on implementing its results commercially; Chair. BRIAN RHOADES; Chief Exec. SHAUN COFFEY.

Libraries and Archives

Auckland

Auckland City Libraries: POB 4138, Shortland St, Auckland 1001; tel. (9) 377-0209; fax (9) 307-7741; e-mail allison.dobbie@ aucklandcity.govt.nz; internet www .aucklandcitylibraries.com; f. 1880; 16 community libraries, 1 mobile library, central library; 1,032,591 vols, 17,450 gramophone records, 24,714 music scores, 12,000 compact discs, 2,000 videos; special collections: Grey and Shaw Collections of MSS and incunabula, Grey Maori Collection, Lewis Eady Music Collection, Reed Dumas Collection; photographic collections; Group Man., Libraries ALLISON DOBBIE.

University of Auckland Library: Private Bag 92019, Auckland; tel. (9) 373-7999; fax (9) 373-7565; internet www.library.auckland .ac.nz; f. 1884; 2,161,000 vols; consists of General Library, 13 divisional libraries and 3

information commons facilities; Librarian JANET COPSEY.

Christchurch

Christchurch City Libraries: POB 1466, Christchurch 8015; tel. (3) 941-7923; fax (3) 941-7848; e-mail library@ccc.govt.nz; internet library.christchurch.org.nz; f. 1859; 1,044,143 items, including 360,000 vols; 12 libraries and one mobile library; Library Man. CAROLYN ROBERTSON; publ. *Connect* (monthly).

Lincoln University Library: POB 64, Lincoln University, Lincoln, Canterbury 7647; tel. (3) 325-2811; fax (3) 325-2944; e-mail library@lincoln.ac.nz; internet www .lincoln.ac.nz/libr; f. 1960; 209,459 books, 2,560 current print periodicals, 16,000 electronic periodicals; specializes in commerce and management, primary production and natural resources, science and engineering, social sciences; University Librarian TERESA HORN.

University of Canterbury Library: Private Bag 4800, Christchurch; tel. (3) 366-7001; fax (3) 364-2055; e-mail helpdesk@libr .canterbury.ac.nz; internet library .canterbury.ac.nz; f. 1873; 1,800,000 items; spec. collns incl. Macmillan Brown Collection of New Zealand and Pacific Materials; Librarian G. PATTIE.

Dunedin

Dunedin Public Libraries: POB 5542, Moray Place, Dunedin; tel. (3) 474-3690; fax (3) 474-3660; e-mail library@dcc.govt.nz; internet www.dunedinlibraries.com; f. 1908; 716,289 vols; heritage collns incl. McNab New Zealand colln (87,000 vols) and numerous special collns, incl. illuminated MSS and Bibles, Samuel Johnson, Sir Walter Scott, Charles Dickens, Walt Whitman, Farjeon, hymn books, autographed letters; Library Services Man. BERNIE HAWKE.

Otago District Law Society Library: Private Bag 1901, Dunedin; tel. (3) 477-0596; fax (3) 474-1886; e-mail library@odls .org.nz; internet www.odls.org.nz/library/ index.html; f. 1859; 13,500 vols, consisting of statutes, regulations, law reports, unreported judgments, treaties; and a representative selection of New Zealand secondary sources (textbooks, law journals, dictionaries and encyclopedias); Librarian ELSJA KINLEY.

University of Otago Library: POB 56, Dunedin 9054; tel. (3) 479-8932; fax (3) 479-8947; e-mail library@otago.ac.nz; internet www.library.otago.ac.nz; f. 1869; Consists of several libraries: Central (arts, humanities, social sciences, commerce), Law, Dental, Medical, Science, Hocken (major NZ and Pacific research collections including archives, pictorial collections, exhibition gallery); Special Collns includes early European imprints, de Beer Exhibition Gallery and Otakou Press; 2,838,816 vols; Librarian SUE PHARO.

Hamilton

University of Waikato Library: Private Bag 3105, Hamilton 3240; tel. (7) 838-4111; fax (7) 838-4017; e-mail library@waikato.ac .nz; internet www.waikato.ac.nz/library; f. 1964; 1,058,000 vols, 2,200 print periodicals, and provides access to 72,000 electronic resources; incorporates Central, Education, Law and Map libraries, and New Zealand Collection; Univ. Librarian ANNETTE MCNICOL.

Palmerston North

Palmerston North City Library: POB 1948, Palmerston North; tel. (6) 351-4100; fax (6) 351-4102; e-mail pncl@pncc.govt.nz; internet citylibrary.pncc.govt.nz; f. 1876;

250,000 vols; lending, reference, children's, audiovisual, archives sections; 3 brs; 1 mobile library; Librarian ANTHONY LEWIS.

Tauranga

Tauranga City Libraries: Private Bag 12022, Tauranga; Located at: Library Arcade, Willow St, Tauranga; tel. (7) 577-7177; fax (7) 578-6787; e-mail library@ tauranga.govt.nz; internet library.tauranga .govt.nz; f. 1906; reference and New Zealand collns; 4 brs, 1 mobile; 300,000 items; General Man., Libraries JILL BEST; publ. *Newsletter*.

Wellington

Archives New Zealand: POB 12-050, Wellington; Located at: 10 Mulgrave St, Wellington; tel. (4) 499-5595; fax (4) 495-6210; e-mail enquiries@archives.govt.nz; internet www.archives.govt.nz; f. 1926; 76,652 linear metres of archives, 1,578,074 photographs, 21,987 films and videos, 534,368 maps and plans; legislative, executive and judicial records of New Zealand government (incl. provincial govts); ministerial papers; National War Art Collection; Treaty of Waitangi; public reference services in Wellington and at regional offices in Auckland, Christchurch and Dunedin; Dir DIANNE MACASKILL.

Museum of New Zealand, Te Papa Tongarewa, Te Aka Matua Library and Information Centre: Cable St, Wellington; tel. (4) 381-7000; fax (4) 381-7370; e-mail mail@tepapa.govt.nz; internet www.tepapa .govt.nz; f. 1990, incorporates Nat. Museum Library, Nat. Art Gallery Library and Royal Soc. of New Zealand Library; 150,000 vols; Man. MANUELA C. ANGELO.

National Library of New Zealand, Te Puna Matauranga o Aotearoa: POB 1467, Wellington 6001; tel. (4) 474-3000; fax (4) 474-3035; e-mail information@natlib.govt.nz; internet www.natlib.govt.nz; f. 1966; 910,247 vols, 8,135 current print periodical titles, 12 main microform collns, 10,790 audio titles in the General Collns; 586,000 items in the Schools Collns; Nat. Librarian P. CARNABY.

Constituent library:

Alexander Turnbull Library: POB 12-349, Wellington 6144; tel. (4) 474-3120; fax (4) 474-3063; e-mail atl@natlib.govt.nz; internet www.natlib.govt.nz; f. 1918; 380,000 vols, including 32,000 rare books, chiefly in English literature; spec. collns incl. New Zealand and the Pacific, Milton, Katherine Mansfield; 30,000 oral history audio cassettes; 8,500 linear m of MSS; 90,000 drawings, paintings, prints and cartoons; 2,620,000 photographic prints, negatives and albums; 58,000 maps; 50,000 sound recordings; 4,500 video cassettes; 1,000 computer files; 150,000 items of ephemera (incl. 19,500 posters); 420,000 newspaper issues; 1,130,000 vols of periodicals; 3,000 music scores; Chief Librarian CHRIS SZEKELY; publs *Off the Record* (annual), *Turnbull Library Record* (annual).

Parliamentary Library: POB 18041, Parliament Bldgs, Wellington 6160; tel. (4) 471-9647; fax (4) 471-2551; e-mail parlinfo@ parliament.govt.nz; internet www .parliament.nz; f. 1858; 750,000 books; exchange and deposit repository; special collns: New Zealand, overseas official and parliamentary materials; services to the public include Parliamentary Information Service and Int. Documents Service; Parliamentary Librarian and Group Man., Information and Knowledge MOIRA FRASER; publs *Bills Digests* (online), *Electorate Profiles* (online), *Research Papers* (online).

Victoria University of Wellington Library: POB 3438, Wellington; tel. (4) 463-5249; fax (4) 471-2070; e-mail library@vuw.ac.nz; internet www.vuw.ac.nz/library; f. 1899; 1,000,000 printed vols; 25,000 current print and electronic periodicals; University Librarian SUE ROBERTS.

Wellington Public Library: POB 1992, Wellington; tel. (4) 801-4040; fax (4) 801-4047; internet www.wcl.govt.nz; f. 1893; 600,000 vols, 450,000 bound periodicals, 85,000 audiovisual items; 12 br. libraries and mobile surburban service; Man., Libraries JANE HILL.

Museums and Art Galleries

Auckland

Auckland Art Gallery Toi o Tāmaki: POB 5449, Auckland 1; tel. (9) 307-7700; fax (9) 302-1096; e-mail gallery@aucklandartgallery.govt.nz; internet www.aucklandartgallery.govt.nz; f. 1888; European paintings since 12th c., sculpture, prints and drawings, Frances Hodgkins collection, Colin McCahon collection, Fuseli drawings, New Zealand painting since 19th c., sculpture and prints; photographs and artists' books, audio- and video-tapes; John Weeks archive; library: research library of 33,000 vols; Dir CHRIS SAINES.

Auckland Museum: Private Bag 92018, Auckland 1; tel. (9) 309-0443; fax (9) 379-9956; e-mail director@aucklandmuseum .com; internet www.aucklandmuseum.com; f. 1852; natural history, ethnology (especially NZ Maori and Oceanic), applied arts (especially Asian, European and NZ ceramics, English furniture, textiles), social and war history; conservation laboratory; library of 100,000 vols; Dir Dr T. L. R. WILSON; Library Services Man. B. RALSTON; publs *Annual Report*, *Records* (annually), *Bulletin* (irregular).

Museum of Transport and Technology (MOTAT): Great North Rd, Western Springs, Auckland; tel. (9) 815-5800; fax (9) 846-4242; e-mail enquiries@motat.org.nz; internet www.motat.org.nz; f. 1960; ontwo sites, exhibiting vehicles, aircraft, machinery and equipment of historical and technical interest, incl. an extensive aircraft colln, vintage agricultural and military vehicles, steam trains, a working tram line and travelling exhibitions; Walsh Memorial Library of 11,000 monographs, 850 serial titles, technical manuals, photographs, maps, plans, archives, spec. collns incl. Whites Aviation Photographic prints, archives of pioneer aviators Jean Batten and Richard Pearse, Les Downey rail photograph colln, Walsh Flying School archives; Dir JEFFREY HUBBARD.

Christchurch

Canterbury Museum: Rolleston Ave, Christchurch 8013; tel. (3) 366-5000; fax (3) 366-5622; e-mail info@canterburymuseum .com; internet www.canterburymuseum .com; f. 1867; library: research library, and spec. research library on the Antarctic; cultural and natural history of the Canterbury region, in NZ and global contexts; Antarctic age of discovery and exploration; archaeology, ethnology, geology, zoology, extinct bird studies; Asian and European arts; Canterbury archives; pictorial history; Dir ANTHONY E. WRIGHT; publ. *Records of the Canterbury Museum* (annual).

Christchurch Art Gallery Te Puna o Waiwhetu: Worcester Blvd, Christchurch 8001; tel. (3) 941-7300; fax (3) 941-7301; e-mail info@christchurchgallery.org.nz; internet www.christchurchgallery.org.nz; f. 1932 as Robert McDougall Art Gallery and McDougall Contemporary Art Annex; present name and location 2003; one of the largest art collections in New Zealand; national and international touring exhibitions; works by local artists; Dir P. ANTHONY PRESTON; publ. *Bulletin* (4 a year).

Dunedin

Dunedin Public Art Gallery: 30 The Octagon, POB 566, Dunedin; tel. (3) 474-3240; fax (3) 474-3250; e-mail dpagmail@dcc .govt.nz; internet www.dunedin.art.museum; f. 1884; maintains a conservation laboratory; holdings include: 14th–19th c. European paintings, New Zealand paintings from 1870, Australian paintings 1900–70, British watercolours, portraits and landscapes; Japanese prints since 18th c., New Zealand prints since 19th c.; old and modern masters, includes oils by Claude Lorrain and Monet; decorative arts collections of furniture, ceramics, glass, oriental rugs, gallery dedicated to works of painter Frances Hodgkins; Dir PRISCILLA PITTS.

Otago Museum: 419 Great King St, POB 6202, Dunedin; tel. (3) 474-7474; fax (3) 477-5993; e-mail mail@otagomuseum.govt.nz; internet www.otagomuseum.govt.nz; f. 1868; natural sciences, NZ and Pacific anthropology, classical archaeology, European and Asian ceramics, 'Discovery World' Science Centre, NZ crafts, southern geology and fossils; Dir S. C. PAUL.

Theomin Gallery, Dunedin: 'Olveston', 42 Royal Terrace, Dunedin; tel. (3) 477-3320; fax (3) 479-2094; e-mail olveston@xtra.co.nz; internet www.olveston.co.nz; built 1904–06; Jacobean-style house designed by British architect Sir Ernest George for David Edward Theomin; bequeathed to the city by his daughter, Dorothy, 1966; opened to the public 1967; antique furniture, ceramics, crystal, bronzes, Persian rugs, silver, early English, European and NZ oils and watercolours; Man. GRANT BARRON.

Gisborne

Tairawhiti Museum: POB 716, Gisborne; Located at: Kelvin Rise, Stout St, Gisborne; tel. (6) 867-3832; fax (6) 867-2728; e-mail info@tairawhitimuseum.org.nz; internet www.tairawhitimuseum.org.nz; f. 1954; social history, Maori treasures (taonga Maori), fine arts, photography, surfboards, 'Star of Canada' wreck colln, natural history, oral history archive, textiles; local archives, cards and postcards, maps, plans, theatrical programmes; Dir Dr MONTY SAUTAR.

Gore

Eastern Southland Gallery (Inc.): Cnr Main and Norfolk Sts, POB 305, Gore, Southland; tel. (3) 208-9907; fax (3) 208-9968; e-mail jgeddes@goredc.govt.nz; f. 1983; exhibitions: art works, craft work, historical displays; cultural centre for presentation of films, lectures, music, poetry, etc.; Dir JIM GEDDES; publ. *Activities Bulletin* (2 a year).

Hokitika

West Coast Historical Museum: Hamilton St, POB 171, Hokitika 7900, Westland; tel. (3) 755-6898; fax (3) 755-5011; e-mail hokimuseum@xtra.co.nz; internet www .westlanddc.govt.nz/main/museum; f. 1960; social and natural history exhibits, working models; audio visual programme on 19th-century West Coast goldmining industry and colonial settlement; Poutini Maori and 19th-century immigrant histories; pounamu (NZ greenstone), gold; maintains research centre with local history archives; Curator JULIA BRADSHAW.

Invercargill

Anderson Park Art Gallery (Inc.): POB 5095, Invercargill; tel. (3) 215-7432; fax (3) 215-7472; e-mail andersonparkgallery@xtra .co.nz; f. 1951; mainly New Zealand works; Dir JOHN HUSBAND.

Southland Museum and Art Gallery: POB 1012, Gala St, Invercargill; tel. (3) 219-9069; fax (3) 218-3872; e-mail info@southlandmuseum.co.nz; internet www .southlandmuseum.com; f. 1915; natural history, Maori and colonial history, 'Victoriana', art gallery, astronomical observatory; live Tuatara enclosure; Sub-Antarctic centre; Man., Library, Museum and Art Gallery KEITH HARRINGTON.

Napier

Hawke's Bay Cultural Trust: POB 248, Napier; tel. (6) 835-7781; fax (6) 835-9249; e-mail enquiries@hbct.co.nz; internet www .hawkesbaymuseum.co.nz; f. 1989; CEO NEIL FERGUS (acting).

Institutions under the Trust's control:

Faraday Centre: 1 Faraday St, Napier; tel. (6) 835-7781; fax (6) 835-9249; e-mail faraday@hbct.co.nz; internet home.clear .net.nz/pages/dprebensen/Faraday; science and technology education (stationary, hot-air and steam engines; steam traction engines, horse-drawn phaetons and hearses, bath-chairs; audio recording and broadcasting equipment; printing presses; early hospital and surgical equipment); workshops for young people; Curator DAVID PREBENSEN.

Hawke's Bay Exhibition Centre: Eastbourne St, Hastings; tel. (6) 876-2077; fax (6) 876-4110; e-mail exhibitionmanager@ hbct.co.nz; regional venue for temporary touring exhibitions related to art, history, science and technology; Exhibition Man. MARGARET CRANWELL.

Hawke's Bay Museum: 9 Herschell St, Napier; tel. (6) 835-7781; fax (6) 835-9249; e-mail enquiries@hbct.co.nz; internet www .hawkesbaymuseum.co.nz; f. 1936; Maori and NZ art and material culture, painting, pottery and sculpture, decorative arts, 1931 earthquake and dinosaur exhibitions; regional archives; Museum Man. DOUGLAS LLOYD JENKINS.

Nelson

Nelson Provincial Museum: Town Acre 445, POB 853, Nelson; tel. (3) 547-9740; fax (3) 547-8549; e-mail enquiries@museumnp .org.nz; internet www.museumnp.org.nz; f. 1841; Maori and European history; reference library, 1,200,000 photographs (since 1860s), archives (since 1840s); CEO (vacant).

The Suter te Aratoi o Whakatu: 208 Bridge St, POB 751, Nelson; tel. (3) 548-4699; fax (3) 548-1236; e-mail info@thesuter .org.nz; internet www.thesuter.org.nz; f. 1895; early New Zealand watercolours; programme of exhibitions, events, performances and films; Dir HELEN TELFORD; publ. *The Suter Newsletter* (quarterly).

Oamaru

Forrester Gallery: Waitaki District Council, Private Bag 50058, Oamaru; tel. (3) 434-1653; fax (3) 434-1654; e-mail info@ forrestergallery.com; internet www .forrestergallery.com; f. 1983; housed in a neo-classical building constructed in 1884; works of art and architectural drawings related to North Otago and New Zealand; programme of exhibitions and cultural events; Dir WARWICK SMITH; publ. *Newsletter* (quarterly).

Paihia

Waitangi Treaty Grounds: Waitangi National Trust, Paihia, Bay of Islands; tel. (9) 402-7437; fax (9) 402-8303; e-mail waitangiestate@waitangi.net.nz; internet www.waitangi.net.nz; f. 1932; historic Treaty House; carved Maori meeting house and war canoe; exhibits of NZ historical interest up to 1840; visitor centre complex and audio-visual programme on signing of Treaty of Waitangi between Maori Chiefs and British Crown on 6 February 1840; live Maori theatre and spec. education programmes; Retail and Business Man. ANDY LARSEN.

Timaru

Aigantighe Art Gallery: 49 Wai-iti Rd, Timaru; tel. (3) 688-4424; fax (3) 684-8346; e-mail gallery@timdc.govt.nz; internet www .timaru.govt.nz/artgallery.html; f. 1956; New Zealand and European paintings, prints, sculpture and ceramics; Dir FIONA CIARAN; publ. *Members' Newsletters* (quarterly).

Wanganui

Sarjeant Gallery: Queen's Park, POB 998, Wanganui; tel. (6) 349-0506; fax (6) 349-0507; e-mail info@sarjeant.queenspark.org.nz; internet www.sarjeant.org.nz; f. 1919; European and English watercolours since 18th c.; representative New Zealand collection; Gilfillan collection, Barraud collection, drawings after Bernardino Poccetti, collection of First World War cartoons; contemporary Maori art; sculpture, particularly wooden photography; Collection Man. DENIS RAINFORTH; publ. *Newsletter*.

Whanganui Regional Museum: POB 352, Watt St, Wanganui; tel. (6) 349-1110; fax (6) 347-6512; e-mail info@museum.queenspark .org.nz; internet www.wanganui-museum .org.nz; f. 1895; Taonga Maori, natural history, local social history; archives; Dir S. E. DELL.

Wellington

New Zealand Academy of Fine Arts: 1 Queens Wharf, Wellington; tel. (4) 499-8807; fax (4) 499-2612; e-mail nzafa@xtra.co.nz; internet www.nzafa.com; f. 1882; art gallery promoting New Zealand artists and the visual arts in New Zealand through 8 annual exhibitions; Man. NAHLEEN MARKHAM; publ. *Academy Arts News* (4 a year).

Te Papa: Cable St, POB 467, Wellington; tel. (4) 381-7000; fax (4) 381-7070; e-mail mail@ tepapa.govt.nz; internet www.tepapa.govt .nz; f. 1992 by merger of the National Art Gallery and the National Museum; art, history, Maori culture, natural environment; collection of Maori taonga, incl. Te Hau-ki-Turanga (oldest extant Maori building in New Zealand); Polynesian, Micronesian and Melanesian art and culture; paintings, drawings, graphic art, photography and sculpture by New Zealand and foreign artists; collections of works by Natalia Gontcharova, Frances Hodgkins, Raymond McIntyre and Colin McCahon; maintains Hector Library (systematic biology, ethnology, early European South Pacific exploration and art reference material); Chief Exec. Dr SEDDON BENNINGTON.

Universities

UNIVERSITY OF AUCKLAND

Private Bag 92019, Auckland 1
Telephone: (9) 373-7999

Fax: (9) 373-7400
E-mail: contactus@auckland.ac.nz
Internet: www.auckland.ac.nz
Founded 1882 as Auckland University College; university status 1962
Academic year: January to November

Chancellor: JOHN GRAHAM
Pro-Chancellor: LYN STEVENS
Vice-Chancellor: STUART MCCUTCHEON
Deputy Vice-Chancellors: Prof. RAEWYN DALZIEL (Academic), Prof. TOM BARNES (Research)
Assistant to the Vice-Chancellor, and Registrar: W. B. NICOLL
Director of Administration: JONATHAN BLAKEMAN

Library: see Libraries and Archives
Number of teachers: 1,700 (full-time)
Number of students: 33,000
Publication: *University of Auckland Research Report* (annually)

DEANS

Faculty of Architecture, Property, Planning and Fine Arts: M. H. PRITCHARD
Faculty of Arts: J. MORROW
Faculty of Business and Economics: B. SPICER
Faculty of Engineering: P. BROTHERS
Faculty of Law: J. K. MAXTON
Faculty of Medical and Health Sciences: Prof. IAN MARTIN
Faculty of Science: A. R. BELLAMY

PROFESSORS AND HEADS OF DEPARTMENTS (H = Head of Department)

ADAMS, P., Applied Behavioural Science
ANAE, M., Pacific Studies (H)
ANDERSON, C. A., Medicine
ASHER, I., Paediatrics (H)
AUSTIN, G. L., Physics
BAKER, E. N., Biological Sciences, Chemistry
BAKER, M., Sociology
BELICH, J. C., History (H)
BELLAMY, A. R., Biological Sciences
BHATTACHARYYA, D., Mechanical Engineering (H)
BISHOP, J. C., Philosophy
BLACK, P. M., Geology
BOOTH, G., Creative and Performing Arts (H)
BOOTH, R., Molecular Medicine and Pathology (H)
BOWMAKER, G., Chemistry (H)
BOWMAN, R. G., Accounting and Finance
BOXALL, P., Management and Employment Relations (H)
BOYS, J. T., Electrical and Electronic Engineering
BRIMBLE, M. A., Chemistry
BRODIE, R. J., Marketing
BROWETT, P., Pathology
BROWNE, P., Geology (H)
BYBLEW, W., Sport and Exercise Science (H)
CALUDE, C. S., Computer Science
CANNELL, M., Physiology (H)
CARMICHAEL, H., Physics
CARTER, I. R., Sociology
CARTWRIGHT, R. W., International Business
CHEN, J. J. J., Chemical and Materials Engineering (H)
CHEN, X. D., Chemical and Materials Engineering
CLARK, G., Chemistry
CLARK, P. J. A., Chinese
CLARK, R. G., Molecular Medicine
COLLINS, I. F., Engineering Science
COOPER, G. J. S., Biological Sciences and Medicine
CORBALLIS, M. C., Psychology
CORRADO, C., Accounting and Finance
COSTER, G. D., General Practice (H)
COVIELLO, N., Marketing

CRAIG, J. L., Geography and Environmental Science
CROSIER, K. E., Molecular Medicine and Pathology
CROSTHWAITE, J., European Languages and Literatures (H)
DANAHER, P. J., Marketing (H)
DAVISON, M. C., Psychology
DENNY, W., Cancer Society Research Centre (H)
DIXON, J., Planning (H)
DRAGUNOW, M., Pharmacology and Clinical Pharmacology
DUFFY, G. G., Chemical and Materials Engineering
DUNN, M. R., Fine Arts (H)
DUNN, W., Business
DURING, M. J., Molecular Medicine
EAGLES, I. G., Commercial Law
ELLIS, R., Applied Language Studies and Linguistics (H)
EMANUEL, D. M., Accounting and Finance
EVANS, P. J., Law
FAULL, R. L. M., Anatomy
FERGUSON, L., Auckland Cancer Society Research Centre
FERGUSON, W. G., Chemical and Materials Engineering
FLAY, R., Mechanical Engineering
FORER, P. C., Geography and Environmental Science
FRASER, J., Molecular Medicine
GAO, W., Chemicals and Materials Engineering
GARDNER, R. C., Biological Sciences
GAULD, D. B., Mathematics (H)
GEERTSHUIS, S., Continuing Education
GILMOUR, R. S., Liggins Institute
GLUCKMAN, P. D., Liggins Institute
GONZALEZ-CASANOVAS, R., Spanish (H)
GORMAN, D., Medicine
GRANTHAM, R., Commerical Law (H)
GRAY, V. J., Classics and Ancient History
GRUNDY, J., Computer Science
GUSTAFSON, B. S., Political Studies (H)
HAARHOF, E. J., Architecture (H)
HARDING, J. E., Obstetrics and Gynaecology
HARRIS, B. V., Law
HARVEY, J. D., Physics
HATCHER, S., Psychiatry (H)
HATTIE, J. A., Education
HAWORTH, N. A. F., International Business (H)
HAZLEDINE, T. J., Economics
HOLLIS, S., English
HOOL, R. B., Economics
HORROCKS, R., Film, Television and Media Studies
HOSKING, J., Computer Science (H)
HOUSLEY, G., Physiology (H)
HUNT, J. G., Architecture (H)
HUNTER, P. J., Bioengineering Institute (H)
HURSTHOUSE, R., Philosophy (H)
IRWIN, G. J., Authropology (H)
JACKSON, M. P., English
JACKSON, P. S., Mechanical Engineering
JACKSON, R., Community Health (H)
JACOBS, R., Optometry and Vision Science (H)
JENSEN, C., Anatomy with Radiology (H)
KALLONIATIS, M., Optometry
KELSEY, J., Law
KILPATRICK, J., Nursing (H)
KIRKNESS, A. C., Applied Language Studies and Linguistics
KISTLER, J., Biological Sciences (H)
KLETTE, R., Computer Science
KYDD, R. R., Psychiatry
LARSEN, K., English (H)
LE HERON, R. B., Geography and Environmental Science
LEES, H., Music
LENNON, D. R., Paediatrics
LIPSKI, J., Physiology
LORRIGAN, G., Business
LUCIANO, B., Italian (H)
MCCARTHY, D. C., Psychology (H)

McCORMICK, R., Goodfellow Unit (H)
McGHEE, C., Ophthalmology (H)
McKECHNIE, P., Classics and Ancient History
McNAUGHTON, S., Education
MACPHERSON, C., Sociology (H)
MANTELL, C. D., Maori and Pacific Health (H)
MARTIN, G. J., Mathematics
MARTIN, I., Surgery
MAXTON, J. K., Law (H)
MELLSOP, G., South Auckland Clinical School (H)
MELVILLE, B., Civil and Resource Engineering (H)
MERRY, A., Anaesthesiology (H)
MITCHELL, E. A., Paediatrics (H)
MITCHELL, M. D., Pharmacology and Clinical Pharmacology (H)
MOLLOY, M. A., Women's Studies
MONTGOMERY, J. C., Biological Sciences (H)
MORIARTY, S., Accounting and Finance
MORROW, J., Political Studies
MUTU, M., Maori Studies (H)
MYERS, M., Management Science and Information Systems
NEICH, R., Anthropology
NEILL, M. A. F., English (H)
NEVILLE, R., Property (H)
NICHOLSON, T., Education
O'CONNOR, C. J., Chemistry
O'SULLIVAN, M., Engineering Science (H)
OWENS, R. G., Psychology
PARRY, B. R., Surgery (H)
PAVLOV, B., Mathematics
PAXTON, J., Pharmacology and Clinical Pharmacology (H)
PENDER, M. J., Civil and Resource Engineering
PERRY, N., Film, Television and Media Studies (H)
PETERS, M., Education
PETRIE, K., Health Psychology (H)
PHILPOTT, A., Engineering Science
POWELL, M. J., Management and Employment Relations
RAMSAY, R. L., French (H)
RANKIN, E. A., Art History (H)
REA, H. H., Medicine
REAY, B. G., History (H)
REID, I. R., Medicine (H)
REILLY, I. L., Mathematics
ROBINSON, V., Education (H)
RUSSELL, D. K., Chemistry
RYAN, D. M., Engineering Science
SALCIC, Z., Electrical and Electronic Engineering
Dame SALMOND, M. A., Anthropology, Maori Studies
SCHWERDTFEGER, P., Chemistry
SCOTT, A. J., Statistics
SCOTT, D., Statistics (H)
SCRIVEN, M., Education
SHARP, R. A., Political Studies
SHAW, J., Pharmacy (H)
SHEPHEARD, C., Fine Arts
SIMPSON, I. J., Medicine
SLEIGH, J., Anaesthesia
SMALL, J., Economics
SMITH, G., Education
SMITH, L., Education
SMITH, W., Geography and Environmental Science (H)
SPALINGER, A., Classics and Ancient History
SPICER, B. H., Accounting and Finance
SRINIVASAN, A., Management Science and Information Systems
STONE, P., Obstetrics and Gynaecology (H)
STURM, T. L., English
SUTTON, D. G., Anthropology
TAGGART, M. B., Law
THOMAS, D. R., Community Health
THOMBORSON, C. D., Computer Science
THORNE, P., Audiology (H)
TIBBLES, J., Music (H)
TINDLE, C., Physics (H)
VALE, B. A., Architecture

VOIT, F., German Languages and Literature (H)
VOWLES, J., Political Studies (H)
WAINWRIGHT, E., Theology (H)
WATTS, P., Law
WELLS, R. M. G., Biological Sciences
WENDT, A., English
WILD, C., Statistics (H)
WILLIAMS, P. W., Geography and Environmental Science
WILLIAMSON, A. G., Electrical and Electronic Engineering
WILSON, M. G., Management and Employment Relations (H)
WILSON, M. J., Classics and Ancient History (H)
WILSON, W., Auckland Cancer Society Research Centre
WILTON, R., Accounting and Finance (H)
WONG, J., Accounting and Finance
ZHANG, Y., Asian Studies (H)

ATTACHED INSTITUTES

Bioengineering Institute: Dir P. J. HUNTER.

Liggins Institute: medical and health research; Dir Prof. PETER GLUCKMAN.

New Zealand Asia Institute: Dir J. KEMBER.

AUCKLAND UNIVERSITY OF TECHNOLOGY

Private Bag, 92006, Auckland 1020
Telephone: (9) 917-9999
Fax: (9) 917-9981
Internet: www.aut.ac.nz
Founded 1895 as Auckland Technical School; became Seddon Memorial Technical College 1913, Auckland Technical Institute 1960, Auckland Institute of Technology 1989; present name 2000
State control
Academic year: January to December
Vice-Chancellor: Dr. JOHN HINCHCLIFF
Pro Vice-Chancellors: Dr. DAVID BROOK (Academic), DEREK McCORMACK (Administration), Prof. PHILIP SALLIS (Research), TOBY CURTIS (Te Ahurei – Maori Development)
Director of University Relations: VIVIEN SUTHERLAND BRIDGWATER
University Librarian: Dr. GRACE SAW
Library of 85,000 vols
Number of teachers: 576
Number of students: 23,288 (22,796 undergraduate, 492 postgraduate)

DEANS

Faculty of Arts: Prof. PETER HARWOOD
Faculty of Business: DES GRAYDON
Faculty of Health Studies: Prof. MAX ABBOTT
Faculty of Science and Engineering: Prof. ROY GEDDES
Te Ara Poutama (Faculty of Maori Development): Assoc. Prof. PARE KEIHA

UNIVERSITY OF CANTERBURY

Private Bag 4800, Christchurch 8002
Telephone: (3) 366-7001
Fax: (3) 364-2999
E-mail: info@canterbury.ac.nz
Internet: www.canterbury.ac.nz
Founded 1873
State control
Academic year: February to November
Chancellor: ROBIN MANN
Vice-Chancellor: Prof. ROY SHARP
Deputy Vice-Chancellor: Prof. IAN TOWN
Assistant Pro-Vice-Chancellor (Academic): Dr J. E. CAMERON
Assistant Pro-Vice-Chancellor (Maori Affairs): Sir T. O'REGAN
Registrar: A. W. HAYWARD

Chief Operating Officer: TOM GREGG
Director of Human Resources: PAUL O'FLAHERTY
Pro-Vice-Chancellors: Prof. KEN STRONGMAN (Arts), Prof. NIGEL HEALY (Business and Economics), Prof. PETER JACKSON (Engineering and Forestry), Prof. IAN SHAW (Science), Prof. SCOTT DAVIDSON (Law)
Senior Maori Member of Staff: JIM ANGLEM
Dean of Postgraduate Studies: Assoc. Prof. D. SHELLEY
Librarian: G. PATTIE
Library: see Libraries and Archives
Number of teachers: 656
Number of students: 13,430

DEANS

College of Commerce: Prof. N. HEALEY
College of Engineering and Forestry: Assoc. Prof. R. DUKE
College of Humanities and Social Sciences: C. G. GOODRICH
College of Science: Assoc. Prof. L. REINISCH
College of Visual and Performing Arts: Assoc. Prof. J. LE COQ (acting)
School of Law: Assoc. Prof. D. WEBB
Postgraduate Studies: Prof. D. GUNBY

PROFESSORS

College of Business and Economics:
CLARKE, B. J., Accountancy, Finance and Information Systems
GIBSON, J., Economics
HAMILTON, R. T., Management
HOLLAND, M., European Studies
MABERLY, E. D., Accountancy, Finance and Information Systems
OXLEY, L., Economics

College of Engineering:
BODGER, P., Electrical and Computer Engineering
BRIDGES, D. S., Mathematics and Statistics
BUCHANAN, A. H., Civil Engineering
BULL, D. K., Civil Engineering
DAVID, T., Mechanical Engineering
GOUGH, P. T., Electrical and Computer Engineering
MANDER, J. B., Civil Engineering
MARSH, K. N., Chemical and Process Engineering
MILLANE, R. P., Electrical and Computer Engineering
PAWLIKOWSKI, K., Computer Science and Software Engineering
SANDS, R., Forestry
STEEL, M., Mathematics and Statistics
TAKOAKA, T., Computer Science and Software Engineering
TAYLOR, D. P., Electrical and Electronic Engineering
WALKER, J. C., Forestry

College of Humanities and Social Studies:
BERCOVITCH, J., Political Science
CARSTAIRS-McCARTHY, A. D., Linguistics
COLE, J. W., Geological Sciences
COOKSON, J. E., History
COPELAND, B. J., Philosophy and Religious Studies
FAIRBURN, M., History
FRANCIS, M., Political Science
HARRISON, P., Philosophy and Religious Studies
HEMPENSTALL, P. J. A., History
HORNBY, G., Education
KUIPER, K., Linguistics
MACDONALD, C., Philosophy
MACDONALD, G. F., Philosophy
McNAUGHTON, H. D., English
MONDRY, H., Russian
NERO, K., Pacific Studies
ROCHFORT, A. D., Fine Arts
THORNS, D. C., Sociology and Anthropology
WILLMOTT, W., Pacific Studies
ZANKER, G., Classics

College of Science:

ABELL, A. D., Chemistry
BAGGALEY, W. J., Physics and Astronomy
BLUNT, J. W., Chemistry
BUTLER, P. H., Physics and Astronomy
BUTTERFIELD, B. G., Plant and Microbial Science
COLE, J. W., Geological Sciences
COXON, J. M., Chemistry
FLETCHER, G., Psychology
HARLAND, P. W., Chemistry
HEARNSHAW, J., Physics and Astronomy
HORNBLOW, A., Health Science
JACKSON, R. R., Biological Sciences
JAMESON, P. E., Biological Sciences
KELLY, D., Biological Sciences
KEMP, S., Psychology
KOKKINIDIS, L., Psychology
McEWAN, M., Chemistry
MUNROE, M. H., Chemistry
PAWSON, E. J., Geography
PHILLIPS, L. F., Chemistry
POWELL, H. K. J., Chemistry
ROBB, M. P., Communication Disorders
ROBINSON, W. T., Chemistry
SCHIEL, D. R, Biological Sciences
Mathematics and Statistics
STEEL, P., Chemistry
STOREY, B., Antarctic Studies
STURMAN, A. P., Geography
WEAVER, S. D., Geology

School of Law:

BURROWS, J. F., Law
JOSEPH, P. A., Law
TODD, S. M. D., Law

LINCOLN UNIVERSITY

POB 94, Lincoln University, Canterbury

Telephone: (3) 325-2811
Fax: (3) 325-2965
Internet: www.lincoln.ac.nz

Founded 1878; formerly the Canterbury Agricultural College and from 1961 to 1989 Lincoln College, a constituent college of the University of Canterbury; from 1990 an autonomous university

State control

Academic year: February to October

Chancellor: Hon. MARGARET AUSTIN
Vice-Chancellor: Dr FRANK WOOD
Deputy Vice-Chancellor: Prof. ROGER FIELD
Librarian: ISOBEL MOSLEY

Library: see Libraries
Number of teachers: 214
Number of students: 3,560

Publications: *Alumni News* (annually), *Infolinc* (monthly), *Lincoln Outlook* (annually)

PROFESSORS

BICKERSTAFFE, R., Food Biochemistry
BYWATER, A. C., Farm Management
CAMERON, K. C., Soil Science
CUSHMAN, J. G., Parks, Recreation and Tourism
DALZIEL, P., Economics
DAVIES, T., Natural Resources Engineering
FIELD, R. J., Plant Science
GOH, K. M., Soil Science
HAMPTON, J., Seed Technology
HILL, M., Seed and Crop Science
JORDAN, B., Plant Biotechnology
KISSLING, C. C., Transport Studies
KULASIRI, D., Computational Modelling and Simulation
LASWAD, F., Accounting
McKINNON, A., Applied Computing
McLAREN, R., Soil Science
MEMON, A., Resource Management
SAUNDERS, A., Trade and Environmental Economics
SIMMONS, D., Tourism
SPELLERBERG, I., Nature Conservation
STEWART, A., Plant Pathology

SWAFFIELD, S., Landscape Architecture
SYKES, A. R., Animal Science
WOODFORD, K., Farm Management and Agribusiness
WRATTEN, S. D., Ecology
ZWART, A. C., Marketing

ATTACHED RESEARCH INSTITUTES

Agribusiness and Economics Research Unit: Dir CAROLINE SAUNDERS.

Centre of Accounting, Education and Research: Dir MURRAY CLARK.

Centre for Advanced Computational Solutions: Dir Prof. DON KULASIRI.

Centre for Environmental Toxicology: Joint Dirs Prof. STEVE WRATTEN, Dr CHARLES EASON.

Centre for Maori and Indigenous Planning and Development: Dir Assoc. Prof. HIRINI MATUNGA.

Centre for Mountain Studies: Dir Dr KEN HUGHEY.

Centre for Soil and Environmental Quality: Dir Prof. KEITH CAMERON.

Centre for Viticulture and Oenology: Dir Dr GLEN CREASY.

Equine Blood Group Typing Unit: Dir Dr ROBIN McFARLANE.

Equine Research Unit: Dir Emeritus Prof. CLIFF IRVINE.

Isaac Centre for Nature Conservation: Dir Prof. IAN SPELLERBERG.

NZ Seed Technology Institute: Dir Prof. MURRAY HILL.

MASSEY UNIVERSITY

Private Bag 11-222, Tennent Drive, Palmerston North 5301

Telephone: (6) 356-9099
Fax: (6) 350-2263
E-mail: contact@massey.ac.nz
Internet: www.massey.ac.nz

Founded 1926 as Massey Agricultural College and merged with the Palmerston North Branch of the Victoria University of Wellington 1963; full autonomy granted 1964; absorbed Wellington Polytechnic 1998

State control

Academic year: February to November

Chancellor: N. J. GOULD
Vice-Chancellor: Prof. JUDITH KINNEAR
Assistant Vice-Chancellor (Academic): Prof. N. LONG (acting)
Assistant Vice-Chancellor (Research and External Relations): Prof. N. LONG
University Registrar: S. D. MORRISS (acting)
Deputy Vice-Chancellor, Auckland: Prof. J. RAINE
Deputy Vice-Chancellor (Palmerston North): Prof. I. WARRINGTON
Deputy Vice-Chancellor (Wellington): Prof. ANDREA McILROY
Librarian: J. W. REDMAYNE

Number of teachers: 1,255
Number of students: 39,657

Publications: *Massey University Annual Report, Massey University Calendar*

PRO VICE-CHANCELLORS

College of Business: Prof. JACK DOWDS
College of Design, Fine Arts and Music: Dr. D. A. JOINER
College of Education: Prof. L. MEYER
College of Humanities and Social Sciences: Prof. B. K. MACDONALD
College of Sciences: Prof. R. D. ANDERSON

PROFESSORS

ANDERSON, R. D., Sciences

BAILEY, W. C., Food Nutrition and Human Health
BARRY, T., Veterinary, Animal and Biomedical Sciences
BIRKBECK, J., Food Nutrition and Human Health
BLAIR, H. T., Veterinary, Animal and Biomedical Sciences
BODDY, J., Health Sciences
BRIGHT, G., Mechatronics
BRODIE, A. M., Fundamental Sciences
BROWN, I., History
CAHAN, S. F., Accountancy
CARRYER, J. B., Health Sciences
CHAPMAN, J. W., Learning and Teaching
CHAMBERLAIN, K. P., Psychology
CHATTERJEE, S., Applied and International Economics
CHETTY, S., Commerce
CHISTI, Y., Biotechnology
CLELAND, D. J., Technology and Engineering
CODD, J. A., Social and Policy Studies in Education
CORBALLIS, R. P., English and Media Studies
CRESSWELL, M. J., History, Philosophy and Politics
CROPP, G. M., Language Studies
CULLEN, J. L., Learning and Teaching
DAVIES, C., Particle Technology
DE BRUIN, A., Commerce
DEVLIN, M., Management
DURIE, M. H., Maori Studies
ENGELBRECHT, H.-J., Applied and International Economics
EVANS, I., Psychology
FIRTH, E. C., Veterinary, Animal and Biomedical Sciences
FLENLEY, J. R., People, Environment and Planning
FREYBURG, C., Information Systems
GARRICK, D. J., Veterinary, Animal and Biomedical Sciences
GENDALL, P. J., Marketing
GILL, H. S., Food, Nutrition and Animal Health
GUILFORD, W. G., Veterinary, Animal and Biomedical Sciences
HARKER, R. K., Education
HARGREAVES, R. V., Finance, Banking and Property Studies
HAWICK, K., Computer Science
HENDY, M. D., Mathematics
HERMANSSON, G. L., Health and Human Development
HEWETT, E. W., Food, Nutrition and Human Health
HODGSON, J., Natural Resources
HODGSON, R. M., Information Sciences and Technology
HOLMES, C. W., Veterinary, Animal and Biomedical Sciences
HOWE, K. R., History, Philosophy and Politics
HUNT, G. J., Aviation
HUNTER, J. J., Information and Mathematical Sciences
INKSON, J. H., Management and International Business
INKSON, K., Management and International Business
JAMESON, P., Plant Biology
LAGROW, S. J., Health Sciences
LAMBERT, D. M., Molecular Biosciences
LASWAD, F., Accountancy
LEATHERN, J., Neuropsychology
LOCK, A. J., Psychology
LONG, N., Psychology
MACDONALD, B. K., Humanities and Social Sciences
McKIBBIN, R., Information and Mathematical Sciences
McLACHLAN, R., Mathematics
MADDOX, I., Industrial Bioscience
MALLON, M., Human Resource Management
MEISTER, A. D., Applied and International Economics

MELLOR, D. J., Food, Nutrition and Human Health
MERRICK, P. L., Psychology
MILNE, K. S., Sciences
MOORE, C. I., Finance, Banking and Property Studies
MORGAN, S., Fine Arts
MORRIS, R. S., Veterinary, Animal and Bio-medical Sciences
MOUGHAN, P. J., Food, Nutrition and Human Health
MUNFORD, R. E., Sociology, Social Policy and Social Work
MURPHY, B., Commerce
NASH, R., Social and Policy Studies in Education
OFFICER, D., Chemistry
ONO, K., Language Studies
OPENSHAW, R., Social and Policy Studies in Education
OVERTON, J. D., People, Environment and Planning
PARRY, D. A., Fundamental Sciences
PEARCE, N. E., Public Health Research
PENNY, E. D., Molecular Biosciences
PERERA, H. M. B., Accountancy
RAE, A. N., Applied and International Economics
REEVES, R., Chemistry
ROCHE, M., Health Sciences
ROSE, L. C., Commerce
SCHEWE, K.-D., Information Systems
SCOTT, D. B., Molecular Biosciences
SHOUKSMITH, G., Psychology
SIGNAL, A., Physics
SINGH, H., Food, Nutrition and Human Health
SISSONS, J. D., People, Environment and Planning
SPOONLEY, P., Social and Cultural Studies
SPRINGETT, B. P., Natural Resources
STABLEIN, R., Management
SULLIVAN, P. A., Molecular Biosciences
TENNANT, M., Health Sciences
THOMSON, D. W., History, Philosophy and Politics
TILLMAN, R. W., Natural Resources
TRAWICK, M. J., People, Environment and Planning
TUNMER, W. E., Learning and Teaching
VAN DER WALT, N. T., Management and International Business
VITALIS, T., Management
WATERS, J., Chemistry
WILLIAMSON, N. B., Veterinary, Animal and Biomedical Sciences
WINGER, R. J., Food, Nutrition and Human Health

ATTACHED RESEARCH INSTITUTES

Animal Health Centre and Animal Research Services: Dir Dr A. E. GOLD-ENTHAL.
Applied Psychology Centre: Dir Assoc. Prof. J. SPICER.
Applied Statistics Consultancy Centre: Dir Assoc. Prof. S. J. HASLETT.
Centre for Agricultural and Veterinary Continuing Education: Dir (vacant).
Centre for Applied Economics and Policy Studies: Dir Prof. A. N. RAE.
Centre for Defence Studies: Dir Dr GLYN HARPER.
Centre for Public Health: Dir Prof. N. PEARCE.
Equine Blood Typing and Research Centre: Dir I. L. ANDERSON.
Fertilizer and Lime Research Centre: Dir Assoc. Prof. M. J. HEDLEY.
Fresh Technologies: Dir Dr M. HERTOG (acting).
Milk and Health Research Centre: Dir Prof. H. GILL.

Molecular Genetics Laboratory: Dir Prof. B. SCOTT.
Monogastric Research Unit: Dir Dr W. HENDRIKS (acting).
New Zealand Natural Heritage Foundation: Dir Prof. B. P. SPRINGETT.
New Zealand Social Research Data Archives: Dir H. G. BARNARD.
Saskawa Fellowship Fund for Japanese Language Education: Dir N. COLLINS.
Social Policy Research Centre: Dir (vacant).

UNIVERSITY OF OTAGO

POB 56, Dunedin 9015
Telephone: (3) 479-1100
Fax: (3) 474-1607
E-mail: university@otago.ac.nz
Internet: www.otago.ac.nz
Founded 1869
Academic year: March to November
Chancellor: L. J. BROWN
Pro-Chancellor: B. A. AITKEN
Vice-Chancellor: D. C. G. SKEGG
Deputy Vice-Chancellors: D. G. JONES (Academic and International), K. G. WHITE (Research)
Assistant Vice-Chancellors: D. H. BUISSON (Division of Commerce), L. J. HOLLOWAY (Division of Health Sciences), A. G. FOX (Division of Humanities), V. A. SQUIRE (Division of Sciences)
Sec. to the Council and Registrar: J. A. FLOOD
Librarian: S. PHARO
Library: see Libraries and Archives
Number of teachers: 1,566 (full-time)
Number of students: 19,707

DEANS

Faculty of Law: R. M. HENAGHAN
Faculty of Medicine: L. J. HOLLOWAY
School of Dentistry: G. J. SEYMOUR
School of Education: G. W. KEARSLEY
School of Language, Literature and Performing Arts: J. D. DRUMMOND
School of Liberal Arts: W. R. GARSIDE
School of Maori, Pacific and Indigenous Studies: T. M. KA'AI
School of Medical Sciences: D. T. JONES
School of Pharmacy: I. G. TUCKER
School of Physical Education: K. DAVIDS
School of Physiotherapy: G. D. BAXTER
School of Social Science: G. W. KEARSLEY
School of Surveying: C. C. HOOGSTEDEN
Christchurch School of Medicine and Health Sciences: G. I. TOWN
Dunedin School of Medicine: J. B. ADAMS
Wellington School of Medicine and Health Sciences: J. N. NACEY

PROFESSORS

ABRAHAM, W. C., Psychology
ADLER, R. W., Accountancy and Business Law
ANDERSON, J. S., Law
ANDERSON, T. J., Medicine
ARDAGH, M. W., Surgery
ATKINSON, M. D., Computer Science
BALLAGH, R. J., Physics
BALLARD, K. D., Education
BANNISTER, P., Botany
BAXTER, G. D., Physiotherapy
BENWELL, G. L., Information Science
BEGG, E. J., Medicine
BINNS, J. A., Geography
BLEY, T. S., Design Studies
BRAITHWAITE, A. W., Pathology
BROOKS, B. L., History
BROOKING, T. W. H., History
BUISSON, D. H., Marketing
BURGESS, C. D., Medicine
BURNS, C. W., Zoology

CAMPBELL, A. J., Medicine
CAMPBELL-HUNT, C., Management
CARRINGTON, C. G., Physics
CHAMBERS, S. T., Pathology
COOPER, A. F., Geology
CRACK, T. F., Finance and Quantitative Analysis
CRANE, J., Medicine
CROOKS, T. J., Education
DARLOW, B. A., Paediatrics
DAVIDS, K., Physical Education
DAVIDSON, I. J., Theology and Religious Studies
DAVIS, D. K., Communication Studies
DAWSON, J. B., Law
DELAHUNT, B., Pathology
DOMINIK, W. J., Classics
DOWELL, A. C., General Practice
DOYLE, T. C. A., Medicine
DRUMMOND, J. D., Music
DUFOUR, J. P., Food Science
ELLIS, P. M., Psychological Medicine
ENDRE, Z. H., Medicine
EVANS, D. M., Biomedical Ethics
FERGUSON, M. M., Stomatology
FERGUSSON, D. M., Psychological Medicine
FIELDING, D. J., Economics
FOX, A. G., English
FRIZELLE, F. A., Surgery
GARSIDE, W. R., History
GEARE, A. J., Economics
GIBSON, R. S., Human Nutrition
GILLETT, G. R., Neurosurgery and Biomedical Ethics
GREEN, D. P. L., Anatomy and Structural Biology
GRIFFIN, J. F. T., Microbiology
GRIMWOOD, K., Paediatrics and Child Health
GROVER, S., Management
HALL, C. M., Tourism
HANNAH, J., Surveying
HARRIS, C. P., Marketing
HARRIS, J. M., English
HAYNE, H., Psychology
HEATH, C. J., Higher Education
HENAGHAN, R. M., Law
HERBISON, A. E., Physiology
HOLLOWAY, L. J., Pathology
HOLTON, D. A., Mathematics and Statistics
HOOD, J. A. A., Oral Sciences and Orthodontics
HORNE, J. G., Surgery and Anaesthasia
HUNTER, K. A., Chemistry
HUTTON, J. D., Obstetrics and Gynaecology
ISICHEI, E., Theology and Religious Studies
JONES, D. G., Anatomy and Structural Biology
JONES, D. T., Microbiology
JOYCE, P. R., Psychological Medicine
KA'AI, T. M., Maori Studies
KARDOS, T. B., Oral Studies and Orthodontics
KEARSLEY, G. W., Social Science
KIESER, J. A., Oral Sciences and Orthodontics
KNIGHT, R. G., Psychology
KYLE, P. M., Obstetrics and Gynaecology
LAING, R. M., Clothing and Textile Science
LANGLEY, J. D., Preventive and Social Medicine
LAWSON, R. W., Marketing
LEACH, H. M., Anthropology
LEES, G., Pharmacology and Toxicology
LE GROS, G. S., Medicine
MACGREGOR, A. C., Accountancy and Business Law
MACLEOD, R. D., General Practice
McNAUGHTON, N., Psychology
MAHONEY, R. R., Law
MANN, J. I., Human Nutrition
MAY, H., Education
MEERSAHAERT, M. M., Mathematics and Statistics
MEHIGAN, T. J., Languages and Cultures
MEIKLE, M. C., Oral Sciences
MERCER, A. R., Zoology
MILLER, J. O., Psychology
MILNE, M. J., Accounting and Business Law

MOLTENO, A. C. B., Ophthalmology
MONTEITH, B. D., Oral Rehabilitation
MOORFIELD, J. C., Maori Studies
MORGAN, R. K., Geography
MULDER, R. T., Psychological Medicine
MURDOCH, D. R., Pathology
MUSGRAVE, A. E., Philosophy
NACEY, J. N., Medicine
NEL, P. R., Political Studies
NICHOLSON, H. D., Anatomy and Structural Biology
NORRIS, R. J., Geology
OLDS, R. J., Pathology
OWEN, P. D., Economics
POULIN, R., Zoology
PRINGLE, K. C., Obstetrics and Gynaecology
PURVIS, M. K., Information Science
RADES, T., Pharmacy
RADNER, H., Communication Studies
REEVE, A. E., Biochemistry
RICHARDS, A. M., Medicine
ROAKE, J. A., Surgery
ROBERTSON, S. P., Paediatrics and Child Health
ROBINSON, B. H., Chemistry
RONSON, C. W., Microbiology
ROTH, P. A., Law
ROTHWELL, A. G., Orthopaedic Surgery
SAINSBURY, R., Medicine
SEYMOUR, G. J., Dentistry
SHIPTON, E. A., Anaesthesia
SIBSON, R. H., Geology
SIMMS, M. J., Political Studies
SIMPSON, J., Chemistry
SKEGG, P. D. G., Law
SMILLIE, J. A., Law
SMITH, A. B., Children's Issues
SMITH, J. K., Education
SMITH, J. M. B., Microbiology
SMITH, P. F., Pharmacology and Toxicology
SMITH, R. A. J., Chemistry
SQUIRE, V. A., Mathematics and Statistics
SULLIVAN, S. J., Physiotherapy
SUMMERHAYER, G. R., Anthropology
SWAIN, M. V., Oral Sciences
TAGG, J. R., Microbiology
TANNOCK, G. W., Microbiology
TATE, W. P., Biochemistry
TAYLOR, B. J., Paediatrics and Child Health
TAYLOR, D. R., Medicine
TILYARD, M. W., General Practice
TOOP, L. J., Public Health and General Practice
TOWN, G. I., Medicine
TOWNSEND, C. R., Zoology
TREBILCO, P. R., Theology and Religious Studies
TRIBBLE, E. B., English
TUCKER, I. G., Pharmacy
VAN RIJ, A. M., Surgery
WALKER, R. J., Medicine
WHEATLEY, A. M., Physiology
WHITE, K. G., Psychology
WICKENS, J. R., Anatomy and Structural Biology
WILSON, J. B., Medicine
WILSON, P. D., Obstetrics and Gynaecology
WINTERBOURN, C. C., Pathology
WYVILL, G., Computer Science

VICTORIA UNIVERSITY OF WELLINGTON

POB 600, Wellington 6005
Telephone: (4) 472-1000
Fax: (4) 499-4601
Internet: www.vuw.ac.nz
Founded 1899
Languages of instruction: English, Maori
Academic year: March to February (3 trimesters)

Chancellor: Emeritus Prof. TIM BEAGLEHOLE
Pro-Chancellor: IAN MCKINNON

Vice-Chancellor: Prof. PAT WALSH
Deputy Vice-Chancellor: Prof. DAVID MACKAY
Pro-Vice-Chancellors: Prof. PIRI SCIASCIA (Maori), Prof. PAT WALSH, Prof. DEBORAH WILLIS, Prof. NEIL QUIGLEY, Prof. DAVID BIBBY, Prof. MATTHEW PALMER, Prof. WARWICK CLEGG, Prof. DUGALD SCOTT
Assistant Vice-Chancellor for Academic Affairs: Assoc. Prof. JENNY HARPER
Chief Financial Officer: WAYNE MORGAN
Dir Facilities Management: PETER FEHL
Dir Human Resources: ANNEMARIE DE CASTRO
Library: see Libraries and Archives
Number of teachers: 698
Number of students: 19,179
Publications: *Victorious* (3 a year), *Staff and Student Research* (annual)

DEANS

Faculty of Architecture and Design: Prof. D. BIBBY
Faculty of Commerce and Admin.: Prof. PETER THIRWELL
Faculty of Education: Prof. DUGALD SCOTT
Faculty of Humanities and Social Sciences: Prof. D. WILLIS
Faculty of Law: Prof. M. PALMER
Faculty of Science: Prof. D. BIBBY

PROFESSORS

Faculty of Architecture and Design (tel. (4) 463-6200; fax (4) 463-6204; e-mail architecture@vuw.ac.nz; internet www.vuw.ac.nz/home/faculties_schools/archdes.html):
  FLEETWOOD, R., Design
  FRASER, S., Design
  HOLDEN, G., Architecture

Faculty of Commerce and Administration (tel. (4) 463-5376; fax (4) 463-5360; e-mail fca-sao@vuw.ac.nz; internet www.vuw.ac.nz/fca/index.html):
  BOSTON, J., Govt
  BOWDEN, R., Econ. and Finance
  BOYLE, G., Econ. and Finance
  BROCKLESBY, J., Management
  CUMMINGS, S., Management
  DUNSTAN, K., Accountancy and Commercial Law
  EVANS, L. T., Econ. and Finance
  GORMAN, G., Information Management
  HALL, V. B., Econ. and Finance
  HAWKE, G., Govt
  HUFF, S., Information Management
  LAFFERTY, G., Management
  LOVE, N., Management
  PEARCE, D., Management
  QUIGLEY, N., Econ. and Finance
  SCOTT, C. D., Govt
  THIRKELL, P. C., Marketing and Int. Business
  VAN ZIJL, T., Accountancy and Commercial Law
  WILEY, J., Marketing and Int. Business

Faculty of Education (tel. (4) 463-9500; fax (4) 463-9649; e-mail teaching@vuw.ac.nz; internet www.vuw.ac.nz/education/about/faculty.aspx):
  HALL, C. G. W.
  MEYER, L.
  MORRIS-MATTHEWS, K.
  WEARMOUTH, J.

Faculty of Humanities and Social Sciences (tel. (4) 463-5208; fax (4) 463-5209; e-mail hum-socsci-office@vuw.ac.nz; internet www.vuw.ac.nz/fhss/index.html):
  BAUER, L., Linguistics and Applied Language Studies
  CLARK, M., History, Philosophy, Political Science and Int. Relations
  DAVIDSON, J. F., Art History, Classics and Religious Studies
  DUKE, J., Nursing and Midwifery
  EASTING, R., English, Film and Theatre

HILL, M., Social and Cultural Studies
HOLMES, J., Linguistics and Applied Language Studies
LEVINE, S., History, Philosophy, Political Science and Int. Relations
MORRIS, P., Art History, Classics and Religious Studies
NATION, P., Linguistics and Applied Languages
PRATT, J., Social and Cultural Studies
STERELNY, K., History, Philosophy, Political Science and Int. Relations
WALSH, K., Nursing and Midwifery

Faculty of Law (tel. (4) 463-6366; fax (4) 463-6365; e-mail law-enquiries@vuw.ac.nz; internet www.vuw.ac.nz/law):
  ANDERSON, G.
  ANGELO, A. H.
  ATKIN, B.
  MCLACHLAN, C.
  MCLAUCHLAN, D. W.
  PREBBLE, J.
  SMITH, T.

Faculty of Science (tel. (4) 463-5101; fax (4) 463-5122; e-mail science-faculty@vuw.ac.nz; internet www.vuw.ac.nz/science):
  BARRETT, P. J., Earth Sciences
  CALLAGHAN, P., Chemical and Physical Sciences
  CROZIER, M., Earth Sciences
  DAUGHERTY, C., Biological Sciences
  DOWNEY, R., Mathematics, Statistics and Computer Science
  GARNOCK-JONES, P., Biological Sciences
  GOLDBLATT, R. I., Mathematics, Statistics and Computer Science
  HINE, J., Mathematics, Statistics and Computer Science
  JOHNSTON, J., Chemical and Physical Sciences
  KAISER, A., Chemical and Physical Sciences
  KHMALADZE, E., Mathematics, Statistics and Computer Science
  LEKNER, J., Chemical and Physical Sciences
  SCHENK, S., Psychology
  SMITH, E., Earth Sciences
  SPENCER, J. L., Chemical and Physical Sciences
  TALLON, J., Chemical and Physical Sciences
  WARD, C., Psychology
  WARD, T., Psychology
  WHITTLE, G., Mathematics, Statistics and Computer Sciences

ATTACHED RESEARCH INSTITUTES

Antarctic Research Centre: Dir Prof. P. J. BARRETT.

Asian Studies Institute: Dir Dr S. EPSTEIN.

Centre for Accounting, Governance and Taxation Research: Dir Prof. K. DUNSTAN.

Centre for Applied Cross-Cultural Research: Dir Prof. C. WARD.

Centre for Biodiscovery: Dir Assoc. Prof. B. JORDAN.

Centre for Building Performance Research: Dir Prof. G. HOLDEN.

Centre for Logic, Language and Computation: Dir Prof. R. GOLDBLATT.

Centre for Mathematics Education: Dir Dr J. HIGGINS.

Centre for Strategic Studies: Dir P. COZENS.

Centre for the Study of Leadership: Dir Dr B. JACKSON.

Climatic and Atmospheric Research Centre: Dir Dr J. MCGREGOR.

Crime and Justice Research Centre: Dir J. PAULIN.

Deaf Studies Research Unit: Dir D. MCKEE.

Earthquake Hazard Centre: Dir A. CHARLESON.

English Language Institute: Dir (vacant).

Health Services Research Centre: Dir Dr J. CUMMING.

He Parekereke: Dir W. PENETITO.

Heritage and Leisure: Dir (vacant).

Industrial Relations Centre: Dir Prof. G. LAFFERTY.

Institute of Criminology: Head Prof. P. STENNING.

Institute for Early Childhood Studies: Dir Dr C. DALLI.

Institute of Geography: Dir Prof. M. J. CROZIER.

Institute of Geophysics: Dir Prof. E. G. C. SMITH.

Institute of Policy Studies: Dir Dr A. LADLEY.

Institute of Professional Legal Studies: Wellington Dir R. FULLER.

International Institute of Modern Letters: Dir Prof. B. MANHIRE.

Language Learning Centre: Dir C. EDWARDS.

MacDiarmid Institute for Advanced Materials and Nanotechnology: Dir Prof. P. CALLAGHAN.

Malaghan Institute of Medical Research: Dir Prof. G. LE GROS.

New Zealand Centre for Conflict Resolution: Dir I. MCDUFF.

New Zealand Centre for Public Law: Dir Dr M. PALMER.

New Zealand Dictionary Centre: Man. Dr D. BARDSLEY.

New Zealand Electronic Text Centre: Dir E. STYRON.

New Zealand Institute for Research on Ageing: Dir Assoc. Prof. J. DAVEY.

New Zealand Institute for the Study of Competition and Regulation: Dir Prof. G. BOYLE.

Roy McKenzie Centre for the Study of Families: Dir Dr J. PRYOR.

Stout Research Centre: Dir Assoc. Prof. L. WEVERS.

Treaty of Waitangi Research Unit: Dir Dr R. HILL.

Wai-te-Ata Press: Dir Dr S. SHEP.

UNIVERSITY OF WAIKATO

Private Bag 3105, Hamilton

Telephone: 856-2889
Fax: 838-4370
E-mail: info@waikato.ac.nz
Internet: www.waikato.ac.nz

Founded 1964
Academic year: February to November

Chancellor: JOHN GALLAGHER
Vice-Chancellor: ROY CRAWFORD
Assistant to the Vice-Chancellor: HELEN PRIDMORE
Librarian: S. PHARO
Library: see Libraries78014,405

DEANS

Faculty of Arts and Social Sciences: Prof. D. ZIRKER
School of Computing and Mathematical Sciences: Prof. M. APPERLEY
School of Education: Prof. N. ALCORN
School of Law: Prof. J. FARRAR (acting)
Waikato Management School: Prof. M. J. PRATT
School of Maori and Pacific Development: Prof. A. YATES-SMITH (acting)

School of Science and TEngineering: Prof. R. PRICE

PROFESSORS

APPERLEY, M. D., Computing and Mathematical Sciences
BARRATT, A. A. T., English
BARTON, B., Law
BEARDON, C., Computer Sciences
BEDFORD, R. D., Geography
BING, D., Political Science and Public Policy
BISHOP, R., Maori Education
BOOTH, D., Sport and Leisure Studies
CARY, C., Biological Sciences
CLARK, D., Management
CLEARY, J. G., Computer Sciences
CORNER, J., Management Systems
CRAIG, I., Mathematics
CUBITT, S., Screen and Media Studies
DANIEL, R. M., Biological Sciences
EGGLETON, I., Accounting
ERICKSEN, N., International Global Change Institute
FARRAR, J. H., Law
FARRELL, R. L., Biological Sciences
FOULDS, L. R., Management Systems
GILLESPIE, A. M., LAw
GILSON, C. H. J., Strategic Management and Leadership
GLYNN, E. L., Human Development and Counselling
GRANT, B., Sport and Leisure Studies
GREEN, T. G. A., Biological Sciences
HAMILTON, D., Biological Sciences
HARCOURT, M., Strategic Management and Leadership
HEALY, T. R., Earth Sciences
HOLMES, M. J., Economics
JOHN, N., Statistics
JONES, A. T., Wilf Malcolm Institute of Educational Research
KALNINS, E. G., Mathematics
KAMP, P. J. J., Earth Sciences
KOOPMAN-BOYDEN, P. G., Arts and Social Sciences
LAWRENCE, S., Accounting
LEITCH, S., Public Relations and Marketing
LOWE, A., Accounting
MCGEE, C., Wilf Malcolm Institute of Educational Research
MCKIE, D., Management Communication
MCQUEEN, B., Management Systems
MAY, S., Arts and Language Education
MIDDLETON, S. C., Policy, Cultural and Social Studies in Education
MOLAN, P. C., Biological Sciences
MORGAN, H. W., Biological Sciences
MOTION, J., Management Communication
NELSON, C. S., Earth Sciences
NICHOLSON, B. K., Chemistry
O'DRISCOLL, M., Psychology
POOL, D. I., Population Studies
POOT, J., Population Studies
PRATT, M. J., Management Studies
PRICE, R., Science and Engineering
QUICK, S. P., Biological Sciences
REEDY, T., Maori Sustainable Enterprise
REEVES, S., Computer Science
RICHARDSON, N. A., Management
RITCHIE, J., Psychology
ROA, T. C., Maori and Pacific Development
RYAN, C. A., Tourism Management
SCARPA, R., Economics
SCRIMGEOUR, F. G., Economics
SILVESTER, W. B., Biological Sciences
SMYTH, J., Wilf Malcolm Institute of Educational Research
SNEYD, A. D., Mathematics
SPILLER, P. R., Law
STOKES, E. M., Geography, Tourism and Environmental Planning
TE AWEKOTUKWU, N. A., Maori and Pacific Development
VAREY, R. J., Marketing and International Management
VOS, E. A. J., Finance

WALKER, G. M., English
WILKINS, A. L., Chemistry
WILKINS, R. J., Biological Sciences
WITTEN, I. H., Computer Science
YATES-SMITH, G. R. A., Maori and Pacific Development
ZIRKER, D., Arts and Social Sciences
ZORN, T. E., Management Communication

Polytechnic Institutions

Central Institute of Technology: Private Box 40740, Upper Hutt; tel. (4) 527-6398; fax (4) 527-6359; f. 1960; full-time technician and professional education; 330 staff; 5,000 enrolments; library: 29,000 vols, 800 periodicals (570 current); CEO T. BOYLE.

Christchurch Polytechnic Institute of Technology: Madras St, POB 22-095, Christchurch 8032; tel. (3) 379-8150; fax (3) 366-6544; e-mail info@cpit.ac.nz; internet www.cpit.ac.nz; f. 1965; courses at trade technician, professional and degree levels, recreational and community courses; specializes in information technology, with pathways to Monash University Master programmes; library: 48,000 items; 1,180 teachers (350 full-time, 830 part-time); 17,600 students; Dir JOHN W. SCOTT; publs *Prospectus* (annually), *Annual Report*.

Hutt Valley Polytechnic: Private Bag 39803, Te Puni Mail Centre, Petone, nr Wellington; tel. (4) 568-3419; fax (4) 568-6849; f. 1976; courses in trades, commercial and technical subjects; 180 staff, 10,000 enrolments; library of 20,000 items; Chief Exec. W. J. MATTHEW.

Manukau Institute of Technology: Private Bag 94006, Manukau City; tel. (9) 968-8000; fax (9) 968-8701; e-mail info@manukau .ac.nz; internet www.manukau.ac.nz; f. 1970; courses in trade, technical and professional subjects; library: 55,000 vols; 409 teachers; 32,674 students; Chief Exec. Dr GEOFFREY PAGE.

Open Polytechnic of New Zealand: Wyndrum Ave, Private Bag 31914, Lower Hutt; tel. (4) 913-5300; fax (4) 913-5308; e-mail brochurecentre@openpolytechnic.ac.nz; internet www.openpolytechnic.ac.nz; f. 1946; certificate- to degree-level courses by distance and open learning methods in business, social science, professional, technical, agriculture/horticulture, trades and self-improvement subjects; 37,000 students; Chief Exec. PAUL GRIMWOOD.

Otago Polytechnic: Private Bag, Dunedin; tel. (3) 477-3014; fax (3) 471-6870; e-mail info@tekotago.ac.nz; internet www.tekotago .ac.nz; f. 1966; degrees, diplomas and certificates in fine arts, business, engineering, architectural technology, health sciences, tourism and sports; 236 teachers; 9,000 students; library: 30,000 vols; CEO PHIL KER.

UNITEC Institute of Technology: Private Bag 92025, Auckland; tel. (9) 849-4180; fax (9) 815-2901; e-mail ceo@unitec.ac.nz; internet www.unitec.ac.nz; f. 1976; faculties of architecture and design, arts and social sciences, business, health and environmental sciences; Applied Technology Institute; library: 88,834 vols; 496 teachers (full-time); 18,179 students; Dir Dr JOHN A. WEBSTER; Registrar REBECCA EWERT.

Waikato Institute of Technology: Private Bag HN 3036, Hamilton 2020; tel. (7) 834-8888; fax (7) 838-0707; e-mail info@wintec.ac .nz; internet www.wintec.ac.nz; f. 1968; courses at Master's degree, diploma, certificate, professional technician and trades levels, also community education; library: 62,800 vols; 365 teachers; 13,100 students

(4,500 full-time, 8,600 part-time); CEO (vacant).

Schools of Art and Music

Elam School of Fine Arts: Faculty of Fine Arts, University of Auckland, Private Bag 92019, Auckland; tel. (9) 373-7599; fax (9) 308-2302; e-mail enquiries@elam.auckland .ac.nz; internet www.elam.auckland.ac.nz; f. 1950; library: 35,000 vols; 35 teachers; 450 students; Head of School Prof. MICHAEL DUNN; publ. *Fine Arts Library Bulletin*.

School of Fine Arts: Faculty of Visual and Performing Arts, University of Canterbury, Christchurch; tel. (3) 364-2161; fax (3) 364-2858; e-mail postmaster@fina-canterbury.ac .nz; internet www.canterbury.ac.nz; f. 1882; BA, BA (Hons), BFA, BFA (Hons), MA, MFA and PhD degrees; courses in art theory, art history, film, graphic design, painting, photography, printmaking and sculpture; library: 10,000 vols, including index of NZ historic buildings, 100,000 slides; 20 teachers; 785 students; Head Prof. DESMOND ROCHFORT (acting).

NICARAGUA

The Higher Education System

The oldest current institution of higher education in Nicaragua is the Universidad Nacional Autónoma de Nicaragua (founded in 1812), which dates from the Spanish colonial period. Nicaragua became part of the Central American Federation in 1821 and declared its independence in 1838. There are many commercial schools and eight universities. In 2002/03 a total of 100,363 students attended universities and other higher education institutes. The National Council of Universities is the body responsible for all strategic planning.

Admission to higher education is on the basis of the Bachillerato, the leading secondary school qualification, and an entrance examination. The Licenciado is the main undergraduate degree is a four- or five-year course of study; a professional title may also be awarded depending on the subject. Following the Licenciado, the first postgraduate degree is the Maestría, which lasts two years and culminates with the submission of a thesis.

Institutions of higher education also offer two- or three-year courses in technical and vocational education. The main qualification studied for is the Técnico Superior.

Learned Societies

BIBLIOGRAPHY, LIBRARY SCIENCE AND MUSEOLOGY

Asociación Nicaragüense de Bibliotecarios y Profesionales afines: Apdo postal 3257, Calle F. Guzman Bolanos, Altamira del Est, Casa 120, Managua; e-mail anibipa@yahoo.com; f. 1983.

LANGUAGE AND LITERATURE

Academia Nicaragüense de la Lengua (Nicaraguan Academy of Letters): Apdo 2711, Managua; Located at: Avda del Campo 42, Las Colinas, Managua; fax (2) 49-5389; e-mail pavsa@munditel.com.ni; internet www.anl.edu.ni; f. 1928; corresp. of the Real Academia Española (Madrid); 13 mems; Dir JORGE EDUARDO ARELLANO SANDINO; Sec. FRANCISCO ARELLANO OVIEDO.

Alliance Française: Apdo 2370, Managua; Located at: Planes de Altamira, De la Embajada de México 1/2 Cuadra al Norte, Managua; tel. (2) 67-2811; fax (2) 67-8287; e-mail alfmanag@cablenet.com.ni; internet www.ambafrance-ni.org/fr/alliance/managua; offers courses and exams in French language and culture and promotes cultural exchange with France; attached teaching centre in León; Dir RAFAEL PONT.

MEDICINE

Sociedad de Oftalmología Nicaragüense: Clínica Especializada, Managua; f. 1949; Pres R. LACAYO G.

Sociedad Nicaragüense de Psiquiatría y Psicología: Centro Médico, Managua; f. 1962; Pres. Dr R. GUTIÉRREZ.

Research Institutes

ECONOMICS, LAW AND POLITICS

Instituto Nicaragüense de Investigaciones Económicas y Sociales (INIES): Apdo postal C-16, Managua; Located at: Avda Bolívar, Antojitos 2 cuadra al sur Managua; tel. (2) 66-2485; fax (2) 66-8503; e-mail inies@sdnnic.apc.org; f. 1981 to inform and conduct research on developing alternatives for the more vulnerable sectors of the national population; documentation centre of 8,000 items, 250 periodicals; Dir BLADIMIR VARELA HIDALGO; publs *Cuadernos de Investigación* (irregular), *Boletín Socioeconómico* (quarterly).

NATURAL SCIENCES

Physical Sciences

Observatorio Geofísico: Apdo postal 1761, Managua; tel. (2) 25-1023; f. 1980; geophysics, geology, seismology, vulcanology; publ. *Boletín Sismológico* (annually).

Libraries and Archives

Bluefields

Biblioteca Raití: Alcaldía Municipal, Bluefields, Zelaya; tel. (8) 22-2502; Librarian JANICE TAYLOR.

Chinandega

Biblioteca 'Eduardo Montealegre': Parque Las Rosas 2 cuadras al sur, Chinandega; tel. (3) 41-2950; Librarian ANA LUISA PANIAGUA GONZÁLEZ.

León

Biblioteca Rubén Dario de la Universidad Nacional Autónoma de Nicaragua: Frente a la panadería León Dorado, León; tel. (3) 11-3508; f. 1816; 36,000 vols; Dir NORMA FLORES.

Managua

Archivo Nacional de Nicaragua: Del Cine Cabrera 2½ Cuadras al Lago, Managua; tel. (2) 22-6290; fax (2) 22-2722; e-mail binanic@tmx.com.ni; internet manfut.org/museos/archivonacional.html; f. 1882; 40,356 vols; Dir ALFREDO GONZÁLEZ VILCHEZ; publs *Boletín Técnico Informativo*, *Gaceta Oficial*.

Biblioteca del Instituto Centroamericano de Administración de Empresas: Campus Francisco de Sola, Montefresco, Managua; tel. (2) 65-8141 ext. 228; fax (2) 65-8617; e-mail biblioteca@mail.incae.edu.ni; internet www.incae.ac.cr/ES/biblioteca/ncbiblio.shtml; specialized library of 40,000 vols and 255 periodical titles on business administration, economic development and Central American social and economic conditions; collection of 15,000 case materials for teaching of management; Dir Lic. ANTONIO ACEVEDO; publs *Bibliografía de Casos* (annually), *Mini-Bibliografía* (monthly), *Nuevas Adquisiciones* (monthly), *Nuevos Artículos* (monthly), *Revistas – Números Temáticos* (irregular).

Biblioteca Nacional 'Rubén Dario': Apdo Postal 3514, Managua; Palacio Nacional de la Cultura, Antigua Catedral, Managua; tel. and fax (2) 22-2722; e-mail binanic@tmx.com.ni; internet www.abinia.org/nicaragua; f.

1880; 80,000 vols; Dir JIMMY ALVARADO MORENO.

Masaya

Biblioteca 'El Ateneo': Masaya; f. 1941; new collection of literature on philately and numismatics; Dir Dr SANTIAGO FAJARDO F.

Nagarote

Biblioteca Municipal: Costado sur Parque Central, Nagarote, León; tel. (3) 13-2244; Dir Prof. JOSÉ ANGEL PALACIOS.

Museums and Art Galleries

Managua

Museo Nacional de Nicaragua: Apdo 416, Colonia Dambach, Managua; tel. (2) 22-5291; internet manfut.org/museos/nacional.html; f. 1896; archaeology, ceramics, zoology, botany and geology; library of 500 vols; Dir LEONOR MARTÍNEZ DE ROCHA.

Masaya

Museo 'Tenderí': Villa Nindirí, Masaya; archaeological remains from the Chorotega Indian culture; coins and medals from the Spanish colonial era.

Universities

ESCUELA INTERNACIONAL DE AGRICULTURA Y GANADERÍA

Apdo postal 5, Rivas

Telephone: (4) 53-3551

Fax: (4) 53-3957

E-mail: eiag@tmx.com.ni

Dir: Fr GREGORIO BARREALES O. D.

Academic programmes in agriculture, management, veterinary science and zootechnology.

UNIVERSIDAD CENTROAMERICANA

Pista de la Resistencia, Apdo 69, Managua

Telephone: (2) 77-3026

Fax: (2) 67-0106

E-mail: asrector@ns.uca.edu.ni

Internet: www.uca.edu.ni

Founded 1961

Private control

Academic year: February to December

Rector: Dra MAYRA LUZ PÉREZ DÍAZ

Vice-Rector (General Affairs): P. JESÚS MANUEL SARIEGO
Vice-Rector (Academic): RENATA RODRIGUEZ
Vice-Rector (Research and Postgraduates): SANDRA RUIZ
Secretary-General: P. MIGUEL ÁNGEL RUIZ
Director of Administration: Lic. RÓGER URIARTE GÓMEZ
Librarian: Lic. GLORIA MARÍA MORALES
Number of teachers: 324 (72 full-time, 252 part-time)
Number of students: 6,401
Publications: *Cuadernos de Sociología*, *Diakonía*, *Encuentro* (24 a year), *Envío* (monthly), *WANI* (4 a year)

DEANS

Faculty of Administration: GUILLERMO BORNEMANN
Faculty of Agriculture and Stockbreeding: VERA AMANDA SOLÍS REYES
Faculty of Communications: Dr GUILLERMO ROTHSCHUH
Faculty of Foreign Languages: RAMÓN BERMÚDEZ
Faculty of Humanities: DONALD MÉNDEZ QUINTANA
Faculty of Law: MANUEL ARKUZ ULLOA

ATTACHED INSTITUTES

Centro de Análisis Sociocultural (CASC).
Instituto de Acción Social 'Juan XXIII'.
Instituto de Educación (IDEUCA).
Instituto de Historia de Nicaragua y Centroamérica (IHNCA).
Instituto de Investigación y Documentación de la Costa Atlántica (CIDCA).
Instituto de Investigación NITLAPAN.

UNIVERSIDAD NACIONAL AGRARIA

Km. 12½ Carretera Norte, Managua
Telephone: (2) 33-1619
Fax: (2) 33-1950
Internet: www.una.edu.ni
Founded 1929; present name and status 1990
Rector: Ing. FRANCISCO TELÉMACO TALAVERA SILES
Vice-Rector General: Ing. ALBERTO SEDILES JAEN
Director, Camoapa Campus: Ing. LUIS HERNÁNDEZ MALUEÑO
Director, Juigalpa Campus: Ing. ARISTIDES TABLADA CALERO
Registrar: Lic. RONALD QUIROZ OCAMPO
Library of 12,000 vols, 500 periodicals
Number of students: 2,217
Publications: *La Calera* (2 a year), *Boletín Informativo* (monthly)

DEANS

Faculty of Agronomy: Dr DENNIS SALAZAR CENTENO
Faculty of Animal Sciences: Ing. ELMER GUILLEN CORRALES
Faculty of Natural Resources and the Environment: Lic. ESTHER CARBALLO MADRIGAL
Faculty of Rural Development: Dr ELGIN VIVAS VILLACHICA

UNIVERSIDAD NACIONAL AUTÓNOMA DE NICARAGUA

Located at: Apdo Postal 663, Managua
De Enel Central 2½ km al sur, Villa Fontana, Managua
Telephone: (2) 78-6769
Fax: (2) 78-2990
E-mail: unan@unan.edu.ni
Internet: www.unan.edu.ni
Founded 1812

Academic year: June to March
State control
Rector: FRANCISCO GUZMÁN PASOS
Vice-Rector (Academic): Dr GUSTAVO SILES GONZÁLEZ
Vice-Rector (Administrative): Lic. JAIME LÓPEZ LOWERY
Vice-Rector (General): ELMER CISNEROS MOREIRA
Registrar: Dra NÍVEA GONZÁLEZ ROJAS
Library Director: SIDAR RIVERA MARÍN
Library: see Libraries and Archives
Number of teachers: 709
Number of students: 24,629
Publications: *Gaceta Universitaria* (every 2 months), *Cuadernos Universitarios* (quarterly), *Revista Médica* (2 a year)

DEANS

Faculty of Economics: ABEL MEMBREÑO GALEANO
Faculty of Education and Humanities: Lic. ALEJANDRO GENET CRUZ
Faculty of Medicine: Dr FRANCISCO CORTÉZ HERNÁNDEZ
Faculty of Sciences: Lic. HUGO GUTIÉRREZ OCÓN

CAMPUS IN LEÓN

Universidad Nacional Autónoma de Nicaragua, Sede León

León
Internet: www.unanleon.edu.ni
Rector: Dr OCTAVIO MARTINEZ ORDÓÑEZ
Faculties of medicine, dentistry, law, chemistry, humanities.

ATTACHED INSTITUTES

Centro de Investigaciones Económicas y Tecnológicas (CINET): Dir M.A. MARIO R. LÓPEZ.
Centro de Investigaciones y Estudios de la Salud (CIES): Dir Dr JULIO PIURA LÓPEZ.
Centro de Investigaciones Geocientíficas (CIGEO).
Centro para la Investigación en Recursos Acuáticos (CIRA).
Centro de Investigaciones Socio-Educativas (CISE).
Instituto Nicaragüense de Investigaciones Económicas y Sociales (INIES).
Instituto Politécnico de la Salud.
Laboratorio de Física de Radiaciones y Metrología.
Observatorio Astronómico.

UNIVERSIDAD NACIONAL DE INGENIERÍA

Avda Universitaria Frente Escuela de Danza, Apdo postal 5595, Managua
Telephone: (2) 77-1650
Fax: (2) 67-3709
Internet: www.uni.edu.ni
Founded 1983
State control
Academic year: March to December
Rector: Ing. ALDO URBINA VILLALTA
Vice-Rector (Academic): Arq. ANA ULMOS VADO
Vice-Rector (Administrative): Ing. NÉSTOR GALLO ZELEDÓN
Vice-Rector (General): Ing. SERGIO ENRIQUE ALVAREZ GARCÍA
Vice-Rector (Research and Development): Lic. SERGIO MARTÍNEZ TRAÑA
Registrar: Ing. DIEGO ALFONSO MUÑOZ LATINO
Librarian: Lic. VIOLETA BONICHE SOMARRIBA
Number of teachers: 409

Number of students: 7,518
Publications: *Campus* (6 a year), *Nexo* (quarterly scientific review), *Teckno* (6 a year)

DEANS

Faculty of Architecture: Arq. VÍCTOR ARCIA GÓMEZ
Faculty of Chemical Engineering: SILVIO ROJAS ZAMBRANA
Faculty of Construction Technology: Ing. JULIO MALTEZ MONTIEL
Faculty of Electrotechnology and Computer Science: Ing. ARIEL ROLDÁN PAREDES
Faculty of Industrial Technology: Ing. DANIEL CUADRA HORNEY
Faculty of Sciences and Systems: RONALD TORRES MERCADO

HEADS OF DEPARTMENTS

Architecture (tel. (2) 78-1467; fax (2) 70-5121):

Design and Expression: Arq. EDUARDO RODRIGUEZ VÁSQUEZ
Research and Development: Arq. FRANCISCO MENDOZA VELÁSQUEZ
Technology: Arq. DANILO RAMÍREZ SILVA
Theory and Planning: Arq. BENJAMÍN ROSALES

Chemical Engineering (tel. (2) 78-1463):

Chemistry: Ing. EDDY CASCO
Research and Development: Ing. ERNESTO ACEVEDO LUGO
Unitary Operation: Ing. MARIA ESTHER BALTODANO PILARTE

Construction Technology (tel. (2) 49-6435; fax (2) 49-6435):

Agricultural Machinery: Ing. GUILLERMO ASEVEDO AMPIÉ
Construction: Ing. MARVIN ROBLETO
Design: Ing. GUSTAVO OCAMPO ELVIR
Hydraulic Engineering: MSc MIGUEL BLANCO CHÁVEZ
Irrigation and Drainage: Ing. JOSEFINA ROMO TRUJILLO
Road Transport: Ing. ALDO ZAMORA LACAYO
Structural Engineering: MSc SERGIO OBREGÓN AGUILAR

Electrotechnology and Computer Science (tel. (2) 78-3134; fax (2) 78-1461):

Architecture of Systems and Applications: Ing. HUMBERTO ZEPEDA
Digital Systems and Telecommunications: Ing. HÉCTOR GUILLÉN NAVARRETE
Electrical: Ing. DANILO MORALES LÓPEZ
Electrotechnology: Ing. JAMIE ALVAREZ CALERO
Maintenance: Ing. CAMILO ROOSVELT LINDO CARRIÓN
Mathematics Simulation and Programming: Ing. MARÍA MERCEDES GARCÍA BUCARDO
Graduate Studies: Lic. MARISELA QUINTANA (Dir)

Industrial Technology (tel. (2) 49-6437; fax (2) 49-6437):

Industrial Studies: Ing. FREDDY BOZA (Co-ordinator)
Mechanical Engineering Studies: Ing. ABELARDO BARRIOS (Co-ordinator)

Sciences and Systems (tel. (2) 49-6429; fax (2) 49-6429):

Administration: MANUEL HUETE CASTILLO
Foreign Languages: GLADYS TÉLLEZ BACA
Informatics: RÓGER MARTÍNEZ MURILLO
Mathematics: Lic. RÓGER GARCÍA GUEVARA
Physics: Lic. HILDA LUVY TORRES CASTILLO
Research and Development: GONZÁLO ZÚNIGA MORALES
Sciences and Systems: Lic. MARÍA AUXILIADORA CORTEDANO LARIOS
Social Sciences: Lic. MARTHA L. PARRALES IBARRA

Graduate Studies: MARIBEL DURIEZ GONZÁLEZ

UNIVERSIDAD POLITÉCNICA DE NICARAGUA

Located at: Apdo 3595, Managua
Costado Sur Colonia Rubén Darío, Managua
Telephone: (2) 89-7740
Fax: (2) 49-9232
E-mail: rectoria@upoli.edu.ni
Internet: www.upoli.edu.ni/default.html
Founded 1967 as institute, university status 1977
Private control
Academic year: March to December
Rector: Ing. EMERSON PÉREZ SANDOVAL
Vice-Rector (Academic): Dra MIRNA CUEVAS RUIZ
Vice-Rector (General): Dra LIDIA RUTH ZAMORA
Vice-Rector (Students): Lic. BLANCA ROSA GALARZA
Registrar: TOMÁS HANDELL TÉLLEZ RUIZ
Librarian: Licda AURA CELA CORTEZ SILVA

Number of teachers: 101
Number of students: 1,475

DEANS
School of Administration, Commerce and Finance: MIGUEL MURILLO
School of Design: D. I. EDUARDO VANEGAS
School of Economics: EYRA REYES
School of Engineering: Licda GLADYS AGUILAR
School of Law: Dr OSCAR CASTILLO GUIDO
School of Nursing: MARGARITA GUEVARA
School of Tourism: AMPARO MENDOZA

ATTACHED INSTITUTES
Bautista Conservatoire of Music: Dir Licda MARÍA CARIDAD ROSADO VILLAFAÑE.
Institute for Gender Studies: Dir BRENDA CONSUELO RUÍZ.
Institute of Humanistic Research and Development (IDEHU): Dir Dr JERJES RUIZ.
Institute for Training and Research in Integral Rural Development: Dir Lic. HUGO SILVA.

Inter-University Centre of Caribbean and Latin American Studies: Exec. Dir GUILLERMO GÓMEZ SANTIBÁÑEZ.
Martin Luther King Centre of Social Research: Dir Lic. DENIS TORRES PEREZ.

College

Instituto Centroamericano de Administración de Empresas (INCAE): Apdo 2485, Managua; Campus Francisco de Sola Montefresco, Km. 15½ Carretera Sur, Managua; tel. (2) 65-8141; fax (2) 65-8617; e-mail incaenic@mail.incae.edu.ni; internet www.incae.ac.cr; f. 1964 with technical assistance from Harvard Business School; 16-month degree programme in business administration; executive training programmes; management research and consulting; 53 teachers; library: see Libraries and Archives; Rector Dr ROBERTO ARTAVIA.

NIGER

The Higher Education System

The Republic of Niger was formerly part of French West Africa and obtained independence from France in 1960. The Ecole Nationale d'Administration du Niger (founded in 1963) is the oldest current institution of higher education and the Université Abdou Moumouni (founded in 1971; formerly Université de Niamey) was the first university-level institution. The other leading institution is the Université islamique du Niger (founded in 1987). In 2004/05 there were 7,374 students enrolled in university-level education.

The principal officer of a university is the President or Rector, elected by the faculty to serve three-year, renewable terms of office. A Vice-President is also elected to assist the President. Deans of Faculty and Heads of Department are also elected to their posts and serve for three years and two years respectively.

The university degree system is based on the French cyclical model. The first cycle lasts two years and leads to the award of the Diplôme Universitaire d'Etudes Littéraires (arts and humanities), the Diplôme Universitaire d'Etudes Scientifiques (mathematics or sciences) or the Diplôme d'Etudes Economiques Générales (economics). The second cycle lasts either one year for the award of the Licence or two years for the award of the Maîtrise. Professional titles are awarded in fields such as agricultural engineering (Diplôme d'Ingénieur des Techniques Agricole), agronomy (Diplôme d'Ingénieur Agronome or Diplôme d'Agronomie Approfondie) and medicine (Doctorat en Médecine).

Specialist non-university education is offered by institutes attached to the relevant Ministries, including schools and centres for administration, public health, civil aviation and information technology.

Learned Society

LANGUAGE AND LITERATURE

Alliance Française: BP 126, Agadez; tel. 20-44-05-82; offers courses and examinations in French language and culture and promotes cultural exchange with France; attached teaching centre in Maradi.

Research Institutes

GENERAL

Institut de Recherche pour le Développement (IRD): Ave de Maradi BP 11416, Niamey; tel. 20-75-38-27; fax 20-75-20-54; e-mail irdniger@ird.ne; internet www.ird.ne; medical entomology, hydrology, genetics, ecology, soil sciences, botany, agronomy, economics, linguistics, sociology; in co-operation with Org. for Co-ordination and Co-operation in the Fight against Endemic Diseases; library: documentation centre of 2,500 vols; Dir FRANCIS KAHN; (see main entry under France).

Institut de Recherches en Sciences Humaines (IRSH) de l'Université Abdou Moumouni: BP 318, Niamey; tel. 20-73-51-41; f. 1975 as successor to Institut Français d'Afrique Noire and Centre Nigérien de Recherches en Sciences Humaines; 6 sections: art and archaeology, history and popular traditions, linguistics and nat. languages, Arabic MSS, geography and environmental devt, sociology of devt, devt econ.; library of 30,000 vols; Dir ABDOULAYE MAGA; publs *Etudes Nigériennes* (irreg.), *Mu Kara Sani* (2 a year).

AGRICULTURE, FISHERIES AND VETERINARY SCIENCE

Institut de Recherches sur les Fruits et Agrumes (IRFA): BP 886, Niamey; Dir C. LENORMAND; (see main entry under France).

Institut National de Recherches Agronomiques au Niger (INRAN): BP 149, Niamey; e-mail inran@intnet.ne; soil science; stations at Tarna and Kolo; Dir J. NABOS.

Laboratoire Vétérinaire de Niamey: Niamey.

Station Avicole et Centre d'Elevage Caprin: Maradi; f. 1961; Dir HASSANE BAZA; publ. *Report* (annually).

Station Sahélienne Expérimentale de Toukounous: Service d'Elevage du Niger, Toukounous/Filingué; f. 1931; selection and breeding of Zebu Azaouak cattle and distribution of selected bulls to improve the local heterogeneous breed; Dir Dr MANFRED LINDAU; publs *Annual Report, Berlin Münchner Tierärztliche Wochenschrift*.

HISTORY, GEOGRAPHY AND ARCHAEOLOGY

Centre d'Etudes Linguistiques et Historiques par Tradition Orale: BP 878, Niamey; tel. 20-73-54-14; fax 20-73-36-54; f. 1974; 25 mems; library of 1,250 vols; oral tradition, African languages and cultures; publishes works in African languages, French and English; publ. *Les Cahiers du CELHTO*.

TECHNOLOGY

Bureau de Recherches Géologiques et Minières (BRGM): BP 11458, Niamey; tel. 20-72-23-25; Dir G. BERNERT; (see main entry under France).

Office National de l'Energie Solaire: BP 621, Niamey; tel. 20-73-45-05; f. 1965; 40 staff; research, post-univ. and technical courses; Dir Eng. ALBERT WRIGHT.

Libraries and Archives

Niamey

Archives de la République du Niger: BP 550, Niamey; tel. 20-72-26-82; fax 20-72-36-54; f. 1913; documents to the end of the 19th century; Dir IDRISSA YANSAMBOU.

Centre d'Information et de Documentation Economique et Sociale (CIDES): Ministère des Finances et du Plan, BP 862, Niamey; tel. 20-72-33-11; fax 20-73-59-83; f. 1988; attached to Min. of Economy, Finance and Planning; 10,500 vols; Dir MALIKI ABDOULAYE; publ. *CIDES-Flash* (6 a year).

Museum

Niamey

Musée National du Niger: BP 248, Niamey; tel. and fax 20-73-43-21; e-mail museengr@intnet.ne; f. 1959; representative colln of tribal costumes, crafts, tribal houses; incl. park and zoo, geological and mineral exhibition, ethnographic museum, palaeontology and pre-history museums; also Handicrafts Centre and Cultural Activities Centre; Curator NÉINO CHAÏBOU.

Universities

UNIVERSITÉ ABDOU MOUMOUNI

BP 237, 10896 Niamey
Telephone: 20-73-27-13
Fax: 20-73-38-62
Founded 1971; univ. status as Univ. de Niamey 1973; present name 1999
State control
Language of instruction: French
Academic year: October to June
Rector: Prof. BOULI ALI DIALLO
Sec.-Gen.: MAÏGA DJIBO
Librarian: SAIDOU HAROUNA
Library of 62,000
Number of teachers: 260
Number of students: 3,700
Publications: *Annales de l'Université Abdou Moumouni* (annual), *Etudes Nigériennes*, *Mu Kara Sani* (2 a year)

DEANS
Faculty of Agronomy, Arts and Humanities: AMOUKOU IBRAHIM
Faculty of Arts and Humanities: ABOUBACAR ADAMOU
Faculty of Econ. and Law: ALHADA ALKACHE
Faculty of Health Sciences: NOUHOU HASSANE
Faculty of Science: FODÉ MADÉ

CONSTITUENT INSTITUTES
Ecole Normale Supérieure: Dir MAMAN SALEY.
Institut de Recherches en Sciences Humaines: Dir BOUBE GADO.

Institut de Recherche sur l'Enseignement des Mathématiques: Dir ABOU TRAORE.

UNIVERSITÉ ISLAMIQUE DU NIGER

BP 11507, Niamey, Say
Telephone: 20-72-39-03
Fax: 20-73-37-96

Founded 1987 by the Islamic Conference Org.
Language of instruction: Arabic
Number of teachers: 20
Number of students: 350
Vice-Chancellor: Prof. ABDELALI OUDHRIRI
Faculties of Arabic Language and Islamic Studies.

College

Ecole Nationale d'Administration du Niger: Rue Martin Luther King Jr, BP 542, Niamey; tel. 20-72-31-83; fax 20-72-43-83; e-mail enaniger@intnet.ne; f. 1963 to train civil servants and other officials; library: 27,000 vols; 116 teachers (56 full-time, 60 part-time); 431 students; Dir DJIBO ISSAKA; publ. *Revue* (2 a year).

NIGERIA

The Higher Education System

The oldest current institution of higher education in Nigeria is the Federal College of Agriculture, Ibadan (founded in 1921) and the oldest university is the University of Ibadan (founded in 1948; formerly University College, Ibadan), originally founded in conjunction with the University of London (United Kingdom). Expansion of the university system began following Nigeria's independence in 1963, and the universities established during 1960–70 are referred to as the 'first generation' universities, among them the University of Nigeria (founded in 1960), Obafemi Awolowo University (founded in 1961; present name since 1987), Ahmadu Bello University (founded in 1962), the University of Lagos (founded in 1962) and the University of Benin (founded in 1970). Education is partly the responsibility of the state Governments, although the Federal Government has played an increasingly important role since 1970, and universities may be federally, state or privately administered. In 1998 there were 411,347 students enrolled in 36 universities, 216,782 students in 45 polytechnics and 105,817 students in 63 colleges of education. In 2001 there were 45 universities (25 federal, 16 state and 4 private).

The Governing Board or Council is the governing body of the Federal universities, and its members are Government appointees. The chief executive role is taken by the Vice Chancellor in universities, the Rector in polytechnics and the Provost in colleges of education. Funding for public universities is channelled through different agencies for different types of institution, namely the National Universities Commission (universities), the National Board for Technical Education (polytechnics) and the National commission for Colleges of Education (colleges). The National Universities Commission is also responsible for accreditation and quality assurance, which takes place on a six-yearly cycle.

Admission to higher education is made on the basis of sufficient passes in the Senior School Certificate and the University Matriculation Examination, administered by the Joint Admissions and Matriculation Board. Most undergraduate Bachelors degrees last four years, but programmes leading to the award of professional titles last five years and degrees in medicine and dentistry take six years to complete. A student awarded a first or second-class Bachelors degree with Honours may be admitted to the first postgraduate degree, the Masters, study for which lasts for one to two years. Following the Masters, the Doctorate is the highest university-level degree, and consists of a two- or three-year period of research, submission of a thesis and an oral examination (viva).

Polytechnics and colleges offer post-secondary technical and vocational education. The most popular qualifications offered by these institutions are the Ordinary National Diploma, Higher National Diploma and Full Professional Diploma.

Learned Societies

GENERAL

UNESCO Office Abuja: PMB 424, Garki, Abuja; Located at: Plot 777, Bouake St (off Herbert Macauley Way), Wuse Zone 6, Abuja; tel. (9) 4618502; fax (9) 5238094; e-mail abuja@unesco.org; Dir HUBERT CHARLES.

AGRICULTURE, FISHERIES AND VETERINARY SCIENCE

Fisheries Society of Nigeria: PMB 12529, Lagos; f. 1976; 500 mems; Pres. OLATUNDE OLANIYI; Gen. Sec. B. B. ADEKOYA; publs *Fishery Bulletin*, *Fish Network* (4 a year), *Proceedings*.

Forestry Association of Nigeria: POB 4185, Ibadan, Oyo State; tel. (64) 626535; f. 1970 to further interest in forests and forest resources management and utilization; 61 life mems; 1,000 ordinary mems; 17 corporate mems; Pres. BELLOI ABBA YAKASA; Sec. P. C. OBIAGA; publs *FAN Newsletter*, *Nigerian Journal of Forestry*, *Proceedings of Annual Conference*.

Nigerian Veterinary Medical Association: c/o Nigerian Veterinary Medical Institute, POB 38, Vom, Plateau State; f. 1963 to advance the science and art of veterinary medicine, including its relationship to public health and agriculture; 891 mems; Pres. Dr L. H. LOMBIN; Sec. Dr L. Y. NYAM; publs *Nigerian Veterinary Journal*, *Tropical Veterinarian* (all every 6 months), *Zariya Veterinarian*.

West African Association of Agricultural Economics: c/o Dept of Agricultural Economics, University of Ibadan, Ibadan, Oyo State; fax (8) 87222872; f. 1972; 250 mems from Benin Republic, Burkina Faso, Cameroon, Côte d'Ivoire, Ghana, Liberia, Mali, Nigeria, Senegal, Sierra Leone and Togo; Pres. Prof. Dr ANTHONY E. IKPI; Sec. Dr THOMAS EPONOU; publ. *West African Journal of Agricultural Economics*.

ARCHITECTURE AND TOWN PLANNING

Nigerian Institute of Architects: 2 Idowu Taylor St, Victoria Island, POB 178, Lagos; tel. (1) 2617940; fax (1) 2617947; e-mail nia@skannet.com; f. 1960; 87 Fellows, 1,370 full mems; 874 graduate mems; Pres. Arc. MOHAMMED JIMOH FAWORAJA; publs *NIA Journals*, *NIA Newsletter*, *NIA Yearbook and Diary*, *Shelter for Nigerians*.

BIBLIOGRAPHY, LIBRARY SCIENCE AND MUSEOLOGY

Nigerian Library Association: c/o National Library of Nigeria, Sanusi Dantata House, Business Central District, PMB 1, Garki GPO 900001, Abuja; tel. (9) 2346773; e-mail info@nla-ng.org; internet www.nla-ng.org; f. 1962; 5,000 mems; established to safeguard and promote the professional interests of librarians; to promote the establishment and development of libraries; to assist in the promotion of legislation considered necessary for the establishment, regulation and management of libraries in Nigeria; to encourage bibliographical study, research and library co-operation; Pres. VICTORIA OKOJIE; publs *Nigerian Libraries* (2 a year), *NLA Newsletter* (2 a year), *occasional papers*.

ECONOMICS, LAW AND POLITICS

Nigerian Bar Association: Plot 1261, Adeola Hopewell St, Victoria Island, Lagos; tel. and fax (1) 4618287; e-mail webmaster@nigerianbar.com; internet www.nigerianbar.com; f. 1962; Pres. Chief BAYO OJO; Gen. Sec. NIMI WALSON-JACK.

Nigerian Economic Society: Department of Economics, University of Ibadan, Ibadan; f. 1957; to advance the study and promote investigation of economic and social problems, with special reference to Nigeria; 2,774 mems comprising 1,768 full mems, 200 assoc. mems, 730 life mems, 23 corporate mems, 40 institutional mems and 13 life corporate mems; Pres. SAM OLOFIN; Sec. Dr P. K. GARBA; publs *Nigerian Journal of Economic and Social Studies* (3 a year), *Proceedings of Annual Conferences, Seminars, Symposia, Workshops*.

Nigerian Institute of International Affairs: 13 Kofo Abayomi Rd, Victoria Island, POB 1727, Lagos; tel. (1) 2615606; fax (1) 2611360; e-mail dg@niianet.org; internet www.niianet.org; f. 1961; a non-political and non-profit-making organization for the study of international affairs, to disseminate and maintain information on intl issues through conferences, lectures and discussions; 2,344 mems; library of 69,324 vols, 1,707 periodicals, 20,509 pamphlets, 333,085 press clippings; Dir-Gen. Prof. JOY U. OGWU; publs *Nigeria: Bulletin on Foreign Affairs* (quarterly), *Nigerian Forum* (monthly), *Nigerian Journal of International Affairs* (4 a year).

Nigerian Institute of Management: Plot 22, Idowu Taylor St, POB 2557, Victoria Island, Lagos; tel. (1) 2615105; fax (1) 614116; e-mail registrar@managementnigeria.org; internet www.managementnigeria.org; f. 1961; a professional body for the management profession; aims to determine standards of knowledge and skills to be attained by persons seeking to become management professionals; and to regulate and control the profession of management; academic programmes offered include the Professional Diploma in Management and Post-Graduate Diploma in Management (with Obafemi Owalowo University, Ile-Ife—see Federal Universities); 20,000 mems; library of 2,300 vols; Dir-Gen. Chief

L. E. A. Aimiuwu; publ. *Management in Nigeria* (4 a year).

Nigerian Political Science Association (NPSA): c/o The Secretariat, School of Social Sciences, University of Port Harcourt, PMB 5323, Port Harcourt; f. 1973 to research in politics and government in Nigeria; 200 mems; Pres. Prof. L. Adele Jinadu; Vice-Pres. Dr Y. R. Barongo; National Sec. Dr Cliff Edogun; publ. *Newsletter*.

EDUCATION

Committee of Vice-Chancellors of Nigerian Federal Universities: PMB 12022, 3 Idowu Taylor St, Victoria Island, Lagos; tel. (1) 2612425; f. 1962; acts as a co-ordinating body for Federal Universities; offers advice to government and university governing councils on educational matters; 24 fed. univ. mems; Sec.-Gen. Prof. Musa Abdullahi.

HISTORY, GEOGRAPHY AND ARCHAEOLOGY

Historical Society of Nigeria: c/o Dept. of History, University of Lagos, Lagos; internet www.hsnonline.org; f. 1955 to encourage interest and work in connection with the study of Nigerian history; Pres. Prof. Monday B. Abasiattai; Sec. Dr I. R. Amadi; publs *Bulletin of News* (quarterly), *Journal*, *Tarikh* (2 a year).

Nigerian Geographical Association: c/o Dept of Geography, University of Ibadan, Ibadan; tel. (22) 400550; f. 1955; to further interest in geography and its methods of teaching with special reference to Nigeria; 500 mems; Pres. Prof. Adetoye Faniran; publ. *Nigerian Geographical Journal*.

LANGUAGE AND LITERATURE

Alliance Française: c/o French Consulate, Maison de France 2, Aromire Rd (on Kingsway Rd, opp. Ikoyi Hotel), Ikoyi, Lagos; tel. (1) 2692365; fax (1) 2694181; e-mail alliance@maison-de-france.ng; internet www.maisondefrance-ng.com; offers courses and exams in French language and culture and promotes cultural exchange with France; attached teaching centres in Enugu, Ibadan, Ikoyi, Ikoyi-Yaba, Ilorin, Jos, Kaduna, Kano, Lagos, Lagos-Yaba, Maiduguri, Owerri and Port Harcourt.

British Council: Plot 2935, IBB Way, Maitama, PMB 550, Garki, Abuja; tel. (9) 41378707; fax (9) 4130902; e-mail info.abuja@ng.britishcouncil.org; internet www.britishcouncil.org/nigeria; offers courses and exams in English language and British culture and promotes cultural exchange with the UK; attached offices in Lagos and Kano; Dir, Nigeria and Regional Dir, West Africa Dr John Richards.

Goethe-Institut: 10, Ozumba Mbadiwe Ave, opp. 1004 Flats, Victoria Island, Lagos State; tel. (1) 2610717; fax (1) 2617916; e-mail verw@lagos.goethe.org; internet www.goethe.de/af/lag/deindex.htm; offers courses and exams in German language and culture and promotes cultural exchange with Germany; library of 6,000 vols; Dir Michael Müller-Verweyen.

MEDICINE

Nigerian Dental Association: c/o Dept of Oral Pathology and Biology, School of Dental Sciences, University of Lagos, PMB 12003, Lagos; fax (1) 5849582; e-mail ndass1966@yahoo.co.uk; Pres. Dr Kofo Winfunke Savage; Sec.-Gen. Dr O. A. Orebanjo.

Nigerian Medical Association: POB 1108, Adeniyi Jones Ave, Ikeja, Marina, Lagos; tel. (1) 4801569; fax (1) 4936854; e-mail info@nigerianma.org; internet www.nigerianma.org

.org; f. 1951; 35,000 mems; Chair. (vacant); Pres. Dr Wole Atoyebi; Sec.-Gen. Dr Wapada Inuwa Balami.

Nigerian Society for Microbiology: c/o Prof. Nduka Okafor, Anambra State University of Technology, PMB 1660 Enugu State; f. 1973 to promote the advancement of medical, veterinary, agricultural and industrial microbiology; holds annual conferences in the Nigerian universities; 130 mems; Pres. Dr A. O. Eiiofor; publ. *Nigerian Journal for Microbiology* (2 a year).

Nutrition Society of Nigeria: c/o Dept of Human Nutrition, Faculty of Public Health, College of Medicine, University of Ibadan, Ibadan, Oyo State; e-mail nutrisocng@yahoo.com; f. 1963; 350 mems; Pres. Prof. Isaac O. Akinyele; publ. *Nigerian Nutrition Newsletter*.

NATURAL SCIENCES

General

Nigerian Academy of Science: NSPRI House, 32–36 Barikisu Iyede St, PMB 1004, University of Lagos Post Office, Akoko, Yaba, Lagos; tel. (1) 7916130; e-mail president@nascience.org; internet www.nascience.org; f. 1977; 45 foundation fellows, 97 current fellows; Pres. Prof. Gabriel B. Ogunmola; Hon. Sec. Prof. T. A. I. Akeju; publs *Discourses* (2 a year), *Newsletter* (2 a year), *Nigerian Journal of Agricultural Sciences* (annually), *Nigerian Journal of Medical Sciences* (annually), *Nigerian Journal of Natural Sciences* (annually), *Texts of Quarterly Lectures* (4 a year).

Biological Sciences

Ecological Society of Nigeria: c/o Department of Biological Sciences, University of Lagos, Lagos; f. 1973; 373 mems; Pres. Prof. J. K. Egunjobi; Sec. C. Chike Okafo; publs *Newsletter*, *Proceedings*.

Entomological Society of Nigeria: c/o Department of Crop Protection, Ahmadu Bello University, PMB 1044, Samaru, Zaria, Kaduna State; f. 1965 to further the study of insects in Nigeria; 250 mems; Pres. Prof. S. N. Okiwelu; Sec. O. O. Adu; publs *Nigerian Entomologists' Magazine* (annually), *Nigerian Journal of Entomology* (annually).

Genetics Society of Nigeria: c/o International Institute of Tropical Agriculture, Oyo Rd, PMB 5320, Ibadan, Oyo State; f. 1972 to further interest in genetics for the benefit of mankind and in the various areas of crops, livestock and medicine; 75 mems; Pres. Dr O. A. Ojomo; Sec. Dr A. O. Abifarin; publ. *Proceedings*.

Physical Sciences

Geological Survey of Nigeria: PMB 2007, Kaduna South; tel. (62) 212003; f. 1919; geological mapping; mineral exploration; geophysical and geochemical surveys and consultation on geological problems; library of 34,000 vols; Chief Officer J. I. Nehikhare; publs *Annual Report*, *Bulletins*, *Occasional Papers*, *Records*, geological maps.

TECHNOLOGY

Nigerian Society of Engineers: 1 Engineering Close, PMB 72667, Victoria Island, Lagos; tel. (1) 2617349; fax (1) 2617315; e-mail se@nse.org.ng; internet www.nse.org.ng; f. 1958; 15,000 mems; library of 1,500 vols; Pres. Eng. Foluseke Abidemi Somolu; publ. *The Nigerian Engineer* (4 a year).

Research Institutes
GENERAL

Lake Chad Research Institute (LCRI): Malamfatori, PMB 1293, Maiduguri, Borno State; tel. (76) 232106; fax (76) 923441; f. 1975; research into the hydrological behaviour and characteristics of Lake Chad and the limnology of the associated surface and ground waters; the abundance, distribution and other biological characteristics of species of fish and other aquatic life in the lake and practical methods of their exploitation; the behaviour and characteristics of the wildlife associated with the lake and its conservation; ecology and methods of control of crop pests and diseases of economic importance; improvement of the methods of control of dry farming and livestock husbandry in the severe environmental condition around the lake; improvement of cultivation of wheat, barley, and other crops by irrigation; the socio-economic and public health effects of the introduction of large-scale irrigation schemes and improved methods of animal husbandry and fishing on the rural populations around the lake; library of 16,000 vols; Dir Dr William Ndahi; publs *Annual Report*, *LCRI Newsletter* (quarterly).

AGRICULTURE, FISHERIES AND VETERINARY SCIENCE

Cocoa Research Institute of Nigeria: Onigambari, PMB 5244, Ibadan, Oyo State; tel. (22) 410040; f. 1964; research into cocoa, cola, coffee, cashew and tea; research aspects include entomology, plant-breeding, plant pathology, soil chemistry and biochemistry; library of 15,000 vols; Dir S. T. Olatoye; publs *Annual Report*, *CRIN News* (monthly), *Progress Report* (4 a year), advisory leaflets, research report papers (both 4 a year)

Forestry Research Institute of Nigeria (FRIN): PMB 5054, Ibadan, Oyo State; tel. (2) 413327; fax (2) 2410515; e-mail Dfrin@skannet.com; internet www.frin-ng.org; f. 1954; conducts intensive research into all aspects of forestry and forest products utilization; Federal Colleges of Forestry at Ibadan and Jos, Federal College of Wildlife Management at New Bussa and Federal College of Forestry Mechanization at Afaka in Kaduna State; library of 14,000 vols, 400 periodicals; Dir Prof. J. J. Owonubi; publs *Annual Report*, *Journal of Forestry Research and Management* (2 a year), *Newsletter* (4 a year).

Institute for Agricultural Research (IAR): Ahmadu Bello University, PMB 1044, Samaru, Zaria, 810261; tel. (69) 551335; fax (69) 550563; e-mail iar20002001@yahoo.com; internet www.iarsamaru.org; f. 1924; improvement of production of sorghum, millet, wheat, groundnuts, cotton and fibres, cowpea, sesame, soyabean and vegetables; maintenance of soil fertility; land resources assessment; crop environment; cropping systems and intercropping; crop–livestock integration; mechanization; soil and water management; socio-economic studies of small farm management, marketing, credit, supply systems and extension; sub-stations at: Kano in Kano State, Kadawa in Kano State and Talata Mafara in Zamfara State; library of 18,000 vols; Dir Prof. Shehu Garki Ado; publs *Samaru Agricultural Newsletter* (6 a year), *Samaru Journal of Agricultural Research* (annual), *Samaru Miscellaneous Papers* (2 a year), *Samaru Research Bulletins* (quarterly), *Soil Survey Reports*.

Institute of Agricultural Research and Training (IART): Obafemi Awolowo University, Moor Plantation, PMB 5029, Ibadan,

Oyo State; tel. (2) 2312523; fax (2) 2316857; e-mail drart@infoweb.abs.net; f. 1921, university institute 1970; comprises research division and two federal colleges of agriculture and animal health production; serves as national centre for research into crops, cereals, grains, soyabean, jute, kenaf, livestock, soils and water management; library of 45,000 vols; Dir Prof. E. A. ADEBOWALE; publs *Annual Report*, *Moor Journal of Agricultural Research* (2 a year), *Newsletter* (4 a year).

National Agricultural Extension and Research Liaison Services: Ahmadu Bello University, PMB 1067, Zaria; tel. (69) 550589; fax (69) 552198; e-mail naqasabu@hotmail.com; f. 1963; conducts research on extension approaches, methodologies and adoption process; also serves as a link between research and extension; packaging of improved technologies in forms of extension publications, training, radio and television programmes, agricultural shows, audiovisual materials; consultancy services; programme areas are Crop and Forestry, Livestock and Fisheries, Agricultural Engineering and Irrigation, Farm Management and Co-operatives, Extension and Rural Youths, Planning and Evaluation, Food Technology and Rural Home Economics, Publications and Publicity, Farm Broadcast; zonal offices in Maiduguri, Zaria, Badeggi, Umudioke and Ibadan; library of 2,000 vols, 1,400 periodicals; Dir S. S. ABUBAKAR; publ. *The Nigerian Journal of Agricultural Extension* (2 a year).

National Animal Production Research Institute (NAPRI): Ahmadu Bello University, Shika, POB 1096, Zaria; tel. (69) 550435; fax (69) 551272; e-mail napri@inet-global.com; f. 1928; research into dairy, beef, sheep, goat, swine, rabbit and poultry production, management and breeding, range and pasture research and improvement, livestock economics and rural sociology of pastoral nomadic peoples; library of 23,624 vols; Dir Prof. L. O. EDUVIE; publs *Annual Report*, *Bulletin* (4 a year), *Journal of Animal Production Research* (annually).

National Centre for Agricultural Mechanization: Federal Ministry of Agriculture, PMB 1525, Ilorin, Kwara State; f. 1977; testing and developing of agricultural machinery; standardization, extension and training services in the field of agricultural mechanization; Dir Prof. KAYODE ONI.

National Centre for Genetic Resources and Biotechnology (NACGRAB): Moor Plantation, PMB 5382, Ibadan, Oyo State; tel. (2) 2312622; e-mail nacgrab@skannet.com; f. 1986; research, data gathering and dissemination of information on matters relating to plant genetic resources, genetic engineering and biotechnology; library of 1,500 vols; Project Man. LANRE GBADAMOSI; publ. *Annual Report*.

National Cereals Research Institute (NCRI): PMB 8, Badeggi, Bida, Niger State; tel. (66) 461233; tel. (66) 461234; e-mail ncri@skannet.com; f. 1975, formerly Federal Department of Agricultural Research; conducts research into the production, processing and industrial capacity utilization of rice, digitaria, oilseeds (soybean and beniseed) and sugarcane; mechanization and improvement of methods of cultivating, harvesting, processing and storage of crops; improving the utilization of by-products; ecology of crop pests and diseases and improved methods of their control; integration of crop cultivation into farming systems in different ecological zones and its socio economic effects on the rural population; distributes farming implements, machinery

and cultivated varieties of rice and soybean; library of 6,078 vols; includes a Plant Quarantine Training Centre; Head of Station A. S. GANA; publs *Annual Report*, *Information Papers* (monthly), *Memoranda* (irregular), *Research Bulletins* (quarterly).

National Horticultural Research Institute (NIHORT): Idi-Ishin, PMB 5432, Ibadan, Oyo State; tel. and fax (2) 2412230; e-mail nihortinfo@yahoo.com; two sub-stations at Mbato, near Okigwe, Imo State and at Bagauda, near Tiga, Kano State; f. 1975; 30 mems; conducts research in fruit and vegetable production and consumption; in particular improvement of the genetic potentials of the cultivated, semicultivated and wild crops; improvement of agronomic and husbandry practices; mechanization and improvement of methods of cultivating, harvesting, processing and storage; improvement of the utilization of by-products; ecology of crop pests and diseases and improved methods of their control; integration of crop cultivation into farming systems in different ecological zones of the country; library of 10,000 vols; Dir J. O. BABATOLA; publs *Annual Report*, *NIHORT Newsletter* (quarterly), *information papers* (monthly).

National Institute for Freshwater Fisheries Research (NIFFR): PMB 6006, New Bussa, Niger State; tel. (31) 670 444; f. 1968; research into the limnological behaviour and characteristics of the man-made lakes and their effects on the fish and other aquatic life; the abundance, distribution and other biological characteristics of species of fish and practical methods of their exploitation; the socio-economic effects of the construction of man-made lakes on rural populations; technical and vocational training in freshwater fishing and related fields; library of 20,000 vols, 40 periodicals; Dir Prof. B. M. B. LADU; publs *Annual Report*, *Newsletter* (quarterly), *Nigerian Fisheries and Aquatic Sciences Abstract* (annually).

National Root Crops Research Institute (NRCRI): Umudike, PMB 7006, Umuahia, Abia State; tel. and fax (82) 440471; e-mail keninwrosu_nrcri@yahoo.com; internet www.nrcri.org.ng; f. 1923; research for the genetic improvement of yams, cocoyams, cassava, sweet potato, Irish potato, ginger and other root-crops; farming systems research and middle manpower training; library of 3,113 books, 25,665 periodicals; Dir Dr KEN I. NWOSU; publs *Advisory Bulletins* (monthly), *Annual Report*, *Gazette*, *News Bulletin* (quarterly), *Newsletter*, *Programmes of Work* (annually).

National Veterinary Research Institute (NVRI): Vom, near Jos, Plateau State; f. 1924; intensive research into all aspects of animal diseases and their treatment and control; all aspects of animal nutrition; production of vaccine and sera; introduction of exotic stock to improve meat, milk and egg production; standardization and quality control of manufactured animal feeds; training livestock superintendents, laboratory technicians and technologists; library of 14,000 vols, 4,000 reports, etc.; Dir Dr LAMI H. LOMBIN; publs *Annual Report*, *Index of Veterinary Research* (annually), *Newsletter* (quarterly), *Research Papers* (irregular).

Nigerian Institute for Oil Palm Research (NIFOR): PMB 1030, Benin City, Edo State; tel. (52) 602485; fax (52) 602486; e-mail nifor@infoweb.abs.net; f. 1939; research into the production and products of oil palm and other palms of cconomic importance and recommendation of improved methods; library of 13,000 vols; Dir Dr U. OMOTI; publs *Annual Report*,

Nigerian Journal of Palms and Oil Seeds (irregular).

Nigerian Stored Products Research Institute (NSPRI): Km. 3, Asa Dam Rd, PMB 1489, Ilorin, Kwara State; tel. (31) 222143; fax (31) 221639; e-mail nspiriheadquarters@yahoo.com; f. 1960; research into stored-product pests and primary processing; training, analytical services and advisory work, design and construction of storage structures; 450 mems; library of 3,610 vols; Exec. Dir Dr M. A. ADESIDA (acting); publs *Annual Report*, *Journal* (4 a year), *Newsletter* (4 a year), *Nigerian Post-Harvest Technology Abstract* (annually), *Research News* (4 a year).

Rubber Research Institute of Nigeria (RRIN): Iyanomo, PMB 1049, Benin City, Bendel State; tel. (52) 244625; f. 1961; research on natural rubber (*Hevea brasiliensis*) production; sub-station at Akwete near Aba in Anambra; library of 1,000 vols; Dir Dr E. K. OKAISABOR; publs *Annual Report*, *RRIN's advisory leaflets* (monthly), *information booklets* (quarterly).

BIBLIOGRAPHY, LIBRARY SCIENCE AND MUSEOLOGY

Institute of Archaeology and Museum Studies: PMB 2031, Jos, Plateau State; tel. (73) 453516; e-mail iamsjos2000@yahoo.co.uk; f. 1963; library of 1,500 vols, 500 journals; Dir MONICA ABADOM; publ. *The Museologist* (annually).

ECONOMICS, LAW AND POLITICS

Centre for Management Development: PMB 21578, Ikeja; tel. (1) 7748165; fax (1) 4978390; e-mail cmd@nipost.com.ng; f. 1973 to promote and co-ordinate the activities of institutions engaged in the education and training of managerial manpower; advises government on policy, formulates policies and guidelines, monitors standards of management education, accredits and registers management trainers, assesses training programmes, provides advisory and consultancy service to Nigerian businesses; library of 30,000 vols, 6,000 periodicals, also general publs and serials, teaching materials library, and audio-visual unit; Dir-Gen. Dr J. Y. MAIYAKI; Chief Librarian TOYIN DINA; publs *Annual Report*, *Nigerian Management Review* (2 a year).

Nigerian Institute of Social and Economic Research: PMB 5, University Post Office, Ibadan; tel. (2) 8102904; fax (2) 8101194; e-mail dg@niser.org.ng; internet www.nisernigeria.org; f. 1950 as WA Institute of Social and Economic Research, present name 1960; government-financed; applied research on problems of immediate and long-term relevance to Nigerian development: economic planning and development, agricultural and industrial development, business and technology, foreign and international trade, public finance and social, physical and manpower planning and development; political development, population studies; training for staff of planning organizations; consultancy service for federal and state governments, private organizations and international bodies; library of 75,000 vols; Dir-Gen. Prof. BANKOLE ONI; publs *Annual Report*, *Research for Development* (annually).

EDUCATION

Nigerian Educational Research Council: POB 8058, Lagos; f. 1965; curriculum development and general educational research; 30 mems; library of 12,000 vols; Chair. Prof. S. N. NWOSU; Sec. J. M. AKINTOLA; publs conference and workshop reports.

MEDICINE

National Institute of Pharmaceutical Research and Development (NIPRD): PMB 21, Idu, Abuja; tel. (9) 5239089; f. 1989; research into medical plants, herbs and drug development and formulary; drug information centre; national centre for drugs; regulates the standardization of pharmaceutical substances; library of 2,350 vols, 2,389 journals, 6,000 CD-ROMs; Dir Dr UFORD S. INYANG; publs *Annual Report, Journal of Phytomedicine and Therapeutics (JOPAT)* (annually).

Nigerian Institute of Medical Research (NIMR): Edmund Crescent, PMB 2013, Yaba, Lagos; tel. (1) 800090; fax (1) 862865; e-mail director@nimr-ng.org; internet www.nimr-ng.org; f. 1973; to identify the major health problems of the country and their determinants; research into environmental hazards and their effect on the population's health; library of 13,000 vols; Dir-Gen. Dr ONI IDIGBE; publs *Annual Report, Newsletter* (4 a year).

Nigerian Institute for Trypanosomiasis Research (NITR): PMB 2077, Kaduna, Kaduna State; tel. (62) 238074; fax (62) 238075; e-mail nitre@linkserve.com.ng; f. 1951; research into trypanosomiasis and onchocerciasis generally; the pathology, immunology and methods of treatment of the diseases; the ecology and life-cycle of the vectors and the mode of transmission of the disease; chemical, biological and other methods of vector control, the socio-economic effects of the disease on the rural populations; maintains 2 brs, 1 field station; library of 4,000 vols; Dir Dr I. HALID; publ. *Annual Report*.

NATURAL SCIENCES

General

Nigerian Institute for Oceanography and Marine Research (NIOMR): Victoria Island, PMB 12729, Lagos; tel. (1) 2617385; fax (1) 2619517; e-mail niomr@linkserve.com .ng; f. 1975; research into the resources and physical characteristics of the Nigerian territorial waters and the high seas beyond; library of 10,000 vols; Dir J. G. TOBOR; publs *Annual Report, Newsletter* (quarterly).

TECHNOLOGY

Federal Institute of Industrial Research (FIIRO): PMB 21023, Ikeja, Lagos; Located at: Blind Centre St, Cappa Bus Stop, off Agege Motor Rd, Oshodi, Ikeja, Lagos; tel. (1) 8947094; fax (1) 4525880; e-mail info@ fiiro-ng.org; internet www.fiiro-ng.org; f. 1956; food technology, industrial fermentation through biotechnology, pulp and paper research, domestic and industrial water treatment, environmental studies, ceramic and eng. materials research, machinery and equipment design and fabrication; consultancy, analytical services, technical services to industry, scientific and industrial information service; 368 mems; library of 14,500 vols; Dir-Gen./CEO Dr OLUWOLE OLATUNJI; publs *Profile on FIIRO Commercializable Technologies* (irreg.), *Research Report* (irreg.), *Journal of Industrial Research and Technology*.

National Centre for Energy Research and Development: University of Nigeria, Nsukka, Enugu State; tel. (42) 771853; fax (42) 771855; e-mail misunn@aol.com; f. 1982; federal government-funded centre for research and development of solar and other renewable and non-renewable energy such as photovoltaic, photothermal, wind energy, radiation measurement, biomass, coal, energy management, etc.; Dir Dr O. V. EKECHUKWU.

National Research Institute for Chemical Technology (NARICT): PMB 1052, Zaria, Kaduna State; tel. (69) 334503; fax (69) 334835; e-mail narict@inet.global.com; f. 1988; research and development work in chemicals, leather and allied fields; short-term training courses in chemical technology, laboratory management, chemistry laboratory practicals, safety; four extension centres, at Kano, Jos, Maiduguri and Sokoto for extension services; serves as national information centre on leather and chemical technology; Dir-Gen. Dr E. M. OKONKWO; publs *Journal of Leather and Chemical Technology* (annually), *NARICT Annual Report, NARICT Bulletin* (annually), *NARICT Newsletter* (monthly).

Nigerian Building and Road Research Institute (NBRRI): PMB 5065, Wuse General Post Ofice, Abuja; premises at: Plot 335 Gabes St, Wuse Zone 2, Abuja; tel. and fax (9) 5237466; e-mail c.ofoegbu@nbrri.rinaf.net .ng; f. 1978; conducts applied research and development into the use of local materials and methods in road and building construction; library of 12,000 vols; Dir-Gen. Prof. CHARLES OFOEGBU; publs *Annual Report, Journal on Construction Management and Engineering Materials* (4 a year), *Technical Digest* (2 a year).

Projects Development Institute (PRODA): Emene Industrial Layout, PMB 01609, Enugu State; tel. (42) 301306; fax (42) 457691; e-mail service@prodaenugu.gov.ng; internet www.prodaenugu.gov.ng; f. 1970, as Project Development Agency, present status 1977; conducts research into various areas of science, ceramics, energy and engineering with the aim of advancing industialization; promotes the establishment of new industrial projects through laboratory and pilot investigations to the construction of large-scale commercial plants, uses local raw materials and labour; library of 4,000 vols; Dir Prof. M. O. CHIJIOKE; publs *Annual Report, PRODA Newsletter* (quarterly).

Raw Materials Research and Development Council (RMRDC): Plot 427, Aguiyi Ironsi St, Maitama District, PMB 232, Garki, Abuja; tel. (1) 2635206; e-mail info@rmrdc .org; internet www.rmrdc.org; f. 1987; supports and expedites industrial development and self-sufficiency through maximum utilization of local materials; library of 3,000 vols; Chief Exec. Dr ABUBAKAR ABDULLAHI; publs *Annual Report, Research Reports* (occasional), *RMRDC Newsletter* (quarterly).

Libraries and Archives

Abeokuta

Ogun State Library: PMB 2060, Abeokuta, Ogun State; f. 1976; 21,736 vols; special collection on Ogun State; Chief Librarian Alhaji BAYO YISA ODULAJA.

Akure

Ondo State Library Board: PMB 719, Akure; tel. (34) 230561; f. 1976, renamed 1985; reading and reference services, mobile- and school-library services, training of library assistants; 62,546 vols; Dir T. A. AJUMOBI.

Bauchi

Bauchi State Library Board: Ministry of Education, Bauchi; f. 1976; lending and reference services, special services to rehabilitation centres, training of library staff; 35,000 vols, 3,475 periodicals; Dir MUSA M. DEDE; publ. *Annual Report*.

Benin

Edo State Library Board: 17 James Watt Rd, PMB 1127, Benin City; tel. (52) 200810; f. 1971; 272,398 vols; Central Reference Library with emphasis on the needs of the State Government; Technical Service Division; School Library Division; Public Library Division (13 brs, 3 Rural Information Centres); Mobile Service to remote areas; hospital and prison services; Dir Dr J. O. U. ODIASE; publs *Annual Reports, Edo Library Accessions List* (2 a year), *Index to The Observer* (2 a year), *Legal Deposit Bulletin* (2 a year), *Newsletters* (monthly).

Enugu

Enugu State Library Board: PMB 01026, Enugu; tel. (42) 334103; f. 1955; Dir of Library Services C. C. UDE.

Attached library:

State Central Library: Market Rd, Enugu; f. 1956; lending and reference library activities; legal deposit and regional centre for bibliographical information and research; c. 83,000 vols; Nigeriana colln; 1 mobile library unit; divisional library at Onueke; zonal libraries at Abakaliki and Nsukka.

Ibadan

Federal Ministry of Science and Technology, Library and Documentation Centre: Moor Plantation, PMB 5382, Ibadan, Oyo State; f. 1973; 2,000 vols, 700 current periodicals, 22 microfiches, 350 reprints; newspaper clippings; the Liaison Office in Nigeria for both AGRIS (International Information System for Agricultural Sciences and Technology) and CARIS (Current Agricultural Research Information Service); Librarian O. A. ADIGUM; publs *List of Reprints, List of Serials* (annually).

Forestry Research Institute of Nigeria Library: PMB 5054, Ibadan; tel. (2) 2414441; fax (2) 2410515; e-mail dfrin@ skannet.com; internet www.frin-ng.org; f. 1954; 14,000 vols, 400 periodicals; special collections: Nigerian silvicultural records and working plans, postgraduate theses collection, and Harold Young Library of rare materials on forest mensuration, biometrics, photogrammetry and technometrics; Head of Library J. A. ADEBOYE; publs *Current Awareness Service on Agricultural Research and Development Bulletin* (monthly), *Current Contents* (monthly), *Library Accession Lists* (4 a year).

Kenneth Dike Library, University of Ibadan: University of Ibadan, Ibadan; tel. (2) 8101100; fax (2) 8103118; e-mail library@ ibadan.ac.ng; internet www.ui.edu.ng/ unitslibrary.htm; f. 1948; 700,000 vols, 1,500 current periodicals; depository for OAU and UN specialized agencies publs; special collection of Africana, private papers of eminent Nigerians; Librarian OLUFUNMILAYO G. TAMUNO; publs *Annual Report, Library Record*.

National Archives of Nigeria: PMB 4, University of Ibadan Post Office, Ibadan; f. 1951, legally recognized 1957; charged with collection, rehabilitation, reproduction and preservation of all public records including private papers under the Ministry of Information and National Orientation; three major (zonal) offices at Enugu, Ibadan and Kaduna; other brs are Located at Abeokuta, Akure, Benin, Calabar, Ilorin, Jos, Lagos Maiduguri, Oweri, Port-Harcourt and Sokoto; 8,500 vols; Dir COMFORT AINA UKWU; publs *Annual Report, Special Lists*.

Ife

Hezekiah Oluwasanmi Library, Obafemi Awolowo University: Ile-Ife; tel. (36) 230290; e-mail ul@library.oauife.edu.ng; f. 1961; 640,567 vols, 6,905 periodicals; spec. collns of Africana, audio-visual materials and govt documents; Librarian M. O. AFOLABI; publs *Abstracts of Theses* (annual), *Research in Progress at the Obafemi Awolowo University* (annual).

Ikeja

Federal Institute of Industrial Research, Oshodi Industrial Information Centre and Extension Services: PMB 21023, Ikeja, Cappa Bus Stop, Agege Motor Rd, Lagos State; tel. (1) 4522905; fax (1) 4525880; f. 1956; scientific, technological and industrial information documentation and dissemination, current awareness, extension and publications services; 12,500 vols; special collections: UNIDO, NTIS and IDRI publs; Librarian I. DEKWE; publs *Annual Report, Industrial Abstracts* (quarterly), *Latest Technology Index* (quarterly).

Ilorin

Kwara State Library Board: Sulu Gambari Rd, PMB 1561, Ilorin, Kwara State; f. 1968; 45,000 vols; Dir Deacon BENSON BABATUNDE ODEWALE; publ. *Annual Report.*

Jos

Plateau State Library Services: c/o Bureau for Information, POB 2053, Jos, Plateau State; f. 1976; 45,293 vols; brs at Akwanga, Keffi, Lafia, Pankshin and Shendam; Librarian TIMOTHY P. A. ANGBA (acting).

Kaduna

Kaduna State Library Board: PMB 2061, Kaduna; f. 1953, renamed 1976; 200,000 vols; Dir JOSEPH AHMADU MAIGARI; publs *Annual Reports, Bibliographies, Current Awareness Bulletin, Legal Deposit Collection, Public Enlightenment, Readers' Guides.*

Kano

Kano State Library Board: PMB 3094, Ahmadu Bello Way, Kano; tel. (64) 645614; e-mail nassarawa2001@yahoo.com; f. 1968; includes mobile and school library services, cultural programmes, outreach services to government departments, reference and documentation services, audiovisual services, internet services; 1,000,000 vols; Exec. Dir Alhaji SANUSI ABDULLAH NASSARAWA.

Lagos

Central Medical Library: Federal Ministry of Health, PMB 2003, Yaba, Lagos; f. 1946; serves the entire country; 30,000 vols, 600 journals; Librarian M. O. ORIMOLADE.

Lagos City Libraries: PMB 2025, Lagos; f. 1950; 229,150 vols; Librarian Mrs B. B. OGUNLANA; publ. *Annual Report.*

National Library of Nigeria: 4 Wesley St, PMB 12626, Lagos; tel. (1) 2600220; fax (1) 2631563; f. 1964; 12 brs; 140,000 vols in main library, 18,000 at branches; special collections of Nigerian and UK government publications, UN documents, Rhodes House Library Collection (private papers of past colonial civil servants), Ranfurly Library Collection; depository for UN, OAU and Canadian publs; Chair. FRANCIS Z. GANA; National Librarian Alhaji MU'AZU H. WALI.

University of Lagos Library: Lagos; tel. and fax (1) 4932552; e-mail library@unilag.edu; internet www.unilag.edu; f. 1962; 375,000 vols, 4,500 periodicals; legal depository for Lagos State; depository for all publications of ECA, GATT, ICJ and ILO; collections on UNESCO, WHO and FAO; Librarian Dr S. O. OLANLOKUN (acting); publs *Annual Report, Library Notes, Reader's Guide, Unilag: Quarterly News Bulletin.*

Maiduguri

Borno State Library Board: PMB 1443, Maiduguri, Borno State; tel. (76) 231389; f. 1968; became library board 1984; 86,535 vols; 11 brs; provides information for the public, trains library staff, organizes school libraries, annual book exhibition, etc.; Dir JOHN YADU MALGWI.

Nsukka

University of Nigeria, Nsukka Libraries: Nnamdi Azikiwe Library, Nsukka, Enugu State; tel. (42) 771444; fax (42) 270644; e-mail misunn@aol.com; f. 1960; 717,000 vols at Nsukka and Enugu campuses, medical library at Enugu with 42,000 vols, Africana collection of 30,000 vols; Librarian EMENIKE IKEGBUNE (acting); publs *Annual Report, Nsukka Library Notes* (irregular), *UNLAN.*

Owerri

Imo State Library Board: PMB 1118, Owerri, Imo State; tel. (83) 230280; f. 1976; lending, reference, children's library and library for the handicapped, bibliographic and information consultancy services, rural library services and school library resource centre; 123,000 vols; Dir of Library Services AGATHA C. NWACHUKWU; publs *Annual Report, The Light* (annually).

Port Harcourt

British Council Information Centre: Plot 127, Olu Obasanjo Way, GRA II, Port Harcourt; tel. (84) 237173; fax (84) 237172; e-mail info.portharcourt@ng.britishcouncil.org; Centre Man. PATIENCE EZINWOKE.

Museums and Art Galleries

Benin

National Museum, Benin: Benin; tel. and fax (52) 252675; e-mail natmusben@yahoo.com; f. 1973; Benin antiquities, bronzes, ivory, terracotta, wood, beads, masks, masquerades, ancestral figures, materials for warfare, etc.; Curator MARTINS OGUNTAYO AKANBIEMU.

Esie

Esie Museum: PMB 301, Kwara State; f. 1945; stone antiquities (800 half life-size human figures); Dir (vacant).

Ife

Natural History Museum, Obafemi Awolowo University: Ile-Ife, Osun State; tel. (36) 230291 ext. 2451; e-mail misawumi@oauife.edu.ng; f. 1971; research, outreach activities, teaching, exhibition and identification of animal and plant specimens; botanical, entomological, geological, palaeontological and zoological collections; archaeological artifacts; offers MSc in conservation and MSc and PhD in biosystematics; Dir Prof. M. A. ISAWUMI.

Jos

National Museum, Jos: PMB 2031, Jos, Plateau State; f. 1982; ethnography, architecture and archaeology of Nigeria; terracotta Nok figurines, modern and traditional Nigerian pottery; zoological and botanical gardens; museum of traditional architecture; transport museum; craft village; open-air theatre; library of 10,000 vols and 2,000 Arabic MSS; Dir M. DANDAURA.

Kaduna

National Museum, Kaduna: PMB 2127, Kaduna; tel. (62) 211180; fax (1) 2633890; f. 1975; archaeology and ethnography; houses the 'Craft Village', where traditional hair-plaiting, weaving, pottery, calabash decoration, wood carving, leather work, brass casting and smithery are done; library of 1,500 vols; Dir Dr K. S. CHAFE; publ. *Tambari.*

Kano

Gidan Makama Museum: POB 2023, Kano; tel. (64) 645170; e-mail yusufadamu2000@yahoo.com; internet www.kanoonline.com/gidan_makama; f. 1959; local art work; history of Kano and the Kanawas from 15th–19th centuries; Curator MUSA O. HAMBOLU.

Lagos

National Museum, Lagos: Onikan Rd, Lagos; tel. (1) 2634045; e-mail natmuslog@yahoo.com; f. 1957; ethnography, archaeology and traditional art; library of 9,076 vols; Dir-Gen. Dr OMOTOSHO ELUYEMI.

Oron

National Museum, Oron: PMB 1004, Oron, Akwa Ibom State; f. 1958; rebuilt after civil war in 1975; wooden sculptures and ethnographic artefacts and materials; Chief Curator ANIEFIOK UDO AKPAN.

Owo

Owo Museum: Federal Dept of Antiquities, POB 84, Owo, Ondo State; f. 1959; arts and crafts; some ethnographic relics mainly from the Eastern part of the Yoruba region; Curator E. OLA ABEJIDE.

Universities

FEDERAL UNIVERSITIES

ABUBAKAR TAFAWA BALEWA UNIVERSITY

PMB 0248, Bauchi

Telephone: (77) 543500

Fax: (77) 542095

E-mail: info@atbunet.org

Internet: www.atbunet.org

Founded 1988

Federal government control

Language of instruction: English

Academic year: October to September

Vice-Chancellor: Prof. A. S. SAMBO

Deputy Vice-Chancellor (Academic): Prof. S. NA'ALLAH

Deputy Vice-Chancellor (Administration): Dr G. A. BABAJI

Registrars: Alhaji AYUBA MOHAMMED GITAL, Alhaji IBRAHIM MUSA

Librarian: Alhaji ZUBAIRU MOHAMMED

Number of teachers: 260

Number of students: 6,000 (4,000 full-time, 2,000 part-time)

Publications: *Annual Report, University Bulletin* (4 a year)

DEANS

School of Agriculture and Agricultural Technology: Prof. S. T. MBAP

School of Engineering Technology: Prof. A. A. ASERE

School of Environment and Environmental Technology: Prof. S. SULAIMAN

School of Management Technology: Prof. S. KUSHWAHA

School of Science and Science Education: Prof. E. J. E. EDEMENANG

PROFESSORS

ABUBAKAR, M. M., Animal Science
ADEGBOLA, T. A., Animal Science
AJAYI, J. O., Chemistry
ALE, S. O., Mathematics Education
ALIYU, U. O., Electrical Engineering
ASERE, A. A., Mechanical Engineering
AUDU, J. A., Biological Science
CHAUDHARY, J. P., Crop Protection
DADA, S. S., Geology
DIKE, E. F. C., Geology
EDEMENANG, E. J. E., Computers
FABIYI, J. P., Microbiology
HAQUE, M. F., Physics
JIDEANI, A. I., Biological Science
KUSHAWA, S., Agricultural Economics
MATAWAL, D. S., Civil Engineering
MBAP, S. T., Animal Production
MSHELIA, E. D., Physics
NA'ALLAH, S., Industrial Design
OLAGBEMIRO, T. O., Chemistry
OLARINOYE, R. D., Physics Education
ONOGU, M. I., Electrical Engineering and
  Electronics
ORAZULIKE, D. M., Geology
OSENI, T. O., Animal Production
OYAWOYE, E. O., Animal Production

UNIVERSITY OF ABUJA

PMB 117, Abuja, Federal Capital City

Telephone: (9) 8821380
Fax: (9) 8821605
E-mail: vc@uniabuja.edu.ng

Founded 1988
Language of instruction: English
Academic year: October to September

Chancellor (vacant)
Vice-Chancellor: Prof. A. L. GAMBO
Registrar: Mallam YAKUBU HASSAN HABI
Librarian: Dr FAB. A. J. AKHIDIME

Number of teachers: 150
Number of students: 5,400

DEANS

College of Arts and Education: Dr JOSEPH N.
  UKWEDEH
College of Law, Management and Social
  Sciences: Dr NANA M. TANKO
College of Science and Agriculture: Prof.
  SIMON I. OKWUTE
Postgraduate School: Dr MICHAEL A. ADE-
  WALE

PROFESSORS

ADELABU, J. A., Physics
AMDII, I. E. S., Political Science
BIRAI, U. M., Political Science
IKEOTUONYE, A. I., Education
OKWUTE, S. I., Chemistry
UJO, A. A., Political Science

UNIVERSITY OF AGRICULTURE, ABEOKUTA

PMB 2240, Abeokuta, Ogun State

Telephone: (39) 245170
Fax: (39) 243045
E-mail: root@unaab.edu.ng
Internet: www.unaab.edu.ng

Founded 1988 (previously a college of Uni-
  versity of Lagos)
Federal control
Language of instruction: English
Academic year: October to July

Chancellor (vacant)
Vice-Chancellor: Prof. ISRAEL FOLORUNSO
  ADU
Deputy Vice-Chancellor: A. R T. SOLARIN
Registrar: ADEMOLA OYERINDE
Librarian: A. T. AGBOOLA

Number of teachers: 278
Number of students: 5,661

Publications: *Agricultural Sciences, Science,
Environment and Technology (ASSET)* (2 a
year), *UNAAB News*

DEANS

College of Agricultural Management, Rural
  Development and Consumer Studies: Prof.
  S. O. AWONORIN
College of Animal Science and Livestock
  Production: Prof. O. A. ADEBAMBO
College of Engineering: Prof. G. A. ADEG-
  BOYEGA
College of Environmental Resources Man-
  agement: Prof. O. MARTINS
College of Natural Sciences: Prof. O. AKIN-
  LADE
College of Plant Science and Crop Produc-
  tion: Prof. M. T. ADETUNJI
College of Veterinary Medicine: Prof. E. B.
  OTESILE
Postgraduate School: Prof. O. ARIYO

PROFESSORS

ADAMSON, I., Chemistry
ADDO, A. A., Home Science and Management
ADEBAMBO, O. A., Animal Breeding and
  Genetics
ADETUNJI, M. T., Soil Science and Agricul-
  tural Mechanisation
ADU, I. F., Animal Nutrition
AKINGBALA, J. O., Food Science and Technol-
  ogy
AKINLADE, O., Physics
ARIYO, O. J., Plant Breeding and Seed
  Technology
AWONORIN, S. O., Food Science and Technol-
  ogy
BAMIRO, F. O., Chemistry
BELLO, N. J., Water Management and Agri-
  cultural Meteorology
EROMOSELE, I. C., Chemistry
ERUVBETINE, D., Animal Nutrition
KADIRI, M., Biological Sciences
LADEINDE, T. A. O., Plant Breeding and Seed
  Technology
MARTINS, O., Water Management and Agri-
  cultural Meteorology
OGUNTONA, C. R. B., Home Science and
  Management
OJANUGA, A. G., Soil Science and Agricultural
  Mechanisation
OKUNEYE, P. A., Agricultural Economics and
  Farm Management
OLADOKUN, M. A. O., Horticulture
OLAGOKE, S. T. O., Crop Protection
OLASANTAN, F. O., Horticulture
ONWUKA, C. F., Animal Nutrition
PHILLIP, D., Agricultural Economics and
  Farm Management
TAYO, T. O., Plant Physiology and Crop
  Production

ATTACHED RESEARCH INSTITUTES

**Agricultural Media Resources and
Extension Centre:** Dir Dr A. E. ADEOTE
(acting).

Research and Development Centre: Dir
Prof. I. ADAMSON.

UNIVERSITY OF AGRICULTURE, MAKURDI

PMB 2373, Makurdi, Benue State

Telephone: (44) 533204

Founded 1988, previously campus of the
  University of Jos, now a fully independent
  university
Federal control
Language of instruction: English
Academic year: October to September

Chancellor: HRH, Igwe (Barr) J. U. NNAJI
  (Eze Odezurigbo III of Nike, Enugu)
Vice-Chancellor: Prof. J. O. I. AYATSE
Registrar: Dr S. A. EDE
Librarian: V. N. OZOWA

Number of teachers: 262
Number of students: 4,023

Publication: *Journal of Agriculture, Science
and Technology* (2 a year)

DEANS

College of Agronomy: Dr M. O. OBASI
College of Agricultural Economics and
  Extension: Prof. C. P. O. OBINNE
College of Agricultural Engineering and
  Engineering Technology: Prof. G. A. IGWUE
College of Animal Science: Prof. J. A. AYOADE
College of Food Technology: Prof. M. A.
  AKPAPUNAM
College of Forestry and Fisheries: Dr P. A.
  ANNUNE
College of Science, Agricultural and Science
  Education: Prof. I. ONYIDO
College of Veterinary Medicine: Prof. A. E. J.
  OKOH
School of Postgraduate Studies: Prof. A. O.
  NWANKITI

ATTACHED CENTRES

Centre for Academic Planning: Head
Prof. E. I. KUCHA.

Centre for Agrochemical Technology:
Head Prof. I. ONYIDO.

**Centre for Food and Agricultural Strat-
egy:** Head Prof. J. C. UMEH.

Centre for Linkages: Head Prof. D. V. UZA.

Centre for Research Development: Head
Prof. B. A. KALU.

Centre for Seed Technology: Head Prof.
A. A. OJO.

Co-operative Extension Centre: Head Dr
D. K. ADEDZWA.

AHMADU BELLO UNIVERSITY

Zaria

Telephone: (69) 550581
Fax: (69) 550022
E-mail: registrar@abu.edu.ng

Founded 1962
Federal control
Language of instruction: English
Academic year: November to June

Chancellor: HRH Alhaji ALIYU MUSTAPHA
Vice-Chancellor: Prof. SHEHU USMAN ABDUL-
  LAHI
Deputy Vice-Chancellor for Academic
  Affairs: Prof. MUSA SHOK
Deputy Vice-Chancellor for Administration:
  Prof. YAKUBU ABDULLAHI NASIDI
Registrar: Alhaji MAIRIGA MANI
Librarian: Prof. D. O. BOZIMO

Number of teachers: 2,064
Number of students: 35,783

Publications: *Inaugural Lectures* (4 a year),
  University Bulletin (every 2 weeks), *University Gazette, University Public Lectures*
  (monthly), *University Research Report*

DEANS

Faculty of Administration: Prof. I. ABDULSA-
  LAM
Faculty of Agriculture: Prof. T. K. ATALA
Faculty of Arts: Dr K. CHAFE
Faculty of Education: Prof F. KOLO
Faculty of Engineering: Prof. M. A. GULMA
Faculty of Environmental Design: Dr A.
  AHUWAN
Faculty of Law: Dr S. G. KANAM
Faculty of Medicine: Prof. H. A. AIKHIONBARE
Faculty of Pharmaceutical Sciences: Dr H.
  KAITA
Faculty of Science: Prof. F. IYUN
Faculty of Social Sciences: Dr F. ODEKUNLE
Faculty of Veterinary Medicine: Dr G. S. A.
  MOHAMMED
Postgraduate School: Prof. I. U. UMOH

PROFESSORS

Faculty of Administration (Kongo Campus, Zaria):

ABDULLAHI, S., Business Administration
ABDULSALAMI, I., Public Administration

Faculty of Agriculture (Agricultural Complex, A. B. U. Main Campus, Zaria):

AHMED, M. K., Agronomy
AMATOSI, C. I., Crop Protection
ATALA, T. K., Rural Sociology
DIKE, M. C., Crop Protection
OGUNBILE, A. O., Agricultural Economics
OGUNLELA, V. B., Agronomy
OLAREWAJU, J. D., Plant Science
OLUFAJO, O. O., Agronomy
OLUKOSI, J. O., Agricultural Economics
VOH, J. P., Rural Sociology

Faculty of Arts (tel. (69) 551540):

AHMED, U. B., African and Nigerian Languages
ABAH, O. S., English
MAHADI, A., History
MOHAMMED, A., English
MOHAMMED, D., African and Nigerian Languages
NASIDI, Y. A., English

Faculty of Education (e-mail deaneduc@yahoo.com):

ADEYANJU, F. B., Physical and Health Education
BOZIMO, D. O., Library Science
CHADO, M. A., Physical and Health Education
KOLO, F. D., Education
LADAN, B. A., Physical and Health Education
OLAOFE, I. A., Education
VENKATESWARLU, K., Physical and Health Education
ZAKARI, M., Library Science

Faculty of Engineering (e-mail deaneng@abu.edu.ng):

ADEFILA, S. S., Chemical Engineering
AKU, S. Y., Mechanical Engineering
BAJOGA, B. J., Electrical Engineering
FOLAYAN, C. O., Mechanical Engineering
GULMA, M. A., Electrical Engineering
OKUOFU, C. A., Water Resources and Environmental Engineering
OYINOLA, A. K., Metallurgical Engineering

Faculty of Environmental Design (e-mail deanen@abu.edu.ng):

MOSAKU, T. O., Building
OGUNTONA, T., Industrial Design
OLORUKOOBA, B. K., Fine Arts
SA'AD, H. T., Architecture
SCHWEDTFEGER, F. W., Architecture

Faculty of Law:

CHUKKOL, K., Public Law
YAKUBU, M. G., Islamic Law

Faculty of Medicine:

ADEKEYE, E. A., Dental Surgery
AHMED, M. H., Psychiatry
AIKHIONBARE, H. A., Paediatrics
ALI, M. A., Human Physiology
OGALA, W. N., Paediatrics
ONYEMELUKWE, G. C., Medicine
SINGH, S. P., Human Anatomy
YAKUBU, A. M., Paediatrics

Faculty of Pharmaceutical Sciences (tel. (69) 951209; e-mail emabdu@abu.edu.ng):

AGUYE, I. A., Pharmacy and Clinical Pharmacy
HUSSEIN, I., Pharmacology and Clinical Pharmacy
ILYAS, M., Pharmacy and Medicinal Chemistry
MUSTAPHA, A., Pharmaceutical and Medicinal Chemistry
OLORINOLA, P. F., Pharmaceutical Microbiology

ONAOLAPO, J. A., Pharmaceutical Science and Microbiology
SHOK, M., Pharmacognosy and Drug Development

Faculty of Science (tel. (69) 551886; e-mail science@abu.edu.ng):

AHMAD, A., Microbiology
AMUPITAN, J. O., Chemistry
ARIYO, J. A., Geography
AWODI, S., Biological Sciences
BELLO, K. O., Textile Science and Technology
HARIHARAN, N. I., Physics
IKE, E. C., Geology
IYUN, J. F., Chemistry
KOLAWOLE, E. G., Textile Science and Technology
NKEONYE, P. O., Textile Science and Technology
OJO, S. B., Physics
OSAZUWA, I. B., Physics

Faculty of Social Sciences (tel. (69) 551540; fax (69) 550022):

AWOGBADE, M., Sociology
DUNMOYE, A., Political Science
KWANASHIE, M., Economics
NKOM, S., Sociology
ODEKUNDE, F., Sociology

Faculty of Veterinary Medicine (tel. (69) 551358; e-mail deanvet@abu.edu.ng):

ABDULLAHI, U., Veterinary Surgery and Medicine
AGBEDE, R. I. S., Parasitology and Entomology
ALIU, Y. O., Physiology and Pharmacology
ESIEVO, K. A. N., Veterinary Pathology and Medicine
GHAJI, A., Veterinary Anatomy
GYANG, E. O., Veterinary Surgery and Medicine
HAMBOLU, J. O., Anatomy
KWAGA, J. P. K., Veterinary Public Health and Preventive Medicine
OGWU, D., Veterinary Surgery and Medicine
OJO, S. A., Veterinary Anatomy
UMOH, J. U., Veterinary Public Health and Preventive Medicine
ZARIA, L. T., Veterinary Pathology and Microbiology

Centres:

ADAMU, A. M., National Animal Production Research Institute
ADEGBEHIN, J. D., National Agricultural Research and Liaison Services
ALIYU, J. S., Institute of Education
BAIKIE, A., Institute of Education
EDUVIE, L. V., National Animal Production Research Institute
GEFU, J. O., National Animal Production Research Institute
OTCHERE, E. O., National Animal Production Research Institute

ATTACHED INSTITUTES

Institute of Administration: PMB 1013, Zaria; f. 1954 and attached to the University in 1962; Dir Prof. K. CHUKKOL.

Institute for Agricultural Research: see under Research Institutes; Dir Dr S. G. ADO.

Institute of Education: Main Campus, Samaru, Zaria; f. 1965; Dir Dr A. NKOM.

Institute of Health: Shika-Zaria; Dir I. ABDU-AGUYE.

Veterinary Teaching Hospital: Dir Dr P. AUDU.

OTHER ATTACHED UNITS

Arewa House (Research Centre): Dir Dr HAMEED BOBBOI.

Biotechnology Centre: Dir Prof. AHMAD A. AHMAD.

Centre for Automotive Design and Development: Exec. Dir (vacant).

Centre for Energy Research and Training: Dir Dr M. I. UMAR.

Centre for Islamic Studies: PMB 1013, Zaria; Dir Dr I. N. SADA.

Division of Agricultural Colleges: PMB 1044, Zaria; f. 1971; incorporates schools of agriculture in Kaduna, Kabba and Samaru; Provost Dr S. DADARI.

Institute for Development Research: Dir M. MODIBBO.

Iya Abubakar Computer Centre: Dir Dr B. K. JAH.

National Agricultural Extension and Liaison Services: Dir Dr U. MOHAMMED.

National Animal Production Research Institute: see under Research Institutes; Dir Prof. A. M. ADAMU.

School of Basic and Remedial Studies: Dandume Rd, Funtua; Dir (vacant).

University Health Services: Dir Dr S. K. MUSA.

BAYERO UNIVERSITY

PMB 3011, Kano

Telephone: (64) 666023

Fax: (64) 665904

E-mail: registrar@buk.edu.ng

Founded 1977

Federal control

Language of instruction: English

Academic year: October to July (2 semesters)

Chancellor: HRH OBA SIJUWADE OKUNADE OLUBUSE II (Ooni of Ife)

Chairman of Council (vacant)

Vice-Chancellor: Prof. DANJUMA ABUBAKAR MAIWADA (acting)

Deputy Vice-Chancellor (Academic) (vacant)

Deputy Vice-Chancellor (Administration): Dr ALI UMAR DIKKO

Registrar: FARUK MUHAMMAD YANGANAU

Librarian: MISBAHU NA'IYA KATSINA

Library of 170,000 vols, 2,200 periodicals

Number of teachers: 478

Number of students: 27,939

Publications: *Bayero University Quarterly News*, *University Public Lectures* (annually)

DEANS

Faculty of Agriculture: Dr ABDU A. MANGA
Faculty of Arts and Islamic Studies: Dr ABUBAKAR A. RASHEED
Faculty of Education: MUSA A. AUYO
Faculty of Law: Dr NASIRUDEEN USMAN
Faculty of Medicine: Dr AMINU T. ABDULLAHI
Faculty of Science: ABDU A. AUDU
Faculty of Social and Management Sciences: Dr KABIR DANDAGO
Faculty of Technology: MUSTAPHA M. BICHI (acting)
Postgraduate School: Prof. MOHAMMED AHMED RUFAI
General Studies Unit: Prof. MUTAPHA C. DUTSE (Dir)

PROFESSORS

ABBA, I. A., History
ABDULKADIR, D., Centre for the Study of Nigerian Languages
ABDULKADIR, M. S., History
ABDULLAHI, M., Sociology
ABUBAKAR, M. A., Arabic
ABUBAKAR, M. M.
ADAMU, U. A., Education
AHMED, K., Geography
AJIBERO, M., Library Science
AYODELE, J. T., Chemistry
AZARE, G. D., Education

BICHI, A. Y., Centre for the Study of Nigerian Languages
BICHI, M. Y., Education
DAMBATTA, B. B., Chemistry
DANGAMBO, A., Nigerian Languages
DISO, S. I., Mechanical Engineering
DUZE, M. C., Sociology
EGBON, M., Mass Communication
ESSIET, E. U., Geography
FAGBEMI, A. O., Education
FALOLA, J. A., Geography
FATOPE, M. O., Physics
GUSAU, S. M., Nigerian Languages
HASHIM, I., Political Science
IBRAHIM, M., Paediatrics
JEGA, A. M., Political Science
JIBRIL, M. M., English Language
JOWITT, D. R., English and European Languages
KATANDE, J., Electrical Engineering
MAIWAQDA, D. A., Education
MUHAMMAD, A. R., History
OCHOGWU, M., Library Science
OLOFIN, E. A., Geography
PEDRO, I. A., Economics
RUJBANI, S. M., Mathematics
SALIHI, A., Mechanical Engineering
SALIM, B. A., Nigerian Languages
SANI, M. A. Z., Nigerian Languages
SHEA, P. J., History
SULEIMAN, M. D., History
TABI'U, M., Islamic Law
UMAR, I. H., Physics
YADUDU, A. H., Law
YAHAYA, D., History
ZAHRADEEN, M. S., Islamic Studies
ZAHRADEEN, U., Management Science

ATTACHED CENTRES

Centre for Democratic Research and Training: Dir Prof. ATTAHIRU M. JEGA.

Centre for the Study of the Nigerian Languages: Dir Dr KARAYE MAIKUDU.

General Studies Unit: Dir Prof. MUSTAPHA C. DUZE.

UNIVERSITY OF BENIN

Ugbowo-Lagos Rd, Ugbowo, PMB 1154, Benin City

Telephone: (52) 600443
Fax: (52) 241156
E-mail: registra@uniben.edu.ng
Internet: www.uniben.edu

Founded 1970
Federal control
Language of instruction: English
Academic year: October to June

Chancellor: Emir of Katsina, HRH Alhaji MUHAMMADU KABIR USMAN
Pro-Chancellor: Prof. M SANNI ZAHRADEEN
Vice-Chancellor: Prof. E. A. C. NWANZE
Deputy Vice-Chancellor (Academic): Prof. AUGUSTINE O. OKHAMAFE
Deputy Vice-Chancellor (Administrative): Prof. BENSON E. BAFOR
Registrar: HENRY O. BAZUAYE
Librarian: S. A. OGUNROMBI (acting)

Library of 265,144 vols
Number of teachers: 848
Number of students: 22,958

Publications: *Benin Journal of Educational Studies, Faculty of Arts Journal* (quarterly), *Faculty of Education Journals* (2 a year), *Journal of the Humanities, Physical Health Education and Recreational Journal, University of Benin Law Journal* (annually)

DEANS

Faculty of Agriculture: Prof. JOHN O. IGENE
Faculty of Arts: Prof. AIGBONA I. IGBAFE
Faculty of Dentistry: Dr MICHAEL A. OJO
Faculty of Education: Prof. DAVID E. AWANBOR
Faculty of Engineering: Prof. THOMAS O. K. AUDU
Faculty of Law: PATRCIK E. OSHIO
Faculty of Medicine: Prof. FRIDAY E. OKONOFUA
Faculty of Pharmacy: Prof. AUGUSTINE O. OKHAMAFE
Faculty of Science: Prof. JOHN A. OKHUOYA
Faculty of Social Sciences: Prof. AMOROSU B. AGBADUDU
School of Postgraduate Studies: Prof. LOUIS I. OJOGWU

PROFESSORS

ABIODUN, P. O., Child Health
ADEMOROTI, C. M. A., Chemistry
AFE, J. O., Educational Psychology and Curriculum Studies
AGBADUDU, A. B., Business Administration
AGBAKWURU, E. O. P., Pharmaceutical Chemistry
AGHENTA, J. A., Educational Administration and Foundations
AHONKHAI, S. I., Chemistry
AJISAFE, M. O., Physical and Health Education
AKERELE, A., Business Administration
ALAKIJA, W., Community Health
ANAO, A. R., Accounting
ASALOR, J. O., Mechanical Engineering
AUDU, T. O. K., Chemical Engineering
AWANBOR, D., Educational Psychology and Curriculum Studies
AWARITEFE, A. A., Mental Health
AYANRU, D. K. G., Microbiology
AYANRU, J. O., Ophthalmology
BADMUS, G. A., Educational Psychology and Curriculum Studies
BAFOR, B. E., Geology
EBEIGBE, A. B., Physiology
EBEWELE, R. O., Chemical Engineering
ECHENIM, K., Modern Languages
EGHAFONA, N. O., Microbiology
EGUDU, R. N., English and Literature
EHIAMETALOR, E. T., Educational Administration and Foundations
EKUNDAYO, J. A., Microbiology
GRILLO, B. O., Anatomy
HUGBO, P. G., Pharmaceutical Microbiology
IGBAFE, A. I., History
IGENE, J. O., Animal Science
IKEDIUGWU, F. E. O., Microbiology
IKENEBOMEH, M. J., Microbiology
IKHATUA, J. U., Animal Science
ILOHA, M. A., Economics and Statistics
IMEOKPARIA, G. E., Geology
IMOGIE, A. I., Educational Psychology and Curriculum Studies
IREMIREN, G. O., Crop Science
IWU, G. O., Chemistry
KUALE, P. A., Civil Engineering
NDIOKWERE, C. L., Chemistry
NWAGWU, N. A., Educational Administration and Foundations
NWANZE, E. C., Biochemistry
NWOKOYE, D. N., Civil Engineering
OBADAN, M. I., Economics and Statistics
OBASEIKI-EBOR, E. E., Pharmaceutical Microbiology
OBASOHAN, A. O., Medicine
OBIANWU, H. O., Pharmacology and Toxicology
OBIKA, L. F., Physiology
OBUEKWE, C. O., Microbiology
ODERINMI, A., Educational Psychology and Curriculum Studies
ODIME, J. O., Surgery
OFOEGBU, R. O., Surgery
OFUANI, O. A., English and Literature
OGBEIDE, N. O., Chemistry
OGBEIDE, O., Community Health
OGBIMI, A. O., General Studies
OGONOR, J. I., Pharmaceutical Chemistry
OGUDE, S. E., English and Literature

OHWOVORIOLE, E. N., Mechanical Engineering
OJOGWU, L. I., Medicine
OKAFOR, F. C., Geography and Regional Planning
OKEH, P. I., Modern Languages
OKEKE, E. O., Mathematics
OKHAMAFE, A. O., Pharmaceutics and Pharmaceutical Technology
OKHUOYA, J. A., Botany
OKIEIMEN, F. E., Chemistry
OKOH, S. E. N., Economics and Statistics
OKOJIE, C. E., Economics and Statistics
OKOLO, A. A., Child Health
OKOLOKO, G., Botany
OKONOFUA, F. E., Obstetrics and Gynaecology
OKOR, R. S., Pharmaceutics and Pharmaceutical Technology
OLA, R. F., Physics
OLOMU, J. M., Animal Science
OMIUNU, F. G. I., Geography and Regional Planning
OMU, F. I. A., History
OMUTA, G. E. D., Geography and Regional Planning
ONOKERHORAYE, A. G., Geography and Regional Planning
OPUTE, F. I., Botany
OROBATOR, S. E., Physics
ORONSAYE, A. U., Obstetrics and Gynaecology
OSAGIE, A. U., Biochemistry
OSAZE, R. E., Business Administration
OSHODIN, O. G., Physical and Health Education
OWIE, I., Physical and Health Education
OYAIDE, W. J., Agricultural Economics and Extension Services
SADA, P. O., Geography and Regional Planning
SALAMI, L. A., Mechanical Engineering
SANNI, B. S., Chemistry
UCHE, C., Sociology and Anthropology
UFOMATA, D., Restorative Dentistry
URAIH, N., Microbiology
WEMAMBU, S. N. C., Medical Microbiology

ATTACHED INSTITUTES

Centre for Adult Education and Extra-Mural Studies: Head Dr S. ONYEMUWA (acting).

Centre for Educational Technology: Dir Dr S. E. ADUWA-OGIEGBAEN (acting).

Institute of Child Health: centre for health research and training; Dir Assoc. Prof. O. OVIAWE (acting).

Institute of Education: runs postgraduate diploma course and Associateship Certificate; Dir Dr A. O. ORUBU.

Institute of Public Administration and Extension Services: runs non-degree and postgraduate courses; Dir Dr S. U. AKPOVI (acting).

UNIVERSITY OF CALABAR

PMB 1115, Calabar, Cross River State

Telephone: (87) 232790
Fax: (87) 231766
E-mail: webadmin@unicaledu.org
Internet: www.unicaledu.org

Founded 1975; previously a campus of the University of Nigeria
Federal control
Language of instruction: English
Academic year: October to July

Chancellor: HRH IGWE KINGSLEY CHIME (Eze of Abia)
Vice-Chancellor: Prof. IVARA EJEMOT ESU
Deputy Vice-Chancellor (Academic): Prof. A. I. ESSIEN
Deputy Vice-Chancellor (Administration): Prof. JOHN O. OFEM
Registrar: E. E. EFFIOM
Librarian: Dr OLU OLAT LAWAL

Number of teachers: 707
Number of students: 22,678 full-time

DEANS

Faculty of Agriculture: Prof. A. I. ESSIEN
Faculty of Arts: Prof. CHRIS NWAMUO
Faculty of Basic Medical Sciences: Prof. I. B. UMOH
Faculty of Clinical Sciences: Dr C. E. ANTIA-OBONG (acting)
Faculty of Education: Prof. S. C. UCHE (acting)
Faculty of Laboratory and Allied Health Sciences: Prof. A. E. UDOH (acting)
Faculty of Law: N. O. ITA (acting)
Faculty of Science: Prof. JOHN O. OFFEM
Faculty of Social Sciences: Prof. JOHN E. NDEBBIO
College of Medical Sciences: Prof. SPENCER EFEM
Graduate School: Prof. EBONG W. MBIPOM

PROFESSORS

Faculty of Agriculture:

AMALU, U. C., Soil Science
ASUQUO, B. O., Animal Science
ESSIEN, A. I., Animal Science
ESU, I., Soil Science

Faculty of Arts:

ABASIATTAI, M. B., History
EKO, E. O., English and Literary Studies
ERIM, E. O, History
ESSIEN, O. E. A., Languages and Linguistics
IKONNE, C. U. E., English and Literary Studies
IWE, N. S. S., Religious Studies and Philosophy
JOHN, E. E., Languages and Linguistics
NOAH, M. E., History
NWAMUO, C. I., Theatre Arts
ORISAWAYI, D., English and Literary Studies
UKA, K., Theatre Arts
UYA, O. E., History

Faculty of Education:

ABODERIN, A. O., Curriculum and Teaching
AMADI, L. E., Curriculum and Teaching
DENGA, D. I., Educational Foundations and Administration
ENUKOHA, O. I.
ESU, A. E.
IKPAYA, B. O.
NWACHUKWU, D. N., Guidance and Counselling
OMOJUWA, J. O.
UCHE, S. C.

College of Medical Sciences:

AKPAN, J. O., Pharmacology
ANDY, J. J., Medicine
ATTAH, E. B., Pathology
BASSEY, O. O., Surgery
BOLARIN, D. M., Chemical Pathology
BRAIDE, V. B., Pharmacology
EFEM, S., Surgery
EJEZIE, G. C., Medical Microbiology and Parasitology
EKA, O. U., Biochemistry
ESSIEN, E. U., Biochemistry
ONUBA, O. O., Surgery
OSIM, E. E., Physiology
OTU, A. A., Surgery
UMOH, I. B., Biochemistry
UTSALO, S. J., Medical Microbiology, Parasitology

Faculty of Science:

AKPAN, E. B., Geology
BRAIDE, E. I., Parasitology
EKPA, O. D., Chemistry
EKPE, U. J., Chemistry
EKWERE, S. J., Geology
EKWUEME, B. N., Geology
IBOK, U. J., Chemistry

LIPCSY, Z.
MBIPOM, E. W., Physics
MENKITI, A. I., Physics
OFFEM, J. O., Chemistry
OKWUEZE, E. E., Physics
PETERS, S. W., Geology
USUA, E. J., Biological Sciences
UWAH, E. J., Physics

Faculty of Social Sciences:

BASSEY, C. O., Political Science
EBONG, M. O., Geography, Regional Planning
ETUK, E. J., Management Studies
NDEBBIO, J. E. U., Economics
OBOT, J. U., Geography, Regional Planning
OTTONG, J. G., Sociology
SULE, R. A. O., Geography, Regional Planning

Institute of Oceanography:

ANTAI, E. E.
HOLZLONER, S.
OBIEKEZIE, A. I.

Institute of Public Policy and Administration:

UYA, O. E.

FEDERAL UNIVERSITY OF TECHNOLOGY, AKURE

PMB 704, Akure, Ondo State

Telephone: (34) 243744
Fax: (34) 230450
Internet: futa-edu.ng

Founded 1981
State control
Language of instruction: English
Academic year: October to September

Chancellor: Emir of Lafia ISA MUSTAPHA AGWAI II
Vice-Chancellor: Prof. PETER O. ADENIYI
Deputy Vice-Chancellor (Academic): Prof. O. C. ADEMOSUN
Deputy Vice-Chancellor (Development): Prof. A. M. BALOGUN
Registrar: Dr E. F. OYEBADE
Librarian: O. A. OKE (acting)

Number of teachers: 442
Number of students: 13,432

Publications: *Journal of Applied Tropical Agriculture* (4 a year), *Journal of Urban and Environmental Research* (every 2 years), *Nigerian Journal of Pure and Applied Physics* (4 a year)

DEANS

School of Agriculture and Agricultural Technology: Prof. J. A. FUWAPE
School of Engineering and Engineering Technology: Prof. C. O. ADEGOKE
School of Environmental Technology: Prof. D. O. OLANREWAJU
School of Mines and Earth Sciences: Prof. J. S. OJO
School of Sciences: Prof. K. O. IPINMOROTI
School of Postgraduate Studies: Prof. V. A. ALETOR

ATTACHED INSTITUTES

Centre for Continuing Education: Dir Prof. A. A. OSHODI.

Centre for Research and Development: Dir Prof. I. B. ODEYEMI.

Computer Centre: Dir J. O. OMOFAYE (acting).

General Studies Unit: Dir Dr R. O. ABIOLA (acting).

F. U. T. A. Business Development: Man. Dir ELDER FESSY OLABODE (acting).

University Teaching and Research Farm: Man. J. A. ADEDAYO (acting).

FEDERAL UNIVERSITY OF TECHNOLOGY, MINNA

PMB 65, Minna, Niger State

Telephone: (66) 222422
Fax: (66) 222422
E-mail: futmx@skannet.com
Internet: www.futminna.net

Founded 1983
Federal control
Language of instruction: English
Academic year: October to September (2 semesters)

Chancellor: The Olu of Warri, HRH OGIAME ATUWASE II
Pro-Chancellor: HRH Dr MUHAMMAD ZAYYANU ABDULLAHI
Vice-Chancellor: Prof. HAMMAN TUKUR SA'AD
Deputy Vice-Chancellor: Dr T. Z. ADAMA
Dean of Students: Dr A. O. OSUNDE
Registrar: MALLAM M. D. USMAN
Librarian: M. A. BELLO

Number of teachers: 265
Number of students: 13,623

Publications: *Journal of Agricultural Technology* (2 a year), *Journal of Science, Technology and Mathematics Education* (2 a year), *Nigeria Journal of Technological Research* (2 a year), *Proceedings of the National Engineering Conference* (annually)

DEANS

School of Agriculture and Agricultural Technology: Prof. E. A. SALAKO
School of Engineering and Engineering Technology: Prof. F. O. AKINBODE
School of Environmental Technology: Prof. O. SOLANKE
School of Science and Science Education: Prof. H. O. AKANYA
Postgraduate School: Prof. J. A. ABALAKA

FEDERAL UNIVERSITY OF TECHNOLOGY, OWERRI

PMB 1526, Owerri, Imo State

Telephone: (83) 233546
E-mail: registrar@futo.edu.ng

Founded 1980
Federal control
Language of instruction: English
Academic year: October to July

Chancellor: HRH Dr SHEKARAU ANGYU MASSA-IBI
Pro-Chancellor: ALHAJI UMARU F. ABDULLAHI
Vice-Chancellor: Prof. B. A. NWACHUKWU (acting)
Deputy Vice-Chancellor (Academic) (vacant)
Deputy Vice-Chancellor (Administration) (vacant)
Registrar: PRINCE J. A. FALEYE (acting)
Bursar: R.-U. AKUJOBI
Librarian: J. E. NWOGU

Library of 40,000 vols
Number of teachers: 550
Number of students: 22,929

Publications: *Annual Review, Centre for Industrial Studies, Erosion News* (4 a year), *Newsletter* (monthly), *University Annual Report*

DEANS

School of Agriculture and Agricultural Technology: Prof E. T. ESHETT
School of Engineering and Engineering Technology: Prof. O. O. ONYEMAOBI
School of Management Technology: Rev. Fr Prof. L. I. ASIEGBU
School of Science: Dr G. E. EHEDURU (acting)
Postgraduate School: Prof. C. I. ANUNUSO

PROFESSORS

ACHI, P. B. U., Mechanical Engineering

ANANABA, S. E., Geophysics
ANUNUSO, C. I., Analytical Chemistry
ANYANWU, B. N., Industrial Microbiology
ASIABAKA, C. C., Agricultural Economics
ASIEGBU, REV. FR. L. C., Ethical Philosophy
BANIGO, E. O. I., Food Processing Technology
DURU, O. J., Agricultural Engineering
EJIKE, U. B. C. O., Applied Mathematics
EJIMANYA, J. I., Communications Engineering
ENYIEGBULAM, E. M., Polymer Science and Technology
ESHETT, E. T., Pedology
IJIOMA, C. I., Agricultural Engineering
ILOEJE, M. U., Animal Production
IWUAGWU, C., Geology
IWUALA, M. E. O., Biology
NDUKA, A., Theoretical Physics and Applied Mathematics
NGOCHINDO, R. I., Chemistry
NJOKU, J. E., Agricultural Economics
NTAMERE, C. C., Economics
NWACHUKWU, B. A., Civil Engineering
NWACHUKWU, M. A., Electrical and Electronics Engineering
NWANKWO, G. I., Geology
NWUFO, M. I., Crop Production
OBAH, B., Petroleum Engineering
OBIEFUNA, J. C., Crop Production
OFOR, O., Chemistry
OGBOBE, O., Polymer and Textile Engineering
OGUOMA, O. N., Mechanical Engineering
OGWUDE, I. C., Transport Management Technology
OKEREKE, C. D., Agricultural Engineering
OKORAFOR, O. E., Metallurgical Engineering
OKPALA, K. O., Chemical Engineering
ONUCHUKWU, A. I., Chemistry
ONWUAGBA, B. N., Physics
ONWUATU, J. U., Mathematics
ONYEMAOBI, O. O., Materials and Metallurgical Engineering
ONYEAGORO, L. A., Mechanical Engineering
ONYEZE, G. O. C., Industrial Microbiology
OSONDU, K. E., Pure Mathematics
OSUJI, G. E., Soil Physics
OZOH, P. T. E., Biological Sciences
UDEDIBIE, A. B. I., Animal Production
UKOHA, A. I., Biochemistry
UKPONNWAN, J. O., Polymer and Textile Technology
UZUEGBU, J. O., Food Microbiology

FEDERAL UNIVERSITY OF TECHNOLOGY, YOLA

PMB 2076, Yola, Adamawa State
Telephone: (75) 624416
Fax: (75) 624416
E-mail: vcfuty@yahoo.com
Internet: www.futy.edu.ng
Founded 1981, present status 1988
Federal control
Language of instruction: English
Academic year: October to September
Chancellor: H. H. Oba GABRIEL ADEKUNLE AROMOLARAN II
Vice-Chancellor: Prof. ABDULLAHI YUSUFU RIBADU
Registrar: Alh. AHMED USMAN W/CHEKKE
Librarian: Prof. B. S. H. WOMBOH
Library of 29,000 vols
Number of teachers: 345
Number of students: 9,701
Publication: *Technology and Development* (annually)

DEANS AND HEADS OF DEPARTMENT

School of Agriculture and Agricultural Technology: Prof. A. KADAMS (Dean)
School of Engineering and Engineering Technology: Prof. P. B. OMAJI (Dean)

School of Environmental Sciences: Dr F. ILLESANMI (Dean)
School of Management and Information Technology: Prof. S. O. ANYANWU (Dean)
School of Pure and Applied Sciences: Dr A. OKOLO (Dean)
School of Technology and Science Education: Dr L. C. EZUGU (Dean)
School of Post-Graduate Studies: Prof. G. FAKUADE (Dean)
Economics: A. BAWA BELLO (Head)
Information Technology: G. MATUDI IKA (Head)
Management: H. ISA MOHAMMED (Head)

HEADS OF DEPARTMENTS

School of Agriculture and Agricultural Technology (tel. (75) 627314; fax (75) 624416; e-mail deansaat@futy.edu.ng):

Agricultural Economics: Mal. S. J. MSHELIA
Animal Science: Dr M. ARDO
Crop Production: Dr D. T. GUNGULA
Food Science: Mal. M. A. USMAN
Forestry and Wildlife: I. O. TELLA
Soil Science: Prof. L. SINGH

School of Engineering and Engineering Technology (tel. (75) 627515; fax (75) 624416):

Agricultural Engineering: Engr. B. ALIYU
Chemical Engineering: Prof. P. B. ONAJI
Civil Engineering: Engr. V. E. ANAMETAN-FIOK
Electrical Engineering: Engr. D. K. RODGERS
Mechanical Engineering: Engr. E. O. ONCHE

School of Environmental Sciences (tel. (75) 627313; fax (75) 624416; e-mail aromofelix@yahoo.com):

Architecture: V. B. RAY
Buildings: N. A. KEFTIN
Geography: Dr M. GALTIMA
Industrial Design: J. EWULE
Surveying: A. A. MUSA
Urban and Regional Planning: Dr F. A. ILOSANMI

School of Pure and Applied Sciences (tel. (75) 627283; fax (75) 624416; e-mail okoloab@yahoo.com):

Biochemistry: Prof. M. S. NADRO
Biological Sciences: Dr I. B. CHIMBEKUJWO
Chemistry: Dr D. KUBMARAWA
Geology: I. A. KWADA
Mathematics and Computer Science: M. O. EGWURUBE
Microbiology: Dr N. DE
Physics: Dr U. USMAN
Statistics and Operations Research: Dr A. OKOLO

School of Technology and Science Education (tel. (75) 627258; fax (75) 624416; e-mail deanstst@futy.edu.ng):

Science Education: Dr J. M. NDAGANA
Technology Education: Dr K. H. BULAMA

UNIVERSITY OF IBADAN

Ibadan
Telephone: (2) 8101100
E-mail: dvcadmin@mail.ui.edu.ng
Internet: www.ui.edu.ng
Founded 1948 as University College, Ibadan, a constituent College of the University of London, UK; present name and status 1962
Federal control
Language of instruction: English
Academic year: September to July
Chancellor: HH ORCHIVIRIGH ALFRED AKAWE, TORKULA TOR TIV IV
Vice-Chancellor: IBIDAPO OBE
Deputy Vice-Chancellor: Prof. JAMES AKINWUMI

Registrar: M. LADIPO
Librarian: A. O. SCOTT-EMUAKPOR
Library: see Libraries and Archives
Number of teachers: 1,077
Number of students: 20,434
Publications: *Annual Report, Calendar, Gazette, Official Bulletin, Research Bulletin of the Centre for Arabic Documentation* (2 a year)

DEANS

Faculty of Agriculture and Forestry: T. IKOTUN
Faculty of Arts: A. ABENIRAN
Faculty of Basic Medical Sciences: ABEYOMBO BOLARINWA
Faculty of Dentistry: J. O. LAWOYIN
Faculty of Education: OLUREMI AYOBELE-BAMSAIYE
Faculty of Law: ABEFOLAKE OKEDIRAN
Faculty of Pharmacy: O. A. ITIOLA
Faculty of Science: L. A. HUSSAIN
Faculty of Social Sciences: A. SOYIBO
Faculty of Technology: B. ALABI
Faculty of Veterinary Medicine: B. O. OKE

PROFESSORS

Faculty of Agriculture and Forestry:

ADEDIPE, N. O., Crop Protection and Environmental Biology
ADEGBOYE, R. O., Agricultural Economics
ADEGEYE, A. J., Agricultural Economics
ADEKANYE, T. O., Agricultural Economics
ADELEYE, I. O. A., Animal Science
ADENEYE, J. A., Animal Science
ADESIYAN, S. O., Crop Protection and Environmental Biology
ADEYOJU, S. K., Forest Resources Management
AGBOOLA, A. A., Agronomy
AJAYI, S. S., Wildlife and Fisheries Management
AKEN'OVA, M. E., Agronomy
AKINSOYINU, A. O., Animal Science
AKINWUMI, J. A., Agricultural Economics
BABALOLA, O., Agronomy
BABATUNDE, G. M., Animal Science
EGBUNIKE, G. N., Animal Science
EGUNJOBI, J. K., Agricultural Biology
EKPERE, J. A., Agricultural Extension Services
ENABOR, E. E., Forest Resources Management
FAGBAMI, A. A., Agronomy
FALUSI, A. O., Agricultural Economics
FASEHUN, F. F., Forest Resources Management
IDACHABA, F. S., Agricultural Economics
IKOTUN, B., Agricultural Biology
IVBIJARO, M. F., Crop Protection and Environmental Biology
LONGE, G. O., Animal Science
LUCAS, E. O., Agronomy
NGERE, L. O., Animal Science
NWOKO, S. G., Agricultural Economics
OBIGBESAN, G. O., Agronomy
ODEBIYI, J. A., Agricultural Biology
ODU, C. T. I., Agronomy
OGUNMODEDE, B. K., Animal Science
OKALI, D. U. U., Forestry
OKUBANJO, A. O., Animal Science
OLAYEMI, J. K., Agricultural Economics
OLOGHOBO, A. D., Animal Science
OLUYEMI, J. A., Animal Science
OMUETI, J. A. I., Agronomy
OYENUGA, V. A., Animal Science
TEWE, O. O., Animal Science
WILLIAMS, C. E., Agricultural Extension Services

Faculty of Arts:

ABOGUNRIN, S. O. K., Religious Studies
ADE-AJAYI, J. F., History
ADELUGBA, D., Theatre Arts

ADENIRAN, A., Linguistics and African Languages
ADEWOYE, O., History
ASEIN, S. O., English
BAMGBOSE, T. A., Linguistics and Nigerian Languages
BANJO, L. A., English
ELUGBE, B. O., Linguistics and African Languages
ILEVBARE, J. A., Classics
IZEVBAYE, D. S., English
KENNY, J., Religious Studies
MALIK, S. H. A., Arabic and Islamic Studies
MUNOZ, L. J., Modern European Languages
ODEJIDE, A. I., Communication and Language Arts
ODUNUGA, O. O., Modern European Languages
OLATUNJI, O. O., Linguistics and Nigerian Languages
OMAMOR, A. P., Linguistics and African Languages
OSOFISAN, B. A., Theatre Arts
OSUNDARE, N., English
OWOLABI, D. K. O., Linguistics and African Languages
SOBOLO, R. S., Philosophy
TAMUNO, T. N., African Studies

Faculty of Basic Medical Sciences:
AGBEDANA, E. O., Chemical Pathology
AJAYI, O. A., Human Nutrition
AKINYELE, I. O., Human Nutrition
ATINMO, T., Human Nutrition
BOLABINWA, A. F., Physiology
DAVID-WEST, T. S., Virology
ELEGBE, R. A., Physiology
EMEROLE, G. O., Biochemistry
FATUNSO, M., Biochemistry
MADUAGWU, C. N., Biochemistry
ODUOLA, A. M. J., Pharmacology and Therapeutics
OLORUNSOGO, O. O., Biochemistry
OKPAKO, D. T., Pharmacology and Therapeutics
OSIFO, B. O. A., Chemical Pathology
OSOTIMEHIN, B. O., Chemical Pathology
OYEBOLA, D. D. O., Physiology
SALIMONU, S. L., Chemical Pathology
SHOKUNBI, M. T., Anatomy
TAYLOR, G. O. L., Chemical Pathology
UWAIFO, A. O., Biochemistry

Faculty of Education:
ADEDEJI, J. A., Physical and Health Education
AIYEPEKU, W. O., Library Studies
AJALA, J. A., Physical and Health Education
AKINBOYE, J. O., Guidance and Counselling
ANYANWU, C. N., Adult Education
AYODELE, S. O., Institute of Education
BAJAH, S. T., Education
DADA, A., Teacher Education
FALAYAJO, A., Institute of Education
FAYOSE, O. P., Library and Archival Studies
GESINDI, S. A., Guidance and Counselling
IGBANUGO, V. C., Physical and Health Education
LONGE, R. S., Educational Management
NZOTTA, B. C., Library, Archival and Information Studies
OBEMEATA, J. O., Institute of Education
OKEDARA, C. A., Teacher Education
OKEDARA, J. T., Adult Education
OMOLEWA, M. A., Adult Education
ONIBOKUN, Y. M., Institute of Education
ONWU, G. O. M., Teacher Education
UBAHAKWE, E. E., Teacher Education
UDOH, C. O., Physical and Health Education
YOLOYE, E. A., Institute of Education

Faculty of Clinical Sciences and Dentistry:
ADEBO, O. A., Surgery

ADEKUNLE, O. O., Surgery
ADENIYI, J. D., Preventive and Social Medicine
ADEUJA, A. O. G., Medicine
AJAGBE, H. A., Oral and Maxillofacial Surgery
AJAYI, O. O., Surgery
AJAO, O. G., Surgery
AKINKUGBE, F. M., Child Health
AKINKUGBE, O. O., Medicine
ANTIA, A. U., Paediatrics
BAMGBOYE, E. A., Preventive and Social Medicine
COLE, T. O., Medicine
FALASE, A. O., Medicine
FAMILUSI, J. B., Paediatrics
IJADUOLA, G. T. A., Otorhinolaryngology
KALE, O. O., Preventive and Social Medicine
LAGUNDOYE, S. B., Radiology
LAWANI, J., Surgery
NOTTIDGE, V. A., Preventive and Social Medicine
ODEJIDE, A. O., Psychiatry
OHAERI, J. U., Psychiatry
OJENGBEDE, A. O., Obstetrics and Gynaecology
OLATAWURA, M. O., Psychiatry
OLUBUYIDE, I. O., Medicine
ONADEKO, B. O., Medicine
OSUNTOKUN, O., Ophthalmology
OTOLORIN, E. O., Obstetrics and Gynaecology
OYEDIRAN, A. B. O. O., Preventive and Social Medicine
OYEMADE, A., Preventive and Social Medicine
SOLANKE, T. F., Surgery
SRIDHAR, M. K. C., Preventive and Social Medicine

Faculty of Law:
ANIFALAJE, J. O., Private and Business Law
OJO, J. D., Public and International Law
SHYLLON, F., Public and International Law

Faculty of Pharmacy:
JAIYEOBA, K. T., Pharmaceutical and Industrial Pharmacy
ODELOLA, H. A., Pharmaceutical Microbiology and Clinical Pharmacy
OLANIYI, A. A., Pharmaceutical Chemistry

Faculty of Science:
ADELEKE, B. B., Chemistry
ADESOGAN, E. K., Chemistry
ADESOMOJU, A. A., Chemistry
AJAYI, S. O., Chemistry
AKIN-OJO, A., Physics
AKINYELE, O., Mathematics
AWE, O., Physics
BABALOLA, I. A., Physics
BADEJOKO, A., Geology
EGUNYOMI, A., Botany
EKHAGUERE, G. O. S., Mathematics
EKUNDAYO, O., Chemistry
EKWEOZOR, L. M., Chemistry
ELUEZE, A. A., Geology
FAGADE, S. O., Zoology
FANIRAN, J. A., Chemistry
FASADI, I. O., Botany and Microbiology
GIWA, F. B. A., Physics
HUSSAIN, L. A., Physics
ILORI, S. A., Mathematics
IWEIBO, I., Chemistry
KOLAWOLE, G. A., Chemistry
KUKU, A. O., Mathematics
LONGE, O., Computer Science
MADUEMEZIA, A., Physics
NWAGWU, M., Zoology
ODERINDE, R. A., Chemistry
ODUNFA, A., Botany and Microbiology
OGUNMOLA, G. B., Chemistry
OJO, A., Physics
OKONJO, K. O., Chemistry
OKORIE, D. A., Chemistry
OKORIE, T. G., Zoology

OLADIRAN, E. O., Physics
ONI, C. E. A., Physics
OSIBANJO, O., Chemistry
OSO, B. A., Botany and Microbiology
OSONUBI, O., Botany and Microbiology
SOWUNMI, M. A., Archaeology
UKOLI, F. M. A., Zoology

Faculty of Social Sciences:
ABUMERE, S. I., Geography
ADEKANYE, J. A., Political Science
AJAYI, S. I., Economics
AREOLA, O. O., Geography
AYENI, M. O., Geography
AYOADE, J. A. A., Political Science
AYOADE, J. O., Geography
EGUNJOBI, T. O., Urban and Regional Planning
FANIRAN, A., Geography
FILANI, M. O., Geography
GBOYEGA, E. A., Political Science
IKPORUKPO, C. O., Geography
INANGA, E. L., Economics
KAYODE, M. O., Economics
MBANEFOH, G. F., Economics
OLOFIN, S. O., Economics
ONIMODE, B., Economics
OTITE, K. J. O., Sociology
OTUBANJO, D. A., Political Science
OYEJIDE, T. A., Economics
SOYIBO, A., Economics
SOYODE, A., Economics
UGWUEGBU, D. C. E., Psychology

Faculty of Technology:
AKINGBALA, J. O., Food Technology
ALABI, B., Mechanical Engineering
AWORH, O. C., Food Technology
BAMIRO, O. A., Mechanical Engineering
FAGBENLE, B. O., Mechanical Engineering
FALADE, G. K., Petroleum Engineering
IGBEKA, J. C., Agricultural Engineering
LUCAS, E. B., Agricultural Engineering
OFI, O., Mechanical Engineering
OLORUNDA, A. O., Food Technology

Faculty of Veterinary Medicine:
ADENE, D. F., Veterinary Medicine
ADETOSOYE, A. I., Veterinary Microbiology and Parasitology
AIRE, T. A., Veterinary Anatomy
AKINBOADE, A. O., Veterinary Microbiology and Parasitology
AKRAVIE, S. O., Veterinary Pathology
AKUSU, M. O., Veterinary Surgery and Reproduction
ALONGE, D. O., Veterinary Public Health and Preventive Medicine
ANOSA, V. O., Veterinary Pathology
AROWOLO, R. O. A., Veterinary Physiology and Pharmacology
AYANWALE, F. O., Veterinary Public Health and Preventive Medicine
ESURUOSO, G. O., Veterinary Public Health and Preventive Medicine
FAGBEMI, B. O., Veterinary Microbiology and Parasitology
JOSHUA, P. A., Veterinary Medicine
NOTTIDGE, H. O., Veterinary Medicine
OBI, T. U., Veterinary Medicine
ODUYE, O. O., Veterinary Medicine
OGUNRINADE, A. F., Veterinary Microbiology and Parasitology
OJO, M. O., Veterinary Microbiology and Parasitology
OLADOSU, L. A., Veterinary Medicine
OLOWOOKORUN, M. O., Veterinary Physiology and Pharmacology
OLUFEMI, B. E., Veterinary Medicine
OSUAGWUH, A. I. A., Veterinary Surgery and Reproduction
OTESILE, E. B., Veterinary Medicine

ATTACHED INSTITUTES
Africa Regional Centre for Information Science: Dir Prof. ENIKHAMENOR.

Institute of African Studies: Dir Prof. M. OMIBIYI-OBIDIKE.

Institute of Child Health: Dir Prof. F. M. AKINKUGBE.

Institute of Education: Dir Prof. S. T. BAJAH.

Postgraduate Institute for Medical Research and Training: Dir Prof. A. M. J. ODUOLA.

UNIVERSITY OF ILORIN

PMB 1515, Ilorin, Kwara State
Telephone: (31) 221691
Fax: (31) 221937
E-mail: registra@unilorin.edu.ng
Internet: www.unilorin.edu.ng
Founded 1975
Federal control
Language of instruction: English
Academic year: September to June
Chancellor: HRH AMBROSE ALLAGOA
Vice-Chancellor: Prof. SHAMSUDEEN ONYI-LOKWU ONCHE AMALI
Deputy Vice-Chancellor (Academic): Prof. ISHAQ OLANREWAJU OLOYEDE
Deputy Vice-Chancellor (Administration): Prof. LUKE DAYO EDUNGBOLA
Registrar: O. O. OYEYEMI
Librarian: Prof. M. I. AJIBERO
Library of 155,000 vols, 2,800 periodicals
Number of teachers: 644
Number of students: 18,488
Publications: *Annual Report, News Bulletin* (weekly), *University Calendar*

DEANS

Faculty of Agriculture: Prof. J. O. ATTEH
Faculty of Arts: Prof. R. D. ABUBAKRE
Faculty of Business and Social Sciences: Prof. I. O. TAIWO
Faculty of Education: Prof. E. A. OGUNSAKIN
Faculty of Engineering and Technology: Prof. O. A. ADETIFA
Faculty of Health Sciences: Prof. M. A. ARAOYE
Faculty of Law: Prof. Z. O. AJE
Faculty of Science: Prof. T. O. OPOOLA
Post-Graduate School: Prof. J. A. MORAKINYO

HEADS OF DEPARTMENTS

Faculty of Agriculture (tel. (31) 221945):
  Agricultural Economics and Farm Management: Dr. O. A. OMOTESHO
  Agricultural Extension and Rural Development: Prof. M. D. AWOLOLA
  Animal Production: Dr B. AWOSANYA
  Crop Production: Dr T. FAGBEMI
Faculty of Arts (tel. (31) 221701):
  History: Prof. R. O. LASISI
  Linguistics and Nigerian Languages: Prof. B. OGUNSINA
  Modern European Languages: Prof. E. E. ADEGBIJA
  Performing Arts: F. O. OMOJOLA
  Religions: Prof. R. A. AKANMIDU
Faculty of Business and Social Science (tel. (31) 221978):
  Accounting and Finance: A. A. OWOLABI
  Business Administration: Dr J. O. OLUJIDE
  Economics: I. O. TAIWO
  Geography: Prof. J. F. OLORUNFEMI
  Political Science: O. L. OVWASA
  Sociology and Social Administration: Prof. A. A. MORDI
Faculty of Science (tel. (31) 221839):
  Biochemistry: Prof. O. B. OLOYEDE
  Biological Sciences: Prof. F. A. OLADELE
  Chemistry: Dr G. O. ADEDIRAN
  Geology and Mineral Science: Prof. O. O. OGUNSANWO
  Mathematics: Prof. T. O. OPOOLA

Physics: Dr C. O. AKOSILE
Statistics: Prof. B. A. OYEJOLA
Faculty of Education (tel. (31) 221706):
  Curriculum Studies and Educational Technology: Dr I. O. ABIMBOLA
  Educational Foundations: Dr A. A. OGUNLADE
  Educational Management: Dr D. O. DUROSARO
  Guidance and Counselling: Dr A. A. ADEGOKE
  Physical and Health Education: Dr O. O. OBIYEMI
Faculty of Health Sciences (tel. (31) 221844):
  Anatomy: Prof. A. O. SOLADOYE
  Behavioural Sciences: Prof. M. L. ADELEKAN
  Chemical Pathology and Immunology: B. A. AIYEDUN
  Child Health: Dr A. OJUAWO
  Clinical Pharmacology: Prof. A. OLATUNDE
  Epidemiology and Community Health: Dr A. O. AWOYEMI
  Haematology: Prof. J. O. ADEWUYI
  Medicine: Dr P. O. OLUBOYU
  Microbiology and Parasitology: B. A. ONILE
  Obstetrics and Gynaecology: Dr M. ANATE
  Pathology and Haematology: Prof. A. S. ANJORIN
  Physiology and Biochemistry: Dr E. A. BALOGUN
  Radiology: Prof. D. A. NZEH
  Surgery: Prof. E. O. O. ODELOWO
Faculty of Engineering and Technology (tel. (31) 221951):
  Agriculture Engineering: Dr K. OJE
  Civil Engineering: Prof. B. F. SULE
  Electrical Engineering: T. S. IBIYEMI
  Mechanical Engineering: Dr J. A. OLORUNMAIYE
Faculty of Law (tel. (31) 226004):
  Business Law: S. A. BELLO
  International Law: A. A. OBA
  Islamic Law: Prof. A. ZUBAIR
  Jurisprudence and Private Law: R. J. L. IJAODOLA
  Public Law: Dr Z. O. AJE

ATTACHED INSTITUTES

Institute of Education: Dir Prof. S. A. JIMOH.

Sugar Research Institute: Dir Dr J. A. OLOFINTOYE.

UNIVERSITY OF JOS

PMB 2084, Jos, Plateau State
Telephone: (73) 610514
Fax: (73) 610514
Internet: www.uiowa.edu/intlinet/unijos
Founded 1975
Federal control
Language of instruction: English
Academic year: September to June (2 semesters)
Chancellor: HRH Oba Dr FESTUS IBIDAPO ADEDINSEWO ADESANOYE OSEMAWE OF ONDOLAND
Pro-Chancellor: Prof. MUSA ABDULLAHI
Vice-Chancellor: Prof. MONDAY MANGYWAT
Deputy Vice-Chancellor (Academic): Prof. A. O. MALU
Deputy Vice-Chancellor (Administration): Prof. J. O. A. ONYEKA
Registrar: Z. D. GALAM
Librarian: Dr A. OCHAI
Number of teachers: 745
Number of students: 14,378

DEANS AND DIRECTORS

Faculty of Arts: Prof. E. B. AJULO
Faculty of Education: Prof. I. J. IHENACHO

Faculty of Environmental Sciences: Prof. A. A. ADEPETU
Faculty of Law: Dr J. M. NASIR
Faculty of Medical Sciences: Prof. J. O. OGUNRANTI
Faculty of Natural Sciences: Prof. M. S. AUDU
Faculty of Pharmaceutical Sciences: Prof. F. OKWUASABA
Faculty of Social Sciences: Prof. S. G. TYODEN
School of Postgraduate Studies: Prof. G. A. UBOM
Institute of Education: Dr A. Y. MALLUM
Centre for Continuing Education: Dr E. A. ABAMA
Centre for Development Studies: Dr J. S. ILLAH

PROFESSORS

Faculty of Arts:
  AIRE, Y. O., Languages and Lingusitics
  AJE, A. O., Languages and Linguistics
  AJULO, E. B., English
  AMALI, S. O. O., Theatre Studies
  BASHIR, I. L., History
  CYRIL, I. O., Religious Studies
  JAMES, I., History
  JEMKUR, J. F., History
  MANGVWAT, M. Y., History
  YAHYA, M. T., Religious Studies

Faculty of Education:
  ABANG, T., Special Education
  ADEWOLE, M. A., Philosophy of Education
  AKINNADE, C. T. O., Science and Technical Education
  AKPAN, E. U. U., Science and Technology Education
  AWOTUNDE, P. O., Science Education
  IHENACHO, I. J., Special Education
  LASSA, P. N., Mathematics Education
  MALLUM, M. P., Guidance and Counselling
  OZOJI, E., Special Education
  UDOH, S. U., Social Science Education

Faculty of Environmental Sciences:
  ADEPETU, A. A., Geography and Planning
  KOLAWOLE, J. O., Building

Faculty of Law:
  ADUBA, J. N., Public and Law

Faculty of Medical Sciences:
  ADOGA, G. I., Biochemistry
  ANAKWE, G. E., Biochemistry
  IDOKO, J. A., Medicine
  IHEZUE, C. H., Surgery
  ISICHEI, H. U., Psychiatry
  MALU, A. O., Medicinal Radiology
  OKOYE, Z. S. C., Biochemistry
  UBOM, G. A., Enzymology and Molecular Biology

Faculty of Natural Sciences:
  AGINA, S. E., Botany
  AJAYI, J., Zoology
  AKUESHI, C. O., Plant Pathology
  AUDU, M. S., Mathematics
  DUHLINSKA, D. D., Protozoology, Insect Pathology
  EGILA, J. N., Chemistry
  EKPENYONG, K. I., Chemistry
  EKWENCHI, M. M., Chemistry
  HUSAINI, S. W. H., Plant Taxonomy and Cytogenetics
  IFENKWE, O. P., Botany
  LIVERPOOL, L. S. O., Mathematics
  NWUFO, B. T., Chemistry
  OGBONNA, C. I., Botany
  OGEZI, I. E., Geology and Mining
  OJOJEKWU, P. C., Zoology
  ONUMANYI, P., Mathematics
  ONWULIRI, C. O. E., Zoology
  ONYEKA, J. O. A., Zoology
  POPOV, T. V., Zoology
  SHAMBE, T. S., Chemistry
  UFODIKE, E. B. C., Zoology
  UTAH, E. U., Physics

Faculty of Pharmaceutical Sciences:
   IRANLOYE, T. A., Pharmacology and Pharmaceutical Technology
   OKWUASABA, F., Pharmacology and Clinical Pharmacy
   SOKOMBA, E. N., Pharmacology
Faculty of Social Sciences:
   ALLI, W. O., International Relations
   ALUBO, S. O., Sociology
   ETANNIBI, E. O., Sociology
   IBANGA, U. A., Sociology
   NWEZE, A., Psychology
   TYODEN, G. S., Political Economy
Centre for Development Studies:
   OJOWU, O., Economics

UNIVERSITY OF LAGOS

Lagos
Telephone: (1) 4932660
Fax: (1) 4932667
E-mail: vc@unilag.edu
Internet: www.unilag.edu

Founded 1962
Federal control
Language of instruction: English
Academic year: October to June

Chancellor: HRH Alhaji Dr ALIYU O. OBAJE (the Attah Igala)
Pro-Chancellor: Chief AFE BABALOLA
Vice-Chancellor: Prof. OYE IBIDAPO-OBE
Deputy Vice-Chancellor (Academic and Research): Prof. OLUSOGA A. SOFOLA
Deputy Vice-Chancellor (Management) (vacant)
Registrar: C. F. A. OLUMIDE
Librarian: S. O. OLANLOKUN
Library: see Libraries and Archives
Number of teachers: 969
Number of students: 39,783

Publications: *Imodoye, A Journal of Africa Philosophy* (annually), *Journal of Economics and Policy Analysis* (annually), *Journal of Engineering Research* (annually), *Journal of Private and Property Law* (annually), *Journal of Society, Development and Public Health* (annually), *LAANGBASA (Jona Ise Akadani Ede Yoruba)* (African Studies, annually), *Lagos Historical Review* (annually), *Lagos Journal of Environmental Studies* (annually), *Lagos Review of English Studies* (annually), *Nigerian Journal of Business and Social Science* (annually), *Nigerian Journal of Health and Biomedical Sciences* (2 a year), *Nigerian Journal of Industrial Relations* (annually), *Nigerian Journal of Management Studies* (annually), *Nigerian Journal of Philosophy* (annually), *UNILAG Communication Review* (annually), *UNILAG Journal of Business* (annually), *UNILAG Journal of Politics* (annually), *UNILAG Sociological Review* (annually)

DEANS

Faculty of Arts: Prof. C. S. MOMOH
Faculty of Business Administration: Prof. W. ADEWUNMI
Faculty of Education: Prof. DURO ADENAYO AJEYALEMI
Faculty of Engineering: Prof. O. O. AKINDELE
Faculty of Environmental Sciences: Prof. R. O. IYAGBA
Faculty of Law: Prof. CHIOMA AGOMO
Faculty of Pharmacy: Prof. H. A. B. COKER
Faculty of Science: Prof. O. O. AMUND
Faculty of Social Sciences: Prof. L. OLURODE
College of Medicine: Prof. S. O. ELEHSA (Provost)
School of Basic Medical Sciences: Prof. S. A. ADIGUN
School of Clinical Sciences: Prof. A. O. GRANGE

School of Dental Sciences: Prof. J. A. AKINWANDE
School of Postgraduate Studies: Prof. F. O. OLATUNJI

PROFESSORS

ABAELU, A. M., Biochemistry
ABASS, O., Computer Science
ABIDOYE, R. O., Community Health
ABUDU, O. O., Obstetrics and Gynaecology
ADEBAYO, N., Sociology
ADEDIMILA, A. S., Civil Engineering
ADEGBOLA, O., Geography
ADEGBENRO, O., Electrical and Electronics Engineering
ADEGOKE, K. A., Curriculum Studies (Education)
ADEJUGBE, M. O. A., Economics
ADEKOLA, S. A., Electrical and Electronics Engineering
ADELEMO, I. A., Geography
ADENIYI, P. O., Geography
ADEOGUN, A. A., Commercial and Industrial Law
ADE-OJO, S., European Languages
ADEPOJU, J. A., Mathematics
ADEROGBA, K., Mathematics
ADEWALE, A. O., Adult Education
ADEWUNMI, W., Banking and Finance
ADEYEMI, A. A., Public Law
ADEYEMI, J. D., Psychiatry
ADEYEMI, S. D., Surgery
ADEYEMI-DORO, H. O., Surgery
ADIGUN, S. A., Physiology
ADU, D. I., Mathematics
AGOMO, C. K., Commercial and Industrial Law
AJAYI, O., Mathematics
AJEYALEMI, S. D., Curriculum Studies (Education)
AKEJU, T. A., Civil Engineering
AKERE, J. F., English
AKINDELE, O. O., Mechanical Engineering
AKINFELEYE, R. A., Mass Communication
AKINGBADE, J. F., Business Administration
AKINOLA, M. O., European Languages (French)
AKINSETE, I., Haematology and Blood Transfusion
AKINTOLA-ARIKAWE, J. O., Geography
AKINTONWA, A., Pharmacology
AKINWANDE, J. A., Oral and Maxillofacial Surgery
AKINWANDE, A. I., Biochemistry
AKO, C. T., Chemical Engineering
AKPATA, T. V. I., Botany and Microbiology
ALABA, I. O., African Languages and Literature (Yoruba)
ALABA OGUNSANWO, Political Science
ALO, B. I., Chemistry
AMUND, O. O., Botany and Microbiology
ARIGBABU, S. O., Surgery
ASIKA, M. N., Business Administration
AWONUSI, V. O., English
AWOSOPE, C. O., Electrical and Electronics Engineering
AYENI, J. O., Computer Science
AYENI, O. O., Surveying
BALOGUN, O. Y., Geography
BALOGUN, S. A., Metallurgical Engineering
BANDELE, E. O., Medicine
BELLO, R. A., Chemical Engineering
COKER, A. O., Medical Microbiology and Parasitology
COKER, H. A. B., Pharmaceutical Chemistry
DANESI, M. A., Medicine
DENLOYE, A. O., Chemical Engineering
DON-PEDRO, K., Zoology, Marine Biology and Fisheries
DUROSIMI-ETTI, F. A., Radiation biology, Radiotherapy and Radiodiagnosis
EDEBIRI, U., European Languages (French)
EGBERONGBE, F. O. A., Surveying and Geoinformatics
EJIOGU, A. M., Educational Administration
ELESHA, S. O., Morbid Anatomy

ERUVBETINE, A. E., English
EZE, L. N., Psychology
EZEIGBO, C. U., Surveying and Geoinformatics
EZEIGBO, T. A., English
FAGBAMIYE, E. O., Educational Administration
FAGBENRO-BEYIOKU, A. F., Microbiology and Parasitology
FAJEMIROKUN, F. A., Surveying and Geoinformatics
FAMUYIWA, O. O., Psychiatry
FOGAM, P. K., Commercial and Industrial Law
FOLARIN, B. A., Psychology
FOLAWIYO, A. F. A., Physical and Health Education
GBADAMOSI, T. G. O., History
GIWA-OSAGIE, O. O. F., Obstetrics and Gynaecology
GRANGE, A. O., Clinical Pathology
IBIDAPO-OBE, O., Systems Engineering
IFUDU, N. D., Pharmacy and Pharmaceutical Technology
IGWILO, C. I., Pharmacy and Pharmaceutical Technology
IJAOLA, O. O., Electrical and Electronics Engineering
IKULAYO, P. B., Physical and Health Education
ISIEKWE, M. C., Dental Sciences
IYAGBA, R. O., Building
IYIEGBUNIWE, W. C., Finance
JEBODA, S. O., Preventive Dentistry
JOHNSON, M. A., European Languages (French)
JOHNSON, T. O., Medicine
KAMMA, C. M., Mechanical Engineering
KAZEEM, A. A., Clinical Pathology
KENKU, M. A., Mathematics
KUKOYI, A. A., European Languages (French)
KUSEMIJU, K., Marine Science
KWOFIE, E. N., European Languages (French)
LAWAL, A. A., History
LAWAL, O. O., Education
MAJEKODUNMI, A. A., Surgery
MAKANJU, O. O. A., Psychology
MAKANJUOLA, W. A., Zoology
MALAKA, S. L. O., European Languages (French)
MOMOH, C. S., Philosophy
MOREGBE, J. I., Philosophy
NINALOWO, A., Sociology
NWANKO, D. I., Zoology, Marine Biology and Fisheries
OBEBE, B. J., Curriculum Studies
ODEIGAH, P. G. C., Zoology, Marine Biology and Fisheries
ODIETE, W. O., Zoology, Marine Biology and Fisheries
ODUGBEMI, T., Medical Microbiology and Parasitology
ODUKOYA, O. O., Oral Pathology
ODUTOLA, T. A., Medicine
OGBOJA, O., Chemical Engineering
OGEDENGBE, O. K., Obstetrics and Gynaecology
OGUNDOWOLE, E. K., Philosophy
OGUNLESI, M. M., Chemistry
OGUNSANWO, A. C. A., Political Science
OGUNTOYE, A. O., Educational Administration
OHWOVORIOLE, A. E., Medicine
OJO, S. A., European Languages (French)
OJO, S. O., Geography
OKENIMKPE, M. N., Adult Education
OKEOWO, P. A., Surgery
OKORO, C. C., Electrical and Electronics Engineering
OKOTORE, R. O., Biochemistry
OLATUNJI, F. O., Chemical Engineering
OLOWOKUDEJO, J. O., Botany and Microbiology
OLUKOJU, A. O., History
OLUMIDE, Y. M., Medicine
OLUNLOYO, V. O. S., Mechanical Engineering

OLURODE, O., Sociology
OLUSANYA, O., Architecture
OLUWAFEMI, C. O., Physics
OMOLUABI, P. F., Psychology
OMO-MALAKA, S. L., Zoology, Marine Biology and Fisheries
OMOTOLA, J. A., Private and Property Law
OMOREGBE, J., Philosophy
OSEGBE, D. N., Surgery
OSIBOGUN, A. O., Community Health
OSINBAJO, Y., Public Law
OSIPITAN, T. A. I., Public Law
OSUNTOKUN, J. O., History
OTOBO, D., Industrial Relations and Personnel Management
OWHOTU, V. B., Curriculum Studies
OWOEYE, I. O., Physiotherapy
OYEBANDE, L., Geography
OYEBODE, A., Jurisprudence and International Law
OYEDIRAN, M. A., Child Health and Primary Care
OYEKANMI, F. A. D., Sociology
OYELELE, D. A., Geography
DA ROCHA-AFODU, J. T., Surgert
SOFOLA, O. A., Physiology
SOFOLUWE, A. B., Computer Science
SOTE, E. O., Child Dental Health
SOTE, G. A., Psychology
SOWEMIMO, G. O. A., Surgery
SUSU, A. A., Chemical Engineering
TALABI, S. O., Mechanical Engineering
TAYO, F., Clinical Pharmacy
TOMORI, S., Economics
UCHE, L. U., Mass Communication
UCHEGBU, A., Jurisprudence and International Law
UNAH, J. I., Philosophy
UTUAMA, A. A., Private and Property Law
UZOCHUKWU, S., African Languages and Literature (Igbo)
UZODIKE, E. N. U., Private and Property Law
VINCENT, T., English
WILLIAMS, G. O., Zoology, Marine Biology and Fisheries

UNIVERSITY OF MAIDUGURI

PMB 1069, Maiduguri, Borno State

Telephone: (76) 232949
E-mail: root@unimaid.edu.ng
Internet: www.unimaid.org

Founded 1975
Federal control
Language of instruction: English
Academic year: October to June

Vice-Chancellor: His Royal Majesty Dr EKPENYONG OKONKO UDOUTUN
Pro-Chancellor and Chairman of Council: Haj. Dr HAMIDU ALKALI
Vice-Chancellor: Prof. JIBRILLA DAHIRU AMIN
Deputy Vice-Chancellor (Academic Services): Prof. SUNDAY ANGAYA BWALA
Deputy Vice-Chancellor (Central Administration): Prof. MOHAMMED MALA DAURA
Registrar: Dr LAWAN BUKAR ALHAJI
Librarian: JAMES ABAYOMI AGAJA (acting)
Number of teachers: 700
Number of students: 25,000

Publications: *Annals of Borno, Inaugural Lecture and Convocation Speeches*

DEANS

Faculty of Agriculture: Prof. B. O. OGUBAMERU
Faculty of Arts: Prof. IDRIS O. AMALI
Faculty of Education: Prof. AYODELE FAJONYOMI
Faculty of Engineering: Prof. M. A. HAQUE
Faculty of Law: Assoc. Prof. ISA CIROMA (acting)
Faculty of Management Sciences: Prof. DAHIRU HASSAN BALAMI (acting)
Faculty of Science: Prof. B. V. GOPAL (acting)

Faculty of Social Sciences: Dr SA'AD (acting)
Faculty of Veterinary Medicine: Prof. S. S. BABA
College of Medical Sciences: Prof. M. A. KHALIL

PROFESSORS

ABUBAKAR, A., Languages and Linguistics
ABUBAKAR, S., History
ADENIJI, F. A., Agricultural Engineering
AGUOLU, C. C., Library Science
AL-AMIN, J.D.
ALKALI, M. NUR, History
AMALI, I. O. O., English
AMBALI, A. G., Veterinary Medicine
ANASO, A. B., Crop Science
AZEKE, T. O., Education
BABU, S. S., Veterinary Medicine, Microbiology and Parasitology
BADEJO, B. R., Languages and Linguistics
BRANN, C. M. B., Language and Linguistics
BWALA, S. A., Medicine
CAREW, P. F. C., Education
CHHANGANI, R. C., Common Law
CHIBUZO, G. A., Veterinary Anatomy
EGWU, G. O., Veterinary Anatomy
ENYIKWOLA, O., Human Physiology
FOLORUNSO, O. A., Soil Science
GOPAL, B. V., Biological Sciences
HARRY, T. O., Microbiology
HASSAN, A. W., Surgery
IGBOKWE, I. O., Veterinary Pathology
IGUN, U. A., Sociology and Anthropology
JIBOYEWA, D. A., Education
KALU, A. U., Veterinary, Public Health and Preventive Medicine
KOROMA, D. S. M., History
MOHAMMED, I., Medicine
MSHELIA, E. D., Physics
MSHELIA, B., P.H.E.
ODO, P. E., Crop Science
OGUNBAMERU, B. O.
OIIU, J. O., Agricultural Engineering
OLOWOKURE, T. O., Accountancy
OMOTARA, B., Community Medicine
ONI, A., Continuing Education
OSIYEMI, T. I. O., Veterinary Microbiology and Parasitology
PADONU, M. K. O., Community Medicine
PRASAD, B., Human Anatomy
RICHARDS, W. S., Biological Sciences
SHEHU, U., Community Medicine
SODIPO, W., Biochemistry
TIJANI, K., Political Science and Administration
UBOSI, C. O., Animal Science
UGHERUGHE, P. O., Crop Science
ZARIA, L. T., Veterinary Microbiology and Parasitology

MICHAEL OKPARA UNIVERSITY OF AGRICULTURE, UMUDIKE

PMB 7267, Umuahia, Umuahia, Abia State

Telephone: (82) 440555
Fax: (82) 440555

Founded 1992 as Federal University of Agriculture, Umudike; present name and status 2000

Vice-Chancellor: Prof. OGBINNAYA C. ONWUDIKE
Deputy Vice-Chancellor: Prof. HILARY O. EDEOGA
Registrar: JULIA N. UCHE
Librarian: ALOYSIUS ONONOGBO

Library of 8,500 vols
Number of teachers: 158
Number of students: 1,248

DEANS

College of Agricultural Economics, Rural Sociology and Extension: Prof. ALOYSIUS NWOSU
College of Animal Science and Animal Health: Prof. JOHN IBEAWUCHI

College of Biological and Physical Sciences: Dr OBIOHA EZEREONYE
College of Crop and Soil Sciences: Dr CHIDA AMADIOHA
College of Food Processing and Storage Technology: Prof. ENOCH AKOBUNDU
College of Natural Resources and Environmental Management: Prof. EME AKACHUKU
School of Postgraduate Studies: Prof. SYLVESTER IBE

PROFESSORS

AKACHUKU, E. A., Natural Resources and Environmental Management
AKOBUNDU, E. N. T., Food Processing and Storage Technology
ALUKO, P., Natural Resources and Environmental Management
ANASO, H. U., Crop and Soil Sciences
ASIEGBU, J. C., Crop and Soil Sciences
CHIBOKA, V. O., Biological and Physical Sciences
EDEOGA, H. O., Biological and Physical Sciences
EKWUEME, B. N., Biological and Physical Sciences
ELUWA, M. C., Biological and Physical Sciences
IBE, S. N., Animal Science and Animal Health
IBEAWUCHI, J. A., Animal Science and Animal Health
MENKITI, A. I., Biological and Physical Sciences
NJOKU, P. C., Animal Science and Animal Health
NWAGBO, E. C., Agricultural Economics, Rural Sociology and Extension
NWOKE, B. E. B., Biological and Physical Sciences
NWOSU, A. C., Agricultural Economics, Rural Sociology and Extension
OBIZOBA, I. C., Food Processing and Storage Technology
OKERE, L. C., Agricultural Economics, Rural Sociology and Extension
OKOH, P. N., Biological and Physical Sciences
ONWUDIKE, O. C., Animal Science and Animal Health
ONYENWEAKU, C. E., Agricultural Economics, Rural Sociology and Extension
UWAEGBUTE, A. C., Food Processing and Storage Technology
UWAKAH, C. T., Agricultural Economics, Rural Sociology and Extension

NATIONAL OPEN UNIVERSITY OF NIGERIA

14–16 Ahmadu Bello Way, PMB 80067, Victoria Island, Lagos

Telephone: (1) 8188849
E-mail: registrar@nou.edu.ng
Internet: www.nou.edu.ng

Founded 1983; suspended by government 1984; re-opened 2001

Vice-Chancellor: Prof. OLUGBEMIRO JEGEDE
Number of students: 32,400

Courses for adults by correspondence and distance teaching at 20 study centres serving each state and local government area of Nigeria; Schools of Arts and Social Sciences, Business and Human Resource Management, Education and Science and Technology; Centre for Continuing Education; Regional Training and Research Institute for Open and Distance Learning (RETRIDAL).

UNIVERSITY OF NIGERIA

Nsukka, Enugu State

Telephone: (42) 771911
E-mail: unmail@unn-edu.net
Internet: www.unn-edu.net

Founded 1960
Federal control
Language of instruction: English
Academic year: September to June

Campus in Enugu

Chancellor: Emir of Zazzau Alhaji Dr SHEHU IDRIS
Pro-Chancellor: Prof. BOLANLE AWE
Vice-Chancellor: Prof. CHINEDU O. NEBO
Deputy Vice-Chancellor (Academic): Prof. K. MOSTO ONUOHA
Deputy Vice-Chancellor (Administration): Prof. F. I. IDIKE
Deputy Vice-Chancellor (Enugu Campus): Prof. PETER O. EBIGBO
Registrar: P. CHINEMERE DIOKA AMNES (acting)
Librarian: EMENIKE IKEGBUNE
Library: see Libraries and Archives
Number of teachers: 1,122
Number of students: 29,482

Publication: *Annual Report*

DEANS

Faculty of Agriculture: Prof. J. S. C. MBAGWU
Faculty of Arts: Prof. E. P. NWABUEZE
Faculty of Biological Sciences: Prof. I. C. ONONOGBU
Faculty of Business Administration: Prof. IKE E. NWOSU
Faculty of Education: Prof. S. C. O. A. EZEJI
Faculty of Engineering: Prof. A. N. NZEAKO
Faculty of Environmental Studies: Prof. L. C. UMEH
Faculty of Health Sciences and Technology: Dr G. U. MADUBUKO
Faculty of Law: Prof. B. O. OKERE
Faculty of Medical Sciences and Dentistry: Prof. B. C. OZUMBA
Faculty of Pharmaceutical Sciences: Prof. G. D. OKIDE
Faculty of Physical Sciences: Prof. C. A. NWADINIGWE
Faculty of Social Sciences: Prof. R. N. C. ANYADIKE
Faculty of Veterinary Medicine: Prof. I. U. ASUZU
School of General Studies: Prof. A. O. OKORE
School of Postgraduate Studies: Prof. S. O. ONYEGEGBU
College of Medicine: Prof. M. A. C. AGHAJI (Provost)

PROFESSORS

ADEILUYI, J. O., Civil Engineering
AGAJELU, S. I., Geoinformatics and Surveying
AGHAJI, M. A. C., Medical Sciences and Dentistry
AGU, C. C., Economics
AGUWA, C. N., Clinical Pharmacy and Pharmacy Management
AKAH, P. A., Pharmacology and Toxicology
AKAMIGBO, F. O. R., Soil Science
Rev. Fr AKUBUE, A. U., Educational Foundations
ALI, A., Institute of Education
AMAZIGO, J. C., Mathematics
AMUCHEAZI, E. C., Political Science
AMUCHIE, F. A., Health and Physical Education
ANATSUI, E. K., Fine and Applied Arts
ANIAKOR, C. C., Fine and Applied Arts
ANIKA, S. M., Veterinary Physiology and Pharmacology
ANYADIKE, R. N. C., Geography
ANYANWU, S. U., Health and Physical Education
ARUA, E. O., Agricultural Economics
ASIEGBU, J. E., Crop Science
ASUZU, I. U., Veterinary Physiology and Pharmacology
ATTAH, C. A., Surgery
AZUBUIKE, J. C., Paediatrics
CHIDEBELU, S. A. N. D., Agricultural Economics

CHIDUME, C. E., Mathematics
CHIEJINA, S. N., Veterinary Parasitology and Entomology
CHIKWENDU, V. E., Archaeology
CHUKWU, C. C., Veterinary Medicine
EBIGBO, P. O., Psychological Medicine
EDOKA, B. E., Library and Information Science
EGBUNIWE, N., Civil Engineering
EGONU, I. T. K., Foreign Languages and Literature
EGWIM, P. O., Medical Biochemistry
Rev. Fr EJIOFOR, L. J. C., Political Science
EKE, E. I., Educational Foundations
EKECHUKWU, O. V., Mechanical Engineering
ENEKWE, O., English
ESEDEBE, P. O., History
EYO, I. E., Psychology
EZEASOR, D. N., Veterinary Anatomy
EZEILO, B. N., Psychology
EZEJI, S. C. O. A., Vocational Teacher Education
EZEKWE, C. I., Mechanical Engineering
EZEOKE, A. C. J., Chemical Pathology
EZEPUE, M. C., Geology
EZE-UZOMAKA, O. J., Civil Engineering
HARBOR-PETERS, V. F., Science Education
IBEMESSI, J. A., Pure and Industrial Chemistry
IGBOELI, G., Animal Science
IGWILO, B. N., Fine and Applied Arts
IHEKORONYE, A. I., Food Science and Technology
IHEZUE, U. H., Psychological Medicine
IJOMA, J. O., History
IKEJIANI-CLARK, M. I. O., Public Administration and Local Government
IKENE, A. I., Home Science and Technology
IKPEZE, A. I., Economics
ILOABACHIE, G. C., Obstetrics and Gynaecology
ILOBA, C., Crop Science
ILOEJE, O. C., Mechanical Engineering
IMAGA, E. U. L., Management
KENE, R. O. C., Veterinary Surgery and Obstetrics
MADUBUNYI, L. C., Veterinary Parasitology and Entomology
MADUEWESI, E. J., Educational Foundations
MBAGWU, J. S. C., Soil Science
MODUM, E. P., Languages
MODUM, U., Accountancy
NGODDY, P. O., Food Science and Technology
NJOKO, O. N., History
NWABUEZE, E. P., Dramatic Arts
NWACHUKWU, P A., Linguistics and Nigerian Languages
NWACHUKWU, T. A., Educational Foundations
NWAFOR, J. C., Geography
NWAGBO, E. C., Agricultural Economics
NWAKOBY, B. A. N., Community Medicine
NWALA, T. U., Philosophy
NWANKITI, O. C., Botany
NWOSU, I. E., Marketing
NZE, C. B., Philosophy
NZEAKO, A. N., Electronic Engineering
OBANU, Z. A., Food Science and Technology
OBI, I. U., Crop Science
OBI, M E., Soil Science
OBI, S. K. C., Microbiology
OBIANYO, N. E. N., Surgery
OBIDOA, O., Biochemistry
OBIKEZE, D. S., Sociology and Anthropology
OBIZOBA, I. C., Home Science and Nutrition
OBOEGBULAM, S. I., Veterinary Pathology and Microbiology
ODIGBOH, E. U., Agricultural Engineering
ODUKWE, A. O., Mechanical Engineering
OGBAZI, J. N., Vocational Teacher Education
OGBUJI, R. O., Crop Science
OHAEGBU, A. U., Languages
OKAFOR, B. C., Otolaryngology
OKAFOR, C. O., Pure and Industrial Chemistry
OKAFOR, E. C., Pure and Industrial Chemistry

OKAFOR, F. C., Zoology
OKAFOR, F. O., Banking and Finance
OKAFOR, F. U., Philosophy
OKEKE, C. E., Physics and Astronomy
OKEKE, E. A. C., Education
OKEKE, F. N., Physics and Astronomy
OKEKE, P. N., Physics and Astronomy
OKOGBUE, C. O., Geology
OKOLI, F. C., Public Administration and Local Government
OKONKWO, P. O., Pharmacology and Therapeutics
OKORAFOR, A. E., Economics
OKORE, A. O., Economics
OKORIE, J. U., Vocational Teacher Education
OKORJI, E. C., Agricultural Economics
OKORO, B. A., Paediatrics
OKORO, O. M., Vocational Teacher Education
OKOYE, J. O. A., Veterinary Pathology and Microbiology
OKPALA, J. I. N., Education
OKPARA, E., Psychology
OKPOKO, A. I., Archaeology
OLAITAN, S. O., Vocational Teacher Education
OLI, J. M., Medicine
OLOIDI, O., Fine and Applied Arts
ONAH, J. O., Marketing
ONONOGBU, I. C., Biochemistry
ONUKOGU, I. B., Statistics
ONUOHA, K. M., Geology
Rev. ONWU, N., Religion
ONYEGEGBU, S. O., Mechanical Engineering
ONYEJEKWE, D. C., Mechanical Engineering
ORANU, R. N., Vocational Teacher Education
OSUAGWU, C. C., Electronic Engineering
OSUALA, E. C., Vocational Teacher Education
OSUALA, J. D. C., Adult Education and Extramural Studies
OYEOKU, O. K., Fine and Applied Arts
OZIOKO, J. O. C., Psychology
OZUMBA, B. C., Obstetrics and Gynaecology
PAL, S., Physics and Astronomy
SOLUDO, C. C., Economics
UCHE, P. I., Statistics
UKAEJIOFO, E. O., Medical Laboratory Science
UME, J. A., Estate Management
UMEH, L. C., Urban and Regional Planning
UMEH, T. A., Adult Education and Extramural Studies

ATTACHED INSTITUTES

Centre for Energy Research and Development: Nsukka; Dir Prof. E. C. OKORJI (acting).

Centre for Equipment Maintenance and Development: Nsukka; Dir Prof. I. C. OBIZOBA.

Institute of African Studies: Nsukka; Dir Prof. O. O. ENEKWE.

Institute for Development Studies: University of Nigeria, Enugu Campus, Enugu; Dir Prof. E. U. L. IMAGA.

Institute of Education: Nsukka; Dir Prof. E. A. C. OKEKE.

Veterinary Teaching Hospital: Nsukka; Dir Dr L. J. E. ORAJAKA (acting).

NNAMDI AZIKIWE UNIVERSITY

PMB 5025, Awka, Anambra State

Telephone: (46) 550082
E-mail: gomach@infoweb.abs.net

Founded 1992
Academic year: October to June
Federal govt control
Languages of instruction: English, French, Igbo

Chancellor: Emir of Ilorin Alhaji SULE GAMBARI
Vice-Chancellor: Prof. ILOCHI A. OKAFOR
Deputy Vice-Chancellor (Academic): Prof. R. I. EGWUATU

Deputy Vice-Chancellor (Administration): Prof. A. N. EBOATU
Registrar: J. N. ANDY-AGBAI
Librarian: Dr M. W. ANYAKOHA
Provost, College of Health Sciences: Prof. B. U. O. UMEH
Bursar: E. N. ATTADO

Library of 65,000 vols
Number of teachers: 500
Number of students: 28,000

Publications: *Journal of Arts and Humanities, Journal of Economic Studies, Journal of Education Management, Journal of Management Studies, Journal of Vocational and Adult Education, Tropical Journal of Medical Research, UNIZIK Law Journal*

DEANS

Faculty of Arts: Prof. C. C. AGBODIKE
Faculty of Education: Prof. S. I. OKWUANASO
Faculty of Engineering and Technology: Prof. D. O. ONUKWULI
Faculty of Environmental Sciences: C. C. AKAGU
Faculty of Health Sciences and Technology: Prof. G. O. C. EKEJINDU
Faculty of Law: Dr G. NWAKOBY
Faculty of Management Sciences: Prof. B. C. OSISIOMA
Faculty of Medicine: Prof. S. N. C. ANYANWU
Faculty of Natural Sciences: Prof. A. N. C. OKAKA
Faculty of Social Sciences: Prof. Canon I. C. OKOYE
Postgraduate School: Prof. B. C. E. EGBOKA

PROFESSORS

Faculty of Education:
AKUEZUILO, E. C.
AKUSOBA, E. U.
EZE, T. I.
IKE, A. O.
NDINECHI, G. I.
NDU, A. N.
NNADOZIE, J. C.
OKAFOR, J. O.
OKONKWO, R. U. N.
OKWUANASO, S. I.
UMEDUM, S. O.
UNACHUKWU, G. C.

Faculty of Engineering and Technology:
NNABUIFE, E. L. C.
OFODILE, E. I. F.
OKEKE, S. I.
OKEKE, S. S. N.
OMENYI, S.
ONUKWULI, D. O.
UBA NWUBA, E. I.

Faculty of Law:
OKAFOR, I.

Faculty of Management Sciences:
EJIOFOR, P., Management Studies
NZE, F., Public Administration
OSISIOMA, B. C., Accountancy

Faculty of Medicine:
ADINMA, J. I. B.
AGBATA, A. I.
AHANEKU, J. E.
EKEJINDU, G. O. C.
IKPEZE, O. C.
MBONU, O. O.
NWOSU, M. C.
OFFIAELI, R. O.
UMEH, B. U. O.

Faculty of Natural Sciences:
ANASO, H. U.
ANENE, G.
EBOATU, A. N.
EGBOKA, B. C. E.
EGWUATU, R. I.
EKEJUBA, I. O. C.

NWAORGU, O. C.
OBIENU, E. U.
ODIBO, F. J. C.
OGUM, G. E. O.
OKAKA, A. N. C.
OKEREKE, G. U.
OLI, B. A.
ONOCHIE, C. C.
ONYALI, I.
OYEKA, A.
OYEKA, C. A.

Faculty of Social Sciences:
NWEKE, C. C., Psychology
OBI, A. W., Economics
OKOYE, I. C., Political Science
OKUNNA, C. S., Mass Communication

OBAFEMI AWOLOWO UNIVERSITY

Ile-Ife

Telephone: (36) 230290
Fax: (36) 232401
E-mail: registra@oauife.edu.ng
Internet: www.oauife.edu.ng

Founded 1961 as University of Ife, present name 1987
Federal control
Language of instruction: English
Academic year: September to July

Chancellor: Alhaji KABIR USMAN
Pro-Chancellor: Alhaji SHETIMA A. M. LIBERTY
Vice-Chancellor: Prof. ROGER MAKANJUOLA
Deputy Vice-Chancellor (Academic): Prof. A. A. ADEDIRAN
Deputy Vice-Chancellor (Administration): Prof. L. O. KEHINDE
Registrar: B. O. ILUYOMADE
University Bursar: O. ODEYEMI
University Librarian: M. O. AFOLABI

Library: see Libraries and Archives
Number of teachers: 1,343
Number of students: 22,742

Publications: *Calendar, Gazette, Handbook, Ife Studies in English Language, Odu: A Journal of West African Studies* (2 a year), *Quarterly Journal of Administration, Second Order* (2 a year), *University Bulletin*

PROVOSTS

College of Health Sciences: M. O. BALOGUN
Postgraduate College: S. K. ADESINA

DEANS

Faculty of Administration: O. OJO
Faculty of Agriculture: R. ADEYEMO
Faculty of Arts: O. T. AKINRINADE
Faculty of Basic Medical Sciences: M. A. DUROSINMI
Faculty of Clinical Sciences: J. A. OWA
Faculty of Dentistry: O. D. OTUYEMI (acting)
Faculty of Education: D. K. AKANBI
Faculty of Environmental Design and Management: C. A. AJAYI
Faculty of Law: M. O. ADEDIRAN
Faculty of Pharmacy: A. O. OGUNDAINI
Faculty of Science: M. A. BADEJO
Faculty of Social Sciences: J. A. FABAYO
Faculty of Technology: M. O. FABORODE

PROFESSORS

Faculty of Administration:
ERERO, E. J., Public Administration
OJO, O., International Relations
OMOPARIOLA, O., Management and Accounting
ORIBABOR, P. E., Management and Accounting
SESAY, A., International Relations
SOREMEKUN, O., International Relations

Faculty of Agriculture:
ADEBAYO, A. A., Soil Science
ADEPETU, J. A., Soil Science

ADERIBIGBE, A. O., Animal Science
ADEYEMO, R., Agricultural Economics
ADUAYI, E. A., Soil Science
AINA, P. O., Soil Science
AJOBO, O., Agricultural Economics
AKINGBOHUNGBE, A. E., Plant Science
AKINYEMIJU, O. A., Plant Science
ALOFE, C. O., Plant Science
FAKOREDE, M. A., Plant Science
ILORI, J. O., Animal Science
JIBOWO, A. A., Agricultural Extension and Rural Sociology
LADIPO, J. L., Plant Science
LAOGUN, E. A., Agricultural Extension and Rural Sociology
MATANMI, B. A., Plant Science
OBISESAN, I. O., Plant Science
OKUSAMI, T. A., Soil Science
OLAYINKA, A., Soil Science
SONAIYA, E. B., Animal Science

Faculty of Arts:
ADEDIRAN, A. A., History
ADEWOLE, L. O., African Languages and Literature
AJUWON, B., African Languages and Literature
AKINRINADE, O. T., History
IBITOKUN, B. M., English
ILESANMI, T. M., Religious Studies
KOLAWOLE, M. E. M., English
MAKINDE, M. A., Philosophy
MANUS, C. U., Modern European Languages
NWEZEH, E. C., Foreign Languages
OLANIYAN, R. A., History
OLAYIWOLA, D. O., Religious Studies
OLOMOLA, G. O. I., History
OLORUNFEMI, A., History
OMOSINI, O., History
ONIBERE, S. G. A., Religious Studies
VIDAL, A. O., Music

Faculties of Basic Medical Sciences, Clinical Sciences and Dentistry:
ADEJUYIGBE, O., Surgery
ADELEKAN, D. A., Community Health
ADEYEMO, A. O., Surgery
AKINOLA, D. O., Surgery
AKINSOLA, A., Medicine
ARIGBABU, O., Surgery
BALOGUN, M. O., Medicine
CAXTON-MARTINS, A. E., Anatomy and Cell Biology
DARE, F. O., Obstetrics and Gynaecology
DUROSINMI, M. A., Haematology and Immunology
ELEGBE, R. A., Physiological Sciences
FAKUNLE, J. B., Chemical Pathology
FAJEWONYOMI, B. A., Community Health
JINADU, M. I., Nursing
MAKANJUOLA, R. O. A., Mental Health
ODESANMI, W. O., Morbid Anatomy and Forensic Medicine
OGUNBODEDE, E. O., Preventive Dentistry
OGUNNIYI, S. O., Obstetrics and Gynaecology
OJO, O. S., Morbid Anatomy and Forensic Medicine
OJOFEITIMI, E. O., Community Health and Nutrition
ONWUDIEGWU, U., Obstetrics and Gynaecology
OTUYEMI, O. D., Child Dental Health
OWA, J. A., Paediatrics and Child Health
OYEDEJI, G. A., Paediatrics and Child Health

Faculty of Education:
ADEYANJU, S. A., Physical and Health Education
AKANBI, D. K., Educational Technology
EHINDERO, O. J., Institute of Education
FASOKUN, T. O., Continuing Education
FAWOLE, J. O., Physical Education
OBIDI, S. S., Education, Foundation and Counselling

OGUNDARI, J. T., Physical and Health Education
OKUNROTIFA, E. B., Physical and Health Education

Faculty of Environmental Design and Management:
AJAYI, C. A., Estate Management
AMOLE, S. A., Architecture
AREMU, P. S. O., Fine Arts
FADARE, S. O., Urban and Regional Planning
IGHALO, J. I., Estate Management
OGUNJUMO, A., Urban and Regional Planning
OLAJUYIN, L. O., Urban and Regional Planning

Faculty of Law:
ADEDIRAN, M. O., Public Law
FABUNMI, J. O., Business Law
OKORODUDU-FUBARA, M. T., International Law

Faculty of Pharmacy:
ADESANYA, S. A., Pharmacognosy
ADESINA, S. K., Drug Research
ADEWUNMI, C. O., Drug Research
ALADESANMI, J. A., Pharmacognosy
ELUJOBA, A. A., Pharmacognosy
LAMIKANRA, A., Pharmaceutics
OGUNBONA, F. A., Pharmaceutical Chemistry
OGUNDAINI, A. O., Pharmaceutical Chemistry
OGUNDARI, O., Pharmaceutical Chemistry
OLUGBADE, T. O., Pharmaceutical Chemistry
ONAWUNMI, G. O., Pharmaceutics
ONYEJI, O. C., Pharmaceutical Chemistry
ORAFIDIYA, O. O., Pharmaceutics
SOFOWORA, E. A., Pharmacognosy

Faculty of Science:
ADEDOKUN, J. A., Physics
ADEGOKE, J. A., Zoology
ADESULU, E. A., Zoology
ADEWUSI, S. R. A., Chemistry
AFOLAYAN, A., Biochemistry
AFUWAPE, M. A., Mathematics
AJAYI, E. O. B., Physics
AJAYI, T. R., Geology
AKANNI, M. S., Chemstry
AKINRELERE, E. A., Mathematics
AKO, B. D., Geology
AKO-NAI, K. A., Microbiology
ALADEKOMO, J. B., Physics
AMIRE, O. A., Chemistry
AMUSA, A., Physics
ARAWOMO, G. A. O., Zoology
ASAOLU, S. O., Zoology
AUBICJO, F. O. I., Chemistry
BALOGUN, E. E., Physics
BALOGUN, R. A., Zoology
FAKUNLE, C. O., Chemistry
IGE, W. J., Chemistry
IMORU, C. O., Mathematics
ISAWUMI, M. A. (Natural History Museum)
ISICHEI, A. O., Botany
KOLAWOLE, D. O., Microbiology
NWACHUKWU, J. I., Geology
OBAFEMI, C. A., Chemistry
ODEYEMI, O., Microbiology
ODU, E. A., Botany
OGUNKOYA, L. O., Chemistry
OJO, J. F., Chemistry
OKON, E. E., Zoology
OLANIYI, H. B., Physics
OLAREWAJU, V. O., Geology
OLOMO, J. B., Physics
OLORODE, O., Botany
OLORUNFEMI, M. O., Geology
OLUTIOLA, P. O., Microbiology
ONAJOBI, F. D., Biochemistry
OSADEBE, F. A. N., Physics
OSHOBI, E. O., Mathematics
RAHAMAN, M. A., Geology
SALAMI, M. B., Geology

SALAU, A. A. M., Physics
SHONUKAN, O. O., Microbiology

Faculty of Social Sciences:
ADEWUYI, A. A., Demography and Social Statistics
ADESINA, F. A., Geography
AFONJA, S., Sociology and Anthropology
EBIGBOLA, J. A., Demography and Social Statistics
EKANADE, O., Geography
FABAYO, J. A., Economics
JEJE, L. K., Geography
ODEBIYI, A. I., Sociology and Anthropology
OGUNBADEJO, F. O., Political Science
OGUNKOYA, O. O., Geography
OLORUNTIMEHIN, O., Sociology and Anthropology
OLOWU, A. A., Psychology
TOGONU-BICKESTETH, T., Psychology

Faculty of Technology:
ADEGBOYEGA, G. A., Electronic and Electrical Engineering
ADEKOYA, L. O., Mechanical Engineering
AFONJA, A. A., Metallurgical and Materials Engineering
AJAYI, G. O., Electronic and Electrical Engineering
AJIBOLA, O. A., Agricultural Engineering
BURAIMAH-IGBO, L. A., Electronic and Electrical Engineering
FABORODE, M. O., Agricultural Engineering
FAPOHUNDA, M. O., Agricultural Engineering
FASHAKIN, J. B., Food Science and Technology
IGE, M. T., Agricultural Engineering
ILLORI, M. O., Technology, Planning and Development Unit
KEHINDE, L. O., Electronic and Electrical Engineering
KUKU, T. A., Electronic and Electrical Engineering
LASISI, F., Agricultural Engineering
LAYOKUN, S. K., Chemical Engineering
MAKANJUOLA, G. A., Agricultural Engineering
MOJOLA, O. O., Mechanical Engineering
OGEDENGBE, M. O., Civil Engineering
OGUNSUA, A. O., Food Science and Technology
SANNI, S. A., Chemical Engineering
SOLOMON, B. O., Chemical Engineering
TAIWO, O., Chemical Engineering

AFFILIATED INSTITUTES

Institute of Agricultural Research and Training Ibadan: see under Research Institutes.

Institute of Education: Ile-Ife; f. 1962; sponsored by the University, the Oyo State Ministry of Education and the Association of Principals of Teacher Training Colleges and Secondary Schools in the State; a mobile library equipped with books, audio-visual aids and film aids demonstration among colleges and secondary schools; Dir O. J. EHINDERO; publ. *News Bulletin* (quarterly).

UNIVERSITY OF PORT HARCOURT

PMB 5323, Port Harcourt, Rivers State
Telephone: (84) 335218
Fax: (84) 230903
E-mail: registrar@uniport.edu.ng
Internet: www.uniport.edu.ng
Founded 1975
Federal control
Language of instruction: English
Academic year: October to July
Chancellor: HRH Alhaji MUSTAPHA UMAR EL-KANEMI (Shehu of Borno)
Pro-Chancellor: Prof. (Emer.) ALHAJI L. A. K. JIMOH
Vice-Chancellor: Prof. NIMI DIMPKA BRIGGS

Deputy Vice-Chancellor (Academic): Prof. J. D. OKOH
Deputy Vice-Chancellor (Administration): Prof. M. O. C. ANIKPO
Registrar: Dr CHRIS ALAFONYEKA TAMUNO
Librarian: Prof. E. O. AYALOGU
Library of 90,000 vols, 220 foreign current journals, depository rights for UN publications
Number of teachers: 560
Number of students: 26,672
Publications: *Biologia Africana* (2 a year), *Journal of Education in Developing Areas—JEDA* (annually), *Kiabara* (2 a year), *Library Waves* (2 a year)

DEANS
Faculty of Basic Medical Sciences: Prof. O. O. EBONG
Faculty of Clinical Sciences: Prof. K. E. O. NKANGINIEME
Faculty of Dentistry: Prof. F. OKOISOR
Faculty of Engineering: Prof. C. UMEZURIKE
Faculty of Humanities: Prof. S. I. UDOIDEM
Faculty of Management Sciences: Prof. D. P. S. ASECHEMIE
Faculty of Pharmacy: Prof. O. K. UDEALA
Faculty of Science: Prof. C. M. OJINNAKA
Faculty of Social Sciences: Prof. W. J. OKOWA
College of Health Sciences: Prof. O. J. ODIA (Provost)
School of Graduate Studies: Prof. W. I. BELL-GAM

PROFESSORS
Faculty of Education:
AWOTUA-EFEBO, E. B., Educational Technology
BARIKOR, C. N., Adult Education
DIENYE, N. E., Science Education
DIKE, H. I., Curriculum and Educational Technology
EHEAZU, B. A., Adult and Non-Formal Education
ENAOWHO, J. O., Educational Management and Planning
GBAMANJA, S. P. T., Curriculum and Educational Technology
JOE, A. I., Psychology, Guidance and Counselling
OKEKE, B. S., Education Administration
OKOH, J. D., History and Philosophy of Education
UKWUIJE, R. P. I., Educational Psychology, Guidance and Counselling

Faculty of Engineering:
AJIENKA, J. A., Petroleum Engineering
EBONG, M. B., Civil Engineering
KUYE, A. O., Chemical Engineering
NWAOGAZIE, I. L., Civil Engineering
ONYEKONWU, M. A., Petroleum Engineering
UMEZURIKE, C., Mechanical Engineering

College of Health Sciences:
ANAH, C. O., Cardiology
ASOGWA, S. E., Preventative and Social Medicine
BRAMBAIFA, N., Pharmacology
BRIGGS, N. D., Obstetrics and Gynaecology
DATUBO-BROWN, D. D., Surgery
EBONG, O. O., Pharmacology
EKE, N., Surgery
ELECHI, E. N., Surgery
EKE, F., Paediatrics
ESSIEN, E. N., Haematology
JOHN, T., Obstetrics and Gynaecology
NKANGINIEME, K. E. O., Paediatrics
NWANKWOALA, R. N. P., Pharmacology
ODIA, O. J., Medicine
OKOISOR, F., Dentistry
ORUAMABO, R. S., Paediatrics
UDEALA, O. K., Pharmacy
WAKWE, V. C., Chemical Pathology

Faculty of Humanities:

BESTMAN, M. T., French
CHUKWUMA, H. O., Oral Literature
EJITUWU, N. C., History
EJIZU, C. I., Religious Studies
EKWELIE, S. A., Linguistics
EMENANJO, E. N., Linguistics
IKONNE, C., English
ILEGA, D., Religious Studies
MADUKA, C. T., Comparative Literature
NNOLIM, C. E., Literature
NWODO, C. S., Philosophy
UDOIDEM, S. I., Philosophy

Faculty of Management Sciences:

ASECHEMIE, D. P. S., Accounting
BARIDAM DON, O. M., Management
NWACHUKWU, C. C., Management

Faculty of Science:

ABBEY, B. W., Biochemistry
AKPOKODJE, E. A., Geology
AMAJOR, L. C., Geology
ANOSIKE, E. O., Enzymology and Protein Chemistry
ANUSIEM, A. C. I., Thermochemistry and Biophysical Chemistry
ARENE, F. O. I., Animal and Environmental Biology
ARINZE, A. E., Plant Science and Biotechnology
AYALOGU, E. O., Biochemistry
EBENIRO, J. O., Physics
EFIU-VWEVWERE, B. J. O., Biodegradation and Environmental Toxicology
EKEKE, G. I., Biochemistry
ETU-EFEOTOR, J. O., Sedimentology, Sedimentary Geochemistry
KINAKO, P. D. S., Botany
LALE, N. E. S., Crop Science
NYANANYO, B. L., Plant Science and Biotechnology
OJINNAKA, C. M., Organic and Natural Products Chemistry
OKIWELU, S. N., Entomology
OKOLI, B. S., Genetics
OKPOKWASILI, G. S. C., Microbiology
OTI, M. N., Geology

Faculty of Social Sciences:

AGIOBENEBO, T. J., Economics
ANIKPO, M. O. C., Sociology
BELL-GAM, W. I., Geography
EKPENYONG, S., Sociology
ETENG, I. A., Sociology
GBOSI, A. A., Economics
IBODJE, S. W. E., Political and Administrative Studies
OKOKO, K. A. B., Political and Administrative Studies
OJO, O. J. B., Political and Administrative Studies
OKOWA, W. J., Economics

USMANU DANFODIYO UNIVERSITY

Dundaye Village, PMB 234, Sokoto

Telephone: (60) 234042
Fax: (60) 235519
E-mail: registrar@udusok.edu.ng
Internet: www.udusok.edu.ng

Founded 1975
Federal control
Language of instruction: English
Academic year: November to July

Chancellor (vacant)
Vice-Chancellor: Prof. A.S. MIKAILA
Deputy Vice-Chancellor: Dr A. A. ZURU (Academic)
Registrar: A. S. USMAN
Librarian: AHMED ABDU BALARABE (acting)

Number of teachers: 371
Number of students: 11,617

Publications: *Annual Report, Calendar, Convocation Speeches, News Bulletin*

(monthly), *Student Handbook* (annually), *University Lecture Series*

DEANS

Faculty of Agriculture: Dr H. M. TUKUR (acting)
Faculty of Arts and Islamic Studies: Dr M. M. DANGANA (acting)
Faculty of Education and Extension Services: Dr F. A. KALGO (acting)
Faculty of Law: Mal. M. I. SAID
Faculty of Management and Administration: Prof. S. A. DIYO
Faculty of Science: Dr U. ABUBAKAR
Faculty of Social Sciences: (vacant)
Faculty of Veterinary Medicine: Dr A. I. DANEJI
College of Health Sciences: Dr W. E. K. OPARA
Postgraduate School: Dr R. A. SHEHU

PROFESSORS

ABDULKAREEM, A., Health Sciences
ABDULRAHMAN, D. A., Sociology
ABDULRAHMAN, F. W., Chemistry
ABUBAKAR, M. K., Biochemistry
ADAMU, M., History
ADEYANJU, J. B., Veterinary Medicine
AGALEA, A. S., Arabic
AUDU, M. S., Mathematics
BADEJO, O. A., Health Sciences
BANDE, T. M., Political Science
BASHAR, M. L. A., Economics
BASHIR, A. M., Accounting
BILBIS, L. S., Biochemistry
BIRNIWA, H. A., Nigerian Languages
DANIEL, S. O., Community Health
DORA, J. S., Geography
ILIYA, M. A., Geography
IPINJOLU, J. K., Forestry and Fisheries
JUNAID, M. I., Education
KALGO, F. A., Education
KAURA, J. M., Islamic Studies
KYIOGWON, U. B., Agricultural Economics and Extension
MAGAJI, M. D., Crop Science
MAJEED, Q., Biological Sciences
MAMMAN, A. B., Geography
MIKAILU, A. S., Business Administration
MUKOSHY, I. A., Nigerian Languages
OBEMBE, A. Y. O., Medicine
OPARA, W. E., Surgery
SALAWU, A. A., Education
SHEHU, B., Surgery
SHEIDU, A. D., Accounting
YAQUB, N. O., Political Science
ZURU, A. A., Chemistry

ATTACHED INSTITUTES

Centre for Hausa Studies: Dir S. OMAR.

Centre for Islamic Studies: Dir Dr M. M. SHUNI.

Sokoto Energy Research Centre: Dir Prof. B. GARBA.

University Translation Bureau (UNESCO).

UNIVERSITY OF UYO

1 Ikpa Rd, PMB 1017, Uyo, Akwa Ibom State

Telephone: (85) 200303
Fax: (85) 202694
E-mail: vc@uniuyo.edu.ng
Internet: www.uniuyo.edu.ng

Founded 1983 as University of Cross River State, then re-named University of Akwa Ibom State; present name 1991
Federal govt control
Language of instruction: English
Academic year: October to July

Chancellor: The Emir of Fika, Haj. Dr ABALI IBN MUHAMMADU
Vice-Chancellor: Prof. AKPAN H. EKPO

Deputy Vice-Chancellor (Academic): Prof. UDO I. ANWANA
Deputy Vice-Chancellor (Administration): Prof. UDO ETUK
Dean of Student Affairs: ETOK O. EKANEM
Registrar: PETER J. EFIONG
Librarian: Dr OFFIONG O. UDOH

Library of 46,745 vols, 271 periodicals
Number of teachers: 769
Number of students: 16,707

Publications: *Journal of Humanities, Journal of Research in Education and the Humanities, Uyo Social Science Journal*

DEANS

Faculty of Agriculture: Prof. BASSEY A. NDON
Faculty of Arts: Prof. UDO A. ETUK
Faculty of Basic Medical Sciences: Prof. A. ABODERIN
Faculty of Business Administration: Prof. EDET B. AKPAKPAN
Faculty of Education: Prof. GEORGE S. IBE-BASSEY
Faculty of Engineering: Prof. E. U. NWA
Faculty of Environmental Studies: AKANINYENE MENDIE
Faculty of Law: Prof. ENEFIOK E. ESSIEN
Faculty of Pharmacy: Prof. ETIENE E. ESSIEN
Faculty of Social Sciences: Prof. IMO E. UKPONG
Postgraduate School: Prof. IME S. IKIDDEH

PROFESSORS

ABASIATTAI, M. B., History
ABASIEKONG, E. M., Sociology
ABODERIN, A., Chemistry
ACHALU, O. E., Health Education
AFOLABI, M., Library Science
ANWANA, U. I., Guidance and Counselling
EKA, D., English
EKONG, E. E., Sociology
EKPENYONG, S., Sociology and Anthropology
EKPO, A. H., Economics
EKPO, N. M., Physics
EKPO, O. E., Curriculum Studies
ENOH, C. O. E., Geography
ESHIET, I. T., Chemistry and Education
ESSIEN, E. E., Pharmaceutical Chemistry
ETTE, S. I., Biochemistry
ETUK, U. A., Philosophy
EZE, O. C., Law
IBE-BASSEY, G. S., Educational Technology
IKKIDEH, I. S., English
IWOK, E. R., Accounting
NWA, E. U., Engineering
OKON, E. D., Zoology
UDO, E. J., Soil Science
UDOFOT, M. A., Curriculum Studies
UKPONG, I. I., Economics
UMOH, J. E., Animal Science
UMOH, P. U., Law
USORO, E., Geography

STATE UNIVERSITIES

ABIA STATE UNIVERSITY

PMB 2000, Uturu, Abia State

Telephone: (88) 220785
Internet: www.abia-state-uni.net

Founded 1981 as Imo State University; present name c. 1993
State control
Language of instruction: English
Academic year: October to August

Chancellor: Ambassador Dr Chief M. T. MBU
Vice-Chancellor: Prof. OGWO E. OGWO
Deputy Vice-Chancellor: Prof. STELLA OGBUAGU
Pro-Chancellor: EMEKA NWANKPA
Registrar: O. E. ONUOHA
Librarian: HERBERT I. IWUJI

Library of 27,000 vols
Number of teachers: 640
Number of students: 7,050

DEANS

College of Agriculture and Veterinary Medicine: Dr V. O. IMOH
College of Biological and Physical Sciences: Dr C. I. OGBONNAYA
College of Business Administration: Dr I. AJA-NWACHUKU
College of Education: Prof. V. C. NWACHUKU
College of Engineering and Environmental Studies: Dr M. A. IJIOMA (acting)
College of Humanities and Social Sciences: Prof. J. O. J. NWACHUKWU-ABADA
College of Legal Studies: M. O. UNEGBU (acting)
College of Medicine and Health Sciences: A. U. MBANASO (Provost)

PROFESSORS

AKPUAKA, F. C., Medicine and Health Sciences
ALEZI, O., Education
EBEOGU, A. N., Humanities and Social Sciences
EKE, F., Medicine and Health Sciences
MADUABUM, M. A., Education
MBATA, G. N., Biological and Physical Sciences
MKPA, M. A., Education
NWACHUKU, V. C., Education
NWACHUKWU-AGBADA, J. O. J., Humanities and Social Sciences
OGBONNAYA, C. I., Biological and Physical Sciences
OGBUAGU, S. C., Humanities and Social Sciences
OGWO, E. O., Marketing
ONOFEGHARA, N., Education
ONOH, J. K., Finance
ONUIGBO, W. I., Medicine and Health Sciences
OPARA-NADI, O. I., Agriculture and Veterinary Medicine
UWAKAH, C. T., Agriculture and Veterinary Medicine

ATTACHED RESEARCH INSTITUTES

Centre for Igbo Studies: Dir Dr C. NWAHUNANYA.
Centre for Population Studies: Dir D. CHIKEZIE.
Institute for Distance Education: Dir I. S. ONWUCHEKWA.
Language Centre: Dir Dr A. R. UHUEGBU.

ADAMAWA STATE UNIVERSITY

PMB 25, Mubi, Adamawa State
Telephone: (75) 883620
E-mail: info@adamawastateuni.net
Internet: www.adamawastateuni.net
Founded 2002
Vice-Chancellor: Prof. ABDURRAHMAN GHAJI
Number of teachers: 40
Number of students: 1,484
Faculties of Agriculture, Science and Social and Management Sciences.

UNIVERSITY OF ADO-EKITI

PMB 5363, Ado-Ekiti, Ekiti State
Telephone: (30) 250026
E-mail: admin@unadportal.com
Internet: www.unadportal.com
Founded 1982
Vice-Chancellor: Prof. ISRAEL O. ORUBULOYE
Deputy Vice-Chancellor: Prof. OLUFUNKE EGUNJOBE
Registrar: M. O. OGUNNIYI
Bursar: F. M. FAPOHUNDA
Librarian: G. O. OGUNLEYE
Library of 100,000 vols
Number of teachers: 492

Number of students: 15,570 (12,340 full-time; 3,230 part-time)
Publications: *Annual Report, Nigerian Journal of Banking and Financial Issues* (2 a year)

DEANS

Faculty of Agriculture: Prof. J. A. OLUYEMI
Faculty of Arts: Dr M. A. ABIODUN (acting)
Faculty of Education: Prof. I. O. AKINDUTIRE
Faculty of Engineering: Dr J. O. ARIBISALA (acting)
Faculty of Law: A. IBIDAPO-OBE
Faculty of Management Sciences: Prof. J. F. AKINGBADE
Faculty of Science: Prof. O. OLAOFE
Faculty of Social Sciences: Prof. J. O. KOLAWOLE (acting)
College of Medicine: Prof. D. D. OYEBOLA
School of Postgraduate Studies: Prof. A. O. AKANDE

PROFESSORS

ABE, O. B., Mathematics
ADELOWO, E. D., Religious Studies
ADERIYE, J. B. I., Microbiology
AKANDE, A. O., Plant Science and Forestry
AKINDUTIRE, I. O., Educational Foundations
ALONGE, M. F., Guidance and Counselling
ALUKO, M. E., Mechanical Engineering
ASHAOLU, A. O., English
EGUNJOBI, O. A., Zoology
FALUYI, M. A., Plant Science and Forestry
KUTI, A. F. D., Law
OJO, S. I. A., Civil Engineering
OLAOFE, O., Chemistry
OMOJOLA, A. F. D., Mathematics
ORUBULOYE, I. O., Sociology
OWUMANAM, D. O., Guidance and Counselling
OYEBODE, A. B., Law
YOLOYE, V. L., Zoology

AMBROSE ALLI UNIVERSITY

PMB 14, Ekpoma, Edo State
Telephone: (55) 98448
Founded 1981
State control
Language of instruction: English
Academic year: September to August
Chancellor: HRH Alhaji Dr UMARU FARUQ BAHAGO (Emir of Minna)
Vice-Chancellor and Chief Executive: Prof. D. O. AIGBOMIAN
Deputy Vice-Chancellor (Academic): Dr G. B. EFOGHE
Deputy Vice-Chancellor (Administration) (vacant)
Provost, College of Medicine: Prof. G. O. AKPEDE
Registrar: G. T. OLAWOLE
Librarian: M. E. OJO-IGBINOBA
Library of 94,000
Number of teachers: 500
Number of students: 18,000
Publications: *AAU* (journal of the Faculty of Education, annually), *Iroro* (journal of the Faculty of Arts and Social Sciences, annually)

DEANS

Faculty of Agriculture: Dr P. O. ONOLEMHEMHEN (acting)
Faculty of Arts: Prof. F. I. EMORDI
Faculty of Clinical Sciences: F. ALUFOHAI
Faculty of Education: Prof. M. O. OMO-OJUGO
Faculty of Engineering and Technology: Prof. C. A. AJUWA
Faculty of Environmental Studies: Dr Ing. S. O. IZOMOH (acting)
Faculty of Law: Prof. A. D. BADAIKI
Faculty of Medicine: Dr C. P. ALOAMAKA
Faculty of Natural Sciences: Prof. F. EGHAREVBA (acting)

Faculty of Social Sciences: Prof. B. E. AIGBOKHAN

PROFESSORS

AGBONLAHOR, D. E., Microbiology
AIGBOKHAN, B. E., Economics
AIGBOMIAN, D. O., Educational Foundations
AKINBODE, A., Geography and Regional Planning
ALOAMAKA, C. P., Physiology
DIME, C. A., Religious and Cultural Management
ECHEKWUBE, A. O., Philosophy
EFOGHE, G. B., Psychology
EGUAVOEN, O. I., Chemistry
EMIOLA, A., Law
EMORDI, F. I., Modern Languages
IJOMAH, B. I. C., Sociology
IMOBIGHE, T. A., Political Science
KURNOW, K., History
LONGE, J. B., Economics
OAIKHINAN, E. P., Engineering, Technology and Development
OKECHA, S. A., Chemistry
OMO-OYUGO, M. O., Curriculum and Instruction
OSEMEIKHIAN, J. E. A., Physics
REMISON, S. U., Crop Science
SEGYNOLA, A. A., Geography and Regional Planning
UNOMAH, A. C., History
YESUFU, A. K., Electrical and Electronic Engineering

ATTACHED INSTITUTES

Centre for Security and Development Studies: Dir T. A. IMOBIGHE.
General Studies: Dir Dr V. O. AGHAYERE (acting).
Institute of Education: Dir Dr S. O. MOMOH (acting).

BENUE STATE UNIVERSITY

PMB 102119, Makurdi, Benue State
Telephone: (44) 533811
Fax: (44) 534040
E-mail: root@bensu.edu.ng
Founded 1992
Vice-Chancellor: Prof. DAVID I. KER
Deputy Vice-Chancellor: Dr YAKUBU A. OCHEFU
Registrar: W. I. MOZEH
Librarian: D. GBAKIGHIR
Library of 52,000 vols
Number of teachers: 324
Number of students: 6,114 (4,851 full-time, 1,263 part-time)

DEANS

Faculty of Arts: Dr CHARITY ANGYA
Faculty of Education: Dr NANCY AGBE
Faculty of Law: PAUL P. V. BELABO
Faculty of Management Science: CLEMENT AJEKWE
Faculty of Science: Prof. SOLOMON ABAA
Faculty of Social Science: Prof. JOSIAH SHINDI
Postgraduate School: Prof. AKASE SORKAA

PROFESSORS

ABAA, S., Physics
AGBO, C. I., Economics
AGISHI, E. C., Biology
AKPA, B., Accounting
AYATSE, J., Chemistry
EGA, L., Sociology
GYUSE, T., Geography
KER, D. I., English
OKITA, S. I. O., History
SAMBA, Law
SHINDI, J., Psychology
TEASYO, J., Sociology

EBONYI STATE UNIVERSITY

PMB 053, Abakaliki, Ebonyi State

Telephone: (43) 221093

Founded 1999

Vice-Chancellor: Prof. FIDELIS OGAH

Deputy Vice-Chancellor: Dr SELINA O. OCHEFU

Registrar: CHRISTIAN A. EZEH

Librarian: LIVINUS O. NWALI

Library of 21,000 vols

Number of teachers: 480

Number of students: 11,342 (8,227 full-time; 3,115 part-time)

DEANS

Faculty of Agriculture and Natural Resources Management: Prof. EKUMA O. EKUMANKAMA

Faculty of Applied and Natural Sciences: Prof. JAMES C. OGBONNA

Faculty of Arts: Dr AUSTIN CHUKWU

Faculty of Basic Medical Sciences: Prof. CLARENCE O. DIRIBE

Faculty of Clinical Medicine: Prof. VINCENT E. EGWUATU

Faculty of Education: Dr EMMANUEL AKUMAH

Faculty of Health Science and Technology: Dr ANTHONY O. AFOKE

Faculty of Law: Prof. MARTIN C. OKANY

Faculty of Management Sciences: Prof. EGWU U. EGWU

Faculty of Postgraduate Studies: Dr ERIC C. OKOLI

PROFESSORS

AKUBILO, C. J. C., Agricultural Economics, Management and Extension

ALAKU, S. O., Animal Production and Fisheries Management

ALI, A., Computer Science Education

AMUCHIE, F. A., Human Kinetics and Health Education

ANEZI-ONWU, O. N., Medicine

ATTAH, C. A., Surgery

AZUBUIKE, M. M., Computer Science Education

DIRIBE, C. O., Medical Biochemistry

EGWU, E. U., Management and Marketing

EGWUATU, V. E., Obstetrics and Gynaecology

EKUMANKAMA, E. O., Food Science

EZEIFEKA, G. O., Applied Microbiology

EZEILO, J. O., Industrial Mathematics and Applied Statistics

IBE, S., Animal Production and Fisheries Management

IBEMISI, J. A., Industrial Chemistry

IHEME, B. A., Law

INYIAMA, H. C., Computer Science

MARIRE, B. N., Animal Production and Fisheries Management

MGBODILE, M. U. K., Chemical Pathology

NDU, U., Applied Biology

NNOKE, F. N., Soil and Environmental Management

OBI, I. U., Crop Production and Landscape Management

OBIAKO, M. N., Surgery

OBIDOA, O., Medical Biochemistry

OBINNA, O. E., Economics

OBIONU, C. N., Community Medicine

OGAH, F., Crop Production and Landscape Management

OGBONNA, J. C., Biochemistrty and Biotechnology

OJI, C., Surgery

OKAGDUE, R. N., Applied Microbiology

OKAKA, A. N. C., Biochemistrty and Biotechnology

OKAKA, J. C., Food Science

OKANY, M. C., Law

OKOGBUE, C. O., Geology and Exploration Geophysics

OKOLI, E. C., Food Science

OKOLI, F. C., Political Science and Public Administration

OKORJI, E. C., Agricultural Economics, Management and Extension

OLUIKPE, B. O., English

ONUAGULUCHI, G., Pharmacology and Therapeutics

ONYENEKE, C. E., Biochemistrty and Biotechnology

OSISIOMA, B. C., Accountancy

UBAH, C. N., History and International Relations

UCHE, C. U., Banking and Finance

UKPABI, S. C., History and International Relations

UKWU, U. I., Economics

UMEH, E. D., Crop Production and Landscape Management

UMEJI, A. C., Geology and Exploration Geophysics

UMEZUIKE, I. A., Law

UMOH, S. M., Management and Marketing

ENUGU STATE UNIVERSITY OF SCIENCE AND TECHNOLOGY

PMB 01660, Enugu

Telephone: (42) 451244

Fax: (42) 335705

E-mail: esut@compuserve.com

Internet: www.esut.edu.ng

Founded 1980

Campuses at Enugu and Nsukka

State control

Academic year: January to October (2 semesters)

Language of instruction: English

Chancellor: Dr Chief ERNEST ADEGUNLE OLADEINDE SHONEKAN

Pro-Chancellor: Igwe Dr C. A. ABANGWU

Vice-Chancellor: Prof. SAMUEL CHUKWU

Deputy Vice-Chancellor: Prof. Rev. Canon CHINEDU NEBO

Registrar: B. N. UZOIGWE

Librarian: Dr N. ENE

Number of teachers: 472

Number of students: 29,827

Publication: *Journal of Science and Technology* (2 a year)

DEANS

Faculty of Agriculture: Prof. B. N. MARIRE

Faculty of Applied Natural Sciences: Prof. A. C. OKONKWO

Faculty of Basic Medical Sciences: Prof. S. E. ASOGWA

Faculty of Education: Prof. O. O. ONOWOR

Faculty of Law: Dr OBI S. OGENE

Faculty of Management Sciences: P. E. EMEKEKWUE

Faculty of Social Sciences: Dr D. N. NWATU

School of Engineering: Prof. G. N. ONOH

School of Environmental Sciences: Prof. A. N. AGU

School of Postgraduate Studies: Prof. R. C. OKAFOR

PROFESSORS

ADIBE, E. C., Geography and Meteorology

AGAJELU, S. I., Surveying and Photography

AGU, N., Geography and Meteorology

AKUBUILO, C. J. C., Agriculture

ALAKU, S. O., Animal Science

ANEKE, L. E., Chemical Engineering

ANOWOR, O. O., Foundations of Education

ASOGWA, S. E., Community Medicine

CHIDOBEM, I. J., Animal Science

CHUKWU, S. C., Co-operatives

ENE, A. C., Applied Natural Sciences

MADUEWESI, J. N. C., Applied Natural Sciences

MARIRE, B. N., Animal Science

MOGBO, J. O., Foundations of Education

NEBO, C. O., Mechanical and Materials Engineering

NWORGY, O. C., Applied Biology

OCHO, L. O., Foundations of Education

OHUCHE, R. O., Industrial Mathematics and Statistics

OKAFOR, N., Applied Microbiology and Brewing

OKAFOR, R. C., Foundations of Education

OKAKA, J. C., Agriculture

OKONKWO, C. A. C., Applied Biology

OKORIE, B. A., Mechanical and Materials Engineering

ONOH, G. N., Electrical and Electronic Engineering

ONYEHALU, A. S., Foundations of Education

UGWU, I. C., Urban and Regional Planning

UMEH, E. D., Applied Biology

ATTACHED INSTITUTES

Biotechnology and Pest Management Centre: Dir Dr A. A. NDUJI.

ESUT Business School, Lagos: Dir Dr I. S. NDOLO.

ESUT Social Research Institute: Dir Dr D. N. NWATU.

Industrial Development Centre: PMB 01660, Enugu; Dir Prof. B. A. OKORIE.

Institute of Education: PMB 01660, Enugu; Dir Dr C. U. UZODIMMA.

Institute of Entrepeneurial Studies: Dir Dr O. J. ONWE.

IMO STATE UNIVERSITY

PMB 2000, Owerri, Imo State

Telephone: (83) 221687

Fax: (83) 232716

Founded 1981

Vice-Chancellor: Prof. TONY G. ANWUKAH

Registrar: FRANCIS E. NWANKWO

Number of teachers: 230

Number of students: 15,991

DEANS

Faculty of Agriculture and Veterinary Medicine: A. ONWEAGBA

Faculty of Business Administration: INNOCENT OKONKWO

Faculty of Education: D. A. ONYEJEMEZI

Faculty of Engineering and Environmental Sciences: U. O. NKWOGU

Faculty of Humanities: ROSE ACHOLONU

Faculty of Law: U. S. F. NNABUE

Faculty of Science: E. N. MGBENU

Faculty of Social Sciences: C. R. NWACHUKWU

College of Medical and Health Sciences: B. C. JIBURUM

Postgraduate School: F. N. MADUBUIKE

KANO STATE UNIVERSITY OF TECHNOLOGY, WUDIL

PMB 3244, Kano, Kano State

Telephone: (64) 241149

Fax: (64) 241175

Founded 2001

Vice-Chancellor: SHAWKI A. A. SEOUD

Registrar: A. U. ABDURAHIM.

LADOKE AKINTOLA UNIVERSITY OF TECHNOLOGY

PMB 4000, Ogbomoso, Oyo State

Telephone: (38) 720285

Fax: (38) 720750

Founded 1990 as Oyo State University of Technology; present name 1991

Vice-Chancellor: Prof. AKINOLA M. SALAU

Registrar: Y. O. GBADAMOSI

Library of 19,604 vols

Number of teachers: 439

Number of students: 12,245

DEANS

Faculty of Agriculture: J. I. OLAIFA
Faculty of Engineering and Technology: J. O. OJEDIRAN (acting)
Faculty of Environmental Sciences: R. O. R. KALILU
Faculty of Medical Sciences: P. O. AKINWISU (acting)
Faculty of Pure and Applied Sciences: R. O. AYENI

LAGOS STATE UNIVERSITY

PMB 1087, Apapa, Lagos State
Telephone: (1) 5884048
Fax: (1) 5884048
E-mail: veecee@lasu.org
Founded 1983
State control
Language of instruction: English
Academic year: October to July
Vice-Chancellor: Prof. ABISOGUN OLUBODE LEIGH
Registrar: OLUWATOYIN GLADSTONE OSHUN
Librarian: T. A. B. SERIKI
Library of 63,000 vols
Number of teachers: 513
Number of students: 35,544 (16,422 full-time, 19,122 part-time)
Publications: ECOFLASH, Educational Perspectives, Enhancing Quality Education in Nigeria, Journal of Humanities (2 a year), Journal of Prospects in Science, LASU Jurist, LASU Law Journal, LASU Social Science Journal, Nigerian Journal of Research & Review in Science

DEANS

Faculty of Arts: Dr KUMLE LAWAL
Faculty of Education: Prof. ADEMOLA ONIFADE
Faculty of Engineering: Prof. P. A. O. ADEGBUYI
Faculty of Law: Prof. B. A. SUSU
Faculty of Management Science: Prof. O. J. FAPOHUNDA
Faculty of Sciences: Prof. MARTIN A. ANATE-KHAI
Faculty of Social Sciences: Prof. TAYO ODU-MOSU
College of Medicine: Prof. WOLE ALAKIJA
Postgraduate School: Prof. C. O. OSHUN

PROFESSORS

ABDUL-KUREEM, H., Medical Biochemistry
ADARAMOLA, F., International Law and Jurisprudence
AJAJA, O., Mechanical Engineering
AJOSE, S. O., Electronics and Computer Engineering
AKINRIMISI, E. O., Haematology and Blood Transfusion
ALAKIJA, W., Community and Primary Healthcare
ANETEKHAI, M. A., Fisheries Science
ASHIRU, O. A., Anatomy
BAMGBOYE, O. A., Chemistry
DADA, O. A., Chemical Pathology
FAPOHUNDA, O. J., Business Administration
HUNPONU-WUSU, O. O., Community and Primary Healthcare
IKHARIALE, M. A., Public Law
MATANMI, S. O., Industrial Relations and Personnel Management
OBAFUNWA, J. O., Pathology
ODERINDE, B. B., Curriculum Studies
ODUBUNMI, E. O., Curriculum Studies
ODUMOSU, A. O., Geography and Planning
ODUMOSU, T., Communications
OKANLAWON, A., Anatomy
OKEBUKOLA, P. A. O., Curriculum Studies
OLUKOYE, A. O., Chemical Pathology
ONABANJO, A. O., Medical Microbiology

ONIFADE, A., Public Law
OSINBAJO, O. O., Public Law
OYERINDE, J. P. O., Medical Biochemistry
SAGOE, A. O., Haematology and Blood Transfusion
TUNDE, S., Communications and Educational Management
YEROKUN, O. A., Business Law

NIGER DELTA STATE UNIVERSITY

PMB 1, Abraka, Delta State
Telephone: (54) 66027
Founded 1992
Vice-Chancellor: Prof. F. M. A. UKOLI
Registrar: E. E. AVBIOROKOMA
Librarian: LAWRENCE OGBENI.

OLABISI ONABANJO UNIVERISTY

PMB 2002, Ago-Iwoye, Ogun State
Telephone: (37) 432384
Fax: (37) 432384
E-mail: info@oou-edu.org
Internet: www.oou-edu.org
Founded 1982
State Government control
Academic year: October to July
Chancellor: Dr AYOOLA OBA OTUDEKO
Pro-Chancellor: Prof. BIYI AFONJA
Vice-Chancellor: Prof. AFOLABI SOYODE
Deputy Vice-Chancellors: Prof. E. O. A. AJAYI, Prof. ODUTOLA OSILESI
Registrar: APOSTLE SAMUEL O. AJAYI
Librarian: O. K. ODUSANYA
Library of 106,709 vols
Number of teachers: 699
Number of students: 43,382 (28,221 full-time, 15,161 part-time)
Publications: Ago-Iwoye Journal of Social and Behavioural Sciences (2 a year), GEGE Journal of English Department (annually), International Journal of Accountancy, Finance and Management Sciences (2 a year), Journals of History and Diplomatic Studies (annually), Journal of Philosophy and Development. (annually), Journal of Public Law and Practice (annually), Journal of Social and Management Sciences (annually), Nigerian Journal of Private and Commercial Law (annually), OSU Journal of Educational Studies (annually), OYE Journal of Arts (annually), Private and Commercial Law Additional Information (annually), Studies in Curriculum (quarterly)

DEANS

Faculty of Agricultural Management and Rural Development: Dr AIHONSU JOHN (Provost)
Faculty of Agricultural Production and Renewable Resources: Prof. S. O. OSUNLAJA
Faculty of Arts: Prof. KAMALDEEN BALOGUN
Faculty of Basic Medical Sciences: Prof. JIDE OLOWOOKERE
Faculty of Clinical Sciences: Prof. FEMI ADELOWO
Faculty of Engineering: Prof. J. AKINYEMI
Faculty of Environmental Technology: Prof. TOYIN OGUNTONA
Faculty of Education: Prof. OLATUNJI ODE-DEYI
Faculty of Law: Prof. JUSTUS SOKEFUN
Faculty of Management Sciences: Dr S. A. TELLA (acting)
Faculty of Pharmacy: Prof. M. N. FEMI-OYEWO
Faculty of Science: Prof. AFOLABI ADEBANJO
Faculty of Social Sciences: Dr WALE OLAITAN
College of Agricultural Sciences: Prof. S. F. ADEDOYIN (Provost)
College of Engineering and Technology: Prof. R. O. FAGBENLE (Provost)

Obafemi Awolowo College of Health Sciences: Prof. M. A. OLANREWAJU (Provost)
Postgraduate School: Prof. O. O. KEHINDE PHILLIPS (Provost)

PROFESSORS

ADEBANJO, A., Chemical Sciences
ADEDIPE, V. O., Educational Foundations and Management
ADEDOYIN, S. F., Agricultural Extension and Rural Sociology
ADEJONWO, K. O., Crop Production
ADESEMOWO, P. O., Educational Foundations and Management
ADESIMI, A. A., Agribusiness and Farm Management
ADETORO, O. O., Obstetrics and Gynaecology
AFEJUKU, D. H., Private and Commercial Law
AJAYI, E. O. A., Educational Foundations and Management
AJIBADE, E. S., Educational Foundations and Management
ALAUSA, O. K., Community Medicine and Primary Care
AWODERU, V. A., Biological Sciences
AYANLAJA, S. A., Soil Science and Farm Mechanisation
BALOGUN, K A., Religious Studies
BENEDICT, J. N., Curriculum Studies and Instructional Technology
DADA, O. A., Haematology and Blood Transfusion
DADA, S. S., Earth Sciences
EJIWUNMI, A. B., Anatomy
ERINOSHO, O. A., Sociology
FEMI, O. M. N., Pharmaceutics and Pharmaceutical Technology
HASSAN, T., Educational Foundations and Management
IYANIWURA, J. O., Mathematical Sciences
JAYESIMI, A. E. A., Medicine
KEHINDE-PHILLIPS, O. O., Earth Sciences
ODEDEYI, TUNJI, Sports Science and Health Education
ODUGBEMI, O. O., Geography and Regional Planning
ODUMUYIWA, E. A., Religious Studies
OGUNBA, OYIN, English
OGUNDERO, V. W., Biological Sciences
OGUNYEMI, E. O., Chemical Pathology and Haematology
OLAGUNJU, O. P., Educational Foundations and Management
OLANREWAJU, D. M., Paediatrics
OLOWOOKERE, J. O., Biochemistry
OLOWU, A. O., Paediatrics
OLUDIMU, O. L., Agricultural Economics
OSILESI, O., Biochemistry
OSONUBI, O., Biological Sciences
OSUNLAJA, S. O., Crop Production
OWORU, O. O., Crop Production
OYEDEJI, O. A., Curriculum Studies and Instructional Technology
OYEGUNLE, O. A., Anaesthesia
OYESIKU, O. O., Geography and Regional Planning
SANWO, J. O., Crop Production
SOSANWO, O. A., Mathematical Sciences
SULE-ODU, A. O., Obstetrics and Gynaecology
TAIWO, A., Educational Foundations and Management

RIVERS STATE UNIVERSITY OF SCIENCE AND TECHNOLOGY

PMB 5080, Port Harcourt, Rivers State
Telephone: (84) 233288
Fax: (84) 230720
E-mail: riversvarsity@yahoo.com
Founded 1971, university status 1980
State control
Language of instruction: English
Academic year: October to July

Chancellor: Maj.-Gen. (rtd) MUHAMMADU SANI SAMI
Pro-Chancellor: Chief OMBO F. ISOKRARI
Vice-Chancellor: Prof. S. C. ACHINEWHU
Deputy Vice-Chancellor: Prof. V. O. T. OMUARU
Registrar: M. Y. OGURU
Librarian: Dr B. E. AHIAUZU

Library of 121,700 vols
Number of teachers: 502
Number of students: 15,342
Publications: *Annual Report, News Bulletin* (monthly)

DEANS

Faculty of Agriculture: Prof. S. N. WEHKE
Faculty of Engineering: Prof. T. JOHNARRY
Faculty of Environmental Sciences: Dr N. O. ORUWARI (acting)
Faculty of Law: U. JACK-OSIMIRI (acting)
Faculty of Management Sciences: Dr D. W. MacCLAYTON (acting)
Faculty of Science: Prof. S. D. ABBEY
Faculty of Technical and Science Education: Prof. W. AMAEWHULE (acting)
Postgraduate School: Prof. E. N. WAMI

HEADS OF DEPARTMENTS

Faculty of Agriculture:

Agricultural Economics and Extension: Prof. M. S. IGBEN
Animal Science: Prof. B. M. ORUWARI
Crop and Soil Science: Dr N. M. OGBURIA (acting)
Fisheries: Chief M. B. INKO-TARIAH
Food Science and Technology: Dr I. S. BARIMALAA (acting)
Forestry and Environment: Dr H. N. UKOIMA (acting)

Faculty of Engineering:

Agricultural Engineering: Dr A. J. AKOR (acting)
Chemical and Petrochemical Engineering: Prof. S. A. AMADI
Civil Engineering: Dr M. E. EPHRAIM (acting)
Electrical Engineering: Dr C. O. AHIAKWO (acting)
Marine Engineering: Dr I. E. DOUGLAS (acting)
Mechanical Engineering: Eng. Dr H. I. HART (acting)

Faculty of Environmental Sciences:

Architecture: F. B. TAOL (acting)
Estate Management: I. I. KAKALU (acting)
Land Surveying: T. A. OPUAJI (acting)
Quantity Surveying: K. N. O. NYENKE (acting)
Urban and Regional Planning: Dr OWEI (acting)

Faculty of Law:

Business Law: G. A. OPARA
Jurisprudence and International Law: N. S. OKOGBULE (acting)
Private and Property Law: A. I. CHUKWUEMERIE (acting)
Public Law: R. U. A. WOKOCHA

Faculty of Management Sciences:

Accountancy: N. A. UKPAI (acting)
Banking and Finance: Dr S. N. AMADI (acting)
Management: Dr SETH ACCRA-JAJA
Marketing: Dr P. P. EKERETE
Mass Communication: Dr A. A. AMAKIRI
Secretarial Administration: Dr E. I. UGOJI (acting)

Faculty of Sciences:

Applied and Environmental Biology: Dr O. K. N. OGBALU
Chemistry: Dr P. U. ADIUKWU
Mathematics and Computer Science: Dr M. A. ALABRABA

Medical Laboratory Sciences: Dr C. K. NWACHUKWU
Physics: Dr F. E. OPARA

Faculty of Technical and Science Education:

Business Education: Dr M. E. AKPOMI
Educational Foundations: Dr N. W. ANDAH (acting)
Science and Technical Education: A. I. A. EKEZIE

PROFESSORS

Faculty of Agriculture:

ALFRED-OCKIYA, J. F., Fisheries
AMAKIRI, M. A., Soil Science
BEREPUBO, N. A., Animal Science
IGBEN, M. S., Agricultural Economics/Extension
ISIRIMAH, N. O., Crop/Soil Science
MONSI, A., Animal Science
ONUEGBU, B. A., Crop/Soil Science
OPUWARIBO, E. E., Crop/Soil Science
ORUWARI, B. M., Animal Science
WAHUA, T. A. T., Crop/Soil Science
WEKHE, S. N, Animal Science
ZUOFA, K, Crop/Soil Science

Faculty of Engineering:

ABOWEI, M. F. N.
CHINWAH, J. G.
IDERIAH, F. J. K., Mechanical Engineering
IDONIBOYE-OBU, K. I., Chemical/Petrochemical Engineering
JOHNARRY, T., Civil Engineering
ODI-OWEI, S., Mechanical Engineering
OGUARA, T. M., Civil Engineering
WAMI, E. N.

Faculty of Environmental Sciences:

FUBARA, D. M. J., Geodesy
ORUWARI, M. O.
TEME, S. C., Geology

Faculty of Management Sciences:

AHIAUZU, A. I., Business Administration
FUBARA, B. A., Business Administration
JOHNNIE, P. B., Business Administration

Faculty of Science:

ABBEY, S. D.
NWANKWO, S. I., Chemistry
OGULU, A.
OKWAKPAM, B. A.
SOKARI, T. G.

Faculty of Technical and Science Education:

AHIAKWO, M. J.
AMAEHULE, W. A.
GEORGEWILL, J. W.

ATTACHED INSTITUTES

Institute of Agricultural Research and Training: Dir Dr Y. GIAMI (acting).

Institute of Education: Dir Prof. J. W. GEORGEWILL.

Institute of Foundation Studies: Dir Dr C. OPARA (acting).

Institute of Geoscience and Space Technology: Dir Prof. S. C. TEME.

Institute of Pollution Studies: Dir Prof. N. O. ISIRIMAH (acting).

PRIVATE UNIVERSITIES

ABTI AMERICAN UNIVERSITY OF NIGERIA

2 Ahmed Onibudo St, POB 73688, Victoria Island, Lagos
Telephone: (1) 3200695
E-mail: abtiuniversity@yahoo.com
Internet: www.abti-american.edu.ng
Founded 2005 in partnership with the American University, Washington, DC, USA
Number of students: 200
President: Dr DAVID HUWILER

Dean of Students and Registrar: Dr BARRY MORRIS.

BABCOCK UNIVERSITY

PMB 21244, Ikeja, Lagos
Telephone: (37) 630148
Fax: (37) 630532
E-mail: babcock@infoweb.abs.net
Internet: www.babcockuni.edu.ng
Founded 1999; fmrly Adventist Seminary of West Africa
Seventh-Day Adventist Church control
Vice-Chancellor: Prof. ADEKUNLE ALALADE
Faculties of Education and Humanities, Management and Social Sciences and Science and Technology.

BENSON IDAHOSA UNIVERSITY

PMB 1100, University Way, Off Upper Adesuwa Grammar School Rd, Benin City
Telephone: (52) 253764
E-mail: webmaster@idahosauniversity.com
Internet: www.idahosauniversity.com
Founded 2002
President: Rev. F. E. B. IDAHOSA II.

COVENANT UNIVERSITY

10 km Idiroko Rd,, Canaan Land, Ota, Ogun State
Telephone: (1) 7900724
E-mail: contact@covenantuniversity.com
Internet: www.covenantuniversity.com
Founded 2002
Chancellor: Dr DAVID OYEDEPO
Vice-Chancellor: Prof. AIZE OLOHIGBE IMOUO-KHOME OBAYAN
Colleges of Business and Social Sciences, Human Development and Science and Technology.

IGBINEDION UNIVERSITY

PMB 0006, Okada, Benin-City
Telephone and fax: (52) 260005
E-mail: pefs@skannet.com
Internet: www.igbinedionuniversity.edu.ng
Founded 1999
Vice-Chancellor: Prof. EGHOSA EMMANUEL OSAGHAE
Deputy Vice-Chancellor: Prof. L. C. CHIEDOZI
Dean of Student Affairs: Prof. GILBERT O. NWOBU
Registrar: Dr SALLY AKWUGO ASAGWARA
Librarian: Dr R. OLORUNSOLA (acting)

DEANS AND PROVOSTS

College of Agriculture: Prof. ADETOKUNBO ADEOLA (Dean)
College of Arts and Social Sciences: Dr ANGELU M. ONWUEJEOGU (Dean)
College of Business and Management Studies: Prof. A. E. OKOYE (Dean)
College of Engineering: Dr T. S. WARA (acting) (Dean)
College of Health Sciences: Prof. TUNDE DARAMOLA (Provost)
College of Law: Prof. M. O. OGUNGBE (Dean)
College of Natural and Applied Sciences: Prof. ALEXANDER E. ODAIBO (Dean)
College of Pharmacy: Prof. SAMSON ESEZOBOR (Dean)
School of Basic Medical Sciences: Prof. A. A. ODUTOGA (Dean)
School of Clinical Medicine: Prof. L. C. CHIEDOZIE (Dean)
School of Postgraduate Studies: Prof. ABAYOMI ONI (Dean)

PROFESSORS

ADELUSI, Pharmacy

ADEOLA, A., Wildlife and Forestry
AGBA, M., Microbiology
AGBONLAHOR, D., Microbiology and Medical Laboratory Sciences
AIBONI, S., Law
AWOGUN, I., Medical Microbiology
BAXTER-GRILLO, D., Anatomy
CHIEDOZIE, L., Surgery
DARAMOLA, T., Community Health
EKEH, J., Electrical and Electronic Engineering
EKUNDARE, R., Economics
ESEZOBOR, S., Pharmacy
NAREBO, D., Law
NWOBU, G., Medical Laboratory Sciences
ODAIBO, A., Biological Sciences: Zoology
ODUTUGA, A., Biochemistry
OFUOROFO, I., Chemical Pathology
OGUNBIYI, J., Morbid Anatomy
OGUNGBE, M., Law
OKOYE, A., Accountancy
OLUOHA, U., Chemical Pathology
ONI, A., Mechanical Engineering
ONWUJEOGWU, A., Sociology and Anthropology
OSAGHAE, Political Science
OSENI, T., Agronomy
OSIFO, N., Pharmacology
PADONU, M., Community Health
YESUFU, English

PAN-AFRICAN UNIVERSITY

2 Ahmed Onibudo St, POB 73688, Victoria Island, Lagos
Telephone: (1) 3200695
Founded 2002
Vice-Chancellor: Prof. ALBERT J. ALOS
Postgraduate degree programmes in business administration and economics.

Polytechnics and Colleges

FEDERAL POLYTECHNIC, ADO-EKITI

PMB 5351, Ado-Ekiti, Ekiti State
Telephone: (30) 250523
E-mail: fedpolyado@fedpolyado.org
Internet: www.fedpolyado.org
Founded 1977
Academic year: February to November
Rector: Prof. O. AJAJA
Registrar: A. I. AJAYI
Librarian: M. O. OLASEHINDE
Library of 15,706 vols, 845 periodicals
Number of teachers: 290
Number of students: 6,161
Publications: *Expertus* (sustainable development, 2 a year), *Research Journal* (annually)

HEADS OF SCHOOLS

Business Studies: A. O. AKINYEMI
Engineering: D. A. T. ADEGBOYEGA
Environmental Studies: G. S. OLORUNOJE
Science and Computer Studies: D. O. ORIMAYE

AKANU IBIAM FEDERAL POLYTECHNIC, UNWANA

PMB 1007, Afikpo, Ebonyi State
Telephone: (90) 500180
Founded 1981
Rector: G. I. AMASIATU
Registrar: IHEANACHOR V. OBI OBI
Librarian: J. A. EKEH (acting)
Library of 12,217 vols
Number of teachers: 132
Number of students: 2,500

Publications: *Annual Report, Information Bulletin* (quarterly), *Student Handbook*

DIRECTORS

School of Business: A. I. IBIAM
School of Engineering: S. EGBUCHULAMI
School of Industrial Technology: M. I. ANUNA
School of Science and General Studies: O. U. L. IBE-URO

FEDERAL POLYTECHNIC, AUCHI

PMB 13, Auchi, Edo State
Telephone: (57) 200148
Fax: (57) 200148
Founded 1973
Rector: Sir O. F. EBOREIME
Registrar: F. O. OGUNBOR
Librarian: J. O. AGHOJA
Library of 38,250 vols
Number of teachers: 305
Number of students: 9,500

DIRECTORS OF SCHOOLS

Applied Sciences and Technology: P. AWERIALE
Art and Design: Prince OSAGIE-ERESE
Business Studies: J. EDEMODE
Engineering: S. OHIMAI
Environmental Studies: C. V. AJOKU

FEDERAL POLYTECHNIC, BAUCHI

PMB 0231, Bauchi
Telephone: (77) 543630
Fax: (77) 540465
E-mail: registrar@bauchipoly.edu.ng
Internet: www.bauchipoly.edu.ng
Founded 1979
Academic year: October to July
Rector: Surv. I. S. JAHUN
Registrar: Alhaji LABARAN IBRAHIM
Librarian: Mallam N. O. TOYYO
Library of 35,900 vols
Number of teachers: 257
Number of students: 8,667

DEANS

School of Business Studies: C. P. EJIKEME
School of Engineering Technology: Engr J. D. KONNI
School of Environmental Technology: J. A. ALEREGE
School of General Studies: Mal. M. L. GARBA
School of Technology: S. M. KUMO

BENUE STATE POLYTECHNIC, UGBOKOLO

PMB 2215, Otukpo, Benue State
Founded 1976
State control
Language of instruction: English
Academic year: October to September
Rector: Dr Y. W. AWODI
Deputy Rector: A. T. IKEREVE
Registrar: D. O. ONA
Librarian: M. A. SHINYI
Number of teachers: 115
Number of students: 1,505
Publication: *New Bulletin* (monthly)

DEANS

School of Art and Design: B. Y. EBUTE (acting)
School of Business and Administrative Studies: E. A. ADEGBE
School of Engineering: P. E. AGBESE
School of Technology: P. U. ANYOGO

FEDERAL POLYTECHNIC, BIDA

PMB 55, Bida, Niger State
Telephone: (66) 461707
Founded 1977
Academic year: October to July
Rector: Engr UMARU SANI-ANGO
Registrar: S. F. IKO
Librarian: S. A. KASIMU
Library of 26,105 vols
Number of teachers: 377
Number of students: 9,097
Publication: *Polymath Journal*

DIRECTORS

School of Applied Arts and Science: Dr S. O. ADEYEMO
School of Business and Management: P. KARICKSON
School of Engineering: Engr A. SULE
School of Environmental Studies: S. M. OB'LAMA
School of Preliminary Studies: ABDULLAHI MANN

POLYTECHNIC, BIRNIN KEBBI

PMB 1034, Birnin Kebbi, Kebbi State
Telephone: (68) 320597
Fax: (68) 320597
E-mail: kbpoly@skannet.com.ng
Founded 1976
Academic year: October to July
Rector: Arc. MUHAMMAD KABIR NABADE
Registrar: BELLO BAGUDU ABUBAKAR
Librarian: YUSUF ABUBAKAR ARGUNGU
Library of 13,761 vols
Number of teachers: 350
Number of students: 3,678
ND and HND courses; Postgraduate diplomas in management and public administration

DEANS

School of Accounting and Finance: UMARU SULE
School of Business and Public Administration: UMAR M. S. RAHA
School of Environmental Design: TIMOTHY O. IBIRONKE
School of Industrial Engineering: ISHAYA H. JOSHUA
School of Natural Resources Engineering: ABUBAKAR MIKAIL
School of Sciences: ABUBAKAR UMAR BASHAR
School of Surveying and Land Administration: (vacant)
School of Vocational and Technical Education: UMAR A. RUFAI

POLYTECHNIC, CALABAR

PMB 1110, Calabar, Cross River State
Telephone: (87) 222303
Founded 1973
State control
Language of instruction: English
Academic year: October to June
Rector: Engr R. E. EKANEM
Deputy Rector: Dr R. A. ITAM
Registrar: G. F. A. ONUGBA
Librarian: J. S. UMOH
Library of 25,000 vols
Number of teachers: 213
Number of students: 5,000

DIRECTORS OF SCHOOLS AND CENTRES

School of Agriculture: Dr E. J. OROK
School of Applied Science: U. U. ASUQUO
School of Business and Management: P. O. N. ABANG
School of Communication Arts: Dr M. E. EKERE

School of Education: Dr Joe Ibanga
School of Engineering: Dr E. U. Uye
School of Environmental Studies: A. Diawuo
Computer Centre: T. O. Eyo (acting)
Continuing Education Centre: N. U. Umoh
Centre for General and Preliminary Studies:
L. O. I. Ogueze
Industrial Co-ordination and Public Relations Unit: M. J. Mbong (acting)
Polytechnic Industrial Consultancy Services Unit: Dr I. U. Ugot

FEDERAL POLYTECHNIC, EDE

PMB 231, Ede, Osun State
Telephone: (35) 360096
Fax: (35) 360640
E-mail: edepoly@pinet.net
Vice-Chancellor: Deacon Joseph S. Oke.

INSTITUTE OF MANAGEMENT AND TECHNOLOGY

PMB 01079, Enugu, Enugu State
Telephone: (42) 250416
Founded 1973
Academic year: October to August
Rector: Dr T. Onyisi
Deputy Rector: Mazi L. O. E. Okata
Registrar: C. E. Attah
Librarian: Moses Idoko
Library of 49,000 vols
Number of teachers: 360
Number of students: 20,539
Publications: *Bulletin* (monthly), *Calendar*, *Journal of Technology Education* (annually), *MANTECH* (quarterly)

DIRECTORS OF SCHOOLS

Business Studies: Bona Ebue
Communication Arts: U. S. Madukwe
Distance Learning and Continuing Education: C. Ejeogu
Engineering: Engr V. C. Okoloekwe
Financial Studies: J. C. Odike
General Studies: F. C. Ndubuisi
Science, Vocational and Technical Education: I. Okafor
Technology: P. Ugwu

POLYTECHNIC, IBADAN

PMB 22, U.I. Post Office, Ibadan
Telephone: (22) 8104095
Fax: (22) 8101122
E-mail: polyibadan@pinet.net
Founded 1961, Polytechnic status 1970
Rector: Prof. A. O. Alabi
Registrar: R. G. Olayiwola
Librarian: O. A. Obikoya
Library of 78,000 vols
Number of teachers: 410
Number of students: 15,000
Publications: *Calendar/Prospectus* (annually), *PolyNews* (irregular)
Ordinary and Higher Diploma courses in commerce and communication sciences, engineering, environmental studies, natural sciences and NCE teacher education; Postgraduate Diploma courses in business studies and in mass communication; and Full Professional Diploma in town and regional planning.

FEDERAL POLYTECHNIC, IDAH

PMB 1037, Idah, Kogi State
Telephone: (58) 800128
Founded 1977
Rector: Dr Joseph Egila
Deputy Rector: Dr D. O. Bello
Registrar: S. A. Ogunleye

Librarian: J. I. Itanyi
Library of 19,489 vols
Number of teachers: 136
Number of students: 3,200
Publication: *News Bulletin* (monthly)

DIRECTORS OF SCHOOLS

School of Business Studies: M. A. Okpanachi
School of Engineering: Surv. P. Iyaji
School of Technology: E. O. Nda-Suleiman

FEDERAL POLYTECHNIC, ILARO

PMB 50, Ilaro, Ogun State
Telephone: (39) 440005
Founded 1979
Rector: Dr Prince S. A. Olateru-Olagbegi
Vice-Rector: Dr K. O. Jibodu
Registrar: R. O. Egbeyemi
Librarian: R. Ola Bello
Library of 16,000 vols
Number of students: 3,000

DIRECTORS

School of Applied Science: Dr J. O. A. Omole
School of Business Studies: J. O. Abibu
School of Engineering: F. O. Aregbe

KADUNA POLYTECHNIC

PMB 2021, Kaduna
Telephone: (62) 211551
Internet: kadpoly.edu.ng
Founded 1968
Rector: Alhaji Yusufu Aboki
Secretary: Abdullahi Ahman
Librarian: S. I. Shika
Library on three campuses of 56,000 vols
Number of teachers: 700
Number of students: 10,000

DIRECTORS

College of Administration and Business Studies: Dr U. Zahradeen
College of Environmental Studies: A. B. Ojo
College of Science and Technology: M. B. Salami (acting)

KANO STATE POLYTECHNIC

PMB 3401, B. U. K. Rd, Kano
Telephone: (64) 666058
Founded 1976
Rector: Arch. Hamza Said
Registrar: Sulaiman Abdullahi
Chief Librarian: Alhaji Wada Tafida Kurawa
Library of 30,276 vols
Number of teachers: 510
Number of students: 12,826
Publication: *News Bulletin* (monthly)

DIRECTORS

School of Management Studies: Hajiya Asabe B. Borodo
School of Social and Rural Development: Sulaiman Hashim
School of Technology: Yusufu Sule Gaya

HASSAN USMAN KATSINA POLYTECHNIC

PMB 2052, Katsina
Telephone: (65) 32816
Founded 1983
Rector: Kabir Ibrahim Matazu
Registrar: Abdu Halliru Abdullahi
Director, Library Services: Mannir Isa Batagarawa
Library of 18,000 vols
Number of teachers: 501
Number of students: 3,506

DIRECTORS OF COLLEGES

College of Administration and Management Studies: Alhaji Abdullahi Bawa
College of Legal and General Studies: Alhaji Musa Sule
College of Science and Technology: Aliyu Abubakar Bakori

FEDERAL POLYTECHNIC, KAURA NAMODA

PMB 1012, Kaura-Namoda, Zamfara State
Telephone: (63) 60452
E-mail: namodapoly@plet.net
Founded 1983
Academic year: October to July
Rector: Engr. Na'inna Mohammad Audi
Vice-Rector: C. Apraku
Registrar: A. Danboyi
Librarian: Alh. Sanusi Umar Ksauri
Library of 11,450 vols
Number of teachers: 152
Number of students: 3,268
Publications: *Kanajoge* (2 a year), *Namoda Telescope* (every six months), *Polytechnic News Bulletin* (monthly)

DIRECTORS

School of Business Management: Amos Oyeyiola
School of Engineering: Engr. Abubakar Lugard
School of Environmental Studies: Mall. Tajudeen Yusuf
School of General Studies: Alh. Ibrahim Kamba
School of Science and Technology: Isa Mohammad Kutigi

KWARA STATE POLYTECHNIC

PMB 1375, Ilorin
Telephone: (31) 221441
Founded 1972
Academic year: October to July
Rector: Prof. M. A. Ozatunji
Registrar: J. F. Ogunrinde
Librarian: E. S. Afolabi
Library of 50,155 vols
Number of teachers: 650
Number of students: 14,000
Publication: *Techforum* (2 a year)

DIRECTORS

Institute of Administration: K. G. Shittu
Institute of Basic and Applied Sciences: A. F. Fatunbi
Institute of Business and Vocational Studies: J. A. Awolola
Institute of Environmental Studies: A. O. Sulyman
Institute of General Studies: M. O. Olasehinde
Institute of Technology: Dr A. A. Saadu

LAGOS STATE POLYTECHNIC

PMB 21606, Ikeja, Lagos State
Telephone: (1) 523528
Founded 1977
Rector: B. Oloro
Deputy Rector: J. B. Agunbiade
Registrar: Oluwole O. Ojikutu
Chief Librarian: E. O. Soyinka
Library of 29,558 vols, 1,880 in special collections
Number of teachers: 222
Number of students: 4,287
Publications: *Laspotech News* (quarterly), *Poly Handbook* (annually).

MOSHOOD ABIOLA POLYTECHNIC, ABEOKUTA

PMB 2210, Abeokuta, Ogun State
Telephone: (80) 33230941
E-mail: mapolylib2002@yahoo.com
Internet: www.mapoly.educ.ng
Founded 1979
Rector: Alhaji WAHEED A. KADIRI
Deputy Rector: Arch. OLATOKUNBO FOWODE
Registrar: Maj. (retd) A. B. BADMOS
Librarian: BOLA ADEOSUN
Library of 22,097 vols
Number of teachers: 165
Number of students: 15,000
Publications: *Liberal Forum* (annually), *Polymath* (annually), *Social Philosophy* (annually)

DIRECTORS
School of Business and Management Studies: O. A. SOBANDE
School of Communication and General Studies: S. O. FAMUYIWA
School of Engineering: Dr M. O. ABDUL
School of Environmental Studies: A. A. JEGEDE
School of Pure and Applied Science: A. S. AROWOLO
Centre for Part-time Studies: O. A. SOILE

FEDERAL POLYTECHNIC, MUBI

PMB 35, Mubi, Adamawa State
Telephone: (75) 882771
Founded 1979
Academic year: October to July
Rector: Alhaji M. A. ABBA
Deputy Rector: E. E. ETUK
Registrar: B. BELLO
Librarian: T. S. TARFA
Library of 23,601 vols
Number of teachers: 184
Number of students: 3,338
Publications: *Applied Science and Management* (annually), *Sabon Dale* (annually)

DIRECTORS
School of Business Studies and General Studies: A. S. YAHAYA
School of Engineering: I. DAGWA
School of Science Technology: A. BAWA

FEDERAL POLYTECHNIC, NASARAWA

PMB 001, Nasarawa, Nasarawa State
Telephone: (47) 66707
E-mail: fpnas@yahoo.com
Founded 1983
Rector: Dr IDRIS BUGAJE.

FEDERAL POLYTECHNIC, NEKEDE

PMB 1036, Owerri, Imo State
Telephone: (83) 231516
Founded 1978
Rector: Engr O. I. NWANKWO
Registrar: C. D. ONUKOGU
Librarian: J. U. OBASI
Library of 24,837 vols
Number of teachers: 257
Number of students: 30,000

DEANS
School of Business and Public Administration: S. C. NSOFOR
School of Engineering Technology: J. N. AMADI
School of Environmental Design: G. O. C. NWACHUKWU
School of General Studies: Dr N. C. ANUMIHE
School of Industrial Sciences: C. A. OMENKA

FEDERAL POLYTECHNIC, OFFA

PMB 420, Offa, Kwara State
Telephone: (31) 800160
Founded 1979
Rector: Dr ABDUL-RAZAQ BELLO.

FEDERAL POLYTECHNIC, OKO

PMB 21, Aguata, Anambra State
Telephone: (48) 911144
Founded 1979
Rector: Dr U. C. NZEWI
Registrar: Sir O. C. A. OFOCHEBE
Librarian: Dr OBIORA NWOSU
Library of 150,000 vols
Number of students: 9,298
Publications: *Federal Polytechnic Library* (4 a year), *Journal of Accountancy* (Nigerian edition, 2 a year), *The Polytechnic Accountant* (annually)

Courses in Business Studies, Information Technology, Environmental Design, Technology, Accountancy, Business Administration and Management, Marketing, Secretarial Studies, Banking and Finance, Mass Communication, Library Science, Architecture, Estate Management and Building Technology.

ONDO STATE POLYTECHNIC

POB 1019, Owo, Ondo State
Telephone: (51) 241045
Founded 1980
Rector: Prof. A. S. ADEDIMILA
Deputy Rector: KEHINDE ALAO
Registrar: R. F. AKERELE
Librarian: M. O. POPOOLA
Library of 25,000 vols
Number of teachers: 173
Number of students: 9,710

DEANS
Business Studies: Chief A. O. OLALEYE
Engineering: Rev. S. A. ADEGBEMIRO
Environmental Studies: E. A. ARIGBEDE
Food Technology: J. K. AJAYI

PETROLEUM TRAINING INSTITUTE

PMB 20, Effurun, Delta State
Telephone: (53) 250774
Fax: (53) 250774
Founded 1972
Academic year: October to July
Principal: Dr S. E. OVURU
Director of Finance and Supplies: Alh. H. A. LABBO
Director of Studies: Dr R. E. AKPOJIVI
Registrar: Dr I. M. ABBASS
Librarian: E. M. A. DUDU
Library of 54,013 vols
Number of teachers: 225
Number of students: 2,520
Publications: *Annual Report*, *PTI News* (4 a year).

PLATEAU STATE POLYTECHNIC, BARKIN LADI

PMB 02023, Bukuru, Plateau State
Founded 1978, present status 1980
Rector: Engr ALEXANDER A. T. KEBANG
Registrar: TIMOTHY A. ANJIDE
Director of Administration: LAMI A. ENATTO
Librarian: J. E. KOTSO
Library of 11,393 vols
Number of teachers: 121
Number of students: 2,260

Publications: *News Bulletins*, *Students' Handbook*

DEANS
School of Administration and General Studies: Mrs. L. A. ENATTO
School of Engineering and Environmental Studies: Dr R. JATAU
School of Management Studies: ELIZABETH PAM
School of Science and Technology: K. D. DABER

DIRECTORS
Centre for Continuing Education: ELIZABETH K. PAM
Consultancy and Applied Research Division: Engr O. O. OLUSANYA

YABA COLLEGE OF TECHNOLOGY

PMB 2011, Yaba, Lagos State 234
Telephone: (1) 7742155
Fax: (1) 7917565
Internet: www.yabatech.edu.ng
Founded 1948
Federal control
Academic year: October to July
Rector: O. OWOSO
Registrar: F. F. TAIWO (acting)
Deputy Rector (Academic): A. O. AGBAJE-WILLIAMS
Deputy Rector (Administration): Eng. A. I. ABIODUN
Polytechnic Librarian: R. I. OLOGBONSAIYE
Library of 70,000 vols
Number of teachers: 800
Number of students: 14,000
Publications: *Newsletter*, *Prospectus* (annually), *Yabatech News* (quarterly), *YCT Academic Journal* (published by various departments, each semester)

DIRECTORS
School of Art, Design and Printing: MAO OMOIGHE
School of Engineering: Eng. P. K. ADEGBOYEGA
School of Environmental Studies: Arch. A. A. ADENIJI
School of Management: IFY MAFINZE
School of Science: I. A. ABIODUN
School of Technology: O. AKINJAIYEJU

Federal College of Agriculture, Akure: Ado-Ekiti Rd, Akure, Ondo State; tel. and fax (34) 240891; f. 1957; library: 10,000 vols; 30 teachers; 1,000 students; Principal Dr A. O. AYODELE.

Federal College of Agriculture, Ibadan: Institute of Agricultural Research and Training, PMB 5029, Moor Plantation, Ibadan; tel. (2) 2312070; f. 1921; 33 teachers; 319 students; Provost Dr D. S. DARAMOLA.

Federal College of Forestry: Forestry Research Institute of Nigeria, PMB 5054, Ibadan; tel. (22) 411035; f. 1941; technical forestry training, National and Higher National Diploma courses; vocational courses; library: 4,800 vols; 20 teachers; 520 students; Dir Dr ISAAC I. ERO.

Federal School of Dental Hygiene: 1 Broad St, PMB 12562, Lagos; f. 1957; Principal Dr S. JOHNSON.

National Eye Centre: Off Nnamdi Azikiwe Way, PMB 2267, Kaduna; tel. and fax (62) 313956; e-mail neckad@yahoo.com; f. 1979; provides postgraduate ophthalmic training (medical and surgical), TOT IOL microsurgical course, ophthalmic nursing training, clinical services; 9 teachers; 16 students; Chief Medical Dir Dr C. P. OZEMELA; publs *Newsletter* (4 a year), *Pharmacy News* (monthly).

NORWAY

The Higher Education System

The oldest current institutions of higher education were founded before Norway declared its independence from Swedish rule in 1905. The state Universitetet i Oslo (founded in 1811) is the oldest university; the next oldest university is the state Universitetet for Miljo- Og Biovitenskap (Norwegian University of Life Sciences—founded in 1859). The first institution founded in the independent period in was the private Teologiske Menighetsfakultet (Norwegian Lutheran School of Theology—founded in 1907). Higher education is administered according to the Universities and Colleges Act (1995). Norway participates in the Bologna Process to establish a European Higher Education Area, the first phase of which is to adopt a credit-based system of comparable degrees with two main cycles (undergraduate and graduate). At 1 October 2003 130,148 students were enrolled at colleges of higher education, with a further 79,611 enrolled at universities and their equivalent.

Admission to higher education is on the basis of successful completion of secondary education, however since 2000 applicants have also been admitted with non-formal qualifications. In 2003 a two-tier Bachelors and Masters degree system was implemented in accordance with the principles of the Bologna Process. Norwegian institutions award degrees on the basis of the European Credit Transfers System (ECTS), and each year is equivalent to 60 'credits'. The standard undergraduate degree is the Bachelors, which lasts three years, and the first postgraduate degree is the Masters, a course lasting one-and-a-half to two years. The final postgraduate and highest university degree is the Doctorate, awarded after three to four years of study. The title of the Doctorate may vary depending on the subject area.

Post-secondary vocational and technical education is available at technical colleges (Teckniske Fagskoler), university colleges and state colleges. Programmes at these institutions last for two to three years.

Regulatory and Representative Bodies

GOVERNMENT

Ministry of Culture and Church Affairs: Akersgt. 59, POB 8030 Dep., 0030 Oslo; tel. 22-24-78-39; fax 22-24-90-10; e-mail postmottak@kkd.dep.no; internet www.regjeringen.no/kkd; Minister TROND GISKE.

Ministry of Education and Research: Akersgt. 44, POB 8119 Dep., 0032 Oslo; tel. 22-24-90-90; fax 22-24-95-40; e-mail postmottak@kd.dep.no; internet www.regjeringen.no/kd; Minister ØYSTEIN KÅRE DJUPEDAL.

ACCREDITATION

ENIC/NARIC Norway: NOKUT – Norwegian Agency for Quality Assurance in Education, POB 1708 Vika, 0121 Oslo; tel. 21-02-18-60; fax 21-02-18-01; e-mail postmottak@nokut.no; internet www.nokut.no/sw335.asp; Deputy Dir Gen IDA LØNNE.

Nasjonalt organ for kvalitet i utdanningen (Norwegian Agency for Quality Assurance in Education): POB 1708 Vika, 0121 Oslo; Kronprinsens gate 9, Oslo; tel. 21-02-18-00; fax 21-02-18-01; e-mail postmottak@nokut.no; internet www.nokut.no; f. 2002; ind. governmental agency; controls and develops the quality of Norwegian higher education instns through the evaluation, accreditation and recognition of quality assurance systems, instns and education programmes; Chair. Prof. PETTER AASLESTAD; CEO PER ARNE SYRRIST.

NATIONAL BODIES

Norsk Forbund for Fjernundervisning (Norwegian Association for Distance Education and Flexible Education): Lilleakerveien 23, 0283 Oslo; tel. 22-51-04-80; fax 22-51-04-81; e-mail nade@nade-nff.no; internet www.nade-nff.no; f. 1968; Dir INGEBORG BOE; publ. *Forum for Fjernundervisning* (newsletter).

Senter for internasjonalisering av høyere utdanning (Norwegian Centre for International Co-operation in Higher Education): POB 7800, 5020 Bergen; Vaskerelven 39, 5014 Bergen; tel. 55-30-88-00; fax 55-30-88-01; e-mail siu@siu.no; internet siu.no; promotes int. co-operation in education and research; Chair. Prof. KNUT BRAUTASET; Dir GUNN MANGERUD.

Universitets- og Høgskolerådet (Norwegian Association of Higher Education Institutes): Pilestredet 46B, 0167 Oslo; tel. 22-45-39-50; e-mail uhr@uhr.no; internet www.uhr.no; f. 2000 by mcrgcr of the Norwegian Council of State Colleges and the Norwegian Council of Univs.

Learned Societies

GENERAL

Kongelige Norske Videnskabers Selskab (Royal Norwegian Society of Sciences and Letters): Erling Skakkesgt. 47C, 7491 Trondheim; tel. 73-59-21-57; fax 73-59-58-95; e-mail postmaster@dknvs.no; internet www.dknvs.no; f. 1760; 617 mems (457 Norwegian, 141 foreign, 1 hon., 18 assoc.); Pres. Prof. STEINAR SUPPHELLEN; Sec.-Gen. YNGVE ESPMARK; publ. *Skrifter*.

Norske Videnskaps-Akademi (Norwegian Academy of Science and Letters): Drammensveien 78, 0271 Oslo; tel. 22-12-10-90; fax 22-12-10-99; e-mail dnva@online.no; internet www.dnva.no; f. 1857; sections of Mathematics and Natural Sciences, of Historical and Philosophical Sciences; 809 mems (452 Norwegian, 357 foreign); Pres. Prof. OLE DIDRIK LÆRUM; Sec.-Gen. Prof. REIDUN SIRVÅG; publs *Skrifter, Avhandlinger, Årbok*.

ARCHITECTURE AND TOWN PLANNING

Norske Arkitekters Landsforbund (Norwegian Architects' Association): Josefines gt. 34, 0351 Oslo 3; tel. 23-33-25-00; fax 23-33-25-01; e-mail nal@arkitektur.no; internet www.arkitektur.no; f. 1911; 3,060 mems; Dir JANNIKE HOVLAND; publs *Arkitektnytt* (20 a year), *Byggekunst* (8 a year), *Norske Arkitektkonkurranser*.

BIBLIOGRAPHY, LIBRARY SCIENCE AND MUSEOLOGY

Norsk Bibliotekforening (Norwegian Library Association): Malerhaugveien 20, 0661 Oslo; tel. 23-24-34-30; fax 22-67-23-68; e-mail nbf@norskbibliotekforening.no; internet www.norskbibliotekforening.no; f. 1913; 3,300 mems; Pres. FRODE BAKKEN; Sec. TORE KR. ANDERSEN; publ. *Bibliotekforum* (10 a year).

Norske Kunst- og Kulturhistoriske Museer (Association of Museums of Art and Cultural History): Ullevålsveien 11, 0165 Oslo; tel. 22-20-14-02; fax 22-11-23-37; f. 1918; 470 mems; library of 1,500 vols; Gen. Sec. SIRI S. VESTERKJAER; publ. *Museumsnytt* (Museum News).

ECONOMICS, LAW AND POLITICS

Norsk Forening for Internasjonal Rett (International Law Association, Norwegian Branch): c/o Wiersholm Mellbye and Bech, POB 1400 Vika, 0115 Oslo; Ruseløkkveien 26, 0115 Oslo; tel. 21-02-10-00; fax 21-02-10-01; e-mail nfir@nfir.no; internet www.nfir.no; f. 1925; 95 mems; Pres HANS WILHELM LONGVA; Sec. ELI ASCHEIM.

Statsøkonomisk Forening (Economic Association of Norway): Ullern Alle 59, 0381 Oslo; tel. 63-90-05-76; f. 1883; approx. 300 mems; Pres. Prof. KJELL STORVIK; Sec. BJÖRN STENSETH.

FINE AND PERFORMING ARTS

Arts Council Norway: POB 101, 0102 Oslo; tel. 22-47-83-30; fax 22-33-40-42; e-mail post@kulturrad.dep.no; internet www.kulturrad.no; f. 1965 in connection with the Cultural Fund to encourage artistic life and cultural activities in Norway and to distribute the resources of the Fund in grants and subsidies; nine mems appointed by the Cabinet and four by the Storting (Parliament) all for a period of four years; Chair. VIGDUS MOE SKARSTEIN; Dir-Gen. OLE JACOB BULL; publs *Notatserien* (2–6 a year), *Rapportserien* (1–4 a year).

Musikkinformasjonssenteret (Music Information Centre Norway): POB 2674 Solli, 0203 Oslo; tel. 23-27-63-00; fax 23-27-

63-01; e-mail info@mic.no; internet www.mic
.no; f. 1979; promotes and offers information
on Norwegian music of all genres, composers,
music institutions, performing groups and
artists; aims to build up a representative
colln of contemporary Norwegian music;
comprises a manuscript library, orchestral
materials, reference library, copying service;
library: 11,000 items of sheet music; 9,500
recordings; Dir SVEIN BJØRKÅS; publ. *Ballade*
(in Norwegian, online).

Norske Billedkunstnere (Association of
Norwegian Visual Arts): Grev Wedels plass
7, 0151 Oslo; tel. 23-35-68-50; fax 23-35-68-
69; e-mail nbk@billedkunst.no; internet www
.billedkunst.no; f. 1889, reorganized 1979
and 1988; a national association of professional artists' organizations; the Norwegian
Government's Advisory Board on questions
relating to graphic arts; 5 mems elected
every other year represent some 2,300 painters, sculptors and artists; Pres. ARNE NØST;
Sec. GJERT GJERTSEN; publ. *Billedkunstneren*
(7 a year).

HISTORY, GEOGRAPHY AND ARCHAEOLOGY

**Foreningen til norske Fortidsminnes-
merkers Bevaring** (Society for the Preservation of Ancient Monuments in Norway):
Dronningensgt. 11, 0152 Oslo; tel. 23-31-70-
70; fax 23-31-70-50; e-mail hovedadm@
fortidsminneforeningen.no; internet www
.fortidsminneforeningen.no; f. 1844; 7,500
mems; to protect and preserve buildings,
sites and monuments of historical value in
Norway; Chair. MARIANNE ROALD YTTERDAL;
Sec.-Gen. BJARTE GULLACHSEN; publs *Arbok*
(annually), *Fortidsvern* (4 a year).

Kirkehistorisk Samfunn (Church History
Society): Markalléen 7, 1368 Stabekk; e-mail
peidbe@frisurf.no; f. 1956; 54 mems; Pres.
Prof. JAN SCHUMACHER; Sec. Prof. Dr PEDER
A. EIDBERG.

Landslaget for Lokalhistorie: Institutt for
historie og klassiske fag, NTNU, 7491 Trondheim; tel. 73-59-64-33; fax 73-59-64-41;
e-mail post@historielag.org; internet www
.historielag.org; f. 1920; local history; 420
mem. historical socs; Pres. KURT TVERLI;
Man. JOSTEIN MOLDE; publs *Heimen* (4 a
year), *Lokalhistorisk* (4 a year).

Norsk Arkeologisk Selskap (Norwegian
Archaeological Society): Huk Aveny 35, 0287
Oslo 2; tel. 22-43-87-92; fax 22-13-52-86;
e-mail nas@arkeologi.no; internet www
.arkeologi.no; f. 1936; 720 mems; Pres.
CHRISTEN AASS; Sec.-Gen. EGIL MIKKELSEN;
publ. *Viking* (annually).

Norsk Lokalhistorisk Institutt: POB 8045
Dep, 0031 Oslo; Observatoriegata 1b, 0254
Oslo; tel. 22-92-51-30; fax 22-92-51-31; e-mail
nli@lokalhistorie.no; internet www
.lokalhistorie.no; f. 1955; guidance for local
historians, research in local history including
publication of sources, etc., valuable for
research; Dir KNUT SPRAUTEN.

Norsk Slektshistorisk Forening (Norwegian Genealogical Society): POB 59, Sentrum, 0101 Oslo; tel. 22-11-14-00; e-mail
sekretar@genealogi.no; internet www
.genealogi.no; f. 1926; approx. 2,000 mems;
Pres. LARS LØBERG; Sec. JAN KRISTIANSEN;
publs *Genealogen* (2 a year), *Norsk Slektshistorisk Tidsskrift* (2 a year).

Norske Historiske Forening (Norwegian
Historical Society): Avdeling for historie,
POB 1008 Blindern, 0315 Oslo; tel. 22-85-
67-59; fax 22-85-52-78; e-mail hifo@sv.uit.no;
internet www.uit.no/hifo; f. 1869; 970 mems;
Pres. VERA SCHWACH; Sec. ANNE IDA RØKE-
NESS; publs *HIFO-nytt* (quarterly), *Historisk
Tidsskrift* (quarterly).

LANGUAGE AND LITERATURE

Alliance Française: Frognersetervein 32,
0776 Oslo; offers courses and exams in
French language and culture and promotes
cultural exchange with France.

British Council: Fridthof Nansens Plass 5,
0160 Oslo; tel. 22-39-61-90; fax 22-42-40-39;
e-mail british.council@britishcouncil.no;
internet www.britishcouncil.no; offers
courses and exams in English language and
British culture and promotes cultural
exchange with the UK; Dir SIMON GIVERIN.

Goethe-Institut: Grønland 16, 0188 Oslo;
tel. 22-05-78-80; fax 22-17-20-04; e-mail
info@oslo.goethe.org; internet www.goethe
.de/oslo; offers courses and exams in German
language and culture and promotes cultural
exchange with Germany; library of 6,000
vols, 30 periodicals; Dir MICHAEL DE LA
FONTAINE.

Norsk PEN (Norwegian Centre of International PEN): Tordenskjoldsgate 6B, 0160
Oslo; tel. 22-47-92-20; fax 22-47-92-01;
e-mail pen@norskpen.no; internet www
.norskpen.no; f. 1922; contact for Norwegian
writers with the rest of the writing world;
defends freedom of expression world-wide,
with a special focus on Afghanistan, Belarus,
China, Tunisia, Turkey and the Middle East;
370 mems; Pres. ANDERS HEGER; Sec.-Gen.
CARL MORTEN IVERSEN.

**Riksmålsforbundet—Det Norske Aka-
demi for Sprog og Litteratur** (Norwegian
Academy for Language and Literature):
Inkognitogaten 24, 0256 Oslo 2; e-mail
ordet@riksmalsforbundet.no; internet www
.riksmalsforbundet.no; f. 1953; protects and
authorizes dictionaries of the traditional
'Riksmaal'; Chair. TROND VERNEGG; Sec.
Prof. SISSEL LANGE-NIELSEN.

Norske Forfatterforening (Norwegian
Authors' Union): POB 327 Sentrum, 0103
Oslo; tel. 23-35-76-20; e-mail post@
forfatterforeningen.no; internet www
.forfatterforeningen.no; f. 1893; 490 mems;
Chair. ANNE OTERHOLM.

MEDICINE

Norsk Farmaceutisk Selskap (Norwegian
Pharmaceutical Society): POB 5070, Majorstua, 0301 Oslo; tel. 21-62-02-23; fax 22-60-
81-73; e-mail farm-sel@online.no; internet
www.nfs.no; f. 1924; to further the scientific
and practical development of pharmacy; 550
mems; Chair. RAGNAR SALMÉN; Sec. KARL
ARNE WÆRNHUS.

Norsk Kirurgisk Forening (Norwegian
College of Surgeons): POB 17, Kjelsås, 0411
Oslo; fax 22-15-33-30; internet www
.legeforeningen.no/nkf; f. 1911; 804 mems;
Chair. TOM GLOMSAKER; Sec. RAGNI SKILLE
BERGER; publ. *Vitenskapelige forhandlinger*
(annually).

Norske Laegeforening (Norwegian Medical Association): POB 1152 Sentrum, 0107
Oslo; tel. 23-10-90-00; fax 23-10-90-10; e-mail
legeforeningen@legeforeningen.no; internet
www.legeforeningen.no; f. 1886; 23,000
mems; Pres. Dr TORUNN JANBU; Sec.-Gen.
Dr TERJE VIGEN; publ. *Tidsskrift for den
norske lægeforening* (2 a month).

Norske Medicinske Selskab (Norwegian
Medical Society): Drammensvn. 44, 0271
Oslo 2; tel. 22-44-06-44; internet www.dnms
.no; f. 1833; 600 mems; Medical Dir ØIVIND
LARSEN; Sec. ASTRID LAVOLL-NYLENNA.

Norske Tannlegeforening (Norwegian
Dental Association): POB 3063 Ellsenberg,
0207 Oslo 1; Frederik Stangsg. 20, 0264 Oslo;
tel. 22-54-74-00; fax 22-55-11-09; e-mail
tannlegeforeningen@tannlegeforeningen.no;
internet www.tannlegeforeningen.no; f.
1884; 4,540 mems; Pres. ARILD VAUGSTEIN;
Sec.-Gen. EIVIND KARLSEN; publ. *Den norske
tannlegeforenings Tidende* (monthly).

NATURAL SCIENCES

General

Polytekniske Forening (Polytechnical
Society): Rosenkrantzgt. 7, 0159 Oslo; tel.
22-42-68-70; fax 22-42-58-87; e-mail
polyteknisk@polyteknisk.no; internet www
.polyteknisk.no; f. 1852; 7,000 mems; Gen.
Sec. FREDRIK EVJEN; publ. *Teknisk Ukeblad*.

Selskapet til Vitenskapenes Fremme
(Society for the Advancement of Science):
Institutt for geografi/miljofag, Universitetet i
Bergen, Hans Holmboesgate 23, 5007 Ber-
gen; f. 1927; 200 mems; objects: to promote
and encourage intellectual activities gener-
ally by regular series of lectures, excursions;
Pres. Prof. KAREN BLAAUW HELLE; Gen. Sec.
Asst Prof. ARNFINN SEIM.

Biological Sciences

Norsk Botanisk Forening (Norwegian
Botanical Association): Naturhistorisk
Museum, POB 1172 Blindern, 0318 Oslo;
tel. 22-85-17-01; fax 22-85-18-35; e-mail
blyttia@nhm.uio.no; internet www.toyen.uio
.no/botanisk/nbf/; f. 1935; 1,100 mems; Pres.
ANDERS LUNDBERG; publ. *Blyttia* (quarterly).

Physical Sciences

Norsk Geologisk Forening (Geological
Society of Norway): NGU, POB 3006, 7002
Trondheim; tel. 73-90-40-68; fax 73-92-16-20;
e-mail ngf@geologi.no; internet www.geologi
.no; f. 1905; 1,400 mems; Chair. HARALD
BREKKE; Gen. Sec. TERJE THORSNES; publ.
Norsk Geologisk Tidsskrift (Norwegian Jour-
nal of Geology, 4 a year).

Norsk Kjemisk Selskap (Norwegian Chemical Society): POB 1107 Blindern, 0317
Oslo; tel. 22-85-55-56; fax 22-85-54-41;
internet www.kjemi.no; f. 1893; 2,100
mems; Pres. TOR HEMMINGSEN; Gen. Sec.
HARALD WALDERHAUG; publs *Kjemi*, *Year
Book*.

TECHNOLOGY

Norges Tekniske Vitenskapsakademi
(Norwegian Academy of Technological
Sciences): Lerchendal Gaard, 7491 Trond-
heim; tel. 73-59-54-63; fax 73-59-08-30;
e-mail ntvamail@ntva.ntnu.no; internet
www.ntva.no; f. 1955; 454 mems; Pres. Prof.
ASBJØRN ROLSTADÅS; Sec.-Gen. HEIN JOHN-
SON.

**Teknisk-Naturvitenskapelig Forening
(Tekna)** (Norwegian Society of Chartered
Technical and Scientific Professionals
(Tekna)): POB 2312, Solli, 0201 Oslo; tel.
22-94-75-00; fax 22-94-75-01; e-mail post@
tekna.no; internet www.tekna.no; f. 1874;
professional society; promotes research and
development; represents engineering profession in its relations with other organizations
and countries; 30,600 mems; Pres. EINAR E.
MADSEN; Sec.-Gen. TRYGVE DAHL; publs *Sivi-
lingeniøren* (10 a year), *Teknisk Ukeblad*
(weekly), *Våre veger* (10 a year).

Research Institutes

GENERAL

Chr. Michelsens Institutt: POB 6033,
Postterminalen, 5892 Bergen; tel. 55-57-40-
00; fax 55-57-41-66; e-mail cmi@cmi.no;
internet www.cmi.no; f. 1930; independent,
non-profit research institution with a focus
on Sub-Saharan Africa, Southern and Central Asia, the Middle East, Balkans and
South America; library of 70,000 vols; Dir
GUNNAR M. SØRBØ.

Norges Forskningsråd (Research Council of Norway): Stensberggata 26, POB 2700, St Hanshaugen, 0131 Oslo; tel. 22-03-70-00; fax 22-03-70-01; e-mail post@forskningsradet.no; internet www.forskningsradet.no; attached to Ministry of Education and Research; promotes and supports basic and applied research in all areas of science, technology, medicine and the humanities; awards research grants and fellowships and runs its own research establishments (see elsewhere under Research Institutes); Dir-Gen. ARVID HALLÉN.

ECONOMICS, LAW AND POLITICS

Institute of Industrial Economics: Breiviken 2A, 5035 Bergen-Sandviken; tel. 55-95-06-60; f. 1975; independent, non-profit research institution, carrying out research into economic and social conditions of importance for industrial development in Norway; c. 30 staff; Pres. ARNE SELVIK; publs reports, books, discussion papers.

International Peace Research Institute, Oslo (PRIO): Hausmanns gt. 7, 0186 Oslo; tel. 22-54-77-00; fax 22-54-77-01; e-mail info@prio.no; internet www.prio.no; f. 1959, ind. institute 1966; library of 20,000 vols, 300 journals; Chair BERNT AARDAL; Dir STEIN TØNNESSON; publs *Journal of Peace Research* (6 a year), *Security Dialogue* (quarterly).

Norsk Utenrikspolitisk Institutt (Norwegian Institute of International Affairs): C. J. Hambros pl. 2D, POB 8159, Dep., 0033 Oslo; tel. 22-99-40-00; fax 22-36-21-82; e-mail info@nupi.no; internet www.nupi.no; f. 1959; international economics, development studies, European integration, collective security, Russian studies, United Nations, peacekeeping; library of 20,000 vols; Dir SVERRE LODGAARD; publs *International Politikk* (quarterly), *Forum for Development Studies*, *Hvor Hender Det?* (weekly), *Nordisk Øst-Forum* (quarterly), *Norwegian Foreign Policy Studies* (monographs), *NUPI Notat*, *NUPI Rapport* (Research reports).

Norske Nobelinstitutt (Norwegian Nobel Institute): Henrik Ibsens gate 51, 0255 Oslo; tel. 22-12-93-00; fax 22-12-93-10; e-mail postmaster@nobel.no; internet www.nobel .no; f. 1903; follows the development of international relations (especially the work for the pacific settlement of them) in order to advise the Nobel Peace Prize Committee; research dept; library of 196,000 vols; Dir GEIR LUNDESTAD.

Statistisk Sentralbyrå (Statistics Norway): Kongens gt. 6, POB 8131, Dep, 0033 Oslo; tel. 21-09-00-00; fax 21-09-49-73; e-mail ssb@ssb.no; internet www.ssb.no; f. 1876; library of 160,000 vols; Dir-Gen. ØYSTEIN OLSEN; publs *Norges offisielle statistikk* (series, Official Statistics of Norway, irreg.), *Økonomiske analyser* (Economic Survey), *Sosiale og Økonomiske Studier* (Social and Economic Studies), *Statistiske analyser* (Statistical Survey).

HISTORY, GEOGRAPHY AND ARCHAEOLOGY

Institute for Pacific Archaeology and Cultural History: Bygdøynesveien 36, 0286 Oslo; tel. 23-08-67-67; fax 23-08-67-60; e-mail kon-tiki@online.no; internet www .kon-tiki.no; f. 1986; attached to Kon-Tiki Museum (Oslo).

NATURAL SCIENCES

Biological Sciences

Havforskningsinstituttet (Institute of Marine Research): POB 1870 Nordnes, 5817 Bergen; tel. 55-23-85-00; fax 55-23-85-31; e-mail post@imr.no; internet www.imr.no; f.

1900; attached to Ministry of Fisheries; applied research related to fisheries; divisions: marine environment, marine living research, aquaculture (with two experimental stations), coastal zone; library of 80,000 vols; Dir ROALD VAAGE; publs *Årsmelding* (annual report), *Facts and Figures* (every 2 years), *Fisken og Havet*.

Physical Sciences

Norges Geologiske Undersøkelse (Geological Survey of Norway): Leiv Eirikssons vei 39, 7491 Trondheim; tel. 73-90-40-00; fax 73-92-16-20; e-mail ngu@ngu.no; internet www .ngu.no; f. 1858; library of 75,000 vols and 950 periodicals; Man. Dir TORE NEPSTAD; publs *Bulletin* (scientific articles in English, irregular), *Gråsteinen* (popular science magazine in Norwegian, irregular).

Norske Meteorologiske Institutt (Norwegian Meteorological Institute): POB 43, Blindern, 0313 Oslo; e-mail met.inst@met.no; internet www.met.no; f. 1866; library of 30,000 vols; Dir-Gen. ANTON ELIASSEN; publs *Årsberetning* (annual report), *Klimatologisk månedsoversikt* (monthly), *Technical Report* (irregular).

Norsk Polarinstitutt (Norwegian Polar Institute): Polar Environmental Centre, 9296 Tromsø; tel. 77-75-05-00; fax 77-75-05-01; e-mail postmottak@npolar.no; internet www.npolar.no; f. 1928; objects: preparation and publication of maps of Norwegian territories in the polar regions; scientific investigations in the fields of geology, geophysics and biology; responsible for Norwegian Antarctic Research expeditions; scientific logistical support; administration and maintenance of an all-year scientific station Ny-Ålesund, Svalbard; library of 20,000 vols and 12,000 pamphlets and authors' MSS; Dir JAN-GUNNAR WINTHER; publs *Polar Research* (2–3 a year), *Rapporter* (5–10 a year), *Research in Svalbard* (annually).

RELIGION, SOCIOLOGY AND ANTHROPOLOGY

Instituttet for sammenlignende kulturforskning (Institute for Comparative Research in Human Culture): POB 2832 Solli, 0204 Oslo; tel. and fax 22-55-42-07; e-mail kulturfo@online.no; internet kulturfo .webhotell.no; f. 1922; comparative study of languages, religions, folklore, law, ethnology, archaeology, and sociology, sponsoring research programmes and publishing; Pres. P. KVÆRNE, Vice-Chair. S. MØNNESLAND; publ. *Institute for Comparative Research in Human Culture. Series B* (2 to 4 a year).

TECHNOLOGY

Institutt for energiteknikk (Institute for Energy Technology): POB 40, 2007 Kjeller; tel. 63-80-60-00; fax 63-81-63-56; e-mail firmapost@ife.no; internet www.ife.no; f. 1948; international research institute for energy and nuclear technology; undertakes research and development within the energy and petroleum sectors, carries out assignments in nuclear technology, safety and environmental research; Man. Dir KJELL H. BENDIKSEN.

NIVA—Norsk Institutt for Vannforskning (NIVA—Norwegian Institute for Water Research): POB 173, Kjelsås, 0411 Oslo; tel. 22-18-51-00; fax 22-18-52-00; internet www .niva.no; f. 1958; research and contract projects on technical, economical and sanitary problems in connection with water supply, waste water and pollution in rivers and lakes/fjords; library of 34,000 vols, 800 periodicals; Dir ODD KARSTEN SKOGHEIM; publ. *Reports*.

Norges Geotekniske Institutt (NGI) (Norwegian Geotechnical Institute): Sognsveien 72, POB 3930, Ullevaal Stadion, 0806 Oslo; tel. 22-02-30-00; fax 22-23-04-48; e-mail ngi@ ngi.no; internet www.ngi.no; f. 1953; soil, rock and snow mechanics, foundation engineering, dams, offshore structures, instrumentation, rock engineering, geoenvironmental engineering; library of 22,500 vols, 300 periodicals, Terzaghi Library, Peck Library; Dir SUZANNE LACASSE.

Norsk institutt for by- og regionforskning (Norwegian Institute for Urban and Regional Research): Gaustadalleen 21, POB 44, Blindern, 0313 Oslo; tel. 22-95-88-00; fax 22-60-77-74; e-mail nibr@nibr.no; internet www.nibr.no; f. 1967; 90 mems; library of 23,000 vols, 200 periodicals; Dir Mag. JON NAUSTDALSLID; publs *NIBR-notat*, *NIBR-rapport*, *Regionale Trender* (2 a year).

Norsk Institutt for Luftforskning (Norwegian Institute for Air Research): POB 100, 2007 Kjeller; tel. 63-89-80-00; fax 63-89-80-50; internet www.nilu.no; f. 1969; national and international research and consultation in air pollution, atmospheric dispersion and measurements, meteorological measurements and analysis, instrumentation and chemical analysis; library of 9,000 vols, 130 periodicals; Dir ØYSTEIN HOV; publs *Annual Report*, scientific reports.

Norsk Regnesentral (Norwegian Computing Centre): POB 114, Blindern, 0314 Oslo 3; tel. 22-85-25-00; fax 22-69-76-60; e-mail nr@ nr.no; internet www.nr.no; f. 1958; contract research and development projects in information and communication technology and applied statistical modelling; library of 4,000 vols, 250 periodicals; Man. Dir LARS HOLDEN.

NUTEC—Norsk Undervannsteknologisk Senter A/S (NUTEC—Norwegian Underwater Technology Centre): Svestadveien 27, 1458 Fjellstrand; tel. 66-96-69-00; fax 66-96-69-01; e-mail shg@nutec.no; internet www .nutec.no; f. 1976, present name 1981; test and research centre for underwater technology, full-scale testing, diving, hyperbaric medicine and physiology, safety analysis, education and training; consulting services; library of 5,000 vols, 170 periodicals; Dir RASMUS D. WOXHOLT; publ. *NUTEC Reports*.

Norwegian Marine Technology Research Institute (MARINTEK): POB 4125 Valentinlyst, 7450 Trondheim; tel. 73-59-55-00; fax 73-59-57-76; e-mail marintek@ marintek.sintef.no; internet www.marintek .sintef.no; f. 1984; mem. of the SINTEF Group; research, development and technical consultancy in the maritime sector for industry and the public sector; develops and verifies technological solutions for the shipping and maritime equipment industries and offshore petroleum production; library of 11,000 vols, 365 periodicals; Pres. ODDVAR AAM; publ. *Marintek Review*.

NORSAR: POB 53, 2007 Kjeller; tel. 63-80-59-00; fax 63-81-87-19; internet www.norsar .no; f. 1968; research on problems in distinguishing between subterranean nuclear explosions and earthquakes; applied seismology research; Dir ANDERS DAHLE; publ. *Technical Summary* (2 a year).

Papirindustriens Forskningsinstitutt (PFI) (Paper and Fibre Research Institute): 7491 Trondheim; tel. 73-55-09-00; fax 73-55-09-99; e-mail firmapost@pfi.no; internet www .pfi.no; f. 1923; Pres. Dr PHILIP ANDRÉ REME.

Senter for Internasjonal Økonomi og Skipsfart (SIØS) (Centre for International Economics and Shipping): Norwegian School of Economics and Business Administration, Helleveien 30, 5045 Bergen; tel. 55-95-95-75; fax 55-95-93-50; f. 1958; research and publication of results, aims to provide a centre for research fellows in sea transport, shipping economics and international economics from Norway and abroad, to promote cooperation with similar institutions; library of 3,500 vols, 1,600 periodicals, reports, etc.; Dir Prof. GUTTORM SCHJELDERUP; Sec. ANNE LIV SCRASE.

SINTEF Byggforsks (SINTEF Building and Infrastructure): POB 123, Blindern, 0314 Oslo 3; tel. 22-96-55-00; internet www .byggforsk.no; f. 1953, reorganized 1985 as an independent institute; library of 25,000 vols, 250 periodicals; Dir BJØRN SVENSVIK; publs *Anvisninger* (Design Manuals, irregular), *Håndbøker* (Handbooks, English summary), *Byggdetaljblad* (Norwegian building detail sheets), *Rapporter* (Reports, English summary, irregular), *Saertrykk* (reprints), technical briefs.

SINTEF Energiforskning (SINTEF Energy Research): 7034 Trondheim; tel. 73-59-72-00; fax 73-59-72-50; e-mail energy .research@sintef.no; internet www.sintef.no; f. 1951; research and development in the field of energy, especially electricity generation, transmission, distribution and consumption; Man. Dir SVERRE AAM.

Stiftelsen for Industriell og Teknisk Forskning ved Norges Tekniske Høgskole (SINTEF) (Foundation for Scientific and Industrial Research at the Norwegian Institute of Technology): Strindveien 4, 7465 Trondheim; tel. 73-59-30-00; fax 73-59-33-50; e-mail info@sintef.no; internet www.sintef .no; f. 1950; undertakes contracts in science and technology research for industry and others; six affiliated research institutes; Pres. UNNI M. STEINSMO.

Transportøkonomisk Institutt (Institute of Transport Economics): POB 6110, Etterstad, 0602 Oslo; tel. 22-57-38-00; fax 22-57-02-90; e-mail toi@toi.no; internet www.toi.no; f. 1964; Norwegian centre for transport research; library of 24,000 vols, 240 periodicals; Dir LASSE FRIDSTROM; publ. *Samferdsel* (Communication, 10 a year).

Libraries and Archives

Arendal

Arendal Bibliotek (Arendal Library): Serviceboks 616, 4809 Arendal; tel. 37-01-39-13; fax 37-01-30-80; e-mail arendal@arendal .folkebibl.no; internet www.arendal.folkebibl .no; f. 1832, incorporated *Aust-Agder Fylkesbibliotek* (East Agder County Library) 1972; 196,720 vols; Head Librarian GURI ERLANDSEN.

Ås

Universitetet for Miljø- og Biovitenskap, Biblioteket (Norwegian University of Life Sciences, Library): POB 5003, 1432 Ås; tel. 64-96-50-00; fax 64-96-55-01; f. 1859; literature concerning all branches of agricultural science and forestry, conservation of natural resources, biology, etc.; 493,000 vols; Head Librarian PAUL STRAY.

Bergen

Bergen offentlige Bibliotek (Municipal and County Library): 5015 Bergen; tel. 55-56-85-95; fax 55-56-85-55; e-mail fido@bergen .folkebibl.no; internet www.bergen.folkebibl .no; f. 1874; 634,000 vols; Grieg collection of 150 MSS and 5,800 letters; City Librarian TRINE KOLDERUP FLATEN.

Universitetsbiblioteket i Bergen (University of Bergen Library): POB 7808, 5020 Bergen; tel. 55-58-25-32; fax 55-58-97-03; e-mail post@ub.uib.no; internet www.ub.uib .no; f. 1825 as Bergens Museums Bibliotek;

1,765,000 vols; spec. collns of newspapers, manuscripts, pictures and maps; Dir Dr KARI GARNES; publs *Norwegian Archaeological Review*, *Sarsia* (Marine Biology).

Drammen

Drammen Bibliotek (Public Library of Drammen): POB 136 Bragernes, 3001 Drammen; Gamle Kirkepl. 7, POB 1136, 3019 Drammen; tel. 32-80-63-00; fax 32-80-64-53; e-mail ref.biblioteket@drammen.kommune .no; internet bibliotek.drammen.kommune .no; f. 1916; municipal library of Drammen and county library of Buskerud; 3 br.libraries, 3 children's brs, 2 bookmobiles; 310,000 vols; Pres. ANNIKKEN SIGHOLT; Chief Librarian CECILIE BRUUN.

Hamar

Statsarkivet i Hamar (Regional State Archives): Lille Strandgt. 3, 2300 Hamar; tel. 62-52-36-42; fax 62-52-94-48; f. 1917; public record office, archives; public reading-room open on weekdays; 13,000 vols; Chief Archivist PER-ØIVIND SANDBERG.

Kristiansand

Kristiansands Folkebibliotek (Municipal Library): POB 476, 4665 Kristiansand; tel. 38-12-49-10; fax 38-12-49-49; e-mail post .folkebibliotek@kristiansand.kommune.no; internet www.kristiansand.folkebibl.no; f. 1909; 290,000 vols; Chief Librarian ANNE KRISTIN UNDLIEN.

Oslo

ABM–utvikling (Norwegian Archive, Museum and Library Authority): POB 8145 DEP, 0033 Oslo; tel. 23-11-75-00; fax 23-11-75-01; e-mail post@abm-utvikling.no; internet www.abm-utvikling.no; f. 2003; Dir JON BIRGER ØSTBY.

Deichmanske Bibliotek (Oslo Public Library): Arne Garborgs 4, 0179 Oslo 1; tel. 23-43-29-00; fax 22-11-33-89; f. 1785; 1,246,000 vols; Chief Librarian LIV SØETEREN.

Riksarkivet (National Archives of Norway): Folke Bernadottes vei 21, 4013 Ullevål Stadion, 0806 Oslo; tel. 22-02-26-00; fax 22-23-74-89; internet www.riksarkivet.no; f. 1817; takes charge of the archives of the ministries and other branches of the central administration; 60,000 vols; Dir JOHN HERSTAD; publ. *Arkivmagasinet* (3 a year).

Statistisk sentralbyrås bibliotek og Informasjonssenter (Statistics Norway, Library and Information Centre): POB 8131 Dep., 0033 Oslo; Kongensgt. 6, Oslo; tel. 21-09-46-42; fax 21-09-45-04; e-mail biblioteket@ssb.no; internet www.ssb.no/ biblioteket; f. 1917; 154,000 vols: mainly economic, demographic and statistical literature (official and int. statistics included); open to the public; OECD deposit library; European Statistical Data Support; publ. *Biblioteksnytt* (electronic edn only, monthly).

Stortingsbiblioteket (Library of the Norwegian Parliament): Stortinget, 0026 Oslo 1; tel. 23-31-36-90; fax 23-31-38-59; e-mail biblioteket-postmottak@stortinget.no; f. 1871; reference library mainly for members of Parliament and govt officials; open to the public on application; 180,000 vols; literature on political and social science, law, and economics; reports from official and semi-official institutions; Head Librarian GRO SANDGRIND; publs *Arsberetning* (Annual Report), *Nytt fra Stortingsbiblioteket* (monthly).

Patentstyret (Norwegian Patent Office): POB 8160 Dep., 0033 Oslo; tel. 22-38-73-00; fax 22-38-73-01; e-mail email@patentstyret .no; internet www.patentstyret.no; f. 1888; 27,000,000 patent specifications; 50,000 vols

of scientific and technical books and periodicals of reference for patent research; Head of Dept TORIL FOSS; publs *Norske mønstertidende*, *Norske Patentskrifter*, *Norsk Patenttidende*, *Norsk varemerketidende*.

Universitetsbiblioteket i Oslo (University of Oslo Library): POB 1085, Blindern, 0317 Oslo; tel. 22-85-50-50; fax 22-84-41-50; e-mail postmottak@ub.uio.no; internet www.ub.uio .no; f. 1811; 3,300,000 vols; spec. collns of papyri and orientalia; the Univ. Library receives by law copies of all Norwegian books; Librarian BENTE ANDREASSEN.

Utenriksdepartementets Dokumentasjonssenter (Documentation Centre of the Ministry of Foreign Affairs): 7 Juni-Plassen 1, Oslo, POB 8114 Dep., 0032 Oslo 1; tel. 22-24-31-30; fax 22-24-31-61; e-mail doksenter@ mfa.no; f. 1900; literature on foreign affairs, international law and international relations; not open to the public; Head Librarian RITA AARS-NICOLAYSEN.

Rjukan

Rjukan Bibliotek (Public Library of Rjukan): POB 54, 3661 Rjukan; tel. 35-08-16-60; fax 35-08-16-65; e-mail utlaan@rjukan .folkebibl.no; internet www.rjukan.folkebibl .no; f. 1914; 117,863 vols; 3 brs; Chief Librarian PER ESPELAND.

Stavanger

Stavanger Bibliotek (Stavanger Library): POB 310, 4001 Stavanger; tel. 51-50-70-90; fax 51-50-70-25; f. 1885; municipal library for the town of Stavanger, central library for the county of Rogaland; 450,432 vols; music and picture collection; Librarian KURT KRISTENSEN.

Tønsberg

Tønsberg og Nøtterøy Bibliotek (Tønsberg and Nøtterøy Public Library): Storgt. 26, 3126 Tønsberg; tel. 33-31-94-85; fax 33-31-64-75; e-mail tbg@tonsberg.folkebibl.no; internet tbg.tonsberg.folkebibl.no; f. 1909; 250,000 vols; Chief Librarian METTE HENRIKSEN AAS.

Trondheim

Universitetsbiblioteket i Trondheim (NTNU library): 7491 Trondheim; tel. 73-59-51-10; fax 73-59-51-03; e-mail ubit@ub .ntnu.no; internet www.ub.ntnu.no; f. 1768; library of the Norges Teknisk-Naturvitenskapelige Universitet (NTNU); receives deposit copies of all Norwegian books; arts, social sciences, science, technology, architecture, medicine; nat. resource library for architecture and technology; 2,500,000 vols, 15,000 periodicals; Dir INGAR LOMHEIM.

Ulefoss

Telemark fylkesbibliotek/Nome folkebibliotek: Ringsevja 2, 3830 Ulefoss; tel. 35-94-89-20; fax 35-94-89-40; e-mail telfy@t-fk .no; internet www.tm.fylkesbibl.no; f. 1942; county library; 152,447 vols, 197 periodicals; Librarian LILLIAN NILSSEN.

Museums and Art Galleries

Bergen

Bergen Museum, Universitetet i Bergen: H. Hårfagresgt. 1, 5020 Bergen; tel. 55-58-93-60; fax 55-58-93-64; e-mail post@bm.uib .no; internet museum.uib.no; f. 1825, part of University 1948; anthropology, archaeology, botany, geology, Norwegian culture and folk art, zoology; Dir SIRI JANSEN; publ. *Årbok for Bergen Museum* (annually).

Vestlandske Kunstindustrimuseum (West Norway Museum of Decorative Art): Nordahl Brungt. 9, 5014 Bergen; tel. 55-33-66-33; fax 55-33-66-30; e-mail post@vk .museum.no; internet www.vk.museum.no; f. 1887; 20,000 objects including Norwegian and European furniture, glass, porcelain, silver and textiles from the renaissance to modern times; Gen. Munthe's collection of Chinese art; library of 20,000 vols; Dir JORUNN HAAKESTAD; Curators ANNE BRITT YLVISÅKER, TROND INDAHL.

Bodø

Salten Museum: Prinsens gt. 116, 8005 Bodø; tel. 75-50-35-00; fax 75-52-58-05; e-mail post@saltenmuseum.no; internet www.saltenmuseum.no; f. 1888; covers most aspects of life in the county of Nordland; 80,000 items, specialities: fisheries, boats, etc.; library of 6,000 vols; Dir HARRY ELLINGSEN.

Drammen

Drammens Museum–Fylkesmuseum for Buskerud: Konnerudgaten 7, 3045 Drammen; tel. 32-20-09-30; e-mail post@ drammens.museum.no; internet www .drammens.museum.no; f. 1908; merged with Drammen Art Collection 1996; large collns of art and cultural history; library of 16,000 vols; Dir ASMUND THORKILDSEN; publ. *Arbok*.

Fredrikstad

Fredrikstad Museum: POB 862, 1670 Kraakeroey; Located at: Isegran, Kraakerroey, Fredrikstad; f. 1903; cultural and military history of the town and district; Curator TOVE M. THØGERSEN; publ. *Yearbook*.

Hamar

Hedmarksmuseet og Domkirkeodden: POB 1053, 2305 Hamar; tel. 62-54-27-00; fax 62-54-27-13; e-mail admin@ hedmarksmuseet.museum.no; internet www .domkirkeodden.no; f. 1906; open-air museum and medieval collection; ruins of the medieval cathedral, bishop's palace (now housing a modern exhibition), and other medieval ruins; excavations in progress; farm buildings depicting local history and domestic life; library of 14,000 vols; Dir STEINAR BJERKESTRAND; Chief Curator RAGNAR PEDERSEN; publ. *Arbok Fra Kaupang og bygd*.

Attached museums:

Kirsten Flagstad Museum: Kirkegt. 11, Hamar; POB 1053, Hamar 2305; tel. 62-54-27-00; fax 62-54-27-13; e-mail post@ kirsten-flagstad.no; internet www .kirsten-flagstad.no; dedicated to the life and work of opera singer Kirsten Flagstad (1895–1962), born in Hamar.

Norsk Utvandrermuseum (Norwegian National Emigrant Museum): Åkershagan, 2312 Ottestad; tel. 62-57-48-50; fax 62-57-48-51; e-mail museum@emigrant.museum .no; internet www.museumsnett.no/ emigrantmuseum; f. 1955; Chair. GEORG A. BROCH.

Lillehammer

Lillehammer Kunstmuseum (Lillehammer Art Museum): Stortorget, 2601 Lillehammer; tel. 61-26-94-44; fax 61-25-19-44; e-mail kunstmus@online.no; f. 1927; contains collections of Norwegian paintings, sculpture and graphic art, historical and contemporary art exhibitions; Dir SVEIN OLAV HOFF; publs catalogues, etc.

Sandvigske Samlinger (Sandvig Collections): Maihaugen, 2600 Lillehammer; tel. 61-28-89-00; fax 61-26-95-93; f. 1887; 185 old houses of historical interest and 30 old workshops in a new exhibition hall; exhibitions of Norwegian history and folk culture; library of 18,000 vols; Dir OLAV AARAAS; publs *Guides*, *De Sandvigske Samlingers Yearbook*.

Oslo

Forsvarsmuseet (Armed Forces Museum): Akershus festning, Oslo Mil, 0015 Oslo; tel. 23-09-35-70; fax 23-09-31-90; e-mail fmu@c2i .net; internet www.fmu.mil.no; f. 1978; library of 175,000 vols; Dir ROLF SCHEEN; publs *Annual Report, Fosvarsmuseets Arbok*, *Forsvarsmuseets skrifter* (4 or 5 a year).

Kon-Tiki Museum: Bygdøynesveien 36, 0286 Oslo; tel. 23-08-67-67; fax 23-08-67-60; e-mail kon-tiki@online.no; internet www .kon-tiki.no; archaeology of Easter Island, eastern Polynesia, the Galapagos Islands and Peru; boats and artefacts from Thor Heyerdahl's expeditions.

Kunstindustrimuseet i Oslo (Museum of Decorative Arts and Design, Oslo): St Olavsgate 1, 0165 Oslo; tel. 22-03-65-40; fax 22-11-39-71; e-mail museum@kunstindustrimuseet .no; internet www.kunstindustrimuseet.no; f. 1876; Norwegian and foreign decorative and applied art, fashion, Scandinavian crafts and design, goldsmith and silversmith work, woven tapestry (incl. 12th-century Baldishol tapestry), glass and faïence, furniture, textiles and costumes, East Asian items; Dir MARTIN BIEHL.

Munch Museum: Tøyengata 53, 0578 Oslo; tel. 23-49-35-00; fax 23-49-35-01; e-mail info@munch.museum.no; internet www .munch.museum.no; f. 1963; colln of 1,000 paintings, 4,500 drawings and 18,000 prints, bequeathed to the city of Oslo by Edvard Munch; library of 22,000 vols, incl. colln of Munch's private letters, notes and diaries and Munch's private book colln; Dir GUNNAR SOERENSEN.

Nasjonalmuseet for Kunst, Arkitektur og Design (National Museum of Art, Architecture and Design): POB 7014, St. Olavs plass, 0130 Oslo; Kristian Augusts gate 23, Oslo; tel. 21-98-20-00; e-mail info@ nasjonalmuseet.no; internet www .nasjonalmuseet.no; f. 2003 by merger of the Norwegian Museum of Architecture, the Museum of Decorative Arts and Design, the Museum of Contemporary Art and the National Gallery; library of 30,000 vols; Dir SUNE NORDGREN.

Naturhistorisk museum, Universitetet i Oslo (Natural History Museum, University of Oslo): Boks 1172 Blindern, 0318 Oslo; tel. 22-85-16-30; fax 22-85-17-09; e-mail posttmottak@nhm.uio.no; internet www .nhm.uio.no.

Constituent museums:

Botanisk hage og Botanisk museum (Botanical Garden and Botanical Museum): Boks 1172 Blindern, 0318 Oslo; Located at: Sarsgt. 1, 0562 Oslo; tel. 22-85-17-00; fax 22-85-18-35; e-mail r.h.okland@ nhm.uio.no; internet www.toyen.uio.no; f. 1814 (garden), 1863 (museum); attached to Universitetet i Oslo; taxonomy and plant ecology; library of 45,000 vols; Dir Prof. RUNE HALVOSEN ØKLAND; publ. *Sommerfeltia* (irregular).

Geologisk museum (Geological Museum): Boks 1172 Blindern, 0318 Oslo; Located at: Sarsgt. 1, 0562 Oslo; tel. 22-85-16-00; fax 22-85-18-00; e-mail nhm-museum@nhm.uio.no; internet www .nhm.uio.no/geomus; f. 1915; attached to Universitetet i Oslo; rocks, minerals and fossils; research laboratories in mineralogy, petrology, geochemistry and palaeontology; library of 75,000 vols; Dir ELEN ROALDSET.

Zoologisk museum (Zoological Museum): Boks 1172 Blindern, 0318 Oslo; Located at: Sarsgt. 1, 0562 Oslo; tel. 22-85-17-00; fax 22-85-18-37; f. c.1813; attached to Universitetet i Oslo; public exhibitions of Norwegian and world fauna; Norwegian vertebrates and invertebrates, Arctic, Antarctic and exotic, particularly Australian, research collections; library: c. 28,000 vols, 53,000 pamphlets; Dir JAN T. LIFJELD.

Norsk Folkemuseum (Norwegian Museum of Cultural History): Bygdøy, Museumsv. 10, 0287 Oslo; tel. 22-12-37-00; fax 22-12-37-77; e-mail post@norskfolkemuseum.no; internet www.norskfolkemuseum.no; f. 1894; consists of indoor and open-air sections comprising more than 230,000 objects; special exhibits in the indoor section include: rural culture (including display of folk dresses and folk art), church history, toys, Lapp collection; open-air museum consists of: 155 old buildings (including 13th c. Gol stave church), examples of different farms, relics from all over Norway arranged as an old town quarter, museum shop, artisans; library of 45,000 vols; Dir OLAV AAVAAS.

Norsk Sjøfartsmuseum (Norwegian Maritime Museum): Bygdøynesvn. 37, 0286 Oslo; tel. 24-11-41-70; fax 24-11-41-51; e-mail fellespost@norsk-sjofartsmuseum.no; internet www.norsk-sjofartsmuseum.no; f. 1914; museum opened 1974; Norwegian maritime history and coastal culture; colln of portraits, models, instruments, historic ships (Amundsen's 'Gjøa' and traditional small craft), full-size original ship interiors; library of 30,000 vols, archives of photographs and plans, MSS, maps; Dir JAN-BØRGE TJÄDER; Head of Research BÅRD KOLLTVEIT; publ. *Norsk Sjøfartsmuseum, Årsberetning* (annually).

Norsk Teknisk Museum (Norwegian Museum of Science and Technology): Kjelsåsveien 143, 0491 Oslo 4; tel. 22-79-60-00; fax 22-79-61-00; e-mail post@norsk-teknisk .museum.no; f. 1914; library of 40,000 vols; Dir GUNNAR NERHEIM; publ. *Yearbook*.

Oslo Kommunes Kunstsamlinger (City of Oslo Art Collections): Tøyengata 53, POB 2812, Tøyen, 0608 Oslo; tel. 22-67-37-74; fax 22-67-33-41; general collns, and spec. collns of works by Munch and Vigeland; Dir RUTH LILIAN BREKKE.

Riksantikvaren (Directorate for Cultural Heritage): Dronningensgt. 13, POB 8196 Dep., 0034 Oslo; tel. 22-94-04-00; fax 22-94-04-04; f. 1912; directorate responsible for national monuments and sites, medieval buildings; archives: c. 700,000 photos; library of 50,000 vols; Dir-Gen. NILS MARSTEIN; publs *Norges Kirker, Norske Minnesmerker, Riksantikvarens Rapporter, Riksantikvarens Skrifter* (Antiquarian Bulletin).

Universitetets kulturhistoriske museer (University Museum of Cultural Heritage): POB 6762 St Olavs plass, 0130 Oslo; Located at Frederiks gt. 2, 0164 Oslo (Historical Museum); Huk Aveny 35, 0287 Oslo (Viking Ship Museum); tel. 22-85-19-00; fax 22-85-97-87; e-mail info@ukm.uio.no; internet www .ukm.uio.no; f. 1999; exhibits from prehistoric and Viking times, including Viking ships (at Bygdøy), and the Middle Ages, Norwegian coins, collns from Africa, South America, North America, east Asia and the Arctic; library of 70,000 vols; Dir Prof. Dr philos. EGIL MIKKELSEN; publs *Universitetets kulturhistoriske museers Skrifter, Norske Oldfunn, Universitetets kulturhistoriske museer Varia*.

Vigeland-museet: Nobelsgate 32, 0268 Oslo; tel. 23-49-37-00; fax 23-49-37-01; e-mail post@vigeland.museum.no; internet www.vigeland.museum.no; f. 1947; life and work of sculptor Gustav Vigeland; Curator TORIL SMIT.

Sandefjord

Kommandør Chr. Christensens Hvalfangstmuseum (Commdr Chr. Christensen's Whaling Museum): Museumsgt. 39, 3210 Sandefjord; tel. 33-48-46-50; fax 33-46-37-84; e-mail museene@sandefjord.kommune .no; f. 1917; shows the development of whaling from primitive to modern times; geography, ethnology, zoology, maritime history, etc.; library of 15,000 vols; Dir SIDSEL HANSEN.

Skien

Fylkesmuseet for Telemark og Grenland (Historical Museum): Övregt. 41, 3700 Skien; f. 1909; conservation and research on items of historical interest from the Telemark region; situated in Brekkeparken, with open air museum (log houses dating from the Middle Ages) and a manor house furnished in 17th-, 18th- and 19th-century styles; collections on folk art, handicrafts, navigation, church art, Ibsen Collection and Ibsen's childhood home, Venstøp Farm; library: c. 6,000 vols; Dir TOR GARDÅSEN.

Stavanger

Arkeologisk Museum i Stavanger (Museum of Archaeology, Stavanger): POB 478, 4002 Stavanger; tel. 51-84-60-00; fax 51-84-61-99; e-mail ams@ark.museum.no; internet www.ark.museum.no; f. 1975; own library, scientific archive; Dir HAROLD JACOBSEN; publs *AmS-skrifter* (record of theses and dissertations, in English), *AmS-varia* (AmS research reports, in Norwegian), *AmS-Småtrykk* (scientific articles), *AmS-Rapport* (institutional research reports), *Fra haug ok heidni* (scientific magazine, 4 a year).

Stavanger Museum: 4010 Stavanger; tel. 51-84-27-00; fax 51-84-27-01; e-mail post@ stavanger.museum.no; f. 1877; urban and rural culture, zoology, ornithology; a maritime museum, a canning museum, a medical museum, a children's museum, a printing museum and the mansions of Ledaal and Breidablikk are in the museum's care; library of 65,000 vols; Dir GUNNAR NERHEIM.

Tromsø

Tromsø Museum (Universitetetsmuseet): 9037 Tromsø; tel. 77-64-50-00; fax 77-64-55-20; internet uit.no/tmu; f. 1872; six sections: Archaeology, Botany, Cultural History, Geology, Sami Ethnography, Zoology; library of 180,000 vols; Dir ELSE BOTTENGÅRD; publs *Acta Borealia* (A and B), *Antikvariske registreringer i Nord-Norge*, *Arsberetninger* (annual report), *Astarte*, *Ottar*, *Skrifter*, *Tromura* (scientific reports).

Trondheim

Nordenfjeldske Kunstindustrimuseum (National Museum of Decorative Arts): Munkegaten 5, 7013 Trondheim; tel. 73-80-89-50; fax 73-80-89-51; e-mail nkmuseum@nkim .museum.no; internet www.nkim.museum .no; f. 1893; depts of furniture, textiles, glass, ceramics, metalwork from the Renaissance period to modern times; Dir JAN-L. OPSTAD.

Vitenskapsmuseet, Norges Teknisk-Naturvitenskapelige Universitet (Museum of Natural History and Archaeology, of the Norwegian University of Science and Technology): 7491 Trondheim; tel. 73-59-21-45; fax 73-59-22-23; e-mail post@vm.ntnu.no; internet www.ntnu.no/vmuseet; f. 1760; graduate and research institution of the univ.; archaeological, botanical and zoological depts; mineralogical and numismatic collections; marine station; schools service; Dir Prof. ASTRID LANGVATN; publ. *Gunneria* (irregular).

Universities

NORGES TEKNISK-NATURVITENSKAPELIGE UNIVERSITET (NTNU)
(Norwegian University of Science and Technology)

7491 Trondheim
Telephone: 73-59-50-00
Fax: 73-59-53-10
E-mail: postmottak@adm.ntnu.no
Internet: www.ntnu.no

Founded 1996 to replace the Univ. of Trondheim (which included the Norwegian Institute of Technology, the College of Arts and Science and the Museum of Natural History and Archaeology)

Academic year: August to June

Rector: TORBJØRN DIGERNES
Pro-Rectors: JULIE FEILBERG, ASTRID LÆGREID
Univ. Dir: PER IVAR MAUDAL
Assistant Univ. Dir: PETER LYKKE

Number of teachers: 1,700
Number of students: 20,000

Publication: *Gemini* (6 a year)

DEANS

Faculty of Architecture and Fine Art: TORE I. HAUGEN
Faculty of Arts: KATHRINE SKRETTING
Faculty of Eng. Science and Technology: INGVALD STRØMMEN
Faculty of Information Technology, Mathematics and Electrical Eng.: ARNE SØLVBERG
Faculty of Medicine: STIG A. SLØRDAHL
Faculty of Natural Sciences and Technology: BJØRN HAFSKJOLD
Faculty of Social Sciences and Technology Management: JAN MORTEN DYRSTAD

PROFESSORS

Faculty of Architecture and Fine Art (tel. 73-59-50-98; fax 73-59-50-94; e-mail fak-adm@ ab.ntnu.no; internet www.ab.ntnu.no/eng):

BERGAUST, K., Fine Art
BJØNNESS, H. C., Urban Design and Planning
BLEIKLIE, S., Architectural Design and Management
BOOKER, C. A., Architectural Design, Form and Colour Studies
BRAND, P., Architectural Design, Form and Colour Studies
FISKAA, H., Urban Design and Planning
FURUNES, A.-K., Fine Art
GAMDRUP, M., Fine Art
GRYTLI, E. R., Architectural Design, History and Technology
GUSTAVSEN, A., Architectural Design, History and Technology
HESTNES, A. G., Architectural Design, History and Technology
HØYEM, H., Architectural Design, History and Technology
JAUKKURI, M. H., Fine Art
LARSEN, K., Architectural Design and Management
LARSEN, K. E., Architectural Design, History and Technology
LUND, F., Architectural Design, Form and Colour Studies
MATUSIAK, B., Architectural Design, Form and Colour Studies
MEDALEN, T., Urban Design and Planning
RØE, B., Urban Design and Planning
SAMBOLEC, D., Fine Art
SHETELIG, C. F. L., Architectural Design and Management
SIEM, J. H., Architectural Design, History and Technology
STEEN, O., Architectural Design and Management

STØA, E., Architectural Design and Management
SVENDSEN, S. E., Architectural Design and Management

Faculty of Arts (tel. 73-59-65-95; fax 73-59-10-30; e-mail hf-fak@ntnu.no; internet www .ht.ntnu.no/eng):

ALTERHAUG, B., Musicology
ANDERSEN, H. W., History
BAKKA, E., Musicology
BENDER JØRGENSEN, L., Archaeology
BERGMANN, S., Religious Studies
BORGERSEN, T., Media Studies
BULL, I, History
DAHL, S. L., History
DOMMELEN, W. A. VAN, Linguistics
DYBVIG, M., Philosophy
ELIASSEN, K. O., Literature
EVENSEN, L. S., Applied Linguistics
FAUSKEVÅG, S. E., Romance Literature
FEIGS, W. G., Germanic Languages
FINDAL, W., History of Art
FINKE, S., Philosophy
FISKUM, B., Musicology
FOSS, G., General Literature
FRETHEIM, T., Literature
GIMNES, S., Scandinavian Literature
HAGLAND, J. R., Scandinavian Literature and Comparative Literature
HALVORSEN, A., Romance Studies
HANKELN, R., Medieval Music
HAUG, A., Medieval Studies
HAWTHORN, J., English Literature
HELLAN, L., Applied Linguistics
HERNÆS, P. O., History
HETLAND, J., Germanic Languages
IMSEN, S., History
IVERSEN, G., Film Studies
JASINSKI, M. E., Maritime Architecture
JONSSON, L. S., Musicology
KALDAL, I., History
KNOWLES, J., Philosophy
LEDANG, O. K., Musicology
LIE, M., Social Anthropology
LIE, S., Literature
MELBY, K., Women's Research, History
MITCHELL, D., English Literature
MOLANDER, B., Philosophy
MÆHLUM, B. K., Norwegian Language
NEUMANN, B. O., German Literature
NILSEN, H. N., Literature
NORDGÅRD, T., Linguistics
NYLANDER, L., Literature
PETERI, G. G., History
RASMUSSEN, B., Drama and Theatre
RISE, H., Church Music
SAWYER, B., History
SHERRY, R. G., English
SIMENSEN, J., History
SKRETTING, K., Media Studies
STUGU, O. S., History
SUPPHELLEN, S., History
SØRENSEN, K. H., History of Technology
SØRENSEN, B., Film Studies
TVINNEREIM, H. S., History of Art
ULRICHSEN, J. H., Religious Studies
VIDEN, G., History
VULCHANOVA, M. D., English Language
WYLLER, T., Philosophy
ØFSTI, A., Philosophy
ØSTBY, P., History of Technology
ØSTERUD, E., Literature
AFARLI, T. A., Scandinavian Studies and Comparative Literature
AARSET, H. E., Literature
AASLESTAD, P., Scandinavian Studies and Comparative Literature

Faculty of Engineering Science and Technology (tel. 73-59-45-01; fax 73-59-45-06; e-mail info@ivt.ntnu.no; internet www.ivt.ntnu.no/ eng):

AMDAHL, J., Marine Structures
ANDERSEN, B., Production and Quality Eng.
ANDERSSON, H. I., Fluids Eng.
ASHEIM, H. A., Petroleum Eng., Production

BAKKEN, L. E., Thermal Eng.

BARDAL, E., Machine Design and Materials Technology

BELL, K., Structural Eng., Structural Mechanics

BERGE, S., Marine Structures

BOLLAND, O., Thermal Eng.

BRATTEBØ, H., Environmental Eng.

BRATTELAND, E., Marine Technology

BRATTLI, B., Eng. Geology

BREDESEN, A. M., Refrigeration Eng.

BREVIK, I. H., Fluids Eng.

BROCH, E., Eng. Geology

BRULAND, A., Project Management and Construction Eng.

DIGERNES, T., Marine Systems Design

EIKEVIK, T. M., Food Eng. in the Marine Sector

ERTESVÅG, I. S., Thermal Energy

ENDAL, A., Marine Systems Design

FALTINSEN, O. M., Marine Hydrodynamics

FIKSDAL, L., Urban Water Systems

FJELDAAS, S., Machine Design

GJØRV, O. E., Structural Eng., Concrete

GOLAN, M., Petroleum Eng., Production

GRANDE, L. O., Marine Geotechnical Eng.

GUDMUNDSSON, J. S., Petroleum Eng. Production

GUNDERSEN, T., Process, Energy and Systems Eng.

GUSTAFSON, C.-G., Materials and Processes, Materials Technology

HALMØY, E., Materials and Processes, Materials Technology

HANSSEN, S. O., Heating, Ventilation and Sanitary Eng.

HERTWICH, E., Thermal Energy

HOLM, K. R., Geomatics

HOLT, R. M., Petroleum Eng., Drilling Technology

HOLTHE, K. H., Structural Eng., Structural Mechanics

HOPPERSTAD, O. S., Structural Eng., Steel and Light Metal

HORVLI, I., Highway Eng.

HOVD, A., Highway Eng.

HOVDE, P. J., Bldg Technologies

HUSTAD, J. E., Thermal Energy

HÅRKEGÅRD, G., Machine Design and Materials Technology

HØISETH, K. V., Structural Eng., Concrete

HAAGENSEN, P. J., Structural Eng., Steel and Light Metal

HAAVALDSEN, T., Bldg Technologies

IRGENS, F., Structural Eng., Structural Mechanics

JELMERT, T. A., Petroleum Eng., Reservoir Technology

JOHANNESSEN, S., Transport Eng.

JOHNSEN, R., Corrosion and Surface Technology

KANSTAD, T., Structural Eng., Concrete

KILLINGTVEIT, Å., Eng. Hydrology

KLEPPE, J., Petroleum Eng., Reservoir Technology

KOCH, W. H., Production and Quality Eng.

KRAMMER, G., Environmental Eng.

KRILL, A., Geology

KRISTIANSEN, S., Marine Systems Design

KROGSTAD, P.-Å., Fluids Eng.

LANDRØ, M., Applied Geophysics

LANGSETH, M., Structural Eng., Sheet and Light Metal

LARSEN, C. M., Marine Structures

LARSEN, P. K., Structural Eng., Sheet and Light Metal

LEIRA, B. J., Marine Structures

LI, C., Mining Eng.

LIEN, T. K., Production and Quality Eng.

LILE, O. B., Petroleum Eng., Applied Geophysics

LIPPARD, S. J., Petroleum Geology

LØSET, S., Arctic Technology

MAGNUSSEN, O. M., Industrial Fish Processing

MALO, K. A., Structural Eng., Sheet and Light Metal

MALVIK, T., Resources Geology

MATHISEN, K. M., Structural Eng., Structural Mechanics

MIDTBØ, T., Geomatics

MINSAAS, K. J., Marine Hydrodynamics

MOAN, T., Marine Structures

MOE, G., Port and Ocean Eng.

MYRAN, T., Eng. Geology

MYRHAUG, D., Marine Hydrodynamics

NIELSEN, K. O., Mining Eng.

NIELSEN, T. K., Fluids Eng.

NILSEN, B., Eng. Geology

NORDAL, S., Geotechnical Eng.

NOREM, H. A., Transport Eng.

NOVAKOVIC, V., Heating, Ventilation and Sanitary Eng.

NYDAL, O. J., Indoor Environmental Eng.

NÆSS, A., Marine Technology

NØRSTRUD, H., Fluids Eng.

OKSMAN, K., Materials and Processes

PETTERSEN, B., Marine Hydrodynamics

PRESTVIK, T., Geology, Petrology

RASCH, F. O., Production and Quality Eng.

RASMUSSEN, M., Marine Eng.

RAUSAND, M., Production and Quality Eng.

REMSETH, S. N., Structural Eng., Structural Mechanics

ROALD, S., Project Management and Construction Eng.

ROKOENGEN, K., Eng. Geology

ROLSTADÅS, A., Production and Quality Eng.

RØDLAND, A., Petroleum Eng. (Drilling Technology)

RØLVÅG, T., Computer-aided Eng.

SAGER, T. Ø., Transport Eng.

SAMSET, K. F., Project Management and Construction Eng.

SANDVIK, K. L., Mineral Dressing

SANGESLAND, S., Petroleum Eng. (Drilling Technology)

SCHILLING, W., Urban Water Systems

SELLEVOLD, E. J., Structural Eng., Concrete

SINDING-LARSEN, R., Resources Geology

SIVERTSEN, O. I., Machine Design

SKALLERUD, B. H., Structural Eng., Structural Mechanics

STEEN, S., Marine Technology and Experience Hydrodynamics

STRØMMEN, E. N., Structural Eng., Structural Mechanics

STRØMMEN, I., Refrigeration Eng.

STØLE, H., Hydro Power Devt

STØREN, S., Materials and Processes, Materials Technology

SYVERTSEN, T. G., Structural Eng., Structural Mechanics

SÆTRAN, L. R., Fluids Eng.

SØNJU, O. K., Thermal Energy

SØRENSEN, A. J., Marine Hydrodynamics

SØRENSEN, S. I., Structural Eng., Concrete

THAULOW, C., Materials Processes, Materials Technology

THUE, J. V., Building Technology

TJELFLAAT, P. O., Indoor Environmental Eng.

TORSÆTER, O., Petroleum Eng., Reservoir Technology

TØNDER, K., Machine Design, Materials Technology

URSIN, B., Petroleum Eng., Seismatics

VALBERG, H. S., Materials and Processes, Materials Technology

VALLAND, H., Marine Eng.

VATN, J., Production and Quality Eng.

VENNESLAND, Ø., Structural Eng., Concrete

WANG, K., Production and Quality Eng.

WESTBY, O., Marine System Design

WHITE, M. F., Marine Eng.

WHITSON, C. H., Petroleum Eng., Reservoir Technology

YTREHUS, T., Fluids Eng.

ZHANG, Z., Solid State Mechanics

ØDEGAARD, H., Environmental Eng., Urban Water Systems

Faculty of Information Technology, Mathematics and Electrical Engineering (tel. 73-59-42-02; fax 73-59-36-28; e-mail adm@ime.ntnu.no; internet www.ime.ntnu.no/eng):

ANDRESEN, S. H., Telematics

BLAKE, R., Image Processing

BRATSBERG, S. E., Database Systems

BRATBERGSENGEN, K., Database Systems

BRÆK, R., Telematics

BAAS, N. A., Mathematics

CONRADI, R., Software Eng.

DIGERNES, T., Mathematics

DIVITINI, M., Software Eng.

DO, V. T., Telematics

DONG, H., Telecommunications

DOWNING, K., Artificial Intelligence

EGELAND, O., Eng. Cybernetics

EMSTAD, P. J., Telematics

ENGAN, H. E., Physical Electronics

ENGEN, S., Mathematical Statistics

FIMLAND, B.-O., Physical Electronics

FJELDLY, T. A., Physical Electronics

FORSSELL, B., Telecommunications

FOSS, B. A., Eng. Cybernetics

FOSSEN, T. I., Eng. Cybernetics

FOSSO, O. B., Electrical Power Eng.

FAANES, H. H., Electrical Power Eng.

GREPSTAD, J., Physical Electronics

GULLA, F. A., Database Systems

GUTTEBERG, O., Satellite Communications

HAG, K., Mathematics

HALAAS, A., Algorithm Theory and Construction

HELVIK, B. E., Telematics

HENRIKSEN, R., Eng. Cybernetics

HOLDEN, H., Mathematics

HOLEN, A. T., Electrical Power Eng.

HOLTE, N., Telecommunications

HOVD, M., Eng. Cybernetics

HOVEM, J. M., Telecommunications

HUGHES, P., Database Systems

HVASSHOVD, S.-O., Database Systems

ILSTAD, E., Electric Power Eng.

JACCHERI, M. L., Software Eng.

JOHANSEN, T. A., Eng. Cybernetics

KNAPSKOG, S. J., Telematics

KRISTIANSEN, L., Telematics

KRISTIANSEN, U. R., Telecommunications

KROGSTAD, H. E., Mathematics

KURE, Ø., Telematics

LANDSTAD, M. B., Mathematics

LINDQVIST, B. H., Mathematical Statistics

LINDQVIST, L. P., Mathematics

LORENTZEN, L., Mathematics

LYUBARSKII, Y., Mathematics

MALVIG, K. E., Eng. Cybernetics

MJØLSNES, S. F., Telematics

MONTEIRO, E., Human–Computer Interaction

MÜLLER, R. R., Wireless Networks

NATVIG, L., Computer Architecture and Design

NILSEN, R., Electrical Power Eng.

NILSSEN, R., Electrical Power Eng.

NORUM, L. E., Electrical Power Eng.

NYGÅRD, M., Database Systems

NYSVEEN, A., Electrical Power Eng.

NÆSS, A., Mathematical Statistics

NØRSETT, S. P., Mathematics

OMRE, K. H., Mathematical Statistics

ONSHUS, T. E., Eng. Cybernetics

OWREN, B., Mathematics

PERKIS, A., Digital Image Processing

PETTERSEN, K. Y., Eng. Cybernetics

PETTERSEN, O., Eng. Cybernetics

RAMSTAD, T. A., Telecommunications

REITEN, I., Mathematics

ROUDAKOV, A., Mathematics

RUE, H., Mathematical Statistics

RØNNEKLEIV, A., Physical Electronics

RØNNINGEN, L. A., Telematics

RØNQVIST, E., Mathematics

SEIP, K., Mathematics

SINDRE, G., Information Systems
SKAAR, J., Photonics
SKAU, C. F., Mathematics
SKRAMSTAD, T., Human–Computer Interaction
SMALØ, S. O., Mathematics
SOLBERG, Ø., Mathematics
STRAUME, E., Mathematics
STÅLHANE, T., Software Eng.
SVENDSEN, T., Telecommunications
SVENSSON, P., Telecommunications
SVAASAND, L. O., Physical Electronics
SÆTHER, T., Physical Electronics
SØLVBERG, A., Information Systems
SØLVBERG, I., Information Management
UNDELAND, T. M., Electrical Power Eng.
WANGENSTEEN, I., Electrical Power Eng.
YTTERDAL, T., Physical Communications
ØIEN, G. E., Telecommunications
AAGESEN, F. A., Telematics
AAMODT, A., Artificial Intelligence
AARNES, J. F., Mathematics
AAS, E. J., Physical Electronics

Faculty of Medicine (tel. 73-59-88-59; fax 73-59-88-65; e-mail dmf-post@medisin.ntnu.no; internet www.medisin.ntnu.no/eng):

ANGELSEN, B. A. J., Biomedical Eng.
AUSTGULEN, R., Cancer Research and Molecular Medicine
BACKE, B., Laboratory Medicine, Children's and Women's Health
BASSØE, C. F., Neuroscience
BENTZEN, N., Public Health and General Practice
BERGH, K., Laboratory Medicine, Children's and Women's Health
BOVIM, G., Neurology
BRATLID, D., Laboratory Medicine, Children's and Women's Health
BRUBAKK, A.-M., Laboratory Medicine, Children's and Women's Health
BRUBAKK, A. O., Physiology
CHEN, D., Cancer Research and Molecular Medicine
CLIFFORD, G., Child Psychiatry
DALE, O., Anaesthesiological Pharmacology
DRABLØS, F., Cancer Research and Molecular Medicine
ELLINGSEN, ø., Physiology
ESPEVIK, T., Cancer Research and Molecular Medicine
FARUP, P. G., Applied Clinical Research
FINSEN, V., Neuroscience
GRILL, V., Cancer Research and Molecular Medicine
GRIMSMO, A., Public Health and General Practice
GRØNBECK, J. E., Surgery Gastroenterology
GØTESTAM, K. G., Neuroscience
HARALDSETH, O., MR/Radiology
HAUGEN, O. A., Morphology
HELGERUD, J., Sports Physiology
HOLMEN, J., Nord-Trøndelag Health Study
IVERSEN, O.-J., Laboratory Medicine, Children's and Women's Health
JACOBSEN, G., Public Health and General Practice
JOHNSEN, R., Public Health and General Practice
JYNGE, P., Physiology
KLEPP, O., Oncology
KLUNGLAND, H., Laboratory Medicine, Children's and Women's Health
KROKAN, H. E., Cancer Research and Molecular Medicine
KAASA, S., Cancer Research and Molecular Medicine
LAMVIK, J., Cancer Research and Molecular Biology
LARSSON, B. S., Child Psychiatry
LEIVSETH, G., Neuroscience
LYDERSEN, S., Cancer Research and Molecular Medicine
LÆGREID, A., Microarray
LØVIK, M., Public Health

MIDELFART, A., Neuroscience
MOSER, M.-B., Neuroscience
NILSEN, O. G., Cancer Research and Molecular Medicine
OTTERLEI, M., Cancer Research and Molecular Medicine
PETERSEN, H., Public Health and General Practice
RYGNESTAD, T., Laboratory Medicine
RØNNINGEN, H., Neuroscience
SAND, T., Neurology
SANDVIK, A. K., Cancer Research and Molecular Medicine
SCHEI, B., Public Health and General Practice
SKORPEN, F., Nord-Trøndelag Health Study
SLUPPHAUG, G., Cancer Research and Molecular Medicine
SLØRDAHL, S. A., Physiology
SLØRDAL, L., Laboratory Medicine, Children's and Women's Health
SONNEWALD, U., Neuroscience
STOVNER, L. J., Neuroscience
SUNDAN, A., Cancer Research and Molecular Medicine
SVEBAK, S., Neuroscience
SYVERSEN, T., Neuroscience
SYVERSEN, U., Cancer Research and Molecular Medicine
TORP, H., Biomedical Eng.
VATTEN, L. J., Public Health and General Practice
VIDEM, V., Laboratory Medicine, Children's and Women's Health
VIK, T., Public Health and General Practice
WALDUM, H., Cancer Research and Molecular Medicine
WESTIN, S., Public Health and General Practice
WIBE, A., Cancer Research and Molecular Medicine
WIDERØE, T.-E., Nephrology
WITTER, M., Neuroscience
WAAGE, A., Haematology
AADAHL, P., Anaesthesiology

Faculty of Natural Sciences and Technology (tel. 73-59-41-97; fax 73-59-14-10; e-mail postmottak@nt.ntnu.no; internet www.nt.ntnu.no/eng):

ALSBERG, B. K., Physical Chemistry
AMUNDSEN, T., Etology
ANDERSEN, R., Terrestrial Ecology
ANDERSEN, R., Zoo Physiology
ANTHONSEN, T., Organic Chemistry
ARMBRUSTER, W. S., Evolution, Ecology
ARNBERG, L., Process Metallurgy
BAKKE, J. M., Organic Chemistry
BAKKEN, J. A., Process Metallurgy
BECH, C., Zoology
BERG, O. K., Freshwater Ecology
BLEKKAN, E. A., Chemical Eng., Catalysis and Petrochemistry
BONES, A., Cell and Molecular Biology
BORG, A., Surface Physics
BRATAAS, A., Theoretical Physics
CARLSEN, P. H., Organic Chemistry
CHEN, D., Chemical Eng., Catalysis and Petrochemistry
CHRISTENSEN, B. E., Biopolymer Chemistry
DAVIES, C., Biophysics and Medical Technology
EINARSRUD, M.-A., Inorganic Chemistry
ELGSÆTER, A., Biological Physics
ENGH, T. A., Metallurgy
FIKSDAHL, A., Organic Chemistry
FOOSNÆS, T., Inorganic Chemistry
FOSSHEIM, K., Material Physics
FOSSUM, J. O., Condensed-Matter Physics
GRANDE, T., Inorganic Chemistry
GREGERSEN, Ø. W., Chemical Eng., Pulp and Paper Technology
GRONG, Ø., Process Metallurgy
HAFSKJOLD, B., Physical Chemistry
HAGEN, K., Physical Chemistry

HANSEN, A., Theoretical Physics
HERTZBERG, T., Chemical Eng., Process Systems Eng.
HOGSTAD, O., Zoology
HOLMEN, A., Chemical Eng., Catalysis and Petrochemistry
HOLMESTAD, R., Material Physics
HUNDERI, O., Surface Physics
HYTTERBORN, H., Plant Ecology
HÆGG, M.-B., Chemical Eng., Separation Technology
HØYE, J. S., Theoretical Physics
HAARBERG, G. M., Electrochemistry
IVERSEN, T.-H., Cell Biology
JAKOBSEN, H. A., Chemical Eng., Reactor Technology
JENSSEN, B. M., Ecotoxicology
JOHANSEN, B., Cell and Molecular Biology
JOHNSSON, A., Biophysics and Medical Technology
KJELSTAD, B. J., Ultraviolet Radiation
KJELSTRUP, S., Physical Chemistry, Thermodynamics
KOCH, H., Physical Chemistry
KOLBEINSEN, L., Process Metallurgy
KOLBENSTVEDT, H., Theoretical Physics
LANGELAND, A. L., Freshwater Ecology
LEVINE, D. W., Biochemical Eng.
LINDGREN, M., Experimental Optics
LINDMO, T., Biophysics and Medical Technology
LJONES, T., Biophysical Chemistry
LOHNE, O., Physical Metallurgy
LØKBERG, O. J., Applied Optics
MARTHINSEN, K., Physical Metallurgy
MELØ, T. B., Biophysics and Medical Technology
MIKKELSEN, A., Biophysics and Medical Technology
MO, F., Crystallography
MOKSNES, A., Terrestrial Ecology
MORK, K. J., Theoretical Physics
MUSTAPARTA, H., Neurophysiology
MYRHEIM, J., Anyons
MØRK, P., Chemical Eng., Polymer and Colloid Chemistry
NAQVI, K. R., Biophysics and Medical Technology
NES, E.-A., Physical Metallurgy
NESSE, N., Chemical Eng., Separation Technology
NICHOLSON, D. G., Materials Science
NILSSEN, K. J., Zoophysiology, Aquaculture
NISANCIOGLU, K., Electrochemistry
OLAUSSEN, K., Anyons
OLSEN, Y., Marine Biology
PREISIG, H., Chemical Eng., Process Systems Eng.
REINERTSEN, H., Aquaculture, Marine Biology
ROSENQVIST, G., Etology
ROVEN, H. J., Physical Metallurgy
RYUM, N., Physical Metallurgy
RØSKRAFT, E., Evolutionary Biology
RAAEN, S., Experimental Condensed Matter Physics
SAKSHAUG, E., Marine Biology
SAMUELSEN, E. J., Material Physics
SCHRØDER, K. H., Analytical Chemistry
SJØBLOM, J., Chemical Eng., Polymer and Colloid Chemistry
SKAGERSTAM, B.-S., Theoretical Physics
SKJÅK-BRÆK, G., Biotechnology, Biopolymer Chemistry
SKOGESTAD, S., Chemical Eng., Process Systems Eng.
SKULLERUD, H., Electron and Ion Physics
SMIDSRØD, O., Biotechnology, Biopolymer Chemistry
SOLBERG, J. K., Physical Metallurgy
STEINNES, E., Environmental Technology
STOKKE, B. T., Biophysics and Medical Technology
STRØM, A. R., Biotechnology, Molecular Genetics
STØLEVIK, R. E., Physical Chemistry

SUDBØ, A., Theoretical Physics
SUNDE, S., Hydrogen Technology
SVENDSEN, H. F., Chemical Eng., Reactor Technology
SÆTHER, B.-E., Terrestrial Ecology
TANGSTAD, M., Process Metallurgy
TUNOLD, R., Electrochemistry
VADSTEIN, O., Biotechnology
VALBERG, A., Biophysics and Medical Technology
VALLA, S., Biotechnology, Molecular Genetics
VÅRUM, K., Marine Biochemistry
WRIGHT, J., Marine Biochemistry
YSTENES, M., Inorganic Chemistry
ZACHARIASSEN, K. E., Zoophysiology
ØSTGAARD, K., Environmental Biotechnology
ØSTVOLD, T., Inorganic Chemistry
ØYE, H. A., Inorganic Chemistry
ÅSTRAND, P. O., Physical Chemistry

Faculty of Social Sciences and Technology Management (tel. 73-59-19-00; fax 73-59-19-01; e-mail postmottak@svt.ntnu.no; internet www.sv.ntnu.no/eng):

ALMÅS, R., Sociology
BERG, N. G., Human Geography
BERGE, E., Sociology
BJØRGEN, I. A., Psychology
BORGE, L.-E., Economics
BRANDTH, B., Sociology
BRØGGER, J. C., Social Anthropology
CHRISTIANSEN, M., Industrial Economics
DAHL-JØRGENSEN, C., Social Anthropology
DALE, B. E., Geography
DYRSTAD, J. M., Economics
ERRING, B. B., Social Anthropology
ESPNES, G. A., Programme for Social Work
ETTERMA, G., Sports Sciences
FET, A. M., Organizational Studies
GAIVORONSKI, A. A., Industrial Economics
HESTAD, K., Psychology
HOEL, T. L., Education
HOPMANN, S., Education
HOVDEN, J., Organizational Studies
HVINDEN, B., Sociology
HAAVELSRUD, M., Education
IMSEN, G. M., Education
INGVALDSEN, R. P., Sports Sciences
JACOBSEN, K. H., Psychology
JENSEN, A.-M., Sociology
JENSSEN, A. T., Political Science
JONES, M. R. H., Geography
KARLSEN, A., Economic Geography
KAUL, H., Psychology
KNUTSEN, T., Political Science
KOLSTAD, A., Psychology
KREKLING, S., Psychology
KVANDE, E., Sociology
LEIULFSRUD, H., Sociology
LEVIN, M., Organizational Studies
LISTHAUG, O., Political Science
LORENTZEN, S., Education
LUND, R., Geography
LUNHEIM, R., Organizational Studies
MARTINUSSEN, W. M., Sociology
MEER, A. L. VAN DER, Psychology
MOSER, E., Neuroscience
MOSER, M.-B., Neuroscience
MOSES, J., Political Science
MOXNES, K., Sociology
NORDAHL, H. M., Psychology
NORDVIK, H., Psychology
NYGREEN, B., Industrial Economics
QVORTRUP, J., Sociology
RAMET, S., Political Science
RASMUSSEN, B., Sociology
RASMUSSEN, K., Psychology
RATTSØ, J. G., Economics
RINGDAHL, G. I., Health Psychology
RINGDAL, K., Sociology
RUNDMO, T., Psychology
SAKSVIK, P. Ø., Psychology
SCHIEFLOE, P.-M., Sociology
SIGMUNDSSON, H., Sociology

SIMKUS, A., Sociology
SJØBERG, B.-M. D., Psychology
SKONHOFT, A., Economics
SKAALVIK, E. M., Education
SOLEM, K. E., Political Science
SOLEM, O., Organizational Studies
STEINSHOLT, K., Education
STILES, T. C., Psychology
SÆTNAN, A. R., Sociology
TORVIK, R., Economics
TØSSEBRO, J., Programme for Social Work
VEREIJKEN, E., Sports Sciences
VIKAN, A., Psychology
WEEL, F. VAN DER, Psychology
WESTGAARD, R. H., Organizational Studies
WICHSTRØM, L., Psychology
WIJST, D. VAN DER, Industrial Economics
WAAGØ, S., Organizational Studies

Museum of Natural History and Archaeology (tel. 73-59-21-45; fax 73-59-22-23; e-mail post@vm.ntnu.no; internet www.ntnu.no/vmuseet/eng):

CHRISTOPHERSEN, A., Archaeology
FLATBERG, K. I., Botany
HOGSTAD, O., Zoology
JASINKSI, M. E., Maritime Archaeology
JOHANSEN, A. B., Archaeology
MOEN, A., Botany
MORK, J., Population Genetics
OLSEN, Y., Marine Physiology
SAKSHAUG, E., Marine Botany
SOGNES, K., Archaeology
SOLEM, J. O., Zoology

UNIVERSITETET I BERGEN
(University of Bergen)

POB 7800, 5020 Bergen
Telephone: 55-58-00-00
Fax: 55-58-96-43
E-mail: post@uib.no
Internet: www.uib.no
Founded 1946
State control
Academic year: August to June

Rector: Prof. KIRSTI KOCH CHRISTENSEN
Deputy Rector: Prof. RUNE NILSEN
Vice-Rector for Education: Prof. LEIV SYDNES
University Director-General: KÅRE ROMMETVEIT
Deputy Director-General: SVERRE SPILDO
Librarian: K. GARNES

Library: see Libraries and Archives
Number of teachers: 1,900
Number of students: 17,000

Publications: *Ilicifolia* (irregular), *Naturen* (a popular scientific review, 6 a year), *Sarsia* (6 a year)

DEANS

Faculty of Arts: Prof. VIGDIS SONGE-MØLLER
Faculty of Dentistry: Prof. MAGNE RAADAL
Faculty of Law: Prof. ERNST NORDTVEIT
Faculty of Mathematics and Natural Sciences: Prof. DAG AKSNES
Faculty of Medicine: Prof. NILS ERIK GILHUS
Faculty of Psychology: Prof. ODD HAVIK
Faculty of Social Sciences: Prof. ALF ERLING RISA

PROFESSORS

Faculty of Arts (tel. 55-58-93-80; fax 55-58-93-83; e-mail post@hffa.uib.no; internet www.hf.uib.no):

ACHEN, H. VON
AKSELBERG, G., Nordic Language
ALVER, B. G., Folklore
ANGVIK, B., Spanish
BAGGE, S. H., History
BELL, J. N., Arabic
BERGGREEN, B., Ethnology
BJØRNSON, Ø., History
BLÜCHER, K., Italian
BONDEVIK, J., Nordic Language

BREIVIK, L. E., English Philology
BROWN, E., Philosophy
BUVIK, P., General Literature
BØRTNES, J., Russian Literature
CHRISTENSEN, K. K., General Linguistics
DANBOLT, G., History of Art
DE SMEDT, K.
DOMMASNES, L. H.
DYRVIK, S., History
DYVIK, H. J., General Linguistics
FJELLAND, R., Philosophy
FLØTTUM, K., French Language
FORSBERG, L. L., Archaeology
FURE, O.-B., History
GILHUS, A. I. S., Religion
GILJE, N., Philosophy
GRØNLIE, T., History
HÄGG, T., Classical Philology
HALMØY, O., French Language
HAUGEN, O. E., Nordic Language
HELLE, L. J., Russian Language
HESTVIK, A., General Linguistics
HOPLAND, K. O., Religion
HOVLAND, E., History
HUBBARD, W. H., History
HÅLAND, R., African Archaeology
INDRELID, S.
JACOBSEN, K. A.
JANICKI, K., English Philology
JOHANNESSEN, K. S., Philosophy
JOHNSEN, K. O., Philosophy
KIILERICH, B. K., Art History
KITTANG, A., General Literature
KOLLER, W., German Language
KRISTOFFERSEN, G., Nordic Language
KROEPELIEN, B., Art History
LEIRBUKT, O., German Language
LIE, R. K., Philosophy
LINNEBERG, A., General Literature
MANDT, G., Archaeology
MEYER, J. C., History of Art
MEYER, S., European Culture
MORTENSEN, E., General Literature
MORTENSEN, L. B., Latin
MUNDAL, E., Nordic Languages
NAGEL, A.-H., History
NES, O., Philology
O'FAHEY, R. S., History
PIERCE, R., Egyptology
QUESEDA-PACHECO, M. A., Spanish
RYDLAND, K., English Philology
RYDVING, L. O. H., Religion
SANAKER, J. K., French Language
SANDBERG, B., German Literature
SANDVIK, G.
SANDØY, H., Nordic Language
SCHRØTER, H. G., History
SELBERG, T., Folklore
SILLARS, S. J., English Philology
SKARSTEN, R., Humanistic Informatics
SKIRBEKK, G., Philosophy
SKÅNLAND, M. H., Linguistics
SOLBERG, B., Archaeology
SONGE-MØLLER, V.
STEGANE, I., Nordic Language
STENSTRØM, A.-B., English Language
SÆTRE, L., General Literature
THOMASSEN, E., Religion
UTAKER, A., Philosophy
VELAND, R. M., French Language
VENNESLAN, K., Philosophy
WINTHER, T., French Language
WÆRNESS, K. E., Sociology
ØSTBY, E., Archaeology
ØVERLAND, O., American Literature
ØYE, I., Archaeology
ÅDLAND, E., General Literature
ÅRSETH, A., Nordic Language

Faculty of Dentistry (tel. 55-58-65-60; fax 55-58-65-77; e-mail post@odont.uib.no; internet www.uib.no/odfa/ENGLISH/index.htm):

BAKKEN, V., Oral Microbiology
BERG, E., Prosthesis
BERGE, M. E., Prosthodontics
BIRKELAND, J. M., Cariology

BJORVATN, K., Dental Research
EIDE, R., Dental Materials
ESPELID, I., Paedodontics
GJERDET, N. R., Dental Materials
GUSTAVSEN, F., Prosthodontics
HALSE, A., Oral Radiology
HAUGEJORDEN, O., Community Dentistry
HELLEM, S., Oral Surgery
JOHANNESSEN, A. C., Oral Pathology
MOLVEN, O., Endodontics
RASMUSSEN, P. A., Paedodontics
RÅDAL, M. J., Odontophobia and Paedo-
dontics
SKAUG, N., Oral Microbiology
TVEIT, A. B., Cariology
WISTH, P. J., Orthodontics

Faculty of Law (tel. 55-58-95-00; fax 55-58-
95-10; e-mail post@jurfa.uib.no; internet
www.jur.uib.no):

ANDERSSON, J. B.
BERNT, J. F.
GIERTSEN, J.
HOLGERSEN, G.
HUSABØ, E. J.
KRÜGER, K.
LILLEHOLT, K.
MÆLAND, H. J.
NORDTVEIT, E.
NYGAARD, N.
RASMUSSEN, Ø.
AALL, J.

Faculty of Mathematics and Natural
Sciences (tel. 55-58-20-62; fax 55-58-96-66;
e-mail post@mnfa.uib.no; internet www.uib
.no/mnfa/index_eng.html):

AKSNES, D., Chemistry
AKSNES, D. L., Fisheries Biology
ANDERSEN, Ø. M., Chemistry
BERG, C. C., Botany
BERGE, G., Mathematics
BERNTSEN, J., Mathematics
BEZEM, M. A., Computer Science
BIRKELAND, N.-K., Microbiology
BIRKS, H. J. B., Botany
BJØRSTAD, P. E., Computer Science
BRATBAK, G., Microbiology
BRIX, O., Zoology
BÅMSTEDT, U., Fisheries Biology
CSERNAI, L., Physics
DAHLE, H. K., Mathematics
DYSTHE, K., Mathematics
ECKHOFF, K. S., Mathematics
ECKHOFF, R. K., Physics
EIGEN, G., Physics
ENDRESEN, C., Fisheries Biology
ENGEVIK, L. E., Mathematics
ESPEDAL, M., Mathematics
ESPELID, T. O., Computer Science
FERNØ, A., Fisheries Biology
FJOSE, A., Molecular Biology
FOSSEN, F., Geology
FRANCIS, G. W., Organic Chemistry
FRODESEN, A. G., Physics
FURNES, H., Petroleum Geology
FYHN, H. J., Milieu Physiology
GABRIELSEN, R., Petroleum Geology
GADE, H. G., Physical Oceanography
GAMMELSRØD, T., Physical Oceanography
GISKE, J., Fisheries Biology
GRAHL-NIELSEN, O., Chemistry
GRAUE, A., Physics
GRØNÅS, S., Meteorology
GUDMUNDSSON, A., Geology
HAMMER, E. A., Physics
HANSEN, J. P., Physics
HANYGA, A., Applied Geophysics
HAUGAN, P. M., Geophysics
HAVSKOV, J., Applied Geophysics
HELLAND, D. E., Molecular Biology
HELLAND-HANSEN, W., Geology
HELLESETH, T., Computer Science
HEUCH, I., Mathematics
HOBÆK, H., Physics
HOFFMAN, A. C., Physics
HOLME, A., Mathematics

HUSEBYE, E., Applied Geophysics
HUSEBYE, S., Chemistry
HØGSTEDT, G., Zoology
HØILAND, H., Physical Chemistry
JAKOBSEN, P. J., Zoology
JANSEN, E., Geology
JENSEN, H. B., Molecular Biology
JOHANNESEN, O. M., Physical Oceanogra-
phy
JOHNSEN, T., Mathematics
JØRGENSEN, P. M., Botany
KALAND, P. E., Botany
KLØVE, T., Computer Science
KNUDSEN, L. R., Computer Science
KNUTSEN, G., Microbiology
KOCBACH, L., Physics
KOLLTVEIT, K., Physics
KRISTOFFERSEN, Y., Seismology
KRYVI, H., Zoology
KVALHEIM, O. M., Chemistry
KVAMME, B., Physics
LARSSON, P., Zoology
LAURITZEN, S.-E., Geology
LIEN, T., Microbiology
LILLEHAUG, J., Molecular Biology
LILLESTØL, E., Physics
LØVLIE, R., Geomagnetism
MALYSHEV, A., Computer Science
MANGERUD, J., Quaternary Geology
MANNE, R. E., Chemistry
MJELDE, R., Applied Geophysics
MOE, D., Botany
MUNTHE-KAAS, H., Computer Science
MYKLEBOST, K., Physics
MÆLAND, E., Applied Geophysics
MAALØE, S. B., Geology
NEMEC, W., Geology
NESJE, A., Geology
NYLUND, A., Fisheries Biology
NÆVDAL, G., Fisheries Biology
OSLAND, P., Physics
PAULSEN, J., Mathematics
PEDERSEN, R.-B., Geology
RAAE, A. J., Molecular Biology
ROBINS, B., Geology
RYE, N. M., Geology
RØDSETH, Ø. J., Mathematics
RØHRICH, D., Physics
SALVANES, A. G. V.
SCHRADER, H., Geology
SEJRUP, H. P., Geology
SKARTVEIT, A., Physical Oceanography
SKOGEN, A., Botany
SKORPING, A., Zoology
SLETTEN, E., Physical Chemistry
SLETTEN, J., Inorganic Chemistry
SONGSTAD, J., Inorganic Chemistry
STAMNES, J. J., Physics
STEFANSSON, S., Fisheries Biology
STEIHAUG, T., Informatics
STORETVEDT, K. M., Geomagnetism
STORØY, S., Computer Science
STRAY, A., Mathematics
STRØMME, S. A., Mathematics
STUGU, B., Physics
SUNDVOR, E., Seismology
SVENDSEN, H., Physical Oceanography
SVENDSEN, J.-I., Geology
SYDNES, L. K., Chemistry
SÆTHER, O. A., Zoology
SØRÅS, F., Physics
SØREVIK, T., Computer Science
SÆTHRE, L. J., Chemistry
TAI, X.-C., Mathematics
TALBOT, M. R., Petroleum Geology
TELLE, J. A., Computer Science
THINGSTAD, T. F., Microbiology
TJØSTHEIM, D. B., Statistics
TORSVIK, V. L., Microbiology
TOTLAND, G. K., Zoology
TVERBERG, H., Mathematics
TØNSBERG, T., Botany
ULLTANG, Ø., Fisheries Biology
VÅGEN, J. S., Physics
WALTHER, B. T., Molecular Biology
WILLASSEN, E., Zoology

YTREHUS, Ø., Computer Science
ØIEN, A. H., Mathematics

Faculty of Medicine (tel. 55-58-20-86; fax 55-
58-96-82; internet www.uib.no/med):

ABRAHAM, K. A., Anatomy
AKSLEN, L. A., Pathology
AKSNES, L., Paediatrics
ANDERSEN, K.-J., Internal Medicine
APOLD, J., Genetics
BAKKE, O.
BERGAMASCHI, R., Surgery
BERGE, R. K., Clinical Biochemistry
BERSTAD, A., Internal Medicine
BINDOFF, L., Neurology
BJELKE, E., Hygiene
BJERKVIG, R., Anatomy and Cell Biology
BJORVATN, B., Tropical Medicine
BOMAN, H., Genetics
BROCH, O. J., Pharmacology
BRUSERUD, Ø., Internal Medicine
DAHL, O., Oncology
DALEN, H., Pathology
DICKSTEIN, K., Internal Medicine
DÆHLIN, L., Surgery
DØSKELAND, S. O., Anatomy
FLATMARK, T., Biochemistry
FUKAMI, M., Biochemistry
GILHUS, N. E., Neurology
GRONG, K., Surgery
GRØNVOLD, M. A. S., Immunology
GULSVIK, A., Internal Medicine
HALSTENSEN, A., Internal Medicine
HAUG, K., Social Medicine
HAUKÅS, S. A.
HEDIN, L. F.
HELLE, K. B., Physiology
HEYERAAS, K. J., Physiology
HOLE, K., Physiology
HOLMSEN, H. A., Biochemistry
HOLSTEN, F., Psychiatry
HOVE, L. M., Orthopaedics
HUNSKÅR, S., General Practice
HUSBY, P., Anaesthesiology
HUSEBYE, E.
HØVDING, G., Clinical Medicine
HAAHEIM, L. R., Virology
HAARR, L., Virology
IRGENS, L., Preventive Medicine
IVERSEN, B. M., Internal Medicine
JØRGENSEN, H. A., Psychiatry
KALLAND, K.-H., Virology
KIRKEBØ, A., Physiology
KRUGER, P. G., Anatomy
KVINNSLAND, I. H., Oral Anatomy
KVÅLE, G., Epidemiology, Health Promo-
tion
LANGELAND, N., Infectious Diseases, Virol-
ogy and Bacteriology
LEKVEN, J., Surgery
LIE, R. T., Medical Statistics and Infor-
matics
LJUNGGREN, A. E., Physiotherapy
LUND, T., Anaesthesiology
LUND-JOHANSEN, P., Clinical Medicine
LÆRUM, O. D., Experimental Pathology
and Oncology
LØNNING, P. E., Oncology
MARCUSSON, J. A.
MARTINEZ, A., Biochemistry
MATRE, R., Immunology
MOEN BENTE, E., General Practice
MORILD, I., Pathology
MØLSTER, A., Orthopaedics
NILSEN, R., Pathology and Immunology
NJØLSTAD, P. R., Paediatrics
NYGÅRD, H., Geriatrics
NYLAND, H. I., Clinical Neurology
NÆSS, A., Internal Medicine
OMVIK, P., Internal Medicine
PRYME, I. F., Biochemistry
REED, R. K., Physiology
REFSUM, H., Pharmacology
RIISE, T., General Practice
SARASTE, J., Anatomy
SCHREINER, A. H., Internal Medicine

SKARSTEIN, A., Surgery, Gastroenterology
SKJÆRVEN, R., Medical Statistics and Informatics
SOMMERFELT, H., Epidemiology and Microbiology
STEEN, V. M., Molecular Medicine
SVENDSEN, E., Pathology
SØVIK GULDBORG, S.-H., Physiology
TELL, G. S., Preventive Medicine
TERLAND, O.
THORSEN, T. E., Clinical Biochemistry
TONNING, F. M., Otorhinolaryngology
TYLLESKAR, T.
UELAND, P. M., Pharmacology
ULSTEIN, M. K., Gynaecology and Obstetrics
URSIN, R., Physiology
VEDELER, C. A., Clinical Neurology
VOLLSET, S. E., Medical Statistics and Informatics
WESTER, K.
WIIG, H., Physiology
AARLI, J. A., Clinical Neurology
AASJØ, E. B., Virology

Faculty of Psychology (tel. 55-58-27-10; fax 55-58-98-71; e-mail post@psyfa.uib.no; internet www.uib.no/psyfa):

ELLERTSEN, B., Clinical Psychology
EVANS, T. D.
FUGLESTAD, O. L., Education
HAUKEDAL, W., Organizational Psychology
HAVIK, O. E., Clinical Psychology
HUGDAHL, K., Somatic Psychology
JOHNSEN, B. H.
LABERG, J. C., Clinical Psychology
LIE, G. T., Social Psychology
LØBERG, T., Clinical Psychology
MITTELMARK, M. B., Social Psychology
MURISON, R., Physiological Psychology
NIELSEN, G. H., Clinical Psychology
NORDBY, H.
SAM, D. L., Personal Psychology
SUNDBERG, H., Physiological Psychology
URSIN, H., Physiological Psychology
VOLLMER, F., Personal Psychology
AARØ, L. E., Social Psychology

Faculty of Social Sciences (tel. 55-58-90-50; fax 55-58-90-52; e-mail post@svfa.uib.no; internet www.svt.uib.no):

AMUNDSEN, E. S., Economics
BAKKE, M., Media Studies
BJELLAND, A. K., Social Anthropology
DAVIDSEN, P., Information Science
EIDE, M., Media Studies
FLÅM, S. D., Economics
GRIPSRUD, J., Media Studies
GRØNHAUG, R., Social Anthropology
GRØNMO, S., Sociology
GULBRANDSEN, Ø., Social Anthropology
HENRIKSEN, G., Social Anthropology
HOLT-JENSEN, A., Geography
HVIDING, E., Social Anthropology
HÅLAND, G., Social Anthropology
JANSEN, A.-I., Administration and Organization Theory
JOHANSEN, A., Media Studies
KAPFERER, B., Social Anthropology
KAPFERER, J., Sociology
KNUDSEN, J. C., Social Anthropology
KORSNES, O., Sociology
KUHNLE, S., Comparative Politics
LARSEN, P. L., Media Studies
LINDSTRØM, U. A., Comparative Politics
LITHMAN, Y., Sociology
LOMMERUD, K. E., Economics
LÆGREID, P., Administration and Organization Theory
MANGER, L. O., Social Anthropology
MIDTBØ, T., Comparative Politics
MORGAN, K.
NILSEN, A., Sociology
OFFERDAL, A. J., Administration and Organization Theory
OPDAHL, A. L., Information Science
RISA, A. E., Economics

RONESS, P. G., Administration and Organization Theory
STRAND, T., Administration and Organization Theory
SVÅSAND, L. G., Comparative Politics
SÆTREN, H., Administration and Organization Theory
TJØTTA, S., Economics
TORSVIK, G., Economics
TVEDT, T., History and Development Studies
UHDE, A., Economics
ØSTBYE, H., Media Studies
ØYEN, E., Sociology
ÅRRESTAD, J., Economics
ÅSE, T. H., Geography

Bergen Museum (tel. 55-58-93-60; fax 55-58-93-64; e-mail bergen.museum@bm.uib.no; internet www.bm.uib.no/home.html):

ACHEN, H. VON, Art History
FOSSEN, H., Geology
INDRELID, S., Archaeology
MOE, D., Botany
SÆTHER, O. A., Zoology
WILLASSEN, E., Zoology

ATTACHED INSTITUTES

Bergen Foundation of Science: HIB, Thormøhlensgt. 55, 5028 Bergen; Dir (vacant).

Bergen High Technology Centre, Limited: HIB, Thormøhlensgt. 55, 5028 Bergen; Dir JAN S. JOHANNESSEN.

Centre for Development Studies: Strømgt. 54, 5007 Bergen; Dir Prof. TERJE TVEDT.

Centre for International Health: Armauer Hansens hus, Haukeland sykehus, 5021 Bergen; Dir GUNNAR KVÅLE.

Centre for Middle Eastern and Islamic Studies: Hans Tanksgt. 19, 5020 Bergen.

Centre for Social Science Research: Professor Keysersgt. 2, 5007 Bergen; Head of Research KARI TOVE ELVBAKKEN.

Centre for Studies of Environment and Resources: HIB, Thormøhlensgt. 55, 5020 Bergen; Chair ULF LIE.

Centre for the Study of the Sciences and Humanities: Allegaten 32, 5007 Bergen; Chair Prof. RAGNAR FJELLAND.

Centre for Virology: HIB, Thormøhlensgt. 55, 5028 Bergen; Chair. LARS HAARR.

Centre for Women and Gender Research: H. Fossgt. 12, 5007 Bergen; Dir Prof. KARI WÆRNESS.

Humanities Information Technology Research Programme (HIT Centre): Harald Hårfagresgt. 31, 5007 Bergen; Chair CLAUS HUITFELDT.

LOS Centre (Norwegian Centre for Research in Organization and Management): Rosenberggt. 39, 5015 Bergen; Dir IVAR BLEIKLIE.

Marine Biological Station: University of Bergen, Espelamdsveien 232, 5258 Blomsterdalen; open to research workers from all countries; 1 research vessel.

Medical Birth Registry of Norway: Haukelandsveien 10, 5021 Bergen; Chair Prof. LORENTZ IRGENS.

Nansen Environmental and Remote Sensing Centre: Edv. Griegsvei 3A, 5037 Solheimsvik; Dir OLA M. JOHANNESSEN.

Norwegian Social Science Data Services: Hans Holmboesgt. 22, 5007 Bergen; Dir BJØRN HENRICHSEN.

Research Centre for Health Promotion: Oistelinsgt. 3, 5007 Bergen; Dir Prof. GRO LIE.

University Media Centre: Nøstegt. 72, 5011 Bergen; Dir STEIN UNGER HITLAND.

See also under Museums and Art Galleries

UNIVERSITETET I OSLO
(University of Oslo)

POB 1072, Blindern, 0316 Oslo
Telephone: 22-85-50-50
Fax: 22-85-44-42
E-mail: informasjon@uio.no
Internet: www.uio.no

Founded 1811
State control
Academic year: August to June (two semesters)

Rector: Prof. Dr ARILD UNDERDAL
Vice-Rector: Prof. Dr ANNE-BRIT KOLSTØ
Librarian: JAN ERIK RØED

Library: see Libraries
Number of teachers: 2,400
Number of students: 32,000

Publications: *Annual Report*, *Apollon* (4 a year in Norwegian, annually in English), *Uniforum* (16 a year)

DEANS

Faculty of Arts: Prof. BJARNE ROGAN
Faculty of Dentistry: Prof. HANS R. HAANAES
Faculty of Education: Prof. BENTE E. HAGTVET
Faculty of Law: Prof. JOHN T. JOHNSEN
Faculty of Mathematics and Natural Sciences: Prof. KNUT FÆGRI
Faculty of Medicine: Prof. STEIN A. EVENSEN
Faculty of Social Sciences: Prof. ASBJØRN RØDSETH
Faculty of Theology: Prof. HELGE S. KVANVIG

PROFESSORS

Faculty of Arts (Administrasjonsbygn., 8 et., POB 1079 Blindern, 0316 Oslo; tel. 22-85-62-93; fax 22-85-45-50):

AKSNES, H., Musical Theory
ALLERN, S., Media and Communication Research
AMUNDSEN, A. B., Folklore
ANDERSEN, Ø., Classical Philology (Greek)
ANDERSEN, P. T., Nordic Literature
ASHEIM, O., Philosophy
ASKEDAL, J. O., German Language
ASZTALOS, M. M., Classical Philology (Latin)
AUESTAD, R. A., Japanese Language
AÚKRÚST, K. H., History of Religions
BAUNE, Ø., Philosophy
BENEDICTOW, O. J., History
BENUM, E., History
BENSKIN, M., English Language
BERGE, K. L., Nordic Language
BJERKE, Ø. L. S., Fine Art History
BJORVAND, H., German Linguistics
BJØRGUM, J., History
BJØRKVOLD, J. R., Musicology
BJØRNFLATEN, J. J., Slavonic Languages
BLIKSRUD, L., Nordic Literature
BRAAVIG, J., History of Religion
BRANDT, J. R., Classical Archaeology
BRENDEMOEN, B., Turkish Language
BRULAND, K., History
BRYNHILDSVOLL, K., Research on Ibsen
BØ, G., Norwegian Literature
BØ-RYGG, A., General Aesthetics
CARTER, M., Arabic
COLLETT, F. P., History
DAHL, H. F., Media and Communication Research
DIMAS, P., Philosophy
EDZARD, L. E., Hebrew and Semitic Languages
EGGE, A., History
EIFRING, H., Modern Chinese Languages
ELSNESS, J., English Language
EMILSSON, E. K., Ancient Philosophy
ERIKSEN, A., Folklore
ERIKSEN, T. B., History of Ideas

FAARLUND, J. T., Nordic Language and Literature
FARNER, G., Dutch
FEHR, D., Literature
FJELD, R. E. V., Lexicography
FRICKE, C., Philosophy
FRIEDMAN, R. M., History
FRØLICH, J., French Literature
FUGLESANG, S., Fine Art History
FUGLESTAD, F., History
FØLLESDAL, A., Philosophy
FØRLAND, T. E., History
GJELSVIK, O., Philosophy
GLAMBEK, I., Art History
GODØY, R. I., Musical Theory
GRIMNES, O. K., History
GUNDERSEN, K., French Literature
GUSTAFSSON, A., Ethnology
HAARBERG, F., Nordic Literature
HAGEBERG, O., Nordic Literature
HAGEMANN, G., History
HANSEN, C. F., German Language
HANSEN, J. E. E., History of Ideas
HARALDSSON, H., Russian
HARBSMEIER, C. H., East Asian Languages
HAREIDE, J., Nordic Literature
HASSELGÅRD, H., English Language
HEDEAGER, L., Nordic Archaeology
HELGHEIM, K., Theatre Research
HELLAND, H. P., French
HEYERDAHL, G. B., History of Ideas
HJELDE, S., History of Religions
HOBÆK HAFF, M., French Language
HODNE, B., Folklore
HOEL, K., Fine Art History
HOVDHAUGEN, E., General Linguistics
IVERSEN, I., General Literary Science
JERVELL, H. R., Computer Science
JOHANNESSEN, F. E., History
JOHANNESSEN, J. B., Linguistics
JOHANSEN, K. E., Philosophy
JOHANSSON, A., Modern Economic History
JOHANSSON, K. A. S., English Language
JØRGENSEN, F. G., Nordic Literature
KAARE, B. H., Folklore
KELLER, J. C., Nordic Archaeology
KIRKEBØEN, G., Psychology, Computer Science
KJELDSTADLI, K., Modern History
KJETSAA, G., Russian Literature
KLEM, L. G., Romance Philology
KOLSTØ, P., Russian and East European Studies
KRISTOFFERSEN, K. E., Linguistics, Philology
KROG, T., History of Ideas
KROGSETH, O., History of Christianity
KVIFTE, T., Folk Music
KVÆRNE, P., History of Religions
LANGE, E., History
LANGHOLM, T., Computer Science
LANZA, E., Linguistics
LAÚK, E., Media and Communication
LIE, S., Norwegian Language
LORENTZ, E., History
LOTHE, J., British Literature
LYCHE, C., French, Phonetics
LØDRUP, H., Linguistics
LØNNING, J. T., Computer Science
MARKUSSEN, I., History of Ideas
MELBERG, B. A. E., Literature
MOEN, I., Linguistics
MORGAN, N., Fine Art History
MYHRE, J., History
MØNNESLAND, S., Slavonic Languages
NAGUIB, S. N., Cultural History, Cultural Analysis
NEDKVITNE, A., History
NYGAARD, J., Theatre Science
OTTOSSON, K., Icelandic
PEDERSEN, A., Philosophy
PETTERSON, E. R., Fine Art History
PHARO, H., History
PRELL, H.-P., German Language
PRICE, P. G., History
QUILLER, B., History of Ideas

RAMBERG, B., Philosophy
RAND, K. A., English Language
RASMUSSEN, T., Media and Communication
REINTON, R., Literary Theory
RIAN, Ø., History
RINDAL, M., Nordic Onomastics
ROGAN, B., Ethnology
ROLL-HANSEN, N., Philosophy
RUUD, E., Musicology
RØNNING, H., Media and Communication Research
SAGMO, I., German Literature
SALBERG, T. K., French
SANDE, S., Classical Archaeology
SAÚGSTAD, F., Philosophy
SCHAANNING, E., History of Ideas
SCHMIDT, R. L., Urdu
SCHMIDT, T., Nordic Literature
SIMONSEN, H. G., Linguistics
SIRGES, T., German Language
SKAUG, E., Art Conservation
SKATTURN, I., Francophone Studies
SKEI, H. H., Literary Theory
SKOGERBØ, E., Media and Communication Research
SKRE, D., Archaeology
SLETSJØE, A., Portuguese Language
STEINFELD, T., Nordic Language and Literature
STEINSLAND, G. S., History of Religions
STENE-JOHANSEN, K., Literary Theory
STENGAARD, B., Ibero-Romance Philology
STENSVOLD, A., History of Religions
SYVERTSEN, T., Media and Communication
SØRENSEN, Ø., Modern History
SÆBØ, K. J., German Language
TEEUWEN, M. J., Japanese
THEIL, R., English Literature
THORSEN, L. E., Ethnology
URSTAD, T. S., British Literature
VANNEBO, K. I., Nordic Languages
VETLESEN, A. J., Philosophy
VIKØR, L. S., Nordic Linguistics
VINJE, F. E., Modern Nordic Language
VOLLSNES, A., Music
WALDAHL, R., Media and Communication Research
WERENSKIOLD, M., Fine Art History
WESSEL, E., German Literature
WICHSTRØM, A., Fine Art History
WIESTAD, E., Philosophy
WIKBERG, K. B., English Literature
WIKSHÅLAND, S., Musicology
WINTHER, P., American Literature
YSTAD, V., Nordic Literature
YTREBERG, E., Media and Communication
ZWARTJES, O., Spanish Language

Faculty of Dentistry (Geitmyrsvn. 69, 3 et., POB 1142 Blindern, 0317 Oslo; tel. 22-85-20-00; fax 22-85-23-32; e-mail infoskranke@odont.uio.no):

BARKVOLL, P., Dental Surgery
BJØRNLAND, T., Oral Surgery and Medicine
BRODIN, P., Physiology
BRYNE, M., Oral Biology
DEMBIK, P., Dentistry
ELLINGSEN, J. E., Prosthetic Dentistry
ERIKSEN, H. M., Cariology
ESPELAND, L. V., Dentistry
ESPELID, L., Dentistry
GRYTTEN, J. I., Community Dentistry, Health Economics
HALTENSEN, T. S., Oral Biology
HANSEN, B., Periodontology
HOLST, D. J., Social Dentistry
HAANÆS, H. R., Dental Surgery
HAAPASALO, M., Endodontics
JACOBSEN, I., Pedodontics
JOKSTAD, A., Dentistry
KLINGE, R. F., General and Oral Anatomy
KOPPANG, H. S., General and Oral Pathology
KOPPANG, R., Material Sciences
LARHEIM, T. A., Dentistry
LYNGSTADAAS, S. P., Dentistry

OLSEN, I., Microbiology
OSMUNDSEN, H., Biochemistry
PREUS, H. R., Periodontology
RISNES, S., General and Oral Anatomy
RYKKE, M., Dentistry
RØED, A., Physiology
SCHEIE, A. AA., Microbiology
SCHENCK, K., Immunology
SKOGLUND, L. A., Dental Pharmacology
SOLHEIM, T., Oral Pathology
STENVIK, A., Orthodontics
THRANE, P. S., Oral Pathology
TRONSTAD, L., Endodontics
TVEIT, A. B., Dentistry
VASSEND, O., Behavioural Science
WÅLER, S. M., Dentistry
ØGAARD, B., Orthodontics

Faculty of Education (Helga Engs hus, POB 1161 Blindern, 0318 Oslo; tel. 22-85-82-76; fax 22-85-82-41; e-mail uv-studentinformasjon@uv.uio.no):

BEFRING, E., Special Education
BIRKEMO, A., Pedagogy
BRÅTEN, I., Pedagogy
BROCK-UTNE, B., Pedagogy
DALE, E. L., Pedagogy
DALEN, M., Special Education
ENGELSEN, B. U., General Didactics
GJESME, T., Pedagogy
GJONE, G., Teacher Education and School Development
HAGTVET, B. E., Education, Dyslexia
HANDAL, G., Pedagogy
HAUGE, T. E., Pedagogy
HERTZBERG, F., Teacher Education
JENSEN, K., Pedagogy
JORDE, D., Teacher Education
JORDELL, K. ø., Pedagogy
LAHN, L. C., Pedagogy
LIE, S., Pedagogy
LIEBERG, S., Pedagogy
LUND, T., Special Education
LYCKE, K. H., Pedagogy
LØVLIE, L., Pedagogy
MARTINSEN, H., Psychology
NIELSEN, H. B., Pedagogy
OSTAD, S., Pedagogy
RUDBERG, M., Pedagogy
RYE, H., Special Education
SIMENSEN, A. M., Teacher Education
SJØBERG, S., Pedagogy (Natural Science)
SKOGEN, K., Special Education
STAFSENG, O., Pedagogy
TELLEVIK, J. M., Special Education
TJELDVOLL, A., Pedagogy
TVEIT, K., Pedagogy
ULVUND, S. E., Pedagogy
VONEN, A. M., Pedagogy, Linguistics
WIGGEN, G., Pedagogy
ØSTERUD, S., Pedagogy
ØZERK, K., Pedagogy

Faculty of Law (Karl Johans g. 47, St Olavs plass, POB 6706, 0130 Oslo; tel. 22-85-93-00; fax 22-85-01-80):

ANDENÆS, K., Sociology of Law
ANDENÆS, M. H., Civil Law
ARNESEN, F., European Law
BING, J., Law
BOE, E., Law
BUGGE, H. CHR., Law
BULL, H. J., Law
BULL, K. STRØM, Law
EIDE, E., Economics and Statistics
ENG, S., Law
ERICSSON, K., Criminology
ESKELAND, S., Law
EVJU, S., Civil Law
FALKANGER, T., Law
FINSTAD, L., Criminology
FLEISCHER, C. A., Law
FØLLESDAL, A., Human Rights Law
GIERTSEN, H., Criminology
GRAVER, H. P., Sociology of Law
HAGSTRØM, V., Civil Law
HELLUM, A., Women's Law

Hov, J., Law
Høigård, I. C., Criminology
Jakhelln, H., Law
Johansen, P. O., Criminology
Johnsen, J. T., Law
Kaasen, K., Law
Kjønstad, A., Law
Michalsen, D., Law
Robberstad, A., European Law
Rognstad, O.-A., Private Law
Røsæg, E., Law
Sand, I. J., Public Law
Schartum, D. W., Administrative Informatics
Simonsen, L., Private Law
Smith, E., Law
Smith, L., Law
Stenvik, A., Private Law
Stridbeck, U., Law
Sverdrup, T., Civil Law
Syse, A., Law
Torvund, O., Law
Ulfstein, G., Law
Wilhelmsen, T. L., Insurance Law
Woxholth, G., Civil Law
Zimmer, F., Law

Faculty of Mathematics and Natural Sciences (Fysikkbygn., POB 1032 Blindern, 0315 Oslo; tel. 22-85-63-44; fax 22-85-43-67):

Aksnes, K., Astrophysics
Albregtsen, F., Computer Science
Alve, E., Geology
Andersen, T. B., Geology
Andersson, K. K., Biochemistry
Andresen, A., Geology
Austrheim, H., Geology
Bakke, O., Biology
Bedos, E. Chr., Mathematics
Benneche, T., Chemistry
Berg, T., Cell Biology
Berg, Y., Informatics
Bertelsen, A., Mechanics
Beuth, F. E., Mathematics
Bjørlykke, K. O., Geology
Borgan, Ø., Statistics
Bravina, L., Physics
Bratteli, O., Mathematics
Brodersen, H., Mathematics
Bugge, L., Physics
Buran, T., Physics
Bye, R., Chemistry
Bølviken, E., Statistics
Carlsson, M., Astrophysics
Christophersen, N., Informatics
Corfu, F., Geology
Dahl, G., Informatics
Dahlback, A., Physics
Dale, B., Geology
Dæhlen, M., Mathematical Modelling
Døving, K., Zoophysiology
Eeg, J. O., Physics
Eliassen, F., Computer Science
Elverhøi, A., Quaternary Geology
Ellingsrud, G., Mathematics
Engvold, O., Astrophysics
Eskild, W., Biochemistry
Faleide, J. I., Geology
Feder, J. G., Physics
Finstad, T., Physics
Fjellvåg, H., Chemistry
Flekkøy, E. G., Physics
Floater, M. S., Informatics
Furuseth, S., Chemistry
Fægri, K., Chemistry
Gabrielsen, O. S., Biochemistry
Galperine, I., Physics
Gelius, L.-J., Geophysics
Gjessing, S., Computer Science
Gjevik, B., Hydrodynamics
Goebel, V. H., Informatics
Gottschalk, L., Geophysics
Gray, J. S., Marine Zoology
Greibrokk, T., Analytical Chemistry
Grue, J., Mechanics
Gundersen, G., Chemistry

Gundersen, K., Biology (Physiology)
Gundersen, L.-L., Chemistry
Guttormsen, M., Physics
Gørbitz, C. H., Chemistry
Hagelberg, E., Zoology
Hagen, J. O. M., Geography
Hansen, E. W., Chemistry
Hansen, F. K., Chemistry
Hanseth, O., Informatics
Hansteen, V., Astrophysics
Helgaker, T., Chemistry
Helland, I., Statistics
Hellesland, J., Mechanics
Hessen, D., Zoology
Hestmark, G., Biology
Hjort, N. L., Statistics
Hjorth-Jensen, M., Nuclear Physics
Hoff, P., Chemistry
Hole, E. O., Physics
Holm, P., Mathematics
Holm, S., Signal Processing
Holtet, J. A., Physics
Humlum, O., Geography
Høeg, K., Geology
Høgåsen, H., Theoretical Physics
Høiland, K., Biology
Haaland, A., Chemistry
Ingebretsen, F., Physics
Isaksen, I., Meteorology
Iversen, T., Geophysics
Jahren, B., Mathematics
Jakobsen, K. S., Biology
Jamtveit, B., Geology
Johansen, H. T., Pharmacy
Johansen, T. H., Physics
Jørgensen, M., Informatics
Karen, P., Chemistry
Karlsen, J., Pharmacy
Kjeldsetii-Moe, O., Astrophysics
Klaveness, D., Biology
Klaveness, J., Pharmacy
Kolstø, A. B., Microbiology
Koomey, J. M., Pharmacology
Kristensen, T. A., Biochemistry
Kristjansson, F. E., Geophysics
Krogdahl, S., Computer Science
Kaartvedt, S., Marine Biology
Kaasbøll, F. F., Informatics
Lambertsson, A., Genetics
Lampe, H. M., Biology
Lande, T. S., Computer Science
Langtangen, H. P., Informatics
Leer, E., Astrophysics
Leinaas, H. P., Zoology
Leinaas, J. M., Physics
Liestøl, K., Mathematical Modelling
Lilje, P. V., Astrophysics
Lillerud, K. P., Chemistry
Lindqvist, B. H., Zoology
Lindstrøm, T., Mathematics
Lund, W., Chemistry
Lundanes, E., Chemistry
Lutken, C. A., Physics
Lyche, T. J. W., Mathematical Modelling
Lysne, O., Communication Systems
Løvhøiden, G., Physics
Løw, E., Mathematics
Laane, C. M., Botany
Malterud, K. E., Pharmacognosy
Martinsen, Ø. G., Physics
Maupin, V., Geophysics
Moen, J. I., Physics
Myhre, A. M., Geology
Møllendal, H., Chemistry
Møller-Pedersen, B., Informatics
Mørken, K., Numerical Analysis
Måløy, K. J., Physics
Nagy, J., Geology
Natvig, B., Mathematical Statistics
Neumann, E. R., Geology
Nielsen, C. J., Chemistry
Nilsson, E. G., Biology (Physiology)
Nissen-Meyer, J., Biochemistry
Norby, P. Æ., Chemistry
Norby, T. E., Chemistry
Nordal, I., Botany

Normann, D., Mathematical Logic
Nystrøm, B., Organic Chemistry
Olsbye, U., Chemistry
Olsen, A., Physics
Omtvedt, F. P., Chemistry
Osnes, E., Physics
Owe, O., Computer Science
Paulsen, B. S., Pharmacognosy
Paulsen, R. E., Pharmacy (Microbiology)
Pecseli, H., Physics
Pedersen, G. K., Mathematics
Pedersen-Bjergaard, S., Pharmacy
Pettersen, E. O., Physics
Piene, R., Mathematics
Plagemann, T. P., Informatics
Podladtchikov, Y., Geology
Prydz, K., Biochemistry
Ranestad, K., Mathematics
Rasmussen, K. E., Pharmaceutical Analysis
Ravndal, F., Theoretical Physics
Read, A. L., Physics
Rekstad, J. B., Physics
Rise, F., Chemistry
Risebro, N. H., Mathematics
Rognes, J., Mathematics
Roos, N., Cell Biology
Roots, J., Chemistry
Rueness, J., Marine Biology
Rustan, A., Pharmacy
Saatcioglu, F., Biology
Sagstuen, E., Physics
Sahay, S., Informatics
Samdal, S., Chemistry
Sand, O., Zoophysiology
Sande, S. A., Pharmacy
Sandholt, P. E., Physics
Sandlie, I., Biology
Schumacher, T., Botany
Seip, H. M., Chemistry
Sirevåg, R., Microbiology
Sjøberg, D., Informatics
Skramstad, J., Chemistry
Skaali, T. B., Physics
Slagsvold, T., Zoology
Smistad, G., Pharmacy
Spilling, P., Telematics and Telecommunications
Stabell, B., Geology
Stabell, R., Astrophysics
Stapnes, S., Physics
Steen, H., Biology
Stenersen, J. H. V., Biology
Stenseth, N. C., Zoology
Stordal, F., Meteorology
Stølen, S., Chemistry
Størmer, E., Mathematics
Sudbø, Aa., Optoelectronics
Svensson, B. G., Physics
Swensen, A. R., Mathematics (Statistics)
Sætre, G.-P., Biology
Søråsen, O., Microelectronics
Taftø, J., Physics
Throndsen, J., Marine Biology
Tilset, M., Chemistry
Tomter, P., Mathematics
Toverud, E., Pharmacy
Trulsen, J., Astrophysics
Tveito, A., Informatics
Tveter, T. S., Physics
Tønnesen, H. H., Clinical Pharmacy
Uggerud, E., Chemistry
Veseth, L., Physics
Vøllestad, A. L., Biology (Zoology)
Weber, J. E., Geophysics
Winther, R., Mathematical Modelling
Øksendal, B., Mathematics
Aagaard, P., Geology
Aalen, R., Biology
Aarnes, H., Biology
Aasen, A. J., Pharmacy
Aashamar, K., Physics

Faculty of Medicine (Søsterhjemmet, Ullevål sykehus, POB 1078 Blindern, 0316 Oslo; tel.

22-85-05-00; fax 22-85-05-01; e-mail delarkiv-sekretariatet@medisin.uio.no):

AGARTZ, I., Psychiatry
AURSNES, I. A., Pharmacology
BENESTAD, H. B., Physiology
BERG, O. T., Health Administration
BERG, T., Physiology
BJERTNESS, E., Epidemiology
BJUNE, G. A., International Health
BJÅLIE, E. G., Anatomy
BLOMHOFF, H. K., Medical Biochemistry
BLOMHOFF, R., Nutrition Research
BOE, J., Respiratory Medicine
BOGEN, B., Immunology
BOTTEN, G. S., Health Administration
BRANTZAEG, P., Immunology
BREIVIK, H., Anaesthesiology
BRODAL, P., Anatomy
BROSSTAD, F. R., Internal Medicine Research
BRUUSGAARD, D., Social Security Medicine
BUKHOLM, G., Bacteriology
CARLSEN, K.-H., Paediatrics
CHRISTOFFERSEN, T., Pharmacology
CLAUSEN, O. P. F., Pathology
COLLAS, P., Biochemistry
COLLINS, A. R., Nutrition Research
DANBOLT, N. C., Physiology
DREVON, C., Nutrition Research
DUTTAVOY, A. K., Nutrition Research
EVENSEN, S. A., Haematology
FINSET, A., Medical Behavioural Research
FOSSUM, S., Anatomy
FRIGESSI, A., Medical Statistics
FRØLAND, S. S., Clinical Medicine
FUGELLI, P., Social Medicine
FYRAND, O. L., Dermatology
GEIRAN, O., Cardiovascular Surgery
GIESDAL, K., Cardiology
GLOVER, J., Physiology
GORDELADZE, J. O., Medical Biochemistry
GRØHOLT, B., Psychiatry
GRØTTUM, P., Medical Computer Science
HAGEN, T. P., Health Administration
HANSSON, V., Medical Biochemistry
HAUG, F. M., Anatomy
HEGGELUND, P., Neurophysiology
HEIBERG, A. N., Psychiatry
HJORTDAHL, P., Medicine
HOLCK, P., Anatomy
HORN, R., Medical Biochemistry
HUITFELDT, H., Pathology
HUSBY, G., Rheumatology
HØGLEND, P. A., Psychiatry
HØSTMARK, T. A., Preventive Medicine
ILEBEKK, A. B., Experimental Medicine
INGSTAD, B., Social Medicine
IVERSEN, I. G. H., Physiology
IVERSEN, P. O., Nutrition Research
IVERSEN, T., Health Economics
JAHNSEN, T., Biochemistry
JELLUM, E., Clinical Biochemistry
KASE, B. F., Paediatrics
KIERULF, P., Clinical Chemistry
KIRKEVOLD, M., Medicine
KJEKSHUS, J., Cardiology
KLEPP, K. I., Nutrition Research
KOLBENSTVEDT, A. N., Radiology
KOLSET, S. O., Nutrition Research
KVITTINGEN, E. A., Clinical Biochemistry
LARSEN, Ø., Medical History
LEVY, F. O., Pharmacology
LIE, S. O., Paediatrics
LINDEGAARD, K., Neurosurgery
LOGE, F. H., Medical Behavioural Research
LORENSEN, M., Nursing Science
LÆRUM, F., Clinical Medicine
LØVSTAD, R., Medical Biochemistry
LAAKE, P., Medical Statistics
MADSHUS, I. H., Molecular Biology
MENGSHOEL, A. M., Health Science
MEYER, H. E., Social Medicine
MOUM, T., Medical Behavioural Research
MULLER, F., Pharmacology
NAFSTAD, P., Social Medicine

NATVIG, J. B., Immunology
NICOLAYSEN, G., Physiology
NJÅ, A., Neurophysiology
NYBERG-HANSEN, R., Neurology
NÆSS, O., Pathology
ORMSTAD, K., Forensic Medicine
OS, I., Pharmacology
OSNES, J. B., Pharmacology
OTTERSEN, O. P., Anatomy
PEDERSEN, J. I., Nutrition Research
REIBERÅS, O., Orthopaedics
REIKVAM, A., Pharmacotherapy
REINHOLT, F. P., Pathology
RINVIK, E., Anatomy
ROGDE, S., Forensic Medicine
ROGNUM, T. O., Forensic Medicine
ROLLAG, H., Bacteriology
ROLSTAD, B., Anatomy
SAGVOLDEN, T., Neurophysiology
SANDANGER, B., Medical Behavioural Research
SANDNES, D. L., Pharmacology
SAUGSTAD, O. D., Paediatrics
SEJERSTED, O. M., Experimental Research
SKOMEDAL, T., Pharmacology
SOLBAKK, J. H., Medical Ethics
SOLLID, L. M., Transplantation Immunology
STEEN, P. A., Anaesthesiology
STOKKE, O., Clinical Biochemistry
STORM, J., Physiology
STORM-MATHISEN, J., Anatomy
STRAAND, F., Social Medicine
STRAY-PEDERSEN, B., Obstetrics and Gynaecology
SØRENSEN, T., Psychiatry
TASKÉN, K., Medical Biochemistry
TELLNES, G., Social Security Medicine
TØNJUM, T., Microbiology
UNDLIEN, D. E., Medical Genetics
URSIN, G., Nutrition Research
VAAGE, I. F., Traumatology
VAGLUM, P., Psychiatry
VATN, M. H., Clinical Epidemiology
VØLLESTAD, N. K., Health Science
WAAL, H., Psychiatry
WALAAS, S. I., Biochemistry
WALLØE, L., Physiology
WANDEL, M., Nutrition Research
ØSTVOLD, A. C., Neurochemistry
AALEN, O. O., Statistics
AASEN, A., Surgery

Faculty of Social Sciences (Eilert Sundts hus, 3. et., POB 1084 Blindern, 0317 Oslo; tel. 22-85-62-64; fax 22-85-48-25; internet www.sv .uio.no):

ALBUM, D., Sociology
ANDRESEN, S. E., Political Science
ARCHETTI, E. P., Social Anthropology
ASHEIM, G., Economics
BALDERSHEIM, H., Political Science
BERKAAK, O. A., Social Anthropology
BIRKELUND, G. E., Sociology
BIØRN, E., Economics
BJERKHOLT, O., Economics
BJØRKLÚND, R., Psychology
BJØRKLÚND, T., Political Science
BLAKAR, R. M., Social Psychology
BORGE, A. I. H., Psychology
BRENNEN, T., Psychology
BROCH, H. B., Social Anthropology
BRÅTEN, S. L., Sociology
CHECKEL, F. T., Political Science
CHRISTENSEN, T., Political Science
CHRISTIANSEN, V., Economics
DUCKERT, F., Psychology
EGEBERG, M., Political Science
ENERSTVEDT, R., Sociology
ERIKSEN, G. T. H., Social Anthropology
FAGERBERG, J., Socio-Economics
FEHR, N. H., Economics
FRØNES, I., Sociology
FURST, E. L., Social Anthropology
FØRSUND, F. R., Economics
GRENNESS, C. E., Psychology

GULLESTAD, S. E., Psychology
HAGTVET, B., Political Science
HAGTVEDT, K. A., Psychology
HANSEN, M. N., Sociology
HANSEN, T., Political Science
HARTMANN, E. F., Psychology
HEIDAR, K., Political Science
HELLEVIK, O., Political Science
HELSTRUP, T., Psychology
HESSELBERG, J., Social Geography
HOEL, M. O., Economics
HOLDEN, S., Economics
HOLTE, A., Psychology
HOVI, J., Political Science
HOWELL, S. L., Social Anthropology
HUNDEIDE, K., Psychology
HVEEM, H., Political Science
HYLLAND, AA., Economics
HØGSNES, G. L., Sociology
HAAVIND, H., Psychology
KALLAND, A., Social Anthropology
KEILMANN, N., Demography
KNUTSEN, O., Political Science
KRAVDAL, Ø., Demographics
LANDRØ, N. I., Psychology
LEIRA, A., Sociology
LIAN, A., Psychology
LINDGREN, M., Psychology
LUND, D., Economics
LUND, S. E., Social Anthropology
MAGNUSSEN, S. J., Psychology
MALNES, R. S., Political Science
MASTEKAASA, A., Sociology
MATLARY, F. H., Political Science
MELHUS, M., Social Anthropology
MJØSET, L., Sociology
MOENE, K. O., Economics and Statistics
MYDSKE, P. K., Political Science
NARUD, H. M., Political Science
NIELSEN, T. H., Social Sciences and Humanities
NILSSEN, T., Economics
NORDBY, T., Political History
NYMOEN, R., Economics
OTNES, P., Sociology
PEDERSEN, W., Social Geography
RASCH, B. E., Political Science
REICHELT, S., Psychology
REINVANG, I., Psychology
ROSE, L. E., Political Science
RUND, B. R., Psychology
RØDSETH, A., Economics
RØNNESTAD, H., Psychology
SCHWEDER, T., Statistics
SEIERSTAD, A., Mathematics
SKJEIE, H., Political Science
SKOE, E. E. A., Psychology
SKOG, O., Sociology
SMITH, L., Psychology
STEEN, A., Political Science
STOKKE, K., Social Geography
STORESLETTEN, K., Economics
STRAND, J., Economics
STRØM, S., Economics and Statistics
SUNDET, J. M., Psychology
SYDSÆTER, K., Mathematics
SØRUM, A., Social Anthropology
TALLE, A., Social Anthropology
TEIGEN, K.-H., Psychology
TETZCHNER, S. V., Psychology
THAGAARD, T., Sociology
TJERSLAND, O. A., Psychology
TORGERSEN, S. O., Psychology
TØRNQUIST, O., Political Science
UNDERDAL, A., Political Science
VISLIE, J., Economics
VOLLRATH, M., Psychology
WESSEL, T., Social Geography
WETTESEN, T. S., Social Geography
WIDERBERG, K., Sociology
WIKAN, U., Social Anthropology
WILLASSEN, Y., Economics
WOLD, A. H., Psychology
ØSTERUD, Ø., Conflict and Peace Research

Faculty of Theology (Domus Theologica, Blindernvn. 9, POB 1023 Blindern, 0315 Oslo; tel. 22-85-03-00; fax 22-85-03-01; internet www.tf.uio.no):

BARSTAD, H. M., Old Testament
CHRISTOFFERSEN, S. A., Systematic Theology
DOKKA, T. S., New Testament and Systematic Theology
FURRE, B., Church History and Systematic Theology
HAFSTAD, K., Systematic Theology
HAUGE, M. R., Old Testament
HELLHOLM, D., New Testament
KVANVIG, H. S., Old Testament
LØNNING, I., Systematic Theology
MOXNES, H., New Testament
RASMUSSEN, T., History of the Church
SEIM, T. K., New Testament
THELLE, N. R., Systematic Theology
THORKILDSEN, D., Church History
WYLLER, T. E., Systematic Theology

Natural History Museums and Botanical Gardens (Sars' gate 1, POB 1172 Blindern, 0318 Oslo; tel. 22-85-50-50; fax 22-85-18-32; e-mail nhm-museum@nhm.uio.no; internet www.nhm.uio.no):

ANDERSEN, K. I., Zoology
BACHMANN, L., Zoology
BAKKE, T. A., Zoology
BJORKLUND, K. R., Palaeontology
BORGEN, L., Botany
BROCHMANN, C., Botany
BRUTON, D. L., Palaeontology
ELVEN, R., Botany
GULDEN, G., Botany
HALVORSEN, O., Zoology
LIEFELD, J. T., Zoology
SUNDING, P., Botany
VAN BERGEN, I. J., Mineralogy
WIIG, Ø., Zoology and Mammalogy
ØKLAND, R. H., Botany

University Museum of Cultural Heritage (POB 6762, St. Olavs plass, 0130 Oslo; tel. 22-85-19-00; fax 22-85-99-20; e-mail info@ukm.uio.no):

CHRISTENSEN, A. E., Scandinavian Archaeology
KNIRK, J. E., Medieval History
MIKKELSEN, E., Nordic Archaeology
PLATHER, U., Art Conservation Chemistry
RESI, H. G., Iron Age
SVENSSON, T. G., Social Anthropology

Biotechnology Centre of Oslo (EMBIO) (Forskringsparken, Gaustadalleen 21, 0349 Oslo; tel. 22-84-05-31; fax 22-84-05-01):

GABRIELSEN, O. S.
TASKÉN, T. (Dir)

Centre for Women's Studies and Gender Research (Sognsvn. 70, 4 et., POB 1040 Blindern, 0315 Oslo; tel. 22-85-89-30; fax 22-85-89-50; e-mail skk-post@skk.uio.no):

NIELSEN, H. B., Women's Studies, Gender Research

UNIVERSITET I STAVANGER

4036 Stavanger
Telephone: 51-83-10-00
Fax: 51-83-30-50
E-mail: post@uis.no
Internet: www.uis.no
Founded 1994 as Høgskolen i Stavanger; present status 2005
State control
Languages of instruction: Norwegian, English

Rector: IVAR LANGEN
Vice-Rector: INGE SÆRHEIM
University Director: INGER ØSTENSJØ
Librarian: ESPEN SKJOLDAL
Number of teachers: 700

Number of students: 7,500
Library of 260,000 vols, 3,000 periodicals

DEANS

Faculty of Arts and Education: MARIT BOYESEN
Faculty of Science and Technology: ARILD BØE
Faculty of Social Sciences: JENS T. LARSEN

UNIVERSITETET I TROMSØ
(University of Tromsø)

9037 Tromsø
Telephone: 77-64-40-00
Fax: 77-64-49-00
E-mail: postmottak@uit.no
Internet: uit.no
Founded 1968
State control
Academic year: August to June (two semesters)

Rector: Prof. JARLE AARBAKKE
Pro-Rector: Prof. GERD BJØRHOVDE
University Director: LASSE LØNNUM
Director of Information: KAREN MARIE CHRISTENSEN
Director of Research and Studies: INGRID BERGSLID SALVESEN
Library Director: HELGE SALVESEN

Number of teachers: 1,002
Number of students: 6,314

Publications: *Nordlyd* (linguistics), *Tromsø Studies in Linguistics*, *Polar Research in Tromsø*, *Nordlit* (literature), *Poljarnyj Vestnik* (Russian language and literature), *Ottar* (popular science), *Ravnetrykk* (university library journal), *Speculum Boreale* (history), *Troll* (literature), Tromsø Geophysical Observatory reports, *Tromura* (Tromsø University Museum reports), *Index seminum* (botany)

DEANS

Faculty of Humanities: Prof. ROLF GAASLAND
Faculty of Law: Prof. HEGE BRÆKHUS
Faculty of Medicine: Prof. TORALF HASVOLD
Faculty of Science: Prof. TORE VORREN
Faculty of Social Sciences: Prof. PETTER NAFSTAD
Norwegian College of Fishery Science: Assoc. Prof. KNUT HEEN (Rector)

PROFESSORS

Faculty of Humanities (tel. 77-64-42-40; e-mail postmottak@hum.uit.no):

ALHAUG, G.
BARSTAD, G.
BJØRHOVDE, G.
BOUVRIE, S. DES
BRØGGER, F. C.
BULL, T.
EGEBERG, E. H.
GAASLAND, R.
HOFSTEN, H. W. VON
KARLSEN, O.
LIEPE, L.
LINDGREN, A.-R.
LUND, N. W.
LÖNNGREN, L.
MØRCK, E.
NESSET, T.
RAMCHAND, G.
RICE, C.
SCHMIDT, M.
STARKE, M.
SVENONIUS, P.
SWAN, T.
TARALDSEN, K. T.
WESTVIK, O. M. J.
WÆRP, H. H.

Faculty of Law (tel. 77-64-41-97; e-mail postmottak@jus.uit.no):

CHRISTIANSEN, P.
HAUGLI, T.

Faculty of Medicine (tel. 77-64-67-50; e-mail post@fagmed.uit.no):

ANDERSEN, T., Community Medicine
ARNESEN, E., Community Medicine
BJØRKLID, E., Medical Biology
BLIX, A. S., Medical Biology
BRANDL, M., Pharmacy
DAHL, S. G., Medical Biology
EL-GEWELY, M. R., Medical Biology
FOLKOW, L., Medical Biology
FØNNEBØ, V., Community Medicine
FØRDE, O. H., Community Medicine
GRAM, I. T., Community Medicine
GREINER-TOLLERSRUD, O. K., Medical Biology
HASVOLD, T., Community Medicine
HOLTEDAHL, K., Community Medicine
HUSEBEKK, A., Medical Biology
HUSEBY, N.-E., Medical Biology
HØYER, G., Community Medicine
JACOBSEN, B. K., Community Medicine
JENSEN, E., Pharmacy
JOHANSEN, S., Medical Biology
JOHANSEN, T., Medical Biology
LARSEN, T., Medical Biology
LOENNECHEN, T., Pharmacy
NIELSEN, K. M., Pharmacy
LUND, E., Community Medicine
MERCER, J., Medical Biology
MELBYE, H., Community Medicine
MJØS, O. D., Medical Biology
MOENS, U., Medical Biology
NIELSEN, K. M., Pharmacy
NJØLSTAD, I., Community Medicine
NORDØY, E., Medical Biology
OLSEN, J. A., Community Medicine
OLSVIK, Ø., Medical Biology
REKVIG, O.-P., Medical Biology
RINNE, A., Medical Biology
SAGER, G., Medical Biology
SMEDSRØD, B., Medical Biology
STOKKAN, K.-A., Medical Biology
SUNDSFJORD, A., Medical Biology
SYLTE, I., Medical Biology
WILLASSEN, N. P., Medical Biology
WINBERG, J.-O., Medical Biology
YTREHUS, K., Medical Biology
ØRBO, A., Medical Biology

Faculty of Sciences (tel. 77-64-40-01; e-mail postmottak@matnat.uit.no):

ANDERSEN, J., Biology
ANSHUS, O. J., Computer Science
ASLAKSEN, T., Physics
BERGH, S., Geology
BHUVANESWARI, T. V., Biology
CARLSON, R., Chemistry
DAHL, D., Chemistry
ELTOFT, T., Physics
ESSER, R., Physics
FLÅ, T., Mathematics and Statistics
FOLSTAD, I., Biology
GHOSH, A., Chemistry
GODTLIBSEN, F., Mathematics and Statistics
HALD, M., Geology
HANSEN, L. K., Chemistry
HANSSEN, A., Physics
HARTVIGSEN, G., Computer Science
HAVNES, O., Physics
HOUGH, E., Chemistry
IMS, R. A., Biology
JACOBSEN, S., Physics
JOHANSEN, D., Computer Science
JOHNSEN, B., Mathematics and Statistics
JUNTILLA, O., Biology
KRUGLIKOV, B., Mathematics and Statistics
LA HOZ, C., Physics
LYCHAGIN, V., Mathematics and Statistics
MELANDSØ, F., Physics
MIENERT, J., Geology

MJØLHUS, E., Mathematics and Statistics
OLSON, L., Mathematics and Statistics
PRASOLOV, A., Mathematics and Statistics
RAVNA, E. K., Geology
RUUD, K., Chemistry
RYPDAL, K., Physics
RØEGGEN, I., Physics
SMALÅS, A., Chemistry
SVENDSEN, J. S., Chemistry
SVENNING, M., Biology
VORREN, K.-D., Biology
VORREN, T., Geology
YOCCOZ, N., Biology

Faculty of Social Sciences (tel. 77-64-42-96; e-mail eksped@sv.uit.no):

ANDERSSON, D. T., Philosophy
BALSVIK, R. R., History
BERTELSEN, R., Archaeology
BLANKHOLM, H. P., Archaeology
BONAUNET, K., Philosophy
DAMM, C., Archaeology
EDVARDSEN, E., Education
EISEMANN, M., Psychology
ENGELSTAD, E., Archaeology
FLATEN, M. A., Psychology
FULSÅS, N., History
GUNERIUSSEN, W., Sociology
HAGA, A., Philosophy
HANSEN, L. I., History
HAUGEN, R., Education
HELLESNES, J., Philosophy
HOLT, R., History
HOLTEDAL, L., Social Anthropology
HØGMO, A., Education
JOHANSEN, T., Sociology
KROGER, J., Psychology
LAENG, B., Psychology
MIDRÉ, G., Sociology
MIKALSEN, K. H., Political Science
MYRSTAD, A., Philosophy
NAFSTAD, P., Philosophy
NERGÅRD, J.-I., Education
NIELSEN, J. P., History
NIEMI, E., History
NERGÅRD, P. M., Education
NERHEIM, H., Philosophy
NORDERVAL, Ø., Religious Studies
OLSEN, B., Archaeology
ROSSVÆR, V., Philosophy
RUDMIN, F., Psychology
RØVIK, K. A., Political Science
SAUGESTAD, S., Social Anthropology
SILVERA, D., Psychology
SVARTDAL, F., Psychology
THUEN, T., Social Anthropology
TJELMELAND, H., History
TRÆEN, B., Psychology
VERPLANKEN, B., Psychology
VITTERSØ, J., Psychology
WATERLOO, K., Psychology
AGMO, A., Psychology
AARSÆTHER, N., Planning and Local Community Research

Norwegian College of Fishery Science (tel. 77-64-60-00; e-mail eksped@nfh.uit.no):

AMUNDSEN, P.-A., Aquatic Biology
BØGWALD, J., Marine Biotechnology
CLARK, D., Economics and Management
EILERTSEN, H. C., Aquatic Biology
ELVEVOLL, E. O., Marine Biotechnology
FALK-PETERSEN, I. B., Aquatic Biology
FEVOLDEN, S.-E., Aquatic Biology
FLÅTEN, O., Economics and Management
GULLIKSEN, B., Aquatic Biology
HERSOUG, B., Economics and Management
HOLM, P., Economics and Management
JENTOFT, S., Economics and Management
JOBLING, M., Aquatic Biology
JOHNSEN, H. K., Aquatic Biology
JØRGENSEN, E., Aquatic Biology
JØRGENSEN, J. B., Marine Biotechnology
JØRGENSEN, T. ø., Marine Biotechnology
KLEMETSEN, J., Aquatic Biology
KRISTIANSEN, S., Aquatic Biology
OLAFSEN, J. A., Marine Biotechnology

OLSEN, K. K., Aquatic Biology
OLSEN, R. L., Marine Biotechnology
OLSEN, S. O., Economics and Management
ROBERTSEN, B., Marine Biotechnology
SCHULZ, C.-E., Economics and Management
TANDE, K., Aquatic Biology
TRONDSEN, T., Social and Marketing Studies
VASSDAL, T., Economics and Management
WASSMANN, P., Aquatic Biology

ATTACHED INSTITUTES

Centre for Advanced Studies in Theoretical Linguistics (CASTL): internet uit.no/castl/4700; Dir Prof. CURT RICE.

Centre for Environment and Development Studies (SEMUT): internet uit.no/semut; Head of Administration HÅKON FOTTLAND.

Centre for Flexible Education (U-VETT): internet uit.no/uvett/193; Head of Administration INGER ANN HANSSEN.

Centre for International Health: internet uit.no/sih/918; Dir Adjunct Prof. TORE GUTTEBERG.

Centre for Peace Studies: internet uit.no/cps/3285; Dir Assoc. Prof. CHARLES P. WEBEL.

Centre for Research on the Elderly in Tromsø: internet uit.no/172; Gen. Man. PÅL VEGAR STOREHEIER.

Centre for Sámi Health Research: internet uit.no/medsamisk/2011; Dir Prof. EILIV LUND.

Centre for Sámi Studies: internet www.sami.uit.no; Head of Administration ELSE GRETE BRODERSTAD.

Centre for Women and Gender Research (KVINNFORSK): internet uit.no/kvinnforsk; Head of Administration LISE NORDBRØND.

National Centre for Rural Medicine: internet uit.no/distriktsmedisin/omnkd; Dir Prof. TORALF HASVOLD.

National Research Centre in Complementary and Alternative Medicine (NAFKAM): internet uit.no/nafkam/omnafkam; Dir Prof. VINJAR FØNNEBØ.

Norwegian Structural Biology Centre (NORSTRUCT): internet uit.no/norstruct/home; Dir Prof. ARNE O. SMALÅS.

Roald Amundsen Centre for Arctic Research: internet uit.no/amundsen/438; Head of Administration GEIR GOTAAS.

Tromsø University Museum: internet uit.no/tmu; Dir DIKKA STORM.

Colleges of University Standing

ARKITEKTHØGSKOLEN I OSLO
(Oslo School of Architecture)

POB 6768, St Olavs plass, 0130 Oslo
Telephone: 22-99-70-00
Fax: 22-99-71-90
E-mail: postmottak@aho.no
Internet: www.aho.no
Founded 1945
State control
Academic year: September to June

Rector: KARL OTTO ELLEFSEN
Pro-Rector: BIRGER SEVALDSON
Chief Administrative Director: OLA STAVE
Librarian: SIDSEL MOUM

Library of 40,000 vols
Number of teachers: 38
Number of students: 400

Publication: *Research Magazine* (annually)

PROFESSORS

DAHLE, E., Architectural Design II
DIGERUD, J., Form and Design
DUNIN-WOYSETH, H., Director of the Doctoral Programme
EGGEN, A., Building Technology
ELLEFSEN, K. O., Urbanism
FJELD, P. O., Architectural Design III
HJELTNES, K., Architectural Design II
KLEVEN, B., Architectural Design I
KLEVEN, T., Architectural Design I
LØKSE, O., Form and Design
MICHL, J., Industrial Design
MUNSHI, K., Industrial Design
SANDAKER, B., Building Technology
SKJØNSBERG, T., Form and Design
THIIS-EVENSEN, T., Architectural Theory and History
TOSTRUP, E., Architectural Design I

HANDELSHØYSKOLEN BI
(Norwegian School of Management)

POB 580, 1301 Sandvika
Telephone: 67-57-05-00
Fax: 67-57-05-70
E-mail: info@bi.no
Internet: www.bi.no
Founded 1943
Private control
Languages of instruction: Norwegian, English
Academic year: September to June

President: TORGE REVE
Provost: JAN GRUND
Vice-President for Graduate Programmes: OLAV DIGERNES
Librarian: BENTE R. ANDREASSEN

Number of teachers: 262
Number of students: 15,123 (8,396 full-time; 6,727 part-time)

Publications: *BI-forum* (quarterly), *Scandinavian Leadership* (annual).

HØGSKOLEN I BODØ
(Bodø University College)

8002 Bodø
Telephone: 75-51-72-00
Fax: 75-51-74-57
Internet: www.hibo.no
Founded 1970
State control
Languages of instruction: Norwegian, English
Academic year: August to June

Rector: FRODE MELLEMVIK
Director: STIG FOSSUM
Registrar: MAGNE RASCH
Librarian: LARS BAUNA

Number of teachers: 270
Number of students: 3,600

DEANS

Department of Education: ELISABETH NILSEN
Department of Fisheries and Natural Sciences: TERJE SOLBERG
Department of Humanities: JO BECH KARLSEN
Department of Nursing: BRITT LILLESTØ
Department of Social Sciences: ØYSTEIN HENRIKSEN
Bodø Graduate School of Business: STIG INGEBRIGTSEN

ATTACHED INSTITUTE

Nordlandsforskning (Nordland Research Institute): Dir BENTE INGEBRIGTSEN.

HØGSKOLEN I NARVIK
(Narvik University College)

Lodve Langes gate 2, POB 385, 8505 Narvik
Alta campus: Follumsvei 33, 9510 Alta
Telephone: 76-96-60-00 (Narvik); 78-45-69-00 (Alta)
Fax: 76-96-68-10 (Narvik); 78-45-69-09 (Alta)
E-mail: postmottak@hin.no
Internet: www.hin.no
Founded 1955
Number of teachers: 90
Number of students: 1,000
Library of 20,000 items
Rector: EDEL STORELVMO.

HØGSKOLEN I TROMSØ
(Tromsø University College)

Mellomveien 110, 9293 Tromsø
Telephone: 77-66-03-00
Fax: 77-68-99-56
E-mail: postmottak@hitos.no
Internet: www.hitos.no
Founded 1994 through merger of four colleges
State control
Academic year: August to June
Rector: ULF CHRISTENSEN
Number of teachers: 260
Number of students: 2,200

DEANS

Faculty of Art (Music Conservatory): IAN RUDGE
Faculty of Education: BJØRG HUNSTAD (Dir)
Faculty of Engineering and Economics: ULF MACK GROWEN
Faculty of Health Sciences: TORIL HANSEN

NORGES HANDELSHØYSKOLE
(Norwegian School of Economics and Business Administration)

Helleveien 30, 5035 Bergen-Sandviken
Telephone: 55-95-90-00
Fax: 55-95-91-00
E-mail: nhh.postmottak@nhh.no
Internet: www.nhh.no
Founded 1936
State control
Academic year: September to June
Rector: CARL J. NORSTRØM
Vice-Rector: ARNE KINSERDAL
Director: GEIR KJELL ANDERSLAND
Librarian: MAGNHILD B. AASE
Library of 244,000 vols, 2,500 periodicals
Number of teachers: 155
Number of students: 2,700
Publication: Publications: exchange list sent on request

DEANS

Faculty of Business Administration: GUNNAR E. CHRISTENSEN
Faculty of Economics: JAN I. HAALAND
Faculty of Languages: EINAR HANSEN

PROFESSORS

Faculty of Business Administration:
BERGSTRAND, J., Economics
BJERKSUND, P., Finance
COLBJOERNSEN, T., Organization
ECKBO, E., Finance
EKERN, S., Finance
ELLING, J., Accounting
GJESDAL, F., Accounting
GJØLBERG, O., Finance
GOODERHAM, P. N., Organization
GRØNHAUG, K., Marketing
GRØNLAND, S., Data Processing
GUNDERSEN, F. F., Law
HANNESSON, R., Fishery Economics

HANSEN, T., Finance
JOHNSEN, A., Accounting
JOHNSEN, T., Finance
JØRESKOG, K. G., Marketing
JØERNSTEN, K., Finance
KIIL, B., Organization
KINSERDAL, A., Accounting
KNUDSEN, K., Organization
KOLLTVEIT, B., Organization
LANGHOLM, O., Accounting
LENSBERG, T., Finance
LILLESTØL, J., Mathematics
MATHIESEN, L., Economics
McKEE, T. E., Accounting
MESSIER, W. T., Accounting
METHLIE, L., Data Processing
NORDHAUG, O., Organization
NORSTRØM, C., Accounting
OLSON, O., Accounting
ROGNES, J. K., Organization
SCHILBRED, C., Finance
STENSLAND, G., Finance
SYVERSEN, J., Law
TROYE, S., Marketing
ÅSE, K., Finance
ØKSENDAL, B., Finance

Faculty of Economics:
BIVAND, R., Geography
BJORNDAL, T., Fishery Economics
GORDON, D., Economics
HAGEN, K. P., Economics
HODNE, F. F., Economic History
HOPE, E., Economics
HÅLAND, J. I., Economics
KLOVLAND, J. T., Economics
KYDLAND, F., Economics
MATHIESEN, L., Economics
NORDVIK, H. W., Economic History
NORMAN, V. D., Economics
SALVANES, K. G., Economics
SANDMO, A., Economics
SCHROTER, H. G., Economic History
SOLHAUG, T., Economic History
STEIGUM, E., Economics
VATNE, E., Geography
VENABLES, A., Economics

Faculty of Languages:
BREKKE, M., English
CHRISTENSEN, C., German
PICHT, H., Languages

ATTACHED INSTITUTES

Administrative Research Foundation:
Dir PER I. STRAND.

Foundation for Research in Economics and Business Administration: Dir PER HEUM.

NORGES IDRETTSHØGSKOLE
(Norwegian School of Sport Sciences)

Ullevål Stadion, POB 4014, 0806 Oslo
Telephone: 22-23-26-00
Fax: 22-23-42-20
E-mail: postmottak@nih.no
Internet: www.nih.no
Founded 1968
State control
Academic year: August to June
Rector: GUNNAR BREIVIK
Director: BAARD WIST
Librarian: HEGE UNDERTHUN
Library of 73,000 vols
Number of teachers: 60
Number of students: 1,000
Publication: *Moving Bodies* (4 a year)

HEADS OF DEPARTMENTS

Coaching and Psychology: LARS TORE RONGLAN
Cultural and Social Studies: SIGMUND LOLAND
Physical Education: EJGIL JESPERSEN

Physical Performance: JOSTEIN HALLÉN
Sport Medicine: ROALD BAHR

UNIVERSITETET FOR MILJØ- OG BIOVITENSKAP (UMB)
(Norwegian University of Life Sciences)

POB 5003, 1432 Ås
Telephone: 64-96-50-00
Fax: 64-96-50-01
E-mail: info@umb.no
Internet: www.umb.no
Founded 1859 as State College
Language of instruction: Norwegian, English
Academic year: August to August
Rector: Prof. KNUT HOVE
Vice-Rectors: Prof. MORTEN BAKKEN, Prof. TRINE HVOSLEF EIDE
Man. Dir: NILS DUGSTAD
Dir of Studies: SIRI LÖKSA
Information Dir: ANITA WATTUM
Number of teachers: 250, incl. 80 full professors
Number of students: 2,900, plus 250 postgraduates
Publication: *Alumni UMB*.

TEOLOGISKE MENIGHETSFAKULTET
(Norwegian Lutheran School of Theology)

Gydas Vei 4, POB 5144, Majorstuen, 0302 Oslo
Telephone: 22-59-05-00
Fax: 22-59-05-05
E-mail: post@mf.no
Internet: www.mf.no
Founded 1907
Private control
Languages of instruction: Norwegian, English
Academic year: August to June
Rector: Prof. VIDAR L. HAANES
Vice-Rector: SVERRE DAG MOGSTAD
Dir of Academic Affairs: Dr theol. ØYSTEIN LUND
Librarian: ELNA STRANDHEIM
Library of 66,000 vols, 280 periodicals
Number of teachers: 45
Number of students: 900
Publications: *Halvårsskrift for Praktisk Teologi Biannual* (2 a year), *Lys og Liv* (5 a year), *Tidsskrift for Teologi og Kirke* (quarterly), *Ung Teologi* (quarterly)

DEANS

Graduate Studies: Prof. TERJE STORDALEN
Ministry Div.: HALVOR NORDHAUG
Postgraduate Studies: Prof. Dr theol. GUNNAR HEIENE
Undergraduate Studies: HANNE BIRGITTE SØDAL TVEITO

PROFESSORS

AUSTAD, T., Dogmatics and Moral Theology
ENGEDAL, L. G., Practical Theology
ENGELSVIKEN, T., Missiology
FURSETH, I., Sociology of Religion
GRAVEM, P., Religious Studies
HAANES, V., Church History
HEGSTAD, H., Practical Theology
HEIENE, G., Ethics and Moral Theory
HENRIKSEN, J. O., Philosophy of Religion
HVALVIK, R., New Testament Exegesis
KROGSETH, O., Religious Studies
KVALBEIN, H., New Testament Exegesis
MOGSTAD, S. D., Philosophy of Religious Education
OFTESTAD, B. T., Church History
SANDNES, K. O., New Testament Exegesis
SANNES, K. O., Dogmatics
SKARSAUNE, O., Church History

STORDALEN, T., Old Testament Exegesis
THORBJØRNSEN, S. O., Ethics
WEYDE, K. W., Old Testament Exegesis
ØSTNOR, L., Ethics and Moral Theology

ATTACHED RESEARCH INSTITUTES

Egede Institute of Missiology and Ecumenical Research: POB 5144, Majorstuen, 0302 Oslo; Dir ROLV OLSEN; publ. *Norwegian Journal of Missiology*.

NORGES VETERINÄRHØGSKOLE
(Norwegian School of Veterinary Science)

POB 8146 Dep, 0033 Oslo

Telephone: 22-96-45-00
Fax: 22-56-57-04
E-mail: sekretariatet@veths.no
Internet: www.veths.no

Founded 1935
Academic year: August to June

Rector: HALLSTEIN GRØNSTØL
Director-General: KJELL GJAEVENES
Registrar: TOVE JENSSEN
Librarian: ANNE CATHRINE MUNTHE

Library of 77,000 vols
Number of teachers: 114
Number of students: 340

PROFESSORS

ALESTRØM, P., Biochemistry
ANDRESEN, Ø., Reproduction
AULIE, A., Physiology
AUNE, T., Food Hygiene
BERG, K. A., Reproduction
BJERKÅS, I., Anatomy
BORREBÆK, B., Biochemistry
DOLVIK, N. I., Large Animal Clinical Sciences
FARSTAD, W., Reproduction
FRØSLIE, A., Forensic Medicine
GJERDE, B., Parasitology
GRANUM, P. E., Food Hygiene
GRØNDALEN, J., Small Animal Clinical Sciences
GRØNSTØL, H., Large Animal Clinical Sciences

HARBITZ, I., Biochemistry
HORSBERG, T. E., Pharmacology
INGEBRIGTSEN, K., Pharmacology and Toxicology
KARLBERG, K., Reproduction
KROGDAHL, Å., Nutrition
LANDSVERK, T., Pathology
LARSEN, J. J., Microbiology
LINGAAS, F., Animal Genetics
LØKEN, T., Large Animal Clinical Sciences
MOE, L., Small Animal Clinical Sciences
POPPE, T., Aquaculture and Fish Diseases
PRESS, CH. McL., Anatomy
REITE, O. B., Aquaculture and Fish Diseases
RIMSTAD, E., Virology
ROPSTAD, E., Reproduction
RØNNINGEN, K., Animal Genetics
SIMENSEN, E., Research Farm
SJAASTAD, Ø., Physiology
SMITH, A., Laboratory Animals
SØLI, N., Pharmacology and Toxicology
TEIGE, J., Pathology
ULVUND, M., Sheep and Goat Research
UNDERDAL, B., Food Hygiene
WALDELAND, H., Sheep and Goat Research
YNDESTAD, M., Food Hygiene
ØDEGAARD, S., Reproduction

Schools of Art and Music

Agder Musikkonservatorium (Agder Conservatory of Music): Kongensgt. 54, 4610 Kristiansand; tel. 38-14-19-00; fax 38-14-19-01.

Grieg Academy: University of Bergen, Lars Hillesgt. 3, 5015 Bergen; tel. 55-58-69-50; fax 55-58-69-60; f. 1905; education of musicians, music teachers and organists; 118 students.

Kunstakademiet i Trondheim, Norges Teknisk-Naturvitenskaplige Universitet: NTNU, Innherredsveien 7, 7034 Trondheim; tel. 73-59-79-00; fax 73-59-79-20; e-mail adm@kit.ntnu.no; internet www.kit.ntnu.no; f. 1946; 8 staff; 70 students; library: 5,500 vols; Pres. IVAR SMEDSTAD;

Registrar HEGE SCHIERNING JOHANSEN; publ. *Kitsch* (quarterly).

Kunsthøgskolen i Bergen: Strømgaten 1, 5015 Bergen; tel. 55-58-73-00; fax 55-58-73-10; e-mail khib@khib.no; internet www.khib.no; university-level courses in fine arts, photography, visual communication, interior and furniture design, ceramics, textiles and printmaking; library: 15,000 vols, 195 periodicals; 45 teachers; 300 students; Rector NINA MALTERUD; Dir JOHAN A. HAARBERG.

Musikkonservatoriet i Trondheim (Trondheim Conservatory of Music): Norges Teknisk-Naturvitenskaplige Universitet, 7491 Trondheim; tel. 73-59-73-00; fax 73-59-73-01; e-mail mit@he.ntnu.no; internet www.he.ntnu.no/mit; f. 1911; 50 teachers; 140 students.

Norges Musikkhøgskole (Norwegian State Academy of Music): POB 5190, Majorstua, 0302 Oslo; tel. 23-36-70-00; fax 23-36-70-01; e-mail mh@nmh.no; internet www.nmh.no; f. 1973, merged with Eastern Norway Conservatory of Music 1996; library: 70,000 books and items of sheet music, 24,000 sound recordings; 170 teachers; 465 students; Dir ERLING W. WIST.

Statens Kunstakademi (National Academy of Fine Arts): St. Olavs gate 32, 0166 Oslo 1; tel. 22-99-55-30; fax 22-99-55-33; e-mail ska@khio.no; internet ska.khio.no; f. 1909; university-level courses in painting, sculpture, print-making and electronic media; library: 13,000 vols, 100 periodicals; 17 teachers; 105 students; Dean MICHAEL O'DONNELL.

Statens Håndverks- og Kunstindustriskole (National College of Art and Design): Ullevålsv. 5, 0165 Oslo; tel. 22-99-55-80; fax 22-99-55-85; e-mail sentralb@khio.no; f. 1818; includes departments of ceramics, fashion and costume design, interior architecture and furniture design, metal and jewellery, painting, textile design and visual communication, lithography and printmaking; library: 50,000 vols; 70 teachers; 380 students; Dean POUL JENSEN.

OMAN

The Higher Education System

Until independence was confirmed in 1951 Oman had a special relationship with the United Kingdom. The first institutions of higher education were founded in the 1980s, notably Sultan Qaboos University (founded 1986). In 2004/05 there were 12,855 students enrolled at the University and a further 23,286 students enrolled in 34 other institutions of higher education (six teacher-training colleges, the College of Shari'a and Law, five technical colleges, the Academy of Tourism and Catering, the College of Banking and Financial Studies, 16 institutes of health and four vocational-training centres). The Ministry of Education has supreme authority over general education, but the Ministry of Higher Education is responsible for tertiary education, the Ministry of Manpower oversees most vocational and technical training and the Ministry of Health co-ordinates health sciences, nursing and pharmaceutical education. The Ministries sponsor an estimated 6,000 students per year to attend high education.

Success in the secondary school leaving certificate (*thanawiya amma*) examinations is the main basis for admission to higher education. Students are required to take a one-year Foundation course prior to commencing the undergraduate Bachelors degree; this consists of English-language, IT and study skills training. The Bachelors degree is usually a four-year course and students must accrue at least 120 'credits' in order to graduate. Medical students must first complete a four-year Bachelor of Health Sciences degree before graduating to a three-year postgraduate programme in Clinical Medicine. The first postgraduate degree is the Diploma, which is approximately equivalent to half a Masters degree. Following completion of the Masters, the PhD is the highest university degree.

Technical and vocational education at the post-secondary level is offered by technical industrial colleges, vocational training centres, professional institutes and a higher college of technology. The technical industrial colleges award National Diplomas after upwards of two years of study and workplace training; admission is on the basis of the *thanawiya amma*. The vocational training centres offer one or two-year programmes of training for skilled and semi-skilled workers, and qualifications are equivalent to the United Kingdom National Vocational Qualification (NVQ). The Ministry of Health administers Institutes of Health Sciences, Pharmacy, Public Health and Medical Records.

Learned Societies

HISTORY, GEOGRAPHY AND ARCHAEOLOGY

Historical Association of Oman: POB 3941, 112 Ruwi; tel. 24795826; fax 24601270; internet www.hao.org.om; f. 1971; study of history, monuments and natural history of Oman; organizes lectures and field trips to places of interest; library of 400 vols; 200 mems; Pres. KAMAL ABDUL-REDHA SULTAN.

LANGUAGE AND LITERATURE

British Council: Road One, Madinat al Sultan, Qaboos West, Muscat, POB 73, Postal Code 115; tel. 24600548; fax 24699163; e-mail bc.muscat@mo .britishcouncil.org; internet www .britishcouncil.org/oman; teaching centre; offers courses and exams in English language and British culture and promotes cultural exchange with the UK; attached office in Seeb; Dir JIM SCARTH; Dir, Teaching and Examination Services MARY STANSFIELD.

Research Institutes

AGRICULTURE, FISHERIES AND VETERINARY SCIENCE

Directorate of Water Resources Research: c/o Ministry of Regional Municipalities, Environment and Water Resources, POB 323, Muscat; activities include hydrological surveys, water conservation, etc.

Marine Sciences and Fisheries Centre: c/o Ministry of Agriculture and Fisheries, POB 467, Muscat; tel. 24740062; fax 24740159; f. 1987; conservation, ecology, oceanography, biological research, food technology; includes a library and aquarium.

Libraries and Archives

Bowshar

Central Medical Library: Ministry of Health–Royal Hospital, POB 1331, Seeb, 111 Bowshar; tel. 24595971 ext. 454; fax 24594247; 7,000 vols, 122 periodicals; special collections: Ministry of Health reports, health reports, WHO collections; Senior Librarian K. W. A. JAYAWARDANE.

Muscat

Archives of the Directorate General of Heritage: Ministry of National Heritage and Culture, POB 668, Muscat 113; f. 1976; 5,000 MSS, 50,000 archives; Dir-Gen. MOHAMMED SAID AL-WOHAIBI.

Museums and Art Galleries

Muscat

Oman Natural History Museum (ONHM): Ministry of National Heritage and Culture, POB 668, Muscat 113; tel. 24605400; fax 24602735; e-mail mnhcgov@ gto.net.om; internet www.htsdevelopment .com/oman/; f. 1983; includes the National Herbarium of Oman and the National Shell and Coral Collection, and the Insect and Osteological Collections.

Qurm

Qurm Museum: c/o Ministry of National Heritage and Culture, POB 668, Muscat 113; historical.

Ruwi

National Museum at Ruwi: c/o Ministry of National Heritage and Culture, POB 668, Muscat 113; historical.

University

SULTAN QABOOS UNIVERSITY

POB 50, 123 Al-Khod

Telephone: 24413333

Fax: 24413391

E-mail: webmaster@squ.edu.om

Internet: www.squ.edu.om

Founded 1986

State control

Academic year: September to May

President: HE Dr SAUD NASSER AL-RIYAMI

Vice-President: Dr HAMED BIN SULAIMAN BIN SALEM AL-SALMEI

Assistant Vice-President for Administration and Financial Affairs: RASHID HAMED AL-KIYUMI

Assistant Vice-President for Humanities College: Dr HAMED SAID AL-OUFI

Assistant Vice-President for Postgraduate Studies and Research: Dr ALI SAOUD ALI AL-BIMANI

Assistant Vice-President for Science Colleges: Dr MOOSA ABDULLAH MOOSA AL-KHINDI

Library Director: Dr MOOSA NASSER AL-MUFARAJI

Library of 120,698 vols

Number of teachers: 964

Number of students: 12,591

Publications: *Journal of Scientific Research: Agricultural Marine Sciences* (2 a year), *Journal of Scientific Research: Medical Sciences* (2 a year), *Journal of Scientific Research: Science and Technology* (2 a year)

DEANS

College of Agriculture: Prof. ANTON McLACHLAN

College of Arts and Social Sciences: Dr ISSAM ALI AL-RAWAS

College of Commerce and Economics: Dr DARWISH AL-MOHARBY

College of Education: Prof. ALI AHMED MADKOUR

College of Engineering: Dr AMER ALI AL-RAWAS
College of Medicine: Dr BAZDAWI AL-RIYAMI
College of Science: Dr ABDULAZIZ AL-KINDI

DIRECTORS

Centre of Educational Technology: KHALID KHAMIS AL-SAADI
Centre for Environmental Studies and Research: Prof. REGINALD VICTOR
Centre for Human Resources and Staff Development: ABDUL BASIT TALIB RAJAB AL-HAMMADI
Centre of Information Systems: ALI OBAID AL-MAJEENI
Language Centre: Dr WILLIAM HARSBARGER
Remote Sensing Centre: Dr ANDY KWARTENG
Student Counselling Centre: SAUD MOHAMMAD ALI SULAIMAN

Colleges

Institute of Health Sciences: POB 3720, 112 Ruwi, Muscat; tel. 24560085; fax 24560384; f. 1982; under the Ministry of Health; library: 5,000 vols; 36 teachers; 244 students; Dean ALYA MOHAMMED MUSALLEM AL-RAWAHY; publ. *Quarterly Medical News Journal.*

Institute of Public Administration: POB 1994, Ruwi 112; tel. 24600205; fax 24602066; f. 1977; training, research and consultancy; library of 12,000 Arabic vols, 3,800 foreign; 70 Arabic periodicals, 5 foreign; 1,000 students per year attend courses; 57 staff; Dir-Gen. SULEIMAN BIN HILAL AL-ALAWI; publ. *Al-Edari* (4 a year).

Muscat Technical Industrial College: POB 3845, 112 Ruwi; tel. 25698280; f. 1984; library: 10,000 vols; 50 teachers; 500 students; Dir Dr MUNEER BIN SULTAN AL-MASKERY.

Vocational Training Centre: c/o Ministry of Social Affairs, Labour and Vocational Training, POB 560, Muscat; f. 1968; attached to the Ministry of Social Affairs, Labour and Vocational Training; technical and commercial diploma courses; 100 staff; 450 full-time, 400 part-time students; Principal HILAL BIN MOHAMMED AL-ADAWI.

PAKISTAN

The Higher Education System

In 1947 Pakistan declared its independence from the former British Indian Empire. The oldest current institutions of higher education were established during the period of British rule, among them the Government College University (founded in 1864), Liaquat University of Medical and Health Sciences (founded in 1881; present name and status since 2001) and the University of the Punjab (founded in 1882). Consequently, the university system is closely based on the late 19th century British model (particularly the University of London) of federal institutions, consisting of a centralized administration and affiliated colleges. Universities and degree-awarding institutions are broadly divided into 'general' and 'professional' categories. In 2005 there were 110 universities and degree-awarding institutions overall (55 private and 55 public), of which 74 were general and 36 were professional.

In late 2002 the Higher Education Committee (HEC) replaced the University Grants Commission (UGC) as the national controlling body of higher education. The HEC is responsible for, *inter alia*, dispersal of Government funding, formation of higher education policy, evaluation, accreditation and quality assurance. It has authority over both public and private institutions, although universities are still autonomous institutions. The chairman of the university is the Chancellor and the chief executive and academic officer is the Vice-Chancellor, aided by Pro Vice-Chancellors. Bodies of institutional and academic control include the Senate, Syndicate, Academic Council, Boards of Faculty and Study, Selection Board, Advanced Studies and Research Board, Finance and Planning Committee, Affiliation Committee and Disciplinary Committee.

Admission to higher education is based on the secondary school leaving certificate. Colleges affiliated to universities conduct most undergraduate teaching, particularly the two-year Bachelors (Pass) degree. The Bachelors (Honours) degree is a three-year course of study conducted by both affiliated colleges and universities. Specialist degrees leading to professional titles in architecture and medicine are five-year programmes of study. Bachelors degrees in law, education and library science are postgraduate degrees taken after the Bachelors (Pass). Postgraduate diplomas are one-year courses taken following a relevant first degree. The Masters is a postgraduate degree requiring two years of study following the Bachelors (Pass) and one year following the Bachelors (Honours); it consists of coursework and final examinations. The Master of Philosophy (MPhil) last two years, and is a research-based degree taken after a Masters in arts, commerce or science. The highest university degree is the PhD, requiring three years of study after award of the Masters.

Technical and vocational education at the post-secondary level is available at polytechnics and colleges of technology, which are the responsibility of the National Institute of Science and Technical Education. At a provincial level Boards of Technical education are the responsible bodies. Polytechnics specialise in three-year Diploma courses and colleges of technology offer degree courses to holders of the Polytechnic Diplomas (in addition to the Diploma). Several professional bodies are authorised to issue Diplomas and certificates, among them the Pakistan College of Physicians and Surgeons, the Institute of Chartered Accountants Pakistan, the Institute of Cost and Management Accountants of Pakistan and the Pakistan Nursing Council.

Learned Societies

GENERAL

Quaid-i-Azam Academy: 297 M. A. Jinnah Rd, Karachi 74800; tel. (21) 7218184; fax (21) 7219175; f. 1976; research on Quaid-i-Azam Mohammad Ali Jinnah, on the historical background (including cultural, religious, literary, linguistic, social, economic and political aspects) of the Pakistan Movement, and various aspects of Pakistan; gives scholarships and professorships; awards Quaid-i-Azam Academic and Literary Prizes for scholarly works; library of 20,000 vols; photostat vols of Archives of Freedom Movement; photostat files of Quaid-i-Azam Papers; 52 photostat vols of Shamsul Hasan collections, Sadar Abdur Rab Nishtar collections, 2,000 microfilms of various pre-partition newspapers and other collections; publs bibliographies, research studies, biographies, monographs and documents (in English, Urdu and dialects); Dir Dr MUHAMMAD ALI SIDDIQUI.

UNESCO Office Islamabad Pakistan: 44000, POB 2034, Islamabad; Located at: Saudi-Pak Tower, 1st Fl., Blue Area, Jinnah Ave, Islamabad 44000; tel. (51) 2873308; fax (51) 2825341; e-mail islamabad@unesco.org; internet undp.un.org.pk/unesco; f. 1945; education, basic sciences, culture, communication, information, social sciences; Dir JORGE SEQUEIRA.

ARCHITECTURE AND TOWN PLANNING

Pakistan Council of Architects and Town Planners: Suite 111, 1st Floor, RSM Square, E-1 Shaheed-e-Millat Rd, Karachi 75350; tel. (21) 4523129; fax (21) 4541099; e-mail mail@pcatp.org.pk; internet www .pcatp.org.pk; f. 1983 as a statutory body by the Government of Pakistan; regulation of the professions of architecture and town planning; Chair. SHAHAB GHANI KHAN.

BIBLIOGRAPHY, LIBRARY SCIENCE AND MUSEOLOGY

Library Promotion Bureau: Karachi University Campus, POB 8421, Karachi 75270; f. 1965; aims to promote librarianship in Pakistan; co-ordinates with all the other organizations engaged in promotional activities; publs reference books, books on library and information science, text books on library science, bibliographies, directories, etc.; Pres. M. ADIL USMANI; Sec.-Gen. Dr NASIM FATIMA; publ. *Pakistan Library Bulletin*.

National Book Foundation: 6-Mauve Area, G-8/4, Taleemi Chowk, Islamabad; tel. (51) 9261533; fax (51) 9261534; e-mail nbf@ isb.paknet.com.pk; internet www.nbf.org.pk; f. 1972; aims to make books available at moderate prices, promotes writing, research and publication, promotes literacy, organizes book festivals and exhibitions, operates book promotion schemes, publishes Braille books; 128 mems; Man. Dir GHIASUDDIN AHMED; Sec. MUHAMMAD ASLAM RAO; publ. *Kitab* (in English and Urdu).

Pakistan Library Association: c/o Pakistan Institute of Development Economics, QAU Campus, POB 1091, Islamabad; tel. (51) 9214041; fax (51) 9210006; e-mail naqvizj@hotmail.com; f. 1957; to advance the cause of the library movement throughout Pakistan; 1,329 mems; Pres. AZMAT ULLAH BHATTI; Sec.-Gen. HAFIZ KHUBAIB AHMAD; publs *Conference Proceedings* (annually), *Journal* (2 a year), *Newsletter* (6 a year).

ECONOMICS, LAW AND POLITICS

Institute of Cost and Management Accountants of Pakistan: ST-18/C, Block-6, Gulshan-e-Iqbal, POB 17642, Karachi 75300; tel. (21) 9243900; fax (21) 9243342; e-mail ed@icmap.com.pk; internet www .icmap.com.pk; f. 1951; regulates management accountancy profession in Pakistan and arranges professional development programmes; 2,700 mems; 15,000 registered students; library of 32,000 vols; Exec. Dir Z. H. SUBZWARI; publs *ICMAP News Letter*, *Industrial Accountant* (quarterly), *Management Accountants Conference Proceedings* (every 3 years), *Professional Information Bulletin* (every 2 months), *Shoaib Memorial Lecture* (every 2 years), *Students' Handbook* (annually).

Pakistan Institute of International Affairs: Aiwan-e-Sadar Rd, POB 1447, Karachi 74200; tel. (21) 5682891; fax (21) 5686069; e-mail piia@cyber.net.pk; f. 1947 to study international affairs and to promote the scientific study of international politics, Pakistan foreign policy, economics and jurisprudence; library: see Libraries and

Archives; 650 mems; Chair. FATEHYAB ALI KHAN; Sec. Dr QAZI SHAKIL AHMAD; publs *Pakistan Horizon* (4 a year), *Aalami Ufaq* (in Urdu, 4 a year).

EDUCATION

Higher Education Commission: Sector H/9, Islamabad; tel. (51) 9040000; fax (51) 9290128; e-mail info@hec.gov.pk; internet www.hec.gov.pk; f. 1974 as University Grants Commission, for the promotion and co-ordination of university education, the maintenance of standards of teaching, examinations and research in universities, and the orientation of university courses to national needs; library of 41,000 vols, 232 periodicals; Chair. Prof. Dr ATTA-UR-RAHMAN; publs *Annual Reports*, *Guide to the Equivalence of Qualifications in Pakistan* (irregular), *Handbook of Centres of Excellence and Advanced Studies*, *Handbook of Colleges*, *Handbook of Universities of Pakistan* (every 2 years), *Higher Education News* (4 a year), *Statistics on Higher Education in Pakistan*.

Punjab Bureau of Education: Punjab Public Service Commission, Lahore; tel. (42) 9202762; fax (42) 9202766; e-mail education@punjab.gov.pk; f. 1958, clearing house for information on education of all aspects and levels, within Pakistan and abroad; Documentation Section, Statistical Section, Publication Section and Research Section; library of 10,000 vols and periodicals; Dir SAJJAD HUSSAIN NAQVI; publ. *Educational Statistics* (annually).

FINE AND PERFORMING ARTS

Arts Council of Pakistan: M. R. Kayani Rd, Karachi; tel. (21) 9213090; fax (21) 9213074; e-mail arts_council_khi@yahoo.com; f. 1956 to foster the development of fine arts and crafts, drama, music, and to promote the study and appreciation thereof by sponsoring exhibitions, lectures, etc.; 2,700 mems; Pres. FAZUL-UR-REHMAN; Dir SHAMIM ALAM; Sec. ANEEQ AHMED; publ. *Khabar Nama*; publ. *Newsletter* (monthly).

Lok Virsa (National Institute of Folk and Traditional Heritage): POB 1184, Shakarparian, Islamabad; tel. (51) 9201651; fax (51) 9203983; f. 1974; museum, publishing house, media centre, sound archive; library: library of over 20,000 vols on Pakistan culture, ethnology, folklore; films, videotapes, cassettes and publications on folk heritage and culture; Dir MAZHAR-UL-ISLAM.

HISTORY, GEOGRAPHY AND ARCHAEOLOGY

Department of Archaeology and Museums: 27-A, Central Union Commercial, Shaheed-e-Millat Rd, Karachi; tel. and fax (21) 4526458; e-mail doam@gem.net.pk; f. 1947; to explore, excavate and scientifically conserve the archaeological, historical and cultural wealth of the country; to develop a documentary and published record; and exhibit material in the museums for the purpose of educational research and amusement; Dir-Gen. Dr SAEED-UR-REHMAN; publ. *Pakistan Archaeology* (annually).

Pakistan Historical Society: Bait al-Hikmah, Hamdard University campus, Madinat al-Hikmah, Karachi 74600; tel. (21) 6440035; fax (21) 6611755; e-mail phs@hamdard.edu.pk; f. 1950; historical studies and research, particularly history of Islam and the Subcontinent; library of 8,000 vols, 80 MSS; Pres. SADIA RASHID; Gen. Sec. Dr ANSAR ZAHID KHAN; publ. *Historicus* (quarterly).

LANGUAGE AND LITERATURE

Alliance Française: House 15, St 18, F 7/2 Islamabad; tel. (51) 2826517; fax (51) 2822176; e-mail alliance@pak-france-coop.org; internet www.pak-france-coop.org; offers courses and exams in French language and culture and promotes cultural exchange with France; attached teaching centres in Karachi, Lahore and Peshawar; library of 1,500 vols.

Anjuman Taraqqi-e-Urdu Pakistan: D-159, Block 7, Gulshan-e-Iqbal, Karachi 75300; tel. (21) 7724023; f. 1903 in pre-partition India, 1948 in Pakistan; promotion of the Urdu language and literature; preparing a 6-volume bibliography of Urdu books, in collaboration with Unesco; library: lending library of 20,000 vols, research library of 26,000 vols and 4,000 MSS; Pres. AFTAB AHMED KHAN; Hon. Sec. JAMILUDDIN A'ALI; publs *Qaumi Zaban* (monthly), *Urdu* (quarterly).

Balochi Academy: Adalat Rd, Quetta, Balochistan; tel. (81) 829566; f. 1958 to promote Baluchi language and literature; publishes books on Balochi history, poetry, culture, folk stories, and a Balochi–Urdu dictionary and encyclopaedia; 48 mems; library of 40,000 vols; Chair. JAN MOHAMMAD DASHTI; Gen. Sec. ABDUL QADIR SHAHWANI ASEER.

British Council: POB 1135, Islamabad; tel. (51) 111425425; e-mail info@britishcouncil.org.pk; internet www.britishcouncil.org/pakistan; offers courses and exams in English language and British culture and promotes cultural exchange with the UK; attached offices in Faisalabad, Karachi, Lahore, Multan, Peshawar and Quetta; Dir Dr TOM CRAIG-CAMERON.

Goethe-Institut: POB 848, GPO Karachi; Located at: 2 Brunton Rd, Civil Lines Karachi 75530; e-mail admin@karachi.goethe.org; internet www.goethe.de/karachi; f. 1956; offers courses and exams in German language and culture and promotes cultural exchange with Germany; library of 5,000 vols, 20 periodicals; Dir Dr PETRA RAYMOND; Chief Librarian ASTRID RÜDIGER.

Institute of Islamic Culture: 2 Club Rd, Lahore 3; tel. (42) 6363127; f. 1950; publications on Islamic subjects in English and Urdu; Dir Dr RASHID AHMAD JULLUNDHRI; publ. *Al-Ma'arif* (quarterly, in Urdu).

Iqbal Academy: POB 1308, GPO, Lahore; tel. (42) 6314510; fax (42) 6314496; e-mail dhikr@lhr.infolink.net.pk; f. 1951; publishes books and pamphlets on Dr Allama Iqbal; library: research library of 30,000 vols; Pres. FEDERAL MINISTER FOR CULTURE, SPORTS, TOURISM AND YOUTH AFFAIRS; Dir MUHAMMAD SUHEYL UMAR; publs *Iqbaliat* (2 a year in Urdu, annually in Arabic, Turkish and Farsi), *Iqbal Review* (2 a year, in English).

National Language Authority: Pitras Bukhari Rd, H-8/4, Islamabad; tel. (51) 9250317; fax (51) 9250310; e-mail nlauit@apollo.net.pk; internet www.nla.gov.pk; f. 1979; promotes Urdu as the nat., official, judicial and instructional language of Pakistan; organizes seminars and conferences; offers courses; develops Urdu terminology in various disciplines; compiles dictionaries; develops Urdu keyboard lay-outs for computers and computer codes (Standardized Urdu Code Plate), and localization of MicroSoft Urdu Office and Windows XP; member of UNICODE, Inc.; library of 25,000 vols; Chair. Prof. FATEH MUHAMMAD MALIK; publ. *Akhbar-e-Urdu* (monthly).

Pakistan Academy of Letters: 401-C Park Tower, Plot 3-F-10/3, Islamabad; tel. (51) 9257432; fax (51) 9257159; internet www.pal.sdnpk.org; f. 1976; promotion of literary works; determination of research priorities in literature; evaluation of the performance of literary bodies; setting up of Bureau of Translation; introduction of Pakistani literature to foreign readers; organizes seminars on literary and academic issues; advises the Government on international literary gatherings; nominates recipients for various literary awards and distinctions; provides financial assistance to scholars; Dir IFTIKHAR HUSSAIN ARIF; publs *Academy* (monthly), *Adbiat* (quarterly), *Pakistani Literature* (2 a year).

Pakistan Writers Guild: 11 Abbok Rd, Anarkali, Lahore; f. 1959; 4 regional offices; promotes authorship, dispenses literary prizes, concerned with welfare of writers; Sec.-Gen. MOHAMED TUFAIL; publ. *Ham Qalam* (monthly).

Pashto Academy: University of Peshawar, Peshawar; tel. and fax (91) 9216486; e-mail pashto@psh.paknet.com.pk; internet www.pashtoacademy.8m.com; f. 1955; research into Pashto language and literature, history, art and culture; a research cell for the study of the life and works of Khushal Khan Khattak and his contemporaries; research library; Dir Dr RAJ WALI SHAH KHATTAK; publ. *Pukhto* (monthly).

Sindhi Adabi Board: POB 12, Jamshoro, Sindh, 76070 92; tel. (222) 771276; fax (222) 771300; e-mail sindhiab@yahoo.com; internet www.sindhiab.com; f. 1951; autonomous literary and cultural institution set up by the government to foster the language, literature and culture of the Sindh region; publishes books in English, Sindhi, Urdu, Persian and Arabic; library of 10,000 vols, 450 MSS; Chair. HAMIDA KHUHRO; Sec. INAMULLAH SHAIKH; publs *Mehran* (quarterly), *Gul Phul* (children's monthly), *Sartyoon* (women's monthly).

Urdu Academy: 33C Model Town 'A', Bahawalpur; f. 1959 to develop Urdu literature and language; publishes books in English and Urdu; Sec. MASUD HASSAN SHIHAB; publ. *Az-Zubair* (Urdu, quarterly).

Urdu Dictionary Board: ST-18/A, Block 5, Gulshan-e-Iqbal, Off Karachi University Rd, Karachi 75300; tel. (21) 4988887; f. 1958 by Government of Pakistan; projects include a comprehensive, 23-vol. Urdu Dictionary; Chair. FEDERAL MINISTER FOR EDUCATION; Pres. Dr JAMILUDDIN AALI.

Urdu Science Board: 299 Upper Mall, Lahore 54000; tel. (42) 5758684; fax (42) 5754281; e-mail info@urduscienceboard.com; internet www.urduscienceboard.com; f. 1962; aims to remove deficiencies in the Urdu language, particularly in the fields of technology, natural and social sciences, so that Urdu can be used as the medium of instruction in higher education, and to co-ordinate the work of other organizations engaged in related fields; to prepare standard dictionaries of scientific and technical terms; library of 10,000 vols; Dir-Gen. KHALID IQBAL YASIR; publ. *Urdu Science Magazine* (quarterly).

MEDICINE

College of Physicians and Surgeons, Pakistan: 7th Central St, Defence Housing Authority Phase II, Karachi 75500; tel. (21) 5892801; fax (21) 5887513; e-mail library@cpsp.edu.pk; internet www.cpsp.edu.pk; f. 1962; aims to promote specialist practice of medicine, surgery and gynaecology and allied disciplines by means of improvement in hospital teaching and methods; arranges postgraduate medical, surgical and other specialist training; provides for medical research and organizes scientific conferences for Pakistani and foreign medical experts;

awards diplomas of MCPS and FCPS; 6,100 members (MCPS), 6,630 fellows (FCPS); short course on research methodology, biostatistics, medical writing and computer learning, CME for medical and allied health teachers, CME in RH primary care providers (medical), computer training workshop for medical librarians in Pakistan, diploma in health system management; library of 8,000 books, 7,000 vols of periodicals, 6,300 dissertations, 62 CD-ROMs, 250 audio journals, medical databases (MEDLINE and ExtraMed) on CD-ROMs; Pres. Prof. M. SULTAN FAROOQUI; Sec. Prof. IRSHAD WAHEED; Registrar Prof. ASADULLAH KHAN; publ. *Journal of the College of Physicians and Surgeons Pakistan* (monthly).

Pakistan Academy of Medical Sciences: 238 Jinnah Colony, Faisalabad; tel. (411) 31795; f. 1975 for the advancement of medical sciences and arts, for the recognition of merit and scholarly achievement, for co-operation among professionals and with other similar orgs; awards annual Gold Medal and holds annual PAMS Lecture; 56 Fellows; Pres. Prof. KHALID J. AWAN; Sec.-Gen. IFTIKHAR A. MALIK; publs *Bulletin* (2 a year), *Pakistan Journal of Ophthalmology* (quarterly).

Pakistan Medical Association: PMA House, Garden Rd, POB 7267, Karachi 74400; tel. and fax (21) 6687506; e-mail care@pma.org.pk; internet www.pma.org.pk; f. 1948; Pres. UMAR AYUB KHAN.

NATURAL SCIENCES
General

Pakistan Academy of Sciences: 3 Constitution Ave, G-5/2, Islamabad; tel. (51) 9204657; fax (51) 9206770; e-mail pasisb@yahoo.com; internet www.paspk.org; f. 1953; to promote research in pure and applied sciences, establish and maintain libraries; awards grants and fellowships and gold medals; 103 mems (80 fellows, 23 foreign fellows); Pres. Prof. Dr ATTA-UR-RAHMAN; Sec.-Gen. Prof. Dr KHALID MAHMOOD KHAN; publs *Proceedings of the Pakistan Academy of Sciences* (4 a year), *Newsletter* (4 a year), *Proceedings of Symposia, Monographs* (irregular), *Yearbook*.

Pakistan Association for the Advancement of Science: 1st Floor, Shadman Plaza, Shadman Market, Lahore; tel. (42) 7532014; fax (42) 7532014; e-mail cmsaleem@wol.net.pk; f. 1947 for the promotion of science in all its branches, including its application to practical problems and research; organizes national conferences; 1,500 mems; Pres. Prof. Dr MUHAMMAD SALEEM CHAUDHRY; Gen. Sec. Dr MUHAMMAD ARSHAD; publs *Pakistan Journal of Science* (4 a year), *Pakistan Journal of Scientific Research* (4 a year), *Proceedings of the All Pakistan Science Conference* (every 3 years), *Proceedings of the National Seminars* (every 3 years).

Scientific Society of Pakistan: Karachi University Campus, Karachi 32; tel. (21) 4463144; f. 1954 to promote science through the national language (Urdu); 3,500 mems; Pres. Dr SYED IRTIFAQ ALI; Sec. Maj. (retd) AFTAB HASAN; publs *Jadeed Science* (every 2 months), *Proceedings of Annual Science Conferences* (all in Urdu), *Science Bachchon Key Liye* (monthly), *Science Nama* (every 2 weeks).

PHILOSOPHY AND PSYCHOLOGY

Pakistan Philosophical Congress: Dept of Philosophy, University of the Punjab, New Campus, Lahore 20; tel. (42) 5863984; f. 1954 for the promotion of philosophical studies; Pres. Dr ABDUL KHALIQ; Sec. Dr NAEEM AHMAD; publs *Annual Proceedings, Pakistan Philosophical Journal* (annually).

RELIGION, SOCIOLOGY AND ANTHROPOLOGY

Hamdard Foundation: Hamdard Centre, Nazimabad, Karachi 74600; tel. (21) 6616001; fax (21) 6611755; e-mail hlpak@paknet3.ptc.pk; f. 1953; administers and controls the charitable and philanthropic work of Hamdard Laboratories (WAQF) Pakistan; oversees the establishment of academic, educational, professional and commercial institutes; library: see Libraries and Archives; Pres. SADIA RASHID; publs *Akhbar-ur-Tib* (every 2 weeks), *Hamdard-i-Sehat* (monthly), *Hamdard Islamicus* (4 a year), *Hamdard Medicus* (4 a year), *Hamdard Naunehal* (monthly), *Khabar Nama Hamdard* (monthly).

Jamiyat-ul-Falah: Akbar Rd, Saddar, POB 7141, Karachi 74400; f. 1950 to work for the exposition, propagation and implementation of Islam; Tamizuddin Khan Memorial Library (8,000 vols), Quran, Tafseer, Hadees, and Seerat collection; Falah Islamic Centre, Falah Social Service Centre, Falah Majlis-e-Adab (literary society), Falah Pakistan Studies Centre, Falah Muslim World Studies Centre, Falah Science Studies Centre; Sec.-Gen. SHAMSUDDIN KHALID AHMED; publ. *Voice of Islam* (English, monthly).

Karachi Theosophical Society: Jamshed Memorial Hall, M. A. Jinnah Rd, Karachi 74200; tel. (21) 7721275; f. 1896; 150 mems; activities include study of comparative religion, philosophy and science; investigation of unexplained laws of nature; library of 20,000 vols; Pres. DARA F. MIRZA; Gen.-Sec. K. J. DINSHAW; publ. *Theosophy in Karachi* (6 a year).

Society for the Preservation of Muslim Heritage: E6 Fourth Gizri St, Karachi 75500; f. 1981; Sec. SUHAIL ZAHEER LARI.

TECHNOLOGY

Institution of Electrical and Electronics Engineers Pakistan: 4 Lawrence Rd, Lahore; tel. (42) 6305289; f. 1969; lectures, seminars and publications on electrical and electronic telecommunication engineering; 2,300 corporate mems, 2,150, individual mems; library of 2,050 vols, 6,000 periodicals; Pres. BASHIR AHMAD ABBASI; publs *The Electrical Engineer* (monthly), *Newsletter*, *Quarterly Electrical Journal*.

Institution of Engineers (Pakistan): IEP HQ Bldg, Engineering Centre, Gulberg III, Lahore 54660; tel. (42) 5756974; fax (42) 5759449; e-mail iephq@lhr.paknet.com.pk; f. 1948; 50,000 mems (corporate and individual); publ. *The Pakistan Engineers* (monthly).

Research Institutes
AGRICULTURE, FISHERIES AND VETERINARY SCIENCE

Central Cotton Research Institute: Sakrand 62710, Nawabshah, Sindh; tel. (244) 322356; internet www.ccri.org.pk; f. 1970; divisions: agronomy, breeding and genetics, cytogenetics, entomology, pathology, physiology, fibre technology, statistics, transfer of technology; processing of cotton varieties and their release for cultivation in the local environment; library of 1,530 vols; Dir Dr AHMED ALI BALOCH; publ. *The Pakistan Cottons*.

Central Cotton Research Institute: Sakrand 67210, Nawabshah, Sindh; tel. and fax (24151) 356; f. 1976; divisions: agronomy, breeding and genetics, cytogenetics, entomology, pathology, physiology, fibre technology, statistics, transfer of technology; research on cotton plant; processing of cotton varieties and their release for general cultivation in the province; library of 1,050 vols; Dir Dr BARKAT ALI SOOMRO.

Pakistan Agricultural Research Council: Headquarters, Plot 20 Sector G-5/1, Islamabad; tel. (51) 9203966; fax (51) 9202968; e-mail chair@comsats.net.pk; internet www.parc.gov.pk; f. 1978; aims to undertake, aid, promote and co-ordinate agricultural research; establish research establishments; arrange the training of high-level scientists in agricultural sciences; and to generate, acquire and disseminate information relating to agriculture; library of 21,000 vols, 1,166 periodicals; Chair. Dr BADARUDDIN SOOMRO; publs *Annual Report*, *Pakistan Journal of Agricultural Research* (quarterly), *Pakistan Journal of Agricultural Social Sciences* (2 a year), *PARC News* (monthly), *Progressive Farming* (every 2 months).

Pakistan Forest Institute: Peshawar University Campus, Peshawar, NWFP 25000; tel. (91) 49580; tel. (91) 71260; f. 1947; library: see Libraries and Archives; Forestry Museum; two training courses leading to BSc and MSc in Forestry; Dir-Gen. Dr K. M. SIDDIQUI; publ. *Pakistan Journal of Forestry* (2 year).

Punjab Veterinary Research Institute: Ghazi Rd, Lahore Cantt.; tel. (42) 9220140; fax (42) 9220142; f. 1963; aims to promote and improve the development of the livestock industry and control diseases; production of vaccines, research on animal health problems; disease diagnosis and investigation; development of improved laboratory techniques; part of the Punjab Livestock and Dairy Development Department.

Rice Research Institute Dokri: Dokri, Larkana, Sindh; tel. (74) 4080328; fax (74) 4080283; f. 1938; research on various aspects of rice incl. varietal improvement, control of insect pests, diseases and weeds, grain quality; library of 4,426 vols, 1,523 periodicals.

Veterinary Research Institute: NWFP, Bacha Khan Chowk, Charsadda Rd, POB 367, Peshawar 25000; tel. (91) 9210218; fax (91) 9210220; e-mail directorvri@hotmail.com; f. 1949 to undertake research on livestock and poultry diseases, production of veterinary biologics and diagnostic agents; 45 mems; library of 1,000 vols on aspects of livestock and poultry; Dir Dr SAADULLAH JAN; publ. *Journal of Animal Health and Production* (quarterly).

ECONOMICS, LAW AND POLITICS

Applied Economics Research Centre: University of Karachi, POB 8403, Karachi 75270; tel. (21) 9243168; fax (21) 4829730; e-mail pjae@cyber.net.pk; internet www.aerc.edu.pk; f. 1982; policy-orientated quantitative research on problems in applied economics; courses leading to MPhil and PhD in Economics; 175 mems; library of 35,000 vols; Sec. Dr TUFAIL HAKEM; publ. *Pakistan Journal of Applied Economics* (2 a year).

Centre for South Asian Studies: University of the Punjab, Quaid-i-Azam Campus, Lahore 54590; tel. and fax (42) 9231143; f. 1973; interdisciplinary research on South Asia, including economics, politics, sociology, foreign affairs, and other social developments of the area; programme includes data collection and analysis; sponsors seminars; library of 12,000 vols; Dir Dr SADIQ ALI GILL; publ. *South Asian Studies* (2 a year, English).

Federal Bureau of Statistics: Statistics Division, Government of Pakistan, SLIC Building No. 5, China Chowk, Islamabad; tel. (51) 9208489; fax (51) 9203233; e-mail techcell@isb.paknet.com.pk; internet www.statpak.gov.pk; f. 1950; library of 4,600 vols, 41,200 periodicals; Dir-Gen. Dr NOOR MUHAMMAD LARIK; publs *Census of Manufacturing Industries* (annually), *Foreign Trade Statistics of Pakistan* (separate series for imports and exports, each annually), *Macro Economic Indicators of Pakistan* (4 a year), *Monthly Statistical Bulletin*, *National Accounts* (annually), *Newsletter* (monthly), *Pakistan Statistical Yearbook* (annually), *Reviews of Foreign Trade* (monthly), *Statistical Pocket Book of Pakistan* (annually).

Institute of Strategic Studies: Sector F-5/2, Islamabad; tel. (51) 9204423; fax (51) 9204658; e-mail strategy@paknet2.ptc.pk; f. 1973; provides a broad-based and informed public understanding of vital strategic and allied issues affecting Pakistan and the international community at large; library of 11,000 vols and 70 foreign periodicals; Dir-Gen. Ambassador (retd) MOHAMMED WALIULLA KHAN KHAISHGI; publ. *Strategic Studies* (quarterly).

National Institute of Public Administration: 78 Shahrah-e-Quaid-e-Azam, Lahore; tel. (42) 9200921; fax (42) 9200926; e-mail nipalhr@oajbet4.ptc.pk; internet www.niplahore.gov.pk; f. 1961; training in public administration for officers of federal and provincial govt; research in public administration; consultancy services to the govt; library of 30,000 vols; Dir-Gen. Maj.-Gen. (Retd) SIKANDAR SHAMI; publ. *Public Administration Review* (quarterly).

Pakistan Economic Research Institute (PERI): 24 Mianmir Rd, Upper Mall Scheme, Lahore 15; f. 1955 to undertake socio-economic investigations and co-ordinate research in economic problems of Pakistan; to collect, compile and interpret statistical data; to publish the results and findings of investigations; Dir AZIZ A. ANWAR; Sec. A. R. ARSHAD; publ. publs Research Papers.

Pakistan Institute of Development Economics: Quaid-i-Azam University campus, POB 1091, Islamabad 44000; tel. (51) 9206610; fax (51) 9210886; e-mail pide@apollo.net.pk; internet www.pide.org.pk; f. 1957; provides in-service training in economic analysis, research methods, and project planning, preparation, appraisal, implementation and evaluation techniques; PhD programme in economics; library of 33,750 vols, 220 current periodicals, 6,200 microfiches, 22,700 research papers and reports; Dir Dr A. R. KEMAL; publ. *Pakistan Development Review* (4 a year).

Pakistan Institute of Human Rights: H No 2-A, 38, F-8/1, Islamabad; tel. (51) 857755; fax (51) 256903; e-mail pihr@pihr.org; internet www.pihr.org; f. 1998, on the 50th anniversary of the Universal Declaration of Human Rights; non-profit, non-aligned research-based academic institution promoting human rights.

HISTORY, GEOGRAPHY AND ARCHAEOLOGY

National Institute of Historical and Cultural Research: POB 1230, Islamabad; tel. (51) 9266395; fax (51) 5551871; f. 1973, name changed 1983; promotes studies on the history and culture of South Asian Muslims, and the genesis and growth of the Muslim freedom movement; publishes research studies in history and culture, bibliographies, indices etc.; library of 17,000 vols, a collection of historical records, old newspapers, jour-

nals, photocopies of rare material, microfilms, microfiches; Dir Dr RIAZ AHMAD; publs *Majallah-i-Tarikh wa Thaqafat* (2 a year, in Urdu), *Pakistan Journal of History and Culture* (2 a year).

Research Society of Pakistan: c/o the Vice Chancellor, University of the Punjab, Lahore; tel. (42) 9211631; f. 1963 to organize research in national affairs, particularly in the national struggle that led to the establishment of Pakistan; research on cultural, political, literary, linguistic, economic, historical, topographical and archaeological features of Pakistan; library: reference library of 12,000 vols; Pres. Lt-Gen. (Ret'd) ARSHAD MAHMOOD (Vice-Chancellor of the University of the Punjab); Dir Dr A. SHAKOOR AHSAN; publs *Journal* (4 a year), research results.

MEDICINE

Cancer Research Institute: Dept and Institute of Radiotherapy, Jinnah Post-graduate Medical Centre, Karachi 75510; f. 1954.

Pakistan Medical Research Council: Shahrah-e-Jamhuriat G-5/2, Islamabad; e-mail pmrc@comsats.net.pk; internet www.pmrc.org.pk; f. 1953; reconstituted 1962; aims to promote research in fields of medicine and public health, to disseminate and arrange for utilization of this research, and to establish liaison with national and international organizations; 19 mems; Exec. Dir Dr HUMA QURESHI; publ. *Pakistan Journal of Medical Research* (quarterly).

NATURAL SCIENCES

General

Fazl-i-Omar Research Institute: Rabwah, Chenabnagar, P.C. 35460, District Jhang; tel. (4524) 211082; fax (4524) 212296; e-mail tjadid@fsd.paknet.com.pk; f. 1946; objectives: to promote the study of science and the development of industries in the country; library of 10,000 vols; Dir MUBARAK MUSLEH-UD-DIN AHMAD.

Pakistan Council for Science and Technology: Off Constitution Ave, Bank Rd, Sector G-5/2, Islamabad; tel. (51) 9205157; fax (51) 9205171; e-mail pcst@isb.comsats.net.pk; internet www.pcst.org.pk; f. 1961; advises the Govt on science and technology policy; devises measures for the promotion, development and application of science and technology in Pakistan; library of 1,200 vols; publs *Science, Science and Technology in the Islamic World* (4 a year), *Technology and Development* (every 2 months).

Pakistan Council of Scientific and Industrial Research (PCSIR): Press Centre, Shahrah-e-Kamal Ataturk, Karachi 74200; tel. (21) 2628763; fax (21) 2636704; internet www.pcsir.gov.pk; f. 1953; promotes scientific and industrial research and its applications to the development of the national industries and the utilization of the natural resources of the country; Scientific Information Centre: see Libraries and Archives; Chair. Dr ANWARUL HAQ; Sec. AHMAD SAGHIR; publs *Pakistan Journal of Scientific and Industrial Research* (6 a year), *PCSIR News Bulletin* (monthly).

Attached research institutes:

Institute of Industrial Electronic Engineering: St-22/C, Block 6, Gulshan-e-Iqbal, Karachi; tel. (21) 4982353; general research and development work, quality control, design and development of electronic components; Principal Dr S. NAIMAT ALI RIZVI.

PCSIR Fuel Research Centre: PCSIR Laboratories Campus, off University Rd, Karachi; tel. (21) 8141738; fax (21) 8141754; e-mail frc@khi.sdnpk.org; coal

analysis, upranking of coal, making of briquettes, hydrogen and alternative fuels division, coal conversion and combustion; Dir Dr M. A. DAMANI.

PCSIR Laboratories Complex Karachi: off University Rd, Karachi; tel. (21) 8141834; fax (21) 8141847; e-mail klcpcsir@khi.paknet.com.pk; fish technology, pharmaceuticals, applied physics, paints, plastics, building materials, chemical engineering; rural technology and water decontamination; library of 45,000 vols, 900 journals and periodicals; Dir-Gen. S. NAEEM MAHMOOD.

PCSIR Laboratories Complex Lahore: Ferozepur Rd, Lahore 54600; tel. (42) 9230704; fax (42) 9230705; e-mail pcsir@brain.net.pk; metallurgical, industrial fermentation, oils and fats, glass and ceramics, food technology research divisions and solar energy and environmental research; Dir-Gen. Dr WAZIR HUSSAIN SHAH.

PCSIR Laboratories Complex Peshawar: Jamrud Rd, POB Peshawar University, Peshawar; tel. (91) 9216240; fax (91) 9216232; e-mail pcsirlp@brain.net.pk; indigenous drugs, fruit technology, minerals evaluation, wool and rural technology, process design and fabrication divisions; Dir Engr MUHAMMAD TARIQ.

PCSIR Laboratories Quetta: POB 387, Mian Ghundi, Mastung Rd, Quetta; tel. (81) 460161; fax (81) 460158; e-mail pcsirqta@qta.paknet.com.pk; mineral processing and fruit technology; Dir Dr K. KHAN.

PCSIR Laboratories Hyderabad: POB 356, GPO Hyderabad, Hyderabad; tel. (221) 871434; product development and dissemination of solar energy technology, solar refrigeration and photovoltaic applications, solar water desalination, solar air-conditioning and solar architecture, solar energy storage and power generation, wind energy converters, development of tidal wave and geo-thermal energy; Officer in Charge Dr RIAZUDDIN ABRO.

PCSIR Leather Research Centre: D/102, SITE, South Ave, Karachi 75700; tel. (21) 2570765; fax (21) 2578748; leather technology, with special reference to tanning and upgrading of leathers, training in leather technology; Dir GHULAM ABBAS.

PCSIR National Physical and Standards Laboratory: 16 Sector H/9, Islamabad; tel. (51) 9257462; fax (51) 9258162; e-mail npsllab@isb.comsts.net.pk; maintains primary standards of physical measurements; develops sets of secondary standards; supplies standard materials for industrial calibration and standardization; Dir KHALID ISLAM.

Biological Sciences

Centre of Excellence in Marine Biology: University of Karachi, Karachi 75270; tel. (21) 470572; fax (21) 4978960; e-mail shameel@super.net.pk; internet www.kudcs.edu.pk; f. 1975; 20 mems; library of 3,000 vols, 50 periodicals; Dir Prof. Dr MUSTAFA SHAMEEL; publs *CEMB News* (2 a year), *Pakistan Journal of Marine Biology* (2 a year).

Department of Plant Protection: Jinnah Ave, Malir Halt, Karachi 27; tel. (21) 9248612; fax (21) 9248673; e-mail locust@plantprotection.gov.pk; internet www.plantprotection.gov.pk; f. 1947; survey and control of desert locust population, control of crop pests by air; executes Plant Quarantine Act 1976 and Pakistan Agriculture Pesticide Ordinance 1971 and its rules 1973; advises Federal and Provincial Govts on plant protection matters; library of 22,085 vols, 13 current periodicals; Dir-Gen. RAASHID BASHIR MAZARI; publ. *Locust Situation Bulletin* (every 2 weeks).

Zoological Survey Department: Block 61, Pakistan Secretariat, Shahrah-e-Iraq, Karachi 74200; tel. (21) 9203334; f. 1948; research in ecology, biodiversity, marine biology, and wildlife of Pakistan; library of 8,368 vols, 123 periodicals, 1,600 reprints; Dir HAMID IQBAL JAVED (acting); publs *Newsletter* (4 a year), *Records/Zoological Survey of Pakistan* (annually).

Physical Sciences

Astronomical Observatory of the University of the Punjab: c/o Department of Space Science, Quaid-i-Azam Campus, University of the Punjab, POB 54590, Lahore; tel. (42) 9231099; f. 1920; works within the University's Dept of Space Science Located at Quaid-i-Azam Campus; undergraduate and postgraduate courses; Dir MUMTAZ ALI SHAUKAT.

Pakistan Atomic Energy Commission (PAEC): POB 1114, Islamabad; tel. (51) 9209032; fax (51) 9204908; f. 1956; responsible for the development of nuclear technology as part of Pakistan's nuclear power programme; operates nuclear power plants in Karachi and Chashma; promotes peaceful use of atomic energy in agriculture, medicine, industry and hydrology; searches for indigenous mineral deposits suitable for the production of atomic energy; trains project personnel, Chair. ANWAR ALI; Co ordination Officer MUMTAZ AHMAD; publ. *The Nucleus* (quarterly).

Attached research institutes:

Atomic Energy Medical Centre (AEMC): Jinnah Post Graduate Medical Centre, Karachi; tel. (21) 9205695; fax (21) 9201354; Dir Dr ABID HAMEED.

Atomic Energy Minerals Centre (AEMC): POB 658, Lahore; tel. (42) 9230746; fax (42) 9230745; Dir- Gen. Dr KHURSHID ALAM BUTT.

Bahawalpur Institute of Nuclear Medicine and Oncology (BINO): POB 35, Noor Mahal Rd, Bahawalpur; tel. (621) 9255327; fax (621) 9255331; Dir Dr NAEEM AHMED LAGHARI.

Centre for Nuclear Medicine (CENUM): Mayo Hospital, POB 53, Lahore; tel. (42) 7324141; fax (42) 7313267; Dir Dr SYED WAQAR HAIDER.

Chasnupp Centre of Nuclear Training (CHASCENT): Chashma Barrage Colony, Kundian District, Mianwali; tel. (4592) 41525; fax (4592) 41505; Training Man. ASAD ULLAH KHAN.

Computer Training Centre (CTC): POB 15659, Islamabad; tel. (51) 9258517; Dir NASEEM AKHTAR BHATTI.

Institute of Nuclear Medicine and Oncology (INMOL): Wahdat Rd, POB 10068, Lahore; tel. (42) 9230274; fax (42) 9230778; Dir MUHAMMAD NAEEM.

Institute of Radiotherapy and Nuclear Medicine (IRNUM): Peshawar; tel. (91) 9216118; fax (91) 9216119; Dir Dr AYUB KHAN.

Karachi Institute of Nuclear Power and Engineering (KINPOE): POB 3183, Karachi; tel. (21) 9202222; fax (21) 9202250; Dir Dr KHALID MEHMOOD BUKHARI.

Karachi Institute of Radiotherapy and Nuclear Medicine (KIRAN): POB 3913, Karachi 75530; tel. (21) 4646609; fax (21) 9261610; Dir Dr SHAHID KAMAL.

Larkana Institute of Nuclear Medicine and Radiotherapy (LINAR): POB 05, Larkana; tel. (741) 9410322; fax (741) 9410729; Dir Dr SIRAJ AHMAD ABBASI.

Multan Institute of Nuclear Medicine and Radiotherapy (MINAR): Nishtar Medical College and Hospital, POB 377, Multan; tel. (61) 9200252; fax (61) 9200942; Dir Dr DURR-E-SABIH.

National Institute for Biotechnology and Genetic Engineering (NIBGE): Jhang Rd, POB 577, Faisalabad; tel. (412) 651471; fax (412) 651472; Dir Dr YUSUF ZAFAR.

Nuclear Institute of Agriculture (NIA): Tandojam; tel. (222) 765514; fax (222) 765284; Dir SYED KHURSHEED HUSSAIN SHAH.

Nuclear Institute for Agriculture and Biology (NIAB): Jhang Rd, POB 128, Faisalabad; tel. (412) 654210; fax (412) 654213; Dir and Chief Scientist Dr IQRAR A. KHAN (acting).

Nuclear Institute for Food and Agriculture (NIFA): POB 446, Peshawar; tel. (91) 2964058; fax (91) 2964059; Dir Dr SANA-ULLAH-KHAN KHATTAK.

Nuclear Medicine, Oncology and Radiotherapy Institute (NORI): POB 1590, Islamabad; tel. (51) 9260620; fax (51) 9260616; Dir Dr SYED RAFFAQAT ALI JAFRI.

Pakistan Institute of Engineering and Applied Sciences (PIEAS): PO Nilore, Islamabad; tel. (51) 2207747; fax (51) 9223727; e-mail basim@pieas.edu.pk; internet www.pieas.edu.pk; f. 1968; Rector Dr M. ASLAM.

Pakistan Institute of Nuclear Science and Technology (PINSTECH): PO Nilore, Islamabad; tel. (51) 2207201; fax (51) 9290275; operates a 10-MW research reactor of swimming-pool type; Dir Gen. Dr MUSTANSAR JEHANGIR (acting).

Punjab Institute of Nuclear Medicine (PINUM): POB 2019, Jail Rd, Faisalabad; tel. (41) 9210177; fax (41) 9210180; Dir Dr JAVED IRFAN ULLAH.

Pakistan Meteorological Department: Headquarters Office, POB 1214, Sector H-8/2, Islamabad; tel. (51) 9250367; fax (51) 9250368; e-mail pakmet@pakmet.com.pk; internet www.pakmet.com.pk; f. 1947; provides effective hydro-meteorological and geophysical services for improved protection of life, property and the environment, increased safety on land, at sea and in the air, enhanced quality of life and sustainable economic growth; ensures the timely issue of different types of weather and flood forecasts, warnings and advisories; investigates the behaviour of the atmosphere and exploits this knowledge for short- and long-term weather predictions; undertakes research and devt activities in various disciplines such as weather modifications and the wind potential of coastal and northern areas of Pakistan; Dir-Gen. Dr QAMAR-UZ-ZAMAN CHAUDHRY; publs *Agromet Bulletin of Pakistan* (monthly), *Pakistan Journal of Meteorology* (2 a year), *Quarterly News Bulletin* (incl. climate news).

RELIGION, SOCIOLOGY AND ANTHROPOLOGY

Institute of Sindhology: Allama I. I. Kazi Campus, University of Sindh, Jamshoro 76070, Sindh; tel. and fax (221) 771386; e-mail sindhology_s@yahoo.com; internet www.sindhology.com.pk; f. 1962 as Sindhi Academy, name changed 1964; aims to interpret Sindh and its contribution to history and civilization, encourage translation and original work in the fields of social

and natural sciences; to project Sindh on an international level by publishing relevant research material in foreign languages, to develop working tools (dictionaries, historical surveys, etc.) for scholars, to advance research in history, culture, literature and fine arts; includes a bureau of production, publication and translation, a documentation, information and research cell, a research library, a dept of preservation of documents and rare material, anthropological research centre with Sindh Art Gallery and Museum, a dept of performing arts, sound and film with ethnomusical gallery; photographic and microform sections; 84 staff; library: see Libraries; Dir SHOUKAT HUSSAIN SHORO; publs *Sindhi Adab* (in Sindhi, annually), *Sindhological Studies* (in English, 2 a year).

Islamic Research Institute: POB 1035, Islamabad 44000; tel. (51) 850751; internet www.iiu.edu.pk/iri/iri.htm; f. 1960, research arm of Islamic International University since 1980; aims to develop and disseminate methodology for research in various fields of Islamic learning, to interpret the teachings of Islam so as to bring out its dynamic character in the context of the intellectual and scientific progress of the modern world; to study contemporary problems of the world of Islam; contribute to the revival of Islamic heritage; organizes study groups, serves as a clearing-house on various aspects of Islam, organizes seminars, conferences, etc.; 24 research staff; library of 55,000 vols and periodicals, 550 microfilms, 140 MSS, 760 photostats, 150 cassettes; Dir-Gen. Z. I. ANSARI; publs *Al-Dirasat ul-Islamiyyah* (quarterly), *Fikr-o-Nazar* (quarterly), *Islamic Studies* (quarterly, in English).

TECHNOLOGY

Hydrocarbon Development Institute of Pakistan: 18, Street 6, Sector H-9/1, POB 1308, Islamabad; tel. (51) 9258301; fax (51) 9258310; e-mail hdip@isb.compol.com; internet www.hdip.com.pk; f. 1975; research and services in petroleum geology and geochemistry, resource estimation, enhanced oil recovery, petroleum products testing and evaluation, petroleum processing technology, coal utilization technology, interfuel substitution, energy conservation, environmental control, compressed natural gas, energy database, oil and gas advisory and training services; 225 mems; library of 1,500 vols, 44 periodicals; Dir-Gen. HILAL A. RAZA; publ. *Pakistan Journal of Hydrocarbon Research* (annually).

Irrigation Research Institute: Shahrah-e-Quaid-e-Azam, Lahore; f. 1925; deals with irrigation and allied engineering problems in Pakistan; 2 field model stations, 2 sub-stations and subsidiary laboratories for soils, foundation engineering, tube well experiments, etc.; library of 20,000 vols; Administrator SAAD HARROON; publs reports, records, memoirs.

Pakistan Council of Research in Water Resources: H. 3 and 5 St 17 F-6/2, Islamabad; tel. (51) 9218980; fax (51) 9218939; e-mail pcrwr@isb.comstats.net.pk; f. 1964; aims to promote research in the fields of water and environment, hydraulics, irrigation, drainage, reclamation, tube wells and flood control; library of 9,820 vols; Chair. Dr MUHAMMAD AKHRAM KHALOOM; Chief of Research Dr ABDUL MAJEED; publs *Annual Report, Fresh Arrivals and Periodicals Content Service* (4 a year), *Journal of Drainage and Water Management* (2 a year), *Reservoir* (newsletter, 4 a year).

Pakistan Institute of Cotton Research and Technology: Moulvi Tamizuddin Khan

Rd, Karachi 1; tel. (21) 9205991; fax (21) 9202558; e-mail picrt@hotmail.com; f. 1956; to carry out fundamental and applied research work on cotton fibres, yarns and fabrics; provides testing facilities and training to agriculture, trade and industry; library of 30,000 vols, 350 periodicals; Dir I. H. RESHAMWALA; publ. *The Pakistan Cottons* (quarterly).

Pakistan Institute of Management: Management House, Shahrah Iran, Clifton, Karachi 75600; tel. (21) 9251711; fax (21) 9251715; internet www.pim.com.pk; f. 1954; 900 institutional and 250 individual mems; dedicated to the management development programme in Pakistan; offers 140 short courses in functional and integrated aspects of management each year; br. in Lahore; library of 6,000 vols, 60 films, 60 periodicals; Dir ZARRAR R. ZUBAIR; publ. *Pakistan Management Review* (quarterly).

Pakistan Standards Institution: 39 Garden Rd, Saddar, Karachi 74400; tel. (21) 7729527; fax (21) 7728124; f. 1951; member of ISO, International Electrotechnical Commission (IEC), Organisation Internationale de Métrologie Légale (OIML); objects: to recommend national standards for the measurement of length, weight, volume and energy, to prepare and promote general adoption of standards on national and international basis relating to materials and commodities, and simplification in industry and commerce, enforcement of standards, etc.; library of 1,852 technical books, 148,955 national and international standards; Dir Dr M. ASAD HASAN; publs *Pakistan Standards Specification, PSI Annual Report, PSI Yearbook, Test Methods and Code of Practice*.

Libraries and Archives

Bahawalpur

Central Library: Bahawalpur; tel. (621) 80658; f. 1948; 105,960 vols (36,070 Urdu, 61,730 English, 8,160 other languages); 175 MSS (120 Arabic, 55 Persian and Urdu); 34 microfilms, 70 films; mobile library; audiovisual and microfiche sections; language laboratory; collections: books, newspapers and periodicals since 1948; some 19th-century newspapers and periodicals; map gallery; children's library of 22,400 vols; Braille library of 1,100 vols; computer training centre; Chief Librarian MUHAMMAD ASHRAF JALAL.

Islamia University Central Library: Bahawalpur; tel. (621) 925122; f. 1975; 92,000 vols, 50 MSS; Librarian ABDUL RASHEED.

Dera Ismail Khan

Gomal University Central Library: D. I. Khan, NWFP; tel. (966) 750351; f. 1974; 60,000 vols; Librarian ABDUL GHAFFAR KHAN.

Faisalabad

University of Agriculture Library: Faisalabad 38040; tel. (41) 9201082; e-mail luaf@fsd.paknet.com.pk; internet www.uaf.edu.pk/lib.htm; f. 1961; internet access, audiovisual section; 213,158 vols, 15,820 MSS, 113 microfilms; Head, Library Department NISAR AHMAD JAMIL; publ. *News Bulletin* (quarterly).

Hyderabad

Pakistan National Centre Library and Culture Centre: Hyderabad, Sindh; f. 1958; 19,000 vols; Dir M. R. SIDDIQI.

Shamsul Ulema Daudpota Sindh Government Library: Hyderabad; f. 1951;

reference and general; 59,000 vols; Librarian KHAIR MOHAMMED MUGHAL.

Islamabad

Allama Iqbal Open University Central Library: Sector H-8, Islamabad; tel. (51) 9250040; e-mail aioucl@asia.com; internet www.aiou.edu.pk; f. 1974; 1,000,000 vols; colln of theses, monographs and term papers; archives and govt papers colln; Librarian Dr MUHAMMAD FAZIL KHAN (acting); publs *Ilm Ki Roshni* (Urdu, 2 a year), *Journal of Social Sciences and Humanities* (2 a year), *Maarif-e-Islami* (Urdu, 2 a year), *Pakistan Journal of Education* (2 a year).

International Islamic University Central Library: POB 1243, Faisal Mosque Campus, Islamabad; tel. (51) 9257955; f. 1980; teaching and research facilities; 1,500,000 vols; 108 periodicals and journals; Senior Librarian SHER NOWROZ KHAN.

Islamabad Public Library: Block 5-B, Super Market, F-6 Markaz, Islamabad; tel. (51) 9221382; f. 1950; spec. collns incl. central and provincial govt publs; Senior Librarian ABDUL LATIF KHAN.

Ministry of Agriculture and Works Library: Ministry of Agriculture, Food and Under-developed Areas, Library, Government of Pakistan, Islamabad; f. 1947; 26,000 vols; 159 periodicals; Librarian S. S. FATIMI; publs *Economic Survey of the Muslim Countries, Food and Forestry*.

National Archives of Pakistan: Administrative Block Area, Block N, Pak Secretariat, Islamabad; tel. (51) 9202044; f. 1951; acquisition, classification and preservation of public and private records of permanent and historical value; provides reference service and assistance to accredited scholars; promotes ideology of Pakistan by projecting the Muslim efforts in acquiring independence; 35,000 vols, 325 MSS, 400 oral archives (250 cassettes, 80 video cassettes), 800 titles of newspapers and periodicals, gazetteers of 80 districts, 20,000 govt publs, Quaid-i-Azam Papers, Muslim League Records; Dir-Gen. ATIQUE ZAFAR SHEIKH; publs *Annual Report, Archival Sources in South Asia, Archives News* (quarterly), *The Pakistan Archives* (2 a year).

National Assembly Library: Islamabad; tel. (51) 9205626; fax (51) 9204673; e-mail assembly@isb.paknet.com.pk; internet www.na.gov.pk; f. 1947; 80,000 vols, 160 current periodicals, United Nations publications; Librarian Haji HATTAR.

National Library of Pakistan: Constitution Ave, POB 1982, Islamabad 44000; tel. (51) 9214523; fax (51) 9221375; e-mail nlpiba@paknet.com.pk; internet www.nlp.gov.pk; f. 1993; depository library for all Pakistani publications, ISBN agency for Pakistani publications, Pakistan National Biography published annually; 140,000 vols, 600 MSS, 80,000 microfiches, 400,000 pages on microfilm; Dir-Gen. MUHAMMAD NAZIR.

Pakistan Scientific and Technological Information Centre (PASTIC): PASTIC National Centre, Quaid-i-Azam University Campus, POB 1217 Islamabad 44000; tel. (51) 9201340; fax (51) 9207211; e-mail pastic@isb.pol.com.pk; internet www.pastic.gov.pk; f. 1956 as PANSDOC under Pakistan Council of Scientific and Industrial Research, reorganized 1974 under Pakistan Science Foundation; sub-centres at Karachi, Lahore, Peshawar, Quetta, Faisalabad and Muzaffarabad; facilities include documentation services, scientific and technical information services, scientific and technical publications and compilation of scientific bibliographies, patent services, environmental information service, reprographic ser-

vices; 8,000 vols, 600 bound periodicals, 300 current periodicals, 300,000 patents, 1,340 NTIS reports; Dir-Gen. Dr S. R. H. BAQRI; publ. *Pakistan Science Abstracts* (agriculture, animal sciences, biology and biotechnology, chemistry, earth sciences, information, communication and space sciences, mathematics and statistics, medicine, pharmaceutics, plant sciences, each annually).

Quaid-i-Azam University Dr Raziuddin Siddiqi Memorial Library: Islamabad; tel. (51) 2872563; fax (51) 2821397; e-mail drsmlib@yahoo.com; f. 1966; 175,000 vols, 223 current periodicals, 11,200 on-line journals; 29,000-vol. special collection on Indo-Pakistani history and Oriental literature; 269 MSS; 20,000 abstracts provided by Higher Education Commission of Pakistan; Librarian MEHBOOB HUSSAIN KHAN.

Jamshoro

Allama I. I. Kazi Library (University of Sindh): Allama I. I. Kazi Campus, Jamshoro, Sindh; tel. (221) 771681 ext. 2058; e-mail aiiklib@hyd.netasia.com.pk; f. 1947; 230,568 vols, 23 current periodicals, 650 MSS; Chief Librarian Prof. Dr RAFIA A. SHEIKH.

Institute of Sindhology Library: Allama I. I. Kazi Campus, University of Sindh, Jamshoro 76070; tel. (221) 771681-9 ext. 2053; fax (221) 771386; e-mail sindhology_s@yahoo.com; internet www.sindhology.com.pk; f. 1962; 109,000 vols (Sindhi, Urdu, English, Pashito, Persian, Balochi, Arabic and other languages); 14,500 periodical bound vols, 32,000 rare books, 500 microfilms; 2,200 audio tapes, 3,500 slides, 1,700 MSS, 700 bound vols, 3,800 bound vols of newspapers; Librarian GUL MUHAMMED N. MUGHAL.

Mehran University of Engineering and Technology Library: Jamshoro, Sindh; tel. and fax (221) 771169; e-mail mumtaz@uunet.uu.net; f. 1977; 125,000 vols, including journals; Librarian MUMTAZ S. MEMON.

Karachi

All Pakistan Educational Conference Library: 1-J, 45/10 Altaf Brelvi Rd, Karachi 18-74600; tel. (21) 621195; 35,000 vols on Aligarh and Pakistan Movement; Sec. SYED MUSTAFA ALI BRELVI.

Bait al-Hikmah–The Hamdard Library: Madinat al-Hikmah, Muhammad bin Qasim Avenue, off Sharae Madinat al-Hikmah, Karachi 74700; tel. (21) 9600000; fax (21) 6641766; e-mail huvc@cyber.net.pk; internet www.hamdard.edu; f. 1989; 434,693 vols, 28,010 periodicals, 2,300 current periodicals, 1,626 MSS, 1,827 rare books, 690 microfilms, 2,163 audiotapes, photographs, 16,357 stamps, maps and charts; 3,610,000 newspaper clippings covering 1,210 subjects; specializes in medicine, science, history, Indo-Pakistan history, Islamic studies, lieterature, management and social sciences; Dir AFZAL AHMED; Chief Librarian S. AKHTAR ALI.

Dr Mahmud Hussain Library, University of Karachi: Karachi 75270; tel. (21) 9243182; fax (21) 9243218; e-mail kulibrarian@yahoo.com; internet www.ku.edu.pk; f. 1952; 35,000 vols, 6,150 microfilms, 110 current periodicals, 200,000 vols in special collections, 25,000 documents and reports; 18,000 vols in seminar libraries; 4,000 research reports; Deputy Librarian SYEDA ARJUMAND.

Islamic Documentation and Information Centre (IDIC): SS College of Liberal Arts and Social Sciences, opp. Safari Park, University Rd, Karachi 75000; tel. (21)

4978274; fax (21) 4976181; e-mail mnz@ usman.khi.sdnpk.undp.org; f. 1983; 5,250 vols in English and Urdu, 60 current periodicals; Dir-Gen. Dr MANZOOR AHMAD.

Khalikdina Hall Library Association: M. A. Jinnah Rd, Karachi; tel. (21) 7732228; fax (21) 2638000; e-mail swo_qari@usa.net; f. 1856; language classes, social and cultural events; 50,218 vols; Pres. TARIQ RAHMANI; Chief Librarian QARI HILAL AHMED RABBANI.

Liaquat Hall Library: Bagh-e-Jinnah, Abdullah Haroon Rd, Karachi 4; f. 1852 as Frere Hall Library; 52,000 vols; Asst Dir SYEDA SHAHANA ALVI.

Liaquat Memorial Library: c/o Tourism and Cultural Department, Govt. of Sindh, Stadium Rd, Karachi 5; tel. (21) 9230116; e-mail librarian@lml.edu.pk; internet www .lml.edu.pk; f. 1950; 150,000 vols; Principal Librarian I. A. S. BOKHARI.

National Bank of Pakistan, Head Office Library: Central Directorate of State Bank of Pakistan, I. I. Chundrigar Rd, Karachi 2; tel. (21) 2414783; f. 1949; 60,000 vols (45,000 English, 15,000 Oriental); colln of books, technical reports, Govt documents, periodicals and magazines relating mainly to the subjects of economics, banking, finance, management and commerce; Librarian SALIHA MOIN; publs *Index of Economic Literature* (monthly), *List of Acquisitions* (quarterly).

NED University of Engineering and Technology Central Library: University Rd, Karachi 75270; tel. (21) 9243261; fax (21) 9243255; e-mail libadmin@neduet.edu.pk; internet www.neduet.edu.pk; f. 1977; 123,361 vols, 121 current periodicals; Chief Librarian MEHER YASMEEN.

Pakistan Institute of International Affairs Library: Aiwan-e-Sadar Rd, POB 1447, Karachi 74200; tel. (21) 5682891; fax (21) 5686069; e-mail piia@cyber.net.pk; f. 1947; 30,820 vols, 44 microfilms, 200 tapes; newspaper clippings on international politics, economics and jurisprudence; Librarian AFSAR MEHDI.

Scientific Information Centre: PCSIR Laboratories Campus, Karachi 75280; tel. (21) 4651739; fax (21) 4651738; e-mail pcsirsys@super.net.pk; f. 1958; attached to Pakistan Council of Scientific and Industrial Research; Dir Dr KANIZ FIZZA AZHAR; publs *Pakistan Journal of Scientific and Industrial Research* (every 2 months), *PCSIR Bulletin* (monthly), *PCSIR Research and Development Programme* (annual).

State Bank of Pakistan Library: POB 5714, I. I. Chundrigar Rd, Karachi 74000; tel. (21) 9212460; fax (21) 9211009; e-mail bashir .zia@sbp.org.pk; internet www.sbp.org.pk; f. 1949; 70,000 books, 37,000 periodicals; spec. collns: annual reports of major banks and financial instns worldwide, news clipping files since 1949; Chief Librarian BASHIR AHMAD ZIA; publs *Current Contents: Subject-wise Index of Periodical Articles* (monthly), *Economic Literature: a selected bibliography* (annual), *Fresh Arrivals* (monthly).

Lahore

Atomic Energy Minerals Centre Library: POB 658, Lahore; tel. (42) 5758661; fax (42) 5757903; f. 1961; Dir MUHAMMAD MANSOOR.

Dyal Singh Trust Library: 25 Nisbet Rd, Lahore; tel. (42) 7229483; fax (42) 7233631; f. 1908; 146,000 vols; Senior Librarian NUSRAT ALI ATHEER; publs *Bulletin*, *Minhaj* (quarterly).

Ewing Memorial Library: Forman Christian College, Ferozepur Rd, Lahore 54600; tel. (42) 9231581; fax (42) 9230703; e-mail formancc@yahoo.com; f. 1864; 96,000 vols;

Chief Librarian MANZOOR AHMAD KHAN ANJUM.

Government College University Central Library: Fazal-i-Hussain (Main Library), Main Building, Lahore 54000; tel. (42) 9213348; fax (42) 9213350; e-mail chieflibrarian@library.gcu.edu.pk; internet www.gcu.edu.pk/library; f. 1872; 235,637 vols; Chief Librarian ABDUL WAHEED.

Islamia College Library: Civil Lines, Lahore; f. 1958 after split of Old Islamia College; 50,061 vols, 53 current periodicals; Librarian MUNIR AHMAD NAEEM; publs *College Bulletin* (every 2 months), *Faran* (annually).

National Library of Engineering Sciences: University of Engineering and Technology, Grand Trunk Rd, Lahore 54890; tel. (42) 6829243; fax (42) 6827503; e-mail lib@uet.edu.pk; internet www.uet.edu .pk; f. 1961; 125,000 vols, 60,000 bound copies of scientific and technical periodicals; Librarian MUHAMMAD SAEED.

Pakistan Administrative Staff College Library: Shahrah-e-Quaid-e-Azam, Lahore; tel. (42) 9202916; f. 1960; 37,000 vols, 150 periodicals, 1,500 audio tapes; Librarian TALAT ALI SHER.

Punjab Public Library: Lahore; tel. (42) 9211649; f. 1884; 300,000 vols, 5,000 bound vols of periodicals, 1,100 MSS, 121 English and 115 Oriental language periodicals; Bait-ul-Quran Section with Quranic MSS, rare material on the Quran, audio-visual units; ladies' and children's section; arranges seminars and lectures for the promotion of library activities; Chief Librarian and Sec. ZIL-E-HASNAIN; publs *Annual Report*, *Bulletin* (4 a year).

Quaid-e-Azam Library, Lahore: Bagh-e-Jinnah, Lahore; tel. (42) 9203371; f. 1984; research and reference facilities; 110,000 vols, 350 current periodicals; special collection: dissertations on Pakistan and Islam; Chief Librarian MUHAMMAD TAJ; publs *Bulletin* (quarterly), *Informit* (quarterly), *Makhzan* (2 a year).

University of the Punjab Library: Quaid-e-Azam Campus, Lahore 54590; tel. (42) 9230834; fax (42) 9230892; e-mail info@ library.pu.edu.pk; internet www.pulibrary .edu.pk; f. 1882; 402,634 vols, incl. 22,000 MSS; Chief Librarian MUHAMMAD HANIF.

Multan

Bahauddin Zakariya University Library: Bosan Rd, Multan; e-mail librarysc@bzu.edu.pk; f. 1975; 109,000 vols, 20 current periodicals, 20 slides; Chair. Dr MUMTAZ HUSSAIN BOKHARI; publs *Journal of Research* (Humanities), *Journal of Research* (Sciences), *Law Research Journal*, *News Bulletin* (monthly).

Muzaffarabad

University of Azad Jammu and Kashmir Central Library: Muzaffarabad; tel. and fax (58810) 44102; e-mail yakub@ajku.sdnpk .undp.org; f. 1980; 120,000 vols; Chief Librarian MUHAMMAD YAQUB CHAUDHARY.

Peshawar

Archival Museum: Directorate of Archives, Govt of NWFP, Peshawar; tel. (521) 274831; f. 1950; library of 71,000 items; Dir TARIQ MANSOOR JALALI.

Central Forest Library: Pakistan Forest Institute, Peshawar; tel. (91) 9216196; fax (91) 9216203; e-mail pfilib@hotmail.com; f. 1947; 25,000 vols, 20,000 periodicals; Librarian YOUSAF KHAN; publ. *Pakistan Journal of Forestry* (2 a year).

Peshawar University Library: Peshawar; tel. (91) 9216701; fax (91) 9216470; f. 1951; 153,652 vols, 10,400 periodicals, 693 Persian, Arabic and Pashto MSS; Librarian MOHAMMAD IBRAR.

Quetta

University of Balochistan Library: Sariab Rd, Quetta; tel. (81) 9211247; fax (81) 9211277; f. 1971; 120,000 vols, 1,000 rare books, 4,000 microfiche cards, periodicals, depository library of World Bank, UNESCO and UNICEF; Librarian ABDUL JALIL KHAN.

Taxila

Archaeological Library: Taxila Museum, Taxila; f. 1960; 1,450 vols on history and arts, especially the ancient history and archaeology of Pakistan; Custodian GULZAR MOHAMMAD KHAN.

Museums and Art Galleries

Harappa

Archaeological Museum: Harappa, Dist. Sahiwal, Punjab; f. 1967; antiquities from site of the prehistoric city; Curator MOHAMMAD BAHADAR KHAN.

Karachi

National Museum of Pakistan: Burns Garden, Karachi 74200; tel. (21) 2628280; f. 1950; Pakistan's cultural heritage from Stone Age to the birth of Pakistan; Supt QASIM ALI QASIM; publs *Museum Journal*, *Pakistan Archaeology*.

Quaid-i-Azam Birthplace, Reading Room, Museum and Library: Wazir Mansion, Chagla St, Kharadar, Karachi; tel. (21) 2434904; f. 1953; library of 5,000 vols (incl. spec. colln on Indo-Pakistani history); Custodian TAHIR SAEE.

Lahore

Directorate of Archives and Archival Museum: Punjab Civil Secretariat, Lahore; tel. (42) 7322381; fax (42) 212693; f. 1924; consists of Historical Record Office, Central Record Office and Museum; library of 150,000 vols; Dir SYED ISHRAT ALI SHAH; publ. *Urdu Nama* (monthly).

Industrial and Commercial Museum: Poonch House, Multan Rd, Lahore; f. 1950; permanent up-to-date collection of the raw material resources, handicrafts, art-ware and manufactured products of Pakistan; industrial library, reading-room and auditorium attached; provides free economic intelligence to trade and industry; Curator MUSHTAQ AHMAD.

Lahore Fort Museum: Lahore 54000; Mughal Gallery: Mughal paintings, coins, calligraphy, MSS, carving; Sikh Gallery: arms and armour, paintings of Sikh period; Sikh Painting Gallery: oil paintings from the Princess Bamba Collection; Dir SAEED-UR RAHMAN; Curator IRSHAD HUSSAIN.

Lahore Museum: Shahrah-i-Quaid-i-Azam, Lahore; tel. (42) 7322835; f. 1864; collections of Graeco-Buddhist sculpture, Indo-Pakistan coins and miniature paintings of the Mughal, Rajput, Kangra and Pahari schools; Hindu, Buddhist and Jaina sculpture, local arts, Chinese porcelain, armoury, fabrics, Pakistan postage stamps, modern paintings, oriental MSS, Islamic calligraphy, archives and photographs on Pakistan Movement; library of 35,000 vols; Dir Dr SAIFUR RAHMAN DAR; publs *Catalogue of Coins*, *Catalogue of Miniatures*, *Guide Book*, *Guide to Gandhara*

Gallery, *Guide to Manuscripts*, *Lahore Museum Bulletin* (2 a year).

Lahore Zoological Gardens: Shahrah-e-Quaid-i-Azam, Lahore; tel. (42) 6314684; fax (42) 6304683; e-mail lhrzoo@pol.com.pk; internet www.lahorezoo.com.pk; f. 1872; Dir RAJA MUHAMMAD JAVED.

Larkana

Archaeological Museum: Moenjodaro, Larkana, Sindh; tel. (741) 459051; f. 1924; a variety of antiquities unearthed from the prehistoric site of Moenjodaro, dating from 3,000 BC; Curator SAEED JATOI.

Peshawar

Peshawar Museum: Peshawar; f. 1906; the collections of this museum are devoted mainly to the sculptures of the Gandhara School; they comprise an unrivalled collection of images of Buddha, the Bodhisattvas, Buddhist deities, reliefs illustrating the life of the Buddha and Jataka stories, architectural pieces and minor antiquities excavated at Charsadda, Sahri-Bahlol, Shahji-ki-Dheri, Takht-i-Bahi and Jamal Garhi; a Muslim gallery of Koranic MSS and MSS in Arabic and Persian languages; ethnological section; Dir AURANGZEB KHAN.

Taxila

Archaeological Museum: Taxila, Rawalpindi; tel. and fax (596) 9314270; e-mail ilyas_bhatti@hotmail.com; f. 1928; Gandhara sculptures in stone and stucco; gold and silver ornaments; household utensils, pottery; antiquities of every description from the sites of Taxila and monastic area from 6th century BC to 5th century AD; library: see Libraries and Archives; Curator MUHAMMAD ILYAS BHATTI (acting).

Universities

AGA KHAN UNIVERSITY

Stadium Rd, POB 3500, Karachi 74800

Telephone: (21) 4930051

Fax: (21) 4934294

E-mail: student.affairs@aku.edu

Internet: www.aku.net

Founded 1983

Private control (Aga Khan Foundation, Geneva)

Language of instruction: English

Academic year: October to August

Chancellor: HH The Aga Khan

President: SHAMSH KASSIM-LAKHA

Provost and Chief Academic Officer: DAVID DENIS TAYLOR (acting)

Vice-Provost (Academic Development and Special Projects): DAVID DENIS TAYLOR

Director-General and Chief Executive Officer, Aga Khan University Hospital: NADEEM MUSTAFA KHAN

Director-General, University Administration: NURALLAH ASHRAF MERCHANT

Chief Financial Officer: AL-KARIM HAJI

Librarian (Faculty of Health Sciences): AZRA QURESHI

Librarian (Institute for Educational Development): MUNOVER AZMATULLAH

Library of 44,558 books (Faculty of Health Sciences 27,000 books, 500 periodicals; Institute for Educational Development 17,558 books, 140 print periodicals, 100 online periodicals, 1,700 reports)

Number of teachers: 526 (399 full-time, 127 part-time, incl. honorary and visiting staff)

Number of students: 1,025

DEANS

School of Nursing (in the Faculty of Health Sciences): YASMIN AMARSI

Medical College (in the Faculty of Health Sciences): MOHAMMAD KHURSHID

Institute for Educational Development: Dr MUHAMMAD MEMON (Dir)

Institute for the Study of Muslim Civilizations: ABDOU FILALI-ANSARY (Dir)

Postgraduate Medical Education Programme, Kenya: JEFFREY REES (Dir)

Advanced Nursing Studies Programme, East Africa: LAETITIA J. KING (Assoc. Dean)

PROFESSORS

AMARSI, Y., Nursing
BADRUDDIN, S. H., Community Health Sciences
BAIG, S. M., Medicine
BHUTTA, A. B., Paediatrics
BILLOO, A. G., Paediatrics
CHOHAN, U., Anaesthesia
CONNOR, J. D., Pharmacology
FARAH, I., Education
FILALI-ANSARY, A., Education (London)
FROSSARD, P., Biochemistry
GILANI, A. H., Pharmacology
HAMID, S., Medicine
HARLEEH-JONES, B. A., Education
HASAN, R., Microbiology
HASAN, S. H., Pathology
HUSSAIN, R., Microbiology
IQBAL, M. P., Biochemistry
JABBAR, A., Medicine
JAFRI, S. M. W., Medicine
KAMAL, R., Anaesthesia
KARIM, M. S., Community Health Sciences
KAYANI, N., Pathology
KHAN, F. A., Anaesthesia
KHAN, F. H., Anaesthesia
KHAN, I. A., Paediatrics
KHAN, J. A., Medicine
KHAN, K. M., Anatomy
KHAN, M. A., Medicine
KHAN, M. M., Psychiatry
KHAN, S. M., Surgery
KHURSHID, M., Pathology
KING, L., Nursing (Kenya)
MACLEOD, G., Education
MEMON, M., Education
NIZAMI, S. Q., Paediatrics
PARDHAN, S., Education
PERVEZ, S., Pathology
QURESHI, R. H., Family Medicine
RAJA, A. J., Surgery (Kenya)
REES, J., Radiology (Kenya)
RIZVI, J. H., Obstetrics and Gynaecology
SIDDIQUI, A. A., Biochemistry
TALATI, J., Surgery
VELLANI, C. W., Medicine
ZUBERI, R. W., Family Medicine

UNIVERSITY OF AGRICULTURE, FAISALABAD

Faisalabad

Telephone: (41) 9200161

Fax: (41) 9200764

E-mail: uaf@fsd.paknet.com.pk

Internet: www.uaf.edu.pk

Founded 1909 as Punjab Agricultural College, present name 1973

Language of instruction: English

Academic year: October to September

Chancellor: THE GOVERNOR OF THE PUNJAB

Vice-Chancellor: Prof. Dr BASHIR AHMED

Registrar: CH. MUHAMMAD HUSSAIN

Library: see Libraries and Archives

Number of teachers: 459

Number of students: 6,504

Publications: *Journal of Agricultural Sciences* (4 a year), *Journal of Veterinary Science*, *Pakistan Entomologist*, *Research Studies*

DEANS

Faculty of Agriculture: Prof. Dr MUHAMMAD ASHFAQ

Faculty of Agricultural Economics and Rural Sociology: Prof. Dr ZAKIR HUSSAIN

Faculty of Agricultural Engineering and Technology: Prof. Dr M. SHAFI SABIR

Faculty of Animal Husbandry: Prof. Dr AHSAN-UL-HAQUE

Faculty of Sciences: Prof. Dr RAKHSHANDA NAWAZ

Faculty of Veterinary Science: Prof. Dr M. SHOAIB AKHTAR

College of Agriculture, Dera Ghazi Khan: Dr M. IQBAL

DIRECTORS

Advanced Studies: Dr TANVIR ALI
Education and Extension: Dr KAUSAR ALMAS
Research: Prof. Dr MAQSOOD AHMAD GILL

PROFESSORS

Faculty of Agriculture (tel. (41) 9200193; fax (41) 614335; e-mail deanagri@fsd.paknet.com.pk):

Department of Agricultural Entomology:
RANA, M. A.

Department of Agronomy:
AKHTAR, M.
ALI, A.
ATTA, Z
HUSSAIN, A.
MALIK, M. A.

Department of Horticulture:
IBRAHIM, M.
KHAN, I. A.
KHAN, M. A.

Department of Plant Breeding and Genetics:
AZHAR, F. M.
ASLAM, M.
KHAN, I. A.
MEHDI, S.
SALEEM, A.
SALEEM, M.

Department of Plant Pathology:
CHOHAN, R. A.
KHAN, S. M.

Department of Soil Science:
ARSHAD, M.
GHAFOOR, A.
GILL, M. A.
HASSAN, A. U.
RANJHA, A. M.

Faculty of Agricultural Economics and Rural Sociology (tel. (41) 9200196):

Department of Agricultural Economics:
HUSSAIN, Z.

Faculty of Agricultural Engineering and Technology (tel. (41) 9200194; e-mail mssabir_uaf@yahoo.com):

Department of Farm Machinery and Power:
SABIR, M. S.

Department of Food Technology:
ANJUM, F. M.

Department of Irrigation and Drainage:
CHAUDHRY, M. R.

Department of Structural and Environmental Engineering:
ALI, M. A.
SIAL, J. K.

Faculty of Animal Husbandry (tel. (41) 9200195):

Department of Animal Nutrition:
SARWAR, M.

Department of Livestock Management:
GONDAL, K. Z.
YOUNAS, M.

Department of Poultry Husbandry:
HAQ, A.
Faculty of Sciences (tel. (41) 9200197):
Department of Botany:
ASHRAF, M.
Department of Chemistry:
NAWAZ, R.
SHEIKH, M. A.
Department of Mathematics and Statistics:
KHAN, M. I.
Department of Physics:
CHAUDHRY, M. A.
Department of Zoology and Fisheries:
QURESHI, J. I.
Faculty of Veterinary Science (tel. (41) 9200725; e-mail drmsakhter@hotmail.com):
Department of Animal Reproduction:
LODHI, L. A.
SAMAD, H. A.
Department of Physiology and Pharmacology:
AKHTAR, M. S.
NAWAZ, M.
Department of Veterinary Microbiology:
SIDDIQU, M.
Department of Veterinary Pathology:
ANJUM, A. D.
Division of Education and Extension (tel. (41) 9200186):
Department of Rural Home Economics:
ALMAS, K
College of Agriculture, Dera Ghazi Khan:
IQBAL, M.

AIR UNIVERSITY

Sector E-9, PAF Complex, Islamabad 44000
Telephone: (51) 920055756
Fax: (51) 9262530
E-mail: admissions@mail.au.edu.pk
Internet: www.au.edu.pk
Founded 2002
State control
Academic year: September to August
Vice-Chancellor: QAZI JAVED AHMED
Director (Academic Affairs): Dr ZULKAIF AHMED
Librarian: MAMOONA KOUSAR
Number of teachers: 78
Number of students: 816

DEANS

Faculty of Administrative Sciences: MUHAMMAD ISMAIL RAMAY (acting)
Faculty of Basic and Applied Sciences: Dr BASHIR AHMAD SALEEMI
Faculty of Engineering: Dr ZAFAR-ULLAH KORESHI
Faculty of Social Sciences: ABIDA HASSAN (acting)

ALLAMA IQBAL OPEN UNIVERSITY

Sector H-8, Islamabad
Telephone: (51) 9250111
Fax: (51) 9250102
E-mail: aiou@paknet.ptc.pk
Internet: www.aiou.edu.pk
Founded 1974 as People's Open University, renamed 1977
Autonomous control
Languages of instruction: Urdu, English
Academic year: April to March
Chancellor: THE PRESIDENT OF PAKISTAN
Pro-Chancellor: THE MINISTER OF EDUCATION
Vice-Chancellor: Dr S. ALTAF HUSSAIN
Registrar: ILYAS AHMAD

Librarian: Prof. Dr MUHAMMAD FAZIL KHAN (acting)
Library: see Libraries and Archives
Number of teachers: 166
Number of students: 512,635
Publications: *Ilm Ki Roshni* (2 a year), *Jamia Nama* (monthly, in English and Urdu), *Journal of Social Sciences and Humanities* (2 a year), *Marif-I-Islami* (2 a year), *Pakistan Journal of Education* (2 a year), *Sehen Ujala* (2 a year)

DEANS

Faculty of Arabic and Islamic Studies: Prof. Dr ALI ASHGAR CHISHTI
Faculty of Education: Prof. Dr MUHAMMAD RASHID
Faculty of Sciences: Prof. Dr N. A. SANGI
Faculty of Social Sciences and Humanities: Prof. NAJEEB A. KHAN

CHAIRS OF ACADEMIC DEPARTMENTS

Faculty of Arabic and Islamic Studies:
Arabic: Prof. Dr ALI ASHGAR CHISHTI
Fiqh and Islamic Law: Dr M. ZIA-UL-HAQ
Hadith and Seerah: Prof. Dr ALI ASHGAR CHISHTI
Islamic Thought, History and Culture: Dr BAKIR KHAN KHAKWANI
Quran and Tafseer: ABDUL HAMEED ABBASI
Faculty of Education:
Distance, Non-Formal and Continuing Education: Prof. Dr MUHAMMAD RASHID
Educational Planning and Management: Dr MUHAMMAD RASHID
Elementary Teacher Education: Dr TANVEER-UZ-ZAMAN
Science Education: Dr QUDSIA
Secondary Teacher Education: Prof. Dr REHANA MASROOR KHAN
Special Education: MAHMOOD HUSSAIN AWAN
Faculty of Sciences:
Agricultural Sciences: Dr NOWSHAD KHAN
Biology: Prof. Dr N. A. SANGI
Chemistry: Prof. Dr KALEEM TAHIR
Computer Science: Prof. Dr N. A. SANGI
Engineering and Technology: Eng. M. YOUSAF SHAIKH
Environment Science: Dr ABDUL RAUF FAROOQI
Home and Health Sciences: Prof. Dr PARVEEN LIAQAT
Mathematics and Statistics: Dr FAQIR MUHAMMAD
Physics: MAZHARUDIN RANA
Faculty of Social Sciences and Humanities:
Business Administration: Prof. NAJEEB A. KHAN
Commerce: NAJEEB A. KHAN
Economics: Dr MUHAMMAD ASHRAF
English Language and Applied Linguistics: ABDUL HAFEEZ
History: NAJEEB A. KHAN
Iqbaliyat: NAJEEB A. KHAN
Institute of Mass Education: Dr SYED ABDUL SIRAJ
Library and Information Sciences: MUHAMMAD FAZIL KHAN
Pakistan Studies: LUBNA SAIF
Urdu: Prof. Dr NISAR AHMAD QURESHI
Sociology, Social Work and Population Studies: Dr RUKHSANA MASOOD
Pakistani Languages: Dr INAM-UL-HAQ JAVED
Women's Studies: Dr QUDSIA RIFFAT

UNIVERSITY OF ARID AGRICULTURE RAWALPINDI

Shamsabad, Muree Rd, Rawalpindi
Telephone: (51) 9290151
Fax: (51) 9290160

E-mail: registrar@uaar.edu.pk
Internet: www.uaar.edu.pk
Founded 1979; present name and status 1994
Vice-Chancellor: Dr KHALID MEHMOOD KHAN
Registrar: HAJI MUHAMMAD ASLAM CHAUDHRY

DEANS

Faculty of Crop and Food Sciences: Prof. Dr MUSHTAQ KHAN
Faculty of Livestock and Range Management: (vacant)
Faculty of Sciences: Prof. Dr AFSAR MIAN
Center for Information Technology: Dr MUHAMMAD AFZAL (Dir)
University Institute of Management Sciences: Dr ZAHEER AKHTAR (Dir)

UNIVERSITY OF AZAD JAMMU AND KASHMIR, MUZAFFARABAD

Muzaffarabad, Azad Jammu and Kashmir
Telephone: (58810) 49166
Fax: (58810) 4717
E-mail: yaqub@ajku.sdnpk.undp.org
Founded 1980
State control
Languages of instruction: English, Urdu
Academic year: September to October
Chancellor: SARDAR MUHAMMAD IBRAHIM KHAN
Vice-Chancellor: KHALIL AHMAD QURESHI
Registrar: MUHAMMAD HANIF KHAWAJA
Chief Librarian: MUHAMMAD YAQUB CHAUDHARY
Library: see Libraries
Number of teachers: 256
Number of students: 1,800
Publications: *Al-Muhaqqiq* (annually), *Kashmir Economics Review* (annually), *Kashmir Journal of Geology* (annually), *Kashmir Journal of Language Research* (annually), *Kashmir Research Journal of Natural Sciences* (annually).

CONSTITUENT INSTITUTES

University College, Muzaffarabad: Dean of Faculty of Science Dr ABDUL RAUF KHAN; Dean of Faculty of Arts Dr MUHAMMAD KHAIRAT CHAUDHARY.

University College of Agriculture and Food Technology, Rawalakot: Dean Dr MUHAMMAD BASHIR CHAUDHARY.

University College of Engineering and Technology, Mirpur: Dean MUHAMMAD NASRULLAH.

University College of Home Economics, Mirpur: Dean SAEEDA JEHAN ARA SHAH.

University College of Management Sciences, Kotli: Dean Dr GHULAM GHOUS.

University College of Textile and Design, Muzaffarabad: Dean SALEEMA ATTA.

Institute of Islamic Studies: Dean Dr KHALID MAHMOOD.

BAHAUDDIN ZAKARIYA UNIVERSITY

University Campus, Bosan Rd, Multan 60800
Telephone: (61) 9210071
Fax: (61) 9210098
E-mail: regbzu@brain.net.pk
Internet: www.bzu.edu.pk
Founded 1975 as University of Multan; present name 1979
State control
Languages of instruction: Urdu, English
Academic year: October to September
Chancellor: Lt-Gen. (Retd) KHALID MAQBOOL
Vice-Chancellor: Prof. Dr KARAMAT ALI
Registrar: KHURSHID AHMAD KHAN
Librarian: MAQBOOL AHMAD CHAUDHRY
Library: see Libraries and Archives

Number of teachers: 360
Number of students: 6,997

Publications: *Journal of Research (Humanities)*, *Journal of Research (Science)*, *Journal of Research of the Faculty of Islamic Studies and Languages*, *Journal of Research of Business Management*, *News Bulletin*

DEANS

Faculty of Arts and Social Science: Prof. Dr KARAMAT ALI

Faculty of Commerce, Law and Business Administration: Prof. Dr MUHAMMAD ZAFARULLAH

Faculty of Engineering and Technology: Prof. Dr KARAMAT ALI

Faculty of Islamic Studies and Languages: Prof. Dr ANWAR AHMAD

Faculty of Medicine and Dentistry: Prof. Dr SHABBIR AHMAD NASIR

Faculty of Pharmacy: Prof. Dr KHALID HUSSAIN JANBAZ

Faculty of Science and Agriculture: Prof. Dr G. R. PASHA

ATTACHED RESEARCH INSTITUTES

Centre for Advanced Studies in Pure and Applied Mathematics: Dir Prof. Dr NAZIR AHMAD MIR.

Centre for Undergraduate Studies: Dir Dr MUHAMMAD ALI.

Institute of Management Sciences: Dir Prof. Dr MUHAMMAD ZAFARULLAH.

Institute of Pure and Applied Biology: Dir Prof. Dr ABDUL SALAM.

Information Technology Centre: Project Man. Prof. Dr ASGHAR ALI.

Siraiki Research Centre: Dir Prof. Dr ANWAR AHMAD.

CONSTITUENT COLLEGES

University College of Agriculture: Multan; f. 1990; Principal Prof. Dr MUSHTAQ AHMAD SALEEM.

University College of Engineering and Technology: f. 1994; Principal Dr MAHBOOB ALI CHAUDRY.

University College of Fine Arts: f. 2004; Principal ZAFAR H. GILANI.

University Gilani Law College: Multan; f. 1971; Principal Prof. Dr ABDUL RASHID.

University College of Textile Engineering: f. 2004; Principal Dr MAHBOOB ALI CHAUDRY.

There are 126 affiliated colleges

BAHRIA UNIVERSITY

Shangrila, Sector E-8, Islamabad 44000

Telephone: (51) 9260002
Fax: (51) 9260885
E-mail: admn@bci.edu.pk
Internet: www.bci.edu.pk

Founded 2000
State control

Director: M. A. KHALID
Librarian: IFTIKHAR ALI.

UNIVERSITY OF BALOCHISTAN

Sariab Rd, Quetta

Telephone: (81) 9211268
Fax: (81) 9211277

Founded 1970
State control
Languages of instruction: English, Urdu
Academic year: March to December

Chancellor: MIAN GUL AURANGZEB
Vice-Chancellor: Prof. BAHADUR KHAN RODINI
Registrar: ABDUL KABIR KHAN BAZAI
Librarian: ABDUL JALIL KHAN BAZAI

Number of teachers: 255
Number of students: 3,650

Publications: *Acta Mineralogica Pakistanica* (2 a year), *Middle East Journal of Area Studies Centre*

DEANS

Faculty of Arts: Prof. GHULAM NABI ACHAKZAI
Faculty of Science: Dr NAEEM M. HASSAN

ATTACHED INSTITUTES

Area Studies Centre: to promote co-operation with the Middle Eastern and Arab countries; Dir Dr MUNIR AHMED BALOCH.

Centre of Excellence in Mineralogy and Postgraduate Studies: Dir AKHTER MOHAMMAD.

Pakistan Study Centre of Languages, Social Structure and Culture: Dir NADIR QAMBRANI.

University Law College: Principal MIR AURANGZEB.

Institute of Biochemistry Research and Postgraduate studies: Dir Dr ABBAS HAIDER.

BALOCHISTAN UNIVERSITY OF ENGINEERING AND TECHNOLOGY

Khuzdar, Balochistan

Telephone: (871) 412834
Fax: (871) 413364
E-mail: info@buet.qta.sdnpk.org
Internet: www.wb.sdnpk.org/buet

Founded 1987 as Balochistan Engineering College; present name and status 1994
State control

Vice-Chancellor: Col MIRZA ANWAR-UL-HAQUE
Registrar: MOHAMMAD ALAM BALOCH
Librarian: ASIF AKHTAR HASHMI.

BALOCHISTAN UNIVERSITY OF INFORMATION TECHNOLOGY AND MANAGEMENT SCIENCES

Sumungli Rd, Jinnah Town, Quetta, Balochistan

Telephone: (81) 9202463
Fax: (81) 9201064
E-mail: info@buitms.edu.pk
Internet: www.buitms.edu.pk

Vice-Chancellor: Prof. Dr MUHAMMAD ABBAS CHAUDHARY
Registrar: MOHAMMAD AZAM BALOCH
Librarian: GULAM MURTAZA SHAHWANI

DEANS

Faculty of Basic Sciences: Prof. Dr SYED ARIF KAZMI
Faculty of Biotechnology and Informatics: Prof. Dr M. K. MALGHANI
Faculty of Computer and Emerging Sciences: Prof. Dr SABIR USMANI
Faculty of Management Sciences: Prof. Dr ZAFFARYAB

UNIVERSITY OF EDUCATION

Lahore 5400, Punjab

Telephone: (42) 5433632
Fax: (42) 5433599
Internet: www.ue.edu.pk

Founded 2002

Vice-Chancellor: Dr G. MUSTAFA HABBIBULLAH.

UNIVERSITY OF ENGINEERING AND TECHNOLOGY, LAHORE

Grand Trunk Rd, Lahore 54890

Telephone: (42) 6829205
Fax: (42) 6822566

E-mail: webmaster@uet.edu.pk
Internet: www.uet.edu.pk

Founded 1961
Language of instruction: English
Academic year: January to December

Chancellor: THE GOVERNOR OF THE PUNJAB
Vice-Chancellor: Lt-Gen. (retd) MUHAMMAD AKRAM KHAN
Registrar: MUHAMMAD ASLAM MALIK
Library: see Libraries and Archives
Number of teachers: 310
Number of students: 8,248

Publications: *ECHO* (annually), *Research Bulletin* (4 a year), *Varsity News* (every 2 weeks)

DEANS

Faculty of Architecture and Planning: Prof. Dr MAHMOOD HUSSAIN
Faculty of Chemical and Metallurgical Engineering: Prof. Dr IQBAL HUSSAIN (additional duty)
Faculty of Civil Engineering: Prof. Dr JAVED ANWAR AZIZ
Faculty of Electrical Engineering: Prof. Dr JAVED ANWAR AZIZ (additional duty)
Faculty of Mechanical Engineering: Prof. Dr IQBAL HUSSAIN
Faculty of Natural Sciences, Humanities and Islamic Studies: Prof. Dr M. NASIR CH.

PROFESSORS

Department of Architecture (tel. (42) 6829223):

AKBAR, S.
AWAN, M. Y.
GELANI, I. A. S.
HUSSAIN, M.
MALIK, R. A.
REHMAN, A.

Department of Chemical Engineering (tel. (42) 6829288):

AHMAD, M. M.
KHAN, J. R.
MAMOOR, G. M.
NAVEED, S.
SALARYA, A. K.
SALEEMI, A. R.

Department of Chemistry (tel. (42) 6829239):

AMJAD, M.
HAQ, I. U.
TAHIRA, F.

Department of City and Regional Planning (tel. (42) 6829203):

ANJUM, G. A.
BAJWA, E. U.
ISLAM, Q. U.
MALIK, T. H.
ZAIDI, S.-UL-H.

Department of Civil Engineering (tel. (42) 6829202):

ASHRAF, M.
CHAUDHRY, M. Y.
CHISHTY, F. A.
ILYAS, M.
MIAN, Z.
RIZWAN, S. A.
SHAKIR, A. S.
SHEIKH, A. S.
TAHIR, M. A.

Department of Computer Science and Information Technology (tel. (42) 6829260):

ASIM, M. R.
MALIK, A. A.

Department of Electrical Engineering (tel. (42) 6829229):

BUKHARI, S H.
CHUGHTAI, M. A.
KHAN, Z. A.
QURESHI, S. A.
SALEEM, M. M.

SHAH, A. H.
SHAMI, T. A.
SHEIKH, N. M.

Department of Humanities and Social Sciences (tel. (42) 6829291):

ZAIDI, M. H.

Department of Islamic Studies (tel. (42) 6829246):

YAHYA, M. A.

Department of Mathematics (tel. (42) 6829210):

AHMAD, M. O.
CH., N. M.
SHAH, N. A.

Department of Mechanical Engineering (tel. (42) 6829265):

ALI, S.
CHAUDHRY, I. A.
HUSSAIN, I.
KHAN, M. I.
MIRZA, M. R.
PIRACHA, J. L.
QURESHI, A. H.
SHAH, F. H.
TABASSUM, S. A.

Department of Metallurgical and Materials Engineering (tel. (42) 6829207):

AJMAL, M.
HASSAN, F.
IQBAL, J.
ZAIDI, S. Q. H.

Department of Mining and Geological Engineering (tel. (42) 6829212):

AKRAM, M.
CHATTAH, N. H.
HUSSAIN, S. A.
KIRMANI, F. A.
RANA, M. T.

Department of Petroleum and Gas Engineering (tel. (42) 6829271):

KHAN, A. S.

Department of Physics (tel. (42) 6829204):

REHMAN, M. K.

Institute of Environmental Engineering and Research (tel. (42) 6829248):

AHMAD, K.
ALI, W.
AZIZ, J. A.
BARI, A. J.
HYAT, S.
ZIAI, K. H.

UNIVERSITY OF ENGINEERING AND TECHNOLOGY, TAXILA

Taxila 47050, Punjab
Telephone: (596) 9314216
Fax: (596) 9047420
E-mail: registrar@uettaxila.edu.pk
Internet: www.uettaxila.edu.pk

Vice-Chancellor: Prof. Dr HABIBULLAH JAMAL
Registrar: AFTAB AHMAD

Library of 25,000 vols

DEANS

Civil Engineering: Prof. ABDUR RAZZAQ GHUMMAN
Computer Engineering: Prof. UMAR FAROOQ (Project Dir)
Electrical Engineering: Prof. UMAR FAROOQ
Mechanical Engineering: Prof. MUKHTAR HUSSAIN SAHIR

PROFESSORS

AHMAD, S., Mechanical Engineering
AHMED, S., Civil Engineering
AMIN, M., Electrical Engineering
CHOWDHRY, M. A., Electrical Engineering
FAROOQ, U., Electrical Engineering
GHUMMAN, A. R., Civil Engineering

IQBAL ALVI, M. S., Mechanical Engineering
JAMAL, H., Electrical Engineering
JAVAID, M. A., Basic Sciences
KAMAL, M. A., Civil Engineering
KHAN, A. K., Electrical Engineering
KHAN, M. A., Mechanical Engineering
KHAN, S. A., Civil Engineering
KHUSHNOOD, S., Mechanical Engineering
NISAR, H., Civil Engineering
SAHIR, M. H., Mechanical Engineering
ZAFRULLAH, Electrical Engineering

FAISALABAD GOVERNMENT COLLEGE UNIVERSITY

Faisalabad
Telephone: (41) 9200670
Fax: (41) 9200671
E-mail: gcuf@fsd.comsats.net.pk

Founded 1897

Vice-Chancellor: Dr ASIF IQBAL
Registrar: MUHAMMAD AKRAM BHATTI.

FATIMA JINNAH WOMEN UNIVERSITY

Old Presidency, The Mall, Rawalpindi, Punjab 4600
Telephone: (51) 9271162
Fax: (51) 9271168
E-mail: fjwuadmin@comsats.net.pk
Internet: www.fjwu.edu.pk

Founded 1998
State control

Vice-Chancellor: Prof. Dr NAJMA NAJAM
Librarian: SHAZIA ISHAQ

Library of 5,000 vols.

ATTACHED RESEARCH INSTITUTES

Canadian Study Resource Center.
Center for Collaboration and Event Management.
Executive Training of Women in Higher Education Center.
Information Technology Center.
Peace and Conflict Resolution Center.
Psychological Research Center.
Women Research and Resource Center.

FEDERAL URDU UNIVERSITY FOR ARTS, SCIENCE AND TECHNOLOGY

Plot ST-1 ST-2, Block 9, Gulshan-e-Iqbal, Karachi 75300
Telephone: (21) 9243986
E-mail: info@fuuast.edu.pk
Internet: www.fuuast.edu.pk

Other campuses in Abdul Haq and Islamabad

Founded 2002

Vice-Chancellor: Dr IQBAL MOHSIN
Registrar: Prof. Dr SYED QAISER ABBAS

DEANS

Faculty of Arts, Commerce and Law (Abdul Haq): Prof. Dr ZAFAR IQBAL
Faculty of Science and Business Management (Islamabad): Dr KHAIRAT CHUDHARY
Faculty of Science and Technology (Gulshan): Prof. MUHAMMAD SAEED

GOMAL UNIVERSITY

Dera Ismail Khan, North West Frontier Province
Telephone: (961) 750235
Fax: (961) 750266
E-mail: vc@gu.edu.pk
Internet: www.gomal.edu.pk

Founded 1974
State control

Language of instruction: English
Academic year: September to June

Chancellor: THE GOVERNOR OF NWFP
Vice-Chancellor: WAZIRZADA MUHAMMAD IDREES SADDOZAI
Registrar: MUHAMMAD JAN KHAN
Librarian: ABDUL GHAFFAR KHAN

Library: see Libraries and Archives
Number of teachers: 359
Number of students: 5,570

Publication: *Gomal University Journal of Research* (2 a year)

DEANS

Faculty of Agriculture: Prof. HAJI KHALIL AHMAD
Faculty of Arts: (vacant)
Faculty of Pharmacy: Prof. Dr MUHAMMAD FARID
Faculty of Sciences: Prof. Dr AHMAD SAEED

PROFESSORS

AHMAD, H. K., Agriculture
BALOCH, J. J., Physics
KHAN, A. G., Agriculture
KHAN, A. S., Pharmacy
KHAN, I. U., Pharmacy
KHAN, K. Z., Economics
KHAN, L. U., Agriculture
KHAN, M. A., Physics
KHAN, M. F., Pharmacy
KHAN, M. K., Chemistry
KHAN, M. Q., Agriculture
KHAN, Z. A., Chemistry
QAZI, N. S., Pharmacy
SAEED, A., Biological Sciences

CONSTITUENT COLLEGES

Gomal College of Veterinary Sciences.
Law College.
University Wensam College.

ATTACHED INSTITUTES

Institute of Computing and Information Technology: Dir BASHIR AHMAD.
Institute of Education and Research: Dir (vacant).

GOVERNMENT COLLEGE UNIVERSITY

Katchery Rd, Lahore 54600, Punjab
Telephone: (42) 9213340
Fax: (42) 9213341
E-mail: registrar@gcu.edu.pk
Internet: www.gcu.edu.pk

Founded 1864

Vice-Chancellor: Dr KHALID AFTAB
Librarian: ABDUL WAHEED

Library of 156,000 vols
Number of teachers: 275
Number of students: 5,000.

HAMDARD UNIVERSITY

Madinat al-Hikmah, Shahra-e-Madinat al-Hikmah, Muhammad bin Qasim Avenue, Karachi 75600
Telephone: (21) 6996001
Internet: www.hamdard.edu

Other campuses in Faisalabad and Islamabad

Founded 1991 by the Hamdard Foundation (see Learned Societies)
Private control

Chancellor: Chief Justice (retd) AJMAL MIAN
Vice-Chancellor: Dr ISMAIL SAAD
Registrar: Col (retd) RAFIQ AHMED

Library of 400,000 vols, 1,629 manuscripts
Number of students: 5,000

DIRECTORS AND PRINCIPALS

Al-Majeed College of Eastern Medicine: HAKIM ABDUL HANNAN
Cisco Regional Academy: SHAZIA HASNIE
College of Medicine and Dentistry: Dr ALAY HASSAN ZAIDI
Institute of Education and Social Sciences: Dr ISMAIL SAAD
Institute of Information Technology: Dr ABU TURAB ALAM
Institute of Management Sciences: Dr SARWAR RIZVI
School of Law: Dr RASHID MUNIR AHMED
Usman Institute of Technology: JAMSHED UR-REHMAN

AFFILIATED INSTITUTES

Institute of Leadership and Management: internet www.ilm.edu.

Islamic International Medical College: internet www.iimc.edu.pk.

Plastic Technology Centre.

Synthetic Fibre Development and Application Centre.

HAZARA UNIVERSITY

Mansehra, North West Frontier Province
Telephone: (997) 530078
Fax: (997) 530046
E-mail: huniversity@hotmail.com
Internet: www.hu.edu.pk
Founded 2002
State control
Academic year: January to December (two semesters)
Vice-Chancellor: Prof. Dr MOHAMMAD DAUD AWAN
Registrar: Dr M. MAQBOOL AHMAD
Publications: *University Magazine and Student Activities Report, Newsletter* (quarterly)
26 Affiliated colleges.

UNIVERSITY OF HEALTH SCIENCES

Shaikh Zayed Hospital Medical Complex, Khayaban-e-Jamia, Lahore, Punjab
Telephone: (42) 9231304
Fax: (42) 9230394
Internet: www.uhs.edu.pk
Vice-Chancellor: Prof. MALIK HUSSAIN MUBBASHAR
Registrar: Prof. MUHAMMAD ZAFAR IQBAL
Vice-Chancellor: MALIK HUSSAIN MUBBASHAR
Librarian: ABID ALI GILL.

ATTACHED RESEARCH INSTITUTES

Allama Iqbal Medical College, Lahore: Principal SYED SIBIT-UL-HASAN NISHTAR.

De Montmorency College of Dentistry, Lahore: Principal Prof. Dr M. RAFIQUE CHATHA.

Nishtar Medical College, Multan: Principal Dr SHABBIR AHMED.

Punjab Medical College, Faisalabad: Principal Dr ABDUL GHAFFAR REHAN.

Quaid-i-Azam Medical College, Bhawalpur: Principal Prof. KHURSHID AHMED.

Rawalpindi Medical College: Principal Prof. Dr MUHAMMAD MUSSADIQ KHAN.

INTERNATIONAL ISLAMIC UNIVERSITY

POB 1243, Islamabad
Telephone: (51) 850751
Fax: (51) 250821
E-mail: iiui@paknet2.ptc.pk
Internet: www.iiu.edu.pk
Founded 1980, present name 1985

Academic year: September to August
Chancellor: THE PRESIDENT OF PAKISTAN
Pro-Chancellor: Dr ABDULLAH MOHSIN AL-TURKI
Rector: MALIK MERAJ KHALID
President: Prof. Dr H. M. A. LATIF SHAFIE
Vice-Presidents: Dr MAHMOOD AHMAD GHAZI (Academic), Dr WAQAR MASOOD (Planning and Administration), Dr AHMED AL-ASSAL (Resource Development)
Library: see Libraries and Archives
Number of teachers: 97
Number of students: 3,458
Publications: *Al-Dirasat Al-Islamiya* (in English, 4 a year), *Fikr-O-Nazar* (in Urdu, 4 a year), *Islamic Studies* (in English, 4 a year)

DEANS AND DIRECTORS

Faculty of Arabic: Prof. Dr RAGGA ABDUL MONEM GABR
Faculty of Shariah and Law: Dr DIAB SALEEM M. OMER
Faculty of Usuluddin: Dr MUHAMMAD ABDUL TAWWAB-HAMID
Department of Business Administration: Prof. M. AMANULLAH
Department of Computer Science: Dr KHALID RASHID
Institute of Languages: Dr KAMAL ABDUL AZIZ
School of Economics: Dr ZAHID ALIM

ATTACHED INSTITUTES

Academy for Dawah andTraining of Imams: Dir Dr ANIS AHMED.

Academy for Shariah: Dir Dr MAHMOOD AHMED GHAZI.

International Institute of Islamic Economics: Dir Dr SAYYED TAHIR.

Islamic Research Institute: Dir Dr ZAFAR ISHAQ ANSARI.

ISLAMIA UNIVERSITY BAHAWALPUR

Bahawalpur
Telephone: (621) 9250231
Fax: (621) 9250232
E-mail: vciub@mul.paknet.com.pak
Internet: iub.edu.pk
Founded 1975
State control
Languages of instruction: Urdu, English
Academic year: September to August
Chancellor: Lt-Gen. (retd) KHALID MAQBOOL
Vice-Chancellor: Prof. Dr MUNIR AKHTAR
Secretary to the Vice-Chancellor: CH. LIAQUAT ALI
Registrar: ASGHAR ALI
Librarian: MUHAMMAD IQBAL ARSHAD (acting)
Library: see Libraries and Archives
Number of teachers: 183
Number of students: 3,907
Publications: *Journal of Pure and Applied Sciences* (2 a year, English), *Mujullah Uloom-e-Islamia* (2 a year, English, Urdu and Persian)

DEANS

Faculty of Arts: Prof. Dr NAJEEB-UD-DIN JAMAL
Faculty of Islamic Learning: Prof. Dr ABDUL RASHID REHMAT
Faculty of Science: Prof. Dr MUNIR AKHTAR
University College of Engineering and Technology: Prof. Dr. SHIEKH AFTAB AHMAD (Principal, acting)

UNIVERSITY OF KARACHI

University Campus, Karachi 75270
Telephone: (21) 9243161
Fax: (21) 9243203
E-mail: vc@ku.edu.pk
Internet: www.ku.edu.pk

Founded 1951
State control
Languages of instruction: Urdu, English
Academic year: September to August
Chancellor: THE GOVERNOR OF SINDH
Vice-Chancellor: Prof. Dr PIRZADA QASIM RAZA SIDDIQUI
Registrar: Prof. Dr SIKANDAR MEHDI
Library: see Libraries
Number of teachers: 479
Number of students: 20,000
Publications: *Jareeda* (Journal of the Bureau of Composition, Compilation and Translation, annually), *Journal of Science* (2 a year), *Pakistan Journal of Botany* (2 a year), *Pakistan Journal of Nematology* (2 a year), *Pakistan Journal of Psychology* (4 a year)

DEANS

Faculty of Arts: Prof. Dr SHAMS UDDIN
Faculty of Education: Prof. Dr M. ISMAIL BROHI
Faculty of Islamic Studies: Prof. Dr ABDUL RASHID
Faculty of Law: Prof. MAMOON HUSSAIN
Faculty of Medicine: Prof. Dr TIPU SULTAN
Faculty of Pharmacy: Prof. Dr ANWAR EJAZ BEG
Faculty of Science: Prof. Dr MUHAMMAD QAISAR

PROFESSORS

Faculty of Arts:

AHMED, N., Islamic History
ANSARI, A. M. S., Urdu
ARAB, A. K., Arabic
FATIMA, N., Library and Information Science
HAQ, I., Arabic
HUMAYUN, S., Public Administration
HUSAIN, F., Sindhi
HUSAIN, S. M. A., Economics
HUSSAIN, J., General History
MEHDI, S. S., International Relations
MEMON, S., Sindhi
MIRZA, S. Q., Mass Communication
MURTAZA, M. R., Mass Communication
REHMAN, K., Sociology
SAJDIN, M., Commerce
SHAHEED, M. A., Arabic
SHAMSUDDIN, M., Mass Communication
SHERWANI, M. K., Library and Information Science
TAFHIMI, S., Persian
WAJIDI, M. A., Public Administration
WAZARAT, T. A., International Relations

Faculty of Islamic Studies:

RASHID, A., Islamic Studies
SIDDIQUI, M. A. S., Islamic Learning

Faculty of Pharmacy:

AHMED, M., Pharmacognosy
AHMED, M. A., Pharmaceutics
AHMED, S. P., Pharmacology
AHMED, T., Pharmaceutics
ALI, S. A., Pharmaceutics
BAIG, A. E., Pharmaceutics
HUSSAIN, W., Pharmaceutical Chemistry
MANZAR, K. N., Pharmaceutical Chemistry
REHMAN, S. B., Pharmacology
SAIFY, S. Z., Pharmaceutical Chemistry
SHAIKH, D., Pharmaceutics
SULTANA, N., Pharmaceutical Chemistry

Faculty of Science:

AFTAB, N., Biochemistry
AHMED, A., Applied Chemistry
AHMED, E., Statistics
AHMED, F., Physics
AHMED, I., Zoology
AHMED, I. K., Physics
AHMED, N., Genetics
AHMED, S., Botany
AKHTAR, S. K., Physics

AKHTAR, W., Physics
ALI, S. I., Applied Chemistry
ANIS, K., Physics
ANSARI, A. A., Applied Physics
ARAYN, M. S., Chemistry
ARSHAD, R., Physiology
ATHAR, H. S. A., Biochemistry
AZEEM, A., Physiology
AZHAR, A., Biochemistry
AZIZ, K., Botany
AZMATULLAH, M., Geology
BARKATI, S., Zoology
BURNI, S. M. A., Computer Science
FAHIMUDDIN, Chemistry
FARID, A., Philosophy
HALEEM, M. A., Biochemistry
HAMEED, S., Applied Chemistry
HASAN, H., Zoology
HASNAIN, S. N., Biochemistry
HASNI, S., Biochemistry
HUSAIN, V., Geology
HUSSAIN, M. R., Physics
IQBAL, M., Zoology
IQBAL, Z., Botany
JABEEN, D., Biochemistry
JAHANGIR, S., Biochemistry
JAVED, W., Zoology
KAZMI, M. A., Zoology
KAZMI, Q. B., Zoology
KAZMI, S. A., Chemistry
KAZMI, S. U., Microbiology
KHAN, A. F., Microbiology
KHAN, F., Applied Chemistry
KHAN, K. R., Physiology
KHAN, M. A., Botany
KHAN, M. ALTAF, Microbiology
KHAN, M. I., Botany
KHAN, N., Mathematics
KHANUM, A., Biochemistry
KHATOON, H., Microbiology
KHATOON, K., Botany
MAHMOOD, Z., Statistics
MALIK, A., Research Institute of Chemistry
MALIK, S. A., Chemistry
MAQSOOD, Z. T., Chemistry
MEHDI, F., Botany
MOHSIN, S. I., Geology
MUHAMMAD, I., Biochemistry
NAEEM, R. K., Mathematics
NAQVI, I. I., Chemistry
NAQVI, S. M. M. R., Physics
NAQVI, S. R. R., Chemistry
NAZAMI, S. S., Chemistry
NOOR, F., Chemistry
NUSRAT, J., Microbiology
QADEER, A., Applied Physics
QADRI, M. U., Geology
QAISER, M., Botany
QAMAR, J., Mathematics
QASIM, R., Biochemistry
QIDWAI, A. A., Physics
QIDWAI, I. M., Biochemistry
QURESHI, M. A., Physiology
QURESHI, N. M., Physiology
RAFI, F., Physiology
RAOOF, M. A., Physics
RASOOL, S. A., Microbiology
RAZZAQI, T. F., Biotechnology
REHMAN, A. U., Research Institute of Chemistry
RIZVI, N., Zoology
SAIFULLAH, S. M., Botany
SHAIKH, S. A., Geology
SHAHEEN, B., Research Institute of Chemistry
SHAMEEL, M. M., Botany
SHAMS, N., Applied Chemistry
SHAUKAT, S. S., Botany
SIDDIQUI, A. J., Statistics
SIDDIQUI, J. S., Statistics
SIDDIQUI, K. A., Physics
SIDDIQUI, N. S., Biochemistry
SIDDIQI, P. A., Zoology
SIDDIQI, P. Q. R., Physiology
SIDDIQI, R., Microbiology
SIDDIQI, S. A., Chemistry

SIDDIQI, Z., Chemistry
ULLAH, N., Geology
USMAN, M., Botany
USMANI, A. A., Chemistry
VAHIDY, A. A., Genetics
VAHIDY, R., Microbiology
YASMEN, N., Zoology
ZAIDGHAM, N. A., Geology
ZAIDI, S. A. H., Applied Chemistry
ZAIDI, S. S. H., Applied Physics
ZEENAT, I., Psychology

ATTACHED INSTITUTES

Applied Economics Research Centre: see under Research Institutes.

Centre for European Studies: Dir Dr NAVID TAHIR.

Centre of Excellence in Marine Biology: see under Research Institutes.

Centre of Excellence in Women's Studies: Dir Dr KHALIDA GHOUS.

Centre for Molecular Genetics: Dir Dr N. AHMED.

Hussein Ibrahim Jamal Research Institute of Chemistry: Dir Prof. Dr A. REHMAN.

Institute of Clinical Psychology: (vacant).

Institute of Environmental Sciences: Dir Dr M. ALTAF KHAN.

Institute of Marine Science: Dir Dr S. N. SAIF ULLAH.

M. A. H. Qadri Biological Research Centre: Dir Dr A. A. VAHIDY.

Marine Reference Collection and Research Centre: Dir Dr QUDDUSI B. KAZMI.

National Nematological Research Centre: Dir Dr M. A. MAQBOOL.

Pakistan Studies Centre: Dir Dr S. AHMED JAFFAR.

Pure and Applied Physics Research Centre: Dir Dr NAQVI RAZA MUNIR MEHDI.

Shahik Zajed Islamic Research Centre: Dir Dr M. A. SHAHEED.

There are 110 affiliated colleges

KARAKURAM INTERNATIONAL UNIVERSITY

Gilgit, North West Frontier Province

Telephone: (5811) 50440

Fax: (5811) 58245

Founded 2002

Vice-Chancellor: MUHAMMAD AZAN KHAN

Departments of Chemistry, Economics, International Relations, Mathematics and Zoology.

KOHAT UNIVERSITY OF SCIENCE AND TECHNOLOGY

Bannu Rd, off Jerma, Kohat 26000, North West Frontier Province

Telephone: (922) 554565

Fax: (922) 554556

Internet: www.kust.edu.pk

Founded 2001

Vice-Chancellor: Dr ZABTA K. SHINWARI

Registrar: Prof. Dr IHSAN ELLAHI

Director (Academic): MUNAWAR ALI SHAH

Director (Administration): Lt Col (Rtd) ABDUL KARIM

Director (Finance and Planning): MUHAMMAD ZAKIR

Librarian: MURAD ALI.

LAHORE COLLEGE FOR WOMEN UNIVERSITY

Jail Rd, Lahore 54600, Punjab

Telephone: (42) 9203072

Fax: (42) 9203077

Internet: www.lcwu.edu.pk

Founded 1922; present name and status 2002

Vice-Chancellor: Prof. Dr BUSHRA MATEEN

Number of teachers: 260

Number of students: 5,000

Faculties of Natural Sciences, Arts and Social Sciences, Islamic and Oriental Learning, Management Sciences and Technology

PROFESSORS

ALI, Y., Physics
CHEEMA, K. J., Environmental Sciences
CHEEMA, K. J., Zoology
GOHAR, K., Economics
MAHMOOD, A. S., Mathematics
MATEEN, B., Environmental Sciences
NAVQI, R. F., Fine Arts
NAWAZ, R., Islamic Studies

LAHORE UNIVERSITY OF MANAGEMENT SCIENCES

Opposite Sector U, DHA, Lahore Cantt., Lahore 54792

Telephone: (42) 5722670

Fax: (42) 5722591

E-mail: admissions@lums.edu.pk

Internet: www.lums.edu.pk

Founded 1985

Private control

Language of instruction: English

Academic year: September to June

Chancellor: PRESIDENT OF PAKISTAN (ex-officio)

Pro-Chancellor: SYED BABAR ALI

Pro-Vice-Chancellor: Dr SYED ZAHOOR HASSAN

Rector: ABDUL RAZAK DAWOOD

Librarian: MUHAMMAD RAMZAN

Library of 47,000 vols

Number of teachers: 123

Number of students: 1,750

Publications: *Asian Journal of Management Cases* (2 a year), *LUMS Business Recorder* (annually), *PLUMS* (annually)

DEANS

School of Arts and Sciences: Dr ANWAR KURSHID

Graduate School of Business Administration: Dr EHSAN UL-HAQUE

PROFESSORS

ALI, I., Business History and Business Policy
BABRI, H. A., Computer Science
BEG, I., Mathematics
GHANI, J. A., Strategy and Marketing
HASSAN, S. Z., Management Information Systems and Management of Technology
IQBAL, M. A., Computer Science and Mathematics
KHURSHID, A., Technology and Organizational Management
MAUD, M. A., Computer Science
NASIM, A., Business–Government Relations
SARWAR, S. M., Computer Science
SIPRA, N., Finance
ZAMAN, A., Econometrics
ZAMAN, A., Mathematics

LIAQUAT UNIVERSITY OF MEDICAL AND HEALTH SCIENCES

Jamshoro, Sindh

Telephone: (221) 772230

Fax: (221) 771303

E-mail: lumhs@hyd.paknet.com.pk

Internet: www.lumhs.edu.pk

Founded 1881; present name and status 2001

Vice-Chancellor: Prof. Dr Jan Mohammad A. Memon

Registrar: Prof. Abdul Latif Soomro

Publication: *Bulletin*

DEANS

Faculty of Basic Medical Sciences: Prof. Shaheen Shah

Faculty of Community Medicine and Public Health Sciences: Prof. Rafique Ahmed Soomro

Faculty of Dentistry: Prof. Rafque Ahmed Memon

Faculty of Medicine and Allied Sciences: Prof. Allah Bachayo Memon

Faculty of Surgery and Allied Sciences: Prof. Ghulam Ali Memon

UNIVERSITY OF MALAKAND

Chakdara, Dir, Malakand, North West Frontier Province

Telephone: (936) 763441

Fax: (936) 763491

Founded 2001

Vice-Chancellor: Prof. Dr Jehandar Shah

Registrar: Amir Zada Asad.

MEHRAN UNIVERSITY OF ENGINEERING AND TECHNOLOGY

Jamshoro, Sindh

Telephone: (221) 771197

Fax: (221) 771382

Internet: www.muet.edu.pk

Founded 1963 as constituent college of University of Sindh; present status 1977

State control

Language of instruction: English

Academic year: October to August

Chancellor: The Governor of Sindh

Vice-Chancellor: Dr Abdul Qadeer Khan Rajput

Registrar: Mehar Ali Halepota

Library: see Libraries and Archives

Number of teachers: 270

Number of students: 3,702

Publication: *Research Journal of Engineering and Technology* (quarterly)

DEANS

Faculty of Architecture: Dr Dost Ali Khowaja

Faculty of Engineering: Dr A. A. Abro

Faculty of Technology: Dr A. A. Abro

DIRECTORS

Institute of Irrigation and Drainage Engineering: Prof. Shah Nawaz Chandio

Institute of Science and Technology Development: Dr S. M. Qureshi

Postgraduate Studies: Dr Ghous Bux Khaskeli

Research and Development: (vacant)

Computer Centre: Shujauddin Siddiqui

Continuing Education: Dr Mujeebuddin Memon

Industrial Liaison: Dr Abdul Karim Baloch

There are two affiliated colleges

NATIONAL TEXTILE UNIVERSITY

Sheikhupura Rd, Faisalabad 37610, Punjab

Telephone: (41) 753743

Fax: (41) 753714

E-mail: info@ntu.edu.pk

Internet: www.ntu.edu.pk

Founded 1954 as Institute of Textile Technology; renamed National College of Textile Engineering 1965; present name and status 2002

Vice-Chancellor: Vice Adml (Retd) Masood Mazhar Biabani

Rector: Tariq Mehmood

Dean: Dr Muhammad Zuber

Number of teachers: 35

Number of students: 600

CHAIRS OF SUBJECTS

Applied Sciences: Javaid Iqbal

Fabric Manufacturing: Fazal Mahmood

Garment Manufacturing: Fazal Mahmood

Textile Chemistry: Dr Muhammad Zuber

Yarn Manufacturing: Baland Iqbal

NATIONAL UNIVERSITY OF MODERN LANGUAGES

Sector H-9, Islamabad 44000

Telephone: (51) 9257636

Fax: (51) 9257679

E-mail: numlpk@apollo.net.pk

Internet: www.numl.edu.pk

Founded 1970; present name and status 2000

Academic year: January to December (two semesters)

Rector: Brig. Dr Aziz Ahmad Khan

Director (Academic Affairs): Riasat Hussain

Director (Administration): Muhammad Yasin

Director (Library): Muhammad Abbas

Director (Planning and Co-ordination): Kamran Jahangir

Director (Project Director): Col Muhammad Naveed

Number of teachers: 315

Number of students: 12,422

Publications: *Research Magazine* (2 a year), *Daryaft* (annually), *Takhleeqi Adab* (annually).

NATIONAL UNIVERSITY OF SCIENCE AND TECHNOLOGY

Tamiz-ud-din Rd, POB 297, Rawalpindi, Punjab

Telephone: (51) 9271581

Fax: (51) 9271577

E-mail: info@nust.edu.pk

Internet: www.nust.edu.pk

Other campuses in Islamabad, Karachi and Risalpur

Rector: Syed Shujaat Hussain

Publication: *Newsletter* (monthly)

Colleges: Aeronautical Engineering (Risalpur), Civil Engineering (Risalpur), Electrical and Mechanical Engineering (Rawalpindi), Marine Engineering (Karachi), Medical Sciences (Rawalpindi), Telecommunication Engineering (Rawalpindi).

UNIVERSITY INSTITUTES

Centre for Cyber Technology and Spectrum Management: 166-A St 9, Chaklala Scheme-III, Rawalpindi; tel. (51) 9267224; fax (51) 9267223.

Institute of Environmental Science and Engineering: Tamiz-ud-din Rd, Rawalpindi; tel. (51) 9271597; fax (51) 9271597.

Institute of Geographical Information System: 112-A St 37, Sector F-10/1, Islamabad; tel. (51) 9267241; fax (51) 9267245; internet www.igis.edu.pk.

Institute of Information Technology: 166-A St 9, Chaklala Scheme-III, Rawalpindi; tel. (51) 9280443; fax (51) 9280782; internet www.niit.edu.pk.

Institute of Management Sciences: Tamiz-ud-din Rd, Rawalpindi; tel. (51) 9271610; fax (51) 9271610.

International Institute for Peace and Conflict Resolution: 112-A St 37, Sector F-10/1, Islamabad; tel. (21) 5892055; fax (51) 9267224; Hon. Chair. Javed Jabbar.

National Institute of Transportation: Risalpur; tel. (923) 631211; fax (923) 631211.

Technology Incubation Centre: 112-B St 37, Sector F-10/1, Islamabad; tel. (51) 9267241; fax (51) 9267245; internet www.tic.org.pk.

NED UNIVERSITY OF ENGINEERING AND TECHNOLOGY

University Rd, Karachi 75270

Telephone: (21) 9243261

Fax: (21) 9243255

E-mail: vc@neduet.edu.pk

Internet: www.neduet.edu.pk

Founded 1922 as NED Government Engineering College, university status 1977

Language of instruction: English

Academic year: February to December

Chancellor: The Governor of Sindh

Vice-Chancellor: Engr Abul Kalam

Pro-Vice Chancellor: Prof. Dr Shamsul Haque

Registrar: Prof. Dr Sarosh Hashmat Lodi

Library: see Libraries and Archives

Number of teachers: 150

Number of students: 4,000

Publications: *NED University of Engineering and Research* (2 a year), *Research Journal* (4 a year), *Versity News* (monthly)

DEANS

Civil Engineering and Architecture: Prof. Dr Sahibzada Farooq Ahmed Rafeeqi

Electrical and Computer Engineering: Prof. Dr Shahid Hafeez Mirza

Mechanical and Manufacturing Engineering: Prof. Dr Nazimuddin Qureshi

Science, Technology and Humanities: Dr Mahmood Khan Pathan

PROFESSORS

Ahmad, A., Mechanical Engineering

Ahmed, S. F., Civil Engineering

Ahsan, P. F., Civil Engineering

Altaf, T., Electrical Engineering

Hussain, S. G., Electrical Engineering

Khan, A. A., Mathematics and Sciences

Khan, A. S., Civil Engineering

Mahmood, K., Mechanical Engineering

Mahmood, M., Mechanical Engineering

Mirza, S. H., Computer Systems Engineering

Qureshi, N., Mechanical Engineering

Shaikh, N., Electrical Engineering

Siddiqui, A. A., Computer Systems Engineering

Soomro, A. G., Mechanical Engineering

AFFILIATED COLLEGES

Dawood College of Engineering and Technology: see under Colleges.

Government College of Technology: SITE, Karachi; Principal Prof. Rasheed Ahmad Khan.

ATTACHED INSTITUTES

Institute of Environmental Engineering and Research: Chair. Saeed Ahmed Khan.

Institute of Industrial Electronics Engineering: Principal Eng. S. A. Rizvi.

Institute of Material Sciences and Research: Principal Moinuddin Ali Khan.

KANUPP Institute of Nuclear Power Engineering: Principal Dr Ansar Pervaiz.

NORTH WEST FRONTIER PROVINCE AGRICULTURAL UNIVERSITY

Peshawar

Telephone: (91) 9216399

Fax: (91) 9216520

E-mail: ayazjan@hotmail.com
Internet: www.aup.edu.pk
Founded 1981
Language of instruction: English
Academic year: January to December

Chancellor: M. ARIF BANGASH
Vice-Chancellor: YAR MUHAMMAD KHAN
Registrar: MALIK ARSHAD SALIM
Librarian: ATTAULLAH

Library of 79,000 vols
Number of teachers: 160
Number of students: 1,452

Publications: *Journal of Development Studies* (irregular), *Sarhad Journal of Agriculture* (every 2 months)

DEANS

Faculty of Animal Husbandry: Prof. S. IQBAL SHAH
Faculty of Crop Production Sciences: Prof. Dr SAEEDUL HASSAN
Faculty of Crop Protection Sciences: Prof. Dr SHER HASSAN
Faculty of Nutrition Sciences: J. K. KHALIL
Faculty of Rural Social Sciences: YAR MUHAMMAD KHAN

CHAIRMEN

AHMAD, S., Plant Pathology
AMJAD, M., Animal Nutrition
ASRAR, M., Agricultural Mechanization
BAYAN, A., Islamic and Pakistan Studies
CHISTI, A. F., Agricultural Economics and Rural Sociology
FIDA, M., English
HATAM, M., Agronomy
HUSSAIN, N., Plant Protection
HUSSAIN, T., Agricultural Chemistry
HUSSAIN, Z., Physics, Mathematics and Computer Science
JAMAL, M., Water Management
KHAN, A., Human Nutrition
KHAN, R., Food Science and Technology
KHATTAK, R. A., Soil Science
MARWAT, K. B., Plant Breeding and Genetics
MIAN, M. A., Poultry Science
MUHAMMAD, W., Horticulture
SHAHID, M., Entomology
SYED, M. D., Livestock Management

ATTACHED INSTITUTE

Institute of Development Studies: f. 1981; Dir J. B. KHAN.

NORTH WEST FRONTIER PROVINCE UNIVERSITY OF ENGINEERING AND TECHNOLOGY

POB 814, University Campus, Peshawar 25120
Telephone: (91) 9216493
Fax: (91) 9216663
E-mail: uetp2003@yahoo.com
Internet: www.nwfpuet.edu.pk

Founded 1980
Language of instruction: English
Academic year: November to September

Chancellor: KHALIL-UR-REHMAN
Vice-Chancellor: IMTIAZ HUSSAIN GILLANI
Registrar: Lt-Col IMTIAZ AHMAD DURRANI
Dean: Prof. ABDUL JABBAR
Librarian: ABDUR RASHID

Library of 85,000 vols
Number of teachers: 244
Number of students: 2,515

Publication: *Journal of Engineering and Applied Sciences* (2 a year)

HEADS OF TEACHING DEPARTMENTS

Agricultural Engineering: Dr ZAHID MAHMOOD
Architecture: Prof. FAZAL KHALIQ

Basic Science and Islamiat: Prof. KHALID PERVES
Chemical Engineering: Prof. ABDUL JABBER
Civil Engineering: Prof. FAZLE KHALIQ
Computer Software Engineering: Prof. Dr MUHAMMAD SIDDIQUE
Electrical and Electronics Engineering: Prof. HAIDER ZAMAN
Mechanical Engineering: Dr M. A. IRFAN MUFTI
Mining Engineering: Dr KHAN GUL JADOON

ATTACHED RESEARCH INSTITUTE

Center for Computer Information System Engineering (CCISE): Dir Dr NAEEM ARBAB.

UNIVERSITY OF PESHAWAR

Peshawar, NWFP
Telephone: (91) 9216701
Fax: (91) 9216470
E-mail: vice_chancellor@upesh.edu.pk
Internet: www.upesh.edu

Founded 1950
State control
Languages of instruction: Urdu, Pashto
Languages of instruction: English, Persian, Arabic
Academic year: September to June

Chancellor: THE GOVERNOR OF THE NORTH WEST FRONTIER PROVINCE
Vice-Chancellor: Lt. Gen. (rtd) MUMTAZ GUL
Director of Planning and Development: IFTIKHAR HUSSAIN KHAN
Registrar: SHER BAHADUR (acting)
Provost: Dr IMTIAZ AHMED
Librarian: MOHAMMAD IBRAR

Library: see Libraries and Archives
Number of teachers: 583
Number of students: 18,500

Publications: *Geological Bulletin* (annually), *Journal of Humanities and Social Sciences* (annually), *Journal of Law and Society* (annually), *Peshawar University Review* (annually)

DEANS

Faculty of Arts: Prof. Dr GHULAM TAQI BANGASH
Faculty of Islamic and Oriental Studies: Prof. Dr QIBLA AYAZ
Faculty of Life and Environmental Sciences: Prof. Dr HAROON UR RASHID
Faculty of Management and Information Sciences: Prof. Dr ABDUL QAIYUM
Faculty of Numerical and Physical Sciences: Prof. Dr MUHAMMAD IQBAL
Faculty of Social Sciences: Prof. AHMAD ALI

PROFESSORS

ABBASI, J. A., Geology
ADEEL, M. A., Institute of Education and Research
ALI, A., Law
ALI, T., Archaeology
AYAZ, Q., Islamic Studies
BANGASH, G. T., History
GILANI, S. Z., Education (Psychology)
HANIF, M., Islamic Studies
HUSSAIN, F., Biotechnology
IQBAL, M., Statistics
JAN, A.-H., Zoology
JAN, M. Q., Geology
KHAN, A., Geography
KHAN, M., Chemistry
KHAN, M. A., Chemistry
KHAN, M. J., Geology
KHAN, Z. A., Mathematics
KHATTAK, N. S., Electronics
MAJID, M., Geology
MIAN, I., Geology
NAWAZ, A., Geography
NASIR, G., Persian

NOOR, I., Mathematics
QAZI, S., Islamic Studies
RAFIQ, M., Geology
RAHMAN, C., English
RAHMAN, F., Physics
RAHMAN, M., English
RASHID, H., Chemistry
REHANA, N., Chemistry
REHMAN, S. S., Environmental Sciences
RIAZ, M., Physics
RIAZ, M. N., Psychology
SHAH, R., Pashto
SULAIMAN, M., Zoology

CONSTITUENT COLLEGES

Centre of Excellence in Geology: Peshawar; Dir Prof. Dr MUHAMMAD ASIF KHAN.
Centre of Excellence in Physical Chemistry: Peshawar; Dir Dr S. MUSTAFA.
College of Home Economics: University of Peshawar; f. 1954; Principal Dr SIMIN MASOOD.
Institute of Education and Research: Peshawar; f. 1980; Dir RAUF JAMIL.
Islamia College: Peshawar; f. 1913; Principal AJMAL KHAN.
Jinnah College for Women: Peshawar; f. 1964; Principal Prof. Dr NASEEM REHANA MUSTAFA.
Quaid-e-Azam College of Commerce: Peshawar; f. 1962; Principal IKHTIAR MUHAMMAD.
Shaikh Zayed Islamic Centre: Peshawar; Dir Prof. Dr ABDUL GHAFOOR.

ATTACHED INSTITUTES

Area Study Centre: Peshawar; f. 1976; Dir Dr AZMAT HAYAT KHAN.
Pakistan Study Centre: Dir PERVAZ AHMAD KHAN TORU.
Pashto Academy: see under Learned Societies.

There are 88 affiliated colleges

UNIVERSITY OF THE PUNJAB

Quaid-e-Azam Campus, Lahore 54590
Telephone: (42) 9231102
Fax: (42) 9231103
E-mail: registrar@pu.edu.pk
Internet: www.pu.edu.pk

Founded 1882
State control
Languages of instruction: Urdu, English
Academic year: begins September

Chancellor: THE GOVERNOR OF THE PUNJAB
Vice-Chancellor: Lt-Gen. (retd) ARSHAD MAHMOOD
Pro-Vice-Chancellor (vacant)
Registrar: Col (retd) MASUD-UL HAQ

Library: see Libraries and Archives
Number of teachers: 381
Number of students: 10,047

Publications: various faculty and institute bulletins

DEANS

Faculty of Arts: Prof. Dr ABDUL RAUF BUTT
Faculty of Chemical Engineering and Technology: Prof. Dr M. ARIF BUTT
Faculty of Commerce: Prof. M. AZHAR IKRAM
Faculty of Education: Prof. Dr MUHAMMAD ZAFAR IQBAL
Faculty of Islamic and Oriental Learning: Prof. Dr M. AKRAM CHAUDHARY
Faculty of Law: Prof. Dr DIL MUHAMMAD MALIK
Faculty of Medicine and Dentistry: (vacant)
Faculty of Pharmacy: (vacant)
Faculty of Science: Prof. Dr MUJAHID KAMRAN

PROFESSORS

Faculty of Arts (Quaid-e-Azam Campus, Lahore; tel. (42) 9231167; e-mail dean.arts@pu.edu.pk; internet www.pu.edu.pk/arts):

ABID, M., Pakistan Studies Centre
ABID, Q., History
AHMAD, A., Philosophy
AHMAD, N., Philosophy
AHSAN, A. S., Research Society of Pakistan
BUTT, A. R., Economics
CHAUDHRY, M. A., Economics
GILL, S. A., History
HAFEEZ, M., Philosophy
HASNAT, S. F., Political Science
JABEEN, N., Administrative Sciences
JADOON, M. Z. I., Administrative Sciences
JAVED, M. A., Sports Sciences and Physical Education
JULLANDHRY, M. S., Mass Communication
MALIK, M. E., Business Administration
MALIK, M. H., Social Sciences
MIRZA, M. S., Women Studies
SHEIKH, M. D., Mass Communication
SIRAJUDDIN, S. S., English Language and Literature
ZAKAR, M. Z., Sociology

Faculty of Chemical Engineering and Technology (Quaid-e-Azam Campus, Lahore; tel. (42) 9230343; fax (42) 9231159; e-mail dean.engg@pu.edu.pk; internet www.pu.edu.pk/engineering):

AHMAD, J.
AKHTAR, N. A.
BUTT, M. A.
BUTT, M. T. Q.
DILAWARI, A. H.
NAWAZ, S.
RIZVI, S. Z. H.

Faculty of Commerce (Quaid-e-Azam Campus, Lahore; tel. (42) 9231154; fax (42) 9231259; e-mail dean.commerce@pu.edu.pk; internet www.pu.edu.pk/commerce):

ALI, L.
BUTT, Z. A.
CHAUDHARY, N. A.
SAEED, K. A.

Faculty of Education (Quaid-e-Azam Campus, Lahore; tel. (42) 9231264; fax (42) 9231156; e-mail dean.education@pu.edu.pk; internet www.pu.edu.pk/education):

HAMEED, A.
IQBAL, M. Z.
KHALID, M. I.
KHAN, Z. A.
MIRZA, M. S.
ZAIDI, S. N. R.

Faculty of Islamic and Oriental Learning (Allama Iqbal Campus, Lahore; tel. (42) 9210837; fax (42) 9210837; e-mail dean.iol@pu.edu.pk; internet www.pu.edu.pk/islamic):

AKHTAR, H. M., Islamic Studies
CHAUDHARY, M. A., Arabic
FATIMA, S., Islamic Studies
HASAN, M., Urdu
HASHMI, R., Urdu
KHAN, S. A., Urdu
MOEEN, M., Arabic
SHAH, M. A., Iqbal Studies
SHAUKAT, J., Islamic Studies

Faculty of Law (Quaid-e-Azam Campus, Lahore; tel. (42) 9231276; fax (42) 9231278; e-mail dean.law@pu.edu.pk; internet www.pu.edu.pk/law):

MALIK, D. M.
NAEEM, M.

Faculty of Pharmacy (Allama Iqbal Campus, Lahore; tel. (42) 9211617; e-mail dean.pharmacy@pu.edu.pk; internet www.pu.edu.pk/pharmacy):

RIAZ, M.

Faculty of Science (Quaid-e-Azam Campus, Lahore; tel. (42) 9231162; fax (42) 9230242; e-mail dean.science@pu.edu.pk; internet www.pu.edu.pk/science):

ABBASI, G. Q., Mathematics
ABDULLAH, T., Solid State Physics
AHMAD, Z., Geology
AKHTAR, M. W., Biochemistry and Biotechnology
AKHTER, A. S., Statistics
ALEEM, F., High Energy Physics
ANWAR, C. J., Chemistry
ASGHAR, R., Business and Information Technology
AZHAR, S., Business and Information Technology
BHATTI, S. A., Mathematics
BUTT, A. R., Business and Information Technology
DIN, S., Business and Information Technology
DIN, S., Mathematics
FAROOQ, U., Geology
GHAZANFAR, M., Geology
GULZAR, F., Geography
HAFEEZ, M., Business and Information Technology
HASNAIN, S., Botany
IDREES, M., Business and Information Technology
IKRAM, N., Solid State Physics
IQBAL, J., Chemistry
JAMAL, K., Business and Information Technology
KAMRAN, M., Physics
KHAN, Z. A., Business and Information Technology
LATIF, S., Business and Information Technology
MANSOOR, G. D., Business and Information Technology
NAZAR, F. M., Solid-State Physics
RAO, A. A., Business and Information Technology
RASHID, K. H., High-Energy Physics
RAZA, A., Business and Information Technology
RIAZUDDIN, S., Advanced Molecular Biology
SHAKOORI, A. R., Microbiology and Molecular Genetics
SIDDIQI, S. A., Solid State Physics
SOHAIL, M., Business and Information Technology
SOHAIL, S., Business and Information Technology
ZAIDI, N. R., Business and Information Technology

Research Departments:

AHSAN, A. R. S., Research Society of Pakistan
AKRAM, S. M., Iqbaliyat
ALEEM, F., Centre for High Energy Physics
ALI, M., Space Sciences
ANWAR, J., Institute of Chemistry
ANWAR, M., Social Sciences Research Centre
ARIF, M., Urdu Encyclopaedia of Islam
FAROOQ, U., Institute of Geology
GILL, S. A., South Asian Study Centre
JADOON, M. Z. I., Institute of Administrative Sciences
JAMSHAID, M., College of Pharmacy
MALIK, D. M., University Law College
MALIK, M. E., Institute of Business Administration
MIRZA, M., Institute of Education and Research
NAZAR, F. M., Centre for Solid State Physics
RAHMAN, N. K., Centre for Clinical Psychology
SHAUKAT, J., Sheikh Zayed Islamic Centre
ZAIDI, H. S., College of Arts and Design

ATTACHED INSTITUTES AND CONSTITUENT COLLEGES

College of Arts and Design: Allama Iqbal Campus, Lahore; f. 1940; Principal HASAN SHAHNAWAZ ZAIDI.

College of Pharmacy: Allama Iqbal Campus, Lahore; f. 1944; Principal Dr MUHAMMAD JAMSHAID.

Hailey College of Banking and Finance: Lahore; f. 2003; Principal Prof. Dr KHAWAJA AMJAD SAEED.

Hailey College of Commerce: Lahore; f. 1927; Principal Prof. NAZIR AHMAD CHAUDHARY.

Institute of Administrative Sciences: Lahore; f. 1962; Dir Dr MUHAMMAD ZAFAR IQBAL JADOON.

Institute of Business and Information Technology: Lahore; f. 2001; Dir Prof. Dr NAYYAR RAZA ZAIDI.

Institute of Biochemistry and Biotechnology: Lahore; f. 1997; Dir Dr MUHAMMAD WAHEED AKHTAR.

Institute of Business Administration: Lahore; f. 1972; Dir Prof. Dr MUHAMMAD EHSAN MALIK.

Institute of Chemical Engineering and Technology: Lahore; f. 1917; Dir Prof. Dr MUHAMMAD ARIF BUTT.

Institute of Chemistry: Lahore; f. 1923; Dir Dr C. JAMIL ANWAR.

Institute of Education and Research: Lahore; f. 1960; Dir Prof. Dr MUNAWAR MIRZA.

Institute of Environmental Science: Lahore; f. 2000; Dir Dr IFTIKHAR HUSSAIN BALOCH.

Institute of Geology: Lahore; f. 1951; Dir Prof. UMAR FAROOQ.

Institute of Statistics: Lahore; f. 1950; Dir Dr SHAHID KAMAL.

Punjab University College of Information Technology: Allama Iqbal Campus, Lahore; f. 1987; Principal Dr MUHAMMAD ANWAR-UR-REHMAN PASHA.

University Law College: Lahore; f. 1968; Dir Dr DIL MUHAMMAD MALIK.

University Oriental College: Allama Iqbal Campus, Lahore; f. 1882; Principal Dr MAZHAR MOEEN.

QUAID-E-AWAM UNIVERSITY OF ENGINEERING, SCIENCES AND TECHNOLOGY

Nawabshah 67480, Sindh

Telephone: (241) 9370373
Fax: (241) 9370367
E-mail: info@quest.edu.pk
Internet: www.quest.edu.pk
State control

Vice-Chancellor: Prof. ANWAR AHMED JUNEJO
Registrar: MAHAR ALI HALEPOTA.

QUAID-I-AZAM UNIVERSITY

Islamabad

Telephone: (51) 827259

Founded 1965; incorporated 1967; name changed 1976

Postgraduate students only
State control
Language of instruction: English

Chancellor: THE PRESIDENT OF THE ISLAMIC REPUBLIC OF PAKISTAN
Vice-Chancellor: Dr USMAN ALI GHANI ISANI
Registrar: MANZOOR HUSSAIN SHEIKH
Librarian: MEHBOOB HUSSAIN KHAN

Library: see Libraries and Archives
Number of teachers: 195

Number of students: 3,995

Publications: *Prospectus, Scrutiny* (2 a year), *Journal of Social Science, Journal of Science* (2 a year)

DEANS

Faculty of Medicine: Dr SYED FAZLE HADI
Faculty of Natural Sciences: Dr KHAWAJA AZAM ALI
Faculty of Social Sciences: Dr IJAZ HUSSAIN

ATTACHED INSTITUTES

Area Study Centre (US Studies).
Centre for Central Asian Studies.
Centre for Nuclear Studies (PIN-STECH).
National Institute of Historical and Cultural Research.
National Institute of Modern Languages.
National Institute of Pakistan Studies.
National Institute of Psychology.
Pakistan Institute of Medical Sciences.

UNIVERSITY OF SARGODHA

Sargodha, Punjab
Telephone: (451) 9230170
Fax: (451) 222121
Internet: www.uos.edu.pk

Founded 2002

Vice-Chancellor: Dr RIAZ AL HAQ TARIQ
Registrar: CH. MUHAMMAD YOUSUF
Teasurer: MIAN MUHAMMAD SARWAR

Number of teachers: 205
Number of students: 7,000

DEANS

Faculty of Arts and Social Sciences: Prof. Dr ISHTIAQ AHMED
Faculty of Islamic and Oriental Learning: Prof. Dr ALAMDAR HUSSAIN BUKHARI
Faculty of Science and Technology: Prof. Dr M. SAEED IQBAL

PROFESSORS

AHMED, I., Arts and Social Sciences
ALI, M., Chemistry
ARIF, S., English
BUKHARI, A., Islamic and Oriental Learning
HAQ, F., Chemistry
IQBAL, M., Science and Technology
SULTANA, N., Mathematics
TAHIR, M., Chemistry

SHAH ABDUL LATIF UNIVERSITY

Khairpur, Sindh
Telephone: (792) 9280115
Fax: (792) 9280060
E-mail: info@salu.edu.pk
Internet: www.salu.edu.pk

Founded 1975 as campus and 1987 as university
State control
Languages of instruction: English, Sindhi, Urdu
Academic year: September to June

Chancellor: THE GOVERNOR OF SINDH
Vice-Chancellor: Dr A. R. MALIK
Registrar: Prof. SYED AHMED HUSSAIN SHAH
Librarian: MUHAMMAD SALEH BHATTI

Library of 40,311 vols
Number of teachers: 186
Number of students: 4,608

Publications: *Aashikar* (research, in Sindhi, annually), *Ancient Sindh* (research, annually), *Bhittai* (research, in Sindh, annually), *The Commerce and Economic Review* (research, annually), *The Diplomat* (2 a year), *Scientific Sindh* (research, annually)

DEANS

Faculty of Arts: Prof. ABDULLAH PHULPOTO
Faculty of Commerce and Business Administration: Prof. SHAH MUHAMMAD LOHRANI
Faculty of Law: MUFTI JAMAL AHMED
Faculty of Science: Prof. K. D. SOOMRO

UNIVERSITY OF SINDH

Jamshoro 76080, District Dadu
Telephone: (221) 771363
Fax: (221) 771372
E-mail: vicechan@hyd.paknet.com.pk
Internet: www.usindh.edu.pk

Founded 1947 in Karachi
Languages of instruction: English, Urdu, Sindhi

Chancellor: THE GOVERNOR OF SINDH
Vice-Chancellor: MAZHARUL HAQ SIDDIQUI
Registrar: Prof. Dr SAEED AHMED SOOMRO
Controller of Examinations: Dr PERVAIZ AHMED PAHTAN
Director of Finance: FAIZ MUHAMMAD HINGORO
Director of Planning: MUHAMMAD HUSSAIN SHAIKH

Library: see Libraries and Archives
Number of teachers: 423
Number of students: 12,800

Publications: *Ariel* (English, annually), *Grassroot* (English, every 6 months), *Kinjhar* (Sindhi, annually), *Sindhi Arab* (Sindhi, annually), *Sindhological Studies* (English, annually), *Sindh University Journal of Education* (English, annually), *Sindh University Research Journal (Science), Sindh University Research Journal (Social Sciences)* (English, annually), *SU Bulletin* (quarterly), *Tahqiq* (Urdu, annually), *University of Sindh Arts Research Journal* (English, annually)

DEANS

Faculty of Arts: Prof. Dr KAZI KHADIM HUSSAIN
Faculty of Commerce and Business Administration: Prof. Dr ANWAR ALI SHAH G. SAYED
Faculty of Education: Prof. ASIF ALI G. KAZI
Faculty of Islamic Studies: Prof. Dr ABDUL SATTAR ANSARI
Faculty of Law: Prof. AHMED ALI SHAIKH
Faculty of Natural Sciences: Prof. ASIF ALI G. KAZI
Faculty of Social Sciences: Prof. Dr RAFIA AHMED SHAIKH

DIRECTORS

Centre for Environmental Sciences: Prof. Dr UBEDULLAH M. ABBASI
Centre for Excellence in Analytical Chemistry: Prof. Dr IQBAL AHMED BHANGAR
Centre for Health and Physical Education: YASMEEN IQBAL QURESHI
Centre for Rural Development Communication: SYED IBADULLAH RASHDI
Far East and South East Asia Study Centre: HIDAYATULLAH SOOMRO
Institute of Art and Design: Dr MUHAMMAD ALI BHATTI
Institute of Biochemistry: Prof. Dr ALLAH NAWAZ MEMON
Institute of Biotechnology and Genetic Engineering: Prof. Dr MUHAMMAD UMAR DAHOT
Institute of Business Administration: Prof. FEROZUDDIN KAZI
Institute of Chemistry: Prof. Dr MUHAMMAD YAR KHUHAWAR
Institute of Information Technology: Prof. Dr HAJI KHAN SOOMRO
Institute of Languages: Prof. Dr ABDUL GHANI SHAIKH
Institute of Mathematics and Computer Science: Prof. NOOR AHMED SHAIKH

Institute of Pharmacy: Prof. Dr MUHAMMAD USMAN MEMON
Institute of Sindhology: SHAUKAT HUSSAIN SHORO
Pakistan Study Centre: Prof. CHAND BIBI SULTANA BAKHTIARZAI
Sindh Development Studies Centre: Prof. Dr ABIDA TAHIRANI
Women Development Studies Centre: Prof. PARVEEN SHAH

PROFESSORS

Department of Botany:
ABRO, H.
AHMED, B.
HASSANI, S. S.
MEMON, A. H.
RAJPUT, M. T.
SAHITO, M. A.
SHAIKH, W.
TIRMIZI, S. A.
YASMIN, S.

Department of Comparative Religion and Islamic Culture:
BHUTTO, S.

Department of Fine Arts:
BHATTI, M. A.

Department of Muslim History:
ANSARI, A. S.
BHUTTO, M.
BUGHIO, M. M.

Department of Sindhi:
BUGHIO, M. Q.
HUSSAIN, K. K.
IMDAD, S.
KHUWAJA, N. A.

Institute of Languages:
SHAIKH, H. A. G.

ATTACHED SCHOOLS

Dr N. A. Baloch Model School, Hyderabad: Principal AKHTAR AHMED MEMON.
Syed Pannah Ali Shah Model School, Jamshoro: Principal Prof. SAHAR IMDAD.

SINDH AGRICULTURE UNIVERSITY, TANDOJAM

Tandojam District, Hyderabad, Sindh
Telephone: (221) 765870
Fax: (221) 765300
Internet: www.sau.edu.pk

Founded 1977
State control
Language of instruction: English
Academic year: October to March

Chancellor: MUHAMMAD MIAN SOOMRO (Governor of Sindh Province)
Vice-Chancellor: Dr BASHIR AHMED SHAIKH
Registrar: SYED MUHAMMAD MUQEEM SHAH RASHDI
Librarian: ABDUL LATIF ANSARI

Number of teachers: 222
Number of students: 3,930

Publications: *Pakistan Journal of Agriculture, Agricultural Engineering and Veterinary Sciences* (in English, every 6 months), *SARANG Magazine* (in English, Sindhi and Urdu, annually), *SAUNI News* (in English, Sindhi and Urdu, 4 a year), *Seerat Supplement* (in English, Sindhi and Urdu, annually), *Zarat Sindh* (4 a year)

DEANS

Faculty of Agricultural Engineering: Dr NAZIR HUSSAIN LEGHARI
Faculty of Agricultural Social Sciences: Prof AMIR ALI KADRI
Faculty of Animal Husbandry and Veterinary Sciences: Dr LAIQUE AHMED SIDDIQUI

Faculty of Crop Production: Prof. KAZI SULE-
MAN MEMON
Faculty of Crop Protection: Dr SHAFI MUHAM-
MAD NIZAMANI

PROFESSORS

ABRO, G. H., Entomology
ABRO, H. K., Plant Breeding and Genetics
ANSARI, N. N., Poultry Husbandry
ARAIN, M. H., Plant Pathology
BALOCH, A. F., Horticulture
BALOCH, G. M., Animal Nutrition
BHUTTO, H. B., Irrigation and Drainage
BURIRO, U. A., Agronomy
CHANDIO, B. A., Land and Water Manage-
ment
CHANG, M. A., Plant Breeding and Genetics
CHANNA, A. N., Plant Physiology and Bio-
chemistry
DEHO, N. A., Horticulture
DEVERAJANI, B. T., Land and Water Manage-
ment
JAKHARO, A. A., Soil Science
KADRI, A. A., English
KALHORO, A. B., Surgery and Obstetrics
KHAN, M. M., Entomology
KUMBAHAR, M. I., Animal Breeding and
Genetics
KUMBHAR, M. B., Plant Breeding and Genet-
ics
LARIK, A. S., Plant Breeding and Genetics
LEGHARI, N. H., Farm Power and Machinery
LOHAR, M. K., Entomology
MAHAR, S., Farm Power and Machinery
MEMON, K. S., Soil Science
MEMON, M. A., Animal Physiology and Bio-
chemistry
MEMON, N. A., Land and Water Management
MEMON, R. A., Agricultural Education Exten-
sion and Short Courses
MIRBAHAR, K. B., Animal Reproduction
MIRBAHAR, R. B., Plant Physiology and
Biochemistry
MIRJAT, M. S., Irrigation and Drainage
MUGHAL, A. Q., Farm Power and Machinery
NENWANI, K. L., Soil Science
NIZAMANI, S. M., Plant Protection
PARDEHI, M., Anatomy and Histology
PATHAN, M. A., Plant Pathology
PHULLAN, M. S., Parasitology
PHULPOTO, P. B., Agricultural Economics
PUNO, H. K., Soil Science
QAYYUN KHAN, S. M., Agronomy
RAHU, G. M., Entomology
RAJPER, M. M., Biotechnology
RIZVI, N.-UL-H., Entomology
SAIF, M. S., Soil Science
SHAH, A. J., Plant Breeding and Genetics
SHAIKH, B. A., Animal Physiology and Bio-
chemistry
SIDDIQUI, L. A., Veterinary Microbiology
SIYAL, N. B., Soil Science
SOOMRO, A. L., Soil Science

SOOMRO, M. S., Energy and Environment
TNIO, K., Agronomy
WAGGAN, M. R., Soil Science

UNIVERSITY OF VETERINARY AND ANIMAL SCIENCES

Syed Abdul Qadir Jillani Rd, Lahore 54600,
Punjab

Telephone: (42) 9211374
Fax: (42) 9211461
E-mail: helpline@uvas.edu.pk
Internet: www.uvas.edu.pk

Founded 1882; present name and status 2002
Vice-Chancellor: Prof. Dr MANZOOR AHMAD
Registrar: ATTIQUE AHMAD
Librarian: MIAN MUHAMMAD ILYAS

DEANS

Faculty of Animal Production and Technol-
ogy: Prof. Dr TALAT NASEER PASHA
Faculty of Biosciences: Prof. Dr MUHAMMAD
ASHRAF
Faculty of Fisheries and Wildlife: Prof. Dr
MUHAMMAD NAEEM KHAN
Faculty of Livestock Business Management:
Prof. Dr MUHAMMAD AKRAM MUNEER
Faculty of Veterinary Sciences: Prof. Dr
MUHAMMAD AKRAM MUNEER

Colleges

**Dawood College of Engineering and
Technology:** M. A. Jinnah Rd, Karachi
74800; tel. (21) 9231195; fax (21) 9230710; f.
1962; library: 30,269 vols; 70 teachers; 1,451
students; Principal Dr MUHAMMAD SALEEM
CHAUDHRY.

Government College of Technology:
Rasul, Mandi Baha-ud-Din, Punjab; tel. and
fax (456) 553216; f. 1912; diploma and degree
courses in technology and civil engineering;
library: 25,076 vols; 90 teachers; 1,200
students; Principal PARVEZ AKHTAR.

Government Polytechnic Institute:
Sialkot; three-year diploma courses in electrical, mechanical, civil engineering, auto
and diesel technologies; library: 12,999 vols.

Jinnah Postgraduate Medical Centre:
Government of Pakistan, Karachi 75510;
tel. (21) 9201300; fax (21) 9201370; f. 1958;
provides postgraduate training and education (including to doctorate) in the basic
medical subjects, leading potentially to Membership of the College of Physicians and
Surgeons (FCPS, MCPS) of Pakistan; also
degrees in medical technology, occupational
therapy and physiotherapy, diplomas in
general and postgraduate nursing, and other

full-time certificate courses; library: 19,000
books, 21,000 bound periodicals, 500,000
loose periodicals; Dir Dr ABDUL SHAKOOR
QAZI; publ. *Annals* (quarterly).

**National College of Textile Engineering,
Faisalabad:** Chak No. 203/R.B. Mananwala,
Sheikhpura Rd, Faisalabad; tel. (41) 753741;
fax (41) 751714; e-mail tcdc@isb.comsats.net
.pk; departments: spinning, weaving, dyeing,
bleaching, finishing, printing, knitting.

Pakistan Administrative Staff College:
Shahrah-i-Quaid-i-Azam, Lahore; tel. (42)
306367; fax (42) 306368; f. 1960; training in
administrative management for senior
executives from govt and public enterprises,
private sector Commonwealth and third
world countries; also research and publications on the subject; consultancy and advisory service in public administration; library:
see Libraries; Principal MUHAMMAD PARVEZ
MASUD; publ. *Pakistan Administration* (2 a
year).

**Pakistani Swedish Institute of Technol-
ogy:** Landhi, GPO Box 186, Karachi 22; f.
1955; training in electrical, mechanical,
woodworking, welding and clothing technology; library: 20,000 vols; 35 teachers; Dir
IMAM ALI SOOMRO.

**Rawalpindi Government College of
Technology:** Shahrah-e-Shershah, Rawalpindi; f. 1958; three-year diploma courses in
various subjects, degree courses in electrical
power technology, electronics and communication technology; library: 22,000 vols; 1,700
students; Principal Col MUHAMMAD AFSAR;
publ. *Technician* (annually).

**Swedish Pakistani Institute of Technol-
ogy:** Gujrat 50700; tel. (433) 524819; fax
(433) 524819; e-mail spitgrtpk@hotmail.com;
f. 1966; three-year diploma courses in electrical engineering, mechanical engineering,
electronics, instrumentation, foundry, pattern making, metallurgy and welding technology, auto and diesel technology,
automation and control technology; one-
year post-diploma course in biomedical technology; 46 teachers; 593 students; Principal
MIR MUHAMMAD YUNUS.

Textile Institute of Pakistan: *City campus*: P.E.C.H.S., Karachi 75400; *Bin Qasim
campus*: EZ/1/P-8, Eastern Zone, Bin Qasim
Karachi; tel. (21) 4549734 (City); tel. (21)
4750611 (Bin Qasim); fax (21) 4533525
(City); e-mail info@tip.edu.pk; internet www
.tip.edu.pk; f. 1994; degree programmes:
textile science, textile design technology,
textile mangagement and marketing, textile
technology; facilities: 2 science laboratories, 3
textile laboratories (spinning, weaving wet
processing), computer laboratories; library:
4,000 books, journals.

PALAU

The Higher Education System

The Republic of Palau's independence in 1994, under a Compact of Free Association with the USA, marked the end of the US-administered Trust Territory of the Pacific Islands, established in 1947. The Ministry of Education is the responsible body of higher education. The Palau Scholarship Program assists those students who wish to pursue their post-secondary education abroad but intend to return to Palau. The Palau Community College (founded in 1993) is accredited by the Western Association of Schools and Colleges (USA). In 2005 there were an estimated 545 students in tertiary education. The Ministry of Education Bureau of Curriculum and Program Development is responsible for providing adult and community education.

Learned Society

NATURAL SCIENCES

Biological Sciences

Palau Conservation Society: POB 1811, Koror 96940; tel. 488-3993; fax 488-3990; e-mail pcs@palaunet.com; internet palau-pcs.org; f. 1994; works with the community to preserve the nation's unique natural environment and perpetuate its conservation ethic for the economic and social benefit of present and future generations of Palauans and for the enjoyment and education of all; Exec. Dir TIARE TURANG HOLM.

Research Institutes

NATURAL SCIENCES

Biological Sciences

Coral Reef Research Foundation (CRRF): POB 1765, Koror 96940; tel. 488-5123; fax 488-5513; e-mail crrf@palaunet.com; internet www.coralreefresearchfoundation.org; f. 1991 to increase knowledge of coral reefs and other tropical marine environments to allow intelligent conservation and management decisions; special emphasis on species diversity work, collection for biomedical screening, environmental monitoring, reef fish spawning biology, and innovative development of new techniques for marine research work; Dir and Pres. Dr PATRICK L. COLIN.

Palau International Coral Reef Center: POB 7086, Koror 96940; tel. 488-6950; fax 488-6951; e-mail picrc@palaunet.com; internet www.picrc.org; f. 1999 to address critical global challenges to protect marine environments and raise awareness about the importance of preserving coral reef ecosystems; centre for marine research, training and educational activities; indoor gallery displays several closed-system aquariums exhibiting marine organisms; outdoor marine park features open-system aquariums that exhibit the different plant and animal dwellers of these habitats; CEO FRANCIS M. MATSUTARO.

Libraries and Archives

Koror

Palau Congress Library: POB 8, Koror 96940; tel. 488-2507; fax 488-5653; f. 1981; 5,000 vols of committee reports, journals and legislative history on all public laws enacted by the Palau Nat. Congress; Librarian HARRY BESEBES.

Palau National Archives: POB 1886, Koror 96940; tel. 488-4720; fax 488-4502; e-mail archives@palaunet.com; internet www.palaugov.net/mincommunity/natlarch.html; f. 1988; 2,200 16-mm and 110 35-mm cartridges/rolls of microfilms processed during the Trust Territory era; Chief Archivist NAOMI NGIRAKAMERANG; publ. *Newsletter* (online, monthly).

Palau Public Library: POB 189, Koror 96940; tel. 488-2973; fax 488-2830; e-mail publiclibrary@palaumoe.net; 17,000 vols; spec. collns: Pacific area, legislative records of Palau House of Delegates, nuclear topics; Librarian BEDEBII SADANG.

Museum

Koror

Belau National Museum: POB 666, Koror 96940; Located at: Ngerbeched Hamlet, Koror; tel. 488-2265; fax 488-3183; e-mail bnm@palaunet.com; internet www.belaunationalmuseum.com; f. 1955; 4,000 cultural objects relating to anthropology, traditional and contemporary art, history and natural history, media colln of 20,000 photographic slides, 6,000 prints, negatives, films, videos and sound recordings, traditional men's meeting hall, botanical garden; library of 2,000 vols, and periodicals, maps, posters, research papers and articles; Dir and Curator FAUSTINA K. REHUHER-MARUGG.

College

Palau Community College: POB 9, Koror 96940; tel. 488-2470; fax 488-2447; e-mail alvina@palau.edu; internet www.palau.edu; f. 1969; independent, two-year post-secondary vocational/technical institution; school of arts and sciences; school of business; school of technical education; library: 26,000 items, incl. books, periodicals, govt documents, videos, maps and CD-ROMs; 34 teachers; 650 students; Pres. Dr PATRICK U. TELLEI.

PANAMA

The Higher Education System

In 1821 Panama became independent from Spain as part of Gran Colombia, declaring its separate independence in 1903. The Universidad de Panamá (founded in 1935) is the oldest university. There are four public universities, with regional centres in the provinces, and 11 private universities, including one specializing in distance learning. In 2004 there were 128,863 students enrolled in university-level education. Higher education is centralized under the authority of the Ministry of Education.

Admission to higher education is made on the basis of a specialized secondary school certificate (Bachillerato) relevant to the intended field of study. Applicants must also pass an entrance examination. Undergradautes study for four or five years for the Licenciado degree or a professional title. Following the Licenciado a further two years of study is required for the postgraduate Masters (Maestría) degree.

Technical and vocational education is offered by institutions of higher education; the leading programme of study is the Técnico, which requires two to three years of study. Adult education is administered by the Institute for Training and Utilization of Human Resources.

Learned Societies

HISTORY, GEOGRAPHY AND ARCHAEOLOGY

Academia Panameña de la Historia (Panama Academy of History): Apdo 973, Zona 1, Panama City; f. 1921; Pres. MIGUEL A. MARTÍN; Sec. ROGELIO ALFARO; publ. *Boletín*.

LANGUAGE AND LITERATURE

Academia Panameña de la Lengua (Panama Academy of Letters): Apdo 1748, Zona 1, Panama City; Located at: Calle Manuel María Icaza, esquina con Calle 50, Panama City; tel. 223-0717; fax 263-3910; e-mail aplengua@tutopia.com; corresp. of the Real Academia Española (Madrid); 4 mems; 12 elected mems; Dir PABLO PINILLA CHIARI; Sec. TOBÍAS DÍAZ BLAITRY; publ. *Boletín*.

Alliance Française: Apdo Postal 4305, Zona 5, Panama City; Located at: Calle 49, por la Avda Federico Boyd, entrando por la bolsa de valores, Bella Vista, Panama City; tel. 223-7376; fax 264-1931; e-mail alliance@cableonda.net; internet www.afpanama.org; offers courses and exams in French language and culture and promotes cultural exchange with France; attached teaching centres in David.

Research Institutes

AGRICULTURE, FISHERIES AND VETERINARY SCIENCE

Instituto de Investigación Agropecuaria de Panamá (Institute of Agricultural Research): Ciudad del Saber, Clayton, Panama City 6-4391; tel. 317-0519; fax 317-0510; f. 1975; to increase the yields and productivity of agricultural producers; establishes rules for agricultural research carried out in the public sector; advises the govt on the formulation and application of scientific policies and on agricultural technology; promotes technical training at all levels in the agricultural sector; Dir Dr REYNALDO PÉREZ-GUARDIA.

EDUCATION

Instituto para la Formación y Aprovechamiento de los Recursos Humanos (Institute for the Training and Development of Human Resources): Apdo 6337, Zona 5, Panama City; Located at: Vìa España, al lado de la agencia Thrifti Car Rental, Panama City; tel. 269-6666; fax 263-6101; e-mail ifarhu@gob.pa; internet www.ifarhu.gob.pa; f. 1965 for the development of technical training and the rational use of the country's human resources in order to improve its economic and social development; 9 regional agencies, 8 student centres and an Information and Documentation Centre (see below); Dir Gen. Licda GLORIA ROVIRA; publs *Cidinforma* (Monthly), *Orientifarhu* (4 a year), *Mujer al Cambio* (annually).

MEDICINE

Instituto Conmemorativo Gorgas de Estudios de la Salud (Gorgas Commemorative Institute of Health Research): Apdo 6991, Zona 5, Panama City; Located at: Avda Justo Arosemena entre Calle 35 y 36, Panama City; tel. 227-4111; fax 225-4366; e-mail igorgas@gorgas.gob.pa; internet www.gorgas.gob.pa; f. 1921; library of 50,000 vols; Dir Dr JORGE MOTTA; publ. *Boletín Informativo* (online, 4 a year).

NATURAL SCIENCES

Biological Sciences

Smithsonian Tropical Research Institute: Apdo Postal 0843-03092, Balboa, Ancón; Located at: Roosvelt Ave, Building 401, Tupper, Balboa, Ancón; tel. 212-8000; fax 212-8148; internet www.stri.org; f. 1923; administered by the Smithsonian Institution; researches and promotes tropical biology, education and conservation; the institute has extensive marine and terrestrial research facilities; library of 66,000 vols, 850 periodicals; Dir Dr IRA RUBINOFF.

Libraries and Archives

Panama City

Archivo Nacional: Apdo 6618, Zona 5, Panama City; Located at: Avda Perú entre Calle 31 y 32, Zona 5, 6618 Panama City; tel. 225-0944; fax 225-1937; e-mail arnapa@cwpanama.net; internet www.registro-publico.gob.pa; f. 1912; 3,400 vols; Dir FLORENCIO R. MUNOZ B.; publ. *Boletín Informativo* (2 a year).

Biblioteca de la Dirección de Estadística y Censo: Apdo 0816-01521, Panama City; tel. 210-4829; fax 210-4826; e-mail cgrdec@contraloria.gob.pa; internet www.contraloria.gob.pa; f. 1949; compiles and publishes statistical information about Panama and its provinces incl. details of the National Census; 86,277 vols; Dir LUIS ENRIQUE QUESADA; Librarian ELSI P. DE MEJÍA; publs *Panamá en Cifras* (annually, also on CD-ROM), *Estadística Panameña* (29 series, each annually), *Censos Nacionales de Población y Vivienda* (every 10 years, also on CD-ROM), *Censos Nacionales Económicos* (every 10 years), *Censo Nacional Agropecuario* (every 10 years, also on CD-ROM), *Compendios Estadísticas Provinciales* (every 2 years), *Informe del Contralor* (annually, also on CD-ROM).

Biblioteca Interamericana Simón Bolívar: Estafeta Universitaria, Panama City; tel. 223-8786; fax 223-3734; e-mail biblis1@ancon.up.ac.pa; f. 1935 as Biblioteca de la Universidad de Panamá, name changed 1978; 285,855 vols including 9,000 vols in medical library; maintains interchange with 200 institutions; Dir Prof. DAYSI DE JEAN FRANÇOISE; publ. *Boletín Bibliográfico* (2 a year).

Biblioteca Nacional (National Library): Apdo 7906, Zona 9, Panama City; Located at: Parque Recreativo y Cultural Omar, Vía Porras, San Francisco, Panama City; tel. 224-9466; fax 224-9988; e-mail referenci@binal.ac.pa; internet www.binal.ac.pa; f. 1892 as Biblioteca Colón, reorganized as Biblioteca Nacional 1942; a branch of the Ministry of Education's Public Libraries system, its special function is to provide a Government information service; 200,000 vols (including bound reviews and periodicals); Admin. Dir MARÍA MAJELA BRENES; publ. *LOTERIA*.

Centro de Información y Documentación Institucional: Apdo 6337, Zona 5, Panama City; tel. 262-2109; fax 262-1179; e-mail cidi@ifarhu.gob.pa; internet www.ifarhu.gob.pa; f. 1980; 5,000 vols; Dir Lic. INES PERALTA DE VARGAS; publs *Orientifarhu*, *Cidinforma* (bibliographical information), *Alertas* (specialized bibliographical information), *Mujer al Cambio* (women's psychological and social issues, annually).

Museums and Art Galleries

Panama City

Dirección Nacional del Patrimonio Histórico: Apdo 0816-07812, Zona 5, Panama City; tel. 232-7485; fax 232-7644; internet www.inac.gob.pa; f. 1974; conservation and admin. of Panama's historical heritage; library of 8,000 vols; Dir Lic. LINETTE MONTENEGRO.

Instituto Panameño de Arte/Museo de Arte Contemporáneo: Apdo 4211, Zona 5, Panama City; tel. 262-8012; fax 262-3376; e-mail info@macpanama.org; internet www .macpanama.org; f. 1962; museum; library of 3,000 vols; Dir REINIER RODRÍGUEZ FERGUSON.

Museo de Arte Religioso Colonial: Apdo 662, Zona 1, Panama City; Located at: Avda A y Calle 3ra., San Felipe, Panama City; tel. and fax 228-2897; f. 1974; sited in restored 17th c. Dominican chapel; varied collection of objects of religious art of the Colonial period; cultural programmes, and lectures; Dir. Prof. NORIS NÚÑEZ DE ALVAREZ.

Museo de Ciencias Naturales: Apdo 662, Zona 1, Panama City; Located at: Avda Cuba, Calle 29 y 30, Calidonia, Panama City; tel. 225-0645; fax 225-0646; e-mail museocienciasnaturales@yahoo.com; internet www.pa/cultura/museos/ciencias; f. 1975; natural history, geology and palaeontology; fauna of Panama and other countries; library of 300 vols; Dir Profa NURIA ESQUIVEL DE BARILLAS.

Museo de Historia de Panamá: Apdo 662, Zona 1, Panama City; Located at: Palacio Municipal, Avda Central, entre Calles 6 y 7 Oeste, Panama City; tel. and fax 228-6231; f. 1977; Dir Licda NILKA FUENTES; publ. publs guide books.

Public Universities

UNIVERSIDAD AUTÓNOMA DE CHIRIQUÍ

El Cabrero, David, Chiriquí
Telephone: 775-1114
Fax: 774-4050
E-mail: rectoria@unachi.ac.pa
Internet: www.unachi.ac.pa
Founded 1994; present name and status 1995
State control

Rector: VIRGILIO A. OLMOS APARICIO
Vice-Rector for Academic Affairs: DANIEL CARRILLO
Vice-Rector for Research and Postgraduate affairs: Dra JUANA RAMOS CHUE
Vice-Rector for Admin.: ETELVINA DE BONAGAS
Sec.-Gen.: BLANCA RÍOS

Number of teachers: 560
Number of students: 8,500

Publications: *Revista*, *Senda Universitaria* (monthly), *El Observator* (social communication), *Bitacora* (society, culture and science, quarterly), *Econometrín* (economics), *Supra* (Spanish language)

Faculties of Business admin. and accountancy, Econ., Education sciences, Humanities, Law, Medicine, Natural sciences, Nursing, Public admin., Social communication; School of Chemistry; campuses in Boquete, Oriente and Barú.

UNIVERSIDAD ESPECIALIZADA DE LAS AMERICAS (UDELAS)
(Specialized University of the Americas)

Albrook Edificio 806, Apdo 0843-01041, Panamá
Telephone: 501-1000
E-mail: sec.secgen@udelas.ac.pa
Internet: www.udelas.ac.pa
Founded 1997
State control
Language of instruction: Spanish

Rector: Dra BERTA T. DE AROSEMENA
Vice-Rector: Dra MARÍA ROSA MONTANARI
Sec.-Gen.: CAROL GUERRA

Extension centres in Chiriquí, Colón and Veraguas.

UNIVERSIDAD DE PANAMÁ

Ciudad Universitaria 'Dr Octavio Méndez Pereira', El Cangrejo, Apdo Estafeta Universitaria, Panama City
Telephone: 263-6133
Fax: 264-3733
Internet: www.up.ac.pa
Founded 1935
State control
Language of instruction: Spanish
Academic year: March to December

Rector: Dr GUSTAVO GARCÍA DE PAREDES
Vice-Rector for Academic Affairs: Dr JUSTO MEDRANO
Vice-Rector for Admin.: Dr CARLOS BRANDARIZ ZÚÑIGA
Vice-Rector for Extension: Dr ARIOSTO E. ARDILLA MARTÍNEZ
Vice-Rector for Research and Graduate Studies: Dra. BETTY ANN ROWE DE CATSAMBANIS
Vice-Rector for Student Affairs: Dr NELSON NOVARRO
Registrar: Mgtr. ONFALA LÓPEZ DE DE BELLO
Librarian: Prof. DAYSI DE JEAN FRANÇOISE

Number of teachers: 3,662
Number of students: 65,225

Publications: *Campus*, *Hacia La Luz*, *Boletines Estadísticos*, *Revistas Jurídicas Panameñas*, *Scientia*, *EDU*, *ECO*, *Revista Universidad*, *Memoria*

DEANS

Faculty of Agriculture: Dr JUAN MIGUEL MIGUEL OSORIO
Faculty of Architecture: Arq. MARÍA T. DE BENAVIDES
Faculty of Business Admin. and Accountancy: Mgtra. RUTH E. MATA
Faculty of Computer Science, Electronics and Communication: Dra. DIANA CHEN
Faculty of Econ.: Prof. GABRIEL VELÁSQUEZ
Faculty of Education: Prof. TOMÁS GARIBALDI
Faculty of Fine Arts: Prof. EFRAIN CASTRO
Faculty of Humanities: Dr MIGUEL ÁNGEL CANDANEDO ORTEGA
Faculty of Law and Political Sciences: Dr ROLANDO MURGAS TORRAZZA
Faculty of Medicine: Dr SERGIO FUENTES
Faculty of Natural and Exact Sciences and Technology: Prof. RAMIRO GÓMEZ
Faculty of Nursing: Mgtra. ELBA E. DE ISAZA
Faculty of Odontology: Dra. OMAR LÓPEZ
Faculty of Pharmacy: Dra ANGELA DE AGUILAR
Faculty of Public Admin.: Mgtr. NICOLÁS JEROME
Faculty of Social Communication: Prof. HARRY IGLESIAS
Faculty of Veterinary Medicine: Dr CARLOS G. MORÁN R.

ATTACHED INSTITUTES

Central American Institute for Educational Administration and Supervision: Dir Prof. FILIBERTO MORALES.

Institute of Analysis: Dir Dr JERÓNIMO AVERZA.

Institute of Criminology: Dir Lic. MARCELA MÁRQUEZ.

Institute of Earth Sciences: Dir Prof. EDUARDO CAMACHO.

Institute of Environmental Sciences and Biodiversity: Dir Dr RAMÓN ANTONIO EHRMAN.

Institute of Ethnic and Cultural Traditions: Dir Profa DOLORES CORDERO PÉREZ.

Institute of Food and Nutrition: Dir Prof. ANIBAL TAYMES.

Institute for the Improvement of Stockbreeding: (vacant).

Institute of National Affairs: Dir Profa. ENILSA DE CEDEÑO.

Institute of the Panama Canal: Dir Dr PABLO ARMUELLES.

Institute of Women's Studies: Dir Dra. LYDIA GORDÓN DE ISAACS.

Pan-American Institute of Physical Education: (vacant).

UNIVERSIDAD TECNOLOGICA DE PANAMA

Campus 'Víctor Levi Sasso', Apdo Postal 6-2894, El Dorado, Panama City
Telephone: 236-1802
Fax: 236-6510
E-mail: utp@utp.ac.pa
Internet: www.utp.ac.pa
Founded 1981
State control
Academic year: March to December

Rector: Ing. SALVADOR ARSENIO RODRÍGUEZ GUERINI
Vice-Rector for Academic Affairs: Ing. MARCELA PAREDES DE VÁSQUEZ
Vice-Rector for Admin. Affairs: Ing. BENIGNO VARGAS
Vice-Rector for Research and Graduate Studies: Dra DELVA B. DE CHAMBERS
Dir of External Affairs: Dr GREGORIO URRIOLA CANDANEDO
Librarian: Lic. EDILDA F. DE MORALES

Number of teachers: 1,200
Number of students: 16,000

Publications: *Boletín Informativo* (annual), *Memorias* (annual), *El Tecnológico* (bulletin, monthly), *I+D Tecnológico* (annual)

DEANS

Faculty of Civil Eng.: Ing. LUIS BARAHONA
Faculty of Computer Science Eng.: Dr MODALDO TUÑÓN
Faculty of Electrical Eng.: Ing. CELSO SPENCER
Faculty of Mechanical Eng.: Ing. LINO RUÍZ
Faculty of Science and Technology: Lic. ALMA URRIOLA DE MUÑOZ

ATTACHED RESEARCH CENTRES

Computing Centre: Dir Ing. JAIME VÁSQUEZ.

Design and Planning Centre: Dir Ing. JAVIER NAVARRO.

Engineering Experimental Centre: Dir Dr. OSCAR RAMÍREZ.

Hydraulic and Hydrotechnical Research Centre: Dir Ing. RICARDO GONZÁLEZ.

Production and Agroindustrial Research Centre: Dir Dr HUMBERTO ALVAREZ.

Private Universities

UNIVERSIDAD ABIERTA Y A DISTANCIA DE PANAMÁ (UNADP)
(Open and Distance University of Panama)

Apdo 87-2526, Panamá 7
Located at: Calle 39 Este, Bella Vista Edif. 5–57 entre Ave Cuba y Ave Perú, Panama
Telephone: 227-7242
Fax: 227-7243

E-mail: generalunadp@cwpanama.net
Internet: www.unadp.ac.pa
Founded 1994
Private control
Language of instruction: Spanish.

UNIVERSIDAD CATÓLICA SANTA MARÍA LA ANTIGUA

Apdo 0819-08550, Panama City
Telephone: 230-8200
Fax: 230-3593
E-mail: secretar@canaa.usma.ac.pa
Internet: www.usma.ac.pa
Founded 1965, reorganized 1973
Private control
Language of instruction: Spanish
Academic year: January to December (3 semesters)

Chancellor: Mons. JOSÉ DIMAS CEDEÑO
Rector: Dr Mons. PABLO VARELA SERVER
Vice-Rector for Academic Affairs: Mgtr MARÍA EUGENIA DE ALEMÁN
Vice-Rector for Admin.: Mgtr HERNÁN SEDDA
Vice-Rector for Postgraduate Affairs and Research: Dr VÍCTOR WILLIAMS
Registrar: Dra MARÍA HELENA REYNA DE MARIÑAS
Librarian: Lic. IRENE DE CARVAJAL
Library of 100,000 vols
Number of teachers: 453
Number of students: 4,500

Publications: *Boletín Informativo* (annual), *Iustitia et Pulchritudo* (annual), *Revista La Antigua* (2 a year)

DEANS
Admin. Sciences: Prof. SAMUEL DÍAZ
Humanities and Religious Studies: Prof. LILIA URRUTIA DE PALACIOS
Law and Political Science: Prof. FRANCISCO VEGA

Social Sciences: Prof. LILIA URRUTIA DE PALACIOS
Technology and Natural Science: Prof. SAMUEL VÁSQUEZ

UNIVERSIDAD DEL ISTMO

Av. Justo Arosemena, Calle 40 y 41, Panama City
Telephone: 227-8822
Fax: 227-8831
E-mail: informacion@udi.edu
Internet: www.udi.edu
Founded 1963
Private control
Rector: PABLO MICHELSEN
Campuses in Chiriquí, David and La Chorrera.

UNIVERSIDAD INTERAMERICANA DE PANAMÁ

Avda Manuel Espinosa Batista, Panamá
Telephone: 208-4444
Internet: www.uip.edu.pa
Founded 1992
Private control
Language of instruction: Spanish
Academic year: January to December
Pres.: WILLIAM J. SALOM
Rector: JAVIER MARTINEZ
Number of teachers: 86
Number of students: 3,500

Graduate School

Edificio Ocean Business Plaza, Piso 26, Calle Aquilino de la Guardia, Marbella
Telephone: 340-6050.

UNIVERSIDAD LATINA DE PANAMÁ

Apdo 87-0887, Via Ricardo J. Alfaro, Calle Aragón, Catilla, Panamá 7
Telephone: 230-8600
Fax: 230-8686
E-mail: web@ulat.ac.pa
Internet: www.ulat.ac.pa
Founded 1989, present status 1991
Private control
Rector: Dr MODALDO TUÑON
Registrar: CLAUDIA MARÍN
Library Dir: AURA AROSEMENA
Number of teachers: 600
Number of students: 7,000
Campuses in Chitré, David and Santiago

DEANS
Faculty of Admin. and Economic Sciences: AUGUSTO A. CORRO
Faculty of Computer Sciences and Telecommunications: LUJAN GONZALES
Faculty of Health Sciences: Dr JORGE MEDRANO
Faculty of Communication Sciences: NEDELKA GALVEZ
Faculty of Education Sciences: GLADYS DE JAÉN
Faculty of Social Sciences: (vacant)
Faculty of Law and Political Sciences: OCTAVIO DEL MORAL

Schools of Arts and Music

Escuela Nacional de Danzas: Apdo 662, Zona 1, Panama City; f. 1948.

Escuela Nacional de Teatro: Apdo 662, Zona 1, Panama City; f. 1974; 10 teachers; 40 students; Dir Prof. IVÁN R. GARCÍA.

PAPUA NEW GUINEA

The Higher Education System

In 1906 the Territory of Papua came under Australian control, and in 1914 the former German possession of New Guinea became a Trust Territory, also under Australian control. A joint administration for the two territories was established by Australia in July 1949, and the name Papua New Guinea was adopted in 1971. Independence was achieved in 1975. Major institutions of higher education were first established in the 1960s, including the Papua New Guinea Institute of Public Administration (founded in 1963), the University of Papua New Guinea, the Papua New Guinea University of Technology and the University of Vudal (all founded in 1965). In addition to the universities there are also teacher-training colleges and higher institutions, which cater for specific professional training, such as a medical school, which had a total enrolment of 656 students in early 2005. In 1999 there were 13,761 students enrolled in tertiary education.

Admission to higher education is on the basis of the Grade 12 Higher School Certificate. In addition to the standard undergraduate Bachelors degree, which is a four-year programme of study, universities offer two- to four-year diploma and certificate-level courses. Degree courses in medicine and law are five years in duration. Following the Bachelors, the Masters is the first postgraduate degree and lasts between one and three years. Finally, the PhD is the highest university-level degree and requires a minimum of three years' study and research for the preparation and submission of a thesis.

Most technical and vocational education starts at the secondary Grade 10-level, and consists of two- to three-year diploma and certificate programmes at technical colleges and specialized professional institutes.

Learned Societies

BIBLIOGRAPHY, LIBRARY SCIENCE AND MUSEOLOGY

Papua New Guinea Library Association: c/o National Library Service, POB 734, Waigani, NCD; f. 1973; 200 mems; Pres. MARGARET J. OBI; Sec. JENNY WAL; publs *Directory of Libraries in Papua New Guinea*, *PNGLA Nius* (2 a year), *PNG Librarians' Calendar* (monthly), *Toktok bilong haus buk* (Journal, quarterly).

ECONOMICS, LAW AND POLITICS

Papua New Guinea Institute of Banking and Business Management: ToRobert Centre, Vanama Crescent, POB 1721, Port Moresby NCD; tel. 3221000; fax 3212960; e-mail info@bbm.com.pg; internet www.ibbm .com.pg; f. 1965; training in all aspects of management and development; Exec. Dir. RAY CLARK.

LANGUAGE AND LITERATURE

Alliance Française: ADF Haus, Musgrave St, POB 5877, Port Moresby; tel. and fax 3210994; e-mail alliance@daltron.com.pg; internet ambfrance-pg.org; offers courses and exams in French language and culture and promotes cultural exchange with France.

NATURAL SCIENCES

General

Papua New Guinea Scientific Society: c/o National Museum, POB 5560, Boroko; f. 1949 to promote the sciences, exchange scientific information, preserve scientific collections and establish museums; 203 mems; Pres. H. SAKULAS; publ. *Proceedings*.

Research Institutes

GENERAL

National Research Institute: POB 5854, Boroko, NCD 111; tel. 3260300; fax 3260213; e-mail nri@global.net.pg; internet www.nri .org.pg; f. 1989; promotion of research into social, political, economic, educational and cultural issues in Papua New Guinea; practical research opportunities for trainee research workers; library of 10,000 vols; Dir

Dr TOM WEBSTER; publs *Post Courier Index* (annually), *TaimLain: A Journal of Contemporary Melanesian Studies*, *Current Issues* (quarterly).

AGRICULTURE, FISHERIES AND VETERINARY SCIENCE

Lowlands Agricultural Experiment Station: Kerevat, POB 204, Kokopo, East New Britain Province; tel. 9839145; fax 9839129; f. 1928; food crops, spices, soil and land management, entomology and plant pathology.

ECONOMICS, LAW AND POLITICS

Institute of National Affairs: POB 1530, Port Moresby; tel. 3211045; e-mail inapng@ daltron.com.pg; internet www.inapg.com; f. 1979; aims to foster the development of the national economy by encouraging discussion and research on issues which are important in the public and private sectors; undertakes research in matters of interest to management in both sectors, the findings of which are published; organizes seminars, public meetings, etc., on matters of importance to economic development; Pres. P. FRANKLIN; Treas. and Sec. M. J. MANNING.

MEDICINE

Papua New Guinea Institute of Medical Research: POB 60, Goroka EHP 441; tel. 7322800; fax 7321998; e-mail general@ pngimr.org.pg; internet www.pmgimr.org.pg; f. 1968; medical, human biological, nutritional and sociological research, all matters relating to research into human health and disease within Papua New Guinea; library of 5,000 vols; Dir Prof. JOHN C. REEDER; publ. *Annual Report*.

Libraries and Archives

Boroko

National Archives and Public Records Service: POB 1089, Boroko; tel. 3256200; fax 3254251; f. 1957; branch of National Library Service, Division of the Department of Education; repository for the public archives and records of Papua New Guinea; Reference Service and Microfilm Unit, Records Management Service and Records

Centre Service for government offices and statutory bodies; branch repository in Lae: 10,000 linear m and 1,000 maps and plans, and photographic archives; Chief Archivist JACOB HELEVAWA; publs *Guides to Groups of Records in the National Archives* (irregular), *Patrol Reports* (microfiche, irregular).

Lae

Matheson Library, Papua New Guinea University of Technology: Private Mail Bag, Lae; fax 4734355; f. 1965; 120,000 monograph vols, 600 serial titles, 4,000 audiovisual items; special collection: Papua New Guinea; microfilm unit produces microfiche edns of all major PNG serial publs; University Librarian D. TEMU.

Waigani

National Library Service: POB 734, Waigani; tel. 3256200; fax 3251331; e-mail ceminoni@online.net.pg; f. 1975; national reference library; legal deposit library; ISBN agency for Papua New Guinea; advisory services, lending and educational services; important holdings of New Guineana, particularly Government publications; Papua New Guinea collection; films and videos of Papua New Guinea; mobile school library service; 50,000 vols, 4,000 films and video recordings; Dir-Gen. DANIEL PARAIDE; publs *Annual Report*, *Directory of Libraries in Papua New Guinea* (irregular), *OLA Nius* (every 2 months), *Papua New Guinea Directory of Information Sources in Science and Technology* (irregular), *Papua New Guinea National Bibliography* (annually), *Selective Times Index to PNG* (annually).

University of Papua New Guinea Michael Somare Library: Box 319, University Post Office, Waigani; tel. 3267280; fax 3267187; e-mail Library@upng.ac.pg; f. 1965; 458,000 vols, 2,000 current periodicals; special collections: law, New Guinea; Librarian IVARATURE KIVIA (acting); publs *New Guinea Archives: A Listing* (microfiche), *New Guinea Photographic Index* (microfiche).

Subordinate library:

Medical Library: POB 5623, Boroko; f. 1976; 65,000 vols; Librarian L. WANGATAU; publ. *Papua New Guinea Medical Journal*.

Museum and Art Gallery
Boroko

Papua New Guinea National Museum and Art Gallery: POB 5560, Boroko; tel. 3250345; fax 3251779; f. 1954; field research in archaeology, cultural anthropology, natural history; educational tours, public programmes, broadcasts, etc.; aims to implement the National Cultural Property (Preservation) Act to protect Papua New Guinea's cultural heritage, and establish museums; library of 4,500 vols; Dir SOROI MAREPO EOE.

Universities

DIVINE WORD UNIVERSITY

POB 483, Madang

Telephone: 8522937

Fax: 8522812

E-mail: info@dwu.ac.pg

Internet: www.dwu.ac.pg

Founded 1979 by the Society of the Divine Word; university status granted by Act of Parliament 1980

Private control (funded by Catholic church)

President: Fr JAN CZUDA

Academic Vice-President: ANDREW SIMPSON

Administrative Vice-President: BENJAMIN NAING (acting)

Dean of Studies: Dr PAMELA NORMAN

Registrar: CECILIA N'DROWER

Head Librarian: MAKIS DUNNI'IB

Library of 30,000 vols

DEANS

Faculty of Arts: Dr MARK SOLON

Faculty of Business and Management: Dr ROMULO LINDION

Faculty of Education: Dr ALFRED TIVINARLIK

Faculty of Health: Dr BILLY SLVE

UNIVERSITY OF GOROKA

POB 1078, Goroka, EHP

Telephone: 7311700

Fax: 7322620

E-mail: amaras@uog.ac.pg

Internet: www.uog.ac.pg

Founded 1995

State control

Language of instruction: English

Academic year: January to December

Chancellor: Sir EBIA OLEWALE

Vice-Chancellor: Dr DAVID RAWLENCE

Pro-Vice-Chancellor (Administration): Dr MUSAVE SINEBARE

Pro-Vice-Chancellor (Academic and Development): JOSEPH KATA

Librarian: N. AMARASINGHE

Library of 107,000 books, 110 periodicals

Number of teachers: 80

Number of students: 1,100

Publication: *Papua New Guinea Journal of Teacher Education* (annually)

DEANS

Faculty of Education: Dr ARNOLD KUKARI

Faculty of Humanities: Dr GAIRO ONAGI

Faculty of Science: (vacant)

PACIFIC ADVENTIST UNIVERSITY

Private Mail Bag, Boroko, National Capital District 111

Telephone: 3280200

Fax: 3281257

E-mail: administration@pau.ac.gp

Internet: www.pau.ac.pg

Founded 1984 as Pacific Adventist College, present status 1997

Private (funded by Church of Christ)

Language of instruction: English

Academic year: February to August

Vice-Chancellor: Dr NEMANI W. TAUSERE

Number of teachers: 41

Number of students: 379.

UNIVERSITY OF PAPUA NEW GUINEA

Box 320, University Post Office, Waigani

Telephone: 3267200

Fax: 3267187

E-mail: pr&m@upng.ac.pg

Internet: www.upng.ac.pg

Founded 1965

Language of instruction: English

State control

Academic year: February to November (two semesters)

Chancellor: Sir ALKAN TOLOLO

Pro-Chancellor: Dr ROSEMARY KEKEDO

Vice-Chancellor: Dr L. R. EASTCOTT

Deputy Vice-Chancellor: N. R. KUMAN

Registrar: VINCENT MALAIBE

Library: see Libraries and Archives

Number of teachers: 700

Number of students: 4,416

Publications: *Calendar, Faculty Research Reports, Handbooks of Courses, Melanesian Law Journal* (2 a year), *PNG Law, Research in Melanesia* (2 a year), *Science in New Guinea* (quarterly), *South Pacific Journal of Psychology* (all annually), *Yagl-Ambu*

DEANS

School of Business Administration: Dr ALBERT MELLAM

School of Humanities and Social Science: Dr KENNETH SUMBUK

School of Law: Prof. LAWRENCE KALINOE

School of Medicine and Health Sciences: Prof. MATHIAS SAPURI

School of Natural and Physical Sciences: Prof. KIRPAL SINGH

School of Research and Postgraduate Studies: Dr SIMON SAULEI

PAPUA NEW GUINEA UNIVERSITY OF TECHNOLOGY

Private Mail Bag, Lae

Telephone: 4734999

Fax: 4757667

Internet: www.unitech.ac.pg

Founded 1965

Language of instruction: English

State control

Academic year: February to November (two semesters)

Chancellor: A. TOLOLO

Pro-Chancellor: R. KEKEDO

Vice-Chancellor: M. BALOILOI

Deputy Vice-Chancellor (vacant)

Registrar: T. CHAN

Librarian: RAPHAEL TOPAGUR (acting)

Library: see Libraries and Archives

Number of teachers: 199

Number of students: 1,653

Publications: *Calendar, Course Handbook, Reporter, Research Report, Student Handbook, Vice-Chancellor's Report.*

UNIVERSITY OF VUDAL

PMB, Rabaul, East New Britain Province

Telephone and fax: 9839252

E-mail: vlibrary@global.net.pg

Founded 1965 as Vudal Agricultural College; present name and status 1997

Language of instruction: English

Academic year: February to November

Vice-Chancellor: Prof. PHILIP SIAGURU

Library of 25,000

Number of teachers: 17

Number of students: 600

DEANS

School of Natural Resources and Environment: Dr ALAN QUARTERMAIN

College

Papua New Guinea Institute of Public Administration: POB 1216, Boroko; tel. 3260433; fax 3261654; f. 1963; diploma, certificate and short courses in public and land administration, public finance and accountancy, local government, management, law, social development, library studies, business development, communication skills, mathematics and statistics, rural development; library: 75,000 vols; 60 teachers; 700 students; Dir GEI ILAGI; publs *Administration for Development* (2 a year), *Handbook* (annually).

PARAGUAY

The Higher Education System

Paraguay, ruled by Spain from the 16th century, achieved independence in 1811. The oldest current institution of higher education is the Universidad Nacional de Asunción (founded in 1889). The next oldest university was not opened until the 1960s, and following the end of military rule in 1989, university-level education expanded in the 1990s with the opening of several universities. The governing law of higher education is Law 136/93 (1993), which led to the creation of the Council of Universities. in 2002/03 there were an estimated 143,913 students enrolled in university-level education.

Applicants must have the Bachillerato in order to gain admission to higher education, and universities may set individual entry requirements. The Título de Licenciatura is the main undergraduate degree, and is awarded after four years of study. Under Law 136/93 Título de Licenciatura is both an academic and a professional title. Undergraduate degrees in professional fields of study, such as engineering, law, economics and medicine, may last upwards of four years. There is no uniform system of postgraduate degrees, which were not available in Paraguay before 1991. However, the Universidad Nacional de Asunción has established a system which is being considered by the Council of Universities, consisting of: Diploma (Diplomado), a post-graduate short-course in a professional field of study; 'Specialization' (Especialización), undertaken as part of the undergraduate degree; Masters (Maestría), which lasts two years; and Doctorate (Título de Doctorado) or Doctor of Sciences (Doctor en Ciencias), which is available at nine universities.

Post-secondary technical and vocational education is available mainly at higher technical institutions (instituciones técnicas superiors) under the authority of the Directorate of Higher Technical Institutes (Dirección de Institutos Técnicos Superiores). The qualification Título de Técnico Superior is awarded after completion of two years or 1,500 classroom hours of study.

The National Agency for Evaluation and Accreditation of Higher Education (Agencia Nacional de Evaluación y Acreditación de la Educación Superior—ANEAES) was founded in 2003 following the enactment of Law 2072/03. ANEAES is the national body for quality assurance and accreditation of higher education at undergraduate and postgraduate levels. Paraguay also participates in El Mecanismo Experimental de Acreditación de Carreras del MERCOSUR.

Learned Societies

GENERAL

Academia de la Lengua y Cultura Guaraní (Academy of the Guaraní Language and Culture): Calle España y Mompox, Asunción; f. 1975; Pres. Dr RUFINO AREVALO PARIS; Sec. ANTONIO E. GONZÁLEZ; publ. *Revista*.

Academia Paraguaya (Paraguayan Academy): Avda España y Mompox, Asunción; f. 1927; corresp. of the Real Academia Española (Madrid); 34 mems; Pres. JULIO CÉSAR CHAVES; Sec. LUIS A. LEZCANO; publ. *Anales*.

HISTORY, GEOGRAPHY AND ARCHAEOLOGY

Instituto de Numismática y Antigüedades del Paraguay: Hernandarias 1313, Asunción; tel. 81855; f. 1943; Pres. CARLOS ALBERTO PUSINERI SCALA.

LANGUAGE AND LITERATURE

Alliance Française: Mariscal Estigarribia 1039, Calle Estados Unidos, Casilla de Correo 2076, Asunción; tel. (21) 21-0503; fax (21) 21-2697; e-mail alfran@pla.net.py; offers courses and exams in French language and culture and promotes cultural exchange with France.

MEDICINE

Sociedad de Pediatría y Puericultura del Paraguay (Paediatrics and Child Welfare Society): 25 de Mayo y Tacuaí, Asunción; f. 1928; 28 mems; Pres. Dr GUIDO RODRÍGUEZ ALCALÁ; Sec. Dr GUSTAVO A. RIART; publ. *Revista Médica del Paraguay*.

RELIGION, SOCIOLOGY AND ANTHROPOLOGY

Asociación Indigenista del Paraguay: Calle España y Mompox, Casilla 1838, Asunción; f. 1942; anthropology, development of indigenous communities; 170 mems; library of 1,640 vols; Pres. Dr RAFAEL REYES PARGA; Exec. Sec. Lic. AMÉRICO PÉREZ PEÑA.

TECHNOLOGY

Unión Sudamericana de Asociaciones de Ingenieros (USAI) (South American Union of Engineers' Associations): Head Office: Casilla de Correos 336, Asunción; f. 1935; mem. countries: Argentina, Bolivia, Brazil, Chile, Colombia, Ecuador, Paraguay, Peru, Uruguay and Venezuela; Dir and Pres. Ing. CARLOS ESPINOZA MACIEL; Sec. Ing. HERMANN BAUMANN.

Research Institutes

ECONOMICS, LAW AND POLITICS

Centro Interdisciplinario de Derecho Social y Economía Política (CIDSEP): Independencia Nacional y Comuneros, Casilla de Correo 1718, Asunción; tel. (21) 97926; f. 1986; Dir CARLOS ALBERTO GONZÁLEZ.

Centro Paraguayo de Estudios de Desarrollo Económico y Social: Mariscal Estigarribia, 1050 Asunción.

HISTORY, GEOGRAPHY AND ARCHAEOLOGY

Instituto Geográfico Militar: Avda Perú y Artigas, Asunción; Dir Gral. Brig. RUBEN ORTIZ P.; Sec. E. LOPEZ MOREIRA.

MEDICINE

Instituto Nacional de Parasitología (National Institute of Parasitology): Instituto de Microbiología, Facultad de Medicina, Casilla Correo 1102, Asunción; f. 1963; 5 mems; library; Dir Dr ARQUIMEDES CANESE; publ. *Revista Paraguaya de Microbiología* (annually).

RELIGION, SOCIOLOGY AND ANTHROPOLOGY

Centro de Estudios Antropológicos de la Universidad Católica–CEADUC: Casilla de Correo 1718, Asunción; fax (21) 441044; e-mail ceaduc@uca.edu.py; f. 1950, affiliated to Universidad Católica 1971; 25 mems; Dir JOSE ZANARDINI; Sec. MYRIAN AURORA GAONA MARTÍNEZ; publs *Estudios Paraguayos*, *Suplemento Antropológico*, *Universidad Católica* (2 a year).

Centro Paraguayo de Estudios Sociológicos: Eligio Ayala 973, Casilla 2157, Asunción; tel. 43734; f. 1964; research and development in social sciences: migration, bilingualism, population structure, rural development, role of women in the work-force, education, etc.; library: specialized library of 5,000 vols, 4,000 documents; 15 staff; Dir DOMINGO M. RIVAROLA; Sec. MIRTHA M. RIVAROLA; publ. *Revista Paraguaya de Sociología* (3 a year).

TECHNOLOGY

Centro Paraguayo de Ingenieros: Avda España 959, Casilla 336, Asunción; tel. 202424; fax 205019; e-mail cpi@supernet .com.py; internet www.cpi.org.py; f. 1939; 1,415 mems; Pres. Ing. NICANOR FLEITAS BAREIRO; Sec. Ing. CÉSAR MANUEL LÓPEZ BOSIO; publ. *Ingeniería 2000* (annually).

Instituto Nacional de Tecnología y Normalización: Avda Artigas y Gral Roa, Asunción; tel. 290160; fax 290873; carries out research and technological studies, and lays down technical norms; publ. *Normas Técnicas Paraguayas*.

Libraries and Archives

Asunción

Biblioteca Americana (American Library): Mariscal Estigarribia e Iturbe, Asunción;

attached to the Museo Nacional de Bellas Artes (*q.v.*).

Biblioteca de la Sociedad Científica del Paraguay (Library of Paraguayan Scientific Society): Avda España 505, Asunción; f. 1921; 29,300 vols on science.

Biblioteca Pública del Ministerio de Defensa Nacional (Public Library of Ministry of Defence): Avda Mariscal López 1040, Asunción; Dir Col MANUEL W. CHAVES.

Biblioteca y Archivo del Ministerio de Relaciones Exteriores (Library of the Ministry of Foreign Affairs): Palacio de Gobierno, Asunción.

Biblioteca y Archivo Nacionales: Mariscal Estigarriba 95, Asunción; f. 1869; 44,000 vols; Dir MANUEL MARÍA PÁEZ MONGES.

Museums and Art Galleries

Asunción

Casa de la Independencia: 14 de Mayo y Pte Franco, Asunción; tel. 493918; f. 1965; historical museum of colonial period; Pres. Dr GERARDO FOGEL; Dir Prof. CARLOS ALBERTO PUSINERI SCALA.

Colección Carlos Alberto Pusineri Scala: Hernandarias 1313, Asunción; tel. 81855; f. 1950; collections of Guaraní archaeology, trophies of Paraguayan wars, colonial objects; small library of Paraguayan history, numismatics and anthropology; Dir CARLOS ALBERTO PUSINERI SCALA.

Jardín Botánico y Museo de Historia Natural (Botanical Gardens and Natural History Museum): Residencia López, Trinidad, Asunción; f. 1914; Dir Ing. GILDO INSFRÁN GUERROS; herbarium, zoological garden and museum, bacteriological laboratory, agricultural experimental station; publ. *Revista*.

Museo de Cerámica y Bellas Artes 'Julián de la Herreria': Estados Unidos 1120, Asunción; f. 1938; ceramics by Herreria; other modern works by Paraguayan artists; Paraguayan folk art; library of 6,000 vols, 1,000 of which concerned with the arts, particularly ceramics; Founder and Dir JOSEFINA PLÁ.

Museo Etnográfico 'Andrés Barbero': España 217, Asunción; tel. (21) 441696; fax (21) 441696; e-mail museoetn@pla.net.py; internet www.museobarbero.org.py; f. 1929; archaeology, ethnography, ethnology, history, archives, manuscripts, photographs, world music; library of 30,000 vols; Dir Lic. ADELINA PUSINERI.

Museo Histórico Militar (Museum of Military History): Avda Mariscal López 140, Asunción; recent war collections; Dir MANUEL WENCESLAO CHAVES.

Museo Nacional de Bellas Artes: Mariscal Estigarriba e Iturbe, Asunción; f. 1887; the paintings and sculpture of Juan Silvano Godoy form the basis of the collection; Dir JOSÉ LATERZA PARODI.

Yaguarón

Museo Doctor Francia: Yaguarón; f. 1968; relics of Paraguay's first dictator, 'El Supremo'; Pres. Dr FABIO RIVAS; Dir Dr JULIO CÉSAR CHAVES.

Universities

UNIVERSIDAD AMERICANA

Avda Brasilia 1100, Asunción

Telephone: (21) 295-710

Fax: (21) 295-710

E-mail: universidad@uamericana.edu.py

Internet: www.uamericana.edu.py

Founded 1994

President: Dr ANDRÉS BENKÖ KAPUVÁRY

Rector: Dr BENJAMÍN FERNÁNDEZ BOGADO

Vice-Rector (Academic): Ing. EDMUNDO DURÁN

Vice-Rector (Administration and Finance): Ing. RODOLFO CORTHORN

Vice-Rector (International Relations): Lic. SERGIO SOMERVILLE

Library of 5,000 vols, 100 periodicals

Number of teachers: 200

Number of students: 4,000

School of Economics and Administration.

UNIVERSIDAD AUTÓNOMA DE ASUNCIÓN

Jejuí 667, entre O'Leary y 15 de Agosto, Asunción

Telephone: (21) 440-980

Fax: (21) 497-299

E-mail: info@uaa.edu.py

Internet: www.uaa.edu.py

Founded 1978 as Escuela Superior de Administración de Empresas; present name and status 1991

Academic year: March to December

Rector: Ing. JULIO MIGUEL MARTÍN PUERTAS

Vice-Rector: Lic. KITTY GAONA FRANCO

Secretary-General: Lic. MARÍA LUISA PUERTAS

Number of teachers: 300

Number of students: 3,500

DEANS

Faculty of Communication and Art: (vacant)

Faculty of Economics and Business Administration: Dr SALVIO GÓMEZ ZORRILLA

Faculty of Health Sciences: Dr NATALIO PANGRAZIO ROUTI

Faculty of Humanities and Educational Sciences: Lic. ANA MARÍA VILLA

Faculty of Law, Politics and Social Science: Abog. JULIO AMERICO CAMPOS

Faculty of Science and Technology: Lic. JUAN DE DIOS GARBETT

UNIVERSIDAD AUTÓNOMA DEL PARAGUAY

Gen. Díaz 1053, Colón 568, Asunción

Telephone: (21) 441-924

Fax: (21) 447-579

E-mail: rectorado@uap.edu.py

Internet: www.uap.edu.py

Founded 1991

Rector: Dr CARLOS LAHAYE AGUIAR

Vice-Rector: Dr ARNALDO LATAZA MIGONE

DEANS

Faculty of Behavioural Sciences: Prof. Dr JOSÉ ANTONIO ARIAS

Pierre Fauchard Faculty of Dentistry: Prof. Dr ARMANDO MERCADO B.

Faculty of Obstetrics: Prof. Dr REINALDO BARRETO M.

Faculty of Optics: Lic. LEONARDO GARCÍA

ATTACHED RESEARCH INSTITUTES

Educational Support Unit: Dir Dra MIRTHIA CABALLERO DE TESSADA.

Institute of Prosthesis: Dir Prof. Dr ORLANDO PUSINERI.

UNIVERSIDAD CATÓLICA 'NUESTRA SEÑORA DE LA ASUNCIÓN'

CC 1718, Independencia Nacional y Comuneros, Asunción

Telephone: (21) 441-044

Fax: (21) 445-245

E-mail: uca6@mmail.com.py

Founded 1960

Private control

Language of instruction: Spanish

Academic year: March to December

Chancellor: Most Rev. Mgr Dr FELIPE SANTIAGO BENÍTEZ (Archbishop of Asunción)

Rector: Dr ANTONIO TELLECHEA SOLÍS

Vice-Rectors: Lic. VITALINA PÁEZ (Academic), Lic. ENRIQUE V. CÁCERES ROJAS (Administrative)

Secretary-General: Abog. SIXTO VOLPE RÍOS

Director of the Office of International Relations: Abog. MINERVA IZQUIERDO

Librarian: Lcda MARGARITA KALLSEN

Number of teachers: 1,922

Number of students: 18,000

Publications: *Anuario* (university), *Anuario* (Faculty of Law and Diplomatic Science), *Anuario* (Faculty of Philosophy and Human Sciences), *Cuadernos de Discusión* (Faculty of Philosophy and Human Sciences), *Estudios Antropológicos* (Anthropological Studies), *Lila* (Faculty of Business, Administration and Accounting), *La Quincena* (Faculty of Philosophy and Human Sciences), *Revista Jurídica* (Juridical Review), *Universitas* (Tomás Moro Institute of the Faculty of Law and Diplomatic Science), *Ventana Abierta* (Faculty of Philosophy and Human Sciences)

DEANS

Faculty of Accounting (Alto Paraná): Lic. GENARO GARCÍA

Faculty of Accounting (Concepción): Lic. MARÍA VICTORIA COELHO DE SOUZA DE PÉREZ

Faculty of Business Administration and Accounting (Asunción): Lic. DARIÓ TURRINI

Faculty of Business, Administration and Accounting (Guairá): Lic. ESTELA FERNÁNDEZ DE DECOUD

Faculty of Chemistry and Pharmacy (Guairá): Quim. NILSA B. DE MARECOS

Faculty of Economics (Itapúa): Lic. FRANCISCO SOLANO MACIEL

Faculty of Education (Concepción): Dra TERESA LÓPEZ DE VALIENTE

Faculty of Education (Guairá): Lic. HERMINIO LEIVA

Faculty of Education (Itapúa): Lic. MARÍA ISABEL MADRAZZO DE GARAY

Faculty of Health Sciences (Alto Paraná): Dra PETRONA DE CARDOZO

Faculty of Law (Alto Paraná): Dr PORFIRIO ZACARÍAS LEÓN

Faculty of Law (Guairá): Abog. ESTHER LISBOA DE BOGADO

Faculty of Law (Itapúa): Abog. MARCIAL CANTERO SILVA

Faculty of Law and Diplomatic Science (Asunción): Abog. ERNESTO VELÁZQUEZ GUIDO

Faculty of Medicine (Guairá): Dr FRANCISCO DUARTE

Faculty of Philosophy and Human Sciences (Asunción): Dra CARMEN QUINTANA DE HORÁK

Faculty of Science and Technology (Alto Paraná): Ing. MANUEL CHAMORRO

Faculty of Science and Technology (Asunción): Ing. CARLOS SÁNCHEZ LEÓN

Faculty of Science and Technology (Itapúa): Arq. MARIO ZAPUTOVICH

Admissions Courses (Asunción): Lic. ELIZABETH TONINA DE ROJAS (Dir)

Department of Theology and Pastoral Action (Asunción): Pbro Dr CARLOS ALBORNO (Dir)
Higher Institute of Theology (Asunción): Pbro Dr MICHEL GIBAUD (Dir)

CAMPUSES

Alto Paraná: Pro-Rector Lic. EMILIO ZARAGOZA.

Asunción: Pro-Rector Ing. GERÓNIMO BELLASSAI BAUDO.

Concepción: Pro-Rector Lic. NERY ANÍBAL SANABRIA SANABRIA.

Guairá: Pro-Rector Lic. MODESTO ESCOBAR AQUINO.

Itapúa: Pro-Rector Dr JESÚS RENÉ HAURÓN.

UNIVERSIDAD COLUMBIA DEL PARAGUAY

25 de Mayo 658 y Antequera, Asunción
Telephone: (21) 222-662
Fax: (21) 490-811
E-mail: jbu@columbia.edu.py
Internet: www.columbia.edu.py

Founded 1991

Rector: ROBERTO ELÍAS CANESE

Courses offered in accountancy and business studies, computer engineering, hotel management and tourism, law, marketing, organizational psychology and social engineering.

UNIVERSIDAD COMUNERA

San José 630 y Artigas, Asunción
Telephone: (21) 223-892

Founded 1992

Rector: ADRIANO IRALA BURGOS

Faculties of Agricultural Administration and Tourism.

UNIVERSIDAD DEL CONO SUR DE LAS AMÉRICAS

Avda España 372 Calle Brasil, Asunción
Telephone: (21) 213-872
Fax: (21) 212-658
E-mail: ucsa@ucsa.py
Internet: www.ucsa.edu.py

Founded 1996

Rector: Ing. LUIS ALBERTO LIMA
Academic Director: Lic. ANDRÉS ANTONIO VILLALBA COLMÁN
Vice-Rector (Administration): Lic. HELGA MARÍA DE SARUBBI
Vice-Rector (Postgraduate Studies): Lic. JUDITH FARIAS DA FONSECA
Vice-Rector (Research and Development): Lic. JOSÉ BLÁS VILLALBA

SUBJECT CO-ORDINATORS

Business: Lic. CLARISSA MELINA RODRÍGUEZ CAÑETE
Engineering: Ing. JOSÉ JUAN RICART BOSSI

Social Studies: Lic. NANCY MIRIAN CAÑETE DE GINZO

UNIVERSIDAD DEL NORTE

Avda España 676, Boquerón, Asunción
Telephone: (21) 229-450
Fax: (21) 228-217
E-mail: info@uninorte.edu.py
Internet: www.uninorte.edu.py

Founded 1991
Academic year: March to December

Rector: JUAN MANUEL MARCOS

Library of 20,000 vols

DEANS

Faculty of Biochemistry: ANA KALENIUSKA
Faculty of Economics and Administration: CARLOS DAHLBECK
Faculty of Education and Humanities: DOMINGO PEDROZO
Faculty of Engineering: JOSÉ LUIS MARCOS
Faculty of Health Sciences: CARLOS MICHELETTO
Faculty of Law and Politics: ANÍBAL CARTAMA
Faculty of Medicine: JUAN CARLOS CHAPARRO
Faculty of Technology: CARLOS CABALLERO
Postgraduate Faculty: JUAN MANUEL MARCOS

UNIVERSIDAD DEL PACÍFICO

México 775, Asunción
Telephone: (21) 450-287.

UNIVERSIDAD EVANGÉLICA DEL PARAGUAY

José Berges 459, Asunción
Telephone: (21) 223-496
Fax: (21) 223-496
E-mail: unievangelica@rieder.net.py
Internet: www.uep.edu.py

Founded 1994
Academic year: February to December

Rector: DIONISIO ÓRTIZ MUTTI
Vice-Rector: MELITA WALL
Secretary-General: ESTEBAN MISSENA DEL CASTILLO

Number of teachers: 193
Number of students: 1,374

Faculties of Accounting, Administration and Economics, Nursing, Modern Languages, Psychology and Human Development, Humanities and Educational Sciences, Theology, Health Sciences and Music.

ATTACHED RESEARCH INSTITUTE

Instituto de Formación Técnica Superior (INFORTES): Dir MELITA WALL.

UNIVERSIDAD NACIONAL DE ASUNCIÓN

Casilla 910, 2064 Asunción
Telephone: (021) 507-080

Fax: (021) 213734
Internet: www.una.py

Founded 1889
State control
Language of instruction: Spanish
Academic year: March to December

Rector: Prof. Dr L. H. BERGANZA
Vice-Rector: Prof. Arq. J. R. UGARRIZA
Secretary-General: Prof. Dr G. B. BARRIENTOS
Librarian: Lic. E. R. DE GONZÁLEZ-PETIT

Number of teachers: 1,789
Number of students: 19,898

Publications: *Guía de cursos y carreras, Mundo universitario, Revista de la Universidad Nacional de Asunción*

DEANS

Faculty of Agricultural Engineering: Ing. PEDRO G. GONZÁLES
Faculty of Architecture: Arq. JUAN R. UGARRIZA
Faculty of Chemistry: Dr RAFAEL CAMPERCHIOLI
Faculty of Dentistry: Dr RUBÉN AYALA ARELLANO
Faculty of Economics: Dr EPIFANIO SALCEDO
Faculty of Exact and Natural Sciences: Dr ELBIO ESQUIVEL
Faculty of Law and Social Sciences: Dr CARLOS A. MERSÁN
Faculty of Medicine: Dr LUIS ALBERTO REYES
Faculty of Philosophy: Dra OLINDA M. DE KOSTIANOVSKY
Faculty of Physical Sciences and Mathematics: Ing. HÉCTOR A. ROJAS
Faculty of Veterinary Sciences: Dr RAMON E. A. PISTILLI
Polytechnic Faculty: Lic. OSCAR BENÍTEZ ROA

DIRECTORS

Andrés Barbero Institute: Lic. YRMA DE SARUBBI
Institute of Electronic Engineering: Ing. EDUARDO KISHI
Institute of Geographical Sciences: Arq. MARÍA A. GONZÁLEZ TORRES
School of Librarianship: YOSHIKO MORIYA DE FREUNDORFER

UNIVERSIDAD NACIONAL DEL ESTE

POB 389, Calle 3 y Los Palmitos, Ciudad del Este, Alto Paraná
Telephone: (61) 63804
Fax: (61) 68664
Internet: www.une.edu.py

Founded 1993

Rector: Dr GLIBERTO RUIZ CARVALLO
Vice-Rector: Lic. VÍCTOR ALFREDO BRÍTEZ CHAMORRO

Faculties of Agricultural Engineering, Economics, Health Sciences, Law and Social Sciences and Philosophy.

PERU

The Higher Education System

From the 16th century Peru was under Spanish control until independence was declared in 1821 and achieved in 1824. The oldest current universities date from the period of Spanish rule, notably the Universidad Nacional Mayor de San Marcos de Lima (founded in 1551) and the Universidad Nacional de San Cristóbal de Huamanga (founded in 1677). The Universidad Nacional de la Libertad (founded in 1824) was the first university established in the independent period; its founder was Simon Bolivar. The Universidad Nacional de San Agustín de Arequipa (founded in 1828) followed shortly after. Higher education consists of pre-university and university levels. The Constitution of 1993 abolished the right to free university education. In 2000 there were 436,637 students in university-level education, and in 2003 there were 389,223 students enrolled at other institutions of higher education. In the same year, 248,003 students were enrolled in vocational institutions and 26,672 students attended specialist institutions.

Students must hold the certificate of completion of secondary education (Certificado de Educación Secundaria Común Completa) in order to sit the university entrance examination. The first undergraduate degree is the Bachelors (Bachiller), awarded after a three- to five-year period of specialization. Upon completion of a thesis the Licenciado or professional title is then awarded. Not every university awards postgraduate degrees, which are primarily the Masters (Maestría) and the Doctorate (Doctorado); both degrees require completion of two years of study.

Post-secondary technical and vocational education is provided by Teacher Training Institutes (Institutos Superiores Pedagógicos) and Higher Technological Institutes (Institutos Superiores Tecnológicos). The The Especialista Profesional and Titulo de Bachiller Profesional are the main qualifications offered by Higher Technological Institutes.

Learned Societies

GENERAL

Academia Peruana de la Lengua (Peruvian Academy of Letters): Jr Conde de Superunda 298, Lima 1; fax 457424; f. 1887; corresp. of the Real Academia Española (Madrid); 30 mems; Dir Dr LUIS JAIME CISNEROS; Sec. Dr MARTHA HILDEBRANDT; publ. *Boletín* (annually).

UNESCO Office Lima: Apdo 41-0192, Lima 41; Located at: Avda Javier Prado Este 2465, 8 piso, Museo de la Nacion, San Borja, Lima 41; tel. (1) 476-9871; fax (1) 476-9872; e-mail unescope@amauta.rcp.net.pe; internet www .unesco.org/lima; Dir PATRICIA URIBE.

ARCHITECTURE AND TOWN PLANNING

Colegio de Arquitectos del Perú: Avda San Felipe 999, Lima 11; tel. (14) 713772; fax (14) 713641; f. 1962; 3,717 mems; library of 3,500 vols; Dean NICANOR A. OBANDO OLIVA; Man. MARIANELLA VEGA JERI.

BIBLIOGRAPHY, LIBRARY SCIENCE AND MUSEOLOGY

Asociación Peruana de Archiveros (Peruvian Association of Archivists): Archivo General de la Nación, Calle Manuel Cuadros s/n, Palacio de Justicia, Apdo 3124, Lima.

Colegio de Bibliotecólogos del Perú: Avda 2 de Mayo 1545, Oficina 218, Lima 27; fax 442-7513; e-mail cbp@peru.com; internet cbp.tripod.com.pe; f. 1990; 680 mems; Dean SEGUNDO SOTO CORONEL.

EDUCATION

Asamblea Nacional de Rectores (Rectors' National Assembly): Calle Aldabas 337, Urb. Las Gardenias, Surco, Lima 33; tel. 495716; fax 496711; f. 1988; 34 mems; library of 30,000 vols; Pres. Dr CÉSAR PAREDES CANTO; Exec. Dir Ing. EDGARDO TORRES VERA; publs *Universidad, Escuelas y/o Carreras Profesionales, Grados y Títulos* (statistical bulletin), *Desarrollo Universitario* (bulletin).

Asociación Nacional de Educadoras Sampedranas: Máximo Abril 695, Jesús María, Lima 11; tel. 310562; f. 1910; aims to contribute to the development and improvement of national education; educa-

tional research, 'Education for Peace', educational innovation, institutional development; 6,200 mems; library of 1,000 vols with special collection: 'Education for Peace'; Pres. PEREGRINA MORGAN DE GOÑI; Sec. NANETE PÉREZ DE PILCO.

FINE AND PERFORMING ARTS

Asociación de Artistas Aficionados: Jr Ica 323, Costado del Municipal, Lima; f. 1938; 254 mems; presentation of plays, classical ballet and varied music programmes.

Instituto de Arte Peruano 'José Sabogal' (José Sabogal Institute of Peruvian Art): Avda Alfonso Ugarte 650, Apdo. 3048, Lima 1; tel. and fax (1) 423-5892; e-mail mncp@ inictel.gob.pe; internet museodelacultura .perucultural.org.pe; f. 1946; under the auspices of the Museo Nacional de la Cultura Peruana; publ. *Revista del Museo Nacional* (annually).

Instituto Nacional de Cultura: Avda Javier Prado este 2465, Lima 41; tel. 476-9933; fax 476-9888; e-mail comunicaciones@ inc.gob.pe; internet www.inc.gob.pe; f. 1971; official cultural institute; 24 brs; Dir Dr LUIS GUILLERMO LUMBRERAS; publs *Revista Arqueologicas, Revista Gaceta Cultural, Revista de Historia y Cultura, Revista del Museo Nacional*.

Instituto Peruano de Cultura Hispánica (Peruvian Institute of Hispanic Culture): Calle de la Riva 426, Lima; f. 1947; 280 mems; publ. *Boletín*.

HISTORY, GEOGRAPHY AND ARCHAEOLOGY

Centro de Estudios Histórico-Militares del Perú (Centre of Historico-Military Studies of Peru): Paseo Colón 190, Lima 1; tel. 230415; f. 1944; 1,098 mems; library of 13,800 vols; publ. *Revista*.

Centro de Investigación y Restauración de Bienes Monumentales del Instituto Nacional de Cultura: Casilla 5247, Jr Ancash 769, Lima.

Instituto Geográfico Nacional (National Geographical Institute): Avda Aramburú 1190, Lima 34; tel. (1) 475-3085; fax (1) 475-3075; e-mail postmast@ignperu.gob.pe; f.

1921; 250 mems; library of 3,200 vols; Dir Brig.-Gen. JOSÉ HERRERA ROSAS; publ. publs topographical, physical and political maps of Peru, *Boletín Informativo*.

Instituto Vizcardo de Estudios Históricos (Vizcardan Institute of Historical Studies): Porta 540, Miraflores, Lima; f. 1954; study of revolutionary movements for Spanish-American independence (1781–1820); publ. *Revista*.

Sociedad Geográfica de Lima (Lima Geographical Society): Jirón Puno 450, Apdo 1176, Lima 100; tel. (1) 427-3723; fax (1) 426-9930; e-mail sgl@geolima.org; f. 1888; library of 7,500 vols, also archives and museum; 750 mems, including corresp. and hon.; Pres. RAÚL PARRA MAZA; Sec. Ing. ZANIEL NOVOA GOICOCHEA; publs *Boletín* (annually), *Anuario Geográfico del Perú, Forjando Los Genios del Mañana* (annually), *Diccionario Geográfico del Perú*.

LANGUAGE AND LITERATURE

Alliance Française: Avda Arequipa 4595, Casilla 18, 1667 Lima; tel. (1) 4465524; fax (1) 4471770; e-mail director@ alianzafrancesalima.edu.pe; internet www .alianzafrancesalima.edu.pe; offers courses and exams in French language and culture and promotes cultural exchange with France; attached teaching centres in Arequipa, Chiclayo, Cusco, Iquitos, Piura and Trujillo; Dir of Operations, Peru PIERRE RIVRON.

British Council: 22nd Fl., Torre Parque Mar, Avda Jose Larco 1301, Miraflores, Lima 18; tel. (1) 617-3060; fax (1) 617-3065; e-mail bc.lima@britishcouncil.org.pe; internet www .britishcouncil.org/peru; offers courses and exams in English language and British culture and promotes cultural exchange with the UK; Dir FRANK FITZPATRICK.

Goethe-Institut: Jr. Nazca 722, Jesús María, Casilla 3042, Lima 100; tel. (1) 433-3180; fax (1) 431-0494; e-mail vl@lima.goethe .org; internet www.goethe.de/hn/lim/deindex .htm; offers courses and exams in German language and culture and promotes cultural exchange with Germany; library of 7,500 vols, 24 periodicals; Dir DR WALTER-JÜRGEN SCHORLIES.

MEDICINE

Academia de Estomatología del Perú (Peruvian Academy of Stomatology): Calle Los Próceres 261, Urb. Sta Constanza, Lima 33; tel. (1) 435-1623; fax (1) 435-1623; f. 1929; 165 mems; library of 600 vols; Pres. Dr JUAN OTAYZAN ARRIETA; Sec. Dr ORLANDO NORIEGA VÁSQUEZ; publ. *Estomatologia Integrada* (2 a year).

Academia Nacional de Medicina (National Academy of Medicine): Apdo 1589, Malecón Armendáriz 791, Miraflores, Lima 18; f. 1884; 40 mems; 40 associate mems; 40 corresp. and hon. mems; Pres. Dr GINO COSTA ELICE; Perm. Sec. Dr JAVIER MARIATEGUI; publ. *Boletín de la Academia Nacional de Medicina*.

Academia Peruana de Cirugía: Malecón Armendáriz 791, Miraflores; e-mail urocca@ amauta.rec.net.pe; f. 1940; activities relate to the development of surgery in Peru; national and foreign membership; 100 titular mems and unlimited number of associates; Pres. Dr LUIS GURMENDI; publ. *Revista*.

Asociación Médica Peruana 'Daniel A. Carrión' (Peruvian Medical Association): Jirón Ucayali 218, Lima; f. 1920; 1,499 mems; Dir Dr MAX ARNILLAS ARANA; Sec. Dr MANUEL PAREDES MANRIQUE; publ. *Revista Médica Peruana*.

Federación Médica Peruana (Peruvian Medical Association): Almte Guisse 2165, Lima; f. 1942; 1,230 mems; Pres. Dr VICENTE UBILLÚS; Sec. Dr ENRIQUE FERNÁNDEZ V.; publ. *Boletín de la Federación Médica Peruana*.

Sociedad Peruana de Tisiología y Enfermedades Respiratorias (Peruvian Phthisiological Society): Domingo Casanova 116, Lince, Lima; f. 1935; 280 mems; Pres. CARLOS MENDOZA EUWING; Sec. RUBEN PAZ ANSSUINI; publ. *Revista Peruana de Tuberculosis y Enfermedades Respiratorias* (2 a year).

NATURAL SCIENCES

Biological Sciences

Sociedad Entomológica del Perú: Apdo 14-0413, Lima 14; f. 1956; 700 mems; library of 9,500 vols; Pres. PEDRO G. AGUILAR F.; Sec. JESÚS ALCÁZAR S.; publ. *Revista Peruana de Entomología* (annually).

Mathematical Sciences

Instituto Nacional de Estadística (National Institute of Statistics): Avda Gral Garzón 662, Jesús María, Lima 11; tel. 4333104; fax 4333159; e-mail infoinei@inei .gob.pe; internet www.inei.gob.pe; f. 1975; involved in population, housing, socio-economic and agricultural censuses and surveys; plans statistical policy of country; library of 9,000 vols; Dir FARID MATUK CASTRO; publs *Indice de precios al consumidor* (monthly), *Compendio Económico* (annually), *Informe Económico Mensual* (monthly), *Cuentas Nacionales – PBI Nacional* (annually).

Physical Sciences

Asociación Peruana de Astronomía: Avda de las Artes Norte 637, Lima 41; fax (1) 431-3084; e-mail apaastro@amauta.rcp .net.pe; f. 1946; 550 mems; library of 1,000 vols, 1,000 periodicals; Pres. JAVIER RAMÍREZ GUIJA; Sec. PATRICIA VIGIL V.; publ. *Boletín* (3 a year).

Sociedad Geológica del Perú (Peruvian Geological Society):; tel. (1) 461-2362; fax (1) 461-5272; e-mail sgp@sgp.org.pe; internet www.sgp.org.pe; f. 1924; 800 mems; library of 40,000 vols; Pres. Ing. CARLOS MORALES BERMÚDEZ LÁMPARO; publs *Boletín*

(annually), *Resumenes Extendidos* (conference proceedings, every 3 years).

Sociedad Peruana de Espeleología (Peruvian Speleological Society): Jr Puno 450, Lima; f. 1965; Pres. Ing. CARLOS MORALES-BERMÚDEZ LÁMPARO; publ. *Cavernas Peruanas*.

Sociedad Química del Perú (Peruvian Chemistry Society): Apdo 14-0576, Lima 14; f. 1933; 1,200 mems; library of 5,600 vols; Pres. OLGA LOCK DE UGAZ; Sec.-Gen. Dr JUAN DE DIOS GUEVARA R.; publ. *Boletín* (quarterly).

RELIGION, SOCIOLOGY AND ANTHROPOLOGY

Centro Amazónico de Antropología y Aplicación Práctica (CAAAP): Apdo 14-0166, Lima 14; tel. 625811; fax 638846; f. 1974; defends the cultural identity and the way of life of marginalized Amazonian people and seeks to protect natural resources in the Amazonian region; library of 5,000 vols; Dir FABIOLA LUNA; publs *Amazonía Peruana* (2 a year), *Nuestra Tierra–Nuestra Vida* (quarterly), *El Trueno* (quarterly).

Instituto de Estudios Etnológicos (Institute of Ethnological Studies): Avda Alfonso Ugarte 650, Apdo. 3048, Lima 1; tel. and fax (1) 423-5892; e-mail mncp@inictel.gob.pe; internet museodelacultura.perucultural.org .pe; f. 1946; under auspices of Museo Nacional de la Cultura Peruana; publ. *Revista del Museo Nacional* (annually).

Instituto de Estudios Islámicos: Calle Rey de Bahamonde 121, Vista Alegre, Surco, Lima 33; tel. 489720; f. 1959; sound archives, numismatic collection, etc.; interests include economics, sociology and politics of contemporary Muslim world, the Palestinian problem, the Iranian Islamic revolution, the al-Fateh (Jamahiriya) revolution, and the diffusion of Islamic religious values in South America; special interest in Islamic-America relations in 16th and 17th centuries and nowadays; Pres. Dr RAFAEL GUEVARA BAZÁN; Chief Officer Prof. ELVA ZEGARRA TORREBLANCA.

Instituto Indigenista Peruano (Peruvian Institute of Indian Affairs): C/o Ministerio de Agricultura, Avda Salaverry s/n, Jesús María, Lima 11; f. 1946; studies the specific problems of indigenous groups; library of 1,500 vols, 1,046 periodicals; Dir Ing. CARLOS EDUARDO MENDOZA SALDIVAR; publ. *Perú-Indígena* (annually).

TECHNOLOGY

Asociación de Ingenieros Civiles del Perú: Nicolás de Piérola 788, 4° piso, Casilla 1314, Lima.

Asociación Electrotécnica Peruana: Avda República de Chile 284, Oficina 201, Lima; f. 1943; Pres. Ing. LEONCIO BARBA ARANJO.

Instituto Peruano de Ingenieros Mecánicos: Avda República de Chile 284, Of. 201, Lima; Dir ROBERTO HEREDIA ZAVADA.

Sociedad de Ingenieros del Perú (Society of Peruvian Engineers): Avda N. de Piérola 788, Casilla 1314, Lima; library of 15,000 vols; Sec. Ing. ADOLFO BUSTAMANTE T.; publ. *Ingenería* (3 a year).

Research Institutes

GENERAL

Institut de Recherche pour le Développement (IRD): Apdo 18-1209, Lima 18; tel. (1) 422-4719; fax (1) 222-2174; f. 1967; research in geology, agronomy, botany, ecol-

ogy, economy, archaeology, geography; 15 staff; library of 950 vols; natural history museum; Dir Rep. RENÉ MAROCCO; publ. *Boletín Sistemas Agrarios*; (see main entry under France).

AGRICULTURE, FISHERIES AND VETERINARY SCIENCE

Estación Experimental Vista Florida: Km 8 Carretera Chiclayo-Ferreñafe, Casilla 116, Chiclayo; f. 1970; crops research (plant protection, rice, corn, beans, sorghum); 26 staff; library of 5,000 vols; Dir JOSÉ HERNÁNDEZ L..

Instituto Nacional de Investigación y Promoción Agropecuaria (National Agricultural Research Institute): Avda Guzmán Blanco 390, Lima 5; tel. 317159; f. 1929; library of 50,000 vols; technical staff 350; Exec. Dir Dr JAVIER GAZZO FERNÁNDEZ DÁVILA; publs *Revista de Investigación Avances en Investigación, Serie de Boletín Investigación, Avances en Investigación, Serie de Boletín Técnico, Informes Especiales, Divulgaciones, Boletín Bibliográfico*.

ECONOMICS, LAW AND POLITICS

Instituto Peruano para la Investigación de la Estadística: Avda Benavides 190, Lima 18; tel. 46-40-64; f. 1974; study of statistics in general, and especially in relation to economics; library of 5,000 vols; organizes symposia, seminars, courses, etc.

EDUCATION

Instituto Experimental de Educación Primaria No. 1: Barranco Avda Miraflores 200, Lima; f. 1940; to study systems and methods for the development of learning and the means to evaluate and control the results; library of scholastic texts; Dir Prof. NARCISO GONZÁLEZ CH; publ. *Boletín*.

MEDICINE

Instituto de Cultura Alimentaria Birchner-Benner: Diez Canseco 487, Miraflores, Lima; fax 444-4250; f. 1979; research into diet, especially of meat-substitutes and high-nutrition and low-cost food mixtures; warns about inadequate diet; promotes agriculture by biological methods; film and sound archives; Pres. CÉSAR MORALES GARCÍA; Sec. MARCELA CÁRDENAS.

Instituto de Investigaciones Alérgicas 'Dr Luis E. Betetta' ('Dr Luis E. Betetta' Allergy Research Institute): Avda La Marina 2501, Maranga, San Miguel, Lima 32.

Instituto Nacional de Salud (National Institute of Health): Cápac Yupanqui No. 1400–Jesús Maria, Lima 11; tel. (1) 4713254; fax (1) 4717443; internet www.ins.gob.pe; f. 1936; communicable diseases, occupational diseases, nutritional disorders, food and drug quality control, research, production of vaccines and reagents, traditional medicine; library of 5,000 books, 30,000 journals, 1,000 theses; Head Dr CÉSAR NÁQUIRA VELARDE; publs *Boletín* (weekly), *Revista Peruana de Medicina Experimental y Salud Pública* (quarterly).

NATURAL SCIENCES

General

Instituto del Mar del Perú (IMARPE) (Peruvian Marine Institute): Esq. Gral. Valle y Gamarra, Apdo 22, Callao; tel. (51) 420-2000; internet www.imarpe.gob.pe; f. 1964; oceanography, marine biology, fisheries, aquaculture, aquatic ecotoxicology, hydroacoustics, biodiversity; library of 75,000 vols; Pres. Contra-Almirante HUGO ARÉVALO ESCARÓ; Exec. Dir Econ. GODOFREDO CAÑOTE SANTAMARINA; Scientific Dir Biol. RENATO

GUEVARA-CARRASCO; publs *Informe* (research results, 6 a year), *Boletín* (scientific papers, 1 or 2 a year), *Informe Progresivo* (current research activities, monthly).

Biological Sciences

Instituto de Biología Andina (Institute of Andean Biology): Apdo 5073, Lima; f. 1930; affiliated to the Faculty of Medicine, San Marcos Univ.; laboratories in Lima, Morococha and Puno; mobile laboratory research on physiology of inhabitants of the Andes and their resistance to high altitudes, acclimatization and fertility of animals taken to high altitudes with a view to industrial use, methods of hygiene, adaptive faculties of men at great heights, chronic mountain sickness and remedies, ecology and sociological problems; library of 1,091 vols, 400 periodicals; Dir Dr TULIO VELÁSQUEZ; publ. *Archivos de Biología Andina* (quarterly).

Physical Sciences

Dirección General de Meteorología del Perú (National Meteorological Service): Jr Cahuide 785, Jesus Maria, Lima 11; tel. 470-4863; fax 470-4863; internet www.senamhi.gob.pe; f. 1928; 79 primary stations; publ. *Boletín* (annually).

Instituto Geofísico del Perú (Geophysical Institute): Apdo 3747, Lima; tel. (014) 365640; fax (014) 370258; f. 1919 as Huancayo Magnetic Observatory of the Carnegie Institution of Washington, transferred to the Peruvian Government 1947; education sector; observatories in Huancayo, Jicamarca, Ancón, Arequipa and Lima; basic and mission-oriented research; international programmes in geomagnetism, seismology, atmospheric sciences, solar activity and natural hazards; Pres. Dr MANUEL CHANG.

TECHNOLOGY

Instituto Geológico, Minero y Metalúrgico (Institute of Geology, Mining and Metallurgy): Apdo 889, Avda Canadá 1470, San Borja, Lima; tel. (1) 224-2965; fax (1) 225-4540; e-mail postmaster@ingemmet.gob.pe; internet www.ingemmet.gob.pe; f. 1978; carries out and co-ordinates geological mapping at regional scale and evaluates mineral resources; environmental assessment and ecological zonification; provides mining and metallurgical information; library of 33,098 vols; Pres. ROMULO MUCHO MAMANI; Dir HUGO RIVERA MANTILLA; publs *Boletín Serie A: Carta Geológica Nacional* (irregular), *Boletín Serie B: Geología Económica* (irregular), *Boletín Serie C: Geodinámica e Ingeniería Geológica* (irregular), *Boletín Serie D: Estudios Regionales* (irregular), *Informes Técnicos* (irregular), *Newsletter* (electronic, monthly).

Instituto Peruano de Energía Nuclear (Peruvian Nuclear Energy Institute): Avda Canadá 1470, San Borja Dist., Lima 41, Apdo 1687, Lima 100; tel. (1) 224-8998; fax (1) 224-8991; f. 1975; research into peaceful uses of nuclear energy in medicine, biology, agriculture and industry, prospecting, mining and processing of uranium ores; management of nuclear reactor and operation of a radioisotope production plant; nucleo-electricity planning; training and research; library: information and documentation centre of 75,000 vols, periodicals, monographs; Pres. JORGE DU BOIS GERVASI; Exec. Dir Dr CONRADO SEMINARIO ARCE; publs *Boletín de Informaciones* (quarterly), *Informes*.

Affiliated institute:

Centro Superior de Estudios Nucleares: Avda Canadá 1470, San Borja, Lima 41; tel. (1) 224-5090; Dir Ing. IGNACIO FRISANCHO PINEDA.

Libraries and Archives

Arequipa

Biblioteca de la Universidad Nacional de San Agustín: Apdo 23, Arequipa; f. 1900; 430,000 vols, 1,204 pamphlets and 535 periodicals; in addition the University has 12 specialized libraries; Dir Dr JORGE DÍAZ ENCINAS; publ. *Revista de Investigación de la Universidad*.

Biblioteca Pública Municipal de Arequipa: Ejercicios 310, Apdo 435, Arequipa; f. 1879; 28,000 vols; Librarian ENRIQUE ALZÁGARA BALLÓN; also houses *Casa de la Cultura*.

Callao

Biblioteca de la Escuela Naval del Perú (Naval School Library): La Punta, Callao; f. 1914; Librarian ABEL ULLOA FERNÁNDEZ-PRADA; specialized library of 6,500 vols.

Biblioteca Pública Municipal Piloto: Esq. Ruiz y Colón, Callao; f. 1936, reorganized 1957; 48,312 vols; 42 mems; Dir ROSA SÁNCHEZ DE WU.

Lima

Archivo General de la Nación (National Archives): Palacio de Justicia, Calle Manuel Cuadros s/n., Apdo 3124, Lima; tel. (1) 275930; fax (1) 426-7221; e-mail agn.peru@mail.pol.com.pe; f. 1861; 2 sections, Administrative and Historical; Dir Dra AIDA MENDOZA NAVARRO; publs *Legislación Archivística Peruana*, *Revista del AGN*.

Archivo Histórico Municipal: Palacio Municipal de Lima, Jirón de la Unión 300, Lima; f. 1963; documents, certificates from the 19th century; Librarian LUIS E. WUFFARDEN.

Biblioteca Central de la Pontificia Universidad Católica del Perú: Apdo 1761, Lima; tel. (1) 460-2870 ext. 176; fax (1) 463-3773; e-mail biblio@pucp.edu.pe; internet www.pucp.edu.pe; f. 1917; 400,000 vols, 30,000 audio-visual items; Dir Dr CARMEN VILLANUEVA.

Biblioteca Central de la Universidad Nacional Mayor de San Marcos (San Marcos National University General Library): Pasaje Simón Rodríguez 697, Lima 1; tel. (14) 428-5210; fax (14) 428-5210; f. 1551; the collection corresponding to the colonial period was incorporated in the *Biblioteca Pública*—now the *Biblioteca Nacional*—when the latter was founded in 1821; the Peruvian Section has valuable material on history, law, and literature; Dir Dr OSWALDO SALAVERRY GARCÍA; 450,000 vols; publ. *Boletín Bibliográfico* (annually).

Biblioteca de la Municipalidad de Lima: Pza. de Armas s/n, Lima; tel. (1) 4279241; fax (1) 4332422; f. 1935; gen. reference about Lima and its municipal govt; 22,000 vols; Librarian LUZMILA TELLO.

Biblioteca de la Universidad Nacional de Ingeniería: Apdo 1301, Lima; 29,000 vols; Librarian JUANA PAREJA MARMANILLO.

Biblioteca del Ministerio de Relaciones Exteriores (Library of the Ministry of Foreign Affairs): Palacio Torre-Tagle, Lima; f. 1921; 12,351 vols; Dir MANUEL G. GALDO; publ. *Maris Aestus*.

Biblioteca Nacional del Perú (National Library): Avda Abancay 4ta Cdra s/n, Lima 01; tel. (1) 4287690; fax (1) 4277331; e-mail sg@binape.gob.pe; internet www.binape.gob.pe; f. 1821 by José de San Martín; possesses copies of the first printed works in Peru and the Americas; 736,465 vols, 32,500 MSS, 12,499 maps, 11,000 photographs, 2,164,413 periodicals; Dir Dr SINESIO LÓPEZ JIMÉNEZ; publs *Fénix* (annually), *Bibliografía Peruana* (annually), *Boletín de la Biblioteca Nacional* (irregular), *Gaceta Bibliotecaria del Perú* (irregular), *Bibliografías de intelectuales Peruanos* (irregular), *Revista Libros y Artes* (quarterly).

Museums and Art Galleries

Arequipa

Museo Arqueológico (Archaeological Museum): Ciudad Universitaria, Pabellón de la Cultura, Altos, Casilla 23, Arequipa; tel. 22-9719; f. 1933; ceramics, mummies; Dir Dr E. LINARES MÁLAGA.

Ayacucho

Museo Histórico Regional de Ayacucho (Regional Historical Museum of Ayacucho): Centro Cultural Simón Bolívar, Avda Los Libertadores s/n, Ayacucho; f. 1954; archaeology, anthropology, history and popular crafts; library of 4,724 vols (including bound periodicals, etc.); Dir CÉSAR O. PRADO; Curator FREDY LAGOS ARRIARÁN; publ. *Anuario*.

Callao

Museo del Ejército del Perú (Army Museum of Peru): Fortaleza del Real Felipe, Plaza Independencia, Callao; f. 1984; Dir LUIS LOAYZA MORALES.

Museo Naval del Perú J. J. Elias Murguía (Naval History Museum): Avda Jorge Chávez 123, Plaza Grau, Callao; tel. 294793; f. 1958; library: specialist library of 7,948 vols; Dir Capitán de Fragata (retd) ALFONSO AGÜERO MORAS; publ. *Fuentes para la Historia Naval*.

Cuzco

Museo Arqueológico: Calle Tigre 165, Cuzco; Dir Dr LUIS A. PARDO.

Museo Histórico Regional de Cuzco: Cuesta del Almirante s/n, Palacio del Almirante s/n, Cuzco; f. 1946; Peruvian colonial art, Cuzco schools of painting affiliated to Inst. Nacional de Cultura; Dir ANTONIA VEGA CENTENO B.; publ. *Revista del Museo Histórico Regional*.

Huancayo

Museo Arqueológico 'Federico Gálvez Durand' de la Gran Unidad Escolar 'Santa Isabel': Pichcus s/n, Huancayo; f. 1952; 1,654 archaeological specimens from Nazca and other Peruvian cultures; examples of weaving, gold and bronze ornaments, fossils.

Huánuco

Museo-Biblioteca 'Leoncio Prado': 2 de Mayo y Tarapacá, Huánuco; f. 1945; natural history; Curator RICARDO E. FLORES.

Huaráz

Museo Arqueologico de Ancash: Avda Luzuriaga 762, Plaza de Armes, Huaráz, Ancash; tel. (43) 42-1551; fax (43) 42-4849; e-mail museoarqueologicodeancash@hotmail.com; internet www.museoarqueologicodeancash.com; f. 1935; pre-Hispanic history of the Ancash region; exhibits include ceramics, metalwork, textiles, human remains collns from the Chavín, Recuay, Moche, Wari, Chimu and Inca cultures; largest Lithic Park in South America, incl. stone carvings and megalithic statues from the Recuay culture; Dir Arq. FERNANDO ENVER GUTIERREZ HONORES; publs *Cuadernillo de Difusión*, *Revista*.

Ica

Museo Cabrera: Plaza de Armas, Bolívar 174, Ica; f. 1966; collection of ancient engraved stones and pottery; library of 100,000 vols; Dir Dr JAVIER CABRERA.

Lambayeque

Museo Regional Arqueológico 'Bruning' de Lambayeque ('Bruning' Archaeological Museum): Calle 2 de Mayo 48, Lambayeque; f. 1924; nearly 8,000 exhibits, of which 1,366 gold, 110 silver; textile, ceramic, wooden and stone pieces; two unique blue and black granite mortars incised with mythological figures in 'Chavin' style; Dir WALTER ALVA.

Lima

Museo Arqueológico 'Rafael Larco Herrera' (Archaeological Museum): Avda Bolívar 1515, Pueblo Libre, Lima 21; tel. (1) 461-1312; fax (1) 461-5640; e-mail webmaster@museolarco.org; internet museolarco.perucultural.org.pe; f. 1926; Peruvian pre-Columbian history; collection of gold, silver, erotica; 45,000 classified archaeological objects; library of 10,000 vols; Exec. Dir ANDRÉS ALVAREZ-CALDERÓN.

Branch museum:

Museo de Arte Precolombino: Plaza de Las Nazarenas 231, Cusco; tel. and fax (84) 233-210; e-mail amap@infonegocio.net.pe; internet map.perucultural.org.pe; f. 2003; arts of ancient Peruvian cultures; 450 objects from 1250 BC–AD 1532; Dir ANDRÉS ALVAREZ CALDERÓN; Exec. Dir EDGAR CASAVERDE.

Museo de Arte de Lima (Museum of Art): Paseo Colón 125, Lima; tel. (1) 423-6332; fax (1) 331-0126; e-mail prensa@museodearte .org.pe; internet www.museodearte.org.pe; inaugurated in its present form in 1961; exhibits of Peruvian art from its origins to the present day; Pre-Colombian Department: ceramics, carvings, Paracas woven material dating from 400 BC; Colonial Department: furniture, sculpture, paintings, religious art, silver; Modern Department: furniture and paintings since 19th c.; an important film archive; studio art courses; library of 4,000 items; restoration and conservation laboratory; Dir NATALIA MAJLUF BRAHIM; publ. *Bulletin* (6 a year).

Museo de Arte Italiano: Paseo de la República 250, Lima 1; tel. (1) 423-9932; fax (1) 423-9932; f. 1923; 1920s Italian art donated by the Italian colony in Peru; organizes courses and conferences; library of 500 vols; Dir IRENE VELAOCHAGA REY.

Museo de Historia Natural de la Universidad Nacional Mayor de San Marcos (Natural History Museum of the National University of San Marcos): Avda Arenales 1256, Apdo 14-0434, Lima 14; tel. (1) 471-0117; fax (1) 265-6819; e-mail museohn@ unmsm.edu.pe; f. 1918; incl. Herbario San Marcos (USM), with 300,000 specimens largely of Peruvian flora and units of zoology, botany, ecology, and geosciences; zoological collns; library of 8,000 vols; Dir Prof. Dr NIELS VALENCIA; publs *Serie 'A' Zoología, Serie 'B' Botánica, Serie 'C' Geología, Memorias, Serie de Divulgación* (irreg.), *Boletín del Museo de Historia Natural UNMSM, Nueva Serie* (irreg.).

Museo del Virreinato (Museum of the Viceroys): Quinta de Presa, Jirón Chira 344, Rímac, Lima; tel. (1) 481-3867; f. 1935; sited in an 18th-century mansion; exhibits relating to the period of the Spanish Viceroys; Dir JOSÉ FLORES ARAOS; publ. *Revista*.

Museo Geológico de la Universidad Nacional de Ingeniería del Perú (Geological Museum of the National University of Engineering): Avda Tupac Amaru, Lima; f. 1891 as Museo de Yacimentos Minerales y Metalíferos de la Escuela Nacional de Ingenieros, name changed 1955; incorporates the Raymondi collections; Chief of Dept. of Geology JULIO DAVILA V.

Museo Nacional de Arqueología, Antropología e Historia del Perú (National Museum of Archaeology, Anthropology and History): Plaza Bolívar s/n, Pueblo Libre, Lima 21; tel. (1) 4635070; fax (1) 4632009; f. 1945; library of 30,000 vols; colln contains pre-Inca and Inca remains, and artefacts from the colonial and republican periods; Dir FERNANDO ROSAS MOSCOSO; publs *Boletines, Arqueológicas, Historia y Cultura, Cuadernos de Investigaciones.*

Museo Nacional de la Cultura Peruana: Avda Alfonso Ugarte 650, Apdo 3048, Lima 1; tel. and fax 4235892; e-mail mncp@inc.gob .pe; internet museodelacultura.perucultural .org.pe; f. 1946; responsible for Instituto de Estudios Etnológicos and the Instituto de Arte Peruano 'José Sabogal'; popular art and ethnography; ethno-historical library and a photographic archive; Dir GLADYS ROQUEZ DIAZ; publs *Revista del Museo Nacional* (annually), *Boletín* (4 a year).

Museo Postal y Filatélico Correo Central de Lima (Postal and Philatelic Museum): Conde Superunda 170, Lima 1; f. 1931; library of 100 vols; Dir DORA IBERICO CASTRO.

Trujillo

Museo de Arqueología de la Universidad de Trujillo: Apdo 299, Calle Bolívar 466, Trujillo; f. 1946; Dir Dr JORGE ZEVALLOS QUIÑONES; publ. *Chimor.*

National Universities

UNIVERSIDAD NACIONAL AGRARIA LA MOLINA

Apdo 456, La Molina, Lima 1

Telephone: (1) 349-5877

Fax: (1) 348-0747

E-mail: orgi@lamolina.edu.pe

Internet: www.lamolina.edu.pe

Founded 1902; formerly Escuela Nacional de Agricultura

Language of instruction: Spanish

Academic year: April to December (two semesters)

Rector: Ing. FRANCISCO DELGADO DE LA FLOR BADARACCO

Director (Postgraduate School): Dr SALOMÓN HELFGOTT

Director (International Office): Ing. ROBERTO UGAS

Number of teachers: 495

Number of students: 4,100

Publication: *Anales Científicos* (3 a year)

DEANS

Agricultural Engineering: Dr ABEL MEJIA MARCACUZCO

Agronomy: Dr LEONOR MATTOS CALDERÓN

Economics and Planning: Ing. LUÍS JÍMENEZ DÍAZ

Fisheries: Ing. RAÚL PORTURAS OLAECHEA

Food Science and Technology: Dr AUGUSTO MONTEZ GUTIERREZ

Forestry: Ing. JOSÉ DANCE CABALLERO

Sciences: Dr EDUARDO GÓMEZ-CORNEJO BELGRANO

Zootechnics: Dr MAÑUEL ROSEMBERG BARRON

Postgraduate School: Dr SALOMÓN HELFGOTT

ATTACHED INSTITUTES

Centro de Investigaciones en Zonas Aridas: Avda Camilo Carrillo 300, Lima 11.

Instituto de Biotecnología: Dir LOURDES TAPIA.

Instituto Nacional de Desarrollo Agroindustrial: Avda La Universidad s/n, La Molina, Lima 12.

Laboratorios La Molina Calidad Total: Dir Dr JAVIER GÓMEZ.

UNIVERSIDAD NACIONAL AGRARIA DE LA SELVA

Apdo 156, Tingo María, Huánuco

Telephone: (64) 562341

Fax: (64) 561156

Internet: www.unas.edu.pe

Founded 1964

State control

Language of instruction: Spanish

Academic year: April to December

Rector: ALBERTO SILVA DEL AGUILA

Vice-Rector (Academic): TEODOLFO VALENCIA CHAMBA

Secretary-General: CLODOALDO CREDO VALDIVIA

Librarian: TULIO JURADO BAQUERIZO

Number of teachers: 190

Number of students: 1,533

Publication: *Tropicultura*

DIRECTORS OF ACADEMIC PROGRAMMES

Agronomy: Ing. ROLANDO RIOS RUIZ

Animal Breeding: Ing. EBER CARDENAS RIVERA

Food Industries: Ing. GUILLERMO DE LA CRUZ CARBANZA

Resources: Dr CESAR AUGUSTO MAZABEL TORRES

Economics and Administration: Lic. JAIME PEÑA CAMARENA

UNIVERSIDAD NACIONAL DEL ALTIPLANO

Avda Ejercito No 329, Apdo 291, Puno

Telephone: 352912

Internet: www.unap.edu.pe

Founded 1856

Academic year: March to December

Rector: Dr VICTOR TORRES ESTEVES

Administrative Vice-Rector Econ.: FRANCISCO GUTIERREZ GUTIERREZ

Academic Vice-Rector: Prof. VICTOR GALLEGOS MONROY

Head of Personnel and General Services: HERMOGENES MENDOZA ANCCO

Librarian: Prof. SERAFÍN CALSIN MAMANI

Number of teachers: 623

Number of students: 10,202

Publications: *Revistas problematicas, Revista Universitaria, Revista Visión Agraria*

DEANS

Agriculture: R. SERRUTO COLQUE

Veterinary Medicine and Stockbreeding: Prof. C. SANCHEZ VIVEROS

Economic Engineering: L. AVILA ROJAS

Accounting and Administration: E. PINEDA QUISPE

Statistics for Engineering: E. CALMET URIA

Social Sciences: M. CANO OJEDA

Mining Engineering: V. NAVARRO TORRES

Metallurgy and Geological Engineering: H. MANRIQUE MEZA

Civil Engineering, Architecture and Systems: P. ARROYO GONZALES

Agricultural Engineering: W. SALAS PALMA

Law and Political Science: J. VALDEZ PEÑARANDA

Chemical Engineering: N. VILLAFUERTE PRUDENCIO

Biological Sciences: S. ATENCIO LIMACHI

Education: J. L. CACERES MONROY

Health Sciences: R. LOPEZ VELASQUEZ

Nursing: N. CALSIN CHIRINOS
Social Work: G. PINTO SOTELO
Postgraduate School: F. CÁCEDA DÍAZ

UNIVERSIDAD NACIONAL DE LA AMAZONÍA PERUANA

Sargento Lores 385, Apdo 496, Iquitos, Loreto
Telephone: 2343657
Fax: 233657
Founded 1962
State control
Language of instruction: Spanish
Academic year: April to February (two terms)
Rector: JOSÉ ROJAS VÁSQUEZ
Academic Vice-Rector: Lic. PEDRO VÁSQUEZ PÉREZ
Librarian: MARGARITA FASANANDO VÁSQUEZ
Number of teachers: 400
Number of students: 3,200
Publication: *Conocimiento*

DEANS

Faculty of Agronomy Science: Ing. JULIO VÁSQUEZ RAMÍREZ
Faculty of Biology: ANDRÉS URTEAGA CAVERO
Faculty of Education and Humanities: Prof. JOSÉ ZUMAETA TORRES
Faculty of Administration and Accountancy: Prof. HEDMER PASQUEL CHONG
Faculty of Nursing: Enf. PABLO CASTRO TRELLES
Faculty of Food Sciences: Ing. JORGE TORRES LUPERDI
Faculty of Forestry: Ing. JOSÉ TORRES VÁSQUEZ
Faculty of Chemistry: Ing. JESÚS LÓPEZ SANGAMA
Faculty of Human Medicine: Dr MARIO THEMME RUNCIMAN
Faculty of Zootechnics: Ing. FERNANDO ARAUJO PAREDES

UNIVERSIDAD NACIONAL DE ANCASH 'SANTIAGO ANTÚNEZ DE MAYOLO'

Apdo 70, Huáraz, Ancash
Telephone: (44) 722085
Fax: (44) 721393
E-mail: jnunez00@yahoo.com
Internet: www.unasam.edu.pe
Founded 1977
State control
Language of instruction: Spanish
Academic year: April to December
Rector: Mag. ENRIQUE HUERTA BERRIOS
Vice-Rector (Academic): Dr JOSE FELIX NUÑEZ CALDERON
Vice-Rector (Administrative): Lic. CARLOS REYES PAREJA
Secretary: Econ. WILMER SICCHA CUSTODIO
Librarian: Ing. OSCAR RUIZ CASIMIRO
Number of teachers: 400
Number of students: 6,500
Publications: *Avance Santiaguino* (monthly), *Informativo UNASAM*, *Revista de Investigacion de la UNASAM* (3 a year)

DEANS

Faculty of Agricultural Sciences: Ing. PEDRO COLONIA CERNA
Faculty of Civil Engineering: Ing. FELISMERO SALINAS FERNANDEZ
Faculty of Economic and Administrative Sciences: Econ. DARIO VAREAS ARCE
Faculty of Education: Lic. VICTOR PAREDES ESTEÍA
Faculty of Environmental Sciences: Ing. CESAR DAVILA PAREDES
Faculty of Food Industry Engineering: Ing. DANIEL REEVES ITA

Faculty of Law and Political Science: Abog. FABIAN ANICETO LUCERO
Faculty of Medicine: Lic. RIBIANA LEÓN HUERTA
Faculty of Mining, Geological and Metallurgical Engineering: Ing. JACINTO ISIDRO GIRALDO
Faculty of Science: Lic. ESMELIN NIGUIN ALAYO

UNIVERSIDAD NACIONAL DE CAJAMARCA

Apdo 16, Jr Lima 549, Cajamarca
Telephone: 2796
Internet: www.unc.edu.pe
Founded 1962
State control
Language of instruction: Spanish
Academic year: March to December (two semesters)
Rector: Prof. CÉSAR A. PAREDES CANTO
Vice-Rectors: Dr HOMERO BAZÁN ZURITA, Ing. AURELIO MARTOS DÍAZ
Librarian: LUIS RONCAL
Number of teachers: 387
Number of students: 5,700
Publications: *Gaceta Universitaria*, *Revista de la UNTC*

DEANS

Agriculture: Dr ISIDORO SÁNCHEZ VEGA
Economics, Administration and Accountancy: Prof. SEGUNDO CIEZA YAÑEZ
Education: Dr JOSUÉ TEJADA ATALAYA
Engineering: Ing. JULIO GUZMÁN PERALTA
Health: Dr JORGE CÉSPEDES ABANTO
Social Sciences: Prof. ALIDOR LUNA TELLO
Veterinary Medicine: Dr ROBERTO ACOSTA GÁLVEZ
Animal Husbandry: Ing. TULIO MONDRAGÓN RONCAL

UNIVERSIDAD NACIONAL DEL CALLAO

Saenz Peña 1060, Apdo 138, Callao
Telephone: 429-1600
Fax: 429-6607
E-mail: rector@redunac.unac.edu.pe
Internet: www.unac.edu.pe
Founded 1966
State control
Language of instruction: Spanish
Academic year: April to December (two terms)
Rector: ALBERTO ARROYO VIALE
Vice-Rectors: VICTOR MEREA LLANOS GLORIA SAENZ ORREGO
Registrar: PABLO ARELLANO UBILLUZ
Librarian: LUIS CARRASCO VEREGAS
Number of teachers: 550
Number of students: 12,000
Publications: *Ciencia y Tecnología* (annually), *Catálogo de Informes de Investigación* (annually)

DEANS

Administration: CÉSAR ANGULO RODRÍGUEZ
Accounting: CARLOS HÚRTADO CRIADO
Chemical Engineering: PABLO DIAZ BRAVO
Economics: JUAN NUNURA CHULLY
Electrical and Electronic Engineering: FRANCO VELIZ LIZÁRRAGA
Environmental Engineering: MARIA TERESA VALDERRAMA ROJAS
Fish and Food Engineering: JUVENCIO VRIOS AVENDOÑO
Health Sciences: ARCELIA ROJAS SALAZAR
Industrial and Systems Engineering: MANUEL MORI PAREDES
Mathematics and Physics: ROEL MARIA VIDAL GUZMÁN

Mechanical Engineering: FELIX GUERRERO ROLDAN
Postgraduate School: LIDA SANÉZ FALCÓN

UNIVERSIDAD NACIONAL DEL CENTRO DEL PERÚ

Calle Real 160, Casilla Postal 138, Huancayo 570, Junín
Telephone: (64) 235531
Fax: (64) 235981
Internet: www.uncp.edu.pe
Founded 1959
State control
Language of instruction: Spanish
Academic year: April to December (two terms)
Rector: Ing. ESAÚ TIBERIO CARO MEZA
Academic Vice-Rector: Ing. HUGO AYALA SÍNCHEZ
Chief Administrative Officer: Prof. KRÚGER SARAPURA YUPANQUI
Librarian: Dr FERNANDO ARAUCO VILLAR
Number of teachers: 705
Number of students: 8,395
Publications: *Boletín Informativo* (monthly), *Proceso* (irregular), *Ciencias Agrarias*

DEANS

Accountancy: CPC HERNANDO PAYANO ROJAS
Administration: Lic. ANDRÉS ILDEFONSO SUÁREZ
Agronomy: Ing. GLICERIO LÓPEZ ORIHUELA
Forestry: Ing. PEDRO ARIZAPANA ANCCASI
Stockbreeding: Ing. HUMBERTO RODRÍGUEZ LANDEO
Economics: Econ. MANUEL LARRAURI ROJAS
Anthropology: Ing. JULIO BARRERA YUPANQUI
Architecture: Arq. FELIPE ARIAS MATOS
Nursing: Lic. HÉCTOR ZAPATA RIVERA
Medicine: Dr RIGOBERTO ZÚÑIGA MERA
Food Engineering: Ing. LIBIA GUTIÉRREZ GONZALES
Mechanical Engineering: Ing. RAÚL MAYCO CHÁVEZ
Mining Engineering: Ing. ÓRISON DELZO SALOMÉ
Electrical, Electronic and Systems Engineering: Ing. HÉCTOR TORRES MARAVÍ
Metallurgical Engineering: Ing. EUGENIO MUCHA BENITO
Education and Humanities: Lic. CARLOS GAMBOA DEL CARPIO
Chemical Engineering: Ing. ANTONIO COCHACHI GUADALUPE
Social Work: Lic. LIDIA LAGONES MIRANDA
Postgraduate School: Dr PABLO MOSOMBITE PINEDO

UNIVERSIDAD NACIONAL 'DANIEL ALCIDES CARRIÓN'

Edif. Estatal 4, Apdo 77, Cerro de Pasco, Pasco
Telephone: 2197
Internet: www.undac.edu.pe
Founded 1965
Rector: Prof. NORBERTO GONZALES PERALTA
Number of teachers: c. 90
Number of students: c. 1,000
Faculties of economics, education, mining and metallurgy.

UNIVERSIDAD NACIONAL DE EDUCACIÓN 'ENRIQUE GUZMÁN Y VALLE'

La Cantuta s/n, Chosica, Lima 15
Telephone: 910052
Internet: www.une.edu.pe
Founded 1967
State control
Language of instruction: Spanish

President: Dra DORALIZA TOVAR TORRES

First Vice-President (Academic): Dra LUZ DORIS SÁNCHEZ PINEDO

Second Vice-President (Administrative): VIDAL BAUTISTA CARRASCO

General Secretary: Dra GLADYS RAMÍREZ ADRIANZÉN

Registrar: Prof. MIREIA SOLÉ ALABART

Librarian: MARGARITA LÓPEZ M.

Library of 16,500 vols

Number of teachers: 190

Number of students: 9,744

Publication: *Cantuta*

DEANS

Faculty of Humanities: HUMBERTO VARGAS SALGADO

Faculty of Sciences: LILIANA SUMARRIVA BUSTINZA

Faculty of Technology: JOSÉ ASTOLAZA DE LA CRUZ

Postgraduate School: Dr JORGE JHONCON KOOYIP (Dir)

UNIVERSIDAD NACIONAL 'FEDERICO VILLARREAL'

Calle Carlos González 285, Maranga, San Miguel, Lima 32

Telephone: (14) 464-1424

Fax: (14) 464-1301

E-mail: postmast@unfv-bib.edu.pe

Internet: www.unfv-bib.edu.pe

Founded 1960

State control

Language of instruction: Spanish

Academic year: April to December

Rector: Dr WILLIAM CAJAS BUSTAMANTE

Vice-Rector (Academic): Dr ERNESTO MELGAR SALMÓN

Vice-Rector (Administrative): Dr OSWALDO ALVARADO SÁNCHEZ

General Secretary: Dra IBETT ROSAS DÍAZ

Librarian (vacant)

Number of teachers: 1,800

Number of students: 25,000

Publications: *Villarreal al Futuro*, *Wiñay Yachay*, *Yachaywasi*, *Hipótesis*

DEANS

Education: Dra NANCY OLIVERO PACHECO

Humanities: Dr GIOVANNI MITROVIC DE RISI

Law and Political Sciences: Dr ALBERTO VÁSQUEZ RÍOS

Social Sciences: Lic. MARÍA RIVADENEIRA RÍOS

Public and Private Administration: Mag. JUAN STROMSDORFER GAMARRA

Economics: Mag. JORGE PASTOR PAREDES

Finance and Accountancy: C.P.C. CARLOS ESPINOZA VÁSQUEZ

Architecture, Town Planning and Plastic Arts: Arq. RODOLFO PAZ FERNÁNDEZ

Odontology: Dr ALEJANDRO SALAZAR FUERTES

Oceanography, Fisheries and Food Sciences: Dr JUAN ACOSTA POLO

Medicine: Dr SEGUNDO GALLARDO VALLEJO

Medical Technology: Lic. ROSA GUTIÉRREZ PAUCAR

Geographical and Environmental Engineering: Mag. JORGE LESCANO SANDOVAL

Electronic Engineering and Information Science: Ing. DARIO BIELLA-BIANCHI DIAMANDESCU

Psychology: Lic. FLORITA PINTO HERRERA

Civil Engineering: Ing. ROQUE SÁNCHEZ CRISTÓBAL

Industrial and Systems Engineering: Mag. JOSÉ BAZAN BRICEÑO

Natural Sciences and Mathematics: Dr CARLOS HUACO OVIEDO

UNIVERSIDAD NACIONAL DE HUANCAVÉLICA

Ciudad Universitaria Paturpampa, Huancavélica

Telephone: (67) 751-380

Fax: (67) 751-551

E-mail: secretaria@unh.edu.pe

Internet: www.unh.edu.pe

Founded 1990

Rector: MANUEL J. BASTO SÁEZ

Vice-Rector (Academic): Dr ALFONSO CORDERO FERNÁNDEZ

Vice-Rector (Administration): ADOLFO R. CORTAVARRIA

Secretary-General: Lic. ALEJANDRO RODRIGO QUILCA

DEANS

Faculty of Engineering: Dr OMAR BURGA MOSTACERO

Faculty of Business Administration: RAÚL RUA SULCA

Faculty of Nursing: Lic. BENJAMINA ORTIZ ESPINAR

Faculty of Education: ZEIDA P. HOCES LA ROSA

UNIVERSIDAD NACIONAL DE HUÁNUCO 'HERMILIO VALDIZÁN'

Jr Dos de Mayo 680, Apdo 278, Huánuco

Telephone: 512341

Fax: 513360

Founded 1964

State control

Language of instruction: Spanish

Academic year: April to July, August to December (2 semesters)

Rector: EDGARDO TORRES VERA

Vice-Rectors: ABNER CHAVEZ LEANDRO (Academic), Lic. LUIS SARA RATO (Administrative)

Head of Administration: ESTEBAN MEDINA AVILA

Librarian: Lic. AURORA AMPUDIA DAVILA

Library of 25,967 vols

Number of teachers: 261

Number of students: 5,637

Publications: *Cuadernos de Investigación*, *Boletines Informativos*, *Visita de la Provincia de León de Huánuco en 1562—Iñigo Ortíz de Zúñiga, visitador—Vols I and II*, *Antología Huanuqueña Vol I* (prose), *Vol II* (poetry) and *Vol III* (essays)

DEANS

Agriculture: N. V. MARCE PEREZ SAAVEDRA

Business Management: CPC ARTURO RIVERA Y CALDAS

Education and Humanities: Lic. JESUS ALFONSO FARFAN GUTIERREZ

Health Sciences: Psic. ROSARIO SANCHEZ INFANTAS

Law and Political Science: Abog. MANUEL CORNEJO HUAPALLA

Engineering: Mg. DORIS ALVARADO LINARES

UNIVERSIDAD NACIONAL DE INGENIERÍA

Casilla 1301, San Martín de Porres, Lima

Telephone: 811035

Internet: www.uni.edu.pe

Founded 1896 as Escuela Nacional de Ingenieros del Perú, present name 1955

State control

Language of instruction: Spanish

Academic year: April to December

Rector: Dr JOSÉ IGNACIO LOPEZ SORIA

Vice-Rectors: Ing. MIGUEL ANGEL SAENZ LIZARZABURU, Dr CASIO ORE ORE

Secretary-General: Dr ABELARDO LUDEÑA LUQUE

Library: see Libraries

Number of teachers: 996

Number of students: 12,241

Publications: *Boletín 'Quilca'*, *Revista Técnica 'Tecnia'*, *Revista Artes y Ciencias 'Amaru'*

DEANS OF FACULTIES

Architecture, Town Planning and Fine Arts: Arq. JAVIER SOTA NADAL

Science: Dr JAIME AVALOS SANCHEZ

Economics and Social Sciences: Lic. JORGE ABADIE LINARES

Civil Engineering: Ing. GENARO HUMALA AYBAR

Geology, Mining and Metallurgical Engineering: Ing. PEDRO MAXIMO ANGELES BETETA

Industrial and Systems Engineering: Ing. LUIS FLORES FONSECA

Mechanical Engineering: Ing. JUAN HORI ASANO

Electrical and Electronic Engineering: Ing. JUBERT CHAVEZ SERRANO

Petroleum Engineering: Ing. ARTURO BURGA ACOSTA

Chemical and Manufacturing Engineering: Ing. LUCIO RAMOS BENAVENTE

Environmental Engineering: Ing. JORGE PFLUCKER

UNIVERSIDAD NACIONAL JORGE BASADRE GROHMANN

Calle Alto Lima 1594, Casilla 316, Tacna

Telephone: (54) 721385 ext. 211

Fax: (54) 714911

E-mail: cote@principal.unjbg.edu.pe

Internet: www.unjbg.edu.pe

Founded 1971 as Universidad Nacional de Tacna

State control

Language of instruction: Spanish

Academic year: April to December

Chancellor: Dr CARLOS VALENTE ROSSI

Rector: Dr hab VICENTE M. CASTAÑEDA CHÁVEZ

Vice-Rectors: Mgr DANTE MANZANARES CÁCERES, Dr ELÍ ESPINOZA ATENCIA

Secretary-General: Lic. CARLOS POLO BRAVO

Librarian: Ing. ALBERTO PACHECO PACHECO

Library of 29,000 vols

Number of teachers: 457

Number of students: 4,903

Publications: *Memoria de Gestión* (annually), *Ciencia y Tecnología* (annually), *Revista Materno Infantil* (annually)

DEANS

Administration: Ing. Eco. JESÚS OLIVERA CÁCERES

Accounting: CPC BETTY COHAILA CALDERÓN

Fishing Engineering: Dr ELÍ ESPINOZA ATENCIA

Obstetrics: Obst. MIRIAM RÍOS MORENO

Food Industry Engineering: Dr MIGUEL LARREA CÉSPEDES

Agriculture: Ing. ELOY CASILLA GARCÍA

Mining Engineering: Ing. DANTE MORALES CABRERA

Metallurgical Engineering: Ing. RAÚL DEL POZO TELLO

Education: Prof. OLIVER BALLÓN MONTESINOS

Science: Lic. RAMÓN VERA ROALCABA

Nursing: Mgr. DALILA SALAS ROMERO

Medicine: Dr JORGE LÓPEZ CLAROS

Law and Arts: Psic. CARLOS PAUCA LAZO

Postgraduate School: Mgr PELAYO DELGADO TELLO

ATTACHED RESEARCH INSTITUTE

Instituto de Investigación Sísmica.

Instituto de Investigacion, Produccion y Extension Agraria: Dir Dr OSCAR FERNÁNDEZ CUTIRE.

UNIVERSIDAD NACIONAL 'JOSÉ FAUSTINO SÁNCHEZ CARRIÓN'

Avda Grau 592, Of. 301, Apdo 81, Huacho, Lima

Telephone: 324741
Internet: www.unjfsc.edu.pe

Founded 1968

Rector: Lic. SEVERO LLANOS BAYONA

Library of 5,000 vols
Number of teachers: 100
Number of students: c. 3,000

Departments of fisheries, administration, engineering, nutrition, sociology.

UNIVERSIDAD NACIONAL DE LA LIBERTAD

Independencia 431, Of. 203, Trujillo

Telephone: 24-3721
Fax: 25-6629
Internet: www.unitru.edu.pe

Founded 1824 by Simón Bolívar
State control
Language of instruction: Spanish
Academic year: April to December

Rector: Dr GUILLERMO GIL MALCA
Vice-Rector (Academic): Dr HUGO REQUEJO VALDIVIESO
Vice-Rector (Administrative): Dr WALTER ARRASCUE VARGAS
Librarian: Dr HUGO CASANOVA HERRERA

Library of 23,806 volumes, 36,001 periodicals and pamphlets
Number of teachers: 845
Number of students: 12,500

Publications: *Memoria Rectoral, Revista de Derecho, Lenguaje y Ciencia, Revista del Museo de Arqueología y Antropología, Amauta—Archivos de Oftalmología del Norte del Perú*

DEANS

Law and Political Sciences: Dr RÓGER ZAVALETA CRUZADO
Education: Dr VÍCTOR BALTODANO AZABACHE
Economic Sciences: Dr EDUARDO UPSON LEÓN
Medical Sciences: Dr RICARDO ROMERO CANO
Engineering: Ing. MANUEL TAM REYES
Biological Sciences: Dr JULIO ARELLANO BARRAGÁN
Physical and Mathematical Sciences: Dr AUGUSTO CHAFLOQUE CHAFLOQUE
Pharmacy and Biochemistry: Dr JOSÉ SILVA LARA
Social Sciences: Dr WEYDER PORTOCARRERO CÁRDENAS
Nursing: Dr ELVIRA RODRÍGUEZ ANTINORI
Chemical Engineering: Dr MARIO ALVA ASTUDILLO

UNIVERSIDAD NACIONAL MAYOR DE SAN MARCOS DE LIMA

Avda República de Chile 295, Of. 506, Casilla 454, Lima

Telephone: 314629
Internet: www.unmsm.edu.pe

Founded 1551

Rector: Dr ANTONIO CORNEJO POLAR
Vice-Rector: Dr GUSTAVO S. MIRÓ QUESADA
Administrative Director: Dr VÍCTOR HONMA SAITO

Number of teachers: 3,150
Number of students: 34,223

Publications: *Boletín Informativo, Boletín Bibliográfico, Revista de San Marcos*, etc

DIRECTORS OF ACADEMIC PROGRAMMES

Mathematics and Physics: Dr R. MOSQUERA RAMÍREZ

Chemistry and Chemical Engineering: Ing D. SÁNCHEZ MANTILLA
Geology and Geography: Dr A. ALBERCA CEVALLOS
Biology: Dra B. LIZÁRRAGA DE OLARTE
Pharmacy and Biochemistry: Dr A. DEL CASTILLO ICAZA
Veterinary Science: Dr V. FERNÁNDEZ ANHUAMÁN
Medicine: Dr J. CAMPOS REY DE CASTRO
Dentistry: Dr B. PEREA RUIZ
Social Science: Dr W. REÁTEGUI CHÁVEZ
Law and Political Science: Dr R. LA HOZ TIRADO
Philosophy, Psychology and Art: Dr A. CASTRILLÓN VIZCARRA
Linguistics, Literature and Philology: Dr M. MARTOS CARRERA
Education: Dr C. BARRIGA HERNÁNDEZ
Accountancy: Dr J. C. TRUJILLO MEZA
Economics: Dr A. MENDOZA DIEZ
Engineering: Dr P. MATÍAS ATÚNCAR
Metallurgy: Ing. M. CHÁVEZ AGUILAR
Nutrition: Dr T. AGUILAR FAJARDO
Administration: Dr A. PAÚCAR CARBAJAL
Completion Studies: Dr M. VELASCO VERÁSTEGUI
National School of Librarianship and Information Science: M. BONILLA DE GAVIRIA

UNIVERSIDAD NACIONAL MICAELA BASTIDAS DE APURIMAC

Avda Arenas 121, Abancay

Telephone: (83) 322577
Internet: www.unamba.edu.pe

Founded 2000
State control

President: Dr CARROLL DALE SALINAS
Vice-President (Academic): DALIN OMAR ENCOMENDEROS
Vice-President (Administration): ALFONSO VÍCTOR BUSTINZA CHOQUE
Secretary-General: Abog. CORINA VELÁSQUEZ SANCHEZ

Number of teachers: 104
Number of students: 1,500

Publication: *Boletín*

CO-ORDINATORS OF ACADEMIC PROGRAMMES

Business Administration: Lic. YUDBERTO VILCA COLQUE
Agricultural Engineering: Ing. FULGENCIO VILCANQUI PEREZ
Mining: Ing. NELSON PALEMON MEZA PEÑA
Education: Ing. JESÚS MANUEL IBARRA CABRERA

UNIVERSIDAD NACIONAL PEDRO RUIZ GALLO

8 de Octubre 637, Apdo 557, Lambayeque

Telephone: 2080
Internet: www.unprg.edu.pe

Founded 1970
State control
Language of instruction: Spanish

Rector: Ing. ANGEL DIAZ CELIS
Vice-Rector: Ing. PEDRO CASANOVA CHIRINOS
Librarian: Dr GUILLERMO BACA AGUINAGA

Number of teachers: 261
Number of students: 5,460

Publications: *Boletín Informativo* (monthly), *Universidad* (annually)

DIRECTORS OF ACADEMIC PROGRAMMES

Administration: Ing. M. MORENO MESTA
Agriculture: Ing. D. OJE DA PEÑA
Biology: Ing. A. DÍAZ CELIS
Accounting: Ing. A. GIRALDO ESPINOSA
Law: Ab. C. VELA MARQUILLO
Economics: Econ. G. NINAHUAMAN MUCHA

Mathematics and Statistics: Mat. N. LÓPEZ SEGURA
Nursing: Enf. C. ROMERO DE CARCELEN
Agricultural Engineering: Ing. O. VIVAR PÁRRAGA
Civil Engineering: Ing. J. SALAZAR CASTILLO
Mechanical and Electrical Engineering: Ing. J. SAENZ QUIROGA
Human Medicine: Dr A. BURGA HERMÁNDEZ
Veterinary Medicine: Vet J. GUTIÉRREZ REYES
Sociology: M. RAMOS BAZÁN
Animal Husbandry: Ing. F. VILLENA RODRÍGUEZ

UNIVERSIDAD NACIONAL DE PIURA

Esquina Apurimac-Tacna 719–743, Apdo 295, Piura

Telephone: 324603
Fax: 321931
E-mail: postmast@tallan.unp.edu.pe
Internet: www.unp.edu.pe

Founded 1961
State control
Language of instruction: Spanish
Academic year: March to December

Rector: Ing. FREDDY APONTE GUERRERO
Vice-Rector (Academic Affairs): Ing. LUÍS GUZMÁN FARFÁN
Vice-Rector (Administrative Affairs): Ing. ORLANDO ZAPATA COLOMA
Administrative Director: Lic. JORGE RODRÍGUEZ RIVERA
Librarian: Dr LUÍS VEGA FARFÁN

Number of teachers: 481
Number of students: 8,503

Publications: *Boletines, Universalia* (scientific journal, 2 a year)

DEANS

Faculty of Agronomy: Dr CÉSAR DELGADILLO FUKUSAKI
Faculty of Administrative Sciences: Lic. VICENTE SÁNCHEZ JUÁREZ
Faculty of Accounting and Finance: MÁXIMO MÁRQUEZ TACURA
Faculty of Sciences: SAUL CÉSPEDES LOMPARTE
Faculty of Social Sciences and Education: Econ. LORENZO ALVILES VALEZMORO
Faculty of Economics: Econ. JOSÉ ORDINOLA BOYER
Faculty of Industrial Engineering: Lic. MARK SADOWSKY SMITH
Faculty of Mining Engineering: Ing. RICARDO DILLON LONG
Faculty of Fisheries Engineering: MANUEL MOGOLLÓN LÓPEZ
Faculty of Human Medicine: Dr RAÚL CASTILLO ZÚÑIGA
Faculty of Animal Husbandry: ADRIÁN GUZMÁN ZAGARRO
Faculty of Law and Political Sciences: Dr CARLOS CORNEJO GUERRERO
Faculty of Civil Engineering: Ing. RICARDO CARRASCO SOTOMAYOR
Faculty of Architecture: MIGUEL ADRIANZÁN HUANCAS

UNIVERSIDAD NACIONAL DE SAN AGUSTÍN DE AREQUIPA

Santa Catalina 117, Cercado, Arequipa

Telephone: (54) 237808
Fax: (54) 237808
Internet: www.unsa.edu.pe

Founded 1828
State control
Language of instruction: Spanish
Academic year: April to December

Rector: Dr JUAN MANUEL GUILLÉN BENAVIDES
Academic Vice-Rector: ROLANDO CORNEJO CUERVO

Administrative Vice-Rector: ROBERTO KOSAKA MASUNO

General Secretary: LUIS ALBERTO VALDIVIA RODRÍGUEZ

Library: see Libraries

Number of teachers: 1,453

Number of students: 22,899

Publications: *Boletín Bibliográfico, Boletín Estadístico* (annually)

DEANS

Architecture and Town Planning: CÉSAR MÁRQUEZ MARES

Biological and Agricultural Sciences: VALDEMAR MEDINA HOYOS

Accounting and Administration: EDGAR RÍOS VILLENA

History and Social Sciences: VÍCTOR RAÚL SACCA ABUSABAL

Education: VÍCTOR HUGO LINARES HUACO

Natural and Formal Sciences: ANDRÉS REYNOSO ORTIZ

Law: RAYMUNDO NÚÑEZ LOZADA

Economics: EDGAR ACOSTA Y GUTIÉRREZ

Nursing: ESPERANZA VALDIVIA AMPUERO

Philosophy and Humanities: TERESA ARRIETA TRONCOSO DE GUZMÁN

Geology and Geophysics: MELECIO LAZO ANGULO

Civil Engineering: ENRIQUE CAMPOS MATTOS

Production and Services Engineering: JOSÉ HERNÁNDEZ VALLEJOS

Process Engineering: MARIO LOZADA REYNOSO

Medicine: BENJAMÍN PAZ ALIAGA

Psychology and Industrial and Public Relations: CÉSAR SALAS MORALES

UNIVERSIDAD NACIONAL DE SAN ANTONIO ABAD

Avda de la Cultura s/n, Apdo 367, Cusco

Telephone: 222271

Internet: www.unsaac.edu.pe

Founded 1962; reorganized 1969

Rector: Ing. CARLOS CHACON GALINDO

Number of teachers: 450

Number of students: c. 16,000

Publication: *Revista Universitaria* (annually)

Departments of economics, accountancy, education, technology, geology and mining, animal husbandry.

UNIVERSIDAD NACIONAL DE SAN CRISTÓBAL DE HUAMANGA

Portal Independencia No. 57, Apdo 220, Ayacucho

Telephone: 912522

Fax: 912510

Founded 1677; reopened 1959

State control

Language of instruction: Spanish

Academic year: March to July, August to December

Rector: Ing. PEDRO VILLENA HIDALGO

Academic Vice-Rector (vacant)

Administrative Vice-Rector: Ing. LUIS LI PONCE

Secretary-General: Ing. MAURO VARGAS CAMARENA

Librarian: MARIA ISABEL MATTA DURAN

Number of teachers: 450

Number of students: 6,000

Publications: *Boletín UNSCH, Guamangengis, Signos y Obras*

DEANS

Agronomy: Ing. CÉSAR ROLANDO RUIZ CANALES

Social Sciences: TULA RUTH ALARCON ALARCON

Law and Political Sciences: Dr DANIEL QUISPE PEREZ

Education: Prof. HECTOR ELIAS VEGA LEON

Economics and Administration: AURELIO ELORRIETA ESPINOZA

Mining and Civil Engineering: Ing. CARLOS AUBERTO PRADO PRADO

Biological Sciences: VICTOR ALEGRIA VALERIANO

Chemical and Metallurgical Engineering: Ing. CLEMENTE LIMAYLLA AGUIRRE

Nursing: Prof. VICENTE VALVERDE BALTAZAR

Obstetrics: Dr SADOT TORRES RAMOS

RESEARCH INSTITUTES

Research Institute of Agriculture and Animal Husbandry: Dir Ing. FERNANDO BARRANTES DEL AGUILA.

Research Institute of Biological Sciences: Dir VÍCTOR CORNEJO ALARCÓN.

Research Institute of Economics at Huamanga: Dir Econ. MARIO BRAVO CHACÓN.

Research Institute of Historico-Social Sciences: Dir JUAN JOSÉ GARCÍA MIRANDA.

Research Institute of Chemical Engineering: Dir Ing. CÉSAR GRANADOS RAFAEL.

Educational Research Institute of the Andean Region: Dir Prof. RANULFO CAVERO CARRASCO.

Research Institute of Mathematics and Physics: Dir Prof. CESAR AUGUSTO ROJAS JURADO.

Research Institute of Health and Population Studies: Dir Dr JESÚS PALACIOS SOLANO.

Research Institute of Linguistics and Literature: Dir Prof. ELMAR ALIAGA APAESTEGUI.

Research Institute of Civil and Mining Engineering: Dir Ing. JULIO CHAVEZ CASTILLO.

Research Institute of Juridical Sciences: Dir Abog. RAÚL PALACIO GARCÍA.

UNIVERSIDAD NACIONAL 'SAN LUIS GONZAGA'

Cajamarca 194, Ica

Telephone: 233201

Founded 1961

Rector: Dr CESAR ANGELES CABALLERO

Secretary-General: Dr MIGUEL CALDERÓN REINA

Number of teachers: 459

Number of students: 6,295

Publications: *Letras y Educación, Educación Dental*

Academic Programmes in agronomy, economic and social sciences, law, arts and education, pharmacy and biochemistry, dentistry, civil engineering, mechanical engineering and electricity, medicine, veterinary medicine, fisheries and biological sciences.

UNIVERSIDAD NACIONAL DE SAN MARTÍN

Martínez de Compagñón 527, Apdo 239, Tarapoto

Founded 1979

Rector: Prof. DALÍN ENCOMENDEROS DÁVALOS

Secretary-General: Ing. ALEJANDRO CRUZ RENGIFO

Librarian: JORGE YUNGBLUTH ZEGARRA

Number of teachers: 41

Number of students: 410.

UNIVERSIDAD NACIONAL DEL SANTA

Avda Pacífico 508, Urb. Buenos Aires Apdo 10, Nuevo Chimbote

Telephone: (44) 311-249

Fax: (44) 311-556

Internet: www.uns.edu.pe

Founded 1984; present status 1998

Rector: ESTEBAN HORNA BANCES

Vice-Rector (Academic): PEDRO MONCADA BECERRA

Vice-Rector (Administration): Ing. PEDRO GAMARRA LEIVA

Number of teachers: 160

Number of students: 3,100

DEANS

Faculty of Engineering: Ing. VICTOR CASTRO ZAVALETA

Faculty of Science: Lic. AMÉRICA ODAR ROSARIO

Faculty of Education and Humanities: Lic. BETTY RISCO RODRÍGUEZ

UNIVERSIDAD NACIONAL DE TUMBES

Apdo 157 Avda Bolognesi 194, Centro Cívico, 3er Piso, Tumbes

Telephone: (74) 523-081

Fax: (74) 523-081

Internet: www.untumbes.edu.pe

Founded 1984

Rector: Dr ADÁN ALVARADO BERNUY

Vice-Rector (Academic): Dr CESAR MANTILLA AVALOS

Vice-Rector (Administration): AUBERTO HIDALGO MOGOLLÓN

DEANS

Faculty of Agrarian Sciences: FRANCISCO ALBURQUEQUE VIERA

Faculty of Fishery: CÉSAR ESTUARDO POMA SÁNCHEZ

Faculty of Health Sciences: GINO ANTONIO MORETTI OTOYA

Faculty of Economics: MANUEL PAZ LÓPEZ

Faculty of Law and Social Sciences: RICARDO NOBLECILLA MORÁN

UNIVERSIDAD NACIONAL DE UCAYALI

Apdo postal 90, Pucallpa

Telephone: (64) 571044

Fax: (64) 571044

Founded 1979

State control

Language of instruction: Spanish

Rector: Dr VICTOR CHÁVEZ VÁSQUEZ

Vice-Rectors: Ing. DANIEL BALAREZO INFANTE (Academic), Dr MIGUEL NOLTE MANZANARES (Administration)

Registrar: Ing. Admin. ROMEL PINEDO RÍOS

Librarian: RAUL JAVIER GUTIÉRREZ PINEDA

Number of teachers: 178

Number of students: 1,400

DEANS

Agronomy: OSCAR LLAPAPASCA PAUCAR

Forest Sciences: Ing. CARLOS FACHIN MATOS

Health: ISABEL ESTEBAN ROBLADILLO

Administration and Accountancy: Lic. Admin. PEDRO ORMEÑO CARMONA

Private Universities

PONTIFICIA UNIVERSIDAD CATÓLICA DEL PERÚ

Apdo 1761, Lima 100
Located at: Avda Universitaria, Cdra 18 s/n, San Miguel, Lima 32
Telephone: (1) 626-20-00
Fax: (1) 626-28-47
E-mail: secgen@pucp.edu.pe
Internet: www.pucp.edu.pe
Founded 1917
Private control
Language of instruction: Spanish
Academic year: March to December (two terms)

Rector: Ing. LUIS GUZMÁN BARRÓN SOBREVILLA
Vice-Rector (Academic): Dr MARCIAL RUBIO CORREA
Vice-Rector (Administrative): EFRAÍN GONZALES DE OLARTE
Secretary-General: Dr RENÉ ORTIZ CABALLERO
Registrar: ANGELITA BASSO
Director of International Relations and Co-operation: LUIS JAIME CASTILLO BUTTERS
Librarian: Dra CARMEN VILLANUEVA

Library: see Libraries
Number of teachers: 2,572
Number of students: 17,000

Publications: *Agenda Internacional* (2 a year), *Análisis Económico de Coyuntura* (monthly), *Anthropológica* (annual), *Areté* (philosophy, 2 a year), *Boletín de Arqueología* (archaeology, annual), *Boletín del Instituto Riva-Agüero* (annual), *Debates en Sociología* (sociology, 2 a year), *Derecho* (law, annual), *Economía* (economics, annual), *Educación* (education, 2 a year), *Electro Electrónica* (2 a year), *Espacio y Desarrollo* (annual), *Histórica* (2 a year), *Lexis* (linguistic and literary review, 2 a year), *Pensamiento Constitucional* (annual), *Pro Matemática* (2 a year), *Revista de Psicología* (psychology, 2 a year), *Revista de Química* (chemistry, 2 a year), *Synergies Pérou* (didactology of languages and cultures, annual), *Tren de Sombras* (cinema, quarterly)

DEANS

Faculty of Administration and Accounting: NELSON SANTOS
Faculty of Architecture and Planning: FREDERICK COOPER (Government Commission's President)
Faculty of Communication Arts and Sciences: Dr LUIS PEIRANO FALCONÍ
Faculty of Education: JORGE CAPELLA
Faculty of Fine Arts: ALEJANDRO ALAYZA
Faculty of Humanities: Dra LILIANA REGALADO DE HURTADO
Faculty of Law: Dr ARMANDO ZOLEZZI MÖLLER
Faculty of Science and Engineering: EDUARDO ÍSMODES
Faculty of Social Sciences: ADOLFO FIGUEROA
Arts (General Studies Programme): Dr ROBERTO CRIADO ALZAMORA
Science (General Studies Programme): Dr LUIS MONTESTRUQUE ZEGARRA
Graduate School: Dr MÁXIMO VEGA CENTENO (Dir)

ATTACHED INSTITUTES

Andean Ethnomusicology Centre: Dir RAÚL ROMERO.
Applied Geographical Research Centre: Dir Dra NICOLE BERNEX.
Centre for Continuing Education: Dir ANA VELAZCO.
Cultural Centre: Dir Dr EDGAR SABA.
International Studies Institute: Dir FABIÁN NOVAK.

Foreign Languages Centre: Dir JULIA ZUCCHETTI.
Centre for the Manufacture of Advanced Technologies: Dir KURT PAULSEN.
Peruvian Music and Dance Centre: Dir ROSA ELENA VÁSQUE.
Oriental Studies Centre: Dir Dr JOSÉ ANTONIO LEÓN HERRERA.
Education and Research Centre: Dir ANA REVILLA.
Institute for Human Rights and Democracy: Pres. SALOMÓN LERNER.
Pre-University Centre: Dir JUAN VEGA.
Centre for the Study, Research and Diffusion of Latin American Music: Dir Dr ARMANDO SÁNCHEZ MÁLAGA.
Centre for Sociological, Economic, Political and Anthropological Research (CISEPA): Dir AUGUSTO CASTRO.
Services and Technology Transfer Centre: Dir CARLOS WENDORFF.
Centre for University Teaching: Dir Dr JUAN CARLOS CRESPO LÓPEZ DE CASTILLA.
Riva-Agüero Institute: Dir Dr JOSÉ ANTONIO DEL BUSTO DUTHURBURU.
Languages Institute: Dir ALDO HIGASHI.
European Studies Institute: Dir Dr MIGUEL GIUSTI.
Environmental Studies Institute: Dir Dr RICHARD KORSWAGEN EDERY.
Corrosion and Protection Institute: Dir Lic. MARÍA ISABEL DÍAZ TANG.
Computing Institute: Dir Ing. JOSÉ FLORES MOLINA.
Institute for Quality: Dir Ing. KURT PAULSEN MOSCOSCO.
Centre for Research on Architecture and Urban Studies: Dir PABLO VEGA.

UNIVERSIDAD FEMENINA DEL SAGRADO CORAZÓN

Avda Los Frutales 954, Urb. Santa Magdalena Sofía, La Molina, Apdo 0005, Lima 41
Telephone: (1) 436-4641
Fax: (1) 436-3247
E-mail: postmast@unife.edu.pe
Internet: www.unife.edu.pe
Founded 1962
Private control
Language of instruction: Spanish
Academic year: April to December (two semesters)

Rector: Dra R. M. ELGA GARCÍA ASTE
Vice-Rector (Administrative): Dra GRACIELA RUIZ DURÁN
Vice-rector (Academic): Dra ROSA MARÍA REUSCHE LARI
Librarian: Lic. MARÍA LA SERNA DE MÁS

Library of 67,340 vols
Number of teachers: 321
Number of students: 2,292

Publications: *Revista de Educación*, *Cuaderno de Psicología*, *Revista de Psicología*, *Puente*, *Consensus*, *Avances en Psicología*, *Comunifé*

DEANS

Psychology and Humanities: Dra. VICTORIA GARCÍA GARCÍA
Education: Dr AGUSTÍN CAMPOS ARENAS
Translation, Interpreting and Communications: Lic. ROSSANA SORIANO VERGARA
Architecture: Arq. CARMEN ÁNGELA SALVADOR WADSWORTH
Law and Political Sciences: Dr LUIS FELIPE ALMENARA BRYSON
Engineering: Mg. JUAN MANUEL FERNÁNDEZ CHAVESTA

Postgraduate School: Dra GLORIA BENAVIDES VÍA

UNIVERSIDAD 'INCA GARCILASO DE LA VEGA'

Avda Arequipa 3610, San Isidro, Lima
Telephone: 711421
Internet: www.uigv.edu.pe
Founded 1964
Private control
Rector (vacant)
Secretary-General: Dr ALFONSO CARRIZALES ULLOA
Librarian: NANCY HARMAN DE ALVARADO
Number of teachers: 240
Number of students: c. 7,000

Publication: *Garcilaso*

DIRECTORS

Education: A. CASTRO URBINA
Economics: M. DELGADO ULLOQUE
Accountancy: T. MOYA DE ROJAS
Administration: G. SUXE MONTERO
Social Sciences: A. CASTRO URBINA
Law: R. CASTRO NESTAREZ
Social Work: B. CORDOVA SUÁREZ
Industrial Engineering: L. TITO ATAURIMA

UNIVERSIDAD DE LIMA

Apdo 852, Lima 100
Telephone: (14) 4376767
Fax: (14) 4378066
E-mail: postmaster@ulima.edu.pe
Internet: www.ulima.edu.pe
Founded 1962
Private control
Language of instruction: Spanish
Academic year: April to July, August to December

Rector: Dra ILSE WISOTZKI LOLI
Vice-Rector: Dr GERMÁN RAMÍREZ-GASTÓN BALLÓN
Director of Administration and General Services: Ing. JOSÉ ANTONIO LIZÁRRAGA
Librarian: NANCY LIZÁRRAGA CANO

Number of teachers: 887
Number of students: 11,053

Publications: *Lienzo* (annually), *Ciencia Económica* (2 a year), *Ius et Praxis* (2 a year), *Persona* (annually), *Noticias* (monthly), *Contratexto* (annually)

DEANS

Accountancy: JAIME VIZCARRA
Administration: CARLOS BRESANI
Communication Sciences: ÓSCAR QUÉZADA
Economics: JAVIER ZÚÑIGA
General Studies: CÉSAR VIALARDI
Industrial Engineering: JAIME LEÓN
Law: OSWALDO HUNDSKOPF
Psychology: EDWIN SALAS
Systems Engineering: JULIO PADILLA
Postgraduate School: EDUARDO CARRILLO

ATTACHED RESEARCH INSTITUTES

Centro de Estudios Ambientales: Dir JAVIER ZÚÑIGA.
Centro Integral de Educación Continua: Dir MÓNICA APARICIO.
Grupo de Opinión Pública: Dir LUIS BENAVENTE.
Instituto de Investigación Científica: Dir FERMÍN CEBRECOS.

UNIVERSIDAD DEL PACÍFICO

Avda Salaverry 2020, Jesús María, Apdo 4683, Lima 11
Telephone: (1) 471-2485
Fax: (1) 219-0140

E-mail: dri@up.edu.pe
Internet: www.up.edu.pe
Founded 1962
Private control
Academic year: April to July, September to December

Rector: Prof. FELIPE ORTIZ DE ZEVALLOS
Vice-Rector: ESTUARDO MARROU LOAYZA
Secretary-General: Prof. CARLOS GATTI MURRIEL
Registrar: Prof. JOSÉ ESPINOZA DURÁN
Librarian: ABRAHAM TELLO CHÁVEZ
Number of teachers: 190
Number of students: 1,681 full-time
Number of students: 1,700 part-time
Publications: *Apuntes*, *Punto de Equilibrio*

DEANS

Administration and Accountancy: Prof. PEDRO FRANCO CONCHA
Economics: Prof. JORGE GONZÁLEZ IZQUIERDO
Post-Graduate School: Mag. ALEJANDRO FLORES CASTRO

UNIVERSIDAD PERUANA 'CAYETANO HEREDIA'

Apdo 4314, Lima 100
Telephone: 82-0252
Fax: 82-4541
E-mail: postmaster@upch.edu.pe
Internet: www.upch.edu.pe
Founded 1961
Private control
Language of instruction: Spanish
Academic year: April to March

Rector: Dr OSWALDO ZEGARRA ROJAS
Vice-Rector for Academic Affairs: Dr DAVID LOZA FERNANDEZ
Vice-Rector for Research: Dr ALBERTO RAMIREZ RAMOS
Vice-Rector for Administrative Affairs: Dr RODOLFO ZAVALA ULFFE
Secretary-General: JUAN JIMENEZ BENDEZU

Number of teachers: 450
Number of students: 4,264

Publications: *Acta Herediana*, *Revista Médica Herediana*, *Revista Estomatológica*, *Revista Acta Andina*, *Boletín UPCH*

DEANS

Faculty of Medicine: Dr LUIS CARAVEDO REYES
Faculty of Sciences and Philosophy: Dr ABRAHAM VAISBERG WOLACH
Faculty of Stomatology: Dr FERNANDO DONAYRE GONZALES
Faculty of Education: Dr MAÑUEL BELLO DOMINGUEZ
Faculty of Public Health and Administration: Dr ALEJANDRO LLANOS CUENTAS
Faculty of Nursing: Dr MARGOT ZARATE LEÓN
School of Postgraduate Studies: Dr ENRIQUE MACHICADO ZAVALA

ATTACHED RESEARCH INSTITUTES

'Alexander von Humboldt' Tropical Medicine Institute: Dir Dr EDUARDO GOTUZZO HERENCIA.

Population Studies Institute: Dir Dra MAGDALENA CHU VILLANUEVA.

Genetics Institute: Dir Dra TERESA PEREZ DE GIANELLA.

Institute of Health and Development: Dir Dr MARCOS CUETO CABALLERO.

Institute of Gerontology: Dir Dr SEGUNDO SECLEN SANTISTEBEN.

Institute of Philosophical Study and Research: Dir Dr FRANCISCO MIRO QUESADA CANTUARIAS.

Institute of Research into Man and Nature: Dir Dr CARLOS MONGE CASSINELLI.

Institute of Altitude Research: Dir Dr GUSTAVO GONZALES RENGIFO.

UNIVERSIDAD DE PIURA

Avda Ramoin Mugica 131, Urbanization San Eduardo, POB 353, Piura
Telephone: (74) 307777
Fax: (74) 308888
E-mail: webmaster@udep.edu.pe
Internet: www.udep.edu.pe
Founded 1968
Private control
Language of instruction: Spanish
Academic year: March to December

President: Dr ANTONIO ABRUÑA PUYOL
Vice-Presidents: Dr ISABEL GALVEZ AREVALO, Dr PAUL CORCUERA GARCIA, Dr SERGIO BALAREZO SALDAÑA
General Secretary: Dr CARLOS HAKANSSON NIETO
Librarian: Dra GENARA CASTILLO CORDOVA

Number of teachers: 280
Number of students: 3,500

Publications: *Revista Amigos*, *Revista de Investigacion de Derecho*, *Revista de Investigacion de Comunicacion*

DEANS

Faculty of Communications: Dra ISABEL GÁLVEZ ARÉVALO
Faculty of Economics and Business Administration: JESUS CHIYON CARRASSCO
Faculty of Education: Mgtr SUSANA TERRONES JUAREZ
Faculty of Engineering: Ing. SUSANA VEGAS CHIYON
Faculty of Law: Dr PERCY GARCIA CAVERO
Faculty of Sciences and Humanities: Arq. ERNESTO MAVILA UGARTE

UNIVERSIDAD PRIVADA VÍCTOR ANDRÉS BELAUNDE

Jirón Pedro Barroso 260, 4° piso, Apdo 241, Huánuco
Telephone: 2496
Founded 1984

Rector: RAUL ISRAEL OLIVERA
Vice-Rector: RAFAEL ISRAEL OLIVERA
Administrative Officer: MANUEL MANRIQUE MARCOS
Librarian: MARY DIAZ PAIVA

Number of teachers: 55
Number of students: 1,700

DEANS

Faculty of Law and Politics: EMERICO ISRAEL OLIVERA
Faculty of Obstetrics: MANUEL ISRAEL OLIVERA
Faculty of Forestry Engineering: NILO LOPEZ TELLO

UNIVERSIDAD RICARDO PALMA

Avda Benavides 5440, Urb. Las Gardenias, Santiago de Surco, Apdo 18-0131, Lima
Telephone: (1) 275-0450
Fax: (1) 275-0468
E-mail: webmaster@urp.edu.pe
Internet: www.urp.edu.pe
Founded 1969
Private control
Language of instruction: Spanish
Academic year: April to December

Rector: Dr IVÁN RODRÍGUEZ CHÁVEZ
Vice-Rectors: Dr HUGO SANCHEZ CARLESSI, Arq. ROBERTO CHANG CHAO
Secretary-General: Lic. GERARDO CHOQUE MARTINEZ
Librarian: Mg. ROSARIO VALDIVIA PAZ SOLDÁN

Number of teachers: 650

Number of students: 9,000

Publications: *Revista*, *Tradición*, *Revista de la Faculdad de Lenguas Modernas*, *Revista Arquitextos*, *Revista Perfiles de Ingeniería*, *Revista de la Facultad de Ciencias Económicas*, *Revista de la Facultad de Psicología*, *Revista Biotempus*

DEANS

Faculty of Architecture and Town Planning: Arq. OSWALDO VELASQUEZ HIDALGO
Faculty of Biological Sciences: Dra REINA ZUÑIGA DE ACLETO
Faculty of Economics: Dr RONALD FIGUEROA AVILA
Faculty of Engineering: Mg. LEONARDO ALCAYHUAMAN ACCOSTUPA
Faculty of Medicine: Dr MANUEL HUAMÁN GUERRERO
Faculty of Modern Languages: Dra DORA BAZÁN DE DEVOTO
Faculty of Psychology: Dr RAÚL YAÑEZ CANNON

UNIVERSIDAD SAN MARTÍN DE PORRES

Ciuadad Universitaria, Avda Las Calandrias s/n, Santa Anita, Lima
Telephone: (1) 478-1001
E-mail: rectorado@usmp.edu.pe
Internet: www.usmp.edu.pe
Founded 1969

Rector: Ing. JOSÉ ANTONIO CHANG ESCOBEDO

Departments of Arts and Education; Institutes of Philosophy and Social Sciences, History and Geography.

College

UNIVERSIDAD ESAN

Apdo 1846, Lima 100
Telephone: (1) 3177200
Fax: (1) 3451328
E-mail: cendoc@esan.edu.pe
Internet: www.esan.edu.pe

Founded 1963, as a jt venture between the Peruvian Govt and the US Dept of State Agency for Int. Devt to promote the socio-economic devt of the region; training in management at graduate level and for executives

Dir: JORGE TALAVERA TRAVERSO

Library of 50,000 vols
Number of teachers: 37
Number of students: 3,000

Publications: *Cuadernos de Difusión* (2 a year), *Documentos de Trabajo*, *INFORME-SAN* (institutional bulletin, fortnightly).

Schools of Art and Music

Conservatorio Nacional de Música (National Conservatory of Music): Jr. Carabaya 429, Lima; tel. (1) 426-9677; fax (1) 426-5658; e-mail cnmdg@terra.com.pe; f. 1908 as Academia Nacional de Música 'Alcedo', autonomous since 1966; performance, musicology, education, composition; choir and orchestra; library: 14,000 books and musical scores, and record library; 87 teachers; 400 students; Dir Gen. ENRIQUE ITURRIAGA ROMERO; Acad. Dir CARMEN ESCOBEDE REVOREDO; publ. *Conservatorio* (annual)..

Affiliated institutes:

Conservatorio Regional de Música del Norte 'Carlos Valderrama': Independencia 572 (2° piso), Trujillo; tel. (44) 235392; fax (44) 235392; e-mail crmncv@ qnet.com.pe; f. 1946; 42 teachers; 450 students; Dir CARLOS E. PAREDES ABAD.

Escuela Regional de Música de Huánuco: Dir JAIME DÍAZ.

Escuela Superior de Formación Artística 'Mario Urteaga': Km. 3.5 Carretera Baños del Inca, Cajamarca; tel. (44) 826010; fax (44) 821209; e-mail esfamusica@yahoo.com; f. 1984; 9 teachers; 89 students; Dir RAMÓN BAZÁN FIGUEROA.

Escuela Superior de Música 'Condorcunca': Jirón 28 de Julio Nro 122, Ayacuche; tel. (64) 812598; e-mail esma@ goalsnet.com.pe; f. 1957; 33 teachers; 152 students; Dir PEDRO RAMÓN CASTILLA HUAYHUA.

Escuela Superior de Música 'José María Valle Riestra': Avda Bolognesi Nro 890, Piura; tel. (74) 322632; e-mail esmjmvr@lanet.com.pe; f. 1951; 23 teachers; 203 students; Dir REYNALDO E. BURGO PÉREZ.

Escuela Superior de Música 'Luis Duncker Lavalle': Calle 4 s/n, Coop. Labramara J.L. Bustamante y Rivero, Arequipa; tel. (54) 424510; fax (54) 425723; e-mail esma@terra.com.pe; f. 1945; 33 teachers; 251 students; Dir ELÍAS ADOLFO CHÁVEZ.

Escuela Superior Pública de Formación Artística 'Francisco Lase': Avda 2 de Mayo Nro 412, Tacna; tel. (54) 711601; fax (54) 711601; e-mail esfafl@correoweb .com; internet www.geocities.com/esfafl; f.

1989; 45 teachers; 315 students; Dir DAVID ORTIZ OVIEDO.

Instituto Superior de Música 'Leandre Alviña Miranda': Tocuyeres 526, San Blas, Cuzco; tel. (84) 231621; fax (84) 231621; e-mail ismlam.cusco@latinmail .com.pe; f. 1950; 36 teachers; 192 students; Dir ESTEBAN ITUPA LLAVINA.

Escuela Nacional Superior Autónoma de Bellas Artes (Autonomous National School of Fine Arts): Ancash 681, Lima; fax 4270799; f. 1918; to train artists and teachers; library: 5,000 vols; Dir PEDRO BENITO ROTTA BISSO; publ. *Anuario Académico*.

Escuela Regional de Bellas Artes 'Diego Quispe Tito': Cuzco.

Instituto Superior de Arte 'Carlos Baca Flor': Calle Sucre 111, Arequipa.

PHILIPPINES

The Higher Education System

From the 16th century until 1898 the Philippines were under Spanish control. They were ceded to the USA under the terms of the Treaty of Paris (1898) and remained under US control until independence was achieved in 1946. The Philippines' colonial inheritance is reflected in its higher education system. The two oldest institutions, the University of San Carlos (founded in 1595; current status since 1948) and the University of Santo Tomás (founded in 1611), are both private Catholic universities, while universities founded during or after the period of US control are modelled on US institutions. The Commission on Higher Education is the supreme national body for public and private universities. In 1998/99 there were 2,481,809 students enrolled in university-level institutions.

Admission to higher education is on the basis of satisfactory performance in the High School Diploma and the university entrance examination. Most Filipino degrees are awarded on a 'credit–semester' basis; students are expected to accrue a specified number of credits each semester throughout the duration of the degree in order to graduate. Associate degrees are offered by community colleges and universities and are two-year programmes of study in the arts and sciences. The first full undergraduate degree is the Bachelors, usually a four-year course, but degrees in certain subjects may require longer periods of study, such as law and medicine (eight years). The postgraduate degrees are the Masters and PhD. The Masters last for two years and consists of full-time study and the submission of a thesis. For a PhD, students are required to undertake at least three years of study and research and complete a dissertation.

The Technical Education and Skills Development Authority is the controlling body of post-secondary technical and vocational education, which is offered by public and private technical/vocational institutes and specialist institutions. The duration of programmes varies from one to three years; in some instances programmes are geared towards a Certificate system of four levels. There is no mandatory system of accreditation for higher education, but the Commission on Higher Education encourages institutions to seek accreditation from one of four agencies, namely Philippine Accrediting Association of Schools, Colleges and Universities, Philippine Association of Colleges and Universities—Commission on Accreditation, Association of Christian Schools and Colleges—Accrediting Agency, Inc. and Accrediting Agency of Chartered Colleges and Universities in the Philippines. All of the above-listed bodies are members of the Federation of Accreditation Agencies of the Philippines.

Learned Societies

GENERAL

Academia Filipina (Philippine Academy): 47 Juan Luna St, San Lorenzo Village, 1200 Makati, Metro Manila; tel. (2) 817-1128; fax (2) 817-1135; f. 1924; corresp. of the Real Academia Española (Madrid); 15 mems; Dir ALEJANDRO ROCES; Sec. SALVADOR B. MALIG.

AGRICULTURE, FISHERIES AND VETERINARY SCIENCE

Crop Science Society of the Philippines: c/o Phil Rice, Los Baños, Pili Drive, College, Laguna; tel. (49) 536-3635; e-mail asian@laguna.net; internet www.cssp.org.ph; f. 1970; 3,000 mems; Pres. NORVIE L. MANIGBAS; Vice-Pres. RENATO A. REANO; publ. *Philippine Journal of Crop Science* (3 a year).

Philippine Society of Agricultural Engineers: ATI Bldg Elliptical Rd, Diliman, Quezon City; tel. and fax (2) 920-4071; e-mail contact@psae.net; internet psae.net; f. 1950; 5,800 mems; Pres. Dr TERESITO G. AGUINALDO.

Philippine Veterinary Medical Association: Unit 233, Union Square Condominium, 15th Ave, Cubao, Quezon City; tel. (2) 911-3159; internet www.prc.gov.ph/portal_articles.asp?pid=73&sid=263&aid=2003; f. 1907; 5,274 mems; Pres. Dr TOMAS C. LAZARO II.

ARCHITECTURE AND TOWN PLANNING

United Architects of the Philippines (UAP): 53 Scout Rallos St, Diliman, Quezon City 1103; tel. (2) 412-6374; fax (2) 372-1796; e-mail uap@united-architects.org; internet www.united-architects.org; f. 1974 following merger of Philippine Institute of Architects, League of Philippine Architects and Association of Philippine Government Architects; Pres. Archt EDRIC MARCO C. FLORENTINO; Sec.-Gen. Archt. GIL C. EVASCO.

BIBLIOGRAPHY, LIBRARY SCIENCE AND MUSEOLOGY

Association of Special Libraries of the Philippines (ASLP): Room 301, National Library Bldg, Kalaw St, Ermita, Manila; tel. (2) 524-4611; e-mail ladladj@dlsu.edu.ph; internet www.aczafra.com; f. 1954; 556 mems; Pres. JOCELYN L. LADAD; Sec. ARLENE Y. GONZALES; publs *ASLP Bulletin* (quarterly), *ASLP Newsletter* (quarterly), *Directory of Special Libraries*.

EDUCATION

Association of Catholic Universities of the Philippines, Inc.: University of Santo Tomas (Room 111, Main Bldg), España, Manila; tel. (2) 731-35-44; fax (2) 740-97-27; f. 1973 to serve the interests of the 21 Catholic univs in the Philippines; Pres. Rev. Fr TAMERLANE R. LANA; Sec. Gen. Prof. GIOVANNA V. FONTANILLA; publ. *ACUP Newsletter* (annually).

Philippine Association of State Universities and Colleges: 2nd Fl., ITC Bldg, EARIST Compound, Valencia St, Sta Mesa, Manila; tel. (2) 716-0944; fax (2) 716-0430; f. 1967; independent but attached to Dept of Education, Culture and Sports; aims to foster excellence in higher education, to promote communication among its mem. institutions, to encourage studies on higher education, to secure adequate government support for education, to encourage inter-institutional assistance through fellowships, grants, teacher exchange, accreditation; 75 mem. institutions; library with special collections on education; Pres. ELDIGARIO D. GONZALES; Exec. Dir Dr FREDERICK S. PADA; publ. *Baliham* (quarterly).

HISTORY, GEOGRAPHY AND ARCHAEOLOGY

Philippine Historical Association: c/o Office of External Affairs, St Mary's College, 37 M. Ignacia Ave, 1103 Quezon City; tel. 413-4076 ext. 222; fax 374-3073; e-mail glo.santos@yahoo.com; f. 1955; 500 mems; Pres. Prof. AMBETH OCAMPO; Exec. Dir Dr GLORIA M. SANTOS; publs *Philippine Historical Bulletin* (annually), *PHA Balita* (2 a year).

LANGUAGE AND LITERATURE

Alliance Française: POB 2899, 128 Manila; Located at: 209 Nicanor Garcia St, Bel Air II, 1209 Makati City; tel. (2) 895-75-85; fax (2) 899-36-54; e-mail info@alliance.ph; internet www.alliance.ph; offers courses and exams in French language and culture and promotes cultural exchange with France; Dir PHILIPPE NORMAND.

British Council: 10th Fl., Taipan Pl., F. Ortigas Jr. Ave, Ortigas Centre, Pasig City 1605, Manila; tel. (2) 914-1011; fax (2) 914-1020; e-mail britishcouncil@britishcouncil.org.ph; internet www.britishcouncil.org/philippines; teaching centre; offers courses and exams in English language and British culture and promotes cultural exchange with the UK; library; Dir GILL WESTAWAY.

Goethe-Institut: POB 1744, Makati Central Post Office, 1257 Makati City; Located at: 4-5/F Adamson Centre, 121 Leviste St., Salcedo Village, 1227 Makati City; tel. (2) 817-0978; fax (2) 817-0979; e-mail goetheinfo@pldtdsl.net; internet www.goethe.de/manila; f. 1961; offers courses and exams in German language and culture and promotes cultural exchange with Germany; library of 3,000 vols; Dir RICHARD KÜNZEL.

Instituto Cervantes: 855 T.M. Kalaw St, Ermita, 1000 Manila; tel. (2) 526-14-82; fax (2) 526-14-49; e-mail cenmni@cervantes.es; internet manila.cervantes.es; f. 1991; offers courses and exams in Spanish language and culture and promotes cultural exchange with Spain and Spanish-speaking Latin and Central America; library: library of 23,000 vols, 1,500 CDs and audio cassettes, 2,000 video cassettes and DVDs; Dir JAVIER GALVÁN.

Komisyon sa Wikang Filipino: Watson Bldg, 1610 J. P. Laurel St, San Miguel, Manila; tel. (2) 734-55-46; fax (2) 736-03-15; internet www.komfil.gov.ph; f. 1991 (fmrly Institute of Philippine Languages); aims to develop, promote and standardize Filipino and other Philippine languages; library of 5,000 vols; Chair. Dr PONCIANO B. P. PINEDA; publ. *Sangwika* (newsletter, quarterly).

MEDICINE

Manila Medical Society: 800 Taft Ave, Manila; tel. (2) 524-9944; fax (2) 525-6771; e-mail mmsi@yahoo.com; internet www .geocities.com/mmsi1902; f. 1902; 1,249 mems; Pres. Dr ASCENSION F. BAUTISTA; Sec. Dr FELICISIMA B. BACON.

Philippine Medical Association: PMA Bldg, North Ave, Quezon City; tel. (2) 929-6366; fax (2) 929-6951; e-mail medical@pma .com.ph; internet www.pma.com.ph; f. 1903; 107 component societies, 60 affiliated speciality societies; Pres. Dr MODESTO O. LLAMAS; Sec.-Gen. Dr REY MELCHOR SANTOS; publ. *Journal.*

Philippine Paediatric Society, Inc.: POB 3527, Manila; f. 1947; 620 mems; Pres. Dr JOEL S. ELISES; Sec. Dr VICTOR S. DOCTOR; publ. *Philippine Journal of Paediatrics* (every 2 months).

Philippine Pharmaceutical Association: 815 R. Papa St. Sampaloc, 1008 Manila; tel. (2) 50-9006; fax (2) 522-3230; f. and incorporated 1920; 8,000 mems; Pres. Dr LOURDES TALAG ECHAUZ; Exec. Sec. Dr NORMA V. LERMA.

NATURAL SCIENCES

General

National Academy of Science and Technology: 2nd Fl., Philippine Science Heritage Center, DOST Complex, Gen. Santos Ave, Bicutan, Taguig City, 1631 Metro Manila; tel. (2) 837-2071; fax (2) 837-3170; e-mail nast@dost.gov.ph; internet www.nast.dost .gov.ph; f. 1976; advises the President and Cabinet on policies concerning science and technology nationally; Pres. Dr EMIL Q. JAVIER; Sec. Dr EVELYN MAE TECSON-MENDOZA.

Physical Sciences

Philippine Council of Chemists: 2227 Severino Reyes St, Sta Cruz, POB 1202, Manila 2805; f. 1958; 200 mems; Nat. Pres. MIGUEL G. AMPIL; Gen. Sec. P. B. CARBONELL; publ. *Bulletin.*

TECHNOLOGY

Philippine Institute of Mining, Metallurgical and Geological Engineers: POB 1595, Manila; f. 1940; 117 mems; Pres. JONES R. CASTRO; Sec.-Treas. LEOPOLDO F. ABAD.

Philippine Society of Civil Engineers: c/o Bureau of Public Works, Bonifacio Drive, Manila; f. 1918; assumed present title 1933; Pres. FLORENCIO MORENO; Sec.-Treas. TOMAS DE GUZMÁN; publ. *The Philippine Engineering Record* (quarterly).

Philippine Society of Mechanical Engineers: 19 Scout Bayoran St, South Triangle, Quezon City; tel. (2) 371-1819; fax (2) 372-4341; e-mail info@psme.org; internet www .psme.org; f. 1952; Pres. Eng EDIMAR V. SALCEDO.

Research Institutes

GENERAL

Advanced Science and Technology Institute: ASTI Bldg., C. P. Garcia Ave., Technology Park Complex, U.P. Campus, Diliman, Quezon City, 1101; tel. (2) 426-9755; fax (2) 925-8598; e-mail info@asti.dost .gov.ph; internet www.asti.dost.gov.ph; conducts research and development in information and communications technology and microelectronics; Dir DENIS F. VILLORENTE.

Institute of Philippine Culture, Ateneo de Manila University: Frank Lynch Hall, Social Devt Complex, Loyola Heights, Quezon City 1108; tel. 426-6067; fax 426-6067 ext. 121; e-mail ipc@admu.edu.ph; internet www.ipc-ateneo.org; f. 1960 as a univ. research org.; undertakes studies directed towards solving devt problems, particularly in the areas of upland devt, local governance, agrarian reform, community health, resources management, irrigation, forestry, women and sustainable agriculture; assists devt agencies; trains agency personnel and local communities in the use of research methodologies; library of 7,000 vols, 3,000 reprints and 104 multimedia vols; Dir Dr WILFREDO F. ARCE; publs *Culture and Development Series, IPC Discussion Papers, IPC Final Reports* (all irreg.), *IPC Monograph Series, IPC Papers, IPC Social Explorations Series.*

National Research Council of the Philippines: General Santos Ave, Bicutan, Taguig City; tel. (2) 837-6141; fax (2) 837-6143; e-mail nrcpinfo@dost.gov.ph; internet mis.dost.gov.ph/nrcp; f. 1933; supports basic research in a wide variety of fields; 12 scientific divisions; 2,250 mems; library of 1,300 vols; Pres. Prof. FORTUNATO T. DELA PEÑA; Exec. Dir Dr PACIENTE A. CORDERO Jr; publs *Annual Report, Newsletter* (4 a year), *NRCP Research Journal* (4 a year), *Technical Bulletin* (irregular).

AGRICULTURE, FISHERIES AND VETERINARY SCIENCE

Bureau of Plant Industry: 692 San Andres St, Malate, Manila; tel. (2) 525-7857; fax (2) 521-7650; e-mail cu.bpi@da.gov.ph; internet bpi.da.gov.ph; f. 1930; conserves and develops Philippine plant genetic resources and ensures the protection and development of the plant industry; library of 10,000 vols; Dir LEALYN A. RAMOS.

Forest Products Research and Development Institute (FPRDI): Narra Rd, Forestry Campus, UP College, Los Baños, Laguna 4031; tel. (49) 536-2630; fax (49) 536-3630; e-mail fprdi@laguna.net; internet www.uplb.edu.ph/fprdi; f. 1957; to conduct basic and applied research on forest products, undertake the transfer of completed research and provide technical services and industrial manpower training; 236 mems; library of 7,000 books, 3,000 reports, 4,000 vols of periodicals; Sec. Dr ESTRELLA F. ALABASTRO; publs *Annual Report, Forest Products Technoflow, FPRDI Journal* (irregular).

Philippine Rice Research Institute: Central Experiment Station Maligaya, Science City of Muñoz, Nueva Ecija; tel. (44) 456-0277; e-mail prri@philrice.gov.ph; internet www.philrice.gov.ph; f. 1960; aims to sustain the country's self-sufficiency in rice; undertakes and funds a national research and development programme for rice and rice-based farming systems; trains scientists, farmer-leaders and agribusiness managers; Exec. Dir Dr LEOCADIO S. SEBASTIAN.

EDUCATION

Science Education Institute: c/o Department of Science and Technology, 3rd PTRI Bldg, Bicutan, Taguig, 1604, Metro Manila; tel. (2) 837-1359; fax (2) 837-1924; e-mail webmaster@sei.dost.gov.ph; internet www .sei.dost.gov.ph; Dir Dr ESTER B. OGENA; publ. *Annual Report.*

SEAMEO Regional Center for Educational Innovation and Technology: University of the Philippines, POB 207, Commonwealth Ave, Diliman, Quezon City 1101; tel. (2) 924-7681; fax (2) 921-0224; e-mail info@seameo-innotech.org; internet www.seameo-innotech.org; f. 1970; identifies basic educational problems common to the Southeast Asian region and assists the Southeast Asian Ministers of Education Organization member countries in the solution of these problems; conducts training, development, research programmes; library of 14,000 vols; Dir Dr ERLINDA C. PEFIANCO; publs *INNOTECH Journal* (2 a year), *INNOTECH Newsletter* (6 a year).

MEDICINE

Food and Nutrition Research Institute: c/o Department of Science and Technology, Gen. Santos Ave, Bicutan, Taguig 1604, Metro Manila; tel. (2) 837-2934; fax (2) 837-3164; e-mail mvc@fnri.dost.gov.ph; internet www.fnri.dost.gov.ph; f. 1987; Dir Dr MARIO V. CAPANZANA; publ. *Annual Report.*

NATURAL SCIENCES

Physical Sciences

Philippine Institute of Volcanology and Seismology: PHIVOLCS Bldg, C. P. Garcia Ave, U.P. Campus, Diliman, Quezon City; tel. (2) 426-14-68; fax (2) 929-83-66; e-mail phivolcs@x5.phivolcs.dost.gov.ph; internet www.phivolcs.dost.gov.ph; f. 1952; library of 3,000 vols; Dir RENATO U. SOLIDUM, Jr.

TECHNOLOGY

Industrial Technology Development Institute: DOST Compound, Gen. Santos Ave, Bicutan, Taguig 1631, Metro Manila; tel. (2) 837-2071; fax (2) 837-6156; e-mail nea@dost.gov.ph; internet www.mis.dost.gov .ph/itdi; f. 1951; carries out research and development in the areas of food processing, materials science, chemicals and minerals, electronics and process control, fuels and energy, microbiology and genetics, and the environment; Dir Dr NUNA E. ALMANZOR.

Metals Industry Research and Development Center: MIRDC Compound, Gen. Santos Ave, Bicutan, Taguig 1604, Metro Manila; tel. (2) 837-0431; fax (2) 837-0430; e-mail rtv@mirdc.dost.gov.ph; internet www .mirdc.dost.gov.ph; f. 1972; research and development, quality control, and testing of metal products; Exec. Dir ROLANDO T. VILORIA; publs *Annual Report, Metals Industry Trends and Events* (newsletter, 4 a year).

Mines and Geosciences Bureau: North Ave, Diliman, Quezon City, 1100, Metro Manila; tel. (2) 920-91-20; fax (2) 920-16-35; e-mail central@mgb.gov.ph; internet www .mgb.gov.ph; f. 1898; administers the utilization and management of the country's mineral wealth; conducts geological, mining, metallurgical, chemical and other research; undertakes geological and mineral exploration surveys; library of 4,200 vols; Dir JEREMIAS DOLINO; publs *Mineral Gazette* (2 a year), *Mineral Industry Indicators* (2 a year), *National Directory of Producing Mines and Quarries in the Philippines* (annually), *Philippine Mineral Industry Review* (quarterly), *Philippine Mineral Statistics* (annually).

Philippine Nuclear Research Institute: Commonwealth Ave, Diliman, Quezon City 1101; tel. (2) 920-8787; fax (2) 920-1646; e-mail info@pnri.dost.gov.ph; internet www .pnri.dost.gov.ph; f. 1958; peaceful applications of nuclear energy; library of 19,069 vols;

Dir Dr ALUMANDA M. DELA ROSA (acting); publs *Philippines Nuclear Journal* (annually), *PNRI Annual Report*.

Philippine Textile Research Institute: Gen. Santos Ave, Bicutan, Taguig City, Metro Manila; tel. and fax (2) 837-1325; e-mail ptri@dost.gov.ph; internet www.ptri .dost.gov.ph; f. 1967; conducts applied research and development for the textile industry; provides technical services and training programmes; Dir Dr CARLOS C. TOMBOC.

Libraries and Archives

Bacalod City

Bacalod City Library: Bacolod City, Negros Occidental; e-mail mcorpuz@ bacolodcity.gov.ph; 50,000 vols.

Cagayan de Oro City

Cagayan de Oro City Public Library: Apolinar Velez St, Cagayan de Oro City; tel. (8822) 72-55-60; Librarian MYRNA F. ACE-DERA.

Xavier University Library: Ateneo de Cagayan, Corrales Ave, Cagayan de Oro City 9000; tel. (8822) 72-31-16 ext. 2302; fax (8822) 72-71-63; e-mail librarytech@xu.edu .ph; internet library.xu.cdu.ph; f. 1933; 121,500 vols, 376 periodicals; Dir, Univ. Libraries ANNABELLE P. ACEDERA; publ. *Kinaadman*.

Cebu City

Cebu City Public Library: Osmeña Blvd., Cebu City; tel. (32) 253-1526; Librarian CIRILA A. DELOS REYES.

University of San Carlos Library: P. del Rosario St, 6000 Cebu City; tel. (32) 253-1000 ext. 133; fax (32) 254-04-32; e-mail direklib@ usc.edu.ph; internet www.usc.edu.ph; f. 1947; 269,705 vols incl. 21,320 vols of Filipiniana, 3,360 titles of periodicals (44,992 vols total); 3,502 audiovisual items; spec. colln for local studies held in Cebuano Studies Center at above address; Dir of Libraries Dr MARILOU P. TADLIP.

Davao City

Davao City Library: 3rd Fl., SP Building, San Pedro St, Davao City; tel. (82) 227-3137; fax (82) 226-8913; Librarian NORA FE ALAJAR.

Dumaguete

Silliman University Library: 6200 Dumaguete City, Negros Oriental; tel. and fax (35) 422-7208; e-mail sulib@su.edu.ph; internet su.edu.ph; f. 1906; 200,000 items; Librarian LORNA YSO; publs *Convergence* (arts and sciences, irregular), *Silliman Journal* (humanities, social sciences and sciences, 2 a year).

Makati City

Asian Institute of Management Library: 123 Paseo de Roxas, POB 2095, Makati City 1260; tel. (2) 892-4011; fax (2) 817-2663; e-mail vong@aim.edu; internet www.aim .edu; f. 1968; 20,000 vols; Knowledge Resource Officer VIRGINIA G. ONG.

Filipinas Heritage Library: Nielson Tower, Ayala Triangle Makati Ave, Makati City, 1224; tel. (2) 892-1801; fax (2) 892-1810; e-mail librarian@filipinaslibrary.org.ph; internet www.filipinaslibrary.org.ph; f. 1996; research library specializing in Philippine art, culture, history, language, religion and social sciences; also covers management, marketing, information technology, human resources and literature; 12,000 vols, 200 periodicals, maps and graphic materials; Dir MA. ANTONIA C. ORTIGAS.

Manila

Adamson University Library: 900 San Marcelino St, Ermita, 1000 Manila; tel. (2) 524-2011 ext. 131; internet www.adamson .edu.ph; f. 1933; Dir of Libraries ERLINDA B. GONZALES.

Ateneo de Manila University Rizal Library: Katipunan Ave, Loyola Heights, Quezon City 1108; tel. (2) 426-6001; fax (2) 426-5961; e-mail ltdavid@ateneo.edu; internet rizal.lib.admu.edu.ph; f. 1967; 200,000 books, 36,000 bound periodicals, 325,000 microforms; preservation of special collns, incl. Filipiniana colln, Rizaliana, American Historical colln, Pardo de Tavera colln and the Ateneo Library of Women's Writings; Dir Prof. LOURDES T. DAVID.

Far Eastern University Library: POB 609, Quezon Blvd, Manila 1008; 3rd Fl., NRH Bldg, Nicanor Reyes Sr St, Sampaloc, Manila 1008; tel. (2) 735-5649; e-mail evelyn_sf@hotmail.com; f. 1928; 82,243 vols; Librarian Dr EVELYN S. FABITO.

Manila City Library: 2nd Fl., Sining Kayumanggi Bldg, Mehan Garden, Malate, Manila; tel. (2) 523-8688; Chief Librarian FILEMON L. GECOLEA.

National Library of the Philippines: POB 2926, T. M. Kalaw St, 1000 Ermita, Manila; tel. (2) 525-3196; fax (2) 524-2329; e-mail amb@nlp.gov.ph; internet www.nlp .gov.ph; f. 1900; 207,703 books, 6,250 periodicals, 813,095 MSS, 51,680 vols of theses and dissertations, 10,332 cassette tapes, 6,004 microfilms, 2,190 sheet maps, 388 CD-ROMs; also 762,459 vols in public libraries and 8,579 vols in bookmobiles; Dir PRUDENCIANA C. CRUZ; publs *Philippine National Bibliography* (annually), *TNL Annual Report*, *TNL Newsletter* (irregular).

Philippine Women's University Library: Taft Ave, Manila 1004; internet www.pwu .edu.ph; nine br. libraries; 87,620 vols; medicine, pure sciences, Filipiniana, music, the arts, literature, archive collection; Librarian DIONISIA M. ANGELES.

Science and Technology Information Institute, Department of Science and Technology: Gen. Santos Ave, Upper Bicutan, Taguig City, Metro Manila; tel. (2) 837-2191; internet www.stii.dost.gov.ph; f. 1974; acquisition of scientific documents, technical information processing, science information services, training in library and information science and computer applications; 28,000 bound vols, 3,047 periodicals, 4,000 microfilms; Chief Dr IRENE D. AMORES; publs *Annual Report*, *ASTINFO Newsletter* (4 a year), *Bulletin of Researches* (4 a year), *Philippine Inventions* (4 a year), *Philippine Men of Science* (annually), *Philippine Science and Technology Abstracts* (4 a year), *Philippine Scientific Bibliographies* (irregular), *Philippine Technical Information Series* (), *R & D Philippines* (annually), *SEA Abstracts* (4 a year), *Technical Tips* (every 2 weeks).

Technological University of the Philippines Library: Ayala Blvd, Ermita, Manila 1000; tel. (2) 302-7750 ext. 601; internet www .tup.edu.ph; 34,170 items; Dir Dr WILHELMINA G. BORJAL.

University of the East Library: 2219 Claro M. Recto Ave, Manila 2806; internet online.ue.edu.ph/manila/library; 183,000 vols; Dir of Libraries NORMA I. JHOCSON.

University of Manila Central Library: 546 Dr M. V. de los Santos St, Sampaloc, Manila; f. 1913; 28,600 vols; other libraries; 23,000 vols; Chief Librarian CORAZON G. PAYTE.

University of the Philippines Manila, University Library: 650 Pedro Gil St, Ermita, Manila 1000; tel. (2) 526-4253; fax (2) 526-5847; e-mail tdugenia@mail.upm.edu .ph; internet lib.upm.edu.ph; main library and nine br. libraries; Librarian THERESA P. DUGENIA.

University of Santo Tomas Library: España St, Manila 1015; tel. (2) 731-30-34; fax (2) 740-97-09; e-mail library@mnl.ust.edu .ph; internet library.ust.edu.ph; 391,120 vols; collections of Filipiniana and rare and ancient books; special libraries of Ecclesiastical Faculties, Medicine, Music, Engineering, Fine Arts and Commerce; High School and Elementary School libraries; Prefect of Libraries Fr ANGEL APARICIO; Chief Librarian Prof. ERLINDA F. FLORES.

Quezon City

Loyola School of Theology Library: POB 240, U.P. Quezon City; tel. (2) 426-5966; e-mail lwakefield@admu.edu.ph; internet www.lst.edu/library.asp; f. 1965; 69,000 vols, 18,000 vols of periodicals; Librarian CRISANTA C. ROSALES; publ. *Landas (The Way)* (2 a year).

University of the Philippines Diliman University Library: Gonzalez Hall, Diliman, Quezon City 1101; tel. (2) 926-1877; fax (2) 926-1876; e-mail salvacion.arlante@up .edu.ph; internet www.mainlib.upd.edu.ph; f. 1922; 1,055,048 vols, 32,671 periodical titles; 26 brs; Dir SALVACION M. ARLANTE; publ. *Index to Philippine Periodicals* (quarterly).

Museums and Art Galleries

Cebu City

CAP Art Center and President Osmeña Memorabilia: 60 Osmena Blvd, Cebu City; tel. (32) 217-519; fax (32) 218-102; f. 1986; work by artists from all parts of the Philippines; memorabilia concerning the late President Osmeña; Curator MARY F. ABAD.

Casa Gorordo Museum: 35 Lopez Jaena St., Cebu City; tel. (32) 255-5645; fax (32) 253-2380; fmr home of the first Filipino Bishop of Cebu, now restored as a typical 19th c. residence; furniture, paintings, religious relics, pottery and ceramics; Curator CHARLES MUERTEGUI.

Southwestern University Museum: Urgello Rd, Cebu City 6000; tel. and fax (32) 253-6500; internet www.cebu-online .com/swum; prehistoric, archaeological, ethnographic, ecclesiastical and art objects; Dir TONETTE S. PAÑARES.

University of San Carlos Museum: P. del Rosario St, Cebu City 6000; tel. (32) 253-1000 loc 191; fax (32) 253-1000; e-mail museum@ usc.edu.ph; internet www.usc.edu.ph; f. 1967; Spanish colonial, ethnographic, archaeological and natural science objects; Curator MARLENE SOCORRO SAMSON.

Davao City

Davao Museum: Zonta Bldg, Insular Village Phase I, Lanang, Davao City; f. 1977; tribal art, local costumes, jewellery, textiles, handicrafts, musical instruments; Curator Dr HEIDI K. GLORIA.

Makati City

Ayala Museum: Makati Avenue, Greenbelt Park, Ayala Center, Makati City 1224; tel. (2) 757-7117; fax (2) 757-3588; e-mail museum_inquiry@ayalamuseum.org; internet www.ayalamuseum.org; f. 1967; archaeological, ethnographic and fine arts collections; paintings by Philippine artists Juan Luna, Fernando Amorsolo and Fernando Zobel; 60 dioramas illustrating Philippine history; models of ships and watercraft; Dir Dr FLORINA H. CAPISTRANO-BAKER.

Makati Museum: J. P. Rizal St, Poblacion, Makati City; tel. (2) 896-0277; native arts and crafts, paintings by contemporary Filipino artists; Curator LINGLING CERVANTES.

Manila

Archdiocesan Museum of Manila: 121 Arzobispo St, Intramuros, Manila; tel. (2) 527-7631 ext. 222; fax (2) 530-4815; f. 1987; history of the Catholic Church in the Philippines; Curator Mgr JOSE ABRIOL.

Lopez Memorial Museum: Benpres Bldg, Ground Floor, Exchange Rd, cnr Meralco Ave, 1600 Pasig City, Metro Manila; tel. (2) 635-95-45; fax (2) 631-24-17; e-mail pezseum@skyinet.net; internet www .lopezmuseum.org.ph; f. 1960; paintings by the Filipino painters Juan Luna, Felix Resureccion Hidalgo and others; letters and MSS of Jose Rizal; library of 16,000 vols, including rare Filipiniana; Dir MERCEDES LOPEZ VARGAS.

Malacañang Palace Presidential Museum: J. P. Laurel St, San Miguel, Manila; tel. 521-2301; internet www.op.gov .ph/museum; f. 1993; memorabilia of all former Philippine presidents; Dir MA. EDNA S. GAFFUD.

Metropolitan Museum of Manila: Central Bank Complex, Roxas Blvd, Manila 1104; tel. (2) 536-1566; fax (2) 523-0613; e-mail info@ metmuseum.ph; internet metmuseum.ph; f. 1976; fine arts museum: painting, sculpture, graphic arts, decorative arts, prehistoric gold, pottery; Pres. CORAZÓN S. ALVINA; Dir (vacant).

Museum of Arts and Sciences: Third Fl., Main Building, University of Santo Tomas, Calle España, Manila 1008; tel. (2) 781-1815; fax (2) 740-9718; e-mail museum@ust.edu .ph; internet www.ustmuseum.com; f. 1870; divisions of natural history, Philippine ethnography, history (including numismatics), archaeology (including Philippine and Chinese ceramics), art gallery and the Hall of Philippine Religious Images; Dir Rev. Fr ISIDRO C. ABAÑO; publ. *UST Museum Newsletter* (4 a year).

National Museum of the Philippines: POB 2659, Padre Burgos St, Manila 1000; tel. (2) 527-1215; fax (2) 527-0306; e-mail nmuseum@i-next.net; internet members .tripod.com/philmuseum/index; f. 1901; divisions of anthropology, archaeology, botany, geology, zoology, museum education, restoration and engineering, arts, cultural properties, planetarium; 21 regional br. museums and sites; library of 5,000 vols; Dir Fr GABRIEL S. CASAL; publs *Artifacts* (newsletter, monthly), *National Museum Papers* (every 2 years).

Attached sites:

Angono Petroglyphs Site: Binangonan, Rizal, Luzon; the most ancient Filipino work of art, dating from c. 1,000 BC; 127 drawings of human and animal figures; declared as a national cultural treasure.

Balanghai Site: Libertad, Butuan City, Mindanao; remains of the earliest known watercraft in the country, dating from 320AD.

Bolinao Branch: Bolinao, Pangasinan, Luzon; archaeological and general museum; Head GINA DE VERA.

Butuan City Branch: Butuan City, Mindanao; archaeological artefacts from Agusan del Norte and ethnographic materials from several local ethnic communities; Head MARGARITA CEMBRANO.

Cagsawa Branch: Albay, Luzon; geological materials from the Mayon volcano,

archaeological and ethnographic collns; Head ALICE ALAURIN.

Cotabato City Branch: Cotabato City, Mindanao; ethnographic colln of local tribal materials; Head DANIEL LACERNA.

Fort Pilar Branch: Zamboanga City, Mindanao; f. 1985; material culture of three ethnic groups, traditional boats; dioramas depicting c. 400 species of marine life; Head EUFEMIA CATOLIN.

Fort San Pedro Branch: Cebu City, Cebu; ceramics, archaeological artefacts depicting the history of a sunken 16th-century Spanish galleon; Head VICENTE SECUYA.

Jolo Branch: Jolo, Sulu, Mindanao; material culture of Sulu; Head BELEN UDDIN.

Kabayan Branch: Kabayan, Benguet, Luzon; material culture of the Ibalois and the Kankana-ey; Head JULIET IGLOSO.

Kiangan Branch: Kiangan, Ifugao, Luzon; anthropological materials, Ifugao house.

Lubuagan Branch: Lubuagan, Kalinga, Luzon; ethnographic colln on culture of the Kalinga.

Magsingal Branch: Vigan City, Ilocos Sur, Luzon; ethnographic colln on the Ilocano people and liturgical arts; Head REMEDIOS PALACPAC.

Peñablanca Branch: Peñablanca, Cagayan, Luzon; finds from the cave sites of Peñablanca.

Puerto Galera Branch: Puerto Galera, Oriental Mindoro, Luzon; archaeological history of Puerto Galera; Head MAMERTO CONTRERAS.

Tabon Caves Branch: Tabon, Quezon, Palawan; natural heritage of the region; ethnographic materials from three local ethnic groups; archaeological artefacts from the Tabon Caves; Head VIVIAN BROWN.

Tuguegarao Branch: Tuguegarao City, Cagayan, Luzon; prehistory of the Cagayan Valley; ethnographic exhibits; Head AIREEN MELAD.

Vigan Branch: Vigan City, Ilocos Sur, Luzon; culture of the Ilocano people through archaeological and ethnographic materials; Head REMEDIOS PALACPAC.

San Agustín Museum: POB 3366, General Luna St, Intramuros, Manila 1002; tel. (2) 527-4060; fax (2) 527-4058; f. 1972; located in 400-year-old San Agustín monastery; Hispano-Philippino religious art (paintings, sculptures, etc.); library of 3,000 vols; Curator Dr PEDRO G. GALENDE.

University of Santo Tomas Museum of Arts and Sciences: 3rd Fl., Main Bldg, University of Santo Tomas, Calle España, Manila 1008; tel. (2) 781-1815; fax (2) 740-9718; e-mail museum@ust.edu.ph; internet www.ustmuseum.com; f. 17th c.; sections on natural history, Philippines religious images, coins, medals and memorabilia, visual arts, ethnography and non-Philippine oriental arts; Dir Rev. Fr ISIDRO C. ABAÑO; publ. *Newsletter* (4 a year).

Marikina City

Philippine Science Centrum: Building D, Riverbanks Center, 84A Bonifacio Ave, Barangka, Marikina City, 1803 Metro Manila; tel. (2) 942-5136; fax (2) 942-5091; e-mail pfst@science-centrum.ph; internet www .science-centrum.ph; f. 1990; interactive museum with sections on earth science, human body, light, vision and perception, mechanics, electricity and magnetism, liquids and mathematics; operated by Philippine Foundation for Science and Technol-

ogy; Head of Operations EDICEL HERRERA; publ. *PFST Update* (4 a year).

Pasay City

Cultural Center of the Philippines Museum/Museo ng Kalinangang Pilipino: CCP Complex, Roxas Blvd, Pasay City, Metro Manila; tel. (2) 832-5094; fax (2) 832-3683; e-mail museo@culturalcenter.gov .ph; internet www.culturalcenter.gov.ph; f. 1988; traditional Filipino art and traditional Asian musical instruments; Officer-in-Charge SONITA MAGANTE-REINOSO.

Quezon City

Ateneo Art Gallery: Ateneo de Manila University, Katipunan Ave, Loyola Heights, Quezon City 1108; tel. (2) 426-6001 ext. 4160; fax (2) 426-6488; e-mail yarambulo@ateneo .edu; internet www.admu.edu.ph/?p=221; f. 1960; works by Filipino artists since 1945; Curator RAMON E. S. LERMA.

Jorge B. Vargas Museum and Filipiniana Research Center: University of the Philippines Diliman, Roxas Ave, Diliman, Quezon City 1101; tel. (2) 928-1927; fax (2) 928-1925; e-mail vargas.museum@up.edu .ph; internet www.vargasmuseum.org; f. 1987; Philippine oil paintings, watercolours, pastels, drawings and sculpture from the 1880s to the 1960s, incl. work by the artists Lorenzo Guerrero, Simon Flores, Juan Luna, Felix Resurrecion Hidalgo, Fabian de la Rosa, Fernando Amorsolo, Jorge Pineda, Vicente Rivera y Mir, Victorio Edades, Juan Aralleno and Diosdado Lorenzo, and by the sculptors Guillermo Tolentino and Graciano Nepomuceno; archives, newspaper cuttings, photographs; library of 3,193 vols, 1,542 vols of periodicals; Curator Dr ANA MARIA THERESA P. LABRADOR.

Universities

ADAMSON UNIVERSITY

900 San Marcelino St, Ermita, 1000 Manila

Telephone: (2) 524-20-11

Fax: (2) 524-73-23

E-mail: belita@netasia.net

Internet: www.adamson.edu.ph

Founded 1932

Private (Roman Catholic)

Language of instruction: English

Academic year: June to March

President: Fr JIMMY A. BELITA

Executive Vice-President: Fr VICENTE PAYUYO

Vice-President for Finance: Fr CONSTANCIO GAN

Vice-President for Academic Affairs: Dr ROSARIO ALBERTO

Vice-President for Pastoral Affairs: Fr GREGORIO BANAGA

Registrar: Sr MAGDALENA BEBIDA

Librarian: ERLINDA B. GONZALES

Library: See Libraries and Archives

Number of teachers: 550

Number of students: 20,028

Publications: *Adamson Chronicle* (monthly), *Adamson Newsletter* (monthly), *Sofia* (annual), *Sci-Tech* (annual), *Law Journal* (annual), *LIA COM* (annual)

DEANS

College of Law: PONCIANO SUBIDO

Graduate School: ROSARIO ALBERTO

College of Liberal Arts: Dr ADELAIDA ALMEIDA

College of Sciences: Dr DULCE CASACLANG

College of Engineering: PETER URETA

College of Education: Dr ADELAIDA ALMEIDA

College of Commerce: Dr JOSÉ GONZÁLEZ

College of Architecture: Dr RAMÓN VICTOR

College of Pharmacy: ELEODORA LORENZO

AKLAN STATE UNIVERSITY

Banga, Aklan 5601, Western Visayas
Telephone: (36) 267-6567
Fax: (36) 267-5801
E-mail: webmaster@asu.edu.ph
Internet: www.asu.edu.ph
Founded 1918 as Capiz Farm School; present name and status 2001
State control
Academic year: June to March
President: Dr BENNY A. PALMA
Vice-President (Academic): Dr EDNA I. GONZALES
Vice-President (Administration): Prof. THEODORE R. ROWAN
University Secretary: MICHELLE M. TAN
Director (Library and Information Technology): EDELINA L. MATEO

DEANS

College of Agriculture, Forestry and Environmental Sciences: Dr DANILO E. ABAYON (acting)
School of Arts and Sciences: Dr CELEDONIA HILARIO (acting)
School of Fisheries and Marine Sciences: Dr ELENITA B. ANDRADE (acting)
School of Industrial Technology: Prof. JOSEFINA F. TUPAS (acting)
School of Rural Resources Development and Management: Prof. JESUS R. NAVARRA (acting)
School of Veterinary Medicine: Dr CECILIA T. REYES (acting)

ANGELES UNIVERSITY FOUNDATION

Angeles City
Telephone: (2) 845-1491
Fax: (2) 845-1491
Internet: www.auf.edu.ph
Founded 1962
Private control
Languages of instruction: English, Filipino
Academic year: June to March
Chancellor: Dr EMMANUEL Y. ANGELES
President: Dr RICARDO P. PAMA
Vice-President for Academic Affairs: Dr RUBEN C. UMALY
Vice-President for Administration: Prof. SYLVIA M. SORIANO
Vice-President for Finance: LORETO A. CANLAS
Registrar: Dr ARCHIMEDES T. DAVID
Librarian: TERESITA M. MANARANG
Library of 38,569 vols
Number of teachers: 317
Number of students: 7,500
Publications: *Alumnews*, *AUF Journal*, *AUF News*, *Datalink*, *MPA Perspective*, *Nurscene*, *The Pioneer*

DEANS

College of Allied Medical Professions: CONSUELO P. MACALALAD
College of Arts and Sciences: Dr NUNILON G. AYUYAO
College of Business Administration: LEONIDA F. CAYANAN
College of Computer Science: CAESAR R. MAÑALAC
College of Criminology: LUCIA M. HIPOLITO
College of Education: LUCENA P. SAMSON
College of Engineering and Technology: Eng. JOSÉ L. MACAPAGAL, Jr
College of Medicine: Dr REYNALDO V. LOPEZ
College of Nursing: ZENAIDA S. FERNANDEZ
Graduate School: Dr CONCESA MILAN BADUEL

AQUINAS UNIVERSITY

Rawis, Legazpi City 4500
Telephone: (52) 482-0540
Fax: (52) 482-0540
E-mail: secgen@aquinas-university.edu.ph
Internet: www.aquinas-university.edu.ph
Founded 1948; University 1968
Private (Roman Catholic) control
Languages of instruction: English, Filipino
Academic year: June to May
President: Very Rev. Fr Dr RAMONCLARO G. MENDEZ
Vice-President: Very Rev. Fr ALFREDO A. FERNANDEZ
Secretary-General: VIRGILIO S. PERDIGON, Jr
Registrar: LETICIA R. ROQUE
Librarian: MARILYN M. BENDICIO
Library of 58,547 vols
Number of teachers: 298
Number of students: 6,374
Publication: *Aquinas University Research Journal*

DEANS

College of Law: Atty EMERSON B. AQUENDE
College of Engineering: Eng. MANUEL T. NAVEA, Jr
College of Architecture and Fine Arts: Arch. ERNESTO M. TIANCO
College of Arts and Sciences: JAZMIN B. LLANA
College of Business Administration: Dr MILAGROS B. RICAFORT
College of Education: Rev. Fr Dr RAMONCLARO G. MENDEZ
College of Nursing: MA. CLARA LL. RUBINO
Graduate Studies and Research: Dr ZORAYDA N. NUYDA

ARELLANO UNIVERSITY

2600 Legarda Street, Sampaloc, Manila
Telephone: 60-74-41
Internet: www.arellano.edu.ph
Founded 1938
Language of instruction: English
Private control
Chairman, Board of Trustees: Atty FLORENTINE CAYCE, Jr
President: JOSE T. ENRIQUEZ
Executive Vice-President: PAULINO F. CAYCO
Registrar: Mrs JOSEFA V. LEBRON
Librarian: ALFREDO C. VALDEZ
Number of teachers: 335
Number of students: 10,326
Publications: *Arellano Standard*, *Philippine Education Quarterly*

DEANS

Graduate School: Dr AMPARO S. LARDIZABAL
Arellano Law College: Atty MARIANO M. MAGSALIN
College of Arts and Sciences: Dr SERGIA G. ESGUERRA
College of Education and Normal College: Dr AMPARO S. LARDIZABAL
College of Commerce: FRANCISCO P. CAYCO
College of Nursing: Dr PRAXEDES S. M. DELA ROSA

ATENEO DE DAVAO UNIVERSITY

E. Jacinto St, 8000 Davao City
Telephone: (82) 221-2411
Fax: (82) 226-4116
E-mail: admissions@addu.edu.ph
Internet: www.addu.edu.ph
Founded 1948
Language of instruction: English
Private control
Academic year: June to March
President: Rev. EDMUNDO M. MARTINEZ
Registrar: Atty RENE ALEXIS VILLARENTE

Librarian: LEONISA P. SALES
Library of 104,857 vols
Number of teachers: 512 (372 full-time, 140 part-time)
Number of students: 7,925
Publications: *Tambara* (annually), *Journal of Business and Governance* (4 a year)

DEANS

School of Arts and Sciences: Dr PERLA E. FUNA
School of Business and Governance: JOSE ISAGANI M. LACSON
Law School: Atty HILDEGARDO F. IÑIGO

ATTACHED INSTITUTES

Center for Business Research and Extension: Dir FREDDIE CERAPIO.
Ignatian Institute for Religious Education: Dir Rev. WILLIAM J. MALLEY.
Institute of Small Farms and Industries: Dir JOCELYN E. CABO.
Regional Science Teaching Center: Dir Dr PERLA E. FUNA.
Resource Center for Local Governance: Dir LOURDES J. MAMAED.

ATENEO DE MANILA UNIVERSITY

POB 154, Manila
Telephone: 924-4601
Internet: www.admu.edu.ph
Founded 1859; University 1959
Languages of instruction: English, Filipino
Private control
Academic year: June to March (two terms) and summer term
President: Rev. BIENVENIDO F. NEBRES
Vice-President for Finance and Treasurer: JOSE M. SANTOS
Academic Vice-President: Dr PATRICIA B. LICUANAN
Librarian: ROGELIO B. MALLILLIN
Number of teachers: 741
Number of students: 12,518
Publications: *Philippine Studies* (quarterly), *Guidon*, *Alumni Guidon*, *Pantas* (2 a year), *Landas—Journal of Loyola School of Theology*, *IPC Reports*

DEANS

School of Arts and Sciences: Dr LEOVINO MA. GARCIA
Graduate School of Business: ENRIQUE H. DAVILA (Assistant Dean)
College of Law: Atty CYNTHIA R. DEL CASTILLO

UNIVERSITY OF BAGUIO

General Luna Rd, Baguio City 2600
Telephone: (74) 4423071
Fax: (74) 4423071
E-mail: ub@ubaguio.edu
Internet: www.ubaguio.edu
Founded 1948 as a Technical School
Private control; granted deregulated status by the Philippine Commission on Higher Education
Languages of instruction: English, Filipino
Academic year: June to March
President: HERMINIO C. BAUTISTA
Vice-President for Academic Affairs: Dr PERFECTO M. LOPEZ
Vice-President for Administration: Dr REBECCA C. CAJILOG
Registrar: Eng. MELBA E. BALIWAN
Librarian: BIRGIT S. SANTIAGO
Library of 75,223 vols
Number of teachers: 415

Number of students: 18,085

Publications: *University of Baguio Journal* (2 a year), *The Leaven* (4 a year)

DEANS

College of Liberal Arts: Dr TERESITA DE GUZMAN

College of Commerce: MARY HAYDEE AGNES E. DABUCOL

College of Education: Dr AGNES T. BAUTISTA

Graduate School: Dr AGNES T. BAUTISTA

College of Engineering: Eng. RENATO D. TANDOC

College of Dentistry: Dr VERONICA S. GARCIA

Law Enforcement Academy: Dr MILLER F. PECKLEY

College of Physical Therapy and Optometry: ESMERELDA M. GATCHALLAN

College of Medical Technology: CONSTANTINO WI

College of Nursing: CATALINA B. ALINDUZA

College of Information and Communications Technology: Eng. LAKAN-ASA R. BAUTISTA

College of Hotel and Restaurant Management: JANE P. LIU

College of Law: DANIEL T. FARIÑAS

BATANGAS STATE UNIVERSITY

Rizal Ave, Batangas City 4200

Telephone: (43) 778-2170

Fax: (43) 778-2170

E-mail: webmaster@batstate-u.edu.ph

Internet: www.batstate-u.edu.ph

Founded 1903 as Manual Training School; present name and status 2001

State control

Academic year: June to March

President: Dr ERNESTO M. DE CHAVEZ

Senior Executive Vice-President: Dr ROLANDO L. LONTOC, Sr

Executive Vice-President: Dr PORFIRIO C. LIGAYA

Vice-Presidents: LUZVIMINDA ROSALES (Administration and Finance), Dr MARITESS D. MANLONGAT (Academic Affairs), Dr FELIX M. PANOPIO (Extension Campus Operation), Dr JESSIE A. MONTALBO (ICT, Infrastructure Development and External Affairs), Dr ROLANDO M. LONTOK, Jr (Research, Public Relations, Planning and Development, and University Secretary)

Director (Library Services): Prof. ARACELI H. LUNA

Central campuses in Batangas City (Don Pablo Borbon Campuses 1 and 2) and extension campuses in Balayan, Calaca, Lipa City (Don Claro M. Recto Campus), Lobo, Malvar (Jose P. Laurel Polytechnic College Campus), Nasugbu (ARASOF Campus), Padre Garcia, Rosario, San Juan and Taysan

DEANS

College of Accountancy (Don Pablo Borbon Campus 1 and Lipa City): Prof. MARIA CARMEN L. VIDAL

College of Arts and Science: Prof. RACHEL EVANGELIO

College of Engineering (Lipa City): Eng. ERMA QUINAY

College of Engineering, Architecture and Fine Arts (Don Pablo Borbon Campus 2): Prof. ROGELIO A. ANTENOR

College of Industrial Technology (Don Pablo Borbon Campuses 1 and 2): Dr ROLANDO M. LONTOK, Jr

College of Industrial Technology (Calaca, Balayan and Lipa City Campuses): Prof. MAXIMO PANGANIBAN

College of Liberal Arts: Dr GLORIA G. MENDOZA

College of Physical Education and Human Kinetics: Prof. EDUARDO EVANGELIO

Graduate School: Dr ROLANDO L. LONTOC

School of Business and Economics: Prof. MARITESS D. MANLONGAT

School of Developmental Communication: Prof. CYNTHIA Q. MANALO

School of Energy, Earth and Transportation Engineering: Dr JESSIE A. MONTALBO

School of Food and International Hospitality Management: Prof. TERESA KALALO

School of Governance, Peace and Development Studies: Prof. RACHEL EVANGELIO

School of Informatics and Computing Sciences: Dr JESSIE A. MONTALBO

ATTACHED RESEARCH CENTRE

Batangas Center for Research and Special Studies: Dir Prof. JOCELYN R. CASTILLO.

BENGUET STATE UNIVERSITY

La Trinidad, Benguet 2601

Telephone: (74) 422-24-01

Fax: (74) 442-22-81

E-mail: cip@bsu.edu.ph

Internet: www.bsu.edu.ph

Founded 1916, university status 1985

Language of instruction: English

Academic year: June to May

President: Dr CIPRIANO C. CONSOLACION

Vice-President: Dr FRANCO T. BAWANG

Designated Vice-Presidents: Dr MARCOS A. BULIYAT (Academic Affairs), Dr ROGELIO D. COLTING (Research and Extension), Dr TESSIE M. MERESTELA (Planning and Development)

Director of Admissions: VIRGINIA R. DUGAT

Director of Student Affairs: Prof. WILFREDO B. MINA

Registrar (vacant)

Librarian: Dr NORA J. CLARAVALL

Library of 34,000 vols

Number of teachers: 290

Number of students: 6,598 on degree courses

Publications: *BSU Research Journal*, *BSU Extension*, *BSU Newsletter*, *Highland Express*, college publications

DEANS

College of Agriculture: Dr DANILO P. PADUA

College of Arts and Sciences: Dr EDNA A. CHUA

College of Forestry: For. MELECIO A. BALANGEN

College of Engineering and Applied Technology: Eng. GENARO W. MACASIEB, Jr

College of Teacher Education: Dr PERCYVERANDA A. LUBRICA

College of Veterinary Medicine: Dr RUTH C. DIEGO

College of Home Economics and Technology: Dr JANE K. AVILA

College of Nursing: Dr FLORENCE C. CAWAON

Graduate School: Dr DOMINADOR S. GARIN

BICOL UNIVERSITY

Rizal St, Legazpi City 4500

Telephone: (5221) 449-13

Internet: www.bicol-u.edu.ph

Founded 1970

State control

Languages of instruction: English, Filipino

Academic year: June to May (2 semesters and a Summer Term)

President: LYLIA CORPORAL-SENA

Vice-President: EMILIANO A. ABERIN

Vice-President for Academic Affairs: NELIA S. CIOCSON

Registrar: CARMELINA O. BALLARES

Librarian: EXALTACION R. RESONTOC

Library of 35,380 vols

Number of teachers: 568

Number of students: 12,572

Publications: *The Bicol Universitarian* (quarterly), *Graduate Forum* (2 a year), *The Gearcast*, *The Net*, *R & D Journal*, *The Cassette*, *The Mentor*, *Research Monitor* (2 a year), *Outreach* (quarterly), *BU Bulletin* (6 a year)

DEANS

Graduate School: NELIA S. CIOCSON

Arts and Sciences: SUSANA C. CABREDO

Agriculture: JUSTINO R. ARBOLEDA

Fisheries: OFELIA S. VEGA

Engineering: EDUARDO M. LORIA

Education: OSCAR L. LANDAGAN

Nursing: PAZ G. MUÑOZ

School of Arts and Trades: EDGAR R. CAMBA

Institute of Communication and Cultural Studies: RAMONA B. RAÑESES

BULACAN STATE UNIVERSITY

Malolos, Bulacan 3000

Telephone: (44) 791-0153

Fax: (44) 791-0153

E-mail: bsu-ice@bulsu.edu.ph

Internet: www.bulsu.edu.ph

Founded 1904 as Bulacan Trade School; present name and status 1993

State control

Academic year: June to March

President: Dr ROSARIO PIMENTEL

Vice-President (Academic Affairs): Dr MARIANO C. DE JESUS

Vice-President (Planning and Development): Dr FRANCISCO L. CRUZ

Dean (Student Affairs): TRINIDAD P. PANGAN

Registrar: LEILANI M. LIZARDO

Librarian: VIRGINIA C. MIRANDA

Regional campuses in Bambang, Bustos, Hagonoy and Sarmiento

DEANS

College of Arts and Sciences: Dr NORMA C. MORALA

College of Education: Dr DANILO D. FAUSTINO

College of Engineering: Dr CECILIA A. GERONIMO

College of Industrial Technology: Dr SALVADOR P. PEREDO

College of Law: (vacant)

Graduate School: Dr DANILO S. HILARIO

DIRECTORS

Distance Education: EDGARDO MATEO

Institute of Architecture and Fine Arts: SATURNINA C. PARUNGAO

Institute of Computer Education: FAUSTO S. HILARIO

Institute of Home Economics: FIDELITA P. ESTRADA

Institute of Physical Education and Sports: RACQUEL M. MENDOZA

CAGAYAN STATE UNIVERSITY

Carig, Tuguegarao City 3500

Telephone: (78) 844-01-07

Fax: (78) 844-41-19

E-mail: abcortes@scan.com.ph

Founded 1978 by merger of Northern Luzon State College of Agriculture and Cagayan Valley College of Arts and Trades

Academic year: June to March

President: Dr ARMANDO B. CORTES

Vice-President for Academic Affairs: Dr ELEUTERIO C. DE LEON

Director for Research: ROMILLO N. TRINIDAD

Number of teachers: 500

Number of students: 10,300

Publications: *Research Journal of the Graduate School*, *Faculty Journal* (annually), *CSU Research Journal* (2 a year)

Colleges of agriculture, arts and sciences, engineering, fisheries, industrial technology, medicine, teacher training, and Graduate School.

CAVITE STATE UNIVERSITY

Bancod, Indang, Cavite 4122

Telephone: (46) 4150-010
Fax: (46) 4150-013
E-mail: cvsu_rc@cavite.net

Founded 1906; fmrly Don Severino Agricultural College; present name and status 1998

President: Dr RUPERTO S. SANGALANG

Colleges of Arts and Trades and Fisheries; courses in agriculture, business administration, development studies, economics, education, engineering, environmental studies, food technology, hotel and restaurant management, mass communication, mathematics and computer science, natural sciences and technology.

CEBU NORMAL UNIVERSITY

Osmeña Boulevard, Cebu City, Cebu 6000

Telephone: (32) 253-9611
Fax: (32) 253-9611
E-mail: info@cnu.vis.ph
Internet: www.cnu.edu.ph

Founded 1915 as Cebu Normal Secondary School; present name and status 1998
State control
Academic year: June to March
President: Dr ESTER B. VELASQUEZ
Vice-President (Academic Affairs): Dr MARCELO T. LOPEZ
Vice President (Administration): Dr PORPONIO B. LAPA, Jr
Registrar: ALFREDO V. ALBARICO
Dean (Student Affairs): Dr FATIMA A. BANZON
University Librarian: PORTIA D. TADENA
Number of students: 5,900

DEANS

College of Arts and Sciences: Dr ANGEL O. PESIRLA
College of Nursing: Dr EMILIA N. BUSTAMENTE (acting)
College of Teacher Education: Dr MERLEA A. CABALQUINTO
Graduate School: Dr BERNADITA M. SOLEDAD

CENTRAL LUZON STATE UNIVERSITY

Muñoz, Nueva Ecija 3120

Telephone: (6344) 456-0107
Fax: (6344) 456-5187
Internet: www.clsu.edu.ph

Founded 1907, attained university status 1964
State control
Languages of instruction: English, Filipino
Academic year: June to March
President: Dr RODOLFO C. UNDAN
Vice-Presidents: Dr RUBEN C. SEVILLEJA (Academic Affairs), Prof. REYNALDO S. GUTIERREZ (Administration), Prof. ONOFRE F. RINGOR (Business Affairs), Dr HONORATO L. ANGELES (Research, Extension and Training), Prof. REYNALDO S. GUTIERREZ (Administration), Prof. REYNALDO S. GUTIERREZ (Administration)
Dean of Students: Dr ZENAIDA M. SERNA
Director of Admissions: Dr MELISSA E. AGULTO
Librarian: Prof. CELIA D. DE LA CRUZ
Number of teachers: 373
Number of students: 6,489
Publications: CLSU Collegian (2 a year), CLSU Newsletter (monthly), CLSU Scien-

tific Journal (2 a year), CLSU Research Digest (2 a year)

DEANS

College of Agriculture: Dr FEDERICO O. PEREZ
College of Arts and Sciences: Dr MARILOU G. ABON
College of Business Administration and Accountancy: Dr DANILO S. CASTRO
College of Education: Dr DANILO G. TAN
College of Engineering: Dr IRENEO C. AGULTO
College of Fisheries: Dr ARSENIA G. CAGAUAN
College of Home Science and Industry: Dr HILARIA T. CUARESMA
College of Veterinary Science and Medicine: Dr JESUS S. DE LA ROSA
Institute of Graduate Studies: Dr CYNTHIA C. DIVINA

AFFILIATED INSTITUTES

Centre for Central Luzon Studies: Dir Prof. MARILOU G. ABON.

Central Luzon Agriculture Resources Research and Development Center: Dir Dr HONORATO L. ANGELES.

Freshwater Aquaculture Center, CLSU: Dir Dr RUBEN C. SEVILLEJA.

Information Systems Institute: Dir Eng. THEODY B. SAYCO.

Environmental Management Institute: Dir Dr ANME MELINDA P. ALBERTO.

CENTRAL MINDANAO UNIVERSITY

University Town, Musuan, Bukidnon 8710

Telephone: (88) 3561910
Fax: (88) 8442520
E-mail: cmu.musuan@eudora.com
Internet: www.cmu.edu.ph

Founded 1952 as the Mindanao Agricultural College; University 1965
State control
Languages of instruction: English, Filipino
Academic year: June to March (two semesters and a summer school)
President: Dr MARDONIO M. LAO
Vice-Presidents: Dr EMMANUEL A. LARIOSA (Academic Affairs), Dr PORFERIO M. BALANAY (Administration), Dr HERMINIO M. PAUA (Research and Extension)
Registrar: Prof. NELLIE C. LASTIMOSA
Librarian: Prof. ESTHER E. DINAMPO
Library of 23,000 vols
Number of teachers: 311
Number of students: 5,371
Publications: CMU Journal of Food, Agriculture and Nutrition (quarterly), Barangay Balita (quarterly), Newsletter (quarterly)

DEANS

College of Arts and Sciences: Dr CECILIA B. AMOROSO
College of Agriculture: Dr CELSO C. TAUTHO
College of Education: Dr MARINA I. LIZARDO
College of Engineering: Prof. REYNALDO G. JUAN
College of Home Economics: Dr NERISSA A. MACARAYAN
College of Forestry: Dr JAMES O. LACANDULA
College of Veterinary Medicine: Dr JOSE ALEXANDER C. ABELLA
Graduate School: Dr EVELYN L. BARRIDO

DEPARTMENT CHAIRMEN

College of Agriculture (tel. (88) 3561881; fax (88) 3561910):

Agribusiness: Dr JOSEFINO M. MAGALLANES
Agricultural Economics: Dr ISABELO O. MUGOT
Agricultural Education: Dr JUDITH O. INTONG
Agronomy: Dr DELFIN UALLADOR
Animal Science: Dr MARIA LUZ L. SORIANO

Development Communication: Prof. NELIA T. ESCARLOS
Entomology: Prof. ESTELITO CATLI
Horticulture: Dr LOUELLA CABAHUG
Plant Pathology: Dr LOLITO CAPILI
Soil Science: Dr NONILONA DAQUIADO

College of Arts and Sciences (tel. (88) 3561911):

Behavioural Sciences: Prof. ZENAIDA CAINTIC
Biological Sciences: Prof. VICTORIA T. QUIMPANG
Chemistry: Dr LORDINO CABIGON
Languages and Literature: Prof. MARICHU CATERIAL
Mathematics: Prof. LETICIA J. TAN
Physics: JUSEMIE V. ORTELANO
Social Science: ELEUTERIO D. TANO

College of Education (tel. (88) 3561890):

Educational Services: Prof. LOURDES BAGO
Business Education: Prof. MAGDALENA R. REDOBLE
Physical Education: Prof. MARYLOU C. VILORIA

College of Engineering (tel. (22) 3561812):

Agricultural Engineering: Prof. ARNOLD VILLAMOR
Civil Engineering: Prof. PAULINO REOMERO
Electrical Engineering: Prof. LESLIE S. CABAÑEZ
Mechanical Engineering: Prof. COSTANCIO VERULA

College of Forestry (tel. (88) 3561872):

Forest Biological Science: Prof. DEOLITO T. CLAVEJO
Forest Resources Management: Prof. ANTONIO O. ECUACION
Wood Science Technology: Prof. GEORGE R. PUNO

College of Home Economics (tel. (88) 3561885):

Education and Family Life: Prof. INES B. GEWAN
Food Science and Nutrition: Prof. ANGELITA R. BOKINGO

College of Veterinary Medicine (tel. (88) 3561883):

Anatomy, Physiology and Pharmacology: JOSE ESCARLOS, Jr
Medicine and Surgery: Prof. PETER R. ORBASE
Microbiology, Parasitology, Pathology and Public Health: Dr ROY V. VILLOREJO

CENTRAL PHILIPPINE UNIVERSITY

POB 231, Iloilo City 5000

Telephone: (33) 7-34-71
Fax: (33) 20-36-85
Internet: www.cpu.edu.ph

Founded 1905
Language of instruction: English
Private control
Academic year: June to March (two terms)
President: AGUSTIN A. PULIDO
Treasurer: ROSALENE J. MADERO
Vice-President for Academic Affairs: ELMA S. HERRADURA
Registrar: ESTHER S. BASIAO
Librarian: VICTORY D. GABAWA
Number of teachers: 280
Number of students: 9,280
Publications: The Central Echo (student paper), Centralite (student annual), Link (Alumni organ), Southeast Asia Journal

DEANS

College of Agriculture: ENRIQUE S. ALTIS
College of Arts and Sciences: LYNN J. PAREJA
College of Commerce: MILAGROS V. DIGNADICE
College of Education: LORNA D. GELLADA

College of Engineering: WALDEN S. RIO
College of Law: JUANITO M. ACANTO
College of Nursing: BETTY T. POLIDO
College of Theology: JOHNNY V. GUMBAN
School of Graduate Studies: MIRIAM M. TRAVIÑA

CENTRO ESCOLAR UNIVERSITY

9 Mendiola St, San Miguel, Manila
Telephone: (2) 735-59-91
Fax: (2) 735-59-91
E-mail: ceu1@galileo.fapenet.org
Internet: www.ceu.edu.ph

Founded 1907
Languages of instruction: English, Filipino
Private control
Academic year: June to March

President: Dr ROSITA L. NAVARRO
Vice-Presidents: Dr ROSITA L. NAVARRO (Academic Affairs, concurrent with University Presidency), LUCILA C. TIONGCO (Alumni Affairs), CARMELITA E. LA O' (Business Affairs), Dr MARIA L. AYUYAO (Executive), JOSEPHINE E. MAPE (Finance)
Registrar: LUCIA D. GONZALES
Librarian: Dr TERESITA G. HERNANDEZ

Number of teachers: 800
Number of students: 22,691

Publications: *Academe*, *Ciencia y Virtud* (quarterly), *The Clarion* (quarterly), *Graduate and Faculty Studies* (annually), *Rose and the Leaf* (annually)

DEANS
School of Arts and Humanities: Dr CECILIA G. VALMONTE
School of Accountancy, Business, Secretarial and Public Administration: Dr CONRADO E. IÑIGO, Jr
College of Dentistry: Dr RENATO M. SISON
School of Education, Music and Social Work: Dr PAZ I. LUCIDO
College of Medical Technology: Dr PRISCILLA A. PANLASIGUI
College of Science: Dr ZENAIDA M. AUSTRIA
College of Nursing: MERLINA V. LOCQUIAO
School of Tourism, Family Economics and Nutrition: Dr CARMINA P. CATAPANG
College of Optometry: Dr JESSICA L. FLOR
School of Pharmacy: Dr OLIVIA M. LIMUACO
Graduate School: Dr ROSITA L. NAVARRO

DE LA SALLE UNIVERSITY

2401 Taft Ave, Malate, Manila 1004
Telephone: (2) 523-4148
Fax: (2) 521-9094
E-mail: quebengcoc@dlsu.edu.ph
Internet: www.dlsu.edu.ph

Founded 1911
Private control
Languages of instruction: English, Filipino
Academic year: June to April

President: Bro. ARMIN A. LUISTRO
Executive Vice-President: Dr CARMELITA I. QUEBENGCO
Vice-President for Academics and Research: Dr ALLAN B. I. BERNARDO
Assistant Vice-President for Administrative Services: ENRICO J. CORDERO
Assistant Vice-President for Academic Services: AGNES G. YUHICO
Registrar: EDWIN P. SANTIAGO
Librarian: PERLA T. GARCIA

Number of teachers: 1,000
Number of students: 14,686 (11,000 undergraduate, 2,000 postgraduate, 1,686 Graduate School of Business)

Publications: *Asia-Pacific Social Science Review* (2 a year), *Ideya* (2 a year), *Philippine Journal of Business and Economics* (2 a year), *DLSU Business and Economics Review* (2 a year), *Journal of Research in Science and Engineering* (3 a year), *Asia-Pacific Education Researcher* (2 a year), *Tanglaw* (2 a year), *URCO Digest* (3 a year), *Malay* (2 a year)

DEANS
College of Business and Economics: Dr MICHAEL M. ALBA
College of Education: Dr BARBARA WONG-FERNANDEZ
College of Engineering: Dr JULIUS B. MARIDABLE
College of Liberal Arts: Dr ANTONIA P. CONTRERAS
College of Science: Dr GERARDO C. JANAIRO
College of Computer Studies: Dr NELSON MARCOS

PROFESSORS
BAUTISTA, C. F., Literature and Philippine Languages
BAUTISTA, M. L. S., English Language Education
BERNARDO, A. B. I., Science Education
CABRERA, E. C., Biology
CALUYO, F. S., Electronics and Communications Engineering
CLAVERIA, F. G., Biology
CLEMEÑA, R. M. S., Counsellor Education
CONTRERAS, A. P., Political Science
CORPUZ, C. C., History
CRUZ, I. R., Literature and Philippine Languages
CULABA, A. B., Mechanical Engineering
DADIOS, E. P., Manufacturing Engineering Management
DE MESA, J. M., Religious Education
DEL MUNDO, C. A., Jr, Communication
DERY, L. C., History
DIESTO, S. D., Mathematics
EDRALIN, D. M., Business Management
ESTAÑERO, R. A., Civil Engineering
EVASCO-PERNIA, M., Literature and Philippine Languages
GALLARDO, S. M., Chemical Engineering
GARCIA, L. R., Jr, Marketing Management
GASPILLO, P. D., Chemical Engineering
GERVACIO, S. V., Mathematics
GONZALEZ, A. B., English Language Education
GRIPALDO, R. M., Philosophy
GRUENBERG, E. V., Literature and Philippine Languages
INTAL, P. S., Jr, Economics
JANAIRO, G. C., Chemistry
KROGER, D. P. O. F. M., Theology and Religious Education
LAMBERTE, E. E., Behavioural Sciences
LICUANAN, W. R. Y., Biology
OLAÑO, S. S. B., Jr, Chemical Engineering
PALISOC, S. T., Physics
PASCASIO, A. A., Mathematics
PATALINGHUG, W. C., Chemistry
PRUDENTE, M. S., Science Education
RAGASA, C. Y., Chemistry
REYES, F. C., Educational Leadership and Management
ROBLES, A. C., Jr, Political Science
ROCES, S. A., Chemical Engineering
SALAZAR, C. M., Chemical Engineering
TRANCE, A. S., Mathematics
TULLAO, T. S., Jr, Economics
UNITE, A. A., Economics
VILLACORTA, W. V., Political Science

DON MARIANO MARCOS MEMORIAL STATE UNIVERSITY

Bacnotan, La Union 2515
Telephone: (72) 888-5677
Fax: (72) 888-3191
Internet: www.dmmmsu.edu.ph

Founded 1960 as La Union Agricultural School; present name and status 1980

State control
Academic year: June to March
President: Dr ERNESTO R. GAPASIN
Vice-President (Academic Affairs): Dr AMELIA O. BACUNGAN
Vice-President (Administration) (vacant)
Vice-President (Planning and Development): Dr ELVI C. BUGAOAN
Vice-President (Research and Public Relations): Dr FLORENTINA S. DUMLAO

HEADS OF OPERATING UNITS
North La Union Campus: Dr ORLANDO O. ALMOITE (Chancellor)
Mid La Union Campus: Dr RODOLFO R. APIGO (Chancellor)
South La Union Campus: Dr INOCENCIO I. MANGAOANG, Jr
Graduate College: Dr NORMA B. NATINO (Dean)
Open University System: Dr CONCEPCION L. BEDERIO (Dir)
Sericulture Research Development Institute: Dr RICARDO C. BRIONES (Dir)
Apiculture Training and Development Center: Dr APOLONIO S. SITO (Dir)

UNIVERSITY OF THE EAST

2219 Claro M. Recto Ave, Manila 1008
Telephone: (2) 741-5471
Fax: (2) 735-6972
E-mail: postmaster@ue.edu.ph
Internet: online.ue.edu.ph/manila
Academic year: June to March

Founded 1946 as the Philippine College of Commerce and Business Administration; University of the East 1951
Private control

Chairman of the Board and Chief Executive Officer: P. O. DOMINGO
President and Chief Academic Officer: Dr JOSEFINA R. CORTES
Executive Vice-President and Chief Administrative Officer: CARMELITA G. MATEO
Chancellor of UE Caloocan: Dr JOSE C. BENEDICTO
Vice-President for Academic Affairs: Atty CARLOS M. ORTEGA
Vice-President for Administration: WILHELMINA A. DE LAS ALAS
Vice-President for Information Technology and Systems: NUMERIANO M. DELA CRUZ
Dean of Students: TRINIDAD O. ABENOJAR
Registrar: ROMEO Q. ARMADA
Director of Libraries: NORMA I. JHOCSON
Library: see Libraries and Archives
Number of teachers: 863
Number of students: 28,125

Publications: *CAS Horizon*, *Graduate School Research Journal*, *Law Update*, *Research Bulletin*

DEANS
Graduate School: Dr ROSARIO E. MAMINTA
College of Arts and Sciences (Caloocan campus): Dr TERESITA E. ERESTAIN
College of Arts and Sciences (Manila campus): CARMELITA S. FLORES
College of Business Administration (Caloocan campus): Dr JOSE C. BENEDICTO
College of Business Administration (Manila campus): Dr RELLITA D. PAEZ
College of Computer Studies and Systems: PRESIDIO R. CALUMPIT, Jr
College of Dentistry: Dr DIAMPO J. LIM
College of Education: Dr LETICIA P. CORTES
College of Engineering: Dr GENARO T. MARZAN
College of Fine Arts: GERARDO M. TAN
College of Law: Justice REYNALDO L. SUAREZ
Elementary and Secondary Laboratory Schools: ESMYRNA F. ESTACIO (Principal)

Physical Education Department: Luz S. Santa Ana (Dir)

AFFILIATED MEDICAL CENTRE

University of the East Ramon Magsaysay Memorial Medical Center: Aurora Blvd, Sta Mesa, Quezon City, Metro Manila; internet www.uerm.edu; f. 1956
Affiliated to University of the East; Chief Librarian: Loretta G. Bautista; library of 31,150 vols, 342 periodicals

DEANS

College of Medicine: Dr Romeo A. Divinagracia
College of Nursing: Dr Carmelita Divinagracia
College of Physical Therapy: (vacant)

UNIVERSITY OF EASTERN PHILIPPINES

University Town, Northern Samar 6400
Founded 1918
State control
Languages of instruction: English, Filipino
President: Dr Pedro D. Destura
Vice-Presidents: Dr Pedro A. Basiloy (Administration), Dr Nilo E. Colinares (Academic Affairs), Dr Nestor L. Rubenecia (External Affairs)
Registrar: Rogelio L. Noble
Librarian: Fe G. Baoy
Number of teachers: 339
Number of students: 7,511
Publications: *UEP Graduate Journal, The Pacific Journal of Science and Technology, The Pillar*

DEANS

College of Agriculture: Prof. Leon A. Guevara
College of Arts and Communication: Dr Lydia E. de la Rosa
College of Business Administration: Dr Lourdes O. Moscare
College of Education: Dr Zenaida S. Lucero
College of Engineering: Engr Romeo D. Atencio
College of Law: Atty Mar P. de Asis
College of Veterinary Medicine: Dr Eduardo L. Alvarez
College of Nursing: Dr Elbie Y. Baldo
College of Science: Dr Nestor L. Rubenecia
Graduate School: Dr Mindanilla B. Broto

FAR EASTERN UNIVERSITY

POB 609, Manila
Telephone: (2) 735-56-21
Fax: (2) 735-02-32
Internet: www.feu.edu.ph
Founded 1928 as Institute of Accountancy, incorporated in 1934 as Far Eastern University
Private control
Language of instruction: English
Academic year: June to March
President: Edilberto C. de Jesus
Vice-President on Academic Affairs: Lydia A. Palaypay
Registrar: John J. Macasio (acting)
Chief Librarian: Zenaida M. Galang
Library: see Libraries
Number of teachers: 1,320
Number of students: 25,106
Publications: *Far Eastern University Journal* (2 a year), *Transition* (annually), *Ambon* (annually), *Arts and Science Review* (2 a year), *Cultural Forum* (irregular), *FEU Newsletter* (4 a year), *Papers Etcetera* (2 a year)

DEANS

Institute of Accounts, Business and Finance: Danny A. Cabulay
Institute of Architecture and Fine Arts: Victoriano O. Aviguetero, Jr
Institute of Arts and Sciences: Angel O. Abaya
Institute of Education: Jovito B. Castillo
Institute of Graduate Studies: Jovito B. Castillo (Co-ordinator)
Institute of Law: Atty Andres D. Bautista
Institute of Nursing: Norma M. Dumadag

FOUNDATION UNIVERSITY

Dumaguete City 6200
Telephone: (35) 422-9167
Fax: (35) 422-9142
E-mail: estertan@eudoramail.com
Internet: www.speed.com.ph/users/fu
Founded 1949
Language of instruction: English
Private control
Academic year: June to March (two semesters)
President: Dr Ester V. Tan (acting)
Vice-President for Academic Affairs: Dr Ester V. Tan
Vice-President for Student Life and External Affairs: Dinno Willie D. Depositario
Registrar: Melodina P. delos Santos
Librarian: Stella P. Micullar
Library of 55,000 vols
Number of teachers: 148
Number of students: 3,931
Publications: *Foundation Time* (monthly), *Graduate Journal* (2 a year), *University Recorder* (2 a year), *Law Forum* (2 a year)

DEANS

Graduate School: Dr Ester V. Tan
College of Arts and Sciences: Dr Mira D. Sinco
College of Education: Dr Thelma E. Florendo
College of Business and Economics: Dr Eva C. Melon
College of Agriculture: Candida S. Basubas
College of Law and Jurisprudence: Atty Joel C. Obar
School of Industrial Engineering: Engr Marlon A. Tanilon

GREGORIO ARANETA UNIVERSITY FOUNDATION

Araneta University Post Office, Malabon, Metro Manila 1404
Telephone: 366-90-53
Fax: 361-90-54
E-mail: gauf@gauf.curricula.net
Internet: www.gauf.curricula.net
Founded 1946; reorganized as a foundation 1965
Private control
Languages of instruction: English, Filipino
Academic year: June to March
President: Dr Manuel D. Punzal
Executive Vice-President: Dr Rosenda A. de Gracia
Director for Academic Affairs: Dr Ma. Corazon V. Tadena
Registrar: Prof. Teresita R. Gutierrez
Librarian: Prof. Felisa W. Dador
Number of teachers: 156 (69 full-time, 87 part-time)
Number of students: 3,012
Publications: *Araneta Research Journal* (4 a year), *Tinig* (monthly), *Harvest* (annually), *Compendium of Veterinary Research* (annually), *The Philippine Veterinarian* (4 a year)

DEANS

College of Agriculture and Forestry: Dr Anastacio T. Mercado
College of Arts and Sciences: Dr Lillian L. Pena
College of Business and Accountancy: Dr Nellie A. Asuncion
College of Education: Dr Lydia S. Jusay
College of Engineering and Technology: Dr Leovigildo A. Manalo
College of Veterinary Medicine: Dr Daniel C. Ventura, Jr
Graduate School: Dr Ma. Corazon V. Tadena

ISABELA STATE UNIVERSITY

San Fabian, Echague, Isabela 1318
Telephone: 22013
Founded 1978
State control
Language of instruction: English
Academic year: June to May
President: Dr Rodolfo C. Nayga
Vice-President: Dr Mariano P. Baluag
Registrar: Thelma T. Lanuza
Librarian: Romula P. Romero
Library of 11,818 vols
Number of teachers: 477
Number of students: 4,340
Publications: *Research Journal, CVIARS Monitor, Forum, Mediator, Hexachord, Geyser*

DEANS

College of Agriculture: Dr Francisco M. Basuel
School of Business Administration: Prof. Relli C. Pableo
School of Development Communication: Prof. Lolita G. Sarangay
School of Engineering: Eng. Jose J. Lorenzana
College of Arts and Sciences: Dr Jesus B. Gollayan
Polytechnic College: Dr Esperanza Bueno
Teachers' College: Dr Sacrificia T. Catabui
College of Forestry: Dr Roberto R. Araño
Graduate Studies: Dr Nelson T. Binag

LEYTE NORMAL UNIVERSITY

Paterno St, Tacloban City, Leyte 6500
Telephone: (53) 321-2176
Fax: (53) 325-6122
Internet: lnu.evis.net.ph
Founded 1921 as Leyte Normal School; present name and status 1995
State control
Academic year: June to March
President: Dr Crescencia V. Chan-Gonzaga
Publication: *LNU Research Journal* (annually)
Colleges of Arts and Sciences, Commerce, Education, Engineering and Management, Development and Entrepreneurship.

LEYTE STATE UNIVERSITY

Visca, Baybay, Leyte 6521
Telephone: (53) 335-2601
Fax: (53) 335-2601
Internet: www.lsu.visayas.org
Founded 1924 as Baybay Agricultural School; present name and status 2001
State control
Academic year: June to March
President: Dr Paciencia P. Milan
Number of teachers: 261
Publication: *Annual Report*
Colleges of Agriculture, Arts and Science, Education, Engineering and Agri-Indus-

tries, Forestry and Veterinary Medicine;
Graduate School; Open University system.

UNIVERSITY OF MANILA

546 Dr M. V. de los Santos St, Sampaloc,
Manila 1008
Telephone: 7413637
Fax: 7413640
Founded 1913
Private, non-sectarian institution
Language of instruction: English
Academic year: June to May (three terms)
President: Dr VIRGILIO DE LOS SANTOS
Executive Vice-President: Atty ERNESTO LL.
DE LOS SANTOS
Vice-President for Academic Affairs: Dr
EMILY D. DE LEON
Registrar: Dr VIRGILIO DE LOS SANTOS
Chief Librarian: CORAZON G. PAYTE
Number of teachers: 250
Number of students: 7,500

Publications: *The University of Manila Graduate School Journal, The UM Law Gazette, The Gold Leaf*

DEANS

College of Law: MICHAEL P. MORALDE
College of Education: EMILY D. DE LEON
College of Liberal Arts: ROSALIA V. MOLINA
College of Business Administration and
Accountancy: NELSON S. ABELEDA
College of Engineering: ARSENIO A. RON-
QUILLO
College of Foreign Service: BENJAMIN D.
QUINERI
College of Criminology: FORTUNATO S. RIVERA
Graduate Studies: EMILY D. DE LEON

MANILA CENTRAL UNIVERSITY

Edsa, 1400 Caloocan
Telephone: 364-10-71
Internet: www.mcu.edu.ph
Founded 1904
Private control
Language of instruction: English
Academic year: June to March
President: LUALHATI TANCHOCO-GONZALEZ
Vice-Presidents: Dr FELICIANA A. REYES (Academic Affairs), Dr ARISTOTLE T. MALABA-
NAN (Administrative Affairs), LEZITA H.
REYES (Finance)
Registrar: CORAZON R. CRUZ
Librarian: ADALGESA MASANGKAY
Number of teachers: 240
Number of students: 9,028

Publications: *The Pharos, Research Journal, Gold and Purple*

DEANS

College of Medicine: Dr LITA BRITANICO
College of Pharmacy: Dr LUZVIMINDA ONG
College of Dentistry: Dr ELIZA PUZON
College of Medical Technology: PETRONA
BENITEZ
College of Arts and Sciences: AMANDA LO-
RENZANA
College of Business Administration: PERCY
GARCIA
College of Nursing: LINA SALARDA
College of Optometry: Dr FRANCISCO BAE-
TIONG, Jr
College of Physical Therapy: Dr JOSÉ REDEN-
TOR C. BUCU
School of Midwifery: LINA SALARDA
Graduate School: Dr FELICIDAD C. ROBLES
High School Principal: RIORICA NAVARRO
Head, Elementary Department: REMEDIOS
BATAC

MARIANO MARCOS STATE UNIVERSITY

Batac, Ilocos Norte
Telephone: 792-31-91
Fax: (77) 792-31-31
Internet: www.mmsu.edu.ph
Founded 1978
State control
Language of instruction: English
Academic year: June to March
President: Dr ELIAS L. CALACAL
Vice-President for Academic Affairs: Dr
NANCY B. BALANTAC
Vice-President for Administration: Dr HE-
RALDO L. LAYAOEM
Vice-President for Research and Extension:
Dr RODOLFO A. NATIVIDAD
Registrar: Dr NENITA P. BLANCO
Administrative Officer: MANUEL B. CORPUZ
Librarian: Prof. BUCALEN C. SABOY
Library of 55,511 vols
Number of teachers: 485
Number of students: 11,761

DEANS

Graduate School: Dr LORENZA S. MATIAS
College of Arts and Sciences: Dr ANABELLE C.
FELIPE
College of Agriculture and Forestry: Dr
SALUD F. BARROGA
College of Education: Dr VICENTE A. BONDAN
College of Business, Economics and Accountancy: Dr MARIETTA M. BONOAN
College of Engineering and Technology: Engr
CARLOS F. UNGSON
Institute of Health Sciences: Prof. VIOLETA
M. GLOVA
College of Technology: Prof. NESTOR M.
AGNGARAYNGAY
College of Aquatic Sciences and Technology:
Prof. RODOLFE V. LADDARAN

ATTACHED CENTRES

Iloko Research and Information Center:
Dir Dr ERNESTO MA. CADIZ.

Regional Science Teaching Center: Dir
Prof. LEO VER DOMINGO.

**Fulbright American Studies Resource
Center:** Dir Prof. BUCALEN C. SABOY.

Business Resource Development Center: Head Prof. LORNA FERNANDEZ.

Center for Applied Research and Technology Transfer: Dir Prof. FELIPE R. ESTA.

PAMANTASAN NG LUNGSOD NG MAYNILA
(University of the City of Manila)

Intramuros, Manila 1002
Telephone: (2) 527-35-51
E-mail: plm@plm.edu.ph
Internet: www.plm.edu.ph
Founded 1967
City government control
Languages of instruction: English, Filipino
Academic year: June to March (2 semesters);
summer term for graduate schools; trimestral for graduate programmes in management and engineering
President: Dr BENJAMIN G. TAYABAS
Vice-President for Academic Affairs: Dr
VIRGINIA N. SANTOS
Vice-President for Administration: ANGELITA
G. SOLIS
Vice-President for Finance and Planning:
ANGELITA G. SOLIS
Registrar: Dr ESTER D. JIMENEZ
Librarian: REBECCA M. JOCSON
Library of 49,400 vols
Number of teachers: 633
Number of students: 10,385

Publications: *Ang Pamantasan, Pamantasan
Star Post, PLM Review*

DEANS

Graduate School of Arts, Sciences, Education
and Nursing: Dr GERALDINE E. TRIA
Graduate School of Business and Government: Dr ROBERT G. ONG
Graduate School of Engineering: Eng. FELIX
F. ASPIRAS
College of Arts and Sciences: Dr DOLORES B.
LIWAG
College of Business and Public Administration: NILO D. BULADACO
College of Education: MYRNA G. GIL
College of Engineering and Technology: Eng.
JUAN C. TALLARA, Jr
College of Law: Atty JOSE M. ROY III
College of Medicine: Dr EUGENIO A. PICAZO
College of Nursing: Dr MARILYN R. COLADILLA
College of Physical Therapy: ANNA MARGAR-
ITA FERMINA G. GUICO
College of Physical Education, Recreation
and Sports: Dr PRISCILLA L. MIÑAS

MINDANAO STATE UNIVERSITY

MSU Campus, Marawi City 9700
Telephone: (63) 3521002
E-mail: op@msumain.edu.ph
Internet: www.msumain.edu.ph
Founded 1961
Language of instruction: English
Academic year: June to May
President: Dr CAMAR A. UMPA
Executive Vice-President and Chancellor: Dr
DATUMANONG A. SARANGANI
Vice-President for Academic Affairs: Prof.
YUSOPH LATIP
Vice-President for Planning and Development: Prof. SAIDALE MOHAMAD
Vice-President for Administration and
Finance: Dr DATUMANONG SARANGANI (acting)
Registrar: JESSIE SILANG
Librarian: LAWANSAN MANGORAC
Number of teachers: 1,220
Number of students: 12,000

Publications: *Mindanao Varsitarian*
(monthly), *Pagsibol, Darangen, Piglas,
Alumni Monitor, OVCRE Bulletin, Unirescent, Mindanao Journal, Mindanao Arts
and Culture Professional Papers Publication, Ongangen, CSSH Graduate Research
Journal*

DEANS

College of Agriculture: Dr CAMAR MIKUNUG
College of Natural Sciences and Mathematics: Prof. RAMBE RAMEL
College of Social Sciences and Humanities:
Prof. BONIFACIO R. TACATA
College of Business Administration: Dr MER-
LYN TAN
College of Public Affairs: Dr NASRODEN GURO
College of Education: Dr PENDILILANG GUNT-
ING
College of Engineering: Prof. RODRIGO BAID
(acting)
College of Fisheries: Dr JULIETA LAGMAY
College of Forestry and Environmental
Sciences: Dr GERARDO GAVINE
College of Health Sciences: Dr MINDAMORA
MUTIN
College of Hotel and Restaurant Management: Dr CECILLE MAMBUAY
College of Law: Atty BASARI D. MAPUPUNO
College of Medicine: Dr ANGELO MANALO
College of Sports and Physical Recreation:
Prof. HASAN MARANDA
Graduate School: Dr COSAIN DERICO
King Faisal Center for Islamic and Arabic
Studies: Prof. TALIB BENITO

Institute of Science Education: Dr EMERITA MOTI
Regional Science Training Center: Dr DOLORES PATTUINAN
School of Information Technology: Dr PEPE L. MADRID

ATTACHED INSTITUTE OF TECHNOLOGY

Iligan Institute of Technology of the Mindanao State University: Andres Bonifacio Ave, Tibanga, Iligan City 9200; tel. (63) 2214056; fax (63) 3516173; e-mail oc-mps@ sulat.msuiit.edu.ph; internet www.msuiit .edu.ph; f. 1968
State control
Languages of instruction: English, Filipino
Academic year: June to April; Chancellor: Prof. MARCELO P. SALAZAR; Vice-Chancellor (Academic Affairs): Dr EDGAR W. IGNACIO; Vice-Chancellor (Research and Extension): Dr JAMAIL A. KAMLIAN; Vice-Chancellor (Administration and Finance): Atty BASHER T. MACAPADO; Registrar: Prof. EVELYN M. JAMBOY; Librarian: ELENA APUGAN-BRANZUELA (acting); library of 58,975 vols; 490 ; 7,778 ; publ. *Gazette* (4 a year), *Mindanao Forum* (annually)

DEANS

College of Arts and Social Sciences: Dr GEOFFREY G. SALGADO
College of Science and Mathematics: Dr ARNULFO P. SUPE
College of Engineering: Dr JERSON N. OREJUDOS
College of Business Administration: Prof. MIGUEL S. MARTINEZ
College of Education: Prof. LEDDY PADERANGA
School of Engineering Technology: Prof. PAULINO T. SANCHEZ
School of Graduate Studies: Dr BRIGIDA A. ROSCOM
Integrated Development School: Prof. DIGNA C. PADURA

UNIVERSITY OF MINDANAO

Bolton St, Davao City, Mindanao
Telephone: (82) 227 54-56
Internet: www.umindanao.edu.ph
Founded 1946
Private control
Language of instruction: English
Academic year: June to March
President: DOLORES P. TORRES
Executive Vice-President for Broadcasting: GUILLERMO P. TORRES
Executive Vice-President for Education: SATURNINO R. PETALCORIN
Senior Vice-President for Academic Affairs: Dr PAQUITA D. GAVINO
Vice-President for Treasury: SANDRA G. ANGELES
Vice-President for Accounting: GLORIA E. DETOYA
Vice-President for Administration: ANTONIO M. PILPIL
Vice-President for MIS/EDP: EDGARDO O. CASTILLO
Registrar: GLORIA E. DETOYA
Number of teachers: 455
Number of students: 22,569
Publications: *UM Faculty Journal, News Bulletin*

DEANS

Post-Doctoral: Dr EFIGENIA C. OCCEÑA
Graduate School: Dr JULIAN RODRIGUEZ, Jr
College of Engineering: CARMENCITA E. VIDAMO
College of Architecture: ILUMINADO C. QUINTO
College of Commerce and Accountancy: VICENTE B. VALDEZ
College of Law: Atty JOSÉ C. ESTRADA

College of Arts and Sciences: Dr HERNANDO ZAMORA
Teachers' College: Dr NECITA I. JOYNO
College of Forestry: DAN D. MITCHAO
College of Criminology: GEOFFREY GIRADO (Asst Dean)

NATIONAL UNIVERSITY

551 Mariano F. Jhocson St, Sampaloc, Manila
Telephone: 61-34-31
Internet: www.nu.edu.ph
Founded 1900
Language of instruction: English
Private control
Academic year: June to March
President: JESUS M. JHOCSON
Registrar: LETICIA J. PAGUIA
Head of Graduate Studies: ZENAIDA N. MAGIBA
Librarian: CONSUELO J. MIGUEL

DEANS

College of Commerce: LETICIA J. PAGUIA (acting)
College of Dentistry: Dr GREGORIO D. GABRIEL
College of Pharmacy: CELIA V. LANSANG
College of Education: DOMINGO L. DIAZ
College of Liberal Arts: ZENAIDA N. MAGIBA
College of Electrical, Industrial and Mechanical Engineering: ROMULO D. COLOMA
College of Civil, Chemical and Sanitary Engineering: ROMULO D. COLOMA
College of Architecture: FERNANDO ABAD

UNIVERSITY OF NEGROS OCCIDENTAL-RECOLETOS

Lizares Ave, POB 214, 6100 Bacolod City
Telephone: 433-2449
Fax: 433-1709
Internet: www.uno-r.edu.ph
Founded 1941
Private control
Language of instruction: English
Academic year: June to March
President: Fr DEMETRIO PEÑASCOZA
Comptroller: Fr WILLIAM VILLAFLOR
Registrar: Eng. ISMAEL L. EXITO
Librarian: ARABELLA M. ANANORIA
Number of teachers: 330
Number of students: 7,879
Publications: *The Tolentine Star* (2 a semester), *UNO-R Journal of the Graduate School (Raison d'Etre)* (quarterly)

DEANS

Graduate School: Dr JOSE B. FERRARIS
School of Agriculture: Dr EVANGELINE O. ABOYO
College of Arts and Sciences: Dr SONIA S. DAQUILA
College of Law: NELSON P. LO
Teachers' Formation Centre: TERESA L. LAGRADILLA
College of Engineering: Eng. CHRISTOPHER G. TACLOBOS
College of Criminology: CARLITO C. MAGBANUA
College of Commerce: CLARITA T. LACSON
High School Department: Fr EDWIN MACMAC
Elementary Department: MARCELA D. YAP

UNIVERSITY OF NORTHERN PHILIPPINES

Vigan, Ilocos Sur
Telephone: 28-10
Internet: www.unp.edu.ph
Founded 1965
State control
Languages of instruction: English, Filipino

Academic year of two semesters
President: Dr DOROTEA C. FILART
Executive Vice-President: Prof. LEO OANDASAN
Vice-President for Academic Affairs: Dr PACITA B. ANTIPORDA
University Secretary: Prof. RAMONA VEGA
Director of Admissions: ELEUTERIA REMUCAL
Director of Research: Prof. NORMA I. CACHOLA
Librarian: PEROMA L. PACIS
Library of 28,369 vols
Number of teachers: 392
Number of students: 7,017
Publications: *Tandem* (every 2 months), *New Vision* (quarterly)

DEANS AND DEPARTMENT HEADS

Faculty of Arts and Sciences: Dr FRANCISCO C. MACANAS
Faculty of Business Administration: Dr LUMEN ALMACHAR
Institute of Criminology: Prof. PLACIDO UNCIANO
Institute of Engineering: Eng. ROGELIO ANINAG
Institute of Fine Arts: Prof. FLORO PERLAS
Institute of Nursing and Paramedical Services: Prof. LILIA SALVADOR
Faculty of Teacher Education: Dr CIRILO PARRA
Institute of Social Work and Community Development: DANIEL COLCOL
Institute of Technical Education and Cottage Industries Development: Prof. WILHELMINA VERGARA
Faculty of the Graduate School: SALVADOR S. EDER

UNIVERSITY OF NUEVA CACERES

Jaime Henandez Ave, Naga City 4400
Telephone: 21-21-84
Internet: www.unc.edu.ph
Founded 1948
Private control
Languages of instruction: English, Filipino
Academic year: June to March (two semesters)
President: Dr DOLORES H. SISON
Executive Vice-President: PERFECTO O. PALMA
Vice-President for Administration: JAIME HERNÁNDEZ, Jr
Registrar: NELIA E. SAN JOSE
Librarian: Dr PERPETUA S. PORCALLA
Number of teachers: 327
Number of students: 8,061
Publications: *Nueva Caceres Review, Nueva Caceres Bulletin* (every 2 months), *Red and Gray* (annually), *The Trailblazer* (monthly)

DEANS

College of Arts and Sciences and Education: LOURDES S. ANONAS
College of Engineering: MAXIMINO O. PANELO, Jr
College of Law and Commerce: PERFECTO O. PALMA
School of Graduate Studies and Research: MILAGROS Z. REYES

PROFESSORS

ANONAS, L. S., Methods of Research
ALMOITE, G. E. O., Public Administration
BARIAS, A. M.
CADAG, D., Engineering Management, Highway Engineering, Water Resources Engineering, Hydrology
CONDA, A., Development of the Novel
ENOJADO, V. F., Human Relations, Principles of Guidance
EVORA, M., Electrical Engineering, Refrigeration Engineering
FORTUNO, R. Z., Production, Planning Control

GROYON, S., Psychology
PALMA, M. B., Civil Procedure, Special Proceedings
PORCALLA, P., Library Science
REYES, M., Educational Planning, Personnel Administration, Inferential Statistics
SEPTIMO, C., Power Plant Design, Steam Power Engineering, Industrial Plant Design

NUEVA ECIJA UNIVERSITY OF SCIENCE AND TECHNOLOGY

Gen. Tinio St, Cabanatuan City 3100, Central Luzon

Telephone: (44) 463-1201
Fax: (44) 463-0226
E-mail: president@nuest.edu.ph
Internet: www.nuest.edu.ph

Founded 1929 as Nueva Ecija Trade School; present name and status 1998
State control
Academic year: June to March

President: Dr GEMILIANO C. CALLING

Campuses at Fort Magsaysay, Gabaldon, San Isidro and Sumacab; Colleges of Arts and Science, Business and Management Technology, Computer Studies, Education, Engineering and Industrial Technology; Graduate School.

PALAWAN STATE UNIVERSITY

Tiniguiban Heights, Puerto Princesa City 5300

Telephone: (48) 433-2379
Fax: (48) 433-5303
E-mail: psu@pal-onl.com
Internet: www.psu.itgo.com

Founded 1972 as Palawan Teacher's College; present name and status 1994
State control
Academic year: June to March

President: Dr TERESITA L. SALVA
Executive Vice-President: Dr CARLOS A. ALCANTARA
Vice-President (Academic Affairs): Dr ELIZABETH J. MAGAY
Vice-President (Administration): MARILYN GONZALES PABLICO
Vice-President (Finance): DESTIDCHADO S. VILLASARIO
Registrar: VENERANDA L. LAGROSA
University Librarian: LOURDES C. SALVADOR.

PANGASINAN STATE UNIVERSITY

Lingayen, Pangasinan

Telephone: (75) 542-6103
Fax: (75) 542-8694
Internet: www.psu.edu.ph

Founded 1979
State control
Languages of instruction: English, Filipino
Academic year: June to May

President: Dr RUFINO O. ESLAO
Vice-President for Academic Affairs: Dr REYNALDO P. SEGUI
Vice-President for Research and Extension: Dr PORFERIO L. BASILIO
Vice-President for Administration: Dr ALFREDO F. AQUINO
Administrative Officer: EMERITO J. URBANO
Librarian (Lingayen): ARACELI P. UNTALAN

Library of 50,000 vols
Number of teachers: 308
Number of students: 5,830

Publications: *PSU Graduate School Journal*, *PSU Annual Reports* (annually), *PSU Chronicle*, *The Technotrends*, *The Reflections*, *The Farm Breeze*, *The Golden Harvest*, *The Green Hills*, *The Technologist*, *The Aqua Sounds*, *The Ocean View*, *Banyuhay* (2 a year), *Research and Extension Bulletin* (quarterly)

DEANS

Graduate School (Urdaneta Center, Bayambang Center, Lingayen Center): Dr RODOLFO C. ASANION
College of Arts, Trades and Technology, PSU-Asingan: Prof. ESTER E. LOMBOY
College of Engineering and Technology, PSU-Urdaneta: Dr EUSEBIO E. MICLAT
College of Fisheries, PSU-Binmaley: Dr PORFERIO L. BASILIO
College of Agriculture, PSU-Santa Maria: Dr LYDIO E. CALONGE
College of Education, PSU-Bayambang: Dr APOLINARIO G. BAUTISTA
College of Agriculture, PSU-Infanta: Prof. ARTEMIO M. REBUGIO
College of Arts, Sciences and Technology, PSU-Lingayen: Dr VICTORIANO C. ESTIRA
College of Agriculture: PSU-San Carlos City: Dr LEONARDO E. MONGE

UNIVERSITY OF PANGASINAN

Arellano St, Dagupan City

Telephone: (75) 522-5635
Fax: (75) 522-2496
E-mail: registrar@upang.edu.ph
Internet: www.upang.edu.ph

Founded 1925; University status 1968
Private control
Languages of instruction: English, Filipino
Academic year: June to March

President: CESAR T. DUQUE
Registrar: TERESITA R. VISTRO
Librarian: IDA F. ROSARIO

Library of 20,500 vols
Number of teachers: 218
Number of students: 10,340

Publication: *The Researcher* (2 a year)

DEANS

School of Graduate Studies: Dr ALELI N. CORNISTA
College of Education: Dr TITO G. ROCABERTE
College of Accountancy, Commerce, Secretarial Administration and Management Accounting: MARIETTA B. SORIO
College of Liberal Arts: Dr OFELIA C. RAYOS
College of Engineering: Dr LUIS M. ORTEGA
College of Law: Atty HERMOGENES S. DECANO
College of Architecture: Arch. FREDDIE O. ARCALAS
College of Nursing: Dr VIRTUD P. OLOAN
College of Physical Therapy: Dr MELECIO M. PENA III
College of Medical Technology: MARIA D. AVELINO
College of Computer Science and Technology: MARIETTA B. SORIO
University High School: NENITA T. RAYOS (Principal)
University Elementary Laboratory School: NENITA Y. VICTORIO

PARTIDO STATE UNIVERSITY

San Juan Bautista, Goa, Camarines Sur 4422

Telephone: (54) 453-0235
Fax: (54) 453-1301
E-mail: psu-goa@asia.com
Internet: ecommunity.ncc.gov/psu

Founded 1941 as Partido High School; present name and status 2001
State control
Academic year: June to March

President: Dr MODESTO D. DETERA
Vice-President (Academic Affairs): Dr MINDA P. FORMALEJO
Vice-President (Administration): LEONCIO P. OBIAS

Campuses in Caramoan, Lagonoy, Sagñay, Salogon, San Jose and Tinambac; Departments of Business Education, Engineering, Graduate Studies, Teacher Education and Technology.

PHILIPPINE NORMAL UNIVERSITY

Taft Ave, Cnr Ayala Blvd, Manila 1000

Telephone: (2) 527-0374
Fax: (2) 536-6471
Internet: www.pnumanila.com.ph

Founded 1901; present name and status 1991
State control
Academic year: June to March

President: Dr NILO L. ROSAS.

PHILIPPINE WOMEN'S UNIVERSITY

Taft Ave, 1004 Manila

Telephone: (2) 526-69-34
Fax: (2) 536-81-69
Internet: www.pwu.edu.ph

Founded 1919
Private control
Language of instruction: English
Academic year: June to March

Chairman of the Board of Trustees: Hon. HELENA Z. BENITEZ
President: Dr JOSE CONRADO BENITEZ
Chancellor, Manila Campus, and Vice-President for Academic Affairs: Dr DOLORES LASAN
Chancellor, Quezon City Campus: Dr SYLVIA MONTES
Chancellor, Cavite Campus: Dr AMELIA REYES
Vice-Presidents: JULITA DADO (Administration and Finance), ENCARNACION RARALIO (Planning, Development and External Affairs)
Registrar: LILIA ROBOSA
Librarian: DIONISIA ANGELES

Library: see Libraries
Number of teachers: 479
Number of students: 10,675

Publications: *The Philwomenian* (monthly), *The Maroon and White* (annually), *PWU Research Journal* (2 a year), *Journal on Women's Health*, *Journal on the Environment and Habitat*, *PWU Bulletin* (quarterly), *Philippine Educational Forum* (2 a year)

DEANS

College of Arts and Sciences: Dr ELIZABETH DELA CRUZ
College of Education: Dr CECILIO DUKA
College of Music: MERCEDES DUGAN (Head)
College of Nursing: CONSTANCIA P. PITPITAN
College of Pharmacy: ZENAIDA SADIWA
Conrado Benitez Institute of Business Education: Dr CONSUELO ANG
Institute of Fine Arts and Design: LORNA SALUTAL (Head)
Institute of Medical Sciences and Technology: Dr NINI FESTIN LIM
Philippine Institute of Nutrition, Food Science and Technology: ROMUALDA GUIRRIEC
Philippine School of Social Work: Dr NENITA M. CURA (Dir)
College of Distance Education: LUMEN LARGOZA

UNIVERSITY OF THE PHILIPPINES SYSTEM

UP Diliman, Quezon City

Telephone: (2) 928-01-10
Fax: (2) 928-01-10
E-mail: op@up.edu.ph
Internet: www.up.edu.ph

Founded 1908
State control
Languages of instruction: English, Filipino
Academic year: June to March (two terms, one summer session)
President: Dr EMERLINDA R. ROMAN
Vice-President (Academic Affairs): Dr MARIA SERENA I. DIOKNO
Vice-President (Administration): Prof. MARTIN V. GREGORIO
Vice-President (Development): Prof. RAFAEL A. RODRIGUEZ
Vice-President for (Planning and Finance): Dr ERLINDA S. ECHANIS
Vice-President (Public Affairs): Dr JOSE Y. DALISAY, Jr
Secretary: Prof. MARTIN V. GREGORIO
Library: see Libraries and Archives
Number of teachers: 4,383
Number of students: 48,090
Publications: *Annual Report, Carillon* (3 a year), *Daluyan* (quarterly), *Facts and Figures* (annually), *Pahinungod Newsletter* (quarterly), *Pananaw* (quarterly), *UP-CIDS Chronicle* (quarterly), *UP Gazette* (quarterly), *UP Newsbriefs* (weekly), *UP Newsletter* (monthly).

CONSTITUENT CAMPUSES

UP at Baguio

Internet: www.upb.edu.ph

Chancellor: PRISCILLA SUPNET-MACANSANTOS
Registrar: FLOR ANGEL HERNANDEZ
Librarian: CRISTINA B. VILLANUEVA

DEANS

College of Arts and Communication: DELFIN L. TOLENTINO
College of Science: TEOFINA A. RAPANUT
College of Social Sciences: LORELIE C. MENDOZA
Institute of Management: BIENVENIDO MARZAN (Dir)

UP at Diliman

Internet: www.upd.edu.ph

Chancellor: CLARO T. LLAGUNO
Registrar: ELENA L. SAMONTE
Librarian: BELEN ANGELES

DEANS

College of Architecture: HONRADO FERNANDEZ
College of Arts and Letters: JOSEFINA A. AGRAVANTE
College of Business Administration: RAFAEL A. RODRIGUEZ
College of Education: LILIA M. RABAGO
College of Engineering: EDGARDO G. ATANACIO
College of Fine Arts: NESTOR O. VINLUAN
College of Home Economics: LYDIA B. ARRIBAS
College of Human Kinetics: LEILANI L. GONZALO
College of Law: MERLIN M. MAGALLONA
College of Mass Communication: LUIS V. TEODORO
College of Music: REYNALDO T. PAGUIO
College of Public Administration: JOSE N. ENDRIGA
College of Science: DANILO M. YANGA
College of Social Science and Philosophy: CONSUELO PAZ
College of Social Work and Community Development: EVELINA A. PANGALANGAN
Asian Centre: ARMANDO MALAY
Extension Program in San Fernando/Olongapo: REYNALDO A. TABBADA
Institute of Islamic Studies: WADJA K. ESMULA
Institute of Library Science: JOSEPHINE C. SISON

School of Economics: FELIPE M. MEDALLA
School of Labour and Industrial Relations: MARAGTAS SOFRONIO V. AMANTE
School of Urban and Regional Planning: BENJAMIN V. CARIÑO
Statistical Centre: LISA GRACE S. BERSALES

DIRECTORS

College of Arts and Letters:

Department of Art Studies: PATRICK D. FLORES
Department of English and Comparative Literature: CORAZON D. VILLAREAL
Department of European Languages: EDGARDO TIAMSON
Department of Filipino and Philippine Literature: LIGAYA T. RUBIN
Department of Speech Communication and Theatre Arts: AMIEL LEONARDIA

College of Business Administration:

Department of Accounting, Finance, Business Economics and Law: ERNESTO P. PINEDA
Department of Business Administration: EMERLINDA R. ROMAN

College of Education:

Division of Curriculum and Instruction: JULIAN E. ABUSO
Division of Educational Leadership and Professional Services: ELIZA PACQUEO ARRE
UP Integrated School: MA. THERESA L. DE VILLA

College of Engineering:

Department of Chemical Engineering: JOSE C. MUÑOZ
Department of Civil Engineering: PETER PAUL M. CASTRO
Department of Computer Science: MARK JAMES K. ENCARNACION
Department of Electrical Engineering: ROWENA CRISTINA L. GUEVARRA
Department of Engineering Sciences: MARK ALBERT H. ZARCO
Department of Geodetic Engineering: ANSELMO D. ALMAZAN
College of Industrial Engineering and Operational Research: EDGARDO G. ATANACIO
Department of Mechanical Engineering: FERDINAND G. MANEGDEG
Department of Metallurgical and Mining Engineering: MANOLO G. MENA

College of Fine Arts:

Department of Arts and Theory: VIRGINIA D. DANDAN
Department of Studio Arts: BENJAMIN CABANGIS
Department of Visual and Communication Arts: LEONARDO C. ROSETE

College of Home Economics:

Department of Clothing, Textiles and Related Arts: RACQUEL B. FLORENDO
Department of Family Life and Child Development: LILIAN L. JUADIONG
Department of Food Science and Nutrition: FLOR CRISANTA F. GALVEZ
Department of Home Economics Education: MARILOU R. LIM

College of Human Kinetics:

Department of Professional Studies: GILDA L. UY
Department of Service Physical Education: RONUALDO U. DIZER
Department of Sports: NOEL K. RIVERA

College of Mass Communication:

Department of Broadcast Communication: ROSA MARIA T. FELICIANO
Department of Communication Research: JOSE R. LACSON
Film and Audiovisual Communication Department: ELLEN J. PAGLINAUAN

Graduate Studies Department: REYNALDO V. GUIOGUIO
Journalism Department: CAROLINA MALAY OCAMPO

College of Music:

Department of Composition and Theory: JOSEFINO J. TOLEDO
Department of Conducting and Choral Ensemble: JOEL P. NAVARRO
Department of Music Education: FE C. NERA
Department of Music Research: FELICIDAD A. PRUDENTE
Department of Piano and Organ: IMELDA ONGSIAKO
Department of Strings and Chamber Music: ARTURO T. MOLINA
Department of Voice and Theatre Music: ELMO Q. MAKIL
Department of Wind and Percussion: ENRIQUE D. BARCELO

College of Science:

Department of Mathematics: VITTORIO D. ALMAZAR
Department of Meteorology and Oceanography: EMMANUEL C. ANGLO

College of Social Science and Philosophy:

Department of Anthropology: FRANCISCO A. DATAR
Department of Geography: DARLENE O. GUTIERREZ
Department of History: MA. LUISA T. CAMAGAY
Department of Linguistics: RICARDO MA. D. NOLASCO
Department of Philosophy: LEONARDO D. DE CASTRO
Department of Political Science: MALAYA C. RONAS
Department of Psychology: ANNADAISY J. CARLOTA
Department of Sociology: LUZVIMINDA C. VALENCIA

College of Social Work and Community Development:

Department of Community Development: ROSARIO S. DEL ROSARIO
Department of Social Work: BENILDA B. TAYAG
Women and Development Program: SYLVIA ESTRADA-CLAUDIO

UP at Los Baños

Internet: www.uplb.edu.ph

Chancellor: RUBEN L. VILLAREAL
Registrar: ERLINDA S. PATERNO
Librarian: LEONOR B. GREGORIO

DEANS

College of Agriculture: CECILIO R. ARBOLEDA
College of Arts and Sciences: PACIFICO C. PAYAWAL
College of Economics and Management: MARIO V. PERILLA
College of Engineering and Agro-Industrial Technology: ERNESTO P. LOZADA
College of Forestry: LUCRECIO L. REBUGIO
College of Human Ecology: FLORENTINO L. LIBRERO
College of Veterinary Medicine: MAURO F. MANUEL
Graduate School: ANN INEZ N. GIRONELLA

DIRECTORS

College of Agriculture:

Institute of Animal Science: DOMINGO B. ROXAS
Institute of Development Communication: MA. CELESTE H. CADIZ
Institute of Food Science and Technology: ERNESTO V. CARPIO

Department of Agricultural Education and Rural Studies: VIRGINIA R. CARDENAS

Department of Agronomy: ENRIQUE C. PALLER

Department of Entomology: ELISEO P. CADAPAN

Department of Horticulture: CALIXTO M. PROTASIO

Department of Plant Pathology: MARINA P. NATURAL

Department of Soil Science: IRENEO MANGUIAT

Rural High School: LEONIDO R. NARANJA

College of Arts and Sciences:

Institute of Biological Sciences: MACRINA T. ZAFARRALA

Institute of Chemistry: ERNESTO J. DEL ROSARIO

Institute of Computer Science: ELIEZER A. ALBACEA

Institute of Environmental Science and Management: BEN S. MALAYANG III

Institute of Mathematical Sciences and Physics: ARTURO S. PACIFICADOR , Jr

Department of Humanities: REMEDIOS V. NARTEA

Department of Human Kinetics: VENERANDA L. GENIO

Department of Social Sciences: DWIGHT DAVID A. DIESTRO

College of Economics and Management:

Institute of Agrarian Studies: RENATO L. TALATALA

Agricultural Credit and Co-operative Institute: SEVERINO L. MEDINA

Department of Development Management: RUFINO S. MANANGHAYA

Department of Agribusiness Management: HIPOLITO C. CUSTODIO , Jr

Department of Agricultural Economics: EUSEBIO P. MARIANO

Department of Economics: ACHILLES C. COSTALES

College of Engineering and Agro-Industrial Technology:

Department of Agricultural Machinery and Engineering Technology: CARLOS R. DEL ROSARIO

Department of Civil Engineering: SENEN M. MIRANDA

Department of Electrical Engineering: MAXIMO G. VILLANUEVA

College of Forestry:

Department of Forest Biological Sciences: MUTYA Q. MANALO

Department of Forest Resources Management: SEVERO R. SAPLACO

Department of Silviculture and Forest Influences: ARTURO SA. CASTILLO

Department of Social Forestry: DAYLINDA B. CABANILLA

Department of Wood Science and Technology: ELVIRA C. FERNANDEZ

College of Human Ecology:

Institute of Human Nutrition and Food: CORAZON V. C. BARBA

Department of Community and Environmental Resources Planning: RAYMUNDO B. MENDOZA , Jr

Department of Human and Family Development Studies: DELFINA M. TORRETA

Department of Social Development Services: EDUARDO A. DACANAY

College of Veterinary Medicine:

Department of Basic Veterinary Sciences: MA. AMELITA C. ESTACIO

Department of Paraclinical Sciences: LOINDA R. BALDRIAS

Department of Veterinary Clinical Sciences: JEZZIE A. ACORDA

UP at Manila

Internet: www.upm.edu.ph
Chancellor: PERLA D. SANTOS OCAMPO
Registrar: LEONOR C. LAGO
Librarian: THERESA P. DUGENIA
Library: Library: see Libraries and Archives

DEANS

College of Arts and Sciences: JOSEFINA G. TAYAG

College of Allied Medical Professions: POLICARPIA M. MAGPILI

College of Dentistry: LEONOR C. LAGO

College of Medicine: RAMON L. ARCADIO

College of Nursing: CECILIA M. LAURENTE

College of Pharmacy: LETICIA-BARBARA B. GUTIERREZ

College of Public Health: BENJAMIN C. VITASA

Graduate School: LILIA A. REYES

National Teacher-Training Centre for the Health Professions: CRISTINA F. MENCIAS

National Institutes of Health: PERLA SANTOS OCAMPO

DIRECTORS

College of Arts and Sciences:

Department of Arts and Communication: RAFAEL A. VILLAR

Department of Biology: MA. OFELIA M. CUEVAS

Department of Physical Education: FLOZERFIDA L. LINSAO

Department of Physical Sciences and Mathematics: MARILOU G. NICOLAS

Department of Social Sciences: SABINO G. PADILLA

Field School: DENNIS N. MILLAN

College of Allied Medical Professions:

Department of Physical Therapy: MA. ELIZA SD. RUIZ

Department of Occupational Therapy: MA. CONCEPCION C. CABATAN

Department of Speech Pathology: JOCELYN CHRISTINA B. MARZAN

College of Dentistry:

Department of Basic Health Sciences: SUSAN S. BANZON

Department of Clinical Health Sciences: NANETTE V. VERGEL DE DIOS

Department of Community Dentistry: ELIZABETH G. DE CASTRO

Graduate Program in Orthodontics: SANDRA REGINA C. HERNANDO

College of Medicine:

Department of Anatomy: NOEL G. GUISON

Department of Anaesthesiology: VIRGILIO T. GENUINO

Department of Biochemistry: JASMYNE C. RONQUILLO

Department of Pharmacology: CLEOTILDE H. HOW

Department of Pathology: ARIEL M. VERGEL DE DIOS

Department of Physiology: XENIA T. TIGNO

College of Pharmacy:

Department of Pharmaceutical Chemistry: ILEANA R. F. CRUZ

Department of Pharmacy: MILDRED B. OLIVEROS

Department of Industrial Pharmacy: MARISSA L. PANGANIBAN

College of Public Health:

Department of Environmental and Occupational Health: BENJAMIN C. VITASA

Department of Epidemiology and Biostatistics: JESUS N. SAROL , Jr

Department of Health Promotion and Education: RAFAELITA A. ONG

Department of Medical Microbiology: ADALBERTO M. ALDAY

Department of Nutrition: EMILIE G. FLORES

Department of Parasitology: LILIAN A. DELAS LLAGAS

Department of Public Health Administration: IRMA L. PARALAJAS

UP on Mindanao

Dean: ROGELIO V. CUYNO.

UP in the Visayas

Internet: www.upv.edu.ph

Chancellor: ARSENIO S. CAMACHO
Registrar: MARILYN Z. ALCARDE
Librarian: TERESITA LEDESMA

DEANS

College of Fisheries: PEPITO M. FERNANDEZ

College of Arts and Sciences: MINDA J. FORMACION

College of Management: EVELYN T. BELLEZA

School of Technology: JOSE ALI F. BEDAÑO

UP Cebu College: JESUS V. JUARIO

UP Tacloban College: VIOLA C. SIOZON

DIRECTORS

College of Fisheries:

Institute of Aquaculture: ARNULFO A. MARASIGAN

Institute of Fish Processing: JOSE P. PERALTA

Institute of Fisheries Policy and Development Studies: CARLOS C. BAYLON

Institute of Marine Fisheries and Oceanology: RICARDO P. BABARAN

College of Management:

Department of Accounting: PERLA D. DE LOS SANTOS

Department of Management: EDUARDO T. CONCEPCION

UP Open University

Internet: www.upou.org

Chancellor: MA. CRISTINA D. PADOLINA.

POLYTECHNIC UNIVERSITY OF THE PHILIPPINES

Anonas St, Santa Mesa, Manila
Telephone: (2) 716-26-44
Fax: (2) 716-11-43
E-mail: omcarague@edsamail.com.ph
Internet: www.pup.edu.ph

Founded 1904
State control
Languages of instruction: English, Filipino
Academic year: June to March

President: Dr OFELIA M. CARAGUE

Vice-President for Academic Affairs: Dr SAMUEL M. SALVADOR

Vice-President for Administration: Dr DANTE G. GUEVARRA

Vice-President for Student Services: Dr MOISES S. GARCIA

Vice-President for Finance: Dr CARMELA S. PEREZ

Vice-President for Research and Development: Dr NORMITA A. VILLA

Registrar: Prof. MELBA D. ABALETA
Library Officer: Dr IRENE D. AMORES

Library of 205,365 vols
Number of teachers: 1,381
Number of students: 42,988

Publications: *PUP Studies, Statistical Bulletin, PUP Monograph* (annually), *The Catalyst* (monthly), *Trends* (quarterly), *Journal of Economics and Politics* (quarterly), *BISIG* (Journal of Labour and Industrial Relations), *Graduate Forum, Campus Circular, CLMC Update, Journal of Open and Distance Education, PUP Open University Newsletter* (monthly)

DEANS

Graduate School: Dr VICTORIA C. NAVAL
College of Accountancy and Law: Dr GLORIA T. BAYSA
College of Arts: Dr AMALIA C. ROSALES
College of Business: Dr ERLINDA C. GARCIA
College of Office Administration and Business Teacher Education: Prof. AVELINA C. BUCAO
College of Computer Management and Information Technology: Prof. GISELA MAY A. ALBANO
College of Economics, Finance and Politics: Dr ROMAN R. DANNUG
College of Engineering and Architecture: VICKY S. CRUZ
College of Languages and Mass Communication: Prof. WILHELMINA N. CAYANAN
College of Physical Education and Sports: Prof. MARIPRES P. PASCUA
College of Architecture and Fine Arts: Arch. GLORIA T. BAYSA
College of Science: ADELA JAMORABO-RUIZ
College of Tourism, Hotel and Restaurant Management: MA. TERESA C. VILLAR
Institute of Co-operatives: ELENITA S. MANTALABA
Open University: Dr CARMENCITA L. CASTOLO
Technical School: JOSEFINA R. TAN
Taguig Campus: AMELITA A. LAURENTE
Commonwealth: DORIS B. GATAN

ATTACHED INSTITUTES

Research Institute for Politics and Economics: Dir Prof. DANILO CUETO.

Institute of Labor and Industrial Relations: Dir Prof. ROGELIO ORDOÑEZ.

Center for International Relations: Dir JOSE D. LAPUZ.

MANUEL L. QUEZON UNIVERSITY

916 R. Hidalgo, Quiapo, Manila

Telephone: (2) 734-0121
Fax: (2) 733-7976
E-mail: mlq@mlqu.edu.ph
Internet: www.mlqu.edu.ph

Founded 1947

President: AMADO C. DIZON
Vice-President for Academic Affairs: MARTHA A. MOGOL
Executive Officer, Regent: MA. VICTORIA O. CHAN
Registrar: Prof. GREGORIO A. DEL VALLE , Jr
Treasurer, Regent: AMADOR P. ALVENDIA
Chief Librarian: Prof. FLORDELIZA M. TORRES

Number of teachers: 291
Number of students: 8,355

Publications: *MLQU Newsletter, Junior Quezonian, MLQU Graduate Journal, MLQU Law Quarterly*

DEANS

Faculty of Law: NORBERTO S. GONZALES
Faculty of Arts and Science: LETICIA L. LAVA
Faculty of Accountancy and Business: ENRIQUE A. B. GABRIEL
Faculty of Education: VIRGINIA P. GANIR
Faculty of Graduate Studies: MARTHA A. MOGOL
Faculty of Engineering: ANTERO P. MANGUNDAYAO
Faculty of Architecture: CARLOS B. BANAAG
Faculty of Criminology: CLETO B. SENOREN
Faculty of Secretarial Education and Technology: PILAR E. SOTO
Faculty of the Institute of Computer Education: JUANITA M. UMAGAT

RAMON MAGSAYSAY TECHNOLOGICAL UNIVERSITY

Iba, Zambales 2201, Central Luzon

Telephone: (47) 811-1683
Fax: (47) 811-1683

Founded 1910; present name and status 2001
State control
Academic year: June to March

President: Dr FELICIANO S. ROSETE

Courses in biology, education, engineering, hotel and restaurant management, mathematics and computer science, psychology, public administration and technology.

RIZAL TECHNOLOGICAL UNIVERSITY

Boni Ave, Mandaluyong City 1550

Telephone: (2) 533-6041
Fax: (2) 532-0665
E-mail: riztech@mnl.cyberspace.com.ph

Founded 1969
State control
Academic year: June to March

President: Dr JOSÉ Q. MACABALLUG

Courses in architecture, business administration, education, engineering, English, industrial and organizational psychology, mathematics, natural sciences, political science, statistics and technology.

UNIVERSITY OF RIZAL SYSTEM

Tanay, Rizal 1980

Telephone: (2) 674-2545
Fax: (2) 674-2543
Internet: ecommunity.ncc.gov.ph/urs

Founded 1959 as Rizal Agricultural School; present name and status 2000
State control
Academic year: June to March

President: Dr OLIVIA F. DE LEON
Vice-President (Academic Affairs): Dr ARACELI M. BOBADILLA
Vice-President (Administration and Development): Dr MILAGROS R. NINONUEVO
Vice-President (Research, Development, Extension and Production): Dr TERESITA F. TRINIDAD

CAMPUS DIRECTORS

URS Main Campus (Tanay): Dr FLORIE B. GAPIDO
URS Angono: Dr ROWENA A. LAROZA
URS Antipolo: Prof. ALLEN U. BAUTISTA
URS Binangonan: Dr DEMETRIA A. SAN JUAN
URS Cainta: Dr MANUEL S. ORDONEZ
URS Morong: Dr HERMY D. ESTRABO
URS Pililla: Dr GLORIA P. SARABIA
URS Rodriguez: Dr TERESITA BUENVIAJE

SAINT LOUIS UNIVERSITY

POB 71, 2600 Baguio City

Telephone: (74) 442-2793
Fax: (74) 442-2842
E-mail: picrodir@slu.edu.ph
Internet: www.slu.edu.ph

Founded 1911
Private control (Roman Catholic)
Languages of instruction: English, Filipino
Academic year: June to March (two semesters)

President: Rev. Fr PAUL VAN PARIJS
Vice-President for Academic Affairs: Engr JOSE MARIA PANGILINAN
Vice-President for Finance: EVANGELINE O. TRINIDAD
Vice-President for Administration: Atty ARNULFO SORIANO
Registrar: VIOLETA GARCIA
Dean, Student Affairs: GIL ESPIRITU
Director of Libraries (College-Level): VIRGILIO C. FUERTE

Library of 107,214 vols
Number of teachers: 669
Number of students: 23,584

Publications: *SLU Research Journal* (2 a year), *SLU Chronicle* (4 a year), *Buhay SLU* (monthly), *Cordillera Researches and Studies* (annually)

DEANS

College of Engineering and Architecture: JOSELITO BUHANGIN
College of Accountancy and Commerce: NOEL B. DE LEON
College of Human Sciences: TERESITA AZARCON
College of Education: ROQUE Q. BERNARDEZ
College of Law: CEAZAR ORACION
College of Natural Science: GAUDELIA A. REYES
College of Medicine: ROBERTO LEGASPI
College of Nursing: MARY GRACE LACANARIA
College of Information and Computing Sciences: RANDY FLORES

DIRECTORS

Saint Louis University Extension Institute for Small-scale Industries: ROBERT ARGUELLES
Institute of Philosophy and Religion: PACITA VIZCARRA
SLU Hospital of the Sacred Heart: MALOU JACINTO
Regional Science Teaching Center: OSCAR BAUTISTA
Regional Science Development Center: OSCAR BAUTISTA

UNIVERSITY OF SAN AGUSTÍN

General Luna St, 5000 Iloilo City

Telephone: (33) 337-4841
Fax: (33) 337-4403
E-mail: info@usa.edu.ph
Internet: www.usa.edu.ph

Founded 1904; University status 1953
Private control
Languages of instruction: English, Filipino
Academic year: June to March

President, and Vice-President for Academic Affairs: Rev. Fr MANUEL M. VERGARA
Vice-President for Administration: Rev. Fr RODOLFO A. BUGNA
Vice-President for Student Affairs: Rev. Fr DENNIS CUERVO
Registrar: MADELA O. DUERO
Librarian: REGINA MALIGAD

Number of teachers: 507
Number of students: 11,408

Publications: *The Augustinian* (6 a year), *The Augustinian Mirror* (2 a year), *Augustinian Interdisciplinary Journal* (2 a year), *Communitas* (4 a year), *Augustinian Research Journal* (annually), *Augustinian Legacy* (annually)

DEANS

Graduate School: Dr REMEDIOS SOMCIO
School of Law: Atty JUANA JUDITA P. NAFARRETE
College of Pharmacy/Medical Technology: GILDA RIVERO
College of Technology: Eng. MAURA BASCO
College of Commerce: NEOMISIA GONZALES
Teachers' College: Dr NORA LEGASPI
College of Nursing: SOFIA COSETTE MONTEBLANCO
Conservatory of Music: SALVACION JARDENIL
College of Liberal Arts: Dr AMORITA RABUCO

UNIVERSITY OF SAN CARLOS

Cebu City 6000

Telephone: (32) 253-1000
Fax: (32) 255-4341
E-mail: president@usc.edu.ph
Internet: www.usc.edu.ph

Founded 1595; University status 1948

Private (Roman Catholic) control
Language of instruction: English
Academic year: June to March (two terms)
President: Fr RODERICK C. SALAZAR, Jr
Vice-President for Academic Affairs: Fr ERNESTO M. LAGURA
Vice-President for Administration: Fr VICENTE UY
Vice-President for Finance: Fr GENEROSO B. REBAYLA, Jr
Registrar: Sencio NORBERTO P. JAYME
Director of Library System: Dr MARIOLOU P. TADLIP

Number of teachers: 868 (635 full-time, 233 part-time)
Number of students: 33,729

Publications: *The University Bulletin* (every 2 weeks), *Philippine Scientist* (annually), *Philippine Quarterly of Culture and Society* (quarterly), *University Journal* (2 a year)

DEANS

College of Law: Atty CORAZON E. VALENCIA
College of Arts and Sciences: Dr RAMON S. DEL FIERRO
College of Education: Dr MARILOU P. GALLOS
College of Commerce: Fr MARK C. MATHIAS
College of Engineering: Eng. NICANOR S. BUENCONSEJO
College of Pharmacy: YOLANDA C. DELIMAN
College of Nursing: CARMELITA C. ALESNA
College of Architecture and Fine Arts: Arch. OMAR MAXWELL P. ESPINA

CHAIRMEN

Graduate Engineering: Eng. LUZ G. PACA
Graduate Business Administration: Dr RENE Y. PAQUIBUT
Biology: Dr DANILO B. LARGO
Chemistry: Dr PATRICK JOHN LIM
Economics: RAMON M. ECHEVARIA, Jr
History: PACUAL EMELIO S. PASCUAL
Library Science: EVELYN A. SANSON
Philosophy: ANTONIO P. DILUVIO
Psychology: Dr ANDRES S. GERONG
Languages and Literature: ISABELITA V. MANGCO
Teachers' Education: MILAGROS L. TABASA
Hospitality Management: Dr CECIL S. GANTALAO
Physical Education: FRANCITA P. PACANA
Accountancy: CHALLONER A. MATERO
Business Administration: Dr RENE Y. PAQUIBUT
Secretarial Administration: JOSEPHINE ABELLA
Chemical Engineering: Eng. AGNES FE L. ALVEAR
Civil Engineering: Eng. MARIO P. DE LEON
Mechanical and Industrial Engineering: Eng. MICHAEL LORETERO
Computer Engineering: Dr JOE MARI J. MAJA
Electrical, Electronics and Communications Engineering: ELLEN AGNES ZAFRA
Fine Arts: JORGE B. LAO
Architecture: Arch. ANTONIO ANDRES L. FLORES
Political Science: FERDINAND S. BONCAYAO
Religious Education: Fr JAIMELITO GEALAN
Mathematics and Computer Science: JOVITA N. RAVINA
Physics: Dr ROLANDO EMERITO S. OTADOY
Sociology and Anthropology: JOSE ELEAZAR L. BERSALES

ATTACHED INSTITUTES

Office of Population Studies: Dir JOSEPHINE L. AVILA.

San Carlos Publications: Dir HAROLD OLOFSON, Editor.

Water Resources Centre: Dir Fr HERMAN VAN ENGELEN.

Cebuano Studies Centre: Dir Dr ERLINDA K. ALBURO.

USC Museum: MARLENE SOCORRO R. SAMSON, Curator.

Academic Extension and Industry Linkage Office: Dir MARILYN Y. TIU.

Business Resource Centre: TERESITA C. ABARQUEZ, Project Officer.

Institute of Planning and Design: Dir ELLIS A. PUERTO.

CHED Zonal Research Centre: Dir Dr VICTORINA H. ZOSA.

Architecture Computer Centre CAD/ CAE Training Centre: Dir JOSEPH MICHAEL P. ESPINA.

UNIVERSITY OF SAN JOSE-RECOLETOS

Corner Magallanes and P. Lopez Sts, 6000 Cebu City
Telephone: (32) 253-7900
Fax: (32) 254-1720
E-mail: usjr@usjr.edu.ph
Internet: www.usjr.edu.ph

Founded 1947, university status 1984
Private (Roman Catholic) control
Language of instruction: English
Academic year: June to March

President: Rev. Fr CONSTANTINO B. REAL
Vice-President for Administration: Rev. Fr CORNELIO E. MORAL
Vice-President for Academics: Rev. Fr SIXTO M. BITANGJOL
Vice-President for Business and Finance: Rev. Fr LEONARDO P. PAULIGUE
Vice-President for Student Welfare: Rev. Fr ANTHONY A. MORILLO
Director of Basak Campus: Rev. Fr RAUL M. BUHAY
Registrar: DEMETRIO QUIRANTE
Librarian: EVELYN A. LIM

Library of 190,000 vols
Number of teachers: 500
Number of students: 13,000

Publications: *Forward* (annually), *USJ-R Journal of Research* (Graduate School publication, 2 a year), *Josenian* (annually), *USJ-R Updates* (newsletter, 4 a year), *Precedent* (2 a year), *Faculty Research Journal* (annually)

DEANS

College of Arts and Sciences: Dr CORAZON A. TAN
College of Commerce: Dr SUSAN CHUNG
College of Education: Dr ALMA ANG
College of Engineering: Dr EVANGELINE EVANGELISTA
College of Law: Atty ALICIA E. BATHAN
College of Nursing: RAOUL
Graduate School: (vacant)
Grade School Department: PURA S. WAGAS
High School Department: SONIA F. PAGLINAWAN
Religious Education Center: Rev. Fr CORNELIO E. MORAL

ATTACHED INSTITUTES

Student Development and Planning Center: Dir Dr VICTORIA D. GABISON.

Research Center: Dir Dr AUDREY BARBARA M. BUCAD.

Institute of Non-formal Education and Community Outreach Project (INFECOP): Supervisor ELIZABETH P. SESTOSO.

CPA Review School: Dir PETER DANTE AMPARADO.

UNIVERSITY OF SANTO TOMÁS

España St, Manila
Telephone: 731-31-01
Fax: 732-74-86
Internet: www.ust.edu.ph

Founded 1611
Private (Roman Catholic) control
Academic year: June to March

Grand Chancellor: Very Rev. Fr TIMOTHY RADCLIFFE
Vice-Chancellor: Very Rev. Fr QUIRICO PEDREGOSA
Rector: Rev. Fr TAMERLANE R. LANA
Vice-Rector: Rev. Fr ERNESTO M. ARCEO
Secretary-General: Fr RODEL ALIGAN
Registrar: Prof. RODOLFO N. CLAVIO
Prefect of Libraries: Fr ANGEL APARICO
Chief Librarian: Prof. ERLINDA FLORES

Number of teachers: 1,438
Number of students: 32,061

Publications: *Academia, Thomasian, Varsitarian, Journal of Medicine, Law Review, Unitas, Boletín Eclesiástico, Commerce Journal, Nursing Journal, Education Journal, Science Journal, Philippiniana Sacra, Acta Manilana, Journal of Graduate Research*

DEANS

Faculty of Sacred Theology: Rev. Fr FAUSTO GOMEZ
Faculty of Canon Law: Rev. Fr JAVIER GONZALES
Faculty of Philosophy: Fr ERNESTO ARCEO
Faculty of Civil Law: Dr AMADO DIMAYUGA
Faculty of Medicine and Surgery: Dr ANGELES TAN-ALORA
Faculty of Pharmacy: Dr ROSALINDA SOLEVILLA
Faculty of Arts and Letters: Dr ARMANDO DE JESUS
Faculty of Engineering: Dr MARILYN MABINI
College of Education: Dr CLOTILDE ARCANGEL
College of Science: Dr GLORIA BERNAS
College of Commerce and Business Administration: Prof. AMELIA HALILI
College of Architecture and Fine Arts: Arch. LUIS FERRER
College of Nursing: Prof. GLENDA VARGAS
Graduate School: Fr JOSE ANTONIO AUREADA
Institute of Religion: Fr RODEL ALIGAN
Conservatory of Music: Prof. ERLINDA FULE

SILLIMAN UNIVERSITY

6200 Dumaguete City, Negros Oriental
Telephone: (35) 4227195
Fax: (35) 2254768
E-mail: pres@su.edu.ph
Internet: www.su.edu.ph

Founded 1901
Private control
Language of instruction: English
Academic year: June to May

President: Dr AGUSTIN A. PULIDO
Vice-President for Academic Affairs: Dr BETTY C. ABREGANA
Vice-President for Finance: JEAN G. ESPINO
Registrar: ANNABELLE E. PAA
Librarian: LORNA TUMULAK-YSO

Library: see Libraries
Number of teachers: 253
Number of students: 6,500

Publications: *Silliman Journal* (humanities, social sciences and sciences, 2 a year), *Sillimanian Magazine* (annually), *Sands and Corals* (literary magazine, annually), *Educator* (every 5 years), *Ingenium* (2 a year), *SUCN Abstracts* (irregular), *Infoline* (monthly), *Insights* (2 a year), *Nurse* (2 a year), *Scoop* (annually), *Stones and Pebbles* (annually), *Convergence* (annually)

DEANS

College of Arts and Sciences: Prof. CARLOS
MAGTOLIS
College of Education: Dr JESUSA CORAZON
GONZALES
College of Law: Atty MYLES BEJAR
College of Engineering: Dr BENJAMIN TOBIAS
Divinity School: Dr NORIEL CAPULONG
College of Nursing and Allied Medical
Sciences: Dr MARIA TERESITA S. SINDA
College of Business Administration: Atty
TABITHA TINAGAN
School of Communication: CELIA ACEDO
College of Agriculture: Prof. EDNA DUMANCAS
College of Performing Arts: Prof. JOSEPH
BASA
School of Basic Education: Prof. LETICIA
ALCALA

ATTACHED INSTITUTES

Center for Tropical Conservation Studies: Dir Dr ELY ALCALA.

Silliman University Angelo King Center for Research and Environmental Management (SUAKCREM): Dir Dr ANGEL C. ALCALA.

Silliman University Marine Laboratory: Dir Dr HILCONIDA CALUMPONG.

UNIVERSITY OF SOUTHEASTERN PHILIPPINES

Bo. Obrero, Davao City 8000
Telephone: (82) 227-4351
Fax: (82) 221-7737
E-mail: registrar@usep.edu.ph
Internet: www.usep.edu.ph
Founded 1978
State control
Academic year: June to March
President: Dr JULIETA I. ORTIZ
Vice-President (Academic Affairs): Dr
ROSARIO E. GARCIA
Vice-President (Administration): Dr RODULFO
C. SUMUGAT
Dean (Bislig Campus): GRACINEE I. TEJANO
(acting)
Dean (Mabini Campus): Dr ADONIAS CAMBAN-
GAY
Dean (Tagum Campus): Dr DANIEL UGAY
Registrar: VIC JEAN SOLLER
Librarian: TERESITA ECO
Publications: *Annual Report, Headlight* (2 a
year)

DEANS

College of Arts and Sciences: Dr HELEN
PONDEVIDA
College of Development and Management:
Dr SURLITA M. SUMUGAT
College of Education: Dr MILAGROS ARQUIL-
LANO
College of Engineering: Eng. ANGEL DE VERA
College of Technology: Dr NIMFA OTANA
Institute of Computing: Eng. ROBERTO CANDA
(acting)
Laboratory School: Prof. JANETTE D. BUTLIG
(Officer-in-Charge)
School of Applied Economics: Dr AGUSTINA
TAN-CRUZ
School of Government and Management: Dr
ROSARIO GARCIA (acting)

ATTACHED RESEARCH INSTITUTES

Affiliated Non-Conventional Energy Center: Dir Eng. FULTON YAP.

Center for Professional Board Review for Teachers: Officer-in-Charge Dr AIDA AGULO.

Center for Technician Education and Staff Development: Exec. Dir Dr PERFECTO A. ALIBIN.

Mindanao Center for Policy Studies: Dir Dr SPHREMIANO B. ANTIPOLO.

Teacher Training Center: Dir Dr EDNA H. JALOTJOT (acting).

UNIVERSITY OF SOUTHERN MINDANAO

Kabacan 9407, North Cotabato
Telephone: (64) 248-21-38
Fax: (64) 248-21-38
Internet: www.usm.edu.ph
Founded 1954 as Institute of Technology,
present name 1980
State control
Languages of instruction: English, Filipino
Academic year: June to December (2 seme-
sters)
President: Dr VIRGILIO G. OLIVA
Vice-President: Dr ROSE MARIE B. BUGARIN
Registrar: Dr ELPIDIO R. BAUTISTA
Librarian: CELIA ORIA
Number of teachers: 434
Number of students: 9,152
Publications: *USMARC Monitor, CA
Research Journal, USM Research and
Development Journal* (every 6 months)
Colleges of agriculture, engineering, home
economics, education, arts and sciences,
trade and industry; institutes of veterinary
science, Middle Eastern and Asian studies,
development economics management, animal
science and aquaculture.

UNIVERSITY OF SOUTHERN PHILIPPINES

Mabini St, Cebu City
Telephone: (32) 232-5939
Fax: (32) 231-0178
Internet: www.usp.ph
Founded 1927; University status 1949
Private control
President: OSCAR JEREZA
Registrar: ERLINDA M. CAMPOS
Number of teachers: 197
Number of students: 7,439

DEANS

College of Arts and Sciences: INOCENTA GO
Graduate School of Law: RONALD DUTERTE
College of Engineering: ROMULO JEREZA
College of Commerce: GERONIMO S. ANA
College of Education: ISABELITA CONALES
(acting)
Graduate School: Dr ROSETTA MANTE
School of Social Work: INOCENTA GO

SOUTHWESTERN UNIVERSITY

Villa Aznar, Urgello St, Cebu City 6000
Telephone: (32) 256-27-43
Fax: (32) 253-75-01
E-mail: president@swu.edu.ph
Internet: www.swu.edu.ph
Founded 1946
Private control
Languages of instruction: English, Filipino
Academic year: June to March
President: Dr ALICIA P. CABATINGAN
Vice-President (Academic): Dr FRANCES F.
LUMAIN
Vice-President (Administration): THELMA G.
GARCIA
Vice-President (Finance): LASSI MATTI A.
HOLOPAINEN
Registrar: FRANCISCO B. BACALLA
Librarian: VIRGINIA P. MOLLANEDA
Number of teachers: 540
Number of students: 10,768

Publications: *SWU Research Digest* (2 a
year), *SWU Graduate School Journal*
(annually)

DEANS

Graduate School: Dr ALICIA P. CABATINGAN
College of Law: Atty JONAH S. VILLAGONZALO
College of Arts and Sciences: CATALINO C.
ABOS
College of Dentistry: Dr CORNELIA R. NOVAL
College of Optometry: Dr ARLEN O. DORIO
College of Commerce: FLORDELIS R. RIVERA
College of Pharmacy: Dr ALTHEA R. ARENAJO
College of Engineering: Eng. CARLOS S. SA-
TIEMBRE
College of Medical Technology: ALMA A.
HOLOPAINEN
College of Veterinary Medicine: Dr JOCELYN
A. TINGSON
College of Medicine: Dr MARILYN T. ZARRAGA
College of Nursing: Dr CARMEN V. N. SAN
LORENZO
Teachers' College: Dr FRANCES F. LUMAIN
Maritime College: Comm. CARMELO T.
SIMOLDE
College of Physical Therapy: DAVID M.
MATHEU
Institute of Computer Science: Engr AL
BENJIE C. LOZADA
Institute of Physical Education and Sports:
MELQUIADES B. GONZALEZ

TARLAC STATE UNIVERSITY

Romulo Blvd, Tarlac City, Tarlac 2300
Telephone: (45) 982-0110
Fax: (45) 982-3317
E-mail: tsu@mozcom.com.ph
Founded 1906 as Tarlac Trade School; pre-
sent name and status 1989
State control
Academic year: June to March
President: Dr DOLORES G. MATIAS
Courses in architecture, business adminis-
tration, education, engineering, fine arts,
journalism, mathematics and computer
science, natural sciences, nutrition, social
sciences, technology and theatre.

TECHNOLOGICAL UNIVERSITY OF THE PHILIPPINES

POB 3171, Ayala Blvd, Ermita, Metro Man-
ila
Telephone: (2) 523-22-93
Fax: (2) 523-22-93
Internet: www.tup.edu.ph
Founded 1901
State control
Languages of instruction: English, Filipino
Academic year: June to March
President: Dr FEDESERIO C. CAMARAO
Vice-President (Academic Affairs): Prof.
JOSEFINO P. GASCON
Vice-President (Administration and
Finance): Prof. RADAMES M. DOCTOR
Vice-President (Planning and Development):
Prof. PERLA S. ROXAS
Vice-President (Research and Extension): Dr
EMILIANA V. R. TADEO
Director, TUP Cavite: Prof. ENRICO R.
HILARIO
Director, TUP Taguig: Dr FEDERICO RAMOS
Director, TUP Visayas: Dr LEONCIO JAMERA
Registrar: Dr MILAGROS I. CACHOLA
Library Director: Dr WILHELMINA G. BORJAL
Library: Library: see Libraries and Archives
Number of teachers: 573
Number of students: 18,915

Publications: *Philippine Journal of Industrial Education and Technology* (2 a year),
TUP.com (4 a year), *TUP Graduate Journal* (annually)

DEANS

College of Sciences: Dr ADORA S. PILI
College of Liberal Arts: Dr MARCELO B. APAR
College of Architecture and Fine Arts: Dr DIONISIO A. ESPRESSION, Jr
College of Engineering: Prof. FLORENCIO G. BALANAY, Jr
College of Industrial Education: Dr OLYMPIO V. CAPARAS
College of Industrial Technology: Prof. BUENAVENTURA V. SABATER

PROFESSORS

AGBAYANI, J., Economics
ALTO, R., Education
APAR, M., Filipino
ARRIETA II, C., Tool and Die Technology
BALUYUT, F., Education
BELEN, V., English
BELGICA, A., Career Education
BUAQUIÑA, V., Mathematics
CACHOLA, M., Foods
CALO, R., Physical Education
CAMARO, G., Research, Life Sciences, Ecology
CAPARAS, O., Industrial Arts
DE LEON, L., Education
DELOS REYES, V., Education
DIMAYUGA, Z., Education
DOMANTAY, D., Education
GABRIEL, P., English
GALANG, E., Family and Community Education
GARINO, N., Electrical Technology, Technology Management
GATMAYTAN, R., Chemistry
GOLLAYAN, R., Chemistry
GRAZA, N., Mechanical Engineering
HILARIO, E., Education
HUANG, A., Mathematics
IGNACIO, M., Mathematics
IMLAN, J., Public Administration
JANIER, J., Mathematics
JOAQUIN, A., Drafting Technology
LABUGUEN, F., Foods
LEJANO, B., Civil Engineering
MACAM, Jr, V., Civil Engineering
MANALASTAS, J., Civil Engineering
MANALASTAS, S., Chemistry Education
MANGAO, F., Mathematics
MATIC, V., Chemistry
MENDOZA, M., Social Studies
OBNAMIA, C., English, Journalism, Education
PACIO, A., Mathematics Education
PANGAN, M., Mathematics
PANGILINAN, M., Social Studies
PEREDA, P., Education
PEREZ, J., Sociology
PILI, A., Chemistry
RIVERA, A., Education
ROLLUQUI, G., Electronic Engineering Technology, Computer Technology
SALTIVAN, L., Physics
TABANERA, M. D., Physics
TRACENA, M., English
VALDERRAMA, L., Public Administration
VELAS, F., Cultural Affairs
VERAYO, E., Education
VILLAMEJOR, S., English
ZARATAN, L., Education Research

UNIVERSITY OF THE VISAYAS

6000 Cebu City
Telephone: (32) 253-28-85
Internet: www.uv.edu
Founded 1919
Private control
Languages of instruction: English, Filipino
Academic year: June to May
President: EDUARDO R. GULLAS
Executive Vice-President: JOSE R. GULLAS
Registrar: JOSEFINA T. ARREZA
Librarian: EDNA CAGA
Number of teachers: 600

Number of students: 18,214
Publications: *The Visayanian, Spectrum* (Graduate Research Journal), *Strategies* (Education Journal), *Statistical Bulletin*, etc

DEANS

College of Commerce: SOLEDAD CUMBRA
College of Criminology: EMMANUEL PEPITO
College of Engineering and Architecture: MARCIALITO VALENZONA
Graduate School: FE NECESARIO
College of Law: AMADEO SENO
College of Arts and Sciences: ERLINDA L. PEPITO
College of Medicine: RENATO ESPINOSA
Nautical School: GODOFREDO COSIDO
College of Nursing: LOURDES FERNAN
College of Pharmacy: CARMEN YAP
Teachers' College: AURORA A. ECONG

DIRECTORS

Research, Development and Planning Centre: NICERIO L. LEANZA
Instructional Media Centre: ALICE RABOR

WEST VISAYAS STATE UNIVERSITY

Luna St, La Paz, Iloilo City, Iloilo 5000
Telephone: (33) 320-0870
Fax: (33) 320-0879
Internet: www.wvsu.edu.ph
Founded 1924 as Iloilo Normal School; present name and status 1986
State control
Academic year: June to March
President: Dr LOURDES C. ARAÑADOR
Colleges of Arts and Sciences, Education, Mass Communications, Medicine and Nursing; Institute of Information and Communications Technology.

WESTERN MINDANAO STATE UNIVERSITY

Normal Rd, Baliwasan, 7000 Zamboanga City
Telephone: 991-1040
Fax: 991-3065
Internet: www.wmsu.edu.ph
Founded 1918
State control
Languages of instruction: English, Filipino
Academic year: June to October, October to March (two semesters)
President: Dr ELDIGARIO D. GONZALES
Vice-President for Academic Affairs: Dr MARLENE C. TILLAH
Vice-President for Research Extension and Training (vacant)
Vice-President for Administration and Finance: Dr CLEMENCIO M. BASCAR
Registrar: JULIETA A. DEL ROSARIO
Librarian: SALUD C. LAQUIO
Library of 50,000 vols
Number of teachers: 436
Number of students: 12,397
Publication: *Bulletin*

DEANS

College of Agriculture: ERIBERTO D. SALANG
College of Arts and Sciences: Dr RAIMUNDA J. BANICO
College of Education: Prof. FELICITAS F. FALCATAN
College of Engineering and Technology: Eng. MOHAMMAD NUR MOHAMMAD
College of Law: Atty EDUARDO F. SANSON
College of Home Economics: Prof. NOEMI S. ENRIQUEZ
College of Forestry: Prof. DINO A. SABELLINA
College of Nursing: Prof. TERESITA C. MARBELLA

College of Science and Mathematics: Dr ELBIA P. AQUINO
College of Social Work: Prof. BAGIAN ABDULKARIM
College of Criminology: Prof. EFFRENDY ESTIPONA
Institute of Asian and Islamic Studies: Prof. NURUDDIN I. UNGGANG
Institute of Physical Education, Sports and Cultural Affairs: Prof. ALICIA LOURDES SORIANO
Extension Services: Dr ABDULAJID A. IBBA
Graduate School: Prof. OFELIO R. MENDOZA
Research Center: Dr ALFREDO DUCANES
Admissions: Prof. RUTH N. JUNIO
Student Affairs: Eng. ARMANDO ARQUIZA

XAVIER UNIVERSITY

Ateneo de Cagayan, Corrales Ave, 9000 Cagayan de Oro City
Telephone: (8822) 72-27-25
Fax: (8822) 72-63-55
E-mail: pres@xu.edu.ph
Internet: www.xu.edu.ph
Founded 1933
Private control
Language of instruction: English
Academic year: June to March (two terms)
President: Fr JOSE RAMON T. VILLARIN
Registrar: AURORA M. GAPUZ
Librarian: ANNABELLE P. ACEDERA
Number of teachers: 407
Number of students: 9,897
Publications: *Kinaadman (Wisdom)* (annually), *XU Graduate School Journal* (2 a year)

DEANS

Faculty of Agriculture: Engr GUADALUPE M. CALALANG
Faculty of Arts and Sciences: Fr ANTONIO F. MORENO
Faculty of Commerce: Dr ALFONSO B. HORTELANO
Faculty of Education: Dr AMOR Q. DE TORRES
Faculty of Engineering: Engr ANTONIO C. SEVILLANO, Jr
Faculty of Law: Atty RAUL R. VILLANUEVA
Faculty of Medicine: Dr CANDIDA D. CANCEKO
Faculty of Nursing: Dr RAMONA HEIDI C. PALAD
Graduate School: Dr ESTER L. RAAGAS

HEADS OF DEPARTMENTS

Faculty of Agriculture (tel. (8822) 72-31-16 ext. 3100; fax (8822) 72-31-16 ext. 3100; e-mail aggies@xu.edu.ph):

Agricultural Engineering: Engl. ALEJANDRO S. VILLAMOR
Agricultural Sciences: Dr DANIEL C. PADUANO, Jr
Development Communication: ESTRELLA T. BORJA
Food Technology: SYLVIA T. AGUHOB

Faculty of Arts and Sciences (tel. (8822) 72-31-16 ext. 3034; fax (8822) 72-31-16 ext. 6; e-mail artscies@xu.edu.ph):

Biology: ANITA S. MABAO
Chemistry: JULIET Q. DALAGAN
Economics: Dr EDUARDO S. CANLAS
English: Dr MARK E. LABUNTOG
Filipino: LILIA T. MACAYA
History and Political Science: HERMINIA Q. YAPTENCO
Mathematics: NESTOR T. FABRE
Philosophy: JANE D. GALLAMASO
Psychology and Guidance: MARIA LEORUPPE V. RAAGAS
Religious Studies: LOVENIA P. NACES
Sociology and Anthropology: LITA P. SEALZA

Faculty of Commerce (tel. (8822) 72-31-16 ext. 3317; e-mail commerce@xu.edu.ph):

Accountancy: MARCO C. ILANO
Business Administration and Agri-Business Management: Dr RUSTUM D. GEVERO
Information Management: BENEFF R. SALINAS

Faculty of Education (tel. (8822) 72-31-16 ext. 3042; fax (8822) 72-31-16 ext. 3035; e-mail education@xu.edu.ph):

Physical Education: ANGELITA SAYOSAY

Faculty of Engineering (tel. (8822) 72-31-16 ext. 1207; fax (8822) 72-31-16 ext. 1209; e-mail tony@miki.eng.xu.edu.ph):

Chemical and Civil Engineering: MA. THERESA I. CABARABAN
Computer Science: GERARDO S. DOROJA
Electrical and Mechanical Engineering: ELISEO B. LINOG, Jr
Physics: JOSEPH L. AGNES

Faculty of Medicine (tel. (8822) 72-31-16 ext. 1104; fax (8822) 72-31-16 ext. 1103; e-mail jprcm@xu.edu.ph):

Eyes, Ears, Nose and Throat: Dr AUGUSTO V. DEJOS
Medicine: Dr MA. TERESA O. DE LA SORNA
Obstetrics and Gynaecology: Dr CYNTHIA S. BACONGA
Paediatrics: Dr EVELYN C. HERNANDEZ
Preventive and Community Medicine: Dr GINA ITCHON
Surgery: Dr NICOLSON S. VALMORIA

DIRECTORS

Research Institute for Mindanao Culture: Dr ISIAS S. SEALZA
Southeast Asia Rural Social Leadership Institute: Dr ANSELMO B. MERCADO
Institute for the Development of Educational Administrators: Dr ALFONSO B. HORTELANO
Philippine Folklife and Folklore Research and Archives: LUIS OSTIQUE
Appropriate Technology for Small Farmers: RACHEL POLESTICO
Legal Aid and Research Center for Human Rights: Atty NEIL Y. PACAMALAN
Mindanao Lumad and Muslim Development Center: Rev. EMETERIO J. BARCELON
Center for Industrial Technology: Engr ANTONIO C. SEVILLANO, Jr
Sustainable Agriculture Center: VICTORIANO I. TAGUPA

Colleges
GENERAL

San Beda College: Mendiola St, Manila; tel. 735-60-11; fax 735-59-94; e-mail sbc@dns.sbc.edu.ph; f. 1901; private control; constituent grade and high schools and colleges of law, arts and sciences; library: 120,464 vols; 276 teachers; 6,006 students; Rector Rev. BERNARDO M. PEREZ; Librarian MARLO CHAVEZ.

St Paul College of Manila: 680 Pedro Gil St, Malate, Manila, POB 3062; tel. (2) 524-56-87; fax (2) 525-66-20; e-mail spcm@spcm.edu.ph; internet www.spcm.edu.ph; f. 1912; private control; first degree courses in computer science, hotel and restaurant management, psychology, education, commerce, secretarial administration, nursing, communication arts, music; library: 47,898 vols; 148 teachers; 2,800 students; Pres. Sister NATIVIDAD DE JESUS FERAREN.

St Scholastica's College: 2560 Leon Guinto St, Malate, Metro Manila 1004, POB 3153; tel. (2) 524-7686; fax (2) 521-2593; e-mail maryjohn@ssc.edu.ph; internet www.ssc.edu.ph; f. 1906; Private control (sectarian); schools of accountancy, arts and sciences, commerce, music, music education; 516 teachers; 6,601 students; Pres. Sister MARY JOHN MANANZAN.

State Polytechnic College of Palawan: Aborlan, 5302 Palawan; tel. 433-4480; f. 1910; courses in agriculture, forestry, fisheries, environmental management, engineering and technology, education, arts, science, rural development; library: 22,500 vols; Pres. Dr CONCEPTO B. MAGAY; publs *SPCP-IMS Research Journal* (2 a year), *SPCP Research Journal* (irregular), *SPCP Newsletter* (monthly).

ECONOMICS

Asian Institute of Management: Eugenio Lopez Foundation Building, Joseph R. McMicking Campus, 123 Paseo de Roxas, Makati City, 1260; tel. (632) 8924011; fax (632) 8179240; e-mail admissions@aim.edu.ph; internet www.aim.edu.ph; f. 1968 by Ateneo de Manila University, De La Salle University, the Harvard Business School and the Ford Foundation; academic units and degree programmes: Washington SyCip Graduate School of Business (MBA, Master in Management), Center for Development Management (Master in Development Management), Asian Center for Entrepreneurship (Master in Entrepreneurship), Executive Education and Life Long Learning Center (Executive MBA, Certificate Programmes); library: more than 25,000 books and periodicals, more than 30,000 learning material items; 61 teachers; Pres. ROBERTO F. DE OCAMPO; Dean VICTORIA S. LICUANAN.

MEDICINE

Bicol Christian College of Medicine: AMEC-BCCM Postal Station, Rizal St, Legazpi City 4901; tel. (5221) 44433; fax (5221) 455058; f. 1980; 4-year undergraduate courses; library: 30,052 vols; Pres. EMMANUEL F. AGO; Dean, College of Medicine Dr ANGELITA F. AGO.

Cebu Doctors' University College of Medicine: CDU Administrative Offices Bldg, Gov. M. Roa St, Cebu City 6000; tel. and fax (32) 253-4919; e-mail cdu-cm@cebudoctorsuniversity.edu; internet www.cebudoctorsuniversity.edu/medicine; f. 1977; library: 11,800 vols; 160 staff; 360 students; President POTENCIANO V. LARRAZABAL; Secretary POTENCIANO S. D. LARRAZABAL, III; Treasurer PHILIP ANTHONY S. D. LARRAZABAL; Dean ENRICO B. GRUET; publ. *Proceedings* (2 a year).

TECHNOLOGY

Leyte Institute of Technology: Salazar St, Tacloban City; f. 1965; courses in engineering, science, industrial technology, education and vocational training; postgraduate courses; 309 staff; library: 17,000 vols; Pres. GREGORIO T. DE LA ROSA; Registrar FRANKLIN A. COLASITO; publs *Annual Report*, *Graduate School Bulletin*, *College Journal*, *Industrial Wheel*.

Lyceum of the Philippines: Real and Muralla Sts, Intramuros, POB 1264, Manila; tel. (2) 527-55-48; fax (2) 527-17-61; internet www.lyceumphil.edu.ph; f. 1952; private control; faculties of law, graduate studies, mechanical engineering, mass communication, journalism, arts and sciences, foreign service, economics, business administration, office management, technical vocational, hotel and restaurant management, secretarial science, computer engineering, electronics and communication engineering, political science, legal studies, Filipino, literature, history, humanities, mathematics, psychology, biology, tourism, accountancy, legal secretarial administration, computer science, secondary education, banking and finance, management, marketing, computer data managment and processing, tax and customs administration, cruise line management, nursing and medical transcription; library: 45,000 vols; 300 teachers; 10,000 students; Pres. ROBERTO P. LAUREL.

Mapùa Institute of Technology: Muralla St, Intramuros, Manila; tel. (832) 527-7916; fax (832) 527-5161; f. 1925; private control; faculties of architecture and planning, industrial design, industrial engineering, mining and metallurgical engineering, civil engineering, electrical engineering, electronics and communications engineering, mechanical engineering, geology, environmental and sanitary engineering, chemical engineering and chemistry, computer engineering; 13,000 students; Pres. OSCAR B. MAPÙA, Sr.

Namei Polytechnic Institute: 123 A Mabini St, Mandaluyong, Metro Manila; tel. 531-73-28; fax 815-63-37; f 1947; private control; courses in Naval Architecture and Marine Engineering, B. S. Marine Transportation, Marine Engineering, Mechanical Engineering and Electrical Engineering; Pres. MARIA VICTORIA P. ESTRELLA; Registrar PERLA G. CRUZ.

Naval Institute of Technology: Naval, Biliran 6543; f. 1972; library: 10,000 vols; 83 teachers; 2,500 students; Pres. Dr JUANITO S. SISON.

Palompon Institute of Technology: Palompon, Leyte; tel. (53) 5559841; fax (53) 3382501; e-mail pit@glinesnx.com.ph; internet foo.ncc.gov.ph/community/pit/; f. 1972; courses in marine transportation and engineering; engineering technology; technical and vocational education; customs administration; radio communication; domestic science; industrial technology, shipping management, teacher education, information technology, industrial engineering, doctor's and master's programmes; library: 10,434 vols; 114 teachers; 2,776 students; Pres. Dr JUANITO S. SISON.

POLAND

The Higher Education System

Higher education in Poland dates from the 14th century, with the establishment of Uniwersytet Jagielloński (Jagiellonian University—founded in 1364), the country's oldest current university. Several institutions of higher education were founded in the 18th and 19th centuries, including Uniwersytet Wrocławski (the University of Wrocław—founded in 1702), Akademia Muzycna im. Fryderyka Chopina w Warszawie (the Frederick Chopin Academy of Music in Warsaw—founded in 1810) and Uniwersytet Warszawki (the University of Warsaw—founded in 1816). Many institutions of higher education were founded during the period of Communist rule (1948–89) and by 2003/04 there were 400 higher education establishments in Poland, including 17 universities and 22 technical universities, with a total of 2m. students.

The Ministry of National Education is the State authority responsible for higher education; most institutions of higher education are funded from the State budget. Higher education is administered according to the Higher Education Act (1990) and Act of Academic Title and Degrees (1990). Higher education is provided by universities (uniwersytet), technical universities (politechnika) and non-university level institutions (wyzsze szkoly zawodowe). Poland participates in the Bologna Process to establish a European Higher Education Area, the first phase of which is to adopt a credit-based system of comparable degrees with two main cycles (undergraduate and graduate).

The main criteria for admission to higher education is the secondary school 'maturity' certificate (swiadectwo dojrzalosci) and some institutions may set entrance examinations. Poland has implemented a two-tier Bachelors and Masters degree system, in accordance with the principles of the Bologna Process, but some old-style degree programmes are still offered, mostly by institutions of professional education. The primary examples of these types of degree are the Licencjat and Inzynier, which are awarded after three- to four-year courses of higher professional education. The undergraduate Bachelors degree is a three- or four-year course of study equivalent to the initial stages of the old-style Masters (Magistr). The new Masters is now a separate postgraduate degree lasting one to two years; however, students in mainly professional fields of study continue to work towards integrated Masters programmes. Admission to the highest level of university degree, the Doctorate (Doktor), requires the Masters. The Doctorate is awarded following the submission and defence of a thesis and success in doctorate examinations.

Technical and vocational education at the post-secondary level is offered by Post-Secondary Schools (Szkoly policealne or Szkoly pomaturalne) and Schools of Higher Professional Education (Wyzsze Szkoly Zawodowe); the latter were established following the Act on Schools of Higher Vocational Education (1997).

Regulatory and Representative Bodies

GOVERNMENT

Ministry of Culture and National Heritage: ul. Krakowskie Przedmieście 15/17, 00-071 Warsaw; tel. (22) 4210100; fax (22) 8260726; e-mail rzecznik@mkidn.gov.pl; internet www.mkidn.gov.pl; Minister KAZIMIERZ MICHAŁ UJAZDOWSKI.

Ministry of National Education: Al. Szucha 25, 00-918 Warsaw; tel. (22) 3474100; fax (22) 5224100; e-mail informacja@men.gov.pl; internet www.men.gov.pl; Minister ROMAN GIERTYCH.

Ministry of Science and Higher Education: ul. Wspólna 1/3, 00-529 Warsaw; tel. (22) 5292718; fax (22) 6280922; e-mail dip@mnii.gov.pl; internet www.nauka.gov.pl; Minister MICHAŁ SEWERYŃSKI.

ACCREDITATION

Centralna Komisja do Spraw Stopni i Tytułów (Central Commission for Degrees and Titles): pl. Defilad 1 (PKiN), 00-091 Warsaw; tel. (22) 826-82-38; fax (22) 620-33-24; e-mail bck@pan.pl; internet www.pan.pl/ck; defines fields and disciplines within sciences and the arts in which academic and professional titles and degrees are awarded; grants relevant instns the right to award such titles and degrees; ratifies awards of Dr Hab. degrees; Pres. Prof. TADEUSZ KACZOREK; Sec. Prof. OSMAN ACHMATOWICZ.

ENIC/NARIC Poland: Bureau for Academic Recognition and Int. Exchange, ul. Smolna 13, 00-375 Warsaw; tel. (22) 828-81-61; fax (22) 828-81-61 ext. 239; e-mail biuro@ buwiwm.edu.pl; internet www.buwiwm.edu .pl/rec; Deputy Dir EWA MAJDOWSKA.

Państwowa Komisja Akredytacyjna (State Accreditation Committee): ul. Żurawia 32/34, 00-515 Warsaw; tel. (22) 622-07-18; fax (22) 621-15-84; internet www.pka.edu.pl; supports Polish public and non-public higher-education instns in the devt of educational standards matching the best models adopted in Europe and the world; conducts obligatory assessments of the quality of education and gives opinions on applications submitted by higher-education instns to provide degree programmes; Pres. Dr Hab. ZBIGNIEW MARCINIAK; Sec. Dr Hab. MIECZYSŁAW WACŁAW SOCHA.

FUNDING

Komitet Badań Naukowych (State Committee for Scientific Research): ul. Wspólna 1/3, 00-529 Warsaw; tel. (22) 529-27-18; fax (22) 628-09-22; e-mail dip@kbn.gov.pl; internet kbn.icm.edu.pl; f. 1991; draws up guidelines on scientific policy, submits plans for budgetary expenditure in the area of science and technology, distributes funds among instns and research teams and controls spending, and signs int. agreements on co-operation in science and technology; Chair. MICHAŁ KLEIBER; Gen. Dir KRYSTYN WEREMOWICZ.

NATIONAL BODIES

Konferencja Rektorów Akademickich Szkół Polskich (Conference of Rectors of Academic Schools in Poland): ul. Wybrzeze Wyspianskiego 27, 50-370 Wrocław; tel. (71) 320-29-60; fax (71) 320-32-22; e-mail krasp@ pwr.wroc.pl; internet www.krasp.org.pl; f. 1997; voluntary asscn of rectors representing those instns of higher education awarding doctorates (or equivalent) in at least one scientific discipline; 105 mems, 3 assoc. instns; Pres. Prof. Dr TADEUSZ LUTY; Sec. Gen. Prof. Dr ANDRZEJ KRASNIEWSKI.

Rada Główna Szkolnictwa Wyższego (Central Council for Higher Education): ul. Wspólna 1/3, 00-529 Warsaw; tel. (22) 529-25-64; fax (22) 529-27-68; e-mail radaglowna@mnisw.gov.pl; internet www .rgsw.edu.pl; formulates opinions on how higher education should be developed and on all proposed legislation concerning higher education; Pres. Prof. Dr Hab JERZY BŁAŻEJOWSKI.

Learned Societies

GENERAL

Bydgoskie Towarzystwo Naukowe (Bydgoszcz Scientific Society): ul. Jezuicka 4, 85-102 Bydgoszcz; tel. and fax (52) 322-22-68; e-mail btn@um.bydgoszcz.pl; f. 1959; 553 mems; library of 17,500 vols; Pres. Prof. Dr hab. HENRYK Z. WREMBEL; Sec.-Gen. Dr GRZEGORZ DOMINIAK; publs *Ekologia i Technika* (every 2 months), *Prace Wydziału Nauk Humanistycznych* (annually), *Prace Wydziału Nauk Przyrodniczych* (annually), *Prace Wydziału Nauk Technicznych* (annually), *Przegląd Bydgoski* (annually), *Bydgostiana Kolokwium Wiedzy o Ziemi* (irregularly).

Gdańskie Towarzystwo Naukowe (Gdańsk Scientific Society): ul. Grodzka 12, 80-841 Gdańsk; tel. (58) 301-21-24; fax (58) 305-81-31; e-mail gtn@3net.pl; f. 1922 as Gdańsk Society of Friends of Science and Art; sections of Social Sciences and Humanities, Biological and Medical Sciences, Mathematical, Physical and Chemical

Sciences, Technical Sciences, Earth Sciences; 572 mems; Pres. Prof. Dr JAN DRWAL; Sec. Prof. Dr JERZY BŁAŻEJOWSKI; publ. *Acta Biologica et Medica*.

Kieleckie Towarzystwo Naukowe (Kielce Scientific Society): ul. Zamkowa 5, 25-009 Kielce; tel. (41) 344-54-53; fax (41) 344-54-53; e-mail ktn@pu.kielce.pl; internet www.pu .kielce.pl/ktn; f. 1958; regional scientific research in history, philology, medicine, geology, geography and nature conservation, psychology, sociology and education, physics, mathematics, engineering; 464 mems; library of 4,620 vols; Pres. Prof. Dr hab. ADAM MASSALSKI; Sec. Prof. Dr hab. MAREK JÓŹWIAK; publs *Rocznik Swiętokrzyski* (Yearbook), *Studia Kieleckie* (irregular).

Łomżyńskie Towarzystwo Naukowe im. Wagów (The Brothers Waga Łomża Scientific Society): ul. Długa 13, 18-400 Łomża; tel. and fax (86) 216-32-56; e-mail zegalska@ poczta.onet.pl; f. 1975; history, ethnology, linguistics, veterinary science, environmental protection, natural history, geography, agriculture, settlement of Northeast Poland, economics; 250 mems; Pres. Prof. Dr hab. MICHAŁ GNATOWSKI; Dir Mgr inż. ELŻBIETA ŻEGALSKA; publs *Polszczyzna Mazowsza i Podlasia* (annually), *Studia Łomżyńskie* (annually).

Lubelskie Towarzystwo Naukowe (Lublin Scientific Society): Pl. Litewski 2, 20-080 Lublin; tel. and fax (81) 532-13-00; e-mail biuro@ltn.lublin.pl; f. 1957; 722 mems; five sections: humanities, biology, mathematics-physics-chemistry, technical science, mining and geography; Pres. Prof. Dr hab. EDMUND K. PROST; Sec.-Gen. Prof. Dr JAN MALARCZYK.

Polska Akademia Nauk (PAN) (Polish Academy of Sciences): Pałac Kultury i Nauki, Plac Defilad 1, POB 24, 00-901 Warsaw; tel. (22) 620-49-70; fax (22) 620-49-10; e-mail barbara.szoltyk@pan.pl; internet www.pan .pl; f. 1952; divisions of Agricultural, Forestry and Veterinary Sciences (Chair. Prof. ANDRZEJ GRZYWACZ), Biological Sciences (Chair. Prof. LESZEK KACZMAREK), Earth and Mining Sciences (Chair. Prof. BOGDAN NEY), Mathematical, Physical and Chemical Sciences (Chair. Prof. HENRYK SZYMCZAK), Medical Sciences (Chair. Prof. ANDRZEJ TRZEBSKI), Social Sciences (Chair. Prof. HENRYK SAMSONOWICZ) and Technical Science (Chair. Prof. WŁADYSŁAW WŁOSIŃSKI); 559 mems (189 ordinary, 142 corresp., 228 foreign); attached research institutes: see Research Institutes; collection: science and technology, future studies, praxiology, library and information science, bibliography; library of 413,697 vols; Pres. Prof. ANDRZEJ B. LEGOCKI; Vice-Presidents Prof. JANUSZ LIPOWSKI, Prof. JAN STRELAU; publs *Academia. The Magazine of the Polish Academy of Sciences* (English and Polish versions, each 4 a year), *Acta Arithmetica* (4 a year), *Acta Biochimica Polonica* (4 a year), *Acta Geologica Polonica* (4 a year), *Acta Neurobiologicale Experimentalis* (4 a year), *Acta Physica Polonica* (4 a year), *Acta Poloniae Historica* (2 a year), *Acta Protozoologica* (4 a year), *Acta Physiologiae Plantarum* (4 a year), *Annual Report*, *Archeologia* (annually), *Archives of Metallurgy and Materials* (4 a year), *Archivum Immunologiae et Therapiae Experimentalis* (6 a year), *Bulletin of the Polish Academy of Sciences:* Series: Technical Sciences (4 a year), *Chemia Analityczna* (4 a year), *Chemical and Process Engineering* (4 a year), *Ethnologia Polonia* (annually), *Etudes et Travaux* (annually), *Folia Neuropathologica* (4 a year), *Fundamenta Mathematicae* (4 a year), *Journal of Animal and Feed Sciences* (4 a year), *Nauka* (4 a year), *Oceanologia* (4 a year), *Onomas-*

tica (annually), *Pamiętnik Literacki* (4 a year), *Polish Journal of Food and Nutrition Sciences* (4 a year), *Polish Journal of Pharmacology* (6 a year), *Polish Journal of Veterinary Sciences* (4 a year), *Studia Logica* (4 a year), *Studia Mathematica* (4 a year).

Poznańskie Towarzystwo Przyjaciół Nauk (Poznań Society of Friends of Arts and Sciences): ul. Sew. Mielżyńskiego 27/29, 61-725 Poznań; tel. (61) 852-74-41; fax (61) 852-22-05; e-mail sekretariat@ptpn.poznan .pl; internet www.ptpn.poznan.pl; f. 1857; 1,070 mems; library of 197,176 books, 5,024 periodical titles, 1,432 MSS, 15,157 old books including incunabula, 1,839 maps and atlases, 711 microfilms; Pres. Prof. Dr hab. LEON KOZACKI; Sec.-Gen. Dr STANISŁAW JAKÓBCZYK; publs *Roczniki Dziejów Społecznych i Gospodarczych, Lingua Posnaniensis, Slavia Antiqua, Slavia Occidentalis, Bulletin de la Société des Amis des Sciences et des Lettres de Poznań—Série D: Sciences Biologiques, Badania Fizjograficzne nad Polską Zachodnią* (Series A (Geography) Series B (Botany) Series C (Zoology)), *Sprawozdania Poznańskiego Towarzystwa Przyjaciół Nauk*.

Szczecińskie Towarzystwo Naukowe (Szczecin Scientific Society): ul. Wojska Polskiego 96, 70-481 Szczecin; tel. (91) 423-18-62; e-mail wtarc@univ.szczecin.pl; internet www .univ.szczecin.pl/stn; f. 1956; Sections (I) Social Sciences, (II) Agriculture and Natural Sciences, (III) Medicine, (IV) Technical Sciences and Mathematics, (V) Maritime Sciences; 292 mems; library of 16,130 vols; Pres. Prof. Dr hab. JANINA JASNOWSKA; Sec.-Gen. Prof. Dr hab. WALDEMAR TARCZYŃSKI; publs in each section Series I, II, III, IV, V, *Szczecińskie Roczniki Naukowe* (Szczecin Scientific Annuals).

Towarzystwo Naukowe Płockie (Płock Scientific Society): plac Narutowicza 8, 09-402 Płock; tel. (24) 366-99-50; fax (24) 262-26-04; e-mail aktnp@interia.pl; internet www .tnp.org.pl; f. 1820; 416 mems; library of 328,149 vols; Pres. Dr hab. inż. ZBIGNIEW KRUSZEWSKI; Sec.-Gen. Dr WIESŁAW KOŃSKI; publs *Notatki Płockie* (quarterly), *Sprawozdanie z działalności* (Yearbook).

Towarzystwo Naukowe w Toruniu (Scientific Society of Toruń): ul. Wysoka 16, 87-100 Toruń; tel. (56) 622-39-41; fax (56) 622-39-41; e-mail tnt.biuro@wp.pl; internet www.tnt.torun.pl; f. 1875; concerned with historical, legal and social studies, philology, philosophy and natural sciences; 490 mems; library of 112,340 vols; Pres. Prof. MARIAN BISKUP; Gen. Sec. Prof. MARIAN KALLAS; publs include *Roczniki, Fontes* (irregular), *Zapiski Historyczne* (quarterly, concerned chiefly with Pomeranian problems), *Prace Wydziału Filologiczno-Filozoficznego* (irregular), *Sprawozdania* (annually), *Studia Iuridica* (irregular), *Studia Societatis Scientiarum Toruniensis* (various series: geography and geology, botany, zoology, astronomy, physiology, medicine, all irregular), *Prace Popularnonaukowe* (irregular), *Prace Archaeologiczne* (irregular).

Towarzystwo Naukowe Warszawskie (Warsaw Scientific Society): ul. Nowy Świat 72, 00-330 Warsaw; tel. and fax (22) 657-28-26; e-mail sekretariat@tnw.waw.pl; internet www.tnw.waw.pl; f. 1907; 420 mems; Pres. Prof. ANDREJ PASZEWSKI; Sec.-Gen. Prof. EWA RZETELSKA-FELESZKO; publ. *Rocznik TNW* (annually).

Towarzystwo Przyjaciół Nauk w Przemyślu (Society of Science and Letters of Przemyśl): ul. Kościuszki 7, 37-700 Przemyśl; tel. (16) 678-56-01; e-mail tpntpn@wp.pl; internet www.tpn.vt.pl; f. 1909; 266 mems; library of 60,000 vols; Pres. Prof. Dr hab. ZDZISŁAW BUDZYŃSKI; Sec.-Gen. Dr MACIEJ

DALECKI; publs *Rocznik Przemyski, Acta Medica Premisliensia, Biblioteka Przemyska, Polska południowo-wschodnia w epoce nowożytnej. Źródła dziejowe*.

Towarzystwo Wiedzy Powszechnej (Universal Education Society): Pałac Kultury i Nauki, Plac Defilad 1, VI flor, Room 602, 00-901 Warsaw; tel. (22) 826-56-30; fax 620-33-06; e-mail twp@twp.pl; internet www.twp.pl; f. 1950; general adult education; runs private schools providing vocational, secondary and post-secondary education; founded five schools of higher education of which two award Masters qualifications; organizes discussions, lectures, seminars, conferences, popular science and training sessions; 6,000 mems; library of 2,000 vols; Pres. EDWARD BALAWEJDER; Gen. Dir ZENON GAWORCZUK; publ. *Edukacja Dorosłych* (monthly).

Towarzystwo Wolnej Wszechnicy Polskiej (Society of the Polish Free University): ul. Górnośląska 20, 00-484 Warsaw; tel. (22) 621-73-55; fax (22) 625-38-34; e-mail mlipowski@mercury.ci.uw.cdu.pl; f. 1882; permanent education, research and application services, specialized interests clubs; 1,000 mems; library of 10,000 vols; Pres. Dr inż. MIKOŁAJ Ł. LIPOWSKI; Sec.-Gen. (vacant); publs *Kalendarz Samorządowy* (annually), *Człowiek w Społeczeństwie* (irregular), *Zeszyty Naukowe* (irregular).

Wrocławskie Towarzystwo Naukowe (Wrocław Scientific Society): ul. Parkowa 13, 51-616 Wrocław; tel. (71) 348-40-61; e-mail wtn@wtn.wroc.pl; internet zts.ita.pwr .wroc.pl/wtn; f. 1946 to study social and exact sciences; 482 mems; Pres. Prof. MARIAN PIEKARSKI; Sec. Prof. JAN ZARZYCKI; publs include *Prace Wrocławskiego Towarzystwa Naukowego* (Series A: Humanistic Sciences, Series B: Exact Sciences), *Annales Silesiae, Litteraria, Rozprawy Komisji Historii Sztuki, Rozprawy Komisji Językowej, Sląskie Prace Bibliologiczne i Bibliotekoznawcze, Sprawozdania* (series A and B).

AGRICULTURE, FISHERIES AND VETERINARY SCIENCE

Polskie Towarzystwo Gleboznawcze (Polish Society of Soil Science): ul. Wiśniowa 61, 02-520 Warsaw; tel. (22) 849-48-16; f. 1937; 750 mems; Pres. Prof. Dr hab. PIOTR SKŁODOWSKI; Sec. Dr hab. JÓZEF CHOJNICKI; publ. *Roczniki Gleboznawcze* (4 a year).

Polskie Towarzystwo Leśne (Polish Forest Society): ul. Bitwy Warszawskiej 1920r. 3, 02-362 Warsaw; tel. (22) 822-14-70; fax (22) 822-49-35; e-mail sylwan@ibles.waw.pl; f. 1882; 3,360 mems; library of 1,700 vols; Pres. Prof. Dr ANDRZEJ GRZYWACZ; Sec. Dr JAN ŁUKASZEWICZ; publ. *Sylwan* (monthly).

Polskie Towarzystwo Nauk Weterynaryjnych (Polish Society of Veterinary Sciences): ul. Grochowska 272, 03-849 Warsaw; tel. (22) 810-33-97; fax (22) 810-33-97; e-mail ptnw@vetclub.pl; internet www .vetcentrum.pl/ptnw; f. 1952; lectures and seminars in 17 divisions throughout Poland; congress every 4 years; 1,500 mems; library of 2,500 vols; Pres. Prof. Dr JERZY KITA; Sec. Dr JAROSŁAW KABA; publ. *Medycyna Weterynaryjna* (monthly).

Polskie Towarzystwo Zootechniczne (Polish Society of Animal Production): Kaliska 9, 02-316 Warsaw; tel. (22) 822-17-23; e-mail ptz_redakcja@alpha.sggw.waw.pl; f. 1922; 1,200 mems; library of 2,630 vols; Pres. Prof. ZYGMUNT REKLEWSKI; Dir Inż. ANNA ZABŁOCKA-IDCZAK; publs *Animal Production Review* (monthly), *Animal Production Review Applied Science Reports* (annually).

ARCHITECTURE AND TOWN PLANNING

Stowarzyszenie Architektów Polskich (Association of Polish Architects): ul. Foksal 2, 00-950 Warsaw; tel. (22) 827-87-12; fax (22) 827-87-13; e-mail sarp@sarp.org.pl; internet sarp.org.pl; f. 1934; 6,040 mems; Sec.-Gen. JERZY GROCHULSKI; publ. *Komunikat SARP* (monthly).

Towarzystwo Urbanistów Polskich (Polish Town Planners' Society): Pl. Zamkowy 10, 00-277 Warsaw; tel. (22) 831-07-73; fax (22) 831-28-30; f. 1923; 1,300 mems; Pres. Dr STANISŁAW WYGANOWSKI; Sec.-Gen. Dr LILIANA SCHWARTZ; publ. *Biuletyn TUP* (2 a year).

BIBLIOGRAPHY, LIBRARY SCIENCE AND MUSEOLOGY

Stowarzyszenie Archiwistów Polskich (Polish Archivists' Association): ul. Długa 6, 00-950 Warsaw; tel. (22) 831-32-08; Pres. Dr WŁADYSŁAW STĘPNIAK; Sec.-Gen. (vacant); publ. *Archiwista* (quarterly).

Stowarzyszenie Bibliotekarzy Polskich (Polish Librarians Association): National Library, al. Niepodleglosci 213, 02-086 Warsaw; tel. (22) 608-24-51; fax (22) 825-91-57; e-mail biurozgsbp@wp.pl; internet ebib.oss .wroc.pl/sbp/english/index_en.html; f. 1917; 8,300 mems in 16 regional divisions; Pres. JAN WOŁOSZ; Sec.-Gen. ELŻBIETA STEFAŃCZYK; publs *Bibliotekarz* (monthly), *Poradnik Bibliotekarza* (monthly), *Przegląd Biblioteczny* (4 a year), *Zagadnienia Informacji Naukowej* (4 a year).

ECONOMICS, LAW AND POLITICS

Polskie Towarzystwo Demograficzne (Polish Demographic Society): al. Niepodległości 164, room 3, 02-554 Warsaw; tel. 48-22-3379273; e-mail ewaf@sgh.waw.pl; f. 1982; 250 mems; Pres. ZBIGNIEW STRZELECKI; Sec. LUCYNA NOWAK; publ. *Polish Population Review* (2 a year).

Polskie Towarzystwo Ekonomiczne (Polish Economic Society): Nowy Swiat 49, 00-042 Warsaw; tel. (22) 827-99-04; fax (22) 827-99-04; e-mail zk@pte.pl; internet www.pte.pl; f. 1945; 6,220 mems; Pres. Prof. Dr hab. ZDZISŁAW SADOWSKI; Gen.-Sec. Prof. Dr hab. URSZULA PŁOWIEC; publ. *Ekonomista* (every 2 months).

Polskie Towarzystwo Towaroznawcze (Polish Society for Commodity Science): ul. Sienkiewicza 4, 30-033 Cracow; tel. (12) 633-08-21; e-mail adamczyw@ae.krakow.pl; internet www.ae.krakow.pl; f. 1963; 500 mems; Pres. Prof. Dr WACŁAW ADAMCZYK; Sec. Dr STANISŁAW POPEK; publ. *Towaroznawstwo—Problemy Jakości* (annually).

EDUCATION

Polskie Towarzystwo Pedagogiczne (Polish Pedagogics Society): ul. Smulikowskiego 6/8, 00-389 Warsaw; tel. (22) 826-10-11, ext. 249; f. 1981; 800 mems; Pres. Prof. Dr hab. ZBIGNIEW KWIECIŃSKI; Sec.-Gen. Prof. Dr hab. MARIAN WALCZAK; publs *Forum Oświatowe* (Educational Forum, 2 a year), *Przegląd Historyczno-Oświatowy* (Historical-Educational Review, quarterly).

FINE AND PERFORMING ARTS

Polskie Stowarzyszenie Filmu Naukowego (Polish Association of Scientific Film): ul. Mokotowska 58 pok. 1, 00-534 Warsaw; tel. (22) 629-08-32; internet galaxy.uci.agh .edu.pl/~kpfn/; Pres. GRZEGORZ KOWALEWSKI; Sec.-Gen. STANISŁAW SLEDŹ; publ. *Film Naukowy* (2 a year).

Stowarzyszenie Historyków Sztuki (Art Historians Association): Rynek Starego Miasta 27, 00-272 Warsaw; tel. (22) 635-96-99; fax (22) 635-90-74; e-mail shs@shs.pl.pl; internet www.shs.pl; f. 1934; search and publication, popularization of art history; 1,406 mems; library of 28,492 vols; Pres. Prof. Dr hab. MARIA POPRZĘCKA; Sec.-Gen. Dr KATARZYNA NOWAKOWSKA-SITO; publs *Materiały Sesii SHS*, *Materiały do Dziejów Rezydencji w Polsce*, *Materiały Seminariów Metodologicznych*, *Materiały Sesji Oddziałowych*.

Towarzystwo im. Fryderyka Chopina (Frederic Chopin Society): Zamek Ostrogskich, ul. Okólnik 1, 00-368 Warsaw; tel. (22) 827-54-71; fax (22) 827-95-99; e-mail info@ chopin.pl; internet www.chopin.pl/tifc; f. 1934; 500 mems; permanent Secretariat of the Int. Chopin Piano Competitions and Int. Chopin Record Competitions 'Grand Prix du Disque-Fryderyk Chopin'; central Chopin museum, library, phototheque and phonotheque for study of Chopin's life and preparation of complete edition of his works; organization of concerts; patronage of Chopin's birth-place in Zelazowa Wola; Gen. Dir ALBERT GRUDZIŃSKI; publs *Annales Chopin*, *Chopin Studies*.

Warszawskie Towarzystwo Muzyczne im. Stanisława Moniuszki (Stanisław Moniuszko Music Society in Warsaw): ul. Morskie Oko 2, 02-511 Warsaw; tel. (22) 49-68-56; 300 mems; Pres. STEFANIA WOYTOWICZ; Sec. ALEKSANDER ROWIŃSKI.

HISTORY, GEOGRAPHY AND ARCHAEOLOGY

Polskie Towarzystwo Geograficzne (Polish Geographical Society): Krakowskie Przedmieście 30, 00-927 Warsaw; tel. (22) 826-17-94; fax (22) 826-17-94; e-mail ptg@ wgsr.uw.edu.pl; f. 1918; 1,500 mems; library of 17,000 vols; Pres. Prof. Dr ANDRZEJ JANKOWSKI; Sec. Dr TOMASZ KOMORNICKI; publs *Czasopismo Geograficzne* (Geographical Journal, 4 a year), *Polski Przegląd Kartograficzny* (Polish Cartographical Review, 4 a year), *Teledetekcja Srodowiska* (annually), *Prace Komisji Geografii Komunikacji* (annually), *Studia Obszarów Wiejskich* (Rural Studies, annually).

Polskie Towarzystwo Historyczne (Polish Historical Society): Rynek Starego Miasta 29/31, 00-272 Warsaw; tel. (22) 831-63-41; e-mail pth@ihpan.edu.pl; internet historicus .umk.pl/pth; f. 1886; 4,137 mems; Pres. Prof. Dr KRZYSTOF MIKULSKI; Sec.-Gen. Mgr ZOFIA T. KOZŁOWSKA; 53 local branches, 4 research centres; publs *Przegląd Historyczny* (quarterly), *Sobótka-Sląski Kwartalnik Historyczny* (quarterly), *Studia i Materiały do dziejów Wielkopolski i Pomorza* (series), *Komunikaty Mazursko-Warmińskie* (quarterly), and several annuals.

Polskie Towarzystwo Numizmatyczne (Polish Numismatic Society): 00-281 Warsaw 40, Skr. poczt. 2; 00-281 Warsaw, ul. Jezuicka 6; tel. and fax (22) 831-39-28; e-mail ptn@ptn.pl; internet www.ptn.pl; f. 1991; 2,200 mems; library of 3,500 vols; Pres. Dr KRZYSZTOF FILOPOW; Sec. ADAM ZAJĄC; publ. *Biuletyn Numizmatyczny* (4 a year).

Stowarzyszenie Miłośników Dawnej Broni i Barwy (Historic Arms and Uniforms Association): al. 3 Maja 1, 30-062 Cracow; tel. (12) 295-55-77; fax (12) 633-97-67; f. 1957; 320 mems; Pres. Prof. Dr hab. ALEKSANDER GUTERCH; publ. *Studia do dziejów dawnego uzbrojenia i ubioru wojskowego*.

Towarzystwo Miłośników Historii i Zabytków Krakowa (Society of Friends of the History and Monuments of Cracow): Sw. Jana 12, 31-018 Cracow; tel. (12) 21-27-83; fax (12) 23-10-74; f. 1896; 650 mems; Pres. Prof. Dr JERZY WYROZUMSKI; Sec. OLGA DYBA; publs *Rocznik Krakowski*, *Biblioteka Krakowska*, *Kraków Dawniej i Dziś*, *Rola Krakowa w dziejach narodu*.

LANGUAGE AND LITERATURE

Alliance Française: ul. Puławska 17, 02-515 Warsaw; tel. (22) 529-31-91; fax (22) 529-31-94; e-mail elisabeth.de-pontbriand@ diplomatie.gouv.fr; internet www .af-enpologne.pl; offers courses and exams in French language and culture and promotes cultural exchange with France; attached offices in Białystok, Cieszyn, Gdańsk, Gorzow, Katowice, Łódź, Lublin, Opole, Poznań, Rybnik, Rzeszów, Szczecin, Toruń, Wałbrzych and Wrocław; Dir ELISABETH DE PONTBRIAND.

British Council: 00-697 Warsaw, Al Jerozolimskie 59; tel. (22) 695-59-00; fax (22) 621-99-55; e-mail bc.warsaw@britishcouncil .pl; internet www.britishcouncil.pl; teaching centre and library; offers courses and exams in English language and British culture and promotes cultural exchange with the UK; attached teaching centre in Kraków; Dir SUSAN MAINGAY.

Goethe-Institut: Located at: ul. Chmielna 11A, 00-021 Warsaw; tel. (22) 505-90-00; e-mail sekretariat@goethe.pl; internet www .goethe.de/ms/war/deindex.htm; offers courses and exams in German language and culture and promotes cultural exchange with Germany; attached centre in Krakow; library of 15,000 vols, 30 periodicals; Dir VERA BAGALIANTZ.

Instituto Cervantes: ul. Myśliwiecka 4, 00-459 Warsaw; tel. (22) 622-54-22; fax (12) 622-54-13; e-mail cenvar@cervantes.es; internet varsovia.cervantes.es; offers courses and exams in Spanish language and culture and promotes cultural exchange with Spain and Spanish-speaking Latin and Central America; library: library of 16,000 vols; Dir JOSEP MARIA DE SAGARRA ÁNGEL.

Polskie Towarzystwo Filologiczne (Polish Philological Society): Al Mickiewicza 9/11, VI p., 31-120 Kraków; tel. (12) 633-63-77 ext. 2324; e-mail ZGPTF@vela.filg.uj.edu.pl; f. 1893; aims to promote classical studies; 500 mems; library of 2,500 vols; Pres. Prof. Dr hab. JERZY STYKA; Sec. Dr JOANNA JANIK; publ. *EOS* (annually).

Polskie Towarzystwo Fonetyczne (Polish Phonetic Association): Instytut Lingwistyki UAM, ul. Międzychodzka 5, 60-371 Poznań; tel. (61) 829-27-06; fax (61) 829-27-00; e-mail fonetyka@amu.edu.pl; internet www.staff .amu.edu.pl/~fonetyka; f. 1980; linguistic phonetics, phonetics in medicine and technology; 112 mems; Pres. GRAŻYNA DEMENKO; Sec. MARIUSZ OWSIANNY.

Polskie Towarzystwo Językoznawcze (Polish Linguistic Society): al. A. Mickiewicza 31, 31-120 Cracow; e-mail ptj@civ.pl; internet www.ptj.civ.pl; f. 1925; 965 mems; Pres. ELŻBIETA MAŃCZAK-WOHLFELD; Sec. JUSTYNA WINIARSKA; publ. *Biuletyn* (annually).

Polskie Towarzystwo Neofilologiczne (Modern Language Association of Poland): ul. Berwińskiego 1, 60-765 Poznań; tel. (61) 866-07-13; internet main.amu.edu.pl/ ~ptnwil; f. 1929; 184 mems; Pres. WERONIKA WILCZYŃSKA; Sec. ANNA BARBARA CIEŚLICKA; publ. *Neofilolog* (2 a year).

Towarzystwo Literackie im. Adama Mickiewicza (Mickiewicz Literary Society): Nowy Swiat 72, 00-330 Warsaw; tel. 26-52-31, ext. 279; f. 1886; 1,600 mems; arranges lectures on literature mainly in the provinces; Pres. Prof. Dr ZDZISŁAW LIBERA; Sec. Dr BARBARA KRYDA; publ. *Rocznik* (Yearbook).

Związek Literatów Polskich (Union of Polish Writers): Krakowskie Przedmieście

87/89, 00-079 Warsaw; tel. (22) 826-57-85; f. 1920; 700 mems; library of 40,000 vols and cuttings; Chair. PIOTR KUNCEWICZ.

MEDICINE

Polskie Lekarskie Towarzystwo Radiologiczne (Polish Medical Society of Radiology): c/o, Dr Anna Siemianowicz, Nuklearnej Śląskiej Akademii Medycznej – SP CSK AM, ul. Medyków 14, 40-752 Katowice; tel. and fax (32) 252-55-66; e-mail gwawrzonek@csk.katowice.pl; internet www .polradiologia.org; f. 1925; 1,700 mems; Pres. Asst Prof. JAN BARON; Sec. Dr ANNA SIEMIANOWICZ; publ. *Polski Przegląd Radiologiczny* (quarterly).

Polskie Towarzystwo Anatomiczne (Polish Anatomical Society): ul. Chałubińskiego 5, 02-004 Warsaw; tel. (22) 629-52-82; fax (22) 629-52-82; e-mail ejank@ib.amwaw.edu .pl; f. 1923; 400 mems; Pres. STANISŁAW SZTEYN; Sec. Dr EWA JANKOWSKA-STEIFER; publs *Folia Morphologica*, *Postępy Biologii Komórki* (Advances in Cell Biology).

Polskie Towarzystwo Anestezjologii i Intensywnej Terapii (Polish Society of Anaesthesiology and Intensive Therapy): Katedra i Klinika Anestezjologii i Intensywnej Terapii AM SPSK Nr 4, ul. Jaczewskiego 8, 20-954 Lublin; tel. (81) 724-43-32; fax (81) 742-52-56; e-mail anest2@am.lublin.pl; internet www.anestezjologia.org.pl; f. 1959; Pres. Prof. Dr hab. n. med. ANDRZEJ NESTOROWICZ; Sec.-Gen. Dr n. med. ANNA FIJAŁKOWSKA; publ. *Anestezjologia Intensywna Terapia* (every 2 months).

Polskie Towarzystwo Badań Radiacyjnych im. Marii Skłodowskiej-Curie (M. Skłodowska-Curie Polish Society for Radiation Research): ul. Chocimska 24, 00-791 Warsaw; tel. (22) 849-77-74; fax (22) 849-29-64; e-mail ptbr@pzh.gov.pl; internet www .ptbr.pzh.gov.pl; f. 1967; 229 mems; Pres. Prof. Dr hab. ANTONI GAJEWSKI; Sec. Dr MAŁGORZATA ROCHALSKA.

Polskie Towarzystwo Chirurgów Dziecięcych (Polish Association of Paediatric Surgeons): Klinika Chirurgii Dziecięcej Instytutu Centrum Zdrowia Matki Polki, ul. Rzgowska 281/289, 93-338 Łódź; tel. (42) 271-13-58; e-mail klinikachirdziec@poczta.onet .pl; f. 1965; 810 mems; Pres. Pers. Prof. Dr CZESŁAW STOBA; Sec.-Gen. Prof. Dr TOMASZ LENKIEWICZ; publs *Chirurgia Dziecięca – Rocznik* (annually), *Surgery in Childhood International* (quarterly), *Rocznik Dziecięcej Chirurgii Urazowej* (annually).

Polskie Towarzystwo Diagnostyki Laboratoryjnej (Polish Laboratory Diagnostics Society): c/o Dr n. med. Andrzej Marszałek, Zakład Diagnostyki Laboratoryjnej 10 WSK z Polikliniką SPZOZ, ul. Powstańców Warszawy 5, 85-680 Bydgoszcz; tel. (52) 378-48-87; fax (52) 377-33-10; e-mail ptdlsekretarz@ptdl.ids.pl; internet www .diagnostykalab.pl/diagnost/ptdl/teren.htm; f. 1963; 3,500 mems; Pres. Prof. Dr n. med. MAREK PARADOWSKI; Sec. Dr n. med. ANDRZEJ MARSZAŁEK; publ. *Diagnostyka Laboratoryjna* (quarterly).

Polskie Towarzystwo Epidemiologów i Lekarzy Chorób Zakaźnych (Polish Society of Epidemiology and Infectious Diseases): ul. Św. Floriana 12, 85-030 Bydgoszcz; tel. (52) 322-48-70; fax (52) 345-71-95; e-mail kikchzak@amb.bydgoszcz.pl; f. 1958; 1,200 mems; Pres. Prof. WALDEMAR HALOTA; Sec. Dr EWA TOPCZEWSKA-STAUBACH; publ. *Przegląd Epidemiologiczny* (quarterly).

Polskie Towarzystwo Farmaceutyczne (Polish Pharmaceutical Society): ul. Długa 16, 00-238 Warsaw; tel. and fax (22) 831-15-42; e-mail zarzad@ptfarm.pl; internet www

.ptfarm.pl; f. 1947; 7,000 mems; Pres. Prof. Dr hab. JANUSZ PLUTA; publs *Farmacja Polska* (every 2 weeks), *Acta Poloniae Pharmaceutica* (every 2 months), *Bromatologia i Chemia Toksykologiczna* (quarterly).

Polskie Towarzystwo Farmakologiczne (Polish Pharmacological Society): Katedra i Zakład Farmakologii Doświadczalnej i Klinicznej, ul. Krakowskie Przedmieście 26/28, 00-927 Warsaw; tel. and fax (22) 826-21-16; e-mail phawar@hotmail.com; internet pharmacology.slam.katowice.pl; f. 1965; 545 mems; Pres. Prof. Dr hab. n. med. MAREK KOWALCZYK; Sec. Dr ADAM PRZYBYŁKOWSKI; publ. *Information Bulletin* (in Polish, 2 a year).

Polskie Towarzystwo Fizjologiczne (Polish Physiological Society): ul. Grzegórzecka 16, 31-531 Kraków; tel. (12) 421-10-06; fax (12) 421-15-78; e-mail mpbrzozo@cyf-kr.edu .pl; internet www.ptf.ifzz.pl; f. 1936 to promote scientific activity in all fields of physiology; 300 mems; Pres. Prof. Dr hab. STANISŁAW KONTUREK; Sec. Prof. Dr hab. TOMASZ BRZOZOWSKI; publ. *Journal of Physiology and Pharmacology*.

Polskie Towarzystwo Fizyki Medycznej (Polish Society of Medical Physics): c/o Dr Ewa Zalewska, Instytut Biocybernetyki i Inżynierii Biomedycznej PAN, ul. Ks. Trojdena 4, 02-109 Warsaw; e-mail k.zaremba@ ire.pw.edu.pl; internet ptfm.irc.pw.edu.pl; f. 1965; 150 mems; Pres. Prof. GRZEGORZ PAWLICKI; Sec. Dr EWA ZALEWSKA; publ. *Polish Journal of Medical Physics and Engineering*.

Polskie Towarzystwo Ftizjopneumonologiczne (Polish Phthisiopneumonological Society): ul. Płocka 26, 01-138 Warsaw; tel. (32) 271-56-08; fax (32) 274-56-64; e-mail ftpulmza@imfomed.slam.katowice.pl; internet www.towarzystwo.witaj.pl; f. 1934; research into tuberculosis and chest diseases; Pres. Prof. Dr hab. med. JERZY KOZIELSKI; publ. *Pneumonologia i Alergologia Polska* (monthly).

Polskie Towarzystwo Gerontologiczne (Polish Society of Gerontology): ul. Fabryczna 27, 15-471 Białystok; tel. and fax (85) 869-49-74; e-mail geronto@amb.edu.pl; internet www.borgis.pl/ptg; f. 1973; 320 mems; Pres. Dr hab. med. BARBARA BIEŃ; Sec. Dr n. med. Z. BEATA WOJSZEL; publ. *Gerontologia Polska* (quarterly).

Polskie Towarzystwo Ginekologiczne (Polish Gynaecological Society): Klinika Onkologii Ginekologicznej Małgorzata Skowrońska, ul. Polna 33, 60-535 Poznań; tel. (61) 841-92-65; fax (61) 841-94-65; e-mail ptgzg@ gpsk.am.poznan.pl; internet www.gpsk.am .poznan.pl/ptg; br. in Wrocław; Pres. Prof. Dr hab. MAREK SPACZYŃSKI; Sec. Prof. Dr hab. LESZEK PAWELCZYK; publ. *Ginekologia Polska* (monthly).

Polskie Towarzystwo Higieniczne (Polish Hygiene Society): ul. Karowa 31, 00-324 Warsaw; tel. (22) 826-63-20; fax (22) 826-82-36; e-mail jsobotka@plearn.edu.pl; internet venus.ci.uw.edu.pl/pth; f. 1898; Pres. Assoc. Prof. CEZARY W. KORCZAK; Sec. Dr PAWEŁ GORYŃSKI; publs *Druk Bibliofilski 'Hygeia'* (all irregular), *Problemy Higieny*, *Problemy Higieny Pracy*.

Polskie Towarzystwo Higieny Psychicznej (Polish Mental Health Society): Targowa 59/16, 03-729 Warsaw; tel. (22) 818-65-99; e-mail pthp@poczta.onet.pl; safeguarding the mental and moral health of the individual; f. 1935; 1,250 mems; library of 2,500 vols; Pres. ANDRZEJ BAŁANDYNOWICZ; publ. *Zdrowie Psychiczne* (quarterly).

Polskie Towarzystwo Immunologii Doswiadczalnej i Klinicznej (Polish Society for Experimental and Clinical Immunology):

ul. Garbary 15, 61-866 Poznań; tel. (61) 854-06-65; fax (61) 852-85-02; e-mail zarzad@ immuno.pl; internet www.immuno.pl; f. 1969; 500 mems; Pres. Prof. Dr hab. ANDRZEJ MACKIEWICZ; Scientific Sec. Dr hab. DARIUSZ KOWALCZYK; Technical Sec. Dr hab. PIOTR WYSOCKI; publs *Central European Journal of Immunology* (quarterly, in English), *Integryna – Biuletyn PTI* (quarterly, in Polish).

Polskie Towarzystwo Kardiologiczne (Polish Cardiological Society): ul. Stawki 3A/1, 00-193 Warsaw; tel. (22) 887-18-56; fax (22) 887-18-58; e-mail zarzad.glowny@ ptkardio.pl; internet www.ptkardio.pl; Pres. Prof. Dr hab. ADAM TORBICKI; Sec. Prof. Dr hab. TOMASZ PASIERSKI; publ. *Kardiologia Polska* (monthly); publ. *Folia Cardiologica* (monthly).

Polskie Towarzystwo Lekarskie (Polish Medical Association): Al. Ujazdowskie 24, 00-478 Warsaw; tel. and fax (22) 628-86-99; e-mail ptl@interia.pl; internet www.ptl.org .pl; f. 1951; 25,000 mems; Pres. Prof. Dr hab. med. JERZY WOY-WOJCIECHOWSKI; Secs Dr FELICJA ŁAPKIEWICZ, Dr ZBIGNIEW MILLER; publs *Polski Tygodnik Lekarski* (weekly), *Wiadomości Lekarskie* (every 2 weeks), *Przegląd Lekarski* (monthly).

Polskie Towarzystwo Medycyny Pracy (Polish Society of Occupational Medicine): ul. Teresy 8, 90-950 Łódź; tel. (42) 631-47-75; fax (42) 631-47-19; e-mail jolantaw@imp.lodz.pl; internet www.imp.lodz.pl/ptmp/ptmp.htm; f. 1969; Pres. Prof. Dr hab. RYSZARD ANDRJEZAK; Sec. Dr JOLANTA WALUSIAK; publs *Medycyna Pracy* (every 2 months), *International Journal of Occupational Medicine and Environmental Health* (quarterly, in English).

Polskie Towarzystwo Medycyny Sądowej i Kryminologii (Polish Society of Forensic Medicine and Criminology): ul. Święcickiego 6, 60-781 Poznań; tel. (61) 869-91-81; fax (61) 866-21-58; e-mail ZMS@amp .edu.pl; Pres. Prof. Dr hab. ZYGMUNT PRZYBYLSKI; publ. *Archiwum Medycyny Sądowej i Kryminologii* (quarterly).

Polskie Towarzystwo Medycyny Społecznej i Zdrowia Publicznego (Polish Society of Social Medicine and Public Health): ul. Chodźki 1, 20-093 Lublin; tel. (81) 740-57-53; fax (81) 740-57-52; e-mail mchbt@eskulap.am.lublin.pl; f. 1916; 1,800 mems; Pres. Prof. Dr hab. n. med. LESZEK WDOWIAK; publ. *Problemy Medycyny Społecznej* (Problems in Social Medicine, 2 or 3 a year).

Polskie Towarzystwo Medycyny Sportowej (Polish Society of Sports Medicine): POB 55, 00-968 Warsaw; ul. Marymoncka 34, 00-968 Warsaw; tel. (22) 834-40-01; e-mail sekretariat@ptms.org.pl; internet www.ptms .org.pl; f. 1937; Pres. Prof. ARTUR DZIAK; Sec. WOJCIECH DRYGAS; publ. *Medycyna Sportowa* (quarterly).

Polskie Towarzystwo Nauk Żywieniowych (Polish Society of Nutritional Sciences): ul. Nowoursynowska 159C, 02-776 Warsaw; tel. and fax (22) 59-37-123; e-mail senger@alpha.sggw.waw.pl; f. 1980; 300 mems; Pres. Prof. Dr hab. ANNA GRONOWSKA-SENGER; Sec. Dr JERZY BERTRANDT; publ. *Polish Journal of Food and Nutrition Sciences* (4 a year).

Polskie Towarzystwo Neurochirurgów (Polish Society of Neurosurgeons): ul. Żeromskiego 113, 90-549 Łódź; tel. (42) 639-35-51; f. 1964; 279 mems; Pres. Prof. Dr hab. ANDRZEJ RADEK; publ. *Neurologia i Neurochirurgia Polska* (every 2 months).

Polskie Towarzystwo Neurologiczne (Polish Neurological Society): ul. Jaczewskiego 8, 20-957 Lublin; tel. (81) 724-47-20; fax (81) 742-55-34; e-mail neurolog@

asklepios.am.lublin.pl; internet www .neurologiapolska.pl; f. 1934; Pres. Prof. ZBIGNIEW STELMASIAK; Sec. ANNA SZCZPAŃSKA-SZEREJ; publ. *Neurologia i Neurochirurgia Polska* (every 2 months).

Polskie Towarzystwo Onkologiczne (Polish Oncological Society): ul. Garncarska 11, 31-115 Cracow; tel. and fax (12) 422-87-60; e-mail pto@io.gliwice.pl; internet www.pto.io .gliwice.pl; f. 1921; 720 mems; Pres. Prof. Dr hab. MARIAN REINFUSS; Sec. Prof. Dr hab. JAN KULPA; publ. *Nowotwory* (quarterly).

Polskie Towarzystwo Ortopedyczne i Traumatologiczne (Polish Orthopaedic and Traumatological Society): Plac Medyków 1, 41-200 Sosnowiec; tel. (32) 368-25-31; fax (32) 368-20-44; internet www.ptoitr.pl; f. 1928; Pres. Prof. Dr hab. TADEUSZ SZYMON GAŹDZIK; Sec. Dr MAREK BOŻEK; publs *Chirurgia Narządów Ruchu i Ortopedia Polska* (6 a year), *Kwartalnik Ortopedyczny* (4 a year).

Polskie Towarzystwo Patologów (Polish Society of Pathologists): ul. Unii Lubelskiej 1, 71-252 Szczecin; tel. and fax (91) 487-00-32; e-mail polpat@ams.edu.pl; internet www .pol-pat.pl; f. 1958; 581 mems; Pres. Prof. Dr hab. WENANCJUSZ DOMAGAŁA; Sec. Dr ELŻBIETA URASIŃSKA; publ. *Patologia Polska* (quarterly, in English).

Polskie Towarzystwo Pediatryczne (Polish Paediatric Society): ul. Sporna 36/50, 91-738 Łódź; tel. (42) 617-29-29; fax (42) 617-28-82; e-mail ptpzg@csk.am.lodz.pl; internet csk .am.lodz.pl/ptpzg; f. 1908; 4,500 mems; Pres. Prof. Dr hab. KRYSTYNA WĄSOWSKA-KRÓLIKOWSKA; Sec. Prof. Dr hab. JERZY STAŃCZYK; publs *Pediatria Polska* (monthly), *Przegląd Pediatryczny* (quarterly).

Polskie Towarzystwo Pielęgniarskie (Polish Nursing Association): Reymonta 8/12, 01-842 Warsaw; tel. and fax (22) 663-63-45; e-mail zgptpiel@wp.pl; internet www .zgptpiel.waw.pl; f. 1924, revived 1957; 6,500 mems; library of 3,000 vols; Pres. KRYSTYNA WOLSKA-LIPIEC; Sec. ELŻBIETA CHRÓŚCICKA; publ. *Biuletyn Polskiego Towarzystwa Pielęgniarskiego* (quarterly).

Polskie Towarzystwo Psychiatryczne (Polish Psychiatric Association): Al. Sobieskiego 1/9, 02-957 Warsaw; tel. and fax (22) 842-40-87; e-mail wciorka@ipin.edu.pl; internet www.psychiatria.org.pl; f. 1920; 1,400 mems; Pres. Prof. Dr JACEK WCIÓRKA; publs *Psychoterapia* (quarterly), *Psychiatria Polska* (every 2 months), *Archives of Psychiatry and Psychotherapy* (4 a year).

Polskie Towarzystwo Stomatologiczne (Polish Dental Association): ul. Krakowska 26, 50-425 Wrocław; tel. (71) 792-40-98; fax (71) 792-40-99; e-mail paradont@stom.am .wroc.pl; internet www.pts.net.pl; f. 1951; 8,000 mems; Pres. Prof. Dr hab. MAREK ZIĘTEK; Sec. Dr MAŁGORZATA RADWAN-OCZKO; publs *Czasopismo Stomatologiczne* (monthly), *Protetyka Stomatologiczna* (every 2 months), *Dental and Medical Problems* (quarterly), *Dental Forum* (2 a year).

Polskie Towarzystwo Toksykologiczne (Polish Toxicological Society): POB 199, 90-950 Łódź; ul. Sw. Teresy od Dzieciątka Jezus 8, 90-950 Łódź; tel. (42) 631-45-02; fax (42) 656-83-31; e-mail impx@imp.lodz.pl; internet www.imp.lodz.pl/nowy_pttox; f. 1978; 305 mems; Pres. Prof. Dr hab. KONRAD RYDZYŃSKI; Sec. Dr JOLANTA GROMADZIŃSKA; publ. *Acta Poloniae Toxicologica* (2 a year).

Polskie Towarzystwo Urologiczne (Polish Urological Society): ul. Burszynowa 2, 04-749 Warsaw; tel. and fax (22) 815-68-61; e-mail info@pturol.org.pl; internet www .pturol.org.pl; f. 1949; 800 mems; Pres. Prof. Dr hab. ANDRZEJ BORÓWKA; Sec. Prof.

ROMUALD ZDROJOWY; publs *Urologia Polska* (4 a year), *Przegląd Urologiczny* (6 a year).

Polskie Towarzystwo Walki z Kalectwem (Polish Society for Rehabilitation of the Disabled): ul. Oleandrów 4 m. 10, 00-629 Warsaw; tel. and fax (22) 825-70-50; e-mail twk@idn.org.pl; internet twk.idn.org.pl; f. 1960; popularizing progressive ideas in prophylaxis and changing social attitudes towards the disabled; Pres. Dr PIOTR JANASZEK; Sec. Dr ZBIGNIEW KAŹMIERAK; publ. *Life of the Polish Society for Rehabilitation of the Disabled Information Bulletin*.

Stowarzyszenie Neuropatologów Polskich (Association of Polish Neuropathologists): ul. Pawińskiego 5, 02-106 Warsaw; tel. (61) 661-92-34; fax (61) 661-98-12; e-mail jszymas@ampat.amu.edu.pl; internet snp .amu.edu.pl; f. 1964; 51 mems; Pres. Prof. Dr JANUSZ SZYMAŚ; Sec. Dr HALINA WEINRAUDER; publ. *Folia Neuropathologica* (quarterly).

Towarzystwo Chirurgów Polskich (Society of Polish Surgeons): ul. Banacha 1A, 02-097 Warsaw; tel. and fax (22) 658-36-62; e-mail tchp@mp.pl; internet tchp.org.pl; f. 1889; 3,150 mems; Pres. Prof. ZBIGNIEW PUCHALSKI; Sec.-Gen. Prof. MAREK KRAWCZYK; publ. *Polski Przegląd Chirurgiczny* (monthly).

Towarzystwo Internistów Polskich (Polish Society of Internal Medicine): ul. Ziołowa 45/47, 40-635 Katowice; tel. (32) 359-82-90; fax (32) 202-99-33; e-mail ekucharz@slam .katowice.pl; internet tip.org.pl; f. 1906 to advance knowledge of internal medicine, and represent Polish internal surgeons; organizes Congress (every 4 years), annual Nat. Educational Conference on Internal Medicine and Polish–Slovak Conference on Internal Medicine; 6,000 mems; Pres. Prof. EUGENIUSZ J. KUCHARZ; Sec. Dr ANNA KOTULSKA; publ. *Polskie Archiwum Medycyny Wewnętrznej* (Polish Archives of Internal Medicine, monthly, in English).

NATURAL SCIENCES
Biological Sciences

Polskie Towarzystwo Biochemiczne (Polish Biochemical Society): ul. Pasteura 3, 02-093 Warsaw; tel. (22) 589-23-52; fax (22) 589-24-99; e-mail ptbioch@nencki.gov.pl; internet www.ptbioch.edu.pl; f. 1958; 1,200 mems; Pres. Prof. LECH WOJTCZAK; Sec. Prof. SLAWOMIR PIKULA; publs *Acta Biochimica Polonica* (online, 4 a year), *Postępy Biochemii* (Advances in Biochemistry, 4 a year).

Polskie Towarzystwo Biofizyczne (Polish Biophysical Society): ul. Chałubińskiego 10, 50-368 Wrocław; tel. (71) 784-14-15; fax (71) 784-00-88; e-mail hendrich@biofiz.am.wroc .pl; internet www.ptbf.am.wroc.pl; f. 1972; 250 mems; Pres. Prof. Dr hab. MARIA KOTER-MICHALAK; Sec. Dr ANETA KOCEVA-CHYLA; publ. *Current Topics in Biophysics* (2 a year, in English, supplement in Polish).

Polskie Towarzystwo Biometryczne (Polish Biometrical Society): Agricultural University, Wojska Polskiego 28, 60-637 Poznan; tel. and fax (61) 848-71-40; e-mail smejza@owl.au.poznan.pl; f. 1961; 230 mems; biometry, applied mathematical statistics in medicine, agriculture, biology, etc.; Pres. Prof. Dr hab. STANISŁAW MEJZA; Sec. Dr DANUTA KACHLICKA; publs *Listy Biometryczne – Biometrical Letters* (2 a year), *Colloquium Biometryczne* (annually).

Polskie Towarzystwo Botaniczne (Polish Botanical Society): Al. Ujazdowskie 4, 00-478 Warsaw; f. 1922; 1,320 mems; library of 24,651 vols; Pres. Prof. Dr JAN J. RYBAZYŃSKI; publs *Acta Agrobotanica*, *Acta Mycologica*, *Acta Societatis Botanicorum Poloniae*, *Biuletyn Ogrodów Botanicznych Muzeów i*

Zbiorów, *Monographiae Botanicae*, *Rocznik Sekcji Dendrologicznej Pol. Tow. Bot.*, *Wiadomości Botaniczne*.

Polskie Towarzystwo Entomologiczne (Polish Entomological Society): ul. Dąbrowskiego 159, 60-594 Poznań; tel. (61) 848-79-16; e-mail carabus@au.poznan.pl; internet pte .au.poznan.pl; f. 1923; theoretical and applied entomology; 700 mems; library of 11,000 vols; Pres. Prof. Dr hab. JANUSZ NOWACKI; Sec. Dr inż PAWEŁ SIENKIEWICZ; publs *Polskie Pismo Entomologiczne-Bulletin Entomologique de Pologne* (4 a year), *Klucze do oznaczania owadów Polski* (Keys to Identification of Polish Insects, irregular), *Wiadomości Entomologiczne* (Entomological News, 4 a year).

Polskie Towarzystwo Fitopatologiczne (Polish Phytopathological Society): ul. Wojska Polskiego 71c, 60-625 Poznań; tel. (61) 848-77-08; fax (61) 848-77-11; e-mail mmanka@owl.au.poznan.pl; internet www .au.poznan.pl/ptfit; f. 1971; 380 mems; Pres. Prof. Dr hab. MAŁGORZATA MAŃKA; Sec. Prof. Dr hab. MONIKA KOZŁOWSKA; publ. *Phytopathologia Polonica* (4 a year, in English).

Polskie Towarzystwo Genetyczne (Polish Genetics Society): ul. Ciszewskiego 8 , 02-786 Warsaw; tel. and fax (22) 853-09-31; fax (22) 853-09-31; e-mail k_charon@hotmail.com; internet jay.au.poznan.pl/PTG; f. 1963; 762 mems; Pres. Prof. Dr hab. MAREK SWITONSKI; Sec. Prof. Dr hab. KRYSTYNA MAŁGORZATA CHARON; publ. *Genetica Polonica* (4 a year).

Polskie Towarzystwo Hydrobiologiczne (Polish Hydrobiological Society): ul. Banacha 2, 02-095 Warsaw; tel. (22) 554-64-43; fax (22) 554-64-26; e-mail igor@hydro.biol.uw .edu.pl; internet www.pth.home.pl; f. 1959; 12 brs nationally; 500 mems; Pres. Prof. Dr hab. ANDRZEJ GÓRNIAK; Sec. Dr JAN IGOR RYBAK; publs *Wiadomości Hydrobiologiczne* (in quarterly *Wiadomości Ekologiczne*), *Fauna Słodkowodna Polski*.

Polskie Towarzystwo Mikrobiologów (Polish Society of Microbiologists): ul. Chocimska 24, 00-791 Warsaw; tel. (22) 542-12-38; fax (22) 542-13-07; internet www .microbiology.pl; f. 1927; 800 mems; Pres. Prof. DANUTA DZIERŻANOWSKA; Sec. Dr JOLANTA SZYCH; publs *Journal of Polish Microbiology* (English, quarterly), *Medycyna Doświadczalna i Mikrobiologia* (Experimental Medicine and Microbiology, Polish, quarterly), *Postępy Mikrobiologii* (Advances in Microbiology, Polish, quarterly).

Polskie Towarzystwo Parazytologiczne (Polish Parasitological Society): Twarda 51–55, 00-818 Warsaw; tel. (22) 697-89-95; fax (22) 620-62-27; internet www.ptparasit.org .pl; f. 1948; 390 mems; Pres. Doc. dr hab. BOŻENA MOSKWA; publs *Wiadomości Parazytologiczne* (quarterly), *Katalog Fauny Pasozytniczej Polski* (irregular), *Monografie Parazytologiczne* (irregular).

Polskie Towarzystwo Zoologiczne (Polish Zoological Society): Sienkiewicza 21, 50-335 Wrocław; tel. (71) 375-40-49; fax (71) 322-50-44; e-mail ptzol@biol.uni.wroc.pl; f. 1935; 750 mems; library of 55,000 vols; Pres. Dr hab. Prof. MARTA BOROWIEC; Sec. ANDRZEJ JABŁOŃSKI; publs *Zoologica Poloniae*, *Przegląd Zoologiczny*, *The Ring* (quarterly), *Notatki Ornitologiczne*.

Mathematical Sciences

Polskie Towarzystwo Matematyczne (Polish Mathematical Society): ul. Sniadeckich 8, 00-950 Warsaw; tel. (22) 629-95-92; e-mail zgptm@impan.gov.pl; internet www .impan.gov.pl/PTM; f. 1919; 2,080 mems; Pres. Prof. Dr KAZIMIERZ GOEBEL; publs *Annales Societatis Mathematicae Polonae: Series I Commentationes Mathematicae, Ser-*

ies II *Wiadomości Matematyczne* (Mathematical News), *Series III Matematyka Stosowana* (Applied Mathematics), *Series IV Fundamenta Informaticae*, *Series V Dydaktyka Matematyki* (Didactics of Mathematics), *Popularny Miesięcznik Matematyczno-Fizyczno-Astronomiczny DELTA* (Mathematical and Physical popular monthly).

Polskie Towarzystwo Statystyczne (Polish Statistical Association): Al. Niepodległości 208, 00-925 Warsaw; tel. (22) 625-42-89; e-mail czedoman@krysia.uni.lodz.pl; f. 1912; statistics, informatics, economics and econometrics; *c.* 1,000 mems; Pres. Prof. CZESŁAW DOMAŃSKI; Sec. JÓZEF GWOZDOWSKI; publs *Biuletyn Informacyjny* (Bulletin of Information, quarterly), *Wiadomości Statystyczne* (Statistics in Transition, journal, monthly).

Physical Sciences

Polskie Towarzystwo Astronomiczne (Polish Astronomical Society): ul. Bartycka 18, 00-716 Warsaw; tel. (22) 841-00-41 ext. 146; fax (22) 841-00-46; e-mail pta@pta.edu.pl; internet www.pta.edu.pl/pta; f. 1923; 219 mems; Pres. Prof. Dr hab. ANDRZEJ WOSZCZYK; Sec. Dr ADAM MICHALEC; publs *Urania – Postępy Astronomii* (Progress in Astronomy), *Delta*.

Polskie Towarzystwo Chemiczne (Polish Chemical Society): ul. Freta 16, 00-227 Warsaw; tel. (22) 831-13-04; fax (22) 831-13-04; e-mail zgptchem@chemix.ch.pw.edu.pl; internet www.ptchem.lodz.pl; f. 1919; 2,350 mcms; library of 2,400 vols; Pres. Prof. JERZY KONARSKI; Sec. Prof. ROMAN MIERZECKI; publs *Wiadomości Chemiczne* (Chemical News), *Polish Journal of Chemistry*, *Orbital* (Society News, 6 a year), *Chemical Analysis* (6 a year).

Polskie Towarzystwo Fizyczne (Polish Physical Society): ul. Hoża 69, 00-681 Warsaw; tel. and fax (22) 621-26-68; e-mail ptf@fuw.edu.pl; internet ptf.fuw.edu.pl; f. 1920; 1,800 mems; library of 1,300 vols; Pres. Prof. Dr hab. MACIEJ KOLWAS; Gen. Sec. Doc. HELENA BIAŁKOWSKA; publs *Postępy Fizyki* (Advances in Physics, every 2 months), *Acta Physica Polonica A and B* (monthly, in English, French, German and Russian), *Reports on Mathematical Physics* (every 2 months, in English), *Delta* (monthly, in Polish).

Polskie Towarzystwo Geofizyczne (Polish Geophysical Society): ul. Podleśna 61, 01-673 Warsaw; tel. (22) 569-45-62; f. 1947; development of geophysical sciences and their popularization; 450 mems; library of 5,000 vols; Pres. Dr ALFRED DUBICKI; Sec.-Gen. Dr JERZY SZKUTNICKI; publ. *Przegląd Geofizyczny* (Geophysical Review, quarterly).

Polskie Towarzystwo Geologiczne (Polish Geological Society): Oleandry 2a, 30-063 Cracow; tel. (12) 633-20-41; fax (12) 22-63-06; e-mail ptg@ing.uj.edu.pl; internet www.uj.edu.pl/ING/PTG; f. 1921; 1,004 mems; library of 9,213 books, 24,591 journals; Pres. Dr hab. Inż. JACEK MATYSZKIEWICZ; Sec. Dr inż. JANUSZ MAGIERA; publ. *Annales Societatis Geologorum Poloniae/Rocznik Polskiego Towarzystwa Geologicznego/ Annals of the Polish Geological Society* (3 a year).

Polskie Towarzystwo Miłośników Astronomii (Polish Amateur Astronomical Society): ul. św. Tomasza 30/8, 31-027 Cracow; tel. (12) 422-38-92; e-mail zg-ptma@astronomia.pl; internet ptma-zg.astronomia.pl; f. 1919; 3,000 mems; amateur observations, instrument-making, popularization of astronomy; Pres. Prof. ZBIGNIEW KOWALSKI; Sec. Dr HENRYK BRANCEWICZ; publ. *Urania* (monthly) and reports.

Polskie Towarzystwo Mineralogiczne (Mineralogical Society of Poland): Al. Mickiewicza 30, 30-059 Cracow; tel. (12) 617-24-36; fax (12) 633-43-30; e-mail szydlak@uci.agh.edu.pl; internet uranos.cto.us.edu.pl/~ptmin; f. 1969; 195 mems; Pres. Prof. PIOTR WYSZOMIRSKI; Sec. Dr TADEUSZ SZYDŁAK; publ. *Mineralogia Polonica* (2 a year).

Polskie Towarzystwo Nautologiczne (Polish Nautological Society): ul. Sienkiewicza 3, 81-374 Gdynia; tel. and fax (58) 620-49-75; f. 1958; history of human involvement with the sea; 150 mems; library of 2,800 vols; Pres. Prof. Dr DANIEL DUDA; Sec. Dr ELŻBIETA SKUPIŃSKA-DYBEK; publ. *Nautologia* (quarterly).

PHILOSOPHY AND PSYCHOLOGY

Polskie Towarzystwo Filozoficzne (Polish Philosophical Society): Nowy Swiat 72, p.160, Warsaw; tel. 26-52-31, ext. 159; f. 1904; study of all traditional philosophical disciplines; 826 mems; library of 7,200 vols; Pres. Prof. Dr WŁADYSŁAW STRÓŻEWSKI; Sec. Doc. Dr hab. BARBARA MARKIEWICZ; publ. *Ruch Filozoficzny* (Philosophical Movement, quarterly).

Polskie Towarzystwo Psychologiczne (Polish Psychological Association): Stawki 5/7, 00-183 Warsaw; tel. and fax (22) 831-13-68; e-mail ptp@engram.psych.uw.edu.pl; internet www.ptp.org.pl; f. 1948; 2,000 mems; Pres. Dr MAŁGORZATA TOEPLITZ-WINIEWSKA; Gen. Sec. BEATA KOZAK; publs *Przegląd Psychologiczny* (Psychological Review, quarterly), *Nowiny Psychologiczne* (Psychological Newsletter, quarterly).

RELIGION, SOCIOLOGY AND ANTHROPOLOGY

Polskie Towarzystwo Antropologiczne (Polish Anthropological Society): Dept of Anthropology, University of Wrocław, ul. Kuźnicza 35, 50-138 Wrocław; tel. (71) 375-25-18; e-mail pta@antropo.uni.wroc.pl; f. 1925; 317 mems; library: *c.* 10,000 vols; Pres. Prof. Dr DANUTA KORNAFEL; Sec. Dr BARBARA KWIATKOWSKA; publ. *Przegląd Antropologiczny* (Anthropological Review, annually).

Polskie Towarzystwo Kryminalistyczne (Polish Society of Criminologists): ul. Zgoda 11 lok. 300, 00-018 Warsaw; tel. (22) 692-43-85; fax (22) 692-83-81; e-mail biuro@kryminalistyka.pl; internet www.kryminalistyka.pl; f. 1973; forensic science; 350 mems; Pres. Prof. Dr hab. MARIUSZ KULICKI; Sec. Mgr inż. TOMASZ BEDNAREK; publ. *Z Zagadnień Współczesnej Kryminalistyki* (irregular).

Polskie Towarzystwo Ludoznawcze (Polish Ethnographical Society): Szczytnicka 11, 50-382 Wrocław; tel. (71) 321-16-10; fax (71) 321-16-14; e-mail ptl@free.ngo.pl; f. 1895; cultural anthropology, folklore; 680 mems; library of 41,432 vols; Pres. DOROTA SIMONIDES; Sec. JERZY ADAMCZEWSKI; publs *Lud* (annually), *Atlas Polskich Strojów Ludowych*, *Prace i Materiały Etnograficzne*, *Prace Etnologiczne*, *Literatura Ludowa* (every 2 months), *Archiwum Etnograficzne*, *Biblioteka Popularna*, *Dzieła Wszystkie O. Kolberga*, *Łódzkie Studia Etnograficzne* (annually), *Biblioteka Zesłańca*, *Komentarze do Polskiego Atlasu Etnograficznego*, *Dziedzictwo Kulturowe*, *Biblioteka Literatury Ludowej*.

Polskie Towarzystwo Orientalistyczne (Polish Oriental Society): c/o Instytut Orientalistyczny UW, ul. Krakowskie Przedmieście 26/28, 00-927 Warsaw; tel. (22) 552-03-53; e-mail pto.orient@uw.edu.pl; internet www.orient.uw.edu.pl/~pto; f. 1922; 124 mems; Pres. MAREK MEJOR; Sec.-Gen. MARIA KOZŁOWSKA; publ. *Przegląd Orientalistyczny* (quarterly).

Polskie Towarzystwo Religioznawcze (Polish Society for the Science of Religions): 30 skr. poczt. 151, Jaracza 1 Lok. 6, 00-959 Warsaw; tel. (22) 625-26-42; e-mail prof2aw@yahoo.com; f. 1958; history, theory, methodology, sociology, psychology of religions; 165 mems; Pres. Prof. Dr hab. ZBIGNIEW STACHOWSKI; Scientific Sec. Prof. Dr hab. ANDRZEJ WÓJTOWICZ; publ. *Przegląd Religioznawczy* (quarterly).

Polskie Towarzystwo Semiotyczne (Polish Semiotics Society): c/o Dept of Logical Semiotics, Warsaw University, ul. Krakowskie Przedmieście 3, 00-927 Warsaw; tel. (22) 826-54-18; fax (22) 826-57-34; e-mail jerzy.pelc@mercury.ci.uw.edu.pl; f. 1968; all aspects of semiotics: signs, sign systems, information, communication, indirect cognition; applied semiotics; 140 mems; library of 1,500 vols; Pres. Prof. Dr JERZY PELC; Sec Dr. WIESŁAWA ŻANDAROWSKA; publs *Polski Biuletyn Semiotyczny* (annually), *Sygnały Semiotyczne*.

Polskie Towarzystwo Socjologiczne (Polish Sociological Association): ul. Nowy Swiat 72, 00-330 Warsaw; tel. (22) 826-77-37; fax (22) 826-77-37; e-mail pts@ifispan.waw.pl; internet www.pts.org.pl; f. 1957; 1,040 mems; Pres. Prof. WLODZIMIERZ WESOTOWSKI; Sec. Prof. KRYSTYNA JANICKA; publs *Polish Sociological Review* (4 a year), *Informacja Bieżąca* (Current News, quarterly).

Polskie Towarzystwo Teologiczne (Polish Theological Society): ul. Kanonicza 3, 31-002 Cracow; tel. (12) 422-56-90; e-mail zarzad@ptt.net.pl; internet www.ptt.net.pl; f. 1924; Pres. Rev. Dr hab. KAZIMIERZ PANUŚ; Sec. Rev. Mgr KAZIMIERZ MOSKAŁA; publ. *Ruch Biblijny i Liturgiczny* (quarterly).

Towarzystwo Naukowe Organizacji i Kierownictwa (Scientific Society for Organization and Management): ul. Koszykowa 6, Box C, 00-564 Warsaw; tel. (22) 625-44-85; fax (22) 629-21-27; e-mail bzg@tnoik.org; internet www.tnoik.org; f. 1925, 32,000 individual mems, 5,000 collective mems; library of 15,000 vols; Pres. Prof. Dr hab. RYSZARD BOROWIECKI; Gen. Sec. Mgr WŁODZIMIERZ HAUSNER; publ. *Przegląd Organizacji* (monthly).

TECHNOLOGY

Akademia Inżynierska w Polsce (Academy of Engineering in Poland): ul. Czackiego 3/5, 00-950 Warsaw; tel. (22) 828-64-45; fax (22) 827-29-49; e-mail aip@aip.medianet.pl; internet www.aip.medianet.pl; f. 1992; Pres. Prof. Dr hab. inz. BOGDAN JERZY NEY; Gen. Sec. Prof. Dr inz. JANUSZ DYDUCH.

Federacja Stowarzyszeń Naukowo-Technicznych–Naczelna Organizacja Techniczna (FSNT-NOT) (Polish Federation of Engineering Associations): ul. Czackiego 3/5, 00-950 Warsaw; tel. (22) 826-74-61; fax (22) 827-29-49; e-mail notdgz@not.org.pl; internet not.org.pl; 230,000 mems; Pres. Dr WOJCIECH RATYŃSKI; Sec.-Gen. KAZIMIERZ WAWRZYNIAK; publ. *Przegląd Techniczny* (weekly).

Polskie Towarzystwo Akustyczne (Polish Acoustical Society): ul. J. Śmidowicza 69, 81-103 Gdynia; tel. (58) 626-28-72; fax (58) 625-48-46; e-mail ekoz@amw.gdynia.pl; internet www.acoustics.org.pl; Pres. Prof. Dr hab. inż. EUGENIUSZ KOZACZKA; Sec.-Gen. Dr inż. GRAZYNA GRELOWSKA; publ. *Archives of Acoustics* (continuous).

Polskie Towarzystwo Astronautyczne (Polish Astronautical Society): Bartycka 18a, Room 137, 00-716 Warsaw; tel. (22) 840-37-66 ext. 214; fax (22) 840-31-31; e-mail

poczta@ptastronaut.org.pl; internet www
.ptastronaut.org.pl; f. 1954; 86 mems; scientific, educational, and popular astronautics,
planetology, bio-astronautics, space physics,
CETI, and space law; Pres. ZBIGNIEW KŁOS;
Exec. Sec. ANDRZEJ KOTARSKI; publ. *Postępy
Astronautyki* (Progress in Astronautics, yearbook).

**Polskie Towarzystwo Elektrotechniki
Teoretycznej i Stosowanej** (Polish Society
for Theoretical and Applied Electrical Engineering): ul. Koszykowa 75, Politechnika
Warszawska, Wydz. Elektryczny, Gmach
Electrotechniki p. 310, 00-662 Warsaw; tel.
and fax (22) 625-67-25; e-mail ptetis@ien.pw
.edu.pl; internet www.ee.pw.edu.pl/ptetis; f.
1961; brs in 13 major towns; 750 mems; Pres.
Prof. Dr hab. inż. KRZYSZTOF KLUSZCZYŃSKI;
Gen. Sec. Dr inż. WŁODZIMIERZ KAŁAT.

Polskie Towarzystwo Ergonomiczne
(Polish Ergonomics Society): ul. Narbutta
85 p. 103, 02-524 Warsaw; tel. and fax (22)
660-82-09; e-mail jerzy.s.marcinkowski@put
.poznan.pl; internet www.ergonomia-polska
.com; f. 1977; Pres. Dr JERZY S. MARCIN-
KOWSKI; Gen. Sec. Prof. Dr hab. med. LUD-
MIŁA BORODULIN-NADZIEJA; publ. *Ergonomia*
(2 a year).

Polskie Towarzystwo Mechaniki Teoretycznej i Stosowanej (Polish Society of
Theoretical and Applied Mechanics): Dept of
Civil Engineering, Warsaw University of
Technology, Al. Armii Ludowej 16, p. 650,
00-637 Warsaw; tel. (22) 825-71-80; fax (22)
825-71-80; e-mail biuro@ptmts.org.pl;
internet www.ptmts.org.pl; f. 1958; 976
mems; brs in 17 other towns; Pres. Prof. Dr
JÓZEF KUBIK; Gen. Sec. Dr WIESŁAW
NAGÓRKO; publ. *Journal of Theoretical and
Applied Mechanics* (4 a year).

Research Institutes
GENERAL

Instytut Kultury (Institute of Culture): ul.
Świetojańska 2, 00-288 Warsaw; tel. (22) 831-
76-98; fax (22) 831-88-98; e-mail instkult@
warman.com.pl; f. 1974; library of 35,000
vols; Dir JAN STANISLAW WOJCLECHOWSKI;
publ. *Prace Instytutu Kultury*.

**Instytut Podstaw Inżynierii Środowiska
PAN** (Institute of Environmental Engineering): ul. M. Skłodowskiej-Curie 34, 41-819
Zabrze; tel. (32) 271-64-81; fax (32) 271-74-
70; e-mail ipis@ipis.zabrze.pl; internet www
.ipis.zabrze.pl; f. 1961; attached to Polish
Acad. of Sciences; air and water pollution
control, land reclamation, energy conservation, influence of pollutants on plants; library
of 14,000 vols; Dir Prof. Dr hab. inż.
CZESŁAWA-ROSIK DULEWSKA (acting); Dir
Doc. Dr hab. inż. JOANNA KYZIOŁ (acting);
publs *Archiwum Ochrony Srodowiska*
(Archives of Environmental Protection, quarterly, with summaries in English and Russian), *Prace i Studia* (irregular).

Instytut Slawistyki PAN (Slavonic Institute): ul. J. Bartoszewicza 1 B m. 17, 00-337
Warsaw; tel. and fax (22) 826-76-88; e-mail
ispan@ispan.waw.pl; internet www.ispan
.waw.pl; f. 1954; attached to Polish Acad. of
Sciences; 88 mems; library of 115,000 vols;
Dir Prof. Dr hab. ZBIGNIEW GREN; publs *Acta
Baltico-Slavica*, *Studia z Filologii Polskiej i
Słowiańskiej*, *Slavia Meridionalis*, *Studia
Literaria Polono-Slavica*.

Instytut Sportu (Institute of Sport): ul.
Trylogii 2/16, 01-982 Warsaw; tel. (22) 834-
08-12; fax (22) 835-09-77; e-mail insp@insp
.waw.pl; internet www.insp.pl/default.htm; f.
1978; library of 6,130 vols; Dir Prof. Dr hab.

RYSZARD GRUCZA; publ. *Biology of Sport* (4 a
year).

Zakład Badań Narodowościowych PAN
(Centre for the Study of Nationalities): Stary
Rynek 78/79, 61-772 Poznań; tel. and fax (61)
852-09-50; e-mail zbnpan@man.poznan.pl; f.
1973; attached to Polish Acad. of Sciences;
library of 1,800 vols; Dir Prof. Dr hab.
WOJCIECH J. BURSZTA; publ. *Sprawy Narodo-
wościowe* (Issues of Nationality, 2 a year).

Zakład Krajów Pozaeuropejskich PAN
(Centre for Studies on Non-European Countries): Nowy Swiat 72, 00-330 Warsaw; tel.
(22) 826-63-56; fax (22) 826-63-56; e-mail
csnec@zkppan.waw.pl; f. 1978; attached to
Polish Acad. of Sciences; library of 16,000
vols; Dir Dr JERZY ZDANOWSKI; publs *Hemi-
spheres* (in English and French, annually),
Acta Asiatica Varsoviensia (in English and
French, annually).

AGRICULTURE, FISHERIES AND
VETERINARY SCIENCE

**Instytut Agrofizyki im. Bohdana Dobr-
zańskiego PAN** (Institute of Agrophysics):
ul. Doświaczalna 4, 20-290 Lublin; tel. (81)
744-50-61; fax (81) 744-50-67; e-mail agrof@
demeter.ipan.lublin.pl; internet www.ipan
.lublin.pl; f. 1968; attached to Polish Acad. of
Sciences; library of 3,000 vols; Dir Prof. Dr
hab. RYSZARD WALCZAK; publs *Acta Agrophy-
sica* (2 a year), *International Agrophysics*
(quarterly), *Polish Journal of Soil Science* (2
a year).

Instytut Badawczy Leśnictwa (Forestry
Research Institute): ul. Bitwy Warszawskiej
1920 r. 3, 00-973 Warsaw; tel. (22) 823-45-65;
fax (22) 822-49-35; e-mail ibl@ibles.waw.pl;
internet www.ibles.waw.pl; f. 1930; comprises 14 scientific sections covering all
aspects of forestry, especially factors of
environment, silviculture and selection,
tree-planting, forest economics, management, forest work organization, protection,
forest plant pathology, game management,
water economy, logging mechanization and
transport; main documentation and information centre of forestry; brs at Cracow,
Białowieża and Katowice; library of 69,000
vols; Dir Prof. Dr hab. eng. A. KLOCEK; publs
Folia Forestalia Polonica (Series A – Forestry, in English, irregular), *Leśne Prace
Badawcze* (Forest Research Papers, 4 a
year), *Notatnik Naukowy*, *Nowości Piśmiennictwa Leśnego* (monthly).

**Instytut Biotechnologii Przemysłu
Rolno-Spożywczego** (Institute of Agricultural and Food Biotechnology): ul. Rakowiecka 36, 02-532 Warsaw; tel. (22) 849-02-
24; fax (22) 849-04-26; e-mail ibprs@ibprs.pl;
internet www.ibprs.pl; f. 1949; biotechnology: improvement of microbial strains, fermentation processes (beer, wine, spirits,
organic acids), malt, yeasts, enzymatic preparations, microbial preparations; technology of fruit and vegetable products, food
analysis, food concentration, storage and
processing of grain, bread and pastry baking;
culture collection of industrial micro-organisms; library of 22,000 vols; Dir Prof. ROMAN
GRZYBOWSKI; publ. *Prace Instytutów i Labor-
atoriów Badawczych Przemysłu Spożywczego*
(in Polish with summaries in English,
annually).

**Instytut Budownictwa, Mechanizacji i
Elektryfikacji Rolnictwa** (Institute for
Building, Mechanization and Electrification
in Agriculture): ul. Rakowiecka 32, 02-532
Warsaw; tel. (22) 49-32-31; fax (22) 49-17-37;
e-mail selian@ibmer.waw.pl; f. 1950;
research into the mechanization of farming,
economics and management, land reclamation, farm building and energy sources;
library of 47,783 vols; Dir ALEKSANDER SZEP-

TYCKI; publs *Prace NaukowoBadawcze
IBMER* (annually), *Przegląd Dokumentacyjny—Technika Rolnicza* (6 a year), *Problemy Inżynierii Rolniczej* (quarterly),
Inżynieria Rolnicza (irregular).

Instytut Celulozowo-Papierniczy (Pulp
and Paper Research Institute): ul. M. Skłodowskiej-Curie 19/27, 90-570 Łódź; tel. (42)
638-03-78; fax (42) 638-03-79; e-mail
kancelaria@icp.lodz.pl; internet www.icp
.lodz.pl; f. 1952; research in pulp, paper,
analysis and testing, protection of the environment; library of 16,000 vols; Dir Dr inż.
TOMASZ MALINOWSKI; publ. *Celuloza i
Papier—Informacja Ekspresowa* (monthly).

**Instytut Ekonomiki Rolnictwa i Gospo-
darki Żywnościowej** (Institute of Agricultural and Food Economics): ul.
Świętokrzyska 20, POB 984, 00-950 Warsaw;
tel. (22) 505-44-44; fax (22) 827-19-60; e-mail
ierigz@ierigz.waw.pl; internet www.ierigz
.waw.pl; f. 1983, fmrly Inst. of Agricultural
Economics; library of 38,000 vols; Dir Prof.
Dr ANDRZEJ KOWALSKI; publs *Zagadnienia
Ekonomiki Rolnej* (Problems of Agricultural
Economics, 6 a year), *Rynek Rolny* (Agricultural Market, monthly), *Raporty Rynkowe*
(Market Reports, 2 a year).

**Instytut Fizjologii i Żywienia Zwierząt
im. Jana Kielanowskiego PAN** (Kielanowski Institute of Animal Physiology and
Nutrition): ul. Instytucka 3, 05-110
Jabłonna; tel. (22) 782-41-75; fax (22) 774-
20-38; f. 1955; attached to Polish Acad. of
Sciences; study of nutrition of ruminants,
pigs and poultry, digestive processes, neuroendocrinology, endocrinology of reproduction; library of 5,000 vols; Dir Dr JACEK
SKOMIAT.

**Instytut Fizjologii Roślin im. Fran-
ciszka Górskiego PAN** (Institute of Plant
Physiology): ul. Niezapominajek 21, 30-239
Cracow; tel. (12) 425-18-33; fax (12) 425-18-
44; e-mail ifr@ifr-pan.krakow.pl; internet
www.ifr-pan.krakow.pl; f. 1956; attached to
Polish Acad. of Sciences; laboratories; plant
growth and development, photosynthesis,
biology of stress, metabolism of fungi; myxomycetes; Dir Prof. Dr hab. FRANCISZEK
DUBERT; publ. *Acta Physiologiae Plantarum*
(quarterly).

**Instytut Genetyki i Hodowli Zwierząt
PAN** (Institute of Genetics and Animal
Breeding): Jastrzębiec ul. Postępu 1, 05-552
Wólka Kosowska; tel. (22) 756-17-11; fax (22)
756-16-99; e-mail e.dymnicki@ighz.pl;
internet www.ighz.edu.pl/index.htm; f.
1955; attached to Polish Acad. of Sciences;
research work in animal genetics with special reference to farm animals; 130 mems;
library of 6,000 vols, 5,640 journals; Dir Prof.
EDWARD DYMNICKI; publs *Prace i Materiały
Zootechniczne* (irregular), *Animal Science
Papers and Reports* (4 a year).

Instytut Genetyki Roślin PAN (Institute
of Plant Genetics): ul. Strzeszyńska 34, 60-
479 Poznań; tel. (61) 823-35-11; fax (61) 823-
36-71; e-mail office@igr.poznan.pl; internet
www.igr.poznan.pl; f. 1961; attached to Polish Acad. of Sciences; basic genetic research
on cultivated plants, genomics, biometrics,
molecular biology, plant stresses; Dir Prof.
WOJCIECH K. SWIĘCICKI; publ. *Journal of
Applied Genetics* (quarterly).

Instytut Melioracji i Użytków Zielonych
(Institute for Land Reclamation and Grassland Farming): Falenty, 05-090 Raszyn; tel.
(22) 628-37-63; fax (22) 628-37-63; e-mail e
.kaca@imuz.edu.pl; internet www.imuz.edu
.pl; f. 1953; grassland farming, water management in agriculture, flood and drought
management, rural sanitation, land development, sustainable development of rural
areas; library of 47,200 vols and 8,900 vols

in special collections; Dir Prof Dr hab. inż. EDMUND KACA; publs *Journal of Water and Land Development* (annually), *Water – Environment – Rural Areas* (2 a year).

Instytut Meteorologii i Gospodarki Wodnej (Institute of Meteorology and Water Management): ul. Podleśna 61, 01-673 Warsaw; tel. (22) 569-42-99; fax (22) 569-43-01; e-mail sekretariat@imgw.pl; internet www .imgw.pl; f. 1973 from former State Institute of Hydrology and Meteorology and the Institute of Water Management; collections of data from 61 meteorological stations, 149 meteorological posts, 893 hydrological posts, 1,027 pluviometric posts and 100 groundwater posts; library of 98,500 vols; Dir Prof. Dr eng. JAN ZIELIŃSKI; publ. *Wiadomości Instytutu Meteorologii i Gospodarki Wodnej* (Reports, quarterly).

Instytut Nawozów Sztucznych (Fertilizers Research Institute): 24-110 Puławy; tel. (81) 887-64-44; fax (81) 887-63-36; e-mail ins@atena.ins.pulawy.pl; internet www.ins .pulawy.pl; f. 1948; research in synthesis gases and hydrogen, nitric acid and its salts, mineral fertilizers, catalysts and sorbents, derivatives of methanol and urea, supercritical carbon dioxide extraction, environmental protection, unit operations, new processes and products; library of 36,700 vols; Dir BOLESŁAW SKOWROŃSKI; publ. *Przemysł Nawozowy* (monthly).

Instytut Przemysłu Cukrowniczego (Institute of the Sugar Industry): ul. Rakowiecka 36, 02-532 Warsaw; tel. (22) 849-00-93; fax (22) 848-09-01; e-mail inspcukr@atos .warman.com.pl; internet www.orgmasz.waw .pl/w/jbr/p2.htm; f. 1898; research into all branches of the sugar industry; Raw Product, Sugar Beet, Technological, Analytical, Mechanical, Environmental Protection Depts; library of 1,500 vols; Dir ANTONI LAUDAŃSKI; publs *Informacja o wynikach produkcyjnych i danych techniczno-technologicznych przemysłu cukrowniczego* (annually), *Informacja dekadowa z przebiegu Kampanii* (9 a year), *Burak cukrowy – gazeta dla plantatorów* (irregular).

Instytut Roślin i Przetworów Zielarskich (Research Institute of Medicinal Plants): ul. Libelta 27, 61-707 Poznań; tel. (61) 852-56-16; fax (61) 852-74-63; e-mail iripz@iripz.pl; internet www.iripz.pl; f. 1947; botany, plant breeding, agrotechnology, pest control, phytochemistry, pharmaceutical analysis, technology of plant drugs, pharmacology; library of 13,000 vols; Dir Prof. Dr hab. Dr h.c. JERZY LUTOMSKI; publ. *Herba Polonica* (quarterly).

Instytut Rozwoju Wsi i Rolnictwa PAN (Institute of Rural and Agricultural Development PAS): Nowy Świat 72, 00-330 Warsaw; tel. (22) 826-63-71; fax (22) 657-27-50; e-mail irwir@irwirpan.waw.pl; internet www .irwirpan.waw.pl; f. 1971; attached to Polish Acad. of Sciences; research into the process of developing agriculture and rural society; 41 mems; library of 5,000 vols; Dir Prof. MAREK KŁODZIŃSKI; publs *Problems of Rural and Agricultural Development* (4 or 5 a year in Polish, summaries in English), *Village and Agriculture* (quarterly in Polish, annual supplement of selected papers in English).

Instytut Rybactwa Śródlądowego im. Stanisława Sakowicza (Inland Fisheries Institute): ul. Oczapowskiego 10, 10-719 Olsztyn; tel. (89) 524-01-71; fax (89) 524-05-05; e-mail irs@infish.com.pl; internet www .infish.com.pl; f. 1951; Dir Prof. Dr hab. BOGUSŁAW ZDANOWSKI; publs *Archives of Polish Fisheries* (2 a year), *Komunikaty Rybackie* (6 a year).

Instytut Sadownictwa i Kwiaciarstwa (Institute of Pomology and Floriculture): ul.

Pomologiczna 18, 96-100 Skierniewice; tel. (46) 833-20-21; fax (46) 833-32-28; e-mail isad@insad.pl; internet www.insad.pl; f. 1951; three divisions; pomology, floriculture, bee-keeping, covering field of applied research; five interdivisional laboratories: chemical, botanical, physiological, biochemical and isotopes; experimental greenhouses, phytotrone, cold storage and freezing facilities; 6 field stations; library of 37,578 vols; Dir Prof. Dr hab. DANUTA GOSZCZYŃSKA; publs *Journal of Fruit and Ornamental Plant Research* (annually), *Zeszyty Naukowe Instytutu Sadownictwa i Kwiaciarstwa* (annually), *Pszczelnicze Zeszyty Naukowe* (Bee Research Bulletin), *Sprawozdanie Roczne* (annually).

Instytut Technologii Drewna (Wood Technology Institute): ul. Winiarska 1, 60-654 Poznań; tel. (61) 849-24-00; fax (61) 822-43-72; e-mail office@itd.poznan.pl; internet www.itd.poznan.pl; f. 1952; responsible for solving problems of the wood processing industry and for developing new technical processes; library of 26,973 vols; Dir Prof. WŁADYSŁAW STRYKOWSKI; publ. *Drewno Wood* (2 a year).

Instytut Uprawy, Nawożenia i Gleboznawstwa—Państwowy Instytut Badawczy (Institute of Soil Science and Plant Cultivation—State Research Institute): Czartoryskich 8, 24-100 Puławy; tel. (81) 886-34-21; fax (81) 886-45-47; e-mail iung@iung.pulawy.pl; internet www.iung .pulawy.pl; f. 1917; pedology; utilization and protection of agricultural land; soil chemistry, plant physiology, biochemistry, microbiology, soil and crop management, production technology of cereals, forage crops, tobacco and hops, etc.; Dir Prof. Dr hab. SEWERYN KUKUŁA; publs *Pamiętnik Puławski* (2 or 3 a year), *Zalecenia Agrotechniczne* (every 5 years).

Instytut Warzywnictwa (Research Institute of Vegetable Crops): ul. Konstytucji 3 Maja 1/3, 96-100 Skierniewice; tel. (46) 833-22-11; fax (46) 833-31-86; e-mail iwarz@ inwarz.skierniewice.pl; internet www.inwarz .skierniewice.pl; f. 1964; research into the development of practical guidelines for the rational and economic development of vegetable production; Dir Prof. Dr hab. STANISŁAW KANISZEWSKI; publs *Biuletyn Warzywniczy* (Vegetable Crops Research Bulletin, 2 a year), *Nowości Warzywnicze* (Vegetable News, 2 a year).

Instytut Zootechniki (Institute of Animal Husbandry): k. Krakowa, 32-083 Balice; tel. (12) 258-81-11; fax (12) 285-67-33; e-mail izooinfo@izoo.krakow.pl; internet www.izoo .krakow.pl; f. 1950; 5 Scientific Depts, 11 Experimental Stations; library of 125,000 vols; Dir Prof. J. KRUPIŃSKI; publs *Annals of Animal Science* (4 a year), *Reports on Animal Performance Testing* (annually), *Wiadomosci Zootechniczne* (4 a year).

Morski Instytut Rybacki (Sea Fisheries Institute): ul. Kołłątaja 1, 81-332 Gdynia; tel. (58) 620-17-28; fax (58) 620-28-31; e-mail sekrdn@mir.gdynia.pl; internet www.mir .gdynia.pl; f. 1923; departments of ichthyology, oceanography, fishing technique, technology of fish processing, sea-fishery economics, scientific information; two branches at Szczecin and Świnoujście; library of 24,000 vols; Dir Doc. Dr hab. TOMASZ LINKOWSKI; publ. *Bulletin of the Sea Fisheries Institute*.

Państwowy Instytut Badawczy (National Veterinary Research Institute): ul. Partyzantów 57, 24-100 Puławy; tel. (81) 886-30-51; fax (81) 886-25-95; e-mail t.wijaszka@piwet .pulawy.pl; internet www.piwet.pulawy.pl; f. 1945; veterinary microbiology, immunology,

parasitology, toxicology, etc.; 16 scientific departments including those at Bydgoszcz and Zduńska Wola, and 4 specialized laboratories; library of 18,345 vols; Dir Dr TADEUSZ WIJASZKA; publ. *Bulletin of the Veterinary Institute in Puławy* (quarterly).

Zakład Badań Srodowiska Rolniczego i Leśnego PAN (Research Centre for Agricultural and Forest Environmental Studies): ul. Bukowska 19, 60-809 Poznań; tel. (61) 847-5603; fax (61) 847-3668; e-mail kedan@man .poznan.pl; internet www.zbsril.poznan.pl; f. 1979; attached to Polish Acad. of Sciences; study of energy flow and cycling of matter, evaluation of ecological guidelines for landscape management, and strategy for nature conservancy; library of 35,000 vols; Dir Prof. Dr hab. ANDRZEJ KĘDZIORA.

ARCHITECTURE AND TOWN PLANNING

Instytut Gospodarki Mieszkaniowej (Housing Research Institute): ul. Filtrowa 1, 00-925 Warsaw; tel. (22) 825-09-53; fax (22) 825-06-83; e-mail igmuchm@polbox.com; internet www.orgmasz.waw.pl/w/jbr/k7.htm; f. 1952; research and development in housing problems: dwelling construction and stock, investment process, construction market; library of 8,770 vols, 76 periodicals; Dir Dr RYSZARD UCHMAN; publs *Problemy Rozwoju Budownictwa* (quarterly), *Sprawy Mieszkaniowe* (quarterly).

Instytut Gospodarki Przestrzennej i Mieszkalictwa (Institute of Spatial Management and Housing): ul. Targowa 45, 03-728 Warsaw; tel. (22) 619-13-50; fax (22) 619-24-84; e-mail igpik@igpik.waw.pl; internet www.igpik.waw.pl; f. 1986; physical planning, architecture, municipal economy; library of 70,000 vols, including several special collections; Dir WŁODZIMIERZ BUCHALSKI; publ. *Geospatial information-key asset of spatial planning* (2 a year).

Instytut Techniki Budowlanej (Building Research Institute): ul. Filtrowa 1, 00-611 Warsaw; tel. (22) 825-04-71; fax (22) 825-52-86; e-mail itb@itb.pl; internet www.itb.pl; f. 1945; research in the use of building materials and methods of construction; library of 90,500 vols; Dir STANISŁAW WIERZBICKI; publ. *Prace Instytutu Techniki Budowlanej* (quarterly).

ECONOMICS, LAW AND POLITICS

Instytut Ekspertyz Sądowych (Institute of Forensic Research): ul. Westerplatte 9, 31-033 Cracow; tel. (12) 422-87-55; fax (12) 422-38-50; e-mail ies@ies.krakow.pl; internet www.ies.krakow.pl; f. 1929; departments of: criminalistics, traffic accident investigation, forensic toxicology, forensic psychology, forensic haemogenetics; 49 mems; library of 9,194 vols; Dir ALEKSANDER GŁAZEK; publs *Z Zagadnień Nauk Sądowych* (Problems of Forensic Sciences, 2 a year), *Paragraf na Drodze* (monthly).

Instytut Finansów (Institute of Finance): ul. Karmelicka 10, pokój 202, 00-163 Warsaw; tel. (22) 831-66-04; fax (22) 831-66 04; e-mail insfin@if.gov.pl; internet www.if.gov .pl; Dir ANDRZEJ WERNIK.

Instytut Funkcjonowania Gospodarki Narodowej (Institute of National Economy): Al. Niepodległości 164, pok. 814, 02-554 Warsaw; tel. and fax 848-59-28; fax 848-59-28; e-mail kkucin@sgh.waw.pl; internet www .sgh.waw.pl; f. 1972; Dir Prof. Dr hab. KAZIMIERZ KUCIŃSKI; publs *Materiały i Prace* (3 or 4 a year), *Mongrafie i Opracowania* (2 a year), *Szara Seria* (3 or 4 a year).

Instytut Koniunktur i Cen Handlu Zagranicznego (Foreign Trade Research Institute): ul. Żurawia 4A, 00-503 Warsaw;

tel. (22) 693-47-67; fax (22) 693-45-57; e-mail koniunkt@ikchz.warszawa.pl; internet handelue.pl/ikchz.pl; f. 1928 as Economic Trends Research Institute; present name 1969; Polish and world economics, European studies, Polish foreign trade, int. trade; library of 24,000 vols; Dir Dr hab. RYSZARD MICHALSKI; publs *Foreign Investments in Poland* (In Polish and English, annually), *Poland's Foreign Economic Policy* (In Polish and English), *Polish Foreign Trade* (In Polish and English).

Instytut Nauk Ekonomicznych PAN (Institute of Economics): Pałac Staszica, ul. Nowy Świat 72, 00-330 Warsaw; tel. (22) 657-27-07; fax (22) 826-72-54; e-mail inepan@inepan.waw.pl; internet www.inepan.waw.pl; f. 1981; attached to Polish Acad. of Sciences; library of 15,000 vols; Dir Prof. ZBIGNIEW HOCKUBA; publs *Studia Ekonomiczne* (4 a year), *Working Papers* (irregular), *Monografie* (irregular), *Opera Minora* (irregular).

Instytut Nauk Prawnych PAN (Institute of Legal Studies): Pałac Staszica, ul. Nowy Świat 72, 00-330 Warsaw; tel. (22) 826-75-71; fax (22) 826-78-53; e-mail inp@inp.pan.pl; internet www.inp.pan.pl; f. 1956; attached to Polish Acad. of Sciences; legal research; 66 mems; library of 44,000 vols; Dir Prof. Dr hab. WŁADYSŁAW CZAPLIŃSKI; publs *Droit Polonais Contemporain* (quarterly, in French and English), *Studia Prawnicze* (quarterly), *Orzecznictwo sądów polskich* (monthly), *Archiwum Kryminologii* (irregular), *Polish Yearbook of International Law* (in English), *Polska Bibliografia Prawnicza* (yearbook).

Instytut Organizacji i Zarządzania w Przemyśle 'ORGMASZ' (Institute of Organization and Management in Industry): ul. Żelazna 87, 00-879 Warsaw; tel. (22) 654-60-61; fax (22) 620-43-60; e-mail instytut@orgmasz.waw.pl; internet www.orgmasz.waw.pl; f. 1953; library of 11,200 vols, special collections; Dir Inż RYSZARD WIECZOR-KOWSKI; publ. *Ekonomika i Organizacja Przedsiębiorstwa* (Business Economics and Organization, monthly).

Instytut Pracy i Spraw Socjalnych (Institute of Labour and Social Studies): Bellottiego 3B, 01-022 Warsaw; tel. (22) 636-72-00; fax (22) 636-72-00; e-mail instprac@ipiss.com.pl; internet www.ipiss.com.pl; f. 1963; research into labour, wages, income distribution, living standards, social security and social insurance, labour law, human resources management, collective labour relations, family problems and family policy; Dir BOŻENNA BALCERZAK-PARADOWSKA; publs *Materiały z Zagranicy* (irregular), *Polityka Społeczna* (Social Policy, monthly), *Raport IPiSS* (irregular), *Opracowania PCZ* (irregular), *Zarządzanie Zasobami Ludzkimi* (Human Resources Management, 6 a year).

Instytut Rynku Wewnętrznego i Konsumpcji (Institute of Home Market and Consumption): al. Jerozolimskie 87, 02-001 Warsaw; tel. (22) 628-55-85; fax (22) 628-24-79; e-mail irwik@irwik.waw.pl; internet www.irwik.waw.pl; f. 1950; 135 mems; library of 40,000 vols; Dir MARIAN STRUŻYCKI; publs *Materiały Informacyjno-Szkolebiowe* (series), *Rocznik IRWIK* (series), *Przedsiębiorstwo i Rynek* (4 a year), *Biuletyn Informacyjny COINTE* (6 a year), *Przegląd Dokumentacyjny* (quarterly), *Bieżąca informacja o publikacjach z zakresu rynku w kraju i na świecie* (monthly).

Instytut Studiow Politycznych PAN (Institute of Political Studies): ul. Polna 18/20, 00-625 Warsaw; tel. (22) 825-52-21; fax (22) 825-21-46; e-mail politic@isppan.waw.pl; internet www.isppan.waw.pl; f. 1990 to develop theoretical work and empirical studies of post-communist societies; attached to Polish Acad. of Sciences; library of 17,330 vols; Dir Prof. WOJCIECH MATERSKI; publs *Kultura i Społeczeństwo* (Culture and Society, 4 a year), *Studia Polityczne* (Political Studies, 2 a year), *Civitas* (4 a year), *Rocznik Polsko-Niemiecki* (Polish-German Yearbook), *Europa Srodkowo-Wschodnia* (Central-Eastern Europe Yearbook).

Instytut Turystyki (Institute of Tourism): ul. Merliniego 9a, 02-511 Warsaw; tel. (22) 844-63-47; fax (22) 844-12-63; e-mail it@intur.com.pl; internet www.intur.com.pl; f. 1972; social, economic and spatial aspects of tourism, professional training and provision of information; library of 12,609 vols, 3,304 periodicals, special collns of 3,280 vols; Dir Dr KRZYSZTOF ŁOPACIŃSKI; publ. *Problemy Turystyki* (4 a year).

Instytut Wymiaru Sprawiedliwości (Institute of Justice): ul. Krakowskie Przedmieście 25, 00-950 Warsaw; tel. (22) 826-03-63; fax (22) 826-24-01; e-mail iws@iws.org.pl; internet www.iws.org.pl; f. 1992; financed and supervised by the Ministry of Justice but operates independently; sections of Civil Law, Criminal Law and Criminology, and Statistical Analysis and Methodology; library of 5,500 vols; Dir Prof. Dr hab. ANDRZEJ SIEMASZKO.

Instytut Zachodni im. Zygmunta Wojcie-chowskiego (Institute for Western Affairs): Mostowa 27, 61-854 Poznań; tel. (61) 852-76-91; fax (61) 852-49-05; e-mail izpozpl@rose.man.poznan.pl; internet www.iz.poznan.pl; f. 1945; for the study of Polish–German relations up to the acquisition of Polish western territories, and since 1945, and of Western European economic, political, historical, juridical, social and cultural matters; library of 100,000 vols; Dir Prof. Dr Hab. ANDRZEJ SAKSON; publ. *Przegląd Zachodni* (quarterly).

Państwowy Instytut Naukowy–Instytut Śląski w Opolu (Government Research Institute–Silesian Institute in Opole): ul. Piastowska 17, 45-081 Opole; tel. and fax (77) 453-60-32; e-mail instytutslaski@wp.pl; internet www.instytutslaski.opole.pl; f. 1957; departments: Historical and German–Polish Relationships Research, Regional Research; library of 72,000 vols (history since 19th c., contemporary history, social economics, Silesiana); Dir Prof. Dr hab. STANISŁAW SENFT; publs *Studia Śląskie* (annually), *Śląsk Opolski* (4 a year), *Zeszyty Odrzańskie* (annually), *Region and Regionalism* (in English, irregular).

Polski Instytut Spraw Międzynarodowych (Polish Institute of International Affairs): 1, POB 1010, ul. Warecka 1, 00-950 Warsaw; tel. (22) 556-80-00; fax (22) 556-80-99; e-mail pism@pism.pl; internet www.pism.pl; f. 1996; research in int. affairs; courses for civil servants, conferences; library of 156,000 vols; Dir Dr SŁAWOMIR DĘBSKI (acting); publs *Biuletyn* (in Polish, irreg.), *Polski Przegląd Dyplomatyczny* (in Polish, 6 a year), *Polish Quarterly of International Affairs* (quarterly), *Europa* (journal, in Russian, 4 a year), *Sprawy Międzynarodowe* (in Polish, 4 a year).

EDUCATION

Centrum Badań Polityki Naukowej i Szkolnictwa Wyższego (Centre for Science Policy and Higher Education): ul. Nowy Świat 69, 00-046 Warsaw; tel. and fax (22) 826-07-46; e-mail CRPHE@plearn.pl; f. 1973; planning and forecasting development of higher education; modernization of instruction and organization of higher education; Dir Prof. IRENEUSZ BIAŁECKI; publ. *Nauka i Szkolnictwo Wyższe* (Science and Higher Education, 2 a year).

Instytut Badań Edukacyjnych (Institute for Educational Research): ul. Górczewska 8, 01-180 Warsaw; tel. (22) 632-18-69; fax (22) 632-18-95; e-mail ibe@medianet.pl; internet www.medianet.pl/~ibe; f. 1950; library of 100,000 vols; depts of fundamental research, vocational education, educational information; Dir Prof. Dr STEFAN KWIATKOWSKI; publ. *Edukacja* (4 a year).

Instytut Kształcenia Zawodowego (Institute of Vocational Education): ul. Mokotowska 16/20, 00-561 Warsaw; tel. 285-661; f. 1972; 113 staff; library of 18,000 vols; Dir STANISŁAW KACZOR; publs *Pedagogika Pracy* (annually), *Biblioteka Kształcenia Zawodowego*, *Szkoła-Zawód-Praca* (annually).

FINE AND PERFORMING ARTS

Instytut Sztuki PAN (Institute of Art): ul. Długa 26/28, 00-950 Warsaw; tel. (22) 504-82-18; fax (22) 831-31-49; e-mail ispan@ispan.pl; internet www.ispan.pl; f. 1949; attached to Polish Acad. of Sciences; fine arts, architecture, music, theatre, film, cultural anthropology; 125 mems; library of 140,000 vols; photographic archive of 450,000 negatives; phonographic library of 80,000 items; 16,000 tapes; Dir Doc. Dr hab. LECH SOKÓŁ; publs *Biuletyn Historii Sztuki* (4 a year), *Konteksty*. *Polska Sztuka Ludowa* (4 a year), *Pamiętnik Teatralny* (4 a year), *Muzyka* (4 a year), *Kwartalnik Filmowy* (4 a year), *Dagerotyp* (Daguerrotype, annually), *Almanach Sceny Polskiej* (Almanack of the Polish Stage, annually), *Rzeczy Teatralne* (Theatre Miscellaneous, annually).

HISTORY, GEOGRAPHY AND ARCHAEOLOGY

Instytut Archeologii i Etnologii PAN (Institute of Archaeology and Ethnology): Al. Solidarności 105, 00-140 Warsaw; tel. (22) 620-28-81; fax (22) 624-01-00; e-mail director@iaepan.edu.pl; internet www.archaeology.pl; f. 1953; attached to Polish Acad. of Sciences; prehistoric, classical, early medieval and industrial archaeology, medieval and modern history of material culture, ethnography, ethnology; library of 185,000 vols; Dir Prof. ROMUALD SCHILD; publs *Archaeologia Polona*, *Archaeology of Poland*, *Archaeology*, *Polish Archaeological Researches*, *Archaeological Reports*, *Archaeological Review*, *Inventaria Archaeologica*, *Archaeologia Urbium*, *Polish Archaeological Abstracts*, *Ethnologia Polona*, *Bibliotheca Antiqua*, *Quarterly Journal of the History of Material Culture*, *Studies and Materials of the History of Material Culture*, *Library of Polish Ethnography*, *Polish Ethnographic Atlas*, *Polish Ethnography*, *Culture of Early Medieval Europe*, *Studia Ethnica*.

Instytut Geodezji i Kartografii (Institute of Geodesy and Cartography): ul. Modzelewskiego 27, 02-679 Warsaw; tel. (22) 329-19-00; fax (22) 329-19-50; e-mail igik@igik.edu.pl; internet www.igik.edu.pl; f. 1945; Dir Prof. Dr ADAM LINSENBARTH; publs *Prace IGIK* (2-3 a year), *Rocznik Astronomiczny* (annually), *Biuletyn Informacyjny Branżowego Ośrodka Informacji Naukowej, Technicznej i Ekonomicznej Geodezji i Kartografii* (4 a year), *Informacja Bibliograficzna Geodezji i Kartografii* (monthly).

Instytut Geografii i Przestrzennego Zagospodarowania im. S. Leszczyckiego PAN (Stanisław Leszczycki Institute of Geography and Spatial Organization): ul. Twarda 51/55, 00-818 Warsaw; tel. (22) 697-88-41; fax (22) 620-62-21; e-mail igipzpan@twarda.pan.pl; internet www.igipz.pan.pl; f. 1953; attached to Polish Acad. of Sciences;

geomorphology, hydrology, climatology, geoecology, economic geography, urban and population studies, geography of agriculture and rural areas, global development, political geography, regional planning, environmental management, ecodevelopment, European studies, cartography, geographic information systems; library of 132,113 vols, 50,804 vols of periodicals, 4,483 atlases, 80,180 maps, 1,149 antique and atlases; Dir Prof. Dr PIOTR KORCELLI; publs *Przegląd Geograficzny* (quarterly), *Prace Geograficzne* (irregular), *Bibliografia Geografii Polskiej* (annually), *Dokumentacja Geograficzna* (irregular), *Geographia Polonica* (2 a year), *Geopolitical Studies* (irregular), *Europa XXI* (irregular), *Monografie* (irregular), *Atlas Warszawy* (irregular).

Instytut Historii im. Tadeusza Manteuffla PAN (Institute of History): Rynek Starego Miasta 29/31, 00-272 Warsaw; tel. and fax (22) 831-36-42; e-mail ihpan@ihpan.edu.pl; internet www.ihpan.edu.pl; f. 1953; attached to Polish Acad. of Sciences; study of political and social history from the Middle Ages to the modern era; specific fields of research: Poland and Central-Eastern Europe; origins and history of modern Poland, history of Polish culture; social changes in post-World War II Poland; history of mass migrations in 19th and 20th c.; history of totalitarian systems and the Second World War; 167 mems; library of 59,000 vols; Dir Prof. STANISŁAW BYLINA; publs *Acta Poloniae Historica* (2 a year, in English), *Czasopismo Prawno-Historyczne* (2 a year), *Dzieje Najnowsze* (4 a year), *Kwartalnik Historyczny* (4 a year), *Odrodzenie i Reformacja w Polsce* (annually), *Roczniki Dziejów Społecznych i Gospodarczych* (annually), *Roczniki Historyczne* (annually), *Studia Zródłoznawcze. Commentationes* (annually), *Studia z Dziejów ZSRR i Europy Srodkowo-Wschodniej* (annually).

Zakład Archeologii Sródziemnomorskiej PAN (Research Centre for Mediterranean Archaeology): Nowy Swiat 72, Pałac Staszica (pok. 33), 00-330 Warsaw; tel. and fax (22) 826-65-60; e-mail zaspan@zaspan.waw.pl; f. 1956; attached to Polish Acad. of Sciences; study, documentation and publication of results of Polish and foreign excavations in the Middle East, Nubian studies, including surveys and excavations; publication of ancient objects in Polish museums; library of 13,600 books, 6,900 vols of periodicals; Dir Prof. Dr KAROL MYŚLIWIEC; publs *Alexandrie* (irregular), *Deir el-Bahari* (irregular), *Etudes et Travaux*, *Nea Paphos* (irregular), *Nubia* (irregular), *Saqqara* (irregular), *Tell Atrib* (irregular), *Travaux du Centre d'Archéologie Méditerranéenne*.

LANGUAGE AND LITERATURE

Instytut Badań Literackich PAN (Institute of Literary Research): Nowy Swiat 72, Pałac Staszica, 00-330 Warsaw; tel. and fax (22) 826-99-45; e-mail ibadlit@ibl.waw.pl; internet www.ibl.waw.pl; f. 1948; attached to Polish Acad. of Sciences; 20 scientific departments, and sections in Poznań, Toruń and Wrocław; research in the theory of literature, history of Polish literature, and sociology of literature; library of 450,000 vols, special collections: 85,000 vols; Dir Prof. ELŻBIETA SARNOWSKA-TEMERIUSZ; publs *Pamiętnik Literacki* (Literary Journal, quarterly), *Teksty Drugie* (Texts, every 2 months).

Instytut Języka Polskiego PAN (Polish Language Institute): al. Mickiewicza 31, 31-120 Cracow; tel. and fax (12) 632-87-13; internet www.ijp-pan.krakow.pl; f. 1973; attached to Polish Acad. of Sciences; library

of 20,000 vols; Dir Prof. Dr hab. IRENEUSZ BOBROWSKI; publs *Polonica* (annually), *Prace* (series), *Słownik gwar polskich* (annually), *Słownik staropolski*, *Atlas gwar mazowieckich* (continuous), *Studia gramatyczne* (series), *Studia leksykograficzne* (series).

MEDICINE

Centrum Onkologii, Instytut im. Marii Skłodowskiej-Curie (Marie Sklodowska-Curie Memorial Cancer Centre and Institute of Oncology): ul. Roentgena 5, 02-781 Warsaw; tel. (22) 546-20-00; e-mail dyrektor@coi.waw.pl; internet www.coi.waw.pl; f. 1932; brs at Cracow and Gliwice; fundamental cancer research, clinical research, diagnosis and treatment, epidemiology; co-ordinates Nat. Cancer Programme; 247 scientific staff; library of 23,458 vols; Dir Prof. Dr hab. MAREK P. NOWACKI; publs *Nowotwory* (quarterly), *Journal of Oncology* (every 2 months).

Instytut Biocybernetyki i Inżynierii Biomedycznej PAN (Institute of Biocybernetics and Biomedical Engineering): ul. Trojdena 4, 02-109 Warsaw; tel. (22) 659-91-43; fax (22) 659-70-30; e-mail ibib@ibib.waw.pl; internet www.ibib.waw.pl; f. 1975; attached to Polish Acad. of Sciences; collaborates with WHO; mem. of UNESCO Global Network for Molecular and Cell Biology; field of activities: biomeasurements, artificial internal organs, mathematical and physical modelling of physiological systems and processes, computerized image analysis, computer-aided medical diagnosis; library of 23,800 vols; Dir Prof. ANDRZEJ WERYŃSKI; publs *Biocybernetics and Biomedical Engineering* (4 a year), *Prace IBIB PAN* (IBIB PAN Reports, irregular).

Attached centre:

Miedzynarodowe Centrum Biocybernetyki (International Centre for Biocybernetics): 02-109 Warsaw, ul. Trojdena 4; tel. (22) 659-91-43; fax (22) 658-28-72; e-mail macicj.nalecz@ibib.waw.pl; internet www.ibib.waw.pl/icb.html; f. 1988; attached to Polish Acad. of Sciences; international centre for research and training in biocybernetics and biomedical engineering; organizes five seminars a year; Dir Prof. MACIEJ NAŁECZ; publ. *Lecture Notes of the ICB Seminars*.

Instytut Farmaceutyczny (Pharmaceutical Research Institute): ul. Rydygiera 8, 01-793 Warsaw; tel. (22) 456-39-00; fax (22) 456-38-38; e-mail kontakt@ifarm.waw.pl; internet www.ifarm.waw.pl; f. 1952; organic synthesis of pharmaceutically active substances, process development, pharmaceutical finished forms, bioequivalence and bioavailability of drug products; library of 12,200 vols, 350 periodical titles; Dir Dr WIESŁAW SZELEJEWSKI.

Instytut Farmakologii PAN (Institute of Pharmacology): ul. Smętna 12, 31-343 Cracow; tel. (12) 637-40-22; fax (12) 637-45-00; e-mail ifpan@if-pan.krakow.pl; internet www.if-pan.krakow.pl; f. 1954; attached to Polish Acad. of Sciences; behavioural, biochemical, molecular, electrophysiological, pharmacokinetic and histochemical aspects of psychopharmacology and neuropsychopharmacology; modelling and synthesis of potential, centrally acting agents; acclimatization of medicinal plants and their phytochemical investigation; library of 11,322 vols, 15,055 periodicals; Dir Prof. Dr hab. EDMUND PRZEGALIŃSKI; publ. *Pharmacological Reviews* (every 2 months).

Instytut Genetyki Człowieka PAN (Institute of Human Genetics): ul. Strzeszyńska 32, 60-479 Poznań; tel. (61) 823-30-11; fax (61) 823-32-35; e-mail igcz@man.poznan.pl; internet www.igcz.poznan.pl; f. 1974;

attached to Polish Acad. of Sciences; Dir Prof. Dr JERZY NOWAK.

Instytut Hematologii i Transfuzjologii (Institute of Haematology and Blood Transfusion): ul. Chocimska 5, 00-957 Warsaw; tel. (22) 849-85-07; fax (22) 848-89-70; e-mail hematol@ihit.waw.pl; internet www.ihit.waw.pl; f. 1951; Dir Prof. KRZYSZTOF WARZOCHA; publs *Acta Haematologica Polonica* (4 a year), *Sprawozdania Roczne z Działalności Instytutu* (annually).

Instytut Immunologii i Terapii Doświadczalnej im. Ludwika Hirszfelda PAN (L. Hirszfeld Institute of Immunology and Experimental Therapy): ul. Rudolfa Weigla 12, 53-114 Wrocław; tel. (71) 337-11-72; fax (71) 337-13-82; e-mail bednorz@iitd.pan.wroc.pl; internet www.iitd.pan.wroc.pl; f. 1952; attached to Polish Acad. of Sciences; research work in basic and clinical immunology, microbiology, immunochemistry, immunogenetics, experimental and bacteriophage therapy; library of 24,000 vols; Dir Prof. Dr ANDRZEJ GÓRSKI; publs *Archivum Immunologiae et Therapiae Experimentalis* (English, 6 a year), *Postępy Higieny i Medycyny Doświadczalnej* (Polish, 6 a year).

Instytut Kardiologii (National Institute of Cardiology): ul. Alpejska 42, 04-628 Warsaw; tel. (22) 815-25-24; fax (22) 343-45-00; e-mail biblnauk@ikard.waw.pl; internet www.ikard.waw.pl; f. 1980; library of 6,487 vols; Dir-Gen. Prof. ZBIGNIEW RELIGA; publ. *Biblioteka Kardiologiczna* (Cardiological Library, irregular).

Instytut Matki i Dziecka (Mother and Child Research Institute): ul. Kasprzaka 17A, 01-211 Warsaw; tel. (22) 327-70-00; fax (22) 327-70-01; internet www.imid.med.pl; f. 1948; research into the physiology and medicine of reproduction; Dir Prof. Dr hab. WOJCIECH WOŹNIAK; publ. *Development Period Medicine* (4 a year).

Instytut Medycyny Doświadczalnej i Klinicznej im. M. J. Mossakowskiego PAN (Medical Research Centre): ul. Pawińskiego 5, 02-106 Warsaw; tel. (22) 608-64-93; fax (22) 668-55-32; e-mail sekretariat@cmdik.pan.pl; internet www.cmdik.pan.pl; f. 1967; attached to Polish Acad. of Sciences; Departments of Physiology and Neurophysiology, Neuroimmunology, Neurochemistry, Neuropathology, Neurology, Neurosurgery, Experimental Transplantology, Endocrinology and Cellular Biology at the Ultrastructural (immunocytochemical and histochemical) level Located at the Ochota campus, attached to the Bielanski Hospital; two further units (Neuromuscular Unit and Department of Endocrinology) Located at the Warsaw Medical University; library of 10,000 vols, 164 periodicals; Dir Prof. Dr hab. n. med. ZBIGNIEW CZERNICKI; publs *Annual Report*, *Folia Neuropathologica* (4 a year).

Instytut Medycyny Morskiej i Tropikalnej (Institute of Maritime and Tropical Medicine): ul. Powstania Styczniowego 9B, 81-519 Gdynia; tel. and fax (58) 622-33-54; e-mail poczta@immt.gdynia.pl; f. 1939; attached to Medical University of Gdańsk; research in maritime occupational health, tropical medicine and epidemiology, toxicology, microbiology, travel medicine; clinic; postgraduate courses; 340 staff; WHO Inter-Regional Collaborating Centre on Maritime Occupational Health; Dir Dr W. NAHORSKI; publ. *International Maritime Health* (quarterly).

Instytut Medycyny Pracy i Zdrowia Srodowiskowego (Institute of Occupational Medicine and Environmental Health): ul. Kościelna 13, 41-200 Sosnowiec; tel. (32) 266-08-85; fax (32) 266-11-24; internet www

.imp.sosnowiec.pl; f. 1950; occupational toxicology; Dir Prof. Dr hab. JERZY A. SOKAL.

Instytut Medycyny Pracy im. prof. dra med. Jerzego Nofera (Nofer Institute of Occupational Medicine): ul. Sw. Teresy 8, POB 199, 90-950 Łódź; tel. (42) 631-45-02; fax (42) 656-83-31; e-mail impx@imp.lodz.pl; internet www.imp.lodz.pl; f. 1954; research in occupational medicine and hygiene, physiology, psychology, toxicology, neurotoxicology, carcinogenesis, pathology and epidemiology, management of occupational health service, radiation protection and the diagnosis and treatment of occupational diseases and acute poisonings, scientific information; Dir Prof. Dr KONRAD RYDZYŃSKI; publs *Medycyna Pracy* (Occupational Medicine, 6 a year), *International Journal of Occupational Medicine and Environmental Health* (in English, 4 a year), *Informacja Expresowa–Ostre Zatrucia* (Express Information–Acute Poisoning, 4 a year).

Instytut Medycyny Wsi im. Witolda Chodźki (W. Chodźko Institute of Agricultural Medicine): POB 185, ul. Jaczewskiego 2, 20-950 Lublin; tel. (81) 747-80-27; fax (81) 747-86-46; e-mail imw@galen.imw.lublin.pl; internet www.imw.lublin.pl; f. 1951; environmental and agricultural medicine, family doctor training, health service organization in rural areas; library of 14,000 vols; Dir Prof. Dr hab. JERZY ZAGÓRSKI; publs *Medycyna Ogólna* (electronic and 4 a year), *Sprawozdania z działalności Instytutu* (annually), *Annals of Agricultural and Environmental Medicine* (electronic and 2 a year), *Zdrowie Publiczne* (electronic and 4 a year).

Instytut Psychiatrii i Neurologii (Institute of Psychiatry and Neurology): ul. Sobieskiego /9, 02-957 Warsaw; tel. (22) 458-28-00; e-mail ipin@ipin.edu.pl; internet www.ipin.edu.pl; f. 1951; library of 26,300 vols; Dir Prof. STANISŁAW PUŻYŃSKI; publs *Postępy Psychiatrii i Neurologii* (4 a year), *Farmakoterapia w Psychiatrii i Neurologii* (4 a year), *Alkoholizm i Narkomania* (4 a year).

Instytut Zdrowia Publicznego (Institute for Public Health): ul. Chełmska 30/34, 00-725 Warsaw; tel. (22) 851-43-69; fax (22) 841-06-52; e-mail sekretariat@il.waw.pl; internet www.il.waw.pl; pharmaceutical microbiology and laboratory accreditation; library of 7,000 vols; Dir Prof. dr hab. ZBIGNIEW E. FIJAŁEK; publs *Biuletyn Informacyjny Instytutu Leków* (irregular), *Biuletyn Leków* (4 a year).

Instytut Żywności i Żywienia (National Food and Nutrition Institute): ul. Powsińska 61/63, 02-903 Warsaw; tel. (22) 842-21-71; fax (22) 842-11-03; e-mail jarosz@izz.waw.pl; internet www.izz.waw.pl; f. 1963; multidisciplinary scientific research in the field of human nutrition; library of 15,000 vols; Dir MIROSŁAW JAROSZ; publs *Żywienie Człowieka i Metabolizm* (4 a year), *Żywność, Żywienie a Zdrowie* (4 a year).

Państwowy Zakład Higieny (National Institute of Hygiene): ul. Chocimska 24, 00-791 Warsaw; tel. (22) 849-76-12; fax (22) 849-74-84; internet www.pzh.gov.pl; f. 1918; 15 departments covering all aspects of epidemiology, bacteriology, virology, parasitology, vaccines and sera control, medical statistics, radiologic control and radiobiology, immunopathology, communal hygiene, foodstuffs, environmental toxicology, school hygiene, health education, biological contamination control; courses in public health; library of 45,000 vols; Dir-Gen. Prof. JAN K. LUDWICKI; publs *Roczniki Państwowego Zakładu Higieny* (4 a year), *Medycyna Doświadczalna i Mikrobiologia* (4 a year), *Przegląd Epidemiologiczny* (4 a year).

NATURAL SCIENCES
General

Instytut Historii Nauki PAN (Institute for the History of Science): Pałac Staszica, Nowy Swiat 72, pok. 9, 00-330 Warsaw; tel. (22) 657-27-46; fax (22) 826-61-37; e-mail ihn@ihnpan.waw.pl; internet www.ihnpan.waw.pl; f. 1954; attached to Polish Acad. of Sciences; library of 20,000 vols; Dir Prof. Dr hab. KALINA BARTNICKA; publs *Kwartalnik Historii Nauki i Techniki* (4 a year), *Organon* (in French, English and Russian, annually), *Archiwum Dziejów Oświaty* (annually), *Analecta* (2 a year), *Medycyna Nowożytna* (2 a year), *Rozprawy z Dziejów Nauki i Techniki* (annually).

Instytut Oceanologii PAN (Institute of Oceanology): ul. Powstańców Warszawy 55, POB 68, 81-712 Sopot; tel. (58) 551-72-81; fax (58) 551-21-30; e-mail office@iopan.gda.pl; internet www.iopan.gda.pl; f. 1953; attached to Polish Acad. of Sciences; marine physics, hydrodynamics, marine chemistry, marine ecology, genetics of marine organisms; library of 7,000 vols, 240 periodicals; Dir Prof. Dr STANISLAW MASSEL; publ. *Oceanologia* (4 a year, in English).

Biological Sciences

Centrum Badań Ekologicznych PAN (Centre for Ecological Research): Dziekanów Leśny, Ul. M. Konopnickiej 1, 05-092 Łomianki; tel. (22) 751-30-46; fax (22) 751-31-00; e-mail cbe@cbe-pan.pl; internet www.cbe-pan.pl; f. 2002; attached to Polish Acad. of Sciences; population and community studies, landscape ecology, ecological bioenergetics, biogeochemistry, agroecology, polar research, hydrobiology, plant ecology, soil ecology, vertebrate ecology, modelling of ecological processes; library of 75,000 vols; Dir Prof. JANUSZ UCHMAŃSKI; publs *Polish Journal of Ecology* (original papers in English, quarterly), *Wiadomości Ekologiczne* (with English summary).

Instytut Biochemii i Biofizyki PAN (Institute of Biochemistry and Biophysics): ul. Pawińskiego 5A, 02-106 Warsaw; tel. (22) 659-70-72; fax (22) 592-21-90; e-mail secretariate@ibb.waw.pl; internet www.ibb.waw.pl; f. 1957; attached to Polish Acad. of Sciences; research work in the fields of molecular genetics, biotechnology, biochemistry, biophysics, bioinformatics; library of 16,000 vols, 140 periodicals, 1,000 online periodicals; Dir Prof. WŁODZIMIERZ ZAGÓRSKI-OSTOJA.

Instytut Biologii Doświadczalnej im M. Nenckiego (M. Nencki Institute of Experimental Biology): ul. Pasteura 3, 02-093 Warsaw; tel. (22) 822-28-31; fax (22) 822-53-42; internet www.nencki.gov.pl; f. 1918; attached to Polish Acad. of Sciences; scientific research work in the fields of biochemistry, cell biology, molecular biology, neurophysiology and experimental psychology; library of 68,000 vols; Dir Prof. JERZY DUSZYŃSKI; publs *Acta Neurobiologiae Experimentalis* (quarterly), *Acta Protozoologica* (quarterly).

Instytut Botaniki im. Władysława Szafera PAN (W. Szafer Institute of Botany): Lubicz 46, 31-512 Cracow; tel. (12) 421-51-44; fax (12) 421-97-90; e-mail office@ib-pan.krakow.pl; internet bobas.ib-pan.krakow.pl; f. 1954; attached to Polish Acad. of Sciences; library of 164,533 vols; Dir Prof. Dr ZBIGNIEW MIREK; publs *Acta Palaeobotanica* (International Journal of Palaeobotany), *Fragmenta Floristica et Geobotanica Polonica* (Material on the Flora and Vegetation of Poland, in Polish), *Polish Botanical Journal*.

Instytut Chemii Bioorganicznej PAN (Institute of Bio-organic Chemistry): ul. Noskowskiego 12/14, 61-704 Poznań; tel. and fax (61) 852-85-03; e-mail ibch@ibch.poznan.pl; internet www.ibch.poznan.pl; f. 1980; attached to Polish Acad. of Sciences; bio-organic chemistry, crystallochemistry of nucleic acids, proteins and their components; molecular biology, genetics and genetic engineering of plants, applied phytochemistry, biochemistry, bioinformatics; library of 3,300 vols; Dir Prof. Dr WOJCIECH T. MARKIEWICZ.

Instytut Dendrologii PAN (Institute of Dendrology): ul. Parkowa 5, 62-035 Kórnik, nr. Poznan; tel. (61) 817-00-33; fax (61) 817-01-66; e-mail idkornik@man.poznan.pl; internet www.idpan.poznan.pl; f. 1952; attached to Polish Acad. of Sciences; dendrology, acclimatization, systematics and geography of woody plants, tree genetics, tree physiology, seed physiology, tree resistance to pathogens, frost and pollution; 40 scientists; library of 40,000 vols; Dir Prof. GABRIELA LORENC-PLUCIŃSKA; publ. *Dendrobiology* (annually).

Instytut Ochrony Przyrody PAN (Institute of Nature Conservation): ul. A. Mickiewicza 33, 31-120 Cracow; tel. (12) 632-22-21; fax (12) 632-24-32; e-mail sekretariat@iop.krakow.pl; internet www.iop.krakow.pl; f. 1920; attached to Polish Acad. of Sciences; research work on all problems relating to nature conservation, biological conservation, landscape ecology, interaction between human activity and the biosphere; field stations in Wrocław and Zakopane; library of 21,000 vols, 19,000 periodicals, 19,000 maps and photographs; Dir Prof. HENRYK OKARMA; publs *Nature Conservation* (in English, annually), *Studia Naturae* (irregular), *Chrońmy Przyrodę Ojczystą* (Let Us Protect the Nature of our Homeland, 6 a year).

Instytut Paleobiologii im. Romana Kozłowskiego PAN (Institute of Palaeobiology): ul. Twarda 51/55, 00-818 Warsaw; tel. (22) 697-88-50; fax (22) 620-62-25; e-mail paleo@twarda.pan.pl; internet www.paleo.pan.pl; f. 1952; attached to Polish Acad. of Sciences; library of 11,000 vols, 27,000 vols of periodicals; Dir Prof. HUBERT SZANIAWSKI; publs *Palaeontologia Polonica* (irregular), *Acta Palaeontologica Polonica* (4 a year).

Instytut Parazytologii im Witolda Stefańskiego PAN (W. Stefański Institute of Parasitology): ul. Twarda 51/55, 00-818 Warsaw; tel. (22) 620-62-26; fax (22) 620-62-27; e-mail iparpas@twarda.pan.pl; f. 1952; attached to Polish Acad. of Sciences; scientific research work in parasitology, including animal parasitism, its origin, prevalence, manifestations and effects in natural and experimental parasite-host systems; departments of biodiversity, molecular biology, epizootiology and pathology, and deer farming; library: documentation centre and library of 25,666 vols (e-mail: libripar@twarda.pan.pl); Dir Prof. Dr ANDRZEJ MALCZEWSKI; Librarian Dr hab. WŁADYSŁAW CABAJ; publ. *Acta Parasitologica* (quarterly).

Instytut Systematyki i Ewolucji Zwierząt PAN (Institute of Systematics and Evolution of Animals): ul. Sławkowska 17, 31-016 Cracow; tel. (12) 422-19-01; fax (12) 422-42-94; e-mail office@isez.pan.krakow.pl; internet www.isez.pan.krakow.pl; f. 1865; attached to Polish Acad. of Sciences; library of 85,000 vols; Dir Prof. ADAM NADACHOWSKI; publs *Folia Biologica* (4 a year), *Acta Zoologica Cracoviensia* (4 a year).

Zakład Badania Ssaków PAN (Mammal Research Institute): ul. Gen. Waszkiewicza 1c, 17-230 Białowieża; tel. and fax (85) 682-77-50; e-mail mripas@bison.zbs.bialowieza.pl; internet bison.zbs.bialowieza.pl; f. 1954; attached to Polish Acad. of Sciences; scientific research in biomorphology, ecology, ecophysiology, genetics, taxonomy and fauna of mammals; collection of 177,000 specimens; library of 34,000 vols; Dir Prof. Dr hab. JAN M. WÓJCIK; publ. *Acta Theriologica* (quarterly).

Zakład Biologii Wód im. Karola Starmacha PAN (Institute of Freshwater Biology): ul. Sławkowska 17, 31-016 Cracow; tel. (12) 421-50-82; fax (12) 422-21-15; e-mail office@zbw.pan.krakow.pl; f. 1952; attached to Polish Acad. of Sciences; study of the plant and animal communities in ponds, rivers and dam reservoirs and productivity of these ecosystems, hydrochemistry and fisheries; hydrobiological station at Goczałkowice; biological fisheries station at Brzączowice; library of 29,000 vols and 1,520 periodicals; Dir Dr GRAŻYNA MAZURKIEWICZ-BOROŃ; publs *Supplementa ad Acta Hydrobiologica, Ecohydrology and Hydrobiology*.

Mathematical Sciences

Instytut Matematyczny PAN (Institute of Mathematics): ul. Sniadeckich 8, POB 21, 00-956 Warsaw; tel. (22) 522-81-00; fax (22) 629-39-97; e-mail im@impan.gov.pl; internet www.impan.gov.pl; f. 1948; attached to Polish Acad. of Sciences; scientific research work in mathematics and applications; local brs in Cracow, Gdańsk, Katowice, Łódź, Poznań, Toruń and Wrocław; 100 mems; library of 134,000 vols; Dir prof. Dr hab. STANISŁAW JANECZKO; publs *Colloquium Mathematicum* (online), *Acta Arithmetica* (online), *Fundamenta Mathematicae* (online), *Studia Mathematica* (online), *Annales Polonici Mathematici* (online), *Dissertationes Mathematicae* (online), *Applicationes Mathematicae* (online), *Bulletin* (online).

Attached centre:

> **Międzynarodowe Centrum Matematyczne im. Stefana Banacha** (Stefan Banach International Mathematical Centre): 00-956 Warsaw, ul. Sniadeckich 8, POB 21; tel. (22) 522-82-32; fax (22) 622-57-50; e-mail office@banach.impan.gov.pl; internet www.impan.gov.pl; f. 1972 by an agreement of Academies of East European countries; branch of the Institute of Mathematics; promotion of international co-operation in mathematics through organizing research-and-training semesters, workshops, conferences and symposia in different fields of mathematics; no permanent staff; Dir Prof. Dr hab. STANISŁAW JANECZKO.

Physical Sciences

Centrum Astronomiczne im. Mikołaja Kopernika PAN (Copernicus Astronomical Centre): ul. Bartycka 18, 00-716 Warsaw,; tel. (22) 841-10-86; fax (22) 841-00-46; e-mail camk@camk.edu.pl; internet www.camk.edu.pl; f. 1957; attached to Polish Acad. of Sciences; astronomy and astrophysics; library of 20,000 vols; Dir Prof. Dr hab. MAREK SARNA.

Centrum Badań Kosmicznych PAN (Space Research Centre): ul. Bartycka 18A, 00-716 Warsaw; tel. (22) 840-37-66; fax (22) 840-31-31; e-mail cbk@cbk.waw.pl; internet www.cbk.waw.pl; f. 1977; attached to Polish Acad. of Sciences; space physics, planetary geodesy, remote sensing; library of 9,000 vols; Dir Dr Hab. MAREK BANASZKIEWICZ; publ. *Artificial Satellites – Journal of Planetary Geodesy* (quarterly).

Centrum Chemii Polimerów PAN (Centre of Polymer Chemistry): Marie Curie-Skłodowskiej 34, POB 20, 41-819 Zabrze; tel. (32) 273-22-14; fax (32) 271-29-69; e-mail polymcr@uranos.cto.us.edu.pl; internet www.cchp-pan.zabrze.pl; f. 1968; attached to Polish Acad. of Sciences; divisions of polymer chemistry (three laboratories), polymer physical chemistry (three laboratories), physics of semiconductors and thin films (one laboratory); library of 22,000 vols; Dir Dr MAREK KOWALCZUK; publ. *Journal of Applied Chemistry* (4 a year).

Centrum Fizyki Teoretycznej PAN (Centre for Theoretical Physics): Al. Lotników 32/46, 02-668 Warsaw; tel. (22) 847-09-20; fax (22) 843-13-69; e-mail cft@cft.edu.pl; internet www.cft.edu.pl; f. 1980; attached to Polish Acad. of Sciences; classical and quantum field theory, general relativity, statistical physics, quantum and atom optics; Dir Prof. MAREK KUŚ.

Institute of High Pressure Physics: POB 65, 01-142 Warsaw; Located at: ul. Sokołowska 29/37, 01-142 Warsaw; tel. (22) 632-50-10; fax (22) 632-42-18; e-mail sylvek@unipress.waw.pl; internet www.unipress.waw.pl; f. 1972; attached to Polish Acad. of Sciences; effects of high pressure on metals and semiconductors, high pressure metal formation and crystal growth, cold isostatic pressing, hot isostatic pressing and sintering; manufacture of high pressure laboratory equipment; Dir Prof. Dr hab. SYLWESTER POROWSKI.

Instytut-Centrum Badań Molekularnych i Makromolekularnych PAN (Centre of Molecular and Macromolecular Studies): ul. Sienkiewicza 112, 90-363 Łódź; tel. (42) 684-71-13; fax (42) 684-71-26; e-mail cbmm@bilbo.cbmm.lodz.pl; internet www.cbmm.lodz.pl; f. 1972; attached to Polish Acad. of Sciences; hetero-organic chemistry, organic chemistry of sulphur, bio-organic chemistry, polymer physics, polymer chemistry, hetero-organic polymers, instrumental and elemental analysis; library: over 15,000 vols; Dir Prof. Dr MARIAN MIKOŁAJCZYK.

Instytut Chemii Fizycznej PAN (Institute of Physical Chemistry): Kasprzaka 44/52, 01-224 Warsaw; tel. (22) 343-31-08; fax (22) 343-33-33; e-mail ichf@ichf.edu.pl; internet ichf.edu.pl; f. 1955; attached to Polish Acad. of Sciences; research work in physico-chemical fundamentals including chemical engineering and chemical technology as follows: physical chemistry of metal-hydrogen systems including surface science and heterogeneous catalysis, analytical physical chemistry and instrumentation, experimental thermodynamics of organic mixtures, spectroscopy, including special-purpose apparatus, calorimetry including special-purpose apparatus and instrumentation, theory of chemical kinetics, electrochemistry and corrosion, fuel cells, molten salts, process kinetics, statistical mechanics and thermodynamics of irreversible phenomena; library of 92,035 vols; Dir Prof. ALEKSANDER JABLONSKI; publ. *Polish Journal of Chemistry* (monthly).

Instytut Chemii Organicznej PAN (Institute of Organic Chemistry): Kasprzaka 44–52, 01-224 Warsaw; tel. (22) 631-87-88; fax (22) 632-66-81; e-mail icho-s@icho.edu.pl; internet www.icho.edu.pl; f. 1954; attached to Polish Acad. of Sciences; research in synthetic organic chemistry and natural products chemistry; library of 19,648 vols; Dir Prof. Dr MAREK CHMIELEWSKI.

Instytut Fizyki Jądrowej im. Henryka Niewodniczańskiego (Henryk Niewodniczanski Institute of Nuclear Physics): ul. Radzikowskiego 152, 31-342 Cracow; tel. (12) 662-80-00; fax (12) 662-84-58; e-mail dyrektor@ifj.edu.pl; internet www.ifj.edu.pl; f. 1955; attached to Polish Acad. of Sciences; high-energy and elementary particle physics, nuclear and strong interactions physics, condensed matter physics, interdisciplinary application of physics (radiation and environmental biology), environmental physics, medical physics, dosimetry, nuclear geophysics, econophysics, radiochemistry and materials engineering; library of 17,000 vols; Dir Prof. MAREK JEŻABEK.

Instytut Fizyki Molekularnej PAN (Institute of Molecular Physics): ul. Smoluchowskiego 17, 60-179 Poznań; tel. (61) 869-51-00; fax (61) 868-45-24; e-mail postmaster@ifmpan.poznan.pl; internet www.ifmpan.poznan.pl; f. 1975; attached to Polish Acad. of Sciences; physics of magnetics, ferroelectrics and liquid crystals; molecular interactions in liquids; molecular electronics; nanostructures; radiospectroscopy (EPR, NMR, NQR); superconductivity and low-temperature physics; library of 23,500 vols; Dir Prof. Dr hab. NARCYZ PIŚLEWSKI; publ. *Molecular Physics Reports* (quarterly).

Instytut Fizyki PAN (Institute of Physics): Al. Lotników 32/46, 02-668 Warsaw; tel. (22) 843-70-01; fax (22) 843-09-26; e-mail director@ifpan.edu.pl; internet www.ifpan.edu.pl; f. 1953; attached to Polish Acad. of Sciences; research in condensed-matter physics: semiconductors, magnetics, superconductors, atomic and molecular physics, quantum optics, spectroscopy, x-ray crystallography, crystal growth; 350 mems; library of 28,000 vols; Dir Prof. Dr hab. JACEK KOSSUT; publs *Actu Physica Polonica* (monthly), *Proceedings of Conferences in Physics* (irregular), *Monographs in Physics* (irregular).

Instytut Fizyki Plazmy i Laserowej Mikrosyntezy im. Sylwestra Kaliskiego (S. Kaliski Institute of Plasma Physics and Laser Microfusion): POB 49, ul. Hery 23, 00-908 Warsaw; tel. (22) 638-14-60; fax (22) 666-83-72; e-mail office@ifpilm.waw.pl; internet www.ifpilm.waw.pl; f. 1976; library of 1,000 vols; Dir Dr ZYGMUNT SKŁADANOWSKI; publ. *IPPLM Annual Report*.

Instytut Geofizyki PAN (Institute of Geophysics): ul. Księcia Janusza 64, 01-452 Warsaw; tel. (22) 691-59-54; fax (22) 691-59-15; e-mail sn@igf.edu.pl; internet www.igf.edu.pl; f. 1952; attached to Polish Acad. of Sciences; seismology and physics of the Earth's interior, geomagnetism, palaeomagnetism, physics of the atmosphere, hydrology and polar research; library of 44,000 vols; Dir Prof. Dr hab. KACPER RYBICKI; publs *Acta Geophysica Polonica* (quarterly), *Publications* (irregular).

Instytut Katalizy i Fizykochemii Powierzchni PAN (Institute of Catalysis and Surface Chemistry): ul. Niezapominajek 8, 30-239 Cracow; tel. (12) 639-51-01; fax (12) 425-19-23; e-mail ncikifp@cyf-kr.edu.pl; internet www.ik-pan.krakow.pl; f. 1968; attached to Polish Acad. of Sciences; kinetics and mechanism of heterogeneous, homogeneous and enzymatic catalytic reactions, solid state chemistry, properties and dynamics of colloids, inter-facial phenomena, electrochemistry of interfaces; library of 9,000 vols; Dir Prof. MAŁGORZATA WITKO.

Instytut Mechaniki Górotworu PAN (Strata Mechanics Research Institute): ul. Reymonta 27, 30-059 Cracow; tel. (12) 637-62-00; fax (12) 637-28-84; e-mail dziurzyn@img-pan.krakow.pl; internet www.img-pan.krakow.pl; f. 1954; attached to Polish Acad. of Sciences; mechanics of granular media, rock deformation, gas and rock-mass outbursts, low-speed flow of fluids, dynamics of air flow, flow through porous media, micromeritics; library of 23,000 vols; Dir Prof. Dr WACŁAW DZIURZYŃSKI; publ. *Archives of Mining Sciences* (quarterly).

Instytut Nauk Geologicznych PAN (Institute of Geological Sciences): Twarda 51/55, 00-818 Warsaw; tel. (22) 697-87-01; fax (22)

620-62-23; e-mail ingpan@twarda.pan.pl; internet www.ing.pan.pl; f. 1956; attached to Polish Acad. of Sciences; stratigraphy, sedimentology, tectonics, petrography, mineralogy and isotope geochemistry, Quaternary geology, hydrogeology, micropalaeontology; runs undergraduate and PhD courses; library: library (in Warsaw and Cracow) of 42,700 books, 100,700 periodicals, 11,030 maps; Dir Prof. TERESA MADEYSKA; publs *Studia Geologica Polonica* (irregular), *Geologia Sudetica* (annually), *Archiwum Mineralogiczne* (irregular), *Studia Quaternaria* (annually).

Instytut Niskich Temperatur i Badań Strukturalnych PAN (Institute of Low Temperature and Structure Research): POB 1410, 50-950 Wrocław 2; Located at: ul. Okólna 2, 50-422 Wrocław; tel. (71) 343-50-21; fax (71) 344-10-29; e-mail intibs@int.pan.wroc.pl; internet www.int.pan.wroc.pl; f. 1966; attached to Polish Acad. of Sciences; physics and chemistry of solids: electronic and crystallographic structure, low temperature phenomena, magnetism, superconductivity; library of 22,000 vols; Dir Prof. Dr hab. JÓZEF SZNAJD; publ. *Physics and Chemistry of Solids* (quarterly).

Instytut Problemów Jądrowych im. Andrzeja Sołtana (A. Sołtan Institute for Nuclear Studies): 05-400 Swierk/Otwock; tel. (22) 718-05-83; fax (22) 779-34-81; e-mail sins@ipj.gov.pl; internet www.ipj.gov.pl; f. 1983, fmrly part of Institute of Nuclear Research; library of 27,000 vols; nuclear physics, elementary particle physics, plasma physics, accelerator physics and technology, material research using nuclear technology, spectrometric technology and nuclear electronics; Dir Prof. ZIEMOWID SUJKOWSKI; publ. *Annual Report*.

Państwowy Instytut Geologiczny (Polish Geological Institute): ul. Rakowiecka 4, 00-975 Warsaw; tel. (22) 849-53-51; fax (22) 849-53-42; e-mail sekretariat@pgi.gov.pl; internet www.pgi.gov.pl; f. 1919, name changed 1987; geological, hydrogeological and geo-environmental mapping; geological and hydrogeological national survey; central chemical laboratory; eight brs; geological museum; library of 160,000 vols, 32,000 bound periodicals, 520,000 maps and atlases, 326,000 geological documents; Dir Prof. Dr TADEUSZ PERYT; publs *Bibliografia Geologiczna Polski* (Geological Bibliography of Poland, annually), *Biuletyn* (irregular), *Geological Quarterly*, *Prace* (Memoirs, irregular).

Zakład Karbochemii PAN (Institute of Coal Chemistry): ul. Sowińskiego 5, 44-121 Gliwice; tel. (32) 238-07-80; fax (32) 231-28-31; e-mail inbox@karboch.gliwice.pl; internet www.karboch.gliwice.pl; f. 1954; attached to Polish Acad. of Sciences; research on structure, properties and reactivity of coals and studies on coal conversion methods; thermodynamics data banks, membrane separation processes, conducting polymers; library of 5,000 vols; Dir Prof. Dr hab. Inż. ZBIGNIEW FLORJAŃCZYK.

PHILOSOPHY AND PSYCHOLOGY

Instytut Filozofii i Socjologii PAN (Institute of Philosophy and Sociology): Nowy Świat 72, 00-330 Warsaw; tel. (22) 826-71-81; fax (22) 826-78-23; e-mail scretar@ifispan.waw.pl; internet www.ifispan.waw.pl; f. 1956; attached to Polish Acad. of Sciences; library of 173,258 vols; Dir Prof. HENRYK DOMAŃSKI; publs *Studia Logica* (in English, quarterly), *Archiwum Historii Filozofii i Myśli Społecznej* (irregular), *Przegląd Filozoficzny* (4 a year), *Studia Mediewistyczne* (irregular), *Studia Socjologiczne* (4 a year), *Mediaevalia Philosophica Polonorum* (irre-

gular), *Prakseologia* (irregular), *Sisyphus* (in English, irregular), *Etyka* (irregular), *ASK— Społeczeństwo—Badania—Metody* (irregular).

Instytut Psychologii PAN (Institute of Psychology): ul. Chodakowska 19/31, 03-815 Warsaw; tel. (22) 517-99-16; fax (22) 517-99-17; e-mail sekretariat@psychpan.waw.pl; f. 1980; attached to Polish Acad. of Sciences; social psychology, personality, general psychology, psycholinguistics, cognitive and decision processes, political psychology, ecological psychology, cross-cultural psychology; library of 8,000 vols; Dir Prof. Dr BOGDAN WOJCISZKE; publ. *Studia Psychologiczne* (quarterly).

RELIGION, SOCIOLOGY AND ANTHROPOLOGY

Zakład Antropologii PAN (Institute of Anthropology): ul. Kuźnicza 35, 50-951 Wrocław 56; tel. (71) 343-86-75; fax (71) 343-81-50; e-mail sekretaria@antro.pan.wroc.pl; internet www.antro.pan.wroc.pl; f. 1952; attached to Polish Acad. of Sciences; biological aspects of social stratification, genetics of growth, developmental norms, craniology, morphology; library of 16,000 vols; Dir Prof. Dr hab. PAWEŁ BERGMAN.

Żydowski Instytut Historyczny w Polsce (Jewish Historical Institute in Poland): ul. Tłomackie 3/5, 00-090 Warsaw; tel. (22) 827-92-21; fax (22) 827-83-72; e-mail zihinb@ikp.atm.com.pl; f. 1947; includes a museum of Jewish art and martyrology, archives; library of 60,000 vols, 600 MSS; Dir Prof. Dr FELIKS TYCH; publ. *Biuletyn* (quarterly, summary in English).

TECHNOLOGY

Centralny Instytut Ochrony Pracy– Państwowy Instytut Badawczy (CIOP-PIB) (Central Institute for Labour Protection—National Research Institute): ul. Czerniakowska 16, 00-701 Warsaw; tel. (22) 623-46-01; fax (22) 623-36-95; e-mail oinip@ciop.pl; internet www.ciop.pl; f. 1950; research and consultancy in occupational safety and health, testing protective equipment, training, certification, standardization, information and promotion; library of 39,000 vols; Dir Prof. DANUTA KORADECKA; publs *Bezpieczeństwo Pracy–Nauka i Praktyka* (Occupational Safety–Science and Practice, monthly), *International Journal of Occupational Safety and Health* (in English, 4 a year), *Podstawy i Metody Oceny Środowiska Pracy* (Principles and Methods of Assessing the Working Environment, 4 a year).

Główny Instytut Górnictwa (Central Mining Institute): Plac Gwarków 1, 40-166 Katowice; tel. (32) 258-16-31; fax (32) 259-65-33; e-mail gig@gig.katowice.pl; internet www.gig.katowice.pl; f. 1945; research work in rock mechanics, mining systems, blasting technique, gas, dust, water and rock burst hazards, clean coal technologies utilization and recovery of waste water, material engineering, noise and vibration control, environmental protection; 608 mems; library of 390,000 vols; Gen. Dir Prof. JÓZEF DUBIŃSKI; publs *Prace Naukowe* (Transactions, irregular, about 20 papers a year), *Annual Report* (in English and Polish), *Prace Naukowe – Górnictwo i Środowisko* (4 a year).

Instytut Automatyki Systemów Energetycznych (Institute of Power Systems Automation): ul. Wystawowa 1, 51-618 Wrocław; tel. (71) 348-42-21; fax (71) 348-21-83; e-mail bujko@iase.wroc.pl; internet www.iase.wroc.pl; f. 1949; automatic control systems, computer systems and networks, database systems, data communication for electric power system operation, expert systems,

exploitation and management; library of 21,000 vols, 5,400 vols of reports; Dir Prof. Dr Ing. JAN BUJKO; publs *Prace IASE* (annually), *Biuletyn IASE* (2 a year in monthly *Energetyka* journal), *Informator Patentowy Energetyki* (4 a year).

Instytut Badań Systemowych PAN (Systems Research Institute): ul. Newelska 6, 01-447 Warsaw; tel. (22) 837-35-78; fax (22) 837-27-72; e-mail olgierd.hryniewicz@ibspan.waw.pl; internet www.ibspan.waw.pl; f. 1977; attached to Polish Acad. of Sciences; control and optimization theory and applications, methods of systems analysis; library of 45,000 vols; Dir Prof. Dr hab. OLGIERD HRYNIEWICZ; publs *Control and Cybernetics* (quarterly), *Working Papers IBS PAN* (continuous), *Badania Systemowe* (series of monographs).

Instytut Badawczy Dróg i Mostów (Road and Bridge Research Institute): ul. Jagiellońska 80, 03-301 Warsaw; tel. (22) 811-32-31; fax (22) 811-17-92; e-mail ibdim@ibdim.edu.pl; internet ibdim.edu.pl; Dir Prof. Dr hab. Inż. LESZEK RAFALSKI; publs *Drogi i Mosty* (Roads and Bridges, 4 a year), *Nowości Zagranicznej Techniki Drogowej* (3-4 a year), *Prace Instytutu Badawczego Dróg i Mostów* (4 a year), *Studia i Materiały* (irregular).

Instytut Budownictwa Wodnego PAN (Institute of Hydroengineering): ul. Kościerska 7, 80-953 Gdańsk; tel. (58) 552-39-03; fax (58) 552-42-11; e-mail sekr@ibwpan.gda.pl; internet www.ibwpan.gda.pl; f. 1953; attached to Polish Acad. of Sciences; river, estuary and reservoir hydraulics, maritime hydraulics, soil mechanics and foundation engineering, environmental engineering; library of 24,000 vols; Dir Prof. WOJCIECH MAJEWSKI; publs *Archives of Hydroengineering and Environmental Mechanics* (4 a year), *Proceedings* (irregular).

Instytut Chemii i Techniki Jądrowej (Institute of Nuclear Chemistry and Technology): ul. Dorodna 16, 03-195 Warsaw; tel. (22) 811-06-56; fax (22) 811-15-32; e-mail sekdyrn@ichtj.waw.pl; internet www.ichtj.waw.pl; f. 1955; library of 41,000 vols; Dir Dr LECH WALIŚ; publs *INCT Reports* (Series A and B, irreg.), *Nukleonika* (quarterly, with 2 or 3 supplements).

Instytut Chemii Nieorganicznej (Institute of Inorganic Chemistry): ul. Sowińskiego 11, 44-100 Gliwice; tel. (32) 231-30-51; fax (32) 231-75-23; e-mail sekret@ichn.gliwice.pl; internet www.ichn.gliwice.pl; f. 1948; library of 18,000 vols; Dir Dr Inż. BOŻENNA PISARSKA; publ. *Bieżąca Informacja Chemiczna seria— NIEORGANIKA* (Bibliography selected from current papers, monthly).

Instytut Chemii Przemysłowej (Industrial Chemistry Research Institute): Rydygiera 8, 01-793 Warsaw; tel. (22) 633-97-98; fax (22) 633-82-95; e-mail ichp@ichp.pl; internet www.ichp.pl; f. 1922; research into carbo- and petrochemistry, organic synthesis, polymer and plastics technology, industrial catalysis, household chemistry products and disinfectants, environmental impact technology, process safety, chemical process engineering, instrumental analysis, medical diagnostic tests, biotechnology; Bureau for Ozone Layer Protection; Nat. Centre for Ecological Management in the Chemical Industry; library of 49,600 vols, 55,540 periodicals; Dir Prof. JACEK KIJEŃSKI; publ. *Polimery* (monthly).

Instytut Elektrotechniki (Electrotechnical Institute): ul. Pożaryskiego 28, 04-703 Warsaw; tel. (22) 812-20-00; fax (22) 615-75-35; e-mail iel@iel.waw.pl; internet www.iel.waw.pl; f. 1946; research and manufacture of electric machines, apparatus and appliances; library of 45,000 vols, 500 periodicals; Gen.

Dir Dr STEFAN PARADOWSKI; publs *Nowa Elektrotechnika* (monthly), *Prace Instytutu Elektrotechniki* (Proceedings of the Electrotechnical Institute).

Instytut Energetyki (Institute of Power Engineering): ul. Mory 8, 01-330 Warsaw; tel. (27) 211-02-00; fax (22) 836-63-63; e-mail instytut.energetyki@ien.com.pl; internet www.ien.com.pl; f. 1953; library of 53,000 vols; Man. Dr JACEK WAŃKOWICZ; publs *Biuletyn Instytutu Energetyki* (6 a year), *Prace Instytutu Energetyki* (irregular).

Instytut Energii Atomowej (Institute of Atomic Energy): 05-400 Otwock-Swierk; tel. (22) 718-00-01; fax (22) 779-38-88; e-mail iea@cyf.gov.pl; internet www.iea.cyf.gov.pl; f. 1983; fmrly Inst. of Nuclear Research; reactor technology, radiation protection and dosimetry, quality standards for nuclear reactors, condensed matter physics, nuclear power plants, radioactive waste management; library of 16,000 vols, 685 periodicals; Dir Prof. Dr hab. KRZYSZTOF WIETESKA; publ. *Annual Report*.

Instytut Informatyki Teoretycznej i Stosowanej PAN (Institute of Theoretical and Applied Informatics): ul. Bałtycka 5, 44-100 Gliwice; tel. (32) 231-73-19; fax (32) 231-70-26; e-mail office@iitis.gliwice.pl; internet www.iitis.gliwice.pl; f. 1969; attached to Polish Acad. of Sciences; 35 staff; research areas: performance evaluation of computer networks, computer vision, quantum informatics; library of 6,000 vols; Dir Prof. Dr TADEUSZ CZACHÓRSKI; publ. *Archiwum Informatyki Teoretycznej i Stosowanej* (quarterly).

Instytut Inżynierii Chemicznej PAN (Institute of Chemical Engineering): ul. Bałtycka 5, 44-100 Gliwice; tel. (32) 234-69-15; fax (32) 231-03-18; e-mail secret@iich.gliwice.pl; internet www.iich.gliwice.pl; f. 1958; attached to Polish Acad. of Sciences; chemical and process engineering: chemical reaction engineering, adsorption, membrane separation, mass and heat transfer, environmental and bioprocess engineering, renewable energy sources; library of 6,580 vols; Dir Prof. Dr hab. inż. KRZYSZTOF WARMUZINSKI; publs *Inżynieria Chemiczna i Procesowa* (4 a year), *Prace Naukowe* (research papers, annually).

Instytut Łączności (National Institute of Telecommunications): ul. Szachowa 1, 04-894 Warsaw; tel. (22) 512-81-00; fax (22) 512-86-25; e-mail info@itl.waw.pl; internet www.itl.waw.pl; f. 1951; telecommunications, data transmission, satellite telecommunications, optical transmission, information technology, radiocommunications, EMC; library of 56,405 vols; Dir ZBIGNIEW KĄDZIELSKI; publs *Journal of Telecommunications and Information Technology* (4 a year), *Telekomunikacja i Techniki Informacyjne* (4 a year).

Instytut Lotnictwa (Institute of Aviation): Al. Krakowska 110/114, 02-256 Warsaw; tel. (22) 846-00-11; fax (22) 846-44-32; e-mail ilot@ilot.edu.pl; internet www.ilot.edu.pl; f. 1926; library of 72,000 vols; Dir Dr WITOLD WIŚNIOWSKI; publs *Prace Instytutu Lotnictwa* (4 a year), *Informacja Ekspresowa Lotnicza i Silnikowa* (monthly), *Przegląd Dokumentacyjny* (monthly), *Tematy Prac Wykonawczych w Instytucie Lotnictwa* (annually), *Prace Przemysłu Lotniczego* (annually), *Opracowania Problemowe* (15–20 a year).

Instytut Maszyn Matematycznych (Institute of Mathematical Machines): ul. Ludwika Krzywickiego 34, 02-078 Warsaw; tel. (22) 621-84-41; fax (22) 629-92-70; e-mail imasmat@imm.org.pl; internet bi.imm.org.pl; f. 1957; computer science and technology, training and education; library of 28,000 vols; Dir ROMAN CZAJKOWSKI; publ. *Techniki*

Komputerowe—Biuletyn Informacyjny (irregular).

Instytut Maszyn Przepływowych im. R. Szewalskiego PAN (R. Szewalski Institute of Fluid Flow Machinery): ul. Gen. J. Fiszera 14, 80-952 Gdańsk; tel. (58) 341-12-71; fax (58) 341-61-44; e-mail imp@imp.gda.pl; internet www.imp.gda.pl; f. 1956; attached to Polish Acad. of Sciences; fundamental research, design methods, construction and development of machines and equipment for energy conversion in flow, measuring techniques and instrumentation in connection with fluid-flow machines, solid-state mechanics, machinery diagnostics, plasma physics; library of 23,000 vols; Dir Prof. Dr hab. JAROSŁAW MIKIELEWICZ; publs *Transactions* (2 a year), *Zeszyty Naukowe* (bulletin, irregular), *Annual Report*, *Archives of Thermodynamics* (4 a year), *Archives of Energetics* (2 a year).

Instytut Maszyn Spożywczych (Institute of Food Processing Machinery): ul. Otwocka 1B, 03-759 Warsaw; tel. (22) 619-12-61; fax (22) 619-87-94; e-mail ims@orgmasz.waw.pl; internet www.orgmasz.waw.pl/w/ims/ims_a.htm; f. 1954; research and application in all fields of food processing, marketing and catering machinery and equipment; automation, energy-saving techniques; library of 4,984 vols, 141 periodicals, 20,066 leaflets; Dir Assoc. Prof. WALDEMAR P. RACZKO; publs *Postępy Techniki* (Developments in Food Processing Technology, 3 a year), *Biuletyn Informacyjny* (Bulletin of Food Processing Machinery, irregular).

Instytut Mechanizacji Budownictwa i Górnictwa Skalnego (Institute for Mechanized Construction and Rock Mining): ul. Racjonalizacji 6/8, 02-673 Warsaw; tel. (22) 843-02-01; fax (22) 843-59-81; e-mail imb@imbigs.org.pl; internet www.imbigs.org.pl; f. 1951; mechanization of building sites, mineral mining processing; earth-moving, construction and mining machinery for quarries, equipment research, development and state quality testing and certifying; training of machinery operators; standardization of construction machinery and equipment; library of 8,800 vols, 54 periodicals; Dir Prof. Dr hab. Inż. EUGENIUSZ BUDNY; publs *Działalność Instytutu Mechanizacji Budownictwa* (annually), *Wiadomości IMB* (4 a year), *Przegląd Mechaniczny*.

Instytut Metali Nieżelaznych (Institute of Non-ferrous Metals): ul. Sowińskiego 5, 44-100 Gliwice; tel. (32) 238-02-00; fax (32) 231-69-33; e-mail imn@imn.gliwice.pl; internet www.imn.gliwice.pl; f. 1952; processing of non-ferrous ores and other mineral materials; pyro-and hydrometallurgical processes of metals recovery from ores and concentrates, and recovery of accompanying metals; waste treatment and utilisation; new alloys and composites; processing of metals and alloys; environmental protection; analytical chemistry of metals; 422 mems; library of 35,000 vols, 270 current periodicals, 15,000 reports; Dir Prof. Dr ZBIGNIEW SMIESZEK; publ. *Biuletyn Instytutu Metali Nieżelaznych* (monthly).

Instytut Metalurgii i Inżynierii Materiałowej im. Aleksandra Krupkowskiego PAN (A. Krupkowski Institute of Metallurgy and Materials): ul. W. Reymonta 25, 30-059 Cracow; tel. (12) 637-42-00; fax (12) 637-21-92; e-mail office@imim-pan.krakow.pl; internet www.imim.pl; f. 1953; attached to Polish Acad. of Sciences; metallurgical thermodynamics, physical metallurgy, metal working; library of 25,000 vols; Dir Prof. Dr hab. Inż. BOGUSŁAW MAJOR; publ. *Archives of Metallurgy and Materials* (4 a year).

Instytut Metalurgii Żelaza im. Stanisława Staszica (Stanislaw Staszic Institute

of Ferrous Metallurgy): ul. K. Miarki 12, 44-100 Gliwice; tel. (32) 234-52-05; fax (32) 234-53-00; e-mail imz@imz.gliwice.pl; internet www.imz.gliwice.pl; f. 1945; library: 37,000 books, 21,000 vols of periodicals; Dir Dr Inż. ADAM SCHWEDLER; publ. *Prace Instytutu Metalurgii Żelaza* (transactions, 4 a year).

Instytut Mineralnych Materiałów Budowlanych (Institute of Mineral Building Materials): ul. Oświęcimska 21, 45-641 Opole; tel. (77) 456-3201; fax (77) 456-2661; e-mail immb@immb.opole.pl; internet www.immb.opole.pl; f. 1954; basic and applied research in mineral building materials technology, thermal engineering and environmental protection; br. in Cracow; library of 11,800 vols, 4,000 vols of reports; Dir Assoc. Prof. JERZY DUDA; publ. *Prace IMMB* (2 a year).

Instytut Morski (Maritime Institute): ul. Długi Targ 41/42, 80-830 Gdańsk; tel. (58) 301-16-41; fax (58) 301-35-13; e-mail jacu@im.gda.pl; internet www.im.gda.pl; f. 1950; economic and technical research in shipping, harbour and coastal engineering, corrosion, maritime law; 120 staff; library of 80,000 vols; Dir Asst Prof. Dr Eng. JAN CURZYTEK; Scientific Dir Prof. zw.Dr hab. Inż. BOLESŁAW MAZURKIEWICZ; publs *Prace Instytutu Morskiego*, *Zeszyty Problemowe Gospodarki Morskiej*, *Materiały Instytutu Morskiego*, *Przegląd Informacji*, *Informacja ekspresowa*.

Instytut Nafty i Gazu (Oil and Gas Institute): ul. Lubicz 25A, 31-503 Cracow; tel. (12) 421-00-33; fax (12) 421-00-50; e-mail office@inig.pl; internet www.igng.krakow.pl; f. 1945; oil and gas recovery industry, gas transport and storage, gas use, and related topics; library of 110,000 vols; Dir Prof. Dr hab Inż. MARIA CIECHANOWSKA; publs *Prace, Nafta Gaz* (monthly), *Przegląd Bibliograficzno-Faktograficzny 'Nafta-Gaz'* (4 a year).

Instytut Obróbki Plastycznej (Metal Forming Institute): ul. Jana Pawła 14, 61-139 Poznań; tel. (61) 657-05-55; fax (61) 657-07-21; e-mail inop@inop.poznan.pl; internet www.inop.poznan.pl; f. 1948; library of 23,500 vols; Dir ANDRZEJ PLEWIŃSKI; publ. *Obróbka Plastyczna Metali* (5 a year).

Instytut Odlewnictwa (Foundry Research Institute): ul. Zakopiańska 73, 30-418 Cracow; tel. (12) 266-26-19; fax (12) 266-08-70; e-mail iod@iod.krakow.pl; internet czapla.iod.krakow.pl/infocast/inst_odl.html; f. 1946; research into foundry materials, technological processes, alloys and additives; library of 10,000 vols, 45 periodicals; Pres. Dr Eng. JERZY TYBULCZUK; publ. *Odlewnictwo – Nauka i Praktyka* (6 a year).

Instytut Podstaw Informatyki PAN (Institute of Computer Science): ul. J. K. Ordona 21, 01-237 Warsaw; tel. (22) 836-28-41; fax (22) 837-65-64; e-mail ipi@ipipan.waw.pl; internet www.ipipan.waw.pl; f. 1976; attached to Polish Acad. of Sciences; library of 16,400 vols, 250 periodicals; research depts of Theoretical Foundations of Computer Science and Artificial Intelligence; Dir–Gen. Prof. JACEK KORONACKI; Dir (Scientific Affairs) BEATA KONIKOWSKA; Dir (Economic Affairs) BOGUSŁAW MARTYNIAK; publs *Prace IPI PAN* (ICS PAS Reports, irreg), *Machine Graphics and Vision* (quarterly).

Instytut Podstawowych Problemów Techniki PAN (Institute of Fundamental Technological Research): ul. Świętokrzyska 21, 00-049 Warsaw; tel. (22) 826-12-81; fax (22) 826-98-15; e-mail director@ippt.gov.pl; internet www.ippt.gov.pl; f. 1953; attached to Polish Acad. of Sciences; applied mechanics, vibrations, ultrasonics, ultrasound in medicine, acoustics, electromagnetic fields, mechanical systems, energy problems, automatics and robotics, building structures, computational science and engineering; library of 80,000 vols; Dir Prof. WOJCIECH KRZYSZTOF NOWACKI; Scientific Council Chair. Prof. KAZIMIERZ SOBCZYK; publs *Archives of Acoustics* (4 a year), *Archives of Civil Engineering* (4 a year), *Archives of Mechanics* (6 a year), *Biblioteka Mechaniki Stosowanej* (Applied Mechanics Series), *CAMES–Computer Assisted Mechanics and Engineering Sciences* (4 a year), *Engineering Transactions* (4 a year), *Journal of Technical Physics* (4 a year), *Prace IPPT* (IFTR Reports).

Instytut Przemysłu Gumowego 'Stomil' ('Stomil' Rubber Research Institute): ul. Harcerska 30, 05-820 Piastów; tel. (22) 723-60-25; fax (22) 723-71-96; e-mail ipgum@ipgum.pl; internet www.ipgum.pl; f. 1953; research in all brs of rubber technology and of its development; library of 6,000 vols; Dir Dr JACEK MAGRYTA; Scientific Board Chair. Prof. Dr hab.Inż. ZBIGNIEW FLORJAŃCZYK; publs *Elastomery* (6 a year), *Guma–Elastomery–Przetwórstwo Informacje bieżace* (monthly), *Rubber–Elastomers–Processing Technology* (in English, monthly).

Instytut Przemysłu Organicznego (Institute of Industrial Organic Chemistry): ul. Annopol 6, 03-236 Warsaw; tel. (22) 811-12-31; fax (22) 811-07-99; e-mail ipo@ipo.waw.pl; internet www.ipo.waw.pl; f. 1947; research on plant pesticides and biocides, auxiliary chemical products, organic intermediate products, blasting materials, chemical safety, toxicology and ecotoxicology; 235 mems; library of 36,700 vols, 171 periodicals; Dir Dr KAROL BUCHALIK; publs *Central European Journal of Energetic Materials* (4 a year), *Organika—Prace Naukowe Instytutu Przemysłu Organicznego* (annually), *Pestycydy* (4 a year).

Instytut Spawalnictwa (Institute of Welding): ul. Bł. Czesława 16/18, 44-100 Gliwice; tel. (32) 231-00-11; fax (32) 231-46-52; e-mail is@is.gliwice.pl; internet www.is.gliwice.pl; f. 1945; fundamental and developmental research, acceptance tests, certification, consulting, training, safety of welders, standardization, manufacture; library of 12,000 vols, 36 periodicals; Dir Prof. JAN PILARCZYK; publs *Biuletyn Instytutu Spawalnictwa* (every 2 months), *Informacja Expressowa* (every 2 months).

Instytut Systemów Sterowania (Institute of Control Systems): ul. Długa 1-3, 41-506 Chorzów; tel. (32) 247-28-20; fax (32) 246-25-91; e-mail office@iss.pl; internet www.iss.pl; f. 1977; Dir LESZEK E. ŻYCHOŃ; publs *Prace Naukowe Instytutu Systemów Sterowania* (irregular), *Komunikaty Naukowe ISS*.

Instytut Szkła i Ceramiki (Institute of Glass and Ceramics): ul. Postępu 9, 02-676 Warsaw; tel. 43-74-21; fax 43-17-89; e-mail home@ceram.isc.ifpan.edu.pl; f. 1952; basic research on all aspects of glass and ceramics technology; library of 15,000 vols and special collections of 5,000 vols; Dir ZBIGNIEW POLESIŃSKI; publ. *Szkło i Ceramika* (every 2 months).

Instytut Technologii Elektronowej (Institute of Electron Technology): Al. Lotników 32/46, 02-668 Warsaw; tel. (22) 548-77-00; fax (22) 847-06-31; e-mail cambroz@ite.waw.pl; internet www.ite.waw.pl; f. 1966; library of 11,000 vols; Dir Prof. Dr hab. inż. C. AMBROZIAK; publs *Electron Technology* (online, 4 a year), *Biblioteka Elektroniki* (irregular).

Instytut Technologii Materiałów Elektronicznych (Institute of Electronic Materials Technology): ul. Wólczyńska 133, 01-919 Warsaw; tel. (22) 835-30-41; fax (22) 864-54-96; e-mail itme@itme.edu.pl; internet www.itme.edu.pl; f. 1979; library of 20,000 vols;

Gen. Man. Dr ZYGMUNT ŁUCZYŃSKI; Scientific Dir Prof. ANDRZEJ JELEŃSKI; publs *Materiały Elektroniczne* (4 a year), *MST News – Poland* (4 a year).

Instytut Technologii Nafty im. Prof. Stanisława Pilata (Institute of Petroleum Processing): ul. Łukasiewicza 1, 31-429 Cracow; tel. (12) 617-75-28; fax (12) 617-75-22; e-mail itn@itn.com.pl; internet www.itn.com.pl; f. 1958; petroleum refining and petrochemistry, standardization of products and testing methods, new methods of analysis and production, fuel and oil additives; library of 20,000 vols; Man. Dir Dr LESZEK ZIEMIAŃSKI; publs *Nafta Gaz* (monthly), *Biuletyn* (4 a year).

Instytut Transportu Samochodowego (Motor Transport Institute): ul. Jagiellońska 80, 03-301 Warsaw; tel. (22) 811-09-44; fax (22) 811-09-06; e-mail awojciech@its.waw.pl; internet www.its.home.pl; f. 1952; focuses on operation of motor transport in the market economy, road traffic organization, and environmental protection; library of 22,000 vols, 50 periodicals; Dir Dr ANDRZEJ WOJCIECHOWSKI; Scientific Cttee Chair. Prof. Dr hab. Inż. JERZY MERKISZ; publs *Transport Samochodowy* (4 a year), *Bezpieczeństwo Ruchu Drogowego* (4 a year), *Biuletyn Informacyjny* (6 a year).

Instytut Biopolimerów i Włókien Chemicznych (Institute of Biopolymers and Chemical Fibres): ul. M. Skłodowskiej-Curie 19/27, 90-570 Łódź; tel. (42) 637-67-44; fax (42) 637-62-14; e-mail ibwch@ibwch.lodz.pl; internet www.ibwch.lodz.pl; f. 1952; chemistry, technology, application of chemical fibres, environmental protection, natural polymers, their modification, applied biotechnology, medical and agricultural applications of polymers and fibres; library of 9,548 vols; Man. Dir Dr DANUTA CIECHAŃSKA; publ. *Fibres and Textiles in Eastern Europe*.

Instytut Włókien Naturalnych (Institute of Natural Fibres): ul. Wojska Polskiego 71b, 60-630 Poznań; tel. (61) 845-58-00; fax (61) 841-78-30; e-mail sekretar@inf.poznan.pl; internet www.inf.poznan.pl; f. 1930; complex research on production and processing of natural fibres (flax, hemp, kenaf, jute, silk), environmental protection, processing of waste products, plant biotechnology, properties of fibre, yarn, fabrics and textiles, composites, flame retardants, plant protection; cultivation and harvesting of fibrous plants and natural dyestuffs; library of 20,278 vols, 7,800 in special collections; Gen. Dir Prof. Dr RYSZARD KOZŁOWSKI; Scientific Board Chair. Prof. Dr BOGUMIŁ LASZKIEWICZ; publs *Euroflax* (2 a year), *Journal of Natural Fibers* (4 a year), *Natural Fibres, Włókna Naturalne* (annually).

Instytut Włókiennictwa (Textile Research Institute): ul. Brzezińska 5/15, 92-103 Łódź; tel. (42) 616-31-95; fax (42) 679-26-38; e-mail info@mail.iw.lodz.pl; internet www.iw.lodz.pl; f. 1945; textile raw materials, technology of yarn manufacturing, non-woven fabrics, textile chemical processing; library of 17,559 vols and 12,879 in special collections; Dir JOLANTA MAMENAS; Scientific Council Chair. Prof. Dr hab. KAZIMIERZ KOPIAS; publ. *Prace Instytutu Włókiennictwa* (annually).

Instytut Wzornictwa Przemysłowego (Institute of Industrial Design): ul. Świętojerska 5/7, 00-236 Warsaw; tel. (22) 860-00-66; fax (22) 831-64-78; e-mail iwp@iwp.com.pl; internet www.iwp.com.pl; f. 1950; research into design and ergonomics of industrial products; ergonomic research and data selection; design for the disabled; standardization; technical information service; organization of national and foreign exhibitions, seminars, conferences etc.;

library of 42,000 vols, 270 titles of periodicals, collection of special editions, etc.; Dir Prof. HALINA WALTER; Scientific Council Pres. Prof. JERZY WUTTKE; publs *Studies and Materials*, *Express News*, *Design Library Series*.

Polski Komitet Normalizacyjny (Polish Committee for Standardization): Świętokrzyska 14, 00-050 Warsaw; tel. (22) 556-76-00; fax (22) 556-77-80; e-mail prezeskr@pkn.pl; internet www.pkn.pl; f. 1924; library has collections of Polish National Standards, ISO, IEC, EN and foreign standards; Pres. JANUSZ SZYMAŃSKI; publ. *Normalizacja* (monthly).

Przemysłowy Instytut Automatyki i Pomiarów (Industrial Research Institute of Automation and Measurements): Al. Jerozolimskie 202, 02-486 Warsaw; tel. (22) 874-00-00; fax (22) 874-02-20; e-mail piap@piap.pl; internet www.piap.pl; f. 1965; development of automation equipment, measuring instruments and industrial robots; library of 24,000 vols; Dir Prof. STANISŁAW KACZANOWSKI; publ. *Pomiary Automatyka Robotyka* (monthly).

Przemysłowy Instytut Elektroniki (Industrial Institute of Electronics): ul. Długa 44/50, 00-241 Warsaw; tel. (22) 831-52-21; fax (22) 831-30-14; e-mail pie@pie.edu.pl; academic year pie.edu.pl; automatic production lines and technical equipment, equipment for thermal and chemical processes, test and measuring systems; Dir Dr Inż. JÓZEF WIECHOWSKI; Scientific Board Chair. Prof. Dr hab. Inż. MIECZYSŁAW HERING; publ. *Prace PIE* (quarterly).

Przemysłowy Instytut Maszyn Budowlanych (Construction Equipment Research Institute): ul. Napoleona 2, 05-230 Kobyłka; tel. (22) 786-23-26; fax (22) 786-18-30; e-mail pimb@pimb.com.pl; internet www.pimb.com.pl; f. 1952; library of 14,000 vols; Dir Dr ANDRZEJ MACHNIEWSKI; publ. *Prace PIMB* (irregular).

Przemysłowy Instytut Maszyn Rolniczych (Industrial Institute of Agricultural Machinery): ul. Starołęcka 31, 60-963 Poznań; tel. (61) 871-22-00; fax (61) 879-32-62; e-mail office@pimr.poznan.pl; internet www.pimr.poznan.pl; f. 1946; design and testing of agricultural machines and equipment; library of 11,000 vols; Man. Dir Dr Inż. TADEUSZ PAWŁOWSKI; Scientific Council Chair. Prof. Zw. Dr Inż. ZDZISŁAW KOŚMICKI; publs *Journal of Research and Applications in Agricultural Engineering* (4 a year), *Katalog – cennik ciągników i maszyn rolniczych* (2 a year), *Ciągniki i maszyny rolnicze. Budowa, przeznaczenie* (every 2 years).

Przemysłowy Instytut Motoryzacji (Automotive Industry Institute): ul. Jagiellońska 55, 03-301 Warsaw; tel. (22) 811-14-21; fax (22) 811-60-28; e-mail info@pimot.org.pl; internet www.pimot.org.pl; f. 1972; Dir Dr Inż LECH SOKALSKI; Scientific Council Chair. Prof. Dr hab. Inz. JERZY BARZYKOWSKI.

Przemysłowy Instytut Telekomunikacji (Telecommunications Research Institute): ul. Poligonowa 30, 04-051 Warsaw; tel. and fax (22) 810-23-81; e-mail office@pit.edu.pl; internet www.pit.edu.pl; f. 1934; radar technology, microwave technology and antennas, command control communication, intelligent systems (C3I); library of 22,000 vols; Dir Dr Inż. ROMAN DUFRENE; Scientific Council Chair. Prof. Dr Inż. STANISŁAW SŁAWIŃSKI; publs *Prace Przemysłowego Instytutu Telekomunikacji* (2 a year), *Postępy Radiotechniki* (2 a year).

Libraries and Archives

Białystok

Biblioteka Główna Politechniki Białostockiej (Main Library of Białystok Technical University): ul. Wiejska 45C, 15-351 Białystok; tel. (85) 746-33-30; fax (85) 746-33-32; e-mail bgpb@pb.bialystok.pl; internet libra .pb.bialystok.pl; f. 1951; 196,496 books, 38,224 periodicals, 89,022 special collections; Chief Custodian BARBARA KUBIAK.

Bydgoszcz

Wojewódzka i Miejska Biblioteka Publiczna im. dr. Witolda Bełzy w Bydgoszczy (Bydgoszcz Dr W. Bełza Voivodship and Public Municipal Library): ul. Długa 39, 85-034 Bydgoszcz; tel. (52) 339-92-00; fax (52) 328-73-90; e-mail wimbp .bydgoszcz@utp.edu.pl; internet www.wimbp .man.bydgoszcz.pl; f. 1903; 1,124,099 vols, incl. 8,214 old books, 6,444 maps and atlases, 1,892 MSS; Dir EWA STELMACHOWSKA; publ. *Bibliotekarz Kujawsko-Pomorski* (2 a year).

Cracow

Biblioteka Główna Akademii Pedagogicznej im. KEN (Main Library of the Pedagogical University of Cracow): ul. Podchorążych 2, 30-084 Cracow; tel. (12) 662-63-61; fax (12) 637-22-43; e-mail info@tessa.wsp .krakow.pl; internet www.ap.krakow.pl/ biblio/; f. 1946; 654,504 vols, 48,526 periodicals, 1,857 sound recordings; also audiovisual materials, CD-ROMs and microforms; Dir TERESA WILDHARDT.

Biblioteka Jagiellońska (Jagiellonian Library): al. Mickiewicza 22, 30-059 Cracow; tel. (12) 633-63-77; fax (12) 633-09-03; e-mail ujbj@if.uj.edu.pl; internet www.bj.uj.edu.pl; f. 1364; collection: national library for old books before 1800, central library of general scientific, Polish affairs, humanities, Polish writing of the 15th–18th c.; 1,943,406 vols, 707,207 periodicals, 7,447 online journals, 105,630 old prints (3,634 incunabula), 28,214 MSS, 37,759 music prints, 49,575 drawings and items of graphic art, 45,759 maps and atlases, and also flysheets and microforms; 46 university institute libraries: 1,782,508 units; Dir Dr HAB. Z. PIETRZYK; publ *Bulletin of the Jagiellonian Library* (annually), *Fontes et Studia Bibliotheca Jagellonica* (irregular).

Biblioteka Naukowa PAU i PAN w Krakowie (Scientific Library of the Polish Academy of Arts and Sciences and the Polish Academy of Sciences in Cracow): ul. Sławkowska 17, 31-016 Cracow; tel. (12) 431-00-21; fax (12) 422-29-15; e-mail biblioteka@pau .krakow.pl; f. 1856; 339,570 annual vols of periodicals relating to the social and biological sciences, 147,066 MSS, old prints, cartography, graphic arts; 674,199 vols; Dir KAROLINA GRODZISKA; publ. *Rocznik Biblioteki Naukowej PAU i PAN w Krakowie* (Yearbook).

Wojewódzka Biblioteka Publiczna w Krakowie (Cracow Voivode Public Library): ul. Rajska 1, 31-124 Cracow; tel. (12) 632-59-07; fax (12) 633-22-10; e-mail biblioteka@wbp .krakow.pl; internet www.wbp.krakow.pl; f. 1945; 550,000 vols; 771 regional brs; Dir Dr ARTUR PASZKO; publ. *Notes Biblioteczny* (2 a year).

Częstochowa

Biblioteka Główna Politechniki Częstochowskiej (Central Library of Częstochowa University of Technology): Al. Armii Krajowej 36, 42-200 Częstochowa; tel. (34) 361-44-73; fax (34) 365-15-07; e-mail bsekret@matinf .pcz.czest.pl; internet www.bg.pcz.czest.pl; f. 1950; 454,259 vols, incl. 138,156 books, 75,498 periodicals ,240,605 standards,

patents, etc.; Dir Mgr MAŁGORZATA HANKIEWICZ; publ. *Wykaz Nabytków Zagranicznych* (List of Foreign Acquisitions, monthly).

Gdańsk

Biblioteka Gdańska PAN (Gdańsk Library of the Polish Academy of Sciences): Wałowa 15, 80–858 Gdańsk; tel. (58) 301-22-51; fax (58) 301-55-23; e-mail bgpan@task.gda.pl; internet www.bgpan.gda.pl; former City Library; f. 1596; collection: humanities, social sciences, maritime, Pomeranian and Gdańsk affairs; 539,542 vols, incl. 55,114 old books, 634 incunabula, 80,284 periodicals, 5,275 MSS, 9,542 maps, 8,000 graphics; Dir Dr MARIA PELCZAR; publ. *Libri Gedanenses* (annually).

Biblioteka Główna Politechniki Gdańskiej (Central Library of Gdańsk Technical University): ul. G. Narutowicza 11/12, 80-952 Gdańsk; tel. 47-25-75; fax 47-27-58; e-mail library@sunrise.pg.gda.pl; 1,096,000 vols incl. 494,000 books, 113,000 periodicals, 491,000 standards, patents; Librarian Mgr JANINA LIGMAN; publs *Bibliografia Publikacji Pracowników Naukowych Politechniki Gdańskiej* (Bibliography of Publications of Scientific Workers of the Technical University of Gdańsk, irregular), *Raport Politechniki Gdańskiej* (Report of the Technical University of Gdansk, annually), *Wykaz Nabytków* (List of Acquisitions, monthly).

Gliwice

Biblioteka Główna Politechniki Śląskiej (Central Library of Silesian University of Technology): ul. Kaszubska 23, 44-100 Gliwice; tel. (32) 237-12-69; fax (32) 237-15-51; e-mail sekr@bibg.polsl.gliwice.pl; internet www.bg.polsl.pl; f. 1945; 570,990 vols in main library and 219,609 vols in departmental libraries; Dir Dr inz. KRZYSZTOF ZIOLO; Vice-Dir Dr inz. MARIA RYCHLEWSKA.

Katowice

Biblioteka Główna Śląskiej Akademii Medycznej (Main Library of the Silesian Medical University): ul. Poniatowskiego 15, 40-055 Katowice; tel. (32) 208-35-37; fax (32) 208-35-87; e-mail biblio@slam.katowice.pl; internet www.slam.katowice.pl; f. 1948; 175,000 vols; Head of Library Dr JERZY M. DYRDA; publs *Bibliografia publikacji pracowników* (annually), *Biuletyn Informacyjny SAM* (irregular).

Biblioteka Śląska (Silesian Library): Plac Rady Europy 1, 40-021 Katowice; tel. (32) 208-37-00; fax (32) 208-37-20; e-mail bsl@bs .katowice.pl; internet www.bs.katowice.pl; f. 1922; collection: social science, economics, literature relating to Silesia; 1,234,477 books (incl. 26,946 old vols), 200,416 vols of periodicals, 13,400 MSS, 17,758 maps and atlases, 8,047 drawings and prints, 26,842 postcards, 15,442 photographs, 242,645 documents of social life; Dir Prof. Dr hab. JAN MALICKI; publs *Książnica Śląska* (irregular), *Bibliografia Śląska* (annually), *Bibliografia Województwa Śląskiego* (annually).

Kielce

Biblioteka Główna Politechniki Świętokrzyskiej (Central Library of Świętokrzyska Technical University): Al. Tysiąclecia Państwa Polskiego 7, 25-314 Kielce; tel. (41) 342-44-83; fax (41) 344-76-35; e-mail library@eden.tu.kielce.pl; internet lib.tu.kielce.pl; f. 1966; 115,425 books, 34,468 vols of periodicals, 50,881 standards; Dir DANUTA KAPINOS.

Łódź

Biblioteka Uniwersytecka w Łódzi (Library of Łódż University): ul. Matejki 34/ 38, 90-237 Łódź; tel. (42) 635-40-29; fax (42)

678-16-78; e-mail bulinf@krysia.uni.lodz.pl; internet www.lib.uni.lodz.pl/library; f. 1945; 1,073,217 books, 423,499 vols of periodicals, 3,676 MSS, 18,847 maps and atlases, 59,017 vols of music, 47,321 iconographic items, 3,026 microfilms, 31,934 microfiches; Dir Dr JAN JANIAK.

Wojewódzka i Miejska Biblioteka Publiczna im. Marszałka Józefa Piłsudskiego (J. Piłsudski Scientific Public Regional Library of Łódź): ul. Gdańska 100/ 102, 90-508 Łódź; tel. (42) 637-30-90; fax (42) 637-21-02; e-mail informacja@hiacynt.wimbp .lodz.pl; internet www.wimbp.lodz.pl; f. 1917; general; special subjects socio-economic science and the arts; 496,278 books, 110,784 periodicals, 60,027 vols in special collns; Dir ELŻBIETA PAWLICKA; publ. *Sprawozdanie z działalności WiMBP* (annually).

Lublin

Biblioteka Główna Uniwersytetu Marii Curie-Skłodowskiej w Lublinie (Central Library of the M. Curie-Skłodowska University): ul. I. Radziszewskiego 11, 20-950 Lublin; tel. and fax (81) 537-58-35; e-mail kasbo@eos.umcs.lublin.pl; internet www.bg .umcs.lublin.pl; f. 1944; general scientific colln of 2,527,251 vols, including 494,867 vols of periodicals, 16,000 online journals, 803 MSS, 369,207 patents, 40,272 maps and atlases, 33,707 drawings and illustrations, 14,954 music scores, 19,215 ancient books, 4 incunabula, 2,814 dissertations, 4,900 audio cassettes and records; Dir Dr BOGUSŁAW KASPEREK.

Wojewódzka i Miejska Biblioteka Publiczna im H. Łopacińskiego (H. Łopacińskiego Voivodship and City Public Library): ul. Narutowicza 4, 20-950 Lublin; tel. (81) 532-39-47; fax (81) 532-39-47; e-mail info@ hieronim.wbp.lublin.pl, f. 1907; scientific and educational collection; 710,000 vols, 16,000 old vols, 35,000 periodicals, 2,800 MSS, 3,500 maps and atlases, 18,000 drawings and illustrations, 2,600 microfilms; Dir ZOFIA CIURUŚ; publs *Bibliotekarz Lubelski* (annually), *Dostrzegacz Biblioteczny* (irregular).

Poznań

Biblioteka Kórnicka PAN (Library of the Polish Academy of Sciences, Kórnik): 62-035 Kórnik, near Poznań; tel. (61) 817-00-81; fax (61) 817-19-30; e-mail bkpan@amu.edu.pl; internet www.bkpan.poznan.pl; f. 1828; 191,784 books, 79,680 periodicals, 15,222 MSS, 30,055 old prints, 14,000 graphics; collections on history, history of Polish literature, history of art, history of culture; attached literary museum; Dir Prof. Dr hab. STANISŁAW SIERPOWSKI; publ. *Pamiętnik Biblioteki Kórnickiej*.

Biblioteka Raczyńskich (Raczyńsky Library): Plac Wolności 19, 61-739 Poznań; tel. (61) 852-94-42; fax (61) 852-98-68; e-mail sekret@bracz.edu.pl; internet www.bracz .edu.pl; f. 1829; scientific and educational collection; 1,592,654 vols, 17,854 old books, 44,851 periodicals, 10,038 MSS, 11,596 maps and atlases, 37,083 ex-libris, 21,374 photos, 1,514 drawings and illustrations, 164 microfilms, 84,517 audio and video items; Dir WOJCIECH SPALENIAK.

Biblioteka Uniwersytecka (Library of Adam Mickiewicz University): Skr. Poczt. 526, ul. Ratajczaka 38/40, 61-816 Poznań; tel. (61) 829-38-20; fax (61) 829-38-24; e-mail library@amu.edu.pl; internet lib.amu.edu.pl; f. 1919; supports the academic programmes of the University and the University's curriculum in natural sciences, the humanities, mathematics, chemistry, physics, social science, law and languages; supports research activity of the academic community;

acquisition, organization and dissemination of information; provides training in computer literacy and web-based searches; 2,731,000 vols in central library, incl. 100,240 ancient vols, 5,600 MSS, 30,000 maps and atlases, 2,059,000 vols in departmental libraries; Dir Dr ARTUR JAZDON; publ. *Biblioteka* (annually).

Rzeszów

Biblioteka Główna Politechniki Rzeszowskiej (Central Library of Rzeszów University of Technology): ul. Pola 2, 35-959 Rzeszów; tel. (17) 854-25-33; fax (17) 854-25-33; e-mail bgprz@prz.rzeszow.pl; internet www.prz.rzeszow.pl/biblio/biblio.htm; f. 1951; 143,500 books, 33,600 vols of periodicals, 139,000 items in special collections; Dir Mgr ELŻBIETA KAŁUŻA.

Sopot

Biblioteka Główna Uniwersytetu Gdańskiego (Central Library of the University of Gdansk): ul. Armii Krajowej 110, 81-824 Sopot; tel. (58) 551-11-17; fax (58) 551-52-21; e-mail bib@bg.univ.gda.pl; internet www.bg.univ.gda.pl; f. 1970; 786,032 books, 140,424 items in special collections, 273,507 vols of periodicals; Dir URSZULA SAWICKA.

Szczecin

Biblioteka Główna Uniwersytetu Szczecińskiego (Library of University of Szczecin): ul. A. Mickiewicza 16, 70-384 Szczecin; tel. (91) 444-23-60; fax (91) 444-23-62; e-mail info@bg.univ.szczecin.pl; internet bg.univ.szczecin.pl; f. 1985; 1,300,000 vols; Dir JOLANTA GOC; publs *Wykaz ważniejszych nabytków* (irregular), *Bibliografia publikacji pracowników Uniwersytetu Szczecińskiego*.

Książnica Pomorska im. Stanisława Staszica (Stanisław Staszic Pomeranian Library): ul. Podgórna 15, 70-205 Szczecin; tel. (91) 481-91-10; fax (91) 481-91-15; e-mail ksiaznica@ksiaznica.szczecin.pl; internet www.ksiaznica.szczecin.pl; f. 1905; 848,087 vols, 157,930 vols of periodicals, 3,243 MSS, 30,410 early books, 250,010 govt documents, 38,287 standards, 9,036 maps and atlases, 19,032 records, 4,755 tapes, 2,407 CDs, 3,986 microforms; Dir LUCJAN BĄBOLEWSKI; publs *Bibliografia Pomorza Zachodniego. Piśmiennictwo polskie i Piśmiennictwo zagraniczne* (Bibliography of Western Pomerania. Polish Literature and Foreign Literature), *Bibliotekarz Zachodniopomorski* (The West Pomeranian Librarian, 4 a year).

Toruń

Wojewódzka Biblioteka Publiczna – Książnica Kopernikańska w Toruniu (Copernicus Library of Toruń): ul. Słowackiego 8, 87-100 Toruń; tel. (56) 622-66-42; fax (56) 622-55-13; e-mail ksiaznica@ksiaznica.torun.pl; internet www.ksiaznica.torun.pl; f. 1923; international exchange of information, bibliographic enquiries, archival research, research on cultural and political history of Pomerania; 769,419 books, incl. 26,300 old books, 92,926 vols of periodicals, 700 MSS, 3,807 cartographic units; Dir Mgr TERESA E. SZYMOROWSKA; publs *Folia Toruniensia* (irregular), *Regional Bibliography of Kujawy-Pomerania* (on CD-ROM, annually).

Warsaw

Archiwum Akt Nowych (Central Archive of Modern Records): ul. Hankiewicza 1, 02-103 Warsaw; tel. (22) 822-52-45; fax (22) 823-00-42; e-mail sekretariat@aan.gov.pl; internet www.aan.gov.pl; f. 1919; Dir JOLANTA LOUCHIN.

Archiwum Główne Akt Dawnych (Central Archives of Historical Records): ul.

Długa 7, 00-263 Warsaw; tel. (22) 831-54-19; fax (22) 831-16-08; e-mail archagad@poczta.onet.pl; internet www.archiwa.gov.pl/agad; f. 1808; archives from 13th century to 1918; 22,946 vols, 412,704 records; Dir Dr HUBERT WAJS.

Archiwum Polskiej Akademii Nauk (Archives of the Polish Academy of Sciences): ul. Nowy Swiat 72, 00-330 Warsaw; tel. (22) 657-28-48; fax (22) 826-81-30; e-mail archiwum@apan.waw.pl; internet www.apan.waw.pl; f. 1953; 26,000 vols; brs in Cracow, Poznań, Katowice; Dir Dr HANNA KRAJEWSKA; publ. *Biuletyn Archiwum PAN* (annually).

Biblioteka Narodowa (National Library): al. Niepodległości 213, 02-086 Warsaw; tel. (22) 608-29-99; fax (22) 825-52-51; e-mail biblnar@bn.org.pl; internet www.bn.org.pl; f. 1928; State central library; collection of writings in Polish and relating to Poland; basic foreign publications in the social sciences and humanities; library science literature; houses the Bibliographic Institute, the Institute of the Book and Reading; 2,362,014 books, 818,811 vols of periodicals, 26,466 MSS, 161616 old books, 113,878 maps and atlases, 476,712 drawings, photographs, illustrations, leaflets and posters, 116,112 music scores, 2,088,752 items of social ephemera, 241,518 reels of microfilm; Dir MICHAŁ JAGIEŁŁO; publs *Biuletyn Informacyjny Biblioteki Narodowej* (Information Bulletin, 4 a year), *Polish Libraries Today* (in English, irregular), *Rocznik Biblioteki Narodowej* (National Library Yearbook, scientific library science periodical, electronic, with English summaries).

Biblioteka Publiczna m. st. Warszawy-Biblioteka Główna Województwa Mazowieckiego (Warsaw Public Library—Central Library of Masovia Province): ul. Koszykowa 26–28, POB 365, 00-950 Warsaw; tel. (22) 621-78-52; fax (22) 621-19-68; e-mail Biblioteka@biblpubl.waw.pl; internet www.biblpubl.waw.pl; f. 1907; general collection; 1,249,083 vols, 13,000 old prints, 4,000 MSS, 18,400 maps and atlases, 39,600 standards, 3,933 drawings, 5,900 records; Dir MICHAŁ STRĄK; publ. *Bibliotekarz* (The Librarian, monthly).

Biblioteka Sejmowa (Sejm Library): ul. Wiejska 4, 00-902 Warsaw; tel. (22) 628-85-45; fax (22) 694-17-78; e-mail parlib@sejm.gov.pl; internet bs.sejm.gov.pl:4001/ALEPH; f. 1919; law, political and social sciences, modern history, economics; 260,000 vols, 112,000 vols of periodicals, 86,000 parliamentary, official and int. publs, 771 metres of archival documents, 35,000 sound and video recordings of Sejm meetings; Dir WOJCIECH KULISIEWICZ.

Biblioteka Szkoły Głównej Handlowej – Centralna Biblioteka Ekonomiczna (Library of Warsaw School of Economics – Central Economics Library): ul. Rakowiecka 22B, 02-521 Warsaw; tel. (22) 849-50-98; fax (22) 849-50-98; e-mail infnauk@sgh.waw.pl; f. 1906; collection: economics, sociology, social policy, geography, economic history, politics, statistics and demography, accounting, finance, co-operative movement, law, labour problems, foreign trade, marketing, industry, agriculture, transport, business and management; 741,693 books, 207,378 periodicals, 69,233 special collections; Dir Mgr ALICJA KENSKA; publs *Przegląd Bibliograficzny Piśmiennictwa Ekonomicznego* (4 a year), *Bibliografia Opublikowanego Dorobku Pracowników Naukowo-Dydaktycznych SGH, Wykaz Nabytków Wybranych Biblioteki SGH*.

Biblioteka Uniwersytecka w Warszawie (Warsaw University Library): Dobra 56–66, 00-312 Warsaw; tel. (22) 552-56-60; fax (22)

552-56-59; e-mail buw@uw.edu.pl; internet www.buw.uw.edu.pl; f. 1817; 2,815,322 vols, incl. 130,287 ancient vols, 652,131 periodicals, 6,534 MSS, 11,414 maps and atlases, 35,384 drawings and prints, 16,869 microforms, 72,208 vols of music, 112,137 documents of social life; Dir EWA KOBIERSKA-MACIUSZKO; publ. *Acta Bibliothecae Universitatis Varsoviensis* (irregular).

Centralna Biblioteka Rolnicza (Central Agricultural Library): POB 360, 00-950 Warsaw; ul. Krakowskie Przedmieście 66, 00-950 Warsaw; tel. (22) 826-60-41; fax (22) 826-01-57; e-mail listy@cbr.edu.pl; internet www.cbr.edu.pl; f. 1955; branch at Puławy; mem. of Agris-FAO; 235,000 vols and 693 current periodical titles on agriculture and related sciences; centre for information and documentation in agriculture and for exchange with scientific institutions abroad; Dir Dr RYSZARD MIAZEK; publs *Bibliography of Polish Agricultural and Food Economy Literature, Modern Agriculture: Science, Advice and Practice.*

Centralna Biblioteka Statystyczna (Central Statistical Library): al. Niepodległości 208, 00-925 Warsaw; tel. (22) 608-31-43; fax (22) 608-31-88; internet statlibr.stat.gov.pl; f. 1918; collection: scientific and specialized (economic and social subjects, with emphasis on statistics); 436,849 books, 1,500 periodical titles, 5,000 maps and atlases; Dir Mgr BOŻENA ŁAZOWSKA; publs *Bibliografia Wydawnictw Głównego Urzędu Statystycznego* (irregular), *Bibliografia Polskiego Piśmiennictwa Statystycznego* (irregular), *Bibliografie Piśmiennictwa Demograficznego, Roczniki zagraniczne w zbiorach Centralnej Biblioteki Statystycznej, Biuletyn Nabytków.*

Centralna Biblioteka Wojskowa (Central Military Library): ul. Ostrobramska 109, 04-041 Warsaw; tel. (22) 681-79-52; fax (22) 681-69-40; internet cbw.wp.mil.pl; f. 1919; 280,842 vols, 143,484 periodicals; special collection: 157,941 vols; Dir Col. Dr ANDRZEJ WESOŁOWSKI; publs *Polska Bibliografia Wojskowa* (Polish Military Bibliography, quarterly), *Biuletyn Nabytków Piśmiennictwa Wojskowego Centralnej Biblioteki Wojskowej* (irregular).

Główna Biblioteka Lekarska (Central Medical Library): Chocimska 22, 00-791 Warsaw; tel. (22) 849-78-51; fax (22) 849-78-02; e-mail gbl@gbl.waw.pl; internet www.gbl.waw.pl; f. 1945; collection of medical items, drawings and illustrations; 422,279 vols, 4,000 old vols, 1,156 MSS and 154,442 periodicals, 44,246 microforms; Dir Dr ALEKSANDER TULCZYŃSKI; publs *Biuletyn Głównej Biblioteki Lekarskiej* (2 a year), *Polska Bibliografia Lekarska* (year book).

Główna Biblioteka Pracy i Zabezpieczenia Społecznego (Central Library of Labour and Social Security): ul. Limanowskiego 23, 02-943 Warsaw; tel. (22) 642-04-73; fax (22) 642-19-27; e-mail gbpizs@gbpizs.gov.pl; internet www.gbpizs.gov.pl; f. 1974; affiliated to Ministry of Labour and Social Policy; collection: labour, wages, social affairs and related problems; 52,300 vols, 14,437 vols of periodicals; Dir Dr MAŁGORZATA KLOSSOWSKA; publs *Bibliography of economic and social problems of labour* (annually), *Documentation Review* (monthly), *special bibliographies* (irregular).

Naczelna Dyrekcja Archiwów Państwowych (Main Directorate of the Polish State Archives): ul. Długa 6, 00-950 Warsaw; tel. (22) 831-32-06; fax (22) 831-75-63; e-mail ndap@archiwa.gov.pl; internet www.archiwa.gov.pl; f. 1945; 19,032 vols; Dir-Gen. Doc. Dr hab. DARIA NAŁĘCZ; publs *Archeion* (2 a year), *Teki archiwalne* (annually), *Miscellanea Historico-Archivistica* (annually), *Colloquia*

Jerzy Skowronek dedicata (conference papers of the archives of Central and Eastern Europe, annually).

Ośrodek Informacji Naukowej Polskiej Akademii Nauk (Scientific Information Centre of the Polish Academy of Sciences): Pałac Kultury i Nauki, 00-901 Warsaw; f. 1953; 23,000 vols, 900 scientific periodicals from all over the world on social science and other scientific disciplines; Dir Dr ANDRZEJ GROMEK; publs *Przegląd Informacji o Naukoznawstwie* (Review of Information on Science of Science, 4 a year), *Zagadnienia Informacji Naukowej* (Problems of Information Science, 2 a year), *Przegląd Literatury Metodologicznej* (Review of Methodological Literature, 2 a year).

Ośrodek Przetwarzania Informacji (Information Processing Centre): al. Niepodległości 188B, 00-950 Warsaw; tel. (22) 825-12-40; fax (22) 825-33-19; e-mail opi@opi.org .pl; internet www.opi.org.pl; f. 1990; international co-operation, technology transfer, information services on research and development; database management; Dir Dr OLAF GAJL; publ. *Informator Nauki Polskiej* (Polish Research Directory, every 2 years).

Wrocław

Biblioteka Uniwersytecka we Wrocławiu (Library of the University of Wrocław): Szajnochy 10, 50-076 Wrocław; tel. (71) 346-31-20; fax (71) 344-49-30; e-mail infnauk@bu .uni.wroc.pl; internet www.bu.uni.wroc.pl; f. 1945; collection: 3,649,000 vols, incl. 14,000 manuscripts, 310,000 old prints, 12,000 cartographic items, 45,000 vols of music, 17,000 items of graphic art; Silesiaca and Lusatica; bibliography, international relations between Poland and other Slavonic countries and Germany; Dir GRAŻYNA PIOTROWICZ; publs *Bibliografia Publikacji Pracowników Uniwersytetu Wrocławskiego* (annually), *Bibliografia Piśmiennictwa o Uniwersytecie Wrocławskim* (irregular), *Bibliothecalia Wratislaviensia* (irregular).

Wojewódzka i Miejska Biblioteka Publiczna im. Tadeusza Mikulskiego we Wrocławiu (T. Mikulski Voivodship and Municipal Public Library): Rynek 58, 50-065 Wrocław; tel. (71) 344-40-01; fax (71) 344-18-08; e-mail wbp@wbp.wroc.pl; 253,000 vols, 128,000 special collections; Dir LEON KRZEMIENIECKI; publ. *Książka i Czytelnik* (2 a year).

Zakład Narodowy im. Ossolińskich (Ossoliński National Institute): ul. Szewska 37, 50-139 Wrocław; tel. (71) 344-44-71; fax (71) 344-85-61; e-mail znio@oss.wroc.pl; internet www.oss.wroc.pl; f. 1817; 1,646,738 vols; colln incl. MSS, old prints, graphics, drawings, bookplates, postcards, numismatic material, decorative items, badges, social documents, microforms, digitalized objects; Dir Dr ADOLF JUZWENKO; publs *Czasopismo Zakładu Narodowego im. Ossolińskich* (annually), *Rocznik Wrocławski* (annually).

Museums and Art Galleries

Bydgoszcz

Muzeum Okręgowe im. Leona Wyczółkowskiego (L. Wyczółkowski Museum): Gdańska 4, 85-006 Bydgoszcz; tel. (52) 585-98-14; fax (52) 585-98-16; f. 1880; Polish art since 19th c.; paintings and graphic art of Leon Wyczółkowski and gallery of contemporary Polish paintings; Archaeological and Local History brs and Coin Room; library of 41,000 vols; Dir Mgr Mgr IWONA LOOSE.

Bytom

Muzeum Górnośląskie w Bytomiu (Upper Silesian Museum): Pl. Jana III Sobieskiego 2, 41-902 Bytom; tel. (32) 281-82-94; fax (32) 281-34-01; e-mail mgbytom@us.edu.pl; internet www.muzeum.bytom.pl; f. 1927 in Katowice, transferred in 1945; history, archaeology, ethnography, natural history, Polish and foreign art; branch museum (ul. W. Korfantego 34, Bytom); library of 51,300 vols; Dir MIECZYSŁAW DOBKOWSKI; publ. *Rocznik Muzeum Górnośląskiego w Bytomiu* (annals).

Cracow

Muzeum Archeologiczne w Krakowie (Archaeological Museum in Cracow): ul. Senacka 3, 31-002 Cracow; tel. (12) 422-75-60; fax (12) 422-77-61; e-mail mak@ma .krakow.pl; internet www.ma.krakow.pl; f. 1850; library of 11,753 vols, 16,726 periodicals; Dir Dr JACEK RYDZEWSKI; publs *Materiały Archeologiczne* (annually), *Materiały Archeologiczne Nowej Huty* (annually).

Muzeum Etnograficzne im. S. Udzieli w Krakowie (Ethnographic Museum in Cracow): ul. Krakowska 46, 31-060 Cracow; tel. (12) 430-60-23; fax (12) 430-63-30; e-mail mek@tele2.pl; internet www.mek.tele2.pl; f. 1910; folk art and folk culture of Poland; also foreign collections from Europe, Asia, Africa, S. America; library of 30,000 vols; archives; Dir MARIA ZACHOROWSKA; publ. *Rocznik Muzeum Etnograficznego w Krakowie* (annually).

Muzeum Historyczne m. Krakowa (History Museum of the City of Cracow): Krzysztofory, Rynek Główny 35, 31-011 Cracow; tel. and fax (12) 422-32-64; e-mail sekretariat@ mhk.pl; internet www.mhk.pl; f. 1899; traditions, history and culture of the city of Cracow, model houses, arms and clocks, history of the theatre in Cracow, history and culture of the Jews in Cracow, history of the Cracow Fowler Brotherhood, upheaval and martyrdom of the Polish people in the period 1936–1956; library of 23,810 vols; special collection of 1,171 items; Dir MICHAŁ NIEZABITOWSKI; publ. *Krzysztofory-Zeszyty Naukowe* (annually).

Muzeum Narodowe w Krakowie (National Museum in Cracow): 3 Maja ave 1, 30-062 Cracow; tel. (12) 295-56-20; fax (12) 295-55-55; e-mail dyrekcja@muz-nar.krakow .pl; internet www.muzeum.krakow.pl; f. 1879; history, fine art, costume and textiles, arms and armour, numismatics, house-museums of Matejko, Wyspiański, Mehoffer and Szymanowski, Japanese art and technology; library of 300,000 vols and Czartoryski Library; Dir ZOFIA GOŁUBIEW; publs *Rozprawy i Sprawozdania Muzeum Narodowego w Krakowie* (Yearbook), *Notae Numismaticae Zapiski Numizmatyczne* (Numismatic Notes, annually).

Zamek Królewski na Wawelu (Wawel Royal Castle): Wawel 5, 31-001 Cracow; tel. (12) 422-51-55; fax (12) 422-19-50; e-mail zamek@wawel.krakow.pl; internet www .wawel.krakow.pl; f. 1930; collections of art in the Royal Castle: Italian Renaissance furniture, King Sigismund August's 16th c. collection of Flemish tapestries, Italian and Dutch painting, Polish carpets; Royal treasury: crown jewels, historical relics, banners, gold objects; Armoury: Polish and West European weapons; objects of Oriental art: Persian and Turkish weaponry and tents; oriental rugs, Chinese and Japanese pottery; collection relating to the history of Wawel Hill, other archaeological materials, Polish stove tiles from 15th–18th c.; 18th c. Meissen porcelain; library of 15,000 vols, 390 periodicals; Dir Prof. Dr hab. JAN OSTROWSKI; publs

Studia Waweliana (annually), *Biblioteka Wawelska, Acta Archaeologica Waweliana.*

Frombork

Muzeum Mikołaja Kopernika (Nicholas Kopernik Museum): ul. Katedralna 8, 14-530 Frombork; tel. (55) 244-00-71; fax (55) 244-00-72; e-mail frombork@frombork.art.pl; internet www.frombork.art.pl; f. 1948; biographical exhibits; history of astronomy; astronomical observatory; example of Foucault's pendulum; planetarium; modern art gallery; history of medicine; herb garden; library of 20,500 vols; Dir Mgr HENRYK SZKOP; publ. *Komentarze Fromborskie* (annual).

Gdańsk

Centralne Muzeum Morskie (Polish Maritime Museum): ul. Ołowianka 9–13, 80-751 Gdańsk; tel. (58) 301-86-11; fax (58) 301-84-53; e-mail info@cmm.pl; internet www.cmm .pl; f. 1960; depts of ports development, history of shipbuilding, history of maritime shipping and trade, marine fine arts, history of yachting, underwater archaeology, educational services; special vessel for underwater archaeological investigations; laboratory for conservation of artefacts recovered from sea; Lighthouse Museum in Rozewie; also br. in Hel (history of Polish fishery; open-air exhibition of types of fishing boats); br. in Tczew (history of Polish inland navigation); four historic ships (incl. sailing ship 'Dar Pomorza', fmr Polish school-ship); library of 42,000 vols, archives: plans, drawings, photos, documents; Dir Dr inż. JERZY LITWIN.

Muzeum Archeologiczne w Gdańsku (Archaeological Museum in Gdańsk): ul. Mariacka 25/26, 80-958 Gdańsk; tel. (58) 301-50-31; fax (58) 301-52-28; e-mail mag@ archeologia.pl; internet www.archeologia.pl; f. 1953; library of 23,000 vols; Dir HENRYK PANER; publs *Pomorania Antiqua*, *Gdańsk Archaeological Museum African Reports.*

Muzeum Historii Miasta Gdańska (History Museum of the City of Gdańsk): Ratusz Głównego Miasta, ul. Długa 47, 80-831 Gdańsk; tel. (58) 301-48-71; fax (58) 301-48-71; f. 1970; Dir ADAM KOPERKIEWICZ.

Muzeum Narodowe w Gdańsku (National Museum in Gdańsk): ul. Toruńska 1, 80-822 Gdańsk; tel. (58) 301-70-61; fax (58) 301-11-25; e-mail info@muzeum.narodowe.gda.pl; internet www.muzeum.narodowe.gda.pl; f. 1872; art since 12th c., craftwork since 15th c., photography, ethnography (collns held at various locations); library of 19,224 vols, 3,506 periodicals; Dir TADEUSZ PIASKOWSKI.

Kielce

Muzeum Narodowe w Kielcach (National Museum in Kielce): Pl. Zamkowy 1, 25-010 Kielce; tel. (41) 344-40-14; fax (41) 344-82-61; e-mail poczta@muzeumkielce.net; internet www.muzeumkielce.net; f. 1908; brs: Museum of Stefan Żeromski's early years, Henryk Sienkiewicz Museum in Oblęgorek; library of 40,000 vols; Dir Prof. Dr KRZYSZTOF URBAŃSKI; publ. *Rocznik Muzeum Świętokrzyskiego* (annual) from vol 10 *Rocznik Muzeum Narodowego w Kielcach.*

Łódź

Centralne Muzeum Włókiennictwa (Central Museum of Textiles): ul. Piotrkowska 282, 93-034 Łódź; tel. (42) 683-26-84; fax (42) 684-33-55; e-mail ctmustex@ muzeumwlokiennictwa.pl; internet www .muzeumwlokiennictwa.pl; f. 1960; collections of textile tools and machines, documents of history of textile industry, Polish and foreign artistic textiles, industrial textiles, ancient and modern clothes, folk textiles; library of 12,000 vols; Dir NORBERT ZAWISZA; publ. *Bulletin*.

Muzeum Archeologiczne i Etnograficzne: Pl. Wolności 14, 91-415 Łódź; tel. (42) 632-84-40; fax (42) 632-97-14; f. 1956; archaeology, ethnography, numismatics; radio-chemical laboratory; library of 47,000 vols; Dir Doc. Dr hab. RYSZARD GRYGIEL; publ. *Prace i Materiały Muzeum Archeologicznego i Etnograficznego* (archaeology, ethnography, numismatics and conservation series).

Muzeum Sztuki w Łodzi (Art Museum): ul. Więckowskiego 36, 90-743 Łódź; tel. (42) 633-97-90; fax (42) 632-99-41; e-mail muzeum@muzeumsztuki.lodz.pl; internet www .muzeumsztuki.lodz.pl; f. 1929; departments: Gothic art; foreign painting of the 15th–19th c.; Polish painting since 17th c.; international modern and contemporary art; Księży Młyn house with late-19th c. interior décor; library of 36,000 vols; Dir MIROSŁAW BORUSIEWICZ.

Lublin

Muzeum Lubelskie w Lublinie (Lublin Provincial Museum): The Castle (Zamek), ul. Zamkowa 9, 20-117 Lublin; tel. and fax (81) 532-17-43; e-mail kancelaria@zamek-lublin .pl; internet www.zamek-lublin.pl; f. 1906; regional archaeological, historical and ethnographic collection, Polish and foreign paintings and decorative art; armoury; numismatics; conservation dept; 14th c. Holy Trinity Chapel, with 15th c. paintings; 13th c. dungeon; library of 20,000 vols; Dir ZYGMUNT NASALSKI; publ. *Studia i Materiały Lubelskie*.

Państwowe Muzeum na Majdanku (State Museum in Majdanek): ul. Droga Męczenników Majdanka 67, 20-325 Lublin; tel. (81) 744-26-47; fax (81) 744-05-26; e-mail dyr@majdanek.pl; internet www.majdanek.pl; f. 1944; former Nazi concentration camp; Dir EDWARD BALAWEJDER; publ. *Zeszyty Majdanka* (annually).

Olsztynek

Muzeum Budownictwa Ludowego— Park Etnograficzny w Olsztynku (Museum of Building, Ethnographic Park in Olsztynek): ul. Sportowa 21, 11-015 Olsztynek; tel. and fax (89) 519-21-64; e-mail mbl_olsztynek@olsztyn.ken.pl; internet www .muzeumbudludolsztynek.republika.pl; f. 1962; library of 9,345 vols; Dir TADEUSZ KUFEL.

Oświęcim

Państwowe Muzeum Auschwitz-Birkenau w Oświęcimiu/Auschwitz-Birkenau Memorial and Museum in Oświęcim: ul. Więźniów Oświęcimia 20, 32-620 Oświęcim; tel. (33) 844-81-02; fax (33) 843-19-34; e-mail muzeum@auschwitz.org.pl; internet www .auschwitz.org.pl; f. 1947; former Nazi concentration camp at Auschwitz-Birkenau, illustrating system of mass extermination; library of 20,000 vols, 2,500 periodicals and archives; Dir Mgr JERZY WRÓBLEWSKI; publ. *Zeszyty Oświęcimskie* (in Polish and German).

Poznań

Muzeum Archeologiczne: ul. Wodna 27, 61-781 Poznań; tel. (61) 852-64-30; fax (61) 853-10-10; e-mail lechk@man.poznan.pl; internet www.muzarp.poznan.pl; f. 1857; archaeology of Greater Poland and the Nile basin; library of 50,000 vols; Dir Prof. Dr LECH KRZYŻANIAK; publs *Fontes Archaeologici Posnanienses* (annually), *Biblioteka Fontes Archaeologici Posnanienses* (irregular), *Studies in African Archaeology* (irregular).

Muzeum Narodowe (National Museum): Al. Marcinkowskiego 9, 61-745 Poznań; tel. (61)) 856-80-00; fax (61) 851-58-98; e-mail

mnp@mnp.art.pl; internet www.mnp.art.pl; f. 1857; Medieval Art, European paintings 14th–19th c., Polish paintings since 15th c., Prints and drawings, Sculpture, Numismatics, Modern art; library of 89,000 vols; br. museums specializing in ethnography, Poznań history, military history, musical instruments, applied arts; Dir Prof. Dr hab. WOJCIECH SUCHOCKI; publs *Studia Muzealne* (annually), *Monographs*.

Sanok

Muzeum Budownictwa Ludowego w Sanoku (Museum of Folk Architecture in Sanok): ul. Traugutta 3, 38-500 Sanok; tel. (13) 463-09-04; fax (13) 463-53-81; e-mail skansen.sanok@pro.onet.pl; f. 1958; traditional architecture, interiors, folk arts and crafts, icons; library of 18,900 vols on the Orthodox church and ethnography; Dir Mgr JERZY GINALSKI; publs *Materiały Muzeum Budownictwa Ludowego w Sanoku* (every 2 years), *Acta Scansenologica* (every 2 years).

Szczecin

Muzeum Narodowe w Szczecinie (National Museum in Szczecin): ul. Staromłyńska 27, 70-561 Szczecin; tel. (91) 431-52-00; fax (91) 431-52-04; e-mail biuro@muzeum .szczecin.pl; internet www.muzeum.szczecin .pl; f. 1945; Pomeranian art and archaeology, Polish art since 19th c., African and Asian art, maritime and ethnological collections; library of 77,831 vols; Dir LECH KARWOWSKI; publs *Mare Articum—The Baltic Art Magazine* (2 a year), *Materiały Zachodniopomorskie* (annually).

Sztutowo

Państwowe Muzeum Stutthof w Sztutowie (State Museum in Sztutowo): ul. Muzealna 6, 82-110 Sztutowo; tel. (55) 247-83-53; fax (55) 247-83-58; e-mail stutthof@stutthof.pl; internet www.stutthof.pl/en/main.htm; former Nazi concentration camp of Stutthof; f. 1962; Dir ROMUALD DRYNKO; publ. *Zeszyty Muzeum Stutthof* (annually).

Toruń

Muzeum Etnograficzne w Toruniu (Ethnographical Museum in Toruń): Wały gen. Sikorskiego 19, 87-100 Toruń; tel. (56) 622-80-91; fax (56) 622-89-44; internet www .zabytki.pl/sources/muzea/t/torun-etnograf .html; f. 1959; folk culture of northern Poland; library of 18,142 vols; Dir ROMAN TÚBAJA; publ. *Rocznik Muzeum Etnograficznego w Toruniu* (annually).

Muzeum Okręgowe w Toruniu (District Museum in Toruń): Rynek Staromiejski 1, Ratusz, 87-100 Toruń; tel. (56) 622-36-84; fax (56) 622-40-29; e-mail muzeum@muzeum .torun.pl; internet www.muzeum.torun.pl; f. 1861; 14th- to 20th-century art (painting, graphics, sculpture, handicrafts), Far-Eastern art, history, archaeology, militaria, numismatics, Copernicus museum; library of 25,000 vols; Dir Dr ANNA KOSICKA; publs *Rocznik Muzeum w Toruniu* (Toruń Museum Yearbook), *Biuletyn* (Bulletin, 4 a year).

Warsaw

Muzeum Historyczne m. st. Warszawy (History Museum of the City of Warsaw): Rynek Starego Miasta 28, 00-272 Warsaw; tel. (22) 635-16-25; fax (22) 831-94-91; e-mail mhw@zabytki.pl; f. 1948; exhibits relating to the history of Warsaw from the 10th century; library of 42,000 vols; Dir Prof. Dr JANUSZ DURKO; publ. *Almanach Muzealny* (every 2 years).

Muzeum i Instytut Zoologii PAN (Institute of Zoology): ul. Wilcza 64, 00-679 Warsaw; tel. (22) 629-32-21; fax (22) 629-63-02; e-mail sekretariat@miiz.waw.pl; internet

www.miiz.waw.pl; f. 1819; attached to Polish Acad. of Sciences; research in various fields of zoology; molecular and three-dimensional morphometrics laboratory; research station at Łomna near Warsaw; zoological collections of 8,178,000 specimens; archives and documents; library of 117,696 vols, 696 current periodicals, 4,953 maps; Dir Prof. WIESŁAW BOGDANOWICZ; publs *Annales Zoologici* (4 a year), *Fragmenta Faunistica* (2 a year), *Acta Ornithologica* (2 a year), *Acta Chiropterologica* (2 a year).

Muzeum Literatury im. Adama Mickiewicza (Adam Mickiewicz Museum of Literature): Rynek Starego Miasta 20, 00-272 Warsaw; tel. (22) 831-40-61; fax (22) 831-76-92; e-mail muzeum.literatury@poczta.wp.pl; f. 1951; museum of literary history of Poland especially 19th and 20th c.; library of 110,000 vols; Dir JANUSZ ODROWĄŻ-PIENIĄŻEK; publ. *Blok-Notes Muzeum Literatury*.

Muzeum Narodowe w Warsawie (National Museum in Warsaw): Al. Jerozolimskie 3, 00-495 Warsaw; tel. (22) 621-10-31; fax (22) 622-85-59; e-mail muzeum@mnw .art.pl; internet www.mnw.art.pl; f. 1862; paintings and sculpture; prints and drawings; numismatics; decorative arts and crafts; photography; Egyptian, Greek, Roman and Byzantine (Nubian) art; medieval and modern Polish art since 12th c.; 14th–19th c. foreign painting; also administers the Poster Museum at Wilanów, Królikarnia palace in Warsaw and, outside Warsaw, Nieborów Palace; Otwock Palace; library of 130,000 vols; Dir FERDYNAND RUSZCYC; Director for Collection, Research and Education Dr DOROTA FOLGA JANUSZEWSKA; publ. *Bulletin du Musée National de Varsovie* (quarterly).

Muzeum Niepodległości (Museum of Independence): Al. Solidarności 62, 00-240 Warsaw; tel. (22) 827-37-70; fax (22) 827-03-23; e-mail promocja@muzeumniepodleglosci.art .pl; internet www.muzeumniepodleglosci.art .pl; f. 1990; history of Polish independence movements; library of 27,600 vols, 3,800 periodicals; Dir Dr ANDRZEJ STAWARZ.

Muzeum Techniki w Warszawie (Warsaw Museum of Technology): Pałac Kultury i Nauki, 00-901 Warsaw; tel. (22) 656-67-59; fax (22) 620-47-10; f. 1875; popularization of science and technology and their history, preservation of monuments of technology; planetarium; cinema; local branches: Museum of Ancient Metallurgy in Nowa Słupia, Museum of the old Polish Basin in Sielpia, water-powered forges in Stara Kuźnica and Gdańsk, 19th-century blast furnace in Chlewiska, Museum of Industry in Old Rolling Mill, Warsaw; library of 17,160 vols; Dir JERZY JASIUK.

Muzeum Wojska Polskiego (Polish Military Museum): 43, Al. Jerozolimskie 3, Warsaw; tel. (22) 629-52-71; fax (22) 629-52-73; e-mail muzeumwp@wp.mil.pl; f. 1920; collection of 79,000 weapons, uniforms, banners, decorations, etc; permanent exhibition showing Polish military history since 10th c.; militaria from Asia, Africa, Australia; collection of modern paintings, sculptures and graphics; iconographic collection; conservation workshops for metal, textile, wooden, leather and paper exhibits; library of 40,000 vols; Dir Colonel JACEK MACYSZYN; publ. *Muzealnictwo Wojskowe* (Military Museology, irregular).

Muzeum Ziemi PAN (Museum of the Earth): al. Na Skarpie 20–26, 00-488 Warsaw; tel. (22) 629-80-63; fax (22) 629-74-97; e-mail mzgeol@warman.com.pl; internet www.mz-pan.pl/menu/start.htm; f. 1932; attached to Polish Acad. of Sciences; most important collections: Polish minerals, rocks, metcorites, fossil flora and fauna, Baltic amber; Dir Doc. KRZYSZTOF JAKUBOWSKI; publ. *Prace Muzeum Ziemi PAN* (1 or 2 a year).

Ogród Botaniczny – Centrum Zachowania Różnorodności Biologicznej PAN (Botanical Garden – Centre for the Conservation of Biological Diversity): 76, ul. Prawdziwka 2, POB 45, 02-973 Warsaw; tel. (22) 648-38-56; fax (22) 757-66-45; e-mail obpan@ ikp.atm.com.pl; internet www.obpanwar.pl; f. 1974; attached to Polish Acad. of Sciences; conservation and evaluation of genetic resources of plants; library of 8,000 vols; Dir JERZY PUCHALSKI; publs *Biuletyn* (annually), *Prace* (reports, irregular).

Państwowe Muzeum Archeologiczne (State Archaeological Museum): ul. Długa 40, 00-950 Warsaw; tel. (22) 831-32-21; fax (22) 831-51-95; e-mail pma@pma.pl; internet www.pma.pl/main.html; f. 1923; prehistoric and proto-historic exhibits; organizes regional and field exhibitions, and carries out archaeological excavations throughout Poland; archaeological stores at Rybno; library of 55,000 vols; Dir Dr WOJCIECH BRZEZINSKI; publ. *Wiadomości Archeologiczne* (irregular).

Państwowe Muzeum Etnograficzne w Warszawie (State Ethnographic Museum in Warsaw): ul. Kredytowa 1, 00-056 Warsaw; tel. (22) 827-76-41; fax (22) 827-66-69; e-mail pme@pme.art.pl; internet www.pme .art.pl; f. 1888; Polish and non-European ethnographical collection; library of 23,000 vols; Dir Dr JAN WITOLD SULIGA; publ. *Zeszyty Państwowego Muzeum Etnograficznego w Warszawie* (Reports, annually).

Zamek Królewski w Warszawie—Pomnik Historii i Kultury Narodowej (Royal Castle in Warsaw, National History and Culture Memorial): Pl. Zamkowy 4, 00-277 Warsaw; tel. (22) 657-21-70; fax (22) 657-21-27; e-mail zamek@zamek-krolewski.art.pl; internet www.zamek-krolewski.art.pl; f. 1980; furniture, carpets and rugs, paintings, sculpture, applied arts, drawings, numismatics; library of 25,000 vols; Dir ANDRZEJ ROTTERMUND; publ. *Kronika Zamkowa* (2 a year).

Wieliczka

Muzeum Żup Krakowskich Wieliczka (Cracow Salt Works Museum in Wieliczka): Zamkowa 8, 32-020 Wieliczka; tel. (12) 422-19-47; fax (12) 278-30-28; e-mail promocja@ muzeum.wieliczka.pl; internet www .muzeum.wieliczka.pl; f. 1951; history, archaeology, geology, history of art and ethnography, archives, metal conservation laboratory; library of 18,000 vols, special collections: photographs, mining maps; Dir Prof. ANTONI JODŁOWSKI; publ. *Studia i Materiały do Dziejów Żup Solnych w Polsce* (annually).

Wrocław

Muzeum Architektury (Museum of Architecture): ul. Bernardyńska 5, 50-156 Wrocław; tel. (71) 343-36-75; fax (71) 344-65-77; e-mail muzeum@ma.wroc.pl; internet www .ma.wroc.pl; f. 1965; Polish and other architecture; modern art; library of 7,000 vols; Dir Dr JERZY ILKOSZ.

Muzeum Historyczne we Wrocławiu (Historical Museum in Wrocław): ul. Sukiennice 14/15, 50-107 Wrocław; tel. (71) 44-57-30; fax (71) 44-47-85; f. 1970; Dir MACIEJ ŁAGIEWSKI.

Muzeum Narodowe we Wrocławiu (National Museum in Wrocław): Pl. Powstańców Warszawy 5, 50-153 Wrocław; tel. (71) 372-51-50; fax (71) 343-56-43; e-mail muzeumnarodowe@wr.onet.pl; internet www

.mnwr.art.pl; f. 1948; collection of medieval art, Polish painting since 17th c., European painting since 16th c., decorative arts, prints, photographs, ethnography and history relating to Silesia, panoramic painting 'Battle of Racławice'; numismatics; library of 92,889 vols; Dir MARIUSZ HERMANSDORFER; publ. *Roczniki Sztuki Śląskiej* (annually).

Zakopane

Muzeum Tatrzańskie im. Tytusa Chałubińskiego (T. Chałubiński Tatra Museum): ul. Krupówki 10, 34-500 Zakopane; tel. (18) 201-52-05; fax (18) 206-38-72; e-mail museum@tatrynet.pl; internet www.muzeum .tatrynet.pl; f. 1888; geology, regional flora, fauna, history and ethnography; glass paintings, pottery, sculpture, wooden, metal and leather ware, costumes, musical instruments, etc.; collection of furniture, textiles, ceramics and jewellery made in the Zakopane style; collection of oriental carpets; contemporary pictures by St. Ignacy Witkiewicz and Marek Zuławsky; Wł. Hasior Art Gallery; library of 50,000 vols; Dir Mgr TERESA JABŁOŃSKA; publ. *Rocznik Podhalański*.

Universities

UNIWERSYTET W BIAŁYMSTOKU
(University of Białystok)

ul. Marii Sklodowskiej-Curie 14 15-097 Białystok

Telephone: (82) 745-70-01
Fax: (82) 744-77-49
E-mail: uniwersytet@uwb.edu.pl
Internet: www.uwb.edu.pl
State control

Rector: Prof. JERZY NIKITOROWICZ
Pro-Rector for Financial Matters and Regional Relations: Dr MAREK PRONIEWSKI
Pro-Rector for Research Matters and International Relations: Dr HALINA PARAFIANOWICZ
Pro-Rector for Teaching Matters and Students' Affairs: Prof. MIROSŁAWA MELEZINI

DEANS

Faculty of Biology and Chemistry: Prof. ANATOL KOJŁO
Faculty of Economics: Dr ROBERT CIBOROWSKI
Faculty of Education and Psychology: Prof. ELWIRA KRYŃSKA
Faculty of History and Sociology: Prof. ANDRZEJ SADOWSKI
Faculty of Law: Prof. LEONARD ETEL
Faculty of Mathematics and Physics: Prof. STANISŁAW UBA
Faculty of Philology: Dr BAZYLI SIEGIEŃ

UNIWERSYTET JAGIELLOŃSKI
(Jagiellonian University)

ul. Gołębia 24, 31-007 Cracow

Telephone: (12) 422-10-33
Fax: (12) 422-63-06
E-mail: rektor@adm.uj.edu.pl
Internet: www.uj.edu.pl
Founded 1364
Academic year: October to June

Rector: Prof. Dr hab. KAROL MUSIOŁ
Vice-Rector (Collegium Medicum): Prof. Dr hab. WIESŁAW PAWLIK
Vice-Rector (Development): Prof. Dr hab. PIOTR TWORZEWSKI
Vice-Rector (Educational Affairs): Prof. Dr hab. MARIA SZEWCZYK
Vice-Rector (Personal and Financial Affairs): Prof. Dr hab. WŁADYSŁAW MIODUNKA
Vice-Rector (Research and International Relations): Prof. Dr hab. SZCZEPAN BILINSKI

Administrator: Dr TADEUSZ SKARBEK
Librarian: Prof. Dr hab. ZDZISŁAW PIETRZYK
Library: see Libraries and Archives
Number of teachers: 3,407
Number of students: 41,086

Publications: *Zeszyty Naukowe Uniwersytetu Jagiellońskiego* (annually in 26 series), *Kronika* (annually), *Alma Mater* (monthly), *Zmieniające się przedsiębiorstwo w zmieniającej się politycznie Europie* (annually), *Materiały Edukacyjne Bibliotekoznawstwa i Informacji Naukowej* (annually), *Management in Culture* (2 a year), *Zeszyty Prasoznawcze* (4 a year), *Acta Physica Polonica B* (monthly), *Ad Americam* (annually), *Biuletyn Biblioteki Jagiellońskiej* (annually), *Romanica Cracoviensia* (annually), *Cracow Indological Studies* (irregular), *Estetyka i Krytyka* (4 a year), *Eurasian Prehistory* (2 a year), *Forum Europejskie* (4 a year), *Foton* (4 a year), *Kwartalnik Religioznawczy NOMOS* (4 a year), *MODUS Prace z Historii Sztuki* (annually), *Nowy Filomata* (4 a year), *Peregrinus Cracoviensis* (irregular), *Politea* (annually), *Prace Archeologiczne* (irregular), *Prace Archeologiczne—Studies in Ancient Art and Civilization* (irregular), *Prace Geograficzne* (irregular), *Prace Historyczne* (annually), *Principia* (2 a year), *Przekładaniec* (literary translation, 2 a year), *Recherches Archéologiques* (irregular), *Reports on Mathematical Logic* (annually), *Reports on Philosophy* (annually), *Schedae Informaticae*, *Studia z zakresu Prawa Pracy i Polityki Społecznej* (annually), *Universitatis Jegellonicae Acta Mathematica* (annually)

DEANS

Faculty of Biology and Earth Sciences: Prof. Dr hab. KAZIMIERZ KRZEMIEŃ
Faculty of Biotechnology: Prof. Dr hab. KAZIMIERZ STRZAŁKA
Faculty of Chemistry: Prof. Dr hab. LEONARD M. PRONIEWICZ
Faculty of Health Care: Prof. Dr hab. JOLANTA JAWOREK
Faculty of History: Prof. Dr hab. ANDRZEJ BANACH
Faculty of International and Political Studies: Prof. Dr hab. WIESŁAW KOZUB-CIEMBRONIEWICZ
Faculty of Law and Administration: Prof. Dr hab. TADEUSZ WŁUDYKA
Faculty of Management and Social Communication: Prof. Dr hab. MICHAŁ DU VALL
Faculty of Mathematics and Computer Science: Prof. Dr hab. MAREK JARNICKI
Faculty of Medicine: Prof. Dr hab. WOJCIECH NOWAK
Faculty of Pharmacy: Prof. Dr hab. JOANNA SZYMURA-OLEKSIAK
Faculty of Philology: Prof. Dr hab. MARCELA SEWIĄTKOWSKA
Faculty of Philosophy: Prof. Dr hab. MARIA FLIS
Faculty of Physics, Astronomy and Applied Computer Science: Prof. Dr hab. JERZY SZWED
Faculty of Polish Studies: Prof. Dr hab. JACEK POPIEL

PROFESSORS

Faculty of Biology and Earth Sciences (tel. (12) 422-63-48; fax (12) 430-14-73; e-mail binoz@adm.uj.edu.pl; internet www.uj.edu .pl/uj-guide/biol.en.html):

BILIŃSKA, B., Animal Physiology
BILIŃSKI, Sz., Cell Biology
BOBEK, B., Wildlife Research
CHEŁMICKI, W., Geography
DĄBROWSKI, Z., Animal Physiology
DOMANSKI, B., Geography
DZWONKO, Z., Plant Ecology

FALNIOWSKI, A., Malacology
GÓRECKI, A., Ecology
GREGORASZCZUK, E., Animal Physiology
GUZIK, CZ., Population and Agricultural Geography
JACKOWSKI, A., Geography of Religion
KACZANOWSKI, K., Anthropology
KOZŁOWSKI, J., Hydrobiology
KRZEMIEŃ, K., Geomorphology
KUTA, E., Cytology and Embryology of Plants
LASKOWSKI, R., Ecology
LITYŃSKA, A., Glycobiology
ŁOMNICKI, A., Population Ecology
MARCHLEWSKA-KOJ, A., Mammalian Reproduction
MORYCOWA, E., Palaeozoology
MYDEL, R., Geographical Studies on Japan
OBRĘBSKA-STARKEL, B., Climatology
OLECH, M., Plant Taxonomy
OSZCZYPKO, N., Geology
PETRYSZAK, B., Systematic Zoology and Zoological Geography
PŁYTYCZ, B., Evolutionary Immunology
PRZYWARA, L., Plant Cytology and Embryology
RADOMSKI, A., Geology
RAFIŃSKI, J., Evolutionary Biology
SAWICKA-KAPUSTA, K., Ecology, Environmental Protection
SKIBA, S., Soil Geography and Pedology
SLĄCZKA, A., Tectonics and Stratigraphy
SZOŁTYS, M., Zoology
SZYMURA, J. M., Zoology
TRZCIŃSKA-TACIK, H., Botany
TURNAU, K., Plant Taxonomy and Phytogeography
UCHMAN, A., Geology, Sedimentology, Ichnology
WEINER, J., Ecological Bioenergetics and Evolutionary Ecosystems
WIDACKI, W., Geography
WOJTUSIAK, J., Zoology
WOYCIECHOWSKI, M., Ecology and Evolution
ŻABIŃSKI, W., Geology
ZAJĄC, A., Plant Taxonomy and Phytogeography
ZAJĄC, M., Phytogeography
ZEMANEK, A., Botany
ZEMANEK, B., Phytogeography
ZUCHIEWICZ, W., Geology

Faculty of Biotechnology (ul. Gronostajowa 7, 30-387 Cracow; tel. (12) 252-60-02; fax (12) 252-69-02; e-mail sekretariat@mol.uj.edu.pl; internet www.mol.uj.edu.pl):

DUBIN, A., Biochemistry
FRONCISZ, W., Biophysics
GABRYŚ, H., Plant Physiology
KLEIN, A., Biochemistry
KOJ, A., Biochemistry
KOROHODA, WŁ., Cell Biology
ŁUKIEWICZ, S., Biophysics
PASENKIEWICZ-GIERULA, M., Molecular Biophysics
POTEMPA, J., Biochemistry, Biotechnology
PRYJMA, J., Microbiology and Immunology
SARNA, T., Biophysics
STRZAŁKA, K., Biochemistry
WASYLEWSKI, Z., Physical Biochemistry
WIĘCKOWSKI, S., Plant Physiology
ŻAK, Z., Animal Biochemistry

Faculty of Chemistry (ul. Ingardena 3, 30-060 Cracow; tel. (12) 633-63-77 ext. 2215; fax (12) 634-05-15; e-mail sekretar@chemia.uj.edu.pl; internet www.ch.uj.edu.pl):

BARAŃSKI, A., Chemical Kinetics
BOGDANOWICZ-SZWED, K., Chemistry of Heterocyclic Compounds
DATKA, J., Inorganic Chemistry and Infrared Spectroscopy
DZIEMBAJ, R., Catalysis, Solid State Chemistry and Technology
HODOROWICZ, S. A., Crystallography and Solid State Chemistry

JUSZKIEWICZ, A., Physical and Environmental Chemistry
KOŚCIELNIAK, P., Analytical and Forensic Chemistry
NAJBAR, J., Physical Chemistry, Photophysics and Photochemistry
NAJBAR, M., Inorganic and Environmental Catalysis
NALEWAJSKI, R. F., Theoretical Chemistry, Quantum Chemistry
NOWAKOWSKA, M., Physical Chemistry, Photochemistry of Polymers
OLEKSYN, B., Crystallography and Crystal Chemistry
PALUCH, M., Physical Chemistry, Surface Chemistry
PARCZEWSKI, A., Chemometrics and Analytical Chemistry
PAWLIKOWSKI, M., Theoretical Chemistry, Molecular Spectroscopy
PETELENZ, P., Theoretical Chemistry
PRONIEWICZ, L.M., Chemical Physics, Molecular Spectroscopy
SILBERRING, J., Biochemistry and Neurochemistry
STASICKA, Z., Inorganic and Coordination Chemistry
STOCHEL, G., Inorganic and Bioinorganic Chemistry
WÓJCIK, M., Physical Chemistry, Molecular Spectroscopy

Faculty of Health Care (ul. Michałowskiego 12, 31-126 Cracow; tel. (12) 421-41-41; fax (12) 421-41-41; e-mail kbrzezns@cm-uj.krakow.pl; internet www.cm-uj.krakow.pl):

CZABAŁA, J., Psychology
GOLINOWSKA, S., Health Economics
HAŁUSZKA, J., Environmental Health
PILC, A., Pharmacology
SPODARYK, K., Physiotherapy
SZAFRAN, Z., Biochemistry
WŁODARCZYK, W., Health Policy

Faculty of History (tel. (12) 422-77-62; fax (12) 430-14-67; e-mail historia@adm.uj.edu.pl; internet www.uj.edu.pl/uj-guide/history.en.html):

BACZKOWSKI, K., General Medieval History
BAŁUS, K., History of Late Modern Art
BRZOZA, CZ., Modern Polish History
CENTAROWICZ, A., General Modern History
CHOCHOROWSKI, J., Archaeology
CHWALBA, A., Documentation of Polish Independence Movements
CIAŁOWICZ, K, Archaeology
DĄBROWA, E., Ancient History
DYBIEC, J., History of Science and Culture
DZIELSKA, M., Byzantine History
FABIAŃSKI, M., History of Modern Art
GĄSOWSKI, T., Polish Modern History
GEDL, M., Archaeology
GINTER, B., Archaeology
GRYGLEWICZ, T., History of Contemporary Art
JARZĘBSKA, A., 20th-century Polish History
KACZANOWSKI, P., Archaeology
KOZŁOWSKI, J., Archaeology
MAŁKIEWICZA, A., History of Modern Art
MICHALEWICZ, A., Economic and Social History
OSTROWSKI, JAN, History of Art
OSTROWSKI, JANUSZ, Classical Archaeology
PAJA-STACH, J., Contemporary Polish Music
PAPUCI-WŁADYKA, E., Archaeology
PARCZEWSKI, M., Polish and Modern Archaeology
PIROŻYŃSKI, J., General Modern History
QUIRINI-POPŁAWSKA, D., Medieval History
ROBOTYCKI, CZ., Polish Ethnography, Anthropology of Culture
ROJEK, W., General Modern History
ŚLIWA, J., Mediterranean Archaeology
ŚNIEŻYŃSKA-STOLOT, E., History of Ideas
SZCZUR, S., Medieval History

Faculty of International and Political Studies (tel. (12) 422-02-25; fax (12) 422-02-25; e-mail wsmip@adm.uj.edu.pl; internet www.uj.edu.pl/WydzMiedzPol):

BABIŃSKI, G., Sociology of Interethnic Relationships
CZIOMER, E., International Relations
FLORKOWSKA-FRANCIĆ, H., History of International Migration Movements
KAPISZEWSKI, A., Middle East Studies
KOZUB-CIEMBRONIEWICZ, M., Modern Political Movements and Political Thought
MACH, Z., Anthropology
MAJCHROWSKI, J. M., Recent Political History of Poland, History of Political and Legal Doctrines, Religious Policy
MANIA, A., World History of the 20th Century
MIODUNKA, W., Applied Linguistics in Polish Language Teaching
PURCHLA, J., Economic History and History of Art
RAŹNY, A., East Slavonic Philology
STAWOWY-KAWKA, I., History of Balkan Countries
SUCHANEK, L., Russian and Soviet Literature
WALASZEK, A., History of International Migration Movements
ZIĘBA, A., Constitutional Law
ZYBLIKIEWICZ, L., International Relations

Faculty of Law and Administration (tel. (12) 422-37-42; fax (12) 423-11-21; e-mail prawo@adm.uj.edu.pl; internet www.uj.edu.pl/uj-guide/law&adm.en.html):

BARAN, KA., General Legal History
BARAN, KRZ., Labour Law
BŁACHUT, J., Criminology
BIERNAT, S., European Law
BRZEZIŃSKI, B., Financial Law
CHOJNICKA, K., History of Political and Legal Thought
ĆWIĄKALSKI, K., Criminal Law
CZAJOWKI, J., Modern Political Systems
DROZD, E., Civil Law, Private International Law
GABERLE, A., Criminology
GAWLIK, B., Civil Law
GIZBERT-STUDNICKI, T., Theory and Philosophy of Law
GRZYBOWSKI, M., Modern Political Systems
HOFMAŃSKI, P., Criminal Procedure
HOŁDA, Z., Sentencing and Penal Procedure
JASKÓLSKI, M., History of Political and Legal Thought
KISIEL, W., Territorial Self-Government
KRAJEWSKLI, K., Criminology
KUBAS, A., Civil Law
LANKOSZ, K., International Public Law
LICHOROWICZ, A., Agricultural Law
MĄCZYŃSKI, A., Civil and International Private Law
MALEC, J., History of Administration
PAŁECKI, K., Theory and Sociology of Law
PŁESZKA, K., Theory and Philosophy of Law
PREUSSNER-ZAMORSKA, J., Civil Law
PYZIOŁ, W., Private Business Law
SARKOWICZ, R., Theory and Philosophy of Law
SARNECKI, P., Constitutional Law
SONDEL, J., Roman Law
STEC, M., Private Business Law
STELMACH, J., Theory and Philosophy of Law
SZEWCZYK, M., Criminal Law
ŚWIĄTKOWSKI, A., Labour Law
SZUMAŃSKI, A., International Business Law
TRAPLE, E., Civil Law
URUSZCZAK, W., History of Ecclesiastical Law
WAGNER, B., Labour Law
WALASZEK-PYZIOŁ, A., Public Business Law
WASILEWSKI, A., Environmental Protection Law

WŁUDYKA, T., Economics Policy
WOJCIKIEWICZ, J., Forensic and Police Science
WOŚ, T., Administration Law, Administration Procedures Law
ZAWADA, K., Civil Law and International Private Law
ZIMMERMAN, J., Administrative Procedures
ZOLL, A., Criminal Law

Faculty of Management and Social Communication (tel. (12) 422-10-33 ext. 1132; fax (12) 421-49-75; e-mail orzech@adm.uj.edu.pl; internet gemini.miks.uj.edu.pl):

BAŃKA, A., Organizational Psychology
BARTA, J., Copyright Law, Press Law and Information Law
BEDNARCZYK, M., Tourism Management
BOBROWSKI, J., Linguistics, Communication
GOBAN-KLAS, T., Theory of Mass Communication, Public Relations
GODZIC, W., Media and Film Studies
HELMAN, A., Film Studies
LASKOWSKI, R., Linguistics, Slavic Language and Social Communication
LIBERSKA, B., International Economics
LUBASZEWSKI, W., Electrical Transformation of Information
LUBELSKI, T., Film Studies
MAREK, T., Psychology of Work, Organization and Management
MARKIEWICZ, R., Copyright Law, Information Law and Industrial Property Law
MATCZEWSKI, A., Industrial Management
NĘCKI, Z., Social Psychology
OKOŃ-HORODYŃSKA, E., Economics, Management
ORZECHOWSKI, E., Arts Management, History of Theatre
PISAREK, W., Media Research, Social Linguistics
PLEŚNIAROWICZ, K., Arts Management, Performance Theory
PRZEWŁOCKI, R., Medical Science, Neuroscience, Pharmacology
SOWA, K., Management of Higher Education, Sociology
STACHÓWNA, G., Film Studies
STĘPNIEWSKI, J., Accounting, Auditing, Operational Management
SURDYKOWSKA, S., International Accounting and Corporate Finance, Management, Accounting, Comparative Economics Systems
SZUMPICH, S., Management, Accounting, Comparative Economics Systems
SZWAJA, J., Civil and Commercial Law, Industrial Property Law
WIDACKI, J., Criminal Law, Management of Public Security
WILK, E., Media and Film Studies
WITKOWSKI, L., Philosophy, Theory of Arts and Education
WOJCIECHOWSKI, J., Communication and Librarianship

Faculty of Mathematics and Computer Science (tel. (12) 422-10-33 ext. 1145; fax (12) 430-14-67; e-mail matinf@adm.uj.edu.pl; internet www.mat-inf.uj.edu.pl):

DENKOWSKI, Z., Optimization and Control Theory
DRUŻKOWSKI, L. M., Analytic and Algebraic Geology
FLASIŃSKI, M., Artificial Intelligence Systems
GANCARZEWICZ, J., Differential Geometry
IDZIAK, P. M, Foundations of Computer Science
JARNICKI, M., Complex Analysis
MROZEK, M., Numerical Methods
OMBACH, J., Dynamical Systems
OPOZDA, B., Differential Geometry
PAWŁUCKI, W., Singularity Theory
PELCZAR, A., Analysis, Differential Equations

PLEŚNIAK, W., Complex Analysis, Theory of Approximations
RUSEK, K., Algebraic Geometry
SĘDZIWY, S., Numerical Methods
SICIAK, J., Complex Analysis
SRZEDNICKI, R., Differential Equations
STOCHEL, J., Functional Analysis, Theory of Operators
SZAFIRSKI, B., Differential Equations, Theory of Turbulence
SZAFRANIEC, F. H., Functional Analysis, Theory of Operators
TWOREWSKI, P., Analytical and Algebraic Geometry
WINIARSKI, T., Analytic and Algebraic Geometry

Faculty of Medicine (ul. Św. Anny 6, 31-008 Cracow; tel. (12) 422-54-44; fax (12) 422-40-06; e-mail dziekwl@cm-uj.krakow.pl; internet www.cm-uj.krakow.pl/pliki/en_lekarski.html):

ADAMEK-GUZIK, T., Internal Medicine
ALEKSANDROWICZ, J., Psychotherapy, Psychiatry
ANDRES, J., Anaesthesiology
BASTA, A., Gynaecology and Oncology
BOGDAŁ, J., Gastroenterology, Internal Medicine
BOGDASZEWSKA-CZABANOWSKA, J., Dermatology
BOMBA, J., Psychiatry
BRZOZOWSKI, T., Physiology
CICHOCKI, T., Histology
DEMBIŃSKA-KIEĆ, A., Clinical Biochemistry
DEMBIŃSKI, A., Physiology
DOBROWOLSKI, Z., Urology
DUBIEL, J. S., Cardiology
GIEROWSKI, J., Pyschiatry
GRODZIŃSKA, L., Pharmacology
HECZKO, P., Microbiology
KACIŃSKI, M., Neurology
KARCZ, D., Surgery
KAWECKA-JASZCZ, K., Cardiology
KLIMEK, R., Gynaecology, Obstetrics
KONIECZNY, L., Biochemistry
KORBUT, R., Pharmacology
KULIG, J., Surgery
LAUTERBACH, R., Paediatrics
LITWIN, J., Histology
MAJEWSKI, S., Dental Prosthetics
MALEC, E., Paediatric Cardiac Surgery
MARCINKIEWICZ, J., Immunology
MIODOŃSKI, A., Laryngology
MIRECKA, J., Histology
MUSIAŁ, J., Internal Medicine
NASKALSKI, J., Clinical Biochemistry
NIŻANKOWSKA-MOGILNICKA, E., Pulmonology
OBTUŁOWICZ, K., Internal Medicine
PACH, J., Toxicology
PAWLĘGA, J., Oncology
PAWLICKI, R., Histology
PAWLIK, W., Physiology
PIETRZYK, J., Paediatrics
PIWOWARSKA, W., Cardiology
POPIELA, T., Gastroenterological Surgery
RATAJCZAK, M., Transplantology
REROŃ, E., Laryngology
ROKITA, E., Medical Physics
RYN, Z., Psychiatry
SIERADZKI, J., Metabolic Diseases
SKŁADZIEŃ, J., Otolaryngology
SKOTNICKI, A., Haematology
SŁADEK, K., Internal Medicine
STACHURA, J., Pathomorphology
STARZYCKA, M., Ophthalmology
SUŁOWICZ, W., Nephrology
SZCZEKLIK, A., Internal Medicine
THOR, P., Physiopathology
TOBIASZ-ADAMCZYK, B., Epidemiology and Preventive Medicine
TRACZ, W., Cardiology
WYSOCKI, A., Surgery
ZARZYCKI, D., Orthopaedics
ZEMBALA, M., Microbiology, Immunology

ZIĘBA, A., Psychiatry

Faculty of Pharmacy (ul. Medyczna 9, 30-688 Cracow; tel. (12) 657-54-56; fax (12) 657-02-62; e-mail mfdmicha@cyf-kr.edu.pl; internet www.cm-uj.krakow.pl):

BOJARSKI, J., Organic Chemistry
BRANDYS, J., Toxicology
BUDAK, A., Pharmaceutical Microbiology
CZARNECKI, R., Pharmacodynamics
JAŚKIEWICZ, J., Biochemical Analysis
KIEĆ-KONOWICZ, K., Chemical Technology of Drugs
PAWŁOWSKI, M., Pharmaceutical Chemistry
RZESZUTKO, W., Inorganic Chemistry
STAREK, A., Biochemical Toxicology
SZYMURA-OLEKSIAK, J., Pharmacokinetics
ZACHWIEJA, Z., Food Chemistry, Nutrition
ZIEJA, A., Pharmaceutical Chemistry

Faculty of Philology (tel. (12) 422-11-03; fax (12) 422-11-03 ext. 1102; e-mail filolog@adm.uj.edu.pl; internet www.filg.uj.edu.pl):

BALBUS, S., Theory of Literature
BOCHENEK-FRANCZAKOWA, R., French Literature
BOROWSKI, A., Polish Philology
BORYŚ, W., Comparative and Historical Slavic Etymology, Serbo-Croatian Linguistics
BRZEZINA, M., Linguistics
BUJNICKI, T., History of Polish Literature
DUNAJ, B., Linguistics
FIUT, A., Polish Philology
GIBIŃSKA-MARZEC, M., English Literature
HOMBEK, D., Polish Philology
JARZĘBSKI, J., History of Polish Literature
JAWORSKI, S., History of Polish Literature
KAPUŚCIK, J., Russian Literature and History
KŁAŃSKA, M., German Philology
KORNHAUSER, J., Slavonic Philology
KORPANTY, J., Classical Philology
KORUS, K., Classical Philology
KORYTOWSKA, M., Comparative Literature
KOWALIKOWA, J., Methodology of Teaching Polish Literature
KULAWIK, A., Theory of Literature
KUREK, H., Polish Philology
LABOCHA, J., Polish Philology
LIPIŃSKI, K., German Philology, History of German Literature, Translation
MAŃCZAK-WOHLFELD, E., English Linguistics
MARKOWSKI, M., History of Polish Literature
MELANOWICZ, M., Japanese Literature
MICHALAK-PIKULSKA, B., Arabic Literature
MICHALIK, J., Theatre Studies
MIODOŃSKA-BROOKES, E., Polish Philology
MUSKAT-TABAKOWSKA, E., Cognitive Linguistics and Theory of Translation 1
NAUMOW, A., Slavonic Philology
NYCZ, R., Polish Philology
PISOWICZ, A., Iranian and Armenian Linguistics
PRZEBINDA, G., Russian Literature and History, Ukrainian Culture and History
SKARŻYŃSKI, M., Polish Philosophy
ŚLIWIŃSKI, W., Polish Philology
SMOCZYŃSKI, W., General and Indo-European Linguistics
STABRYŁA, S., Classical Philology
STACHOWSKI, M., Turkic and Altaic Linguistics
STALA, M., History of Polish Literature
STYKA, J., Classical Philology
SUGIERA, M., Theatre Studies
ŚWIĄTKOWSKA, M., Romance Philology
SZCZUKIN, W., Russian Literature, Culture and History, Theory of Literature
SZTURC, W., Comparative Literature
WALECKI, W., History of Polish Literature
WIDŁAK, S., Romance Philology
WŁODARSKI, M., History of Polish Literature
WRÓBEL, H., Polish and Czech Philology

WYKA, M., History of Polish Literature
ZABORSKI, A., Chamito-Semitic Linguistics
ZAJADA, A., Polish Philology
ZARĘBIANKA, Z., History of Polish Language
ZIEJKA, F., History of Polish Philology

Faculty of Philosophy (tel. (12) 422-11-36; fax (12) 430-14-75; e-mail filozof@adm.uj.edu.pl; internet www.phils.uj.edu.pl):

ALEKSANDER, T., Adult Education
DRABINA, J., History of Christianity
FLIS, A., Sociology of Culture
FLIS, M., Sociology of Culture, Anthropology
FRYSZTACKI, K., Sociology
GALEWICZ, W., Philosophy
GORLACH, K., Sociology
GROTT, B., Religious Studies
GRYZMAŁA-MOSZCZYŃSKA, H., Psychology of Religion
KOCIK, L., Sociology
KUBIAK, H., Sociology of Politics
LEGUTKO, R., Political Philosophy
LIPIEC, J., Philosophy
MIKLASZEWSKA, J., Philosophy
NĘCKA, E., Psychology
OCHMANN, J., Religious Studies
PACZKOWSKA-ŁAGOWSKA, E., Philosophy
PALKA, S., Methodological Elements of Education
PALUCH, A., Sociology
PERZANOWSKI, J., Philosophy and Logic
PIĄTEK, Z., Philosophy of Natural Sciences
PILECKA, W., Psychology
RODZIŃSKI, S., Pedagogy
SKOCZYŃSKI, J., Philosophy
SLANY, K., Sociology
STRÓŻEWSKI, W., Philosophy, Ontology
SUCHOŃ, W., Philosophy
SZTOMPKA, P., Sociological Theory
SZYMAŃSKA-ALEKSANDROWICZ, B., Philosophy
SZYMAŃSKI, M., Pedagogy, Sociology
URBAN, B., Pedagogy
WILKOSZEWSKA, K., Philosophy of Aesthetics
WOLEŃSKI, J., Philosophy, Epistemology
WROŃSKI, A., Logic and Philosophy

Faculty of Physics, Astronomy and Applied Computer Science (ul. Reymonta 4, 30-059 Cracow; tel. (12) 632-48-88 ext. 5703; fax (12) 433-70-86; e-mail fais@adm.uj.edu.pl; internet www.fais.uj.edu.pl):

ARODŹ, H., Field Theory
BAŁANDA, A., Nuclear Physics
BARA, J., Nuclear Physics
BIAŁAS, A., Theory of Elementary Particles, Astrophysics
BLICHARSKI, J. S., Radiospectroscopy, Biophysics
BODEK, K., Nuclear Physics
DOHNALIK, T., Atomic and Optical Physics
FIAŁKOWSKI, K., Theoretical Physics
FULIŃSKI, A., Statistical Physics
GAWLIK, W., Atomic and Optical Physics, Photonics
JURKIEWICZ, J., Theoretical Physics
KAMYS, B., Nuclear Physics
KOTAŃSKI, A., Computer Science, High Energy Physics
KRÓLAS, K., Nuclear Physics
KULESSA, R., Nuclear Physics
KUTSCHERA, M., Astrophysics
LONGA, L., Statistical Physics
ŁĄTKA, K., Experimental Physics
MACHALSKI, J., Radioastronomy and Extragalactic Astronomy
MAJKA, Z., Hot Matter
MALEC, E., Relativity, Astrophysics
MASŁOWSKI, J., Radioastronomy and Cosmic Physics
MICEK, S., Experimental Computer Physics
MOŚCICKI, J., Soft Matter Physics
MUSIOŁ, K., Atomic Physics
NOWAK, M., Theoretical Physics
OLEŚ, A. M., Theoretical Physics

OSTROWSKI, M., Astronomy
PĘDZIWIATR, A., Experimental Physics
RICHTER-WĄS, E., Applied Numerical Methods, High Energy Physics
ROKITA, E., Medical Physics, Environmental Physics
ROŚCISZEWSKI, K., Condensed Matter Theory
SPAŁEK, J., Condensed Matter Theory
STANEK, J., Solid State Physics
STARUSZKIEWICZ, A., General Relativity, Electrodynamics, Astrophysics
SZWED, J., Applied Numerical Methods, High Energy Physics
SZYMOŃSKI, M., Experimental Physics
SZYTUŁA, A., Solid State Physics, Magnetism
TOMALA, K., Radiospectroscopy
URBAN, S., Solid State Physics
WALUŚ, W., Nuclear Physics
WARCZAK, A., Experimental Physics
WITAŁA, H., Nuclear Physics
WOSIEK, J., Theoretical Computer Physics
WRÓBEL, S., Solid State Physics
ZAKRZEWSKI, J., Atomic and Optical Physics, Photonics
ZALEWSKI, K., Particle Theory

UNIWERSYTET GDAŃSKI
(University of Gdańsk)

Ul. Bażyńskiego 1A, 80-952 Gdańsk
Telephone: (58) 552-91-00
Fax: (58) 552-03-11
E-mail: rekug@ug.gda.pl
Internet: www.ug.gda.pl
Founded 1970
State control
Academic year: October to June

Rector: Prof. Dr hab. ANDRZEJ CEYNOWA
Pro-Rectors: Prof. Dr hab. JERZY BIELIŃSKI, Prof. Dr hab. BERNARD LAMMEK, Prof. Dr hab. ANNA SZANIAWSKA, Dr JACEK TARASZKIEWICZ
Administrative Director: Mgr PIOTR ŻERKO
Librarian: Mgr URSZULA SAWICKA

Library: see Libraries and Archives
Number of teachers: 1,611
Number of students: 30,000

Publications: *Prace Habilitacyjne*, *Skrypty*, *Zeszyty Naukowe*

DEANS

Faculty of Biology, Geography and Oceanology: Prof. Dr hab. GRZEGORZ WĘGRZYN
Faculty of Biotechnology: Prof. Dr hab. EWA ŁOJKOWSKA
Faculty of Business Management: Prof. Dr hab. MIROSŁAW SZREDER
Faculty of Chemistry: Prof. Dr hab. inż. LECH CHMURZYŃSKI
Faculty of Economics: Prof. Dr hab. STANISŁAW SZWANKOWSKI
Faculty of Languages and History: Prof. Dr hab. JÓZEF ARNO WŁODARSKI
Faculty of Law and Administration: Prof. Dr hab. JAROSŁAW WARYLEWSKI
Faculty of Mathematics, Physics and Informatics: Prof. Dr hab. ANDRZEJ KOWALSKI
Faculty of Social Sciences: Prof. Dr hab. HENRYK MACHEL

ATTACHED INSTITUTES

Biological Station: 80-680 Gdańsk-Górki Wschodnie; Dir Prof. Dr hab. EDWARD SKORKOWSKI.

Bird Migration Station: 84-210 Choczewo, Przebędowo; Dir Prof. Dr hab. PRZEMYSŁAW BUSSE.

Limnological Station: Województwo Gdańskie 83-300 Borucino; Dir Dr hab. WŁADYSŁAW LANGE.

Maritime Field Laboratory: ul. Morska 2, 84-150 Hel; Dir Dr hab. KRZYSZTOF SKÓRA.

UNIWERSYTET ŚLĄSKI
(University of Silesia)

Bankowa 12, 40-007 Katowice
Telephone: (32) 359-13-67
Fax: (32) 359-20-52
E-mail: adku@adm.us.edu.pl
Internet: www.us.edu.pl
Founded 1968
State control
Language of instruction: Polish
Academic year: October to June

Rector: Prof. Dr hab. JANUSZ JANECZEK
Pro-Rectors: Prof. Dr hab. WIESŁAW BANYŚ, Prof. Dr hab. WOJCIECH ŚWIĄTKIEWICZ, Prof. Dr hab. JERZY ZIOŁO, Dr hab. HALINA RUSEK
Registrar and Chief Administrative Officer: Dr JAN JELONEK
Librarian: Dr DARIUSZ PAWELEC

Library of 271,000 vols, 15,300 periodicals
Number of teachers: 2,020
Number of students: 45,579

Publication: *Zeszyty Naukowe Wydziałów*

DEANS

Faculty of Biology and Environmental Protection: Prof. Dr hab. PAWEŁ MIGULA
Faculty of Computer and Materials Sciences: Prof. US Dr hab. Ing ZYGMUNT WRÓBEL
Faculty of Earth Sciences: Prof. Dr hab. JACEK JANIA
Faculty of Education and Psychology: Prof. Dr hab. STANISŁAW JUSZCZYK
Faculty of Ethnology and Sciences of Education: Prof. Dr hab. ZIGMUNT KŁODNICKI
Faculty of Fine Arts and Music: Prof. EUGENIUSZ DELEKTA
Faculty of Law and Administration: Prof. UŚ Dr hab. KAZIMIERZ ZGRYZEK
Faculty of Mathematics, Physics and Chemistry: Prof. Dr hab. STANISŁAW KUCHARSKI
Faculty of Philology: Prof. US Dr hab. PIOTR WILCZEK
Faculty of Radio and Television: Prof. BOGDAN DZIWORSKI
Faculty of Social Sciences: Prof. Dr hab. JÓZEF BANKA
Faculty of Theology: Prof. Dr hab. WINCENTY MYSZOR

PROFESSORS

Faculty of Arts (ul. Bielska 62, 43-400 Cieszyn; tel. (33) 854-62-40 ext. 135; fax (33) 858-11-28; e-mail wart@mail.filus.edu.pl):

BANASZKIEWICZ, G., Graphics
DELEKTA, E., Graphics
FILIPOWSKA, K., Graphics
FOBER, J., Sculpture
GONIEWICZ-URBAŚ, H., Music
GRABOWSKI, T., Graphics
HERMA, J., Sculpture
KOWALCZYK-KLUS, A., Graphics
LIS, Z., Graphics
PITSCH, A., Graphics
STARAK, R., Graphics
STARCZEWSKI, A., Graphics
STOMPEL, J., Music
SWIDER, J., Music
TUREK, K., Music
WROŃSKI, J., Music

Faculty of Biology and Environmental Protection (ul Jagielońska 28, 40-032 Katowice; tel. (32) 200-94-61; fax (32) 200-93-61; e-mail biologia@us.edu.pl):

CABAŁA, S., Biology
HEJNOWICZ, Z., Biophysics
HERCZEK, A., Biology
KARCZ, W., Biology
KLAG, J., Zoology
MAŁUSZYŃSKA, J., Biology
MAŁUSZYŃSKA, M., Genetics
MIGULA, P., Biology
ROSTAŃSKI, K., Botany

SZAREJKO, I., Genetics
STOLAREK, J., Botany
WIKA, S., Botany
WOJCIECHOWSKI, W., Zoology

Faculty of Computer and Materials Sciences
(ul. Żeromskiego 3, 41-200 Sosnowiec; tel.
(32) 291-84-59; fax (32) 291-85-49; e-mail
dwt@us.edu.pl):

BOJARSKI, Z., Chemistry
BUDNIOK, A., Materials Science
CZECH, Z., Computer Science
ŁĄGIEWKA, E., Physics
MORAWIEC, H., Materials Science
MOSHKOV, M., Computer Science
PIECHA, J., Computer Science
RASEK, J., Technology
STOLARZEWICZ, A., Chemistry and Technology

Faculty of Earth Sciences (ul. Będzińska 60,
41-200 Sosnowiec; tel. (32) 291-83-81 ext.
324; fax (32) 291-58-65; e-mail dz-wnoz@
ultra.cto.us.edu.pl):

IDZIAK, A., Geology
JACHOWICZ, S., Geology
JANECZEK, J., Geology
JANIA, J., Geography
JANKOWSKI, A. T., Geography
KLIMEK, K., Geology
KRUSZEWSKA, K., Geology
NIEDŹWIEDŹ, J., Climatology, Meteorology
OSTAFICZUK, S., Geology
PULINA, M., Geography
RACKI, G., Geology
RÓŻKOWSKI, A., Geology
SZCZYPEK, T., Geography
TKOCZ, J., Geography
ZUBEREK, W., Geophysics

Faculty of Education and Psychology (ul.
Grażyńskiego 53, 40-126 Katowice; tel. (32)
258-94-82; fax (32) 258-94-82; e-mail pips@us
.edu.pl):

BAŃKA, A., Psychology
BOROWSKA, T., Education
JUSZCZYK, S., Education
KOJS, W., Education
PETLAK, E., Education
PILCH, T., Education
RADZIEWICZ-WINNICKI, A., Education
RATAJCZAK, Z., Psychology
TOKARZ, M., Logic
VASEK, A., Education
ZIELIŃSKI, J., Education

**Faculty of Ethnology and Science of Educa-
tion** (ul. Bielska 62, 43-400 Cieszyn; tel. (33)
854-61-14; fax (33) 858-11-28; e-mail artped@
mail.filus.edu.pl):

BOROWSKA, T., Pedagogy
KADŁUBIEC, D., Polish Philology
KANTOR, R., Ethnology
KOJS, W., Pedagogy
KOPOCZEK, A., Music
LEWOWICKI, T., Pedagogy
LOTKO, E., Polish and Czech Philology
OBER, J., Information Engineering
OLBRYCHT, K., Pedagogy

Faculty of Law and Administration (ul.
Bankowa 11b, 40-007 Katowice; tel. (32)
359-20-60; fax (32) 359-20-61; e-mail
akrawcz@us.edu.pl):

CHEŁMICKI-TYSZKIEWICZ, L.
CIĄGWA, J.
DOLNICKI, B.
FELUŚ, A.
GÓRNIOK, O.
GRABOWSKA, G.
GRABOWSKI, J.
KAŁUS, S.
KNOSALA, E.
KRAJEWSKI, K.
KUDEJ, M.
LIPIŃSKI, A.
LITYŃSKI, A.
MAŁAJNY, R.

MARSZAŁ, K.
NOWACKI, J.
PAZDAN, M.
SOBAŃSKI, R.
STRZĘPKA, J.
WIDŁA, T.
ZWIERZCHOWSKI, E.

**Faculty of Mathematics, Physics and Chem-
istry** (ul. Bankowa 14, 40-007 Katowice; tel.
(32) 359-16-52; e-mail basia@dz.wmfch.us
.edu.pl):

BŁASZCZYK, A., Mathematics
BUHL, F., Chemistry
BURIAN, A., Physics
DEC, J., Physics
DŁOTKO, T. W., Mathematics
DRZAZGA, Z., Physics
ERNST, S., Chemistry
GBURSKI, Z., Physics
GER, R., Mathematics
HANDEREK, J., Physics
JEŻEBEK, M., Physics
KOCOT, A., Physics
KOŁODZIEJ, K., Physics
KOWALSKA, T., Chemistry
KUCHARSKI, S., Chemistry
KULPA, W., Mathematics
LASOTA, A., Mathematics
ŁUCZKA, J., Physics
MAŃKA-MARCISZ, R., Physics
MATLAK, M., Physics
MATKOWSKI, J., Mathematics
POLAŃSKI, J., Chemistry
RATUSZNA, A., Physics
ROLEDER, K., Physics
RZOSKA, S., Physics
RUDNICKI, R., Mathematics
SZYMICZEK, K., Mathematics
ŚLEBARSKI, A., Physics
ŚLIWIOK, J., Chemistry
TALIK, E., Physics
UJMA, Z., Physics
WARCZEWSKI, J., Physics
WESTWAŃSKI, B., Physics
ZAREK, W., Physics
ZIOŁO, J., Physics
ZIPPER, E., Physics
ZIPPER, W., Physics
ZRAŁEK, M., Physics

Faculty of Philology (plac Sejmu Śląskiego 1,
40-032 Katowice; tel. (32) 255-12-60 ext. 267;
fax (32) 255-32-29; e-mail filologia@homer.fil
.us.edu.pl):

ABŁAMOWICZ, A., French Philology
ARABSKI, J., English Philology
BANYŚ, W., French Philology
BEDNARSKI, M., Philology
CZAPIK-LITYŃSKA, B., Slavonic Philology
CZERWIŃSKI, P., Russian Philology
FAST, P., Russian Philology
FONTAŃSKI, H., Russian Philology
GONDEK, E., Philology
GWÓŹDŹ, A., Philology
HESKA-KWAŚNIEWICZ, K., Polish Philology
HUCZEK, M., Economics
ILUK, J., German Philology
JĘDRZEJKO, E., Polish Philology
KALAGA, W., English Philology
KAKIETEK, P., English Philology
KLESZCZ, K., Polish Philology
KŁOSIŃSKI, K., Polish Philology
KORPANTY, J., Classical Philology
KOSOWSKA, E., Philology
MALICKI, J., Polish Philology
MICZKA, T., Polish Philology
OCIECZEK, R., Polish Philology
OPACKA, A., Polish Philology
OPACKI, I., Polish Philology
PASZEK, J., Polish Philology
PIECHOTA, M., Philology
PIKAŁA-TOKARZ, B., Slavonic Philology
POLAŃSKI, E., Polish Philology
POLAŃSKI, K., English Philology
ROSTROPOWICZ, J., Classical Philology
SIERADZKA, D., Philology

SŁAWEK, T., English Philology
SOCHA, I., Philology
STEFANIAK, B., Philology
STYKA, J., Classical Philology
SZEWCZYK, G., German Philology
UDALSKA, E., Philology
WANDZIOCH, M., French Philology
WILKOŃ, A., Philology
WILKOSZEWSKA, K., Polish Philology
WÓJCIK, W., Polish Philology
WOJTYNEK-MUSIK, K., French Philology
WRÓBEL, H., Polish Philology

Faculty of Radio and Television (ul. Targowa
1, 41-503 Chorzów; tel. (32) 258-70-70; fax
(32) 258-70-70):

BIENIOK, H., Economics
CZYŻEWSKI, S., Film Arts
DUDA-GRACZ, J., Fine Arts
DUDEK, W., Political Science
DZIWORSKI, B., Film Arts
MORSKI, K., Musical Education
NOWICKI, M., Film Arts
STUHR, J., Film Arts
SZCZECHURA, D., Film Arts
ZAJICEK, E., Economics
ZANUSSI, K., Film Arts

Faculty of Social Sciences (ul. Bankowa 11,
40-007 Katowice; tel. (32) 258-04-11; fax (32)
258-04-11; e-mail dziekan@wns.us.edu.pl):

BAŃKA, J., Philosophy
DOBROWOLSKI, P., Political Science
DŁUGAJCZYK, E., History
FRĄCKIEWICZ, L., Political Science
GŁOMBIK, C., Philosophy
GLUCHAŁA, J., History
JACHER, W., Sociology
KACZANOWICZ, W., History
KANTYKA, J., History
KIEPAS, A., Philosophy
KRAKOWSKI, J., Economics and Finance
MIKUŁOWSKI-POMORSKI, J., Political Science
PANIC, I., History
PROMIEŃSKA, H., Philosophy
PRZEWŁOCKI, J., History
SZCZEPAŃSKI, M., Sociology
SZTUMSKI, J., Sociology
ŚLĘCZKA, K., Philosophy
ŚWIĄTKIEWICZ, W., Sociology
WANATOWICZ, M., History
WÓDZ, J., Sociology
WÓDZ, K., Sociology
ŻECHOWSKI, Z., Sociology

Faculty of Theology (ul. Wita Stwosza 17A,
40-042 Katowice; tel. (32) 257-20-67; e-mail
wtl@quest.kuria.katowice.pl):

MYSZOR, J., Theology
MYSZOR, W., Theology
ROOS, L., Theology
UGLORZ, M., Theology
ULRICH, L., Theology

**UNIWERSYTET ŁÓDZKI
(University of Łódź)**

Narutowicza 65, 90-131 Łódź
Telephone: (42) 365-40-02
Fax: (42) 678-39-58
E-mail: rektorat@uni.lodz.pl
Internet: www.uni.lodz.pl
Founded 1945
State control
Language of instruction: Polish
Academic year: October to September
Rector: Prof. Dr hab. WIESŁAW PUŚ
Pro-Rector (Research): Prof. Dr hab. HENRYK
PIEKARSKI
Pro-Rector (Teaching): Prof. Dr hab. ELIZA
MAŁEK
Pro-Rector (Students): Prof. Dr hab. ANDRZEJ
NOWAKOWSKI
Pro-Rector (Economic Relations): Prof. Dr
hab. EUGENIUSZ KWIATKOWSKI

Pro-Rector (International Relations): Prof. Dr hab. PIOTR DARANOWSKI

Administrative Director: ALICJA KORYT-KOWSKA

Librarian: Dr JAN JANIAK

Library: see Libraries and Archives

Number of teachers: 2,173

Number of students: 42,027

Publications: *Acta Universitatis Lodziensis* (Research Bulletin), *Kronika Uniwersitetu Łódzkiego*

DEANS

Faculty of Philology: Prof. Dr hab. BOHDAN MAZAN

Faculty of Philosophy and History: Prof. Dr hab. STEFAN PYTLAS

Faculty of Educational Sciences: Prof. Dr hab. JACEK PIETKARSKI

Faculty of Physics and Chemistry: Prof. Dr hab. BOGUSŁAW KRYCZKA

Faculty of Mathematics: Prof. Dr hab. MARCIN STUDNIARSKI

Faculty of Biology and Environmental Protection: Prof. Dr hab. ANTONI RÓŻALSKI

Faculty of Law and Administration: Prof. Dr hab. MAREK ZIRK-SADOWSKI

Faculty of Economics and Sociology: Prof. Dr hab. PAWEŁ STAROSTA

Faculty of Management: Prof. Dr hab. TADEUSZ MARKOWSKI

Faculty of International and Political Studies: Prof. Dr hab. ELŻBIETA H. OLEKSY

Faculty of Geographical Sciences: Prof. Dr hab. KAZIMIERZ KŁYSIK

PROFESSORS

Faculty of Philology (ul. Kościuszki 65, 90-514 Łódź; tel. (42) 639-02-53; fax (42) 639-02-54; e-mail filolog@uni.lodz.pl):

BIEŃKOWSKA, D., Polish Language
BOLECKI, W., Romance Literature and Contemporary Literature
CYBULSKI, M., Polish and Slavonic Languages
CZYŻEWSKI, S., Theory of Literature
DEJNA, K., Polish and Slavonic Languages
DUNIN-HORKAWICZ, J., Research on Books
GALA, A., Polish Language
GAZDA, G., Theory of Literature
HELMAN, A., Film
JABŁKOWSKA, J., German Philology
JANICKA-SWIDERSKA, I., English Philology
JANISZEWSKA-ZEIDLER, A., Theory of Literature, Theatre and Film
KAMIŃSKA, M., Polish and Slavonic Languages
KORYTKOWSKA, M., Slavonic Studies
KULIGOWSKA-KORZENIEWSKA, A., History of Theatre
LEWANDOWSKA-TOMASZCZYK, B., English Language
MAŁEK, E., Russian Literature
MUCHA, B., Russian Literature
NOWIKOW, W., Spanish Philology
NURCZYŃSKA-FIDELSKA, E., Theory of Literature
OKOŃ, J., Old Polish Literature
POKLEWSKA, K., Polish Literature
PUSZ, W., History of Polish Literature
RATAJCZAK, D., Theory of Literature
SADZIŃSKI, R., German Philology
STARNAWSKI, J., Old Polish Literature
SYPNICKI, J., French Language
TADEUSIEWICZ, H., Research on Books
TARANTOWICZ, A., German Philology
UMIŃSKA-TYTOŃ, E., Polish Language
WIŚNIEWSKI, B., Classical Philology
WOLSKA, B., History of 18th- and 19th-century Polish Literature
WRÓBLEWSKI, W., Classical Philology and Philosophy

Faculty of Philosophy and History (ul. Lindleya 3/5, 90-131 Łódź; tel. (42) 635-43-50; fax (42) 678-39-58):

BRZEZIŃSKI, A., Archaeology
CERAN, W., Prehistory and Medieval History
GAJDA-KRYNICKA, J., Philosophy
GŁOSEK, M., Prehistory
GROMCZYŃSKI, W., History of 19th- and 20th-century Philosophy
HASSAN ALI JAMSHEER, Near East Studies
HUNGER, R., History of Art
KAJZER, L., Medieval History, Archaeology
KRAWCZYK-WASILEWSKA, V., Cultural Anthropology, Ethnography
LIPIŃSKA, J., History of Art
MALINOWSKI, G., Logic
MATERSKI, W., Recent World History
MĄCZYŃSKA, M., Archaeology
NOWACZYK, A., Logic
PANASIUK, R., History of 19th-century Philosophy
PIÓRCZYŃSKI, J., Philosophy
PUŚ, P., 19th- and 20th-century Economic History of Poland
SAMUŚ, W., Recent Polish History
STYCZYŃSKI, M., History of Russian Philosophy
SZCZYGIELSKI, W., Modern Polish History
SZTABIŃSKI, G., Aesthetics
SZYNKIEWICZ, S., Ethnology
TUCHAŃSKA, B., Philosophy of Science
WIERUSZEWSKA-ADAMCZYK, M., Ethnography
WIŚNIEWSKI, E., Russian History
ZAJĄCZKOWSKI, S. M., Medieval Polish History

Faculty of Educational Sciences (ul. Kopernika 55, 90-553 Łódź; tel. (42) 639-07-76; fax (42) 639-07-77):

BŁASZCZYK, J., Physical Education
BŁASZCZYK, T., Science of Art
BUCZYŃSKI, A., Physical Education
DOWLASZ, B., Music Education
FLORKOWSKI, A., Psychology
JAŁMUŻNA, T., Pedagogy
KACZOROWSKI, S., Science of Art
KĘDZIORA, J., Biochemistry
KOCUR, J., Psychiatry
MARYNOWICZ-HETKA, E., Social Pedagogy
ORKISZ, S., Physical Education and Health
PAŃCZYK, J., Pedagogy
ŚLIWERSKI, B., Pedagogy
WIERZBIŃSKI, A., Music Education
WÓDKA, B., Science of Art

Faculty of Physics and Chemistry (ul. Pomorska 149/153, 90-236 Łódź; tel. (42) 635-57-00; fax (42) 678-70-87; e-mail dziekanat@fic.uni.lodz.pl):

BALD, E., Chemistry, Analysis
BARTCZAK, W., Theoretical Physics
BARTNIK, R., Organic Chemistry
CIBOROWSKI, J., Theoretical Physics
EPSZTAJN, J., Organic Chemistry
GILLER, M., Experimental Physics
JANKOWSKI, J., Experimental Nuclear Physics
KAPUŚCIK, E., Physics
KOSIŃSKI, P., Theoretical Physics
ŁAWRYNOWICZ, J., Complex Analysis
MAŚLANKA, P., Theoretical Physics
MLOSTOŃ, G., Organic Chemistry
PIEKARSKI, H., Physical Chemistry
PŁAŻA, S., Inorganic Chemistry
REMBIELIŃSKI, J., Theoretical Physics
ROMANOWSKI, S., Physical and Theoretical Chemistry
SCHOLL, H., Physical Chemistry
SKOWROŃSKI, R., Organic Chemistry
SUKIENNICKI, A., Solid State Physics
TYBOR, W., Theoretical Physics
WOJTCZAK, L., Solid State Physics
ZAKRZEWSKI, J., Organic Chemistry

Faculty of Mathematics (ul. Banacha 22, 90-238 Łódź; tel. (42) 635-59-49; fax (42) 635-42-66; e-mail facmath@imul.uni.lodz.pl):

BALCERZAK, M., Real Analysis

CHĄDZYŃSKI, J., Complex Variables
GOLDSTEIN, S., Functional Analysis
JAJTE, R., Probability Theory
JAKUBOWSKI, Z., Analytical Functions
MIKOŁAJCZYK, L., Analytical Functions
NOWAKOWSKI, A., Optimization Theory
PASZKIEWICZ, A., Functional Analysis
PAWLAK, R., Functional Analysis
WALCZAK, P., Geometry
WALCZAK, S., Analytical Functions
WALISZEWSKI, W., Geometry
WILCZYŃSKI, W., Real Analysis
WŁODARCZYK, K., Functional Analysis, Complex Analysis

Faculty of Biology and Environmental Protection (ul. Pilarskiego 14, 90-231 Łódź; tel. (42) 635-40-16; fax (42) 635-45-06; e-mail dziekan@biol.uni.lodz.pl):

BAŃBURA, J., Biology, Ecology
BARTOSZ, G., Biophysics
BŁASIAK, J., Molecular Genetics
BRYSZEWSKA, M., Biophysics
DŁUGOŃSKI, J., Microbiology
DUDA, W., Biochemistry
GABARA, B., Cytology and Cytochemistry
GALICKA, W., Ecology and Zoology of Vertebrates
GAŹDZICKI, A., Geology
GRZYBKOWSKA, M., Zoology, Ecology
GWOŹDZIŃSKI, K., Molecular Biology
HEREŹNIAK, J., Biology
JAKUBOWSKA-GABARA, J., Geobotany
JANAS, K., Plant Physiology
JAWORSKI, A., Microbiology
JAŻDŻEWSKI, K., Zoology
JÓŻWIAK, Z., Biochemistry
KACA, W., Microbiology
KILIAŃSKA, Z., Biochemistry
KONOPACKI, J., Neurophysiology
KRAJEWSKA, W., Biochemistry
KUKULSKA-GOŚCICKA, T., Immunology
KWIATKOWSKA, M., Plant Cytology and Cytochemistry
LIGOWSKI, R., Biology, Oceanography
LIPIŃSKA, A., Biochemistry
LISZEWSKI, S., Economic Geography
ŁAWRYNOWICZ, M., Botany, Mycology
MARKOWSKI, J., Biology, Theriology
MASZEWSKI, J., Cell Biology
OLACZEK, R., Plant Systems and Geography
PENCZAK, T., Zoology, Fish Ecology
PIECHOCKI, A., Zoology
ROMANIUK, A., Animal Physiology and Neurophysiology
RÓŻALSKA, B., Infectious Biology
RÓŻALSKI, A., Microbiology
RUDNICKA, W., Immunology
SIDORCZYK, Z., Microbiology
SZWEDA-LEWANDOWSKA, Z., Molecular Biophysics
URBANEK, H., Biochemistry
WACHOWICZ, B., Biochemistry
ZALEWSKI, M., Biology

Faculty of Law and Administration (ul. Składowa 43, 90-127 Łódź; tel. (42) 635-40-21; fax (42) 678-45-33; e-mail dziekanat@wpia.uni.lodz.pl):

BIŃCZYCKA-MAJEWSKA, T., Labour Law
BORKOWSKI, J., Administrative Law
BRONIEWICZ, W., Civil Procedure
CHRÓŚCIELEWSKI, W., Administrative Procedure
DĘBOWSKA-ROMANOWSKA, T., Financial Law
GRZEGORCZYK, T., Penal Procedure
HOŁYST, B., Criminology
JANKOWSKI, J., Civil Law
KATNER, W., Civil Law
KMIECIAK, Z., Administrative Procedure
LELENTAL, S., Penal Law
LEWANDOWSKI, H., Labour Law
LEWASZKIEWICZ-PETRYKOWSKA, B., Civil Law
MARCINIAK, A., Civil Procedure

MATUSZEWSKI, J., Medieval History, History of Law
MATUSZEWSKI, J., History of State and Law
NYKIEL, W., Financial Law
PYZIAK-SZAFNICKA, M., Civil Law
RYMASZEWSKI, Z., History of State and the Law
SEWERYŃSKI, M., Labour Law
SZYMCZAK, T., Constitutional Law
TYLMAN, J., Penal Procedure
WŁODARCZYK, W., Social Insurance and Social Policy Law
ZIRK-SADOWSKI, M., Theory of State and Law

Faculty of Economics and Sociology (ul. Polskiej Organizacji Wojskowej 3/5, 90-255 Łódź; tel. (42) 635-51-12; fax (42) 635-50-32; e-mail dziekes@uni.lodz.pl):

BOKSZAŃSKI, Z., Cultural Sociology
BORKOWSKA, S., Business Administration
BUCHNER-JEZIORSKA, A., Sociology
DĘBSKI, W., Commerce and International Finance
DOKTÓR, K., Industrial Sociology
DOMAŃSKI, C., Statistics
DURAJ, J., Economics and Organization of Industry
GAJDA, J., Economics
JÓZEFIAK, C., Economics
KOCIK, L., Sociology
KRYŃSKA, E., Economics, Economic Policy
KUCHARSKA-STASIAK, E., Economics of Urban Development
KULPIŃSKA, J., Industrial Sociology
KWIATKOWSKI, E., Theory of Economy
LEWANDOWSKA, L., Economics, Industrial Economics
MARSZAŁEK, A., Economics
MILO, W., Econometrics, Statistics
MORTIMER-SZYMCZAK, H., Planning and Economic Policy
PIĄTKOWSKI, W., History of Economic Theory
PIOTROWSKA-MARCZAK, K., Finance
RUDOLF, S., Political Economy of Capitalism
SKODLARSKI, J., International Economic Relations
SUCHECKA, J., Economics
SUŁKOWSKI, B., Cultural Sociology
TOMASZEWICZ, Ł., Econometrics
TRZASKALIK, T., Economics
WARZYWODA-KRUSZYŃSKA, W., Sociology
WELFE, A., Econometrics
WELFE, W., Econometrics and Statistics
WOJCIECHOWSKI, E., Economics of Urban Development

Faculty of Management (ul. Matejki 22/26, 90-237 Łódź; tel. (42) 635-50-50; fax (42) 635-53-06; e-mail wzdziek@uni.lodz.pl):

DIETL, J., Commercial Economics
GREGOR, W., Organization and Management, Marketing
GREGORCZYK, B., Organization and Management, Banking
JANOWSKA, Z., Human Resources, Management Accountancy
JARUGA, A., Cost Accounting, Management Accountancy
KOBYLIŃSKI, W., Quality Management
ŁAŃCUCKI, J., Management
MARKOWSKI, T., Economics of Urban Development
MIKOŁAJCZYK, Z., Theory of Organization and Management
PIASECKI, B., Economics and Organization of Industry
SIKORSKI, C., Organization and Management
SZYMCZAK, J., Management
ZIELIŃSKI, J. S., Computer Science

Faculty of International and Political Studies (ul. Składowa 41/43, 90-127 Łódź; tel. (42) 675-42-74; fax (42) 678-49-16; e-mail interul@uni.lodz.pl):

DE LAZARI, A., Eastern Studies
DOMAŃSKI, T., Euromarketing
DUBICKI, T., History
DZIEKAN, M., History of Arabic Literature
KMIECIŃSKI, J., Archaeology
KUCZYŃSKI, K. A., German Literature
MICHOWICZ, W., History of International Relations (Dir)
OLEKSY, E., American Literature
PRZEBINDA, G., Russian Philology

Faculty of Geographical Sciences (ul. Pilarskiego 14/16, 90-231 Łódź; tel. (42) 635-45-09; e-mail dziekan@geo.uni.lodz.pl):

BACHVAROV, M., Urban Geography and Tourism
HEFFNER, K., Political Geography and Regional Studies
JELONEK, A., Social and Economic Geography
KŁYSIK, C., Climatology and Meteorology
KOTER, M., Environmental Biophysics
KOWALCZYK, A., Urban Geography and Tourism
KOŻUCHOWSKI, K., Physical Geography
LASKOWSKI, S., Pedology
LISZEWSKI, S., Economic Geography
MARSZAŁ, T., Social and Economic Geography
MATCZAK, A., Urban Geography
WERWICKI, A., Economic Geography

UNIWERSYTET MEDYCZNY W ŁODZI
(Medical University of Łódź)

al. Kościuszki 4, 90-419 Łódź

Telephone: (42) 632-51-00
Fax: (42) 630 07-07
E-mail: rektor@rkt.am.lodz.pl
Internet: www.umed.lodz.pl

Founded 2002 by the merger of Łódź Medical Academy and Łódź Military Medical Academy
State control

Rector: Prof. ANDRZEJ LEWIŃSKI

Number of teachers: 1,177
Number of students: 23,127

DEANS

Faculty of Medicine: Prof. KAZIMIERZ JĘDRZEJEWSKI
Faculty of Medicine and Dentistry: Prof. WIELISŁAW PAPIERZ
Faculty of Military Medicine: Prof. JAN BŁASZCZYK
Faculty of Pharmacy: Prof. JADWIGA SZYMAŃSKA
Faculty of Physiotherapy: Prof. JUREK OLSZEWSKI
Faculty of Public Health: Prof. ANNA JEGIER

KATOLICKI UNIWERSYTET LUBELSKI JANA PAWŁA II
(John Paul II Catholic University of Lublin)

20-950 Lublin, Al. Racławickie 14

Telephone: (81) 445-41-05
Fax: (81) 445-41-91
E-mail: dwz@kul.lublin.pl
Internet: www.kul.lublin.pl

Founded 1918
Private control
Academic year: October to June

Chancellor: Archbp Prof. Dr hab. JÓZEF ŻYCIŃSKI
Rector: Rev. Prof. Dr hab. STANISŁAW WILK
Vice-Rector (Personnel and Financial Management): Prof. Dr hab. ROMAN DOKTÓR

Vice-Rector (Research, and International and Public Relations): Rev. Prof. Dr hab. MIROSŁAW KALINOWSKI
Vice-Rector (Student Affairs): Prof. Dr hab. JÓZEF FERT
Librarian: Rev. Dr TADEUSZ STOLZ
Library of 1,800,000 vols (including department libraries) of which 1,000,000 books, 50,000 old books, 35,000 vols of periodicals, 5,000 MSS, 3,000 maps and atlases, 10,000 music scores, 10,000 audio cassettes and records, 15,000 graphic items
Number of teachers: 1,012
Number of students: 20,340

Publications: *Zeszyty Naukowe KUL* (4 a year), *Roczniki Teologiczne* (annually), *Roczniki Filozoficzne* (annually), *Roczniki Humanistyczne* (annually), *Roczniki Nauk Społecznych* (annually), *Ethos* (4 a year), *Przegląd Uniwersytecki* (6 a year), *Roczniki Nauk Prawnych* (annually), *Law–Administration–Church* (4 a year), *Studia Norwidiana* (annually), *Studia Polonijne* (annually), *Vox Patrum* (2 a year), *Roczniki Psychologiczne* (annually), *KERYGS* (2 a year), *Człowiek i Przyroda* (2 a year), *Acta Mediaevalia, Summarium*

DEANS

Faculty of Humanities: Prof. Dr hab. JANUSZ DROB
Faculty of Law, Canon Law and Administration: Rev. Prof. Dr hab. ANTONI DĘBIŃSKI
Faculty of Mathematics and Natural Sciences: Rev. Prof. Dr hab. STANISŁAW ZIĘBA
Faculty of Philosophy: Prof. Dr hab. STANISŁAW KICZUK
Faculty of Social Sciences: Prof. Dr hab. ANDRZEJ SĘKOWSKI
Faculty of Theology: Rev. Prof. Dr hab. JERZY PAŁUCKI
Off-Campus Faculty of Legal and Economic Sciences: Prof. Dr hab. JAN ŚWITKA
Satelllite Faculty of Social Sciences: Rev. Prof. Dr hab. MARIAN WOLICKI

PROFESSORS

Faculty of Humanities (tel. (81) 445-41-45; fax (81) 445-41-90):

BORKOWSKA, U., History of Medieval Culture
CHODKOWSKI, R., Classical Linguistics, Greek Literature
DEPTUŁA, C., History of Medieval Culture
ECKMANN, A., Classical Linguistics, Ancient Christian Literature
FITA, S., History of Polish Literature
KNAPIŃSKI, R., Art History
LITAK, S., History of Education
MACIEJEWSKI, M., Literature of the Enlightenment and Romantic Periods in Polish Literature
MAKARSKI, W., Linguistics
PODBIELSKI, H., Classical Greek Philology
POPOWSKI, R., Classical Philology, Greek Linguistics
WOLICKA-WOLSZLEGER, E., Theory of Art and History of Artistic Theories
ZIÓŁEK, J., Modern History

Faculty of Law, Canon Law and Administration (tel. (81) 445-37-31; fax (81) 445-37-26; e-mail prawa@kul.lublin.pl):

CIOCH, H., Civil Law
KOŚĆ, A., Philosophy of Law
KRUKOWSKI, J., Canon Law
ŁĄCZKOWSKI, W., Financial Law, Administrative Law
MISZTAL, H., Canon Law, Law and Religion
SZAJKOWSKI, A., Commercial Law
TYSZCZYK, B., History of State and Law
WITCZAK, W., Forensic Medicine
ZUBERT, B., Canon Law

Faculty of Mathematics and Natural Sciences (tel. (81) 445-45-52; fax (81) 445-35-36):

ANDRZEJEWSKI, R., Ecology
CICHOCKA, E., Agriculture
FISCHER-MALANOWSKA, Z., Ecology
GOSZCZYŃSKI, W., Horticulture
MAGOMEDOW, M. R., Ecology
MATUS, P., Mathematics
SKOWRONSKI, T., Toxicology
STĘPNIEWSKA, Z., Agricultural Engineering
SZESZKO, M., Mathematics and Computer Science
URBANOWICZ, P., Computer Science
WOJCIECHOWSKA, W., Ecology, Hydrobiology
ZIĘBA, S., Humanistic Ecology

Faculty of Philosophy (tel. (81) 445-42-51; fax (81) 445-41-90; e-mail filozofia@kul.lublin.pl):

BRONK, A., Philosophy of Science
CZERKAWSKI, J., History of Philosophy
GAŁKOWSKI, J., Ethics, Political Philosophy
HAJDUK, Z., Philosophy of Nature, Philosophy of Science
HERBUT, J., Methodology of Philosophy
KICZUK, S., Logic
MARYNIARCZYK, A., Metaphysics
SZOSTEK, A., Ethics
WIELGUS, S., History of Philosophy, Medieval Philosophy
ZIELIŃSKI, E., History of Ancient and Medieval Philosophy
ŻYCIŃSKI, J., Philosophy of Nature, Philosophy of Science

Faculty of Social Sciences (tel. (81) 445-35-48; fax (81) 445-42-93; e-mail wns@kul.lublin.pl):

BIELA, A., Experimental Psychology, Industrial Psychology, Environmental Psychology
BRAUN-GAŁKOWSKA, M., Educational Psychology, Family Psychology
CHUDY, W., Education
CZUMA, Ł., Social Economics
DYCZEWSKI, L., Sociology of Culture, Sociology of Family
DZWONKOWSKI, R., Sociology of Ethnic Groups
GILOWSKA, Z., Economics, Local Finance
KADER, A., Economics
KOWALCZYK, S., Theoretical Philosophy, Social Philosophy
KRYCZKA, P., Urban Sociology, Sociology of the Family
MARIAŃSKI, J., Sociology of Religion, Sociology of Morals
MAZUREK, F., Catholic Social Thought
PRĘŻYNA, W., Social Psychology, Psychology of Religion
RAVEN, J., Economics
SĘKOWSKI, A., Rehabilitative Psychology
WÓJCIK, S., Sociology, Local Policy
ZALESKI, Z., Experimental Psychology

Faculty of Theology (tel. (81) 445-38-41; fax (81) 445-38-45; e-mail teolog@kul.lublin.pl):

DRĄCZKOWSKI, F., Patristics
DZIUBA, A., Moral Theology
GŁOWA, W., Pastoral Theology, Liturgy
HRYNIEWICZ, W., Ecumenism, Orthodox Theology
KAMIŃSKI, R., Pastoral Theology, Organization of Pastoral Care
KAWCZYŃSKA-BUTRYM, Z., Social Life of the Family
KULPACZYŃSKI, S., Pastoral Theology
MISIUREK, J., Dogmatic Theology, History of Spirituality
NAGÓRNY, J., Moral Theology
NOWAK, A., Spirituality
PACIOREK, A., Biblical Studies
PAWLAK, I., Musicology
RUBINKIEWICZ, R., Biblical Studies
RUSECKI, M., Fundamental Theology
TRONINA, A., Biblical Studies

WITCZYK, H., Biblical Studies
WILK, S., History of Monasteries
ZAHAJKIEWICZ, M., Medieval Church History
ZASĘPA, T., Contemporary Forms of Communication of the Faith
ZIMOŃ, H., Religious Studies

Off-Campus Faculty of Legal and Economic Sciences (ul. Lwowska 68, 22-600 Tomaszow Lubelski; tel. and fax (84) 664-45-74):

ANTONOWICZ, L., International Public Law
CZEREWKO, G., Theory of Economics
DYONIZIAK, R., Sociology of Work
JAROSZ, A., Economics and History of Economic Thought
KOSSAK, W., Civil Law
KRUKOWSKI, J., Theory of Law
MISZTAL, H., Canon Law
ŚRUTWA, J., Church History of Law
WOJCIECHOWSKI, W., Econometrics and Statistics

Satellite Faculty of Social Sciences (ul. Ofiar Katynia 6, 37-450 Stalowa Wola; tel. (15) 642-25-35):

KASJANOW, W., Economics
KOZORIZ, M., Economics
NYCZKAŁO, N., Education
WOLICKI, M., Education

UNIWERSYTET MARII CURIE-SKŁODOWSKIEJ
(Marie Curie-Skłodowska University)

Plac Marii Curie-Skłodowskiej 5, 20-031 Lublin

Telephone: (81) 537-51-07
Fax: (81) 537-51-02
E-mail: rector@ramzes.umcs.lublin.pl
Internet: www.umcs.lublin.pl

Founded 1944
Academic year: October to June

Rector: Prof. Dr hab. WIESŁAW ANDRZEJ KAMIŃSKI
Pro-Rector (Development): Prof. Dr hab. JERZY WĘCŁAWSKI
Pro-Rector (General): Prof. Dr hab. TADEUSZ BOROWIECKI
Pro-Rector (Scientific Research, International Relations and Off-Campus Centres): Prof. Dr hab. ANNA TUKIENDORF
Pro-Rector (Students and Teaching): Prof. Dr hab. ANNA PAJDZIŃSKA
Chief Administrative Officer: Inż. MACIEJ GRUDZIŃSKI
Librarian: Dr BOGUSŁAW KASPEREK

Library: general scientific colln of 2,528,340 vols, including 338,853 vols of periodicals, 10,168 online journals, 803 MSS, 369,207 patents, 40,272 maps and atlases, 14,954 music scores, 19,215 ancient books, 2,814 dissertations, 4,822 audio cassettes and records
Number of teachers: 1,805
Number of students: 34,758

Publication: *Annales Universitatis Mariae Curie-Skłodowska*

DEANS

Faculty of Biology and Earth Sciences: Prof. Dr hab. RYSZARD DĘBICKI
Faculty of Chemistry: Prof. Dr hab. ANDRZEJ DĄBROWSKI
Faculty of Economics: Prof. Dr hab. ELŻBIETA SKRZYPEK
Faculty of Fine Arts: Prof. Dr hab. URSZULA BOBRYK
Faculty of Humanities: Prof. Dr hab. HENRYK GMITEREK
Faculty of Law and Administration: Prof. Dr hab. ANTONI PIENIĄŻEK
Faculty of Mathematics, Physics and Computer Science: Prof. Dr hab. KRZYSZTOF POMORSKI

Faculty of Philosophy and Sociology: Prof. Dr hab. JACEK PAŚNICZEK
Faculty of Political Science: Prof. Dr hab. STANISŁAW MICHAŁOWSKI
Faculty of Psychology and Pedagogy: Prof. Dr hab. ZDZISŁAW BARTKOWICZ

PROFESSORS

Faculty of Biology and Earth Sciences (ul. Akademicka 19, 20-030 Lublin; tel. (81) 537-52-16; fax (81) 537-52-14; internet binoz .umcs.lublin.pl):

BEDNARA, J., Anatomy and Plant Cytology
BYSTREK, J., Plant Systematics
DĘBICKI, A., Soil Science
DERNAŁOWICZ-MALARCZYK, E., Biochemistry
DROŻAŃSKI, W., Microbiology
FIEDERUK, J., Microbiology
GRANKOWSKI, N., Molecular Biology
HARASIMIUK, M., Geomorphology
JAKUBOWICZ, T., Biochemistry and Immunology
KAŁKOWSKA, K., Animal Physiology
KANDEFER-SZERSZEŃ, M., Microbiology
KRUPA, Z., Plant Physiology
KUREK, E., Environmental Microbiology
LEONOWICZ, A., Biochemistry
MICHALCZYK, Z., Hydrography
PĘKALA, K., Physical Geography and Geomorphology
ROGALSKI, J., Molecular Biology
RUSSA, R., Microbiology
SIRKO, M., Cartography
SKORUPSKA, A., Microbiology
ŚNIEZKO, R., Botany
ŚWIĘS, F., Botany
SZCZODRAK, J., Microbiology
TRĘBACZ, K., Biology and Biophysics
WOJCIECHOWSKI, K., Geography
WOJTANOWICZ, J., Physical Geography and Geomorphology
ZAWADZKI, T., Plant Physiology

Faculty of Chemistry (Plac Marii Curie-Skłodowskiej 3, 20-030 Lublin; tel. (81) 537-57-16; fax (81) 533-33-48; e-mail chemia@ hermes.umcs.lublin.pl; internet chemia.umcs .lublin.pl):

BOROWIECKI, T., Chemical Technology
BORÓWKO, M., Physical Chemistry
CHIBOWSKI, E., Physical Chemistry
CHIBOWSKI, S., Physical Chemistry
DAWIDOWICZ, A., Physical Chemistry
DĄBROWSKI, A., Theoretical Chemistry
FERENC, W., Inorganic Chemistry
GAWDZIK, B., Physical Chemistry
GOWOREK, J., Physical Chemistry
HUBICKA, H., Inorganic Chemistry
HUBICKI, Z., Inorganic Chemistry
JAŃCZUK, B., Physical Chemistry
KOZIOŁ, A., Chemistry, X-ray Crystallography
LEBODA, R., Physical Chemistry of Surfaces and Chromatography
MACHOKI, A., Heterogeneous Catalysis, C1 Chemistry
MATYNIA, T., Organic Chemistry
NARKIEWIEZ-MICHAŁCK, J., Theoretical Chemistry
NAZIMEK, D., Physical Chemistry
PATRYKIEJEW, A., Physical Chemistry
PIETRUSIEWICZ, K., Organic Chemistry
PIKUS, S., X-ray Crystallography-powder Diffraction
PODKOŚCIELNY, W., Organic Chemistry
RAYSS, J., Physical Chemistry
RÓŻYŁŁO, J., Physical Chemistry
RUDZINSKI, W., Theoretical Chemistry
SOKOLOWSKI, S., Theoretical Chemistry
STASZCZUK, P., Physical Chemistry
WOLIŃSKI, K., Quantum Chemistry, Methods and Applications
WÓJCIK, W., Physical Chemistry

Faculty of Economics (tel. (81) 537-54-62; fax (81) 537-54-62; e-mail ekonomia@ramzes .umcs.lublin.pl; internet ekonomia.umcs .lublin.pl):

GRABOWIECKI, J., Political Economy
KARPUŚ, P., Economics
KOZŁOWSKI, S., Economics
MAMEARZ, M., Economics, Financial Markets
MUCHA-LESZKO, B., Political Economy, Economic Planning
POMORSKA, A., Finances
RONCK, H., Economics
RUDNICKI, M., Economics of Agriculture
SIKORSKI, C., Economics
SKOWRONEK, Cz., Industrial Ecomomics
SKRZYPEK, E., Economics
SOBCZYK, G., Economics
SZYMAŃSKI, Z., Economics, History of Economic Thought
SZYNAL, J., Economics, Banking
WĘCŁAWSKI, J., Economics, Banking
WICH, U., Urban Planning
ZALEWA, J., Agricultural Economics
ZUKOWSKI, M., Economics

Faculty of Fine Arts (al. Kraśnicka 2b, 20-718 Lublin; tel. (81) 523-53-91; fax (81) 523-53-91; e-mail warto@klio.umcs.lublin.pl):

BERNATOWICZ, M., Conducting
BOBRYK, U., Conducting
DĄBROWSKA, B., Conducting
GÓRSKI, K., Conducting
GRYKA, J., Graphics
HERMAN, M., Painting
JAWORSKA, A., Conducting
JAWORSKI, L., Conducting
KIERSKI, J., Sculpture
KOŁODZIEJ, R., Graphics
LECH, P., Graphics
MAZUREK, G., Graphics
MIELESZKO, S., Teaching of Sculpture
NALEPKA, J., Music Education
NAWROT-TRZCINSKA, I., Photographics
NIEDŹWIEDŹ, Z., Graphics
ORDYK-CZYZŻEWSKA, E., Conducting
POPEK, A., Graphics
PRZYCHODZIŃSKA-KACICZAK, M., Music Education
RZECHOWSKA-KLAUZA, G., Conducting
SMOCZYŃSKI, M., Painting
SNOCH, M., Graphics
STYKA, A., Painting
SWIECA, C., Music Education
WOJCIECHOWSKI, J., Painting
WRÓBLEWSKI, W., Painting
ZAWADZKI, T., Painting
ZUKOWSKI, S., Painting

Faculty of Humanities (Plac Marii Curie-Skłodowskiej 4, 20-031 Lublin; tel. (81) 537-54-66; fax (81) 537-54-66; internet www.umcs .lublin.pl):

BARTMIŃSKI, J., History of Polish Literature
BLAIM, A., English Literature
BONIECKA, B., History of Polish Literature
GMITEREK, M., Modern History
GRABIAS, S., Applied and Sociolinguistics
KARDELA, H., English Philology
KĘSIK, M., French Linguistics
KOKOWSKI, A., Archaeology
KOLEK, L., English Literature
KOLODZIEJ, E., Archiving
KORDELA, H., English Philology
KOSYL, Cz., Polish Philology
KRAJKA, W., Theory of Literature, History of English Literature
KRUK, S., History of Polish Theatre
LEWANDOWSKI, J., Modern History
LEWICKI, R., Linguistics
MAZUR, J., Polish Linguistics
MIKULEC, B., Modern History
MISIEWICZ, J., Theory of Literature
MYRDZIK, B., History of Polish Literature
NIEZNANOWSKI, S., Old Polish Literature

ORŁOWSKI, J., History of Russian Literature
PLISIECKI, J., Film
POMORSKI, J., Methodology and History of Historiography
RADZIK, T., Contemporary History
SAWECKA, H., Theory of Romance Literature
ŚLADKOWSKI, W., Modern History
ŚWIĘCH, W., Modern Polish Literature
STĘPNIK, K., Polish Literature
SZCZYGIEŁ, R., Medieval History
SZYMAŃSKI, J., Auxiliary Sciences of History
TOKARSKI, R., Polish Language
TRELIŃSKA, B.
WIŚNIEWSKA, H., Polish Linguistics
WOŹNIAKIEWICZ-DZIADOSZ, M., Theory of Literature

Faculty of Law and Administration (tel. (81) 537-51-26; fax (81) 537-54-05; internet pia .umcs.lublin.pl):

BOJARSKI, T., Penal Law
CHORĄŻY, K., Administrative Law
GDULEWICZ, E., Constitutional Law
KIDYBA, A., Economic Law
KMIECIK, R., Penal Law
KOROBOWICZ, A., History of State and Law
KURYŁOWICZ, M., Roman Law
LESZCZYNSKI, L., Theory of State and Law
OLESZKO, A., Civil Law
POŹNIAK-NIEDZIELSKA, M., Economic Law
SAWCZUK, M., Civil Procedure
SKRĘTOWICZ, E., Penal Law
SKUBISZ, R., European Community Law
SZRENIAWSKI, J., Administrative Law and Administrative Science
TOKARCZYK, R., History of Political Thought
WĄSEK, A., Penal Law and Criminology
WITKOWSKI, W., History of State and Law
WÓJTOWICZ, W., Financial Law
WRÓBEL, A., European Community Law
ZDYB, M., Administrative Law

Faculty of Mathematics, Physics and Computer Science (Plac Marii Curie-Skłodowskiej 2, 20-031 Lublin; tel. (81) 537-52-12; fax (81) 537-52-71; internet mfi.umcs.lublin.pl):

ADAMCZYK, B., Physics
BARAN, A., Computer Science
BUDZYŃSKI, M., Experimental Physics
GLADYSZEWSKI, L., Theoretical Physics
GOEBEL, K., Differential Equations
GOWOREK, T., Nuclear Physics
GÓŹDŹ, A., Theoretical Physics
GRUSZECKI, W., Biophysics
HAŁAS, St., Experimental Physics
JAŁOCHOWSKI, M., Experimental Physics
KAMIŃSKI, W., Nuclear Physics
KOMOROWSKI, T., Differential Equations
KORCZAK, Z., Solid Body Physics
KOZICKI, J., Computer Science
KRAWCZYK, W., Biophysics
KRZYŻ, J., Analytic Functions
KUCZUMOW, T., Differential Equations
KUREK, J., Differential Geometry
MĄCZKA, D., Experimental Physics
MICHALAK, L., Experimental Physics
MIKOŁAJCZAK, P., Solid Body Physics
MURAWSKI, K., Computer Science
NOWAK, M., Analytic Functions
POMORSKA, B., Theoretical Physics
POMORSKI, K., Theoretical Physics
PRUS, S., Functional Analysis
RYCHLIK, Z., Probability Theory
RZYMOWSKI, W., Differential Equations
SIELANKO, J., Nuclear Physics
SIELEWIESIUK, J., Physics and Biophysics
SZEZERBA, J., Computer Science
SYZNAL, D., Probability Theory
TARANKO, E., Theoretical Physics
TARANKO, R., Theoretical Physics
WANIURSKI, J., Analytical Functions
WÓJCIK, L., Experimental Physics
WYSOKIŃSKI, K., Theoretical Physics
ZĄBEK, S., Numerical Methods

ZAŁUŻNY, M., Theoretical Physics
ZIĘBA, W., Probability Theory
ZŁOTKIEWICZ, E., Analytic Functions
ŻUK, J., Experimental Physics)

Faculty of Philosophy and Sociology (Plac Marii Curie-Skłodowskiej 4, 20-030 Lublin; tel. (81) 537-54-79; fax (81) 537-54-81; e-mail dziekfis@ramzes.umcs.lublin.pl; internet bacon.umcs.lublin.pl):

CZARNECKI, Z., History of Philosophy
FILIPIAK, M., Sociology
JEDYNAK, S., Ethics
KOSIŃSKI, S., Sociology
LIBISZEWSKA-ZÓŁTKOWSKA, M., Sociology
MIZIŃSKA, J., Epistemology
OGRYZKO-WIEWIÓROWSKA, M., Sociology
PAŚNICZEK, J., Logic
STYK, J., Sociology
SYMOTIUK, S., Philosophy of Culture
TOKARSKI, S., Sociology of Medicine

Faculty of Political Science (Plac Litewski 3, 20-080 Lublin; tel. (81) 532-42-78; fax (81) 533-66-10; e-mail poldziek@sokrates.umcs .lublin.pl; internet www.politologia.pl):

CHAŁUPCZAK, H., International Relations
CZARNOCKI, A., International Relations
HOŁDA, Z., Human Rights
HUDZIK, J., Political Philosophy
JACHYMEK, J., Political Thought
JANUSZ, G., International Relations
JELENKOWSKI, M., Political Doctrines
KUCHARSKI, W., National Minorities
MAJ, Cz., International Relations
MAJ, F., Contemporary History
MICH, W., Contemporary History
MICHAŁOWSKI, S., Local Government
MIECZKOWSKI, A., Contemporary History
OLSZEWSKI, E., Political Movements
PIETRAŚ, M., International Relations
PIETRAŚ, Z., J., International Relations
STĘPICŃ, S., Contemporary History
SZELIGA, Z., Constitutional Law
WÓJCIK, A., Contemporary History
ŻMIGRODZKI, M., Political Systems

Faculty of Psychology and Pedagogy (ul. Narutowicza 12, 20-950 Lublin; tel. (81) 537-63-04; fax (81) 537-04-27; internet pip .umcs.lublin.pl):

BARTKOWICZ, Z., Pedagogy
CACKOWSKA, M., Didactics
CHODKOWSKA, M., Sociology
GAJDA, M., Pedagogy
GAŚ, Z., Psychopathology
GUZ, S., Pedagogy
HERZYK, A., Neuropsychology
KACZMAREK, B., Psychology
KĘPSKI, Cz., Pedagogy
KIRENKO, J., Pedagogy
KRASOWICZ-KUPIS, G., Psychology
KUCHA, R., History of Learning and Education
KWIATKOWSKA, G., Philosophy
OCHMAŃSKI, M., High School Pedagogy
PALAK, Z., Pedagogy
POPEK, S., Psychology
SARAN, J., Pedagogy
STACHYRA, J., Pedagogy
WĘGLIŃSKI, A., Pedagogy

UNIWERSYTET WARMIŃSKO-MAZURSKI W OLSZTYNIE
(University of Warmia and Mazury in Olsztyn)

ul. M. Oczapowskiego 2, 10-957 Olsztyn

Telephone: (89) 523-33-30

Fax: (89) 523-04-08

E-mail: bwz@uwm.edu.pl

Internet: www.uwm.edu.pl

Founded 1999 through merger of Olsztyn University of Agriculture and Technology, Higher School of Pedagogy, and Warmian Theological Institute

State control

Rector: Prof. RYSZARD J. GÓRECKI
Deputy Rector: Prof. JÓZEF GÓRNIEWICZ
Pro-Rector (Doctoral Studies): Prof. STANIS-
ŁAW ACHREMCZYK
Pro-Rector (Staff Affairs): Prof. GABRIEL FOR-
DOŃSKI
Pro-Rector (Research and Economic Co-
operation): Prof. JAN JANKOWSKI
Pro-Rector (Student Affairs): Prof. JANUSZ
PIECHOCKI
Director of Administration: Dr ALEKSANDER
SOCHA

Library of 823,374 vols, 1,811 periodicals
Number of teachers: 1,680
Number of students: 30,000

Publications: *Forum Oświatowe* (1 or 2 a
year), *Humanistyka i Przyrodoznawstwo* (1
or 2 a year), *Prace Językoznawcze* (1 or 2 a
year), *Echa Przeszłości* (1 or 2 a year),
Forum Teologiczne (1 or 2 a year), *Acta
Polono-Ruthenica* (1 or 2 a year), *Acta
Neophoilologica* (1 or 2 a year), *Economic
Sciences* (1 or 2 a year), *Technical Sciences*
(1 or 2 a year), *Natural Sciences* (1 or 2 a
year)

DEANS

Faculty of Animal Bioengineering: Prof.
MANFRED LOREK
Faculty of Biology: Prof. JADWIGA PRZAŁA
Faculty of Geodesy and Land Management:
Dr RYSZARD ŻRÓBEK
Faculty of Humanities: Prof. ANDRZEJ STA-
NISZEWSKI
Faculty of Veterinary Medicine: Prof. TOMASZ
JANOWSKI
Faculty of Engineering and Technical
Sciences: Prof. KAZIMIERZ WIERZBICKI
Faculty of Food Sciences: Prof. ZBIGNIEW
SMIETANA
Faculty of Environmental Sciences and Fish-
eries: Dr IRENA WOJNOWSKA-BARYŁA
Faculty of Arts and Educational Sciences: Dr
EUGENIUSZ ŁAPIŃSKI
Faculty of Agriculture and Environmental
Management: Prof. JAN KUCHARSKI
Faculty of Theology: Rev. Prof. ALOJZY SZORC
Faculty of Management and Business
Administration: Dr HENRYK LELUSZ

UNIWERSYTET OPOLSKI
(Opole University)

pl. Kopernika 11a, 45-058 Opole

Telephone: (77) 454-58-71
Fax: (77) 454-51-22
E-mail: sekretariat@uni.opole.pl
Internet: www.uni.opole.pl

Founded 1994 by the merger of Opole
Teacher Training College and the Theolo-
gical-Pastoral Institute of Opole
State control

Chancellor: ANDRZEJ KIMLA
Deputy Chancellor: GRZEGORZ KŁOSIŃSKI

DEANS

Faculty of Economics: Prof. JANUSZ SŁODCZYK
Faculty of History and Education: Prof.
STEFAN MAREK GROCHALSKI
Faculty of Mathematics, Physics and Chem-
istry: Prof. HUBERT WOJTASEK
Faculty of Natural Sciences and Technology:
Prof. ANDRZEJ GAWDZIK
Faculty of Philology: Prof. IRENA JOKIEL
Faculty of Theology: Prof. TADEUSZ DOLA

UNIWERSYTET IM. ADAMA
MICKIEWICZA W POZNANIU
(Adam Mickiewicz University in
Poznań)

ul. H. Wieniawskiego 1, 61-712 Poznań

Telephone: (61) 852-64-25
Fax: (61) 829-41-11

E-mail: rectorof@amu.edu.pl
Internet: www.amu.edu.pl

Founded 1919

Rector: Prof. Dr hab. STANISŁAW LORENC
Pro-Rectors: Prof. Dr hab. BRONISŁAW MARCI-
NIAK, Prof. Dr hab. BOGUSŁAW MRÓZ, Prof.
Dr hab. KAZIMIERZ PRZYSZCZYPKOWSKI, Prof.
Dr hab. BOGDAN WALCZAK, Prof. Dr hab.
JANUSZ WIŚNIEWSKI
Registrar: Mgr STANISŁAW WACHOWIAK
Librarian: Dr ARTUR JAZDON

Library: see Libraries
Number of teachers: 2,634
Number of students: 51,677

DEANS

Faculty of Law and Administration: ANDRZEJ
SZWARC
Faculty of History: DANUTA MINTA-TWOR-
ZOWSKA
Faculty of Modern Languages and Litera-
ture: Prof. Dr hab. JÓSEF DARSKI
Faculty of Polish and Classical Philologies:
Prof. Dr hab. ANTONI SMUSZKIEWICZ
Faculty of Mathematics and Computer
Science: Prof. Dr hab. ZBIGNIEW PALKA
Faculty of Chemistry: Prof. Dr hab. GRZE-
GORZ SCHROEDER
Faculty of Biology: Prof. Dr hab. ANDRZEJ
LESICKI
Faculty of Physics: Prof. Dr hab. ANDRZEJ
DOBEK
Faculty of Geography and Geology: Prof. Dr
hab. JANUSZ CHOIŃSKI
Faculty of Social Sciences: Prof. Dr hab. JAN
GRAD
Faculty of Educational Studies: Prof. Dr hab.
WIESŁAW AMBROZIK
Faculty of Theology: Prof. Dr hab. PAWEŁ
BORTKIEWICZ
Faculty of Education and Fine Arts in Kalisz:
Prof. JERZY RUBIŃSKI

PROFESSORS

Faculty of Law and Administration (ul. Św.
Marcin 90, 61-809 Poznań; tel. (61) 853-68-
43):

CHOBOT, A., Labour Law
GOMUŁOWICZ, A., Financial Law
GULCZ, M., Economics
KĘPIŃSKI, M., European Law
KIJOWSKI, A., Labour Law
KOŁECKI, H., Criminal Law
ŁĄCZKOWSKI, W., Financial Law
MAŁECKI, J., Financial Law
NIEDBAŁA, Z., Labour Law
OWOC, M., Criminal Law
PATRYAS, W., Theory of State and Law
SMYCZYŃSKI, T., Civil Law
SOŁTYSIŃSKI, S., Civil Law
STACHOWIAK, S., Criminal Procedure
SZWARC, A. J., Criminal Law
TYRANOWSKI, J., International Law
WRONKOWSKA-JAŚKIEWICZ, S., Theory of
State and Law
ZEDLER, F., Civil Procedure

Faculty of History (ul. Sw. Marcin 78, 61-809
Poznań; tel. (61) 852-87-79; fax (61) 852-47-
82; e-mail dhist@amu.edu.pl):

BŁASZCZYK, G., East European History
BUCHOWSKI, M., European Ethnology, The-
ory of Anthropology
FOGEL, J., Bronze and Early Iron Age
Prehistory
HAUSER, P., Contemporary History
JASIEWICZ, Z., Ethnology of Poland and
Central Asia
JASIŃSKI, T., Medieval History
KOŚKO, A., Prehistory of Poland
KOTŁOWSKI, T., Contemporary History
KOWAL, S., Economic History
LABUDA, A., History of Art
ŁAZUGA, W., Modern History
MOLIK, W., Modern Polish History

MROZEWICZ, L., Ancient History
OLEJNIK, K., Military History
OLSZEWSKI, W., Modern and Contemporary
History
PIOTROWSKI, P., History of Contemporary
Art
POSERN-ZIELIŃSKI, A., Ethnology of the
Americas, Anthropology of Ethnicity
SCHRAMM, T., Modern History
SERWAŃSKI, M., Modern History
SIERPOWSKI, S., Contemporary History
SKIBIŃSKI, S., History of Medieval Art
STRZELCZYK, J., Medieval History
WYRWA, A., History
ZAWADZKI, S., Ancient History

Faculty of Modern Languages and Literature
(al. Niepodległości 4, 61-874 Poznań; tel. (61)
852-22-03; fax (61) 853-69-33; e-mail
spuppel@amu.edu.pl):

ANDRUSZKO, Cz., Russian Literature
BAŃCZEROWSKI, J., General Linguistics
DARSKI, J., German Linguistics
DZIUBALSKA-KOŁACZYK, K., English Lin-
guistics
FISIAK, J., English Linguistics
GUSSMANN, E., English Linguistics
KALISZAN, J., Russian Linguistics
KAROLAK, Cz., German Literature
KASZYŃSKI, S., Austrian Literature and
Culture
KOPCEWICZ, A., American Literature
KOPYTKO, R., English Linguistics
KRYSZTOFIAK-KASZYŃSKA, M., Danish Lit-
erature
ŁABĘDZKA, I., Romance Literature
LIPOŃSKI, W., Anglo-Saxon Studies
ŁOBACZ, P., General Linguistics
MAJEWICZ, A., Oriental Linguistics
MALINOWSKI, W., Romance Literature
MARKUNAS, A., Methodology of Russian
Language Teaching
ORŁOWSKI, H., German Literature
PAPIÓR, J., German Literature and Culture
PFEIFFER, W., Applied Linguistics
PIOTROWSKI, B., History of Scandinavia
POGONOWSKI, J., Mathematical Linguistics
PUPPEL, S., English Linguistics
SCHATTE, CH., German Linguistics
SIEK-PISKOZUB, T., English Linguistics
SIKORSKA, L., English Literature
SOBKOWIAK, W., English Linguistics
STEFFEN-BATOGOWA, M., General Linguis-
tics
SYPNICKI, J., Romance Linguistics
TOMASZKIEWICZ, T., Romance Linguistics
WĄSIK, Z., General Linguistics
WILCZYŃSKA, W., Applied Linguistics
WÓJTOWICZ, M., Russian Linguistics
ZGÓŁKA, T., General Linguistics

Faculty of Polish and Classical Philologies
(al. Niepodległości 4, 67-874 Poznań; tel. (61)
852-71-27; fax (61) 852-71-27):

ABRAMOWSKA, J., Polish Literature, Histor-
ical Poetics
ADAMCZYK, M., Old Polish Literature
BĄBA, S., Idioms and Culture of Polish
Language
BAKUŁA, B., 20th-century Literature
BALCERZAN, E., Polish Literature, Theory of
Literature and 20th-century Literature
BARTOL, K., Classical Philology
BOREJSZO, M., Polish Linguistics
CHRZĄSTOWSKA, B., New Teaching Meth-
ods, History of Polish Literature
CZAPLIŃSKI, P., Theory of Literature, Lit-
erary Criticism
DANIELEWICZ, J., Hellenistic Philology
DWORACKI, S., Hellenistic Philology
HENDRYKOWSKA, M., Film History and
Theory
HENDRYKOWSKI, M., Film History and The-
ory
KRĄŻYŃSKA, Z., Polish Linguistics
LEGEŻYŃSKA, A., Theory of Literature
LEWANDOWSKI, I., Latin Philology

LEWANDOWSKI, T., Polish Literature
NOWAK, H., Polish Dialectology
POKRZYWNIAK, J. T., Old Polish Literature
PRZYBYLSKI, R. K., Theory of Literature, History of Literature
RATAJCZAK, D., Polish Drama
RZEPKA, W., Polish Linguistics
SMUSZKIEWICZ, A., Teaching of Polish Language and Literature
TROJANOWICZ, Z., 19th-century Polish Literature
WALCZAK, B., Polish Linguistics
WIEGANDT, E., History of Contemporary Literature
WYDRA, W., Editorial and Bibliography
WYSŁOUCH, S., Polish Literature, Theory of Literature and 20th-Century Literature
ZGÓŁKA, T., General Linguistics
ZGÓŁKOWA, H., Polish Linguistics

Faculty of Mathematics and Information Sciences (ul. Umultowska 87, 61-614 Poznań; tel. (61) 829-53-11; fax (61) 829-53-15; e-mail wmiuam@math.amu.edu.pl):

BATÓG, T., Mathematical Logic, Mathematical Linguistics
BUSZKOWSKI, W., Logic, Linguistics, Computation Theory
DOMAŃSKI, P., Functional Analysis
DREWNOWSKI, L., Functional Analysis
HUDZIK, H., Functional Analysis
KACZOROWSKI, J., Number Theory
KĄKOL, J., Functional Analysis, Topology
KAROŃSKI, M., Discrete Mathematics and Probability
KRZYŚKO, M., Mathematical Statistics
KUBIACZYK, I., Mathematics
ŁUCZAK, T., Discrete Mathematics and Probability
MARZANTOWICZ, W., Mathematics
MASTYŁO, M., Functional Analysis
MURAWSKI, R., Mathematical Logic, Philosophy of Mathematics
PYCH-TABERSKA, P., Approximation Theory
RUCIŃSKI, A., Discrete Mathematics and Probability
SZUFLA, ST., Differential Equations
WASZAK, A., Functional Analysis

Faculty of Chemistry (ul. Grunwaldzka 6, 60-780 Poznań; tel. (61) 829-13-35; fax (61) 865-80-08; e-mail depchem@amu.edu.pl):

BRZEZIŃSKI, B., Bio-organic Physical Chemistry
BUREWICZ, A., Teaching of Chemistry
DEGA-SZAFRAN, Z., Physical Organic Chemistry
FIEDOROW, R., Catalysis
GAWROŃSKI, J., Organic Chemistry, Stereochemistry
JARCZEWSKI, A., Physical Organic Chemistry
JASKÓLSKI, M., Crystallography and Biological Chemistry
KATRUSIAK, A., Crystallography
KONARSKI, J., Theoretical Chemistry
KOPUT, J., Physical Chemistry
KORONIAK, H., Synthesis and Structure of Organic Compounds
KOWALAK, S., Catalysis
LIS, S., Rare Earths
ŁOMOZIK, L., Co-ordination Chemistry, Bioinorganic Chemistry
MARCINIAK, B., Photochemistry
MARCINIEC, B., Organometallic Chemistry, Molecular Catalysis
NAWROCKI, J., Water Treatment Technology
PARYZEK, Z., Organic and Natural Products Chemistry
RADECKA-PARYZEK, W., Co-ordination and Macrocyclic Chemistry, Bioinorganic Chemistry
ROZWADOWSKA, M., Asymmetric Synthesis, Alkaloid Chemistry
RYCHLEWSKA, U., Crystallography

SARBAK, Z., Adsorption and Catalysis, Environmental Protection
SCHROEDER, G., Organic Chemistry
SIEPAK, J., Water and Soil Analysis
SZAFRAN, M., Physical Organic Chemistry
WACHOWSKA, H., Chemistry of Coal
WASIAK, W., Instrumental Analysis
WOJCIECHOWSKA, M., Heterogeneous Catalysis
WOLSKA, E., Solid-state Chemistry and Magnetochemistry
WYRZYKIEWICZ, E., Mass Spectrometry of Organic Compounds
WYSOCKA, W., Natural Products Chemistry
ZIOŁEK, M., Heterogeneous Catalysis

Faculty of Biology (ul. Umultowska 89, 61-614 Poznań; tel. (61) 829-55-52; fax (61) 829-55-50; e-mail dziekan@amu.edu.pl):

AUGUSTYNIAK, H., Biochemistry
BALCERKIEWICZ, S., Plant Ecology
BEDNORZ, J., Animal Ecology
BIELAWSKI, J., Animal Cytology
BŁASZAK, Cz., Animal Ecology
BOBOWICZ, M., Plant Genetics
BUJAKIEWICZ, A., Mycology
BURCHARDT, L., Hydrobiology
CIEŚLIK, J., Anthropology
GOŹDZICKA-JÓZEFIAK, A., Biochemistry
GWÓŹDŹ, E., Plant Ecophysiology
HRYNIEWIECKA, L., Biochemistry
JACKOWIAK, B., Botany
KRASKA, M., Hydrobiology
KRZAK, M., Plant Genetics
LATOWSKI, K., Plant Taxonomy
LISIEWSKA, M., Mycology
NIEDBAŁA, W., Animal Ecology
PIONTEK, J., Anthropology
PRUS-GŁOWACKI, W., Plant Genetics
RATAJCZAK, L., Plant Physiology
RATAJCZAK, W., Plant Physiology
STĘPCZAK, K., Zoology
STRZAŁKO, J., Anthropology
SZWEYKOWSKA-KULIŃSKA, Z., Biochemistry
WOJTASZEK, P., Biochemistry
WOŹNY, A., Plant Cytology
ŻUKOWSKI, W., Plant Taxonomy

Faculty of Physics (ul. Umultowska 85, 61-614 Poznań; tel. (61) 829-51-56; fax (61) 829-51-55; e-mail dobek@amu.edu.pl):

BARNAS, J., Solid-state Physics
BŁASZAK, M., Mathematical Physics
BŁASZCZAK, Z., Molecular Optics
DOBEK, A., Biophysics
HOJAN, E., Electroacoustics
JACYNA-ONYSZKIEWICZ, Z., Quantum Physics
JURGA, K., Radiospectroscopy
JURGA, S., Radiospectroscopy and Molecular Physics
KAMIENIARZ, G., Computer Physics
KOZIEROWSKI, M., Nonlinear Optics
KURZYŃSKI, M., Statistical Physics
ŁABOWSKI, M., Molecular Acoustics
MAKAREWICZ, R., Environmental Acoustics
MICNAS, R., Solid-state Physics
MRÓZ, B., Ferroelectrics
NAWROCIK, W., Physics
OZIMEK, E., Psychoacoustics
PARZYŃSKI, R., Quantum Electronics
PATKOWSKI, A., Molecular Biophysics
PUSZKARSKI, H., Solid-state Physics
ROBASZKIEWICZ, S., Solid-state Physics
SCHWARZENBERG-CZERNY, A., Astronomy
STANKOWSKA, J., Molecular Physics
ŚLIWIŃSKA-BARTKOWIAK, M., Physics
TANAŚ, R., Nonlinear Optics
WĄSICKI, J., Physics
WNUK, E., Astronomy

Faculty of Geography and Geology (ul. Fredry 10, 61-701 Poznań; tel. (61) 852-02-98; fax (61) 853-02-10; e-mail dziego@amu.edu.pl):

CHOIŃSKI, J. A., Hydrology
CIERNIEWSKI, J., Remote Sensing

FEDOROWSKI, J., Palaeozoology
GŁAZEK, J., Dynamic and Regional Geology
GŁĘBOCKI, B., Economic Geography
GÓRSKI, J., Hydrogeology
KANIECKI, A., Hydrology
KOSTRZEWSKI, A., Dynamic Geomorphology, Geoecology
KOZACKI, L., Integrated Physical Geography
LORENC, S., Geology, Petrography
MUSZYŃSKI, A., Mineralogy, Petrography
NOWACZYK, B., Geomorphology
PARYSEK, J., Socioeconomic Geography
ROGACKI, H., Spatial Management
SKOCZYLAS, J., Petroarchaeology, Archometry
TOBOLSKI, K., Palaeobotany
WOŚ, A., Climatology, Meteorology

Faculty of Social Sciences (ul. Szamarzewskiego 89, 60-568 Poznań; tel. (61) 847-25-71; fax (61) 847-15-55; e-mail socuam@amu.edu.pl):

ANDRZEJEWSKI, B., History of German Philosophy
BRZEZIŃSKA, A., Development
BRZEZIŃSKI, J., Methodology of Psychology
BUKSIŃSKI, T., Social Philosophy, Philosophy of History
CHYŁA, W., Culture
DROZDOWICZ, Z., Philosophy of Religion
GOLKA, M., Sociology of Culture, Social Anthropology
JAMROZIAKOWA, A., Aesthetics
KOSMAN, M., History
KOSMANOWA, B., History of Science
KOSZEL, B., History and Political Science
MALENDOWSKI, W., Political Science
NOWAK, L., Philosophy of Science, Political Philosophy
NOWAKOWA, I., Philosophy of Science
ORCZYK, J., Economics and History
PAŁUBICKA, A., Theory of Culture
PUŚLECKI, Z., International Economic Relations
SAKSON, A., Sociology of Ethnic Minorities, Sociology of Youth
SĘK, H., Health and Clinical Psychology
SOBCZAK, J., Law
STACHOWSKI, R., History of Psychological Thought
TITTENBRUN, J., Theory and Practice of Privatization
WOŹNIAK, Z., Sociology of Medicine
ZAMIARA, T., Philosophy of Science
ZIÓŁKOWSKI, M., Sociological Theory

Faculty of Educational Studies (ul. Szamarzewskiego 89, 60-569 Poznań; tel. (61) 847-49-00; fax (61) 847-49-00):

DUDZIKOWA, M., School Education
FRĄCKOWIAK, T., Social Education
GNITECKI, J., Methodology of Education
MELOSIK, Z., Comparative Education
POTULICKA, E., Comparative Education
PRZYSZCZYPKOWSKI, K., Adult Education
SKRZYPCZAK, J., Adult Education
STRYKOWSKI, W., Educational Technology
ZANDECKI, A., Youth Educational Problems
ŻOŁĄDŹ-STRZELCZYK, D., Pedagogy, History of Education

Faculty of Theology (ul. Wieżowa 2–4, 61-111 Poznań; tel. (61) 829-39-90; fax (61) 851-97-35; e-mail thfac@man.poznan.pl):

BRANIAK, J., Sociology
CZĘSZ, B., Theology, Patristic Theology
LEWEK, A., Theology, Religious Communication
NIPARKO, R., Christian Pedagogy
PONIŻY, B., Theology, Old Testament Exegisis
PYTEL, J., Theology, New Testament Exegisis
STEFAŃSKI, J., Theology
SZPET, J., Theology, Religious Education
TARNOWSKI, K., Philosophy

WĘCŁAWSKI, T., Theology, Fundamental Theology
WEJMAN, H., Theology of Spirituality

Faculty of Education and Fine Arts in Kalisz (62-800 Kalisz; tel. (62) 767-07-30; fax (62) 764-57-21; e-mail wpa@amu.edu.pl):

JANKOWSKI, D., Education
NAWROT, A., Fine Arts
NIEKRASZ, A., Methodology of Art
WERNER, B., Music Arts

UNIWERSYTET RZESZOWSKI
(Rzeszów University)

al. Rejtana 16C, 35-959 Rzeszów

Telephone: (17) 872-10-00
Fax: (17) 852-20-44
E-mail: rektor@univ.rzeszow.pl
Internet: www.univ.rzeszow.pl

Founded 2001 through the merger of the Pedagogical University of Rzeszów, the Marie Curie Skłodowska University, Lublin (Rzeszów branch) and the Economics Faculty of the Agricultural Academy of Krakow

State control

Rector: Prof. WŁODZIMIERZ BONUSIAK
Pro-Rector for Education: Prof. STANISŁAW KRAWCZYK
Pro-Rector for Foreign Relations: Prof. STANISŁAW SAGAN
Pro-Rector for Scientific Research and Finances: Prof. JERZY KITOWSKI
Pro-Rector for Student Affairs and Accreditation: Prof. EWA ORLOF

DEANS

Faculty of Agriculture and Biology: Prof. CZESŁAW PUCHALSKI
Faculty of Arts and Education: Prof. MIECZYSŁAW RADOCHOŃSKI
Faculty of Economics: Prof. SYLWESTER MAKARSKI
Faculty of Health Sciences: Prof. RYSZARD CIEŚLIK
Faculty of History and Sociology: Prof. ALEKSANDER BOBKO
Faculty of Law: Prof. JAN ŁUKASIEWICZ
Faculty of Mathematics and Natural Sciences: Prof. JERZY TOCKI
Faculty of Philology: Prof. STANISŁAW ULIASZ
Faculty of Physical Education: Prof. KAZIMIERZ OBODYŃSKI
External Faculty of Biotechnology (Kolbuszowa): Prof. IGOR Z. ZUBRZYCKI

UNIWERSYTET SZCZECIŃSKI
(Szczecin University)

Al. Jedności Narodowej 22A, 70-453 Szczecin

Telephone: (91) 434-25-36
Fax: (91) 434-29-92
E-mail: rektorat@univ.szczecin.pl
Internet: www.univ.szczecin.pl

Founded 1985
State control
Language of instruction: Polish
Academic year: October to September

Rector: Prof. Dr hab. ZDZISŁAW CHMIELEWSKI
Vice-Rectors: Prof. Dr hab. WALDEMAR TARCZYŃSKI (Academic Affairs), Prof. Dr hab. HENRYK BABIS (Education Affairs), Prof. Dr hab. STANISŁAW CZEPITA (Development and Organisation)
Administrative Officer: EUGENIUSZ KISIEL
Library: see Libraries
Number of teachers: 1,008
Number of students: 26,793

Publication: *Przegląd Uniwersytecki* (The University Review, 6 a year)

DEANS

Faculty of Arts: Prof. Dr hab. EDWARD WŁODARCZYK
Faculty of Economics and Management: Prof. Dr hab. TERESA LUBIŃSKA
Faculty of Mathematics and Physics: Prof. Dr hab. RYSZARD LEŚNIEWICZ
Faculty of Natural Sciences: Prof. Dr hab. LUCJAN AGAPOW
Faculty of Law and Administration: Prof. Dr hab. ZBIGNIEW OFIARSKI
Faculty of Management and Economics of Services: Prof. Dr hab. JÓZEF PERENC

PROFESSORS

ALEKSIEJENKO, M., Arts
BĄKOWSKI, W., Economics
BIAŁECKI, T., Arts
BRONK, H., Economics
CHMIELEWSKI, Z., Arts
CHWESIUK, K., Economics
CZAPLEWSKI, R., Economics
CZERNIATIN, W., Mathematics
DEPTUŁA, W., Natural Sciences
DOROZIK, L., Economics
DUDZIŃSKI, J., Economics
DZIEDZICZAK, I., Economics
FARYŚ, J., Arts
GIZA, A., Arts
GŁODEK, Z., Economics
GŁOWACKI, A., Arts
GÓRBIEL, A., Law
GRANOWSKI, J., Physics
GRZYWACZ, W., Economics
HADACZEK, B., Arts
HŁYŃCZAK, A. J., Natural Sciences
HOZER, J., Economics
JANASZ, W., Economics
JASKOT, K., Arts
JASZCZANIN, J., Natural Sciences
KARWOWSKI, J., Economics
KĘPCZYŃSKI, J., Natural Sciences
KIZIUKIEWICZ, T., Economics
KOPYCIŃSKA, D., Economics
KOROBOW, W., Mathematics
KOŹMIAN, D., Arts
KUCHARSKA, E., Arts
LUKS, K., Economics
MEJBAUM, W., Arts
MOŁCZANOWA, O., Arts
NOWAKOWSKI, A., Economics
PERENC, J., Economics
PRUSAK, F., Law
RADOMSKA-TOMCZUK, M., Fine Arts
ROGALSKA, S., Natural Sciences
ROGALSKI, M., Natural Sciences
RZEPA, T., Social Sciences
SIERGIEJEW, N., Physics
SŁAWIK, K., Law
ŚLIAŻAS, J., Natural Sciences
STANIELEWICZ, J., Arts
SULIKOWSKI, A., Arts
SUŁKOWSKI, Cz., Economics
SYGIT, M., Medical Sciences
SZAŁEK, B., Economics, Arts
SZLAUER, L., Natural Sciences
URBAŃCZYK, E., Economics
WAŚNIEWSKI, T., Economics
WIERZBICKI, T., Economics
WOŹNIAK, R., Arts
ZALEWSKI, P., Economics
ZAWADZKI, J., Economics

UNIWERSYTET MIKOŁAJA KOPERNIKA W TORUNIU
(Nicholas Copernicus University of Toruń)

ul. Gagarina 11, 87-100 Toruń

Telephone: (56) 654-29-51
Fax: (56) 654-29-44
E-mail: rektor@uni.torun.pl
Internet: www.uni.torun.pl

Founded 1945
State control

Language of instruction: Polish
Academic year: October to September (two terms)

Rector: Prof. Dr hab. JAN KOPCEWICZ
Vice-Rectors: Prof. Dr hab. MAREK ZAIDLEWICZ, Prof. Dr hab. ANDRZEJ RADZIMIŃSKI, Prof. Dr hab. JERZY W. WIŚNIEWSKI, Prof. Dr hab. GRZEGORZ JARZEMBSKI
Registrar: Dr STEFAN NIELEK
Librarian: Dr MIROSŁAW A. SUPRUNIUK

Library of 933,277 books, 493,503 vols of periodicals, 53,422 old books, 5,283 MSS, 11,552 cartographic publications, 228,668 graphics and posters, 98,802 musical scores, 9,216 records; 608,000 vols in departmental libraries; special collns: Pomeranica, Copernicana, Baltica, Polish Emigration Archives
Number of teachers: 1,400
Number of students: 31,625

Publications: *Reports on Mathematical Physics, Open Systems and Information Dynamics, Comparative Law Review, Topological Methods in Nonlinear Analysis, Eastern European Countryside, Logic and Logical Philosophy, Theoria et Historia Scientiarum, Toruński Rocznik Praw Człowieka i Pokoju, Prussia Sacra* (published jointly with Max-Planck-Institut, Göttingen)

DEANS

Faculty of Biology and Earth Sciences: Prof. Dr hab. ANDRZEJ TRETYN
Faculty of Chemistry: Prof. Dr hab. JÓZEF CEYNOWA
Faculty of Economics and Management: Prof. Dr hab. WŁODZIMIERZ KARASZEWSKI
Faculty of Fine Arts: Prof. Dr hab. JÓZEF FLIK
Faculty of History: Prof. Dr hab. WALDEMAR REZMER
Faculty of Humanities: Prof. Dr hab. WITOLD WOJDYŁO
Faculty of Languages: Prof. Dr hab. ADAM BEDNAREK
Faculty of Law and Administration: Prof. Dr hab. ZBIGNIEW WITKOWSKI
Faculty of Mathematics and Computer Science: Prof. Dr hab. ADAM JAKUBOWSKI
Faculty of Physics, Astronomy and Informatics: Prof. Dr hab. JÓZEF SZUDY
Faculty of Theology: Rev. Prof. Dr hab. JERZY BAGROWICZ

PROFESSORS

Faculty of Biology and Earth Sciences (ul. Gagarina 9, 87-100 Toruń; tel. (56) 611-44-41; fax (56) 611-47-72; e-mail baranow@biol.uni.torun.pl; internet www.biol.uni.torun.pl):

BEDNAREK, R., Soil Science
BEDNARSKA, E., Plant Cytology
BUSZKO, J., Entomology, Zoogeography
CAPUTA, M., Animal Physiology
CEYNOWA-GIEŁDON, M., Plant Taxonomy, Geobotany
CHWIROT, B., Plant and Animal Cytology
DAHM, H., Microbiology
DONDERSKI, W., Microbiology, Biotechnology
FALKOWSKI, J., Economic Geography, Spatial Management
GIZIŃSKI, A., Hydrobiology
GNIOT-SZULŻYCKA, J., Biochemistry
GÓRSKA-BRYLASS, A., Plant Cytology
KOPCEWICZ, J., Plant Physiology
KRIESEL, G., Anthropology
MAIK, W., Social Geography
NIEWAROWSKI, W., Physical Geography, Palaeogeography
REJEWSKI, M., Plant Ecology
SADURSKI, A., Hydrobiology and Environmental Protection
SZUPRYCZYŃSKI, J., Geomorphology
TRETYN, A., Plant Physiology

Faculty of Chemistry (ul. Gagarina 7, 87-100 Toruń; tel. (56) 654-29-38; fax (56) 654-24-77; e-mail wydzial@chem.uni.torun.pl; internet www.chem.uni.torun.pl):

BUSZEWSKI, B., Analytical Chemistry
CHOSTENKO, A., Nuclear Chemistry
GRODZICKI, A., Inorganic Chemistry
KITA, P., Inorganic Chemistry
ROZWADOWSKI, M., Physical Chemistry
RYCHLICKI, G., Physical Chemistry
SADLEJ, A., Theoretical Chemistry
TRYPUĆ, M., Chemical Technology
ZAIDLEWICZ, M., Organic Chemistry

Faculty of Economics and Management (ul. Gagarina 13A, 87-100 Toruń; tel. (56) 611-46-08; fax (56) 654-24-50; e-mail krystyna@econ.uni.torun.pl; internet www.econ.uni.torun.pl):

BOGDANIENKO, J., Investment Economics
DREWIŃSKI, M., Management
GŁUCHOWSKI, J., Finance Management
JAWOROWSKI, P., Agricultural Economics
KACZMARCZYK, S., Marketing
MELLER, J., Human Resources Management
SMOLEŃSKI, S., Marketing
SOJAK, S., Accounting
STANKIEWICZ, M., Strategic Management and Planning
SUDOŁ, S., Industrial Management
SZULCE, H., Marketing
WIŚNIEWSKI, Z., Employment Policy
ZIELIŃSKI, Z., Econometrics

Faculty of Fine Arts (ul. Sienkiewicza 30/32, 87-100 Toruń; tel. (56) 622-70-51; fax (56) 622-59-71; internet www.uni.torun.pl/wydzialy/wszp):

BEBARSKA, J., Sculpture
CANDER, K., Painting
CHMIELEWSKI, B., Drawing
CHMIELEWSKI, W., Drawing
FLIK, J., Painting
GUTTFELD, A., Painting
KILJAŃSKI, L., Graphics
KRUSZELNICKI, Z., History of Art
LIMONT, W., Art Education
MALINOWSKI, J., History of Art
PAWŁOWSKI, M., Graphics
PRĘGOWSKI, J., Painting
PRZYBYLIŃSKI, B., Graphics
ROUBA, B., Restoration of Painting
SKIBIŃSKI, S., Medieval Art and Architecture
SŁOBOSZ, J., Graphics
STRZELCZYK, A., Conservation on Painting and Leather
SZAŃKOWSKI, M., Sculpture
TAJCHMAN, J., Restoration of Architectural Monuments
WOLSKI, L., Painting
ZIOMEK, M., Painting

Faculty of History (Pl. Teatralny 2A, 87-100 Toruń; tel. (56) 622-62-03; fax (56) 622-28-44; e-mail atom@his.uni.torun.pl; internet www.his.uni.torun.pl):

CHUDZIAK, J., Archaeology of Buildings
DYGDAŁA, J., 16th- to 18th-century Polish History
KALEMBKA, S., Polish and General History
KOZŁOWSKI, R., Modern Polish History
KUTZNER, M., Polish and General Medieval History of Art
MALISZEWSKI, K., 16th- to 18th-century Polish and General History
MAŁŁEK, K., 16th- to 18th-century Polish and General History
MIELCZAREK, M., Classical Archaeology and Numismatics
NOWAKOWSKI, A., Medieval Archaeology and Military History
OLCZAK, J., Medieval Archaeology and History of Glass
POMIAN, K., Polish and General Modern History of Art and Culture

RADZIMIŃSKI, A., Medieval Church History
REZMER, W., Polish Army between the Two World Wars
STASZEWSKI, J., 16th- to 18th-century Polish and General History
SUDZIŃSKI, R., Modern Polish History
SYMONIDES, J., EU and International Law
TANDECKI, J., Polish-German Relationship
TONDEL, J., History of the Book
WAŻBIŃSKI, Z., History of Art
WENTA, J., Medieval History
WOJCIECHOWSKI, M., 19th- and 20th-century Polish and General History
WOŹNICZKA-PARUZEL, B., Bibliotherapy
ZAREMSKA, H., Cultural History

Faculty of Humanities (ul. Fosa Staromiejska 1A, 87-100 Toruń; tel. (56) 611-36-10; fax (56) 652-27-69; e-mail whminus@ped.uni.torun.pl; internet www.uni.torun.pl/wydzialy/wh):

ADAMSKI, W., Social Structures and Transformations
BAŃKA, A., Psychology
BOROWICZ, R., Sociology of Education
BYBLUK, M., Teaching of Languages
HUBNER, P., History of Science, Sociology of Institutions
KALETA, A., Rural Sociology
KOWALIK, S., Special Education
KWIECIŃSKI, Z., Sociology of Education
ŁUKASZEWICZ, R., School Education
MELOSIK, Z., General Education
MUCHA, J., Social Anthropology and History of Sociology
NALASKOWSKI, A., General Education
PAWLAK, J., History of Philosophy and Social Thought
PERZANOWSKI, J., Logic and Philosophy
PÓŁTURZYCKI, J., General Education
SCHULZ, R., General Education
SIEMIENIECKI, B., Technology in Education
SZAHAJ, A., Political Philosophy, Philosophy of Culture
SZULAKIEWICZ, M., Political Culture
TEMPCZYK, M., Philosophy of Natural Science
TYBURSKI, W., Ethics
WINCŁAWSKI, W., History of Sociology
ZANDECKI, A., General Education
ŻELAZNY, M., Aesthetics, History of Philosophy

Faculty of Languages (Coll. Maius, ul. Fosa Staromiejska 3, 87-100 Toruń; tel. (56) 611-35-10; fax (56) 622-66-59; internet www.uni.torun.pl/wydzialy/wf):

BEZWIŃSKI, A., Russian Literature
BRZOZA, H., Russian Literature
FRIEDEL, T., Slavonic and Polish Linguistics
GROCHOWSKI, M., General Linguistics, Semiotics
HARTMANN, H., German Literature
KALLAS, K., Contemporary Polish Syntax
KRYSZAK, J., Contemporary Polish Poetry
SAUERLAND, K., German Literature
SAWICKA, I., Slavonic Linguistics
SKUCZYŃSKI, J., History of Polish Literature and Theatre
SPEINA, J., 20th-century Polish Prose
SZARMACH, M., Greek Literature, Second Sophistry
SZUPRYCZYŃSKA, M., Contemporary Polish Syntax
WĄSIK, Z., English Linguistics
WISZNIOWSKA-MAJCHRZYK, M., English Drama
WRÓBLEWSKI, W., Classical Philology

Faculty of Law and Administration (ul. Gagarina 15, 87-100 Toruń; tel. (56) 611-41-10; fax (56) 611-40-05; e-mail kandydat_WPiA@cc.uni.torun.pl; internet www.law.uni.torun.pl):

BORODO, A., Financial Law
BRZEZIŃSKI, B., Public Finance Law

BULSIEWICZ, A., Criminal Law
FILAR, M., Penal Law
JASUDOWICZ, T., Human Rights
JUSTYŃSKI, J., Political and Legal Doctrines
KALLAS, M., History of the Polish State
KOLASIŃSKI, K., Labour Law
KULICKI, M., Crime Detection
LANG, A., Theory of Law and State
ŁASZEWSKI, R., History of Law
LUBIŃSKI, K., Civil Law
MAREK, A., Criminal Law
MIK, C., European Law, Human Rights
MORAWSKI, L., Theory of Law and State
NESTEROWICZ, M., Civil Law
OCHENDOWSKI, E., Administrative Law

Faculty of Mathematics and Computer Science (ul. Chopina 12/18, 87-100 Toruń; tel. (56) 611-34-10; fax (56) 622-89-79; e-mail wmii@mat.uni.torun.pl; internet www.mat.uni.torun.pl):

GÓRNIEWICZ, L., Nonlinear Analysis
JAKUBOWSKI, A., Theory of Probability
KAMIŃSKI, B., Ergodic Theory
KWIATKOWSKI, J., Ergodic Theory
LEMAŃCZYK, M., Ergodic Theory
NAGAJEW, A., Theory of Probability, Statistics
SIMSON, D., Algebra
SKOWROŃSKI, A., Algebra
TYC, A., Algebra

Faculty of Physics, Astronomy and Informatics (ul. Grudziądzka 5/7, 87-100 Toruń; tel. (56) 611-33-10; fax (56) 611-53-97; e-mail lidia@phys.uni.torun.pl; internet www.phys.uni.torun.pl):

BĄCZYNSKI, A., Molecular Spectroscopy, Optoelectronics
BALTER, A., Molecular Spectroscopy, Photophysics, Molecular Biophysics
BIELSKI, A., Atomic and Molecular Physics, History of Physics
CHWIROT, S., Atomic and Optical Physics
DEMBIŃSKI, S., Quantum Optics, Chaos Theory
DUCH, W., Computational Intelligence, Cognitive Science and Theoretical Physics
JANKOWSKI, K., Atomic and Molecular Physics, Computational Methods in Physics
JASKÓLSKI, W., Atomic and Molecular Physics, Physics of Low-dimensional Structures
KARWOWSKI, J., Atomic and Molecular Physics
KOSSAKOWSKI, A., Theoretical Physics, Statistical Physics
KREŁOWSKI, J., Astrophysics
KUS, A., Radio Astronomy
MĘCZYŃSKA, H., Solid State Physics
RACZYŃSKI, A., Atomic and Molecular Physics
ROZPŁOCH, F., Condensed Matter Physics, Physics of Carbon
SZUDY, J., Atomic and Molecular Physics, Optical Collisions
WOJTOWICZ, A., Solid State Physics, Optoelectronics
WOLSZCZAN, A., Radio Astronomy, Pulsars
WOSZCZYK, A., Astrophysics, Physics of Comets
WYBOURNE, B., Atomic and Molecular Physics
ZAREMBA, J., Atomic and Molecular Physics

Faculty of Theology (ul. Mickiewicza 121, 87-100 Toruń; tel. (56) 611-49-90; fax (56) 611-49-91; internet www.uni.torun.pl/wydzialy/wt):

BAGROWICZ, J., Catechetic and Religious Education
GRABOWSKI, M., Christian Philosophy
RYCHLICKI, C., Dogmatic and Ecumenical Theology

UNIWERSYTET WARSZAWSKI
(University of Warsaw)

Krakowskie Przedmieście 26–28, 00-927 Warsaw

Telephone: (22) 552-00-00

Fax: (22) 826-32-62

Internet: www.uw.edu.pl

Founded 1816

Academic year: October to June

Rector: Prof. Dr hab. PIOTR WĘGLEŃSKI

Vice-Rectors: Prof. Dr hab. MAREK WĄSOWICZ, Prof. Dr hab. WŁODZIMIERZ BORODZIEJ, Prof. Dr hab. JAN MADEY, Prof. Dr hab. WOJCIECH MACIEJEWSKI

Administrative Director: JERZY PIESZCZURYKOW

Librarian: Dr HENRYK HOLLENDER

Library: see Libraries

Number of teachers: 2,602

Number of students: 55,790

Publications: *Acta Philologica* (irregular), *American Studies* (irregular), *Stosunki Międzynarodowe* (irregular), *Japonica* (irregular), *Przegląd Humanistyczny* (4 a year), *Phytoocenosis* (irregular), *Przegląd Glottodydaktyczny* (irregular), *Barok* (2 a year), *Novensia* (irregular), *Journal of Juristic Papyrology* (irregular), *Studia Palmyreńskie* (irregular), *Przegląd Historyczny* (4 a year), *Kwartalnik Pedagogiczny* (4 a year), *Africana Bulletin* (irregular), *Studia Europejskie* (4 a year), *Biuletyn Centrum Europejskiego Uniwersytetu Warszawskiego* (irregular), *Orientalia Varsoviensia* (irregular), *Ikonotheka* (irregular), *Polityka Wschodnia* (irregular), *Studia Politologiczne* (irregular), *Filozofia Nauki* (irregular)

DEANS

Faculty of Biology: Prof. Dr hab. MICHAŁ KOZAKIEWICZ

Faculty of Chemistry: Prof. Dr hab. STANISŁAW GŁĄB

Faculty of Journalism and Political Science: Prof. Dr hab. GRAŻYNA ULICKA

Faculty of Physics: Prof. Dr hab. KATARZYNA CHAŁASIŃSKA-MACUKOW

Faculty of Geography and Regional Studies: Prof. Dr hab. MARIA SKOCZEK

Faculty of Geology: Prof. Dr hab. BRONISŁAW MATYJA

Faculty of History: Prof. Dr hab. PIOTR BIELIŃSKI

Faculty of Mathematics, Informatics and Mechanics: Prof. Dr hab. STEFAN JACKOWSKI

Faculty of Economic Science: Prof. Dr hab. MARIAN WIŚNIEWSKI

Faculty of Philosophy and Sociology: (vacant)

Faculty of Modern Languages and Oriental Studies: Prof. Dr EMMA HARRIS

Faculty of Polish Philology: Prof. Dr hab. STANISŁAW DUBISZ

Faculty of Law and Administration: Prof. Dr hab. MIROSŁAW WYRZYKOWSKI

Faculty of Education: Prof. Dr hab. ALICJA SIEMAK-TYLIKOWSKA

Faculty of Applied Linguistics and East Slavonic Languages: Prof. Dr hab. ANTONI SEMCZUK

Faculty of Psychology: Prof. Dr hab. DANUTA KĄDZIELAWA

Faculty of Management: Prof. Dr hab. KAZIMIERZ RYĆ

Faculty of Applied Social Sciences and Social Rehabilitation: Prof. Dr hab. MARCIN KRÓL

PROFESSORS

Faculty of Biology (Miecznikowa 1, 02-096 Warsaw; tel. (22) 554-11-03; fax (22) 554-11-06; internet www.biol.edu.pl):

BARTNIK, E., Molecular Biology, Genetics

BRYŁA, J., Biochemistry—Metabolism

CHARZYŃSKA, M., Embryology

CHRÓST, R., Microbiology

CYMBOROWSKI, B., Animal Physiology

DOBROWOLSKI, K., Zoology Ecology

DOBRZAŃSKA-KACZANOWSKA, J., Zoology

FALIŃSKI, J., Botany, Ecology

GLIWICZ, M., Zoology, Hydrobiology

HREBENDA, J., Microbiology

JERZMANOWSKI, A., Biochemistry

KACPERSKA-LEWAK, A., Plant Physiology, Biochemistry

KACZANOWSKI, A., Zoology

KŁOSOWSKI, S., Ecology of Water Plants

KOZAKIEWICZ, M., Ecology

KURAŚ, M., Experimental Biology

MARKIEWICZ, Z., Microbiology

MORACZEWSKI, J., Zoology

MYCIELSKI, R., Microbiology

PIECZYŃSKA, E., Zoology, Hydrobiology

PIEKAROWICZ, A., Microbiology

POSKUTA, J., Plant Physiology

PREJS, A., Zoology, Hydrobiology

RYCHTER, A., Plant Physiology

SIŃSKI, E., Zoology

STAROŃ, K., Molecular Biology

STĘPIEŃ, P., Molecular Biology, Genetics

SYMONIDES, E., Botany, Ecology

TARKOWSKI, A., Embryology

TOMASZEWICZ, H., Botany

WĘGLEŃSKI, P., Molecular Biology, Genetics

WIŁKOMIRSKY, B., Botany

WŁODARCZYK, M., Microbiology

WOJCIECHOWSKI, Z., Biochemistry

ZIELENKIEWICZ, P., Experimental Biology

Faculty of Chemistry (Pasteura 1, 02-096 Warsaw; tel. (22) 822-02-11; fax (22) 822-59-96; e-mail dziekan@chem.uw.edu.pl; internet www.chem.uw.edu.pl):

BILEWICZ, R., Analytical Chemistry

BORUCKA-BUKOWSKA, J., Physical Chemistry and Molecular Spectroscopy

CHAŁASIŃSKI, G., Theoretical Chemistry

CZERWIŃSKI, A., Physical Chemistry

FIGASZEWSKI, Z., Physical Chemistry

GADOMSKI, W., Physical Chemistry, Optics

GALUS, Z., Mineral Chemistry

GŁĄB, B., Analytical Chemistry

GOLIMOWSKI, J., Analytical Chemistry

IZDEBSKI, J., Organic Chemistry

JAWORSKI, J., Chemistry and Food Technology

JEZIORSKI, B., Analytical Chemistry

JURCZAK, J., Organic Chemistry

KALINOWSKI, M., Physical Chemistry

KASPRZYCKA-GUTTMAN, T., Chemical Technology

KOCZOROWSKI, Z., Electrochemistry

KOLIŃSKI, A., Theoretical Chemistry

KRYGOWSKI, T., Physical Chemistry

KULESZA, P., Electrochemistry

LEŚ, A., Theoretical Chemistry

NIEDZIELSKI, J., Organic Chemistry

OSZCZAPOWICZ, J., Organic Chemistry

PIELA, L., Theoretical Chemistry

SADLEJ, J., Physical Chemistry

SAMOCHOCKA, K., Radiochemistry

STOJEK, Z., Electrochemistry

SZYDŁOWSKI, J., Radiochemistry

TEMERIUSZ, A., Organic Chemistry

TROJANOWICZ, M., Analytical Chemistry

WRONA, P., Analytical Chemistry

ŻYLICZ, M., Biochemistry

Faculty of Geography and Regional Studies (Krakowskie Przedmieście 30, 00-927 Warsaw; tel. (22) 552-06-31; fax (22) 552-15-21; e-mail globus@wgsr.uw.edu.pl; internet www.wgsr.uw.edu.pl):

CIOŁKOSZ, A., Cartography, GIS

DEMBICZ, A., Economic Geography, Socioeconomic Geography of Latin America

GRYGORENKO, W., Cartography

GUDOWSKI, J., Economic Geography

GUTRY-KORYCKA, M., Hydrogeology, Hydrology

KOSTROWICKA, A., Economic Geography, Geography of Tourism

KOWALCZYK, A., Economic Geography

MAKOWSKI, J., Regional Geography

MIKULSKI, Z., Hydrogeography, Hydrology

MYCIELSKA-DOWGIAŁŁO, E., Geomorphology

PLIT, F., Regional Geography of Africa

RICHLING, A., Physical Geography, Landscape Ecology

SOCZYŃSKA, U., Hydrology

STOPA-BORYCZKA, M., Climatology

Faculty of Philosophy and Sociology (00-046 Warsaw, Nowy Świat 69; tel. (22) 826-09-62; fax (22) 826-09-62; internet www.is.uw.edu.pl/wfis):

AUGUSTYNEK, Z., Philosophy

CIUPAK, E., Sociology

DEMBIŃSKA-SIURY, D., Philosophy

JADACKI, J., Philosophy

JANKOWSKI, H., Sociology

JASIŃSKA-KANIA, A., Sociology

KOŹMIŃSKI, A., Sociology

KUCZYŃSKA, A., Philosophy

KUCZYŃSKI, J., Philosophy

MARKIEWICZ, B., Philosophy

MARODY, M., Sociology

MORAWSKI, W., Sociology

NOWICKA-RUSEK, E., Sociology

OMYŁA, M., Logic Philosophy

PELC, J., Logic

ROSIŃSKA-ZIELIŃSKA, Z., Philosophy

SIEMEK, M. J., Philosophy

SIEMIEŃSKA-ŻOCHOWSKA, R., Sociology

SMOLICZ, J. J., Sociology

STANISZKIS, J., Sociology

WIATR, J., Sociology

Faculty of Journalism and Political Science (Krakowskie Przedmieście 3, 00-047 Warsaw; tel. (22) 552-02-18; fax (22) 828-94-99; e-mail wdinp@mail.uw.edu.pl; internet www.wdinp.uw.edu.pl):

AULEYTNER, J., Economy

BASZKIEWICZ, J., Political Science

BRALCZYK, J., Journalism

DANECKI, J., Political Economy

DOBRZYCKI, W., Law and International Relations

FILIPIAK, T., Political Science

FILIPOWICZ, S., History of Social-Political Thought

GOLKA, B., Journalism

GOŁĘBIOWSKI, B., Political Science

GOŁEMBSKI, F., Political Science

HALIŻAK, M., Political Science

KASPRZYK, L., International Relations

KUKUŁKA, J., Political Science

KUŹNIAR, R., International Relations

ŁUKASZUK, L., International Law

MICHALSKI, B., Journalism

MROZEK, A. B., Political Science

PARZYMIES, S., International Relations

PIEKARA, A., Social Politics

PRZYBYSZ, K., Political Science

RAJKIEWICZ, A., Political Science

SATKIEWICZ, A. H., Theory of Style, Polish Language

SKRZYPEK, A., History

SOBCZAK, J., Law

SYMONIDES, J., International Relations

WŁADYKA, W., Political History

WOJTASZCZYK, K., Political Science

ZIELIŃSKI, E., Modern Political Systems

Faculty of Polish Philology (Oboźna 8, 00-927 Warsaw; tel. (22) 552-04-28; fax (22) 826-07-83; internet www.polon.uw.edu.pl):

BARTNICKA, B., Polish Philology, Linguistics

CZAPLEJEWICZ, E., Polish Literature

DOMAŃSKI, J., Classical Philology

DREWNOWSKI, T., History of Polish Literature

DUBISZ, S., Polish Philology

FRYBES, S., Polish Literature

GRZEGORCZYKOWA, R., Polish Philology

HANDKE, R., Theory of Literature
KARWACKA, H., Polish Literature
KOWALCZYK, A., History of Literature
KUPISZEWSKI, W. M., Polish Philology, Linguistics
LAM, A., Polish Philology, Literature
MACIEJEWSKI, J., History of Polish Literature
MAKOWSKI, S., History of Literature
MARKOWSKI, A., Polish Philology, Linguistics
MENCWEL, A., Science of Culture
MITOSEK, Z., Theory of Literature
NOWICKA-JEŻOWA, A., Literature, History of Polish Literature
OSIŃSKI, Z., Science of Culture
OWCZAREK, B., Theory of Literature
PELC, J., History of Literature
PUZYNINA, J., Polish Philology, Linguistics
SIATKOWSKA, E., Slavonic Philology, Linguistics
SIATKOWSKI, J., Slavonic Philology, Linguistics
SMOCZYŃSKI, W., Linguistics
SMUŁKOWA, E., Slavonic Philology, Linguistics
STAROWIEYSKI, M., Classical Philology
SUDOLSKI, Z., Polish Philology, Literature
SULIMA, R., Science of Culture
ŚWIDZIŃSKI, M., Polish Literature, Linguistics
TABORSKI, R., Polish Literature
WOJTCZAK-SZYSZKOWSKI, J., Classical Philology

Faculty of Applied Linguistics and East Slavonic Languages (Szturmowa 4, 02-678 Warsaw; tel. (22) 553-42-23; fax (22) 553-42-24; internet www.uw.edu.pl/wlsifw):

GRUCZA, F., Linguistics
KIELAR, B., Linguistics
KOZAK, S., Ukrainian Philology
KRZESZOWSKI, T., Linguistics
LUKSZYN, J., Russian Philology
NAMOWICZ, T., German Philology
SEMCZUK, A., Russian Philology
ŚLIWOWSKI, R., Russian Philology
SZYSZKO, T., Russian Philology
WAWRZYŃCZYK, J., Linguistics
ZMARZER, W., Linguistics

Faculty of Modern Languages and Oriental Studies (Browarna 8/10, 00-311 Warsaw; tel. (22) 552-09-50; fax (22) 826-75-28; e-mail dznfilol@mail.uw.edu.pl; internet www .neofilologia.uw.edu.pl):

ASZYK-BANGS, U., Linguistics
BOGACKI, B. K., Italian Philology
BOGUSŁAWSKI, A., Russian Philology
BOJAR, B., Formal Linguistics
BYRSKI, M. K., Oriental Philology
BYSTYDZIEŃSKA, G., English Studies
CZOCHRALSKI, J., German Philology
DANECKI, J., Oriental Philology
KAŁUŻYŃSKI, S., Oriental Philology
KOMOROWSKA-JANOWSKA, H., Linguistics
KOTAŃSKI, W., Oriental Philology
KÜNSTLER, M., Sinology
ŁYCZKOWSKA, K., Oriental Philology
MAJDA, T., Oriental Philology
MAŁCUŻYŃSKI, P., Literature
MANTEL-NIEĆKO, J., Ethiopian Philology
MELANOWICZ, M., Oriental Philology
PIŁASZEWICZ, S., African Philology
POPKO, M., Oriental Philology
RUBACH, J., English Philology
RUSIECKI, J., English Linguistics
SALWA, P., Italian Literature
SAUERLAND, K. K., German Philology
SEMENIUK-POLAKOWSKA, M., Linguistics
SKARŻYŃSKA-BOCHEŃSKA, K., Oriental Philology
SKŁADANEK, B., Iranian Philology
SKŁADANEK, M., Oriental Philology
SŁUPSKI, Z., Oriental Philology
TUBIELEWICZ, J., Oriental Philology

UGNIEWSKA-DOBRZAŃSKA, J., Italian Philology
WEŁNA, J. A., English Philology
WESELIŃSKI, A., English Literature
WIKTOROWICZ, J., German Philology
WIŚNIEWSKI, J., English Literature
ŻABOKLICKI, K., French Philology

Faculty of Geology (Żwirki i Wigury 93, 02-089 Warsaw; tel. (22) 822-58-84; fax (22) 554-00-01; e-mail dziekstu@geo.uw.edu.pl; internet www.geo.uw.edu.pl):

BAŁUK, W. A., Palaeontology
DRĄGOWSKI, A., Environmental Protection
GRABOWSKA-OLSZEWSKA, B., Engineering Geology
KACZYŃSKI, R., Engineering Geology
KOWALSKI, W., Geochemistry, Mineralogy
KRAJEWSKI, S., Hydrogeology
KUTEK, J., Tectonics, Stratigraphy
LINDNER, L., Quaternary Geology
MACIOSZCZYK, A., Hydrogeology
MACIOSZCZYK, T., Hydrogeology
MAŁECKA, D., Hydrogeology
MARCINOWSKI, R., Stratigraphy
MARKS, L., Quaternary Geology
MATYSIAK, S., Mechanics of Solids
MYŚLIŃSKA, E., Engineering Geology
ORŁOWSKI, S., Stratigraphy
PININSKA, J., Engineering Geology, Geomechanics
RADWAŃSKI, A., Geology
RONIEWICZ, P., Sedimentology
SPECZIK, S., Geology of Ore Deposits
SZULCZEWSKI, M., Stratigraphy, Sedimentology
WIERZBOWSKI, A., Stratigraphy
WYRWICKI, R., Geology of Ore Deposits

Faculty of History (tel. (22) 552-05-45; fax (22) 826-21-30; internet www.his.uw.edu.pl/wh):

AUGUSTYNIAK, U., History of Culture
BANASZKIEWICZ, J., Modern History
BIEŃKOWSKA, B., History of Culture, Library Science
BRAVO, B., Ancient History
BUCHWALD-PELC, P., Library Science
BUKO, A., Archaeology
BUKOWSKI, Z., Archaeology
CHMIELEWSKI, W., Archaeology
CHRÓŚCICKI, J., History of Art
CZEKANOWSKA-KUKLIŃSKA, A., Musicology
DASZEWSKI, W., Archaeology
FIAŁKOWSKI, K., Library Science
GARLICKI, A., History
GAWLIKOWSKI, M., Archaeology
GODLEWSKI, W., Archaeology
GOŁĄB, M., Musicology
HELMAN-BEDNARCZYK, Z., Musicology
JAŚKIEWICZ, D., History of the USSR
JUSZCZAK, W., History of Art
KARPOWICZ, M., History of Art
KIZWALTER, T., 19th-Century History
KOLENDO, J., Archaeology
KOŁODZIEJSKA, J., Library Science
KOZŁOWSKI, S., Archaeology
KULA, M., General History
LASOTA-MOSKALEWSKA, A., Biology, Archaeozoology
LENGAUER, W., History
ŁUKASIEWICZ, J., History
MACISZEWSKI, J., History
MĄCZAK, A., Modern History
MICHAŁEK, K., Modern History, History of the USA
MIKOCKI, T., History of Art
MIŁOBĘDZKI, J. A., History of Art
MODZELEWSKI, K., Medieval History
MURASZKIEWICZ, M., Library Science
MYŚLIWIEC, K., Archaeology
NIWIŃSKI, A. S., History, Egyptology
NOWAKOWSKI, W., Archaeology
OKULICZ-KOZARYN, J., Archaeology
PAPUZIŃSKA-BEKSIAK, J., Literature
PERZ, M., Musicology
POKROPEK, M., Ethnography

PONIATOWSKA, I., History of Music
POPPE, A., Medieval History
POPRZĘCKA, M., History of Art
POTKOWSKI, E., History
RAKOWSKI, A., Musical Acoustics
RUDNICKI, S., 19th- and 20th-century Polish History
RUSINOWA, J., Modern History
SAMSONOWICZ, H., Medieval History
SKUBISZEWSKI, P., Medieval History of Art
SOCHACKI, Z., Archaeology
SOKOLEWICZ, Z., Ethnography
SUCHODOLSKI, S., Archaeology
SZAFLIK, J., History
ŚWIDERKÓWNA, A., Papyrology
TANTY, M., History of Slavonic Countries
TOMASZEWSKI, J., Political Science
TYMOWSKI, M., Modern History
TYSZKIEWICZ, J., Medieval History
WASILEWSKI, T., Medieval History
WAWRYKOWA, M., Modern History
WIERCIŃSKI, A., Archaeology
WIPSZYCKA-BRAVO, E., Ancient History
WOJCIECHOWSKI, M., Modern History
WYROBISZ, A., Medieval History
ZADROŻYŃSKA-BARĄCZ, A., Ethnography
ŻARNOWSKA, A., Modern Polish History
ŻERAŃSKA-KOMINEK, S., Musicology

Faculty of Mathematics, Informatics and Mechanics (Banacha 2, 02-097 Warsaw; tel. (22) 554-42-14; fax (22) 554-42-00; e-mail mim@mimuw.edu.pl; internet www.mimuw .edu.pl):

BESSAGA, C., Mathematical Analysis
BIAŁYNICKI-BIRULA, A., Mathematics
BOJDECKI, T., Theory of Elasticity
BROWKIN, J., Mathematics
DRYJA, M., Informatics
ENGELKING, R., Mathematics
GRABOWSKI, J., Mathematics
JACKOWSKI, S., Mechanics
KREMPA, J., Mathematics
KWAPIEŃ, S., Mathematics
LIGOCKA, E., Mathematics
MOSZYŃSKA, M., Mathematics
PALCZEWSKI, A., Mathematics
PERADZYŃSKI, Z., Mathematics
POL, R., Mathematics
PUCZYŁOWSKI, E., Mathematics
RYTTER, W., Informatics
SEMADENI, Z., Mathematics
SIEKLUCKI, K., Mathematics
SKOWRON, A., Mathematics
SZAŁAS, A., Informatics
TARLECKI, A., Informatics
TIURYN, J., Mathematics
TORUŃCZYK, H., Mathematics
TURSKI, W., Informatics
WOJTASZCZYK, P., Mathematics
WOŹNIAKOWSKI, H., Informatics
ZBIERSKI, P., Mathematics
ŻOŁĄDEK, H., Mathematics

Faculty of Physics (Hoża 69, 00-681 Warsaw; tel. (22) 553-21-23; fax (22) 625-23-36; e-mail dziekfiz@fuw.edu.pl; internet www.fuw.edu .pl):

BADEŁEK, B., Experimental Physics
BAJ, M., Solid Body Physics
BARANOWSKI, J., Experimental Physics
BAŻAŃSKI, S., Theoretical Physics
BIAŁYNICKI-BIRULA, I., Optics and Mechanics
BLINOWSKI, J., Solid Body Physics
CHAŁASIŃSKA-MACUKOW, K., Optics
CIBOROWSKI, J. A., Experimental Physics
CIEŚLAK-BLINOWSKA, K., Medical Physics
DEMIAŃSKI, M., Theoretical Physics
DOBACZEWSKI, J., Theoretical Physics
DZIEMBOWSKI, W., Astronomy
ERNST, K., Atomic Physics
GAJ, J., Solid Body Physics
GRAD, M., Geophysics
GRYNBERG, M., Solid Body Physics
HAMAN, K., Geophysics

KALINOWSKI, J., Molecule Elementary Physics
KAMIŃSKA, M., Solid Body Physics
KIJOWSKI, J., Theoretical Physics
KOPCZYŃSKI, W., High Energy Physics
KOWALCZYK, P., Experimental Physics
KRÓLIKOWSKI, J., High Energy Physics
KRÓLIKOWSKI, W., Atomic Physics
KRUSZEWSKI, A., Astronomy
KUBIAK, M., Astrophysics
KURCEWICZ, W., Nuclear Physics
LELIWA-KOPYSTYŃSKI, J., Geophysics
LESYNG, B., Biophysics
MAURIN, K., Mathematical Methods in Physics
MIELNIK, B., Theoretical Physics
NAMYSŁOWSKI, J., Theoretical Physics
NAPIÓRKOWSKI, M., Statistics Physics
NAZAREWICZ, W., Solid Body Physics
PIASECKI, J., Theoretical Physics
POKORSKI, S., Theoretical Physics
RADZEWICZ, C., Experimental Physics
ROHOZIŃSKI, ST., Atomic Physics
RYKACZEWSKI, K., Experimental Physics
SHUGAR, D., Biophysics
SKRZYPCZAK, E., High Energy Physics
SOSNOWSKA, I., Experimental Physics
STĘPIEŃ, K., Astronomy
STĘPNIEWSKI, R., Solid Body Physics
SYM, A., Physics
SZOPLIK, T., Optics
SZYMACHA, A., Atomic Physics
TRAUTMAN, A., Electrodynamics and Theory of Relativity
TWARDOWSKI, A., Solid Body Physics
UDALSKI, A., Astrophysics
WILHELMI, Z., Atomic Physics
WORONOWICZ, S., Mathematical Methods in Physics
WÓDKIEWICZ, K., Optics
WRÓBLEWSKI, A., Experimental Physics
ZAKRZEWSKI, J., High Energy Physics
ŻYLICZ, J., Experimental Physics

Faculty of Education (Mokotowska 16/20, 00-561 Warsaw; tel. (22) 553-08-18; fax (22) 629-89-79; e-mail pedagog@mail.uw.edu.pl; internet www.pedagog.uw.edu.pl):

BARTNICKA, K., Education History
FRĄCZEK, A., Psychology
KRUSZEWSKI, K., Education
KUPISIEWICZ, C., Didactics, Comparative Education
KWIATKOWSKA, H., Education
LEWOWICKI, T., Adult Education
MIESZALSKI, S., Didactics
POŁTURZYCKI, J., Education
PRZECŁAWSKA, A., Social Education
THEISS, W., Education
WILGOCKA-OKOŃ, B., Education
WOJNAR, I., Education
WOYNAROWSKA, B., Social Medicine
ZACZYŃSKI, W., Didactics

Faculty of Psychology (Stawki 5/7, 00-183 Warsaw; tel. (22) 554-97-00; fax (22) 635-79-91; e-mail dean@sci.psych.uw.edu.pl; internet www.psych.uw.edu.pl):

GAŁKOWSKI, T., Educational Psychology
GRZELAK, J., Social Psychology
GRZESIUK, L., Psychopathology and Psychotherapy
JARYMOWICZ, M., Personality Psychology
KOFTA, M., Personality Psychology
KOŚCIELSKA, M., Clinical Psychology
KOZIELECKI, J., Cognitive Psychology
MATCZAK, A., Individual Differences
MATYSIAK, J., Biological Psychology
MIKA, S., Social Psychology
STRELAU, J., Individual Differences
WIECZORKOWSKA-NEJTARDT, G., Social Psychology
ZALEWSKA, M., Clinical Psychology

Faculty of Law and Administration (tel. (22) 552-03-95; fax (22) 826-99-25; internet www.uw.edu.pl/wpia):

BARDACH, J., History of Law
BŁESZYŃSKI, J., Civil Law
DYBOWSKI, T., Civil Law
ERECIŃSKI, T., Civil Law
FLOREK, L., Labour Law
GARDOCKI, L., Penal Law
GARLICKI, L., Constitutional Law
IZDEBSKI, H., History of Law
JĘDRASIK-JANKOWSKA, I., Labour Law
JĘDRZEJEWSKA, M., Civil Law
KRUSZYŃSKI, P., Penal Law
OKOLSKI, J., Civil Law
PIETRZAK, M., History of Law
PIETRZYKOWSKI, K., Civil Law
PIONTEK, E., International Law
RAJSKI, J., Civil Law
REJMAN, G., Penal Law
SAFJAN, M., Civil Law
SALWA, Z., Labour Law
SKOWROŃSKA-BOCIAN, E., Civil Law
SÓJKA-ZIELIŃSKA, K., History of Law
SZYSZKOWSKA, M., Philosophy of Law
TOMASZEWSKI, T., Penal Law
TRZCIŃSKI, J., Constitutional Law
TURSKA, A., Sociology of Law
WĄSOWICZ, M., History of Law
WIERZBOWSKI, M., Administrative Law
WINCZOREK, P., Theory State and Law
ZABŁOCKA, M., Roman Law
ZIELIŃSKI, A., Civil Law

Faculty of Economic Sciences (Długa 44/50, 00-241 Warsaw; tel. (22) 554-91-44; fax (22) 831-28-46; internet www.wne.uw.edu.pl):

BAKA, W., Banking and Finance
DANILUK, M., Public Finance
DOBROCZYŃSKI, M., International Economics
GMYTRASIEWICZ, M., Economics, Business
GÓRECKI, B., Econometrics
JEZIERSKI, A., Economic History
KASPRZAK, T., Business, Informatics
KLEER, J., Economics
KOTOWICZ-JAWOR, J., Economics
KOZIŃSKI, W., Banking and Finance
LUBBE, A., International Economics
ŁUKASZEWICZ, A., Economic Policy
MACIEJEWSKI, W., Econometrics
MORECKA, Z., Political Economy
OKÓLSKI, M., Statistics, Demography
OPOLSKI, K., Banking and Finance
RUTKOWSKI, J., Political Economy
SADOWSKI, Z., Theory of Economic Development
SIWIŃSKI, W., International Economics
SZEWORSKI, A., Political Economy
SZTYBER, W., Political Economy, Public Finance
TIMOFIEJUK, I., Statistics
WIECZORKIEWICZ, A., Banking and Finance
WILKIN, J., Political Economy, Agricultural Economics

Faculty of Management (Szturmowa 3, 02-678 Warsaw; tel. (22) 553-40-00; fax (22) 553-40-01; internet www.wz.uw.edu.pl):

BOLESTA-KUKUŁKA, K., Sociology of Management
BUCZKOWSKI, L., Techniques of Management
GŁOWACKI, R., Marketing
JAROSZYŃSKI, A., Administrative Law
KISIELNICKI, J., Industrial Economy and Informatics
KRZYŻANOWSKI, R., Social Economics
KWIATKOWSKI, S., Theory of Management
MAJCHRZYCKA-GUZOWSKA, A., Financial Law
MUSZALSKI, W., Employment
OBŁÓJ, K., Organization and Management
RYĆ, K., Economic Theory
ŚLIWA, J., Planning
SOBCZAK, K., Administrative Law

SOPOĆKO, A., Theory of Organization
SZPRINGER, W., Administrative Law
ZAWIŚLAK, A., Theory of Management

Faculty of Applied Social Sciences and Social Rehabilitation (Żurawia 4, 00-503 Warsaw; tel. (22) 621-91-22; fax (22) 625-40-86):

BAŁANDYNOWICZ, A., Resocialization, Prevention
BOKSZAŃSKI, Z., Sociology
JAWŁOWSKA, A., Sociology
KACZYŃSKA, E., History of Social Economics
KICIŃSKI, K., Sociology of Morals
KRÓL, M., History of Ideas
KULPIŃSKA, J., Sociology
KURCZEWSKI, J., Sociology, Sociology of Law
KWAŚNIEWSKI, J., Labour Law, Deviation Sociology
MISIAK, W., Sociology
PILCH, T., Education
PRZECŁAWSKI, K., Sociology
RZEPLIŃSKI, A., Law, Criminology
SWIDA-ZIEMBA, H., Sociology
SZYMANOWSKI, T., Penal Law
TYMOWSKI, A., Social Politics
WOJCIK, P., Political Science, Social Politics
ZABOROWSKI, Z., Psychology
ZIEMBA, Z., Philosophy

UNIWERSYTET KARDYNAŁA STEFANA WYSZYŃSKIEGO W WARSZAWIE
(Cardinal Stefan Wyszyński University in Warsaw)

ul. Dewajtis 5, 01-815 Warsaw

Telephone: (22) 839-52-21
Fax: (22) 839-52-45
E-mail: rektorat@uksw.edu.pl
Internet: www.uksw.edu.pl

Founded 1954 as Akademia Teologii Katolickiej; present name and status 1999
Academic year: October to June

Rector: Rev. Prof. Dr hab. ROMAN BARTNICKI
Vice-Rector (General Affairs and Scientific Research): Rev. Prof. Dr hab. RYSZARD RUMIANEK
Vice-Rector (Education and International Cooperation): Rev. Prof. Dr hab. JAN BIELECKI
Vice-Rector (Development and Student Affairs): Prof. Dr hab. ZBIGNIEW CIEŚLAK
Administrative Director: Mgr inż MAREK LEPA
Librarian: Mgr PIOTR LATAWIEC

Library of 200,000 vols
Number of teachers: 520
Number of students: 15,392

Publications: *Collectanea Theologica* (4 a year), *Prawo Kanoniczne* (4 a year), *Studia Philosophiae Christianae* (2 a year), *Studia Theologica Varsaviensia* (2 a year), *Saeculum Christianum* (2 a year), *Kroniki UKSW* (4 a year), *Maqom* (2 a year), *Jus Matrimoniale* (annually), *Studia nad Rodziną* (2 a year), *Wiadomości UKSW* (monthly), *Studia Psychologica* (annually), *Zeszyty Prawnicze* (annually)

DEANS

Faculty of Theology: Rev. Prof. Dr hab. STANISŁAW URBAŃSKI
Faculty of Canon Law: Rev. Prof. Dr hab. JULIAN KAŁOWSKI
Faculty of Christian Philosophy: Rev. Prof. Dr hab. JÓZEF DOŁĘGA
Faculty of History and Social Sciences: Rev. Prof. Dr hab. HENRYK SKOROWSKI
Faculty of Law: Prof. Dr hab. CEZARY MIK
Faculty of Humanities: Dr TOMASZ CHACHULSKI
Faculty of Mathematics and Science: Prof. Dr hab. MAREK KOWALSKI

PROFESSORS

Faculty of Theology (tel. (22) 839-92-82; e-mail wtdz@uksw.edu.pl):

BALTER, L., Dogmatic Theology
BARTNICKI, R., Biblical Studies
BEŁCH, K., Pastoral Theology
BOKWA, I., Dogmatic Theology
CHROSTOWSKI, W., Biblical Studies
CZAJKOWSKI, M., Biblical Studies
DECYK, J., Liturgy
DURAK, A., Liturgy
DZIUBA, A., Moral Theology
GACKA, B., Dogmatic Theology
GÓRALCZYK, P., Moral Theology
GRACZYK, M., Moral Theology
JABŁOŃSKI, S., Mariology
KARWACKI, R., Fundamental Theology
KULISZ, J., Fundamental Theology
LEWANDOWSKI, J., Dogmatic Theology
LEWEK, A., Theology of Mass Media
MATWIEJUK, K., Liturgics
MĘDALA, S., Biblical Studies
MIERZWIŃSKI, B., Pastoral Theology
MISIASZEK, K., Catechesis
MROCZKOWSKI, I., Moral Theology
MURAWSKI, R., Catechesis
NOWAK, J., Liturgy
OGÓREK, P., Theology of Spirituality
OZOROWSKI, E., Dogmatic Theology
PAZERA, W., Homiletics
PIETRZYK, Z., History of the Church
PIKUS, T., Fundamental Theology
PRZYBYŁOWSKI, J., Pastoral Theology
RUMIANEK, R., Biblical Studies
SAKOWICZ, E., Religion
SALIJ, J., Dogmatic Theology
SEWERYNIAK, H., Fundamental Theology
TYLKI-SZYMAŃSKA, A., Family Studies
URBAŃSKI, S., Theology of Spirituality
WARCHOŁ, E., History of the Church
WARZESZAK, J., Dogmatic Theology
ZABIELSKI, J., Moral Theology
ZAŁĘSKI, J., Biblical Studies

Faculty of Canon Law (tel. (22) 839-52-64; fax (22) 561-88-12; e-mail prawokan@uksw.edu.pl):

BŁESZYŃSKI, J., Civil Law
BRZOZOWSKI, A., Civil Law
DĘBIŃSKI, A., Roman Law
DYBOWSKI, T., Civil Law
GÓRALSKI, W., Ecclesiastical Matrimonial and Family Law
GRĘŹLIKOWSKI, J., History of Law
JEMIELITY, W., History of Ecclesiastical Polish Law
KAŁOWSKI, J., Law of Consecration Life Institutes and Apostolic Life Associations
KIWIOR, W., Procedural Law
KRUKOWSKI, J., Religion and Concordat Law
PASTUSZKO, M., Law of Sacraments
SOBAŃSKI, R., Theory of Ecclesiastical Law
STAWNIAK, H., Law of Teaching Services
SYRYJCZYK, J., Ecclesiastical Criminal Law
SZTYCHMILER, R., Ecclesiastical Procedural Law
WROCEŃSKI, J., Ecclesiastical Law of Persons

Faculty of Christian Philosophy (tel. (22) 561-88-53; fax (22) 561-88-53; e-mail wfch@uksw.edu.pl):

ANDRZEJUK, A., Philosophy
ARANOWSKA, E., Methodology of Psychological Sciences
BIELECKI, J., Psychology of Religion
BOLOZ, J., Bioethics
BOMBIK, M., Logic
DOŁĘGA, J., Philosophy of Nature
GAŁUSZKO, K., Preservation of Nature
GASIUL, H., Psychology of Personality
GERAS, G., Judicial and Penitentiary Psychology

HAŁACZEK, B., Anthropology, History and Philosophy of Science
JAKUBIK, A., Clinical Psychology
KLIMSKI, T., History of Philosophy
LATAWIEC, A., Philosophy of Nature
LEMAŃSKA, A., Philosophy of Nature
MACEWICZ, J., Genetics
MATCZAK, A., Developmental Psychology
MORAWIEC, E., Philosophy, Metaphysics
NIEZNAŃSKI, E., Logic, Methodology of Sciences
NOWICKA, G., Biochemistry
PODREZ, E., Ethics
PORĘBSKI, S., History of Polish Philosophy
RYŚ, M., Psychology of Marriage and Family
SARELO, Z., Ethics
SINIARSKA-WOLAŃSKA, A., Ecology
SOCHOŃ, J., History of Philosophy, Philosophy of Religion
STOJANOWSKA, E., Social Psychology
STRZAŁECKI, A., General Psychology, Psychodiagnosis
TERELAK, J., Psychology of Labour and Stress
TYLKA, J., Clinical Psychology
ZABŁOCKI, K., Pedagogy, Psychology of Revalidation and Rehabilitation

Faculty of History and Social Sciences (tel. (22) 561-88-10; fax (22) 561-88-10; e-mail wnhis@uksw.edu.pl):

BALICKI, J., Political Science
BANIA, Z., History of Medieval and Modern Architecture
CYWIŃSKI, B., Contemporary History
DADAK-KOZICKA, K., Musicology
DĄBEK, S., Musicology
DĄBROWSKA, T., Archaeology
DELUGA, W., History of Art
DROZD, J., International Relations
DYLUS, A., Philosophy and Ethics
GRONKIEWICZ-WALTZ, H., Administrative and Banking Law
GROSFELD, J., Political Economy
JANOCHA, M., History of Art
JUROS, H., Moral Theology, Ethics
KOBIELUS, S., History of Art
KOBYLIŃSKI, Z., Archaeology
KOŁOSOWSKI, T., History of Early Christian Literature
KORAL, J., Political Science
KOZŁOWSKI, S., Archaeology
KRASNODĘBSKI, Z., Philosophy and Sociology
MAJKOWSKI, W., Sociology of the Family
MANDZIUK, J., History of the Church
MAZURKIEWICZ, P., Political Science
MIŚKIEWICZ, M., Archaeology
MOISAN-JABLONSKI, CH., History of Art
NAUMOWICZ, J., History of Early Christian Literature
NAWROT, E., History
OCHOCKI, A., Demography
ODZIEMKOWSKI, J., History
POKORA, H., History of Art
POTOCKI, A., Sociology
REKŁAJTIS, E., Arabic Philology
SKOROWSKI, H., Political Science
SZYMONIK, K., Arts of Music
TRZECIAK, M., Sociology
UERTZ, R., Political Science
WILSKA, M., Archaeology
WÓJTOWICZ, A., Sociology
WYSOCKI, W., History
ZBUDNIEWEK, J., History of the Church
ZIEMER, K., Political Science
ŻYRO, T., Political Science

Faculty of Law (ul. Wóycickiego 1/3, 01-938 Warsaw; tel. (22) 569-96-50; fax (22) 569-97-45; e-mail prawo@uksw.edu.pl):

BORUTA, M., Labour Law
CIEŚLAK, Z., Administrative Law
GRANAT, M., Constitutional Law
JĘDRZEJEWSKA, M., Civil Proceedings
JURCEWICZ, A., Agrarian Law

KACZYŃSKI, L., Labour Law
KALLAS, M., History of the Political System and Law in Poland
LIPOWICZ, I., European Administrative Law
MAJEWSKI, J., Criminal Law
MIK, C., International and European Law
MORAWSKI, L., Theory and Philosophy of Law
NOWAK-FAR, A., Financial Law
OMYŁA, M., Logic and Methodology of Legal Sciences
PRUSAK, F., Criminal Procedure
STOJANOWSKA, W., Family Law
STRZYCZKOWSKI, K., Private Economic Law
SZAJKOWSKI, A., Private Economic Law
SZPOR, G., Informatics Law
ZABŁOCKI, J., Roman Law
ZIELIŃSKI, A., Civil Proceedings

Faculty of Humanities (tel. (22) 839-77-63; e-mail polonistyka@uksw.edu.pl):

BIEŃKOWSKA, E., History of 19th- and 20th-century Literature, Comparative Literature, Literary Criticism
BOBROWSKA, B., History of Literature of the Second Half of the 19th Century
DOPART, B., Romantic Literature
DUMA, J., History of Language
DYBCIAK, K., History of 20th-century Literature, Literary Criticism
JANUS, E., History of Language
KOSTKIEWICZOWA, T., History of 18th-century Literature, Theory of Literature
KUCZYŃSKA-KWAPISZ, J., Education for Handicapped People
ŁUKASZUK-PIEKARA, M, 20th-century Literature
PAWŁOWSKI, K., Classical Philology, Theory of Literature
PISKUREWICZ, J., History of Child-rearing
PRUSSAK, M., Science of Theatre, History of Literature of the Second Half of the 19th Century, Science Publications
SMOLIŃSKA-THEISS, B., Education
SURZYSZKIEWICZ, J., Education
THEISS, W., Social Education
WARZECHA, J., Biblical Studies
WOLNICZ-PAWŁOWSKA, E., History of Language
ZIELIŃSKA, A., Linguistics

Faculty of Mathematics and Natural Science (tel. (22) 561-89-29; e-mail matematyka@uksw.edu.pl):

ALSTER, K., Mathematics
CHEŁMIŃSKI, K., Mathematics
CHOJNACKI, W., Mathematics
CYTOWSKI, J. W., Computer Science
GAJDA, M., Physics
GÓRECKI, J., Chemistry
GODLEWSKI, M., Physics
HERBICH, J., Chemistry
HOŁYST, R., Chemistry
JABŁOŃSKI, A., Chemistry
KARPIŃSKI, Z., Chemistry
KIJOWSKI, J., Physics
KORYBUT-DASZKIEWICZ, B., Chemistry
KOTLARSKI, H., Mathematics
KOWALSKI, M. A., Mathematics
KRYNICKI, M., Mathematics
KULPA, W., Mathematics
KUŚ, M., Physics
KUTNER, W., Chemistry
ŁUNARSKA-BOROWIECKA, E., Chemistry
MACEK, W., Physics
MAINARDI, S., Economy
MAZUR, T., Mathematics
MOSTOWSKI, J., Physics
NANIEWICZ, Z., Mathematics
NOWICKA-TARASZEWSKA, J., Chemistry
RUSINEK, J., Mathematics
RZĄŻEWSKI, K., Physics
SKOŚKIEWICZ, T., Physics
SKWARCZYŃSKI, M., Mathematics
SOCHA, L., Computer Science
TURSKI, L. A., Physics
TURZAŃSKI, M., Mathematics

WALUK, J., Chemistry
ZAGRODNY, D., Mathematics
ZAREMBA, L., Mathematics

UNIWERSYTET WROCŁAWSKI
(University of Wrocław)

pl. Uniwersytecki 1, Wrocław
Telephone: (71) 343-68-47
Fax: (71) 3744-34-21
E-mail: rektorat@adm.uni.wroc.pl
Internet: www.uni.wroc.pl
Founded 1702, rebuilt 1945
State control
Language of instruction: Polish
Academic year: October to June (two terms)
Rector: Prof. Dr hab. ZDZISŁAW LATAJKA
Vice-Rector (Scientific Research and Foreign Relations): Prof. Dr hab. KRZYSZTOF WÓJTOWICZ
Vice-Rector (General Affairs) (vacant)
Vice-Rector (Teaching Affairs): Prof. Dr hab. KRYSTYNA GABRYJELSKA
Vice-Rector (Student Affairs): Prof. Dr hab. JERZY MARÓN (acting)
Administrative Officer: Dr BEATA LENKIEWICZ
Librarian: Mgr Inż. GRAŻYNA PIOTROWICZ
Library: see Libraries and Archives
Number of teachers: 1,720
Number of students: 41,663

Publication: *Acta Universitatis Wratislaviensis*

DEANS

Faculty of Chemistry: Prof. Dr hab. JERZY PIOTR HAWRANEK
Faculty of Historical and Pedagogical Sciences: Prof. Dr hab. BOGDAN ROK
Faculty of Law and Administration: Prof. Dr hab. MAREK BOJARSKI
Faculty of Mathematics and Computer Science: Prof. Dr hab. RYSZARD SZEKLI
Faculty of Natural Sciences: Prof. Dr hab. ANDRZEJ WITKOWSKI
Faculty of Philology: Prof. Dr hab. WŁADYSŁAW DYNAK
Faculty of Physics and Astronomy: Prof. Dr hab. HENRYK CUGIER
Faculty of Social Sciences: Prof. Dr hab. BERNARD ALBIN

PROFESSORS

Faculty of Chemistry (ul. F. Joliot-Curie 14, 50-383 Wrocław; tel. (71) 375-72-90; fax (71) 375-74-20; e-mail dziekanat@wchuwr.chem.uni.wroc.pl; internet www.chem.uni.wroc.pl/indexpol.htm):

HAWRANEK, J., Electronic Data Processing
JAKUBAS, R., Physical Chemistry
JEZIERSKI, A., Inorganic Chemistry
KISZA, A., Physical Chemistry
KOLL, A., Physical Chemistry
KONOPIŃSKA, D., Organic Chemistry
KOZŁOWSKI, H., Bioinorganic and Biomedicinal Chemistry
LATAJKA, Z., Theoretical Chemistry and Chemical Physics
LATOS-GRAŻYŃSKI, L., General Chemistry
LIS, T., Crystallography
MROZIŃSKI, J., Methodology of Chemistry
PRUCHNIK, F., Environmental Chemistry and Protection
RATAJCZAK, H., Theoretical Chemistry and Chemical Physics
SIEMION, I., Organic Chemistry
SKRZYPIEC-LEGENDZIEWICZ, J., Analytical Chemistry
SOBOTA, P., Inorganic Chemistry for Natural Scientists
SOBCZYK, L., Physical Chemistry
ZIÓŁKOWSKI, J., Inorganic Chemistry

Faculty of Historical and Pedagogical Sciences (ul. Szewska 48, 50-139 Wrocław; tel. (71) 375-22-23; fax (71) 343-28-55; e-mail dziekan@hist.uni.wroc.pl; internet www.wnhip.hist.uni.wroc.pl):

ADAMCZYK, M., Comparative Pedagogy
BANAŚ, P., Science of Art
CIESIELSKI, M., History of Eastern Europe
CZAPLIŃSKI, M., History of Silesia
DERWICH, M., Centre for Studies of Religious Orders and Church Congregations
KULAK, T., General and Polish History since 19th c.
KUSIAK, F., Economic History, Demography and Statistics
MATWIJOWSKI, K., 16th–18th c. General and Polish History
OCHMAN-STANISZEWSKA, S., 16th–18th c. General and Polish History
PIETRZAK, J., 16th–18th c. General and Polish History
POTYRAŁA, B., General Pedagogy
ROK, B., 16th–18th c. General and Polish History
WACHOWSKI, K., Medieval Archaeology
WRZESIŃSKI, W., Contemporary History
ZABSKI, E., Philosophical and Methodological Foundations of Psychology
ŻERELIK, R., Centre for Studies of Religious Orders and Church Congregations

Faculty of Law and Administration (ul. Uniwersytecka 22–26, 50-145 Wrocław; tel. (71) 343-71-64; fax (71) 375-27-84; internet www.prawo.uni.wroc.pl):

ADAMIAK, B., Administrative Proceedings and Judicial Control of Administrative Activity
BANASZEK, B., Constitutional Law
BŁAS, A., Administrative Law
BEDNARSKI, T., Statistics and Operation Researches
BOĆ, J., Administrative Law
BOGUNIA, L., Criminal Law Practice
BOJARSKI, M., Law of Petty Offences and Penal Fiscal Law
DZIAŁOCHA, K., Constitutional Law
FOJCIK-MASTALSKA, E., Financial Law
FRĄCKOWIAK, J., Economic and Commercial Law
GNIEWEK, E., Civil Law and International Private Law
JENDROŚKA, J., Administrative Proceedings and Judical Control of Administrative Activity
JONCA, K., Political and Legal Doctrines
KACZMAREK, T., Substantive Penal Law
KAŹMIERCZYK, S., Theory and Philosophy of Law
KEGEL, Z., Crime Detection
KIERES, L., Administrative Economic Law
KOLASA, J., International Economic Relations
KONIECZNY, A., History of Administration
MACIEJEWSKI, M., Political and Legal Doctrine
MASTALSKI, R., Financial Law
MĄDRZAK, H., Civil Procedure
OLSZEWSKI, L., International Economic Relations
ORZECHOWSKI, K., History of Polish State and Law
POŁOMSKI, F., History of Polish State and Law
SZURGACZ, H., Labour Law
ŚWIDA, Z., Penal Proceedings
TRZCIŃSKI, J., Crime Detection

Faculty of Mathematics and Computer Science (pl. Grunwaldzki 2–4, 50-384 Wrocław; tel. and fax (71) 375-74-91; e-mail dziekan@math.uni.wroc.pl; internet www.math.uni.wroc.pl/wydzial/index.php):

BILER, P., Differential Equations
BOŻEJKO, M., Mathematical Analysis
DAMEK, E., Geometry
DUDA, R., History and Methodology of Mathematics
HULANICKI, A., Functional Analysis
KISIELEWICZ, A., Algebra and Theory of Numbers
KOPOCIŃSKI, B., Applied Mathematics
NARKIEWICZ, W., Algebra and Theory of Numbers
NEWELSKI, Algebra and Theory of Numbers
PACHOLSKI, L., Programming Languages
PYTLIK, T., Functional Analysis
ROLSKI, T., Stochastic Processes
SYSŁO, M., Programming Methods
SZCZOTKA, W., Applications of Mathematics
SZWARC, R., Mathematical Analysis
URBANIK, K., Theory of Probability

Faculty of Natural Sciences (ul. Kuźnicza 35, 50-138 Wrocław; tel. and fax (71) 343-57-28):

BOROWIEC, L., Animal Systematics
CEBRAT, S., Genome Studies
DZUGAJ, A., Animal Physiology
KOZUBEK, A., Lipids and Liposomes
KUPRIŃSKI, T., Anthropology
ŁOBODA, J., Social and Economic Geography
OGORZAŁEK, A., Zoology
OTLEWSKI, J., Protein Engineering
POLANOWSKI, A., Biotechnology of Proteins
SACHANBIŃSKI, M., Museum of Mineralogy and Section of Gemmology
SADOWSKA, A., Geology (Palaeobotany)
SIKORSKI, A., Cell Biology
SZOPA-SKÓRKOWSKI, J., Genetic Biochemistry
TOMIAŁOJĆ, L., Natural Museum
WESOŁOWSKI, T., Bird Ecology
WILUSZ, T., Enzymology
WITKOWSKI, A., Avian Ecology
WYRZYKOWSKI, J., Regional Geography and Tourism

Faculty of Philology (pl. Biskupa Nankiera 15, 50-140 Wrocław; tel. and fax (71) 343-30-29; e-mail dziekanat.fil@uni.wroc.pl):

DĄBROWSKA, A., Applied Linguistics
DEGLER, J., Theory of Culture and Performing Arts
DYNAK, W., Methodology of Teaching Polish Language and Literature
JANIKOWSKI, K., Scandinavian Studies, German Language
JASTRZĘBSKI, J., Theory of Culture
KAMIŃSKA-SZMAJ, I., Contemporary Polish
KLIMOWICZ, T., Russian Literature and Culture
KOLBUSZEWSKI, J., History of Polish Literature before 1918
KUNICKI, W., German Literature before 1848
ŁAWIŃSKA-TYSZKOWSKA, J., New Latin Philology
ŁUGOWSKA, J., Theory of Culture and Performing Arts
MIGOŃ, A., Theory and History of Books
MIGOŃ, K., Theory and History of Books
MIODEK, J., History of Polish
PISAREK, L., Russian Studies
PRĘDOTA, S., Dutch Lexicology and Lexicography
PYSZNY, J., Polish Literature since 1918
SAWICKI, P., Italian Studies
SOKOLSKI, J., History of Early Polish Literature
SZASTYŃSKA-SIEMION, A., Greek Philology
TOMICZEK, E., Applied Linguistics
WIECZOREK, D., Ukrainian Studies
ZAWADA, A., Polish Literature since 1918
ZABSKI, T., History of Polish Literature before 1918

Faculty of Physics and Astronomy (pl. M. Borna 9, 50-204 Wrocław; tel. (71) 375-94-04; fax (71) 321-76-82; e-mail dziekan@ift.uni.wroc.pl; internet www.wfa.uni.wroc.pl):

CZAPLA, Z., Experimental Physics (Dielectrics Physics)
CISZEWSKI, A., Microstructure Surface Experimental Physics

CUGIER, H., Astrophysics and Classical Astronomy

HABA, Z., Theoretical Physics (Field Theory)

KIEJNA, A., Absorption Experimental Physics

KOŁACZKIEWICZ, J., Experimental Physics (Spectroscopy of Field Emission)

LUKIERSKI, J., Theoretical Physics (High-Energy Physics and Theory of Fundamental Particles)

ŁOPUSZAŃSKI, J., Theoretical Physics (Mathematical Methods in Physics)

MRÓZ, S., Experimental Physics (Electron Spectroscopy)

POPOWICZ, Z., Theoretical Physics (Field Theory)

PĘKALSKI, A., Theoretical Physics (Nonlinear Dynamics and Complex Systems)

REDLICH, K., Theoretical Physics (High-Energy Physics and Theory of Fundamental Particles)

Faculty of Social Sciences (ul. Koszarowa 3, 51-149 Wrocław; tel. (71) 375-51-92; fax (71) 326-10-11; e-mail sekretariat@wns.uni.wroc.pl; internet www.wns.uni.wroc.pl):

ALBIN, B., International Studies (Eastern Europe Research)

ANTOSZEWSKI, A., Political Sciences (Political Systems)

BAL, K., Philosophy (German Philosophy)

BOKAJŁO, W., Contemporary Political Ideas

DĄBROWSKI, S., Political Sciences (Contemporary History and Social Movements)

GAJDA-KRYNICKA, J., Philosophy (History of Philosophy)

GELLES, R., International Studies

HULANICKA, B., Sociology of Political Relations

JABŁONSKI, A., Theory of Politics

KOSIAN, J., History of Philosophy in Silesia

ŁOS-NOWAK, T., International Relations

ŁUKASZEWICZ, R., Studies in Alternatives of Human Education

PISAREK, H., Epistemology and Ontology

SIEMIANOWSKI, A., Philosophy of Science and Culture

STANDTMUELLER, E., Studies on European Union

SURMACZYŃSKI, M., Sociology (Sociology of Political Relations)

WOLAŃSKI, M., Research in East European Studies

UNIWERSYTET ZIELONOGÓRSKI
(University of Zielona Góra)

ul. Podgórna 50, 65-246 Zielona Góra

Telephone: (68) 328-20-00
Fax: (68) 324-55-97
E-mail: rektor@uz.zgora.pl
Internet: www.uz.zgora.pl

Founded 2001 through merger of Politechnika Zielonogórska and Wyższa Szkoła Pedagogiczna im. Tadeusza Kotarbińskiego
State control

Rector: Prof. Dr hab. MICHAŁ KISIELEWICZ
Pro-Rector for Science and Foreign Relations: Prof. Dr hab. inż JÓZEF KORBICZ
Pro-Rector for the School of Exact and Economic Sciences: Prof. Dr hab. MARIAN NOWAK
Pro-Rector for the School of Technical Sciences: Prof. Dr hab. inż FERDYNAND ROMANKIEWICZ
Pro-Rector for Student Affairs: Prof. Dr hab. KRZYSZTOF URBANOWSKI
Pro-Rector for the School of Humanities and Social Sciences: Prof. Dr hab. ZDZISŁAW WOŁK

Library of 425,255 vols
Number of teachers: 1,177
Number of students: 23,127

Publications: Zeszyty Naukowe (irregular), Discussiones Mathematicae (4 series, each 2 a year), Applied Mathematics and Computer Science (4 a year), Management (2 a year), Applied Mechanics and Engineering (4 a year), Studia Zachodnie (annually)

DEANS

Faculty of Arts: Prof. Dr hab. ANDRZEJ TUCHOWSKI
Faculty of Electrotechnology, Informatics and Telecommunications: Prof. Dr hab. inż. JERZY BOLIKOWSKI
Faculty of Humanities: Prof. Dr hab. ANDRZEJ KSENICZ
Faculty of Land and Environmental Engineering: Prof. Dr hab. inż. HENRYK GREINERT
Faculty of Mechanical Engineering: Prof. Dr hab. inż. RYSZARD ROHATYŃSKI
Faculty of Education and Social Sciences: Prof. Dr inż. WIELISŁAWA OSMAŃSKA-FURMANEK
Faculty of Exact Sciences: Prof. Dr hab. MIECZYSŁAW BOROWIECKI
Faculty of Management: Prof. Dr hab. DANIEL FIC

Technical Universities

AKADEMIA GÓRNICZO-HUTNICZA IM. STANISŁAWA STASZICA W KRAKOWIE
(AGH University of Science and Technology)

ul. Mickiewicza 30, 30-059 Cracow

Telephone: (12) 617-20-02
Fax: (12) 633-46-72
E-mail: rektorat@uci.agh.edu.pl
Internet: www.agh.edu.pl

Founded 1919
State control
Languages of instruction: Polish, English
Academic year: October to June

Rector: Prof. Dr RYSZARD TADEUSIEWICZ
Vice-Rectors: Prof. Dr ANTONI TAJDUŚ (General Affairs), Prof. Dr ANDRZEJ ŁĘDZKI (Education), Prof. Dr ANDRZEJ KORBEL (International Affairs), Prof. Dr JANUSZ KOWAL (Science)
Chief Administrative Officer: MSc HENRYK ZIOŁO
Librarian: Mgr EWA DOBRZYŃSKA-LANKOSZ

Library of 407,247 vols, 138,287 vols periodicals, 769,333 items special collections
Number of teachers: 2,014
Number of students: 29,237

Publications: Elektrotechnika i Elektronika (Electrical Engineering, 2 a year), Geologia (Geology, 4 a year), Górnictwo (Mining, 4 a year), Mechanika (Mechanics, 4 a year), Metallurgy and Foundry Engineering (2 a year), Opuscula Mathematica (annually), Telekomunikacja Cyfrowa (annually), Inżynieria Środowiska (Environmental Engineering, 2 a year), Automatyka (Automatics, 2 a year), Geodezja (Mining Surveying, 2 a year), Computer Science (annually), Kliertnictwo Nafta Gaz (Drilling Oil and Gas, annually)

DEANS

Faculty of Applied Mathematics: Prof. Dr ADAM PAWEŁ WOJDA
Faculty of Applied Social Sciences: Dr ANNA SIWIK
Faculty of Drilling, Oil and Gas: Prof. Dr STANISŁAW STRYCZEK
Faculty of Electrical Engineering, Automatics, Computer Science and Electronics: Prof. Dr TADEUSZ ORZECHOWSKI

Faculty of Foundry Engineering: Prof. Dr STANISŁAW RZADKOSZ
Faculty of Fuels and Energy: Prof. Dr JANINA MILEWSKA-DUDA
Faculty of Geology, Geophysics and Environmental Protection: Prof. Dr TADEUSZ SŁOMKA
Faculty of Management: Prof. Dr WIESŁAW WASZKIELEWICZ
Faculty of Materials Science and Ceramics: Prof. Dr JERZY LIS
Faculty of Mechanical Engineering and Robotics: Prof. Dr WŁODZIMIERZ KOWALSKI
Faculty of Metallurgy and Materials Science: Prof. Dr ZBIGNIEW MALINOWSKI
Faculty of Mining and Geoengineering: Prof. Dr JERZY KLICH
Faculty of Mining Surveying and Environmental Engineering: Prof. Dr JAN GOCAŁ
Faculty of Non-Ferrous Metals: Prof. Dr WOJCIECH LIBURA
Faculty of Physics and Applied Computer Science: Prof. Dr KAZIMIERZ JELEŃ

POLITECHNIKA BIAŁOSTOCKA
(Białystok Technical University)

ul. Wiejska 45A, 15-351 Białystok

Telephone: (85) 742-23-93
Fax: (85) 742-23-93
E-mail: rektorat@pb.bialystok.pl
Internet: www.pb.bialystok.pl

Founded 1949
State control
Languages of instruction: Polish, Russian, English
Academic year: October to June

Rector: Prof. Dr hab. Inż. MICHAŁ BOŁTRYK
Vice-Rectors: Prof. Dr hab. Inż. SŁAWOMIR ADAM SORKO, Prof. Dr hab. Inż. FRANCISZEK SIEMIENIAKO, Prof. Dr hab. Inż MIKOŁAJ BUSŁOWICZ
Registrar: Inż. MIROSŁAW MILEWSKI
Librarian: Mgr BARBARA KUBIAK
Library: see Libraries and Archives
Number of teachers: 773
Number of students: 16,500

Publications: Zeszyty Naukowe (irregular), Matematyka, Fizyka, Chemia (irregular), Elektryka (irregular), Mechanika (irregular), Budownictwo (irregular), Inżynieria Środowiska (irregular), Budowa i Eksploatacja Maszyn (irregular), Architektura (irregular), Ekonomia i Zarządzanie (irregular), Informatyka (irregular)

DEANS

Faculty of Architecture: Prof. Dr hab. Inż. arch. ANDRZEJ BASISTA
Faculty of Civil Engineering and Environmental Sciences: Prof. Dr hab. Inż. CZESŁAW MIEDZIAŁOWSKI
Faculty of Electrical Engineering: Prof. Dr hab. Inż. BRUNON LEJDY
Faculty of Mechanics: Prof. Dr hab. Inż. ANDRZEJ SEWERYN
Faculty of Computer Science: Prof. Dr hab. Inż. LEON BOBROWSKI
Faculty of Management: Prof. zw. Dr hab. Inż. JOANICJUSZ NAZARKO
Institute of Mathematics and Physics: Prof. Dr hab. TADEUSZ ŁUKASZEWICZ

PROFESSORS

Faculty of Architecture (ul. Krakowska 9, 15-875 Białystok; tel. (85) 742-29-29; fax (85) 742-29-29; e-mail arch@pb.bialystok.pl):

AGRANOWICZ-PONOMARIEWA, E., Interior Design
BASISTA, A., Architecture
BISSENIK, A., Interior Design
BORKOWSKA-LARYSZ, B., Interior Design
DEBIS, J., Painting
DURMANOW, W., Urban Design

DWORAKOWSKI, A., Architecture and Graphics
IODO, I., Town Planning
KALISZUK, H., Interior Design
KUKAWSKI, T., Architecture and Graphics
PINIŃSKI, Z., Architecture
RYCHTER, Z., Theory of Building
RYMASZEWSKI, B., Preservation of Monuments
SAWCZUK, H., History of Architecture
SZCZYKOWSKA-ZALESKA, J., Sculpture
WŁODARCZYK, J., Architecture

Faculty of Civil Engineering and Environmental Engineering (ul. Wiejska 45E, 15-351 Białystok; tel. (85) 742-04-18; fax (85) 742-24-13; e-mail malasz@pb.bialystok.pl):

BĄK, G., Building Engineering
BANASZUK, H., Environmental Protection
BOŁTRYK, M., Civil Engineering
BRYŁKA, J., Physical Chemistry
CZERWIŃSKI, A., Forest Botany, Phytosociology
DENCZEW, S., Water Supply and Sewer Systems
DZIENIS, L., Waterworks and Sewerage
GARNCAREK, R. J., Building Engineering, Mechanical Engineering
GRABOWSKI, R. J., Geodesy and Cartography
JEZIERSKI, W., Physics of Building
KRÓLIKOWSKI, A., Waterworks and Sewerage
LEWANDOWSKI, W., Inorganic Chemistry
ŁAPKO, A., Civil Engineering
MIEDZIAŁOWSKI, Cz., Building Construction
OWCZAREK, S., Bridge Construction
PIEŃKOWSKI, K., Fluid Mechanics, Thermal Mechanics
RADZISZEWSKI, P., Road Engineering
ROSOCHACKI, ST. J., General Chemistry
SORKO, S. A., Thermal Techniques
STACHURSKI, W., Building Construction
TRIBIŁŁO, R., Theory of Building Structures
WIATER, J., Agricultural Technology
WIERZBICKI, T., Environmental Engineering, Water and Waste Technology

Faculty of Electrical Engineering (ul. Wiejska 45D, 15-351 Białystok; tel. (85) 742-05-66; fax (85) 742-16-57; e-mail welpb@pb.bialystok.pl):

BADURSKI, J., Internal Medicine, Laboratory Diagnostics
BOLKOWSKI, ST., Electrotechnics and Metrology
BUSŁOWICZ, M., Control Theory, Automatics
CITKO, T., Electrical Engineering, Automatics
CYWIŃSKI, K., Electrotechnology
CZAWKA, G., Electronic Systems
DOROSZ, J., Chemical Technology
DYBCZYŃSKI, W., Lighting
GOŁĄBIOWSKI, J., Electrotechnology
GRISZYN, J., Radiation and Navigation Technology
JORDAN, A., Electrical Engineering, Electrical Metrology
KORNILUK, W., Safety in Electroenergetics
NIEBRZYDOWSKI, J., Electrical Engineering
RAFAŁOWSKI, M., Applied Optics
SIKORSKI, A., Power Electronics
SOWA, A., Electrotechnology
ŚWIERC, M., Biocybernetics, Biomedical Engineering
TWARDY, L., Electro-energetics
ZAJĄC, A., Optoelectronics

Faculty of Mechanics (ul. Wiejska 45C, 15-351 Białystok; tel. (85) 742-15-41; fax (85) 742-11-12; e-mail w.mechaniczny@pb.bialystok.pl):

CZECH, M., Mechanics, Materials Rheology
DĄBROWSKI, J. R., Chemical Engineering, Machine Construction

GAWRYSIAK, M., Mechanical Engineering, Mechatronics
HEJFT, R., Mechanics, Machine Construction
JAWOREK, K., Automatic Control and Robotics
KARPOWICZ, Ś., Automation Engineering
KOWALEWSKI, Z., Applied Mechanical Engineering
KURZYDŁOWSKI, K., Materials Technology
ŁACH, J., Mechanics, Machine Construction
LINDSTEDT, P., Automatic Control and Robotics
MATYSIAK, ST., Computer Techniques
MIATLUK, M., Machine Construction
OSIPIUK, W., Mechanics, Machine Construction
PIWNIK, J., Mechanics, Plastics
PUCIŁOWSKI, K., Mechanics
RAWSKI, F., Automobile Engineering
SEWERYN, A., Mechanics, Resistance of Materials
SIEMIENIAKO, F., Automatic Control and Robotics
SKIEPKO, T., Thermodynamics and Fluid Mechanics
SULYM, H., Applied Mechanical Engineering

Faculty of Computer Science (tel. (85) 742-82-06; fax (85) 742-34-23; e-mail sekretar@ii.pb.bialystok.pl):

BOBROWSKI, L., Biocybernetics
DAŃKO, W., Mathematical Logic
GRZESZCZUK, P., Mathematics
GUŁAKOW, I., Optoelectronics
JARMOLIK, W., Technical Informatics
OSTANIN, A., Computer Science
PIOTROWSKI, A., Technical Informatics
STEPANIUK, J., Mathematics
SZODA, Z., Mathematics
TRZĘSICKI, K., Logic
WIERZCHOŃ, S., Computer Science

Faculty of Management (ul.Ojca Tarasiuka 2, 06-001 Kleosin; tel. (85) 663-22-08; fax (85) 663-19-88; e-mail magda@pb.bialystok.pl):

BARSZCZAK, T., Agricultural Technology
CELMAROWSKI, Cz., Machine Construction
GARBACZEWSKA, G., Biology
IGNATIUK, S., Agricultural Engineering
JĘDRUSZCZAK, M., Agricultural Technology and Agribusiness
JUREWICZ, S., Economics, Mechanics
KLEMENTOWICZ, T., History of Political and Economic Doctrines
KORZUCH, A., Finance and Accountancy
KORZUCH, B., Management
KOWALCZEWSKI, W., Organization and Management, Economics
KUBICKA, H., Agricultural Technology
KURLISZYN-MOSKAL, A., Environment and Tourism Management
ŁAGOWSKA, B., Horticulture
ŁOBODA, T., Biology
MĄDRY, W., Mathematics
MICHAŁOWSKI, K., Environment and Tourism Management
MIŁASZEWSKI, P., Economics, Environmental Engineering and Environmental Protection
NARUSZEWICZ, S., Law, International Economics
NAZARKO, J., Electrical Power Engineering
NICZYPORUK, A., Agricultural Technology
POPŁAWSKI, W. T., Sociology
SADOWSKI, M., Environmental Protection
SASINOWSKI, H., Economics
SOKÓŁ, J., Animal Science
ŚLUSARCZYK, J., Humanities
TOMCZONEK, Z., Humanities, History
WASIAK, A., Chemistry, Materials Engineering, Mechanical Engineering

Institute of Mathematics and Physics (tel. (85) 742-82-00; fax (85) 742-23-93; e-mail wrobi@pb.bialystok.pl):

BARTOSIEWICZ, Z., Mathematical Theory and Control
ŁUKASZEWICZ, T., Physics
MARCZENKO, WŁ., Control Theory
REWIŃSKI, A., Physics

POLITECHNIKA CZĘSTOCHOWSKA (Częstochowa University of Technology)

ul. Dąbrowskiego 69, 42-200 Częstochowa

Telephone: (34) 325-04-98
Fax: (34) 361-23-85
E-mail: rektor@adm.pcz.czest.pl
Internet: www.pcz.pl
Founded 1949
State control
Academic year: October to June

Rector: Prof. Dr hab. Inż. HENRYK DYJA
Pro-Rectors: Prof. Dr hab. Inż. ANDRZEJ RUSEK, Prof. Dr hab. Inż. MARIA NOWICKA-SKOWRON, Prof. Dr hab. Inż. JÓZEF KOSZKUL
Executive Director: Mgr MAREK REMBISZ
Librarian: Mgr MAŁGORZATA HANKIEWICZ
Library: see Libraries and Archives
Number of teachers: 878
Number of students: 20,975

Publication: *Turbulence* (annually)

DEANS

Faculty of Mechanical Engineering and Computer Science: Prof. Dr hab. Inż. JERZY WŁODARSKI
Faculty of Materials Processing Technology and Applied Physics: Prof. Dr hab. Inż. JERZY SIWKA
Faculty of Electrical Engineering: Prof. Dr hab. Inż. ANDRZEJ ROMAN
Faculty of Civil Engineering: Prof. Dr hab. Inż. SŁAWOMIR KOSIŃSKI
Faculty of Management: Prof. Dr hab. JANUSZ SZOPA
Faculty of Environmental Protection and Engineering: Prof. Dr hab. Inż. MARTA JANOSZ-RAJCZYK

PROFESSORS

Faculty of Mechanical Engineering and Computer Science (al. Armii Krajowej 21, 42-200 Częstochowa; tel. (34) 325-05-61; fax (34) 325-05-04; e-mail dziekanat@itm.pcz.czest.pl):

CUPIAŁ, K., Machines and Internal Combustion Engines
DOMAŃSKI, Z., Physics, Biophysics
DROBNIAK, S., Fluid Mechanics, Fluid Flow Machines
GAJEWSKI, W., Thermodynamics
GIERZYŃSKA-DOLNA, M., Mechanical Engineering, Plastics Processing Machines and Technology
JARŻA, A., Fluid Mechanics
KENSIK, R., Welding
KLAJNY, R., Fluid Mechanics
KOMPANEC, L., Informatics
KOSZKUL, J., Plastics Materials
KRIVOI, S., Mathematics
KUBARSKI, J., Mathematics
KUKLA, S., Mathematics, Mechanics
KUKURYK, B., Plastic Working of Metals
MAJCHRZAK, E., Mathematics
MAZANEK, E., Machine Design
MELECHOW, R., Machine Building Technology
MENDERA, K., Machines and Internal Combustion Engines
MIRKOWSKI, J., Mechanics and Internal Combustion Engines
MOCHNACKI, B., Mathematics
NIESZPOREK, T., Machine-building Technology

PARKITNY, R., Applied Mechanics and Foundry Technology
PIECH, H., Computer Engineering
POSIADAŁA, B., Applied Mechanics
RUTKOWSKA, D., Informatics
RUTKOWSKI, L., Informatics, Cybernetics
SCZYGIOL, N., Applied Mechanics
SEWASTJANOW, P., Mathematics
SUBERLAK, O., Plastics Materials
SZOPA, R., Mathematics
TOMSKI, L., Machine Design, Applied Mechanics
TUBIELEWICZ, K., Machine Building Technology
WIERZBICKI, E., Applied Mathematics, Mechanics
WŁODARSKI, J., Plastics Processing Machines and Technology
WOLAŃSKI, R., Thermodynamics, Thermal Processes in Welding
WOŹNIAK, C., Mathematics, Mechanics
WYRZYKOWSKI, R., Informatics

Faculty of Materials Processing Technology and Applied Physics (al. Armii Krajowej 19, 42-200 Częstochowa; tel. (34) 325-07-13; fax (34) 361-38-88; e-mail dziekanat@mim.pcz .czest.pl; internet www.mim.pcz.czest.pl):

BALA, H., Corrosion of Metals
BOCHENEK, A., Metallurgy, Materials Science
BRASZCZYŃSKI, J., Metallurgy, Foundry Technology
BUDZIK, R., Metallurgy of Ferrous Metals
DYJA, H., Plastic Working of Metals
DZILIŃSKI, K., Physics
GOLIS, B., Plastic Working of Metals
HRABAŃSKI, R., Physics
JEZIORSKI, L., Metallurgy, Metals Science
JOWSA, J., Metallurgy
KNAP, F., Plastic Working of Metals
KONOPKA, Z., Metallurgy, Foundry Technology
ŁĘDZKI, A., Metallurgy, Steelmaking
LESIK, L., Metallurgy
LIS, A., Materials Engineering, Metallurgy
MIELCZAREK, E., Thermodynamics in Power Engineering, Heat Engineering
MOREL, S., Heat Engineering
NITKIEWICZ, Z., Metallurgy, Materials Engineering
PIETRZYK, M., Metallurgy
PILARCZYK, J., Metallurgy, Materials Science
PIŁKOWSKI, Z., Foundry, Steelmaking
SIWKA, J., Metallurgy, Steelmaking
SŁUPEK, S., Metallurgy, Heat Engineering
STACHURA, S., Metals Science
WASZKIELEWICZ, W., Organization and Management, Metallurgy
WIERZBICKA, B., Metallurgy, Casting of Non-ferrous Metals
WOLKENBERG, A., Metals Science
WYSŁOCKI, B., Physics of Magnetic Materials
WYSŁOCKI, J., Physics, Physics of Magnetic Materials
ZAPART, M., Physics
ZAPART, W., Physics of Magnetic Materials
ZBROSZCZYK, J., Physics

Faculty of Electrical Engineering (al. Armii Krajowej 17, 42-200 Częstochowa; tel. (34) 325-08-22; fax (34) 325-08-23; e-mail dziekanat@el.pcz.czest.pl; internet www.el .pcz.czest.pl):

BIERNACKI, Z., Electrotechnics, Measurements, Design of Measuring Equipment
BRZOZOWSKI, W., Electrical Engineering, Power Stations
DOBRZAŃSKA, I., Electrical Engineering, Electrical Power Management
ISKIERKA, S., Electrotechnics
JANICZEK, R., Electrotechnology
KRAWCZYK, A., Electrotechnics
KRUCZININ, A. M., Electrotechnology
MINKINA, W., Electronics

POPOV, B., Informatics
ROJEK, R., Electronics, Automatics
ROLICZ, P., Electrotechnics
ROMAN, A., Electronics, Magnetic Materials
RUSEK, A., Electric Motors
SAWICKI, A., Electrotechnology
SOIŃSKI, M., Magnetic Materials, Material Engineering
SOKALSKI, K., Physics
SOWA, P., Electroenergetics
WYSOCKI, J., Electronics, Computer Engineering
ZĄBKOWSKA-WACŁAWEK, M., Electrotechnology

Faculty of Civil Engineering (ul. Akademicka 3, 42-200 Częstochowa; tel. (34) 325-09-30):

BOBKO, T., Technology, Organization of Building
CZECH, L., Geometrical Construction, Civil Engineering
DREWNOWSKI, S., Materials Engineering, Structural Engineering
KLEIBER, M., Structural Engineering
KONIECZNY, S., Structural Mechanics
KOSIŃSKI, S., Structural Mechanics
KOZŁOWSKI, R., Civil Engineering
KWIATEK, J., Civil Engineering, Geotechnology
PRZYBYŁO, W., Structural Mechanics, Civil Engineering
PUSZKARIOWA, E., Building Materials
RAJCZYK, J., Civil Engineering
SŁUŻALEC, A., Mathematics, Mechanics
SYGUŁA, S., Bridge Construction, Civil Engineering

Faculty of Management (al. Armii Krajowej 19B, 42-200 Częstochowa; tel. (34) 325-03-25; e-mail wz@zim.pcz.czest.pl; internet zim.pcz .czest.pl):

ANTOSZKIEWICZ, J., Organization and Management
BARTZ, B., Economics, Logistics
BORKOWSKI, S., Organization and Management, Metallurgy
BOROWIECKI, R., Organization and Management
BUKOWSKI, L., Machine Building Technology, Management
BUKUVKA, O., Production Engineering
CHRZAN, P., Econometrics, Statistics
DURAJ, J., Organization and Management
DURLIK, I., Marketing
FIEDOROWICZ, K., Economics
GOŁUCHOWSKI, J., Informatics
GORCZYCKA, E., Economics, Organization and Management
GRZESZCZYK, T., Economics, Law
GUBARIENI, N., Informatics
GURGUL, E., Agrotechnology
JASTRZĘBOWSKI-HOFFMAN, Z., History, Politics
KATKOW, A., Informatics
KIEŁTYKA, L., Automatics in Management
KLIBER, J., Materials Engineering, Metallurgy
KLISIŃSKI, J., Economics, Marketing
KONODYBA-SZYMAŃSKI, B., Metallurgy
LEWANDOWSKI, J., Organization and Management, Machine Building Technology
MALISZEWSKI, J., Economics, Organization and Management
MILIAN, L., Sociology, Organization and Management
MOSZKIEWICZ, M., Economics
NOWAK, C., Agricultural Technology
NOWICKA-SKOWRON, M., Economics, Organization and Management
NOWICKI, A., Organization and Management, Informatics
PABIAN, A., Organization of Building
PARTYKA, M., Mathematics, Informatics
RUBACHOW, A., Organization and Management Economics
SITEK, E., Economics

SOBOLAK, L., Organization and Management
SUCHECKA, J., Economics
SZOPA, J., Theoretical and Applied Mechanics, Applied Mathematics, Computers
SZTUKA, J., Marketing
SZUWALSKI, K., Organization and Management
VARKOLY, L., Materials Engineering, Computer Engineering
WOŹNIAK-SOBCZAK, B., Economics, Organization and Management
ZACHOROWSKA, A., Economics
ZAWISŁAWSKA, D., Economics
ŻÓŁTOWSKI, B., Process Engineering and Organization

Faculty of Environmental Protection and Engineering (tel. (34) 325-04-62; fax (34) 325-04-63; e-mail wiis@adm.pcz.czest.pl):

BIEŃ, J., Geology, Hydrogeology
BIS, Z., Mechanics, Thermodynamics
BOHDZIEWICZ, J., Environmental Engineering
DEWIATOW, W., Mechanics, Structural Engineering
GIRCZYS, J., Sanitary Engineering
GODZIK, S., Environmental Engineering
GUMNITSKY, J., Biochemistry, Biotechnology
HŁAWICZKA, S., Environmental Engineering
JAGIEŁA, K., Electrotechnology
JANIKOWSKI, R., Environmental Engineering
JANOSZ-RAJCZYK, M., Environmental Engineering
KISIEL, A., Sanitary Engineering
KOSIŃSKI, W., Environmental Engineering
KUCHARSKI, R., Environmental Engineering
MALINA, G., Sanitary Engineering
NOWAK, W., Sanitary Engineering
PISAREK, J., Mechanics, Machine Building Technology
SANITSKY, M., Environmental Engineering

POLITECHNIKA GDAŃSKA
(Gdańsk University of Technology)

ul. G. Narutowicza 11/12, 80-952 Gdańsk

Telephone: (58) 341-57-91
Fax: (58) 341-58-21
E-mail: rektor@pg.gda.pl
Internet: www.pg.gda.pl

Founded 1945
Academic year: October to July

Rector: Prof. JANUSZ RACHOŃ
Vice-Rectors: Prof. RYSZARD KATULSKI, Prof. ROMUALD SZYMKIEWICZ, Prof. WOJCIECH SADOWSKI, Prof. WŁADYSŁAW KOC
Chief Administrative Officer: EWA MAZUR
Librarian: BOŻENA HAKUĆ

Library: see Libraries and Archives
Number of teachers: 1,123
Number of students: 18,093

Publications: *Zeszyty Naukowe Politechniki Gdańskiej* (Scientific Papers of the Technical University of Gdańsk, irregular), *Wykazy Nowych Nabytków Biblioteki* (Library Acquisitions Lists, quarterly), *Pismo PG* (Journal, monthly)

DEANS

Faculty of Applied Physics and Mathematics: J. GODLEWSKI
Faculty of Architecture: A. BARANOWSKI
Faculty of Chemistry: J. NAMIEŚNIK
Faculty of Electrical and Control Engineering: K. JAKUBIUK
Faculty of Electronics, Telecommunications and Informatics: H. KRAWCZYK
Faculty of Environmental Engineering: K. WILDE

Faculty of Management and Economics: P. DOMINIAK

Faculty of Mechanical Engineering: A. BARYLSKI

Faculty of Ocean Engineering and Ship Technology: (vacant)

PROFESSORS

Faculty of Architecture (Narutowicz 11/12, 80-952 Gdańsk; tel. and fax (58) 347-13-15; e-mail dziekanarch@pg.gda.pl; internet www .pg.gda.pl/architektura):

GÓRA, J., Painting
KITA, A., Painting
STAWICKA-WAŁKOVSKA, M., Healthy Housing (Urban and Building) and Environmental Assessment of Buildings (Sustainable Buildings)

Faculty of Civil and Environmental Engineering (Narutowicz 11/12, 80-952 Gdańsk; tel. (58) 347-22-05; fax (58) 347-20-44; e-mail biuruyd@pg.gda.pl; internet cenwil.bl.pg.gda .pl/wilis/):

BOGDANIUK, B., Traffic Engineering
GODYCKI ĆWINKO, T., Theory of Reinforced and Prestressed Concrete Structures
JUDYCKI, J., Road Construction
KOWALCZYK, Z., Technology and Management in Civil Engineering
KOWALIK, P., Geodesy
KRYSTEK, R., Traffic Engineering
OLAŃCZUK-NEYMAN, K., Environmental Engineering
OBARSKA-PEMPKOWIAK, H., Environmental Engineering
SIKORA, Z., Civil Engineering, Soil Mechanics and Geomechanical Computation
SZYMCZAK, Cz., Structural Mechanics
SZYMKIEWICZ, R., Hydrology
ZADROGA, B., Soil Mechanics and Foundation Engineering
ZIÓŁKO, J., Steel Structures

Faculty of Chemistry (Narutowicz 11/12, 80-952 Gdańsk; tel. (58) 347-13-45; fax (58) 347-26-94; e-mail dzknt@chem.pg.gda.pl; internet www.pg.gda.pl/chem):

BALAS, A., General Chemistry
BIERNAT, J., General Chemistry
BIZIUK, M., Environmental Analytical Chemistry, Elemental Analysis, Spectrophotometric Analysis
BOROWSKI, E., Biochemistry
DAROWICKI, K., Electrochemistry, Corrosion and Corrosion Protection
HĘDRZYCKA, K., Biochemistry
HUPKA, J., Chemical Engineering
KAMIŃSKI, M., Chemical Technology
KAWALEC-PIETRENKO, B., Chemical Engineering
KOŁODZIEJCZYK, A., Organic Chemistry
KONOPA, J., Organic Chemistry
KUR, J., Molecular Biology
LEWANDOWSKI, W., Heat Technology, Chemical Engineering
MAZERSKI, J., Molecular Modelling, Chemometrics, Biophysics
MILEWSKI, S., Biochemistry
NAMIEŚNIK, J., Analytical Chemistry
PACYNA, J., Environmental Chemistry, Environmental Engineering, Environmental Analysis and Monitoring
POŁOŃSKI, T., Organic Chemistry, Stereochemistry, Molecular Modelling, Chiroptical Spectroscopy
RACHOŃ, J., Organic Chemistry
SYNOVIEĆKI, J., Technical Science
WOJNOWSKI, W., Inorganic Chemistry

Faculty of Electrical and Control Engineering (Narutowicz 11/12, 80-952 Gdańsk; tel. (58) 347-12-58; fax (58) 347-18-02; e-mail dean@ely.pg.gda.pl; internet www.ely.pg.gda .pl):

BRDYŚ, M., Control Systems

JAKUBIUK, K., Principles of Electrotechnics, Electrical Apparatus
KOWALSKI, Z., Industrial Automation
KRAWĆZUK, M., Mechanics
KRZEMIŃSKI, Z., Electrical Drives and Power Electronics
MARECKI, J., Electrical Power Engineering
PAZDRO, P., Electrical Apparatus and Traction
SZCZERBA, Z., Electrical Power Engineering
WOLNY, A., High-Voltage Current Switching
ZAJCZYK, R., Power Engineering
ZIMNY, P., Theoretical Electromagnetic Field

Faculty of Electronics, Telecommunications and Informatics (Narutowicz 11/12, 80-952 Gdańsk; tel. (58) 347-12-45; fax (58) 341-61-32; e-mail deans@eti.pg.gda.pl; internet www .eti.pg.gda.pl):

CZYŻEWSKI, A., Sound Engineering
GÓRSKI, J. K., Software Engineering, Informatics
KOWALCZUK, Z., Automatic Control and Robotics
KRAWCZYK, H., Computer Science, Parallel, Architectures and Fault-Tolerance
KUBALE, M., Discreet Optimization
MALINA, W., Computer Science and Pattern Recognition
MAZUR, J., Microwave Techniques
MROZOWSKI, M., Electromagnetic Field Theory, Microwaves
NIEDŹWIECKI, MACIEJ, Automatic Control
NOWAKOWSKI, A., Electronics Technology
POLOWCZYK, M., Telecommunications Technology
RUTKOWSKI, D., Principles of Telecommunications
SOBCZAK, W., Cybernetics
SPIRALSKI, L., Electronic Equipment
STEPNOWSKI, A., Marine Acoustics, Telecommunications
WOŹNIAK, J., Telecommunications, Computer Communication Systems
ZIELONKO, R., Electronic Equipment Technology
ZIENTALSKI, M., Electronic Equipment Technology

Faculty of Management and Economics (Narutowicz 11/12, 80-952 Gdańsk; tel. (58) 347-18-99; fax (58) 347-18-61; e-mail dziekani@mech.pg.gda.pl; internet www.zie .pg.gda.pl):

ADAMKIEWICZ, A., Research and Development of Social, Economic and Technological Systems
DASZKOWSKA, M., Principles of Marketing, Services Marketing, the Service Economy

Faculty of Mechanical Engineering (Narutowicz 11/12, 80-952 Gdańsk; tel. (58) 347-20-32; fax (58) 347-10-25; e-mail dziekani@mech .pg.gda.pl; internet www.mech.pg.gda.pl):

BALCERSKI, A., Marine Diesel Engines and Ship Power Plants
EJSMONT, J., Machine Building and Maintenance
NEYMAN, A., Tribology
PRZYBYLSKI, W., Manufacturing Engineering
PUZYREWSKI, R., Fluid Mechanics
STĄSIEK, J., Thermodynamics and Heat Transfer
WALCZAK, W., Welding
WITTBRODT, E., Mechanics and Machine Dynamics, Applied Mechanics
ZIELIŃSKI, A., Materials Engineering

Faculty of Ocean Engineering and Ship Technology (Narutowicz 11/12, 80-952 Gdańsk; tel. (58) 347-16-62; fax (58) 341-47-12; e-mail sekoce@pg.gda.pl; internet www .oce.pg.gda.pl/wydziai):

BRANDOWSKI, A., Engineering Safety and Reliability, Ship Technology
DOMACHOWSKI, Z., Automatic Control of Power Engineering Plants
GIRTLER, J., Ship Power Plants and Diesel Engines
KOLENDA, J., Mechanics of Ship Structures
ROSOCHOWICZ, K., Ship Technology
SZANTYR, J., Mechanics, Ship Hydrodynamics

Faculty of Applied Physics and Mathematics (Narutowicz 11/12, 80-952 Gdańsk; tel. (58) 347-13-10; fax (58) 347-28-21; internet www .mif.pg.gda.pl):

GŁAZUNOW, J., Mathematical Analysis, Applied Mathematics
GODLEWSKI, J., Physics
MURAWSKI, L., Physics, Solid State Physics
KALINOWSKI, J., Physics
KAMONT, Z., Differential Equations
LEBLE, S., Theoretical and Mathematical Physics
ROMANOWSKI, A., Algebra
SADOWSKI, W., Solid State Physics
SIENKIEWICZ, J., Physics, Applied Informatics
SZMYTKOWSKI, Cz., Atomic and Molecular Physics

POLITECHNIKA KRAKOWSKA IM. TADEUSZA KOŚCIUSZKI
(Cracow University of Technology)

Warszawska 24, 31-155 Cracow

Telephone: (12) 628-20-00
Fax: (12) 628-20-71
E-mail: r-0@admin.pk.edu.pl
Internet: www.pk.edu.pl

Founded 1945
State control

Language of instruction: Polish

Academic year: October to June (two semesters)

Rector: Prof. zw. Dr hab. Inż. JÓZEF GAWLIK
Pro-Rectors: Dr hab. Inż. RAFEŁ PALEJ, Dr hab. Inż. Arch. WOJCIECH KOSINSKI, Prof. Zw. Dr hab. Inż. KAZIMIERZ FURTAK, Prof. Zw. Dr hab. Inż. JOZEF GAWLIK, Dr hab. Inż. Arch. WACŁAW CELADYN
Chief Administrative Officer: Mgr Inż. ZBIGNIEW SKAWICKI
Librarian: Mgr MAREK GÓRSKI

Library of 234,600 vols, 81,221 periodicals, 422,127 standards, patents, etc.
Number of teachers: 1,167
Number of students: 17,357

Publications: *Czasopismo Techniczne* (Technical Bulletin, irregular; series on Architecture, Civil Engineering, Chemistry, Mechanics, Electrotechnics, Environmental Science), *Zeszyty Naukowe i Monografie Politechniki Krakowskiej* (Scientific Papers, irregular; series on Architecture, Civil Engineering, Environmental Engineering, Mechanics, Electrical and Computer Engineering, Chemical Engineering and Technology, Basic Technical Sciences, Human, Economic and Social Sciences)

DEANS

Faculty of Applied Physics and Computer Modelling: Dr hab. RYSZARD ZACH
Faculty of Architecture: Prof. Zw. Dr hab. Inż. arch. DARIUSZ KOZŁOWSKI
Faculty of Ciyil Engineering: Prof. Dr hab. Inż. JACEK SLIWIŃSKI
Faculty of Chemical Engineering and Technology: Prof. Zw. Dr hab. Inż. ZBIGNIEW ŻUREK
Faculty of Electrical and Computer Engineering: Dr hab. Inż. PIOTR DROZDOWSKI
Faculty of Environmental Engineering: Dr hab. Inż. KRZYSZTOF KNAPIK

Faculty of Mechanical Engineering: PDr hab. Inż. KRZYSZTOF SZUWALSKI

PROFESSORS

Faculty of Architecture (tel. (12) 628-20-20; fax (12) 628-20-20; e-mail a-0@admin.pk.edu .pl; internet www.pk.edu.pl/arch):

BARTKOWICZ, B., Urban Design and Spatial Planning

BIEDA, K., Urban Design Theory and Practice

BÖHM, A., Architecture, Landscape Architecture

BULIŃSKI, W., Architectural Design

DOUSA, S., Sculpture

GOŁOGÓRSKA-KUCIA, E., Painting and Drawing

KADŁUCZKA, A., History of Architecture and Monument Preservation

KOZŁOWSKI, D., Architectural Design and Theory

KUŚNIERZ, K., History of Urban Design

LENARTOWICZ, J. K., Design of Industrial Architecture

MITKOWSKA, A., History of Architecture and Urban Design

SERUGA, W., Urban and Architectural Design

SIEWNIAK, M., Landscape Architecture

WYŻYKOWSKI, A., Urban and Architectural Design

Faculty of Civil Engineering (tel. (12) 628-20-23; fax (12) 628-20-23; e-mail l-0@admin.pk .edu.pl; internet www.pk.edu.pl/wil):

ADAMSKI, A., transport Control Computer Systems, Management and Control Decision-Making, Optimisation Problems

CHRZANOWSKI, M., Fracture Mechanics and Rheology

CICHOŃ, C., Theory of Structure, Numerical Analysis

CZYCZUŁA, W., Rail and Air Transport Infrastructure, Transportation Systems

DYDUCH, K., Reinforced and Prestressed Concrete Structures, Industrial Buildings, Modernization

FLAGA, A., Structural Mechanics, Building Aerodynamics, Wind Engineering

FLAGA, K., Bridges, Tunnels, Concrete Structures, Technology of Concrete, Nondestructive Testing

FURTAK, K., Bridges, Tunnels, Concrete Structures

KAWECKI, J., Structural Mechanics

ORKISZ, J., Theory of Structure, Structural Mechanics

RUDNICKI, A., Traffic and Highway Engineering, Transportation Systems

ŚLIWIŃSKI, J., Concrete Technology, Building Materials

STACHOWICZ, A., Structural Mechanics, General and Industrial Building, Concrete Structures

SZEFER, G., Solid and Structural Mechanics

TRACZ, M., Traffic and Highway Engineering

WASZCZYSZYN, Z., Structural Mechanics, Strength of Materials, Artificial Intelligence, Neurocomputing and Microcomputing

Faculty of Chemical Engineering and Technology (tel. (12) 628-20-35; fax (12) 628-20-35; e-mail wiitch@indy.chemia.pk.edu.pl; internet www.chemia.pk.edu.pl):

BARAŃSKI, A., Organic Chemistry and Physical Organic Chemistry

KOWALSKI, Z., Inorganic Chemical Technology

PIELICHOWSKI, J., Chemistry and Technology of Polymers, Organic Synthesis

STOKŁOSA, A., Physical Chemistry, Solid State Physical Chemistry

TABIS, B., Chemical Engineering

ŻUREK, Z., Solid State Chemistry, Materials Science

Faculty of Environmental Engineering (tel. (12) 628-28-01; fax (12) 628-20-40; e-mail s-0@admin.pk.edu.pl; internet www.wis.pk .edu.pl):

BRYŚ, H., Surveying in Engineering

DĄBROWSKI, W., Water Supply, Waste Water Disposal, Sanitary Engineering

KANDEFER, S., Thermal Engineering, Combustion Processes, Use of Thermal Waste, Air Protection Systems

KOCWA-KALUCH, R., Environmental Biology, Microbiology of Water, Waste Water and Air

MACZEK, K., Refrigeration, Air Conditioning, Environmental Engineering

NACHLIK, E., Hydraulics and Water Management

PIASEK, Z., Geodesy and Cartography for Environmental Engineering, Numerical Geodesy

SŁOTA, H., Water Management

WYSOKIŃSKI, L., Geotechnics, Environmental and Geological Engineering, Civil Engineering

Faculty of Mechanical Engineering (Jana Pawła II 37, 31-864 Cracow; tel. (12) 648-14-32; fax (12) 648-14-32; e-mail m-0@admin .pk.edu.pl; internet www.mech.pk.edu.pl):

CYKLIS, J., Production Engineering

DYLĄG, M., Chemical Engineering, Chemical Industry Equipment, Environmental Engineering

GAWLIK, J., Machining, Design of Cutting Tools

GOLEC, K., Internal Combustion Engines, Engine Cold-starting, Feeding Systems, Turbocharging

KAMIEŃSKI, J., Industrial Equipment

KAZIOR, J., Machine Technology, Powder Metallurgy, Stainless Steels

KNAPCZYK, J., Motor Vehicles and Tractors, Robotics, Theory of Machines and Mechanisms

KOZŁOWSKI, R., Physical Metallurgy and Heat Treatment, Power Engineering Materials Science

MATRAS, Z., Fluid Mechanics, Rheology, Chemical Engineering, Power Engineering

MAZURKIEWICZ, S., Experimental Mechanics, Biomechanics

MICHAŁOWSKI, S., Machine Dynamics, Robotics

MUC, A., Plate and Shell Structures, Mechanics of Composite Materials

NIZIOŁ, J., Theoretical and Applied Mechanics, Machine Dynamics

OPRZĘDKIEWICZ, J., Reliability of Mechanical Devices

RUP, K., Fluid Mechanics, Heat and Mass Transfer

RYŚ, J., Machine Design, Gears, Pressure Vessels

SENDYKA, B., Internal Combustion Engines

SKRZYPEK, J., Theory of Plasticity, Rheology, Damage

TALER, J., Power Machines and Engineering, Heat Transfer, Thermodynamics

WANTUCH, E., Production Engineering

WOJNAR, L., Trybology

WOŁKOW, J., Hydraulic and Pneumatic Control and Drives

ZALEWSKI, W., Power Equipment and Systems, Refridgerating and Air-conditioning Systems

ZIELINSKI, A., Computer Methods of Structural Mechanics, Computer-aided Machine Design

Faculty of Electrical and Computer Engineering (tel. (12) 628-20-43; fax (12) 628-20-43; e-mail e-0@admin.pk.edu.pl; internet www.elektron.pk.edu.pl):

JAGIEŁŁO, A., Electrical Machines

LAYER, E., Electrical Metrology

MALECKI, P., Experimental Particle Physics, Online Computing, Detector Control Systems

MOŚCIŃSKI, J., Computer Systems, Large-scale Computing, Network Security, Wireless Networking

SAPIECHA, K., Computer Architecture and Programming

SIWCZYŃSKI, M., Electrotechnics, Circuit Theory and Signals

SOBCZYK, T., Electrical Machines

SZARANIEC, E., Mathematical Geophysics

Faculty of Applied Physics and Computer Modelling (Podchorążych 1, 30-084 Cracow; tel. (12) 638-07-28; fax (12) 638-07-28; e-mail f-0@admin.pk.edu.pl; internet www.pk.edu .pl/wftimk):

ARTEMOWICZ, O., Algebra

CISOWSKI, J., Solid State Physics

GRAFIJCZUK, W., Mechanics

KOZARZEWSKI, B., Theoretical Physics, Quantum Computation

ŁAWRENIUK, S., Differential Equations

ŁOPUSZAŃSKI, O., Spectral Theory of Operators

OSTOJA-GAJEWSKI, A., Applied Mechanics

PLICZKO, A., Mathematics

POLITECHNIKA ŁÓDZKA
(Technical University of Łódź)

ul. Ks. I. Skorupki 6/8, 90-924 Łódź

Telephone: (42) 631-20-01

Fax: (42) 636-85-22

E-mail: rector@sir.p.lodz.pl

Internet: www.p.lodz.pl

Founded 1945

Academic year: September to June (2 semesters)

Rector: Prof. Dr hab. JAN KRYSIŃSKI

Pro-Rectors: Prof. Dr hab. STANISŁAW BIELECKI, Prof. Dr hab. STANISŁAW MITURA, Prof. Dr hab. EDWARD JEZIERSKI, Prof. Dr hab. ANDRZEJ NAPIERALSKI

Administrative Director: Dr hab. JERZY PRYWER

Librarian: Mgr Inż. BŁAŻEJ FERET

Library of 285,200 vols, 801 current periodicals, 223,300 patents and standards

Number of teachers: 1,600

Number of students: 21,000

Publications: *Zeszyty Naukowe Politechniki Łódzkiej, Bulletin*

DEANS

Faculty of Biotechnology and Food Science: Prof. Dr hab. J. ICIEK

Faculty of Chemistry: Prof. Dr hab. M. ZABORSKI

Faculty of Civil Engineering, Architecture and Environmental Engineering: Prof. Dr hab. W. BARAŃSKI

Faculty of Electrical and Electronic Engineering: Prof. Dr hab. A. MATERKA

Faculty of Mechanical Engineering: Prof. Dr hab. P. KULA

Faculty of Organization and Management: Prof. Dr hab. K. BARANOWSKI

Faculty of Process and Environmental Engineering: Prof. Dr hab. A. HEIM

Faculty of Technical Physics, Informatics and Applied Mathematics: Prof. Dr hab. L. GAJEK

Faculty of Textile Engineering and Marketing: Prof. Dr hab. I. KRUCIŃSKA

Institute of Papermaking and Paper Machines: Prof. Dr hab. B. SURMA-SLUSARSKA

PROFESSORS

Faculty of Biotechnology and Food Science
(Wólczańska 171/173, 90-924 Łódź; tel. (42)
631-34-01; fax (42) 631-34-02; e-mail
deanbiof@sir.p.lodz.pl; internet snack.p.lodz
.pl):

BIELECKI, S., Technical Biochemistry
ICIEK, J., Chemical Food Technology, Food
Engineering
LIBUDZISZ, Z., Technical Microbiology
OKRUSZEK, A., Biotechnology, Organic
Chemistry
SZOPA, J., Technical Microbiology
TURKIEWICZ, M., Biochemistry, Enzymology
TWARDOWSKI, T., Technical Biochemistry
WYSOCKI, S., Physical and Theoretical
Chemistry

Faculty of Chemistry (Zeromskiego 116, 90-
924 Łódź; tel. (42) 631-31-00; fax (42) 631-31-
03; e-mail deanchem@ck-sg.p.lodz.pl;
internet www.p.lodz.pl/chemia):

ABRAMCZYK, H., Molecular Spectroscopy,
Laser Spectroscopy, Physical and Theo-
retical Chemistry
BARTCZAK, T., X-ray Structure Analysis,
Bioinorganic Chemistry
BARTCZAK, W., Radiation Chemistry, Com-
putation Chemistry
BEM, H., Physical and Nuclear Chemistry
GĘBICKI, J. M., Organic Physical Chemis-
try, Photochemistry, Spectroscopy,
Radiation Chemistry, Biocrystallogra-
phy
GŁÓWKA, M., Biocrystallography
HAWLICKA, E., Physical and Theoretical
Chemistry, Computation Chemistry
KAROLAK-WOJCIECHOWSKA, J., Physical
Chemistry
MAŁKIEWICZ, A., Organic Chemistry
MAYER, J., Physical Chemistry, Radiation
Chemistry
PAKUŁA, T., Physics of Polymers
PANETH, P., Physical and Theoretical
Chemistry
PARYJCZAK, T., Chemical Catalysis
ROSIAK, J. M., Biomaterials Engineering,
Polymer Chemistry, Radiation Technol-
ogy
RYNKOWSKI, J., General Chemistry, Chemi-
cal Catalysis, Environmental Protection
ŚLUSARSKI, L., Rubber Chemistry and
Technology
ULAŃSKI, J., Physics and Physical Chem-
istry of Polymers
ZABORSKI, M., Rubber Chemistry and Tech-
nology
ZABROCKI, J., Organic Chemistry

**Faculty of Civil Engineering, Architecture
and Environmental Engineering** (Politechniki 6, 90-924 Łódź; tel. (42) 631-35-00; fax
(42) 636-00-00; e-mail deanarch@sir.p.lodz
.pl; internet www.p.lodz.pl/baisl):

JOCZ, J., Sculpture
JUZWA, J., Industrial Architecture, Plan-
ning of Industrial Areas
KAMIŃSKA, M., Concrete Structures
KLEMM, P., Building Physics, Building
Materials, Acoustics of the Architectural
and Urban Environment
LEBIEDOWSKI, M., Environmental Engi-
neering
PAWŁOWSKI, P., History of Town Planning,
Planning for Urban Revitalization
PRZEWŁOCKI, P., Engineering Geodesy,
Building Metrology, Cartography,
Descriptive Geometry
SIEMIŃSKI, S., Town Planning
SUCHAR, S., Theoretical and Applied
Mechanics
ZABŁOCKI, W., Architecture

**Faculty of Electrical and Electronic Engi-
neering** (B. Stefanowskiego 18/22, 93-924
Łódź; tel. (42) 631-25-02; fax (42) 636-47-02;

e-mail deanelec@sir.p.lodz.pl; internet wee.p
.lodz.pl):

JANUSZKIEWICZ, K., Electrothermal Science,
Numerical Simulation in Electrothermal
Science
KACPRZAK, T., Telecommunications, Elec-
tronic Devices and Systems, Neural Net-
works
KOŁACIŃSKI, Z., Electrical Apparatus,
Plasma Tecnologies
KOSZMIDER, A., Instrument Transformers,
Applied Electrical Engineering
KUŚMIEREK, Z., Electrical Metrology
KUŹMIŃSKI, K., Control Theory, Automa-
tion
LESZCZYŃSKI, J., Electrotechnology, Mate-
rials Science, Superconductivity
MATERKA, A., Telecommunications, Signals
Processing, Medical Electronics
MIELCZARSKI, W., Power Engineering
MOSIŃSKI, F., Stochastic Processes, High
Voltage Engineering
NAPIERALSKI, A., Microelectronics, Electro-
nic Circuits, Power Electronics, Compu-
ter Engineering, Thermography
NOWACKI, Z., Electrical Drive Control,
Power Electronics
PAWELSKI, W., Electronic Devices and Cir-
cuits, Power Electronics
PAWLIK, M., Thermal Power Plant Energy
Economics
SANKOWSKI, D., Computerized Data Mea-
surement, Identification and Control of
Electrothermal Systems
SUBIETA, K., Databases, Object-oriented
Systems, Software Engineering
TADEUSIEWICZ, M., Circuit Theory, Theore-
tical Electrotechnology
WALCZUK, E., Electrical Apparatus
WIAK, S., Computer-aided Design, Electro-
dynamics
ZAKRZEWSKI, K., Electric Machines and
Transformers, Applied Electrodynamics

Faculty of Mechanical Engineering (B. Stefanowskiego 1/15, 90-924 Łódź; tel. (42) 631-
22-00; fax (42) 631-22-03; e-mail deanmech@
sir.p.lodz.pl; internet www.p.lodz.pl/
mechaniczny):

AWREJCEWICZ, J., Dynamics, Control, Bio-
mechanics
CZOŁCZYŃSKI, K., Mechanics, Machine
Dynamics
FODEMSKI, T., Thermodynamics, Heat
Transfer
GOŁĄBCZAK, A., Production Engineering
KAPITANIAK, T., Mechanics, Machine
Dynamics
KAZIMIERSKI, Z., Applied Fluid Mechanics
KOŁAKOWSKI, Z., Applied Mechanics
KRÓLAK, M., Applied Mechanics
KRUSZYŃSKI, B., Machining, Manufactur-
ing and Machine Tools Surface Technol-
ogy
KRYSIŃSKI, J., Fluid-Flow Machinery
KULA, P., Machine Design, Materials Engi-
neering
KWAPISZ, L., Machine Mechanics
MITURA, S., Materials Engineering
PIETROWSKI, S., Materials Engineering,
Foundry
SZCZEPANIAK, C., Theory and Design of
Land Vehicles
TOMCZYK, I., Machine Design, Control
WALKOWIAK, B., Medical Engineering
WIŚNIEWSKI, M., Machine Design, Tribol-
ogy

Faculty of Organization and Management
(Piotrkowska 266, 90-361 Łódź; tel. (42) 631-
37-68; fax (42) 684-79-93; e-mail dz-w9-4@sir
.p.lodz.pl; internet oizet.p.lodz.pl/oiz):

BARANOWSKI, K., Humanities
LEWANDOWSKI, J., Management
MARTIN, C., Management
PENC, J., Strategy Management

POMYKALSKI, A., Economics
WŁODARCZYK, M., Management

**Faculty of Process and Environmental Engi-
neering** (Wólczańska 213, 90-924 Łódź; tel.
(42) 631-37-00; fax (42) 636-56-63; e-mail
deanev@wipos.p.lodz.pl; internet wipos.p
.lodz.pl):

HEIM, A., Mechanical Engineering, Chemi-
cal Engineering
KAMIŃSKI, W., Environmental Engineer-
ing, Chemical Engineering
LEDAKOWICZ, S., Chemical Engineering and
Bioprocess Engineering, Environmental
Engineering, Chemical Technology
MUCHA, M., Chemical Engineering, Che-
mical Technology
PIDDUBNIAK, D., Mechanics
TYCZKOWSKI, J., Materials Science, Chemi-
cal Engineering, Chemistry
WODZIŃSKI, P., Chemical Engineering,
Mechanical Engineering
ZARZYCKI, R., Environmental Engineering
ZBICIŃSKI, I., Chemical Engineering, Envir-
onmental Engineering

**Faculty of Technical Physics, Informatics
and Applied Mathematics** (Wólczańska 215,
93-005 Łódź; tel. (42) 631-36-01; fax (42) 631-
36-02; e-mail dz-w7-3@sir.p.lodz.pl; internet
www.ftims.p.lodz.pl):

BALCERZAK, M., Real Analysis
DZIUBIŃSKI, I., Differential Equations,
Complex Mathematics
GAJEK, L., Statistics, Financial and Actuar-
ial Mathematics
JACYMIRSKI, M., Signal Processing Methods
and Algorithms, Technical and Medical
Diagnosis
JEMEĆ, W., Cytography, Asymptotic Meth-
ods, Integral Equations
KUCHARCZYK, W., Solid State Physics
MIŚKIEWICZ, L., Artistic Composition of
Images and Virtual Spaces, Computer
Graphics, Visualization
NAKWASKI, N., Semiconductor Laser Phy-
sics, Computer Physics
OPANOWICZ, A., Physics of Semiconductors
and Insulators
PRZANOWSKI, M., Theory of Relativity,
Mathematical Physics
STACHIW, P., Numerical Methods, Methods
of Optimization, System Theory
STARKOV, V., Complex Analysis

**Faculty of Textile Engineering and Market-
ing** (Zeromskiego 116, 90-543 Łódź; tel. (42)
631-33-00; fax (42) 631-33-01; e-mail dzw4@
sir.p.lodz.pl):

CYGAN, W., Tapestry
DEMS, K., Structural Mechanics
KOPIAS, K., Knitting Technology
KRUCIŃSKA, I., Mechanical Technology of
Textiles, Metrology
LIPP-SYMONOWICZ, B., Chemical Technol-
ogy of Textiles
MASAJTIS, J., Mechanical Technology of
Textiles
RYBICKI, F. E., Chemical Technology of
Textiles
WYSOKIŃSKA, Z., Economics
ZAJACZKOWSKI, J., Mechanics, Textiles

Institute of Papermaking and Printing
(Wólczańska 223, 93-005 Łódź; tel. (42) 636-
88-22; fax (42) 631-38-03; e-mail bsurma@
ck-sg.p.lodz.pl; internet inpap.p.lodz.pl):

KAWKA, W., Processes and Equipment in
the Paper Industry
LUTSKIV, M., Processes and Equipment in
the Paper Industry
PRZYBYSZ, K., Paper Technology
TARNAWSKI, W. Z., Processes and Equipment in the Paper Industry

POLITECHNIKA LUBELSKA
(Technical University of Lublin)

ul. Nadbystrzycka 38D, 20-618 Lublin
Telephone: (81) 538-11-00
Fax: (81) 532-26-12
E-mail: politechnika@pollub.pl
Internet: www.pollub.pl
Founded 1953
State control
Language of instruction: Polish
Academic year: October to June (two semesters)

Rector: Prof. JOZEF KUCMASZEWSKI
Vice-Rectors: Prof. WITOLD STEPNIEWSKI, Prof. MAREK OPIELAK, Prof. ANDRZEJ WACW-LORDARCZYK
Chief Administrative Officer: MIECZYSLAW HASIAK
Library Dir: Mgr Inż. STEFAN WÓJTOWICZ
Library of 172,000 vols, 97,000 standards and technical catalogues
Number of teachers: 566
Number of students: 12,000

DEANS

Faculty of Civil and Sanitary Engineering: Prof. BOGUSLAV SZMYGIN
Faculty of Electrical Engineering and Computer Science: Prof. WOLDEMAR WOJCIK
Faculty of Environmental Engineering: Prof. LUCJAN PAWLOWSKI
Faculty of Management Sciences and Principles of Technology: Prof. JERZY LIPSKI
Faculty of Mechanical Engineering: Prof. HENRYK KOMSTA

PROFESSORS

Faculty of Civil and Sanitary Engineering:
  BUREK, R., Heating, Ventilation and Automation
  CIEŚLAK, W., Mathematics and Engineering Geometry
  CIĘZAK, T., Institute of Civil Engineering and Architecture
  FLAGA, A., Structural Mechanics
  HALICKA, A., Civil Engineering Structures
  KRZOWSKI, Z., Geotechnics
  KUKIEŁKA, J., Highway Engineering
  OLSZTA, W., Water Supply and Waste Water Removal
  POMORSKA, K., Chemical Engineering
  SADOWSKI, T., Solid Mechanics

Faculty of Electrical Engineering:
  BOBROWSKI, A., Mathematics
  GRZEGÓRSKI, S., Informatics
  JANOWSKI, T., Institute of Electrical Engineering and Electrotechnologies
  KOLANO, J., Electrical Drive Systems
  KOSMULSKI, M., Electrochemistry
  LOZBIN, V., Automatics and Metrology
  MAJKA, K., Power Plants and Energy Management
  PIETRZYK, W., Computer and Electrical Engineering
  RUTKA, Z., Power Networks and Protection
  WOJCIK, W., Electronics
  ZIELENSKI, W., Mechanics, Polymer Processing
  ŻUKOWSKI, P., Electrical Devices and High-Tech Engineering

Faculty of Environmental Engineering:
  KWIETNIEWSKI, M., Water Supply and Sewage Disposal
  OLSZTA, W., Water Management
  OZONEK, J., Indoor Environment Engineering
  PAWLOWSKI, L., Institute of Environmental Production Engineering
  PAWLOWSKI, L., Water, Waste Water and Waste Technology
  SOBCZUK, H., Thermal Techniques
  SOLDATOV, V., Sustainable Development
  STEPNIEWSKI, W., Land Protection

Faculty of Management and Principles of Technology:
  BANEK, T., Quantitative Methods
  BAUM, T., Ergonomics
  BOJAR, E., Economics
  LENIK, K., Principles of Technology
  LIPSKI, J., Enterprise Organization
  OLCHOWIK, J., Institute of Physics
  PAWLAK, M., Organization and Management
  SITKO, W., Management
  SKOWRON, S., Marketing
  WANIURSKI, J., Applied Mathematics

Faculty of Mechanical Engineering:
  JONAK, J., Machine Design
  KOCZAN, L., Mathematics, Analytical Functions
  KUCZMASZEWSKI, J., Production Engineering
  NIEWCZAS, A., Internal Combustion Engines and Transportation
  OPIELAK, M., Food Processing Engineering
  SIKORA, R., Mechanics, Polymer Processing
  SWIC, A., Institute of Technical Systems of Information
  SZABELSKI, K., Applied Mechanics
  TARKOWSKI, P., Tribology, Motor Vehicles and Internal Combustion Engines
  WEROŃSKI, A., Physical Metallurgy, Heat Treatment
  WEROŃSKI, W., Metal Forming

POLITECHNIKA POZNAŃSKA
(Poznań University of Technology)

Pl. Marii Skłodowskiej-Curie 5, 60-965 Poznań
Telephone: (61) 665-35-37
Fax: (61) 665-37-70
E-mail: rector@put.poznan.pl
Internet: www.put.poznan.pl
Founded 1919
State control
Academic year: October to September

Rector: Prof. JERZY DEMBCZYŃSKI
Vice-Rector (Scientific and International Affairs): Prof. ANNA CYSEWSKA-SOBUSIAK
Vice-Rector (Educational Affairs): Prof. TOMASZ ŁODYGOWSKI
Vice-Rector (General Affairs): Prof. BOGDAN MARUSZEWSKI
Chief Administrative Officer: Dr MIROSŁAW STROIŃSKI
Registrar: Mgr KRYSTYNA DŁUGOSZ
Librarian: Mgr HALINA GANIŃSKA
Library of 237,680 vols, 74,668 vols of periodicals, 46,811 standards, 154,358 patents
Number of teachers: 1,200
Number of students: 20,000
Publications: *Zeszyty Naukowe Politechniki Poznańskiej* (Faculty Bulletins, in Polish and English), *Foundations of Computing and Decision Sciences* (in English, 4 a year), *Fasciculi Mathematici* (in English)

DEANS

Faculty of Architecture: Prof. WOJCIECH BONENBERG
Faculty of Chemical Technology: Prof. ADAM VOELKEL
Faculty of Civil and Environmental Engineering and Architecture: Prof. JÓZEF JASICZAK
Faculty of Computer Science and Management: Prof. LESZEK PACHOLSKI
Faculty of Electrical Engineering: Prof. RYSZARD NAWROWSKI
Faculty of Mechanical Engineering and Management: Prof. ADAM HAMROL
Faculty of Technical Physics: Prof. DANUTA BAUMAN
Faculty of Working Machines and Transportation: Prof. KAROL NADOLNY

CHAIRS

Atomic Physics: Prof. EWA STACHOWSKA
Basics of Machine Design: Prof. MARIAN DUDZIAK
Drawing, Painting, Sculpture and Visual Arts: Prof. WŁODZIMIERZ WŁOSZKIEWICZ
Optical Spectroscopy: Prof. MIROSŁAW DROZDOWSKI
Public Architecture and Housing: Prof. MARIAN FIKUS
Thermal Engineering: Prof. LEON BOGUSŁAWSKI

ATTACHED INSTITUTES

Institute of Structural Engineering: Dir Prof. JERZY RAKOWSKI.
Institute of Civil Engineering: Dir Prof. WITOLD WOŁOWICKI.
Institute of Environmental Engineering: Dir Prof. EDWARD SZCZECHOWIAK.
Institute of Architecture and Spatial Planning: Dir Dr hab. EWA CICHY-PAZDER.
Institute of Applied Mechanics: Dir Prof. WACŁAW SZYC.
Institute of Management Engineering: Dir Prof. MAREK FERTSCH.
Institute of Mechanical Technology: Dir Prof. JAN ŻUREK.
Institute of Materials Technology: Dir Prof. MICHAŁ SZWEYCER.
Institute of Materials Science and Engineering: Dir Prof. MIECZYSŁAW JURCZYK.
Institute of Electric Power Engineering: Dir Dr JÓZEF LORENC.
Institute of Computing Science: Dir Prof. JAN WĘGLARZ.
Institute of Industrial Electrical Engineering: Dir Dr hab. KONRAD SKOWRONEK.
Institute of Electronics and Telecommunications: Dir Prof. ANDRZEJ DOBROGOWSKI.
Institute of Machines and Motor Vehicles: Dir Prof. WIESŁAW ZWIERZYCKI.
Institute of Internal Combustion Engines and Transport: Dir Prof. JERZY MERKISZ.
Institute of Chemistry and Technical Electrochemistry: Dir Prof. ALEKSANDER CISZEWSKI.
Institute of Technology and Chemical Engineering: Dir Prof. ANDRZEJ KRYSZTAFKIEWICZ.
Institute of Mathematics: Dir Prof. JAROSŁAW WERBOWSKI.
Institute of Physics: Dir Prof. BRONISŁAW SUSŁA.
Institute of Control and Systems Engineering: Dir Prof. KRZYSTOF KOZŁOWSKI.
Institute of Automatic and Computer Engineering: Dir Prof. ANDRZEJ KASIŃSKI.

POLITECHNIKA RZESZOWSKA
(Rzeszów University of Technology)

POB 85, ul. W. Pola 2, 35-959 Rzeszów
Telephone: (17) 854-12-60
Fax: (17) 854-12-60
E-mail: rektor@prz.rzeszow.pl
Internet: www.prz.rzeszow.pl
Founded 1963 as High School of Engineering; University status 1974
Academic year: October to September
Rector: Assoc. Prof. ANDRZEJ SOBKOWIAK
Vice-Rector (Education): Prof. LESZEK WOŹNIAK
Vice-Rector (General Affairs): Prof. TADEUSZ MARKOWSKI
Vice-Rector (International Co-operation): Assoc. Prof. ALEKSANDER KOZŁOWSKI
Vice-Rector (Research): Asst. Prof. JACEK KLUSKA

Administrative Director: Mgr WACŁAW GAWEŁ

Library Director: Mgr ELŻBIETA KAŁUŻA

Library: see Libraries and Archives

Number of teachers: 680

Number of students: 11,680

Publications: *Zeszyty Naukowe, Folia Scientiarum Universitatis Technicae Resoviensis*

DEANS

Faculty of Chemistry: Prof. HENRYK GALINA

Faculty of Civil and Environmental Engineering: Prof. LEONARD ZIEMIAŃSKI

Faculty of Electrical and Computer Engineering: Assoc. Prof. KAZIMIER BUCZEK

Faculty of Management and Marketing: Assoc. Prof. KAZIMIERZ RAJCHEL

Faculty of Mechanical Engineering and Aeronautics: Prof. FELIKS STACHOWICZ

HEADS OF DEPARTMENTS

Faculty of Chemistry (Powstańców Warszawy 6, 35-959 Rzeszów; tel. (17) 854-36-55; fax (17) 854-36-55; e-mail chemia@prz.rzeszow.pl):

Inorganic and Analytical Chemistry: Prof. S. KOPACZ

Computer Chemistry: Assoc. Prof. B. DĘBSKA

General Chemistry and Electrochemistry: Prof. S. WOTOWIEC

Organic Chemistry: Assoc. Prof. JACEK LUBCZAK

Chemical Engineering and Process Control: Prof. R. PETRUS

Polymer Technology: Assoc. Prof. P. KRÓL

Industrial and Materials Chemistry: Prof. H. GALINA

Physical Chemistry: Assoc. Prof. A. SOBKOWIAK

Biochemistry and Biotechnology: Assoc. Prof. E. WATAJTYS-RODE

Faculty of Civil and Environmental Engineering (Powstańców Warszawy, 35-959 Rzeszów; tel. (17) 865-16-70; fax (17) 865-16-70; e-mail rb@prz.rzeszow.pl):

Building Structures: Assoc. Prof. S. WOLIŃSKI

Physics: Prof. TADEUSZ PASZKIEWICZ

Structural Mechanics: Prof. L. ZIEMIAŃSKI

Descriptive Geometry: Assoc. Prof. B. JANUSZEWSKI

Geodesy: Prof. ROMAN KADAJ

Town Planning and Architecture: Assoc. Prof. A. RYBKA

Building Engineering: Assoc. Prof. LECH LICHOŁAI

Geotechnic and Hydraulic Engineering: Assoc. Prof. JAN JAREMSKI

Water Supply and Sewage Systems: Assoc. Prof. J. RAK

Materials Engineering and Building Technology: Assoc. Prof. G. PROKOPSKI

Environmental Engineering and Chemistry: Assoc. Prof. J. TOMASZEK

Water Purification and Protection: Prof. W. NIEMIEC

Bridges: Prof. A. JAROMINIAK

Heat Engineering and Air Conditioning: Assoc. Prof. J. GÓRSKI

Structural Research: Assoc. Prof. W. ŁAKOTA

Faculty of Electrical and Computer Engineering (tel. (17) 854-98-33; fax (17) 854-20-88; e-mail dwe@prz.rzeszow.pl):

Control and Computer Engineering: Prof. L. TRYBUS

Distributed Systems: Assoc. Prof. F. GRABOWSKI

Principles of Electrical and Computer Engineering: Assoc. Prof. J. BAJOREK

Electrodynamics and Electrical Machinery: Prof. S. APANASEWICZ

Electronic and Communication Systems: Assoc. Prof. W. KALITA

Principles of Electronics: Assoc. Prof. A. KOLEK

Metrology and Measurement Systems: Asst Prof. A. KOWALCZYK

Power Electronics and Power Engineering: Asst Prof. K. BUCZEK

Faculty of Management and Marketing (Powstańców Warszawy 8, 35-959 Rzeszów; tel. (17) 865-13-83; fax (17) 862-81-93; e-mail rz@prz.rzeszow.pl):

Organization and Management: Prof. L. WOŹNIAK

Marketing: Prof. J. ADAMCZYK

Humanities: (vacant)

Mathematical Methods in Economics: Assoc. Prof. L. LAUDAŃSKI

Law and Administration: Assoc. Prof. K. RAJCHEL

Finance and Banking: Assoc. Prof. WŁ. FILAR

Mathematics: Prof. J. BANAŚ

Economics: Prof. K. STOKŁOSA

Faculty of Mechanical Engineering and Aeronautics (Powstańców Warszawy 8, 35-959 Rzeszów; tel. (17) 854-31-16; fax (17) 854-31-16; e-mail rm@prz.rzeszow.pl):

Manufacturing Techniques and Automation: Assoc. Prof. J. BUREK

Machine Design: Prof. T. MARKOWSKI

Manufacturing Processes and Production Organization: Prof. J. ŁUNARSKI

Motor Vehicles and Internal Combustion Engines: Assoc. Prof. K. LEJDA

Materials Forming and Processing: Prof. F. STACHOWICZ

Computer Science: Assoc. Prof. S. WOŁEK

Applied Mechanics and Robotics: Prof. H. KOPECKI

Avionics and Control Systems: Prof. J. GRUSZECKI

Thermodynamics: Assoc. Prof. B. BIENIASZ

Aircraft and Aircraft Engines: Prof. M. ORKISZ

Fluid Mechanics and Aerodynamics: Assoc. Prof. Ł. WĘSIERSKI

Materials Science: Prof. J. SIENIAWSKI

Casting and Welding: Prof. W. ORŁOWICZ

POLITECHNIKA ŚLĄSKA
(Silesian University of Technology)

ul. Akademicka 2A, 44-100 Gliwice

Telephone: (32) 231-23-49

Fax: (32) 237-16-55

E-mail: rek.sekr@polsl.gliwice.pl

Internet: www.polsl.gliwice.pl

Founded 1945

State control

Academic year: October to June

Rector: Prof. Dr WOJCIECH ZIELIŃSKI

Vice-Rector (Research and Industrial Co-operation): Prof. Dr MARIAN DOLIPSKI

Vice-Rector (Organization and Development): Prof. Dr WOJCIECH CHOLEWA

Vice-Rector (Education): Prof. Dr RYSZARD K. WILK

Chief Administrative Officer: WOJCIECH WYDRYCHIEWICZ

Library: see Libraries and Archives

Number of teachers: 1,707

Number of students: 30,042

Publication: *Zeszyty Naukowe Politechniki Śląskiej* (Research Review—various titles)

DEANS

Faculty of Architecture: Prof. Dr NINA JUZWA

Faculty of Automatic Control, Electronics and Computer Science: Prof. Dr JERZY RUTKOWSKI

Faculty of Chemistry: Prof. Dr JERZY SUWIŃSKI

Faculty of Civil Engineering: Prof. Dr STANISŁAW MAJEWSKI

Faculty of Electrical Engineering: Assoc. Prof. Dr BOGUSŁAW GRZESIK

Faculty of Materials Science and Metallurgy: Dr. LESZEK BLACHA

Faculty of Mathematics and Physics: Dr. STANISŁAW KOCHOWSKI

Faculty of Mechanical Engineering: Prof. Dr LESZEK DOBRZAŃSKI

Faculty of Mining and Geology: Assoc. Prof. Dr KRYSTIAN PROBIERZ

Faculty of Organization and Management: Prof. Dr ANDRZEJ KARBOWNIK

Faculty of Power and Environmental Engineering: Prof. Dr MICHAŁ BODZEK

Faculty of Transport: Prof. Dr ANDRZEJ WILK

POLITECHNIKA ŚWIĘTOKRZYSKA
(Kielce University of Technology)

Al. Tysiąclecia Państwa Polskiego 7, 25-314 Kielce

Telephone: (41) 342-41-00

Fax: (41) 344-29-97

E-mail: rek@tu.kielce.pl

Internet: www.tu.kielce.pl/en

Founded 1965

State control

Academic year: October to June

Rector: Prof. Dr hab. WIESŁAW TRĄMPCZYŃSKI

Vice-Rector (Staff Development): Prof. Dr hab. ANDRZEJ RADOWICZ

Vice-Rector (Research): Prof. Dr hab. JAN STĘPIEŃ

Vice-Rector (Education): Prof. Dr hab. MARIA ŻYGADŁO

Administrative Officer: ZYGMUNT PAPROS

Library: see Libraries and Archives

Number of teachers: 407

Number of students: 7,263

DEANS

Faculty of Civil and Environmental Engineering: Prof. Dr hab. ZBIGNIEW RUSIN

Faculty of Mechatronics and Machinery Design: Prof. Dr hab. STANISŁAW ADAMCZAK

Faculty of Electrical and Computer Engineering: Prof. Dr hab. TADEUSZ STEFAŃSKI

Faculty of Management and Computer Modelling: Prof. Dr hab. WACŁAW GIERULSKI

PROFESSORS

Faculty of Civil and Environmental Engineering (tel. (41) 342-45-41; fax (41) 344-37-84; e-mail Zbigniew.Rusin@tu.kielce.pl; internet www.tu.kielce.pl/en/faculties/WBiIS):

BARTKIEWICZ, B., Water and Sewer Engineering

BEZAK-MAZUR, E., Environmental Protection

BOROWICZ, T., Structural Mechanics

CZYŻYK, F., Water and Sewer Engineering

DĄBKOWSKI, SZ., Water Engineering

DĄBROWSKI, W., Water Supply and Sewerage

FARYNIAK, L., Civil Engineering

GOŁASKI, L., Strength of Materials

GOMULIŃSKI, A., Structural Mechanics

GOSZCZYŃSKI, S., Reinforced Concrete Structures and Industrial Building

KOCWA-HALUCH, E., Water and Sewer Engineering

KOWAL, Z., Metal Constructions and Theory of Structures

KOZŁOWSKI, T., Geotechnology

KULICZKOWSKI, A., Water Supply and Sewerage

LEWINOWSKI, C., Road and Bridge Engineering

ŁOMOTOWSKI, J., Water and Sewer Engineering

NITA, P., Airfield Construction and Maintenance

PAUK, W., Geotechnology

PIASTA, J., Concrete Technology and Prefabrication

PIASTA, W., Concrete Technology and Prefabrication

RAKOWSKI, G., Structural Mechanics

RUDZIŃSKI, L., Building Repair and Maintenance

RUSIN, Z., Building Materials

SABINIAK, H., Water and Sewer Engineering

SIKORSKI, M., Water and Sewer Engineering

TRĄMPCZYŃSKI, W., Geotechnology

WOŹNIAK, M., Sanitation and Waste Management

WYSOCKI, J., Geotechnology

ŻYGADŁO, M., Sanitation and Waste Management

Faculty of Mechatronics and Machinery Design (tel. (41) 342-44-20; fax (41) 344-86-98; e-mail adamczak@tu.kielce.pl; internet www.tu.kielce.pl/en/faculties/WMiBM):

ADAMCZAK, S., Mechanical Engineering and Metrology

AMBROZIK, A., Vehicles and Mechanical Equipment

ANTOSZEWSKI, B., Operation Engineering

BODASZEWSKI, W., Strength of Materials

CHAŁUPCZAK, J., Metals and Materials Technology

DINDORF, R., Mechanical Engineering and Metrology

DZIADOŃ, A., Metals and Materials Technology

JANECKI, D., Centre for Laser Technology of Metals

KORUBA, Z., Vehicles and Mechanical Equipment

KUNDERA, C., Vehicles and Mechanical Equipment

MĄCZYŃSKI, J., Centre for Laser Technology of Metals

NEIMITZ, A., Principles of Machine Design

OKNIŃSKI, A., Physics

OSIECKI, J., Vehicles and Mechanical Equipment

OTMIANOWSKI, T., Operation Engineering

PŁONECKI, L., Centre for Laser Technology of Metals

PONIEWSKI, M., Thermodynamics and Fluid Mechanics

PRZYBYŁOWICZ, K., Metals and Materials Technology

RADOWICZ, A., Mechanics

STAŃCZYK, T., Vehicles and Mechanical Equipment

SZADKOWSKI, J., Centre for Laser Technology of Metals

WESOŁOWSKI, Z., Centre for Laser Technology of Metals

Faculty of Electrical and Computer Engineering (tel. (41) 342-41-29; fax (41) 344-77-58; e-mail stefan@tu.kielce.pl; internet www.tu.kielce.pl/en/faculties/WEAiI):

BOBROWSKI, C., Modern Physics

GAD, S., Power Engineering Electronics

GORZAŁCZANY, M., Electronics and Intelligent Systems

JASTRIEBOW, A., Automatic Control Devices and Systems

KACZMAREK, Z., Theoretical Electrical Engineering and Metrology

KOWALSKI, Z., Power Engineering

NADOLSKI, R., Electrical Machines

POPŁAWSKI, E., Power Engineering Electronics

SAPIECHA, K., Computer Science

STACHULEC, K., Modern Physics

STEFAŃSKI, T., Management and Control Systems

STĘPIEŃ, J., Power Engineering

SUCHAŃSKA, M., Telecommunications and Photonics

TUNIA, H., Power Engineering Electronics

WCIŚLIK, M., Automatic Control Devices and Systems

Faculty of Management and Computer Modelling (tel. (41) 342-44-40; fax (41) 342-43-06; e-mail gierulski@tu.kielce.pl; internet www.tu.kielce.pl/en/faculties/WZiMK):

BEDNARCZYK, J., Institute of Economics and Management

BOJCZUK, D., Institute of Production Engineering

CICHOŃ, C., Computer Science Fundamentals

GIERULSKI, W., Institute of Economics and Management

GRYSA, K., Mathematics

JASTRZĘBSKA-SMOLAGA, H., Institute of Economics and Management

KOCAŃDA, A., Institute of Production Engineering

KOTOWSKA-JELONEK, M., Institute of Economics and Management

LINCZOWSKI, C., Institute of Production Engineering

MEDUCKI, S., Institute of Economics and Management

NAUMIUK, J., Institute of Economics and Management

OKSANYCZ, A., Institute of Economics and Management

PŁOSKI, A., Mathematics

RADZISZEWSKI, B., Institute of Production Engineering

POLITECHNIKA SZCZECIŃSKA
(Technical University of Szczecin)

al. Piastów 17, 70-310 Szczecin
Telephone: (91) 434-67-51
Fax: (91) 449-40-14
E-mail: rector@ps.pl
Internet: www.ps.pl
Founded 1946
Academic year: October to September
Rector: Prof. Dr hab. Inż. MIECZYSŁAW WYSIECKI
Pro-Rectors: Prof. Dr hab. Inż. WŁODZIMERZ KIERNOŻYCKI, Prof. Dr hab. Inż. WALERIAN ARABCZYK, Dr hab. Inż. RYSZARD GETKA
Registrar: Mgr Inż. FRANCISZEK KAMOLA
Librarian: Mgr ANNA GRZELAK-ROZENBERG
Library of 273,500 books, 134,000 vols of periodicals, 4,700,000 patents, standards and catalogues
Number of teachers: 710
Number of students: 12,415
Publications: *Inżynier* (4 a year), *Eco Plast* (2 a year), *Polish Journal of Chemical Technology* (4 a year), *Prace Naukowe Politechniki Szczecińskiej* (4 a year)

DEANS

Faculty of Civil Engineering and Architecture: Dr hab. Inż. WŁADYSŁAW SZAFLIK

Faculty of Mechanical Engineering: Prof. Dr hab. Inż. STEFAN BERCZYŃSKI

Faculty of Chemical Engineering: Prof. Dr hab. Inż. EUGENIUSZ MILCHERT

Faculty of Electrical Engineering: Dr hab. Inż. ANDRZEJ BRYKALSKI

Faculty of Maritime Technology: Prof. Dr hab. Inż. MIECZYSŁAW HANN

Faculty of Computer Science and Information Technology: Prof. Dr hab. Inż. ANDRZEJ PIEGAT

PROFESSORS

Faculty of Civil Engineering and Architecture (al. Piastów 50, 70-311 Szczecin; tel. (91) 449-42-21; fax (91) 433-86-42; e-mail wbia@main.tuniv.szczecin.pl):

MEYER, Z., Hydro-engineering, Applied Hydraulics, Hydromechanics

ORŁOVICH, R., Building Construction

PĘSKI, W., Architecture and Urban Planning

RACINOWSKI, R., Quaternary Geology, Engineering Geology, Geomorphology

STEFAŃCZYK, B., Technology of Road and Building Materials

TOKARCZYK, R., Painting

WILK, R., Sculpting

Faculty of Mechanical Engineering (al. Piastów 19, 70-310 Szczecin; tel. (91) 484-57-17; fax (91) 449-43-46; e-mail wm@ps.pl; internet www.wm.ps.pl):

BERCZYŃSKI, S., Machine Technology

BES, T., Power Engineering, Thermodynamics, Heat Exchange, Thermal Energy Management

BŁĘDZKI, A., Material Engineering

HONCZARENKO, J., Bases of Constructing Machine Tools

MARCHELEK, K., Machining Processes

MYSŁOWSKI, J., Construction and Operating Machines

NOWACKI, J., Surface Engineering, Materials Science, Composite Materials, Heat Treatment

ROMANÓW, F., Thin-walled and Multilayer Constructions, Automotive Vehicles, Strength of Vehicles and Machines

WYSIECKI, M., Material Engineering, Copper Alloys

ZALEWSKI, P., Automotive Engineering

Faculty of Chemical Engineering (al. Piastów 42, 70-065 Szczecin; tel. (91) 434-30-86; fax (91) 449-46-36; e-mail wtiic@main.tuniv.szczecin.pl; internet www.ps.pl/wchem):

ARABCZYK, W., Inorganic Technology, Technology of Catalysts and Catalytic Processes

GRECH, E., Physical Organic Chemistry

KAŁUCKI, K., Chemical Technology, Catalysis and Engineering

KARCZ, J., Chemical Engineering, Mixing of Liquids in Single and Multiphase Systems

KURZAWA, M., Inorganic Chemistry, Solid State Chemistry of Inorganic Compounds

MASIUK, S., Chemical Engineering

MILCHERT, E., Organic Technology and Engineering

MORAWSKI, A., Technology of Water and Atmosphere Protection, Catalytic Processes, Water and Waste Water Technology

MYSZKOWSKI, J., Organic Technology, Environment Engineering

SPYCHAJ, T., Polymer Chemistry and Technology

STRASZKO, J., Physical-chemical Bases of Reactor Processes

SZAFKO, J., Physical Chemistry of Polymers and Polymer Technology

Faculty of Electrical Engineering (ul. Gen. Sikorskiego 37, 70-313 Szczecin; tel. (91) 434-09-26; fax (91) 434-09-26; e-mail dziekanat.we@ps.pl; internet www.we.ps.pl):

AFONON, A., Electrical Machines

JAKOWLEW, B., Electrical Materials

KUBISA, S., Electrical Engineering, Electric and Electronic Metrology

LIPIŃSKI, W., Electronics, Electrical Engineering

PURCZYŃSKI, J., Electronics, Electrical Engineering, Numerical Methods

SIDELNIKOV, B., Electrical Machines

SIKORA, R., Electrical Engineering

SKOCZOWSKI, S., Automation and Robotics, Electrical Engineering

VALOZHYN, A., Polymer Chemistry

ŻUCHOWSKI, A., Automation and Robotics, Electrical Engineering

Faculty of Maritime Technology (al. Piastów 41, 71-065 Szczecin,; tel. (91) 449-49-20; fax (91) 433-27-49; e-mail wtm@ps.pl; internet www.wtm.ps.pl):

HANN, M., Deck Equipment, Transport Engineering, Offshore Machinery, Reliability and Safety of Technical Systems
SEMENOV, I., Shipbuilding and Ship Design, Systems Engineering
ŻMUDZKI, S., Engines

Faculty of Computer Science and Information Technology (71-210 Szczecin, ul. Żołnierska 49; tel. (91) 449-56-70; fax (91) 487-64-39; e-mail wi@wi.ps.pl; internet www.wi.ps.pl):

BELETSKY, V., Programming and Information Security
BUDZIŃSKI, R., Company Financial Databases, Econometrical Analyses of Development in Efficiency, Models and Methods for Multicriterial Optimization
KOROSTIL, Y., Architecture, Security in Informatics
NOWAKOWSKI, A., Economic Analysis of Companies, Computer Science in Economics, Virtual Organization
OCHIN, E., Computer Network Architecture and Design
PIEGAT, A., Artificial Intelligence and Robotics
POPOV, O., Mathematical Methods, Systems Theory and Simulation
ROGOZA, V., Numerical Algorithms, Modelling and Simulation, Computation Theory and Models
ZAIKINE, O., Computer Network Systems and the Community

Institute of Economics and Management (al. Piastów 17, 71-311 Szczecin; tel. (91) 449-48-32; fax (91) 434-10-92; e-mail iekoiz@arcadia.tuniv.szczecin.pl):

CZEREPANIAK-WALCZAK, M., Social Education
SUŁKOWSKI, Cz., Managerial Economics, Investment Management, Macroeconomics
ZAWADZKI, J., Econometrics, Theory of Projection

Institute of Physics (al. Piastów 17, 70-311 Szczecin; tel. (91) 449-45-85; fax (91) 434-21-13; e-mail if@main.tuniv.szczecin.pl):

GUSKOS, N., Physics of Solid Bodies
KRUK, I., Biophysics, Molecular Optics

POLITECHNIKA WARSZAWSKA
(Warsaw University of Technology)

Pl. Politechniki 1, 00-661 Warsaw

Telephone: (22) 660-72-11
Fax: (22) 621-68-92
E-mail: soltyski@rekt.pw.edu.pl
Internet: www.pw.edu.pl

Founded 1826
State control
Academic year: October to September

Rector: Prof. Dr STANISŁAW MAŃKOWSKI
Vice-Rector (General Affairs): Prof. Dr WŁODZIMIERZ KURNIK
Vice-Rector (Scientific Affairs): Prof. Dr PIOTR WOLAŃSKI
Vice-Rector (Academic Affairs): Prof. Dr LECH CZARNECKI
Vice-Rector (Student Affairs): Prof. Dr ANDRZEJ JAKUBIAK
Vice-Rector (Płock Campus): Prof. Dr JANUSZ ZIELIŃSKI (acting)
Registrar (vacant)
Librarian: Mgr JOLANTA STĘPNIAK

Library of 780,000 books, 1,200 periodical titles, 7,500 electronic periodical titles, 220,000 special collns, including 34,000 Polish, European and international standards

Number of teachers: 2,301
Number of students: 31,808

Publication: *Prace naukowe — Politechnika Warszawska* (Scientific Works — Warsaw University of Technology)

DEANS

Faculty of Architecture: Prof. Dr MACIEJ KYSIAK
Faculty of Automobile and Construction Machinery Engineering: Prof. Dr JAN SZLAGOWSKI
Faculty of Chemical and Process Engineering: Prof. Dr LEON GRADOŃ
Faculty of Chemistry: Prof. Dr WŁADYSŁAW WIECZOREK
Faculty of Civil Engineering: Prof. Dr GRZEGORZ JEMIELITA
Faculty of Civil Engineering, Mechanics and Petrochemistry (Płock Campus): Prof. Dr JANUSZ ZIELIŃSKI
Faculty of Electrical Engineering: Prof. Dr ROMAN BARLIK
Faculty of Electronics and Information Technology: Prof. Dr JÓZEF LUBACZ
Faculty of Environmental Engineering: Prof. Dr MARIAN ROSIŃSKI
Faculty of Geodesy and Cartography: Prof. Dr WITOLD PRÓSZYŃSKI
Faculty of Materials Science and Engineering: Prof. Dr TADEUSZ KULIK
Faculty of Mathematics and Information Science: Prof. Dr ZBIGNIEW LONC
Faculty of Mechatronics: Prof. Dr JERZY E. KUREK
Faculty of Physics: Prof. Dr FRANCISZEK KROK
Faculty of Power and Aeronautical Engineering: Prof. Dr KRZYSZTOF KĘDZIOR
Faculty of Production Engineering: Prof. Dr KRZYSZTOF SANTAREK
Faculty of Transport: Prof. Dr ANDRZEJ CHUDZIKIEWICZ
Business School: Dr ZBIGNIEW TUROWSKI (Dir)
College of Economics and Social Sciences (Płock Campus): Dr IRENA BIELECKA (Dir)
College of Social Science and Administration: Prof. HELENA KISILOWSKA (Dir)

PROFESSORS

Faculty of Architecture (Koszykowa 55, 00-659 Warsaw; tel. (22) 628-28-87; fax (22) 628-32-36; e-mail dziekan@arch.pw.edu.pl; internet www.arch.pw.edu.pl):

BENEDEK, W., Housing Design and Public Utilities
BRYKOWSKA, M., History of Towns and Architecture
CHMIELEWSKI, J. M., Urban Design and Town Planning
GAWLIKOWSKI, A. Z., Urban Design and Town Planning
GZELL, S., Urban Design and Town Planning
HRYNIAK, Z., Urban Design and Town Planning
KŁOSIEWICZ, L., Contemporary Architecture
KUBICA, B., Fine Arts – Sculpture
KUCZA-KUCZYŃSKI, K., Housing Design and Public Utilities
PAWŁOWSKI, Z., Building Structures
ROGUSKA, J., History of Towns and Architecture
SZPARKOWSKI, Z., Industrial Buildings
SZULBORSKI, K., Building Structures
TOMASZEWSKI, A., Conservation of Monuments, History of Architecture
WIŚNIEWSKA, M., Housing Design and Public Utilities
WERNER, W., Economics of Investment Processes and Management
WRONA, S., Computer-Aided Architectural Design

Faculty of Automobile and Construction Machinery Engineering (Narbutta 84, 02-524 Warsaw; tel. (22) 849-03-01; fax (22) 849-03-06; e-mail dzk@simr.pw.edu.pl; internet www.simr.pw.edu.pl):

BIAŁAS, S., Geometrical Accuracy in Machinery Design, Tolerance Technology
BOGACZ, R., Dynamics of Means of Transport
DĄBROWSKI, Z., Machine Design, Vibroacoustics
GOŁOŚ, K., Fatigue in Materials
KURNIK, WŁ., Dynamics of Mechanical Systems, Mechatronics
MADEJ, J., Mechanics of Rail Vehicles
OSIŃSKI, J., Dynamics of Mechanical Systems
RADKOWSKI, ST., Safety in Technical Systems, Technical Diagnostics
STARCZEWSKI, Z., Dynamics of Mechanical Systems, Dynamics of Rotors and Journal Bearing System
SZLAGOWSKI, J., Plastics Design of Structures, Automation of Construction Machinery
SZUMANOWSKI, A., Electromechanical Propulsion Systems, Energy Storage, Hybrid and Electric Vehicles
TYLIKOWSKI, A., Dynamics of Mechanical Systems, Mechatronics
WICHER, J., Mechanics, Dynamics of Mechanical Systems
WRÓBEL, J., Theory of Machine Design

Faculty of Chemical and Process Engineering (Waryńskiego 1, 00-645 Warsaw; tel. and fax (22) 825-14-40; e-mail dziekan@ichip.pw.edu.pl; internet www.ichip.pw.edu.pl):

BAŁDYGA, J., Chemical Reactor Engineering
BIŃ, A. K., Process Kinetics, Environmental Protection Processes
CHMIELEWSKI, A. G., Environmental Engineering, Separation Processes
GAWROŃSKI, R., Membrane Processes
GRADOŃ, L., Chemical Engineering, Aerosol Mechanics
POHORECKI, R., Chemical Reactor Engineering, Bioprocess Engineering
SIENIUTYCZ, S., Process Thermodynamics, Non-equilibrium Thermodynamics
SZEWCZYK, K. W., Biochemical Technology, Bioprocess Engineering
SZWAST, Z., Process Optimization
WOLNY, A., Chemical Engineering

Faculty of Chemistry (Noakowskiego 3, 00-664 Warsaw; tel. and fax (22) 628-27-41; e-mail dziekan@ch.pw.edu.pl; internet www.ch.pw.edu.pl):

BRZÓZKA, Z., Analytical Chemistry
DOMAŃSKA-ŻELAZNA, U., Physical Chemistry
FLORJAŃCZYK, Z., Organic Chemistry, Polymer Science
GRYFF-KELLER, A., Organic Chemistry
GRZYWA, E., General Chemistry
JAROSZ, M., Analytical Chemistry
JOŃCZYK, A., Organic Chemistry and Technology
KASIURA, K., Inorganic and Analytical Chemistry
KLJEŃSKI, J., Organic Chemistry, Catalysis
KSIĄŻCZAK, A., Theory and Technology of Explosives
ŁOBIŃSKI, R., Analytical Chemistry
MĄKOSZA, M., Organic Chemistry and Technology
PLENKIEWICZ, J., Biotransformation in Organic Chemistry
PROŃ, A., Polymer Science, Solid State Technology
ROKICKI, G., Organic Chemistry, Polymer Science

SERWATOWSKI, J., Physical Organic Chemistry
WIECZOREK, W., Solid State Technology

Faculty of Civil Engineering (Armii Ludowej 16, 00-637 Warsaw; tel. (22) 825-59-37; fax (22) 825-88-99; e-mail dziekanat@il.pw.edu.pl; internet www.il.pw.edu.pl):

ABRAMOWICZ, M., Reinforced Concrete Structures
CHRABACZYŃSKI, G., Building Production and Prefabrication
CZARNECKI, L., Technology of Building Materials
GOMULIŃSKI, A., Structural Mechanics
JAWORSKI, K., Technology of Building Materials
KARCZEWSKI, J., Metal Constructions, Spatial Structures
KNAUFF, M., Building Construction
NAGÓRSKI, R., Structural Mechanics
OBRĘBSKI, J., Structural Mechanics
RADOMSKI, W., Bridge Engineering
RUNKIEWICZ, L., Building Construction
SUCHORZEWSKI, W., Construction of Roads, Streets and Bridges
SZCZEŚNIAK, W., Structural Mechanics
WITKOWSKI, M., Structural Mechanics, Computers in Civil Engineering
WOJEWÓDZKI, W., Theory of Elasticity and Plasticity
ŻÓŁTOWSKI, W., Metal Constructions

Faculty of Civil Engineering, Mechanics and Petrochemistry (Płock Campus) (Łukasiewicza 17, 09-400 Płock; tel. (24) 262-62-54; fax (24) 367-22-25; e-mail zielinski@pw.plock.pl; internet www.pw.plock.pl):

BOCHEŃSKI, C., Agricultural Engineering
BUKOWSKI, A., Technology of Plastics
CHOCHOWSKI, A., Solar Power Engineering
DWILIŃSKI, L., Construction and Reliability of Agricultural Machinery
FRĄCZEK, K., Carbon Derivatives Technology, Polymer Chemistry
KAJDAS, Cz., Technology and Processing of Petroleum and its Products, Tribopolymerization
KAMIŃSKI, E., Mechanical Appliances and Machinery
KOSIŃSKI, W., Cartography and Surveying
PONIEWSKI, M., Heat Engines and Thermal Equipment
POWIERŻA, L., Systems Engineering
PYSIAK, J., Physical Solid-state Chemistry
RÓŻYCKI, C., Trace Analysis, Chemometrics
ŚCIŚLEWSKI, Z., Durability
URBANIEC, K., Food Industry Machinery
WŁODARCZYK, W., Building Constructions
WOLSKI, L., Physics of Buildings, Sanitary Systems
ZIELIŃSKI, J., Technology of Petroleum and Plastics
ŻUK, D., Agricultural Engineering

Faculty of Electrical Engineering (pl. Politechniki 1, 00-661 Warsaw; tel. (22) 629-25-31; fax (22) 625-75-24; e-mail ura@dean.ee.pw.edu.pl; internet www.ee.pw.edu.pl):

BĄK, J., Lighting Technology
BARLIK, R., Industrial Electronics and Electrical Drives, Power Electronics
BOLKOWSKI, S., Circuit Theory and Electromagnetic Fields
CELIŃSKI, Z., Nuclear Technology
CICHOCKI, A., Circuit Theory
CIOK, Z., High-voltage Technology
DMOWSKI, A., Industrial Electronics
FLISOWSKI, Z., High-voltage Technology
HERING, M., Electro-heating Technology
KACZOREK, T., Linear Control Systems
KAŹMIERKOWSKI, M., Industrial Electronics and Intelligent Control
KOCZARA, N., Electrical Drives and Generation of Power
KRZEMIŃSKI, S., Circuit Theory

KUJSZCZYK, S., Power Systems and Electrical Networks
MACHOWSKI, J., Power Systems and Electrical Networks
MAKSYMIUK, J., Electrical Apparatus
MIKOŁAJUK, K., Circuit Theory and Electromagnetic Fields
OSOWSKI, S., Artificial Intelligence – Neural Networks
RAWA, H., Circuit Theory and Electromagnetic Fields
SIKORA, J., Circuit Theory and Electromagnetic Fields
SUPRONOWICZ, H., Industrial Electronics
TRZASKA, Z., Circuit Theory and Electromagnetic Fields
TUMAŃSKI, S., Electrical Measurements
WINCENCIAK, S., Circuit Theory and Electromagnetic Fields

Faculty of Electronics and Information Technology (Nowowiejska 15–19, 00-665 Warsaw; tel. (22) 825-37-58; fax (22) 825-19-84; e-mail dziekan@elka.pw.edu.pl; internet www.elka.pw.edu.pl):

DĄBROWSKI, M., Computer Networks and Switching
DOBROWOLSKI, J., Computer-aided Design of Microwave Circuits, Monolithic Microwave Integrated Circuits
EBERT, J., High-power Radiotechnology
GALWAS, B., Microwave Electronics and Photonics
GWAREK, P., Microwave Technology
HOLEJKO, K., Telecommunications and Opto-electronics
JACHOWSKI, R., Measurement Systems and Sensors
JAKUBOWSKI, A., Microelectronics, Metaloxide-semiconductor Devices
KUDREWICZ, J., Theory of Electronic Systems
KUŹMICZ, W., Microelectronics
ŁUBA, T., Computer Engineering, Digital Systems Design
LUBACZ, J., Information and Communication Technologies
MAJKUSIAK, B., Microelectronics
MALINOWSKI, K., Information Engineering and Control Systems
MODELSKI, J., Microwaves, Satellite and Cable Television
MORAWSKI, R. Z., Measurement and Instrumentation
MORAWSKI, T., Microwave Technology
MULAWKA, J., Computer Science, Artificial Intelligence
MURASZKIEWICZ, M., Information and Knowledge Systems, Databases, Networking
PAWŁOWSKI, Z., Medical and Nuclear Electronics
PIÓRO, M., Information and Communication Technologies
ROSŁONIEC, S., Microwave Technology
RYBIŃSKI, H., Information Systems, Databases
SZCZEPAŃSKI, P., Optoelectronics, Laser Physics
TRACZYK, W., Knowledge-based Systems
WIERZBICKI, A., Optimization and Decision Theory
WOJCIECHOWSKI, J., Electronics, Telecommunication Networks, Signals and Systems
WOŹNICKI, J., Electronics, Optoelectronics
ZABRODZKI, J., Computer Science, Computer Graphics

Faculty of Environmental Engineering (Nowowiejska 20, 00-653 Warsaw; tel. (22) 621-45-60; fax (22) 625-73-77; e-mail dziekan@is.pw.edu.pl; internet www.is.pw.edu.pl):

BIEDUGNIS, S., Water Supply and Sewerage Systems, Sanitary and Environmental Engineering

JĘDRZEJEWSKA-ŚCIBAK, T., Indoor Air Quality, Ventilation and Air Conditioning
KINDLER, J., Water Resources Management and Environmental Systems
MAŃKOWSKI, S., Heat Engineering
MITOSEK, M., Hydraulics, Fluid Mechanics
MIZIELIŃSKI, B., Ventilation and Air Conditioning
NAWALANY, M., Environmental Engineering, Groundwater Protection
OSIADACZ, A., Gas Engineering
PISARCZYK, S., Building Engineering, Geotechnology
ROMAN, M., Water Supply and Sewerage Systems, Sanitary and Environmental Engineering

Faculty of Geodesy and Cartography (pl. Politechniki 1, 00-661 Warsaw; tel. (22) 660-72-23; fax (22) 621-36-80; e-mail dziekanat@gik.pw.edu.pl; internet www.gik.pw.edu.pl):

ADAMCZEWSKI, Z., Theory of Adjustment, Geodetic Computation
BARLIK, M., Geodesy, Gravimetry
BIAŁOUSZ, S., Soil Mapping and Remote Sensing, Geographical Information Systems
CZARNECKI, K., Geodesy
CZICHON, H., Technology of Printing
MACIEJEWSKA, A., Soil Conservation and Land Protection
MAKOWSKI, A., Cartography
MARTUSEWICZ, J., Surveying for Tunnelling
MERWIŃSKI, R., Printing Technology
PRÓSZYŃSKI, W., Engineering Surveying, Theory of Adjustment
ROGOWSKI, J., Geodetic Astronomy, Satellite Geodesy
SKŁODOWSKI, P., Soil Science, Soil Conservation
SKÓRCZYŃSKI, A., Surveying, Theory of Adjustment
ŚLEDZIŃSKI, J., Satellite Geodesy
WILKOWSKI, W., Rural Land Management

Faculty of Materials Science and Engineering (Wołoska 141, 02-507 Warsaw; tel. (22) 849-99-29; fax (22) 660-85-14; e-mail wim@inmat.pw.edu.pl; internet www.inmat.pw.edu.pl):

GRABSKI, M. W., Physics of Plastic Deformation
KURZYDŁOWSKI, K. J., Materials Characterization and Modelling
LEONOWICZ, M., Magnetic Materials
OLSZYNA, A., Ceramic Materials
MICHALSKI, A., Surface Engineering
SZUMMER, A., Functional Construction of Materials
WIERZCHOŃ, T., Surface Engineering

Faculty of Mathematics and Information Science (pl. Politechniki 1, 00-661 Warsaw; tel. (22) 621-93-12; fax (22) 625-74-60; e-mail sekretariat@mini.pw.edu.pl; internet www.mini.pw.edu.pl):

JANECZKO, S., Singularity Theory and Symplectic Geometry
KLEIBER, M., Computer Methods in Mechanics
LONC, Z., Discrete Mathematics
MACUKOW, B., Artificial Intelligence
MĄCZYŃSKI, M., Algebra, Mathematical Foundations of Quantum Theory
MARCINIAK, K., Computer Graphics and Geometry
MUSZYŃSKI, J., Differential Equations
PLUCIŃSKA, A., Probability and Stochastic Processes
ROMANOWSKA, A., Algebra
SPIEŻ, S., Topology

Faculty of Mechatronics (Św. A. Boboli 8, 02-525 Warsaw; tel. (22) 849-07-11; fax (22) 849-99-36; e-mail dean@mchtr.pw.edu.pl; internet www.mchtr.pw.edu.pl):

CIEŚLICKI, K., Fluid Mechanics
DUNAJSKI, Z., Biomedical Engineering

GAMBIN, W., Mechanics
JANISZOWSKI, K., Automatic Control and Robotics, System Identification
JÓŹWICKI, R., Design of Optical Instruments
KOŚCIELNY, J. M., Automatic Control, Fault Detection
KUJAWIŃSKA, M., Applied Optics, Machine Vision
KUREK, J., Automatic Control and Robotics, Control Theory
MRUGALSKI, Z., Design of Precision Devices
OLEKSIUK, T., Design of Precision Devices
PAŁKO, T., Biomedical Engineering
PATORSKI, K., Applied Optics, Design of Optical Instruments
PAWLICKI, W. G., Biomedical Engineering
RATAJCZYK, E., Measuring Apparatus

Faculty of Physics (Koszykowa 75, 00-662 Warsaw; tel. (22) 660-72-67; fax (22) 628-21-71; e-mail dziekan@if.pw.edu.pl; internet www.if.pw.edu.pl):

ADAMCZYK, A., Liquid Crystals
BACEWICZ, R., Solid State Physics
BOGUSZ, W., Solid State Physics
ĆWIOK, S., Nuclear Physics
HOŁYST, J., Physics of Complex Systems
KOSIŃSKI, R., Physics of Magnetism
KROK, F., Solid State Physics
SŁOWIŃSKI, B., Nuclear Physics
STRZAŁKOWSKI, I., Solid State Physics
SUKIENNICKI, A., Physics of Magnetism
WOLIŃSKI, T., Optoelectronics
ŻEBROWSKI, J., Physics of Complex Systems

Faculty of Power and Aeronautical Engineering (Nowowiejska 24, 00-665 Warsaw; tel. (22) 621-53-10; fax (22) 625-73-51; e-mail dziekan@meil.pw.edu.pl; internet www.meil .pw.edu.pl):

ARCZEWSKI, K., Analytical Mechanics, Multibody Systems
BANASZEK, J., Thermodynamics, Mathematical Methods of Heat Transfer
DIETRICH, M. (acting), Mechanical Engineering, Biomedical Engineering
DOMANSKI, R., Heat Transfer, Thermodynamics, Environmental Engineering
FURMAŃSKI, P., Heat Transfer, Thermodynamics, Thermal Properties of Materials
GORAJ, Z., Aerodynamics, Flight Dynamics, Aircraft Design
JEDRAL, W., Power Engineering, Pumping Machinery and Installations
KĘDZIOR, K., Modelling of Human Movement, Systems Dynamics, Robotics and Biomechanics
LEWANDOWSKI, J., Environmental Engineering, Power Engineering, Control of Power Plants
LEWITOWICZ, J., Aircraft Maintenance, Aerospace Engineering
MARYNIAK, J., Flight Mechanics
MILLER, A., Power Engineering, Gas and Steam Turbines
PORTACHA, J., Power Engineering, Power Plants
RYCHTER, T., Internal Combustion Engines, Combustion
SADO, J., Thermodynamics, Refrigeration, Plasma Physics
STUPNICKI, J., Fundamentals of Machine Construction
STYCZEK, A., Mathematical Methods of Fluid Mechanics
SZOPA, T., Safety Engineering
SZUMOWSKI, A., Fluid Mechanics, Gas Dynamics, Aerodynamic Noise Control
WOLAŃSKI, P., Combustion, Aero Engines
ŻOCHOWSKI, M., Strength of Materials

Faculty of Production Engineering (Narbutta 85, 02-524 Warsaw; tel. (22) 849-97-95; fax (22) 849-94-34; e-mail dean@wip.pw.edu.pl; internet www.wip.pw.edu.pl):

BOSSAK, M., Computational Mechanics, Computer-aided Design
GRUDZEWSKI, W., Organization and Management
HEJDUK, J., Organization and Management
JEMIELNIAK, K., Production Engineering
KACZOROWSKI, M., Materials Science and Engineering
KISIELNICKI, J., Organization and Management
KLASZTORNY, M., Applied Mechanics
KOCAŃDA, A., Metal-forming
KOZAK, J., Production Engineering
MASŁOWSKI, A., Automation and Robotics
LEWANDOWSKI, J., Economics
MASŁYK-MUSIAŁ, E., Organization and Management
MONKIEWICZ, J., Organization and Management
NOWICKI, B., Production Engineering
PERZYK, M., Casting Technology
SANTAREK, K., Organization and Management
SZAFARCZYK, M., Machine Tools Control and Drive
SZENAJCH, W., Mechanical Engineering, Automatic Control of Industrial Processes
TKACZYK, S., Organization and Management
WILCZYŃSKI, A., Mechanical Engineering
WŁOSIŃSKI, W., Materials Technology

Faculty of Transport (Koszykowa 75, 00-662 Warsaw; tel. (22) 660-73-11; fax (22) 621-56-87; e-mail dziekan@it.pw.edu.pl; internet www.it.pw.edu.pl):

BORGOŃ, J., Air Traffic Control
CHUDZIKIEWICZ, A., Dynamics and Diagnostics of Means of Transport
DĄBROWA-BAJON, M., Rail Traffic Control
DYDUCH, J., Control Systems
KISILOWSKI, J., Dynamics and Diagnostics of Mechanical Systems
LESZCZYŃSKI, J., Organization and Technology of Transport
MANEROWSKI, J., Flight Mechanics
NIEDZIELA, T., Image Processing
SMALKO, Z., Maintenance and Operation of Vehicles

College of Economics and Social Sciences (Płock Campus) (Łukasiewicza 17, 09-400 Płock; tel. (24) 367-21-26; fax (24) 262-90-08; e-mail knes@pw.plock.pl):

BIAŁOŃ-SOCZYŃSKA, L., Economics of Industry, Economics of Science, Marketing
GÓRALSKI, W., Domestic Relations Law, Canon Law
KRAJEWSKA, A., Economics, Fiscal Policy and Taxation Theory
KRAJEWSKI, S., Innovative and Structural Policies, Enterprise Operation and Privatization
MARCINIAK, S., Economics of Innovation, Macroeconomics
OBRĘBSKI, T., Labour Economics, Industrial Relations
PACHO, W., Financing Strategies of Public Limited Companies
SPYCHALSKI, G., History of Economics, Modern Economics
STAWICKI, J., Econometrics and Statistics
WĄSOWICZ, M., Economic Theory, Environmental Economics
WITKOWSKA, J., International Economics, European Integration
ZIELIŃSKI, R., Economic Theory, Defence Economics

College of Social Science and Administration (Noakowskiego 18/20, 00-668 Warsaw; tel. (22) 621-36-92; fax (22) 825-37-46; e-mail kolegium@kns.pw.edu.pl; internet www.kns .pw.edu.pl):

BIAŁOŃ-SOCZYŃSKA, L., Economics of Industry, Economics of Science, Marketing
MARCINIAK, S., Economics of Innovation, Macroeconomics
NIEWIADOMSKI, Z., Public Administration, Self-government, Physical Planning
OBRĘBSKI, T., Economics, Labour Economics, Industrial Relations
ZAWADZKA, Z., Economics, Finance, Banking

POLITECHNIKA WROCŁAWSKA
(Wrocław University of Technology)

Wybrzeże Wyspiańskiego 27, 50-370 Wrocław

Telephone: (71) 320-22-77
Fax: (71) 322-36-64
E-mail: sekrpwr@ac.pwr.wroc.pl
Internet: www.pwr.wroc.pl

Founded 1945
State control
Language of instruction: Polish
Academic year: October to June

Rector: Prof. ANDRZEJ MULAK
Vice-Rector (Scientific): Prof. JERZY ZDANOWSKI
Vice-Rector: Prof. LUDWIK KOMOROWSKI
Vice-Rector: Dr LUDOMIR JANKOWSKI
Vice-Rector (Teaching): Prof. JERZY ŚWIĄTEK
Chief Administrative Officer: Mgr Inż. ANDRZEJ KACZKOWSKI
Librarian: Dr HENRYK SZARSKI

Library of 900,000 vols, including 4,500 periodical titles
Number of teachers: 1,996
Number of students: 29,519

Publications: *Environmental Protection Engineering* (4 a year), *Optica Applicata* (4 a year), *Studia Geotechnica et Mechanica* (4 a year), *Systems Science* (4 a year), *Badania Operacyjne i Decyzje* (4 a year), *Fizykochem. Problemy Mineralurgii* (annually), *Architectus Systems* (2 a year), *Pryzmat* (monthly), *Semestr* (monthly), *Acta – Bioengineering and Biomechanics* (2 a year), *Systems – Journal of Transdisciplinary Systems Science* (2 a year), *Geometria Wykreślna i Grafika Inżynierska* (annually), *Materials Science* (4 a year)

DEANS

Faculty of Architecture: Prof. ELŻBIETA TROCKA-LESZCZYŃSKA
Faculty of Basic Problems of Technology: Prof. RYSZARD GRĄŚLEWICZ
Faculty of Civil Engineering: Prof. ERNEST KUBICA
Faculty of Chemistry: Prof. HENRYK GÓRECKI
Faculty of Computer Science and Management: Prof. TADEUSZ GALANC
Faculty of Electronics: Prof. JANUSZ BIERNAT
Faculty of Electrical Engineering: Prof. JANUSZ SZAFRAN
Faculty of Environmental Engineering: Prof. KRZYSZTOF BARTOSZEWSKI
Faculty of Mechanical Engineering: Prof. WACŁAW KOLLEK
Faculty of Mechanical and Power Engineering: Prof. ZBIGNIEW GNUTEK
Faculty of Microsystem Electronics and Photonics: Prof. BENEDYKT LICZNERSKI
Faculty of Mining Engineering: Prof. MONIKA HARDYGÓRA

Higher Institutes

AGRICULTURE

SZKOŁA GŁÓWNA GOSPODARSTWA WIEJSKIEGO W WARSZAWIE
(Warsaw Agricultural University)

ul. Nowoursynowska 166, 02-787 Warsaw
Telephone: (22) 843-85-88
Fax: (22) 843-85-88
E-mail: rektor@alpha.sggw.waw.pl
Internet: www.sggw.waw.pl
Founded 1816
Academic year: October to June

Rector: Prof. Dr. hab. TOMASZ BORECKI
Pro-Rector (Science): Prof. Dr hab. KATARZYNA NIEMIROWICZ-SZCZYTT
Pro-Rector (Development): Prof. Dr hab. ALOJZY SZYMAŃSKI
Pro-Rector (Teaching): Prof. Dr hab. SŁAWOMIR PODLASKI
Chief Administration Officer: Dr WŁADYSŁAW SKARŻYŃSKI
Librarian: Mgr JERZY LEWANDOWSKI
Library of 180,000 books, 110,500 vols of periodicals
Number of teachers: 1,081
Number of students: 20,362
Publication: *Annals* (in 8 series)

DEANS

Faculty of Agriculture: Prof. Dr hab. JAN LABĘTOWICZ
Faculty of Veterinary Medicine: Prof. Dr hab. WŁODZIMIERZ KLUCIŃSKI
Faculty of Forestry: Prof. Dr hab. HERONIM OLENDEREK
Faculty of Horticulture and Landscape Architecture: Prof. Dr hab. KAZIMIERZ TOMALA
Faculty of Engineering and Environmental Science: Prof. Dr hab. KAZIMIERZ BANASIK
Faculty of Wood Technology: Dr hab. KRYSZTOF KRAJEWSKI
Faculty of Animal Science: Prof. Dr hab. JÓZEF KULISIEWICZ
Faculty of Agricultural Economics: Prof. Dr hab. MARIAN PODSTAWKA
Faculty of Food Technology: Prof. Dr hab. ANDRZEJ LENART
Faculty of Human Nutrition and Consumer Sciences: Dr hab. KRYSTYNA GUTKOWSKA
Faculty of Production Engineering: Prof. Dr hab. CZESŁAW WASZKIEWICZ

PROFESSORS

Faculty of Agriculture (02-528 Warsaw, ul. Rakowiecka 26–30; tel. (22) 849-97-20; fax (22) 849-93-20; e-mail rol_dziekan@sggw .waw.pl):

BIELAWSKI, W., Biochemistry
GOLINOWSKI, W., Botany
GWOREK, B., Soil Science
ŁABĘTOWICZ, Z., Soil Science
MĄDRY, W., Mathematical Statistics and Experimentation
OSTROWSKA, D., Crop Production
PRACZ, J., Soil Science
RADECKI, A., Soil and Land Management
RUSSEL, S., Agricultural Microbiology

Faculty of Veterinary Medicine (tel. (22) 847-37-56; fax (22) 847-20-12; e-mail wet_dziekan@sggw.waw.pl):

BORYCZKO, Z., Animal Gynaecology, Animal Reproduction
FRYMUS, T., Epizootiology
HARTWIG, A., Bee Pathology
KANIA, B., Physiology, Biochemistry, Pharmacology and Toxicology
KLECZKOWSKI, M., Clinical and Laboratory Diagnostics
KLUCIŃSKI, W., Physiopathology, Internal Medicine
KOBRYŃ, H., Anatomy
KULASEK, G., Animal Physiology
LECHOWSKI, R., Internal Medicine
LEONTOWICZ, H. J., Dietetics
MOTYL, T., Animal Physiology
NIEMIAŁTOWSKI, M., Animal Immunology
OSTASZENSKI, P., Animal Physiology
SITARSKA, E., Pathophysiology, Veterinary Laboratory Diagnostics
SYSA, P., Histology and Embryology
SZCZAWIŃSKI, J., Hygiene of Food of Animal Origin
WIECHETEK, M., Veterinary Pharmacology and Toxicology, Environmental Protection
WĘDRYCHOWICZ, H., Parasitology
ZABIELSKI, R., Forest Management

Faculty of Forestry (02-528 Warsaw, ul. Rakowiecka 26–30; tel. (22) 849-11-79; fax (22) 849-13-75; e-mail les_dziekan@sggw .waw.pl; internet wl.sggw.waw.pl/indexpl .html):

BORECKI, T., Forest Management
BRUCHWALD, A., Forest Mensuration and Productivity
BRZEZIECKI, B., Silviculture
DUDZIŃSKA, T., Forest Mensuration and Productivity
GOSZCZYŃSKI, J., Ecology, Game Management
GRZYWACZ, A., Forest Phytopathology
MAZUR, S., Entomology and Forest Protection
MIŚCICKI, S., Forest Management
MOZGAWA, J., Forest Management, Forest Economics
OLENDEREK, H., GIS in Forestry
PASCHALIS-JAKUBOWICZ, P., Forest Resources Utilisation
STĘPIEŃ, E., Forest Management, Forest Economics
TRACZ, H., Forestry Entomology and Ecology
ZAJĄCZKOWSKI, S., Tree Physiology
ŻYBURA, H., Silviculture

Faculty of Horticulture and Landscape Architecture (tel. (22) 843-07-17; fax (22) 843-07-17; e-mail ogr_dziekan@sggw.waw .pl):

CIECHOMSKI, W., Horticultural Economics
DĄBROWSKI, Z. T., Applied Entomology, Resistance of Plants to Pests
DAMIĘCKI, J., Design
GAWROŃSKI, S., Pomology
IGNATOWICZ, S., Applied Entomology
JADCZUK, E., Pomology and Basic Natural Science in Horticulture
KOBRYN, J., Medicinal and Vegetable Plants
KROPCZYŃSKA-LINKIEWICZ, D., Applied Entomology
KRYCZYŃSKI, S., Phytopathology
ŁUKASZEWSKA, A. J., Ornamental Plants
MAJEWSKI, T., Phytopathology, Mycology, Taxonomy
MALEPSZY, S., Plant Genetics, Biotechnology
NIEMIROWICZ-SZCZYTT, K., Plant Genetics and Breeding, Biotechnology
PRZYBECKI, Z., Plant Genetics and Breeding, Biotechnology
RYLKE, J., Landscape Planning and Design
SADOWSKA, A., Medicinal and Anticancer Plants, Plant Propagation, Environmental Protection
SUCHORSKA-TROPIŁO, K., Medicinal and Spice Plants
SZYSZKO, J., Landscape Architecture
TOMALA, K., Horticulture, Fruit Storage Quality
TOMCZYK, A., Applied Entomology
WEGLARZ, Z., Medicinal and Spice Plants
WYSOCKI, Cz., Environment Protection
ZAMORSKI, Cz., Phytopathology

Faculty of Engineering and Environmental Science (tel. (22) 847-24-53; fax (22) 847-24-53; e-mail iks_dziekan@sggw.waw.pl):

BANASIK, K., Hydraulics
BIERNACKA, E., Soil Science, Environmental Protection
BRANDYK, T., Soil Physics
DĄBKOWSKI, S., Hydraulics
IGNAR, S., Hydraulics
KUBRAK, J. R., Hydraulics
ŁYKOWSKI, B., Meteorology and Climatology
PAWŁAT, H., Natural Bases of Environmental Engineering
PIERZGALSKI, E., Environmental Science and Engineering
SZYMAŃSKI, A., Geotechnics
ZELAZO, J., Hydraulics

Faculty of Wood Technology (02-528 Warsaw, ul. Rakowiecka 26–30; tel. (22) 849-12-09; fax (22) 849-12-09; e-mail tdr_dziekan@sggw .waw.pl):

BAJKOWSKI, B., Mechanical Wood Processing
DOŁOWY, K., Physics
DZBEŃSKI, W., Wood Materials Engineering, Sawmilling
KRUTIL, D., Wood Sciences and Wood Protection
MATEJAK, M., Drying of Wood
STARECKI, A. W., Wood Technology
SWACZYNA, J., Technology, Organization and Management in the Wood Industry

Faculty of Animal Science (02-528 Warsaw, ul Rakowiecka 26–30; tel. (22) 849-07-84; fax (22) 849-07-84; e-mail zoo_dziekan@sggw .waw.pl):

BRZOZOWSKI, P., Animal Breeding
CHARON, K., Animal Genetics
CHRZANOWSKI, S., Horse Breeding
FABIJAŃSKA, M., Animal Nutrition and Feed Management
GRODZKI, H., Animal Breeding
JASIŃSKI, Z., Beneficial Insects
JURCZAK, M., Animal Breeding
KOŚLA, T. Z., Animal Hygiene
KRYŃSKI, A., Animal Hygiene
KULISIEWICZ, J., Animal Breeding
NIEMIEC, J., Poultry Breeding
NIŻNIKOWSKI, R., Animal Breeding
REKLEWSKA, B., Animal Breeding
ROKICKI, E., Animal Hygiene
SOKÓZ, J., Animal Nutrition and Feed Management
SWIERCZEWSKA, E., Animal Breeding
WOJDA, R., Ichthyobiology and Fishery
ŻARSKI, T., Animal Hygiene

Faculty of Agricultural Economics (tel. (22) 843-11-73; fax (22) 847-11-73; e-mail ekr_dziekan@sggw.waw.pl):

ADAMOWICZ, M., Agricultural Economics
GÓRECKI, J., Worldwide Agriculture
HYBEL, J., Economy and Economic Policy
KLEPACKI, B., Farm Economics and Organization
LEWANDOWSKI, J., Farm Economics and Organization
PODSTAWKA, M., Agrarian Policy and Marketing
PRZYCHODZEN, Z., Agricultural Pedagogics
RUNOWSKI, H., Farm Economics and Organization
WIECZOREK, T., Agricultural Pedagogics, History of Education
ZIĘTARA, W., Farm Economics and Organization

Faculty of Food Technology (02-528 Warsaw, ul. Rakowiecka 26–30; tel. (22) 849-66-36; fax (22) 849-66-36; e-mail tzy_dziekan@sggw .waw.pl):

DRZAZGA, B., Fruit and Vegetable Technology
HABER, T. A., Technology of Cereals

KRYGIER, K., Fat and Oil Technology

LENART, A., Food Technology

LEWICKI, P., Food Technology

MROCZEK, J., Poultry and Meat Technology

PISULA, A., Meat Technology

SOBCZAK, E., Technology of Industrial Fermentation and Technical Microbiology

WZOREK, W., Wine, Juice and Beer Technology

ZMARLICKI, S., Milk Technology

Faculty of Human Nutrition and Consumer Sciences (tel. (22) 847-00-12; fax (22) 847-00-12; e-mail zcz_dziekan@sggw.waw.pl):

BRZOZOWSKA, A., Human Nutrition

GRONOWSKA-SENGER, A., Human Nutrition

KELLER, J. S., Physiology of Nutrition

KOŁOZYN-KRAJEWSKA, D., Gastronomic Technology

NERYNG, A., Human Nutrition

ROSZKOWSKI, W., Human Nutrition

ŚWIDERSKI, F., Human Nutrition

Faculty of Production Engineering (tel. (22) 847-23-42; fax (22) 847-23-42; e-mail wip_dziekan@sggw.waw.pl):

BOCHEŃSKI, C., Machine and Vehicle Management, Environmental Protection

CHOCHOWSKI, A., Electronics and Automation

KAMIŃSKI, E., Farm and Forestry Machinery

MAJEWSKI, Z., Farm Machinery, Field Operation Organization

SKROBACKI, A., Farm Machinery and Equipment

WASZKIEWICZ, Cz., Farm Machinery

WIĘSIK, J., Forestry Engineering

Akademia Rolnicza im. Augusta Cieszkowskiego (August Cieszkowski Agricultural University): ul. Wojska Polskiego 28, 60-637 Poznań; tel. (61) 847-03-34; fax (61) 848-71-46; f. 1951; faculties of horticulture, agronomy, animal breeding and biology, forestry, wood technology, food technology, land reclamation and environmental engineering; library: 641,000 vols; 782 teachers; 9,016 students; Rector Prof. Dr JERZY PUDEŁKO; publ. *Annals* and other irregular works.

Akademia Rolnicza im. Hugona Kołłątaja w Krakowie (Agricultural University of Cracow): al. Mickiewicza 21, 31-120 Cracow; tel. (12) 662-42-60; fax (12) 633-62-45; e-mail recint@ar.krakow.pl; internet www.ar.krakow.pl; f. 1890; State control; faculties of Agriculture and Economics, Food Technology, Animal Science, Environmental Engineering and Land Surveying, Forestry, Horticulture, Agricultural Engineering; language of instruction: Polish; library: 618,576 vols; 747 teachers; 12,646 students; Rector Prof. Dr JANUSZ ŻMIJA; publs *Zeszyty Naukowe* (in Polish or English), *Acta Scientiarum Polonorum* (irregular).

Akademia Rolnicza w Lublinie (University of Agriculture in Lublin): ul. Akademicka 13, 20-033 Lublin; tel. and fax (81) 533-35-49; f. 1955; faculties of veterinary science, agriculture, animal husbandry, agricultural engineering, horticulture; library: 336,000 vols; 640 teachers; 6,000 students; Rector Prof. Dr hab. MARIAN WESOŁOWSKI; publs *Annales UMCS, Sectio DD Medicina Veterinaria, Sectio E Agricultura, Sectio EE Zootechnica, Sectio EEE Horticulture, Excerpta Veterinaria Lublin* (in English).

Akademia Rolnicza w Szczecinie (Szczecin Agricultural University): ul. Janosika 8, 71-424 Szczecin; tel. (91) 422-35-15; fax (91) 423-24-17; e-mail rektor@ar.szczecin.pl; internet www.ar.szczecin.pl; f. 1954; faculties: environmental management and agriculture, economics and organization of food economy, biotechnology and animal science,

food sciences and fisheries; library: 307,572 vols; 463 teachers; 10,427 students; Rector Prof. Dr hab. JAN BRONISŁAW DAWIDOWSKI; publs *Acta Ichthyologica et Piscatoria* (in English), *Acta Scientiarum Polonorum-Piscaria* (Zootechnics, in English), *Advances in Agricultural Sciences* (in English), *Folia Universitatis Agriculturae Stetinensis* (Scientific Papers, in Polish, with English summary), *Rozprawy* (Treatises, in Polish, with English summary).

Akademia Rolnicza we Wrocławiu (Agricultural University of Wrocław): Norwida 25, 50-375 Wrocław; tel. (71) 320-51-01; fax (71) 320-54-04; e-mail rektor@ozi.ar.wroc.pl; internet www.ar.wroc.pl; f. 1951; faculties of biology and animal science, environmental engineering and geodesy, veterinary medicine, food science, agriculture; library: 180,000 vols; 750 teachers; 11,500 students; Rector Prof. Dr hab. MICHAŁ MAZURKIEWICZ; publs *Zeszyty Naukowe, Electronic Journal of Polish Agricultural Universities* (online), *Acta Scientiarum Polonorum* (online).

Akademia Techniczno-Rolnicza im. J. J. Śniadeckich w Bydgoszczy (University of Technology and Agriculture in Bydgoszcz): ul. Kordeckiego 20, 85-225 Bydgoszcz; tel. (52) 373-14-50; fax (52) 373-03-70; e-mail rektor@atr.bydgoszcz.pl; internet www.atr.bydgoszcz.pl; f. 1951; agriculture, animal husbandry, civil engineering, electronics and telecommunication, chemical technology and engineering, environmental engineering, management and marketing, mechanics and machine construction, technical physics; library: 239,706 vols, 51,243 periodicals; 656 teachers; 9,900 students; Rector Prof. JANUSZ SEMPRUCH; publs *Zeszyty Naukowe* (in Polish, with Russian and English summaries, irregular), *Image Processing and Communications* (in English, 4 a year).

ECONOMICS, SOCIAL SCIENCES

Akademia Ekonomiczna w Krakowie (Cracow University of Economics): Rakowicka 27, 31-510 Cracow; tel. (12) 293-57-00; fax (12) 293-50-17; e-mail akademia@ae.krakow.pl; f. 1925; faculties of economics, management and commodity science; library: 530,000 vols, 1,630 periodicals; 630 teachers; 20,000 students; Rector Prof. Dr hab. TADEUSZ GRABIŃSKI; publs *Zeszyty Naukowe* (Scientific Papers), *Argumenta Oeconomica Cracoviensia*.

Akademia Ekonomiczna im. Karola Adamieckiego w Katowicach (Karol Adamiecki University of Economics in Katowice): 1 Maja 50, 40-287 Katowice; tel. and fax (32) 59-99-72; e-mail wojtyla@ae.katowice.pl; f. 1937; faculties of management and economics; library: 330,000 vols; 446 teachers; 9,784 students; Rector Prof. JAN WOJTYŁA; publ. *Studia Ekonomiczne* (Economic Studies, irregular).

Akademia Ekonomiczna w Poznaniu (University of Economics in Poznań): al. Niepodległości 10, 60-967 Poznań; tel. (61) 856-90-00; fax (61) 866-89-24; internet www.ae.poznan.pl; f. 1926; faculties of management, economics and commodity science; library: 439,356 vols; 608 teachers; 16,860 students; Rector Prof. Dr WITOLD JUREK; publs *Prace Doktorskie Obronione v Akademii Ekonomicznej w Poznaniu* (annually), *Zeszyty Naukowe Seria I, Zeszyty Naukowe Seria II–Prace habilitacyjne, Podręczniki, The Poznan University Review, Debiuty Ekonomiczne*.

Akademia Ekonomiczna im. Oskara Langego we Wrocławiu (Wrocław University of Economics): Komandorska 118/120, 53-345 Wrocław; tel. (71) 368-01-00; fax (71)

367-27-78; e-mail www@ae.wroc.pl; internet www.ae.wroc.pl; f. 1947; faculties: engineering and economics, national economy, computer science and management, regional economy and tourism; library: 350,000 vols; 683 teachers; 18,644 students (16,144 undergraduate, 2,500 postgraduate); Rector Prof. zw. Dr hab. MARIAN NOGA; publs *Argumenta Oeconomica* (4 a year), *Prace Naukowe Akademii Ekonomicznej im O. Langego we Wrocławiu*.

Szkoła Główna Handlowa (Warsaw School of Economics): Al. Niepodległości 162, 02-554 Warsaw; tel. (22) 337-90-00; fax (22) 849-53-12; e-mail information@sgh.waw.pl; internet www.sgh.waw.pl; f. 1906; economics, European studies, spatial economy, public administration, quantitative methods and information systems, finance and banking, international relations, management and marketing; library: see Libraries and Archives; 900 teachers; 16,451 students (6,544 full-time, 6,131 extra-mural, 2,626 postgraduate, 1,150 PhD); Rector Prof. MAREK ROCKI; Exec. Dir Dr PIOTR WACHOWIAK; publs *Poland: International Economic Report* (annually), *National Economy* (monthly).

Wyższa Szkoła Przedsiębiorczości i Zarządzania im. Leona Koźmińskiego (Leon Kozminski Academy of Entrepreneurship and Management): ul. Jagiellońska 59, 03-301 Warsaw; tel. (22) 519-21-00; fax (22) 811-30-64; e-mail wspiz@wspiz.edu.pl; internet www.wspiz.edu.pl; f. 1993; MBA degree courses; library: 35,000 vols; 240 teachers; 5,170 students (3,400 undergraduate, 1,770 postgraduate); Rector Prof. Dr ANDRZEJ K. KOŹMIŃSKI.

MEDICINE

Akademia Medyczna w Białymstoku (Medical Academy of Białystok): Ul. Kilińskiego 1, 15-230 Białystok; tel. (85) 742-17-05; fax (85) 742-49-07; e-mail dzialnau@amb.ac.bialystok.pl; f. 1950; medical faculty and division of stomatology; pharmaceutical faculty and divisions of pharmacy and laboratory medicine; library: 235,000 vols; 660 teachers; 1,762 students; Rector Prof. Dr hab. ZBIGNIEW PUCHALSKI; publ. *Annals*.

Akademia Medyczna im. Ludwika Rydygiera w Bydgoszczy (Ludwik Rydygier Medical University in Bydgoszcz): ul. Jagiellońska 13, 85-067 Bydgoszcz; tel. (52) 585-33-00; fax (52) 585-33-08; e-mail rektor@amb.bydgoszcz.pl; internet www.amb.bydgoszcz.pl; f. 1984; library: 64,000 vols, 16,000 periodicals; 545 teachers; 3,714 students; Rector Prof. Dr hab. DANUTA MIŚCICKA ŚLIWKA

DEANS

Faculty of Health Sciences: Prof. Dr hab. ZBIGNIEW BARTUZI

Faculty of Medicine: Prof. Dr hab. GERARD DREWA

Faculty of Pharmacy: Prof. Dr hab. ALEKSANDER GUTSZE

Akademia Medyczna w Gdańsku (Medical University of Gdańsk): ul. Marii Skłodowskiej-Curie 3a, 80-210 Gdańsk; tel. (58) 349-10-00; fax (58) 349-12-00; e-mail rektor@amg.gda.pl; internet www.amg.gda.pl; f. 1945; faculties of medicine with sub-faculties of dentistry and nursing), health sciences, pharmacy and (jointly with Univ. of Gdańsk) biotechnology; library: 544,316 vols; 915 teachers; 2,700 students; Rector Prof. Dr WIESŁAW MAKAREWICZ; publ. *Annales Academiae Medicae Gedanensis* (annually).

Akademia Medyczna w Lublinie (Medical University in Lublin): ul. Aleje Racławickie 1, 20-059 Lublin; tel. (81) 532-00-61; fax (81) 532-89-03; e-mail eskulap@am.lublin.pl; internet eskulap.am.lublin.pl/~am; f. 1950; faculties of medicine, pharmacy and nursing; library: 250,000 vols; 1,180 teachers; 3,535 students; Rector Prof. Dr hab. MACIEJ LATALSKI.

Akademia Medyczna w Łodzi (Medical University of Łódź): Al. Kościuszki 4, 90-419 Łódź; tel. (42) 632-21-13; fax (42) 632-23-47; e-mail akmed@rkt.am.lodz.pl; f. 1945; faculty of medicine (Dean Prof. ANDRZEJ JOSS) with sub-faculties of stomatology, public health, and nursing; faculty of pharmacy (Dean Prof DARIA ORSZULAK-MICHALAK) with sub-faculty of laboratory medicine and college of cosmetology; library: 291,309 vols; 935 teachers; 3,058 students; Rector Prof. HENRYK STĘPIEŃ; publ. *Annales Academiae Medicae Lodziensis* (irregular).

Akademia Medyczna im. Karola Marcinkowskiego w Poznaniu (Karol Marcinkowski University of Medical Sciences in Poznań): ul. Fredry 10, 61-701 Poznań; tel. (61) 852-03-42; fax (61) 852-04-55; e-mail info@usoms.poznan.pl; internet www.usoms .poznan.pl; f. as University faculty 1920; University status 1950; faculties of medicine, pharmacy, health sciences (with nursing, physiotherapy, public health); sections of stomatology, clinical analysis; library: 328,773 vols; 1,013 teachers; 3,714 students; Rector Prof. Dr LEON DROBNIK; publs *Annual* (with supplements), *Annual Medical News*.

Akademia Medyczna w Warszawie (Medical University of Warsaw): 02-032 Warsaw, Filtrowa 30; tel. (22) 825-19-04; fax (22) 825-73-00; f. 1789; faculties of medicine, dentistry and pharmacy; library: 400,000 vols; 1,185 teachers; 3,200 students; Rector Prof. Dr ANDRZEJ GÓRSKI; publ. *Medycyna-dydaktyka-wychowanie* (Medicine-Didactics-Education, quarterly).

Akademia Medyczna we Wrocławiu (Wrocław Medical University): 50-367 Wrocław, ul. Pasteura 1; tel. (71) 784-10-01; fax (71) 784-01-09; e-mail rektor@am.wroc.pl; internet www.am.wroc.pl; f. 1950; faculties of medicine, dentistry, nursing and pharmacy, postgraduate training; library: 190,367 books, 76,322 papers; 884 teachers; 3,900 students; Rector Prof. Dr hab. LESZEK PARADOWSKI; publ. *Advances in Clinical and Experimental Medicine* (4 a year).

Centrum Medyczne Kształcenia Podyplomowego (Medical Centre for Postgraduate Education): ul. Marymoncka 99, 01-813 Warsaw; tel. (22) 834-68-47; fax (22) 834-04-70; f. 1970; faculties of basic sciences, clinical medicine, stomatology, pharmacy, family medicine; school of public health and social medicine; library: 46,000 vols; Dir Prof. Dr hab. med. JAN DOROSZEWSKI.

Collegium Medicum Uniwersytetu Jagiellońskiego (Jagiellonian University, Medical College): ul. Sw. Anny 12, 31-008 Cracow; tel. (12) 422-04-11; fax (12) 422-25-78; e-mail mabertma@cyf-kr.edu.pl; internet www.cm-uj.krakow.pl; f. 1364; faculties of Medicine (with Division of Dentistry), Pharmacy (with Division of Medical Analysis), Health Care (with Institute of Nursing and Institute of Public Health); Vice-Rector Prof. MAREK ZEMBALA; Representatives of the Rector Prof. JACEK S. DUBIEL (General Affairs), Prof. JANUSZ PACH (Clinical Affairs), Prof. WIESŁAW PAWLIK (Education and Foreign Co-operation), Prof. RYSZARD LAUTERBACH (Scientific Research and Postgraduate Training); library 210,000 vols; 1,200 staff, 100 full professors; 4,600 students; publs *Annales Collegii Medici Universitatis Jagiel-*

Ionicae Cracoviensis (annually), *The Methodical Review* (annually)

DEANS

Faculty of Health Care: Assoc. Prof. ANTONI CZUPRYNA
Faculty of Medicine: Prof. JERZY STACHURA
Faculty of Pharmacy: Prof. JOANNA SZYMURA-OLEKSIAK

Pomorska Akademia Medyczna w Szczecinie (Pomeranian Academy of Medicine in Szczecin): ul. Rybacka 1, 70-204 Szczecin; tel. (91) 433-63-03; fax (91) 433-56-60; e-mail pastupam@r.1pam.szczecin.pl; f. 1948; 1,094 teachers; 1,743 students; Rector Prof. Dr hab. KRZYSTOF MARLICZ; publs *Annales Academiae Medicae Stetinensis*, *Biuletyn* (monthly).

Śląska Akademia Medyczna w Katowicach (Medical University of Silesia in Katowice): ul. Warszawska 14, 40-006 Katowice; tel. (32) 251-49-64; fax (32) 208-35-61; e-mail rektor@slam.katowice.pl; internet www.slam .katowice.pl; f. 1948; medical, dental, pharmaceutical and nursing faculties; research in medicine and medical analysis, with special interest in cardiology, cardiac surgery, nephrology, gastroenterology, pulmonary diseases, environmental and occupational medicine; library: see Libraries; 1,517 teachers; 4,682 students; Rector Prof. Dr hab. TADEUSZ WILCZOK; publs *Annales Academiae Medicae Silesiensis* (annually), *Annales Societatis Doctrinae Studentium* (irregular), *Wiadomości Lekarskie* (monthly).

Szkoła Wyższa Psychologii Społecznej (School of Social Psychology): Chodakowska 19/31, 03-815 Warsaw; tel. (22) 517-96-00; fax (22) 517-99-21; e-mail centrum .informacji@swps.edu.pl; internet www.swps .edu.pl; f. 1996; library: 12,000 vols; 243 teachers; 8,314 students; Pres. Prof. ANDRZEJ ELIASZ; publs *Studia Psychologiczne* (joint publ., 2 a year), *Czasopismo Psychologiczne* (joint publ., 2 a year), *Psychologia Jakości Życia* (2 a year), *Kultura Popularna* (2 a year), *Charaktery* (joint publ., monthly).

TECHNOLOGY AND ENGINEERING

Akademia Morska w Gdyni (Gdynia Maritime University): ul. Morska 83, 81-225 Gdynia; tel. (58) 620-75-12; fax (58) 620-67-01; e-mail rector@am.gdynia.pl; internet www.am.gdynia.pl; f. 1920; mechanics, navigation, management and marketing, electrical engineering; library: 84,000 vols, 7,000 in special collections; 370 teachers; 8,500 students; Rector Prof. JÓZEF LISOWSKI; publs *Zeszyty Naukowe*, *Scientific Journal*, *Joint Proceedings*.

Politechnika Koszalińska (Technical University of Koszalin): Sniadeckich 2, 75-453 Koszalin; tel. (94) 342-60-20; fax (94) 342-03-74; e-mail kupk@tu.koszalin.pl; internet www.tu.koszalin.pl; f. 1968; depts of mechanical engineering, civil and environmental engineering, electronics, and economics and management; Institute of Design; library: 99,800 vols; 512 teachers; 15,767 students; Rector Prof. Dr hab. KRZYSZTOF WAWRYN; publs *Zeszyty Naukowe* (Research Review, annually), *Koszalińskie Studia i Materiały* (2 a year), *Na Temat* (6 a year).

Politechnika Opolska (Technical University of Opole): ul. Stanisława Mikołajczyka 5, 45-271 Opole; tel. (77) 400-60-00; fax (77) 400-60-50; e-mail rektor@po.opole.pl; internet www.po.opole.pl; f. 1966; academic year October to September (first semester); Rector Prof. Dr PIOTR WACH; Pro-Rector for Science Prof. JERZY SKUBIS; Pro-Rector for Students Dr hab. STANISŁAW WITCZAK; Pro-Rector for Organizational Affairs Dr ZYG-

MUNT KASPERSKI; Director of Administration LEON PRUCNAL; library: 370,000 vols; 429 teachers; 12,224 students; publs *Skrypty* (annually), *Studies and Monographs* (annually), *Wiadomości Uczelniane* (University Newsletter, monthly), *Zeszyty Naukowe* (Scientific Papers, annually)

DEANS

Faculty of Building Engineering: Prof. Dr TADEUSZ CHMIELEWSKI
Faculty of Electrical Engineering Automatic Control: Prof. Dr JÓZEF KĘDZIA
Faculty of Management and Production Engineering: Dr hab. AGATA ZAGÓROWSKA
Faculty of Mechanical Engineering: Prof. Dr LEON TRONIEWSKI
Faculty of Physical Education and Physiotherapy: Prof. Dr JÓZEF WOJNAR.

Attached Research Institute:

Institute of Mathematics, Physics and Chemistry: Luboszycka 5, 45 036 Opole; tel. (77) 453-84-47 ext. 171; fax (77) 453-84-47 ext. 172; e-mail imfiche@po.opole.pl.

Politechnika Radomska im. Kazimierza Pułaskiego (K. Pułaski Technical University in Radom): ul. Malczewskiego 29, 26-600 Radom; tel. (48) 361-70-10; fax (48) 361-70-12; e-mail rektor@kiux.man.radom.pl; internet www.man.radom.pl; f. 1950; faculties of mechanical engineering, transport, materials science and footwear production technology, economics, teacher training, labour, business and finance, banking, mathematics, physics, chemistry, plastics, cosmetic chemistry, art, food industry, fine art education, history, information technology, sociology, statistics, politics, geography, ecology, foodstuffs economy, law; library: 144,000 vols, 66,000 in special collections; 506 teachers; 12,500 students; Rector Prof. Dr hab. Inż. WINCENTY LOTKO; publs *Economics* (2 series), *Mechanics* (1 series), *Pedagogics* (2 series), *Prace Naukowe* (4 series, 1, 2, 3 or 4 of each a year), *Transport* (4 series).

Wyższa Szkoła Morska w Szczecinie (Maritime University Szczecin): Wały Chrobrego 1, 70-500 Szczecin; tel. (91) 34-42-26; fax (91) 33-81-23; f. 1969; faculties of navigation and marine engineering; 200 staff; library: 93,000 vols; 1,871 students; Rector Prof. Dr Capt. STANISŁAW GUCMA; publ. *Zeszyty Naukowe* (quarterly).

THEOLOGY

Chrześcijańska Akademia Teologiczna (Christian Theological Academy): ul. Miodowa 21, 00-246 Warsaw; tel. (22) 831-95-97; fax (22) 635-95-44; e-mail chat@chat.edu.pl; internet www.chat.edu.pl; f. 1954; library: 55,000 vols; 76 teachers; 955 students; Rector Archbishop Prof. Dr hab. JEREMIASZ JAN ANCHIMIUK; publ. *Rocznik Teologiczny* (2 a year).

Schools of Art and Music

Akademia Muzyczna im. Feliksa Nowowiejskiego w Bydgoszczy (F. Nowowiejski Academy of Music in Bydgoszcz): ul. Słowackiego 7, 85-008 Bydgoszcz; tel. (52) 321-11-42; fax (52) 321-23-50; e-mail sekr@ amuz.bydgoszcz.pl; internet www.amuz .bydgoszcz.pl; f. 1979; 100 teachers; 402 students; Rector Prof. JERZY KASZUBA.

Akademia Muzyczna im. Stanisława Moniuszki w Gdańsku (Stanisław Moniuszko Academy of Music in Gdańsk): ul. Łagiewniki 3, 80-847 Gdańsk; tel. (58) 301-77-15; fax (58) 301-43-65; f. 1947; faculties of composition and theory, music performance, music education; 165 teachers; 433 students; library: 92,000 vols; Rector Prof. Dr ANTONI POSZOWSKI; publs *Rocznik Informacyjny* (annually), *Zeszyty Naukowe* (irregular), *Prace Specjalne* (irregular), *Kultura Muzyczna Północynch Ziem Polski* (irregular), *Muzyka Pomorza* (irregular), *Skrypty i Podręczniki* (irregular), *Bibliografia* (irregular).

Akademia Muzyczna im. Karola Szymanowskiego w Katowicach (Academy of Music in Katowice): ul. Zacisze 3, 40-025 Katowice; tel. (32) 255-40-17; fax (32) 256-44-85; internet www.am.katowice.pl; f. 1929; faculties of composition, music theory and education, instrumental music, vocal music and theatrical art, jazz and popular music; library: 100,000 vols; special collection: music in Silesia; 170 teachers; 745 students; Rector Prof. JULIAN GEMBALSKI.

Akademia Muzyczna w Krakowie (Academy of Music in Cracow): ul. Sw. Tomasza 43, 31-027 Cracow; tel. (12) 422-32-50; fax (12) 422-23-43; e-mail zbrektor@cyf-kr.edu.pl; internet www.amuz.krakow.pl; f. 1888; faculties of composition, theory and conducting; instrumental performance; vocal technique; teacher training and choir conducting; also postgraduate studies; library: 47,000 vols; 365 teachers; 644 students; Rector Prof. STANISLAW KRAWCZYNISKI.

Akademia Muzyczna w Łodzi (Academy of Music in Łódź): Gdańska 32, 90-716 Łódź; tel. (42) 632-67-40; fax (42) 639-99-60; e-mail rektorat@cytra.amuz.lodz.pl; internet www .amuz.lodz.pl; f. 1945; composition, theory, eurhythmics, music education; instrumental and vocal technique, performance; library: 32,000 scores, 8,000 vols, 6,000 records and CDs, 300 periodicals; 208 teachers; 574 students; Rector Prof. ANNA WESOŁOWSKA-FIRLEJ.

Akademia Muzyczna im. Ignacego Jana Paderewskiego w Poznaniu (Academy of Music in Poznań): ul. Sw. Marcin 87, 61-808 Poznań; tel. (61) 53-67-55; fax (61) 53-66-76; f. 1920; faculties of composition, theory, conducting, instrumental technique, vocal technique, music teaching; Rector Prof. MIECZYSŁAW KOCZOROWSKI.

Akademia Muzyczna im. Fryderyka Chopina w Warszawie (Frederick Chopin Academy of Music in Warsaw): ul. Okólnik 2, 00-368 Warsaw; tel. (22) 827-72-41; fax (22) 827-83-10; e-mail info@chopin.edu.pl; internet www.chopin.edu.pl; f. 1810; 7 faculties: composition, conducting and theory of music, keyboard instruments, orchestral instruments, vocal performance, general music education, sound engineering; teacher training; library: 20,000 books and 71,000 scores; 330 teachers; 814 students; Rector Prof. RYSZARD ZIMAK; publs *Zeszyty Naukowe*, *Prace Biblioteki Głównej*.

Akademia Muzyczna im. Karola Lipińskiego we Wrocławiu (Academy of Music in Wrocław): pl. 1-go Maja 2, 50-043 Wrocław; tel. (71) 355-55-53; fax (71) 355-91-05; e-mail info@amuz.wroc.pl; internet www

.amuz.wroc.pl; f. 1948; departments of composition, conducting, music theory and music therapy, instrumental music, vocal music, music education; library: 113,015 vols; 185 teachers; 685 students; Rector Prof. GRZEGORZ KURZYŃSKI.

Akademia Sztuk Pięknych im. Jana Matejki w Krakowie (Academy of Fine Arts in Cracow): pl. Matejki 13, 31-157 Cracow; tel. (12) 422-24-50; fax (12) 422-65-66; e-mail zerektor@cyf-kr.edu.pl; internet www.asp.krakow.pl; f. 1818; faculties of painting, sculpture, conservation and restoration of works of art, graphic arts, industrial design, interior design; postgraduate studies in theatre, film and television stage design; European poster collection up to 1939; library: 86,500 vols, 21,000 graphic items, 7,500 posters; 244 teachers; 845 students; Rector Prof. STANISŁAW RODZIŃSKI; Library Dir JADWIGA WIELGUT-WALCZAK; publ. *Studia i materiały konserwatorskie* (annually).

Akademia Sztuk Pięknych w Gdańsku (Academy of Fine Arts in Gdańsk): Targ Węglowy 6, 80-836 Gdańsk; tel. (58) 301-44-40; fax (58) 301-22-00; e-mail office@asp.gda .pl; internet www.asp.gda.pl; f. 1945; faculties of painting, graphics, sculpture, architecture and industrial design; library: 10,450 vols; 130 teachers; 875 students; Rector Prof. TOMASZ BOGUSŁAWSKI.

Akademia Sztuk Pięknych w Poznaniu (Academy of Fine Arts in Poznań): Al. Marcinkowskiego 29, 60-967 Poznań; tel. (61) 855-25-21; fax (61) 852-80-91; e-mail office@asp.poznan.pl; internet www.asp .poznan.pl; f. 1919, state-controlled from 1921; faculties of painting, printmaking, sculpture, interior architecture and design, art education, multimedia communication; library: 60,000 vols; 189 full-time teachers; 1,264 full-time students; Rector Prof. WOJCIECH MÜLLER; Vice-Rectors Prof. ANDRZEJ WIELGOSZ, Prof. ASP MARCIN BERDYSZAK, Prof. PIOTR KURKA; Administration Dir WIESŁAWA SZOKALEWICZ

DEANS

Painting Faculty: Prof. ASP TOMASZ PSUJA
Printmaking Faculty: Prof. MIROSŁAW PAWŁOWSKI
Sculpture Faculty: Prof. ASP WOJCIECH KUJAWSKI
Interior Architecture and Design Faculty: Prof. ZDZISŁAW ŁOSIŃSKI
Art Education Faculty: Prof. ASP JACEK JAGIELSKI
Multimedia Communication Faculty: Prof. ASP ANDRZEJ SYSKA

Akademia Sztuk Pięknych w Warszawie (Academy of Fine Arts in Warsaw): Krakowskie Przedmieście 5, 00-068 Warsaw; tel. (22) 826-19-72; fax (22) 826-21-14; f. 1904 as Szkoła Sztuk Pięknych (School of Fine Arts), renamed 1927; departments of painting, sculpture, interior design, graphics, industrial design, conservation of works of art; special studies: tapestry, scenography;

library: 24,500 books, 5,578 vols of periodicals; 296 teachers; 1,020 students; Rector Prof. ADAM MYJAK; Library Dir Mgr IRENA KURNICKA-KĘPA; publs *Rocznik* (annually, in English and Russian), *Zeszyty Naukowe ASP* (Scientific Copy Books ASP).

Akademia Sztuk Pięknych we Wrocławiu (Academy of Fine Arts in Wrocław): Plac Polski 3/4, 50-156 Wrocław; tel. (71) 343-15-58; fax (71) 343-15-58; f. 1946; faculties of painting, sculpture, graphic arts, glass and ceramics design, interior architecture, industrial design; library: 14,000 vols; Rector KONRAD JARODZKI.

Akademia Teatralna im. Al. Zelwerowicza w Warszawie (A. Zelwerowicz Academy of Theatre in Warsaw): ul. Miodowa 22/24, 00-246 Warsaw; tel. (22) 831-69-25; fax (22) 831-91-01; e-mail rektorat@at.edu.pl; internet www.at.edu.pl; f. 1932; faculties of acting, directing, theatre studies, puppetry; library: 39,000 vols; 110 teachers; 360 students; Rector Prof. LECH SLIWONIK

DEANS

Acting Faculty: BOŻENA SUCHOCKA
Directing Faculty: WOJCIECH ADAMCZYK
Puppetry Faculty: WOJCIECH KOBRZYŃSKI
Theatre Studies Faculty: ANDRZEJ KRUCZYŃSKI

Państwowa Wyższa Szkoła Filmowa Telewizyjna i Teatralna im. Leona Schillera w Łodzi (National School of Film, Television and Theatre in Łódź): Targowa 61/63, 90-323 Łódź; tel. (42) 674-39-43; fax (42) 674-81-39; e-mail swzfilm@filmschool .lodz.pl; internet www.filmschool.lodz.pl; f. 1948; faculties of film and television direction, film and television camerawork, acting, production; courses in screen-writing, television production, photography; library: 40,000 vols; 118 teachers (96 full-time, 22 part-time); 825 students (incl. 600 extra-mural); Rector Prof. HENRYK KLUBA.

Akademia Sztuk Pięknych im. Władysława Strzemińskiego w Łodzi (Władysław Strzemiński Academy of Fine Arts in Łódź): Ul. Wojska Polskiego 121, 91-726 Łódź; tel. (42) 656-10-56; fax (42) 656-21-92; e-mail rektorat@asp.lodz.pl; internet www .asp.lodz.pl; f. 1945; textile faculty (depts of textile, fashion, painting, sculpture, drawing and composition); faculty of graphic art and painting (depts of graphic design, printmaking, painting, visual problems); faculty of visual education; faculty of industrial design; library: 30,000 vols; 240 teachers; 1,500 students; Rector Prof. GREG CHOJNACKI; Librarian KRYSTYNA LOREK.

Państwowa Wyższa Szkoła Teatralna im. Ludwika Solskiego w Krakowie (State Theatre Academy in Cracow): ul. Strasewskiego 21–22, 31-109 Cracow; tel. (12) 422-81-96; fax (12) 422-02-09; e-mail rektor@pwst.krakow.pl; f. 1945; faculties of acting and stage craft; puppet theatre section (Wrocław); Rector Prof. Dr hab. JACEK POPIEL.

PORTUGAL

The Higher Education System

Portugal was ruled by a monarchy from the 11th century until it was overthrown in 1910 and a republic was declared. The two oldest current universities, Universidade de Lisboa (founded 1288) and Universidad de Coimbra (founded 1290), date from the late 13th century and were the only such institutions until 1911, when Universidade do Porto was founded. Portugal was governed by a dictatorship during 1932–74, the later years of which saw the establishment of several prominent universities, but most institutions of higher education were founded after the restoration of civilian government in 1975. Higher education is divided into two strands, universities and other institutions (polytechnic institutes, higher schools, professional institutes, schools of art and music). Universities offer undergraduate and postgraduate degrees while other institutions offer three-year degrees and one- or two-year diploma programmes.

Universities became autonomous institutions under the University Autonomy Law (1988), which granted them the power to devise curricula, award degrees and define the equivalency of foreign awards. The Ministry of Science, Technology and Higher Education oversees state universities and other institutions of higher education. The Statute of the Private Higher Education Institution is the legislation governing private institutions, which are not allowed to offer degree-level programmes but instead offer five-year diploma courses.

Portugal participates in the Bologna Process to establish a European Higher Education Area, the first phase of which is to adopt a credit-based system of comparable degrees with two main cycles (undergraduate and graduate). In 2005/06 there were 367,934 students at 333 institutions of higher education (including the Azores and Madeira).

Portuguese students are admitted to higher education on the basis of two examinations, the prova de afericção (counter test) for secondary education and the provas específicas (specific examination) for the intended course of study. In 2006 a two-tier Bachelors (Licenciatura) and Masters (Mestrado) degree system was introduced in both universities and polytechnic institutes in accordance with the principles of the Bologna Process. The Bachelors degree is usually a three-year programme of study, although courses in some subjects may last longer, such as medicine and dentistry (six years). Under the new system some degrees are integrated courses of study culminating with award of the Masters degree, which is otherwise a separate postgraduate degree lasting up to two years. The Doctorate (Doutor) is the highest university-level degree and students may spend up to five or six years in study and research. The Ministry of Labour and Social Solidarity is responsible for vocational and technical education. The Decree Law 26/89 (1989) legislated the creation of professional schools (Escolas Profissionais) and primarily aimed at upper secondary-level students.

Regulatory and Representative Bodies

GOVERNMENT

Ministry of Culture: Palácio Nacional da Ajuda, 1349-021 Lisbon; tel. (21) 361-45-00; fax (21) 364-98-72; e-mail infocultura@min-cultura.pt; internet www.min-cultura.pt; Minister MARIA ISABEL DA SILVA PIRES DE LIMA.

Ministry of Education: Av. 5 de Outubro 107, 1069-018 Lisbon; tel. (21) 781-16-90; fax (21) 797-80-20; e-mail cirep@min-edu.pt; internet www.min-edu.pt; Minister MARIA DE LURDES REIS RODRIGUES.

Ministry of Labour and Social Solidarity: Praça de Londres 2, 1049-056 Lisbon; tel. (21) 844-11-00; fax (21) 842-41-08; e-mail gmtss@mtss.gov.pt; internet www.mtss.gov.pt; Minister JOSÉ ANTÓNIO FONSECA VIEIRA DA SILVA.

Ministry of Science, Technology and Higher Education: Palácio de Laranjeiras, Estrada de Laranjeiras 197–205, 1649-018 Lisbon; tel. (21) 723-10-00; fax (21) 727-14-57; e-mail mctes@mctes.gov.pt; internet www.mctes.pt; Minister JOSÉ MARIANO REBELO PIRES GAGO.

ACCREDITATION

ENIC/NARIC Portugal: NARIC Centre, Ministério da Educação, Direcção-Geral do Ensino Superior/Divisão de Reconhecimento e Intercâmbio, 137 Av. Duque d'Ávila – 4o, 1069-016 Lisbon; tel. (21) 312-60-00; fax (21) 312-60-41; e-mail manuela.paiva@desup.min-edu.pt; internet www.naricportugal.pt/naric_en; Head MANUELA PAIVA.

NATIONAL BODIES

Associação Portuguesa de Ensino Superior Privado (Portuguese Association of Private Higher-Education Institutions): Av. da República, 47 1o Dto, 1050-188 Lisbon; tel. (21) 799-48-60; fax (21) 799-48-69; e-mail contactos@apesp.pt; internet www.apesp.pt; works towards the full integration of non-state higher education in the Portuguese educational system; Pres. Prof. JACINTO JORGE CARVALHAL; Dir Prof. Dr VENTURA MELLO SAMPAYO.

Conselho Coordenador do Ensino Particular e Cooperativo (Co-ordinating Council for Private and Co-operative Education): Av. 5 de Outubro 89-2o, 1050-050 Lisbon; tel. (21) 797-29-10; fax (21) 795-67-93; e-mail ccepc@mail.telepac.pt; internet www.sg.min-edu.pt/ccepc; f. 1980; works for the integration of private and co-operative education into the nat. educational and training system; Pres. Dr ANTÓNIO DE ALMEIDA COSTA.

Conselho Coordenador dos Institutos Superiores Politécnicos (Co-ordinating Council for Polytechnic Institutes): Av. 5 de Outubro, 89-3o, 1050-050 Lisbon; tel. (21) 792-83-50; fax (21) 792-83-69; e-mail ccisp@ccisp.pt; internet www.ccisp.pt; f. 1979; representative body for public polytechnic instns with influence in all aspects of their operation; Pres. Prof. LUCIANO RODRIGUES DE ALMEIDA; Sec. Gen. Prof. MÁRIO SIMÕES BARATA.

Conselho Nacional de Avaliação do Ensino Superior (National Council for the Evaluation of Higher Education): Praça das Indústrias, Edifício Rosa, 2o andar , 1300-307 Lisbon; tel. (21) 361-61-40; fax (21) 361-61-49; e-mail cnaves@cnaves.pt; internet www.cnaves.pt; f. 1998; fosters and supervises evaluation procedures throughout the higher-education system; Pres. Prof. Dr ADRIANO JOSÉ ALVES MOREIRA; Sec. Gen Prof. Dr JOSÉ FONTES.

Conselho Nacional de Educação (National Council for Education): Rua Florbela Espanca, 1700-195 Lisbon; tel. (21) 793-52-45; fax (21) 797-90-93; e-mail cnedu@mail.telepac.pt; internet www.cnedu.pt; f. 1982; ind. advisory body on all aspects of the Portuguese educational system; 68 mems; Pres. Prof. Dr JÚLIO PEDROSA DE JESUS; publ. Pareceres e Recomendações (Opinions and Recommendations, annual).

Conselho de Reitores das Universidades Portuguesas (Council of Rectors of the Portuguese Universities): Quinta de S. Miguel dos Arcos, Rua Visconde de Porto Salvo 24, 2780-683 Paço d'Arcos; tel. (21) 361-17-91; fax (21) 361-17-95; e-mail crup@crup.pt; internet www.crup.pt; Pres. Prof. Dr JOSÉ DIAS LOPES DA SILVA; Sec.-Gen. Dr JOÃO CARLOS LOPES DE MELO BORGES.

Direcção Geral do Ensino Superior (Directorate-General for Higher Education): Av. Duque D'Ávila, 137, 1069-016 Lisbon; tel. (21) 312-60-00; fax (21) 312-60-01; e-mail dges@dges.mctes.pt; internet www.dges.mctes.pt; establishes and carries out nat. policy on higher education; Dir Gen. Prof. ANTÓNIO MORÃO DIAS.

Direcção-Geral de Inovação e de Desenvolvimento Curricular (DGIDC) (Department for Innovation and Curricular Development): Av. 24 de Julho 140, 1399-025 Lisbon; tel. (21) 393-45-00; fax (21) 393-46-95; e-mail dgidc@dgidc.min-edu.pt; internet www.dgidc.min-edu.pt; educational research, innovation in teaching practice, curriculum devt and evaluation, spec. education, and distance learning; library of 23,000 vols, 1,500 periodicals; Pres. MARIA EMÍLIA BREDEROLE SANTOS; publs Inovação (3 a year), Noesis (quarterly).

Learned Societies

GENERAL

Academia das Ciências de Lisboa (Lisbon Academy of Sciences): Rua da Academia das Ciências 19, 1o, 1249-122 Lisbon; tel. (21) 321-97-30; fax (21) 342-03-95; e-mail geral@acad-ciencias.pt; internet www.acad-ciencias.pt; f. 1779; attached to Min. of Science, Technology and Higher Education; Class of Sciences (Pres. Prof. Eng. E. R ARANTES E OLIVEIRA) and Class of Arts (Pres.. Prof. BRAZ TEIXEIRA); weekly lectures on science and arts topics; 56 mems; attached research institutes: see Research Institutes; library: see Libraries and Archives; Pres. Prof. Eng. EDUARDO ROMANO ARANTES E OLIVEIRA; Sec.-Gen. Prof. Dr ANTÓNIO DIAS FARINHA; publs *Memórias da Classe de Ciências*, *Memórias da Classe de Letras*.

Sociedade Científica da Universidade Católica Portuguesa (Scientific Society of the Portuguese Catholic University): Universidade Católica Portuguesa, Palma de Cima, 1649-023 Lisbon; tel. (21) 721-41-36; fax (21) 721-41-59; internet www.ucp.pt; f. 1980 to advance the intellectual, artistic, moral and spiritual forms of a Christian-inspired culture as a means to the fulfilment of man, and to promote research in a perspective of interdisciplinarity aiming at a synthesis of knowledge; 14 sections: arts, philosophy, law, history, economics, environmental sciences, literature and linguistics, education, theology, exact and natural sciences, applied sciences and engineering, health sciences and technology, social sciences and politics, communication and information sciences; 200 mems; Pres. Prof. Dr ANÍBAL PINTO DE CASTRO.

AGRICULTURE, FISHERIES AND VETERINARY SCIENCE

Sociedade Portuguesa de Ciências Veterinárias (Portuguese Society of Veterinary Science): Escola Superior de Medicina Veterinária, Rua Gomes Freire, 1169-014 Lisbon; tel. (21) 358-02-22; fax (21) 358-02-21; e-mail spcvet@spcvet.pt; internet www.spcvet.pt; f. 1902; organizes veterinary scientific congresses every three years and regular technical and scientific meetings; makes awards to veterinary students in Portugal; 685 mems; library of 3,210 vols, 43,500 periodicals; Pres. Dr LUÍS MANUEL DOS ANJOS FERREIRA; Gen. Sec. Dr ALEXANDRE LEITÃO; publ. *Revista Portuguesa de Ciências Veterinárias* (quarterly).

Affiliated societies:

Sociedade Portuguesa de Patologia Animal (Portuguese Society of Animal Pathology): Lisbon; Pres. Profa ANABELA GOUVEIA ANTUNES ALVES.

Sociedade Portuguesa de Reprodução Animal (Portuguese Society of Animal Reproduction): Lisbon; Pres. Dr ANTÓNIO MITTERMAYER ROCHA.

Sociedade Portuguesa Veterinária de Anatomia Comparativa (Portuguese Veterinary Society of Comparative Anatomy): Av. E.U.A. 96-RC-D, 1700 Lisbon; f. 1974; 47 mems; Pres. Dr FERNANDO BRILHANTE SIMÕES.

Sociedade Portuguesa Veterinária de Estudos Sociológicos (Portuguese Society of Sociological Veterinary Studies): Av. E.U.A. 96-RC-D, 1700 Lisbon; f. 1965; 39 mems; Pres. Profa Dra MARIA-ANA MARQUES.

BIBLIOGRAPHY, LIBRARY SCIENCE AND MUSEOLOGY

Associação Portuguesa de Bibliotecários, Arquivistas e Documentalistas (Portuguese Association of Librarians, Archivists and Documentalists): Rua Morais Soares, 43C-1° Dt°, 1900-341 Lisbon; tel. (21) 816-19-80; fax (21) 815-45-08; e-mail apbad@apbad.pt; internet www.apbad.pt; f. 1973; 1,500 mems; Pres. ANTÓNIO JOSÉ DE PINA FALCÃO; publ. *Cadernos BAD*.

ECONOMICS, LAW AND POLITICS

Ordem dos Economistas (Economists' Association): Rua da Estrela 8, 1200-669 Lisbon; tel. (21) 392-94-70; fax (21) 396-14-28; e-mail cdoc@ordemeconomistas.pt; internet www.ordemeconomistas.pt; f. 1976; 6,000 mems; Pres. ANTÓNIO SIMÕES LOPES; Sec. MARIA ISAURA DOS ANJOS LOPES TRINDADE CALHA, JOSÉ MARIA DA CUNHA RÊGO DE AMORIM; publs *Anuário do Economista* (annually), *Cadernos de Economia* (4 a year), *Carta Informativa* (4 a year).

EDUCATION

Instituto Açoriano de Cultura (Azorean Institute of Culture): Apdo 67, 9700-220 Angra do Heroísmo, Terceira, The Azores; tel. (295) 21-58-25; fax (295) 21-44-42; e-mail iac@iac-azores.org; internet www.iac-azores.org; f. 1956; Pres. Dr JORGE A. PAULUS BRUNO; Sec. Dr JOSÉ AVELINO ROCHA DOS SANTOS; publs *Atlântida* (annually), *Insula* (annually).

Instituto Camões (Camões Institute): Rua Rodrigues Sampaio 113, 1150-279 Lisbon; tel. (21) 310-91-00; fax (21) 314-39-87; e-mail icgeral@instituto-camoes.pt; internet www.instituto-camoes.pt; f. 1929 as Junta de Educação Nacional, present name 1992; attached to the Ministry of Foreign Affairs; promotes teaching of Portuguese language and culture abroad; awards grants to foreign students in Portugal; publs works on Portuguese language and culture; 250 mems; library of 4,500 vols; Pres. SIMONETTA LUZ AFONSO; publ. *Camões* (irregular).

Instituto de Coimbra (Coimbra Institute): Rua da Ilha, Coimbra; f. 1851; 150 mems; 13 hon., 156 correspondents in Portugal, 280 foreign corresponding; library of 21,000 vols; Pres. Prof. LUIS GUILHERME MENDONÇA DE ALBUQUERQUE; Sec. ARMANDO CARNEIDA SILVA; publ. *O Instituto* (scientific and literary).

FINE AND PERFORMING ARTS

Academia Nacional de Belas Artes (National Academy of Fine Arts): Largo da Academia Nacional de Belas Artes, 1200-005 Lisbon; tel. (21) 346-70-91; fax (21) 342-75-00; e-mail geral@academiabelasartes.pt; f. 1932; library of 25,000 vols, including some 16th c. work; 20 mems; Pres. Prof. Arq. AUGUSTO PEREIRA BRANDÃO; Sec. Arq. ANTÓNIO MARQUES MIGUEL; publs *Inventário Artístico de Portugal*, *Revista-Boletim de Belas Artes*.

Instituto Gregoriano de Lisboa (Lisbon Institute of Gregorian Studies): Av. 5 de Outubro 258, 1600-038 Lisbon; tel. (21) 793-00-04; fax (21) 795-04-15; e-mail secretaria@inst-gregoriano.rcts.pt; internet www.inst-gregoriano.rcts.pt; f. 1976; Dir Dra MARIA LUÍSA MACHADO NUNES DE OLIVEIRA; publs *Modus* (musicology), *Musica Lusitaniae Sacra*.

Sociedade Nacional de Belas Artes (National Society of Fine Arts): Palacio das Belas Artes, Rua Barata Salgueiro 36, 1250-044 Lisbon; tel. (21) 313-85-10; fax (21) 313-85-19; e-mail geral@snba.pt; internet www.snba.pt; f. 1901; exhibitions of painting, sculpture, drawing, etc.; organises courses in design, painting, drawing, visual education, sociology and history of art; 1,350 associates; library of 5,000 vols; Pres. FERNANDO DE AZEVEDO; publ. *Boletim Informativo* (2 a year).

HISTORY, GEOGRAPHY AND ARCHAEOLOGY

Academia Portuguesa da História (Portuguese Academy of History): Palácio dos Lilases, Alameda das Linhas de Torres 198–200, 1769-024 Lisbon; tel. (21) 754-90-60; fax (21) 759-13-82; e-mail acad.port.historia@sapo.pt; internet www.aph.com.pt; f. 1720; research on historical topics; providing historical information; 40 mems; 190 corresp. mems; library of 180,000 vols; Pres. Profa Dra MANUELA MENDONÇA; Sec.-Gen. Prof. Dr MIGUEL CORRÊA MONTEIRO; publs *Anais*, *Boletim*, *Documentos Medievais Portugueses*, *Fontes Narrativas da História Portuguesa*, *Itinerários Régios*, *Subsídios para a História Portuguesa*.

Associação dos Arqueólogos Portugueses (Association of Portuguese Archaeologists): Largo do Carmo 4, 1a Dto, 1200-092 Lisbon; tel. and fax (21) 346-04-73; internet www.museusportugal.org/AA; f. 1863; 640 mems; library of 10,500 vols; Pres. Dr JOSÉ MORAIS ARNAUD; Sec. Dr JACINTA BUGALHÃO; publ. *Arqueologia e História* (irregular).

Instituto Geográfico Português (Portuguese Geographical Institute): Rua Artilharia Um 107, 1099-052 Lisbon; tel. (21) 381-96-00; fax (21) 381-96-99; e-mail igeo@igeo.pt; internet www.igeo.pt; f. 2002 by merger of the Instituto Português de Cartografia e Cadastro and the Centro Nacional de Informação Geográfica; attached to the Ministry of the Environment, Territorial Planning and Regional Devt; is the country's national cartographic authority, provides official geographical information, fosters training and research; main brs in Ponta Delgada, Beja, Faro, Castelo Branco, Santarém, Funchal and Mirandela; Pres. Col Eng. Geógrafo ARMÉNIO DOS SANTOS CASTANHEIRA.

Instituto Histórico da Ilha Terceira (Terceira Historical Institute): Convento de São Francisco, Ladeira de São Francisco, 9700 Angra do Heroísmo, The Azores; tel. (295) 21-31-47; e-mail ihit@ihit.pt; internet www.ihit.pt; f. 1942; 20 mems; Pres. Dr FRANCISCO DOS REIS MADURO DIAS; Sec. Dr ANTÓNIO BENTO FRAGA BARCELOS; publ. *Boletim* (annually).

Instituto Português de Arqueologia (Portuguese Archaeological Institute): Av. da Índia 136, 1300-300 Lisbon; tel. (21) 361-65-00; fax (21) 361-65-59; e-mail ipa@ipa.min-cultura.pt; internet www.ipa.min-cultura.pt; Dir Dr FERNANDO REAL.

Real Instituto Arqueológico de Portugal (Royal Archaeological Institute of Portugal): Praça Rainha D. Filipa 4, 6°, Dto, 1600 Lisbon; tel. (21) 759-11-09; f. 1868; Pres. Dr JOÃO PAULO CAXARIA; Sec.-Gen. Dr JOSÉ ANTÓNIO FALCÃO; publs *Actas*, *Trabalhos*.

Real Sociedade Arqueológica Lusitana (Royal Lusitanian Archaeological Society): Hospital do Espírito Santo, Praça Conde do Bracial 3, 7540 Santiago do Cacém; tel. (269) 82-63-80; f. 1849; archaeological, historical and ethnological studies; has own museum, archives and library; 50 fellows; 150 mems; 97 corresp. mems; Pres. Dr JOSÉ ANTÓNIO FALCÃO; Gen.-Sec. Dr LÍLIA RIBEIRO DA SILVA TAVARES; publs *Anais*, *Boletim*, *Memórias*, *Repertorium Fontium Studium Artis Historiae Portugaliae Instaurandum*, *Trabalhos*.

Sociedade de Geografia de Lisboa (Lisbon Geographical Society): Rua das Portas de Santo Antão 100, 1150-269 Lisbon; tel. (21) 342-54-01; fax (21) 346-45-53; e-mail soc .geografia.lisboa@clix.pt; internet planeta .clix.pt/socgeografia-lisboa; f. 1875; library of 205,240 vols, 2,020 periodicals, 6,000 MSS, 155 theses/dissertations, 3 sheets printed music, 10,050 maps; 1,500 mems; Pres. Prof. JOÃO PEREIRA NETO; Sec.-Gen. Eng. EUGÉNIO TERRA DA MOTTA; publs *Boletim* (scientific and literary journal, annually), *Memórias* (irregular), *Relatório* (annually).

Sociedade Martins Sarmento (Martins Sarmento Society): Rua Paio Galvão, 4814-509 Guimarães; tel. (253) 41-40-11; fax (253) 41-59-69; e-mail casa.sarmento@csarmento .uminho.pt; internet www.csarmento .uminho.pt; f. 1881; archaeology and culture; 600 mems; library of 100,000 vols; Pres. ANTÓNIO AMARO DAS NEVES; publs *Boletim* (quarterly), *Revista de Guimarães* (annually).

LANGUAGE AND LITERATURE

Alliance Française: Rua Pinheiro Chagas 60, Apdo 2049, 3000-333 Coimbra; tel. (239) 70-12-52; fax (239) 40-48-50; e-mail dgafportugal@alliancefr.pt; internet www .alliancefr.pt; offers courses and exams in French language and culture and promotes cultural exchange with France; attached offices in the Algarve, Beja, Caldas da Rainha, Entroncamento, Évora, Guimarães, Leiria, Lisbon, Monção, Portalegre, Setúbal, Vila Real and Viseu; Dir of Operations ALAIN DIDIER.

Associação Portuguesa de Escritores (Portuguese Writers' Association): Rua de S. Domingos à Lapa 17, 1200-832 Lisbon; tel. (21) 397-18-99; fax (21) 397-23-41; e-mail a.p .escritores@oninet.pt; f. 1973; protects the interests of Portuguese writers, promotes Portuguese literature abroad, supports cultural activities, conferences, debates, confers several literary prizes, etc; over 600 mems; library of 7,500 vols; Pres. Dr JOSÉ MANUEL MENDES.

British Council: Rua Luís Fernandes, 1–3, 1249-062 Lisbon; tel. (21) 3214500; fax (21) 3476151; e-mail lisbon.enquiries@pt .britishcouncil.org; internet www .britishcouncil.org/portugal; teaching centre; offers courses and exams in English language and British culture and promotes cultural exchange with the UK; attached teaching centres in Almada, Alverca, Cascais, Coimbra, Foz do Douro, Miraflores, Parede and Porto; Dir ROSEMARY HILHORST.

Goethe-Institut: Campo dos Mártires da Pátria 37, 1169-016 Lisbon; tel. (21) 882-45-10; fax (21) 885-00-03; e-mail info@lissabon .goethe.org; internet www.goethe.de/ lissabon; offers courses and exams in German language and culture and promotes cultural exchange with Germany; attached centre in Porto; library of 14,000 vols, 50 periodicals; Dir RONALD GRÄTZ.

Instituto Cervantes: Rua Santa Marta 43 F r/c, 1169-119 Lisbon; tel. (21) 310-50-20; fax (21) 315-22-99; e-mail cenlis@cervantes .es; internet lisboa.cervantes.es; offers courses and exams in Spanish language and culture and promotes cultural exchange with Spain and Spanish-speaking Latin and Central America; library of 20,000 vols; Dir RAMIRO ANDRÉS FONTE CRESPO.

Sociedade Portuguesa de Autores (Portuguese Society of Authors): Av. Duque de Loulé 31, 1069-153 Lisbon; tel. (21) 359-44-00; fax (21) 353-02-57; e-mail geral@ spautores.pt; internet www.spautores.pt; f. 1925; copyright protection and authors' rights; cultural activities; 500 full, 18,000 assoc. mems; library of 20,000 vols; Pres. MANUEL FREIRE; publ. *Autores* (quarterly).

MEDICINE

Ordem dos Farmacêuticos (Pharmaceutical Society): Rua da Sociedade Farmacêutica 18, 1169-075 Lisbon; tel. (21) 319-13-70; fax (21) 319-13-99; e-mail dirnacional@ ordemfarmaceuticos.pt; internet www .ordemfarmaceuticos.pt; f. 1835; 9,950 mems; library of 5,040 vols; famous collection of Portuguese pharmacopoeias; unique MS *Historia Pharmaceutica das Plantas Exóticas* by Frei João de Jesus Maria, with permit to print from the Holy Office; Pres. Prof. JOSÉ A. ARANDA DA SILVA; publ. *Revista do Ordem dos Farmacêuticos* (6 a year).

Ordem dos Médicos (Medical Association): Av. Almirante Gago Coutinho 151, 1749-084 Lisbon; tel. (21) 842-71-00; fax (21) 842-71-99; e-mail ordemmedicos@omsul.com; internet www.ordemdosmedicos.pt; f. 1938; 24,851 mems; Pres. PEDRO MANUEL MENDES HENRIQUES NUNES; publs *Acta Médica Portuguesa* (6 a year), *Revista* (monthly).

Sociedade Anatómica Portuguesa (Portuguese Anatomical Society): Lab. de Anatomia Normal, Faculdade de Medicina de Coimbra, 3049 Coimbra Codex; f. 1930; 184 mems; Pres. Prof. Dr ANTÓNIO CARLOS MIGUÉIS.

NATURAL SCIENCES
General

Serviço de Informação e Documentação (Information and Documentation Service): Av. D. Carlos I 126, 7°, 1249-074 Lisbon; tel. (21) 392-44-41; fax (21) 395-72-84; e-mail sid@fct.mctes.pt; internet www.fct.mces.pt; f. 1936; national centre of scientific and technical information; attached to Fundação para a Ciência e a Tecnologia; 3,000 Portuguese, 5,000 foreign books, 350 periodicals; Dir GABRIELA LOPES DA SILVA.

Biological Sciences

Sociedade Broteriana (Botanical Society): Instituto Botânico, Universidade de Coimbra, 3049 Coimbra; tel. (239) 82-28-97; fax (239) 82-07-80; e-mail socbrot@ci.uc.pt; f. 1880; 300 mems; library of 122,000 vols; Chair. Prof. JOSÉ F. M. MESQUITA; publs *Anuário*, *Boletim* (annually), *Memórias* (irregular).

Sociedade Portuguesa de Ciências Naturais (Portuguese Natural Science Society): Faculdade de Ciências, Campo Grande, 1749-016 Lisbon; tel. (21) 750-00-00 ext. 22310; fax (21) 750-00-09; e-mail spcn@fc.ul.pt; internet spcn.fc.ul.pt; f. 1907; 938 mems; library of 30,000 vols; Pres. HUMBERTO ROSA; publs *Boletim*, *Natura*, *Naturalia*.

Mathematical Sciences

Instituto Nacional de Estatística (National Statistical Institute): Av. António José de Almeida, 1000-043 Lisbon; tel. (21) 842-61-00; fax (21) 842-63-80; e-mail ine@ine .pt; internet www.ine.pt; f. 1935; 750 mems; library of 12,000 books, 2,500 periodicals; Pres. Dra ALDA CARVALHO; publs *Statistical Review*, *Statistical Yearbook* (in English and Portuguese).

Physical Sciences

Sociedade Geológica de Portugal (Geological Society): Departamento de Ciências da Terra, Universidade Nova de Lisboa, Quinta da Torre, 2829-516 Caparica; tel. and fax (21) 294-83-49; e-mail rbr@fct.unl.pt; f. 1940; 600 mems; library of 1,000 vols; Pres. Prof. Dr ROGÉRIO ROCHA; Sec. Dra FILOMENA DINIZ; publs *Boletim*, *Maleo*.

Sociedade Portuguesa de Química (Portuguese Chemical Society): Av. da República 37-4°, 1050-187 Lisbon; tel. (21) 793-46-37; fax (21) 795-23-49; e-mail sede@spq.pt; internet www.spq.pt; 2,800 mems; Pres. Prof. JOSÉ GASPAR MARTINHO; Gen. Sec. Prof. FERNANDO PINA; publ. *Química* (quarterly).

RELIGION, SOCIOLOGY AND ANTHROPOLOGY

Academia Internacional da Cultura Portuguesa (International Academy of Portuguese Culture): Rua das Portas de Santo Antão 110, 1150-269 Lisbon; tel. (21) 342-10-81; fax (21) 342-10-33; e-mail aicportuguesa@ clix.pt; f. 1965; seeks to promote research into the culture of Portuguese communities living outside the national territory; 50 mems; Pres. Prof. Dr ADRIANO MOREIRA; publ. *Boletim*.

Sociedade Portuguesa de Antropologia e Etnologia (Portuguese Anthropological and Ethnological Society): Faculdade de Ciências, Univ. do Porto, Praça Gomes Teixeira, 4099-002 Porto; tel. (22) 208-71-49; fax (22) 202-69-03; e-mail vojsoj@sapo.pt; internet spae.no.sapo.pt; f. 1918; 300 mems; library of 10,000 vols; Pres. Prof. VÍTOR OLIVEIRA JORGE; Sec. PAULO CASTRO SEIXAS; publ. *Trabalhos de Antropologia e Etnologia* (2 a year).

TECHNOLOGY

Ordem dos Engenheiros (Portuguese Association of Engineers): Av. Sidónio Pais 4E, 1050-212 Lisbon; tel. (21) 313-26-00; fax (21) 352-46-32; e-mail secretariageral@cdn .ordeng.pt; internet www.ordemengenheiros .pt; f. 1936; 28,000 mems; library of 23,000 vols, 500 periodical titles; Pres. Eng. FERNANDO FERREIRA SANTO; publ. *Ingenium* (review, monthly).

Research Institutes
GENERAL

Fundação para a Ciência e a Tecnologia (Science and Technology Foundation): Av. D. Carlos I 126, 1249-074 Lisbon; tel. (21) 392-43-00; fax (21) 390-74-81; e-mail presidencia@fct.mctes.pt; internet www.fct .mces.pt; f. 1997; attached to the Ministry of Science, Technology and Higher Education; evaluates, finances and promotes institutions, programmes and projects in the fields of science and technology; also concerned with the education and qualifications in human resources; library of 15,500 vols; Pres. Prof. JOÃO JOSÉ DOS SANTOS SENTIEIRO.

Instituto de Altos Estudos (Institute for Advanced Studies): c/o Academia das Ciências de Lisboa, Rua da Academia das Ciências 19, 1249-122 Lisbon; tel. (21) 321-97-30; fax (21) 342-03-95; e-mail geral@ acad-ciencias.pt; internet www.acad-ciencias .pt; f. 1931; attached to Lisbon Acad. of Sciences; Pres. Prof. MANUEL JACINTO NUNES.

Instituto de Investigação Científica Tropical (Tropical Science Research Institute): Rua da Junqueira 86–1°, 1300-344 Lisbon; tel. (21) 361-63-40; fax (21) 363-14-60; e-mail iict@iict.pt; internet www.iict.pt; f. 1883; Documentation and Information Centre (Palácio dos Condes da Calheta, Rua General João de Almeida 15, 1300-266 Lisbon; tel. (21) 361-97-30; fax (21) 361-97-39; e-mail cdi@iict.pt); Garden and Museum of Tropical Agriculture: see Museums and Art Galleries; Overseas Historical Archives (Calçada da Boa-Hora 30, 1300-095 Lisbon; tel. (21) 361-63-30; fax (21) 361-63-39; email ahu@iict.pt);

Pres. Prof. Dr JORGE BRAGA DE MACEDO; publs *Boletim da Filmoteca Ultramarina Portuguesa, Comunicações do IICT* (series: Agrarian Sciences; Biological Sciences; Ethnological and Ethnomuseological Sciences; Geographical Sciences; Earth Sciences), *Estudos de Antropologia Cultural e Social, Estudos de Ciências Políticas e Sociais, Estudos de História e Cartografia Antiga – Memórias, Estudos e Ensaios e Documentos, Index Seminum, Leba* (quaternary, prehistory, archaeology), *Memórias, Revista Internacional de Estudos Africanos, Separatas do Centro de Estudos de História e Cartografia Antiga, Studia.*

Research centres:

Centro de Ambiente e Ciências da Terra do Instituto de Investigação Científica Tropical (Environment and Earth Sciences Centre): Al. D. Afonso Henriques 41, 4° Dt°, 1000-123 Lisbon; tel. (21) 847-64-05; fax (21) 840-79-65; e-mail cgeol@iict.pt; internet www.iict.pt.

Centro de Antropobiologia do Instituto de Investigação Científica Tropical (Anthropobiology Centre): Av. Óscar Monteiro Torres 34–1° Esq°, 1000-219 Lisbon; tel. (21) 796-66-70; e-mail cantp@iict.pt; internet www.iict.pt; f. 1954; Dir (vacant).

Centro de Antropologia Cultural e Social do Instituto de Investigação Científica Tropical (Cultural and Social Anthropology Centre): Av. Ilha da Madeira, Edifício Museu, 1400-203 Lisbon; tel. (21) 301-52-64; fax (21) 301-19-45; e-mail cacst@iict.pt; internet www.iict.pt; f. 1962; Dir Dra CLARA SARAIVA.

Centro de Botânica do Instituto de Investigação Científica Tropical (Botany Centre): Travessa Conde da Ribeira 9, 1300-142 Lisbon; tel. (21) 361-63-40; e-mail cbotn@iict.pt; internet www.iict.pt; f. 1948; Dir Dra MARIA ADÉLIA DINIZ.

Centro de Cartografia do Instituto de Investigação Científica Tropical (Cartography Centre): Travessa Conde da Ribeira 7–9, 1300-007 Lisbon; tel. (21) 361-63-40; fax (21) 363-14-60; e-mail ccart@iict.pt; internet www.iict.pt; f. 1946; Dir Prof. Eng. ARMANDO SEPÚLVEDA.

Centro de Cristalografia e Mineralogia do Instituto de Investigação Científica Tropical (Crystallography and Mineralogy Centre): Alameda D. Afonso Henriques 41–4° Esq°, 1000-123 Lisbon; tel. (21) 847-65-96; fax (21) 840-79-65; e-mail ccris@iict.pt; internet www.iict.pt; f. 1957; Dir Prof. Dra MARIA ONDINA FIGUEIREDO.

Centro de Desenvolvimento Global do Instituto de Investigação Científica Tropical (Global Development Centre): Rua João de Barros 27, 1300-319 Lisbon; tel. (21) 364-27-32; e-mail cfotg@iict.pt; internet www.iict.pt.

Centro de Detecção Remota para o Desenvolvimento do Instituto de Investigação Científica Tropical (Remote Sensing for Development Centre): Travessa Conde da Ribeira 9, 1300-142 Lisbon; tel. (21) 361-63-40; fax (21) 364-00-46; e-mail ccart@iict.pt; internet www.iict.pt.

Centro de Ecofisiologia, Bioquímica e Biotecnologia Florestal do Instituto de Investigação Científica Tropical (Ecophysiology, Biochemistry and Forest Biotechnology Centre): Av. da República, Quinta do Marquês, 2780-155 Oeiras; tel. (21) 454-46-82; fax (21) 454-46-89; e-mail cochichor@mail.telepac.pt; internet www.iict.pt.

Centro de Estudos Africanos e Asiáticos do Instituto de Investigação Científica Tropical (African and Asian Studies Centre): Rua da Junqueira 30–1°, 1349-007 Lisbon; tel. (21) 362-26-21; fax (21) 362-26-26; e-mail cestaa@iict.pt; internet www.iict.pt; f. 1983; Dir Prof. Dra JILL REANEY DIAS.

Centro de Estudos de Fitossanidade do Armazenamento do Instituto de Investigação Científica Tropical (Research Centre on Plant Health during Storage): Travessa Conde da Ribeira 9, 1300-142 Lisbon; tel. (21) 361-63-40; e-mail cefa@iict.pt; internet www.iict.pt; f. 1955; Dir Prof. Dr ANTÓNIO MARQUES MEXIA.

Centro de Estudos de História e Cartografia Antiga do Instituto de Investigação Científica Tropical (History and Early Cartography Research Centre): Rua da Junqueira 30 r/c, 1349-007 Lisbon; tel. (21) 360-05-82; e-mail cesth@iict.pt; internet www.iict.pt; f. 1961; history of Portuguese expansion overseas, African history; library of 9,200 vols, 430 periodicals; Dir Dra MARIA EMÍLIA MADEIRA SANTOS; publs *Boletim da Filmoteca Ultramarina Portuguesa* (irregular), *Studia* (2 a year).

Centro de Estudos de Pedologia do Instituto de Investigação Científica Tropical (Pedology Studies Centre): Tapada da Ajuda, 1349-018 Lisbon; tel. (21) 365-31-00; e-mail cestp@iict.pt; internet www.iict.pt; f. 1960; Dir Prof. Eng. RUI PINTO RICARDO.

Centro de Estudos de Produção e Tecnologia Agrícolas do Instituto de Investigação Científica Tropical (Agricultural Technology and Production Studies Centre): Tapada da Ajuda, Edifício das Agro-Indústria e Agronomia Tropical, 1349-018 Lisbon; tel. (21) 361-72-40; e-mail cestt@iict.pt; internet www.iict.pt; f. 1960; Dir (vacant).

Centro de Etnologia Ultramarina do Instituto de Investigação Científica Tropical (Overseas Ethnology Centre): Av. Ilha da Madeira, 1400-203 Lisbon; tel. (21) 301-21-18; fax (21) 301-19-45; e-mail cetno@iict.pt; internet www.iict.pt; f. 1962; Dir Dra MARGARIDA LIMA DE FARIA.

Centro de Florestas e Produtos Florestais do Instituto de Investigação Científica Tropical (Forests and Forest Products Centre): Tapada da Ajuda, 1349-018 Lisbon; tel. (21) 363-46-62; fax (21) 364-50-00; e-mail cestf@iict.pt; internet www.iict.pt; f. 1948; Dir Prof. Dra HELENA PEREIRA.

Centro de Fotogrametria do Instituto de Investigação Científica Tropical (Photogrammetry Centre): Rua João de Barros 27, 1300-319 Lisbon; tel. (21) 364-27-32; e-mail cfotg@iict.pt; internet www.iict.pt; f. 1983; Dir Prof. Dr ARMANDO SEPÚLVEDA.

Centro de Geodesia do Instituto de Investigação Científica Tropical (Geodesy Centre): Rua da Junqueira 534, 1300-341 Lisbon; tel. (21) 363-18-62; fax (21) 364-19-47; e-mail cgeod@iict.pt; internet www.iict.pt; f. 1983; Dir Eng. JOSÉ FRIAS DE BARROS.

Centro de Geografia do Instituto de Investigação Científica Tropical (Geography Centre): Rua Ricardo Espírito Santo 7 c/v Esq°, 1200-790 Lisbon; tel. and fax (21) 395-67-72; e-mail cgeog@iict.pt; internet www.iict.pt; f. 1983; Dir Prof. Dr ILÍDIO DO AMARAL.

Centro de Geologia do Instituto de Investigação Científica Tropical (Geol-

ogy Centre): Alameda D. Afonso Henriques 41–4° Dt°, 1000-123 Lisbon; tel. (21) 847-64-05; fax (21) 840-79-65; e-mail cgeol@iict.pt; internet www.iict.pt; f. 1958; Dir Prof. Dr RICARDO AUGUSTO QUADRADO.

Centro de Investigação das Ferrugens do Cafeeiro do Instituto de Investigação Científica Tropical (Coffee Rusts Research Centre): Av. da República, Quinta do Marquês, 2780-155 Oeiras; tel. (21) 454-46-80; fax (21) 454-46-89; e-mail cferc@iict.pt; internet www.iict.pt; f. 1955; Dir Dr CARLOS RODRIGUES JÚNIOR.

Centro de Pré-História e Arqueologia do Instituto de Investigação Científica Tropical (Prehistory and Archaeology Centre): Travessa Conde da Ribeira 7, 1300-142 Lisbon; tel. (21) 361-63-40; e-mail cphst@iict.pt; internet www.iict.pt; f. 1954; Dir Prof. Dr A. TEODORO DE MATOS.

Centro de Sociedades e Culturas Tropicais do Instituto de Investigação Científica Tropical (Societies and Tropical Cultures Centre): R. da Junqueira 30, 1°, 1349-007 Lisbon; tel. (21) 360-05-81; fax (21) 360-05-87; e-mail cestaa@iict.pt; internet www.iict.pt.

Centro de Sócio-Economia do Instituto de Investigação Científica Tropical (Socio-Economics Centre): Travessa Conde da Ponte 9–1°, 1300-141 Lisbon; tel. (21) 363-57-48; fax (21) 363-96-03; e-mail csoec@iict.pt; internet www.iict.pt; f. 1956; Dir Prof. Dr JORGE BRAGA DE MACEDO.

Centro de Veterinária e Zootecnia do Instituto de Investigação Científica Tropical (Veterinary and Zootechnics Centre): Rua Prof. Cid dos Santos, Alto da Ajuda, 1300-477 Lisbon; tel. (21) 365-28-00; fax (21) 365-28-15; e-mail cvetz@iict.pt; internet www.iict.pt; f. 1983; Dir Dr LUÍS ALFARO CARDOSO.

Centro de Zoologia do Instituto de Investigação Científica Tropical (Zoology Centre): Rua da Junqueira 14, 1300-343 Lisbon; tel. (21) 363-70-55; e-mail czool@iict.pt; internet www.iict.pt; f. 1948; Dir Dr LUÍS F. MENDES.

AGRICULTURE, FISHERIES AND VETERINARY SCIENCE

Estação Agronómica Nacional (National Agronomical Research Station): Av. República, Quinta do Marquês, Nova Oeiras, 2784-505 Oeiras; tel. (21) 440-35-00; fax (21) 441-60-11; e-mail dir.ean@iniap.min-agricultura.pt; internet www.iniap.min-agricultura.pt/default.aspx?uni=9; f. 1937; comprises departments of agronomy, entomology, experimental statistics, genetics and plant breeding, pedology, phytopathology, plant physiology, microbiology, systematic botany and plant sociology; library of 172,000 vols; Dir ANTÓNIO M. MARQUES MEXIA; Librarian NAIR SÁ; publs *Agronomia Lusitana, Index Seminum.*

Estação Florestal Nacional (National Forestry Research Station): Quinta do Marquês, Oeiras; tel. (21) 446-37-00; fax (21) 446-37-01; e-mail silva.lusitana@efn.com.pt; f. 1979; forestry research unit of the Instituto Nacional de Investigação Agrária e das Pescas; 4 research departments; 105 staff; library of 3,500 vols; Dir Dr RUI OLIVEIRA E SILVA; publ. *Silva Lusitana.*

HISTORY, GEOGRAPHY AND ARCHAEOLOGY

Centro de Estudos do Baixo Alentejo (Centre for Lower Alentejo Studies): c/o Real Sociedade Arqueológica Lusitana, Hospital do Espírito Santo, Praça Conde do Bracial 3,

7540 Santiago do Cacém; tel. (269) 82-63-80; f. 1944; Dir The Pres. of the Royal Lusitanian Archaeological Soc. (*q.v.*); Sec.-Gen. The Gen.-Sec. of the Royal Lusitanian Archaeological Society (*q.v.*).

Centro de Estudos Geográficos (Centre for Geographical Studies): Faculdade de Letras, Alameda da Universidade, 1600-214 Lisbon Codex; tel. (21) 794-02-18; fax (21) 793-86-90; e-mail ceg@mail.telepac.pt; internet www.ceg.ul.pt; f. 1943; funded by the Fundação para a Ciência e Tecnologia (*q.v.*); research into geoecology, physical and environmental geography, and human and regional geography; library of 35,000 vols; Dir Prof. Dr DIOGO JOSÉ BROCHADO DE ABREU; publ. *Finisterra* (2 a year).

Centro de Estudos Históricos e Etnológicos (Centre for Historical and Ethnological Studies): Serra do Balas, Areias, 2240 Ferreira do Zêzere; tel. (249) 39-14-08; f. 1983; Pres. Dr JORGE M. RODRIGUES FERREIRA; Sec. ANABELA BENTO; publs *Boletim, Série Arqueológica*.

LANGUAGE AND LITERATURE

Instituto de Lexicologia e Lexicografia da Língua Portuguesa (Institute of Lexicology and Lexicography of the Portuguese Language): c/o Academia das Ciências de Lisboa, Rua da Academia das Ciências 19, 1249-122 Lisbon; tel. (21) 321-97-30; fax (21) 342-03-95; e-mail geral@acad-ciencias.pt; internet www.acad-ciencias.pt; f. 1987; attached to Lisbon Acad. of Sciences; Pres. Prof. Dr JOÃO MALACA CASTELEIRO.

Instituto Português da Sociedade Científica de Goerres (Portuguese Institute of the Goerres Research Society): c/o Universidade Catolica Portuguesa, Palma de Cima, 1649-023 Lisbon; tel. (21) 721-40-00 ext. 1115; fax (21) 726-05-46; e-mail mrato@reitoria.ucp.pt; internet www.libri.ucp.pt/biblioteca.htm; f. 1962; research into the language and literature of the 17th–18th c. in Portugal and Brazil; library of 9,000 vols; publ. *Portugiesische Forschungen*.

MEDICINE

Centro de Estudos de Vectores e Doenças Infecciosas do Instituto Nacional de Saúde (Centre for Research into Vectors and Infectious Diseases of the National Institute of Health): Av. da Liberdade 5, 2965-575 Águas de Moura; tel. (21) 750-81-22; fax (21) 750-81-21; e-mail cevdi@insa.min-saude.pt; internet www.insarj.pt; f. 1938; study of arboviruses Lyme disease, rickettsias and rickettsioses, rodent-borne diseases and haemorrhagic fevers; library of 3,400 vols; Dir Prof. ARMINDO R. FILIPE.

Instituto de Medicina Molecular (Institute of Molecular Medicine): Faculdade de Medicina da Universidade de Lisboa, Av. Professor Egas Moniz, 1649-028 Lisbon; tel. (21) 799-94-11; fax (21) 799-94-12; e-mail imm@fm.ul.pt; internet www.imm.ul.pt; f. 2001; attached to Ministry of Science, Technology and Higher Education; research into cell and development biology, immunology and infectious diseases, neurosciences and oncology; Exec. Co-ordinator Profa Dra M. CARMO-FONSECA.

NATURAL SCIENCES
General

Instituto de Investigação Científica 'Bento da Rocha Cabral' (Institute of Scientific Research): Calçada de Bento da Rocha Cabral 14, 1250-047 Lisbon; e-mail shfc@ircabral.org; internet www.ircabral.org/shfc/node6.html; f. 1922; biochemical research, histology and embryology, bacter-

iology, physiology, history and philosophy of science; Dir J. MIRABEAU CRUZ; publs *Relatórios, Travaux de Laboratoire*.

Sociedade Afonso Chaves (Afonso Chaves Society): Edifício do Museu Carlos Machado, Rua de Santo André, Apdo 258, 9500-903 Ponta Delgada Codex, The Azores; tel. (296) 28-38-14; e-mail frias@notes.uac.pt; f. 1932; 15 Fellows, 290 mems; main interests of the Society are ethnography, natural history, geophysics and geology of the Azores; Pres. Prof. ANTÓNIO MANUEL DE FRIAS MARTINS; Sec. Dr CARLOS MEDEIROS; publ. *Açoreana* (annually).

Biological Sciences

Instituto de Investigação das Pescas e do Mar (Institute of Fisheries and Maritime Research): Av. de Brasília, 1449-006 Lisbon; e-mail ipimar@ipimar.pt; internet ipimar-iniap.ipimar.pt; f. 1978; attached to Min. of Agriculture, Rural Devt and Fisheries; marine biology, fisheries, aquaculture, marine environment, aquatic products technology; library of 9,000 vols, 1,400 periodicals; Pres. Dr MARCELO VASCONCELOS; publs *IPIMAR Divulgação, Publicações Avulsas, Relatórios Científicos e Técnicos*.

Jardim Botânico (Botanical Gardens): Rua da Escola Politécnica 58, 1250-102 Lisbon; tel. (21) 392-18-02; fax (21) 397-08-82; e-mail jb@fc.ul.pt; internet www.jb.ul.pt; f. 1878; attached to University of Lisbon; taxonomy and systematics, biomonitoring, biodiversity and conservation; library of 18,000 vols; Dir Profa Dra MARIA AMÉLIA LOUÇÃO; publs *Delectus Sporarum et Seminum* (annually), *Portugaliae Acta Biologica* (irregular), *Revista de Biologia* (irregular).

Physical Sciences

Instituto de Meteorologia (Institute of Meteorology): Rua C do Aeroporto, 1749-077 Lisbon; tel. (21) 844-70-00; fax (21) 840-23-70; e-mail informacoes@meteo.pt; internet www.meteo.pt; f. 1946; library of 34,000 vols; Pres. ADÉRITO VICENTE SERRÃO; publs *Açores* (annually), *Anuário Climatológico de Portugal, Anuário Sismológico de Portugal* (annually), *Boletim Actinométrico de Portugal* (monthly), *Boletim do Centro de Física da Atmósfera de Lisboa/Gago Coutinho* (monthly), *Boletim da Estação de Aeronomia de Lisboa* (monthly), *Boletim Geomagnético Prelimar* (monthly), *Boletim Informativo* (monthly), *Boletim Meteorológico* (daily), *Boletim Meteorológico para a Agricultura* (3 a month), *Observações magnéticas de S. Miguel, Projecto 12 do PIDDAC* (monthly), *Resumos Meteorológicos para a Aeronáutica* (monthly), *Revista do Instituto Nacional de Meteorologia e Geofísica* (quarterly).

Observatório Astronómico da Universidade de Coimbra (Coimbra Univ. Astronomical Observatory): Almas de Freire, Santa Clara, 3000 Coimbra; tel. (239) 81-49-47; fax (239) 81-49-35; f. 1772; library of 3,500 vols; publs *Comunicações, Efemérides Astronómicas* (annually), *Longitudinal Position of Sunspots and Chromospheric Filaments* (monthly).

Observatório Astronómico de Lisboa (Lisbon Astronomical Observatory): Tapada da Ajuda, 1349-018 Lisbon; tel. (21) 361-67-30; fax (21) 361-67-50; e-mail info@oal.ul.pt; internet www.oal.ul.pt; f. 1861; part of the Faculty of Sciences, Univ. of Lisbon, since 1995; the country's official timekeeper; carries out scientific research through its attached site; provides astronomical information to the public and civilian society; promotes teaching of astronomy in schools; 6 mems; library of 11,696 items; Dir Prof. RUI JORGE AGOSTINHO; publs *Dados Astronómicos* (annually), *O Observatório* (monthly).

Attached site:

Centro de Astronomia e Astrofísica da Universidade de Lisboa (Astronomy and Astrophysics Centre of the University of Lisbon): Tapada da Ajuda, 1349-018 Lisbon; tel. (21) 361-67-30; fax (21) 361-67-52; e-mail rui.agostinho@oal.ul.pt; internet www.oal.ul.pt/caaul; research into extragalactic and galactic astrophysics, the Sun, planetary and space sciences, cosmology and gravitational physics; Scientific Co-ordinator Prof. RUI JORGE AGOSTINHO.

RELIGION, SOCIOLOGY AND ANTHROPOLOGY

Centro de Investigação em Antropologia (Anthropological Research Centre): Departamento de Antropologia, Universidade de Coimbra, Rua do Arco da Traição, 3000-056 Coimbra; tel. (239) 82-90-51; fax (239) 82-34-91; e-mail cpadez@antrop.uc.pt; internet www.uc.pt/cia; f. 1994; African and Amerindian studies, anthropology of past populations, genetics and dynamics of human populations, and material, visual and performative cultures; library of 44,790 vols, 330 periodicals; Pres. Prof. Dra CRISTINA PADEZ; publ. *Antropologia Portuguesa*.

Comissão Nacional de Arte Sacra e do Património Cultural da Igreja (National Committee for Sacred Art and the Cultural Heritage of the Church): Santuário de Fátima, Apdo 31, 2496 Fátima Codex; tel. (249) 53-33-47; fax (249) 53-33-43; f. 1989; research centre; Pres. ANTÓNIO FRANCISCO MARQUES; Gen. Sec. Dr JOSÉ ANTÓNIO FALCÃO.

Instituto Português de Artes e Tradições Populares (Portuguese Institute of Folk Arts and Traditions): Travessa do Passadiço 1, 7540 Santiago do Cacém; tel. (269) 82-63-80; f. 1979; Dir Prof. Dr PERE FERRÉ; Gen. Sec. Dr JOSÉ ANTÓNIO FALCÃO; publs *Biblioteca de Artes e Tradições Populares, Novos Inquéritos*.

TECHNOLOGY

Centro Aquícola do Rio Ave (Inland Fisheries Station): 4481 Vila do Conde Codex; tel. (252) 63-12-41; f. 1886; fresh water fisheries and aquaculture; 15 staff; library of 1,000 vols; Dir EUARDO LENCASTRE.

Instituto Hidrográfico (Hydrographic Institute): Rua das Trinas 49, 1249-093 Lisbon; tel. (21) 094-30-00; fax (21) 094-32-99; e-mail mail@hidrografico.pt; internet www.hidrografico.pt; f. 1960; hydrographic surveys, physical oceanography, magnetic compass adjustments, laboratory; library of 11,000 vols; Dir-Gen. Vice-Admiral VIEGAS FILIPE; publ. *Anais*.

Instituto Nacional de Engenharia, Tecnologia e Inovação (INETI) (National Institute of Engineering, Technology and Innovation): Estrada do Paço do Lumiar 22, 1649-038 Lisbon; tel. (21) 092-46-00; fax (21) 716-09-01; e-mail geral@ineti.pt; internet www.ineti.pt; f. 1977; attached to Min. of the Economy and Innovation; research and development in technological innovation for application in the fields of energy, new systems, processes and products, environmental management and sustainability, geological resources and hazards, public health and safety, defence and space, laboratory support and testing; library of 38,000 vols; Pres. Dr ALCIDES RODRIGUES PEREIRA.

Attached centres:

Campus de Coimbra (Coimbra Branch): Rua Coronel Júlio Veiga Simão-Loreto, 3020 Coimbra; tel. (239) 82-37-97; fax (239) 82-90-00; e-mail atendimento.drc@ineti.pt; internet www.ineti.pt.

Centro de Dados Geológico-Mineiro Alfragide (Geological and Mining Data Centre, Alfragide): Estrada da Portela, Zambujal-Alfragide, Apdo 7586, 2720-866 Amadora; tel. (21) 470-54-00; fax (21) 471-90-18; e-mail geral@ineti.pt; internet www .ineti.pt.

Centro de Estudos Geológicos e Mineiros de Beja (Geological and Mining Studies Centre, Beja): Rua Frei Amador Arrais 39 r/c, Apdo 104, 7801-902 Beja Codex; tel. (284) 31-13-10; fax (284) 32-59-74; e-mail inetibeja@ineti.pt; internet www .ineti.pt; f. 1944.

Laboratorio de S. Mamede de Infesta (Laboratory, S. Mamede de Infesta): Rua da Amieira, Apdo 1089, 4466-956 S. Mamede de Infesta; tel. (22) 951-19-15; fax (22) 951-40-40; internet www.ineti.pt.

Museu Geológico de Lisboa (Geological Museum): see under Museums and Arts Galleries.

Laboratório Nacional de Engenharia Civil (National Civil Engineering Laboratory): Av. do Brasil 101, 1700-066 Lisbon Codex; tel. (21) 844-30-00; fax (21) 844-30-11; e-mail lnec@lnec.pt; internet www.lnec.pt; f. 1947; attached to Min. of Public Works, Transport and Communications; library of 140,000 vols; Pres. CARLOS ALBERTO MATIAS RAMOS; publs *Especificações* (standards, regulations), *Memórias* (technical papers).

Libraries and Archives

Agualva-Cacém

Biblioteca Municipal de Agualva-Cacém (Agualva-Cacém Municipal Library): Praceta das Descobertas 20A, 2735-095 Caçem; tel. (21) 432-80-39; f. 1997; 11,452 vols, 21 periodicals.

Amadora

Biblioteca Municipal da Amadora (Amadora Municipal Library): Rua Capitão Plácido de Abreu, Venteira, 2700 Amadora; tel. (21) 494-80-40; fax (21) 491-49-50; e-mail biblioteca.amadora@clix.pt; internet www .bibliotecas.cm-amadora.pt; f. 1960.

Angra do Heroísmo

Biblioteca Pública e Arquivo de Angra do Heroísmo (Public Library and Archives): Palácio Bettencourt, Rua da Rosa 49, 9700-171 Angra do Heroísmo, The Azores; tel. (295) 21-26-90; fax (295) 21-28-21; e-mail bpaah@mail.telepac.pt; f. 1957; 147,000 vols, 3.5m. MSS; Dir Dr MARCOLINO CANDEIAS COELHO LOPES; publs *Arquivo Distrital de Angra do Heroísmo*, *Boletim da Biblioteca Pública*.

Braga

Arquivo Distrital de Braga (Braga District Archives): Universidade do Minho, Largo do Paço, 4704-553 Braga; tel. (253) 60-11-78; fax (253) 60-11-80; e-mail adb@ uminho.pt; internet www.adb.uminho.pt; f. 1917; 1,498 m of documents since the 6th c.; Dir Dra MARIA ASSUNÇÃO CARDOSO JACOME VASCONCELOS CHAVES.

Biblioteca Pública de Braga (Braga Public Library): Largo do Paço, 4704-553 Braga; tel. and fax (253) 60-11-35; e-mail bpb@bpb .uminho.pt; internet www.bpb.uminho.pt; f. 1841; attached to the Universidade do Minho; 500,000 vols, 27,000 periodicals, 53 incunabula; Dir Dr HENRIQUE BARRETO NUNES.

Bragança

Arquivo Distrital de Bragança (Bragança District Archives): Convento de S. Francisco, Apdo 125, 5301-902 Bragança; tel. (273) 30-02-70; fax (273) 30-02-79; e-mail geral@ adbraganca.org; internet www .empresasglobais.com/adbraganca; f. 1916; 2,072 m of documents; Dir ANA MARIA AFONSO.

Cascais

Biblioteca 'Condes de Castro Guimarães': Av. Rei Humberto II de Itália, Parque Marechal Carmona, 2750 Cascais; tel. (21) 482-54-02; fax (21) 483-69-70; f. 1930; 25,000 vols; history, art, philosophy, literature, archaeology, local history; Librarian ANTÓNIO MANUEL GONÇALVES DE CARVALHO; publ. *Arquivo de Cascais—Boletim Cultural do Município* (annually).

Coimbra

Arquivo da Universidade de Coimbra (Archives of Coimbra University): The University, Rua de S. Pedro 2, 3000-370 Coimbra; tel. (239) 85-98-55; fax (239) 82-09-87; e-mail secauc@ci.uc.pt; internet www.uc.pt/ auc; f. 1901; Dir Prof. Dra MARIA JOSÉ AZEVEDO SANTOS; publ. *Boletim* (annually).

Biblioteca Municipal (Municipal Library): Rua Pedro Monteiro, 3000-329 Coimbra; fax (239) 70-24-96; f. 1922; 526,000 vols, 1,300 video cassettes, 5,500 audio cassettes and CDs; public library comprising a network of small annex libraries and a mobile library; Dir PINTO LOUREIRO; Librarian J. BRANQUINHO DE CARVALHO; publ. *Arquivo Coimbrão* (irregular).

Universidade de Coimbra: Biblioteca Geral (University of Coimbra: General Library): Largo da Porta Férrea, 3000-447 Coimbra; tel. (239) 85-98-00; fax (239) 82-71-35; e-mail bguc@ci.uc.pt; internet www.uc.pt/ bguc; f. 1291; 800,000 vols, 27,300 periodicals; 7 faculty br. libraries; Dir Prof. Dr CARLOS FIOLHAIS; publs *Acta Univ. Conimbrigensis*, *Boletim da Biblioteca Geral da Universidade de Coimbra* (annually), *Divulgação Bibliográfica*, *Revista da Universidade de Coimbra* (annually), *Sumários das Publicações Periódicas Portuguesas* (10 a year).

Attached library:

> **Biblioteca Joanina:** Largo da Porta Férrea, 3000-447 Coimbra; tel. (239) 85-98-41; fax (239) 82-71-35; e-mail bguc@ci .uc.pt; internet www.uc.pt/bguc/011joa .htm; f. 1777; 200,000 vols; Dir Prof. Dr CARLOS FIOLHAIS.

Évora

Biblioteca Pública de Évora (Évora Public Library): Largo Conde de Vila Flor, 7000-804 Évora; tel. (266) 76-93-30; fax (266) 76-93-31; e-mail bpevora@ptnetbiz.pt; internet www.evora.net/bpe/; f. 1805; 644,000 vols; Dir JOSÉ ANTÓNIO CALIXTO.

Funchal

Arquivo Regional da Madeira (Madeira Regional Archives): Caminho dos Álamos 35, Santo António, 9020-064 Funchal, Madeira; tel. (291) 70-84-00; fax (291) 70-84-02; e-mail arm@arquivo-madeira.org; internet www .arquivo-madeira.org; f. 1931; 8,500 vols on specialized history, 300,000 MSS; Dir MARIA FÁTIMA ARAÚJO DE BARROS FERREIRA; publ. *Arquivo Histórico da Madeira*.

Biblioteca Municipal do Funchal (Municipal Library): Palácio de São Pedro, Rua da Mouraria 31, 9050 Funchal, Madeira; tel. (291) 22-28-49; fax (291) 22-77-30; e-mail bmfunchal@gmail.com; f. 1838; 35,318 vols; Librarian RUI DE ORNELAS GONÇALVES.

Biblioteca Pública Regional da Madeira (Madeira Regional Public Library): Caminho dos Álamos 35, 9020-064 Funchal; tel. (291) 70-84-10; fax (291) 70-84-12; e-mail bprm@ bprmadeira.org; internet www.bprmadeira .org; f. 1979; legal deposit library; 150,000 units; Supervising Librarian JULIANA DE JESUS.

Guimarães

Biblioteca Municipal Raul Brandão (Municipal Library): Largo Cónego José Maria Gomes, 4800-419 Guimarães; tel. (253) 51-57-10; e-mail secretaria@ bib-raul-brandao.rcts.pt; internet www .bib-raul-brandao.rcts.pt; f. 1992; incl. local studies library; 70,000 vols.

Horta

Biblioteca Pública e Arquivo Regional da Horta (Horta Public Library and Regional Archive): Rua D. Pedro IV 25, 9901-852 Horta, Faial, The Azores; tel. (292) 20-81-90; fax (292) 20-81-99; e-mail bpar.horta.info@ azores.gov.pt; internet www.azores.gov.pt/ Portal/pt/entidades/drcultura-bpah; f. 1886; 31,000 vols; Librarian LUÍS MANUEL PITA SÃO BENTO.

Leiria

Arquivo Distrital de Leiria (District Archives): Rua Marcos Portugal 4, Apdo 1145, 2400-179, Leiria; tel. (244) 82-00-50; fax (244) 82-00-59; e-mail adlra@adleiria .iantt.pt; internet adleiria.iantt.pt; f. 1916; 30,000 books, 496 microfilms; Dir ACÁCIO FERNANDO DOS SANTOS LOPES DE SOUSA.

Lisbon

Arquivo Histórico Militar (Military Historical Archives): Largo dos Caminhos de Ferro 2, 1100-105 Lisbon; tel. (21) 884-25-63; fax (21) 884-25-14; e-mail ahm@mail.exercito .pt; internet www.exercito.pt/ahm; f. 1921; Dir Tenente-Coronel ANICETO AFONSO; publs *Boletim*, *Noticias* (2 a year).

Arquivo Histórico Parlamentar (Parliamentary Historical Archives): Palácio de S. Bento, 1249-068 Lisbon; tel. (21) 391-95-21; fax (21) 391-74-70; e-mail leonor.borges@ar .parlamento.pt; internet www.parlamento .pt/conhecer; Dir LEONOR CALVÃO BORGES.

Arquivo Municipal de Lisboa (Municipal Archives): internet arquivomunicipal .cm-lisboa.pt; f. f. 12th century; publ. *Cadernos*.

Constituent centres:

> **Arquivo do Arco do Cego:** Rua Nunes Claro 8A, 1000-209 Lisbon; tel. (21) 841-11-70; fax (21) 848-46-38; e-mail arqmun .acego@cm-lisboa.pt; f. 1919; documents since 1834.

> **Arquivo Fotográfico:** Rua da Palma 246, 1100-394 Lisbon; tel. (21) 886-23-32; fax (21) 886-16-14; e-mail arqmun.fotografico@ cm-lisboa.pt; f. 1942; images since end of 19th c.

> **Arquivo Histórico:** Rua B, Bairro da Liberdade, lote 3 a 6, piso 1, 1070-017 Lisbon; tel. (21) 380-71-00; fax (21) 380-71-12; e-mail dba.dga@cm-lisboa.pt; f. 1931; documents since 12th c.

> **Arquivo Intermédio:** Rua B, Bairro da Liberdade, lote 3 a 6, piso 0, 1070-017 Lisbon; tel. (21) 380-71-03; fax (21) 380-71-99; e-mail arqmun.intermedio@cm-lisboa .pt; f. 1985; city administration documents.

Biblioteca Central da Marinha (Naval Library): Praça do Império, 1400-206 Lisbon; tel. (21) 365-85-20; fax (21) 365-85-23; e-mail biblioteca.marinha@marinha.pt; internet www.marinha.pt/Marinha/PT/Extra/Biblioteca; f. 1835; valuable editions; 126,616 vols; Dir C/Alm. JOSÉ LUÍS FERREIRA LEIRIA PINTO.

Biblioteca da Academia das Ciências de Lisboa (Library of the Academy of Sciences): Rua da Academia das Ciências 19, 1249-122 Lisbon; f. 1779; 1,000,000 vols, 3,000 MSS, 63 incunabula; Dir Prof. Dr JUSTINO MENDES DE ALMEIDA.

Biblioteca da Assembleia da República (Library of the Assembly of the Republic): Palácio de S. Bento, 1249-068 Lisbon Codex; tel. (21) 391-94-52; fax (21) 391-74-47; e-mail bib@ar.parlamento.pt; internet www .parlamento.pt; f. 1836; 200,000 vols; special collections: national legislation and old books from the libraries of religious orders; Dir JOSÉ LUÍS M. TOMÉ.

Biblioteca de Ajuda (Ajuda Library): Palácio da Ajuda, Calçada da Ajuda, 1349-021 Lisbon; tel. and fax (21) 363-85-92; e-mail ajuda.lib@ippar.pt; internet www.ippar.pt/ sites_externos/bajuda/index.htm; f. 1756; 100,000 vols, 30,000 MSS, 5,000 music MSS, 213 incunabula; Dir Dra CRISTINA PINTO BASTO.

Biblioteca de Arte da Fundação Calouste Gulbenkian: Av. de Berna 45A, 1067-001 Lisbon; tel. (21) 782-30-00; fax (21) 782-30-44; e-mail artlib@gulbenkian.pt; internet www.biblarte.gulbenkian.pt; 200,000 vols specializing in art; Dir Dr JOSÉ AFONSO FURTADO.

Biblioteca do Exército (Army Library): Rua Museu deArtilharia, 1149-065 Lisbon; tel. (21) 884-24-56; e-mail bibex@mail .exercito.pt; internet www.exercito.pt; f. 1837; 100,000 vols; Dir Col FRANCISCO DIAS COSTA.

Biblioteca e Arquivo Histórico do Ministério das Obras Públicas, Transportes e Comunicações (Library and Historical Archive of the Ministry of Public Works, Transport and Communications): Avda da Liberdade 193, 1250-149 Lisbon; tel. (21) 319-42-00; fax (21) 319-42-18; e-mail biblioteca@sg.moptc.pt; internet www.moptc .pt; f. 1852; 13,000 vols, documents since 16th c.; 200,000 textual documents on industry, agriculture, forestry, trade, public works, etc.; 1,100 periodicals; Dir Dra MARIA TERESA AZEVEDO MENEZES.

Biblioteca Francisco Pereira de Moura (Higher Institute of Economics and Management Library): Instituto Superior de Economia e Gestão, Rua do Quelhas 6, 1200-781 Lisbon; tel. (21) 392-28-88; fax (21) 397-26-84; e-mail biblio@iseg.utl.pt; internet www .iseg.utl.pt/biblioteca; attached to Universidade Técnica de Lisboa.

Biblioteca Municipal Central (Central Municipal Library): Palácio Galveias, Largo do Campo Pequeno, 1049-064 Lisbon; tel. (21) 797-13-26; fax (21) 793-71-58; e-mail bib .galveias@cm-lisboa.pt; f. 1931; 332,673 vols; Dir Dra MANUELA RÊGO.

Biblioteca Nacional (National Library): Campo Grande 83, 1749-081 Lisbon; tel. (21) 798-20-00; fax (21) 798-21-40; e-mail bn@bn.pt; internet www.bn.pt; f. 1796; 2,489,018 vols, 50,000 periodicals, 36,000 MSS; Dir Dr JORGE COUTO; publ. *Leituras* (2 a year).

Biblioteca Popular de Lisboa: Rua Ivens 35, and Rua da Academia das Ciências 19, 1200 Lisbon; tel. (21) 346-98-83; f. 1918; 97,774 vols, 835 periodicals; Librarian DURVAL PIRES DE LIMA; Principal Officers CARLOS ALBERTO DE MESQUITA, MARIA TERESA PIRES DE LIMA, JOSÉ PAULO RIBEIRO.

Instituto dos Arquivos Nacionais, Torre do Tombo (National Archives, Torre do Tombo): Alameda da Universidade, 1649-010 Lisbon; tel. (21) 781-15-00; fax (21) 793-72-30; e-mail dc@iantt.pt; internet www .iantt.pt; f. 1378; collection dates since 9th c.;

Dir MIRIAM HALPERN PEREIRA; publ. *Boletim* (news and information, 4 a year).

Serviço de Biblioteca e Documentação Diplomática (Library and Diplomatic Documentation Service): Palácio das Necessidades, Lisbon; tel. (21) 394-62-65; fax (21) 394-60-28; f. 1736; 80,000 vols; Dir MARIA HELENA LOPES DE NEVES PINTO.

Mafra

Biblioteca do Palácio Nacional de Mafra (Mafra National Palace Library): Terreiro de D. João V, 2640-492 Mafra; tel. (261) 81-75-50; fax (261) 81-19-47; e-mail pnmafra@ippar .pt; internet www.ippar.pt/english/ monumentos/palacio_mafra.html; f. 18th c.; 40,000 vols; notable collection of rare books (esp. incunabula and 17th–18th c. books); Dir MARIA MARGARIDA MONTENEGRO.

Ponta Delgada

Biblioteca Pública e Arquivo Regional de Ponta Delgada (Ponta Delgarda Public Library and Regional Archive): Largo do Colégio, 9500 Ponta Delgada, São Miguel, The Azores; tel. (296) 28-20-85; fax (296) 28-12-16; e-mail info@bparpd.pt; f. 1841; 120,000 vols in special collections, 40,000 monographs, 5,000 serials, 3,000 metres of archive material; Dir VALTER M. DE MELO REBELO.

Porto

Arquivo Distrital do Porto (District Archives): Rua das Taipas 90, 4050-598 Porto; tel. (22) 339 51-70; fax (22) 339-51-79; e-mail info@adporto.org; internet www .adporto.org; f. 1931; 200,000 vols; Dir MARIA JOÃO PIRES DE LIMA; publ. *Boletim do Arquivo Distrital do Porto.*

Arquivo Histórico Municipal do Porto (Municipal Historical Archives): Rua da Alfândega 10, 4050-029 Porto; tel. (22) 206-04-00; fax (22) 206-04-01; e-mail dmah@ cm-porto.pt; internet www.cm-porto.pt; f. 1980; Head of Section MARIA HELENA DE PAIVA GIL BRAGA.

Biblioteca Pública Municipal do Porto (Municipal Library): Rua D. João IV (ao Jardim de São Lázaro), 4049-017 Porto; tel. (22) 519-34-80; fax (22) 519-34-88; e-mail bpmp@cm-porto.pt; internet www.cm-porto .pt; f. 1833; 1,390,000 vols, 9,411 MSS, 246 incunabula; Dir ISABEL SANTOS; publ. *Biblioteca Portucalensis* (annually).

Santarém

Biblioteca Municipal de Santarém (Santarém Municipal Library): Rua Braamcamp Freire, 2000-094 Santarém; tel. (24) 330-44-81; fax (24) 330-44-79; e-mail biblioteca@ cm-santarem.pt; internet www.cm-santarem .pt/santarem/geral/destaques; f. 1880; 100,000 vols; Librarian Dr LUIS NAZARÉ FERREIRA.

Setúbal

Arquivo Distrital de Setúbal (District Archives): Rua Prof. Borges de Macedo, Manteigadas Sul, 2910-001 Setúbal; tel. (265) 70-99-00; fax (265) 70-99-35; e-mail adstb@adsetubal.iantt.pt; internet www .iantt.pt; f. 1965; documents since 16th c.

Sintra

Arquivo Municipal de Sintra/Arquivo Histórico (Sintra Municipal Archives/Historical Archives): Palácio Valenças, Rua Visconde de Monserrate 1, 2710-591 Sintra; tel. (21) 923-88-21; fax (21) 923-87-78; e-mail geral@cm-sintra.pt; internet www.cm-sintra .pt; f. 1939; 60,000 documents since 14th c.

Biblioteca Municipal de Sintra: Rua Gomes de Amorim 12/14, 2710-569 Sintra; tel. (21) 923-61-70; fax (21) 923-61-79; e-mail

geral@cm-sintra.pt; internet www.cm-sintra .pt; f. 1939; 60,000 vols.

Torres Novas

Biblioteca Gustavo Pinto Lopes: Largo do Salvador 6, 2350-415 Torres Novas; tel. (249) 81-24-80; e-mail bmtorresnovas@mail .telepac.pt; internet www.cm-torresnovas.pt/ biblioteca/biblioteca.asp; f. 1937; 31,200 vols; Dir Dr JOÃO CARLOS LOPES.

Vila Nova de Gaia

Biblioteca Municipal de Vila Nova de Gaia (Municipal Library): Rua de Angola, 4430-014 Vila Nova de Gaia; tel. (22) 374-56-70; fax (22) 374-56-79; e-mail bmgaia@ gaianima.pt; internet www.bmgaia.net; f. 1933; 101,000 vols, 2,246 periodicals; Co-ordinator CRISTINA MARGARIDE.

Vila Real

Arquivo Distrital de Vila Real (Vila Real District Archives): Av. Almeida Lucena 5, 5000-660 Vila Real; tel. (259) 33-08-20; fax (259) 32-57-12; e-mail correio@advrl.org.pt; internet www.advrl.org.pt; f. 1965; 31,590 vols, 1,500 m of documents, 180 m of Portuguese legislation since 1715; Dir MANUEL SILVA GONÇALVES.

Viseu

Arquivo Distrital de Viseu (Viseu District Archives): Largo de Santa Cristina, 3504-515 Viseu; tel. (232) 43-03-80; fax (232) 42-18-00; e-mail mdoresah@ad-viseu.com; internet www.ad-viseu.com; f. 1932; 450,000 documents; Dir MARIA DAS DORES ALMEIDA HENRIQUES; publ. *Boletim Informativo.*

Museums and Art Galleries

Alenquer

Museu Municipal 'Hipólito Cabaço' (Municipal Museum): Rua Maria Milne e Carmo 2, 2580-318 Alenquer; tel. (263) 73-09-06; fax (263) 71-15-04; f. 1945; archaeological, historical and ethnographical collections; 4,000 exhibits; Dir JOÃO JOSÉ FERNANDES GOMES.

Alpiarça

Casa dos Patudos—Museu de Alpiarça (Alpiarça Museum): Rua José Relvas, 2090-100 Alpiarça; tel. (243) 55-83-21; fax (243) 55-64-44; e-mail cm.alpiarca@mail.telepac.pt; internet www.cm-alpiarca.pt; f. 1904; fine and applied arts, archaeology; library of 41,000 vols incl. historical archive; Dir Dr JOSÉ ANTÓNIO FALCÃO; publ. *Boletim.*

Amadora

Centro Ciência Viva de Amadora (Living Science Centre): Rua Gonçalves Ramos 54B, 2700-036 Amadora; tel. (21) 491-13-14; fax (21) 493-09-00; e-mail info@amadora .cienciaviva.pt; internet amadora.cienciaviva .pt; f. 2003; interactive displays on scientific and technological topics, incl. town planning and electricity; Exec. Dir JOSÉ ALBERGARIA.

Angra do Heroísmo

Museu de Angra do Heroísmo (Angra do Heroísmo Museum): Edifício de São Francisco, Angra do Heroísmo, Ilha Terceira, The Azores; tel. (295) 21-31-47; fax (295) 21-31-37; e-mail info@museuangraheroismo.org; internet www.museuangraheroismo.org; f. 1949 in a 17th c. Franciscan monastery; historical museum; permanent exhibition on the history of the Azores Islands; paintings, ceramics, furniture, sculpture, ethnography, arms, guns, carriages; Dir Dr FRANCISCO DOS REIS MADURO-DIAS.

Braga

Museu Regional de Arqueologia 'D. Diogo de Sousa' (Regional Archaeological Museum): Rua dos Bombeiros Voluntários, 4700-025 Braga; tel. (253) 27-37-06; fax (253) 61-23-66; e-mail mdds@um.geira.pt; internet www.ipmuseus.pt; f. 1918; colln ranges from the Palaeolithic to the Middle Ages; visits to local archaeological sites; public library; (museum temporarily closed to the public); Dir Dra MARIA ISABEL CUNHA E SILVA.

Bragança

Museu do Abade de Baçal (Abbot of Baçal Museum): Rua Conselheiro Abílio Beça 27, 5300-011 Bragança; tel. (273) 33-15-95; fax (273) 32-32-42; e-mail info@ museu-abade-bacal.rcts.pt; internet www .ipmuseus.pt; f. 1915; archaeology, epigraphy, sacred art, paintings, gold items, numismatics, furniture, ethnography; Dir JOÃO MANUEL NETO JACOB.

Cascais

Museu 'Condes de Castro Guimarães': Av. Rei Humberto II de Itália, Parque Marechal Carmona, 2750 Cascais; tel. (21) 482-54-07; fax (21) 482-54-04; e-mail cmc .museus@mail.telepac.pt; internet www .cm-cascais.pt; f. 1931; *Crónica* about the kings of the first dynasty of Duarte Galvão, 16th-century illuminated *Codex* on parchment, 17th-century Indo-Portuguese counting frames, paintings, oriental porcelain; furniture, silverware; library of 2,826 vols; Curator MARIA JOSÉ REGO DE SOUSA.

Castelo Branco

Museu de Francisco Tavares Proença Júnior: Largo Dr. José Dias Lopes, 6000-462 Castelo Branco; tel. (272) 34-42-77; fax (272) 34-78-80; e-mail mftpj@ipmuseus.pt; internet www.ipmuseus.pt; f. 1910; important archaeological collection of objects found in megalithic tombs at Beira Baixa; Bronze-Age weapons and objects from a complete workshop found at Castelo Novo; illustrations of rupestral art in the Tagus sanctuary; Roman epigraphy; art gallery (16th c. Portuguese School, 16th c. Brussels tapestries); Bishop's Gallery (18th and 19th c. paintings); ethnographic collections; ceramic collections; regional embroidery workshop; textiles, incl. oriental and Indo-Portuguese embroidered bedcovers; Dir AIDA RECHENA.

Coimbra

Museu Nacional de Ciência e Técnica 'Dr Mário Silva' (National Museum of Science and Technology): Palacete Sacadura Botte, Rua dos Coutinhos 23, 3000 Coimbra; tel. (239) 85-19-40; fax (239) 85-19-49; e-mail mnct@mnct.mces.pt; internet www.mnct.mct .pt; f. 1971; attached to the Ministry of Science, Technology and Higher Education; information science, medicine, physics, graphic arts, photography, cinema, radio, industrial technology; Dir Prof. Dr PAULO GAMA MOTA.

Museu Nacional de 'Machado de Castro' (Machado de Castro National Museum): Largo Dr José Rodrigues, 3000-236 Coimbra; tel. (239) 82-37-27; fax (239) 82-27-06; e-mail mnmc@ipmuseus.pt; internet www.ipmuseus .pt; f. 1911; established in the old Bishop's Palace built over Roman galleries, renewed in the 16th c. and recently adapted; antiquities, sculpture, paintings, silver-work, priests' vestments, tapestries, ceramics, glass, furniture; (closed until 2007 for renovations); Dir PEDRO REDOL.

Évora

Museu de Évora: Largo do Conde de Vila Flor, 7000-804 Évora; tel. (266) 70-26-04; fax (266) 70-80-94; e-mail mevora@ipmuseus.pt; internet www.ipmuseus.pt; f. 1915; paintings: large collections of 16th-century Flemish and Portuguese works; 17th-century works; local prehistoric tools and Roman art and archaeology; sculpture from middle ages to the 19th century; 18th-century Portuguese furniture and silver; (closed temporarily for reorganization); Dir JOAQUIM OLIVEIRA CAETANO.

Faro

Museu Arqueológico e Lapidar Infante D. Henrique (Infante D. Henrique Archaeological and Geological Museum): Convento de N.S. da Assunção, Largo Afonso III, 8000-167 Faro; tel. (289) 89-74-00; fax (289) 89-74-19; e-mail dmm.drp@cm-faro.pt; internet www.cm-faro.pt; f. 1894; history, archaeology, ethnography, art from 16th–19th c., photography, toys; Dir Dra DÁLIA PAULO; publ. *Anais do Municipio do Faro* (annually).

Museu Marítimo 'Almirante Ramalho Ortigão' (Maritime Museum): Departamento Marítimo do Sul, Faro; f. 1931; regional methods of fishing, instruments, models of ships and equipment, paintings of marine fauna, sailors' handicrafts; Curator Capt. LUÍS FERNANDO TAVARES DOS BEIS ÁGOAS.

Figueira da Foz

Museu Municipal 'Santos Rocha' (Municipal Museum): Rua Calouste Gulbenkian, 3080-084 Figueira da Foz; tel. (233) 40-28-40; fax (233) 40-28-57; e-mail museu@cm-figfoz .pt; internet www.cm-figfoz.pt/museu; f. 1894; art, archaeology, ethnology, coins and medals, Indo-Portuguese furniture, weapons; library of 14,300 vols; Managers ANA PAULA CARDOSO, SÓNIA PINTO, MANUELA SILVA, SÓNIA PINTO.

Funchal

Museu de Arte Contemporânea (Museum of Contemporary Art): Fortaleza de São Tiago, Rua do Portão de São Tiago, 9050-031 Funchal, Madeira; tel. (291) 21-33-40; fax (291) 21-33-48; e-mail mac.funchal@sapo .pt; internet www.rpmuseus-pt.org/Pt/cont/ fichas/museu_18.html; f. 1966; Portuguese art since the 1960s; Dir JOSÉ MANUEL DE FREITAS SAINZ-TRUEVA.

Museu de Arte Sacra (Museum of Sacred Art): Rua do Bispo 21, 9000 Funchal, Madeira; tel. (291) 22-89-00; fax (291) 23-13-41; f. 1955; diocesan museum; art of the 15th–18th c., Flemish art of the 15th and 16th c., sculpture, jewellery.

Museu Municipal do Funchal (Historia Natural) (Funchal Municipal Museum—Natural History): Rua da Mouraria 31, 9004-546 Funchal, Madeira; tel. (291) 22-97-61; fax (291) 22-51-80; e-mail ciencia@ mail.cm-funchal.pt; f. 1929; Natural History Museum and Marine Aquarium; large collection of marine animals, especially deep-sea fish and crustaceans; library on marine biology; Curator Dr MANUEL JOSÉ BISCOITO; publs *Bocagiana* (irregular), *Boletim* (annually).

Museu da Quinta das Cruzes: Calçada do Pico 1, 9000-206 Funchal, Madeira; tel. (291) 74-06-70; fax (291) 74-13-84; e-mail mqc@ netmadeira.com; f. 1946; decorative arts; Dir MARIA TERESA MENDES AZEREDO PAIS; publs *Catalogue of Temporary Exhibitions, Porcelana da China—Colecção do Museu Quinta das Cruzes, Um Olhar do Porto.*

Guimarães

Museu de Alberto Sampaio (Alberto Sampaio Museum): Rua Alfredo Guimarães, 4810-251 Guimarães; tel. (253) 42-39-10; fax (253) 42-39-19; e-mail masampaio@ipmuseus .pt; internet www.ipmuseus.pt; f. 1928; religious painting and sculpture, goldsmiths' and silversmiths' art, priestly garments, ceramics; research on industrial archaeology and anthropology; Dir Dra ISABEL MARIA FERNANDES.

Museu da Sociedade Martins Sarmento (Museum of the Martins Sarmento Society): Rua Paio Galvão, 4814-509 Guimarães; tel. (253) 41-40-11; fax (253) 41-59-69; e-mail casa.sarmento@csarmento.uminho.pt; internet www.csarmento.uminho.pt; f. 1885; archaeology; numerous exhibits relating to Portuguese Celtic, Roman and Visigothic periods; ethnography, numismatics, contemporary art; Dir Dr J. SANTOS SIMÕES.

Paço dos Duques de Bragança (Palace of the Dukes of Bragança): Rua Conde D. Henrique, 4810-245 Guimarães; tel. (253) 41-22-73; fax (253) 51-72-01; e-mail paco .duques@ippar.pt; internet www.geira.pt/ pduquesbraganca; f. 1910; 15th-century palace and national monument attached to the Portuguese Institute of Architectural Heritage; 17th- and 18th-century art, tapestries, ceramics, faïence, furniture; Dir Dra MARIA DA CONCEIÇÃO MARQUES.

Lamego

Museu de Lamego: Largo de Camões, 5100-147 Lamego; tel. (254) 60-02-30; fax (254) 65-52-64; e-mail mlamego@ipmuseus.pt; internet www.ipmuseus.pt; f. 1917; important collection of 16th-century Brussels tapestries, Portuguese painting of 16th–18th centuries, sculpture, religious ornaments; Dir Dr AGOSTINHO RIBEIRO.

Leiria

Museu da Imagem em Movimento (Museum of the Moving Image): Centro Cultural de Sant'Ana 1, Leiria; tel. (244) 83-85-11; internet www.rt-leiriafatima.pt/ destaques.php?idreg=40; f. 1995; commemorates the centenary of the creation of cinema; photographic archive, documentation centre.

Lisbon

Centro de Arte Moderna José de Azeredo Perdigão, Fundação Calouste Gulbenkian (Centre for Modern Art): Rua Dr Nicolau de Bettencourt, 1050-078 Lisbon; tel. (21) 782-34-74; fax (21) 782-30-34; e-mail camjap@gulbenkian.pt; internet www .camjap.gulbenkian.pt; f. 1979; Portuguese and foreign modern art; documentation and research depts, workshops, outdoor amphitheatre; Dir Dr JORGE MOLDER.

Jardim e Museu Agrícola Tropical do Instituto de Investigação Científica Tropical (Garden and Museum of Tropical Agriculture): Largo dos Jerónimos, 1400-209 Lisbon; tel. and fax (21) 362-02-10; e-mail jmat@iict.pt; f. 1906; Dir MARIA CÂNDIDA LIBERATO.

Museu Arqueológico do Carmo (Archaeological Museum): Largo do Carmo, 1200-092 Lisbon; tel. (21) 347-86-29; fax (21) 324-42-55; internet www.museusportugal.org/AAP; f. 1863; administered by Associação dos Arqueólogos Portugueses; prehistoric, Roman, Visigothic and medieval collections; sarcophagi, religious sculpture, coins, etc.; Curator (vacant).

Museu Calouste Gulbenkian: Av. de Berna 45A, 1067-001 Lisbon Codex; tel. (21) 782-30-00; fax (21) 782-30-32; e-mail info@ gulbenkian.pt; internet www.museu .gulbenkian.pt; f. 1969; Gulbenkian art collection containing works since 2800BC; antique classical and oriental art, Egyptian, Assyrian, Greek, Roman, Islamic and Far Eastern art; European painting, sculpture, illuminated MSS, tapestries and fabrics, furniture, silverware, jewellery, glass, medals, coins; Dir Dr João Castel-Branco Pereira.

Museu da Cidade (City Museum): Palácio Pimenta, Campo Grande 245, 1700-091 Lisbon; tel. (21) 751-32-00; fax (21) 757-18-58; e-mail museudacidade@cm-lisboa.pt; f. 1942; history of development of Lisbon shown by archaeological, historical, artistic and ethnological documents and exhibits; an 'ensemble' of the 18th-century period and a large model of Lisbon before the earthquake of 1755; Dir Ana Cristina Leite.

Museu da Música (Music Museum): Estação do Metropolitano Alto dos Moinhos, Rua João de Freitas Branco, 1500-359 Lisbon; tel. (21) 771-09-90; fax (21) 771-09-99; e-mail mmusica@ipmuseus.pt; internet www.museudamusica-ipmuseus.pt; f. 1994; more than 1,000 instruments of both classical and popular traditions, European wind, key and percussion instruments of the 16th–19th c-, Portuguese clavichords, harpsichords and 19th c. string instruments, also African, Asian and Portuguese folk instruments; iconography; sound archive of 6,000 items; printed documents and MSS; Dir Maria Helena Trindade.

Museu de Arte Popular (Museum of Folk Art): Av. Brasília, 1400-038 Lisbon; tel. (21) 301-12-82; fax (21) 301-11-28; e-mail martepopular@ipmuseus.pt; internet www.ipmuseus.pt; f. 1948; folk art, ethnology; (temporarily closed for renovation); Dir Dra Elisabete Costa.

Museu de Artes Decorativas (Museum of Decorative Arts): Fundação Ricardo do Espírito Santo Silva, Largo das Portas do Sol 2, 1100-411 Lisbon; tel. (21) 886-21-83; fax (21) 887-49-30; e-mail geral@fress.pt; internet www.fress.pt; f. 1953; includes Ricardo do Espírito Santo Silva's private collection of Portuguese furniture, silver, china, paintings, rugs, tapestries etc., and workshops in which craftsmen are trained in all aspects of traditional interior arts.

Museu de São Roque (St Roque Museum): Largo Trindade Coelho, 1200-470 Lisbon; tel. (21) 323-53-80; fax (21) 323-50-60; e-mail museus.roque@scml.pt; internet www.scml.pt; f. 1905; collections of religious paintings, Church vessels in precious metals, embroidered vestments by Italian artists of the 18th c.; works from the chapel of St John the Baptist in the adjacent museum of the 16th c. Church of St Roque; (closed for alterations and extension work; expected to reopen in late 2007); Curator Teresa Freitas Morna.

Museu do Chiado (Chiado Museum): Rua Serpa Pinto 4, 1200-444 Lisbon; tel. (21) 343-21-48; fax (21) 343-21-51; e-mail mchiado@ipmuseus.pt; internet www.museudochiado-ipmuseus.pt; f. 1911; painting and sculpture since 1850; library of 6,000 vols; Dir Pedro Lapa.

Museu Etnológico da Sociedade de Geografia de Lisboa (Ethnological Museum): Rua das Portas de Santo Antão 100, 1150-269 Lisbon; tel. (21) 342-50-68; fax (21) 346-45-53; e-mail soc.geografia.lisboa@clix.pt; internet socgeografia-lisboa.planetaclix.pt; f. 1875; native arts, arms, clothing, musical instruments from Africa, India, China, Indonesia and Timor, statues of navigators and historians, relics of voyages of discovery, scientific instruments; Curator Dr José de Queiroz Soares.

Museu Geológico de Lisboa: Rua Academia das Ciências 19, 1200-003 Lisbon; tel.

(21) 346-39-15; fax (21) 342-46-09; e-mail museugeol@ineti.pt; internet www.ineti.pt; f. 1848; paleontology, stratigraphy, archaeology and mineralogy; fossils from the Tertiary period.

Museu Militar (Military Museum): Largo do Museu de Artilharia, 1100 Lisbon; e-mail mmilitar@um.geira.pt; f. 1851; exhibits of Portuguese military history, light arms, ancient artillery and other equipment, paintings since 18th c.; Dir Col Manuel Ribeiro de Falla.

Museu Mineralógico e Geológico (Museum of Mineralogy and Geology): Rua da Escola Politécnica 58, 1250-102 Lisbon; tel. (21) 392-18-36; fax (21) 390-58-50; e-mail smineralogia@fc.ul.pt; internet www.mnhn.ul.pt/geologia/geologia.htm; f. 1837; attached to Museu Nacional de História Natural; geology, petrology, mineralogy, palaeontology and museology; Dir Prof. Fernando José Arraiano de Sousa Barriga; Curators Dr César Lopes, Dra Liliana Póvoas; publs *Gaia* (journal of geosciences), *Memórias de Geociencias* (irregular).

Museu Nacional de Arqueologia do Dr Leite de Vasconcelos (National Museum of Archaeology): Praça do Império, 1400-206 Lisbon; tel. (21) 362-00-00; fax (21) 362-00-16; e-mail mnarqueologia@ipmuseus.pt; internet ww.mnarquelogia-ipmuseus.pt; f. 1893; attached to Inst. Português de Museus; library of 25,000 vols; Dir Dr Luís Raposo; publ. *O Arqueólogo Português*.

Museu Nacional de Arte Antiga (National Museum of Ancient Art): Rua das Janelas Verdes, 1249-017 Lisbon; tel. (21) 391-28-00; fax (21) 397-37-03; e-mail mnarteantiga@ipmuseus.pt; internet www.mnarteantiga-ipmuseus.pt; f. 1884; Portuguese and foreign plastic and ornamental art from the 12th–19th c.; library of 36,000 vols; Dir Dra Dalila Rodrigues.

Museu Nacional de Etnologia (National Ethnological Museum): Av. Ilha da Madeira, 1400-203 Lisbon; tel. (21) 304-11-60; fax (21) 301-39-94; e-mail mnetnologia@ipmuseus.pt; internet www.ipmuseus.pt; f. 1965; Portuguese rural artefacts; collns representing the people and cultures of Lusophone Africa, Mali, Côte d'Ivoire, Ghana, Nigeria, Cameroon, Indonesia, Timor, Macau, and the Amazonian Indians; library: 20,000 books and periodicals; Dir Prof. Dr Joaquim Pais de Brito.

Museu Nacional de História Natural (National Museum of Natural History): Universidade de Lisboa, Rua da Escola Politécnica 58, 1250-102 Lisbon; tel. (21) 392-18-90; fax (21) 392-18-41; internet www.mnhn.ul.pt; f. 1859; library of 27,000 vols; Dirs Profa Maria Amelia Martins-Loução (Botany), Prof. Fernando Barriga (Mineralogy and Geology), Dra. Maria Graça Ramalhinho (Zoology and Anthropology); publs *Arquivos do Museu Bocage*, *Boletim*, *Gaia* (journal of geosciences), *Portugaliae Acta Biologica*, *Revista de Biologia (Lisboa)* (annually).

Museu Nacional dos Coches (National Coach Museum): Praça Afonso de Albuquerque, Belém, 1300-004 Lisbon; tel. (21) 361-08-50; fax (21) 363-25-03; e-mail mncoches@ipmuseus.pt; internet www.museudoscoches-ipmuseus.pt; f. 1905 by Queen Amélia in the Riding School of the Royal Palace; comprehensive collection of carriages and coaches since 1619, many by famous craftsmen, including those of the Portuguese ex Royal Family; sedan chairs, harness and equipment, royal liveries, etc., silver trumpets; section of portraits, paintings and engravings; Dir Dra Silvana Bessone.

Museu Numismático Português (Portuguese Numismatic Museum): Imprensa Nacional-Casa da Moeda, Av. Dr A. J. de Almeida, 1000-042 Lisbon; tel. (21) 789-07-00; fax (21) 789-07-08; e-mail mramos@incm.pt; internet www.incm.pt; f. 1933; important collns of Portuguese and Colonial, Iberian, Roman and Visigothic coins; also Portuguese and foreign medals; temporarily closed to the public; library of 20,000 vols; consists of Documentation and Information Centre, and Historical Archives of the Nat. Press and the Lisbon Mint; Dir Dr Margarida Ramos; publ. *Diário da República*.

Museu Rafael Bordalo Pinheiro: Campo Grande 382, 1700-097 Lisbon; tel. (21) 755-04-68; fax (21) 757-18-58; e-mail museu.bordalopinheiro@cm-lisboa.pt; internet www.museubordalopinheiro.pt; f. 1916 as a biographical museum; originals and reproductions of famous caricatures, ceramics, satirical documents; Chief Man. Ana Cristina Leite.

Odivelas

Núcleo Museológico do Posto de Comando do Movimento das Forças Armadas (Command Post of the Armed Forces Movement): Rua José Gomes Monteiro 3D–Loja B, 2675-372 Odivelas; tel. (21) 934 61-00; fax (21) 934-61-98; e-mail cultura@cm-odivelas.pt; internet www.cm-odivelas.pt; f. 2001; commemorates the revolution of 25 April 1974, covering the main events during 24–26 April 1974.

Porto

Museu de Arte Contemporânea de Serralves (Serralves Museum of Contemporary Art): Rua D. João de Castro 210, 4150-417 Porto; tel. (22) 615-65-00; fax (22) 615-65-33; e-mail serralves@serralves.pt; internet www.serralves.com; f. 1999; Portuguese and international art since the late 1960s; library: reference library; Dir João Fernandes.

Museu de Etnologia do Porto (Ethnological Museum): Largo de S. João Novo 11, 4050-554 Porto; internet www.ipmuseus.pt; f. 1945; ethnology, archaeology and history; (temporarily closed to the public); Dir (vacant).

Museu Nacional de Soares dos Reis (National Museum): Palacio dos Carrancas, Rua D. Manuel II, 4050-342 Porto; tel. (22) 339-37-70; fax (22) 208-28-51; e-mail mnsr@ipmuseus.pt; internet www.mnsr-ipmuseus.pt; f. 1833; paintings, sculpture, jewellery, furniture, pottery, glass, metalwork; Dir Dra Teresa Viana.

Setúbal

Museu de Setúbal (Setúbal Museum): Rua do Balneário Dr Paulo Borba, 2900-261 Setúbal; tel. (265) 53-78-90; fax (265) 53-78-93; internet www.rpmuseus-pt.org/Pt/cont/fichas/museu_92.html; f. 1961; 16th c. art, sacred sculpture, decorative arts, archaeology, numismatics; Dir Fernando António Baptista Pereira.

Sintra

Museu Arqueológico de São Miguel de Odrinhas (Archaeological Museum): Av. Prof. Dr. D. Fernando d'Almeida, Odrinhas, 2710 Sintra; tel. (21) 961-35-74; fax (21) 961-35-78; internet museudeodrinhas.no.sapo.pt; f. 1955; epigraphs from Etruscan times to the modern age, important colln of Roman inscriptions and carved stones; archaeological artifacts from the Middle Palaeolithic to the 18th c.

Sintra Museu de Arte Moderna (Museum of Modern Art): Av. Heliodoro Salgado, 1270 Sintra; tel. (21) 924-81-70; fax (21) 924-81-77; e-mail info@sintramodernart.com; internet www.berardomodern.com; art representing 14 movements.

Torres Novas

Museu Municipal Carlos Reis (Municipal Museum): Rua do Salvador 10, 2350-415 Torres Novas; tel. (249) 81-25-35; fax (249) 81-16-96; e-mail bmtorresnovas@mail .telepac.pt; internet www.cm-torresnovas.pt/ museu; f. 1937; archaeological, historical, fine arts, ethnographical, religious art, numismatics; Dir Dr JOÃO CARLOS LOPES.

Vila Nova de Gaia

Casa Museu Teixeira Lopes (Teixeira Lopes House and Museum): Rua Teixeira Lopes 32, 4430 Vila Nova de Gaia; tel. (22) 375-12-24; fax (22) 375-20-95; e-mail cmteixeiralopes@gaianima.pt; internet www .cm-gaia.pt; f. 1933; comprises the home of the sculptor António Teixeira Lopes (1866–1942) and the adjacent Galerias Diogo de Macedo; sculpture and paintings since 19th c; furniture, ceramics, tapestries, decorative arts.

Vila Viçosa

Museu-Biblioteca da Casa de Bragança (Museum and Library of the House of Braganza): Paço Ducal, Terreiro do Paço 7160-251 Vila Viçosa; tel. (268) 98-06-59; fax (268) 98-98-08; e-mail palacio .vilavicosa@mail.telepac.pt; internet www .fcbraganca.pt; f. 1933; tapestry, furniture, tiles, European and Chinese ceramics, portraits of the Royal Family, arms, photographs, coaches and carriages; rare 16th c. printed books, Italian 16th c. majolica, and 17th and 18th c. musical archives; library of 76,000 vols; Curator Dra MARIA DE JESUS MONGE; Librarian Dr JOÃO LUÍS DA COSTA RUAS.

Viseu

Museu Grão Vasco: Paço dos Três Escalões, 3500-195 Viseu; tel. (232) 42-20-49; fax (232) 42-12-41; e-mail mgv@ipmuseus.pt; internet www.ipmuseus.pt; f. 1916; furniture, tapestry, plate, ceramics and glassware, prints and Portuguese paintings; Dir Dra ANA PAULA ABRANTES.

Universities

UNIVERSIDADE DOS AÇORES

Apdo 1422, 9501-801 Ponta Delgada (Açores)

Telephone: (296) 65-00-00
Fax: (296) 65-00-05
E-mail: uac@notes.uac.pt
Internet: www.uac.pt

Founded 1976, university status 1980
State control
Academic year: October to July

Rector: Prof. Dr VASCO MANUEL VERDASCA DA SILVA GARCIA
Academic Vice-Rector: Prof. Dr ERMELINDO MANUEL BERNARDO PEIXOTO
Administrative Vice-Rector: Prof. Dr JOSÉ ESTEVAM DE MATOS
Pro-Rectors: Dr JOÃO ANTÓNIO CÂNDIDO TAVARES (Departmental Co-ordination and Scientific Research), Prof. Dra MARIA AUGUSTA CAVACO MIGUEL (External Relations), Prof. Dr JOÃO GIL PEREIRA (Remote Regions Affairs), Prof. Dr JORGE ROSA MEDEIROS (Remote Regions Affairs), Prof. Dr JOÃO DA SILVA MADRUGA (University Relations)
Administrator: Dr VAGNER CORDERIO DA SILVA
Librarian: Dra MARIA JOÃO MOTA MELO

Library of 160,000 vols
Number of teachers: 283

Number of students: 3,532

Publication: *Archipélago* (series on human sciences, natural sciences)

DIRECTORS

Department of Agriculture: Prof. Dr ALFREDO E. S. BORBA
Department of Biology: Dr ANTÓNIO DOS SANTOS PIRES MARTINS
Department of Economics and Administration: Prof. Dr MÁRIO JOSÉ AMARAL FORTUNA
Department of Education: Prof. Dra ISABEL CONDESSA
Department of Earth Sciences: Prof. Dra GABRIELA QUEIROZ
Department of History, Philosophy and Social Sciences: Prof. Dr CARLOS CORDEIRO
Department of Literature and Modern Languages: Prof. Dr ANTÓNIO MACHADO PIRES
Department of Mathematics: Prof. Dra ISAURA RIBEIRO
Department of Oceanography and Fisheries: Prof. Dr RICARDO SERRÃO SANTOS
Department of Technological Sciences: Prof. Dra ELIZABETE LIMA

UNIVERSIDADE DO ALGARVE

Quinta da Penha, 8000 Faro

Telephone: (289) 800100
Fax: (289) 801575
E-mail: info@ualg.pt
Internet: www.ualg.pt

Founded 1979
State control
Language of instruction: Portuguese
Academic year: September to July

Rector: Prof. Dr EUGÉNIO MARIA ALTE DA VEIGA
Administrator: Dra MARIA CÂNDIDA RICO SOARES BARROSO
Librarian: Dra MARGARIDA VARGUES

Number of teachers: 575
Number of students: 7,971

DEANS

Faculty of Agricultural Science and Technology: Prof. Dra MARIA EMILIA LIMA COSTA
Faculty of Aquatic Science and Technology: Prof. Dra MARIA JOÃO BEBIANO
Faculty of Economics and Administration: Prof. Dr JOÃO ALBINO DE MATOS SILVA
Faculty of Exact Sciences and Humanities: Prof. Dr ANTÓNIO EDUARDO DE BARROS RUANO
Higher School of Education: Profa Adjunta MARIA ISABEL SANTANA DA CRUZ
Higher School of Management and Tourism: Prof. LUDGERO SEQUEIRA
Higher School of Technology: Prof. JOSÉ ANTÓNIO SILVESTRE

UNIVERSIDADE AUTÓNOMA DE LISBOA

Rua de Santa Marta 56, 1150 Lisbon

Telephone: (21) 317-76-00
E-mail: secgeral@universidade-autonoma.pt
Internet: www.universidade-autonoma.pt

Founded 1985
Private control

Rector: Prof. Dr JUSTINO MENDES DE ALMEIDA
Registrar: Prof. Dr JORGE TRACANA DE CARVALHO
Librarian: Prof. Dr MIGUEL FARIA

Library of 20,000 vols
Number of teachers: 500
Number of students: 8,700

HEADS OF DEPARTMENTS

Applied Mathematics: Profa Dra FERNANDA LENCASTRE BERNARDO
Business Studies: Prof. Dr J. A. ALMAÇA
Economics: Prof. Dr ARLINDO DONÁRIO

Engineering: Prof. Dr JOÃO TRAVASSOS
History: Prof. Dr A. CARVALHO HOMEM
Informatics: Prof. CARLOS BILELO GONÇALVES
Information Sciences: Prof. Dr ANTÓNIO LENCASTRE BERNARDO
International Relations: Prof. Dr R. LADEIRO MONTEIRO
Law: Prof. Dr F. LUCAS PIRES
Modern Languages and Literature: Prof. Dr ÁLVARO MANUEL MACHADO
Sociology: Prof. Dr POLICARPO LOPES

UNIVERSIDADE DE AVEIRO

Campus Universitario de Santiago, 3810-193 Aveiro

Telephone: (234) 37-02-00
Fax: (234) 37-09-85
E-mail: sre@adm.ua.pt
Internet: www.ua.pt

Founded 1973
State control
Academic year: September to July

Rector: Prof. MARIA HELENA VAZ DE CARVALHO NAZARÉ
Vice-Rectors: Prof. FERNANDO MANUEL BICO MARQUES, Prof. FRANCISCO ANTÓNIO CARDOSO VAZ, Prof. MANUEL ANTÓNIO COTÃO DE ASSUNÇÃO, Prof. ANTÓNIO MANUEL DE BRITO FERRARI DE ALMEIDA, Prof. JOSÉ ALBERTO DOS SANTOS RAFAEL
Chief Administrative Officer: Dr JOSÉ DA CRUZ COSTA
Librarian: Dra MARIA EMÍLIA M. FERREIRA ARAÚJO

Number of teachers: 952
Number of students: 11,905

Publication: *Lineas* (4 a year)

HEADS OF DEPARTMENTS

Biology: Prof. Dr V. M. DOS SANTOS QUINTINO
Ceramics and Glass Engineering: Prof. Dr J. A. L. BAPTISTA
Chemistry: Prof. Dr F. M. DOMINGUES
Didactics and Educational Technology: Profa Dra I. DA S. C. SÁCHAVES
Education Sciences: Prof. Dr A. R. DA COSTA
Electronics and Telecommunications: Prof. Dr F. M. S. RAMOS
Environment and Planning: Prof. Dr E. A. CASTRO
Geosciences: Prof. Dr F. T. ROCHA
Languages and Cultures: Prof. Dr J. M. N. TORRÃO
Mathematics: Prof. Dr H. R. MALONEK
Physics: Prof. Dr J. L. PINTO
Section of Civil Engineering: Prof. Dr J. C. CARDOSO
Section of Economy, Management and Industrial Engineering: Prof. Dr R. A. G. SANTIAGO
Section of Mechanical Engineering: Prof. Dr J. J. DE A. GRÁCIO

ATTACHED POLYTECHNIC SCHOOLS

Águeda Higher School of Technology and Management.
Aveiro North Higher School.
Higher Institute of Accountancy and Administration.
Higher School of Health Sciences.

UNIVERSIDADE DA BEIRA INTERIOR

Rua Marquês de Ávila e Bolama, 6200 Covilhã

Telephone: (275) 31-90-00
Fax: (275) 31-90-57
E-mail: ubiserct@ubi.pt
Internet: www.ubi.pt

Founded 1986

Rector: Prof. Dr MANUEL JOSÉ DOS SANTOS SILVA

Administrative Officer: Dr José Esteves Correia Pinheiro
Librarian: Dra Joana Lopes Dias
Library of 74,000 vols
Number of teachers: 460
Number of students: 5,443
Publication: *Boletim Informativo 'Urbi@Orbi'*

HEADS OF DEPARTMENTS

Department of Aerospace Science: Prof. Dr Ivan de Azevedo Camelier
Department of Business Administration: Profa Dra Zélia Maria da Silva Serrasqueiro
Department of Chemistry: Prof. Dr Paulo Jorge da Silva Almeida
Department of Civil Engineering: Prof. Dr Vitor Manuel Pissarra Cavaleiro
Department of Communication and Arts: Prof. Dr José Manuel Boavida Santos
Department of Computer Science: Prof. Dr Abel João Padrão Gomes
Department of Electromechanical Engineering: Prof. Dr Silvio José Pinto Simões Mariano
Department of Mathematics: Prof. Dr António Jorge Gomes Bento
Department of Paper Science and Technology: Prof. Dr Rogério Manuel dos Santos Simões
Department of Physics: Prof. Dr João Pinheiro Providência e Costa
Department of Psychology and Education: Prof. Dr Manuel Joaquim da Silva Loureiro
Department of Sociology: Prof. Dr Alcides Almeida Monteiro
Department of Sports Science: Prof. Dr Fernando Franco de Almada
Department of Textile Science and Technology: Prof. Dr Rui Alberto Lopes Miguel

UNIVERSIDADE CATÓLICA PORTUGUESA

Palma de Cima, 1649-023 Lisbon
Telephone: (21) 721-40-00
Fax: (21) 727-02-56
E-mail: info@reitoria.ucp.pt
Internet: www.ucp.pt
Founded 1968
Private control
Language of instruction: Portuguese
Academic year: September to July
Chancellor: Patriarch José Policarpo
Rector: Prof. Manuel Braga da Cruz
Vice-Rectors: Prof. Fernando Branco, Prof. João Duarte Lourenço, Prof. Luísa Leal de Faria
Librarian: Prof. Luísa Leal de Faria
Number of teachers: 850
Number of students: 10,500
Publications: *Didaskalia* (2 a year), *Direito e Justiça* (3 a year), *Economia* (3 a year), *Gestão e Desenvolvimento*, *Humanística e Teológica*, *Lusitania Sacra*, *Máthesis*, *Povos e Culturas*, *Revista Portuguesa de Filosofia* (4 a year), *Revista Portuguesa de Humanidades*, *Theologica* (4 a year)

DIRECTORS

Faculty of Arts: Prof. Aires do Couto
Faculty of Economics and Management (Lisbon): Prof. Fátima Barros
Faculty of Economics and Management (Porto): Prof. Alberto Coraceiro de Castro
Faculty of Engineering: Prof. Manuel Barata Marques
Faculty of Human Sciences: Prof. Isabel Capeloa Gil
Faculty of Law: Prof. Rui Medeiros
Faculty of Philosophy: Prof. Nuno da Silva Gonçalves

Faculty of Social Sciences: Prof. A. Oliveira Ramos
Faculty of Theology: Prof. Peter Stilwell
Castro College of Biotechnology: Francisco Xavier Malcata
Castro College of Science and Technology: C. Passos Morgado
Education Institute: Joaquim Azevedo
European Studies Institute: Ernáni Lopes
Institute of Bioethics: Walter Osswald
Institute for Canon Law: Prof. M. Saturnino Gomes
Institute for Distance Learning: Roberto Carneiro
Institute of Health Sciences: Prof. A. Castro Caldas
Oriental Studies Institute: Luis Filipe Thomaz
Political Studies Institute: João Carlos Espada
School of Fine Arts: Prof. Francisco Carvalho Guerra
University Institute for Development and Social Progress: Prof. J. Ribeiro Gomes

ATTACHED RESEARCH INSTITUTES

Cardinal Hoeffner Centre for Social and Pastoral Studies: Dir Luís Marinho Antunes.
Centre for Applied Economic and Managerial Studies: Dir Alberto Coraceiro de Castro.
Centre for Applied Studies: Dir Fernando Machado.
Centre for Canon Law: Dir Manuel Saturino Gomes.
Centre for Opinion Polls: Dir Mário Lages.
Centre for Portuguese and Brazilian Literature and Culture: Dir Manuel Cândido Pimentel.
Centre for Portuguese-speaking Peoples and Cultures: Dir Roberto Carneiro.
Centre for Religious History: Dir Manuel Clemente.
Centre for Studies on Ethical, Political and Religious Philosophy: Dir Mendo de Castro Henriques.
Centre for Studies on Portuguese Thought: Dir Ângelo Alves.
Human Rights Institute: Dir Jorge Miranda.
Information Problems Centre: Dir Luís Valadares Tavares.
International Studies Centre: Exec. Dir Nuno Pinheiro Torres.

UNIVERSIDADE DE COIMBRA

Paço das Escolas, 3004-531 Coimbra
Telephone: (239) 85-98-00
Fax: (239) 82-58-41
E-mail: info@ci.uc.pt
Internet: www.uc.pt
Founded 1290 (in Lisbon)
State control
Language of instruction: Portuguese
Academic year: September to July
Rector: Prof. Dr Fernando Jorge Rama Seabra Santos
Vice-Rectors: Prof. Dr António José Avelãs Nunes, Prof. Dr João Carlos Marques, Prof. Dr Antonio Manuel de Oliveira Gomes Martins, Prof. Dra Cristina Maria Silva Robalo Cordeiro
Pro-Rectors: Prof. Dr Francisco José de Baptista Veiga, Prof. Dr José António Raimundo Mendes da Silva, Prof. Dr Fernando Alberto Deométrio Rodrigues Alves Guerra
Registrar: Dr Carlos José Luzio Vaz

General Library Director: Prof. Dr Carlos Manuel Carlos Manuel
Director of University Archives: Dra Maria José Azevedo Santos
Library: see Libraries and Archives
Number of teachers: 1,472, including 494 professors
Number of students: 21,165
Publications: *Acta Universitatis Conimbrigensis*, *Anuário da Universidade*, *Biblos*, *Boletim do Arquivo da Universidade*, *Boletim da Biblioteca da Universidade de Coimbra*, *Boletim do Centro de Estudos Geográficos*, *Boletim das Ciências Económicas*, *Boletim da Faculdade de Direito*, *Boletim do Laboratório de Fonética Experimental*, *Brasilia*, *Conimbriga*, *Humanitas*, *Revista Ciência Biológica*, *Revista de História Literária de Portugal*, *Revista Portuguesa de Filologia*, *Revista Portuguesa de História*, *Revista Portuguesa de Pedagogia*, *Revista da Universidade*

DEANS

Faculty of Arts: Prof. Dr Lúcio José Sobral da Cunha
Faculty of Economics: Prof. Dr Pedro Augusto de Melo Lopes Ferreira
Faculty of Law: Prof. Dr Manuel Carlos Lopes Porto
Faculty of Medicine: Prof. Dr Francisco José Franqueira de Castro e Sousa
Faculty of Pharmacy: Prof. Dr Adriano Teixeira Barbosa de Sousa
Faculty of Psychology and Education: Prof. Dr José Manuel Tomás da Silva
Faculty of Science and Technology: Prof. Dr Lélio Quaresma Lobo
Faculty of Sports Science and Physical Education: Profa Dra Ana Maria Miranda Botelho Teixeira

ATTACHED INSTITUTES

Centro de Estudos Sociais da Faculdade de Economia da Universidade de Coimbra (Social Studies Centre): Colégio de São Domingos, Largo de Dom Dinis, Apdo 3087, 3000 Coimbra; tel. (239) 82-64-59; Dir Prof. Dr Boaventura Sousa Santos; publ. *Revista Crítica de Ciências Sociais* (quarterly).
Instituto Botânico 'Dr Júlio Henriques' (Botanical Institute): Arcos do Jardim, 3049 Coimbra Codex; tel. (239) 82-28-97; f. 1775; library of 114,000 vols; Dir Prof. Dr J. Firmino Moreira Mesquita; publ. *Boletim*, *Index Seminum*, *Memórias* and *Anuário* of Sociedade Broteriana.
Instituto de Climatologia e Hidrologia (Climatological and Hydrological Institute): Faculdade de Medicina, Universidade de Coimbra, 3000 Coimbra; f. 1930; Pres. Prof. Dr Frederico Teixeira; publ. *Publicações do Instituto de Climatologia e Hidrologia*.
Instituto de Estudos Clássicos (Classical Studies Institute): Faculdade de Letras, Universidade de Coimbra, 3049 Coimbra Codex; tel. (239) 410-99-00; f. 1947; library of 15,000 vols, 500 periodicals; Dir Prof. Dr José Ribeiro Ferreira.
Instituto Geofísico (Geophysical Institute): Av. Dias da Silva, 3030 Coimbra; f. 1864; library of 16,000 vols; meteorological, magnetic and seismological observatory; Dir Prof. Dr António Ferreira Soares; publ. *Observações Meteorológicas, Magnéticas e Sismológicas* (annually).
Instituto Nacional de Medicina Legal (National Institute of Legal Medicine): Largo da Sé Nova, 3000-213 Coimbra; tel. (239) 85-42-20; fax (239) 83-64-70; e-mail correio@inml.mj.pt; internet www.inml.mj.pt; f. 1919; library of 5,000 vols, 45 periodicals; Dir Prof. Dr Duarte Nuno Pessoa Vieira.

Museums: see under Museums and Art Galleries

UNIVERSIDADE DE ÉVORA

Largo dos Colegiais, Apdo 94, 7002-554 Évora
Telephone: (266) 74-08-00
Fax: (266) 74-08-04
Internet: www.uevora.pt
Founded 1973, university status 1979
State control
Language of instruction: Portuguese
Academic year: September to September
Rector: MANUEL FERREIRA PATRÍCIO
Vice-Rectors: JOSÉ ANTUNES AFONSO DE ALMEIDA, DIEGO CAEIRO FIGUEIREDO, AMÍLCAR JOAQUIM DA CONCEIÇÃO SERRÃO, MANUEL RIJO
Number of teachers: 574
Number of students: 7,449

PROFESSORS

BRAUMANN, C. A. S., Stochastic Processes
CARVALHO, M. J. G. P. R., Agricultural Sciences
CLARA, M. I. E. DA, Plant Pathology
CORTE-REAL, J. A. M., Physics
FERREIRA, A. A. C. G., Soil Conservation
LOPES, R. M. E. J., Natural Resource Economics
LOURENÇO, M. E. V., Plant Physiology
MACHADO, J. A. S. G., History of Art
MARQUES, C. A. F., Agricultural Economics
MORAIS, J. M. C., Toxicology
OLIVEIRA, M. R. G., Phytotechnics
PINHEIRO, A. C. A., Agricultural Economics
RAMOS, F. M., Social and Cultural Anthropology
ROSA, R. M. V. N., Energetics, Climatology and Materials
SANTOS, M. A. O. P., Physics
SERRALHEIRO, R. P., Soil and Water Engineering
ZORRINHO, J. C. D., Information Systems Analysis

UNIVERSIDADE DE LISBOA

Alameda da Universidade, 1649-004 Lisbon
Telephone: (21) 793-91-93
Fax: (21) 796-36-24
E-mail: reitoria@reitoria.ul.pt
Internet: www.ul.pt
Founded 1288, restored 1911
State control
Academic year: October to July
Rector: Prof. JOSÉ BARATA MOURA
Vice-Rectors: Prof. ANTÓNIO M. DE ALMEIDA, Prof. JOÃO S. LOPES, Prof. ANTÓNIO S. NÓVOA
Administrator: Dra MARIA LUISA CERDEIRA
Librarian: Dra MARIA LEAL VIEIRA
Number of teachers: 1,853
Number of students: 19,917
Publications: *Agenda* (monthly), *Boletim*

PRESIDENTS OF DIRECTIVE COUNCILS

Faculty of Dental Medicine: Prof. ANTÓNIO V. TAVARES
Faculty of Fine Arts: Prof. CRISTINA A. TAVARES
Faculty of Humanities: Prof. ISABEL C. HENRIQUES
Faculty of Law: Prof. ANTÓNIO SOUSA FRANCO
Faculty of Medicine: Prof. J. MARTINS E SILVA
Faculty of Pharmacy: Prof. JOSÉ MORAIS
Faculty of Psychology and Education: Prof. TERESA V. CARVALHO
Faculty of Science: Prof. NUNO GUIMARÃES

HEADS OF DEPARTMENTS

Faculty of Humanities (Alameda da Universidade, 1649-214 Lisbon; tel. (21) 792-00-00;

fax (21) 796-00-63; e-mail flul.informacoes@mail.fl.ul.pt; internet www.fl.ul.pt):

Anglo-American Studies: Prof. ÁLVARO PINA
Classical Languages and Literatures: Prof. ARNALDO ESPÍRITO SANTO
Geography: Prof. JORGE GASPAR
German Studies: Prof. TERESA SERUYA
History: Prof. JOSÉ A. RAMOS
Linguistics: Prof. IVO CASTRO
Literatures: Prof. ALBERTO CARVALHO
Philosophy: Prof. JOÃO BRANQUINHO
Portuguese Language and Culture for Foreign Students: Prof. MALACA CASTELEIRO
Postgraduate Course of Librarianship and Information Sciences: Prof. AIRES NASCIMENTO

Faculty of Law (Alameda da Universidade – Cidade Universitária, 1649-014 Lisboa; tel. (21) 797-70-51; fax (21) 795-03-03; e-mail webmaster@correio.fd.ul.pt; internet www.fd.ul.pt):

Historical and Judicial Sciences: Prof. Dr RUI DE ALBUQUERQUE
Judicial and Economic Sciences: Prof. PITTA E CUNHA
Judicial and Political Sciences: Prof. JORGE MIRANDA
Judicial Sciences: Prof. OLIVEIRA ASCENÇÃO

Faculty of Medicine (Av. Prof. Egas Moniz, HSM – Cidade Universitária, 1649-028 Lisbon; tel. (21) 797-43-65; fax (21) 796-40-59; e-mail utm@fm.ul.pt; internet www.fm.ul.pt):

Institutes:

Anatomy: Prof. ANTÓNIO G. FERREIRA
Biochemistry: Prof. J. MARTINS E SILVA
Biomathematics: Prof. HELENA NICOLAU
Genetics: Prof. MANUEL PIRES BICHO
Histology and Embriology: Prof. MARIA DO CARMO FONSECA
Immunology: Prof. ANTÓNIO COUTINHO
Legal Medicine: Prof. JOÃO LOBO ANTUNES
Medical Deontology: Prof. LESSEPS DOS REYS
Medical Psychology: Prof. LUISA FIGUEIRA
Microbiology: Prof. MELO CRISTINO
Museum (History of Medicine): Prof. GOMES PEDRO
Neurological Therapy: Prof. J. ALEXANDRE RIBEIRO
Nutrition: Prof. ERMELINDA CAMILO
Nuclear Medicine: Prof. FERNANDO GODINHO
Pathological Anatomy: Prof. MARIA JOSÉ FORJAZ LACERDA
Pharmacology: Prof. J. A. RIBEIRO
Physiological Chemistry: Prof. J. MARTINS E SILVA
Physiology: Prof. SILVA CARVALHO
Preventive Medicine and Public Health: Prof. J. PEREIRA MIGUEL

University Clinics:

Cardiology: Prof. MARIA CELESTE VAGUEIRO
Cardio-Thoracic Surgery: Prof. RUI DE LIMA
Dermatology: Prof. Dr GUERRA RODRIGO
Gynaecology: Prof. MADALENA BOTELHO
Infectious Diseases: Prof. FRANCISCO ANTUNES
Medicine I: Prof. Dr A. G. PALMA CARLOS
Medicine II: Prof. Dr M. CARNEIRO DE MOURA
Medicine III: Prof. LUCIANO RAVARA
Neurology: Prof. Dr CASTRO CALDAS
Neurosurgery: Prof. Dr LOBO ANTUNES
Ophthalmology: Prof. Dr RIBEIRO DA SILVA
Orthopaedics: Prof. A. RODRIGUES GOMES
Otorhinolaryngology: Prof. Dr MÁRIO ANDREA
Paediatrics: Prof. JOÃO GOMES PEDRO
Plastic Surgery: Prof. A. CORDEIRO FERREIRA
Chest Medicine: Prof. ANTÓNIO RODRIGUES COUTO

Psychiatry: Prof. J. SIMÕES DA FONSECA
Radiology: Prof. JORGE CABRAL CAMPOS
Surgery I: Prof. Dr VEIGA FERNANDES
Surgery II: Prof. H. BICHA CASTELO
Surgery III: Prof. FERNANDO PAREDES
Urology: Prof. J. CARNEIRO DE MOURA
Vascular Surgery: Prof. Dr A. DINIS DA GAMA

Faculty of Science (Campo Grande – Cidade Universitária, 1749-016 Lisbon; tel. (21) 757-31-41; fax (21) 759-77-16; e-mail info.fcul@fc.ul.pt; internet www.fc.ul.pt):

Animal Biology: Prof. MARIA JOSÉ R. COSTA
Chemistry and Biochemistry: Prof. HELENA FLORÊNCIO CASTRO
Geology: Prof. JOSÉ MUNHÁ
Education: Prof. MARIA ODETE VALENTE
Informatics: Prof. PEDRO B. VEIGA
Mathematics: Prof. TERESA LEMOS
Physics: Prof. FELIPE D. SANTOS
Plant Biology: Prof. JOSÉ ALBERTO FEIJÓ
Statistics and Operational Research: Prof. ANTÓNIA TURKMAN

ATTACHED RESEARCH INSTITUTES

'Cámara Pestana' Bacteriological Institute: R. do Instituto Bacteriológico, 1169-410 Lisbon; Dir Prof. JOSÉ MELO CRISTINO.
'Infante D. Luis' Geophysical Institute: Rua da Escola Politécnica 58, 1250-102 Lisbon; Dir Prof. ILÍDIO MARTINS.
Institute of Careers Guidance: Largo Trindade Coelho 21, 1200-470 Lisbon; Dir Prof. HELENA REBELO PINTO.
Institute of Social Sciences: Av. Prof. Aníbal de Bettencourt 9, 1600-189 Lisbon.

UNIVERSIDADE LUSÍADA

Rua da Junqueira 190/198, 1300 Lisbon
Campuses in Lisbon, Oporto and Vila Nova de Famalição
Telephone: (21) 363-99-44
Fax: (21) 363-83-07
E-mail: info@lis.ulusiada.pt
Internet: www.ulusiada.pt
Founded 1986 by Cooperativa de Ensino Universidade Lusíada
Private control
Academic year: October to June
Rector: Prof. Dr ANTÓNIO JORGE MARTINS DA MOTTA VEIGA
Vice-Rector: Prof. Dr JOSÉ J. GONÇALVES DE PROENÇA
Librarian: Dr MADALENA FERNANDES
Library of 15,000 vols
Number of teachers: 986
Number of students: 17,041
Publications: *Boletim Informativo*, *CDE Bulletin*, *Pólis* (legal-political studies), *Revista Lusíada de Ciência e Cultura*

HEADS OF DEPARTMENTS

Accountancy: Prof. Dr ARMANDINO ROCHA (Famalição)
Architecture: Prof. Arqto CARLOS SANTOS (Famalição): Prof. Dr Arqto JOAQUIM BRAIZINHA (Lisbon): Prof. Dr Arqto MANUEL DIOGO (Oporto)
Economics: Prof. Dr E. RAPOSO DE MEDEIROS (Lisbon): Prof. Dr LUÍS MARIA TEIXEIRA PINTO (Oporto)
Economics and Business Studies: Prof. Dr FRANCISCO V. S. MARTINS
Electronic and Computer Science Engineering: Prof. Dr J. CAMPOS NEVES (Famalição)
History: Prof. Dr JOÃO CASTRO NUNES
Industrial Design: Prof. Dr Arqto MANUEL DIOGO (Porto): Prof. Dr Arqto JOAQUIM BRAIZINHA (Lisbon)
Industrial Engineering and Management: Prof. Dr J. SANTOS CRUZ (Famalição)

International Relations: Prof. Dr José Manuel Durão Barroso (Lisbon): Prof. Dr Fernando Roboredo Seara (Oporto)
Law: Prof. Dr Duarte Nogueira (Lisbon): Prof. Dr Rogério Soares (Oporto)
Management: Prof. Dr Mário Patinha Antão (Lisbon): Profa Dra Isabel Soares (Oporto)
Mathematics: Prof. Dr A. Pereira Gomes (Lisbon): Profa Dra Margarida Barros (Oporto)
Textile Engineering: Prof. Dr Gustavo da Costa Pereira (Famalicão)

ATTACHED INSTITUTES

Archaeology and History of Art Centre: Dir Prof. Dr Luís Raposo.

Architecture Technologies Research Centre: Dir Prof. Arqto. N. Santos Pinheiro.

Business Institute: Dir Prof. Dr P. Rebelo de Sousa.

Centre for the Study and Research of Drug Addiction: Dir Prof. Dr António Martins da Cruz.

Consumer Law Institute: Dir Prof. Dr Mário Frota.

Cultural Institute: Dir Prof. Dr António Martins da Cruz.

Environmental Law Institute: Dir Prof. Dr B. Martins da Cruz.

Environment Research Centre: Dir Prof. Dr G. Costa Pereira.

European Studies Institute: Dir Prof. Dr José Luís da Cruz Vilaça.

Historical Research Centre: Dir Prof. Dr Fernando Castelo Branco Chaves.

Housing Research Centre: Dir Prof. Arqto. José Callado.

Information, Communication and Computer Research Centre: Dir Prof. Eng. António Brito.

International Relationships Research Centre: Dir Prof. Dr Joaquim de Carvalho.

Language Institute: Dir Prof. Dra Maria Emília Galvão.

Law and Mental Health Institute: Dir Prof. Dr António Martins da Cruz.

Law Research Centre: Dir Prof. Dr Inocêncio Galvão Telles.

Management Research Centre: Dir Prof. Dr Mário Patinha Antão.

Mathematics Research Centre: Dir Prof. Dr Nuno da Costa Pereira.

UNIVERSIDADE DA MADEIRA

Edifício da Penteada (3° Andar), Penteada, 9000 Funchal, Madeira
Telephone: (291) 70-50-70
Fax: (291) 70-50-89
E-mail: sda@uma.pt
Internet: www.uma.pt
Founded 1988
State control
Academic year: September to August
President: Prof. Dr Pedro Pereira Telhado
Vice-Rectors: Profa Dr Nuno Jardim, Profa Dra Isabel Torres
Administrator: Dra Graça Moniz
Librarian: Dra Maria Yolanda Pereira da Silva

Library of 95,400 vols
Number of teachers: 200
Number of students: 2,528

PRESIDENTS AND DIRECTORS

Department of Biology: Prof. Dr António Brehm
Department of Chemistry: Profa Dra Paula Castilho (Pres.)

Department of Education: Prof. Dr Carlos Fino
Department of Mathematics: Prof. Dr José Carmo
Department of Physics: Prof. Dr Mikhail Benilov (Pres.)
Department of Romance Studies: Prof. Dr Minh Há Lo Geero
Section of Management: Prof. Dr Pedro Telhado Pereira
Section of Physical Education: Prof. Dr Sena Lino
Section of Systems Engineering and Computers: Prof. Dr Joaquim Amandio Rodrigues de Azuedo
Autonomous Section of Classical and Humanistic Studies: Prof. Dr Glório Franco

UNIVERSIDADE DO MINHO

Largo do Paço, 4704-553 Braga
Telephone: (253) 60-41-00
Fax: (253) 61-69-36
E-mail: gcii@reitoria.uminho.pt
Internet: www.uminho.pt
Founded 1973
State control
Language of instruction: Portuguese
Academic year: October to July

Rector: Prof. António Guimarães Rodrigues
Vice-Rectors: Prof. Viriato Capela, Prof. José Mendes, Prof. Manuel Mota, Prof. Acílio Rocha
Pro-Rector: Prof. Irene Montenegro
Chief Administrative Officer: Eng. José F. Aguilar Monteiro
Librarian: Dr Eloy Rodrigues

Number of teachers: 1,200
Number of students: 16,000

Publications: *Cadernos do Noroeste, Ciência Jurídica, Fórum, Revista Portuguesa de Educação, UM Boletim, UM Jornal*

DEANS

Architecture: Prof. Paulo Cruz
Arts, Humanities and Human Sciences: Prof. Fernando Augusto Machado
Childhood and Elementary Education: Prof. António Sousa Fernandes
Economics, Business and Political Sciences: Prof. Margarida Almeida
Education and Psychology: Prof. Leandro Almeida
Engineering: Prof. António Cunha
Health School: Prof. Sérgio Machado dos Santos
Law: Prof. Luís Gonçalves
Nursing School: Prof. Ana Maria Pacheco
Sciences: Prof. João Ferreira

PROFESSORS

Alves Bernardo, C. A., Polymer Engineering
Alves Ferreira, J. F., Physics
Alves Pereira, P. A., Civil Engineering
Araújo, M. D., Textile Engineering
Assunção Montenegro, M. I., Chemistry
Barbosa Freitas, V. L., Computer Science
Borges Almeida, J. M., Physics
Cabeço Silva, A. A., Textile Engineering
Cadima Ribeiro, J. A., Economics
Calado Ferreira, M. I., Physics
Carvalho Proença, A. J., Computer Science
Couto Teixeira, J. A., Biological Engineering
Duarte Pousada, A. S., Polymer Engineering
Eiras Capela, J. V., History
Esgalhado Valença, J. M., Computer Science
Estanqueiro Rocha, A., Philosophy
Estrela Leão, M. C., Biology
Farhangmehr, M., Management and Public Administration
Gomes Correia, A., Civil Engineering
Gomes Covas, J. A., Polymer Engineering
Gomes Mendes, J. F., Civil Engineering

Gomes Mota, M. J., Biological Engineering
Guimarães Almeida, L. M., Textile Engineering
Guimarães Rodrigues, A. J., Industrial Engineering
Lemos Martins, M., Communication Science
Machado Santos, S., Computer Science
Magalhães Cunha, A. A., Polymer Engineering
Monteiro Couto, C. A., Electronics Engineering
Oliveira Campos, A. M., Chemistry
Oliveira Rocha, J. A., Management and Public Administration
Pereira Carmelo, J. M., Physics
Pereira Vieira, J. M., Civil Engineering
Ramos Morgado, R. J., Electronics Engineering
Rego Paiva Proença, M. F., Chemistry
Rocha Armada, M. J., Management and Public Administration
Rocha Gomes, J. I., Textile Engineering
Rodrigues Vaz, E. G., Mathematics
Salvador Pinheiro, J. D., Biological Engineering
Sanches Simões, J. M., Childhood Studies
Santos Soares, L. J., Biological Engineering
Silva Ferraz, A. M., Economics
Silva Lima, N. M., Childhood Studies
Silva Maia, H. L., Chemistry
Simões Carvalho, M. G., Childhood Studies
Tavares Oliveira, D. R., Biological Engineering
Varela Freitas, C. M., Childhood Studies

ATTACHED RESEARCH INSTITUTES

3Bs Research Group (Biomaterials, Biodegradables and Biomimetics): Dir Prof. Rui Reis.

Algorithmic–Centre of Information Technology and Electronics: Dir J. Monteiro.

Anthropology Research Institute: Dir L. Cunha.

Archaeology Unit: Dir M. Martins.

Biological Engineering Research Centre: Dir Prof. Manuel Mota.

Centre for Biology: Dir Prof. Maria Manuela Samsonetty G. Côrte-Real.

Centre for Chemistry: Dir Prof. Ana Maria Campos.

Centre for Children's Studies: Dir Dr Ana Maria Almeida.

Centre for Civil Engineering: Dir António Gomes Correia.

Centre for Communication and Society Studies: Dir M. Martins.

Centre for Computation Sciences and Technologies: Dir Prof. Alexandre Santos.

Centre for Earth Sciences: Dir Prof. Graciette Tavares Dias.

Centre for Economics and Management: Dir C. Machado.

Centre for Geological Research, Mapping and Resources Valorisation: Dir Prof. Carlos Leal Gomes.

Centre for Humanistic Studies: Dir E. Keating.

Centre for Law Studies: Dir Prof. Gravato Morais.

Centre for Literacy Promotion and Child Well-Being: Dir M. Carvalho.

Centre for Mathematics: Dir Prof. Rui Ralha.

Centre for Physics: Dir Prof. Sérgio Miguel Nascimento.

Centre for Population and Society Studies: Dir M. Durães.

Centre for Production Systems Engineering: Dir Prof. Madalena Araújo.

Centre for Research in Education: Dir Prof. MARIA DE FÁTIMA SEQUEIRA.

Centre for Research in Psychology: Dir Prof. PAULO MANUEL MACHADO.

Economics Politics Research Institute: Dir L. VEIGA.

European, International and Industrial Economics Research Institute: Dir M. PROENÇA.

Geography Research Centre: Dir J. SARMENTO.

Health and Life Sciences Research Institute: Dir C. LEÃO.

Historic Studies Institute: Dir J. CAPELA.

History and Social Sciences Centre: Dir E. LEANDRO.

Management and Public Policy Research Institute: Dir S. CAMÕES.

Management Studies Institute: Dir M. CORTEZ.

Mechanical Engineering Centre: Dir J. TEIXEIRA.

Micro-economics Research Institute: Dir L. PINTO.

'Officina Mathematica' Research Institute: Dir Prof. WOLFRAM ERLHAGEN.

Political Science and International Relations Research Institute: Dir L. PEREIRA.

Polymer Engineering Research Institute: Dir C. BERNARDO.

Sociology Studies Institute: Dir C. SILVA.

Textile Science and Technology Centre: Dir F. FERREIRA.

UNIVERSIDADE NOVA DE LISBOA
(New University of Lisbon)

Campus de Campolide, 1099-085 Lisbon

Telephone: (21) 371-56-00
Fax: (21) 371-56-14
E-mail: reitoria@unl.pt
Internet: www.unl.pt
Founded 1973
State control
Academic year: October to July

Rector: Prof. Dr LEOPOLDO GUIMARÃES
Vice-Rectors: Prof. Dra SALWA CASTELO-BRANCO, Prof. Dr JOSÉ RUEFF
Pro-Rectors: Prof. Dr JOSÉ ANTÓNIO GIRÃO, Prof. Dr ANTÓNIO PORTO, Prof. Dra MARIA ROSÁRIO SENTIERO, Prof. Dr ÁLVARO F. SILVA
Administrator: Dra FERNANDA ANTÃO

Number of teachers: 1,410
Number of students: 14,580

Publications: *Faculdade de Ciências Médicas: Annual Report, Faculdade de Ciências Médicas: Nova Medicina* (quarterly), *Faculdade de Ciências Sociais e Humanas: Bulletin, Portuguese and Japanese Studies* (annually), *Faculdade de Ciências Sociais e Humanas: Cadernos de Cultura* (irregular), *Faculdade de Ciências Sociais e Humanas: Cadernos de Filosofia* (2 a year), *Faculdade de Ciências Sociais e Humanas: Ethnologia* (irregular), *Faculdade de Ciências Sociais e Humanas: Faces de Eva: estudos sobre a mulher* (2 a year), *Faculdade de Ciências Sociais e Humanas: Fórum Sociológico* (2 a year), *Faculdade de Ciências Sociais e Humanas: Geolnova* (2 a year), *Faculdade de Ciências Sociais e Humanas: Revista de Estudos Anglo-Portugueses* (annually), *Faculdade de Ciências Sociais e Humanas: Revista da FCSH* (annually), *Faculdade de Direito Cultura: Revista de História e Teoria das Ideias* (annually), *Faculdade de Ciências Sociais e Humanas: Working Paper* (irregular),

Frontal (irregular), *Instituto de Tecnologia Química e Biológica: Revista Portuguesa de Saúde Pública* (2 a year, one annual themed journal), *Thémis* (2 a year)

DIRECTORS

Faculty of Economics: Prof. Dr VASCO BORGES SANTOS
Faculty of Law: Prof. Dr JOÃO CAUPERS
Faculty of Medical Sciences: Prof. Dr ANTÓNIO M. RENDAS
Faculty of Sciences and Technology: Prof. Dr ANTÓNIO NUNES DOS SANTOS
Faculty of Social and Human Sciences: Prof. Dr JORGE CRESPO
Institute of Chemical and Biological Technology: Prof. Dr PETER F. LINDLEY
Institute of Hygiene and Tropical Medicine: Prof. Dr JORGE TORGAL
Institute of Statistics and Information Management: Prof. Dr MARCO PAINHO
National School of Public Health: Prof. Dr FERNANDO GALVÃO DE MELO

UNIVERSIDADE DO PORTO

Rua D. Manuel II, 4050-345 Porto Codex

Telephone: (22) 607-35-00
Fax: (22) 609-87-36
E-mail: grp@reit.up.pt
Internet: www.up.pt
Founded 1911
State control
Academic year: October to July

Rector: JOSÉ NOVAIS BARBOSA
Vice-Rectors: ISABEL AZEVEDO, JOSÉ FERREIRA GOMES, JOSÉ MARQUES DOS SANTOS, FRANCISCO RIBEIRO DA SILVA

Number of teachers: 1,896 (full-time)
Number of students: 27,050 (23,624 undergraduate, 3,426 postgraduate)

Publications: *Arquivos de Medicina* (medicine), *Arquivos Portugueses de Cirurgia* (surgery), *Cadernos de Consulta Psicológica* (consultant psychology), *Cadernos de Literatura Comparada* (comparative literature), *Douro, Estudos CEJD* (sport), *Mediaevalia* (medieval studies), *Revista Africana Studia* (African studies), *Revista de Filosofia* (philosophy), *Revista de Geografia* (geography), *Revista de História* (history), *Revista de Línguas e Literaturas* (languages and literature), *Revista Educação Sociedade e Cultura* (education, society and culture), *Revista Estudos, Revista Património* (national heritage), *Revista População e Sociedade* (population and society), *Revista Portugália, Revista Portuguesa de Ciências do Desporto* (sports sciences), *Sociologia* (sociology), *Terceira Margem* (Brazilian studies)

DEANS

Faculty of Architecture: DOMINGOS TAVARES
Faculty of Arts: ANA MONTEIRO
Faculty of Dental Medicine: FERNANDO PERES
Faculty of Economics: JOSÉ DA SILVA COSTA
Faculty of Engineering: CARLOS A. VEIGA DA COSTA
Faculty of Fine Arts: RODRIGO A. PINA CABRAL
Faculty of Law: CÂNDIDO AGRA
Faculty of Medicine: JOSÉ M. TEIXEIRA AMARANTE
Faculty of Nutrition and Food Sciences: MARIA D. VAZ DE ALMEIDA
Faculty of Pharmacy: JORGE M. MOREIRA GONÇALVES
Faculty of Psychology and Education: PEDRO N. A. LOPES DOS SANTOS
Faculty of Science: JOSÉ M. MACHADO DA SILVA
Faculty of Sport Science and Physical Education: JORGE OLÍMPIO BENTO
Porto Business School: DANIEL BESSA

Abel Salazar Institute of Biomedical Sciences: CORÁLIA VICENTE

ATTACHED RESEARCH INSTITUTES

Animal Science Research Centre: Dir JOSÉ M. CORREIA DA COSTA.

Archaeological Research Centre of Coimbra and Porto Universities: Dir MARIA DE J. SANCHES.

Artificial Intelligence and Computer Science Laboratory: Dir MIGUEL FILGUEIRAS.

Centre for African Studies: Dir ANTÓNIO CUSTÓDIO GONÇALVES.

Centre for Applied Mathematics: Dir ISABEL SALGADO LABOURIAU.

Centre for Architectural and Urban Design: Dir NUNO R. MARTINS PORTAS.

Centre for Astrophysics: Dir TERESA LAGO.

Centre for Fluids and Energy: Dir EDUARDO G. OLIVEIRA FERNANDES.

Centre for Judicial and Economic Research: Dir GLÓRIA M. ALVES TEIXEIRA.

Centre for Macroeconomic and Forecast Studies: Dir ÁLVARO AGUIAR.

Centre for Marine and Environmental Research: Dir JOÃO J. O. DIAS COIMBRA.

Centre for Mathematics: Dir JOÃO NUNO TAVARES.

Centre for Numerical Methods in Mechanics and Structural Engineering: Dir ROGÉRIO A. FERNANDES MARTINS.

Centre for Pharmacology and Chemical Biopathology: Dir MARIA I. AMORIM AZEVEDO.

Centre for Psychology: Dir MARIANNE LACOMBLEZ.

Centre for Research and Intervention in Education: Dir STEPHEN R. STOER.

Centre for Studies in Industrial, Labour and Managerial Economics: Dir MARIA M. FERNANDES RUIVO.

Centre for Studies on Population, Economics and Society: Dir FERNANDO A. PEREIRA SOUSA.

Centre for Studies on Territory Development and Planning: Dir ROSA F. MOREIRA SILVA.

Centre for Studies on Transport Phenomena: Dir JOÃO B. L. MOREIRA CAMPOS.

Chemistry Centre: Dir BALTAZAR DE CASTRO.

Chemistry Research Centre: Dir MANUEL A. V. RIBEIRO SILVA.

Civil Engineering Department Research Centre: Dir FERNANDO F. VELOSO GOMES.

Cognition and Affect in Psychology: Dir FÉLIX F. MONTEIRO NETO.

Design and Experimental Validation Group: Dir ANTÓNIO A. FERNANDES.

Diabetes, Growth, Growth Factors and Diabetic Nephropathy: Dir ÁLVARO MACHADO DE AGUIAR.

Electrical Systems Research Centre: Dir ANTÓNIO ALMEIDA DO VALE.

Experimental Mechanics and New Materials: Dir JOAQUIM F. SILVA GOMES.

Experimental Morphology Centre: Dir MANUEL M. PAULA BARBOSA.

Geology Research Unit: Dir MANUEL J. LEMOS SOUSA.

Geo-Space Sciences Research Centre: Dir JOSÉ J. S. PEREIRA OSÓRIO.

Institute for Biomedical Engineering: Dir MÁRIO A. BARBOSA.

Institute of Comparative Literature: Dir GONÇALO J. V. P. VILAS BOAS.

Institute of English Studies: Dir GUALTER CUNHA.

Institute of Modern History: Dir LUÍS A. OLIVEIRA RAMOS.

Institute for Molecular and Cell Biology: Dir ALEXANDRE TIEDTKE QUINTANILHA.

Institute for Molecular Pathology and Immunology: Dir MANUEL SOBRINHO SIMÕES.

Institute of North American Studies: Dir CARLOS M. R. BORGES AZEVEDO.

Institute for Systems and Computer Engineering: Dir PEDRO GUEDES DE OLIVEIRA.

Institute for Systems and Robotics: Dir SEBASTIÃO J. C. FEYO AZEVEDO.

Interacademic Centre for the History of Spirituality: Dir JOSÉ A. M. FREITAS CARVALHO.

Laboratory for Catalysis and Materials: Dir JOSÉ L. C. CONCEIÇÃO FIGUEIREDO.

Laboratory for Process, Environmental and Energy Engineering: Dir LUÍS F. MELO.

Laboratory for Separation and Reaction Engineering: Dir ALÍRIO E. RODRIGUES.

Laboratory of Pure and Interdisciplinary Applied Inorganic Chemistry: Dir ADÉLIO A. S. CASTRO MACHADO.

Linguistics Centre: Dir FERNANDA I. A. BARROS FONSECA.

Management and Industrial Engineering Unit: Dir RUI M. CAMPOS GUIMARÃES.

Material Physics Institute: Dir JOSÉ M. MACHADO DA SILVA.

Metallic Materials Group of the Materials Institute: Dir CARLOS A. SILVA RIBEIRO.

Multidisciplinary Unit for Biomedical Research: Dir NUNO L. P. RODRIGUES GRANDE.

New Technologies and Advanced Production Processes: Dir ANTÓNIO P. BARBEDO MAGALHÃES.

Philosophy Institute: Dir MARIA C. PACHECO.

Physics, Acoustics and Telecommunications Research Centre: Dir FRANCISCO C. VELEZ GRILO.

Physics Research Centre: Dir MARIA A. SANTOS.

Research Centre for Organic Chemistry, Phytochemistry and Pharmacology: Dir MADALENA M. MAGALHÃES PINTO.

Study Group of the History of Viticulture of the Douro Region: Dirs FRANCISCO R. DA SILVA, ANTÓNIO M. BARROS CARDOSO.

System Integration and Process Automation Unit: Dir FERNANDO GOMES ALMEIDA.

Unit for Cardiovascular Research and Development: Dir MÁRIO CERQUEIRA GOMES.

UNIVERSIDADE PORTUCALENSE INFANTE D. HENRIQUE

Rua Dr António Bernardino de Almeida 541–619, 4200-072 Porto

Telephone: (22) 557-20-00
Fax: (22) 557-20-10
E-mail: up@upt.pt
Internet: www.upt.pt

Founded 1986
Private control
Language of instruction: Portuguese
Academic year: September to July

Rector: Prof. Dr FRANCISCO DA COSTA DURÃO
Vice-Rector: Prof. Dr AMÍLCAR DA COSTA PEREIRA MESQUITA

General Secretary: Prof. Dr JOSÉ MANUEL TEDIM
Chief Administrative Officer: ANTÓNIO ALVES MONTEIRO
Librarian: Profa Dra CRISTINA ABREU

Library of 46,150 vols
Number of teachers: 230
Number of students: 3,100

Publications: *Africana, Revista de Ciências da Educação, Revista de Ciências Históricas, Revista Jurídica*

HEADS OF DEPARTMENTS

Computer Science: Prof. Dr JORGE REIS LIMA
Economics: Prof. Dr JOÃO DE ALMEIDA GARRETT
History and Education: Prof. Dr HUMBERTO BAQUERO MORENO
Law: Prof. Dr JOAQUIM MOREIRA DA SILVA CUNHA
Management: Prof. Dr RUI CONCEIÇÃO NUNES
Mathematics: Prof. Dr FRANCISCO DA COSTA DURÃO

ATTACHED INSTITUTES

Centre for African and Eastern Studies: Dir Prof. Dr JOAQUIM DA SILVA CUNHA.

Centre for Computer Science Development: Dir Prof. Dr ARMANDO J. MESQUITA DE CARVALHO.

Centre for Computer Science Technology: Dir Prof. Dr JORGE REIS LIMA.

Centre for Information Systems: Dir Prof. Dr JORGE REIS LIMA.

Centre for Medieval History Research: Dir Prof. Dr HUMBERTO BAQUERO MORENO.

Centre for the Study of Pure and Applied Mathematics: Dir Prof. Dr FRANCISCO DA COSTA DURÃO.

Heritage Institute: Dir Prof. Dr JOSÉ MANUEL TEDIM.

Institute of Finance and Marketing: Dir Prof. Dr RUI CONCEIÇÃO NUNES.

Institute of Ibero-American Studies: Dir Prof. Dr HUMBERTO BAQUERO MORENO.

Institute for Training and International Co-operation (IFCOOP): Dir Prof. Dr PAULO DELGADO.

Juridical Institute: Dir Prof. Dr JOAQUIM DA SILVA CUNHA.

Research Centre for Applied Economics: Dir Prof. Dr JOÃO DE ALMEIDA GARRETT.

UNIVERSIDADE TÉCNICA DE LISBOA

Alameda de Santo António dos Capuchos 1, 1649-047 Lisbon

Telephone: (21) 881-19-00
Fax: (21) 881-19-91
E-mail: rutl@reitoria.utl.pt
Internet: www.utl.pt

Founded 1930
State control
Academic year: September to July

Rector: Prof. Dr JOSÉ DIAS LOPES DA SILVA
Vice-Rectors: Prof. Dr RAUL F. X. BRUNO DE SOUSA, Prof. Dr ANTÓNIO FRANCISCO ESPINHO ROMÃO, Prof. Dr MANUEL F. O. DE SEABRA PEREIRA
Pro-Rectors: Profa Dra MARIA MARQUES CALADO ALBUQUERQUE GOMES, Prof. Dr JORGE ALBERTO CADETE AMBRÓSIO, Prof. Dr JOÃO MANUEL CUNHA DA SILVA ABRANTES
Administrator: Dra MARIA CLARA PETRA VIANA
Librarian: D. UMBELINA NASCIMENTO

Number of teachers: 1,833
Number of students: 22,236

Publications: *DAXIYANGGUO, Portuguese Review of Asiatic Studies, Episteme Review, European Review of Economics and Finance, ISEG—Estudes de Economia, ISCSP—Estudes Politicos e Sociais, Portuguese Economic Journal, Portuguese Review of International and Community Relations, Portuguese Review of Veterinary Sciences*

PRESIDENTS OF THE DIRECTIVE COUNCILS

Faculty of Architecture: Prof Dr FERNANDO ANTÓNIO MATOS CARIA
Faculty of Human Kinetics: Prof. Dr JOSÉ MANUEL FRAGOSO ALVES DINIZ
Faculty of Veterinary Medicine: Prof. Dr LUÍS MANUEL MORGADO TAVARES
Higher Institute of Agronomy: Prof. Dr P. M. L. RODRIGUES DE SOUSA
Higher Institute of Economics and Business Administration: Prof. Dr VITOR F. DA CONCEIÇÃO GONÇALVES
Higher Institute of Engineering: Prof. Dr CARLOS RENATO A. MATOS FERREIRA
Higher Institute of Social and Political Sciences: Prof. Dr JOÃO MANUEL DE FARIA BILHIM

UNIVERSIDADE DE TRÁS-OS-MONTES E ALTO DOURO

POB 202, 5001-911 Vila Real Codex

Telephone: (259) 35 00-00
Fax: (259) 35-04-80
E mail: elibar@utad.pt
Internet: www.utad.pt

Founded 1973, university status 1986
State control
Language of instruction: Portuguese
Academic year: September to July

Rector: Prof. Dr ARMANDO MASCARENHAS FERREIRA
Registrar: Dr FRANCISCO MIGUEL RODRIGUES
Academic Director: LUCINDA MACHADO RODRIGUES
Librarian: Dra MARGARIDA CARVALHO

Number of teachers: 543
Number of students: 6,033

Publications: *Annals of UTAD, Boletim Informativo da UTAD, Yearbook of UTAD*

HEADS OF DEPARTMENTS

Animal Science: Prof. Dr JORGE MANUEL TEXEIRA DE AZEVEDO
Arts and Workmanship: Prof. Dr CARLOS JOSÉ MENDES CARDOSO
Biological and Environmental Engineering: Prof Dr JOSÉ FONTAINHAS FERNANDES
Chemistry: Prof. Dr LUCINDA VAZ DOS REIS
Crop Science and Rural Engineering: Prof. Dr MANUEL TELES DE OLIVEIRA
Economics, Sociology and Management: Prof. Dr ARTUR ARÉDE CRISTÓVÃO
Educational and Psychology Sciences: Prof. Dra MARIA DA CONCEIÇÃO AZEVEDO
Engineering: Prof. Dr JOSÉ BULAS CRUZ
Food Technology: Profa Dra MARIA ARLETE FAIA
Forestry: Prof. Dr. CARLOS PACHECO MARQUES
Genetics and Biotechnology: Prof. Dr. HENRIQUE GUEDES PINTO
Geology: Prof. Dr ALCINO DE SOUSA OLIVEIRA
Literature: Prof. Dr JOSÉE MANUEL CARDOSO BELO
Mathematics: Profa Dra ELZA MARIA SOUSA AMARA
Physics: Prof. Dr JOSÉ MANUEL ALMEIDA
Plant Protection: Profa Dra ANA MARIA NAZARÉ PEREIRA
Soils: Profa Dra ESTER MARIA PORTELA
Sports: Prof. Dr MIGUEL VIDEIRA MONTEIRO
Veterinary Sciences: Prof. Dr JORGE DE ALMEIDA RODRIGUES

Colleges

Instituto Nacional de Administração: Palácio dos Marqueses de Pombal, 2784-540 Oeiras; tel. (21) 446-53-00; fax (21) 446-54-44; e-mail ina@ina.pt; internet www.ina.pt; f. 1979; 373 teachers; 11,473 students; training and research in public administration, law, European affairs, management, computer science, human resources management; European Documentation Centre; library: documentation centre with 19,000 vols, 250 periodicals; Pres. Prof. LUÍS VALADARES TAVARES; publ. *Legislação: Cadernos de Ciência de Legislação* (3 a year).

Instituto Piaget: Quinta de Arreinela de Cima, 2800-303 Almada; internet www.ipiaget.pt; courses: clinical analysis and public health, social sciences, communications science and intercultural development, chemical sciences and the environment, complementary studies, education, artistic and industrial design, design and management of teaching materials, economics and business, economics and management of health sciences, infant education, nursing, food engineering, civil engineering, contract engineering and maintenance management, electrical engineering, physiotherapy, music, human, social and school nutrition, basic education, psychology, environmental health, sociology.

National campuses:

Campus Académico de Almada: Quinta de Arreinela de Cima, 2800-303 Almada; tel. (21) 294-62-50; fax (21) 294-15-84; e-mail caalmada@ipiaget.pt; internet almada.ipiaget.org.

Complexo de Ensino Superior de Macedo de Cavaleiros: tel. (278) 42-00-40; fax (278) 42-54-30; e-mail cmacedo@ipiaget.pt; internet macedo.ipiaget.org.

Campus de Ensino Superior de Viseu: Estrada do Alto Gaio, Lordosa, 3510-655 Viseu; tel. (232) 91-00-00; fax (232) 91-18-70; e-mail cesviseu@ipiaget.pt.

Escola Superior de Saúde—Jean Piaget Silves: tel. (282) 44-10-72; fax (282) 44-10-77.

ISEIT Mirandela: Instituto Piaget, ISEIT Mirandela, Avda 25 de Abril, 5370 Mirandela; tel. (278) 20-01-50; fax (278) 26-52-03; e-mail cesmirandela@ipiaget.pt.

Santo André: tel. (269) 70-87-10; fax (269) 70-87-27.

Vila Nova de Gaia: Alameda Jean Piaget 100, 4405-111 Arcozelo, Vila Nova de Gaia; tel. (22) 762-53-03; fax (22) 753-30-46 Rua António Sérgio, 4406-401 Canelas, Vila Nova de Gaia; tel. (22) 753-76-00; fax (22) 753-76-80; e-mail cesgaia@ipiaget.pt; internet gaia.ipiaget.org.

International campuses:

Universidade Jean Piaget de Angola: see separate entry in Angola chapter.

Universidade Jean Piaget de Cabo Verde: see separate entry in Cape Verde chapter.

Instituto Politécnico de Beja: Rua de Santo António 1A, 7800 Beja; tel. (284) 32-93-27; fax (284) 32-57-71; e-mail centrais@ipbeja.pt; internet www.ipbeja.pt; f. 1987; 231 teachers; 3,143 students; library: 35,000 vols; Dir Dr JOSÉ LUÍS RAMALHO.

Instituto Politécnico de Bragança: Apdo 172, 5300 Bragança; tel. (273) 30-32-00; fax (273) 32-54-05; e-mail dionisio@ipb.pt; internet www.ipb.pt; f. 1983; 310 teachers; 4,000 students; Dir Prof. DIONÍSIO A. GONÇALVES.

Instituto Politécnico de Castelo Branco, Escola Superior Agrária: Quinta de N. Sra. de Mércules, 6001-909 Castelo Branco; tel. (272) 33-99-00; fax (272) 33-99-01; e-mail eduarda@esa.ipcb.pt; f. 1983; higher courses in agriculture (vegetable production, animal production, forestry production, natural resources management, edible oil production); 70 teachers; 1,400 students; library: 22,000 vols; Dir J. C. DUARTE GONÇALVES; publs *AGROforum, Bibliografia Temática, Boletim Bibliográfico, Folha Bibliográfica Mensal.*

Instituto Politécnico da Guarda: Av. Dr Francisco Sá Carneiro 50, 6300 Guarda; tel. (271) 22-01-11; fax (271) 22-26-90; internet www.ipg.pt; f. 1980; 258 teachers; 3,700 students; courses in education, public relations, computer science, civil engineering, mechanical engineering, and business management; Pres. Prof. Dr JOSÉ AUGUSTO ALVES; publ. *Educação e Tecnologia* (2 a year).

Instituto Politécnico de Lisboa: Rua Professor Reinaldo dos Santos 5A, 1500 Lisbon; tel. (21) 778-64-41; fax (21) 778-64-48; e-mail iplsc@mail.esoterica.pt; f. 1985; state control; Pres. Dr ALBERTO A. ANTAS DE BARROS JÚNIOR; Administrator Dr ANTÓNIO JOSÉ CARVALHO MARQUES.

constituent institutes:

Escola Superior de Communicação Social: Rua Carolina Michaelis de Vasconcelos, 1500 Lisbon; tel. (21) 711-90-00; fax (21) 716-48-77; f. 1987; academic year September to July; library of 3,919 vols, 8,799 periodicals; 62 teachers; 866 students; Pres. Dr ALBERTO A. ANTAS DE BARROS.

Escola Superior de Dança: Rua do Século 89–93, 1200 Lisbon; tel. (21) 342-53-55; fax (21) 342-02-71; f. 1983; academic year September to July; 17 teachers; 83 students; library of 1,270 vols; Dir Prof. WANDA RIBEIRO DA SILVA; publ. *Dança.*

Escola Superior de Educação: Av. Carolina Michaelis de Vasconcelos (Junto à Est. de Benfica), 1500 Lisbon; tel. (21) 711-55-00; fax (21) 716-61-47; f. 1985; academic year September to July; library of 28,000 vols, 8,500 periodicals; 96 teachers; 1,065 students; Pres. Dra AMÁLIA GARRIDO BÁRRIOS.

Escola Superior de Música: Rua do Ataíde 7, 1200 Lisbon; tel. (21) 322-49-40; fax (21) 347-14-89; f. 1983; academic year October to June; library of 1,500 vols and 5,000 music scores; 43 teachers; 140 students; Dir Prof. CHRISTOPHER CONSITT BOCHMANN.

Escola Superior de Teatro e Cinema: Rua dos Caetanos 29, 1200 Lisbon; tel. (21) 346-17-94; fax (21) 347-02-73; f. 1983; academic year September to July; library of 10,000 vols, 2,000 periodicals; 43 teachers; 208 students; Pres. Prof. JOÃO M. MOTA RODRIGUES.

Instituto Superior de Contabilidade e Administração de Lisboa (ISCAL): Av. Miguel Bombarda 20, 1050 Lisbon; tel. (21) 798-45-51; fax (21) 797-70-79; f. 1754 as Aula de Comércio, present name 1976; academic year September to July; library of 6,566 vols, 211 periodicals; 202 teachers; 3,334 students; Administrator Dr VICTOR MACIEIRA.

Instituto Superior de Engenharia de Lisboa (ISEL): Rua Conselheiro Emídio Navarro, 1900 Lisbon; tel. (21) 831-70-00; fax (21) 859-70-46; f. 1852 as Instituto Industrial de Lisboa, present name 1974; academic year September to July; library

of 9,388 vols, 312 periodicals; 551 teachers; 5,495 students; Pres. Enga MARIA DA GRAÇA PAES DE FARIA.

Instituto Politécnico de Portalegre: Apdo 84, 7301 Portalegre Codex; tel. (245) 33-00-34; fax (245) 33-03-53; f. 1980; state control; Pres. Prof. Dr F. A. FORTUNATO QUEIRÓS.

constituent schools:

Escola Superior Agrária de Elvas (ESAE): Apdo 254, 7350 Elvas; 5 teachers; 25 students; Dir Eng. GONÇALO J. P. ANTUNES BARRADAS.

Escola Superior de Educação (ESE): Apdo 125, 7301 Portalegre Codex; 72 teachers; 671 students; Pres. Dr ABÍLIO JOSÉ M. AMIGUINHO; Librarian Dr DOMINGOS BUCHO; publ. *Aprender.*

Escola Superior de Tecnologia e Gestão (ESTG): Apdo 148, 7301 Portalegre Codex; 45 teachers; 695 students; Pres. Dr FRANCISCO J. C. TOMATAS; Librarian Bac. CATARINA ELIAS BARRADAS.

Instituto Politécnico de Santarém: Complexo Andaluz, Apdo 279, 2001-904 Santarém; tel. (243) 30-95-20; fax (243) 33-23-84; e-mail relacoes.publicas@ipsantarem.pt; internet www.ipsantarem.pt; f. 1979; library: 38,900 vols; 270 teachers; 3,936 students; Dir Prof. J. A. GUERRA JUSTINO.

Instituto Politécnico de Setúbal: Largo dos Defensores da República 1, 2910-470 Setúbal; tel. (265) 54-88-20; fax (265) 23-11-10; e-mail gire.ni@spr.ips.pt; internet www.ips.pt; f. 1987; courses in education, management and technology; Pres. Prof. Eng. JOÃO DUARTE SILVA.

Instituto Politécnico de Viana do Castelo: Apdo 51, 4901 Viana do Castelo Codex; tel. (258) 80-96-10; fax (258) 82-90-65; e-mail geral@ipvc.pt; internet www.ipvc.pt; f. 1980; first degree courses; Pres. Prof. A. LIMA DE CARVALHO.

Instituto Politécnico de Viseu: Rua Maximiano Aragão, 3504-501 Viseu; tel. (232) 42-20-28; fax (232) 42-57-60; e-mail ipv@ipv.pt; internet www.ipv.pt; f. 1979; 311 teachers; 4,637 students; Dir Prof. JOÃO P. DE BARROS; publs *Forum Media* (2 a year), *Millenium* (4 a year).

Instituto Superior de Línguas e Administração (ISLA): Rua do Sacramento à Lapa 14–16, 1200 Lisbon; tel. (21) 395-51-04; fax (21) 396-67-36; f. 1962; private control; business management, marketing, human resources, computer science for management, applied mathematics, translation, tourism, secretarial studies; library: 13,300 vols; 260 teachers; 3,000 students; Sec.-Gen. MIGUEL P. G. RODRIGUES.

Instituto Superior Politécnico Portucalense: Rua do Paço 3, 4560 Penafiel; tel. (255) 71-10-54; fax (255) 71-10-53; f. 1990; courses in local govt administration, accounting, management, computer studies; library: 5,000 vols; 73 teachers; 620 students; Dir Dr JOAQUIM M. SILVA CUNHA.

School of Art

Escola Superior de Belas-Artes (Higher School of Fine Arts): Av. Rodrigues de Freitas, Oporto; tel. (22) 536-52-35; fax (22) 536-70-36; e-mail expediente@fba.up.pt; internet www.fba.up.pt; f. 1836; attached to University of Porto; Dir Prof. ANTÓNIO QUADROS FERREIRA.

QATAR

The Higher Education System

Qatar was part of the Ottoman Turkish Empire until 1916 when it came under British protection. British control was extended in 1934 and in 1971 independence was achieved. The traditional education system was based on Koranic and Shari'a (Islamic law) studies, but in 1973 the largely secular College of Education was founded and it became the University of Qatar in 1977. The University consists of six Colleges and degrees are approved by the United Kingdom Quality Assurance Agency. In 2004, 9,452 students were enrolled at the Univeristy of Qatar.

Admission to undergraduate courses at the University of Qatar is based upon results achieved in the General Secondary Certificate (*Al-Thanawaya Al-Amah*) examinations. Students are admitted to the University before their applications are considered by the Colleges. Degrees are awarded on a 'credit' basis and students are required to accumulate a specified amount of credits before graduating, depending on the degree applied for. There are mandatory Foundation courses for students in engineering, science, economics and administration, consisting of English, mathematics and IT training. The foremost undergraduate degree is the Bachelors, and the main postgraduate courses are the Postgraduate Diplomas and Certificates, Masters and PhDs. Postgraduate Certificates and Diplomas are between two and five semesters in duration and are available in education, library science and architectural planning. Masters degrees last one year and students are required to maintain a specified grade point average (GPA). Doctoral degrees (mainly PhD) are not yet widespread.

The main post-secondary qualification for technical and vocational education is the Diploma in Technology, available from Colleges of Technology.

Learned Society

GENERAL

UNESCO Office Doha: 57 Al-Jazira Al-Arabia St, POB 3945, Doha; tel. 4867707; fax 4867644; e-mail doha@unesco.org; internet www.unesco.org/doha; designated Cluster Office for Bahrain, Kuwait, Oman, Qatar, Saudi Arabia and United Arab Emirates; Dir ABDALLA BUBTANA.

Research Institute

HISTORY, GEOGRAPHY AND ARCHAEOLOGY

Gulf Co-operation Council Folklore Centre: POB 7996, Doha; tel. 4861999; fax 4867170; e-mail info@gccfolklore.org; internet www.gccfolklore.org; f. 1982 to collect, study, disseminate and protect indigenous local folklore mainly in the fields of literature, customs and traditions, music and dance, arts and crafts; mem. states: Bahrain, Kuwait, Oman, Qatar, Saudi Arabia, UAE; library of 4,853 vols, 110 journals, also video cassettes, cassette recordings and photographic material; Dir-Gen. ABDULRAHMAN AL-MANNAI; publ. *Al Ma'thurat Al Sha'biyyah* (4 a year).

Libraries and Archives

Doha

National Library: POB 205, Doha; tel. 4429955; fax 4429976; e-mail qanaly@qatar.net.qa; f. 1962; 218,600 vols in Arabic, 33,800 vols in English, 1,300 Arabic MSS, 454 on microfilm, 1,288 periodicals on microfilm and 10,248 on microfiche, bibliographic services on subjects of local interest; 5 brs; Dir ABDULLA NASSER AL-ANSARI.

Research and Documents Section: POB 923, Amir's Office, Doha; tel. 4434624; fax 4310518; f. 1975; Dir MUHAMMAD KHALIFA AL-ATTIYAH.

Museum

Doha

Qatar National Museum: Doha; tel. 4442911; e-mail qnm2000@hotmail.com; internet www.qnm.8m.com; opened 1975; consists of five major sections: the old Amiri Palace (nine 19th c. buildings), the new palace, aquarium, lagoon, botanical garden; collections: ethnography, archaeo-history, geology, botany, zoology, jewellery, numismatics, perfumery; Dir IBRAHIM JABER AL-JABER.

University

UNIVERSITY OF QATAR

POB 2713, Doha
Telephone: 4852222
Fax: 4835111
E-mail: prd@qu.edu.qa
Internet: www.qu.edu.qa
Founded 1973 as Faculties of Education, University status 1977
State control
Language of instruction: Arabic
Academic year: September to June
Supreme Head: HH Sheikh HAMAD BIN KHALIFA AL THANI (Amir of Qatar)
President: Prof. Dr SHEIKHA ABDULLA AL-MISNAD
Vice-President (Academic Affairs): Dr SHEIKHA JABOR AL-THANI
Vice-President (Administrative and Financial Affairs): Dr HUMAID ABDULLA MOHAMMED AL-MIDFAA
Library Director: AHMED M. AL-QATTAN
Library of 360,000 vols (Arabic and English), 1,040 periodicals
Number of teachers: 705
Number of students: 8,235
Publications: Faculty bulletins (annually), *Fruits of Knowledge* (annually)

DEANS

College of Arts and Science: Dr SHAIKHA JABOR AL-THANI
College of Business and Economics: Dr KHALID NASSIR AL-KHATER (acting)
College of Education: Prof. Dr ALI ABDEL MONEIM
College of Engineering: Prof. Dr NABEEL AL-SALEM
College of Shari'a Law and Islamic Studies: Dr AISHA YOUSIF AL MANNAI

HEADS OF DEPARTMENTS

College of Business and Economics (POB 2713, Doha; tel. 4851576; fax 4930927):
  Accountancy: Dr AHMED SUBAI QATOB
  Business Administration: Prof. Dr ADEL HARNOOSH SALEH
  Economics: Prof. Dr RIYADH ABDULLA AL MUMENI
  General Administration: Dr LUAY YOUNIS BAHARI

College of Education (POB 2713, Doha; tel. 4852220; fax 4835104):
  Art Education: Prof. Dr HANNA HABEEB RAMLA
  Curriculum and Methods of Teaching: Dr GHADNANA SAID AL NOQBIL AL BIN ALI
  Educational Psychology: Dr YOSSUF MOHAMMED ABDULLA
  Educational Technology: Dr NAJAH MOHAMMED ABDUL LATIF AL NAIMI
  Foundations of Education: Prof. Dr ISMAIL MOHAMMED DHYAB
  Home Economics: Dr MARIAM MAGED AL BUFLASA
  Mental Health: Prof. Dr ALAA-ELDIN A. KAFAFI
  Physical Education: Dr QADRI BAKRI

College of Engineering (POB 2713, Doha; tel. 4852107; fax 4852491):
  Chemical Engineering: Dr HASSAN EASSA AL FADHALA
  Civil Engineeering: Dr KHALED KAMAL NAJI
  Electrical Engineering: Dr SULAIMAN ABDUL HADY SULAIMAN
  Mechanical Engineering: Prof. Dr USAMA AHMED BADER
  Foundation Year Unit: Dr ABDUL HAMEED MEREFIA

College of Humanities and Social Sciences (POB 2713, Doha; tel. 4852227; fax 4835107; e-mail humanities@qu.edu.qa):
  Arabic Language: Prof. Dr OMAR SABER ABDUL JALEEL
  Arabic Language Teaching Unit: Dr ADAM AHMAD ADAM MAHMOUD

English Language Teaching Unit: AMNA SAUD FAHED AL THANI

Geography: Dr NASSER ABDURRAHMAN FAKHROO

History: Dr MUSTAFA AKEEL AL KHATEEB

Information and Library Science: Prof. Dr USAMA AL SAYED MAHMOUD

Mass Communication: Dr ABDUL RAHEEM NOURIDDIN HAMED

Philosophy: Dr MOZA MOHAMMED YOUSUF OBAIDAN (acting)

Social Work: Dr KALTHAM JABOR MOHAMMED AL-KAWARI

Sociology: Prof. Dr KALTHAM ALI GHANEM AL GHANEM

College of Science (POB 2713, Doha; tel. 4852139; fax 4835061):

Biological Science: Prof. Dr FAYSAL TAJELD-EEN ABU SHAMA

Chemistry: Dr SIHAM YOSSUF AL QARADAWI

Computer Science: Dr AHMED MIJAHED OMAR HASNAH (acting)

Environmental Studies Unit: Dr LATIFA SHAHEEN AL NAIMI

Geology: Dr HAMAD ABDUURRAHMAN AL SAAD (acting)

Marine Sciences: Dr JASSIM ABDULLA AL KHAYAT

Physics: Dr ATTA AL MANNAN JAFFER ATTA AL MANNOM

College of Shari'a Law and Islamic Studies (POB 2713, Doha; tel. 4852255; fax 4835105):

Foundations of Religion: Dr MOHAMMED ABDULLA AL SHARQAWI

Islamic Culture, Theology and Comparative Religion: Prof. Dr HASSAM EASSA ABDUL DHAHER

Law: Dr ALI HASSAN NAJEEDA

Philology and Foundations: Prof. Dr ALI MUHEY EL DIN AL QORRA DAGHI

ATTACHED INSTITUTES

Computer Centre: Dir Dr JIHAD MOHAMMED AL-JAAM.

Documentation and Humanities Research Centre: collection, classification and preparation of documents pertaining to the field of humanities as a basic source of research, and the issuing of documented research papers; specialized research on the heritage of the Gulf area in all its aspects: social, cultural, linguistic and literary; Dir Dr SAIF AL MEREIKHI.

Educational Research Centre: educational research and studies which contribute to the development of education in the State of Qatar, oriented among other things toward improvement of the educational process, curricula and textbooks; Dir Dr NASRA REDA BAGHER.

Educational Technology Centre: Dir Dr JIHAD MOHAMMED AL-JAAM.

Gulf Studies Centre: Dir Dr HASSAN AL-ANSARI.

Scientific and Applied Research Centre: to develop experience in scientific, industrial and agricultural fields with special reference to industries, natural resources, agriculture and animal resources of Qatar; and to contribute to the transfer of technology and adapt it for application in Qatar; Dir Dr MOHSIN ABDULLA AL-ANSI.

Sirra and Sunna Research Centre: research related to the *Sirra* of the Prophet Mohamed, i.e. his preaching, moral and spiritual values, and his life, and the *Sunna* of the Prophet Mohamed, i.e. his sayings and acts which are the second source of guidance for the practice of Islam after the holy Koran; Dir Prof. YOUSEF AL-QARADAWI.

Colleges

Language Teaching Institute: POB 3224, Doha; tel. 4657690; fax 4665465; f. 1972; library: 6,000 vols; 29 teachers; 504 students; part-time courses in Arabic, Persian, English, French, for mature students already in employment; Dir MOHAMED HASSAN AL-SIDDIQI.

Regional Training Centre: POB 1300, Doha; tel. 4870000; f. 1970 with UNDP technical aid; library: 2,500 vols; 700 students; Dir F. KADDOURA.

ROMANIA

The Higher Education System

Formerly part of the Ottoman Turkish Empire, Romania became an independent kingdom in 1881. In 1947 King Michael was forced to abdicate and the Romanian People's Republic was proclaimed. Romania became a one-party state under the communist Romanian Workers' Party. Communist rule ended in 1989, when the regime of President Ceaușescu was overthrown in a revolution; multi-party democracy was established in 1991. The oldest current institutions of higher education are mostly specialist establishments dating from the first half of the 19th century, among them the Universitatea 'Politehnica' din București (founded in 1818), the Academia de Muzică 'Georghe Dima' (founded in 1819), the Universitatea de Științe Agronomice și Medicine Veterinara București (founded in 1852) and the Universitatea de Medicină și Farmacia 'Carol Davila' (founded in 1857; current name since 1990). There was an expansion of higher education during the period of reform (1859–66) initiated by Alexander Ioan Cuza, the first elected Domnitor of the United Principalities of Wallachia and Moldova (which later became independent Romania). Current institutions established during that period include the Unversitatea 'Alexandru Ioan Cuza' Iași (founded in 1860), the Universitatea de Arte 'George Enescu' (founded in 1860; current name since 1960), the Universitatea Națională de Muzica din București (founded in 1863) and the Universitaea din București (founded in 1864). The Ministry of Education and Research is responsible for higher education, which is governed by the Constitution (1991) and the Education Act (1995). Education at public institutions is free. Romania participates in the Bologna Process to establish a European Higher Education Area, the first phase of which is to adopt a credit-based system of comparable degrees with two main cycles (undergraduate and graduate). In 2003/04 there were 30,137 students enrolled in 122 institutions of higher education.

Admission to higher education is on the basis of the secondary school diploma (Bacalaureat) and success in the university entrance examination. Higher education is divided into short- and long-term courses. Short-term courses consist solely of the thee-year Diploma de Absolvire and are offered by university colleges (Colegii Universitare). Long-term higher education consists of undergraduate and postgraduate degrees, principally the undergraduate Bachelors and postgraduate Masters degrees, in accordance with the principles of the Bologna Process. The Bachelors degree (Diploma de Licenta) is a programme of study lasting four to six years, depending on the field of study. Following the Bachelors degree, graduates may study for one or two years for the award of, principally, the Masters degree or Professional Postgraduate Diploma (Diploma de Studii postuniversitare). Finally, the highest university-level degree is the Doctorate (Doktorat), a programme of study lasting three to seven years.

Post-secondary technical and vocational education (scoala postliceala) consists of two- to three-year training courses at three levels of specialization.

The academic year in Romania usually runs from October until June (the exact date varies from one university—or even one faculty—to another). It is divided into two semesters of approximately 14 weeks each. An examination period of about four weeks follows each semester. The first semester lasts from October until mid-February, with the examination period starting after the Christmas holiday (beginning of January). The second semester (or the Spring semester) starts at the beginning of March. It includes the Easter holiday and a four-week examination session in May–June. Some faculties organize practical activities with compulsory attendance at the end of the second semester. There is also a re-examination period, in September, for students who did not pass their examinations during the previous academic year.

Learned Societies

GENERAL

Academia Română (Romanian Academy): Calea Victoriei 125, 010093 Bucharest; tel. (21) 212-86-40; fax (21) 312-02-09; e-mail esimion@acad.ro; internet www .academiaromana.ro; f. 1866; sections of Philology and Literature (Chair. EUGEN SIMION), Historical Sciences and Archaeology (Chair. DAN BERINDEI), Mathematical Sciences (Chair. ROMULUS CRISTESCU), Physical Sciences (Chair. MARIUS PECULEA), Chemical Sciences (Chair. MARIA BREZEANU), Biological Sciences (Chair. GHEORGHE ZARNEA), Geonomical Sciences (Chair. MIRCEA SĂNDULESCU), Technical Sciences (Chair. RADU VOINEA), Agricultural Sciences and Forestry (Chair. VALERIU COTEA), Medical Sciences (Chair. vacant), Economics, Legal Sciences and Sociology (Chair. TUDOREL POSTOLACHE), Philosophical, Theological and Psychological Sciences and Education (Chair. ALEXANDRU SURDU), Arts, Architecture and Audiovisual (Chair. MIHNEA GHEORGHIU), Science and Technology of Information (Chair. MIHAL DRĂGĂNESCU); 167 mems (77 ordinary, 90 corresp.); attached research institutes: see Research Institutes; library: see Libraries and Archives; Pres. EUGEN SIMION; Sec.-Gen. ANDREI ȚUGULEA; publs *Studii și cercetări matematice* (Studies and Research in Mathematics), *Revue Roumaine de mathématiques pures et appliquées*, *Math-ematica*, *Revue d'analyse numérique et de théorie de l'approximation*, *Romanian Astronomical Journal*, *Romanian Reports of Physics*, *Revue Roumaine de chimie*, *Romanian Chemical Quarterly Review*, *Cellulose Chemistry and Technology*, *Studii și cercetări de mecanică aplicată* (Studies and Research in Applied Mechanics), *Revue Roumaine des sciences techniques: Série de mécanique appliquée*, *Revue Roumaine des sciences techniques: Série électrotechnique et énergétique*, *Functional and Architectural Electronics*, *Studii și cercetări de biochimie* (Studies and Research in Biochemistry), *Revue Roumaine de biochimie*, *Studii și cercetări de biologie: Seria biologie vegetală* (Studies and Research in Biology: Series of Plant Biology), *Revue Roumaine de biologie: Série de biologie végétale*, *Studii și cercetări de biologie: Seria biologie animală* (Studies and Research in Biology: Series of Animal Biology), *Revue Roumaine de biologie: Série de biologie animale*, *Romanian Neurosurgery*, *Romanian Journal of Biophysics*, *Revue Roumaine des sciences économiques*, *Studii și cercetări de antropologie* (Studies and Research in Anthropology), *Annuaire Roumain d'Anthropologie*, *Ocrotirea naturii și a mediului înconjurător* (The Protection of Nature and of the Environment), *Travaux de l'Institut de Spéléologie 'Emile Racovitza'*, *Studii și cercetări de geologie, geofizică și geografie* (Studies and Research in Geology, Geophysics and Geography, 3 series), *Revue Roumaine de géologie, géophysique et géographie* (3 series), *Studii și cercetări lingvistice* (Studies and Research in Linguistics), *Revue Roumaine de Linguistique*, *Cahiers de linguistique théorique et appliquée*, *Cercetări de linguistică* (Linguistic Researches), *Limba română* (The Romanian Language), *Nyelv- és Irodalomtudományi Köziemények*, *Fonetică și dialectologie* (Phonetics and Dialectology), *Anuar de lingvistică și istorie literară* (Yearbook of Linguistics and Literary History), *Synthesis – Bulletin du Comité National de Littérature comparée*, *Revista de etnografie și folclor* (Journal of Ethnography and Folklore), *Revue des études sud-est européennes*, *Historia Urbana*, *Revue Roumaine des sciences juridiques*, *Romanian Journal of Sociology*, *Revista română de demografie* (Romanian Journal of Demography), *Calitatea vieții* (Quality of Life), *Revue Roumaine de philosophie*, *Revista de psihologie* (Journal of Psychology), *Revue Roumaine de psychologie*.

Asociația Culturală 'Pro Basarabia și Bucovina' (Bessarabia and Bucovina Cultural Association): Bdul Mihail Kogălniceanu 19, 050102 Bucharest; tel. (21) 614-03-59; f. 1990; 60,000 mems; Exec. Pres. NICOLAE RADU HALIPPA.

Centrul European de Cultură, București (European Cultural Centre, Bucharest): Str. Sfinții Voievozi 49–51, 4th Floor, Apt. 16, 010965 Bucharest; tel. (21) 650-81-45; fax

(21) 650-32-80; e-mail office@studyabroad.ro; internet www.studyabroad.ro; f. 1990; organizes int. postgraduate seminars on European issues; promotes Romania as an attractive cultural tourist destination, through research, publs and study tours; promotes colleges and univs in Western Europe, the USA, Canada and Australia, which offer int. programmes related to undergraduate and postgraduate studies in Romania; 1,300 mems; library of 3,000 vols, 40 periodicals; Pres. Acad. DAN BERINDEI; Exec. Dir MARIA BURS-POPESCU.

Institutul Cultural Român (Romanian Cultural Institute): Aleea Alexandru 38, 011824 Bucharest; tel. (21) 230-13-73; fax (21) 230-75-59; e-mail icr@icr.ro; internet www.icr.ro; f. 1990; promotes Romanian culture abroad; publishes works by Romanian and foreign authors, dictionaries, history texts and other literature; 130 mems; Pres. HORIA-ROMAN PATAPIEVICI; publs *Curierul Românesc* (monthly), *Dilema* (weekly), *Contrafort* (monthly), *Destin Românesc* (quarterly), *Glasul Bucovinei* (quarterly), *Lettres internationales* (quarterly), *Transylvanian Review* (quarterly), *Plural* (2 a year).

Societatea Cultural-Ştiinţifică 'Getica' (Getica Cultural Scientific Society): POB 37-149, 70060 Bucharest 37; Str. Plantelor 8–10, 023974 Bucharest; tel. (21) 318-47-57; f. 1990; 87 mems; library of 5,000 vols; Pres. GABRIEL GHEORGHE; publ. *Getica* (irreg.).

AGRICULTURE, FISHERIES AND VETERINARY SCIENCE

Academia de Ştiinţe Agricole şi Silvice 'Gheorghe Ionescu-Şişeşti' (Gheorghe Ionescu-Şişeşti Academy of Agricultural and Forestry Sciences): Bdul Mărăşti 61, 011464 Bucharest 1; tel. (21) 222-78-34; fax (21) 222-91-39; e-mail asas@digi.ro; internet www.asas.ro; f. 1969; sections of Soil Science, Land Reclamation and Environmental Protection in Agriculture, Field Crops, Horticulture, Animal Husbandry, Veterinary Medicine, Forestry Science, Agrarian Economics and Rural Development, Food Industry, Agricultural Mechanization; 316 mems (88 full, 94 corresp., 49 hon., 85 assoc.); attached research institutes: see Research Institutes; library: see Libraries and Archives; Pres. CHRISTIAN IOAN HERA; Gen. Sec. GHEORGHE SIN; publs *Buletinul informativ al Academiei de Ştiinţe Agricole şi Silvice* (annual), *Bulletin de l'Académie des Sciences Agricoles et Forestières* (annual), *Bulletin of the Academy of Agricultural and Forestry Sciences* (annual).

Asociaţia Economiştilor Agrarieni din România (Agrarian Economists' Association of Romania): Bdul Mărăşti 61, 011464 Bucharest; tel. (21) 617-21-80; f. 1990; 42 mems; library of 4,000 vols; Pres. Prof. N. N. CONSTANTINESCU; Gen. Sec. RADU COTIANU.

Societatea Inginerilor Agronomi (Agronomists' Society): Bdul Mărăşti 59, 011464 Bucharest; tel. (21) 618-22-30; f. 1990; 3,500 mems; Pres. Prof. Dr MIHAI VĂJIALĂ; Gen. Sec. Dr RUXANDRA CIOFU.

Societatea Naţională Română pentru Ştiinţa Solului (Romanian National Soil Science Society): Bdul Mărăşti 61, 011464 Bucharest; tel. (21) 224-17-90; fax (21) 222-59-79; e-mail lacatusu@icpa.ro; f. 1962; 494 mems; library of 3,142 vols; Pres. Dr RADU LĂCĂTUŞU; Gen. Sec. CONSTANTIN CRĂCIUN; publs *Ştiinţa Solului* (2 a year), *Bulletin Informativ* (annual).

Societatea Română de Zootehnie (Romanian Society of Animal Production): Bdul Mărăşti 59, 011464 Bucharest; tel. (21) 618-22-30; fax (21) 312-56-93; f. 1990; 4,500 mems; Pres. Prof. STEFAN POPESCU-VIFOR; Sr Sec. Dr AGATHA POPESCU.

ARCHITECTURE AND TOWN PLANNING

Uniunea Arhitecţilor din România (Union of Architects of Romania): Str. Academiei 18–20, 010014 Bucharest; fax (21) 312-30-53; e-mail ma@com.pcnet.ro; f. 1891; 2,010 mems; library of 13,000 vols; Pres. Arch. ALEXANDRU BELDIMAN; publs *Architectura* (quarterly), *Buletin Informativ* (monthly).

ECONOMICS, LAW AND POLITICS

Asociaţia de Drept Internaţional şi Relaţii Internaţionale (Association of International Law and International Relations): Şoseaua Kiseleff 47, 011314 Bucharest; tel. (21) 222-44-22; fax (21) 222-74-62; f. 1965; 500 mems; library of 8,000 vols; Pres. CORNELIU MĂNESCU; Sec.-Gen. MIRCEA MALIŢA.

Asociaţia Română de Drept Umanitar (Romanian Association of Humanitarian Law): Calea Rahovei 147–151, 050892 Bucharest; fax (21) 335-41-75; f. 1990; 200 mems; library of 5,000 vols; Pres. Dr IONEL CLOŞCĂ; Gen. Sec. GHEORGHE BĂDESCU; publ. *Revista română de drept umanitar*.

FINE AND PERFORMING ARTS

Asociaţia Artiştilor Fotografi (Art Photographers' Association): Calea Victoriei 107, POB 1–223, 010069 Bucharest; f. 1956; 1,500 mems; library of 12,000 photographic magazines; publ. *Fotografia şi Video* (6 a year).

Asociaţia Artiştilor Plastici – Bucureşti (Artists' Association of Bucharest): Str. Nicolae Balcescu 18, 021051 Bucharest; tel. (21) 613-38-60; f. 1973; 1,800 mems; Pres. Dr Eng. IOAN CEZAR CORÁCI; Gen. Sec. DAN SEGĂRCEANU.

Uniunea Artiştilor Plastici din România (Romanian Union of Fine Arts): Str. Nicolae Iorga 21, 010433 Bucharest; tel. (21) 650-49-20; fax (21) 311-35-72; e-mail agildus@arexim.ro; internet www.uap.ro; f. 1950; 4,170 mems; library of 12,000 vols; Pres. ALEXANDRU GHILDUS; publs *Arta* (art review, quarterly), *Info* (monthly).

Uniunea Cineaştilor din România (Romanian Film Makers' Union): Str. Mendeleev 28–30, 010365 Bucharest; tel. (21) 212-79-63; fax (21) 311-12-46; e-mail czucin@rnc.ro; f. 1963; 710 mems; Pres. MIHNEA GHEORGHIU; Dir CONSTANTIN PIVNICIERU.

Uniunea Compozitorilor şi Muzicologilor din România (Composers' and Musicologists' Union of Romania): Calea Victoriei 141, 010071 Bucharest; tel. (21) 650-28-38; fax (21) 650-28-25; f. 1920; 432 mems; library of 50,000 vols incl. spec. colln of Romanian music (printed scores and MSS); Pres. ADRIAN IORGULESCU; publs *Muzica* (quarterly), *Actualitatea Muzicală* (fortnightly).

Uniunea Teatrală din România (Theatre Union of Romania): Str. George Enescu 2–4, 010306 Bucharest; tel. (21) 315-36-36; fax (21) 312-09-13; e-mail uniter@fx.ro; f. 1990; 900 mems; Pres. ION CARAMITRU; publs *Semnal teatral* (Theatre Signal, quarterly), *Anuarul teatrului românesc* (Romanian Theatre Yearbook).

HISTORY, GEOGRAPHY AND ARCHAEOLOGY

Comitetul Naţional al Istoricilor (National Committee for Historical Sciences): Calea Victoriei 125, 010071 Bucharest; tel. (21) 212-86-29; fax (21) 312-02-09; f. 1955; Pres DAN BERINDEI; Sec.-Gen. CONSTANTIN BUŞE; publ. *Nouvelles d'études d'histoire* (irreg.).

Federaţia Filatelică Română (Romanian Philatelic Federation): Str. Boteanu 6, 010027 Bucharest; tel. (21) 313-89-21; fax (21) 310-40-04; f. 1891; 25,000 mems; library of 3,000 vols; Pres. LEONARD PASCANU; publ. *Filatelia* (monthly).

Societatea de Ştiinţe Geografice din România (Society of Geographical Sciences of Romania): Bdul Bălcescu 1, 010041 Bucharest; tel. (21) 614-93-50; f. 1875; 5,000 mems; library of 4,000 vols; Exec. Pres. POSEA GRIGORE; publs *Terra*, *Bulletin*.

Societatea de Ştiinţe Istorice din România (Society of Historical Sciences of Romania): Bdul Republicii 13, Bucharest; tel. (21) 313-13-29; fax (21) 321-05-35; f. 1949; 5,000 mems; Chair. N. ADĂNILOAIE; Sec.-Gen. B. TEODORESCU; publ. *Studii şi articole de istorie* (annual).

Societatea Numismatică Romană (Romanian Numismatic Society): Str. Popa Tatu 20, 010805 Bucharest; tel. (21) 642-26-02; f. 1903; 2,405 mems; library of 4,010 vols; Pres. Dr CONSTANTIN PREDA; Sec.-Gen. AURICĂ SMARANDA; publ. *Buletinul* (annual).

LANGUAGE AND LITERATURE

Alliance Française: Str. Emile Zola 6, 011847 Bucharest; tel. (21) 231-05-15; fax (21) 231-05-19; e-mail thierry.dumas@diplomatie.fr; offers courses and examinations in French language and culture and promotes cultural exchange with France; attached offices in Braşov, Constanţa, Craiova, Medgidia, Piteşti and Ploieşti.

British Council: Calea Dorobantilor 14, 010572 Bucharest; tel. (21) 307-96-00; fax (21) 307-90-01; e-mail bc.romania@britishcouncil.ro; internet www.britishcouncil.org/ro/romania.htm; teaching centre; offers courses and examinations in English language and British culture and promotes cultural exchange with the UK; attached offices in Brasov, Cluj, Iaşi, and Timişoara; library of 16,000 vols; Regional Dir, South-Eastern Europe STEPHAN ROMAN; Teaching Centre Man. SILVIA BERNY.

Goethe-Institut: Str. Henri Coanda 22, 010668 Bucharest; tel. (21) 210-40-47; fax (21) 312-05-85; e-mail info@bukarest.goethe.org; internet www.goethe.de/ms/buk/deindex.htm; offers courses and examinations in German language and culture and promotes cultural exchange with Germany; also responsible for Goethe-Institut work in Moldova; library in Chisinau; library of 12,000 vols; Dir HEIDEGERT A. HOESCH.

Instituto Cervantes: Str. Marin Serghiescu 12, 021016 Bucharest; tel. (21) 230-13-54; fax (21) 230-15-67; e-mail cenbuc@cervantes.es; internet bucarest.cervantes.es; offers courses and examinations in Spanish language and culture and promotes cultural exchange with Spain and Spanish-speaking Latin and Central America; library of 12,000 vols, 152 periodicals; Dir IOANA ZLOTESCU SIMATU.

PEN Club: Str. Transilvaniei 56, 010799 Bucharest; tel. (21) 312-58-54; fax (21) 311-11-12; e-mail acivica@fx.ro; f. 1924, re-f. 1990; 50 mems; Pres. ANA BLANDIANA; Sec. DENISA COMANESCU.

Societatea Română de Lingvistică (Romanian Society of Linguistics): Calea 13 Septembrie 13, 050711 Bucharest; tel. (21) 641-27-57; f. 1941; Pres. Prof. EMANUEL VASILIU; Sec. LAURENŢIU THEBAN.

Societatea Română de Lingvistică Romanică (Romanian Society of Romance Linguistics): Str. Edgar Quinet 7, 010017 Bucharest; tel. (21) 650-28-38; f. 1962; 250 mems; library of 2,000 vols; Pres. Dr MARIUS SALA; Gen. Sec. SANDA REINHEIMER RÎPEANU; publ. *Bulletin* (irreg.).

Uniunea Scriitorilor din România (Romanian Writers' Union): Calea Victoriei 115, 010071 Bucharest; tel. (21) 650-72-45; fax (21) 312-96-34; f. 1949; Pres. LAURENTIU ULICI; publs *România Literară, Luceafărul, Viaţa Românească, Secolul 20, Contrapunct, Caiete Critice, Memoria, Apostrof, Ramîuri, Helikon, Lato.*

MEDICINE

Academia de Ştiinţe Medicale (Academy of Medical Sciences): Bdul 1 Mai 11, 061621 Bucharest; f. 1969; sections of Biomedical Research (Sec. Dr C. TAŞCĂ), Clinical Medicine (Sec. Prof. Dr L. GHERASIM), Prophylactic Medicine and Public Health (Sec. Dr TR. IONESCU), Pharmaceutical Research (Sec. Prof. Dr EMANOIL I. MANOLESCU); attached research institutes: see Research Institutes; 82 mems, 14 corresp. mems; Pres. Prof. Dr ŞTEFAN M. MILCU; Gen. Sec. Dr MIHAI ZAMFIRESCU.

Asociaţia Medicală Romană (Romanian Medical Association): Str. Ionel Perlea 10, 010209 Bucharest; tel. (21) 314-10-71; fax (21) 312-13-57; f. 1873; 38 affiliated socs; Pres. Prof. Dr VALERIU POPESCU; Sec.-Gen. Prof. Dr EMANOIL POPESCU; publ. *Buletin A.M.R.* (quarterly).

Societatea de Medici şi Naturalişti Iaşi (Society of Physicians and Naturalists in Iaşi): Bdul Independenţei 16, POB 25, 700098 Iaşi; tel. (232) 14-29-80; f. 1830; medicine, pharmacy, dentistry; 1,640 mems; Chair. Prof. ION HĂULICĂ; publ. *Revista Medico-Chirurgicală* (multi-lingual, English abstracts, quarterly).

Societatea Romană de Stomatologie (Romanian Society of Stomatology): Str. Ionel Perlea 10, 010209 Bucharest; tel. (21) 314-10-62; fax (21) 312-13-57; f. 1923; Pres. Prof. Dr EMILIAN HUTU; Sec. Dr MARION VLADIMIR CONSTANTINESCU; publ. *Stomatologia* (quarterly)

NATURAL SCIENCES

General

Asociaţia Oamenilor de Ştiinţă din România (Scientists' Association of Romania): Calea Griviţei 21 (Fl. 5), 010702 Bucharest; tel. (21) 613-62-34; fax (21) 613-62-34; f. 1956; Pres. Prof. Dr VASILE CÂNDEA; Scientific Sec.-Gen. Prof. Dr Ing. ION HOHAN.

Biological Sciences

Societatea de Ştiinţe Biologice din România (Society of Biological Sciences of Romania): Intrarea Portocalelor 1–3, 060101 Bucharest; f. 1949; 9,000 mems; library of 6,100 vols; Chair. Prof. Dr ION ANGHEL; Sec.-Gen. Dr CONSTANTIN VOICA; publ. *Natura* (quarterly).

Mathematical Sciences

Societatea de Ştiinţe Matematice din România (Romanian Mathematical Society): Str. Academiei 14, 010014 Bucharest; tel. (21) 314-46-53; fax (21) 312-40-72; e-mail office@rms.unibuc.ro; internet www .rms.unibuc.ro; f. 1895; 8,000 mems; Pres. DORIN POPESCU; Sec.-Gen. MIRCEA TRIFU; publs *Bulletin Mathématique* (quarterly), *Gazeta Matematică Seria A, Revista de cultura matematica* (quarterly), *Gazeta Matematică Seria B, Revista de cultura matematica pentru tineret* (monthly).

Physical Sciences

Societatea Geologică a României (Geological Society of Romania): Str. Caransebeş, 012271 Bucharest; f. 1930; 500 mems; Pres. Prof. DAN RĂDULESCU; Gen. Sec. TITUS BRUSTUR; publ. *Buletinul* (annual).

RELIGION, SOCIOLOGY AND ANTHROPOLOGY

Asociaţia Slaviştilor din România (Slav Studies Association of Romania): Str. Pitar Moş 7–13, 010451 Bucharest; tel. (21) 211-1820; fax (21) 211-9940; e-mail slava@lls .unibuc.ro; internet www.unibuc.ro; f. 1956; 150 mems; Pres. Prof. Dr DORIN GĂMULESCU; Sec.and Treas. Dr MARIANA MANGIULEA; publ. *Romanoslavica* (annual).

Institutul Biblic şi de Misiune al Bisericii Ortodoxe Romăne (Biblical and Missionary Institute of the Romanian Orthodox Church): Intrarea Patriarhiei 9, 040162 Bucharest; tel. (21) 406-71-92; fax (21) 300-05-05; e-mail eibmbor@rdslink.ro; internet www.editurapatriarhiei.ro; f. 1925; publishes the synodal Romanian versions of the Holy Scripture, liturgical books, patristic texts, handbooks and treatises for Romanian theological schools, contemporary Orthodox literature; 14 mems; Dir. AURELIAN MARINESCU; Sec. Fr EUGEN MORARU; publs *Biserica Ortodoxa Româna* (quarterly), *Ortodoxia* (2 a year).

Societatea de Etnologie din România (Ethnology Society of Romania): Str. Zalomit 12, 010151 Bucharest; tel. and fax (21) 311-03-23; e-mail rica_org@yahoo.com; f. 1990; 200 mems; library; Pres. Dr. GEORGE ANCA; Sec. ION MOANŢA; publs *Etnologie românească* (quarterly), *Liber* (quarterly), *Trivium* (quarterly), *School of Indology* (quarterly).

TECHNOLOGY

Asociaţia Generală a Inginerilor din România (General Association of Engineers of Romania): Calea Victoriei 118, 010093 Bucharest; tel. (21) 212 8106; fax (21) 312-55-31; e-mail office@agir.ro; internet www .agir.ro; f. 1881; 16,300 mems; library of 32,000 vols; Pres. Prof. Dr Ing. MIHAI MIHĂIŢĂ; publs *Univers Ingineresc* (24 a year), *Buletinul Tehnic AGIR* (quarterly), *Anuarul AGIR* (annual).

Research Institutes

AGRICULTURE, FISHERIES AND VETERINARY SCIENCE

Aquaproiect, SA: Spl. Independenţei 294, 060031 Bucharest; tel. (21) 316-00-35; fax (21) 316-00-42; e-mail office@aquaproiect.ro; internet www.aquaproiect.ro; f. 1953; design institute for water resources eng. and environmental eng.; library of 10,000 vols; Technical Dir Dipl. Eng. GHEORGHE BRĂTIANU.

Centrul de Cercetare şi Producţie pentru Piscicultură, Pescuit şi Industrializarea Pestelui (Research and Production Centre for Fish Culture, Fisheries and the Fish Industry): Str. Portului 2–4, 800032 Galaţi; tel. (236) 41-69-14; fax (236) 41-42-70; attached to Acad. of Agricultural and Forestry Sciences; Dir Dr Eng. CONSTANTIN PECHEANU; Scientific Sec. Dr Eng. NECULAI PATRICHE.

Centrul de Cercetăre-Dezvoltare pentru Cultura Plantelor pe Nisipuri (Central Research Station for Plant Cultivation on Sand): Jud. Dăbuleni, 207220 Dolj; tel. (251) 33-44-02; fax (251) 33-43-47; e-mail sccpndabuleni@rol.ro; f. 1959; attached to Acad. of Agricultural and Forestry Sciences; 111 mems; library of 14,315 vols; Dir Dr Eng. DUMITRU GHEORGHE; publ. *Anales* (annual).

Centrul de Cercetări pentru Protecţia Plantelor (Research Centre for Plant Protection): Bdul Ion Ionescu de la Brad 8, 013813 Bucharest; tel. (21) 269-32-34; fax

(21) 269-32-39; e-mail icpp@com.pcnet.ro; f. 1967; attached to Acad. of Agricultural and Forestry Sciences; library of 8,000 vols; Dir Prof. Dr HORIA ILIESCU; publs *Analele* (annual), *Pesticide Tests, Plant Protection Bulletin* (quarterly).

Centrul Naţional de Geodezie, Cartografie, Fotogrammetrie şi Teledecţie (National Centre of Geodesy, Cartography, Photogrammetry and Remote-Sensing): Bdul Expoziţiei 1A, 012101 Bucharest; fax (21) 224-42-84; fax (21) 224-19-96; f. 1958; library of 6,000 vols; Dir Eng. IOAN STOIAN; publ. *Analele CNGCFT* (annual).

Institutul de Biologie şi Nutriţie Animală Baloteşti (Institute of Biology and Animal Nutrition Baloteşti): Sect. Agricol Ilfov, 077015 Baloteşti; tel. (21) 266-12-28; fax (21) 222-44-10; e-mail ibna@pcnet.ro; f. 1970; attached to Acad. of Agricultural and Forestry Sciences; library of 5,000 vols; Dir Dr DOINA VALENTINA GROSSU; publs *Anale* (annual), *Archiva Zootechnica* (in English, annual).

Institutul de Cercetare-Dezvoltare pentru Apicultură (Research and Development Institute for Beekeeping): Bdul Ficusului 42, 013975 Bucharest; tel. (21) 232-50-60; fax (21) 232-02-87; e-mail icda@rdsmail.ro; internet www.icda.go.ro; f. 1974; attached to Acad. of Agricultural and Forestry Sciences; library of 11,300 vols, 4,400 periodicals; Dir Dipl. Eng. AUREL MĂLAIU; publ. *România apicolă* (monthly).

Institutul de Cercetare-Dezvoltare pentru Cultura şi Industrializarea Sfeclei de Zahăr şi Substanţelor Dulci (Research and Development Institute for the Cultivation and Processing of Sugar Beet and Sweet Substances): Judeţul Călarasi, 915200 Fundulea; tel. and fax (242) 64-24-23; f. 1981; attached to Acad. of Agricultural and Forestry Sciences; Dir Dr Ing AURELIAN POPA; publs *Scientific Works – Beet and Sugar* (annual), *Health of Plants* (1–3 a year), *Cereal and Technical Plants* (1–3 a year), *Agricultural Papers* (1–4 a year).

Institutul de Cercetare şi Dezvoltare pentru Bovine (Institute for Bovine Research and Development): Sect. Agricol Ilfov, 077015 Baloteşti; tel. (21) 266-12-02; fax (21) 266-12-06; e-mail icpcb@k.ro; f. 1970; attached to Acad. of Agricultural and Forestry Sciences; library of 11,000 vols; Dir Dr Ing. IOAN CUREU; publs *Taurine—Scientific Works* (annual), *Presentation* (every 5 years).

Institutul de Cercetare şi Dezvoltare pentru Valorificarea Produselor Horticole (Institute of Research and Development for Marketing Horticultural Products): Intrarea Binelui 1A, POB 1-93, 042146 Bucharest; tel. (21) 312-90-37; fax (21) 330-36-85; f. 1967; attached to Acad. of Agricultural and Forestry Sciences; library of 3,575 vols; Dir Dr Eng. ANDREI GHERGHI; publs *Lucrări ştiinţifice* (annual), *Horticultura* (monthly).

Institutul de Cercetare şi Inginerie Tehnologică pentru Irigaţii şi Drenaje (Research and Technological Engineering Institute for Irrigation and Drainage): Judeţul Giurgiu, 087010 Băneasa; tel. (246) 28-50-23; fax (246) 28-50-24; e-mail scdid@ easynet.ro; f. 1977; attached to Acad. of Agricultural and Forestry Sciences; library of 5,700 vols, 763 periodicals; Dir Dr Ing. GHEORGHE CRUTU; publ. *Scientific Papers on Irrigation and Drainage* (annual).

Institutul de Cercetare-Dezvoltare pentru Cartof si Sfeclă de Zahar (Research and Development Institute for Potato and Sugar Beet): Str. Fundăturii 2, 500470 Braşov; tel. (268) 47-46-47; fax (268) 47-66-08; e-mail icpc@potato.ro; internet www

.potato.ro; f. 1967; attached to Acad. of Agricultural and Forestry Sciences, Bucharest; 55 mems; library of 10,000 vols; Gen. Dir Dr SORIN CHIRU; Scientific Dir GH. OLTEANU; publs *Anale* (scientific papers, annual), *Cartoful în România* (The Potato in Romania, quarterly).

Institutul de Cercetare și Producţie pentru Creşterea Ovinelor şi Caprinelor (Research and Production Institute for Sheep and Goat Breeding): Str. I. C. Brătianu 248, Judeţul Constanţa Palas, 900316 Constanţa; tel. and fax (241) 63-95-06; e-mail icdcoc@relsys.ro; f. 1897; attached to Acad. of Agricultural and Forestry Sciences; Dir Ing. RADU RĂDUCU.

Institutul de Cercetare și Producţie pentru Creşterea Păsărilor şi Animalelor Mici (Research and Production Institute for Poultry and Small Animal Breeding): Sect. Agricol Ilfov, 077015 Baloteşti; fax (21) 795-10-23; f. 1970; attached to Acad. of Agricultural and Forestry Sciences; Dir Ing. GRIGORE MUSCALU.

Institutul de Cercetare şi Producţie pentru Cultura Pajiştilor (Grassland Research and Production Institute): Str. Cucului 5, 500128 Braşov; tel. (268) 165-03-79; fax (268) 15-06-50; f. 1969; attached to Acad. of Agricultural and Forestry Sciences; library of 7,000 vols; Dir-Gen. Dr MIRCEA NEAGU; publ. *Lucrări ştiinţifice* (annual).

Institutul de Cercetare Dezvoltare pentru Pomicultura (Fruit-Growing Research Institute): Mărăcineni, 117450 Argeş; tel. (248) 27-80-66; fax (248) 27-84-77; e-mail icpp_mar@geostar.ro; internet www.icdp.ro; f. 1967; attached to Acad. of Agricultural and Forestry Sciences; 10 experimental fruit stations; research areas incl. breeding studies, biotechnology, pest control and virology; 33 mems; library of 25,000 vols; Dir Dr DORIN SUMEDREA.

Institutul de Cercetări pentru Cereale şi Plante Tehnice (Research Institute for Cereals and Industrial Crops): Judeţul Fundulea, 915200 Călăraşi; tel. (242) 311-07-22; fax (242) 311-07-22; f. 1957; attached to Acad. of Agricultural and Forestry Sciences; library of 12,000 vols; Dir GHEORGHE SIN; publs *Analele* (annual), *Probleme de genetică teoretică şi aplicată*, *Probleme de agrofitotehnie teoretică şi aplicată*, *Probleme de protecţia plantelor* (quarterly), *Romanian Agricultural Research* (every 2 years).

Institutul de Cercetări pentru Ingineria Mediului (Research Institute for Environmental Engineering): Splaiul Independenţei 294, 060031 Bucharest; f. 1990; library of 5,000 vols; Dir IOAN JELEV.

Institutul de Cercetări pentru Legumicultură şi Floricultură (Research Institute for Vegetable and Flower Growing): Judeţul Ilfov, 077185 Vidra; tel. and fax (21) 361-20-94; e-mail inclf@mediasat.ro; internet www.icdlfvidra.ro; f. 1967; attached to Acad. of Agricultural and Forestry Sciences; research into plant breeding and seed production, soil science, plant protection and flower-growing; library of 500 vols; Dir Dr MARCEL COSTACHE; publ. *Annals*.

Institutul de Cercetări-Dezvoltare pentru Pedologie, Agrochimie şi Protecţia Mediului (Research Institute for Soil Science and Agrochemistry): Bdul Mărăşti 61, 060031 Bucharest; tel. (21) 222-94-42; fax (21) 222-59-79; e-mail icpa@icpa.ro; internet www.icpa.ro; f. 1969; attached to Acad. of Agricultural and Forestry Sciences; library of 9,000 vols; Dir Dr Ing. MIHAIL DUMITRU; publ. *Anale* (annual).

Institutul de Cercetări pentru Viticultură şi Vinificaţie (Research Institute for Viticulture and Wine-Making): Str. Valea Mantei 1, Judeţul Valea Călugărească, 107620 Prahova; tel. (244) 23-66-90; fax (244) 23-63-89; e-mail icvv@xnet.ro; f. 1967; Man Dr Eng. NICOLAE VARGA; attached to Acad. of Agricultural and Forestry Sciences; library of 14,000 vols; publ. *Anale* (research papers).

Institutul de Cercetări şi Amenajări Silvice (Forest Research and Management Institute): Şoseaua Stefăneşti 128, 077190 Bucharest; tel. (21) 240-68-45; e-mail icas@com.pcnet.ro; f. 1933; attached to Acad. of Agricultural and Forestry Sciences; library of 32,000 vols; Dir Dr ROMICA TOMESCU; publs *Anale*, *Revista pădurilor* (quarterly).

Institutul de Chimie Alimentară (Research Institute for Food Chemistry): Str. Gârlei 1, 013721 Bucharest; tel. (21) 230-50-90; fax (21) 230-03-11; e-mail ica@sunu.rnc.ro; f. 1950; attached to Acad. of Agricultural and Forestry Sciences; library of 25,000 vols; Dir Prof. Dr GHEORGHE MENCINICOPSCHI; publ. *Ştiinţe şi Tehnologii Alimentare* (Food Sciences and Technology, quarterly).

Institutul de Economie Agrară (Institute of Agrarian Economics): Bdul Mărăşti 61, 011464 Bucharest; tel. (21) 224-17-90; f. 1928; attached to Acad. of Agricultural and Forestry Sciences; library of 42,000 vols; Dir Dr TRAIAN LAZĂR; publ. *Annual Report on the Marketing of Agricultural Products*.

Institutul de Economie Agrară (Institute of Agrarian Economics): Calea 13 Septembrie 13, 050711 Bucharest; tel. (21) 410-07-76; fax (21) 410-32-00; attached to Romanian Acad.; Dir DUMITRU DUMITRU.

Institutul Naţional de Medicină Veterinară Pasteur (Pasteur National Institute of Veterinary Medicine): Calea Giuleşti 333, 060269 Bucharest; tel. (21) 220-64-86; fax (21) 220-69-15; f. 1909; attached to Acad. of Agricultural and Forestry Sciences; library of 30,000 vols; Dir Dr C. ŞTIRBU; publ. *Studies and Research in Veterinary Medicine* (annual).

Institutul Român de Cercetări Marine (Romanian Institute of Marine Research): Bdul Mamaia 300, POB 3, 900001 Constanţa; tel. (41) 54-32-88; fax (41) 83-12-74; e-mail rmri@alpha.rmri.ro; f. 1970; attached to Min. of Water, Forests and Environmental Protection; library of 38,000 vols and periodicals; Dir Eng. S. NICOLAEV; publ. *Cercetări Marine* (annual).

Societatea Comerciala Romsuintest Periş S. A. (Trade Society Romsuintest Periş S. A.): Judeţul Ilfov, 077150 Periş; tel. (21) 796-07-05; fax (21) 796-07-01; f. 1970; attached to Acad. of Agricultural and Forestry Sciences; research into pig-breeding; library of 8,000 vols; Dir Dr ŞTEFAN MANTEA; publ. *Lucrări ştiinţifice* (Scientific Work, annual).

Staţiunea Centrală de Cercetări pentru Combaterea Eroziunii Solului (Central Research Station for Soil Erosion Control): Judeţul Perieni, 737405 Vaslui; attached to Acad. of Agricultural and Forestry Sciences; Dir Eng. D. NISTOR.

Staţiunea Centrală de Cercetări pentru Cultura şi Industrializarea Tutunului (Central Research Station for Tobacco Growing and Industrialization): Str. Gârlei 1, 013721 Bucharest; tel. (21) 230-45-75; fax (21) 230-51-58; f. 1929; attached to Acad. of Agricultural and Forestry Sciences; Dir MARIANA TIGĂU; publ. *Buletinul tutunului* (annual).

Staţiunea Centrală de Producţie şi Cercetări pentru Sericicultură (Central Production and Research Station for Sericulture): Şoseaua Bucureşti-Ploieşti 69, 013685 Bucharest; tel. (21) 633-42-20; f. 1906; attached to Acad. of Agricultural and Forestry Sciences; library of 16,000 vols; Dir Eng. ION DOGARU; publ. *Sericulture* (quarterly).

Staţiunea de Cercetăre-Dezvoltare Agricola Brăila (Brăila Agricultural Research and Development Station): Şoseaua Vizirului km. 9, Judeţul Brăila, 810008 Brăila; tel. (239) 68-46-95; fax (239) 68-47-44; e-mail scda@flox.ro; f. 1954; attached to Acad. of Agricultural and Forestry Sciences; 12 mems; Dir Dr Ing. MARCEL BULARDA; publ. *Scientific Works* (annual).

ARCHITECTURE AND TOWN PLANNING

Centrul pentru Noi Arhitecturei Electronice (Centre for New Electronic Architecture): Bdul Armata Poporului 1–3, Bucharest; tel. (21) 631-78-00; attached to Romanian Acad.; Dir ŞTEFAN GHEORGHE.

Prodomus SA – Institut de Studii şi Proiectare pentru Construcţii Civile (Institute of Research and Design for Civil Engineering Works): Str. Nicolae Filipescu 53–55, 020961 Bucharest; tel. (21) 211-78-40; f. 1949; housing, social bldgs; Dir Eng. CORNELIU VELICU; publs *Prodomus – SA*, *'bdi'* (bulletin of documentation and information).

Proed SA – Institut de Studii şi Proiectare pentru Lucrări Tehnico-Edilitare (Studies and Design Institute for Public Works): Str. Tudor Arghezi 21, 020943 Bucharest; tel. (21) 211-55-10; fax (21) 210-18-01; f. 1949; water, sewerage and other public facilities, traffic organization and public transport; Man. Dir Eng. VICTOR MOLDOVEANU; publ. *'bdi'* (bulletin of documentation and information, quarterly).

ECONOMICS, LAW AND POLITICS

Institutul de Cercetări Economice 'Gheorghe Zane' (Gheorghe Zane Institute for Economic Research): Str. Theodor Codrescu 2, 700481 Iaşi; tel. (232) 11-59-84; f. 1992; attached to Romanian Acad.; library of 40,000 vols; Dir Prof. Dr ALECSANDRU TACU.

Institutul de Cercetări Juridice (Institute of Judicial Research): Calea 13 Septembrie 13, 050711 Bucharest; tel. (21) 410-40-59; fax (21) 411-44-96; e-mail juridic@racai.ro; internet www.icj.ro; f. 1954; attached to Romanian Acad.; domestic, comparative and int. law; library of 7,120 vols, 2,210 periodicals; Dir Prof. GEORGE ANTONIU; publ. *Studii de drept românesc* (quarterly).

Institutul de Economie a Industriei (Institute of Industrial Economics): Casa Academiei, Calea 13 Septembrie 13, 050711 Bucharest; tel. (21) 410-32-00; fax (21) 410-32-00; f. 1977; attached to Romanian Acad.; Dir Prof CORNELIU RUSSU; publ. *Economic Problems* (monthly).

Institutul de Economie Mondială (Institute of Global Economics): Calea 13 Septembrie 13, POB 42-13, 050711 Bucharest; tel. (21) 410-61-76; fax (21) 410-50-20; e-mail office@iem.ro; internet www.iem.ro; f. 1967; attached to Romanian Acad.; library of 21,500 vols, 320 periodicals, World Bank depository library; Dir Dr VIRGINIA CÂMPEANU; publs *Conjunctura economiei mondiale* (annual), *Evoluţia preţurilor internaţionale* (2 a year), *Piaţa internaţională* (2 a week), *Buletin de preţuri şi cotaţii pe piaţa internaţională* (3 a week), *Eurolex* (quarterly), *Euroinfo* (2 a year).

Institutul de Economie Naţională (Institute of National Economy): Calea 13 Septembrie 13, 050711 Bucharest; tel. (21) 411-97-

32; fax (21) 411-97-33; e-mail ien@fx.ro; f. 1953; attached to Romanian Acad.; Dir GHEORGHE ZAMAN; publ. *Revista Româna de Economie* (Romanian Economic Review, 2 a year).

Institutul de Finanțe, Prețuri și Probleme Valutare 'Victor Slavescu' (Victor Slavescu Institute of Finance, Prices and Foreign Exchange Issues): Calea 13 Septembrie 13, 5th Fl., 050711 Bucharest; tel. (21) 410-55-99; f. 1953; attached to Romanian Acad.; library of 40,000 vols; Dir Prof. Dr GHEORGHE MANOLESCU; publs *Buletin Financiar* (Financial Survey, quarterly), *Revista Română de Științe Economice* (Romanian Economic Review).

Institutul de Prognoză Economică (Institute of Economic Forecasting): Str. Mendeleev 34–36, 010365 Bucharest; tel. (21) 659-42-65; attached to Romanian Acad.; Dir MARIN COMȘA.

Institutul Național de Cercetări Economice (National Institute of Economic Research): Calea 13 Septembrie 13, 050711 Bucharest; tel. (21) 410-33-55; fax (21) 411-49-16; e-mail ciumara@zappmobile.ro; internet www.ince.ro; f. 1990; attached to Romanian Acad.; Dir MIRCEA CIUMARA; publs *Romanian Economic Research Observer* (monthly), *Romanian Economic Review* (2 a year).

EDUCATION

Centrul de Cercetări Avansate în Învățarea Automată, Prelucrarea Limbajului Natural și Modelarea Conceptuală (Centre for Advanced Research on Automatic Learning, Natural Language Processing and Conceptual Modelling): Calea 13 Septembrie 13, 050711 Bucharest; tel. (21) 410-29-53; fax (21) 411-39-16; attached to Romanian Acad.; Dir DAN TUFIS.

FINE AND PERFORMING ARTS

Institutul de Arheologic și Istoria Artei (Institute of Archaeology and History of Art): Str. C. Daicoviciu 2, 400020 Cluj-Napoca; tel. (264) 59-11-25; fax (264) 59-44-70; e-mail iaiacluj@personal.ro; f. 1990; attached to Romanian Acad.; library of 20,000 vols; Dir Dr MARIUS PORUMB; publs *Ephemeris Napocensis* (annual), *Ars Transilvaniae* (annual).

Institutul de Istoria Artei 'George Oprescu' (George Oprescu Institute of the History of Art): Calea Victoriei 196, 010098 Bucharest; tel. (921) 223-41-75; f. 1949; attached to Romanian Acad.; Romanian and European architecture, painting, sculpture, Romanian theatre, music, cinematography; library of 69,400 vols, 81,000 negatives, 80,300 photographs; Dir SILVIU ANGELESCU; publs *Revue Roumaine d'Histoire de l'Art* (annuall with 2 series, on fine arts and on theatre, music and cinema), *Studii și cercetări de istoria artei.*

HISTORY, GEOGRAPHY AND ARCHAEOLOGY

Centrul de Istorie și Civilizație Europeană (Centre for History and European Civilization): Str. Cuza Vodă 41, 700038 Iași; tel. (232) 21-24-41; fax (232) 21-24-41; f. 1992; attached to Romanian Acad.; Dir GHEORGHE BUZATU; publ. *Europa XXI* (every 2 years).

Centrul pentru Studiul Istoriei Evreilor din România (Centre for the Study of the History of Jews in Romania): Str. Mămulari 4, 1st Fl., Apt. 1, 030772 Bucharest; tel. and fax (21) 315-10-45; f. 1977; attached to the Fed. of Jewish Communities in Romania; Dir Dr DUMITRU HÎNCU; publ. *Buletinul* (bulletin, 2 a year).

Institutul de Arheologie (Institute of Archaeology): Str. Henri Coandă 11, 010667 Bucharest; tel. (1) 650-34-10; fax (1) 650-34-10; f. 1956; attached to Romanian Acad.; library of 200,000 vols; Dir Prof. Dr PETRE ALEXANDRESCU; publs *Dacia—Revue d'Archéologie et d'Histoire Ancienne* (annual), *Studii și cercetări de istorie veche* (quarterly), *Studii și cercetări de numismatică* (every 2 years), *Materiale și cercetări arheologice* (annual).

Institutul de Arheologie (Institute of Archaeology): Str. Lascăr Catargi 18, 700107 Iași; tel. and fax (232) 21-19-10; f. 1990; attached to Romanian Acad.; Dir VICTOR SPINEI; Asst Dir VIRGIL MIHAILESCU-BÎRLIBA; publs *Arheologia Moldovei* (annual), *Bibliotheca Archaeologica Iassiensis* (irreg.), *Studia Archaeologica* (irreg.), *Studia Honoraria* (irreg.).

Institutul de Geografie (Institute of Geography): Str. Dimitrie Racoviță 12, 023993 Bucharest; tel. (21) 313-59-90; fax (21) 311-12-42; e-mail geoinst@fx.ro; f. 1944; attached to Romanian Acad.; library of 50,000 vols, 200 periodicals, 1,900 atlases and maps; Dir Prof. DAN BĂLTEANU; publ. *Revista Geografică* (annual).

Institutul de Istorie 'A. D. Xenopol' (A.D. Xenopol Institute of History): Str. Lascăr Catargi 15, 700107 Iași; tel. (232) 21 26-14; fax (232) 21-26-14; e-mail xeno@mail.cccis.ro; f. 1941; attached to Romanian Acad.; Romanian and world history; library of 110,000 vols; Dir Dr ALEXANDRU ZUB; Sec. Dr GHEORGHE ONIȘORU.

Institutul de Istorie 'Nicolae Iorga' (Nicolae Iorga Institute of History): Bdul Aviatorilor 1, 011851 Bucharest; tel. (21) 212-53-37; fax (21) 311-03-71; e-mail institnul.iorga@email.ro, internet www.iini .bravehost.com; f. 1936; attached to Romanian Acad.; library of 200,000 vols; Dir Prof. Dr EUGEN BERNARD DENIZE; Deputy Dir Dr OVIDIU CRISTEA; Scientific Sec. Dr ILEANA CAZAN; publs *Studii și materiale de istorie medie* (annual), *Studii și materiale de istorie modernă* (annual), *Revista istorică* (6 a year), *Revue roumaine d'histoire* (quarterly).

LANGUAGE AND LITERATURE

Institutul de Filologie Română 'Al. Philippide' (Al. Philippide Institute of Romanian Philology): Str. Theodor Codrescu 2, 700481 Iași; tel. (232) 26-75-97; fax (232) 21-11-50; e-mail secretariat@philippide.is.edu .ro; internet www.philippide.is.edu.ro; f. 1927; attached to Romanian Acad.; depts of Lexicology and lexicography, Dialectology, Toponimy, Literature, Ethnology; 41 mems; library of 60,000 vols; Dir Prof. DAN MĂNUCĂ; publs *Anuar de Lingvistică și Istorie Literară*, *Buletinul* (quarterly).

Institutul de Istorie și Teorie Literară 'G. Călinescu' (G. Călinescu Institute of Literary History and Theory): Calea 13 Septembrie 13, 050711 Bucharest; tel. (21) 410-32-00 ext. 2023; fax (21) 312-53-42; f. 1949; attached to Romanian Acad.; library of 15,000 vols; Dir Prof. Dr DAN GRIGORESCU; publs *Revista de Istorie și Teorie Literară* (quarterly), *Synthesis* (annual).

Institutul de Lingvistica 'Iorgu Iordan–Al. Rosetti' (Iorgu Iordan–Al. Rosetti Institute of Linguistics): Calea 13 Septembrie 13, 050711 Bucharest; tel. (21) 411-36-98; e-mail inst@iordan.lingv.ro; f. 1949; attached to Romanian Acad.; Dir MARIUS SALA; publs *Studii și Cercetări Lingvistice* (2 a year), *Revue Roumaine de Linguistique* (quarterly), *Limba Română* (6 a year), *Fonetică și Dialectologie* (annual).

MEDICINE

Centrul de Sănătate Publică (Public Health Centre): Str. Gh. Marinescu 40, 540136 Târgu-Mureș; f. 1956; attached to Acad. of Medical Sciences; library of 12,000 vols; Dir Dr FRANCISC JESZENSZKY.

Centrul Metodologic de Parodontologie (Paradontology Methodological Centre): Str. 11 Iunie 10, 040172 Bucharest; tel. (21) 641-20-79; f. 1968; library of 326 vols; Dir Dr THEODORA GUȚU.

Centrul Național de Fono-Audiologie și Chirurgie Funcțională ORL (National Centre for Phono-Audiology and ENT Surgery): Mihai Cioranu 21, 050751 Bucharest; tel. (21) 31-59-80; f. 1972; attached to Acad. of Medical Sciences; library of 2,000 vols; Dir Dr ROMEO CĂLĂRAȘU.

Institutul de Endocrinologie 'C.I. Parhon' (C.I. Parhon Institute of Endocrinology): Bdul Aviatorilor 34–36, 011863 Bucharest; tel. (21) 33-40-10; f. 1946; attached to Acad. of Medical Sciences; library of 65,800 vols; Dir Dr CONSTANTIN DUMITRACHE; publ. *Romanian Journal of Endocrinology* (quarterly).

Institutul de Fiziologie Normală și Patologică 'D. Danielopolu' (D. Danielopolu Institute of Normal and Pathological Physiology): Bdul Ion Mihalache 11A, 011171 Bucharest; tel. (21) 312-89-38; fax (21) 312-59-37; e-mail ifnp@home.ro; internet www .rol.ro/ifnp; f. 1949; attached to Acad. of Medical Sciences; library of 49,000 vols; Dir Prof. Dr MARCEL ULUITU; publ. *Romanian Journal of Physiology* (quarterly).

Institutul de Medicină Internă 'Nicolae Gh. Lupu' (Nicolae Gh. Lupu Institute of Internal Medicine): Șoseaua Ștefan cel Mare 19–21, 020125 Bucharest; tel. (21) 611-13-70; f. 1949; attached to Acad. of Medical Sciences; library of 72,000 vols; Dir Prof. S. PURICE; publ. *Revue Roumaine de Médecine Interne* (quarterly).

Institutul de Neurologie și Psihiatrie (Institute of Neurology and Psychiatry): Șoseaua Berceni 10–12, 041915 Bucharest; tel. (21) 683-78-31; f. 1950; attached to Acad. of Medical Sciences; library of 7,957 vols; Dir Prof. V. VOICULESCU; publ. *Neurologie et Psychiatrie* (series of *Revue Roumaine de Médecine*, quarterly).

Institutul de Patologie și Genetică Medicală 'V. Babeș' (V. Babeș Institute of Pathology and Medical Genetics): Splaiul Independenței 99–101, 050096 Bucharest; tel. (21) 411-51-52; fax (21) 411-51-05; f. 1887; attached to Acad. of Medical Sciences; genetics, immunology, pathology and ultrastructure; library of 20,000 vols; Dir Prof. Dr L. M. POPESCU; publ. *Romanian Journal of Morphology and Embryology* (quarterly).

Institutul de Sănătate Publică (Institute of Public Health): Str. Dr V. Babeș 14, 700465 Iași; tel. (232) 14-15-20; fax (232) 21-03-99; f. 1930; attached to Min. of Health; library of 17,000 vols; Dir LUMINIȚA SMARANDA IANCU; publ. *Journal of Preventive Medicine* (quarterly).

Institutul de Sănătate Publică, București (Institute of Public Health, Bucharest): Str. Dr Leonte 1–3, 080463 Bucharest; tel. (21) 212-62-10; fax (21) 312-34-26; e-mail directie@ispb.ro; internet www.ispb.ro; f. 1927; library of 36,000 vols; separate medical history library of 41,000 vols; Dir Dr OCTAVIAN LUCHIAN; publ. *Sănătate și Prevenție* (quarterly).

Institutul de Sănătate Publică 'Prof. Dr Iuliu Moldovan' (Prof. Dr Iuliu Moldovan Institute of Public Health): Str. Pasteur 4–6, 400349 Cluj-Napoca; tel. (264) 59-42-52; fax (264) 59-98-91; e-mail isbocsan@ispcj.ro;

internet www.ispcj.ro; f. 1930; monitors public health in 11 Transylvanian counties, provides technical assistance, continuing education, field applied scientific research, public health services; 102 mems; library of 30,150 vols; Dir Prof. Dr IOAN STELIAN BOCȘAN.

Institutul de Sănătate Publică 'Prof. Dr Leonida Georgescu', Timișoara (Prof. Dr Leonida Georgescu Institute of Public Health, Timișoara): Bdul Dr Victor. Babeș 16, 300226 Timișoara; tel. and fax (256) 49-21-01; e-mail office@ispt.ro; internet www.ispt.ro; f. 1946; attached to Acad. of Medical Sciences; library of 14,966 vols; Dir Conf. Dr EMILIAN DAMIAN POPOVICI; publs *Annals of the Institute of Public Health, Timișoara* (annual), *Documentary Booklet* (annual).

Institutul de Virusologie 'Ștefan S. Nicolau' (IVN) (Ștefan S. Nicolau Institute of Virology): Șoseaua Mihai Bravu 285, 030304 Bucharest; tel. and fax (21) 324-25-90; e-mail cernescu@valhalla.racai.ro; internet www.virology.ro; f. 1949; attached to Romanian Acad.; WHO Virus Collaborating Centre; research on respiratory viral infections, arboviral infections, viral hepatitis, AIDS; 60 mems; library of 60,000 vols, 200 periodicals; Dir Dr MIHAI STOIAN; publs *Proceedings of the Romanian Academy, series B, Science and Life* (in English, 2 a year), *Studii și Cercetări de Virusologie* (in Romanian, 2 a year).

Institutul Național de Cercetare-Dezvoltare 'Dr I. Cantacuzino' (Dr I. Cantacuzino National Research and Development Institute): Spl. Independenței 103, CP 1-525, 050096 Bucharest; tel. (21) 411-38-00; fax (21) 411-56-72; e-mail office@cantacuzino.ro; f. 1921; attached to Acad. of Medical Sciences; microbiology, immunology and epidemiology of communicable diseases; library of 109,000 vols; Dir Dr ANDREI AUBERT-COMBIESCU; publ. *Romanian Archives of Microbiology and Immunology* (quarterly).

Institutul Național de Medicină Legală 'Mina Minovici' (Mina Minovici National Institute for Forensic Medicine): Șoseaua Vitan-Bârzești 9, 042122 Bucharest; tel. (21) 332-50-08; fax (21) 334-62-60; e-mail danderme@rnc.ro; internet www.legmed.ro; f. 1892; library of 21,000 vols; Dir Prof. Dr DAN DERMENGIU; publ. *Romanian Journal of Legal Medicine* (quarterly).

Institutul Oncologic (Institute of Oncology): Șoseaua Fundeni 252, 022328 Bucharest; f. 1949; attached to Acad. of Medical Sciences; library of 41,144 vols; Dir Prof. ION PANĂ; publ. *Oncologia* (quarterly).

Institutul pentru Controlul de Stat al Medicamentului și Cercetări Farmaceutice 'Petre Ionescu-Stoian' (Petre Ionescu-Stoian State Institute for Drug Control and Pharmaceutical Research): Str. Aviator Sănătescu 48, 011478 Bucharest; tel. (21) 224-10-79; fax (21) 230-50-83; e-mail dd@ns.icsmcf.ro; f. 1929; Dir Prof. Dr DUMITRU DOBRESCU; publ. *Farmaco-vigilența* (Drug Monitoring,quarterly).

NATURAL SCIENCES
Biological Sciences

Institutul de Biochimie (Institute of Biochemistry): Spl Independenței 296, 060031 Bucharest; tel. (21) 223-90-69; fax (21) 223-90-68; internet www.biochim.ro; f. 1990; attached to Romanian Acad.; research into protein science, particularly the biosynthesis and function of proteins and glycoproteins; 47 mems; Dir Dr STEFANA PETRESCU; publ. *Romanian Journal of Biochemistry* (2 a year).

Institutul de Biologie (Institute of Biology): Splaiul Independenței 296, 060031 Bucharest; tel. (21) 637-34-70; fax (21) 310-24-10; e-mail biolog@linux.biochim.ro; attached to Romanian Acad.; Dir Dr MARIN FALCĂ.

Institutul de Biologie și Patologie Celulară 'Nicolae Simionescu' (Nicolae Simionescu Institute of Cellular Biology and Pathology): Bogdan Petriceicu Hașdeu 8, POB 35-14, 050568 Bucharest; tel. (21) 411-08-60; fax (21) 412-11-43; internet www.icbp.ro; f. 1979; 100 mems; attached to Romanian Acad.; Dir MAYA SIMIONESCU.

Institutul de Cercetare și Proiectare Delta Dunării (Danube Delta Research and Design Institute): Str. Babadag 165, 022817 Yulcea; tel. (240) 53-15-20; fax (240) 53-35-47; e-mail icpdd@tlx.ssitl.ro; f. 1970; promotes the conservation of biodiversity and the sustainable devt of wetlands in Romania and the Danube Delta area; library of 40,000 vols; Dir Eng. ROMULUS ȘTIUCĂ; publs *Annals, Review of Ecological Restoration in the Danube Delta Biosphere Reserve*.

Institutul de Cercetări Biologice Cluj-Napoca (Biological Research Institute of Cluj-Napoca): Str. Republicii 48, 400015 Cluj-Napoca; tel. (264) 19-80-84; fax (264) 19-12-38; e-mail icb@mail.dntcj.ro; f. 1958; biology, biotechnology, plant and animal ecology, soil enzymology; library of 9,000 vols, 24,000 periodicals; Dir Dr GHEORGHE COLDEA; publ. *Contribuții Botanice* (annual).

Institutul de Cercetări Biologice Iași (Iași Biological Research Institute): Bdul Carol I 20A, 700505 Iași; tel. (232) 21-82-03; fax (232) 21-81-21; e-mail amanoliu@uaic.ro; f. 1970; library of 35,000 vols; Dir Dr ALEXANDRU MANOLIU.

Institutul de Cercetări Eco-Muzeale Tulcea (Tulcea Institute of Ecological Museum Research): Str. 14 Noiembrie 3, 820009 Tulcea; tel. (240) 51-53-75; fax (240) 51-53-75; e-mail icemtl@tlx.ssitl.ro; f. 1950; archaeology, natural history, history, ethnography, art; library of 92,000 vols; Dir GAVRILĂ SIMION; publ. *Peuce*.

Mathematical Sciences

Institutul de Matematică 'Octav Mayer' (Octav Mayer Institute of Mathematics): Bdul Carol 8, 700505 Iași; tel. (232) 14-75-70; f. 1948; attached to Romanian Acad.; Dir VIOREL BARBU.

Institutul de Matematică 'Simion Stoilow' (Simion Stoilow Institute of Mathematics): POB 1-764, 014700 Bucharest; tel. (21) 319-65-06; fax (21) 319-65-05; e-mail vasile.brinzanescu@imar.ro; internet www.imar.ro; f. 1949, ref. 1990; 128 mems; attached to Romanian Acad.; library of 35,000 vols, 121,000 journals; Dir Prof. Dr ȘERBAN A. BASARAB; publs *Revue Roumaine de Mathématiques Pures et Appliquées* (6 a year), *Mathematical Reports* (quarterly).

Institutul de Statistică Matematică și Matematică Aplicată (Institute of Mathematical Statistics and Applied Mathematics): Calea 13 Septembrie 13, Casa Academiei Române, 050711 Bucharest; tel. (21) 411-49-00; e-mail chief@csm.ro; internet www.csm.ro; f. 1964; attached to Romanian Acad.; Dir MARIUS IOSIFESCU.

Physical Sciences

Institutul Astronomic (Institute of Astronomy): Str. Cuțitul de Argint 5, 040557 Bucharest; tel. (21) 335-68-92; fax (21) 337-33-89; e-mail magda@aira.astro.ro; internet www.astro.ro; f. 1908, re-f. 1990; attached to Romanian Acad.; Dir Dr MAGDA STAVINSCHI; publs *Romanian Astronomical Journal* (2 a year), *Anuarul Astronomic* (Astronomical Yearbook, annual).

Institutul de Cercetări Chimice (Institute of Chemical Research): Splaiul Independenței 202, 060021 Bucharest; tel. (21) 315-32-99; fax (21) 312-34-93; e-mail ssever@chimfiz.icf.ro; f. 1950; natural and bioactive products, technological engineering, chemical products and technologies; Gen. Man. SEVER ȘERBAN.

Institutul de Chimie Fizică (Institute of Physical Chemistry): Splaiul Independenței 202, 060021 Bucharest; tel. (21) 312-61-52; fax (21) 312-11-47; e-mail mpopa@chimfiz.icf.ro; f. 1963; attached to Romanian Acad.; Dir MIHAI VASILE POPA; publs *Revue Roumaine de Chimie* (monthly), *Roumanian Chemical Quarterly Review*.

Institutul de Chimie Macromoleculară 'Petru Poni' (Petru Poni Institute of Macromolecular Chemistry): Aleea Grigore Ghica Vodă 41A, 700487 Iași; tel. (232) 21-74-54; fax (232) 21-12-99; f. 1949; attached to Romanian Acad.; research in polymer chemistry and physics; library of 89,000 vols; Dir CRISTOFOR SIMIONESCU.

Institutul de Chimie Organică 'Costin D. Nenițescu' (Costin D. Nenițescu Institute of Organic Chemistry): Splaiul Independenței 202B, 060021 Bucharest; tel. (21) 224-83-48; fax (21) 312-16-01; e-mail pfilip@cco.ro; internet wwww.cco.ro; f. 1949; attached to Romanian Acad.; Dir PETRE FILIP.

Institutul de Chimie Timișoara (Timișoara Institute of Chemistry): Bdul Mihai Viteazul 24, 300223 Timișoara; tel. (256) 19-18-18; fax (256) 19-18-18; e-mail mracec@acad-tim.utt.ro; f. 1967; attached to Romanian Acad.; library of 10,000 vols; Dir Prof. Dr MIRCEA MRACEC; publ. *Annals of the West University of Timișoara, Chemistry Series* (2 or 3 a year).

Institutul de Fizică Atomică 'Horia Hulubei' (Horia Hulubei Institute of Atomic Physics): 707 Atomistilor, MG-6, 077125 Bucharest-Măgurele; tel. (21) 404-23-01; fax (21) 404-44-40; f. 1949; library of 385,000 vols; Dir-Gen. Prof. Dr NICOLAE VICTOR ZAMFIR; publs *Conference Proceedings, IFA-Preprints, Romanian Journal of Physics* (monthly), *Romanian Reports in Physics* (monthly).

Institutul de Geodinamică 'Sabba S. Ștefănescu' (Sabba S. Ștefănescu Institute of Geodynamics): Str. Jean Louis Calderon 19–21, 020032 Bucharest; tel. (21) 317-21-26; fax (21) 317-21-20; attached to Romanian Acad.; Dir Prof. DOREL ZUGRĂVESCU.

Institutul de Speologie 'Emil Racoviță' (Emil Racoviță Institute of Speleology): Calea 13 Septembrie 13, 050711 Bucharest; tel. (21) 311-08-29; fax (21) 318-81-32; e-mail iser_b@yahoo.com; f. 1920; attached to Romanian Acad.; biospeleology, phreatobiology, edaphobiology, paleobiology, sedimentology, geohydrochemistry, karstology, geospeleology, paleoclimatology, karst protection, arheometry; br. in Cluj Napoca; library of 5,500 vols, 700 periodicals; Man. IOAN POVARA; publs *Travaux* (annual), *Theoretical and Applied Karstology* (annual).

Institutul Geologic al României (Romanian Geological Institute): Str. Caransebeș 1, 012271 Bucharest; tel. (21) 224-20-93; fax (21) 224-04-04; e-mail geol@igr.ro; f. 1906; library of 270,000 vols; museum; Dir Dr ȘERBAN VELICIU; publs Romanian journals of mineralogy, petrology, mineral deposits and environmental geochemistry, stratigraphy, palaeontology, tectonics and regional geology, geophysics (all annual), *Memorii* (irreg.).

Institutul Național de Cercetare-Dezvoltare pentru Fizică Tehnică – IFT

Iaşi (National Institute of Research and Development for Technical Physics): Bdul Mangeron 47, 700050 Iaşi; tel. (232) 13-06-80; fax (232) 23-11-32; e-mail hchiriac@ phys-iasi.ro; internet www.phys-iasi.ro; f. 1951; library of 60,000 vols; Dir Prof. Dr HORIA CHIRIAC; publ. *Proceedings* (every 4 years).

Institutul Naţional de Meteorologie şi Hidrologie (National Institute of Meteorology and Hydrology): Şoseaua Bucureşti-Ploieşti 97, 013686 Bucharest; f. 1884; Dir M. IOANA; publs daily weather reports, *Studii şi Cercetări* (in 2 parts: Meteorology, Hydrology; 1 vol. annually), *Meteorology Journal* (2 a year), *Hydrology Journal* (2 a year), *Bibliografia hidrologică* (annual), *Bibliografia meteorologică* (annual).

Institutul Naţional de Metrologie (National Institute of Metrology): Şoseaua Vitan-Bîrzeşti 11, 042122 Bucharest; tel. (21) 334-55-20; fax (21) 334-55-33; f. 1951; library of 15,000 vols; Dir D. BOICIUC; publ. *Metrologie* (quarterly).

PHILOSOPHY AND PSYCHOLOGY

Institutul de Filosofie şi Psihologie 'C. Rădulescu-Motru' (C. Radulescu-Motru Institute of Philosophy and Psychology): Calea 13 Septembrie 13, POB 1-137, 050711 Bucharest; tel. and fax (21) 318-24-42; f. 1948; attached to Romanian Acad.; Dir ALEXANDRU SURDU; Academic Sec. MIHAIL VASILE; publs *Revista de Filosofie* (6 a year), *Revista de Psihologie* (quarterly), *Revue roumaine de Philosophie* (quarterly).

Institutul de Psihologie (Institute of Psychology): Calea 13 Septembrie 13, O.P. 5, POB 5-8, 050711 Bucharest; tel. (21) 410-30-99; attached to Romanian Acad.; Dir Dr CONSTANTIN VOICU; publs *Revista de Psihologie* (quarterly), *Revue Roumaine de Psychologie* (2 a year).

RELIGION, SOCIOLOGY AND ANTHROPOLOGY

Centrul de Cercetări Antropologice Francisc Rainer (Francisc Rainer Centre for Anthropological Research): Bdul Eroilor Sanitari 8, POB 35-13, 050474 Bucharest; tel. (21) 212-66-63; fax (21) 212-66-63; e-mail rainer@sunu.rnc.ro; f. 1937; attached to Romanian Acad.; library of 7,000 vols, 25 periodicals; Dir Dr CRISTIANA GLAVCE; publ. *Annuaire d'Etudes Anthropologiques* (annual).

Institutul de Cercetare a Calităţii Vieţii (Institute of Research on the Quality of Life): Calea 13 Septembrie 13, 050711 Bucharest; tel. (21) 411-48-05; fax (21) 411-48-00; e-mail iccv@iccv.ro; internet www.iccv.ro; f. 1990; attached to Romanian Acad.; Dir CĂTĂLIN ZAMFIR; publ. *Quality of Life Review* (quarterly).

Institutul de Cercetări Socio-Umane (Institute for Research in Social and Human Sciences): Str. Lucian Blaga 13, 550169 Sibiu; tel. (269) 21-26-04; fax (269) 21-66-05; f. 1956; attached to Romanian Acad.; library of 6,000 vols, 300 periodicals; Dir Dr PAUL NIEDERMAIER; publs *Forschungen zur Volks- und Landeskunde* (2 a year), *Historia Urbana* (2 a year), *Anuarul* (annual), *Studii şi Comunicări de Etnologie* (annual).

Institutul de Cercetări Socio-Umane (Institute for Research in Social and Human Sciences): Str. Mihai Viteazul 24, 300223 Timişoara; tel. (256) 19-40-68; f. 1970; attached to Romanian Acad.; library of 8,000 vols; Dir EUGEN TODORAN; publs *Caietul Cercului de Studii* (2 a year), *Poetică* (annual), *Dialectologie* (annual), *Studii de*

istorie a Banatului (annual), *Toponimie* (annual), *Limbăliterară* (annual).

Institutul de Cercetări Socio-Umane (Institute for Research in Social and Human Sciences): Str. Bolyai 17, 540067 Târgu-Mureş; tel. (265) 42-01-38; f. 1957; attached to Romanian Acad.; history, history of literature, folklore, sociology; library of 338,290 vols; Dir Dr IOAN CHIOREAN.

Institutul de Cercetări Socio-Umane 'C. S. Nicolaescu-Plopsor' (Institute for Research in Social and Human Sciences): Str. Unirii 102, 200330 Craiova; tel. (251) 12-33-30; fax (251) 12-57-02; f. 1965; attached to Romanian Acad.; library of 300,000 vols; Dir Dr AVRAM CEZAR GABRIEL; publs *Arhivele Olteniei* (annual), *Anuarul* (annual).

Institutul de Etnografie şi Folclor 'Constantin Brăiloiu' (Constantin Brăiloiu Institute of Ethnography and Folklore): Str. Take Ionescu 25, 010353 Bucharest; tel. (21) 659-37-48; e-mail etnograf@sunu.rnc.ro; f. 1949; library of 44,000 vols; Nat. Folk Archives of sound, image and MSS; Dir Dr SABINA ISPAS; publ. *Revista de etnografie şi folclor* (6 a year).

Institutul de Sociologie (Institute of Sociology): Calea 13 Septembrie 13, 050711 Bucharest; tel. (21) 312-41-88; f. 1965; attached to Romanian Acad.; Man. Dir Prof. Dr ION DRAGAN; publs *Revue Roumaine des Sciences Sociales — série de Sociologie* (quarterly, English edn every 6 months), *Sociologie Românească* (6 a year).

Institutul de Ştiinţe Politice şi Relaţii Internaţionale (Institute of Political Sciences and International Relations): Bdul Iuliu Maniu 1–3, 061071 Bucharest; tel. (21) 410-10-05; fax (21) 410-10-05; f. 1990, as Institute of Social Theory and Political Science; attached to Romanian Acad.; Dir Prof. Dr STELIAN NEAGOE; publs *Revista de Teorie Socială* (quarterly), *Romanian Review of Social Theory* (3 a year).

Institutul de Ştiinţe Socio-Umane (Institute of Social and Human Sciences): Str. T. Codrescu 2, 700481 Iaşi; tel. (232) 11-59-87; f. 1969; attached to Romanian Acad.; library of 35,000 vols; Dir TUDOREL DIMA; publ. *Anuar de Ştiinţe Socio-Umane*.

International Association for South-East European Studies: Str. Nicolae Racota 12–14, Apt. 14 Bucharest 011393; tel. (21) 224-29-65; fax (21) 224-29-64; e-mail aiesee@rdslink.ro; f. 1963; attached to Romanian Acad.; social sciences; 23 mems; library of 40,000 vols; Pres. Prof. ANDRÉ GUILLOU; publ. *Revue de l'AIESEE* (quarterly).

TECHNOLOGY

Institutul de Informatică Teoretică (Institute of Theoretical Informatics): Bdul Copou 11, 700497 Iaşi; tel. (232) 14-65-34; attached to Romanian Acad.; Dir DAN GÂLEA.

Institutul de Mecanica Solidelor (Institute of Solids Mechanics): Str. Constantin Mille 15, 010141 Bucharest; tel. (21) 614-40-36; attached to Romanian Acad.; Dir TUDOR SIRETEANU.

Institutul Naţional de Cercetare-Dezvoltare pentru Protecţia Mediului (ICIM Bucureşti) (National Research and Development Institute for Environmental Protection (ICIM Bucharest)): Splaiul Independenţei 294, 060031 Bucharest; tel. (21) 221-57-70; fax (21) 220-38-05; e-mail daescu@ icim.ro; internet www.icim.ro; f. 1952; library of 6,000 vols and journals; Dir Prof. OVIDIU IANCULESCU; publs *The Environment* (quarterly), *An Environment for the Future* (annual).

Institutul Naţional de Informare şi Documentare (National Institute for Informa-

tion and Documentation): Str. I. D. Mendeleev 21–25, 010362 Bucharest; tel. (21) 315-87-65; fax (21) 312-67-34; e-mail inid_bucuresti@home.ro; internet www.inid .ro; f. 1949; promotes the use of modern equipment for automatic data processing in the area of documentary information; library: see Libraries and Archives; Gen. Dir ANA EUGENIA NEGULESCU; publs *Management şi marketing coentemporan* (quarterly), *Asigurerea şi promovarea calităţii* (quarterly), *Informarea şi documentarea modernă* (quarterly).

Libraries and Archives

Alba Iulia

Biblioteca Judeţeană 'Lucian Blaga' Alba (Alba 'Lucian Blaga' District Library): Trandafirilor 22, 510113 Alba Iulia; tel. (258) 81-14-43; f. 1943; 159,509 vols; Dir MIOARA POP.

Biblioteca Naţională a României, Filiala Batthyancum (National Library of Romania, Batthyaneum Branch): Str. Gabriel Bethlen 1, 510009 Alba Iulia; tel. (258) 81-19-39; fax (258) 81-19-39; f. 1798; attached to Biblioteca Naţională; 70,782 vols, 4,169 periodicals; spec. collns of MSS since 9th century, 609 incunabula, documents, rare books, ex-libris; mineralogical and numismatic colln; scientific instruments, clocks; religious art; 18th-century astronomical observatory; Dir-Gen. DAN ION ERCEANU.

Alexandria

Biblioteca Judeţeană 'Marin Preda' Teleorman (Teleorman 'Marin Preda' District Library): Str. Mitiţă Filipescu 9, 140056 Alexandria; tel. (247) 32-28-94; fax (247) 32-28-94; f. 1949; 130,000 vols; Dir MARIA NEDELEA.

Arad

Biblioteca Judeţeană 'A. D. Xenopol' Arad (Arad District A. D. Xenopol Library): Str. Gh. Popa 2–4, 310022 Arad; tel. (257) 25-65-10; f. 1913; 507,450 vols; Dir LIANA DRIG.

Bacău

Biblioteca Judeţeană 'C. Sturdza' Bacău (Bacău 'C. Sturdza' District Library): Bdul Ioniţă Sandu Sturdza 1, 600269 Bacău; tel. (234) 11-31-26; fax (234) 11-31-36; f. 1893; 430,000 vols and periodicals; Dir ECĂTERINA ŢURCANU.

Baia Mare

Biblioteca Judeţeană 'Petre Dulfu' Maramureş (Maramureş 'Petre Dulfu' District Library): Bdul Independenţei 4B, 430123 Baia Mare; tel. (262) 27-55-83; fax (262) 27-58-99; e-mail biblioteca@bibliotecamm.ro; internet www.bibliotecamm.ro; f. 1951; 433,828 vols; Dir-Gen. TEODOR ARDELEAN.

Bistriţa

Biblioteca Judeţeană Bistriţa-Năsăud (Bistriţa-Năsăud District Library): Str. Gării 2, 420041 Bistriţa; tel. (263) 22-29-30; fax (263) 22-29-30; f. 1951; 184,000 vols; Dir OLIMPIA POP.

Blaj

Biblioteca Documentară 'Timotei Cipariu' ('Timotei Cipariu' Documentary Library): Str. Armata Roşie 2, 515400 Blaj; f. 1754; attached to Cluj-Napoca br. library of Romanian Academy; 30,000 vols in humanities and sciences; spec. colln of rare and ancient books on history of the Romania people.

Botoşani

Biblioteca Judeţeană 'Mihai Eminescu' Botoşani (Botoşani 'Mihai Eminescu' District Library): Str. Calea Naţională 62, 710028 Botoşani; tel. (231) 51-46-86; fax (231) 53-56-68; e-mail biblioteca@petar.ro; f. 1882; 430,003 vols; Dir CORNELIA VIZITEU.

Brăila

Biblioteca Judeţeană 'Panait Istrati' Brăila (Brăila 'Panait Istrati' District Library): Calea Călăraşilor 52, 810010 Brăila; tel. (239) 61-95-90; fax (239) 61-95-88; e-mail bjpi@bjbraila.ro; internet www.bjbraila.ro; f. 1881; 388,968 vols; Dir RODICA DRĂGHICI; publ. *Ex-libris* (annual).

Braşov

Biblioteca Centrală a Universităţii 'Transilvania' din Braşov (Transylvania University of Braşov Central Library): Str. Iuliu Maniu 41A, 500091 Braşov; tel. (268) 47-60-50; fax (268) 47-60-51; e-mail biblio@unitbv.ro; internet www.unitbv.ro; f. 1948; 708,106 vols; Dir Prof. Dr Eng. ANGELA REPANOVICI.

Biblioteca Judeţeană 'George Bariţiu' Braşov (Braşov 'George Bariţiu' District Library): Bdul Eroilor 33–35, 500036 Braşov; tel. (268) 41-93-38; fax (268) 41-50-79; e-mail biblgb@rdsbv.ro; internet www.bjbv.ro; f. 1835; 800,000 vols; Dir VETURIA VOINESCU.

Bucharest

Arhivele Naţionale (National Archives): Bdul Regina Elisabeta 49, 050013 Bucharest; tel. (21) 315-25-03; fax (21) 312-58-41; f. 1831; 1,221,500 medieval documents, 22,000 seals, 12,820 MSS, 816,929 ft modern documents, 735,680 vols of plans and maps; documentary libraries; Dir-Gen. Prof. Dr CORNELIU MIHAIL LUNGU; publ. *Revista Arhivelor* (annual).

Attached library:

Biblioteca Documentară a Arhivelor Naţionale (Documentary Library of the National Archives): Bdul Regina Elisabeta 49, 050013 Bucharest; tel. (21) 315-25-03; fax (21) 312-58-41; f. 1862; 162,000 vols; Dir-Gen. Prof. Dr CORNELIU MIHAIL LUNGU.

Biblioteca Academiei Române (Library of the Romanian Academy): Calea Victoriei 125, 010071 Bucharest; tel. (21) 212-82-84; fax (21) 212-58-56; e-mail biblacad@bar.acad.ro; internet www.bar.acad.ro; f. 1867; legal nat. deposit for Romanian and UN publs; produces Romanian nat. bibliography of books and serials; 9,965,000 vols, 500,000 historical documents, 350,000 photographs; spec. collns incl. Romanian, Greek, Slavonic, Oriental and Latin MSS; drawings, engravings, photographs, music MSS, maps; numismatic colln; Dir Prof. GABRIEL STREMPEL; publs *Cărţi intrate în reţeaua bibliotecilor Academiei Române* (annual), *Periodice intrate în reţeaua bibliotecilor Academiei Române* (annual).

Biblioteca Centrală a Academiei de Ştiinţe Agricole şi Silvice 'Gheorghe Ionescu-Şişeşti' (Central Library of the Gheorghe Ionescu-Şişeşti Academy of Agricultural and Forestry Sciences): Bdul Mărăşti 61, 011464 Bucharest; f. 1928; 136,000 vols; Chief Librarian N. FLORESCU; publs *Bibliografia agricolă curentă romănă* (quarterly), *Noutăţi documentare FAO* (monthly), *Cărţi străine intrate in bibliotecile din România—seria Agricultură* (monthly).

Biblioteca Centrală a Academiei de Studii Economice (Central Library of the Academy of Economic Studies): Piaţa Romană 6, 010374 Bucharest; f. 1913; 900,000 vols; Chief Librarian VLADIMIR IOVANOV.

Biblioteca Centrală a Universităţii 'Politechnica' din Bucureşti (Central Library of Bucharest Polytechnic University): Splaiul Independenţei 313, 060042 Bucharest; tel. (21) 312-70-44; fax (21) 411-53-65; e-mail dr_popescu@chim.upb.ro; f. 1868; 1,407,000 vols and periodicals; Dir DAN-RADU POPESCU; publ. *Scientific Bulletin* (4 series: mechanical eng., electrical eng., chemistry and materials science, applied mathematics and physics).

Biblioteca Centrală Universitară (Central University Library): Str. Boteanu 1, 010027 Bucharest; tel. (21) 312-01-08; fax (21) 312-08-44; e-mail stoica@bcub.ro; internet www.bcub.ro; f. 1891; 1,821,823 vols; Dir-Gen. Prof. Dr ION STOICA; publ. *Ghidul lucrărilor de referinţe în colecţiile Bibliotecii Centrale Universitare din Bucureşti* (Guide to Reference Works in the Collections of the Library of Bucharest University, 2 a year).

Biblioteca de Documentare Medicală 'Dr Dimitrie Nanu' (Dr Dimitrie Nanu Medical Documentation Library): Str. Pitar Moş 7–15 010451 Bucharest; tel. (21) 211-04-30; fax (21) 211-11-45; f. 1951; attached to Centrul de Calcul, Statistică Sanitară şi Documentare Medicală; 310,556 vols; Dir FELICIA-IOANA DOBRESCU.

Biblioteca Documentară de Istorie a Medicinei (Documentary Library of the History of Medicine): Str. Dr Leonte 1–3, 050463 Bucharest; tel. (21) 638-40-10; fax (21) 312-34-26; f. 1953; 50,200 vols, 1,100 periodicals, 3,500 MSS and documents, 5,200 museum pieces; Dir Prof. MARIOARA GEORGESCU.

Biblioteca Institutului Naţional de Informare şi Documentare (Library of the National Institute for Information and Documentation): Str. I. D. Mendeleev 21–25, 010362 Bucharest; tel. (21) 313-40-10; fax (21) 312-67-34; e-mail inid_bucuresti@home.ro; internet www.inid.ro; f. 1949; 743,000 vols incl. 135,000 periodicals; Chief Librarian DACIA CRISTIANA STATIE.

Biblioteca Metropolitană Bucureşti (Bucharest Metropolitan Library): Str. Take Ionescu 4, 701661 Bucharest; tel. (21) 211-36-25; fax (21) 211-36-25; e-mail biblioteca@email.ro; f. 1938; 1,417,057 vols, periodicals, newspapers, musical scores; Dir FLORIN ROTARU; publs *Bibliografia oraşului Bucureşti* (annual), *Biblioteca Bucureştilor* (monthly).

Biblioteca Naţională a României (National Library of Romania): Str. Ion Ghica 4, 030046 Bucharest; tel. (21) 315-70-63; fax (21) 312-33-81; e-mail go@bibnat.ro; internet www.bibnat.ro; f. 1836; 12,000,000 vols; acts as copyright deposit library and nat. bibliographic agency; incorporates research centre for librarianship and book pathology and restoration; spec. collns of MSS, old and rare books, musical scores, photographs, maps, prints, old illustrated postcards and drawings; Dir-Gen. ION DAN ERCEANU; publs *Bibliografia Naţională Română* (6 series), *Catalogul colectiv al cărţilor străine intrate în bibliotecile din România* (quarterly), *Repertoriul periodicelor străine intrate în bibliotecile din România* (annual), *ABSI – Abstracte în bibliologie şi ştiinţa informării* (monthly), *Biblioteconomie – Culegere de traduceri prelucrate* (quarterly), *Revista Bibliotecii Naţionale a Romăniei* (2 a year), *Aniversări culturale* (2 a year).

Biblioteca Pedagogică Naţională (National Education Library): Str. Zalomit 12, 010151 Bucharest; tel. and fax (40) 311-03-23; e-mail pedagogical-library@yahoo.com; internet www.bpn.ro; f. 1880; 480,000 educational vols and periodicals; methodological centre for the nat. network of school libraries; Dir-Gen. Dr GEORGE ANCA; publs *Éducation en Roumanie* (Education in Romania, annual), *Modernizarea învăţămîntului* (annual), *Informare tematică* (annual), *Bibliografia pedagogică* (annual), *LIBER. Revistă pentru bibliotecile pedagogice şi şcolare* (quarterly), *Studii de biblioteconomie şi informare documentară* (irreg.).

Biblioteca Universitaţii de Arte Bucureşti (Library of the Bucharest University of Fine Arts): Str. Gen. Budişteanu 19, 010773 Bucharest; tel. (21) 314-32-11; f. 1864; 60,000 vols, 261,262 slides and photographs; spec. colln: 19th- and 20th-century European fine-art periodicals; Dir GABRIELA BĂJENARU.

Biblioteca Universităţii de Ştiinţe Agronomice şi Medicina Veterinară (Library of the University of Agronomic Sciences and Veterinary Medicine): Bdul Mărăşti 59, 011460 Bucharest; tel. (21) 318-25-67; fax (21) 318-28-88; e-mail biblioteca_usamv@yahoo.com; f. 1868; 480,000 vols; Dir CARMEN CONSTANTIN; publs *Agronomy, Biotechnology, Horticulture, Land Reclamation, Veterinary Medicine, Zootechnics.*

Centrul de Documentare pentru Construcţii, Arhitectură, Urbanism şi Amenajarea Teritoriului (Documentation Centre for Building, Architecture, Urban Studies and Town Planning): Şoseaua Pantelimon 266, POB 3-5, 021652 Bucharest; tel. (21) 255-50-22; fax (21) 255-50-22; e-mail cdcas@cons.incerc.ro; f. 1957; 350,000 vols, 200 current periodicals; Dir-Gen. ELENA TÎRZIMAN.

Centrul de Informare şi Documentare Economică (Centre of Economic Information and Documentation): Casa Academiei Române, Calea 13 Septembrie 13, 050711 Bucharest; tel. (21) 411-60-75; fax (21) 411-54-86; e-mail cide@zappmobile.ro; internet www.ince.ro; f. 1990; attached to Romanian Acad.; Dir IOAN FRANC VALERIU; publs *Probleme Economice* (weekly), *Studii şi Cercetări Economice* (monthly), *Romanian Economic Research Observer* (monthly), *Analele INCE* (quarterly), *Marketing Management* (6 a year), *Caiete Critice* (monthly), *Romanian Journal of Economic Forecasting* (quarterly), *Revista Română de Economie* (2 a year).

Mediateca Universităţii Naţionale de Muzică din Bucureşti (Media Library of the Bucharest University of Music): Str. Ştirbei Vodă 33, 010102 Bucharest; e-mail eva78ro@yahoo.com; f. 1864; 39,150 vols, 82,190 scores, 16,545 recordings, 7,200 tapes, 12,871 periodicals, 8,003 theses; Dir ŞTEFANA SAVU.

S. C. Biblioteca Chimiei SA (S. C. Chemistry Library SA): Calea Plevnei 139B, 060011 Bucharest; tel. (21) 310-26-78; fax (21) 222-91-76; e-mail syscom@syscom.ro; internet www.bch.ro; f. 1956; provides access to nat. and foreign scientific and technical literature; 41,000 vols, 141,000 vols of periodicals; Gen. Man. Ing. ION ANDRONACHE; publs *Revista de Chimie* (monthly), *Materiale Plastice* (quarterly).

Serviciul de Documentare al Ministerului Învăţământului (Documentation Service of the Ministry of Education): Str. Spiru Haret 12, 010716 Bucharest; tel. (21) 614-26-80; fax (21) 312-47-53; f. 1971; information and documentation on teaching and educational management abroad; Romanian legislation on education; Head EUGENIU TOMA; publs *Educaţie-Învăţământ* (2 a year), *Buletinul Ministerului Învăţământului* (quarterly).

Serviciul de Informare, Documentare şi Informatizare al Academiei de Ştiinţe

Agricole şi Silvice 'Gheorghe Ionescu-Şişeşti' (Information, Documentation and Electronic Information Service of the Gheorghe Ionescu-Şişteşti Academy of Agricultural and Forestry Sciences): Bdul Mărăşti 61, 011464 Bucharest; tel. (21) 618-25-54; fax (21) 617-01-55; f. 1928; attached to Acad. of Agricultural and Forestry Sciences; 147,000 vols and CD-ROMs; Head Dr C. KEVORCHIAN; publ. *Curierul ASAS* (quarterly).

Buzău

Biblioteca Judeţeană 'V. Volcalescu' Buzău (Buzău 'V. Volcalescu' District Library): Str. Unirii 140, 120238 Buzău; tel. (238) 72-15-09; fax (238) 71-72-83; f. 1873; 250,000 vols; Dir ALEXANDRU OPROESCU.

Călăraşi

Biblioteca Judeţeană 'Al. Odobescu' Călăraşi (Călăraşi 'Al. Odobescu' District Library): Str. Bucureşti 102, 910161 Călăraşi; tel. (242) 31-67-57; fax (242) 31-67-57; f. 1884; 150,000 vols; Dir GHIŢĂ DUMITRU.

Cluj-Napoca

Biblioteca Centrală Universitară 'Lucian Blaga' (University 'Lucian Blaga' Central Library): Str. Clinicilor 2, 400006 Cluj-Napoca; tel. (264) 11-70-92; fax (264) 11-76-33; f. 1872; 3,553,596 vols; Dir DORU RADOSAV.

Biblioteca Filialei Cluj-Napoca a Academiei Românc (Library of the Cluj-Napoca Branch of the Romanian Academy): Str. M. Kogălniceanu 12–14, 400084 Cluj-Napoca; f. 1950; 760,000 vols and periodicals on the humanities and science, 179 incunabula, 2m. documents; spec. collns incl. Romanian, Latin, Hungarian, Slavonic MSS; Dir NICOLAE BOŞCAIU.

Biblioteca Judeţeană 'Octavian Goga' Cluj ('Octavian Goga' Cluj County Library): Calea Dorobanţilor f. n., 400691 Cluj-Napoca; tel. (264) 43-03-23; fax (264) 59-54-28; e-mail bjc@bjc.ro; internet www.bjc.ro; f. 1921; 4 br. libraries; 733,576 vols; Dir DOINA POPA; publ. *Lectura* (quarterly).

Biblioteca Universiţaţii de Medicină şi Farmacie (Library of the University of Medicine and Pharmacy): Avram Iancu 31, 400083 Cluj-Napoca; tel. (264) 19-26-29; fax (264) 46-01-06; e-mail irobu@umfcluj.ro; internet www.umfcluj.ro; f. 1775; 321,000 vols and periodicals; Dir IONA ROBU; publ. *Clujul Medical* (quarterly).

Biblioteca Universităţii Tehnice din Cluj-Napoca (Library of Cluj-Napoca Technical University): Str. Constantin Daicoviciu 15, 400020 Cluj-Napoca; tel. (264) 43-04-08; fax (264) 19-20-55; e-mail biblio@utcluj.ro; f. 1884; 650,000 vols and periodicals; Dir Dipl. Eng. CĂLIN CÂMPEAN; publ. *Acta Technica Napocensis* (in English, annual).

Constanţa

Biblioteca Judeţeană 'Ioan N. Roman' Constanţa ('Ioan N. Roman' Constanţa County Library): Str. Mircea cel Bătrân 104A, 900663 Constanţa; tel. and fax (241) 61-44-82; e-mail bjc@biblioteca.ct.ro; internet www.biblioteca.ct.ro; f. 1931; 650,000 vols; Dir Dr LILIANA LAZIA; publs *Bibliografia Dobrogei* (annual), *Biblion* (2 a year).

British Council Library: Bdul Mircea cel Batran 104A, 900663 Constanţa; tel. (241) 61-83-65; e-mail bc.constanta@biblioteca.ct.ro; Librarian CONSTANTINA MOTOC.

Craiova

Biblioteca Judeţeană 'Al. şi Aristia Aman' Dolj (Dolj 'Al. and Aristia Aman' District Library): Str. M. Kogălniceanu 9, 200390 Craiova; tel. (251) 13-22-67; f. 1908; 466,000 vols; Dir MARIANA LEFERMAN.

Biblioteca Universităţii din Craiova (University of Craiova Library): Str. Al. I. Cuza 13, 200585 Craiova; tel. (251) 41-24-79; fax (251) 41-24-79; e-mail lohon@central.ucv.ro; f. 1966; 1,135,000 vols; Dir OCTAVIAN LOHON.

Deva

Biblioteca Judeţeană 'O. Densusianu' Hunedoara-Deva (Hunedoara-Deva 'O. Densusianu' District Library): Str. 1 Decembrie 28, 330025 Deva; tel. (254) 21-94-40; fax (254) 21-64-57; e-mail bibjud_hd@smart.ro; f. 1949; 306,878 vols and periodicals; Dir VALERIA STOIAN.

Drobeta-Turnu Severin

Biblioteca Judeţeaňa 'I. G. Bibicescu' Mehedinţi (Mehedinţi 'I.G. Bibicescu' District Library): Str. Traian 115, 220134 Drobeta-Turnu Severin; tel. (252) 31-56-82; f. 1921; 264,300 vols; Dir ELENA ROMAN.

Focşani

Biblioteca Judeţeană 'Duiliu Zamfirescu' Focşani (Focşani 'Duiliu Zamfirescu' District Library): Str. M. Kogălniceanu 12, 620036 Focşani; tel. (237) 61-54-68; f. 1910; 198,000 vols; Dir Prof. VICTOR RENEA.

Galaţi

Biblioteca Judeţeană 'V. A. Urechia' Galaţi (Galaţi 'V. A. Urechia' County Library): Str. Mihai Bravu 16, 800222 Galaţi; tel. (236) 41-10-37; fax (236) 31-10-60; e-mail bvau@bvau.ro; internet www.bvau.ro; f. 1890; 626,000 vols; Dir EUGEN IORDACHE; publ. *Buletinul Fundaţiei Urechia* (2 a year).

Biblioteca Universităţii 'Dunarea de Jos' din Galaţi (University of Galaţi 'Dunarea de Jos' Library): Str. Domnească 47, 800008 Galaţi; f. 1948; 480,000 vols mainly on science, technology and eng., food industry, history, theology, languages and literature, econ.; Dir MARIA CALIOPIA UDRESCU.

Giurgiu

Biblioteca Judeţeană 'J. A. Bassarabescu' Giurgiu (Giurgiu District 'J. A. Bassarabescu' Library): Str. Mircea cel Bătrân 23, 080033 Giurgiu; tel. (246) 21-23-46; f. 1951; 182,000 vols and periodicals; Dir ION MIHAI.

Iaşi

Biblioteca Centrală a Universiţaţii de Medicină şi Farmacie 'Gr. T. Popa' Iaşi (Central Library of the Gr. T. Popa University of Medicine and Pharmacy in Iaşi): Str. Vasile Alecsandri 7, 700054 Iaşi; tel. (232) 21-82-24; fax (232) 21-18-20; e-mail vscutaru@asklepios.umfiasi.ro; f. 1879; central library with 90 brs; 373,000 vols; Dir VIORICA SCUTARIU; publ. *Buletin Bibliografic* (quarterly).

Biblioteca Centrală Universitară 'Mihai Eminescu' (University 'Mihai Eminescu' Central Library): Str. Păcurari 4, 700551 Iaşi; tel. (232) 26-42-45; fax (232) 26-17-96; e-mail alcalinescu@bcu-iasi.ro; internet www.bcu-iasi.ro; f. 1640; 2,900,000 vols; Dir Prof. Dr ALEXANDRU CĂLINESCU.

Biblioteca Judeţeană 'Gh. Asachi' Iaşi (Iaşi 'Gh. Asachi' District Library): Str. Palat 1, 700019 Iaşi; tel. (232) 11-51-59; fax (232) 21-21-70; e-mail icpopa@tuiasi.ro; f. 1920; 600,000 vols, 12,000 records; Dir Prof. NICOLAE BUSUIOC; publ. *Bibliographical Annual of the Iaşi District.*

Biblioteca Universităţii Tehnice 'Gheorghe Asachi' Iaşi (Library of the Iaşi Gheorghe Asachi Technical University): Bdul Carol I 11, 700506 Iaşi; tel. and fax (232) 21-17-73; e-mail library@tuiasi.ro; internet www.library.tuiasi.ro; f. 1937; 556,074 vols, 135,116 periodicals, 311,707 standards and patents; Dir MIHAELA STIRBU; publ. *Iaşi Polytechnic Magazine* (quarterly).

Miercurea-Ciuc

Biblioteca Judeţeană Harghita (Harghita District Library): Piaţa Libertăţii 1, 530100 Miercurea-Ciuc; tel. (266) 17-19-88; f. 1950; 209,289 vols and periodicals; Dir KATALIN KOPACZ.

Năsăud

Biblioteca Documentară Năsăud (Năsăud Documentary Library): Str. Grănicerilor 41, 425200 Năsăud; f. 1931; attached to Cluj-Napoca br. library of Romanian Academy; 53,323 vols; Dir MARIA ŞUTEU.

Oradea

Biblioteca Judeţeană 'Gheorghe Şincai' Bihor (Bihor 'Gheorghe Şincai' District Library): Piaţa Unirii 3, 410100 Oradea; tel. (259) 23-12-57; fax (259) 23-12-57; e-mail bjbihor@roetco.ro; f. 1912; 642,317 vols; Dir CONSTANTIN MĂLINAŞ.

Piatra-Neamţ

Biblioteca Judeţeană 'G. T. Kirileanu' Neamţ (Neamţ 'G.T. Kirileanu' District Library): Str. Republicii 15, 610005 Piatra-Neamţ; tel. (233) 21-15-24; fax (233) 21-03-79; e-mail bib_gtk_neamt@yahoo.com; internet www.bibgtkneamt.org; f. 1956; 286,424 vols and periodicals; Dir CONSTANTIN BOSTAN.

Piteşti

Biblioteca Judeţeană Argeş 'Dinicu Golescu' (Argeş District Library 'Dinicu Golescu'): Str. Victoriei 18, 110017 Piteşti; tel. (248) 22-30-30; fax (248) 22-34-16; e-mail bjdgarges@gmail.com; internet www.bjarges.ro; f. 1880; 404,849 vols and periodicals, 2,018 audiovisual items, 120 electronic documents; Dir MIHAIL OCTAVIAN SACHELARIE.

Ploieşti

Biblioteca Centrală Universiţaţii 'Petrol-Gaze' ('Petrol-Gaze' University Central Library): Bdul Bucureşti 39, POB 22, 100520 Ploieşti; tel. (244) 17-31-71; fax (244) 17-58-47; f. 1948; 357,675 vols; Dir Prof. DAN EMIL.

Biblioteca Judeţeană 'N. Iorga' Prahova (Prahova 'N. Iorga' District Library): Str. Sublocotenent Erou Călin Cătălin 1, 100066 Ploieşti; tel. (244) 12-24-92; fax (244) 11-83-43; f. 1921; 389,000 vols; Dir Prof. NICOLAE BOARU.

Râmnicu Vâlcea

Biblioteca Judeţeană 'Antim Ivireanul' Vâlcea (Vâlcea 'Antim Ivireanul' District Library): Str. Carol I, 2-6 , 240591 Râmnicu-Vâlcea; tel. and fax (250) 73-92-21; internet www.bjul.go.ro; f. 1950; 400,000 vols; Dir Prof. DUMITRU LAZĂR.

Reşiţa

Biblioteca Judeţeană 'Paul Iorgovici' Caraş-Severin (Caraş-Severin 'Paul Iorgovici' District Library): Str. Paul Iorgovici 50, 320026 Reşiţa; tel. (55) 21-16-87; f. 1952; 287,000 vols; Dir NICOLAE SĂRBU; publ. *Revista Noastră.*

Satu Mare

Biblioteca Judeţeană Satu Mare (Satu Mare District Library): Str. Decebal 2, 440006 Satu Mare; tel. (261) 71-11-99;

e-mail santa@p5net.ro; internet www
.bibliotecasatumare.ro; f. 1951; 379,553 vols;
Dir VOICU D. RUSU.

Sf. Gheorghe

Biblioteca Judeţeană Covasna (Covasna
District Library): Gabor Aron 14, 520008 Sf.
Gheorghe; tel. (267) 35-16-09; fax (267) 35-
16-09; e-mail biblio@mk.cosys.ro; f. 1927;
215,000 vols; Dir JENŐ KISS.

Sibiu

Biblioteca Judeţeană 'Astra' Sibiu (Sibiu
'Astra' District Library): Str. Gh. Bariţiu 5,
550178 Sibiu; tel. (269) 21-05-51; fax (269)
21-57-75; f. 1861; 759,000 vols, 34,966 documents and MSS, 12,325 iconographies; 10
brs; Dir Prof. ION MARIS.

Biblioteca Muzeului Brukenthal (Library
of Brukenthal Museum): Piaţa Mare 4,
550163 Sibiu; tel. (269) 21-76-91; fax (269)
21-15-45; e-mail info@brukenthalmuseum.ro;
internet www.brukenthalmuseum.ro; f.
1817; 280,000 vols; Chief Librarian Dr
ALEXANDRU AVRAM.

British Council Library: Biblioteca Brit-
anica, Bdul Victoriei 5–7, 550024 Sibiu; tel.
(269) 21-10-56; e-mail bc.sibiu@sibiu.rdsnet
.ro; Librarian CARMEN BOKOR.

Slatina

**Biblioteca Judeţeană 'Ion Minulescu'
Olt** (Olt 'Ion Minulescu' District Library):
Bdul Al. I. Cuza 3B, 230025 Slatina; tel. and
fax (249) 43-51-46; e-mail paul.matiu@
hotmail.ro; f. 1931; 231,667 vols and periodicals; Dir PAUL MATIU.

Slobozia

Biblioteca Judeţeană Ialomiţa (Ialomiţa
District Library): Bdul Matei Basarab 26,
920031 Slobozia; tel. (243) 23-00-55; f. 1951;
132,242 vols and periodicals; Dir DENCĂ
ŞERBAN.

Suceava

**Biblioteca Bucovinei 'I. G. Sbierea'
Suceava** (Suceava 'I. G. Sbierea' Library of
Bucovina): Str. Mitropoliei 4, 720035
Suceava; tel. and fax (230) 53-07-98; f. 1923;
335,000 vols and periodicals; Dir GHEORGHE-
GABRIEL CĂRĂBUŞ.

Târgovişte

**Biblioteca Judeţeană 'Ion Heliade
Rădulescu' Dâmboviţa** (Dâmboviţa 'Ion
Heliade Rădulescu' District Library): Str.
Stelea 2, 130018 Târgovişte; tel. (245) 61-
23-16; f. 1944; 273,000 vols and periodicals;
Dir VICTOR PETRESCU.

Târgu Jiu

**Biblioteca Judeţeană 'Christian Tell'
Gorj** (Gorj 'Christian Tell' District Library):
Str. Eroilor 23, 210135 Târgu Jiu; tel. (253)
21-49-04; fax (253) 21-49-04; f. 1934; 273,542
vols; Dir ALEXANDRA ANDREI.

Târgu Mureş

Biblioteca Documentară Teleki-Bolyai
('Teleki-Bolyai' Documentary Library): Str.
Bolyai 17, 540067 Târgu Mureş; tel. (265) 16-
18-57; f. 1802; books in the natural and social
sciences before 19th century; maps, incunabula and MSS; Dir DIMITRIE POPTĂMAŞ.

Biblioteca Judeţeană Mureş (Mureş
County Library): Str. Georges Enescu 2,
540052 Târgu Mureş; tel. (265) 16-26-31;
fax (265) 26-43-84; f. 1913; 846,660 vols,
6,949 periodicals, 125 electronic books,
1,925 microfilms, 53 maps, 70 incunabula,
13,398 MSS, 5,428 other documents; Dir Dr
CORINA THEODOR; publs *Biblitheca Marisi-
ana, Libraria*.

Timişoara

Biblioteca Judeţeană Timiş (Timiş District Library): Piaţa Libertăţii 3, 300077
Timişoara; tel. (256) 43-07-40; fax (256) 43-
39-98; e-mail paulbanciu@yahoo.com; f. 1904;
731,000 vols, periodicals and MSS; Dir PAUL-
EUGEN BANCIU.

Biblioteca Universităţii Timişoara (University of Timişoara Library): Bdul V. Pârvan 4, 300223 Timişoara; tel. (256) 19-03-53;
fax (256) 19-40-04; f. 1948; 780,000 vols and
periodicals; Dir V. ŢARA.

Tulcea

**Biblioteca Judeţeană 'Panait Cerna'
Tulcea** (Tulcea 'Panait Cerna' District
Library): Str. Isaccei 20, 820241 Tulcea; tel.
(240) 51-38-33; f. 1900; 295,000 vols and
periodicals; Dir Prof. DOINA LELIA POSTO-
LACHE.

Vaslui

**Biblioteca Judeţeană 'Nicolae Milescu
Spătarul' Vaslui** (Vaslui 'Nicolae Milescu
Spătarul' District Library): Hagi Chiriac 2,
730129 Vaslui; tel. (35) 31-37-67; f. 1951;
158,788 vols and periodicals; Dir ELENA
POAMA.

Zalău

**Biblioteca Judeţeană 'Ioniţă Scipione
Bădescu' Sălaj** (Sălaj 'Ioniţă Scipione
Bădescu' District Library): Str. Iuliu Maniu
13, 450016 Zalău; tel. (260) 63-20-07; f. 1954;
150,000 vols; Dir SILVIA COSMA.

Museums and Art Galleries

Aiud

Muzeul de Istorie Aiud (Aiud Museum of
History): Piaţa Consiliul Europei 24, Judeţul
Alba, 515200 Aiud; tel. (258) 86-12-80 ext. 30;
e-mail office@aiud.ro; internet www.aiud.ro;
f. 1796; archaeology of the primitive commune, the Dacian-Roman period and the pre-
feudal period; library of 1,800 vols; Dir PAUL
SCROBOTĂ.

Muzeul de Ştiinţele Naturii Aiud (Aiud
Natural History Museum): Str. Bethlen
Gabor 1, 515200 Aiud; tel. (258) 86-17-48; f.
1796; library of 500 vols; Dir ANA HERTA.

Alba Iulia

Muzeul Naţional al Unirii (National
Museum of Union): Str. Mihai Viteazul 12–
14, 510010 Alba Iulia; tel. (258) 81-33-00; fax
(258) 81-18-53; e-mail mnu@muzeu.uab.ro; f.
1887; exhibits relating to prehistoric and
Roman archaeology, medieval era, ecclesiastical history, ethnography and to Romanian
Union; library of 55,000 vols; Dir SOFIA
ŞTIRBAN; publs *Apulum—Acta Musei Apulensis* (annual), *Bibliotheca Musei Apulensis*
(annual).

Alexandria

Muzeul Judeţean de Istorie Teleorman
(Teleorman District Museum of History): Str.
Dunării 137, 140038 Alexandria; tel. (247)
32-21-41; f. 1951; history, numismatics, ethnography; Dir ECATERINA ŢÂNŢĂREANU.

Arad

Complexul Muzeal Arad (Arad Museum
Complex): Piaţa George Enescu 1, 310131
Arad; tel. (257) 28-18-47; fax (257) 28-01-14;
e-mail muzeumarad@inext.ro; internet
muzeularad.inext.ro; f. 1893; archaeology,
history, ethnology, natural sciences, fine
and applied art; Dir PETER HÜGEL; publs
Ziridava (archaeology and history, every 2

years), *Studii şi Comunicări* (architecture
and art history, every 2 years), *Armonii
Naturale* (natural history, every 2 years),
Zarandul (ethnology, every 2 years).

Bacău

**Muzeul Judeţean de Istorie 'Iulian Anto-
nescu' Bacău** (Bacău 'Iulian Antonescu'
District Museum of History): Str. Nicolae
Titulescu 23, 600049 Bacău; tel. (234) 11-24-
44; f. 1957; history, art, ethnography, literature; library of 9,000 vols; Dir Dr VIOREL
CĂPITANU; publ. *Carpica* (annual).

**Muzeul Judeţean de Ştiinţele Naturii
Bacău** (Bacău District Natural History
Museum): Str. Gheorghe Vrânceanu 44,
600402 Bacău; tel. (234) 11-20-06; fax (234)
11-20-06; f. 1964; library of 17,000 vols; Dir
Dr NECULAI BARABAŞ; publ. *Studii şi Comunicări*.

Baia Mare

Muzeul Judeţean Maramureş (Maramureş District Museum): Bdul Traian 8,
430212 Baia Mare; tel. (262) 41-19-27; f.
1899; history, Romanian art; library of
20,000 vols; Dir IOAN IGNA; publ. *Marmaţia*
(annual).

Associated museum:

Muzeul de Mineralogie Baia Mare
(Baia Mare Mineralogical Museum): Bdul
Traian 8, 430212 Baia Mare; tel. and fax
(262) 22-75-17; e-mail muzmin@rdslink.ro;
f. 1989; exhibition of minerals; mineralogical and crystallographic research; library
of 900 vols; Dir VICTOR GORDUZA.

Bistriţa

Muzeul Judeţean Bistriţa (Bistriţa
County Museum): Str. Gen. Grigore Bălan
19, 420016 Bistriţa; tel. (263) 21-10-63; fax
(263) 21-10-63; f. 1950; Dir Dr IOAN CHIN-
TAUAN; publs *Studii şi Cercetări Etnocultur-
ale, Revista Bistriţei* (history), *Studii şi
Cercetări Ştiinţele Naturii*.

Botoşani

Muzeul Judeţean Botoşani (Botoşani District Museum): Str. Unirii 13, 710221 Botoşani; tel. (231) 51-34-46; f. 1955; history,
archaeology, ethnography, fine arts; incl.
'Nicolae Iorga' and 'George Enescu' memorial
houses; library of 10,000 vols; Dir ALEXANDRU
SANDU.

Brad

Muzeul de Istorie şi Etnografie Brad
(Brad History and Ethnography Museum):
335200 Brad; f. 1987; traditional arts and
crafts, spec. colln of wooden objects; Curator
MIHAI DAVID.

Brăila

Muzeul Brăilei (Brăila Museum): Piaţa
Traian 3, 810153 Brăila; tel. (339) 40-10-02;
fax (339) 40-10-03; e-mail sediu@
MuzeulBrailei.ro; internet www
.muzeulbrailei.ro; f. 1881; history, fine arts,
ethnography, natural sciences; library of
26,000 vols and periodicals; Dir Dr IONEL
CÂNDEA; publs *ISTROS* (every 2 years),
Analele Brăilei (every 2 years).

Bran

Muzeul Bran (Bran Museum): Str. Princi-
pală 460, Judeţul Braşov, 507025 Bran; tel.
(268) 23-65-38; f. 1957; history, ethnography,
feudal art; Dir RAUL MIHAI.

Braşov

**Muzeul, Biblioteca şi Arhiva Istorică a
Primei Şcoli Româneşti din Scheii Bra-
şovului** (Museum, Library and Historical
Archive of First Romanian School of Braşov):
Piaţa Unirii 1, 500123 Braşov; tel. (268) 14-

38-79; f. 1933; historical museum in building of first Romanian school (15th century); Dir Dr VASILE OLTEANU.

Muzeul de Artă (Art Museum): Bdul Eroilor 21, 500030 Braşov; tel. (268) 14-43-84; fax (268) 47-51-72; e-mail mab@rdsbv.ro; internet www.mab.ro; f. 1950; decorative arts, Romanian fine arts; Dir VERONICA BODEA TATULEA.

Muzeul de Etnografie (Ethnographical Museum): Bdul Eroilor 21A, 500030 Braşov; tel. (268) 15-22-52; Dir LIGIA FULGA.

Muzeul Judeţean de Istorie Braşov (Braşov District History Museum): Nicolae Bălcescu 67, 500019 Braşov; tel. (268) 47-23-50; fax (268) 47-23-50; f. 1908; library of 15,500 vols, archives; Dir Prof. RADU ŞTEFĂNESCU.

Bucharest

Muzeul Căilor Ferate Române (Romanian Railway Museum): Calea Griviţei 193A, 010711 Bucharest; tel. (21) 618-01-40.

Muzeul de Istorie al Evreilor din România 'Dr Moses Rosen' (Dr Moses Rosen History Museum of the Jews in Romania): Str. Mămulari 3, 030771 Bucharest; tel. (21) 315-08-37; fax (21) 312-08-69; e-mail comppceb@kappa.ro; f. 1978; Dir BEATRICE STAMBLER.

Muzeul Literaturii Române (Museum of Romanian Literature): Bdul Dacia 12, 010412 Bucharest; tel. (21) 650-33-95; fax (21) 650-33-95; f. 1957; library of 80,000 vols and periodicals and 46,000 MSS and photographs; Dir ALEXANDRU DAN CONDEESCU; publ. *Manuscriptum* (quarterly).

Muzeul Municipiului Bucureşti (Bucharest Museum of History and Art): Bdul I. C. Brătianu 2, 030174 Bucharest; tel. (21) 315-68-58; fax (21) 613-85-15; e-mail mmb@b.astral.ro; f. 1921; library of 55,000 vols; Dir IONEL IONIŢĂ.

Muzeul Naţional Cotroceni (Cotroceni National Museum): Bdul Geniului 1, 060116 Bucharest; tel. (21) 637-46-11; fax (21) 312-16-18; f. 1991; Romanian art, medieval architecture, decorative art, history; Dir Dr ELEONORA COFAS.

Muzeul Naţional de Artă al României (National Museum of Art of Romania): Calea Victoriei 49–53, 030026 Bucharest; tel. (21) 315-51-93; fax (21) 312-43-27; e-mail national@art.museum.ro; internet art.museum.ro; f. 1950; European art since 14th century, Romanian religious and lay works of art from 14th–18th centuries, Romanian modern art since 19th century; also administers the Arts Collns Museum, Theodor Pallady Museum and the K. H. Zambaccian Museum (all in Bucharest); library of 40,000 vols; Dir ROXANA THEODORESCU.

Muzeul Naţional de Istorie a României (National History Museum of Romania): Calea Victoriei 12, 030026 Bucharest; tel. (21) 315-82-07; fax (21) 311-33-56; e-mail direct@mnir.ro; internet www.mnir.ro; f. 1972; library of 45,000 vols; Dir Dr CRIŞAN MUŞEŢEANU; publs *Muzeul Naţional, Cercetări arheologice, Cercetări numismatice, Cercetări istorice* (annual), *Cercetări de conservare şi restaurare a patrimoniului muzeal* (annual).

Muzeul Naţional de Istorie Naturală 'Grigore Antipa' ('Grigore Antipa' National Natural History Museum): Şoseaua Kiseleff 1, 011341 Bucharest; tel. (21) 312-88-26; fax (21) 312-88-86; e-mail dmurariu@antipa.ro; internet www.antipa.ro; f. 1834; zoology, hydrobiology, anatomy, oceanography, ecology, zoogeography, ethnography, anthropology; library of 30,200 vols, 20,000 periodicals; Dir Dr DUMITRU MURARIU; publ. *Travaux* (annual).

Muzeul Naţional 'Georges Enescu' ('Georges Enescu' National Museum): Calea Victoriei 141, 010071 Bucharest; tel. (21) 659-63-65; fax (21) 312-91-82; f. 1956; Dir ILINCA DUMITRESCU.

Muzeul National al Satului 'Dimitrie Gusti' (National Village Museum 'Dimitrie Gusti'): Şoseaua Kiseleff 28–30, 011342 Bucharest; tel. (21) 317-90-68; e-mail muzeulsatalui@xnet.ro; internet www.muzeul-satalui.ro; f. 1936; open-air nat. museum of village life since 17th century; library of 30,000 vols, 130,000 photographs; Dir-Gen. Dr PAULA POPOIU; publ. *Ethnos* (ethnographical and ethnological studies).

Muzeul Ţăranului Român (Romanian Peasant Museum): Şoseaua Kiseleff 3, 011341 Bucharest; tel. (21) 212-96-61; fax (21) 312-98-75; e-mail mtr@digicom.ro; internet www.muzeultaranului.ro; f. 1906; c. 100,000 items on peasant art and traditions; Dir DINU C. GIURESCU; publ. *MARTOS* (review, in French and English, annual).

Muzeul Tehnic 'Prof. Ing. Dimitrie Leonida' (Prof. Eng. Dimitrie Leonida Museum of Technology): Str. Candiano Popescu 2, 040583 Bucharest; tel. (21) 623-77-77; f. 1909; library of 25,000 vols; Dir Dipl. Eng. NICOLAE DIACONESCU.

Buzău

Muzeul Judeţean Buzău (Buzău District Museum): Str. Nicolae Bălcescu 50, 120246 Buzău; tel. (238) 43-51-27; fax (238) 71-06-38; f. 1951; history, folk art, contemporary decorative arts; Dir DOINA CIOBANU; publ. *Musaios* (annual).

Călăraşi

Muzeul Dunării de Jos (Museum of the Lower Danube): Str. Progresului 4, 910079 Călăraşi; tel. (242) 31-31-61; fax (242) 31-19-74; e-mail muzdj@nexdns.nex.ro; f. 1951; archaeology, numismatics, medieval history, modern arts, natural history, ethnography of the area; Dir MARIAN NEAGU.

Câmpulung

Muzeul Zonal Câmpulung (Câmpulung Zonal Museum): Str. Negru Vodă 119, 115100 Câmpulung; tel. (248) 11737; f. 1880; history, arts, natural science, ethnography, folk art; Dir ŞTEFAN TRÂMBACIU; publs *Studii şi comunicări, Istoria Câmpulungului şi a zonei Muscel.*

Câmpulung Moldovenesc

Muzeul Artei Lemnului (Wooden Art Museum): Calea Transilvaniei 10, 725100 Câmpulung Moldovenesc; tel. (230) 31-13-78; f. 1936; ethnography, history, arts, folk art; Dir MARCEL ZAHANICIUC.

Caracal

Muzeul Romanaţiului Caracal (Caracal Museum of the Romanaţi): Str. Libertăţii 26, 235200 Caracal; tel. (249) 51-13-44; f. 1951; history, ethnography, art, lapidarium; Dir PAUL LICĂ.

Caransebeş

Muzeul Judeţean de Etnografie şi a Regimentului de Graniţă-Caransebeş (Caransebeş Border District Ethnographic and Regimental Museum): Piaţa Gen. Ion Dragalina 2, 325400 Caransebeş; tel. (255) 51-41-73; fax (255) 51-21-93; f. 1929; history, ethnography, folk-art; incl. Tibiscum archaeological site; Dir Prof. Dr NICOLETA GUMĂ; publs *Tibiscum, Studii şi Comunicări de Etnografie şi Istorie.*

Cluj-Napoca

Grădina Botanică a Universităţii Babeş-Bolyai (Botanical Garden of Babeş-Bolyai University): Str. Republicii 42, 400015 Cluj-Napoca; tel. (264) 59-21-52; fax (264) 43-18-58; e-mail grbot@grbot.ubbcluj.ro; internet www.ubbcluj.ro/facilitati/facilitati.html#gr-bot; f. 1920; 51 mems; library of 25,000 vols; Dir Dr VASILE CRISTEA; publs *Contribuţii botanice, Flora Romaniae Exsiccata, Delectus seminum.*

Muzeul Etnografic al Transilvaniei (Transylvanian Museum of Ethnography): Str. Memorandumului 21, 400114 Cluj-Napoca; tel. (264) 59-23-44; fax (264) 59-21-48; e-mail contact@muzeul-etnografic.ro; internet www.muzeul-etnografic.ro; f. 1922; incl. open-air nat. ethnographic park; Dir SIMONA MUNTEANU.

Muzeul Naţional de Artă Cluj: Piaţa Unirii 30, 400098 Cluj-Napoca; tel. (264) 11-69-52; f. 1951; Romanian and foreign art from 16th to 20th centuries; library of 9,000 vols; Dir Dr LIVIA DRĂGOI.

Muzeul Naţional de Istorie a Transilvaniei (National History Museum of Transylvania): Str. Constantin Daicoviciu 2, 400020 Cluj-Napoca; tel. (264) 19-56-77; fax (264) 19-17-18; e-mail secretariat@mnit.museum.utcluj.ro; internet www.museum.utcluj.ro; f. 1859; library of 28,000 vols; Dir IOAN PISO; publ. *Acta Musei Napocensis* (annual).

Muzeul Zoologic al Universităţii 'Babeş Bolyai' Cluj-Napoca (Zoological Museum of the Cluj-Napoca 'Babeş Bolyai' University): Str. Clinicilor 5–7, 400006 Cluj-Napoca; tel. (264) 19-14-83; f. 1859; Dir Dr ITON COROIU; publ. *Studia* (annual).

Constanţa

Complexul Muzeal de Ştiinţe ale Naturii (Natural History Museum Complex): Bdul Mamaia 255, 900522 Constanţa; tel. (241) 48-12-30; fax (241) 48-12-36; e-mail office@delfinariu.ro; internet www.delfinariu.ro; f. 1958; aquarium, dolphinarium, planetarium, astronomical observatory, micro-reservation; Dir GABRIELA PLOTOAGĂ; publ. *Pontus Euxinus.*

Muzeul de Artă (Art Museum): Bdul Tomis 84, 900657 Constanţa; tel. (241) 61-70-12; f. 1961; Romanian paintings and other works of art; Dir DOINA PAULEANU.

Muzeul de Artă Populară (Folk Art Museum): Bdul Tomis 32, 900742 Constanţa; tel. (241) 61-61-33; fax (241) 61-61-33; e-mail muzeuartapop@from.ro; internet www.muzeuartapopct.from.ro; Dir MARIA MAGIRU.

Muzeul de Istorie Naţională şi Arheologie (National History and Archaeology Museum): Piaţa Ovidiu 12, 900745 Constanţa; tel. (241) 61-39-25; fax (241) 61-87-63; e-mail archmus@minac.ro; internet www.minac.ro; f. 1879; affiliated archaeological museums of Histria, Tropaeum Traiani and Capidava; library of 37,000 vols; Dir GHEORGHE PAPUC; publ. *Pontica* (annual).

Muzeul Marinei Române (Romanian Naval Museum): Str. Traian 53, 900725 Constanţa; tel. (241) 61-90-35; fax (241) 61-90-35; e-mail muzeu.marina@rdslink.ro; internet www.cjc.ct.ro/institutii-regii-cultura/m.marinei; f. 1969; history of Romanian navy and merchant fleet; Dir Cmdr Dr MARIAN MOŞNEAGU.

Corabia

Muzeul de Arheologie şi Etnografie Corabia (Corabia Archaeological and Ethnographical Museum): Str. Cuza Vodă 65, 235300 Corabia; tel. (249) 56-13-64; Dir FLOREA BĂCIU.

Craiova

Muzeul Olteniei (Oltenia Museum): Str. Popa Şapcă 4, 200416 Craiova; tel. (251) 11-86-31; f. 1951; incorporates museums of art, ethnography, natural history, and archaeology and history; library of 12,000 vols; Dir MIHAI DUTESCU; publ. *Oltenia—Studii și cercetări*.

Curtea de Argeș

Muzeul de Istorie și Etnografie (History and Ethnography Museum): Str. Negru Vodă 2, 115300 Curtea de Argeș; tel. (248) 1-14-46; Dir N. MOISESCU.

Deva

Muzeul Civilizației Dacice și Romane Deva (Deva Museum of Dacian and Roman Civilization): Str. 1 Decembrie 39, 330005 Deva; tel. (254) 21-22-00; fax (254) 21-22-00; e-mail muzeucdr_deva@smart.ro; f. 1882; archaeology, history, natural sciences, numismatics, art, ethnography; incorporates museum of Roman archaeology at Sarmizegetusa and the ethnographical museums at Orăștie and Brad; library of 30,980 vols; Dir ADRIANA RUSU-PESCARU; publ. *Sargetia. Acta Musei Devensis*.

Drobeta-Turnu Severin

Muzeul Regiunii 'Porțile de Fier' ('Iron Gates' Regional Museum): Str. Independenței 2, 220171 Drobeta-Turnu Severin; tel. (262) 81-21-77; f. 1882; natural history, ethnography, archaeology and Roman ruins; aquarium; Dir ION STÎNGĂ; publ. *Drobeta* (annual).

Focșani

Muzeul Vrancei (Vrancea Museum): Bdul Gării 5, 620012 Focșani; tel. (237) 22-28-90; f. 1951; incorporates museums of ethnography (open-air), natural history, and history and archaeology; Dir HORIA DUMITRESCU.

Galați

Muzeul Județean de Istorie (District Museum of History): Str. Maior Iancu Fotea 2, 800017 Galați; tel. (236) 41-42-28; f. 1939; library of 8,000 vols; Dir ȘTEFAN STANCIU; publ. *Danubius*.

Attached museums:

Complexul Muzeal de Științele Naturii (Natural Science Museum Complex): Str. Regiment 11 Siret, 800340 Galați; tel. (236) 41-18-98; fax (236) 41-44-75; e-mail contact@cmsngl.ro; f. 1956; flora and fauna of the region, botanical and zoological gardens, aquarium; Dir Ing. CAMELIA GROSU.

Muzeul de Arta Vizuala (Visual Art Museum): Str. Domnească 141, 800163 Galați; tel. (236) 41-34-52; fax (236)-31-25-02; e-mail contact@mavgl.ro; internet www.mavgl.ro; f. 1956; Dir DAN BASARAB NANU.

Gherla

Muzeul de Istorie Gherla: Str. Mihai Viteazul 6, Județul Cluj, 405300 Gherla; tel. (264) 24-19-47; fax (264) 24-16-66; f. 1881; library of 4,221 vols; Dir RODICA PINTEA.

Giurgiu

Muzeul Județean Giurgiu (Giurgiu District Museum): Str. Constantin Dobrogeanu Gherea 3, 080024 Giurgiu; tel. (246) 21-68-01; f. 1950; history, ethnography; Dir VASILE BARBU; publ. *File de istorie*.

Golești

Complexul Muzeal Golești (Golești Museum Complex): Ștefănești Commune, Județul Argeș, 117715 Golești; tel. and fax (248) 26-63-64; e-mail cmngolesti@yahoo.com; f. 1939; history of fruit and vine-growing; library of 9,100 vols; Dir CONSTANTIN ILIESCU.

Gura Humorului

Muzeul Obiceiurilor Populare din Bucovina (Museum of Bucovinean Folk Traditions): Piața Republicii 2, 725300 Gura Humorului; tel. (230) 23-11-08; f. 1956; library of 2,415 vols; Dir ELVIRA ROMANIUC.

Iași

Complexul Național Muzeal 'Moldova' Iași (Iași 'Moldova' National Museum Consortium): Piața Ștefan cel Mare și Sfânt 1, 700028 Iași; tel. (232) 21-83-83; fax (232) 21-83-83; e-mail palatulculturii@home.ro; internet www.palatulculturii.home.ro; f. 1992; Dir VAL CONDURACHE; publs *Cercetări istorice* (annual), *Buletinul Ioan Neculce* (annual), *Anuarul Muzeului Etnografic al Moldovei* (annual), *Buletinul Centrului de Restaurare-Conservare* (2 a year).

Selected constituent museums:

Muzeul de Artă din Iași (Iași Art Museum): Piața Ștefan cel Mare și Sfânt 1, 700028 Iași; tel. (232) 31-41-36 ext. 124; fax (232) 21-83-83; e-mail palatulculturii@home.ro; internet www.palatulculturii.home.ro; f. 1860; Curator IVONA ARAMĂ.

Muzeul Etnografic al Moldovei (Ethnographic Museum of Moldavia): Piața Ștefan cel Mare și Sfânt 1, 700028 Iași; tel. (232) 31-41-36 ext. 144; fax (232) 21-83-83; e-mail palatulculturii@home.ro; internet www.palatulculturii.home.ro; f. 1943; Curator VASILE MUNTEANU.

Muzeul de Istorie a Moldovei (History Museum of Moldavia): Piața Ștefan cel Mare și Sfânt 1, 700028 Iași; tel. (232) 31-41-36 ext. 135; fax (232) 21-83-83; e-mail palatulculturii@home.ro; internet www.palatulculturii.home.ro; f. 1916; incl. Al. I. Cuza Memorial Museum, in Ruginoasa, Mihail Kogalniceanu Memorial Museum in Iași, Museum of the Union in Iași (dedicated to the period of creating and maintaining the union of the Romanian lands), History Museums in Hârlău and Pașcani, and archaeological sites at Cucuteni and Cotnari; Curator SENICA TURCANU.

Muzeul Științei și Tehnicii 'Ștefan Procopiu' ('Stefan Procopiu' Museum of Science and Technology): Piața Ștefan cel Mare și Sfânt 1, 700028 Iași; tel. (232) 31-41-36 ext. 145; fax (232) 21-83-83; e-mail palatulculturii@home.ro; internet www.palatulculturii.home.ro; f. 1955; incl. Iași Memorial Museum 'Poni-Cernatescu'; Curator LENUȚA CHIRIȚĂ.

Muzeul de Istorie Naturală Iași (Iași Natural History Museum): Str. Română 40, 700312 Iași; f. 1834; attached to Iași University; geology, palaeontology, zoology; Dir Dr C. MÂNDRU.

Mangalia

Muzeul de Arheologie 'Callatis' (Callatis Archaeological Museum): Șoseaua Constanței 23, 905500 Mangalia; tel. (241) 75-35-80; f. 1928; prehistory, Greek and Roman periods, ancient Greek colony of Callatis; library of 500 vols; Dir Prof. NICOLAE GEORGESCU-CHELUȚĂ.

Mediaș

Muzeul Municipal Mediaș (Mediaș Municipal Museum): Str. M. Viteazu 46, 551034 Mediaș; tel. (269) 84-12-99; fax (269) 83-64-75; f. 1950; history, natural history, ethnography; Dir Dr PETER WEBER.

Miercurea Ciuc

Muzeul Secuiesc al Ciucului/Csiki Székely Múzeum (Ciuc Szekler Museum): Piața Cetății 2, 530110 Miercurea Ciuc; tel. (266) 11-17-27; fax (266) 17-20-24; e-mail muzeu@cemc.topnet.ro; f. 1930; history, ethnography,

archaeology, 20th-century art history; library of 9,000 vols; Dir SZABÓ ANDRÁS.

Mogoșoaia

Centrul Național de Cultura Mogoșoaia (Mogoșoaia National Cultural Centre): Brâncoveanu Palace, Ilfov, Str. Valea Parcului 1, Com., 077135 Mogoșoaia; tel. (21) 490-40-22; fax (21) 225-66-90; e-mail pbpb@xnet.ro; f. 1702; medieval Romanian art; Dir DOINA MANDRU.

Năsăud

Muzeul Năsăudean (Năsăud Museum): Str. Grănicerilor 19, 425200 Năsăud; tel. (263) 36-29-67; history, ethnography; Dir IOAN RADU NISTOR.

Oradea

Muzeul Țării Crișurilor (Criș County Museum): Bdul Dacia 1–3, 410464 Oradea; tel. (259) 47-99-17; fax (259) 47-99-18; e-mail mtariicrisurilor@yahoo.com; internet www.mtariicrisurilor.ro; f. 1971; history, art, ethnography and natural science; library of 30,000 vols; Dir Dr AUREL CHIRIAC; publs *Biharea* (ethnography, annual), *Crisia* (history, annual), *Nymphaea* (natural sciences, annual).

Orăștie

Muzeul de Etnografie și Artă Populară (Ethnography and Folk Art Museum): Str. Aurel Vlaicu 17, 335700 Orăștie; f. 1952; Curator COSMA AURELIAN.

Petroșani

Muzeul Mineritului (Mining Museum): Str. N. Bălcescu 12, 332026 Petroșani; tel. (254) 54-17-44; f. 1961; history of mining in the Jiu Valley; Dir DUMITRU PELIGRAD.

Piatra-Neamț

Complexul Muzeal Județean Neamț (Neamț District Museums Complex): Bdul Mihai Eminescu 10, 610029 Piatra-Neamț; tel. (233) 21-74-96; e-mail muzeu.pneamt@csc.ro; Dir GHEORGHE DUMITROAIA.

Selected affiliated museums:

Muzeul de Artă Piatra-Neamț (Piatra-Neamț Art Museum): Piața Libertății 1, 610100 Piatra-Neamț; tel. (233) 21-68-08; f. 1980; Romanian art; Curator VIOLETA DINU.

Muzeul de Etnografie Piatra-Neamț (Piatra-Neamț Ethnography Museum): Piața Libertății 1, 610100 Piatra-Neamț; tel. (233) 21-68-08; Curator FLORENTINA COSTAN.

Muzeul de Istorie și Arheologie Piatra-Neamț (Piatra-Neamț History and Archaeology Museum): Bdul Mihai Eminescu 10, 610029 Piatra-Neamț; tel. (233) 21-81-08; f. 1934; Curator GHEORGHE DUMITROAIA; publ. *Memoria Antiquitatis* (annual).

Muzeul de Științele Naturii Piatra-Neamț (Piatra-Neamț Natural History Museum): Str. Petru Rareș 26, 610119 Piatra-Neamț; tel. (233) 22-42-11; f. 1960; Curator MARIA APETREI; publ. *Studii și comunicări* (annual).

Pitești

Muzeul Județean Argeș (Argeș County Museum): Str. Armand Călinescu 44, 110047 Pitești; tel. (248) 22-02-54; fax (248) 22-02-54; e-mail muzeuarg@geostar.ro; f. 1928; history, art, natural history; library of 18,000 vols; Dir RADU STANCU; publs *Argessis – Studii și comunicări* (Studies and Reports), *Argessis – Studii și comunicări* (history series and natural science series, annual), *Naturalia* (annual).

Ploieşti

Muzeul de Biologie Umană (Human Biology Museum): Str. Călin Cătălin 1, 100066 Ploieşti; tel. (244) 12-19-00; f. 1956; Dir Prof. EMILIA IANCU; publ. *Comunicări şi referate*.

Muzeul Judeţean de Artă Prahova: Bdul Independenţei 1, 100028 Ploieşti; tel. (244) 52-22-64; fax (244) 51-13-75; e-mail office@artmuseum.ro; internet www.artmuseum.ro; f. 1931; Dir FLORIN SICOIE.

Muzeul Judeţean de Istorie şi Arheologie Prahova (Prahova District Museum of History and Archaeology): Str. Toma Caragiu 10, 100042 Ploieşti; tel. and fax (244) 51-44-37; e-mail histmuseumph@yahoo.com; internet www.histmuseum.ro; f. 1953; library of 60,247 vols; Dir-Gen. LIA MARIA DULGHERU; publ. *Studii şi comunicări* (annual).

Muzeul Naţional al Petrolului (National Oil Museum): Str. Dr Bagdazar 8, 100575 Ploieşti; tel. (244) 59-75-85; fax (244) 51-95-42; e-mail mnpetrol@go.ro; internet www.mnpetrol.go.ro; f. 1961; history of the Romanian oil industry; library of 3,000 vols; Dir GABRIELA TĂNĂSESCU.

Rădăuţi

Muzeul Etnografic Rădăuţi (Rădăuţi Ethnographic Museum): Piaţa Unirii 63, 725400 Rădăuţi; tel. (230) 46-25-65; f. 1920; Dir DRAGOŞ CUSAC.

Râmnicu Vâlcea

Muzeul Judeţean Râmnicu Vâlcea (Râmnicu Vâlcea District Museum): Calea Traian 159, 240284 Râmnicu Vâlcea; tel. (250) 71-81-21; f. 1950; history, art, ethnography; Dir PETRE BARDASU.

Reghin

Muzeul Etnografic Reghin (Reghin Ethnographic Museum): Str. Vînătorilor 51, Judeţul Mureş, 545300 Reghin; tel. (265) 52-14-48; f. 1960; library of 2,336 vols, 3,186 slides, 128 ethnological films; Dir MARIA BORZAN.

Reşiţa

Muzeul Banatului Montan (Museum of the Mountainous Banat): Bdul Republicii 10, 320151 Reşiţa; tel. (255) 23-14-69; fax (255) 22-65-00; f. 1959; Dir Dr ŢEICU DUMITRU; publs *Banatica, Arheologia Medievală*.

Roman

Muzeul de Istorie Roman (Roman Museum of History): Str. Cuza Vodă 19, 611009 Roman; tel. (233) 72-77-26; fax (233) 72-77-26; f. 1957; Curator Dr VASILE URSACHI.

Satu Mare

Muzeul Judeţean Satu Mare (Satu Mare District Museum): Bdul Vasile Lucaciu 21, 440031 Satu Mare; tel. (261) 73-75-26; fax (261) 76-87-61; e-mail muzeu@p5net.ro; f. 1891; history, ethnography, paintings by Aurel Popp; library of 50,000 vols; Dir VIOREL CIUBOTA; publ. *Studii şi comunicări*.

Sf. Gheorghe

Muzeul Naţional Secuiesc (National Szekler Museum): Str. Kos Karoly 10, 520055 Sf. Gheorghe; tel. (267) 31-24-42; fax (267) 31-24-42; e-mail office@szekelynemzetimuzeum.ro; internet www.szekelynemzetimuzeum.ro; f. 1875; history, ethnography, archaeology, natural history, icons, classical and modern Hungarian art; library of 110,000 vols; Dir ZOLTÁN KATÓ; publ. *Acta Margitensia* (annual).

Sibiu

Complexul Naţional Muzeal 'Astra' (Astra National Museum Complex): Piaţa Mică 11, 550182 Sibiu; tel. (269) 21-81-95; fax (269) 21-80-60; e-mail office@muzeulastra.ro; internet www.muzeulastra.ro; f. 1963; library of 10,000 vols; Dir Prof. Dr CORNELIU BUCUR; publ. *Cibinium* (Romanian museology and the history of traditional folk civilization, every 2 years).

Muzeul Naţional Brukenthal (Brukenthal National Museum): Piaţa Revoluţiei 4 Sibiu; tel. (269) 41-76-91; e-mail info@brukenthalmuseum.ro; internet www.brukenthalmuseum.ro; f. 1817; history, ethnography, 15th- to 18th-century European painting; library: see Libraries and Archives; Dir AL. LUNGU; publs *Cibinium, Studii şi Communicări*.

Affiliated museum:

Muzeul de Istorie Naturală din Sibiu (Sibiu Natural History Museum): Str. Cetăţii 1, 550160 Sibiu; tel. (69) 43-68-68; f. 1849; library of 65,000 vols; Curator GH. BAN; publ. *Studii şi Comunicări de Ştiinţe Naturale*.

Sighetu Marmaţiei

Muzeul Maramureşan Sighetu Marmaţiei (Sighetu Marmaţiei Museum of Maramureş): Str. Libertăţii 16, 435500 Sighetu Marmaţiei; tel. (262) 51-15-21; f. 1873; history, ethnography, natural history, open-air museum; Dir MIHAI DĂNCUŞ.

Sighişoara

Muzeul de Istorie Sighişoara (Sighişoara History Museum): Piaţa Muzeului 1, 545400 Sighişoara; tel. (265) 77-11-08; fax (265) 77-15-14; f. 1899; Dir ADRIANA ANTIHI.

Slatina

Muzeul Judeţean Olt (Olt District Museum): Str. Ana Ipătescu 1, 230079 Slatina; tel. (249) 41-52-79; fax (249) 41-52-79; e-mail muzeu_olt@yahoo.com; internet www.clicknet.ro/muzeu_olt; f. 1951; Dir LAURENTIU GUTICA-FLORESCU.

Slobozia

Muzeul Judeţean Ialomiţa (Ialomiţa District Museum): Str. Matei Basarab 30, 920055 Slobozia; tel. (243) 23-00-54; history, ethnography, archaeology, and plastic art; Dir VLĂDĂRCANU ALEXANDRU.

Suceava

Muzeul Naţional al Bucovinei (Bucovina National Museum): Str. Ştefan cel Mare 33, 720003 Suceava; tel. (230) 71-64-39; f. 1900; folk art, history, natural history, astronomical observatory, planetarium, Romanian fine arts; library of 91,000 vols; Dir PAVEL BLAJ; publ. *Suceava—Anuarul Muzeului judeţean* (History and Natural Sciences sections).

Târgovişte

Complexul Muzeal Judeţean Dâmboviţa (Dâmboviţa District Museum Complex): Str. Justiţiei 3–5, 130017 Târgovişte; tel. (245) 61-28-77; f. 1940; archaeology, ethnography, fine arts, history of books and printing in Romania; Dir CII. BULEI; publ. *Vallachica*.

Târgu Jiu

Muzeul Judeţean Gorj (Gorj District Museum): c/o Muzeul de Istorie şi Arheologie, Str. Geneva 8, 210136 Târgu Jiu; tel. (253) 21-20-44; fax (253) 21-20-44; Dir Prof. VASILE MARINOIU.

Constituent museums:

Muzeul Arhitecturii Populare din Gorj (Gorj Museum of Folk Architecture): open-air Curtişoara village, 215101 Bumbeşti-Jiu; f. 1968; Curator Prof. VASILE PETRE.

Muzeul de Artă (Art Museum): Parcul Central, 210132 Târgu Jiu; tel. (253) 21-85-50; f. 1982; Romanian contemporary art; sculptures by Brâncuşi; Curator CARMEN SILVIA ŞOCU.

Muzeul de Istorie şi Arheologie (History and Archaeology Museum): Str. Geneva 8, Jud. Gorj, 210136 Târgu Jiu; tel. (253) 21-20-44; f. 1894; library of 10,000 vols.

Târgu Mureş

Muzeul Judeţean Mureş (Mureş District Museum): Str. Horea 24, 540036 Târgu Mureş; tel. (265) 42-56-34; Dir VALER POP; publ. *Marisia* (annual).

Attached museums:

Muzeul de Arheologie şi Istorie (Archaeology and History Museum): Str. George Enescu 2, 540052 Târgu Mureş; tel. (265) 43-25-12.

Muzeul de Artă (Art Museum): Str. George Enescu 2, 540052 Târgu Mureş; tel. (265) 43-21-79; f. 1913; art of the 19th and 20th centuries.

Timişoara

Muzeul Banatului Timişoara (Timiş Museum of the Banat): Piaţa Huniade 1, 300052 Timişoara; tel. (256) 19-13-39; fax (256) 20-13-21; e-mail root@mbt.dnttm.ro; internet www.infotim.ro/mbt; f. 1872; archaeology, natural history, ethnography, art; Dir OCTAVIAN DOGARIU; publ. *Analele Banatului* (annual).

Vaslui

Muzeul Judeţean 'Ştefan cel Mare' Vaslui (Vaslui District 'Stephen the Great' Museum): Piaţa Independenţei 1, 730240 Vaslui; tel. (235) 31-16-26; e-mail museumvs@yahoo.com; f. 1975; ancient history and archaeology, ethnography and folk art, modern Romanian art; library of 5,000 vols; Dir IOAN MANCAŞ; publ. *Acta Moldaviae Meridionalis* (5–10 a year).

Zalău

Muzeul Judeţean de Istorie şi Artă Sălaj (Sălaj District Museum of History and Art): Str. Unirii 9, 450042 Zalău; tel. (260) 61-22-23; fax (260) 66-17-06; e-mail muzeu@zalau.astral.ro; f. 1951; library of 14,975 vols; Dir DUMITRU GHEORGHE TAMBA; publ. *Acta Musei Porolissensis* (annual).

Universities

UNIVERSITATEA '1 DECEMBRIE 1918' DIN ALBA IULIA
(1 December 1918 University, Alba Iulia)

Nicolae Iorga 11–13, 510009 Alba Iulia

Telephone: (258) 81-15-12
Fax: (258) 81-26-07
E-mail: cond@uab.ro
Internet: www.uab.ro

Founded 1991
State control
Language of instruction: Romanian
Academic year: October to July

Gen. Man. Dir: Eng. VASILE MARCULET
Chief Accountant: SOFIA MIHALACHE
Sec.-in-Chief: CRISTINA HAVA

Library of 50,000 vols
Number of teachers: 163
Number of students: 7,935

Publications: *Acta Universitatis Apulensis* (annual), *RevCad* (annual), *Pro Cont* (every 2 years)

DEANS

Faculty of History and Philology: Prof. Dr IACOB MARZA

Faculty of Law and Social Sciences: Prof. Dr ADRIAN TULBURE

Faculty of Orthodox Theology: Prof. Dr ANDREI ANDREICUT

Faculty of Sciences: Prof. Dr NICOLAE TODEA

ATTACHED RESEARCH INSTITUTES

Institute of Systemic Archaeology: Mihai Viteazul 12, 510010 Alba Iulia; tel. (258) 81-70-71; fax (258) 81-84-59; e-mail bcum@bcum .uab.ro; internet www.bcum.uab.ro; Dir Prof. Dr IULIU PAUL.

UNIVERSITATEA 'ALEXANDRU IOAN CUZA' IAŞI

Bdul Carol I 11, 700506 Iaşi

Telephone: (232) 20-10-00

Fax: (232) 20-11-21

E-mail: rectorat@uaic.ro

Internet: www.uaic.ro

Founded 1860

State control

Academic year: October to July

Rector: Prof. Dr DUMITRU OPREA

Vice-Rector for Academic Affairs: Prof. Dr CONSTANTIN SĂLĂVĂSTRU

Vice-Rector for Int. Co-operation and Univ. Image): Prof. Dr HENRI LUCHIAN

Vice-Rector for Scientific Research and Post-graduate Studies: Prof. Dr GHEORGHE POPA

Vice-Rector for Student Affairs: Prof. Dr LUMINIŢA MIHAELA IACOB

Vice-Rector for Univ. Strategy: Prof. Dr ALEXANDRU CECAL

Univ. Chief Sec.: OANA CEICĂ

Gen. Admin. Man.: BOGDAN-EDUARD PLEŞCAN

Int. Relations Officer: LIVIA VRĂNESCU

Dir of Central Univ, Library: Prof. Dr ALEXANDRU CĂLINESCU

Library: see Libraries and Archives

Number of teachers: 935

Number of students: 40,000

Publication: *Analele Universităţii*

DEANS

Faculty of Mathematics: Prof. Dr OVIDIU CÂRJĂ

Faculty of Physics: Prof. Dr MIHAI TOMA

Faculty of Biology: Prof. Dr ION BĂRA

Faculty of Geography and Geology: Prof. Dr CONTANTIN RUSU

Faculty of Letters: Prof. Dr IULIAN POPESCU

Faculty of History: Prof. Dr ALEXANDRU FLORIN PLATON

Faculty of Philosophy: Prof. Dr ŞTEFAN AFLOROAIEI

Faculty of Law: Prof. Dr TUDOREL TOADER

Faculty of Econ.: Prof. Dr VASILE COCRIŞ

Faculty of Chemistry: Prof. Dr GELU BOUR-CEANU

Faculty of Psychology and Education Sciences: Prof. Dr TEODOR COZMA

Faculty of Computer Science: Prof. Dr GHEORGHE GRIGORAŞ

Faculty of Orthodox Theology: Rev. Prof. Dr GHEORGHE POPA

Faculty of Roman Catholic Theology: Rev. Assoc. Prof. EMIL DUMEA

Faculty of Physical Education and Sport: Prof. Dr IOAN IACOB

PROFESSORS

Faculty of Mathematics (tel. (232) 20-10-60; fax (232) 20-11-60; e-mail ocarja@uaic.ro; internet math.uaic.ro):

ANASTASIEI, M., Geometry

ANICULĂESEI, GH., Applied Mathematics

ANIŢA, S., Applied Mathematics

ARNĂUTU, V., Applied Mathematics

BARBU, V., Applied Mathematics

BRÂNZEI, D., Geometry

CÂRJĂ, O., Mathematical Analysis

CHIRIŢĂ, S., Applied Mathematics

IEŞAN, D., Applied Mathematics

ILIOI, C., Applied Mathematics

FLORESCU, L., Mathematical Analysis

FRUNZĂ, ŞT., Mathematical Analysis

MOROŞANU, P., Applied Mathematics

OPROIU, V., Geometry

POP, I., Geometry

POPA, E., Mathematical Analysis

PRECUPANU, A., Mathematical Analysis

PRECUPANU, T., Mathematical Analysis

RADU, GH., Algebra

RĂŞCANU, A., Applied Mathematics

TOFAN, I., Algebra

TURINICI, M., Applied Mathematics

VRABIE, I., Applied Mathematics

ZĂLINESCU, C., Mathematical Analysis

Faculty of Physics (tel. (232) 20-10-50; fax (232) 20-11-50; e-mail admphys@uaic.ro; internet physics.uaic.ro):

BIBOROSCH, L., Plasma Physics

DARIESCU, C., Quantum Mechanics

DARIESCU, M. A., Quantum Mechanics

DOROHOI, O. D., Plasma Physics

GEORGESCU, V., Solid State Physics

IGNAT, E. M., Theoretical Physics

LOZNEANU, E., Plasma Physics

MERCHEŞ, I., Theoretical Physics

POPA, G., Plasma Physics

RUSU, G., Solid State Physics

RUSU, M., Solid State Physics

SINGUREL, G., Spectroscopy and Quantum Optics

STANCU, A., Electricity and Magnetism

STRAT, M., Optics and Spectroscopy

SULIŢANU, N., Solid State Physics

TOMA, M., Plasma Physics

Faculty of Biology (Bdul Carol I 20A, 700505 Iaşi; tel. (232) 20-10-72; fax (232) 20-14-72; e-mail admbio@uaic.ro; internet biology.uaic .ro):

AILIESEI, O., Microbiology, Immunology

ARTENIE, V., Biochemistry

BĂRA, I., Genetics

CHIFU, T., Environmental Protection and Nature Preservation, Environmental Biodiversity, Phylogenesis

COJOCARU, D., Enzymology, Biochemistry

HEFCO, V., Animal Physiology

ION, I., Vertebrate Zoology

MIRON, I., Aquaculture, Limnology

MISĂILĂ, C., Animal Physiology

MITITIUC, M., Phytopathology, Biogeography

MURARIU, A., Vegetal Physiology, Basis of Environment Protection

MUSTAŢĂ, GH., Evolutionary Biology

NEACŞU, I., Biophysics, Molecular Biology

NIMIŢAN, E., Microbiology, Biotechnology

ŞTEFAN, N., Vegetal Taxonomy, Phytosociology, Phytocenology

TOMA, C., Plant Anatomy, Vegetal Cytology, Phylogenesis

TOMA, O., Structural Organization of Proteins and Nucleic Acids

Faculty of Geography and Geology (Bdul Carol I 20A, 700505 Iaşi; tel. (232) 20-10-74; fax (232) 20-14-74; e-mail cvusu@uaic.ro; internet geography.uaic.ro):

BAICAN, V., Environmental Geography

BRÂNZILĂ, M., Geology and Palaeontology

GANDRABURA, E., Geochemistry

IONIŢĂ, I., Geomorphology

LĂCĂTUŞU, R., Physical Geography

MUNTELE, I., Human Geography

MURARIU, T., Geology and Geochemistry

NIMIGEANU, V., Physical Geography

POPA, GH., Geochemistry

ROMANESCU, GH., Physical Geography

RUSU, C., Physical Geography of Romania

RUSU, E., Human Geography

UNGUREANU, A., Human Geography

UNGUREANU, I., Environmental Geography

Faculty of Letters (tel. (232) 20-10-52; fax (232) 20-11-52; e-mail iulianp@uaic.ro; internet letters.uaic.ro):

AVĂDANEI, ST., English and American Literature

BĂLĂNESCU, S., Russian Literature

BLUMENFELD, O., English Language and Literature

CĂLINESCU, A., French Literature

CĂRCĂLEANU, E., Italian and Spanish

CIUBOTARU, I., Romanian Literature

CIUBOTARU, M., Romanian Language

CONSTANTINESCU, V., Comparative Literature

COTORCEA, L., Russian Literature

DIACONESCU, T., Latin Literature

DIACONU, D., Italian and Spanish

DIMITRIU, C., Romanian Language

DOROBĂŢ, D., English Literature

DUMISTRĂCEL, S., Romanian Language

FRÎNCU, C., Romanian Language

GOGĂLNICEANU, C., English Language

HAGIU, A., French Language

HOIŞIE, A., German Literature

HULBAN, H., English Language

IORDACHE, E., Russian Literature

IRIMIA, D., Romanian Language

LOBIUC, I., Romanian Language and Literature

MACARIE, G., Comparative Literature

MĂNUCĂ, D., Romanian Literature

MOLDOVANU, D., Romanian Language and Literature

MUNTEANU, E., Romanian Language

MUREŞANU, M., French Literature

PÂRVU, S., English Literature

PAVEL, M., French Language

PORUCIUC, A., English Language

SÂRBU, A., French Literature

SPÂNU, P., French Literature

ŢUGUI, G., Romanian Literature

ZUGUN-ELOAE, P., Romanian Linguistics

Faculty of History (tel. (232) 20-10-56; fax (232) 20-11-56; internet history.uaic.ro):

AGRIGOROAIEI, I., Romanian Contemporary History

CIUPERCĂ, I., Contemporary World History

CLIVETTI, G., World History

CRISTIAN, V., Modern World History

GOROVEI, S., Medieval History

IACOB, G., Contemporary History

LÁSZLÓ, A., Ancient World History

PLATON, F., Medieval History

PUNGĂ, G., Medieval History

RUSU, D., Romanian Modern and Contemporary History

SPINEI, V., Medieval History

TEODOR, D., Ancient World History

TODERAŞCU, I., Medieval Romanian History

URSULESCU, N., Ancient History

ZUGRAVU, N., Ancient History

Faculty of Philosophy (Bdul Carol I 11, 700506 Iaşi; tel. (232) 20-10-54; fax (232) 20-11-54; e-mail admfil@uaic.ro; internet philosophy.www.uaic.ro):

ADĂMUŢ, A., History of Philosophy

AFLOROAEI, ST., Ontology, Hermeneutics, Metaphysics

BALAHUR, D., Sociology

CARPINSCHI, A., Political Science

CELMARE, ŞT., Systematic Philosophy

COZMA, C., Ethics

DIMA, T., Logic and Epistemology

DUMITRESCU, D., History of Philosophy

GHIDEANU, T., History of Philosophy

IOAN, P., Logic

IONESCU, I., Sociology

MARIN, C., History of Philosophy

MIFTODE, V., Sociology, Social Anthropology

NISTOR, M., Aesthetics, History and Philosophy of Religions

RAVEICA, T., History of Philosophy

RÂMBU, N., Philosophy of Culture and Hermeneutics

SĂLĂVĂSTRU, C., Logic and Semiology

STĂNCIULESCU, T. D., Semiotics and Philosophy of Creation

Faculty of Law (tel. (232) 20-10-58; fax (232) 20-11-58; internet www.laws.uaic.ro):

MACOVEI, I., Private International Law, International Commercial Law

RĂUSCHI, S., Civil Law

Faculty of Economics (Bdul Carol I 22, 6600 Iaşi; tel. (232) 20-10-70; fax (232) 21-70-00; e-mail vcocris@uaic.ro; internet www.feaa.uaic.ro):

AIRINEI, D., Programming Languages

ANDONE, I., Accounting Information Systems and Financial Analysis

BRINZA, A., Marketing

CIOBANU, I., Management and Marketing

COCRIŞ, V., Finance and Banking

COSTE, V., Management

DUMITREAN, E., Financial and Managerial Accounting

FĂTU, T., Principles of Computers

FILIP, G., Finance

FILIP, M., Computer Programming

FLOREA, I., Accounting and Financial Control

IACOB, GH., Management and Marketing

IGNAT, I., Economics

JABA, E., Statistics

JABA, O., Management

MAXIM, E., Management and Marketing

NEAGU, T., Computer Programming

NECHITA, V., Political Economy

NICA, P., Management

OPREA, D., Business Information Systems

PEKAR, V., Agricultural Economics

PETRESCU, S., Economic Analysis

PETRIŞ, R., Accounting

POHOAŢĂ, I., Contemporary Economic Thought

PRALEA, S., International Economic Relations

PRUTEANU, S., Marketing

SASU, C., Marketing and Management

SCORŢESCU, GH., Accounting, Information Systems and Financial Analysis

TABĂRĂ, N., Accounting, Information Systems and Financial Analysis

TACU, A., Economic Statistics and Demography

ŢARCĂ, M., Economic Statistics and Demography

TOFAN, A., Management

VOINEA, G., Finance

ZAIŢ, D., Econometrics

Faculty of Chemistry (Splaiul Bahlui 71, 6600 Iaşi; tel. (232) 20-13-63; fax (232) 20-13-13; e-mail acecal@ch.tuiasi.ro; internet www.chemistry.uaic.ro):

BÂLBA, N., Material Sciences

BERDAN, I., Inorganic and Co-ordination Chemistry

BOURCEANU, G., Physical Chemistry

CAPROŞU, M., Organic Chemistry

CAŞCAVAL, A., Organic Chemistry

CECAL, A., Inorganic and Nuclear Chemistry

CIUGUREANU, C., General Chemistry

DRUŢĂ, I., Organic Chemistry and Structural Analysis

GHIRVU, C., Quantum Chemistry and Physical Chemistry

IORDAN, A., Inorganic Chemistry

MANGALAGIU, I., Organic Chemistry

MIHĂILĂ, G., Chemical Technology

MOCANU, R., Analytical Chemistry

NEMŢOI, G., Electrochemistry

NICOLAESCU, T., Organic Chemistry

ODOCHIAN, L., Physical Chemistry

ONOFREI, T., Analytical Chemistry

ONU, A., Physical Chemistry

PALAMARU, M., Inorganic Chemistry

POPOVICI, E., Material Sciences

SUNEL, V., Organic Chemistry

VASILE, A., Chemical Technology

Faculty of Psychology and Education (Str. Toma Cozma 3, 6600 Iaşi; tel. (232) 20-10-28; fax (232) 21-06-60; e-mail gratiela@uaic.ro; internet www.psychology.uaic.ro):

COZMA, T., General Education

CREŢU, C., Psycho-pedagogy of Excellence and Creativity

CUCOŞ, C., Pedagogy

MOISE, C., Education

NECULAU, A., Social Psychology

ŞOITU, L., Pedagogy

Faculty of Computer Science (Str. Berthelot 16, 6600 Iaşi; tel. (232) 20-10-90; fax (232) 20-14-90; e-mail dcristea@infoiasi.ro; internet www.infoiasi.ro):

CRISTEA, D., Artificial Intelligence

CROITORU, C., Algorithms

FELEA, V., Theory of Data Bases, Operating Systems

JUCAN, T., Formal Languages

LUCHIAN, H., Computer Design

MASALAGIU, C., Logic

ŢIPLEA, F. L., Algebraic Principles of Computer Science

Faculty of Orthodox Theology (Bdul Ştefan cel Mare şi Sfânt 45, 6600 Iaşi; tel. (232) 20-13-28; fax (232) 21-12-32; e-mail mary@theo.uaic.ro; internet www.teologie.uaic.ro):

ACHIMESCU, N., History and Philosophy of Religions

SANDU, I., Branch Orthodox Theology – Cultural Inheritance

Faculty of Roman Catholic Theology (tel. (232) 20-11-14; fax (232) 20-11-15; e-mail ftrc@uaic.ro):

LUCACI, B., Roman Catholic Theology

Faculty of Physical Education and Sport (Str. Toma Cozma 3, 6600 Iaşi; tel. (232) 20-10-26; fax (232) 20-11-26; e-mail admefs@uaic.ro; internet www.sport.uaic.ro):

FIEDLER, P., Methodology of Physical Education

IACOB, I., Methodology of Physical Education

LUCA, A., Acrobatic Gymnastics

ATTACHED INSTITUTES

Astronomical Observatory: Aleea M. Sadoveanu 5, 700490 Iaşi.

Botanical Garden: Str. Dumbrava Roşie 7–9, 700487 Iaşi; Dir Prof. Dr M. MITITIUC.

Natural History Museum: see under Museums and Art Galleries.

'Ion Borcea' Black Sea Biological Marine Research Station at Agigea, Constanţa: Dir Prof. Dr G. MUSTAŢĂ.

Biological Research Station at Potoci-Bicaz, Neamţ: Dir Prof. Dr I. MOGLAN.

'Simion Mehedinţi' Scientific Research Center and University Practice at Tulnici, Vrancea: Dir D. JURAVLE.

'Ion Gugiuman' Scientific Research Center and University Practice at Rarău, Suceavu: Dir Prof. C. RUSU.

UNIVERSITATEA DE ARTĂ ŞI DESIGN DIN CLUJ-NAPOCA

Piaţa Unirii 31, 400098 Cluj-Napoca

Telephone: (264) 59-32-14

Fax: (264) 59-28-90

E-mail: rector@uartdcluj.ro

Internet: www.uartdcluj.ro

Founded 1925

Rector: Dr IOAN SBÂRCIU

DEANS

Faculty of Applied Arts and Design: Dr ALEXANDRU ALAMOREANU

Faculty of Fine Arts: Dr RADU SOLOVASTRU

DIRECTORS

Dept for Teacher Training: Prof. MARIOARA PETCU

Fine and Decorative Arts Colleges: Dr DOREL MOISE

UNIVERSITATEA DE ARTĂ TEATRALĂ ŞI CINEMATOGRAFICĂ 'I. L. CARAGIALE' (I. L. Caragiale University of Drama and Cinematography)

Str. Matei Voievod 75–77, 021452 Bucharest

Telephone: (21) 252-80-20

Fax: (21) 252-54-55

E-mail: ri@unatc.ro

Internet: www.unatc.ro

Founded 1950

Rector: Prof. Dr FLORIN ZAMFIRESCU

Library of 95,000 vols (incl. English theatre library of 5,000 vols)

Number of teachers: 190

Number of students: 680.

UNIVERSITATEA DE ARTĂ TEATRALĂ TÂRGU-MUREŞ (University of Dramatic Art of Târgu-Mureş)

Str. Köteles Sámuel 6, 540057 Târgu Mureş

Telephone: (265) 26-62-81

Fax: (265) 26-62-81

E-mail: uat.ms@rdslink.ro

Internet: www.uat.ro

Founded 1954 as Institutul de Teatru 'Szentgyörgyi István'

Rector: Prof. Dr BÉRES ANDRÁS

Chancellor: Dr OANA LEAHU

Library of 40,000 vols

Number of teachers: 81

Number of students: 130.

UNIVERSITATEA DE ARTE 'GEORGE ENESCU'

Str. Horia 7–9, 700126 Iaşi

Telephone: (232) 21-25-49

Fax: (232) 21-25-51

E-mail: enescu@arteiasi.ro

Internet: www.arteiasi.ro

Founded 1860, renamed 1960

Academic year: October to May

Rector: Prof. Dr VIOREL MUNTEANU

Librarian: IOAN BĂDULEŢ

Library of 142,000 vols, 7,000 records, 1,500 cassette tapes

Number of teachers: 134

Number of students: 1,279

Publication: *Byzantion* (Byzantine studies)

DEANS

Faculty of Composition, Musicology and Musical and Theatrical Education: Dr LAURA OTILIA VASILIU

Faculty of Fine and Decorative Arts and Desiign: Prof. Dr DUMITRU N. ZAHARIA

Faculty of Musical Interpretation: Prof. Dr CORNELIU GHEORGHE SOLOVĂSTRU

UNIVERSITATEA 'AUREL VLAICU' DIN ARAD

Bdul Revoluţiei 81, Arad

Telephone: (257) 28-30-10

Fax: (257) 28-00-70
State control
Rector: Prof. Dr LIZICA MIHUT.

UNIVERSITATEA 'BABEŞ-BOLYAI' CLUJ-NAPOCA

Str. M. Kogălniceanu 1, 400084 Cluj-Napoca
Telephone: (264) 19-43-15
Fax: (264) 19-19-06
Internet: www.ubbcluj.ro
Founded 1919
Languages of instruction: Romanian, Hungarian, German
Academic year: October to July (2 semesters)
Rector: Prof. Dr ANDREI MARGA
Pro-Rectors: Prof. Dr N. BOCŞAN, Prof. Dr W. W. BRECKNER, Prof. Dr M. MUTHU, Prof. Dr N. PAINA, Prof. Dr S. ŞIMON, Prof. Dr. P. SZILÁGYI
Sec.-Gen.: MARIA BOIAN
Librarian: Prof. Dr DORU RADOSAV
Library: see Libraries
Number of teachers: 1,083
Number of students: 20,183

Publications: *Studia Universitatis Babeş-Bolyai, Judaic Library Collection, Colloquia: Journal of Central European History, Studi Italo-Romeni, Brain and Cognition and Behaviour, Botanical Contributions, Papers of Transition*

DEANS

Faculty of Mathematics and Computer Science: L. TÂMBULEA
Faculty of Physics: E. BURZO
Faculty of Chemistry and Chemical Eng.: S. MAGER
Faculty of Biology and Geology: V. CRISTEA
Faculty of Geography: I. MAC
Faculty of History and Philosophy: M. BĂRBULESCU
Faculty of Letters: I. POP
Faculty of Law: L. POP
Faculty of Psychology and Education: M. IONESCU
Faculty of Econ.: D. RACOVIŢAN
Faculty of Orthodox Theology: I. ICĂ
Faculty of Greek Catholic Theology: A. GOŢIA
Faculty of Protestant Theology: Z. GÁLFI
Faculty of Roman Catholic Theology: J. MARTON
Faculty of Physical Education and Sports: M. ALEXEI
Faculty of European Studies: N. PĂUN
Faculty of Political Science and Public Administration: V. BOARI
Faculty of Business: I. A. GIURGIU

PROFESSORS

Faculty of Mathematics and Computer Science:

ANDRICA, D., Geometry
BLAGA, P., Numerical Analysis
BOIAN, F. M., Informatics
BOTH, N., Algebra
BRECKNER, W. W., Functional Analysis and Optimization
CĂLUGĂREANU, G., Algebra
COBZAŞ, Ş., Functional Analysis
COMAN, G., Numerical Analysis
DUCA, D., Mathematical Analysis
DUMITRESCU, D., Informatics
FRENŢIU, M., Informatics
KOLUMBÁN, I., Mathematical Analysis
MICULA, G., Differential Equations
MIHOC, I., Probability Theory
MOCANU, P., Mathematical Analysis
MOLDOVAN, G., Informatics
MUNTEAN, E., Informatics
MUREŞAN, A., Applied Mathematics
NÉMETH, A., Mathematical Analysis
PÂRV, B., Informatics
PETRILA, T., Fluid Mechanics

POP, M. I., Fluid Mechanics
POP, V., Astronomy
PURDEA, I., Algebra
RUS, A. I., Differential Equations
SĂLĂGEAN, G. Ş., Mathematical Analysis
SZILÁGYI, P., Differential Equations
TÂMBULEA, L., Informatics
TRIF, D., Differential Equations
URECHE, V., Astronomy
VASIU, A., Geometry

Faculty of Physics:

ARDELEAN, I., Materials Science
BARBUR, I., Solid State Physics
BURZO, E., Solid State Physics
COLDEA, M., Solid State Physics
COSMA, C., Physics of Radiation
COZAR, O., Atomic and Molecular Physics
CRIŞAN, M., Theoretical Physics
CRIŞAN, V., Solid State Physics
CRISTEA, G., Solid State Physics
ILIESCU, T., Optics and Spectroscopy
ILONCA, G., Solid State Physics
POP, I., Solid State Physics
ŞIMON, S., Solid State Physics
TATARU, E., Electronics
ZNAMIROVSCHI, V., Atomic and Nuclear Physics

Faculty of Chemistry and Chemical Engineering:

AGACHI, P. Ş., Chemical Engineering
BÂLDEA, I., Physical Chemistry
CORDOŞ, E., Analytical Chemistry
DIUDEA, M., Organic Chemistry
GROSU, I., Organic Chemistry
HOROVITZ, O., Physical Chemistry
MAGER, S., Organic Chemistry
POPESCU, C., Physical Chemistry
SILAGHI-DUMITRESCU, I., Inorganic Chemistry
SILBERG, I. A., Organic Chemistry
SILVESTRU, C., Inorganic Chemistry
VLASSA, M., Organic Chemistry

Faculty of Biology and Geology:

BALINTONI, I. C., Geotectonics
BEDELEAN, I., Mineralogy
BUCUR, I., Palaeontology
COMAN, N., Genetics
CRISTEA, V., Botany
DRĂGAN BULARDA, M., Microbiology
MUREŞAN, I., Mineralogy
PÉTERFI, L. S., Botany
PETRESCU, I., Palaeobotany
POPESCU, O., Cell Biology
TARBA, C., Biophysics
TOMESCU, N., Zoology
TRIFU, M., Plant Physiology
TUDORANCEA, C., Ecology
VLAD, Ş. N., Petrology

Faculty of Geography:

CIANGĂ, N., Human Geography
COCEAN, P., Regional Geography
GÂRBACEA, V., Regional Geography
MAC, I., Physical Geography
POP, G., Human Geography
RABOCA, N., Economic Geography
SOROCOVSCHI, V. E., Hydrology
SURD, V., Rural Geography

Faculty of History and Philosophy:

BĂRBULESCU, M., Ancient History and Archaeology
BOCŞAN, N., Modern History
CIPĂIANU, G. A., Contemporary History
CODOBAN, A. T., Philosophy
CSUCSUJA, Ş., Contemporary History
EDROIU, N., Medieval History of Romania
GLODARIU, I., Ancient History
ILUŢ, P., Sociology
MAGYARI, A., Modern History
MUSCĂ, V., History of Philosophy
PAVEL, T., Modern History
PISO, I., Ancient History and Archaeology
POP, I. A., Medieval History
PUŞCAŞ, V., Contemporary History

ROTARIU, T., Sociology
TEODOR, P., Medieval History of Romania
ŢOCA, M., History of Art
VESE, V., Contemporary History

Faculty of Letters:

BACIU, I., French Language
BORCILĂ, M., General Linguistics
CĂPUŞAN, M., French Literature
CSEKE, É., Hungarian Literature and Society
DRAGOŞ, E., History of the Romanian Language
FANACHE, V., History of Romanian Literature
GRUIŢA, G., Contemporary Romanian Language
KOZMA, D., Hungarian Literature
MUTHU, M., Theory of Literature and Aesthetics
OLTEAN, Ş., History of the English Language
PAPAHAGI, M. D., Italian Literature
PÉNTEK, J., General Linguistics
PETRESCU, I., History of Romanian Literature
POP, I., History of Romanian Literature
POP, R., French Literature
ŞEULEAN, I., Folklore and Cultural Anthropology
STANCIU, V., English Literature
VARTIC, I., Comparative Literature and Theory of Drama
ZDRENGHEA, M., Contemporary English Literature

Faculty of Law:

COSTIN, M. N., Commercial Law
POP, L., Civil Law
URSA, V., Criminal Law
ZĂPÎRŢAN, L., Political Science

Faculty of Psychology and Education:

GOIA, V., Methodology
IONESCU, M., Education
LĂSCUŞ, V., Education
MICLEA, M., Psychology
PITARIU, H., Psychology
PREDA, V., Psychology for Teaching

Faculty of Economics:

AVORNICULUI, C., Data Processing in Economics
AVRAM-NIŢCHI, R., Data Processing in Economics
BĂTRÎNCEA, I., Economic Analysis
BEJU, V., Finance
CĂINAP, I., Economic Analysis
CISTELECAN, L., Finance
DIŢU, G., Political Economy
DRĂGOESCU, A., Political Economy
DRĂGOESCU, E., Finance
DUMBRAVĂ, P., Accountancy
FLOREA, I., Statistics
FRĂŢILĂ, R., Manufacture and Marketing of Products
GHIŞOIU, N., Data Processing in Economics
GORON, S., Data Processing in Economics
ILIEŞ, L., Transport Management
IONESCU, T., Political Economy
LAZĂR, D., Marketing
LAZĂR, I., Agricultural Management
MIHUŢ, I., Management
NAGHI, M., Management
NISTOR, I., Finance
NISTOR, L. I., Macroeconomic Forecasting
NIŢCHI, I. Ş., Data Processing in Economics
OPREAN, D., Data Processing in Economics
OPREAN, I., Accountancy
OPREAN, V., Data Processing in Economics
PAINA, N., Marketing
PÂNTEA, P., Accountancy
PLĂIAŞ, I., Marketing
POP, S. I., Management
POPESCU, G., Political Economy
POSTELNICU, G., Political Economy
PURDEA, D., Management

RACOVIȚAN, D., Data Processing in Economics
ROȘCA, T., Finance
STĂNEANU, G., Finance
TEMEȘ, I., Accountancy
TULAI, C., Finance
VINCZE, M., Agricultural Economics
VORZSÁK, A., Marketing

Faculty of Orthodox Theology:

ICĂ, I., Fundamental Theology
MORARU, A., History of the Orthodox Church

Faculty of Greek Catholic Theology:

GOȚIA, A., Catechetical Theology
GUDEA, N., History of the Greek Catholic Church

Faculty of Roman Catholic Theology:

MARTON, J., Ecclesiastical History

Faculty of Physical Education and Sport:

BENGEANU, C., Volleyball
BRĂTUCU, L. S., Anatomy and Physiology
MAROLICARU, M., Methodology of Scientific Research
NETA, G., Football

Faculty of European Studies:

BÎRSAN, M., Management of European Institutions
GYEMANT, L., European Studies
MARGA, A., Philosophy
PĂUN, N., Management of European Institutions

Faculty of Political Science and Public Administration:

BOARI, V., Political Ideology
STEGĂROIU, D. C., Management of Human Resources

Faculty of Business:

GIURGIU, A., Finance
VORZSÁK, M., Micro- and Macroeconomics

ATTACHED INSTITUTES

Computer Science Research Institute: Dir Prof. M. FRENȚIU.

Institute of Physics: Dir Prof. I. ARDELEAN.

Centre for Electrochemical Research: Dir Prof. L. ONICIU.

Institute of Gemmology: Dir Prof. I. MÂRZA.

Institute of Geography: Dir Prof. I. MAC.

Institute of Central European History: Dir Prof. P. TEODOR.

Institute of Oral History: Dir Prof. D. RADOSAV.

Institute of Anthropology: Dir I. CUCEU.

Institute of Classical Studies: Dir Prof. M. BÁRBULESCU.

Centre for Documentation and Comparative Studies of Universities: Dir Prof. M. MICLEA.

Dr. Moshe Carmilly Institute of Jewish Studies and History: Dir Prof. L. GYEMANT.

Institute for Modernity Research: Dir I. COPOERU.

Centre for Interethnic Relationship Studies: Dir Asst Prof. M. LAZĂR.

Social Research Centre: Dir Prof. V. BOARI.

Centre of Post-Totalitarian Society Studies: Dir Asst Prof. O. PECICAN.

CONCORD-ERCIR Centre of Text Analysis: Dir Prof. M. PAPAHAGI.

UNIVERSITATEA BACĂU
(University of Bacău)

Calea Marașești 157, 600115 Bacău
Telephone: (234) 14-24-11
Fax: (234) 14-57-53

E-mail: rector@ub.ro
Internet: www.ub.ro

Founded 1961 as Pedagogical Institute; became Bacău Institute of Higher Education 1974; present name and status 1990
State control
Language of instruction: Romanian
Academic year: October to June

Rector: Prof. VICTOR BLANUȚA
Vice-Rector for Admin. Affairs): Prof. VASILE PUIU
Vice-Rector for Int. Relations: Prof. CONSTANTIN MĂZĂREANU
Gen. Man.: Ing. SORIN BOICIUC
Registrar: Ing. ADRIAN APAVALOAIE
Head of Int. Relations: Ing. OANA BUCĂTARU
Librarian: Ing. CECILIA ANGHEL

Library of 250,000 vols, 1,370 periodicals
Number of teachers: 226
Number of students: 6,281 (5,416 undergraduate, 865 postgraduate)
Publications: *Cultural Perspectives: the Semiology of Culture* (3 a year), *Economic Revue* (2 a year), *Scientific Studies and Research – Mathematics* (monthly)

DEANS

Faculty of Eng.: Prof. GHEORGHE PINTILIE
Faculty of Letters: DOINA CMECIU
Faculty of Physical Education: Prof. ELEONORA CONSTANTINESCU
Faculty of Sciences: Prof. LUCIAN ȘARADICI

UNIVERSITATEA DIN BUCUREȘTI

Bdul Mihail Kogălniceanu 34–46, 050107 Bucharest
Telephone: (21) 307-73-01
Fax: (21) 313-17-60
E-mail: secretariat@unibuc.ro
Internet: www.unibuc.ro

Founded 1864
State control
Academic year: October to July

Rector: Prof. Dr IOAN PÂNZARU
Pro-Rectors: Prof. Dr CONSTANTIN BUȘE, Prof. Dr DANA MARINESCU, Prof. Dr IOAN MIHĂILESCU, Prof. Dr ION MUNTEANU
Registrar: MARIA PRUNĂ
Librarian: Prof. Dr MIRCEA REGNEALĂ

Library: see Libraries and Archives
Number of teachers: 1,490
Number of students: 24,650
Publications: *Analele Universității din București* (Chemistry, Law, Geology, Geography, History, Romanian Language and Literature, Physics, each annual), *Euroatlantic Studies* (in English, 2 a year), *Geography Communications* (in French and English, annual), *Revue Roumaine d'Egyptologie, Science and Technology of Environmental Protection*

DEANS

Faculty of Baptist Theology: Prof. Dr O. BUNACIU
Faculty of Biology: Prof. Dr TATIANA VASSU
Faculty of Chemistry: Prof. Dr DIMITRU OANCEA
Faculty of Foreign Languages and Literature: Prof. Dr ALEXANDRA CORNILESCU
Faculty of Geography: Prof. Dr ILEANA PĂTRU
Faculty of Geology and Geophysics: Prof. Dr LUCIAN MATEI
Faculty of History: Prof. Dr VLAD NISTOR
Faculty of Political Sciences and Admin.: Prof. Dr CRISTIAN PREDA
Faculty of Journalism and Communication Sciences: Prof. Dr MIHAI COMAN
Faculty of Law: Prof. Dr V. CIOBANU
Faculty of Letters: Prof. Dr LIVIU PAPADIMA
Faculty of Mathematics: Prof. Dr ION CHIȚRSCU

Faculty of Orthodox Theology: Prof. Dr N. NECULA
Faculty of Philosophy: Dr M. DUMITRU
Faculty of Physics: Prof. Dr S. ANTOHE
Faculty of Psychology and Education: Prof. Dr D. POTOLEA
Faculty of Roman Catholic Theology and Social Work: Prof. Dr I. MĂRTINCĂ
Faculty of Sociology and Social Work: Prof. Dr C. ZAMFIR
Dept of Public Admin.: Dr MAGDALENA PLATIS
Dept of Open and Distance Education: Dr BOGDAN LOGOFĂTU

PROFESSORS

Faculty of Baptist Theology (Str. Berzei 29, Bucharest; tel. (21) 638-44-00; fax (21) 638-44-00; e-mail bbts@astral.ro):

BUNACIU, I., New Testament
TALPOȘ, V., Old Testament

Faculty of Biology (Splaiul Independenței 91–95, Bucharest; tel. (21) 411-52-07; fax (21) 411-23-10; e-mail web@bio.bio.unibuc.ro; internet www.bio.unibuc.ro):

BOTNARIUC, N., Ecology
COSTACHE, M., Biochemistry
CRISTUREAN, I., Botany
DINISCHIOTY, A., Biochemistry
FLONTA, M. L., Animal Physiology and Biophysics
GAVRILĂ, L., Plant Genetics
GEORGESCU, D., Anatomy
IGA, D. P., Anatomy
IORDĂCHESCU, D., Biochemistry
LAZĂR, V., Microbiology
MAILAT, I. E., Anatomy
MANOLACHE, V., Animal Biology
MARIN, A., Botany
MEȘTER, L. E., Animal Biology
MIHĂESCU, G., Microbiology
MIȘCALENCU, D., Anatomy
NĂSTĂSESCU, M., Animal Biology
SÂRBU, A., Botany
SESAN, T., Botany
STOIAN, V., Genetics
TEODORESCU, I., Ecology
TESIO, C., Animal Biology
TOMA, N., Botany
VĂDINEANU, A., Ecology
VASSU, T., Genetics
VOICA, C., Plant Physiology
ZĂRNESCU, O., Histology

Faculty of Chemistry (Bdul Regina Elisabeta 4–12, Bucharest; tel. (21) 315-92-49; fax (21) 315-92-49; e-mail doan@gw-chimie.math.unibuc.ro; internet www.chimie.math.unibuc.ro):

ANDRUH, M., Inorganic Chemistry
ANGELESCU, E., Chemical Technology and Catalysis
BACIU, I., Organic Chemistry
BALA, C., Analytical Chemistry
BĂIULESCU, G.-E., Analytical Chemistry
BREZEANU, M., Inorganic Chemistry
CENUȘE, A., Physical Chemistry
CERCASOV, C., Organic Chemistry
CIOACĂ, C., Physics
CIOBANU, A., Organic Chemistry
CIOCĂZANU, I., Physical Chemistry
CIUCU, A., Analytical Chemistry
CONSTANTINESCU, E., Physical Chemistry
CONTINEANU, M., Physical Chemistry
CRISTUREAN, E., Inorganic Chemistry
DĂNEȚ, A. F., Analytical Chemistry
DAVID, V., Analytical Chemistry
DUMITRESCU, V., Analytical Chemistry
FIFIRIG, M., Physics
GĂINAR, I., Physical Chemistry
HILLEBRAND, M., Physical Chemistry
IVAN, L., Organic Chemistry
KRIZA, A., Inorganic Chemistry
LECA, M., Physical Chemistry
MAGEARU, V., Analytical Chemistry
MANDRAVEL, L. C., Physical Chemistry

MARIAN, P., Physics
MARINESCU, D., Inorganic Chemistry
MEDVEDOVICI, A., Analytical Chemistry
MELTZER, V., Physical Chemistry
MIHALCEA, I., Physical Chemistry
MUTIHAC, L., Analytical Chemistry
NEGOIU, D., Inorganic Chemistry
NEGOIU, M., Inorganic Chemistry
NICOLAE, A., Organic Chemistry
OANCEA, D., Physical Chemistry
OLTEANU, M. V., Physical Chemistry
ONCESCU, T., Physical Chemistry
PÂRVULESCU, V., Chemical Technology and Catalysis
PATROESCU, C., Analytical Chemistry
PAULINA, M., Physics
POPA, N., Inorganic Chemistry
ROȘU, T., Inorganic Chemistry
SAHINI, V., Physical Chemistry
SĂNDULESCU, I., Chemical Technology and Catalysis
SEGAL, E., Physical Chemistry
SZABÓ, A., Chemical Technology and Catalysis
TĂNASE, I., Analytical Chemistry
UDREA, I., Organic Chemistry
VÂLCU, R., Physical Chemistry
VLĂDESCU, L., Analytical Chemistry
VOLANSCHI, E., Physical Chemistry

Faculty of Foreign Languages and Literature (Str. Edgar Quinet 5–7, Bucharest; tel. (21) 312-13-13; fax (21) 312-13-13; internet www .unibuc.ro/ro/fac_flls_ro):

ANGHELESCU, N., Oriental Languages
BACIU, I., English
BĂDESCU, I., French
BĂLUȚĂ-SKULTETY, M., Classical Languages
BARBORICĂ, C., Slovak Language
CĂLIN, G., Slavic Languages
CIZEK, E. A., Classical Languages
CORNILESCU, A., English
CREȚIA, G., Classical Languages
CUNIȚĂ, A., French
DERER, D., Italian
DOBREA, A., Russian
DOBRIȘAN, N., Oriental Languages
DUMITRIU, G., English
GĂMULESCU, D., Serbo-Croat Language
GUȚU, G., German
HOGEA-VELISCU, I., Oriental Languages
IONESCU, A.-I., Slavic Languages
IRIMIA, M. L., English
MICLĂU, P., French
MIHĂILĂ, GH., Slavic Languages
MIHĂILĂ, R., American Literature
MITU, M., Slavic Languages
MOLNAR, S., Hungarian
MURVAI, O., Hungarian
NICOLAESCU, M., English
NICOLESCU, A., English
PANĂ, I., English
PÂNZARU, I., French
PETRICĂ, I., Slavic Languages
REBUȘAPCĂ, I., Slavic Languages
RÎPEANU, S., Romance Languages
ROȘIANU, N., Russian
SANDU, D., German
SĂULESCU, M., English
SLUȘANSCHI, D. M., Classical Languages
ȘOPTEREANU, V., Russian
ȘTĂNESCU, C., German
SURDULESCU, R., English
SZOBOLCS, A., Hungarian
TOMA, D., French
TOMA, R., French
TUPAN, M., English
TUȚESCU, M., French
VIANU, L., English
VISAN, F., Oriental Languages
VIȘAN, V., French
WALD, L., Classical Languages

Faculty of Geography (B-dul Nicolae Bălcescu 1, Bucharest 1; tel. (21) 315-30-74; fax (21) 315-30-74; e-mail secretariat@geo .unibuc.ro; internet www.unibuc.ro/ro/fac_fgeogr_ro):

BĂLTEANU, D., Geomorphology
CÂNDEA, M., Human and Economic Geography
CIULACHE, S., Meteorology and Hydrology
ERDELI, G., Human and Economic Geography
GEANANĂ, M., Geomorphology and Pedology
GRECU, F., Geomorphology and Pedology
GRIGORE, M., Geomorphology and Pedology
IANOȘ, I., Human and Economic Geography
IELENICZ, M., Geomorphology and Pedology
MARIN, I., Regional Geography
POPESCU, N., Geomorphology and Pedology
VESPREMEANU, E., Meteorology and Hydrology

Faculty of Geology and Geophysics (Str. Traian Vuia 6, Bucharest 6; tel. (21) 211-31-20; fax (21) 211-31-20; e-mail Secr@gg.unibuc .ro; internet www.gg.unibuc.ro):

ANASTASIU, N., Mineralogy
CONSTANTINESCU, E., Mineralogy
DANCHIV, A., Geological Engineering
DINU, C., Geology and Palaeontology
DRĂGĂSTAN, O., Geology and Palaeontology
GEORGESCU, P., Geophysics
GRIGORESCU, D., Geology and Palaeontology
IVAN, M., Geophysics
MĂRUNȚEANU, C., Geological Engineering
MATEI, L., Mineralogy
POPESCU, R., Mineralogy
SCRĂDEANU, D., Geological Engineering
ZAMFIRESCU, F., Geological Engineering

Faculty of History (5, B-dul Regina Elisabeta 4–12, Bucharest; tel. (21) 314-53-89; fax (21) 310-06-80; e-mail historybucharest@hotmail .com; internet www.unibuc.ro/ro/fac_fistr_ro):

BABEȘ, M., Prehistory and Archaeology
BARNEA, A., Ancient History, Archaeology and Epigraphy
BOIA, I., Historiography and Modern History
BREZEANU, S., Byzantine History
BULEI, I., Modern Romanian History
BUȘE, C., Contemporary History, Euro-Atlantic Studies
CIUCĂ, M., Medieval Romanian History
GIURESCU, D. C., Contemporary Romanian History
ISAR, N., Modern Romanian History
LUKACZ, A., Medieval History
MAIOR, L., Modern Romanian History
MAXIM, M., Ottoman History
MURGESCU, B., Modern and Economic History
NISTOR, V., Ancient Roman History
PANAITE, V., Ottoman History
PETOLESCU, C. C., Ancient Roman History and Epigraphy
PETRE, Z., Ancient Greek History
PIPPIDI, A., Medieval History
RETEGAN, M., Contemporary Romanian History
SCURTU, I., Contemporary Romanian History
ȘTEFĂNESCU, ȘT., Medieval Romanian History
TEOTEOI, T., Medieval Romanian and Byzantine History
VULPE, A., Prehistory and Archaeology
ZBUCHEA, GH., South-east European History

Faculty of Journalism and Communication Sciences (Bucharest, B-dul Iuliu Maniu 1–3, A Building, 6th Floor; tel. (21) 410-06-43; fax (21) 410-06-43; e-mail mcoman53@yahoo .com; internet www.fjsc.ro):

COMAN, M., Journalism
FRUMUȘANI, D., Journalism
ZOLTAN, R., Communications

Faculty of Law (B-dul Mihail Kogălniceanu 36–46, Bucharest; tel. (21) 312-07-19; fax (21) 312-07-19; internet www.unibuc.ro/ro/fac_fdrept_ro):

ATHANASIU, A., Private Law
BÂRSAN, C., Private Law
BESTELIU, R., Public Law
BIZIM, A., Sports
BUCUR, I., Economic Sciences
CĂRPENARU, ST., Private Law
CIOBANU, V., Private Law
CIOCLEI, V., Criminal Law
CORNESCU, V., Economic Sciences
CREȚOIU, GH., Economic Sciences
FILIPAȘ, A., Criminal Law
IORGOVAN, A., Constitutional Law
MARINESCU, D., Private Law
MITRACHE, C., Criminal Law
MOLCUȚ, E., Public Law
MURARU, I., Public Law
NĂSTASE, A., Public Law
NEAGU, I., Public Law
POPA, N., Public Law
ȘAGUNA, D., Public Law
SITARU, D., Private Law
STANCIU, S., Economic Sciences
STANCU, E., Criminal Law
VOLONCIU, N. D., Criminal Law

Faculty of Mathematics and Informatics (Str. Academiei 14, Bucharest 1; tel. (21) 314-35-08; fax (21) 315-69-90; e-mail chitesu@fmi .unibuc.ro; internet www.unibuc.ro/ro/fac_fmat_ro):

ALBU, T., Algebra
ATANASIU, A., Theoretical Computer Science
BĂDESCU, L., Geometry
BOBOC, N., Mathematical Analysis
BUCUR, GH., Mathematical Analysis
CAMENSCHI, G., Mechanics and Equations
CĂZĂNESCU, V., Theoretical Computer Science
CHIȚESCU, I., Mathematical Analysis
CRISTEA, M., Mathematical Analysis
CUCULESCU, I., Probability Theory, Statistics and Operational Research
DĂSCĂLESCU, S., Algebra
DINCĂ, G. I., Mechanics and Equations
DUMITRESCU, M., Probability Theory, Statistics and Operational Research
GEORGESCU, G., Theoretical Computer Science
GEORGESCU, H., Computer Science
IANUȘ, S., Geometry
IFTIMIE, V., Mechanics and Equations
ION, I., Algebra
IONESCU, P., Algebraic Geometry
MIHĂILĂ, I., Mechanics and Equations
MILITARU, G., Algebra
MIRICĂ, S., Mechanics and Equations
MITRANA, V., Theoretical Computer Science
NĂSTĂSESCU, C., Algebra
NICOLESCU, L., Geometry
NIȚĂ, C., Algebra
POPA, N., Mathematical Analysis
POPESCU, D., Algebra
POPESCU, I., Information Technology
POPESCU, L., Informatics
PREDA, V., Probability Theory, Statistics and Operational Research
PROPOAIE, G., Geometry
RUDEANU, S. A., Computer Science
SABAC, M., Mathematical Analysis
ȘANDRU, N., Mechanics and Equations
ȘTEFĂNESCU, A., Probability Theory, Statistics and Operational Research
ȘTEFĂNESCU, GH., Computer Science
STRĂTILĂ ȘERBAN, V., Mathematical Analysis
ȚIGOIU, S., Mechanics and Equations
TOMESCU, I., Computer Science
TUDOR, C., Probability Theory, Statistics and Operational Research
VĂDUVA, I., Statistics and Stochastic Models

Faculty of Letters (Str. Edgar Quinet 5–7, Bucharest 1; tel. (21) 313-43-36; fax (21) 313-43-36; internet www.unibuc.ro/ro/fac_litr_ro):

ANGELESCU, S., Folklore
ANGHELESCU, M., Romanian Literature
BĂLTĂCEANU, I., Hebrew Studies
BANCIU, D., Communication and Public Relations
BERCIU, A., College of Administration
BIDU VRÂNCEANU, A., Romanian Language
BRÎNCUȘI, GR., Romanian Language
CAZIMIR, ȘT., Romanian Literature
CHIVU, GH., Romanian Language
CONSTANTINESCU, N., Folklore
CORNEA, L. P., Romanian Literature
DINDELEGAN, G., Romanian Language
DINU, M. C., Communication and Public Relations
DOCA, GH., Romanian Language
DOMINTE, C., Romanian Language
FILIPAȘ, E., Romanian Literature
FORASCU, N., Romanian Language
GANĂ, G., Romanian Literature
GRIGORESCU, D., Comparative Literature
GUȚU ROMALO, V., Romanian Language
HANȚĂ, A., Romanian Literature
HRISTEA, TH., Romanian Language
MANOLESCU, N. A., Romanian Literature
MANZAS, Z., Romanian Language
MARTIN, M. A., Theory of Literature
MAZILU, D. H., Romanian Literature
MELIAN, A., Romanian Literature
MICU, D., Romanian Literature
MIHĂILESCU, F., Romanian Literature
MORARU, M., Romanian Language
MUNTEANU, R., Comparative Literature
NEGRICI, E., Romanian Literature
NICULESCU, F., Romanian Language
REGNEALA, M., Communication and Public Relations
RUXANDOIU, L., Romanian Language
SARAMANDU, N., Romanian Language
ȘERBAN, I. V., European Studies
SIMION, E., Romanian Literature
SLAMA CAZACU, T., Romanian Language
SPIRIDON, M., Communication and Public Relations
STOICA, I., Library and Information Science
TĂNĂSESCU, A., Theory of Literature
VRÂNCEANU, A., Romanian Language
ZAMFIR, M., Romanian Literature

Faculty of Orthodox Theology (Str. Sfânta Ecaterina 2, Bucharest 4; tel. (21) 335-07-75; fax (21) 335-41-83; internet www.unibuc.ro/stuffteologie-romano-catolic):

CORNIȚESCU, C., Biblical Theology, Cultural Heritage and Church Painting
CORNIȚESCU, E., Biblical Theology, Cultural Heritage and Church Painting
DAVID, P., Systematic Theology
DURA, N., Practical Theology
IONIȚĂ, V., Church History
MOLDOVEANU, N., Practical Theology
NECULA, N., Practical Theology
RĂDUCĂ, P., Systematic Theology
RUS, R., Systematic Theology

Faculty of Philosophy (Splaiul Independenței 204, Bucharest 5; tel. (21) 410-29-59; fax (21) 411-52-89; e-mail matei@fil.unibuc.ro; internet www.unibuc.ro/ro/fac_filozof_ro):

BĂNȘOIU, I., History of Philosophy and Philosophy of Culture
DUMITRU, M., Logic and Theoretical Philosophy
FLONTA, M., Logic and Theoretical Philosophy
IANOȘI, I., History of Philosophy and Philosophy of Culture
ILIESCU, A., Political and Moral Philosophy
MORAR, V., History of Philosophy and Philosophy of Culture
MUREȘAN, V., Political and Moral Philosophy

PÂRVU, I., Logic and Theoretical Philosophy
STOIANOVICI, D., Logic and Theoretical Philosophy
SURDU, A., History of Philosophy and Philosophy of Culture
TONOIU, V., Logic and Theoretical Philosophy
ȚURLEA, M., Logic and Theoretical Philosophy
VIERU, S., Political and Moral Philosophy
VLĂDUȚESCU, GH., History of Philosophy and Philosophy of Culture

Faculty of Physics (Str. Atomistilor 405, 077125 Platforma Magurele, Bucharest; tel. (21) 457-44-18; fax (21) 457-44-18; e-mail Secretariat@fizic.unibuc.ro; internet www.fizica.unibuc.ro):

ALEXANDRU, H., Solid State Physics
ANGELESCU, T., Nuclear Physics and Particle Physics
ANTOHE, ST., Electricity, Solid State Physics
ARMEANU, I., Mathematical Physics
BEȘLIU, C., Nuclear Physics
BORȘAN, D., Atmospheric Physics
BRÂNCUȘ, D., Solid State Physics
CIOBANU, GH., Statistical Physics and Thermodynamics
CONSTANTINESCU, A., Nuclear Physics, Computational Physics
CONSTANTINESCU, L. M., Physics of Polymers
COSTESCU, A., Theoretical Physics
COTFAS, N., Mathematical Physics
DOLOCAN, V., Solid State Physics, Electrophysics
DRAGOMAN, D., Solid State Physics
DULIU, O., Nuclear Physics
FLORESCU, V., Quantum Mechanics
GEORGESCU, L., Polymer Physics
GHIORDĂNESCU, N., Nuclear Physics
GHEORGHE, V., Biophysics
GRECU, V., Atomic Physics
IONESCU, A., Atomic Physics
IOVA, I., Optics, Spectroscopy
JIPA, A., Relativistic Nuclear Physics
LAZANU, I., Nuclear Physics
LICEA, I., Solid State Physics
MARIAN, T., Quantum Mechanics
MIHUL, A., Nuclear Physics
MUNTEANU, I., Solid State Physics
MUTIHAC, R., Electricity
NENCIU, GH., Quantum Mechanics
PĂTRAȘCU, ȘT., Earth Physics
PLĂVIȚU, C., Molecular Physics, Polymers
POPA-NIȚA, V., Polymer Physics
POPESCU, A., Biophysics
POPESCU, F., Atomic Physics
POPESCU, I., Optics, Spectroscopy, Plasma, Lasers
RĂDUȚĂ, A., Theoretical Physics
REVEICA, I. M., Nuclear Physics
RUXANDRA, V., Electricity
SIMA, O., Nuclear Physics
ȘTEFĂNESCU, D., Mathematical Physics
TOADER, E., Optics, Plasma Physics
TUDOR, T., Optics, Lasers, Holography
TURCU, G., Biophysics
TURBATU, S., Mathematical Physics
VLĂDUCĂ, G., Nuclear Physics

Faculty of Political Sciences (Str. Sfântul Ștefan 24, Bucharest 2; tel. (21) 310-08-94; fax (21) 312-53-78; e-mail fspub@fspub.ro):

ANDREESCU, Ș., International Relations
BARBU, D., Political Sciences
FIDULU, P., International Relations
MELEȘCANU, T., International Relations
MOTOC, I., International Relations
PREDA, C., Political Sciences
STOICA, G., Political Sciences
VLAD, L., International Relations

Faculty of Psychology and Education (B-dul Iuliu Maniu 1–3, A Building, 5th Fl.,

Bucharest 6; tel. (21) 410-27-40; fax (21) 411-68-90; internet www.unibuc.ro/ro/fac_fpse_ro):

CREȚU, T., Psychology
CRISTEA, S., Teacher Training
ENĂCHESCU, S., Special Education
FĂTU, S., Teacher Training
LERGHIT, I., Education
MITROFAN, I., Psychology
MITROFAN, N., Psychology
NEACȘU, I., Education
NICOLESCU, V., Education
PĂUN, E., Education
POPESCU, E., Education
POTOLEA, D., Education
RĂȘCANU, R., Psychology
ROCO, M., Psychology
SCHIOPU, U., Psychology
STANCIU, I., Education
TOMȘA, G., Education
VERZA, E., Special Education
ZLATE, M., Psychology

Faculty of Public Administration (tel. (21) 312-49-31; fax (21) 312-16-50; e-mail mihaela.dutulescu@drept.unibuc.ro):

BUCUR, I., Public Administration
CORNESCU, V., Public Administration

Faculty of Roman Catholic Theology and Social Work (Str. General Berthelot 19, Bucharest 1; tel. (21) 314-86-10; fax (21) 314-86-10; internet www.unibuc.ro/stuff/teologie-romano-catolica):

FERENȚ, E., Theology
MĂRTINCĂ, I., Theology
PETERCĂ, V., Theology
ROBU, I., Theology

Faculty of Sociology and Social Work (Str. Schitu Magureanu 9, Bucharest 5; tel. (21) 315-31-22; fax (21) 315-83-91; e-mail secretar@sas.unibuc.ro; internet www.sas.swork.unibuc.ro):

ABRAHAM, P., Social Work
ANGHEL, P., Social Work
BĂDESCU, I., Sociology
CHELCEA, S., Sociology
DRĂGAN, I., Sociology
GEANĂ, GH., Sociology
GHEȚĂU, V., Sociology
LARIONESCU, M., Sociology
MĂRGINEAN, I., Sociology
MIHĂILESCU, I., Sociology
SANDU, D., Sociology
VOINEA, M., Sociology
ZAMFIR, C., Sociology
ZAMFIR, E., Social Work

UNIVERSITATEA 'CONSTANTIN BRÂNCUSI' DIN TÂRGU JIU

Bdul Republicii 1, Târgu Jiu
Telephone: (253) 21-43-07
Fax: (253) 21-57-94
E-mail: univ@utgjiu.ro
Internet: www.utgjiu.ro
State control

Rector: Prof. Dr ADRIAN GORUN
Prorector: Prof. Dr Ing. ONISIFOR OLARU

FACULTIES

Faculty of Engineering (Str. Geneva 3, Targu-Jiu; tel. (253) 21-35-09; fax (253) 21-44-62; e-mail ing@utgjiu.ro; internet www.utgjiu.ro/ing):

Faculty of Law and Administration (Str. Victoriei 24, Targu-Jiu; tel. (253) 21-92-68; fax (253) 21-92-41; e-mail fsj@utgjiu.ro; internet www.utgjiu.ro/fsj):

Faculty of Economics (Str. Victoriei 24, Targu-Jiu; tel. (253) 21-10-12; fax (253) 21-

30-12; e-mail fse@utgjiu.ro; internet www
.utgjiu.ro/fse_new):

Faculty of Physical Education and Sport (Str.
Victoriei 24, Targu-Jiu; tel. (253) 21-43-07;
fax (253) 21-57-97; e-mail fefs@utgjiu.ro;
internet www.utgjiu.ro/fefs):

Faculty of Letters and Social Sciences (Str.
Grivitei 1, Targu-Jiu; tel. (253) 21-44-52; fax
(253) 21-44-52; e-mail flss@utgjiu.ro; internet
www.utgjiu.ro/flss):

Dept of Mathematics (Str. Geneva 3, Targu-
Jiu; tel. (253) 21-35-09; fax (253) 21-44-62;
e-mail math@utgjiu.ro; internet www.utgjiu
.ro/math):

UNIVERSITATEA DIN CRAIOVA

Str. A. I. Cuza 13, 200585 Craiova
Telephone: (251) 41-43-98
Fax: (251) 41-16-88
E-mail: relint@central.ucv.ro
Internet: www.central.ucv.ro

Founded 1947
State control
Academic year: October to July

Rector: ION VLADIMIRESCU
Vice-Rectors: NICU PANEA, DUMITRU TOPAN,
RADU CONSTANTINESCU, LUCIAN BUŞE
Scientific Sec.: DAN CLAUDIU DANISOR
Gen. Sec.: MIRCEA ZĂVĂLEANU
Librarian: OCTAVIAN LOHON

Library: see Libraries
Number of teachers: 1,200
Number of students: 25,000

Publications: *University Bulletin* (annual, in
16 series according to subject), *Revista de
Stiinte Juridice, Studii si Cercetari de
Onomastica, Viitorul, Revista Forum Geo-
grafic – Studii si Cercetari de Geografie si
Protectia Mediului*

DEANS
Faculty of Mathematics and Computer
Science: DUMITRU BUSNEAG
Faculty of Chemistry: MIRCEA PREDA
Faculty of Physics: ECATERINA MARINESCY
Faculty of Letters: CRISTIANA TEODORESCU
Faculty of History, Philosophy and Geogra-
phy: VLADIMIR OSIAC
Faculty of Law: SORIN IOANESCU
Faculty of Econ.: CONSTANTIN TUMBAR
Faculty of Electrotechnology: ELEONOR STOE-
NESCU
Faculty of Automation, Computers and Elec-
tronics: DAN POPESCU
Faculty of Electromechanics: ALEXANDRU
BITOLEANU
Faculty of Mechanics: MARINA BICĂ
Faculty of Horticulture: ION OLTEANU
Faculty of Agriculture: MIRCEA BADESCU
Faculty of Theology: STEFAN RESCEANU
Faculty of Physical Education and Sports:
CORNELIU STROE
Faculty of Economic Sciences of Dobreta-
Turnu Severin: AUREL PIŢURCĂ
Faculty of Eng. and Management of Techno-
logical Systems of Dobreta-Turnu Severin:
MIHAIL MANGRA

PROFESSORS
Faculty of Mathematics and Computer
Science (tel. (251) 41-37-28; fax (251) 41-26-
73; e-mail facmatinf@central.ro; internet inf
.ucv.ro):

AVRAMESCU, C., Differential Equations
BĂLAN, T., Special Mathematics
BUSNEAG, D., Algebra
DINCĂ, AL., Algebra, Formal Languages
KESSLER, P., Mathematical Analysis
LEONTE, A., Theory of Probability

MURĂRESCU, G., Geometry
NICULESCU, C., Mathematical Analysis
RĂDULESCU, V., Differential Equations
TANDAREANU, N., Systems, Informatics
VLADIMIRESCU, I., Statistics
VRACIU, G., Algebra

Faculty of Chemistry (107 Calea Bucureşti
St, 200479 Craiova; tel. and fax (251) 59-70-
48; e-mail office@chimie.ucv.ro; internet
chimie.ucv.ro):

BLEJOIU, S., Physical Chemistry
FLOREA, S., Organic Chemistry
GLODEANU, E., Organic Chemistry, Bio-
chemistry
MARINESCU, G., Organic Chemistry, Bio-
chemistry
MUREŞAN, N., Chemistry
MUREŞAN, V., Inorganic Chemistry
PLENICEANU, M., Analytical Chemistry
POPESCU, A., Analytical Chemistry
PREDA, M., Physical Chemistry

Faculty of Physics (tel. and fax (251) 41-50-
77; e-mail fizica@central.ucv.ro; internet
fizica.ucv.ro):

BIZDADEA, C., Classical Mechanics, Analy-
tical Mechanics
SOCACIU, M., Liquid Crystals, Dielectrics
ULIU, F., Coherent Optics
URSACHE, M., Optics, Lasers

Faculty of Letters (tel. (251) 41-44-68; fax
(251) 41-66-88; e-mail litere@central.ucv.ro;
internet www.ucv.ro):

AFANA, E., General Linguistics, Classical
Languages
BEŞTELIU, M., Romanian Literature
DUMITRESCU, E., Romanian Literature
DUMITRASCU, K., General Linguistics, Clas-
sical Languages
FIRAN, F., Romanian Literature
GHIDIRMIC, O., Romanian Literature
ILIESCU, M., French Language
IVĂNUŞ, D., Romanian Language
MAVRODIN, I., French Literature
PANEA, N., Romanian Literature
SORESCU, G., Romanian Literature
SUTEU, F., General Linguistics, Classical
Languages
TRĂISTARU, I., Romanian Literature
TROCAN, D., French Language

Faculty of History, Philosophy and Geography (tel. and fax (251) 41-85-15; e-mail
osiac@central.ucv.ro; internet www.ucv.ro):

BUZATU, GH., History
CEAPRAZ, I., Logics
DOBRINESCU, V., History
OSIAC, V., History
OTOVESCU, D., Sociology
PATROI, I., History

Faculty of Law:

BELU, C., Private Law
DIACONESCU, H., Public Law
DOGARU, I., Private Law
GAINA, V., Private Law
NEDELCU, I., Public Administration
NICULEANU, C., Public Law
PREDESCU, B., Private Law
SĂMBRIAN, T., Private Law
SANDU, A., Public Administration
SCURTU, S., Private Law
TĂNĂSESCU, I., Public Law

Faculty of Economic Sciences (tel. and fax
(251) 41-13-17; e-mail stec@central.ucv.ro;
internet stec.central.ucv.ro):

BĂBEANU, M., Political Economics
BĂRBĂCIORU, V., Financial Accountancy
BICA, F., Languages for Computer Pro-
grammes
BUSE, L., Economic and Financial Analysis
CIURLĂU, C., Macroeconomic Analysis
CONSTANTINESCU, D., Industrial Manage-
ment and Organization
DRAGOMIR, G., Management
FOTA, C., International Economic Relations

GEORGESCU, P., Statistics
HOBEANU, T., Management
LOLESCU, J., History of the National Econ-
omy
MARIN, E., Political Economics
MEGLISAN, GH., Marketing
MITROI, N., Informatics
NISTORESCU, T., Management
OPRITESCU, M., Currency and Credits
PÂRVU, V., History of Economics
PIRVU, G., Political Economics
POPA, A., Investment Efficiency
RADU, F., Economic Activities of Industrial
Units
RICU, L., Informatics
ROŞU-HAMZESCU, I., International Eco-
nomic Relations
STAICU, C., Accountancy
STEFAN, V., History of Economics
STEFANESCU, I., Informatics
TORNIŢĂ, I., Prices and Competitiveness
TRANDAFIR, D., Accountancy
TRAŞCĂ, M., Accountancy
TUMBĂR, C., Management
VANCEA, I., Statistics
VASILESCU, N., Statistics

Faculty of Electrotechnology:

ARON, I., Basic Electrical Engineering
BADEA, M., Basic Electrical Engineering
CIVIDJAN, G., Electrical Apparatus
FETIŢĂ, I., Basic Electrical Engineering
LUNGU, R., Basic Electrical Engineering
MIRCEA, I., Power Plants
PUŞCAŞU, S., Basic Electrical Engineering
TOPAN, D., Basic Electrical Engineering
TUSALIU, P., Electrical Apparatus

Faculty of Automatics, Computers and Electronics:

AMBROZIE, C., Electric and Electronic Mea-
surement
BURDESCU, D., Data Structures
IVĂNESCU, M., Discrete Industrial Auto-
matics
MARIAN, GH., Computer Programming
MARIN, C., Automatic Regulators
NICULESCU, E., Electrical Devices
RĂSVAN, V., Theory of Automatic Systems
VÎNĂTORU, M., Ruling Systems for Contin-
uous Industrial Processes

Faculty of Electromechanics:

BRITOLEANU, A., Electrical Drives
CAMPEANU, A., Electrical Machinery
CIOC, I., Design and Building of Electrical
Machinery
DEGERATU, P., Automatization of Electrical
Machinery
DRAGANESCU, O., Electrical Machinery
FLORIGANŢĂ, G., Design and Building of
Electrical Machinery
MANOLEA, G., Electromechanics
NICA, C., Electrical Machinery
NICOLA, D., Electrical Machinery and Elec-
trical Traction
SAVIUC, V., Special Machinery
VINTILĂ, N., Electrical Machinery

Faculty of Mechanics:

CARAMAVRU, N., Thermotechnics and Ther-
mic Machinery
CERNĂIANU, E., Resistance of Materials
ENE, AL., Descriptive Geometry and Draw-
ing
MANGRA, M., Science of Materials
POPESCU, I., Mechanisms
ŞONTEA, S., Technology
TÎRPE, GH., Technology of Machine Build-
ing

Faculty of Horticulture:

ANTON, D., Floriculture
BALASA, M., Vegetable Garden
BOBIRNAC, B., Plant Protection
COSTESCU, C., Entomology
GHEORGHIŢĂ, M., Oenology
GLODEANU, C., Phytopathology

GODEANU, I., General Pomiculture
MILITIU, I., Tropical Horticulture
OLTEANU, I., General Viticulture
POPA, A., Microbiology
ROSU, L., Horticultural Technology
SORESCU, C., Anatomy of Vertebrates
TUȚĂ, V., Viticulture
ZĂVOI, A., Plant Improvement

Faculty of Agriculture:

GĂNGIOVEANU, I., Agrotechnology
IONESCU, I., Meadow Cultivation
MARIN, A., Agrochemistry
MATEI, I., Agrotechnics
MOCANU, R., Agrochemistry
PANĂ, D., Management
NICOLESCU, M., Phytotechnics
POP, L., Agrotechnics
ȘOROP, G., Pedology
VASILE, D., Pedology
VOICA, N., Genetics

Faculty of Theology:

BUZERA, A., Ritual
DAMASCHIN, C., History of the Romanian Orthodox Church
IRINEU, P., Dogmatic and Symbolistic Theology

UNIVERSITATEA 'DUNAREA DE JOS' DIN GALAȚI

Str. Domnească 47, 800008 Galați
Telephone: (236) 41-36-02
Fax: (236) 46-13-53
Internet: www.ugal.ro

Founded 1948, Univ. status 1974
State control
Languages of instruction: Romanian, English, French
Academic year: October to July

Rector: ALEXANDRU EPUREANU
Pro-Rectors: Prof. MIRCEA BULANCEA, Prof. EMIL CONSTANTIN, Prof. VIOREL MINZU, Assoc. Prof. DANIELA SARPE
Registrar: BEATRICE BIANCA DRAȘOVEAN
Librarian: MIOARA VONCILA

Number of teachers: 583
Number of students: 8,869

DEANS

Faculty of Econ. and Admin. Sciences: EMILIA TANASESCU
Faculty of Eng. in Brăila: ADRIAN GOANTA
Faculty of Food Science, Aquaculture and Fisheries: PETRU ALEXE
Faculty of Letters, History and Theology: NICOLAE IOANA
Faculty of Mechanical Eng.: PANAIT TANASE
Faculty of Metallurgy and Materials Science: NICOLAE CANANAU
Faculty of Naval and Electrical Eng.: ADRIAN FILIPESCU
Faculty of Physical Education and Sport: TOMA BADIU
Faculty of Sciences: ION MIRICA

PROFESSORS

Faculty of Economics and Administrative Sciences:

COSTESCU, C., Management
GEORGESCU, T., World Economy
OLARU, A., Marketing and Economic Analysis
PANȚIRU, P., Political Economy
PĂTRAȘC, A., Management in Industry
STOICA, A., Political Economy
VRABIE, D., Psychology and Education

Faculty of Engineering (in Brăila):

AXINTI, G., Hydraulic Equipment
BRATU, P., Engineering Mechanics and Vibration
CONSTANTINESCU, F., Civil Engineering
OPROESCU, GH., Cutting

Faculty of Food Science, Aquaculture and Fisheries:

ADAM, A., Fishing Materials, Mechanization in Pisciculture
BANU, C., Meat Technology
BORDEI, D., Baking Technology and Equipment
BULANCEA, M., Oenology
COSTIN, G. M., Milk Technology
CULACHE, D., Technology of Sugar Production
DAN, V., Microbiology
HOPULELE, T., Fermentation Technology and Equipment
MORARU, C., Mill Bread Processing
RĂUȚA, M., Hydrology and Oceanography
ROTARU, G., Milk Technology and Equipment
TOFAN, I., Cereals and Flour Preservation
VASILESCU, G., Hydrobiology, Aquatic Exploitation, Biological Non-piscatorial Resources

Faculties of Letters, History and Theology:

BARNA, D., Education
BRUDIU, M., Ancient Romanian History
CANDEA, I., Medieval History
CIOCALTAN, V., Medieval World History
CROITORU, M., Modern Foreign Languages and Literature
DIMA, T., Logic and Epistemology
DUMISTRACEL, C., Social Anthropology
LICA, V., Ancient World History
ONISORU, G., Contemporary World History
SANDRU, D., Contemporary Romanian History
TIUTIUCA, D., Comparative Literature
TOFAN, S., Philosophy of Culture and Hermeneutics
ȚURLAN, V., Linguistics
VOICU, V., History of Philosophy

Faculty of Mechanical Engineering:

ANDREI, V., Mechanics of Fluids and Hydraulic Machines
BALAN, G., Mechanics
BARSAN, I. G., Vibrations and Friction
CHIRICA, I., Resistance of Materials
CONSTANTIN, E., Machine Tool Design, Equipment and Welded Constructions
CONSTANTIN, V., Machine Parts and Mechanisms
CRUDU, I., Machine Design, Tribology
DUMITRU, G., Internal Combustion Engines
EPUREANU, A., Machine Building Technology
FĂLTICEANU, C., Mechanics, Strength, Machine Parts
GEORGESCU, V., Pressure Welding Technology
GHEORGHIU, C., Design and Structure of Internal Combustion Engines
IONIȚĂ, I., Steam Boilers and Thermal Equipment
IORDACHESCU, D., Industrial Robots and Welding
IOSIFESCU, C., Refrigeration Techniques
JĂSCANU, M., Machine Parts
MATULEA, I., Mechanics and Vibrations
MITU, S., Machine Tools
MODIGA, M., Ship Structures
MUȘAT, S., Mechanics
OANCEA, N., Cutting and Surface Generation
PALAGHIAN, L., Machine Parts
PANAIT, T., Turbines
PÂNTURU, D., Food Equipment
PORNEALA, S., Heat Pumps
STEFANESCU, I., Machine Parts
STOICESCU, L., Strength of Materials
TARĂU, I., Quality Control
TĂRU, E., Tool-cutting Design

Faculty of Metallurgy and Materials Science:

DRUGESCU, E., Physical Metallurgy and Heat Treatments
GROȘU, V., Metallurgical Implements

MITOSERIU, O., Crystallography and Mineralogy

Faculty of Naval and Electrical Engineering:

BUMBARU, S., Computer Programming and Artificial Intelligence
CĂLUEANU, D., Electrical Engineering and Electrical Machines
CEANGĂ, E., Electronics and Automation
CEANGĂ, V., Shipboard Installations
MODIGA, M., Ship Structure
POPOVICI, O., Shipbuilding
VASILESCU, A., Hydromechanics

Faculty of Physical Education and Sport:

BALAIS, F., Volleyball
SÂRBU, D., Physical Education

UNIVERSITATEA ECOLOGICA DIN BUCURESTI
(Ecological University of Bucharest)

Str. Franceza 22, 030104 Bucharest
Telephone: (21) 312-12-50
Fax: (21) 315-77-30
E-mail: rectorat@ueb.ro
Internet: www.ueb.ro

Founded 1990
Private control

Rector: Prof. Dr MIRCEA DUTU.

UNIVERSITATEA 'EFTIMIE MURGU' REȘIȚA

Piața Traian Vuia 1–4, Reșița
Telephone: (255) 21-02-27
Fax: (255) 21-02-30
Internet: www.uem.ro
State control

Faculties of Eng., Admin. and economic sciences.

UNIVERSITATEA 'LUCIAN BLAGA' DIN SIBIU
(Lucian Blaga University of Sibiu)

Bdul Victoriei 10, 550024 Sibiu
Telephone: (269) 21-60-62
Fax: (269) 21-78-87
Internet: www.ulbsibiu.ro

Founded 1990
State control
Academic year: October to June

Rector: Prof. Dr DUMITRU CIOCOI-POP
Vice-Rectors: Prof. Dr VIOREL FLOREA, Prof. Dr CONSTANTIN OPREAN, Prof. Dr DOINA PETICĂ-ROMAN
Dir-Gen.: Econ. EMANOIL MUSCALU
Scientific Sec. to the Senate: Prof. Dr GHEORGHE DORIN STOICESCU

Library of 475,000 vols
Number of teachers: 486
Number of students: 8,940 (8,573 undergraduate, 367 postgraduate)

DEANS

Faculty of Eng.: Prof. Dr DAN MANIU-DUȘE
Faculty of Food and Textile Processing Technology: Prof. Dr VASILE JĂSCANU
Faculty of Law and Public Admin.: Prof. Dr IOAN SANTAI
Faculty of Letters, History and Journalism: Prof. Dr NICOLAE JURCA
Faculty of Medicine: Assoc. Prof. ILIE CRĂCIUN
Faculty of Sciences: Prof. Dr DAN POPESCU
Faculty of Theology: Prof. Dr Rev. MIRCEA PĂCURARIU
Univ. College: Prof. Dr NICOLAE TODERICIU (Dir)

UNIVERSITATEA NATIONALA DE ARTE BUCUREŞTI
(National University of Arts Bucharest)

Str. Gl. Budişteanu 19, 010773 Bucharest
Telephone: (21) 312-51-97
Fax: (21) 312-54-29
E-mail: rectorat@unarte.ro
Internet: www.unarte.ro

Founded 1864 as Scoala Nationala de Arte Frumoase
Academic year: October to June
State control

Rector: Dr RUXANDRA DEMETRESCU
Chancellor: Dr CATALIN BALESCU

Library: see Libraries and Archives
Number of teachers: 274
Number of students: 1,000

Depts of Ceramics, glass and metal, Design (industrial and graphic), Graphic fine art, History and theory of art, Mural art, Painting, Pedagogy of art, Photography, video and new media, Sculpture, Stage design and scenography, Textile arts, Work of art restoration

DEANS

Faculty of Fine Arts: MIHAIL MANESCU
Faculty of Applied Arts and Design: ALEXANDRU GHILDUS
Faculty of Art History and Theory: CORINA POPA

UNIVERSITATEA NAŢIONALĂ DE MUZICĂ DIN BUCUREŞTI

Ştirbei Vodă 33, 010102 Bucharest
Telephone: (21) 314-63-41
Fax: (21) 314-63-41
E-mail: international@unmb.ro
Internet: www.unmb.ro

Founded 1864
Languages of instruction: Romanian, English
Languages of instruction: French, German
Academic year: October to July

Rector: Prof. Dr DAN BUCIU
Pro-Rectors: Prof. Dr DOREL PAŞCU RĂDULESCU, Prof. Dr VALENTINA SANDU-DEDIU

Library of 249,000
Number of teachers: 165
Number of students: 1,230 (full-time)

Depts of Composition, Musicology, Music theory, Conducting (orchestra and choir) and church music, General piano, Keyboard instruments, Stringed instruments, Wind and brass instruments and percussion, Chamber music and orchestral ensemble, Vocal studies and opera direction

DEANS

Faculty of Composition, Musicology and Musical Education: Prof. Dr THEODOR TUTUIANU
Faculty of Performing Arts: Prof. Dr SERBAN DIMITRIE SOREANU

UNIVERSITATEA DE NORD, BAIA MARE
(University of the North, Baia Mare)

Str. Victor Babes 62A, 430083 Baia Mare
Telephone: (262) 42-27-78
Fax: (262) 27-61-53
E-mail: dcpeter@ubm.ro
Internet: www.ubm.ro

Founded 1961 as Institute of Higher Education; univ. status 1990
State control
Academic year: October to June

Rector: Prof. Dr DAN CALIN PETER
Vice-Rectors: Prof. Dr NICOLAE FELCAN, NICOLAE POP

Chief Sec.: MARIANA DOBRA
Chief Librarian: MAXIM MARIA
Library of 217,000 vols
Number of teachers: 216
Number of students: 4,500

Publications: *Scientific Bulletin of Philology, Scientific Bulletin of Foreign Languages, Scientific Bulletin of Pedagogy, Psychology and Methodology, Scientific Bulletin of Philosophy and Theology, The Maramureş Orthodoxy, Scientific Bulletin of Economics, Scientific Bulletin of Mathematics and Informatics, Proceedings of the Mathematical Creativity Seminar, Scientific Bulletin of Chemistry and Biology, Physics Journal, Scientific Bulletin of Electrotechnology, Electronics, Automation, Scientific Bulletin of Tribology and Machine Construction Technology*

DEANS

Faculty of Eng.: Prof. Dr RADU COTETIU
Faculty of Letters: Prof. Dr GEORGETA CORNITA
Faculty of Mineral Resources and Environment: Prof. Dr NICOLAE BĂNCILĂ-AFRIM
Faculty of Sciences: Assoc. Prof. Dr VASILE VIMAN
Univ. College: Prof. Dr CEZAR TOADER

PROFESSORS

Faculty of Engineering:

COTETIU, R. CRACIUN, I. FILIP, D. LOBONTIU, M. NASUI, V. PAY, E. PETER, D. C. PEREAN, L. TIPLEA, V. TISAN, V. TOADER, C.

Faculty of Letters (Str. Victoriei 76, 430122 Baia Mare):

CORNITA, G.
FELECAN, N.
GLODEANU, G.
IANCU, V.
ISTRATE, A.
OLOS, A.

Faculty of Mineral Resources and Environment:

BANCILA-AFRIM, N. OROS, V.

Faculty of Sciences (Str. Victoriei 76, 430122 Baia Mare):

ARDELEAN, G.
BERINDE, V.
HUTIRA, T.
MORAR, G.
POP, I.

UNIVERSITATEA DIN ORADEA
(University of Oradea)

Str. Armatei Române 5, 410087 Oradea
Telephone: (259) 43-28-89
Fax: (259) 43-27-89
E-mail: rectorat@uoradea.ro
Internet: www.uoradea.ro

Founded 1990
State control
Academic year: October to July

Rector: Prof. Dr Ing. TEODOR MAGHIAR
Vice-Rectors: Prof. Dr NICOLAE JOSAN, Prof. Dr PAUL MAGHERU, Assoc. Prof. Dr IOAN MANG, Prof. Dr IOAN PUSCAS
Scientific Sec.: Assoc. Prof. Dr Ing. CORNEL ANTAL
Gen. Admin. Dir: Ing. VIOREL GHERGHELEŞ
Number of teachers: 1,237
Number of students: 33,000

DEANS

Faculty of Architecture and Construction: Dr VASILE MITREA
Faculty of Letters: Prof. Dr IOAN DERŞIDAN
Faculty of Social Humanistic Science: Prof. Dr FLORICA CHIPEA

Faculty of Physical Education and Sport: Assoc. Prof. Dr IACOB HANŢIU
Faculty of History and Geography: Prof. Dr BARBU ŞTEFĂNESCU
Faculty of Political Science and Communication Sciences: Prof. Dr LIA POP
Faculty of Science: Prof. Dr TEODOR JURCUŢ
Faculty of Electrotechnics and Informatics: Prof. Dr Ing. TEODOR LEUCA
Faculty of Management and Technological Engineering: Prof. Dr Ing. IOAN EUGEN RADU
Faculty of Energy Eng.: Prof. Dr Ing. IOAN FELEA
Faculty of Medicine and Pharmacy: Prof. Dr MIRCEA IFRIM
Faculty of Orthodox Theology: Archdeacon Prof. Dr CONSTANTIN VOICU
Faculty of Econ.: Prof. Dr GHEORGHE OLAH
Faculty of Law and Jurisprudence: Assoc. Prof. Dr OVIDIU ŢINCA
Faculty of Environmental Protection: Prof. Dr VASILE BARA
Faculty of Fine Arts: Assoc. Prof. CORNELIU T. DURGHEU
Faculty of Music: Prof. Dr AVRAM GEOLDEŞ
Faculty of Textiles and Leatherwork: Prof. Dr Ing. VASILE IOVAN
Univ. College of Technology, Econ. and Admin.: Prof. Dr Ing. DINU MIRCEA FODOR
Univ. Medical College: Prof. Dr MIRCEA IFRIM
Univ. College of Education: Dr IOAN SABĂU
Teacher Training Dept: Prof. Dr VASILE MARCU
Dept of Distance Learning Education: Assoc. Prof. Dr ANCA DODESCU

UNIVERSITATEA OVIDIUS CONSTANŢA

Bdul Mamaia 124, Constanţa
Aleea Universitatii 1, 900527 Constanţa
Telephone and fax: (241) 61-83-72
E-mail: intaff@univ-ovidius.ro
Internet: www.univ-ovidius.ro

Founded 1990
State control

Rector: Prof. VICTOR CIUPINA
Vice-Rectors: Prof. TASIM GEMIL, Prof. NICULAE PERIDE, Prof. VICTOR PLOAE

Number of teachers: 857
Number of students: 16,702

DEANS

Faculty of Letters: ADINA CIUGUREANU
Faculty of Theology: MARIANA JUGANARU
Faculty of History: WLADIMIR GEORGES BOSKOFF
Faculty of Law and Public Admin.: DANUT MANDALOPOL
Faculty of Economic Sciences: GEORGE STANCULESCU
Faculty of Physics: DRAGOMIR COPREAN
Faculty of Chemistry: ANA RODICA STAICULESCU
Faculty of Petroleum Technology: MARIAN COJOC
Faculty of Mathematics and Informatics: MACEDON TEODOSIE
Faculty of Natural Sciences: PETRE BORDEI
Faculty of Sports: IONEL NICOLAE
Faculty of General Medicine: VIRGIL BREABAN
Faculty of Dental Medicine and Pharmacy: CORNELIU AMARIEI
Faculty of Arts: ANCA DRAGU
Faculty of Pedagogy: FLORENTA MARINESCU

ATTACHED RESEARCH INSTITUTES

Center for Interdisciplinary Research on Micro and Nanostructures.

Center for Applied Mathematics.

Center for Research of the Black Sea History and Civilisation during the 19th to 21st Centuries.

Center for Research on Modern Technologies of Depollution and Waste Management.

Center for Research on Economy and Business Administration.

Center for Research on Oral Health.

Center for Advanced Engineering Sciences: organized under the framework of the Black Sea Universities Network.

Center of Excellency on Pancreas Islet Cells Transplant in Diabetus Mellitus.

UNIVERSITATEA 'PETROL-GAZE' DIN PLOIEŞTI

Bdul Bucureşti 39, 100680 Ploieşti

Telephone: (244) 57-54-50
Fax: (244) 57-58-47
E-mail: mail@upg-ploiesti.ro
Internet: www.upg-ploiesti.ro

Founded 1948 as Institutul de Petrol şi Gaze; present name 1994
State control
Academic year: October to July

Pres.: Prof. Dr Ing. VLAD ULMANU
Vice-Pres: Prof. Dr Ing. ION BOLOCAN, Prof. Dr Ing. MIHAI PASCU COLOJA, Prof. Dr Ing. LIVIU DUMITRAŞCU, Prof. Dr Ing. GHEORGHE ZECHERU
Librarian: E. DAN

Number of teachers: 750
Number of students: 9,500

DEANS

Faculty of Well-Drilling and Petroleum Reservoir Engineering: Prof. Dr Ing. ION MĂLUREANU
Faculty of Petroleum Technology and Petrochemistry: Assoc. Prof. Dr Ing. PAUL ROSCA
Faculty of Mechanical and Electrical Eng.: Prof. Dr Ing. ION VOICU
Faculty of Letters and Sciences: Assoc. Prof. Dr CHRISTIAN MARINOIU
Faculty of Economical Sciences: Prof. Dr ION IARCA

PROFESSORS

ANGHEL, A.
ANTONESCU, L.
ANTONESCU, N. N.
AVRAM, L.
BADOIU, D.
BALU, I.
BOLOCAN, I.
BUCUR, C.
CARTOAJE, V.
COLOJA, M. P.
CUTU, I.
DUDA, G.
DUMITRASCU, L.
FRUZESCU, D.
GEORGESCU, D.
GEORGESCU, O.
GHEORGHITOIU, M.
GRIGORE, N.
IARCA, I.
IONESCU, M.
IORDACHE, G.
MALUREANU, I.
MARIN, C.
MINESCU, F.
MINESCU, M.
NISTOR, I.
OPREA, M.
PANAIT, G.
PARASCHIV, N.
PATARLAGEANU, M.
PETCU, A.
POPA, C.
ROSCA, P.
SIRO, B.
SOARE, A.
STEFAN, G.
STOICESCU, C. C.

STRATULA, C.
TALLE, V.
TOMESCU, D.
TUDOR, I.
ULMANU, V.
VASILESCU, S.
VOICU, I.
ZECHERU, G.

UNIVERSITATEA DIN PETROŞANI
(University of Petroşani)

Str. Universităţii 20, 332006 Petroşani

Telephone: (254) 54-90-12
Fax: (254) 54-29-94
E-mail: m_georgescu@upet.ro
Internet: www.upet.ro

Founded 1864; became Coal Institute 1948, Mining Institute 1957 and Technical Univ. of Petroşani 1991; present name 1995
State control
Academic year: October to July

Rector: Prof. Dr Eng. NICOLAE DIMA
Vice-Rectors: Prof. Dr Eng. MIRCEA GEORGESCU, Prof. Dr Eng. EMIL POP
Scientific Sec.: Assoc. Prof. Dr Eng. Ec. IOAN CUCU
Chief Registrar: MARIA ZAPARTAN
Librarian: Eng. LUMINIŢA DANCIU

Library of 305,172 vols
Number of teachers: 215
Number of students: 6,341

Publications: Annals of Economics (annual.), Annals of Electrical Engineering (annual), Annals of Mechanical Engineering (annual), Annals of Mining Engineering (annual), Annals of Physics (annual), Annals of Social Sciences (annual), Informative Gazette (monthly), Library's Informative Gazette (quarterly), Mining Magazine (monthly)

DEANS

Faculty of Machine and Electrical Eng.: Prof. Dr Eng. ARON POANTA
Faculty of Mining: Prof. Dr Eng. IOAN DUMITRESCU
Faculty of Science: Assoc. Prof. Dr Eng. ILIE MITRAN
Univ. College: Prof. Dr Eng. MIHAI PASCULESCU (Dir)

UNIVERSITATEA 'PETRU MAIOR' DIN TÂRGU-MUREŞ
(Petru Maior University of Târgu-Mureş)

Str. Nicolae Iorga 1, 540088 Târgu-Mureş

Telephone and fax: .(265) 21-18-38
E-mail: rectorat@upm.ro
Internet: www.upm.ro

Founded 1960
State control
Academic year: October to July

Rector: Prof. Dr. Eng. LIVIU MARIAN
Vice-Rectors: Prof. Dr. Eng. VASILE BOLOS, Assoc. Prof. Dr CĂLIN ENĂCHESCU
Chancellor: Assoc. Prof. Dr CORNEL SIGMIREAN

Library of 120,000 vols,000 periodicals
Number of teachers: 333 (133 full-time, 200 part-time)
Number of students: 6,200

Publications: Buletinul Ştiinţific (annual), Studia Universitatis–Filologia (annual), Studia Universitatis–Istoria (annual)

DEANS

Faculty of Econ. and Admin. Sciences: Assoc. Prof. ZSUZANNA SZABO
Faculty of Eng.: Prof. Dr. Eng. DUMITRU ŞOAITA

Faculty of Sciences and Letters: Prof. Dr IULIAN BOLDEA
Univ. College: Assoc. Prof. Dr MARIA GEORGESCU

UNIVERSITATEA DIN PITEŞTI

Piaţa Gen. V. Milea 1, Piteşti

Telephone: (248) 62-40-00
Fax: (248) 62-22-89
Internet: www.upit.ro
State control

Faculties of Sciences, Eng., Orthodox theology.

UNIVERSITATEA 'ŞTEFAN CEL MARE'
('Stephen the Great' University)

Str. Universităţii 9, 720225 Suceava

Telephone: (230) 52-00-81
Fax: (230) 52-00-80
E-mail: dep.rel.int@eed.usv.ro
Internet: www.usv.ro

Founded 1963 as Pedagogical Institute; became Institute of Higher Education 1976; univ. status 1990
State control
Academic year: October to July

Rector: Prof. ADRIAN GRAUR
Vice-Rector for Academic Services: Prof. EMANUEL DIACONESCU
Vice-Rector for Int. Relations: Prof. SANDA-MARIA ARDELEANU
Vice-Rector for Material Resources: Prof. AUREL BURCIU
Gen. Admin. Dir: Ing. EMIL NECHIFOR
Registrar: Ing. MARIA MUSCĂ
Library Dir: Prof. VASILE DOSPINESCU

Library of 292,000 vols, 2,350 periodicals
Number of teachers: 320
Number of students: 11,573 vols

Publications: Acta Tribologica (annual), Annals (philosophy and socio-human disciplines, geography, philology (literature), philology (linguistics), mechanics, electrical eng., forestry, economic sciences and public admin., education; each annual; annals of univ. college, annual), Atelier de Traduction (twice in a year), ISTECFILO (2 a year), La Lettre 'R' (2 a year)

DEANS

Faculty of Economic Sciences and Public Admin.: Prof. ELENA HLACIUC
Faculty of Education: Assoc. Prof. RODICA NAGY
Faculty of Electrical Eng.: Assoc. Prof. LEON MANDICI
Faculty of Food Eng.: Prof. SONIA GUTT
Faculty of Forestry: Prof. RADU CENUSA
Faculty of History and Geography: Assoc. Prof. MIHAI LAZAR
Faculty of Letters and Communication Sciences: Prof. ION HORIA BIRLEANU
Faculty of Mechanical Eng.: Prof. IOAN MIHAI
Faculty of Physical Education and Sport: PETRU GHERVAN

PROFESSORS

Faculty of Economic Sciences and Public Administration (tel. (230) 52-02-63; fax (230) 52-02-63):

BURCIU, A.
HLACIUC, E.
PRELIPCEAN, G.
SANDU, G.

Faculty of Education Sciences (tel. (230) 21-61-47; fax (230) 52-00-80):

NAGY, R.

Faculty of Electrical Engineering (tel. (230) 52-02-77; fax (230) 52-02-77):

CERNOMAZU, D.
GAITAN, V.

GRAUR, A.
PENTIUC, GH.
PENTIUC, R.
POPA, V.
POTORAC, A.

Faculty of Food Engineering (tel. (230) 52-02-67; fax (230) 52-00-80):

GUTT, S.

Faculty of Forestry (tel. (230) 52-16-64; fax (230) 52-00-80):

HOREANU, C.

Faculty of History and Geography (tel. (230) 52-37-42; fax (230) 52-37-42):

BRANDUS, C.
GULICIUC, E.
GULICIUC, V.
MAXIM, S.-T.
RADOANE, M.
RADOANE, N.
VITCU, D.

Faculty of Letters and Communication Sciences (tel. (230) 52-40-97; fax (230) 52-40-97):

ARDELEANU, S.-M.
BIRLEANU, I.-H.
CONSTANTINESCU, M.
DIACONU, M.
DOSPINESCU, V.
MOLDOVEANU, GH.
OPREA, I.
STEICIUC, B.

Faculty of Mechanical Engineering (tel. (230) 52-37-43; fax (230) 52-37-43):

AMARANDEI, D.
BANCESCU, N.
CEFRANOV, E.
CIOBANU, M.
DIACONESCU, E.
GRAMATICU, M.
GUTT, GH.
IACOB, D.
IONESCU, R.
MIHAI, I.
MUSCA, I.
RATA, V.
SEVERIN, L.
TARASI, P.

UNIVERSITATEA 'TITU MAIORESCU'

Str. Dionisie Lupu 70, 010458 Bucharest
Telephone: (213) 16-16-43
E-mail: international@utm.ro
Internet: www.utm.ro
Founded 1990
Private control

Rector: Prof. IOSIF R. URS
Vice-Rector: Prof. VALENTIN CORNELIU PAU
Scientific Sec. of the Senate: Prof. PETRE BIELTZ

Library of 1,500,000 vols (central library; there are also separate faculty libraries)

DEANS

Faculty of Economic Sciences: Prof. MAGDALENA NEGRUTIU
Faculty of Information Sciences and Technology: Prof. EMIL CRETU
Faculty of Law: Prof. SMARANDA ANGHENI
Faculty of Medicine: Prof. DAN FLORIN UNGUREANU
Faculty of Dental Medicine: Prof. DAN-DUMITRU SLAVESCU
Faculty of Psychology: Prof. DUMITRU GHEORGHIU

UNIVERSITATEA 'TRANSILVANIA' DIN BRAŞOV

Bdul Eroilor 29, 500036 Braşov
Telephone: (268) 41-20-88
Fax: (268) 41-05-25

E-mail: rectorat@unitbv.ro
Internet: www.unitbv.ro
Founded 1971 by merger of Polytechnical and Pedagogical Institutes of Braşov
State control
Languages of instruction: Romanian, English
Academic year: October to July

Rector: Prof. Dr Eng. SERGIU CHIRIACESCU
Vice-Rectors: Prof. Dr Math. ELEONOR CIUREA, Prof. Dr Eng. VICTOR DOGARU, Prof. Dr STELA DRĂGULIN, Prof. Dr Eng. RADU IOVĂNAŞ
Chancellor: Prof. Dr Eng. ARCADIE CIUBOTARU
Registrar: Mat. FLOAREA CERNAT
Scientific Sec.: Prof. Dr Eng. ARCADIE CIUBOTARU
Library Dir: Dr Eng. ANGELA REPANOVICI
Library: see Libraries and Archives
Number of teachers: 2,022
Number of students: 15,192

Publication: *Buletinul Universităţii 'Transilvania' din Braşov*

DEANS

Faculty of Mechanics: Prof. Dr Eng. GHEORGHE RADU
Faculty of Technical Eng.: Prof. Dr Eng. ION VIŞA
Faculty of Electrical Eng.: Prof. Dr Eng. WILIBALD SZABO
Faculty of Forestry and Forest Exploitation: Prof. Dr Eng. GHEORGHIŢA IONAŞCU
Faculty of Wood Technology: Prof. Dr Eng. IVAN CISMARU
Faculty of Materials Science and Eng.: Prof. Dr Eng. IOAN GIACOMELLI
Faculty of Mathematics and Computing: Prof. Dr Mat. NICOLAE PASCU
Faculty of Economic Sciences: Prof. Dr DORIN LIXĂNDROIU
Faculty of Letters: Dr OVIDIU MOCEANU
Faculty of Physical Training and Sport: Dr DRAGOŞ IONESCU-BONDOC
Faculty of Music: Dr HORIA CRISTIAN
Faculty of Medicine: Prof. Dr TEODOR LEAŞU
Faculty of Law and Sociology: Prof. Dr NICOLAE BUJDOIU
Univ. College of Technology: Prof. Dr Eng. ION BALCU
Univ. College of Forestry, Econ. and Computing: Prof. Dr Eng. IOSIF LEAHU
Univ. College of Education and Philology: DOINA USACI
Univ. College of Medicine: Dr LILIANA MARCELA ROGOZEA

PROFESSORS

Faculty of Technical Engineering (Str. Colina Universităţii 1, 500036 Braşov; tel. (268) 41-46-90; fax (268) 41-46-90; e-mail f2-itehn@unitbv.ro; internet www.unitbv.ro/tech):

ALEXANDRU, P., Mechanisms
BOBANCU, Ş., Mechanisms
BONCOI, GH., Automatic Machine Tools
BRANA, M. A., Descriptive Geometry and Technical Drawing
BUZATU, C., Automation of Technological Processes
CALEFARIU, G.
CHIŞU, E., Machine Components
CIOBOTĂ, M., Precision Mechanics
CRUCIAT, P., Technical Measurements
DAJ, I., Machine Components
DEACONESCU, T.
DELIU, M.
DIACONESCU, D. V., Mechanisms
DIŢU, V., Car Construction Technology
DUDIŢA, F., Mechanisms
DUMITRU, S., Physics
GAGIONEA, E. L., Descriptive Geometry and Technical Drawing
INŢA, I., Physics
IVAN, M., Machine Tools and Dimensional Control

IVAN, N. V., Machine Eng. Technology
JULA, A., Machine Elements
LUPULESCU, N.-B., Car Construction Technology
MĂNIUŢ, P.
MĂRĂSCU KLEIN, V., Unconventional Materials, Computer-Aided Production Systems Design
MARTINESCU, I., Technology of Cold-pressing
MOGAN, GH. L., Machine Elements
MOLDOVEAN, GH., Machine Elements
NEDELCU, A.
OBACIU, GH., Electric Drive and Machine Tools
PĂUNESCU, T., Car Construction Technology
POPESCU, I., Technical Measurement and Tolerance
ROŞCA, D. M., Metal-cutting Theory
SĂVESCU, D., Machine Elements
SECARĂ, GH., Metal Cutting, Tool Design
SOFONEA, L., Physics
STAREŢU, I., Machine Components
STROE, I., Machine Components
TALABĂ, D., Machine Components
TĂNĂSESCU, I., Machine Elements and Mechanisms
TUREAC, I., Machines for Processing by Deformation
URSUŢIU, D., Physics
VĂSÎI-ROŞCULEŢ, S., Design of Devices
VELICU, D., Descriptive Geometry and Technical Drawing
VIŞA, I., Mechanisms

Faculty of Mechanics (Str. Politehnicii 1, 500036 Braşov; tel. (268) 47-47-61; fax (268) 47-47-61; e-mail f1-mecanica@unitbv.ro; internet www.unitbv.ro/mechanics):

ABĂITĂNCEI, D., Automotive Technology
BĂCANU, GH., Physics
BALCU, I., Strength of Materials and Vibration
BENCHE, V., Heat Eng. and Fluid Mechanics
BIŢ, C. S., Strength of Materials and Vibration
BOBESCU, GH., Automotive Technology
BOLFA, T. E., Strength of Materials and Vibration
BRĂTUCU, GH., Agricultural and Food-processing Machinery
CÂMPIAN, V., Automotive Technology
CÂNDEA, I., Mechanics
CHIRIACESCU, T. S., Strength of Materials and Vibration
CHIRU, A., Automotive Technology
CIOFOAIA, V., Strength of Materials and Vibration
CIOLAN, GH., Automotive Technology
COFARU, C., Automotive Technology
CONSTANTIN, F., Mechanics
CRISTEA, L., Precision Eng. and Mechatronics
CURTU, T. I., Strength of Materials and Vibration
DELIU, GH., Mechanics
DUMITRIU, A., Precision Eng. and Mechatronics
FETCU, D., Heat Eng. and Fluid Mechanics
GOIA, A.I, Strength of Materials and Vibration
IONESCU, EMIL GH., Precision Eng. and Mechatronics
IONESCU, ENACHE, Agricultural and Food-processing Machinery
MUNTEANU, GH. M., Strength of Materials and Vibration
MUREŞAN, M., Heat Eng. and Fluid Mechanics
NAGY, T., Automotive Technology
NĂSTĂSOIU, S., Automotive Technology
OLTEANU, C., Precision Eng. and Mechatronics

POPA, V. A., Strength of Materials and Vibration
POPARAD, H., Precision Eng. and Mechatronics
POPESCU, S., Agricultural and Food-processing Machinery
POSTELNICU, A., Heat Eng. and Fluid Mechanics
PREDA, I., Automotive Technology
RADU, GH. A., Automotive Technology
RADU, N. GH., Strength of Materials and Vibration
ROȘCA, ILEANA C., Strength of Materials and Vibration
ROȘCA, IOAN C., Precision Mechanics and Mechatronics
RUS, F., Agricultural and Food-processing Machinery
SĂLĂJAN, C., Automotive Technology
SECARA, E. M., Mechanics
SEITZ, N., Automotive Technology
ȘERBĂNOIU, N., Heat Eng. and Fluid Mechanics
SOARE, I., Automotive Technology
ȘOVA, M., Heat Eng. and Fluid Mechanics
ȘOVA, V., Heat Eng. and Fluid Mechanics
SZÁVA, I., Strength of Materials and Vibration
ȚANE, N., Agricultural and Food-processing Machinery
TOFAN, M., Mechanics
ȚUREA, N., Automotive Technology
ULEA, M., Strength of Materials and Vibration
UNGUREANU, V. B., Heat Eng. and Fluid Mechanics
VEȘTEMEAN, N., Heat Eng. and Fluid Mechanics
VLASE, S., Mechanics

Faculty of Forestry and Forest Exploitation (Str. Șirul Beethoven 1, 500123 Brașov; tel. (268) 47-57-05; fax (268) 47-57-05; e-mail f5-silvic@unitbv.ro; internet www.unitbv.ro/silvic):

ALEXANDRU, V. M., Forest Exploitation
BELDEANU, E., Forest Exploitation
BOȘ, N.
CHIȚEA, GH., Biostatistics
CIORTUZ, I., Silviculture
CIUBOTARU, A., Forest Exploitation
CLINCIU, I., Flood Control
COSTEA, C.
DANCIU, M. A., Silviculture
FLORESCU, I. I., Silviculture
IONAȘCU, GH., Forest Exploitation
KISS, A., Topography
LEAHU, I., Dendrometry
MARCU, M., Silviculture
MARCU, O., Silviculture
NEGRUȚIU, A., Silviculture
NEGRUȚIU, F., Silviculture
OLTEANU, N., Forest Exploitation
OPREA, I., Forest Exploitation
PARASCAN, D., Silviculture
POPESCU, I., Forest Exploitation
RUSU, A.
SIMON, D., Silviculture
ȘOFLETEA, N., Silviculture
SPÂRCHEZ, GH., Silviculture
TAMAȘ, Ș., Operations Research
TÂRZIU, D., Silviculture
UNGUREANU, ȘT., Forest Exploitation

Faculty of Wood Technology (Str. Colina Universității 1, 500068 Brașov; tel. (268) 41-53-15; fax (268) 41-53-15; e-mail f6-ilcmn@unitbv.ro; internet www.unitbv.ro/il):

BĂDESCU, L. A.-M., Wood-processing Machinery
BARBU, M. C., Wood Technology
BUDĂU, G., Wood-processing Machinery
CISMARU, I., Wood Technology
DOGARU, V., Wood-processing Machinery
ISTRATE, V., Wood Technology

LĂZĂRESCU, C., Wood-processing Machinery
MIHAI, D., Wood Technology
MITIȘOR, A., Wood Technology
NĂSTASE, V., Wood Technology
PETROVICI, V., Wood Technology
ȚARAN, N., Wood-processing Machinery
TUDOR, E., Wood-processing Machinery
ZLATE, GH., Wood Technology

Faculty of Materials Science and Engineering (Str. Colina Universității 1, 500068 Brașov; tel. (268) 47-16-26; fax (268) 47-16-26; e-mail f3-simat@unitbv.ro):

ANDREESCU, F. G., Welding Equipment
BEJAN, V., Technology of Fabrication and Maintenance of Equipment
BOT, D., Heating Equipment, Foundry Technology
CÂNDEA, V. N., Welding Technology
CHICHERNEA, F., Technological Equipment and Materials Science
CIOBANU, I., Fundamentals of Foundry
CONSTANTINESCU, A., Foundry Equipment
CRIȘAN, A., Technological Equipment and Materials Science
DUȚA-CAPRĂ, A., Chemistry
EFTIMIE, L., Welding Technology
ENE, V., Special Proceedings for Foundry
FĂTU, S., Study of Metals
FLOREA, R. G., Welding Technology
GEAMĂN, V., Technological Equipment and Materials Science
GIACOMELLI, I., Equipment and Technologies for Thermal Treatments
IOVANĂȘ, R., Technology of Welding by Pressing
LUCA, V., Study of Metals
MACHEDON, T., Welding Equipment, Non-Destructive Testing, Hydraulic and Pneumatic Engines
MARKOS, Z., Welding Technology
MILOȘAN, I.
MUNTEANU, A., Thermal Treatments and Heat Processing
NOVAC, GH., Welding Equipment
PAȚACHIA, S., Chemistry
POPA, A., Technology of Plastic Deformation
POPESCU, R. M., Welding Technology
SAMOILĂ, C., Furnaces and Equipment for Heating
SCOROBEȚIU, L., Fundamentals of Welding Processes
ȘERBAN, C., Study of Metals
ȚICĂ, E.-R., Chemistry
ȚIEREAN, M., Welding Technology
TRIF, N., Mechanization, Automation and Robots for Welding Processing
TUDORAN, P., Study of Metals
VARGA, B., Technological Equipment
VEȚELEANU, A.

Faculty of Mathematics and Computing (Str. Iuliu Maniu 27, 500091 Brașov; tel. (268) 41-40-16; fax (268) 41-40-16; e-mail f7-stiinte@unitbv.ro; internet info.unitbv.ro):

ATANASIU, GH., Geometry
CIUREA, E., Computing
COCAN, M., Computing
LUPU, M., Differential Equations
MARIN, M., Differential Equations
MARINESCU, C., Differential Equations
MUNTEANU, GH., Differenctial Equations
ORMAN, G., Mathematical Analysis and Probability
OVESEA, H., Mathematical Analysis and Probability
PASCU, N., Mathematical Analysis and Probability
PESCAR, V., Geometry
PITIȘ, GH., Differential Equations
RADOMIR, I., Mathematical Analysis and Probability
SCHEIBER, E., Computing
ȚIȚA, N., Mathematical Analysis and Probability

Faculty of Electrical Engineering (Str. Politehnicii 1, 500024 Brașov; tel. (268) 47-47-18; fax (268) 47-47-18; e-mail f4-electro@unitbv.ro; internet www.vega.unitbv.ro):

ANDONIE, R., Electronics
BIDIAN, D. Ș., Electrical Eng.
BORZA, P. N., Electronics
CERNAT, M., Electrical Eng.
DAN, ȘT., Automation
FRATU, A., Automation
GEORGESCU, M., Electrical Eng.
GOGIOIU, A., Electrical Eng.
HELEREA, E., Electrical Eng.
MĂRGINEANU, I., Automation
MARINESCU, C., Electrical Eng.
MATLAC, I. V., Electrical Eng.
NICOLAIDE, A. C., Electrical Eng.
OLTEAN, I. D., Electronics
PEȘTEANU, O., Electrical Eng.
SCUTARU, GH., Electrical Eng.
SISAK, F., Automation
STOIA, D. D., Electrical Eng.
SZABO, W., Electronics
SZEKELY, I., Electronics
ȚAȚA, M. S., Electrical Eng.
TOACȘE, GH., Electronics
TOPA, I., Automation

Faculty of Economic Sciences (tel. (268) 41-93-04; fax (268) 41-93-04; e-mail f8-economic@unitbv.ro; internet econ.unitbv.ro):

BĂCANU, V. B., Finance, Accounting and Economic Theory
BRÂNZAN, I., Management and Computing
BRĂTUCU, G., Marketing and Tourism
DUGULEANĂ, L., Management and Computing
FORIȘ, T., Management and Computing
LEFTER, C., Marketing and Tourism
LIXĂNDROIU, D. I., Management and Computing
OPREI, I., Management and Computing
POPA, M., Management and Computing
POPESCU, M., Management and Computing
SAON, S., Finance, Accounting and Economic Theory

Faculty of Medicine (Str. N. Bălcescu 56, 500019 Brașov; tel. (268) 41-21-85; fax (268) 41-21-85; e-mail f10-medicina@unitbv.ro):

COMAN, GH., Preclinical Medicine
LEAȘU, T., Specialized Medicine
RĂDOI, M., Internal Medicine
RADU, I., Preclinical Medicine

Faculty of Music (Str. Lungă 5, 500035 Brașov; tel. (268) 47-88-86; fax (268) 41-05-25; e-mail f9-muzica@unitbv.ro; internet www.unitbv.ro/muzica):

BICA, N., Teaching Music
DRĂGULIN, S. D., Instrumental Interpretation
IACOBESCU, L., Instrumental Interpretation

Faculty of Law and Sociology (B-dul Eroilor 27, 500030 Brașov; tel. (268) 47-40-17; fax (268) 47-40-17):

BUJDOIU, N., Sociology, Philosophy and Law
CHIRIȚĂ, R., Sociology, Philosophy and Law
POENARU, E., Sociology, Philosophy and Law

UNIVERSITATEA 'VALAHIA' DIN TÂRGOVIȘTE

Bdul Regele Carol I 2, 130024 Târgoviște
Telephone: (245) 20-61-01
Fax: (245) 21-76-92
E-mail: rectorat@valahia.ro
Internet: www.valahia.ro
Founded 1989

Rector: Prof. Dr ION CUCUI
Pro-Rectors: Prof. Dr MARIN CIRCIUMARU, Prof. Dr CONSTANTIN GHITA, Prof. Dr

GHEORGHE IONITA, Prof. Dr CONSTANTIN GHITA

Librarian: AGNES ERICH

Number of teachers: 400
Number of students: 10,000

DEANS

Faculty of Arts and Sciences: Dr CALIN OROS
Faculty of Econ.: Prof. Dr ION STEGAROIU
Faculty of Environmental Eng. and Biotechnology: Prof. Dr STEFANIA IORDACHE
Faculty of Humanities: Prof. Dr ION STANCIU
Faculty of Law: Dr SACHE NICOLAESCU
Faculty of Material Sciences, Mechatronic Eng. and Robotics: Prof. Dr AUREL GABA
Faculty of Theology: Prof. Dr MIHAITA NIFON

DIRECTORS OF COLLEGES

Univ. College of Econ. and Admin.: Dr VIRGIL POPA
Univ. College of Education: (vacant)
Univ. College of Technology: Dr CORNEL MARIN

UNIVERSITATEA DE VEST DIN TIMIȘOARA

V. Pârvan 4, 300223 Timișoara
Telephone: (256) 19-00-09
Fax: (256) 19-00-09
E-mail: rector@rectorat.uvt.ro
Internet: www.uvt.ro

Founded 1944
State control
Academic year: October to June

Rector: Prof. Dr IOAN MIHAI
Pro-Rectors: Prof. Dr NICOLAE AVRAM (Postgraduate Study Programmes and Scientific Research), Prof. Dr ȘTEFAN BALINT (Int. Relations), Prof. Dr ADRIAN CHIRIAC (Undergraduate Study Programmes and Student Affairs), Prof. Dr HORIA CRISTEA (Financial Affairs)
Scientific Sec.: Prof. Dr ȘTEFAN BALINT
Sec.-Gen.: VIRGIL DEBREȚIN
Librarian: Prof. VASILE ȚARA

Number of teachers: 722
Number of students: 14,243

Publication: Analele Universității din Timișoara (mathematics, physics, philology, econ. and social sciences)

DEANS

Faculty of Mathematics: Prof. Dr MIHAIL MEGAN
Faculty of Physics: Prof. Dr DORINA VANGHELI
Faculty of Chemistry, Biology and Geography: Assoc. Prof. Dr AUREL FAUR
Faculty of Letters, Philosophy and History: Prof. Dr ILEANA OANCEA
Faculty of Econ.: Assoc. Prof. Dr EMIL CAZAN
Faculty of Sociology and Psychology: Prof. ȘTEFAN BUZĂRNESCU
Faculty of Law: Prof. Dr RADU MOTICA
Faculty of Arts: Assoc. Prof. DUMITRU ȘERBAN
Faculty of Music: Assoc. Prof. FELICIA STANCOVICI
Faculty of Political Sciences and Communication: (vacant)
Faculty of Physical Education and Sports: Prof. MARIA GÖNCZI-RAICU

PROFESSORS

Faculty of Mathematics (tel. (256) 19-40-02; fax (256) 19-40-02; e-mail mihmeg@info.uvt.ro; internet www.math.uvt.ro.):

ALBU, A., Differential Geometry
BALINT, Ș., Mathematical Equations
BOROȘ, E., Algebra
CONSTANTIN, GH., Probability Theory
CRAIOVEANU, M., Spectral Geometry
GAȘPAR, D., Functional Analysis, Spectral Theory
IVAN, GH., Algebra

MĂRUȘTER, Ș., Non-Linear Optimization and Computer Science
MEGAN, M., Mathematical Analysis
OBĂDEANU, V., Theoretical Mechanics and Differential Geometry, Operational Research
OPRIȘ, D., Operational Research
PAPUC, D. I., Differential Geometry
PREDA, P., Mathematical Analysis
PUTA, M., Differential Equations in Geometry
RADU, V., Stochastic Analysis and Probability Theory
REGHIȘ, M., Differential Equations
SCHWAB, E., Homological Algebra
STRĂTILĂ, Ș., Mathematical Analysis and Operator Algebras
SUCIU, N., Complex Analysis

Faculty of Physics (tel. (256) 19-60-88; fax (256) 19-60-88; e-mail vangheli@quasar.physics.uvt.ro; internet quasar.physics.uvt.ro/physics):

AVRAM, N., Atomic and Molecular Physics and Spectroscopy
BIRĂU, O., Thermodynamics and Molecular Physics
HRIANCA, I., Electricity and Magnetism
MUSCUTARIU, I., Electricity and Magnetism, Solid State and Semiconductor Physics
NICOARĂ, I., Laser Crystals
SCHLETT, Z., Plasma Physics, Semiconductor Materials and Devices

Faculty of Chemistry, Biology and Geography (Str. I. Pestalozzi 16, 300115 Timișoara; tel. (256) 19-03-77; fax (256) 19-03-33; e-mail afaur@cbg.uvt; internet www.cbg.uvt.ro):

CHIRIAC, A., Physical Chemistry
DOCA, N., Chemical Eng.
MRACEC, M., Physical Chemistry
NUȚIU, R., Organic Chemistry
TRUȚI, S., Geography

Faculty of Letters, Philosophy and History (tel. (256) 19-38-86; fax (256) 19-38-86; internet www.litere.uvt.ro):

BENEA, D., Ancient History
BIRIȘ, I., History of Culture and Civilization
BUCA, M., Russian Language
CHEIE, I., Romanian Literature
CIOCÂRLIE, L., French Literature
EVSEEV, I., Russian Language
FRĂTILĂ, V., Dialectology
GRECU, C., Philosophy of Logic
GYURCSIK, M., French Literature
HARANGUȘ, C., Ontology
MIOC, S., Romanian Literature
MUNTEANU, I., Modern Romanian History
OANCEA, I., Romance Philology
PÂRLOG, H., English Linguistics
SÂRBU, R., Russian Language
ȚARA, V., History of the Romanian Language

Faculty of Economics (Str. I. Pestalozzi 16, 300115 Timișoara; tel. (256) 19-84-99; fax (256) 19-06-98; e-mail decanat@fse1.uvt.ro):

BĂBĂIȚĂ, I., Political Economy
BĂBĂIȚĂ, V., Accounting
BĂILEȘTEANU, GH., Business Econ.
BURTICĂ, M., Macroeconomic Forecasting
CĂTINIANU, FL., Prices and Tariffs
CERNA, S., Currency and Credits
CRĂCIUNESCU, V., Management
CRISTEA, H., Business Finance
DĂNĂIAȚĂ, I., Management
EPURAN, M., Accounting
FALNIȚĂ, E., Science of Commodities
GOIAN, M., Management
IONESCU, GH., Marketing
IVAN, ȘT., Informatics
LĂDAR, L., Marketing
LUPULESCU, M., Computer Programming
MARTIN, I., Microeconomic Analysis
MIHAI, I., Financial Analysis

NEGRUT, C., Agrarian Economics and Policy
OPRIȘ, L., Agrarian Policies in the World
POPOVICI, AL., Programming of Production
PUTZ, E., Transport in Tourism
ROTARIU, I., Management of Foreign Trade
SILAȘI, GR., Regional and World Economy
ȘOȘDEANU, A., Accounting
TALPOȘ, I., Public Finance
TRANDAFIR, N., Political Economy
VÂRLAN, GH., Economic Forecasting

Faculty of Sociology and Psychology (tel. (256) 19-07-70; fax (256) 19-07-70; e-mail steb@socio.uvt.ro; internet www.socio.uvt.ro):

DABU, R., Sociology
POENARU, R., Pedagogy, Deontology
VINTILESCU, D., Educational Theory

Faculty of Law (Bdul Eroilor 9A, 300575 Timișoara; tel. (256) 20-11-54; fax (256) 20-11-54; e-mail ramar@isel.uvt.ro; internet www.drept.uvt.ro):

DRESSLER, M., Forensic Medicine
MIHAI, GH., Philosophy of Law
MOTICA, R. I., Law
POPA, V., Roman Law, Labour Law

Faculty of Arts (Calea Bogdanesti 32A, Timișoara; tel. (256) 19-66-50; fax (256) 19-66-50):

FÂNTĂNARIU, S., Graphic Arts
FLONDOR, C., Painting
JECZA, P., Sculpture
NUȚIU, R., Painting
SULEA, I., Painting
ZIMAN, M., Textile Arts

Faculty of Music (Piața Libertatii 1, 300077 Timișoara; tel. (256) 13-32-05; fax (256) 13-32-05; internet rectorat.uvt.ro/musica/muzw.html):

STANCOVICI, F., Piano
VULPE, D., Choral Conducting

Faculty of Political Sciences and Communication (tel. (256) 19-40-68 ext. 172; fax (256) 19-00-33; e-mail gcoltescu@yahoo.com):

COLTESCU, G., Political Sciences

Faculty of Physical Education and Sport (tel. (256) 19-60-92; fax (256) 19-03-33):

GÖNCZI-RAICU, M., Gymnastics
IONESCU, I., Football

Technological Universities

UNIVERSITATEA DE ARHITECTURA ȘI URBANISM 'ION MINCU'

Str. Academiei 18-20, 010014 Bucharest
Telephone: (21) 315-54-82
Fax: (21) 312-39-54
Internet: www.iaim.ro

Founded 1892 by the Romanian Society of Architects as a private school of architecture
Academic year: October to July

Rector: Prof. Dr EMIL BARBU POPESCU

DEANS

Faculty of Architecture: Prof. Dr STEFAN SCAFA UDRISTE
Faculty of Interior Architecture: Dr IULIUS IONESCU
Faculty of Urbanism: Prof. Dr ALEXANDRU M. SANDU

DIRECTORS

Univ. College: Prof. Dr NICULAE GRAMA
School of Advanced Studies: Prof. Dr SORIN VASILESCU

UNIVERSITATEA MARITIMĂ DIN CONSTANŢA

Str. Mircea cel Bătrân 104, 900663 Constanţa

Telephone: (241) 66-47-40
Fax: (241) 61-72-60
E-mail: info@imc.ro
Internet: www.imc.ro

Founded 1972

Rector: Prof. Dr DUMITRU DINU

Library of 35,000 vols.

UNIVERSITATEA DE MEDICINĂ ŞI FARMACIE 'CAROL DAVILA'

Str. Dionisie Lupu 37, Bucharest

Telephone: (21) 318-07-18
Fax: (21) 318-07-19
Internet: www.univermed-cdgm.ro

Founded 1857 (fmrly Institutul de Medicina şi Farmacie, renamed 1990)

Rector: Prof. Dr FLORIAN POPA
Pro-Rectors: Prof. Dr CONSTANTIN VIRGILIU ARION, Prof. Dr MIHAIL COCULESCU, Prof. Dr IOAN LASCAR, Prof. Dr MONICA DANIELA POP, Prof. Dr IOANEL SINESCU

Library of 700,000 vols
Number of teachers: 1,189
Number of students: 7,039

DEANS

Faculty of Dentistry: Prof. Dr AUGUSTIN MIHAI
Faculty of Medicine: Prof. Dr MIRCEA CINTEZA
Faculty of Pharmacy: Prof. Dr CONSTANTIN MIRCIOIU

UNIVERSITATEA DE MEDICINĂ ŞI FARMACIE DIN CRAIOVA

Petru Rareş 2, 200349 Craiova

Telephone: (251) 522458
Fax: (251) 593077
E-mail: rector@umfcv.ro
Internet: www.umfcv

Rector: Prof. Dr TUDOREL CIUREA
Vice-Rector for Academic and Scientific Affairs: Prof. Dr AUGUSTIN CUPSA
Vice-Rector for Student Affairs: Prof. Dr TUDOR UDRISTOIU
Scientific Sec.: Prof. Dr FLORINEL BĂDULESCU
Head of Library Services: Prof. ALINA CROITORU

Library of 80,000 vols, 51 periodicals
Number of teachers: 337
Number of students: 4,500

Publications: *Craiova Medicala* (quarterly), *Journal of Pharmacology* (quarterly)

DEANS

Faculty of Medicine: Prof. Dr ION GEORGESCU
Faculty of Pharmacy: Prof. Dr FLORICA POPESCU
Faculty of Stomatology: Prof. Dr MIHAI SURPĂTEANU
Univ. College of Medicine: Assoc. Prof. IULIANA NICOLESCU

PROFESSORS

Faculty of Medicine:
BADULESCU, F.
BULUCEA, D.
CIUREA, T.
CUPSA, A. M.
FERESCHIN, A.-E.
GEORGESCU, I.
ILIE, C.
MARINESCU, D. C.
MELINTE, V.
MOGOANTA, L.
POGOVEANU, I.
POPESCU, R. S.

STOICA, Z.
UDRISTOIU, T.
VRABETE, M. E.

Faculty of Pharmacy:
NEAMTU, J.
PISOSCHI, C. G.
POPESCU, F.
RADU, S.

Faculty of Stomatology:
BANITA, I. M.
DIACONESCU, G. I.
PATROI, G.
SIMIONESCU, C. E.
SURPATEANU, M.

University College of Medicine:
MANEA, M.
NICOLESCU, I.

UNIVERSITATEA DE MEDICINĂ ŞI FARMACIE 'GR. T. POPA'

Str. Universităţii 16, 700115 Iaşi

Telephone: (232) 21-18-18
Fax: (232) 21-41-46
E-mail: rectorat@asklepios.umfiasi.ro
Internet: www.umfiasi.ro

Founded 1879
State control
Languages of instruction: Romanian, English
Academic year: October to July

Pres.: Prof. Dr CAROL STANCIU
Vice-Pres: Prof. Dr DUMITRU BUIUC, Prof. Dr CRISTIAN DRAGOMIR, Prof. Dr EUGEN TÎRCOVEANU, Prof. Dr EUSEBIE ZBRANCA
Registrar: Eng. DANA BUGEAC
Librarian: Prof. VIORICA SCUTARU

Library of 373,000 vols
Number of teachers: 1,373
Number of students: 5,334

Publication: *Buletin Bibliografic* (quarterly)

DEANS

Faculty of Medical Bioengineering: Prof. Dr FLORIN TOPOLICEANU
Faculty of Medicine: Prof. Dr VALERIU RUSU
Faculty of Pharmacy: Prof. Dr URSULA HELENA STĂNESCU
Faculty of Stomatology: Prof. Dr VASILE BURLUI

PROFESSORS

Faculty of Medical Bioengineering (tel. (232) 21-35-73; fax (232) 21-35-73; e-mail pasimin@umfiasi.ro; internet www.umfiasi.ro/umf120/facbio.html):

APOSTOL, I., Clinical Physiology
BALTAG, O., Exact, Metrological and Informatics Sciences
CHIRIAC, H., Biomedical Eng.
DIACONU, I., Exact, Metrological and Informatics Sciences
GROSU, I., General and Applied Physics
PETRESCU, GH., General Management and Marketing
POEATA, I., Biomaterials and Techniques of Prosthetic Systems
UGLEA, C., Applied Chemistry and Physical Chemistry
UNGUREANU, M., Synthetic and Bioactive Substance

Faculty of Medicine (tel. (232) 21-53-50; fax (232) 21-52-88; e-mail gabic@umfiasi.ro; internet www.umfiasi.ro/umf120/facmed.html):

ALDEA, A. S., Thoracic Surgery
ANTOHE, D. S., Anatomy
ARSENESCU, C., Internal Medicine
ASTARASTOAIE, V., Forensic Medicine
BĂDESCU, A., Histology
BĂDESCU, M., Physiopathology
BALAN, G., Internal Medicine
BILD, E., Oncology and Radiotherapy

BOISTEANU, P., Psychiatry
BRĂNIŞTEANU, D., Physiology
BRUMARU, O., Paediatrics
BUIUC, D., Microbiology
CARASIEVICI, E., Immunology
CHIRIAC, R. M., Rheumatology and Balneophysiotherapy
CHIRIŢA, V., Psychiatry
CHISĂLIŢA, D., Ophthalmology
CIORNIA, T., Forensic Medicine
COLEV, V., Physiopathology
COMAN, G., Microbiology
COSOVANU, A., Internal Medicine
COSTĂCHESCU, GH., Obstetrics and Gynaecology
COSTINESCU, V., Otorhinolaryngology
COTRUTZ, C., Cell Biology
COTUŢIU, C., Histology
COVIC, M., Genetics
COVIC, M., Internal Medicine
DANIIL, C., Radiology
DATCU, G., Internal Medicine
DATCU, M. D., Internal Medicine
DIACONU, C., Surgery
DIMITRIU, A. G., Paediatrics
DRAGOMIR, C., Infant Care
DRAGOMIR, C., Surgery
DRAGOMIR, D., Obstetrics and Gynaecology
FRÎNCU, D. L., Anatomy
FRÎNCU, D. L., Physical Education
GAVĂT, V., Hygiene
GEORGESCU, G., Internal Medicine
GEORGESCU, N. M., Orthopaedics and Traumatology
GHEORGHIŢĂ, N., Biochemistry
GOŢIA, D. G., Paediatric Surgery
GOŢIA, S., Paediatrics
IANOVICI, N., Neurosurgery
IONESCU, C., History of Medicine
IVAN, A., Epidemiology
LUCA, M., Parasitology and Mycoses
LUCA, V., Infectious Diseases
LUCA, V., Physiopathology
MĂTĂSARU, S., Paediatrics
MIHAILOVICI, M. S., Pathological Anatomy
MIHAIESCU, T., Pneumophtisiology
MIHALACHE, C., Occupational Medicine
MIHALACHE, ST., Surgery
MOGOŞ, V., Endocrinology
MORARU, D., Paediatrics
MORARU, E., Paediatrics
MUNGIU, C. O., Pharmacology
PANDELE, G. I., Internal Medicine
PETRESCU, GH., Physiology
PETRESCU, Z., Dermatology
PETROVANU, R., Family Practice Medicine
PLAHTEANU, M., Forensic Medicine
PLEŞA, C., Surgery
POPESCU, D. C., Neurobiology
PRELIPCEAN, C., Internal Medicine
PRICOP, F., Obstetrics and Gynaecology
PRICOP, M., Obstetrics and Gynaecology
RADULESCU, D., Pathological Anatomy
RUSU, V., Biophysics
SINIŢCHI, G., Family Practice Medicine
SLĂTINEANU, S., Physiology
STAN, M., Internal Medicine
STANCIU, C., Internal Medicine
ŞTEFANACHE, F., Neurology
STOIAN, M., Surgery
STRATONE, A., Exploration Physiology
TÎRCOVEANU, E., Surgery
TOPOLICEANU, F., Exploring Physiology
UNGUREANU, G., Internal Medicine
ZAMFIR, M., Anatomy
ZBRANCA, E., Endocrinology

Faculty of Pharmacy (tel. (232) 26-77-46; fax (232) 21-18-20; e-mail v_dorica@yahoo.com; internet www.umfiasi.ro/umf120/facfarm.html):

CARAMAN, C., Inorganic Chemistry
CUCIUREANU, R., Environmental Chemistry
DĂNILĂ, GH., Pharmaceutical Chemistry
DORNEANU, M., Organic Chemistry
DORNEANU, V., Analytical Chemistry

GAFIŢEANU, E., Pharmaceutical Technology
HRISCU, A., Pharmacodynamics
LAZAR, M., Drug Control
PĂDURARU, I., Pharmaceutical Biochemistry
PAVELESCU, M. D. G., Pharmacology
POPOVICI, I., Pharmaceutical Technology
PROCA, M., Toxicology
SCUTARIU, M. D., Anatomy and Physiology
STAN, M., Analytical Chemistry
STĂNESCU, U. H., Pharmacognosy
ŞTEFĂNESCU, E., Organic Chemistry

Faculty of Stomatology (tel. (232) 26-76-86; fax (232) 21-18-20; internet www.umfiasi.ro/umf120/facstom.html):

ALDEA, M.-J., Obstetrics and Gynaecology
ALDESCU, C., Radiology
ANDRIAN, S., Cariology
BURLEA, M., Paediatrics
BURLUI, V., Prosthetics
CHIRITA, R., Psychiatry
COSTIN, D., Ophthalmology
COSTULEANU, M., Physiopathology
COTRUTZ, E. C., Cell Biology
DĂNILĂ, I., Preventative Stomatology
DIACONESCU, M. R., Surgery
DOROBĂŢ, V., Infant Stomatology
FĂTU, C., Anatomy
FOMA, N., EPI Therapy
FRATU, A., Orthodontics
GOGĂLNICEANU, D., Dental Surgery
HURJUI, J., Internal Medicine
IFTENI, G., L.O.C. Prosthetic Therapy
LABA, E., Pathological Anatomy
LĂCĂTUŞU, ST., Cariology
MARIN, G., Community Dentistry
MAXIM, A., Pedodontics
MIHALACHE, G., Anatomy
MÎRŢU, D. V., Otorhinolaryngology
MORARASU, C., Oral Complex Rehabilitation
NEAMŢU, C., Physiology
NECHIFOR, M., Pharmacology
NIŢĂ, M., Histology
PANAITE, ST., Technology of Dental Processes
PAVEL, M., Biochemistry
PENDEFUNDA, L., Neurology
POPESCU, E., Oral Surgery
URSACHE, M., Oral Semiology
VICOL, H. C., Oro-Maxillo-Facial Pathology
VORONEANU, M., Anaesthesiology

UNIVERSITATEA DE MEDICINĂ ŞI FARMACIE 'IULIU HAŢIEGANU' CLUJ-NAPOCĂ

Str. Emil Isac 13, 400023 Cluj-Napoca
Telephone: (264) 19-55-24
Fax: (264) 19-72-57
E-mail: dri@umfcluj.ro
Internet: www.umfcluj.ro
Founded 1872
Languages of instruction: Romanian, English, French
Academic year: October to July (2 semesters)
Rector: Prof. Dr MARIUS BOJIŢĂ
Vice-Rector for Academic Affairs: Prof. Dr VACILE SURCEL
Vice-Rector for Academic Organization and Devt: Prof. Dr ANDREI ACHIMAŞ
Vice-Rector for Scientific Affairs: Prof. Dr MIRCEA GRIGORESCU
Registrar: RADU HRINIUC
Librarian: IOANA ROBU
Library: see Libraries and Archives
Number of teachers: 600
Number of students: 3,500

Publications: *Acta Neurologica Transilvanicae, Anuarul Universităţii, Applied Medical Informatics, Clujul Medical, Diabetes Management, The Heart, Minimally Invasive Surgery, Quo Vadis, Radiology and Medical Oncology, Romanian Journal of Angiology and Vascular Surgery, Romanian Journal of Gastroenterology, Romanian Journal of Pathology, Romanian Journal of Reconstructive Microsurgery*

DEANS

Faculty of Medicine: Prof. Dr NICOLAE MIU
Faculty of Pharmacy: Prof. Dr ROBERT SĂNDULESCU
Faculty of Stomatology: Assoc. Prof. Dr GRIGORE BĂCIUŢ

PROFESSORS AND HEADS OF DEPARTMENT

Faculty of Medicine:

ACALOVSCHI, I., Anaesthesiology and Intensive Care
ANDERCOU, A., Surgery
BADEA, R., Medical Imaging
BÂRSAN, M., Cardiology
BENGA, G., Cellular and Molecular Biology
BENGA, I., Paediatric Neurology
BOCŞAN, I., Epidemiology
BOLOSIU, H. D., Internal Medicine
CĂLUGĂRU, M., Ophthalmology
CĂPÂLNEANU, R., Cardiology
CÂRSTINA, D., Infectious Diseases
COCÂRLĂ, A., Occupational Health
COSTIN, N., Gynaecology
DEJICA, D., Clinical Immunology
DRAGHICI, A., Internal Medicine
DUNCEA, C., Internal Medicine
FUNARIU, GH., Surgery
GHERMAN, M., Nephrology
GHILEZAN, N., Oncology
GRIGORESCU-SIDO, F., Anatomy
GRIGORESCU-SIDO, P., Paediatrics
HANCU, N., Nutrition and Metabolic Diseases
IONUT, C., Hygiene
JEBELEANU, GH., Biochemistry
KORY, S., Neurology
LAZĂR, L., Oncology
LUCAN, M., Urology
MACREA, R., Paediatric Psychiatry
MAIER, N., Dermatology
MIU, N., Paediatrics
MUREŞAN, A., Physiology
NANULESCU, M., Paediatrics
OLINIC, N., Internal Medicine
OLINICI, C., Morphopathology
PARAIAN, N., Paediatric Surgery
PASCU, O., Gastroenterology
PLESCA-MANEA, L., Physiopathology
POPESCU, A., Neonatology
SANDOR, V., Pharmacology
SASCA, C., Microbiology
SURCEL, I. V., Gynaecology
ŢIGAN, S., Medical Informatics
TOADER RADU, M., Histology
TOMESCU, E., Otorhinolaryngology
TURDEANU, N., Surgery
VLAD, L., Surgery
ZAMORA, C., Pneumophthisiology
ZDRENGHEA, D., Cardiology

Faculty of Pharmacy:

BOJIŢĂ, M., Drug Control
COMAN, M., Drug Industry
LEUCUŢA, S., Pharmaceutical Technology
MOLDOVAN, M., Dermatopharmacy and Cosmeticology
ONIGA, I., Pharmacognosy
ONIGA, O., Pharmaceutical Chemistry
OPREAN, L., Inorganic Chemistry
POLICINENCU, C., Pharmaceutical Legislation, Marketing and Management
PRODAN, A., Informatics
SĂNDULESCU, R., Analytical Chemistry
TĂMAŞ, M., Pharmaceutical Botany
TĂRMURE, C., Biochemistry

Faculty of Stomatology:

BĂCUIŢ, G., Oral and Maxillofacial Surgery
BORZEA, D., Stomatological Propaedeutics
COCÂRLĂ, E., Orthodontics, Pedodontics
FILDAN, F., Oral Radiology

NEGUCIOIU, M., Dental Propaedeutics
POPA, S., Dental Propaedeutics
ROTARU, A., Oral and Maxillofacial Surgery

UNIVERSITATEA DE MEDICINĂ ŞI FARMACIE TÂRGU MUREŞ

Str. Gheorghe Marinescu 38, 540139 Târgu Mureş
Telephone: (265) 21-31-27
Fax: (265) 21-04-07
E-mail: rectorat@umftgm.ro
Internet: www.umftgm.ro
Founded 1948
State control
Languages of instruction: Romanian, Hungarian
Academic year: October to September
Rector: Prof. Dr CONSTANTIN COPOTOIU
Vice-Rectors: Assoc. Prof. Dr KLARA BRÎNZANIUC, Prof. Dr ÖRS ŞTEFAN NAGY
Chief Sec.: ELENA NISTOR
Scientific Sec.: Prof. Dr IOAN NICOLAESCU
Int. Relations Officer: ANNAMÁRIA GYÖRFI
Librarian: FLORIN DAMIAN
Library of 283,000 vols
Number of teachers: 381
Number of students: 2,559

Publication: *Revista de Medicină şi Farmacie/Orvosi és Gyógyszerészeti Szemle* (quarterly)

DEANS

Faculty of Dentistry: Prof. Dr SORIN POPŞOR
Faculty of General Medicine: Dr VIRGIL TITUS GLIGA
Faculty of Pharmacy: Prof. Dr MARIA TITICA DOGARU

PROFESSORS

Faculty of Dentistry (tel. (265) 21-55-51 ext. 130; fax (265) 21-04-07; e-mail decanatstoma@umftgm.ro):

KOVÁCS, D.
MONEA, A., Odontology
POPŞOR, S.

Faculty of General Medicine (tel. (265) 21-55-51 ext. 110; fax (265) 21-04-07; e-mail decanatmg@umftgm.ro):

BANCU, S., Surgery
BOJA, R., Urology
BORDA, A., Histology
BRASSAI, Z., Internal Medicine
BRATU, D., Internal Medicine
BURIAN, M., Radiology
CARASCA, E., Internal Medicine
COPOTOIU, C., Surgery
DEAC, R., Cardiac Surgery
DRAŞOVEANU, C., Otorhinolaryngology
EGYED, Z., Pathomorphology
GEORGESCU, C., Internal Medcine
GEORGESCU, L., Physiotherapy
HOBAI, S., Biochemistry
INCZE, A., Internal Medicine
JUNG, I., Pathology
KIKELI, P. I., Family Medicine
KUN, I. Z., Endocrinology
MATHE, I., Biochemistry
MONEA, M., Pharmacology
MUNTEANU, I., Paediatrics
NAGY, Ö., Orthopaedics
NICOLAESCU, I., Biophysics
NIRESTEAN, A., Psychiatry
OLTEANU, G., Internal Medicine
PASCU, I., Neurology
PASCU, R., Infectious Diseases
SABĂU, M., Physiology
SABĂU, M., Epidemiology
SCHIOPU, A., Physiopathology
SIN, A., Cell Biology
URECHE, R., Hygiene

Faculty of Pharmacy (tel. (265) 21-55-51 ext. 111; fax (265) 21-04-07; e-mail rectorat@umftgm.ro):

AJTAI, M., General and Industrial Toxicology
CSEDÖ, C., Pharmacognosy
DOGARU, M. T.
DUDUCZ, G., Medicinal Biotechnology
DUSA, S.
GYÉRESI, A., Pharmaceutical Chemistry
OROIAN, S.
POPOVICI, A., Pharmaceutical Technology
TÖKÉS, B., Physico-Chemistry

ATTACHED RESEARCH INSTITUTE
Academy of Research of the University of Medicine and Pharmacy.

UNIVERSITATEA DE MEDICINĂ ŞI FARMACIE 'VICTOR BABEŞ'

Piăta Eftimie Murgu 2, 300041 Timişoara
Telephone: (256) 29-33-89
Fax: (256) 49-06-26
E-mail: relint@umft.ro
Internet: www.umft.ro

Founded 1945 as Institutul de Medicină
Academic year: October to July

Rector: Prof. Dr STEFAN IOSIF DRAGULESCU
Pro-Rectors: Prof. Dr POMPILIA DEHELEAN, Prof. Dr MARIUS RAICA, Prof. Dr DAN V. POENARU
Scientific Sec. of the Senate: Prof. Dr DAN GAIŢA

Library of 195,000 vols
Number of teachers: 963
Number of students: 4,028

Publications: *Cercetări Medico-Chirurgicale* (quarterly), *Timişoara Medicală* (quarterly)

DEANS
Medicine: Prof. Dr FLORIN MICLEA
Dental Medicine: Prof. Dr VIRGIL CARLIGERIU
Pharmacy: Prof. Dr CARMEN CRISTESCU

UNIVERSITATEA 'POLITEHNICA' DIN BUCUREŞTI

Splaiu Independenţei 313, 060042 Bucharest
Telephone: (21) 402-91-00
Fax: (21) 411-53-65
E-mail: dv_ionescu@rectorat.pub.ro
Internet: www.pub.ro

Founded 1818
State control
Academic year: October to July (2 semesters)

Rector: Prof. Dr ECATERINA ANDRONESCU
Vice-Rector for (Scientific Research: Prof. Dr SERBAN RAICU
Vice-Rector for Graduate Education: Prof. Dr MARIN DRAGULINESCU
Vice-Rector for Financial Affairs: Prof. Dr MIHAI OCTAVIAN POPESCU
Vice-Rector for Undergraduate Education: Prof. Dr DUMITRU CEZAR IONESCU
Vice-Rector forInt. Relations, European Integration and Partnership: Prof. Dr MARIAN GHEORGHE
Scientific Sec.: Prof. Dr IULIAN RIPOSAN
Chief Admin. Officer: Prof. Dr GABRIEL IACOBESCU
Dir of the Int. Co-operation Dept (vacant)
Librarian: Dr DUMITRU RADU POPESCU

Library: see Libraries and Archives
Number of teachers: 1,590
Number of students: 22,000

DEANS
Faculty of Aircraft Eng.: Prof. Dr STELIAN GALETUSE
Faculty of Automatic Control and Computer Science: Prof. Dr DUMITRU POPESCU
Faculty of Biotechnical Systems Eng.: Prof. Dr IOAN PAUNESCU
Faculty of Electrical Eng.: Prof. Dr MIHAI IORDACHE
Faculty of Electronics and Telecommunications: Prof. Dr TEODOR PETRESCU
Faculty of Eng. and Management of Technological Systems: Prof. Dr CONSTANTIN MINCIU
Faculty of Eng. Sciences Taught in Modern Languages: Prof. Dr ADRIAN PASCU
Faculty of Industrial Chemistry: Prof. Dr HORIA IOVU
Faculty of Materials Science and Eng.: Prof. Dr RAMI SABAN
Faculty of Mechanical Eng.: Prof. Dr IOAN VOICA
Faculty of Power Eng.: Prof. Dr ADRIAN BADEA
Faculty of Transport Eng.: Prof. Dr CORNELIU MIHAIL ALEXANDRESCU

DIRECTORS
Technical College No. 1 (Mechanical College): Prof. Dr GHEORGHE SOLOMON
Technical College No. 2 (Electrical College): Dr ISTVAN SZTOJANOV

PROFESSORS

Basic Training:
BLANDU, M., Modern Languages
CRAIU, M., Mathematical Analysis
ENESCU, N., Mechanics
FLONDOR, P., Mathematical Analysis
STAICU, M., Mechanics
STĂNĂŞILĂ, O., Algebra, Mathematical Analysis
UDRIŞTE, C., Special Mathematics

Faculty of Electrical Engineering (tel. (21) 402-95-57; fax (21) 410-43-55; e-mail iordache@hertz.pub.ro):
CRĂCIUNESCU, A., Drive Systems
CRISTEA, P., Basic Electrical Eng.
FLUERAŞU, C., Basic Electrical Eng.
GALAN, N., Electrical Machines
GAVRILĂ, H., Basic Electrical Eng.
GOLOVANOV, C., Theory and Design of Electrical Apparatus
HĂNŢILĂ, I. F., Basic Electrical Eng.
IOAN, C. D., Basic Electrical Eng.
IONESCU, F., Theory and Design of Electrical Apparatus
MĂGUREANU, R., Micromachines and Drive Systems
MOREGA, AL., Electrical Materials
NOŢINGHER, P., Electrical Materials
POPESCU, M. O., Theory and Design of Electrical Apparatus
SPINEI, F., Basic Electrical Eng.
TĂNĂSESCU, F., Electrical Eng.
TOMESCU, F., Basic Electrical Eng.
TRUŞCĂ, V., Theory and Design of Electrical Apparatus

Faculty of Automatic Control and Computer Science (tel. (21) 402-91-79; fax (21) 410-10-44; e-mail dpopescu@router.indinf.pub.ro):
ATHANASIU, I., Computer Science
BORANGIU, T., Robotics
CRISTEA, V., Computer Science
CUPCEA, N., Computer Science
DUMITRACHE, I., Control Eng.
GIUMALE, C., Computer Science
ILIESCU, S., Control Eng.
IONESCU, T., Control Eng.
IORGA, V., Computer Science
MOISA, T., Computer Science
NIŢU, C., Control Eng.
PETRESCU, A., Computer Science
POPEEA, C., Control Eng.
POPESCU, D., Control Eng.
STANESCU, A., Control Eng.
TĂPUŞ, N., Computer Science

Faculty of Electronics and Telecommunications (061071 Bucharest, B-dul Iuliu Maniu 1–3; tel. (21) 410-33-30; fax (21) 411-33-73; e-mail teodor.petrescu@munde.pub.ro):
BĂNICĂ, I., Telecommunications
BODEA, M., Electronic Devices and Circuits
BORCOCI, E., Telecommunications
BREZEANU, GH., Electronic Devices and Circuits
BURILEANU, L., Telecommunications
BUZULOIU, V., Information Theory
CONSTANTIN, I., Telecommunications
DASCĂLU, D., Electronic Devices and Circuits
DRAGULANESCU, N., Reliability
DRAGULIMISCU, M., Reliability
IANCU, O., Reliability
LĂZĂRESCU, V., Information Theory
MANOLESCU, A., Electronic Devices and Circuits
MANOLESCU, A. M., Electronic Devices and Circuits
PROFIRESCU, M., Electronic Devices and Circuits
RUSU, A., Electronic Devices and Circuits
STRUNGARU, R., Medical Eng.
SVASTA, P., Reliability

Faculty of Power Engineering (tel. (21) 402-94-33; fax (21) 410-43-50; e-mail badea@study.energ.pub.ro):
ATHANASOVICI, V., Electric Power Plants
BADEA, A., Electric Power Plants
COATU, S., High Voltage Technology
CRISTESCU, D., High Voltage Technology
EREMIA, M., High Voltage Technology
GOLOVANOV, N., High Voltage Technology
HURDUBETIU, S., High Voltage Technology
IONESCU, D. C., Reliability
ISBĂŞOIU, E., Hydraulics
NISTREANU, V., Hydraulics
PANAITESCU, V., Hydraulics
POSTOLACHE, P., High Voltage Technology
ROBESCU, D. N., Hydraulics
SETEANU, I., Hydraulics
VASILIU, N., Hydraulics

Faculty of Mechanical Engineering (tel. (21) 402-96-11; fax (21) 410-42-51; e-mail i.voica@deca.ing-mec.pub.ro):
ALEXANDRESCU, N., Fine Mechanics
BRĂTIANU, C., Thermomechanical Equipment
JINESCU, V., Thermomechanical Equipment
MARINESCU, M., Thermodynamics
MICU, C., Fine Mechanics
MIHAIESCU, L., Thermomechanical Equipment
PANA, C., Internal Combustion Engines
PASCOVICI, M., Machine Elements
PASCU, A., Fine Mechanics
PETRESCU, S., Thermodynamics
TUDOR, A., Machine Elements

Faculty of Engineering and Management of Technological Systems (tel. (21) 402-94-57; fax (21) 411-42-67; e-mail minciu@imst.msp.pub.ro):
ANTONESCU, P., Mechanism Theory
AURITE, T., Machine Tools
CONSTANTINESCU, I., Strength of Materials
DORIN, A., Machine Tools
GHEORGHE, M., Machine-Building Technology
ILIESCU, N., Strength of Materials
ISPAS, C., Machine Tools
MINCIU, C., Machine Tools
NEAGU, C., Machine-Building Technology
POPESCU, I., Machine-Building Technology
RADEŞ, M., Strength of Materials
ZGURĂ, GH., Technology of Materials

Faculty of Transport Engineering (tel. (21) 402-96-53; fax (21) 411-16-59; e-mail cm_alexandrescu@rectorat.pub.ro):

ALEXANDRESCU, C., Remote Controls and Electronics
FRĂȚILĂ, GH., Automotive Eng.
NEGRUȘ, E., Automotive Eng.
RAICU, Ș., Transport Eng.
SEBEȘAN, I., Railway Vehicles
STOICESCU, A., Automotive Eng.
TANASUICA, I., Transport Eng.

Faculty of Biotechnical Systems Engineering (tel. (21) 402-96-75; fax (21) 411-62-53; e-mail paunescu@ma.pub.ro):

DAVID, L., Agricultural Machines
MURAD, E., Agricultural Machines
PAUNESCU, I., Agricultural Machines

Faculty of Aircraft Engineering (Bucharest, Str Polizu 1; tel. and fax (21) 650-23-87; e-mail s_galetuse@aero.pub.ro):

BERBENTE, C., Aircraft Eng.
GĂLETUȘE, S., Aircraft Eng.
STANCIU, V., Aircraft Eng.

Faculty of Materials Science and Engineering (tel. (21) 402-94-19; fax (21) 410-39-85; e-mail decanat@sim.pub.ro):

BOJIN, D., Metallurgy of Non-Ferrous Metals
BRATU, C., Forge and Foundry Technology
BUNEA, D., Forge and Foundry Technology
COJOCARU, M., Metallurgy of Non-Ferrous Metals
MOLDOVAN, P., Metallurgy of Non-Ferrous Metals
PANAIT, N., Metallurgy of Non-Ferrous Metals
RIPOȘAN, I., Forge and Foundary Technology
TALOI, D., Metallurgy of Non-Ferrous Metals
ZAMFIR, S., Metallurgy of Non-Ferrous Metals

Faculty of Industrial Chemistry (Bucharest, Str. Polizu 1; tel. and fax (21) 223-09-03):

ANDRONESCU, E., Silicate and Oxide Compounds Chemistry
BANCIU, M., Organic Chemistry
BOZGA, GH., Chemical Reactors
CONSTANTINESCU, I., Inorganic Chemical Technology
DIMONIE, M., Polymer Science
FILIPESCU, L., Inorganic Chemical Technology
GEANĂ, D., Physical Chemistry
GEORGESCU, M., Silicate and Oxide Compounds Chemistry
GURAN, C., Inorganic Chemistry
JINESCU, GH., Chemical Eng.
JITARU, I., Inorganic Chemistry
MEGHEA, A., Physical Chemistry
MUNTEAN, M., Silicate and Oxide Compounds Chemistry
RADU, C., Management in the Chemical Industry
RADU, D., Silicate and Oxide Compounds Chemistry
ROȘCA, S., Organic Chemistry
TARABAȘANU, C., Dyes
VASILESCU, D. S., Polymer Science
VIȘAN, T., Physical Chemistry and Electrochemical Technology
WOINAROSCHY, E. A., Chemical Eng.

UNESCO Department (tel. (21) 402-94-75; fax (21) 402-93-87; e-mail leca@eeee.unesco.pub.ro):

LECA, A., Environment

UNIVERSITATEA 'POLITEHNICA' TIMIȘOARA

Piața Victoriei 2, 300006 Timișoara
Telephone: (256) 22-03-76
Fax: (256) 19-03-21

E-mail: rectorat@rectorat.utt.ro
Internet: www.utt.ro
Founded 1920
State control
Academic year: October to July
Rector: Prof. Dr Ing. IOAN GHEORGHE CARTIȘ
Pro-Rectors: Prof. Dr Ing. T. E. MAN, Prof. Dr Ing. V. POPESCU, Prof. Dr Ing. N. ROBU
Scientific Sec.: Prof. Dr Ing. A. NICHICI
Chief Sec.: Prof. A. GASPAR
Admin. Dir: F. STAICU
Librarian: E. OTESTEANU

Number of teachers: 887
Number of students: 9,293

Publications: *Anuarul Didactic* (2 a year), *Anuarul Stiinţific* (research summary, 2 a year), *Buletinul Ştiinţific şi Tehnic* (Scientific and Technical Bulletin, 2 a year)

DEANS

Faculty of Mechanical Eng.: G. URDEA
Faculty of Electrotechnical Eng.: M. NEMEȘ
Faculty of Computers and Automatization: ST. HOLBAN
Faculty of Electronics and Telecommunications: A. IGNEA
Faculty of Civil Eng.: I. COSTESCU
Faculty of Hydrotechnics and Environmental Eng.: GH. POPA
Faculty of Chemical Eng.: O. DAVIDESCU
Faculty of Management in Production and Transport: M. IZVERCIAN
Faculty of Eng. (Hunedoara): S. JIȚIAN

PROFESSORS

Faculty of Mechanical Engineering:

ANCUSA, V., Fluid Mechanics, Transport Phenomena
BABEU, T., Theory of Elasticity and Strength of Materials
BACRIA, V., Mechanics
BAGIU, L., Electromechanical Eng.
BALAȘOIU, V., Hydropneumatic Equipment
BALEKICS, M., Machine Elements
BĂRGLĂZAN, M., Hydraulic Turbines
BRESTIN, A., Technology of Materials
BRÎNDEU, L., Mechanics and Vibration
BUDĂU, V., Materials, Quality Control
CARTE, I., Hydraulic Machines
CARTIS, I., Heat Treatment
CHIRIAC, A., Robotics and Automation in the Textile Industry
CRISTUINEA, C., Theory of Elasticity
CRUDU, M., Mechanisms
CUCURUZ, L., Materials, Casting
DAVID, I., Tolerances
DOBRE, I., Theory of Elasticity and Strength of Materials
DOLGA, V., Mechanical Eng.
DRĂGHICI, G., Manufacturing Eng.
DRĂGULESCU, D., Mechanical Eng.
DUMITRU, I., Technical Mechanics, Strength of Materials
DUNGAN, M., Calculus and Construction of Weight-bearing Structures of Railway Rolling Stock
FAUR, N., Elasticity and Strength of Materials
FLESER, T., Quality Control
GHEORGHIU, M., Mechanics of Fluids and Hydraulic Machines
GLIGOR, O., Components for Precision Mechanics Devices
GLIGOR, T., Mechanics
GLITA, G., Non-Conventional Welding Technologies
HEGEDUS, A., Mechanics
HERMAN, R., Technology Systems and Adjustments
HOANCĂ, V., Thermal Engines
ICLĂNZAN, T., Plastics Manufacturing
IONEL, I., Combustion and Environmental Impact of Stationary Combustion Facilities

IONESCU, N., Mechanisms
IORGA, D., Internal Combustion Engines
JADANEANȚ, M., Thermotechnics
KOVACS, A., Mathematics
LĂNCRĂNGEAN, Z., Technology of Materials
MĂDĂRAS, L., Machine Elements
MANIU, I., Dynamics, Construction and Design of Robotic Systems
MARCUSANU, A., Tolerances
MARINA, M., Mechanisms
MARINCA, V., Mechanics
MESAROȘ, A., Mechatronics, Mechanics
MILOȘ, L., Welding
MITELEA, I., Materials Science
NAGI, M., Thermic Devices, Heat and Mass Transfer
NEGREA, V. D., Internal Combustion Engines
NEGUT, N., Elasticity and Strength of Materials
NICA, C. M., Basic Experimental Research
NICHICI, A., Technology of Materials
NICOARĂ, I., Optical Devices
OPREA, M., Anti-Corrosive Protection Technologies, Materials Technology
PERJU, D., Mechanisms
POMMERSHEIM, A., Programming Languages
POPOVICI, I., Technology of Materials
POPOVICI, V., Welding Equipment
RADULESCU, C., Robotics, Industrial Robots
SAFTA, V., Welding Control and Welded Constructions
SANTĂU, I., Pumping Services
SAVII, G., Computer Aided Design
SERBAN, V., Materials and Primary Technologies
SMICALĂ, I., Mechanics
SPOREA, I., Materials Technology
SURU, P., Management and Marketing, Computer-Aided Design
TOADER, M., Mechanics
TUCU, D., Technologies and Machines for the Food Industry
URDEA, G., Machine Tools
VACARESCU, I., Biomedical Apparatus

Faculty of Electrotechnical Engineering:

ANDEA, P., Electrical Apparatus Technology
ATANASIU, G., Special Electrical Machines
BABESCU, M., Electrical Machines
BANZAR, T., Mathematics
BARTZER, S., Technology of Electrical Products
BIRIESCU, M., Electromechanical Systems Testing
BOJA, N., Mathematics
BOLDEA, I., Electrical Machines
BUTTA, A., Power Delivery
CONSTANTIN, I., Mathematics
CRĂCIUN, P., Physics
CRISTEA, M., Physics
DABA, D., Theoretical Electrotechnics
DELESEGA, I., Electrical Apparatus and Equipment Testing
DOBRE, S., Electrotechnics
DUȘA, V., Optimization Techniques in Industrial Energetics
GHEJU, P., Industrial Power Systems and Networks
HEINRICH, I., Stations and Transformation Posts
HELER, A., Electrotechnics and Electric Machines
IVASCU, C., Automation and Power Systems Protection
KILYENI, S., Numerical Methods in Eng.
LIPOVAN, O., Mathematics
LUSTREA, B., Basis of Energetics and Energy Conversion
MARCU, C., Physics
MIHALCA, I., Physics
MOGA, B., Microprocessors in Electroenergetics
MOLDOVAN, L., Electric Equipment

NEAGU, M., Mathematics
NEGRU, V., High-Voltage Eng.
NEMEŞ, M., Electrical Power Systems
NICA, E., Electrical Machines
POPOVICI, D., Electrical Drives
RADU, D., Non-linear Electrotechnics
SORA, I., Electroheat, Electrotechnology, Electrical Lighting
TOADER, D., Electromechanical Eng.
VASILIEVICI, A., Electrical Equipment
VELICESCU, C., Power Systems and Network Viability
VETRES, I., Basis of Electrotechnics

Faculty of Computers and Automatization:

BREABAN, F., Biomedical Eng.
CIOCARLIE, H., Numerical Processing of Signals
CRETU, V., Advanced Data Structures and Programming Techniques
CRIŞAN, M., Artificial Intelligence
DRAGOMIR, T.-L., Systems Theory
ELES, P., Programming Techniques
HOLBAN, S., Basis of Artificial Intelligence
JIAN, I., Database Design and Use
JURCĂ, I., Operating Systems Design
PREITL, S., Automatic Adjustment Eng.
PROSTEAN, O., System Identification
ROBU, N., Neuronal Networks
STRATULAT, M., Creation of Interfaces, Circuits
STRUGARU, C., Peripheral Devices and Data Transmission
VLĂDUTIU, M., Computer Reliability

Faculty of Electronics and Telecommunications:

BOGDANOV, I., Robotics
CARSTEA, H., Electronic Equipment Testing and Control
CHIVU, M., Electric and Electronic Measurements
CIUGUDEAN, M., Integrated Circuits and Electronics
CRIŞAN, S., Electronic Measurements
IGNEA, A., Electric and Electronic Measurements
IONEL, S., Statistics Processing of Signals
ISAR, A., Signals, Circuits, Systems
MUREŞAN, T., Integrated Circuits and Electronics
NAFORNIȚĂ, I., Signals Processing
NAFORNIȚA, M., Data Transfer, Modern Communications Networks
OTESTEANU, M., Television
POLICEC, A., Communications Systems and Techniques
POPESCU, V., Power Electronics
TĂNASE, M., Electronics
TIPONUT, V., Electronic Devices
TOMA, C., Television
TOMA, L., Data Acquisition Systems

Faculty of Civil Engineering:

BĂNCILĂ, R., Steel Structures
BOB, C., Chemistry and Construction Materials
BOTICI, A., Statics, Stability and Dynamics of Constructions
CADAR, I., Reinforced Concrete Structures
CARABA, I., Steel Structures
CIOBANU, G., English
CLIPII, T., Reinforced Concrete Structures
COSTESCU, I., Road Design and Construction
CUTEANU, E., Strength of Materials
DIMOIU, I., Earthquake Eng.
DUBINA, D., Construction
FURDUI, C., Civil Construction
GĂDIANU, L., Steel Structures
GAVRA, C. S., History of Architecture
GHEORGHIU, T., Urbanism, Architecture Design
GIONCU, V. M., Structures
GRUIA, A., Soil Mechanics and Foundation Eng.

HAIDA, V., Soil Mechanics and Foundation Eng.
IANCA, S., Civil Eng., Architecture and Urbanism
IVAN, M., Statics, Stability and Dynamics
JIVA, C., Concrete Bridges
MARIN, M., Soil Mechanics and Foundation Eng.
MERCEA, G., Steel Structures
NEAMȚU, M., Topography
PATCAS, I., Steel Structures
PODRUMAR, D. G., Heating Installations
REGEP, Z., Steel Structures
RETEZAN, A., Installations
SÂRBU, I., Numerical Methods in Installations Optimization
SCHEIN, T., Soil Mechanics and Foundation Eng.
STOIAN, V., Civil Construction
TOMA, A., Technologies and Mechanization in Civil Eng.
TUDOR, D., Civil Construction

Faculty of Hydrotechnics and Environmental Engineering:

CIOMOCOS, F., Strength of Materials
CRETU, G., Hydrology, Water Resources Supply
DANILESCU, A., Statics, Stability and Dynamics of Construction
DAVID, A., Hydraulics, Transport, Groundwater Pollution Modelling
DOANDES, V., Topography, Road Topography
ION, M., Hydrotechnical Construction
IONESCU, N., Machines for Construction, Irrigation and Drainage
MAN, E. T., Irrigation and Drainage
MARTON, A., Ecology, Ecotoxicology
MIREL, I., Water Supply and Town Drainage
NICOARĂ, T., Hydraulics
POPA, G., Hydrotechnical Construction
PRELUSCHEK, E., Hydrotechnic Constructions
ROGOBETE, G., Improvement of Soils and Polluted Areas
WEHRY, A., Irrigation and Drainage

Faculty of Chemical Engineering:

BURTICA, G., Mineral Salts Technology
CSUNDERLIK, C., Organic Chemistry
DAESCU, C., Pharmaceutical Products
IOVI, A., Technology of Mineral Fertilizers
LAZĂU, I., Physical Chemistry
LUPEA, A. X., Pharmaceutical Products
NUȚIU, M., Organic Chemistry
OPRESCU, D., General Chemistry
PERJU, D., Process Modelling
PETCA, G., Technology of General Chemistry, Water and Waste Water Technology
PUGNA, I., Chemical Industry

Faculty of Management in Production and Transport:

DĂNILĂ, C., Harvesting Machines
DUMITRESCU, C., Ergonomics, Quality Eng.
GLĂVAN, S., Agrobiological Basis of Agricultural Mechanics
IZVERCIAN, M., Management
NICA, C., Zootechnical Machines
POCINOG, G., Modelling, Simulation and Study of Production
POPA, H., Management and Industrial Eng.
SABAU, C., Finances, Accounting, Ergonomic Analysis, Management
ŞTEFAN, C., Agricultural Eng.
TAROATA, A., Marketing, Industrial Eng.

Faculty of Engineering (Hunedoara):

ILCA, I., Technology of Plastic Deformation
SAIMAC, A., Electrotechnics

UNIVERSITATEA DE ŞTIINŢE AGRICOLE ŞI MEDICINĂ VETERINARĂ A BANATULUI DIN TIMIŞOARA

Calea Aradului 119, 300645 Timişoara
Telephone: (256) 49-40-23
Fax: (256) 20-02-96
E-mail: usabtm@mail.dnttm.ro
Internet: www.usab-tm.ro
Founded 1945
State control
Academic year: October to September
Rector: Acad. Prof. Dr Dr H. C. PAÚ ION OTIMAN
Vice-Rectors: Prof. Dr HORIA CERNESCU, Prof. Dr VASILE GOSA, Prof. Dr ALEXANDRU MOISUC, Prof. Dr VALERIU TABARA
Gen. Admin. Dir: Ing. TRAINA BERAR
Admin. Officer: ENIKO NĂDĂŞAN
Scientific Advisor: Prof. Dr VIOREL BERAR
Head of Int. Relations Office: Dr COSMIN SALASAN

Library of 300,000 vols
Number of teachers: 544
Number of students: 6,302

Publication: *Lucrări Ştiinţifice* (series Agronomy, Veterinary Medicine and Animal Sciences, Food Technology, Horticulture, Agricultural Management, annual)

DEANS

Faculty of Agricultural Management: Prof. Dr LIVIU SÂMBOTIN
Faculty of Agriculture: Prof. Dr PAUL PARSAN
Faculty of Animal Sciences and Biotechnologies: Prof. Dr MARIAN BURA
Faculty of Food Technologies: Prof. Dr DOREL PARVU
Faculty of Horticulture: Prof. Dr AUREL LAZUREANU
Faculty of Veterinary Medicine: Prof. Dr GHEORGHE BARABUS

PROFESSORS

Faculty of Agronomy (tel. (256) 14-38-19):

BORCEAN, I., Phytotechnology
BORZA, I., General Ecology and Environmental Protection
COSTE, I., Botany and Plant Systematics
GOIAN, M., Agrochemistry
MOISUC, A., Food Cultivation and Fodder Plants
ONU, N., Land Improvement
PĂLĂGEŞIU, I., Entomology and Invertebrate Zoology
PALICICA, R., Comparative Anatomy
POPESCU, GH., Phytopathology
RUSU, I., Pedology

Faculty of Animal Sciences (tel. (256) 14-28-21):

BURA, M., Breeding of Fur-bearing Animals, Bees and Small Animals
DRAGOMIR, N., Fodder Production and Conservation
DRÂNCEAN, D., Biotechnology in Animal Nutrition
GRIGOROIU, E., Management, Marketing, Zooeconomy and Legislation
LIXANDRU, B., Ecology, Environmental Protection and Animal Hygiene
LUNGULESCU, GH., Horse Breeding and Equestrian Sports
NĂFORNIȚĂ, M., Biology of Animal Reproduction and Artificial Insemination
POPA, I. C., Agricultural Equipment and Zootechnical Installations
STANCIU, G., Technology of Cattle Breeding
VINTILĂ, C., Biotechnologies in the Processing of Animal Products
VINTILĂ, I., Genetics and Animal Improvement

Faculty of Food Technology (tel. (256) 12-79-84):

GĂRBĂN, Z., Food Biochemistry
JIANU, I. V., General Technology in the Food Industry

Faculty of Horticulture (tel. (256) 12-49-73):

AUNGURENCE, N., Agricultural Machines
BERAR, V., General Vegetable Crops
BUTNARU, G., Genetics
BUTNARU, H., Vegetable Growing
DRĂGĂNESCU, E., Orchards
GHINEA, L., Microbiology and Soil Biology
LĂZUREANU, A., Agrotechnology and Weeds
NEDELEA, G., Plant Improvement
NISTOR, GH., Animal Husbandry and Animal Nutrition
POP, A., Plant Physiology
TONEA, C., Tractors, and Agricultural and Horticultural Machinery

Faculty of Veterinary Medicine (tel. (256) 12-37-82):

BOLTE, S., Surgical Pathology
CERNESCU, H., Animal Reproduction, Obstetrics and Gynaecology
CHIȘU, I., Biochemistry
COMAN, M., Morphopathology
COSOROABĂ, I., Parasitology and Parasitological Diseases
CRĂINICEANU, E., Nutrition and Fodder Control
DECUN, M., Hygiene and Environmental Protection
FALCĂ, C., Semiology and Laboratory Diagnosis
MÂNZAT, R. M., Infectious Diseases
POP, P., Medical Pathology, Nutrition and Diseases of the Metabolism
SĂRĂNDAN, H., Physiology
SAS, E., Zootechnics
ȘINCAI, M., Cell Biology, Histology and Embryology
STUPARIU, A., Toxicology and Toxosis
TRIF, R., Microbiology

UNIVERSITATEA DE ȘTIINȚE AGRICOLE ȘI MEDICINĂ VETERINARĂ CLUJ-NAPOCA

Calea Mănăștur 3–5, 400372 Cluj-Napoca
Telephone: (264) 59-63-84
Fax: (264) 59-37-92
E-mail: staff@usamvcluj.ro
Internet: www.usamvcluj.ro
Founded 1869 as Institutul Agronomic; present name and status 1992

Rector: Prof. Dr LIVIU AL. MARGHITAS
Pro-Rectors: Prof. Dr IOAN GROZA, Prof. Dr DORU PAMFIL, Prof. Dr MIHAI RUSU

Library of 207,000 vols
Number of teachers: 208
Number of students: 1,903

Publication: *Buletinul* (agricultural-horticultural series, animal husbandry-veterinary medicine series)

DEANS

Faculty of Agriculture: Prof. Dr IOAN ROTAR
Faculty of Animal Science and Biotechnology: Prof. Dr GHEORGHE MURESAN
Faculty of Horticulture: Prof. Dr ALEXANDRU SILVIU APAHIDEAN
Faculty of Veterinary Medicine: Prof. Dr VASILE COZMA

UNIVERSITATEA DE ȘTIINȚE AGRICOLE ȘI MEDICINĂ VETERINARĂ 'ION IONESCU DE LA BRAD' DIN IAȘI

Al. Mihail Sadoveanu 3, 700490 Iași
Telephone: (232) 27-49-33
Fax: (232) 26-06-50
E-mail: rectorat@univagro-iasi.ro

Internet: www.univagro-iasi.ro
Founded 1912; present name 1990

Rector: Prof. Dr GERARD JITĂREANU

Library of 112,597 vols, incl. 6,655 periodicals

Publication: *Lucrări Științifice Editura* (annual)

DEANS

Faculty of Agriculture: Prof. Dr CONSTANTIN LEONTE
Faculty of Animal Science: Prof. Dr MIRCEA-IOAN POP
Faculty of Horticulture: Prof. Dr GICĂ GRĂDINARIU
Faculty of Veterinary Medicine: Prof. Dr MIHAI CARP CARARE

UNIVERSITATEA DE ȘTIINȚE AGRONOMICE ȘI MEDICINĂ VETERINARĂ BUCUREȘTI

Bdul Mărăști 59, 011464 Bucharest
Telephone: (21) 224-25-76
Fax: (21) 224-28-15
E-mail: post@info.usamv.ro
Internet: www.usab.ro
Founded 1852 Institutul Agronomic 'N. Bălcescu'

Rector: NICOLAI POMOHACI

Library: see Libraries and Archives
Number of teachers: 495
Number of students: 4,573 (4,298 undergraduate, 275 postgraduate)

Publication: *Lucrări Științifice* (annual)

Faculties of Agriculture, Animal husbandry, Biotechnology, Horticulture, Land reclamation and environmental eng., Veterinary medicine.

UNIVERSITATEA TEHNICA DIN CLUJ-NAPOCA

Str. Constantin Daicoviciu 15, 400020 Cluj-Napoca
Telephone: (264) 19-56-99
Fax: (264) 19-20-55
E-mail: int.rel.office@staff.utcluj.ro
Internet: www.utcluj.ro
Founded 1948
Academic year: October to July

Rector: Prof. Dr Eng. GHEORGHE LAZEA
Pro-Rectors: Prof. Dr Eng. PETRU BERCE, Prof. Dr Eng. VASILE IANCU, Prof. Dr Eng. MIHAI ILIESCU
Registrar: ELENA FĂRĂGĂU

Library: see Libraries and Archives
Number of teachers: 660
Number of students: 13,000

Publications: *ACAM-Automation, Computer Science and Applied Mathematics, Acta Technica Napocensis, Logi A, Scientific Bulletin of the Cluj-Napoca Technical University* (annual)

DEANS

Faculty of Architecture and Urban Planning: Prof. Dr Eng. MIRCEA SERGIU MOLDOVAN
Faculty of Automation and Computer Science: Prof. Dr Eng. KALMAN PUSZTAI
Faculty of Civil Eng.: Prof. Dr Eng. IOAN POP
Faculty of Electrical Eng.: Prof. Dr Eng. RADU MUNTEANU
Faculty of Electronics and Telecommunications: Prof. Dr Eng. AUREL VLAICU
Faculty of Machine Building: Prof. Dr Eng. GHEORGHE ACHIMAS
Faculty of Materials Science: Prof. Dr Eng. TIBERIU RUSU
Faculty of Mechanical Eng.: Prof. Dr Eng. NICOLAE CORDOS

College for Technical, Economic and Business Administration Studies: Dr Eng. SORIN GROZAV

PROFESSORS

Faculty of Civil Engineering (tel. (264) 19-48-16; fax (264) 19-49-67; e-mail ioan.pop@cif.utcluj.ro; internet www..utcluj.ro/utcn/civeng):

ALEXA, P., Theoretical Mechanics, Structural Dynamics, Structural Stability
ANDREICA, H., Timber Structures
BADEA, G., Water Supplies and Sewerage
BÂRSAN, G., Theoretical Mechanics, Structural Dynamics, Structural Stability
BIA, C., Strength of Materials, Theory of Elasticity
BORȘ, I., Theoretical Mechanics, Numerical Methods
BRUMARU, M., Buildings
BUCUR, I., Reinforced Concrete Structures
CĂTĂRIG, A., Structural Analysis
CHIOREAN, T., Economics of the Construction Industry, Management and Organization
CHISĂLIȚĂ, A., Theoretical Mechanics, Numerical Methods, Cable and Hinged Structures, Non-Linear Analysis
COMȘA, E., Buildings
CORDOȘ, GH., Sociology
DOMȘA, J., Construction Technology
DUMITRAȘ, M., Buildings
HOSSU, T., Management in Civil Eng.
ILIESCU, M., Road Eng.
IOANI, A., Strength of Materials, Theory of Elasticity
IONESCU, A., Reinforced Concrete Structures
JURCĂU, N., Psychology
KOPENETZ, L., Computer-Aided Eng. and Design, Structural Analysis, Lightweight Structures
MĂGUREANU, C., Reinforced and Prestressed Concrete
MARȚIAN, I., Strength of Materials, Theory of Elasticity
MOGA, A., Construction Technology
MOGA, I., Thermotechnology
MOGA, P., Metal Bridges
NISTOR, I., History of Culture and Civilization
OLARIU, I., Structural Analysis
ONEȚ, T., Reinforced and Prestressed Concrete
OPRIȚOIU, A., Heat Eng.
PĂCURAR, V., Steel Structures
PANȚEL, E., Strength of Materials, Theory of Elasticity, Numerical Methods
PETRINA, M., Structural Analysis, Computer Programming
POP, F., Electric Installation
POP, I., Seismic Eng.
POPA, A., Soil Mechanics and Foundations
VERDEȘ, D., Agricultural Buildings, Physics of Construction
VIOREL, G., Concrete Bridges

Faculty of Control and Computer Engineering (Str. G. Barițiu 26–28, 400027 Cluj-Napoca; tel. (264) 19-48-35; fax (264) 19-48-35; e-mail kalman.pusztai@cs.utcluj.ro; internet www.utcluj.ro/utcn/AC):

CÂMPEANU, V., Mathematical Analysis
COLOSI, T., Theory of Systems, Automation
COROVEI, I., Algebra, Special Mathematics
CRIVEI, I., Algebra, Mathematical Analysis
DĂDÂRLAT, T., Digital Circuits
FEȘTILĂ, C., Control Structures and Algorithms
GANSCA, I., Mathematical Analysis
GAVREA, I., Calculus
GORGAN, D., Fundamentals of Computer Graphics
IGNAT, I., Operating Systems
IVAN, D. M., Numerical Analysis, Mathematical Analysis

LAZEA, GH., Theory of Robot Control
LEŢIA, I. A., Real Time Control
LUNG, N., Special Mathematics
NEDEVSCHI, S., Design with Microchips
OPRIŞ, GH., Special Mathematics, Differential Equations
PUSZTAI, K., Computer Networks
RASA, I., Numerical Mathematics
SALOMIE, I., Design Techniques
TOADER, GH., Mathematical Analysis
VORNICESCU, N., Differential Equations, Mathematical Analysis

Faculty of Electrical Engineering (Str. G. Bariţiu 26–28, 400027 Cluj-Napoca; tel. (264) 19-48-45; fax (264) 19-48-45; e-mail radu .munteanu@mas.utcluj.ro; internet www .utcluj.ro/utcn/ETEL/et):

BĂLAN, H., Electrical Equipment
BIRO, K., Electrical Machines
CATANĂ, D., Marketing
CATANĂ, GH., Marketing
CHINDRIŞ, M., Technological Design of Management Systems
CIUPA, R., Principles of Electronics
DARIE, S., Electrical Power Stations, Electrical Apparatus
DRAGOMIR, N., Electrical Measuring
IANCU, V., Electrical Machines
IMECS, M., Theory of Automatic Control Systems
IUGA, A., Electrotechnical Eng.
MAIER, V., Electrothermics
MAN, E., Elements of Electrotechnics
MARSCHALKO, R., Electronics
MICU, D., Electrical Eng.
MUNTEANU, R., Data Acquisition, Sensors and Control
RĂDULESCU, M., Electrical Drives
SIMION, F., Non-linear Circuits, Basic Electrical Eng.
TĂRNOVAN, I. G., Electronic Measurements
TODORAN, GH., Electrical Measurements
TRIFA, V., Applied Informatics and Microprocessor Systems
VIOREL, A., Electrical Machines

Faculty of Electronics and Telecommunications (Str. G. Bariţiu 26–28, 400027 Cluj-Napoca; tel. (264) 19-48-31, fax (264) 19-20-55; e-mail aurel.vlaicu@com.utcluj.ro; internet www.utcluj.ro/utcn/ELTC):

BORDA, M., Information Theory
DOBROTĂ, V., Telecommunications
FEŞTILĂ, L., Analogical Integrated Circuits
LUNGU, Ş., Electronics
MIRON, C., Electronics
PITICĂ, D., Applied Electronics
RUSU, C., Signal Processing
TODEREAN, G., Communications Eng.
VAIDA, M., Informatics
VLAICU, A., Multimedia Systems
VOICULESCU, E., Optoelectronics
ZĂHAN, S., Telecommunications

Faculty of Machine Building (Bdul Muncii 103–105, 400641 Cluj-Napoca; tel. (264) 41-50-51; fax (264) 41-50-54; e-mail gheorghe .achimas@tcm.utcluj.ro; internet zeus.east .utcluj.ro/mb):

ABRUDAN, I., Production Systems
ACHIMAŞ, GH., Metal Forming
ANTAL, A., Machine Components
ARGHIR, M., Computer Programming
BANABIC, D., Manufacturing Technologies
BERCE, P., Manufacturing Technologies
BLEBEA, I., Industrial Robots
BOJAN, I., Management Information Systems
CÂNDEA, D., Industrial Management
CĂZILĂ, A., Machine Components
CREŢU, M., Machine Tools and Industrial Robots
DEACU, L., Hydraulics
GALIŞ, M., Design of Machine Tools
GYENGE, Cs., Manufacturing Technologies
IANCĂU, H., Plastics

ISPAS, V., Mechanics, Robotics
ITU, T., Technical Measurements
MORAR, L., Numerical Control
NEGREAN, L., Mechanics
OLTEANU, R., Manufacturing Technology
PLITEA, N., Mechanics
POP, D., Machine Components
POP, I., Hydraulics
POPA, M., Unconventional Technologies
POPESCU, S., Mechanics
PRUNEA, P., Economics
ROŞ, O., Manufacturing Technologies
SUCALĂ, F., Machine Components
URSU-FISCHER, N., Computer Programming

Faculty of Materials Science (Bdul Muncii 103–105, 400641 Cluj-Napoca; tel. (264) 41-50-51; fax (264) 41-50-54; e-mail trusu@sim .east.utcluj.ro; internet www.utcluj.ro/utcn/ Facsim):

ARGHIR, G., Crystallography
BICSAK, E., Science of Materials, Welded Constructions Technology
BIRIŞ, I., Heat Processes in Metallurgical Furnaces
CÂNDEA, V., Materials Science
CANTA, T., Plastic Deformation Theory
COMAN, S., Mechanical Eng., Mechanical Technology
COSMA, I., Physics
CULEA, E., Physics
DEMCO, D., Physics
DOMŞA, S., Materials Technology
IANCU, D., Heat and Thermochemical Treatment Technologies
LUCACI, P., Physics
LUPŞA, I., Physics
MILEA, I., Physics
MILITARU, V., Physics
NAGY, E., Steel Casting
NAŞCU, H., Chemistry
ORBAN, R., Materials Technology
PICĂ, M., Chemistry
POP, O., Physics
RUSU, T., Quality Management, Environmental Protection
SOPORAN, V., Technology for Casting Alloys
SPÂRCHEZ, Z., Composite Materials, Metallurgical Physics
VERMEŞAN, G., Heat and Thermochemical Treatment Technologies
VIDA, S., Materials Manufacturing Technology

Faculty of Mechanical Engineering (Bdul Muncii 103–105, 400641 Cluj-Napoca; tel. (264) 41-50-51; fax (264) 41-50-54; e-mail cordos_n@yahoo.fr; internet www.east.utcluj .ro/mec):

APAHIDEAN, B., Thermodynamics
BĂŢAGĂ, N., Heat Machines
BEJAN, M., Strength of Materials
BRÂNZAŞ, P., Management and Marketing
BURNETE, N., Automobiles and Tractors
CORDOŞ, N., Vehicle Dynamics
CREŢU, A., Strength of Materials
HĂRDĂU, M., Strength of Materials
MĂDĂRĂŞAN, T., Thermodynamics and Thermal Machines
MĂTIEŞ, V., Mechanics
ROŞ, V., Forming Machines

Faculty of Architecture and Urban Planning (Str. Observator 32–34, Cluj-Napoca; tel. (264) 19-02-55; fax (264) 19-02-55; e-mail moldovanms@hotmail.com; internet www .utcluj.ro/utcn/arch):

MATEI, A., Architectural Composition
MOLDOVAN, M., History of World Architecture, Aesthetics, History of Arts
MURADIN, C., Styles of Furniture
SZABO, B., Theory of Structures and Renovation of Constructions

UNIVERSITATEA TEHNICĂ DE CONSTRUCŢII BUCUREŞTI
(Bucharest Technical University of Civil Engineering)

Bdul Lacul Tei 124, 020396 Bucharest

Telephone: (21) 242-12-08
Fax: (21) 242-07-81
E-mail: stematiu@utcb.ro
Internet: www.utcb.ro

Founded 1864

Rector: Prof. Dr DAN STEMATIU
Pro-Rectors: Prof. Dr EUGEN CHESARU, Prof. Dr NICULAE MIRA, Prof. Dr IORDAN PETRESCU
Scientific Sec.: Prof. Dr DUMITRU ONOSE

Library of 560,000 vols
Number of teachers: 530
Number of students: 6,964

Publication: *Buletin Ştiinţific* (Scientific Bulletin, quarterly)

DEANS

Faculty of Bridges, Roads and Railways: Prof. Dr ANTON CHIRICA
Faculty of Building Services: Prof. Dr RADU MIRCEA DAMIAN
Faculty of Construction Technology: Prof. Dr FLORIN PETRESCU
Faculty of Geodesy: Prof. Dr JOHAN NEUNER
Faculty of Hydraulic Eng.: Prof. Dr OVIDIU IANCULESCU

UNIVERSITATEA TEHNICĂ 'GHEORGHE ASACHI' IAŞI

Bdul D. Mangeron 67, 700050 Iaşi

Telephone: (232) 21-23-22
Fax: (232) 21-16-67
E-mail: rectorat@staff.tuiasi.ro
Internet: www.tuiasi.ro

Founded 1937
State control
Languages of instruction: Romanian, English, French
Academic year: October to October

Rector: Prof. Dr Ing. NICOLAE BADEA
Pro-Rectors: Prof. Dr Ing. MIRCEA COZMÎNCĂ, Prof. Dr Ing. ION GIURMA, Prof. Dr Ing. VALENTIN I. POPA, Prof. Dr Ing. MIHAIL VOICU
Registrar: GABRIELA IURCAN
Librarian: MIHAELA ŞTIRBU

Library: see Libraries and Archives
Number of teachers: 1,164
Number of students: 10,117

Publications: *Review Magazine* (2 a year), *Scientific Bulletin* (2 a year)

DEANS

Faculty of Architecture: Prof. Dr arch. VIRGILU ONOFREI
Faculty of Chemical Eng.: Prof. Dr ION BALASANIAN
Faculty of Civil Eng.: Prof. Dr NICOLAE TĂRANU
Faculty of Control Systems and Computer Eng.: Prof. Dr DAN GÂLEA
Faculty of Electrical Eng.: Prof. Dr MIHAI CRETU
Faculty of Electronics and Telecommunications: MIHAI LUCANU
Faculty of Mechanical Eng.: Prof. Dr SPIRIDON CRETU
Faculty of Hydrotechnical Eng.: IOSIF BARTHA
Faculty of Machine Building: Prof. Dr VIOREL CHIRILĂ
Faculty of Materials Science and Eng.: Prof. Dr DAN GELU GĂLUŞCĂ
Faculty of Textiles and Leather Technology: ROMEO BUTNARU
Cross-Border Faculty of Eng. (in collaboration with Technical University of Moldova): Prof. GH. NISTOR

PROFESSORS

Faculty of Architecture (Bdul D. Mangeron 43, 700050 Iaşi; tel. and fax (232) 43-78-38; e-mail arhitect@ce.tuiasi.ro; internet www.tuiasi.ro):

BLIUC, I., Building Elements
ONOFREI, V., Architectural Theory

Faculty of Automatic Control and Computer Engineering (Bdul Mangeron 53A, 700050 Iaşi; tel. (232) 23-13-43; fax (232) 21-42-90; e-mail decanat@ac.tuiasi.ro):

BALABAN, E., Digital Control Systems, Control of Electrical Drives
BOŢAN, C., Optimization Techniques, Optimal Control
BOTEZ, C., Databases and Computer Programming, Software Eng.
GÂLEA, D., Artificial Intelligence
GANCIU, T., Systems Identification, Data Processing
HOZA, F., Digital Computers, Microcontrollers
HUŢANU, C., Multiprocessor Systems, Microprocessor Systems
ILINCA, M., Computer Programming
LAZĂR, C., Control Eng., Data Transmission
OLAH, I., Electrical and Electronic Control Equipment, Servomechanisms
PAL, C., Robot Control Systems
PĂNESCU, A. D., Knowledge-Based Systems, Robot Control Systems
PĂSTRĂVANU, O. C., Discrete Event Systems, Neural Networks in Control Eng.
VALACHI, A., Digital Logic Design, Digital Systems Design
VOICU, M., Systems Theory, Principles of Feedback Control

Faculty of Chemical Engineering (Bdul D. Mangeron 71A, 700050 Iaşi; tel. (232) 27-86-80 ext. 2135; fax (232) 27-13-11; e-mail decanat@ch.tuiasi.ro; internet www.tuiasi.ro):

AELENEI, N., Physical Chemistry
APOSTOLESCU, M., Mineralogy
BALASANIAN, I., Technology of Inorganic Substances
BEZDADEA, M., General Chemistry
BOBU, E., Equipment in the Pulp and Paper Industry
BULACOVSCHI, V., Macromolecular Chemistry
CIOVICĂ, S., Paper Technology
CRISTIAN, GH., Equipment for Organic Industry
DĂRÂNGĂ, M., Physical Chemistry of Polymers
DUMITRIU, E., Organic Technology
GAVRILESCU, D., Pulp and Paper Technology
GORDUZA, V., Technology of Dyes
GRIGORIU, I., Equipment for Inorganic Technology
IVĂNOIU, M., Physical Chemistry of Polymers
LAZĂR, D., Electrochemistry
LUCA, C., General Chemistry
LUNGU, M., Rheology of Polymers
MACOVEANU, M., General Technology
MIHĂILESCU, C., Physico-Chemistry of Polymers
NICU, M., Technology of Polymers
NICU, V., General Technology
OBROCEA, P., Pulp and Paper Technology
ONISCU, C., Technology of Synthetic and Biosynthetic Drugs
ONU, P., General Chemistry
OPREA, CL., Mechano-chemistry of Polymers, Monomers and Polymer Technology
OPREA, SP., Chemical Organic Technology
PETRESCU, S., Materials Science
POPA, I. M., Physical Chemistry
POPA, M., Polymer Technology

POPA, V., Wood Chemistry
ROŞCA, I., Inorganic Chemistry
RUSU, M., Rubber and Plastic Materials Processing
SCUTARU, D., Organic Chemistry
SIMINICEANU, I., Technology of Inorganic Substances
SIMIONESCU, B., Physical Chemistry of Polymers
SÎRGHIE, I., Analytical Chemistry
STANCU, A., Transport Phenomena in the Chemical Industry
SZEP, A., Technology of Inorganic Substances
UNGUREANU, ŞT., Automation in the Chemical Industry
VĂTĂ, M., Organic Chemistry

Faculty of Civil Engineering (Bdul D. Mangeron 43, 700050 Iaşi; tel. (232) 27-86-83; fax (232) 23-33-68; e-mail decanat@ce.tuiasi.ro):

AMARIEI, C., Structural Mechanics, Plastic Design
ANDREI, R., Transport Infrastructure
ATANASIU, M. G., Structural Mechanics, Computer-Aided Design, Earthquake Eng.
AXINTE, E., Steel Structures
BOBOC, V., Road Eng.
BROŞTEANU, M., Buildings
BUDESCU, M., Structural Mechanics, Computer-Aided Design, Earthquake Eng.
CIONGRADI, I., Structural Mechanics, Computer-Aided Design, Earthquake Eng.
CIORNEI, AL., Buildings
COROBCEANU, S., Concrete and Reinforced Concrete Construction
COSOSCHI, B., Road Eng.
DUMITRAŞ, A., Structural Mechanics
FLOREA, N., Hydrotechnical Structures
GAVRILAŞ, I., Construction
GIUŞCĂ, N., Construction Technology
GORBĂNESCU, D., Strength of Materials, Theory of Elasticity and Plasticity
GRECU, V., Soil Mechanics and Foundation Eng.
GROLL, L., Building Materials
GUGIUMAN, G., Road Eng.
HAGIU, V., Management of Construction Works
HIRHUI, I., Building Materials
IGNAT, J., Electrical Installations
IONESCU, C., Structural Mechanics, Earthquake Eng.
ISOPESCU, D., Wooden Constructions, Composite Structures
JANTEA, C., Bridge Eng.
MATEESCU, TH., Water Supply and Sewerage Installations, Installations for Buildings
MIHALACHE, N., Strength of Materials, Theory of Elasticity and Plasticity, Numerical Methods
MUŞAT, V., Soil Mechanics and Foundation
NOUR, S., Concrete and Reinforced Concrete Constructions
PESCARU, V., Steel Structures
POPOVICI, D., Highways
PRECUPANU, D., Strength of Materials, Theory of Elasticity and Plasticity
RĂILEANU, P., Soil Mechanics and Foundations
SECU, AL., Industrial and Agricultural Constructions
ŞERBANOIU, I., Managerial Analysis of the Building Process, Management of Construction Work
STANCIU, A., Soil Mechanics and Foundations
ŞTEFĂNESCU, D., Buildings
ŢARANU, N., Industrial Buildings and Composite Structures, Steel Structures
UNGUREANU, N., Strength of Materials, Theory of Elasticity and Plasticity, Numerical Methods
VARLAM, F., Concrete Bridge Eng.

VELICU, C., Thermal Eng., Rehabilitation of Buildings
VEREŞ, AL., Buildings and Architectural Acoustics
VLAD, I., Strength of Materials, Theory of Elasticity and Plasticity
VLAD, N., Road Technology Eng.

Faculty of Electrical Engineering (Bdul D. Mangeron 53, 700050 Iaşi; tel. and fax (232) 23-76-27; e-mail decanat@ee.tuiasi):

ADAM, M., Electrical Equipment
ALEXANDRESCU, V., Power Systems
ANDRONE, C., Principles of Electrical Eng.
ASAFTEI, C., Power Plants
ASANDEI, D., Power Plants
BALAN, T., Electrical Materials
BALUTA, GH., Principles of Electrical Eng.
BARABOI, A., Electrical Equipment, EMC, Power Electronics
CANTEMIR, L., Electric Traction, Uses of Electrical Energy in Modelling, Electrical Drives, Systems Theory, Intelligent Control
CÂRŢÎNĂ, GH., Optimal Control and Computer Applications in Energetics
CIOBANU, L., Electrical Drives of Robots, Reliability
CIOBANU, R. C., Electrical Materials
CREŢU, A., Electrical Eng.
CREŢU, M., Electrical Measurements and Transducers
DIACONESCU, M., Electrical Drives, Electronics and Power Electronics
GAVRILAŞ, M., Power Plants
GEORGESCU, GH., Power Networks
GRAUR, I., Power Electronics, Vector Control of AC Drives
GUŞĂ, M., High-Voltage Eng.
HNATIUC, E., Electrical Apparatus Design, Environmental Protection
IVAS, D., Power Systems Reliability
LEONTE, P., Electrical Equipment
LIVINŢ, GH., Systems Theory, Automatic Control
MITREA, S., Principles of Electrical Eng.
MUNTEANU, F., Power Systems Reliability
NEMESCU, M., Systems Theory and Industrial Automation
OLAH, R., Overvoltages and Insulation Eng.
OLARU, R., Industrial Automation
POPESCU, I., Fundamentals of Electrical Eng.
SIMION, A., Electrical Machines
SUCHAR, I., Electrical Eng. and Electronics
TEODORU, E., Electrical Machines and Drives

Faculty of Electronics and Telecommunications (Bdul Copou 11, 700506 Iaşi; tel. (232) 27-00-41; fax (232) 21-77-20; e-mail decanat@etc.tuiasi.ro):

ALEXA, D., Microwave Eng., Power Electronics
ALEXANDRU, D. N., Telecommunications, Communications Systems
BÂRSAN, T., Mathematics
BEJANCU, A., Mathematics
BOGDAN, I., Mobile Communications, Antennas
CASSIAN, I., Fibre-optic Communications, Microwave Technology
CEHAN, V., Radio Transmitters, Satellite Communications
CIOBANU, GH., Mathematics
CORDUNEANU, A., Mathematics
COTAE, P., Digital Communication
CRĂCIUN, I., Mathematics
DIMITRIU, L., Electronic Measurement and Control Apparatus, Automotive Electronics
DUMA, P., Microprocessors, Microcontrollers, Electronic Telephone Exchanges
FETECĂU, C., Mathematics
GORAS, L., Signals, Circuits and Systems

GRIGORAS, V., Signals, Circuits and Systems

LUCANU, M., Industrial Electronics, PWM Techniques for Converters

MUNTEANU, V., Information Theory

NEAGU, AL., Mathematics

NEGOESCU, N., Mathematics

PAPAGHIUC, N., Mathematics

SAVA, V., Mathematics

SÎRBU, A., Software Eng., Computer-Aided Design

STIURCĂ, D., Analogue Integrated Circuits

TALPALARU, P., Mathematics

TARNICERIU, D., Signal Processing

TEODORESCU, H., Medical Electronics, Image Processing, Neural Networks and Fuzzy Systems

Faculty of Hydrotechnical Engineering (Bdul D. Mangeron 63–65, 700050 Iaşi; tel. and fax (232) 27-08-04; e-mail decanat@hidro.tuaisi.ro):

ALEXANDRESCU, O., Pumping Installations

AXINTE, S., Ameliorative Agriculture

BÂRSAN, E., Water Supply

BARTHA, I., Hydraulics

BLĂGOI, O., Hydraulics

CISMARU, C., Irrigation and Drainage

COJOCARU, I., Irrigation and Drainage

DIMA, M., Sewerage, Waste Water Treatment

GIURMĂ, I., Hydrology and Water Management

HOBJILĂ, V., Construction Technology

LUCA, M., Hydraulics

MANOLOVICI, M., Hydrotechnical Constructions

NISTOR, GH., Surveying

NIŢESCU, E., Work Technology and Mechanization in Land Reclamation

PATRAŞ, M., Reinforced Concrete

POPESCU, ST., Numerical Methodology, Dispersion

POPOVICI, N., Soil Erosion Control, Regulation and Management of Watercourses

STĂTESCU, F., Soil Science

Faculty of Machine Building (Bdul D. Mangeron 63, 700050 Iaşi,; tel. (232) 24-21-09; fax (232) 21-16-67; e-mail secretariat@tcm.tuiasi.ro):

AGOP, M., Physics

BOHOSIEVICI, C., Technology of Machine Building

BRAHA, V., Mechanical Eng.

CĂLUGĂRU, GH., Physics

CARATA, E., Machine Tools

CHIRILĂ, V., Technology of Machine Building

CIUBOTARIU, C., Physics

CONSTANTINESCU, C., Machine Tools

COZMÎNCĂ, M., Metal Cutting

DUSA, P.

FETECĂU, C., Theoretical Mechanics

GHERGHEL, N., Design of Mechanical Devices

GRĂMESCU, TR., Technology of Machine Building

IBĂNESCU, I., Theoretical Mechanics

LUNGU, GH., Machine Tools

MUSCĂ, G., Computer-Aided Manufacturing

NEAGU, E., Physics

NEAGU, R., Physics

PANAIT, S., Metal Cutting

PARASCHIV, DR., Machine Repairing Technology

PLĂHTEANU, B., Machine Tools

RUSU, E., Theoretical Mechanics

SLĂTINEANU, L., Machine Building Technology

UNGUREANU, GH., Computer-Aided Design

URSU, D., Physics

ZET, GH., Physics

ZETU, D., Design of Automatic Machine Tools

Faculty of Materials Science and Engineering (Bdul D. Mangeron 63, 700050 Iaşi; tel. and fax (232) 23-00-09; e-mail decanat@sim.tuiasi.ro):

ALEXANDRU, I., Technology of Materials

BACIU, C., Technology of Materials

BULANCEA, V., Rolling

CARCEA, I., Composites

COJOCARU FILIPIUC, V., Metallurgy

DIMA, A., Technology and Applied Metallurgy

FLORESCU, A., Materials Technology

GĂLUSCĂ, D. G., Technology of Thermal Treatment

MĂLUREANU, I., Technology of Metals

MUNTEANU, C., Materials Technology

PETRUŞ, O., Computational Metallurgy

SUSAN, M., Applied Metallurgy

Faculty of Mechanical Engineering (Bdul D. Mangeron 61–63 700050 Iaşi; tel. and fax (232) 23-23-37; e-mail decanat@mec.tuaisi.ro):

AMARIEI, N., Strength of Materials

ATANASIU, V., Mechanical Transmissions

BÂRSĂNESCU, P., Strength of Materials

BERCEA, M., Machine Design

COMANDAR, C., Strength of Materials

COZMA, D., Agricultural Machines

CRĂCIUN, V., Agricultural Machines

CREŢU, SP., Machine Design, Tribology and Vibration

DĂSCĂLESCU, D., Internal Combustion Engines

DRĂGAN, B., Machine Vibrations

DUCA, C., Mechanisms

DUMITRAŞCU, GH., Thermotechnics and Heat Engines

GAFIŢANU, M., Machine Design, Tribology and Vibration

GAIGINSCHI, R., Internal Combustion Engines

GRIGORAS, S., Machine Design and Reliability

HAGIU, GH., Machine Design and Vibration

HORBANIUC, G., Thermotechnology and Heat Engines

HOSTIUC, L., Machine Design

LEON, D., Strength of Materials

LOZONSCHI, GH., Thermotechnics and Heat Engines

MERTICARU, V., Machine Dynamics

MOCANU, F., Strength of Materials

NECULĂIASA, V., Agricultural Machines

OLARU, D., Tribology and Machine Design

OPRIŞAN, C., Mechanisms

PALIHOVICI, VAL., Strength of Materials

POPOVICI, A., Mechanisms

RACOCEA, C., Machine Design

RECEANU, D., Mechanisms

ŢENU, I., Equipment for the Food Industry

ŽUBCU, V., Gas and Steam Turbines

Faculty of Textiles and Leather Technology (Bdul D. Mangeron 53, corp TEX 1, 700050 Iaşi; tel. (232) 23-04-91; fax (232) 23-04-91; e-mail decanat@tex.tuiasi.ro):

ANTONIU, GH., Textile Raw Materials

AVRAM, D., Structure of Textile Yarns

BADEA, N., Leather and Furs Chemistry and Technology

BORDEIANU, D., Technology and Equipment for Spinning Mills

BRUDARU, O., Fuzzy Systems

BUCEVSCHI, D., Technology of Leather Substitutes

BUDULAN, C., Equipment and Automation in the Knitwear Industry

BUTNARU, R., Chemistry and Technology of Textile Materials

CIOCOIU, M., Weaving Process and Machinery, Statistical Methods in Textiles

CONDUCARCHE, GH., Management

DRĂGOI, L., Weaving Machinery Design and Automation

GRIBINCEA, V., Textile Raw Materials

GRIGORIU, A., Special Technologies of Textile Products Finishing

ILIESCU, E., Principles of Chemical Technology

IRIMIA, M., Economics and Accountability

LEONTE, R., Marketing

LIUŢE, D., Preparatory Weaving Processes, Weaving Technology

LUCA, G., Management

MĂLUREANU, G., Footwear Design

MITU, S., Clothing

MUNTEANU, A., Marketing and Economics

MUNTEANU, V., Marketing

MUREŞAN, A., Equipment for Textile Finishing

MUSTAŢĂ, A., Bast Fibre Spinning

NECULĂIASA, M., Textile Metrology, Textile Quality Control

PINTILIE, E., Computer-Aided Design in Ready-Made Clothing, Design of Ready-Made Clothing Machinery

RUSU, C., Total Quality Management, Human Resources Management

VÎLCU, M., Theoretical Bases of Spinning

VITAN, F., Transfer Phenomena and Equipment

VOICU, M., Interpersonal Communication

Other Institutes of Higher Education

Academia de Arte Vizuale 'Ioan Andreescu' (Academy of Visual Arts 'Ioan Andreescu'): Piaţa Unirii 31, 400098 Cluj-Napoca; tel. (264) 19-15-77; fax (264) 19-28-90; f. 1950; faculties of Fine arts, Decorative arts and design; library: 52,000 vols; 75 teachers; 553 students; Rector IOACHIM NICA.

Academia Naţională de Educaţie Fizică şi Sport (National Academy of Physical Education and Sport): Str. Constantin Noica 140, 060057 Bucharest; tel. (21) 638-53-15; fax (21) 312-04-00; e-mail anefs@kappa.ro; internet www.kappa.ro/clients/anefs/anefs/htm; f. 1922 (fmrly Institutul de Educaţie Fizica şi Sport, renamed 1992); teacher training and army officer training, coaches and physiotherapists; library: 145,000 vols; 99 teachers; 887 students; Rector Prof. Dr IOAN SABĂU; publ. *Discobolul*.

Academia de Muzică: Str. Stirbei Vodă 33, 010102 Bucharest; tel. (21) 614-63-41; fax (21) 615-83-96; f. 1864; faculties of Performance and composition, Musicology, Musical pedagogy; library: see Libraries and Archives; 186 teachers; 800 students; Rector Prof. PETRE LEFTERESCU.

Academia de Muzică 'Gheorghe Dima': Str. I.C. Brătianu 25, 400079 Cluj-Napoca; tel. and fax (264) 19-38-79; e-mail amgd@amgd.utcluj.ro; internet www.amgd.ro; f. 1819, reorganized 1919; faculties of Instrumental performance, Music theory, Singing and stage art; library: 188,000 vols; 250 teachers; 1,182 students; Rector Prof. AUREL MARC; publ. *Lucrări de Muzicologie* (Musicology Articles, annual).

Academia de Studii Economice (Academy of Economic Studies): Piaţa Romană 6, 010374 Bucharest; tel. (21) 211-26-50; fax (21) 312-95-49; e-mail rectorat@crc.ase.ro; internet www.ase.ro; f. 1913; faculties of Management, Econ., Agricultural and food production, Economy and admin., Finance and banking, Admin. and accounting, Cybernetics, Statistics and computer science for econ., Trade, Int. economic relations, Economic studies in foreign languages; college of econ. at Buzău; library: see Libraries and Archives; 765 teachers; 20,000 students; Rector Prof. Dr PAUL BRAN; publs *Economic*

Journal (in Romanian and English, quarterly), *Informatica Economică* (quarterly)..

Attached Centre:

Bulgaria–Romania Interuniversity Europe Center/BRIE–Giurgiu: Str. Negru Voda 8, 080036 Giurgiu; tel. (21) 211-07-97; fax (21) 312-95-49; e-mail brie@ase.ro; internet www.brie.ase.ro; f. 2001;

operates through collaboration between Rusenski Universitet 'Angel Kanchev' (see Bulgaria chapter) and the Academia de Studii Economice; Dir Prof. Dr CONSTANTIN APOSTOL.

Institutul de Arhitectură 'Ion Mincu': Str. Academiei 18–20, 010014 Bucharest; tel. 315-54-82; fax 312-39-54; e-mail mac@iaim

.ro; internet www.iaim.ro; f. 1892; architecture and town-planning; library: 203,000 vols; 228 teachers (incl. 80 part-time); 2,000 students; Rector Prof. Dr BARBU POPESCU; Chancellor Assoc. Prof. Dr ZENO BOGDANESCU; publs *Analele Arhitecturii, Arhitext Design*.

RUSSIA

The Higher Education System

In March 1917 the last Tsar of the Romanov dynasty, which had ruled Russia as an autocracy since 1613, was forced to abdicate and a liberal Provisional Government took power. The Bolsheviks overthrew the Provisional Government in November of the same year and the Russian Soviet Federative Socialist Republic (RSFSR) was proclaimed. In 1922 the RSFSR joined the Union of Soviet Socialist Republics (USSR), which disintegrated in 1991, when the Russian Federation, as the RSFSR was formally renamed, was founded. The oldest current institutions of higher education date from the 18th century, notably St Petersburg State University (founded 1724) and Moscow State University 'M. V. Lomonsov' (founded 1755). Several specialist institutions were founded during the reign of Catherine the Great (1762–96). Major institutions founded during the 19th century include Moscow Agricultural Academy 'K. A. Tirmiyazev' (founded 1865), Tomsk Polytechnic University (founded 1896) and Nizhnii Novgorod State Technical University (founded 1898 in Warsaw, Poland). Universal education was a fundamental Bolshevik principle, and during the period of Soviet rule (1917–91) more than 340 institutions of higher education were founded. In 2004/05 there were 7m. students enrolled in institutions of higher education, of which there were 1,061 in 2005/06.

Higher education institutions are categorised as Academies, Universities, Institutes and Conservatories. Universities are sub-divided by subject area: Agriculture, Humanities and Sciences, Medical, Pedagogical and Technical. The Ministry of Education and Science has overall responsibility for higher education, particularly the licensing and accreditation of institutions. Russia participates in the Bologna Process to establish a European Higher Education Area, the first phase of which is to adopt a credit-based system of comparable degrees with two main cycles (undergraduate and graduate). This system was to be fully implemented by 2010.

Admission is made on the joint basis of the Certificate of Secondary Education (Attestat o srednem obrazovanii) and performance in a competitive entrance examination. However, a system of Single Entry University Examinations is gradually being adopted by the administrative regions (48 by 2003), which will test students in a range of compulsory and designated subjects (the latter depending on the institution's requirements). The undergraduate degree is the Bachelors (Baklavr), a four-year programme of study divided into two years of general studies and two years of specialized studies. Graduates holding the Bachelors are eligible to study for the Masters (Magistr), the first postgraduate degree, which is either a one-year taught course or a two-year period of research. Doctoral-level studies consist of Aspirantura and Doktorantura. Aspirantura is a period of study following the Masters lasting a minimum of three years and culminating with the defence of a thesis and the award of the title Candidate of Sciences (Kandidat Nauk). Following Aspirantura, Doktorantura lasts for an unspecified period of time that, upon completion, results in the title Doctor of Sciences (Doktor Nauk).

Technical and vocational education is largely offered by specialist institutions and technical colleges at the upper secondary level. The primary qualifications are the Diploma of Completed Specialized Secondary Education (advanced level) and Diploma of Completed Specialized Secondary Education (basic level).

Regulatory and Representative Bodies

GOVERNMENT

Ministry of Culture and the Mass Media: 109074 Moscow, Kitaigorodskii proyezd 7; tel. (495) 928-38-72; internet www.mkmk.ru; Minister ALEKSANDR S. SOKOLOV.

Ministry of Education and Science: 103905 Moscow, ul. Tverskaya 11; tel. (495) 237-97-63; internet www.mon.gov.ru; Minister ANDREI A. FURSENKO.

ACCREDITATION

ENIC/NARIC Russia: 117593 Moscow, Nat. Information Centre for Academic Recognition and Mobility, Mikluho-Maklaya St. 6, RUDN; tel. (095) 958-28-81; fax (095) 433-15-11; e-mail RussianENIC@sci.pfu.edu.ru; internet www.russianenic.ru; Dir GENNADY LUKICHEV.

Federal Service of Supervision in Education and Science: 115998 Moscow, ul. Shabolovka 33; tel. (495) 208-68-38; internet www.obrnadzor.gov.ru; provides supervision and guidance in the sphere of education and science; monitors the quality of education in instns; organizes licensing, attestation and accreditation of educational instns; Head VIKTOR ALEKSANDROVICH BOLOTOV.

National Accreditation Agency: 424000 Yoshkar-Ola, 3 Lenin Sq.; tel. (8362) 41-61-94; fax (8362) 41 38-84; e-mail uno@nica.ru; internet www.nica.ru; f. 1995; supports higher-education instns, vocational-training establishments and the educational authorities in carrying out their state accreditation procedures; Dir VLADIMIR NAVODNOV.

NATIONAL BODIES

Association of Non-State Higher Education Establishments: 107005 Moscow, Radio St 22; tel. (495) 105-03-83; fax (495) 105-03-81; e-mail va_zernov@mtu-net.ru; Pres. VLADIMIR ZERNOV.

Association of Russian Higher Education Institutions: 105064 Moscow, 4 Gorokhovsky per.; tel. (495) 2613152; fax 495) 2674681; e-mail svp@miigaik.ru; Pres. VIKTOR SAVINYKH.

Federal Agency for Education: 115998 Moscow, Lyusinovskaya ul. 51; tel. (495) 237-97-63; fax (495) 236-01-71; e-mail bicab@ed.gov.ru; internet www.ed.gov.ru; manages state property, implements education and training policies, funds higher-education instns; Head GRIGORI ARTEMOVICH BALYKHIN.

Russian Academy of Education: 119905 Moscow, Pogodinskaya ul. 8; tel. (495) 245-16-41; fax (495) 246-81-77; e-mail vadimil@mailru.com; f. 1943; br. depts of Philosophy of education and theoretical pedagogy, Psychology and physiology in education, General secondary education, Culture and education, Basic vocational training, Higher education; regional depts: Northwest (St Petersburg), Siberia (Krasnoyarsk), Southern (Rostov-on-Don), Central (Moscow), Povolzhskoe (Kazan), Urals (Ekaterinburg); 14 experimental schools; attached research institutes: see Research Institutes; library: see Libraries and Archives; Pres. Prof. Dr N.D. NIKANDROV; Chief Learned Sec. Prof. Dr S.V. DARMODEKHIN; publs *Pedagogika* (Pedagogics, monthly), *Voprosy Psikhologii* (Problems of Psychology, monthly), *Defektologiya* (Defectology, every 2 months), *Izvestiya* (News, quarterly).

Russian Rectors' Union: 119991 Moscow, V-234, Vorobievy Gory, Lomonosov Moscow State Univ., Glavnoe Zdanie, Rooms 1001–1003; tel. and fax (495) 939-20-32; e-mail office@rsr-online.ru; internet rsr-online.ru; f. 1992; c. 800 mems; Pres. VIKTOR A. SADOVNICHY; Sec. Gen. OLGA V. KASHIRINA.

Learned Societies

GENERAL

Russian Academy of Natural Sciences: 113105 Moscow, Varshavskoye shosse 8; tel. (495) 954-26-11; fax (495) 954-73-05; e-mail presidium@raen.ru; internet www.raen.ru; f. 1990; organizes and co-ordinates pure and applied research; sections: Mathematics; Physics; Chemistry; Earth Sciences; Mining and Metallurgy; Issues in Education; Informatics; Biomedicine; Biology and Ecology; Russian Encyclopedia; Economics and Sociology; Issues in Macroeconomics; Geopolitics and Security; Noosphere Knowledge and Technology; Humanities and Creative Work; Interbranch Ecological and Economic Systems Research; Environmental Sciences; depts: St Petersburg Branch for Education and Science Development; Oil and Gas;

Forest Sciences; Eurasia Concept and Culture; Ecology, Hydrogeology, Engineering Geology and Geocryology; Applied Mathematics and Mathematical Physics; Class and National Traditions; 2,500 mems (incl. 100 hon., 250 foreign); Pres. Prof. Dr OLEG L. KUZNETSOV; Chief Scientific Sec. LIDA V. IVANITSKAYA.

Russian Academy of Sciences: 119991 Moscow, Leninsky pr. 14; tel. (495) 954-29-05; fax (495) 954-33-20; e-mail uvs@pran.ru; internet www.pran.ru; f. 1724; depts of Mathematics (Academician-Sec. L. D. FADEYEV), Physics (Academician-Sec. A. F. ANDREEV), Power Engineering, Mechanics and Control Processes (Academician-Sec. V. E. FORTOV), Information Science and Computer Technology (Academician-Sec. E. P. VELIKHOV), Chemistry and Materials (Academician-Sec. V. A. KABANOV), Biology (Academician-Sec. A. I. GRIGORIEV), Earth Sciences (Academician-Sec. O. A. BOGATIKOV), Social Sciences (Academician-Sec. V. L. MAKAROV), History and Philology (Academician-Sec. A. P. DEREVYANKO); Siberian division (Pr. Akademika Lavrenteva 17, 630090 Novosibirsk; tel. 30-05-67; Chair. N. L. DOBRETSOV), incl. centres in Krasnoyarsk, Irkutsk, Kemerovo, Omsk, Tomsk and Tumen; Far Eastern division (Svetlanskaya 50, 690600 Vladivostok; tel. 2-25-28; Chair. V. J. SERGIENKO); Urals division (Pervomaiskaya 91, 620219 Ekaterinburg; tel. 74-02-23; Chair. V. A. CHERESHNEV), incl. centres in Perm and Komi; additional centres in Makhachkala, Petrozavodsk, Kazan, Nalchik, Ufa and Apatity; 1,429 mems (501 academicians, 720 corresp. mems, 208 foreign mems); attached research institutes: see Research Institutes; libraries and archive: see Libraries and Archives; Pres. YU. S. OSIPOV; Chief Learned Sec. V. V. KOSTYUK; publs *Izvestiya Rossiiskoi Akademii Nauk* (Bulletin of the Russian Academy of Sciences, in 16 series: Biology, Geography, Literature and Language, Mathematics, Metals, Economics and Society, Mechanics of Liquids and Gases, Solid State Mechanics, Technical Cybernetics, Energy and Transport (6 a year); Geology, Inorganic Materials, Physics of Atmosphere and Ocean, Earth Physics, Physics, Chemistry (monthly)), *Doklady Rossiiskoi Akademii Nauk* (Proceedings of the Academy, 3 a month), *Izvestiya Sibirskogo otdeleniya Rossiiskoi Akademii Nauk* (Bulletin of the Siberian Branch of the Russian Academy of Sciences, in 5 series: Biological and Medical Sciences, History, Philology and Philosophy, Economics and Applied Sociology (quarterly); Technical Sciences, Chemical Sciences (6 a year)), *Nauka v Rossii* (Science in Russia, in Russian and English, 6 a year), *Vestnik Rossiiskoi Akademii Nauk* (Journal of the Russian Academy of Sciences, monthly), *Vestnik Dalnevostochnogo otdeleniya RAN* (Journal of the Far Eastern Division of the Russian Academy of Sciences).

UNESCO Office Moscow: 119331 Moscow, ul. Mytnaya 1; tel. (495) 230-10-65; fax (495) 238-60-85; e-mail moscow@unesco.org; internet www.unesco.ru; designated Cluster Office for Armenia, Azerbaijan, Belarus, Moldova and Russia; Dir BADARCH DENDEV.

Union of Scientific and Engineering Associations: 119034 Moscow, Kursovoi per. 17; tel. (495) 290-62-86; fax (495) 291-85-06; e-mail sitsev@mail.sitek.ru; Pres. Acad. I. GULIAEV; Learned Sec. S. V. PRYANISHNIKOV; Sec.-Gen. V. SITSEV.

AGRICULTURE, FISHERIES AND VETERINARY SCIENCE

Russian Academy of Agricultural Sciences: 107814 Moscow, Bolshoi Kharitonevsky per. 21; tel. (495) 207-39-42; f. 1992; depts of Plant Breeding and Genetics (Academician-Sec. V. S. SHEVELUKHA), Arable Farming and the Use of Agricultural Chemicals (Academician-Sec. I. P. MAKAROV), Feed and Fodder Crops Production (Academician-Sec. (vacant)), Plant Protection (Academician-Sec. N. M. GOLYTSIN), Livestock Production (Academician-Sec. (vacant)), Veterinary Science (Academician-Sec. V. P. SHISHKOV), Mechanization, Electrification and Automation in Farming (Academician-Sec. G. E. LISTOPAD), Forestry (Academician-Sec. V. N. VINOGRADOV), the Economics and Management of Agricultural Production (Academician-Sec. (vacant)), Land Reform and the Organization of Land Use (Academician-Sec. (vacant)), Land Reclamation and Water Resources (Academician-Sec. B. B. SHUMAKOV), the Storage and Processing of Agricultural Products (Academician-Sec. (vacant)); regional depts in St Petersburg (Non Black Soil Zone), Novosibirsk (Siberia), Khabarovsk (Far East); 150 mems; 128 corresp. mems; 73 foreign corresp. mems; attached research institutes: see Research Institutes; library: see Libraries and Archives; Pres. A. A. NIKONOV; Chief Learned Sec. V. P. SHISHKOV; publs *Vestnik selskokhozyaistvennoi nauki* (Agricultural Science Journal), *Doklady* (Proceedings), *Mekhanizatsiya i elektrificatsiya selskogo khozyaistva* (Mechanization and Electrification of Agriculture), *Selskokhozyaistvennaya biologiya* (Agricultural Biology), *Selektsiya i Semenovodstvo* (Selection and Seed Science), *Sibirskii vestnik selskokhozyaistvennoi nauki* (Siberian Agricultural Science Journal).

Society of the Timber and Forestry Industry: 103062 Moscow, Ul. Chernyshevskogo 29; tel. (495) 923-95-70; Chair. YU. A. YAGODNIKOV.

Soil Science Society: 109017 Moscow, Pyzhevskii per. 7; tel. (495) 231-43-59; attached to Russian Acad. of Sciences; Pres. G. V. DOBROVOLSKY.

ARCHITECTURE AND TOWN PLANNING

Union of Russian Architects: 123001 Moscow, Granatni per. 22; tel. (495) 291-55-78; fax (495) 202-81-01; e-mail sarrus@rambler.ru; f. 1981; 12,000 mems; Pres. YU. P. GNEDOVSKIY; publ. *Vesti SAR* (4 a year).

ECONOMICS, LAW AND POLITICS

Association of International Law: 119841 Moscow, ul. Frunze 10; attached to Russian Acad. of Sciences; Chair. Prof. G. I. TUNKIN.

Association of Orientalists: 103753 Moscow, ul. Rozhdestvenka 12; tel. (495) 928-57-64; attached to Russian Acad. of Sciences; Chair. M. S. KAPITSA.

Association of Political Sciences: 118941 Moscow, ul. Znamenka 10; attached to Russian Acad. of Sciences; Pres. Dr G. K. SHAKHNAZAROV.

Economics Society: 117259 Moscow, B. Cheremushkinskaya ul. 34; tel. (495) 120-13-21; Chair. V. S. PAVLOV.

Municipal Economy and Services Society: 103001 Moscow, Trekhprudny per. 11/13; tel. (495) 299-83-00; Chair. A. F. PORYADIN.

Russian Association of Sinologists: 117218 Moscow, Nakhimovsky pr. 32; tel. (495) 124-08-35; fax (495) 310-70-56; e-mail ifes@cemi.rssi.ru; f. 1992; 700 mems; attached to Russian Acad. of Sciences; Pres. V. S. MYASNIKOV.

EDUCATION

All-Russia 'Znanie' Society: 101814 Moscow, Novaya pl. 3/4; tel. (495) 621-90-58; fax (495) 625-42-49; e-mail znanie@znanie.org; internet www.znanie.org; f. 1947; adult education; 101,990 mems; Pres. Acad. S. N. BAGAEV; publ. *New Knowledge* (4 a year).

FINE AND PERFORMING ARTS

Russian Academy of Arts: 119034 Moscow, Ul. Prechistenka 21; tel. (495) 201-39-71; fax (495) 201-39-71; f. 1757; depts of Painting (Academician-Sec. E. N. MAXIMOV), Sculpture (Academician-Sec. A. A. BICHUKOV), Graphic Art (Academician-Sec. M. P. MITURICH-KHLEBNIKOV), Decorative Arts (Academician-Sec. L. A. SOKOLOVA), Architecture and Monumental Art (Academician-Sec. M.M. POSOKHIN); 218 mems (100 ordinary, 118 corresp.); attached research institutes: see Research Institutes; library: see Libraries and Archives; Pres. Z. K. TSERETELY; Chief Learned Sec. M. M. KURILKO-RYUMIN; publ. *Informatsionny Byulleten* (Information Bulletin, 4 a year).

Russian Union of Composers: 103009 Moscow K9, per. Bryusova 8/10; tel. (495) 229-52-18; fax (495) 229-52-18; f. 1960; 1,415 mems; Chair. VLADISLAV KAZENIN; publs *Muzikalnaya Akademia, Musical Life, Musical Review* (newsletter, in Russian).

Theatre Union of the Russian Federation: 103009 Moscow, ul. Gorkogo 16/2; tel. (495) 229-91-52; 30,124 mems; library of 300,000 vols; Chair. M. A. ULYANOV; publs *Information from the Secretariat* (quarterly), *Problems of Contemporary Theatre.*

Union of Arts of the Russian Federation: 103062 Moscow, ul. Pokrovka 37.

Union of Russian Filmmakers: 123825 Moscow, Vasilevskaya 13; tel. (495) 251-53-70.

HISTORY, GEOGRAPHY AND ARCHAEOLOGY

Russian Geographical Society: 190000 St Petersburg, tsentr, per. Grivtsova 10; tel. (812) 315-85-35; fax (812) 315-63-12; e-mail rgo@spb.org.ru; internet spb.org.ru/rgo; f. 1845; attached to Russian Acad. of Sciences; 20,000 mems; library of 470,000 vols, archive of 600,000 units; Pres. Prof. SERGEI B. LAVROV; publ. *Izvestiya RGS* (6 a year).

LANGUAGE AND LITERATURE

Alliance Française: 191186 St Petersburg, ul. Zhukovskogo 16; tel. (812) 272-08-60; e-mail info@af.spb.ru; internet www.af.spb.ru; offers courses and exams in French language and culture and promotes cultural exchange with France; attached offices in Ekaterinburg, Irkutsk, Kazan, Nizhnii Novgorod, Novosibirsk, Rostov-on-Don, Samara and Yakutsk; Dir of School GALINA DRAGAN.

British Council: 109189 Moscow, ul. Nikoloyamskaya 1; tel. (495) 782-02-00; fax (495) 782-02-01; e-mail bc.moscow@britishcouncil.ru; internet www.britishcouncil.ru; teaching centre; offers courses and exams in English language and British culture and promotes cultural exchange with the UK; attached centres in Ekaterinburg, Irkutsk, Krasnoyarsk, Nizhnii Novgorod, Novosibirsk, Rostov-on-Don, Samara, Sochi, Tomsk, Yaroslavl and Yuzhno-Sakhalinsk; Dir ADRIAN GREER; Training Centre Man. CLARE JEFFS.

Instituto Cervantes: 121069 Moscow, Novinski bul. 20 bl. 1–2; tel. (495) 937-19-52; fax (495) 937-19-51; e-mail cenmos@cervantes.es; internet moscu.cervantes.es; offers courses and exams in Spanish language and culture and promotes cultural exchange with Spain and Spanish-speaking

Latin and Central America; library of 12,000 vols; Dir Juan Carlos Vidal García.

International Community of Writers' Unions: 121825 Moscow, Povarskaya ul. 52; tel. (495) 291-63-07; f. 1992; 7,000 mems; Chair. G. M. Markov; First Sec. Timur Pulatov; publs *Literaturnaya Gazeta* (weekly), *Novyi Mir* (monthly), *Inostrannaya Literatura* (monthly).

Press Society: 103051 Moscow, Petrovka 26; tel. (495) 921-82-98; Chair. B. A. Kuzmin.

Russian Association for Comparative Literature: 121069 Moscow, ul. Vorovskogo 25A; tel. (495) 290-17-09; attached to Russian Acad. of Sciences; Chair. Acad. Yu. B. Vipper.

Russian Linguistics Society: 103009 Moscow, ul. Semashko 1/12; attached to Russian Acad. of Sciences; Chair. Acad. T. V. Gamkrelidze.

Russian PEN Centre: 103031 Moscow, ul. Neglinnaya 18/1, str. 2; tel. (495) 209-45-89; fax (495) 200-02-93; e-mail 7416.g23@g23 .relcom.ru; f. 1989; protection of freedom of expression, international exchange; writers in prison committee; 160 mems; Pres. Andrei Bitov; Gen. Dir Alexandr Tkachenko; publ. newsletter.

Union of Writers of the Russian Federation: 119087 Moscow, Komsomolsky pr. 13; tel. (495) 246-43-50.

MEDICINE

Federation of Anaesthesiologists and Reanimatologists: 125284 Moscow, POB 87, Botkin Hospital K. 14; tel. and fax (095) 945-97-25; e-mail igormol@orc.ru; f. 1991 (fmrly All-Union Society, f. 1959); 600 mems; Chair. I. Molchanov.

International Society for Pathophysiology: 125315 Moscow, ul. Baltiiskaya 8; tel. (095) 151-17-56; fax (095) 151-95-40; e-mail 4909.g23@g23.relcom.ru; internet home.ptt .ru/pathophysiology; f. 1991; 1,200 mems; Pres. Prof. Osmo Hänninen; Sec. Gen. L. Szollar; publ. *Pathophysiology* (4 a year).

National Immunological Society: 115478 Moscow, Kashirskoe shosse 24/2; tel. (095) 111-83-33; fax (095) 117-10-27; f. 1983; 500 mems; Chair. R. V. Petrov; Gen. Sec. S. Yu. Sidorovich; publ. *Immunologiya* (every 2 months).

National Medical and Technical Scientific Society: 129301 Moscow, ul. Kasatkina 3; tel. (095) 283-97-84; fax (095) 187-37-34; f. 1968; 55,000 mems and 512 organizations; library: Central State Scientific Medical Library of 3,000,000 vols; Pres. B. I. Leonov; Chief Learned Sec. B. E. Belousov; publ. *Biomedical Engineering* (bi-monthly).

National Ophthalmological Society: 103064 Moscow, ul. Sadovo-Chernogryazskaya 14/19; Chair. E. S. Avetisov; Chief Learned Sec. T. I. Forofonofa; publ. *Vestnik oftalmologii* (every 2 months).

National Pharmaceutical Society: 117418 Moscow, ul. Krasikova 34; Chair. M. T. Alyushin; Chief Learned Sec. R. S. Skulkova.

National Scientific Medical Society of Anatomists, Histologists and Embryologists: 117869 Moscow, ul. Ostrovityanova 1; Chair. V. V. Kupriyanov; Chief Learned Sec. V. V. Korolev.

National Scientific Medical Society of Endocrinologists: 117036 Moscow, ul. Dm. Ulyanova 11; Chair. V. G. Baranov; Chief Learned Sec. N. T. Starkova.

National Scientific Medical Society of Haemotologists and Transfusiologists: 125167 Moscow, Novozykovskii pr. 4-a; Chair. V. N. Shabalin; Chief Learned Sec. M. P. Khokhlova.

National Scientific Medical Society of the History of Medicine: 101838 Moscow, Petrovirigskii per. 6/8; Chair. Yu. P. Lisitsyn; Chief Learned Sec. I. V. Vengrova.

National Scientific Medical Society of Hygienists: 103064 Moscow, Mechnikova per. 5; Chair. G. N. Serdyukovskaya; Chief Learned Sec. A. G. Sukharev.

National Scientific Medical Society of Infectionists: 125284 Moscow, 1 Botkinskii pr. 3; Chair. V. N. Nikiforov; Chief Learned Sec. N. M. Belyaeva.

National Scientific Medical Society of Nephrologists: 119021 Moscow, ul. Rossolimo 11-a; tel. (095) 248-53-33; f. 1969; holding of conferences, congresses, symposia; 1,200 mems; Chair. N. A. Mukhin; Chief Learned Sec. S. O. Androsova.

National Scientific Medical Society of Neuropathologists and Psychiatrists: 119034 Moscow, Kropotkinskii per. 23; Chair. G. V. Morozov; Chief Learned Sec. G. Y. Lukacher.

National Scientific Medical Society of Obstetricians and Gynaecologists: 113163 Moscow, ul. Shabolovka 57; Chair. G. M. Saveleva; Chief Learned Sec. T. V. Chervakova.

National Scientific Medical Society of Oto-Rhino-Laryngologists: 119435 Moscow, Bol. Pirogovskaya 6; Chair. N. A. Preobrazhenskii; Chief Learned Sec. N. P. Konstantinova.

National Scientific Medical Society of Paediatricians: 117963 Moscow, Lomonosovskii pr. 2/62; Chair M. Yu. Studenikin; Chief Learned Sec. G. V. Yatsyk.

National Scientific Medical Society of Phthisiologists: 107564 Moscow, platforma Yauza, ul. 6 km Severnoi Zheleznoi Dorogi; Chair. A. G. Khomenko; Chief Learned Sec. V. V. Erokhin.

National Scientific Medical Society of Physical Therapists and Health-Resort Physicians: 121099 Moscow, Kalinina pr. 50; Chair. A. N. Obrosov; Chief Learned Sec. V. D. Grigoreva.

National Scientific Medical Society of Physicians-Analysts: 123242 Moscow, ul. Sadovaya-Kudrinskaya 3; Chair. B. F. Korovkin; Chief Learned Sec. R. L. Martsishevskaya.

National Scientific Medical Society of Physicians in Curative Physical Culture and Sports Medicine: 117963 Moscow, Lomonosovskii pr. 2/62; Chair. S. V. Kruzshev; Chief Learned Sec. A. V. Sokova.

National Scientific Medical Society of Roentgenologists and Radiologists: 117837 Moscow, ul. Profsoyuznaya 86; Chair. A. S. Pavlov; Chief Learned Sec. V. Z. Agranat.

National Scientific Medical Society of Stomatologists: 119435 Moscow, ul. Pogodinskaya 5; Chair. N. N. Bazhanov; Chief Learned Sec. V. M. Bezrukov.

National Scientific Medical Society of Surgeons: 119874 Moscow, Abrikosovskii per. 2; Chair. B. V. Petrovskii; Chief Learned Sec. M. I. Perelman.

National Scientific Medical Society of Therapists: 121500 Moscow, 3 Cherepkovskaya 15; Chair. A. S. Smetnev; Chief Learned Sec. B. A. Sidorenko.

National Scientific Medical Society of Toxicologists: 193019 St Petersburg, ul. Bekhtereva 1; Chair. S. N. Golikov; Chief Learned Sec. L. A. Timofeevskaya.

National Scientific Medical Society of Traumatic Surgeons and Orthopaedists: 125299 Moscow, ul. Priorova 10; tel. (095)

450-24-72; fax (095) 154-31-39; e-mail cito@ cito-priorov.ru; f. 1921; Chair. S. P. Mironov; Chief Learned Sec. V. V. Trotsenko; publ. *N. N. Priorov Journal of Traumatology and Orthopaedics* (4 a year).

National Scientific Medical Society of Urological Surgeons: 105483 Moscow, ul. 3-ya Parkovaya 51; tel. (095) 367-62-62; fax (095) 164-76-60; e-mail urology@cdromclub .ru; f. 1925; 5,506 mems; Chair. N. A. Lopatkin; Chief Learned Sec. L. M. Gorilovski; publ. *Urology and Nephrology* (every 2 months).

National Scientific Medical Society of Venereologists and Dermatologists: 107076 Moscow, ul. Korolenko 3; Chair. O. K. Shaposhnikov; Chief Learned Sec. V. N. Mordovtsev.

Russian Academy of Medical Sciences: 109801 Moscow, ul. Solyanka 14; tel. (095) 298-21-37; fax (095) 921-56-15; e-mail orlov@ ramn.ru; f. 1944; depts of Preventive Medicine (Academician-Sec. N. F. Izmerov), Clinical Medicine (Academician-Sec. E. I. Gusev), Medical and Biological Sciences (Academician-Sec. K. V. Sudakov); Siberian dept (Academician-Sec. V. A. Trufakin), Northwest dept (Academician-Sec. B. I. Tkachenko); 496 mems (191 ordinary, 232 corresp., 73 foreign); 60 specialist research ccls; attached research institutes: see Research Institutes; library: see Libraries and Archives; Pres. V. I. Pokrovsky; Gen. Sec. V. A. Tutelian; publs *Vesti Meditsyny* (Medical News), *Vestnik Rossiiskoi Akademii Meditsinskikh Nauk* (Journal of the Russian Academy of Medical Sciences), *Arkhiv Patologii* (Pathology Archive), *Byulleten Eksperimentalnoi Biologii i Meditsiny* (Bulletin of Experimental Biology and Medicine), *Voprosy Virusologii* (Problems in Virology), *Voprosy Meditsinskoi Khimii* (Problems in Medical Chemistry), *Immunologiya* (Immunology), *Meditsinskaya Radiologiya* (Medical Radiology and Radiation Safety), *Morfologia* (Morphology), *Patologicheskaya Fiziologiya i Eksperimentalnaya Terapiya* (Pathological Physiology and Experimental Therapy), *Eksperimentalnaya i Klinicheskaya Pharmakologiya* (Experimental and Clinical Pharmacology), *Byulleten Sibirskogo Otdeleniya Rossiiskoi AMN* (Bulletin of the Siberian Division of the Russian Academy of Medical Sciences).

Russian Gastroenterological Association: 119881 Moscow, ul. Pogodinskaya 5; tel. (095) 248-38-00; fax (095) 248-36-10; f. 1995; 2,500 mems; Pres. Prof. Dr V. T. Ivashkin; Sec. Dr A. S. Trukhmanov; publs *Journal of Gastroenterology, Hepatology and Coloproctology* (6 a year).

Russian Medical Association: 125315 Moscow, ul. Baltiskaya 10/3; tel. (095) 151-27-67; fax (095) 151-55-25; e-mail rmass@ online.ru; internet www.rmass.ru; f. 1993; 262,000 mems; Chair. Prof. A. G. Sarkisian; Learned Sec. Dr Lev Malyshev; publ. *Vrachebnaya Gazeta* (monthly).

Russian Neurosurgical Association: 603600 Nizhnii Novgorod, Verkhne-Volskaya nab. 18; tel. (8312) 46-36-48; fax (8312) 36-05-95; Pres. A. P. Fraerman; Sec. S. N. Kolesov.

Russian Oncological Society (St Petersburg branch): 197758 St Petersburg, pos. Pesochnyi-2, ul. Leningradskaya 68; tel. (812) 596-86-54; fax (812) 596-89-47; f. 1954; 460 mems; Chair. Prof. Dr Vladimir F. Semiglazov; Sec.-Gen. Dr Evgenia V. Tsyrlina; publ. *Voprosi oncologii* (6 a year).

Russian Pharmacological Society: 125315 Moscow, ul. Baltiiskaya 8; tel. (095) 151-18-81; fax (095) 151-12-61; f. 1958 (fmrly All-Union Scientific Medical Soc. of Pharmacologists); 295 mems; library of 10,000 vols; Chair. D. A. KHARKEVICH; Chief Learned Sec. S. A. BORISENKO; publ. *Russian Journal of Experimental and Clinical Pharmacology*.

Russian Rheumatological Association: 115522 Moscow, Kashirskoye shosse 34A; tel. (495) 114-44-90; fax (495) 114-44-68; e-mail sokrat@irramn.ru; internet www .rheumatolog.ru; f. 1928; 1,860 mems; library of 102,000 vols; Chair. E. NASONOV; Gen. Sec. I. ALEXEEVA; publ. *Clinical-practical Rheumatology* (6 a year).

Russian Society of Medical Genetics: 115478 Moscow, Moskvorechie ul. 1; tel. (499) 612-81-04; fax (095) 324-07-02; internet www.med-gen.ru/rsmg/rsmgen .htm; f. 1993; human genome project, human genetics, cytogenetics, clinical genetics, genetic counselling, experimental genetics, ecogenetics and human molecular genetics; 500 mems; Chair. E. K. GINTER; Chief Learned Sec. V. I. IZHEVSKAYA; publ. *Medical Genetics* (monthly).

Scientific Medical Society of Anatomists-Pathologists: 109801 Moscow, ul. Bolshaya Serpuhovskaya 27; Chair. D. S. SARKISOV.

Society of Cardiology: 101953 Moscow, Petroverigskii ul. 10; tel. (095) 623-86-36; e-mail info@cardiosite.ru; internet www .cardiosite.ru; f. 1963; cardiology, diagnosis, treatment and prevention of cardiovascular disease; training courses; 188 mems; Pres. Dr RAFAEL OGANOV; Sec.-Gen. Prof. SVETLANA A. SHALNOVA; publs *Cardiovascular Therapy and Prevention* (6 a year), *Russian Journal of Cardiology* (6 a year).

NATURAL SCIENCES
General

Moscow House of Scientists: 119821 Moscow, Kropotkinskaya ul. 16; tel. (095) 201-45-55; attached to Russian Acad. of Sciences; Dir A. I. DERGACHEV.

St Petersburg M. Gorky House of Scientists: 191065 St Petersburg, Dvortsovaya nab. 26; tel. (812) 315-88-14; attached to Russian Acad. of Sciences; Dir L. M. ANISIMOVA.

Biological Sciences

Biochemical Society: c/o Prof. M. B. Agalarova, Ovchinnikov Institute of Bio-organic Chemistry, 117871 Moscow, Miklukho-Maklaya 16/10; tel. (095) 429-8040; e-mail biosoc@mail.ibch.ru; attached to Russian Acad. of Sciences; Pres. Acad. S. E. SEVERIN.

Biotechnology Society: 109044 Moscow, Bol. Kommunisticheskaya ul. 27; tel. (095) 272-67-49; Chair. V. E. MATVEYEV.

Hydrobiological Society: 103050 Moscow, Tverskaya ul. 27; tel. (095) 299-65-04; attached to Russian Acad. of Sciences; Pres. L. M. SUSHCHENYA.

Microbiological Society: 117811 Moscow, pr. 60-letiya Oktyabrya 7, korp. 2; tel. (095) 939-27-63; attached to Russian Acad. of Sciences; Pres. E. N. KONDRATEVA.

Moscow Society of Naturalists: 103009 Moscow, ul. Gertsena 6; tel. (095) 203-67-04; f. 1805; sections for zoology, botany, geology, hydrobiology, geography, biophysics, palaeontology, histology, experimental morphology, genetics, etc.; 2,700 mems; library of 500,000 vols; Chair A. L. YANSHIN; publ. *Byulleten Moskovskogo Obshchestva Ispytatelei prirody* (every 2 months).

Palaeontological Society: 199106 St Petersburg, Srednii pr. 74; tel. (812) 328-91-56; fax (812) 321-30-23; f. 1916; attached to Russian Acad. of Sciences; 800 mems; Pres.

Acad. B. S. SOKOLOV; publ. *Abstracts of Annual Meetings* (annually).

Russian Botanical Society: 197376 St Petersburg, ul. Prof. Popova 2; tel. (812) 234-96-02; fax (812) 234-45-12; attached to Russian Acad. of Sciences; Pres. R. V. KAMELIN.

Russian Entomological Society: 199034 St Petersburg, Universitetskaya nab. 1; tel. (812) 328-12-12; fax (812) 114-04-14; e-mail reo@zisp.spb.su; f. 1859; attached to Russian Acad. of Sciences; 2,000 mems; library of 80,000 vols; Pres. G. S. MEDVEDEV; publs *Entomologicheskoe obozrenie* (4 a year), *Trudy Russkogo Entomologicheskogo Obschestva* (irregular), *Chtenia pamyati N.A. Kholodkovskogo* (annually).

Russian Society of Geneticists and Breeders: 117312 Moscow, ul. Fersmana 11, korp. 2; tel. 124-59-52; attached to Russian Acad. of Sciences; Pres. Acad. V. A. STRUNNIKOV.

Society of Helminthologists: 117259 Moscow, Bol. Cheremushkinskaya 28; attached to Russian Acad. of Sciences; Pres. A. S. BESSONOV.

Society of Ornithologists: c/o Russian Academy of Sciences, 117901 Moscow, Leninsky pr. 14; attached to Russian Acad. of Sciences; Pres. V. D. ILICHEV.

Society of Protozoologists: 194064 St Petersburg, Tikhoretsky pr. 4; tel. (812) 247-18-36; fax (812) 247-03-41; e-mail tamara@tb10336.spb.edu; f. 1968 as All-Union Society of Protozoologists; present name 1991; attached to Russian Acad. of Sciences; 200 mems; Pres. (vacant); Sec.-Gen. Prof. Dr TAMARA V. BEYER; publs *Tsitologiya* (Cytology, in Russian with English summaries, monthly), *Protistology* (4 a year).

Physical Sciences

Astronomical and Geodesical Society: 103001 Moscow, Sadovo-Kudrinskaya ul. 24; attached to Russian Acad. of Sciences; Pres. YU. D. BULANZHE.

Ferrous Metallurgy Society: 129812 Moscow, pr. Mira 101; tel. (095) 287-83-80; Chair. N. I. DROZDOV.

Gubkin, Acad. I. M., Petroleum and Gas Society: 117876 Moscow, 12-ya Parkovaya ul. 5; tel. (095) 463-93-72; Chair. S. T. TOPLOV.

Mendeleev, D. I., Chemical Society: 101907 Moscow, Krivokolennyi per. 12; tel. (095) 928-43-51; fax (095) 928-43-54; f. 1868; 45 regional orgs; 1,800 mems; Sec.-Gen. NATATYA KOSSINOVA; publ. *Russian Chemical Journal* (every 2 months); publ. *Chemistry in Russia* (monthly bulletin).

Russian Geological Society: 113191 Moscow, 2-aya Roshinskaya ul. 10; tel. (095) 954-96-34; fax (095) 954-96-22; f. 1988; 1,025 mems; Pres. V. P. ORLOV.

Russian Mineralogical Society: 199026 St Petersburg, V. O., 21 liniya 2; tel. (812) 218-86-40; e-mail vmo@mineral.ras.spb.ru; f. 1817; attached to Russian Acad. of Sciences; 1,700 mems; library: 83,000 units; Pres. Acad. D. V. RUNDKVIST; publ. *Zapiski*.

Society of Non-Ferrous Metallurgy: 103001 Moscow, Sadovaya-Kudrinskaya ul. 18; tel. (095) 291-29-87; Chair. V. S. LOBANOV.

PHILOSOPHY AND PSYCHOLOGY

Russian Philosophical Society: ul. Volhonka 14, Room 102, Moscow 119992; tel. (095) 201-24-02; e-mail rphs@iph.ras.ru; internet www.logic.ru/~phil-soc; f. 1972; attached to Russian Acad. of Sciences; 4,000 mems; Pres. V. S. STEPIN; Vice-Pres. A. N.

CHUMAKOV; publ. *Bulletin of the Russian Philosophical Society*.

Society of Psychologists: 129366 Moscow, Yaroslavskaya ul. 13; tel. (095) 282-45-03; attached to Russian Acad. of Sciences; Chair. E. V. SHOROKHOVA.

RELIGION, SOCIOLOGY AND ANTHROPOLOGY

Russian Society of Sociologists: 117259 Moscow, ul. Krzhizhanovskogo 24/35 str. 5; tel. (095) 719-09-71; fax (095) 719-07-40; e-mail mansurov@isras.rssi.ru; internet www.isras.rssi.ru; f. 1989; attached to Russian Acad. of Sciences; 1,350 mems; Chair. VALERY A. MANSUROV; publ. *Vestnik* (Newsletter, 4 a year).

TECHNOLOGY

Aircraft Building Society: 125040 Moscow, Leningradskii pr. 24a; tel. (095) 214-22-88; Chair. A. M. BATKOV.

Civil Engineering Society: 103062 Moscow, Podsosensky per. 25; tel. (095) 297-07-29; Chair. I. I. ISHENKO.

Computers and Informatics Society: 127486 Moscow, Deguninskaya ul. 1, korp. 4; tel. (095) 487-31-61; Chair. I. N. BUKREYEV.

Mapping and Prospecting Engineering Society: 117801 Moscow, ul. Krzhizhanovskogo 14, korp. 2; tel. (095) 124-35-60; Chair. A. A. DRAZHNYUK.

Mechanical Engineering Society: 109004 Moscow, ul. Zemlyanoi Val 64, korp. 1; tel. (095) 297-93-00; Chair. B. N. SOKOLOV.

Mining Engineers' Society: 103006 Moscow, Karetnyi ryad 10/18; tel. (095) 299-88-15; Chair. A. P. FISUN.

Popov, A. S., Radio Engineering, Electronics and Telecommunications Society: 103897 Moscow, Kuznetskii Most 20/6; tel. (095) 921-71-08; Chair. YU. V. GULYAEV.

Power and Electrical Power Engineering Society: 191025 St Petersburg, Stremyannaya ul. 10; tel. (095) 311-32-77; Chair. N. N. TIKHODEYEV.

Scientific-Technical Association: 198103 St Petersburg, pr. Ogorodnikova 26; tel. (812) 251-28-50; attached to Russian Acad. of Sciences; General Dir M. L. ALEKSANDROV.

Shipbuilding Engineering Society: 191011 St Petersburg, Nevskii pr. 44; tel. (095) 315-50-27; Chair. I. V. GORYNIN.

Society of the Food Industry: 103031 Moscow, Kuznetskii Most 19, pod. 2; tel. (095) 924-49-30; Chair. A. N. BOGATYREV.

Society of the Instrument Manufacturing Industry and Metrologists: 103009 Moscow, Tverskaya ul. 12, str. 2; tel. (095) 209-47-98; Chair. G. I. KAVALEROV.

Society of Light Industry: 117846 Moscow, ul. Vavilova 69; tel. (095) 134-90-01; Chair. R. A. CHAYANOV.

Vavilov, S. I., Society of Instrument Manufacturers: 121019 Moscow, Mokhovaya ul. 17, str. 2; tel. (095) 203-34-65.

Water Transport Society: 103012 Moscow, Staropansky per. 3; tel. (095) 921-18-12; Chair. (vacant).

Research Institutes
AGRICULTURE, FISHERIES AND VETERINARY SCIENCE

Adygea Agricultural Research Institute: 352764 Krasnodar krai, Maikop, Podgornoe; attached to Russian Acad. of Agricultural Sciences.

Afanasev, V. A., Research Institute of Fur-Bearing Animals and Rabbits: 140143 Moscow oblast, Ramensky raion, p/o Rodniki; tel. (095) 501-53-55; fax (095) 501-53-55; f. 1932; attached to Russian Acad. of Agricultural Sciences; Dir N. A. BALAKIREV.

Agrarian Institute: 103064 Moscow, Bol. Kharitonevskaya per. 21, korp. 2, POB 34; tel. (095) 207-70-75; fax (095) 928-22-90; e-mail agrin@glas.apc.org; f. 1990; attached to Russian Acad. of Agricultural Sciences; Dir Dr A. V. PETRIKOV.

Agricultural Research Institute for the Central Areas of the Non-Black Soil (Nechernozem) Zone: 143104 Moscow oblast, Odintsovsky raion, Nemchinovka, ul. Agrokhimikov 6; tel. (095) 591-83-91; attached to Russian Acad. of Agricultural Sciences.

Agrophysical Research Institute: 195220 St Petersburg, Grazhdanskii Pp.14; tel. (095) 543-46-30; attached to Russian Acad. of Agricultural Sciences; Dir I. B. USKOV.

All-Russia Horticulture Institute for Breeding, Agrotechnology and Nursery: 115598 Moscow, Birulevo-Zagorie, ul. Zagorievskogo; tel. and fax (095) 329-51-66; e-mail vstisp@vstisp.org; internet www.vstisp.org; Dir IVAN KULIKOV; publ. *Fruit Trees and Small Fruits of Russia* (2 a year); attached to Russian Acad. of Agricultural Sciences.

All-Russia Institute of Plant Protection: 196608 St Petersburg, Pushkin, shosse Podbelskogo 3; tel. (812) 470-43-84; fax (812) 470-51-10; e-mail vizrspb@mail333.com; internet www.vizrsph.chat.ru; f. 1929, attached to Russian Acad. of Agricultural Sciences; Dir V. A. PAVLYUSHIN; publ. *Plant Protection News* (3 a year).

All-Russia Legumes and Pulse Crops Research Institute: 302502 Orel, P/O Streletskoe; tel. (0862) 403-224; fax (0862) 403-130; e-mail office@vniizbk.orel.ru; attached to Russian Acad. of Agricultural Sciences; Dir Prof. V. I. ZOTIKOV.

All-Russia Maize Research Institute: 860022 Nalchik, ul. Mechnikova 130A; tel. (86622) 5-03-16; attached to Russian Acad. of Agricultural Sciences.

All-Russia Meat Research Institute: 109316 Moscow, ul. Talilikhina 26; tel. (095) 276-95-11; fax (095) 276-95-51; e-mail vniimp@glasnet.ru; f. 1930; attached to Russian Acad. of Agricultural Sciences; Dir L. A. BORISOVICH; publ. *Proceedings* (annually).

All-Russia Potato Research Institute: 140052 Moscow oblast, Lyuberetsky raion, pos. Korenevo, ul. Lorkha; tel. (095) 557-10-11; fax (095) 557-10-11; f. 1930; attached to Russian Acad. of Agricultural Sciences; library of 500,000 vols; Dir Prof. A. V. KORSHUNOV; publ. *Proceedings* (annually).

All-Russia Poultry Research and Technology Institute: Moscow oblast, Sergiev pos.; attached to Russian Acad. of Agricultural Sciences.

All-Russia Rapeseed Research and Technological Institute: 398037 Lipetsk, Boevoi pr. 26, kod 074; tel. (0742) 26-08-64; attached to Russian Acad. of Agricultural Sciences.

All-Russia Research and Technological Institute for Chemical Land Reclamation: 189520 St Petersburg, Pushkin, ul. Lermontova 9; tel. (812) 465-58-75; attached to Russian Acad. of Agricultural Sciences.

All-Russia Research and Technological Institute for Chemicalization in Agriculture: 143013 Moscow oblast, Odinstsovsky raion, Nemchinovka, ul. Agrokhimikov 6; tel. (095) 591-91-73;

attached to Russian Acad. of Agricultural Sciences.

All-Russia Research and Technological Institute for Mechanization in Livestock Raising: 142004 Moscow oblast, Podolsky raion, p/o Znamya Oktyabrya; 31; tel. (095) 119-74-97; fax (095) 119-75-17; f. 1969; attached to Russian Acad. of Agricultural Sciences; Dir N. M. MOROZOV; publ. *Scientific Research Problems of Mechanization and Automation of Livestock Farming.*

All-Russia Research and Technological Institute for Organic Fertilizers: 601242 Vladimir oblast, Vyatkino; attached to Russian Acad. of Agricultural Sciences.

All-Russia Research Institute for Agricultural Biotechnology: 127550 Moscow, Timiryazevskaya ul. 42; tel. (095) 976-65-44; fax (095) 977-09-47; e-mail iab@iab.ac.ru; internet www.agrobiotech.ru; f. 1974; attached to Russian Acad. of Agricultural Sciences; Dir P. N. KHARCHENKO.

All-Russia Research Institute for Agricultural Economics and Standards and Norms: 344006 Rostov on Don, pr. Sokolova 52; tel. (8632) 65-31-81; fax (8632) 64-89-61; f. 1980; attached to Russian Acad. of Agricultural Sciences; Dir Dr VLADIMIR V. KUZNETSOV.

All-Russia Research Institute for Beef Cattle Breeding and Production: Orenburg, Yanvarskaya ul. 29; attached to Russian Acad. of Agricultural Sciences.

All-Russia Research Institute for Biological Control: 350039 Krasnodar, a/ya 39; tel. (8612) 50-81-91; attached to Russian Acad. of Agricultural Sciences.

All-Russia Research Institute for Cybernetics in the Agro-industrial Complex: 117218 Moscow, ul. Krzhizhanovskogo 14/1; tel. (095) 124-76-02; attached to Russian Acad. of Agricultural Sciences.

All-Russia Research Institute for Economics, Labour and Management in Agriculture: 111621 Moscow, Orenburgskaya ul. 15; tel. (095) 550-06-71; attached to Russian Acad. of Agricultural Sciences.

All-Russia Research Institute for Electrification in Agriculture: 109456 Moscow, 1-i Veshnyakovskii pr. 2; tel. (095) 171-19-20; fax (095) 170-51-01; e-mail viesh@dol.ru; f. 1930; attached to Russian Acad. of Agricultural Sciences; library of 135,000 vols; Dir Acad. D. S. STREBKOV; publ. *Scientific Proceedings* (2 a year).

All-Russia Research Institute for Farm Animal Genetics and Breeding: 196600 St Petersburg-Pushkin, Moskovskoye shosse 55a; tel. (812) 470-76-63; fax (812) 465-99-89; e-mail spbvniigen@mail.ru; attached to Russian Acad. of Agricultural Sciences; Dir Acad. P.N. PROCHORENKO.

All-Russia Research Institute for Flowers and Tropical Crops: 354002 Sochi, ul. Fabrikiusa 2/28; tel. (8622) 92-73-61; attached to Russian Acad. of Agricultural Sciences.

All-Russia Research Institute for Horse Breeding: 391105 Ryazan oblast, Rybnoyek raion; tel. (0912) 24-02-65; fax (0912) 24-02-65; e-mail vniik@rinf.ryazan.ru; internet www.ruhorses.ru; f. 1930; attached to Russian Acad. of Agricultural Sciences; library of 47,000 vols; Dir Prof. Dr V. V. KALASHNIKOV; publs *Stud Book* (every 4 years, with annual supplement), *Scientific Works* (annually).

All-Russia Research Institute for Irrigated Arable Farming: 400002 Volgograd, Timiryazevskaya ul. 9; tel. (8442) 43-49-79; fax (8442) 43-34-75; e-mail vniioz@avtlg.ru; f. 1967; attached to Russian Acad. of Agricul-

tural Sciences; library of 138,000 vols; Dir Dr V. V. MELIKHOV.

All-Russia Research Institute for Irrigated Horticulture and Vegetable Crops Production: 416300 Astrakhan oblast, Kamyziak, ul. Lubicha 13; attached to Russian Acad. of Agricultural Sciences.

All-Russia Research Institute for Mechanization in Agriculture: 109389 Moscow, 1-i Institutskii pr. 5; tel. (095) 171-19-33; attached to Russian Acad. of Agricultural Sciences; Dir Acad. V. A. KUIBYSHEV.

All-Russia Research Institute for Sheep and Goat Breeding: 355014 Stavropol, Zootekhnichesky per. 15; tel. (8652) 34-76-88; fax (8652) 34-76-88; e-mail vniiok@minas.rosmail.com; f. 1932; attached to Russian Acad. of Agricultural Sciences; Dir. Prof. VASILY MOROZ; publs *Proceedings* (annually), *Conference Materials* (2 a year).

All-Russia Research Institute for the Agricultural Use of Reclaimed and Improved Land: 170530 Tver oblast, Emmaus; tel. (0822) 37-15-46; fax (0822) 36-07-63; e-mail vniimz@mail.ru; internet www.vniimz.newmail; f. 1977; attached to Russian Acad. of Agricultural Sciences; library of 20,000 vols; Dir Dr N. KOVALEV; publ. *Proceedings.*

All-Russia Research Institute for the Biosynthesis of Protein Substances: 109004 Moscow, Bol. Kommunisticheskaya 27; tel. (095) 912-70-09; fax (095) 911-39-23; e-mail bclok@rutenia.ru; attached to Russian Acad. of Agricultural Sciences; Dir Dr ALEXANDER P. ZAKHARYCHEV.

All-Russia Research Institute for Vegetable Breeding and Seed Production: 143080 Moscow oblast, Odintsovsky raion, Lesnoi gorodok; tel. (095) 599-24-42; fax (095) 599-22-77; e-mail vniissok@cea.ru; f. 1920; attached to Russian Acad. of Agricultural Sciences; Dir. Prof. VICTOR F. PIVOVAROV.

All-Russia Research Institute for Veterinary Sanitation, Hygiene and Ecology: 123022 Moscow, Zvenigorodskoe shosse 5; tel. (095) 256-35-81; attached to Russian Acad. of Agricultural Sciences.

All-Russia Research Institute of Agricultural Microbiology: 189620 St Petersburg, Pushkin 8, shosse Podbelskogo 3; tel. (812) 470-51-00; fax (812) 470-43-62; f. 1930; attached to Russian Acad. of Agricultural Sciences; Dir Prof. I. A. TIKHONOVICH.

All-Russia Research Institute of Animal Husbandry: 142023 Moscow oblast, Podolskii raion, pos. Dubrovitsy; tel. (095) 546-63-35; attached to Russian Acad. of Agricultural Sciences; Dir Acad. A. P. KALASHNIKOV.

All-Russia Research Institute of Arable Farming and Soil Erosion Control: 305021 Kursk, ul. Karla Marksa 70B; tel. (0712) 53-42-56; fax (0712) 53-67-29; e-mail vnizem@kursknet.ru; f. 1970; attached to Russian Acad. of Agricultural Sciences; library of 20,000 vols, 40 periodicals; Dir G. N. CHERKASOV; publs *Proceedings of an International Conference* (annually), *Scientific Bulletin* (annually).

All-Russia Research Institute of Economics in Agriculture: 123007 Moscow, Khoroshevskoe shosse 35, korp 3; tel. (095) 195-60-16; attached to Russian Acad. of Agricultural Sciences; Dir I. G. USHCHACHEV.

All-Russia Research Institute of Information, Technological and Economic Research on the Agro-Industrial Complex: c/o Russian Academy of Agricultural Sciences, 107814 Moscow, Bolshoi Kharitonevsky per. 21; attached to Russian Acad. of Agricultural Sciences; Dir Acad. V. I. NAZARENKO.

All-Russia Research Institute of Marine Fisheries and Oceanography: 107140 Moscow, Verkhnyaya Krasnoselskaya 17; tel. (095) 264-93-87; Dir A. S. BOGDANOV.

All-Russia Research Institute of Medicinal and Aromatic Plants: 113628 Moscow, ul. Grina 7; tel. 382-83-18; attached to Russian Acad. of Agricultural Sciences.

All-Russia Research Institute of Phytopathology: 143050 Moscow oblast, Vyazemy; tel. (095) 592-92-87; attached to Russian Acad. of Agricultural Sciences.

All-Russia Research Institute of Plant Quarantine: 140150 Moscow oblast, Ramensky raion, pos. Bykovo, Pogranichnaya 32; tel. (095) 556-23-29; f. 1979; library of 10,000 vols; Dir Dr ANATOLIY I. SMETNIK; Scientific Sec. Dr ELENA V. TERESHKOVA; publ. *Problems of Plant Quarantine*.

All-Russia Research Institute of Pond Fishery: 141821 Moscow oblast, Dmitrovsky raion, p/o Rubnoe; tel. (095) 587-21-98; attached to Russian Acad. of Agricultural Sciences.

All-Russia Research Institute of Tobacco, Makhorka and Tobacco Products: 350072 Krasnodar, Moskovskaya ul. 42; tel. (861) 57-88-82; attached to Russian Acad. of Agricultural Sciences.

All-Russia Rice Research Institute: 353204 Krasnodar krai, Dinskoi raion, pos. Belozernoe; tel. (8612) 56-65-96; fax (8612) 50-91-24; attached to Russian Min. of Agriculture; Dir Prof. E. P. ALESHIN.

All-Russia Vegetable Production Research Institute: 141018 Moscow oblast, Mytishchi, Novomytishchinsky pr. 82; tel. (095) 582-00-15; attached to Russian Acad. of Agricultural Sciences.

All-Russia Veterinary Research Institute for Poultry Diseases: St Petersburg, Moskovsky pr. 99; attached to Russian Acad. of Agricultural Sciences.

Altai Experimental Farm: 659739 Altai krai, Gorno-Altaisky autonomous oblast, Shebalinsky raion, selo Cherga; attached to Russian Acad. of Sciences; Dir YU. S. ZEMIROV.

Bashkir Research and Technological Institute for Animal Husbandry and Feed Production: Bashkortostan, 450025 Ufa, Pushkinskaya ul. 86; tel. (3472) 22-17-23; attached to Russian Acad. of Agricultural Sciences.

Bashkir Research Institute for Arable Farming and Field Crops Breeding: 450059 Ufa, ul. Zorge 19; tel. (3472) 24-07-08; attached to Russian Acad. of Agricultural Sciences.

Caspian Research Institute for Arid Arable Farming: 431213 Astrakhan, Solenoe zaimishche; tel. (851) 24-38-36; fax (851) 192-17-00; f. 1991; attached to Russian Acad. of Agricultural Sciences; library of 30,000 vols.

Chelyabinsk Agricultural Research Institute: 436404 Chelyabinsk oblast, Chebarkulsky raion, Timiryazevsky; tel. (35168) 33-23-16; attached to Russian Acad. of Agricultural Sciences.

Dagestan Agricultural Research Institute: 367014 Makhachkala, pr. K. Marksa, Nauchnyi park; tel. (8722) 3-66-60; attached to Russian Acad. of Agricultural Sciences.

Dokuchaev, V. V., Central Black Soil (Chernozem) Agricultural Research Institute: 397463 Voronezh oblast, Talov raion; attached to Russian Acad. of Agricultural Sciences.

Dokuchaev, V. V., Institute of Soil Science: 109017 Moscow, Pyzhevsky per. 7; tel. (095) 231-50-37; attached to Russian Acad. of Agricultural Sciences; Dir Acad. V. V. YEGOROV.

Don Zone Agricultural Research Institute: 346714 Rostov oblast, Aksai raion, Rassvet; attached to Russian Acad. of Agricultural Sciences.

Flax Research Institute: 172060 Tverskii raion, Torzhok, ul. Lunacharskogo 35; tel. (08251) 5-16-45; fax (08251) 5-44-58; e-mail vniil@tver.dep.ru; f. 1930; library of 50,000 vols; Dir ANATOLI N. MARCHENKOV; publ. *Trudy VNIL* (annually).

Forest Research Institute: 185035 Petrozavodsk, Pushkinskaya ul. 11; tel. and fax (8142) 76-81-60; e-mail vitaly.krutov@krc.karelia.ru; internet www.krc.karelia.ru; f. 1957; attached to Russian Acad. of Sciences; Dir Dr VITALY KRUTOV.

Institute of Forest Research: 143030 Moscow oblast, Odintsovsky raion, p/o Uspenskoe; tel. (095) 419-52-57; fax (095) 419-52-57; e-mail root@ilan.msk.su; f. 1958; attached to Russian Acad. of Sciences; library of 51,400 vols; Dir Prof. S. E. VOMPERSKY; publ. *Lesovedenie* (Russian Forest Science, 6 a year).

Institute of Forestry: 620134 Ekaterinburg, Bilimbaevskaya ul. 32A; tel. (3432) 52-08-80; attached to Russian Acad. of Sciences; Dir. S. A. MAMAEV.

Institute of Soil Science and Agrochemistry: 630099 Novosibirsk, Sovetskaya 18; tel. (3832) 22-53-58; attached to Russian Acad. of Sciences; Dir I. M. GADZHIEV.

Kovalenko, Ya. R., All-Russia Institute of Experimental Veterinary Science: 109472 Moscow, Kuzminki; tel. (095) 377-29-79; attached to Russian Acad. of Agricultural Sciences; Dir G. F. KOROMYSLOV.

Krasnodar Scientific Research Institute of the Storage and Processing of Agricultural Produce: 350072 Krasnodar, Topolinskaya ul. 2; tel. (8612) 57-95-93; fax (8612) 57-98-44; e-mail kisp@kubannet.ru; attached to Russian Acad. of Agricultural Sciences.

Krasnodar Scientific Research Institute of Vegetable and Potato Production: 350921 Krasnodar Belozerny; tel. (8612) 229-54-90; f. 1931; attached to Russian Acad. of Agricultural Sciences; library of 10,000 vols.

Kursk Research Institute of the Agro-industrial Complex: 307026 Kursk oblast, Cheremushki; attached to Russian Acad. of Agricultural Sciences.

Lukianenko, P. P., Krasnodar Agricultural Research Institute: 350012 Krasnodar; tel. (8612) 56-28-15; attached to Russian Acad. of Agricultural Sciences.

Michurin, I. V., All-Russia Research Institute for Genetics and Breeding in Horticulture: 393740 Tambov oblast, Michurinsk; tel. (47545) 5-78-87; fax (47545) 5-79-29; e-mail cglm@rambler.ru; attached to Russian Acad. of Agricultural Sciences; Dir SAVELYEV NIKOLAI IVANOVICH.

Michurin, I. V., All-Russia Research Institute for Horticulture: 393740 Tambov oblast, Michurinsk, ul. Michurina 30; tel. (07545) 4-21-32; attached to Russian Acad. of Agricultural Sciences.

Nizhne-Volzhsky Agricultural Research Institute: 404013 Volgograd oblast, Nizheznensky; attached to Russian Acad. of Agricultural Sciences.

North Caucasus Mountains and Foothills Agricultural Research Institute: 363110 North Ossetia, Prigorny raion, Mikhailovskoe; attached to Russian Acad. of Agricultural Sciences.

North Caucasus Research Institute for Horticulture and Viticulture: 350029 Krasnodar, ul. 40-letiya Pobedy 9; tel. (8612) 54-06-74; attached to Russian Acad. of Agricultural Sciences.

Orenburg Agricultural Research Institute: 460051 Orenburg, ul. Gagarina 27/1; tel. (3532) 3-86-94; attached to Russian Acad. of Agricultural Sciences.

Pacific Fisheries Research Centre (TINRO): 690950 Vladivostok, ul. Shevchenko 4; tel. (4232) 400921; fax (4232) 300752; e-mail tinro@tinro.ru; f. 1925; ichthyology, oceanography, commercial invertebrates, commercial marine algae, parasitology of marine animals, commercial fisheries, mechanization of fish processing, technology of fish and marine production, aquaculture (marine and freshwater), study of marine pollution; brs at Amur (Khabarovsk) and Chukotka; library of 61,500 vols, 11,000 MSS; Dir Dr L. N. BOCHAROV; publ. *Izvestiya TINRO* (1–3 a year).

Potapenko, Ya. I., All-Russia Research Institute for Viticulture and Winemaking: Rostovsky raion, 346421 Novocherkassk, pr. Baklanovsky 166; tel. (86352) 6-70-88; fax (86352) 6-64-59; fax ruswine@yandex.ru; internet www.rusvine.com; f. 1936; attached to Russian Acad. of Agricultural Sciences; Dir Dr LEONID VASILIEVICH KRAVCHENKO.

Povolzhsky Research Institute for the Economics and Development of the Agro-industrial Complex: 410020 Saratov, ul. Shekhurdina 12; tel. (8452) 64-06-47; attached to Russian Acad. of Agricultural Sciences.

Pryanishnikov, D. N., All-Russia Research Institute of Fertilizers and Agropedology: 127550 Moscow, ul. Pryanishnikova 31; tel. (095) 976-01-75; attached to Russian Acad. of Agricultural Sciences; Dir N. Z. MILASHENKO.

Pustovoit, V. S., All-Russia Research Institute of Oil Crops: 350038 Krasnodar, ul. Filatova 17; tel. (861) 255-59-33; fax (861) 259-79-14; e-mail vniimk-center@mail.ru; internet pustovoit.narod.ru; f. 1912; attached to Russian Acad. of Agricultural Sciences; library of 100,300 vols; Dir-Gen. Dr VYACHESLAV M. LUKOMETS; publ. *Oil Crops Scientific Bulletin* (2 a year).

Research and Technological Institute for Agricultural Biotechnology: 410020 Saratov, ul. Tulaikova 7; tel. (8452) 64-04-31; attached to Russian Acad. of Agricultural Sciences.

Research Institute for Animal Nutrition: Moscow oblast, Dmitrovsky raion, pos. Ermolovo.

Research Institute for Breeding and Diversity in Horticulture: 303130 Orel, Zhilina; attached to Russian Acad. of Agricultural Sciences.

Research Institute of Agricultural Forest Reclamation: 400062 Volgograd, Universitetsky pr. 97; tel. (8442) 46-25-67; fax (8442) 46-25-10; e-mail vnialmi@avtlg.ru; internet www.avtlg.ru/~vnialmi; f. 1931; attached to Russian Acad. of Agricultural Sciences; library of 93,700 vols; Dir Acad. KONSTANTIN N. KULIK; publ. *Scientific Papers* (2 a year).

Research Institute of Chemical Means of Plant Protection: 109088 Moscow, Ugreshskaya 31; tel. (095) 279-55-40; Dir N. N. YUKHTIN.

Research Institute of Farm Animal Physiology, Biochemistry and Nutrition: 249010 Kaluzhskaya oblast, Borovsk; attached to Russian Acad. of Agricultural Sciences; Dir Acad. V. I. GEORGIEVSKII.

Research Institute of Non-infectious Animal Diseases: Moscow oblast, Istrinsky raion.

Research Institute of Technological Studies in Agricultural Cybernetics: c/o Russian Academy of Agricultural Sciences, 107814 Moscow, Bolshoi Kharitonevsky per. 21; attached to Russian Acad. of Agricultural Sciences.

Research Institute of the Economics and Development of the Agro-industrial Complex in the Central Black Soil (Chernozem) Zone: 394042 Voronezh, ul. Sarafimovicha 26A; tel. and fax (0732) 22-99-40; e-mail niieoapk@vmail.ru; internet web .vrn.ru/niieoapk; f. 1930; attached to Russian Acad. of Agricultural Sciences; Dir V. MERNAYA.

Research Institute of Veterinary Entomology and Arachnology: 625010 Tyumen, Institutskaya ul. 2; attached to Russian Acad. of Agricultural Sciences; Dir V. Z. YAMOV.

Russian Institute of Agricultural Radiology and Agroecology: 249032 Kaluga oblast, Obninsk, Kievskoe shosse; tel. (08439) 6-48-02; fax (095) 255-22-25; e-mail riar@ obninsk.org; f. 1971; attached to Russian Acad. of Agricultural Sciences; 300 mems; library of 70,000 vols; Dir RUDOLF M. ALEXAKHIN; Deputy Dir NATALYA I. SANZHAROVA.

St Petersburg Forestry Research Institute: 194021 St Petersburg, Institutsky pr. 21; tel. (812) 552-80-21; fax (812) 552-80-42; e-mail spbfriin@nm10043.spb.cdu; internet www.spbniilh.ru; f. 1929; 130 mems; library of 90,000 vols; Dir ALEXANDER B. EGOROV (acting); publ. *Proceedings* (annually).

Samoilov, Ya. V., Research Institute of Fertilizers and Insectofungicides: 117333 Moscow, Leninskii pr. 55; tel. (095) 135-20-32; Dir V. M. BORISOV.

Skryabin, K. I., All-Russia Institute of Helminthology: 117259 Moscow, Bol. Cheremushkinskaya, 28; tel. (095) 124-56-55; attached to Russian Acad. of Agricultural Sciences; Dir Acad. V. S. ERSHOV.

South-East Agricultural Research Institute: 410020 Saratov, ul. Tulaykova 7; tel. (8452) 64-76-88; fax (8452) 64-76-88; e-mail ariser@mail.saratov.ru; f. 1910; attached to Russian Acad. of Agricultural Sciences; library of 350,000 vols; Dir NIKOLAI I. KOMAROV.

South Urals Agricultural Research Institute: 454002 Chelyabinsk, Shershni; tel. (3512) 42-42-01; attached to Russian Acad. of Agricultural Sciences.

Stavropol Agricultural Research Institute: 356200 Stavropol krai, Shpakovskoe; attached to Russian Acad. of Agricultural Sciences.

Sukachev, V. N., Institute of Forestry: 660036 Krasnoyarsk, Akademgorodok; tel. and fax (3912) 43-36-86; e-mail dndr@ifor .krasnoyarsk.su; f. 1944; attached to Russian Acad. of Sciences; library of 200,000 vols; Dir Dr ANATOLY SUKHININ.

Tula Agricultural Research Institute: 301053 Tula oblast, Molochnye dvory; tel. (08752) 5-23-41; fax (08752) 2-30-15; f. 1956; attached to Russian Acad. of Agricultural Sciences; Dir Prof. V. I SEVEROV.

Tulaikov, M. M., Samara Agricultural Research Institute: 446080 Samara oblast, Bezenchuk, ul. K. Marksa 41; attached to Russian Acad. of Agricultural Sciences.

Ulyanovsk Agricultural Research Institute: 433115 Ulyanovsk oblast, Timiryazevskoe; tel. (8422) 31-78-58; attached to Russian Acad. of Agricultural Sciences.

Vavilov, N. I., Research Institute of the Plant Industry: 190000 St Petersburg, ul. Bolshaya Morskaya 44; tel. (812) 315-50-93; fax (812) 311-87-62; e-mail v.dragavtsev@vir .nw.ru; internet vir.nw.ru; f. 1894; attached to Russian Acad. of Agricultural Sciences; departments: computerized information systems; plant biochemistry and molecular biology; laboratory for long-term storage of seeds; rye, barley and oats; fruit crops; industrial crops; experimental stations: Astrakhan, Daghestan, Far East, Krymsk, Kuban, Maikop, Moscow, Pavlovsk, Polar, Volgograd, Yekaterinino, Zeya; herbarium of 250,000 specimens; Dir Prof. Dr VICTOR A. DRAGAVTSEV.

Vilyams, V. R., All-Russia Fodder Research Institute: 141055 Moscow oblast, Lobnia raion, Lugovaya stantsiya; tel. (095) 577-73-37; fax (095) 577-01-07; e-mail vniicorm@mtu-net.ru; f. 1922; attached to Russian Acad. of Agricultural Sciences; Dir Dr ANATOLY SV. SHPATSOV; publs *Fodder Production* (monthly), *Achievements of the Agricultural Industry Complex* (monthly).

ARCHITECTURE AND TOWN PLANNING

Central Research and Design Institute of Dwellings: 127434 Moscow, Dmitrovskoe shosse 9, korp. 8; tel. (095) 976-28-19; fax (095) 976-37-82; f. 1962; Dir STANISLAV V. NIKOLAEV.

Central Research and Design Institute of Town Planning: 117944 Moscow, pr. Vernadskogo 29; tel. (095) 138-28-06; fax (095) 133-11-29; f. 1963; library of 25,000 vols; Dir YU. N. MAXIMOV.

Kucherenko, V. A., State Central Research and Experimental Design Institute for Complex Problems of Civil Engineering and Building Structures: 109428 Moscow, 2-ya Institutskaya 6; tel. (095) 171-26-50; fax (095) 171-28-58; f. 1927; Dir VASIL GORPINCHENKO; publs *Strength and Reliability of Structures, Numerical Methods of Analysis and Optimization of Building Structures, Investigations into Structural Earthquake Resistance, Timber Structures, Structural Dynamics* (all every 2 years), *New Forms and Strength of Metal Structures, Large-Panel and Masonry Structures* (both every 3 years), *Phosphate Materials, Investigation into Building Structures* (both annually), *Earthquake Engineering* (6 a year).

Panfilov, K. D., Academy of Municipal Economics: 123371 Moscow, Volokolamskoe shosse 116; tel. (095) 490-31-66; fax (095) 490-36-00; f. 1931; depts of scientific-technical co-ordination, municipal electrical supply, urban electric transport, anti-corrosion protection of underground metal structures, urban roads maintenance, municipal sanitation, urban landscaping, housing and municipal buildings, information, automation of technological processes, ecology; 6 research institutes (Moscow, St Petersburg, Rostov on Don, Tomsk, Ekaterinburg); 2 experimental factories (Moscow, St Petersburg); library of 740,000 vols; Dir V. F. PIVOVAROV; Scientific Sec. A. N. PROKHOROV.

Research Institute of Foundations and Underground Structures: 109428 Moscow, 2-ya Institutskaya 6; tel. (095) 171-22-40; fax (095) 171-37-01; f. 1931; Dir Prof. V. A. ILYICHEV; publ. *Soil Mechanics and Foundation Engineering* (every 2 months).

Scientific and Research Institute for Architecture and Town Planning Theory: 121019 Moscow, pr. Vozdvizhenka 5; tel. (095) 290-36-80; fax (095) 290-36-80.

BIBLIOGRAPHY, LIBRARY SCIENCE AND MUSEOLOGY

All-Russia Research Institute of Restoration: 109172 Moscow, Krestyanskaya ul. 10; tel. (095) 276-99-90.

Book Research Institute: 103473 Moscow, 2-i Volkonsky per. 10; tel. (095) 281-72-58; Dir A. I. SOLOVEV.

Library Association of Dagestan: 367026 Dagestan, ul. Batyraya 1; tel. (8722) 68-02-74; President KAZIM OMAROV.

ECONOMICS, LAW AND POLITICS

All-Russia Research and Design Institute of the Statistical Information System: 127486 Moscow, Deguninskaya ul. 1/3; tel. (095) 488-14-04.

All-Russia Research Institute of Economic Problems in Development of Science and Technology: 111024 Moscow, Aviamotornaya ul. 26/5; tel. (095) 273-52-31; f. 1986; library of 15,000 vols.

Bank Credit and Finance Research Institute: 103016 Moscow, ul. Alekseya Tolstogo 30/1; tel. (095) 925-61-18.

Central Economics and Mathematics Institute: 117418 Moscow, Nakhimovsky pr. 47; tel. (095) 129-16-44; fax (095) 310-70-15; e-mail director@cemi.rssi.ru; internet www.cemi.rssi.ru; f. 1963; attached to Russian Acad. of Sciences; Dir V. L. MAKAROV; publs *Economics and Mathematical Methods* (4 a year), *Economics of Contemporary Russia* (4 a year).

Central Economics Research Institute: 119898 Moscow, Smolensky bul. 3/5; tel. (095) 246-84-63.

Central Laboratory of Socio-Economic Measurements: c/o Russian Academy of Sciences, 117418 Moscow, ul. Krasikova 32; attached to Russian Acad. of Sciences; Dir A. YU. SHEVYAKOV.

Centre for the Study of Nationality Problems: 117036 Moscow, ul. Dm. Ulyanova 19; tel. (095) 123-90-61; attached to Russian Acad. of Sciences; Head M. N. GUBOGLO.

Federal Service of State Statistics: 107450 Moscow, ul. Myasnitskaya 39; tel. (095) 207-49-02; fax (095) 207-40-87; e-mail stat@gks.ru; internet www.gks.ru; f. 1918 as Central Statistical Board; present name 1991; provides demographic and economic statistical information and analysis to state authorities, the scientific community and commercial and international organizations; Dir VLADIMIR SOKOLIN.

Financial Research Institute: 103006 Moscow, Nastasinsky per. 3 korp. 2; tel. (095) 299-74-14; fax (095) 299-31-69; f. 1937.

Institute for African Studies: 123001 Moscow, ul. Spiridonovka 30/1; tel. (095) 290-27-52; fax (095) 202-07-86; e-mail dir@ inafr.ru; f. 1959; attached to Russian Acad. of Sciences; Dir A. M. VASILIEV; publs *Vostok-Orience* (jointly with Institute of Oriental Studies, 6 a year), *Asia and Africa Today* (jointly with Institute of Oriental Studies, monthly), *IAS Newsletter* (4 a year).

Institute for Comparative Political Studies: 101831 Moscow, Kolpachnyi per. 9a; tel. (095) 916-37-03; fax (095) 916-03-01; f. 1966; attached to Russian Acad. of Sciences; library of 50,000 vols; Dir T. T. TIMOFEEV; publs *Forum* (annually), *Polis* (6 a year).

Institute for Economics and Mathematics at St Petersburg:; e-mail korbut@ emi.nw.ru Tchaikovski ul. 1, St Petersburg 191187; tel. and fax (812) 273-7953; e-mail emi@emi.spb.ru; internet www.spbrc.nw.ru; f. 1990; attached to Russian Acad. of Sciences; Dir Prof. LEONID A. RUKHOVETS.

Institute for International Economic and Political Studies: 117418 Moscow, Novocheremushkinskaya 46; tel. (095) 128-91-57; fax (095) 120-83-71; e-mail imepi@transecon.ru; internet www.transecon.ru; f. 1960; attached to Russian Acad. of Sciences; Dir Prof. Dr RUSLAN GRINBERG; publ. *The World of Transformations* (4 a year).

Institute for Legislation and Comparative Law: 103728 Moscow, Vozdvizhenka 4/22; tel. (095) 291-02-07; fax (095) 290-58-56; f. 1925 (fmrly All-Union Research Institute of Soviet Legislation); library of 180,000 vols; Dir LEV A. OKUNKOV; publs *Problems of Perfecting Legislation* (3 a year), *Commentary on New Russian Legislation* (annually), *Materials of Foreign Legislation and International Private Law* (annually), *Legislation of Foreign Countries* (6 or 7 a year).

Institute for Socio-Economic Studies of Population: 117218 Moscow, Nakhimovsky pr. 32; tel. (095) 129-04-00; fax (095) 129-08-01; e-mail isesp_ras@mtu-net.ru; internet www.cemi.rssi.ru/isesp; f. 1988; attached to Russian Acad. of Sciences; Dir NATALIA RIMASHEVSKAYA; publ. *Population* (4 a year).

Institute of Economic and Social Problems of the North: 167610 Syktyvkar, Kommunisticheskaya ul. 26; tel. (8212) 42-42-67; fax (8212) 42-42-67; e-mail iespn@ksc.komi.ru; attached to Russian Acad. of Sciences; Dir V. N. LAZHENTSEV.

Institute of Economic Problems: 184209 Murmansk oblast, Apatity, ul. Fersmana 24a; tel. (81555) 7-64-72; fax (81555) 7-48-44; e-mail selin@iep.kolasc.net.ru; internet www.ksc.ru; f. 1986; attached to Kola Science Centre (Russian Acad. of Sciences); Dir Prof. VLADIMIR S. SELIN; publ. *Sever i rynok* (The North and the Market, in Russian, 3 a year).

Institute of Economic Research: 680042 Khabarovsk, Tikhookeanskaya ul. 153; tel. (421) 272-48-88; fax (421) 272-48-07; e-mail minakir@ecrin.ru; internet www.ecrin.ru; f. 1976; attached to Russian Acad. of Sciences; Dir Prof. P. A. MINAKIR; publ. *Spatial Economics* (quarterly).

Institute of Economics: 620219 Ekaterinburg, Moskovskaya ul. 29; tel. (3432) 51-45-36; fax (3432) 51-45-36; e-mail green@uran.ru; f. 1971; attached to Russian Acad. of Sciences; Dir A. I. TATARKIN.

Institute of Economics: 117218 Moscow, Nakhimovskiy pr. 32; tel. (095) 129-06-09; attached to Russian Acad. of Sciences; Dir Acad. RUSLAN S. GRINBERG.

Institute of Europe: 103873 Moscow, Mokhovaya 8–3; tel. (095) 203-73-43; fax (095) 200-42-98; f. 1988; attached to Russian Acad. of Sciences; library of 3,000 vols; Dir VITALY V. ZHURKIN; publ. *Reports* (6 a year).

Institute of Far Eastern Studies: 117218 Moscow, Nakhimovsky pr. 32; tel. (095) 124-01-17; fax (095) 310-70-56; e-mail ifes@cemi.rssi.ru; f. 1966; attached to Russian Acad. of Sciences; Dir M. L. TITARENKO; publ. *Far Eastern Affairs* (6 a year).

Institute of Foreign Economic Research: c/o Russian Academy of Sciences, 117418 Moscow, ul. Krasikova 32; attached to Russian Acad. of Sciences; Dir S. A. SITARYAN.

Institute of National Economic Forecasting: 117418 Moscow, Nakhimovsky pr. 47; tel. (495) 129-34-22; fax (495) 718-97-71; e-mail office@ecfor.ru; internet www.ecfor.ru; f. 1986; attached to Russian Acad. of Sciences; undertakes macroeconomic analysis; short-, medium-, and long-term forecasting of the Russian economy; Dir Prof. VICTOR V. IVANTER; publs *Problemy Prognozirovaniya* (in Russian, 6 a year), *Studies on Russian Economic Development* (in English, 6 a year).

Institute of Philosophy and Law: 620144 Ekaterinburg, ul. 8 Marta 68; tel. (3432) 22-23-46; attached to Russian Acad. of Sciences; Dir S. S. ALEKSEEV.

Institute of Problems of Assimilation of the North: 625003 Tyumen, a/ya 2774; tel. (3452) 7-82-76; attached to Russian Acad. of Sciences; Dir V. P. MELNIKOV.

Institute of Problems of the Marketplace: 117418 Moscow, Nakhimovsky pr. 47; tel. (095) 129-10-00; attached to Russian Acad. of Sciences; Dir N. YA. PETRAKOV.

Institute of Social Sciences: 670042 Ulan-Ude, ul. Marii Sakhyanovoi 6; tel. (3012) 3-66-25; attached to Russian Acad. of Sciences; Dir V. T. NAIDAKOV.

Institute of Socio-Economic Problems of the Development of the Agroindustrial Complex: 401600 Saratov, pr. Lenina 94; tel. (8452) 24-25-38; attached to Russian Acad. of Sciences; Dir V. B. OSTROVSKY.

Institute of Socio-Political Research: 119991 Moscow, Leninsky pr. 32A; tel. (095) 938-58-39; fax (095) 938-18-86; e-mail info@ispr.ru; internet www.ispr.ru; f. 1991; attached to Russian Acad. of Sciences; Dir Prof. Dr GENNADY OSIPOV; publs *Eurasia* (annually), *Science, Culture, Society* (4 a year), *Social and Demographic Policies*.

Institute of State and Law: 119841 Moscow, ul. Znamenka 10; tel. (095) 291-33-81; attached to Russian Acad. of Sciences; Dir B. N. TOPORNIN.

Institute of the Economics of the Comprehensive Assimilation of the Natural Resources of the North: 677891 Yakutsk, ul. Petrovskogo 2; tel. (4112) 3-52-46; attached to Russian Acad. of Sciences; Dir N. V. IGOSHIN.

Institute of USA and Canada Studies: 121814 Moscow, Khlebnyi per. 2/3; tel. (095) 291-20-52; fax (095) 200-12-07; e-mail iskran@glasnet.ru; attached to Russian Acad. of Sciences; Dir SERGEI ROGOV; publs *US: Economy, Policy, Ideology* (monthly).

Institute of World Economics and International Relations: 117957 Moscow, Profsoyuznaya 23; tel. (095) 120-43-32; fax (095) 120-65-75; e-mail imemoran@imemo.ru; internet www.imemo.ru; attached to Russian Acad. of Sciences; 545 mems; Dir Prof. SIMONIA A. NODARI (acting); publs *World Economics and International Relations* (monthly, in Russian), *Russian Economic Barometer* (quarterly, in English).

International Research Institute for Management Sciences: 117312 Moscow, Pr. 60-letiya Oktyabrya 9; tel. (095) 137-28-57.

Latin America Institute: 115035 Moscow, Bol. Ordynka 21; tel. (095) 951-53-23; fax (095) 953-40-70; e-mail ilac-zan@mtu-net.ru; internet www.mtu-net.ru/ilaran; f. 1961; attached to Russian Acad. of Sciences; Dir Dr V. M. DAVYDOV; publ. *Iberoamerica* (in Spanish, 4 a year).

Peace Research Center of IMEMO: 117859 Moscow, ul. Profsoyuznaya 23; tel. (095) 128-93-89; fax (095) 120-65-75; e-mail imemoran@online.ru; attached to Russian Acad. of Sciences; Dir A.K. KISLOV; publ. *Ways to Security* (in Russian, 2 or 3 a year).

Pricing Research Institute: 107078 Moscow, Kirovsky pr-d 4/3; tel. (095) 925-50-56.

Research Institute for the Strengthening of the Legal System and Law and Order: 123805 Moscow, GSP 2-ya Zvenigorodskaya ul. 15; tel. (095) 256-54-63.

Research Institute of Planning and Normatives: 125319 Moscow, Kochnovsky pr. 3; tel. (095) 152-45-91; attached to Russian Acad. of Sciences; Dir B. V. GUBIN (acting).

Sochi Research Centre: 354000 Sochi, Teatralnaya 8a; tel. (862) 92-37-71; fax (862) 292-44-11; e-mail snic@sochi.ru; f. 1988; attached to Russian Acad. of Sciences; research into management of the development of recreational areas and tourism; Dir M. M. AMIRKHANOV.

Survey Technique and Applied Research (STAR) Centre of the Institute of Sociology: 117259 Moscow, ul. Krzhizhanovskogo 24/35, str. 5; tel. (095) 719-09-71; fax (095) 719-07-40; e-mail valman@socio.msk.su; f. 1983; attached to Russian Acad. of Sciences; opinion survey design, data collection; Dir Prof. V. MANSUROV.

EDUCATION

Central Sports Research Institute: 107005 Moscow, Elizavetinsky per. 10; tel. (095) 261-50-76.

Centre for Pre-School Education: 113035 Moscow, ul. Osipenko 21; tel. (095) 231-49-28; attached to Russian Acad. of Education; Dir A. S. SPIVAKOVSKAYA.

Centre for Social Pedagogics: 119905 Moscow, Pogodinskaya ul. 8; tel. (095) 246-44-58; attached to Russian Acad. of Education; Dir V. G. BOCHAROVA.

Institute for Advanced Training: 109180 Moscow, ul. Bol. Polyanka 58; tel. (095) 237-31-51; attached to Russian Acad. of Education; Dir Y. A. ROODIE.

Institute for Educational Innovation: 117449 Moscow, ul. Vinokurova 3-B; tel. (095) 126-26-30; attached to Russian Acad. of Education; Dir V. I. SLOBODCHIKOV.

Institute for School Development in Siberia, the Far East and the North: 634050 Tomsk, ul. Gertsena 68; tel. (3822) 21-28-21; attached to Russian Acad. of Education; Dir G. V. ZALEVSKY.

Institute for the Occupational Training of Youth: 119903 Moscow, Pogodinskaya ul. 8; tel. (095) 245-05-13; attached to Russian Acad. of Education; Dir V. A. POLYAKOV.

Institute of Developmental Physiology: 119869 Moscow, ul. Pogodinskaya 8, korp. 2; tel. (095) 245-04-33; attached to Russian Acad. of Education; Dir Dr M. M. BEZRUKIKH.

Institute of Higher Education: 111024 Moscow, Tretya Kabelynaya ul. 1; tel. (495) 273-48-19; e-mail sav@niivo.hetnet.ru; attached to Russian Acad. of Education; Dir ALEXANDER SAVELIEV.

Institute of National Problems of Education: 105077 Moscow, Pervomayskaya 101; tel. (095) 461-92-45; fax (095) 461-92-45; f. 1991; (fmrly Research Institute of National Schools, f. 1949); Dir Prof. M. N. KOUZMIN; publ. *Uchenye Zapiski* (annually).

Institute of Secondary Education: 119906 Moscow, ul. Pogodinskaya 8; tel. (095) 245-37-33; attached to Russian Acad. of Education; Dir. V. S. LEDNEV.

Institute of Secondary Specialized Education: Tatarstan, 420039 Kazan, ul. Isayeva 12; tel. (8432) 42-63-24; fax (8432) 42-46-80; e-mail postmaster@isee.kcn.ru; f. 1976; attached to Russian Acad. of Education; Dir G. V. MUKHAMETZYANOVA; publ. *Professional Education* (4 a year).

Institute of Teaching and Learning Resources: 119903 Moscow, ul. Pogodinskaya 8; tel. (095) 246-35-90; attached to Russian Acad. of Education; Dir T. S. NAZAROVA.

Institute of Theoretical Pedagogics and International Research in Education:

129278 Moscow, ul. Pavla Korchagina 7; tel. (095) 283-09-55; attached to Russian Acad. of Education; Dir B. S. GERSHUNSKY.

Institute of Vocational Education: 119186 St Petersburg, nab. Moiki 48; tel. (812) 311-60-88; attached to Russian Acad. of Education; Dir A. P. BELYAEVA.

Psychological Institute: 103009 Moscow, Mokhovaya ul. 9, korp. B; tel. (095) 202-88-76; attached to Russian Acad. of Education; Dir V. V. RUBTSOV.

Research Centre for Aesthetic Education: 119034 Moscow, Kropotkinskaya nab. 15; tel. (095) 202-25-97; attached to Russian Acad. of Education; Dir B. P. YUSOV.

Research Centre for the Teaching of Russian: 119903 Moscow, Pogodinskaya ul. 8; tel. (095) 246-05-59; attached to Russian Acad. of Education; Dir E. A. BYSTROVA.

Research Institute of Remedial Education: 119869 Moscow, ul. Pogodinskaya 8, korp. 1; tel. (095) 245-04-52; attached to Russian Acad. of Education; Dir N. N. MALOFEEV.

Siberian Institute of Educational Technologies: 630098 Novosibirsk, Primorskaya ul. 22; tel. (3832) 45-18-32; fax (3832) 45-87-51; f. 1985; attached to Russian Acad. of Education; Dir I. M. BOBKO; publ. *Information Technologies in Education* (2 a year).

State Research Institute for the Family and Education: 119906 Moscow, ul. Pogodinskaya 8; tel. (095) 247-06-06; fax (095) 247-04-77; e-mail isv@niisv.ru; internet www.niisv.ru; f. 1998; attached to Russian Acad. of Education; Dir SERGEI VLADIMIROVICH DARMODECHIN.

FINE AND PERFORMING ARTS

Art Research Museum: St Petersburg, Universitetskaya nab. 17; tel. (812) 328-27-19; fax (812) 323-61-69; f. 1758; attached to Russian Acad. of Arts; laboratories and bronze-casting studios; 3 brs; Dir E. V. GRISHINA.

Research Institute of Film Art: 125009 Moscow, Degtyarny per. 8; tel. and fax (095) 299-56-79; e-mail cineaste@mail.ru; f. 1974; 65 mems; library of 60,000 vols; still photos archive; research in the field of history and theory of film and monitoring of the situation in Russian and world cinema; Dir LIUDMILA BUDYAK; Deputy Dirs DMITRY KARAVAEV, MARK ZAK; publs *Kinograph* (almanac), *Kinovedcheskie Zapisky* (Film Notebooks, 4 a year).

Research Institute of the Theory and History of Fine Arts: 119034 Moscow, ul. Prechistenka 21; tel. (095) 201-42-91; attached to Russian Acad. of Arts; Dir V. V. VANSLOV.

State Institute for Art Studies: 103009 Moscow, Kozitsky per. 5; tel. (095) 200-03-71; fax (095) 785-24-06; e-mail a.komech@sias.ru; f. 1944; research in fine art, theatre, music, architecture, folklore, mass media; studies in sociology, economics and the politics of culture; library of 70,000 vols; Dir Dr A. I. KOMECH; publs *World of Arts* (annually), *Theory of Culture* (annually), *Occidental Art of the 20th Century* (every 2 years), *Cultural Transactions* (every 2 years).

HISTORY, GEOGRAPHY AND ARCHAEOLOGY

Institute of Archaeology: 117036 Moscow, Ul. Dm. Ulyanova 19; tel. (095) 126-47-98; fax (095) 126-06-30; e-mail ia.ras@mail.ru; internet archaeolog.ru; f. 1919; attached to Russian Acad. of Sciences; Dir N. A.

MAKAROV; publ. *Russiyskaya Archeologia* (4 a year).

Institute of Geography: 664033 Irkutsk, Ulanbatorskaya 1; tel. (3952) 46-43-20; attached to Russian Acad. of Sciences; Dir V. V. VOROBEV.

Institute of Geography: 109017 Moscow, Staromonetnii per. 29; tel. (495) 959-00-32; fax (495) 959-00-33; e-mail igras@igras.geonet.ru; f. 1918; attached to Russian Acad. of Sciences; library of 10,000 vols; Dir Acad. V. M. KOTLYAKOV; publs *Geomorphology* (4 a year), *Izvestiya Akademii Nauk – Seriya Geograficheskaya* (6 a year), *Materialy Glyatsiologicheskikh Issledovanii* (2 a year).

Institute of History and Archaeology: 620219 Ekaterinburg, ul. R. Lyuksemburg 56; tel. (3432) 22-14-02; fax (3432) 22-42-30; e-mail istor@uran.ru; internet www.uran.ru/structure/institutions/history/index.htm; f. 1988; attached to Russian Acad. of Sciences; Dir Prof. V. V. ALEKSEEV; publ. *Ural Historical Journal* (annually).

Institute of History, Language and Literature: 450054 Ufa, pr. Oktyabrya 71; tel. (3472) 35-60-50; fax (3472) 35-60-77; e-mail ilishev@anrb.ru; f. 1932; attached to Russian Acad. of Sciences; Dir ILDUS Y. ILISHEV.

Institute of History, Philology and Philosophy: 630090 Novosibirsk, pr. Akad. Lavrenteva 17; tel. (3832) 35-05-37; fax (3832) 35-77-91; attached to Russian Acad. of Sciences; Dir Acad. A. P. DEREVYANKO.

Institute of Language, Literature and Arts: 367025 Makhachkala 25, ul. Magomeda Gadjieva 45; tel. (872) 267-06-21; fax (872) 267-06-21; f. 1924; attached to Russian Acad. of Sciences; library of 160,000 vols; Dir M. I. MAGOMEDOV.

Institute of Language, Literature and History: 167610 Syktyvkar, Kommunisticheskaya ul. 26; tel. (8212) 24-55-64; fax (8212) 44-21-97; e-mail smetanin@mail.komisc.ru; internet www.komisc.ru/illh; f. 1970; attached to Russian Acad. of Sciences; Dir ALEXANDR F. SMETANIN.

Institute of Linguistics, Literature and History: 185610 Petrozavodsk, Pushkinskaya ul. 11; tel. (8142) 77-44-96; e-mail nikitina@post.krc.karelia.ru; attached to Russian Acad. of Sciences; Dir YU. A. SAVVATEEV.

Institute of Military History: 117330 Moscow, Universitetskii pr. 14; tel. (095) 147-45-65; attached to Russian Acad. of Sciences; Dir A. N. BAZHENOV.

Institute of Oriental Studies: 103777 Moscow, Rozhdestvenka 12; tel. (095) 925-64-61; fax (095) 312-14-65 br. in St Petersburg: 192041 St Petersburg, Dvortsovaya nab. 18; tel. (812) 315-87-28; e-mail invost@mail.convey.ru; f. 1818; attached to Russian Acad. of Sciences; Dir R. B. RYBAKOV; Head E. I. KICHANOV; publ. *Manuscripta Orientalia* (4 a year).

Institute of Research in the Humanities: 677007 Sakha Republic, Yakutsk, Petrovskaya ul. 1; tel. (41122) 5-49-96; fax (41122) 5-49-96; f. 1935; attached to Acad. of Sciences of the Sakha Republic; history, language and culture of the peoples of the Sakha Republic; Dir VASILY N. IVANOV.

Institute of Russian History: 117036 Moscow, ul. Dm. Ulyanova 19; tel. (095) 126-94-49; fax (095) 126-39-55 br. at St Petersburg: 197110 St Petersburg, Petrozavodskaya 7; tel. (812) 235-41-98; fax (812) 235-64-85; attached to Russian Acad. of Sciences; Dir A. N. SAKHAROV.

Institute of Slavonic Studies: 117334 Moscow, Leninsky pr. 32A; tel. (095) 938-17-80; fax (095) 938-00-96; e-mail ritlen@mail

.ru; f. 1947; attached to Russian Acad. of Sciences; Dir V. K. VOLKOV; publ. *Slavyanovedeniye* (4 a year).

Institute of the History, Archaeology and Ethnography of the Peoples of the Far East: 690950 Vladivostok, ul. Pushkinskaya 89; tel. (4232) 22-05-07; fax (4232) 26-82-11; e-mail ihae@eastnet.febras.ru; internet www.febras.ru/~ihae; f. 1971; attached to Russian Acad. of Sciences; Dir Dr V. L. LARIN; publ. *Russia and the Pacific* (in Russian, 4 a year).

Institute of the History of Material Culture: 191065 St Petersburg, Dvortsovaya nab. 18; tel. (812) 312-14-84; attached to Russian Acad. of Sciences.

Institute of World History: 117036 Moscow, ul. Dm. Ulyanova 19; tel. (095) 126-94-21; attached to Russian Acad. of Sciences; Dir A. O. CHUBARYAN.

Krasovsky, F. N., Central Research Institute for Geodesy, Aerial Photography, and Cartography: 125413 Moscow, Onezhskaya 26; tel. (095) 456-95-31.

Oceanography Research Institute: 190121 St Petersburg, nab. Moiki 120; Dir I. S. GRAMBERG.

Pacific Institute of Geography: 690041 Vladivostok, ul. Radio 7; tel. (4232) 32-06-72; fax (4232) 31-21-59; f. 1971; attached to Russian Acad. of Sciences; library of 28,000 vols; Dir Prof. P. YA. BAKLANOV; publ. *Zov Taigi*.

State Oceanography Institute: 119838 Moscow, Kropotkinskii per. 6; tel. (095) 246-72-88 br. 199026 St. Petersburg, V.O., 23-ya liniya 2-a; tel. (812) 218-81-23; Dir F. S. TERZIEV.

Udmurt Institute of History, Language and Literature: 426004 Izhevsk, ul. Lomonosova 4; tel. (3412) 75-53-21; fax (3412) 75-39-94; f. 1931; attached to Russian Acad. of Sciences; library of 60,000 vols; Dir KUZMA I. KULIKOV.

LANGUAGE AND LITERATURE

Gorky, A. M., Institute of World Literature: 121069 Moscow, ul. Vorovskogo 25a; tel. (095) 290-50-30; attached to Russian Acad. of Sciences; Dir F. F. KUZNETSOV.

Ibragimov, G., Institute of Language, Literature and Art: 420503 Kazan, ul. Lobachevskogo 2/31; tel. (8432) 38-70-59; fax (8432) 38-74-79; attached to Acad. of Sciences of the Republic of Tatarstan; Dir M. Z. ZAKIEV.

Institute of Linguistic Research: 199053 St Petersburg, Tuchkov per. 9; tel. (812) 328-16-11; fax (812) 328-46-11; f. 1921; attached to Russian Acad. of Sciences; Dir Prof. Dr ANATOLY DOMASHNEV.

Institute of Linguistics: 125009 Moscow, ul. Bol. Kislovsky per. 1/12; tel. (095) 290-35-85; fax (095) 290-05-28; e-mail iling@iling-ran.ru; internet www.iling-ran.ru; f. 1950; attached to Russian Acad. of Sciences; Dir V. A. VINOGRADOV; publs *Caucasology* (2 a year), *Voprosy Filologii* (3 a year), *Voprosy Psikholingvistiki* (2 a year).

Institute of Russian Literature (Pushkin House): 199034 St Petersburg, nab. Makarova 4; tel. (812) 328-19-01; fax (812) 328-11-40; e-mail irli@mail.ru; f. 1905; attached to Russian Acad. of Sciences; Dir N. N. SKATOV; publ. *Russian Literature* (4 a year).

Russian Institute for Cultural Research: 109072 Moscow, Bersenevskaya nab. 20; tel. (095) 959-09-08; fax (095) 959-10-17; e-mail riku@dol.ru; internet www.riku.ru; f. 1932; attached to Ministry for Culture and Mass Communication of the Russian Federation;

library: library of 67,000 books and periodicals; Dir Prof. KIRILL E. RAZLOGOV.

Vinogradov Institute of the Russian Language: 121019 Moscow, Volkhonka 18/2; tel. (095) 202-65-40; fax (095) 291-23-17; e-mail irlras@irl.msk.su; f. 1944; attached to Russian Acad. of Sciences; library of 110,000 vols; Dir Dr A. M. MOLDOVAN; publs *Rusistics Today* (4 a year), *Russian Speech* (6 a year).

MEDICINE

All-Russia Antibiotics Research Institute: 113105 Moscow, Nagatinskaya ul. 3a; tel. (095) 111-42-38; fax (095) 118-93-66; f. 1947; library of 65,000 vols; br. in Penza; Dir Prof. S. M. NAVASHIN; publ. *Antibiotics and Chemotherapy.*

All-Russia Research Institute of Eye Diseases: 119021 Moscow, ul. Rossolimo 11; tel. (095) 248-01-25; f. 1973; microsurgery of the eye, therapeutic ophthalmology, laser ophthalmology, new technical equipment in ophthalmology; 550 mems; 150 scientific staff; Chief officers ALEKSEEV, KRASNOV, KUZNETSOVA, MUSTAEV; publ. *Vestnik Oftalmologii* (bi-monthly).

All-Russia Research Institute of Pharmaceutical Plants: 113628 Moscow, ul. Grina 7; tel. (095) 382-83-18; Dir P. T. KONDRATENKO.

All-Russia Research Institute of the Technology of Blood Substitutes and Hormonal Preparations: 109044 Moscow, per. Lavrov 6; tel. (095) 276-43-60.

Allergen State Unitary Enterprise: 355019 Stavropol, Biologicheskaya ul. 20; tel. (8652) 24-40-84; fax (8652) 25-31-46; e-mail allergen@z-com.ru; f. 1918; vaccines and sera, allergens, nutrient media, pharmaceuticals; library of 39,500 vols and periodicals; Dir-Gen. V. V. ERMELOV.

Anokhin, P. K., Institute of Normal Physiology: 103009 Moscow, ul. Bolshaya Nikitskaya 6; tel. (095) 203-66-70; fax (095) 203-54-32; attached to Russian Acad. of Medical Sciences; Dir K. V. SUDAKOV.

Bakulev Scientific and Research Centre for Cardiovascular Surgery: 117049 Moscow, Leninskii pr. 8; tel. (095) 236-13-61; fax (095) 237-21-72; e-mail leoan@online.ru; internet www.bakoulev.sovintel.ru; f. 1956; attached to Russian Acad. of Medical Sciences; Head Acad. L. A. BOKERIYA; publs *Journal of Thoracic and Cardiovascular Surgery* (in Russian, 6 a year), *Annals of Surgery* (in Russian, 6 a year), *Bulletin* (in Russian, 6 a year), *Annals of Arrhythmology* (in Russian, 6 a year).

Blokhin, N. N., Cancer Research Center: Kashirskoe shosse 24, 115478 Moscow; tel. (095) 324-11-14; fax (095) 323-53-55; e-mail info@eso.ru; internet www.cancercenter.ru; f. 1951; attached to Russian Acad. of Medical Sciences; Dir MIKHAIL V. DAVYDOV; publs *Journal* (quarterly), *Herald of Moscow Cancer Society* (monthly), *Journal of Biotherapy* (2 a month), *Pediatric Oncology* (2 a month).

Attached institutes:

Research Institute of Carcinogenesis: Kashirskoe shosse 24, 115478 Moscow,; tel. (095) 324-14-70; attached to Russian Acad. of Medical Sciences; Dir DAVID G. ZARIDZE.

Russian Institute of Clinical Oncology: Kashirskoe shosse 24, 115478 Moscow; tel. (095) 324-44-16; attached to Russian Acad. of Medical Sciences; Dir MIKHAIL I. DAVYDOV.

Research Institute of Experimental Therapy and Tumour Diagnosis: Kashirskoe shosse 24, 115478 Moscow; tel. (095) 324-22-74; attached to Russian Acad. of Medical Sciences; Dir ANATOLY Y. BARYSHNIKOV.

Research Institute of Pediatric Oncology: Kashirskoe shosse 24, 115478 Moscow; tel. (095) 324-43-09; attached to Russian Acad. of Medical Sciences; Dir LEV A. DURNOV.

Blood Transfusion Research Institute: 125167 Moscow, Novozykovsky pr-d 4A; tel. (095) 212-45-51; fax (095) 212-42-52.

Burdenko Neurosurgical Institute: 125047 Moscow, ul. Fadeeva 5; tel. (095) 251-65-26; fax (095) 250-93-51; attached to Russian Acad. of Medical Sciences; Dir A. N. KONOVALOV.

Cardiological Research Centre: 121552 Moscow, 3°, Cherepkovskaya ul. 15; tel. (095) 415-13-47; fax (095) 415-29-62; attached to Russian Acad. of Medical Sciences; Dir E. I. CHAZOV.

Attached institutes:

Institute of Experimental Cardiology: 121552 Moscow, 3 Cherepkovskaya ul. 15A; tel. 415-00-35; attached to Russian Acad. of Medical Sciences; Dir V. N. SMIRNOV.

Myasnikov, A. L., Institute of Cardiology: 121552 Moscow, 3°, Cherepkovskaya ul. 15; tel. 415-52-05; attached to Russian Acad. of Medical Sciences; Dir YU. N. BELENKOV.

Central Institute of Traumatology and Orthopaedics: 125299 Moscow, ul. Priorova 10; tel. (095) 450-24-72; fax (095) 154-31-39; e-mail cito@cito-priorov.ru; f. 1921; 12 clinics; library of 40,000 vols; Dir Prof. S. P. MIRONOV; publ. *N. N. Priorov Journal of Traumatology and Orthopaedics* (4 a year).

Central Research Institute for the Evaluation of Working Capacity and Vocational Assistance to Disabled Persons: 127486 Moscow, ul. Susanina 3; tel. (095) 906-18-31; fax (095) 906-18-32; f. 1930; library of 50,000 vols; Dir D. I. LAVROVA.

Central Research Institute of Dermatology and Venereal Diseases: 107076 Moscow, ul. Korolenko 3; tel. (095) 964-43-22; fax (095) 964-26-20; e-mail info@cnikvi.ru; internet www.cnikvi.ru; f. 1921; publ. *Vestnik Dermatologii i Venerologii* (Journal of Dermatology and Venereology, 6 a year).

Central Research Institute of Epidemiology: 111123 Moscow, Novogireevskaya 3-a; tel. (095) 176-02-19; Dir A. SUMAROKOV.

Central Research Institute of Gastroenterology: 111123 Moscow, shosse Entuziastov 86; tel. and fax (095) 304-19-42; e-mail gastroenter@mtu-net.ru; internet www.gastro-online.ru; f. 1973; Dir Prof. L. B. LAZEBNIK; publs *Experimental and Clinical Gastroenterology* (6 a year), *Hepatology* (4 a year).

Central Research Institute of Roentgenology and Radiology: 197758 St Petersburg, Pesochny, ul. Leningradskaya 70/4; tel. (812) 596-84-62; fax (812) 596-67-05; e-mail crirr@peterlink.ru; internet www.private.peterlink.ru/crirr; f. 1918; Dir Prof. ANATOLY M. GRANOV; publ. *Volume of Conference Reports* (annually).

Central Research Institute of Tuberculosis: 107564 Moscow,Yauzskaya alleya 2; tel. (095) 268-49-60; fax (095) 268-49-40; attached to Russian Acad. of Medical Sciences; Dir A. G. KHOMENKO.

Centre for the Chemistry of Drugs—All-Russia Chemical and Pharmaceutical Research Institute: 119815 Moscow, ul. Zubovskaya 7; tel. (095) 246-97-68; fax (095) 246-78-05; f. 1920; research on drugs; library of 150,000 items; Dir R. G. GLUSHKOV; publ. *Collection of Proceedings* (annually).

Chumakov, M. P., Institute of Poliomyelitis and Virus Encephalitis: 142782 Moscow oblast, Kievskoe shosse, 27 km; tel. (095) 439-90-07; attached to Russian Acad. of Medical Sciences; Dir S. G. DROZDOV.

Chuvash Eye Diseases Research Institute: 428028 Cheboksary, Traktorostroitelei 10; tel. (8350) 26-05-75; fax (8350) 26-52-13; f. 1987; Dir Dr NIKOLAI PASHTAEV.

Dagestan Medical Research Centre: 367020 Makhachkala, ul. Gorikogo 53; tel. (87200) 7-49-97; attached to Russian Acad. of Medical Sciences; Dir S.-M. A. OMAROV.

Eastern Siberian Research Centre: 664003 Irkutsk, ul. Timiryazeva 16; tel. (3952) 27-54-48; fax (3952) 27-48-13; e-mail scippnw@sbamsr.irk.ru; attached to Russian Acad. of Medical Sciences; Chair. of Presidium Acad. S. I. KOLESNIKOV.

Attached institutes:

Institute of Epidemiology and Microbiology: 664000 Irkutsk, ul. Karla Marksa 3; tel. (3952) 33-34-23; fax (3952) 33-34-45; attached to Russian Acad. of Medical Sciences; Dir Prof. V. I. ZLOBIN.

Institute of Industrial Medicine and Human Ecology: 665827 Irkutskaya oblast, Angarsk 27, a/ya 1170; tel. (218) 55-90-70; fax (218) 55-40-77; e-mail rvc@iimhe.irk.ru; attached to Russian Acad. of Medical Sciences; Dir V. S. RUKAVISHNIKOV.

Institute of Paediatrics and Human Reproduction: 664003 Irkutsk, ul. Timiryazeva 16; tel. (3952) 34-73-67; fax (3952) 27-48-13; e-mail scippnw@sbamsr.irk.ru; attached to Russian Acad. of Medical Sciences; Dir Acad. S. I. KOLESNIKOV.

Institute of Surgery: 664047 Irkutsk, Yubileiny mikroraion 100; tel. (3952) 38-53-31; fax (3952) 38-53-31; attached to Russian Acad. of Medical Sciences; Dir Prof. E. G. GRIGOREV.

Institute of Traumatology and Orthopaedics: 664003 Irkutsk, ul. Bortsov Revolyutsii 1; tel. (3952) 27-54-30; fax (3952) 27-54-30; attached to Russian Acad. of Medical Sciences; Dir Prof. A. P. BARABASH.

Ekaterinburg Institute of Restorative Surgery, Traumatology and Orthopaedics: Ekaterinburg, Bankovsky per. 7.

Ekaterinburg Region Institute of Dermatology and Venereal Diseases: Ekaterinburg, ul. K. Libknekhta 9.

Ekaterinburg Viral Infections Research Institute: 620030 Ekaterinburg, Letnyaya ul. 23; tel. (3432) 61-99-60; f. 1920; Dir Prof. NINA P. GLINSKIKH; publ. *Viral Infections: Urgent Problems* (annually).

Endocrinology Research Centre: 117036 Moscow, ul. Dm. Ulyanova 11; tel. (095) 124-43-00; fax (095) 718-05-22; e-mail post@endocrincentr.ru; internet www.endocrincentr.ru; f. 1925; attached to Russian Acad. of Medical Sciences; Dir I. I. DEDOV; publ. *Diabetes Mellitus* (in Russian, 4 a year).

Attached institutes:

Institute of Clinical Endocrinology: Institute of Clinical Endocrinology: Moscow; tel. (095) 126-96-70; fax (095) 718-05-22; e-mail melnich@endocrincentr.ru; f. 1988; Dir J. A. MELNICHENKO.

Institute of Experimental Endocrinology: 112255 Moscow, ul. Moskvorechie 1; tel. (095) 324-93-25; f. 1965; Dir V. N. BABICHEV.

Institute of Diabetes: Moscow; tel. (095) 1244500; fax (095) 7180522; f. 1988; Dir M. I. BALABOLKIN.

Ersman Hygiene Research Institute: 141000 Mytishchi, ul. Semashko 2; tel. (095) 583-82-14.

Federal Bureau for Medical and Social Expertise: 127486 Moscow, ul. Ivana Susanina 3; tel. (095) 487-57-11; fax (095) 487-81-81; e-mail fbmse@inbox.ru; f. 2000 as Federal Scientific and Practical Centre for Medico-Social Expertise and Rehabilitation of Invalids (formed by merger of Central Research Institute of Prosthetics and Prosthesis Design and Central Research Institute for the Evaluation of Working Capacity and Vocational Assistance to Disabled Persons); present name 2005; library of 45,000 vols; Dir Prof. Dr S. N. PUZIN; publ. *Journal of Medical and Social Expertise and Rehabiliation* (4 a year).

Federal Research Institute for Health Education and Health Promotion: 103101 Moscow, ul. A. Mitskevicha 3; tel. (095) 202-18-13; fax (095) 202-54-08; f. 1927; library of 10,000 vols; Dir Dr V. A. POLESKY.

Federal Research Institute of Paediatric Gastroenterology: 603950 Nizhnii Novgorod, ul. Semashko 22; tel. (8312) 36-66-35; fax (8312) 36-56-59; e-mail niidegastro@mail.ru; f. 1929; Dir Prof. Dr ANATOLY I. VOLKOV.

Gamalei, N. F., Institute of Epidemiology and Microbiology: 123098 Moscow, ul. Gamalei 18; tel. (095) 193-30-01; fax (095) 305-67-38; attached to Russian Acad. of Medical Sciences; Dir S. V. PROZOROVSKII.

Haematological Research Centre: 125167 Moscow, Novozykovsky pr-d 4A; tel. (095) 212-21-23; fax (095) 212-42-52; attached to Russian Acad. of Medical Sciences, Dir A. I. VOROBIEV.

Herzen, P. A., Moscow Cancer Research Institute: 125284 Moscow, 2-i Botkinsky pr-d 3; tel. (095) 945-19-35; f. 1903; library of 19,336 vols; Dir Prof. V. I. CHISSOV.

Institute for the Protection of the Mother and Baby: 680028 Khabarovsk, ul. Istomina 85, korp. 13; tel. (4212) 35-71-37; fax (4212) 34-08-88; attached to Russian Acad. of Medical Sciences; Dir V. K. KOZLOV.

Institute of Biochemistry: 630117 Novosibirsk, ul. Akad. Timakova 2; tel. (3832) 32-27-35; f. 1989; attached to Russian Acad. of Medical Sciences; Dir L. E. PANIN.

Institute of Biomedical Chemistry: 119121 Moscow, ul. Pogodinskaya 10; tel. (495) 246-69-80; fax (495) 245-08-57; e-mail inst@ibmc.msk.ru; internet www.ibmc.msk.ru; f. 1944; attached to Russian Acad. of Medical Sciences; library of 136,000 vols; Dir Prof. ALEXANDER IVANOVICH ARCHAKOV; publ. *Voprosy meditsinskoy khimii* (6 a year).

Institute of Biomedical Problems: 123007 Moscow, Khoroshevskoe shosse 76A; tel. (095) 195-23-63; fax (095) 195-22-53; f. 1963; environmental effects on the human body, with emphasis on the effect of space flights; library of 80,000 vols; Dir ANATOLY I. GRIGORIEV; publ. *Aerospatial and Environmental Medicine* (every 2 months).

Institute of Biomedical Research and Therapy: 113149 Moscow, Simferopolsky bul. 8; tel. (095) 113-23-51; Dir A. V. KARAULOV.

Institute of Clinical and Experimental Lymphology: 630117 Novosibirsk, ul. Akad. Timakova 2; tel. (3832) 32-56-53; fax (3832) 32-95-31; f. 1991; attached to Russian Acad. of Medical Sciences; library of 1,000 vols; Dir YU. I. BORODIN; publ. *Bulletin* (3 or 4 a year).

Institute of Clinical and Preventive Cardiology: 625026 Tyumen, ul. Melnikaite 111, POB 4312; tel. (3452) 22-76-08; fax (3452) 22-53-49; e-mail kuznets@sbtx.tmn

.ru; f. 1985; attached to Russian Acad. of Medical Sciences; Dir V. A. KUZNETSOV.

Institute of Clinical Immunology: 630091 Novosibirsk, ul. Yadrintsovskaya 14; fax (3832) 22-70-28; attached to Russian Acad. of Medical Sciences; Dir V. A. KOZLOV.

Institute of Epidemiology and Microbiology: 690028 Vladivostok, ul. Selskaya 1; tel. (4232) 29-43-03; attached to Russian Acad. of Medical Sciences; Dir N. N. BESEDNOVA.

Institute of Experimental Medicine: 197376 St Petersburg, ul. Akad. Pavlova 12; tel. (812) 234-54-01; fax (812) 234-94-89; attached to Russian Acad. of Medical Sciences; Dir B. I. TKACHENKO.

Institute of Eye Diseases: 119021 Moscow, ul. Rossolimo 11; tel. (095) 248-78-92; fax (095) 248-01-25; attached to Russian Acad. of Medical Sciences; Dir M. M. KRASNOV.

Institute of General Pathology and Pathological Physiology: 125315 Moscow, ul. Baltiiskaya 8; tel. (095) 151-17-56; fax (095) 151-95-40; attached to Russian Acad. of Medical Sciences; Dir G. N. KRYZHANOVSKII.

Institute of Human Morphology: 117418 Moscow, ul. Tsyuryupy 3; tel. (095) 120-80-65; fax (095) 120-14-56; attached to Russian Acad. of Medical Sciences; Dir N. K. PERMYAKOV.

Institute of Immunology: 142380 Moscow oblast, Chekhovsky raion, Lyubuchany; tel. (095) 546-15-55; fax (095) 546-15-55; f. 1980; library of 2,800 vols; Dir V. P. ZAVYALOV.

Institute of Immunology: 115478 Moscow, Kashirskoe shosse 24, korp. 2; tel. (095) 111-83-01; fax (095) 117-10-27, Dir R. M. KHAITOV.

Institute of Influenza: 197022 St Petersburg, ul. Prof. Popova 15/17; tel. (812) 234-58-75; fax (812) 234-01-50; attached to Russian Acad. of Medical Sciences; Dir O. I. KISELEV.

Institute of Internal Medicine: 630089 Novosibirsk, ul. Bogatkova 175/1; tel. (3832) 22-55-11; fax (3832) 22-28-21; e-mail zima_iim@issa.nsc.ru; f. 1981; attached to Russian Acad. of Medical Sciences; Dir M. I. VOEVODA; publ. *Interpress* (4 a year).

Institute of Medical and Biological Cybernetics: 630117 Novosibirsk, ul. Akad. Timakova 2; tel. (3832) 32-12-56; fax (3832) 32-55-58; f. 1992; attached to Russian Acad. of Medical Sciences; Dir M. B. SHTARK; publ. *Biofeedback* (every 3 years).

Institute of Medical Climatology and Rehabilitation: 690025 Vladivostok, Sadgorod 25; tel. (4232) 33-05-22; fax (4232) 25-11-83; f. 1984; attached to Russian Acad. of Medical Sciences; library of 20,000 vols; Dir Prof. Dr E. M. IVANOV.

Institute of Medical Problems of the Extreme North: 629730 Tyumen oblast, Yamalo-Nenets Autonomous Okrug, Nadym, km 107; tel. (34995) 3-03-20; fax (34995) 9-74-53; e-mail nii_mpks@nadym.ru; internet www.nii_mpks; f. 1994; attached to Russian Acad. of Medical Sciences; Dir Prof. A. A. BUGANOV; publ. *Public Health Service of Yamal* (2 a year).

Institute of Medical Problems of the North: 660022 Krasnoyarsk, ul. Partizana Zheleznyaka 3G; fax (3912) 23-19-63; e-mail rimpn@scn.ru; f. 1976; attached to Russian Acad. of Medical Sciences; Dir VALERY T. MANCHUK.

Institute of Neurology: 123367 Moscow, Volokolamskoe shosse 80; tel. (095) 490-21-11; fax (095) 490-22-10; e-mail institute@neurology.med.ru; internet www.neurology.ru; f. 1945; attached to Russian Acad. of Medical Sciences; Dir N. V. VERESHCHAGIN.

Institute of Nutrition: 109240 Moscow, Ustinskii pr-d 2/14; tel. (095) 917-44-85; attached to Russian Acad. of Medical Sciences; Dir M. N. VOLGAREV.

Institute of Occupational Health: 105275 Moscow, pr. Budennogo 31; tel. (095) 365-02-09; fax (095) 366-05-83; attached to Russian Acad. of Medical Sciences; Dir Prof. N. F. IZMEROV.

Institute of Paediatrics: 117296 Moscow, Lomonsovskii pr. 2/62; tel. (095) 134-03-61; fax (095) 134-13-08; attached to Russian Acad. of Medical Sciences; Dir M. YA. STUDENIKIN.

Institute of Paediatrics and Child Surgery of the Ministry of Public Health of the Russian Federation: 127412 Moscow, Taldomskaya ul. 2; tel. (095) 484-02-92; fax (095) 438-62-32; Dir Prof. YURI E. VELTISCHEV; publ. *Vestnik* (Annals of Perinatology and Paediatrics).

Institute of Pharmacology: 125315 Moscow, ul. Baltiiskaya 8; tel. (095) 151-18-41; fax (095) 151-12-61; attached to Russian Acad. of Medical Sciences; Dir S. B. SEREDENIN.

Institute of Physiology: 630117 Novosibirsk, ul. Akad. Timakova 4; fax (3832) 32-42-54; attached to Russian Acad. of Medical Sciences; Dir V. A. TRUFAKIN.

Institute of Regional Pathology and Pathological Morphology: 630117 Novosibirsk, ul. Akad. Timakova 2; tel. (3832) 32-31-56; fax (3832) 33-48-45; e-mail pathol@cyber.ma.nsc.ru; f. 1992; attached to Russian Acad. of Medical Sciences; Dir L. M. NEPOMNYASHCHIKH.

Institute of Rheumatology: 115552 Moscow, Kashirskoe shosse 34-a; tel. (095) 114-44-90; fax (095) 114-44-68; f. 1959; attached to Russian Acad. of Medical Sciences; br. at Volgograd; Dir V. A. NASONOVA; publ. *Revmatologia* (6 a year).

Institute of the Brain: 107120 Moscow, per. Obukha 5; tel. (095) 917-80-07; fax (095) 916-05-95; attached to Russian Acad. of Medical Sciences; Dir N. N. BOGOLEPOV.

Institute of the Molecular Pathology and Biochemistry of Ecology: 630117 Novosibirsk, ul. Akad. Timakova 2; fax (3832) 32-31-47; attached to Russian Acad. of Medical Sciences; Dir V. V. LYAKHOVICH.

Institute of the Physiology and Pathology of Breathing: 675000 Blagoveshchensk, ul. Kalinina 22; tel. (4162) 42-32-33; fax (4162) 42-12-28; f. 1981; attached to Russian Acad. of Medical Sciences; Dir M. T. LUTSENKO; publ. *Bulletin* (4 a year).

Institute of Viral Preparations: 109088 Moscow, 1 Dubrovskaya ul. 15; tel. (095) 274-81-45; fax (095) 274-57-10; attached to Russian Acad. of Medical Sciences; Dir O. G. ANDZHAPARIDZE.

Irkutsk Antiplague Research Institute of Siberia and the Far East: 664047 Irkutsk, ul. Trilissera 78; tel. (3952) 22-01-35; fax (3952) 22-01-40; e-mail adm@chumin.irkutsk.ru; internet www.irkutsk.ru/chumin; f. 1934; library of 55,000 vols; Dir Prof. E. P. GOLUBINSKY.

Irkutsk Institute of Orthopaedics and Traumatology: 664003 Irkutsk, ul. Bortzov Revoliutsii 1; tel. (3952) 27-54-30; f. 1946; diseases of the skeleton and bone tissue regeneration; library of 32,000 vols; Dir Prof. A. P. BARABASH.

Irkutsk Research Institute of Epidemiology and Microbiology: 664000 Irkutsk, ul. Karla Marksa 3; tel. (3952) 24-42-30; Dir V. I. ZLOBIN.

Ivanovskii, D. I., Institute of Virology: 123098 Moscow, ul. Gamalei 16; tel. (095)

190-28-74; fax (095) 190-28-67; attached to Russian Acad. of Medical Sciences; Dir D. K. LVOV.

Kazan Institute of Epidemiology, Microbiology and Hygiene: 420015 Kazan, Bol. Krasnaya ul. 67; tel. (8432) 32-25-80; Dir F. Z. KAMALOV.

Kazan State Institute of Orthopaedics and Traumatology: 420015 Kazan, ul. Gorkogo 3; tel. (8432) 38-59-05; f. 1945; library: 13,500 units; publ. *Transactions* (annually).

Khabarovsk Institute of Epidemiology and Microbiology: Khabarovsk, ul. Shevchenko 2; tel. (4212) 33-52-28; Dir T. P. VLADIMIROVA.

Laboratory of Experimental Biological Models: 143412 Moscow oblast, PO Otradnoe, pos. Svetlye Gory; tel. (095) 561-53-70; attached to Russian Acad. of Medical Sciences; Dir T. I. ZAITSEV.

Laboratory of Polar Medicine: 663310 Norilsk 10, ul. Talnakhskaya 7A, p/ya 625; fax (3919) 34-47-19; attached to Russian Acad. of Medical Sciences; Dir L. A. NADTO-CHII.

Martsinovsky, I. E., Institute of Medical Parasitology and Tropical Medicine: 119435 Moscow, Mal. Pirogovskaya ul. 20; tel. (095) 246-80-49; fax (095) 246-90-47; f. 1920; library of 70,000 vols; Dir Prof. V. P. SERGIEV; publ. *Medical Parasitology and Parasitic Diseases* (quarterly).

Mechnikov I. I., Institute of Vaccines and Sera: 103064 Moscow, Mal. Kazenny per. 5A; tel. (095) 917-49-00; fax (095) 917-54-60; e-mail instmech@iitp.ru; f. 1919; attached to Russian Acad. of Medical Sciences; Dir B.F. SEMENOV.

Medical Research Centre for Preventive Medicine and the Protection of the Health of Industrial Workers: 620014 Ekaterinburg, ul. Popova 30; tel. (3432) 71-87-54; fax (3432) 71-87-40; e-mail mrc@etel.ru; f. 1929; Dir SERGEY V. KUZMIN; publs *Balneology and Physiotherapy* (annually), *Urgent Issues of Preventive Medicine in the Urals* (annually).

Moscow G. N. Gabrichevskii Institute of Epidemiology and Microbiology: 125212 Moscow, ul. Admirala Makharova 10; tel. (095) 452-18-16; fax (095) 452-18-30; f. 1895; library of 8,922 vols; Dir Prof. BORIS A. SHENDEROV; publ. *Medical Aspects of Microecology* (annually).

Moscow Helmholtz Research Institute of Eye Diseases: 103064 Moscow, ul. Sadovaya-Chernogryazskaya 14/19; tel. (095) 207-23-19; fax (095) 975-24-00; f. 1900; library of 69,445 vols; Dir ALEXANDER M. YUZHAKOV.

Moscow Municipal Research First Aid Institute: 129010 Moscow, Sukharevskaya pl. 3; tel. (095) 925-38-97; f. 1923; library of 30,000 vols; Dir Prof. B. D. KOMAROV.

Moscow Research Institute of Psychiatry: 107076 Moscow, Poteshnaya ul. 3; tel. (095) 963-76-26; fax (095) 162-10-03; e-mail krasnov@mtu-net.ru; internet www.psychiatr.ru; f. 1920; social and biological psychiatry; treats alcohol and drug addiction; Dir Prof. V. N. KRASNOV; publ. *Social and Clinical Psychiatry* (in Russian, 4 a year).

Nizhnii Novgorod Institute for Skin and Venereal Diseases: Nizhnii Novgorod, ul. Kovalikhinskaya 49; f. 1930; library of 10,000 vols; Dir Prof. T. A. GLAVINSKAYA.

Nizhnii Novgorod Institute of Industrial Hygiene and Occupational Diseases: Nizhnii Novgorod, ul. Semashko 20.

Nizhnii Novgorod Research Institute of Traumatology and Orthopaedics: 603155 Nizhnii Novgorod, V. Volzhskaya nab. 18; tel.

(8312) 36-01-60; fax (8312) 36-05-91; e-mail gito@pop.sci-nnov.ru; internet www.nniito.ru; f. 1945; 222 mems; library of 38,035 vols; Dir Prof. V. AZOLOV.

Novosibirsk Institute of Tuberculosis: Novosibirsk, ul. Chaplygina 75.

Omsk Research Institute of Naturally Occurring Infections: 644080 Omsk 80, pr. Mira 7; tel. (3812) 65-06-33; Dir A. A. MATUSHENKO.

Ott, D. O., Research Institute of Obstetrics and Gynaecology: 199034 St Petersburg, Mendeleevskaya liniya 3; tel. (812) 328-14-02; fax (812) 328-23-61; f. 1797; attached to Russian Acad. of Medical Sciences; Dir Prof. EDWARD K. AILAMAZYAN.

Pharmacy Research Institute: 117418 Moscow, ul. Krasikova 34; tel. (095) 128-57-88; Dir A. I. TENTSOVA.

Plague Prevention Research Institute for the Caucasus and Transcaucasia: 355106 Stavropol, Sovetskaya ul. 13; tel. (8652) 3-13-12; Dir V. I. EFREMENKO.

Research Centre for Medical Genetics: 115478 Moscow, Moskvorechie 1; tel. (095) 111-85-80; fax (095) 324-07-02; e-mail ekginter@mail.ru; internet www.medgen.ru; f. 1969; attached to Russian Acad. of Medical Sciences; Dir EVGENY K. GINTER; publ. *Medical Genetics* (monthly).

Attached institutes:

Institute of Clinical Genetics: Moscow; tel. (095) 111-85-94; attached to Russian Acad. of Medical Sciences; Dir E. K. GINTER.

Institute of Human Genetics: Moscow; tel. (095) 111-85-87; attached to Russian Acad. of Medical Sciences; Dir S. S. SHISHKIN.

Research Centre for Molecular Diagnostics and Therapy: 117638 Moscow, Simferopolsky bul. 8; tel. (095) 113-23-51; fax (095) 113-26-33; e-mail e.severin@mtu-net.ru; f. 1985; Dir E. S. SEVERIN; publs *Problems of Biological, Medical and Pharmaceutical Chemistry* (4 a year), *Molecular Medicine* (4 a year).

Research Centre for Obstetrics, Gynaecology and Perinatology: 117815 Moscow, GSP-7, ul. Akademika Oparina; tel. (095) 438-51-71; e-mail centre@pregnancy.ru; internet www.pregnancy.ru; Dir Prof. VLADIMIR I. KULAKOV; Scientific Sec. Dr TATYANA V. LEOPATINA.

Research Centre of Medical Radiology: 249020 Kaluga oblast, Obninsk, ul. Koroleva 4; tel. (095) 956-14-39; fax (095) 956-14-40; f. 1958; attached to Russian Acad. of Medical Sciences; library of 121,000 vols; Dir A. F. TSYB; publ. *Radiation and Risk* (2 a year).

Research Centre of Mental Health: 115552 Moscow, Kashirskoe shosse 34; tel. (095) 117-61-83; fax (095) 952-89-40; attached to Russian Acad. of Medical Sciences; Dir A. S. TIGANOV.

Research Centre of Obstetrics, Gynaecology and Perinatology: 117815 Moscow, ul. Akad. Oparina 4; tel. (095) 438-18-00; fax (095) 438-18-00; attached to Russian Acad. of Medical Sciences; Dir VLADIMIR KULAKOV.

Research Centre of Surgery: 119874 Moscow, Abrikosovski per. 2; tel. and fax (495) 246-95-63; attached to Russian Acad. of Medical Sciences; Dir B. A. KONSTANTINOV.

Research Institute for Complex Problems of Hygiene and Occupational Diseases: 654041 Novokuznetsk, ul. Kutuzova 23; tel. (3843) 79-69-79; fax (3843) 79-66-69; e-mail zacharenkov@nvkz.kuzbass.net; internet www.ni-kpg.ru; f. 1976; attached to Russian Acad. of Medical Sciences; Dir Dr V. V. ZAKHARENKOV.

Research Institute of Children's Infections: 197022 St Petersburg, ul. Prof. Popova 9; tel. (812) 234-18-62; f. 1927; library of 25,000 vols; Dir V. V. IVANOVA; publ. *Infectious Diseases of Childhood* (1 or 2 a year).

Research Institute of Epidemiology and Microbiology: 603600 Nizhnii Novgorod, Gruzinskaya ul. 44; tel. (8312) 33-40-07; fax (8312) 35-64-80; f. 1929; library of 10,000 vols; Dir I. N. BLOKHINA; publ. *Annual Collection of Research Articles*.

Research Institute of Forensic Medicine: 123242 Moscow, ul. Sadovaya-Kudrinskaya 3, Korp. 2; tel. (095) 254-32-49; Dir Prof. V. I. PROZOROVSKY.

Research Institute of Haematology and Intensive Therapy: 125167 Moscow, Novozykovsky pr-d 4A; tel. (095) 212-45-51; fax (095) 212-42-52; f. 1926; library of 50,000 vols; publ. *Sovremennye Problemy Gematologii i Perelivaniya Krovi* (monthly).

Research Institute of Laser Medicine: 121165 Moscow, Studencheskaya ul. 40; tel. (095) 249-39-05.

Research Institute of Medical Primatology: 354376 Sochi-Adler, Veseloye 1; tel. (8622) 42-28-62; fax (8622) 42-22-39; e-mail iprim@mail.sochi.ru; internet iprim.sochi.net; f. 1927; attached to Russian Acad. of Medical Sciences; Dir Prof. BORIS ARKADIEVICH LAPIN.

Research Institute of Occupational Safety under the auspices of the Independent Russian Trade Unions: 191187 St Petersburg, ul. Gagarinskaya 3; tel. (812) 279-08-13; fax (812) 275-42-48; f. 1927; noise control, respiratory protection, air conditioning, ventilation, air pollution analysis, hygiene and VDUs, certification of personal protective equipment and workplaces; library of 47,000 vols; Dir E. A. KOLODIN.

Research Institute of Radiation Hygiene: 197101 St Petersburg, ul. Mira 8; tel. (812) 233-53-63; fax (812) 233-26-12; e-mail irii@ek6663.spb.edu; f. 1956.

Research Institute of the Technology and Safety of Medicines: 142450 Moscow oblast, Noginsky raion, pos. Staraya Kupavna, ul. Kirova 23; tel. (095) 524-09-36; attached to Russian Acad. of Sciences; Dir YU. V. BUROV.

Research Institute of Traditional Methods of Treatment: 103051 Moscow, Petrovsky bul. 8; tel. (095) 200-27-91.

Research Institute of Transplants and Artificial Organs: 123436 Moscow, Shchukinskaya ul. 1; tel. (095) 190-29-71.

Research Institute of Vaccines and Sera: 614089 Perm, GSP, NIIVS.

Research Institute of Vaccines and Sera: 634004 Tomsk, ul. Lenina 32; tel. (3822) 22-45-12; Dir N. B. CHERNY.

Rostov Institute of Radiology and Oncology: Rostov-on-Don, Voroshilovsky pr. 119; affiliated to the Chelyabinsk Radiation Hygiene Institute.

Rostov Region Paediatric Research Institute: Rostov-on-Don, Dolomanovsky per. 142.

Rostov Research Institute for Plague Control: 344007 Rostov on Don, ul. M. Gorkogo 117; tel. (8632) 66-57-03; fax (8632) 34-13-76; f. 1934; library of 52,300 vols; Dir Prof. YU. M. LOMOV.

Russian Anti-plague Research Institute 'Microbe': 410005 Saratov, ul. Universitetskaya 46; tel. (8452) 26-21-31; fax (8452) 51-52-12; e-mail microbe@san.ru; internet www.microbe.ru; f. 1918; library of 95,000 vols; Dir Dr V. V. KUTYREV; publ. *Problems of Particularly Dangerous Infections* (2 a year).

Russian Institute of Medical Parasitology: Rostov-on-Don, Moskovskaya 67.

Russian Polenov, A. L., Neurosurgical Institute: 191104 St Petersburg, ul. Mayakovskogo 12; tel. (812) 272-98-79; fax (812) 275-56-03; e-mail igor@rnsi.spb.su; f. 1926; library of 36,000 vols; Dir V. P. BERSNEV; publ. *Neurosurgery* (annually).

Russian Research Centre of Rehabilitation and Physiotherapy: 121099 Moscow, Novy Arbat 32; tel. (095) 252-18-83; fax (095) 292-65-11; f. 1920; library of 73,500 vols; Dir Dr V. M. BOGOLYUBOV; publs *Problems of Health Resorts, Physiotherapy and Exercise Therapy* (every 2 months).

Russian Research Institute of Haematology and Transfusiology: 191024 St Petersburg, 2-a Sovetskaya ul. 16; tel. (812) 274-56-50; fax (812) 274-92-27; e-mail bloodscience@mail.ru; internet www .bloodscience.ru; f. 1932; Dir Dr E. A. SELIVANOV.

Russian Research Institute of Phthisiopulmonology: 103030 Moscow, ul. Dostoevskogo 4; tel. (095) 281-84-22; fax (095) 281-45-37; e-mail logosoev@glasnet.ru; f. 1918; library of 55,019 vols; Dir Prof. A. A. PRYMAK; publ. *Tuberculosis and Ecology* (6 a year).

Russian Research Institute of Traumatology and Orthopaedics 'Vreden, R. R.': 195427 St Petersburg, Baykova ul. 8; tel. (812) 556-08-28; fax (812) 556-79-01; e-mail rniito@aotrf.org; f. 1906; orthopaedic clinical research centre; postgraduate training; library of 57,000 vols; Dir RASHID TIKHILOV; publ. *Travmatologia i Ortopedia Rossii* (Traumatology and Orthopaedics of Russia, quarterly).

Russian Scientific Centre of Roentgenoradiology: 117837 Moscow, ul. Profsoyuznaya 86; tel. (095) 333-94-39; fax (095) 334-79-24; e-mail mailbox@rncrr.rssi.ru; internet www.space.ru/rncrr; f. 1924; laser diagnosis and treatment of malignant tumours; library of 51,700 vols; Dir Prof. V.P. KHARCHENKO.

St Petersburg Artificial Limb Research Institute: St Petersburg, pr. K. Marxa 9/12.

St Petersburg Institute of Ear, Throat, Nose and Speech: St Petersburg, Bronnitskaya 9; tel. (812) 292-54-29; f. 1930; library of 45,000 vols; Dir A. A. LANTSOV.

St Petersburg Institute of Eye Diseases: St Petersburg, Mokhovaya 38.

St Petersburg Institute of Phthisiopulmonology: 193036 St Petersburg, Ligovsky pr. 2–4; tel. (812) 279-25-54; fax (812) 279-25-73; f. 1923; library of 26,000 vols; Dir Prof. ALEXANDR V. VASILEV.

St Petersburg Institute of Tuberculosis: 193130 St Petersburg, Ligovsky pr. 2/4.

St Petersburg Institute of Vaccines and Sera: 198320 Krasnoe Selo, ul. Svobody 52; tel. (812) 132-19-78; Dir R. N. RODIONOVA.

St Petersburg Pasteur Institute of Epidemiology and Microbiology: 197101 St Petersburg, ul. Mira 14; tel. (812) 233-20-92; fax (812) 232-92-17; e-mail intdep@ok7368 .spb.edu; internet www.pasteur.soc.ru; f. 1923; library of 60,000 vols; Dir ANATOLY ZHEBRUN.

St Petersburg Petrov, N. N., Research Institute of Oncology: 188646 St Petersburg, Pesochny 2, St Petersburgskaya ul. 68; tel. (812) 237-89-94.

St Petersburg Research Institute of Industrial Hygiene and Occupational Diseases: 193036 St Petersburg, 2-a Sovetskaya ul. 4; tel. (812) 279-40-11; f. 1924.

Samara Institute of Epidemiology, Microbiology and Hygiene: Samara, Chapaevskaya 87.

Saratov Institute of Restorative Surgery, Traumatology and Orthopaedics: Saratov, ul. Chernyshevskogo 148.

Scientific Centre of Clinical and Experimental Medicine: ul. Akad. Timakova 2, 630117 Novosibirsk; tel. (3832) 33-64-56; fax (3832) 33-64-56; e-mail sck@cyber.ma.nsc.ru; f. 1970; attached to Russian Acad. of Medical Sciences; Dir Dr V. A. SHKURUPY; publ. *Siberian Consilium* (medical pharmaceuticals, 6 a year).

Scientific Research Institute for General Reanimatology: 103031 Moscow, ul. Petrovka 25; tel. (095) 200-27-08; fax (095) 209-96-77; e-mail miiorramn@mediann.ru; f. 1936; attached to Russian Acad. of Medical Sciences; Dir Prof. V. V. MOROZ; br. at Novokuznetsk.

Scientific Research Institute for the Investigation of New Antibiotics: 119867 Moscow, Bol. Pirogovskaya 11; tel. (095) 246-99-80; fax (095) 245-02-95; attached to Russian Acad. of Medical Sciences; Dir YU. V. DUDNIK.

Semashko, N. A., Research Institute of Social Hygiene, Health Service Economics and Management: 103064 Moscow, ul. Vorontsovo Pole 12; tel. (095) 917-48-86; fax (095) 916-03-98; f. 1944; attached to Russian Acad. of Medical Sciences; Dir O. P. SHCHEPIN; publs *Bulletin, Journal of Social Hygiene and the History of Medicine*.

Serbsky National Research Centre for Social and Forensic Psychiatry: 119034 Moscow, Kropotkinsky per. 23; tel. (095) 201-52-62; fax (095) 201-72-31; e-mail dmitrieva@ psi.med.ru; internet www.psi.med.ru/sspcen .htm; f. 1921; forensic psychiatry, social and clinical issues of psychiatry; library of 74,000 vols; Dir T. B. DMITRIEVA; publ. *Russian Psychiatric Journal* (contents and summaries in English, 6 a year).

Sochi Health Research Institute: Sochi, Kurortny pr. 110.

State Institute of Natural Curative Factors: 357500 Pyatigorsk, pr. Kirova 30; tel. (87933) 50-050; fax (87933) 55-618; f. 1920; neurology, rheumatology, pain assessment and management, behavioural therapy; library of 120,000 vols; Dir Prof. KRIVOBOROV.

State Research Institute for the Standardization and Control of Drugs: 117246 Moscow, Nauchni pr-d 14A; tel. (095) 128-26-32; Dir Prof. YU. F. KRYLOV.

State Scientific Research Institute of Medical Polymers: 117246 Moscow, Nauchni pr-d 10; tel. (095) 120-21-62; fax (095) 120-05-61; e-mail medpol@dol.ru; internet www.medpol.ru; f. 1966; library of 15,000 vols; Dir Prof. G. A. MATJUSHIN.

Sysin, A. N., Institute of Human Ecology and Environmental Hygiene: 119833 Moscow, ul. Pogodinskaya 10; tel. (095) 246-58-24; fax (095) 247-04-28; f. 1931; attached to Russian Acad. of Medical Sciences; Dir G. I. SIDORENKO.

Tarasevich, L. A., State Research Institute for the Standardization and Control of Medical Biological Preparations: 121002 Moscow, Sivtsev-Vrazhek 41; tel. (095) 241-39-22; fax (095) 241-39-22; e-mail gisk@glasnet.ru; f. 1919; library of 20,000 vols; Dir Prof. N. V. MEDUNTSIN.

Technological Research Institute for Antibiotics and Medical Enzymes: 198020 St Petersburg, Ogorodnikov pr. 41; tel. (812) 251-19-44; f. 1956; antifungal antibiotics, enzymes for medical use, nucleoside preparation of cardiovascular action; library of 55,000 vols; Dir Dr B. V. MOSKVICHEV.

Tomsk Institute of Physiotherapy and Spa Treatment: Tomsk, ul. Rosa Luxembourg 1.

Tomsk Research Centre: 634012 Tomsk, Kievskaya ul. 111/2; fax (3822) 44-50-57; attached to Russian Acad. of Medical Sciences; Chair. of the Presidium R. S. KARPOV.

Attached institutes:

Institute of Cardiology: 634012 Tomsk, Kievskaya ul. 111/2; tel. (3822) 44-33-97; attached to Russian Acad. of Medical Sciences; Dir R. S. KARPOV.

Institute of Medical Genetics: 634050 Tomsk, pos. Sputnik, nab. Ushaika 10; tel. (3822) 22-22-28; attached to Russian Acad. of Medical Sciences; Dir V. P. PUZYREV.

Institute of Oncology: 634001 Tomsk, Kooperativnyi per. 5; tel. (3822) 23-04-86; attached to Russian Acad. of Medical Sciences; Dir B. N. ZYRYANOV.

Institute of Pharmacology: 634028 Tomsk, pr. Lenina 3; fax (3822) 41-83-79; attached to Russian Acad. of Medical Sciences; Dir E. D. GOLDBERG.

Laboratory of Experimental Biomedical Models: 634009 Tomsk, Kooperativny per. 7B; tel. (3822) 22-36-26; attached to Russian Acad. of Medical Sciences; Dir S. A. KUSMARTSEV.

SI Mental Health Research Institute: 634014 Tomsk, Sosnovy Bor; tel. (3822) 72-43-79; fax (3822) 72-44-25; e-mail redo@ mail.tomsknet.ru; internet www.niipz.nm .ru; f. 1981; attached to Russian Acad. of Medical Sciences; library of 8,120 vols; Dir Acad. VALENTIN SEMKE; publ *Siberian Journal of Psychiatry and Addiction Psychiatry* (quarterly).

Toxicological Institute: 193019 St Petersburg, ul. Bekhtereva 1; tel. (812) 265-06-80; Dir S. N. GOLIKOV.

Turner Scientific Research Institute of Child Orthopaedics and Traumatology: 189620 St Petersburg, ul. Parkovaya 64–68; tel. (812) 465-28-57; f. 1932; library of 33,600 vols; Dir Prof. V. L. ANDRIANOV; publ. scientific papers (2–3 a year).

Ufa Eye Research Institute: 450025 Ufa, ul. Pushkinskaya 90; tel. (3472) 22-37-75; fax (3472) 22-08-52; e-mail eye@academy .bashnet.ru; f. 1926; Dir Prof. M. T. AZNABAYEV; publ. *Collected Articles* (annually).

Ufa Research Institute of Occupational Health and Human Ecology: 450106 Ufa, ul. Kuvykina 94; tel. (3472) 28-53-19; fax (3472) 28-49-16; f. 1955; complex development of scientific fundamentals of labour hygiene and physiology, industrial toxicology, occupational pathology, environmental hygiene and aspects of hygiene in juvenile vocational training and the workplace in the oil, petrochemical, gas and microbiological industries; library of 63,000 vols; Dir A. B. BAKIROV; publ. *Production and Environmental Hygiene: Workers' Health Care in Oil and Gas Extracting and Petrochemical Industries* (annually).

Ufa Skin and Venereal Diseases Institute: Ufa, ul. Frunze 43.

Urals Research Institute of Maternity and Childhood Care: 620028 Ekaterinburg, ul. Repina 1; tel. (3432) 51-42-02; fax (3432) 51-22-12; f. 1877; library of 30,000 vols; Dir Dr G. A. CHERDANTSEVA.

Urals Research Institute of Phthisiopulmonology: 620039 Ekaterinburg, ul. 22 Partsezda 50; tel. (3432) 32-72-20; fax (3432) 31-80-41; e-mail urniif@mail.ur.ru; internet www.urniif.okb1.mplik.ru; f. 1931; library of 5,000 vols; Dir V. A. SOKOLOV.

Urology Research Institute: 105425 Moscow, 3-ya Parkovaya ul. 51; tel. (095) 367-62-62; fax (095) 367-62-62; e-mail urology@cdromclub.ru; f. 1979; Dir Acad. NIKOLAI A. LOPATKIN.

Vishnevsky, A. V., Institute of Surgery: 113811 Moscow, Bol. Serpukhovskaya 27; tel. (095) 236-72-90; fax (095) 237-08-14; attached to Russian Acad. of Medical Sciences; Dir V. D. FEDOROV.

Volgograd Plague Prevention Research Institute: 400131 Volgograd, Golubinskaya ul. 7; tel. (8442) 37-37-74; fax (8442) 32-33-36; e-mail vari2@sprint-v.com.ru; f. 1970; library of 13,320 vols; Dir V. V. ALEKSEEV.

Voronezh Region Radiological and Oncological Institute: Voronezh, ul. Kalyaeva 2.

NATURAL SCIENCES
General

Arctic and Antarctic Research Institute: 199397 St Petersburg, ul. Beringa 38; tel. (812) 352-00-96; fax (812) 352-26-88; Dir I. YE. FROLOV.

Institute of Economic and International Problems of the Assimilation of the Ocean: 690600 Vladivostok, ul. Sukhanova 5-a; tel. (4232) 5-77-31; attached to Russian Acad. of Sciences; Dir. R. SH.-A. ALIEV.

Institute of Global Climate and Ecology: 107258 Moscow, Glebovskaya 20B; tel. (095) 169-01-43; attached to Russian Acad. of Sciences; Dir YU. A. IZRAEL.

Institute of Limnology: 664033 Irkutsk, Ulan-Batorskaya ul. 3; fax (3952) 46-04-05; e-mail root@lin.irkutsk.su; attached to Russian Acad. of Sciences; Dir M. A. GRACHEV.

Institute of Limnology: 196199 St Petersburg, ul. Sevastyanova 9; tel. (812) 297-22-97; attached to Russian Acad. of Sciences; Dir V. A. RUMYANTSEV.

Institute of Natural Sciences: 670042 Ulan-Ude, ul. M. Sakhyanovoi 6; tel. (3012) 3-01-62; attached to Russian Acad. of Sciences; Dir K. A. NIKIFOROV.

Institute of the History of Science and Technology: 103012 Moscow, Staropanskii per. 1/5; fax (095) 925-99-11; e-mail postmaster@ihst.ru; internet www.ihst.ru; f. 1953; attached to Russian Acad. of Sciences; library of 70,000 vols; Dir Prof. V. M. OREL; publ. *Voprosy istorii estestvoznaniya i tekhniki* (4 a year).

Branch:

> **Institute for the History of Science and Technology – St Petersburg Branch:** Universitetskaya nab. 5, 199034 St Petersburg; tel. (812) 328-47-12; fax (812) 328-46-67; e-mail ihst@ihst.nw.ru; internet sciencehistory.org.ru; Dir Prof. E. I. KOLCHINSKY.

Mountain Taiga Station: 692533 Primorskii krai, Ussuriisky raion, pos. Gornotaezhnoe; tel. (42341) 9-11-10; attached to Russian Acad. of Sciences; Dir P. S. ZORIKOV.

North-East Interdisciplinary Science Research Institute: 685010 Magadan, Portovaya 16; tel. (41322) 3-06-11; fax (41322) 3-00-51; e-mail director@neisri.magadan.su; f. 1960; attached to Russian Acad. of Sciences; geology, geophysics, metallogeny, history, archaeology, economics; library of 450,000 vols; Dir Dr V. I. GONCHAROV; publ. *Kolymskie Vesti* (Kolyma News, 4 a year).

Pacific Oceanological Institute: 690041 Vladivostok, Baltiiskaya ul. 43; tel. (4232) 31-14-00; fax (4232) 31-25-73; attached to Russian Acad. of Sciences; Dir Prof. V. A. AKULICHEV.

Pushchino Scientific Centre: 142290 Moscow oblast, Pushchino, pr. Nauki 3; tel. (095) 923-80-03; fax (095) 923-80-03; e-mail nazarova@psn.ru; internet www.psn.ru; f. 1963; attached to Russian Acad. of Sciences; Dir VLADIMIR A. SHUVALOV.

Shirshov, P. P., Institute of Oceanology: 117997 Moscow, Nakhimovsky pr. 36; tel. (095) 124-59-96; fax (095) 124-59-83; e-mail office@ocean.ru; internet www.ocean.ru; f. 1946; attached to Russian Acad. of Sciences; brs in Kaliningrad, Gelendzhik, St Petersburg; Dir Prof. S. S. LAPPO.

Biological Sciences

All-Russia Research Institute for Nature Conservation: 113628 Moscow, Znamenskoe-Sadki, VNII Priroda; tel. (095) 423-03-22; fax (095) 423-23-22; f. 1981; research, general methodology, environmental protection strategy and co-ordination at home and internationally; five departments: animal protection, plant protection, ecosystem protection and recovery (including aquatic ecosystems), utilization of natural resources and nature reserves; library (books, journals, theses); Dir Prof. V. A. KRASILOV.

All-Russia Research Institute of Applied Microbiology: 142279 Moscow oblast, Serpukhovsky raion, Obolensk; tel. (0967) 2-77-61; Dir N. N. URAKOV.

All-Russia Research Institute of Especially Pure Biopreparations: 197110 St Petersburg, Pudozhskaya ul. 7; tel. (812) 230-12-25; fax (812) 230-49-48; e-mail onir@inshpb.spb.su; f. 1974; Dir E. N. SVENTITSKY.

Bakh, A. N., Institute of Biochemistry: Leninsky Pr. 33, 119071 Moscow; tel. (095) 952-34-41; fax (095) 952-27-32; e-mail inbi@inbi.ras.ru; internet www.inbi.ras.ru; attached to Russian Acad. of Sciences; 255 mems; Dir Prof. V. O. POPOV; Vice-Director Prof. B. B. DZANTIEV; publs *Applied Biochemistry and Microbiology* (every 2 months), *Uspekhi Biologicheskoi Khimii* (Progress of Biological Chemistry, in Russian, annually).

Bioengineering Research Centre: 117984 Moscow, ul. Vavilova 34/5; tel. (095) 135-73-19; fax (095) 135-05-71; attached to Russian Acad. of Sciences; Dir K. G. SKRYABIN.

Biotechnical Research Institute: 119034 Moscow, ul. Prechistenka 38; tel. (095) 246-16-56; Dir A. M. KARPOV.

Biotechnologia JSC: 117246 Moscow, Nauchny pr-d 8; tel. (095) 332-34-20; fax (095) 331-01-01; f. 1993 as private company (fmrly state enterprise, f. 1986); biotechnology, pharmaceuticals; Gen. Dir RAIF G. VASILOV.

Engelhardt Institute of Molecular Biology: 117984 Moscow, ul. Vavilova 32; tel. (095) 135-23-11; fax (095) 135-14-05; attached to Russian Acad. of Sciences; Dir Acad. A. D. MIRZABEKOV.

Institute of Bio-organic Chemistry: 630090 Novosibirsk, pr. Akad. Lavrenteva 8; tel. (3832) 35-64-41; fax (3832) 35-16-65; e-mail vlasov@modul.bioch.nsk.su; attached to Russian Acad. of Sciences; Dir Prof. V. V. VLASOV.

Institute of Biological Problems of the North: 685000 Magadan, pr. K. Marksa 24; tel. (41322) 2-47-30; fax (41322) 2-01-66; e-mail ibpn@ibpn.magadan.su; f. 1972; attached to Russian Acad. of Sciences; Dir Prof. F. B. CHERNYAVSKY.

Institute of Biology: 630091 Novosibirsk, ul. Frunze 11; tel. (3832) 20-96-14; attached to Russian Acad. of Sciences; Dir V. I. EVSIKOV.

Institute of Biology: 185610 Petrozavodsk, Pushkinskaya ul. 11; tel. (8142) 7-36-15;

attached to Russian Acad. of Sciences; Dir S. N. DROZDOV.

Institute of Biology: 167610 Syktyvkar, Kommunisticheskaya ul. 28; tel. (8212) 42-52-02; fax (8212) 42-01-63; e-mail taskaev@biology.komitex.ru; f. 1962; attached to Russian Acad. of Sciences; Dir Dr A. I. TASKAEV.

Institute of Biology: 450054 Ufa, 25, pr. Oktyabrya 69; tel. (3472) 34-34-01; attached to Russian Acad. of Sciences; Dir V. M. KORSUNOV.

Institute of Biology: 670042 Ulan-Ude, ul. M. Sakhyanovoi 6; tel. (3012) 3-36-75; attached to Russian Acad. of Sciences; Dir V. M. KORSUNOV.

Institute of Biology: 677891 Yakutsk, pr. Lenina 41; tel. (4112) 2-77-81; attached to Russian Acad. of Sciences; Dir. N. G. SOLOMONOV.

Institute of Biology and Soil Science: 690022 Vladivostok, pr. Stoletiya Vladivostoka 159; tel. (4232) 31-04-10; fax (4232) 31-01-93; e-mail ibss@eastnet.febras.ru; internet www.ibss.febras.ru; f. 1962; attached to Russian Acad. of Sciences; library of 80,000 vols; Dir Prof. YU. N. ZHURAVLEV; publ. *Proceedings* (in Russian, annually).

Institute of Biophysics: 660036 Krasnoyarsk, Akademgorodok; tel. (3912) 43-15-79; fax (3912) 43-34-00; attached to Russian Acad. of Sciences; Dir Dr A. G. DEGERMENDZHY.

Institute of Biophysics: 123182 Moscow, Zhivopisnaya ul. 46; tel. (095) 190-56-51; fax (095) 190-35-90; e-mail ibphgen@rcibph.dol.ru; f. 1946; radiobiology, radiation protection, health physics, medical radiology, non-ionizing radiation; Dir L. A. ILYIN.

Institute of Cell Biophysics: 142290 Moscow oblast, Pushchino, Institutskaya ul. 3; tel. (495) 625-59-84; fax (496) 733-05-09; e-mail admin@icb.psn.ru; f. 1991; attached to Russian Acad. of Sciences; Dir Prof. EVGENII FESENKO.

Institute of Cytology: 194064 St Petersburg, Tikhoretsky pr. 4; tel. (812) 247-18-29; fax (812) 247-03-41; attached to the Soc. of Protozoologists, affiliated with the Russian Acad. of Sciences; Dir Prof. Dr VLADIMIR N. PARFENOV.

Institute of Cytology and Genetics: 630090 Novosibirsk, pr. Akad. Lavrenteva 10; tel. (3832) 35-12-65; fax (3832) 35-65-68; attached to Russian Acad. of Sciences; Dir V. K. SHUMNY.

Institute of Food Substances: c/o Russian Academy of Sciences, 117901 Moscow, Leninsky pr. 14; attached to Russian Acad. of Sciences; Dir M. N. MANAKOV.

Institute of Higher Nervous Activity and Neurophysiology: 117865 Moscow, ul. Butlerova 5a; tel. (095) 334-70-00; attached to Russian Acad. of Sciences; Dir Acad. P. V. SIMONOV.

Institute of Marine Biology: Petropavlovsk-Kamchatskii; attached to Russian Acad. of Sciences; Dir (vacant).

Institute of Marine Biology: 690041 Vladivostok, ul. Palchevskogo 17; tel. (4232) 31-09-05; fax (4232) 31-09-00; e-mail inmarbio@mail.primorye.ru; internet www.imb.dvo.ru; f. 1970; attached to Russian Acad. of Sciences; library of 40,000 vols; Dir Prof. VLADIMIR L. KASYANOV; publs *Biologiya morya* (6 a year), *Russian Journal of Marine Biology* (online, 7 a year).

Institute of Microbiology: 117811 Moscow, pr. 60-letiya Oktyabrya 7, korp. 2; tel. (095) 135-45-66; attached to Russian Acad. of Sciences; Dir Acad. M. V. IVANOV.

Institute of Molecular Biology of the Gene: 117333 Moscow, ul. Vavilova 34/5;

tel. (095) 135-60-89; attached to Russian Acad. of Sciences; Dir Acad. G. P. GEORGIEV.

Institute of Molecular Genetics: 123182 Moscow, pl. Kurchatova 2; tel. (095) 196-00-00; fax (095) 196-02-21; e-mail img@img.ras.ru; internet www.img.ras.ru; f. 1978; 260 mems; attached to Russian Acad. of Sciences; Dir EVGENY D. SVERDLOV.

Institute of Parasitology: 117071 Moscow, Leninskii pr. 33; tel. (095) 952-57-46; attached to Russian Acad. of Sciences; Dir M. D. SONIN.

Institute of Physicochemical and Biological Problems in Soil Science: 142290 Moscow oblast, Serpukhovskii raion, Pushchino; tel. (0967) 73-36-34; fax (0967) 79-05-32; e-mail vnk@issp.serpukhov.su; internet www.issp.serpukhov.su; f. 1999; attached to Russian Acad. of Sciences; Dir V. N. KUDEYAROV.

Institute of Physiologically Active Substances: 142432 Moscow oblast, Noginskii raion, p/o Chernogolovka; tel. (096) 524-50-62; attached to Russian Acad. of Sciences; Dir Acad. N. S. ZEFIROV.

Institute of Physiology: c/o Russian Academy of Sciences, 117901 Moscow, Leninsky pr. 14; attached to Russian Acad. of Sciences; Dir O. G. GAZENKO.

Institute of Physiology: 167982 Syktyvkar, Pervomayskaya 50; tel. (8212) 24-16-83; fax (8212) 44-78-90; e-mail secr@physiol.komisc.ru; internet physiol.komisc.ru; f. 1988; attached to Russian Acad. of Sciences; Dir Prof. Dr M. P. ROSHCHEVSKY.

Institute of Plant and Animal Ecology: 620008 Ekaterinburg, ul. 8 Marta 202; tel. (3732) 60-82-55; fax (3732) 60-65-00; e-mail common@ipal.uran.ru; f. 1944; attached to Russian Acad. of Sciences; Dir Acad. V. N. BOLSHAKOV; publ. *Russian Journal of Ecology* (6 a year).

Institute of Problems of the Industrial Ecology of the North (INEP KSC): 184200 Murmansk oblast, Apatity, ul. Fersmana 14; tel. (81555) 7-95-94; fax (81555) 7-49-64; e-mail nikolay@inep.ksc.ru; f. 1989; attached to Russian Acad. of Sciences; library of 400,000 vols; Dir Dr. VLADIMIR A. MASLOBOEV.

Institute of Protein Research: 142292 Moscow oblast, Serpukhovskii raion, Pushchino; tel. (095) 924-04-93; fax (095) 924-04-93; e-mail protres@sun.ipr.serpukhov.su; attached to Russian Acad. of Sciences; Dir Prof. A. S. SPIRIN.

Institute of the Biochemistry and Physiology of Micro-organisms: 142292 Moscow oblast, Serpukhovskii raion, Pushchino; tel. (277) 3-05-26; attached to Russian Acad. of Sciences; Dir A. M. BORONIN.

Institute of the Biochemistry and Physiology of Plants and Micro-organisms: 410049 Saratov, pr. Entuziastov 13; tel. (8452) 97-04-44; fax (8452) 97-03-83; e-mail institute@ibppm.sgu.ru; internet www.ibppm.saratov.ru; f. 1980; attached to Russian Acad. of Sciences; library of 30,000 vols; Dir V. V. IGNATOV.

Institute of the Biology of Inland Waters: 152742 Yaroslavskaya oblast, Nekouzsky raion, p/o Borok; tel. (08547) 24-042; fax (08547) 24-042; e-mail ibiw@mail.ru; internet www.ibiw.yaroslavl.ru; f. 1956; attached to Russian Acad. of Sciences; Dir Dr SERGEI I. GENKAL; publ. *Biology of Inland Waters* (3 a year).

Institute of the Ecology and Genetics of Micro-organisms: 614081 Perm, ul. Goleva 13; tel. (3422) 44-67-12; fax (3422) 44-67-11; e-mail conf@ecology.psu.ru; internet www.ecology.psu.ru; f. 1988; attached to Russian

Acad. of Sciences; library of 3,000 vols; Dir V. A. CHERESHNEV; publ. *Proceedings of Scientific Research* (annually).

Institute of the Ecology of Natural Complexes: Tomsk; attached to Russian Acad. of Sciences; Dir V. N. VOROBEV.

Institute of the Ecology of the Volga Basin: 445003 Togliatti; tel. (8469) 23-54-78; fax (8469) 48-95-04; attached to Russian Acad. of Sciences; Dir G. S. ROZENBERG.

Institute of Theoretical and Experimental Biophysics: 142290 Moscow oblast, Serpukhovsky raion, Pushchino; tel. (095) 632-78-69; fax (096) 733-05-53; e-mail office@iteb.ru; attached to Russian Acad. of Sciences; Dir Prof. G. R. IVANITSKY.

Institute of Water and Ecological Problems: 680063 Khabarovsk, ul. Kim Yu Chena 65; tel. (4212) 22-75-73; fax (4212) 22-70-85; e-mail dmitry@ivep.khv.ru; f. 1968; attached to Russian Acad. of Sciences; Dir Dr B. A. VORONOV; publ. *Biogeochemical and Hydroecological Peculiarities of the Amur River Watershed Ecosystems* (annually).

Institute for Water and Environmental Problems: 656038 Barnaul, Molodyozhnaya ul. 1; tel. (3852) 66-64-60; fax (3852) 24-03-96; e-mail iwep@iwep.asu.ru; internet www.iwep.asu.ru; f. 1987; research into hydrology, physical geography, cartography, biogeochemistry, geomorphology, limnology, air and water quality, mathematical modelling of contaminant transport in the environment; attached to Russian Acad. of Sciences, library of 37,000 vols; Dir Prof. YURI I. VINOKUROV; publ. *Polzunovsky Vestnik* (in Russian, 6 a year).

Kazan Institute of Biology: 420111 Kazan, ul. Lobachevskogo 2/31; tel. (8432) 32-64-91; attached to Russian Acad. of Sciences; Dir Dr A. I. TARCHEVSKY.

Koltsov, A. N., Institute of Developmental Biology: 117808 Moscow, ul. Vavilova 26; tel. (095) 135-64-83; attached to Russian Acad. of Sciences; Dir N. G. KHRUSHCHOV.

Komarov, V. L., Botanical Institute: 197376 St Petersburg, ul. Prof. Popova 2; tel. (812) 234-12-37; fax (812) 234-45-12; e-mail binadmin@ok3277.spb.edu; internet www.binran.spb.ru; f. 1713; attached to Russian Acad. of Sciences; 460 mems; Dir V. T. YARMISHKO; publs *Botanichesky Zhurnal* (12 a year), *Rastitelnost Rossii* (2 or 3 a year).

Murmansk Marine Biological Institute: 183010 Murmansk, Vladimirskaya ul. 17; tel. (8152) 56-52-32; fax (512) 951-02-88; e-mail mmbi@online.ru; internet www.mmbi.murman.ru; f. 1935; attached to Russian Acad. of Sciences; library of 70,000 vols; Dir Acad. G. G. MATISHOV.

Pacific Institute of Bio-organic Chemistry: 690022 Vladivostok, pr. 100-letiya Vladivostoka 159; tel. (4232) 31-14-30; fax (4232) 31-40-50; e-mail piboc@eastnet.febras.ru; f. 1964; attached to Russian Acad. of Sciences; Dir Prof. A. STONIK.

Palaeontological Institute: 117647 Moscow, Profsoyuznaya 123; tel. (095) 339-05-77; fax (095) 339-12-66; e-mail admin@paleo.ru; internet www.paleo.ru; f. 1930; attached to Russian Acad. of Sciences; library of 20,000 vols; attached museum: see Museums and Art Galleries; Dirs Prof. A. YU. ROZANOV, Prof. S. V. ROZHNOV, Prof. A. V. LOPATIN; publs *Journal* (6 a year), *Paleontological Journal* (supplementary issues, 6 a year), *Transactions* (3 or 4 a year).

Pavlov Institute of Physiology: 199034 St Petersburg, nab. Makarova 6; tel. (812) 328-07-01; fax (812) 328-05-01; e-mail krylov@infran.ru; internet www.infran.ru; f. 1925;

attached to Russian Acad. of Sciences; Dir Prof. D. P. DVORETSKY.

Research Institute for Monitoring Land and Ecosystems: 101000 Moscow, Bolshevistaky per. 11; tel. (095) 924-55-52.

Research Institute for the Biological Testing of Chemical Compounds: Moscow oblast, Kupavna, ul. Kirova 23; Dir L. A. PIRUZYAN.

Research Institute for the Genetics and Selection of Industrial Micro-organisms: 113545 Moscow, 1-i Dorozhnyi per. 1; tel. (095) 315-37-47; Dir V. G. DEBABOV.

Research Institute of Food Biotechnology: 109033 Moscow, Samokatnaya 4в; tel. (095) 362-44-95.

Scientific Centre of Biological Research: Moscow oblast, Serpukhovskii raion, Pushchino; attached to Russian Acad. of Sciences; Dir E. L. GOLOVLEV.

Sechenov, I. M., Institute of Evolutionary Physiology and Biochemistry: 194223 St Petersburg, pr. M. Toreza 44; tel. (812) 552-79-01; attached to Russian Acad. of Sciences; Dir Acad. V. L. SVIDERSKY.

Severtsov, A. N., Institute of Ecology and Evolution: 117071 Moscow, Leninskii pr. 33; tel. (095) 952-20-88; fax (095) 954-55-34; e-mail sevin@glas.aps.org; attached to Russian Acad. of Sciences; Dir Acad. DMITRI S. PAVLOV; publs *Russian Journal of Aquatic Ecology* (2 a year), *Lutreola* (2 a year).

Shemyakin-Ovchinnikov Institute of Bio-organic Chemistry: 117871 Moscow, ul. Miklukho-Maklaya 16/10; tel. (095) 335-01-00; fax (095) 310-70-07; e-mail ivavt@ibch.siobc.ras.ru; f. 1959; attached to Russian Acad. of Sciences; library of 250,000 vols; br. at Pushchino; Dir Prof. V. T. IVANOV; publ. *Journal of Bio-organic Chemistry* (in Russian and English, monthly).

Siberian Institute of Plant Physiology and Biochemistry: 664033 Irkutsk 33, POB 317; tel. (3952) 42-67-21; fax (3952) 51-07-54; e-mail matmod@sifibr.irk.ru; internet sifibr.irk.ru; f. 1961; attached to Russian Acad. of Sciences; research on plant physiology and biochemistry, microbiology and soil science, entomology, botany, geobotany and forestry; Dir Dr VICTOR VOINIKOV; publ. *Journal of Stress Physiology & Biochemistry*.

State Research Centre of Virology and Biotechnology (Vector): 630559 Novosibirsk oblast, Koltsovo; tel. (3832) 36-60-10; fax (3832) 36-74-09; e-mail vector@vector.nsk.su; internet www.vector.nsc.ru; f. 1974; library of 90,000 vols; Dir Acad. LEV S. SANDAKHCHIEV.

Timiryazev, K. A., Institute of Plant Physiology: 127276 Moscow, Botanicheskaya 35; tel. (095) 977-80-22; fax (095) 977-80-18; e-mail ifr@ippras.ru; internet www.ippras.ru; f. 1890; attached to Russian Acad. of Sciences; library of 83,000 vols; Dir Prof. VL. V. KUZNETSOV; publ. *Russian Journal of Plant Physiology* (6 a year).

Vavilov Institute of General Genetics: 119991 Moscow, ul. Gubkina 3; tel. (095) 135-62-13; fax (095) 135-12-89; e-mail iogen@vigg.ru; internet www.vigg.ru; f. 1966; attached to Russian Acad. of Sciences; library of 5,000 vols; Dir Prof. YU. P. ALTUKHOV; publs *Russian Journal of Genetics* (monthly), *Advances in Current Biology* (6 a year).

Zoological Institute: 199034 St. Petersburg, Universitetskaya nab. 1; tel. (812) 218-02-11; attached to Russian Acad. of Sciences; Dir O. A. SKARLATO.

Mathematical Sciences

Euler, L., International Institute of Mathematics: 197022 St Petersburg,

Pesochnaya nab. 10; tel. (812) 234-05-74; fax (812) 234-58-19; e-mail admin@euler.pdmi.ras.ru; internet www.pdmi.ras.ru/eimi; f. 1988; attached to Russian Acad. of Sciences; Dir Acad. L. D. FADDEEV.

Institute of Mathematics: 630090 Novosibirsk, pr. Akad. Koptyuga 4; tel. (3832) 33-28-92; fax (3832) 33-25-98; e-mail gelios@math.nsc.ru; f. 1957; attached to Russian Acad. of Sciences; library of 120,000 vols; Dir Acad. M. M. LAVRENTEV; publs *Sibirsky Matematichesky Zhurnal* (6 a year), *Diskretny Analiz i Issledovanie Operatsii* (series 1, 4 a year, series 2, 2 a year), *Matematicheskie Trudy* (2 a year), *Sibirsky Zhurnal Industrialnoy Matematiki* (4 a year).

Institute of Mathematics: 450057 Ufa, ul. Tukaeva 50; tel. (3472) 22-59-36; attached to Russian Acad. of Sciences; Dir V. V. NAPALKOV.

Steklov, V. A., Institute of Mathematics: 119991 Moscow, ul. Gubkina 8; tel. (095) 135-22-91; fax (095) 135-05-55; e-mail steklov@mi.ras.ru; internet www.mi.ras.ru; attached to Russian Acad. of Sciences; Dir Acad. YU. S. OSIPOV.

Steklov, V. A., Institute of Mathematics, St Petersburg Branch: 191011 St Petersburg, nab. Fontanki 25–27; tel. (812) 312-40-58; attached to Russian Acad. of Sciences; Dir Acad. L. D. FADDEEV.

Physical Sciences

All-Russia Geological Oil Research Institute (VNIGNI): 105819 Moscow, shosse Entuziastov 36; tel. (095) 273-26-51; fax (095) 273-55-38; f. 1953; library of 80,000 vols; Dir Dr K. A. KLESCHEV; publs *Geology of Oil and Gas* (annually), *Proceedings* (6 a year).

All-Russia Research Institute for the Geology and Mineral Resources of the World's Oceans: 190121 St Petersburg, Angliisky 1; tel. (812) 113-83-79; fax (812) 114-14-70; f. 1948; library of 60,500 vols; Dir Prof. I. S. GRAMBERG.

All-Russia Research Institute of Chemical Technology: 115409 Moscow, Kashirskoe shosse 33; tel. (095) 324-61-55.

All-Russia Research Institute of Geological, Geophysical and Geochemical Systems (VNIIgeosystem): 117015 Moscow, Varshavskoe shosse 8; tel. (495) 954-53-50; fax (495) 958-37-11; e-mail vniigeosystem@geosys.ru; internet www.geosys.ru; f. 1961; fundamental and applied scientific research; experimental design and technological research in earth sciences and geological exploration; library of 38,000 vols; Dir LEONID E. CHESALOV; publ. *Geoinformatika* (6 a year).

All-Russia Research Institute of Hydrolysis: 198099 St Petersburg, ul. Kalinina 13; tel. (812) 186-29-22; Dir O. I. SHAPOVALOV.

All-Russia Research Institute of Natural Gases and Gas Technology: 142717 Moscow oblast, Leninsky raion, pos. Razvilka; tel. (095) 355-92-06; fax (095) 399-16-77; e-mail samsr@gazprom.ru; f. 1948; library of 100,000 vols.

All-Russia Research Institute of Optical and Physical Measurements: 103031 Moscow, ul. Rozhdestvenka 27; tel. (095) 208-41-83; attached to Russian Acad. of Sciences; Gen. Dir I. G. BARANNIK.

All-Russia Research Institute of Physical-Technical and Radiotechnical Measurements: 147570 Moscow oblast, Solnechnogorsky raion, p/o Mendeleevo; tel. (095) 535-92-78; attached to Russian Acad. of Sciences; Dir B. I. ALSKIN.

All-Russia Scientific Research Institute of Mineral Resources: 109017 Moscow,

Staromonetni per. 31; tel. (095) 231-50-43; fax (095) 238-19-21; f. 1918; prospecting for and estimating ore deposits, research in processing; library of 345,000 vols; Dir Prof. A. N. EREMEEV.

Amur Complex Research Institute: 675000 Amur oblast, Blagoveshchensk, per. Relochnyi 1; tel. (4162) 42-72-32; fax (4162) 42-59-31; e-mail root@intpmr.amur.su; f. 1980; attached to Russian Acad. of Sciences; geology, minerals; library of 26,000 vols; Dir V. G. MOISEENKO.

Andreev Acoustics Institute: 117036 Moscow, ul. Shvernika 4; tel. (095) 126-74-01; fax (095) 126-84-11; e-mail dubrov@akin.ru; internet www.akin.ru; f. 1953; attached to Russian Acad. of Sciences; Dir N.A. DUBROVSKY.

Arbuzov, A. E., Institute of Organic and Physical Chemistry: 420088 Kazan, ul. Akad. Arbuzova 8; tel. (8432) 73-93-65; fax (8432) 73-22-53; e-mail arbuzov@iopc.kcn.ru; internet www.iopc.kcn.ru; f. 1965; attached to Russian Acad. of Sciences; Dir O. G. SINYASHIN.

Baikov, A. A., Institute of Metallurgy: 117911 Moscow, Leninskii pr. 49; tel. (095) 135-86-11; attached to Russian Acad. of Sciences; Dir Acad. N. P. LYAKISHEV.

Bardin, I. P., Central Research Institute of Ferrous Metallurgy: 107005 Moscow, 2-ya Baumanskaya 9/23; tel. (095) 265-72-04; fax (095) 267-48-27; e-mail ferrum.sc@online.ru; f. 1944; library of 65,000 vols; Dir-Gen. VLADIMIR I. MATORIN.

Bochvar, A. A., All-Russia Research Institute of Inorganic Materials: 123060 Moscow, ul. Rugova 5a; tel. (095) 190-82-97; fax (095) 196-41-68; e-mail post@bochvar.ru; internet www.bochvar.ru; f. 1945; Dir-Gen. ALEKSANDR VIKTOROVICH VATULIN; publ. *Materialovedeniye i Novye Materialy* (Materials Science and New Materials, annually).

Boreskov Institute of Catalysis: 630090 Novosibirsk, pr. Akad. Lavrenteva 5; tel. (383) 330-82-69; fax (383) 330-47-19; e-mail bic@catalysis.ru; internet www.catalysis.ru; attached to Russian Acad. of Sciences; Dir V. N. PARMON.

Central Aerological Observatory: 141700 Moscow, Dolgoprudny, Pervomayskaya ul. 3; tel. (095) 408-61-48; fax (095) 576-33-27; e-mail info@cao.su; f. 1941; atmospheric physics and chemistry up to 100km, study and monitoring of ozone layer, cloud physics, applied meteorology, weather modification; use of aircraft, rocket, satellite, radar and other facilities; upper-air sounding methods; library of 61,000 vols; Dir A. CHERNIKOV; publ. *CAO Proceedings*.

Central Seismological Observatory: Obninsk; attached to Russian Acad. of Sciences.

Chita Institute of Natural Resources: 672014 Chita, ul. Nedorezova 16, POB 147; tel. (302) 221-25-82; fax (302) 221-25-82; e-mail root@cinr.chita.su; internet www.chita.ru/public_htm/cinr.htm; f. 1981; attached to Russian Acad. of Sciences; library of 6,000 vols; Dir A. B. PTITSYN; publ. *Report on Environmental Conditions in Zabailkalye* (annually).

Far Eastern Institute of Geology: 690022 Vladivostok, pr. Stoletiya Vladivostoka 159; tel. (4232) 31-87-50; fax (4232) 31-78-47; e-mail fegi@online.marine.su; f. 1959; attached to Russian Acad. of Sciences; Dir A. I. KHANCHUK.

General Physics Institute: 119991 Moscow, ul. Vavilova 38; tel. (495) 135-82-96; fax (495) 234-31-96; e-mail director@gpi.ru; internet www.gpi.ru; f. 1983; attached to

Russian Acad. of Sciences; brs in Tarusa and Troitsk; Dir Prof. IVAN A. SHCHERBAKOV.

Geological Institute: 670047 Ulan-Ude, ul. Sakhyanova 6; tel. (3012) 33-09-55; fax (3012) 33-60-24; e-mail gin@bsc.buryatia.ru; f. 1973; attached to Russian Acad. of Sciences; Dir A. G. MIRONOV.

Graphite Research Institute: 111524 Moscow, Elektrodnaya 2; tel. (095) 176-13-06; fax (095) 176-12-63; Dir V. I. KOSTIKOV.

Grebenshchikov, I. V., Institute of Silicate Chemistry: 199155 St Petersburg, ul. Odoevskogo 24, korp. 2; tel. (812) 350-65-16; fax (812) 328-54-01; e-mail ichsran@isc.nw.ru; attached to Russian Acad. of Sciences; Dir Acad. V. J. SHEVCHENKO.

High-Mountain Geophysical Institute: 360030 Nalchik, pr. Lenina 2; tel. (866) 247-00-31; fax (866) 247-00-24; e-mail vgikbr@rambler.ru; f. 1963; meteorology, climatology, glaciology, geophysics, ecology; library of 17,230 vols, 26,288 periodicals; Dir Dr VALERY O. TAPASKHANOV.

Institute for Geothermal Research: 367030 Makhachkala, pr. Shamila 39-A; tel. and fax (8722) 62-93-57; e-mail danterm@xtreem.ru; f. 1980; attached to Russian Acad. of Sciences; Dir A. B. ALKHASOV.

Institute for Superplasticity Problems in Metals: 450001 Ufa, ul. St Khalturina 39; tel. (3472) 24-64-07; fax (3472) 25-37-59; e-mail nail@ipsm.bashkiria.su; f. 1985; attached to Russian Acad. of Sciences; library of 7,000 vols; Dir Prof. O. A. KAIBYSHEV.

Institute of Applied Astronomy: 197110 St Petersburg, ul. Zhdanovskaya 8; tel. (812) 275-11-18; fax (812) 275-11-19; e-mail ipa@ipa.rssi.ru; internet www.ipa.rssi.ru; f. 1988; attached to Russian Acad. of Sciences; Dir Dr A. M. FINKELSTEIN; publs *Trudy IPA RAN* (in Russian, 2 a year), *Communications* (in Russian and English, 10 a year).

Institute of Applied Physics: 603600 Nizhnii Novgorod, ul. Ulyanova 46; tel. (8312) 38-90-91; attached to Russian Acad. of Sciences; Dir Acad. A. V. GAPONOV-GREKHOV.

Institute of Astronomy: 109017 Moscow, Pyatnitskaya ul. 48; tel. (095) 951-54-61; fax (095) 230-20-81; e-mail postmaster@inasan.rssi.ru; internet www.inasan.rssi.ru; f. 1936; attached to Russian Acad. of Sciences; Dir Acad. A. A. BOYARCHUK.

Institute of Atmospheric Optics: 634055 Tomsk, Akademicheskii pr. 1; tel. (382) 249-27-38; fax (382) 249-20-86; e-mail mgg@iao.ru; internet www.iao.ru; f. 1969; research and development in physics, laser engineering, aerosol technology and ozone; attached to Siberian br. of the Russian Acad. of Sciences; Dir Prof. GENNADY GRIGOREVICH MATVIENKO.

Institute of Atmospheric Physics: 119017 Moscow, Pyzhevskii per. 3; tel. (095) 951-55-65; fax (095) 953-16-52; e-mail mail_adm@omega.ifaran.ru; f. 1956; attached to Russian Acad. of Sciences; library of 4,000 vols, 40 periodicals; Dir Acad. G. S. GOLITSYN; publ. *Izvestiya – Atmospheric and Oceanic Physics* (6 a year).

Institute of Chemical Kinetics and Combustion: 630090 Novosibirsk, Institutskaya 3; tel. (3832) 34-41-50; fax (3832) 34-23-50; e-mail root@kinetics.nsk.su; f. 1957; attached to Russian Acad. of Sciences; library of 88,000 vols; Dir Prof. YU. D. TSVETKOV.

Institute of Chemical Physics: Chernogolovka; attached to Russian Acad. of Sciences; Dir S. M. BATURIN.

Institute of Chemistry: 690022 Vladivostok, pr. Stoletiya Vladivostoka 159; tel. (4232) 31-25-90; fax (4232) 31-18-89; e-mail chemi@online.ru; f. 1971; attached to Russian Acad. of Sciences; library of 5,000 vols; Dir Prof. Dr V. Yu. GLUSHCHENKO.

Institute of Coal and Coal Chemistry: 650610 Kemerovo GSP, ul. Rukavishnikova 21; tel. (3842) 28-14-33; fax (3842) 21-18-38; e-mail pvp@kemsc.ru; internet www.kemsc.ru; f. 1983; attached to Russian Acad. of Sciences; library of 40,000 vols; Dir G. I. GRITSKO; publ. *Coalbed Methane* (4 a year).

Institute of Cosmophysical Research and Aeronomy im. Yu. G. Shafer: 677980 Yakutsk, pr. Lenina 31; tel. (4112) 33-50-26; fax (4112) 33-55-51; e-mail ikfia@ysn.ru; internet ikfia.ysn.ru; f. 1962; attached to Russian Acad. of Sciences; library of 40,000 vols; Dir Dr EVGENY. G. BEREZHKO.

Institute of Electrophysics: 620219 Ekaterinburg, Komsomolskaya ul. 34; tel. (3432) 44-18-53; attached to Russian Acad. of Sciences; Dir Acad. G. A. MESYATS.

Institute of Energy Problems of Chemical Physics: 117829 Moscow, Leninskii pr. 38, korp. 2; tel. (095) 137-34-79; attached to Russian Acad. of Sciences; Dir V. L. TALROZE.

Institute of Experimental Meteorology: Obninsk; Dir M. A. PETROSYANTS.

Institute of Experimental Mineralogy: 142432 Moscow oblast, Noginskii raion, Chernogolovka, Institutskaya ul. 4; tel. (096) 524-44-25; fax (096) 524-44-25; e-mail shap@iem.ac.ru; internet www.iem.ac.ru; f. 1969; attached to Russian Acad. of Sciences; 206 mems; Dir YURI B. SHAPOVALOV; publ. *Experiments in Geosciences* (annually).

Institute of Geochemistry: 664033 Irkutsk, ul. Favorskogo 1a; tel. (3952) 46-05-00; attached to Russian Acad. of Sciences; Dir M. I. KUZMIN.

Institute of Geology: 184209 Murmansk oblast, Apatity, ul. Fersmana 14; tel. (81555) 76567; fax (81555) 76481; e-mail felix@geoksc.apatity.ru; internet geoksc.apatity.ru; f. 1951; attached to Russian Acad. of Sciences; Dir F. P. MITROFANOV.

Institute of Geology: 367025 Makhachkala, ul. Gadzhieva 45; attached to Russian Acad. of Sciences; Dir V. V. SUETNOV.

Institute of Geology: 109017 Moscow, Pyzhevskii per. 7; tel. (095) 230-80-29; fax (095) 231-04-43; f. 1930; attached to Russian Acad. of Sciences; Dir Y. G. LEONOV.

Institute of Geology: 185610 Petrozavodsk, Pushkinskaya ul. 11; tel. (8142) 78-27-53; fax (8142) 77-06-02; e-mail geology@krc.karelia.ru; internet geoserv.krc.karelia.ru; f. 1946; attached to Russian Acad. of Sciences; Dir K. I. HEISKANEN (acting).

Institute of Geology: 167610 Syktyvkar, Pervomaiskaya ul. 54; tel. (8212) 42-00-37; fax (8212) 42-53-46; e-mail institute@geo.komi.ru; f. 1958; attached to Russian Acad. of Sciences; Dir N. P. YUSHKIN; publs *Vestnik* (monthly), *Proceedings* (4 a year).

Institute of Geology: 450000 Ufa 25, ul. K. Marxa 16/2; tel. (3472) 22-82-56; fax (3472) 23-03-68; attached to Russian Acad. of Sciences; Dir V. N. PUCHKOV.

Institute of Geology: 677891 Yakutsk, pr. Lenina 39; tel. (4112) 3-53-81; attached to Russian Acad. of Sciences; Dir B. V. OLEINIKOV.

Institute of Geology and Precambrian Geochronology: 199034 St Petersburg, nab. Makarova 2; tel. (812) 218-47-01; attached to Russian Acad. of Sciences; Dir V. A. GLEBOVITSKY.

Institute of Geomechanics: c/o Russian Academy of Sciences, 117333 Moscow, ul. Vavilova 44 (korp. 2, komn. 86); attached to Russian Acad. of Sciences.

Institute of Geophysics: 620016 Ekaterinburg, ul. Amundsena 100; tel. (343) 267-88-68; attached to Russian Acad. of Sciences; Dir P. S. MARTYSHKO.

Institute of High-Energy Physics: 142281 Moscow oblast, Protvino; tel. (095) 924-67-52; fax (0967) 74-28-24; e-mail alexandrov@mx.ihep.ru; internet www.ihep.ru; f. 1963; library of 300,000 vols; Dir A. A. LOGUNOV.

Institute of High-Pressure Physics: 142092 Moscow oblast, Troitsk; tel. (095) 334-00-10; fax (095) 334-00-12; e-mail hpp@hppi.troitsk.ru; internet www.hppi.troitsk.ru; f. 1958; attached to Russian Acad. of Sciences; Dir Prof. S. M. STISHOV.

Institute of High-Temperature Electrochemistry: 620219 Ekaterinburg, S. Kovalevskaya 22; tel. (343) 374-50-89; fax (343) 374-59-92; e-mail head@ihte.uran.ru; internet www.ihte.uran.ru; f. 1958; attached to Russian Acad. of Sciences; Dir Prof. V. A. KHOKHLOV.

Institute of High-Temperature Physics: 127412 Moscow, Izhorskaya 13/19; tel. (095) 485-83-45; attached to Russian Acad. of Sciences; Dir V. M. BATENIN.

Institute of Hydrodynamics: 630090 Novosibirsk, pr. Akad. Lavrenteva 15; tel. (3832) 33-16-12; fax (3832) 33-16-12; e-mail root@hydro.nsc.ru; f. 1957; attached to Russian Acad. of Sciences; library of 87,000 vols; Dir Acad. V.M. TITOV; publs *Combustion Explosions and Shock Waves* (6 a year), *Continuum Dynamics* (1 or 2 a year), *Journal of Applied Mechanics and Technical Physics* (6 a year).

Institute of Macro-Molecular Compounds: 199004 St Petersburg, Bolshoi pr. 31; tel. (812) 213-10-70; fax (812) 218-68-69; attached to Russian Acad. of Sciences; Dir E. F. PANARIN.

Institute of Marine Geology and Geophysics: 693002 Yuzhno-Sakhalinsk, ul. Nauki 5; tel. (4242) 2-21-28; attached to Russian Acad. of Sciences; Dir K. F. SERGEEV.

Institute of Metal Physics: 620041 Ekaterinburg, GSP-170, ul. Sofia Kovalevskaya 18; tel. (343) 374-02-30; fax (343) 374-52-44; e-mail physics@imp.uran.ru; internet www.imp.uran.ru; f. 1932; attached to Russian Acad. of Sciences; library of 18,000 vols, 92,000 periodicals; Dir Prof. Dr V. V. USTINOV; publs *Fizika metallov i metallovedenie* (Physics of Metals and Metallography, monthly), *Defectoscopiya* (Journal of Non-Destructive Testing, monthly).

Institute of Metallo-organic Chemistry: 603600 Nizhnii Novgorod, ul. Tropinina 49; tel. (8312) 66-27-09; fax (8312) 66-14-97; f. 1989; attached to Russian Acad. of Sciences; library of 50,000 vols; Dir G. A. ABAKUMOV.

Institute of Metallurgy: 620016 Ekaterinburg, ul. Amundsena 101; tel. (3432) 28-53-00; fax (3432) 28-61-30; e-mail imet@imet.uran.ru; f. 1955; attached to Russian Acad. of Sciences; Dir Acad. L. I. LEONTIEV.

Institute of Mineralogy: 456301 Chelyabinsk oblast, Miass; tel. (35135) 5-35-62; attached to Russian Acad. of Sciences; Dir V. N. ANFILOGOV.

Institute of New Chemical Problems: 142432 Moscow oblast, Noginsky raion, Chernogolovka; tel. (095) 524-50-24; attached to Russian Acad. of Sciences; Dir V. N. TROITSKII.

Institute of Nuclear Physics: 630090 Novosibirsk, pr. Akad. Lavrenteva 11; tel. (3832) 35-97-77; fax (3832) 35-21-63 br. in Protvin; attached to Russian Acad. of Sciences; Dir Acad. A. N. SKRINSKY.

Institute of Nuclear Research: 117312 Moscow, pr. 60-letiya Oktyabrya 7A; tel.

(095) 135-77-60; attached to Russian Acad. of Sciences; Dir Dr V. A. MATVEEV.

Institute of Oil Chemistry: 634055 Tomsk, Akademicheskii pr. 3; tel. (3822) 1-86-23; attached to Russian Acad. of Sciences; Dir E. E. SIROTKINA.

Institute of Organic Chemistry: 630090 Novosibirsk, Akademgorodok, pr. Akad. Lavrenteva 9; tel. (3832) 35-16-52; attached to Russian Acad. of Sciences; Dir Acad. G. A. TOLSTIKOV.

Institute of Organic Chemistry: 450054 Ufa, pr. Oktyabrya 71; tel. and fax (3472) 35-60-66; attached to Russian Acad. of Sciences; Dir M. S. YUNUSOV.

Institute of Organic Synthesis: 620219 Ekaterinburg, ul. S. Kovalevskoi 20; tel. (3432) 74-11-89; fax (3432) 74-11-89; e-mail chupakhin@ios.uran.ru; f. 1993; attached to Russian Acad. of Sciences; Dir Prof. OLEG N. CHUPAKHIN.

Institute of Permafrost: ul. Merzlotnaya 36, 677010 Yakutsk; tel. and fax (4112) 33-44-76; e-mail mpi@ysn.ru; f. 1961; attached to Russian Acad. of Sciences; library of 40,000 vols; Dir RUDOLF V. ZHANG.

Institute of Physical Chemistry: 117915 Moscow, Leninskii pr. 31; tel. (095) 955-46-36; attached to Russian Acad. of Sciences; Dir YU. M. POLUKAROV.

Institute of Physics: 367003 Makhachkala 3, ul. 26 Bakinskikh Komissarov 94; tel. (8722) 2-51-60; attached to Russian Acad. of Sciences; Dir I. K. KAMILOV.

Institute of Problems of the Geology and Extraction of Oil and Gas: 117917 Moscow, Leninskii pr. 65; tel. (095) 135-75-66; attached to Russian Acad. of Sciences; Dir V. N. VINOGRADOV.

Institute of Semiconductor Physics: 630090 Novosibirsk, pr. Akad. Lavrenteva 13; tel. (383) 333-39-50; fax (383) 333-27-71; f. 1962; attached to Russian Acad. of Sciences; Dir Prof. A. L. ASEEV.

Institute of Solid State Chemistry: 620219 Ekaterinburg, ul. Pervomaiskaya 91; tel. (3432) 74-52-19; fax (3432) 74-44-95; e-mail server@ihim.uran.ru; internet www.uran.ru/structure/institutions/chimtt/issc.htm; f. 1932; attached to Russian Acad. of Sciences; Dir V. G. BAMBUROV.

Institute of Solid State Physics: 142432 Moscow oblast, Chernogolovka; tel. (095) 993-27-55; fax (096) 524-97-01; e-mail adm@issp.ac.ru; internet www.issp.ac.ru; f. 1963; attached to Russian Acad. of Sciences; Dir Prof. V. V. KVEDER.

Institute of Solution Chemistry: 153045 Ivanovo, Akademicheskaya ul. 1; tel. (0932) 37-85-21; fax (0932) 37-85-09; e-mail adm@isc-ras.ru; internet www.isc-ras.ru; f. 1981; attached to Russian Acad. of Sciences; library of 70,000 vols; Dir Prof. ANATOLY ZAKHAROV; publs *Problems of Solution Chemistry* (4 a year), *Proceedings* (annually), *Textile Chemistry* (2 a year), *Chemical Thermodynamics and Thermochemistry* (2 a year).

Institute of Space Physics Research and the Diffusion of Radio Waves: 684034 Kamchatka obl., Elizovsky raion, Paratunka, Mirnaya ul. 7; tel. (41531) 9-31-93; attached to Russian Acad. of Sciences; Dir I. N. AMIANTOV.

Institute of Space Research: 117810 Moscow, Profsoyuznaya 84/32; tel. (095) 333-20-88; fax (095) 310-70-23; attached to Russian Acad. of Sciences; Dir A. A. GALEEV.

Institute of Spectroscopy: 142092 Moscow oblast, Troitsk; tel. (095) 334-05-79; fax (095) 334-08-86; attached to Russian Acad. of Sciences; Dir E. A. VINOGRADOV.

Institute of Strength Physics and Materials Science: 634021 Tomsk, Akademicheskii pr. 2/1; tel. (3822) 25-94-81; fax (3822) 25-95-76; e-mail ispms@ispms.tomsk.su; internet www.ispms.tsc.ru; f. 1984; attached to Russian Acad. of Sciences; Dir Acad. V. E. PANIN; publ. *Physical Mesomechanics* (6 a year).

Institute of Structural Macrokinetics and Materials Science: 142342 Moscow oblast, Noginsky raion, Chernogolovka; tel. (095) 962-80-00; fax (095) 962-80-40; e-mail merzh@ism.ac.ru; internet www.ism.ac.ru; f. 1988; attached to Russian Acad. of Sciences; Dir A. G. MERZHANOV.

Institute of Tectonics and Geophysics: 680022 Khabarovsk, ul. Kim Yu Chena 65; tel. (4212) 22-71-89; fax (4212) 22-76-84; e-mail tectonic@itig.khabarovsk.su; attached to Russian Acad. of Sciences; Dir N. P. ROMANOVSKY; publ. *Tikhookeanskaya Geologiya* (in Russian and English, 6 a year).

Institute of Terrestrial Magnetism, the Ionosphere and Radio Wave Propagation: 142092 Moscow oblast, Troitsk; tel. (095) 334-01-20; fax (095) 334-01-24; f. 1940; attached to Russian Acad. of Sciences; library of 100,000 vols; br. in St Petersburg; Dir Prof. VICTOR N. ORAEVSKY.

Institute of the Chemistry and Technology of Rare Elements and Mineral Raw Materials: 184200 Apatity, ul. Fersmana 26a; tel. (81555) 7-95-49; fax (81555) 7-94-14; e-mail office@chemy.kolasc.net.ru; internet www.kolasc.net.ru/chemy; f. 1957; attached to Russian Acad. of Sciences; Dir V. T. KALINNIKOV.

Institute of the Chemistry of High-Purity Substances: 603950 Nizhnii Novgorod, ul. Tropinina 49, GSP-75; tel. (8312) 62-56-70; fax (8312) 62-56-66; e-mail victor@ihps.nnov.ru; internet www.ihps.nnov.ru; f. 1988; fundamental and applied research of high-purity substances; production of zinc selenide, quartz and chalcogenide optical fibres; attached to Russian Acad. of Sciences; Dir Prof. M. F. CHURBANOV; publs *Journal of Optoelectronics and Advanced Materials*, *Optical Letters*.

Institute of the Earth's Crust: 664033 Irkutsk, ul. Lermontova 128; tel. (3952) 46-40-00; fax (3952) 46-29-00; e-mail drf@crust.irk.ru; internet earth.crust.irk.ru; f. 1949; attached to Russian Acad. of Sciences; library of 318,000 vols; Dir E. V. SKLYAROV.

Institute of the Geology of Ore Deposits, Petrography, Mineralogy and Geochemistry: 119017 Moscow, Staromonetnyi per. 35; tel. (495) 951-45-79; fax (495) 230-21-79; e-mail director@igem.ru; internet www.igem.ru; f. 1955; attached to Russian Acad. of Sciences; Dir NIKOLAY BORTNIKOV.

Institute of the Mineralogy, Geochemistry and Crystal Chemistry of Rare Elements: 121357 Moscow, ul. Veresaeva 15; tel. (095) 443-84-28; fax (095) 443-90-43; e-mail krem@imgre.iitp.ru; f. 1956; attached to Russian Acad. of Sciences and Min. of Natural Resources; Dir A. A. KREMENETSKY; publ. *Applied Geochemistry* (annually).

Institute of Theoretical and Experimental Physics: 117259 Moscow, Bol. Cheremushkinskaya ul. 25; tel. (095) 123-31-95; fax (095) 883-95-92; e-mail director@itep.ru; internet www.itep.ru; f. 1945; Dir M. V. DANILOV.

Institute of Theoretical Astronomy: 191187 St Petersburg, nab. Kutuzova 10; tel. (812) 279-06-67; e-mail ita@ita.spb.su; attached to Russian Acad. of Sciences; Dir A. G. SOKOLSKII.

Institute of Thermal Physics: 620016 Ekaterinburg, Amundsena 106; tel. (3432) 67-88-01; fax (3432) 67-88-00; e-mail itp@itp.uran.ru; f. 1988; attached to Russian Acad. of Sciences; Dir V. G. BAIDAKOV.

Institute of Thermophysics: 630090 Novosibirsk, pr. Akad. Lavrenteva 1; tel. (3833) 30-70-50; fax (3833) 30-84-80; e-mail web@itp.nsc.ru; internet www.itp.nsc.ru; f. 1957; attached to Russian Acad. of Sciences; undertakes research in the fields of heat and mass transfer, physical hydrodynamics and gas dynamics, thermal physics of ionized gases and physics of low-temperature plasma; library of 100,000 vols; Dir Dr S. V. ALEKSEENKO; publs *Thermophysics and Aeromechanics* (4 a year), *Journal of Engineering Thermophysics* (4 a year).

Institute of Volcanology and Seismology: 683006 Petropavlovsk-Kamchatsky, bul. Piipa 9; tel. (4152) 25-95-13; fax (4152) 25-47-23; e-mail volcan@kcs.iks.ru; internet www.kcs.iks.ru; 130 mems; attached to Russian Acad. of Sciences; Dir EVGENY I. GORDEEV.

Institute of Water Problems: 107078 Moscow, Novaya Basmannaya ul. 10, POB 231; tel. (095) 265-97-57; fax (095) 265-18-87; e-mail iwapr@iwapr.msk.su; f. 1968; attached to Russian Acad. of Sciences; library of 35,000 vols; Dir M. G. KHUBLARYAN; publ. *Water Resources* (6 a year).

Institute of Water Problems of the North: Petrozavodsk, pr. Uritskogo 50; tel. (8142) 5-34-71; attached to Russian Acad. of Sciences; Head N. N. FILATOV (acting).

International Institute of Earthquake Prediction Theory and Mathematical Geophysics: 117556 Moscow, Varshavskoe shosse 79, korp. 2; tel. (095) 110-77-95; fax (095) 310-70-32; e-mail mitpan@mitp.ru; internet www.mitp.ru; f. 1990; attached to Russian Acad. of Sciences; Dir A. A. SOLOVIEV; publ. *Computational Seismology* (annually).

Irkutsk Institute of Organic Chemistry 'A. E. Favorsky': 664033 Irkutsk, ul. Favorskogo 1; tel. (3952) 42-44-11; f. 1957; attached to Russian Acad. of Sciences; library of 9,200 vols, 52,500 periodicals; Dir BORIS A. TROFIMOV.

Joint Institute for Nuclear Research: 141980 Moscow oblast, Dubna; tel. (09621) 65-059; fax (09621) 65-599; e-mail post@jinr.ru; internet www.jinr.ru; f. 1956; conducts studies on the structure of matter, high- and low-energy physics, condensed matter, heavy ion and neutron physics; education programme; languages of instruction: Russian, English; 18 mem. states; library of 422,000 vols; Dir V. G. KADYSHEVSKY; publs *JINR Annual Report*, *JINR News* (4 a year), *Journal of Elementary Particles and the Atomic Nucleus* (6 a year), *Particles and Nuclei – Letters* (6 a year).

Kapitza, P. L., Institute of Physical Problems: 117973 Moscow, GSP-1, ul. A. N. Kosygina 2; tel. (095) 137-32-48; fax (095) 938-20-30; e-mail andreev@kapitza.ras.ru; attached to Russian Acad. of Sciences; Dir Acad. A. F. ANDREEV.

Karpinsky, A. P., All-Russia Geological Research Institute: 199106 St Petersburg, Vasilevsky ostrov, Sredny pr. 74; tel. (812) 321-57-06; fax (812) 321-30-23; e-mail vsegei@mail.wplus.net; f. 1882; Dir O. V. PETROV; publ. *Regional Geology and Metallogeny* (2 a year).

Karpov Institute of Physical Chemistry: ul. Vorontsovo Pole 10, 105064 Moscow,; tel. (095) 917-32-57; fax (095) 975-24-50; e-mail simonov@cc.nifhi.ac.ru; internet www.nifhi.ac.ru; f. 1918; 900 mems; library of 38,000 vols; Exec. Dir Prof. ALEXANDER PAVLOVICH SIMONOV.

Khlopin, V. G., Radium Institute: 194021 St Petersburg, 2-i Murinskiy pr. 28; tel. (812) 247-56-41; fax (812) 247-57-81; e-mail moshkov@atom.nw.ru; f. 1922; radiochemistry, nuclear physics; library of 170,000 vols; Dir Dr ALEXANDER A. RIMSKY-KORSAKOV; publ. *Radiochemistry* (in Russian, 6 a year).

Kirensky Institute of Physics: 660036 Krasnoyarsk; tel. (3912) 43-26-35; fax (3912) 43-89-23; e-mail dir@iph.krasn.ru; internet www.kirensky.ru; f. 1956; attached to Russian Acad. of Sciences; 300 mems; main fields of activity: physics, magnetic phenomena and magnetic materials; condensed matter physics and materials for electronics; design and engineering of new active elements; components and devices for radio-electronics, acousto-electronics, optoelectronics and quantum electronics; training of higher level material science specialists; Dir Acad. Prof. VASILY F. SHABANOV; Scientific Sec. Dr KIRILL A. SHAIKHUTDINOV.

Konstantinov, B. P., St Petersburg Institute of Nuclear Physics: 188350 Leningrad oblast, Gatchina, Orlova Roscha; tel. (812) 297-91-25; fax (812) 713-71-96; attached to Russian Acad. of Sciences; Dir ANSELM.

Krylov, A. P., All-Russia Oil and Gas Research Institute: 125422 Moscow, Dmitrovsky pr. 10; tel. (095) 976-83-01.

Kurchatov, I. V., Institute of Atomic Energy: 123182 Moscow, ul. Kurchatova 46; tel. (095) 196-61-07; fax (095) 943-00-74; Dir Acad. EVGENII P. VELIKHOV.

Kurnakov, N. S., Institute of General and Inorganic Chemistry: 117907 Moscow, Leninskii pr. 31; tel. (095) 952-07-87; fax (095) 954-12-79; f. 1918; attached to Russian Acad. of Sciences; Dir Acad. NIKOLAI T. KUZNETSOV.

Landau, L. D., Institute of Theoretical Physics: 117940 Moscow V-234, ul. A. N. Kosygina 2; tel. (095) 137-32-44; fax (095) 938-20-77; attached to Russian Acad. of Sciences; Dir Acad. I. M. KHALATNIKOV.

Lebedev, P. N., Physics Institute: 117924 Moscow, Leninskii pr. 53; tel. (095) 135-14-29; fax (095) 135-85-33; attached to Russian Acad. of Sciences; br. in Kuibyshev; Dir Acad. L. V. KELDYSH.

Lithosphere Institute: 109180 Moscow, Staromonetnyi per. 22; tel. (095) 233-55-88; attached to Russian Acad. of Sciences; Dir N. A. BOGDANOV.

Main Astronomical Observatory: 196140 St Petersburg, Pulkovo; tel. (812) 297-98-41; attached to Russian Acad. of Sciences; br. in Nikolaev oblast; Dir V. K. ABALAKIN.

Mendeleev, D. I., Research Institute of Metrology: 198005 St Petersburg, Moskovskii pr. 19; tel. (812) 251-76-01; fax (812) 113-01-14; e-mail hal@onti.vniim.spb.su; f. 1842; attached to Russian Acad. of Sciences; library of 80,000 vols; Dir N. I. KHANOV.

Moscow Radiotechnical Institute: 117519 Moscow, Varshavskoe shosse 132; tel. (095) 315-31-11; fax (095) 314-10-53; e-mail mrti_r@fsuemrti.ru; internet www.fsuemrti.ru; f. 1946; attached to Russian Acad. of Sciences; devt of particle accelerators for industrial and medical applications; high-power SHF and x-ray technologies and installations; plasma technologies and installations; computer control and data-processing systems for applications such as accelerators, medicine, ecology and safety; Dir Dr B. MAKAROV.

Nesmeyanov, A. N., Institute of Elementary Organic Compounds: 117813 Moscow V-334, GSP 1, ul. Vavilova 28; tel. (095) 135-92-02; fax (095) 135-50-85; e-mail dir@ineos

.ac.ru; f. 1954; attached to Russian Acad. of Sciences; Dir Prof. YU. N. BUBNOV.

Nikolaev Institute of Inorganic Chemistry: 630090 Novosibirsk, pr. Akad. Lavrenteva 3; tel. (3832) 34-44-90; fax (3832) 34-44-89; e-mail sam@she.nsk.su; internet www .che.nsk.su; f. 1958; attached to Russian Acad. of Sciences; Dir Acad. F. A. KUZNETSOV; publ. *Journal of Structural Chemistry* (6 a year).

Noginsk Research Centre: c/o Institute of Solid State Physics, 142342 Moscow oblast, Chernogolovka; attached to Russian Acad. of Sciences; Chair. Acad. YU. A. OSIPYAN.

Polar Geospace Physics Observatory 'Tiksi': 678400 Bulunsky raion, Tiksi, Leninskaya ul. 25; tel. (41167) 2-17-89; fax (41167) 5-39-94; e-mail common@pgo.ysn.ru; attached to Russian Acad. of Sciences; Dir V. N. MEDVEDEV.

Polar Institute of Geophysics: 183023 Murmansk, ul. Khalturina 15; tel. (8152) 6-58-29; attached to Russian Acad. of Sciences; br. in Apatity; Dir V. G. PIVOVAROV.

Radiophysics Research Institute: 603950 Nizhnii Novgorod, Bol. Pecherskaya ul. 25; tel. (8312) 36-72-94; fax (8312) 36-99-02; e-mail sneg@nirfi.sci-nnov.ru; internet www .nirfi.sci-nnov.ru; f. 1956; library of 250,000 vols; Dir Dr S.D. SNEGIREV; publ. *Izvestiya vysshikh uchebnykh zavedenii – Radiofizika* (monthly).

Research Centre for the Study of Properties of Surfaces and Vacuums: c/o Russian Academy of Sciences, 117901 Moscow, Leninsky pr. 14; attached to Russian Acad. of Sciences; Dir L. E. LAPIDUS.

Research Institute of Experimental Physics: 607190 Nizhegorodskaya oblast, Sarov, pr. Mira 37; tel. (83130) 4-44-68; fax (83130) 5-38-08; e-mail osv@dc.vniief.ru; f. 1946; Dir Dr RADY I. ILKAEV; publs *Questions of Atomic Science and Technics* (4 a year), *Atom* (4 a year).

Research Institute of Geophysical Research on Exploration Wells: Bashkortostan, 452620 Oktyabrsky, ul. Gorkogo 1; tel. (34767) 5-30-24; fax (34767) 5-50-16; e-mail vniigis@poikc.bashnet.ru; internet www.vniigis.bashnet.ru; f. 1956; geophysical well logging; library of 177,000 vols; Dir A. P. POLIAKOV.

Research Institute of Geophysical Shock Waves: Moscow oblast, Ramenskoe, Pryamolineinaya ul. 26.

Research Institute of Gold and Rare Metals: Magadan, ul. Gagarina 2.

Research Institute of the Geochemistry of the Biosphere: 353918 Novorossiisk, Leninsky pr. 54; tel. (8617) 23-03-03; fax (8617) 23-03-03; e-mail niigb@mail .kubtelecom.ru; f. 1992; attached to Rostov on Don State University; Dir V. A. ALEKSEENKO; publs *Geochemistry of the Biosphere* (annually), *Ecology: Experience, Problems* (irregular).

Russian Research Institute for Integrated Water Management and Protection: 620062 Ekaterinburg, ul. Mira 23; tel. and fax (343) 374-26-79; e-mail wrm@wrm .ru; internet www.wrm.ru; f. 1969; 98 ; library of 30,000 vols; Dir Prof. Dr N. B. PROKHOROVA; Deputy Dir Y. A. PODZINA; publs *Water of Russia* (monthly), *Water Sector of Russia* (2 a year).

Semenov, N. N., Institute of Chemical Physics: 117977 Moscow, ul. A. N. Kosygina 4; tel. (095) 137-29-51; fax (095) 938-21-56; e-mail berlin@chph.ras.ru; internet www .chph.ras.ru; f. 1931; attached to Russian Acad. of Sciences; Dir A. A. BERLIN; publ. *Khimicheskaya fizika* (monthly).

Shmidt, O. Yu., Institute of Earth Physics: 123810 Moscow, Bol. Gruzinskaya ul. 10; tel. (095) 254-27-10; fax (095) 253-92-83; attached to Russian Acad. of Sciences; Dir M. S. ZHDANOV.

Shubnikov, A. V., Institute of Crystallography: 117333 Moscow, Leninskii pr. 59; tel. (095) 135-63-11; fax (095) 135-10-11; attached to Russian Acad. of Sciences; br. in Kaluga; Dir V. I. SIMONOV (acting).

Siberian Institute of Terrestrial Magnetism, the Ionosphere, and Radio Wave Propagation: 664033 Irkutsk, ul. Lermontova 126; tel. (3952) 46-08-65; attached to Russian Acad. of Sciences; Dir G. A. ZHEREBTSOV.

Siberian Research Institute of Geology, Geophysics and Mineral Raw Materials: 630104 Novosibirsk, Krasny pr. 67; tel. (3832) 22-45-03.

Special Astrophysical Observatory: 357147 Karachai-Cherkessian Republic, pos. Nizhnii Arkhyz; tel. (901) 498-29-31; fax (901) 498-29-31; e-mail adm@sao.ru; internet www.sao.ru; f. 1966; attached to Russian Acad. of Sciences; Dir YU. YU. BALEGA; publ. *Bulletin* (4 a year).

State Hydrological Institute: 199053 St Petersburg, V.O., 2-ya liniya 23; tel. (812) 213-89-16; Dir I. A. SHIKLOMANOV.

State Research Institute of Non-ferrous Metals: 129515 Moscow, ul. Akad. Koroleva 13; tel. (095) 215-61-73; fax (095) 215-34-53; e-mail gin@gintsvet.msk.ru; f. 1918; library of 500,000 vols; Dir ANDREI TARASOV; publ. *Gintsvetmet Proceedings* (annually).

Titanium Research Institute: 117393 Moscow, ul. Obrucheva 52; tel. (095) 332-95-55.

Troitsk Research Centre: 142092 Moscow oblast, Troitsk, Yubileinaya 3; tel. (095) 334-06-35; fax (095) 334-06-32; e-mail laptev@inr .troitsk.ru; attached to Russian Acad. of Sciences; Chair. Acad. VICTOR A. MATVEEV.

United Institute of Geology, Geophysics and Mineralogy: 630090 Novosibirsk, pr. Akad. Koptyuga 3; tel. (3832) 33-26-00; fax (3832) 33-27-92; attached to Russian Acad. of Sciences; Dir-Gen. Acad. N. L. DOBRETSOV.

Vernadsky, V. I., Institute of Geochemistry and Analytical Chemistry: 119991 Moscow, ul. A. N. Kosygina 19; tel. (095) 137-41-27; fax (095) 938-20-54; e-mail geokhi .ras@relcom.ru; internet www.geokhi.ru; f. 1947; attached to Russian Acad. of Sciences; library of 33,000 vols, 230 periodicals; Dir Prof. ERIC M. GALIMOV; publs *Geochemical International* (monthly), *Journal of Analytical Chemistry* (monthly).

Voeikov, A. I., Main Geophysical Observatory: 194018 St Petersburg, ul. Karbysheva 7; tel. (812) 297-01-03; fax (812) 297-86-61; f. 1849; climatology, atmospheric physics, air pollution; library of 380,000 vols; Dir Dr V. M. KATTSOV; publ. *Trudy GGO*.

Zavaritsii, Acad. A. N., Institute of Geology and Geochemistry: 620219 Ekaterinburg, Pochtovy per. 7; tel. (3432) 51-80-40; attached to Russian Acad. of Sciences; Dir V. A. KOROTEEV.

Zelinsky, N. D., Institute of Organic Chemistry: 119991 Moscow, Leninskii pr. 47; tel. (095) 137-29-44; fax (095) 135-53-28; e-mail secretary@ioc.ac.ru; internet www.ioc .ac.ru; f. 1934; attached to Russian Acad. of Sciences; Dir M. P. EGOROV; publs *Mendeleev Communication* (6 a year), *Russian Chemical Bulletin* (monthly), *Russian Chemical Reviews* (monthly).

PHILOSOPHY AND PSYCHOLOGY

Institute of Philosophy: 119991 Moscow, Volkhonka ul. 14; tel. (495) 203-92-17; fax (495) 609-93-50; e-mail iph@iph.ras.ru; internet www.iph.ras.ru; f. 1929; attached to Russian Acad. of Sciences; 300 mems; library of 89,500 vols; Dir A. A. GUSEINOV; Acad. Sec. B. O. NIKOLAICHEV; publs *Personality, Culture, Society* (quarterly), *Epistemology and Philosophy of Science* (quarterly).

Institute of Psychology: 129366 Moscow, Yaroslavskaya ul. 13; tel. (095) 282-51-49; attached to Russian Acad. of Sciences; Dir A. V. BRUSHLINSKY.

RELIGION, SOCIOLOGY AND ANTHROPOLOGY

Institute of Sociology: 117259 Moscow, ul. Krzhizhanovskogo 24/35, korp. 5; tel. (095) 128-91-09 br. in St Petersburg: 198147 St Petersburg, ul. Serpukhovskaya 38; tel. (812) 292-27-65; fax (812) 292-29-29; attached to Russian Acad. of Sciences; Dir V. A. YADOV.

Miklukho-Maklai, N. N., Institute of Ethnology and Anthropology: 117334 Moscow, Leninsky pr. 32A; tel. (095) 938-17-47; fax (095) 938-06-00; e-mail anthpub@iea .ras.ru; internet www.iea.ras.ru; f. 1933; attached to Russian Acad. of Sciences; library of 60,000 vols; Dir V. A. TISHKOV; publs *Etnograficheskoe obozrenie* (Ethnographic Review, 6 a year), *Bulletin of Ethnological Monitoring* (6 a year).

Research and Training Centre for Problems of Human Activity: 117279 Moscow, ul. Profsoyuznaya 83B; tel. (095) 333-01-02; attached to Russian Acad. of Sciences; Gen. Dir V. A. SHESTAKOV.

TECHNOLOGY

Accounting Machine Building Research Institute: 115230 Moscow, Varshavskoe shosse 42; tel. (095) 111-51-61.

All-Russia Electrotechnical Institute (VEI): 111250 Moscow, Krasnokazarmennaya ul. 12; tel. (095) 362-55-08; fax (095) 362-56-17; e-mail vkozlov@online.ru.

All-Russia Logachev Scientific Research Institute of Exploration Geophysics (VIRG-Rudgeofizika): 193019 St Petersburg, Fayansovaya ul. 20; tel. (812) 567-68-03; fax (812) 567-87-41; e-mail virg@lek.ru; internet www.virg.spb.ru; f. 1945; development of instruments and technology for predicting, exploring, evaluating and mining ores and diamonds, drilling for oil and gas; solving environmental problems; provision of services in these areas; library of 54,000 vols; Dir G. N. MIKHAILOV; publs *Geophysical Instruments, Russian Journal of Geophysics* (both every 6 months).

All-Russia Oil Geological Prospecting Institute: 191104 St Petersburg, Liteinyi pr. 39; tel. (812) 273-43-83; fax (812) 273-73-87.

All-Russia Railway Transport Research Institute: 129851 Moscow, 3-ya Mytishchinskaya ul. 10; tel. (095) 687-64-23; fax (095) 687-65-48; internet www.vniizht.ru; f. 1917; Dir A. E. SEMECHLIN; publ. *Vestnik VNIIZhT* (monthly).

All-Russia Research and Design Institute for Atomic Power Station Equipment: 125171 Moscow, ul. Volkova Kosmonavta 6A; tel. (095) 150-83-55.

All-Russia Research and Design Institute for Problems of the Development of Oil and Gas Resources on the Continental Shelf: 107078 Moscow, Kalanchevskaya ul. 11; tel. (095) 971-51-03; fax (095) 280-23-57; Dir I. B. DUBIN.

All-Russia Research and Design Institute of Electroceramics: 111024 Moscow, shosse Entuziastov 17; tel. (095) 273-13-34.

All-Russia Research and Design Institute of Metallurgical Engineering: 109428 Moscow, Ryazansky pr. 8A; tel. (095) 174-37-00; attached to Russian Acad. of Sciences; Gen. Dir V. M. SINITSKY.

All-Russia Research and Design Institute of the Oil-Refining and Petrochemical Industry: 107005 Moscow, ul. Fridrikha Engelsa 32; tel. (095) 261-96-26; fax (095) 261-66-44; e-mail vnipineft@vnipineft.ru; internet www.vnipineft.ru; f. 1929; Dir V. M. NIKITIN.

All-Russia Research, Design and Technological Institute of Lighting Technology: 129626 Moscow, pr. Mira 106; tel. (095) 287-13-52; fax (095) 287-08-91; e-mail vnisi@com2com.ru; f. 1953.

All-Russia Research Institute for Nuclear Power Plant Operation: 109507 Moscow, Ferganskaya 25; tel. (095) 376-15-43; fax (095) 376-83-33; f. 1979; Dir-Gen. Prof. A. A. ABAGYAN.

All-Russia Research Institute for Oil Refining JSC: 111116 Moscow, Aviamotornaya ul. 6; tel. (095) 261-52-02; fax (095) 261-02-95; f. 1933; Dir E. F. KAMINSKY; publ. *Mir Nefteproduktov* (The World of Oil Products, 4 a year).

All-Russia Research Institute for the Canned and Vegetable Dry Products Industry: 142703 Moscow oblast, Vidnoe, Shkolnaya 78; tel. (095) 541-08-72; attached to Russian Acad. of Agricultural Sciences.

All-Russia Research Institute for the Dairy Industry: 113093 Moscow, Lyusinovskaya 35; tel. (095) 236-31-64; attached to Russian Acad. of Agricultural Sciences.

All-Russia Research Institute for the Protection of Metals from Corrosion: 125209 Moscow, Baltiiskaya ul. 14; tel. (095) 151-55-01.

All-Russia Research Institute for the Refrigeration Industry: 125422 Moscow, ul. Kostyakova 12; tel. (095) 216-00-04; attached to Russian Acad. of Agricultural Sciences; Dir V. F. LEBEDEV.

All-Russia Research Institute of Electrical Insulating Materials and Foiled Dielectrics: 111250 Moscow, Krasnokazarmennaya ul. 12; tel. (095) 273-24-78.

All-Russia Research Institute of Electromechanics (VNIIEM): 101000 Moscow, Glavpochtamt Box 496 VNIIEM, Khoromny Tupik 4; tel. (095) 208-84-67; fax (095) 207-49-62; f. 1941; research and development in space technology, monitoring and control systems for nuclear reactors, electromechanical systems, devices and materials; library of 200,000 vols; Dir Dr S. A. STOMA; publ. *Trudy VNIIEM* (proceedings, 3 a year).

All-Russia Research Institute of Exploration Geophysics: 101000 Moscow, ul. Pokrovka 22; tel. (095) 925-45-13; fax (095) 956-39-38; f. 1944; library of 50,000 vols; Dir A. V. MIKHALTSEV; publs *Prikladnaya Geofizika* (2 a year), *Razvedochnaya Geofizika*.

All-Russia Research Institute of Fibre-Optic Systems of Communication and Data Processing: 107066 Moscow, Khiznyaya Krasnoselskaya ul. 13, korp. 1; tel. (095) 267-20-31.

All-Russia Research Institute of Food Biotechnology: 109033 Moscow, Samokatnaya ul. 4B; tel. (095) 362-44-95; attached to Russian Acad. of Agricultural Sciences.

All-Russia Research Institute of Fuel and Energy Problems (VNIIKTEP): 117259 Moscow, Bol. Cheremushkinskaya 34; tel. (095) 128-90-14; fax (095) 128-85-91; f. 1975; library of 63,000 vols; Dir N. K. PRAVEDNIKOV; publ. *The Fuel and Energy Complex of Russia* (annually).

All-Russia Research Institute of Helium Technology: 119270 Moscow, Luzhnetskaya nab. 10A; tel. (095) 242-50-77; fax (095) 234-91-11.

All-Russia Research Institute of Mineral Resources and the Use of the Subsurface: 123007 Moscow, 3-ya Magistralnaya 38; tel. (095) 259-69-88; fax (095) 259-91-25; e-mail info@viems.ru; internet www.viems.ru; f. 1964; attached to Russian Acad. of Sciences and Russian Min. of Natural Resources; Dir-Gen. M.A. KOMAROV.

All-Russia Research Institute of Organic Synthesis (VNIIOS): 105005 Moscow, ul. Radio 12; tel. (095) 261-96-88; fax (095) 261-07-77; e-mail vniios@aha.ru; internet www.vniios.ru; f. 1949; Dir-Gen. V. K. S. CHERNYKH.

All-Russia Research Institute of Problems of Computer Technology and Information Science: 113114 Moscow, 2-i Kozhevnichesky per. 4/6; tel. (095) 235-58-09; Dir V. ZAKHAROV.

All-Russia Research Institute of Radiotechnology: 107055 Moscow, Bol. Pochtovaya ul. 55–59; tel. (095) 267-66-04.

All-Russia Research Institute of Refractory Metals and Hard Alloys: 115430 Moscow, Varshavskoe shosse 56; tel. (095) 113-55-72.

All-Russia Research Institute of Starch Products: 140052 Moscow oblast, pos. Korenevo, ul. Nekrasova; tel. (095) 557-15-00; attached to Russian Acad. of Agricultural Sciences.

All-Russia Research Institute of Television and Radio Broadcasting JSC: 123298 Moscow, 3-ya Khoroshevskaya ul. 12; tel. (095) 192-90-02; fax (095) 943-00-06; e-mail vniitr@online.ru; internet www.vniitr.com; f. 1934; Gen. Dir ALEXANDER S. MKRTUMOV; publ. *Teleraidoveshchaniye* (4 a year).

All-Russia Research Institute of the Cable Industry: 111112 Moscow, shosse Entuziastov 5; tel. (095) 278-02-16.

All-Russia Research Institute of Trunk Pipeline Construction: 105058 Moscow, Okruzhnoi pr-d 19; tel. (095) 366-68-39.

All-Russia Scientific Research Institute for Exploration Methods and Engineering: 199106 St Petersburg, Veselnaya ul. 6; tel. (812) 322-78-53; fax (812) 322-79-37; e-mail vitr@spb.cityline.ru; f. 1955; drilling equipment and techniques for minerals and water; library of 30,000 vols, patents; Dir IVAN S. AFANASYEV; publ. *Collection of Scientific Works* (4–6 a year).

All-Russia Scientific Research Institute of Aviation Materials (VIAM): 107005 Moscow, ul. Radio 17; tel. (095) 261-86-77; fax (095) 267-86-09; e-mail admin@viam.ru; internet www.viam.ru; f. 1932; Dir-Gen. EVGENY N. KABLOV; publ. *Aircraft Materials and Technology* (annually).

All-Russia Scientific Research Institute of Fats: 191119 St Petersburg, ul. Chernyakovskogo 10; tel. (812) 164-15-24; fax (812) 112-25-74; e-mail wniig@peterlink.ru; f. 1933; attached to Russian Acad. of Agricultural Sciences; Dir ALEXANDER N. LISITSYN; publs *Vestnik* (newsletter, 2 a year), *Trudy* (works, irregular).

All-Russia Scientific Research Institute of Natural and Synthetic Diamonds and Tools: 129110 Moscow, ul. Giliarovskogo 65; tel. (095) 281-59-07; fax (095) 288-99-42; f. 1948; library of 25,000 vols; Dir N. A. KOLCHEMANOV; publ. *Works of VNIIALMAZ* (annually).

All-Russia Scientific Research Institute of Technical Physics and Automation: 115230 Moscow, Varshavskoe shosse 46; tel. (095) 111-9811; fax (095) 111-5431; e-mail vniitfa@tsmail.ru; internet www.vniitfa.ru; f. 1960 as Research Institute of Radiation Technology; Dir NIKOLAY KUZELEV.

Blagonravov, A. A., Institute of Machine Science: 101830 Moscow, ul. Griboedova 4; tel. (095) 924-98-00; attached to Russian Acad. of Sciences; brs in St Petersburg, Samara, Saratov, Nizhnii Novgorod; Dir Acad. K. V. FROLOV.

Budnikov, P. P., All-Russia Research Institute of Construction Materials and Structures: 140080 Moscow, pos. Kraskovo, ul. Karla Marksa 117; tel. (095) 557-30-66; fax (095) 557-30-09; f. 1931; library of 180,000 vols; Dir YU. GUDKOV; publs *Ceramic Materials*, *Gypsum binders and products*, *Autoclaved Materials* (all annually).

Burenie Scientific and Production Co.: 350624 Krasnodar, ul. Mira 34; tel. (8612) 62-23-34; fax (8612) 62-23-34; f. 1970; drilling and maintenance of wells; library of 100,000 vols; Gen. Dir Dr SERGEI A. RYABOKON.

Central Automobile and Automobile Engine Scientific Research Institute: 125438 Moscow, Avtomotornaya ul. 2; tel. (095) 456-36-91; fax (095) 943-00-30; e-mail root@gnc.nami.extech.msk.su; f. 1918; library of 106,000 vols, special collections 93,600 vols; Dir Prof. V. KUTENEV; publ. various journals.

Central Boiler and Turbine Institute: 194021 St Petersburg, Politekhnicheskaya ul. 24; tel. (812) 277-95-64; fax (812) 277-40-95; e-mail ckti@neva.spb.ru; internet www.ckti.ru; f. 1927; Dir-Gen E. K. CHAVCHANIDZE.

Central Design and Research Institute of the Standard and Experimental Design of Livestock Units for the Production of Milk, Beef and Pork: 121002 Moscow, Maly Mogiltsevsky per. 3; tel. (095) 241-36-82.

Central Diesels Research and Development Institute: 196158 St Petersburg, Moskovskoe shosse 25, korp. 1; tel. (812) 291-65-81; fax (812) 291-22-73; f. 1924; library of 62,000 vols; Dir V. BORDUKOV; publ. *Dvigatelestroynie* (4 a year).

Central Electronics Research Institute: 117415 Moscow, pr. Vernadskogo 39; tel. (095) 432-93-30; fax (095) 431-58-86; f. 1964; Dir B. N. AVDONIN.

Central Institute of Aviation Engines: 111116 Moscow, Aviamotornaya ul. 2; tel. (095) 361-64-81; fax (095) 267-13-54; f. 1930; Dir V. SKIBIN.

Central Marine Research and Design Institute Ltd (CNIIMF): 193015 St Petersburg, Kavalergardskaya ul. 6; tel. (812) 271-12-83; fax (812) 274-38-64; f. 1929; shipbuilding, marine equipment, navigation, transport technology; library of 312,000 vols; Dir VSEVOLOD I. PERESYPKIN; publ. *Transactions*.

Central Paper Research Institute: 141290 Moscow oblast, Pushkinsky raion, pos. Pravdinsky, ul. Lenina 15/1; tel. (095) 584-36-23; fax (095) 292-65-11; f. 1918; library of 90,000 vols; Dir B. V. OREKHOV; publs *Research Papers of ZNIIB* (annually), *Pulp, Paper, Board* (monthly).

Central Research and Design Institute of Fuel Apparatus and Vehicle and Tractor Engines and Stationary Engines: 192102 St Petersburg, Volkovskii pr-d 102; tel. (812) 166-91-11.

Central Research Institute for Machine Building: 141070 Moscow oblast, Korolev, Pionyerskaya ul. 4; tel. (095) 513-50-00; fax (095) 187-03-22; e-mail anfimov@mcc.rsa.ru; f. 1946; spacecraft and rocket engineering, aero and gas dynamics, heat and mass exchange, strength of materials, reliability, mission control for spacecraft and space stations; library of 100,000 vols; Dir NIKOLAI A. ANFIMOV; publs *Astronautics and Rocket Engineering* (3 or 4 a year), *Rocketry and Space Technology* (weekly).

Central Research Institute of Coating Materials and Artificial Leathers: 113184 Moscow, ul. Bakhrushina 11; tel. (095) 953-23-55; fax (095) 951-39-27; e-mail cniipik@mail.ru; Dir Dr C. N. KOZLOV.

Central Research Institute of Engineering Technology: 109088 Moscow, Sharikopodshipnikovskaya ul. 4; tel. (095) 275-83-00.

Central Research Institute of Geological Prospecting for Base and Precious Metals: 113545 Moscow, Varshovskoe shosse 129b; tel. (095) 313-18-18; fax (095) 315-28-74; e-mail tsnigri@tsnigri.ru; internet www.tsnigri.ru; f. 1935; forecasting, prospecting, exploration and assessment of deposits of base and precious metals; 400 mems; Dir Dr IGOR MIGACHEV; publs *Otechestvennaya Geologia* (6 a year), *Rudy i Metally* (in Russian with English abstracts, 6 a year).

Central Research Institute of Telecommunications: 111141 Moscow, 1-i pr-d Perova Polya 8; tel. (095) 304-57-97; fax (095) 274-00-67.

Central Research Institute of the Ministry of Defence: 141090 Moscow oblast, Bolshevo, V/Ch 25840; tel. (095) 472-92-12; Dir L. I. VOLKOV.

Central Research Laboratory for the Introduction of Personal Computers: c/o Russian Academy of Sciences, 117901 Moscow, Leninsky pr. 14; attached to Russian Acad. of Sciences; Dir A. N. ILIN.

Central Scientific Research and Design Institute of the Wood Chemical Industry: 603603 Nizhnii Novgorod, Moskovskoe shosse 85, GSP 703; tel. (8312) 41-36-98; fax (8312) 41-36-90; f. 1932; library of 146,000 vols; Dir VICTOR YA. BONDAREV; publ. *Scientific Works* (annually).

Concrete and Reinforced Concrete Research Design and Technological Institute: 109428 Moscow, Vtoraya Institutskaya ul. 6; tel. (095) 171-26-69; fax (095) 174-77-24; e-mail niizhb@niizhb.ru; internet www.niizhb.ru; f. 1927; development of standards and norms for concrete construction and design; certification testing; postgraduate courses; 400 mems; library of 200,000 vols; Dir Dr A. I. ZVEZDOV; Deputy Dir Dr V. FALIKMAN; Scientific Dir Dr T. MOUKHAMEDIEV; publs *Proceedings of NIIZLB* (annually), *Beton i Zhelezobeton* (Concrete and Reinforced Concrete, 6 a year).

Design and Research Institute of the Synthetic Rubber Industry: 105318 Moscow, ul. Ibragimova 15; tel. (095) 366-43-44; fax (095) 369-52-55; Dir S. I. KARTASHOV.

Design and Technological Institute of Monocrystals: 630058 Novosibirsk, Russkaya ul. 43; tel. (3832) 33-22-39; fax (3832) 33-22-59; e-mail chepurov@crystal.nsk.su; f. 1978; attached to Russian Acad. of Sciences; Head ANATOLY I. CHEPUROV.

Dollezhal, N. A. Research and Development Institute of Power Engineering: 101000 Moscow, POB 788; tel. (095) 263-73-13; fax (095) 975-20-19; e-mail nikiet@nikiet.ru; internet www.nikiet.ru; f. 1952; nuclear power, thermal physics and hydrodynamics; radiation, nuclear and environmental safety of nuclear reactors; strength, reliability and material science; conversion of nuclear technologies; library of 200,000 vols; Dir B. A. GABARAEV.

Dorodnitsyn Computing Centre of the Russian Academy of Sciences (CC RAS): 119991 Moscow, GSP-1, ul. Vavilova 40; fax (095) 135-61-59; e-mail wcan@ccas.ru; internet www.ccas.ru; attached to Russian Acad. of Sciences; scientific divisions: mechanics and mathematical physics, informatics and mathematical cybernetics, mathematical systems and decisions modelling, mathematical and programming software, computational technique; Dir Prof. YU. G. EVTUSHENKO.

Constituent centres of the Theoretical and Applied Informatics and Mechanics Research and Educational Centre of CC RAS:

Theoretical and Applied Mechanics Research and Education Centre: Head Acad. V. RUMYANTSEV.

Informatics, Pattern Recognition, Image Analysis, Intelligent Information Technologies and Systems Research and Education Centre: Head Acad. YU. ZHURAVLEV.

New Computer Technology Research and Education Centre: Head Acad. YU. ZHURAVLEV.

Computer Education and New Information Technology Research and Education Centre: Head YU. PAVLOVSKY.

Intelligent Systems and Fuzzy Logic Research and Education Centre: Head Dr A. AVERKIN.

Applied Mathematics and Informatics Research and Education Centre: Head YU. EVTUSHENKO.

Pure and Applied Mathematics Research and Education Centre: Head YU. EVTUSHENKO.

Thermal Physics of Gasdynamic Systems Research and Education Centre: Head Dr N. SEVERTSEV.

Efremov, D. V., Institute of Electrophysical Apparatus: 196641 St Petersburg, Sovetsky pr. 1; tel. (812) 464-89-63; fax (812) 464-79-79; e-mail glukhikh@niiefa.spb.su; internet www.niiefa.spb.su; f. 1945; Dir V. A. GLUKHIKH; publ. *Plasma Devices and Operations*.

Electronic Control Machines Research Institute: 117812 Moscow, ul. Vavilova 24; tel. (095) 135-32-21; Dir N. L. PROKHOROV.

Energy Systems Institute: 664033 Irkutsk, Lermontova ul. 130; tel. (3952) 42-47-00; fax (3952) 42-44-44; e-mail root@isem.sei.irk.ru; internet www.sei.irk.ru; f. 1960; attached to Russian Acad. of Sciences; Dir N. I. VOROPAI.

Ershov, A. P., Institute of Informatics Systems: 630090 Novosibirsk, pr. Akad. Lavrenteva 6; tel. (3832) 35-56-52; fax (3832) 32-34-94; f. 1990; attached to Russian Acad. of Sciences; library of 100,000 vols; Dir Prof. ALEXANDER G. MARCHUK; publ. *Systems Informatics* (annually).

Experimental Factory for Analytical Instrumentation: 198510 St Petersburg, Lomonosov, ul. Fedyuninskogo 3; tel. (812) 473-06-48; attached to Russian Acad. of Sciences; Dir V. I. STEPANOV.

Experimental Factory for Scientific Instrumentation: 142342 Moscow oblast, Noginsk raion, p/o Chernogolovka; tel. (095) 524-50-05; attached to Russian Acad. of Sciences; Dir L. P. KOKURIN.

Experimental Research Institute of Metal-Cutting Machine Tools: 117419 Moscow, 5-i Donskoi pr-d 21B; tel. (095) 952-39-63; Dir V. S. BELOV.

Far Eastern Research Institute of Mineral Raw Materials: 680005 Khabarovsk, ul. Gerasimova 31; tel. (4212) 34-28-43; Dir YU. I. BAKULIN.

Fedorov, E. K., Institute of Applied Geophysics: 129128 Moscow, Rostokinskaya ul. 9; tel. (095) 181-37-14; Dir S. I. AVDYUSHIN.

Gubkin, I. M., Institute of the Petrochemical and Gas Industry: 117917 Moscow, Leninsky pr. 65; tel. (095) 234-22-92.

High-Technology Ceramics Research Centre: 119361 Moscow, Ozernaya ul. 48; tel. (095) 430-77-70; fax (095) 437-98-93; attached to Russian Acad. of Sciences; Dir V. YA. SHEVCHENKO.

Hydrochemical Institute: 344090 Rostov on Don, pr. Stachki 198; tel. (8632) 22-44-70; fax (8632) 22-44-70; e-mail ghi@aaanet.ru; f. 1920; library of 40,000 vols; Dir A. M. NIKANOROV; publ. *Gidrokhimicheskiye Materialy* (3 a year).

Image Processing Systems Institute: 44300 Samara, ul. Molodogvardeya 151; tel. (8462) 32-57-83; fax (8462) 32-27-63; e-mail soifer@space.samara.su; f. 1988; attached to Russian Acad. of Sciences; library of 1,000 vols; Dir Prof. V. A. SOIFER; publ. *Computer Optics* (in Russian, 2 a year).

Institute for Systems Analysis: 117312 Moscow, pr. 60-letia Oktyabrya 9; tel. (095) 135-42-22; fax (095) 938-22-09; e-mail isa@isa.ru; internet www.isa.ru; f. 1976; attached to Russian Acad. of Sciences; Dir YU. S. POPKOV.

Institute of Analytical Instrumentation: 198103 St Petersburg, Rizhsky pr. 26; tel. (812) 251-86-00; fax (812) 251-70-38; e-mail iap@ianin.spb.su; internet www.iai.rssi.ru; f. 1977; attached to Russian Acad. of Sciences; Dir N. I. KOMYAK; publ. *Scientific Instrumentation* (4 a year).

Institute of Applied Mathematics: 690041 Vladivostok, ul. Radio 7; tel. (4232) 31-33-30; fax (4232) 31-18-56; f. 1988; attached to Russian Acad. of Sciences; library of 21,000 vols; Dir Prof. N. V. KUZNETSOV.

Institute of Applied Mechanics: c/o Russian Academy of Sciences, 119991 Moscow, Leninsky pr.; tel. (095) 938-18-45; fax (095) 938-07-11; e-mail iam@ipsun.ras.ru; attached to Russian Acad. of Sciences; Dir YU. G.YANOVSKY; publ. *Journal on Composite Materials and Design* (4 a year).

Institute of Applied Mechanics: 426067 Izhevsk, T. Baramzinoy 34; tel. (3412) 50-88-10; fax (3412) 50-79-59; e-mail foipm@udm.ru; internet www.udman.ru; f. 1989; attached to Russian Acad. of Sciences; physics and mechanics of heterogenous media; problems of mechanics of deformed solid and material tribo-technology; new materials; 150 mems; Dir A. M. LIPANOV; publ. *Chemical Physics and Mezoscopy* (4 a year).

Institute of Automation and Control Processes: 690041 Vladivostok, ul. Radio 5; tel. (4232) 31-04-39; fax (4232) 31-04-52; e-mail director@iacp.vl.ru; internet www.dvo.ru/iacp; f. 1971; attached to Russian Acad. of Sciences; Dir V. P. MYASNIKOV.

Institute of Automation and Electrometry: 630090 Novosibirsk, Universitetskii pr. 1; tel. (3832) 35-10-52; fax (3832) 35-48-51; e-mail malinovsky@iae.nsk.su; attached to Russian Acad. of Sciences; Dir Prof. S. T. VASKOV.

Institute of Biological Instrumentation: 123373 Moscow, Volokalamskoe shosse 91; tel. (095) 491-73-72; Dir V. N. ZLOBIN.

Institute of Chemistry and Chemical Technology: 660049 Krasnoyarsk, ul. K. Marksa 42; tel. (3912) 27-38-31; fax (3912)

23-86-58; e-mail chem@krsk.info; internet krsk.info/icct; f. 1981; attached to Russian Acad. of Sciences; Dir Prof. G.L. PASHKOV; publs *Proceedings of Workshops* (every 3 years), *Siberian Gold* (symposium proceedings, every 2 years).

Institute of Computational Technologies: 630090 Novosibirsk, pr. Akad. Lavrenteva 6; tel. (3833) 30-61-50; fax (3833) 30-63-42; e-mail shokin@ict.nsc.ru; internet www.ict.nsc.ru; f. 1990; attached to Russian Acad. of Sciences; Head YU. I. SHOKIN; publ. *Journal of Computational Technologies* (10 a year).

Institute of Continuous Media Mechanics: 614013 Perm, ul. Akad. Koroleva 1; tel. (3422) 33-07-21; fax (3422) 33-69-57; e-mail mvp@admin.icmm.perm.su; f. 1971; attached to Russian Acad. of Sciences; Dir V. P. MATVEYENKO.

Institute of Control Sciences, Automation and Telemechanics: 117806 Moscow, ul. Profsoyuznaya 65; tel. (095) 334-89-10; fax (095) 334-93-40; e-mail vasmac@ipu.rssi.ru; attached to Russian Acad. of Sciences; Dir Acad. I. V. PRANGISHVILI.

Institute of Electronic Measurement 'Kvarz': 603009 Nizhnii Novgorod, pr. Gagarina 176; tel. (8312) 66-70-93; fax (8312) 66-55-62; e-mail nnipi_kvarz@sinn.ru; internet www.kvarz.ru; f. 1949; research, development and manufacture of electronic measurement equipment; 1,200 mems; Dir-Gen. A. M. KUDRIAVTSEV; publ. *Electronic Measurements* (in Russian, annually).

Institute of Energy Research: 117333 Moscow, ul. Vavilova 44, korp. 2; tel. (095) 127-48-34; attached to Russian Acad. of Sciences; Dir A. A. MAKAROV.

Institute of Engineering Science: 620219 Ekaterinburg, Komsomolskaya ul. 34, GSP-207; tel. (343) 374-47-25; fax (343) 374-53-30; e-mail ges@imach.uranru; internet www.imach.uran.ru; f. 1986; attached to Russian Acad. of Sciences; research into mechanics of solids and structures, advanced materials and technologies; automated systems of measurements, nondestructive testing and diagnostics of machine life; mechanics and control of transportation and traction machines; creation of basic algorithms, software and hardware for systems of automated control of compound objects; library of 16,700 vols; Dir Prof. E. S. GORKUNOV.

Institute of High Current Electronics: 634055 Tomsk, pr. Akademichesky 2–3; tel. (3822) 49-15-44; fax (3822) 49-24-10; e-mail contact@hcei.tsc.ru; internet www.hcei.tsc.ru; f. 1977; attached to Russian Acad. of Sciences; library of 50,000 vols; Dir Academician SERGEI D. KOROVIN.

Institute of Informatics Problems of the Russian Academy of Sciences (IPIRAN): 119333 Moscow, ul. Vavilova 44-2; tel. (095) 137-34-94; fax (095) 930-45-05; e-mail sshorgin@ipiran.ru; internet www.ipiran.ru; f. 1983; attached to Russian Acad. of Sciences; fundamental and applied research and development in integrated information-telecommunication networks and systems and stochastic systems; theoretical problems and applied technologies in accumulation, processing and representation of information; creation of computerized information systems; Dir IGOR SOKOLOV; publs *Systems and Methods of Informatics* (annual), *Informatics and Its Applications* (quarterly).

Institute of Information Science and Automation: 199178 St Petersburg, 14 liniya 39; tel. (812) 218-03-82; attached to Russian Acad. of Sciences; Dir V. M. PONOMAREV.

Institute of Information Transmission Problems: 127994 Moscow GSP-4, Bol. Karetny per. 19; tel. (095) 209-42-25; fax (095) 209-05-79; e-mail director@iitp.ru; internet www.iitp.ru; f. 1961; attached to Russian Acad. of Sciences; Dir N. A. KUZNETSOV; publs *Automation and Remote Control* (monthly), *Problems in Information Transmission* (4 a year).

Institute of Laser and Information Technology: 140700 Moscow oblast, Shatura, Svyatoozerskaya ul. 1; tel. (09645) 2-59-95; fax (09645) 2-25-32; e-mail ilit@laser.ru; internet www.laser.ru; f. 1979; attached to Russian Acad. of Sciences; library of 35,000 vols; Dir Prof. V. YA. PANCHENKO.

Institute of Mathematics and Mechanics: 620219 Ekaterinburg, ul. S. Kovalevskoi 16; tel. (3432) 374-83-32; fax (3432) 374-25-81; e-mail bvi@imm.uran.ru; internet www.imm.uran.ru; f. 1956; attached to Ural Branch of the Russian Acad. of Sciences; Dir Prof. V. I. BERDYSHEV; publ. *Proceedings* (in Russian, annually; in English, 2 a year).

Institute of Medical Instrument Making: 125422 Moscow, Timiryazevskaya ul. 1; tel. (095) 211-09-65; fax (095) 200-22-13; attached to Russian Acad. of Medical Sciences; Dir V. A. VIKTOROV.

Institute of Mining, Khabarovsk: 680000 Khabarovsk, ul. Turgeneva 51; tel. (4212) 33-79-27; attached to Russian Acad. of Sciences; Dir G. V. SEKISOV.

Institute of Mining, Novosibirsk: 630091 Novosibirsk, Krasny pr. 54; tel. (3832) 17-05-36; fax (3832) 17-06-78; e-mail admin@misd.nsc.ru; internet www.misd.nsc.ru; f. 1944; attached to Russian Acad. of Sciences; library of 40,000 vols; Dir OPARIN VICTOR NIKOLAEVICH; Academic Sec. TARASIK T. MIKHAILOVNA; publ. *Journal of Mining Science* (6 a year).

Institute of Mining of the North: 677018 Yakutsk, ul. Lenina 43; tel. (4112) 44-59-30; fax (4112) 44-59-30; e-mail igds@sci.yakutia.ru; f. 1980; attached to Russian Acad. of Sciences; Dir Dr M. D. NOVOPASHIN.

Institute of Mining, Perm: 614007 Perm, Sibirskaya ul. 78A; tel. (3422) 16-75-02; fax (3422) 16-09-69; e-mail arc@mine.perm.su; f. 1988; attached to Russian Acad. of Sciences; library of 3,000 vols; Dir Prof. ARKADI E. KRASNOSHTEIN; publs *Mining Echo* (4 a year), *Collection of Scientific and Research Works* (annually), *Proceedings* (irregular).

Institute of Monitoring of Climatic and Ecological Systems: 634055 Tomsk, Akademicheskii pr. 10/3; tel. (3822) 492265; fax (3822) 491950; e-mail post@iom.tomsknet.ru; internet www.imces.tsc.ru; f. 1972; attached to Russian Acad. of Sciences; fmrly the Institute of Optical Monitoring; Dir M. V. KABANOV.

Institute of Petrochemistry and Catalysis: 450075 Bashkortostan, Ufa, pr. Oktyabrya 141; tel. and fax (3472) 31-27-50; e-mail ink@anrb.ru; internet www.anrb.ru/ink/index.html; f. 1992; Dir USAIN M. DZHEMILEV.

Institute of Petroleum Refining and Petrochemistry: 450065 Bashkortostan, Ufa, Initsiativnaya ul. 12; tel. (3472) 43-31-17; fax (3472) 43-31-17; e-mail ipnhp@anrb.ru; f. 1956; Dir E. G. TELIASHEV.

Institute of Physical and Technical Problems of the North: 677891 Yakutsk, Oktyabrskaya ul. 1; tel. (4112) 44-66-65; fax (4112) 44-66-65; e-mail v.p.larionov@sci.yakutia.ru; attached to Russian Acad. of Sciences; f. 1970; Dir Acad. V. P. LARIONOV.

Institute of Physics and Power Engineering: Bondarenko pl. 1, 249033 Kaluga oblast, Obninsk; tel. (08439) 98250; fax (08439) 58545; e-mail avzrod@ippe.obninsk.ru; internet www.ippe.ru; f. 1946; nuclear systems for civil and defence purposes; nuclear, laser and reactor physics; thermal physics, hydro-, gas and plasma-dynamics, liquid-metal coolant technologies; radiation material science; 3,800 mems; library of 320,000 vols; Dir-Gen. ANATOLY V. ZRODNIKOV.

Institute of Problems in Cybernetics: 117312 Moscow, ul. Vavilova 37; tel. (095) 124-77-67; attached to Russian Acad. of Sciences; Dir (vacant).

Institute of Problems in the Complex Utilization of Mineral Resources: 111020 Moscow, Kryukovskii tupik 4; tel. and fax (095) 360-89-60; e-mail info@ipkonran.ru; internet www.ipkonran.ru; f. 1977; attached to Russian Acad. of Sciences; Dir V. A. CHANTURIA.

Institute of Problems in the Safe Development of Nuclear Energy: 113191 Moscow, Bol. Tulskaya ul. 52; tel. (095) 955-26-47; attached to Russian Acad. of Sciences; Dir L. A. BOLSHOV.

Institute of Problems of Marine Technology: 690600 Vladivostok, ul. Sukhanova 5A; tel. (4232) 22-64-16; fax (4232) 22-64-51; e-mail ageev@marine.febras.ru; f. 1988; attached to Russian Acad. of Sciences; Dir M. D. AGEEV.

Institute of Problems of Mechanics: 119526 Moscow, pr. Vernadskogo 101; tel. (495) 434-32-38; fax (495) 938-20-48; f. 1965; attached to Russian Acad. of Sciences; library of 150,000 vols; Dir Prof. F. L. CHERNOUSKO.

Institute of Programmable Systems: 152140 Pereslavl-Zalesskii; tel. (08535) 9-81-21; attached to Russian Acad. of Sciences; Dir A. K. AILAMAZYAN.

Institute of Radio Engineering and Electronics: 103907 Moscow, Mokhovaya ul. 8; pr. K. Marksa 18; tel. (095) 203-52-93; fax (095) 200-52-58; attached to Russian Acad. of Sciences; br. in Saratov; Dir Acad. YU. V. GULYAEV.

Institute of Regional Systems Research: Birobidzhan; attached to Russian Acad. of Sciences; (in process of formation).

Institute of Remote Sensing Methods for Geology (VNIIKAM): 199034 St Petersburg, Birzhevoi pr-d 6; tel. (812) 218-28-01; fax (812) 218-39-16; Dir ALEXEI V. PERTSOV.

Institute of Solid State Chemistry and Mechanochemistry: 630128 Novosibirsk, Kutateladze ul. 18; tel. (3832) 32-96-00; fax (3832) 32-28-47; e-mail root@solid.nsk.su; internet www.solid.nsc.ru; f. 1944; attached to Russian Acad. of Sciences; library of 50,000 vols; 230 mems; Dir Prof. N. Z. LYAKHOV; publ. *Chemistry for Sustainable Development* (every 2 months).

Institute of Synthetic Polymer Materials: 117393 Moscow, Profsoyuznaya 70; tel. (095) 335-91-00; attached to Russian Acad. of Sciences; Dir (vacant).

Institute of Technical Chemistry: 614013 Perm, ul. ak. Koroleva; tel. and fax (342) 237-82-90; e-mail techem@permonline.ru; internet www.itch.permonline.ru; f. 1985; attached to Russian Acad. of Sciences; Dir Dr V. N. STRELNIKOV.

Institute of the Automation of Design: 123056 Moscow, 2-ya Brestskaya; tel. (095) 250-02-62; attached to Russian Acad. of Sciences; Dir O. M. BELOTSERKOVSKY.

Institute of the Economics and Organization of Industrial Production: 630090 Novosibirsk, pr. Akad. Lavrenteva 17; tel. (3832) 35-05-36; fax (3832) 35-55-80; attached to Russian Acad. of Sciences; Dir (vacant).

Institute of the Geology and Exploitation of Fossil Fuels: 117312 Moscow, ul. Fersmana 50; tel. (095) 124-91-55; attached to Russian Acad. of Sciences; Dir N. KRYLOV.

Institute of Informatics and Mathematical Modelling of Technological Processes: 184200 Murmansk oblast, Apatity, ul. Fersmana 24A; tel. (81555) 7-40-50; fax (81555) 7-42-26; e-mail putilov@iimm.kolasc.net.ru; f. 1989; attached to Russian Acad. of Sciences; Dir Dr V. A. PUTILOV; publ. *Computer-Aided Simulation*.

Institute of Theoretical and Applied Mechanics: 630090 Novosibirsk, Institutskaya ul. 4/1; tel. (3832) 33-35-34; fax (3832) 34-22-68; e-mail fomin@itam.nsc.ru; internet www.itam.nsc.ru; f. 1957; attached to Russian Acad. of Sciences; library of 87,000 vols; Dir Prof. V. M. FOMIN; publs *Journal of Applied Mechanics and Technical Physics* (6 a year), *Combustion, Explosion and Shock Waves* (6 a year), *Thermophysics and Aeromechanics* (4 a year), *Physical Mesomechanics* (4 a year).

Institute of Trade Machinery: 127521 Moscow, Scheremetevskaya ul. 47; tel. (095) 218-51-47; fax (095) 219-73-21; f. 1961; Dir VYACHESLAV LVOVICH UMANSKY.

Ioffe, Acad. A. F., Physical-Technical Institute: 194021 St Petersburg, Politeckhnicheskaya ul. 26; tel. (812) 247-21-45; fax (812) 247-10-17; attached to Russian Acad. of Sciences; br. in Shuvalovo; Dir Acad. ZH. I. ALFEROV.

Joint Russian-Vietnamese Tropical Research and Testing Centre: 117071 Moscow, Leninsky pr. 33; tel. (095) 954-12-19; f. 1987; attached to Russian Acad. of Sciences; long-term health consequences of Agent Orange, ecology, tropical resistance of materials and equipment; Head Acad. V. E. SOKOLOV.

Kargin, V. A., Polymer Research Institute: 606006 Nizhegorodskaya oblast, Dzerzhinsk; tel. (8313) 25-50-00; fax (8313) 33-13-18; e-mail niip@kis.ru; internet www.advtech.ru/Nipolymer/nipolymer1.htm; f. 1949; library of 142,000 vols; Gen. Dir Prof. V. V. GUZEEV.

Kazan Physical-Technical Institute: 420029 Kazan, ul. Sibirskii trakt 10/7; tel. (8432) 76-50-44; attached to Russian Acad. of Sciences; Dir K. M. SALIKHOV.

Keldysh, M.V., Institute of Applied Mathematics: 125047 Moscow, Miusskaya pl. 4; tel. (095) 972-37-14; attached to Russian Acad. of Sciences; Dir S. P. KURDYUMOV.

Kostyakov, A. N., All-Russian Research Institute of Hydraulic Engineering and Land Reclamation: 127550 Moscow, Bol. Akademicheskaya 44; tel. (095) 153-72-70; fax (095) 153-73-70; library of 8,000 vols; Dir Prof. Dr B. M. KIZYAEV; publ. *Transactions* (1 or 2 a year).

Krylov Shipbuilding Research Institute: 196158 St Petersburg, Moskovskoe shosse 44; tel. (812) 127-93-48; fax (812) 127-93-49; e-mail krylov@krylov.spb.ru; internet www.krylov.com.ru; f. 1894; Science Principal and Dir V. M. PASHIN; publ. *Proceedings* (annually).

Krzhizhanovsky, G. M., State Energy Research Institute: 117927 Moscow, Leninsky pr. 19; tel. (095) 954-37-32; attached to Russian Acad. of Sciences; Dir E. P. VOLKOV.

Lebedev, S. A., Institute of Precision Mechanics and Computing Technology: 117333 Moscow, Leninsky pr. 51; tel. (095) 137-15-67; attached to Russian Acad. of Sciences; Dir G. G. RYABOV.

Lebedev, S. V., All-Russia Synthetic Rubber Research Institute: 198035 St Petersburg, Gapsalskaya ul. 1; tel. (812) 251-40-28; fax (812) 251-48-13; f. 1928; synthetic elastomeric materials, production processes, applications; Dir Prof. VITALY A. KORMER.

Mining Institute: 184200 Murmansk oblast, Apatity, ul. Fersmana 24; tel. (81555) 3-75-20; attached to Russian Acad. of Sciences; Dir N. N. MELNIKOV.

Mints, Acad. A. L., Institute of Radio Technology JSC: 127083 Moscow, ul. 8 Marta 10/1; tel. (095) 214-04-51; fax (095) 214-06-62; e-mail spz@newmail.ru; Gen.l Dir V. I. SHUSTOV.

Moscow Scientific-Industrial Association 'Spektr': 119048 Moscow, ul. Usacheva 35; tel. (095) 245-56-56; fax (095) 246-88-88; f. 1964; attached to Russian Acad. of Sciences; research, development and manufacture of non-destructive-testing equipment and instruments; Gen. Dir V. V. KLYUEV.

National Institute of Aviation Technology: 127051 Moscow, Petrovka 24; tel. (095) 311-05-41; fax (095) 311-03-23; e-mail info@niat.ru; internet www.niat.ru; f. 1920; Dir. O. S. SIROTKIN; publ. *Aviation Industry* (in Russian and English).

Paper Research Institute: 194018 St Petersburg, pr. Shvernika 49; tel. (812) 247-17-03; Dir A. IVANOV.

Pechora Research and Design Institute for the Oil Industry: 169400 Komi, Ukhta, Oktyabrskaya ul. 11; tel. (82147) 6-16-63; fax (82147) 6-03-36; Dir A. N. ILIN.

Physical-Technical Institute: 42600 Izhevsk, ul. Kirova 132; tel. (3142) 43-02-03; fax (3142) 25-06-14; e-mail fti@fti.udm.ru; internet fti.udm.ru; attached to Russian Acad. of Sciences; Dir Dr VLADIMIR LADYANOV.

Plastics Research Institute: 111112 Moscow, Perovskii pr. 35; tel. (095) 361-64-21; Dir V. I. ILICH.

Polymer Plastics Research Institute: St Petersburg, Polyustrovskii pr. 32; Dir Z. N. POLYAKOV.

Polzunov, I. I., Scientific and Development Association for Research and Design of Power Equipment JSC: 194021 St. Petersburg, Politekhnicheskaya ul. 24; tel. (812) 277-95-64; fax (812) 277-40-95; f. 1927; attached to Russian Acad. of Sciences; Dir V. K. RYZHKOV; publ. *Proceedings*.

Republic Engineering-Technical Centre for the Restoration and Strengthening of Components of Machines and Mechanisms: 634067 Tomsk, Khim ploshchadka; tel. (3822) 1-45-04 br. at Novosibirsk: 630055 Novosibirsk, ul. Musy Dzhalilya 9; tel. (3832) 32-12-49; attached to Russian Acad. of Sciences; Dir V. F. PINKIN (Tomsk); Dir V. M. NEZAMUTDINOV (Novosibirsk).

Research and Design Institute for the Mechanical Processing of Minerals: 199026 St Petersburg, V. O., 21-ya liniya 8a; tel. (812) 321-97-29; fax (812) 325-62-02; f. 1920; Dir VASILY ARSENTIEV; publ. *Obogashcheniye Rud* (Mineral Processing Journal, 6 a year).

Research and Design Institute of Artificial Fibres: 141009 Moscow oblast, Mytishchi, ul. Kolontsova 5; tel. (095) 284-44-78; Dir V. SMIRNOV.

Research and Design Institute of Autogenous Engineering: 109004 Moscow, Shelaputinsky per. 1; tel. (095) 915-09-60; fax (095) 915-09-60; e-mail vniiautogen@newmail.ru; f. 1944; equipment for thermal cutting and spraying; Dir NIKOLAI I. NIKIFOROV; publ. *Research Work* (irregular).

Research and Design Institute of Chemical Engineering: 125015 Moscow, Bol. Novodmitrovskaya 14; tel. (095) 285-29-23; Dir N. SAMSONOV.

Research and Design Institute of Management Information Technology: 125083 Moscow, ul. Yunnatov 18; tel. (095) 212-60-60.

Research and Design Institute of Metallurgical Engineering: 109428 Moscow, Ryazanskii pr. 8A; tel. (095) 174-37-00.

Research and Design Institute of Polymer Construction Materials: 117419 Moscow, 2-i Verkhny Mikhailovsky pr. 9; tel. (095) 952-30-68; fax (095) 954-40-91; attached to Polymerstroymateriali JSC; Dir ALEXANDER V. POGORELOV.

Research and Design Institute of the Bearings Industry: 109088 Moscow, 2-ya ul. Mashinostroeniya 27; tel. (095) 275-11-59.

Research and Design Institute of Woodworking Machinery: 107082 Moscow, Rubtsovskaya nab. 3; tel. (095) 261-16-73; f. 1948; library of 50,000 vols; publ. *Catalogue of Woodworking Machines* (annually).

Research and Design Technological Institute of Heavy Engineering: Ekaterinburg, pl. 1-i Pyatiletki.

Research and Experimental Design Institute of Machinery for the Food Industry: 123308 Moscow, pr. Marshala Zhukova 1.

Research Centre for Fundamental Problems of Computer Technology and Control Systems: 117218 Moscow, ul. Krasikova 25a; tel. (095) 125-77-09; attached to Russian Acad. of Sciences; Chair. of Presidium K. A. VALIEV.

Attached institutes:

Institute of Computer Technology Problems: 150007 Yaroslavl, Universitetskaya 21; tel. (0852) 35-52-83; attached to Russian Acad. of Sciences; Dir YU. A. MAMATOV.

Institute for Problems in Microelectronics Technology and Ultra-pure Materials: 142432 Moscow oblast, Chernogolovka; tel. (095) 962-80-47; fax (095) 292-65-11; attached to Russian Acad. of Sciences; Dir V. V. ARISTOV.

Microelectronics Institute: 150007 Yaroslavl, Universitetskaya 21; tel. (0852) 11-65-52; attached to Russian Acad. of Sciences; Dir V. A. KURCHIDIS.

Physical Technological Institute: 117218 Moscow, ul. Krasikova 25-a; tel. (095) 125-77-09; attached to Russian Acad. of Sciences; Dir K. A. VALIEV.

Research Institute of Systems of Automated Designing of Radioelectronic Apparatus and Very Large Scale Integrated Circuits: 103681 Moscow, Zelenograd, ul. Sovetskaya 3; tel. (095) 531-56-45; attached to Russian Acad. of Sciences; Dir A. L. STEMPKOVSKY.

Special Design Bureau for Microelectronics and Computer Technology: 15007 Yaroslavl, Universitetskaya 21; tel. (0852) 11-81-73; attached to Russian Acad. of Sciences; Dir A. M. GLUSHKOV.

Research Centre for Space Probes: 117810 Moscow, Profsoyuznaya ul. 84/32; attached to Russian Acad. of Sciences; Head N. A. DOLGIKH (acting).

Research, Design and Technological Institute of Electrothermic Equipment: 109052 Moscow, Nizhegorodskaya 29; tel. (095) 278-75-09.

Research Design-Technological Institute for Coal Machinery: 109193 Moscow, ul. Petra Romanova 7; tel. (095) 279-47-66.

Research Institute for Food Concentrates and Food Technologies and Special Food Technology: 117279 Moscow, Miklukho-Maklaya ul. 32; tel. and fax (495) 429-04-11; e-mail niispt@yandex.ru; internet www.niippspt.ru; f. 1981; attached to Russian Acad. of Agricultural Sciences; develops food concentrates, cereal snacks; food rations for Armed Forces and cosmonauts; tea and coffee products, infant foods; library of 7,000 vols; Dir Dr VICTOR F. DOBROVOLSKY; publ. *Tea and Coffee in Russia* (4 a year).

Research Institute for Instrumentation: 125124 Moscow, ul. Raskovoi 20; tel. (095) 214-55-88.

Research Institute for Systems Research: 109280 Moscow, Avtozavodskaya 23; tel. (095) 277-87-31; attached to Russian Acad. of Sciences; Dir V. B. BETELIN.

Research Institute for the Bakery and Confectionery Industry: 107553 Moscow, Bol. Cherkizovskaya ul. 26A; tel. (095) 161-41-44; attached to Russian Acad. of Agricultural Sciences.

Research Institute for the Beer, Soft Drinks and Wine Industry: 119021 Moscow, ul. Rossolimo 7; tel. (095) 246-67-69; attached to Russian Acad. of Agricultural Sciences.

Research Institute for the Organization, Management and Economics of the Oil and Gas Industry: 117420 Moscow, ul. Nametkina 14; tel. (095) 332-00-22.

Research Institute for the Processing of Casing Head Gas: 350550 Krasnodar, Krasnaya ul. 118; tel. (8612) 55-85-52; Dir N. I. KORSAKOV.

Research Institute of Abrasives and Grinding: 197342 St Petersburg, Beloostrovskaya ul. 17; tel. (812) 245-33-05; fax (812) 245-47-90; f. 1931; library of 62,000 vols; Dir S. MOLCHANOV.

Research Institute of Agricultural Engineering: 127427 Moscow, Dmitrovskoe shosse 107; tel. (095) 485-55-81.

Research Institute of Applied Automated Systems: 103009 Moscow, ul. Nezhdanovoi 2A; tel. (095) 229-78-46; attached to Russian Acad. of Sciences; Dir O. L. SMIRNOV.

Research Institute of Atomic Reactors: Ulyanovsk oblast, 433510 Dimitrovgrad; tel. (84235) 3-20-21; fax (84235) 3-56-48; e-mail adm@niiar.ru; internet www.pub.niiar.ru; f. 1956; library of 96,000 vols; Dir Prof. A. F. GRACHEV.

Research Institute of Automobile Electronics and Electrical Equipment: 105187 Moscow, Kirpichnaya 39–41; tel. (095) 365-25-66.

Research Institute of Automobile Industry Technology: 115333 Moscow, pr. Andropova 22/30; tel. (095) 118-20-00; Dir S. V. PODOBLYAEV.

Research Institute of Building Ceramics: 143980 Moscow oblast, Zheleznodorozhnyi-1; tel. (095) 527-73-73.

Research Institute of Chemical Fibres and Composite Materials: 195030 St Petersburg, ul. Khimikov 28; tel. (812) 227-61-48; Dir P. E. MIKHAILOV.

Research Institute of Chemical Reagents and Ultrapure Chemical Substances: 107258 Moscow, Bogorodskii val 3; tel. (095) 963-70-70; Dir E. A. RYABENKO.

Research Institute of Chemicals for Polymer Materials: 392680 Tambov, ul. Montazhnikov 3; tel. (0752) 29-51-52; attached to

Syntez joint-stock company; Dir B. N. GORBUNOV.

Research Institute of Construction and Road Machinery: 123424 Moscow, Volokolamskoe shosse 73; tel. (095) 491-10-33.

Research Institute of Construction Physics: 127238 Moscow, Lokomotivny pr. 21; tel. (095) 482-40-76; fax (095) 482-40-60; e-mail niisf@ipc.ru; f. 1956; library of 2,000 vols; Dir G. L. OSIPOV.

Research Institute of Current Sources: 129626 Moscow; tel. (095) 287-97-42; attached to Russian Acad. of Sciences; Dir YU. V. SKOKOV.

Research Institute of Drilling Technology: 117957 Moscow, Leninsky pr. 6; tel. (095) 236-01-70; Dir A. V. MNASHCHAKOV.

Research Institute of Earthmoving Machinery: c/o VNIIZEMMASH, 198005 St Petersburg, Petrovskii pr. 2; tel. (812) 235-57-84; fax (812) 235-57-84; attached to VNIIZEMMASH; Dir V. P. KORNEEV.

Research Institute of Elastic Materials and Products: 119048 Moscow, Mal. Trubetskaya ul. 28; tel. (095) 242-53-42; fax (095) 245-62-10; Dir S. V. REZNICHENKO.

Research Institute of Electrical Engineering: 191186 St Petersburg, Dvortsovaya nab. 18; tel. (812) 387-55-22; fax (812) 387-55-22; e-mail jandan@peterlink.ru; f. 1992; attached to Russian Acad. of Sciences; Dir Acad. Y.B. DANILEVICH; publs *Electrichestvo* (monthly), *Energetics News of RAS* (6 a year).

Research Institute of Electro-welding Technology: 194100 St Petersburg, Litovskaya ul. 10; tel. (812) 245-40-95; Dir V. V. SMIRNOV.

Research Institute of Electromeasuring Equipment: 195267 St Petersburg, pr. Prosveshcheniya 85; tel. (812) 559-51-41.

Research Institute of Foundry Machinery and the Technology and Automation of Foundry Production: 123557 Moscow, Presnenskii val 14; tel. (095) 252-27-25; Dir E. KRAKOVSKII.

Research Institute of Gas Use in the Economy and Underground Storage of Oil, Oil Products and Liquefied Gases: 123298 Moscow, ul. Berzarina 12; tel. (095) 946-89-11.

Research Institute of Hydrogeology and Engineering Geology (VSEGINGEO): 142452 Moscow oblast, Noginskii raion, p/o Kupavna, pos. Zelenyi; tel. (095) 521-20-00; fax (095) 913-51-26; e-mail gvartany@online.ru; f. 1939; Dir Acad. G.S. VARTANYAN.

Research Institute of Instrumentation Technology: 113191 Moscow, Gamsonovskii per. 9; tel. (095) 232-10-41.

Research Institute of Light Alloys: Moscow, ul. Gorbanova 20; Dir N. I. KORYAGINA.

Research Institute of Light and Textile Machinery: 113105 Moscow, Varshavskoe shosse 33; tel. (095) 111-00-30; fax (095) 958-58-41; e-mail vniiltek@mail.magelan.ru; internet www.vimi.ru/vniiltekmash; f. 1932; library of 30,000 vols; Dir Prof. Dr R. M. MALAFEYEV.

Research Institute of Organizational Technology: 119146 Moscow, Komsomolskii pr. 9A; tel. (095) 246-41-21.

Research Institute of Road Traffic Safety: 109389 Moscow, Mal. Lubyanka 16/4.

Research Institute of Rubber and Latex Products: 107564 Moscow, Krasnobogatyrskaya ul. 42; tel. (095) 161-02-92; fax (095) 963-49-11; Dir V. A. BERESTENEV.

Research Institute of Rubber Technical Products: 141300 Moscow oblast, Sergievsky Posad; tel. (09654) 4-57-59; fax

(09654) 4-10-52; f. 1960; library of 15,000 vols; Dir V. V. SHVARTS.

Research Institute of Special Engineering: 107082 Moscow, Cheshikhinsky pr-d 18/20; tel. (095) 261-50-76.

Research Institute of Synthetic Fibres: 170613 Tver, ul. Pashi Savelevoi 45; tel. (08222) 5-36-10; Dir V. F. LOSKUTOV.

Research Institute of Technical Physics: 454070 Chelyabinsk oblast, Chelyabinsk 70; Dir V. Z. NECHAI.

Research Institute of the Cement Industry OJSC (NIICement): 107014 Moscow, 3-i Luchevoy prosek 12; tel. (095) 268-27-21; fax (095) 268-27-26; e-mail riicement@mtu-net.ru; f. 1947; formerly State Research Institute of the Cement Industry; Dir-Gen. Prof. Dr V.I. SHUBIN.

Research Institute of the Chemistry and Technology of Elementary Organic Compounds: 111123 Moscow, shosse Entuziastov 38; tel. (095) 273-72-50; fax (095) 273-13-23; e-mail eos@eos.incotrade.ru; f. 1945; Dir E. A. CHERNYSHEV.

Research Institute of the Clock and Watch Industry: 125315 Moscow, Chasovaya 24/1; tel. (095) 151-15-01.

Research Institute of the Factory Technology of Prefabricated Reinforced Concrete Structures and Items: 111524 Moscow, ul. Plekhanova 7; tel. (095) 176-27-04.

Research Institute of the Gas Industry: 142700 Moscow oblast, Vidnoe.

Research Institute of the Metrology Service: 119361 Moscow, G-361, Ozernaya ul. 46; tel. (095) 437-55-77; fax (095) 437-56-66; e-mail office.vniims@relcom.ru; attached to Russian Acad. of Sciences; Dir V. V. SAZHIN.

Research Institute of the Tyre Industry: 105118 Moscow, ul. Burakova 27; tel. (095) 273-69-01; fax (095) 176-37-42; Dir A. A. VOLNOV.

Research Institute of Tooling: 105023 Moscow, Bol. Semenovskaya 49; tel. (095) 366-94-11.

Research Institute of Transport Construction: 129329 Moscow, Kolskaya 1; tel. (095) 180-20-42; fax (095) 189-72-53; e-mail mail@tsniis.com; internet www.tsniis.com; f. 1935; research on bridges, tunnels, railways and associated structures, and development of standards and codes of practice; Dir-Gen. ANATOLY SYCHEV.

Research Institute of Vehicle and Tractor Materials: 113184 Moscow, Ozerkovskaya nab. 22/24; tel. (095) 230-94-59.

Research-Training Centre 'Robototekhnika': 105037 Moscow, Izmailovskaya pl. 7; tel. (095) 165-17-01; fax (095) 367-06-36; e-mail robot@bmstu.ru; internet www.robot.bmstu.ru; f. 1983; attached to Russian Acad. of Sciences and Bauman Moscow State Technical University; Head Prof. A. S. YUSCHENKO.

Russian Research, Design and Technological Institute for Crane and Traction Electrical Equipment: 109280 Moscow, ul. Masterkova 4; tel. (095) 275-61-66; fax (095) 275-49-03; f. 1960; library of 160,000 vols; Dir ANATOLY D. MASHIKHIN.

Russian Research Institute of Industrial Design: 129223 Moscow, pr. Mira, VVTs, korp. 312; tel. (095) 216-90-10; fax (095) 216-88-10; f. 1962; Dir LEV A. KUZMICHEV; publs *Tekhnicheskaya Estetika* (2 a year), *Designer's Library* (2 a year).

Russian Research Institute of Information Technology and Automated Design

Systems: 129090 Moscow, ul. Shchepkina 22; tel. (095) 288-19-24.

Russian Scientific Centre of Applied Chemistry: 197198 St Petersburg, pr. Dobrolyubova 14; tel. (812) 325-66-45; fax (812) 325-66-48; f. 1919; library of 500,000 vols; Gen. Dir Prof. G. F. TERESHCHENKO; publ. *Annual Proceedings*.

Science Production Association 'Orgstankinprom': 105264 Moscow, 5-ya Parkovaya 37, korp. 2; tel. (095) 164-56-53.

Scientific and Engineering Centre 'SNIIP': 123060 Moscow, ul. Raspletina 5; tel. (095) 943-00-62; fax (095) 943-00-63; f. 1954; systems and instrumentation connected with nuclear power production, electronics and space research; Dir Dr S. B. CHEBYSHOV; publ. *Proceedings* (annually).

Scientific and Research Institute for Standardization and Certification in the Engineering Industry: 123007 Moscow, ul. Shenogina 4; tel. (095) 256-04-49; fax (095) 943-00-78; f. 1957; standardization, certification of products.

Scientific and Technical Complex 'Progress': 119034 Moscow, Kropotkinskaya ul. 13/7; tel. (095) 301-23 25; attached to Russian Acad. of Sciences; General Dir L. N. LUPICHEV.

Scientific Centre of Complex Transportation Problems: 113035 Moscow, Sofiiskaya nab. 34, korp. V; tel. (095) 233-89-13; fax (095) 231-14-54; f. 1955; Dir V. ARSENOV.

Scientific-Experimental Centre for the Automation of Air Traffic Control: 123182 Moscow, Volokolamskoe shosse 26; tel. (095) 190-42-18; attached to Russian Acad. of Sciences; Head T. G. ANODINA.

Scientific Research Institute for Systems Studies: 117218 Moscow, pr. Nakhimovsky 36, korp. 1; tel. (095) 719-76-51; fax (095) 719-76-81; e-mail betelin@sistyd.msk .su; internet www.niisi.ru; f. 1989; attached to Russian Acad. of Sciences; Dir V. B. BETELIN; publs *Issues in Cybernetics* (annually), *Issues of SRISA* (2 a year).

Scientific Research Institute of Comprehensive Engineering Problems in Animal Husbandry and Fodder Production (VNIIKOMZH): 101509 Moscow, Lesnaya 43; tel. (095) 250-37-90; fax (095) 978-91-38; f. 1974; library of 40,000 vols; Dir-Gen. I. V. ILIN; publ. *Scientific Research Works of VNIIKOMZH* (annually).

Scientific Research Institute of Multiprocessor Computer Systems of the Taganrog State University of Radio Engineering: 347928 Taganrog, ul. Chekhova 2; tel. (86344) 36-07-57; fax (86344) 36-03-76; e-mail mvs@tsure.ru; internet www.mvs.tsure.ru; f. 1972; attached to Russian Acad. of Sciences; Dir I. A. KALIAEV; publ. *Multiprocessor Computer Structures* (annually).

Scientific-Technical Co-operative 'Problems of Mechanics and Technology': 109180 Moscow, ul. Bol. Polyanka 2/10; tel. (095) 251-52-08; attached to Russian Acad. of Sciences; Chair. Acad. V. V. STRUMINSKY.

Siberian Research Institute of the Oil Industry: 625016 Tyumen, ul. 50-let Oktyabrya 118; tel. (3452) 21-19-16; Dir R. I. KUZOVATKIN.

Skochinsky Institute of Mining: 140004 Moscow, Lyubertsy 4; tel. (095) 554-85-13; fax (095) 554-52-47; e-mail igd@igd.ru; internet www.igd.ru; f. 1927; attached to Russian Acad. of Sciences; technology of opencast and underground coal mining; certification of mine electrical equipment and explosion-proof equipment; library of 40,000 vols; Dir ANATOLY DMITRIEVICH RUBAN;

publs *Technology of Opencast and Underground Coal Mining* (4 a year), *Economics of the Coal Industry* (1 or 2 a year).

Special Design Bureau for Applied Geophysics: 630058 Novosibirsk, Russkaya ul. 35; tel. (3832) 32-36-45; e-mail geophys@ hydromet.ru; attached to Russian Acad. of Sciences; Head N. P. RASHENTSEV.

Special Design Bureau for Automation of Marine Research: 693023 Yuzhno-Sakhalinsk, ul. Gorkogo 25; tel. and fax (424) 255-49-66; e-mail skb-sami@sakhalin .ru; f. 1972; attached to Russian Acad. of Sciences; Head ANATOLY E. MALASHENKO.

Special Design Bureau for High Capacity Electronics: 634055 Tomsk, Akademicheskii pr. 4; tel. (3822) 1-84-59; attached to Russian Acad. of Sciences; Head A. P. KHUZEEV.

Special Design Bureau for Hydroimpulse Technology: 630090 Novosibirsk, ul. Tereshkovoi 29; tel. (3832) 35-72-91; attached to Russian Acad. of Sciences; Head A. A. DERIBAS.

Special Design Bureau for Scientific Instruments: 630058 Novosibirsk, Russkaya ul. 41; tel. (3832) 35-30-41; attached to Russian Acad. of Sciences; Head YU V. CHUGUI.

Special Design-Technological Bureau for Special Electronics and Analytical Instrumentation: 630090 Novosibirsk, ul. Akad. Nikolaeva 8; tel. (3832) 32-24-40; attached to Russian Acad. of Sciences; Head K. K. SVITASHCHEV.

Special Design-Technological Bureau 'Nauka': 66049 Krasnoyarsk, pr. Mira 53; tel. (3912) 27-29-12; attached to Russian Acad. of Sciences; Head V. F. SHABANOV.

State Design and Research Institute for the Design of Research Institutes, Laboratories and Research Centres of the Academy of Sciences: 117971 Moscow, ul. Gubkina 3; tel. (095) 135-73-01; fax (095) 135-02-20; e-mail gp@gpran.msk.ru; f. 1938; attached to Russian Acad. of Sciences; Dir A. S. PANFIL.

State Design and Research Institute of Power Systems and Electricity Networks: 107884 Moscow, 2-ya Baumanskaya 7; tel. (095) 261-98-21.

State Institute of Mined Chemical Raw Materials: 140000 Moscow oblast, Lyubertsy, Oktyabrsky pr. 259; tel. (095) 554-42-46.

State Research and Project Development Institute of Maritime Transport: 125319 Moscow, Bol. Koptevsky pr-d 6; tel. (095) 152-36-51; fax (095) 152-09-16; f. 1939; design of port structures and ship repair yards; economic problems of maritime transport; maritime law; Dir FELIX G. ARAKELOV.

State Research Institute for the Nitrogen Industry and the Products of Organic Synthesis: 109815 Moscow, Zemlyanoi val 50; tel. (095) 227-00-04; Dir N. D. ZAICHKO.

State Research Institute for the Operation and Repair of Civil Aviation Equipment: Moscow, ul. Krzhizhanovskogo 7.

State Research Institute of Automobile Transport: 123514 Moscow, ul. Geroev-Panfilovtsev 24; tel. (095) 496-57-22.

State Research Institute of Civil Aviation: 103340 Moscow oblast, Sheremetevo Airport; tel. (095) 578-48-01.

State Research Institute of the Rare Metals Industry: 109017 Moscow, Bol. Tolmachevsky per. 5; tel. (095) 239-90-66.

'Submicron' Research Institute: 103482 Moscow, Zelenograd, korp. 331A; tel. (095) 536-26-17.

Topchiev, A. V., Institute of Petro-Chemical Synthesis: 117912 Moscow, Leninskii pr. 29; tel. (095) 954-22-92; attached to Russian Acad. of Sciences; Dir Acad. N. A. PLATE.

Tractor Research and Development Institute: 125040 Moscow, Verkhnyaya 34; tel. (095) 257-01-10; fax (095) 973-20-23; e-mail nati@ccas.ru; f. 1925; Dir NIKOLAI A. SHCHELTSIN.

Vavilov State Optical Institute: 199034 St Petersburg, Birzhevaya Liniya 12; tel. (812) 328-48-92; fax (812) 328-37-20; e-mail leader@soi.spb.ru; internet soi.srv.pu.ru; f. 1918; library of 600,000 vols; Dir Dr G. PETROVSKY; publ. *Journal of Optical Technology* (monthly).

'VNIPIenergoprom' Association JSC: 105094 Moscow, Semenovskaya nab. 2/1; tel. (095) 360-76-40; fax (095) 366-36-25; internet www.vnipiep.ru; f. 1942; design, research and development of energy transmission systems, combined heating and power plants, project management, development of heat and power-supply schemes for municipal areas, principally Moscow.

Vologdin, V. P., Research Institute of High-Frequency Currents: 197376 St Petersburg, ul. L. Tolstogo 7; tel. (812) 234-69-57; fax (812) 234-46-52; e-mail vniitvch@ mail.ru; internet www.vniitvch.spb.ru; f. 1947; Dir F. V. BEZMENOV.

Zhukovsky, N. E., Central Aero- and Hydro-dynamics Institute: 140160 Moscow oblast, Zhukovsky 3; tel. (095) 556-41-79; Dir G. P. SVISHCHEV.

Libraries and Archives

Arkhangelsk

Dobroliubov Arkhangelsk Regional Research Library: 163061 Arkhangelsk, ul. Loginova 2; tel. (8182) 65-11-28; fax (8182) 43-97-39; e-mail library@dvinalend .ru; internet www.dvinalend.ru; Dir OLGA STIUPINA.

Barnaul

Altai State University Library: 656099 Barnaul, Sotsialisticheskii pr. 68; 159,000 vols; Dir GALINA TRUSHNIKOVA.

Cheboksary

Chuvash State University Library: 428015428034 Cheboksary, Moskovskii pr. 15Universitetskaya 38; tel. 248320(8835) 49-79-88; e-mail library@chuvsu.ru; internet library.chuvsu.ru; 1,703,091 vols; Dir NINA D. NIKITINA.

Ekaterinburg

Urals A. M. Gorkii State University Library: 620083 Ekaterinburg, Pr. Lenina 51; tel. (3432) 50-75-65; fax (3432) 50-75-65; e-mail library@usu.ru; internet www2.usu .ru/library; f. 1920; 1,200,000 vols; Dir K. P. KUZNETSOVA.

Elista

Kalmyk State University Library: Elista, Ul. R. Lyuksemburg 4; c. 350,000 vols; Dir P. A. DOLINA.

Grozny

Checheno-Ingush State University Library: 364907 Grozny, Ul. N. Buachidze 34/96; tel. 24548; 460,000 vols; Dir R. M. NAZARETYANI.

Ingushetia

National Library of Ingushetia: 366700 Ingushetia, Sunezhsky district, ul. Lunacharskogo 106; Dir RADIMA GAZDIEVA.

Irkutsk

Irkutsk State University Library: 664695 Irkutsk, Bulvar Gagarina 24; 3,200,000 vols; Dir R. V. PODGAICHENKO.

Ivanovo

Ivanovo State University Library: 153377 Ivanovo, Ul. Ermaka 37; 410,000 vols; Dir A. N. KRUPPA.

Library of Ivanovo State Chemistry and Technology University: 153460 Ivanovo, Ul. Friedrich Engels 7; tel. 32-73-54; fax 32-95-02; e-mail ruut@ifti.ivanov.ru; Dir VERA DMITRIEVA.

Izhevsk

Udmurt State University Library: 426034 Izhevsk, Universitetskaya ul. 1; tel. (3412) 52-60-89; fax (3412) 75-58-66; e-mail admin@lib.udsu.ru; internet lib.udsu.ru; f. 1932; 970,647 vols; Librarian L. P. BESKLINSKAYA.

Kaliningrad

Kaliningrad State University Library: 236040 Kaliningrad, Universitetskaya ul. 2; tel. (0112) 43-31-29; fax (0112) 46-58-13; e-mail alexandra@library.albertina.ru; internet www.albertina.ru; f. 1968; 539,000 vols; Dir A. D. SHKITSKAYA.

Kazan

Kazan State University N. I. Lobachevsky Library: 420008 Kazan, Kremlevskaya 18; tel. 64-47-54; e-mail lsl@ksu.ru; internet www.lsl.ksu.ru; f. 1804; 4,886,359 vols; Dir GALINA A. AUKHADIEVA; publs *Opisaniya rukopisei, Retrospektivnye bibliograficheskie ukazately.*

Kemerovo

Kemerovo State University Library: 650043 Kemerovo, Krasnaya ul. 6; tel. (3842) 23-14-26; e-mail nb@kemgu.kemerovo.su; f. 1928; 350,000 vols; Librarian N. P. KONOVALOVA.

Krasnodar

Kuban State University Library: 350049 Krasnodar, Stavropolskaya ul. 149; tel. (8612) 69-95-52; fax (8612) 69-95-17; e-mail gsol@pop.kubsu.ru; internet www.library.kubsu.ru; f. 1920; 1,030,215 vols; Dir G. V. SOLOVEVA.

Krasnoyarsk

Krasnoyarsk State University Library: 660049 Krasnoyarsk, Ul. Maerchaka 6; tel. 90414; 166,000 vols; Librarian E. G. KRIVONOSOVA.

Makhachkala

Dagestan State University Library: Makhachkala, Sovetskaya ul. 8; tel. 7213; 780,000 vols; Dir A. M. SHAKHSHAEVA.

Moscow

All-Russia Patent Technical Library: 121857 Moscow, Berezhkovskaya nab. 24; tel. 240-64-25; fax 240-44-37; f. 1896; the only Russian library which receives Russian and all foreign patents; copies of 105,000,000 patent descriptions; Dir V. I. AMELKINA.

All-Russia Scientific and Research Institute of Patent Information (VNIIPI): 113035 Moscow, Raushskaya nab. 4; tel. (095) 959-33-13; fax (095) 959-33-04; f. 1964; Dir V. D. ZINOVIEV; publs *Inventions* (36 a year), *Utility Models. Industrial Designs* (monthly), *Trademarks, Service Marks. Appellations of Origin of Goods* (monthly).

Archives of the Russian Academy of Sciences: 117218 Moscow, Novocheremushkinskaya ul. 34; tel. 129-19-10; fax 129-19-66; f. 1728; 90 mems; 9,000 vols; Dir B. V. LEVSHIN; publs *Proceedings, Scientific Heritage.*

Central Library for the Blind: 129010 Moscow, Bezbozhnyi per. 9; tel. 280-26-14; f. 1954; 630,000 vols; acts as loan centre for special libraries throughout Russia; Dir A. D. MAKEEVA; publ. *Life of the Blind in Russia and Abroad* (monthly).

Central Library of the Academy of Medical Sciences: 125874 Moscow, Baltiiskaya ul. 8; tel. 155-47-93; f. 1935; 640,000 vols; acts as an enquiry, loan, research and guide centre for 42 libraries in the institutes and laboratories of the Academy of Medical Sciences; Dir G. I. BAKHEREVA.

Central Scientific Agricultural Library of the Russian Academy of Agricultural Sciences: 107139 Moscow, Orlikov per. 3 Korpus V; tel. (095) 207-54-48; fax (095) 207-89-72; e-mail dir@cnshb.msk.ru; f. 1930; centre for bibliographical information on national and foreign agricultural literature, and for scientific and methodological work of agricultural libraries in Russia; 3,000,000 vols, 3,300 periodicals; Dir V. POZDNYAKOV; publs *Selskokhozyaistvennaya literatura* (monthly), *Selskoe khozyaistvo* (monthly), *Subject Bibliographic Lists* (15 titles annually), *Bibliographic Information* (weekly).

Central State Archives: 125212 Moscow, Vyborgskaya 3; tel. 159-73-83; Dir A. PROKOPENKO.

Centre for the Preservation of Historical Documentary Collections: Moscow, Vyborgskaya ul. 3; tel. 159-74-71; Dir V. BONDAREV; formerly Central State Archive of the USSR (TsGA SSSR) Special Archive.

Federal Archival Service of Russia: 103132 Moscow, Ul. Ilyinka 12; tel. (095) 206-35-31; fax (095) 206-55-87; e-mail rosarhiv@rusarchives.ru; internet www.rusarchives.ru; f. 1996; Head V. P. KOZLOV; publ. *Otechestvenniye archivy* (6 a year).

Gorky, A. M., Archives: 121069 Moscow, Ul. Vorovskogo 25A.; tel. 291-19-23; fax 200-32-16; f. 1937; Dir VLADIMIR S. BARAKHOV.

Institute for Scientific Information on the Social Sciences of the Russian Academy of Sciences: 117418 Moscow, Ul. Krasikova 28/21; tel. 128-88-81; fax 420-22-61; f. 1969; sections on philosophy, history, economics, sociology, politology, culturology, global problems and international relations, law, science of sciences, linguistics, theory of literature; 13,500,000 vols; Dir V. A. VINOGRADOV; publs *The Human Being: Image and Essence* (annually), *Theory and Practice of Information in Social Sciences* (annually), various periodicals on social sciences and other subjects.

Institute of Scientific and Technical Information: 125219 Moscow, Ul. Usievicha 20A; tel. 155-43-96; attached to Russian Acad. of Sciences; Dir P. V. NESTEROV.

International Centre for Scientific and Technical Information: 125252 Moscow, Ul. Kuusinena 21 B; tel. (095) 198-70-21; fax (095) 943-00-89; e-mail alsor@icsti.su; internet www.icsti.su; f. 1969; Dir Dr ZURAB A. YAKOBASHVILI.

Library for Natural Sciences of the Russian Academy of Sciences: 119890 GSP Moscow 919, Ul. Znamenka 11/11; tel. (095) 291-22-89; fax (095) 291-91-93; e-mail rapoport@ben.irex.ruhead@benran.ru; internet www.benvan.ruwww.benran.ru; f. 1973; 12,549,000 items in main and associated libraries; Dir N. YE. KALENOV; publ. *Libraries of Academies of Sciences* (in Russian, annually).

Library of the State A. S. Pushkin Museum of Fine Arts: 121019 Moscow, Ul. Volkhonka 12; tel. (095) 203-97-28; fax (095) 203-46-74; e-mail bib@gmii.museum.ru; f. 1898; 200,000 vols, 100,000 reproductions on paper and canvas, 120,000 negatives and photographs, 70,000 slides; Dir O. B. MALINKOVSKAYA.

Library of the State Central Museum of the Contemporary History of Russia: 103050 Moscow, Tverskaya ul. 21; tel. (495) 299-52-17; fax (495) 299-85-15; e-mail sovrhistory@mtu-net.ru; internet www.sovr.ru; f. 1917 as Museum of the Russian Revolution; 360,000 vols, 825,000 periodicals; Chief Librarian TATYANA N. EREMEEVA.

Library of the State Literature Museum: Moscow, Rozhdestvenskii Bulvar 16; f. 1926; collection of 180,000 books, 27,644 periodicals; Russian and foreign works from 16th to 20th centuries; letters and autographed works; folklore works; periodical collection; Dir ANNA IVANOVNA NIKULINA.

Library of the State Museum of Oriental Arts: 103064 Moscow, Vorontsovo pole 16-A; tel. (095) 916-34-29; fax (095) 916-48-46; f. 1918; 70,000 vols; Dir LUDMILA VOLKOVA; publ. *Scientific reports* (annually).

Library of the State Theatrical A. Bakhrushin Museum: 113054 Moscow, Ul. Bakhrushina 31/12; tel. 233-44-18; fax 233-54-48; f. 1894; 120,000 vols on theatrical art; Dir T. B. BONILYA.

Library of the Tolstoy State Museum: 119034 Moscow, Ul. Prechistenka 11; tel. (095) 202-78-51; fax (095) 202-93-38; f. 1911; 76,000 vols, 86,000 newspaper cuttings; Dir L. M. LUBIMOVA.

Moscow State University Scientific Library: 103009 Moscow, Mokhovaya 10.

Rudomino, M. I., State Library for Foreign Literature: 109189 Moscow, Nikoloyamskaya 1; tel. (095) 915-36-21; fax (095) 915-36-37; e-mail vgbil@libfl.ru; internet www.libfl.ru; f. 1922; exchange arrangements with 1,300 libraries, publishing houses and universities in 92 countries; 4,400,000 vols in 140 foreign languages; Dir E. YU. GENIEVA; publ. *Biblioteki za rubezhom.*

Russian National Public Library for Science and Technology: 103031 Moscow, Kuznetskii most 12; tel. 925-92-88; fax 921-98-62; e-mail root@gpntb.ru; internet www.gpntb.ru; f. 1958; permanent contacts with 7,000 enterprises in Russia and other republics of the former USSR; 8,000,000 books, periodicals and documents on natural sciences, technology, agriculture and medicine; special collection of domestic literature of limited distribution; 24 original databases; Dir Dr A. I. ZEMSKOV; publs *Proceedings of Crimea Conferences, Journal of Research, Scientific and Technical Libraries.*

Russian Peoples' Friendship University Library: 117198 Moscow, Miklukho-Maklaia 6; f. 1960; 1,350,000 vols; Dir A. N. SHUMILOV.

Russian State Archive of Modern History: 103132 Moscow, Ul. Ilinka 12; tel. (095) 206-50-06; fax (095) 206-23-21; f. 1991; based on the Archive of the General Department of the Communist Party of the fmr USSR; Dir N. G. TOMILINA.

Russian State Archive of Social-Political History: 103009 Moscow, Bolshaya Dmitrovka 15; tel. (095) 229-97-26; fax (095) 292-90-17; e-mail rchidni1@online.ru; internet www.rusarchives.ru; f. 1920s; 10,000 vols; incl. colln from Central Archive of Komsomol; Dir Dr K. M. ANDERSON; publ. *Scientific Information Bulletin* (annually).

Russian State Archives of Ancient Acts: 119992 GSP-2 Moscow, G-435, Bolshaya Pirogovskaya ul. 17; tel. 245-83-23; fax 245-30-98; e-mail rgada@rusarchives.ru; annals, charts of grand dukes and independent princes, legal documents of Early Russia (11th–15th c.), documents of central and local Russian institutions (16th–18th c.), personal and patrimonial archives of nobility and gentry, archives of church establishments and the largest monasteries of Russia; Dir MICHAIL R. RYZENKOV.

Russian State Archives of Sound Recording: 107005 Moscow, 2-ya Baumanskaya ul. 3; tel. 261-13-00; f. 1932; sound recordings from 1902 of artistic and documentary nature; Dir V. A. KOLIADA.

Russian State Archives of the National Economy: 119435 Moscow, Bolshaya Pirogovskaya ul. 17; tel. 245-26-64; documents of the state bodies in charge of management of industries, agriculture, transportation, communication, construction and of central bodies of financing, planning and statistics (1917–); Dir E. A. TYURINA.

Russian State Army Archives: 125212 Moscow, Ul. Admirala Makarova 29; tel. 159-80-91; documents of military authorities of the RSFSR and the USSR, of the military areas, detachments, units and establishments of the Soviet Army and Frontier Guards (1918–40); Dir V. D. ZAPOROZHNI-CHENKO.

Russian State Art Library: 103031 Moscow, B. Dmitrovka 8/1; tel. (095) 292-06-9253; fax (095) 292-06-53; e-mail bisk@liart.ru; internet www.liart.ru; f. 1922; 1,701,000 items (books, periodicals, press cuttings, engravings, sketches, postcards, photographs, posters); Dir A. A. KOLGANOVA; publ. *Yearbook.*

Russian State Library: 101000 Moscow, Ul. Vozdvizhenka 3–5; tel. (095) 202-35-65; fax (095) 913-69-33; e-mail mbs@rsl.ru; internet www.rsl.ru; f. 1862 as the Rumyantsev Library; acts as enquiry, loan and reference centre throughout Russia, as international book exchange centre and state national book depository, as information centre on culture and arts, as leading research institution in library science, bibliography and history of printing, and as methodological library centre; 43,000,000 books, periodicals and serials; complete files of newspapers in all the 91 languages of the fmr USSR and 156 foreign languages; 450,000 MSS; 860 archival collections; Department of Rare Books includes incunabula, Aldines, palaeotypes, Elzevirs, specimens of earliest Slavonic printing, rare editions of Russian secular works; Dir Dr VICTOR V. FEDOROV; publs *Novosti* (News), *Zapiski otdela rukopisei* (Memoirs of the Manuscript Divison), *Bibliotekovedenie* (Library Science), *Vestochnaya Kollektsia* (Eastern Collection).

Russian State Literature and Art Archives: 125212 Moscow, Vyborgskaya 3, kor. 2; tel. (095) 150-78-10; fax (095) 159-73-81; e-mail rgali@satel.ru; f. 1941; documents of prominent Russian and Soviet writers, composers, artists, theatrical and cinema workers; documents of state and public organizations concerned with the arts (mid-18th century–present day); 1,154,000 vols; Dir T. M. GORJAEVA; publ. *Vstrechi s proshlym* (irregular).

Russian State Military Historical Archives: 107005 Moscow, Ul. 2-ya Baumanskaya 3; tel. (095) 261-20-70; fax (095) 267-18-66; f. 1797; documents of central and district military administrations and estab-

lishments of the Russian Army, private collections of prominent generals, military leaders and historians (end 17th century–1918); Dir I. O. GARKUSHA.

Scientific Library of the State Tretyakov Gallery: 113035 Moscow, 1-i Kadashevskii per. 14; tel. (095) 953-41-85; fax (095) 953-10-51; f. 1899; stock relating to Russian and Soviet art; 400,000 vols; Dir Z.P. SHERGINA.

Scientific S. I. Taneev Library of the Moscow P. I. Tchaikovsky State Conservatoire: 103871 Moscow, Ul. Gertsena 13; f. 1866; Russian and foreign music and books on music; complete files of many Russian and foreign musical periodicals; 1,250,941 vols; Dir A. F. CHERKASOVA.

State Archives of the Russian Federation: 119992 Moscow, Bolshaya Pirogovskaya ul. 17; tel. (095) 245-12-87; fax (095) 245-12-87; e-mail garf@online.ru; internet www.garf.narod.ru; f. 1992; 5,513,107 items; Dir SERGEY V. MIRONENKO; publ. *Archive of Contemporary Russian History* (3 series: catalogues, documents, research).

State Central Polytechnic Library: 101000 Moscow, Politekhnicheskii proezd 2; tel. 928-64-65; f. 1964; 3,000,000 vols, including periodicals; Dir N. G. REINBERG.

State Medical Library of Russia: 117418 Moscow, Nakhimovskaya ul. 49; tel. 128-33-46; fax 128-87-39; e-mail loginov@server .scsml.rssi.ru; f. 1919; 3,000,000 vols; Dir Dr B. R. LOGINOV; publs *Medicine and Public Health* (bibliographical index), *New Medical Books.*

State Public Historical Library of Russia: 101990 Moscow, Starosadskii per. 9; tel. 925-65-14; fax 928-02-84; e-mail maf@shpl .ru; internet www.shpl.ru; f. 1938, 3,229,696 vols, including 74,695 in the Department of Rare Books, 1,107,604 items in the Serials Department; special collection of 10,119 unofficial publications; Dir Dr MIKHAIL AFANASIEV.

Turgenev Library No. 13: 101000 Moscow, Bobrov per. 6, Building 2; tel. 921-00-52; fax 921-99-17; e-mail biblioteka@turgenev.ru; Dir TATYANA KOROBKINA.

Ushinsky State Pedagogical Library: 109017 Moscow, Bolshoi Tolmachevskii per. 3; tel. (095) 951-05-85; fax (095) 951-73-56; e-mail gnpbu@gnpbu.ru; internet www .gnpbu.ru; f. 1925; 2,000,000 units; Dir BORIS N. SIZOV (acting); publ. *Literatura po pedagogicheskim naukam i narodnomu obrazovaniyu* (4 a year).

Nalchik

Kabardino-Balkar State University Library: 360004 Nalchik, ul. Chernyshevskogo 173; 738,000 vols; Dir E. D. MIGUCHKINA.

Nizhnii Novgorod

Nizhnii Novgorod N. I. Lobachevsky State University Central Library: 603091 Nizhnii Novgorod, pr. Gagarina 23; tel. (8312) 31-11-54; 1,210,470 vols; Dir A. I. SAVENKOV.

Novosibirsk

Novosibirsk State University Library: 630090 Novosibirsk, Akademgorodok; tel. (3832) 65-62-60; 450,000 vols; Dir L. G. TORSHENOVA.

Scientific-Technical Centre for Chemical Information: 630090 Novosibirsk, pr. Akad. Lavrenteva 9; tel. (3832) 35-64-40; attached to Russian Acad. of Sciences; Head Acad. V. A. KOPTYUG.

State Public Scientific and Technical Library of the Siberian Department of

the Russian Academy of Sciences: 630200 Novosibirsk, Voskhod 15; tel. (3832) 66-18-60; fax (3832) 66-33-65; e-mail office@ spsl.nsc.ru; internet www.spsl.nsc.ru; f. 1918; 13,000,000 vols; acts as reference, loan, research and co-ordinating centre for 64 Academy institutes located in Siberia and the Far East; Dir Prof. B. S. ELEPOV.

Omsk

Omsk State University Library: 644077 Omsk, pr. Mira 55a; 182,000 vols; Dir L. A. BALAKINA.

Perm

Perm State University Scientific Library: 614990 Perm, ul. Bukireva 15; tel. (3422) 39-64-80; e-mail library@psu.ru; internet www.psu.ru; f. 1916; 1,400,000 vols; Dir RAISA NIKOLAYEVNA.

Petrozavodsk

Petrozavodsk State University Library: 185640 Petrozavodsk, pr. Lenina 33; tel. (8142) 71-10-44; 850,000 vols; Dir MARINA P. OTLIVANCHIK.

Rostov-on-Don

Rostov State University Library: 344049 Rostov-on-Don, Pushkinskaya 148; tel. and fax (8632) 64-08-56; e-mail fld@lib.rsu.ru; internet www.rsu.ru; f. 1915; attached Museum of the History of Books; 2,411,520 vols; Dir SVETLANA A. BONDARENKO; publ. *Donskaya Speech.*

St Petersburg

All-Russian Geological Library: 199106 St Petersburg, Srednii pr. 74; tel. and fax (812) 321-72-12; e-mail vgb@vsegei.ru; f. 1882; scientific and technical literature; 1,000,000 books, monographs, periodicals and special maps; Dir L. M. ILAKAVICHUS; publ. *Geologicheskaya literatura* (Geological Literature, annually).

Central Music Library attached to the S. M. Kirov State Academic Theatre of Opera and Ballet: St Petersburg, ul. Zodchego Rossi 2; contains one of the largest collections in the world of Russian music in MSS, single copies, first editions, etc, 1,500 copies of Russian vaudeville scores, 200 MSS of ballet scores, and a large collection of opera scores including 1,000 foreign operas; Dir S. O. BROG.

Department of the Art and Museum Book Collections of the State Russian Museum: 191011 St Petersburg, Inzhenernaya ul. 4; tel. (812) 219-16-12; fax (812) 314-14-53; f. 1898; 160,000 vols on fine arts, history, philosophy; Dir I. F. SOKOLOVA.

Library of the National Pushkin Museum: 191186 St Petersburg, nab. Moiki 12; tel. (812) 571-06-19; fax (812) 315-73-79; e-mail vmp@mail.admiral.ru; internet www .museumpushkin.ru; f. 1953; collections of works by Russian authors incl. Pushkin, V. A. Krylov and S. Mazkov; 80,000 vols; Dir M. V. BOKARIUS.

Library of the Russian Academy of Sciences: 199034 St Petersburg, Birzhevaya liniya 1; tel. (812) 328-35-92; fax (812) 328-74-36; e-mail ban@rasl.nw.ru; internet www .ban.ru; f. 1714; 20,353,000 vols; collection of 19,000 MSS, 250,000 rare books, including 834 incunabula; 123,000 maps, 1,800,000 publications of the Russian Academy of Sciences; acts as inter-library loan and reference service, exchange centre and book publisher; conducts research in library science, bibliography, palaeography and conservation; co-ordinates network of 31 specialized libraries in the Academy's research institutes; Dir Dr VALERII P. LEONOV; publs *Bibliography of Publications of the Russian*

Academy of Sciences (annually), *Book in Russia* (annually), *Quarterly Bibliography*.

Library of the State Hermitage Museum: St Petersburg, Dvortsovaya nab. 34; f. 1762; over 500,000 vols; on painting, sculpture and all branches of graphic arts throughout the centuries; Dir MAKAROVA.

Music Library of the St Petersburg Conservatoire: St Petersburg, Teatralnaya pl. 3; fax (812) 312-89-74; e-mail admlib@conservatory.ru; internet biblio.conservatory.ru; f. 1862; 500,000 vols, including 180,000 Russian and foreign works on music, 306,000 scores, 7,600 MSS, 490 incunabula; Dir E. NEKRASOVA.

Music Library of the St Petersburg Dmitri Shostakovich State Philharmonic Society: 191011 St Petersburg, Mikhailovskaya ul. 2; f. 1882; 200,000 scores and books on music, 40,000 engravings, lithographs and paintings of musicians, composers, etc; 1,000,000 newspaper cuttings; Dir G. L. RETROVSKAYA.

National Library of Russia: 191069 St Petersburg, Sadovaya ul. 18; tel. (812) 310-98-50; fax (812) 310-61-48; internet www.nlr.ru; f. 1795; 32,064,000 items, including a large collection of incunabula and MSS; Dir VLADIMIR N. ZAITSEV; publ. *PNB-Informazia* (monthly).

Russian State Historical Archives: 190000 St Petersburg, Angliiskaya nab. 4; tel. (812) 311-09-26; fax (812) 311-22-52; f. 1918; documents of central state bodies of the Russian Empire, state and private banks, railways, industrial, trade and other companies; private collections of prominent political and public figures, etc. (18th century–1917); 350,000 vols; Dir A. R. SOKOLOV; publ. *Herald* (irregular).

Russian State Naval Archives: St Petersburg, Millionnaya ul. 36; tel. (812) 315-90-54; f. 1724; documents of central institutions of the Russian pre-revolutionary and Soviet Navy and prominent naval officers (17th century–1940); 1,219,454 vols; Dir V. G. MISHANOV.

St Petersburg State University M. Gorky Scientific Library: 199034 St Petersburg, Universitetskaya nab. 7/9; tel. (812) 328-27-41; fax (812) 328-27-41; e-mail marina@lib.pu.ru; internet www.lib.pu.ru; f. 1783; 7,000,000 vols; Dir N. A. SHESHINA; publs *Pravovedenie* (every 2 months), *Vestnik* (every 2 weeks).

St Petersburg Theatrical Library: St Petersburg, ul. Zodchego Rossi 2; f. 1756; 800,000 vols of plays and works on theatrical subjects, department of French works with first editions of Corneille; MSS and letters by Chekhov, Turgenev, Diaghilev, Fokine; department of stage designs by Bakst, Benoit, etc; department of classical and contemporary fiction; Dir R. A. MIKHALIOVA.

Scientific Library attached to the Russian Institute for the History of Arts: 190000 St Petersburg, Isaakievskaya pl. 5; tel. (812) 315-55-87; fax (812) 315-72-02; e-mail art@union.nit.spb.su; f. 1912; 300,000 books and periodicals on theatre, music, cinematography, history of literature and art, fiction, philosophy, aesthetics, folklore; Chief Librarian I. V. KYTMANOVA.

Scientific Library of the Russian Academy of Arts: 199034 St Petersburg, Universitetskaya nab. 17; Moscow Branch: 119034 Moscow, ul. Prechistenka 21; f. 1757; 471,445 vols on art, architecture, applied and folk arts, including rare 16th and 17th c. vols and a notable collection of 18th c. works on architecture; Dir L. S. POLAYKOVA; Dir N. V. KOMAROVA.

Samara

Russian State Scientific and Technical Archives: 443096 Samara, ul. Michurina 58; tel. (8462) 36-17-81; fax (8462) 36-17-85 also: Moscow, Profsoyuznaya ul. 82; tel. (095) 335-00-95; f. 1964; documentation of research and development projects in industry, construction, transport and communications; invention applications; Dir YURI A. SHASHARIN.

Samara State University Library: 443086 Samara, ul. Potapova 64/163; 245,000 vols; Dir N. I. PARANINA.

Saransk

Mordovian N. P. Ogarev State University Library: 430000 Saransk, Bolshevistskaya ul. 68; tel. (8342) 4-49-91; f. 1931; 1,954,861 vols; Dir Doc. A. V. SMOLYANOV.

Saratov

V. A. Artisevich Zonal Scientific Library: 410000 Saratov, Universitetskaya ul. 42; tel. (845) 227-14-80; fax (845) 251-40-00; e-mail library@sgu.ru; internet library.sgu.ru/nbsgu; f. 1909; 2,861,763 vols; Dir IRINA V. LEBEDEVA.

Syktyvkar

Syktyvkar State University Library: 167001 Syktyvkar, Oktyabrskii pr. 55; tel. (8212) 43-94-51; fax (8212) 43-72-86; f. 1972; 560,980 vols; 812 MSS and books published in Russia before the 18th century; 22 personal archives of scientists; Dir NONNA F. AKOPOVA; publs *Rubezh* (4 a year), *Vestnik* (annually).

Tomsk

Russian State Historical Archive of the Far East: Tomsk, ul. K. Marksa 26; tel. (3822) 2-29-15; formerly Central State Archive of the RSFSR of the Far East (TsGA RSFSR DV).

Tomsk State University Library: 634010 Tomsk, Leninskii pr. 34-a; tel. (3822) 2-44-69; 3,320,000 vols; Dir E. SYNTIN.

Tver

Tver State Medical Academy Library: 170000 Tver, ul. Sovetskaya 4; tel. (822) 33-27-26; fax (822) 33-43-09; e-mail post@tgmi.tunis.tver.su; f. 1954; 468 vols; Dir O. V. TULTSEVA.

Tyumen

Tyumen State University Library: 625036 Tyumen, ul. Volodarskogo 38; 382,000 vols; Dir L. P. KRYUKOVA.

Ufa

Bashkir State University Library: 450074 Ufa, ul. Frunze 32; tel. (3472) 23-66-26; 780,000 vols; Dir E. G. GUIVANOVSKAYA.

National Library of Bashkortostan: 450000 Ufa, ul. Lenina 4; tel. (3472) 22-04-89; fax (3472) 22-04-89; e-mail filib@rb.ru; Dir ILGIZ UTIAGANOV.

Vladikavkaz

North-Ossetian State University Library: 362000 Vladikavkaz, ul. Vatutina 46; 76,000 vols; Dir K. L. KOCHISOV.

Vladimir

Central State Archives of the Nation's Documentary Films and Photographs: Vladimir, Letneperevozinskaya ul. 9; tel. (0922) 2-79-95 also: Moscow oblast, Krasnogorsk, Rechnaya ul. 1; tel. (095) 563-08-45; topical films, newsreels and historical material which was not included in finished films, negatives of documentary photographs (1854–); Dir L. P. ZAPRYAGAEVA.

Vladivostok

Far Eastern State University Central Library: 690652 Vladivostok, Okeanskii pr. 37/41; 700,000 vols; Dir A. G. TRETYAKOVA.

Voronezh

Scientific Library of Voronezh State University: 394000 Voronezh, pr. Revolyutsii 24; tel. (4732) 55-35-59; fax (4732) 20-82-58; e-mail nmo_znb@lib.vsu.ru; internet www.lib.vsu.ru; f. 1918; 3,033,285 vols; Dir OLGA ZAITSEVA (acting).

Yakutsk

Yakutsk State University Library: 677891 Yakutsk, Leninskii pr. 33; tel. (4112) 2-87-49; 429,000 vols; Dir A. P. SEMENOV.

Yalutorovsk

Centre for the Preservation of the Reserve Collection: Tyumen oblast, Yalutorovsk, Ishimskaya ul. 136; tel. (34535) 2-29-87; formed from Central State Archive Reserve Collection of Documents of the State Archive Collection of the USSR (TsGA SF SSSR).

Yaroslavl

Yaroslavl State University Library: 150000 Yaroslavl, ul. Kirova 8/10; tel. (0852) 32-11-94; 263,000 vols; Dir V. A. DOKTOROVA.

Museums and Art Galleries

Arkhangelsk

Arkhangelsk State Museum: 163061 Arkhangelsk, pl. V. I. Lenina 2; tel. (8182) 3-66-79; f. 1737; contains 150,000 items featuring the history of the North coast area of Russia, since ancient times; large collection of archaeology, ethnography, documents and photographs; library of 30,000 vols; Dir YU. P. PROKOPEV.

Arkhangelsk State Museum of Fine Arts: 163061 Arkhangelsk, nab. Lenina 79; tel. (8182) 3-26-73; e-mail m1444@mail.museum.ru; internet www.museum.ru/m1444; contains over 150,000 items of ancient North and Western European art; library of 30,000 vols; Dir M. V. MITKEVICH.

Ashaga-stal

Stalsky Memorial Museum: 368765 Dagestan, Suleiman-Stalskii raion, Ashaga-stal; e-mail m1802@museum.ru; internet www.museum.ru/m1802; f. 1950; exhibits on the history of Dagestan literature, former home of poet Suleiman Stalskii; library of 20,000 vols; Dir LIDIYA M. STALSKAYA.

Astrakhan

Astrakhan State B. M. Kustodiev Gallery: Astrakhan, ul. Sverdlova 81; tel. (8512) 22-66-65; fax (8512) 22-66-65; f. 1918; fine arts; library of 15,000 vols; Dir L. J. ILINA.

Barnaul

State Art Museum of Altai Territory: Barnaul, pr. Lenina 88; tel. (3852) 61-25-10; fax (3852) 61-06-70; e-mail muzei@ab.ru; internet muzei.ab.ru; f. 1959; large collection since 16th c., of icons, paintings, sculptures, wood carvings, ceramics, national costumes; library of 13,526 vols; Dir I. K. GALKINA.

Belinsky

Belinsky, V. G., State Museum: Penza oblast, Belinsky, ul. Belinskogo 11; f. 1938; 31,280 exhibits on the life and work of the literary critic V. G. Belinsky; Curator I. A. GERASEKIN.

Borodino

Borodino State War and History Museum: 143240 Moscow oblast, Mozhaisk, selo Borodino; tel. (09638) 6-32-23; fax (09638) 6-32-22; e-mail borodino@mozhaysk.net; internet www.borodino.ru; f. 1839; research into 1812 campaign, the Battle of Borodino and the 1941–45 war; 60,000 exhibits include material on the Battle of Borodino; library of 12,000 vols; Dir ALICE D. KACHALOVA; Curator GALINA N. NEVSKAYA.

Bryansk

Bryansk State Museum of Soviet Fine Arts: Bryansk, ul. Gagarina 19; Dir B. F. FAENKOV.

Cheboksary

Chuvash Art Museum: 428008 Cheboksary, Kalinina 60; tel. (8352) 22-07-04; f. 1939; 12,000 exhibits, mainly modern Russian, Soviet and Chuvash artists and traditional Chuvash decorative art; library of 15,000 vols; Dir N. SADYUKOV.

Chelyabinsk

Chelyabinsk State Picture Gallery: Chelyabinsk, ul. Truda 92-a; 5,000 items; Dir I. F. TKACHENKO.

Ekaterinburg

Ekaterinburg Picture Gallery: Ekaterinburg, ul. Vainera 11; f. 1746; Western European, Russian and Soviet artists and objects from the Kishisk foundries; Dir E. V. KHAMTSOV.

State Amalgamated Museum of the Writers of the Urals: 620151 Ekaterinburg, Tolmacheva ul. 41; tel. (3432) 51-72-81; f. 1940 (amalgamated 1980); study and popularization of the heritage of the writers of the Urals, collections include the personal belongings and archives of Mamin-Sibiryak, Bazhov and other Ural writers, illustrations to editions of their works and various other artworks, 34,723 items in all; incorporates the House of D. N. Mamin-Sibiryak in Ekaterinburg, the House of P. P. Bazhov, the House of F. M. Reshetnikov; library of 37,700 vols; Dir L. A. KHUDYAKOVA.

Ural Geological Museum: 620144 Ekaterinburg, ul. Kuibysheva 30; tel. (343) 257-31-09; fax (343) 257-48-38; f. 1937; Dir YURI A. POLENOV.

Gagarin

Yurii Gagarin Memorial Museum: 215010 Gagarin, ul. Gerzena 7; tel. (08135) 4-88-37; fax (08135) 4-88-37; f. 1970; exhibits depicting the life and career of Yurii Alekseevich Gagarin (the first man in space) and other early Soviet cosmonauts, and the designers of the spaceships; Dir MARIA STEPANOVA.

Ivanovo

Ivanovo Museum of Art: 153002 Ivanovo, pr. Lenina 33; tel. (0932) 32-65-04; f. 1960; Greek, Roman and Ancient Egyptian art, icons, 18th–20th-century Russian art; library of 7,500 vols; Dir L. W. WOLOWENSKAYA.

Kaluga

Kaluga Museum of Art: Kaluga, ul. Lenina 104; 2,700 exhibits; Dir. A. V. KAZAK.

Tsiolkovsky, K. E., State Museum of the History of Cosmonautics: Kaluga, ul. Koroleva 2; tel. (842) 57-43-33; fax (842) 57-43-33; e-mail director@mkosmos.kaluga.ru; internet www.museum.ru/gmik; f. 1967; contains K. E. Tsiolkovsky's scientific works, history of rocket technique and cosmonau-

tics, large collection of objects relating to astronautics and rocket technology, including the first experimental rocket launched in 1933, the *Sputniks* and *Luniks*, models of orbital stations; library of 35,600 vols; Dir EVGENY KOUZIN.

Kazan

Kazan State A. M. Gorky Memorial Museum: Kazan, ul. Gorkogo 10; exhibits illustrating Gorky's life in the flat where he lived and wrote.

National Museum of the Republic of Tatarstan: Tatarstan, 420111 Kazan, Kremlevskaya ul. 2; tel. (8432) 92-71-62; fax (8432) 92-14-84; e-mail tatar_museum@mail.ru; internet www.tatar.museum.ru; f. 1894; history, archaeology, ethnography, natural resources and decorative applied art of Tatarstan, Russia and other countries; library of 12,000 vols; 54 brs; Gen. Man. G. S. MYKHANOV.

State Museum of Fine Arts of the Republic of Tatarstan: 420015 Kazan, ul. K. Marksa 64; tel. (8432) 36-69-21; fax (8432) 36-18-65; e-mail museum@mfa.kcn.ru; internet www.kcn.ru/tat_en/culture/art_museum/home.htm; f. 1958; large collections of Russian, West European and Soviet paintings; 10,000 exhibits; Dir ANATOLIY A. SLASTUNIN.

Tatar Historical Museum (House of V. I. Lenin): Tatarstan, Kazan, ul. Ulyanova 58; 10,000 exhibits including documents, photographs, works of art and other exhibits relating to Lenin's life.

Kirov

Kirov Victor and Apollinaris Vasnetsov Museum: 610000 Kirov, ul. K. Marksa 70; tel. (8332) 62-26-46; f. 1910; Russian and West European sculpture, paintings, engravings and decorative arts; library of 14,000 vols; Dir ALLA A. NOSKOVA.

Kirovsk

Polar Alpine Botanical Garden Institute: 184230 Murmansk region, Kirovsk; tel. (81555) 63350; fax (81555) 79448; e-mail pabgi@aprec.ru; attached to Russian Acad. of Sciences; Dir Prof. VLADIMIR K. ZHIROV.

Klin

Tchaikovsky House-Museum: 141600 Klin, ul. Tchaikovskogo 48; tel. (49624) 5-81-96; fax (49624) 5-84-67; e-mail gdmch@dol.ru; internet www.museum.ru/m443; f. 1894; composer's last residence and first Russian musical museum; contains 204,549 documents and museum treasures associated with the life and work of Tchaikovsky and other Russian musicians; library of 56,952 vols; Dir GALINA I. BELONOVICH.

Komsomolsk-on-Amur

Komsomolsk-on-Amur Museum of Soviet Fine Arts: Komsomolsk-on-Amur, pr. Mira 50; 5,000 exhibits; Dir E. Y. TURCHINSKAYA.

Konchanskoe-Suvorovskoe

Suvorov Museum: 174435 Novogorodskaya oblast, Borovichskii raion, selo Konchanskoe-Suvorovskoe; tel. (81664) 9-85-33; internet www.museum.ru/m669; the museum features the main periods in the life of General A. V. Suvorov; Dir V. P. MALYSHEVA.

Kostroma

Kostroma Museum of Fine Arts: Kostroma, pr. Mira 5; f. 1913; 5,700 items; collecting, exhibitions, sales, scientific and historical Russian art research, art restoration; library of 6,410 vols; special collections

of Ancient Russian religious books and the work of Y. Chestnyakov; Dir V. Y. IGNATEV.

Krasnoyarsk

Krasnoyarsk Arts Museum: 660097 Krasnoyarsk, Parizhskoi Kommuny ul. 20; tel. (3912) 27-25-58; f. 1958; Russian art (including icons), Russian pre-revolutionary applied art, Siberian folk art and Soviet art; painting, sculpture, graphic art, applied arts; library of 7,700 vols; Dir A. F. EFIMOVSKII; publ. *Surikov Readings* (2 a year).

Krasnoyarsk Museum and Historical Centre: Krasnoyarsk, pl. Mira 1; tel. (3912) 23-82-02; f. 1987; Dir MIKHAIL SHUBSKY.

Kursk

Kursk Art Gallery: 305016 Kursk, ul. Sovetskaya 3; tel. and fax (4712) 54-87-21; e-mail gallery@sovtest.ru; internet www.kursk.amr-museum.ru; f. 1935; Russian, Soviet and European painting and sculpture; library of 50,000 vols; Dir I. A. PRIPACHKIN.

Lermontovo

Lermontov State Museum 'Tarkhany': Penza oblast, Belinskii raion, Lermontovo 442280; tel. (84153) 2-22-34; fax (84153) 2-12-03; e-mail muslerm@sura.ru; internet www.sura.ru/tarhany; f. 1939; life and work of M. Yu. Lermontov; library of 14,000 books; Dir T. M. MELNIKOVA; publ. *Tarkhansky vestnik* (2 a year).

Makhachkala

Dagestan Museum of Fine Arts: Makhachkala, ul. Markova 45; 7,000 exhibits.

Maloyaroslavets

Maloyaroslavets Museum of Military History of 1812: 249050 Maloyaroslavets, Moskovskaya ul. 27; tel. (08431) 2 27-11; f. 1939; collection and study of exhibits of the 1812 war; library of 1,100 vols; Dir N. V. KOTLYAKOVA; publ. *Nashe Nasledie* (Our Heritage, every 2 months).

Melikhovo

Chekhov, A. P. Literature and Memorial Museum-Reserve: 142326 Moscow oblast, Chekhovskii raion, Melikhovo; tel. (272) 3-64-73; fax (272) 3-64-53; f. 1944; the house where the writer lived and worked; library of 14,200 vols and documents; Dir K. V. BOBKOV.

Miass

Natural Science Museum of the Ilmen State Reserve: 456301 Chelyabinsk oblast, Miass 1; tel. (35135) 5-48-90; fax (35135) 5-02-86; e-mail founds@imin.urc.ac.ru; f. 1930; the museum shows the mineralogical resources of the Ilmen State Reserve, the grounds of which contain more than 250 minerals; library of 17,000 vols; Dir Dr S. N. NIKANDROV; publs *Trudy Ilmenskogo Zapovednika, Uralsky mineralogichesky Sbornik*.

Moscow

Anuchin, D. N., Anthropological Institute and Museum: 103009 Moscow, Institute of Anthropology, Moscow State University, Mokhovaya ul. 18; tel. (095) 203-66-09; f. 1879; about 470,000 items; anthropology and archaeology of the Stone Age; collections from outstanding Russian explorers; Mousterian Man from Teshik-Tash and Staroselyie; Mesolithic burials from the Dnieper Region in the Ukraine; library of 30,000 vols; Dir Prof. Dr V. P. CHTETSOV.

Central A. A. Bakhrushin State Theatrical Museum: 113054 Moscow, ul. Bakhrushina 31/12; tel. (095) 953-48-70; fax (095) 953-

54-48; e-mail gctm@ncport.ru; internet www
.gertstein.org/bakhrushin/index.htm; f. 1894;
to collect, house, study and exhibit varied
materials on history and theory of theatre;
approx. 1,300,000 exhibits; library of 120,000
vols; archives of original MSS of Ostrovsky,
Lensky, Stanislavsky, Meyerhold, etc.; Dir V.
V. GUBIN.

**Central Museum of Aviation and Cos-
monautics:** 125167 Moscow, Krasnoarmeiskaya 4; tel. (095) 212-73-01; f. 1924; to record
the national development of aeronautics and
astronautics; contains original full-size aircraft, spacecraft, recovered space exploration
vehicles, instruments, flight clothing, accessories of technical, historical and biographical interest; library of 15,800 vols; Dir P. F.
VYALIKOV.

Central Museum of the Armed Forces:
129110 Moscow, I-110, ul. Sovetskoi Armii 2,
a/ya 125; tel. and fax (495) 281-18-80; f. 1919;
military exhibits; library of 90,000 vols; Dir
A.K. NIKONOV.

Chekhov, A. P., House-Museum: 103001
Moscow, Sadovaya-Kudrinskaya 6; tel. (095)
291-61-54; f. 1954; flat where the writer lived
from 1886–1890; branch of the State Literature Museum.

Dostoevsky, F. M., Museum: 103030 Moscow, ul. Dostoyevskogo 2; tel. (095) 281-10-
85; f. 1928; affiliated to the State Literature
Museum; exhibits illustrating Dostoyevsky's
life, organized in the flat where he lived until
sixteen years old; Dir GALINA B. PONOMAR-
EVA.

Fersman Mineralogical Museum: 119071
Moscow, Leninsky pr. 18, korp. 2; tel. (095)
954-39-00; fax (095) 952-48-50; e-mail
mineral@fmm.ru; internet www.fmm.ru; f.
1716; attached to Russian Acad. of Sciences;
150,000 mineral samples from throughout
the world; library of 16,700 vols; Dir Prof. M.
I. NOVGORODOVA; publ. *New data on minerals*
(annually).

**'Glinka, M. I.', State Central Museum of
Musical Culture:** 125047 Moscow, ul.
Fadeeva 4; tel. (095) 972-32-37; fax (095)
972-32-55; e-mail glinka@cityline.ru;
internet www.museum.ru/glinka; f. 1943;
based on the Museum of the Moscow Conservatoire; collects archives, MSS and memorabilia; musical instruments; musical
iconography; records and tape recordings;
music, books, posters, programmes—in all,
800,000 items; exhibits: musical instruments
of the world; Russian musical culture; Dir-
Gen. A. D. PANIUSHKIN.

**Gogol, N. V., House-Museum and Gogol
Study Centre:** 121019 Moscow, Nikitsky
bul. 7; tel. (095) 291-15-50; fax (095) 291-15-
50; e-mail vik@systel.ru; f. 1974; library of
200,000 vols, Gogol spec. colln of 600 vols and
manuscript room; also exhibits illustrating
life and work of Gogol; Dir VERA P. VIKULOVA.

Gorky, A. M., Memorial Museum: Moscow
121069, Malaya Nikitskaya ul. 6/2; tel. (095)
290-05-35; f. 1965 in the house where the
author lived; contains Gorky's private library
of 10,000 vols, and his collection of Oriental
arts (ivory); Dir L. P. BYKOVTSEVA.

Gorky, A. M., Museum: 121069 Moscow, ul.
Povarskaya 25A; tel. (095) 291-51-30; f. 1937;
44,500 items, including literary and photographic documents, works of art, memorabilia; Dir L. P. BYKOVTSEVA.

Kremlin Museums: 103073 Moscow,
Kreml; tel. (095) 924-55-03; fax (095) 921-
63-23; e-mail head@kremlin.museum.ru;
internet www.kreml.ru; Dir YELENA GAGAR-
INA.

Attached sites:

Armoury: 103073 Moscow, Kreml; f. 1857;
100,000 items: weapons, arms and jewels
from the 12th century to the Revolution.

Kremlin Cathedrals: 103073 Moscow,
Kreml; The cathedrals around the Cathedral Square (Sobornaya ploshchad)
include, among others, the following:
Cathedral of the Assumption (f. 1479);
icons of the 14th–17th centuries; throne
of Ivan the Terrible. Cathedral of the
Annunciation (f. 1489); iconostasis by
leading artists of the 15th century. Arch-
angel Cathedral (1508); tombs of Ivan
Kalita and other Russian Grand Dukes
and Czars. Rizpolozhenskii Cathedral (f.
1485). Cathedral of the Twelve Apostles
and Patriarch's Palace; 17th-century items
of applied decorative art.

Main Botanical Garden 'N. V. Tsitsin':
127276 Moscow, Botanicheskaya ul. 4; tel.
(095) 977-84-18; fax (095) 977-91-72; e-mail
lander@aha.ru; internet www.gbsad.ru; f.
1945; attached to Russian Acad. of Sciences;
br. in Cheboksary; Dir Dr ALEXANDER S.
DEMIDOV; publs *Bulletin* (2 a year), *Newsletter* (2 a year).

Marx-Engels Museum: c/o Russian State
Archive of Modern History, 103132 Moscow,
ul. Ilinka 12; f. 1962; 2,000 exhibits descriptive of the lives of Marx and Engels; Dir V. N.
KUZNETSOV.

Moscow Arts Theatre Museum: 103009
Moscow, pr-d Khudozhestvennogo Teatra 3A;
tel. (095) 229-00-80; f. 1923; Dir V. S.
DAVIDOV.

Attached museums:

**Nemirovich-Danchenko, V., Flat-
Museum:** 103009 Moscow, Ul. Nemirovi-
cha-Danchenko 5/7, kv. 52; tel. 209-53-91;
f. 1944; illustrating career of Nemirovich-
Danchenko.

Stanislavsky, K. S., House-Museum:
103009 Moscow, Ul. Stanislavskogo 6; tel.
229-28-55; affiliated to Theatre Museum; f.
1948; deals with Stanislavsky's work and
the theatrical career of People's Artist, M.
P. Lilina.

**Moscow State University Museum of
Zoology:** 125009 Moscow, ul. Bol. Nikitskaya 6; tel. (095) 203-64-93; fax (095) 203-27-
17; e-mail zmmu@zmmu.msu.ru; internet
zmmu.msu.ru; f. 1791; systematics, specia-
tion, zoogeography, fauna research, phyloge-
netics; library of 190,000 vols; Dir Dr OLGA L.
ROSSOLIMO; publs *Archives* (annually), *Zool-
ogicheskie Issledovania (Zoological
Research)*.

**Museum of Earth Science of the Moscow
State M. V. Lomonosov University:**
119899 Moscow, Universitetskaya pl. 1,
MGU; tel. (095) 939-14-15; fax (095) 939-15-
94; f. 1955; includes material on the origin of
the face of the earth, its geospheres, surface
landscape sphere, earth crust, climates,
waters, soils, plants, animals, economic
resources; on the conservation, utilization
and reconstruction of nature; complex geological and geographical characteristics of
Russia and of the earth; science-teaching,
geological-geographical museum for students
of the Geological, Geographical, Biological
and Pedological departments of Moscow
University; library of 10,000 vols in library;
Dir Prof. S. A. USHAKOV; publ. *Zhizn Zemli*
(The Life of the Earth, 1 vol. every 1–2
years).

Museum of Frontier Guards: Moscow, ul.
Bol. Bronnaya 23; 110,000 exhibits featuring
the history of Soviet frontier guards.

**Museum of the History of the City of
Moscow:** 103012 Moscow, Novaya pl. 12; tel.

(095) 924-31-45; fax (095) 924-31-45; f. 1896;
Dir G. I. VEDEZNIKOVA.

**Museum of the Palaeontological Insti-
tute:** 117647 Moscow, Profsoyuznaya ul. 123;
tel. (095) 339-05-77; fax (095) 339-12-66;
e-mail admin@paleo.ru; internet www.paleo
.ru; f. 1930; Dir A. YU. ROZANOV.

**Museum of the State Academic Malyi
Theatre:** 103009 Moscow, Malyi teatr, Teatralnaya pl. 1/6; tel. (095) 921-85-48; f. 1932,
being developed out of 1927 exhibition;
illustrates and studies history of the Theatre;
Dir YU. M. STRUTINSKAYA.

Nikolai Rubinstein Museum: c/o Moscow
P. I. Tchaikovsky State Conservatoire,
103871 Moscow, Bol. Nikitskaya 13; tel.
(095) 229-90-98; fax (095) 229-90-98;
internet www.mosconsv.ru; colln incl. musical instruments and portraits and sculptures
of Russian composers; documents, photographs, phonographs, antique furniture.

Novodevichii Monastery Museum:
119435 Moscow, Novodevichii pr. 1; tel.
(095) 246-22-01; fax (095) 246-85-26; e-mail
m337@mail.museum.ru; internet www.shm
.ru/filials/novodev/fil_nov.htm; Smolensky
Cathedral (1524) and other monuments of
Russian architecture form the architectural
ensemble of the monastery; Russian fine and
decorative art (16th and 17th centuries); Dir
IRINA G. BORISENKO.

**Obraztsov Central State Puppet Thea-
tre Museum:** 103473 Moscow, Sadovo Samo-
technaya ul. 3; tel. (095) 299-89-10; fax (095)
299-89-10; e-mail museum@obraztsov.ru;
internet www.puppet.ru/museum; f. 1937;
Central Puppet Theatre; 5,600 dolls from 50
countries; puppet theatres of the fmr USSR
and many other countries; colln of cartoons,
sketches, MSS and other documents; library
of 15,000 books; Dir Dr BORIS GOLDOVSKY.

**Permanent Tchaikovsky Exhibition in
the Tchaikovsky Concert Hall:** 125047
Moscow, pl. Triumfalnaya 4/31; exhibits of
the composer's life and works.

Petrographic Museum: 109017 Moscow,
Staromonetnyi per. 35; tel. (095) 230-82-92;
fax (095) 230-21-79; e-mail pavlov@igem.ru;
internet www.museum.ru/M417; f. 1934; Dir
V. A. PAVLOV.

**Pharmaceutical Museum of the Central
Drug Research Institute:** 117418 Moscow,
ul. Krasikova 34; tel. (095) 120-91-51; unique
collection of about 6,000 items on the history
of pharmacy in Russia and the fmr USSR;
Dir B. M. SALO.

Polytechnical Museum: 101000 Moscow,
Polytekhnicheskii pr-d 2; tel. (095) 928-64-
65; fax (095) 923-51-60; e-mail CPB@polymus
.ru; internet www.polymus.ru; f. 1864; over
100,000 exhibits; features history and latest
developments in science and technology;
belongs to the Ministry of Culture; library
of 3m. vols; Dir Prof. G. G. GRIGORIAN.

**Rublev, Andrei, Central Museum of
Ancient Russian Culture and Art:**
107120 Moscow, Andronevskaya pl. 10; tel.
(095) 278-14-89; fax (095) 278-50-55; e-mail
rublevmu@aha.ru; f. 1947; Russian art,
icons, applied art, manuscripts, old printed
books; library of 23,000 vols; Dir Dr G. V.
POPOV.

Shchukin, B. V., Museum-Room: Moscow,
Flat 11, ul. Shchukina 8; contains material
he had about him during his lifetime as a
great actor at the Vakhtangov Theatre.

**Shchusev, A. V., State Research Archi-
tectural Museum:** 121019 Moscow, ul.
Vozdvizhenka 5/25; tel. (095) 291-21-09; fax
(095) 291-21-09; e-mail schusev@muar.ru;
internet www.muar.ru; f. 1934; objects:
study, collection, care and popularization of
historical architecture, outstanding contem-

porary work, monumental sculpture and painting; collection and care of documents on architecture and town planning; over 70,000 sheets of architectural drawings; over 300,000 negatives and 400,000 photographs of architectural monuments throughout the world; library of 50,000 vols; Dir D. A. SARKISIAN; Curator I. V. SEDOVA.

Skryabin, A. N., Museum: 121002 Moscow, ul. Vakhtangova 11; tel. (095) 241-19-01; f. 1919, opened in 1922 in flat where the composer lived and died; MSS, letters, Skryabin's personal library and magnetic-tape archive of Skryabin's compositions performed by the composer and famous artists; excursions, lectures and concerts; library of 287 vols in Skryabin's personal library, 2,149 vols in scientific library; Dir RYBAKOVA.

State Academic Bolshoi Theatre Museum: 103009 Moscow, Bolshoi Teatr, Okhotnyi Ryad 8/2; tel. (095) 292-00-25; f. 1920; objects: documentation of the work of the Bolshoi Theatre, collection of materials and documents on its history and work, study of history of the theatre; Dir V. I. ZARUBIN.

State Central Museum of Contemporary Russian History: 125009 Moscow, Tverskaya ul. 21; tel. (095) 299-52-17; fax (095) 299-85-15; e-mail 9055.g23@g23.relcom.ru; internet www.sovr.ru; f. 1917; social and political history of Russia since 1850; library of 360,000 vols and 825,000 periodicals; Dir Dr TAMARA SHUMNAYA; publ. *Trudy* (Proceedings).

State Darwin Museum: 117292 Moscow, Vavilova 57; tel. (095) 135-33-76; fax (095) 135-33-84; e-mail darwin@museum.ru; internet www.darwin.museum.ru; f. 1907; natural history and evolution; total holdings of 360,065 items; library of 30,000 vols; Dir A. I. KLUKINA.

State Historical Museum: 103012 Moscow, Krasnaya pl. 1/2; tel. (095) 924-45-29; fax (095) 925-95-27; e-mail shkurko@shm.ru; internet www.shm.ru; f. 1872; 4,500,000 exhibits covering Russian history from prehistory to the present; library of 229,000 vols, 29,000 MSS, 25,000 rare books; collection of birch-bark writings; Dir-Gen. ALEXANDER SHKURKO; publs *Trudy GIM, Ezhegodnik GIM, Numizmaticheskii sbornik* (irregular).

State Literature Museum: 103051 Moscow, Petrovka ul. 28; tel. (095) 921-38-57; fax (095) 923-30-22; f. 1934; the museum is a research and educational centre which collects, studies and publishes material on the history of Russian and Soviet literature; br. (museums of Lermontov, Herzen, Dostoevsky, Chekhov, Tolstoy, Pasternak, Prishvin, Aksakov and Bryusov); library of 250,000 vols; Gen. Dir NATALYA V. SHAKHALOVA.

State Museum of Ceramics (country-seat Kuskovo): 111402 Moscow Yunosti ul. 2; tel. (095) 370-01-50; fax (095) 918-65-40; e-mail kuskovo@kuskovo.ru; internet www.kuskovo.ru; large collection of Russian art: paintings, furniture, porcelain, pottery; collection of West European art, tapestries, furniture, paintings, porcelain, pottery, etc.; Dir YELENA S. YERITSYAN.

State Museum of Oriental Art: 107120 Moscow, Nikitsky bul. 12A; tel. (095) 291-96-14; fax (095) 202-48-46; e-mail info@orientalart.ru; internet www.orientalart.ru; f. 1918; large collection of Middle and Far Eastern art, art of the fmr Soviet Central Asian Republics and Transcaucasia, carpets, fabrics, ceramics, etc.; Dir-Gen. V. A. NABACHIKOV.

State Pushkin Museum: 119034 Moscow, ul. Prechistenka 12/2; tel. (095) 202-43-54; fax (095) 202-43-54; f. 1958; 200,000 exhibits;

library of 51,000 vols; maintains br. in Pushkin's former home (Arbat 53); Dir E. BOGATYREV.

State Pushkin Museum of Fine Arts: 121019 Moscow, Volkhonka 12; tel. (095) 203-58-09; fax (095) 203-46-74; e-mail finearts@gmii.museum.ru; internet www.museum.ru/gmii; f. 1912; about 558,000 items of ancient Eastern, Graeco-Roman, Byzantine, European and American art; numismatic colln of 200,000 items; library of 200,000 vols; Dir I. A. ANTONOVA; Chief Conservator GALINA ERSHOVA.

State Tretyakov Gallery: 117049 Moscow, Lavrushinskii per. 10; tel. (095) 230-77-88; fax (095) 231-10-51; e-mail tretyakov@tretyakov.ru; internet www.tretyakov.ru; f. 1856; collection of 130,000 Russian icons and works of Russian and Soviet painters, sculptors and graphic artists since 11th c.; also 3,200 items from the former Pyotr Zakharov Fine Arts Museum in Grozny; new building at Krymskiy Val houses an exhibition of Russian art from 20th c.; Dir VALENTIN A. RODIONOV.

State V. V. Mayakovsky Museum: 101000 Moscow, pr. Serova 3/6; tel. (095) 921-93-87; f. 1974 in the building where Mayakovsky lived 1919–30; manuscripts, documentary material, notebooks, memorial items; library and reading room with c. 200,000 vols, including periodicals; Dir S. E. STRIZHNIKOVA.

S. T. Morozov Folk-Art Museum: 103009 Moscow, Leontyevskii per. 7; tel. (095) 290-52-22; f. 1885; three sections devoted to (*a*) handicrafts connected with peasant daily life; (*b*) applied arts both ancient and contemporary; (*c*) experimental decorative applied art; about 800,000 exhibits; under the jurisdiction of the Russian Council of Local Industries; Dir G. A. YAKOVLEVA.

Timiryazev, K. A., Apartment Museum: 103009 Moscow, Romanovski per. 2, str. 2, kv. 29; tel. (095) 202-80-64; fax (095) 976-29-10; f. 1942; cultural and historical memorial to K. A. Timiryazev; 7,545 exhibits and archives on his life and work; library: personal library of 4,871 vols; Dir A.A. DRUCHEK.

Timiryazev State Museum of Biology: 123242 Moscow, Mal. Gruzinskaya 15; tel. (095) 252-55-42; fax (095) 255-63-21; e-mail gbmt@cea.ru; internet www.museum.ru/timiryazev; f. 1922; origin and evolution of life on earth; library of 11,500 vols; Dir E. A. CHUSOVA.

Tolstoy Residence Museum: 119021 Moscow, ul. Lva Tolstogo 21; tel. (095) 246-94-44; rooms arranged as they were when the author lived there; 4,200 exhibits; Dir A. V. SALOMATIN.

Tolstoy State Museum: 119034 Moscow, ul. Prechistenka 11; tel. (095) 201-58-11; fax (095) 202-93-38; f. 1911; MSS section contains 170,000 sheets of Tolstoy's writings and nearly 600,000 MSS and archive material on Tolstoy and his circle; library of 76,800 works by or about Tolstoy; nearly 87,000 newspaper cuttings, and over 42,000 exhibits in the form of painting, sculpture, photographs, etc.; Dir L. M. LUBIMOVA.

Vakhtangov Theatre Museum: Moscow; history of the Vakhtangov Theatre; Dir I. L. SERGEEVA.

Vernadsky State Geological Museum: 103009 Moscow, Mokhovaya ul. 11, korp. 2; tel. (095) 203-52-87; fax (095) 203-47-98; e-mail info@sgm.ru; internet www.sgm.ru; f. 1755; Dir Prof. D. V. RUNDQVIST.

Zhukovskii, N. E., Memorial Museum: 107005 Moscow, ul. Radio 17; tel. (095) 267-50-54; 25,000 items feature the work of N. E.

Zhukovskii, and Soviet contributions to aviation and astronautics; Dir V. I. MASLOV.

Nalchik

Kabarda-Balkar Art Museum: Nalchik, pr. V. I. Lenina 35; 3,500 exhibits; Dir I. Z. BATASHOV.

Nizhnii Novgorod

Nizhnii Novgorod Historical Museum: Nizhnii Novgorod, nab. Zhdanova 7; 160,000 exhibits including collections of archaeology, featuring the history of the Central Volga area since ancient times.

Nizhnii Novgorod State Museum of Art: 603082 Nizhnii Novgorod, korp. 3 Kremlya; tel. (8312) 39-08-55; fax (8312) 19-20-85; e-mail art@museum.nnov.ru; internet www.museum.nnov.ru/art; f. 1896; Dir VALENTINA N. KRIVOVA.

State A. M. Gorky Museum of Literature: 603155 Nizhnii Novgorod, ul. Minina 26; tel. and fax (8312) 36-15-29; e-mail danco6@yandex.ru; internet www.museum.nnov.ru/danco; f. 1928; 102,000 exhibits, illustrating the life and work of the writer; library of 40,000 vols; Dir T. A. RIZHOVA.

Novocherkassk

Novocherkassk Museum of the History of the Don Cossacks: 346430 Rostov oblast, Novocherkassk, Atamanskaya ul. 38; tel. (86352) 4-80-59; e-mail m838@mail.museum.ru; internet www.doncossacks.ru; f. 1899; deals with the traditions and exploits of the Don Cossacks; collections of porcelain and painting; library of 17,000 vols; Dir SVETLANA A. SEDINKO.

Novosibirsk

Central Siberian Botanical Garden: 630090 Novosibirsk, Zolotodolinskaya ul. 101; tel. (3832) 30-41-01; fax (3832) 30-19-86; e-mail root@botgard.nsk.su; internet www.cbsg.narod.ru; f. 1946; attached to Russian Acad. of Sciences; Dir Prof. V. P. SEDELNIKOV.

Omsk

Omsk Fine Art Museum: Omsk, ul. Lenina 23; 3,780 exhibits; Dir A. A. GERZON.

Orel

Turgenev, I. S., State Literary Museum: 302000 Orel, ul. Turgeneva 11; tel. (08622) 6-27-37; f. 1918; library of 60,000 vols; Dir V. V. SAFRONOVA.

Branch museums:

Granovsky, T. N., Museum: Orel, ul. 7 Noyabrya 24; tel. (08622) 6-34-65; f. 1985; devoted to public figures born in Orel; Man. E. A. IVUSHKINA.

Literary Museum: 302000 Orel, ul. Turgeneva 11; tel. (08622) 6-35-28; f. 1957; devoted to writers born in Orel; Man. L. E. URAKOVA.

Leskov, N. S., House Museum: 301028 Orel, ul. Oktyabrskaya 9; tel. (08622) 6-33-04; f. 1974; Man. L. S. KAMYSHALOVA.

Bunin Museum: 302000 Orel, Oktyabrsky pr. 1; tel. (08622) 6-07-74; f. 1991; Man. I. A. KOSTOMAROVA.

Andreev, N., House Museum: Orel, Pushkarnaya 41; tel. (08622) 6-48-24; f. 1991; Man. O. Y. VOLOGINA.

Orenburg

Orenburg Fine Art Museum: Orenburg, ul. Pravdy 6; 3,500 items; Dir L. B. POPOVA.

Palekh

State Museum of Palekh Art: 155620 Ivanovo oblast, Palekh ul. Bakanova 50; tel. (09334) 2-20-54; fax (09334) 2-26-41; e-mail m1571@mail.museum.ru; internet www .museum.ru/m1571; Dir ALEVTINA G. STRAKHOVA.

Pavlovsk

Museum Palaces and Parks in Pavlovsk: 196621 Leningrad oblast, Pavlovsk, ul. Revolyutsii 20; tel. (812) 470-21-55; fax (812) 465-11-04; e-mail pavlovsk@mail.ru; internet www.pavlovskart.spb.ru; f. 1918; many examples of Russian garden architecture, sculpture by 18th-century Italian and French masters; European paintings of the 16th to 19th centuries, Russian portraits of the 18th century, Russian decorative art of the 18th and 19th centuries; furniture, porcelain, bronzes and textiles; library of 17,000 vols; Dir N. S. TRETYAKOV.

Penza

Penza Picture Gallery: 660026 Penza, Sovetskaya ul. 3; tel. (8412) 66-64-00; f. 1892; library of 3,200 vols; 7,700 exhibits; also 3 memorial museums; Dir VALERYI SAZONOV.

Perm

Perm State Art Gallery: 614045 Perm, Komsomolsky pr. 4; tel. (3422) 12-23-95; fax (3422) 12-22-50; e-mail pgallery@perm.raid .ru; internet www.gallery.permonline.ru; f. 1922; library of 27,800 vols; Dir NADEZHDA V. BELYAEVA.

Petrodvorets

Peterhof State Museum Reserve: 198516 St Petersburg, Petrodvorets, ul. Rasvodnaya 2; tel. (812) 427-74-25; fax (812) 427-93-30; e-mail admin@peterhof.org; internet www .peterhof.org; f. 1918; 18th- to 20th-century architecture, painting and landscape gardening; 18th- and 19th-century sculpture, furniture, porcelain, clocks and jewellery; library of 21,000 books, special collection of 2,000 rare books, 7,000 Russian book-plates, 1,300 printed graphics; Dir V. V. ZNAMENOV.

Petrozavodsk

Karelian Museum of Fine Arts: 185035 Republic of Karelia, Petrozavodsk, pr. K. Marksa 8; tel. (8142) 77-98-60; fax (8142) 78-25-78; e-mail pictures@sampo.ru; internet artmuseum.karelia.ru; f. 1960; Karelian iconic paintings from 15th–19th c., Karelian folk art, modern Karelian art, Russian art from the 18th c. to present, western European art; library of 21,000 vols; Dir NATALIA I. VAVILOVA.

Karelian State Regional Museum: 185035 Republic of Karelia, Petrozavodsk, pl. Lenina 1; tel. (8142) 78-02-40; fax (8142) 78-02-40; e-mail kgkm@karelia.ru; internet karelia.ru/~kgkm; f. 1871; history, economy, science, culture, and natural history of the area; 3 brs; library of 25,700 vols; Dir ELENA ZARINA; publs *Museum Herald* (annually), *Museums of Karelia* (4 a year), *Vestnik* (annually).

Kizhi State Open-Air Museum of History, Architecture and Ethnography: 185610 Republic of Karelia, Petrozavodsk, Neglinskaya nab. 23; tel. (8142) 76-57-66; e-mail olga@kizhi.karelia.ru; f. 1961; wooden architecture, history, ethnography, early Russian and Karelian painting and folklore; library of 8,500 vols; Dir O. A. NABOKOVA.

Pushkin

Tsarskoe Selo State Museum: 189690 Leningrad oblast, Tsarskoe Selo, Sadovaya ul. 7; tel. (812) 466-66-69; fax (812) 465-21-96; e-mail tzar@spb.cityline.ru; internet www.tzar.ru; f. 1918; former imperial summer residence, incl. Catherine and Alexander Palaces; park and garden architecture and 100 architectural ornaments from 18th to 20th centuries, esp. in Baroque and Classical styles; library of 18,041 vols including collection of rare books of 2,375 vols; Dir I.P. SAUTOV.

Pushkinskie Gory

State Pushkin Memorial Museum-Reserve 'Mikhailovskoe': Pskovskaya oblast, Pushkinskie Gory, Novorzhevskaya 21; tel. and fax (81146) 2-23-21; e-mail pgmuseum@ellink.ru; internet www.pushkin .ellink.ru; f. 1922; 33,000 exhibits on the life in exile of the poet, Aleksandr Pushkin (1799–1837); the preserve includes the family lands at Mikhailovskoe, Trigorskoe and Petrovskoe, the ancient towns of Voronich and Savkina Gorka, and the grave of Pushkin; library of 21,000 vols; Dir G. N. VASILEVICH.

Pyatigorsk

State Lermontov Literary Memorial Museum: Pyatigorsk, Lermontovskaya ul. 4; tel. (87933) 5-27-10; f. 1912; exhibits feature the life and work of M. Yu. Lermontov in the Caucasus; library of 14,000 vols; Dir L. MOROZOVA.

Roslavl

Roslavl Historical Museum: Roslavl, ul. Proletarskaya 63; tel. (08134) 3-18-49; f. 1920; collection tracing the history, economy and culture of Russian people from the earliest times; library of 1,300 vols; Dir M. I. IVANOVA.

Rostov-on-Don

Rostov Museum of Fine Art: 344007 Rostov-on-Don, ul. Pushkinskaya 115; tel. (8632) 66-59-07; f. 1938; old Russian, Soviet and foreign descriptive art; library of 14,507 vols; Dir G. S. ALIMURZAEVA; publ. *Khudozhnik.*

Ryazan

Ryazan Kremlin Historical and Architectural Museum Reserve: Ryazan, Kreml 118; tel. (0912) 27-60-65; fax (0912) 21-56-70; e-mail root@riamz.ryazan.ru; internet www .ryazankreml.ru; f. 1884; over 220,000 items describing the history, culture and art of the peoples of Russia; Dir LUDMILA MAKSIMOVA; publs *Yakhontovsky's Readings* (every 2 years), *Scientific Works* (every 5 years).

Ryazan Regional Art Museum: Ryazan, Svoboda ul. 57; tel. (0912) 77-95-00; f. 1913; old Russian (15th–20th centuries), European (16th–19th centuries) and Soviet art; library of 17,000 vols; Dir V. A. IVANOV.

St Petersburg

Acad. F. N. Chernyshev Central Scientific Geological and Prospecting Museum: 199026 St Petersburg, Vasilevskii ostrov, Srednii pr. 74; fax (812) 321-53-99; e-mail cnigr@mail.room.ru; f. 1882, opened 1930; c. 1m. geological specimens incl. examples of mineral deposits from all over the fmr Soviet Union; monographic and palaeontological collns; popularization of geological knowledge; Dir Dr ALEKSEY RYURIKOVICH.

Botanical Museum: 197022 St Petersburg, ul. Prof. Popova 2; tel. (812) 234-84-39; f. 1823; over 60,000 specimens; br. of V. L. Komarov Botanical Institute of Academy of Sciences; Dir L. YU. BUDANTSEV.

Central Museum of Railway Transport of Russia: St Petersburg, Sadovaya ul. 50; fax (812) 315-14-76; f. 1813; traces the history of railway transport in Russia; includes unique colln of miniature models of engines and carriages; Dir G. ZAKREVSKAYA.

Central Naval Museum: 199034 St Petersburg, Birzhevaya pl. 4; tel. (812) 328-27-02; fax (812) 328-27-01; e-mail museum@mail .admiral.ru; internet www.museum.navy.ru; f. 1709; relics and other materials from the Russian and Soviet Navies; departments of history of the Russian Navy, history of the Soviet Navy, history of the Navy in the 1941–45 period, history of the Navy in the post-war period; responsible for Kronstadt Fortress, cruiser Aurora and submarine Narodovolets; library of 16,000 vols; Dir E. N. KORCHAGIN.

Dokuchaev Central Soil Museum: St Petersburg, Birzhevoi pr-d 6; tel. (812) 218-56-02; f. 1904; about 5,000 specimens of soil from nearly every soil zone in the world; library of 14,000 vols (Dokuchaev personal library); Dir Dr B. F. APARIN.

Dostoevsky Memorial Museum: 191002 St Petersburg, Kuznechnyi per. 5/2; tel. (812) 571-40-31; e-mail ashimbaeva@md.spb.ru; internet www.md.spb.ru; f. 1971; the house where the author lived 1878–81; MSS, documentary material, memorial items; library of 23,000 vols; Dir Dr NATALIA ASHIMBAEVA.

Literary Museum of the Institute of Russian Literature: 199034 St Petersburg, Pushkinskii Dom, nab. Makarova 4; tel. (812) 328-19-01; fax (812) 328-11-40; e-mail irliran@mail.ru; internet www.pushkinhouse .spb.ru; based on the material of the Pushkin Anniversary Exhibition of 1899; contains 95,000 exhibits and over 120,000 items of reference material; seven halls containing permanent exhibitions devoted to Radishchev, Lermontov, Gogol, Dostoevsky, I. S. Turgenev, and other Russian writers; Dir T. A. KOMAROVA.

Lomonosov, M. V., Museum: 199164 St Petersburg, Universitetskaya nab. 3; tel. (812) 218-12-11; f. 1947; 3,000 exhibits; Dir E. P. KARPEEV.

Military Medical Museum: 191180 St Petersburg, Lazaretny per. 2; tel. (812) 315-53-58; fax (812) 310-20-25; e-mail m170@mail .museum.ru; internet www.museum.ru/ m170; f. 1942; history of Russian and Soviet military medicine; library: research library of 50,000 vols, also collections of rare books; 60 million archive docs on citizens of 45 countries in Europe, Asia, America and Africa; Dir Prof. Dr A. A. BUDKO; publs *History of Military Medicine in Russia* (annually), *History of Medicine in St Petersburg* (annually), *Military Medicine Abroad* (6 a year), *Memorial Dates of Military Medicine* (annually), *Review of the History of Military Medicine* (annually).

Mining Museum of the St Petersburg State Mining Institute (Technical University): 199106 St Petersburg, 21-ya liniya 2; tel. (812) 328-84-29; fax (812) 327-73-59; e-mail rectorat@spmi.ru; internet www .gorny-ins.ru; f. 1773; specimens of minerals, rocks, ores, fossils, meteorites; historical mining techniques illustrated by models of the 19th and early 20th c.; colln of edged weapons from the Zlatoust Arms Factory; Dir J. POLYARNAYA.

Museum of Artillery, Engineers and Signal Corps: 197046 St Petersburg, Aleksandrovsky park 7; tel. (812) 238-47-04; fax (812) 238-47-04; f. 1703; library of 115,000 vols; Dir Col V. M. KRYLOV.

Museum of Sculpture: St Petersburg, pl. A. Nevskogo 1; largest collection of Russian sculpture, collection and care of documents on architecture and town planning; over 150,000 sheets of architectural drawings; Dir N. H. BELOVA.

Museum of the Gorky Bolshoi Drama Theatre: St Petersburg, ul. Fontanka 65.

Museum of the History of Religion: 191186 St Petersburg, Kazanskaya pl. 2;

fax (812) 311-94-83; f. 1932; 186,000 exhibits on Russian Orthodox Church, Roman Catholic and other Christian churches, Judaism, Islam and Buddhism; library of 170,000 vols; Dir S. A. KUCHINSKY; publ. *Theses* (annually).

Museum of the Mariinsky State Academic Theatre of Opera and Ballet: 190000 St Petersburg, ul. Zodchego Rossi 2, Teatralnaya pl.; tel. (812) 326-41-64; e-mail cml@mariinsky.ru; library consists of repertoire and archive sections; Dir MARIYA N. SCHERBAKOVA.

Museum of the St Petersburg Mussorgsky Academic Opera and Ballet Theatre: St Petersburg, pl. Iskusstv 1; tel. (812) 595-43-13; fax (812) 314-36-53; e-mail reserve@sp.ru; internet www.reserve.sp.ru; f. 1935; colln of materials (sketches, posters, photographs, costumes) depicting the history of the theatre and its work; Dir M. KORTUNOVA.

Museum of Zoology: 199034 St Petersburg, Universitetskaya nab. 1; tel. (812) 328-01-12; fax (812) 328-29-41; e-mail museum@zin.ru; internet www.zin.ru; f. 1832; over 30,000 items describe the origin and evolution the animal world; attached to Zoological Institute of the Russian Acad. of Sciences (see Research Institutes); Chief R.L. POTAPOV.

National Pushkin Museum: 191186 St Petersburg, nab. Moiki 12; tel. (812) 571-38-01; fax (812) 315-73-79; e-mail vmp@mail .admiral.ru; internet www.museumpushkin .ru; f. 1879; under supervision of Ministry of Culture; exhibits illustrating the life and work of the poet and his epoch; Dir S. M. NEKRASOV.

Annexes:

Museum of Derzhavin and Russian Literature of the 18th Century: 198005 St Petersburg, nab. Fontanki 118; tel. (812) 713-07-17; fax (812) 315-73-79; e-mail vmp@mail.admiral.ru; internet www.museumpushkin.ru; f. 2003; Chief Curator N. P. MOROZOVA.

Lyceum Museum: 196600 Pushkin, Sadovaya 2; tel. (812) 476-64-11; fax (812) 315-73-79; e-mail vmp@mail.admiral.ru; internet www.museumpushkin.ru; f. 1949; Chief Curator M. N. PETAI.

Main Literary Exposition–Life and Creative Work of Alexander Pushkin: 191186 St Petersburg, nab. Moiki 12; tel. (812) 314-00-07; fax (812) 315-73-79; e-mail vmp@mail.admiral.ru; internet www .museumpushkin.ru; f. 1999; Chief Curator N. L. PETROVA.

Nekrasov Apartment Museum: 191104 St Petersburg, Liteiny pr. 36; tel. (812) 272-01-65; fax (812) 315-73-79; e-mail vmp@mail.admiral.ru; internet www .museumpushkin.ru; f. 1946; Chief Curator E. YU. GLEVENKO.

Pushkin Apartment Museum: 191186 St Petersburg, nab. Moiki 12; tel. (812) 117-35-31; fax (812) 315-73-79; e-mail vmp@mail.admiral.ru; internet www .museumpushkin.ru; f. 1925; Chief Curator G. M. SEDOVA.

Pushkin Country House Museum: 196607 Pushkin, Pushkinskaya ul. 2; tel. (812) 476-69-90; tel. (812) 315-73-79; e-mail vmp@mail.admiral.ru; internet www.museumpushkin.ru; f. 1958; Chief Curator T. I. GALKINA.

Permanent Exhibition of Musical Instruments: St Petersburg, 5 Isaakievskaya pl.; about 3,000 exhibits, including a large collection of instruments made by the outstanding Russian and foreign craftsmen: Batov, Leman, Nalimov, Krasnoshchekov, Fedorov, Amati, Villaume, Tilke and Denner.

Peter the Great Museum of Anthropology and Ethnography: 199034 St Petersburg, Universitetskaya nab. 3; tel. (812) 328-14-12; fax (812) 328-08-11; e-mail info@ kunstkamera.ru; internet www .kunstkamera.ru; f. 1714; attached to Russian Acad. of Sciences; ethnographical, archaeological, and anthropological material on the native peoples of all continents; anatomical colln; scientific instruments; Dir Prof. YURI K. CHISTOV; publs *Etnograficheskiye tetradi* (annually), *Kuryer* (2 a year), *Sbornik* (annually).

Popov, A. S., Central Museum of Communications: 190000 St Petersburg, Pochtamtskaya ul. 7; tel. and fax (812) 315-48-73; e-mail bakayutova@telecommuseum.sp.ru; internet www.rustelecom-museum.ru; f. 1872; over 8 million items representing the development of all types of communication used in Russia and the former USSR; includes the national postage stamp collection; Dir L. BAKAYUTOVA.

Russian Ethnographic Museum: St Petersburg, Inzhenernaya ul. 4/1; tel. (812) 210-47-68; fax (812) 315-85-02; e-mail rme@ infopro.spb.ru; internet www.ethnomuseum .ru; f. 1902; library of 105,000 vols; 150,000 photographs; Dir V. M. GRUSMAN; publ. *Collected Articles* (every 6 months).

Russian State Museum of the Arctic and the Antarctic: 191040 St Petersburg, ul. Marata 24A; tel. (812) 113-19-98; fax (812) 164-68-18; e-mail vicaar@mail.wplus.net; internet www.polarmuseum.sph.ru; f. 1930; exploration, history, environment, culture and economics of the polar regions; library of 4,900 vols; Dir V. I. BOYARSKY; Scientific Sec. M. V. GAVRILO.

St Petersburg State Museum of Theatre and Music: 191011 St Petersburg, pl. Ostrovskogo 6; tel. (812) 315-52-43; fax (812) 314-77-46; e-mail theatre@museums .org.ru; internet www.theatremuseum.ru; f. 1918; over 440,000 exhibits depicting the history of Russian, Soviet and foreign theatre; 31,000 stage designs, 7,000 prints, 900 sculptures, 240,000 photographs, 24,000 MSS and documents, 62,000 posters and programmes, 4,000 theatre costumes; library of 5,000 vols; museum branches: *Rimsky-Korsakov Museum:* f. 1971; memorial museum in house where the composer lived; *F. I. Chaliapin Museum:* f. 1975; museum of history of Russian opera, in former house of Chaliapin; *Music Museum at the Sheremetev Palace:* f. 1991; museum of music incl. 3,000 instruments, and international music centre; *Samoilov Family Museum:* f. 1994; museum of a dynasty of Russian actors; Dir IRINA V. YEVSTIGNEYEVA.

State Circus Museum: 191011 St Petersburg, ul. Fontanka 3; tel. (812) 313-44-13; fax (812) 314-80-59; e-mail circusmuseum@aport .ru; internet www.circus.spb.ru; f. 1928; 80,000 exhibits of plans, sketches, paintings; section on the circus in Western Europe since 18th c. and on Russian and fmr Soviet state circus; library of 4,000 items, Russian and foreign works; 300 videocassettes of circus material; Dir NATALIA KUZNETSOVA.

State Hermitage Museum: 190000 St Petersburg, Dvortsovaya nab. 34; tel. (812) 110-90-79; e-mail chancery@hermitage.ru; internet www.hermitagemuseum.org; f. 1764 as a court museum; opened to public 1852; richest collection in fmr Soviet Union of the art of pre-historic, ancient Eastern, Graeco-Roman and medieval times; preserves 2,800,000 *objets d'art*, including 600,000 drawings and engravings; works by Leonardo da Vinci, Raphael, Titian, Rubens and Rembrandt; collection of coins, weapons and applied art; Dir MIKHAIL PETROVSKY.

State Museum of the History of St Petersburg: 197046 St Petersburg, Petropavlovskaya Krepost 3; tel. (812) 238-05-11; fax (812) 238-02-43; e-mail mail@spbmuseum .ru; internet www.spbmuseum.ru; f. 1918; more than 1m. exhibits; the museum shows the history and architectural development of St Petersburg; brs at Oreshek fortress, memorial flat of A. Blok, Museum of Printing, S. M. Kirov Museum, Monument and Memorial Hall to the Heroic Defenders of Leningrad, Rumyantsevsky Palace, Museum of the Gas Dynamics Laboratory; Dir B. S. ARAKCHEEV.

State Museum of the Political History of Russia: 197046 St Petersburg, ul. Kuybysheva 2–4; tel. (812) 233-70-48; fax (812) 233-73-00; e-mail polithist@cards.lanck.net; internet www.museum.ru/museum/ polit_hist; f. 1919; history of Russia in the 19th and 20th centuries with particular reference to political and social development; Dir E. G. ARTEMOV.

State Russian Museum: St Petersburg, Inzhenernaya 2; tel. (812) 318-16-08; fax (812) 314-41-53; e-mail info@rusmuseum.ru; internet www.rusmuseum.ru; f. 1895; Russian icons, folk and applied arts, painting, sculpture, 10th- to 20th-century drawings; Dir V. A. GUSEV.

Summer Garden and Museum Palace of Peter the Great: 191186 St Petersburg, Letny Sad; tel. (812) 312-77-15; fax (812) 312-96-66; e-mail m126@mail.museum.ru; f. 1934; 18th-century architecture and sculpture; Dir T. D. KOZLOVA.

Samara

Samara A. M. Gorky Memorial Museum: Samara, ul. S. Razina 126; f. 1946; literary museum devoted to the life and work of Gorky; exhibits in the house and furniture which belonged to him; Chief Curator YELENA KOTELNIKOVA.

Samara Art Museum: 443001 Samara 10, pl. Kuibysheva, Palace of Culture; f. 1897; fine arts museum with 11,000 exhibits; library of 7,000 vols; Dir ANNETA YU. BASS.

Saransk

Mordovian Republic S. D. Erzi Museum of Fine Arts: 430000 Mordoviya Saransk, Kommunisticheskaya ul. 61; tel. (8342) 17-56-38; fax (8342) 17-56-38; e-mail m1451@ mail.museum.ru; internet www.museum.ru/ m1451; f. 1960; painting, sculpture, prints, decorative arts; library of 10,000 vols; Dir M. N. BARANOVA.

Saratov

Chernyshevsky Memorial Museum: 410002 Saratov, ul. Chernyshevskogo 142; tel. (8452) 26-35-83; fax (8452) 26-33-67; e-mail musey@rol.ru; internet www .chernishevsky.ru; f. 1920; study of N. G. Chernyshevsky's life, times and literary inheritance; library of 14,232 vols; Dir GALINA P. MURENONA; publs *Propagandist Velikovo Naslediya* (Publicist of the Great Inheritance, every five years), *N. G. Chernyshevsky Articles, Investigations and Materials* (every three years).

Saratov A. N. Radishchev State Art Museum: 410031 Saratov, Pervomaiskaya 75; tel. and fax (8452) 26-12-09; e-mail radmuseumart@radmuseumart.ru; internet www.radmuseumart.ru; f. 1885; library of 34,000 vols; brs: Victor Borisov-Musatov and Pavel Kuznetsov memorial museums (Saratov), Kuzma Petrov-Vodkin memorial museum (Khvalynsk, Saratov region), Balakovo art gallery (Balakovo, Saratov region), A. A. Mylnikov Engels Art Gallery (Engels, Saratov region); Dir T. V. GRODSKOVA.

Sergievsky Posad

Sergiev Posad State History and Art Museum: 141300 Moscow oblast, Sergiev Posad, pr. Krasnoi Armii 144; tel. (09654) 4-13-58; fax (09654) 4-13-58; e-mail sergiev@divo.ru; internet www.musobl.divo.ru; f. 1920; items dealing with the development of Russian art from the 14th century to the present; icons, embroidery, jewellery, porcelain, glass, vestments; secular applied arts, folk arts; library of 17,000 vols; Dir FELIKS KH. MAKOYEV; Scientific Sec. Dr S. V. NIKOLAEVA.

Starki

Far Eastern State Marine Reserve: 690601 Vladivostok, o. Popova, pos. Starki, Olkhovaya 11; tel. (4232) 9-66-82; attached to Russian Acad. of Sciences; Head V. V. GORLACH.

Stavropol

Stavropol Museum of Fine Arts: Stavropol, ul. Dzerzhinskogo 115–119; tel. (8652) 26-54-78; fax (8652) 26-54-78; e-mail izomuz@iskra.stavropol.ru; internet www.museum.ru/m1608; f. 1962; Dir Z. A. BELAYA.

Syktyvkar

National Gallery of the Komi Republic: 167981 Komi Republic, Syktyvkar, ul. Kirova 44; tel. and fax (8212) 42-60-66; e-mail nrgk@online.ru; internet www.komi.com/NGall; f. 1943; Komi, Russian, Soviet and Western European fine art; Dir SVETLANA BELYAEVA.

Taganrog

Chekhov, A. P., Museum: Taganrog, ul. Oktyabrskaya 9; tel. (86344) 6-27-45; rooms arranged as they were when Chekhov lived there in his childhood.

Tambov

Tambov Picture Gallery: 392000 Tambov, Sovetskaya ul. 97; tel. (0752) 2-36-95; f. 1960; 3,500 exhibits; library of 7,000 vols; Dir T. N. SHESTAKOVA.

Tikhvin

Rimsky-Korsakov House-Museum: 187500 Leningrad oblast, Tikhvin, ul Rimskogo Korsakova 12; tel. (81267) 1-15-09; f. 1944 in house where composer was born; main exhibition devoted to composer's childhood; also material on his later life; special collections: original scores, etc.

Tobolsk

Tobolsk Picture Gallery: Tobolsk, Krasnaya pl. 2; 1,800 items.

Tula

Tula Art Museum: 300012 Tula, ul. Engelsa 64; tel. (0872) 35-42-72; fax (0872) 35-42-72; f. 1919; library: specialist art library of 15,000 vols; Dir M. N. KUSINA.

Tula Museum of Regional Studies: Tula, ul. Sovetskaya 68; tel. (0872) 36-22-08; f. 1919; natural sciences, archaeology, literature, architecture, art, history of Tula region; library of 10,806 vols; Dir N. B. NEMOVA.

Tver

Tver Art Gallery: 170640 Tver, ul. Sovetskaya 3; tel. and fax (822) 33-25-61; e-mail art@tversu.ru; internet www.gallery.tversu.ru; f. 1937; library of 33,000 vols; Dir TATYANA S. KUYUKINA.

Tyumen

Tyumen Picture Gallery: Tyumen, ul. Republiki 29; Dir I. S. TERENTEV.

Uglich

Uglich Historical Museum: Uglich, Kreml 3; tel. (08532) 5-17-57; fax (08532) 5-36-78; e-mail uglmus@yaroslavl.ru; f. 1892; exhibits on the history of the Russian people; Dir VALERY DENISOV.

Vladikavkaz

North-Ossetian K. L. Khetagurov Memorial Museum: Vladikavkaz, Butirina 19; tel. (86722) 3-62-22; f. 1979; collection of materials on Caucasian poetry and literature; Dir E. A. KESAYEVA.

Vladivostok

Botanical Garden: 690024 Vladivostok, ul. Makovskogo 142; tel. (4232) 33-14-32; fax (4232) 33-14-36; internet www.fegi.ru; f. 1949; attached to Russian Acad. of Sciences; Dir Prof. Dr V. A. NEDOLUZHKO.

Oceanarium of the Pacific Research Fisheries Centre: 690950 Vladivostok, Batareinaya ul. 4; tel. (4232) 40-19-65; fax (4232) 30-07-52; e-mail tinro@tinro.ru; internet www.tinro-center.ru; f. 1991; marine and freshwater aquarium; 1,600 exhibits of flora and fauna of the Pacific Ocean; study of hydrobiology and aquaculture; maintenance of zoological colln; library of 3,242 rare vols; Dir B. K. RAZUVAEV.

Voeikovo

Meteorological Museum of the Central Geophysical Observatory: Leningrad oblast, Vsevolozhskii raion, Voeikovo; Dir A. A. VASILIEV.

Volgograd

Volgograd State Museum and Panorama of the Battle of Stalingrad: 400053 Volgograd, ul. Marshal Chuykov 47; tel. (8442) 34-72-72; fax (8442) 34-72-41; e-mail panorama@volgadmin.ru; internet www.volgadmin.ru/panorama; f. 1937; exhibits feature the defence of the city during the Civil War (1918–20) and the Battle of Stalingrad (1942–43); library of 14,450 vols; Dir B. G. USIK.

Vologda

Vologda Historical, Architectural and Artistic Museum Reserve: 160035 Vologda, Orlov 15; tel. (8172) 72-22-83; f. 1885; history, archaeology, ethnography, nature, literature, handicrafts, folk art, decorative and applied art, old Russian painting, modern art of the Vologda region, architecture; library of 40,000 vols; Dir L. D. KOROTAYEVA; publ. catalogues.

Vologda Picture Gallery: Vologda, Kremlevskaya pl.; 6,500 exhibits; Dir S. G. IVENSKII.

Voronezh

Voronezh Art Museum: Voronezh, pr. Revolyutsii 18; tel. (0732) 55-28-43; f. 1933; 22,065 exhibits; library of 18,800 vols; Dir VLADIMIR Y. USTINOV.

Yakutsk

Yakutsk Museum of Fine Arts: 677000 Yakutsk, ul. Khabarova 27; tel. (4112) 2-77-98; f. 1928; folk art, Western European, Russian and Soviet art of 17th to 20th centuries; Dir N. M. VASILEVA.

Yaroslavl

Yaroslavl Historical and Architectural Museum: 150000 Yaroslavl, pl. Bogoyavlenskaya 25; tel. (0852) 30-56-30; fax (0852) 30-57-55; e-mail mp@yarmp.yar.ru; internet www.yarmp.yar.ru; f. 1865; over 370,000 exhibits on the history of the Russian people from ancient times to the present; library of 42,000 vols; Dir YELENA A. ANKUDINOVA; publ. *Kraevedcheskiye Zapiski* (irregular).

Yasnaya Polyana

Leo Tolstoy Museum and Estate: Tulskaya oblast, Shchekinsky raion, Yasnaya Polyana; tel. (0872) 38-67-10; fax (0872) 38-67-10; e-mail yaspol@tula.net; internet yasnayapolyana.ru; f. 1921; house and estate belonging to L. N. Tolstoy; literary museum devoted to his life and work; estate with park and forest; Dir VLADIMIR I. TOLSTOY; publ. *Yasnaya Polyana* (4 a year).

Universities

AGRICULTURAL UNIVERSITIES

ALTAI STATE AGRARIAN UNIVERSITY

656099 Barnaul, Krasnoarmeisky pr. 98

Telephone: (3852) 62-83-96

Fax: (3852) 62-83-96

E-mail: rector@asau.ru

Internet: www.asau.ru

Founded 1943 as Altai Agricultural Institute; present name and status 1991

Rector: Prof. SERGEI V. ZOLOTAREV

Library of 360,430 vols

Number of teachers: 508

Number of students: 10,010

Departments: Agronomy, Animal Production, Veterinary, Zoology, Irrigation and Land Reclamation, Mechanization, Economics and Management, Accounting.

BASHKIR STATE AGRARIAN UNIVERSITY

450001 Ufa, 50 let Oktyabrya ul. 34

Telephone: (3472) 28-08-98

Fax: (3472) 28-08-98

E-mail: bgau@ufanet.ru

Internet: www.bsau.ru

Rector: Prof. VLADIMIR D. NEDOREZKOV

Number of teachers: 685.

CHELYABINSK STATE AGRO-ENGINEERING UNIVERSITY

454080 Chelyabinsk, pr. Lenina 75

Telephone: (3512) 66-65-30

Fax: (3512) 66-65-35

E-mail: kbv@agroun.urc.ac.ru

Internet: www.agroun.urc.ac.ru

Founded 1930

Rector: VASILY V. BLEDNYKH

Library of 400,000 vols

Number of teachers: 400

Number of students: 4,000

Publications: *Trudy Chimeskh*, *Vestnik Universiteta*

Training of engineers, economists, agronomists, teachers and agro-ecologists for state and private farms and businesses.

DON STATE AGRARIAN UNIVERSITY

346493 Rostov oblast, Oktyabrsky r-n, pos. Persianovsky

Telephone: (86360) 35-150

Fax: (86360) 36-450

E-mail: dgau@kamenolomni.donpac.ru

Internet: www.dongau.ru

Founded 1916

Rector: Prof. ANATOLY I. BARANIKOV

Library of 400,000 vols

Number of teachers: 272

Number of students: 4,500

Fields of study: agronomy, animal husbandry, veterinary science.

FAR EAST STATE AGRARIAN UNIVERSITY

675005 Blagoveshchensk, Politekhnicheskaya ul. 86

Telephone: (4162) 42-32-06

Fax: (4162) 42-31-79

E-mail: dgu@inbox.ru

Founded 1950

Rector: BORIS I. KASHPURA

Library of 398,000 vols

Number of teachers: 570

Number of students: 8,000

Publications: *Amur Researcher* (2 a year), *Collection of Scientific Publications* (separate series published by each of 14 institutes, each 1 or 2 a year), *Science to Production* (conference report, annually), *Students' Research to Production* (annually)

Institutes of agronomy, mechanization, finance and economics, civil engineering, technology, veterinary science and animal husbandry, electrification and the automation of agriculture, forestry, humanities; research institutes of stockbreeding, selection and technology in plant breeding, construction, systems of machinery, technology of the processing of agricultural production.

GORSKY STATE AGRICULTURAL UNIVERSITY

362040 Vladikavkaz, ul. Kirova 37

Telephone: (8672) 3-23-04

Fax: (8672) 53-90-04

Library of 208,000 vols

Rector: BORIS B. BASAEV

Number of teachers: 412

Number of students: 6,500

Fields of study: agronomy, animal husbandry, mechanization, economics and management, accounting.

KRASNOYARSK STATE AGRARIAN UNIVERSITY

660049 Krasnoyarsk, pr. Mira 88

Telephone: (3912) 27-36-09

Fax: (3912) 27-03-86

E-mail: info@kgau.krasedu.ru

Internet: www.kgau.ru

Founded 1953

Rector: Prof. NIKOLAI V. TSUGLENOK

Library of 318,000 vols

Number of teachers: 408

Number of students: 6,800

Programmes of study: agroecology, agronomy, animal husbandry, economics, electroenergetics, land exploitation, law, management, mechanization, technology, veterinary medicine.

KUBAN STATE AGRARIAN UNIVERSITY

350044 Krasnodar, ul. Kalinina 13

Telephone: (8612) 56-49-42

Fax: (8612) 50-29-35

E-mail: inform@kubagro.ru

Internet: www.kubagro.ru

Founded 1922

Library of 635,000 vols

Number of teachers: 1,070

Number of students: 17,496

Rector: Dr IVAN T. TRUBILIN

Fields of study: agrochemistry and soil science, agronomy, tropical and sub-tropical agriculture, veterinary, horticulture and viticulture, animal husbandry, mechanization, plant protection, electrification, construction, law, economics and management, accountancy.

MICHURINSK STATE AGRARIAN UNIVERSITY

393760 Tambov oblast, Michurinsk, ul. Internatsionalnaya 101

Telephone: (07545) 5-26-35

Fax: (07545) 5-26-35

E-mail: mgau@mich.ru

Internet: www.mgau.ru

Founded 1931

Rector: ANATOLY I. ZAVRANZHOV

Library of 300,000 vols

Number of teachers: 350

Number of students: 4,000

Fields of study: fruit and vegetable production, viticulture, agronomy, selection and genetics of crops, storing and processing of produce, agroecology, commodity research, gardening, economics and management of agricultural production, livestock production, commerce, book-keeping and auditing, finance and credit.

MOSCOW STATE AGRO-ENGINEERING UNIVERSITY, V. P. GORYACHKIN

127540 Moscow, ul. Timiryazevskaya 58

Telephone: (095) 976-36-40

Fax: (095) 976-78-74

E-mail: rkt@mail.msau.ru

Internet: www.msau.ru

Founded 1930

Rector: MIKHAIL N. EROKHIN

Library of 1,000,000 vols

Number of teachers: 400

Number of students: 5,500

Faculties of Agricultural Mechanization, Farm Electrification, Agricultural Technical Services, Engineering, Economics.

MOSCOW STATE UNIVERSITY OF LAND MANAGEMENT

105064 Moscow, ul. Kazakova 15

Telephone: (095) 261-31-46

Internet: www.guz.ru

Founded 1779

Rector: Prof. SERGEI N. VOLKOV

Library of 220,000 vols

Publications: *Land Boundary Register* (annually), *Rural Architecture* (annually)

Faculties of Land Management, Land Tenure, Municipal Land Tenure, Law, Architecture, Correspondence, Retraining, Further Training.

NOVOSIBIRSK STATE AGRARIAN UNIVERSITY

630039 Novosibirsk, ul. Dobrolyubova 160

Telephone: (3832) 67-38-11

Fax: (3832) 67-39-22

E-mail: public@nsau.edu.ru

Internet: www.nsau.edu.ru

Rector: Prof. ANATOLY F. KONDRATOV

Library of 252,000 vols

Number of teachers: 437

Number of students: 9,400

Fields of study: agronomy, plant protection, mechanization, economics and management, accounting.

OMSK STATE AGRARIAN UNIVERSITY

644008 Omsk, Institutskaya pl. 2

Telephone: (3812) 65-17-72

Fax: (3812) 65-10-72

E-mail: adm@omgau.ru

Internet: www.omgau.ru

Founded 1918

Rector: NIKOLAI M. KOLYCHEV

Library of 622,000 vols

Number of teachers: 979

Number of students: 10,357

Publications: *Kirovets* (monthly), *Vestnik OmGAU* (4 a year)

Faculties of Agronomy, Agrochemistry, Soil Science and Environment, Water Resource Engineering, Humanities, Mathematics and Social Studies, Agricultural Engineering, Dairy Production Technology, Institute of Economics and Finance, Institute of Land Use Planning and Tenure; Institute of Veterinary Medicine; Institute of Part-Time and Continued Education.

OREL STATE AGRARIAN UNIVERSITY

302019 Orel, ul. Generala Rodina 69

Telephone: (0862) 29-40-50

Fax: (0862) 29-40-79

E-mail: pnv@orel.ru

Internet: www.orelsau.ru

Founded 1975 as Orel Agricultural Institute; present name and status 1999

Rector: Prof. NIKOLAI V. PARAKHIN.

ORENBURG STATE AGRARIAN UNIVERSITY

460795 Orenburg, ul. Chelyuskintseva.18

Telephone: (3532) 77-52-30

Fax: (3532) 77-23-30

E-mail: ogau@mail.esoo.ru

Internet: www.orensau.ru

Founded 1930

Rector: SERGEI A. SOLOVYEV

Library of 586,541 vols

Number of teachers: 557

Number of students: 7,486

Publication: *Works*

Faculties of Agronomy, Veterinary Medicine and Biotechnology, Information Technology, Forestry, Mechanization of Agriculture, Economics and Law.

ST PETERSBURG STATE AGRARIAN UNIVERSITY

189620 St Petersburg, Pushkin, Peterburgskoe shosse 2

Telephone: (812) 470-04-22

Fax: (812) 465-05-05

Founded 1904

Rector: VLADIMIR S. SHKRABAK

Library of 782,700 vols

Number of teachers: 473

Number of students: 7,865

Br. in Polessk

Publication: *Collection of Scientific Research Works* (8 a year)

Departments of agroecology and soil science, agronomy, vegetable growing, plant protection, animal husbandry, farm electrification, economics, engineering and law.

SARATOV STATE AGRARIAN UNIVERSITY, N. I. VAVILOV

410034 Saratov, Teatralnaya pl. 1

Telephone: (8452) 26-32-92

Fax: (8452) 72-30-42

E-mail: rector@ssau.saratov.ru
Internet: www.ssau.saratov.ru
Founded 1997
Rector: NIKOLAI I. KUZNETSOV

Library of 1,500,000 vols
Number of teachers: 1,189
Number of students: 19,036

Fields of study: agronomy, plant protection, forestry, economics, amelioration and village arrangement, forestry, agricultural mechanization, technical service, agricultural electrification and automation, technology, mechanization of farm production processing, veterinary, biotechnology.

STAVROPOL STATE AGRARIAN UNIVERSITY

355014 Stavropol, Zootekhnichesky per. 10
Telephone: (8652) 35-22-82
Fax: (8652) 34-58-70
E-mail: rector@stgau.ru
Internet: www.stgau.ru

Founded 1930

Rector: VLADIMIR I. TUKHACHEV
Vice-Rector: YURI A. LOBEIKO

Library of 1,980,000 vols
Number of teachers: 650
Number of students: 12,000

Publication: *Collection of Scientific Works* (annually)

Faculties of Accounting, Agriculture, Economics, Electrification, Banking and Finance, Mechanization, Plant Protection, Veterinary and Zoology.

VORONEZH STATE AGRARIAN UNIVERSITY, K. D. GLINKA

394087 Voronezh, ul. Michurina 1
Telephone: (0732) 52-86-31
Fax: (0732) 52-86-31
E-mail: an@vsau.ru
Internet: www.vsau.ru

Founded 1913

Rector: VLADIMIR E. SHEVCHENKO

Library of 870,000 vols
Number of teachers: 528
Number of students: 8,663

Publication: *Zapiski* (Notes)

Fields of study: agrochemistry and soil science, agronomy, land surveying, agricultural engineering, agricultural economics, veterinary science, animal sciences, agribusiness, food-processing technology.

HUMANITIES AND SCIENCES UNIVERSITIES

ADYGHE STATE UNIVERSITY

352700 Republic of Adygheya, Maykop, ul. Universitetskaya 208
Telephone: (87722) 7-02-73
Fax: (87722) 7-02-73
E-mail: adsu@adygnet.ru
Internet: www.adygnet.ru
State control

Founded 1941; present name and status 1993

Rector: Prof. RASHID D. KHUNAGOV

Library of 529,000 vols
Number of teachers: 550
Number of students: 7,547

Branches in Apsheronsk, Belorechensk, Eisk, Novokubansk, Sochi and Koshekhabl.

DEANS

Faculty of Economics: RAMAZAN M. TESHEV
Faculty of Law: AZAMAT M. SHADZHE

Faculty of Foreign Languages: SUSANNA K. BEDANOKOVA
Faculty of Pedagogy: FATIMA P. KHAKNOVA
Faculty of Philology: UCHUZHUK M. PANESH

DIRECTORS

Institute of Arts: NATALYA L. CHEPNIYAN
Institute of Physical Culture and Judo: YAKUB K. KOBLEV

ALTAI STATE UNIVERSITY

656049 Altai Krai, Barnaul, pr. Lenina 61
Telephone: (3852) 66-75-84
Fax: (3852) 66-76-26
E-mail: rector@dcn-asu.ru
Internet: www.asu.ru

Founded 1973
State control
Language of instruction: Russian
Academic year: September to June

Rector: YURI KIRUSHIN
Vice-Rector for Academic Affairs: GENNADY LAVRENTIEV
Vice-Rector for Finance: VITALY MISHCHENKO
Vice-Rector for International Affairs: VALERY NEVINSKY
Vice-Rector for Science: NIKOLAI MIKHAILOV
Librarian: GALINA TRUSHNIKOVA

Library of 1,000,000 vols, 1,400 periodicals; 6 museums; art gallery
Number of teachers: 750
Number of students: 18,000

Publications: *Chemistry of Vegetative Raw Materials* (on-line, 4 a year), *Proceedings* (4 a year), *Turchaninovia* (on-line, 4 a year)

DEANS

Faculty of Arts: T. STEPANSKAYA
Faculty of Biology: G. SOKOLOVA
Faculty of Chemistry: N. BAZARNOVA
Faculty of Distance Learning: D. RUDER
Faculty of Economics: O. MAMCHENKO
Faculty of Geography: V. REVYAKIN
Faculty of History: V. VLADIMIROV
Faculty of Journalism: V. MANSUROVA
Faculty of Law: V. MUZYUKIN
Faculty of Mathematics: S. KUZIKOV
Faculty of Pedagogical Education: G. SPITSKAYA
Faculty of Philology: N. KUZNETSOVA
Faculty of Physics: A. SHATOKHIN
Faculty of Political Science: E. PRITCHINA
Faculty of Preliminary Training: N. YAKOVLEVA
Faculty of Psychology and Philosophy: L. DEMINA
Faculty of Sociology: S. GRIGORIEV

PROFESSORS

ALGAZIN, G., Mathematical Methods in Sociology
BARUSHNIKOV, G., Geography
BAZARNOVA, N., Chemistry
BELYAEV, V., Marketing
BEZNOSUK, S., General Physics
BOBROV, M., Sociology
BUDKIN, A., Algebra and Mathematical Logic
BUKATY, V., General Physics
BURDASOV, V., Biology
CHERNUSHOV, Y., Ancient History
CHERVYAKOV, V., Economic Geography
CHUVAKIN, A., Philology
DEMCHIK, E., Sociology
DEMINA, L., Psychology and Philosophy
ELCHANINOV, V., Philosophy
FEDYUKIN, V., Philosophy
GAVLO, V., Criminology
GLUSHANIN, E., History
GOLEV, N., Russian Language
GRIGORYEV, S., Sociology
GUBAR, A., Economics
GUSLYAKOVA, L., Social Work

IVANOV, A., Philosophy
IVOLGIN, A., Political Science
KHALINA, N., Linguistics
KIRUSHIN, Y., Archaeology
KISELEV, V., Human and Animal Physiology
KOMAROV, S., Radio Physics
KOZLOVA, S., Philology
KUPRIYANOV, A., Biology
LAGUTIN, A., Theoretical Physics
LAVRENTIEV, G., Education
MALOLETKO, A., Nature Management
MALTSEV, Y., Algebra and Mathematical Logic
MAMCHENKO, O., Information Systems
MEDVEDEV, N., Algebra and Mathematical Logic
MELNIKOV, A., Philosophy
MELNIKOVA, L., Regional Economics
MIRONOV, V., Radiophysics
MISCHENKO, V., Regional Economics
MOISEEV, V., Oriental History
NEVINSKY, V., Constitutional Law
NOVOZHENOV, ., Constitutional Law
OSKORBIN, N., Cybernetics and Applied Mathematics
PETROV, B., Analytical Chemistry
POLYAKOV, V., Applied Physics
RASTOV, Y., Empiric Sociology
RAZGON, V., History
REVYAKIN, V., Geography
REVYAKINA, N., Geography
ROGOVSKY, E., Management
SAGALAKOV, A., Experimental Physics
SEMILET, T., Psychology
SENKO, Y., Education
SHAIDUK, A., General Physics
SHELEPOVA, L., Philology
SKUBNEVSKY, V., History
STARTSEV, O., Applied Physics
STEPANSKAYA, T., Art
TROTSKOVSKY, A., Theory of Economics
TRUKHINA, V., Art
TSUB, S., History
USHAKOVA, E., Philosophy
VASILYEV, V., Biochemistry
YELCHANINOV, V., Philosophy
ZEMLYUKOV, S., Criminal Law

ATTACHED INSTITUTES

Ecological Monitoring Research Institute: Dir A. LAGUTIN.

Humanistic Research Institute: Dir A. SHAMSHIN.

Thermoplastic Materials Research Institute: Dir V. NOVOZHENOV.

AMUR STATE UNIVERSITY

675027 Amurskaya oblast, Blagoveshchensk, Ignatevskoye shosse 21
Telephone: (4162) 39-46-86
Fax: (4162) 39-45-25
E-mail: master@amursu.ru
Internet: www.amursu.ru

Founded 1975
State control
Language of instruction: Russian
Academic year: September to July

President: ANDREY D. PLUTENKO
Vice-President: ELENA S. ASTAPOVA
Pro-Rectors: LUDMILA N. GERASIMOVA, ANDREW P. ZABEAKO
Chief Administrative Officer: TATYANA V. ASTAFUROVA
Librarian: NATALYA P. UDALOVA

Library of 232,000 vols
Number of teachers: 600
Number of students: 8,500

Publication: *Bulletin* (3 a year)

DEANS

Applied Arts: ALEXANDER M. MEDVEDEV
Economics: GALINA F. CHECHETA

Engineering and Physics: VERA F. ULYANY-CHEVA
International Relations: SVETLANA S. KOSIKHINA
Law: ALEXANDER A. GERASIMENKO
Mathematics and Computer Science: EVGENY L. EREMIN
Philology: IRINA I. LEIFA
Power Engineering: LYUDMILA A. VILESOVA
Social Sciences: NELLE K. SCHEPKINA

BASHKIR STATE UNIVERSITY

450074 Bashkortostan, Ufa, ul. Frunze 32

Telephone: (3472) 22-63-70
Fax: (3472) 22-61-05
E-mail: interdpt@bsu.bashedu.ru
Internet: www.bashedu.ru

Founded 1957
Language of instruction: Russian
Academic year: September to June

Rector: Prof. MUKHAMET KH. KHARRASOV
First Vice-Rector: Prof. BAYAZIT S. GALIMOV
Vice-Rectors for Academic Affairs: Prof. NIKOLAI D. MOROZKIN, Prof. YAUDAT T. SULTANAEV
Vice-Rector for Admininstration and Finance: KHAYRULLA KH. MUROV
Vice-Rector for Science: Prof. RIFKAT F. TALIPOV
University Librarian: E. G. GUIVANOVSKAYA

Number of teachers: 525
Number of students: 8,300

DEANS

Faculty of Biology: Prof. RINAT I. IBRAHIMOV
Faculty of Chemistry: Prof. ALEXANDER YA. GERCHIKOV
Faculty of Economics: Prof. FANIYA S. ISKHAKOVA
Faculty of Geography: Prof. RADIK G. SAFIULLIN
Faculty of History: Prof. MARAT M. KULSHARIPOV
Faculty of Mathematics: Prof. YAUDAT T. SULTANAEV
Faculty of Philology: Prof. ALEXANDER A. FEDOROV
Faculty of Philosophy and Sociology: Prof. DAMIR A NURIEV
Faculty of Physics: Prof. ROBERT A. YAKSHIBAEV

BELGOROD STATE UNIVERSITY

308015 Belgorod, ul. Pobedy 30

Telephone: (0722) 30-12-11
Fax: (0722) 30-10-12
E-mail: info@bsu.edu.ru
Internet: www.bsu.edu.ru
State control

Founded 1876 as Belgorod Teaching Institute; 1939–1957 as Belgorod State Teaching Institute; 1957–1994 as Belgorod State Pedagogical Institute; as Belgorod State Pedagogical University 1994–1996; present name and status 1996

Rector: Prof. LEONID YA. DYATCHENKO
First Pro-Rector for Administration, Finance and Security: MIKHAIL V. KOSTROV
First Pro-Rector and Pro-Rector for Science: TATYANA M. DAVYDENKO
Pro-Rector for Academic Affairs: VIKTOR N. TKACHEV
Pro-Rector for Distance and Evening Education: VLADIMIR A. SHAPOVALOV
Chief Accountant: NATALYA P. KOZYREVA

Branches in Alekseevka and Stary Oskol, both f. 1999.

Library of 987,987 vols
Number of teachers: 717
Number of students: 13,015

DEANS

Faculty of Biology and Chemistry: GENNADY M. FOFANOV
Faculty of Computer Science and Telecommunications: EVGENY G. ZHILYAKOV
Faculty of Economics: VLADIMIR I. BOLTENKOV
Faculty of Geology and Geography: ALEXANDER N. PETIN
Faculty of History: ELENA YU. PROKOFIEVA
Faculty of Law: EVGENY E. TONKOV
Faculty of Management and Business: VIKTORIA B. TARABAEVA
Faculty of Medicine: YURI I. AFANASEV
Faculty of Pedagogy: NIKOLAI V. PODDUBNY
Faculty of Philology: SVETLANA P. GRINEVA
Faculty of Physical Culture: VASILY V. SOKOREV
Faculty of Physics and Mathematics: OLEG M. PENKIN
Faculty of Psychology: NADEZHDA I. ISAEVA
Faculty of Romance and Germanic Philology: OLGA N. PROKHOROVA
Faculty of Socio-Theology: SERGEI A. KOLESNIKOV
International Faculty: MIKHAIL A. TRUBITSYN

BELGOROD UNIVERSITY OF CONSUMER CO-OPERATIVES

308023 Belgorod, ul. Sadovaya 116a

Telephone: (0722) 6-08-48
Fax: (0722) 6-49-65
E-mail: bupk@intbel.ru
Internet: www.bupk.ru

Rector: VITALY I. TEPLOV

Number of teachers: 326
Number of students: 8,030

Faculties of Economics, Trade Management; br. in Stavropol.

BRATSK STATE UNIVERSITY

665709 Bratsk, Makarenko ul. 40

Telephone: (3953) 33-20-08
Fax: (3953) 33-20-08
E-mail: rector@brstu.ru
Internet: www.brstu.ru

Founded 1980 as Bratsk Industrial Institute; 1994–1999 as Bratsk State Technical University; present name and status 2004

Number of teachers: 337teachers
Number of students: 9,823students

Rector: Prof. SERGEI V. DELOKOBYLSKY

Library of 448,851 vols
Number of teachers: 337
Number of students: 9,823

Faculties of Power, Mechanics, Forestry Engineering, Construction, Economics, Humanities, Distance Learning, International Education.

BRYANSK STATE UNIVERSITY

241036 Bryansk, Bezhitskaya ul. 14

Telephone: (083) 246-65-38
Fax: (083) 246-63-53
Internet: www.bgunet.com
State control

Founded 1974

Rector: Prof. ANDREI V. ANTYUKHOV
Pro-Rector of Academic Affairs: Prof. VLADIMIR V. SHLYK

Number of teachers: 515
Number of students: 15,712.

BURYAT STATE UNIVERSITY

670000 Ulan-Ude, ul. Smolina 24a

Telephone: (3012) 21-15-80
Fax: (3012) 21-05-88
E-mail: univer@bsu.ru
Internet: www.bsu.ru

State control

Founded 1995 following the merger of State Teachers Training Institute and the Ulan-Ude Branch of Novosibirsk State University

Rector: Prof. STEPAN V. KALMYKOV
First Pro-Rector: Prof. YURI P. SHAGDUROV
Pro-Rector for Academic Affairs: IRINA S. BATUEVA
Pro-Rector for Administration and Finance: Prof. VITALY M. TSINKER
Pro-Rector for International Co-operation: Dr ANATOLY S. KARPOV
Pro-Rector for Science: Prof. BIMBA-TSYREN B. NAMZALOV
Academic Secretary: Prof. VITALY M. TSINKER

DEANS

Faculty of Biology and Geography: VALERY N. KHERTUEV
Faculty of Chemistry: VYACHESLAV V. KHAKHINOV
Faculty of Eastern Studies: DIMITRY I. BURAEV
Faculty of Economics and Management: GALINA I. ROLAGEVA
Faculty of Foreign Languages: NINA ZH. DAGBAEVA
Faculty of History: KONSTANTIN B.-M. MITUPOV
Faculty of Law: YURI N. FEDOROV
Faculty of Medicine: SERGEI M. NIKOLAEV
Faculty of Physics and Technology: A. V. NOMOEV
Faculty of Primary Education: TSYREN R. BAZAROV
Faculty of Qualifications Advancement: LUDMILA S. VASILYEVA
Faculty of Socio-Psychology: ANDREI YU. MATSKEVICH

CHELYABINSK STATE UNIVERSITY

454021 Chelyabinsk, ul. Bratev Kashirinykh 129

Telephone: (3512) 42-05-31
Fax: (3512) 42-09-25
E-mail: postmaster@csu.ru
Internet: www.csu.ru

Founded 1976
Academic year: September to July

Rector: Prof. V. D. BATUKHTIN
Registrar: A. YU. SHATIN
Librarian: L. M. KISELYOVA

Number of teachers: 1,760 (1,410 full-time, 350 part-time)
Number of students: 14,369 (7,800 full-time, 6,569 correspondence)

Publication: *Vestnik*

DEANS

Faculty of Access to Higher Education: E. A. MARTYNOVA
Faculty of Biology: A. L. BURMISTROVA
Faculty of Chemistry: A. V. BELIK
Faculty of Continuing Education: V. A. BURMISTROV
Faculty of Ecology: S. G. AGEEV
Faculty of Economics: T. A. VERESHCHAGINA
Faculty of Eurasia and the East: G. V. SACHKO
Faculty of History: G. A. GONCHAROV
Faculty of Journalism: B. N. KIRSHIN
Faculty of Law: V. A. LEBEDEV
Faculty of Linguistics and Translation: L. A. NEFYODOVA
Faculty of Management: L. A. KUZNETSOVA
Faculty of Mathematics: O. N. DEMENTIEV
Faculty of Original Professions: T. M. KUYASHEVA
Faculty of Philology: I. YU. KARTASHOVA
Faculty of Physics: V. D. BUCHELNIKOV
Institute of Psychology and Pedagogics: S. A. REPIN

PROFESSORS

ABRAMOVSKY, A. P., History
AKHMEDZIANOV, M. G., Physical Education
ALEEV, Physics and Mathematics
ALEVRAS, N. N., History
AZNACHEEVA, E. N., Linguistics
BALYKIN, V. P., Chemistry
BATUKHTIN, V. D., Mathematical Theory of Optimization and Control
BELANKOV, Physics and Mathematics
BELIK, A. V., Chemistry
BENT, M. I., Philology
BLUDENOV, A. F., Economics
BUCHELNIKOV, V. D., Physics and Mathematics
BURMISTROV, V. A., Physics and Mathematics
BURMISTROVA, A. L., Biology
BYCHKOV, I. V., Physics and Mathematics
CHERNETSOV, P. I., Education
DARANKOV, A. Y., Economics
DEMENTIEV, O. N., Physics and Mathematics
DUDOROV, A. Y., Physics and Mathematics
GALIULINA, G. S., History
GOLIKOV, A. A., Economics
GOLOVANOV, V. I., Technology
GORSHKOV, A. V., Economics
GRUDZINSKY, V. V., History
ILYIN, A. M., Physics and Mathematics
JEYT, Physics and Mathematics
KOLOSOVA, O. S., Medicine
KORNEV, N. I., Economics
LAPPA, A. V., Physics and Mathematics
LEBEDEV, V. A., Law
LEZHNEVA, Pedagogics
MARTYNOVA, Pedagogics
MATUSHKIN, S. I., Didactics
MATVEEV, S. V., Topology
MIKHNUKEVICH, V. A., Philology
NARSKY, I. V., History
NEFYODOVA, L. A., Linguistics
NEVELEV, A. B., Philosophy
PAVLENKO, V. N., Physics and Mathematics
PISCHCLIULIN, Pedagogics
PITINA, S. A., Linguistics
PLOKHIKH, N. A., Geology and Mineralogy
POPOV, V. I., Law
POPOVA, N. B., Philology
PRIVEZENTSEV, A. P., Physics and Mathematics
RATANOV, N. E., Physics and Mathematics
REPIN, S. A., Didactics
ROZKOV, A. V., Physics and Mathematics
SABITOV, P. A., Law
SEDOV, V. V., Political Economy
SHATIN, A. YU., Economics
SHISHMARENKOVA, G. YA., Education
SHKATOVA, L. A., Russian Language
SINYAVSKY, V. A., Geology and Mineralogy
SMIRNOV, S. S., History
SOLOVIEV, A. A., Physics and Mathematics
SUKHANOV, K. N., Philosophy
SUROV, Physics and Mathematics
SVIRIDUK, G. A., Physics and Mathematics
TANANA, V. P., Mathematics
TYUMENTSEV, V. A., Physics and Mathematics
UCHOBOTOV, V. I., Physics
YALOVETS, A. P., Physics
YARTSEV, V. M., Physics and Mathematics
ZAGIDULLINA, M. V., Linguistics

CHECHEN STATE UNIVERSITY

Chechnya, 364907 Groznyi, ul. Sheripova 32
Telephone: (87322) 23-40-89
Founded 1972

Rector: ADNAN D. KHAMZAYEV
Number of teachers: 620
Number of students: 8,000

Faculties of Philology, Romance and Germanic Philology, History, Mathematics, Physics, Chemistry and Biology, Economics and Geography.

CHEREPOVETS STATE UNIVERSITY

162600 Cherepovets, ul. Lunacharskogo 5
Telephone: (8202) 55-65-97
Fax: (8202) 55-70-49
E-mail: chsu@chsu.ru
Internet: www.chsu.ru
Founded 1919

Rector: Prof. VLADIMIR S. GRYZLOV
First Pro-Rector: Prof. EVGENY V. ERSHOV
Library of 437,168 vols

HEADS OF DEPARTMENTS

Institute of Engineering Economics: Prof. VALERY V. PLASHENKOV
Institute of Humanities: Prof. ALEXANDER V. CHERNOV
Institute of Mathematics, Physics and Information Science: Prof. EVGENY B. OSIPOV
Institute of Metallurgy and Chemistry: Prof. ALEXANDER L. KUZMINOV
Institute of Pedagogy and Psychology: Prof. VLADIMIR G. MARALOV

CHITA STATE UNIVERSITY

672039 Chita, Aleksandro-Zavodskaya ul. 30
Telephone: (3022) 26-43-93
Fax: (3022) 26-24-38
E-mail: root@chitgu.ru
Internet: www.chitgu.ru
State control
Academic year: September to June (two semesters)
Founded 1974, as a branch of Irkutsk State Polytechnic Institute

Rector: Prof. YURI N. REZNIK
Vice-Rector: Prof. SERGEI A. IVANOV
Number of teachers: 547
Number of students: 14,910

Publications: Science: the 21st Century (annually), Social Anthropology of Transbaikal (annually), Vestnik ChitGU (Scientific, 6 a year)

DEANS

Automobile Transportation: SERGEI P. OZORNIN
Computer Science and Economy: TATYANA A. PLUSNINA
Construction Engineering: VALENTINA V. YEMELIANIVICH
Ecology Engineering: VLADIMIR V. ZVYAGINTSEV
Economics and Management: GALINA YU. POPOVA
Geology: SERGEI V. SMOLICH
Humanitarian Culture: MARINA N. FOMINA
Law: VICTORIA I. SUBBOTINA
Machine Building Engineering: VITALY V. GRUSHEV
Mining Engineering: LUDMILA G. NIKITINA
Power Engineering: YURI V. ERMOLAYEV

HEADS OF DEPARTMENTS

School of Adult Education: OLGA RIBAKOVA
Ecology and Construction: YURI KON
School of Economics and Management: ANDREI LAVROV
School of Law: ANDREI MAKAROV
Mining Engineering: PAVAL AVDEEV
Power Supply: OLEG KUPRYANOV
School of Socio-Political Systems: MICHAEL SHVETSOV
Transportation Systems and Technologies: ANDREI LESKOV

PROFESSORS

ABAKHUMOV, Y. G., Power Engineering
BALANDIN, O. A., Construction Engineering
BEYDINA, T. E., Law
ERDYNEYEVA, K. G., Socio-Psychology
FOMINA, M. N., Humanitarian Culture
KONDRATYEV, V. G., Geology

LYUBIMOVA, L. M., Humanitarian Culture
MYAZIN, V. P., Mining Engineering
NARKELYUN, L. F., Mining Engineering
RASHKIN, A. V., Mining Engineering
SALIKHOV, V. S., Geology
SINITSA, S. M., Geology
ZASLONOVSKY, V. N., Ecology Engineering

CHUVASH STATE UNIVERSITY

428015 Chuvash Autonomous Republic, Cheboksary, Moskovsky pr. 15
Telephone: (8352) 24-03-79
Fax: (8352) 42-80-90
E-mail: oper@chuvsu.ru
Internet: www.chuvsu.ru
Founded 1967
State control
Languages of instruction: Chuvash, Russian
Academic year: September to July

Rector: Prof. Dr LEV P. KURAKOV
First Vice-Rector: NIKOLAI F. GRIGORIEV
Vice-Rectors for Academic Affairs: ANNA V. ARSENTIEVA, LYUDMILA P. PROKOSHENKOVA
Librarian: NINA D. NIKITINA

Library: see Libraries and Archives
Number of teachers: 940
Number of students: 10,600
Publication: Ulyanovets (weekly)

DEANS

Faculty of Chemistry: O. Y. NOSAKIN
Faculty of Chuvash Philology and Culture: V. I. SERGEEV
Faculty of Construction: Y. V. CHERNOV
Faculty of Economics: V. G. KHIRBY
Faculty of Electrical and Power Engineering: G. A. BELOV
Faculty of History: A. V. ARSENTEVA
Faculty of Law: V. G. TIMOFEEV
Faculty of Mathematics: V. G. AGAKOV
Faculty of Mechanical Engineering: Y. P. KUZNETSOV
Faculty of Medicine: V. Y. VOLKOV
Faculty of Philology: Z. F. MYSHKIN
Faculty of Physics: A. I. KOROTKOV
Higher Business School: L. P. KURAKOV (Dir)
Higher School for Training Engineers: V. A. CHEDRIN (Dir)

DAGESTAN STATE UNIVERSITY

Dagestan, 367025 Makhachkala, Gadzhiyeva ul. 8
Telephone: (87200) 68-23-26
Fax: (87200) 67-06-33
E-mail: dgu@dgu.ru
Internet: www.dgu.ru
Founded 1931
State control
Language of instruction: Russian
Academic year: September to July

Rector: Prof. O. A. OMAROV
Vice-Rector: Prof. E. Z. EMIRBEKOV
Registrar: Prof. M. I. ABAKAROV
Librarian: L. I. ALIEVA
Number of teachers: 1,000
Number of students: 20,000
Publication: Transactions

DEANS

Faculty of Biology: Dr KH. M. RAMAZANOV
Faculty of Chemistry: Dr K. M. YUNUSOV
Faculty of Culture: Dr M. A. ISRAFILOV
Faculty of Dagestan Philology: Dr Z. A. MAGOMEDOV
Faculty of Finance and Economics: Dr R. K. KADIEV
Faculty of History: Dr B. B. BULATOV
Faculty of Law: Dr A. R. OMAROV
Faculty of Management in Economics: Dr M. M. MAGOMAEV
Faculty of Mathematics: Dr M. G. MEKHTIEV

Faculty of Physics: Dr KH. A. MAGOMEDOV

Faculty of Romance and Germanic Philology: Dr M. M. ABDULSALAMOV

Faculty of Russian Language and Literature: Dr SH. A. MAZANAEV

ELETS STATE UNIVERSITY 'I. A. BUNIN'

399770 Lipetsk Region, Elets, ul. Kommunarov 28

Telephone: (07467) 2-21-93

Fax: (07467) 2-04-63

E-mail: main@elsu.ru

Internet: www.elsu.ru

State control

Founded 1939

Rector: VALERY P. KUZOVLEV

First Pro-Rector for Academic Affairs: TATYANA A. POZNYAK

Second Pro-Rector for Academic Affairs: OLGA N. SARYCHEVA

Pro-Rector for Administration and Finance: STANISLAV A. KLEIMENOV

DEANS

Faculty of Design: NADEZHDA P. LOGINOVA

Faculty of Economics: SVETLANA A. VOROTYNTSEVA

Faculty of Engineering and Physics: NATALYA A. FORTUNOVA

Faculty of Foreign Languages: ALEXANDER S. ERENKOV

Faculty of Further Pedagogic Training: EKATERINA V. CHERNYKH

Faculty of History: OLEG A. POZDNYAKOV

Faculty of Law: ELENA V. SAFRONOVA

Faculty of Pedagogy and Primary Education: VIKTORIA YU. BABAITSEVA

Faculty of Pedagogy and Psychology: IRINA D. EMELYANOVA

Faculty of Philology: IRINA M. KURNOSOVA

Faculty of Physics and Mathematics: OLGA A. SAVVINA

Faculty of Sport: ALEXANDER I. PROKOFIEV

FAR EASTERN STATE UNIVERSITY

690600 Vladivostok, ul. Sukhanova 8

Telephone: (4232) 26-12-80

Fax: (4232) 25-72-00

E-mail: office@dip.dvgu.ru

Internet: www.dvgu.ru

Founded 1899

State control

Language of instruction: Russian

Academic year: September to June

Rector: V. I. KURILOV

Pro-Rectors: V. P. DIKAREV, N. M. PESTEREVA, B. L. REZNIK, R. M. SAMIGULIN, R. P. SHEPELEVA, G. S. VOROPAYEV

Librarian: N. N. GAIDARENKO

Library: see Libraries

Number of teachers: 993

Number of students: 16,000

Publications: *News of the Institute of International Studies* (4 a year), *News of the Institute of Oriental Studies* (annually), *The Russian Far East* (4 a year)

DEANS

Chemistry and Chemical Ecology: A. A. KAPUSTINA

Correspondence Programme: L. I. ROMANOVA

Academy of Ecology, Marine Biology and Biotechnology: V. A. KUDRYASHOV

Economics: R. V. SABITOVA

Entrepreneurial Law: A. S. SHEVCHENKO

Institute of Environment: YU. B. ZONOV (Dir)

Institute of Foreign Languages: L. P. BONDARENKO (Dir)

German Philology: L. P. BONDARENKO

History and Philosophy: O. V. SIDORENKO

Information Technology: I. V. SOPPA

International Economic Relations and Management: A. A. KHAMATOVA

International Law: V. V. GAVRILOV

International Relations: T. D. KHUZIYATOV

Institute of International Tourism and Hospitality: N. M. PESTEREVA (Dir)

Investigation and Public Prosecution: A. F. REKHOVSKY

Japanese Studies: A. G. SHNYRKO

Journalism: V. V. BAKSHIN

Jurisprudence: A. G. KORCHAGIN

Higher College of Korean Studies: V. V. VERKHOLYAK (Dir)

Law (in Petropavlovsk-Kamchatsky): L. A. ZAKHOZHY

Law (in Yuzhno-Sakhalinsk): M. G. SEREBRENNIKOV

Institute of Law: V. I. KURILOV (Dir)

Management and Business: S. B. GOLOVACHEV

Institute of Management and Business: A. A. BELUSOV (Dir)

Mathematics and Computer Science: V. B. OSIPOV

Institute of Military Programmes: S. A. BOGATYRENKO (Dir)

Institute of Oriental Studies: A. A. KHAMATOVA (Dir)

Pacific Institute of Distance Education and Technology: V. I. VOVNA (Dir)

Physics: P. N. KORNYUSHIN

Physics and Engineering: V. G. LIFSHITS

Institute of Physics and Information Technology: V. I. BELOKON (Dir)

Political Science and Public Administration: A. M. KUZNETSOV

Institute of Pre-University Training: N. A. SMAL (Dir)

Institute of Professional Development and In-Service Training: E. M. CHUKHRAYEV (Dir)

Psychology and Social Work: A. V. STETSIV

Research Institute of Chemistry: N. P. SHAPKIN (Dir)

Research Institute of Regional Studies: B. K. STAROSTIN (Dir)

Romance Philology: N. S. MOREVA

Russian Philology: V. I. SHESTOPALOVA

Sinology: O. V. KUCHUK

State Law: V. F. SHEKHOVTSOV

Institute for Training Highly Qualified Specialists: B. L. REZNIK (Dir)

Vladivostok Institute for International Studies of the Asia-Pacific Region: M. YU. SHINKOVSKY (Dir)

FESU branch in Artem: P. V. KHARITONSKY (Dir)

FESU branch in Hakodate: S. N. ILYIN (Dir)

FESU branch in Nakhodka: A. I. RAZGONOV (Dir)

PROFESSORS

ABAKUMOV, A. I., Mathematics

ABRAMOVA, L. A., Economics

AFINOGENOV, YU. A., Law

AKIMOVA, L. V., Economics

AKIMOVA, T. I., Chemistry

ALEXANDROVSKAYA, L. V., Economics

ALEXEYEV, G. V., Mathematics

ANIKONOV, D. S., Mathematics

ANISIMOV, A. P., Biology

ANISIMOV, N. A., Mathematics

ASHCHEPKOV, L. T., Mathematics

BAKLANOV, P. YA., Physical Geography

BAKSHIN, V. V., Journalism

BELOKON, V. I., Physics

BELOUSOV, A. A., Economics

BEREZNIKOV, K. P., Geophysics

BESSONOVA, V. I., Chemistry

BINDER, A. I., Economics

BINEVSKY, A. A., Philosophy

BONDARENKO, L. P., English Philology

BRESLAVETS, T. I., Japanese Philology

BRODYANSKY, D. L., History

BROVKO, P. F., Geography

BUKIN, O. A., Physics

CHEBOTKEVICH, L. A., Physics

CHIZHOV, L. N., Management

CHUVAKIN, A. A., Russian Philology

DASHKO, N. A., Geophysics

DERBENTSEVA, A. M., Biology

DROZDOV, A. L., Chemistry

DUBININ, V. N., Mathematics

DYUZHIKOVA, E. A., English

EFIMENKO, V. F., Physics

ELANTSEVA, O. P., History

ELYAKOV, G. B., Chemistry

FISENKO, A. I., Economics

FROLOV, N. N., Mathematics

GALKINA, L. V., Korean Philology

GAVRILOVA, T. L., Mathematics

GERASIMENKO, M. D., Physics

GLUSHCHENKO, I. I., History

GRAMM-OSIPOV, L. M., Chemistry

GRAMM-OSIPOVA, V. N., Chemistry

IGNATYUK, V. A., Physics

ILYUSHIN, I. A., Journalism

ISAYEVA, T. S., Law

ISAYEVA, V. V., Biology

IVANKOV, V. N., Biology

IVLEV, A. M., Biology

KAMINSKY, V. A., Chemistry

KAPUSTINA, A. A., Chemistry

KARTAVTSEV, YU. F., Biology

KHAMATOVA, A. A., International Economic Relations and Management

KHRISTOFOROVA, N. K., Biology

KILMATOV, T. R., Oceanology

KLESHCHEV, A. S., Mathematics

KNYAZEV, S. D., Law

KOCHETKOV, V. P., English Language

KOGAN, B. I., Mathematics

KOMAROVA, T. A., Biology

KONDRIKOV, N. B., Chemistry

KORNYUSHIN, P. N., Physics

KOROBEYEV, A. I., Law

KOROTKY, A. M., Physical Geography

KOSTETSKY, E. YA., Biology

KRIVSHENKO, S. F., Russian Philology

KUDRYASHOV, V. A., Biology

KULEBYAKIN, YE. V., Social Work

KULESHOV, YE. L., Physics

KURILOV, V. I., Law

KUSAKIN, O. G., Biology

KUZNETSOV, A. M., Political Science

KUZNETSOV, N. V., Mathematics

KUZNETSOVA, N. V., Economy and Finance of Asian Pacific Countries

LEBEDEV, M. G., English

LIFSHITS, V. G., Physics

MEDVEDEVA, E. S., Economics

MEDVEDEVA, K. A., Russian Philology

MEGRABOVA, E. G., English

MELNIKOVA, T. N., English

MIKHAILOV, V. S., International Law

MIKHEEV, R. I., Law

MIRONETS, YU. A., English

NEDOLUZHKO, A. V., Biology

NELEZIN, A. D., Oceanology

NEMOV, R. S., Psychology

NESTERENKO, A. D., Economics

NOMOKONOV, V. A., Law

NURMINSKY, YE. A., Mathematics

OSIPOV, V. B., Mathematics

OSTANIN, V. A., Economics

OVRAKH, G. P., Political Science

PAK, G. K., Mathematics

PECHERITSA, V. F., International Relations

PESTEREVA, N. M., Geophysics

PRIYATKINA, A. F., Russian Philology

PROSHINA, Z. G., English

PSCHENICHNIKOV, B. F., Biology

RAGULIN, P. G., Economics

REZNICHENKO, I. M., Law

REZNIK, B. L., Physics

ROMANOVA, L. I., Law

SABITOVA, R. G., Economics

SAMIGULIN, R. M., History

SARANIN, A. A., Physics

SAZONOV, V. G., International Economics

SEROV, V. M., Japanese Studies

SHAKHOV, V. N., Economics

SHAPKIN, N. P., Chemistry
SHASHKOV, N. I., Philosophy
SHAVKUNOV, E. V., History
SHCHETINNIKOV, P. S., Economics
SHEKHOVTSOV, V. A., Law
SHEPELEVA, R. P., Mathematics
SHEVCHENKO, A. S., Law
SHEVCHENKO, D. K., Mathematics
SHISHMARYOV, YU. E., Mathematics
SHLYK, V. A., Mathematics
SHNYRKO, A. A., Japanese Studies
SOLONITSYNA, A. A., Sociocultural Service and
  Tourism
SONIN, V. V., Law
SOVASTEEV, V. V., History
STARODUMOVA, YE. A., Russian Philology
STONIK, V. A., Chemistry
SUKHANOV, V. V., Biology
SVYATETSKAYA, T. K., Law
TEREKHOVA, E. V., Foreign Languages
TITOV, A. I., Physics
TKACHEV, V. A., Journalism
TSITSIASHVILI, G. SH., Mathematics
TURCHIN, D. A., Law
VANEEVA, L. A., Law
VASKOVSKY, V. E., Chemistry
VELIKAYA, N. I., Russian Philology
VERISOTSKAYA, YE. V., Japanese Studies
VOLOSHIN, G. YA., Mathematics
VOVNA, V. I., Physics
VYSOTSKY, V. I., Chemistry
YACHIN, S. E., Philosophy
YAKUNIN, L. P., Oceanology
YAROVENKO, V. V., Law
YELANTSEVA, O. P., Economics
YERMAKOVA, E. V., History
YUDIN, V. V., Physics
YUDINA, L. A., Physics
ZAKHOZHY, L. A., Law
ZAYATS, T. S., Chinese Philology
ZHARIKOV, E. P., International Economics
ZHIRMUNSKY, A. V., Biology
ZHURAVLEV, YU. N., Biology
ZOLOTAR, G. YA., Chemistry
ZONOV, YU. B., Geophysics
ZUS, L. B., Law

GORNO-ALTAISK STATE UNIVERSITY

Altai Republic, 649000 Gorno-Altaisk, Len-
  kina ul. 1

Telephone: (38822) 2-25-67
Fax: (38822) 9-51-28
E-mail: office@gasu.ru
Internet: www.gasu.ru
State control

Founded 1949; present name and status 1993

Rector: Prof. YURI V. TABAKAEV
Pro-Rector for Academic Affairs: OLGA A.
  GONCHAROVA
Librarian: NATALYA N. VAKHRENEVA

Library of 2,812,090 vols
Number of teachers: 365
Number of students: 5,375, of whom 2,207
  external

DEANS

Faculty of Agriculture: LUDMILA I. SURTAEVA
Faculty of Biology and Chemistry: VERA N.
  ALEYNIKOVA
Faculty of Economics: VLADIMIR G. ZHDANOV
Faculty of Foreign Languages: VIKTOR N.
  LUKYANENKO
Faculty of Geography: ALEXEI V. BONDAR-
  ENKO
Faculty of History: OLGA A. GONCHAROVA
Faculty of Law: VERA S. IVANOVA
Faculty of Philology: TATYANA N. NIKONOVA
Faculty of Physics and Mathematics: SERGEI
  P. SOLOVEV
Faculty of Psychology and Pedagogy: VALEN-
  TINA A. CHISTYAKOVA
College of Agriculture: VLADIMIR G. ZHDANOV

HEADS OF DEPARTMENTS

Department of General Pedagogy: Prof.
  AVGUSTA P. BELIKOVA
Department of Philosophy: Dr VITALY S.
  POLYANSKY
Department of Physical Education: Dr ANA-
  TOLY G. GONOKHOV

INGUSH STATE UNIVERSITY

Republic of Ingushetia, 366700 Magas, Aleksandro-Zavodskaya ul. 30

Telephone: (87345) 5-12-64
Fax: (87345) 5-12-64

Founded 1994

Rector: ARSAMAK MARTAZANOV
First Pro-Rector: AKHMED MATIYEV
Pro-Rector for International Relations: ZAHI-
  DAT SULTYGOVA

Number of teachers: 316
Number of students: 2,752.

IRKUTSK STATE UNIVERSITY

664003 Irkutsk, 3, K. Marksa ul. 1

Telephone: (3952) 24-34-53
Fax: (3952) 24-22-38
E-mail: rector@isu.ru
Internet: www.isu.ru

Founded 1918
State control
Language of instruction: Russian
Academic year: September to May

Rector: Prof. ALEXANDER I. SMIRNOV
Vice-Rector (Academic): I. GUTNIK
Vice-Rector (Development): V. SAUNIN
Vice-Rector (Finance and General Affairs): V.
  GLEBETS
Librarian: R.V. PODGAICHENKO

Number of teachers: 853
Number of students: 12,230

Publications: *Collected Short Scientific
  Papers*, *Proceedings of the Applied Physics
  Research Institute*, *Proceedings of the Biological Research Institute*, *Proceedings of
  the Oil and Coal Products Research Institute*, *Transactions*

DEANS

Faculty of Biology and Soil Sciences: Assoc.
  Prof. N. I. GRANINA
Faculty of Chemistry: Prof. Dr A. YU.
  SAFRONOV
Faculty of Geography: Asst Prof. A. V.
  ARGUCHINTSOVA
Faculty of Geology: Asst Prof. S. P. PRIMINA
Faculty of History: Prof. S. I. KUZNETSOV
Faculty of Law: Assoc. Prof. O. P. LICHICHAN
Siberian-American Joint Faculty of Manage-
  ment: Asst Prof. A. V. DIOGENOV
Faculty of Philology: Prof. A. S. SOBENNIKOV
Faculty of Physics: Prof. YU. V. PARFENOV
Faculty of Psychology: Assoc. Prof. I. A.
  KOPONAK
Faculty of Service Industries and Advertis-
  ing: Assoc. Prof. V. K. KARNAUKHOVA
Faculty of Social Sciences: Prof. V. A.
  RASHETNIKOV
International Faculty: Asst Prof. V. YA.
  ANDRUKHOVA

ATTACHED RESEARCH INSTITUTIONS

Astronomical Observatory: Dir Assoc.
Prof. S. A. YAZEV.

Applied Physics Research Institute: Dir
Prof. YU. V. PARFENOV.

Biological Research Institute: Dir Asst
Prof. L.R. IZMESTIEVA.

Botanical Garden: Dir Assoc. Prof. V. YA.
KUZEVANOV.

**Centre of New Information Technolo-
gies:** Dir Prof. A. V. MANTSYVODA.

Computing Centre: Dir Asst Prof. V. B.
MANTSYVODA.

Lake Baikal Biological Station.

**Oil and Coal Products Research Insti-
tute:** Dir Dr V.A. KOZLOV.

IVANOVO STATE UNIVERSITY

153025 Ivanovo, ul. Ermaka 39

Telephone: (932) 32-62-10
Fax: (932) 32-46-77
E-mail: rector@ivanovo.ac.ru
Internet: www.ivanovo.ac.ru

Founded 1974
State control

Number of teachers: 429
Number of students: 7,919 (4,452 full-time
  and 3,467 by correspondence)

Rector: Prof. VLADIMIR N. YEGOROV
Pro-Rectors: ALEXEY I. SCHEGLOV (Academic),
  Dr VLADIMIR S. RADNYUK (Administration
  and Finance), Dr VLADIMIR I. NAZAROV
  (Distance Learning and Further Educa-
  tion), Dr NADEZHDA V. USOLTSEVA (Inter-
  national Affairs), Dr OLGA M. KARPOVA
  (Public Relations), Dr DMITRY I. POLY-
  VYANNY (Scientific)

Faculties of Biology and Chemistry, Economics, History, Law, Mathematics, Philology,
Physics and Romance and Germanic Philology.

KABARDINO-BALKARIAN STATE UNIVERSITY

360004 Kabardino-Balkar Republic, Nalchik,
  ul. Chernyshevskogo 173

Telephone: (095) 337-99-55
Fax: (095) 337-99-55
E-mail: bsk@ns.kbsu.ru
Internet: www.kbsu.ru

Founded 1932
State control
Language of instruction: Russian
Academic year: September to June

Rector: BARASBI S. KARAMURZOV
Vice-Rectors: KARNYSH (Extramural Studies),
  HAZESHA T. TAOV (Foreign Affairs), SVE-
  TLANA K. BASHIEVA (Postgraduate and
  Scientific Studies), HAZESHA T. TAOV (For-
  eign Affairs)
Registrar: I. SHOMAKHOVA
Librarian: ROSA N. UNACHEVA

Library: see Libraries
Number of teachers: 790
Number of students: 10,120

DEANS

Faculty of Biology: S. H. SHKHAGAPSOEV
Faculty of Chemistry: A. M. KHARAEV
Faculty of Computer Science and Systems
  Control: YU. K. TLOSTANOV
Faculty of Economics: V. Z. SHEVLOKOV
Faculty of Law: A. Z. DOLOVA
Faculty of Mathematics: M. ABREGOV
Faculty of Mechanical Engineering: V. D.
  BATYROV
Faculty of Medicine: ZAKHOKHOV
Faculty of Microelectronics: R. SH. TESHEV
Faculty of Pedagogy and Methods of Primary
  Education: B. T. SOZAEV
Institute of Philology: H. T. TAOV
Faculty of Physical Education and Sport: M.
  N. KHAUPSHEV
Faculty of Physics: M. H. KHOKONOV
Institute of Social Sciences and Humanities:
  M. Z. SOBLIROV

KALININGRAD STATE UNIVERSITY 'IMMANUEL KANT'

236041 Kaliningrad, ul. A. Nevskogo 14

Telephone: (112) 46-59-17

Fax: (112) 46-58-13
E-mail: rector@admin.albertina.ru
Internet: www.albertina.ru
Founded 1967
Academic year: September to June

Rector: Dr A. P. KLEMESHEV
Pro-Rector: Dr V. N. KHUDENKO
Librarian: A. D. SHKITSKAYA

Library: see Libraries and Archives
Number of teachers: 807
Number of students: 10,821

Publication: *Proceedings*

Faculties of Physics, Mathematics, History, Chemistry, Biology, Geography, Economics, Law; English, German and French Philology, Russian Philology, Teacher Training and Physical Training and Sport.

KALMYK STATE UNIVERSITY

358000 Elista, ul. Pushkina 11

Telephone: (84722) 5-34-31
Fax: (84722) 5-37-29
E-mail: uni@kalmsu.ru
Internet: www.kalmsu.ru

Founded 1970

Rector: G. M. MANDZHIYEVICH
Vice-Rector (Academic): Prof. ANATOLY V. RUDENKO
Vice-Rector (Administration and Finance): Prof. VLADIMIR V. UCHUROV
Vice-Rector (Scientific): Prof. ALEKSANDR A. SOLOVEV
Vice-Rector (Social-Economic Affairs): Prof. VALERY U. MANDZHIEV
Vice-Rector (University–Industry Liaison): Prof. ARKADY K. NATYROV

Number of students: 5,000

Faculties of General Engineering, Philology, Biology, Physics, Mathematics, Oriental Studies and Agriculture.

KAZAN STATE UNIVERSITY

420008 Tatarstan, Kazan, ul. Kremlevskaya 18

Telephone: (8432) 38-70-69
Fax: (8432) 38-74-18
E-mail: public.mail@ksu.ru
Internet: www.kcn.ru/tat_en/university/index.php3

Founded 1804
State control
Languages of instruction: Russian, Tatar
Academic year: September to June

Rector: M. SALAKHOV
Librarian: ZHANA V. SHCHELYVANOVA

Number of teachers: 1,075
Number of students: 10,151

Publication: *Mathematics*

DEANS

Department of Biology: A. I. GOLUBEV
Department of Chemistry: N. A. ULAKHOVICH
Department of Computer Sciences: YA. I. ZABOTIN
Department of Ecology: YU. S. KOTOV
Department of Geography: O. P. PEREVEDENTSEV
Department of Geology: R. K. TUKHVATULLIN
Department of History: I. R. TAGIROV
Department of Journalism: F. I. AGZAMOV
Department of Law: I. A. TARKHANOV
Department of Mathematics: V. V. VISHNEVSKII
Department of Philology: YA. G. SAFIULLIN
Department of Physics: A. V. AGANOV
Department of Tatar Studies: T. N. GALIULLIN

PROFESSORS

AGANOV, A. V., Physics

AKHMADULLIN, A. G., Philology
ALATYREV, V. I., Physiology
ANDRAMONOVA, N. A., Russian Philology
ANDREEV, V. I., Education
ARSLANOV, M. M., Mathematics
BAKHTIN, A. I., Mineralogy
BALALYKINA, E. A., Philology
BARABANSHIKOV, B. I., Genetics
BASHKIROV, SH. SH., Physics
BUDNIKOV, G. K., Chemistry
BUKHARAEV, R. G., Cybernetics
BUROV, B. V., Lithology
BUSYGIN, E. P., History
BUTAKOV, G. P., Geomorphology
CHERKASOV, R. A., Chemistry
ERMOLAEV, I. P., History
FARUKSHIN, M. H., Sociology
GABDULKHAEV, B. G., Mathematics
GALIULLIN, T. N., Philology
GOLUBEV, A. I., Zoology
KAIGORODOV, V. R., Physics
KHAIRUTDINOV, R. G., History
KHAKOV, V. H., Turkic Languages
KHALYMBADYA, V. G., Palaeontology
KHOKHLOVA, L. P., Plant Physiology
KOCHELAEV, B. I., Physics
KONOPLEV, YU. G., Mechanics
KOPOSOV, G. F., Soil Studies
KURDYUKOV, G. I., Law
KUZNETSOV, V. A., Ichthyology
LESHCHINSKAYA, I. B., Microbiology
LIASHKO, A. D., Computing Mathematics
LITVIN, A. L., History
LYUBARSKI, E. L., Botany
MAKLAKOV, A. I., Physics
MALKOV, V. P., Law
NAFIGOV, R. I., History
NEPRIMEROV, N. N., Electronics
NIKOLAEV, G. A., Philology
PEREVEDENTSEV, YU. P., Meteorology
RAKHMATULLIN, E. S., Sociology
RESHETOV, YU. S., Law
RYABOV, A. A., Law
SADYKOV, M. B., Philosophy
SAKHIBULLIN, N. A., Astrophysics
SALNIKOV, YU. I., Chemistry
SEMENOV, V. F., Political Economy
SHARIFYANOV, I. I., History
SHERSTNEV, A. N., Mathematics
SHIROKOV, A. P., Geometry
SIDOROV, V. V., Radiophysics
TAGIROV, I. R., History
TEPLOV, M. A., Physics
TEPTIN, G. M., Meteorology
TORSUEV, N. P., Geomorphology
TROFIMOV, A. M., Geomorphology
TUMASHEVA, D. G., Turkic Languages
USMANOV, M. A., History
YEGALOV, V. I., Differential Equations
YIGUNIN, V. D., History
ZABOTIN, YA. I., Computing Mathematics

ATTACHED RESEARCH INSTITUTIONS

A. M. Butlerov Research Institute of Chemistry: Dir V. D. KISELEV.

N. G. Chebotarev Research Institute of Mathematics and Mechanics: Dir A. V. KOSTERIN.

KEMEROVO STATE UNIVERSITY

650043 Kemerovo, Krasnaya ul. 6

Telephone: (3842) 23-12-26
Fax: (3842) 23-30-34
E-mail: rector@kemsu.ru
Internet: www.kemsu.ru

Founded 1974
State control
Language of instruction: Russian
Academic year: September to July

Rector: YU. A. ZAKHAROV
Pro-Rectors: K. E. AFANASIEV, T. M. CHUREKOVA, B. P. NEVZOROV, T. M. PANINA, B. A. SECHKARYOV, V. A. VOLCHEK
Librarian: N. P. KONOVALOVA

Number of teachers: 780
Number of students: 8,834

Faculties of Biology, Chemistry, Economics, Law, History, Mathematics, Philology, Foreign Languages, Physics, Social Sciences and Sport.

KHAKASSIA STATE UNIVERSITY 'N. F. KATANOV'

Khakassia Republic, 655000 Abakan, Lenina pr. 90

Telephone: (39022) 6-30-55
Fax: (39022) 6-35-65
E-mail: univer@khsu.ru
Internet: www.khsu.ru

State control
Founded 1974

Rector: VALENTIN A. KUZMIN
Pro-Rector for Academic Affairs: LYUBOV V. ARKHIPOVA
Pro-Rector for Administration and Finance: SERGEI V. SHVETS
Pro-Rector for Science and International Affairs: GENNADY S. SURVILLO

Number of teachers: 496
Number of students: 11,587, (of whom 5,287 external).

KOSTROMA STATE UNIVERSITY 'N. A. NEKRASOV'

156001 Kostroma, ul. Pervogo Maya 14

Telephone: (0942) 31-82-91
Fax: (0942) 31-65-61
E-mail: ksu@ksu.kostroma.net
Internet: www.ksu.kostroma.net

State control

Rector: Prof. NIKOLAI M. RASSADIN
First Pro-Rector: SERGEI N. NIKOLAEV
Pro-Rector for Academic Affairs: IRINA G. ASADULINA
Pro-Rector for Admin. and Finance: VYACHESLAV V. ROGACHEV
Pro-Rector for Computerisation: VLADIMIR N. ERSHOV
Pro-Rector for Science: VASILY V. CHEKMAREV
Pro-Rector for Social Affairs: ALEXEI E. PODOBIN

Number of teachers: 706
Number of students: 5,827.

KRASNOYARSK STATE UNIVERSITY

660041 Krasnoyarsk, Svobodny pr. 79

Telephone: (3912) 44-82-13
Fax: (3912) 44-86-25
E-mail: kon@lan.krasu.ru
Internet: www.krasu.ru

Founded 1969
State control
Language of instruction: Russian
Academic year: September to July

Rector: A. S. PROVOROV
Vice-Rectors: Y. ZH. BELOV, Y. Y. LOGINOV, V. V. MOLODKINA, B. V. OLEINIKOV, O. A. OSIPENKO V. A. SAPOZHNIKOV
Librarian: E. G. KRIVONOSOVA

Number of teachers: 720
Number of students: 12,500

Publications: *University Life* (every 2 weeks), *Vestnik KGU* (6 a year)

Faculties of Philology, Economics, Law, Physics, Mathematics, Chemistry, Biology, Modern Languages, Psychology and Education, Physical Training, History and Philosophy.

KUBAN STATE UNIVERSITY

350040 Krasnodar, ul. Stavropolskaya 149

Telephone: (8612) 69-95-02
Fax: (8612) 69-95-17

E-mail: rector@kubsu.ru
Internet: www.kubsu.ru
Founded 1924
State control
Languages of instruction: Russian, English
Academic year: September to July
President: VLADIMIR A. BABESHKO
Chief Vice-President and Vice-President for Information: ALEXANDER G. IVANOV
Vice-President for Academic Affairs: NATALYA V. KRASNOVA
Vice-President for Additional Education: ELENA A. ZHURAVLEVA
Vice-President for Capital Construction and Repairs: ELENA N. SAVENKO
Vice-President for Distance Education: IGOR D. BREGEDA
Vice-President for Science and Research: ALEXANDER A. GAVRILOV
Vice-President for Social Affairs: VIKTOR V. MOMOTOV
Secretary of the University Academic Council: TATYANA M. BELOKON
Librarian: G. V. SOLOVIEVA

Number of teachers: 1,000 including 144 Professors and 506 Associate Professors
Number of students: 16,770

Publications: *Ekologichesky vestnik nauchnykh tsentrov TchES* (Letters of BSEC Research centres, 4 a year), *Ekonomika* (annually), *Filologiya* (Philology, 2 a year), *Golos Minuvshego* (The Voice of the Past, 4 a year), *Obshchestvo i Chelovek* (Society and Mankind, 4 a year), *Priroda* (Nature, 4 a year), *Terra Incognita* (2 a year), *Upravleniye* (Management, annually)

DEANS

Faculty of Applied Mathematics: YU. V. KOLTSOV
Faculty of Architecture and Design: S. YU KOCHETKOVA
Faculty of Biology: V. YA. NAGALEVSKY
Faculty of Chemistry: V. D. BUYKLISKY
Faculty of Economics: I. V. SHEVCHENKO
Faculty of Geography: M. YU. BELIKOV
Faculty of Graphic Art: YU. V. KOROBKO
Faculty of History, Sociology and International Relations: G. M. ACHAGU
Faculty of Journalism: V. V. ROUNOV
Faculty of Law: I. A. NIKOLAYCHUK
Faculty of Management: A. M. ZHDANOVSKY
Faculty of Mathematics: G. F. SOKOL
Faculty of Philology: V. P. ABRAMOV
Faculty of Physics and Technics: N. A. YAKOVENKO
Faculty of Romano-Germanic Philology: V. I. TKHORIK

ATTACHED INSTITUTES

College of Economics, Law and Science.
Kuban Branch of Rostov Research Institute of Mechanics and Applied Mathematics.
Socio-Pedagogical College.

KURGAN STATE UNIVERSITY

640669 Kurgan, ul. Gogolya 25
Telephone: (3522) 43-26-52
Fax: (3522) 43-20-51
E-mail: rektor@kgsu.ru
Internet: www.kgsu.ru
Founded 1952
Rector: Prof. OLEG I. BUKHTOYAROV
Library of 1,000,000 vols
Number of teachers: 700
Number of students: 8,000

Faculties of Mathematics and Information Technology, Natural Sciences, History, Law, Philology, Economics, Health Protection, Psychology and Sport, Pedagogy, Technology, Transport Systems.

KURSK STATE UNIVERSITY

305000 Kursk, ul. Radischeva 33
Telephone: (0712) 56-84-61
E-mail: kgpu@kgpu.kursk.ru
Internet: www.kursk-uni.ru
State control
Founded 1934 as Kursk State Pedagogical Institute
Rector: Prof. VYACHESLAV V. GVOZDEV
First Pro-Rector: Dr NIKOLAI N. GREBENKOV
Pro-Rector for Academic Affairs: Dr YURI F. MELIKHOV
Pro-Rector for Administration and Finance: Dr VIKTO N. RUDMAN
Pro-Rector for International Communications: Dr ELENA I. MIKHAILINA
Pro-Rector for Science and Research: Dr ALEXANDER N. KHUDIN
Chief Accountant: GALINA E. KLOCHKOVA
Number of teachers: 500
Number of students: 6,500 (of which 4,000 internal and 2,500 external students)

DEANS

Faculty of Art and Design: ANATOLY P. BREDIKHIN
Faculty of Foreign Languages: NIKOLAI A. SMAKHTIN
Faculty of Geography: IRINA P. BALABINA
Faculty of History: VIKTOR V. RAKOV
Faculty of Philology: SERGEI P. PRAVEDNIKOV
Faculty of Physics and Mathematics: YURI A. SMIRNITSKY
Faculty of Primary Education: MARINA A. LUKINA

LENINGRAD STATE UNIVERSITY 'A. S. PUSHKIN'

196605 St Petersburg, Pushkin, Peterburgskoe shosse 10
Telephone: (812) 466-65-58
Fax: (812) 466-49-99
E-mail: pushkin@infos.ru
Internet: www.lgu-edu.spb.ru
State control
Founded 1992 as Leningrad Regional Pedagogical Institute; as Leningrad State Regional University 1996–1999; as A. S. Pushkin Leningrad State Regional University 1999–2003; present name and status 2003
Rector: Prof. VYACHESLAV N. SKVORTSOV
First Pro-Rector: Prof. GALINA P. CHEPURENKO
Pro-Rector for Academic Affairs: Prof. TATYANA V. MALTSEVA
Pro-Rector for Economic and International Affairs: Dr LEONID L. BUKIN
Pro-Rector for External and Further Professional Education: Prof. TATYANA S. KOMISSAROVA
Pro-Rector for Science: Dr EKATERINA S. NERYSHKINA
Number of teachers: 361
Number of students: 13,403

DEANS

Faculty of Arts: Dr SVETLANA I. NAZAROVA
Faculty of Foreign Languages: Prof. SVYATOSLAV I. ALATORTSEV
Faculty of Law: Prof. GALINA P. CHEPURENKO
Faculty of Mathematics, Physics and Information Science: Dr SERGEI D. BORONENKO
Faculty of Natural Sciences, Geography and Tourism: Dr ANATOLY M. MAKARSKY
Faculty of Philology: Prof. TATYANA V. MALTSEVA

MAGNITOGORSK STATE UNIVERSITY

455043 Magnitogorsk, Lenina pr. 114
Telephone: (3511) 35-15-32

Fax: (3511) 35-15-32
E-mail: masu@masu.ru
Internet: www.masu.ru
State control
Founded 1932
Rector: Prof. VALENTIN F. ROMANOV
First Pro-Rector: Prof. VLADIMIR P. SEMENOV
Librarian: LUDMILA V. KOTELNIKOVA
Library of 443,335 vols

DEANS

Faculty of Advancement of Qualifications and Training of Specialists: Prof. LUDMILA A. MIROSHNICHENKO
Faculty of Art and Design: Prof. VLADIMIR M. BELY
Faculty of History: Prof. MIKHAIL G. ABRAMZON
Faculty of Information Technology: Prof. ELMIRA R. IPATOVA
Faculty of Linguistics and Translation: Prof. GALINA I. VASINA
Faculty of Pedagogy and Methods of Primary Education: Prof. YURI D. KOROBKOV
Faculty of Philology: Prof. LYUBOV D. PONOMAREVA
Faculty of Physics and Mathematics: Prof. VIKTOR A. KUZNETSOV
Faculty of Pre-School Education: Prof. BORIS D. KULANIN
Faculty of Psychology: Prof. ELENA D. PETROVA
Faculty of Social Work: Prof. FLYURA A. MUSTAEVA

MARI STATE UNIVERSITY

424001 Mari-El Republic, Yoshkar-Ola, pl. Lenina 1
Telephone: (8362) 12-59-20
Fax: (8362) 45-45-81
E-mail: postmaster@marsu.ru
Internet: www.marsu.ru
Founded 1972
State control
Academic year: September to July
Rector: V. I. MAKAROV
Vice-Rector: V. I. CHEMODANOV
Chief Administrative Officer: L. N. STRELNIKOVA
Number of teachers: 384
Number of students: 4,055
Publication: *Arkheografichesky vestnik* (Archaeological News, 2 a year)

DEANS

Faculty of Agriculture: G. S. YUNUSOV
Faculty of Biology and Chemistry: M. G. GRIGORIEV
Faculty of Culture and Arts: R. L. YASHMETOVA
Faculty of Economics: K. V. SHAKIROV
Faculty of Electric Power Technology: L. M. RIBAKOV
Faculty of History and Philology: A. N. CHIMAEV
Faculty of Law: A. M. LOMONOSOV
Faculty of Linguistics and Intercultural Communication: Z. G. ZORINA
Faculty of Physics and Mathematics: G. A. SITNIKOV

MORDOVIAN STATE UNIVERSITY

430000 Mordovian Republic, Saransk, Bolshevistskaya ul. 68
Telephone: (83422) 4-17-77
Fax: (8342) 32-75-27
E-mail: makarkin@mrsu.ru
Internet: www.mrsu.ru
Founded 1931
State control
Academic year: September to June

Rector: Prof. NIKOLAI P. MAKARKIN
Vice-Rectors: Prof. V. D. CHERKASOV, Prof. SERGEI A. FEDOSIN, Prof. N. E. FOMIN, Prof. N. D. KULIKOV, Prof. SERGEI A. FEDOSIN
Registrar: MIKHAIL M. GOUDOV
Librarian: I. V. OTSTAVNOVA

Library of 2,196,381 vols, 731 periodicals
Number of teachers: 2,042 (1,610 full-time, 432 part-time)
Number of students: 27,257

Publications: *Integration of Education* (4 a year), *Regionologiya* (4 a year), *Vestnik Mordovskogo Universiteta* (4 a year)

DEANS

Faculty of Biology: Prof. V. W. REVIN
Faculty of Economics: Prof. N. D. GUSKOVA
Faculty of Electronics: I. V. GULAYEV
Faculty of Foreign Languages: Prof. YU. K. VOROBIYU
Faculty of Geography: N. A. KILDISHOVA
Faculty of Industrial and Civil Construction: Prof. V. T. EROFEYEV
Faculty of Law: Prof. V. F. LEVIN
Faculty of Mathematics: Prof. I. I. CHU-CHAYEV
Faculty of Medicine: Prof. M. D. ROMANOV
Faculty of National Culture: B. S. BRYZ-HINSKY
Faculty of Philology: Prof. M. V. MOSIN
Lighting Engineering Department: Prof. L. V. ABRAMOVA

DIRECTORS

Institute of Agrocomplex: SAMIL I. AKHMETOV
Institute of Economics: NIKOLAI P. MAKARKIN
Institute of Man and Light: LUDMILA V. ABRAMOVA
Science and Research Institute of Ecology: VICTOR N. MASKAIKIN
Science and Research Institute of Industrial and Civil Construction: VLADIMIR P. SELYAYEV
Science and Research Institute of Mathematics: EVGENY V. VOSKRESENSKY
Science and Research Institute of Regional Studies: ALEXANDR I. SOUKHAREV

MOSCOW STATE REGIONAL UNIVERSITY

107005 Moscow, ul. Radio 10a
Telephone: (095) 261-22-28
Fax: (095) 261-22-28
E-mail: mgou@mgou.ru
Internet: www.mgou.ru
State control
Founded 1923 as Moscow State Pedagogical Technical College

Rector: Prof. VLADIMIR V. PASECHNIK
First Pro-Rector (Academic): Dr SERGEI G. DEMBITSKY
Pro-Rector (Administration and Finance): Dr MIKHAIL V. YUDIN
Pro-Rector (Distance Learning): Prof. NINA G. GOLTSOVA
Pro-Rector (Education and Youth Politics): Dr MIKHAIL V. YUDIN
Pro-Rector (Scientific and International Cooperation): Prof. YURI I. YAMALOV

Number of teachers: 586

Faculties of Pedagogy, Linguistics, Translation, Further Education for Higher Education Specialists, Economics, Law, Military Education, Decorative Arts, Politics, Business and Technology, Mathematics and Physics, Physical Education and Philology; 73 departments.

MOSCOW STATE UNIVERSITY 'M. V. LOMONSOV'

119992 Moscow, Leninskie Gory
Telephone: (095) 939-10-00

Fax: (095) 939-01-26
E-mail: rector@rector.msu.ru
Internet: www.msu.ru
Founded 1755
Academic year: September to June
Rector: Acad. VIKTOR SADOVNICHY
Pro-Rectors: VLADIMIR MIRONOV (Academic), YURY ZINCHENKO (Administration), ALEXANDER SALETSKY (Educational Standards and Programmes), VICTOR TROFIMOV (General Affairs and Celebration for 250th Anniversary of the University's Foundation), MIKHAIL SOKOLOV (Health Affairs), ALEXANDER SIDOROVICH (International Co-operation), VLADIMIR MAMONTOV (Personnel), VLADIMIR BELOKURAOV (Science Policy and Scientific Research), ALEXANDER MIKHALEV (University Extension)

Number of teachers: 9,800
Number of students: 40,000

Publications: *Moscow State University* (weekly), *Vestnik MGU* (20 series, 2 a year)

DEANS

Faculty of Art: ALEKSANDER LOBODANOV
Faculty of Bioengineering and Bioinformatics: VLADIMIR SKULACHEV
Faculty of Biology: MIKHAIL GUSEV
Faculty of Chemistry: VALERY LUNIN
Faculty of Computing Mathematics and Cybernetics: YEVGENY MOISEEV
Faculty of Continuing Education: DMITRY KLEMENTYEV
Faculty of Foreign Languages: SVETLANA TER-MINASOVA
Faculty of Fundamental Medicine: VSEVOLOD TKACHUK
Faculty of Geography: NIKOLAI KASIMOV
Faculty of Geology: DMITRY PUSHCHAROVSKY
Faculty of History: SERGEY KARPOV
Faculty of Journalism: YASEN ZASURSKY
Faculty of Law: ALEXANDER SOLICHENKOV
Faculty of Material Sciences: YURY TRETYAKOV
Faculty of Mechanics and Mathematics: OLEG LUPANOV
Pedagogical Faculty: NIKOLAI ROZOV
Faculty of Philology: MARINA REMNEVA
Faculty of Philosophy: VLADIMIR MIRONOV
Faculty of Physics: VLADIMIR TRUKHIN
Faculty of Psychology: ALEKSANDR DONTSOV
Faculty of State Government: ALEKSEI SURIN
Faculty of Sociology: VLADIMIR DOBRENKOV
Faculty of Soil Science: SERGEY SHOBA
Faculty of Continuing Education: ALEKSANDR MIKHALEV
Centre for Intenational Education: VLADIMIR KOCHETOV
Higher School of Business: OLEG VIKHANSKY
Institute of Asian and African Studies: MIKHAIL MEYER

ATTACHED INSTITUTES

Anuchin Research Institute of Anthropological Studies and Anthropology Museum: Dir VLADIMIR CHTEKOV.

P. K. Shernberg State Astronomy Institute: Dir ANATOLY CHEREPASHCHUK.

Research Institute of Mechanics: Dir YURY OKUNEV.

D. V. Skobeltsyn Research Institute of Nuclear Physics: Dir MIKHAIL PANASUK.

A. N. Belozersky Institute of Physico-Chemical Biology: Dir VLADIMIR SKULACHEV.

Research Computing Centre: Dir ALEKSANDR TIKHONRAVOV.

French University College: Dir MICHEL ELTCHENINOFF.

International Laser Centre: Dir VLADIMIR SHUVALOV.

MOSCOW UNIVERSITY OF CONSUMER CO-OPERATIVES

141014 Moscow oblast, Mytischi, ul. V. Voloshinoi 12
Telephone: (095) 582-97-37
Fax: (095) 582-93-10
E-mail: muller@mupk.ru
Internet: www.mupk.ru
Founded 1913

President and Rector: Prof. MARIA V. SEROSHTAN

Number of teachers: 500
Number of students: 12,000

Areas of study: global economics, jurisprudence, finance and credit, management, marketing, accounting and auditing, economics, commodity science, commerce, economic information systems.

NIZHNII NOVGOROD STATE UNIVERSITY 'N. I. LOBACHEVSKY'

603950 Nizhnii Novgorod, pr. Gagarina 23
Telephone: (8312) 65-84-90
Fax: (8312) 65-85-92
E-mail: rector@unn.ru
Internet: www.unn.ru
Founded 1916
State control
Language of instruction: Russian
Academic year: September to June

Rector: Prof. ROMAN G STRONGIN
Vice-Rector (Academic): Assoc. Prof. ALEXANDER V. PETROV
Vice-Rector (Development): Dr SERGEI N. GURBATOV
Vice-Rector (International Relations): ALEXANDER O. GRUDZINSKY
Vice-Rector (Scientific): Prof. GEORGY A. MAKSIMOV
Librarian: Dr YURI M. SOKIN

Number of teachers: 1,250
Number of students: 25,000

DEANS

Faculty of Biology: Dr A. P. VESELOV
Faculty of Business and Management: Dr A. O. GRUDZINSKY
Faculty of Chemistry: Dr N. G. CHERNORUKOV
Faculty of Computer Science and Cybernetics: Dr V. P. SAVELYEV
Faculty of Economics: Dr YU. V. TRIFONOV
Faculty of Finance: Dr V. N. YASENEV
Faculty of History: Dr E. A. MOLEV
Faculty of International Relations: Dr O. A. KOLOBOV
Faculty of Law: Dr P. I. MILKOV
Faculty of Mechanics and Mathematics: Dr A. K. LYUBIMOV
Faculty of Philology: Dr L. I. RUCHINA
Faculty of Physical Training and Sport: Dr V. G. KUZMIN
Faculty of Physics: Dr E. V. CHUPRUNOV
Faculty of Radiophysics: Dr A. V. YAKIMOV
Faculty of Social Sciences: Dr V. A. BLONIN
Advanced School of General and Applied Physics: Dr A. G. LITVAK

ATTACHED RESEARCH INSTITUTES

Research Institute for Chemistry: Dir Dr D. F. GRISHIN.

Research Institute for Applied Mathematics and Cybernetics: Dir Dr YU. G. VASIN.

Research Institute for Mechanics: Dir Dr V. G. BAZHENOV.

Research Institute for Molecular Biology and Regional Ecology: Dir Dr V. V. NOVIKOV.

Physico-Technical Research Institute: Dir Dr O. N. GORSHKOV.

Botanical Garden: Dir Dr E. V. SINEVA.

NORTH OSSETIAN STATE UNIVERSITY

362025 Vladikavkaz, ul. Vatutina 46
Telephone: (8672) 53-09-04
Fax: (8672) 74-05-79
E-mail: webmaster@nosu.ru
Internet: www.nosu.ru

Founded 1969
Language of instruction: Russian
Academic year: September to June

Rector: AKHURBEK M. MAGOMETOV
First Pro-Rector, Pro-Rector for Academic Affairs: ANATOLY V. RAITSEV
Pro-Rector for International Affairs: OLEG S. KHATSAYEV
Pro-Rector for Science: VALERY G. SOZNANOV
Librarian: KLARA K. KOKAYEVA

Number of teachers: 833
Number of students: 11,718

DEANS

Faculty of Arts and Design: V. N. TSALAGOV
Faculty of Biology and Soil Studies: R. G. ZANGIONOVA
Faculty of Chemistry and Technology: N. I. KALOYEV
Faculty of Economics: Z. G. TEDEEV
Faculty of Education and Elementary Education: V. K. KOCHISOV
Faculty of Foreign Languages: T. T. KAMBOLOV
Faculty of Geography: B. M. BEROYEV
Faculty of History: A. I. ABAYEV
Faculty of Law: E. G. PLIYEV
Faculty of Management: V. G. TSOGOYEV
Faculty of Mathematics: A. A. AZIYEV
Faculty of Ossetian Philology: R. Z. KOMAYEVA
Faculty of Philology: L. M. BESOLOV
Faculty of Physical Education and Sports: F. G. KHAMIKOYEV
Faculty of Physics: A. P. BLIYEV

NORTHERN INTERNATIONAL UNIVERSITY

685014 Magadan, ul. Portovaya 13
Telephone: (41322) 3-00-21
Fax: (41322) 3-42-37
Internet: www.niu.ru.

NOVGOROD STATE UNIVERSITY

173003 Novgorod, St Petersburgskaya ul. 41
Telephone: (816) 222-37-07
Fax: (816) 222-41-10
E-mail: tel@novsu.ac.ru
Internet: www.novsu.ac.ru
Founded 1993
Academic year: September to June

Rector and President: Prof. ANATOLY L. GAVRIKOV

Number of teachers: 1,000
Number of students: 19,000

Faculties of Physics and Technology, Engineering and Technology, Architecture, Arts and Design, Economics, Finance, Administration, Law, History, Foreign Languages, Philosophy, Medicine, Stomatology, Pharmacy, Higher Nursing Education, Child Education and Psychology, Arts and Technology, Agricultural Production Technology, Agricultural Engineering, Biology, Chemistry and Environmental Science

Publications: *Chelo* (quarterly), *Vestnik Novgorodskogo Gosudarstvennogo Universiteta* (quarterly).

NOVOSIBIRSK STATE UNIVERSITY

630090 Novosibirsk, ul. Pirogova 2
Telephone: and fax (3832) 39-73-78
E-mail: inter@nsu.ru

Internet: www.nsu.ru
Founded 1959
State control
Language of instruction: Russian
Academic year: September to June

Rector: Prof. NICOLAY S. DICANSKY
Vice-Rector for International Activities: ELENA M. LISMAN
Vice-Rector for Research: Prof. GENNADY YU. SHVEDENKOV
Vice-Rector for Studies: Prof. NATALIA V. DULEPOVA
Registrar: N. I. BOIKOVA
Librarian: L. A. LYAGUSHINA

Library of 815,051 vols
Number of teachers: 2,226
Number of students: 6,038

Publications: *Algebra and Logics* (6 a year), *Critics and Semiotics* (annually), *Philosophy of Science* (4 a year), *Siberian Philological Journal* (2 a year), *Vestnik NGU* (3 a year)

DEANS

Department of Economics (tel. (3832) 39-72-42; e-mail dekeko@lab.nsu.ru; f. 1967):
Prof. GAGIK M. MKRTCHAN

Department of Foreign Languages:
Prof. G. G. KURKINA

Department of Geology and Geophysics (tel. (3832) 39-72-18; e-mail shatsky@uiggm.nsu.ru; internet ggd.nsu.ru; f. 1962):
Prof. VLADISLAV S. SHATSKY

Department of the Humanities (tel. (3832) 30-08-62; e-mail info@gf.nsu.ru; internet www.gf.nsu.ru; f. 1962):
Prof. LEONID G. PANIN

Department of Information Technologies (tel. (3832) 39-77-95; e-mail dekanat@ccfit.nsu.ru; internet www.fit.nsu.ru; f. 2000):
Dr MICHAIL M. LAVRENTIEV

Department of Mechanics and Mathematics (tel. (3832) 39-75-81; e-mail mmf@msu.ru; internet mmfd.nsu.ru):
Prof. SERGUEY S. GONCHAROV

Department of Natural Sciences (tel. (3832) 39-74-30; e-mail decan@fen.nsu.ru; internet www.fen.nsu.ru; f. 1959):
Prof. VLADIMIR A. REZNIKOV

Department of Physics (tel. (3832) 39-78-00; e-mail dean@phys.nsu.ru; internet www.phys.nsu.ru; f. 1961):
Prof. ANDREY V. ARZHANNIKOV

ATTACHED RESEARCH INSTITUTES

Advanced College of Information Science of NSU: tel. (3832) 33-21-31; e-mail valishev@ci.nsu.ru; f. 1991; Dir Asst Prof. ABRIK I. VALISHEV.

Specialised Scientific Study Centre: tel. (3832) 30-30-11; e-mail fmsh@ssc.nsu.ru; f. 1988; Dir Dr ALEXANDR A. NIKITIN.

OMSK STATE UNIVERSITY

644077 Omsk, pr. Mira 55a
Telephone: (3812) 67-01-04
Internet: www.omsu.ru

Founded 1974
State control
Language of instruction: Russian
Academic year: September to June

Rector: Prof. GENNADY I. GERING
Pro-Rectors: Dr MIKHAIL V. KHOROSHEVSKY, Dr VALERY V. DUBITSKY (Academic), Dr VLADIMIR P. AVILOV (Finance and Administration), Dr VLADIMIR I. STRUNIN (Scientific)
Librarian: LYUDMILA A. BALAKINA

Number of teachers: 640

Number of students: 10,000

Publications: *Omsky Universitet* (28 a year), *Vestnik Omskogo Universiteta* (4 a year)

DEANS

Faculty of Arts and Culture: NINA M. GENOVA
Faculty of Chemistry: IRINA V. VLASOVA
Faculty of Economics: LYUDMILA N. IVANOVA
Faculty of Foreign Languages: NATALYA G. GICHEVA
Faculty of History: ALEXEY V. YAKUB
Faculty of International Business: YURI P. DRUS
Faculty of Law: MAXIM S. FOKIN
Faculty of Mathematics: VLADIMIR B. NIKOLAEV
Faculty of Philology: NIKOLAI N. MISYUROV
Faculty of Physics: KLIMENTY N. YUGAI
Faculty of Psychology: LYUDMILA I. DEMENTY
Faculty of Theology and World Culture: DMITRY P. SINELNIKOV

PROFESSORS

ADEEV, G. D., Theoretical Nuclear Physics
AKELKINA, E. A., Literature
AZAROV, V. A., Law
BABOURIN, S. N., Law
BORBAT, V. F., Chemistry and Technology of Non-ferrous and Noble Metals
DUBENSKY, U. P., Pedagogics
ELOVIKOV, L. A., Methodology of Local Labour Management
FAIZULLIN, R. T., Mathematics
FISYUK, A. S., Chemistry
FOMENKO, S. V., History
GERING, G. I., Physics
GOOTS, A. K., Geometry
GRIN, A. G., Mathematics
GRINBERG, M. S., Criminal Law
GRISHKOV, A. N., Mathematics
ISSERS, O. S., Linguistics
KASANNIK, A. I., Ecological Law
KLEIMENOV, M. P., Law
KUKIN, G. P., Algebra
KUZMINA, N. A., Linguistics
LAVROV, E. I., Political Economy
MATYUSCHENKO, V. I., Archaeology
MILLER, A. E., Economy
NOVATOROV, V. E., Pedagogics
OSIPOV, B. I., Linguistics
OSTROVSKY, N. M., Chemistry
OVSIANNIKOVA, I. N., Philosophy
PERTSEV, N. V., Mathematics
POSDNIAKOV, N. K., Politology
PRUDNIKOV, V. V., Physics
RAZUMOV, V. I., Philosophy
REMNEV, A. V., History
ROMANKOV, V. A., Mathematics
ROY, O. M., Sociology
SAGITULLIN, R. S., Chemistry of Heterocyclic Compounds
SEMIKOLENOVA, N. A., Physics
SHIROKOV, I. V., Physics
SKOBELKIN, V. V., Labour Law
SOROKIN, U. A., History
STRUGOV, U. F., Mathematics
TIPUKHIN, V. N., Philosophy
TOLOCHKO, A. P., Pre-Revolutionary Native History
TOMILOV, N. A., Ethnography
VERSHININ, V. I., Analytical Chemistry
YUGAI, K. N., Physics
ZOLOTARYOV, I. D., Physics

OREL STATE UNIVERSITY

302015 Orel, Komsomolskaya ul. 95
Telephone: (0862) 77-73-18
Fax: (0862) 77-73-32
Internet: www.osu.edu.ru
State control

Founded 1974

Rector: Prof. FEDOR S. AVDEEV
Pro-Rector for Academic Affairs: Prof. NADEZHDA A. ILYINA

Pro-Rector for External Education and International Relations: Prof. NADEZHDA A. ILYINA

Pro-Rector for Science: Prof. GENNADY P. VERKEENKO

Number of teachers: 668
Number of students: 11,203.

ORENBURG STATE UNIVERSITY

460352 Orenburg, pr. Pobedy 13

Telephone: (3532) 72-37-01
Fax: (3532) 72-37-01
E-mail: post@mail.osu.ru
Internet: www.osu.ru

Founded 1971

Rector: VICTOR A. BONDARENKO
First Pro-Rector: VLADIMIR P. KOVALEVSKY

Number of teachers: 1,448
Number of students: 32,842

Faculties of Food Industry, Aerospace, Law, Medicine and Biophysics, Finance, Natural Sciences, Information Technology, Transport, Power and Electrical Engineering, Architecture and Civil Engineering, Industrial Management, Humanities, Business Administration, Physics and Mathematics, Philology and Journalism, Economics; brs in Orsk, Buzuluk, Buguruslan, Ufa, Akbulak and Novotroitsk.

PACIFIC STATE UNIVERSITY

680035 Khabarovsk, ul. Tikhookeanskaya 136

Telephone: (4212) 72-07-12
Fax: (4212) 72-07-12
E-mail: info@khstu.ru
Internet: www.khstu.ru

Founded 2005, formerly Khabarovsk State University (f. 1958)

Academic year: September to June

Rector: SERGEI N. IVANCHENKO

Library of 1,000,000 vols
Number of teachers: 800
Number of students: 19,000

Faculties of Economics and Management, Architecture and Civil Engineering, Law, Information Technologies, Highways, Forestry, International Studies, Mathematical Modelling and Modelling of Management Processes.

PACIFIC STATE UNIVERSITY OF ECONOMICS

690950 Vladivostok, Okeansky pr. 19

Telephone: (4232) 26-62-21
E-mail: web@psue.ru
Internet: www.psue.ru
State control

Founded 1964

Rector: Prof. VIKTOR G. BELKIN.

PENZA STATE UNIVERSITY

440026 Penza, Krasnaya ul. 40

Telephone: (8412) 66-29-27
Fax: (8412) 66-29-27
E-mail: cnit@stup.ac.ru
Internet: www.stup.ac.ru
State control

Founded 1943; present name and status 1998

Rector: Prof. VLADIMIR VOLCHIKHIN
First Pro-Rector: VICTOR A. MESCHERYAKOV
Pro-Rector for Academic Affairs: VICTOR B. MEKHANOV
Pro-Rector for Administration and Finance: BORIS V. MALSANOV
Pro-Rector for Governance and Personnel: YURI V. KLOCHKOV

Pro-Rector for Science: MIKHAIL A. SCHERBAKOV

Number of teachers: 725
Number of students: 13,895.

Serdobsk Branch: 442890 Penza Region, Serdobsk, Lenina ul. 285A; Dir IVAN I. IVANOV..

Kuznetsk Institute for Information and Administrative Technologies: 442530 Penza Region, Kuznetsk, Mayakovskogo ul. 57A; Dir PETR P. PETROV.

Penza Technological Institute: 440605 Penza, Baidukova ul. 1A.

PEOPLES' FRIENDSHIP UNIVERSITY OF RUSSIA

117198 Moscow, Miklukho-Maklaya ul. 6

Telephone: (095) 434-70-27
Fax: (095) 433-15-11
E-mail: druzhba@rudn.ru
Internet: www.rudn.ru

Founded 1960 as Patrice Lumumba Peoples' Friendship University

Self-governing

Language of instruction: Russian
Academic year: September to July

Rector: Prof. VLADIMIR M. FILIPPOV (acting)
Vice-Rectors: N. A. CHICHULIN, A. D. GLADUSH, V. F. PONYKA, V. D. PROTSENKO, E. L. SHESHNYAK, G. G. SOKOLOV, N. V. VENSKOVSKY, A. P. YEFREMOV
Librarian: A. N. SHUMILOV

Number of teachers: 2,112
Number of students: 4,000

Publications: *Druzhba* (weekly university newspaper), *Vestnik Rossiiskogo Universiteta Druzhby Narodov* (4 a year)

Faculty of Agriculture: Prof. V. V. GORCHAKOV
Faculty of Ecology: Prof. S. N. SIDORENKO
Faculty of Economics: Prof. N. P. GUSAKOV
Faculty of Engineering: Prof. N. K. PONOMAREV
Faculty of Foreign Languages and General Educational Disciplines: Prof. V. V. YAKUSHEV
Faculty of Humanities and Social Sciences: Prof. N. S. KIRABAEV
Faculty of Law: Prof. A. Y. KAPUSTIN
Faculty of Medicine: Prof. V. A. FROLOV
Faculty of Philology: Prof. V. N. DENISENKO
Faculty of Physical, Mathematical and Natural Sciences: Prof. V. V. DAVYDOV
Academic and Scientific Institute of Information Technology in Physics and Chemistry: Prof. S. N. SIDORENKO
Institute of Distance Learning: Prof. G. A. KRASNOVA
Institute of Foreign Languages: Prof. N. L. SOKOLOVA
Institute of Hotel Business and Tourism: Prof. S. V. DIKHTYAR
Institute of World Economy and Business (International School of Business): Prof. N. P. GUSAKOV

PERM STATE UNIVERSITY

614600 Perm, GSP, ul. Bukireva 15

Telephone: 33-61-83
Fax: 33-80-14
Internet: www.psu.ru

Founded 1916
State control

Language of instruction: Russian
Academic year: September to June

Rector: V. V. MALANIN
Vice-Rectors: Prof. V. I. KACHEVROVSKY, Prof. V. I. KOSTYTSIN, Prof. B. M. OSOVETSKY
Librarian: R. N. ROGALNIKOVA

Number of teachers: 683
Number of students: 9,167

Publications: *Uchenye Zapiski* (Transactions), *Mechanics of Controlled Movement Problems, Statistical Methods of Verifying and Estimating Hypotheses, Computer Systems and Processes Modelling, Radiospectroscopy, Caves Research Problems, Geophysical Methods of Oil and Gas Exploration* (all annually)

Faculties of history, philology, law, economics, mechanics and mathematics, physics, chemistry, biology, geology, geography.

Computing Centre.

Institute of Karstology and Speleology.

Institute of Natural Sciences.

Laboratory of Radiospectroscopy.

PETROZAVODSK STATE UNIVERSITY

185640 Republic of Karelia, Petrozavodsk, pr. Lenina 33

Telephone: (8142) 78-51-40
Fax: (8142) 77-10-21
E-mail: postmaster@mainpgu.karelia.ru
Internet: petrsu.karelia.ru

Founded 1940
State control

Language of instruction: Russian
Academic year: September to June

Rector: VICTOR VASILYEV
Pro-Rector: ANATOLY VORONIN
Librarian: MARINA OTLIVANCHIK

Number of teachers: 694
Number of students: 7,300

Publications: *Petrozavodsk University* (weekly), *Trudy* (Works, annually), *Uchenye Zapiski* (annually)

Faculty of Agriculture: NIKITA ONISCHENKO
Faculty of Baltic and Finnish Philology and Culture: TAMARA STARSHOVA
Faculty of Biology: ERNEST IVANTER
Faculty of Economics: VLADIMIR AKULOV
Faculty of Forestry Engineering: ALEXANDER PITUKHIN
Faculty of History: SERGEI VERIGIN
Faculty of Industrial and Civil Engineering: YURY MARKADANOV
Faculty of Law: SERGEI CHERNOV
Faculty of Mathematics: VLADIMIR SHESTAKOV
Faculty of Medicine: YURI LUPANDIN
Faculty of Philology: ALEKSANDR DVORETSKY
Faculty of Physics: VALEREI SYSUN
Faculty of Political and Social Sciences: VALENTINA MAKSIMOVA

POMORSKY STATE UNIVERSITY 'M. V. LOMONSOV'

163002 Arkhangelsk, Lomosova pr. 4

Telephone: (8182) 28-07-80
Fax: (8182) 28-07-80
E-mail: dit@pomorsu.ru
Internet: www.pomorsu.ru
State control

Founded 1991; present name and status 1996

Rector: Prof. VLADIMIR N. BULATOV
First Pro-Rector: YURI V. KUDRYASHOV
Pro-Rectors for Academic Affairs: IRINA R. LUGOVSKAYA, LEONID N. SHESTAKOV
Pro-Rector for Administration and Finance: ALEXANDER G. LESCHIKOV
Pro-Rector for External Academic Affairs: ANATOLY A. SEMIN

Pro-Rector for International Affairs: ALEXAN-
DER S. KRYLOV
Pro-Rector for Science: VLADISLAV I. GOLDIN
Library of 700,000 vols
Number of students: 12,419.

ROSTOV STATE UNIVERSITY

344711 Rostov-on-Don, Bolshaya Sadovaya
ul. 105

Telephone: (8632) 65-31-58
Fax: (8632) 64-52-55
E-mail: rektorat@mis.rsu.ru
Internet: www.mis.rsu.ru

Founded 1915
State control
Language of instruction: Russian
Academic year: September to June

Rector: Prof. Dr A. V. BELOKON
Pro-Rector for Academic Affairs: Prof. Dr A.
M. YURKOV
Pro-Rector for Admin. and Facilities Main-
tenance: A. M. CHOLIDI
Pro-Rector for Finance: Prof. Dr A. I. NAR-
EZHNY
Pro-Rector for International Affairs: Assoc.
Prof. Dr V. V. ZHUKOV
Pro-Rector for Part-time and Distance Edu-
cation: Assoc. Prof. Dr N. V. IZOTOVA
Pro-Rector for Research: Assoc. Prof. Dr A. T.
USHAK
Dir of Institute for Retraining and the
Improvement of Teachers' Proficiency in
the Humanities and Social Sciences: Prof.
Dr YU. G. VOLKOV
Library Dir: S. V. BEREZOVSKAYA

Library of 3,000,000 vols
Number of teachers: 2,260
Number of students: 12,580

Publications: *Donskaya arkheologia* (quar-
terly), *Filologichesky vestnik* (quarterly),
Izvestiya vyschikh uchebnykh (quarterly),
Valeologia (quarterly)

DEANS

Faculty of Advanced Technology: Prof. A. E.
PANICH
Faculty of Biology and Soil Science: Prof. Dr
V. N. DUMBAY
Faculty of Chemistry: Assoc. Prof. Dr. YE. B.
TSUPAK
Faculty of Econ.: Dr V. A. ALESHIN
Faculty of Geology and Geography: Assoc.
Prof. Dr N. I. BOIKO
Faculty of History: Prof. Dr I. M. UZNARODOV
Faculty of Law: Assoc. Prof. Dr V. T. GAIKOV
Faculty of Mechanics and Mathematics:
Assoc. Prof. Dr YA. M. YERUSALIMSKY
Faculty of Physics: Prof. Dr. L. M. RABKIN
Faculty of Philology and Journalism: Prof. Dr
YE. A. KORNILOV
Faculty of Philosophy and Cultural Studies:
Prof. Dr G. V. DRACH
Faculty of Psychology: Prof. Dr P. N. ERMA-
KOV
Faculty of Sociology and Politology: Prof. Dr
V. I. KURBATOV
Department of Area Studies: Assoc. Prof. T.
F. ERMOLENKO

ATTACHED INSTITUTES

Biological Research Institute: 344090
Rostov-on-Don, Pr. Stachki 194/1; Dir Prof.
Y. P. GUSKOV.
**North Caucasus Research Institute of
Economic and Social Problems:** 344006
Rostov-on-Don, Ul. Pushkinskaya 160; Dir
Prof. V. N. OVCHINNIKOV.
**Research Institute for Mechanics and
Applied Mathematics:** 344090 Rostov-on-
Don, Pr. Stachki 200/1; Dir Prof. I. I.
VOROVICH.

**A. B. Kogan Research Institute for
Neurocybernetics:** 344090 Rostov-on-Don,
Pr. Stachki 194/1; Dir Prof. B. M. VLADI-
MIRSKY.
Research Institute for Physics: 344090
Rostov-on-Don, Pr. Stachki 194; Dir Prof. V.
P. SAKHNENKO.
**Research Institute for Physical and
Organic Chemistry:** 344090 Rostov-on-
Don, Pr. Stachki 194/2; Dir Prof. V. I.
MINKIN.
**Piezopriber Scientific and Technologi-
cal Design Office:** 344104 Rostov-on-Don,
Ul. Milchakova 10; Dir A. Y. PANICH.
**South Russia Regional Centre for Estab-
lishments of Higher Education:** 344090
Rostov-on-Don, Pr. Stachki 200/1; Dir Prof.
Dr L. A. KROUKIER.
**Research Institute of the Geochemistry
of the Biosphere:** 353918 Novorosiisk, Pr.
Lenina 54; Dir Prof. V. A. ALEXEENKO.
**Research Institute of Carbohydrated
Raw Materials:** 344090 Rostov-on-Don, Ul.
Zorge 40; Dir Prof. E. S. SIANISIAN.
**Research Institute of the Geoecology
and Forecasting of Extreme Situations:**
344090 Rostov-on-Don, Pr. Stachki 194/2; Dir
Prof. ZAKRUTIN.
**Academic-Scientific Research Institute
of Valeology:** 344711 Rostov-on-Don, Ul.
Bolshaya Sadovaya 105; Dir Prof. G. A.
KURAEV.
Botanic Garden: 311007 Rostov-on-Don,
Ul. Lasoparkovaya; Dir Prof. V. G. SIDOR-
ENKO.

ROSTOV STATE UNIVERSITY OF
ECONOMICS (RINKH)

344007 Rostov-on-Don, Bol. Sadovaya ul. 69

Telephone: (8632) 66-51-23
Fax: (8632) 65-45-21
E-mail: rector@rseu.ru
Internet: www.rseu.ru

Founded 1931

Rector: VLADIMIR S. ZOLOTAREV

Library of 750,000 vols
Number of teachers: 400
Number of students: 15,830

Publications: *Bulletin* (4 a year), *Scientific
Notes* (4 a year).

RUSSIAN STATE SOCIAL
UNIVERSITY

107150 Moscow, ul. Losinoostrovskaya 24
Moscow, ul. Vilgelma Pika ul., korp. 1

Telephone: (095) 187-60-25
Fax: (095) 783-71-25
E-mail: info@mgsu.info
Internet: www.rgsu.net

Founded 1991 as Russian State Social Institute; accredited with university status as
Moscow State Social University 1994; present name 2004

Rector: Prof. VASILY I. ZHUKOV
Vice-Rector: GENNADY V. SAENKO

DEANS

Faculty of Foreign Languages: IRINA N.
TUPITSYNA
Faculty of Further Education: TAMARA S.
SUMSKAYA
Faculty of Humanities: LEONID G. LAPTEV
Faculty of Law: DIMITRY V. ILYAKOV
Faculty of Personnel Training and Qualifica-
tion Improvement: TATYANA V. SHELYAG
Faculty of Socioeconomics: NIKOLAI N. PILI-
PENKO
Faculty of Social Information Technologies:
VITALY M. ARISTOV

Faculty of Social Insurance and Finance:
ALEXANDER A. GRUNIN
Faculty of Social Management: OLGA A.
URZHA
Faculty of Social Medicine and Rehabilita-
tion Technologies: VALENTINA V. CHESHI-
KHINA
Faculty of Sociology: DINA T. KABDULLINOVA
Faculty of Social Work, Pedagogy and Psy-
chology: VLADISLAV A. NIKITIN
Faculty of Work and Employment Security:
YURI G. SOROKIN

RUSSIAN STATE TRADE AND
ECONOMICS UNIVERSITY

125817 Moscow, ul. Smolnaya 36

Telephone: (095) 458-94-79
Fax: (095) 458-72-47
E-mail: mail@rsute.ru
Internet: www.rsute.ru

Founded 1930

President: Prof. Dr SERGEI N. BABURIN
Number of students: 30,000

Library of 500,000 vols

22 Brs located across Russia.

RUSSIAN STATE UNIVERSITY FOR
THE HUMANITIES

125267 Moscow, Miusskaya pl. 6

Telephone: (095) 250-61-18
Fax: (095) 250-51-09
E-mail: afn@rggu.msk.su
Internet: www.rsuh.ru

Founded 1991

Rector: Prof. YURI N. AFANASYEV

Library of 1,500,000 vols
Number of teachers: 484
Number of students: 4,120.

ST PETERSBURG STATE UNIVERSITY

199034 St Petersburg, Universitetskaya nab.
7/9

Telephone: (812) 328-20-00
Fax: (812) 328-13-46
E-mail: office@inform.pu.ru
Internet: www.spbu.ru

Founded 1724
State control
Academic year: September to June (two
terms)

Rector: Dr L. A. VERBITSKAYA
Vice-Rector: Dr I. V. MURIN
Librarian: N. A. SHESHINA

Library: see Libraries and Archives
Number of teachers: 4,205
Number of students: 25,423

Publications: *Jurisprudence*, *Vestnik* (Journal, in seven series)

DEANS

Faculty of Applied Mathematics: Dr L. A.
PETROSIAN
Faculty of Biology and Soil Science: Dr I. A.
GORLINSKY
Faculty of Chemistry: Dr A. YU. BILIBIN
Faculty of Economics: Dr I. P. BOYKO
Faculty of Geography and Geo-Ecology: Dr V.
V. DMITIREV
Faculty of Geology: Dr I. V. BULDAKOV
Faculty of History: Dr A. YU. DVORNICHENKO
Faculty of International Relations: Dr K. K.
KHUDOLEY
Faculty of Journalism: Dr M. A. SHISHKINA
Faculty of Law: Dr N. M. KROPACHEV
Faculty of Management: Dr V. S. KATKALO
Faculty of Mathematics and Mechanics: Dr
G. A. LEONOV
Faculty of Medicine: Dr S. V. PETROV

Faculty of Oriental Studies: Dr I. M. STEBLIN-KAMENSKY

Faculty of Philology: Dr S. I. BOGDANOV

Faculty of Philosophy: Dr YU. N. SOLONIN

Faculty of Physics: Dr A. S. CHIRTSOV

Faculty of Psychology: Dr L. A. TSVETKOVA

Faculty of Sociology: Dr N. G. SKVORTSOV

ATTACHED INSTITUTES

Institute of Astronomy: Dir Dr V. V. VITYAZEV.

Botanical Gardens: Dir V. N. NIKITINA.

Institute of Applied Mathematics: Dir Dr D. A. OVSIANNIKOV.

Institute of Biology: Dir Dr D. V. OSIPOV.

Institute of Chemistry: Dir Dr YU. E. ERMOLENKO.

Institute of Complex Social Research: Dir Dr V. E. SEMENOV.

Institute of Geography: Dir Dr A. I. CHISTOBAEV.

Institute of the Earth's Crust: Dir Dr V. V. KURILENKO.

Institute of Mathematics and Mechanics: Dir Dr G. A. LEONOV.

Institute of Physics: Dir Dr YE. I. RYUMTSEV.

Institute of Physiology: Dir Dr I. YE. KANUNIKOV.

Institute of Radiophysics: Dir O. V. SOLOVIEV.

Institute of Information Technology: Dir Dr A. N. TEREKHOV.

Institute of Laser Research: Dir Dr YU. S. TVERIANOVICH.

ST PETERSBURG STATE UNIVERSITY OF CINEMA AND TELEVISION

191126 St Petersburg, ul. Pravdy 13

Telephone: (812) 315-74-83

E-mail: info@gukit.ru

Internet: www.gukit.ru

Founded 1918

Rector: Prof. ALEXANDER A. BELOUSOV

Library of 500,000 vols

Number of students: 4,500

Publication: *Proceedings*

Study areas include film equipment, electrical engineering, film and photographic materials, economics, art of cinema and television.

ST PETERSBURG STATE UNIVERSITY OF ECONOMICS AND FINANCE

191023 St Petersburg, ul. Sadovaya 21

Telephone: (812) 310-38-23

Fax: (812) 110-56-74

E-mail: rector@finec.ru

Internet: www.finec.ru

Founded 1930; present name and status 1997

Rector: LEONID S. TARASEVICH

Number of teachers: 2,000

Number of students: 12,000

Library of 1,000,000 vols

Faculties of Economic Theory, Industrial Economics, Finance, Accounting, Statistics, International Economic Relations, Marketing, Management, Banking; also comprises a Higher Economics School.

SAKHALIN STATE UNIVERSITY

693008 Yuzhno-Sakhalinsk, ul. Lenina 290

Telephone: (424) 42-43-57

E-mail: admin@sakhgu.sakhalin.ru

Internet: www.sakhgu.sakhalin.ru

State control

Founded 1949 as Yuzhno-Sakhalinsk Teachers Training College; as Yuzhno-Sakhalinsk State Pedagogical Institute 1954; present name and status 1998

Rector: Dr BORIS R. MISIKOV

Library of 576,818 vols

Number of teachers: 313

Number of students: 6,384

Publications: *Law Journal, Maymanovsky Readings, Philological Journal, Regional Studies Bulletin, Scientists of Note of SahGU*

HEADS OF DEPARTMENTS

Institute of Economy and Oriental studies: VALENTINA V. KOLEGANOVA

Institute of History, Sociology and Management: MIKHAIL S. VYSOKOV

Institute of Law: TATYANA V. KUKHARK

Institute of Natural Sciences: NATALYA V. VALVAKOVA

Institute of Philology: TATYANA E. SHUMILOVA

Institute of Pedagogy: MARINA A. ROMANOVA

Institute of Technology: VALERY N. BELOUSOV

SAMARA STATE UNIVERSITY

443011 Samara, ul. Akademika Pavlova 1

Telephone: (8462) 34-54-02

Fax: (8462) 34-54-17

E-mail: avn@ssu.samara.ru

Internet: www.ssu.samara.ru

Founded 1969

State control

Language of instruction: Russian, English

Academic year: September to June

Rector: GENNADY P. YAROVOY

First Pro-Rector: PETR S. KABYTOV

Pro-Rector for Education: VITALY P. GARKIN

Pro-Rector for Science: YURI N. GORELOV

Chief Librarian: GALINA A. BARSUKOVA

Library of 900,000 vols

Number of teachers: 820

Number of students: 14,000

Publications: *Bulletin* (8 a year), *Physics of Wave Processes and Radio-Technical Systems* (4 a year), *Samara Zemsky Collection* (4 a year)

DEANS

Faculty of Biology: G. L. RYTOV

Faculty of Chemistry: S. V. KURBATOVA

Faculty of History: U. N. SMIRNOV

Faculty of Languages and Literature: A. A. BEZRUKOVA

Faculty of Law: A. A. NAPREENKO

Faculty of Mathematics and Mechanics: V. M. KLIMKIN

Faculty of Physics: V. V. IVAKHNIK

Faculty of Psychology: K. S. LISETSKY

Faculty of Sociology: V. YA. MACHNEV

PROFESSORS

ASTAFIEV, V. I., Mechanics

BLATOV, V. A., Inorganic Chemistry

BREUSOV, Y. G., Economics

BULANOVA, A. V., General Chemistry and Chromatography

FILATOV, O. P., Equations of Mathematical Physics

GIZATULLIN, M. H., Physics and Mathematics

GOLUBKOV, S. A., Russian and Foreign Literature

GORELOV, Y. N., Differential Equations

KABYTOV, P. S., History of Russia

KHRAMKOV, I. V., History of Russia

KLIMKIN, V. M., Functional Analysis

KOMOV, A. N., Electronics

KONEV, V. A., Philosophy of the Humanities Faculties

KOZENKO, B. D., World History

KOZHEVNIKOV, Y. N., Physics and Mathematics

LEONOV, M. I., Russian History

LOBACHEV, A. L., Chemistry and Chromatography

MATVEEV, N. M., Ecology, Botany and Environmental Protection

MERKULOVA, N. A., Human and Animal Physiology

MOLEVICH, E. F., Sociology and Political Science

PLAKSINA, T. I., Ecology, Botany and Environmental Protection

PODKOVKIN, V. G., Biochemistry

PURYGIN, P. P., Organic Chemistry

RUDNEVA, T. I., Education

RYMAR, N. T., Russian and Foreign Literature

SARAEV, L. A., Mathematics and Computers

SEREZHKIN, V. N., Inorganic Chemistry

SEREZHKINA, L. B., Inorganic Chemistry

SHEIFER, S. A., Criminal Court Proceedings and Investigation

SHESTAKOV, A. A., Philosophy

SIKORA, P. E., State and Administrative Law

SKOBELEV, V. P., Russian and Foreign Literature

SKOBLIKOVA, Y. S., Philology, Russian Language

SOBOLEV, V. A., Differential Equations

SOLODYANNIKOV, Y. V., Functional Analysis and Theory of Functions

VOSKRESENSKY, V. E., Algebra and Geometry

YAROVOY, G. P., Radiophysics and Computers

ZAGUZOV, I. S., Mechanics

ATTACHED RESEARCH INSTITUTES

Institute of Applied Ecology: Dir P. P. PURYGIN.

Institute of the History and Archaeology of the Volga Region: Dir I. B. VASILIEV.

Institute of Sociological Research: Dir E. G. MOLEVICH.

SARATOV STATE UNIVERSITY 'N. G. CHERNYSHEVSKY'

410026 Saratov, Astrakhanskaya ul. 83

Telephone: (8452) 24-16-96

Fax: (8452) 24-04-46

E-mail: ied@sgu.ru

Internet: www.sgu.ru

Founded 1909

State control

Academic year: September to July

Rector: LEONID YU. KOSSOVICH

Vice-Rectors: IRINA YU. IVANYUSHINA (Academic Affairs), DIMITRY V. PROKHOROV (International Affairs), DIMITRY A. USANOV (Science)

Registrars: YURI SKLYAROV, SVETLANA MUSHTAKOVA

Librarian: VERA A. ARTISEVICH

Library of 3,000,000 vols

Number of teachers: 1,951

Number of students: 28,075

Publications: *Applied Nonlinear Dynamics, Problems of Applied Physics, News of Saratov University, News of Higher Educational Institutions, Electrochemical Energetics, Mechanics of Deformable Environments, Numbers Theory Research, Differential Equations and Functions Theory, Entomological and Parasitological Research in the Volga Region, Contemporary Herpetology*

Branch in Astrakhan; colleges and institutes: College of Radioelectronics, P. N. Yablochkov; Geological College; College of Management and Service; Pedagogical Institute in Balashov.

DEANS

Biology: Dr GENNADIY V. SHLYAKHTIN

Chemistry: Dr OLGA V. FEDOROVA

Computer Sciences and Information Technologies: Dr DMITRY V. SPERANSKY

Geography: Dr ALEXEY N. CHUMACHENKO
Geology: Dr EVGENY M. PERVUSHOV
History: Dr VELIKHAN S. MIRZEKHANOV
Humanities and Social Sciences: Dr YURI P. SUSLOV
Mechanics and Mathematics: Dr ANDREY M. ZAKHAROV
Non-Linear Processes: Dr YURIY I. LEVIN
Philology: Dr VALERY V. PROZOROV
Philosophy: Dr VLADIMIR N. BELOV
Physics: Dr IGOR N. SALY
Sociology: Dr GENNADIY V. DYLNOV

SOUTH URAL STATE UNIVERSITY

454080 Chelyabinsk, pr. Lenina 76

Telephone: (3512) 65-65-04
Fax: (3512) 65-38-04
E-mail: iao@susu.ac.ru
Internet: www.susu.ac.ru

Founded 1943; present name and status 1997 (formerly Chelyabinsk State Technical University)

State control

Academic year: September to June

Consists of 33 faculties, 13 branches and 8 regional campuses

Rector: Prof. GERMAN P. VYATKIN
First Vice-Rector (Academic): Prof. GENNADY G. MIKHAILOV
Vice-Rector (Academic): Prof. SERGEY Y. GUREVICH
Vice-Rector (Administration and Finance): Prof. VADIM A. TROFIMYCHEV
Vice-Rector (Scientific): Prof. ALEXANDER L. SHESTAKOV
Registrar: IGOR V. SIDOROV
Director of International Relations Department: SERGEY G. BARYSHNIKOV
Director of Library: IRINA P. BERGER
Number of teachers: 5,000
Number of students: 55,000

Publication: *Bulletin* (monthly)

DEANS

Architecture Faculty: SALAVAT G. SHABIEV
Architecture and Construction Faculty: VLADIMIR V. SPASIBOZHKO
Automobile and Tractor Faculty: YURI V. ROZHDESTVENSKY
Commerce Faculty: VALENTINA Y. LOPATINA
Economics and Business Faculty: VALENTINA A. KISELEVA
Economics and Management Faculty: VICTOR I. BARHATOV
Electronics Faculty: LEV S. KAZARINOV
International Faculty: VLADIMIR P. GORSHENIN
Law Faculty: VLADIMIR I. MAYOROV
Law and Finance Faculty: BORIS I. ROVNY
Linguistics Faculty: TAMARA N. HOMUTOVA
Mechanical-Mathematical Faculty: ALEXANDR D. DROZIN
Mechanical-Technological Faculty: ALEXANDR I. SIDOROV
Physical Faculty: NATALIA D. KUNDIKOVA
Physical and Metallurgical Faculty: YURI D. KORIAGIN
Power Engineering Faculty: YURI I. HOKHLOV
Faculty of Psychology: NICOLAY A. BATURIN
Service and Light Industry Faculty: VICTOR A. LIVSHITC
Social and Humanitarian Faculty: VICTOR S. BALAKIN
Rocket Space Technology Faculty: YURI S. PAVLYUK
Valeology, Physical Training and Sports Faculty: YURI M. CHERNECKY

ATTACHED RESEARCH INSTITUTES

Institute of the Chemical Problems of Industrial Ecology: Dir Prof. YURI I. SUKHAREV.

Institute of Radio-electronic Systems: Dir Prof. YURI T. KARMANOV.

STATE UNIVERSITY FOR THE HUMANITIES

119334 Moscow, Leninsky pr-t, 32A

Telephone: (095) 938-10-09
Fax: (095) 938-22-88
E-mail: gugn@gugn.info
Internet: www.gugn.ru

State control

Founded 1992 as the Republican Centre for Humanities Education; present name 1998

Rector: Prof. ALEXANDER O. CHUBARYAN
First Pro-Rector: Prof. NATALYA N. NIKITINA
Pro-Rector for General Affairs: GEORGY N. KRASNOV
Pro-Rector for Science: Prof. MIKHAIL V. BIBIKOV
Academic Secretary: DENIS V. FOMIN-NILOV

Institutes of History, Culture, World Politics, Politology, Law, Psychology, Sociology, Philosophy, Economics, Literary Culture and Management, Advancement of Qualifications and Teacher Training.

STATE UNIVERSITY OF MANAGEMENT

109542 Moscow, Ryazansky pr. 99

Telephone: (095) 371-13-22
Fax: (095) 174-62-81
E-mail: rectorat@guu.ru
Internet: www.guu.ru

Founded 1919

Rector: ANATOLY G. PORSHNEV

Library of 280,000 vols
Number of teachers: 700
Number of students: 10,000.

STAVROPOL STATE UNIVERSITY

355009 Stavropol, ul. Pushkina 1

Telephone: (8652) 35-72-65
Fax: (8652) 35-40-33
E-mail: info@stavsu.ru
Internet: www.stavsu.ru

State control

Founded 1930 as Stavropol Agro-Pedagogical Institute; 1932–1994 as Stavropol Pedagogical Institute; 1994–1996 as Stavropol State Pedagogical University; present name 1996

Rector: Prof. VALDIMIR A. SHAPOVALOV
Vice-Rector for Academic Affairs: Prof. VITALY S. BELOZEROV
Vice-Rector for Administration and Finance: ANATOLY K. VASILENKO
Vice-Rector for Building Projects: YURI P. LUBENTSEV
Vice-Rector for Economic Affairs: Prof. ALEXEY M. EROKHIN
Vice-Rector for Information Systems: Prof. YURI S. BRANOVSKY
Vice-Rector for Sciences: Prof. VIKTOR M. ISHCHENKO
Academic Secretary: Dr ALEXEY E. TREGUBOV
Dean of External Students: Dr TATYANA N. TARANOVA

Number of teachers: 650.

SURGUT STATE UNIVERSITY

628400 Tyumen oblast, Surgut, ul. Energetikov 30

Telephone: (3462) 52-47-00
Fax: (3462) 52-47-29
E-mail: info@inao.surgu.ru
Internet: www.surgu.ru

Founded 1993

Private control

Rector: Prof. GEORGY I. NAZIN
Vice-Rector for Academic Affairs: Prof. YURI V. KUZNETSOV
Vice-Rector for Administration and Finance: Dr BORIS U. SERAZETDINOV
Vice-Rector for Capital Construction: KONSTANTIN S. MOKHOV
Vice-Rector for Distance Learning: Prof. SERGEI F. KOZHUKOV
Vice-Rector for Economic and Social Affairs: VIKTOR I. LYUTY
Vice-Rector for Information Resources: Dr NIKOLAI G. SHEVCHENKO
Vice-Rector for Science: Dr VIKTOR P. SAMSONOV
Vice-Rector for Student Affairs: Dr BORIS U. SERAZETDINOV
Librarian: VALENTINA N. SHEVCHENKO

Library of 282,354 vols

DEANS

Biology: VLADIMIR P. STARIKOV
Economics: LEONID A. AVDEEV
Engineering and Physics: NIKOLAI N. BADULIN
History: ALEXANDER I. PRISCHEPA
Information Technology: FEDOR F. IVANOV
Law: VLADIMIR V. CHERUSHEV
Linguistics: SVETLANA G. KULAGINA
Medicine: LUDMILA V. KOVALENKO
Physical Culture: SERGEI M. OBUKHOV
Psychology: IRINA P. GREKHOVA

SYKTYVKAR STATE UNIVERSITY

167001 Syktyvkar, Oktyabrskii pr. 55

Telephone: (8212) 43-68-20
Fax: (8212) 43-68-20
E-mail: ssu@syktsu.ru
Internet: www.syktsu.ru

Founded 1972

State control

Languages of instruction: Russian, Komi

Academic year: September to July

Rector: VASILY N. ZADOROZHNY
Vice-Rector: NIKOLAI A. TIKHONOV
Chief Administrative Officer: LUBOV S. SHABALOVA
Librarian: NONNA F. AKOPOVA

Number of teachers: 370
Number of students: 4,500

Publications: *Rubezh* (4 a year), *Vestnik* (annually)

DEANS

Faculty of Arts: LUDMILA V. GURLENOVA
Faculty of Chemistry and Biology: IRINA V. PIYR
Faculty of Finance and Economics: TATIANA A. PADERINA
Faculty of Finno-Ugric Studies: NATALIA S. SERGIEVA
Faculty of History: VALTER N. KHUDYAEV
Faculty of Law: ALEXANDER Y. EPIKHIN
Faculty of Management: EKATERINA E. PETRAKOVA
Faculty of Mathematics: ILYA I. BAZHENOV
Faculty of Philology: VLADIMIR P. EFIMENKO
Faculty of Physics: KONSTANTIN YU. BAZHUKOV
Faculty of Physical Training and Sport: ELENA E. SHOMYSOVA
Faculty of Psychology and Social Work: ALBINA V. SOKOLOVA
Centre for Studies in Humanities: NATALI V. PURISH

PROFESSORS

ARAPOV, N. T., Jurisprudence
BOBKOV, S. G., Mathematics
BOCHAROV, M. I., Physical Education
BOLOTOV, S. P., Management
BRACH, B. Y., Chemistry
DOLGIN, M. M., Zoology

IGUSHEV, E. A., Komi and Finno-Ugrian Languages
IRZHAK, L. I., Physiology
KHUDYAEV, S. I., Mathematical Physics
MIKHAILOVSKY, E. I., Computer Science
NAGAEV, V. V., Psychology
NAIDENOV, N. D., Management
NIKETENKOV, V. L., Mathematics
POROSHKIN, A. G., Mathematical Analysis
POTAPOV, S. G., Chemistry
PUNEGOV, V. I., Physics
RAPOPORT, Y. M., Political Science
ROSHEVSKAYA, L. P., History
RYAZANOV, M. A., Chemistry
SEMENOV, V. A., History
SOLOVIEV, V. A., Zoology
SUTKIN, V. N., Chemistry
TIKHOMIROV, A. N., Mathematics
VITYAZEVA, V. A., Economics
VLASOV, A. N., Russian Literature
ZADOROZHNY, V. N., Economics
ZHIDELEVA, V. V., Management
ZOLOTAREV, V. V., History

TAMBOV STATE UNIVERSITY 'G. R. DERZHAVIN'

392622 Tambov, Internatsionalnaya ul. 33
Telephone: (0752) 72-12-29
Fax: (0752) 71-03-07
E-mail: rector@tsu.tmb.ru
Internet: tsu.tmb.ru
State control
Founded 1994 on the basis of Tambov State Pedagogical Institute and Tambov State Institute of Culture

Rector: VLADISLAV M. YURIEV
First Pro-Rector: VLADIMIR N. OKATOV
Pro-Rector for Academic Affairs and New Technologies: ALEXEI A. SLETKOV
Pro-Rector for Administration, Finance and Social Affairs: ALEXEI P. POZDNYAKOV
Pro-Rector for Economic and Social Affairs: IGOR V. OSAULENKO

Library of 850,000 vols
Number of teachers: 650
Number of students: 10,500.

TOGLIATTI STATE UNIVERSITY

445667 Togliatti, ul. Belorusskaya 14
Telephone: (8482) 48-14-75
Fax: (8482) 22-95-22
E-mail: office@tltsu.ru
Internet: www.tltsu.ru

Founded 1951 as Togliatti Polytechnic Institute; present name and status 2001 following merger with Togliatti State Pedagogical University (f. 1988)
Academic year: September to June
Rector: Prof. Dr SERGEI F. ZHILKIN
First Vice-Rector: Dr OLGA A. LYSHOVA

Library of 800,000 vols
Number of teachers: 758
Number of students: 13,000

Faculties of Chemistry and Biology, Economics, Management and Law, Electrical Engineering, Mathematics and Information Science, History, Foreign Languages, Psychology, Philology and Journalism, Graphic Arts and Design and Physical Training and Sports.

ATTACHED INSTITUTES

Automotive Institute: 445667 Togliatti, Belorusskaya ul. 14; Dir Prof. Dr. OLEG I. DRATCHEV.

Institute of Physics and Engineering: 445667 Togliatti, Belorusskaya ul. 14; Dir Prof. Dr. ANATOLY A. VIKARTCHUK.

Pedagogical Institute: 445667 Togliatti, Frunze ul. 2G; Dir Prof. Dr. IRINA V. NEPROKINA.

TOMSK STATE UNIVERSITY

634050 Tomsk, pr. Lenina 36
Telephone: (3822) 52-95-58
Fax: (3822) 52-95-85
E-mail: rector@tsu.ru
Internet: www.tsu.ru
Founded 1878
State control
Academic year: September to June
Rector: Prof. GEORGY V. MAYER
Senior Vice-Rector: Dr MIKHAIL D. BABANSKY
Vice-Rectors: Prof. ALEXANDER S. REVUSHKIN (Academic Affairs), Dr SERGEY N. KIRPOTIN (International Affairs), Prof. GRIGORY E. DUNAEVSKY (Research and Postgraduate Studies)
Registrar: N. BUROVA
Librarian: EVGENY N. SYNTIN

Library: see Libraries and Archives
Number of teachers: 1,410
Number of students: 14,000 (10,000 full-time, 4,000 part-time)

Publications: *Krylovia: Siberian Botanical Journal* (2 a year), *Physics* (4 a year), *Vestnik* (4 a year)

Faculties of biology and soil science, geology and geography, chemistry, history and international relations, philology, journalism, economics, law, philosophy, sociology and political science, mechanics and mathematics, applied mathematics and cybernetics, computer science, physics, radiophysics, technical physics, psychology, foreign languages; institute of culture; international faculty of public and business administration.

ATTACHED INSTITUTES

Institute of Applied Mathematics and Mechanics.

Institute of Biology and Biophysics.

Institute of Socio-Economic Problems of Siberia.

Siberian Physical Technical Institute.

TVER STATE UNIVERSITY

170000 Tver, ul. Zhelyabova 33
Telephone: (0822) 33-15-50
Fax: (0822) 33-12-74
E-mail: uni@tversu.ru
Internet: university.tversu.ru
Founded 1971
Rector: ALEXEY N. KUDINOV
Pro-Rector: VIKTOR P. GAVRIKOV
Librarian: OLGA V. VERSHININA

Number of teachers: 720
Number of students: 10,000

Faculties of Mathematics, Cybernetics, Physics, Chemistry, Biology and Geography, Philology, Modern Languages, Pedagogics, Economics, History, Law, Management and Sociology, Psychology and Social Work and Physical Education.

TYUMEN STATE UNIVERSITY

625003 Tyumen 3, ul. Semakova 10
Telephone: (810) 46-01-41
Fax: (810) 46-19-30
E-mail: international@utmn.ru
Internet: www.utmn.ru
Number of teachers: 792
Number of students: 13,685
Rector: GENNADY F. KUTSEV

Faculties of History, Philology, Romance and Germanic Philology, Physics and Mathematics, Chemistry and Biology, Economics and Geography.

UDMURTIA STATE UNIVERSITY

426034 Udmurtiya, Izhevsk, Universitetskaya ul. 1
Telephone: (3412) 75-16-10
Fax: (3412) 75-58-66
E-mail: inter@uni.udm.ru
Internet: www.udsu.ru
Founded 1931
State control
Language of instruction: Russian
Academic year: September to June
Rector: Prof. VITALY A. ZHURAVLEV
First Vice-Rector: Dr SEMION D. BUNTOV
Vice-Rector for Finance and Economics: GERMAN S. SERGEEV
Vice-Rector for International Relations: MARIA I. BESNOSOVA
Vice-Rector for Public Relations: Prof. SERGEY M. RESHETNIKOV
Vice-Rector for Research and Development, Business and Manufacturing Integration: Dr NATALYA S. LADYZHETS
Director of the University Library: LYUDMILA P. BESKLINSKAYA

Library of 700,000 vols, 400 periodicals, 50 newspapers
Number of teachers: 956
Number of students: 27,255

Attached museums: Museum of Ancient and Medieval History of the Kama-Vyatka Region (140 sq. m, 160,000 artefacts); Museum of Natural Sciences and Zoology (52 sq. m, 3,000 artefacts); Museum of Arts (255 sq. m 2,500 artefacts)

Publications: *Collected Scientific Articles on the Professional Training of Experts* (4 a year), *Herald* (monthly)

DEANS

Faculty of Biology and Chemistry: N. E. ZUBTSOVSKY
Faculty of Geography: I. I. RYSSIN
Faculty of History: M. Y. MALYSHEV
Faculty of Journalism: A. S. IZMAYLOVA-ZUEVA
Faculty of Mathematics: N. N. PETROV
Faculty of Medical Biotechnology: A. K. BARSUKOV
Faculty of Oil and Gas: A. YA. VOLKOV
Faculty of Philosophy and Sociology: Prof. M. N. MAKAROVA
Faculty of Physics: V. P. BOVIN
Faculty of Professional Foreign Language Study: R. G. SHISHKINA
Faculty of Psychology and Pedagogics: N. I. LEONOV
Faculty of Russian Philology: E. A. PODSHIVALOVA
Faculty of Udmurt and Finno-Ugric Philology: L. P. FYODOROVA
Pedagogical Faculty of Physical Training: A. E. ALABUZHEV
Institute of Arts and Design: A. E. ANIKIN
Institute of Civil Defence: A. A. PROSANDEEV
Institute of Economics and Management: O. D. GOLOVINA
Institute of Foreign Languages and Literature: T. I. ZELENINA
Institute of Law, Social Management and Security: V. IVSHIN
Institute of Social Communications: G. V. MERZLYAKOVA

PROFESSORS

Faculty of Geography (tel. (3412) 526170).
PUCHKOVSKY, S. V., Natural Use and Geo-Ecological Cartography
RYSSIN, I. I., Physical Geography and Landscape Ecology
STURMAN, V. I., Natural Use and Geo-Ecological Cartography

Faculty of History (tel. (3412) 255088):

VLADYKIN, V. E., Ethnology and Regional Study

Faculty of Mathematics (tel. (3412) 501188):

BELTYUKOV, A. P., Mathematical Supply of Electronic Computers
CHUBURIN, YU. P., Mathematical Analysis
DERR, V. YA., Mathematical Analysis
GRYZLOV, A. A., Algebra and Topology
ISLAMOV, G. G., Computing Mathematics
KONDRATYEV, B. P., Astronomy and Mechanics
NEPEYVODA, N. N., Algebra and Topology
TONKOV, E. L., Differential Equations
YASHIN, A. D., Algebra and Topology

Faculty of Udmurt and Finno-Ugric Philology (tel. (3412) 755920):

KARPOVA, L. L., Udmurt Language and Pedagogy
KELMAKOV, V. K., General and Finno-Ugric Linguistics
SHUTOV, A. F., Udmurt Language and Pedagogy
TARAKANOV, I. V., Udmurt Language and Pedagogy
VANYUSHEV, V. M., Udmurt Literature and Folk Literature of the Russian Federation
VLADYKINA, T. G., Russian Philology

Institute of Economics and Management (tel. (3412) 500266):

BOTKIN, O. I., Economic Theory
LETCHIKOV, A. V., Mathematical Methods in Economics
MATVEYEV, V. V., Business Economics
MOKRUSHIN, YU. A., Regional and Municipal Economics
PEREVOSCHIKOV, YU. S., Business Economics

Institute of Foreign Languages and Literature (tel. (3412) 754635):

AVETISYAN, V. A., Foreign Literature
LASHKEVITCH, A. V., Foreign Literature
PUSHINA, N. I., Grammar and History of English
UTEKHINA, A. N., German Philology
ZELENINA, T. I., Philology

Institute of Law, Social Management and Security (tel. (3412) 526398):

KAMINSKY, M. K., Criminology and Court Examination
MALKOV, V. P., Criminal Law and Criminology
POSKONIN, V. V., Philosophy and Sociology of Law
POSKONINA, O. V., Philosophy and Sociology of Law
SHUMILOV, E. F., Legal Basis of State and Municipal Services
VITRUK, N. V., Theory and History of State and Law
VOYTOVICH, V. YU., Legal Basis of State and Municipal Services
YAKOVLEV, V. N., Ecological, Agrarian and Natural Resources Law
ZINATULLIN, Z. Z., Criminal Procedure

ATTACHED INSTITUTES

Centre for Surface Physics: Dir V. A. TRAPENZNIKOV.

Institute of Applied Ecology and Bioresources: Dir N. E. ZUBTSOVSKY.

Institute of Crisis Process Research: Dir A. N. DANILOV.

Institute of Distance Education: Dir I. Z. YUSUPOV.

Institute of Ecology, and Agrarian and Natural Resources: Dir V. N. YAKOVLEV.

Institute of Economics and Management: Dir Prof. G. Y. GALUSHKO.

Institute of Experimental Natural Sciences: Dir Prof. V. V. SOBOLEV.

Institute of Foreign Languages and Foreign Literature: Dir T. I. ZELENINA.

Institute of the History and Culture of the Finno-Ugric Peoples of the Urals: Dir Prof. R. D. GOLDINA.

Institute of Law, Social Management and Security: Dir S. D. BUNTOV.

Institute of Mankind: Dir A. A. RASIN.

Institute of Man-made Disasters: Dir V. M. KOLODKIN.

Institute of Mathematics and Informatics: Dir Prof. E. L. TONKOV.

Institute of Public Relations: Dir G. V. MERZLYAKOVA.

Institute of Thermophysics of New Materials: Dir V. I. LADYANOV.

ULYANOVSK STATE UNIVERSITY

432700 Ulyanovsk, ul. L. Tolstogo 42
Telephone: (8422) 41-20-88
Fax: (8422) 41-23-40
E-mail: contact@ulsu.ru
Internet: www.ulsu.ru
State control
Founded 1974

Rector: Prof. YURI V. POLYANSKOV
First Pro-Rector and Pro-Rector for Academic Affairs: TOFIK Z. BIKTIMINOV
Pro-Rector for Administration and Finance: VALERY V. NEFEDKIN
Pro-Rector for Economic and Legal Affairs: NATALYA N. LOMOVYEVA
Pro-Rector for New Information and Teaching Technologies: DIMITRY YU. SHABALKIN
Pro-Rector for Pre-University Education: SERGEI N. MITIN
Pro-Rector for Research: SERGEI V. BULYARSKY
Pro-Rector for Social Development, Internal Communication and Marketing: TATYANA E. NIKITINA

Number of teachers: 635
Number of students: 10,695.

URALS STATE UNIVERSITY

620083 Ekaterinburg, pr. Lenina 51
Telephone: (3432) 55-74-20
Fax: (3432) 55-59-64
E-mail: doc_office@usu.ru
Internet: www.usu.ru
Founded 1920
State control
Language of instruction: Russian
Academic year: September to July

Rector: Prof. VLADIMIR E. TRETYAKOV
Vice-Rectors: Prof. VITALY P. PROKOPEV (Academic), Prof. EVGENY A. PAMYATNYKH (Research), ANATOLY N. YAKOVLEV (Social Affairs)
Librarian: KLAVDIYA P. KUZNETSOVA

Library of 1,064,789 vols
Number of teachers: 900
Number of students: 12,400

DEANS

Faculty of Art Criticism and Culture: Asst Prof. T. A. RUNEVA
Faculty of Biology: Asst Prof. N. N. FIRSOV
Faculty of Chemistry: Assoc. Prof. A. A. VSHIVKOV
Faculty of Economics: Prof. D. V. NESTEROVA
Faculty of History: Asst Prof. D. V. BUGROV
Faculty of Journalism: Asst Prof. B. N. LOZOVSKY
Faculty of Mathematics and Mechanics: Assoc. Prof. M. O. ASANOV
Faculty of Philology: Prof. V. V. BLAZHES
Faculty of Physics: Prof. A. N. BABUSHKIN

Faculty of Philosophy: Prof. A. V. PERTSEV
Faculty of Psychology: Prof. G. A. GLOTOVA
Faculty of Sociology and Politics: Asst Prof. B. B. BAGIROV

PROFESSORS

Faculty of Art Criticism and Culture:

GOLINETS, S. V., History of Art
MIKHAILOV, S. A., Cultural Studies
PIVOVAROV, D. V., History and Philosophy of Religion
TROSHINA, T. M., Museology

Faculty of Biology:

BIBIN, I. A., Human and Animal Physiology
MUKHIN, V. A., Botany
NOVOZHENOV, Y. I., Zoology
PYANKOV, V. I., Plant Physiology

Faculty of Chemistry:

NEUCHADINA, L. N., Analytical Chemistry
NEYMAN, A. YA., Inorganic Chemistry
PETROV, A. N., Physical Chemistry
SUVOROVA, A. I., Higher Molecular Compounds
VSHIVKOV, A. A., Organic Chemistry

Faculty of Economics:

AKBERDINA, R. A., Economics
GREBENKIN, A. V., History and Theory of Management
IVANTSOV, G. B., Theory of Economics
MAZUROV, V. D., Economic Models and Information
NESTEROVA, D. V., Economic History and World Economics
SEMYAKIN, M. N., Economics and Law

Faculty of History:

CHERNOUKHOV, A. V., Archives
CHEVTAEV, A. G., Modern History
MIKHAILENKO, V. I., Theory and History of Foreign Affairs
MINENKO, N. A., Ethnology and Special Historical Sciences
POLYAKOVSKAYA, M. A., Ancient and Medieval History
ROMANCHUK, A. I., Archaeology
SHASHKOV, A. G., Russian History

Faculty of Journalism:

BRODSKY, I. S., Television, Radio and Technical Methods of Journalism
KOVALEVA, M. M., History of the Press
LAZAREVA, E. H., Stylistics and Russian Language
OLESHKO, V. F., Periodical Press

Faculty of Mathematics and Mechanics:

ALBREKHT, E. G., Applied Mathematics
ARESTOV, V. V., Mathematical Analysis and Theory of Functions
ASANOV, M. O., Mathematics for Economics
IVANOV, A. O., Mathematical Physics
PROKOPIEV, V. P., Theoretical Mechanics
RYASHKO, L. V., Computational Mathematics
SHEVRIN, L. N., Algebra of Discrete Mathematics
TRETYAKOV, V. E., Computer Information Science and Management Processes

Faculty of Philology:

BABENKO, L. G., Modern Russian Language
BLAZHES, V. V., Folklore
BIKOV, L. P., Criticism of 20th-century Literary Theory
MATVEEV, A. V., General Linguistics
MIKHAILOVA, O. A., Rhetoric and Stylistics of Russian Language
PAVERMAN, V. M., Foreign Literature
SIDOROVA, O. G., Romance and Germanic Philology

Faculty of Philosophy:

BRYANIK, N. V., Ontology and Theory of Cognition
EREMEEV, A. P., Ethics, Aesthetics, History and Theory of Culture

KEMEROV, V. E., Social Philosophy
LYUBUTIN, K. N., History of Philosophy

Faculty of Physics:

BABUSHKIN, A. N., Low-Temperature Physics
BARANOV, N. V., Condensed Matter
BORISOV, S. F., General and Molecular Physics
GULYAEV, S. A., Astronomy and Geodesy
IVANOV, O. A., Magnetic Phenomena
MOSKVIN, A. S., Theoretical Physics
ZVEREV, L. P., Semiconductor Physics, Radiospectroscopy

Faculty of Psychology:

GLOTOVA, G. A., General Psychology and Psychology of Personality
LUPANDIN, V. I., Psychophysiology

Faculty of Sociology and Politics:

BAGIROV, B. B., Social Politics
BARAZGOVA, E. S., Theory and History of Sociology
MERENKOV, A. V., Sociology
MIRONOV, D. A., History of Politics

RESEARCH INSTITUTES

Institute for Advanced Education in the Humanities and Socioeconomic Sciences: Dir N. N. TSELISHEV.

Institute of Economics and Law: Rector D. V. NESTEROVA.

Institute of Russian Culture: Dir Prof. B. V. EMELYANOV.

Research Institute of Physics and Applied Mathematics: Dir L. P. ZVEREV.

URALS STATE UNIVERSITY OF ECONOMICS

620219 Ekaterinburg, ul. 8 Marta 62

Telephone: (343) 257-02-46
Fax: (343) 257-71-47
E-mail: usue@usue.ru
Internet: www.usue.ru

Founded 1967
Academic year: September to June

Rector: VALENTIN M. KAMYSHOV

Library of 600,000 vols
Number of teachers: 472
Number of students: 12,000

Faculties of Commerce, Economics and Engineering.

ATTACHED RESEARCH INSTITUTES

Institute of Corporate Governance: Dir Dr I. N. TKACHENKO.

Retraining Institute: Dir Dr E. G. KNYAZEVA.

VLADIMIR STATE UNIVERSITY

600000 Vladimir, ul. Gorkogo 87

Telephone: (0922) 23-25-75
Fax: (0922) 23-33-58
E-mail: prorms@vpti.vladimir.ru
Internet: www.vpti.vladimir.ru

Founded 1958

Rector: Prof. ALEXEI G. SERGEEV
Vice Rector: Prof. VLADIMIR A. KECHIN
Vice Rector for Academic and International Affairs: Prof. LYDUMILA T. SUSHKOVA
Vice Rector for Construction: Dr IGOR A. GANDELSMAN
Vice Rector for Education: Dr ANZOR M. SARALIDZE
Vice Rector for General Affairs: Dr ALEXANDER V. CHUB
Vice Rector for Information and Informational Technologies: Dr VLADIMIR A. NEMENTOV
Vice Rector for Science: Prof. VLADIMIR F. KOROSTELEV

Number of teachers: 640
Number of students: 22,242

DEANS

Faculty of Architecture and Civil Engineering: Prof. B. G. KIM
Faculty of Automobile Transport: Prof. S. G. DRAGOMIROV
Faculty of Chemistry and Ecology: Prof. A. A. KHRISTOFOROV
Faculty of Economics: Prof. S.A. MAXIMOV
Faculty of Foreign Students: Dr A. A. PANFILOV
Faculty of Humanities: Dr M. A. BARASHEV
Faculty of Informatics and Applied Mathematics: Dr A. A. GALKIN
Faculty of Mechanical Technology: Prof. V. V. MOROZOV
Faculty of Part-Time Education: Dr N. P. ABARIHIN
Faculty of Radiophysics, Electronics and Medical Engineering: Prof. A. G. SAMOILOV

VLADIVOSTOK STATE UNIVERSITY OF ECONOMICS

690600 Vladivostok, ul. Gogolya 41

Telephone: (4232) 25-08-53
Fax: (4232) 25-09-54
E-mail: international@vvsu.ru
Internet: www.vvsu.ru

Founded 1967

Rector: Prof. GENNADY I. LAZAREV

Library of 258,170 vols
Number of teachers: 410
Number of students: 5,986

Publication: *Russia–21st Century* (4 a year)

Fields of study: politics and law of Asian-Pacific countries, business administration, information technology and technical systems, service, fashion and design, social and political studies, culture, tourism and hospitality.

VOLGOGRAD STATE UNIVERSITY

400062 Volgograd, 2-ya Prodolnaya ul. 30

Telephone: (8442) 43-81-24
Fax: (8442) 43-81-24
E-mail: admin@volsu.ru
Internet: www.volsu.ru

Founded 1980
State control
Languages of instruction: Russian, English, German, French
Academic year: September to June

Rector: OLEG V. INSHAKOV
First Vice-Rector: BORIS N. SIPLIVY
Chief Administrative Officer: SERGEI G. SIDOROV
Librarian: LARISA E. YAKOVLEVA

Library of 700,000 vols
Number of teachers: 612
Number of students: 11,409

Publications: *Vestnik VolGU* (10 series, annually), *Proceedings of the Annual Scientific Conference* (annually), *Proceedings of International Conferences* (5 a year), *Junior Faculty and Students' Papers and Reports* (annually), *Economic History of Russia* (annually), *Strezhen* (annually), *The Region's Economic Development: Problems, Searches, Prospects* (2 a year), *Archaeological Vestnik of the Lower Volga* (annually)

DEANS

Faculty of Continuing Education: Dr ELLA V. ISKRENKO
Faculty of History and International Relations: Dr ANDREW V. LUNOCHKHIN
Faculty of Information Technology and Telecommunications: Dr IGOR V. SHARKEVICH

Faculty of International Economics and Finance: Dr ELENA G. RUSSKOVA
Faculty of Law: Dr ALEXANDER G. EGOROV
Faculty of Linguistics and Intercultural Communication: Dr NIKOLAI L. SHAMNE
Faculty of Mathematics: Dr ALEXANDER G. LOSEV
Faculty of Philology and Journalism: Dr DMITRY YU. ILYIN
Faculty of Philosophy and Social Technology: Dr NIKOLAI V. OMELCHENKO
Faculty of Physics: Dr VALERY V. YATSYSHEN
Faculty of Regional Economics and Management: Dr VLADIMIR V. FESENKO

ATTACHED RESEARCH INSTITUTES

'Americana' Centre for American Studies: Dir Dr ALEXANDER I. KUBYSHKIN.

Centre for Regional and Cross-border Studies: Dir Dr SERGEI V. GOLUNOV.

Innovative Research Laboratory for Radioelectronics: Dir Dr BORIS N. SIPLIVY.

Laboratory for Philosophical and Anthropological Research: Dir Dr NIKOLAI V. OMELCHENKO.

Research Institute of the Archaeology of the Lower Volga Region: Dir Dr IGOR V. SERGATSKOV.

Research Institute of the History of the Russian Language: Dir Dr SOFIA P. LOPUSHANSKAYA.

Research Institute of Regional Studies: Dir Dr VLADIMIR V. KURCHENKOV.

Research Institute of the Russian Economic History of the Twentieth Century: Dir Dr MAXIM M. ZAGORULKO.

Research Laboratory for High-Temperature Superconductivity: Dir Dr VYACHESLAV K. IGANTIEV.

Research Laboratory for Laser Metrology: Dir Dr ALEXEI M. CHMUTIN.

Research Laboratory for Mathematical Physics: Dir Dr ANATOLY I. IVANOV.

Research Laboratory for Quantum Electronics: Dir Dr BORIS V. ANIKEYEV.

VORONEZH STATE UNIVERSITY

394006 Voronezh, Universitetskaya pl. 1

Telephone: (0732) 20-75-22
Fax: (0732) 20-87-55
E-mail: office@main.vsu.ru
Internet: www.vsu.ru

Founded 1918
State control
Academic year: September to July

Rector: Prof. IVAN I. BORISOV
First Vice-Rector: SERGEY A. ZAPRYAGAEV
Vice-Rector: VLADIMIR T. TITOV
Vice-Rector (Administration and Finance): ANATOLY N. PODOBEDOV
Vice-Rector (Information Services): ALEXANDER P. TOLSTOBROV
Vice-Rector (Major Construction Projects): ANATOLY I. BIRYUKOV
Vice-Rector (Organisational and Legal Matters): VALERY P. TROFIMOV
Vice-Rector (Pre-University Training): VLADIMIR N. GLAZYEV
Vice-Rector (Research): ALEXANDER S. SIDORKIN
Librarian: SVETLANA V. YANTS

Library of 3,000,000 vols
Number of teachers: 1,300
Number of students: 21,000

Publication: *Vestnik Voronezhskogo Universiteta*

DEANS

Faculty of Applied Mathematics and Mechanics: A. I. SHASHKIN

Faculty of Biology and Soil Science: V. G. ARTYUKHOV

Faculty of Chemistry: YU. P. AFINOGENOV

Faculty of Computer Science: E. A. ALGAZINOV

Faculty of Economics: V. P. BOCHAROV

Faculty of Geography and Geo-Ecology: V. I. FEDOTOV

Faculty of Geology: V. M. NENAKHOV

Faculty of History: A. Z. VINNIKOV

Faculty of Journalism: V. V. TULUPOV

Faculty of Law: V. A. PANYUSHKIN

Faculty of Mathematics: V. A. KOSTIN

Faculty of Pharmaceutics: A. I. SLIVKIN

Faculty of Philology: V. M. AKATKIN

Faculty of Philosophy and Psychology: YU A. BUBNOV

Faculty of Physics: A. M. VOROBEV

Faculty of Romance and Germanic Philology: N. A. FENENKO

ATTACHED RESEARCH INSTITUTES

Botanical Gardens: f. 1936; Dir D. I. SHCHEGLOV.

Venevitinovo Biological Educational and Research Centre: f. 1946; Dir S. G. REZVAN.

Research Institute of Chemistry and Pharmacy: f. 1963; Dir Prof. VLADIMIR F. SELEMENEV.

Research Institute of Physics: f. 1963; Dir Dr ANATOLY A. CHURIKOV.

Research Institute of Mathematics: f. 1968; Dir Prof. VICTOR G. ZVYAGIN.

Research Institute of Geology: f. 1970; Dir Prof. ARKADY D. SAVKO.

Educational Research and Innovation Centre of Pharmacy: f. 2000; Dir SERGEY A. ZAPRYAGAEV, V. F. DZYUBA.

Educational Research and Production Centre of Geology: f. 2000; attached to Geological Institute of the Russian Academy of Sciences; Dir Prof. YURI G. LEONOV, A. V. SHOSTAK.

Educational Research and Production Centre of Space and Rocket Engineering: f. 2001; Dir SERGEY A. ZAPRYAGAEV.

Centre for Advanced Study and Education: f. 2001; Acad. Dir Prof. ALEXANDER KRAVETS.

Educational Research and Innovation Centre of Radio Engineering and Electronics: f. 2001; Dir A. S. SIGOV.

Educational Research and Production Complex for Ecology and Harmonious Exploitation: f. 2001; Dir Prof. IVAN I. BORISOV, V. S. MALIKOV.

Chemical Physics Educational Research Complex: f. 2001; attached to Institute for Problems of Chemical Physics of the Russian Academy of Sciences; Dir Prof. IVAN I. BORISOV, S. M. ALDOSHIN.

Educational Research Complex of Geography and Geo-Ecology: f. 2001; attached to Institute of Geography of the Russian Academy of Sciences; Dirs Prof. IVAN I. BORISOV, V. M. KOTLYAKOV.

Research and Educational Centre for Wave Processes in Non-linear and Non-Uniform Environments: f. 2001; Dir A. S. SIDORKIN.

YAKUTSK STATE UNIVERSITY

Republic of Sakha (Yakutia), 677000 Yakutsk, ul. Belinskogo 58

Telephone: (4112) 26-33-44

Fax: (4112) 26-14-53

E-mail: oip@sitc.ru

Founded 1956

State control

Languages of instruction: Russian, Yakut

Academic year: September to July

Chancellor: ANATOLY N. ALEXEEV

Vice-Chancellor: EGOR E. PETROV

Librarian: ANATOLY P. SEMENOV

Number of teachers: 950

Number of students: 10,000

Publication: *Nauka i obrazovaniye* (4 a year)

DEANS

Faculty of Biology and Geography: BORIS M. PESTRYAKOV

Faculty of Engineering Technology: ANATOLY T. KOPYLOV

Faculty of Foreign Languages: LUDMILA S. ZAMORSHIKOVA

Faculty of Geology: IGOR I. KOLODEZNIKOV

Faculty of History: YURI D. PETROV

Faculty of Law: ALBINA A. STEPANOVA

Faculty of Philology: VLADIMIR M. PEREVERZIN

Faculty of Yakut Philology and Native Culture: GAVRIL G. FILIPPOV

Institute of Applied Mathematics and Computer Science: VASILY I. VASILIEV

Institute of Economics: ANATOLY A. POPOV

Institute of Education: INNOKENTY A. GOLIKOV

Institute of Medicine: PALMIRA G. PETROVA

Institute of Physics and Technology: INNOKENTY A. GOGOLEV

Teacher-Training Institute: RAISA E. TIMOFEEVA

Mirny Polytechnic Institute: ALBINA A. GOLDMAN

Neryungri Technical Institute: ANATOLY M. SAMOKHIN

PROFESSORS

ALEXEEV, A. N., History

ANDREEV, V. S., Engineering

ANISIMOV, V. M., Education

ANTONOV, N. K., Philosophy

BASHARIN, K. G., Medicine

BEGIEV, V. G., Medicine

BLOKHIN, I. P., Biology

BURTSEV, A. A., Philology

BURYANINA, N. S., Geology

BUSHKOV, P. N., Surgery

CHEMEZOV, E. N., Geology

DANILOV, D. A., Pedagogics

DIACHKOVSKY, N. D., Yakut Language and Literature

DOBROVOLSKY, G. N., Engineering

EGOROV, I. E., Mathematics

FEDOROV, M. M., Law

FOMIN, M. M., Pedagogics

FRIDOVSKY, V. Y., Geology

GOGOLEV, A. I., General History

GOGOLEV, M. P., Medicine

ILLARIONOV, V. V., Philology

IVANOV, A. I., Medicine

IVANOVA, A. V., Education

IZAKSON, V. Y., Mathematics

KERSHENGOLTS, B. M., Biology

KHANDY, M. V., Medicine

KHATYLAEV, M. M., History

KOCHNEV, V. P., Education

KOLODEZNIKOV, I. I., Geology and Mineralology

KORNILOVA, A. G., Education

KOZHEVNIKOV, N. N., Philosophy

KYCHKIN, I. S., Theoretical Physics

KYLACHANOV, A. P., Engineering

LUKOVTSEV, V. S., Philosophy

MAKAROV, V. M., Medicine

MAKHAROV, Y. M., Philosophy

MAKSIMOV, G. N., Philosophy

MIKHAILOV, V. D., Philosophy

MISHLIMOVICH, M. Y., Philology

MORDOSOV, I. I., Biology

NEUSTROEV, N. D., Education

NIKOLAEV, N. S., Engineering

NOVIKOV, A. G., Philosophy

OKONESHNIKOVA, A. P., Psychology

PETROV, E. E., Mathematics

PETROV, N. E., Philology

PETROVA, P. G., Medicine

PETROVA, S. M., Education

POPOV, A. A., Economics

POPOV, B. N., Philosophy

PROKOPIEVA, S. M., Philology

SAMOKHIN, A. V., Mining

SAMSONOV, N. G., Philology

SHAMAEV, N. R., Education

SHEPELEV, V. S., Geology

SIVTSEV, I. S., History

SLASTENA, YU. L., Geology

SMIRNOV, V. P., Engineering

SOLOMONOV, N. G., Biology

STOGNY, V. V., Geology

TAZLOVA, R. S., Psychiatry

TIKHONOV, D. G., Medicine

TOBUROKOV, N. N., Linguistics

TOLSTIKHIN, O. N., Permafrost

TOMSKY, I. E., Economics

TYRLYGIN, M. A., Medicine

VASILIEV, E. P., Medicine

VASILIEV, V. I., Mathematics

VASILIEVA-KRALINA, I. I., Biology

VIKULOV, M. A., Engineering

VINOGRADOV, A. V., Chemistry

YAKIMOV, O. D., Journalism

ZAROVNYAEV, B. N., Geology

YAROSLAVL STATE UNIVERSITY

150000 Yaroslavl, ul. Sovetskaya 14

Telephone: (0852) 72-51-38

Fax: (0852) 30-75-15

E-mail: depint@uniyar.ac.ru

Internet: www.uniyar.ac.ru

Founded 1970

Academic year: September to July

Rector: Prof. G. S. MIRONOV

First Vice-Rector: A. I. RUSAKOV

Vice-Rector (Economy): R. P. USATYUK

Vice-Rector (Education): I. M. LOKHANINA

Vice-Rector (Innovation): S. A. KASHCHENKO

Vice-Rector (Science): Y. A. BRUKHANOV

Registrar: V. P. ISAYEVA

Librarian: I. V. DENEZHKINA

Number of teachers: 530

Number of students: 6,500

Publications: *Yuridicheskiye zapiski* (Judicial Notes, annually), *Ocherki po Torgovomy Pravu* (Sketches on Trade Law, 1 or 2 a year), *Modelirovaniye i Analiz Informatsionnykh System* (Modelling and Analysis of Information Systems, 1 or 2 a year), *Ekonomichesky Vestnik* (Bulletin on Economics, annually), *Put v Nauku* (Road to Science, annually), *Sovremennye Problemy Matematiki i Informatiki* (Modern Problems of Mathematics and Informatics, annually), *Aktualnye Problemy Fiziki* (Current Problems of Physics, annually), *Problemy Novoi i Noveishei Istorii* (Issues of Modern and Contemporary History)

DEANS

Faculty of Biology: A. V. EREMEISHVILI

Faculty of Economics: L. B. PARFIONOVA

Faculty of History: N. P. RYAZANTSEV

Faculty of Information Science and Computing Technology: A. V. ZAFIEVSKY

Faculty of Law: N. N. TARUSINA

Faculty of Mathematics: V. G. DURNEV

Faculty of Physics: V. P. ALEKSEYEV

Faculty of Psychology: A. V. KARPOV

Faculty of Social Sciences: G. M. NAZHMUTDINOV

HEADS OF DEPARTMENTS

Faculty of Biology and Ecology (150057 Yaroslavl, Matrosova ul. 9; tel. (0852) 47-82-98; e-mail dean@bio.uniyar.ac.ru):

Botany and Microbiology: N. V. SHEKHOVTSOVA

Ecology and Zoology: M. V. YASTREBOV

General and Bio-organic Chemistry: V. Y. ORLOV

Human and Animal Physiology: I. Y. MYSHKIN

Morphology: A. V. EREMEISHVILI

Faculty of Economics (150000 Yaroslavl, Komsomolskaya ul. 3; tel. (0852) 30-50-32; fax (0852) 30-33-44; e-mail decan@econom .uniyar.ac.ru):

Accounting and Finance: I. G. KUZMIN

Economic Analysis and Informatics: T. V. PLATOVA

Management and Entrepreneurship: I. V. RAZUMOV

World Economics and Statistics: F. N. ZAVYALOV

Faculty of History (150000 Yaroslavl, ul. Sovetskaya 10; tel. (0852) 30-85-50; e-mail jerin@univ.uniyar.ac.ru):

Contemporary Russian History: V. P. FEDYUK

Medieval and Modern Russian History: Y. Y. YERUSALIMSKY

Museum Management and Regional Studies: A. M. SELIVANOV

World History (Laboratory of Eastern and African Studies and Laboratory of Military History): M. Y. YERIN

Faculty of Information Sciences and Computing Technology (150007 Yaroslavl, Soyuznaya ul. 144; tel. (0852) 24-04-30; internet www.csd.uniyar.ac.ru):

Computing and Software Systems: V. V. VASILCHIKOV

Computer Networks: V. V. MAYOROV

Discrete Analysis: V. A. BONDARENKO

Information and Networking Technology: A. V. ZAFIEVSKY

Theoretical Informatics: V. A. SOKOLOV

Faculty of Law (150000 Yaroslavl, Sobinova ul. 36a; tel. (0852) 72-83-82; e-mail jurfac@ uniyar.ac.ru):

Civil Law and Procedure: V. V. BUTNEV

Criminal Law and Procedure: L. L. KRU-GLIKOV

History and Theories of State and Law: V. N. KARTASHOV

Faculty of Mathematics (150007 Yaroslavl, Soyuznaya ul. 144; tel. (0852) 24-86-17; e-mail durnev@univ.uniyar.ac.ru):

Algebra and Mathematical Logic: L. S. KAZARIN

Differential Equations: E. I. BEREZHNOI

General Mathematics: V. A. KUZNETSOVA

Mathematical Analysis: V. A. KRASNOV

Mathematical Cybernetics: V. G. DURNEV

Mathematical Modelling: S. A. KASH-CHENKO

Theory of Functions and Functional Analysis: N. A. STRELKOV

Faculty of Physics (150000 Yaroslavl, Kirova ul. 8/10, Office 214; tel. (0852) 30-32-62; e-mail avp@uniyar.ac.ru; internet fiziki .uniyar.ac.ru):

Dynamics of Electronic Systems: Y. A. BRUKHANOV

General and Experimental Physics: V. P. ALEKSEYEV

Microelectronics: A. S. RUDY

Radiophysics: K. S. ARTIOMOV

Theoretical Physics: N. V. MIKHEEV

Faculty of Psychology (150057 Yaroslavl, Matrosova ul. 9; tel. (0852) 44-17-71):

General Psychology: Y. K. KORNILOV

Pedagogics and Pedagogical Psychology: S. N. BATRAKOVA

Psychology of Labour and Engineering Psychology: A. V. KARPOV

Social and Political Psychology: V. V. NOVIKOV

Faculty of Social Sciences (150000 Yaroslavl, ul. Sovetskaya 10; tel. (0852) 32-96-05; e-mail gadji@univ.uniyar.ac.ru):

Economics and Social and Economic Policy: V. M. MELIKHOVSKY

History of Russia: V. T. ANISKOV

Philosophy and Cultural Studies: G. M. NAZHMUTDINOV

Social and Political Theories: Y. A. GOLO-VIN

Social Technologies: I. F. ALBEGOVA

Unaffiliated Departments:

Foreign Languages: T. V. SHULDESHOVA

Physical Education: S. M. VORONIN

YUGORSKY STATE UNIVERSITY

672039 Khanty-Mansiysk, ul. Chekhova 16

Telephone: (34671) 211-86

E-mail: ugrasu@ugrasu.ru

Internet: www.ugrasu.ru

State control

Founded 2001

Rector: Prof. YURI I. REUTOV

Faculties of Humanities, Engineering, Information Technology and Applied Mathematics, Natural Resources, Arts, Physical Culture, Sport and Tourism, Law and External Education.

MEDICAL UNIVERSITIES

ALTAI STATE MEDICAL UNIVERSITY

656099 Barnaul, pr. Lenina 40

Telephone: (3852) 36-88-48

Fax: (3852) 22-14-21

E-mail: info@agmu.ru

Internet: www.agmu.ru

Founded 1954

Rector: VALERY M. BRYUKHANOV

Library of 121,000 vols

Number of teachers: 489

Number of students: 4,396.

BASHKIR STATE MEDICAL UNIVERSITY

450092 Bashkortostan, Ufa, ul. Lenina 3

Telephone: (3472) 22-41-73

Fax: (3472) 22-37-51

E-mail: admin@bsmu.anrb.ru

Internet: www.bsmu.anrb.ru

Founded 1932

Rector: VIL M. TIMERBULATOV

Library of 600,000 vols

Number of teachers: 650

Number of students: 4,175.

IRKUTSK STATE MEDICAL UNIVERSITY

664003 Irkutsk, ul. Krasnogo Vosstaniya 1

Telephone: (3952) 24-38-25

Fax: (3952) 340336

E-mail: rector_ismu@bk.ru

Internet: www.ismu.baikal.ru

Founded 1919

Rector: Prof. ASKOLD A. MAIBORODA.

KAZAN STATE MEDICAL UNIVERSITY

420012 Kazan, ul. Butlerova 49

Telephone: (8432) 36-06-52

Fax: (8432) 36-03-93

E-mail: office@intdept.kcn.ru

Internet: www.kgmu.kcn.ru

Founded 1814

Rector: Prof. NAIL KH. AMIROV

Library of 10,000 vols

Number of teachers: 500

Number of students: 4,500

Publication: *Kazan Medical Journal* (6 a year)

Faculties of Medicine, Prophylactic Medicine, Paediatrics, Dentistry, Pharmaceutics, Social Work, Management and Graduate Nursing.

KURSK STATE MEDICAL UNIVERSITY

305041 Kursk, ul. Karla Marksa 3

Telephone: (0712) 22-56-12

Fax: (0712) 56-73-99

E-mail: main@kgmu.kursknet.ru

Internet: www.kgmu.kursknet.ru

Founded 1935

Rector: Prof. ALEXANDER V. ZAVYALOV

Library of 320,214 vols.

MOSCOW STATE MEDICAL-STOMATOLOGICAL UNIVERSITY

127473 Moscow, ul. Delegatskaya 20/1

Telephone: (095) 631-25-44

Fax: (095) 973-37-26

E-mail: mmsi@online.ru

Internet: www.msmsu.ru

Founded 1922

Academic year: September to June

Rector: Prof. NIKOLAI D. YUSHCHUK

Library of 549,979 vols

Number of teachers: 1,147

Number of students: 6,000

Faculties of General Medicine, Stomatology, Clinical Psychology, Postgraduate Education, Advanced Training in Dentistry; Institute of Orthodontics, State Stomatological Research Institute.

NORTHERN STATE MEDICAL UNIVERSITY

163001 Arkhangelsk, Troitsky pr. 51

Telephone: (8182) 21-00-00

E-mail: info@nsmu.ru

Internet: www.nsmu.ru

Founded 1932 as Arkhangelsk State Medical Institute; present name and status 2000

Rector: PAVEL I. SIDOROV

Library of 400,000 vols

Number of students: 5,500

Publications: *Human Ecology* (quarterly), *Medik Severa* (monthly)

Faculties of General Practice, Paediatrics, Stomatology, Social Work, Medical Management, Medical Clinical Psychology, Prophylactic Medicine, Pharmaceutics, Ecology, Adaptive Physical Training; institutes: Management, Information Technology, Medical Education.

ROSTOV STATE MEDICAL UNIVERSITY

344022 Rostov-on-Don, Nakhichevansky per. 29

Telephone: (863) 265-23-91

Fax: (863) 253-06-11

Internet: www.rgmu.al.ru

Founded 1931

Rector: Prof. VIKTOR N. CHERNYSHOV

Library of 340,000 vols.

RUSSIAN STATE MEDICAL UNIVERSITY

117869 Moscow, ul. Ostrovityanova 1

Telephone: (095) 434-03-29

Fax: (095) 434-47-87

E-mail: rgmu@rsmu.ru

Internet: www.rsmu.ru

Founded 1906; present name and status 1991

Rector: Prof. Dr VLADIMIR N. YARYGIN

Library of 900,000 vols
Number of teachers: 1,200
Number of students: 6,300

Publication: *Vestnik* (4 a year)

Faculties of Biomedicine, Medicine and Paediatrics.

ST PETERSBURG STATE MEDICAL UNIVERSITY 'ACAD. I. P. PAVLOV'

197022 St Petersburg, ul. L. Tolstogo 6/8

Telephone: (812) 238-71-12

Fax: (812) 234-08-97

E-mail: admission@spmu.rssi.ru

Internet: www.spmu.runnet.ru

Founded 1897

Rector: Prof. NIKOLAI A. YAITSKY

Vice-Rectors: Prof. U. D. IGNATOV (Academic Affairs), Prof. S. H. AL-SHUKRI (International Affairs), Prof. E. E. ZVARTAU (Research), Prof. S. H. AL-SHUKRI (International Affairs)

Dean of Faculty of General Medicine: Prof. N. N. PETRISHEV

Dean of Foreign Students Affairs: Prof. M. SH. VAKHITOV

Library of 1,000,000 vols

Number of professors: 65

Publications: *Arterial Hypertension* (4 a year), *Nephrology* (4 a year), *St Petersburg Medical News* (6 a year), *Scientific Items* (4 a year)

Areas of study: medicine, dentistry, sports medicine, basic sciences.

ATTACHED RESEARCH INSTITUTES

Bone Marrow Transplantation Institute.

Cardiology Institute.

Nephrology Institute.

Pharmacology Institute.

Pulmonology Institute.

SAMARA STATE MEDICAL UNIVERSITY

443099 Samara, ul. Chapaevskaya 89

Telephone: (8462) 32-16-34

Fax: (8462) 33-29-76

E-mail: info@samsmu.ru

Internet: samsmu.ru

Founded 1919

Rector: Prof. Dr GENNADY P. KOTELNIKOV

Library of 570,183 vols
Number of teachers: 700
Number of students: 4,015

Publications: *Annals of Traumatology and Orthopaedics* (6 a year), *Aspirant Herald of Volga Region* (monthly), *Older Generation* (monthly), *Samara Medical Archive* (6 a year), *Transregional Association 'Povolzhye Healthcare' Herald* (4 a year)

Fields of study: general medicine, paediatrics, dentistry, pharmaceutics, gerontology, ionizing radiation, psychology, medical management, nursing, military medicine, medical prophylactics, therapy, healthcare, surgery, cardiology, traumatology; tissue bank.

SARATOV STATE MEDICAL UNIVERSITY

410012 Saratov, Bol. Kazachya 112

Telephone: (8452) 27-33-70

Fax: (8452) 51-15-34

E-mail: meduniv@sgmu.ru

Internet: www.sgmu.ru

Founded 1909

Rector: Dr PETR V. GLYBOCHKO

Library of 950,000 vols.

SIBERIAN STATE MEDICAL UNIVERSITY

534050 Tomsk, Moskovsky Trakt 2

Telephone: (3822) 53-04-23

Fax: (3822) 53-33-09

E-mail: office@ssmu.net.ru

Internet: www.ssmu.ru

Founded 1888

President: Prof. Dr VYACHESLAV V. NOVITSKY

Library of 500,000 vols
Number of teachers: 676
Number of students: 3,445

Publications: *Bulletin of Siberian Healthcare* (4 a year), *Questions of Reconstructive and Plastic Surgery* (4 a year), *Siberian Magazine of Gastroenterology and Haematology* (4 a year)

Faculties of Medicine, Paediatrics, Pharmaceutics, Military Medicine, Nursing, Biological Medicine, Postgraduate Education, Preparatory Education; Institutes: Cardiology, Oncology, Pharmacology, Genetics, Psychiatric Health; attached hospital.

VLADIVOSTOK STATE MEDICAL UNIVERSITY

690600 Vladivostok, pr. Ostryakova 2

Telephone: (4232) 45-16-24

Fax: (4232) 45-17-19

E-mail: webadmin@vgmu.ru

Internet: www.vgmu.ru

Founded 1958

Rector: Prof. YURI V. KAMINSKY

Number of teachers: 400
Number of students: 2,717

Faculties of Therapeutics, Paediatrics, Medicine and Prophylaxis, Qualification Improvement.

VOLGOGRAD STATE MEDICAL UNIVERSITY

400066 Volgograd, pl. Pavshikh Bortsov 1

Telephone: (8442) 38-50-05

Fax: (8442) 38-50-05

E-mail: cved@volgmed.ru

Internet: www.volgmed.ru

Founded 1935

Rector: Prof. VLADIMIR I. PETROV

Number of teachers: 657
Number of students: 5,070

Colleges of General Medicine, Dentistry, Paediatrics, Pharmacy, Medical Biology, Advanced and Continuing Education, Social Work and Clinical Psychology.

PEDAGOGICAL AND LINGUISTIC UNIVERSITIES

BARNAUL STATE PEDAGOGICAL UNIVERSITY

656031 Altai Region, Barnaul, ul. Molodezhnaya 55

Telephone: (3852) 22-85-52

Fax: (3852) 26-08-36

E-mail: rector@bspu.secna.ru

Internet: www.bspu.secna.ru

Rector: Prof. VLADIMIR N. LOPATKIN

Number of teachers: 563
Number of students: 8,534.

BLAGOVESHCHENSK STATE PEDAGOGICAL UNIVERSITY

675015 Blagoveshchensk, ul. Lenina 104

Telephone: (4162) 42-41-49

Fax: (4162) 42-41-64

E-mail: root@chitgu.ru

Internet: www.bspu.tsl.ru

State control

Founded 1930

Rector: Prof. YURI P. SERGIENKO

Library of 500,000 vols
Number of teachers: 350
Number of students: 6,455.

IRKUTSK STATE LINGUISTIC UNIVERSITY

664000 Irkutsk, ul. Lenina 8

Telephone: (3952) 20-03-61

E-mail: islu@islu.irk.ru

Internet: www.islu.ru

Founded 1948

Rector: Prof. GRIGORY D. VOSKOBOYNIK

Faculties of English Language, German Language, Romance Languages, Eastern Languages, Foreign Languages and Social Science, Training of Foreign Students and Advancement of Qualifications; External Faculty.

MOSCOW STATE LINGUISTICS UNIVERSITY

119837 Moscow, ul. Ostozhenka 38

Telephone: (095) 246-86-03

Fax: (095) 246-83-66

E-mail: info@linguanet.ru

Internet: www.linguanet.ru

Founded 1930; present name and status 1990

Rector: Prof. IRINA I. KHALEEVA

Library of 1,000,000 vols
Number of teachers: 1,500
Number of students: 10,000

Fields of study: humanities and applied science, English, German and French teaching, interpretation and translation, international economics, management, law, international relations, political studies, public relations, cultural studies, regional studies; in-service training for foreign-language teachers and advanced training for interpreters; Interdisciplinary In-Service Training Institute; Foreign Language Methodology Centre for Non-Philological Universities; Russian language programmes.

NIZHNII NOVGOROD STATE LINGUISTICS UNIVERSITY 'N. A. DOBROLYUBOV'

603155 Nizhnii Novgorod, ul. Minina 31A

Telephone: (8312) 36-15-75

Fax: (8312) 36-20-49

E-mail: admdep@lunn.sci-nnov.ru

Internet: www.lunn.sci-nnov.ru

Founded 1937

Rector: Prof. GENNADY P. RYABOV

Library of 400,000 vols
Number of teachers: 400
Number of students: 4,000

Faculties of Pedagogy, Philology, Translation and Interpretation, Business Administration, Law, Economics, Public Relations, Journalism, Office Management, International Relations, Hotel and Tourism Management.

PYATIGORSK STATE LINGUISTIC UNIVERSITY

357532 Pyatigorsk, pr. Kalinina 9

Telephone: (87933) 32-94-74
Fax: (87933) 32-94-58
E-mail: ums@pglu.ru
Internet: www.pglu.ru

Founded 1939
State control
Academic year: September to June

Rector: Prof. YURI S. DAVYDOV
First Vice-Rector: Prof. NIKOLAI V. BARYSHNI-
KOV

Library of 840,000 vols
Number of teachers: 580
Number of students: 3,520

Publication: *PSLU Herald* (quarterly)

Educational programmes: English, French, German, Spanish, Arabic and Chinese languages, Russian as a second language, government and public administration, business administration, tourism management, international relations, public relations, journalism and psychology.

ATTACHED INSTITUTE

Institute of Additional Academic Programmes: 357532 Pyatigorsk, Kalinina pr. 9; Dir Dr LARISA I. ERMAKOVA.

RUSSIAN STATE VOCATIONAL PEDAGOGICAL UNIVERSITY

620012 Ekaterinburg, ul. Mashinostroitelei 11

Telephone: (3432) 31-04 36
Fax: (3432) 31-94-63
E-mail: webmaster@rsvpu.ru
Internet: www.rsvpu.ru

Founded 1979

Rector: GENNADY M. ROMANTSEV

Library of 333,800 vols
Number of teachers: 331
Number of students: 12,239

Publications: *Bulletin of the Association of Russian Educational Institutions on Vocational Pedagogics* (annually), *Bulletin of Teaching Research* (2 a year), *Improvement of Educational Processes in Vocational Schools* (annually), *Innovations in Industry and Education* (annually), *Integrational Processes in Pedagogical Theory and Practice* (annually), *Problems of Public Development in the Fields of Sociology and Economics*.

URALS STATE PEDAGOGICAL UNIVERSITY

620219 Ekaterinburg, GSP 135, pr. Kosmonavtov 26

Telephone: (343) 34-12-59
Fax: (343) 34-97-71
E-mail: root@uspu.ru
Internet: www.uspu.ru

Founded 1930 as Urals Industrial Pedagogical Institute; as Urals State Pedagogical Institute 1932–1993; present name and status 1994
State control

Rector: Prof. VLADIMIR D. ZHAVORONKOV

Number of teachers: 720
Number of students: 7,600.

VOLGOGRAD STATE PEDAGOGICAL UNIVERSITY

400013 Volgograd 13, pr. V. I. Lenina 104

Telephone: (8442) 30-28-12
Fax: (8442) 24-13-68
E-mail: vspu@vspu.ru
Internet: www.vspu.ru

State control
Rector: VALERY I. DANILCHUK
Number of teachers: 596
Number of students: 6,455.

VORONEZH STATE PEDAGOGICAL UNIVERSITY

394043 Voronezh, ul. Lenina 86

Telephone: (0732) 55-19-49
Fax: (0732) 55-17-50
E-mail: rector@vspu.ac.ru
Internet: www.vspu.ac.ru

Founded 1930
State control

Rector: Prof. VYACHESLAV V. PODKOLZIN

Library of 600,000 vols
Number of teachers: 473.

TECHNICAL UNIVERSITIES

ALTAI STATE TECHNICAL UNIVERSITY

656099 Barnaul, Lenina pr. 46

Telephone: (3852) 26-09-17
Fax: (3852) 36-78-64
E-mail: rector@agtu.secna.ru
Internet: astu.secna.ru

Founded 1942

Rector: Prof. VLADIMIR V. EVSTIGNEEV

Library of 1,250,000 vols
Number of teachers: 1,113
Number of students: 14,414

Faculties of Mechanical Technology, Civil Engineering, Power Engineering, Motor Car and Tractor Engineering, Food Technology, Automated Manufacturing, Engineering Pedagogics and Informatics, Chemical Technology, Information Technology and Business, Humanities, Engineering and Economics; Academy of Law And Economics; brs In Rubtsovsk and Biisk.

ARKHANGELSK STATE TECHNICAL UNIVERSITY

163002 Arkhangelsk, Severnaya Dvina nab. 17

Telephone: (8182) 21-89-20
Fax: (8182) 28-07-14
E-mail: info@agtu.ru
Internet: www.agtu.ru

Founded 1929

Rector: OLEG M. SOKOLOV

Library of 629,023 vols
Number of teachers: 525
Number of students: 12,500

Publication: *Lesnoi Zhurnal* (Forestry Journal, 6 a year)

Faculties of Forestry, Natural Resources, Mechanical Engineering, Mechanical Wood Technology, Chemical Technology, Industrial Power Engineering, Construction, Distance Learning, Law, Re-training and Preparatory Studies; Institutes of Economics, Finance and Business, Law and Entrepreneurship, Oil and Gas, Information Technology and Chemical Technology; Colleges of Business, Law, Information Technology; Centres of Innovative Technologies and Information Science; brs in Naryan-Mar, Kotlas, Velsk, Novodvinsk and Mirny.

ASTRAKHAN STATE TECHNICAL UNIVERSITY

414025 Astrakhan, ul. Tatishcheva 16

Telephone: (8512) 25-14-90
Fax: (8512) 25-64-27

E-mail: astu@astu.org
Internet: www.astu.org

Founded 1930

Rector: Prof. Y. T. PIMENOV

Library of 700,000 vols
Number of teachers: 450
Number of students: 7,000

Publications: *ASTU Herald* (annually), *Proceedings*

Faculties of Mechanics, Marine Technology, Transport, Automatics and Electromechanics, Law, Fisheries, Chemical Technology; Institutes of Economics, Information Technology and Service Lines, Biology and Nature Usage.

BALTIC STATE TECHNICAL UNIVERSITY 'D. F. USTINOV' (VOENMEKH)

198005 St Petersburg, ul. 1-ya Krasnoarmeiskaya 1/21

Telephone: (812) 316-26-13
E-mail: zag@insu.ru
Internet: www.insu.ru

Founded 1930

Rector: Prof. YURI V. ZAGASHVILI

Departments of Rocketry and Aircraft, Applied Mechanics and Automation, International Industrial Management, Humanities, Aerospace, Guidance Systems, Natural Sciences

Library of 1,100,000 vols
Number of teachers: 600
Number of students: 5,300.

BELGOROD STATE TECHNOLOGICAL UNIVERSITY 'V. G. SHOUKOV'

308012 Belgorod, ul. Kostyukova 46

Telephone: (722) 54-20-87
Fax: (722) 25-71-39
E-mail: rektor@intbel.ru
Internet: www.bstu.ru

Founded 1970
Academic year: September to June

Rector: Prof. ANATOLY M. GRIDCHIN

Library of 600,000 vols
Number of teachers: 540
Number of students: 9,152

Publication: *Tekhnolog* (newspaper, every 2 months)

Institutes of Building Materials, Economics and Management, Mechanical Equipment in the Building Industry; Departments: Machine Building, Civil Engineering, Architecture and Building Technologies, Production Automation and Information Technologies, Highways, Engineering and Ecology; four brs across Russia.

ATTACHED INSTITUTE

Belgorod Institute of Engineering and Economics: Belgorod, Kostyukov ul. 44; Rector NIKOLAI VOROBYOV.

BRYANSK STATE TECHNICAL UNIVERSITY

241035 Bryansk, bul. 50-let. Oktyabrya 7

Telephone: (0832) 56-09-05
Fax: (0832) 56-24-08
E-mail: rector@tu-bryansk.ru
Internet: www.tu-bryansk.ru

Founded 1929

Rector: Prof. ALEXANDER V. LAGEREV

Library of 554,700 vols
Number of teachers: 368
Number of students: 6,188

Faculties of Transport Engineering, Power Engineering and Engineering Technology.

DAGESTAN STATE TECHNICAL UNIVERSITY

367015 Makhachkala, pr. Imama Shamilya 70

Telephone: and fax (8722) 62-37-61
E-mail: dstu@dstu.ru
Internet: www.dstu.ru

Founded 1972 as Dagestan Polytechnic Institute

Academic year: September to June

Rector: Prof. TAGIR A. ISMAILOV

Vice-Rector: Prof. MAGOMEDOV G. AZAEV

Library of 730,583 vols
Number of teachers: 500
Number of students: 11,000

DEANS

Construction: Prof. ABAKAR D. ABAKAROV
Engineering and Economics: Prof. DZHAV-GARAT M. OMAROVA
Finance and Audit: Asst Prof. MAKHMUD G. AMIRALIEV
Hydraulic Engineering: Prof. AVES I. IBRA-GHIMOV
Informatics and Management: Prof. EMRAN E. ILYASOV
Information Systems: Prof. TADZHIDIN E. SARKAROV
Law and Customs Affairs: Prof. MAGOMED E. AKHMEDOV
Public and Municipal Management: Prof. RASUL M. MAGOMEDOV
Radio Engineering: Asst Prof. SHIRALY A. YUSUPHOV
Skill Improvement and Personnel Retraining: Asst Prof. AISHAT R. SHAKHMAEVA
Social Humanities: Prof. GULNARA N. ALIEVA
Technology: Prof. AMMAKADY R. RABADANOV
Transport: Asst Prof. GUSEIN M. MAGOMEDOV

DON STATE TECHNICAL UNIVERSITY

344010 Rostov-on-Don, pl. Gagarina 1

Telephone: (822) 38-15-25
Fax: (822) 32-79-53
E-mail: root@sintez.rud.su

Founded 1930 as Rostov Institute of Agricultural Engineering, present name 1992

Rector: Prof. Dr ANATOLY A. RYZHKIN

Library of 837,000 vols
Number of teachers: 650
Number of students: 6,000.

EASTERN SIBERIAN STATE UNIVERSITY OF TECHNOLOGY

670013 Ulan-Ude, ul. Klyuchevskaya 40b

Telephone: (3012) 37-56-00
Fax: (3012) 44-14-15
E-mail: office@esstu.ru
Internet: www.esstu.ru

Founded 1962

Rector: Prof. VLADIMIR E. SAKTOYEV

Library of 715,246 vols
Number of teachers: 868
Number of students: 10,640

Fields of study: mechanics and technology of light industry, construction, mechanical engineering, electrical engineering, power engineering, preparatory faculty; institutes: sustainable development, economics and law, food industry and biotechnology; postgraduate courses, Russian language courses, Russian language summer school, pre-university training courses.

FAR EASTERN STATE TECHNICAL FISHERIES UNIVERSITY

690600 Vladivostok, ul. Lugovaya 52b

Telephone: (4232) 44-03-06
Fax: (4232) 44-24-32

E-mail: support@dalrybvtuz.ru
Internet: www.dalrybvtuz.ru

Founded 1930

Rector: Prof. GEORGY N. KIM

Library of 450,000 vols
Number of teachers: 266
Number of students: 6,264

Publications: *Dalrybvtuz* (2 a year), *Scientific Papers* (2 a year).

FAR EASTERN STATE TECHNICAL UNIVERSITY

690950 Vladivostok, ul. Pushkinskaya 10

Telephone: (4232) 26-16-89
Fax: (4232) 26-69-88
E-mail: festu@festu.ru
Internet: www.festu.ru

Founded 1899

Rector: GENNADY P. TURMOV

Library of 2,300,000 vols
Number of teachers: 800
Number of students: 16,500

Publications: *Pacific Science Review* (jointly with Kangnam University, Republic of Korea, annually), *Proceedings* (annually)

Institutes of Civil Engineering, Economics and Management, Maritime Engineering, Mining Engineering, Mechanics, Automatics and Advanced Technologies, Architecture, Information Science, Radioelectronics and Electrical Engineering, Natural Sciences, Politics and Law, Humanities, Continuing and Distance Education, Oriental Studies, Engineering, Social Ecology; brs in Nakhodka, Arseniev, Petropavlovsk-Kamchatsky, Dalnegorsk, Dalnerechensk, Bolshoi Kamen, Artyom, Lesozavodsk, Yuzhno-Sakhalinsk and Kirovsky.

FAR EASTERN STATE TRANSPORT UNIVERSITY

680021 Khabarovsk, ul. Serysheva 47

Telephone: (4212) 34-30-76
Fax: (4212) 34-08-08
E-mail: root@habiigt.khv.ru
Internet: www.dvgups.ru

Founded 1937

Rector: VICTOR G. GRIGORENKO

Director of International Affairs: SERGEY N. TRETIYAK

Faculties of Natural Sciences, Humanities, Aerial Communication, Preparatory Studies, Foreign Students and Military Education; Institutes of Locomotives and Rolling Stock; Management, Automation and Telecommunications, Economics, Transport Construction Engineering, Integrated Forms of Education, Enhancement of Qualifications, Department of Electric Power; International Educational Programmes and Academic Exchange

Library of 960,000 vols
Number of teachers: 520
Number of students: 15,000

Domestic brs: Tynda, Svobodny, Yuzhno-Sakhalinsk. Foreign brs: Harbin (People's Republic of China), Seoul (Republic of Korea).

IRKUTSK STATE TECHNICAL UNIVERSITY

664074 Irkutsk, ul. Lermontova 83

Telephone: (3952) 40-52-00
Fax: (3952) 40-51-00
E-mail: oms@istu.edu
Internet: www.istu.edu

Founded 1930

State control
Academic year: September to June

Rector: Prof. Dr IVAN M. GOLOVNYKH

Vice-Rector for Int. Relations: Prof. Dr OLEG V. REPETSKIY

Library of 1,500,000 vols
Number of teachers: 1,450
Number of students: 33,000

Publications: *DAAD Scholars' Bulletin, Geology, Search and Prospecting for Oil and Mineral Deposits, Higher Educational Institutes' News: Geoscience, ISTU Bulletin, Ore Dressing, Problems of the Development of Eastern Siberia's Mineral Base*

Provides evening education and distance-learning, upgrading of professional skills and re-training of specialists

DEANS

Faculty of Applied Linguistics: Prof. OLGA V. DEMENTIEVA
Faculty of Architecture: Prof. VALERIY V. KOZLOV
Faculty of Business and Management: Prof. GENNADIY E. DYKUSOV
Faculty of Chemical Eng. and Metallurgy: Prof. ELENA V. ZELINSKAYA
Faculty of Civil Eng. and Municipal Economy: Prof. VIKTOR R. CHUPIN
Faculty of Computer Eng.: Prof. ALEXANDER V. PETROV
Faculty of Fine Arts: (vacant)
Faculty of Geology, Geoinformatics and Geoecology: Prof. IVAN I. VERKHOZIN
Int. (Preparatory) Faculty: Prof. VITALIY V. EFREMOV
Faculty of Law, Sociology and Mass Media: Prof. ARTUR V. KHARINSKIY
Faculty of Mining Eng.: Prof. BORIS L. TALGAMER
Faculty of Power Eng.: Prof. VADIM V. FEDCHISHIN
Faculty of Technology and Computerization of Mechanical Eng.: Prof. VLADIMIR P. KOLTSOV
Faculty of Transportation: Prof. IGOR N. GUSEV

IVANOVO STATE ENERGY UNIVERSITY

153548 Ivanovo, ul. Rabfakovskaya 34

Telephone: (0932) 32-72-43
Fax: (0932) 38-57-01
E-mail: nvn@ispu.ru
Internet: www.ispu.ru

Rector: VLADIMIR N. NUZHDIN

Number of teachers: 1,500
Number of students: 8,000

Faculties of Heat and Power Engineering, Industrial Heat and Power Engineering, Power Engineering, Electrical Engineering.

IVANOVO STATE UNIVERSITY OF CHEMISTRY AND TECHNOLOGY

153460 Ivanovo, pr. F. Engelsa 7

Telephone: (0932) 32-92-41
Fax: (0932) 41-79-95
E-mail: rektor@isuct.ru
Internet: www.isuct.ru

Founded 1918 as Ivanovo-Vosnessensk Polytechnic Institute; Ivanovo Institute of Chemistry and Technology 1930–1992; as Ivanovo State Academy of Chemistry and Technology 1992–1998; present name and status 1998

Rector: OSCAR I. KOIFMAN

Faculties of Inorganic Chemistry, Inorganic Chemistry Technology, Silicates and Engineering.

IZHEVSK STATE TECHNICAL UNIVERSITY

426069 Izhevsk, ul. Studencheskaya 7

Telephone: (3412) 59-25-55
Fax: (3412) 58-88-52
E-mail: info@istu.ru
Internet: www.istu.ru

Founded 1952

Rector: Prof. IVAN V. ABRAMOV

Library of 700,000 vols
Number of teachers: 760
Number of students: 11,300

Faculties of Civil Engineering, Mechanical Engineering, Robotics Engineering, Quality Management, Instrumentation Engineering, Computer Science, Management and Marketing, Education, Humanities, Applied Mathematics and Mechanics, Sport; brs in Votkinsk, Glazov, Tchaikovsky and Sarapul.

KALININGRAD STATE TECHNICAL UNIVERSITY

236000 Kaliningrad, Sovietsky pr. 1

Telephone: (0112) 27-22-55
Fax: (0112) 27-95-11
E-mail: ivanov@klgtu.ru
Internet: www.klgtu.ru

Founded 1930
Academic year: September to June

Rector: Prof. VICTOR E. IVANOV

Library of 530,000 vols
Number of teachers: 560
Number of students: 7,000

Publication: *Izvestiya KGTU* (monthly)

Faculties of Biological Resources and Water Usage, Commercial Fisheries, Mechanics and Technology, Naval and Power Engineering, Production Automation and Control, Economics and Humanities.

KAZAN STATE TECHNICAL UNIVERSITY 'A. N. TUPOLEV'

420111 Kazan, ul. K. Marksa 10

Telephone: (8432) 38-50-44
Fax: (8432) 38-50-44
E-mail: rector@rectorat.kstu-kai.ru
Internet: www.kai.ru

Founded 1932; present name and status 1992

Library of 2,000,000 vols
Number of teachers: 1,200
Number of students: 14,000

Rector: Prof. GENNADY L. DEGTYARNY

Publications: *Aviatsionaya Tekchnika: Izvestia VUZov* (Russian Aeronautics, in Russian and English, 4 a year), *Problemy Nelineinogo Analiza v Inzhenernykh Sistemakh* (Non-Linear Analysis Problems in Engineering Systems, in Russian and English, 2 a year), *Radioelectronnye Ustroistva* (Radioengineering Instruments, in Russian, 2 a year), *Vestnik KGTU* (Proceedings of KSTU, in Russian, 4 a year).

KAZAN STATE TECHNOLOGICAL UNIVERSITY

420015 Kazan, ul. K. Marksa 68

Telephone: (8432) 38-56-94
Fax: (8432) 19-42-16
E-mail: office@kstu.ru
Internet: www.kstu.ru

Founded 1919

Rector: SERGEI G. DYAKONOV

Library of 1,600,000 vols
Number of teachers: 950
Number of students: 25,000

Publications: *Economy of Industrial Production, Heat and Mass Transfer in Chemical Engineering*

Faculties of Light Industry Engineering, Mechanics, Chemical Engineering, Oil and Oil Refining, Polymers, Chemical Technology, Energy Engineering and Technological Engineering, Power Machinery Construction and Process Equipment, Management and Automation, Humanities and Food Technology

Branch at Nizhnekamsk.

KAZAN STATE UNIVERSITY OF ARCHITECTURE AND CIVIL ENGINEERING

420043 Kazan, ul. Zelenaya 1

Telephone: (8432) 10-46-48
Fax: (8432) 38-79-72
E-mail: rector@ksaba.ru
Internet: www.ksaba.ru

Founded 1930 as Kazan Engineering and Civil Engineering Institute; later Kazan State Academy of Architecture and Civil Engineering; present name 2005
Academic year: September to June

Rector: VALERY N. KUPRIYANOV
Vice Rector: VLADIMIR N. SUCHKOV
Vice Rector (Academic): DAMIR K. SHARAFUTDINOV

Library of 557,000 vols
Number of teachers: 411
Number of students: 5,200

DEANS

Architecture: G. N. AIDAROVNA
Civil Engineering: V. SH. FATKHULLIN
Constructional Technology: R. K. NIZAMOV
Design: S. M. MIKHAILOV
Economics: G. M. ZAGIDULLINA
Engineering Systems and Ecology: R. S. SAFIN
Highway Engineering: E. M. KHABIBULLINA

ATTACHED RESEARCH INSTITUTES

Institute of Architecture and Design: Dir EVGENY M. UDLER.

Institute of Transport Construction: Dir ALEXANDER I. BREKHMAN.

KOMSOMOLSK-ON-AMUR STATE TECHNICAL UNIVERSITY

681013 Komsomolsk-on-Amur, pr. Lenina 27

Telephone: (4217) 53-23-04
Fax: (4217) 53-61-50
E-mail: office@knastu.ru
Internet: www.knastu.ru

Founded 1955

Rector: Prof. YURI KABALDIN
Number of students: 3,500.

KOSTROMA STATE TECHNOLOGICAL UNIVERSITY

156005 Kostroma, ul. Dzerzhinskogo 17

Telephone: (0942) 57-48-14
Fax: (0942) 57-69-91
E-mail: inter@kstu.edu.ru
Internet: www.kstu.edu.ru

Founded 1932 as Kostroma Textile Institute; as Kostroma Technological Institute 1962; present name and status 1995

Rector: VLADISLAV N. KROTOV

Library of 500,000 vols
Number of teachers: 400
Number of students: 6,000

Faculties of Mechanical Engineering, Industrial Economics, Automotive Systems and Technology, Forestry Engineering, Textile Technology and Law.

KRASNOYARSK STATE TECHNICAL UNIVERSITY

660074 Krasnoyarsk, ul. Kirenskogo 26

Telephone: (3912) 91-21-01
Fax: (3912) 43-06-92
E-mail: info@krgtu.ru
Internet: www.krgtu.ru

Founded 1956 as Krasnoyarsk Polytechnic Institute, present name 1993

Rector: Prof. SERGEY A. PODLESNY

Library of 802,000 vols
Number of teachers: 900
Number of students: 17,000

Publication: *Bulletin* (irregular)

Faculties of Electrical Engineering, Mechanical Engineering, Machinery for the Petroleum and Gas Industries, Automation and Computer Technology, Thermal Power Engineering, Motor Vehicle Engineering, Informatics and Computer Science, Radio Engineering, Economics and Management, Engineering, Physics and Humanities.

KUBAN STATE TECHNICAL UNIVERSITY

350072 Krasnodar, ul. Moskovskaya 2

Telephone: (861) 255-84-01
Fax: (861) 257-65-92
E-mail: adm@kgtu.kuban.ru
Internet: www.kubstu.ru

Founded 1918

Rector: Prof. A. A. PETRIK

Library of 720,000 vols
Number of teachers: 800
Number of students: 13,000

Publications: *Izvestiya Vuzov*, *Pishevaya Teckhnologiya* (Food Technology, 6 a year)

Faculties of Oil, Gas and Power Engineering, Mechanical Engineering, Computer Technology and Automated Systems, Chemical Engineering, Technology of Grain Products, Food Technology, Civil Engineering, Highway Engineering, Economics; Institute of Mechanical Engineering in Armavir, br. in Novorossiisk.

KURSK STATE TECHNICAL UNIVERSITY

305040 Kursk, ul. 50-letiya Oktyabrya 94

Telephone: (0712) 22-57-43
Fax: (0712) 56-18-85
E-mail: rector@kstu.kursk.ru
Internet: www.kstu.kursk.ru

Founded 1964

Rector: Prof. IVAN S. ZAKHAROV

Library of 536,000 vols
Number of teachers: 530
Number of students: 4,400

Publication: *Izvestia* (2 a year)

Faculties of Machine-Building, Textile Technology, Civil and Industrial Construction Engineering, Computer Engineering and Automation Systems, Law, Management, Economics, Finance and Auditing and Environmental Protection.

KUZBASS STATE TECHNICAL UNIVERSITY

650026 Kemerovo, ul. Vesennyaya 28

Telephone: (3842) 23-33-80
Fax: (3842) 36-16-87
E-mail: rector@kuzstu.ru
Internet: www.kuzstu.ru

Founded 1950

Rector: VALERY I. NESTEROV

Library of 611,057 vols

Number of teachers: 678

Number of students: 20,078

Faculties of Mine Construction, Mechanical Engineering, Electrical and Mechanical Engineering, Mining Engineering, Construction, Economics, Chemical Engineering, Biotechnology and Humanities.

LIPETSK STATE TECHNICAL UNIVERSITY

398055 Lipetsk, ul. Moskovskaya 30

Telephone: (0742) 25-00-61

Fax: (0742) 31-04-73

E-mail: mailbox@stu.lipetsk.su

Internet: www.stu.lipetsk.ru

Founded 1956

Rector: Prof. MIKHAIL P. KUPRYANOV

Number of teachers: 500

Number of students: 5,000.

MAGNITOGORSK STATE TECHNICAL UNIVERSITY 'G. I. NOSOV'

455000 Magnitogorsk, pr. Lenina 38

Telephone: (3519) 22-12-87

Fax: (3519) 29-84-26

E-mail: mgtu@magtu.ru

Internet: www.magtu.ru

Founded 1932

Rector: Dr BORIS A. NIKIFOROV

Library of 846,656 vols

Br. in Beloretsk.

MARI STATE TECHNICAL UNIVERSITY

424024 Yoshkar-Ola, pl. Lenina 3

Telephone: (8362) 68-60-61

E-mail: rector@marstu.mari.ru

Internet: www.marstu.mari.ru

Founded 1932

Rector: GENNADY S. OSHEPKOV

Library of 1,000,000 vols

Number of teachers: 548

Number of students: 5,228.

MOSCOW AVIATION INSTITUTE (STATE TECHNICAL UNIVERSITY)

125993 Moscow, A-80, GSP-3, Volokolamskoe shosse 4

Telephone: (095) 158-04-65

Fax: (095) 158-29-77

E-mail: aet@mai.ru

Internet: www.mai.ru

Founded 1930

Rector: Prof. Dr ALEXANDR M. MATVEENKO

Library of 909,000 vols

Number of teachers: 2,000

Number of students: 14,000

Schools of Aircraft Engineering, Flight Vehicle Engines, Control Systems, Informatics and Electric Power Engineering, Vehicle Flight Radioelectronics, Economics and Management, Aerospace Engineering, Robotics and Intelligent Systems, Applied Mathematics and Physics, Applied Mechanics, Humanities and Preparatory Studies.

MOSCOW ENGINEERING PHYSICS INSTITUTE (STATE UNIVERSITY)

115409 Moscow, Kashirskoe shosse 31

Telephone: (095) 324-74-91

Fax: (095) 324-85-20

E-mail: degnn@mephi.ru

Internet: www.mephi.ru

Founded 1942

Rector: Prof. BORIS N. ONYKY

Library of 1,000,000 vols

Number of teachers: 880

Number of students: 6,000.

MOSCOW INSTITUTE OF ELECTRONIC TECHNOLOGY (TECHNICAL UNIVERSITY)

103498 Moscow, Zelenograd, pr-d 4806, 5

Telephone: (095) 531-4441

Fax: (095) 530-2233

E-mail: netadm@miee.ru

Internet: www.miee.ru

Founded 1965

Rector: Prof. YURI A. CHAPLYGIN

Library of 680,000 vols

Number of teachers: 530

Number of students: 4,350

Publication: *Collection of Research Work* (monthly)

Faculties of Microtechnology, Micro-Devices and Technical Cybernetics, Electronics and Computer Technology, Automation and Electronic Engineering, Economics and Humanities.

MOSCOW INSTITUTE OF PHYSICS AND TECHNOLOGY (STATE UNIVERSITY)

141700 Moscow oblast, Dolgoprudny, Institutsky per. 9

Telephone: (095) 408-57-00

Fax: (095) 408-68-69

E-mail: rector@mipt.ru

Internet: www.mipt.ru

Founded 1951

Rector: Prof. NIKOLAY N. KUDRYAVTSEV

Library of 733,000 vols

Number of teachers: 470 full-time, 1,090 part-time

Number of students: 3,500

Departments of Radio Engineering and Cybernetics, General and Applied Physics, Aerophysics and Space Research, Molecular and Biological Physics, Physical and Quantum Electronics, Aeromechanics and Flight Engineering (located in Zhukovsky), Applied Mathematics and Economics and Problems of Physics and Power Engineering.

MOSCOW POWER ENGINEERING INSTITUTE (TECHNICAL UNIVERSITY)

111250 Moscow, ul. Krasnokazarmennaya 14

Telephone: (095) 362-56-45

Fax: (095) 362-89-38

E-mail: suvs@mpei.ru

Internet: www.mpei.ru

Founded 1930

Rector: Prof. EVGENY V. AMETISTOV

Library of 2,000,000 vols

Number of teachers: 1,500

Number of students: 10,000

Publication: *Vestnik MPEI* (6 a year)

Institutes of Power Mechanical Engineering and Mechanics, Heat-Power Engineering and Technical Physics, Power Engineering Efficiency Problems, Electrical Engineering, Electrical Power Engineering, Automatics and Computer Engineering and Radio Engineering and Electronics; brs in Smolensk and Volzgsky.

MOSCOW STATE ACADEMY OF FINE CHEMICAL TECHNOLOGY 'M. V. LOMONOSOV'

117571 Moscow, pr. Vernadskogo 86

Telephone: (095) 434-71-55

Fax: (095) 434-87-11

E-mail: mitht@mitht.ru

Internet: www.mitht.ru

Founded 1930

Rector: Prof. ALLA K. FROLKOVA

Library of 220,000 vols

DEANS

Faculty of Biotechnology and Organic Synthesis: Prof. A. F. MIRONOV

Faculty of Chemistry and Technology Polymer Processing: Prof. E. E. POTAPOV

Faculty of Chemistry and Technology of Rare Elements and Materials for Electronic Technology: Prof. D. V. DROBOT

Faculty of Engineering: Prof. G. I. LAPSHENKOV

Faculty of Management, Ecology and Economics: Doc. I. H. ROZDIN

Faculty of Natural Sciences: Prof. E. M. KARTASHOV

Preparatory Faculty: V. B. MARGULIS

Evening Classes: Doc. A. P. PETRUSENKO

MOSCOW STATE AUTOMOBILE AND ROAD TECHNICAL UNIVERSITY

125829 Moscow, Leningradsky pr. 64

Telephone: (095) 151-03-71

E-mail: info@madi.ru

Internet: www.madi.ru

Founded 1930

Rector: Prof. VYACHESLAV M. PRIKHODKO

Library of 1,000,000 vols

Number of teachers: 850

Number of students: 10,000

Faculties of Motor Transport, Road, Building and Technological Machines, Energy and Ecology, Road Building, Economics, Management, Natural Sciences, Design and Mechanical Engineering, Humanities, Military Training, Foreign Citizen Preparation, Pre-Admission Preparation and Correspondence Learning; Institute for the Improvement of Professional Skills and Retraining of Personnel in the Transport and Road Infrastructure; Moscow Transport Institute; Centre of Engineering Pedagogy; Centre of Innovations in Engineering Education.

MOSCOW STATE FORESTRY UNIVERSITY

141005 Moscow oblast, Mytischi, 1-ya Institutskaya ul. 1

Telephone: (095) 588-55-78

E-mail: mgul@mgul.ac.ru

Internet: www.mgul.ac.ru

Founded 1919

Rector: Prof. VIKTOR G. SANAEV

Library of 550,000 vols

Number of teachers: 627

Number of students: 10,000

Faculties of Forestry, Mechanical and Chemical Wood Technology, Electronics and Technical Systems, Economics and Foreign Relations, Humanities, Landscape Architecture, International School of Business and Management.

MOSCOW STATE INDUSTRIAL UNIVERSITY

109068 Moscow, ul. Avtozavodskaya 16

Telephone: (095) 675-52-37

Fax: (095) 674-63-92

E-mail: topstaff@msiu.ru
Internet: www.msiu.ru

Founded 1960

Rector: Prof. NIKOLAI G. KHOKHLOV

Number of teachers: 790
Number of students: 7,000

Faculties of Automotive Engineering, Applied Mathematics and Engineering Physics, Management and Information Technology and Law.

MOSCOW STATE INSTITUTE OF ELECTRONICS AND MATHEMATICS (TECHNICAL UNIVERSITY)

109028 Moscow, Bolshoi Trekhsvyatitelsky per. 1-3/12

Telephone: (095) 917-90-89
Fax: (095) 916-28-07
E-mail: lenor@miem.edu.ru
Internet: www.miem.edu.ru

Founded 1962

Rector: Dr DMITRY V. BYKOV

Library of 600,000 vols
Number of students: 5,000.

MOSCOW STATE INSTITUTE OF RADIO TECHNOLOGY, ELECTRONICS AND AUTOMATION (TECHNICAL UNIVERSITY)

119454 Moscow, pr. Vernadskogo 78

Telephone: (095) 433-00-44
Fax: (095) 434-86-65
E-mail: rector@mirea.ru
Internet: www.mirea.ru

Founded 1947

Rector: ALEXANDER S. SIGOV

Library of 1,100,000 vols
Number of teachers: 1,200
Number of students: 16,000

Publication: *Proceedings of MIREA* (irregular)

Faculties of Cybernetics, Electronics, Radio Engineering Systems, Computing Machines and Systems; International Faculty of Informatics, Economy and Management; brs at Dubna, Friazino and Makhachkala.

MOSCOW STATE MINING UNIVERSITY

117049 Moscow, Leninsky pr. 6

Telephone: (095) 236-94-80
Fax: (095) 237-31-63
Internet: www.msmu.ru

Founded 1918

Rector: Prof. Dr LEV A. PUCHKOV

Library of 800,000 vols
Number of teachers: 540
Number of students: 5,270

Publications: *Gornyatskaya Smena* (weekly), *Scientific Papers* (2 a year)

Faculties of Coal Mining and Underground Construction, Mining of Mineral and Non-Mineral Deposits, Mining Electrification and Mechanization, Mining Automation and Control and Applied Physics.

MOSCOW STATE TECHNICAL UNIVERSITY 'MAMI'

107023 Moscow, ul. Bol. Semenovskaya 38

Telephone: (095) 369-91-53
Fax: (095) 918-29-75
E-mail: decinter@mami.ru

Founded 1865

Rector: Prof. ANATOLY L. KARUNIN

Library of 1,000,000 vols

Number of teachers: 800
Number of students: 7,500

Faculties of Motor Vehicles and Tractors, Power Engineering, Automation and Control, Mechanical Engineering, Design and Technology, Machine-Building, Economics and Engineering Economics.

MOSCOW STATE TECHNICAL UNIVERSITY OF CIVIL AVIATION

125838 Moscow, GSP-47, Kronshtadtsky bul. 20

Telephone: (095) 459-07-07
Fax: (095) 457-12-01
E-mail: rectorat@mail.mstuca.ru
Internet: www.mstuca.ru

Founded 1971 as Moscow Institute of Civil Aviation Engineers, present name and status 1992

Rector: Prof. VLADIMIR G. VOROBIEV

Library of 1,100,000 vols
Number of teachers: 300
Number of students: 5,300

Publication: *Proceedings* (annually)

Faculties of Maintenance of Aircraft and Engines, Maintenance of Aircraft Electrical Systems and Avionics, Maintenance of Transport Radio Equipment, Management, Applied Mathematics, Computer Systems and Networks, Technological Processes and Safety in the Aviation Industry.

MOSCOW STATE TECHNICAL UNIVERSITY 'N. E. BAUMAN'

107005 Moscow, 2-ya Baumanskaya ul. 5

Telephone: (095) 261-40-55
Fax: (095) 267-98 93
E-mail: irina@interd.bmstu.ru

Founded 1830

Rector: Prof. IGOR B. FEDOROV

Library of 3,000,000 vols
Number of teachers: 2,500
Number of students: 18,000

Publications: *Izvestiya Vuzov* (mechanical engineering), *Vestnik MGTU* (issues each on instrumental engineering and mechanical engineering)

Faculties of Informatics and Control Systems, Electronics and Laser Technology, Robotics and Complex Automation, Power Engineering, Materials and Technology, Special Machinery, Basic Sciences, Engineering Business and Management and Humanities; br. in Kaluga.

MOSCOW STATE TECHNOLOGICAL UNIVERSITY, STANKIN

101472 Moscow, Vadkovsky per. 3-a

Telephone: (095) 973-30-66
Fax: (095) 973-38-85
E-mail: rector@stankin.ru
Internet: www.stankin.ru

Founded 1930

Rector: Prof. YURY M. SOLOMENTSEV

Library of 700,000 vols
Number of teachers: 677
Number of students: 5,873

Faculties of Technology, Information Technology, Mechanics and Control, Metrological Informatics, Economics and Innovation Technology Management.

MOSCOW STATE TEXTILE UNIVERSITY

119991 Moscow, ul. Malaya Kaluzhskaya 1

Telephone: (095) 954-70-73
Fax: (095) 952-14-40

E-mail: office@msta.ac.ru
Internet: www.msta.ac.ru

Founded 1919

Rector: SERGEI D. NIKOLAEV

Library of 780,000 vols
Number of teachers: 530
Number of students: 5,000

Publication: *Vestnik MGTU* (journal, 2 a year)

Faculties of Mechanical Technology, Textile Machinery, Chemical Technology, Applied Arts, Economics and Management, Information, Automation and Energetics.

MOSCOW STATE UNIVERSITY OF CIVIL ENGINEERING

129337 Moscow, Yaroslavskoe shosse 26

Telephone: (095) 183-44-38
Fax: (095) 183-48-01
E-mail: kanz@mgsu.ru
Internet: www.mgsu.ru

Founded 1921

Rector: Prof. VALERY I. TELICHENKO

Library of 1,600,000 vols
Number of teachers: 1,300
Number of students: 11,000

Publication: *Proceedings of MSUCE* (4 a year)

Faculties of Hydraulic Engineering, Heat and Ventilation, Water and Sewerage, Constructional Technology, Mechanization and Automation of Construction, Economics Organization and Management of Construction, Industrial and Civil Construction, Heat and Power Construction, Urban Construction and Services.

MOSCOW STATE UNIVERSITY OF ENGINEERING ECOLOGY

105066 Moscow, ul. Staraya Basmannaya 21/4

Telephone: (095) 267-07-01
Fax: (095) 261-49-61
Internet: www.msuie.ru

Founded 1920 as Moscow State Academy of Chemical Engineering; present name and status 1997

Rector: Prof. MIKHAIL B. GENERALOV

Library of 650,000 vols
Number of teachers: 400
Number of students: 3,000

Faculties of Chemical Machine Building, Cryogenic Technology, Chemical Apparatus Manufacture, Technical Cybernetics and Automation of Technological Processes, Chemical and Biological Engineering and Economics.

MOSCOW STATE UNIVERSITY OF ENVIRONMENTAL ENGINEERING

127550 Moscow, ul. Pryanishnikova 19

Telephone: (095) 976-29-62
Fax: (095) 976-21-79
E-mail: mailbox@msuee.ru
Internet: www.msuee.ru

Founded 1930

Chancellor: Prof. IGOR S. RUMIANTSEV

Number of teachers: 325
Number of students: 3,100

Faculties of Ecology and Irrigation, Economics, Civil Engineering, Mechanics, Professional Development and Distance Education.

MOSCOW STATE UNIVERSITY OF GEODESY AND CARTOGRAPHY

105064 Moscow, Gorokhovsky per. 4

Telephone: (095) 261-31-52

Fax: (095) 267-46-81

E-mail: rector@miigaik.ru

Internet: www.miigaik.ru

Founded 1779

Academic year: September to June

Rector: Prof. VIKTOR P. SAVINYKH

Library of 800,000 vols

Number of teachers: 400

Number of students: 5,000

Publication: *Geodeziya i Aerofotosiomka* (6 a year)

Faculties of Geodesy, Space Surveying and Photogrammetry, Cartography, Applied Cosmonautics, Territorial Economics and Land Management, Optical Instrument Manufacture and Humanities.

MOSCOW STATE UNIVERSITY OF RAILWAY ENGINEERING

103055 Moscow, ul. Obraztsova 15

Telephone: (095) 681-3177

Fax: (095) 681-1340

E-mail: mgups@online.ru

Internet: www.miit.ru

Founded 1896; present name and status 1993

Rector: Prof. BORIS A. LEVIN

Library of 2,000,000 vols

Number of teachers: 1,300

Number of students: 12,000

Publications: *Inzhener Transporta*, *MREI* (Collection of Works)

Faculties of Mechanical Engineering, Mechanical Engineering Technology, Railway Automation, Telemechanics and Communication, Technical Cybernetics, Industrial and Civil Construction, Traffic Management, Electrification of Railways, Railway Construction, Bridges and Tunnels Engineering and Economics.

MOSCOW TECHNICAL UNIVERSITY OF COMMUNICATION AND INFORMATICS

111024 Moscow, ul. Aviamotornaya 8a

Telephone: (095) 957-77-09

Fax: (095) 274-00-32

E-mail: mtuci@mtuci.ru

Internet: www.mtuci.ru

Founded 1921 as Moscow Institute of Electrical Engineering and Communications; present name and status 1992)

Rector: Prof. VAGAN V. SHAKHGILDYAN

Library of 1,300,000 vols

Number of teachers: 850

Number of students: 14,000

Faculties of Radio Communication and Radio and Television Broadcasting, Multi-Channel Communications, Postal Services Automation, Automatic Telecommunications and Engineering and Economics; brs in Rostov-on-Don, Nizhnii Novgorod.

MURMANSK STATE TECHNICAL UNIVERSITY

183010 Murmansk, Sportivnaya ul. 13

Telephone: (8152) 45-46-09

E-mail: webmaster@mstu.edu.ru

Internet: www.mstu.edu.ru

Founded 1950

Rector: Dr ALEXANDER ERSHOV

Library of 350,000

Number of teachers: 394

Number of students: 4,458.

NIZHNII NOVGOROD STATE TECHNICAL UNIVERSITY

603600 GSP 41, Nizhnii Novgorod, ul. Minina 24

Telephone: (8312) 36-23-25

Fax: (8312) 36-05-69

E-mail: nntu@nntu.nnov.ru

Internet: www.nntu.nnov.ru

Founded 1898 in Warsaw as Warsaw Polytechnic Institute; relocated to Moscow 1916, then Nizhnii Novgorod in 1917; re-established as Nizhnii Novgorod Polytechnic Institute; present name and status 1992

Rector: VLADIMIR P. KIRIENKO

Number of teachers: 1,166

Number of students: 12,310.

NIZHNII NOVGOROD STATE UNIVERSITY OF ARCHITECTURE AND CIVIL ENGINEERING

603950 Nizhnii Novgorod, ul. Ilyinskaya 65

Telephone: (8312) 33-82-47

Fax: (8312) 33-73-66

E-mail: srec@nngasu.ru

Internet: www.nngasu.ru

Founded 1930

State control

Academic year: September to June

Rector: Prof. VALENTIN V. NAIDENKO

Vice-Rector for International Relations: Dr ALEXANDER PALEEV

Library of 800,000 vols

Number of teachers: 890

Number of students: 8,000

Publication: *Collected Papers and Proceedings of Scientific Conferences* (2 a year)

Fields of study: architecture, design, urban development, environmental engineering, economics, law, industrial management, environmental management and occupational safety; distance learning programmes..

ATTACHED RESEARCH INSTITUTES

Centre for Pre-University Training of Foreign Students: 603950 Nizhnii Novgorod, Gogolya ul. 3.

International Institute for Economics, Law and Management: 603950 Nizhnii Novgorod, Gogolya ul. 1; Dir Dr IGOR ARZHENOVSKY.

NORTH CAUCASIAN INSTITUTE OF MINING AND METALLURGICAL (STATE TECHNOLOGICAL UNIVERSITY)

362021 North-Ossetian Republic, Vladikavkaz, ul. Kosmonavta Nikolaeva 44

Telephone: (8672) 74-93-79

Fax: (8672) 74-99-45

E-mail: skgtu@skgtu.ru

Internet: www.skgtu.ru

Founded 1931 as the North Caucasian Institute of Non-Ferrous Metals

Rector: Dr VLADIMIR S. VAGIN

Library of 520,000 vols

Number of teachers: 500

Number of students: 4,000

Publications: *Izvestiya Vuzov*, *Tsvetnaya Metallurgia* (6 a year)

Faculties of Mining, Electromechanical, Metallurgical, Electronic Engineering, Construction and Management.

NORTH CAUCASIAN STATE TECHNICAL UNIVERSITY

362021 Stavropol, pr. Kulakova 2

Telephone: (8652) 95-68-08

Fax: (8652) 95-68-08

E-mail: info@ncstu.ru

Internet: www.ncstu.ru

Founded 1958

Rector: Prof. BORIS M. SINELNIKOV.

NORTH-WEST STATE TECHNICAL UNIVERSITY

191186 St Petersburg, ul. Millionnaya 5

Telephone: (812) 312-94-84

Fax: (812) 312-94-84

E-mail: office@nwpi.ru

Internet: www.nwpi.ru

Founded 1930

Rector: VALERY V. GURETSKY

Library of 1,544,698 vols

Number of teachers: 400.

NOVOSIBIRSK STATE TECHNICAL UNIVERSITY

630092 Novosibirsk, pr. Karla Marksa 20

Telephone: (3832) 46-50-01

Fax: (3832) 46-02-09

Internet: www.nstu.ru

Founded 1953

Rector: Prof. NIKOLAI V. PUSTOVOI

Number of teachers: 1,105

Number of students: 9,354

11 Faculties; 80 departments.

NOVOSIBIRSK STATE UNIVERSITY OF ARCHITECTURE AND CIVIL ENGINEERING

630008 Novosibirsk-8, ul. Leningradskaya 113

Telephone: (3832) 66-41-25

Fax: (3832) 16-11-07

E-mail: uungas@sibstrin.ru

Internet: www.sibstrin.ru

Founded 1930

Rector: Prof. ARKADY P. YANENKO

Library of 553,000 vols

Number of teachers: 580

Number of students: 6,700

Publication: *Izvestiya vuzov – Stroitelstvo* (Higher School News – Civil Engineering, monthly)

Faculties of Architecture and Construction, Environmental Engineering, Construction Technology, First Stage of Higher Education, Preliminary Training, Part-time and Correspondence Education, Training of Overseas Students, Building Specialists Refresher Programmes and Further Training; Institutes: Architecture and Civil Engineering, Economics and Management, General and Basic Education and Humanities.

OBNINSK STATE TECHNICAL UNIVERSITY FOR NUCLEAR POWER ENGINEERING (TECHNICAL UNIVERSITY)

249020 Kaluga Region, Obninsk, Studgorodok 1

Telephone: (08439) 7-01-31

Fax: (08439) 7-08-22

E-mail: priem@iate.obninsk.ru

Internet: www.iate.obninsk.ru

Founded 1953 as a branch of Moscow Engineering and Physics Institute; as Obninsk Institute for Nuclear Power Engineering 1985–2002; present name and status 2002

Rector: Prof. NIKOLAI L. SALNIKOV

Library of 140,000 vols
Number of teachers: 340
Number of students: 2,100

Faculties of Physics and Power Engineering, Cybernetics, Natural Science, Economics, Evening Education, Advanced Education, Distance Education.

OMSK STATE TECHNICAL UNIVERSITY

644050 Omsk, Mira pr. 11

Telephone: (3812) 65-33-43
Fax: (3812) 65-26-98

Founded 1942

Rector: Prof. N. S. ZHILIN

Library of 1,186,000 vols
Number of teachers: 620
Number of students: 11,000

Publications: *Analysis and Synthesis of Mechanical Systems* (annually), *Dynamics of Machines and Mechanisms* (every 2 years), *Omsk Scientific Bulletin* (4 a year)

Fields of specialization: mechanical engineering, machine building, automation and information technology, electrical engineering, radio engineering, thermal energy, aerospace, cryogenics, economics, sociology and philosophy.

OMSK STATE TRANSPORT UNIVERSITY

644046 Omsk, pr. Karla Marksa 35

Telephone: (3812) 31-42-13
Fax: (3812) 31-42-13
E-mail: omgups@omgups.ru
Internet: www.omgups.ru

Founded 1930

Rector: Prof. ILKHAM I. GALIEV

Library of 700,000 vols
Number of teachers: 310
Number of students: 6,000

Faculties of Locomotives, Railway Rolling Stock, Electric Transport, Power Supply for Railways, Automation, Telemechanics And Communication Facilities for Railway Vehicles, Technology of Machine-Building, Heat and Power Engineering, Control and Information Technology in Technical Systems, Information Systems, World Economy, Management, Marketing, Finance and Credit, Quality Control.

PENZA STATE UNIVERSITY OF ARCHITECTURE AND CONSTRUCTION

440028 Penza, ul. Titova 28

Telephone: (8412) 48-74-76
Fax: (8412) 48-27-77
E-mail: relay@gasa.penza.com.ru
Internet: www.gasa.penza.com.ru

Founded 1958

Rector: ALEXANDER I. EREMKIN

Library of 370,000 vols
Number of teachers: 395
Number of students: 5,735

Faculties of Architecture, Construction, Technology, Engineering Ecology, Economics and Management and Automotive Engineering.

PERM STATE TECHNICAL UNIVERSITY

614600 Perm, Komsomolsky pr. 29A

Telephone: (3422) 12-87-53

Fax: (3422) 12-11-47
E-mail: rector@pstu.ac.ru
Internet: www.pstu.ac.ru

Founded 1953 as Perm Mining Institute

Rector: VASILY YU. PETROV

Library of 1,400,000 vols
Number of teachers: 932
Number of students: 12,500

Faculties of Mining, Electrical Engineering, Mechanical Technology, Applied Mathematics and Mechanics, Road Transport, Aerospace Technology, Chemical Technology, Construction and Humanities.

PETERSBURG STATE TRANSPORT UNIVERSITY

190031 St Petersburg, Moskovsky pr. 9

Telephone: (812) 310-25-21
Internet: www.pgups.ru

Founded 1809

Rector: Prof. VALERY I. KOVALEV

Library of 1,500,000 vols
Number of teachers: 700

Publication: *Proceedings* (annually)

Faculties of Construction, Electrification, Traffic Management, Mechanics, Electrical Engineering and Bridge and Tunnel Construction.

Branch in Velikie Luki.

ROSTOV STATE UNIVERSITY OF CIVIL ENGINEERING

344022 Rostov-on-Don, Sotsialisticheskaya ul. 162

Telephone: (8632) 65-50-76
Fax: (8632) 65-57-31
E-mail: rgsu@jeo.ru
Internet: www.rgsu.ru

Founded 1943

Rector: VIKTOR I. SHUMEIKO

Library of 710,000 vols

Publication: *Izvestiya* (4 a year)

Institutes of Industrial and Civil Engineering, Civil Engineering Technology and Materials, Environmental Engineering, Highways and Transport and Economics and Management.

ROSTOV STATE UNIVERSITY FOR RAILWAY TRANSPORTATION

344038 Rostov-on-Don, pl. Narodnogo Opolcheniya 2

Telephone: (8632) 45-06-13
Fax: (8632) 45-06-13
E-mail: rek@rgups.ru
Internet: www.rgups.ru

Founded 1929

Rector: VLADIMIR I. KOLESNIKOV

Library of 980,000 vols
Number of teachers: 550
Number of students: 5,000

Fields of study: automation and telemechanics, power engineering, electromechanical engineering, railway construction, traffic and transport management, road building machinery, humanities; Institute of Management and Law.

RUSSIAN STATE HYDROMETEOROLOGICAL UNIVERSITY

195196 St Petersburg, Malookhtinsky pr. 98

Telephone: (812) 444-41-63
Fax: (812) 444-60-90
E-mail: rector@rshu.ru
Internet: www.rshu.ru

Founded 1930

Library of 300,000 vols
Number of teachers: 250
Number of students: 5,500

Rector: Prof. LEV N. KARLIN

Vice-Rectors: Prof. ANDREI V. BELOTSERKOVSKY (Academic Associations), Dr ANATOLY I. BOGUSH (International Relations), VLADIMIR N. VOROBYEV (Research), Dr VLADIMIR M. SAKOVICH (Undergraduate and Graduate Education)

Publication: *Proceedings* (quarterly)

DEANS

Faculty of Ecology and Natural Physics: Dr ANNA L. SKOBLIKOVA

Economic and Social-Humanitarian Faculty: Prof. MIKHAIL M. GLAZOV

Hydrological Faculty: Dr ARKADY DOGANOVSKY

Meteorological Faculty: Prof. LEONID DIVINSKY

Oceanological Faculty: Dr ALEXANDER S. AVERKIYEV

Correspondence Education: Prof. VADIM G. ORLOV

BRANCHES

RSHU Aleksin: 301351, Tula oblast, Aleksin District, Kolosovo; tel. (8753) 7-34-17; Dir VALERY M. BORTYAKOV.

RSHU Rostov-on-Don: 344025 Rostov-on-Don, 31-aya Liniya 4; tel. (8632) 91-41-05; Dir SERGEY S. ANDREEV.

RSHU Tuapse: 352800 Krasnodar Region, Tuapse, ul. Morskaya 4; tel. (8616) 72-37- 63; Dir YARVANT O. YAILY.

RUSSIAN STATE OPEN TECHNICAL UNIVERSITY OF RAILWAY TRANSPORT

125993 Moscow, ul. Chasovaya 22/2

Telephone: (095) 151-14-51
Fax: (095) 151-18-37
E-mail: org@rgotups.ru
Internet: www.rgotups.ru

Founded 1951

Rector: Prof. Dr A. T. DEMCHENKO
Vice-Rector: Prof. Dr V. I. APATZEV

Library of 930,453 vols
Number of teachers: 508
Number of students: 21,573

Faculties of Railway Traffic and Management, Railway Construction and Civil Engineering, Economics and General Technology; brs in Nizhnii Novgorod, Voronezh, Yaroslavl, Smolensk, Saratov, Bryansk, Tula, Novomoscovsk, Ryazan, Murom, Elets, Vologda, Vladimir, Kirov, Izhevsk, Lisky, Kotlas, Kaliningrad, Orel, Rtitshevo, Labytnangy, Astrakhan, Volgograd, Uhta.

RUSSIAN STATE TECHNOLOGICAL UNIVERSITY 'K. E. TSIOLKOVSKY' (MATI)

103767 Moscow, ul. Orshanskaya 3

Telephone: (095) 141-18-40
Fax: (095) 141-19-50
E-mail: intdep@intedu.mati.msk.ru
Internet: www.mati.ru

Founded 1932

Rector: ANATOLY P. PETROV

Library of 800,000 vols
Number of teachers: 1,103
Number of students: 9,000

Faculties of Aerospace Engineering and Technology, Materials Science and Technology, Avionics, Computer Science, Economics and Business, Ecology, Satellite

Communications and Technology, Applied Mathematics and Mechanics.

RUSSIAN STATE UNIVERSITY OF OIL AND GAS 'I. M. GUBKIN'

119991 Moscow, Leninsky pr. 65

Telephone: (095) 137-81-08
Fax: (095) 135-88-95
E-mail: com@gubkin.ru
Internet: www.gubkin.ru

Founded 1930
Academic year: September to June

Rector: ALBERT I. VLADIMIROV
Vice-Rector for Academic Affairs: VICTOR G. MARTYNOV
Vice-Rector for International Affairs: DMITRY N. LEVITSKY

Library of 1,000,000 vols
Number of teachers: 900
Number of students: 8,000

Faculties of Petroleum Geology and Geophysics, Oil And Gas Fields Development, Pipeline Network Design, Construction and Operation, Chemical and Environmental Engineering, Mechanical Engineering, Automation and Computer Science, Economics and Management and Law; br. in Orenburg.

RUSSIAN UNIVERSITY OF CHEMICAL TECHNOLOGY 'D. MENDELEEV'

125047 Moscow, Miusskaya pl. 9

Telephone: (095) 978-87-33
Fax: (095) 200-42-04
E-mail: rector@muctr.edu.ru
Internet: www.muctr.edu.ru

Founded 1920

Rector: Dr PAVEL D. SARKISOV

Library of 1,700,000 vols
Number of teachers: 1,003
Number of students: 8,416

Publication: *Trudy* (every 2 months)

Faculties of Chemical Technology of Organic Substances, Chemical Technology of Inorganic Substances, Chemical Technology of Polymers, Chemical Technology Engineering, Physical Chemistry Engineering, Ecological Engineering, Cybernetics of Chemical Technological Processes, General Engineering and Economics; br. in Novomoskovsk.

ST PETERSBURG ELECTROTECHNICAL UNIVERSITY 'LETI' (ETU)

197376 St Petersburg, ul. Prof. Popova 5

Telephone: (812) 346-44-87
Fax: (812) 234-54-05
E-mail: intdep@eltech.ru
Internet: www.eltech.ru

Founded 1886

Rector: DIMITRY V. PUZANKOV

Library of 1,063,000 vols
Number of teachers: 1,000
Number of students: 8,000

Publications: *Izvestiya ETU* (14 a year), *Izvestiya Vuzov Rossii – Radioelektronika*

Schools of Radio Engineering and Telecommunications, Electronics, Computer Technology and Informatics, Electrical Engineering and Automation, Instrumentation, Biomedical and Ecological Engineering, Economics and Management and Humanities.

ST PETERSBURG STATE MARINE TECHNICAL UNIVERSITY

190008 St Petersburg, ul. Lotsmanskaya 3

Telephone: (812) 114-41-68
Fax: (812) 318-52-27
E-mail: inter@smtu.ru
Internet: www.smtu.ru

Founded 1930

Rector: Dr KONSTANTIN P. BORISENKO

Library of 862,380 vols
Number of teachers: 600
Number of students: 5,500

Faculties of Natural and Social Sciences and Humanities, Naval Architecture and Ocean Engineering, Marine Engineering, Marine Electronics and Control Systems, Business and Management.

ST PETERSBURG STATE MINING INSTITUTE (TECHNICAL UNIVERSITY)

199026 St Petersburg, Vasilevskii ostrov, 21-ya Liniya 2

Telephone: (812) 213-60-78
Fax: (812) 327-73-59
E-mail: rectorat@spmi.ru
Internet: www.spmi.ru

Founded 1773

Rector: Prof. VLADIMIR S. LITVINENKO

Library of 1,209,266 vols
Number of students: 8,000.

ST PETERSBURG STATE POLYTECHNICAL UNIVERSITY

195251 St Petersburg, Politekhnicheskaya ul. 29

Telephone: (812) 247-1616
Fax: (812) 552-6080
E-mail: rector@stu.neva.ru
Internet: www.spbstu.ru

Founded 1899
State control
Languages of instruction: Russian, English
Academic year: September to July

President: Prof. MIKHAIL P. FIODOROV

Library of 2,500,000 vols
Number of teachers: 2,000
Number of students: 16,000

Publications: *Scientific and Engineering News*, *Transactions*

Faculties: of Hydraulic Engineering, Electrical Engineering, Power Engineering, Mechanical Engineering, Physics and Mechanical Sciences, Technology and Materials Science, Economics and Management, Computer Science and Engineering, Radiophysical Science and Engineering, Physical Science and Engineering, Industrial Engineering, Biomedical Engineering and Humanities; brs at Pskov, Cherboksary and Orsk.

ST PETERSBURG STATE TECHNOLOGICAL UNIVERSITY OF PLANT POLYMERS

198095 St Petersburg, ul. Ivan Chernykh 4

Telephone: (812) 786-57-44
Fax: (812) 786-86-00
E-mail: zsv@gturp.spb.ru
Internet: www.gturp.spb.ru

Founded 1931; present name and status 1993
Academic year: September to June

Rector: VYACHESLAV A. SUSLOV (acting)
Vice-Rector for Economics and Development: ALEXANDER L. ASHKALUNIN
Vice-Rector for Innovations: ALEXANDER N. IVANOV
Vice Rector for International Relations: NADEZHDA V. KHODYREVA

Vice-Rector for Research: VICTOR S. KUROV
Vice-Rector for Studies: PAVEL V. LUKANIN

Library of 740,000 vols
Number of teachers: 300
Number of students: 5,000

Publications: *JPPS*, *Pulp Paper Board Magazine*, *TAPPI*

Integrated training of specialists for enterprises in the pulp and paper industry and the fuel and power sector; Departments of Chemical Engineering, Economics and Management, Environmental Engineering, Mechanical, Heat and Power Engineering, Automated Control Systems and Part-Time Studies.

ST PETERSBURG STATE UNIVERSITY OF ARCHITECTURE AND CIVIL ENGINEERING

198005 St Petersburg, 2-ya Krasnoarmeiskaya ul. 4

Telephone: (812) 316-99-65
Fax: (812) 316-58-72
E-mail: rector@spice.spb.su
Internet: www.spbgasu.ru

Founded 1832

Rector: Prof. YURI P. PANIBRATOV

Library of 870,737 vols
Number of teachers: 800
Number of students: 6,000

Publication: *University Scientific Work* (10 a year)

Faculties of Economics and Management, Correspondence, Advanced Training; Institutes of Architecture, Civil Engineering, Environmental Engineering and Protection and Automobile Engineering.

ST PETERSBURG STATE UNIVERSITY OF INFORMATION TECHNOLOGY, MECHANICS AND OPTICS

197101 St Petersburg, ul. Sablinskaya 14

Telephone: (812) 233-00-89
Fax: (812) 232-23-07
E-mail: rector@mail.ifmo.ru
Internet: www.ifmo.ru

Founded 1900

Rector: Prof. VLADIMIR N. VASILEV

Library of 900,000 vols
Number of teachers: 500
Number of students: 4,000

Publication: *Izvestiya Vuzov (Priborostroenie)* (4 a year).

ST PETERSBURG STATE UNIVERSITY OF REFRIGERATION AND FOOD ENGINEERING

191002 St Petersburg, ul. Lomonosova 9

Telephone: (812) 315-36-17
Fax: (812) 315-05-35
E-mail: refr@sarft.spb.ru
Internet: www.sarft.spb.ru

Founded 1935
Academic year: September to June

Rector: ALEXANDER V. BARANENKO
First Vice-Rector: EVGENY I. BORZENKO

Library of 850,000 vols
Number of teachers: 337
Number of students: 5,615

DEANS

Faculty of Correspondence and External Courses: Prof. D. P. MALYAVKO
Faculty of Cryogenics and Conditioning Systems: Dr A. U. BARANOV
Faculty of Economics and Management: Dr V. L. VASILYONOK

Faculty of Food Manufacturing Engineering: Prof. G. I. MALUGHIN

Faculty of Food Technologies: Dr A. L. IZHEVSKY

Faculty of Refrigeration Engineering: Prof. L. S. TIMOFEYEVSKY

ST PETERSBURG STATE UNIVERSITY OF TECHNOLOGY AND DESIGN

191186 St Petersburg, Bol. Morskaya ul. 18

Telephone: (812) 315-75-25

Fax: (812) 117-85-94

E-mail: inter@sutd.ru

Internet: www.sutd.ru

Founded 1930; present name and status 1992

Rector: Prof. VIKTOR E. ROMANOV

Library of 700,000 vols

Number of teachers: 490

Number of students: 5,000 (of whom 2,700 full-time)

Faculties of Design, Textiles, Engineering, Environmental Science, Economics and Management.

ST PETERSBURG STATE UNIVERSITY OF TELECOMMUNICATIONS 'PROF. M. A. BONCH-BRUYEV'

191065 St Petersburg, nab. Moiki 61

Telephone: (812) 315-01-18

Fax: (812) 315-32-27

E-mail: rector@sut.ru

Internet: www.sut.ru

Founded 1930

Rector: Prof. ALEXANDER A. GOGOL

Library of 90,000 vols

Faculties of Telecommunication Networks, Switching Systems and Computer Technology, Multi-channel Telecommunication Systems, Radio Communication, Radio Broadcasting and Television, Telecommunication Technologies and Biomedical Electronics and Economics and Management.

ST PETERSBURG STATE UNIVERSITY OF WATER COMMUNICATIONS

198035 St Petersburg, ul. Dvinskaya 5/7

Telephone: (812) 251-12-21

Fax: (812) 251-01-14

E-mail: sudomeh@mail.ru

Internet: www.spbuwc.ru

Founded 1809

Rector: Prof. ANATOLY S. BUTOV

Library of 906,535 vols

Number of teachers: 350

Number of students: 7,580 (3,880 full-time, 3,700 corresp.)

Faculties of Waterways and Ports, Marine Engineering, Electrical Engineering, Port Handling and Transport Facilities, Navigation, Humanitarian Sciences, Information Technology, Marine Law, Economics and Finance.

SAMARA STATE AEROSPACE UNIVERSITY 'S. P. KOROLEV'

443086 Samara, Moskovskoye shosse 34

Telephone: (8462) 35-18-51

Fax: (8462) 35-18-36

E-mail: ssau@ssau.ru

Internet: www.ssau.ru

Founded 1942

Rector: VICTOR A. SOIFER

Library of 1,092,955 vols

Number of teachers: 750

Number of students: 10,500

Faculties of Aircraft Construction, Flying-Vehicle Engines, Air Transport Engineers, Plastic Working of Metals, Radio Engineering, Information Science, Economics and Management, Aircraft Engines (Evenings), Aircraft Production Technology and Organization (Evenings), Correspondence Education, Information Science and Pre-University Training.

SAMARA STATE TECHNICAL UNIVERSITY

443010 Samara, ul. Molodogvardeiskaya 244

Telephone: (8462) 78-43-00

Fax: (8462) 78-44-00

E-mail: postman@samgtu.ru

Internet: www.samgtu.ru

Founded 1914

Rector: VLADIMIR V. KALASHNIKOV

Number of students: 10,000

Faculties of Machine Building, Oil Technology, Engineering Technology, Thermal Power, Electrotechnology, Automation and Information Technology, Physical Technology, Chemical Technology, Economics and Humanities.

SAMARA STATE UNIVERSITY OF ARCHITECTURE AND CIVIL ENGINEERING

443001 Samara, Molodogvardeiskaya ul. 194

Telephone: (8462) 42-17-84

Fax: (8462) 32-19-65

E-mail: sgasu@sgasu.smr.ru

Internet: www.sgasu.smr.ru

Founded 1930 as Samara State Academy of Architecture and Civil Engineering; present name and status 2004

Rector: Prof. VIKTOR P. BALZANNIKOV

Library of 1,000,000 vols, incl 300,000 specialist books

Number of teachers: 420

Number of students: 7,500

Faculties of Design, Industrial and Civil Engineering, Construction Engineering, Transport and Town Development, Engineering Life-Support Systems, Information Systems and Technologies, Engineering Economics; Correspondence Faculties of Economics, and Engineering; Institutes of Construction, Ecology and Engineering Life Support Systems, Economics and Management and Pre-University Training; Lyceum of Architecture and Civil Engineering; Centre for Linguistic Training.

SARATOV STATE TECHNICAL UNIVERSITY

410054 Saratov, ul. Politekhnicheskaya 77

Telephone: (8452) 50-77-40

Fax: (8452) 50-75-40

E-mail: sstu_office@sstu.saratov.su

Internet: www.sstu.ru

Founded 1930

Rector: Prof. YURI V. CHEBOTAREVSKY

Library of 2,000,000 vols

Number of teachers: 1,100

Number of students: 13,000

Faculties of Electronics and Instrument-Making, Power Engineering, Motor Vehicles, Architecture and Construction, Mechanical Engineering, Highways and Transport Construction, Social Work, Business and Social Systems Management; Computer Training Centre.

SIBERIAN STATE AEROSPACE UNIVERSITY 'I. F. RESHETNEV'

660014 Krasnoyarsk, pr. im. gaz. Krasnoyarsky Rabochy 31

Telephone: (3912) 62-95-95

E-mail: info@sibsau.ru

Internet: www.sibsau.ru

Founded 1959

Rector: Prof. GENNADY P. BELYAKOV

Library of 484,000 vols

Number of teachers: 503

Number of students: 7,000

Departments of Aerospace, Informatics and Control Systems, Civil Aviation, Finance and Economics, International Business, Humanities and Physical Culture and Sport; Institutes of Civil Aviation and of Management and Social Technologies.

SIBERIAN STATE TECHNOLOGICAL UNIVERSITY

660049 Krasnoyarsk, pr. Mira 82

Telephone: (3912) 276382

Fax: (3912) 274440

E-mail: repyakh@sibstu.kts.ru

Internet: www.sibstu.kts.ru

Founded 1930

Rector: Prof. EDUARD S. BUKA

Library of 243,000 vols

Number of teachers: 682

Number of students: 12,912

Faculties of Forestry, Automation and Robot Technology, Timber Technology and Equipment, Engineering for Chemical Technology, Engineering Economics, Woodworking Technology, Chemical Technology, Humanities and Mechanics; brs in Lesosibirsk and five representative offices in major Siberian cities.

SIBERIAN STATE UNIVERSITY OF TELECOMMUNICATIONS AND INFORMATICS

630102 Novosibirsk, ul. Kirova 86

Telephone: (3832) 66-10-38

Fax: (3832) 66-10-39

E-mail: rectorat@neic.nsk.su

Internet: www.sibsutis.ru

Founded 1953

Rector: Prof. VALERY P. BAKALOV

Library of 463,638 vols

Number of teachers: 650

Number of students: 10,000

Faculties of Radio Communication and Broadcasting, Automatic Electrical Communication, Multi-channel Electrical Communication, Engineering Economics and Informatics; brs in Khabarovsk, Ekaterinburg, Ulan-Ude.

SIBERIAN TRANSPORT UNIVERSITY

630023 Novosibirsk, ul. D. Kovalchuk 191

Telephone: (3832) 28-74-70

Fax: (3832) 26-79-78

Founded 1932

Rector: Dr VLADIMIR D. VERESKUN

Library of 773,000 vols

Number of teachers: 600

Number of students: 12,000

Publication: *Proceedings* (5 or 6 a year)

Faculties of Railway Traffic Management, Railway Construction, Construction and Track Machinery, Civil Engineering, Water Supply and Sewerage, Bridges And Tunnels, Economics and Transport Management, Economics and Building Management, Accounting and Auditing, Management and World Economics.

SOUTH RUSSIA STATE TECHNICAL UNIVERSITY (NOVOCHERKASSK POLYTECHNIC INSTITUTE)

346400 Novocherkassk, ul. Prosveshcheniya 132

Telephone: (86352) 5-51-79
Fax: (86352) 2-84-63
E-mail: postmaster@srstu.novoch.ru
Internet: www.srstu.novoch.ru

Founded 1907

President: Prof. VALENTIN E. SHUKSHUNOV
Rector: Prof. LEONID S. LUNIN

Library of 3,100,000 vols
Number of teachers: 2,000
Number of students: 22,000

Publications: *Elektromekhanika* (monthly), *Izvestiya SK NC Visshey Shkoly* (4 a year)

Faculties of Mining and Geology Prospecting, Manufacturing Machines and Robots, Mechanics, Power, Electrical Engineering, Chemical Technology, Construction, Computer Systems and Robotics, Humanities and Social Economic Education.

TAGANROG STATE UNIVERSITY OF RADIO ENGINEERING

Rostov Region, 347928 Taganrog, GSP-17a, Nekrasovsky pr. 44

Telephone: (8634) 31-05-99
Fax: (8634) 31-05-98
E-mail: rector@tsure.ru
Internet: www.tsure.ru

Founded 1952
Academic year: September to June

Rector: VLADISLAV G. ZAKHAREVICH
Vice-Rector: ANATOLY I. KALYAKIN
Vice-Rector for International Relations: VADIM P. POPOV

Library of 980,000 vols
Number of teachers: 1,032
Number of students: 11,320

Publications: *Proceedings of TSURE* (6 a year), *Radiosignal* (weekly)

DEANS

Faculty of Automation and Computer Engineering: YURI M. VISHNYAKOV
Faculty of Economics, Management and Law: GENNADY I. IVANOV
Faculty of Electronics and Manufacturing Engineering: BORIS G. KONOPLIEV
Faculty of Radio Engineering: SERGEY G. GRITCHENKO

ATTACHED RESEARCH INSTITUTE

Research Institute for Multi-processor Computing Systems: Dir IGOR A. KALYAEV.

TAMBOV STATE TECHNICAL UNIVERSITY

392000 Tambov, Sovetskaya ul. 106

Telephone: (0752) 72-10-19
Fax: (0752) 71-02-16
E-mail: postmaster@admin.tgtu.tambov.su
Internet: www.tstu.ru

Founded 1958

Rector: SERGEI V. MISCHENKO

Library of 940,000 vols
Number of teachers: 630
Number of students: 7,000

Publication: *Transactions* (4 a year)

Faculties of Transport and Agricultural Services, Mechanical Engineering, Architecture and Civil Engineering, Technical Cybernetics, Power Engineering, Economics, Humanities, Information Technology,

International Education, Pre-University Training, Advanced Training and Re-Training.

TOMSK POLYTECHNIC UNIVERSITY

634050 Tomsk, pr. Lenina 30

Telephone: (3822) 56-34-70
Fax: (3822) 56-38-65
E-mail: tpu@tpu.ru
Internet: www.tpu.ru

Founded 1896

Rector: YURI P. POKHOLKOV

Library of 2,700,000 vols
Number of teachers: 1,924
Number of students: 22,876

Faculties of Applied Physics and Engineering, Electrophysics and Electronic Equipment, Mechanical Engineering, Chemistry and Chemical Engineering, Thermal Power Engineering, Economics and Management, Humanities, Natural Science and Mathematics; Institutes of International Education, Languages and Communication, Geology and Oil And Gas Industries, Electrical Engineering, Cybernetics, Distance Learning, Continuing Education of Specialists and Engineering Education.

TOMSK STATE UNIVERSITY OF CONTROL SYSTEMS AND RADIOELECTRONICS

634050 Tomsk, pr. Lenina 40

Telephone: (3822) 51-05-30
Fax: (3822) 51-32-62
E-mail: office@tusur.ru
Internet: www.tusur.ru

Founded 1962

Dir: ANATOLY V. KOBZEV

Library of 620,000 vols
Number of teachers: 500
Number of students: 15,000

Faculties of Design Technology, Radio Engineering, Computer Systems, Control Systems and Electronic Equipment.

TULA STATE UNIVERSITY

300600 Tula, pr. Lenina 92

Telephone: (0872) 35-21-55
Fax: (0872) 33-13-05
E-mail: info@uic.tula.ru
Internet: www.tsu.tula.ru

Founded 1930

Rector: Prof. EDUARD M. SOKOLOV

Library of 1,000,000 vols
Number of teachers: 1,036
Number of students: 10,000

Publication: *Izvestiya* (4 a year)

Faculties of Mechanics and Mathematics, Applied Physics, Engineering, Cybernetics, Mining and Construction, Medicine, Humanities, Economics and International Students.

TVER STATE TECHNICAL UNIVERSITY

170026 Tver, nab. A. Nikitina 22

Telephone: (0822) 31-15-09
Fax: (0822) 31-43-07
E-mail: common@tstu.tver.ru
Internet: www.tstu.tver.ru

Founded 1922

Rector: Prof. VYACHESLAV A. MIRONOV

Library of 2,000,000 vols

Faculties of Machine Building, Automatic Control Systems, Civil and Industrial Engineering, Environmental Engineering,

Humanities, Postgraduate, Evening and Distance Education.

TYUMEN STATE OIL AND GAS UNIVERSITY

625000 Tyumen, ul. Volodarskogo 38

Telephone: (3452) 25-08-61
Fax: (3452) 25-08-25
E-mail: general@tgngu.tyumen.ru
Internet: www.tgngu.tyumen.ru

Founded 1963

Rector: NIKOLAI N. KARNAUKHOV

Library of 677,000 vols
Number of teachers: 1,230
Number of students: 30,000

Faculties of Geology and Geoinformatics, Oil and Gas Fields, Pipeline Engineering, Transport, Technical Cybernetics, Oil and Gas Refining, Management, Drilling and Mechanical Engineering.

UFA STATE AVIATION TECHNICAL UNIVERSITY

450000 Bashkortostan, Ufa, ul. K. Marksa 12

Telephone: (3472) 56-96-93
Fax: (3472) 56-96-93
E-mail: root@admin.ugatu.ac.ru
Internet: www.ugatu.ac.ru

Founded 1932

Rector: Prof. MURAT B. GUZAIROV

Library of 700,000 vols

Publications: *Higher School Collections on Research* (irregular), newspaper (weekly)

Faculties of Aircraft Engines, Aircraft Machine Building Technology, Informatics and Robotics, Aircraft Technological Systems, Economics, Management and Finance, Social Sciences and General Sciences.

UFA STATE PETROLEUM TECHNOLOGICAL UNIVERSITY

450062 Bashkortostan, Ufa, ul. Kosmonavtov 1

Telephone: (3472) 42-03-70
Fax: (3472) 43-14-19
E-mail: info@rusoil.net
Internet: www.ugntu.ru

Founded 1941

Rector: AYRAT M. SHAMMAZOV

Library of 1,031,930 vols
Number of teachers: 802
Number of students: 14,000

Faculties of Oil and Mining, Pipeline Transport, Petrochemical, Oil Equipment, Construction, Technology, Economics and Management, Automation of Production Processes, Humanities, Military Studies; brs in Oktyabrsky, Salavat, Sterlitamak.

ULYANOVSK STATE TECHNICAL UNIVERSITY

432027 Ulyanovsk, ul. Severny Venets 32

Telephone: (8422) 43-90-43
Fax: (8422) 43-02-37
E-mail: rector@ulstu.ru
Internet: www.ulstu.ru

Founded 1957 as Ulyanovsk Polytechnic Institute; present name and status 1994

Rector: Prof. ALEXANDER D. GORBOKONENKO

Library of 1,047,000 vols
Number of teachers: 500
Number of students: 14,000

Publication: *Vestnik* (4 a year)

Faculties of Information Systems and Technology, Radio Engineering, Power Engineering, Civil Engineering, Mechanical

Engineering, Aircraft Engineering, Humanities, Economics and Mathematics; br. at Dimitrovgrad.

URALS STATE FORESTRY ENGINEERING UNIVERSITY

620100 Ekaterinburg, ul. Sibirsky Trakt 37

Telephone: (343) 224-23-73
Fax: (343) 224-03-37
E-mail: general@usfeu.ru
Internet: www.usfeu.ru

Founded 1930

Rector: Prof. VALENTIN N. STARZHINSKY

Library of 780,000 vols
Number of teachers: 504
Number of students: 9,927

Faculties of Forestry Engineering, Forestry Economics, Forestry Machinery, Timber Technology, Chemical Technology, Economics and Management, Ecological Engineering, Complementary Education, Correspondence Studies and Humanities; Highways Institute, Ecotoxicological Research Institute; Garden of Curative Plants; Vocational Forestry Enterprise.

URALS STATE MINING UNIVERSITY

620144 Ekaterinburg, ul. Kuibysheva 30

Telephone: (3432) 22-25-47
Fax: (3432) 29-48-38
E-mail: office@usmga.ru
Internet: www.usmga.ru

Founded 1914 as Ekaterinburg Mining Institute; as Sverdlovsk Mining Institute 1934–1993; as Urals State Academy of Mining and Geology 1993–2004; present name and status 2004

Rector: Prof. NIKOLAI P. KOSAREV

Library of 800,000 vols
Number of teachers: 1,500
Number of students: 6,000

Faculties of Geology, Geophysics, Mining Technology, Mining Engineering, Economics and Environmental Engineering.

URALS STATE TECHNICAL UNIVERSITY

620002 Ekaterinburg, ul. Mira 19

Telephone: (343) 374-54-34
Fax: (343) 374-38-84
E-mail: inter@inter.ustu.ru
Internet: www.ustu.ru

Founded 1920

Rector: Prof. STANISLAV S. NABOICHENKO

Library of 2,000,000 vols
Number of teachers: 2,233
Number of students: 35,000

Faculties of Metallurgy, Mechanical Engineering, Heat and Power engineering, Radio Engineering, Chemical Technology, Construction Materials, Civil Engineering, Economics and Management, Physical Engineering, Humanities, Physical Training and Sport and Electrical Engineering.

URALS STATE UNIVERSITY OF RAILWAY TRANSPORT

620034 Ekaterinburg, ul. Kolmogorova 66

Telephone: (343) 245-34-67
Fax: (343) 245-34-67
E-mail: rector@usart.ru
Internet: www.usart.ru

Founded 1956
State control; attached to the Ministry of Transport of the Russian Federation
Academic year: September to June

Rector: Prof. ALEXANDER V. EFIMOV

Vice-Rector for International Affairs: BORS M. GOTLIB

Library of 600,000 vols
Number of teachers: 580
Number of students: 10,186; 6,000 full-time, 4,186 correspondence

Publications: *Annual Report*, *Research Reviews* (every 2 years)

Faculties of Mechanics, Electrical Engineering, Electrification, Construction, Traffic Management and Economics.

VOLGOGRAD STATE TECHNICAL UNIVERSITY

400131 Volgograd, pr. Lenina 28

Telephone: (8442) 23-66-35
Fax: (8442) 23-41-21
E-mail: rector@vstu.ru
Internet: www.vstu.ru

Founded 1930
Academic year: September to June

Rector: Prof. IVAN A. NOVAKOV
Vice-Rector for International Relations and Co-operation: Prof. ALEXANDER A. CHUGUNOV

Library of 1,235,810 vols
Number of teachers: 1,112
Number of students: 18,000

Publication: *Polytekhnik* (every 2 weeks)

Faculties: Automobile Transport, Chemical Technology, Construction Materials Technology, Economics and Business Administration, Electronics and Computer Science, Evening Faculty (Kirovsky District), Machine Building, Preparatory Faculty for Foreign Students, Preparatory Training Faculty, Training and Retraining Evening Faculty (Traktorzavodsky District).

DEANS

A. V. BELOV
A. E. GODENKO
V. F. KABLOV
VASILIY G. KARABAN
YURI Y. KOMAROV
OLEG D. KOSOV
S. M. LEDENEV
A. P. MANTOROSHIN
YURI P. MUKHA
YURI I. OSADSHY
O. P. OTCHENASHEV
A. N. SAVKIN
N. I. ZUBAN

VOLGOGRAD STATE UNIVERSITY OF ARCHITECTURE AND CIVIL ENGINEERING

400074 Volgograd, Akademicheskaya ul. 1

Telephone: (8442) 97-48-72
Fax: (8442) 97-49-33
E-mail: postmaster@vgasu.ru
Internet: www.vgasu.ru

Founded 1952; present name and status 2003

Rector: VLADMIR A. IGNATYEV

Library of 1,019,284 vols
Number of teachers: 487
Number of students: 13,143

Faculties of Civil Engineering, Roads, Architecture, Water Ecology and Hydraulic Engineering, Environmental Engineering, Heat and Energy Supply, Economics and Law; brs in Volzhsky and Mikhailovka.

VOLOGDA STATE TECHNICAL UNIVERSITY

160000 Vologda, ul. Lenina 15

Telephone: (8172) 72-46-45
E-mail: rector_s@mh.vstu.edu.ru
Internet: www.vstu.edu.ru

Founded 1975 as Vologda Polytechnic Institute

Rector: Prof. RUSLAN V. DERYAGIN

Library of 1,200,000 vols

Branches in Cherepovets and Veliky Ostyug.

VORONEZH STATE TECHNICAL UNIVERSITY

394026 Voronezh, Moskovsky pr. 14

Telephone: (0732) 21-09-19
Fax: (0732) 78-38-91
E-mail: rector@vorstu.ru
Internet: www.vorstu.ru

Rector: Prof. VADIM N. FROPOV

Library of 700,000 vols

Faculties of Automation and Mechanization of Engineering, Aviation, Radio Engineering, Automation and Electrical Engineering, Physical Engineering and Engineering Economics.

VYATKA STATE TECHNICAL UNIVERSITY

610601 Kirov, GSP (Centre), Moskovskaya ul. 36

Telephone: (8332) 62-65-71
Fax: (8332) 62-65-71
E-mail: root@kpicnit.vyatka.su

Founded 1963

Rector: Prof. VASILY M. KONDRATOV

Library of 1,000,000 vols

Faculties of Electrical Engineering, Automation and Computer Technology, Chemical Technology, Construction Engineering, Socioeconomics and Machine Engineering

Publication: *Transactions*.

YAROSLAVL STATE TECHNICAL UNIVERSITY

150053 Yaroslavl, Moskovsky pr. 88

Telephone: (0852) 44-15-19
E-mail: webmaster@ystu.ru
Internet: www.ystu.ru

Founded 1944; present name and status 1994

Rector: Prof. YURI A. MOSKVICHEV
Number of students: 5,000.

Academies
ARCHITECTURE AND CIVIL ENGINEERING

Ivanovo Academy of Civil Engineering and Architecture: 153002 Ivanovo, ul. 8 Marta 20; tel. (0932) 32-85-40; fax (0932) 30-00-74; e-mail post@iisi.asinet.ivanovo.su; f. 1981; facilities: construction technology, economics, architecture; library: 250,000 vols; Rector Prof. Dr S. V. FEDOSOV.

Krasnoyarsk State Academy of Civil Engineering and Architecture: 660041 Krasnoyarsk, pr. Svobodnyi 82; tel. (3912) 44-69-40; fax (3912) 44-58-60; e-mail root@kici.krasnoyarsk.su; internet www.gasa.krs.ru; f. 1982; faculties: construction, economics, highway engineering, architecture, engineering services; library: 429,000 vols; 402 teachers; 3,702 students; Rector V. D. NADELYAEV.

Rostov State Academy of Architecture and Art: 344082 Rostov-on-Don, Budennovsky pr. 39; tel. (8632) 39-09-43; fax (8632) 40-81-31; e-mail rai@icomm.ru; f. 1988; architecture, environmental design, arts and crafts, history of art, fashion design, management in architecture; library: 300,000 vols; 181 teachers; 1,091 students;

Rector V. A. Kolesnik; publ. *Problems of Architectural Education* (annually).

Tomsk State Academy of Civil Engineering: 634003 Tomsk, Solyanaya pl. 2; tel. 75-39-30; fax 75-33-58; f. 1952; faculties: architecture, civil and industrial construction engineering, road building, mechanical engineering, technology; library: 638,000 vols; 458 teachers; 5,086 students; Rector G. M. Rogov.

Tyumen Civil Engineering and Architectural Academy: 625001 Tyumen, ul. Lunacharskogo 2; tel. (3452) 46-10-10; fax (3452) 46-23-90; e-mail tumgasa@sbtx.tmn.ru; internet www.tumgasa.ru; f. 1971; faculties: construction, engineering networks and systems, road building, economics and management; 360 teachers; 5,000 students; Rector Dr Tchikichev.

Ural State Academy of Architecture and Arts: 620075 Ekaterinburg, ul. Karla Libknekhta 23; tel. (3432) 51-33-69; fax (3432) 51-95-32; e-mail vgafurov@usaaa.ru; internet www.usaaa.ru; f. 1972 (fmrly Sverdlovsk Architectural Institute); depts of architecture, design, fashion design, monumental decorative art, applied decorative art, urban planning; library: 80,000 vols; 1,100 students; Rector A. A. Starikov; publ. *Architecton* (4 a year).

Voronezh State University of Architecture and Civil Engineering: 394006 Voronezh, 20-Letiya Oktyabrya ul. 84; tel. (0732) 71-52-68; fax (0732) 71-58-54; e-mail rectorat@vgasu.vrn.ru; internet www.vgasu.vrn.ru; f. 1930; academic year September to July; faculties: arts, mechanical engineering and highway construction, engineering systems and buildings, architecture, construction, construction technology, engineering economics, automation and information systems; distance learning courses available; Rector Igor S. Surovtsev; library: 500,000 vols; 485 teachers; 7,981 students; publ. *Scientific Bulletin* (collection of scientific articles, annually).

VGASU Borisoglebsk: 397140, Voronezhskaya Oblast, Borisoglebsk, Sovietskaya ul. 123; Rector Valery A. Lebedev.

AGRICULTURE AND VETERINARY SCIENCE

Belgorod State Agricultural Academy: 309103 Belgorod Region, pos. Maiskii, Vavilova ul. 1; tel. (0722) 39-21-79; fax (0722) 39-11-74; e-mail bsaa@csn.ru; internet www.bsaa.edu.ru; f. 1978; 490 teachers; 4,500 students; Rector Alexandr V. Turiansky.

Bryansk State Agricultural Academy: 243365 Bryansk oblast, Vygonichesky r-n, pos. Kokino; tel. (8341) 2-43-21; e-mail bgsha@bitmcnit.bryansk.su; internet www.bgsha.com; f. 1980; library of 385,000 vols, 150 periodicals; Rector Prof. Nikolai M. Belous; publ. *Collection of Scientific Papers* (annually).

Buryat State Agricultural Academy: 670024 Ulan-Ude, Pushkina ul. 8; tel. (3012) 34-26-11; fax (3012) 34-22-54; e-mail bgsha@eastsib.ru; f. 1932; depts: animal husbandry, agronomy, veterinary medicine, economics, farm mechanization, land tenure regulations, accounting, management; library of 582,000 vols; 325 teachers; 4,800 students; Rector Prof. Alexander P. Popov.

Chuvash State Agricultural Academy: 428000 Cheboksary, K. Marksa ul. 29; tel. (8352) 22-23-34; depts: agronomy, mechanization, animal husbandry; library of 83,000 vols; Rector Nikolai K. Kirillov.

Dagestan State Agricultural Academy: 367032 Makhachkala, M. Gadzhieva ul. 180; tel. (8722) 68-24-70; f. 1932; Rector Magomed M. Dzhambulatov; library of 200,000 vols; publ. *Works*; fields of study: zootechnics, veterinary, fruit and vegetable growing, accountancy.

Irkutsk State Agricultural Academy: 664038 Irkutsk, pos. Molodozhny; tel. (3952) 39-93-30; fax (3952) 39-94-18; e-mail rector@ishi.baikal.ru; internet www.irgsha.narod.ru; f. 1934; depts at main campus: economics, accounting, computer engineering, agronomy, agroecology, soil management, energy engineering, mechanization, zoological engineering, veterinary science, wildlife management; Chita campus: economics, accounting, agronomy, mechanization, zoological engineering; library of 504,814 vols; 357 teachers; 7,736 students; br. in Chita; Rector Alexander A. Dolgopolov.

Ivanovo Agricultural Academy: 153012 Ivanovo, Sovetskaya ul. 45; tel. and fax (0932) 32-81-44; e-mail ivgsha@tpi.ru; f. 1918; depts: agronomy, zootechnics, veterinary medicine, mechanization in agriculture, service and exploitation of farm machines and equipment, land use and land distribution, economics and management in rural production, agroecology; library of 260,364 vols; 211 teachers; 3,328 students; Rector V.F. Tsaryov.

Izhevsk State Agricultural Academy: Udmurt Republic, 426069 Izhevsk, Studencheskaya ul. 11; tel. (3412) 58-99-48; fax (3412) 58-99-47; e-mail root@isa.udm.ru; internet isa.udm.ru; f. 1954; depts: agronomy, animal husbandry, veterinary science, forestry, mechanization, bookkeeping and agricultural analysis, economics, mechanization of the processing of farm produce; library of 500,000 vols; 357 teachers; 6,038 students; extra-mural faculty; Pres. Prof. V. V. Fokin.

Kazan State Academy of Veterinary Medicine 'N. E. Bauman': Tatarstan, 420074 Kazan, Sibirsky trakt ul.; tel. (8432) 76-15-05; f. 1873; advanced training of veterinary and animal husbandry specialists; library of 410,000 vols; 230 teachers; 3,700 students; Rector Acad. G. Z. Idrisov; publ. *Nauchnye Trudy* (4–5 a year).

Kazan State Agricultural Academy: 420015 Kazan, Karla Marksa ul. 65; tel. (8432) 36-65-22; fax (8432) 36-66-51; internet www.ksha.ru; fields of study: agronomy, mechanization, economics and management, accounting; library of 135,000 vols; Rector Prof. Dzhaudat I. Faizrakhmanov.

Kostroma State Agricultural Academy: 156530 Kostroma, P/O Karavaevo; tel. (0942) 54-12-63; fax (0942) 54-34-23; e-mail mobot@ksaa.edu.ru; internet www.ksaa.edu.ru; f. 1949; depts: agronomy, zootechnics, veterinary science, farm mechanization, automobiles and automobile facilities, service and operation of vehicles and machines, electrification and automation of agricultural production, application of computers, architecture, industrial and civil engineering, economics and management, accountancy and auditing, finance and credit, fundamentals of law in agriculture, agricultural management; library of 510,000 vols; 370 teachers; 5,100 students; Rector V. I. Vorobev.

Kursk State Agricultural Academy 'I. I. Ivanov': 305034 Kursk, Karla Marksa ul. 70; tel. (0712) 33-06-05; fax (0712) 23-13-30; e-mail academy@kgsha.ru; internet www.kgsha.ru; f. 1956; fields of study: agronomy, plant protection, zootechnics, mechanization, economics and management, accounting, agroecology, veterinary medicine, seed pro-

cessing and storage; library of 130,000 vols; Rector Vladimir D. Flour.

Moscow Agricultural Academy 'K. A. Timiryazev': 127550 Moscow, Timiryazevskaya ul. 49; tel. (095) 976-04-80; fax (095) 976-29-10; e-mail info@timacad.ru; internet www.timacad.ru; f. 1865; library of 1,500,000 vols; 650 teachers; 10,000 students; Rector Prof Vladimir M. Bautim; publ. *Papers of TSHA* (annually), *Proceedings of TSHA* (6 a year); faculties of agronomy, agricultural chemistry, soil science and ecology, zootechnics, economics, horticulture, agropedagogy; 33 attached research stations and 5 experimental and instructional farms; br. in Kaluga.

Moscow State Academy of Veterinary Medicine and Biotechnology 'K. I. Skryabin': 100472 Moscow, Akad. K. I. Skryabina 23 ul.; tel. (095) 377-91-17; f. 1919; faculties: veterinary biological science, animal husbandry, pedagogical, animal products; library of 500,000 vols; 360 teachers; 3,500 students; Rector Acad. A. D. Belov.

Nizhnii Novgorod State Agricultural Academy: 603078 Nizhnii Novgorod pr. Gagarina 97; tel. (8312) 66-07-30; fax (8312) 66-06-84; f. 1930; fields of study: agrochemistry, agronomy, animal husbandry, mechanization, accounting, veterinary medicine; library of 500,000 vols; 5,000 students; Rector Alezey Galkin; publ. *Scientific Works* (annually).

Penza State Agricultural Academy: 440014 Penza, Botanicheskaya ul. 30; tel. (8412) 59-63-54; fax (8412) 59-63-54; e-mail psaca@penza.com.ru; internet pgsha.penza.com.ru; f. 1951; fields of study: agronomy, agroecology, animal husbandry, mechanization of agriculture, machine repairing, bookkeeping and auditing, economics, administration, farm production technology, motor vehicles and motor vehicle management; library of 264,000 vols; 264 teachers; 3,500 students; Rector Prof. Vladimir D. Korotnev.

Perm Agricultural Academy 'Acad. D. N. Pryanishnikov': 614600 Perm, Kommunisticheskaya ul. 23; tel. and fax (3422) 12-53-94; e-mail pgsha@permregion.ru; f. 1918; depts: agrochemistry and soil science, agronomy, animal husbandry, mechanization, economics and management, accounting, forestry, food technology, applied informatics; library of 320,000 vols; 376 teachers; 9,000 students; Rector Yu. N. Zubarev.

Primorsky State Agricultural Academy: 692510 Ussuriisk, pr. Blyukhera 44; tel. (42341) 6-33-91; fax (42341) 6-03-13; e-mail agracad@hotbox.ru; internet www.primacad.ru; institutes: land management and farming, animal husbandry and veterinary medicine, forestry, economics and business, farm mechanization, staff upgrading and retraining for the agro-industrial complexf. 1957; library of 380,000 vols; 500 teachers; 5,000 students; Rector A. A. Dyomin.

Ryazan State Agricultural Academy: 390044 Ryazan, Kostycheva ul. 1; tel. (0912) 55-35-01; fax (0912) 55-10-70; e-mail rsaa@narod.ru; internet www.rsaa.narod.ru; fields of study: agronomy, animal husbandry, mechanization, economics and management, accounting; library of 94,000 vols; Rector Gennady M. Tunikov.

St Petersburg Academy of Forestry Technology: 194018 St Petersburg, Institutsky per. 5; tel. (812) 550-07-00; fax (812) 550-08-15; f. 1803; faculties: forestry, forestry engineering, forest machinery, mechanical technology of timber, chemical technology, engineering economics; library of 1,400,000 vols; 613 teachers; 9,000 students; br. in

Syktyvkar; Rector Prof. V. I. ONEGIN; publ. *Nauchnye trudy* (annually).

Tyumen State Agricultural Academy: 625003 Tyumen, Respubliki ul. 7; tel. (3452) 46-16-50; fax (3452) 46-16-50; e-mail acadagro@tmn.ru; internet www.tgsha.ru; f. 1879; attached Institutes of Agronomy and Ecology, Finance and Management, Veterinary Medicine and Aquaculture; library of 700,000 vols; 250 teachers; 5,000 students; Rector Dr NIKOLAI V. ABRAMOV.

Ulyanovsk State Agricultural Academy: 432601 Ulyanovsk, bul. Novy Venets 1; tel. (88422) 31-42-72; fax (88422) 31-42-72; e-mail academy@mv.ru; internet www .academy.mv.ru; f. 1943; depts: agronomy, animal husbandry, mechanization, veterinary, medicine, economics; library of 452,000 vols; 312 teachers; 4,248 students; Rector B. I. ZOTOV.

Urals State Academy of Veterinary Medicine: 457100 Chelyabinsk oblast, Troitsk, Gagarina ul. 13; tel. (3516) 32-00-10; fax (3516) 32-04-72; internet www.ugavm.boom .ru; f. 1929; library of 200,000 vols; 180 teachers; 1,434 students; Rector Prof. V. LAZARENKO.

Urals State Agricultural Academy: 620219 Ekaterinburg, K. Libknekhta ul. 42; tel. (3432) 51-33-63; fax (3432) 51-24-80; e-mail academy@usaca.ru; internet www .usaca.ru; f. 1940; library of 450,000 vols; 700 teachers; 2,500 students; Rector ALEXANDER N. SEMIN.

Velikie Luki State Agricultural Academy: 182100 Pskov oblast, Velikie Luki, pl. V. I. Lenina 1; tel. (81153) 3-77-28; fax (81153) 3-26-73; e-mail vgsha@mart.ru; f. 1958; depts: agronomy and ecology, economics, animal husbandry, engineering; library of 390,000 vols; 291 teachers; 4,114 students; Rector Prof. V. P. SPASOV; publ. *Works* (annually).

Volgograd State Agricultural Academy: 400041 Volgograd, Institutskaya ul. 8; tel. (8442) 43-08-45; fax (8442) 43-18-07; f. 1944; depts: agronomy, animal husbandry, farm mechanization, farm electrification, ecology and land reclamation, accounting; library of 568,000 vols; 4,000 students; Rector Acad. A. M. GAVRILOV; publ. *Scientific Information* (2 a year).

Vologda State Dairy Academy 'N. V. Vereschagin': 160555 Vologda pos. Molochnoe, Shmidta ul. 2; tel. (8172) 76-17-30; fax (8172) 76-10-69; e-mail rector@molochnoe.ru; internet www.molochnoe.ru; f. 1911; library of 420,000 vols; 270 teachers; 4,000 students; Rector Dr VLADIMIR N. OSTRETSOV; publ. *Works*.

Voronezh State Academy of Forestry Engineering: 394613 Voronezh, Timiryazeva ul. 8; tel. (0732) 53-74-98; fax (0732) 53-86-10; e-mail postmaster@julygb.vsi.ru; internet vglta.vrn.ru; f. 1918; faculties: forest engineering, forestry, wood-processing technology, motor-vehicle engineering, forest industry economics and management, furniture design, forest machinery and equipment, safety traffic regulation, landscape gardening, gamekeeping and national parks management, international wood trade, industrial process automation; library of 568,000 vols; 397 teachers; 5,500 students; Rector Prof. V. K. POPOV.

Vyatka State Agricultural Academy: 610017 Kirov, Oktyabrsky pr. 133; tel. (8332) 62-97-19; fax (8332) 62-23-17; e-mail vsaa@vit.kirov.ru; f. 1930; depts: agronomy, biology, economics, veterinary medicine, mechanization; library of 407,000 vols; Rector A. K. BOLOTOV.

ECONOMICS, LAW AND POLITICS

Academy of Social Sciences: 117606 Moscow, pr. Vernadskogo 84; tel. (095) 436-93-30; f. 1946; library of 2,000,000 vols; Rector R. G. YUNOVSKII.

Finance Academy under the Government of the Russian Federation: 125468 Moscow, Leningradsky pr. 49; tel. (095) 943-98-55; fax (095) 157-70-70; e-mail academy@ fa.ru; internet www.fa.ru; f. 1918; institutes and depts: finance, credit, financial management, insurance, taxes and taxation, accounting and audit, international economic relations, mathematical methods in economics and crisis management, tax police, evening school, distance learning, short-term retraining and skill development; 21st-Century International Finance University; MBA Business School; 650 teachers; 10,000 students; Rector A. G. GRYAZNOVA.

Irkutsk State Academy of Economics: 664015 Irkutsk, ul. Lenina 11; tel. (3952) 24-10-55; fax (3952) 24-28-38; e-mail kvm@cc .isea.baikal.ru; f. 1930; faculties: law, world economics, finance, economics of mining industry and construction, economics of engineering and road transport, accounting, information systems, labour economics, public administration, management, economics of using natural resources; library of 530,000 vols; Rector M. A. VINOKUROV.

Khabarovsk State Academy of Economics and Law: 680042 Khabarovsk, Tikhookeanskaya ul. 134; tel. (4212) 35-87-37; fax (4212) 72-79-14; auditing and accounting, finance, management, commerce, law, foreign economic relations; library of 400,000 vols; 220 teachers; 7,000 students; Rector Prof. V. A. LIKHOBABIN.

Polar Academy: 192007 St Petersburg, Voronezhskaya ul. 79, A/Ya 533; tel. (812) 167-04-52; fax (812) 167-08-50; f. 1992; Master-level training of students from native Siberian peoples, who are expected to be appointed to high administrative posts in northern and far eastern Siberia; 60 teachers; 100 students; Rector AZURGET CHAUKENVAEVA; publ. *Polarnaya Akademia* (2 a year).

Russian Academy of Economics 'G. V. Plekhanov': 115998 Moscow M-54, Stremyannyi per. 36; tel. (095) 237-85-17; fax (095) 237-95-18; e-mail inter@rea.ru; internet www.rea.ru; f. 1907; faculties: general economics, finance, taxation, national economy, trade in commodities, economics and mathematics, economics and engineering, international economic relations; graduate school; library of 815,000 vols; 1,000 teachers; 12,000 students; Rector V. I. VIDYAPIN.

St Petersburg State Academy of Engineering and Economics: 191002 St Petersburg, ul. Marata 27; tel. (812) 112-06-33; fax (812) 112-06-07; e-mail oms@engec.ru; internet www.engec.ru; f. 1930; institutes: industrial economics and management, regional economics and management, transport economics and management, management information systems, general management of business and finance, tourism and hotel management; library of 370,000 vols; 310 teachers; 3,540 students; Rector A. I. MIKHAILUSHKIN; publ. *Scientific Proceedings of the Institute* (annually).

Samara State Academy of Economics: 443090 Samara, ul. Sovetskoi Armii 141; tel. (8462) 22-15-42; fax (8462) 22-09-53; f. 1931; faculties: finance, industrial economics, commerce and marketing, agribusiness, law, management, accounting; library of 596,000 vols; Rector Prof. A. I. NOSKOV.

Saratov State Academy of Law: 410720 Saratov, GSP, Chernyshevskogo ul. 104; tel. (8452) 25-04-86; fax (8452) 25-32-78; e-mail post@sgap.ru; internet www.sgap.ru; f. 1931; library of 500,000 vols; 300 teachers; 3,000 students; Rector FEDOR A. GRIGORYEV; publ. *Vestnik Saratovskoi gosudarstvennoi academii prava*.

Urals State Academy of Law: 620066 Ekaterinburg, Komsomolskaya ul. 21; tel. (3432) 74-43-63; fax (3432) 74-50-34; e-mail rektorat@usla.ru; internet www.usla.ru; f. 1931; library of 850,000 vols; 327 teachers; 7,310 students; Rector Prof. VIKTOR D. PEREVALOV; publ. *Russian Law Journal* (quarterly).

Volgograd Academy of Public Administration: 400131 Volgograd Gagarina ul. 8; tel. (8442) 33-58-39; fax (8442) 36-29-51; e-mail rector@vags.ru; internet www.vags .ru; f. 1992 to prepare and develop qualified administrators for government and non-profit positions; br. in Astrakhan; 250 teachers; 3,000 students; Rector MIKHAIL A. SUKIASYAN.

ENGINEERING AND INDUSTRY

Ivanovo State Textile Academy: 153000 Ivanovo, pr. F. Engels 21; tel. (0932) 32-85-45; fax (0932) 41-21-08; e-mail rector@igta .ru; internet www.igta.ru; f. 1918; Rector Prof. VLADIMIR V. ZRYUKIN; Vice-Rectors Prof. ALEXANDER A. TUVIN (Complementary Education), Prof. ALEXANDER N. SMIRNOV (Information and International Relations), Prof. GRIGORY I. CHRISTOBORODOV (Scientific and Industrial Activity), Prof. VLADIMIR V. LYUBIMTSEV (Studies); library of 740,911 vols; 388 teachers (incl. 51 professors); 8,488 students; publ. *Technology of Textile Industry* (every 2 months)

DEANS

Faculty of Clothing Manufacture: NATALIA V. YEVSEEVA

Faculty of Complementary Education: ALEXANDER A. TUVIN

Faculty of Correspondence Studies: BORIS V. SOLOVYEV

Faculty of Design and Cultural Service: DMITRY E. YEFREMOV

Faculty of Economic and Management: SVETLANA I. MEDZHIBOVSKAYA

Faculty of Mechanical Engineering and Automation: YEVGENY N. KALININ

Faculty of Preliminary Studies: VALENTIN N. GARELIN

Faculty of Textile Technology: ALEXANDER M. OSIPOV.

Branches of the Ivanovo State Textile Academy:

Kineshma Textile Secondary Technical School: Ul. Korolev 10, 155800 Kineshma; Dir GENNADY M. POSPELOV.

Krasnodar Branch: Ul. Sadovaya 11, 350911 Krasnodar; Dir OLGA B. ULYANOVA.

Nizhnii-Novgorod Branch: Pr. Gagarin 100, 603009 Nizhnii Novgorod; Dir GENNADY E. BUCHAROV.

Ryazan Branch: Bldg 1G, Ul. 12 Linia, 390026 Ryazan; Dir YELENA P. PROTASOVA.

Teikovo Textile Secondary Technical School: Ul. Sergeyevskaya 1, 155048 Teikovo; Dir VLADIMIR S. MITROFANOV.

Vichuga Textile Secondary Technical School: Ul. Pokrovsky 6, 155300 Vichuga; Dir VERA N. YASNIKOVA.

Moscow State Academy of Light Industry: 113127 Moscow, ul. Osipenko 33; tel. (095) 231-58-01; faculties: chemical technology, sewn goods technology, mechanical, leather goods technology, engineering economics; library of 392,000 vols; br. in Novosibirsk; Rector V. A. FUKIN.

Siberian State Academy of Mining and Metallurgy: 654007 Kemerovo oblast, Novokuznetsk, pr. Kirova 42; tel. (3843) 46-35-02; fax (3843) 46-57-92; faculties: mining, metallurgy, electrometallurgy, foundry work, mechanical, technology, construction; library of 1,010,000 vols; 620 teachers; 6,000 students; Rector N. M. KULAGIN.

MEDICINE

Astrakhan State Medical Academy: 414000 Astrakhan, Bakinskaya ul. 121; tel. (8512) 22-70-16; fax (8512) 39-41-30; e-mail agma@astranet.ru; internet www.agma.astranet.ru; f. 1918; library of 700,000 vols; 520 teachers; 3,500 students; Rector Prof. VALENTIN M. MIROSHNIKOV.

Blagoveshchensk State Medical Academy: 675006 Blagoveshchensk, Gorkogo ul. 95; tel. (4162) 2-27-13; tel. (4162) 2-28-68; 264 teachers; 1,681 students.

Chelyabinsk State Medical Academy: 454092 Chelyabinsk, Vorovskogo ul. 64; tel. (3512) 34-16-86; fax (3512) 34-03-36; internet www.vita.chel.su; library of 500,000 vols; 3,000 students; Rector Prof. YURI S. SHAMUROV.

Chita State Medical Academy: 672090 Chita, Gorkogo ul. 39a; tel. (3022) 23-41-63; fax (3022) 32-30-58; e-mail macadem@mail.chita.ru; f. 1953; library of 387,000 vols; 311 teachers; 2,400 students; Rector VLADIMIR N. IVANOV.

Dagestan State Medical Academy: 367025 Dagestan Autonomous Republic, Makhachkala, pl. Lenina 6; tel. (8722) 67-07-94; fax (8722) 68-12-80; e-mail dgma@iwt.ru; internet www.dgma.ru; Rector ABDURAKHMAN O. OSMANOV.

Ivanovo State Medical Academy: 153462 Ivanovo, pr. F. Engelsa 8; tel. (0932) 30-17-66; fax (0932) 32-66-04; e-mail adm@isma.ivanovo.ru; internet www.isma.ivanovo.ru; f. 1930; library of 545,059 vols; 578 teachers; 2,084 students; Rector Prof. RUDOLF R. SHILYAEV.

Izhevsk State Medical Academy: 426034 Udmurt Republic, Izhevsk, Revolyutsionnaya ul. 199; tel. (3412) 52-62-01; fax (3412) 65-81-67; e-mail rector@igma.udm.ru; internet www.igma.udm.ru; f. 1933; library of 402,000 vols; 387 teachers; 2,500 students; Rector Prof. NIKOLAI S. STRELKOV.

Kemerovo State Medical Academy: 650029 Kemerovo, Voroshilova ul. 22A; tel. (3842) 73-48-55; fax (3842) 73-48-55; e-mail ksma@ksma.kuzstu.ac.ru; internet ksma.kuzstu.ac.ru; f. 1956; library of 390,681 vols; 461 teachers; 3,573 students; Rector ALEXANDER YA. EVTUSHENKO.

Krasnoyarsk State Medical Academy: 660022 Krasnoyarsk, Partizana Zheleznyaka ul. 1; tel. (3912) 27-49-24; fax (3912) 23-78-35; e-mail onmpi@krsk.infotel.ru; internet www.krasgma.ru; f. 1942; library of 472,000 vols; 609 teachers; 3,270 students; Rector Prof. VICTOR I. PROKHORENKOV; publ. *Medical Man* (monthly).

Kuban State Medical Academy: 350614 Krasnodar, Sedina ul. 4; tel. (8612) 68-34-57; fax (8612) 68-34-57; e-mail corpus@ksma.kubannet.ru; internet www.ksma.ru; f. 1920; present name and status 1994; library of 560,000 vols; 600 teachers; 5,000 students; Rector BORIS G. ERMOSHENKO.

Nizhnii Novgorod State Medical Academy: 603005 Nizhny Novgorod, pl. Minina i Pozharskogo 10/1; tel. and fax (8312) 39-06-43; e-mail nnsma@sandy.ru; internet www.n-nov.mednet.com; f. 1920; 645 teachers;

3,542 students; library of 480,000 vols; publ. *Zhurnal* (quarterly); Rector Prof. VYACHESLAV V. SHKARIN.

North Ossetia State Medical Academy: 362019 North Ossetia, Vladikavkaz, Pushkinskaya ul. 40; tel. (8672) 53-42-21; fax (8672) 53-03-97; e-mail nosma@dol.ru; f. 1796; library of 265,000 vols; Rector Prof. KAZBEK D. SALBIEV.

Novosibirsk State Medical Academy: 630091 Novosibirsk, Krasnyi pr., 52; tel. and (3832) 22-32-04; e-mail rector@medin.nsc.ru; internet www.medin.nsc.ru; f. 1935; academic year September to June (two semesters); faculties of medicine, paediatrics, stomatology, international physicians, ecology, traditional medicine, nurses' training, pharmaceutical science, clinical psychology, social activity, laboratory medicine, physicians' and professors' improving and retraining and preparatory studies; Evening Lyceum, Institute of Public Health Economics and Management; library of 400,000 specialized vols and periodicals; 784 teachers; 4,500 students; Rector Prof. ANATOLY V. EFREMOV; publ. *Eksperimentalnaya klinicheskaya medicina* (Experimental Clinical Medicine, quarterly), *Meditsinskaya Gazeta* (Medical Newspaper, every 2 weeks).

Omsk State Medical Academy: 644099 Omsk, Lenina ul. 12; tel. (3812) 23-32-89; fax (3812) 23-14-57; e-mail osma@omsk-osma.ru; internet www.omsk-osma.ru; f. 1921; faculties: therapeutic and preventive medicine, paediatrics, stomatology; library of 573,199 vols; Rector Prof. ALEXANDER I. NOVIKOV.

Orenburg State Medical Academy: 460014 Orenburg, Sovetskaya ul. 6; tel. (3532) 77-61-03; fax (3532) 77-94-08; library of 160,000 vols; Rector SERGEI A. PAVLOVICHEV.

Perm State Medical Academy: 614600 Perm, Kuybyshevskaya ul. 39; tel. (3422) 90-44-53; fax (3422) 33-84-55; e-mail med@psma.ru; internet www.psma.ru; library of 541,000 vols; Rector Prof. VLADIMIR A. CHERKASSOV.

St Petersburg State Academy of Paediatric Medicine: 194100 St Petersburg, Litovskaya ul. 2; tel. (812) 245-06-46; fax (812) 245-40-85; f. 1925; library of 600,000 vols; Rector V. V. LEVANOVICH.

St Petersburg State Chemical-Pharmaceutical Academy: 197376 St Petersburg, Ul. Professora Popova 14; tel. (812) 234-57-29; fax (812) 234-60-44; e-mail rector@spcpa.ru; internet www.spcpa.ru; f. 1919; faculties: drug industry technology, pharmacy, further education; library of 334,200 vols; 250 teachers; 2,000 students; Rector G.P. YAKOVLEV.

St Petersburg State Medical Academy 'I. I. Mechnikov': 195067 St. Petersburg, Piskarevsky pr. 47; tel. (812) 543-50-14; fax (812) 140-15-24; e-mail mechnik@westcall.net; internet www.mechnik.spb.ru; f. 1907; faculties: pre-medical training, general medical, preventative medicine, advanced nursing, foreign students, further training, advanced training; library of 556,000 vols; 361 teachers; 4,500 students; Rector Prof. ALEXANDER V. SHABROV.

Smolensk State Medical Academy: 214019 Smolensk, Krupskoi ul. 28; tel. (0812) 55-26-92; fax (0812) 55-26-92; e-mail admsgma@sci.smolensk.ru; internet www.sgma.ru; library of 207,000 vols; Rector Prof. VLADIMIR G. PLESHKOV.

Stavropol State Medical Academy: 355017 Stavropol, Mira ul. 310; tel. (8652) 37-06-92; fax (8652) 37-06-42; e-mail sgma@statel.stavropol.ru; internet www.stgma.ru; f. 1937; languages of instruction: English,

Russian; academic year September to July; faculties: general medicine, stomatology, paediatrics, medical college teaching skills, nursing, postgraduate studies; 2 attached museums; clinics of ophthalmology, neurology and vertebraneurology; library of 345,000 vols; 525 teachers; 3,500 students; Rector Prof. B. D. MINAEV; publ. *South Russia Medical Magazine* (6 a year).

Tver Medical Academy: 170642 Tver, Sovetskaya ul. 4; tel. (0822) 33-17-79; fax (0822) 33-57-59; library of 446,000 vols; Rector BORIS N. DAVYDOV.

Tyumen Medical Academy: 625023 Tyumen, Odesskaya ul. 54; tel. (3452) 22-62-00; fax (3452) 25-23-19; e-mail tgma@tgma.info; internet www.tgma.info; f. 1963; 515 teachers; 3,256 students.

Urals State Medical Academy: 620219 Ekaterinburg, Repina ul. 3; tel. (3432) 51-14-90; fax (3432) 51-64-00; e-mail info@usma.ru; internet www.usma.ru; f. 1931; areas of study: therapeutics, surgery paediatrics, paediatric surgery, anaesthesiology, obstetrics, gynaecology, pathology, otolaryngology, ophthalmology, epidemiology, dentistry; library of 600,000 vols; Rector Prof. ANATOLY P. YASTREBOV; publ. *Herald* (monthly).

Voronezh State Medical Academy 'N. N. Burdenko': 394036 Voronezh, Studencheskaya ul. 10; tel. and fax (0732) 53-03-98; e-mail foreign@vsma.ac.ru; internet www.vsma.ac.ru; f. 1918; academic year September to June (two semesters); library of 500,000 vols; 1,105 teachers; 3,850 students; Rector Prof. Dr I. E. YESAULENKO; publ. *Applied Informational Aspects in Medicine* (4 a year), *Medical Staff* (monthly).

Yaroslavl State Medical Academy: 150000 Yaroslavl, Revolutsionnaya ul. 5; tel. (0852) 30-56-41; fax (0852) 30-50-13; e-mail rector@yma.ac.ru; internet www.yma.ac.ru; Rector YURI V. NOVIKOV.

SCIENCE AND TECHNOLOGY

Moscow State Academy of Applied Biotechnology: 109029 Moscow, ul. Talalikhina 33; tel. (095) 276-19-10; fax (095) 276-14-23; f. 1931; faculties: dairy industry technology, meat industry technology, food production, automation, plastics processing, low-temperature technology, veterinary sanitation, book-keeping, management; library of 611,000 vols; Rector IOSIF A. ROGOV.

Moscow State Academy of Food Industry: 125080 Moscow, Volokolamskoe shosse 11; tel. (095) 158-03-71; fax (095) 158-03-71; f. 1931; food technology, chemical engineering and biotechnology, information systems in economics, management and marketing, machinery, informatics, power engineering, agricultural engineering; 500 teaching staff; library of 1,000,000 vols; 6,000 students; Pres. Prof. V. I. TUZHILKIN.

Moscow State Academy of Instrumentation and Informatics: 107076 Moscow, ul. Stromynka 20; tel. (095) 268-01-01; faculties: engineering, automation in instrument making, transport and power machine building; library of 250,000 vols; Rector Prof. BORIS M. MIKHAILOV.

Moscow State Geological Prospecting Academy: 117873 Moscow, ul. Miklukho-Maklaya 23; tel. (095) 433-62-56; fax (095) 433-56-33; faculties: geology, geophysics, hydrogeology, prospecting engineering and mining, economics; library of 410,335 vols; 439 teachers; 3,964 students; Rector L. G. GRABCHAK; publ. *Geology and Prospecting* (6 a year).

Ryazan State Radio Engineering Academy: 390005 Ryazan, ul. Gagarina 59/1; tel. (0912) 72-18-44; fax (0912) 72-22-15; f. 1951;

faculties: radio equipment design, radio engineering, electronics, automation and telemechanics, computer technology, engineering economics, humanities; library of 720,000 vols; Rector V. K. ZLOBIN.

Rybinsk State Academy of Aviation Technology: 152934 Rybinsk, ul. Pushkina 53; tel. (0855) 52-09-90; fax (0855) 21-39-64; e-mail root@rgata.adm.yar.ru; internet www .rgata.yaroslavl.ru; f. 1955; faculties: aerotechnology, rocket technology, radioelectronics and informatics; library: c. 500,000 vols; 230 teachers; 4,000 students; Rector Prof. V. F. BEZYAZICHNY; publ. *Scientific Notes* (annually), *Vestnik* (annually).

St Petersburg Academy of Civil Aviation: 196210 St Petersburg, ul. Pilotov 38; tel. (812) 291-28-43; faculty: air traffic control; Rector P. V. KARTAMYSHEV.

St Petersburg State Academy of Aerospace Instrumentation: 190000 St Petersburg, Bol. Morskaya ul. 67; tel. (812) 117-15-22; fax (812) 313-70-18; e-mail common@ aanet.ru; internet www.suai.ru; Rector Prof. ANATOLY A. OVODENKO; library of 1,000,000 vols; publ. *V polet* (monthly); Fields of study: instrumentation, informatics and computer systems, automation, information systems in economics, management, law and radio engineering.

St Petersburg State Academy of Refrigeration and Food Technology: 191002 St Petersburg, ul. Lomonosova 9; tel. (812) 315-36-17; fax (812) 315-05-35; depts of refrigeration engineering, equipment for food manufacturing and commerce, cryogenics and conditioning systems; faculties: refrigeration equipment, equipment for food industry, trade and public catering, cryogenic technology and conditioning; library of 850,000 vols; Rector A. V. BARANENKO.

Siberian State Academy of Geodesy: 630108 Novosibirsk, Plakhotnogo ul. 10; tel. (3832) 43-39-37; fax (3832) 44-30-60; e-mail rektorat@ssga.ru; internet www.ssga.ru; f. 1932; faculties: geodesy and economics, aerial phototopography, cadastre and regional planning, management and regulation of land relations, optics and optoelectronic instruments, correspondence, evening, preliminary training; institutes: surveying and management, cadastre and geographic information systems, remote sensing and natural resources management, optics and optical technologies, distance education; library of 267,000 vols; 345 teachers; 9,500 students; Rector Prof. IVAN V. LESNYKH.

Volga Region State Academy of Telecommunications and Informatics: 443010 Samara, ul. L. Tolstogo 23; tel. and fax (8462) 33-58-56; internet www.psati.ru; f. 1956; faculties: radio engineering, radio communication and television, general engineering, economics, telecommunications and informatics, electrical communication, continuing education, extra-mural; Telecom College of PSATI, regional telecommunications training centre; brs in Stavropol and Orenburg; library of 461,000 vols; 298 teachers; 4,100 students; Rector VLADIMIR A. ANDREEV.

Voronezh State Technological Academy: 394040 Voronezh, pr. Revolyutsii 19; tel. and fax (0732) 55-42-67; e-mail rector@vgta.vrn .ru; internet www.vgta.vrn.ru; f. 1930; present name and status 1994; faculties: mechanical, automation, chemical, technological, technology of meat and dairy products; library of 850,000 vols; 491 teachers; 4,800 students; Rector Vitaly K. VITALY K. BITYUKOV.

TRANSPORT

Admiral Makarov State Maritime Academy: 199026 St Petersburg, Vasilevskii ostrov, Kosaya Liniya 15A; tel. (812) 217-19-34; fax (812) 217-07-82; f. 1876; faculties: arctic, navigation, radio engineering, international transport management, electrical engineering, marine engineering; library of 762,000 vols; 380 teachers; 4,400 students; brs in Arkhangelsk, Murmansk; Pres. IVAN I. KOSTYLEV.

Baltic Fishing Fleet State Academy: 236029 Kaliningrad oblast, Molodezhnaya ul. 6; tel. (0112) 21-72-04; fax (0112) 51-66-90; e-mail rector@bga.gazinter.net; f. 1966; faculties: navigation, marine engineering, radio engineering, economics; library of 165,426 vols; 253 teachers; 3,000 students; Dir Prof. A. PIMOSHENKO; publ. *Research Work* (annually).

Far-Eastern State Maritime Academy: Vladivostok, Verkhneportovaya ul. 50A; tel. (4232) 22-49-58; fmrly Far Eastern Higher School of Marine Engineering; faculties: navigation, ship engineering, management of marine transport, electrical engineering, practical psychology; library of 360,000 vols; Rector V. I. SEDYKH.

Kamchatka State Fishing Fleet Academy: 683003 Petropavlovsk-Kamchatsky, Klyuchevskaya ul. 35; tel. and fax (41500) 22-45-38; e-mail rektor@marine.kamchatka .su; f. 1987; trains specialists for the fishing industry, navigators, marine engineers, electrical engineers, radio engineers, technologists and refrigeration engineers; library of 70,000 vols; 250 teachers; 2,000 students; Rector BORIS I. OLEINIKOV; publ. *Conference Papers* (annually).

Moscow State Academy of Water Transport: 115407 Moscow, ul. Sudostroitelnaya 46; tel. (095) 116-30-88; fax (095) 118-31-11; f. 1980; faculties: marine engineering, operations, navigation, mechanization and automation of ports, hydrotechnical construction, engineering economics, legislation, international economic management for water transport; library of 106,000 vols; 5,000 students; Rector Prof. N. P. GARANIN.

Novorossiisk State Maritime Academy: 353918 Novorossiisk, pr. Lenina 93; tel. (8617) 23-03-93; fax (8617) 23-22-95; f. 1975; trains specialists in navigation, ship power plant operation, ship electrical and automated equipment operation, economics and management for the merchant marine; library of 267,000 vols; Dir VASILY GUTSULYAK.

Novosibirsk State Academy of Water Transport: 630099 Novosibirsk, Ul. Shchetinkina 33; tel. (3832) 22-24-28; fax (3832) 22-49-76; e-mail vyacheslavh@mail.ru; f. 1951; faculties: hydroengineering for waterways and ports, navigation and operation of water transport, ship engineers, electrical engineering, water transport management and economics; library of 450,000 vols; 380 teachers; 10,000 students; Dir I. A. RAGULIN.

Volga State Academy of Water Transport: 603600 Nizhnii Novgorod, ul. Nesterova 5; tel. (8312) 36-37-80; fax (8312) 32-17-91; courses in: transport operation and navigation, shipbuilding and ocean technology, land transport systems, electromechanics, electrical engineering, hydrotechnical construction, economics, business management, law; library of 500,000 vols.

Institutes of Higher Education: ARCHITECTURE AND CIVIL ENGINEERING

Moscow Architectural Institute: 103754 Moscow Centre GSP, ul. Rozhdestvenka 11; tel. (095) 924-79-90; fax (095) 921-12-40; e-mail marhi@marhi.ru; internet www

.miarch.ru; f. 1866; library of 400,000 vols; 400 teachers; 2,000 students; Pres. ALEKSANDR P. KUDRYAVTSEV.

Moscow Institute of Municipal Economy and Construction: 109807 Moscow, Srednyaya Kalitnikovskaya ul. 30; tel. (095) 278-32-05; fax (095) 278-15-10; f. 1944; faculties: construction, technology, mechanical engineering, urban construction, ecology and sanitary engineering, engineering, management and economic, commerce; 500 teachers; 13,000 students; library of 600,000 vols; Rector N. V. KOLKUNOV.

Novosibirsk Architectural Institute: 630008 Novosibirsk, Belinskogo 151; tel. and fax (3832) 66-42-64; f. 1989; architecture, design; library of 50,000 vols.

AGRICULTURE AND VETERINARY SCIENCE

All-Russian Extra-Mural Agricultural Institute: 143900 Moscow oblast, Balashikha 8; tel. (095) 521-24-64; fax (095) 521-24-56; f. 1930; depts: agriculture, zoological engineering, mechanization, economics and management, electrification, information technology in economics and law; library of 517,000 vols; Rector L. Y. KISELEV; publ. collections of scientific works of the institute (annually).

Azov-Black Sea Institute of Agricultural Mechanization: 347720 Rostov oblast, Zernograd, ul. Lenina 21; tel. (08536) 3-18-31; library of 192,000 vols; Rector B. M. TITOV.

Kabardino-Balkar Land Improvement Institute: 360004 Nalchik, ul. L. Tolstogo 185; tel. (86600) 5-69-43.

Kurgan Agricultural Institute: 641311 Kurgan oblast, Ketovskii raion, selo Lesnikovo; tel. (35222) 9-41-40; f. 1944; depts: agronomy, zootechnics, economics, mechanization, industrial and civil construction; library of 358,600 vols; Rector V. D. PAVLOV.

Omsk Veterinary Institute: 664007 Omsk, Oktyabrskaya ul 92; tel. and fax (3812) 24-15-35; f. 1918; library of 205,000 vols; 229 teachers; 2,600 students, Dir Prof. GENNADY A. KHONIN.

St Petersburg Veterinary Institute: 196006 St Petersburg, Moskovskii pr. 112; tel. (812) 298-36-31; f. 1919; library of 194,000 vols; 140 teachers; 1,340 students; Rector G. S. KUZNETSOV; publ. *Trudy* (Works).

Samara Agricultural Institute: 446400 Kinel, Poselok Ust-Kinelskii; tel. (8462) 4-68-72; f. 1919; depts: agronomy, animal husbandry, mechanization; library of 215,000 vols; 210 teachers; 3,500 students; Rector N. S. SHIBRAEV.

Saratov Animal Husbandry and Veterinary Institute: 410071 Saratov, Bol. Sadovaya 220; tel. (8452) 24-45-32; f. 1918; library of 376,500 vols; 213 teachers; 4,500 students; Rector V. I. VOROBJEV.

Saratov Institute of Agricultural Engineering: 410740 Saratov, Sovetskaya ul. 60; tel. (8452) 24-37-66; f. 1932; library of 550,000 vols; 320 teachers; 3,500 students; Rector A. G. RYBALKO.

Tver Agricultural Institute: 171314 Tver, P/O Sakharovo; tel. (0822) 39-92-32.

Yakutsk Agricultural Institute: 677891 Yakutsk, ul. P. Morozova 2; tel. (41122) 2-23-20.

ECONOMICS, LAW AND POLITICS

All-Russian Distance Institute of Finance and Economics: 121807 Moscow, Ul. Oleko Dundicha 23; tel. (095) 144-85-19; fax (095) 144-86-19; faculties: finance and credit, accounting, management, marketing;

library of 1,500,000 vols; depts and brs in 21 Russian cities.

Far Eastern Institute of Trade: 690600 Vladivostok, Okeanskii pr. 19; tel. (4232) 2-50-89; f. 1964; faculties: economics, accounting, foodstuffs and non-foodstuffs sciences, technology, organization of public catering; library of 220,000 vols; 572 teachers; 2,760 students; Rector Prof. L. S. PUZYREVSKY.

Institute of Business Studies: 117571 Moscow, pr. Vernadskogo 82; tel. (095) 434-92-53; fax (095) 434-11-48; e-mail ibs@ane.ru; f. 1989; independent; library of 10,500 vols; 182 teachers (32 full-time, 150 part-time); 1,500 students; Pres. Dr SERGEI MIASOEDEV.

Kazan Finance and Economics Institute: 420012 Tatarstan, Kazan, ul. Butlerova 4; tel. (8432) 36-54-41; fax (8432) 38-30-54; e-mail rector@kfei.kcn.ru; internet kfei .kcn.ru; f. 1932; faculties: general economics, business economics, finance and credit, distance learning, advanced training for professionals; 240 teachers; 5,000 students; library of 330,000 vols; Rector N. G. KHAIRULLIN.

Krasnoyarsk Institute of Commerce: 660049 Krasnoyarsk, ul. L. Prushinskoi 14; tel. (3912) 21-93-33; f. 1989; 135 mems; library of 205,835 vols; Chief officers Y. L. ALEXANDROV, B. K. GUSEV.

Moscow Institute of Economics, Statistics and Informatics: 119501 Moscow, Nezhinskaya ul. 7; tel. (095) 442-65-77; fax (095) 442-65-88; e-mail office@rector.mesi.ru; internet www.mesi.ru; f. 1932; faculties: economics and finance, management, law and humanities, statistics and economics, computer technology, Masters programmes; MBA; Open Education and Distance Learning Systems; Institute of Professional Development; library of 269,000 vols; 6,110 teachers (425 in Moscow, 5,685 in Russian regions); 65,000 students (10,000 in Moscow, 55,000 in Russian regions); Rector Prof. VLADIMIR P. TIKHOMIROV.

Moscow State Institute of International Relations: 117454 Moscow, pr. Vernadskogo 76; tel. (095) 434-91-74; fax (095) 434-90-66; internet www.mgimo.ru; f. 1944; faculties: international relations, international economic relations, international law, international business and business administration, international journalism, political science; library of 750,000 vols; 974 teachers; 2,848 students; Rector A. V. TORKUNOV.

Novosibirsk Institute of Commerce: 630087 Novosibirsk, pr. K. Marksa 26; tel. (3832) 46-58-52; f. 1956; faculties: trade economics, trade, accounting, technology; library of 197,000 vols; 240 teachers; 7,500 students; br. in Chita; Rector N. N. PROTOPOPOV.

Novosibirsk Institute of National Economy: 630070 Novosibirsk, Kamennaya ul. 56; tel. (3832) 24-27-22; f. 1968; faculties of industrial economics, economics and planning of supply, financial economics, accounting and statistics; library of 250,000 vols; 4,800 students; Rector V. N. SHCHUKIN.

St Petersburg Institute of Trade and Economics: 194018 St Petersburg, Novorossiiskaya 50; tel. (812) 247-78-06; f. 1930; faculties: trade economics, accounting, trade in industrial goods, trade in foodstuffs, technology; library of 595,300 vols; br. in Krasnoyarsk; Rector V. A. GULIAEV.

Saratov Institute of Economics: 410760 Saratov, ul. Radishcheva 89; tel. (8452) 26-38-50; f. 1918; faculties: industry, agriculture, credit and economics, accounting; library of 255,000 vols; 160 teachers; 4,000 students; Rector K. I. BABAYTSEV.

ENGINEERING AND INDUSTRY

Grozny State Oil Institute: 364051 Grozny, pl. Ordzhonikidze 100; tel. and fax (8712) 22-31-20; f. 1920; faculties: geology, petroleum technology, mechanical engineering, construction engineering, automation and applied informatics; library of 175,864 vols; 340 teachers; 5,565 students; Rector I. A. KERIMOV.

Moscow Institute of Printing: 127550 Moscow, ul. Pryanishnikova 2A; tel. (095) 216-07-46; faculties: printing equipment, printing technology, engineering economics, book trade, layout; br. in St Petersburg.

Norilsk Industrial Institute: 663310 Norilsk, ul. 50-let Oktyabrya 7; tel. (3919) 42-16-31; fax (3919) 42-17-41; f. 1961; faculties: mining, metallurgy, economics, mechanical technology, civil and electrical engineering; library of 300,000 vols; 500 teachers; 3,500 students; Rector A. A. KOLEGOV.

Novocherkassk Institute of Engineering Amelioration: 346409 Novocherkassk, Pushkinskaya 111; tel. (86352) 5-57-56; f. 1907; depts: irrigation and land reclamation, forestry; library of 170,000 vols; 250 teachers; 5,100 students.

Rostov-on-Don Automation and Mechanical Engineering Institute: 344023 Rostov-on-Don, pl. Strany Sovetov 2; tel. (8632) 52-93-51; fax (8632) 54-84-11; f. 1960; faculties: agricultural engineering, mechanical engineering, automation and robotics; library of 237,424 vols; 565 teachers; 1,730 students; Rector N. G. CHERED-NICHENKO; publ. *Economics and Industrial Management*.

Rubtsovsk Industrial Institute: 658207 Rubtsovsk, Traktornaya ul. 2/6; tel. (38557) 3-26-29; fax (38557) 3-54-22; e-mail rii@inst .rubtsovsk.ru; f. 1946; br. of Altai State Technical University; machine technology, motor car and tractor construction, motor vehicles and vehicle equipment, foundry machinery and technology, applied mathematics, management, industrial and civil engineering; library of 130,000 vols; 193 teachers; 1,950 students; Rector S. A. GURCHENKOV.

St Petersburg Institute of Engineering (LMZ-VTUZ): 195197 St Petersburg, Polyustrovsky pr. 14; tel. (812) 540-01-54; fax (812) 540-01-59; f. 1930; faculties: mechanical engineering, nuclear power engineering, turbine manufacture, management; library of 185,000 vols; 350 teachers; 5,000 students; Rector Prof. M. A. MARTYNOV.

Ukhta Industrial Institute: 169400 Komi Autonomous Republic, Ukhta, Pervomaiskaya ul.13; tel. (82147) 6-06-10.

MEDICINE

Khabarovsk State Pharmaceutical Institute: 680000 Khabarovsk, ul. K. Marksa 30; tel. (4210) 34-68-26.

Perm Pharmaceutical Institute: 614600 Perm, GSP-277, ul. Lenina 48; tel. (3422) 12-34-45; fax (3422) 12-94-76; e-mail pfa@ degacom.ru; f. 1937; library of 80,000 vols; 220 teachers; 3,500 students; Rector Prof. Y. OLESHKO.

Pyatigorsk Pharmaceutical Institute: 357533 Pyatigorsk, pr. Kalinina 11; tel. (8790) 9-44-74; f. 1943; library of 370,000 vols; 308 teachers; 2,300 students; Rector V. G. BELIKOV.

SCIENCE AND TECHNOLOGY

Bryansk Technological Institute: 241037 Bryansk, ul. Stanke Dimitrova 3; tel. (0832) 1-19-12; faculties: forestry engineering, for-

estry machinery, timber technology, forestry management.

Kemerovo Institute of Food Science and Technology: 650056 Kemerovo, bul. Stroitelei 47; tel. (3842) 73-40-40; fax (3842) 73-41-03; e-mail office@kemtipp.ru; internet www.kemtipp.ru; f. 1972; divisions: mechanics, refrigeration machines, food products technology, meat and dairy products, technology and organisation of public catering; 480 teachers; 10,000 students; Rector VLADIMIR PETROVITCH YOUSTRATOV.

Moscow State Food Institute: 109803 Moscow, Zemlynoi Val 73; tel. (095) 915-03-40; fax (095) 915-08-77; f. 1953; faculties: fish breeding and biotechnology, mechanical engineering, bread products, industrial economics; 211 teachers; library of 380,000 vols; brs in Krasnoyarsk, Vyazma and Rostov; Rector O. K. FILATOV.

Moscow Technological Institute: 141220 Moscow oblast, Pushkinskii raion, pos. Cherkizovo 1, Glavnaya ul. 99; tel. (095) 584-30-86; faculties: mechanical and radio engineering, chemical technology, engineering economics, art and technology; brs in St Petersburg, Ufa and Tolyatti.

Omsk Technological Institute for Service Industries: 644099 Omsk, Krasnogvardeiskaya 9; tel. (3812) 24-16-93; faculties: art and technology, engineering economics.

Penza Technological Institute: 440600 Penza, pr. Baidukova 1A; tel. (8412) 55-60-86; e-mail rector@vmis.pti.ac.ru; faculties: mechanical engineering, computer science, economics; library of 140,000 vols; Rector Prof. V. B. MOISEEV.

Russian Extra-Mural Institute of the Textile and Light Industries: 123298 Moscow, ul. Narodnogo Opolcheniya 38, korp. 2; tel. (095) 943-63-59; f. 1932; faculties: textile industry technology, light industry technology, chemical technology, electrical engineering, engineering economics; library of 780,000 vols; 350 teachers; 13,000 students; brs in Barnaul, Ufa, Kemerovo and Omsk; Rector V. S. STRELYAEV.

Shakhty Technological Institute for Service Industries: 346500 Rostov oblast, Shakhty, ul. Shevchenko 147; tel. (08536) 2-20-37; f. 1969; courses in fields of service industries, municipal finance and planning, light industry; library of 370,000 vols, 250,000 patent documents; 300 teachers; 2,000 full-time students; Rector Prof. VICTOR ROMANOV; publ. *Sbornik rabot instituta* (collected works, annually).

TRANSPORT

Irkutsk Institute of Railway Engineers: 664074 Irkutsk, ul. Chernyshevskogo 15; tel. (3952) 28-27-12; faculties: electromechanical, construction, traffic management; library of 116,000 vols; 497 teachers; Rector L. P. SURKOV.

Samara Institute of Railway Engineers: 443066 Samara 9, Pervyi Bezymyannyi per. 18; tel. (8462) 51-75-09; fax (8462) 51-77-90; faculties: construction, electromechanical, electrotechnical, operating; library of 260,000 vols; 6,000 students; Rector Prof. V. V. IVANOVICH.

Siberian Motor and Highway Institute: 644080 Omsk, pr. Mira 5; tel. (38112) 65-03-02; fax (38112) 65-03-23; e-mail info@sibadi .omsk.ru; internet www.sibadi.omsk.ru; f. 1930; faculties: road-building machinery, highway and airport building, bridges and tunnels, industrial and civil engineering, vehicles and vehicle services, traffic organization and services management, road transport economics and management; library of

747,000 vols; 500 teachers; 5,000 students; Rector V. A. SALNIKOV.

Schools of Art and Music:CONSERVATOIRES AND SCHOOLS OF MUSIC

Astrakhan State Conservatoire: 414000 Astrakhan, Sovetskaya ul. 23; tel. (8510) 2-93-11; f. 1969; courses: choral conducting, orchestral instruments, piano, folk instruments, singing, musicology; 450 students; Rector GEORGI I. SLAVNIKOV.

Kazan State Conservatoire: 420015 Tatarstan, Kazan, Bol. Krasnaya ul. 38; tel. (8432) 36-55-33; fax (8432) 36-56-41; f. 1945; piano, organ, orchestral and folk instruments, composition, singing, choral conducting, musicology; library of 223,000 vols; 178 teachers; 659 students; Rector R. K. ABDULLIN.

Moscow State Conservatoire 'P. I. Tchaikovsky': 103871 Moscow, ul. Bolshaya Nikitskaya 13; tel. (095) 229-06-41; fax (095) 229-96-59; internet www.mosconsv.ru; f. 1866; faculties: piano, orchestral instruments, singing, operatic and symphonic conducting, choral conducting, composition, musicology; 386 teachers; 865 students; library of 1,244,412 vols; Rector M. A. OVCHINNIKOV (acting).

Nizhnii Novgorod State Conservatoire 'M. I. Glinka': 603600 Nizhnii Novgorod GSP-30, ul. Piskunova 40; tel. (8312) 36-45-27; fax (8312) 36-42-37; f. 1946; piano, orchestral and folk instruments, singing, choral conducting, opera and symphony conducting, composition, musicology; library of 130,000 vols; 170 teachers; 700 students; Rector E. B. FERTELMEISTER.

Novosibirsk State Conservatoire 'M. I. Glinka': 630099 Novosibirsk, Sovetskaya ul. 31; tel. (3832) 22-25-22; fax (3832) 23-95-37; f. 1956; piano, orchestral and folk instruments, singing, symphony and choral conducting, composition, musicology; library of 104,000 vols; Rector Prof. Dr E. G. GURENKO.

Rostov State Conservatoire 'S. V. Rakhmaninov': 344008 Rostov-on-Don, Budennovsky pr. 23; tel. (8632) 62-36-14; fax (8632) 62-35-84; e-mail rostcons@aaanet.ru; internet www.rostcons.aaanet.ru; f. 1967 (fmrly Rostov Musical Pedagogical Institute, present name c. 1992); courses: piano, orchestral instruments, folk instruments, singing, choral conducting, orchestral conducting, composition, musicology, jazz; library of 204,000 vols; 124 teachers; 630 students; Principal Prof. A. S. DANILOV.

Russian State Academy of Music 'Gnesins': 121069 Moscow, Povarskaya ul. 30–36; tel. (095) 291-15-54; fax (095) 290-17-65; f. 1944; 476 teachers; 1,337 students; Principal Prof. S. M. KOLOBKOV.

St Petersburg State Conservatoire 'N. A. Rimsky-Korsakov': 190000 St Petersburg, Teatralnaya pl. 3; tel. (812) 314-96-93; fax (812) 311-82-88; e-mail info@conservatory.ru; internet www.conservatory.ru; f. 1862; piano, orchestral instruments, singing, operatic, symphonic and choral conducting, composition, musicology, opera and ballet direction, musical comedy, folk instruments; library of 462,000 vols, 2,431 incunabula, 7,000 MSS of Russian and European composers; 266 teachers; 1,000 students; Rector S. P. ROLDUGIN; publ. Teatralnaya ploshchad (6 a year).

Saratov State Conservatoire 'L. V. Sobinov': 410600 Saratov, pr. Kirova 1; tel. (8452) 26-06-38; fax (095) 975-09-33; piano, orchestral and folk instruments, choral conducting, singing, composition, musicology, theatre and cinema acting, musical comedy acting; library of 54,065 vols; Rector Prof. VALERY P. LOMAKO.

Urals State Conservatoire 'M. P. Mussorgsky': 620014 Ekaterinburg, pr. Lenina 26; tel. (3432) 71-21-80; fax (3432) 71-21-80; e-mail mail@uscon.ru; internet www.uscon.ru; f. 1934; piano, orchestral and folk instruments, singing, choral conducting, composition, musicology, sound production; library of 130,000 vols; 190 teachers; 700 students; Rector Prof. MIKHAIL V. ANDRIANOV.

SCHOOLS OF ARTS AND CULTURE

Altai State Institute of Culture: 656055 Barnaul, ul. Yurina 277; tel. (3852) 44-57-09; tel. (3852) 44-54-57; librarianship, cultural and educational work; br. in Omsk.

Chelyabinsk State Institute of Art and Culture: 454091 Chelyabinsk, ul. Ordzhonikidze 36A; tel. (3512) 33-89-32; f. 1968; training in theatre direction, choreography, ballet, conducting, library science; library of 301,000 vols; 508 teachers; 2,700 students; Rector A. P. GRAI.

Eastern Siberian State Institute of Culture: 670005 Buryat Autonomous Republic, Ulan-Ude, ul. Tereshkovoi 1; tel. (31022) 3-33-22; f. 1960; faculties: library science, bibliography; library of 420,000 vols.

Far-Eastern State Academy of Arts: 690600 Vladivostock, Petr Veliky 3; tel. (4232) 26-49-22; fax (4232) 26-44-88; e-mail dvgii@fastmail.vladivostock.ru; f. 1962; piano, orchestral instruments, folk instruments, singing, choral conducting, musicology, drama, painting, directing; library of 102,000 vols; 100 teachers; 450 students.

Kazan State Institute of Culture: 420059 Kazan, Orenburgskii trakt 3a; tel. (8432) 37-31-27; librarianship, cultural and educational work.

Kemerovo State Academy of Culture and Arts: 650029 Kemerovo, ul. Voroshilova 17; tel. (3842) 73-29-67; fax (3842) 73-28-08; e-mail kemgaki@mail.ru; internet www.art.kemerovonet.ru; f. 1969; library sciences, information technology, social education, music, theatre, video art, design, art management, worldwide art studies; library of 249,000 vols; 210 teachers; 3,000 students; Rector Prof. EKATERINA L. KUDRINA.

Khabarovsk State Institute of Culture: 680045 Khabarovsk, Krasnorechenskaya ul. 112; tel. (4210) 36-30-39; department: library science.

Krasnodar State Institute of Culture and Art: 350072 Krasnodar, ul. 40-letiya Pobedy 33; tel. (8612) 55-30-63; f. 1967; departments: library science, folk culture; library of 152,500 vols; 267 teachers; 2,800 students; Dir IRINA I. GORLOVA.

Krasnoyarsk State Institute of Fine Arts: 660049 Krasnoyarsk, ul. Lenina 22; tel. (3912) 23-35-02; courses: piano, orchestral instruments, folk instruments, singing, choral conducting, musicology, theatre and cinema acting.

Moscow Higher School of Industrial Art: 125080 Moscow A-80, Volokolamskoe shosse 9; tel. (095) 158-01-33; f. 1825; refounded 1945; faculties: industrial arts, decorative and applied art, interior design, monumental art; library of 50,000 vols; 1,300 students; Rector A. S. KVASOV.

Moscow Literary Institute of the Union of Writers 'M. Gorky': 103104 Moscow, Tverskoi bul. 25; tel. (095) 291-22-66; library of 106,000 vols.

Moscow State Art Institute 'V. I. Surikov': 109004 Moscow, Tovarishchesky per. 30; tel. (095) 912-39-32; fax (095) 912-18-75; e-mail artinst@online.ru; f. 1843; depts: painting, graphic arts, sculpture, architecture, and theory and history of art; library of

154,000 vols; 103 teachers; 450 students; Dir A. A. BICHUKOV.

Moscow State Institute of Culture: 141400 Moscow oblast, Khimki 6, Bibliotechnaya ul. 7; tel. (095) 570-31-33; f. 1930; librarianship, bibliography, information science, cultural studies, museum studies; library of 786,814 vols; 6,000 students; Rector L. P. BOGDANOV.

Perm State Institute for Arts and Culture: 614000 Perm, ul. Gazety 'Zvezda' 18; tel. and fax (3422) 12-45-93; fax (3422) 12-45-93; f. 1975; educational and cultural work; 156 teachers; 1,814 students; library of 170,000 vols; Rector Y. A. MALYANOV.

Samara State Institute of Culture: 443010 Samara, ul. Frunze 167; tel. (8462) 32-76-54; f. 1971; librarianship, educational and cultural work; library of 239,100 vols; 200 teachers; Dir Prof. I. M. KUZMIN; publ. Culture, Creative Activity, Humanity.

St Petersburg Academy of Art and Design: 191028 St Petersburg, Solyanoi per. 13; tel. (812) 273-38-04; fax (812) 272-84-46; f. 1876 (fmrly St Petersburg V. I. Mukhina Higher Industrial Art School, present name c. 1992); faculties: decorative and applied art, monumental arts, design; library of 140,000 vols; 230 teachers; 1,100 students; Rector Prof. A. Y. TALASCHUK.

St Petersburg Institute of Painting, Sculpture and Architecture 'I. E. Repin': 199034 St Petersburg, Universitetskaya nab. 17; tel. (812) 213-61-89; fax (812) 213 65-48; f. 1757; attached to the Academy of Arts of Russia; departments: painting, sculpture, graphic art, architecture, theory and history of art; library of 500,000 vols; 160 teachers; 1,370 students; Rector Prof. O. A. YEREMEYEV.

St Petersburg State Institute of Culture: 191065 St Petersburg, Dvortsovaya nab. 4; tel. (812) 314-11-21; f. 1918; librarianship, cultural, musical and theatrical studies, cinema and television; library of 600,000 vols; 492 teachers; 5,000 students; Rector Prof. P. A. PODBOLOTOV; publ. Trudy Instituta (Proceedings).

Ufa State Institute of Fine Arts: 450025 Bashkortostan, Ufa, ul. Lenina 14; tel. (3472) 23-49-56; departments: piano, orchestral instruments, folk instruments, choral conducting, singing, composition, musicology, theatre and cinema acting, folk theatre, painting; Rector Prof. Z. A. NURGALIN.

Voronezh State Institute of Fine Arts: 394088 Voronezh, ul. Lizyukova 42; tel. (0732) 13-14-81; tel. (0732) 13-08-90; piano, orchestral instruments, folk instruments, singing, choral conducting.

SCHOOLS OF FILM AND THEATRE

Drama School attached to the E. B. Vakhtangov State Theatre 'B. V. Shchukin': 121002 Moscow, ul. Vakhtangova 12a; tel. (095) 241-56-44; theatre and cinema acting.

Drama School attached to the Maly Theatre 'M. S. Shchepkin': 103012 Moscow, Pushechnaya ul. 2/6; tel. (095) 923-18-80; tel. (095) 924-38-89; theatre and cinema acting.

Ekaterinburg State Theatrical Institute: 620151 Ekaterinburg, ul. K. Libknechta 38; tel. (3432) 51-36-90; f. 1985; 350 students; Rector Prof. V. BABENKO.

Moscow Choreographic Institute: 119146 Moscow, 2-ya Frunzenskaya ul. 5; tel. (095) 247-37-80.

Russian Academy of Theatre Arts: 103888 Moscow, Mal. Kislovsky per. 6; tel. (095) 291-91-92; fax (095) 290-05-97; e-mail info@gitis.net; internet www.gitis.net; f. 1878; faculties and departments: Acting, Directing (directing dramatic theatre, circus direction), Musical Theatre (musical theatre direction and acting), Theatre History and Criticism (world theatre history, Russian theatre history), Ballet-master Faculty (choreography), Variety Theatre (variety arts), Theatre Management and Production (performing arts management), Set Design; Inter-Faculty Departments: voice and speech training, vocal training, dance training, movement training, history of the arts, history and theory of music and musical performance, history, philosophy and literature, foreign languages, Russian as a foreign language; Rector Prof. MARINA KHMELNITSKAYA.

St Petersburg State Theatre Arts Academy: 192028 St Petersburg, ul. Mokhovaya 34; tel. (812) 273-15-81; fax (812) 272-17-89; e-mail international@tart.spb.ru; internet www.tart.spb.ru; f. 1779; drama and cinema acting, rock opera acting, puppet theatre, stage directing, theatre planning and organization, theatrical equipment and stage planning; research dept; library of 350,000 vols; 150 teachers; 1,160 students; Rector Prof. Dr L. G. SOUNDSTREM.

State Institute of Cinematography: 129226 Moscow, ul. Vilgelma Pika 3; tel. (095) 181-38-68; f. 1919; direction, shooting, screen play and script writing, cinema studies, economics of cinematography, arts; library of 300,000 vols; 200 teachers; 1,550

students; Rector ALEXANDER NOVIKOV; publ. *Tvorchestvo Molodykh* (Creations of Young Artists), etc.

Studio-School of the Moscow Arts Theatre 'V. I. Nemirovich-Danchenko': 103009 Moscow, Tverskaya ul. 6, str. 7; tel. (095) 229-39-36; fax (095) 200-42-41; f. 1943; drama and cinema acting, theatre directing, theatre technology, set and costume design, theatre management; library of 20,000 vols; 80 teachers; 230 students; Rector Prof. O. P. TABAKOV.

Yaroslavl State Theatre Institute: 150000 Yaroslavl, Pervomaiskaya ul. 43; tel. and fax (0852) 22-23-11; f. 1980; theatrical art; library of 25,300 vols; 300 students; Rector Prof. STANISLAV KLITIN.

RWANDA

The Higher Education System

In 1962 Rwanda became independent from Belgium, and in 1963 the Université Nationale du Rwanda, its oldest current institution of higher education, was founded. In 2003 the number of students at the six public higher education institutions was 12,211, with a further 8,182 attending about seven private institutions. The Ministry of Education, Science, Technology and Research is the national co-ordinating body for higher education. The Minister of Education, Science, Technology and Research is the Chairman of the Governing Council of Université Nationale du Rwanda. The Council's leading officers, including the Rector and Vice-Rectors, are Government appointees.

The secondary school Diplôme des Humanités Complètes is required for admission to higher education. University degrees are divided into two cycles: the first cycle lasts two years and leads to the award of the Baccalauréat in most subjects (engineering lasts three years); the second cycle is between two and four years in duration, following the award of the Baccalauréat, and leads to the award of either the Licence or a professional title. Students studying medicine are awarded the title of Docteur en Médecine after seven years.

The universities and specialist institutes offer post-secondary technical and vocational education. Courses last two years and students receive (usually) the Diplôme de Technicien Supérieur or Ingénieur Technicien.

Learned Society

GENERAL

UNESCO Office Kigali: BP 2502, Kigali; MINEDUC Compound, Kigali; tel. 513845; fax 513844; e-mail kigali@unesco.org; Programme Specialist CONSTANTINO CONSTATINI.

Research Institutes

GENERAL

Institut de Recherche Scientifique et Technologique: BP 227, Butare; tel. 530395; fax 530939; f. 1989; pharmacology, energy, social sciences; library of 9,500 vols; Dir-Gen. Prof. Dr CHRYSOLOGUÉ KOURANGUIÉ; Dir of Pharmacology Centre POLYCARPE NYE-TERO; Dir of Energy Centre DÉO NKRORUM-ZIZA; Dir of Centre for Rwanda Studies JEAN MARARA.

AGRICULTURE, FISHERIES AND VETERINARY SCIENCE

Institut des Sciences Agronomiques du Rwanda (ISAR): BP 138, Butare; tel. 530145; fax 530642; internet www.isar.cgiar.org; f. 1962; attached to Min. of Agriculture; 1,000 personnel; library of 2,500 vols; Dir Dr ELIE MUGUNGA MUHINDA; publs *Annual Report, Technical Letters.*

Attached research stations:

Agricultural Research Institute of Rwanda–Ruhande Station: BP 617, Butare; forestry; Dir ATHANASE MUKURAR-INDA.

Centre de Sélection Bovine de Songa: BP 138, Butare; stockbreeding (cattle, sheep, poultry); Dir (vacant).

Station ISAR/PNAP: BP 73, Ruhengeri; Dir GERVAIS NGERERO.

Station Karama: BP 121, Kigali; plant breeding (living plants, irrigation), stockbreeding (cattle, goats); Dir Ir LAMBERT MAYALA.

Station Rubona: BP 138, Butare; laboratories (chemistry, technology, phytopathology), environmental studies, phytotechnics (living plants, cash crops: coffee, tobacco), zootechnics.

Station Rwerere: BP 73, Ruhengeri; high altitude cultures (wheat, peas, potato); Dir C. SEHENE.

Station Tamira: BP 69, Gisenyi; high altitude cultures (pyrethrum); Dir C. NTAMBABAZI.

TECHNOLOGY

Direction des Mines et de la Géologie: Ministère de l'Energie, de l'Eau et des Ressources Naturelles, BP 447, Kigali; tel. 570496; f. 1962; geological services to the Government and private industry; to prepare a geological map of Rwanda; prospecting; library of 6,000 vols; Dir EMMANUEL BIZI-MANA; publ. *Bulletin du Service Géologique* (annually).

Libraries and Archives

Butare

Bibliothèque Universitaire: Université Nationale du Rwanda, BP 117, Butare; tel. 530330; fax 530210; e-mail biblio@nur.ac.rw; internet www.lib.nur.ac.rw; f. 1964; 206,000 vols; Dir EMMANUEL SERUGENDO.

Kigali

Archives Nationales du Rwanda: BP 1044, Kigali; tel. 83525; fax 83518; f. 1979; 7 staff; 600 vols; Dir ELIAS KIZARI; publ. *Presidential Speeches* (annually).

Bibliothèque Nationale du Rwanda: BP 1044, Kigali; tel. 572730; fax 83518; f. 1989; 6,000 vols; Dir. SÉVERIM SEKUBUMBA.

Universities

INSTITUT DES SCIENCES, TECHNOLOGIE ET DE GESTION DE KIGALI (KIST)
(Kigali Institute of Science, Technology and Management (KIST))

Ave de l'Armée, BP 3900, Kigali

Telephone: 574696

Fax: 571924

E-mail: info@kist.ac.rw

Internet: www.kist.ac.rw

Founded 1997

Academic year: February to November

Rector: Prof. Dr SILAS LWAKABAMBA

Vice-Rector (Academic): Ing. ALBERT BUTARE

Vice-Rector (Finance and Administration): Dr NELSON LUJARA

Director of Academic Services: Prof. ELIPHAZ BISANDA

Director of Administration: ANSELME SANO

Director of Finance: CALISTUS OBIERO

Chief Librarian: ALPHONSE NGABONZIZA

Number of teachers: 165

Number of students: 2,416

DEANS

Faculty of Management: Dr IBRAHIM MUSOBO

Faculty of Science: Dr DESIRÉ KARANGWA

Faculty of Technology: Prof. GRANT MONNEY

Centre for Continuing Education: ANTONIA MUTORO NSANGANO

School of Language Studies: TEMBWE Z. WA OLOLO

UNIVERSITÉ NATIONALE DU RWANDA

BP 56, Butare

Telephone: 530122

Fax: 530121

E-mail: rector@nur.ac.rw

Internet: www.nur.ac.rw

Founded 1963

Languages of instruction: French, English

State control

Academic year: January to October (two semesters)

Rector: Dr EMILE RWAMASIRABO

Vice-Rectors: Prof. SILAS MURERAMANZI (Academic), CANISIUS KARURANGA (Administration and Finance)

Library: see Libraries

Number of teachers: 384

Number of students: 7,240

Publications: *Etudes Rwandaises* (1 each term), *Annuaire, Revue Juridique*

DEANS

Faculty of Agriculture: Dr CANISIUS KANAN-GIRE

Faculty of Arts and Humanities: DÉO BYANA-FASHE

Faculty of Economics, Social Sciences, and Management: Dr JEAN BOSCO MUTAJOGIRE

Faculty of Education: Dr JEAN-PIERRE DUSIN-GIZEMUNGU

Faculty of Law: Dr NGAGI ALPHONSE

Faculty of Medicine: Dr ALEXIS NYAKAYIRO

School of Journalism: JEAN-PIERRE GATSINZI

School of Modern Languages: DEO HODARI

School of Public Health and Nutrition: Dr JOSEPH NTAGANIRA

Colleges

Institut Africain et Mauricien de Statistique et d'Economie Appliquée: BP 109, Kigali; tel. 84989; f. 1975 by the OCAM states; 3-year diploma course; library: 9,184 vols; 7 teachers; 38 students; Dir Sérigne T. Diasse; publ. *Rapport d'enquête* (annually).

Institut Supérieur des Finances Publiques (ISFP): BP 1514, Kigali; tel. 574302; f. 1987; attached to the Ministry of Finance; offers 2-year courses in the financial aspects of public administration; library; Dir Jean-Baptiste Byilingiro.

SAINT CHRISTOPHER AND NEVIS

The Higher Education System

The islands of St Christopher and Nevis were settled by the British in the 1620s and remained under British control until 1983, when they jointly became an independent state and joined the Commonwealth as a full member. The College of Further Education was founded in 1988 as an amalgamation of previously existing institutions and was renamed Clarence Fitzroy Bryant College in 1996. In 2000 a privately financed 'offshore' medical college, the Medical University of the Americas, opened in Nevis. There is also a branch campus of the University of the West Indies located in Basseterre. In 2000/01 there were 1,235 students in tertiary education. All institutions of higher education are recognized and accredited by the Ministry of Education's Accreditation Board.

Admission to Bachelors degree requires sufficient passes in the Caribbean Examinations Council Secondary Education Certificate or GCE A-level. The Bachelors degree at the University of the West Indies last three to four years while the Masters degree takes two years and is mostly coursework based. Following completion of the Masters, the Doctorate requires two to four years of further study, culminating with the submission and defence of a thesis.

Clarence Fitzroy Bryant College and other colleges offer post-secondary vocational and technical education, leading to the award of qualifications such as Diplomas, Technician Diplomas and Associate Degrees.

Learned Societies

HISTORY, GEOGRAPHY AND ARCHAEOLOGY

Nevis Historical and Conservation Society: POB 563, Charlestown, Nevis; tel. 469-5786; fax 469-0274; e-mail museums@nevis-nhcs.org; internet www.nevis-nhcs.org; f. 1980; administers Nevis Field Study Centre, Museum of Nevis History (birthplace of Alexander Hamilton), Horatio Nelson Museum; 650 mems; library: materials on history and culture of Nevis, St Kitts and West Indies, Alexander Hamilton, Horatio Nelson, and Amerindians; Archives of Nevis, newspapers, and civil, parish and government records, maps; Pres. HALSTEAD BYRON; Sec. SUZANNE GORDON, Exec. Dir JOHN GUILBERT; publ. *Newsletter* (4 a year).

LANGUAGE AND LITERATURE

Alliance Française: 1 Orchid St, Greenlands, POB 93, Basseterre, St Kitts; tel. 465-9415; fax 465-0478; e-mail allfrskn@caribsurf.com; offers courses and exams in French language and culture and promotes cultural exchange with France.

Library
Charlestown

Nevis Public Library: Prince William St, Charlestown, Nevis; tel. 469-0421; fax 469-1207; e-mail nepublib@caribsurf.com; Librarian HAZEL FRANCIS (acting).

Universities and Colleges

Clarence Fitzroy Bryant College: Burdon St Campus, POB 268, Basseterre, St Kitts; tel. 465-2856; fax 465-8279; e-mail info@cfbc.edu.kn; internet www.cfbc.edu.kn; f. 1988 as College of Further Education by merger of 4 instns; present name 1996; Principal MARILYN ROGERS (acting); Registrar VENETTA MILLS; Librarians LORREL BRADSHAW, LEAH LIBURD.

Medical University of the Americas: POB 701, Charlestown, Nevis; tel. 469-9177; fax 469-9180; e-mail admissions@mua.edu; internet www.mua.edu; f. 1998; Private control; library: 2,950 books, 110 periodicals; 80 teachers; 600 students (postgraduate); President Dr DAVID L. FREDRICK; Executive Dean Dr SEWELL DIXON; Dean, Basic Sciences Dr RAY LASH.

University of West Indies Branch: Basseterre; tel. 465-6583; fax 465-2190; e-mail ewiskn@caribsurf.com; Dir OLIVIA EDGECOMBE-HOWELL.

SAINT LUCIA

The Higher Education System

The island became a British colony in 1814 and remained under British rule until 1979, when it became independent (but remaining within the Commonwealth). Tertiary education is principally offered by a branch campus of the University of the West Indies. In 2000/01 there were 1,403 students enrolled in tertiary education and 729 students in adult education. The Ministry of Education and Culture is the government agency responsible for higher education.

Sir Arthur Lewis Community College offers qualifications at the upper-secondary and tertiary levels. The Associate degree is a two- or three-year programme of study, depending on the subject. Undergraduate Bachelors and postgraduate Masters degrees are available at the University of the West Indies.

Learned Societies

EDUCATION

National Research and Development Foundation: La Clery, POB 3067, Castries; tel. 452-4253; fax 453-6389; e-mail info@nrdf .org.lc; internet www.nrdf.org.lc; f. 1983 to promote research and the expansion of economic devt in St Lucia; provides technical assistance, training and consultancy; offers short courses in business management and admin.; Exec. Dir GERALD MORRIS.

HISTORY, GEOGRAPHY AND ARCHAEOLOGY

St Lucia Archaeological and Historical Society: Vigie, POB 3060, La Clery, Castries; tel. 453-2519; f. 1954; organizes public lectures, exhibitions and educational activities; Pres. FORTUNA ANTHONY; Admin. Sec. ERIC BRANFORD.

LANGUAGE AND LITERATURE

Alliance Française: La Pyramide, Pointe Séraphine, POB 898, Castries; tel. 452-6602; fax 452-1871; e-mail alliancefrancaise@ candw.lc; f. 1994; offers courses and examinations in French language and culture, and promotes cultural exchange with France; library of 3,792 vols; Dir FRANCK LELARGE.

NATURAL SCIENCES
Biological Sciences

St Lucia Naturalists' Society: POB 783, Castries; tel. 451-6957; conservation and educational activities; Chair. CRISPIN D'AUVERGNE.

RELIGION, SOCIOLOGY AND ANTHROPOLOGY

Folk Research Centre: Mount Pleasant, POB 514, Castries; tel. 453-1477; fax 451-9365; e-mail frc@candw.lc; internet www .stluciafolk.org; f. 1973 to preserve and promote the cultural heritage of St Lucia; Chair. VICTOR POYOTTE; Exec. Dir KENNEDY SAMUEL.

Libraries and Archives
Castries

Central Library of St Lucia: POB 103, Castries; tel. 452-2875; e-mail central .library@candw.lc; internet www.educ.gov.lc; f. 1847; dept of Min. of Education, Human Resource Development, Youth and Sports; government public library; 160,000 vols; Dir of Library Services JOHN ROBERT LEE.

National Archives of St Lucia: POB 3060, La Clery, Castries; tel. 452-1654; fax 453-1405; e-mail stlunatarch_mt@candw.lc; internet www.stluciaarchives.org; f. 1995; 6,000 vols; unselected govt records; spec. historical collns, multimedia; Archivist MARGOT THOMAS.

Museum
Castries

St Lucia National Trust: POB 595, Castries; tel. 452-5005; fax 453-2791; e-mail natrust@candw.lc; internet www.slunatrust .org; f. 1975; responsible for the protected areas of Pigeon Island (history, archaeology, geology, natural history), Fregate Islands Nature Reserve and the proposed Praslin Protected Landscape (archaeology, history, coastal resources, geology, flora and fauna), the Anse Galet Nature Reserve (flora and fauna, history) and several offshore islands (bird nesting sites) and other sites; 600 mems; Dir BISHNU TULSIE; publ. *Conservation News* (quarterly).

College

University of the West Indies, School of Continuing Studies: University Centre, POB 306, The Morne, Castries; tel. 452-3866; fax 452-4080; e-mail uwislu@candw.lc; f. 1948; continuing education; houses the University's Distance Education Centre (UWIDEC) linking the university campuses with eight university centres; Resident Tutor and Head MATTHEW VERNON ROBERTS.

SAINT VINCENT AND THE GRENADINES

The Higher Education System

From the 18 century the islands were under British control until they became fully independent, within the Commonwealth, as Saint Vincent and the Grenadines in 1978. The Vincentian education system is modelled on the British system. Post-secondary education is provided through the Kingstown Medical College, a campus of St. George's University (Grenada), located near Kingstown. The University maintains affiliations with hospitals in the USA, the UK and the Caribbean for clinical programmes. There are also teacher-training, technical, nursing and community colleges, with total enrolment in 2000 of 804 students. The Ministry of Education is the national body responsible for higher education.

Learned Societies

ARCHITECTURE AND TOWN PLANNING

Saint Vincent National Trust: POB 1538, Kingstown; tel. 456-1787; fax 456-2733; works to protect the country's natural and historical areas.

FINE AND PERFORMING ARTS

Saint Vincent and the Grenadines Visual Arts Society: POB 2303, Kingstown; tel. 457-4454; f. 2003 to encourage the local devt of the visual arts; organizes exhibitions and other events; Sec. CÉCILE COMBLEN.

LANGUAGE AND LITERATURE

Alliance Française: POB 560, Kingstown; Located at: Old Public Library Bldg, Victoria Park, Kingstown; tel. 456-2095; fax 456-2080; e-mail afsvg@vincysurf.com; f. 1969; organizes conferences, exhibitions, seminars, films and lectures; Dir MANUEL GUILLON.

Libraries and Archives

Kingstown

Department of Libraries, Archives and Documentation Services: Lower Middle St, Kingstown; tel. and fax 457-2022; e-mail publiclibrary@caribsurf.com; f. 1893; oversees 18 br. libraries containing 262,000 vols; part of the Ministry of Education; Dir JOAN L. O'GARRO.

Principal attached centres:

Kingstown Public Library: Lower Middle St, Kingstown; tel. 456-1111; fax 457-2022; e-mail publiclibrary@caribsurf.com; f. 1893; 32,321 vols, 66 periodicals; Librarian DANA NEVERSON.

National Archives: Richmond Hill, Kingstown; tel. 450-0485; e-mail archives@vincysurf.com; f. 1990; 15,000 vols; Archivist TRISHA-ANN JOB.

Documentation Centre: Richmond Hill, Kingstown; tel. 456-1689; e-mail document@caribsurf.com; 15,000 vols.

Museums and Galleries

Kingstown

Botanical Gardens: New Montrose, Kingstown; tel. 457-1003; f. 1763, the oldest botanical gardens in the Western Hemisphere; conservation of rare species of plants; aviary containing St Vincent parrots; Dir EMMETT DOYLE.

Dr Cecil Cyrus Museum: Montrose, Kingstown; tel. 457-8981; fax 457-0812; e-mail cyrusclinic@caribsurf.com; f. 2002; colln of medical exhibits, 1,000 pathological specimens, 3,000 photographs; memorabilia of Vincentian life and history, historical maps; Keeper Dr A. CECIL CYRUS.

Fort Charlotte: Berkshire Hill, Kingstown; f. 1806; contains a museum depicting the history of the Black Caribs.

College

Kingstown Medical College: POB 585, Ratho Mill, Kingstown; tel. 456-4832; fax 456-9670; e-mail sgu_info@mssl.com; internet www.sgu.edu; f. 1979; preclinical school affiliated to St George's Univ., Grenada; Dean Dr EDWARD S. JOHNSON.

The Higher Education System

In 1962 Western Samoa (as it was then known) gained independence, having been governed by New Zealand since 1919, first as a League of Nations mandate and then as a UN Trust Territory. The current name was adopted in 1997. The National University of Samoa was founded in 1988 and other institutions of higher education include a branch campus of the University of the South Pacific. In 2001 some 1,179 students were enrolled in higher education.

Admission to non-university level higher education is on the basis of the Samoa School Certificate, while admission to university-level higher education requires completion of Senior Secondary school and award of the Pacific Senior Secondary School Certificate. The National University of Samoa and University of the Pacific also offer one-year pre-university preparation and foundation courses. Sub-degree level qualifications include one-year Certificates and one- or two-year Diplomas. Undergraduate Bachelors degrees at the National University of Samoa and the University of the South Pacific last three years and qualify students for the postgraduate Masters, which follows a two-year programme of study.

Learned Society

GENERAL

UNESCO Office Apia: Box 5766, Mata'utu-Uta Post Office, Apia; tel. 24276; fax 22253; e-mail apia@unesco.org; f. 1984; designated Cluster Office for Australia, Cook Islands, Fiji, Kiribati, Marshall Islands, Federated States of Micronesia, Nauru, New Zealand, Niue, Palau, Papua New Guinea, Samoa, Solomon Islands, Tonga, Tuvalu and Vanuatu; documentation centre; Dir VISESIO PONGI.

Libraries and Archives

Apia

Avele College Library: POB 45, Apia; tel. 20831; 5,000 vols serving 520 students.

Nelson Memorial Public Library: POB 598, Apia; tel. and fax 21208; e-mail jpgodinet@lesamoa.net; f. 1959; 92,000 vols; 1 branch library on Savaii island; 1 bookmobile; special collections: R. L. Stevenson, Samoa and Pacific; Sr Librarian JACINTA P. GODINET.

Museum

Apia

Robert Louis Stevenson Museum: POB 850, Apia; tel. 20798; fax 25428; e-mail rlsm@ipasifika.net; f. 1990; writer Robert Louis Stevenson's (1850–1894) restored house and estate; Manager SOLOIA M. FRITZ.

University

IUNIVESITE AOAO O SAMOA
(National University of Samoa)

POB 1622, Apia
Telephone: 20072
Fax: 20938
E-mail: registrar@nus.edu.ws
Internet: www.nus.edu.ws

Founded 1984
Academic year: February to November

Vice-Chancellor: MAGELE MAUILIUA MAGELE
Registrar: FALANA'IPUPU TANIELU AIAFI
Librarian: AIFA'I TOGI TUNUPOPO

Number of teachers: 91
Number of students: 1,400

Publications: *Jafnus* (arts, annually), *Prismcs* (science, annually)

HEADS OF FACULTIES

Faculty of Arts: TUILOMA SUSANA TAUA'A
Faculty of Commerce: WOOD SALELE
Faculty of Education: GATOLOAIFA'AANA TILIA-NAMUA AFAMASAGA
Faculty of Nursing: FULISIA PITA-UO AIAVAO
Faculty of Science: IOANA CHAN MOW
Institute of Samoan Studies: Prof. LEAPAI LAU ASOFOU SO'O

Colleges

Avele College: POB 45, Apia; tel. 20831; f. 1924, under Education Department from 1966; five-year courses; 520 students, including students from the Tokelau Islands; Principal L. A. SANERIVI.

University of the South Pacific, Alafua Campus: Private Bag, Apia; tel. 21671; fax 22933; e-mail enquiries@samoa.usp.ac.fj; internet www.usp.ac.fj/soa; f. 1977; academic year February to December; diploma, degree and higher degree courses; library: 15,000 vols, 1,000 periodicals; 19 teachers; 200 students; Pro-Vice-Chancellor Dr RUBY VA'A (acting); publs *IRETA South Pacific Agriculture News* (monthly), *Journal of South Pacific Agriculture* (quarterly), *South Pacific Agricultural Teacher* (quarterly); (see also Fiji chapter).

SAN MARINO

The Higher Education System

San Marino evolved as a city-state in the early Middle Ages and is the sole survivor of the numerous independent states that existed in Italy before its unification in the 19th century. A treaty of friendship and co-operation with Italy was signed in 1862, renewed in March 1939 and revised in September 1971. The only institution of higher education is the Università degli Studi di San Marino (founded 1985). In 2005/06 19 students attended the Università, and another 843 students were attending courses outside San Marino.

The Rector is the university's senior administrative and academic officer and is responsible for its internal affairs and external relations. The Departments, Centres and Schools constitute the university's academic division, while the Administrative Directorate deals with its financial affairs.

Learned Society

LANGUAGE AND LITERATURE

Alliance Française: Via Prato di Paolo 3, 47872 Acquaviva, San Marino; tel. and fax 0549-882256; e-mail alliancefrsm@yahoo.fr; internet www.alliancefr.it; offers courses and exams in French language and culture and promotes cultural exchange with France.

Library

San Marino

Biblioteca di Stato: Palazzo Valloni, Contrada Omerelli 13, 47890 San Marino; tel. 0549-882248; fax 0549-882295; e-mail biblioteca@omniway.sm; 10,000 vols since 15th c.; Dir ELISABETTA RIGHI IWANEJKO.

Museum

San Marino

Museo di Stato–Galleria d'Arte Moderna e Contemporanea:; tel. 0549-882670; fax 0549-882679; e-mail info@museidistato.sm; internet www.museidistato.sm; 5,000 objects; archaeological finds from the Neolithic to early Middle Ages; architectural remains of the ancient Basilica; paintings and objects from the 17th c. convent of the Clarisse; works of art of the Republic; San Marino coins and medals (1865–1938); Egyptian, Etruscan and Roman archaeological finds donated to the State; Dott.ssa FRANCESCA MICHELOTTI.

University

UNIVERSITÀ DEGLI STUDI DI SAN MARINO

Contrada del Collegio, 47890 San Marino
Telephone: 0549-882541
Fax: 0549-882545
E-mail: rettorato@unirsm.sm
Internet: www.unirsm.sm
Founded 1985
State control

Rector: Prof. GIORGIO PETRONI
Administrative Secretary: Avv. MARIA SCIARRINO
Librarian: Dr ALESSIA GHIRONZI
Library of 40,000 vols, 550 periodicals
Publication: *L'Ateneo del Citano* (annually)

DEANS

Department of Biomedical Studies: Prof. IPPOLITO GIUSEPPE DONINI
Department of Communication: Prof. PATRIZIA VIOLI
Department of Economics and Technology: Prof. VITO ALBINO
Department of Education: Prof. LUIGI GUERRA
Department of Historical and Law Studies: Prof. PIER GIORGIO PERUZZI

SÃO TOMÉ E PRÍNCIPE

The Higher Education System

The Democratic Republic of São Tomé and Príncipe is a group of islands lying in the Gulf of Guinea, off the west coast of Africa, which achieved independence from Portugal in 1975. The Government has made higher education a national priority, however São Tomé e Príncipe is a small, poor and isolated nation, and as such faces many challenges in progressing towards its strategic goals. The Instituto Superior Politécnico de São Tomé e Príncipe was founded in 1997 and is administered by the Government. It offers Bachelors degrees, particularly in teacher training although its curriculum has recently expanded to include areas such as business administration, languages, literature and technology.

Learned Society

LANGUAGE AND LITERATURE

Alliance Française: CP 974, São Tomé; tel. 242300; fax 242309; e-mail alliancefr@cstome .ne.

Libraries and Archives

São Tomé

Arquivo Histórico de São Tomé e Príncipe: CP 87, São Tomé; tel. 222306; fax 224201; e-mail ahstp@cstome.net; f. 1969; 60,000 boxes of documents; 5,000 vols of bibliography; Dir MARIA NAZARÉ DE CEITA.

Biblioteca do Ministério de Agricultura e Pesca: CP 47, São Tomé; tel. 224657; f. 1973; 1,750 vols; Librarian TOMÉ DE SOUSA DA COSTA.

Biblioteca Municipal: São Tomé.

Centro de Documentação Técnica e Científica: São Tomé; 45,000 vols of specialized documents on agriculture, fisheries, economics; 2,000 periodicals; Dir MARIA ROSÁRIO ASSUNÇÃO.

Museum

São Tomé

Museu Nacional: CP 87, São Tomé; tel. 221874; history, ethnography, religious art.

College

Instituto Superior Politécnico de São Tomé e Príncipe: Endereço Ministério da Educação, Quinta de Santo António, CP 41, Príncipe; tel. and fax 223896; e-mail isptsp@ cstome.net; internet www.stome.net/educa/ isp.htm; f. 1997; Dir LÚCIO LIMA VIEGAS PINTO.

SAUDI ARABIA

The Higher Education System

The Kingdom of Saudi Arabia was proclaimed in 1932 following the unification of the central Najd (Nejd) and western Hedjaz regions of the Arabian peninsula under the rule of Ibn Sa'ud, who also established the current ruling Saudi dynasty. The oldest existing institution of higher education is the Madrasat Ahl al-Hadith (founded 1933), a school of Islamic studies. King Saud University (founded 1957; current name 1982) was the first university-level institution, and by 2004 there were 573,736 students enrolled in higher education. Universities mostly consist of colleges and male and female students are often segregated; there are three single-sex institutions. Tertiary institutions in 2004 also included 108 university colleges and 87 colleges exclusively for women. Construction of the first private university, King Faisaliyah University, in partnership with a US technology institute, commenced in 2006. The Council for Higher Education is the supreme national body of post-secondary, non-military education. Quality assurance and accreditation is undertaken by the National Commission for Academic Accreditation and Assessment (founded 2002).

Admission to higher education is based on award of the general Secondary Education Certificate (Tawjihiyah) and performance in the General Aptitude Tests. The Associate degree and undergraduate Diploma are pre-university qualifications offered by community colleges (the undergraduate Diploma is also offered by universities) and are four-semester (two-year) programmes of study. Saudi degrees are awarded on a 'credit–semester' system, whereby students are required to accrue a specified number of credits each semester in order to graduate. Both the Associate degree and undergraduate Diploma require 48–70 credits for graduation. The undergraduate Bachelors degree is often a four-year programme of study, although degrees in professional fields of study such as medicine, pharmacy, engineering and architecture last upwards of five years. 120 credits is the minimum requirement for graduation. Graduates holding the Bachelors degree are eligible for admission to the postgraduate Diploma or Masters degree. The postgraduate Diploma lasts one year (30 credits) and the Masters degree is a two-year course (42 credits), including submission of a dissertation. The highest university degree is the Doctorate, which requires a minimum of three years of study and research, culminating in the public defence of a dissertation.

Post-secondary technical and vocational education is supervised by the General Organization for Technical Education and Vocational Training, and the admission criteria are the same as university education. Institutions offering technical and vocational education include Colleges of Technology, Higher Technical Institutes, Pre-Vocational and Vocational Training Centres, Trade Schools and Junior Health Colleges. Colleges of Technology provide two-year courses of education leading to the award of the Technical College Certificate; Higher Technical Institutes offers a Diploma programme; Trade Schools specialise in programmes of study relating to trades and professions; and Junior Health Colleges train technicians for the health services profession.

Learned Societies

BIBLIOGRAPHY, LIBRARY SCIENCE AND MUSEOLOGY

Arab Regional Branch of the International Council on Archives (ARBICA): Institute of Public Administration, POB 205, Riyadh 11141; tel. (1) 476-1600, ext. 462; close collaboration with ICA, UNESCO and other international organizations; mems: 20 Arab countries; Pres. A. TAMINI (Tunisia); Sec.-Gen. FAHD AL-ASKAR (Saudi Arabia); publ. *Arab Archives Journal* (annually).

LANGUAGE AND LITERATURE

British Council: Tower B, 2nd Fl., Al Mousa Centre, Olaya St, POB 58012, Riyadh 11594; e-mail riyadh@sa.britishcouncil.org; internet www.britishcouncil.org/saudiarabia; teaching centre (men's and women's sections); offers courses and exams in English language and British culture and promotes cultural exchange with the UK; attached teaching centres in Jeddah and Dammam; Dir ALAN SMART; Teaching Centre Man. (Men's section) MALCOLM JARDINE; Teaching Centre Man. (Women's section) DORA GARRY.

NATURAL SCIENCES

Biological Sciences

Saudi Biological Society: King Saud University, POB 2455, Riyadh 11451; tel. (1) 467-5835; fax (1) 467-5833; f. 1975; 350 mems; Pres. Dr I. A. IRIF; Sec.-Gen. Dr F. AL-MANA; publs *Proceedings*, *Abstract and Programme of Annual Conference*, *Journal of the Saudi Biological Society*.

Research Institutes

GENERAL

King Faisal Centre for Research and Islamic Studies: POB 51049, Riyadh 11543; tel. (1) 465-2255; fax (1) 465-9993; e-mail skheragi@kff.com; internet www.kff.com; f. 1983; part of King Faisal Foundation; research in various fields of Islamic civilization; library of 85,000 books, 2,400 periodicals, 23,833 original MSS, 13,000 microfilm and microfiche; audiovisual library of 10,000 vols; children's library of 17,000 vols; Chair. HRH Prince TURKI AL-FAISAL; Sec.-Gen. Dr YAHYA MAHMOUD AL-JUNAID; publs *Al-Faisal* (monthly), *Journal of Linguistic Studies* (in arabic, 6 a year).

ECONOMICS, LAW AND POLITICS

Islamic Research and Training Institute: POB 9201, Jeddah 21413; tel. (2) 636-1400; fax (2) 637-8927; e-mail irti@isdb.org; internet www.irti.org; f. 1982; part of Islamic Development Bank; research to enable the economic and financial activities of the IDB's mem. countries to conform to the Islamic Sharia; research into all aspects of mem. countries' economic and financial systems; training of personnel (but no formal teaching courses); language of instruction: Arabic; library of 9,000 vols; Dir Prof. Dr MABID ALI AL-JARHI.

EDUCATION

Centre for Research in Islamic Education: POB 1034, Mecca; tel. (2) 556-5677; fax (2) 558-6707; f. 1980 by the Organization of the Islamic Conference, affiliated 1982 to Umm Al-Qura University; aims to promote Islamic values in education through research, development and training; Dir Dr ABDURRAZZAK AHMED ZAFAR.

HISTORY, GEOGRAPHY AND ARCHAEOLOGY

King Abdul Aziz Research Centre: POB 2945, Riyadh 11461; fax (1) 441-7020; f. 1972 in memory of the late king; historical, geographical, literary and cultural material; library of 28,000 vols, 200 periodicals; also the private library of the late king (2,000 vols); historical archive including documents in various languages, especially Turkish and English, and Arabic MSS; King Abdul Aziz Memorial Hall shows events in the late king's life, especially his military battles; Sec.-Gen. Dr FAHD AL-SEMMARI; publ. quarterly cultural magazine.

TECHNOLOGY

Bureau de Recherches Géologiques et Minières (BRGM): POB 1492, Jeddah; (see main entry under France).

Libraries and Archives

Jeddah

Educational Library: General Directorate of Broadcasting, Press and Publications, Jeddah.

Mecca

Abbas Kattan Library: Mecca; 7,800 vols, 200 MSS.

Library of Alharam: Mecca; 6,000 vols.

Madrasat Ahl Al Hadith Library: Mecca.

Medina

Islamic University Library: POB 170, Medina; tel. (4) 847-4080; fax (4) 847-4560; f. 1961; consists of a central library and eleven brs; 143,000 vols, 27,772 MSS, 8,761 microfilms, 3,247 theses.

King Abdul Aziz Library: Medina; tel. (4) 823-2134; fax (4) 823-2126; f. 1983; 120,000 vols and MSS; Dir D. ABDULRAHMAN BIN SULIMAN ALMUZINY.

Riyadh

Institute of Public Administration Library: POB 205, Riyadh 11141; tel. (1) 476-8888; fax (1) 479-2136; e-mail library@ipa.edu.sa; internet www.ipa.edu.sa; f. 1961; 240,000 vols in Arabic, English and French, 1,088 periodical titles, 55,000 Saudi public records, 4,953 official publications, 33,420 microforms, 712 CD-ROMs; Dir-Gen. EN MOSTAFA SADHAN.

King Abdulaziz Public Library: POB 86486, Riyadh 11622; tel. (1) 491-1300; fax (1) 491-1949; f. 1985; 275,000 vols (Arabic and non-Arabic), 1,100 current periodicals, 2,500 MSS, 53,000 historic documents on microform, 5,000 audiovisual items, doctoral dissertations; equestrian information; Supervisor-Gen. FAISAL A. AL-MUAAMMAR.

King Saud University Libraries: POB 22480, Riyadh 11495; tel. (1) 467-6148; fax (1) 467-6162; e-mail f10L001@ksu.edu.sa; f. 1957; central library and 7 branches; 1.1 million vols, 3,000 periodicals, 20,000 MSS, 90,000 government publications, 22,000 microfilm items, 4,000 microfiche items, 16,000 audiovisual items; Dean Dr SULAIMAN AL-OGLA; publ. journals.

Library of the King Abdulaziz City for Science and Technology: POB 6086, Riyadh 11442; tel. (1) 488-3555; fax (1) 488-3118; 50,000 vols, 75,000 technical reports; Director, Information Systems HAMAD AL-SADOUN.

National Library: King Faisal St, Riyadh; f. 1968; c. 37,000 vols in Arabic, English, French; 150 MSS; Dir ABDUR RAHMAN AL SARRA.

Saudi Arabian Standards Organization Information Centre: POB 3437, Riyadh 11471; tel. (1) 452-0000; fax (1) 452-0193; f. 1972; 10,000 vols, 650,000 nat., int. and foreign standards; Dir MOHAMMAD ALMESHARI.

Museum

Riyadh

National Museum, Riyadh: POB 3734 Riyadh 11481; tel. (1) 403-0104; fax (1) 404-1391; e-mail info@saudimuseum.com; internet www.saudimueum.com; f. 1999; Saudi history, archaeology, geology, trade, social life and ethnography, and man's relationship with the Universe; language of instruction: Arabic; Dir-Gen. Dr ALI SALEH AL-MOGHANNAM.

Universities

ISLAMIC UNIVERSITY OF IMAM MUHAMMAD IBN SAUD

POB 5701, Riyadh 11432
Telephone: (1) 258-0812
Fax: (1) 259-0271
Founded 1953, University status 1974
State control

Language of instruction: Arabic
Academic year: August to June
President: Dr ABDULLAH IBN YOUSUF AL-SHIBL
Vice-Presidents: Dr SULAIMAN IBN ABDULLAH ABA AL-KHALIL, Dr MOHAMMAD IBN ABDUL-RAHMAN AL-RUBAYE
Vice-Rector for the Islamic Institutes: Dr SALEH IBN MOHAMMAD AL-HASSAN
Dean of Academic Research: Dr ABDULLAH IBN ABDULLRAHMAN AL-RABEE
Dean of Admission and Registration: Dr ABDULAZIZ IBN RASHID AL-OBAIDI
Dean of Admission and Students' Affairs in Qassim: Dr MEZAYAD IBN IBRAHIM AL-MEZAYAD
Dean of Admission and Students' Affairs in the South: Dr SAAD IBN HUSAIN OTHMAN
Dean of Institutes Abroad: Dr BANDAR IBN FAHAD AL-SEWILEM
Dean of Libraries: Dr KHALID IBN ABDULATIF AL-ARFAJ
Dean of Postgraduate Studies: Dr ABDUL AZIZ IBN MUHAMMED AL-FAISAL
Dean of Students: Sheikh ALI IBN SULAIMAN AL-SALHI
Dean of University Centre for Community Service and Continuing Education: Dr ALI IBN ABDULLAH AL-ZIBEN
Number of teachers: 1,648
Number of students: 39,938
Publication: *University Bulletin*

DEANS AND DIRECTORS

College of Arabic Language: Dr AHMED IBN HAFEZ AL-HAKAMI
College of Arabic and Social Sciences (Qassim): Dr MOHAMMAD IBN SULAIMAN-RAJHI
College of Arabic and Social Sciences (in the South): Dr ALI IBN MUHAMMAD ARISH
College of Fundamentals of Religion: Dr MOHAMMAD IBN ABDULLAH AL-FEHAID
College of Islamic Law and Fundamentals of Religion (in the South): Dr ABDULAZIZ IBN ALI AL-GHAMDI
College of Islamic Law and Islamic Studies (Ahsaa): Dr MOHAMMAD IBN ALI AL-MULHIM
College of Islamic Call Dawa (Medina): Dr MOSTAFA IBN OMAR HALABI
College of Islamic Call and Mass Communication: Dr ABDULAZIZ IBN IBRAHIM AL-ASKAR
College of Islamic Law and Fundamentals of Religion (Al-Qassim): Dr ABDUL RAHMAN AL-MEZAINI (acting)
College of Islamic Law (Sharia): Dr ABDUL-RAHMAN IBN MOHAMMAD AL-SADHAN
College of Social Sciences: Dr ASSAF IBN ALI AL-HAWASS
Female University Study Centre: Dr ABDUL-KARIM IBN MOHAMMAD ABDUL KARIM AL-HEMEDI
Higher Judiciary Institute: Dr IBRAHIM IBN ABDULLAH AL-BARAHIM
Institute for Teaching Arabic to Non-Arabs (Riyadh): Dr MOHAMMAD IBN IBRAHIM AL-UHAIDIB

ISLAMIC UNIVERSITY AT MEDINA

POB 170, Medina
Telephone: (1) 847-4080
Fax: (1) 827-4560
Internet: www.iu.edu.sa
Founded 1961
State control
Language of instruction: Arabic
Chancellor: Dr ABDULLAH BIN SALAH AL-ABID
Vice-Rector: ABDUL MUHSIN BEN HAMAD AL-ABBAD
Number of teachers: 620
Number of students: 3,140.

COLLEGES

College of the Arabic Language.
College of Dawa and Usul-Al-Din.
College of the Holy Koran and Islamic Studies.
College of Islamic Law (Sharia).
College of Prophet Sayings (Hadeith) and Islamic Studies.

KING ABDULAZIZ UNIVERSITY

POB 1026, Jeddah 21441
Telephone: (2) 695-1995
Fax: (2) 640-5974
Internet: www.kaau.edu.sa
Founded 1967
State control
Languages of instruction: Arabic, English
Academic year: September to June
President: Prof. GHAZIO O. MADANI
Vice-President: Prof. OSAMA S. TAYEB
Vice-President for Graduate Studies and Academic Research: Prof. FOUAD M. GHAZALI
Supervisor-General for Administration and Financial Affairs: Dr SAMIR A. MURSHID
Librarian: Dr MOFAKHAR H. KHAN
Library of 500,000 vols
Number of teachers: 1,145
Number of students: 30,773
Publication: Publications: research publications, bulletins

DEANS

Faculty of Arts and Humanities: Dr M. A. ABOZEID
Faculty of Dentistry: Prof. H. H. FATANI
Faculty of Earth Sciences: Dr M. O. NASSIEF
Faculty of Economics and Administration: Prof. A. A. SOFI
Faculty of Education: Dr A. I. HAFIZ
Faculty of Engineering: Dr M. S. AL-JIFFRI
Faculty of Marine Science: Dr O. A. HASHIM
Faculty of Medicine and Allied Sciences: Dr S. A. MIRA
Faculty of Meteorology, Environment and Arid Land Agriculture: Dr R. A. KABLI
Faculty of Science: Prof. M. A. ALHARBI

PROFESSORS

Faculty of Arts and Humanities:

AL-BAGHDADI, M. M., Arabic Literature
AL-DIGS, K. S., Islamic Literature
AL-JERASH, M. A., Climatology and Quantitative Methods
AL-KHERIJI, A. M., Social Development
AL-ZEID, I. M., History
ANQAWI, A. A., Medieval Islamic History
BAGADER, A. A., Social Changes
OMER, M. Z., Modern History
TASHKANDI, A. S., Arabic Manuscripts

Faculty of Dentistry:

ABDULRAHMAN, A., Paediatric Dentistry
AL-JEYAR, I. L., Operative
AL-KHATEB, M. M., Fixed Prosthodontics
AL-SABBAGH, A. M., Oral Surgery
FARGHALY, M. M., Dental Public Health
KAMAR, A. A., Dental Biomaterials
KATALDO, A., Oral Pathology
MASOUD, A. J., Endodontics
MOHAMED, M. A., Operative
MOUSTAFA, M. A., Removable Prosthodontics, Partial Dentures
NADA, A. M., Removable Prosthodontics, Partial Dentures
OMAR, T. A., Oral Pathology
SAMAH, A., Paediatric Dentistry
SHARQAWI, M. M., Operative
SHOUKRY, M. M. S., Periodontics

Faculty of Earth Sciences:

ALLOUSH, M. A., Building Materials
AL-MAHDI, O. R., Mineral Resources

AL-NASSER, H. S., Geophysics
AL-SHANTI, A. M., Mineralogy
BASAHEL, A. N., Structural Geology
MARZOUKI, M. H., Petrology and Mineralogy
NASSIEF, A. O., Petrology and Mineralogy
RADEEN, A. A., Petrology and Mineralogy
SHAREEF, F. A., Petroleum and Stratigraphy
SHEHATA, W. M., Engineering Geology

Faculty of Economics and Administration:

AL-AMRI, B. O., Civil Law
AL-SOBIANI, A. A., Administration and Management Planning
ALAKI, M. A., Administration and Management Relations
AL-JEFRI, Y. A., Business Administration
ALSABBAB, A. A., Administration and Management Relations
BAIOUMI, A. M., Cost and Management Accounting
BAMOKHRAMA, A. S., Economics
FADEL, S. Y., International Relations
HASANAIN, O. S., Cost Accounting
MADANI, G. O., Finance and Investment
OMRAN, O. A., Law
SOFI, A. A., Financial Administration
ZA'ED, M. E., Cost Accounting
ZOBAIR, M. O., Monetary Theory

Faculty of Education:

ABDULRADHI, H. M., Physics and Theory
AL-MOJADDADI, M. H. M., Shariah and Legal System
AL-OQABI, A. H., Modern History
AL-SHATAIRI, B. A., Chemistry
BADAWI, A. A., History
BADAWI, F. A., Ancient History
BAMASHMOOS, S. M., Educational Planning
BEDAIR, A. H. M., Biochemistry
HAMID, M. A. I., Weaving
HASSAN, N. M. A., Psychology
JALLOON, A. D., Archery
KHALIL, M. S. M., Fish Anatomy
KHATIR, K. I. M., Tradition of the Prophet
KHOGALI, M. M., Human Geography
MADBROOK, N. A., Principles of Language
REDWAN, M. N., Wrestling
SHAIKH, A. A., English Language Teaching Methods
SHEHATAH, M. N., Entomology

Faculty of Engineering:

ABD. EL-LATIF, A. K., Mechanical Design and Stress Analysis
ABDEL RAHMAN, M. M., Aerodynamics
ABDIN, M. F., Metrology and Advanced Manufacturing Technology
ABDUL-MAJID, S., Nuclear Instrumentation
ABOKHASHABA, A., Metal Cutting and Spare Parts
ABOLANIN, G. M., Heat and Energy Transfer
ABOLFARAJ, W. H., Industrial Engineering
ABORAZIZAH, O. S., Civil Engineering
AHMED, K. M., Structure and Construction
AKYURT, M., Mechanisms and Robotics
AL-IDRISI, M. M., Operational Research
AL-NOURY, S. I., Structure
ALP, T. Y., Physical Metallurgy
ALY, S. E., Desalination Technology and Two-Phase Flow
AWAD, A. E., Biotechnology, Floriculture
DARWISH, M. A., Rock Blasting
ELGILLANI, D. A., Mineral Processing and Metallurgy
EL-NAGGAR, M. M., Extractive Metallurgy
FATHALAH, K., Heat and Mass Transfer
FATTAH, A. A., Nuclear Reactor Safety and Nuclear Desalination
FOUAD, A. A., Nuclear Desalination
GHAZALI, F. M., Geotechnics
HAQUE, M. Z., Mine Management and Mining Law
KUTBI, I. I., Nuclear Desalination

MOHAMED, S. E., Electrical Power Engineering
NAHHAS, M. N., Aviation Engineering
MOUSSA, H. A., Electrical Power Engineering
NAHHAS, M. N., Aviation Engineering
NAJJAR, Y., Gas Turbines, Engines and Energy Systems
NAWAIR, M. H., Human Factors
RAIH, M. A., Aviation Engineering
RUSHDI, A. M., Computer Engineering and Electrical Communication
SABBAGH, J. A., Heat and Energy Transfer
WAFA, F. F., Structural Engineering
WANAS, M. A., Electronics
YORULMAZ, Y. K., Petroleum Refining and Petrochemicals

Faculty of Marine Sciences:

AHMAD, F., Residual and Tidal Currents
BEHAIRY, A. K. A., Modern Marine Sediments
EL-NAKKADI, A. N., Biochemistry
KHAFAJI, A. K., Marine Plant Physiology
NIAZ, G. R., Marine Biochemistry

Faculty of Medicine and Allied Sciences:

ABDULMONAM, N. A., Community Medicine
AHMAD, A. O., Haematology
AJABNOOR, M. A., Biochemistry
AL-ARDAWI, M. S., Biochemistry
AL-AWWAD, A. M., Chemistry
AL-BADWI, A. A., Surgery
AL-JOHARI, K. M., Anatomy
AL-KHATEEB, A. M., Physics
AL-MATRAWI, U. M., Parasitology
AL-QADASI, A. A., Biochemistry
AL-SHAIKH, S. A., Paediatrics
ALI, F. M., Medical Technology
ATTALLAH, A. A., Physiology
BASALAMAH, A. H., Obstetrics and Gynaecology
FATANI, H. H., Medicine
ISLAM, S. I., Pharmacology
KHAN, N. M., Anatomy
MATIX, F. A., Microbiology
MUKHTAR, A. M., Surgery
OSMAN, O. O., Pharmacology
RAFFAII, H. M., Surgery
RAZIK, S. M., Surgery
SAJINEE, S. A., Haematology
SALAMA, H. S., Biology
SALMAN, KH. M., Surgery
SHARIF, M. A., Radiology
SHARIF, M. T., Anatomy
SHOBOKSHI, O. A., Medicine
SIRAJ, A. A., E.N.T.
SOLIMAN, S. A., Chemistry
SUKKAR, M. Y., Physiology
SULAIMAN, N. K., Community Medicine
TAYEB, O. S., Pharmacology
TILMISANY, A. M., Pharmacology
YOUSIF, K. M., Surgery
ZAFAR, M. N., Radiology
ZAHRAN, F. M., E.N.T.

Faculty of Meteorology, Environment and Arid Land Agriculture:

ABDURAZZAK, M. G., Water Resources
ABOHASSAN, A. A., Forest Management
AL-HASHIM, G. M., Environmental Toxicology and Health
AL-HIFNY, A. M., Entomology (Bees)
ARAFA, A. S., Environmental Health
EL-AGAMY, S. A., Horticulture
GOKNIL, M. H., Air Pollution
SAMARRAI, S. M., Genetics and Plant Breeding
SHAHEEN, M. A., Genetics and Fruit Breeding

Faculty of Science:

ABOU-ZAID, A. A., Fermentation
AHMAD, I., Theoretical Nuclear Physics
AL-DESSOUKI, T. A., Laser Optics
ALHARBI, M. A., Theoretical Nuclear Physics
AL-SAYAD, G. M., Statistics

BAESHIN, N. A., Genetics
BANAGAH, A. A., Parasitology
BAGHLAF, A. O., Chemistry
BASAHEL, S. N., Chemistry
ELDIN, H. M., Environmental Microbiology
EL-MASHAK, E. M., Biophysics
EZMIRLI, T. S., Chemistry
FARAG, A. A., Vertebrate Zoology
GHANEM, K. M., Biotechnology
KHOJA, S. M., Enzymes and Metabolic Regulation
MAGHRABI, Y. M., Plant Physiology
MELIBARI, A. A., Biology
RAFI, M., Experimental Molecular Physics
SABBAK, O. A., Chemistry
SAHAB, S. M., Mathematics
SEJININ, M. J., Plant Pathology
SHAHAB, F., Theoretical Particle Physics
SOLEIMAN, A. H., Chemistry
TAHER, M. O., Entomology (Bionomics)
TAWFIK, K. A., Plant Pathology

ATTACHED RESEARCH INSTITUTES

Islamic Economics Research Centre: Dir Dr M. A. ELGARI.

King Fahd Medical Research Centre: Dir Dr Z. M. BANJAR.

KING FAHD UNIVERSITY OF PETROLEUM AND MINERALS

POB 5082, Dhahran 31261

Telephone: (3) 860-0000

Fax: (3) 860-3018

E-mail: rector@kfupm.edu.sa

Internet: www.kfupm.edu.sa

Founded 1963, University status 1975

State control with semi-autonomous operation under a Board of the University

Languages of instruction: English, Arabic

Academic year: September to June (summer semester: June to August)

Chair. of Board of Trustees: HE The Minister of Higher Education Dr KHALID M. AL-ANGARY

Rector: Dr KHALED S. AL-SULTAN

Vice-Rectors: Dr ABDULAZIZ A. AL-SUWAYAN (Academic Affairs), Dr SALEH A. BAKHREBAH (Applied Research), Dr MOHAMMAD O. BUDAIR (Scientific Research and Graduate Studies)

Dean, Admissions and Registration: Dr MAMDOUH M. NAJJAR

Dean of Library Affairs: Dr IBRAHIM M. AL-JABRI

Library of 355,700 vols

Number of teachers: 950

Number of students: 8,155

Publications: *Arabian Journal for Science and Engineering* (6 a year), *CED Newsletter* (2 a year), *CIM Trends* (2 a year), *Engineering Newsletter* (2 a year), *Future* (2 a month), *Graduate Bulletin* (every 2 years), *ITC In-Focus* (4 a year), *Library Newsletter* (2 a year), *Research Newsletter* (2 a year), *Science Newsletter* (2 a year), *Undergraduate Bulletin* (every 2 years)

DEANS

Computer Science and Engineering: Dr JARALLAH S. AL-GHAMDI
Educational Services: Dr MUHAMMAD S. AL-MULHEM
Engineering Sciences and Applied Engineering: Dr SAMIR A. AL-BAIYAT
Environmental Design: Dr SOLAIMAN A. AL-MOHAWIS
Industrial Management: Dr AREF A. AL-ASHBAN
Sciences: Dr MAHMOUD A. NAGADI
Scientific Research: Dr OSAMA A. JANNADI
Graduate Studies: Dr OSAMA A. JANNADI

DEPARTMENTAL CHAIRMEN

College of Computer Science and Engineering (KFUPM Box 5064, Dhahran 31261; tel. (3) 860-2140; fax (3) 860-2366; e-mail dean@ccse.kfupm.edu.sa; internet www.ccse.kfupm.edu.sa/ccse):

Computer Engineering: Dr SADIQ S. MOHAMMED
Information and Computer Science: Dr KANAAN A. FAISAL
Systems Engineering: Dr UMAR M. AL-TURKI

College of Engineering Sciences (KFUPM Box 5056, Dhahran 31261; tel. (3) 860-2500; fax (3) 860-2345; e-mail ces@kfupm.edu.sa; internet www.kfupm.edu.sa/ces/index.htm):

Chemical Engineering: Dr MOHHAMED B. AMIN
Civil Engineering: Dr HAMAD I. AL-ABDUL-WAHHAB
Electrical Engineering: Dr JAMIL M. BAKHESHWAIN
Mechanical Engineering: Dr FALEH A. AL-SULAIMAN
Petroleum Engineering: Dr SIDQI A. ABU-KHAMSIN

College of Environmental Design (KFUPM Box 5051, Dhahran 31261; tel. (3) 860-2580; fax (3) 860-2539; e-mail d-ced@kfupm.edu.sa; internet www.kfupm.edu.sa/ced):

Architectural Engineering: Dr ISMAIL M. BUDAIWI (Dir)
Architecture: Dr ABDULGADER O. AMIR
City and Regional Planning: Dr ADEL S. AL-DOSARY
Construction Engineering and Management: Dr SOLIMAN A. AL-MOHAWIS

College of Industrial Management (KFUPM Box 5073, Dhahran 31261; tel. (3) 860-2700; fax (3) 860-2772; e-mail d-cim@kfupm.edu.sa; internet www.kfupm.edu.sa/cim):

Management and Marketing: Dr EID S. AL-SHAMMARI
Accounting and Management Information Systems: Dr JASSEM S. AL-RUMAIHI
Finance and Economics: Dr IBRAHIM M. AL-GAHTANI

College of Sciences (KFUPM Box 5057, Dhahran 31261; tel. (3) 860-2600; fax (3) 860-2652; e-mail d-cs@kfupm.edu.sa; internet www.kfupm.edu.sa/cs):

Chemistry: Dr ASSAD AHMAD AL-THUKAIR
Earth Sciences: Dr MUSTAFA M. AL-HARIRI
Islamic and Arabic Studies: Dr SULTAN K. HETHLEN
Mathematical Sciences: Dr KHALID M. FURATI
Physics: Dr ALI M. AL-SHUKRI

Research Institute (KFUPM Box 5003, Dhahran 31261; tel. (3) 860-2200; fax (3) 860-3661; e-mail vrar@kfupm.edu.sa; internet www.kfupm.edu.sa/ri):

Centre for Applied Physical Sciences: Dr ABDULRAHMAN A. AL-ARFAJ
Centre for Communications and Computer Research: Dr ADIL S. BALGHONAIM
Centre for Economic and Management Systems: Dr MOHAMMED A. AL-BURAEY
Centre for Engineering Research: Dr ALI A. SHASH
Centre for Environment and Water: Dr ALAADIN A. BUKHARI
Centre for Petroleum and Minerals: Dr ABDULAZIZ A. AL-MAJED
Centre for Refining and Petrochemicals: Dr MOHAMMAD A. AL-SALEH

KING FAISAL UNIVERSITY

POB 380, Al-Hassa 31982
and POB 1982, Dammam 31441
Telephone: (Dammam) (3) 587-7000

Fax: (Dammam) (3) 587-6748
Telephone: (Al-Hassa) (3) 850-0000
Fax: (Al-Hassa) (3) 580-1243
Internet: www.kfu.edu.sa
Founded 1975
State control
Languages of instruction: Arabic, English
Academic year: September to June
President: Prof. Dr YUSSUF M. AL-GINDAN
Vice-President: Dr ABDULAZIZ al-SAATI (Dammam)
Vice-President for Academic Affairs: Dr SAAD M. AL-HAREKY (Al-Hassa)
Vice-President for Graduate Studies and Scientific Research: Dr ABDULLAH I. AL-SAADAT (Al-Hassa)
Secretary-General: Dr SAAD MUHAMMAD AL-HAREKY
Librarian: Dr FADEL M. HOUSAWI (Al-Hassa)
Number of teachers: 717
Number of students: 12,880
Publications: *Basic and Applied Sciences* (2 a year), *Humanities and Management Sciences* (2 a year)

DEANS

College of Agricultural and Food Sciences (Al-Hassa): Dr ABDULLAH S. AL-GAMDI
College of Applied and Community Service (Al-Hassa): Dr ADNAN AL-MULHIM
College of Applied Medical Sciences (Dammam): Dr BASIL A. AL-SHIAKH
College of Architecture and Planning (Dammam): Dr MOHAMMAD MASOUD AL-ABDUL-LAH
College of Clinical Pharmacy (Al-Hassa): Dr AHMED A. AL-SHAOIBY
College of Computer Science and Information Tecnology (Al-Hassa): Dr BADIR AL-GOHAR
College of Dentistry (Dammam): Dr ABDUL-SALAM A. AL-SULIAMAN
College of Education (Al-Hassa): Dr MOHAMMAD AL-OMARE
College of Management Sciences and Planning (Al-Hassa): Dr HASSAN AL-HAJHOOJ
College of Medicine (Al-Hassa): Dr ALI AL-SULTAN
College of Medicine (Dammam): Dr ABDUL-LAH M. AL-ROBIASH
College of Nursing (Dammam): Dr NAIF I. AL-AWAAD
College of Science (Al-Hassa): Dr SHAR A. AL-SHIHRY
College of Veterinary Medicine and Animal Resources (Al-Hassa): Dr ABDULLAH AL-AZRAGY

KING KHALID UNIVERSITY

Abha 418, Asir Province
Telephone: (7) 339-0641
Fax: (7) 339-0531
E-mail: kku@kku.edu.sa
Internet: www.kku.edu.sa
Founded 1998
State control
Rector: Dr ABDULLAH al-RASHID
Faculties of Arabic Language, Computer Science, Dentistry, Engineering, Science and Sharia Law; Colleges of Education, Medicine and Medicinal Science and Pharmacy; Institute of English and Translation.

KING SAUD UNIVERSITY

POB 2454, Riyadh 11451
Telephone: (1) 467-0000
Fax: (1) 467-8301
Internet: www.ksu.edu.sa
Founded 1957 as Riyadh University, present name 1982
State control

Language of instruction: Arabic (English in Medicine and Engineering)
Academic year: October to June
President: Dr AHMED MOHAMMAD AL-DHOBAIB
Vice-Presidents: Dr KHALED BIN ABDULRAHMAN FAHAD AL-HAMOUDI, Dr IBRAHIM ABDULRAHMAN AL-MISHAEL
Vice-President, Abha and Qasim Branches: Dr KHALED BIN ABDULRAHMAN FAHAD AL-HAMOUDI (acting)
Registrars and Deans of Admissions: Dr ALI BIN ESA AL-SHABI (Abha Branch): Dr AHMED BIN SALEH AL-TAMI (Qasim Branch): Dr ABDULHALIM ABDULAZIZ MAZI (Riyadh Branch)
Dean of Student Affairs: Dr ABDULELAH BIN SAAD BIN SAIED (acting)
Dean of Library Affairs: Dr SAAD ABDULLAH AL-DHOBYAN
Library: see Libraries and Archives
Number of teachers: 2,768
Number of students: 37,324
Publications: *Journal of King Saud University, Statistical Yearbook, University Bulletin*

DEANS

College of Administrative Sciences: Dr ABDULLAH BIN MOHAMMAD AL-FAISAL
College of Agriculture: Dr SALEH ABDULRAHMAN AL-SEHIBANI
College of Agriculture and Veterinary Medicine: Dr AHMED BIN ALI AL-RUGEIBAH
College of Applied Medical Sciences: Dr FAHD IBN JABER EL-SHAMMARI
College of Architecture and Planning: Dr SULEMAN BIN TURKI AL-SEDAIRY
College of Arts: Dr MOHAMMED BIN MANSHET AL-SHAFY
College of Computer and Information Sciences: Dr ABDULLAH IBRAHIM AL-SALA-MAH
College of Dentistry: Dr ABDULLAH BIN MOHAMMED AL-DOUSARY
College of Economics and Administration (Al-Qasim Campus): Dr HAMED BIN SULAIMAN AL-BAZAE
College of Education: Dr MOHAMMAD BIN SHAT HUSSEIN AL-KHATIB
College of Education in Abha: Dr ABDUL WAHHAB IBN SALEH BABEER
College of Engineering: Dr ABDULAZIZ SALEM AL-ROWEIS
College of Languages and Translation: Dr JASER BIN ABDULRAHMAN AL-JASER
College of Medicine: Dr ABDULRAHMAN BIN SALEH AL-FERAIH
College of Medicine in Abha: Dr MOHAMMAD YEHIA AL-SHEHRI
College of Pharmacy: Dr KHALED ABDUL MUHSAN EL-RUSHUD
College of Science: Dr ABDULRAHMAN BIN MOHAMMED ABU EMMA
College of Graduate Studies: Dr ALI BIN ABDULLAH FAWAZ AL-FERAIH
Arabic Language Institute: Dr MOHAMMAD IBN YASIN ULFI
Centre of Continuing Education and Community Services: Dr ABDULRAHMAN BIN IBRAHIM AL-SHARE
Centre of Women's University Studies: Dr KHAIRIEH IBRAHIM EL-SAGGAF

UMM AL-QURA UNIVERSITY

POB 715, Mecca
Telephone: (2) 557-4644
Fax: (2) 556-4560
E-mail: webmaster@uqu.edu.sa
Internet: www.uqu.edu.sa
Founded 1979 from existing faculties of King Abdulaziz University
Rector: Dr NASIR BIN ABDULLAH al-SALEH
Vice-Rector: Dr SULTAN BIN SAIED BUKHARI

Secretary-General: Dr ABDULLAH BIN ABDUL-REHMAN ABDUH

Library of 450,000 vols
Number of teachers: 1,408
Number of students: 32,000

Publications: *Journal of Arabic Language and Shariah Sciences, Journal of Engineering, Medicine and Applied Sciences, Journal of Social Sciences and Education*

DEANS

Faculty of Applied Sciences: Dr EISA MUHAMMAD RAWAS
Faculty of Arabic Language: Dr SALEH JAMAL BADAWI
Faculty of Dawa and Usul al-Din: Dr MUHAMMAD TAHIR NOOR WALI
Faculty of Education (Mecca): Dr SALEH MUHAMMAD AL-SAIF
Faculty of Education (Taif): Dr SUBHI ABDULHAFEEZ QADI
Faculty of Engineering: Dr TARIG MUHAMMAD NAHASS
Faculty of Medicine: Dr ABDULRAZAG MUHAMMAD NOOR SULTAN
Faculty of Science (Taif): Dr BAKHIT NAFIE AL-MATRAFI
Faculty of Sharia and Islamic Studies: Dr MUHAMMAD ALI AL-UGLA
Faculty of Social Sciences: Dr MUHAMMAD MOSLEH AL-THOMALI
Arabic Language Institute: Dr ABDULLAH AHMAD ATTAS

ATTACHED CAMPUS

Umm Al-Qura University, Taif Campus
Al-Saddad Rd, Shihar, Taif
Telephone: (2) 749-1917
Fax: (2) 746-3008
Founded 1981
President: Dr RASHID BIN RAJIH
Vice-Presidents: Dr MUHAMMAD IBRAHIM AHMED ALI, Higher Studies and Research: Dr SAAD AL-SOBAI, Finance and Administration
Registrar: ALI F. AL-FAER
Librarian: MOHD ADIL USMANI
Library of 50,000 vols
Number of teachers: 90
Number of students: 2,000

DEANS

Faculty of Education: Dr ABDULLAH ABDUL KARIM AL-ABBADI
Faculty of Library Studies: Dr HAMMAD MUHAMMAD AL-SOMALI

Institutes of Higher Education

English Language Teaching Institute: POB 58012, Al Mousa Bldg, Olaya Main Rd, Riyadh 11594; tel. (1) 462-1818; fax (1) 462-0663; f. 1969 by Ministry of Education and directed by the British Council; brs in Jeddah and Dammam; Direct Teaching Operations Man. KEVIN SMITH.

Institute of Public Administration: POB 205, Riyadh 11141; tel. (1) 476-8888; fax (1) 479-2136; f. 1961; conducts training courses for govt and private-sector employees; researches into and offers advice on administrative problems; Dir-Gen. HAMAD I. AL-SALLOOM; publ. *PA Journal* (quarterly, in Arabic).

Jeddah Health Institute: Jeddah; provides basic medical training; similar Institutes at Riyadh and Hofouf.

King Abdulaziz Military Academy: POB 5969, Riyadh; tel. (1) 465-4244; f. 1955; courses given in modern languages, including English, French and Hebrew, science and military subjects; library: 20,000 vols; 1,300 students; publ. *Journal.*

Madrasat Ahl Al Hadith: Mecca; f. 1933; the College provides instruction in the Hadith, Koran, Fiqh, Tawheed and other Islamic religious studies; Principal Sheikh MUHAMMAD ABDUL RAZZAQ; Sec. MUHAMMAD OMAR ABDULHADI.

Technical Institute: Riyadh; f. 1964; 1,000 students.

Yanbu Industrial College: POB 30436, Yanbu al-Sinaiyah; tel. (4) 394-6111; fax (4) 392-0213; e-mail rc_yic@hotmail.com; internet www.yic.edu.sa; f. 1989; engineering technology; library: 11,570 vols; 127 teachers; 1,400 students; Man. Dir BASSAM ABDULLAH YAMANI; Registrar HAMZA ATIK.

SENEGAL

The Higher Education System

Senegal was a French colony from the 17th century until independence was achieved in 1960. The first institution of higher education, a School of Medicine, was founded in 1915; this later became an Institute of Higher Education in 1950 and was incorporated into the new Université Cheikh Anta Diop de Dakar in 1957. Université Cheikh Anta Diop de Dakar is one of the three public universities, the others being Université de Saint-Louis (or Université de Gaston-Berger—founded 1990) and Université de Sahel (founded 1998). Other institutions of higher education, which mirror the French system, include Schools of Science and Veterinary Medicine, Agriculture and Health. In 2003/04 there were 52,300 students in tertiary education. higher education is largely State funded, although some funding is provided by major international organizations such as USAID, the EU and the World Bank.

The secondary school Baccalauréat is the main qualification required for admission to higher education, although applicants without the Baccalauréat can sit an alternative entrance examination. University degrees are divided into three cycles, in accordance with the old French system. The first cycle is an undergraduate course of study lasting two years and leading to the award of one of the following diplomas, depending on the subject area: Diplôme Universitaire d'Etudes Littéraires (humanities), Diplôme Universitaire d'Etudes Scientifiques (sciences), Diplôme d'Etudes Juridiques Générales (law) and Diplôme d'Etudes Economiques Générales (economics). Alternatively, the Ecole Nationale Supérieure de Technologie offers a two-year Diplôme Universitaire de Technologie. The second cycle follows the award of the Diplômes and is, firstly, a one-year programme of study culminating with the award of the Licence degree and, secondly, another year of study after the Licence leading to the award of the Maîtrise. In law and economics the Maîtrise is an integrated second-cycle degree awarded after two years, while in pharmacy, dentistry and medicine the first degrees are, respectively, Diplôme de Pharmacien, Diplôme de Docteur en Chirurgie Dentaire and Diplôme d'Etat de Docteur en Médecine. Finally, the third cycle consists of doctoral-level studies, leading to the award of Diplôme d'Etudes Approfondies after one year and Doctorat de Troisième Cycle after an additional two years. The highest doctoral-level degree is the Doctorat d'Etat, which is awarded following a minimum of two years research in law, economics, pharmacy, arts or science after the award of Doctorat de Troisième Cycle.

The primary qualification for post-secondary technical and vocational education is currently the Brevet de Technicien Supérieur en Maintenance.

Learned Societies

BIBLIOGRAPHY, LIBRARY SCIENCE AND MUSEOLOGY

Association Sénégalaise de Bibliothécaires, Archivistes et Documentalistes: ASBAD, BP 3252, Dakar; tel. 864-27-73; fax 824-23-79; e-mail asbad2000@hotmail.com; internet www.ebad.ucad.sn/asbad; f. 1988; 200 mems; Pres. DJIBRIL NDIAYE; Sec. BERNARD DIONE; publ. *Canal I. S. T.* (3 a year).

EDUCATION

UNESCO Office Dakar and Regional Bureau for Education in Africa: BP 3311, Dakar; Located at: 12 ave L. S. Senghor, Dakar; tel. 823-83-93; fax 849-23-23; e-mail dakar@unesco.org; internet www.dakar.unesco.org; f. 1970; designated Cluster Office for Cape Verde, Gambia, Guinea, Guinea-Bissau, Liberia, Senegal, and Sierra Leone; Dir ARMOOGUM PARSURAMEN.

LANGUAGE AND LITERATURE

Alliance Française: 3, Rue Parchappe, BP 1777, Dakar; tel. 821-08-22; fax 822-12-25; e-mail alliancefg@gamtel.gm; internet www.alliancefr-senegalgambie.org; offers courses and exams in French language and culture and promotes cultural exchange with France; attached teaching centres in Kaolack, St Louis, Tambacounda and Ziguinchor; also responsible for operations in Gambia; Dir of Office and of Operations in Senegal and Gambia SERGE AYASSE.

British Council: 34–36 Blvd de la République, Immeuble Sonatel, BP 6232 Dakar; tel. 822-20-15; fax 821-81-36; e-mail postmaster@britishcouncil.sn; internet www.britishcouncil.org/senegal; teaching centre; offers courses and exams in English language and British culture and promotes cultural exchange with the UK; library of 3,500 vols; Dir ANDREW McNAB.

Goethe-Institut: 2, Ave Hassan II (ex Sarraut), BP 3264, Dakar; tel. 823-04-70; fax 822-34-82; e-mail info@dakar.goethe.org; internet www.goethe.de/dakar; offers courses and examinations in German language and culture and promotes cultural exchange with Germany; Dir ULRICH RIEKEN.

Research Institutes

GENERAL

Institut de Recherche pour le Développement, Centre de Dakar (IRD): BP 1386, Route des Pères Maristes, Dakar; tel. 832-34-80; fax 832-43-07; e-mail durand@orstom.sn; internet www.ird.sn; f. 1950; soil biology, pedology, medical entomology, hydrology, geology, nematology, demography, economics, zoology, botany, agronomy, geography, sociology, nutrition, marine fisheries, public health, tree viruses, vegetal ecology, geophysics, microbiology; library of 10,000 vols; Dir J. R. DURAND; (see main entry under France).

Institut Fondamental d'Afrique Noire Cheikh Anta Diop: BP 206, Université Cheikh Anta Diop de Dakar, Dakar; tel. 824-16-52; fax 824-49-18; e-mail bifan@ucad.sn; internet www.refer.sn; f. 1936, reconstituted 1959; scientific and humanistic studies on Black Africa; library and museums (see below); Dir DJIBRIL SAMB; publs *Bulletin de l'IFAN, Série A—Sciences Naturelles, Série B—Sciences Humaines, Notes Africaines* (quarterly), *Mémoires de l'IFAN, Initiations et Etudes Africaines, Instructions Sommaires, Catalogues et Documents,* etc.

AGRICULTURE, FISHERIES AND VETERINARY SCIENCE

Institut Sénégalais de Recherches Agricoles (ISRA): BP 3120, Route des Hydrocarbures, Bel-Air, Dakar; tel. 832-24-31; fax 832-24-27; e-mail bakhayok@isra.refer.sn; f. 1974; research in all fields of agriculture, forestry and pisciculture; Dir Dr MOUSSA BAKHAYOKHU; publ. *Rapport Annuel.*

Attached centres:

Centre pour le Développement de l'Horticulture (CDH): BP 2619, Dakar; tel. 835-06-10; fax 835-10-75; f. 1972; market garden research; Dir Dr ALAIN MBAYE.

Centre National de Recherches Agronomiques (CNRA): BP 53, Bambey; tel. 973-60-50; fax 973-60-52; e-mail isracnra@telecomplus.sn; f. 1921; applied agricultural research; 45 research mems; library of 6,700 vols; stations at Louga and Thilmakha; Dir Dr DOGO SECK; publs *Rapport de synthèse, Annuaire analytique des travaux de l'IRAT au Sénégal.*

Centre de Recherche Agronomique de Djibélor: BP 34, Ziguinchor; tel. 991-12-05; fax 991-12-93; Dir SAMBA SALL.

Centre de Recherche Agronomique de Kaolack: BP 199, Kaolack; tel. 941-29-16; fax 941-29-02; Dir Dr MODOU SENE.

Centre de Recherche Agronomique de Saint-Louis: BP 240, Richard-Toll; tel. 961-17-51; fax 961-18-91; Dir Dr SIDY SECK.

Centre de Recherches Océanographiques de Dakar-Thiaroye (CRODT): BP 2241, Dakar; tel. 834-05-36; f. 1956; for the study of oceanographic physics and biology; 67 scientists; library of 450 vols and 74 periodicals; Dir DIAFARA TOURE.

Centre de Recherches Zootechniques de Dahra-Djoloff: BP 01, Dahra-Djoloff; tel. 968-61-11; fax 968-62-71; f. 1950; amelioration of local bovine and ovine breeds, rearing and cross-breeding; Dir TAMSIR DIOP.

Centre de Recherches Zootechniques de Kolda: BP 53, Kolda; tel. 996-11-52; fax

996-11-52; f. 1972; amelioration of local bovine and ovine breeds; fodder cultivation; Dir Dr DEMBA FARBA MBAYE.

Direction des Recherches sur les Productions Forestières: BP 2313, Route des Pères Maristes, Dakar-Hann; tel. 832-32-19; fax 832-96-17; Dir Dr PAPE NDIENGOU SALL.

ECONOMICS, LAW AND POLITICS

Institut Africain de Développement Economique et de Planification des Nations Unies (United Nations African Institute for Economic Development and Planning): BP 3186, Dakar; tel. 823-10-20; fax 822-29-64; e-mail idep@sonatel.senet.net; f. 1962 under the aegis of the Economic Comm. for Africa; financed jointly by African states, the UN, and bilateral and multilateral partners; provides training through the organization of courses, seminars, etc., and undertakes research; library of 25,000 vols, 1,400 periodicals; Dir Dr JEGGAN C. SENGHOR; publ. *IDEP Newsletter* (in English and French, 2 a year).

MEDICINE

Institut d'Hygiène Sociale: Ave Blaise-Diagne, Dakar.

Institut Pasteur: BP 220, Dakar; tel. 839-92-00; fax 839-92-10; e-mail pasteur.dakar@pasteur.sn; internet www.pasteur.sn; f. 1896; medical research, microbiology, virology, immunology; library of 2,030 vols, 88 periodicals; Dir Dr CHRISTIAN MATHIOT; publ. *Annual Report.*

Organisme de Recherches sur l'Alimentation et la Nutrition Africaines (ORANA): BP 2089, 39 ave Pasteur, Dakar; tel. 822-58-92; f. 1956; research of African foods and nutritional values, investigations, documentation, teaching; 30 mems; Dir Dr AMADOU MAKHTAR NDIAYE.

TECHNOLOGY

African Regional Centre for Technology/Centre Régional Africain de Technologie: BP 2435, Dakar; tel. 823-77-12; fax 823-77-13; f. 1977 as an intergovernmental institution under the auspices of the OAU and UNECA; aims to promote the use of technology to improve the socio-economic development of Africa; advises and sets up national institutions, holds training seminars and workshops; activities include food science and technology, energy technology, technological consulting and advisory services, training and information and documentation; 31 mem. states; library of 6,000 vols, patents, microfiches, video cassettes; Exec. Dir Dr OUSMANE KANE; publs *African Technodevelopment Bulletin* (English and French, 2 a year), *Alert Africa Newsletter* (quarterly), *Infonet* (irregular).

Bureau de Recherches Géologiques et Minières (BRGM): BP 268, Dakar; tel. 822-72-19; mining, hydrogeology, irrigation; also directs research in Mali and Mauritania; Dir D. FOHLEN.

Libraries and Archives
Dakar

Archives du Sénégal: Immeuble administratif, Ave Léopold Sédar Senghor, Dakar; tel. 823-50-72; fax 822-51-26; e-mail pmarchi@primature.sn; f. 1913; 26,000 vols, 1,500 periodicals, 8,000 official publs, 12 km. of documents; Dir SALIOU MBAYE; publs *Bibliographie du Sénégal* (2 a year), *Rapport Annuel.*

Bibliothèque Centrale, Université Cheikh Anta Diop de Dakar: BP 2006, Dakar; tel. 824-69-81; fax 824-23-79; e-mail hsene@ucad.sn; internet www.bu.ucad.sn; f. 1952; higher education, human and social sciences, law and economics, medicine and pharmacy, science and technology, veterinary science, information science; 353,000 vols, 5,000 periodicals (of which 1,000 are current); Dir HENRI SENE.

Bibliothèque de l'Alliance Française: BP 1777, 2 rue Assane Ndoye, Dakar; tel. 821-08-22; f. 1948; 12,000 vols; Dir PATRICK MANDRILLY.

Bibliothèque de l'Institut Fondamental d'Afrique Noire: BP 206, Dakar; tel. 825-00-90; e-mail bibifan@ifan.refer.sn; f. 1936; research in humanities and natural sciences; 70,000 vols, 8,200 brochures, 4,036 collections of periodicals, 1,600 microfilms, 2,566 maps, 32,000 photographs, 2,100 slides, 12,200 files of documents; Librarian GORA DIA.

Centre National de Documentation Scientifique et Technique (CNDST): Ministère de la Recherche Scientifique et de la Technologie (MRST), 61 Blvd Djily Mbaye, BP 3218, Dakar; tel. 822-96-19; fax 822-61-44; e-mail cndst1@primature.sn; f. 1977; maintains a database each of research institutions, researchers, research projects and research results, and a socioeconomic databank on Senegal; Dir MOHAMED FADHEL DIAGNE; publs *Répertoire des sources d'information sur l'environnement*, *Répertoire des organismes de documentation au Sénégal*, *Répertoire des textes législatifs et réglementaires dans le domaine de l'environnement au Sénégal* (annually), *Répertoire des textes législatifs et réglementaires au Sénégal* (annually).

Centre Régional de Recherche et de Documentation pour le Développement Culturel (CREDEC) (Regional Research and Documentation Centre for Cultural Development): 13 ave du Pdt Bourguiba, Dakar; tel. 827-80-59; fax 821-75-15; e-mail fdiallo@infomie.fr; f. 1976; mems: 20 African states; part of African Cultural Institute (see under International); *c.* 3,200 vols, special collections on African crafts; Co-ordinator FALILOU DIALLO; publ. *ICA-Information* (quarterly).

Museums and Art Galleries
Dakar

Musée d'Art Africain de Dakar: BP 6167, Dakar-Étoile; f. 1936; administered by Institut Fondamental d'Afrique Noire; ethnography and African art; Curator Dr TAHIROU DIAW.

Gorée

Musée de la Mer: Gorée; f. 1959; administered by Institut Fondamental d'Afrique Noire; sea sciences, oceanography, fishing; Curator Dr SECK.

Musée Historique: Gorée; administered by Institut Fondamental d'Afrique Noire; Curator Dr ABDOULAYE CAMARA.

Universities

UNIVERSITÉ CHEIKH ANTA DIOP DE DAKAR

BP 5005, Dakar-Fann
Telephone: 825-75-28

Fax: 825-37-24
E-mail: info@ucad.sn
Internet: www.ucad.sn

Founded 1915 as École de Médecine, became Institut des Hautes Études 1950; university status 1957
State control
Language of instruction: French
Academic year: October to July

Rector: ABDEL KADER BOYE
Vice-President: MOUSTAPHA SOURANG
Secretary-General: ALIOUNE BADARA DIAGNE
Librarian: HENRI SENE

Library: see Libraries and Archives
Number of teachers: 700
Number of students: 22,000

Publications: *Annuaire* (periodical), *Bulletin de l'IFAN* (periodical, 3 a year), *Dakar médical* (periodical, 3 a year), *Journal de la Faculté des Sciences et Techniques* (periodical, 2 a year), *Notes Africaines* (periodical), *Revue de l'Ecole Normale Supérieure* (periodical, 2 a year), *Revue de la Faculté des Lettres* (periodical)

DEANS

Faculty of Arts and Humanities: MAMADOU KANDJI
Faculty of Economics and Management: MOUSTAPHA KASSE
Faculty of Law and Political Science: MOUSTAPHA SOURANG
Faculty of Medicine, Pharmacy and Odonto-Stomatology: RENÉ NDOYE
Faculty of Science and Technology: LIBASSE DIOP

ATTACHED RESEARCH INSTITUTES

Centre d'Etudes des Sciences et Techniques de l'Information: f. 1965; offers diploma courses in journalism; Dir BIRAHIM MOUSSA GUEYE.

Ecole des Bibliothécaires, Archivistes et Documentalistes: BP 3252, Dakar; tel. 825-76-60; f. 1963, attained present status as university institute 1967; provides a two-year librarianship course, giving priority to students from Francophone countries in Africa; 15 teachers; 200 students; Dir MBAYE DIAM.

École Normale Supérieure: Dir VALDIODIO NDIAYE.

École Supérieure Polytechnique: Dir ABIB NGOM.

Institut Fondamental d'Afrique Noire Cheikh Anta Diop (see Research Institutes).

Institut National Supérieur de l'Education Populaire et du Sport: Dir DJIBRIL SECK.

Institut de Recherches sur l'Enseignement de la Mathématique, de la Physique et de la Technologie: Dir MAMADOU SANGHARE.

Institut des Sciences de l'Environnement: Dir AMADOU TIDIANE BA.

Institut des Sciences de la Terre: Dir ABDOULAYE DIA.

UNIVERSITÉ DU SAHEL

BP 5355 33, Sotrac-Mermoz, Dakar

Telephone: 860-99-75
Fax: 860-99-75
E-mail: unis@refer.sn
Internet: www.unis.sn

Founded 1998
State control

President: ISSA SALL

Number of teachers: 80
Number of students: 400

Publications: *Les Annales du Sahel, Le Sahalien* (monthly)

DIRECTORS

School of Economics and Administration: MOUSTAPHA THIOUINE
School of Educational Sciences: BADARA SALL
School of Humanities and Civilization: BADARA SALL
School of Law and Political Science: MARIE-PIERRE TRAORÉ SARR
School of Science, Engineering and Technology: KHADIR DIOP
School of Social Sciences: MAME DEMBA THIAM

UNIVERSITÉ DE SAINT-LOUIS
(Université Gaston-Berger)

BP 234, Saint-Louis
Telephone: 961-19-06
Fax: 961-18-84
E-mail: webmaster@ugb.sn
Internet: www.ugb.sn
Founded 1990
State control
Language of instruction: French
Academic year: October to July
Rector: Prof. NDIAWAR SARR
Secretary-General: PAPA SÉKOU SONKO
Librarian: MAMADOU LAMINE NDOYE
Library of 18,500 vols

Number of teachers: 237
Number of students: 2,663

HEADS OF TEACHING AND RESEARCH UNITS

Applied Mathematics and Computer Science: MARY TEUW NIANE
Arts and Humanities: GORA MBODJ
Economics and Management: ADAMA DIAW
Law: SAMBA TRAORÉ

Colleges

Ecole Inter-Etats des Sciences et Médecine Vétérinaires (EISMV): BP 5077, Dakar; tel. 865-10-08; fax 825-42-83; e-mail mariamd@eismv.refer.sn; internet www .refer.sn/sngal_ct/edu/eismv/eismv.htm; f. 1968; representing 13 French-speaking African countries; 36 teachers (17 full-time, 19 part-time); 232 students; Dir Prof. FRANÇOIS ADÉBAYO ABIOLA.

Ecole Nationale d'Administration du Sénégal: BP 5209, Dakar; f. 1959; Dir A. N'DENE N'DIAYE.

Ecole Nationale d'Economie Appliquée: BP 5084, Dakar/Fann; tel. 824-79-28; f. 1963; library: 4,500 vols; 147 students; Dir SAMBA DIONE; publ. *Bulletin de Recherche Appliquée.*

Ecole Nationale Supérieure d'Agriculture: BP A 296, Thiès; tel. 951-12-57; fax 951-15-51; e-mail ensath@sentoo.sn; internet www.refer.sn/ensa/accueil.htm; f. 1980; 5-year courses in agricultural engineering; training for members of the agricultural sector; library: 6,000 vols; 10 full-time teachers; 132 students; Dir Prof. PAPA IBRA SAMB.

Ecole Supérieure Polytechnique: BP 5085, Dakar; tel. 825-08-79; fax 825-55-94; e-mail esp@ucad.sn; internet www.esp.sn; second campus in Thiès; f. 1994; 5-year diploma courses in engineering; library: 22,378 vols; 116 teachers; 2,105 students, (913 undergraduate, 1192 postgraduate); Dir ABIB NGOUM; Registrar MARIE NOËLLE MBENGUE; Vice-Dean MAMADOU ADJ; Librarians PHILOMÈNE FAYE, EMMANUEL CABOU

HEADS OF DEPARTMENTS

Chemical Engineering: ABDOULAYE SOW
Civil Engineering: MAMADOU SARR
Computer Engineering: SAMUEL OUYA
Electrical Engineering: GUSTAVE SOW
Mechanical Engineering: YOUSSOUPH MANDIANG

Institut de Technologie Alimentaire: BP 2765, Hann, Dakar; tel. 832-00-70; fax 832-32-95; e-mail ita@metissacana.sn; internet www.ita.sn; f. 1963; Dir Dr AMADOU TIDIANE GUIRO.

SERBIA

The Higher Education System

Following the dissolution of the Socialist Federal Republic of Yugoslavia in 1992, Serbia became part of the Federal Republic of Yugoslavia, which was renamed the State Union of Serbia and Montenegro in 2003. In 2006 Montenegro declared independence from the State Union of Serbia and Montenegro. There are six universities in Serbia, the oldest of which is Univerzitet u Beogradu (university of Belgrade—founded 1865). Serbian is the main language of instruction, but Hungarian and Albanian are also used at, respectively, Univerzitet u Novum Sadu (University of Novi Sad) and Universiteti i Prishtinës (University of Priština). In addition to the universities, higher education is offered by university faculties, specialist institutes and high schools. The New University Law (2002) initiated several new reforms, including adoption of the European Credit Transfer System (ECTS) and increased autonomy for universities; additionally, Serbia participates in Bologna Process to establish a European Higher Education Area, the first phase of which is to adopt a credit-based system of comparable degrees with two main cycles (undergraduate and graduate). In 2002/03 207,082 students were enrolled in 150 institutes of higher education. In 2003 an accreditation committee was established.

Under the old system, admission to higher education was based on completion of general secondary education or four-year vocational certificate programmes and award of the Secondary School Leaving Diploma. Universities also set their own entrance examinations. Quotas for admissions were set by the Government. The new undergraduate Bachelors degree (four years) replaces the old-style awards of Diplom Višeg Obrazovanje (two to three years) and Diplom Visokog Obrazovanja (four to six years). The Masters degree (Magistarska Dimploma) is a one-year programme of study following the Bachelors. Finally, the Doctorate (Doktorat Nauka) is the highest university-level degree and is awarded after a period of research culminating with defence of a thesis.

Learned Societies

GENERAL

Matica srpska (Serbian Cultural and Scientific Association): Matice Srpske 1, 21000 Novi Sad; tel. (21) 527-622; fax (21) 528-901; e-mail ms@maticasrpska.org.yu; internet www.maticasrpska.org.yu/; f. 1826; literary, scientific, cultural and publishing society; 2,830 mems; library of 2,900,000 vols; Pres. BOŽIDAR KOVAČEK; Sec. DRAGAN STANIĆ; publs *Letopis Matice srpske*, *Proceedings* (in the following series: natural sciences, history, social sciences, literature and language, philology and linguistics, art, Slavonic studies, theatre and music, classical studies).

Srpska Akademija Nauka i Umetnosti (Serbian Academy of Sciences and Arts): Knez Mihailova 35, POB 366, 11000 Belgrade; tel. (11) 334-2400; fax (11) 182-825; e-mail presidency@sanu.ac.yu; internet www.sanu.ac.yu; f. 1886; sections of Mathematics, Physics and Geosciences (Sec. ZORAN MAKSIMOVIĆ), Chemical and Biological Sciences (Sec. DRAGOMIR VITOROVIĆ), Technical Sciences (Sec. PETAR MILJANIĆ), Medical Sciences (Sec. IVAN SPUŽIĆ), Literature and Language (Sec. PREDRAG PALAVESTRA), Social Sciences (Sec. KOSTA MIHAILOVIĆ), Historical Sciences (Sec. VASILIJE KRESTIĆ), Fine Arts (Sec. DEJAN DESPIĆ); 143 mems (111 ordinary, 32 corresp.); Pres. DEJAN MEDAKOVIĆ; Gen. Sec. STEFAN KOIČKI; Exec. Sec. VLADIMIR DAVIDOVIĆ; publs *Godišnjak* (Yearbook), *Glas* (Review), *Posebna izdanja* (Monographs), *Spomenik* (Monument), *Srpski etnografski zbornik* (Serbian Ethnographic Collection), *Srpski dijalektološki zbornik* (Serbian Dialectology Collection), *Naučni skupovi* (Scientific Conferences), *Muzička izdanja* (Musical Editions), *Bulletin*, *Galerija* (Gallery), *Iz teorije prava* (Theory of Law), *Ekonomski zbornik* (Collection of Economic Works).

BIBLIOGRAPHY, LIBRARY SCIENCE AND MUSEOLOGY

Bibliotekarsko društvo Srbije (Library Association of Serbia): Skerlićeva 1, 11000 Belgrade; tel. (11) 451-242; fax (11) 452-952; f. 1947; Pres. DOBRIVOJE MLADENOVIĆ; Sec. VERA CRLJIĆ; publ. *Bibliotekar* (The Librarian, 2 a year).

ECONOMICS, LAW AND POLITICS

Association of Jurists of Serbia: Proleterskih brigada 74, Belgrade; f. 1946; Pres. Prof. Dr MIODRAG ORLIĆ; publ. *Pravni život*.

Economists' Society of Serbia: Nusićeva 6/III, POB 490, Belgrade; f. 1944; Pres. BOGOLJUB STOJANOVIĆ; publ. *Ekonomika preduzeća* (monthly).

Jurists' Association of Yugoslavia: Proleterskih brigada 74, POB 179, Belgrade; tel. (11) 444-8459; f. 1947; 30,000 mems; Pres. Prof. Dr SLOBODAN PEROVIĆ; Sec.-Gen. Prof. Dr STEVAN LILIĆ; publ. *Arhiv*.

EDUCATION

Pedagoško društvo Srbije (Pedagogical Society of Serbia): Terazije 26, 11000 Belgrade; tel. and fax (11) 268-7749; e-mail pds_bgd@eunet.yu; internet www.pedagog.org.yu; f. 1923, reorganized 1950 and 1977; 2,000 mems; Pres. SONJA ŽARKOVIĆ; Sec. MILENA DJOKIĆ; publs *Nastava i vaspitanje* (Teaching and Education, 5 a year), *Pedagoška Biblioteka* (Pedagogical Library, irregular).

HISTORY, GEOGRAPHY AND ARCHAEOLOGY

Historical Society of Serbia: Faculty of Philosophy, Čika Ljubina 18–20, Belgrade; f. 1948; 1,500 mems; Pres. Prof. Dr LJUBOMIR MAKSIMOVIĆ; publ. *Istoriski glasnik* (2 a year).

Serbian Geographical Society: Studenski trg 3/III, Belgrade; f. 1910; 1,500 mems; library of 4,500 vols; Chair. Prof. Dr STEVAN M. STANKOVIĆ; Sec. BORKA RADOVANOVIĆ; publs *Bulletin* (2 a year), *Terre et Hommes* (annually), *Globus* (annually), *Editions Spéciales* (1 or 2 a year), *Mémoires*, *Géographique Actualité*.

LANGUAGE AND LITERATURE

British Council: Terazije 8/I, 11000 Belgrade; tel. (11) 302-3800; fax (11) 302-3898; e-mail info@britishcouncil.org.yu; internet www.britishcouncil.org.yu; f. 1940; teaching centre; offers courses and exams in English language and British culture and promotes cultural exchange with the UK; attached centres in Priština and Podgorica (Montenegro); library of 9,000 vols, 30 periodicals; Dir and Cultural Attaché CHRIS GIBSON.

Društvo za Srpski Jezik i Književnost (Society of Serbian Language and Literature): University, Studenski trg 1, Belgrade; f. 1910; Pres. P. STEVANOVIĆ; Sec. D. PAVLOVIĆ; publ. *Pritozi za književnost, jezik, istorija i folklor*.

Goethe-Institut: Knez Mihailova 50, 11000 Belgrade; tel. (11) 262-2823; fax (11) 636-746; e-mail info@belgrad.goethe.org; internet www.goethe.de/belgrad; offers courses and exams in German language and culture and promotes cultural exchange with Germany; library of 12,000 vols; Dir VOLKER MARWITZ.

Serbian PEN Centre: Francuska 7, 11000 Belgrade; f. 1926, re-f. 1962; 83 mems; Pres. MIODRAG PERIŠIĆ; Sec. KOSTA ČAVOŠKI; publ. *Relations* (quarterly, in English, with Assen of Serbian Writers).

Srpska književna zadruga (Serbian Literary Association): Srpskih vladara 19/I, 11000 Belgrade; tel. (11) 330-305; f. 1892; publishing of literary, historical and other learned works; c. 2,500 mems; library of 12,000 vols; special collection of 19th-century periodicals; Pres. (vacant); Sec.-Gen. RADIVOJE KONSTANTINOVIĆ; publ. *Glasnik* (annually).

MEDICINE

Serbian Society for the Fight against Cancer: Pasterova 14, 11000 Belgrade; tel. (11) 656-386; fax (11) 656-386; e-mail pbrzakov@eunet.yu; f. 1927; 30,000 mems; Pres. Dr PREDRAG BRZAKOVIĆ; publ. *Bolje Sprečiti nego Lečiti* (The Best Cure is Prevention, 4 a year).

NATURAL SCIENCES

Mathematical Sciences

Society of Mathematicians of Serbia: Knez Mihailova 35, POB 791 Belgrade; tel. (11) 638-263; f. 1948; Pres. Dr DJORDJE KARAPANDŽIĆ; publ. *Matematički Vesnik* (quarterly).

Physical Sciences

Serbian Chemical Society: Karnegijeva 4, POB 35-08, 11120 Belgrade; tel. and fax (11) 337-0467; e-mail shd@tmf.bg.ac.yu; internet www.shd.org.yu; f. 1897 to promote chemical research and education; 1,000 mems; Pres. Prof. Dr BRANISLAV NIKOLIĆ; Vice-Presidents Prof. Dr IVANKA POPOVIĆ, Dr SLOBODAN MILONJIĆ; Secs Prof. Dr DRAGICA ŠIŠOVIĆ, Prof. Dr DJORDJE JANAĆKOVIĆ; publs *Journal* (in English, monthly), *Hemijski pregled* (in Serbian, 6 a year).

Serbian Geological Society: Kamenička 6, POB 227, Belgrade; f. 1891; 500 mems; library of 3,500 vols; Pres. Dr NIKOLA PANTIĆ; publ. *Zapisnici srpskog geološkog društva* (Reports, annually).

TECHNOLOGY

'Nikola Tesla' Association of Societies for Promotion of Technical Sciences in Yugoslavia: POB 359, Belgrade; organizes an international festival of scientific and technical films, held every two years.

Union of Engineers and Technicians of Serbia: Kneza Miloša 7, Belgrade; tel. and fax (11) 323-0067; e-mail sits@yuonline.net; internet www.sits.org.yu; f. 1868; 36 mem. orgs; Pres. STEVAN SAMŠALOVIĆ; Sec. BRANISLAV VUJINOVIĆ.

Union of Engineers and Technicians of Yugoslavia: Kneza Miloša 9/II, Belgrade; tel. (11) 324-3653; fax (11) 324-3652; e-mail internet@eunet.yu; internet www.sitj.org.yu; f. 1919; mem. assocs in most brs of engineering; Chair. Prof. Dr DEJAN MILOVANOVIĆ; Gen. Sec. Dr KAZIMIR KURIJ; publs *Tehnika* (6 a year), *It Bulletin* (6 a year).

Research Institutes

AGRICULTURE, FISHERIES AND VETERINARY SCIENCE

Institute for Agricultural Mechanization: Zemun, POB 41, Belgrade; f. 1947; 30 mems; library of 6,000 vols; Dir DJORDJE DJURDJEVIĆ; publ. *Poljoprivredna Tehnika* (Agricultural Engineering, annually).

Institute for Plant Protection and the Environment: T. Drajzera 9, POB 936, 11000 Belgrade; tel. (11) 660-049; fax (11) 669-860; e-mail info@izbis.co.yu; internet www.izbis.co.yu; f. 1945; depts of Phytopathology, Phytopharmacy, Biological Control, Toxicology and Environmental Protection; library of 7,000 books, 12,650 periodicals; Dir Dr DIMITRIJE MATIJEVIĆ; publ. *Zaštita bilja* (Plant Protection, 4 a year).

BIBLIOGRAPHY, LIBRARY SCIENCE AND MUSEOLOGY

Jugoslovenski Bibliografsko-Informacijski Institut (Yugoslav Institute for Bibliography and Information): Terazije 26, 11000 Belgrade; tel. (11) 687-836; fax (11) 687-760; e-mail yubin@jbi.bg.ac.yu; internet www.jbi.bg.ac.yu; f. 1949; nat. mem. of the International ISSN System; nat. ISBN agency; nat. centre for the international exchange of publications; maintains Union Catalogue of Foreign Books and Serials; library of 12,000 books, 40 periodicals; Dir Dr RADOMIR GLAVIČKI; publs *Bibliography of Yugoslavia*, *Bibliography of Articles* (social sciences 6 a year, pure and applied sciences 6 a year, humanities, arts and sports 6 a year), *Bibliography of Periodicals*.

Republički zavod za zaštitu spomenika kulture (Institute for the Protection of Cultural Monuments of Serbia): Božidara Adžije 11, 11118 Belgrade; tel. (11) 454-786; fax (11) 344-14-30; e-mail rzzsk@eunet.yu; internet www.heritage.org.yu; f. 1947; research, documentation, conservation and restoration, legal protection and maintenance of central registers of immovable cultural property; specialized training of personnel, publication of books and periodicals; Dir MILETA MILIĆ; Head, Architecture Dept BRANA STOJKOVIĆ PAVELKA; Head, Paintings Dept RADIŠA ŽIKIĆ; Head, Physical and Chemical Laboratory (vacant); Head of Dept of History of Art, Ethnology and Archaeology RADOJKA ZARIĆ; Depts of Law, Documentation, Photographic Laboratory; library of 21,000 vols; publ. *Saopštenja* (Communications).

ECONOMICS, LAW AND POLITICS

Institute of International Politics and Economics: POB 750, Makedonska 25, 11000 Belgrade; tel. (11) 337-3824; fax (11) 337-3835; f. 1947; international relations, world economy, international law, social, economic and political development in all countries; library of 250,000 vols; Dir ALEKSANDAR FATIĆ; publs *International Problems* (quarterly), *Meetunarodna Politika* (quarterly), *Pregled evropskog zakonodavstva* (Survey of European Legislations, 6 a year), *Review of International Affairs* (quarterly).

FINE AND PERFORMING ARTS

Institute of Musicology of the Serbian Academy of Sciences and Arts: Knez Mihailova 35, 11000 Belgrade; tel. (11) 639-033; fax (11) 182-825; e-mail music.inst@bib.sanu.ac.yu; f. 1948; history of Serbian and Yugoslav music, Balkan folk music, medieval and traditional Orthodox church music, music theory and aesthetics; library of 5,500 vols; Dir Prof. Dr DANICA PETROVIĆ; publs *Musicology* (annually), *Sources for the History of Serbian Music* (annually).

HISTORY, GEOGRAPHY AND ARCHAEOLOGY

Arheološki Institut (Archaeological Institute): Knez Mihailova 35/IV, Belgrade; tel. (11) 637-191; fax (11) 180-189; e-mail biblioteka@ai.sanu.ac.yu; internet www.ai.sanu.ac.yu; f. 1947; study of prehistoric, classical and medieval archaeology in the Central Balkan area; library of 13,700 books, 23,440 vols of periodicals; Dir Dr MILOJE VASIĆ; publs *Starinar* (annually), *Djerdapske sveske – Cahiers des Portes de Fer*, *Singidunum* (irregular).

MEDICINE

Zavod za zaštitu zdravlja Srbije (Institute of Public Health of Serbia): Dr Subotića 5, Belgrade; tel. (11) 685-476; fax (11) 685-735; e-mail info@batut.org.yu; f. 1924; library of 40,000 vols; Dir Asst Prof. Dr DRAGOLJUB DJOKIĆ; publ. *Glasnik* (2 a year).

NATURAL SCIENCES

Biological Sciences

Botanical Institute and Garden of the University of Belgrade: Takovska 43, 11000 Belgrade; tel. (11) 767-988; fax (11) 638-500; f. 1874; library of 7,000 vols; Dir Prof. Dr JELENA BLAŽENČIĆ; publ. *Bulletin* (annually).

Physical Sciences

Astronomska Opservatorija u Beogradu (Astronomical Observatory of Belgrade): Volgina 7, 11160 Belgrade; tel. and fax (11) 241-9553; e-mail zoran@aob.bg.ac.yu; internet www.aob.bg.ac.yu; f. 1887, re-formed 1932; astrometry, astrophysics, astrodynamics, solar physics; library of 15,000 vols; Dir Dr ZORAN KNEŽEVIĆ; Chief Officer SRETEN STEPANOVIĆ; publs *Publications* (irregular), *Serbian Astronomical Journal* (2 a year).

Hidrometeorološki Zavod Republike Srbije (Hydrometeorological Service of Serbia): Kneza Višeslava 66, 11000 Belgrade; tel. (11) 544-775; fax (11) 545-378; e-mail vucinicz@eunet.you; f. 1888; Dir NIKOLA DUTINA.

Attached observatory:

Meteorološka opservatorija Beograd (Belgrade Meteorological Observatory): Bul. JNA 8, 11000 Belgrade; tel. (11) 685-770; fax (11) 685-840; f. 1887; Chief Officer SLOBODAN HADŽIVUKOVIĆ; publ. *Observations Météorologiques à Belgrade*.

Seismological Institute: Tašmajdan, POB 351, Belgrade; f. 1906; Dirs Dr B. A. SIKOŠEK, Dr M. N. VUKAŠINOVIĆ; 12 mems; publs *Annuaire macroséismique et microséismique*, *Bulletin mensuel*, *Studies*.

TECHNOLOGY

Institut za nuklearne nauke 'Vinča' (Vinča Institute of Nuclear Sciences): Vinča, POB 522, 11001 Belgrade; tel. (11) 458-222; internet www.vin.bg.ac.yu; f. 1948; basic and applied research in natural, technological and nuclear sciences, and consulting and research programmes in physics, chemistry, physical chemistry, biology, technical sciences, nuclear energy, electronics, computing, material sciences; production and application of radio isotopes; information systems and data processing; library of 30,000 vols; Dir-Gen. Dr MIROSLAV KOPEČNI.

Institut za Tehnologiju Nuklearnih i Drugih Mineralnih Sirovina (Institute for Technology of Nuclear and Other Mineral Raw Materials): Franše D'Epere 86, POB 390, 11000 Belgrade; tel. (11) 648-455; f. 1948; research and application of technology in the field of processing nuclear, metallic and non-metallic mineral raw materials; environmental protection; training; 168 staff; library: *c.* 3,600 vols, 30,000 periodicals; Dir-Gen. Dr RADE ĆOSOVIĆ.

Libraries and Archives

Belgrade

Arhiv Jugoslavije: Vase Pelagića 33, POB 65, 11000 Belgrade; tel. (11) 369-0252; fax (11) 652-740; e-mail arhiv@gov.yu; internet www.arhiv.sv.gov.yu; f. 1950; 16,760 vols; Dir MOMČILO MIĆOVIĆ.

Arhiv Srbije: Karnegijeva 2, 11000 Belgrade; tel. (11) 337-0781; fax (11) 337-0246; f. 1900; history of Serbia; 75,000 vols; Dir MILORAD M. RADEVIĆ; publ. *Arhivski pregled* (annually).

Biblioteka grada Beograda (Belgrade City Library): Zmaj Jovina 1, Belgrade; tel. (11) 639-518; f. 1929; 400,000 vols, 399 MSS; Head SIMEON BABIĆ.

Biblioteka Srpske akademije nauka i umetnosti (Library of the Serbian Academy of Sciences and Arts): Knez Mihailova 35, 11001 Belgrade; tel. (11) 639-120; fax (11) 182-825; e-mail admin@bib.sanu.ac.yu; internet www.sanu.ac.yu; f. 1842 by the Serbian Learned Society; information service, inter-library loan scheme; prepares bibliographies and edits special publications; 1,200,000 vols; Dir Dr NIKŠA STIPČEVIĆ.

Narodna biblioteka Srbije (National Library of Serbia): Skerlićeva 1, 11000 Belgrade; tel. (11) 245-1242; fax (11) 245-1289; e-mail nbs@nbs.bg.ac.yu; internet www.nbs.bg.ac.yu; f. 1832; 5,500,000 vols, incl.

electronic titles; large colln of medieval Cyrillic MSS; large federal copyright and deposit library, national agency for CIP, ISBN, ISSN, ISMN, DOI numbers, Centre for National Current Bibliography, national centre for conservation and preservation, national digital library centre; Dir SRETEN UGRIČIĆ; publs *Arheografski prilozi* (annually), *Glasnik narodne biblioteke Srbije* (Herald of the National Library of Serbia, annually), *Srpska bibliografija* (Serbian national bibliography, 17 volumes).

Univerzitetska biblioteka 'Svetozar Marković' (University Library 'Svetozar Marković'): Bulevar Kralja Aleksandra 71, 11000 Belgrade; tel. (11) 337-0509; fax (11) 337-0354; e-mail info@unilib.bg.ac.yu; internet www.unilib.bg.ac.yu; f. 1921 as successor to the library of the Serbian Lyceum (1844); centre of the network of university libraries in Serbia; 1,428,000 vols (books, periodicals, newspapers), 548 Serbian and other MSS 12th–18th c., 5,000 old documents; Dir BOGOLJUB MAZIĆ; publ. *Infoteka* (2 a year).

Kragujevac

Narodna biblioteka (Public Library): Kragujevac; f. 1866; 50,000 vols.

Niš

Narodna Biblioteka 'Stevan Sremac' ('Stevan Sremac' Public Library): Dušana Kostića 9, 18000 Niš; tel. (18) 511-410; e-mail nbss@eunct.yu; internet www.biblioteke.org.yu/nis/index.html; f. 1879; collection of the Serbian Academy of Science and Art, collection of Serbian graphics, depts of ancient and rare books; local history; 450,315 vols; Dir LJUBINKO VELICKOVIC.

Novi Sad

Arhiv Vojvodine: Dunavska 35, 21000 Novi Sad; tel. (21) 21-244; fax (21) 22-332; f. 1926; 30,000 vols; Dir PAVLE STANOJEVIĆ; publs *Naučno-informativna sredstva o arhivskoj gradji u arhivima Vojvodine* (Scientific information on the Vojvodina archives, quarterly), *Izveštaji o naučno-istraživačkom rudu u inostranstvu* (Research reports from archives abroad).

Biblioteka Matice srpske (Matica Srpska Library): Ul. Matice srpske 1, 21000 Novi Sad; tel. (21) 420-199; fax (21) 528-574; e-mail bms@bms.ns.ac.yu; internet www.bms.ns.ac.yu; f. 1826 in Budapest, opened 1838 and transferred to Novi Sad in 1864; 975,000 books, 200,000 units of periodicals, 17 incunabula, 671 manuscript books, 500 paleotype, 35,000 old and rare books, 700,000 units of special library material (maps, posters, leaflets, music records, cassettes, etc.); copyright and deposit library for Serbia; regional information centre of Science and Technology Information Network; depository library for FAO and UNESCO; Dir MIRO VUKSANOVIĆ; publs *Godišnjak Biblioteke Matice srpske* (Matica Srpska Library Yearbook, annually), *Bibliografija knjiga u Vojvodini* (Bibliography of Books in Vojvodina, annually), *Analiza rada visokoškolskih biblioteka u Vojvodini* (Analysis of the Work of Academic Libraries in Vojvodina, annually), *Analiza rada narodnih biblioteka u Vojvodini* (Analysis of the Work of Public Libraries in Vojvodina, annually), *Bilten prinovljenih knjiga na stranim jezicima* (Bulletin of Acquired Books in Foreign Languages, *News* (4 a year).

Požarevac

Narodna biblioteka (Public Library): Požarevac; f. 1847; 30,000 vols.

Priština

Biblioteka Kombëtare dhe Universitare e Kosovës (National and University Library of Kosovo): Sheshi Nëna Tereza 5, Kosovo Priština; f. 1944; 600,000 vols; Dir BEDRI HYSA.

Sabac

Narodna biblioteka 'Žika Popovič' (Public Library 'Zika Popović'): Masarikova 18, 15000 Sabac; f. 1847; c. 200,000 vols.

Museums and Art Galleries

Belgrade

Etnografski muzej u Beogradu (Ethnographical Museum): Studentski trg. 13, p.p. 357, Belgrade; tel. (11) 328-1888; fax (11) 621-284; e-mail etnomuzej@yubc.net; f. 1901; library of 30,000 vols; Dir MITAR MIHIĆ; publ. *Glasnik etnografskog muzeja* (annually).

Istorijski muzej Srbije (Historical Museum of Serbia): Nemanjina 24, 11000 Belgrade; tel. (11) 266-7735; fax (11) 361-6268; e-mail imus@yubc.net; internet www.imus.org.yu; f. 1963; Senior Curator ANDREJ VUJNOVIĆ; publ. *Zbornik* (annually).

Museum of Yugoslav History: Trg Nikole Pašića 11, 11000 Belgrade; tel. (11) 3398-532; fax (11) 3398-916; f. 1982 as Josip Broz Tito Memorial Centre, a collection of museums and buildings connected with the life and work of Josip Tito (1892–1980), President of Yugoslavia 1953–1980; present name 1996; history of the peoples of the fmr Yugoslavia since 1918; Dir LJILJANA CETINIĆ.

Museum of Contemporary Art: Ušće Save b.b., 11070 Belgrade; tel. (11) 311-5713; fax (11) 311-2955; e-mail msub@eunet.yu; f. 1958; opened 1965; exhibitions of Yugoslav and foreign art; library of 4,500 vols, 22,000 catalogues; Dir RADISLAV TRKULJA; publ. *World Art Critics* (annually).

Muzej grada Beograda (Belgrade City Museum): Zmaj Jovina Sl 1, POB 87, 11000 Belgrade; tel. (11) 637-954; f. 1903; history of the city from prehistory to the present; depts of archaeology, numismatics, history, art, literature, science; library (15,580 vols, 300 rare books) and documentation centre; conservation laboratory; Dir BOŽIDAR SUJICA; publ. *Godišnjak Grada Beograda* (annually).

Muzej Nikole Tesle (Nikola Tesla Museum): Krunska 51, 11000 Belgrade; tel. (11) 243-3886; fax (11) 243-6408; e-mail info@tesla-museum.org; internet www.tesla-museum.org; f. 1952; library: preserves legacy of the engineer and inventor, Nikola Tesla (1856–1943); 155,000 pages of his original documents and 1,000 of his personal items; Dir VLADIMIR JELENKOVIĆ.

Muzej Pozorišne Umetnosti Srbije (Serbian Museum of Theatre): Gospodar Jevremova 19, 11000 Belgrade; tel. (11) 626-630; fax (11) 628-920; e-mail mpus@eunet.yu; internet www.theatremuseum.org.yu; f. 1950; documents, photos, newspaper cuttings on the theatre, costumes, decorations, audiovisual documentation; library of 7,500 vols; Dir KSENIJA RADULOVIĆ; publ. *Teatron* (4 a year).

Muzej primenjene umetnosti (Museum of Applied Art): Vuka Karadžića 18, 11000 Belgrade; tel. (11) 262-6841; fax (11) 262-9121; e-mail mpu@yubc.net; internet www.mpu.org.yu; f. 1950; ceramics, porcelain, glass, metalwork, jewellery, period furniture, woodwork, textiles and costume, photography, book layout, modern architecture and design; library of 24,906 vols; Dir IVANKA ZORIĆ; publ. *Journal* (annually).

Narodni muzej (National Museum): Trg Republike 1A, 11000 Belgrade; tel. (11) 330-60-00; fax (11) 627-721; e-mail na.muzej@eunet.yu; internet www.narodnimuzej.yu; f. 1844; archaeological collections and art collections (medieval, Yugoslav and foreign collections), numismatics; library of 85,000 vols; Dir TATJANA CVJETIĆANIN; publs *Zbornik, Numizmatičar, Kovčežić, Glasnik*.

Prirodnjački muzej u Beogradu (Belgrade Natural History Museum): Njegoševa 51, POB 401, 11000 Belgrade; tel. (11) 344-2265; fax (11) 344-6580; e-mail nhmbeo@nhmbeo.org.yu; f. 1895; botanical, environmental, geological, mineralogical, palaeontological, petrological and zoological studies and collections; library of 64,000 vols; Dir Dr GORDANA JOVANOVIĆ; publ. *Bulletin* (separate series on biology and geology).

Vojni Muzej (Military Museum): Kalemegdan bb, 11000 Belgrade; tel. (11) 33-44-915; fax (11) 33-44-915; f. 1878; military history of Serbia and Montenegro; library of 16,000 vols; Dir Col MIROSLAV KNEŽEVIĆ; publ. *Vesnik* (annually).

Zeljeznicki Muzej (Railway Museum of Serbia): 6 Nemanjina ul., Belgrade; f. 1950; library of 20,000 vols; library: archives section being formed; Dir MILAN RADIVOJEVIĆ.

Novi Sad

Galerija Matice Srpska (Art Gallery of Matica Srpska). Trg Galerija 1, 21000 Novi Sad; tel. (21) 421-455; fax (21) 421-456; e-mail galmats@cunet.yu; f. 1847; fine art; paintings, graphics, sculptures and drawings from the 16th to 20th centuries; Dir LEPOSAVA ŠELMIĆ.

Muzej Vojvodine (Museum of Vojvodina): Dunavska 35–37, 21000 Novi Sad; tel. (21) 420-566; fax (21) 520-135; e-mail musejvojvodine1@ns.cable.net; f. 1947; sections: archaeology, ethnology, history, applied art; library of 80,000 vols; Dir Prof. Dr RANKO KONČAR; publs *Posebna izdanja* (irregular), *Rad vojvodjanskih muzeja* (annually).

Subotica

Gradski muzej—Városi Múzeum: Trg Slobode 1, 24000 Subotica; tel. (24) 555-128; fax (24) 555-228; e-mail sumuseum@subotica.co.yu; internet www.gradskimuzej.subotica.co.yu; f. 1892; sections: archaeology, local history, art, ethnology (collections from Africa and Southeast Asia and Oceania), biology, coins (Hungarian and Roman); library of 12,000 vols; Dir Mgr ISTVÁN HULLÓ.

Universities

UNIVERZITET U BEOGRADU
(University of Belgrade)

Studentski trg 1, 11000 Belgrade 6

Telephone: (11) 635-163
Fax: (11) 638-912
E-mail: ubginfo@rect.bg.ac.yu
Internet: www.bg.ac.yu

Founded 1863; reorganized 1905 and 1954
Academic year: October to September

Rector: DEJAN POPOVIĆ
Vice-Rectors: BOGDAN ĐURIČIĆ, IVAN JURANIĆ, ZARKO SPASIĆ
Secretary-General: SILVIA ZDRAVKOVIĆ
Librarian: DEJAN AJDAČIĆ

Library of 700,000 vols, 10,000 periodicals
Number of teachers: 2,552
Number of students: 92,652 (90,152 undergraduate, 2,500 postgraduate)

Publications: *Acta Veterinaria, Annals of the Faculty of Law* (in Serbian), *Annals of the Faculty of Philology, Bulletin Astronomique de Belgrade, Collection of Works of the Faculty of Mining and Geology* (in Serbian), *Collection of Works of the International Slavistics Center, Contemporary Research in Physics* (in Serbian), *Contributions to Language, Literature and Folklore, Economic Annals* (in Serbian, 4 a year), *Education – the Theory and the Practice* (in English, Russian and Serbian), *Gazette of the Faculty of Forestry* (2 a year), *Geological Annals of the Balkan Peninsula* (in Serbian), *Germanica Belgradensia, Headmaster* (in Serbian), *Information Bulletin* (Faculty of Agriculture, in Serbian, monthly), *Innovations in the Field of Instruction* (in Serbian), *Italica Belgradensia, Journal of Automatic Control* (in English), *Journal of Mining and Metallurgy* (in Serbian), *Lectures in Physical Sciences, Management, Mathematics* (in Serbian), *Medical Research* (in Serbian), *Medical Students, Miscellaneous Studies of the Faculty of Philosophy* (series A: culture and history; series B: social sciences), *October Symposium of Miners and Metallurgists* (annual collection of works, in Serbian), *Philosophical Yearbook* (in Serbian), *Philosophy and Society* (in Serbian), *Physical Education, Physical Engineering* (in English), *Population, Power Engineering* (in English), *Problems of Ethnology and Anthropology, Psychological Research, Review of Research Work at the Faculty of Agriculture* (in English), *Sociological Review, Studies of Adult Education Topics, Transactions* (mechanical engineering, in Serbian and English, 2 a year), *Transport and Traffic in Cities* (in Serbian), *Underground Works* (in Serbian), *The Veterinary Herald* (in Serbian), *Yugoslav Journal of Operations Research* (in English), *Zograf* (iconography)

DEANS

Faculty of Agriculture: NEBOJŠA RALEVIĆ
Faculty of Architecture: ZORAN NIKEZIĆ
Faculty of Biology: MIRKO CVIJAN
Faculty of Chemistry: SOFIJA SOVILJ
Faculty of Civil Engineering: ALEKSANDAR CVETANOVIĆ
Faculty of Defectology: ZORAN ILIĆ
Faculty of Defence and Protection: DRAGANA DULIĆ
Faculty of Economics: BOŽIDAR CEROVIĆ
Faculty of Electrical Engineering: BRANKO KOVAČEVIĆ
Faculty of Engineering in Bor: ZVONIMIR STANKOVIĆ
Faculty of Forestry: LJUBODRAG MIHAILOVIĆ
Faculty of Geography: STEVAN STANKOVIĆ
Faculty of Law: VLADIMIR MILIĆ
Faculty of Mathematics: ALEKSANDAR LIPOVSKI
Faculty of Mechanical Engineering: MILOŠ NEDELJKOVIĆ
Faculty of Medicine: VLADIMIR KOSTIĆ
Faculty of Mining and Geology: NIKOLA LILIĆ
Faculty of Organizational Sciences: NEVENKA ŽARKIĆ-JOKSIMOVIĆ
Faculty of Pharmacy: Prof. Dr DARKO IVANOVIĆ
Faculty of Philology: RATKO NEŠKOVIĆ
Faculty of Philosophy: ŽIVAN LAZOVIĆ
Faculty of Physical Chemistry: VERA DONDUR
Faculty of Physics: MILAN KNEŽEVIĆ
Faculty of Political Sciences: MIJAT DAMJANOVIĆ
Faculty of Sport: MILOŠ KUKOLJ
Faculty of Stomatology: VOJISLAV LEKOVIĆ
Faculty of Teacher Training: SVETLANA BEZDANOV-GOSTIMIR
Faculty of Technology and Metallurgy: BRATISLAV JOVANOVIĆ

Faculty of Transport and Traffic Engineering: MOMČILO MILJUŠ
Faculty of Veterinary Medicine: MILIJANA KNEŽEVIĆ

PROFESSORS

Faculty of Agriculture (Nemanjina 6, 11080 Zemun; tel. (11) 615-315; fax (11) 193-659; e-mail office@agrifaculty.bg.ac.yu; internet www.agrifaculty.bg.ac.yu):

BLAGOJEVIĆ, S., Agricultural Chemistry
ČANAK, M., Mathematics
ĆOROVIĆ, M., Market and Turnover of Agricultural and Agroindustrial Products
ELEZOVIĆ, I., General Phytopharmacy
ERCEGOVIĆ, Đ., Elements and Agricultural Machinery Mechanics
GLAMOČLIJA, Đ., Crop Farming
GRUBIĆ, G., Ruminant Nutrition
IVANOVIĆ, M., Plant Mycosis
JAKOVLJEVIĆ, M. D., Soil and Water Chemistry
JANKOVIĆ, M., Cooling Technology
JELIĆ, M. P., Mathematics
KOSI, F., Thermodynamics and Thermotechnics
KOSTIĆ, N. M., Agrogeology
KOVAČEVIĆ, D., General Crop Farming
LATINOVIĆ, D., Population Genetics and Fertilization of Domestic Animals
LESKOŠEK ČUKALOVIĆ, I., Malt and Beer Technology
MAČEJ, O., Milk Proficiency and Preparation
MITROVIĆ, S., Zootechnics
MRATINIĆ, E., Special Fruit Growing
NEDIĆ, M. J., Special Crop Farming
OBRADOVIĆ, D. B., Technological Microbiology
OSTOJIĆ, M., Milk Production
PAVASOVIĆ, V. L., Technological Operations
PEKIĆ, S., Botany
PERIĆ, V. T., Meat Proficiency and Preparation
PEŠIĆ, R., Macroeconomic Analysis
PETANOVIĆ, R., Acarology
PETKOVIĆ, S., Hydraulics
PETROVIĆ, M., Cattle Breeding
RADOVANOVIĆ, R. M., Meat Industry Follow-Up Products Technology
RAIČEVIĆ, D., Agricultural Machinery
RALEVIĆ, N., Statistics
RALEVIĆ LJUBANOVIĆ, I., Statistics and Operational Research
RISTIĆ, N., Organic Chemistry
RUDIĆ, D. V., Drainage
SKALICKI, Z., Zootechnics
SPALEVIĆ, B., Soil and Water Conservation
SPASIĆ, R., Special Entomology
STEVANOVIĆ, Đ., Sociology
STEVANOVIĆ, D. R., Agrochemistry
ŠTIKIĆ, R., Plant Physiology
ŠESTOVIĆ, M. B., Special Phytopharmacy
ŠEVRALIĆ, M., Field and Co-operative Movement Economics
ŠINŽAR, B. C., Botany
ŠURLAN MOMIROVIĆ, G., Genetics
TODOROVIĆ, M. S., Thermodynamics
VASIĆ, G., Reclamation Systems Production and Maintenance
VELIČKOVIĆ, M., General Fruit Growing
VEREŠ, M., Plant Products Technology
VITOROVIĆ, S. L., Agricultural Toxicology
VUKIĆ, Đ., Agricultural Electrical Technology
VUKŠA, P., Plant Protection Technology
ŽEŽELJ, M., Wheat and Flour Technology

Faculty of Architecture (Bulevar Kralja Aleksandra 73, 11000 Belgrade; tel. (11) 322-5254; fax (11) 322-4122; e-mail deanoffc@arh.arh.bg.ac.yu; internet www.arh.arh.bg.ac.yu):

BADOVINC, P., Urban Functions

BAJIĆ BRKOVIĆ, M., Urban and Regional Planning
CAGIĆ, P. R., Architectural Design, Design Studio
ĐORDEVIĆ, D., Construction Management and Utilities Management in Architecture
JOVANOVIĆ POPOVIĆ, M., Architectural Construction and Principles of Bioclimatic Design
KRUNIĆ, S., Design Studio
KUJUNDŽIĆ, V. B., Wood and Metal Structures
KURTOVIĆ FOLIĆ, N., History of Architecture and Settlements
LAZAREVIĆ BAJEC, N., Urban Structures and Zoning
LOJANICA, M. M., Design Studio, Process in Architectural Design
MARUŠIĆ, D. M., Architectural Design, Design Studio
MIHAJLOVIĆ, M., Physics and Materials in Architectural Building Physics
MIHALJEVIĆ, G. P., Built Environment Economics
MITROVIĆ, B., Architectural Design, Design Studio
NESTOROVIĆ, M., Structural Systems, Spatial Structures
PEROVIĆ, M. R., History of Modern Architecture and Town Planning
RAJIĆ, D., Mechanics and Strength of Materials
RAJOVIĆ, S., Architectural and Urban Design
RAKOČEVIĆ, M., Architectural Design
RIBAR, M., Architectural Design, Specific Design Problems
RISTIĆ, M., Analysis of Metal Structures

Faculty of Biology (Studentski trg 3, 11000 Belgrade; tel. (11) 186-635; fax (11) 638-500; e-mail dekanat@bf.bio.bg.ac.yu; internet www.bio.bg.ac.yu):

ANĐELKOVIĆ, M. L., Population Genetics
ČURČIĆ, B., Pedology and Pedobiology with Soil Protection
CVIJIĆ, G., Experimental Physiology
KALEZIĆ, M., Vertebrate Comparative Morphology
KEKIĆ, V., Behavioural Genetics
KONJEVIĆ, R., Plant Physiology
PETKOVIĆ, B., Plant Morphology, General Botany, Botany with Mycology
RADOVIĆ, I., Principles of Ecology
ROMAC, S., Eucariote Molecular Biology
SIMIĆ, D., Microbiology, Microbiology and Microbial Ecology Genotoxicology, Water Microbiology
STEVANOVIĆ, B., Plant Ecology and Phytogeography, Plant Ecology, Physiology and Physiological Ecology of Plants, Plant Adaptive Types, Physiological Ecology of Plants, Aquatic Botany
STEVANOVIĆ, V., Plant Ecology and Phytogeography, Principles of Ecology, Biogeography, Biodiversity Protection and Revival, Ecosystems of Yugoslavia and the Balkan Peninsula
TOPISIROVIĆ, LJ., Biochemistry
TUĆIĆ, N., Organic Evolution Theory

Faculty of Chemistry (Studentski trg 16, 11000 Belgrade; tel. (11) 328-211; fax (11) 638-785; e-mail dekan@chem.bg.ac.yu; internet www.chem.bg.ac.yu):

BOJOVIĆ, S., Chemical Education
DOŠEN-MIĆOVIĆ, L., Organic Chemistry
GRŽETIĆ, I., Applied Chemistry
JANKOV, R., Biochemistry
JOVANČIĆEVIĆ, B., Applied Chemistry
JURANIĆ, I., Organic Chemistry
MARKOVIĆ, R., Organic Chemistry
MILOSAVLJEVIĆ, S., Organic Chemistry
NIKETIĆ, S., Inorganic Chemistry
NIKETIĆ, V., Biochemistry
PAVLOVIĆ, V., Organic Chemistry

ŠAIČIĆ, R., Organic Chemistry
SOLAJA, B., Organic Chemistry
SOVILJ, S., Inorganic Chemistry
TEŠIĆ, Ž., Analytical Chemistry
VRVIĆ, M., Biochemistry
VUČKOVIĆ, G., Inorganic Chemistry

Faculty of Civil Engineering (Bulevar Kralja Aleksandra 73, 11000 Belgrade; tel. (11) 322-3557; fax (11) 337-0223; e-mail acacv@grf.bg.ac.yu; internet www.grf.bg.ac.yu):

ANĐUS, V., Road Design
BAJIĆ, D., Concrete Structures
BRČIĆ, S., Engineering Mechanics and Strength of Materials
BUĐEVAC, D., Metal Structures
ĆORIĆ, B., Theory of Structures
CVETANOVIĆ, A., Elements of Transportation, Roads
ĐORDJEVIĆ, B., Water Power Engineering, Water Resource Systems
DUNICA, Š., Engineering Mechanics and Strength of Materials
GEORGIJEVIĆ, V., Technical Physics, Building Physics, Introduction to Electronics
IVKOVIĆ, B., Construction Management and Technology, Construction Project Management
JOKSIĆ, D., Geodesy, Geodesy on Roads and Railways, Engineering, Geodesy in City Infrastructure Systems, Photogrammetry, Remote Sensing
JOVANOVIĆ, M., River Engineering, Waterways and Ports
KLEM, N., Automatic Data Processing in Geodesy
KOLUNDŽIJA, B., Structural Theory
LJUBISAVLJEVIĆ, D., Municipal Hydraulic Engineering, Water Quality
MAKSIMOVIĆ, C., Fluid Mechanics, Hydraulic Measurement, Engineering
MAKSIMOVIĆ, M., Soil Mechanics
MALETIN, M., Urban Streets
MURAVLJOV, M., Building Materials
NADJANOVIĆ, D., Concrete Structures
OPRICOVIĆ, S., Systems Optimization
PEROVIĆ, G., Calculus, Congruence Theory
PRAŠČEVIC, Ž., Construction Management and Technology, Special Construction Problems
ŠEKULOVIĆ, M., Structural Theory
ŠUMARAC, D., Engineering Mechanics and Strength of Materials
VRAČARIĆ, K., Geodesy
VUKSANOVIĆ, Đ., Structural Theory

Faculty of Defectology (Visokog Stevana 2, 11000 Belgrade; tel. (11) 183-066; fax (11) 183-081; e-mail handicap@eunet.yu; internet www.defektoloski.bg.ac.yu):

ANDREJEVIĆ, I., Professional and Occupational Training of Persons with Mental Retardation, Professional Training of Deaf and Hard of Hearing Persons
ANIČIĆ, L., Pedagogy of Mentally Retarded Persons, Methodology of Preschool Work with Mentally Retarded Persons
GOLOBOVIĆ, S., Clinical Logopaedia
ILANKOVIĆ, V., Basics of Kinesitherapy
ISPANOVIĆ RADOJKOVIĆ, V., Neurology and Psychiatry, Neuropsychiatry with Re-educational Methods
JOVANOVIĆ, T., Medical Psychology with Basics of Anatomy
KAŠIĆ, Z., Phonetics, Linguistics
KRAJGER GUZINA, A., Neurology and Psychiatry
MATEJIĆ ČURIČIĆ, Ž., Developmental Psychology, Psychology of Blind and Low Vision Persons
MILANDINOVIĆ, V., Serbian Language Methodology for Children with Mental Retardation, Mathematical Methodology for Children with Mental Retardation
POPOVIĆ KANDIĆ, Z., Criminal Law

RADOMAN, V., Psychology of Deaf and Hard of Hearing Persons, Psychology of Persons with Speech Disturbances
RADOVANOVIĆ, D., Psychology of Persons with Behavioural Disturbances
RADULOVIĆ, K., Psychology of Persons with Mental Retardation, Psychology of Physically Challenged Persons
RAPAIĆ, D., Clinical Somatopaedia
STANKOV, B., Basics of Strabology with Orthoptics and Pleoptics
TREBJEŠANIN, Ž., General Psychology with Personality Psychology

Faculty of Defence and Protection (Gospodara Vučića 50, 11000 Belgrade; tel. (11) 451-843; fax (11) 457-685; e-mail fcivod@afrodita.rcub.bg.ac.yu; internet www.fco.bg.ac.yu):

CVETKOVIĆ, M., Contemporary Combat Systems and Devices
KANDIĆ, D., Introduction to Philosophy and Ethics, Ethics
MILAŠINOVIĆ, R., Conflict Theory
MIŠOVIĆ, S., Violent Conflict Theory
PLAVŠIĆ, M., Macroeconomics

Faculty of Economics (Kamenička 6, 11000 Belgrade; tel. (11) 627-866; fax (11) 639-560; e-mail ekof@one.ekof.bg.ac.yu; internet www.ekof.bg.ac.yu):

ANIČIĆ, R. M., Methods of Economic Analysis
ARSENIĆ, Ž., Vehicle Design, Experimental Methods
BABIĆ, S. L., Price Theory, Industrial Organization
BAJEC, J. M., Contemporary Economic Systems, Public Sector Economy
BAKIĆ, O., Tourism Marketing, Tourist Organization Business Operations
BORIČIĆ, B., Mathematics, Program Languages
BOŽIĆ, V. S., Transport Economics, Marketing Logisitics
ČAČIĆ, K. T., Tourism and Catering Business Management, Tourism Economics, Tourism Marketing
CEROVIĆ, B. D., Transition Economics
CVIJETIĆANIN, D., Operational Research, Economic and Mathematical Methods and Models
DEVETAKOVIĆ, S. R., National Economy, Technological Development and Policy, Agrarian Policy
ĐOLEVIĆ, V. R., Economic Statistics, Bases of Statistical Analysis
ĐUKIĆ, Đ., Banking, Securities Trading
ĐURIČIN, D., Strategic Management
EREMIĆ, M. B., Market Research, Bases of Statistical Analysis, Theoretical Statistics
ILIĆ, B. B., Political Economy
IVANIŠEVIĆ, M., Business Finance, Business Financial Restructuring
JAKŠIĆ, M. P., Development and Contemporary Economic Thought, Macroeconomic Analysis
JOKSIMOVIĆ, L., Contemporary Economic Systems, Public Sector Economics
JOVANOVIĆ GAVRILOVIĆ, B., National Economy, Development Theory and Planning, Industrial Economics
JOVANOVIĆ GAVRILOVIĆ, P. R., Yugoslav Economic Relations with Foreign Countries, International Business Finance, International Financing
JOVIČIĆ, M. M., Econometry, Times Series Analysis
KOČOVIĆ, J., Financial and Actuary Mathematics, Insurance, Insurance Tariffs
KOVAČ, O., International Finances, Yugoslav Economic Relations with Foreign Countries, European Union Economics
LOVRETA, S. M., Trade and Sales Management, Trade Economics
LOVRIĆ, M., Bases of Statistical Analysis
MALENOVIĆ, N., Business Economics

MARIČIĆ, B. R., Marketing, Consumer Behaviour
MEDOJEVIĆ, B. V., Political Economy
MILOVANOVIĆ, M. R., Price Theory, Macroeconomic Analysis
NIKOLIĆ, M. M., Business Economic, Energy Economics
PAVLIČIĆ, D., Bases of Statistical Analysis, Decision Making Theory
PETKOVIĆ, M., Business Organization, Human Resources Management, Organizational Development
PETKOVIĆ, V. V., Sociology with Labour Sociology, Tourism Sociology
PETROVIĆ, L., Samples Theory and Experiment Planning, Mathematics, Theoretical Statistics
PETROVIĆ, P. D., Econometry, Open Economy Macroeconomics
RIKALOVIĆ, G., National Economy, Agrarian Economics, Transport Economics
ŠKARIĆ JOVANOVIĆ, K. I., Financial Accounting, Balance Theory and Policy, Special Balances
STANIŠIĆ, M., Accounting Information Systems, Auditing Theory, Auditing
STEVANOVIĆ, N., Cost Accounting Systems, Management Accounting
ŠUVAKOVIĆ, DJ. M., Price Theory, Production Theory
TODOROVIĆ, J. B., Marketing Research and Marketing Information Systems, Mangement Information Systems, Price Theory
ZARIĆ, S., Economic Analysis Methods, Market and Market Institutions

Faculty of Electrical Engineering (Bulevar Kralja Aleksandra 73, 11000 Belgrade; tel. (11) 322-9212; fax (11) 324-8681; e-mail dckanat@etf.bg.ac.yu; internet www.etf.bg.ac.yu):

CVETKOVIĆ, D. M., Mathematics
ĐORDJEVIĆ, A. R., Microwave Technology, Electromagnetics, Fundamentals of Electrical Engineering
DRAJIĆ, D. B., Statistical Telecommunication Theory, Computer Telecommuncations, Digital Transfer Techniques, Transfer and Recording Codes
DUKIĆ, M., Signal Processing and Transfer, Telecommunications, Radio Systems
ĐURIĆ, M., Power System Components, Power Engineering System Regulation, Replay Protection, Power Stations and Distribution Plants
KOSTIĆ, M., Electrical Lighting, Electrical Installations with Lighting
KOVAČEVIĆ, B. D., Automatic Control, Stochastic Systems and Estimation
LACKOVIĆ, I. B., Mathematics
LAZIĆ, B., Fundamentals of Computer Technology, Computer Architecture, Operating Systems
MARJANOVIĆ, S. N., Electronics
MATAUŠEK, M. R., Optimal Process Control, Automatic Control Systems, Process Control, Process Identification
MERKELE, M., Mathematics, Probability and Statistics
MIKIČIĆ, D. J., Technical Mechanics with Hydraulics, Fundamentals of Mechanical Engineering
MILANOVIĆ, V., Quantum Mechanics, Electronic Device Components, Solid State Physical Electronics, Semiconducting Microstructures
MILUTINOVIĆ, V., Microprocessing Systems, Computer VLSI Systems
OSMOKROVIĆ, P., Electrical Engineering Materials, Dosimetry and Radiation Protection, Nuclear Physics
PAUNOVIĆ, Đ., Radio Systems, Telecommunication Electronics, Radio Relay Systems, Design and Simulation Methods, Radiotechnics

PETROVIĆ, D., A.C. Electrical Machinery, Electromechanical Power Conversion

PETROVIĆ, G., Digital Telecommunications, Digital Telephone Exchange Design, Telecommunication Networks, Digital Transfer Technology, Communication System Simulation, Computational Systems

PETROVIĆ, T., Simulation and Modelling, Nonlinear Control Systems, Automatic Control Robust Systems Regulation

PETROVIĆ, Z., Satellite Systems, Fundamentals of Telecommunications, Integrated Telecommunications Networks

POPOVIĆ, B. D., Electrical Measurements, Biomedical Engineering, Biomedical Instrumentation

POTKONJAK, V. N., Robots and Automation

PRAVICA, P. B., Telecommunications

RADUNOVIĆ, J. B., Materials Physics, Optoelectronic Devices and Systems, Optoelectronic and Laser Systems, Electro-optics, Statistical Physics

RAJAKOVIĆ, N., Distributive and Industrial Networks, Power Systems Analysis, Power Systems Exploitation, Power Systems Analysis

RAKOVIĆ, D., Materials Physics, Biophysics

RAMOVIĆ, R., Microelectronics, Electronic Device Components, Semiconductor Analysis and Modelling

REIJIN, B., Electrical Circuit Theory, Medical Informatics, Digital Information Processing, Electrical Circuit Theory

SAVIĆ, M. S., High Voltage Technology, High Voltage Equipment

SIMIĆ, S. K., Mathematics

ŠKOKLJEV, I., General Power Engineering, Power Engineering System Planning

SREĆKOVIĆ, M., Laser Technics, Quantum Electronics

STANKOVIĆ, D. K., Sensors and Converters, Physico-Technical Measurement, Sensors and Actuators

STANKOVIĆ, S. S., Stochastic Signal Processing, Artificial Intelligence and Neural Networks, Automatic Control Systems, Digital Signal Processing

STOJIĆ, M. R., Automatic Control, Digital Control Systems

VASILJEVIĆ, D. M., Digital System Design

VELAŠEVIĆ, D. M., Programming Compilers, Expert Systems, Digital Programming

ZLATANOVIĆ, M. D., Sensors and Convertors, Atomic and Molecular Spectroscopy, Fundamentals of Mechanical Engineering

ŽIVKOVIĆ, D. B., Computer System Control, Pulse and Digital Electronics

Faculty of Engineering in Bor (Vojske Jugoslavije 12, 19210 Bor; tel. (30) 24-555; fax (30) 21-078; e-mail tfb@tf.bor.ac.yu; internet www.tf.bor.ac.yu):

IVANIĆ, L., Casting, Theory of Casting

MAGDALINOVIĆ, N. M., Comminution and Classification

MARKOVIĆ, D., Metals Testing

MILIĆEVIĆ, Ž. M., Underground Mining Technology

MILJKOVIĆ, M. A., Mine Ventilation, Technical Safety Precautions

RAJČIĆ VUJASINOVIĆ, M., Theory of Hydro- and Electrometallurgical Processes

STANKOVIĆ, R., Transport and Haulage, Transport in Mineral Technologies

STANKOVIĆ, V., Metallurgical Operations

STANKOVIĆ, Z. D., Physical Chemistry

STANOJLOVIĆ, R. D., Physical Concentration Methods, Mineral Processing

ŽIVKOVIĆ, Ž. D., Metallurgy of Non-Ferrous Metals and Alloys, Pyrometallurgical Process Theory

Faculty of Forestry (Kneza Višeslava 1, 11000 Belgrade; tel. (11) 553-122; fax (11) 545-485; e-mail sf.bg@sezampro.yu; internet www.rcub.bg.ac.yu/~sfb):

BAJIĆ, V., Forest Utilization, Forestry Mechanization

BANKOVIĆ, S. V., Dendrometry, Geodesy

DANON, G., Basics of Mechanical Engineering, Wood Processing Tool Machinery

ĐOROVIĆ, M., Agricultural Field Improvement

ISAJEV, V., Seed Production, Nursery Practice and Afforestation, Genetics with Plant Breeding

JAIĆ, M., Surface Wood Processing

JOKSIMOVIĆ, V., Erosion Control Agroecosystems

KARADŽIĆ, D., Forest Phytopathology, Ornamental Plant Diseases

KOLIN, B., Hydrothermic Wood Processing, Veneers and Composite Boards

KOSTADINOV, S., Torrents and Erosion

KOSTADINOVIĆ, A., Sociology

KRSTIĆ, M., Siviculture, Forest Improvement

LETIĆ, L., Woodland Water Exploitation, Forest Hydrology

MARJANOV, M., Engineering Mechanics

MATIĆ, V., Materials in Erosion Control Works, Ecological Materials

MIHAJLOVIĆ, L., Forest Protection, Forest Entomology

MILJKOVIĆ, J. P., Chipboards, Particle Boards and Wood-Based Materials

NEŠIĆ, M., Wood Processing Production Management, Change Control, Wood Processing Management

PETKOVIĆ, S. D., Hydraulics with Hydrology, Water Management Basics

RANKOVIĆ, N., Forest Economics, Forest Organization and Management, Timber Trade, Forest Economic Geography

SKAKIĆ, D., Final Wood Processing, Timber Construction

SOKOLOVIĆ, S., Design, Furniture Design

STOJANOVIĆ, L., Silviculture, Forest Improvement

ŠOŠKIĆ, B. M., Wood Properties, Mill Conversion of Wood

ŠULETIĆ, R., Wood Processing Enterprise Design, Project and Investment Management, Enterprise Development Management

TODOROVIĆ, P. S., Wood Industry Control System Technology, Engineering Physics

TODOROVIĆ, T. N., Geotechnics in Flood Control, Geodynamics, Hydrogeology with Geomorphology

TOMIĆ, Z. S., Dendrology, Forest Phytocenology

VUČKOVIĆ, M., Increment Study

VOJKOVIĆ, L., Landscape Design, History of Landscape Architecture

VUKIĆEVIĆ, M., Wood Processing Production Organization, Operational Research

Faculty of Geography (Studentski trg 3, 11000 Belgrade; tel. (11) 637-421; fax (11) 182-889; e-mail dekanat@gef.bg.ac.yu; internet www.gef.bg.ac.yu):

DERIĆ, B., Regional Planning

GRČIĆ, M., Political Geography, Industrial and Transport Geography

KUKRIKA, M., Computing, Information Technology

LJEŠEVIĆ, M., Environment

MANOJLOVIĆ, P., Geomorphology, Mathematical Geography

PAVLOVIĆ, M., Yugoslav Geography, Yugoslav Regional Geography

SPASOVSKI, M., Population Geography, Demography

STAMENKOVIĆ, S., Urban Geography, Applied Urban Geography

STANKOVIĆ, S. M., Tourism Geography, World Tourism Geography

STOJKOV, B., Spatial Planning Analysis and Synthesis Methods, Urban and Rural Spatial Planning

ŽIVKOVIĆ, D., Cartography, Topical Mapping

Faculty of Law (Bulevar Kralja Aleksandra 67, 11000 Belgrade; tel. (11) 324-1501; fax (11) 322-1299; e-mail pravni@ius.bg.ac.yu; internet www.ius.bg.ac.yu):

ANTIĆ, O., Succession Law

AVRAMOVIĆ, S. D., General History of Law

BASTA, D. N., Legal Philosophy

BESAROVIĆ, V. M., Commercial Law, Copyright and Intellectual Property Law

BRAJIĆ, V. M., Labour Law

ČAVOŠKI, K. S., Introduction to Law

ĐUKIĆ VELJOVIĆ, Z., Constitutional Law

IGNJATOVIĆ, Đ., Criminology and Penology

JANJIĆ KOMAR, M., Family Law

JEKIĆ, Z. M., Criminal Procedure

KOŠUTIĆ, B. P., Introduction to Law

KREĆA, M. D., International Public Law

LABUS, M. Z., Political Economy

LILIĆ, S., Administrative Law and Governance

MARKOVIĆ, R. Č., Constitutional Law, Administrative Law

MARKOVIĆ, S., Copyright and Intellectual Property Law

MILIĆ, V. B., Sociology

MITROVIĆ, D., Introduction to Law, Autonomy Law

MITROVIĆ, M., Sociology

ORLIĆ, M. V., Introduction to Civil Law, Real Law

POPOVIĆ, D. M., Public Finances and Financial Law

POPOVIĆ, D. M., General History of Law

STOJANOVIĆ, Z., Criminal Law

SUNDEROVIĆ, B., Labour Law

TABOROŠI, S. A., Law of the Economic System

TODOROVIĆ, M., Sociology

TRKULJA, J., Political Systems

VASILJEVIĆ, M. S., Commercial Law and Traffic Law

VUKADIN, E., Economic Policy

Faculty of Mathematics (Studentski trg 16, 11000 Belgrade; tel. (11) 630-151; fax (11) 630-151; e-mail matf@matf.bg.ac.yu; internet www.matf.bg.ac.yu):

ANGELOV, T., Stellar Astronomy, Stellar Structure and Evolution

BOKAN, N., Differential Geometry

JARIĆ, J. P., Continuum Mechanics, Tensor Calculus

JEVTIĆ, M. J., Complex Analysis

JOVANOVIĆ, B. S., Numerical Analysis

KADELBURG, Z. L., Analysis

KNEŽEVIĆ, J., Differential Equations

KUZMANOVSKI, M., Positional Astronomy

LAŽETIĆ, N., Analysis

MATELJEVIĆ, M. S., Complex Analysis

MIJAJLOVIĆ, Ž. D., Algebra, Mathematical Logic

PAVLOVIĆ, M., Complex and Functional Analysis

RADOJČIĆ, M., Algebra, Mathematical Logic

VREĆICA, S., Topology

Faculty of Mechanical Engineering (27 marta 80, 11000 Belgrade; tel. (11) 337-0761; fax (11) 337-0364; e-mail dekan@alfa.mas.bg.ac.yu; internet www.mas.bg.ac.yu):

ADŽIĆ, M., Fuels, Industrial Water, Lubricants, Combustion

BENIŠEK, M. H., Hydraulic Machinery, Measurement Techniques

BLAGOJEVIĆ, Đ., Rocket Propulsion, Flight Dynamics with Aerodynamics

BOGNER, M. G., Process Equipment Mechanical Design and Selection

BOJANIĆ, P. O., Computer Graphics

BRKIĆ, L. D., Steam Boilers, Thermal Power

ČANTRAK, S., Hydraulics and Pneumatics, Hydromechanics
ČOVIĆ, V. M., Mechanics
DEBELJKOVIĆ, D. L., Linear System Design, Object and Process Dynamics
ĐORDEVIĆ, S., Mechanism Design
ĐORDJEVIĆ, V. D., Fluid Mechanics
DUBOKA, Č. V., Vehicle Maintenance Technology, Experimental Methods
DUBONJIĆ, R. R., Economy
GAJIĆ, A., Turbomachinery, Hydraulic Torque Converters
GEORGIJEVIĆ, D., Mathematics
GOLUBOVIĆ, Z., Mechanics
HOFMAN, M., Ship Theory, Ship Behaviour in Waves
IVANOVIĆ, G., Theory of Vehicle Motion, Theory of Effectiveness
JAĆIMOVIĆ, B., Process Planning, Heat and Mass Transfer Equipment
JANKES, G., Industrial Furnaces and Boilers, Furnace Design
JANKOVIĆ, J., Aircraft Equipment and Systems
JANKOVIĆ, M., Fundamentals of Machine Design
JARAMAZ, S., Interior Ballistics, Projectile Design
JOJIĆ, B. Ž., Aircraft Propulsion, Rocket Propulsion
KALAJDŽIĆ, M. J., Production Process Automation
KLARIN, M. M., Production Organization, Terotechnology
KORUGA, D., Bioautomatic Control
KOZIĆ, Đ., Thermodynamics, Heat and Mass Transfer
KRIVOŠIĆ, I. N., Aircraft Structure
KUBUROVIĆ, M., Environmental Engineering, Drying Equipment
MAJSTOROVIĆ, V., Quality Management
MARKOSKI, M. J., Cooling Devices, Pipelines
MARKOVIĆ, D., Agricultural Machines
MILINOVIĆ, M., Rocket and Launcher Design, Fire Control Systems
MILOSAAVLJEVIĆ, A., Engineering Materials
MILUTINOVIĆ, D., Manufacturing Technology, Industrial Robots
MLADENOVIĆ, N., Mechanics
NEDELJKOVIĆ, M., Hydraulic Machinery, Pumps and Fans
OGNJANOVIĆ, M., Machine Elements, Machine Design
PAVLOVIĆ, M., Fluid Mechanics, Gas Dynamics
PEŠIĆ, S., Aerodynamics, Propellers and Rotors
PETKOVIĆ, Z., Material Handling Machines, Steel Structures
PETROVIĆ, S. V., Internal Combustion Engine Theory and Design
PETROVIĆ, Z., Computer Aided Design, Aircraft Armament
PILIPOVIĆ, M., Manufacturing Systems, Production Process Automation
PLAVŠIĆ, N. I., Machine Elements, Fundamentals of Machine Design
POKRAJAC, S., Sociology, Industrial Management
RAC, A. A., Tribology
RADENOVIĆ, S., Mathematics
RADOJČIĆ, D., Resistance, Propulsion Steering of Ships
RADOVANOVIĆ, M. R., Fuels, Industrial Water, Lubricants
RAŠUO, B., Aircraft Maintenance, Flight Mechanics
RIBAR, Z., Pneumoelectric Control Systems, Hydroelectric Control Systems
RUŽIĆ, D. B., Strength of Materials
SAVIĆ, B., Heat Turbomachines, Thermal Power Plants
SEDMAK, A., Engineering Materials

SEKULIĆ, A., Mechanism Design, Technical Drawing with Engineering Design Graphics
ŠIJAČKI ŽERAVČIĆ, V., Engineering Materials
SPASIĆ, Ž., Computer-Integrated Manufacturing
STEFANOVIĆ, Z., Aerodynamic Construction
STUPAR, S., Computer Aided Design, Aircraft Armament
TANOVIĆ, L., Tools and Tooling, Manufacturing Technology
TOMIĆ, M., Internal Combustion Engines, Internal Combustion Engine Equipment
TOPIĆ, R., Agricultural Machinery Design and Construction
TOŠIĆ, S., Conveyors and Lifting Devices, Material Handling System Design
VELJIĆ, M., Agricultural Machinery Design and Construction
VUKOVIĆ, J. U., Mechanics
ŽEKOVIĆ, D., Mechanics
ŽIVANOVIĆ, T., Power Steam Boilers, Plant Boilers

Faculty of Medicine (Dr Subotića 8, 11000 Belgrade; tel. (11) 685-158; fax (11) 684-053; e-mail dknmed@rcub.bg.ac.yu; internet www .med.bg.ac.yu):

ALEKSANDRIĆ, B., Forensic Medicine
ANTUNOVIĆ, V., Surgery
APOSTOLSKI, S., Neurology
ARSOV, V. J., Surgery
ASIĆ RADOSAVLJEVIĆ, G., Internal Medicine
AVRAMOVIĆ, D. M., Internal Medicine
BACETIĆ, D., Pathological Anatomy
BANIĆEVIĆ, M., Paediatrics
BLAGOTIĆ, M. Ž., Anatomy
BOGDANOVIĆ, R., Paediatrics
BOŠKOVIĆ, D., Internal Medicine
BOŠNJAK, V. I., Internal Medicine
BOŽANIĆ, M., Internal Medicine
BOŽIĆ, M., Infectious Diseases
BRKIĆ POPOVIĆ, V., Internal Medicine
BULAJIĆ, M., Internal Medicine
BUMBAŠIREVIĆ, V., Histology and Embryology
BUNJEVAČKI, G., Paediatrics
BUTKOVIĆ, I., Surgery
ČEBEŠEK, R., Internal Medicine
ČEMERIKIĆ, D. A., Pathological Physiology
ČOLOVIĆ, M., Internal Medicine
ČOLOVIĆ, R., Surgery
CUCIĆ, V. S., Social Medicine
CVEJIĆ, V., Biochemistry
CVETKOVIĆ, D. H., Pathological Anatomy
CVETKOVIĆ, M., Gynaecology and Obstetrics
DENIĆ DJORDJEVIĆ, G., Pathological Physiology
ĐERIĆ, D., Otolaryngology and Maxillofacial Surgery
DJORDJEVIĆ, L. V., Anatomy
DJURIČIĆ, B., Biochemistry
ĐORĐEVIĆ, M., Surgery
ĐORĐEVIĆ, P., Internal Medicine
DOTLIĆ, R., Statistics and Informatics in Medicine
DRAŠKOVIĆ MAŠIREVIĆ, G., Physiology
DREZGIĆ, M., Internal Medicine
ĐUKIĆ, P., Surgery
ĐUKIĆ, V., Surgery
DUNJIĆ, D., Forensic Medicine
ERIĆ MARINKOVIĆ, J., Statistics and Informatics in Medicine
GANOVIĆ, R., Gynaecology and Obstetrics
GLEDOVIĆ, Z., Epidemiology
GLIŠIĆ, S., Surgery
GOLUBOVIĆ, G., Internal Medicine
GOLUBOVIĆ, S., Ophthalmology
GRBOVIĆ, L. Ć., Pharmacology and Toxicology
GRUJIĆ, M., Internal Medicine
HADŽI ĐOKIĆ, J. B., Surgery
HAN, R., Nuclear Medicine
HAVELKA, M., Pathological Anatomy

IGNAJČEV, M., Ophthalmology
ILANKOVIĆ, N., Psychiatry
ILIĆ, A. B., Anatomy
JAKOVIĆ, M., Surgery
JANIĆIJEVIĆ, M., Surgery
JANKOVIĆ, S., Epidemiology
JANOŠEVIĆ, L., Otolaryngology and Maxillofacial Surgery
JANOŠEVIĆ, S., Statistics and Informatics in Medicine
JAREBINSKI, M. S., Epidemiology
JAŠOVIĆ, M., Psychiatry
JEVREMOVIĆ, I., Epidemiology
JORGA, I., Physiology
JORGA, V., Hygiene and Medical Ecology
JOVANOVIĆ, T. M., Physiology
JOVANOVIĆ, T. P., Microbiology and Immunology
KALEZIĆ, V., Surgery
KAŽIĆ, T. M., Pharmacology and Toxicology
KOCIJANČIĆ, M., Internal Medicine
KOCIJANČIĆ, R., Hygiene and Medical Ecology
KONTIĆ, Đ., Ophthalmology
KOSTIĆ, V., Neurology
KOVAČEVIĆ, N., Internal Medicine
KOVAČEVIĆ, S. J., Forensic Medicine
LABAN, A. I., Pathological Anatomy
LAČKOVIĆ, V. B., Histology and Embryology
LASTIĆ, S. S., Anatomical Pathology
LATKOVIĆ, Z., Ophthalmology
LONČAR STEVANOVIĆ, H., Physiology
LOTINA, S., Surgery
LUKIĆ, V. S., Neurology
MAGLAJIĆ, S., Paediatrics
MAKSIMOVIĆ, Ž., Surgery
MANČIĆ, J., Paediatrics
MARIĆ, J., Psychiatry
MARINKOVIĆ, S. V., Anatomy
MARŠEVALSKI, A., Physical Medicine and Rehabilitation
MARTINOVIĆ, Ž., Neurology
MATIĆ, M., Internal Medicine
MICIĆ, D., Internal Medicine
MICIĆ, S., Surgery
MIJAĆ, M., Anatomy
MILENKOVIĆ, S., Ophthalmology
MILIČEVIĆ, N., Histology and Embryology
MILIČEVIĆ, R., Surgery
MILIČEVIĆ, Ž., Histology and Embryology
MILIKIĆ MITIĆ, M., Internal Medicine
MILOVIĆ, I., Surgery
MILUTINOVIĆ, D., Surgery
MIMIĆ OKA, J. I., Biochemistry
MISITA, V., Ophthalmology
MITROVIĆ, M. M., Surgery
MUJOVIĆ, V. M., Physiology
MUNJIZA, M., Psychiatry
NEDELKJOV, V., Pathological Physiology
NEŠIĆ, V., Internal Medicine
NIKOLIĆ, G., Physical Medicine and Rehabilitation
NIKOLIĆ, S., Infectious Diseases
NIKOLIĆ, P. L., Infectious Diseases
OBRADOVIĆ, M., Forensic Medicine
OBRADOVIĆ, V., Nuclear Medicine
OCIĆ, G., Neurology
OSTOJIĆ, M., Internal Medicine
OŠTRIĆ, V., Internal Medicine
PANTELIĆ ATANACKOVIĆ, M., Pathological Anatomy
PANTIĆ, S., Histology and Embryology
PAOVIĆ STANOJEVIĆ, A., Ophthalmology
PAPOVIĆ, R., Biology and Human Genetics
PAUNOVIĆ, V., Psychiatry
PAVLOVIĆ, M. D., Infectious Diseases
PAVLOVIĆ, M. R., Physiology
PAVLOVIĆ, M. Ž., Occupational Medicine
PAVLOVIĆ, S., Nuclear Medicine
PEJOVIĆ, M., Psychiatry
PERIŠIĆ, M., Internal Medicine
PERIŠIĆ, V., Paediatrics
PEŠIĆ, B., Pathological Physiology
PETKOVIĆ, S., Gynaecology and Obstetrics
PILIPOVIĆ, N., Internal Medicine
PLEĆAŠ, D., Hygiene and Medical Ecology

Popović, G., Physical Medicine and Rehabilitation
Popović, M. R., Surgery
Popović, M. R., Surgery
Potić Vesović, V., Physical Medicine and Rehabilitation
Prostran, M., Anatomy
Prostran, M., Pharmacology and Toxicology
Radević, B., Surgery
Radonjić, V., Anatomy
Radulović, N., Paediatrics
Radulović, R., Otolaryngology and Maxillofacial Surgery
Ramić, Z., Microbiology and Immunology
Ranković, A., Anatomy
Rebić, P., Internal Medicine
Repac, R. M., Surgery
Ristić, M., Surgery
Runić, S., Gynaecology and Obstetrics
Samardžić, M., Surgery
Samardžić, R. G., Pharmacology and Toxicology
Šašic, M., Infectious Diseases
Savič Djurković, R. M., Biochemistry
Šeferović, P., Internal Medicine
Šikić, B., Pathological Physiology
Simeunović, S. D., Paediatrics
Simić, S., Social Medicine
Sindelić, R., Surgery
Skender, M., Pathological Anatomy
Slavković, S., Surgery
Stanimirović, B., Gynaecology and Obstetrics
Starčević, V., Physiology
Starović, D., Surgery
Stefanović, B., Histology and Embryology
Stevović, D. M., Surgery
Stojković Mostarica, M., Microbiology and Immunology
Subotić, S. L., Surgery
Suzić, S., Physiology
Talić, B. S., Surgery
Teofilovskid, G. E., Anatomy
Timotijević, I., Psychiatry
Todorović, S., Neurology
Trpinac, D., Histology and Embryology
Vasiljević, J., Pathological Anatomy
Vasiljević, Z., Internal Medicine
Velimirović, D., Surgery
Velimirović, D., Pathological Anatomy
Veljković, S. D., Forensic Medicine
Vidaković, A. R., Occupational Medicine
Vlahović Švabić, M., Microbiology and Immunology
Vlajinac, H. D., Epidemiology
Vučković, V., Physiology
Vučović, D., Surgery
Vulović, D. M., Pathological Physiology
Vulović, Z., Chemistry in Medicine
Zamaklar, D., Surgery
Zec Kranjčić, I., Microbiology and Immunology
Živković, S., Surgery

Faculty of Mining and Geology (Đušina 7, 11000 Belgrade; tel. (11) 323-7321; fax (11) 323-5539; e-mail dean@rgf.bg.ac.yu; internet www.rgf.bg.ac.yu):
Babić, D., Genetic Mineralogy, Mineralogy, Technical Mineralogy
Batalović, V., Hydraulic and Pneumatic Machines in Mining, Boring Machines and Equipment, Exploitation and Oil and Gas Transport
Blečić, N., Coal Deposits, Mining Geology
Ćalić, N. M., Theoretical Bases of Mineral Processing, Mineral Processing
Čokorilo, V., Underground Mining Mechanization
Ćorić, S., Geostatic Calculation
Cvetković Mrkić, S., Ground Improvement Methods and Engineering Geology
Đajić, N., Thermodynamics, Heat Engines and Energy Plants, Automation and Process Control

Dangić, A. V., Geochemistry, Mineral Raw Material Deposits, Geology and Environmental Protection
Deušić, S., Mineral Processing Machinery and Equipment
Dimitrijević, S., Surveying, Mining Photogrammetry
Đoković, I. M., Geological Mapping, Environmental Geology
Dragišić, V., Mineral Deposit Hydrogeology, General Hydrogeology
Gagić, D., Methods and Technology for Underground Excavation of Bedded Deposits, Underground Excavation Methods
Grubor, D., Physics
Grujić, M., Mine Transport and Hoisting
Gržetić, I., Physical Chemistry of Ore Deposits, Geology and Environmental Protection, Laboratory Investigation of Mineral Resources
Ilić, M. M., Exploration of Building Material Deposits, Nonmetallic Mineral Deposits
Ivić, A. P., Mathematics
Ivković, S. Ž., Elements of Machines, Machine Design, Metalworking
Janićević, D., Historical Geology, Geology of Yugoslavia
Jelenković, R., Metallic Mineral Deposits, Mineral Deposits
Jevremović, D., Engineering Geological Investigation, Geological Construction Materials
Karanović, L., X-Ray Structural Analysis, Applied Crystallography
Knežević, S., Historical Geology, Quaternary Geology, Stratigraphy of Yugoslavia
Kostić Pulek, A., Chemistry
Lazić, M., Special Hydrogeology, Exploratory Drilling
Lilić, N., Mine Ventilation, Mine Safety, Environmental Impact of Surface Drilling
Logar, M., Silicate Classification, Industrial Product Mineralogy, Geology and Environmental Protection, Mineral Raw Materials in Technology
Lokin, P. M., Principles of Geotechnics, Geotechnical Investigation Methods
Marinković, S., Chemistry, Oil Chemistry with Basic Refining
Marović, M. S., Neotectonics, Geotectonics, Geology of Yugoslavia
Mihajlović, Đ., Palaeobotany, Palaeoecology, Evolutionary Palaeontology, Fossil Organism Comparative Morphology, Micropalaeontology
Miličić, M., Mathematics, Numerical Analysis
Milovanović, D. J., Metamorphic Rock Petrology, Technical Petrology, Yugoslav Rock Formation Geology
Mitrović, V., Reservoir Physics, Fluid Mechanics, Oil and Gas Reservoir Engineering
Pavlović, V., Open Pit Exploitation Technology, Open Pit Exploration Technology, Removal of Water in Open Pit Mining
Pešić, L., Essentials of Geology, Principles of Geology
Petković, Z., Basics of Deposit Exploitation, Mineral Resource Deposit Exploitation
Poharac Logar, V., Instrumental Mineralogy, Mineralogy
Popov, S. R., Physical Chemistry, Fundamentals of Inorganic Chemistry
Prohaska, S. J., Hydrogeology
Purtić, N. M., Drilling and Blasting
Pušić, M., Ground Water Dynamics and Hydrology
Rabrenović, D., Historical Geology, Palaeogeography

Radojević, J. R., Rock Mechanics, Geomechanics, Rock and Soil Mechanics
Simeunović, D. M., Underground Mine Design, Mine Organization, Underground Excavation Methods
Simić, R., Surface Mining Methods, Removal of Water in Open Pit Mining
Stajević, B., Solid Mineral Deposit Prospecting and Exploration, Geological and Geochemical Prospecting
Starčević, M., Gravity Methods for Investigation, Geophysical Investigation Methodology, Seismology, Geophysical Electronic Instruments, Geophysics
Stevanović, Z., Hydrogeological Investigation Methods, Hydrogeological Investigation
Sudar, M., Micropalaeontology, Palaeontological and Biostratigraphic Research Methodology
Sunarić, D., Engineering Geology, Engineering Geodynamics
Tansković, T., Mining Equipment Maintenance, Thermodynamic Machinery
Tomanec, R., Raw Material Testing Methods for Mineral Processing Technology
Tomić, V., Hydrogeological Mapping
Trifunović, P., Mining Materials Technology
Vujasinović, S. O., Ground Water Protection, Geology and Environmental Protection
Vujić, S. B., Application of Computers in Mining, Programming
Zajić, B., Hoisting Equipment

Faculty of Organizational Sciences (Jove Ilića 154, 11000 Belgrade; tel. (11) 395-0800; fax (11) 461-221; e-mail radaks@fon .fon.bg.ac.yu; internet www.fon.bg.ac.yu):
Ćamilović, S. V., Human Resources Management
Čangalović, M., Operations Research, Discrete Mathematics
Ćirić, V. V., Computer Program Design Principles
Čupić, M. E., Decision Making Theory, Decision Support Systems
Dabić, S., Stock Exchanges and Shareholding
Dajović, S. V., Mathematics
Drakulić, M., Information Systems and Law, Business Law
Dulanović, Ž., Basics of Organization, Organization Projects
Filipović, V., Marketing, Strategic Marketing
Jovanov, Đ., Mathematics, Numerical Analysis
Kostić, K., Management Systems
Krčevinac, S. B., Operations Research, Econometric Methods
Lazarević, B. J., Information System Design
Levi Jakšić, M. I., Technology Management
Milićević, V., Management Economics and Business Planning, International Management
Mitrović, Ž. V., Quality Management, Quality Control
Pešaljević, M., Quality Management, Standardization Systems, Metrology Systems
Petrović, B. M., Work Studies
Petrovic, M. M., Manpower Planning
Radenković, B., Simulation and Simulation Languages
Radović, M. K., Fundamentals of Production Systems, Production Systems
Starčević, D., Distributed Information Systems
Todorović, J. M., Production Management
Vučić, V. V., Mathematics, Operations Research
Vujošević, M., Optimization Methods

VUKOVIĆ, N. A., Probability and Statistics
ŽARKIĆ JOKSIMOVIĆ, N., Financial Mangement and Accounting, Management Accounting

Faculty of Pharmacy (Vojvode Stepe 450, 11000 Belgrade; tel. (11) 473-224; fax (11) 397-2840; e-mail info@pharmacy.bg.ac.yu; internet www.pharmacy.bg.ac.yu):

AGBABA, D., Pharmaceutical Chemistry
DIMITRIJEVIĆ, M., Immunology
ĐURIĆ, Z., Pharmaceutical Technology with Biopharmacy, Industrial Pharmacy with Cosmetology
JANČIĆ, R., Botany
JELIĆ IVANOVIĆ, Z., Medicinal Biochemistry and Clinical Chemistry
JELIKIĆ STANKOV, M., Analytical Chemistry
JOVANOVIĆ, M., Pharmaceutical Technology with Biopharmacy, Industrial Pharmacy with Cosmetology
JOVANOVIĆ, T., General and Inorganic Chemistry
KORIĆANAC, Z, General and Inorganic Chemistry
KRSTIĆ, S., Pharmacology
LEPOSAVIĆ, G., Pathophysiology
MAJKIĆ SINGH, N., Medicinal Biochemistry and Clinical Enzymology
MALEŠEV, D., Physical Chemistry, Instrumental Methods, Chemical Laboratory Methods
MEDENICA, M., Physical Chemistry, Instrumental Methods, Chemical Laboratory Methods
MILETIĆ, I., Bromatology, Quality and Food Safety Control
POKRAJAC, M., Analytical Chemistry
RISTOVSKI, L., Physics
SPASIĆ, S., Medical Biochemistry, Statistics in Pharmacy
SPASOJEVIĆ KALIMANOVSKA, V., Medicinal Biochemistry and Clinical Enzymology
STOJANOV, M., General Biochemistry and Medicinal Biochemistry
STUPAR, M., Pharmaceutical Technology with Biopharmacy, Industrial Pharmacy with Cosmetology
UGREŠIĆ, N., Pharmacology
VLADIMIROV, S., Pharmaceutical Chemistry
VULETA, G., Industrial Pharmacy with Cosmetology
ŽIVANOVIĆ, L., Drugs Analysis

Faculty of Philology (Studentski trg 3, 11000 Belgrade; tel. (11) 638-666; fax (11) 630-039; internet www.fil.bg.ac.yu):

BOGOSAVLJEVIĆ, S., German Literature
BOJOVIĆ, Z., Yugoslav Literature from the Renaissance to Romanticism
BOZOVIĆ, R. N., Arabic Language and Literature
BOZOVIĆ, Z. N., Russian Literature
ĆORIĆ, B., History of the Serbian Language
DERETIĆ, J. R., Serbian and South-Slav Literature
DESIĆ, M. P., Serbo-Croat Language Teaching Methodology
DJINDJIĆ, S. M., Albanian Studies
GRUBAČIĆ, S. K., German Language
HLEBEC, B., English Language
IVANIĆ, D., Modern Serbian Literature
JANIĆEVIĆ, J., Cultural Studies
JANKOVIĆ, V. D., Literary Theory
JEREMIĆ, L., World Literature and Literary Theory
JOVANOVIĆ, G. M., Polish Literature
KOJEN, L., Aesthetics and Literary Theory
MAROJEVIĆ, R. N., Russian Literature
NESKOVIĆ, R. R., Philosophical Fundamentals of Marxism
NIKOLIĆ, M., Contemporary Serbian Language
NOVAKOVIĆ, J. R., French Literature
PETKOVIĆ, N. B., Modern Yugoslav Literature, Twentieth Century Literature

PETROVIĆ, S. D., Sociology of Culture and Art
PIPER, P. J., Russian Literature
POLOVINA, V., General Linguistics
RADIĆ DUGONJIĆ, M., Russian Language
SIMIĆ, R. D., Contemporary Serbo-Croatian Language with Stylistics
STANKOVIĆ, B. D., Russian Language
STOJANOVIĆ, D. S., World Literature with Literary Theory
TANASKOVIĆ, D. R., Arabic Language and Literature
TRNAVCI, H. I., Albanian Language and Literature
VUKOBRAT, S., English Literature

Faculty of Philosophy (Čika Ljubina 18–20, 11000 Belgrade; tel. (11) 639-119; fax (11) 639-356; e-mail info@f.bg.ac.yu; internet www.f.bg.ac.yu):

ALIBABIĆ, Š., Theory of Educational Organization
BANDIĆ, D. I., Ethnology of Yugoslavia (Spiritural Culture)
BOGDANOVIĆ, M. I., Social Research Methodology
BOGOSAVLJEVIĆ, S., Statistics in Psychology
BOJANOVIĆ, R. Ž., Psychology of Interpersonal Relations
BOLČIĆ, S. I., Sociology of Work
BULATOVIĆ, R. N., Andragogy of Work
ĆUPURDIJA, B., Social Anthropology
DENEGRI, J., History of Modern Art
DIMIĆ, L., Yugoslav History
DOŠEN, K., Philosophy
DUŠANIĆ, S. S., Ancient History
ELAKOVIĆ, S., History of Philosophy
HRNJICA, S., General Psychology with Personality Psychology
JELIĆ, V., History of Greek Literature
KAČAVENDA RADIĆ, N., Andragogy of Free Time
KOCIĆ, L. P., General Pedagogy
KOVAČEVIĆ, I., Methodology of Ethnology and Anthropology
KULJIC, T., Political Sociology
KUZMANOVIĆ, B., Social Psychology
LAZIĆ, M., Sociology
LJUŠIĆ, R., National History of the New Age
LOMA, A., Historical Grammar of the Greek Language
MAKSIMOVIĆ, I. M., Byzantine History
MEDIĆ, S., Family Andragogy
MIKIĆ, Ž. M., Physical Anthropology
MILIĆ, A., Family Sociology
MILIN, M., Introduction to the Classics
MIMICA, A., History of Social Theory
MITROVIĆ, A., General History of the New Age
OPALIĆ, P., Social Pathology
PAJEVIĆ, D., Work Psychology
PEŠIĆ, M., Preschool Pedagogy
RADOŠ, K., Educational Psychology
RICL, M., Ancient History
RISTOVIĆ, M., General Modern History
ŠARANOVIĆ BOŽANOVIĆ, N., General Pedagogy
SPREMIĆ, M. M., General History of the Middle Ages
STANKOVIĆ, DJ. DJ., Yugoslav History
ŠUPUT, M., History of Architecture
TODIĆ, B., Introduction to Art History
TRNAVAC, N., School Pedagogy
VOJVODIĆ, M. S., General History of the New Age
VUJOVIĆ, S., Urban Sociology
ZEC, M., Introduction to Economics
ZUROVAC, M. M., Aesthetics

Faculty of Physical Chemistry (Studentski trg 16, 11000 Belgrade; tel. (11) 635-545; fax (11) 187-133; e-mail dekan@ffh.bg.ac.yu; internet www.ffh.bg.ac.yu):

ANIĆ, S., Physical Chemistry
BAČIĆ, G., Physical Chemistry of Fluids, Nuclear Spectrometry

DONDUR, V., Chemical Kinetics, Catalysis
HOLCLAJTNER ANTUNOVIĆ, I., General Physical Chemistry, Plasma Physical Chemistry
JEREMIĆ, M., Physical Chemistry
MARKOVĆ, D., Physical Chemistry, Physical Chemistry in Environmental Protection
MENTUS, S. V., Electrochemistry, Physical Chemistry of Solid Electrolytes
MILJANIĆ, Š., Radiochemistry and Nuclear Chemistry
MIOČ, U., Physico-Chemical Analysis, Applied Spectroscopy
PERIĆ, M. N., Quantum Chemistry and Molecular Structures, Spectra and Structures

Faculty of Physics (Studentski trg 12–16, 11000 Belgrade; tel. (11) 630-152; fax (11) 328-2619; e-mail knez@ff.bg.ac.yu; internet www.ff.bg.ac.yu):

ANIČIN, I., Nuclear Physics
BELIĆ, D. S., Atomic and Molecular Physics, Applied Physics
ĆURIĆ, M. B., Dynamic Meteorology, Cloud Physics
DAMNJANOVIĆ, M., Quantum and Mathematical Physics, Condensed Matter Physics
ĐENIŽE, S. I., Ionized Gas and Plasma Physics, Atomic and Molecular Physics
DRNDAREVIĆ, S., Nuclear Physics, Particle and Field Physics
JANJIĆ, Z. I., Dynamic Meteorology
KNEŽEVIĆ, M., Statistical Physics
KONJEVIĆ, N., Classical and Quantum Optics, Lasers
KRPIĆ, D., Nuclear Physics, Particle and Field Physics
MILOŠEVIĆ, S., Statistical Physics
PURIC, J. M., Ionized Gas and Plasma Physics
SAVIĆ, I., Nuclear Physics, Condensed Matter Physics
SREKOVIĆ, A., Ionized Gas and Plasma Physics
STAMATOVIĆ, A. S., Applied Physics, Atomic and Molecular Physics
ZEKOVIĆ, L., Applied Physics, Condensed Matter Physics

Faculty of Political Sciences (Jove Ilića 165, 11000 Belgrade; tel. (11) 471-911; fax (11) 491-501; e-mail fpn@fpn.bg.ac.yu; internet www.fpn.bg.ac.yu):

DAMJANOVIĆ, M. D., Organization and Management Studies
JEVTIĆ, M., Religious and Political Studies
KECMANOVIĆ, N., Family Sociology
LAKIĆEVIĆ, M., Social Development and Planning
MILOSAVLJEVIĆ, M. V., Social Pathology
PAVLOVIĆ, V. D., Political Sociology of Modern Society
PEŠIĆ, M. D., General Sociology
PODUNAVAC, M. L., Theory of Political Systems
RADOJKOVIĆ, M. J., Communication Studies
SAMARDŽIĆ, S., European Relations and European Union Studies
SIMEUNOVIĆ, D., Foundations of Political Science
SIMIĆ, M., Rehabilitation of Disabled Persons, Public Health
SLAVUJEVIĆ, Z., Political Marketing and Public Relations
SOKIĆ, S. R., Yugoslav Economy, National Economic Studies
ŠTAMBUK, V. Z., Cybernetics and Informatics
TRGOVČEVIĆ, L., Contemporary Political History
VASILJEVIĆ, B., Contemporary Political Economy
VESELINOV, D. S., Political Economy
VIDANOVIĆ, I., Social Case Work
VUKOVIĆ, D., Systems of Social Welfare

Faculty of Sport (Blagoja Parovića 156, 11000 Belgrade; tel. (11) 555-000; fax (11) 555-474; internet www.dif.bg.ac.yu):

ALEXSIĆ, V., Football
BOKAN, B., Physical Culture Theory
ĆIRKOVIĆ, Z., Martial Arts
ILIĆ, N., Physiology
JOVANOVIĆ, S., Martial Arts
KARALEJIĆ, M., Basketball
KUKOLJ, M., General Anthropology
LAZAREVIĆ, L., Psychology
NIKOLIĆ, Z., Physiology
PETROVIĆ, Z., Physical Culture Facilities
RADISAVIJEVIĆ, L., Rhythmic-Sports Gymnastics
RADISAVIJEVIĆ, M., Corrective Gymnastics
RADOJEVIĆ, J., Sports Gymnastics
ŠTAKIĆ, Đ., General Sociology and Physical Culture Sociology
STEFANOVIĆ, Đ., Athletics
UGARKOVIĆ, D., Human Development Biology with Elements of Sports Medicine

Faculty of Stomatology (Dr Subotića 8, 11000 Belgrade; tel. (11) 685-288; fax (11) 685-361; e-mail stomfak@rcub.bg.ac.yu; internet www .stomf.bg.ac.yu):

BELOICA, D. Ć., Paediatrics, Preventive Dentistry
DAPČEVIĆ, B., Internal Medicine
DERGENC, R, Otorhinolarnygology
DIMITRIJEVIĆ, B. B., Periodontology, Oral Medicine
DIMITRIJEVIĆ, B. R., Maxillofacial Surgery
GAVRIĆ, M. M., Maxillofacial Surgery
IVANOVIĆ, V., Conservation Dentistry Endodontics
JANKOVIĆ, L., Periodontology, Oral Medicine
KONTIĆ, M., General Surgery
LEKOVIĆ, V. M., Periodontology, Oral Mechine
MIJANOVIĆ, B., General Surgery
MIKOVIĆ, M. D., Forensic Medicine
MILENKOVIĆ, P. B., Pathophysiology
NIKODIJEVIĆ, M., General Surgery
NIKOLIĆ, L., Ophthalmology
PAP, K., Conservation Dentistry Endodontics
POTIĆ, J. B., Neurology and Psychiatry
SJEROBABIN, I., Maxillofacial Surgery
STAMENKOVIĆ, D., Prosthodontics
STANIŠIĆ-SINOBAD, D. N., Prosthodontics
STOJIĆ, D., Pharmacology, Toxicology
TODOROVIĆ, L. M., Oral Surgery
URSU MAGIDU, I., Periodontology, Oral Medicine
VRANJEŠ, D., Neurology and Psychiatry
VULOVIĆ, M. D., Paediatric Preventive Dentistry
ZELIĆ, O. B., Periodontology, Oral Medicine

Faculty of Teacher Training (Narodnog frontna 43, 11000 Belgrade; tel. (11) 235-1033; e-mail ufbg@tehnicom.net):

BANDJUR, V. B., Didactics
JOVANOVIĆ, A., Literature
KECMANOVIĆ, N., Sociology

Faculty of Technology and Metallurgy (Karnegijeva 4, 11000 Belgrade; tel. (11) 337-0425; fax (11) 322-0847; e-mail tmf@elab.tmf .bg.ac.yu; internet www.tmf.bg.ac.yu):

IVANIĆ, L., Casting, Theory of Casting
MAGADALINOVIĆ, D., Communition and Classification
MARKOVIĆ, D., Materials Testing
MILIĆEVIĆ, Ž., Underground Mining Technology
MILJKOVIĆ, M., Mine Ventilation, Technical Safety Precautions
RAJČIĆ VUJASINOVIĆ, M., Hydro- and Electrometallurgical Process Theory
STANKOVIĆ, R., Transport and Haulage, Transport in Mineral Technologies
STANKOVIĆ, V., Metallurgical Operations
STANKOVIĆ, Z., Physical Chemistry

STANOJLOVIĆ, R., Physical Methods of Concentration, Mineral Processing
STAVRIĆ, B. J., Economics and Production Organization
ŽIVKOVIĆ, Ž., Nonferrous Metal and Alloy Metallurgy, Pyrometallurgical Process Theory

Faculty of Transport and Traffic Engineering (Vojvode Stepe 305, 11000 Belgrade; tel. (11) 397-6017; fax (11) 466-294; e-mail dean@sf.sf .bg.ac.yu; internet www.sf.bg.ac.yu):

BABIĆ, O., Air Traffic Control, Air Cargo Transport
BAKMAZ, M. R., Telecommunications Switching Technology, Telecommunications Traffic and Networks
BOJKOVIĆ, Z. S., Electrical Engineering, Basic Telecommunications Technology, Telecommunications Traffic Exploitation
BUKUMIROVIĆ, M. M., Cybernetics, Cybernetics in Transport and Traffic, Computer Simulation, System Modelling on Computer, Programming Languages in Postal and Telecommunications Traffic
ČOLIĆ, V., Ships and Vessels, Ship Resistance and Propulsion, Basics of Water Transport
CVETKOVIĆ, P. A., Fluid Mechanics, Mechanics, Materials Strength
KUZMANOVIĆ, D., Mechanics
LAZOVIĆ, S. M., Telecommunication Systems
MANDIĆ, D., Railway Traction, Urban Rail Systems, Rail Traffic Operation, Application of Telematics and Process Automation in Railway Traffic
MILORADOVIĆ, S., Mathematics
PANTELIĆ VUJANIĆ, S., Sociology, Traffic and Transport Engineering Law, Navigable Waterways Law, Air Transport Law, Traffic Law, Postal and Telecommunications Law, Railway Transport Law
PAPIĆ, V., Motor Vehicle Maintenance, Transport Vehicles and Maintenance
POPOVIĆ, J., Probability and Statistics, Operations Research
PUTNIK, N. D., Terminals
RADMILOVIĆ, Z., Port Planning and Design, Fleet Operation and Management, Water Transport Basics
RADOJKOVIĆ, Z., Roads, Civil Engineering Basics
ŠELMIĆ, R. R., Elements of Transport Devices and Installations, Thermodynamics
SRETENOVIĆ, M., Materials Handling, Fundamentals in Materials Handling
TOŠIĆ, V. S., Airports
VEŠOVIĆ, V. B., Transport and Traffic Organization and Manangement, Transport and Traffic, Transport and Traffic Work Organization, Postal and Telecommunications Organization and Management
VUJANIĆ, M., Traffic Safety, Accident Prevention, Accident Reconstruction
VUKANOVIĆ, S. V., Traffic Management and Control, Intelligent Transport Systems
VUKOBRAT, M. D., Mechanics
ŽEŽELJ, S., Motor Vehicles

Faculty of Veterinary Medicine (Bulevar JNA 18, 11000 Belgrade; tel. (11) 685-666; fax (11) 685-936; e-mail mara@vet.bg.ac.yu; internet www.vet.bg.ac.yu):

ALEKSIĆ, Z., Forensic Veterinary Medicine
AŠANIN, R. M., Microbiology and Immunology
BALTIĆ, M., Fish, Crab and Shellfish Food Quality and Hygiene
BALGOJEVIĆ, Z., Anatomy
BOŽIĆ, T., Pathophysiology
BUNIĆIĆ, O., Meat Hygiene and Meat Technology

DJURIČIĆ, B., Infectious Diseases of Domestic Animals
DOBRIĆ, Đ., Infectious Diseases of Domestic Animals
DREKIĆ, D. M., Anatomy
GLEDIĆ, D. S., Histology and Embryology
IVANOV, I., Ruminant and Swine Diseases, Clinical Diagnostics
JEZDIMIROVIĆ, M., Pharmacology and Toxicology
JOVANOVIĆ, M., General Pathology and Pathological Morphology
JOVANOVIĆ, S. J., Animal Breeding
KATIĆ, V., Dairy Product Hygiene
KATIĆ RADIVOJEVIĆ, S., Parasitology
KNEŽEVIĆ, M. A., General Pathology and Pathological Morphology
KULIŠIĆ, Z., Parasitology
LAZAREVIĆ, M., Physiology
MIJAČEVIĆ, Z. M., Dairy Product Technology
NIKOLIĆ, Z., Anatomy
NIKOLOVSKI STEFANOVIĆ, Z., Equine and Small Animal Disease, Clinical Propedeutics
PALIĆ, T. D., Avian Diseases, Equine and Small Animal Diseases
PAVLOVIĆ, V., Domestic Animal Reproduction, Artificial Insemination
PEJIN, I., Statistics
PETRUJKIĆ, T., Domestic Animal Reproduction, Artificial Insemination
POPOVIĆ, D., Biophysics
POPOVIĆ, N., Wild Animal Diseases, Equine and Small Animal Diseases
RADENKOVIĆ DAMNJANOVIĆ, B., Animal Hygiene and General Hygiene
ŠAMANC, H., Ruminant and Swine Diseases
ŠĆEPANOVIĆ, D., Sociology and Ethics
ŠIMIĆ, M., Histology and Embryology
SINOVEC, Z., Animal Nutrition Physiology and Pathology
SMILJANIĆ, D., Unit Operations
STOJANOVIĆ, L. V., Dairy Product Hygiene
STOJIĆ, V., Physiology
TRAILOVIĆ, D., Cattle Production Economics and Organization, Health Care, Cattle and Food Marketing and Transfer, Equine and Small Animal Diseases, Clinical Propedeutics
VASIĆ, J., Surgery, Orthopaedics, Ophthalmology
VICKOVIĆ, D., Forensic Veterinary Medicine
VUKOVIĆ, I., Meat Technology

ATTACHED INSTITUTES

Institute for the Application of Nuclear Technology: Dir Dr SLOBODANKA STANKOVIĆ.

Institute of Chemistry, Technology and Metallurgy: Dir Dr ŽARKO JOVANOVIĆ.

Institute of Philosophy and Social Theory: Dir Dr SVETOZAR STOJANOVIĆ.

Institute of Physics: Dir Dr DRAGAN POPOVIĆ.

Institute of Social Sciences: Dir Dr DRAGOMIR PANTIĆ.

Mihajlo Pupin Institute: Dir VLADAN BATANOVIĆ.

Siniša Stankovic Institute for Biological Reseach: Dir Dr RANKA POPOVIĆ.

Vinča Institute of Nuclear Sciences: Dir-Gen. Dr MIROSLAV M. KOPEČNI.

UNIVERZITET UMETNOSTI U BEOGRADU
(University of Arts in Belgrade)

Kosančićev venac 29, 11000 Belgrade

Telephone: (11) 262-5166
Fax: (11) 629-785
E-mail: rektorat@arts.bg.ac.yu
Internet: www.arts.bg.ac.yu

Founded 1957 as Academy of Arts; became University 1973

Academic year: October to September

President: Dr ČEDOMIR VASIĆ

Vice-President: Prof. ANDRIJA DJUKIĆ, Prof. NEBOJSA IGNJATOVIĆ, Prof. KOSTA KRSMANOVIĆ

Secretary-General: OLGA LEČIĆ PAVLOVIĆ

Library of 197,800

Number of teachers: 498

Number of students: 2,539

Publication: *Bilten INFO* (dramatic arts, monthly)

DEANS

Faculty of Applied Arts and Design: Prof. VLADIMIR KOSTIĆ DIVAĆ

Faculty of Dramatic Arts: Prof. Dr PREDRAG POPOVIĆ

Faculty of Fine Arts: Prof. NIKOLA VUKOSAVLJEVIĆ

Faculty of Music: Prof. MILAN MIHAJLOVIĆ (acting)

PROFESSORS

Faculty of Applied Arts and Design (Kralja Petra 4, 11000 Belgrade; tel. (11) 3285-065; fax (11) 182-047; e-mail fpu@eunet.yu):

ANDJELKOVIC, M.
BAJIC, M.
BERBEROVIC, M.
BLAZINA, Z.
BOCINA, R.
CIRIC, R.
DEDIC, B.
DIMITRIJEVIC, D.
DJOLIC, S.
DJURICKOVIC, S.
DRAGOVIC, J.
DRAGUTINOVIC, A.
GAVRIC, Z.
IZVONAR, D.
JANKOVIC, Z.
KAJTEZ, S.
KARANOVIC, B.
KNEZEVIC, I.
KOMAD ARSENIJEVIC, G.
KOSTIC, M.
KOSTIC, V.
KRSMANOVIC, K.
LALIC, R.
MARCIKIC, I.
NAKICENOVIC, M.
NESIC, D.
NINCIC, O.
PAJVANCIC, A.
PETROVIC, D.
RAKIC, I.
RANKOVIC, D.
SIMOVIC, J.
STAMENKOVIC, M.
STOJADINOVIC, O.
STOJANOVIC, D.
TODIC, M.
VELJOVIC, I.
VLAHOVIC, J.
VUCKOVIC, M.
VUKICEVIC, V.
VUKSAN, D.
ZARIC, G.
ZECEVIC, S.
ZIKIC, S.

Faculty of Dramatic Arts (Bulevar umetnosti 20, 11000 Belgrade; tel. (11) 140-419; fax (11) 130-862; e-mail fduinfo@afrodita.rcub.bg.ac.yu; internet www.fdu.bg.ac.yu):

BABAC, M.
BAJIC, D.
BARAC, S.
BOGOEVA SEDLAR, L.
DAKOVIC, N.
DAUTOVIC, F.
DAVID, F.
DEJANOVIC, V.

DIMITRIJEVIC, A.
DJOKIC, J.
DJUKIC, A.
DRAGICEVIC SESIC, M.
GADJANSKI, M.
GLUSICA, M.
IMAMI, P.
JEVTIC, N.
JEVTOVIC, V.
JEZERKIC, V.
JOVANOVIC, D.
JOVICEVIC, A.
KARAJICA, F.
KARANOVIC, S.
KNEZEVIC, R.
LORENCIN, N.
MANDIC, A.
MANDIC, T.
MARIC, G.
MARICIC, N.
MARKOVIC, G.
MARKOVIC, M.
MERC, R.
MILETIN, M.
MRKIC POPOVIC, L.
OPSENICA, V.
PAJKIC, N.
PEKOVIC, G.
PERISIC, P.
POPOV, D.
POPOVIC, P.
POPOVIC, Z.
PROKIC, N.
RANKOVIC, R.
RAPAJIC, S.
SALETOVIC, S.
SAVIN, E.
SAVKOVIC, M.
SIJAN, S.
STOJANOVIC, N.
TABACKI, M.
TERZIC, G.
TODOROVIC, R.
VESELINOVIC, D.
VOLK ZIVKOVIC, M.
VUJIC, I.

Faculty of Fine Arts (Rajićeva 10, 11000 Belgrade; tel. (11) 630-635; fax (11) 328-4569; e-mail fludekan@yubc.net):

BAJIC, M.
BOJOVIC, A.
DRAGOJLOVIC, M.
DRAGOJLOVIC, M.
GROZDANIC, M.
JOVANOVIC, D.
KACIC, D.
KNEZEVIC, R.
KRSTIC, V.
LALIC, V.
NIKOLIC, G.
PAJIN, D.
RADOJCIC, S.
RADOJEV, N.
ROKSANDIC, S.
SIMEONOVIC CELIC, I.
SIVACKI, J.
SMILJANIC, Z.
SUICA, N.
TEPAVAC, M.
VASIC, C.
VUKOSAVLJEVIC, N.
VUKOVIC, B.
VUKOVIC, Z.
ZIVKOVIC, V.

Faculty of Music (Kralja Milana 50, 11000 Belgrade; tel. (11) 361-0960; fax (11) 643-598; e-mail fmuinfo@afrodita.rcub.bg.ac.yu):

ARSIKIN, I.
BELIC, S.
BOZIC, S.
CETKOVIC, Z.
DJURKOVIC, B.
DORIC, R.
ERIC, Z.
GALUN, A.

GOLEMOVIC, D.
GRBIC, S.
GRGIN, A.
HUMO RAJEVAC, T.
IGNJATOVIC, N.
ISAESKI, M.
IVANOVIC, M.
IVANOVIC, M.
JEVTOVIC MINOV, G.
JOKANOVIC, M.
JOVANOVIC, L.
JOVICIC, D.
KARLOVIC, M.
KOSANOVIC, M.
KRSIC, V.
MAKSIMOVIC, J.
MARINKOVIC, S.
MATORKIC IVANOVIC, B.
MEZEI, L.
MIHAJLOVIC, J.
MIHAJLOVIC, M.
MILANKOVIC, V.
MLADJENOVIC, D.
NIKOLIC, M.
OGRIZOVIC, V.
OLUJIC, T.
PERIC, D.
PESIC, U.
PETROVIC, M.
POPOVIC, N.
POPOVIC GROS, L.
RACKOV, N.
RAJIC, I.
RASKOVIC, F.
SABO, A.
SANDOROV, A.
SEPIC, S.
SERDAR, A.
SMILJANIC, R.
SOBAJIC, D.
STANKOVIC, L.
SUVAKOVIC, M.
TOSIC, V.
TRAJKOVIC, V.
VASIC, O.
VUJIC, A.
ZIVKOVIC, N.

ATTACHED INSTITUTES

Centre for Continuing Professional Development in Culture and Media: Dir Prof. GORAN PEKOVIĆ.

Centre for Digital Creativity: Head Prof. ALEKSANDAR KAJEVIĆ.

Centre for Graphic and Visual Research: Dir Prof. NEBOJŠA RADOJEV.

Institute for Theatre, Film, Radio and Television: Head Prof. Dr NEVENA DAKOVIĆ.

UNIVERZITET U KRAGUJEVCU
(University of Kragujevac)

34000 Kragujevac

Telephone: (34) 370-270

Fax: (34) 370-168

Internet: www.kg.ac.yu

Founded 1976

State control

Academic year: October to June

Rector: Prof. Dr MILOŠ DJURAN

Vice-Rector (Finance and Student Affairs): Prof. Dr MILENTIJE STEFANOVIĆ

Vice-Rector (International Relations): Prof. Dr DRAGUTIN DJUKIĆ

Vice-Rector (Teaching and Scientific Research): Prof. Dr ZORAN POWJAVIĆ

General Secretary: JOVAN KUMBUROVIC

Librarian: RUŽICA IGNJATOVIĆ

Number of teachers: 950

Number of students: 14,000

Publication: *LIPAR* (cultural and literary themes, 4 a year)

DEANS

Faculty of Agriculture in Čačak: Prof. Dr MIROSLAV SPASODEVIĆ

Faculty of Economics in Kragujevac: Prof. Dr SLOBADAN MALINIĆ

Faculty of Law in Kragujevac: Prof. Dr SVETA PURIĆ

Faculty of Mechanical Engineering in Kragujevac: Prof. Dr RADOVAN SLAVKOVIĆ

Faculty of Mechanical Engineering in Kraljevo: Assoc. Prof. Dr MILOMIR GAŠIC

Faculty of Medicine in Kragujevac: Assoc. Prof. Dr HEBOJŠA ARSENIJEVIĆ

Faculty of Science and Mathematics in Kragujevac: Assoc. Prof. Dr SRECKO TRIFUNVIĆ

Faculty of Technology in Čačak: Prof. Dr JEROSLAV ZIVANIĆ

Teacher-Training Faculty in Jagodina: Prof. Dr SPETKO DIVDAN

Teacher-Training Faculty in Užice: Prof. Dr KRSTIVOJE SPIJUNOVIC

UNIVERZITET U NIŠU
(University of Niš)

Univerzitetski trg 2, 18000 Niš

Telephone: (18) 547-970

Fax: (18) 547-950

E-mail: uniuni@ni.ac.yu

Internet: ni.ac.yu

Founded 1965

State control

Rector: Prof. Dr ZORAN MILENKOVIĆ

Vice-Rectors: Prof. Dr IGOR MILOVANOVIĆ, Prof. Dr MARKO SEKULOVIČ, Prof. Dr VLADISAV STEFANOVIĆ

Secretary-General: DRAGOSLAV DJOKIĆ

Number of teachers: 1,490

Number of students: 24,529

Publications: *Facta Universitatis* (scientific journal, irregular), *Teme* (journal for social theory and practice, 4 a year)

DEANS

Faculty of Civil Engineering and Architecture: Prof. Dr DRAGAN ARANDJELOVIĆ

Faculty of Economics: Prof. Dr JOVAN KRSTIĆ

Faculty of Electronic Engineering: Prof. Dr GRANIMIR MILOVANOVIĆ

Faculty of Fine Arts: Prof. DJURO RADONJIĆ (acting)

Faculty of Law: Prof. Dr MILORAD BOŽIĆ

Faculty of Mechanical Engineering: Prof. Dr ZORAN BORIČIĆ

Faculty of Medicine: Prof. Dr MILAN VIŠNJIĆ

Faculty of Occupational Safety: Prof. Dr MIROLJUB GROZDANOVIĆ

Faculty of Philosophy: Prof. Dr DRAGAN ŽUNIČ

Faculty of Physical Culture: Prof. Dr DOBRICA ŽIVKOVIČ

Faculty of Science and Mathematics: Prof. Dr TOMISLAV PAVLOVIĆ

Faculty of Technology: Prof. Dr JAKOV STAMENKOVIĆ

Teacher-Training Faculty: Prof. Dr STOJAN CENIĆ

PROFESSORS

Faculty of Civil Engineering and Architecture (Beogradska 14, 18000 Niš; tel. (18) 524-923; fax (18) 524-920; internet www.gaf.ni.ac.yu):

ANDJELKOVIĆ, H., Descriptive Geometry

ANDJELKOVIĆ, M., Industrial Facilities Design, Public Facilities Design

ARANDJELOVIĆ, D., Hydraulic Engineering

CEKIĆ, N., Public Facilities Design, Essential Designing

DAMNJANOVIĆ, M., Architectural Structures, Metal Structures, Metal Structures in Buildings

DRENIĆ, D., Structure Testing, Coupled and Special Structures

IGIĆ, T., Strength of Materials, Structure Plasticity and Limitation Analysis

ILIĆ, Č., Railway Engineering, Superstructures and Stations

ILIĆ, D., Housing Design, Project Development

MARKOVIĆ, M., Descriptive Geometry

MARKOVIĆ, V., Dams and Water Potential Utilization

MILENKOVIĆ, S., Urban Water Supply and Sewerage Systems Engineering

MITKOVIĆ, P., Urbanism, Area Planning

PETKOVIĆ, D., Concrete Structures, Concrete Bridges

POPOVIĆ, B., Structure Plasticity and Limitation Analysis, Structure Statics

PROLOVIĆ, V., Foundation Engineering

PROTIĆ, P., Mathematics

RADIVOJEVIĆ, G., Statics of Architectural Structures, Construction Systems

SPASOJEVIĆ, N., Concrete Bridges, Concrete Structures

STOJIĆ, D., Timber Structures and Scaffolds, Timber and Masonry Structures

TRAJKOVIĆ, D., Organization of Construction Works

VELIČKOVIĆ, D., Metal Structures

ZDRAVKOVIĆ, S., Structural Stability and Dynamics, Theory of Surface Girders

ZLATANOVIĆ, M., Organization of Construction Works, Elements of Road Engineering

ŽIVKOVIĆ, D., Hydrotechnical Structures

Faculty of Economics (Trg Kralja Aleksandra 11, 18000 Niš; tel. (18) 528-876; fax (18) 523-859; internet www.eknfak.ni.ac.yu):

ARANDJELOVIĆ, Z., Yugoslav Economy, Economic Policy

BARAC, N., Business Logistics Management

BOGDANOVIĆ, S., Mathematics

CVETANOVIĆ, S., Theory and Policy of Economic Development

ČUZOVIĆ, S., Trade Economics, Trade Management

DJEKIĆ, S., Agricultural Economics, Agricultural Management

FIGAR, N., Business Economics

GLIGORIJEVIĆ, Ž., Industrial Economics, Industrial Management

GROZDANOVIĆ, D., Business Economics

HAFNER, P., Sociology

JOVANOVIĆ, R., Informatics

KITANOVIĆ, D., Political Economy

KOSTIĆ, V., Russian Language

KRSTIĆ, B., Banking, Banking Management

KRSTIĆ, J., Financial Accounting, Auditing

NIKOLIĆ, S., Business Organization

NOVIĆEVIĆ, B., Managerial Accounting

PREDIĆ, B., Business Planning and Development Policy

SEKULOVIĆ, M., Economic Doctrines, Transition Economics

STANKOVIĆ, L., Marketing, International Marketing

TODOROVIĆ, E., Business Finance

TODOROVIĆ, O., Operations Research, Financial Mathematics

ZDRAVKOVIĆ, D., Theory of Prices and Pricing Policy

Faculty of Electronic Engineering (Beogradska 14, 18000 Niš; tel. (18) 529-100; fax (18) 524-931; internet www.elfak.ni.ac.yu):

ARSIĆ, M., Measurements in Electronics, Telemetry

DAMNJANOVIĆ, M., VLSI Design, Electronic System Design

DANKOVIĆ, B., Methods of Intelligent Control, Process Control, Process Identification

DELETIĆ, S., Theory of Social Development

DIMITRIJEVIĆ, B., Electrical Measurement, Intelligent Instrumentation, Measurement in Microelectronics

DJORDJEVIĆ, B., Digital Electronics, Electronic Circuits

DJORDJEVIĆ KAJAN, S., Computer Graphics, Systems Software, Data Structures and Databases, Software Engineering

GMITROVIĆ, M., Network Synthesis and Signal Processing

JANKOVIĆ, N., Power Components and Circuits, Sensors and Convertors

KOCIĆ, LJ., Mathematics, Numerical Mathematics

KOVAČEVIĆ, M., Mathematics, Numerical Mathematics

KRSTIĆ, D., Wireless Engineering, High-Frequency Electronics

LITOVSKI, V., Electronics, Neural Networks, Electronic Circuit Design

MARKOVIĆ, V., Microwave Electronics, Satellite Communications

MILOSAVLJEVIĆ, Č., Elements of Automatic Control, EMP Regulation

MILOŠEVIĆ, M., Electroacoustics, Audiotechnics

MILOVANOVIĆ, B., Microwave Technology, Microwave Systems, Mobile Telecommunications

MILOVANOVIĆ, D., Electronics, Analogue Electronics

MILOVANOVIĆ, G., Mathematics, Mathematical Methods, Numerical Mathematics

MILOVANOVIĆ, I., Mathematics, Discrete Mathematics

MITIĆ, D., Elements of Electrical Engineering, Electromagnetics

NAUMOVIĆ, M., SAU Design, Automatic Control Theory, Intelligent Control Methods

NIKOLIĆ, Z., Quality and Reliability

NIKOLIĆ, Z., Mobile Telecommunications, Basic Telecommunications, Telecommunications in Electronic Power Engineering

PEJČIĆ, M., Philosophy and Sociology

PEJOVIĆ, M., Physics

PETKOVIĆ, M., Mathematics

PETKOVIĆ, P., Computer-Aided Design, Electronics Circuit Design, Integrated Circuit Design

RADENKOVIĆ, V., Electrical Measurement, Measurement in Electric Power Engineering

RANČIĆ, P., Electrical Installations and Illumination, Special Electrical Installations

RISTIĆ, S., Electronic Components, Semiconducting Components, Power Components and Circuits

STANKOVIĆ, M., Basic Computer Technology, Programming Languages, Assemblers

STANKOVIĆ, R., Logic Design, Pattern Recognition

STEFANOVIĆ, D., Optoelectronics

STEFANOVIĆ, M., Optic Telecommunications, Telecommunication Theory, Digital Telecommunications, Telecommunication System Design, Radar Systems and Radiolocation

STOJADINOVIĆ, N., Quality and Reliability, Physical Electronics, Failure Physics and Diagnostics, Components Characterization, Basic Microelectronics

STOJANOVIĆ, V., Circuit Theory, Television Systems, Television, Digital Picture Processing

STOJČEV, M., Microprocessing Technology, Microprocessing Systems

STOJILKOVIĆ, S., Low Temperature Electronics

TOKIĆ, T., Microcomputers and Programming, Microcomputer Systems and I/O Devices

VELIČKOVIĆ, D., Electromagnetics, Basic Electrical Engineering

ŽIVKOVIĆ, LJ., Materials for Electronics

Faculty of Fine Arts (Knjeginje Ljubice 10, 18000 Niš; tel. and fax (18) 522-396):

CEKIĆ, N., Forms Design

Faculty of Law (Trg Kralja Aleksandra 11, 18000 Niš; tel. (18) 500-203; fax (18) 523-747; internet www.prafak.ni.ac.yu):

BOŽIĆ, M., Economic Policy

ĆIRIĆ, A., International Trade Law

DJURDJIĆ, V., Criminal Procedural Law with Crime Investigation and Law Enforcement

GORČIĆ, J., Financial Law

KONSTANTINOVIĆ-VILIĆ, S., Criminology, Penology

KOVAČEVIĆ-KUŠTRIMOVIĆ, R., Introduction to Civil and Property Law

MIJAČIĆ, M., Law of Obligation

MILENOVIĆ, D., Trade Law

NIKOLIĆ, D., General Legal History

PETROVIĆ, M., Administrative Law, Management Science with Legal Informatics

RADIVOJEVIĆ, Z., Public International Law

ROČKOMANOVIĆ, M., Private International Law

SERJEVIĆ, V., Political Economy

SIMIĆ, M., Introduction to Law

STANIMIROVIĆ, D., Sociology

STANKOVIĆ, G., Civil Procedural Law, Arbitration Law

STOJANOVIĆ, D., Constitutional Law

STOJIČIĆ, S., National Legal History

Faculty of Mechanical Engineering (Beogradska 14, 18000 Niš; tel. (18) 524-914; fax (18) 524-930; internet www.masfak.ni.ac.yu):

BLAGOJEVIĆ, B., Aeration and Ventilators, Cooling Techniques

BOGDANOVIĆ, B., Hydro-Power Transmitters, Compressors and Ventilators, Piping

BORIČIĆ, Z., Fluid Mechanics, Hydraulic and Pneumatic Systems of Automatic Control

ĆOJBAŠIĆ, LJ., Basic Processing Technology, Prime Materials

DJOKIĆ, V., Theory and Methods of Mechanical Systems Design, Elements of Construction Theory, Construction Methods, Welded Constructions, Rubber Construction Machines

DJORDJEVIĆ, D., Sociology and Philosophy of Natural Sciences, Basic Labour Sociology and Economics

DJURDJANOVIĆ, M., Welding, Welding Technology, Machine Systems Tribology

DOMAZET, D., Modelling and Optimization of Production Systems, Computer-Aided Production Design

HEDRIH, K., Elastodynamics

ILIĆ, G., Measurement Technology, Thermodynamics

JEVTIĆ, V., Technical Logistics, Mining and Building Machinery, Continuous Transport Machinery, Mining Mechanization, Driving System Dynamics, Fundamentals of Technical Logisitics

JOVANOVIĆ, M., Computer-Aided Design, Information Technologies, Structure Analysis, Geometric Modelling, Metal Construction

LAKOVIĆ, S., Thermal Plants, Thermal Power Plants, Boilers

LAZAREVIĆ, D., Tools, Non-Conventional Methods, Polymer Modelling Tools

MARINKOVIĆ, V., Machining, Processing Tribology

MILENKOVIĆ, D., Turbomachine Theory and Fundamentals, Hydraulic Machines, Special Pumps

MILOVANČEVIĆ, D., Mathematics

MILTENOVIĆ, V., Machine Parts, Reliability of Machine Systems, Integral Product Development, Machine System Supervision and Protection

NIKODIJEVIĆ, D., Fluid Mechanics, Oil Hydraulics and Pneumatics, Hydraulic Components, Hydro-Pneumatic Elements in Mechatronics, Physics

NIKOLIĆ, V., Automatic Control, Automatic Control Discrete Systems, Systems of Control in Mechatronics, Optimal Control, Nonlinear Control Systems, Neural and Fuzzy Modelling and Control

PAVLOVIĆ, N., Mechanisms in Mechatronics, Micromechanics, Elements of Fine Mechanics, Optical Elements in Mechatronics

PAVLOVIĆ, R., Mechanics, Plate and Shell Theory

PETKOVIĆ, LJ., Mathematics, Numerical Mathematics and Programming

PETROVIĆ, T., Measurement Techniques, Basic Mechatronics, Mechanical Elements in Mechatronics, Mechatronic System Design, Special Design Methods

RADOJKOVIĆ, N., Thermodynamics, Thermal and Diffusing Apparatus

STEFANOVIĆ, A., Internal Combustion Engines

STOJILJKOVIĆ, M., Automation of Production, Packing Machines, Pneumatic and Hydraulic Components, Assembling and Packing Technology, Digital Control Techniques

STOJILJKOVIĆ, V., Production Management, Processing by Plastic Deformation, Management in Mechanical Engineering, Production Process Statistical Control

TASIĆ, Ž., Electrical Engineering and Electronics, Basic Mechatronics

TEMELJKOVSKI, D., Machines for Processing by Deformation

VULIĆ, A., Power Conveyors, Quality of Machine Systems, Technical Diagnostics, Special-Purpose Machines, Agricultural Machines

ŽIVKOVIĆ, D., Hydromechanics of Mixtures, Thermal Turbomachines

ŽIVKOVIĆ, Ž., Theory of Machines and Mechanisms, Technical Drawing, Mechantronic System Modelling

Faculty of Medicine (Braće Tasković 81, 18000 Niš; tel. (18) 570-029; fax (18) 338-770; internet www.medfak.ni.ac.yu):

ANTIĆ, M., Medical Sociology

BABIĆ, M., Neurosurgery

BAŠIĆ, H., Pathological Anatomy

BJELAKOVIĆ, G., Biochemistry

BOGIĆEVIĆ, M., Nuclear Medicine

BOŠNAKOVIĆ, P., Radiology

BURAZOR, M., Internal Medicine, Cardiology

DAČIĆ-SIMONOVIĆ, D., Dental Pathology

DENOVIĆ, B., Forensic Medicine

DIMOV, D., Pathological Anatomy

DJORDJEVIĆ, D., Internal Medicine, Pneumophysiology

DJORDJEVIĆ, V., Biochemistry

DJORDJEVIĆ, V., Internal Medicine, Nephrology

FILIPOVIĆ, S., Elements of Clinical Oncology

IGIĆ, A., Prosthodontics

IGIĆ, S., Prosthodontics

ILIĆ, R., Pathological Anatomy

ILIĆ, S., Internal Medicine, Cardiology

ILIĆ, SL., Nuclear Medicine

JEREMIĆ, M., Surgery, General Surgery

JOVANOVIĆ, D., Physiology

JOVČIĆ, S., Paediatric Surgery

KAMENOV, B., Paediatrics

KATIĆ, V., Pathological Anatomy

KOCIĆ, B., Microbiology and Immunology

KOJOVIĆ, Z., Physical Medicine and Rehabilitation

KONSTANTINOVIĆ, LJ., Infectology

KOSTIĆ, V., Infectology

KOSTIĆ, Ž., Hygiene and Medical Ecology

KRSTIĆ, M., Infectology

KUTLEŠIĆ, Č., Pathological Anatomy

LOVIĆ, B., Internal Medicine, Cardiology

MALOBABIĆ, Z., Pharmacology and Toxicology

MARKOVIĆ, V., Internal Medicine, Cardiology

MARKOVIĆ, Z., Internal Medicine, Rheumatology

MIHAJLOVIĆ, D., Pathological Anatomy

MIHAJLOVIĆ, M., Physiology

MIHAJLOVIĆ, P., Physics

MILADINOVIĆ, P., Gynaecology and Obstetrics

MILATOVIĆ, S., Radiology

MILENKOVIĆ, Z., Surgery, Neurosurgery

MILIĆEVIĆ, R., Paediatric Surgery

MILOSAVLJEVIĆ, LJ., Otorhinolaryngology

MILOSAVLJEVIĆ, M., Gynaecology and Obstetrics

MILJKOVIĆ, S., Psychiatry with Medical Psychology

MIRKOVIĆ, B., Oral and Periodontal Diseases

MITIĆ, N., Dental Pathology

MITIĆ, S., Dental Pathology

MITROVIĆ, M., Surgery, Orthopaedics

MITROVIĆ, R., Hygiene, Medical Ecology

NIKOLIĆ, J., Biochemistry

NOVAK, D., Paediatrics

ORLOV, S., Oral and Periodontal Diseases

PARAVINA, M., Dermatovenereology

PAVLOVIĆ, D., Biochemistry

PEROVIĆ, M., Histology and Embryology

POP-TRAJKOVIĆ, Ž., Gynaecology and Obstetrics

RADENKOVIĆ, S., Pathological Physiology

RADIĆ, S., Pathological Physiology

RAIČEVIĆ, R., Internal Medicine, Nephrology

RANKOVIĆ, Ž., Infectology

SAVIĆ, M., Paedodontics and Preventive Stomatology

SAVIĆ, V., Pathological Anatomy

SKOČAJIĆ, S., Dental Pathology

SPALEVIĆ, M., Forensic Medicine

SPASIĆ, M., Epidemiology

STAMENKOVIĆ, I., Internal Medicine, Gastroenterology

STANIŠIĆ, V., Medical Statistics and Informatics

STANKOVIĆ, A., Internal Medicine, Rheumatology

STANKOVIĆ, D., Prosthodontics

STEFANOVIĆ, N., Anatomy

STEFANOVIĆ, V., Internal Medicine, Nephrology

STOJILJKOVIĆ, M., General Surgery

STOJILJKOVIĆ, S., Pathological Physiology

TIODOROVIĆ, B., Epidemiology

VELJKOVIĆ, S., Physiology

VIŠNJIĆ, M., Plastic Surgery

VUČETIĆ, D., Gynaecology and Obstetrics

VUČETIĆ, R., Anatomy

VUJIČIĆ, B., Oral Surgery

ZLATANOVIĆ, G., Opthalmology

ŽIVKOVIĆ, DJ., Internal Medicine, Pneumophysiology

Faculty of Occupational Safety (Čarnojevića 10A, 18000 Niš; tel. (18) 523-821; fax (18) 49-962; internet www.znrfak.ni.ac.yu):

ANDJELKOVIĆ, B., Protection against Fire in Technical Processes, Introduction to Working and Living Environment Protection, Technological Processes in the Living Environment

CVETKOVIĆ, D., Noise and Vibrations, Noise in the Living Environment

DJORDJEVIĆ, J., Sociology, Social Ecology

IVANJAC, M., Labour Law

JANKOVIĆ, Ž., Safety at Work with Machines and Devices, Fire Extinguishing Processes and Methods

JOVANOVIĆ, D., Protection against Fire and Explosions, Uncontrolled Combustion Processes

MITIĆ, D., Ignition and Combustion Theory, Engineering Materials

NEDELJKOVIĆ, V., Ventilation and Air-Conditioning Systems, Energy and Living Environment

SPASIĆ, D., Economics of Occupational Safety, Economics of Environmental Protection

STANKOVIĆ, M., Mathematics, Mathematical Modelling

ŽIVKOVIĆ, LJ., Safety at Work with Thermal Plants

ŽIVKOVIĆ, N., Systems and Equipment for Industrial Waste Treatment, Air Protection

Faculty of Philosophy (Ćirila i Metodija 2, 18000 Niš; tel. (18) 527-649; fax (18) 46-460; internet www.filfak.ni.ac.yu):

BOGDANOVIĆ, N., History of Serbian Language, Dialectology

BUTIGAN, Z., Sociology of Politics

DJORDJEVIĆ, Z., Introduction to History with Methodology

DJUROVIĆ, R., Serbian Language (Phonology with Accentology)

IVKOVIĆ, M., Sociology of Education, Social Sciences Teaching Methods

MAŠOVIĆ, D., Introduction to American Studies, American Literature

MILOSAVLJEVIĆ, LJ., History of Social Theories, Introduction to Philosophy

MITROVIĆ, LJ., General Sociology

NAUMOVIĆ, M., Sociology of Rural Areas, Sociology of Urban Areas

NEŠIĆ, B., Pedagogical Psychology

NEŠIĆ, V., Social Psychology

PETROVIĆ, Č., Political Economy with Elements of Economic Systems

RISTIĆ, R., Introduction to Canadian and Australian Studies

STOJADINOVIĆ, M., Yugoslav Literature

STOJANOVIĆ, M., Yugoslav Literature

STOJKOVIĆ, M., Sociology of Morals, Labour Sociology

VELIČKOVIĆ, D., Russian Language

VIDANOVIĆ, DJ., English Morphology and Teaching Methods

ŽUNIĆ, D., Sociology of Art, Sociology of Culture and Arts with Serbian Cultural History

Faculty of Physical Culture (Čarnojevića 10A, 18000 Niš; tel. (18) 510-900; fax (18) 42-482; e-mail info@ffk.ni.ac.yu; e-mail faksfiz@ni.ac.yu; internet ni.ac.yu/Prez/ffk):

BUBANJ, R., Biomechanics

DJURAŠKOVIĆ, R., Biology of Human Development with Sports Medicine

JOKSIMOVIĆ, S., Football, Skiing

KOSTIĆ, R., Dancing

KOSTIĆ, R., Volleyball

PETKOVIĆ, D., Sports Gymnastics

POPOVIĆ, R., Rhythmical and Sports Gymnastics

VUČKOVIĆ, S., Recreation Theory and Teaching Methods, Activities in Nature

ŽIVANOVIĆ, N., Theory and History of Physical Education

ŽIVKOVIĆ, D., Theory of Corrective Gymnastics, Corrective Gymnastics Teaching Methods

Faculty of Science and Mathematics (Višegradska 33, 18000 Niš; tel. (18) 533-015; fax (18) 533-014; internet www.pmf.ni.ac.yu):

ĆIRIĆ, M., Mathematical Logic, Computer Technology Teaching Methods, Philosophy and History of Mathematics

DIMITRIJEVIĆ, P., Electromagnetism and Optics, Physics

JANKOVIĆ, S., Differential and Integral Equations, Theory of Probability and Random Processes

KOČINAC, LJ., Linear Algebra and Analytical Geometry, Topology

MILETIĆ, G., Instrumental Analytical Chemistry

MILJKOVIĆ, LJ., Solid State Physics, Physics of Materials

NIKOLIĆ, R., Higher Inorganic Chemistry

NOVAKOVIĆ, N., Physics, Plasma Physics

OBRADOVIĆ, M., Physical Chemistry

PALIĆ, R., Organic Chemistry

PAVLOTIĆ, T., Mechanics and Thermodynamics, Physics of Surfaces and Thin Layers

PECEV, T., Analytical Chemistry

PREMOVIĆ, P., General and Inorganic Chemistry

PURENOVIĆ, M., Industrial Chemistry

RADOVANOVIĆ, B., Instrumental Methods of Structural Analysis, Mechanisms of Organic Reactions

RAKOČEVIĆ, V., Functional Analysis, Theory of Measures and Integrals

STANIMIROVIĆ, P., Programming Languages, Mathematical Programming

URSIĆ-JANKOVIĆ, J., Biochemistry

Faculty of Technology (Bulevar oslobodjenja 124, 16000 Leskovac; tel. (16) 247-203; fax (16) 242-859; e-mail info@tehfin.tehfak.ni.ac.yu; internet www.tehfak.ni.ac.yu):

CAKIĆ, M., Physical Chemistry, Instrumental Analysis

CVETKOVIĆ, D., Organic Chemistry, Organo-Chemical Technology

CVETKOVIĆ, LJ., Production Management and Basic Marketing, Product Management

DJORDJEVIĆ, G., Mathematics

DJORDJEVIĆ, S., Organic Chemistry

GLIGORIJEVIĆ, V., Planning of Textile Processes, Knitting Technology

ILIĆ, P., General Chemistry

KOCIĆ, M., Physics

MARKOVIĆ, D., Instrumental Analysis, Organic Analysis, Chemical-Engineering Thermodynamics

NOVAKOVIĆ, M., Dyeing and Printing Technology

STANKOVIĆ, M., Biochemistry, Technology of Natural Organic Products

STANKOVIĆ, S., Analytical Chemistry

STOJILJKOVIĆ, D., Elements of Equipment in Processing Industry, Engineering Drawing, Mechanics

STOJILJKOVIĆ, S., Thermodynamics and Thermotechnics, Construction Materials, Process Analysis and Simulation, Chemical-Engineering Thermodynamics

TRAJKOVIĆ, C., Clothing Production Technology, Textile Quality Control and Testing

VELJKOVIĆ, V., Unit Operations in Chemical Engineering

Teacher-Training Faculty (Partizanska 14, 17500 Vranje; tel. (17) 22-962; fax (17) 21-633):

CENIĆ, S., General Pedagogy, History of Pedagogy

MALINOVIĆ, T., Mathematics, Mathematical Teaching Methods

UNIVERZITET U NOVOM SADU
(University of Novi Sad)

Trg Dositeja Obradovića 5, 21000 Novi Sad

Telephone: (21) 6350-622

Fax: (21) 450-418

E-mail: rektorat@uns.ns.ac.yu

Internet: www.ns.ac.yu

Founded 1960

State control

Academic year: October to July

Rector: Prof. Dr RADMILA MARINKOVIĆ-NEDUČIN

Vice-Rector: Prof. Dr TODOR ATANACKOVIĆ

General Secretary: PETAR RADONJANIN

Number of teachers: 2,703

Number of students: 38,169

Publication: *Glas Univerziteta* (newspaper, monthly)

DEANS

Faculty of Agriculture: Prof. Dr VLANDAN MARKOVIĆ

Faculty of Civil Engineering: Prof. Dr SRDJAN KOLAKOVIĆ

Faculty of Economics: Prof. Dr STEVAN VASILJEV

Faculty of Engineering Sciences: Prof. Dr ILIJA ĆOSIĆ

Faculty of Law: Prof. Dr SRDJAN ŠARKIĆ

Faculty of Medicine: Prof. Dr STEVAN POPOVIĆ

Faculty of Natural Sciences and Mathematics: Prof. Dr PAVLE TOMIĆ

Faculty of Philosophy: Prof. Dr TOMISLAV BEKIĆ

Faculty of Physical Education: Prof. Dr DRAGOSLAV JAKONJIĆ

Faculty of Technology: Prof. Dr MIRJANA DJURIĆ

Faculty of Education: Prof. Dr DJORDJE DJURIĆ

Technical Faculty 'Mihajlo Pupin': Prof. Dr VELIMIR SOTIROVIĆ

Academy of Arts: Prof. NENAD OSTOJIĆ

PROFESSORS

Faculty of Agriculture (Poljoprivredni Fakultet, Trg Dositeja Obradvića 8, 21000 Novi Sad; tel. (21) 450-355; fax (21) 59761; e-mail dean@polj.ns.ac.yu; internet www.polj.ns.ac.yu):

ALMAŠI, R., Special Entomology

ANTOV, G., Cattle Breeding, Animal Husbandry

BABIĆ, LJ., Drying and Storage, Basic Agricultural Engineering

BAJKIN, A., Agricultural Machinery

BALAŽ, F., Mycoses of Plants, Pant Protection

BALAŽ, J., Mycoses and Bacterioses of Plants

BELIĆ, S., Water Management, Irrigation and Drainage Engineeering

BOGDANOVIĆ, D., Agrochemistry

BOŠNJAK, DJ., Crop Irrigation

BOŽIDAREVIĆ, D., Marketing of Agricultural and Food Products

BRKIĆ, M., Elements of Agricultural Technology, Thermotechnology in Agriculture

ČINDRIĆ, P., Fruit Growing and Viticulture

ČOBANOVIĆ, K., Statistics, Statistical Methods

DJUKIĆ, D., Forage Crop Production

DJUKIĆ, NI., Agricultural Machinery

DJUROVKA, M., Vegetable Crop Production

ERIĆ, P., Forage Crops

GOVEDARICA, M., Microbiology

GVOZDENOVIĆ, D., Pomology, Picking and Storage of Fruit

HADŽIĆ, V., Pedology

JARAK, M., Microbiology

JASNIĆ, S., Plant Pathology, Plant Viruses

JOVANOVIĆ, M., Economics of Agricultural Estates, Economics of Agricultural Engineering

KEVREŠAN, S., Chemistry

KNEŽEVIĆ, A., Botany

KONSTANTINOVIĆ, B., Special Phytopharmacy, Control of Weeds

KORAĆ, M., Pomology, Viticulture

KOVČIN, S., Nutrition of Nonruminant Animals

KRAJINOVIĆ, M., Animal Husbandry

KRALJEVIĆ-BALALIĆ, M., Genetics

LAZIĆ, B., Vegetable Crop Production

LAZIĆ, V., Agricultural Machinery

MALETIN, S., Agricultural Zoology

MALINOVIĆ, N., Agricultural Machinery

MARINKOVIĆ, B., Arable Crop Production, Agronomy

MARKOVIĆ, V., Vegetable Crop Production

MIHAILOVIĆ, D., Meteorology

MIHAJLOVIĆ, L., Agricultural Co-operative Economics, Agrarian Policy

MIHALJEV, I., Seed Production

MILIĆ, D., Organization of Fruit and Vine Production, Business Organization and Economics

MOLNAR, I., Agronomy

NIKOLIĆ, R., Agricultural Tractors, Agricultural Machinery

NOVKOVIĆ, N., Planning Theory and Methodology of Organization

OBRENOVIĆ, D., Business Analysis, Bookkeeping

PAPRIĆ, DJ., General Viticulture

PEJANOVIĆ, R., Economy

PEJIĆ, N., Nutrition of Ruminant Animals

PEKANOVIĆ, V., Botany

PETRIĆ, D., General Entomology

PETROVIĆ, N., Plant Physiology, Protection of Ecosystems

PETROVIĆ, S., Genetics

POKRIĆ, V., Land Reclamation

POPOVIĆ, M., Plant Biochemistry, Biochemistry of Farm Animals

POTKONJAK, S., Economics of Melioration and Mechanization, Economics of Water Resources

POTKONJAK, V., Mechanization in Animal Breeding, Means of Transportation in Agriculture

RATAJAC, R., Agricultural Zoology, Ecology

SAVIĆ, S., Fodder, Feeding Technology

SRDJEVIĆ, B., Informatics

STANČIĆ, B., Breeding of Farm Animals

STARČEVIĆ, LJ., Arable Crop Production

STEVANOVIĆ, M., Agronomy

STOJANOVIĆ, S., Botany

SUPIĆ, B., Poultry Production, Animal Husbandry

ŠTAJNER, D., Chemistry

STRBAC, P., Special Entomology, Plant Protection

TEODOROVIĆ, M., Pig Breeding

UDAVIĆ, M., Agrochemistry

VIDOVIĆ, V., Improvement of Farm Animals

ŽIVANOVIĆ, M., Special Phytopharmacy

Faculty of Civil Engineering (Gradjevinski Fakultet, Kozaračka 2a, 24000 Subotica; tel. (24) 554-300; fax (24) 554-580; e-mail dekanat@gf.su.ac.yu; internet www.gf.su.ac.yu):

BENAK, J., Water Refinement and Water Quality

ĆULIBRK, R., Earthworks, Elements of Traffic Arteries

DELEVIĆ, K., Organization in Building

GOSTOVIĆ, M., Engineering Geodesy

KLEIN, R., Architecture

MEŠTER, DJ., Technical Mechanics

MIHAILOVIĆ, V., Concrete Structures

MILAŠINOVIĆ, D., Resistance of Materials, Theory of Surface Bearers

SAM, A., Social Sciences

STOJKOVIĆ, S., Watercourses, Flood Management

VLAJIĆ, LJ., Experimental Analysis of Construction

ZELENHASIĆ, E., Hydrology and Elements of Hydrotechnology

Faculty of Economics (Ekonomski Fakultet, Moše Pijade 9–11, 24000 Subotica; tel. (24) 552-494; fax (24) 546-486; e-mail dekanat@eccf.su.ac.yu; internet www.eccf.su.ac.yu):

ACIN, DJ., International Economic Relations

ACIN SIGULINSKI, S., International Trade, Management in International Trade

ADŽIĆ, S., Economic System and Economic Policy, National Economy

AHMETAGIĆ, E., Theory of an Organization

ANDRIĆ, M., Accountancy and Revision, Financial Control and Revision

BALABAN, N., Principles of Informatics, Support Systems in Decision Making

BALJ, B., Philosophy

BANDIN, J., Accountancy and Bookkeeping

BANDIN, T., Business Economics

ČILEG, M., Operational Research

DJURKOVIĆ, J., Principles of Informatics, Analysis and Planning of Information Systems

DMITROVIĆ, LJ., Management Accounting

GABRIĆ MOLNAR, I., Sociology

JAKOVČEVIĆ, K., Business Economics

JOSIFIDIS, K., Macroeconomics

KALINIĆ, V., Trade Company Management, Marketing in Trade

KIŠ, T., Econometrics

KONČAR, J., Economics of Domestic Commerce and Commercial Politics

KRMPOTIĆ, T., Agrotechnology

LEKIĆ, T., Development of Technology and Commercial Recognition of Goods

LEKOVIĆ, B., Principles of Management

LJUBOJEVIĆ, C., Marketing Services

LOVRE, K., Programming of Agricultural Development

MALEŠEVIĆ, DJ., Analysis of Business Enterprise Operations

MESAROŠ, K., Mathematics for Economists

SALAI, S., Marketing of Research, Market Communications

STOJKOVIĆ, M., Statistics

ŠAGI, A., Microeconomics

ŠUŠNJAR, G., Human Resources Management

ŠUVAKOV, T., Microeconomics

TODOSIJEVIĆ, R., Strategic Management, Investments

TOT, A., History of Economic Thought

VASILJEV, S., Marketing

VUGDELIJA, D., Mathematics for Economists

VUNJAK, N., Finance, Banking

Faculty of Technical Sciences (Fakultet Tehničkih Nauka, Trg Dositeja Obradovića 6, 21000 Novi Sad; tel. (21) 350-122; fax (21) 58133; e-mail ftndean@uns.ns.ac.yu; internet www.ns.ac.yu):

ATANACKOVIĆ, T., Material Resistance

BABIN, N., Transport Machines

BAČLIĆ, B., Mechanics and Thermodynamics of Continuum

BANJANIN, M., Theory of Communications

BAŠIĆ, DJ., Thermoprocessing Systems

BOROVAC, B., Industrial Robots

BUKUROV, Ž., Fluid Mechanics

ČASNJI, F., Motor Vehicles

ĆIRIĆ, D., Physics

ČOMIĆ, I., Mathematics

ĆOSIĆ, I., Planning of Production Systems

CVETIĆANIN, L., Mechanics

DIMIĆ, M., Mass Transfer, Heat Apparatus

DJORDJEVIĆ, R., Construction Theory

DJORDJEVIĆ, T., Theory of Traffic Flow and Capacity

DJUKIĆ, DJ., Mechanics

DOROSLOVAČKI, R., Discrete Mathematics

DOVNIKOVIĆ, L., Descriptive Geometry

FOLIĆ, R., Concrete Structures and Structural Theory

GAJIĆ, V., Logistics of Enterprise

GALOGAŽA, M., Technology of Prediction, Marketing and Enterprise

GATALO, R., Machine Tools, Flexible Technological Systems

GEORGIJEVIĆ, M., Storage, Equipment and Simulations

GERIĆ, LJ., Distributive Installations

GRKOVIĆ, V., Turbines

GVOZDENAC, D., Thermal Energy and Measurement in Thermal Engineering

HAJDUKOVIĆ, M., Architecture of Computer Systems

HODOLIĆ, J., Productive Engineering Equipment

INIĆ, M., Traffic Safety

KAKAŠ, D., Heat Treatment

KISIN, S., Metal Constructions

KLINAR, I., Motor Equipment

KOPIĆ, DJ., Technology of Railway Transport

KOVAČ, P., Welding

KOVAČ, R., Casting Technology

KOVAČEVIĆ, I., Mathematics

KOVAČEVIĆ, V., Logical Planning of Computing Systems

KOZIMIDIS-LUBURIĆ, U., Physics

KOZIMIDIS-PETROVIĆ, A., Physics

KUZMANOVIĆ, S., Mechanical Elements

LIČEN, H., Automation of Measuring Processes

LUKIĆ, S., Elements of Building Planning

MALBAŠA, V., Electronic Systems and Communication Networks

MALBAŠKI, D., Elements of Computer Programming and Programme Languages

MARIĆ, M., Heat Science, Drying Technology

MARINIĆ, I., Sociology and Economy

MARTINOV, M., Agricultural Machines

MILIDRAG, S., Motor Vehicles

MILIKIĆ, D., Treatment Methods by Material Removal

MILINSKI, N., Physics

MILOŠEVIĆ, V., Digital Telecommunication

MOGIN, P., Databases

NIKIĆ, J., Mathematics

NOVAK, L., Circuit and Systems Theory

OBRADOVIĆ, D., Digital Communications

OBRADOVIĆ, M., Intercomputer Communications

PEKARIĆ-NADJ, N., Principles of Electrical Engineering

PERUNOVIĆ, P., Boilers

PEŠALJEVIĆ, M., Engineering Communications and Logistic Control

PETROVAČKI, D., Automatic Control

PLANČAK, M., Technology of Plasticity and Cold Extrusion

POPOVIĆ, D., Synthesis of Complex Systems in Automatic Control

PRODANOVIĆ, M., City and Spatial Planning

RADIVOJEVIĆ, R., Sociology, Sociology of Work

RADOVIĆ, R., Urban Planning, Contemporary Architecture

SABO, B., Welding Technology

SATARIĆ, M., Physics

SAVIĆ, V., Logistic Technical Systems

ŠEŠIĆ, Ž., Internal Combustion Engines

SIDJANIN, L., Materials Science, Engineering Materials

SOVILJ, B., Technoeconomic Optimization

STANIVUKOVIĆ, D., Reliability of Mechanical Systems

STOJAKOVIĆ, M., Mathematics, Statistical Methods in Planning

STREZOSKI, V., Elements of Electroenergetics

TEŠIĆ, M., Agricultural Machinery

TODIĆ, V., Technological Processes

TOROVIĆ, T., Internal Combustion Engine

UZELAC, Z., Mathematical Methods

VILOTIĆ, D., Plasticity Technology

VLADIĆ, J., Uninterrupted and Automatic Transport

VLAHOVIĆ, M., Recognition of Goods in Transport

VUKOVIĆ, S., Architectural Construction

VUKOVIĆ, V., Fluid Mechanics

ZLOKOLICA, M., Theory of Mechanisms and Machines

ŽIVANOV, LJ., Microelectronics, Principles of Electronics

ŽUPUNSKI, I., Electrical Measurements

Faculty of Law (Pravni Fakultet, Trg Dositeja Obradovića 1, 21000 Novi Sad; tel. (21)

350-377; fax (21) 450-427; e-mail pravni@pf
.ns.ac.yu):

ARSIĆ, Z., Economic Law
BOŠKOVIĆ, M., Criminology, Penology
CARIĆ, S., Economic Law
CVEJIĆ-JANČIĆ, O., Family Law, Inheritance Law
DJURDJEV, A., Constitutional Law
DJURDJEV, D., International Public Law
ETINSKI, R., International Public Law
GRUBAČ, M., Criminal Procedural Law
JOVANOVIĆ, PA., Contemporary Political Systems
JOVANOVIĆ, PR., Labour Law
KEČA, R., Civil Procedural Law
KRKLJUŠ, LJ., History of Yugoslav State and Law
MALENICA, A., Roman Law
MARJANOVIĆ, M., Sociology
MILKOV, D., Administrative Law
PAJVANČIĆ, M., Constitutional Law
PERIĆ, O., Criminal Law
PIHLER, S., Criminal Law
POPOV, DJ., Principles of Economics
POPOVIĆ, M., Theory of State and Law
SALMA, J., Law of Obligation
STANKOVIĆ, F., Principles of Economics
ŠARKIĆ, S., History of State and Law
SOGOROV, S., Economic Law
VRANJEŠ, M., Financial Law
VUČKOVIĆ, M., Law of Obligation
VUKADINOVIĆ, G., Theory of State and Law
VUKIĆEVIĆ, M., Introductory Economics

Faculty of Medicine (Medicinski Fakultet,
Hajduk Veljkova 3, 21000 Novi Sad; tel. (21)
420-677; fax (21) 624-153; e-mail medicins@
eunet.yu; internet www.medical.ns.ac.yu):

ALEKSIĆ, S., Gynaecology and Obstetrics
AVRAMOV, S., Surgery
BABIĆ, LJ., Pathology
BALTIĆ, V., Internal Medicine
BUDAKOV, P., Pathology
BUJAS, M., Gynaecology and Obstetrics
BORIŠEV, V., Surgery
BOROTA, J., Biochemistry
ČVEJANOV, M., Surgery
ČIKOŠ, J., Internal Medicine
ĆURIĆ, S., Internal Medicine
DJAKOVIĆ-ŠVARCER, K., Pharmacology and Toxicology
DJILAS-TODOROVIĆ, LJ., Internal Medicine
DOKMANOVIĆ-DJORDJEVIĆ, M., Gynaecology and Obstetrics
DŽOLEV, A., Maxillofacial Surgery
ERI, Ž., Pathology
FILIPOVIĆ, D., Physiology
GEBAUER, E., Paediatrics
GRUJIĆ, N., Physiology
GRUJIĆ, V., Social Medicine
GUDOVIĆ, R., Anatomy
GUDURIĆ, B., Surgery
HADŽIĆ, B., Pathology
HADŽIĆ, M., Pathology
IVETIĆ, V., Physiology
IVKOVIĆ-LAZAR, T., Internal Medicine
JANJIĆ, DJ., Surgery
JERANT-PATIĆ, V., Microbiology with Parasitology and Immunology
JEŠIĆ-VINDIŠ, M., Internal Medicine
JOVANOVIĆ, J., Infectious Diseases
KNEŽEVIĆ, A., Psychiatry and Medical Psychology
KOVAČEVIĆ, Ž., Biochemistry
KRISTIFOROVIĆ-ILIĆ, M., Hygiene
KRSTIĆ, A., Paediatrics
KRSTIĆ-BOŽIĆ, V., Biology
KULAUZOV, M., Pathological Physiology
KULAUZOV, M., Microbiology with Parasitology and Immunology
LATINOVIĆ, S., Ophthalmology
LAŽETIĆ, B., Physiology
LUČIĆ, A., Pathological Physiology
LUČIĆ, Z., Radiology
LUKAČ, I., Radiology
MAČVANIN, N., Occupational Medicine

MARTINOV-CVEJIN, M., Social Medicine
MIHALJ, M., Anatomy
MIHALJEV-MARTINOV, J., Neurology
MIKOV, M., Pharmacology and Toxicology
MILIČIĆ, A., Surgery
MIROSAVLJEV, M., Hygiene
MILOŠEVIĆ, D., Otorhinolaryngology
MILUTINOVIĆ, B., Physiology
MIRKOVIĆ, M., Surgery
MIROSAVLJEV, M., Hygiene
OBRADOVIĆ, D., Anatomy
PAVLOV-MIRKOVIĆ, M., Gynaecology and Obstetrics
PAVLOVIĆ, S., Internal Medicine
PEJIN, D., Internal Medicine
PJEVIĆ, M., Gynaecology and Obstetrics
PJEVIĆ, M., Surgery
POLZOVIĆ, A., Anatomy
POPOV, I., Psychiatry, Medical Psychology
POPOVIĆ, D., Forensic Medicine
POPOVIĆ, J., Pharmacology and Toxicology
POPOVIĆ, LJ., Surgery
POPOVIĆ, M., Chemistry
RISTIĆ, J., Maxillofacial Surgery
RONČEVIĆ, N., Paediatrics
SABO, A., Pharmacology and Toxicology
SAVIĆ, K., Medical Rehabilitation
SAVIĆ, M., Occupational Medicine
SEDLAK-VADOC, V., Pathological Physiology
SEGEDI, D., Obstetrics and Gynaecology
SIMIČ, M., Forensic Medicine
SOMER, LJ., Histology and Embryology
SOMER, T., Surgery
STANKOVIĆ, S., Biophysics
STANULOVIĆ, M., Pharmacology and Toxicology
STOJANOVIĆ, S., Surgery
STOJKOV, J., Surgery
STOJŠIĆ, DJ., Internal Medicine
ŠĆEKIĆ, V., Internal Medicine
ŠEGULJEV, Z., Epidemiology
ŠLJAPIĆ, N., Pathology
TASIĆ, M., Forensic Medicine
TOPALOV, V., Internal Medicine
VADOC-SEDLAK, V., Pathological Physiology
VOJINOVIĆ-MILORADOV, M., Chemistry
VUKADINOVIĆ, S., Surgery
VUKOVIĆ, B., Epidemiology
ZAMUROVIĆ, A., Medical Rehabilitation
ZORIČIĆ, D., Surgery
ŽIKIĆ, M., Neurology

Faculty of Natural Sciences and Mathematics (Prirodno-Matematički Fakultet, Trg
Dositeja Obradovića 3, 21000 Novi Sad; tel.
(21) 55630; fax (21) 55662; e-mail dekan@im
.ns.ac.yu; internet www.im.ns.ac.yu):

ABRAMOVIĆ, B., Microanalysis
ACKETA, D., Informatics and Numerical Mathematics
BIKIT, I., Nuclear Physics
BJELICA, L., Physical Chemistry
BOGDANOVIĆ, Ž., Physical Geography
BOŽIĆ-KRSTIĆ, V., Biology with Human Genetics
BUDIMAC, Z., Informatics and Numerical Mathematics
BUDINČEVIĆ, M., Analysis and Geometry
BUGARSKI, D., Geography
CRVENKOVIĆ, S., Mathematics
CVETKOVIĆ, LJ., Informatics and Numerical Mathematics
ĆURČIĆ, S., Social Geography
DALMACIJA, B., Chemical Technology and Environmental Protection
DAVIDOVIĆ, R., Regional Geography
DIVJAKOVIĆ, V., Physics of Condensed Matter
DJURDJEV, B., Social Geography
DJUROVIĆ, S., Atomic Physics, Physical Electronics
GAAL, F., Analytical Chemistry
GAJIĆ, LJ., Analysis and Probability
GAJIN, S., Microbiology
GRUBOR-LAJŠIĆ, G., Biochemistry, Physiology, Histology

HADŽIĆ, O., Probability and Statistics, Mathematics
HALAŠI, R., Organic Analysis
HERCEG, D., Numerical Mathematics
JANJIĆ, J., Physics
JOVANOVIĆ, LJ., Chemistry
KAPOR, A., Physics of Condensed Matter
KAPOR, D., Theoretical Physics
KARLOVIĆ, E., Chemical Technology and Environmental Protection
KOSANIĆ, M., General Chemistry
KOVAČEVIĆ, R., Biochemistry
KUHAJDA, K., Chemistry of Natural Products
KRSTIĆ, B., Plant Physiology
LEOVAC, V., Inorganic Chemistry
LOZANOV-CRVENKOVIĆ, Z., Analysis and Probability
MADARASZ-SZILAGYI, R., Algebra and Mathematics
MAŠKOVIĆ, LJ., Classical Theoretical Mechanics
MATAVULJ, M., Microbiology
MERKULOV, LJ., Botany, Plant Anatomy and Morphology
MILJKOVIĆ, LJ., Physical Geography
MILJKOVIĆ, N., Physical Geography
NIKOLIĆ, A., Physical Chemistry
OBADOVIĆ, D., Physics, Physics of Liquid Crystals
PAP, E., Mathematics, Analysis and Geometry
PAUNIĆ, DJ., Informatics and Numerical Mathematics
PENOV-GAŠI, O., Organic Chemistry
PERIŠIĆ-JANJIĆ, N., General and Inorganic Chemistry
PETROVIĆ, D., Biophysics, Medical Physics
PETROVIĆ, J., Organic Chemistry
PETROVIĆ, O., Microbiology, Bacteriology
PETROVIĆ, V., Algebra and Mathematics
PILIPOVIĆ, S., Analysis and Probability
POPSAVIN, V., Chemistry of Natural Products
STANKOVIĆ, S., Biophysics, Medical Physics
STANKOVIĆ, Ž., Plant Physiology
STEVANOVIĆ, D., Morphology and Taxonomy of Invertebrates
STOJAKOVIĆ, Z., Linear Algebra
STOJANOVIĆ, S., Theoretical Mechanics and Electrodynamics
SURLA, D., Computer Science
SURLA, K., Numerical Mathematics
SEŠELJA, B., Mathematical Logic and Algebra, Mathematical Elements of Informatics
ŠETRAJČIĆ, J., Theoretical Physics
ŠIMIĆ, S., Biology, Zoology
ŠKRINJAR, M., Theoretical Physics
ŠURANJI, T., Analytical Chemistry
TAKAČI, A., Mathematics
TAKAČI, DJ., Mathematics, Analysis and Geometry
TERZIĆ, M., Atomic and Isotopic Molecular Spectroscopy
TOMIĆ, P., Geography
TOŠIĆ, B., Theoretical Physics
TOŠIĆ, R., Combinatorics
VAPA, LJ., Biochemistry, Physiology, Histology, Genetics
VOJINOVIĆ-MILORADOV, M., General Chemistry
VOJVODIĆ, G., Algebra and Logic
VRBAŠKI, Ž., Chemical Technology
VUČKOVIĆ, M., Botany, Plant Ecology, Ecology of Medicinal Herbs
VUJIČIĆ, B., Physical Electronics
ZDERIĆ, M., Biology
ŽIGRAI, I., Analytical Chemistry

Faculty of Philosophy (Filozofski Fakultet,
Stevana Musića 24, 21000 Novi Sad; tel. (21)
450-690; fax (21) 450-690; e-mail dekanat@
unsff.ns.ac.yu; internet www.ff.ns.ac.yu):

BANJAI, J., Literary Theory
BEKIĆ, T., German Literature

BERIĆ, V., History of German Language
BIRO, M., Elements of Clinical Psychology, Elements of Psychotherapy and Consulting
BOŠNJAK, I., Hungarian Literature
BURZAN, M., Serbian Language
ČAKI, P., Introduction to Expert and Scientific Work, Library Science
ČELOVSKI, S., Slovak Studies
ČOVIĆ, B., Russian Literature
DINIĆ-KNEŽEVIĆ, D., Medieval History of Yugoslav Nations
DJOŠIĆ, D., Demography with Statistics
DUDOK, D., History of Slovak Language and Literature
EGERIĆ, M., Modern Serbian Literature
GADJANSKI-MARICKI, K., Classical Languages, Ancient History
GENC, L., Genetics and Educational Psychology
GEROLD, L., Hungarian Literature
GORDIĆ, S., Serbian and Yugoslav Literature, Serbian Critics
GRANDIĆ, R., Theory of Education, Family Pedagogy
GRKOVIĆ, M., History of Serbian and Comparative Grammar of Slavic Languages
HARPANJI, M., Slovak Literature, Literary Theory
IGNJATOVIĆ, I., General Psychology, Psychology of Personality
IVANOVIĆ, R., History of Yugoslav Literature
JUKIĆ, S., Elements of Pedagogy, Methodical Bases of Educational Work
JUNG, K., Ethnology, Hungarian Folk Literature
KAIĆ, K., History of Hungarian Culture
KAMENOV, E., Pre-School Education
KAPOR-STANULOVIĆ, P., Development of Psychology, Mental Health
KARANOVIĆ, Z., Serbian Folk Literature
KLEUT, M., Serbian Literature
KOKOVIĆ, D., Sociology and Sociology of Culture
KOSANOVIĆ, B., Russian Literature
KULIĆ, M., Philosophy
LANC, I., Introduction to General and Hungarian Linguistics
MATIĆ, LJ., French Literature
MATIJAŠEVIĆ, J., Modern Russian Language
MILOSAVLJEVIĆ, P., Methodology of Literary Studies
MILOŠEVIĆ, B., Introduction to Sociology, Occupational Sociology
MLADENOVIĆ, U., Pedagogic Psychology, Genetic and Pedagogic Psychology
MOLNAR-ČIKOŠ, L., Syntax of Hungarian Language, Phonetics of Hungarian Language
MOMČILOVIĆ, B., English Literature
OLJAČA, M., Educational System
PEROVIĆ, M., Philosophy
PETROVIĆ, D., Dialectology of Serbian and Standard Serbian Language
PIŽURICA, M., History of Serbian Language
POPOV, Č., Modern History
PUŠIĆ, LJ., Urban Sociology
RADOVANOVIĆ, M., General Linguistics
RADOVIĆ, M., Comparative Literature
RAMAČ, J., Ruthenian Language, Ukrainian Language
REDJEP, J., Medieval Literature
RISTIĆ, Ž., Methodology of Psychology
RODIĆ, R., School Education
ROKAI, P., Medieval History
SAVIĆ, S., Sociolinguistics and Discourse Analysis
SIMEUNOVIĆ, V., Philosophy
STEFANOVIĆ, M., Literary Theory, Serbian Literature
STEPANOV, R., Theory of Law and Politics
STOJAKOV, S., Introduction to Education Science

ŠTRAJNIĆ, N., Comparative Literature
ŠIPKA, M., Statistical Psychology
TAMAŠ, J., Ruthenian Literature, Ukrainian Literature
TOČANAC, D., Modern French Language
TRIPKOVIĆ, M., Sociology and Sociological Theories
UTAŠI, Č., History of Hungarian Literature
VUKOVIĆ, G., Modern Serbian Language

Faculty of Physical Education (Fakultet Fizičke Kulture, Lovćenska 16, 21000 Novi Sad; tel. (21) 450-188; fax (21) 450-199; e-mail ffkns@eunet.yu; internet www.ffk.ns.ac.yu):

BALA, G., Kinesiology of Individual Sports
BJELICA, S., Sociological and Psychological Elements of Kinesiology
DIMOVA, K., Kinesiology of Individual Sports
DUNDJEROVIĆ, R., Kinesiology of Individual Sports
KALAJDŽIĆ, J., Kinesiology of Sports Games
KRSMANOVIĆ, B., Theory and Methods of Physical Education
LUKAČ, D., Sports Medicine
MALACKO, J., Kinesiology of Sports
NIĆIN, DJ., Kinesiology
RADOSAV, M., Football
RAIČ, A., Economical and Political Elements of Kinesiology
SAVIĆ, M., Martial Sports
TONČEV, I., Kinesiology of Individual Sports
ULIĆ, D., Kinesitherapy

Faculty of Technology (Tehnološki Fakultet, Bulevar Cara Lazara 1, 21000 Novi Sad; tel. (21) 58044; fax (21) 450-413; e-mail deantf@uns.ns.ac.yu):

CARIĆ, M., Milk and Dairy Technology
CURAKOVIĆ, M., Wrapping and Packaging
DOKIĆ, P., Chemistry and Technology of Emulsions and Cosmetics, Colloid Chemistry
DJILAS, S., Organic Chemistry
DJURIĆ, M., Engineering Thermodynamics
GRUJIĆ-IVKOV, O., Malt and Beer Technology
JAKOVLJEVIĆ, J., Starch Technology
KIŠ, E., Physical Chemistry Catalysis
LOMIĆ, G., Physical Chemistry, Catalysis
MARINKOVIĆ-NEDUČIN, R., Physical Chemistry, Catalysis
MARJANOVIĆ, N., Food Analysis
PAUNOVIĆ, R., Mathematical Modelling in Industrial Processes
PEJIN, D., Yeast and Alcohol Technology, Industrial Microbiology
PERIČIN, D., Biochemistry, Industrial Enzymology
PERUNIČIĆ, M., Process Dynamics and Control, Process Control Systems
PETROVIĆ, LJ., Meat Processing Technology
POPOV-RALJIĆ, J., Ready-Made Food Technology
PRIBIŠ, V., Meat Processing Technology, Sensory Evaluation of Food
RADONJIĆ, LJ., Construction Materials, Inorganic Materials
RANOGAJEC, J., Ceramics Technology, Inorganic Raw Materials and Products
RAZMOVSKA, R., Yeast and Alcohol Technology
RUŽIĆ, N., Technology of Wine Production
SOKOLOVIĆ, S., Petroleum Refining Technology, Petrochemical Products Applications
SOVILJ, M., Unit Operations, Measurement Techniques
SOVILJ, V., Colloid Chemistry, Physical Chemistry of Macromolecules
STOILJKOVIĆ, D., Physical Chemistry of Polymer Materials, Plastics Materials Technology

ŠEĆEROV-SOKOLOVIĆ, R., Industrial Processes Design, Environmental Protection in the Chemical Industry
ŠKRBIĆ, B., Natural Gas Engineering
ŠKRINJAR, M., Food Microbiology
TEKIĆ, M., Design of Equipment for the Chemical Industry, Separation Processes
TOJAGIĆ, S., Ready-Made Food Technology

Faculty of Education (Učiteljski Fakultet, Podgorička 4, 25000 Sombor; tel. (25) 22030; fax (25) 26641):

BERBER, S., School Hygiene with Ecology
DJURIĆ, DJ., Social Psychology, Educational Psychology
ERAKOVIĆ, T., Defectology
GRHOVAC, S., Teaching Methods in Serbian Language and Literature, Performing Arts
JANKOVIĆ, P., General Pedagogy
LIPOVAC, M., Pedagogy, Didactics
LJUBOJEV, P., Mass Communication, Film and Television Culture
MALEŠEVIĆ, J., Elements of Natural Sciences
NENADIĆ, M., General Sociology, Sociology of Education
PETROVIĆ, N., Mathematics and Teaching Methods in Mathematics
PINTER, J., Teaching Methods in Mathematics, Informatics in Education

Technical Faculty 'Mihajlo Pupin' (Tehnički Fakultet 'Mihajlo Pupin', Djure Djakovića b.b., 23000 Zrenjanin; tel. (23) 550-515; fax (23) 565-520; e-mail www@tf.zr.ac.yu; internet www.tf.zr.ac.yu):

ADAMOVIĆ, Ž., Mechanics, Maintenance, Hydraulics and Pneumatics
ČERNIČEK, I., Theory of Systems, Theory of Management and Decision Making
DJARMATI, Z., Chemistry with Chemical Technology, Chemistry and Biochemistry
HOTOMSKI, P., Informatics
LAMBIĆ, M., Mechanical Engineering, Energetics
MITROVIĆ, Ž., Mathematics
SOTIROVIĆ, V., Informatics
STOJADINOVIĆ, V., Industrial Engineering
ŠUNJKA, S., Textile Technology

Academy of Arts (Akademija Umetnosti, Djure Jakšića 7, 21000 Novi Sad; tel. (21) 422-177; fax (21) 420-187; e-mail aofarts@uns.ns.ac.yu):

BLANUŠA, M., Painting and Painting Technology
ČERNOGUBOV, B., Choir
DENKOVIĆ, LJ., Sculpture
DOBANOVAČKI, B., Poster Arts
DRAŠKOVIĆ, B., Acting, Directing
DJAK, Ž., Graphics and Graphic Technology
GILIĆ, V., Directing
HORVAT, L., Viola
JANKETIĆ, M., Acting
JOVANOVIĆ, V., Elements of Vocal Technique
JOVANOVIĆ, Z., Chamber Music
KATUNAC, D., History of Music, History of Performing
KINKA, R., Piano
KLEMENC, I., Stage Movement
KNEŽEVIĆ, S., Graphics and Graphic Technology
LAZIĆ, R., History and Aesthetics of Directing
MARINKOVIĆ, O., Diction
MIŠIĆ, LJ., Dance
OGNJENOVIĆ, V., Acting
OSTOJIĆ, N., Tone Syllable
OSTOJIĆ, T., Conducting
PREDOJEVIĆ-MILOVANOVIĆ, V., Voice Technique

RAKIDŽIĆ, J., Painting and Painting Technology

RNJAK, D., History of World Drama and Theatre

SIMONOVIĆ, M., Voice Technique

SRDIĆ, N., Clarinet

STANOJEV, M., Graphics and Graphic Technology

STAŠEVIĆ, M., Drawing and Drawing Technology

ŠUBOTIĆ, I., History of Art

ŠTATKIĆ, M., Composition

TODOROVIĆ, D., Painting and Painting Technology

UZELAC, M., Aesthetics

VARGA, I., Cello

There are research institutes attached to each faculty

UNIVERSITETI I PRISHTINËS
(University of Priština)

Sheshi Nëna Tereze 5, Priština 38000, Kosovo

Telephone: (38) 244-183
Fax: (38) 244-187
E-mail: rektorati@uni-pr.edu

Internet: www.uni-pr.edu
Founded 1970
State control
Academic year: September to June
Rector: Prof. Dr JAHI HOXHA
Library: see Libraries and Archives
Number of teachers: 756
Number of students: 14,000
Publications: *Acta Biologiae et Medicinae Experimentalis, Pregled Predavanja, Univerzitetska Misao*

DEANS

Faculty of Agriculture: Prof. SHUKRI FETAHU
Faculty of Arts: Prof. Dr HIVZI MUHARREMI
Faculty of Business: (vacant)
Faculty of Civil Engineering and Architecture: Prof. Dr MUSA STAVILECI
Faculty of Economics: Prof. Dr IBRAHIM KUKA
Faculty of Electrical Engineering and Computing: Dr LUAN AHMA
Faculty of Journalism: (vacant)
Faculty of Law: Prof. Dr BEQIR SADIKAJ
Faculty of Mechanical Engineering: Prof. Dr ISMAJL GOJANI
Faculty of Medicine: Prof. Dr BAJRAM NURAJ

Faculty of Mining and Metallurgy: Prof. Dr KADRI BERISHA
Faculty of Natural Sciences and Mathematics: Prof. Dr MUSTAFË BYTYÇI
Faculty of Philology: Prof. Dr NUHI REXHEPI
Faculty of Philosophy: Dr SELIM DACI
Faculty of Physical Education and Sport: Prof. Dr MUSTAFË ALIU
Faculty of Political Science: (vacant)
Faculty of Teacher Training: Prof. Dr SADIK RASHITI

College

Belgrade Business School: 27 Marta 149, Belgrade; tel. (11) 404-450; fax (11) 424-069; e-mail bbsse@eunet.yu; internet www.bpsbg .com; f. 1956; three-year diploma courses in finance, accounting, marketing, foreign and domestic trade, commerce, management, business informatics and computers, banking and insurance, customs, taxes and budget; library: 20,000 vols; 90 teachers (60 full-time, 30 part-time); 2,000 students; Dir Prof. Dr RADOVAN KNEŽEVIĆ.

SEYCHELLES

The Higher Education System

The Republic of Seychelles comprises some 115 islands in the western Indian Ocean. Seychelles achieved full independence from Britain, as a sovereign republic within the Commonwealth, in 1976. There are no university-level institutions of higher education in the Seychelles, but the Seychelles Polytechnic (founded 1983) offers one- to three-year Diploma and Certificate courses, and the National College of the Arts (founded 1997) offers one- and two-year programmes of study. There are several professional institutes of training and an Adult Learning and Distance Education Centre. The Ministry of Education and Youth is responsible for post-secondary, tertiary and adult education. The Ministry offers scholarships for students wishing to pursue tertiary education overseas. There were 1,837 students in post-secondary (non-tertiary) education in 2005.

Learned Societies

LANGUAGE AND LITERATURE

Alliance Française: Ave Bois de Rose, BP 210, Victoria; tel. 282424; fax 225172; e-mail info@alliancefr.sc; internet www.alliancefr.sc; offers courses and exams in French language and culture and promotes cultural exchange with France.

British Council: see chapter on Mauritius.

Research Institute

GENERAL

National Heritage: POB 573, Victoria, Mahé; tel. 321333; fax 322531; e-mail heritage@seychelles.net; f. 1987; controlled by Culture Division of the Ministry of Education and Culture; carries out research into the cultural heritage of Seychelles; Advisor MARCEL BARRY ROSALIE.

Libraries and Archives

Victoria

National Archives: POB 720, 5th June Ave, Victoria, Mahé; tel. 321333; fax 322113; e-mail pmlalande@hotmail.com; Archivist PETER LALANDE.

Seychelles National Library: POB 45, Francis Rachel St, Victoria, Mahé; tel. 321333; fax 323183; e-mail natlib@seychelles.net; internet www.national-library.edu.sc; f. 1910 as Carnegie Library; 75,000 vols (including branch libraries); 3 brs; special collections: documents on the Indian Ocean region, FAO, UNESCO, IMO and ILO publications; Principal Librarian ANNE-MARY ROBERT.

Museum

Victoria

National Museum: POB 720, 5th June Ave, La Bastille, Victoria, Mahé; tel. 321333; fax 322113; e-mail seymus@seychelles.net; f. 1964; Dir ALAIN LUCAS.

Polytechnic

SEYCHELLES POLYTECHNIC

POB 77, Anse Royale, Victoria
Telephone: 371188
Fax: 371545
E-mail: info@seypoly.edu.sc
Internet: www.seypoly.edu.sc
Founded 1983

State control
Language of instruction: English
Academic year: January to December

Director: JEAN RASSOOL
Assistant Director (Administration): HELENE BELMONT
Assistant Director (Studies): AUDREY NANON
Senior Librarian: MARIE-FRANCE LOZÉ

Library of 9,500 vols
Number of teachers: 56
Number of students: 578

HEADS OF PROGRAMMES
Academic Studies: SHELLA MOHIDEEN
Business and Secretarial Studies: ALPHONSO RODRIGUES
Technical Studies: JAYAH HARRIS
Manchester Training Programme: LIAM CAMPLING

School of Music

National College of the Arts: Ministry of Youth and Culture, POB 1383, Mahé; tel. 224777; fax 321591; e-mail acollart@hotmail.com; f. 1997; depts of music, dance, visual arts, drama; 33 teachers (28 full-time, 5 part-time); 720 students (120 full-time, 600 part-time); Dir DAVID CHETTY.

SIERRA LEONE

The Higher Education System

Formerly a British colony and protectorate, Sierra Leone gained independence from the United Kingdom in 1961. Fourah Bay College (founded 1827), a constituent college of the University of Sierra Leone (founded 1967), is the oldest current institution of higher education. Before joining the University, degrees from Fourah Bay College were awarded by the University of Durham (United Kingdom). The University of Sierra Leone is the only university, and consists of six colleges and institutes. In 2000/01 a total of 8,795 students were enrolled in tertiary education. The Ministry of Education, Science and Technology is responsible for higher education.

Admission to the University is on the basis of the Senior School Certificate examination. The University offers two- and three-year Certificate and Diploma courses in mostly professional fields of study, such as agriculture, engineering and marine biology. The undergraduate Bachelors is either a three-year 'General' degree or a four-year 'Honours' degree. At postgraduate level, students first take the Masters degree, which is awarded after one year following the Bachelors (Honours) or two years following the Bachelors (General), and then after the award of the Masters the Doctor of Philosophy is the highest university degree, requiring three years of research leading to submission of a thesis.

Technical and vocational education at the post-secondary level is available from technical institutes in Kenema and Freetown and the Institute of Public Administration and Management attached the University of Sierra Leone. The technical institutes offer a range of British-accredited qualifications, including City & Guilds certificates, London Chamber of Commerce and Industry examinations and Royal Society of Arts secretarial examinations. The Institute of Public Administration and Management (founded 1980) specializes in continuing education and workplace-based training.

Learned Societies

BIBLIOGRAPHY, LIBRARY SCIENCE AND MUSEOLOGY

Sierra Leone Association of Archivists, Librarians and Information Scientists: 7 Percival St, Freetown; f. 1970; 90 mems; Pres. OLATUNGIE CAMPBELL; Sec. AGNES MOROVIA; publ. *SLAALIS Bulletin* (quarterly).

HISTORY, GEOGRAPHY AND ARCHAEOLOGY

Historical Society of Sierra Leone: c/o Dept of History, Fourah Bay College, University of Sierra Leone, Freetown; f. 1975; 30 mems; Pres. G. S. ANTHONY; publ. *Journal* (2 a year).

LANGUAGE AND LITERATURE

Alliance Française: 30 Howe St, POB 510, Freetown; tel. (76) 683523; e-mail alliancefreetown@yahoo.fr; offers courses and exams in French language and culture and promotes cultural exchange with France.

British Council: Tower Hill, POB 124, Freetown; tel. (22) 222223; fax (22) 224123; e-mail info.enquiry@sl.britishcouncil.org; internet www.britishcouncil.org/sierraleone; offers courses and exams in English language and British culture and promotes cultural exchange with the UK; Dir RAJIV BENDRE.

MEDICINE

Sierra Leone Medical and Dental Association: POB 850, Freetown; tel. (22) 229825; fax (22) 228430; f. 1961; 220 mems; library of 3,000 vols (shared with main hospital); Pres. Dr S. U. M. JAH; Sec. Dr DESMOND WRIGHT; publs *Journal* (annually), *SLMDA Information Newsletter* (quarterly).

NATURAL SCIENCES

General

Sierra Leone Science Association: c/o Dept of Physics, Fourah Bay College, University of Sierra Leone, Freetown; tel. (22) 231617; fax (22) 224439; f. 1960; Hon. Pres. Prof. Dr ERNEST H. WRIGHT; Hon. Sec. (vacant).

Research Institutes

GENERAL

Institute of African Studies: c/o University of Sierra Leone, Fourah Bay College, Freetown; f. 1962; undertakes research in sociology, history and culture of Sierra Leone; offers undergraduate and postgraduate courses in cultural studies; Dir Dr ARTHUR ABRAHAM; publ. *Africana Research Bulletin* (2 a year).

NATURAL SCIENCES

Biological Sciences

Institute of Marine Biology and Oceanography: Fourah Bay College, University of Sierra Leone, Freetown; tel. (22) 250775; f. 1966; 4-year degree programme in marine science, undergraduate diploma in aquatic biology and fisheries; research and training in oceanography, marine algae and ecology, fishery biology and management, aquaculture, marine pollution, estuarine dynamics, and coastal processes; Dir Dr I. W. O. FINDLAY; publ. *Annual Bulletin*.

Physical Sciences

Geological Survey Division: Ministry of Mines, Youyi Bldg, Brookfields, Freetown; f. 1918; to locate mineral deposits and to advise on all matters relating to the earth; library of 16,000 vols including periodicals; Dir A. H. GABISI; publs *Annual Report, Bulletin, Short Papers* (all annually).

Libraries and Archives

Freetown

Fourah Bay College Library: University of Sierra Leone, Freetown; tel. (22) 229471; f. 1827; 200,000 vols, 330 current periodicals; Librarian D. E. THOMAS.

Public Archives of Sierra Leone: c/o Fourah Bay College, Freetown; f. 1965; 63,000 linear ft of records; Sr Archivist ALBERT MOORE.

Sierra Leone Library Board: POB 326, Freetown; tel. (22) 223848; f. 1959; nationwide public library service; also acts as a national library (legal deposit); 80,000 vols; 3 regional libraries, 10 brs; Chief Librarian IRENE O'BRIEN-COKER; publs *Annual Report, Sierra Leone Publications* (annually).

Museum

Freetown

Sierra Leone National Museum: Cotton Tree Building, POB 908, Freetown; tel. (22) 223555; fax (22) 224439; e-mail cabnicol70@yahoo.co.uk; historical, ethnographical and archaeological collection; Curator CELIA NICOL.

University

UNIVERSITY OF SIERRA LEONE

Private Mail Bag, Freetown

Telephone: (22) 226859

Founded 1967

State control

Language of instruction: English

Academic year: October to June

Chancellor: The President of the Republic of Sierra Leone

Vice-Chancellor: Prof. ERNEST H. WRIGHT

Pro-Chancellor: Dr ARTHUR PORTER

Pro-Vice-Chancellor: Prof. A. M. ALGHALI

Secretary and Registrar: J. A. G. THOMAS

Librarian: GLADYS JUSU-SHERIFF

Number of teachers: 301

Number of students: 4,310 (full-time)

Publications: *African Research Bulletin* (2 a year), *Calendar and Prospectus* (annually), *Varsity Update* (monthly), *Vice-Chancellor's Annual Report*.

CONSTITUENT COLLEGES

Fourah Bay College

POB 87, Mount Aureol, Freetown

Telephone: (22) 227924

Internet: fbcusl.8k.com

Founded by the Church Missionary Society in 1827, it was affiliated to the University of Durham in 1876 and became a constituent college of the University in 1966

Principal: Prof. V. E. H. STRASSER-KING
Vice-Principal: Prof. A. J. G. WYSE

DEANS

Faculty of Arts: Rev. Dr L. E. T. SHYLLON
Faculty of Economic and Social Sciences:
Prof. A. ABRAHAM
Faculty of Engineering: Prof. O. R. DAVIDSON
Faculty of Law: Prof. H. M. JOKO-SMART
Faculty of Pure and Applied Science: Prof. V.
E. GODWIN
Postgraduate Studies: Prof. A. J. G. WYSE

PROFESSORS

Faculty of Arts:
WYSE, A. J. G., History
Faculty of Economic and Social Sciences:
ABRAHAM, A., Institute of African Studies
Faculty of Engineering:
DAVIDSON, O. R., Mechanical Engineering
Faculty of Law:
JOKO-SMART, H. M.
Faculty of Pure and Applied Science:
AWUNOR-RENNER, E. R. T., Physics
COLE, N. H. A., Botany
STRASSER-KING, V. E. H., Geology
WILLIAMS, M. O., Zoology

DIRECTORS

Institute of Adult Education and Extra-
Mural Studies: E. D. A. TURAY
Institute of African Studies: Prof. A. ABRA
HAM
Institute of Marine Biology and Oceanogra-
phy: Dr I. W. O. FINDLAY
Institute of Population Studies: Dr A. C.
THOMAS

Njala University College

Telephone: (22) 228788
E-mail: NUC@sierratel.sl

Internet: www.nuc-online.com
Founded 1964
Principal: Prof. A. M. ALGHALI
Vice-Principal: P. K. SAIDU

DEANS

Faculty of Agriculture: Prof. E. R. RHODES
Faculty of Education: Dr T. M. DUGBA
Faculty of Environmental Sciences: Dr G. M.
T. ROBERT

PROFESSORS

Faculty of Agriculture:
KOROMA, J. P. C., Crop Science
RHODES, E. R., Soil Science
Faculty of Education:
BOMAH, A. K., Geography and Rural Devel-
opment

College of Medicine and Allied Health Sciences

Telephone: (22) 240884
Founded 1987
Principal: Prof. A. M. TAQI
Vice-Principal: Assoc. Prof. F. D. R. LISK

DEANS

Faculty of Basic Medical Sciences: Dr J. K.
GEORGE
Faculty of Clinical Sciences: Dr. L. GORDON-
HARRIS
Faculty of Pharmaceutical Sciences: Prof. E.
AYITEY-SMITH

PROFESSORS

Faculty of Basic Medical Sciences:
GEORGE, J. K., Anatomy
Faculty of Clinical Sciences:
TAQI, A. M., Paediatrics

Faculty of Pharmaceutical Sciences:
AYITEY-SMITH, E., Pharmacology.

OFF-CAMPUS INSTITUTES

Institute of Education: Private Mail Bag,
Tower Hill, Freetown; tel. (22) 226874; Dir
MELISSA F. JONAH (acting).

Institute of Library Studies: Mount Aureol, Freetown; tel. (22) 240290; Dir GLADYS
JUSU-SHERIFF.

**Institute of Public Administration and
Management:** Private Mail Bag, Tower Hill,
Freetown; tel. (22) 224801; Dir I. I. MAY-
PARKER.

Colleges

**Milton Margai College of Education and
Technology:** Goderich, nr Freetown; f. 1960;
trains secondary school teachers; library:
23,000 vols; 55 teachers; 624 students;
Principal Dr DENIS KARGBO; Registrar J. U.
WRIGHT (acting).

Paramedical School: POB 50, Bo; f. 1979
with funds from the Government and the
EEC; trains primary health workers; Principal Dr V. O. COLE.

Technical Institute: Congo Cross, Freetown; tel. (22) 231368; fax (22) 231368; f.
1952; 80 teachers; 980 students; City and
Guilds Craft and Technical Courses and
Commercial Education; certificate, diploma
and higher diploma courses in engineering,
business, secretarial work and education;
focal point for the UNEVOC project; Principal MOHAMED A. JALLOH.

Technical Institute: Kenema; vocational
courses.

SINGAPORE

The Higher Education System

In 1826 the East India Company formed the Straits Settlements by the union of Singapore and the dependencies of Penang and Malacca on the Malay Peninsula. They came under British rule in 1867. In 1946 Singapore became a separate crown colony, and in 1959 achieved complete internal self-government. After seceding from the Federation of Malaysia in 1965, Singapore became an independent republic. There are four universities, the oldest of which is National University of Singapore (founded 1980). In 2005 the Open University Centre (founded 1992), affiliated with the Open University (United Kingdom), was elevated to university status and renamed SIM University; it specializes in adult education and correspondence courses. All the universities are publicly funded, but the Singapore Management University (founded 2000) is under private management. In 2005 the total number of students enrolled in university-level education was 59,441 (excluding SIM University), with a further 64,442 students enrolled at the country's five polytechnics.

Admission to university undergraduate degrees is on the basis of results in A-Level examinations. The undergraduate Bachelors degree lasts three years at 'Pass' level and four years at 'Honours' level. Degrees in professional fields of study, such as dentistry, law, engineering and construction, last longer. Both postgraduate Diplomas and Masters degrees are one- or two-year programmes of study, and the Doctor of Philosophy, the highest university degree, lasts three years.

Post-secondary technical and vocational education is offered by the polytechnics and the Institute of Technical Education. The five polytechnics offer three levels of qualification, Certificate, Diploma and Advanced Diploma, in a range of professional fields of study. The Institute of Technical Education (founded 1992) replaced the former Vocational and Industrial Training Board and consists of 10 centres on two campuses; it specializes in full- and part-time training, workplace-based traineeships and continuing education. Qualifications offered include the Industrial Technician Certificate and National Technical Certificate.

Learned Societies

GENERAL

Singapore National Academy of Science: 1st Floor, Singapore Science Centre Building, off Jurong Town Hall Rd, Singapore 2260; established to promote the advancement of science and technology and to represent the mem. societies, institutes and other founder/affiliate mems of the Academy; Pres. Prof. Leo Tan Wee Hin; Sec. Dr Chia Woon Kim.

Singapore Society of Asian Studies: Kent Ridge, POB 1076, Singapore 9111; f. 1982 to promote the study of Asian culture and heritage, with special emphasis on the Southeast Asian region; 130 mems; Pres. Lim Guan Hock; Sec. Dr Yeo Mang Thong; publ. *Asian Culture* (annually).

ARCHITECTURE AND TOWN PLANNING

Singapore Institute of Architects: 79 Neil Rd, Singapore 088904; tel. 62262668; fax 62262663; e-mail info@sia.org.sg; internet www.sia.org.sg; f. 1923; 1,000 mems; Pres. Edward D'Silva; Hon. Sec. Johnny Tan; publs *Singapore Architect* (4 a year), *SIA Year Book*.

BIBLIOGRAPHY, LIBRARY SCIENCE AND MUSEOLOGY

Library Association of Singapore: Bukit Merah Central, POB 0693, Singapore 9115; internet www.las.org.sg; f. 1955; 328 mems; Pres. Choy Fatt Cheong; Hon. Sec. Lim-Yeo Pin Pin; publs *Singapore Libraries* (2 a year), *Singapore Libraries Bulletin* (quarterly).

ECONOMICS, LAW AND POLITICS

Singapore Institute of International Affairs: 2 Nassim Rd, Singapore 258370; tel. 67349600; fax 67336217; e-mail research@siiaonline.org; f. 1961; organizes talks, conferences etc.; commissions research on east-Asian economic integration, sustainable development and governance issues and peace and development in south-east Asia; 379 mems; Chair. Assoc. Prof. Simon Tay; Dir Yeo Lay Hwee.

FINE AND PERFORMING ARTS

Singapore Art Society: 6001 Beach Rd, No 18–08, Golden Mile Tower, Singapore 0719; tel. 62924244; f. 1949 to foster the practice and appreciation of art in Singapore; 325 mems; Pres. Ho Kok Hoe; Hon. Sec. Quek Kian Guan.

LANGUAGE AND LITERATURE

Alliance Française: 1 Sarkies Rd, Singapore 258130; tel. 67378422; fax 67333023; e-mail afsing@alliancefrancaise.org.sg; internet www.alliancefrancaise.org.sg; offers courses and exams in French language and culture and promotes cultural exchange with France; Dir Pascale Fabre.

British Council: 30 Napier Rd, Singapore 258509; tel. 64731111; fax 64721010; e-mail enquiries@britishcouncil.org.sg; internet www.britishcouncil.org.sg; f. 1947; teaching centre; offers courses and exams in English language and British culture and promotes cultural exchange with the UK; attached teaching centres in Holland Village, Marsiling and Tampines; Dir Les Dangerfield; Dir, Teaching Centre Martin Hope.

Goethe-Institut: 163 Penang Rd 05-01, Winsland House II, Singapore 238463; tel. 67354555; fax 67354666; e-mail director@goethe.org.sg; internet www.goethe.de/so/sin/deindex.htm; offers courses and exams in German language and culture and promotes cultural exchange with Germany; library of 8,000 vols; Dir Dr Michael de la Fontaine.

MEDICINE

Academy of Medicine, Singapore: College of Medicine Bldg, Level 1, Left Wing, 16 College Rd, Singapore 0316; tel. 62238968; fax 62255155; f. 1957; professional corporate body of medical and dental specialists; also involved in the postgraduate training of doctors; Master Dr N. C. Tan; Chief Administrator Y. L. Lam; publ. *Annals* (quarterly).

Singapore Medical Association: Level 2, 2 College Rd, Alumni Medical Centre, Singapore 169850; tel. 62231264; fax 62247827; e-mail sma@sma.org.sg; internet www.sma.org.sg; f. 1959; 3,900 mems; Pres. Prof. C. H. Low; Hon. Sec. Dr W. M. Yue; publs *Singapore Medical Journal* (monthly), *SMA Newsletter* (monthly).

NATURAL SCIENCES

General

Singapore Association for the Advancement of Science: 1st Floor, Singapore Science Centre Bldg, off Jurong Town Hall Rd, Singapore 2260; f. 1976 for the dissemination of science and technology; Pres. Prof. Ang Kok Peng; Sec. Dr Leo Tan Wee Hin.

Mathematical Sciences

Singapore Mathematical Society: Mathematics Dept, National University of Singapore, Kent Ridge, Singapore 119260; tel. 68742394; fax 67795452; e-mail smsuser@math.nus.edu.sg; internet sms.math.nus.edu.sg; f. 1952; aims to maintain the status and advance the interests of the profession of mathematics, to improve the teaching of mathematics, and to provide means of intercourse between students, teachers and others interested in mathematics; 620 mems; Pres. Prof. Tan Eng Chye; Sec. Prof. Tang Wee Kee; publ. *Mathematical Medley* (2 a year).

Physical Sciences

Institute of Physics, Singapore: c/o Dept of Physics, National University of Singapore, Kent Ridge, Singapore 119260; tel. 67722604; fax 67776126; f. 1973 to promote study of and research in physics in Singapore; organizes conferences, talks, seminars, exhibitions, visits to industrial and commercial establishments and educational tours abroad; 180 mems; Pres. Prof. Bernard Tan; Sec. Assoc. Prof. Andrew T. S. Wee; publs *Singapore Journal of Physics* (2 a year), *Physics Update* (2 a year).

Research Institutes

ECONOMICS, LAW AND POLITICS

Asian Media Information and Communication Centre: Jurong Point POB 360, Singapore 916412; tel. 67927570; fax

67927129; e-mail amicline@singnet.com.sg; internet www.amic.org.sg; f. 1971; non-profit regional documentation centre; works in co-operation with UNESCO and other int. orgs to promote the understanding and development of communication and its application in the Asia-Pacific region with regard to economic, social and cultural progress; organizes seminars, workshops, refresher courses; convenes conferences; conducts communication research; library of 35,000 records in databases, 350 journals; regional centre for Japan Prize Circulating Library; Sec.-Gen. VIJAY MENON; publs *Media Asia* (quarterly), *AMCB* (every 2 months), *Mass Communication Periodical Literature Index* (every 6 months), *Asian Journal of Communication* (every 6 months).

Institute of Southeast Asian Studies: Heng Mui Keng Terrace, Pasir Panjang, Singapore 119614; f. 1968 to undertake research on South-East Asia, especially problems of development, modernization, political and social change; library of 400,000 vols; Dir Prof. CHIA SIOW YUE; Head of Administration Y. L. LEE; Librarian CH'NG KIM SEE; publs *Contemporary Southeast Asia* (3 a year), *Regional Outlook*, *Southeast Asian Affairs* (annually), *SOJOURN, Social Issues in Southeast Asia* (2 a year), *ASEAN Economic Bulletin* (3 a year).

EDUCATION

Institute of Technical Education (ITE): 10 Dover Drive, Singapore 138683; tel. 67757800; fax 67762172; e-mail itehq@ite .edu.sg; internet www.ite.edu.sg; Chair. ERIC GWEE TECK HAI; Dir Dr LAW SONG SENG; publ. *The Quality Workforce* (6 a year).

Libraries and Archives
Singapore

National Archives of Singapore: National Heritage Board, 1 Canning Rise, Singapore 179868; fax 63393583; f. 1968; 3,400 vols, 43 current periodicals, 1,500,000 photographs, 128,200 building plans, 6,630 maps, 66,427 microfilm rolls, 18,000 tapes of recorded interviews; Senior Dir LILY TAN; publ. *National Heritage Board Annual Report.*

National Library Board: 100 Victoria St, 14-01, Singapore 188064; tel. 63323133; fax 63323332; e-mail helpdesk@nlb.gov.sg; internet www.nlb.gov.sg; f. 1995; 1,053,811 vols (67% of the colln in English, 17% in Chinese, 6% in Malay, 3% in Tamil), 106,910 serial titles; 94,908 audio-visual and other spec. materials; spec. collns incl. Singapore and Southeast Asia, Business, Arts, Languages; oversees the management of the Nat. Library, including the Lee Kong Chian Reference Library, 3 regional libraries, 20 community libraries, 15 community children's libraries and over 30 libraries belonging to govt agencies, schools and private institutions; Chief Exec. Dr N. VARAPRASAD; publs *Singapore Periodicals Index* (annual), *Books about Singapore* (every 3 years), *Singapore National Bibliography* (quarterly).

National University of Singapore Libraries: 12 Kent Ridge Crescent, Singapore 119275; tel. 65162069; fax 67771272; e-mail clbsec@nus.edu.sg; internet www.lib .nus.edu.sg; f. 1905; 2,372,172 vols (Central Library 1,125,675 vols; Japanese Resources 51,955 vols; Chinese Library 465,644 vols; C. J. Koh Law Library 157,087 vols; Hon Sui Sen Memorial Library 90,992 vols; Medical Library 170,040 vols; Science Library 286,221 vols), 23,844 electronic titles, 27,423 audiovisual items, 24,266 microforms;

Director, NUS Libraries SYLVIA YAP; publs *Guide to NUS Libraries* (annually), *LINUS: Newsletter of the NUS Libraries* (quarterly).

Museums and Art Galleries
Singapore

National Heritage Board: 93 Stamford Rd, Singapore 78897; tel. 63361460; fax 63323568; f. 1849; consists of Asian Civilizations Museum, Singapore History Museum, Singapore Art Museum, Children's Discovery Gallery; library of 25,000 vols; history and oral history archives; CEO LIM SIAM KIM.

Singapore Art Museum: 71 Bras Basah Rd, Singapore 189555; tel. 63323222; fax 63347919; internet www.museum.org.sg/ SAM/sam.shtml; f. 1996; modern and contemporary Southeast Asian art.

Singapore Botanic Gardens: National Parks Board, Cluny Rd, Singapore 259569; tel. 64717361; fax 64671832; internet www .nparks.gov.sg; f. 1859; botanical and horticultural research with particular reference to South-East Asia and the tropics; library of 24,000 vols; CEO Dr TAN WEE KIAT; Dir of Gardens Dr CHIN SEE CHUNG; Keeper of Herbarium and Library Dr RUTH KIEW; publ. *The Gardens Bulletin Singapore* (2 a year).

Universities
NANYANG TECHNOLOGICAL UNIVERSITY

Nanyang Ave, Singapore 639798

Telephone: 67911744
Fax: 67911604
E mail: ntu@edu.sg
Internet: www.ntu.edu.sg

Founded 1981 as Nanyang Technological Institute; present name and status 1991
Academic year: July to July

Chancellor: S. R. NATHAN
President: Dr SU GUANING
Deputy Presidents: Prof. LIM MONG KING, Prof. ER MENG HWA
Registrar and Vice President (Academic Services): Dr FOO CHEK FOK
Bursar and Vice President (Finance): TAN EN LIN
Vice-President (Facilities Planning and Management): CHIA OI LENG (acting)
Vice-President (Human Resources): ANGELA LIM SAU TING
Vice-President (Information Technology Services): LOW KIN KIONG
Vice-President (Plans): PEK SIOK CHING
Vice-President (Research): Prof. TONY WOO
Vice-President (Student Affairs): CHONG PENG JEK
Director (Corporate Communications): TAN SU YUEN
Librarian: CHOY FATT CHEONG

Number of teachers: 1,352
Number of students: 33,109

Publications: *Asian Journal of Communication* (3 a year), *Media Asia* (4 a year), *Asian Mass Communication Bulletin* (6 a year), *Electrical and Electronic Engineering Bulletin* (annually), *Nanyang Business Review* (2 a year), *Asian Business Law Review* (4 a year), *Mechanical and Aerospace Engineering Research Bulletin* (annually), *Asia Pacific Journal of Education* (2 a year), *Pedagogies: An International Journal* (2 a year), *Singteach* (4 a year), *Teaching Education* (4 a year), *Technical*

Reports (monthly), *School of Computer Engineering Research Report* (annually)

DEANS

School of Art, Design and Media: Prof. ISAAC KERLOW
School of Biological Sciences: Prof. JAMES PINGKWAN TAM
School of Chemical and Biomedical Engineering: Prof. CHING CHI BUN
School of Civil and Environmental Engineering: Prof. PAN TSO-CHIEN
School of Communication and Information: Assoc. Prof. ANG PENG HWA
School of Computer Engineering: Assoc. Prof. SEAH HOCK SOON
School of Electrical and Electronic Engineering: Prof. KAM CHAN HIN
School of Humanities and Social Sciences: Prof. EDDIE KUO CHEN-YU
School of Materials Science and Engineering: Prof. FREDDY BOEY YING CHIANG (acting)
School of Mechanical and Aerospace Engineering: Prof. LAM KHIN YONG (acting)
School of Mechanical and Production Engineering: Prof. LENNIE LIM (acting)
School of Physical and Mathematical Sciences: Prof. ALEX LAW SAI-KIT
College of Engineering: Prof. LIM MONG KING
Nanyang Business School: Prof. HONG HAI

DIRECTORS

National Institute of Education: Prof. LEO TAN WEE HIN
Institute of Defence and Strategic Studies: BARRY DESKER

PROFESSORS

School of Biological Sciences (60 Nanyang Dr., SBS-01n-21, Singapore 637551; tel. 63162800; fax 67913856; e-mail d-sbs@ntu .edu.sg; internet www.ntu.edu.sg/sbs):

LAW, A. S. K., Molecular and Cell Biology
LUN, K. C., Structural and Computational Biology
NORDENSKLOLD, L., Structural and Computational Biology
TAM, J. P. K.

School of Civil and Environmental Engineering (Block N1, 50 Nanyang Ave, Singapore 639798; tel. 67905265; fax 67910676; e-mail d-cee@ntu.edu.sg; internet www.ntu.edu.sg/ cee):

CHIEW, Y. M., Environmental and Water Resources Engineering
CHOA, V. C. E., Geotechnical Engineering
CHOI, E. C. C., Construction Technology and Management
FAN, H. S. L., Transportation Engineering
FAN, S. C., Structures and Mechanics
PAN, T. C., Structures and Mechanics
RAHARDJO, H., Geotechnical and Transportation Engineering
SOH, C. K., Structures and Mechanics
TAY, J. H., Environmental and Water Resources Engineering

School of Computer Engineering (Block N4, 2A-32, Nanyang Ave, Singapore 639798; tel. 67905786; fax 67926559; e-mail wwwsce@ntu .edu.sg; internet www.ntu.edu.sg/sce):

GOH, A. E. S., Information Systems

School of Communication and Information (31 Nanyang Link, Singapore 637718; tel. 67904577; fax 67943662; e-mail wwwsci@ntu .edu.sg; internet www.ntu.edu.sg/sci):

FOO S. B., Information Studies
KUO C. Y. E., Communication Research

School of Electrical and Electronic Engineering (Block S2.1, 50 Nanyang Ave, Singapore 639798; tel. 67905367; fax 67912687; e-mail wwweee@ntu.edu.sg; internet www.ntu.edu .sg/eee):

CHOI, S. S., Power Engineering

Do, M. A., Circuits and Systems
Er, M. H.
Gay, R. K. L., Information Communication Institute of Singapore
Kam, C. H., Microelectronics
Koh, S. N., Communication Engineering
Kot, C. C., Information Engineering
Lim, Y. C., Information Engineering
Soh, Y. C., Control and Instrumentation
Sundararajan, N., Control and Instrumentation
Xie, L. H., Control and Administration
Yoon, S. F., Microelectronics
Zhu, W. G., Microelectronics

School of Humanities and Social Sciences (Block S3.2, Level B2, 50 Nanyang Ave, Singapore 639798; tel. 67906983; fax 67942830; e-mail d-hss@ntu.edu.sg; internet www.hss.ntu.edu.sg):

Chew, S. B., Economics
Koh, T. A., English
Kuo, C. O. E., Sociology
Lim, C. Y., Economics
Reisman, D. A., Economics

School of Materials Science and Engineering (Block N4.1, #01-30, Nanyang Ave, Singapore 639798; tel. 67904142; fax 67909081; e-mail wwwsme@ntu.edu.sg; internet www.ntu.edu.sg/sme):

Boey, F. Y. C.

School of Mechanical and Production Engineering (Block N3, 50 Nanyang Ave, Singapore 639798; tel. 67905486; fax 67911859; e-mail wwwmae@ntu.edu.sg; internet www.ntu.edu.sg/mae):

Asundi, A. K., Engineering Mechanics
Helander, M. E. G., Systems and Engineering Management
Khoo, L. P., Mechatronics and Design
Khor, K. A., Manufacturing Engineering
Lam, Y. C., Manufacturing Engineering
Liew, K. M., Engineering Mechanics
Lim, L. E. N., Manufacturing Engineering
Lim, M. K., Engineering Mechanics
Ling, S. F., Engineering Mechanics
Lye, S. W., Manufacturing Engineering
Meguid, S. A., Engineering Mechanics
Shang, H. M., Engineering Mechanics
Tam, K. C., Manufacturing Engineering
Yue, C. Y.

School of Physical and Mathematical Sciences (Block 5, Level 3, 1 Nanyang Walk, Singapore 637616; tel. 67903754; fax 67906984; e-mail spms-v1@ntu.edu.sg; internet www.ntu.edu.sg/SPMS/home):

Lee, S. Y.
Leung, P. H., Physical and Mathematical Sciences
Ling, S., Mathematical Sciences
Loh, T. P., Chemistry and Biological Chemistry

College of Chemical and Biomedical Engineering (Block 1 Innovation Centre, 16 Nanying Dr., Unit 100, Level 1, Singapore 637722; tel. 67906743; fax 67947553; e-mail cbe@ntu.edu.sg; internet www.ntu.edu.sg/cbme):

Ching, C. B.

College of Engineering (Block S3.2, Level B1, 50 Nanyang Ave, Singapore 639798; tel. 67906706; fax 67912523; e-mail d-coe@ntu.edu.sg; internet www.ntu.edu.sg/coe):

Lim, E. N.
Lim, M. K.

Nanyang Business School (Block S3, 50 Nanyang Ave, Singapore 639798; tel. 67904636; fax 67913697; e-mail wwwnbs@ntu.edu.sg; internet www.nbs.ntu.edu.sg):

Ang, S., Strategy, Management and Organization
Dufey, G., Banking and Finance
Hong, H.

Neo, B. S.
Sethi, V., Information Technology and Operations Management
Siguaw, J. A., Cornell-Nanyang Institute of Hospitality Management
Tan, H. T., Accounting
Wee, C. H., Strategy, Management and Organization
Williams, J. J., Accounting
Yeo, F. H. H., Accounting

National Institute of Education (1 Nanyang Walk, Singapore 637616; tel. 67903888; fax 68968874; e-mail niepr@nie.edu.sg; internet www.nie.edu.sg):

Chew, C. H.
Gan, L. H.
Goh, K. C.
Gopinathan, S.
Hogan, D. J.
Lee, S. K.
Luke, A. A. J.
Matthews, J. S.
Tan, L. W. H.
Xu, S. Y.

ATTACHED RESEARCH CENTRES

Advanced Materials Research Centre: Dir Assoc. Prof. Subodh Mhaisalkar.

Bioinformatics Research Centre: Dir Assoc. Prof. Liao Kin.

BioMedical Engineering Research Centre: Dir Assoc. Prof. Lim Chu Sing Daniel.

Centre for Advanced Numerical Engineering Simulations: Dir Prof. Liew Kim Meow.

Centre for Financial Engineering: Dir Assoc. Prof. Ho Kim Wai.

Centre for Graphics and Imaging Technology: Dir Assoc. Prof. Wong Kok Cheong.

Centre for High-Performance Embedded Systems: Dir Assoc. Prof. Thambipillai Srikanthan.

Environmental Engineering Research Centre: Dir Assoc. Prof. Stephen Tay Tiong Lee.

Maritime Research Centre: Dir Assoc. Prof. Tan Soon Keat.

Nanyang Technopreneurship Centre: Dir Assoc. Prof. Tan Teng Kee.

Network Technology Research Centre: Dir Assoc. Prof. Shum Ping.

NTU-BCA Centre for Advanced Construction Studies: Dir Assoc. Prof. Ting Seng Kiong.

NTU-MINDEF Protective Technology Research Centre: Dir Assoc. Prof. Pan Tso-Chien.

Positioning and Wireless Technology Centre: Dir Assoc. Prof. Law Choi Look.

Robotics Research Centre: Dir Assoc. Prof. Gerald Seet Gim Lee.

NATIONAL UNIVERSITY OF SINGAPORE

10 Kent Ridge Crescent, Singapore 119260

Telephone: 67756666

Internet: www.nus.edu.sg

Founded 1980 by merger of former University of Singapore and Nanyang University. (The University of Singapore had its origins in the King Edward VII College of Medicine, Raffles College and the University of Malaya in Singapore.)

State control

Language of instruction: English

Academic year: July to June (two semesters)

Chancellor: S. R. Nathan

Pro-Chancellors: Dr M. Baker, Ridzwan bin Haji Dzafir, Dr Andrew Chew Guan

Khuan, Dr Cheong Siew Keong, Ngiam Tong Dow
President: Prof. Shih Choon Fong
Deputy Vice-Chancellor: Prof. Chong Chi Tat
Registrar: Christine Chen (acting)
Librarian: Jill Quah
Library: see Libraries and Archives
Number of teachers: 1,820
Number of students: 30,698
Publications: *Annual Report*, *Knowledge Enterprise* (10 year)

DEANS

Faculty of Arts and Social Sciences: Lily Kong
Faculty of Dentistry: Keson Tan
Faculty of Engineering: Ng Wun Jern
Faculty of Law: Tan Cheng Han
Faculty of Medicine: Lee Eng Hin
Faculty of Science: Lai Choy Heng
School of Business: Leong Siew Meng
School of Computing: Jonan Jaffar
School of Design and Environment: Cheong Hin Fatt

PROFESSORS

Faculty of Arts and Social Sciences:

Chan, H. C., Political Science
Kapur, B. K., Economics
Mohanan, K. P., English Language and Literature
Mukul, A., Public Policy
Ng, C. K., History
Quah, S. T. J., Political Science
Sidle, R. C., Geography
Singh, R., Social Work and Psychology
Suryadinata, L., Political Science
Wang, G. W., East Asian Institute
Wong, K. L. C. A., Sociology
Wong, Y. W., Chinese Studies

Faculty of Business Administration:

Kau, A. K., Marketing
Leong, S. M., Marketing
Tan, C. H., Management and Organization
Wong, K. A., Finance and Accounting

Faculty of Dentistry:

Chew, C. L., Restorative Dentistry
Loh, H. S., Oral and Maxillofacial Surgery

Faculty of Engineering:

Ang, B. W., Industrial and Systems Engineering
Arun, S. M., Mechanical Engineering
Chan, S. H. D., Electrical and Computer Engineering
Cheong, H. F., Civil Engineering
Chew, Y. T., Mechanical Engineering
Ching, C. B., Chemical and Environmental Engineering
Chow, Y. K., Civil Engineering
Chua, S. J., Electrical and Computer Engineering
Chung, T. S. N., Chemical and Environmental Engineering
Fwa, T. F., Civil Engineering
Goh, T. N., Industrial and Systems Engineering
Hang, C. C., Electrical and Computer Engineering
Kam, P. Y., Electrical and Computer Engineering
Kang, E. T., Chemical and Environmental Engineering
Kooi, P. S., Electrical and Computer Engineering
Lam, K. Y., Mechanical Engineering
Lee, T. H., Electrical and Computer Engineering
Leong, M. S., Electrical and Computer Engineering
Li, M. F., Electrical and Computer Engineering

LIEW, A. C., Electrical and Computer Engineering
LIM, S. C., Mechanical Engineering
LIM, Y. C., Electrical and Computer Engineering
LING, C. H., Electrical and Computer Engineering
LOW, T. S., Electrical and Computer Engineering
LYE, K. M., Electrical and Computer Engineering
NEE, Y. C. A., Mechanical Engineering
NEOH, K. G., Chemical and Environmental Engineering
NHAN, P. T., Mechanical Engineering
NG, W. J., Civil Engineering
PARAMASIVAM, P., Civil Engineering
PHANG, C. H. J., Electrical and Computer Engineering
POO, A. N., Mechanical Engineering
SHANG, H. M., Mechanical Engineering
SHANKAR, N. J., Civil Engineering
SHANMUGAM, N. E., Civil Engineering
SHIH, C. F., Engineering
TAN, T. C., Chemical and Environmental Engineering
TAY, A. O. A., Electrical and Computer Engineering
TOYOAKI, N., Civil Engineering
VISWANADHAM, N., Mechanical Engineering
WIJEYSUNDERA, N. E., Mechanical Engineering
WONG, L., Electrical and Computer Engineering
YAP, M., Chemical and Environmental Engineering
YEO, S. P., Electrical and Computer Engineering
YONG, K. Y., Civil Engineering

Faculty of Law:
JAYAKUMAR, S.
KOH, T. B. T.
PINSLER, J.
SORNARAJAH, M.
TAN, Y. L.
WOON, C. M. W.

Faculty of Medicine:
AW, T. C., Pathology
BOSE, K., Orthopaedic Surgery
CHAN, H. L., Medicine
CHAN, S. H., Microbiology
CHIEW, Y. C., Medicine
GOPALAKRISHNAKONE, P., Anatomy
GWEE, M., Pharmacology
HALLIWELL, B., Biochemistry
HWANG, L. H. P., Physiology
KOH, S. Q. D., Community, Occupational and Family Medicine
KUA, E. H., Psychological Medicine
LEE, E. H., Orthopaedic Surgery
LEE, H. P., Community, Occupational and Family Medicine
LEE, J. D. E., Pharmacology
LEE, T. L., Anaesthesia
LEE, Y. S., Pathology
LIM, P., Medicine
LING, E. A., Anatomy
LIU, E., Medicine
LOW, P. S., Paediatrics
NG, S. C., Obstetrics and Gynaecology
OH, M. S. V., Medicine
ONG, C. N., Community, Occupational and Family Medicine
PHO, W. H. R., Orthopaedic Surgery
PRASAD, R. N. V., Obstetrics and Gynaecology
SATKUNANANTHAM, K., Orthopaedic Surgery
SHAMAL, D. D., Orthopaedic Surgery
SIT, K. H., Anatomy
SIT, K. P., Biochemistry
TAN, C. C., Medicine
TAN, K. A. L., Diagnostic Radiology
TAN, W. C., Medicine
TAN, Y. H., Medicine

WEE, A., Pathology
WONG, E. L. J., Medicine
YAP, H. K., Paediatrics

Faculty of Science:
BAI, Z., Statistics and Applied Probability
BERRICK, A. J., Mathematics
CHAN, S. O. H., Chemistry
CHEN, H. Y. L., Mathematics
CHONG, C. T., Mathematics
CHOU, L. M., Biological Sciences
CHOW, S. N., Mathematics
DING, J. L., Biological Sciences
GOH, S. H., Chemistry
HEW, C. L., Biological Sciences
HOR, T. S. A., Chemistry
IP, Y. K. A., Biological Sciences
KOH, K. M., Mathematics
LAI, C. H., Physics
LAM, T. J., Biological Sciences
LEE, C. K., Chemistry
LEE, S. L., Mathematics
LEE, S. Y., Chemistry
LI, F. Y. S., Chemistry
LIM, C. S., Mathematics
LIM, H., Physics
NIEDERREITER, H., Mathematics
OH, C. H., Physics
ONG, C. K., Physics
ONG, P. P. P., Physics
PHILPOTT, M. R., Materials Science
SY, H. K., Physics
TANG, S. H., Physics
TANG, S. M., Physics
TRUONG, Y. K.-N., Statistics and Applied Probability
WATT, F., Physics

School of Computing:
JAFFAR, J., Computer Science
LING, T. W., Computer Science
LU, H. J., Computer Science
OOI, B. C., Computer Science
PNG, P. L. I., Information Systems
WEI, K. K., Information Systems
YUEN, C. K., Computer Science

School of Design and Environment:
BROWN, G. R., Real Estate
OFORI, G., Building

ATTACHED RESEARCH INSTITUTES

Asia Research Institute: Dir Prof. ANTHONY REID.

Bioinformatics Institute: Dir Dr GUNARETNAM RAJAGOPAL.

Bioprocessing Technology Centre: Dir Prof. MIRANDA YAP.

Bioscience Centre: Dir Assoc. Prof. LIM TIT MENG.

Centre for Bone Banking Research: Dir Assoc. Prof. AZIZ NATHER.

Centre for Building Performance and Construction: Dir Dr TEO HO PIN.

Centre for Business Research and Development: Dir CHOW KIT BOEY.

Centre for Entrepreneurship: Dir Assoc. Prof. WONG POH KAM.

Centre for Instructional Technology: Dir RAVI CHANDRAN (acting).

Centre for Integrated Circuit Failure Analysis and Reliability: Dir Assoc. Prof. JOHN THONG.

Centre for Internet Research: Dir Assoc. Prof. A. L. ANANDA.

Centre for Natural Product Research: Dir Prof. MIRANDA YAP.

Centre for Optoelectronics: Dir Prof. CHUA SOO JIN.

Centre for Real Estate Studies: Dir Dr SING TIEN FOO.

Centre for Remote Imaging, Sensing and Processing: Dir KWOH LEONG KEONG.

Centre for Transportation Research: Dir Prof. FWA TIEN FANG.

Data Storage Institute: Dir Assoc. Prof. CHONG TOW CHONG.

East Asian Institute: Dir Prof. WANG GUNGWU.

Genome Institute of Singapore: Dir Prof. EDISON LIU.

Institute for Communications Research: Dir Prof. LYE KIN MUN.

Institute of High-Performance Computing: Dir Prof. LAM KHIN YONG.

Institute of Materials Research and Engineering: Dir Prof. ALBERT YEE.

Institute of Microelectronics: Dir Dr TAN KHEN SANG.

Institute of Molecular Agrobiology: Dir Assoc. Prof. ZHANG LIAO HUI (acting).

Institute of Molecular and Cell Biology: Dir Prof. CHRIS TAN YIN HWEE.

Institute of Systems Science: Dir LIM SWEE CHEANG.

National University Medical Institutes: Dir Prof. CHAN SOH HA.

NUS-SPRING Centre for Best Practices: Dir Dr CHONG CHEE LEONG.

Surface Science Laboratory: Dir Assoc. Prof. ANDREW WEE.

World Health Organization Collaborating Centre for Clinical Research in Human Reproduction: Dir Assoc. Prof. WONG PENG CHEONG.

World Health Organization Collaborating Centre for Dementia Research: Dir Prof. KUA EE HEOK.

World Health Organization Collaborating Centre for Maternal and Child Health/Family Planning Services, Research and Training: Dir Assoc. Prof. WONG PENG CHEONG.

World Health Organization Collaborating Centre for Occupational Health: Dir Assoc. Prof. CHIA SIN ENG.

World Health Organization Collaborating Centre for Research and Training in Immunology: Dir Prof. CHAN SOH HA.

SINGAPORE MANAGEMENT UNIVERSITY

Tanglin, POB 257, Singapore 912409
Bukit Timah Campus, 469 Bukit Timah Rd, Oei Tiong Ham Bldg, Singapore 259756
Telephone: 68220100
Fax: 68220101
E-mail: enquire@smu.edu.sg
Internet: www.smu.edu.sg
Founded 2000
Private control

President: HOWARD HUNTER
Provost: Prof. CHIN TIONG TAN
Registrar: TAN LEE CHUAN
Chief Librarian: KOH BEE CHIN

DEANS

School of Accountancy: Assoc. Prof. PANG YANG HOONG
Lee Kong Chian School of Business: Prof. DAVID B. MONTGOMERY
School of Economics and Social Sciences: Prof. ROBERTO S. MARIANO
School of Information Systems: STEVEN MILLER

PROFESSORS

School of Accountancy (Accountancy Bldg, 469 Bukit Timah Rd, Singapore 259756; tel. 68220610; fax 68220600; e-mail adelineheng@smu.edu.sg; internet www.accountancy.smu.edu.sg):

TAN, T. M.
YOUNG, K. K.

Lee Kong Chian School of Business (Business Bldg, 469 Bukit Timah Rd, Singapore 259756; e-mail dmontgomery@smu.edu.sg; internet www.business.smu.edu.sg):

LIM, K. G.
MONTGOMERY, D.
PANG, E. F.
PHANG, A.
TAN, C. T.
YANG, K. K.

School of Economics and Social Sciences (The Federal Bldg, 469 Bukit Timah Rd, Singapore 259756; tel. 68220832; fax 68220833; e-mail sess@smu.edu.sg; internet www.sess.smu.edu.sg):

KUEN, T. S.
MARIANO, R. S.

School of Information Systems (Raffles Bldg, 469 Bukit Timah Rd, Singapore 259756; tel. 68220903; fax 68220919; e-mail sis@smu.edu.sg; internet www.sis.smu.edu.sg):

DENG, R. H.
LEE, J. K.

Polytechnics

NANYANG POLYTECHNIC

180 Ang Mo Kio Ave 8, Singapore 569830
Telephone: 64515115
Internet: www.nyp.edu.sg
Founded 1992
President: TAN PHENG HOCK
Principal and CEO: LIN CHENG TON
Deputy Principal (Academic) and Registrar: CHAN LEE MUN
Deputy Principal (Development): BRUCE POH GEOK HUAT
Deputy Principal (Technology): EDWARD HO SZE LEUNG
Chief Librarian: WONG CHIEW AUN

DIRECTORS

School of Business Management: V. SESHAMANI
School of Chemical and Life Sciences: Dr JOEL LEE
School of Engineering: CHAN YEW MENG
School of Health Sciences: LONG CHOOI FONG
School of Information Technology: JOHN TAN

NGEE ANN POLYTECHNIC

535 Clementi Rd, Singapore 599489
Telephone: 64666555
Fax: 64687326
E-mail: dept-cc@np.edu.sg
Internet: www.np.edu.sg
Founded 1963
State control
Language of instruction: English
Academic year: June to May
Chairman: TAN HUP FOI
Principal: CHIA MIA CHIANG
Deputy Principal (Academic Planning): LEE TUCK SENG
Deputy Principal (Engineering): TAN HAN CHEONG
Director of the Library: DAVID CHAN FATT CHOW
Library of 224,000 vols, 1,100 periodicals, 290 online books, 26 databases, 23,000 audio-visual items

Number of teachers: 800
Number of students: 14,500

DIRECTORS

School of Business and Accountancy: ONG-LUNG FUNG
School of Engineering: TAN HANG CHEONG
School of Film and Media Studies: Dr VICTOR VALBUENA
School of Health (Nursing): Dr PHANG CHIEW HUN
School of Information and Communications Technology: ANGELA WEE LI KWANG
School of Interdisciplinary Studies: PEE-KOH SEE HUA
School of Life Sciences and Chemical Technology: Dr SUSHILA CHANG-KRISHNASWAMY (acting)
Building and Environment Division (School of Engineering): GRACE QUAH-OON GEK NEO
Electrical Engineering Division (School of Engineering): KOH WEE HIONG
Electronic and Computer Engineering Division (School of Engineering): Dr LIM CHOO MIN
Marine and Offshore Technology Programme (School of Engineering): TAN KIM PONG
Mathematics, Science and Computing Programme (School of Engineering): Dr POK YANG MING
Mechanical Engineering Division (School of Engineering): FOO SEE MENG
Multidisciplinary Engineering Division (School of Engineering): WANG CHIN CHONG
Centre for Professional Development: YOLA LIM CHUAN YUNG
Early Childhood Education Programme: Dr KATHLEEN TERESA WALSH

REPUBLIC POLYTECHNIC

1 Kay Siang Rd, Singapore 248922
Telephone: 63768000
Fax: 64151310
E-mail: gsm@rp.edu.sg
Internet: www.rp.edu.sg
Founded 2002
Principal and Chief Executive: Prof. LOW TECK SENG
Deputy Registrar: SEAN TAY
Library Manager: YEE WAI FUN

DIRECTORS

School of Applied Science: Dr TERENCE CHONG
School of Engineering: FONG YEW CHAN
School of Information Technology and Communications Technology: TAY KHENG TIONG
Centre for Culture and Communication: GAN SU-LIN
Centre for Educational Development: GLEN O'GRADY
Centre for Innovation and Enterprise: CHANG YORK BOON (Man.)

SINGAPORE POLYTECHNIC

500 Dover Rd, Singapore 139651
Telephone: 67751133
Fax: 67806189
E-mail: info@sp.edu.sg
Internet: www.sp.edu.sg
Founded 1954
Language of instruction: English
Academic year: July to May (four terms)
Chairman: TAN KAY YONG
Principal: LOW WONG FOOK

Deputy Principal (Academic): YEOW KIAN PENG
Deputy Principal (Administration): EDWARD QUAH KOK WAH
Registrar: TAN PENG ANN
Librarian: FANG SIN GUEK
Library of 183,000 vols, 7,700 multi-media titles, 760 periodicals and serials
Number of teachers: 878
Number of students: 16,832 (14,438 full-time, 2,394 part-time)
Publications: *fullstop* (8 a year), *Technical Journal* (annually)

DIRECTORS

School of Business: V. MAHEANTHARAN
School of Chemical and Life Sciences: Dr CHENG SIONG
School of Design and the Environment: PETER LEE HOONG FATT
School of Electrical and Electronic Engineering: Dr DAVE CHONG TAD WENG
School of Info-Communications Technology: SONG NAY HAY
School of Mechanical and Manufacturing Engineering: ONG ENG CHAN
Singapore Maritime Academy: SWAPAN DAS SARMA

TEMASEK POLYTECHNIC

21 Tampines Ave 1, Singapore 529757
Telephone: 67882000
Fax: 67898220
E-mail: corporate.communication@tp.edu.sg
Internet: www.tp.edu.sg
Founded 1990
Principal: BOO KHENG HUA
Registrar: SOH ENG KHIM
Library Director: ESTHER ONG
Library of 104,300 vols
Number of teachers: 634
Number of students: 11,560
Publications: *Prospectus* (annually), *Annual Report*, *In Tempo* (4 a year), *Temasek Journal*, *T's* (2 a year)

DIRECTORS

Applied Science School: SOON-ONG MENG WAN
Business School: YEO LI PHEOW
Design School: WONG CHIAT CHANG
Engineering School: LAY-TAN SIOK LEE
Information Technology School: TAN DEK YAM

College

Southeast Asian Ministers of Education Organization (SEAMEO) Regional Language Centre (RELC): 30 Orange Grove Rd, Singapore 258352; tel. 68857888; fax 67342753; e-mail admin@relc.org.sg; internet www.relc.org.sg; f. 1968; aims to improve the teaching of languages in the SEAMEO countries; conducts 6 courses, including MA in applied linguistics; research, regional conferences; provides technical services to national programmes of 10 mem. countries; library: 50,000 vols; 45 teachers; 500 students; Dir MAUREEN NG BOEY LIN; publs *RELC Journal* (3 a year), *Guidelines* (2 a year).

SLOVAKIA

The Higher Education System

Many of Slovakia's higher education institutions predate the foundation of the former Czechoslovakia in 1918, with the oldest being the Univerzita Komenského v Bratislave (Comenius University in Bratislava—founded 1465). The next oldest university is the Univerzita Pavla Jozefa Šafárika v Košiciach (Šafárik University of Košice—founded 1657). In 1990, following the removal of the communist Government which had been in power since 1948, Czechoslovakia was replaced by the Czech and Slovak Federative Republic (CzSFR). In turn, the CzSFR was dissolved in 1993 and the Czech Republic and Slovakia became independent sovereign states. In addition to the universities, higher education is offered by academies of art, military and police academies, technical universities, universities of economics and universities of pedagogy.

Higher education is administered according to the Higher Education Act (No. 172) of 1990, and following ratification of later legislation in 2002 Slovakia now participates in the Bologna Process to establish a European Higher Education Area, the first phase of which is to adopt a credit-based system of comparable degrees with two main cycles (undergraduate and postgraduate). In 2004 there were 24 institutions of higher education, with a total enrolment of 108,608 students.

The Secondary School Leaving Certificate (Vysvedcenie o Maturitnej Skúške) is the main requirement for admission to higher education; additionally, many institutions administer entrance examinations. The Bachelors (Bakalár) is the undergraduate degree and is awarded after three years' study. Graduates holding the Bakalár are eligible for admission to the first postgraduate degree, the Masters (Magister), which lasts between one and three years depending on the subject. Professional titles awarded at this level include Inzinier (Engineer), Doktor Medicíny (Doctor of Medicine) and Doktor Veterinárnej Medicíny (Doctor of Veterinary Medicine). Doctoral-level studies last at least three years and lead to the award of the Doctorate (Doktor).

Learned Societies

GENERAL

Slovenská Akadémia Vied (Slovak Academy of Sciences): Štefánikova 49, 814 38 Bratislava; tel. (2) 52-49-56-34; fax (2) 52-44-49-28; internet www.savba.sk; f. 1953; depts of Exact and Technical Sciences, Natural Sciences and Chemistry, and Social Sciences; attached research institutes: see Research Institutes; library: see Libraries and Archives; Pres. STEFAN LUBY; publs *Acta Hydrologica* (2 a year), *Acta Montanistica Slovaca* (quarterly), *Acta Physica Slovaca* (6 a year), *Acta Virologica* (quarterly), *Architektúra a urbanizmus* (quarterly), *ARS* (3 a year), *Asian and African Studies* (2 a year), *Biologia* (6 a year), *Building Research Journal* (quarterly), *Computing and Informatics* (6 a year), *Contributions of the Astronomical Observatory Skalnaté Pleso* (quarterly), *Contributions to Geodesy and Geophysics* (quarterly), *Casopis pre Politické Vedy* (2 a year), *Clovek a Spoločnosť* (e-journal), *Ekológia* (quarterly), *Ekonomický časopis* (10 a year), *Endocrine Regulations* (quarterly), *Entomological Problems* (every 2 months), *Filozofia* (10 a year), *Folia Œcologica* (2 a year), *General Physiology and Biophysics* (4 a year), *Geografický časopis* (quarterly), *Geographia Slovaca* (1–2 a year), *Geologica Carpathica* (6 a year), *Geologica Carpatica Clays* (2 a year), *Helminthologia* (quarterly), *Historický časopis* (quarterly), *Human Affairs* (2 a year), *Chemical Papers* (6 a year), *Jazykovedný časopis* (2 a year), *Journal of Electrical Engineering* (monthly), *Journal of Hydrology and Hydromechanics* (quarterly), *Kovové materiály* (6 a year), *Kultúra slova* (6 a year), *Mathematica Slovaca* (5 a year), *Neoplasma* (6 a year), *Organon F* (quarterly), *Power Metallurgy Progress* (quarterly), *Právny obzor* (6 a year), *Slavica Slovaca* (2 a year), *Slovak Review* (2 a year), *Slovenská archeológia* (2 a year), *Slovenská literatúra* (6 a year), *Slovenská reč* (6 a year), *Slovenské divadlo* (quarterly), *Slovenské štúdie* (2 a year), *Slovenský národopis* (quarterly), *Sociológia* (6 a year), *Studia Psychologica* (4 a year), *Systematische Musikwissenschaften* (2 a year), *Tatra Mountains—Mathematical Publications* (3 a year), *Životné prostredie* (6 a year).

AGRICULTURE, FISHERIES AND VETERINARY SCIENCE

Slovenská spoločnosť pre polnohospodárske, lesnícke a potravinárske vedy (Slovak Society for Agriculture, Forestry and Food): Radlinskeho 9, 812 37 Bratislava; tel. (2) 52-92-60-55; fax (2) 52-49-31-89; e-mail dandar@chtf.stuba.sk; f. 1968; 564 mems; Pres. Prof. Dr A. DANDAR; Sec. Assoc. Prof. Dr M. TAKÁCSOVA.

ARCHITECTURE AND TOWN PLANNING

Spolok architektov Slovenska (Slovak Architects' Society): Panská 15, 811 01 Bratislava; tel. (2) 54-43-14-31; fax (2) 54-43-57-44; e-mail sas@euroweb.sk; internet www.archinet.sk; 1,900 mems; library of 2,700 vols; Pres. Prof. Dr Ing. Arch. ŠTEFAN SLACHTA; Dir Dr FRANTIŠEK KYSELICA; publs *Projekt* (review of Slovak architecture, 6 a year), *Fórum architektúry* (monthly).

EDUCATION

Slovenská pedagogická spoločnosť (Slovak Education Society): Filozofická fakulta UPJŠ, 080 01 Prešov; internet www.ucm.sk/FF/Slovensky/SPS/; f. 1965; 365 mems; Pres. Prof. Mgr. LADISLAV MACHÁCEK; Sec. Doc. PhDr JÁN DANEK.

FINE AND PERFORMING ARTS

Slovenská výtvarná únia (Slovak Union for the Visual Arts): Partizánská 21, 813 51 Bratislava; tel. (2) 54-41-36-23; f. 1990; 1,800 mems; Pres. VIKTOR HULÍK; publs *Profil*, *Výtvarný život*.

HISTORY, GEOGRAPHY AND ARCHAEOLOGY

Slovenská archeologická spoločnosť (Slovak Archaeological Society): Akademická 2, 949 21 Nitra; tel. (37) 733-57-38; fax (37) 733-56-18; e-mail nrauklku@savba.savba.sk; f. 1956; 300 mems; library of 860 vols; Pres. Dr JAN RAJTÁR; Sec. Dr KLÁRA KUZMOVÁ; publs *Informator* (2 a year), *Bibliografia Slovensky Archeologie* (irregular).

Slovenská geografická spoločnosť pri SAV (Slovak Geographical Society): Štefánikova 49, 814 73 Bratislava; tel. (2) 57-51-02-32; e-mail geognovo@savba.sk; internet www.sgs.sav.sk; f. 1945; 250 mems; Pres. Prof. RENÉ MATLOVIČ; Sec. Dr JÁN NOVOTNÝ.

Slovenská historická spoločnosť pri SAV (Slovak Historical Society): Klemensova 19, 813 64 Bratislava 1; tel. (2) 52-92-57-53; fax (2) 52-96-16-45; e-mail histcica@savba.sk; internet www.dejiny.sk; f. 1946; sections devoted to Modern History, Economic History, Urban History, Military History, Gender Studies, Literature, History of Religion; regional divisions in Trenčín, Topolčany, Košice, Banská Bystrica and Prešov; 340 mems; Pres. PhDr VILIAM ČICAJ; Sec. PhDr KATARÍNA HRADSKÁ.

LANGUAGE AND LITERATURE

Alliance Française: 812 83 Bratislava 1, Palais Kutscherfeld, Sedlarska 7, POB 152; tel. (2) 59-34-77-77; fax (2) 59-34-77-05; e-mail culturel@ifb.sk; internet slovaquie.alliance.free.fr; offers courses and exams in French language and culture and promotes cultural exchange with France; Dir JEAN-PIERRE MEULLENET.

British Council: 814 99 Bratislava, Panská 17, POB 68; tel. (2) 54-43-10-74; fax (2) 54-43-47-05; e-mail info.bratislava@britishcouncil.sk; internet www.britishcouncil.org/slovakia; teaching centre; offers courses and exams in English language and British culture and promotes cultural exchange with the UK; attached centres in Banská Bystrica and Košice; Dir HUW JONES.

Goethe-Institut: 81482 Bratislava, Panenská 33; tel. (2) 54-43-31-30; fax (2) 54-43-31-34; e-mail verw@bratislava.goethe.org; internet www.goethe.de/ms/brl/deindex.htm; offers courses and exams in German language and culture and promotes cultural exchange with Germany; library of 11,500 vols; Dir Dr MANFRED HEID.

Slovenská jazykovedná spoločnosť (Slovak Linguistics Society): Panská 26, 813 64 Bratislava; tel. (2) 54-33-17-61; fax (2) 54-33-17-56; e-mail mirod@juls.savba.sk; f. 1957; 266 mems; Pres. Prof. PhDr MIROSLAV

DUDOK; Sec. Mgr GABRIELA MÚCSKOVÁ; publs *Spisy SJS, Varia, Zápisník slovenského jazykovedca*.

Spoločnosť učiteľov nemeckého jazyka a germanistov Slovenska (SUNG) (Verband der Deutschlehrer und Germanisten der Slowakei/Union of German Teachers and Germanists of Slovakia): Tomášikova 4, POB 14, 820 09 Bratislava 29; tel. (2) 43-42-22-53; fax (2) 48-20-94-28; internet www.sung.sk; f. 1991 as the successor organization to Krúžok moderných filológov (Union of Modern Philology); Pres. Prof. Dr HELENA HANULJAKOVÁ; Gen. Sec. NADEŽDA ZEMANÍKOVÁ; publs *Begegnungen* (1 or 2 a year), *Zeitschrift für Germanistische Sprach- Literaturwissenschaft in der Slowakei, Zeitschrift Mosaik* (annually).

Spolok slovenských spisovateľov (Slovak Writers' Society): Laurinská 2, 815 84 Bratislava 1; tel. (2) 54-41-86-70; fax (2) 54-43-53-71; e-mail spolspis@stonline.sk; f. 1923; 350 mems; Pres. Mgr art. PAVOL JANÍK; Sec. JOZEF ZAVARSKÝ; publs *Literárny týždenník* (Literary Weekly), *Dotyky* (literature by young writers).

MEDICINE

Slovenská parazitologická spoločnosť (Slovak Society for Parasitology): Hlinkova 3, 040 01 Košice; tel. (55) 633-44-55; fax (55) 633-14-14; e-mail pausav@saske.sk; internet www.saske.sk/~pauwww/Helminth.htm; f. 1993; 92 mems; Pres. Prof. Dr P. DUBINSKÝ; Sec. Prof. Dr V. LETKOVÁ; publ. *Správy slovenskej parazitologickej spoločnosti* (irregular).

NATURAL SCIENCES
General
Rada vedeckých spoločností (Council of Scientific Societies): Stefánikova 49, 814 38 Bratislava; tel. (2) 52-49-61-48; fax (2) 52-49-61-48; f. 1990; 45 Slovak mem. socs; Pres. Prof. Dr Ing. JOZEF BRILLA.

Biological Sciences
Slovenská biologická spoločnosť (Slovak Biological Society): Sasinkova 4, 811 08 Bratislava; f. 1967; 180 mems; Pres. Asst Prof. Dr IGOR M. TOMO; publ. *Bulletin* (2 a year).

Slovenská botanická spoločnosť pri SAV (Slovak Botanical Society): Dúbravská cesta 14, 845 23 Bratislava; fax (2) 54-77-19-48; internet www.ibot.sav.sk/sbs/index.html; f. 1955; 450 mems; Pres. Doc. RNDr IGOR MISTRÍK; Sec. RNDr PAVOL MEREDA; publ. *Bulletin* (annually).

Slovenská ekologická spoločnosť (Slovak Ecological Society): Kolpašská 9B, 969 01 Banská Štiavnica; tel. (45) 694-11-01; fax (45) 692-01-17; e-mail sekos@savba.sk; internet 193.87.34.171/sekos.htm; f. 1992; 192 mems; Pres. Prof. Ing. IVAN VOLOŠČUK; Sec. Ing. BRANISLAV OLAH; publs *SEKOS Bulletin* (2 a year), *Ekologické Štúdie* (Ecological Studies, annually).

Slovenská entomologická spoločnosť (Slovak Entomology Society): c/o Dept of Zoology, Univerzita Komenského, Mlynská dolina, 842 15 Bratislava 4; tel. (2) 60-29-62-49; internet www.ses.sav.sk; f. 1957; 235 mems; Pres. Dr STANISLAV KALUZ; Sec. Dr LADISLAV ROLLER; publs *Entomofauna carpathica* (quarterly), *Entomological Problems* (every 6 months).

Slovenská spoločnosť pre biochémiu a molekulárnu biológiu (Slovak Society for Biochemistry and Molecular Biology): Vlárska 3, 833 06 Bratislava 3; internet www.ssbmb.sav.sk; f. 1959; 220 mems; Pres.

Dr JÁN TURŇA; Sec. Ing. Dr ALBERT BREIER; publ. *Newsletter* (6 a year).

Slovenská zoologická spoločnosť pri SAV (Slovak Zoological Society): Mlynská dolina B-2, 842 15 Bratislava; tel. (2) 60-29-66-80; e-mail talka@zoznam.sk; internet www.szs.sav.sk; f. 1956; 200 mems; Pres. Mgr JÁN KAUTMAN; Sec. Dr LUCIA KRŠKOVÁ; publ. *Správy Slovenskej zoologickej spoločnosti* (annual).

Mathematical Sciences
Jednota slovenských matematikov a fyzikov (Union of Slovak Mathematicians and Physicists): Faculty of Mathematics Physics and Informatics, Univerzita Komenského, Mlynská dolina F2, 842 48 Bratislava; tel. (2) 60-29-50-00; fax (2) 65-42-58-82; e-mail jsmf@fmph.uniba.sk; internet www.uniba.sk/~jsmf/en_jsmf.htm; f. 1969; 1,500 mems; Pres. Prof. VICTOR BEZÁK; Sec. Dr IMRICH MORVA; publ. *Obzory matematiky, fyziky a informatiky* (4 a year).

Physical Sciences
Slovenská astronomická spoločnosť (Slovak Astronomical Society): 059 60 Tatranská Lomnica; tel. (52) 446-78-66; fax (52) 446-76-56; e-mail sas@ta3.sk; internet www.ta3.sk/sas; f. 1959; 270 mems; Pres. RNDr VLADIMÍR PORUBČAN; Sec. RNDr LADISLAV HRIC.

Slovenská chemická spoločnosť (Slovak Chemical Society): Radlinského 9, 812 37 Bratislava; tel. (2) 59-32-52-99; fax (2) 52-49-52-05; e-mail schs@chtf.stuba.sk; internet schs.chtf.stuba.sk; f. 1929; 935 mems; Pres. Assoc. Prof. DUŠAN VELIČ; Sec. Dr DALMA GYEPESOVÁ; publs *Bulletin* (2 a year), *Chemical Papers* (6 a year).

Slovenská geologická spoločnosť (Slovak Geological Society): Mlynská dolina 1, 817 04 Bratislava; tel. (2) 59-37-52-25; fax (2) 37-19-40; e-mail takacova@gssr.sk; f. 1965; 350 mems; Pres. RNDr P. REICHWALDER; Sec. RNDr M. ELEČKO; publ. *Mineralia slovaca* (quarterly).

Slovenská meteorologická spoločnosť (Slovak Meteorological Society): c/o Slovenský hydrometeorologický ústav, Jeséniova 17, 833 15 Bratislava; tel. (2) 54-77-20-04; fax (2) 54-77-20-34; f. 1960; 175 mems; Pres. PAVEL ŠŤASTNÝ; Sec. MARIAN OSTROŽLÍK.

PHILOSOPHY AND PSYCHOLOGY
Slovenské filozofické združenie (Slovak Philosophical Association): Klemensova 19, 813 64 Bratislava; tel. (2) 52-92-64-48; fax (2) 52-92-12-15; e-mail sfz@sfz.sk; internet www.sfz.sk; f. 1990; 292 mems; Pres. Mgr Dr SLAVOMÍR GÁLIK; Sec. Mgr. PhDr ERIKA LALÍKOVÁ.

RELIGION, SOCIOLOGY AND ANTHROPOLOGY
Národopisná spoločnosť Slovenska (Slovak Ethnography Society): Klemensova 19, 813 64 Bratislava; tel. and fax (2) 52-96-47-07; e-mail nss@savba.sk; internet www.etnologia.sk; f. 1958; 250 mems; Chair. Dr ZUZANA BEŇUŠKOVÁ; Scientific Sec. Dr ZITA ŠKOVIEROVÁ; publ. *Etnologické rozpravy* (Ethnological Review, 2 a year).

Slovenská antropologická spoločnosť (Slovak Anthropological Society): Mlynská dolina B2, 842 15 Bratislava; f. 1965; 137 mems; Pres. Prof. RNDr M. POSPÍŠIL; Sec. RNDr EVA NEŠČÁKOVÁ.

Slovenská orientalistická spoločnosť (Slovak Society for Oriental Studies): Klemensova 19, 813 64 Bratislava; tel. (2) 52-92-63-26; fax (2) 52-92-63-26; e-mail koholla@klemens.savba.sk; f. 1960; 42 mems; Pres.

Doc. Dr KAROL SORBY; Sec. Dr GABRIEL PIRICKÝ; publs *Asian and African Studies* (2 a year), *Human Affairs* (2 a year).

Slovenská sociologická spoločnosť (Slovak Sociological Society): Klemensova 19, 813 64 Bratislava; tel. (2) 52-92-63-21; fax (2) 52-92-33-12; e-mail sociolog@klemens.savba.sk; internet www.savba.sk/sav/inst/sociolog; f. 1964; 170 mems; Pres. Doc. JAN SOPOCI; Scientific Sec. Dr BOHUMIL BÚZIK; publ. *Sociologicky Zapisník* (4 a year).

TECHNOLOGY
Slovenská spoločnosť pre mechaniku (Slovak Society for Mechanics): Dúbravská cesta 9, 845 03 Bratislava; tel. (2) 54-78-86-62; fax (2) 54-77-35-48; e-mail usarslad@savba.sk; internet mppserv.utc.sk; f. 1967; 252 mems; Pres. Dr J. SLADEK; Sec. Ing. O. IVANKOVA.

Research Institutes
ARCHITECTURE AND TOWN PLANNING
Institute of Construction and Architecture: Dúbravská cesta 9, 845 03 Bratislava; tel. and fax (2) 54-77-35-48; e-mail usarslad@savba.sk; f. 1953; attached to Slovak Acad. of Sciences; Dir Dr JAN SLADEK; publs *Architektura a urbanizmus* (4 a year), *Building Research Journal* (4 a year).

ECONOMICS, LAW AND POLITICS
Ekonomický ústav (Institute of Economic Research): Šancova 56, 811 05 Bratislava; tel. (2) 52-49-82-14; fax (2) 52-49-51-06; e-mail milan.sikula@savba.sk; internet www.ekonom.sav.sk; f. 1953; attached to Slovak Acad. of Sciences; library of 30,000 vols, 1,200 periodicals; Dir Prof Ing. MILAN ŠIKULA; publ. *Ekonomický Časopis* (Journal of Economics, 10 a year).

Institute of Political Science: Dúbravská cesta 9, 813 64 Bratislava; tel. (2) 54-78-97-24; fax (2) 54-78-97-26; internet nic.savba.sk/sav/inst/poli/index.html; f. 1990; attached to Slovak Acad. of Sciences; Dirs PhDr JOZEF JABLONICKÝ, PhDr MIROSLAV PEKNÍK; publ. *Politické vedy* (Political Sciences, 4 a year).

Institute of State and Law: Klemensova 19, 813 64 Bratislava; tel. (2) 52-96-18-33; fax (2) 52-96-23-25; e-mail usap@klemens.savba.sk; internet klemens.savba.sk/usap; f. 1953; attached to Slovak Acad. of Sciences; Dir JUDr EDUARD BARÁNY; publ. *Právny odbor* (6 a year).

Prognostického ústavu (Institute of Forecasting): Šancova 56, 811 05 Bratislava; tel. (2) 39-51-14; fax (2) 39-50-29; e-mail progasis@savba.sk; internet progeko.savba.sk/pu/pu.htm; attached to Slovak Acad. of Sciences; Dir Ing. ŠTEFAN ZAJAC.

EDUCATION
Ústav informácií a prognóz školstva (Institute of Information and Prognoses of Education): Staré grunty 52, 842 44 Bratislava 4; tel. (2) 65-42-51-66; fax (2) 65-42-10-48; e-mail zverka@uips.sk; internet www.uips.sk; f. 1976; library of 4,691 vols; Dir PhDr PETER ZVERKA; publs *Academia* (4 a year), *Mládež a spoločnosť* (Youth and Society, 4 a year), *Informatika v škole* (Informatics in Education, 2 a year), *Prevencia* (Prevention, 4 a year).

FINE AND PERFORMING ARTS
Institute of Art History: Dúbravská cesta 9, 841 04 Bratislava; tel. and fax (2) 54-79-38-95; e-mail dejusekr@savba.sk; internet www.dejum.sav.sk; f. 1953 as Department for

Theory and History of Art of the Institute of History of the Slovak Acad. of Sciences; present name 1990; attached to Slovak Acad. of Sciences; research into the history of Slovak art and architecture since the Middle Ages; Dir Prof. PhDr JÁN BAKOŠ; publ. *ARS* (Journal, 2 a year).

Institute of Musicology: Dúbravská cesta 9, 841 04 Bratislava; tel. and fax (2) 54-77-35-89; e-mail musicology@savba.sk; internet www.uhv.sav.sk; f. 1943; attached to Slovak Acad. of Sciences; Dir Prof. PhDr JURAJ LEXMANN; publs *Systematische Musikwissenschaft* (Systematic Musicology, irregular), *Ethnomusicologicum* (irregular).

Institute of Theatre and Film (Kabinet divadla a filmu SAV): Dúbravská cesta 9, 841 04 Bratislava; tel. (2) 54-77-71-93; fax (2) 54-77-35-67; internet www.kadf.sav.sk; f. 1953; attached to Slovak Acad. of Sciences; Dir PhDr MILOŠ MISTRÍK; publ. *Slovenské divadlo* (4 a year).

HISTORY, GEOGRAPHY AND ARCHAEOLOGY

Institute of Archaeology: Akademická 2, 949 21 Nitra; tel. (37) 733-56-17; fax (37) 733-56-18; e-mail nraurut@savba.sk; internet www.sav.sk; attached to Slovak Acad. of Sciences; Dir Prof. PhDr ALEXANDER RUTTKAY; publs *AVANS* (annually), *Slovenská archeológia* (2 a year), *Študijné zvesti AU SAV* (6 a year), *Východoslovenský pravek* (irregular), *Slovenská numizmatika* (jtly with Nat. Numismatic Cttee, every 2 years).

Institute of Geography: Ul. Štefánikova 49, 814 73 Bratislava; tel. (2) 52-49-55-87; fax (2) 52-49-13-40; e-mail geogsav@savba.sk; internet www.geography.sav.sk; f. 1943; attached to Slovak Acad. of Sciences; Dir Assoc. Prof. JAN FERANEC; publs *Geografický časopis* (4 a year), *Geographia Slovaca* (annually).

Institute of Historical Studies: Klemensova 19, 813 64 Bratislava; tel. (2) 52-92-63-21; fax (2) 52-96-16-45; e-mail histor@klemens.savba.sk; internet klemens.savba.sk/husav/prac.htm; f. 1942; attached to Slovak Acad. of Sciences; library of 75,000 vols; Dir PhDr VALERIAN BYSTRICKÝ; publs *Historický časopis* (Journal of History, 4 a year), *Historické štúdie* (Historical Studies, annually), *Studia Historica Slovaca* (annually), *Slovanské štúdie* (Slavonic Studies, 2 a year), *Z dejín vied a techniky* (Studies in the History of Science and Technology, annually), *Human Affairs* (2 a year).

LANGUAGE AND LITERATURE

Institute of Slovak Literature: Konventná 13, 813 64 Bratislava; tel. and fax (2) 54-41-60-25; e-mail usllnada@savba.sk; internet www.uslit.sav.sk; f. 1943; attached to Slovak Acad. of Sciences; library of 50,000 vols; Dir Doc. PhDr JELENA PASTEKOVA; Sec. Doc. PhDr NADEŽDA BUGÁROVÁ; publ. *Slovenská literatúra* (6 a year).

Institute of World Literature: Konventná 13, 813 64 Bratislava; tel. (2) 54-41-33-91; fax (2) 54-43-19-95; e-mail usvlust@savba.sk; internet www.usvl.sav.sk; attached to Slovak Acad. of Sciences; 30 mems; Dir PhDr JÁN KOŠKA; publ. *Slovak Review* (2 a year).

Ľudovít Štúr Institute of Linguistics: Panská 26, 813 64 Bratislava; tel. (2) 54-43-17-61; fax (2) 54-43-17-56; e-mail slavoo@juls .savba.sk; f. 1943; attached to Slovak Acad. of Sciences; library of 22,000 vols; Dir PhDr SLAVO ONDREJOVIČ; publs *Jazykovedný časopis* (2 a year), *Kultúra slova* (6 a year), *Slovenská reč* (6 a year).

MEDICINE

Cancer Research Institute: Vlárska 7, 833 91 Bratislava; tel. (2) 59-32-72-60; fax (2) 59-32-72-50; e-mail exonalt@savba.sk; internet www.exon.sav.sk; f. 1946; attached to Slovak Acad. of Sciences; Dir Doc. Ing. ČESTMÍR ALTANER; Scientific Sec. Dr ALENA GABELOVA; publ. *Neoplazma* (6 a year).

Institute of Experimental Endocrinology: Vlárska 3, 833 06 Bratislava; tel. (2) 54-77-28-00; fax (2) 54-77-42-47; e-mail ueenregu@savba.sk; internet www.elis.sk; f. 1969; attached to Slovak Acad. of Sciences; Dir RNDr RICHARD KVETŇANSKÝ; publ. *Endocrine Regulations* (4 a year).

Institute of Experimental Pharmacology: Dúbravská cesta 9, 842 16 Bratislava; tel. (2) 54-77-35-86; fax (2) 54-77-59-28; e-mail exfastol@savba.sk; internet nic.savba .sk/sav/insl/exfa/index.htm; f. 1969; attached to Slovak Acad. of Sciences; Scientific Sec. Ing. MÁRIA ĎURIŠOVÁ.

Institute for Heart Research: Dúbravská cesta 9, 842 33 Bratislava; tel. (2) 54-77-44-05; fax (2) 54-77-66-37; e-mail usrdsekr@ savba.sk; internet www.usrd.sav.sk; attached to Slovak Acad. of Sciences; Dir Dr JAN STYK; Scientific Sec. Dr MIROSLAV BARANČÍK.

Institute of Neurobiology: Šoltésovej 4, 040 01 Košice; tel. (55) 678-50-69; fax (55) 678-50-74; e-mail vanicky@saske.sk; internet www.saskc.sk/inb; f. 1977; attached to Slovak Acad. of Sciences; Dir Dr IVO VANICKÝ.

Institute of Normal and Pathological Physiology: Sienkiewiczova 1, 813 71 Bratislava; tel. (2) 52-92-66-18; fax (2) 52-96-85-16; e-mail postmast@unpf.savba.sk; internet nic.savba.sk/sav/inst/unpf/index.html; f. 1953; attached to Slovak Acad. of Sciences; Dir MUDr FEDOR JAGLA.

Institute of Parasitology: Illinkova 3, 040 01 Košice; tel. (55) 633-44-55; fax (55) 633-14-14; e-mail pausav@saske.sk; internet www .saske.sk/~pauwww/Helminth.htm; f. 1953; attached to Slovak Acad. of Sciences; library of 8,000 vols; Dir Prof. Dr P. DUBINSKÝ; publ. *Helminthologia* (4 a year).

Institute of Virology: Dúbravská cesta 9, 842 46 Bratislava; tel. (2) 54-77-42-68; fax (2) 54-77-42-84; e-mail virufcem@savba.savba .sk; internet www.nic.savba.sk/sav/ins/viru; f. 1953; attached to Slovak Acad. of Sciences; Dir Doc. MUDr FEDOR ČIAMPOR; publ. *Acta Virologia* (6 a year).

NATURAL SCIENCES
Biological Sciences

Institute of Animal Biochemistry and Genetics: Moyzesova 61, 900 28 Ivanka pri Dunaji; tel. (2) 45-94-30-52; fax (2) 45-94-39-23; e-mail greksak@ubgz.savba.sk; f. 1990; attached to Slovak Acad. of Sciences; Dir Doc. RNDr MILOSLAV GREKSÁK.

Institute of Animal Physiology: Šoltésovej 4, 040 01 Košice; tel. (55) 728-78-41; fax (55) 728-78-42; e-mail ufhzsav@saske.sk; internet www2.saske.sk/iap; f. 1964; attached to Slovak Acad. of Sciences; Dir MVDr JURAJ KOPPEL.

Institute of Botany: Dúbravská cesta 14, 845 23 Bratislava; tel. (2) 54-77-35-07; fax (2) 54-77-19-48; e-mail botuinst@savba.savba .sk; internet ibot.sav.sk; f. 1953; attached to Slovak Acad. of Sciences; library of 22,000 vols; Dir IVAN JAROLÍMEK; publ. *Biologia* (2 a year).

Institute of Experimental Phytopathology and Entomology: Nádražná 52, 900 28 Ivanka pri Dunaji; tel. (2) 45-94-33-31; fax (2) 45-94-34-31; e-mail postmaster@uefe.savba .sk; internet nic.savba.sk/sav/inst/uefe/

informatclip.htm; f. 1953; attached to Slovak Acad. of Sciences; Dir Doc. Ing. ANTON JANITOR; publ. *Entomological Problems* (2 a year).

Institute of Forest Ecology: Štúrova 2, 960 53 Zvolen; tel. (45) 533-09-14; fax (45) 547-94-85; e-mail valka@sav.savzv.sk; internet www.savzv.sk; f. 1983; attached to Slovak Acad. of Sciences; Dir Prof. Ing. JOZEF VAĽKA; publ. *Folia Oecologica*.

Institute of Landscape Ecology: Štefánikova 3, POB 254, 814 99 Bratislava; tel. (2) 52-49-38-82; fax (2) 52-49-45-08; e-mail director@uke.savba.sk; attached to Slovak Acad. of Sciences; Dir Ing. JÚLIUS OSZLÁNYI; publs *Životné postredie* (6 a year), *Ecology* (4 a year).

Institute of Molecular Biology: Dúbravská cesta 9, 842 51 Bratislava; tel. (2) 59-30-74-11; fax (2) 59-30-74-16; internet imb.savba.sk; f. 1976; incorporated Institute of Microbiology 2000; attached to Slovak Acad. of Sciences; Dir Prof. Ing. Dr JOZEF TIMKO; Scientific Sec. RNDr GABRIELA BUKOVSKA; publ. *Biologia*.

Institute of Molecular Physiology and Genetics: Vlárska 5, 833 34 Bratislava; tel. (2) 54-77-52-66; fax (2) 54-77-36-66; e-mail usrdtylo@savba.savba.sk; internet nic.savba .sk/sav/inst/umfg; f. 1990; attached to Slovak Acad. of Sciences; library of 1,000 vols; Dir Dr ALBERT BREIER; publ. *General Physiology and Biophysics* (4 a year).

Institute of Plant Genetics and Biotechnology: Akademická 2, POB 39A, 950 07 Nitra; tel. (37) 733-66-59; fax (37) 733-66-60; internet pribina.savba.sk/ughr/sk/; f. 1990; present name 1998; attached to Slovak Acad. of Sciences; Dir RNDr ANNA PREŤOVÁ.

Institute of Zoology: Dúbravská cesta 9, 842 06 Bratislava; tel. (2) 59-30-26-01; fax (2) 59-30-26-46; internet www.zoo.sav.sk; attached to Slovak Acad. of Sciences; Dir RNDr MILAN LABUDA; publs *Biologia* (6 a year), *Entomological Problems* (2 a year).

Mathematical Sciences

Institute of Mathematics: Ul. Štefánikova 49, 814 73 Bratislava; tel. (2) 52-49-73-16; internet www.mat.savba.sk; attached to Slovak Acad. of Sciences; Dir Prof. RNDr ANATOLIJ DVUREČENSKIJ; publs *Mathematica Slovaca* (5 a year), *Tatra Mountains Mathematical Publications*.

Physical Sciences

Astronomical Institute: Slovak Academy of Sciences, 059 60 Tatranská Lomnica; tel. (52) 446-78-66; fax (52) 446-76-56; e-mail astrinst@astro.sk; internet www.astro.sk; f. 1943; attached to Slovak Acad. of Sciences; library of 9,000 vols, 6,000 vols of periodicals; Dir Dr JÁN SVOREŇ; Scientific Sec. Dr JÁN RYBAK; publ. *Contributions of Skalnaté Pleso Observatory* (3 a year).

Institute of Chemistry: Dúbravská cesta 9, 845 38 Bratislava; tel. (2) 54-77-20-80; fax (2) 59-41-02-22; e-mail chemsekr@savba.sk; internet chem.sav.sk; f. 1953; attached to Slovak Acad. of Sciences; Dir Dr JÁN HIRSCH; publ. *Chemical Papers* (6 a year).

Institute of Experimental Physics: Watsonova 47, 040 41 Košice; tel. (55) 792-22-01; fax (55) 633-62-92; e-mail sekr@saske.sk; internet www.saske.sk/Uef/index.php; f. 1969; attached to Slovak Acad. of Sciences; research into the fields of sub-nuclear physics, condensed-matter physics, space physics, theoretical physics and biophysics; Dir Doc. RNDr PETER KOPČANSKÝ.

Institute of Geology: Dúbravská cesta 9, 842 26 Bratislava; tel. (2) 54-77-39-41; fax (2) 54-77-70-97; e-mail geolinst@savba.savba.sk;

internet nic.savba.sk/sav/inst/geol/index .html; f. 1952; attached to Slovak Acad. of Sciences; Dir Dr JOZEF MICHALÍK; publ. *Geologica Carpathica* (6 a year).

Institute of Geophysics: Dúbravská cesta 9, 845 28 Bratislava; tel. (2) 59-41-06-26; fax (2) 59-41-06-26; e-mail geoflabi@savba.sk; internet gpi.savba.sk; f. 1953; attached to Slovak Acad. of Sciences; Dir Dr IGOR TUNYI; publ. *Contributions to Geophysics and Geodesy* (4 a year).

Institute of Geotechnics: Watsonova 45, 043 53 Košice; tel. (55) 633-40-49; fax (55) 632-34-02; e-mail ugtsekr@saske.sk; f. 1957; attached to Slovak Acad. of Sciences; Dir Dr VITÁZOSLAV KRÚPA.

Institute of Hydrology: Račianská 75, 830 08 Bratislava; tel. and fax (2) 44-25-94-04; e-mail supervisor@uh.savba.sk; internet www.ih.savba.sk; f. 1955 as Water Management Laboratory; present name 1989; attached to Slovak Acad. of Sciences; Dir Dr V. STEKAUEROVA; publ. *Journal of Hydrology and Hydromechanics* (produced jtly with the Institute of Hydrodynamics of the Academy of Sciences of the Czech Republic, 6 a year).

Institute of Inorganic Chemistry: Dúbravská cesta 9, 845 36 Bratislava; tel. (2) 59-41-04-01; fax (2) 59-41-04-44; e-mail uachsekr@savba.sk; internet www.uach.sav .sk; f. 1953; attached to Slovak Acad. of Sciences; Dir Prof. PAVOL ŠAJGALÍK.

Institute of Materials Research: Watsonova 47, 043 53 Košice; tel. (55) 633-71-07; fax (55) 633-71-08; e-mail imrsas@imrnov .saske.sk; internet www.imrnov.saske.sk; f. 1955 to develop new materials and technologies; attached to Slovak Acad. of Sciences; conducts research on the nature of transformations and transport processes which occur within the structures of materials of varying chemical character (metals, ceramics, plastics, etc.) and internal composition (crystalline, amorphous, composite, etc.); also conducts research on the mechanical and physical properties of materials; 84 mems; Dir LUDOVÍT PARILÁK; Scientific Sec. LUBOMÍR MEDVECKÝ; publs *Kovové materiály* (Metallic Materials, 6 a year), *Acta Metallurgica Slovaca* (4 a year), *Powder Metallurgy Progress* (4 a year).

Institute of Measurement Science: Dúbravská cesta 9, 841 04 Bratislava; tel. (2) 54-77-40-33; fax (2) 54-77-59-43; e-mail umersekr@savba.sk; internet www.um.savba .sk; f. 1953; attached to Slovak Acad. of Sciences; scientific departments: optoelectronic measuring methods, magnetometry, theoretical methods, imaging methods, biomeasurements; 76 mems; library of 8,000 vols; Dir Prof. IVAN FROLLO; Scientific Board Chair. Dipl. Ing. MILAN TYŠLER; publ. *Measurement Science Review* (online, www.measurement.sk).

Institute of Physics: Dúbravská cesta 9, 842 28 Bratislava; tel. (2) 59-41-05-00; fax (2) 54-77-60-85; e-mail fyzihaso@nic.savba.sk; internet nic.savba.sk/sav/inst/fyzi; f. 1955; attached to Slovak Acad. of Sciences; Dir RNDr EVA MAJKOVÁ; publ. *Acta Physica Slovaca* (6 a year).

Institute of Polymer Research: Dúbravská cesta 9, 842 36 Bratislava; tel. (2) 54-77-34-48; fax (2) 54-77-59-23; e-mail upolsekr@savba.sk; internet www.savba.sk/ polymer; f. 1963; attached to Slovak Acad. of Sciences; Dir RNDr PAVOL HRDLOVIČ.

PHILOSOPHY AND PSYCHOLOGY

Institute of Experimental Psychology: Dúbravska cesta 9, 813 64 Bratislava; tel. (2) 54-77-56-25; fax (2) 54-77-55-84; e-mail expspro@savba.sk; internet www.sav.sk/

index.php?lang=en&charset=ascii&doc=or-g-ins&institute_no=44; f. 1955; attached to Slovak Acad. of Sciences; Dir Prof. PhDr IMRICH RUISEL; publ. *Studia Psychologica* (quarterly).

Institute of Philosophy: Klemensova 19, 813 64 Bratislava; tel. (2) 52-96-15-27; fax (2) 52-92-12-15; e-mail filosekr@savba.sk; internet sav.sk; f. 1946; attached to Slovak Acad. of Sciences; Dir Prof. TIBOR PICHLER; publs *Filozofia* (10 a year), *Organon F* (4 a year).

RELIGION, SOCIOLOGY AND ANTHROPOLOGY

Department of Social and Biological Communication: Klemensova 19, 813 64 Bratislava; tel. (2) 54-77-56-83; fax (2) 54-77-34-42; e-mail kvsbk@savba.sk; internet kvsbk.sav.sk; f. 1990; attached to Slovak Acad. of Sciences; Dir PhDr GABRIEL BIANCHI; publs *Human Affairs* (2 a year), *Human Communication Studies* (annually).

Institute of Ethnology: Klemensova 19, 813 64 Bratislava; tel. (2) 52-96-47-07; fax (2) 52-96-47-07; e-mail uetgk@klemens.savba .sk; internet www.savba.sk/sav/inst/etnol/ index.html; f. 1946; attached to Slovak Acad. of Sciences; library of 10,000 vols, 63 periodicals; Dir Dr GABRIELA KILIÁNOVÁ; publs *Slovenský národopis* (4 a year), *Etnologické rozpravy* (2 a year).

Institute of Oriental Studies: Klemensova 19, 813 64 Bratislava; tel. (2) 52-92-63-26; fax (2) 52-92-63-26; e-mail kaoreast@savba.sk; internet www.orient.sav.sk; f. 1960; attached to Slovak Acad. of Sciences; history, linguistics, literature, religion, ethnography, philosophy; library of 12,500 vols; 19 mems; Dir Doc. PhDr DrSc KAROL SORBY; publ. *Asian and African Studies* (2 a year).

Institute of Social Sciences: Karpatská 5, 040 00 Košice; tel. (55) 625-58-56; fax (55) 625-58-56; e-mail gajdosm@saske.sk; f. 1975; attached to Slovak Acad. of Sciences; library of 7,000 vols; Dir Dr MARIÁN GAJDOŠ; publ. *International Journal of Transdisciplinary Studies* (4 a year).

Institute of Sociology: Klemensova 19, 813 64 Bratislava; tel. (2) 52-96-43-55; fax (2) 52-96-23-15; e-mail sociolog@savba.sk; internet www.sociologia.sav.sk; f. 1990; attached to Slovak Acad. of Sciences; Dir Dr LUBOMIR FALŤAN; publ. *Sociológia* (6 a year).

TECHNOLOGY

Institute of Electrical Engineering: Dúbravská cesta 9, 842 39 Bratislava; tel. (2) 54-77-58-06; fax (2) 54-77-58-16; e-mail elusav@savba.sk; internet www.elu.sav.sk; f. 1963; attached to Slovak Acad. of Sciences; Dir Dr KAROL FROHLICH; publ. *Journal of Electrical Engineering* (monthly).

Institute of Informatics: Dúbravská cesta 9, 845 07 Bratislava; tel. (2) 54-77-10-04; fax (2) 54-77-10-04; e-mail upsysekr@savba.sk; internet www.ui.sav.sk; f. 1991; attached to Slovak Acad. of Sciences; research and education in informatics, nano- and microtechnology, cybernetics; Dir Dr LADISLAV HLUCHÝ; publ. *Computing and Informatics* (6 a year).

Institute of Materials and Machine Mechanics: Račianska 75, 831 02 Bratislava 3; tel. (2) 44-25-47-51; fax (2) 44-25-33-01; e-mail ummjerz@savba.sk; internet www .immm.sav.sk; f. 1980; attached to Slovak Acad. of Sciences; library of 13,000 vols; Dir Dr FRANTIŠEK SIMANČÍK; publs *Kovové materiály* (Metallic Materials, 6 a year), *Strojnícky časopis* (Journal of Mechanical Engineering, 6 a year).

Transport Research Institute, Inc.: Veľký Diel 3323, 010 08 Žilina; tel. (41) 565-28-19; fax (41) 565-28-83; e-mail management@vud.sk; internet www.vud.sk; f. 1954; Man. Dir Ing. LUBOMIR PALČÁK; publ. *Horizonty dopravy* (quarterly).

Vúje Trnava Inc.: Okružná 5, 918 64 Trnava; tel. (33) 599-13-56; fax (33) 599-11-93; e-mail vuje@vuje.sk; internet www.vuje .sk; f. 1977; library: library of 23,000 items; engineering design and research; Man. Dir Ing. MARIAN DUGOVIČ; publ. *Spravodajca VÚJE* (annually).

Libraries and Archives

Banská Bystrica

Štátna vedecká knižnica (State Scientific Library): Lazová 9, POB 205, 975 58 Banská Bystrica; tel. (48) 415-51-11; fax (48) 412-40-96; e-mail svkbb@svkbb.sk; internet www.svkbb.sk; f. 1924; 2,000,000 vols; Dir Mgr Dr OĽGA LAUKOVÁ.

Bratislava

Archív hl. mesta SR Bratislavy (Archives of the Capital of the Slovak Republic, Bratislava): Gorkého 5, 815 20 Bratislava; tel. (2) 54-43-32-48; fax (2) 54-43-08-48; e-mail archiv@samb.vs.sk; f. 13th century (archives); 1923 (library); attached to Min. of Interior; 95,000 vols; Dir Dr ANNA BUZINKAYOVÁ.

Centrum vedecko-technických informácií Slovenskej republiky (Slovak Centre for Scientific and Technical Information): Nám. Slobody 19, 812 23 Bratislava; tel. (2) 36-24-19; fax (2) 32-35-27; e-mail cvti@cvtisr .sk; internet www.cvtisr.sk; f. 1938; 362,000 books, 144,000 vols of periodicals, 28,000 trade publs, 239,000 patents, 90,000 standards; Dir ULRICH KOLOMAN; publs *Bulletin Centra VTI SR* (4 a year), *Euro-Info* (10 a year), *Infotrend* (4 a year), *Signálne informácie* (monthly).

Mestská knižnica Bratislava (Bratislava Municipal Library): Klariská 16, 814 79 Bratislava; tel. (2) 54-43-32-44; fax (2) 54-43-51-48; e-mail bratislava@mestskakniznica .sk; internet www.mestskakniznica.sk; f. 1900; 310,000 vols; Dir PhDr ELENA VEĽASOVÁ.

Slovenská ekonomická knižnica (Slovak Economic Library): Dolnozemská cesta 1, 852 35 Bratislava; e-mail ka@sek.euba.sk; internet www.sek.euba.sk; f. 1948; 333,000 vols, 434 periodicals; Dir Dr D. KRAUSOVÁ.

Slovenská pedagogická knižnica (Slovak Education Library): Hálova 16, 851 01 Bratislava 5; tel. (2) 62-41-09-92; fax (2) 62-41-09-92; e-mail postmast@spgk.sk; internet www.spgk.sk; f. 1956; 296,000 vols; Dir PhDr HELENA PANGRÁCOVÁ.

Univerzitná knižnica v Bratislave (University Library of Bratislava): Michalská 1, 814 17 Bratislava 1; tel. (2) 59-80-42-22; fax (2) 54-43-42-46; e-mail ukb@ulib.sk; internet www.ulib.sk; f. 1919; 2,414,641 vols; Dir PhDr TIBOR TRGIŇA.

Ústredná knižnica Slovenskej akadémie vied (Central Library of the Slovak Academy of Sciences): Klemensova 19, 814 67 Bratislava; tel. (2) 52-92-17-33; fax (2) 52-92-17-33; e-mail andrea.doktorova@savba.sk; internet www.uk.sav.sk; f. 1953; 520,000 vols; Dir Mgr ANDREA DOKTOROVÁ.

Košice

Štátna vedecká knižnica (State Scientific Library): Hlavná 10, 042 30 Košice; tel. (55) 622-67-24; fax (55) 622-23-31; e-mail svkk@ ke.sanet.sk; f. 1657; 3,354,000 vols; Dir Mgr

DANIELA DŽUGANOVÁ; publs *Zoznam zahraničných časopisov objednaných na východné Slovensko* (annually), *Súpis bibliografií a rešerší vypracovaných v ŠVK Košice* (annually).

Verejná knižnica Jána Bocatia (Ján Bocatius Public Library): Hlavná 48, 042 61 Košice; tel. (55) 622-32-91; fax (55) 622-32-92; f. 1924; 476,000 vols; Dir Dr KLÁRA KERNEROVÁ.

Martin

Matica slovenská (Slovak National Library): Nam. J. C. Hronskeho 1, 036 52 Martin; tel. (43) 430-18-03; fax (43) 430-18-02; e-mail snk@snk.sk; internet www.snk.sk; f. 1863; 4,500,000 vols; literary archives and museum documents, and complete Slovak printed production; Dir Dr DUŠAN KATUŠĖÁK; publs *Biografické štúdie* (annually), *Genealogicko-heraldický hlas* (2 a year), *Inventar rukopisov ALU MS* (annually), *Knižnica* (Library, monthly), *Slovenská národná bibliografia* (CD-ROM, quarterly; print, annually).

Nitra

Slovenská poľnohospodárska knižnica (Slovak Agricultural Library): Štúrova 51, POB 20B, 949 59 Nitra; tel. (37) 651-77-43; fax (37) 651-77-43; e-mail slpk@uniag.sk; internet www.slpk.sk; f. 1946; 530,000 vols; Dir BEÁTA BELLÉROVÁ.

Prešov

Štátna vedecká (State Scientific Library): Hlavná ul. 99, 081 89 Prešov; tel. (51) 772-49-60; fax (51) 772-49-60; e-mail kniznica@svkpo.sk; internet www.svkpo.sk; f. 1952; 450,000 vols; Dir PhDr ANNA HUDÁKOVÁ.

Zvolen

Slovenská lesnícka a drevárska knižnica (Slovak Library for Forestry and Wood Technology): Masarykova 20, 961 02 Zvolen; tel. (45) 520-66-41; fax (45) 547-99-42; e-mail sldk@sldk.tuzvo.sk; internet sldk.tuzvo.sk; f. 1952; attached to the Technical Univ. in Zvolen; 360,000 vols; Dir Ing. ALENA POLÁČIKOVÁ; publs *Bibliography of the Technical University in Zvolen* (annually), *Ecology Bulletin* (6 a year), *Forestry Bulletin* (monthly), *Wood Sciences Bulletin* (monthly).

Museums and Art Galleries

Banská Bystrica

Múzeum Slovenského národného povstania (Slovak National Uprising Museum): Kapitulská č. 23, 974 00 Banská Bystrica; tel. (48) 415-20-70; fax (48) 412-37-16; e-mail MuzeumSNP@isternet.sk; internet www.muzeumsnp.sk; f. 1955; anti-fascist struggle of the Slovak people during the Second World War; library of 17,000 vols; Dir Dr JÁN STANISLAV.

Stredoslovenské múzeum (Central Slovakia Museum): Nám. Slovenského národného povstánia 4, 974 00 Banská Bystrica; tel. (48) 412-58-97; fax (48) 415-50-77; e-mail smbb@stonline.sk; internet www.stredoslovenske.muzeum.sk; f. 1889; natural sciences, history, ethnography; library of 12,000 vols; Dir MILAN ŠOKA; publ. *Stredné Slovensko* (annually).

Banská Štiavnica

Slovenské banské múzeum (Slovak Mining Museum): Kammerhofská 2, 969 01 Banská Štiavnica; tel. (45) 694-94-22; e-mail sbm@muzeumbs.sk; internet www.muzeumbs.sk; f. 1900; library of 21,000 vols; Dir Dr JOZEF LABUDA; publ. *Zborník SBM* (bulletin).

Bratislava

Galéria mesta Bratislavy (Municipal Gallery of Bratislava): Mirbachov palác, Františkánske nám. 11, 815 35 Bratislava; tel. (2) 54-43-51-02; fax (2) 54-43-26-11; e-mail gmb@nextra.sk; internet www.gmb.sk; f. 1961; Slovak and Central European art; library of 12,000 vols; Dir Dr IVAN JANČÁR.

Mestské muzeum v Bratislave (Bratislava City Museum): Primaciálne nám. 3, 815 18 Bratislava; tel. (2) 54-43-47-42; fax (2) 54-43-46-31; e-mail mmba@bratislava.sk; f. 1868; archaeology, history, art history, applied arts, numismatics, history of pharmacy, ethnography; library of 21,000 vols; Dir PhDr PETER HYROSS.

Slovenská národná galéria (Slovak National Gallery): Riečna 1, 815 13 Bratislava; tel. (2) 54-43-20-81; fax (2) 54-43-39-71; e-mail info@sng.sk; internet www.sng.sk; f. 1948; art, applied art; library of 92,200 vols, 80,000 documents; Dir-Gen. KATARÍNA BAJCUROVÁ; publ. *Yearbook.*

Slovenské národné múzeum (Slovak National Museum): Vajanského nábrežie 2, 814 36 Bratislava; tel. (2) 52-96-68-67; fax (2) 52-92-43-44; e-mail riad@snm.sk; internet www.snm.sk; f. 1893; history, natural history, art, archaeology; Dir PhDr PETER MARÁKY; publs *História* (annually), *Prírodné vedy* (annually), *Etnografia* (annually), *Archeológia* (annually), *Annotationes Zoologicae et Botanicae, Pamiatky a múzeá* (Cultural Heritage Review, 4 a year), *Múzeum* (guidance for museum and art gallery workers, 4 a year).

Košice

Východoslovenské múzeum (Museum of Eastern Slovakia): Hviezdoslavová 3, 041 36 Košice; tel. (55) 622-03-09; fax (55) 622-86-96; f. 1872; history, natural sciences, art, ethnography; library of 53,000 vols; Dir PhDr RÓBERT POLLÁK; publs *Historica Carpatica* (annually), *Natura Carpatica* (annually).

Kremnica

NBS—Múzeum mincí a medailí (National Bank of Slovakia—Museum of Coins and Medals): Štefánikovo nám. 10, 967 01 Kremnica; tel. (45) 678-03-01; fax (45) 674-21-21; e-mail muzeum@nbs.sk; internet www.nbs.sk/mmm/; f. 1890; Dir MARIANA NOVOTNÁ.

Piešťany

Balneologické múzeum (Museum of Balneology): Beethovenova 5, 921 01 Piešťany; tel. (33) 772-28-75; fax (33) 772-28-75; internet www.balneomuzeum.sk; f. 1928; history of Slovak spas, regional history; Dir PhDr VLADIMÍR KRUPA.

Svidník

Múzeum ukrajinsko-rusínskej kultúry (Museum of Ukrainian-Ruthenian Culture): Centrálna 258, 089 01 Svidník; tel. (54) 752-13-65; fax (54) 752-15-69; f. 1956; history and culture of the Ukrainians and Ruthenians in Slovakia; library of 44,354 vols; Dir PhDr MIRÓSLAV SOPÓLIGA.

Vojenské historické múzeum (Military Historical Museum): Bardejovská 14, 089 01 Svidník; tel. (54) 752-13-98; f. 1965; history of the military in eastern Slovakia 1914-1945; library of 3,225 vols; Dir Dr JOZEF RODÁK.

Tatranská Lomnica

Múzeum Tatranského národného parku (Tatras National Park Museum): 059 60 Tatranská Lomnica; tel. (52) 446-79-51; fax (52) 446-79-58; e-mail sl@tanap.sk; f. 1957; geology, botany, zoology, natural history; ethnography, history; library of 19,520 vols; Dir Ing. MIKULÁŠ MICHELČIK.

Universities

EKONOMICKÁ UNIVERZITA V BRATISLAVE
(University of Economics in Bratislava)

Dolnozemská cesta 1/B, 852 35 Bratislava 5

Telephone: (2) 62-41-14-78
Fax: (2) 62-24-73-48
E-mail: kollar@dec.euba.sk
Internet: www.euba.sk

Founded 1940, became State School 1945
State control
Languages of instruction: Slovak, English, French, German
Academic year: September to June,

Rector: Prof. Dr Ing. VOJTECH KOLLÁR
Vice-Rectors: Assoc. Prof. Dr MARIÁN GOGA, Assoc. Prof. Dr Ing. KAJETANA HONTYOVÁ, Assoc. Prof. Ing. GIZELA LÉNÁRTOVÁ, Prof. Dr Ing. KAROL ZALAI, Assoc. Prof. Ing. PETER ZÁVODNÝ
Registrar: Dr MÁRIA DZIUROVÁ
Librarian: Dr DARINA KRAUSOVÁ

Number of teachers: 624
Number of students: 13,205

Publications: *Central European Journal of Operation Research and Economics* (quarterly), *Dialógy o ekonomike a riadení, Economic Review* (quarterly), *Economics and Management* (2 a year), *Ekonóm* (3 a year), *Ekonomika a informatika* (quarterly), *Medzinárodné vz ahy* (2 a year), *Nová ekonomika* (quarterly), *Podniková* (quarterly)

DEANS

Faculty of Business Economics (in Košice): Assoc. Prof. Ing. ŠTEFAN ČARNICKÝ
Faculty of Business Management. Assoc. Prof. Dr ĽUBOMÍR STRIEŠKA
Faculty of Commerce: Assoc. Prof. Dr FERDINAND DAŇO
Faculty of Economic Informatics: Prof. Ing. STOJAN RUSSEV
Faculty of International Relations: Assoc. Prof. Dr Ing. LUDMILA LIPKOVÁ
Faculty of National Economy: Assoc. Prof. Dr RUDOLF SIVÁK

HEADS OF DEPARTMENTS

Faculty of Business Economics (in Košice) (Tajovského 13, 041 30 Košice; tel. (55) 622-38-14; fax (55) 678-59-75; e-mail carnicky@economy.euke.sk; internet phf.euke.sk):
Economics: Ing. E. KAFKOVÁ
Finance and Accounting: Assoc. Ing. V. BOBÁKOVÁ
Foreign Languages: Mgr K. RADVANSKÁ
Informatics and Mathematics: Prof. Dr M. TKÁČ
Management: Assoc. Ing. A. ČEPELOVÁ
Marketing: Ing. M. POLÁK

Faculty of Business Management (Dolnozemská cesta 1, 852 35 Bratislava 5; tel. (2) 62-41-23-51; fax (2) 62-41-22-05; e-mail strieska@dec.euba.sk; internet fpm.euba.sk):
Business Management: Prof. Dr Ing. S. MAJTÁN
Corporate Finance. Prof. Dr Ing. J. KRÁLOVIČ
Informatics Management: Assoc. Prof. Dr Ing. M. KOKLES
Management: Prof. Dr Ing. Š. SLÁVIK
Production Management and Logistics: Assoc. Prof. Dr Ing. A. DUPAĽ

Faculty of Commerce (Dolnozemská cesta 1, 852 35 Bratislava 5; tel. (2) 62-41-19-67; fax

(2) 62-41-23-02; e-mail dano@dec.euba.sk; internet of.euba.sk):

Business Computing: Assoc. Prof. Dr Ing. G. KRISTOVÁ
Commercial Law: Assoc. Prof. Dr M. SABO
Commodities Science and Quality of Goods: Dr Ing. RASTISLAV STRHAN
International Business: Prof. Ing. P. BALÁŽ
Marketing: Assoc. Prof. Dr Ing. J. LIPIANSKA
Tourism: Assoc. Ing. M. PACHINGEROVÁ

Faculty of Economic Informatics (Dolnozemská cesta 1, 852 35 Bratislava 5; tel. (2) 62-41-23-59; fax (2) 62-41-21-95; e-mail russev@dec.euba.sk; internet fhi.euba.sk):

Accounting: Prof. Dr Ing. B. SOUKUPOVÁ
Applied Informatics: Assoc. Prof. Ing. A. KVIETIKOVÁ
Mathematics: Prof. Dr Ing. F. PELLER
Operations Research and Econometrics: Prof. Dr Ing. M. FENDEK
Statistics: Assoc. Prof. Dr Ing. E. SODOMOVÁ

Faculty of International Relations (Dolnozemská cesta 1, 852 35 Bratislava 5; tel. (2) 62-41-18-56; fax (2) 62-24-97-50; e-mail lipkova@dec.euba.sk; internet alpha.euba.sk/~fmv/):

Diplomacy and World History: Assoc. Prof. Dr Ing. L. LIPKOVÁ
Human Sciences: Assoc. Prof. Dr M. MÁRTON
International and European Law: Dr S. MRÁZ
Political and Social Sciences: Assoc. Prof. Dr Ing. J. LIĎÁK
World Economy: Prof. Dr Ing. J. FILIP

Faculty of the National Economy (Dolnozemská cesta 1, 852 35 Bratislava 5; tel. (2) 62-41-23-91; fax (2) 62-41-15-13; e-mail sivak@dec.euba.sk; internet nhf.euba.sk):

Applied Informatics and Computer Technology: Ing. I. ŠÓŠ
Economic Policy: Prof. Dr Ing. P. VINCÚR
Economic Theory: Prof. Dr Ing J. LISÝ
Education: Assoc. Prof. Dr Ing. R. SLOSÁR
Insurance: Assoc. Prof. Dr Ing. A. MAJTÁNOVÁ
Monetary Science: Prof. Ing. A. JANKOVSKÁ
Public Finance: Ing. M. BORODOVČÁK
Regional Development and Geography: Prof. Dr Ing. M. BUČEK
Social Development and Labour: Assoc. Prof. Dr V. STANEK

ATTACHED INSTITUTES

Centre for Further Education: Dir Prof. Dr Ing. JÁN PORVAZNÍK.

Centre for Physical Training and Sports: Dir Mgr IGOR PARTL.

Computer Technology Centre: Dir Ing. ANTON ZDARÍLEK.

International Programmes Institute: Dir Assoc. Prof. Dr JANA LENGHARDTOVÁ.

Language Institute: Dir Assoc. Prof. Dr DANUŠA LIŠKOVÁ.

KATOLÍCKA UNIVERZITA V RUŽOMBERKU
(Catholic University in Ružomberok)

Nám. Andreja Hlinku 60, 034 01 Ružomberok

Telephone: (44) 431-62-00
Fax: (44) 431-62-07
E-mail: rektorat@ku.sk
Internet: www.ku.sk
Founded 2000
Joint control of Slovak state and the Catholic Church
Language of instruction: Slovak

Rector: Prof. Dr BORIS BANÁRY

Vice-Rectors: Prof. Dr JÁN KURUCZ, Prof. Dr DALIBOR MIKULÁS, Prof. Dr ĽUBOMÍR STANČEK
Librarian: Mag. PETER DVORSKÝ
Library of 17,000 vols
Number of teachers: 300
Number of students: 3,000
Publication: *Disputationes Scientificae Universitatis Catholicae in Ružomberok*

DEANS

Faculty of Health Service: Dr ANTON LACKO
Faculty of Pedagogy: Prof. Dr AMANTIUS AKIMJAK
Faculty of Philosophy: Prof. Dr IMRICH VAŠKO
Faculty of Theology: ANTON KONEČNY

PREŠOVSKÁ UNIVERZITA
(University of Prešov)

Nám. Legionárov 3, 080 01 Prešov

Telephone: (51) 756-31-10
Fax: (51) 756-31-47
E-mail: intoff@unipo.sk
Internet: www.unipo.sk
Founded 1997
State control
Academic year: September to June

Rector: Prof. Dr FRANTIŠEK MIHINA
Vice-Rector (Academic): Prof. Dr ZUZANA STANISLAVOVÁ
Vice-Rector (Development): Doc. Ing. PETER KUZMIŠIN
Vice-Rector (International Relations): Doc. PhDr MICHAL VARCHOLA
Vice-Rector (Science and Research): Doc. PhDr VIERA BAĆOVÁ
Library of 300,000 vols
Number of students: 9,129

DEANS

Faculty of Arts (ul. 17 novembra 1, 080 78 Prešov; tel. (51) 773-10-64):

Prof. PhDr RUDOLF DUPKALA

Faculty of Education (ul. 17 novembra 1, 081 16 Prešov; tel. (51) 747-05-50; fax (51) 747-05-51):

Doc. PhDr MILAN PORTIK

Faculty of Greek Catholic Theology (ul. bisbupa Gojdića 2, 080 01 Prešov; tel. (51) 772-51-66; fax (51) 773-38-40; e-mail gkbfpu@unipo.sk):

Doc. ThDr VOJTECH BOHÁC

Faculty of Health (ul. Sládkovićova 36, 080 24 Prešov; tel. (51) 773-33-04; fax (51) 773-37-06; e-mail lackovak@unipo.sk):

PhDr ANNA ELIÁŠOVÁ

Faculty of Humanities and Natural Sciences (ul. 17 novembra 1, 081 16 Prešov; tel. (51) 772-53-62; fax (51) 772-53-61):

Prof. RnDr IVAN BERNASOVSKÝ

Faculty of Orthodox Theology (Masarykova 15, POB 60, 081 60 Prešov; tel. (51) 772-47-29; fax (51) 773-26-77):

Prof. ThDr PETER KORMANÍK

SLOVENSKÁ POĽNOHOSPODÁRSKA UNIVERZITA
(Slovak Agricultural University)

Tr. A. Hlinku 2, 949 76 Nitra

Telephone: (37) 650-81-11
Fax: (37) 741-26-26
E-mail: postmaster@uniag.sk
Internet: www.uniag.sk
Founded 1946 as Vysoká Škola Poľnohospodárska; new name *c.* 1996
State control
Languages of instruction: Slovak, English
Academic year: September to June

Rector: Prof. Dr Ing. IMRICH OKENKA

Vice-Rectors: Prof. JAROSLAV ANTAL, Assoc. Prof. JOZEF BAJLA, Prof. ANNA BANDLEROVÁ, Assoc. Prof. JÁN BRINDZA, Assoc. Prof. EDITA ROHALOVÁ
Senior Administrative Officer: Ing. JOZEF BEĽA
Library: see 'Slovenská poľnohospodárská knižnica', under Libraries and Archives
Number of teachers: 454
Number of students: 9,900
Publications: *Acta Fytotechnica, Acta Horticulturae et Regio Tecturae, Acta OperativoOeconomica, Acta Technologica Agriculturae, Acta Zootechnica* (all annually)

DEANS

Faculty of Agricultural Engineering: Prof. JOZEF LOBOTKA
Faculty of Agronomy: Prof. MAGDALENA LACKO-BARTOSOVÁ
Faculty of Economics and Management: Prof. VLADIMÍR GOZORA
Faculty of Gardening and Landscape Engineering: Prof. DUŠAN HÚSKA

PROFESSORS

Faculty of Agricultural Engineering (tel. (37) 651-32-44; fax (37) 741-70-03; e-mail dekmf@uniag.sk):

BALLA, J., Agricultural Engineering
JECH, J., Technology and Mechanization of Agriculture
LOBOTKA, J., Technology and Mechanization of Agriculture
PÁLTIK, J., Technology and Mechanization of Agriculture
PETRANSKÝ, I., Technology and Mechanization of Agriculture
SEMETKO, J., Technology and Mechanization
ŠESTÁK, J., Technology and Mechanization of Agriculture
TOLNAI, R., Agricultural Engineering
ŽIKLA, A., Technology and Mechanization

Faculty of Agronomy (tel. (37) 651-12-44; fax (37) 741-14-51; e-mail dekaf@uniag.sk):

BEŽO, M, Plant Genetics
BULLA, J., Fundamental Zootechnics
FECENKO, J., Special Plant Production
GÁLIK, R., Fundamental Zootechnics
HALAJ, M., Special Zootechnics
HANES, J., Pedology
HOLÚBEK, R., Special Plant Production
KOVÁČ, L, Fundamental Zootechnics
KOVÁČIK, J., General Zootechnics
KÚBEK, A., Fundamental Zootechnics
KULICH, J., Plant Production
LÍŠKA, E., General Plant Production
MICHALÍK, I., Plant Production
MICHALÍKOVÁ, A., Plant Protection
PAJTÁŠ, M, General Zootechnics
PAŠKA, I., Special Zootechnics
PIVKO, J., General Zootechnics
POLÁČEK, S., Plant Production
PRASLIČKA, J., Plant Protection
ŠTASTNÝ, P., Fundamental Zootechnics

Faculty of Economics and Management (tel. (37) 651-11-51; fax (37) 651-15-89; e-mail dekfem@uniag.sk):

BANDLEROVÁ, A., Economics and Management
BIELIK, P., Food Industry Management
GOZORA, V., Economics and Management
HRONEC, O., Management
HRUBÝ, J., Economics
HUDÁK, J., Sectorial Economics
KABÁT, L., Economics
KUZMA, F., Economics
OKENKA, I., Economics and Management
PODOLÁK, A., Economics
REPKA, I., Economics
ŠIMO, D., Economics
VIŠNOVSKÝ, J., Economics
ZOBORSKÝ, I. M., Economics

Faculty of Gardening and Landscape Engineering (Ul. Tulipanová 7, 949 76 Nitra; tel. (37) 652-27-41; fax (37) 652-27-41; e-mail dekfzki@uniag.sk):

ANTAL, J., Land Improvement
DEMO, M., Plant Production
HRICOVSKY, I., Plant Production
HRUBÍK, P., Horticulture
HUSKA, D., Land Improvement
MACHOVEC, J., Horticulture
ŠPÁNIK, F., Special Plant Production
STRED'ANSKY, J., Land Improvement
SUPUKA, J., Phytopathology
VREŠTIAK, P., Special Plant Production

SLOVENSKÁ TECHNICKÁ UNIVERZITA
(Slovak University of Technology)

Vazovova 5, 812 43 Bratislava
Telephone: (2) 52-49-71-96
Fax: (2) 57-29-43-33
E-mail: zahran@vm.stuba.sk
Internet: www.stuba.sk
Founded 1938
State control
Languages of instruction: Slovak, English
Academic year: September to July

Rector: Prof. Dr Ing. VLADIMÍR BÁLEŠ
Vice-Rector (Economy and Development): Assoc. Prof. Dr ERNEST BUČKO
Vice-Rector (Education): Prof. RNDr JÁN KALUŽNÝ
Vice-Rector (International Relations): Assoc. Prof. Dr arch. ROBERT ŠPAČEK
Vice-Rector (Marketing): Prof. Dr Ing. VOJTECH MOLNÁR
Vice-Rector (Science and Research): Assoc.-Prof. Dr ROBERT REDHAMMER
Bursar: Prof. Dr PETER VIEST
Librarian: VIERA POLČÍKOVÁ

Number of teachers: 1,390
Number of students: 15,328

Publications: *Architektonické listy FA STU* (in Slovak with summary in English, 4 a year), *AT & P Journal* (in Slovak with summary in English, 6 a year), *EE–Journal for Electrical and Power Engineering* (in Slovak with summary in English, 6 a year), *IB–Informačný bulletin FA STU* (in Slovak, monthly), *Journal of Electrical Engineering* (in English, monthly), *Kovové materiály* (in Slovak, monthly), *Slovak Journal of Civil Engineering* (in English, 4 a year), *Spektrum* (in Slovak, 10 a year), *Strojnícky časopis* (in Slovak, monthly), *Vlákna a textil–Fibres and Textiles* (in co-operation with the Slovak Academy of Sciences, in Slovak and English, 4 a year)

DEANS

Faculty of Architecture: Prof. Dr Ing. Arch. PETER GÁL
Faculty of Chemical and Food Technology: Prof. Dr Ing. DUŠAN BAKOŠ
Faculty of Civil Engineering: Prof. Dr Ing. DUŠAN PETRÁŠ
Faculty of Electrical Engineering and Information Technology: Prof. Dr Ing. FRANTIŠEK JANÍČEK
Faculty of Materials Science and Technology: Prof. Dr Ing. JOZEF SABLIK
Faculty of Mechanical Engineering: Assoc. Prof. Dr KAROL JELEMENSKÝ

PROFESSORS

Faculty of Architecture:

ALEXY, T., Town Planning
ANTAL, E., Art Design
ANTAL, J., Architecture, Civic Buildings
DULLA, M., Architecture
FINKA, M., Town Planning
GÁL, P., Town Planning
HAVAŠ, P., Civic Buildings

KAVAN, J., Town Planning
KEPPL, J., Architecture
KOVÁČ, B., Town Planning
PETRÁNSKY, L'., Theory and History of Art Design
ŠARAFÍN, M., Housing Design
TRNKUS, F., Town Planning
TUŽINSKÝ, I., Building Structures

Faculty of Chemical Engineering:

AUGUSTÍN, J., Fermentation Chemistry and Technology
BAJUS, M., Fuel Technology
BAKOŠ, D., Macromolecular Chemistry and Engineering
BÁLEŠ, V., Chemical Engineering and Process Control
BAXA, J., Chemical Processing of Fuels
BISKUPIČ, S., Physical Chemistry and Chemical Physics
BOČA, R., Inorganic Chemistry
BORSIG, E., Macromolecular Chemistry and Engineering
BUSTIN, D., Analytical Chemistry
DANDÁR, A., Chemistry and Foodstuffs Technology
FELLNER, P., Technology of Inorganic Chemistry
FIŠERA, L., Organic Chemistry
GRACZA, T., Organic and Bio-organic Chemistry
HORÁKOVÁ, K., Biology
HRONEC, M., Organic Technology
KOMAN, M., Inorganic Chemistry
KOPRDA, V., Environmental Chemistry and Engineering
KRUPČÍK, J., Analytical Chemistry
KRUTOŠÍKOVÁ, A., Organic Chemistry
KVASNIČKA, V., Chemical Physics
LEHOTAY, J., Analytical Chemistry
MALÍK, F., Biochemical Technology
MARCINČIN, A., Technology of Macromolecular Materials
MATISOVÁ, E., Analytical Chemistry
MELNÍK, M., Inorganic Chemistry
MIKLEŠ, J., Technical Cybernetics
MIKO, M., Biochemistry
MOCÁK, J., Analytical Chemistry
ONDREJOVIČ, G., Inorganic Chemistry
PELIKÁN, P., Physical Chemistry
PRÍBELA, A., Chemistry and Technology of Foodstuffs
ŠAJBIDOR, J., Biochemical Technology
ŠIMA, J., Inorganic Chemistry
ŠIMKOVIČ, J., Mathematics in Economics
ŠIMON, P., Physical Chemistry
STAŠKO, A., Physical Chemistry
TÖLGYESSY, J., Nuclear Chemistry and Environmental Engineering
UHER, M., Organic and Bio-organic Chemistry
VALACH, F., Physical Chemistry and Chemical Physics
VALKO, L., Physical Chemistry

Faculty of Civil Engineering:

AGÓCS, Z., Steel and Timber Structures
BAJZA, A., Non-Metallic Materials and Construction Materials
BALÁŽ, I., Construction Engineering
BARTOŠ, P., Geodesy and Cartography
BET'KO, B., Engineering Theory and Construction Engineering
BIELEK, M., Building Construction
BILČÍK, J., Construction Engineering
DUDA, E., Humanities
FILLO, L., Construction Engineering
GAŠPARÍK, J., Construction Technology
GSCHWENDT, I., Transport Engineering
HRAŠKA, J., Engineering Theory and Construction Engineering
HULLA, J., Geotechnology
HYKŠ, P., Building Construction
IVANIČKA, I., Economics and Management in the Building Industry
KAMENSKÝ, J., Hydraulic Engineering
KLEPSATEL, F., Building Construction

KOMORNÍKOVÁ, M., Applied Mathematics
KRIŠ, J., Construction in Health-care Sector
KUCBEL, J., Building Construction
KYSELKA, M., Architecture
LOVÍŠEK, J., Mechanics of Solid and Pliable Bodies
LUKÁČ, M., Hydraulic Engineering
MAJDÚCH, D., Concrete Structures and Bridges
MARTON, J., Sanitary Engineering Structures
MELICHER, J., Geodesy and Cartography
MESIAR, R., Applied Mathematics
OBOŇA, J., Economics and Building Industry Management
OHRABLO, F., Building Construction
OLÁH, J., Building Construction
PETRÁŠ, D., Engineering Theory and Construction Engineering
PUŠKÁR, A., Engineering Theory and Construction Engineering
PUŠKÁŠ, J., Building Construction
RAVINGER, J., Applied Mechanics
ŠIRÁŇ, J., Applied Mathematics
STAŇEK, V., Geodesy and Cartography
SUMEC, J., Building Construction
SZOLGAY, J., Hydrology and Water Management
TOMAŠOVIČ, P., Engineering Theory and Construction Engineering
TRÁVNIK, I., Economics and Management in the Building Industry
TURČEK, P., Building Construction
VALÁŠEK, J., Building Construction
ZAJAC, J., Building Construction
ZÁMEČNÍK, J., Building Construction
ZAPLETAL, I., Technology and Materials Engineering

Faculty of Electrical Engineering and Information Technology:

ANDRÁŠIK, L., Economics
RAJCSY, J., Measurement Engineering
BALÁŽ, I., Electronics
BARANČOK, D., Condensed Matter Physics and Acoustics
BARTA, Š., Solid State Physics
BÍZIK, J., Technical Cybernetics
BOCK, I., Applied Mathematics
CSABAY, O., Microelectronics
DONOVAL, D., Electronics
ĎURNÝ, R., Solid State Physics
FARKAŠ, P., Telecommunications
FECKO, S., Energy
FRIŠTACKÝ, N., Technical Cybernetics
GATIAL, J., Mathematics
GROŠEK, O., Applied Information Science
HORŇÁK, P., Energy
HORVÁTH, P., Applied Information Science
JANÍČEK, F., Electrical Energy
JURIŠICA, L., Technical Cybernetics
KALAŠ, V., Technical Cybernetics
KLUG, L., Electrical Energy and Electrical Engineering
KOLESÁR, M., Applied Information Science
KOVÁČ, J., Electronics
KREMPASKÝ, J., Experimental Physics
LIPKA, J., Condensed Matter Physics and Acoustics
MAKÁŇ, F., Telecommunications Engineering
MIGLIERINI, M., Solid State Physics
MOLNÁR, L'., Computer Engineering
MURGAŠ, J., Automation and Control
MURÍN, J., Applied Mechanics
NÁVRAT, P., Applied Information Science
NEČAS, V., Nuclear Energetics
PODHRADSKÝ, P., Telecommunications
RIEČANOVÁ, Z., Mathematical Analysis
SITEK, J., Condensed Matter Physics and Acoustics
SLÁMA, J., Theoretical Electrical Engineering
ŠMIEŠKO, V., Measurement Engineering
ŠAFAŘÍK, J., Applied Information Science

TVAROŽEK, V., Electronics
VESELÝ, V., Technical Cybernetics
VOJTEK, V., Applied Information Science
ŽALMAN, M., Automation and Management

Faculty of Materials Science and Technology in Trnava:

BAČA, J., Mechanical Engineering Technology
BALOG, K., Fire Safety and Safety at Work
BÉKES, J., Machinery and Machine Tools
BLAŠKOVITŠ, P., Mechanical Engineering Technology
DRIENSKY, D., Engineering Education
GARAJ, J., Applied Physics
GLESK, P., Teaching of Physical Training
GRGAČ, P., Materials Engineering
HRIVŇÁK, I., Physical Metallurgy and Materials Engineering
HRIVŇÁKOVÁ, D., Physical Metallurgy
HRUBEC, J., Machinery
JANAČ, A., Machinery
KALUŽNÝ, J., Materials Engineering
KOVÁČ, J., Physics
LINCZÉNYI, A., Economics and Management in the Building Industry
MORAVČÍK, O., Applied Information Science and Automation in Industry
MURGAŠ, M., Mechanical Production Engineering
POLÁK, K., Mechanical Engineering Technology
SABLIIK, J., Management in Industrial Engineering
ŠIMA, R., Humanities
ŠKARKA, B., Biochemistry
TUREK, I., Education
TURŇA, M., Welding and Welding Machines
VRBAN, A., Applied Information Science and Automation
ŽITŇANSKÝ, M., Materials Science and Heat Processing

Faculty of Mechanical Engineering:

BENKO, B., Machine Technology
BUKOVECZKÝ, J., Machine Parts
CHUDÝ, V., Automatic Control
DÚBRAVEC, B., Electrical Engines and Equipment
GANČO, M., Hydraulic Machines and Equipment
HAVALDA, A., Physical Metallurgy and Material Structures
HAVELSKÝ, V., Heat Energetics and Environmental Technology
HULKÓ, G., Automatic Control
JAŠŠO, I., Machines for Chemical and Food Industry
JAVORČÍK, L., Machines for Engineering Production
KNEPPO, I., Theoretical Electrotechnology
KRÁL, Š., Machine Parts
KRSEK, A., Production Systems
MOLNÁR, V., Thermal and Nuclear Machines
NOHEL, J., Thermal and Nuclear Machines
PALENČÁR, R., Instrumentation, Informatics and Automation Technology
RUŽIČKA, K., Machines for Engineering Production
SKÁKALA, J., Automatic Control
SLAVKOVSKÝ, J., Materials and Technologies
STAREK, L., Applied Mechanics
STRÝČEK, O., Hydraulic Machines and Equipment
TICHÝ, J., Transport and Manipulation Technology
URBAN, J., Transport and Manipulation Technology
VALČUHA, S., Machines for Engineering Production
VAVRO, K., Machines and Equipment for the Food Industry
ZÁHOREC, O., Applied Mechanics
ZONGOR, J., Engineering Technologies and Materials

SLOVENSKÁ ZDRAVOTNÍCKA UNIVERZITA
(Slovak Medical University)

Limbová 12, 883 03 Bratislava
Telephone: (2) 59-37-01-11
E-mail: info@szu.sk
Internet: www.szu.sk

Founded 2002
State control
Language of instruction: Slovak

Rector: Prof. JÁN ŠTENCL
First Pro-Rector and Pro-rector for Educational Affairs: Prof. Dr DANA FARKAŠOVÁ
Pro-Rector for International Relations: Prof. Dr JURAJ ŠVEC
Pro-Rector for Pedagogical and Academic Affairs: Prof. Dr JAROSLAV HINŠT
Pro-Rector for Preventive Medicine: Prof. Dr JAN BREZA
Pro-Rector for Public Relations: Prof. Dr VILIAM FISCHER
Pro-Rector for Research: Prof. Dr TOMÁŠ TRNOVEC
Questor: Ing. MILAN CAGÁŇ

Library of 15,700 vols, 129 periodicals
Number of teachers: 395
Number of students: 19,436

DEANS

Faculty of Nursing and Special Medical Studies: Prof. PhDr DANA FARKAŠOVÁ
Faculty of Public Health: Prof. Dr MARGARÉTA ŠULCOVÁ
Faculty of Public Health (Banskej Bystrici): Prof. Dr SVETOZÁR DLUHOLUKCÝ
Faculty of Specialized Medical Training: Dr ALOJZ RAKÚS

PROFESSORS

Faculty of Nursing and Special Medical Studies:

KOVÁČ, G., Laboratory Research Methods

Faculty of Public Health:

HEGYI, L., Medical Teaching
ŠAJTER, V., Theoretical Science
ŠULCOVÁ, M., Health in the Workplace

Faculty of Specialized Medical Training:

BREZA, J., Urology
ČERNÁK, A., Ophthalmology
FISCHER, V., Cardiosurgery
GERINEC, A., Paediatric Ophthalmology
HARUŠTIAK, S., Surgery and Thoracic Surgery
HOLOMÁŇ, J., Clinical Pharmacology
HRUŠKOVIČ, I., Paediatric Clinical Immunology and Allergology
KOTHAJ, P., Gastroenterological Surgery
KOVÁČ, G., Clinical Biochemistry and Laboratory Medicine
KOZA, I., Clinical Oncology
KRAJČÍK, S., Geriatrics
KRČMÉRY, V., Tropical Medicine and Chemotherapy
KRISTÚFEK, P., Functional Diagnostics
LECHTA, V., Logopaedia
LISÝ, L., Neurology
MAKAI, F., Orthopaedics
MOKÁŇ, M., Diabetology, Digestion and Nutrition
PETROVIČ, S., Emergency Medicine
RIEČANSKÝ, I., Cardiology and Angiology
ROVENSKÝ, J., Rheumatology
ŠAGÁT, T., Paediatric Anaesthiology and Intensive Medicine
ŠEFRÁNEK, V., Vascular Surgery
ŠIMAN, J., Paediatric Surgery
ŠIMKO, P., Injury-related Surgery
ŠTENCL, J., Obstetrics and Gynaecology
ŠTEŇO, J., Neurosurgery
VAVREČKA, A., Gastroenterology

TECHNICKÁ UNIVERZITA V KOŠICIACH
(Technical University of Košice)

Letná 9, 042 00 Košice
Telephone: (55) 602-11-11
Fax: (55) 633-27-48
E-mail: rektor@tuke.sk
Internet: www.tuke.sk

Founded 1952
State control
Languages of instruction: Slovak, English
Academic year: September to August

Rector: Prof. Dr JURAJ SINAY
Vice-Rector (Development): Prof. Dr DUŠAN MALINDŽÁK
Vice-Rector (Education): Assoc. Prof. Dr VLADIMÍR PENJAK
Vice-Rector (Informatics): Prof. Dr ANTON ČIŽMÁR
Vice-Rector (Science, Research and International Relations): Prof. Dr KAROL FLÓRIÁN
Questor: Ing. GABRIEL FISCHER
Librarian: Dr VALÉRIA KROKAVCOVÁ

Number of teachers: 850 (820 full-time, 30 part-time)
Number of students: 13,351

Publications: *Acta Electrotechnica et Informatica* (4 a year), *Acta Mechanica Slovaca* (4 a year), *Acta Metallurgica Slovaca* (4 a year), *Acta Montanistica Slovaca* (4 a year), *Halo TU* (monthly)

DEANS

Faculty of Arts: Assoc. Prof. Dr JAROSLAV JAREMA
Faculty of Civil Engineering: Prof. Dr STANISLAV KMEŤ
Faculty of Economics: Prof. Dr TOMÁŠ SABOL ŠOLTÉS
Faculty of Electrical Engineering and Informatics: Assoc. Prof. Dr DUŠAN KOCUR
Faculty of Mechanical Engineering: Prof. Dr MIROSLAV BADIDA
Faculty of Metallurgy: Prof. Dr KAREL TOMÁŠEK
Faculty of Mining, Ecology, Control and Geotechnology: Prof. Dr PAVOL RYBÁR
Faculty of Production Technology: Assoc. Prof. Dr SLAVKO PAVLENKO

PROFESSORS

Faculty of Arts (tel. and fax (55) 602-21-77; e-mail dekan.fuu@tuke.sk; internet www.fu.tuke.sk):

BARTUSZ, J., Fine Art

Faculty of Civil Engineering (Vysokoškolská 4, 042 00 Košice; tel. (55) 633-53-11; fax (55) 623-32-19; e-mail Stanislav.Kmet@tuke.sk; internet svfweb.tuke.sk):

HORNIAKOVÁ, L., Theory of Construction of Overground Buildings
HUDÁK, J., Theory of Construction of Engineering Structures
JUHÁS, P., Theory of Construction of Engineering Structures
KMEŤ, S., Theory of Construction of Engineering Structures
ŠTEVULOVÁ, N., Environmental Studies
TKÁČOVÁ, K., Mineralogy and Ecotechnology

Faculty of Economics (B. Němcovej 32, 040 01 Košice; tel. and fax (55) 633-09-83; e-mail ekfdec@tuke.sk; internet www.tuke.sk/ekf/ekf.html):

ŠAMSON, Š., Economic Theory
ŠOLTÉS, V., Mathematics

Faculty of Electrical Engineering and Informatics (tel. (55) 632-24-83; fax (55) 633-01-15; e-mail Dusan.Kocur@tuke.sk):

BANSKÝ, J., Radio Electronics, Electronic Technology

ČIŽMÁR, A., Electronics and Telecommunications Engineering
HUDÁK, S., Computers and Informatics
JELŠINA, M., Electronic Computers
KOLCUM, M., Energetics, High Voltage Engineering
KOVÁČ, D., Energetics, High Voltage Engineering
KROKAVEC, D., Technology and Automation
KROKAVEC, M., Computers and Informatics
LEVICKÝ, D., Radio Electronics
MADARÁSZ, L., Technical Cybernetics
MARCHEVSKÝ, S., Electronics and Telecommunications Engineering
MARTON, K., Energetics, High Voltage Engineering
MICHAELI, L., Radio Electronics
MIHALÍK, J., Electronics and Telecommunications Engineering
SARNOVSKÝ, J., Technical Cybernetics
SINČÁK, P., Artificial Intelligence
ŠOMORA, M., Materials Engineering
ŠPÁNY, V., Radio Electronics
TIMKO, J., Electrical Engineering
TURÁN, J., Radio Electronics
ZBORAY, L., Electrical Engineering

Faculty of Mechanical Engineering (tel. (55) 625-78-25; fax (55) 633-47-38; e-mail Miroslav.Badida@tuke.sk; internet www.sjf.tuke.sk):

BADIDA, M., Environmental Protection
BIGOŠ, P., Construction of Transport Machinery
ČOP, V., Robots and Manipulators
HAJDUK, M., Manufacturing Systems with Robots and Manipulators
HRIVŇÁK, A., Technology of Mechanical Engineering
IMRIŠ, I., Non-Ferrous Metallurgy
KAŽIMÍR, I., Technology of Mechanical Engineering
KLIMO, V., Machine Parts
KNIEWALD, D., Technology of Mechanical Engineering
KOVÁČ, J., Automation and Management
KOVÁČ, M., Robots and Manipulation Devices
LACHVÁČ, J., Production Machines and Equipment
LIBERKO, I., Industrial Engineering and Management
MAJERNÍK, M., Environmental Studies
POLLÁK, L., Technology of Mechanical Engineering
RITÓK, Z., Machine Parts
SALOKY, T., Automation and Control in Mechanical Engineering
ŠIMŠÍK, D., Automation and Management
SINAY, J., Transport and Manipulation
SMRČEK, J., Manufacturing Systems with Robots and Manipulators
SPIŠÁK, E., Engineering Technology and Materials
TAKÁČ, K., Technology of Mechanical Engineering
TREBUŇA, F., Mechanics

Faculty of Metallurgy (tel. (55) 633-18-14; fax (55) 633-70-48; e-mail dhf@hfnov.tuke.sk; internet www.tuke.sk/tu/hf):

BURŠÁK, M., Physical Metallurgy and Materials Science
FLÓRIÁN, K., General and Analytical Chemistry
HAVLIK, T., Non-Ferrous Metallurgy
HOLOUBEK, D., Thermal Power Engineering
KRAKOVSKÁ, E., Analytical Chemistry
KVAČKAJ, T., Ferrous Metallurgy
LUKÁČ, I., Physical Metallurgy and Materials Science
MICHEL', J., Materials Science
MIHOK, L., Ferrous Metallurgy
ŠTOFKO, M., Non-Ferrous Metallurgy
TOMÁŠEK, K., Non-Ferrous Metallurgy
VARGA, A., Thermal Power Engineering

VIRČÍKOVÁ, E., Non-Ferrous Metallurgy
ZRNÍK, J., Physical Metallurgy and Materials Science

Faculty of Mining, Ecology, Control and Geotechnology (tel. (55) 633-00-18; fax (55) 633-66-18; e-mail Pavol.Rybar@tuke.sk; internet www.tuke.sk/fberg):

BOROŠKA, J., Mining, Mechanization, Transport and Deep Well Drilling
DOJČÁR, O., Mining
FABIÁN, J., Mining
FARYAD, S. W., Mining Geology and Geological Prospecting
JACKO, S., Geological Prospecting, Geological Engineering
KOŠTIAL', I., Production Control
KOSTÚR, K., Control of the Acquiring and Processing of Raw Materials
KUNÁK, L., Mining Surveying and Geodesy
LEŠKO, M., Minerals Processing
MALINDŽÁK, D., Control of Acquiring and Processing of Raw Materials
PINKA, J., Mining, Mechanization, Transport and Deep Well Drilling
PODLUBNÝ, I., Control of Acquiring and Processing of Raw Materials
RYBÁR, P., Mining and Geotechnology
SASVÁRI, T., Mining Geology and Geological Prospecting
SEKULA, F., Mining
STROFFEK, E., Mining, Mining Mechanization
ŠÚTTI, J., Three-Dimensional Geodesy
VODZINSKÝ, V., Economy and Management
WEISS, G., Mining Surveying and Geodesy
ZÁBRANSKÝ, F., Petrology

Faculty of Production Technology (Plzenská 10, 080 01 Prešov; tel. (51) 772-30-12; fax (51) 773-34-53; e-mail pavlenko.slavko@fvt.sk; internet www.tuke.sk/fvtpo):

NOVÁK-MARCINČIN, P., Production Engineering
RAGAN, E., Mechanical Technology
VASILKO, K., Mechanical Technology

ATTACHED CENTRE

Computer Centre: Dir Prof. Dr JÁN SARNOVSKÝ.

TECHNICKÁ UNIVERZITA VO ZVOLENE
(Technical University in Zvolen)

T. G. Masaryka 24, 960 53 Zvolen
Telephone: (45) 520-61-03
Fax: (45) 533-00-27
E-mail: rektor@vsld.tuzvo.sk
Internet: www.tuzvo.sk
Founded 1807, reorganized 1952 as University of Forestry and Wood Technology, renamed 1991
State control
Languages of instruction: Slovak, Czech; for graduate studies, also English, German and Russian
Academic year: September to June
Rector: Prof. Ing. JÁN TUČEK
Vice-Rectors: Assoc. Prof. JURAJ MAHÚT, Assoc. Prof. JÁN ŠIMKO, Prof. ŠTEFAN ŽÍHLAVNÍK
Questor: Dr MÁRIA BÍZIKOVÁ
Librarian: Dr ĽUBICA LUDVIGHOVÁ
Library of 359,000 vols
Number of teachers: 243
Number of students: 2,200
Publications: *Acta Facultatis Forestalis* (annually), *Acta Facultatis Xylologiae* (annually), *Proceedings of Research Works of the Faculty of Ecology and Environmental Sciences* (annually), *Scientific and Pedagogical News* (annually)

DEANS

Faculty of Ecology and Environmental Science: Assoc. Prof. Dr IMRICH BESEDA
Faculty of Environmental and Manufacturing Technology: Assoc. Prof. JÁN ZELENÝ
Faculty of Forestry: Assoc. Prof. MILAN HLADÍK
Faculty of Wood Sciences and Technology: Assoc. Prof. MIKULÁŠ SUPÍN

PROFESSORS

Faculty of Ecology and Environmental Science:

CHRAPAN, J., Radioecology
KOŠTÁLIK, J., Physical Geography
MIDRIAK, R., Landscape Ecology
MIKLOS, J., Landscape Ecology
SUPUKA, J., Landscape Ecology

Faculty of Environmental and Manufacturing Technology:

DANKO, M., Processes and Technology of Forest Production
MIKLEŠ, M., Processes and Technology of Forest Production

Faculty of Forestry:

BUBLINEC, E., Nature and Environment
GARAJ, P., Forest Protection and Game Management
HLADÍK, M., Forest Management
KODRÍK, J., Forest Protection and Game Management
KOLENKA, I., Forest Economics
PAGAN, J., Silviculture
PAULE, L., Forest Genetics
SANIGA, M., Silviculture
ŠMELKO, Š., Biometry and Forest Management
VALTÝNI, J., Forest Hydrology – Torrent Control
ŽIHLAVNÍK, S., Geodesy and Photogrammetry

Faculty of Wood Sciences and Technology:

BOROTA, J., Management of Tropical Forests
BUČKO, J., Chemistry and Chemical Technology
DEKRÉT, A., Mathematics
DUBOVSKÁ, R., Metal Processing Technology
HORSKÝ, D., Mechanical Technology of Wood
KURJATKO, S., Wood Science
LIPTÁKOVÁ, E., Wood Products Manufacturing
MARČOK, M., Physics and Applied Mechanics
OSVALD, A., Fire Protection
PETRANSKY, L., Design
RAJČAN, E., Physics and Applied Mechanics
REINPRECHT, L., Wood Technology Engineering
ŠUPÍN, M., Forestry Policy, Trade, Marketing
TREBULA, P., Technology of Wood
VINCÚR, P., Economics

TRENČIANSKA UNIVERZITA ALEXANDRA DUBČEKA
(Alexander Dubček University in Trenčín)

Študentská 2, 911 50 Trenčín
Telephone: (32) 740-01-08
Fax: (32) 740-01-02
E-mail: slabeycius@tnuni.sk
Internet: www.tnuni.sk
Founded 1997
State control
Academic year: September to June
Rector: Assoc. Prof. Dr JURAJ WAGNER
Vice-Rector (Education): Dr ERNEST BROSKA
Vice-Rector (Investment and Development): Assoc. Prof. IGNÁC PRNO

Vice-Rector (Science, Research and International Co-operation): Prof. JURAJ SLABEYCIUS
Vice-Rector (Social Care): Dr ERNEST BROSKA
Chief Librarian: Mgr MÁRIA REHUŠOVÁ
Library of 13,663 vols
Number of teachers: 245
Number of students: 5,393
Publications: *Socialno-ekonomicka Revue* (quarterly), *TnU Trendy* (4 a year)

DEANS

Faculty of Industrial Technology: Assoc. Prof. Dr ONDREJ NEMČOK
Faculty of Mechatronics: Prof. Dr DUŠAN MAGA
Faculty of Social and Economic Relations: Prof. Dr MIROSLAV MEČÁR
Faculty of Special Technologies: Prof. BOHUMIL BÁTORA

PROFESSORS

Faculty of Industrial Technology:

CAPEK, I.
JAMBRICKY, M.
KOPECKY, M.
KOSTIAL, P.
LETKO, I.
MACKO, V.
SLABEYCIUS, J.
STEFANIK, J.
YONA, E.

Faculty of Mechatronics:

BORSC, M.
KNEPPO, I.
KNEPPO, P.
PLANDER, I.
RACEK, V.
TKAC, M.
WAGNER, J.

Faculty of Social and Economic Relations:

ALEXY, J.
BARÁNIK, M.
BARTAK, P.
BENCO, J.
BLAZEJ, A.
CAMPAI, O.
LIPTAK, J.
STRAZOVSKA, H.
VOJTOVIC, S.

Faculty of Special Technologies:

BATORA, B.
DUBOVSKA, R.
VARKOLY, L.

ATTACHED INSTITUTE

Institute of Natural and Human Sciences.

TRNAVSKÁ UNIVERZITA
(University of Trnava)

Hornopotočná 23, 918 43 Trnava

Telephone: (33) 593-92-03
Fax: (33) 551-11-29
E-mail: rektor@truni.sk
Internet: www.truni.sk

Founded 1992
State control
Academic year: October to August

Rector: Prof. JUDr PETER BLAHO
Vice-Rectors: Doc. ThDr ANDREJ FILIPEK (Academic), Prof. MVDr ALEXANDER SABÓ (Development and Foreign Relations), Dr Ing. MARTIN MIŠÚT (Information Systems and Publishing), Doc. PhDr JOZEF MATULNÍK (Science and Research)
Librarian: Mgr ZUZANA MARTINKOVIČOVÁ

Library of 38,069 books, 200 periodicals
Number of teachers: 262
Number of students: 5,526

DEANS

Faculty of Arts: Doc. PhDr EVA NANIŠTOVÁ
Faculty of Education: Doc. RNDr PETER ČERŇANSKÝ
Faculty of Health and Social Work: Prof. MUDr VLADIMÍR KRČMÉRY
Faculty of Law: Prof. JUDr JOZEF PRUSÁK
Faculty of Theology: Prof. RNDr JURAJ DOLINSKÝ

UNIVERZITA J. SELYEHO V KOMÁRNE
(University of J. Selyeho in Komárno)

Ul. roľníckej školy 1519, 945 01 Komárno

Telephone: (35) 790-17-30
Fax: (35) 790-17-13
E-mail: info@selyeuni.sk
Internet: www.selyeuni.sk

Founded 2004
State control
Language of instruction: Hungarian

Rector: Dr Ing. SÁNDOR ALBERT
Vice-Rectors: MIHÁLY FÜLÖP, Prof. Ing. VERONIKA STOFFOVA

Library of 150,000 vols, 40 periodicals
Number of teachers: 80
Number of students: 1,450

DEANS

Faculty of Economy: Prof. Dr. habil SIKOS T. TAMÁS
Faculty of Pedagogy: Dr MARGITY ERDÉLYI
Faculty of Reformed Theology: Dr JÁNOS MOLNÁR

UNIVERZITA KOMENSKÉHO V BRATISLAVE
(Comenius University in Bratislava)

Šafárikovo nám. 6, 818 06 Bratislava 16

Telephone: (2) 52-92-15-94
Fax: (2) 52-96-38-36
E-mail: kr@rec.uniba.sk
Internet: www.uniba.sk

Founded 1465 as Academia Istropolitana; reopened with present name 1919
State control
Languages of instruction: Slovak, English
Academic year: October to June

Rector: Prof. PhDr FRANTIŠEK GAHÉR
Vice-Rector (Development): Assoc. Prof. RNDr IVAN OSTROVSKÝ
Vice-Rector (Education): Prof. RNDr PAVEL SÛRA
Vice-Rector (International Relations): MUDr PETER OSUSKÝ
Vice-Rector (Legislation and Public Relations): JUDr MÁRIA DURAČINSKÁ
Vice-Rector (Science): Prof. RNDr DUŠAN MLYNARČÍK
Bursar: Ing. ZORA DOBRÍKOVÁ

Number of teachers: 2,092
Number of students: 27,000

Publication: numerous faculty publications

DEANS

Faculty of Education: Prof. RNDr OTO MAJZLAN
Faculty of Law: Assoc. Prof. JUDr MARIÁN VRABKO
Faculty of Management: Prof. RNDr JOZEF KOMORNIK
Faculty of Mathematics, Physics and Informatics: Assoc. Prof. RNDr JÁN BOĎA
Faculty of Medicine in Bratislava: Prof. MUDr PAVEL TRAUBNER
Jessenius Faculty of Medicine in Martin: Prof. MUDr JÁN DANKO
Faculty of Natural Sciences: Assoc. Prof. RNDr ANTON GÁPLOVSKÝ
Faculty of Pharmacy: Assoc. Prof. RNDr JOZEF SEGINKO

Faculty of Philosophy: Assoc. Prof. PhDr ANTON ELIÁŠ
Faculty of Physical Education and Sport: Assoc. Prof. PedDr DUŠAN KUTLÍK
Faculty of Protestant Theology: Prof. ThDr IGOR KIŠŠ
Faculty of Roman Catholic Theology: Prof. ThDr VILIAM JUDÁK
Faculty of Social and Economic Sciences: Prof. Ing. LADISLAV KABÁT

PROFESSORS

Faculty of Education (Račianska 59, 813 34 Bratislava; tel. (2) 44-25-49-60; fax (2) 44-25-49-56; e-mail sd@fedu.uniba.sk; internet www.fedu.uniba.sk):

BLANÁR, V., Slovak Language
ČIŽMÁR, J., Teaching of Mathematics
CVRKAL, I., Modern Non-Slavonic Philology, German Literature
KAČALA, J., Slovak Language
KOVÁČ, D., Educational Psychology
KUSIN, V., Philosophy
LECHTA, V., Special Education
MAJZLAN, O., Ecology
MARČOK, V., Theory and History of Slovak Literature
MISTRÍK, E., Synthetic Philosophy
OBDRŽÁLEK, Z., Education
ONDREIČKA, K., Graphics
PAŽITKA, M., Modern Non-Slavonic Philology
PIKÁLEK, Š., Social Work
POVCHANIČ, S., Modern Non-Slavonic Philology
POŽÁR, L., Psychology
RANINEC, J., Music Education
REPKA, R., Linguistics of Concrete Language Groups
ŠEDIVÝ, O., Descriptive Geometry
SLIACKY, O., Theory and History of Slovak Literature
ŠTRAUS, F., Theory and History of Slovak Literature
ŠULKA, R., Descriptive Geometry
ŠUPŠÁKOVÁ, B., Arts and Crafts
ŠVEC, M., Mathematics
TRUP, L., Modern Non-Slavonic Philology
VAŠEK, S., Special Education
VIETOROVÁ, N., Modern Non-Slavonic Philology
ZELINA, M., Education

Faculty of Law (tel. (2) 59-24-41-03; fax (2) 59-24-42-16; e-mail sd@flaw.uniba.sk; internet www.flaw.uniba.sk):

CÚTH, J., International Law
HUSÁR, E., Penal Law
KLIMKO, J., History of State and Law
MAMOJKA, M., Commercial Law
MATHERN, V., Penal Law
OVEČKOVÁ, O., Economic and Financial Law
PLANKOVÁ, O., Civil Law
POSLUCH, M., State Law
STRAKA, J., Czechoslovak History
SKULTÉTY, P., Administrative Law

Faculty of Management (POB 95, Odbojárov 10, 820 05 Bratislava; tel. (2) 55-56-67-02; fax (2) 55-56-67-03; e-mail sd@fm.uniba.sk; internet www.fm.uniba.sk):

HLAVATÁ, I., Finance
KOMORNÍK, J., Probability and Mathematical Statistics
KORČEK, Ľ., Economics
PIŠKANIN, A., Economics and Industrial Management
RALBOVSKÝ, M., Finance
RUDY, J., Business Management
ZAPLETAL, V., Economics

Faculty of Mathematics, Physics and Informatics (Mlynská dolina, 842 48 Bratislava; tel. (2) 65-42-67-20; fax (2) 65-42-58-82; e-mail sd@fmph.uniba.sk; internet www.fmph.uniba.sk):

Bezák, V., Condensed Matter Physics
Brunovský, P., Mathematics
Chorvát, D., Biophysics
Čižmár, J., Teaching Mathematics
Dubničková, A., Physics
Gruska, J., Informatics
Hianík, T., Biophysics
Hubač, I., Biophysics
Kabát, L., Economics
Kačur, J., Mathematics
Katriňák, T., Mathematics
Kodnár, R., Mathematics
Kostyrko, P., Mathematics
Lukáč, P., Plasma Physics
Masarik, J., Physics
Medveď, M., Mathematics
Moczo, P., Physics
Noga, M., Theoretical Physics
Pázmán, A., Mathematics
Pišút, J., Theoretical Physics
Plesník, J., Mathematics
Povinec, P., Physics
Prešnajder, P., Physics
Rovan, B., Informatics
Ružička, J., Physics
Šalát, T., Mathematics
Šáro, S., Nuclear Physics
Sitár, B., Physics
Skalný, J., Physics
Štrba, A., Experimental Physics
Tomlain, J., Meteorology and Climatology

Faculty of Medicine in Bratislava (Špitálska 24, 813 72 Bratislava; tel. (2) 52-96-17-36; fax (2) 59-35-72-70; e-mail sd@fmed.uniba.sk; internet ww.fmed.uniba.sk):

Ághová, Ľ., Public Health
Bada, V., Internal Medicine
Bakoss, P., Epidemiology
Balažovjech, I., Internal Medicine
Bálint, O., Infectious Diseases
Beniak, M., Social Medicine
Beňuška, J., Normal Anatomy, Histology and Embryology
Bergendi, Ľ., Biochemistry
Bilický, J., Radiology
Borovský, M., Gynaecology and Obstetrics
Breza, J., Urology
Buc, M., Immunology
Buchvald, J., Dermatovenereology
Cársky, J., Medicinal Chemistry and Biochemistry
Danihel, Ľ., Pathological Anatomy and Forensic Medicine
Ďuračková, Z., Biochemistry
Ďuriš, I., Internal Medicine
Ferenčík, M., Immunology and Immunochemistry
Gerinec, A., Ophthalmology
Holomáň, K., Gynaecology and Obstetrics
Horňák, M., Urology
Hulín, L., Normal and Pathological Anatomy
Jakubovský, J., Pathological Anatomy and Forensic Medicine
Kapellerová, A., Paediatrics
Kotulová, D., Microbiology
Kovács, L., Paediatrics
Kriška, M., Pharmacology
Makai, F., Orthopaedics and Traumatology
Michalková, D., Paediatrics
Mikeš, Z., Internal Medicine, Cardiology
Mráz, P., Anatomy
Oláh, Z., Ophthalmology
Ondruš, D., Oncology
Pontuch, P., Internal Medicine
Profant, M., Otorhinolaryngology
Redhammer, R., Internal Medicine
Remková, A., Internal Medicine
Satko, I., Stomatology
Šiman, J., Surgery
Šimko, F., Normal and Pathological Physiology
Štrmeň, P., Ophthalmology
Štvrtinová, V., Internal Medicine
Suška, P., Gynaecology and Obstetrics

Švec, J., Oncology
Traubner, P., Neurology
Turčáni, M., Normal and Pathological Physiology
Turčáni, P., Neurology
Varsík, P., Neurology
Vaško, J., Stomatology
Vojtassak, J., Surgery
Zaviačič, M., Pathological Anatomy and Forensic Medicine
Zlatoš, J., Normal Anatomy, Histology and Embryology
Zlatoš, L., Normal and Pathological Physiology
Žucha, L., Psychiatry

Jessenius Faculty of Medicine in Martin (POB 34, Záborského 2, 036 45 Martin; tel. (43) 413-33-05; fax (43) 413-63-32; e-mail sd@jfmed.uniba.sk; internet www.jfmed.uniba.sk):

Bánovčin, P., Paediatrics
Buchancová, J., Internal Medicine
Buchanec, J., Paediatrics
Danko, J., Gynaecology and Obstetrics
Drobný, M., Neurology
Hajtman, A., Otorhinolaryngology
Hanáček, J., Physiology and Pathophysiology
Jakuš, J., Pathophysiology
Javorka, K., Physiology and Pathophysiology
Jurko, A., Paediatrics
Kliment, J., Urology
Korpáš, J., Pathological Physiology
Kubisz, P., Internal Medicine
Lehotský, J., Biochemistry
Mazúch, J., Surgery
Meško, D., Internal Medicine
Mezeš, V., Medicinal Biochemistry
Mokáň, D. M., Internal Medicine
Nosaľová, G., Pharmacology
Novomeský, F., Forensic Medicine
Péč, J., Dermatovenereology
Plank, L., Pathological Anatomy
Sámel, M., Epidemiology
Straka, S., Epidemiology
Stránsky, A., Physiology and Pathophysiology
Tatár, M., Normal and Pathological Physiology
Zibolen, M., Paediatrics

Faculty of Natural Sciences (Mlynská dolina, 842 15 Bratislava; tel. (2) 60-29-66-71; fax (2) 65-42-90-64; e-mail sd@fns.uniba.sk; internet www.fns.uniba.sk):

Adamčíková, Ľ., Physical Chemistry and Chemical Physics
Ebringer, L., Microbiology
Grolmus, J., Genetics
Hensel, K., Zoology
Holba, V., Physical Chemistry
Hovorka, D., Petrology
Hudák, J., Plant Physiology
Jedlička, L., Zoology
Juráni, B., Pedology
Kellö, V., Physical Chemistry and Chemical Physics
Kettner, M., Microbiology
Kminiak, M., Ecology
Kolarov, J., Biochemistry
Kollárová, M., Biochemistry and Molecular Biology
Kováč, L., Biochemistry
Kováč, M., Stratum Geology, Geology and Palaeontology, Applied Geophysics
Kraus, I., Applied Geophysics
Krcho, J., Cartography
Macášek, F., Nuclear Chemistry
Masarovičová, E., Plant Physiology
Matys, M., Engineering Geology
Miadoková, E., Genetics
Mládek, J., Human and Regional Geography
Ondrášik, R., Hydrology and Engineering Geology

Országh, L., Zoology
Paulov, J., Human and Regional Geography
Rojkovič, I., Stratum Geology, Geology and Palaeontology, Applied Geophysics
Schwendt, P., Inorganic Chemistry
Šefara, J., Stratum Geology, Geology and Palaeontology, Applied Geophysics
Ševčík, P., Physical Chemistry
Silný, P., Theory of Teaching Chemistry
Soják, L., Analytical Chemistry
Šomšák, L., Botany
Šubík, J., Biochemistry
Sucha, V., Stratum Geology
Toma, Š., Organic Chemistry
Urban, M., Chemical Physics
Vlček, D., Genetics
Vozárová, A., Mineralogy, Petrology and Geochemistry
Zatko, M., Geography
Žúrková, Ľ., Inorganic Chemistry

Faculty of Pharmacy (Odbojárov 10, 832 32 Bratislava; tel. (2) 55-57-20-22; fax (2) 55-57-20-65; e-mail sd@fpharm.uniba.sk; internet www.fpharm.uniba.sk):

Balgavý, P., Physics
Čižmárik, J., Pharmaceutical Chemistry
Devínsky, F., Pharmaceutical Chemistry
Foltán, V., Public Health
Grančai, D., Pharmacognosis
Havránek, E., Pharmaceutical Chemistry
Kovács, P., Biochemistry
Mlynarčík, D., Galenic Pharmacy
Psenák, M., Biochemistry
Rak, J., Galenic Pharmacy
Remko, M., Physical Chemistry and Chemical Physics
Sarka, K., Physical Chemistry and Chemical Physics
Springer, V., Social Pharmacy
Švec, P., Pharmacology

Faculty of Philosophy (Gondova 2, 818 01 Bratislava; tel. (2) 52-92-10-78; fax (2) 52-96-60-16; e-mail sd@fphil.uniba.sk; internet www.fphil.uniba.sk):

Baďurík, J., History
Bajzíková, E., Slovak Language
Bakoš, J., Fine Art
Chalupka, L., Music
Dolník, J., General Linguistics
Dudok, M., Slavonic Philology
Heretík, A., Psychology
Holec, R., History
Hrčková, N., Music
Hvišč, J., Slavonic Philology
Kimlička, Š., Librarianship and Information Science
Kollárik, T., Psychology
Krekovič, E., Archaeology
Kuklica, P., Classical Philology
Kusý, M., Philosophy
Marcelli, M., Philosophy
Mészáros, O., Modern Non-Slavonic Philology
Michálek, J., Ethnography
Mikula, V., Slovak Literature
Mlacek, J., Slovak Language
Paulíny, J., Modern Non-Slavonic Philology
Perhács, J., Pedagogy
Potzlová-Malíková, M., Fine Art
Povchanič, Š., Modern Non-Slavonic Philology
Psenák, J., Pedagogy
Schenk, J., Sociology
Sokolovský, L., History
Švec, S., Pedagogy
Szomlányiová, S., Political Science
Tandlichová, E., Theory of English Language Teaching
Tušer, A., Journalism
Vojtek, J., General History
Zambor, M., Philosophy
Žigo, M., Philosophy
Žigo, P., Slovak Language

ŽILINEK, M., Pedagogy

Faculty of Physical Education and Sport (Nábrežie arm. generála L. Sobodu, 814 69 Bratislava; tel. (2) 54-41-19-09; fax (2) 54-41-33-27; e-mail sd@fsport.uniba.sk; internet www.fsport.uniba.sk):

GREXA, J., History
HAMAR, D., Sport Kinanthropology
HELLEBRANDT, V., Sport Kinanthropology
KAMPMILLER, T., Sport Kinanthropology
KASA, J., Sport Kinanthropology
LABUDOVÁ, J.
MORAVEC, R., Sport Kinanthropology
ŠTULRAJTER, V., Physiology

Faculty of Protestant Theology (Bartókova 8, 811 02 Bratislava; tel. (2) 67-28-82-50; fax (2) 62-80-39-51; e-mail sd@fevth.uniba.sk; internet www.fevth.uniba.sk):

BÁNDY, J., Protestant Theology
KIŠŠ, L., Protestant Theology

Faculty of Roman Catholic Theology (Kapitulska 26, 814 58 Bratislava; tel. (2) 54-43-51-09; fax (2) 54-43-51-09; e-mail sd@frcth .uniba.sk; internet www.frcth.uniba.sk):

BOŠMÁNSKY, K., Catholic Theology
ĎURICA, M., Catholic Theology
JUDÁK, V., Catholic Theology
KUTARŇA, J., Theology
VRAGAŠ, Š., Catholic Theology

Faculty of Social and Economic Sciences (Odbojárov 10A, 820 05 Bratislava; tel. (2) 55-56-67-18; fax (2) 55-42-36-02; e-mail sd@ fses.uniba.sk; internet www.fses.uniba.sk):

KABÁT, L., Economics
KLEIN, F., Therapeutics and Special Education
KOLLÁRIK, T., Psychology
KUSÝ, M., Philosophy
KVASNIČKA, V., Informatics

UNIVERZITA KONŠTANTÍNA FILOZOFA V NITRE
(University of Constantine the Philosopher in Nitra)

Trieda A. Hlinku 1, 949 01 Nitra

Telephone: (37) 651-13-30
Fax: (37) 651-12-43
E-mail: rektor@ukf.sk
Internet: www.ukf.sk

Founded 1992, from existing faculties

Rector: Prof. RNDr Ing. DANIEL KLUVANEC

DEANS

Faculty of Natural Sciences: Doc. RNDr MÁRIA BAUEROVÁ
Faculty of Pedagogy: Doc. PhDr IVAN J. SZABÓ
Faculty of Philosophy: Doc. PhDr EVA TUČNÁ
Faculty of Social Sciences: (vacant)

UNIVERZITA MATEJA BEL
(Matej Bel University)

Národná 12, 974 01 Banská Bystrica

Telephone: (48) 446-11-52
Fax: (48) 415-31-80
Internet: www.umb.sk

Founded 1992 following merger of Pedagogic Faculty and School of Economics
Academic year: September to June

Rector: Doc. Ing. MILAN MURGAŠ
Vice-Rector (Education and Development): Prof. Ing. JOZEF BENČO
Vice-Rector (Research and International Relations): Doc. PaedDr PAVOL ODALOŠ
Number of students: 7,500

DEANS

Faculty of Economics: Prof. Ing. MILOTA VETRÁKOVÁ
Faculty of Finance: Prof. Ing. JURAJ NEMEC

Faculty of Humanities: Doc. PhDr VLADIMÍR VARINSKÝ
Faculty of Law: Prof. JuDR MOJMÍR MAMOJKA
Faculty of Natural Sciences: Doc. RnDR STANISLAV HOLEC
Faculty of Pedagogy: Prof. PhDr BEATA KOSOVÁ
Faculty of Philology: Doc. PhDr FRANTIŠEK ALABÁN
Faculty of Political Sciences and International Relations: Doc. PhDr PETER KULAŠIK

UNIVERZITA PAVLA JOZEFA ŠAFÁRIKA V KOŠICIACH
(Šafárik University of Košice)

Šrobárova 2, 041 80 Košice

Telephone: (55) 622-26-08
Fax: (55) 622-81-09
E-mail: zahrodd@kosice.upjs.sk
Internet: www.upjs.sk

Founded 1959
State control
Languages of instruction: Slovak, English
Academic year: September to July

Rector: Prof. Dr DUŠAN PODHRADSKÝ
Pro-Rectors: Prof. Dr IGOR PALÚŠ, Doc. Dr PAVOL PETROVIČ, Doc. Dr LEONARD SIEGFRIED, Prof. Dr JÚLIUS VAJÓ
Registrar: Dr Ing. JOZEF LOKŠA
Librarian: Dr DARINA KOŽUCHOVÁ

Number of teachers: 400
Number of students: 4,100

Publications: *Acta iuridica Cassoviensia, Folia Facultatis Medicae Universitatis Šafarikianae Cassoviensia, Thaiszia*

DEANS

Faculty of Law: Doc. Dr PETER VOJČÍK
Faculty of Medicine: Doc. Dr LADISLAV MIROSSAY
Faculty of Natural Sciences: Prof. Dr ALEXANDER FEHER
Faculty of Public Administration: Doc. Dr LADISLAV LOVAŠ

PROFESSORS

Faculty of Law:

GAŠPAR, M., Administrative Law
PALÚŠ, I., Administrative Law

Faculty of Medicine:

JURKOVIČ, I., Pathology
KAFKA, J., Psychiatry
KALINA, I., General Biology
KOHÚT, A., Pharmacology
MYDLÍK, M., Internal Medicine
PAČIN, J., Gynaecology and Obstetrics
ŠAŠINKA, A., Paediatrics
SULLA, I., Neurosurgery
TOMORI, Z., Physiology
VAJÓ, J., Surgery

Faculty of Natural Sciences:

AHLERS, I., General Biology
AHLERSOVÁ, E., Animal Physiology
BUKOVSKÝ, L., Mathematics
CHALUPKA, S., Theoretical Physics
FEHER, A., Physics
GÁLOVÁ, M., Analytical Chemistry
GYÖRYOVÁ, K., Inorganic Chemistry
HONČARIV, R., Genetics
JENDROĽ, S., Mathematics
KRISTIÁN, F., Organic Chemistry
MIŠUROVÁ, E., General Biology
PODHRADSKÝ, D., Biochemistry
SÍLEŠ, E., Physics

Department of Languages:

RYBÁK, J., Slavonic Languages

ATTACHED INSTITUTES

Botanic Garden: Košice, Mánesova 23; Dir Dr SERGEJ MOCHNACKÝ.

Christian Academy: Košice, Šrobárova 2; Dir Ing. JOZEF PALAŠČÁK.

Computer Centre: Košice, Park Angelinum 9; Dir Ing. JOZEF HUGEC.

UNIVERZITA SV. CYRILA A METODA V TRNAVA
(University of Saints Cyril and Methodius in Trnava)

Námestie Jozefa Herdu 2, 917 01 Trnava

Telephone: (33) 556-51-11
Fax: (33) 556-51-20
E-mail: info@ucm.sk
Internet: www.ucm.sk

Founded 1997
State control
Academic year: October to June

Rector: Assoc. Prof. Dr EDUARD KOSTOLANSKÝ
Vice-Rector (Education): Dr DAGMAR VALENTOVIČOVÁ
Vice-Rector (International Relations): Assoc. Prof. Dr JÁN DANEK
Vice-Rector (Investment and Development): Assoc. Prof. Ing. ERNEST ŠTURDÍK
Vice-Rector (Research): Prof. Dr RASTISLAV TOTH

Number of teachers: 221
Number of students: 3,130

DEANS

Faculty of Mass Media and Communications: Doc. Dr VIERA GAŽOVÁ
Faculty of Natural Sciences: Prof. Dr Ing. JOZEF OBOŇA
Faculty of Philosophy: Assoc. Prof. Dr RUŽENA KOZMOVÁ

UNIVERZITA VETERINÁRSKEHO LEKÁRSTVA V KOŠICIACH
(University of Veterinary Medicine in Košice)

Komenského 73, 041 81 Košice

Telephone: (55) 633-01-27
Fax: (55) 633-56-41
E-mail: rektor@uvm.sk
Internet: www.uvm.sk

Founded 1949
State control
Languages of instruction: Slovak, English
Academic year: September to June

Rector: Prof. Dr RUDOLF CABADAJ
Vice-Rectors: Prof. Dr VIERA BAJOVÁ, Assoc. Prof. Dr EMIL PILIPČINEC, Assoc. Prof. Dr EMIL SVICKÝ
Chief Administrative Officer: Ing. RUDOLF LUKÁČ
Librarian: Assoc. Prof. Dr MARTA PROSBOVÁ

Number of teachers: 153
Number of students: 785

Publications: *Folia veterinaria* (4 a year), *Slovenský veterinársky časopis* (6 a year)

PROFESSORS

BAJOVÁ, V., Infectious Diseases
BÍREŠ, J., Internal Diseases of Ruminants and Swine
BLAHOVEC, J., Biochemistry
CABADAJ, R., Food Hygiene and Food Technology
DANKO, J., Anatomy and Histology
KAČMÁRIK, J., Obstetrics and Gynaecology
KOVÁČ, G., Internal Diseases of Ruminants and Swine
LEGÁTH, J., Toxicology
LENARTOVÁ, V., Chemistry and Biophysics
LEŠNÍK, F., Biology
LEVKUT, M., Pathological Anatomy
MARÁČEK, I., Physiology
MARETTA, M., Anatomy and Histology
MESÁROŠ, P., Andrology
MIKULA, I., Microbiology and Immunology

PAULÍK, Š., Infectious Diseases
VAJDA, V., Nutrition and Veterinary Dietetics
VÁRADY, J., Comparative Physiology
ZIBRÍN, M., Anatomy and Histology

ŽILINSKÁ UNIVERZITA
(University of Žilina)

Univerzitná 1, 010 26 Žilina
Telephone: (41) 513-51-01
Fax: (41) 513-50-56
E-mail: info@rekt.utc.sk
Internet: www.utc.sk
Founded 1953 as Vysoká Škola Dopravy a Spojov; present title 1996
State control
Language of instruction: Slovak
Academic year: September to June
Rector: Prof. Dr JÁN BUJŇÁK
Vice-Rector (Development): Prof. Dr MILAN DADO
Vice-Rector (Education): Assoc. Prof. Dr MICHAL POKORNÝ
Vice-Rector (Foreign and Public Relations): Prof. Dr MARIÁN DZIMKO
Vice-Rector (Science and Research): Prof. Dr PAVEL SUROVEC
Registrar: MSc. LADISLAV CIMERÁK
Librarian: PhDr MARTA SAKALOVÁ

Library of 215,137 vols
Number of teachers: 696
Number of students: 10,154

Publications: *Komunikácie – vedecké listy ŽU* (Communications – Scientific Letters, 4 a year), *Krizový Manažment* (Crisis Management), *Materiálové inžinierstvo* (Materials Engineering, annually), *Pokrok v Elektrikom a Elektromikrom Inžinigrstve* (Advances in Electrical and Electronic Engineering), *Práce a štúdie ŽU* (Works and Studies, annually), *Zborník z konferencie TRANSCOM* (Proceedings of the TRANSCOM Conference, every 2 years), *Zborník z vedeckých konferencií ŽU* (Proceedings of the Scientific Conferences, every 5 years), *Znalectvo-Cestná doprava, elektrotechnika, strojarstvo* (Expertise in Road Traffic, Electrotechnology and Mechanical Engineering, 4 a year), *Znalectvo-Stavebnictvo a Podnikové Hospodárstvo* (Expertise in Civil Engineering and Economics of Enterprise, 4 a year)

DEANS

Faculty of Civil Engineering: Prof. Dr JÁN CELKO
Faculty of Electrical Engineering: Assoc. Prof. Dr JÁN MICHALÍK
Faculty of Management Science and Informatics: Assoc. Prof. VLADIMR JAMRICH
Faculty of Mechanical Engineering: Prof. ŠTEFAN MEDVECKÝ
Faculty of Operation and Economics of Transport and Communications: Prof. Dr TATIANA COREJOVÁ
Faculty of Science: Assoc. Prof. Dr MIROSLAVA RŮŽIČKOVÁ
Faculty of Special Engineering: Prof. Dr PAVEL POLEDŇÁK

PROFESSORS

Faculty of Civil Engineering (Komenského 52, 010 26 Žilina; tel. (41) 513-55-01; fax (41) 723-35-02; e-mail education@fstav.utc.sk; internet svf.utc.sk):

BENČAT, J., Structural Mechanics
BUJŇÁK, J., Theory and Construction of Engineering Structures
ČELKO, J., Theory and Construction of Engineering Structures
ČOREJ, J., Theory and Construction of Engineering Structures
KOVAŘÍK, K., Theory and Construction of Engineering Structures
MELCER, J., Structural Mechanics
MIKOLAJ, J., Theory and Construction of Engineering Structures
MORAVČÍK, M., Applied Mechanics
SCHLOSSER, F., Theory and Construction of Engineering Structures
VIČAN, J., Theory and Construction of Engineering Structures

Faculty of Electrical Engineering (Univerzitná 1, 010 26 Žilina; tel. (41) 513-20-51; fax (41) 513-15-15; e-mail education@fel.utc.sk; internet fel.utc.sk):

BLUNÁR, K., Communications Engineering
BURY, P., Physics of Condensed Matter and Acoustics
ČÁPOVÁ, K., Theoretical Electrotechnology
DADO, M., Telecommunications
DOBRUCKÝ, B., Electric Traction and Electric Drives
HRABOVCOVÁ, V., Electric Traction and Electric Drives
NEVESELÝ, M., Theoretical Electrotechnology
TRSTENSKÝ, D., Communications Engineering
VITTEK, J., Electric Traction and Electric Drives

Faculty of Management Science and Informatics (Univerzitná 1, 010 26 Žilina; tel. (41) 513-40-51; fax (41) 565-20-44; e-mail education@fri.utc.sk; internet www.fri.utc.sk):

ALEXÍK, M., Information and Control Systems
CENEK, P., Transport and Communications Technology
HITTMÁR, S., Management in Transport
JANÁČEK, J., Transport and Communications Technology
MANULIAK, I., Information and Control Systems
MARČEK, D., Management
SKÝVA, L., Technical Cybernetics

Faculty of Mechanical Engineering (Univerzitná 1, 010 26 Žilina; tel. (41) 513-25-00; fax (41) 565-29-40; e-mail education@dsjf.utc.sk; internet fstroj.utc.sk):

BOKUVKA, O., Materials Engineering
DZIMKO, M., Machine Elements and Mechanisms
GREGOR, M., Industrial Engineering and Management
HLAVŇA, V., Transportation and Handling Technologies
HONNER, K., Workplace Arrangement
KONEČNÁ, R., Material Engineering
KOŠTURIAK, J., Industrial Engineering and Management
KUKUČA, P., Transportation and Handling Technologies
KURIC, I., Mechanical Engineering
MÁLIK, L., Machine Elements and Mechanisms
MEDVECKÝ, Š., Machine Elements and Mechanisms
MEŠKO, J., Mechanical Engineering
MIČIETA, B., Industrial Management
OBMAŠČÍK, M., Mechanical Engineering
PALČEK, P., Materials Engineering
SKOČOVSKÝ, P., Materials Engineering
SLÁDEK, G., Mechanical Engineering
ZVOLENSKÝ, P., Transport and Handling Technologies

Faculty of Operation and Economics of Transport and Communications (Univerzitná 1, 010 26 Žilina; tel. (41) 513-30-50; fax (41) 565-14-99; e-mail education@fpedas.utc.sk; internet fpedas.utc.sk):

CISKO, Š., Economics
COREJOVÁ, T., Transport and Communications Technology
GNAP, J., Economics
HAVEL, K., Transport and Communications Technology
HOLLAREK, T., Transport Engineering
KAZDA, A., Transport and Communications Technology
KEVICKÝ, D., Transport and Communications Technology
KRÁLOVENSKÝ, J., Economics
KŘÍŽ, J., Transport and Communications Technology
LIŠČÁK, S., Transport and Communications Technology
NEDELKA, M., Transport and Communications Technology
SEDLÁČEK, B., Economics
ŠTOFKOVÁ, J., Economics
SUROVEC, P., Transport and Communications Technology
VOLESKÝ, K., Transport and Communications Technology

Faculty of Science (Hurbanova 15, 010 26 Žilina; tel. (41) 513-61-01; fax (41) 564-30-85; e-mail education@fpv.utc.sk; internet www.fpv.utc.sk):

BAJÁK, I., Physics
BOICHUK, O., Mathematics
ČÁP, I., Physics
DIBLÍK, J., Applied Mathematics
KONVIT, M., Transport and Communications Technology
KURCZ, J., Musicology
OBERUČ, J., Education and Psychology
POLONSKÝ, D., Education and Psychology
VOLF, I., Teaching of Physics

Faculty of Special Engineering (Ul. 1. mája 32, 011 17 Žilina; tel. (41) 513-66-01; fax (41) 513-66-20; e-mail education@fsi.utc.sk; internet www.utc.sk/fsi):

MACA, J., Operational Research, Stochastic Dynamics of Systems
MIKOLAJ, J., Transport Economics
POLEDŇÁK, P., Fire Protection
SEIDL, M., Logistics, Transport Technology
ŠIMÁK, L., Crisis Management

ATTACHED INSTITUTES

Institute of Competitiveness and Innovations: Dir Prof. ŠTEFAN MEDVECKÝ.

Institute of Forensic Engineering: Dir Prof. Dr GUSTÁV KASANICKÝ.

Institute of Information and Communication Technologies: Dir MSc. JOZEF MUŽÍK.

Institute of Life-Long Learning: Dir Dr RENÁTA ŠVARCOVÁ.

Institute of Physical Education: Dir Dr ROBERT JANIKOVSKÝ.

Research Institute of Alpine Biology: Dir Assoc. Prof. MARIÁN JANICA.

Schools of Art and Music

VYSOKÁ ŠKOLA MÚZICKÝCH UMENÍ
(Academy of Music and Dramatic Arts)

Ventúrska 3, 813 01 Bratislava
Telephone: (2) 54-43-21-72
Fax: (2) 54-43-01-25
E-mail: rektorat@vsmu.sk
Internet: www.vsmu.sk
Founded 1949
Academic year: September to June
Rector: Prof. ONDREJ ŠULAJ
Library of 65,000 vols
Number of teachers: 220
Number of students: 880

DEANS

Faculty of Drama and Puppetry: Assoc. Prof. JURAJ LETENAY
Faculty of Film and Television: Prof. STANISLAV PÁRNICKÝ

Faculty of Music and Dance: Prof. JÁN VLADIMÍR MICHALKO

VYSOKÁ ŠKOLA VÝTVARNÝCH UMENÍ
(Academy of Fine Arts and Design)

Hviezdoslavovo nám. 18, 814 37 Bratislava

Telephone: (2) 54-43-24-40
Fax: (2) 54-43-23-31
E-mail: rektor@vsvu.sk
Internet: www.afad.sk

Founded 1949
Academic year: October to July

Rector: Assoc. Prof. JÁN HOFFSTÄDTER
Vice-Chancellor (Academic Affairs): Asst. Prof. BOHUNKA KOKLESOVÁ

Vice-Chancellor (Foreign Relations): Asst. Prof. ANNA DAUČÍKOVÁ
Vice-Chancellor (Research and Development): Assoc. Prof. ŠTEFAN KLEIN
Registrar: LÝDIA MACUROVÁ

Library of 32,580 vols
Number of teachers: 84
Number of students: 635

HEADS OF DEPARTMENTS

Applied Arts: Assoc. Prof. KAROL WEISSLECHNER
Architectural Creation: Assoc. Prof. IMRICH VAŠKO
Conservation and Restoration: Prof. DANA SALAMONOVÁ
Graphic Design: Asst Prof. STANISLAV STANKOCI

History and Theory of Art: Prof. IVAN RUSINA
Industrial Design: Assoc. Prof. ŠTEFAN KLEIN
Painting and other Media: Assoc. Prof. DANIEL FISCHER
Photography and New Media: Prof. MILOTA HAVRÁNKOVÁ
Printmaking: Assoc. Prof. RÓBERT JANČOVIČ
Sculpture, Objects and Installation: Assoc. Prof. ANTON ČIERNY
Textile Creation: Asst. Prof. JÚLIA SABOVÁ

Konzervatórium: Timonova 2, 042 03 Košice; tel. (55) 622-19-67; fax (55) 622-20-92; e-mail kon-ke@stonline.sk; internet www.cassovia.sk/konzervatorium; f. 1951; library: 20,185 vols, 3,079 records; 103 teachers; 262 students; Dir Mag. BARTOLOMEJ BURÁŠ.

SLOVENIA

The Higher Education System

Slovenia's higher education institutions predate the foundation of the former Yugoslavia in 1918, with the oldest being Univerza v Ljubljani (University of Ljubljana), which was founded in 1595. In 1991 Slovenia declared independence from the Socialist Federal Republic of Yugoslavia. There are three universities, and in 2004/05 91,229 undergraduates were enrolled in tertiary education.

Higher education is organized according to the terms of the Higher Education Act (1994, amended 2004 and 2006) and in addition to the universities, other institutions of higher education include university faculties (fakultet), art academies (urnetniske akademije), high schools (visoke skole) and professional institutes. The Council for Higher Education was founded in 1994 as the main accreditation body and since 2006 has been responsible for quality assurance. In 1998 a 'credit' system for awarding postgraduate degrees was introduced and extended to undergraduate degrees in 2002. Following amendments to the Higher Education Act in 2004, Slovenia now participates in the Bologna Process to establish a European Higher Education Area, the first phase of which is to adopt a credit-based system of comparable degrees with two main cycles (undergraduate and graduate). The Professional and Scientific Titles Act (2006) laid out the new system of degrees and titles to be awarded in accordance with the principles of the Bologna Process.

The secondary school leavers' diploma (Matura) is the main requirement for admission to higher education. University places are offered on a quota basis (numerus clausus). Higher education degrees are now divided into three cycles. The first cycle consists of either academic or professional undergraduate degrees, equivalent to Bachelors, requiring 180–240 credits during two to four years of study. The second cycle degree is the Masters (Magister), lasting up to two years and requiring 60–120 credits. Doctoral studies (Doctorat) constitute the third cycle of university degrees and usually last three years.

Post-secondary technical and vocational education is provided by vocational colleges (visje strokovne sole). The primary qualification is the Post-Secondary Diploma.

Learned Societies

GENERAL

Slavistično društvo Slovenije (The Society for Slavic Studies of Slovenia): Aškerčeva 2/II, 1000 Ljubljana; internet www.ff.uni-lj.si/slovjez/sds/sds.html; f. 1935; a forum for professional Slavists, to provide a link between research and professional practice, to nurture cultural values regarding Slovene language and literature and awareness of Slovene history; to organize support for and publish Slavic research in academic and popular books and periodicals; 900 mems; Chair. MIRAN HLADNIK; publs *Kronike Slavističnega Društva* (monthly, online), *Slavistična revija* (Slavonic Review, quarterly), *Jezik in slovstvo* (Language and Literature, 8 a year).

Slovenska Akademija Znanosti in Umetnosti (Slovenian Academy of Sciences and Arts): Novi trg 3, 1000 Ljubljana; tel. (1) 470-61-00; fax (1) 425-34-23; e-mail sazu@sazu.si; internet www.sazu.si; f. 1938; 60 full mems, 30 assoc. mems; library; see Libraries and Archives; Pres. BOŠTJAN ŽEKŠ; Sec.-Gen. Prof. Dr LIDIJA ANDOLŠEK-JERAS; publs *Annual Report*, *Opera*, *Acta Archaeologica*, *Acta Geographica*, *Acta Carsologica*, *Traditiones*.

BIBLIOGRAPHY, LIBRARY SCIENCE AND MUSEOLOGY

Zveza bibliotekarskih društev Slovenije (Union of Associations of Slovene Librarians): Turjaška 1, 1000 Ljubljana; tel. (1) 200-11-93; fax (1) 251-30-52; e-mail zveza-biblio.ds-nuk@guest.arnes.si; internet www.zbds-zveza.si; f. 1947; 1,000 mems, co-ordinates activities with 8 regional library assocs; Pres. MELITA AMBROŽIĆ; Treas. ZDENKA RUDOLF; publ. *Knjižnica* (Library, 4 a year).

ECONOMICS, LAW AND POLITICS

Society of Jurists of Slovenia: Dalmatinova 4, Ljubljana; f. 1947; 1,073 mems; Pres. JOŽE PAVLIČIČ; publ. *Jurist*.

FINE AND PERFORMING ARTS

Društvo slovenskih skladateljev (Society of Slovene Composers): Trg francoske revolucije 6, Ljubljana; tel. (1) 241-56-60; fax (1) 241-56-66; e-mail info@drustvo-dss.si; internet www.drustvo-dss.si; f. 1945; represents and promotes Slovene composers; promotes the creation of new Slovene music; organize concerts of contemporary Slovene music; 106 mems; Pres. JANI GOLOB; Sec. SOJAR VOGLAR; publ. *Edicije DSS* (printed scores, etc., of its mems).

Slovensko umetnostnozgodovinsko društvo (Slovenian Society of Historians of Art): Aškerčeva 2, 1000 Ljubljana; tel. (1) 241-12-10; fax (1) 241-12-11; e-mail majca .korosaj@ff.uni-lj.si; internet www.gov.si/ukd; f. 1921; excursions, symposia, congresses; 300 mems; library of 22,000 vols; Chair. NACE ŠUMI; publs *Archives d'Histoire de l'Art*, *Zbornik za umetnostno zgodovino* (annually).

HISTORY, GEOGRAPHY AND ARCHAEOLOGY

Zveza geografskih društev Slovenije (Association of the Geographical Societies of Slovenia): Filozofska fakulteta, Aškerčeva 2, 1000 Ljubljana; tel. (1) 241-12-1248; fax (1) 425-93-37; e-mail geografija@ff.uni-lj.si; internet www.ff.uni-lj.si/geo; f. 1922; 700 mems; Pres. MATEJ GABROVEC; Secs KATJA VRTAČNIK GARBAS, MATEJA BREG; publs *Geografski vestnik* (annual), *Geografski obzornik* (quarterly).

Zveza zgodovinskih društev Slovenije (Slovenian Historical Association): Aškerčeva 2, 1000 Ljubljana; tel. (1) 241-12-00; fax (1) 425-93-37; f. 1839; 1,649 mems; library of 5,215 vols; Pres. Dr JURIJ PEROVŠEK; publs *Zgodovinski časopis* (Historical Review, 4 a year), *Kronika* (3 a year), *Časopis za zgodovino in narodopisje* (2 a year).

LANGUAGE AND LITERATURE

Goethe-Institut: Tivolska 30, 1000 Ljubljana; tel. (1) 426-95-00; e-mail naumann@ljubljana.goethe.org; internet www.goethe .de/ins/si/lju/ktn/deindex.htm; offers courses and exams in German language and culture and promotes cultural exchange with Germany; Dir ABED NAUMANN.

Slovenska Matica (Slovenian Society): Kongresni trg 8, 1000 Ljubljana; tel. (1) 251-42-00; fax (1) 251-42-00; e-mail drago .jancar@siol.net; f. 1864; literary and publishing society; 2,800 mems; library of 10,000 vols; Pres. Prof. Dr JOŽA MAHNIČ; Sec. DRAGO JANČAR.

NATURAL SCIENCES

General

Društvo matematikov, fizikov in astronomov Slovenije (Society of Mathematicians, Physicists and Astronomers of Slovenia): POB 2964, 1001 Ljubljana; tel. (1) 476-65-00; fax (1) 251-72-81; e-mail tajnik@dmfa.si; internet www.dmfa.si; f. 1949; 1,200 mems; Chair. Prof. Dr ZVONKO TRONTELJ; publs *Obzornik mat. fiz.* (6 a year), *Presek* (6 a year).

Prirodoslovno Društvo Slovenije (Natural History Society of Slovenia): Salendrova ul. 4, 1573 Ljubljana; tel. (1) 252-19-14; fax (1) 421-21-21; e-mail prirodoslovno.drustvo@guest.arnes.si; internet www.proteus.si; f. 1934; 2,500 mems; Pres. RADOVAN KOMEL; Sec. Gen. JANJA BENEDIK; publ. *Proteus* (10 a year).

Physical Sciences

Jamarska zveza Slovenije (Speleological Association of Slovenia): Lepi pot 6, POB 2544, 1109 Ljubljana; tel. (1) 429-34-44; e-mail predsedstvo@jamarska-zveza.si; internet www.jamarska-zveza.si; f. 1889; 43 caving societies and research groups with a total of 1,000 mems; Pres. JORDAN GUSTIN; publ. *Naše jame* (2 a year).

Research Institutes

GENERAL

Inštitut za Antropološke in Prostorske Študije (Institute of Anthropological and Spatial Studies): Novi trg 2, 1000 Ljubljana; tel. (1) 470-64-95; fax (1) 425-77-95; e-mail iaps@zrc-sazu.si; internet iaps.zrc-sazu.si; f. 1995; attached to Scientific Research Centre of SASA (ZRC SAZU); Dir Dr IVAN ŠPRAJC.

Znanstvenoraziskovalni Center SAZU (ZRC SAZU) (Scientific Research Centre of SASA): Novi trg 2, 1000 Ljubljana; tel. (1) 425-52-26; fax (1) 425-52-53; e-mail zrc@zrc-sazu.si; internet www.zrc-sazu.si; f. 1981 by Slovenian Acad. of Sciences and Arts; now an independent body with a network of research institutes (listed individually in this section of Research Institutes) in the humanities and natural sciences; Dir Dr OTO LUTHAR.

BIBLIOGRAPHY, LIBRARY SCIENCE AND MUSEOLOGY

Inštitut za Biografiko in Bibliografijo ZRC SAZU (Institute of Biographical and Bibliographical Studies at ZRC SAZU): Novi trg 2, 1000 Ljubljana; tel. (1) 470-62-95; fax (1) 425-77-54; e-mail ibb@zrc-sazu.si; internet www.zrc-sazu.si; f. 1999; attached to Scientific Research Centre of SASA (ZRC SAZU); Dir Dr ANDREJ VOVKO; publ. *Življenja in Dela* (Lives and Deeds, irregular).

FINE AND PERFORMING ARTS

Glasbenonarodopisni Inštitut ZRC SAZU (Institute of Ethnomusicology at ZRC SAZU): Novi trg 2, 1000 Ljubljana; tel. (1) 470-62-65; fax (1) 425-77-53; e-mail gn@alpha.zrc-sazu.si; internet www.zrc-sazu.si/www/gni/gni-s.htm; f. 1934; attached to Scientific Research Centre of SASA (ZRC SAZU); Dir Dr MARJETKA GOLEŽ KAUČIČ; publ. *Traditiones* (annually).

Muzikološki inštitut ZRC SAZU (Institute of Musicology at ZRC SAZU): Novi trg 2, 1000 Ljubljana; tel. (1) 470-61-00; fax (1) 425-77-99; e-mail mi@zrc-sazu.si; internet www.zrz-sazu.si/www/mi/mii-s.htm; f. 1972; attached to Scientific Research Centre of SASA (ZRC SAZU); library of 15,000 vols; Head Dr METODA KOKOLE; publ. *Monumenta Artis Musicae Sloveniae* (2 a year).

Umetnostnozgodovinski inštitut Franceta Steleta ZRC SAZU (France Stele Institute of Art History at ZRC SAZU): Novi trg 2, POB 306, 1001 Ljubljana; tel. (1) 470-61-00; fax (1) 425-78-00; e-mail umzg@zrc-sazu.si; internet odmev.zrc-sazu.si/instituti/uzifs/; f. 1972; attached to Scientific Research Centre of SASA (ZRC SAZU); library of 17,000 vols; Dir Dr BARBARA MUROVEC (acting); publs *Acta historiae artis Slovenica* (annually), *Umetnosta Kronika* (quarterly).

HISTORY, GEOGRAPHY AND ARCHAEOLOGY

Geografski inštitut Antona Melika ZRC SAZU (Anton Melik Geographical Institute at ZRC SAZU): Gosposka ul. 13, 1000 Ljubljana; tel. (1) 470-61-54; fax (1) 425-77-93; e-mail gi@zrc-sazu.si; internet www.zrc-sazu.si/gi; f. 1946; attached to Scientific Research Centre of SASA (ZRC SAZU); depts of physical, social, regional geography, natural disasters, geographical information system, thematic cartography, environmental protection; geographical museum and library; also houses a cartographic colln and 3 spec. geographical collns: Landscapes of Slovenia, Settlements of Slovenia and Glaciers of Slovenia; headquarters of the Com-

mission for the Standardization of Geographical Names; 26 mems; library of 41,000 vols and periodicals; Dir Dr DRAGO PERKO; publs *Geografija Slovenije* (Geography of Slovenia, in Slovene, 2 a year), *Geografski zbornik* (Acta Geographica Slovenica, in English, 2 a year), *Georithem* (in Slovene, 2 to 5 a year), *GIS v Sloveniji* (GIS in Slovenia, in Slovene, every 2 years).

Inštitut za arheologijo ZRC SAZU (Institute of Archaeology at ZRC SAZU): Novi Trg 2, 1000 Ljubljana; tel. (1) 470-63-80; fax (1) 425-77-57; e-mail iza@zrc-sazu.si; internet www.zrc-sazu.si/iza; f. 1947; attached to Scientific Research Centre of SASA (ZRC SAZU); library of 35,000 vols; Dir Dr JANA HORVAT; publs *Arheološki vestnik* (annually), *Opera Instituti archaeologici Sloveniae*.

Uprava Republike Slovenije za kulturno dediščino (Cultural Heritage Office of the Republic of Slovenia): Plečnikov trg 2, 1000 Ljubljana; tel. (1) 251-32-87; fax (1) 425-54-71; e-mail urskd@gov.si; internet www.gov.si/ukd; f. 1913, to preserve and study historical and archaeological monuments, and sites of historical, artistic, scientific, ethnological and sociological interest; a complete register of historical monuments in Slovenia; library of 13,500 books; Dir STANE MRVIČ; publs *Varstvo spomenikov* (Preservation of Monuments, annually), *Vestnik* (Bulletin), *Kulturni in naravni spomeniki Slovenije* (series of guides to the historical and natural monuments of Slovenia, 10 a year).

Zgodovinski inštitut Milka Kosa ZRC SAZU (Milko Kos Institute of History at ZRC SAZU): Novi trg 2, 1000 Ljubljana; tel. (1) 470-62-00; fax (1) 425-78-01; e-mail zi@zrc-sazu.si; internet www.zrc-sazu.si; f. 1947; attached to Scientific Research Centre of SASA (ZRC SAZU); Head Prof. Dr DARJA MIHELIČ.

LANGUAGE AND LITERATURE

Inštitut za slovenski jezik Frana Ramovša ZRC SAZU (Fran Ramovš Institute of the Slovenian Language at ZRC SAZU): Novi trg 2, p. p. 306, 1001 Ljubljana; tel. (1) 470-61-60; fax (1) 425-77-96; e-mail isj@zrc-sazu.si; internet www.zrc-sazu.si/isjfr; f. 1945; attached to Scientific Research Centre at SASA (ZRC SAZU); Head Dr VARJA CVETKO OREŠNIK; publs *Jezikoslovni Zapiski* (2 a year), *Slovenski Jezik* (Slovene Linguistic Studies, every 2 years).

Inštitut za slovensko literaturo in literarne vede ZRC SAZU (Institute of Slovene Literature and Literary Sciences at ZRC SAZU): Novi trg 2, 1000 Ljubljana; tel. (1) 470-63-00; fax (1) 425-77-54; e-mail lit@zrc-sazu.si; internet www.zrc-sazu.si/slolit; f. 1948; attached to Scientific Research Centre of SASA (ZRC SAZU); library of 40,000 vols; Dir Dr DARKO DOLINAR.

MEDICINE

Inštitut za medicinske vede ZRC SAZU (Institute of Medical Sciences at ZRC SAZU): Novi trg 2, 1000 Ljubljana; tel. (1) 470-61-00; fax (1) 426-14-93; e-mail imv@zrc-sazu.si; internet www.zrz-sazu.si/imv; f. 1987; attached to Scientific Research Centre of SASA (ZRC SAZU); Dir Dr MARJAN KORDAŠ.

NATURAL SCIENCES

Biological Sciences

Biološki inštitut Jovana Hadžija ZRC SAZU (Jovan Hadži Institute of Biology at ZRC SAZU): Novi trg 2, 1000 Ljubljana; tel. (1) 470-63-10; fax (1) 425-77-97; e-mail carni@zrc-sazu.si; internet www.zrc-sazu.si/bi; f. 1950; attached to Scientific Research

Centre of SASA (ZRC SAZU); Dir Dr ANDRAŽ ČARNI.

Paleontološki inštitut Ivana Rakovca ZRC SAZU (Ivan Rakovec Institute of Palaeontology at ZRC SAZU): Novi trg 2, 1000 Ljubljana; tel. (1) 470-63-71; fax (1) 425-77-55; e-mail spela@zrc-sazu.si; internet www.zrc-sazu.si/www/piir/piir-a.htm; f. 1949; attached to Scientific Research Centre of SASA (ZRC SASA); Dir Dr ŠPELA GORIČAN.

Physical Sciences

Geološki Zavod Slovenije (Geological Survey of Slovenia): Dimičeva 14, 1009 Ljubljana; tel. (1) 280-97-00; fax (1) 280-97-53; e-mail w@geo-zs.si; internet www.geo.zs.si; f. 1946; geology, geotechnology, geophysics, mining, soil and rock mechanics, drilling and blasting, manufacturing and maintenance of drilling equipment; 1,300 mems; library of 15,000 vols, 300 periodicals, 30,000 reports; Dir Dr BOJAN OGORELEC; publ. *Geologija* (2 a year).

Inštitut za raziskovanje krasa ZRC SAZU (Institute for Karst Research at ZRC SAZU): Titov trg 2, 6230 Postojna; tel. (5) 700-19-00; fax (5) 700-19-99; e-mail izrk@zrc-sazu.si; internet www.zrc-sazu.si; f. 1947; karstology and speleology; attached to Scientific Research Centre of SASA (SRC SAZU); Dir Dr TADEJ SLABE; publs *Acta Carsologica* (2 a year), *Annotated Bibliography of Karst Publications* (annual).

PHILOSOPHY AND PSYCHOLOGY

Filozofski inštitut ZRC SAZU (Institute of Philosophy at ZRC SAZU): Novi trg 2, POB 306, 1001 Ljubljana; tel. (1) 470-64-70; fax (1) 425-77-92; e-mail fi@zrc-sazu.si; internet fi.zrc-sazu.si; f. 1979; attached to Scientific Research Centre at SASA (ZRC SAZU); 10 mems; Head Dr RADO RIHA; publ. *Filozofski vestnik* (3 a year).

RELIGION, SOCIOLOGY AND ANTHROPOLOGY

Inštitut za narodnostna vprašanja (Institute for Ethnic Studies): Erjavčeva 26, 1000 Ljubljana; tel. (1) 200-18-70; fax (1) 251-09-64; e-mail inv@inv.si; internet www.inv.si; f. 1925; study of inter-ethnic relations in Slovenia and abroad and of Slovene ethnic minorities in neighbouring countries; sociolinguistics, human rights, migration, general ethnic issues; library of 37,000 vols; Pres. Dr BORIS JESIH; Dir Dr MITJA ŽAGAR; publ. *Razprave in gradivo* (Treatises and Documents, 2 a year).

Inštitut za slovensko izeljenstvo ZRC SAZU (Institute for Slovene Emigration Studies at ZRC SAZU): Novi trg 2, 1000 Ljubljana; tel. (1) 470-64-85; fax (1) 425-78-02; e-mail izi@zrc-sazu.si; internet www.zrc-sazu.si/isi; f. 1986; attached to Scientific Research Centre of SASA (ZRC SAZU); Dir Dr MARINA LUKŠIČ-HACIN; publs *Bilten* (Newsletter, annual), *Dve Domovini* (Two Homelands, 2 a year).

Inštitut za slovensko narodopisje ZRC SAZU (Institute of Slovene Ethnology at ZRC SAZU): Novi trg 2, 1000 Ljubljana; tel. (1) 470-62-80; fax (1) 425-77-52; e-mail monika@zrc-sazu.si; internet www.zrc-sazu.si/isn; f. 1951; attached to Scientific Research Centre of SASA (ZRC SAZU); Dir Dr MONIKA KROPEJ; publs *Traditiones* (annually), *Studia Mythologica Slavica* (annually).

Libraries and Archives

Celje

Osrednja knjižnica Celje (Public Library of Celje): Muzejski trg 1a, 3000 Celje; tel. (3) 426-17-10; e-mail sikce@ce.sik.si; internet www.ce.sik.si; f. 1946; 365,000 vols; Librarian BRANKO GOROPEVŠEK.

Koper

Osrednja knjižnica Srečka Vilharja (Srečko Vilhar Public Library): Trg Brolo 1, 6000 Koper; tel. (5) 663-26-00; fax (5) 663-26-15; e-mail info@kp.sik.si; internet sikkp.kp.sik.si; f. 1951; 270,000 vols; Librarian Prof. EVGEN KOŠTIAL.

Ljubljana

Arhiv Republike Slovenije (Archives of the Republic of Slovenia): Zvezdarska 1, p.p. 21, 1127 Ljubljana; tel. (1) 241-42-00; fax (1) 241-42-69; e-mail ars@gov.si; internet www.gov.si/ars; f. 1887; collection of important archives, especially those connected with the territory populated by Slovenes since 12th c.; archive of Slovene film production since 1905; Dir DRAGAN MATIĆ.

Biblioteka Slovenske akademije znanosti in umetnosti (Library of the Slovenian Academy of Sciences and Arts): Novi trg 3–5, POB 323, 1000 Ljubljana; tel. (1) 470-62-46; fax (1) 425-34-62; e-mail marija@zrc-sazu.si; internet www.sazu.si/biblioteka_sazu.htm; f. 1938; 505,100 vols; Librarian MARIJA FABJANČIČ; publs *Kratko poročilo o delu v letu* (annual), *Mesečni seznam novosti* (monthly), *Objave* (irreg.).

British Library: 1000 Ljubljana, Center Tivoli, Tivolska 30; tel. (1) 300-20-30; fax (1) 300-20-44; e-mail info@britishcouncil.si; internet www.britishcouncil.si; offers courses and exams in English language and British culture and promotes cultural exchange with the UK; 400 vols; Dir STEVE GREEN.

Centralna ekonomska knjižnica (Central Economic Library): Kardeljeva ploščad 17, 1000 Ljubljana; tel. (1) 589-25-91; fax (1) 589-26-98; e-mail cek@ef.uni-lj.si; internet www.ef.uni-lj.si/cek; f. 1946; library and information centre for business, economics and related sciences; European documentation centre; 238,000 vols and periodicals, 420 current periodicals; Dir Prof. Dr IVAN KANIČ; publ. *Mesečni pregled novih knjig* (monthly).

Centralna medicinska knjižnica, Medicinska fakulteta (Central Medical Library, Faculty of Medicine): Vrazov trg 2, 1000 Ljubljana; tel. (1) 543-77-30; fax (1) 543-77-45; e-mail infocmk@mf.uni-lj.si; internet www.mf.uni-lj.si/cmk; f. 1945; central library for the Faculty of Medicine, Slovene healthcare organizations and biomedical research institutions; literature of biomedicine; 209,227 books and periodicals, 437 current print journals, 660 e-journals; Dir Dr ANAMARIJA ROŽIĆ-HRISTOVSKI.

Centralna tehniška knjižnica Univerze v Ljubljani (Central Technical Library of the University of Ljubljana): Trg republike 3, 1000 Ljubljana; tel. (1) 251-40-72; fax (1) 425-66-67; e-mail post@ctk.uni-lj.si; internet www.ctk.uni-lj.si; f. 1949; central technical library for the university; specialized information centre for engineering, civil engineering and standards; information and referral centre for science and technology; interlibrary loan centre; 200,000 vols, research papers, standards, patents, regulations; Chief Librarian Dr MATJAŽ ŽAUCER; publs *Annual Report*, *New Books Accession List* (quarterly).

Knjižnica Narodnega Muzeja Slovenije (Library of the National Museum of Slovenia): Prešernova 20, POB 1967, 1000 Ljubljana; tel. (1) 241-44-68; fax (1) 241-44-00; e-mail anja-dular@narmuz-lj.si; internet www.narmuz-lj.si/anj/odd/knj/knj.html; f. 1821; 150,000 vols; special collection of Slovene prints from 16th c.; Librarian ANJA DULAR.

Knjižnica Pravne fakultete (Library of the Faculty of Law): Poljanski Nasip 2, Ljubljana; tel. (1) 420-32-31; f. 1920; 118,400 vols; Librarian MIRA VRHOVNIK.

Narodna in univerzitetna knjižnica (National and University Library): Turjaška 1, POB 259 1001 Ljubljana; tel. (1) 200-11-10; fax (1) 251-30-52; e-mail uprava@nuk.uni-lj.si; internet www.nuk.uni-lj.si; f. 1774; incorporates state copyright and deposit library, National Slovene library, University of Ljubljana library, library promotion and consultancy centre, permanent education centre and library research centre; UNESCO deposit library; incorporates Information and Documentation Centre on the Council of Europe, and EU Colln; 2,458,000 vols, incl. 1,190,000 books, 324,000 serials; 80,000 printed music items, 23,700 sound recordings, 13,800 audiovisual items, 7,400 MSS (incl. 85 parchments and 508 incunabula), 74,000 maps, 170,000 pictorial items, 3,800 microforms; Man. Dir LENART ŠETINC; publs *Knjižničarske novice* (print, monthly; online), *Novice NUK* (newsletter, 2 a year), *Signalne informacije* (print, monthly; online), *Slovenska bibliografija* (print, 4 a year; also online).

Slovanska knjižnica Ljubljana (Slavic Library): Einspiclerjeva ul 1, 1000 Ljubljana; tel. (1) 236-38-50; fax (1) 236-38-51; e-mail slovanska.knjiznica@guest.arnes.si; internet www.slovanskaknjiznica.si; f. 1901; language, literature, history and culture of the Slavs; 160,000 vols; Dir Prof. MATEJA KOMEL SNOJ.

Maribor

Univerzitetna knjižnica Maribor (University of Maribor Library): Gospejna 10, 2000 Maribor; tel. (2) 250-74-00; fax (2) 252-60-87; e-mail ukm@uni-mb.si; internet www.ukm.uni-mb.si; f. 1903; 841,099 vols; Dir Dr IRENA SAPAČ.

Novo Mesto

Knjižnica Mirana Jarca ('Milan Jarc' Regional Library): Rozmanova ul. 26, 8000 Novo Mesto; tel. (7) 393-46-00; fax (7) 393-46-01; e-mail web@gea.nm.sik.si; internet www.nm.sik.si; f. 1946; 400,000 vols; Dir ANDREJA PLENIČAR.

Museums and Art Galleries

Brežice

Posavski muzej (Regional Museum): Cesta prvih borcev 1, 8250 Brežice; tel. (7) 496-12-71; fax (7) 466-05-16; internet www.posavski-muzej.si; f. 1949; collection of archaeological exhibits from Neolithic times to the early Middle Ages; also ethnographical collection; historical section: from Slovene-Croat peasants' revolt of 1573 to the present; Baroque festival hall with frescoes (1703) and Baroque gallery; memorial room of painter Franjo Stiplovšek; library of 7,350 vols, 35 periodicals; Curator IVAN KASTELIC.

Celje

Pokrajinski muzej (Regional Museum): Muzejski trg 1, 3000 Celje; tel. (3) 544-26-33; fax (3) 544-33-84; e-mail pokrajinski-muzej-celje@guest.arnes.si; f. 1882; collections of archaeology, art and cultural history, ethnography and history; library of 8,456 vols; Dir DARJA PIRKMAJER.

Ljubljana

Mednarodni Grafični Likovni Center (MGLC) (International Graphics and Art Centre): Pod turnom 3, 1000 Ljubljana; tel. (1) 241-38-00; fax (1) 241-38-21; e-mail info@mglc-lj.si; internet www.mglc-lj.si; f. 1986; permanent collection of contemporary international graphics; organizes the International Biennial of Graphics; exhibitions of prints, drawings; print workshop; Dir Dr LILIJANA STEPANČIČ.

Mestni muzej (Municipal Museum): Gosposka 15, 1000 Ljubljana; tel. (1) 241-25-00; fax (1) 241-25-40; e-mail info@mm-lj.si; internet www.mm-lj.si; f. 1935; cultural history museum of Ljubljana; collections include archaeological dept, containing articles from lake dwellings of the chalcolithic period, cemeteries of the Illyrian-Celtic period and of Roman domination (Emona), and from the Old Slavic period; cultural historical collection; modern history; also fine arts exhibitions; information centre about the cultural and natural heritage in the Ljubljana area; library of 9,324 vols; Dir TAJA VOVK ČEPIČ; publs various guides.

Moderna galerija (Museum of Modern Art): Tomšičeva 14, 1000 Ljubljana; tel. (1) 241-68-00; fax (1) 251-41-20; e-mail info@mg-lj.si; internet www.mg-lj.si; f. 1948; permanent colln of contemporary Slovene art from the Impressionists to the present day and worldwide modern art; organizes regular art exhibitions; photographic archive; library: art library of 50,000 vols; Dir ZDENKA BADOVINAC.

Muzej novejše zgodovine slovenije (Museum of Contemporary History): Celovška c. 23, 1000 Ljubljana; tel. (1) 300-96-11; fax (1) 433-82-44; e-mail uprava@muzej-nz.si; internet www.muzej-nz.si; f. 1948 to collect all important archives, museum objects and library material of Slovene history since 1914; Dir Dr MARJETA MIKUŽ.

Narodna galerija (National Gallery): Puharjeva 9, 1000 Ljubljana; tel. (1) 241-54-34; fax (1) 241-54-03; e-mail info@ng-slo.si; internet www.ng-slo.si; f. 1918; colln of Gothic sculptural arts, medieval frescoes and copies of Gothic frescoes from Slovenia; colln of Slovenian Renaissance, Baroque and 19th-century paintings and sculptures; paintings by Slovenian impressionists; European painters since the 14th century; colln of Slovenian graphic arts from the 18th to the early 20th century; photo-documentation of works of art from Slovenia; library of 34,000 vols; Dir Dr BARBARA JAKI.

Narodni muzej Slovenije (National Museum of Slovenia): Prešernova ul. 20, POB 1967, 1000 Ljubljana; tel. (1) 241-44-00; fax (1) 241-44-22; e-mail info@nms.si; internet www.nms.si; f. 1821; depts of archaeology, history, history of applied arts; coins and medals; graphic arts; library of 150,000 vols; branch: Museum of Bled (medieval castle); Dir Prof. Dr PETER KOS; publs *Situla* (annual), *Catalogi et Monographiae* (annual), *Argo* (2 a year), *Viri* (irreg.).

Prirodoslovni muzej Slovenije (Slovenian Natural History Museum): Prešernova 20, POB 290, 1001 Ljubljana; tel. (1) 241-09-40; fax (1) 241-09-53; e-mail stome@pms-lj.si; internet www2.pms.lj.si; f. 1821; zoology, botany, geology; library of 12,500 books and periodicals; Dir Prof. MATIJA GOGALA; publs *Scopolia* (3 a year), *Acta Entomologica Slovenica* (2 a year).

Slovenski etnografski muzej (Slovenian Ethnographical Museum): Metelkova 2, 1000

Ljubljana; tel. (1) 300-87-00; fax (1) 300-87-36; e-mail etnomuz@etno-muzej.si; internet www.etno-muzej.si; f. 1923; Slovenian and non-European ethnographic collections; library of 30,000 vols; Dir INJA SMERDEL; publs *Etnolog* (annually), *Knjižnica Slovenskega etnografskega muzeja* (library newsletter, 1 or 2 a year).

Slovenski šolski muzej (Slovenian School Museum): Plečnikov trg 1, 1000 Ljubljana; tel. and fax (1) 251-30-24; e-mail solski .muzej@guest.arnes.si; internet www .ssolski-muzej.si; f. 1898 to collect school documents and educational books since 16th century; exhibition about the devt of schools in Slovenia; library of 59,000 vols, 542 fascicules; 17,084 documents for all schools in Slovenia; Dir Mag. STANKO OKOLIŠ; publ. *Šolska kronika* (School Chronicle, 2 a year).

Zemljepisni muzej Geografskega inštituta Antona Melika (Geographical Museum of the Anton Melik Geographical Institute): Gosposka ul. 13, 1000 Ljubljana; f. 1946; attached to the Anton Melik Geographical Institute; maps of Slovenia, geographical collns; Head PRIMOŽ GAŠPERIČ.

Maribor

Pokrajinski muzej Maribor (Regional Museum of Maribor): Grajska ul. 2, 62000 Maribor; tel. (2) 228-35-51; fax (2) 252-77-77; e-mail info@pmuzej-mb.si; internet www .pmuzej-mb.si; f. 1903 from collections of the Maribor Museum, the historical societies and the Episcopal Museum; archaeological, ethnological, historical, fine and applied art, costume collection exhibits; library of 12,000 vols; Dir MIRJANA KOREN.

Ptuj

Pokrajinski muzej Ptuj (Regional Museum): Muzejski trg 1, 2250 Ptuj; tel. (2) 787-92-30; fax (2) 787-92-45; e-mail muzej-ptuj.uprava@siol.net; internet www .pok-muzej-ptuj.si; f. 1893; history, archaeology, art, ethnography, numismatics, musical instruments, lapidary; reconstructions of 4 temples of Mithras; library of 15,000 vols; Dir Prof. ALEŠ ARIH; publs *Archaeologia Poetovionensis, Zbornik*.

Škofja Loka

Loški Muzej: Grajska pot 13, 4220 Škofja Loka; tel. (4) 517-04-00; fax (4) 517-04-12; e-mail loski.muzej@guest.arnes.si; internet www.loski-muzej.si; f. 1939 by the Museum Association of Škofja Loka; special collection of exhibits relating to the Freising dominion (973–1803); ethnographic, topographic, natural history and historical exhibits; records of altars since 17th c., exhibits of medieval guilds; relics of the struggle for national liberation; art gallery; open-air museum; library of 18,000 vols; Pres. JANA MLAKAR; publ. *Loški razgledi*.

Universities

UNIVERZA V LJUBLJANI
(University of Ljubljana)

Kongresni trg 12, 1000 Ljubljana

Telephone: (1) 241-85-00
Fax: (1) 241-86-60
E-mail: rektorat@uni-lj.si
Internet: www.uni-lj.si

Founded 1595, reconstituted 1809, reopened 1919
State control
Language of instruction: Slovene
Academic year: October to September (two terms)

Rector: Prof. Dr ANDREJA KOCIJANČIČ

Vice-Rectors: Prof. Dr JULIJANA KRISTL, Prof. Dr PETER MAČEK, Prof. Dr IVAN SVETLIK
Secretary-General: MIHAELA KRANJC
Librarians: Dr MATJAŽ ŽAUCER (Central and Technical Library), LENART ŠETINC (National and University Library)

Number of teachers: 3,500
Number of students: 56,000

Publications: *Objave* (irregular), *Seznam predavanj* (annually), *Vestnik* (monthly)

DEANS

Faculty of Architecture: Prof. PETER GABRIJELČIČ
Faculty of Arts: Prof. Dr BOŽIDAR JEZERNIK
Biotechnical Faculty: Prof. Dr JOŽE OSTERC
Faculty of Chemistry and Chemical Technology: Prof. Dr STANE PEJOVNIK
Faculty of Civil Engineering and Geodesy: Prof. Dr BOJAN MAJES
Faculty of Computer and Information Science: Prof. Dr BOŠTJAN VILFAN
Faculty of Economics: Prof. Dr MAKS TAJNIKAR
Faculty of Education: Prof. Dr CVETA RAZDEVŠEK PUČKO
Faculty of Electrical Engineering: Prof. Dr TOMAZ SLIVNIK
Faculty of Law: Prof. Dr RAJKO PIRNAT
Faculty of Maritime Studies and Transport: Prof. Dr JURIJ KOLENC
Faculty of Mathematics and Physics: Prof. Dr SLOBODAN ŽUMER
Faculty of Mechanical Engineering: Prof. Dr KARL KUZMAN
Faculty of Medicine: Prof. Dr DUŠAN ŠUPUT
Faculty of Natural Sciences and Technology: Prof. Dr RADOMIR TURK
Faculty of Pharmacy: Prof. Dr ALBIN KRISTL
Faculty of Public Administration: Prof. Dr SREČKO DAVJAK
Faculty of Social Sciences: Prof. Dr ZINKA KOLARIČ
Faculty of Social Work: Prof. Dr VITO FLAKER
Faculty of Sport: Prof. Dr BOJAN JOŠT
Faculty of Theology: Prof. Dr BOGDAN KOLAR
Faculty of Veterinary Medicine: Prof. Dr MILAN POGAČNIK
Academy of Fine Arts: Prof. BERNIK STANE
Academy of Music: Prof. PAVEL MIHELČIČ
Academy of Theatre, Radio, Film and Television: Prof. ALEŠ VALIČ
University College of Health Care: Prof. Dr FRANCE SEVŠEK

UNIVERZA V MARIBORU
(University of Maribor)

Slomškov trg 15, 2000 Maribor

Telephone: (2) 235-52-80
Fax: (2) 235-52-11
E-mail: rektorat@uni-mb.si
Internet: www.uni-mb.si

Founded 1975
State control
Language of instruction: Slovene
Academic year: October to September

Rector: Prof. Dr IVAN ROZMAN
Vice-Rector for International and Inter-University Co-operation: Assoc. Prof. Dr MARKO JESENŠEK
Vice-Rector for Scientific Research and Rehabilitation: Prof. Dr ŽELJKO KNEZ
Vice-Rector for Student Affairs: Prof. Dr DUŠAN RADONJIČ
Vice-Rector for Students: MARKO PUKJŠIČ
Secretary-General: BOŠTJAN BRUMEN
Librarian: Dr IRENA SAPAČ

Number of teachers: 1,204
Number of students: 20,572

Publications: *Časopis za zgodovino in narodopisje, Naše gospodarstvo* (published by the Faculty of Economics and Business, 6 a year), *Organizacija in Kadri* (published by the Faculty of Organizational Sciences, 10 a year), *Univerzitetna revija, Znanstvena revija*

DEANS

Faculty of Agriculture: Dr BOŽIDAR KRAJNČIČ
Faculty of Business and Economics: Dr LEO GUSEL
Faculty of Chemistry and Chemical Engineering: Prof. Dr VALTER DOLEČEK
Faculty of Civil Engineering: Prof. Dr LUDVIK TRAUNER
Faculty of Criminal Justice: Prof. Dr MILAN PAGON
Faculty of Education: Prof. Dr JOSO VUKMAN
Faculty of Electrical Engineering and Computer Sciences: Prof. Dr IGOR TIČAR
Faculty of Law: Prof. Dr ŠIME IVANJKO
Faculty of Mechanical Engineering: Prof. Dr ANDREJ POLAJNAR
Faculty of Organizational Sciences: Dr JOŽE FLORJANČIČ
College of Nursing Studies: Dr DUŠANKA MIČETIĆ-TURK

PROFESSORS

Faculty of Agriculture (Vrbanska 30, 2000 Maribor; tel. (2) 250-58-00; fax (2) 229-60-71; e-mail fk@uni-mb.si; internet www.uni-mb .si/new/fk/okv_sl.htm):

KRAJNČIČ, B., Plant Physiology, Biology, Botany

Faculty of Business and Economics (Razlagova 14, 2000 Maribor; tel. (2) 229-00; fax (2) 227-056; e-mail dekan.epf@uni-mb.si; internet www.uni-mb.si/new/epf/okv_an .htm):

BOBEK, D., Business Administration in Banking
BELAK, J., Economics
FILIPIČ, D., Finance
GUSEL, L., Yugoslav Import-Export System
HAUC, A., Project Management
INDIHAR, S., Mathematics
KENDA, V., International Trade
KOKOTEC-NOVAK, M., Economics
KOLETNIK, F., Accounting, Auditing
MULEJ, M., Dialectical Theory of Systems
MUSIL, V., Polymeric Materials
OVIN, R., Economic Policy
PAUKO, F., Tourism
PIVKA, H., Business Law
RADONJIČ, D., Market Research
SAVIN, D., Political Economy
SRUK, V., Sociology, Philosophy and Political Science
ŽIŽMOND, E., Economic Policy

Faculty of Chemistry and Chemical Engineering (Smetanova ul. 17, 2000 Maribor; tel. (2) 229-44-00; fax (2) 252-77-74; e-mail fkkt@ uni-mb.si; internet www.atom.uni-mb.si):

DOBČNIK, D., Analytical Chemistry
DOLEČEK, V., Physical Chemistry
DROFENIK, M., Inorganic Chemistry
GLAVIČ, P., Inorganic Technology
KNEZ, Z, Separation Process
KROPE, J., Thermoenergetics

Faculty of Civil Engineering (Smetanova ul. 17, 2000 Maribor; tel. (2) 229-43-00; fax (2) 222-41-79; e-mail fg@uni-mb.si; internet kamen.uni-mb.si):

CVIKL, B., Physics
ILIĆ, R., Materials
LEP, J., Mathematics
PŠUNDER, M., Building Economics
TRAUNER, L., Soil Mechanics, Geotechnics
UMEK, A., Earthquake Engineering

Faculty of Education (Koroska 160, 2000 Maribor; tel. (2) 229-36-00; fax (2) 251-81-80; internet www.pfmb.uni-mb.si):

BELEC, B., Geography
BREŠAR, M., Mathematics
BOKOR, J., Hungarian Linguistics

BRUMEN, M., Physics
FLERE, S., Sociology
JAUŠOVEC, N., Psychology
JUTRONIĆ-TIHOMIROVIĆ, D., English Linguistics
KLAVŽAR, S., Mathematics
KLEMENČIČ, M., Contemporary History
MIŠČEVIĆ, N., History of Philosophy
MLINARIČ, J., History of Middle Ages
PANDUR, L., Painting Design
ROZMAN, F., History of Southeast Europe
VAUHNIK, J., Special Didactics of Sports Education
VUKMAN, J., Mathematics
ZORKO, Z., History of Language, Dialectology

Faculty of Electrical Engineering and Computer Science (Smetanova ul. 17, 2000 Maribor; tel. (2) 220-70-00; fax (2) 251-11-78; e-mail feri@uni-mb.si; internet www.feri.uni-mb.si):

BREŠAR, F., Mathematics
DOLINAR, D., Electro-Mechanical Control Systems
GRČAR, B., Control and Regulation Systems
GUID, N., Computer Graphics
HORVAT, B., Computing and Microcomputer Systems
JEZERNIK, K., Robotics
KUMPERŠČAK, V., Physics
ROZMAN, I., Information Systems
ZAGRADIŠNIK, I., Electrical Machines
ZAZULA, D., Systems Software
ŽUMER, V., Programming Languages

Faculty of Law (Mladinska 9, 2000 Maribor; tel. (2) 250-420; fax (2) 223-245; internet www.pf.uni-mb.si):

DEVETAK, S., Public International Law
FLERE, S., Sociology
GEČ-KOROŠEC, M., Family Law
IVANJKO, Š., Company Law, Insurance Law
KRANJC, J., Roman Law
OJNIK, S., History of Law
PERNEK, F., Financial Law
RUPNIK, J., Constitutional Law
TOPLAK, L., International Business Law

Faculty of Mechanical Engineering (Smetanova ul. 17, 2000 Maribor; tel. (2) 220-75-00; fax (2) 220-79-00; e-mail fs@uni-mb.si; internet www.fs.uni-mb.si/en):

ALUJEVIĆ, A., Mechanics, Thermodynamics
BALIČ, J., Manufacturing Technologies, Theory of Systems, Computer Integrated Manufacturing, Manufacturing Systems

FLAŠKER, J., Machine Elements II, Mechanical Design of Devices I, Technical Regulations
JEZERNIK, A., CAD/CAM
KRIŽMAN, A., Industrial Engineering, Metal Heat Processing
MAJCEN LE MARECHAL, A., Chemistry, Organic Chemistry I
OBLAK, M., Mechanics and Hydrodynamics
POLAJNAR, A., Work Study and Manufacturing Systems Planning
ŠKERGET, L., Fluid Mechanics amd Heat Transfer, Transport Phenomena, Eco-Engineering in Manufacturing
ŠOSTAR, A., Technological Measurements

Faculty of Organizational Sciences (Kidričeva cesta 55A, 4000 Kranj; tel. (4) 237-42-00; fax (4) 237-42-99; e-mail dekanat@fov.uni-mb.si; internet www.fov.uni-mb.si):

FLORJANČIČ, J., Personnel Administration
GRIČAR, J., Analysis and Design of Organizational Systems
JEREB, J., Human Resources Management
JESENKO, J., Quantitative Methods
JUG, J., Andragogy and Human Relations, Human Resources
KLJAJIČ, M., Systems Theory
RAJKOVIČ, V., Management Information Systems
VILA, A., Production Process Management
VRŠEC, E., Production Systems

College of Nursing Studies (Zitna 15, 2000 Maribor; tel. (2) 300-47-00; fax (2) 300-47-47; e-mail vzs@uni-mb.si; internet sola.vzdr.uni-mb.si):

BERVAR, M., Surgery
BORKO, E., Gynaecology and Obstetrics
BRUMEC, V., Physiology
GOLOUH, R., Pathology
HREN-VENCELJ, H., Microbiology, Parasitology
KAJZER, Š., Elements of Administration and Management
KRAJNC-SIMONETTI, S., Social Medicine and Statistics in Health Care
MULEJ, M., Anaesthesiology and Reanimatology
POKORN, D., Medical Diatetics
RAIŠP, I., Internal Medicine

ATTACHED CENTRES

Centre for Applied Mathematics and Theoretical Physics: Krekova 2, 2000 Maribor; Dir Dr MARKO ROBNIK.

European Centre for Ethnic and Regional Studies: Mladinska 9, 2000 Maribor; Dir Dr SILVO DEVETAK.

UNIVERZA V PRIMORSKA
(University of Primorska)

Titov Trg 4, 6000 Koper
Telephone: (5) 611-75-00
Fax: (5) 611-75-30
E-mail: info@upr.si
Internet: www.upr.si
Founded 2003
State control
Languages of instruction: Slovenian, English
Rector: Dr LUCIJA ČOK
Vice-Rector for Education: Dr ANDREJ BRODNIK
Vice Rector for Science and Research: Dr MILAN BUFON
Secretary-General: ANTON BALOH
Library of 40,000 vols, 400 periodicals across 5 libraries
Number of teachers: 260, 81 research staff
Number of students: 5,338

DEANS

Faculty of Education (Koper): Dr RADO PIŠOT
Faculty of Humanities (Koper): Dr VESNA MIKOLIĆ
Faculty of Management (Koper): Dr EGON ŽIŽMOND
College of Health Care (Izola): Dr MARIJA OVSENIK
College of Tourism—Touristica (Portoroz): Dr MARIJA OVSENIK

PROFESSORS

FILIPI, G., Applied Linguistics
ROTAR, D., Anthropology
ŽAGAR, I. Z., Slovenian Language and Literature

ATTACHED RESEARCH INSTITUTES

Primorska Institute of Natural Sciences and Technology: Dir Prof Dr TOMAŽ PISANSKI.

Science and Research Centre of Koper: Dir Dr DARKO DAROVEC.

SOLOMON ISLANDS

The Higher Education System

Formerly a British protectorate since 1900, Solomon Islands became independent, within the Commonwealth, in 1978. Solomon Islands College of Higher Education (founded 1984) and the University of the South Pacific Solomon Islands Centre (founded 1977) are the principal institutions of higher education. Scholarships are available for higher education at various universities overseas. Higher Education is the responsibility of the Ministry of Education and Human Resources Development.

The Pacific Senior Secondary Certificate or the Solomon Islands School Certificate are the main requirements for admission to the University of the South Pacific (and also to the University of Papua New Guinea). Preliminary and Foundation programmes are available to prepare students for admission to degree courses. The Bachelors is the main undergraduate degree, and lasts for three years in most subjects except medicine, which lasts four years and is taught at the Fiji School of Medicine. After the Bachelors, the first postgraduate degree is the one- to two-year Masters, which is followed by the two-year Doctorate, the highest university degree.

Solomon Islands College of Higher Education is principally an institution of technical and vocational education offering certificate and diploma courses.

Libraries and Archives

Honiara

Solomon Islands National Archives: Ministry of Education and Training, POB 781, Honiara; tel. 21426; f. 1979; British Solomon Islands Protectorate records 1900–78, Solomon Islands Government records since 1978; collections of records, microfilm, film and sound recordings on Solomon Islands and Western Pacific; Government Archivist JOSEPH P. WALE.

Solomon Islands National Library: POB 165, Ministry of Education and Training, Honiara; tel. 21601; fax 25366; f. 1974; 120,000 vols; Solomon Islands collection and central reference collection; Dir WALTER HUBERTS-RHEIN; publ. *Solomon Islands National Library Newsletter*.

Museum

Honiara

Solomon Islands National Museum and Cultural Centre: POB 313, Honiara; tel. 22309; fax 23351; part of Dept of Culture, Tourism and Aviation; collection began in 1950s, permanent site 1969; research into all aspects of Solomons culture (pre-history, language, oral tradition, music, dance, architecture, etc.); promotes traditional crafts, music and dance; Dir LAWRENCE FOANAOTA; publs *Journal*, *Custom Stories*, *Taem bifo Newsletter*.

Colleges

Solomon Islands College of Higher Education: POB R113, Honiara; tel. 30111; fax 30390; e-mail siche@solomon.com.sb; f. 1984; library: 2,500 vols; 135 teachers; 1,200 students; Dir G. TALOIKWAI; Registrar LUCIEN KII

HEADS OF SCHOOLS

Education: PATRICIA RODI
Finance and Administration: JOHN IPO
Humanities and Science: NORMAN HATIGEVA (acting)
Industrial Development: DONALD DUNA
Marine and Fisheries Studies: Capt. STARLING DAEFA
Natural Resources: ALEX MAKINI (acting)
Nursing: VEZERLYN ISOM (acting)

University of the South Pacific Solomon Islands Centre: POB 460, Honiara; tel. 21307; fax 21287; e-mail galo_g@usp.ac.fj; f. 1971; responsible for providing USP courses through extension; developing national continuing education courses; promoting research on subjects of national interest; library: 9,000 vols; 4 teachers; 600 students (mostly distance-learning); Dir GLYNN GALO.

SOMALIA

The Higher Education System

The union of former British and Italian Somaliland took effect in 1960, when the independent Somali Republic (Somalia) was proclaimed. In 1954 the Italian Government established institutes of law, economics and social studies, and in 1969 these institutions were incorporated into the National University of Somalia. However, in the early 1990s the campus of the National University of Somalia in Mogadishu was largely destroyed during civil war. In 1997 Mogadishu University was established as a private institution due to lack of government funding. Until mid-2005 the Somali Government was based in Nairobi, Kenya, for security reasons; hence there was no direct government control over higher education prior to this. Two universities have been founded in Somaliland, Amoud University and the University of Hargeisa.

The Secondary School Certificate is the main requirement for admission to higher education; other criteria include two years' national youth service and a competitive entrance examination. The Bachelors (Laurea) is the main undergraduate degree, and lasts four years. There are numerous institutions of professional education offering post-secondary vocational and technical qualifications.

Research Institutes

MEDICINE

Institute for the Preparation of Serums and Vaccines: Mogadishu.

Laboratory of Hygiene and Prophylaxis: Mogadishu; sections of medicine and chemistry.

NATURAL SCIENCES

Physical Sciences

Geological Survey Department: Ministry of Water Development and Mineral Resources, POB 744, Mogadishu; library of 500 vols; Dir V. N. KOZERENKO.

Libraries and Archives

Mogadishu

National Library of Somalia: POB 1754, Mogadishu; tel. (1) 22758; f. 1970; research, legal deposit; 30,000 vols, 75 periodicals; training in library science; Dir HASSAN NOOR FARAH.

Somali Institute of Public Administration Library: Mogadishu.

Museum

Mogadishu

Somali National Museum: Corso Republica, POB 6917, Mogadishu; tel. 21041; f. 1934; ethnographical, historical and natural science collections; library of 3,000 vols; Dir AHMED FARAH.

Universities

AMOUD UNIVERSITY

Borama, Awdal
Internet: www.amoud-university.borama.ac .so
Private control
President: Prof. SULEIMAN AHMED GULAID

Vice President (External Affairs): Prof. ABDILLAHI HASHI ABIB
1st Vice-President (Planning) and Registrar: Prof. AHMED HASHI ABIB
2nd Vice-President (Academic and Students): prof. AHMED A. BOQORE
Librarian: QABUL NUH ALI

Library: main campus library: 65,000 vols, all subjects; Borama City campus: 30,000 vols, all subjects; medical and allied health sciences library of 20,000 vols

DEANS

Agriculture and Environmental Sciences: Prof. ABUBAKAR SH. ABDI
Business and Public Administration: Prof. HASSAN OMAR HALAS
Education: Prof. FARAH ABDILLAHI FARID
Medicine and Allied Health Sciences: Dr SAEED WALHAD

SOMALI NATIONAL UNIVERSITY

POB 15, Mogadishu
Telephone: (1) 80404
Founded 1954, University status 1969
Languages of instruction: Somali, Arabic, Italian, English
Rector: MOHAMED GANNI MOHAMED
Vice-Rector for Academic Affairs: MOHAMED ELMI BULLALE
Registrar: NUREYN SHEIKH ABRAR
Librarian: Mrs SIRAD YUSUF ISMAIL

Number of teachers: 549
Number of students: 4,640

DEANS

Faculty of Agriculture: MOHAMED ALI MOHAMED
Faculty of Economics: MOHAMED ISMAIL SHEIKH
Faculty of Education: HUSSEIN MUSA ALI
Faculty of Engineering: ABDULLAHI JIMALE MOHAMED
Faculty of Geology: MOHAMMOUD ABDI ARUSH
Faculty of Industrial Chemistry: AHMED MAYE ABDURAHMAN
Faculty of Islamic and Arabic Studies: SHARIF MOHAMED ALI ISAAK

Faculty of Journalism: MOHAMOUD ISMAIL ABDIRAHMAN
Faculty of Languages: (vacant)
Faculty of Law: ABUD MUSAD ABUD
Faculty of Medicine: ABDI AHMED FARAH
Faculty of Political Science: ADEN ABDULLAHI NUR
Faculty of Technical Teacher Education: ABDULLAHI MOHAMUD WARSAMME
Faculty of Veterinary Medicine: ABDULHAMID HAJI MOHAMED
Somali Institute of Development Administration and Management: IBRAHIM MOHAMUD ABYAN

UNIVERSITY OF HARGEISA

University Avenue Rd, Hargeisa
Telephone: (2) 422166
E-mail: contact@hargeisauniversity.net
Internet: www.hargeisauniversity.net
Founded 2000
Private control
Academic year: September to July, 2 semesters
Vice-Pres. for Admin.: MOHAMED MOHAMOUD FARAH
Registrar: YUSUF AINAB
Library of 15,000 vols.

Colleges

School of Industrial Studies: Mogadishu; departments of radio, carpentry, mechanics, electricity, building construction.

School of Islamic Disciplines: Mogadishu; includes a faculty of law.

School of Public Health: Mogadishu.

School of Seamanship and Fishing: Mogadishu; 170 students.

Technical College: Burgo; f. 1965; 4-year courses.

Veterinary College: Mogadishu; 30 students; 10 teachers; Projects Dir Dr J. NEILSEN.

SOUTH AFRICA

The Higher Education System

Higher education institutions predate the formation of the Union of South Africa in 1910, with the oldest being University of Cape Town (formerly South African College), which was founded in 1829. The development of the higher education system in the 20th century was affected by the 'apartheid' (segregation) laws imposed by the National Party in the period 1948–91, which resulted in the emergence of historically 'white' and 'black' universities and technikons (tertiary education institutions offering technological and commercial vocational training). In 1986 the 'quota clause' of the governing Universities Act was abolished and institutions were free to admit students regardless of race or ethnicity; by 1991 all the apartheid laws had been repealed. In 1999 there were 21 universities and 15 technikons. In 2002 it was announced that the number of universities was to be reduced to 11, the number of technikons reduced to six, and that four comprehensive institutions and two national higher education institutes would be created. These changes were implemented during 2004–05. In 2004 there were 744,488 students enrolled in 29 public institutions of higher education.

Higher education is principally funded by the Government and administered by the Ministry of Education, under the terms of Higher Education Act (1997). The government of a University is the duty of the Council, which comprises senior officers, such as the Vice-Chancellor, staff representatives, students, alumni and local government officials, among others. The Senate is the supreme academic body, and is made up of Heads of Department and Professors. Faculty Boards are subordinate to the Senate. The Vice-Chancellor, Rector or Principal is the chief executive officer. The government budget and students' tuition fees are the main sources of higher education funding.

The Senior Certificate is being phased out in favour of the National School Certificate as the main criteria for admission to higher education; this process is expected to be completed by 2009. Undergraduate admissions are administered by the Matriculation Board of the South African Universities Vice Chancellors Association. The main undergraduate degree is the 'Ordinary' or 'Honours' Bachelors, which is often a three-year programme of study, although some professionally-related fields of study, such as architecture, dentistry and medicine, last upwards of five years. A Bachelors with 'Honours' is required for admission to the postgraduate Masters degree, a one- or two-year course of research. Finally, the Doctorate is the highest university degree, and requires a minimum research period of two years after the award of the Masters.

Tertiary-level technical and vocational education is principally offered by the technikons. In addition to non-university Certificates and Diplomas, the technikons offer university-level degrees with a professional or technical focus. The Bachelors of Technology is a four-year undergraduate degree, the Masters of Technology is a one-year postgraduate research degree and the Doctor of Technology is a two-year research project following the award of the Masters of Technology.

Regulatory and Representative Bodies

GOVERNMENT

Ministry of Arts and Culture: Private Bag X899, Pretoria 0001; 481 Church St, 10th Floor, cnr Church and Beatrix Sts, Kingsley Centre, Arcadia, Pretoria; tel. (12) 32440968; fax (12) 3242687; e-mail sandile.memela@dac .gov.za; internet www.dac.gov.za; Minister Dr Z. PALLO JORDAN.

Ministry of Education: Private Bag X895, Pretoria, 0001; Sol Plaatje House, 123 Schoeman St, Pretoria 0002; tel. (12) 3125911; fax (12) 3256260; e-mail webmaster@doe.gov.za; internet www.education.gov.za; Minister G. NALEDI PANDOR.

ACCREDITATION

Council for Quality Assurance in General and Further Education and Training: Post Net Suite 102, Private Bag X 1, Queenswood, Pretoria 0120; 37 General Van Ryneveld St, Persequor Techno Park, Pretoria; tel. (12) 349-1510; fax (12) 349-1511; e-mail info@umalusi.org.za; internet www .umalusi.org.za; monitors and improves the quality of gen. and further education and training in SA; CEO PELIWE LOLWANA.

Higher Education Quality Committee: POB 13354, The Tramshed, Pretoria 0126; Didacta Bldg, 211 Skinner St, Pretoria 0001; tel. (12) 392-9100; fax (12) 392-9110; e-mail admin@che.ac.za; internet www.che.ac.za/ heqc/heqc.php; the HEQC is in the process of implementing new audit and accreditation systems as well as supporting capacity devt in a number of areas; Exec. Dir Dr LIS LANGE (acting).

NATIONAL BODIES

Council on Higher Education: POB 13354, The Tramshed, Pretoria 0126; Didacta Bldg, 211 Skinner St, Pretoria 0001; tel. and fax (12) 392-9100; e-mail admin@che.ac.za; internet www.che.ac.za; f. 1998; aims to contribute to the devt of a higher education system characterized by quality and excellence, equity, responsiveness to economic and social devt needs, and effective and efficient provision, governance and management; CEO Dr MALA SINGH.

Higher Education South Africa: POB 27392, Sunnyside, Pretoria 0132; UNISA Sunnyside Campus, Bldg 3, Level 1, cnr Rissik and Mears St, Sunnyside, Pretoria; tel. (12) 481-2842; fax (12) 481-2843; e-mail admin@hesa.org.za; internet www.hesa.org .za; f. 2005; works to enhance the role and contribution of higher education in society; aims to contribute to nat. devt goals through critical enquiry, and scholarly and intellectual leadership; 23 mems (public univs and univs of technology); CEO Prof. DUMA MALAZA.

International Education Association of South Africa: POB 65099, Reservoir Hills, Durban 4090; Room 413, 4th Floor, Rick Turner Student Union, Univ. of Natal, King George V Ave, Durban 4041; tel. (31) 260-3077; fax (31) 260-2136; e-mail aieasa@ukzn .ac.za; internet www.ukzn.ac.za/ieasa; f. 1997; advocates, promotes and supports the internationalization of higher education by providing a professional forum for instns and individuals to address challenges and develop opportunities in int. education; Pres. FAZELA HANIFF; Exec. Dir Dr ROSHEN KISHUN.

Matriculation Board: POB 3854, Pretoria 0001; Ground Floor, Bldg 3, Unisa Sunnyside North Campus, cnr Rissik and Mears St, Sunnyside, Pretoria; tel. (12) 481-2848; fax (12) 481-2922; e-mail exemption@hesa-enrol .ac.za; internet www.hesa-enrol.ac.za/mb; f. 1997; advisory cttee on minimum gen. univ. admission requirements to Higher Education South Africa; 19 mems; Chair. HUGH AMOORE (acting).

National Association of Distance Education and Open Learning in South Africa (NADEOSA): POB 31822, Braamfontein, Johannesburg 2017; tel. (11) 403-2813; fax (11) 403-2814; e-mail info@saide.org.za; internet www.nadeosa.org.za; f. 1996; 55 mem. orgs; Pres. OUPA MASHILE.

South African Universities' Vice-Chancellors' Association: POB 27392, Sunnyside 0132; tel. (12) 481-2842; fax (12) 481-2843; e-mail admin@sauvca.org.za; internet ww.sauvca.org.za; f. 1955 as Committee of Univ. Principals, present name 1998; 21 mems; Chief Exec. PIYUSHI KOTECHA; publ. IZWI (quarterly).

Learned Societies

GENERAL

Royal Society of South Africa: P. D. Hahn Bldg, POB 594, Cape Town 8000; tel. (21) 650-2543; fax (21) 650-2710; e-mail roysoc@ science.uct.ac.za; internet www.rssa.uct.ac .za; f. 1877 to advance all aspects of science; Royal Charter 1908; 490 mems (193 fellows, 40 hon. foreign fellows, 257 ordinary mems);

library of 33,000 vols of scientific periodicals; Pres. Prof. D. E. RAWLINGS; Gen. Sec. Prof. R. L. CHRISTIE; Foreign Sec. Prof. M. N. BRUTON; publ. *Transactions* (annually).

South African Academy of Science and Arts/Suid-Afrikaanse Akademie vir Wetenskap en Kuns: Private Bag X11, Arcadia, Pretoria 0007; tel. (12) 328-5082; fax (12) 328-5091; e-mail akademie@akademie.co.za; internet www.akademie.co.za; f. 1909 for the promotion of science, technology, arts and the Afrikaans language; 1,000 mems; Chair. Prof. T. ERASMUS; Sec. Prof. L. R. MCFARLANE; publs *Nuusbrief* (2 a year), *SA Tydskrif vir Natuurwetenskappe en Tegnologie* (4 a year), *Tydskrif vir Geesteswetenskappe* (4 a year).

AGRICULTURE, FISHERIES AND VETERINARY SCIENCE

South African Society for Animal Science/Suid-Afrikaanse Vereniging vir Veekunde: POB 13884, Hatfield, Pretoria 0028; tel. (12) 420-5017; fax (12) 420-3290; e-mail secretary@sasas.co.za; internet www.sasas.co.za; f. 1961 to advance animal science and promote viable animal production systems; 400 mems; Pres. P. BEVAN; Sec. Prof. J. B. J. VAN RYSSEN; publ. *South African Journal of Animal Science* (4 a year).

South African Society of Dairy Technology: POB 1853, Silverton 01217; tel. (12) 804-0818; fax (12) 804-9692; e-mail dairy-foundation@pixie.co.za; f. 1967; 400 mems; Pres. A. P. DE KLERK; Sec. Y. E. STEYN.

Southern African Institute of Forestry/Suider-Afrikaanse Instituut van Boswese: Postnet Suite 329, P/Bag X4, Menlo Park 0102; tel. (12) 348-1745; fax (12) 348-1745; e-mail forestry@mweb.co.za; internet www.saif.org.za; f. 1937; aims to collect and publish information on all aspects of forestry, to conserve the forest estate, to encourage the practice of scientific forestry, to create a forum for discussion of topics related to forestry; 560 mems; Chair. G. MARAIS; Sec.-Treas. C. VILJOEN; publ. *Southern African Forestry Journal* (3 a year).

ARCHITECTURE AND TOWN PLANNING

South African Institute of Architects: Private Bag X10063, Randburg 2125; Bouhof, 31 Robin Hood Rd, Robindale, Randburg; tel. (11) 782-1315; fax (11) 782-8771; e-mail admin@saia.org.za; internet www.saia.org.za; f. 1996 by merger of existing organisations; 2,380 mems; Exec. Officer S. LINNING; publs *Architecture South Africa* (6 a year), *Digest of South African Architecture* (annually).

BIBLIOGRAPHY, LIBRARY SCIENCE AND MUSEOLOGY

Library and Information Association of South Africa (LIASA): POB 1598, Pretoria 0001; Vista Campus, 263 Skinner St, Pretoria Central; tel. (12) 337-6129; fax (12) 337-6108; e-mail liasa@liasa.org.za; internet www.liasa.org.za; f. 1997 by merger of existing organizations; 3,000 mems; Pres. TOMMY MATTHEE; Chair. DORA ACKERMANN; publ. *LIASA-In-Touch* (4 a year); publ. *LIASA News* (4 a year); publ. *South African Journal of Libraries and Information Science* (2 a year).

Southern African Museums Association: POB 15899, Emerald Hill, Port Elizabeth 6011; tel. (41) 366-1751; fax (86) 503-4521; e-mail sama@futurserve.co.za; internet www.samaweb.org.za; f. 1936; 400 mems incl. 150 institutional mems; Pres. BEVERLEY THOMAS; National Office Mgr MARC CATTANEO; publs *Samab Bulletin* (annual), *Samantics* (quarterly).

ECONOMICS, LAW AND POLITICS

Economic Society of South Africa: Department of Economics, University of South Africa, POB 302, Pretoria 0001; tel. (11) 429-4878; internet www.essa.org.za; f. 1925 to promote the thorough discussion of and research into economic questions, in particular those affecting South Africa; 550 mems, incl. 6 honorary mems, 14 life members; 22 foreign members; brs in Bloemfontein, Cape Town, Eastern Cape, Johannesburg, Kwazulu-Natal, Limpopo, North-West, Pretoria and Stellenbosch; Pres. Prof. ELSABÉ LOOTS; publ. *The South African Journal of Economics* (quarterly).

Institute of Bankers in South Africa: POB 61420, Marshalltown 2107; 1st Fl., Sunnyside Ridge Bldg, Sunnyside Office Park, 32 Princess of Wales Terrace, Parktown; tel. (11) 481-7000; fax (11) 484-8716; e-mail iobinfo@iob.co.za; internet www.iob.co.za; f. 1904; 20,000 mems; Chief Exec. PHIL MNISI; Pres. T. A. BOARDMAN; publ. *South African Banker* (quarterly).

South African Institute of International Affairs: POB 31596, Braamfontein, Johannesburg 2017; Jan Smuts House, East Campus, University of the Witwatersrand, Johannesburg; tel. (11) 339-2021; fax (11) 339-2154; e-mail saiiagen@global.co.za; internet www.saiia.org.za; f. 1934 to promote understanding of international issues among South Africans; 3,500 mems; library: Jan Smuts Library; 10,000 books, 2,000 journals; spec. collns incl. UN depository colln, World Bank regional depository library, Martin Edmonds colln; Chair. of the Nat. Council FRED PHASWANA; Nat. Dir ELIZABETH SIDIROPOULOS; publs *eAfrica* (online, monthly), *SADC Barometer* (online, monthly), *South African Foreign Policy Monitor* (online, 6 a year)), *South African Journal of International Affairs* (2 a year), *South African Yearbook of International Affairs*.

FINE AND PERFORMING ARTS

Federasie van Afrikaanse Kultuurvereniginge (Association of Afrikaans Cultural Societies): POB 73169, Lynnwoodrif 0040; Gerard Moerdyk-huis, Voortrekkermonumentterrein Eeufeesweg, Pretoria; tel. (12) 326-8646; fax (12) 326-9171; e-mail fak@mweb.co.za; internet www.fak.org.za; f. 1929; 2,300 affiliated socs; Chair. Prof. DANIE GOOSEN; Dir Dr CAREL STANDER; publ. *Handhaaf Newsletter* (3 a year).

South African National Association for the Visual Arts (SANAVA): POB 6188, Pretoria 0001; tel. (12) 460-5862; fax (12) 323-1275; f. 1851 as the Cape Fine Arts Society; became the South African Fine Arts Asscn in 1871; became the South African Asscn of Arts in 1945; mem. of Int. Asscn of Art; present name 1998; encourages visual arts nationally and internationally; 23 autonomous brs with individual galleries, management cttees, as well as 22 affiliated orgs; 5,500 mems; Nat. Pres. ANTON LOUBSER; Vice-Pres LYNETTE DEN KROODEN, HELEN WELDRICK; Hon. Consultant for Social Devt AVITHA SOOFUL; Treas. BASIE BOTHA.

HISTORY, GEOGRAPHY AND ARCHAEOLOGY

Genealogical Society of South Africa: Suite 143, Postnet X2600, Houghton 2041; internet www.ggsa.info; f. 1964 to promote and facilitate interest in genealogy and family history; brs in Pretoria, Cape Town, Johannesburg, Western Gauteng, Vanderbijlpark, Bloemfontein, Durban, Pietermar-

itzburg, Port Elizabeth; 900 mems; Pres. JOHANN JANSE VAN VUUREN; Sec. MARILYN COETZEE; publ. *Familia* (4 a year).

Nederlands Cultuurhistorisch Instituut: University of Pretoria, Pretoria 0002; tel. (12) 420-2808; fax (12) 362-5100; e-mail malanc@ais.up.ac.za; internet www.up.ac.za; f. 1931; offers books and information on Dutch culture, history and art; 250 mems; library of 32,000 vols; Dir Prof. J. A. BOON.

Society of South African Geographers: Department of Geography (53), POB 339, University of the Free State, Bloemfontein 9301; tel. (51) 401-2184; fax (51) 401-3816; e-mail bitss.sci@mail.uovs.ac.za; internet www.ssag.co.za; f. 1994 by merger of existing organizations; 400 mems; Pres. Prof. M. E. MEADOWS; Hon. Sec. Lt-Col J. A. JACOBS; publ. *South African Geographical Journal* (2 a year).

South African Archaeological Society: POB 15700, Vlaeberg 8018; tel. (21) 481-3886; fax (21) 481-3993; e-mail archsoc@iziko.org.za; internet www.archaeology.org.za; f. 1945; 1,000 mems; library of 1,000 vols, 5,000 periodicals; Hon. Sec. J. DEACON; publs *The Digging Stick* (3 a year), *Goodwin Series* (irregular), *South African Archaeological Bulletin* (2 a year).

Van Riebeeck Society: POB 15151, Vlaeberg 8018; Located at: Centre for the Book, 82 Queen Victoria St, Cape Town, 8000; tel. (21) 423-8424; fax (21) 424-1484; e-mail vanriebk@mweb.co.za; internet www.vanriebeecksociety.co.za; f. 1918; 1,075 mems; publishes and republishes original and rare documents, books and pamphlets relating to the history of southern Africa; Chair. Prof. H. PHILLIPS; Sec. P. E. WESTRA.

LANGUAGE AND LITERATURE

Alliance Française: POB 72067, Parkview 2122; 17 Lower Park Dr., Cnr Kerry Rd, Johannesburg; tel. (11) 646-1169; fax (11) 646-4521; e-mail info@alliance.org.za; internet www.alliance.org.za; f. 1936; offers courses and exams in French language and culture and promotes cultural exchange with France; attached teaching centres in Bloemfontein, Bosmont, Cape Town, Diepkloof, Durban, East London, Florida Hills, Klersdorp, Lowveld, Mitchell's Plain, Nelspruit, Parkview, Pietermaritzburg, Port Elizabeth, Potchefstroom, Pretoria, Somerset West, Soweto, Stellenbosch, Vaal Triangle, Vanderbiljpark, Vlaeberg and Welkom; also responsible for Alliance Française operations in Botswana, Lesotho and Swaziland.

British Council: Ground Fl., Forum 1, Braampark, 33 Hoofd St, Braamfontein, Johannesburg; tel. (860) 01-22-33; fax (860) 10-35-25; e-mail information@britishcouncil.org.za; internet www.britishcouncil.org/southafrica; offers courses and exams in English language and British culture and promotes cultural exchange with the UK; attached offices in Johannesburg (teaching centre), Cape Town and Durban; responsible for British Council activities in Botswana, Lesotho, Malawi, Mauritius, Mozambique, Namibia, Swaziland, Zambia and Zimbabwe; Regional Dir, Southern Africa ROSEMARY ARNOTT; Dir of Operations, South Africa DAVID HIGGS.

Classical Association of South Africa: c/o Academia Latina, University of Pretoria, Pretoria 0002; tel. (12) 420-2368; fax (12) 420-4008; internet www.casa-kvsa.org.za; f. 1965 to promote the study and appreciation of classical antiquity; 350 mems; Chair. J. L. HILTON; Sec. M. R. DIRCKSEN; publs *Acta Classica* (annually), *Akroterion* (annually).

English Academy of Southern Africa:
POB 124, WITS, Johannesburg 2050; tel.
(11) 717-9339; fax (11) 717-9339; e-mail
englishacademy@societies.wits.ac.za; internet www.englishacademy.co.za; f. 1961; concerned with all forms and uses of English;
promotes education, research and debate;
organizes lectures and promotes creative,
critical and scholarly talents of users of
English in Southern Africa; awards the
English Academy Medal, the Olive Schreiner
Prize, the Thomas Pringle Awards, the Percy
FitzPatrick Prize, and the Sol Plaatje Prize
for Translation; 306 mems (270 full mems, 30
associate mems and 6 corporate mems); Pres.
ROSEMARY GRAY; Hon. Sec. R. V. SHARMAN;
publ. *The English Academy Review*
(annually).

Goethe-Institut: 119 Jan Smuts Ave, Parkwood 2193, Johannesburg; tel. (11) 442-3232;
fax (11) 442-3738; e-mail info@johannesburg
.goethe.org; internet www.goethe.de/af/joh/
enindex.htm; offers courses and exams in
German language and culture and promotes
cultural exchange with Germany; attached
centre in Cape Town; library of 2,300 vols, 70
periodicals; Dir and Regional Dir for Sub-Saharan Africa Dr BERND PIRRUNG.

South African PEN Centre: POB 732,
Constantia 7848; f. 1960; 70 full and 30
associate mems; Sec. DEBORAH HORN-BOTHA;
publ. *Newsletter*.

MEDICINE

**Association of Surgeons of South Africa/
Chirurgiese Vereniging van Suid-
Africa:** POB 1105, Johannesburg, Cramerview 2132; tel. (11) 706-4815; fax (11) 463-1041; e-mail surgicom@worldonline.co.za;
internet www.surgeon.co.za; f. 1945; 250
mems; Pres. Prof. M. R. Q. DAVIES; Chair.
Dr S. S. PILLAY; publ. *South African Journal
of Surgery*.

Colleges of Medicine of South Africa: 17
Milner Rd, Rondebosch 7700; tel. (21) 689-9533; fax (21) 685-3766; e-mail admin@
colmedsa.co.za; internet www.collegemedsa
.ac.za; f. 1954; provides postgraduate examinations in all branches of medicine for all
doctors and dentists in South Africa; 9,000
mems; library: small archive and reference
library; CEO and Sec. BERNISE BOTHMA; publ.
Transactions (2 a year).

Nutrition Society of Southern Africa:
POB 1697, Brits 0250; tel. (82) 667-4723;
fax (12) 521-3510; e-mail info@
nutritionsociety.co.za; internet www
.nutritionsociety.co.za; f. 1955 to advance the
scientific study of nutrition; 235 mems; Pres.
Prof. ESTÉ VORSTER; Chair. Dr MARIUS SMUTS;
Sec. P. M. N. KUZWAYO; publ. *The South
African Journal of Food Science and Nutrition*.

South African Medical Association: Private Bag X1, Pinelands 7430, Cape Town;
Block F, Castle Walk, Office Park, Nossob St,
Erasmuskloof Ext 3, Pretoria; tel. (21) 481-2000; fax (21) 481-2100; e-mail publishing@
samedical.org; internet www.samedical.org;
f. 1998 from existing organizations; 16,000
mems; professional organization for medical
practitioners in South Africa; Pres. Dr LASIE
MOGUDI; Chair. Dr KGOSIETSILE LETLAPE;
publs *Continued Medical Education*
(monthly), *South African Medical Journal*
(monthly).

South African Pharmacology Society:
Box 16, Pharmacology, North-West University, Potchefstroom 2520; tel. (18) 299-4015;
fax (18) 293-5219; e-mail office@sapharmacol
.co.za; internet www.sapharmacol.co.za; f.
1966; 154 mems; Pres. Prof. DOUGLAS OLIVER;
Sec. Prof. TIAAN BRINK.

**South African Society of Obstetricians
and Gynaecologists:** Dept of Obstetrics
and Gynaecology, POB 339, Bloemfontein
9300; tel. (51) 405-3444; fax (51) 444-2660;
internet www.sasog.co.za; f. 1946; 571 mems;
Pres. Prof. F. GUIDOZZI; Sec. Dr M. PILLAY.

NATURAL SCIENCES
General

**Associated Scientific and Technical
Societies of South Africa:** POB 93480,
Yeoville 2143; Located at: 18A Gill St,
Observatory 2198; tel. (11) 487-1512; fax
(11) 648-1876; e-mail asts@global.co.sa; f.
1920; to promote the interests of scientific,
professional and technical societies; to
advance the knowledge of scientific and
technical subjects; to assist in raising the
standard of mathematics and science for
underprivileged scholars; to raise awareness
of career prospects in technology; and to
provide secretarial, liaison, and meeting
facilities, etc., for its member societies;
60,000 mems in 51 mem. socs; Pres. A. S.
MEYER; Man. ERROL H. VAN ROOY; publ.
Annual Proceedings.

**Southern Africa Association for the
Advancement of Science:** POB 366, Irene
0062; tel. and fax (12) 667-2544; e-mail s2a3@
global.co.za; internet s2a3.up.ac.za; f. 1902;
76 mems; Pres. Dr I. RAPER; Hon. Sec. S. A.
KORSMAN.

Biological Sciences

BirdLife South Africa: POB 515, Randburg 2125, Johannesburg; 239 Barkston
Drive, Blairgowrie, Johannesburg; tel. (11)
789-1122; fax (11) 789-5188; e-mail info@
birdlife.org.za; internet www.birdlife.org.za;
f. 1930; 6,000 mems; Pres. Prof. LES UNDER-
HILL; Dir Prof. GERHARD VERDOORN; publs
Africa Birds and Birding (6 a year), *Ostrich*
(quarterly).

Botanical Society of South Africa: Private Bag X10, Claremont 7735; tel. (21) 797-2090; fax (21) 797-2376; e-mail info@
botanicalsociety.org.za; internet www
.botanicalsociety.org.za; f. 1913; 15,000
mems; aims to promote the conservation,
cultivation, wise use and study of the
indigenous flora of southern Africa; Pres.
Adv. A. B. MEIRING; Dir Dr BRUCE MCKENZIE;
publ. *Veld & Flora* (quarterly).

Herpetological Association of Africa:
Dept of Herpetology, National Museum,
POB 266, Bloemfontein 9300; e-mail herp@
nasmus.co.za; internet www.wits.ac.za/haa;
promotes the study and conservation of
reptiles and amphibians, especially African
species; Chair. MICHAEL F. BATES; Sec. ROSE
SEPHTON-POULTNEY; publs *African Herp
News*, *African Journal of Herpetology*.

**South African National Biodiversity
Institute:** Head Office: Private Bag X101,
Pretoria 0001; tel. (12) 843-5000; fax (12)
804-3200; e-mail info@sanbi.org; internet
www.sanbi.org; f. 1913 as the Nat. Botanical
Institute; present name 2004; promotes the
conservation, sustainable use and appreciation of South Africa's biodiversity; library:
libraries at Pretoria and Kirstenbosch with
15,500 vols; Chief Exec. SUNJIT SINGH (acting); publs *Bothalia* (2 a year), *Strelitzia*
(irreg.), *Flowering Plants of Africa* (2 a year).

**South African Society of Biochemistry
and Molecular Biology:** c/o Dept of Biochemistry, Microbiology and Biotechnology,
Rhodes Univ,. Grahamstown 6140; tel. (46)
603-8262; fax (46) 622-3984; e-mail g.blatch@
ru.ac.za; internet www.sasbmb.org.za; f.
1973; 450 mems; Pres. Prof. GREG BLATCH;
Sec. FOURIE JOUBERT; publ. *SASBMB Newsletter* (2 a year).

**Southern African Society of Aquatic
Scientists:** c/o Dr V. Wepener, Department
of Zoology, RAU, POB 524, Auckland Park
2006; tel. (11) 341-1111; fax (11) 341-1349;
internet www.dwaf.gov.za/iwqs/sasaqs; f.
1964 as Limnological Society of South Africa;
holds annual congresses and general meetings; 250 mems; Pres. Prof. DIGBY CYRUS;
Hon. Sec. Dr RODNEY OWEN; publs *African
Journal of Aquatic Science*, *Newsletter* (4–6 a
year).

South African Society for Microbiology:
Dept of Biotechnology, University of the Free
State, POB 339, Bloemfontein 9300; tel. (51)
401-2223; fax (51) 444-3219; e-mail albertynj
.sci@mail.co.za; internet www.sasm.za.net;
420 mems; Pres. Dr KOOS ALBERTYN; Sec.
Dr EVODIA SETATI.

**Southern African Wildlife Management
Association:** POB 217, Bloubergstrand
7436; tel. (21) 554-1297; fax (86) 672-9882;
e-mail elma@mweb.co.za; internet www
.sawma.co.za; f. 1970; 370 mems; Pres. Dr
CHRISTO MARAIS; Vice-Pres. and Treasurer
JULIUS KOEN; publs *Newsletter* (annual,
online), *South African Journal of Wildlife
Research*.

**Wildlife and Environment Society of
South Africa (WESSA):** 1 Karkloof Rd,
POB 394, Howick 3290; tel. (33) 330-3931;
fax (33) 330-4576; e-mail alisonk@wessa.co
.za; internet www.wildlifesociety.org.za; f.
1926; 11,000 mems; Chair. JOHN GREEN;
Hon. Treasurer JAMES PINNELL; publs *African
Wildlife* (in English, 4 a year), *EnviroKids* (in
English, 4 a year).

Physical Sciences

**Astronomical Society of Southern
Africa:** POB 9, Observatory 7935; tel. (21)
447-0025; e-mail assa@saao.ac.za; internet
assa.saao.ac.za; f. 1922; 250 mems; Dir T. P.
COOPER; Hon. Sec. L. SIMONE; publs *Monthly
Notes* (6 a year), *SkyGuide* (annual).

Geological Society of South Africa: POB
61809, Marshalltown 2107; Located at:
Chamber of Mines Bldg, 5th Fl., 5 Hollard
St, Marshalltown; tel. (11) 492-3370; fax (11)
492-3371; e-mail info@gssa.org.za; internet
www.gssa.org.za; f. 1895; promotes the study
of the earth sciences, facilitates the professional development of its members, and
advances the use of geoscience in the academic, professional, and public sectors; 2,300
mems, icl. 400 student mems; Exec Mgr
LEOPOLD BOSCH; publs *Geobulletin* (quarterly), *South African Journal of Geology*
(quarterly).

South African Chemical Institute: POB
407, Witwatersrand 2050; Humphrey Raikes
Bldg, Rm 500, Wits Campus, Witwatersrand;
tel. (11) 717-6741; fax (11) 717-6779; e-mail
saci@aurum.wits.ac.za; internet www.saci.co
.za; f. 1912; promotes chemistry and the
chemical industry in South Africa; 755
mems; Pres. Prof. TONY FORD; Vice-Pres.
Prof. NEIL COVILLE; publ. *South African
Journal of Chemistry* (quarterly).

South African Institute of Physics: Postnet Suite 228, Private Bag X10, Musgrave
4062; e-mail secretary@saip.org.za; internet
www.saip.org.za; f. 1955; 490 mems; Pres.
Prof. HARM MORAAL; Sec. JAYNIE PADAYECHEE.

RELIGION, SOCIOLOGY AND ANTHROPOLOGY

South African Institute of Race Relations: POB 31 044, Braamfontein, 2017
Johannesburg; tel. (11) 403-3600; fax (11)
403-3671; e-mail sairr@sairr.org.za; internet
www.sairr.org.za; f. 1929; research, publishing, bursary administration; library: J. H.
Hofmeyr Library specialising in South African current affairs incl. 120 journals, histor-

ical documents, statistics, biographies; Pres. H. GILIOMEE; Dir J. KANE-BERMAN; publs *Fast Facts* (monthly), *Frontiers of Freedom* (4 a year), *South Africa Survey* (annually), *Spotlight* (irregular).

TECHNOLOGY

Aeronautical Society of South Africa (AeSSA): POB 14717, Sinoville 0129; tel. and fax (12) 808-1359; internet www.aessa .org.za; f. 1911 to advance the growth and scientific study of aeronautics; merged with South African Institute of Aerospace Engineering and the Royal Division of AeSSA 2001, to form Royal Aeronautical Society of South Africa (RAeSSA); present name 2005 (while retaining Royal Division status); theoretical and practical research; offers advice, instruction and facilities for those studying the subject; organizes meetings, lectures, etc.; 20,000 mems; Chair. Dr ROB HURLIN; Hon. Sec. Dr C. LAW; publ. *Newsletter*.

Chartered Institute of Transport in Southern Africa: POB 95327, Grant Park 2051; tel. (11) 888-1813; fax (11) 782-8265; e-mail citsa@global.co.za; f. 1993; 700 mems; Pres. MALCOLM F. MITCHELL; Exec. Man. C. LARKIN; publs *CITSA Handbook* (annually), *Pegasus* (quarterly).

Institution of Certificated Mechanical and Electrical Engineers, South Africa: POB 93480, Yeoville 2143; 18 A Gill St, Observatory, Johannesburg 2198; tel. (11) 487-1683; fax (8667) 18533; e-mail icmee@ pixie.co.za; internet www.icmeesa.com; f. 1912; 1,444 mems; Pres. CHRIS SCHNEHAGE; Hon. Treasurer ROBBY HOLMWOOD; publ. *Vector Magazine* (monthly).

South African Institute of Agricultural Engineers/Suid-Afrikaanse Instituut van Landbou-Ingenieurs: POB 912-719, Silverton 0127; tel. (12) 804-1540; fax (12) 804-0753; f. 1964; 500 mems; meetings, lectures, symposia, etc.; awards study bursaries; Pres. Prof. P. W. L. LYNE; Sec. F. B. REINDERS; publs *Agricultural Engineering in South Africa* (annually), *Newsletter* (quarterly).

South African Institute of Assayers and Analysts: c/o The Secretary, South African Chemical Institute, POB 407, Witwatersrand 2050; e-mail saci@aurum.wits.ac.za; f. 1919 to uphold the status and interests of the profession of assaying in all its branches; attached to the South African Chemical Institute; 181 mems; Pres. J. W. BARNETT; publ. *Bulletin* (4 a year).

South African Institute of Electrical Engineers: POB 751253, Gardenview 2047; Innes House, 18A Gill St, Observatory, Johannesburg; tel. (11) 487-3003; fax (11) 487-3002; e-mail info@saiee.org.za; internet www.saiee.org.za; f. 1909; 6,000 mems; Pres. VIV CRONE; Hon. Treasurer LES JAMES; publs *Elektron* (11 a year), *Energize* (11 a year), *SAIEE Transactions* (4 a year).

South African Institute of Mining and Metallurgy: POB 61127, Marshalltown 2107; 5th Fl., Chamber of Mines Bldg, 5 Hollard St, Johannesburg; tel. (11) 834-1273; fax (11) 838-5923; e-mail carina@saimm.co .za; internet www.saimm.co.za; f. 1884; 3,000 mems; Pres. Dr WILLEM VAN NIEKERK; Man. CARINA REYNDERS; publ. *Journal* (6 a year).

South African Institution of Civil Engineering (SAICE): Private Bag X200, Halfway House 1685, Located at: Building 19, Thornhill Office Park, Bekker St, Vorna Valley, Midrand; tel. (11) 805-5947; fax (11) 805-5971; e-mail civilinfo@saice.org.za; internet www.civils.org.za; f. 1903; represents the civil engineering profession in

South Africa; 6,571 mems; Exec. Dir D. B. BOTHA; publs *Civil Engineering* (magazine, 11 a year), *Journal* (technical journal for research papers, 4 a year).

South African Institution of Mechanical Engineering: POB 511, Bruma 2026; tel. (11) 615-5660; fax (11) 388-5356; e-mail saimeche@iafrica.com; internet www .saimeche.org.za; f. 1892; 4,500 mems; Pres. Prof. H. L. T. JEFFERY; Hon. Treasurer G. BARBIC; publs *R&D Journal* (4 a year), *SA Mechanical Engineer* (monthly).

Research Institutes

GENERAL

Africa Institute of South Africa: POB 630, Pretoria 0001; Located at: Embassy House, cnr of Edmond St and Bailey Lane, Arcadia, Pretoria; tel. (12) 304-9760; fax (12) 323-8153; e-mail ai@ai.org.za; internet www .ai.org.za; f. 1960; applied research and the collection of information in the fields of politics, socio-economics, development and international relations on the African continent and its diaspora; Exec. Dir Dr EDDY MALOKA; publs *Africa Insight* (quarterly), *Inside AISA* (newsletter, every 2 months).

Council for Scientific and Industrial Research (CSIR): POB 395, Pretoria 0001; Located at: Meiring Naudé Rd, Brummeria, Pretoria; tel. (12) 841-2911; fax (12) 349-1153; e-mail query@csir.co.za; internet www .csir.co.za; f. 1945; directed and multi-disciplinary research in areas of biosciences, built environment, natural resources and the environment, defence, peace, safety and security, materials science and manufacturing; and in emerging research areas of nanotechnology, synthetic biology, and mobile autonomous intelligent systems; library: see Libraries and Archives; Pres. and CEO Dr SIBUSISO SIBISI; Chief Financial Officer CHRIS STURDY (acting); Group Exec. for Operations HOFFIE MAREE; Dir. Services RAYNOLD ZONDO; Group Exec. for Research and Development Outcomes and Strategic Human Capital Development KHUNGEKA NJOBE; publs *CSIR eNews* (every 2 months), *ScienceScope* (4–5 a year), research reports.

AGRICULTURE, FISHERIES AND VETERINARY SCIENCE

Agricultural Research Council: POB 8783, Pretoria 0001; 1134 Park St, Hatfield, Pretoria; tel. (12) 427-9700; fax (12) 342-3948; e-mail nkami@arc.agric.za; internet www.arc.agric.za; f. 1992; Pres. and CEO Dr N. TAU-MZAMANE.

Attached research institutes:

Agrimetrics Institute: Private Bag X640, Pretoria 0001; tel. (12) 342-9968; fax (12) 342-9969; interdisciplinary service of biometrical and datametrical input to all institutes of the Agricultural Research Council; planning of scientific experiments, analysis and interpretation of research results; datametric service for devt and application of scientific data and management of computer systems; Dir Dr PIET JOOSTE.

Animal Improvement Institute, Irene: ARC Livestock Division, Private Bag X2, Irene 0062; tel. (12) 672-9055; fax (12) 665-1550; e-mail andrew@arc.agric.za; internet www.arc.agric.za; research and devt in animal breeding and genetics; nutrition and food science; library of 10,000 vols; Dir Dr M. A. MAGADLELA.

Animal Nutrition and Animal Products Institute, Irene: Private Bag X2, Irene 1675; tel. (12) 672-9111; fax (12) 665-

1609; research and devt in animal nutrition, meat and dairy products; Dir Dr HEINZ MEISSNER.

Grain Crops Institute: Private Bag X1251, Potchefstroom 2520; tel. (18) 299-6100; fax (18) 294-7146; f. 1981; research on grain crops and oil and protein seeds; Dir Dr P. J. A. VAN DER MERWE.

ARC Infruitec-Nietvoorbij: Private Bag X5026, Stellenbosch 7599; tel. (21) 809-3100; fax (21) 809-3400; e-mail breedtk@ arc.agric.za; internet www.arc.agric.za; f. 1960; research on the cultivation and postharvest technology of deciduous fruit, on all aspects of cultivation of table, raisin and wine grapes, and on production of wine and brandy; library of 5,000 vols; Research Man. Dr JOHAN VAN ZYL.

Institute for Agricultural Engineering: Private Bag X519, Silverton 0127; tel. (12) 842-4000; fax (12) 804-0753; f. 1961; research on agricultural mechanization, farm structures, irrigation, resource conservation, energy, aquaculture and product processing; Dir Prof. TIMOTHY SIMALONGA.

Institute for Soil, Climate and Water: Private Bag X79, Pretoria 0001; tel. (12) 310-2500; fax (12) 323-1157; e-mail iscwinfo@arc.agric.za; f. 1902; soil science, agrometeorology, water utilization, remote sensing, analytical services; library of 10,000 vols; Research and Technology Man. Prof. T. SIMALENGAI.

Institute of Tropical and Subtropical Crops: Private Bag X11208, Nelspruit 1200; tel. (13) 753-2071; fax (13) 752-3854; f. 1926; research on fruit, cocoa, and exotic crops; Dir Dr JOHANN VAN ZYL.

Onderstepoort Institute for Exotic Diseases: Private Bag X6, Onderstepoort 0110; tel. (12) 529-9501; fax (12) 529-9543; diagnostic service and research on infectious diseases and production of foot-and-mouth vaccine; Dir Dr GAVIN THOMPSON.

Onderstepoort Veterinary Institute: Private Bag X5, Onderstepoort 0110, Pretoria; tel. (12) 529-9111; fax (12) 565-6573; f. 1908; research on animal diseases; production of vaccines; diagnostic service; library of 96,000 vols; Dir Dr DAAN VERWOERD; publ. *Onderstepoort Journal of Veterinary Research* (quarterly).

Plant Protection Research Institute: Private Bag X134, Pretoria 0001; tel. (12) 808-0952; fax (12) 808-1489; promotes economically and environmentally acceptable pest control and sustainable farming; research on invertebrates, fungi, bacteria and viruses; advisory service on aspects of biological control; library of 9,000 vols; Dir MIKE WALTERS.

Range and Forage Institute: Private Bag X05, Lynn East, Pretoria 0039; tel. (12) 841-9611; fax (12) 808-2155; research on sustainable livestock and rangeland management systems; Head Dr AIMIE AUCAMP.

Roodeplaat Vegetable and Ornamental Plant Institute: Private Bag X293, Pretoria 0001; tel. (12) 841-9611; fax (12) 808-0844; f. 1949; research on vegetables, and on cut flowers, pot plants and other ornamental plants; Dir Dr SONJA VENTER; publ. *Roodeplaat Bulletin*.

Small Grain Institute: Private Bag X29, Bethlehem 9700; tel. (58) 303-5686; fax (58) 303-3952; research on improvement and cultivation of small grain crops; Dir COBUS LE ROUX.

Tobacco and Cotton Research Institute: Private Bag X82075, Rustenburg 0300; tel. (142) 993150; fax (142) 993113;

basic and applied research on tobacco and cotton; Dir DEON JOUBERT.

Attached unit:

Plant Genetic Resources Unit: c/o The Division Manager, Private Bag X05, Lynn East 0039; tel. (12) 841-9716; fax (12) 808-1001; centralizes and co-ordinates plant genetic resources activities within the plant science institutes and liaises with regional and int. agencies; responsible for documenting Agricultural Research Council germplasm and for arranging safety base collection facilities; Man. Dr ROGER ELLIS.

MEDICINE

National Health Laboratory Service: POB 1038, Johannesburg 2000; Located at: 1 Modderfontein Rd, Sandringham, Johannesburg; tel. (11) 386-6000; fax (11) 386-6002; e-mail info@nhls.ac.za; internet www.nhls.ac.za; f. 1912, formerly South African Institute for Medical Research; national network of approx 250 regional pathology laboratories, situated in all provinces except KwaZulu-Natal; co-ordinates diagnostic pathology services, research, teaching, training and production of anti-snake sera, reagents and media; member institutions include the pathology departments and laboratories of the medical schools of the universities of the Witwatersrand, Pretoria, Cape Town, Free State and Transkei and the Medical University of South Africa; library of 17,500 vols, 250 periodical titles, 5,000 reprint titles of staff papers; Chair. of Board of Management SESI BALOYI; CEO JOHN ROBERTSON; Head of Dept of Anatomical Pathology Prof. A. PATTERSON; Head of Dept of Chemical Pathology (vacant); Head of Dept of Clinical Microbiology and Infectious Diseases Prof. A. DUSE; Head of Dept of Haematology Prof. WENDY STEVENS; Head of Dept of Human Genetics Prof. D. VILJOEN; Head of Dept of Immunology Prof. A. A. WADEE; Head of Dept of Medical Entomology Prof. M. COETZEE.

South African Brain Research Institute: 6 Campbell St, Waverley, Johannesburg 2090; tel. (11) 786-2912; fax (11) 786-1766; e-mail mag@iafrica.com; internet www.sabri.org.za; f. 1981; all aspects of pure and applied brain research; 12 mems; library of 10,000 vols; Exec. Dir Dr M. A. GILLMAN.

South African Medical Research Council: POB 19070, Tygerberg 7505; Located at: Francie van Zijl Drive, Parowvallei, Western Cape; tel. (21) 938-0911; fax (21) 938-0200; e-mail info@mrc.ac.za; internet www.mrc.ac.za; f. 1969; nat. research programmes: environment and development, health systems and policy, infection and immunity, molecules to disease, non-communicable diseases, and women and child health; Pres. Prof. ANTHONY MBEWU.

NATURAL SCIENCES

Biological Sciences

Municipal Botanic Gardens: 70 St Thomas Rd, Durban, KwaZulu-Natal; tel. (31) 201-1303; fax (31) 201-7382; e-mail sandig@prcsu.durban.gov.za; f. 1849, for the propagation, display and landscape of ornamental, exotic and southern African indigenous flora, and as a place for the study of and instruction in botany and horticulture and potential agricultural crops; extensive collections of orchids, cycads, palms and bromeliads; herb garden; garden for the blind; water lily pond, fern garden; indigenous medicinal plants; Dir Parks Dept G. H. KLOPPENBORG (acting); Curator, Durban Botanic Gardens C. G. M. DALZELL.

National Zoological Gardens of South Africa: POB 754, Pretoria 0001; Located at: 232 Boom St, Pretoria 0001; tel. (12) 328-3265; fax (12) 323-4540; e-mail zoologic@cis.co.za; internet www.zoo.ac.za; f. 1899; attached to National Research Foundation; library of 4,000 vols, 40 periodicals; CEO WILLIE LABUSCHAGNE; publ. *Zoön.*

Physical Sciences

Council for Geoscience: Private Bag X112, Pretoria 0001; Located at: 280 Pretoria St, Silverton, Pretoria 0001; tel. (12) 841-1911; fax (12) 841-1221; internet www.geoscience.org.za; f. 1912; applied and fundamental geological research, mapping; library of 200,000 books, 10,000 maps; CEO THIBEDI RAMONTJA; publs annual reports, bulletins, biographies, handbooks, *Groundwater Series*, *Memoirs*, *Seismological Series.*

Hartebeesthoek Radio Astronomy Observatory: POB 443, Krugersdorp 1740; tel. (12) 326-0742; fax (12) 326-0756; e-mail info@hartrao.ac.za; internet www.hartrao.ac.za; f. 1961, since 1988 a national facility under Foundation for Research Development (now National Research Foundation); radio telescope 26m in diameter used for observations of Local Galaxy, spectroscopy of interstellar and circumstellar atoms and molecules, masers, pulsars, quasars and active galaxies; collaborates in global VLBI Networks; library of 1,000 vols, 75 periodicals; Dir Prof. ROY BOOTH.

NECSA (South African Nuclear Energy Corporation): POB 582, Pretoria 0001; Located at: Church St W Extension, Pelindaba, Brits District; tel. (12) 305-4911; fax (12) 305-3111; e-mail info@necsa.co.za; internet www.necsa.co.za; f. 1982 as Atomic Energy Corporation of South Africa Ltd (AEC); 10 mems; operates UF6 conversion, fuel fabrication facilities, isotope production centre, hot cell facility and food radurization plant; enrichment research; operates 20 MW ORR type research reactor (SAFARI-1); 3.75 MV Van der Graaff accelerator; CEO Dr ROB ADAM.

Satellite Applications Centre: Division of Microelectronics and Communications Technology, CSIR, POB 395, Pretoria 0001; tel. (12) 334-5000; fax (12) 334-5001; e-mail webmaster@csir.co.za; internet www.sac.co.za; f. 1961 as part of US Satellite Tracking and Data Network; since 1975 part of CSIR; receives, archives and processes METEOSAT, LANDSAT, NOAA and SPOT data; on-line LANDSAT data catalogue; 45 staff; library: c. 500 vols, 30 periodicals; Operations Man. RAOUL HODGES; publ. *Remote Sensing Newsletter for South Africa.*

South African Astronomical Observatory: POB 9, Observatory 7935; outstation: POB 25, Sutherland 6920; tel. (21) 447-0025; fax (21) 447-3639; e-mail enquiries@saao.ac.za; internet www.saao.ac.za; f. 1972 by a merger of the Royal Observatory Cape of Good Hope and the Republic Observatory, Johannesburg; equipment incl. 11-, 1.9-, 1.0-, 0.75- and 0.5-m reflectors; library of 30,000 vols; Dir Prof. P. A. CHARLES.

RELIGION, SOCIOLOGY AND ANTHROPOLOGY

Human Sciences Research Council (HSRC): Private Bag X41, Pretoria 0001; Located at: 134 Pretorius St, Pretoria 0002; tel. (12) 302-2000; fax (12) 326-2001; e-mail rpcf@hsrc.ac.za; internet www.hsrc.ac.za; f. 1969; promotes, supports and co-ordinates research in the human sciences, advises the govt on research priorities, disseminates research findings, promotes the training of people for research work and makes avail-

able to all South Africans the full range of disciplines in the human sciences; Pres. and CEO Dr OLIVE SHISANA; publs *HSRC Annual Report*, *HSRC Review* (3 a year).

Institute for the Study of Mankind in Africa: School of Anatomical Sciences, University of the Witwatersrand Medical School, 7 York Rd, Parktown 2193; tel. (11) 647-2203; fax (11) 643-4318; e-mail kuykendallkl@anatomy.wits.ac.za; internet www.wits.ac.za/isma; f. 1960 to perpetuate the work of Prof. Raymond A. Dart on the study of mankind in Africa, past and present, in health and disease; serves as a centre of anthropological and medical field work; it functions partly through the auspices of the University of the Witwatersrand; Pres. Dr KEVIN KUYKENDALL.

TECHNOLOGY

MINTEK: PMB X3015, Randburg 2125; tel. (11) 709-4111; fax (11) 793-2413; e-mail info@mintek.ac.za; internet www.mintek.co.za; f. 1934; research, devt and technology transfer to promote mineral technology and to foster the establishment and expansion of industries in the fields of minerals and mineral products; investigates all aspects of mineral beneficiation, especially areas such as new alloys and chemical products; divs specializing in mineralogy, minerals eng., hydrometallurgy, pyrometallurgy, measurement and control, analytical science, physical metallurgy, analytical and process chemistry; sponsors univ. research groups; library of 30,000 vols; CEO Dr PAUL JOURDAN; publs *Mintek Bulletin* (monthly), *Research Reports* (irreg.).

South African Bureau of Standards: Private Bag X191, 1 Dr Lategan Rd, Groenkloof, Pretoria 0001; tel. (12) 428-7911; fax (12) 344-1568; e-mail info@sabs.co.za; internet www.sabs.co.za; f. 1945; draws up national standards, administers the SABS mark and listing schemes; Pres. M. J. KUSCUS (acting); publ. *Standards Bulletin: Official information* (online).

Libraries and Archives

Alice

University of Fort Hare Library: Private Bag X1322, Alice 5700; tel. (40) 602-2612; fax (40) 653-1423; f. 1916; 165,000 vols; contains the Howard Pim Library of Rare Books; University Librarian YOLISA K. SOUL.

Bloemfontein

Free State Library and Information Services: Private Bag X20606, Bloemfontein 9300; tel. (51) 405-4680; fax (51) 403-3567; e-mail jacomien@majuba.ofs.gov.za; internet mangaung.ofs.gov.za; f. 1948; 3,000,000 books; serves 135 public libraries; Dir T. A. LUBBE; publ. *Free State Libraries* (4 a year).

Mangaung Library Services: POB 1029, Bloemfontein, 9301; tel. (51) 405-8241; fax (51) 405-8604; e-mail mpumie@civic.mangaung.co.za; f. 1875; Legal Deposit, National Drama Library, and Public Library; 500,000 vols, 65,000 plays; Man., Education, Library, Arts and Culture N. L. MOHLAODI; publ. *Catalogue of the National Drama Library.*

University of the Free State Library and Information Services: POB 301, Blomfontein 9300; tel. (51) 401-3488; fax (51) 448-2879; e-mail crn.bib@mail.ufs.ac.za; internet www.ufs.ac.za; f. 1904; the colln includes rare pamphlets and other early South African pbls of the Dreyer-Africana Colln and items on the South African War; 576,000 vols (3,000 periodicals); Dir C. R. NAMPONYA.

Cape Town

Cape Town City Libraries: POB 4728, Cape Town 8000; tel. (21) 462-4400; fax (21) 461-5981; e-mail hheymann@ctcc.gov.za; f. 1952; free municipal public library service; central library and 32 suburban brs, travelling, hospital, old age homes, homebound library services; 1,500,000 vols; special art, music and business collections; Librarian H. C. F. HEYMANN; publ. *Annual Report*.

Library and Information Unit of Parliament: POB 18, Cape Town 8000; Located at: Ground Fl., NCOP Wing, Parliament St, Cape Town 8000; tel. (21) 403-2140; fax (21) 461-4331; e-mail library@parliament.gov.za; internet www.parliament.gov.za; f. 1857; provides general and legislative reference services and a press-cutting service to members and officers of Parliament; legal deposit library and depository for UN publs; 350,000 items, including the Mendelssohn Africana Collection; 2,700 current periodicals; local and foreign government and parliamentary publs; Librarian ALBERT NTUNJA.

Royal Society of South Africa Library: c/o University of Cape Town, Rondebosch 7700; f. 1877, Royal Charter 1908; 33,000 vols of scientific periodicals; Hon. Librarian Prof. J. R. E. LUTJEHARMS; publ. *Transactions of the Royal Society of South Africa* (irregular).

South African Library: POB 496, Cape Town 8000; 5 Queen Victoria St, POB 496, Cape Town 8000; tel. (21) 424-6320; fax (21) 423-3359; internet www.nlsa.ac.za; f. 1818; national reference and preservation library with legal deposit privileges; 750,000 books and official publs, 200,000 bound periodicals, 8,000 current periodicals, 45,000 bound newspapers, 300 current newspapers, 20,000 maps, 100,000 iconographic items; MS collections of Cape and early SA; comprehensive Africana collection pertaining to South Africa, with materials on neighbouring Southern African countries; UN and World Bank depository library; special collections incl. Grey Collection of 115 medieval MSS, 5,000 vols incl. incunabula and early South African imprints; Dessinian (17th–18th c.); Nourse Cromwelliana (17th c.); Fairbridge (19th c.); reference room for research; regular exhibitions of library material; microfilming, photographic and copying services; Dir JOHN KGWALE TSEBE; publs *Grey Bibliographies*, *Quarterly Bulletin*.

University of Cape Town Libraries: Private Bag X3, Rondebosch 7701; tel. (21) 650-3134; fax (21) 689-7568; e-mail selref@uctlib.uct.ac.za; internet www.lib.uct.ac.za; f. 1905; 1,062,000 vols, 34,000 periodicals; J. W. Jagger Linear Library and branches: African Studies (Southern Africa), Architecture, Botany (Bolus), Education, Fine Arts and Drama (Hiddingh Hall), Institute of Child Health, Jewish Studies, Law, Medical, Music; special collections incl. rare books (incl. fore-edge paintings, Kipling, pre-1925 Africana, Bolus (antiquarian botanical), history of medicine, Van Zyl (antiquarian legal works), material relating to the history of Cape Province (incl. archives of the Black Sash (Cape Western Region), the Cape Chamber of Industries, Syfrets and various trade unions), the papers of C. Louis Leipoldt, Pauline Smith and Olive Schreiner, and Bleek/Lloyd and G. P. Lestrade African language collections; Exec. Dir JOAN RAPP.

Western Cape Education Library and Information Service (EDULIS): Private Bag X9099, Cape Town 8000; Located at: 15 Kruskal Ave, Bellville 7530; tel. (21) 957-9618; fax (21) 948-0748; e-mail edulis@pgwc.gov.za; internet wced.wcape.gov.za/planning&devel/support/media_serv/edulis.html; f. 1859; ; 8,000 mems; 60,000 vols, 150 current periodicals; Head LYNE MCLENNAN.

Western Cape Provincial Library Service: POB 2108, Cape Town 8000; Located at: cnr of Chiappinni and Alfred Sts, Cape Town 8001; tel. (21) 483-2273; fax (21) 483-2031; e-mail capelib@pgwc.gov.za; internet www.capegateway.gov.za; f. 1945; 14 regional libraries, 309 affiliated libraries; collections of art prints, phonographic records, CDs, audio cassettes, 16mm films, videos; 7,000,000 vols; Central Information Service; Dir, Library and Archival Services JOHAN SWIEGELAAR; publ. *Cape Librarian / Kaapse Bibliotekaris* (6 a year).

Durban

eThekwini Municipal Library Service: City Hall, Smith St, POB 917, Durban 4000; tel. (31) 311-2401; fax (31) 311-2403; e-mail ref@prcsu.durban.gov.za; internet www.durban.gov.za; f. 1853; approx. 1,500,000 vols; special collections of African Studies and Shakespeareana; 89 brs; Dir R. NYONGWANA (acting).

University of KwaZulu-Natal Library, Durban Campus: King George V Ave, Glenwood, Durban 4041; tel. (31) 260-2317; fax (31) 260-2051; e-mail buchanan@ukzn.ac.za; internet www.library.und.ac.za; Campus Librarian NORA BUCHANAN.

East London

Buffalo City Municipal Library Service: Gladstone St, POB 652, East London; tel. (43) 722-4991; fax (43) 743-1729; f. 1876; 30,000 mems; 225,000 vols; Librarian Mrs M. M. DAVIDSON.

Grahamstown

Grahamstown Public Library: POB 180, Grahamstown 6140; tel. (46) 603-6040; fax (46) 622-9488; e-mail library@makana.gov.za; internet www.makana.gov.za; f. 1842; 81,053 vols; Librarian C. CLACK.

National English Literary Museum: Private Bag 1019, Grahamstown 6140; tel. (46) 622-7042; fax (46) 622-2582; e-mail nelm@ru.ac.za; internet www.rhodes.ac.za/nelm; f. 1972; 21,000 vols; research collns of books, literary manuscripts, photographs, journal articles, academic theses and press cuttings; Dir MALCOLM HACKSLEY; publ. *NELM News* (2 a year).

Rhodes University Library: Rhodes Univ., POB 184, Grahamstown 6140; tel. (46) 603-8436; fax (46) 622-3487; e-mail library@ru.ac.za; internet www.rhodes.ac.za/library; f. 1904; 400,000 vols; Dir, Library Services GWENDA THOMAS.

Johannesburg

City of Johannesburg Library and Information Services: Beyers Naude Square, Cnr of Market and Fraser Sts, Johannesburg 2001; tel. (11) 870-1222; fax (11) 870-1252; e-mail crefindex@joburg.org.za; f. 1890; 1,916,162 vols; Regional Man. G. SHENKER; publs *Annual Report*, *Local Government Library Bulletin* (monthly).

Library of the South African Institute of Race Relations: POB 97, Johannesburg 2000; tel. (11) 403-3600; fax (11) 403-3671; e-mail sairr@icon.co.za; internet www.sairr.org.za; f. 1929; 7,030 vols; valuable archival and documentary material; newspaper clippings from 1930 on race relations, politics, labour and economics; bibliographies on race relations; Information Dir T. DIMANT.

University of the Witwatersrand Library: Private Bag XI, PO Wits, 2050; tel. (11) 717-1901; fax (11) 717-1065; e-mail felixu@library.wits.ac.za; internet www.wits.ac.za/library; f. 1922; 1,069,000 vols; two central libraries (undergraduate and research), also br. libraries: architecture, biological and physical sciences, management, geological and mathematical sciences, education and commerce, engineering, law, health sciences, nuclear sciences; spec. collns incl. Africana, Hebraica and Judaica, Portuguese, Archaeology and Egyptology, Historical and Literary Papers (incl. Church of the Province of South Africa), Early Printed Books; Librarian FELIX N. UBOGU.

Kimberley

Kimberley Public Library: POB 627, Kimberley 8300; tel. (53) 830-6241; fax (53) 833-1954; e-mail fritz@kbymun.org.za; internet home.global.co.za/~afrilib; f. 1882; 127,000 vols; Africana Library of 20,000 vols, 545 MSS, 1,145 photographs (North Cape and Diamond Fields); Judy Scott Library of 43,000 vols; Librarian F. VAN DYK.

Mmabatho

North-West Provincial Library Services: Private Bag X2044, Mmabatho 2735; tel. (18) 392-2060; f. 1978; under Dept of Arts, Culture and Sport; 75 public libraries, 7 college libraries, 1,000 school libraries, 7 govt dept libraries; 1,600,000 vols; Deputy Dir N. B. NOMNGA.

Pietermaritzburg

KwaZulu-Natal Provincial Library Service: Private Bag X9016, Pietermaritzburg; tel. (33) 341-3000; fax (33) 394-2237; e-mail slaterc@plho.kzntl.gov.za; f. 1952; consists of central organization and reference library at Pietermaritzburg; four regional offices for Coast, South Coast, Midlands and Northern areas, serving 172 public libraries; 3,000,000 vols, 21,000 CDs, 32,000 video cassettes, 6,500 DVDs; Dir CAROL SLATER; Ref. Librarian SUE DAVIES; publ. *KZN Librarian* (4 a year).

Natal Society Library: POB 415, Pietermaritzburg 3200, Natal; tel. (33) 345-2383; fax (33) 394-0095; e-mail nsl@futurenet.co.za; f. 1851; lending, children's, reference, legal deposit, school assignments, music, special collections, map collections, Africana collection; 6 brs, hospital, housebound and travelling library services; 600,000 vols; 6,332 current legal deposit periodicals and newspapers, 122 current overseas periodicals, numerous bound legal deposit and overseas periodicals and newspapers; Dir J. C. MORRISON; publs *Annual Report*, *Natalia* (annually), *AIDS Bibliography*.

University of KwaZulu-Natal Library, Pietermaritzburg Campus: Private Bag X014, Scottsville 3209; tel. (33) 260-5054; fax (33) 260-5260; e-mail brammage@ukzn.ac.za; internet www.library.unp.ac.za; f. 1909; 375,000 vols; Librarian CAROL BRAMMAGE (acting).

Port Elizabeth

Nelson Mandela Metropolitan Libraries: POB 66, Port Elizabeth 6000; tel. (41) 506-1373; fax (41) 506-1390; e-mail kdeklerk@mandelametro.gov.za; f. 1901; public library with extensive Africana, genealogical and maritime collections; research and orientation workshops for scholars; 500,000 vols; Head of Libraries BONGIWE CHIGUMBU; publ. *Annual Report*.

Nelson Mandela Metropolitan University Library and Information Services: POB 77700, Port Elizabeth 6000; tel. (41) 504-2281; fax (41) 504-2280; internet www.nmmu.ac.za; f. 1964; 507,356 vols; L. C. Steyn Collection of Roman Dutch Law; Director MARJORY EALES.

Potchefstroom

Ferdinand Postma Library, Potchefstroom University for Christian Higher Education: Private Bag X05, Noordbrug 2522; tel. (18) 299-2000; fax (18) 299-2999; e-mail fpbalg@puknet.puk.ac.za; internet www.puk.ac.za/library; f. 1869; 543,290 vols, 1,637 current periodicals; Main Library (Ferdinand Postma Library), Library of the Theological School of the Reformed Churches in South Africa (Jan Lion Cachet Library), Music Library, Natural Sciences Library, Vaal Triangle Campus Library at Vanderbijlpark; special collections: Carney Africana Collection, Hertzog Law Collection, Collection of the Institute for Research in Children's Literature; Dir TOM LARNEY (acting).

Pretoria

Council for Scientific and Industrial Research (CSIR) Information Services: POB 395, Pretoria 0001; tel. (12) 841-2911; fax (12) 841-4405; e-mail csiris@csir.co.za; internet www.csir.co.za; f. 1945; 90,000 bound vols, 4,000 serial titles and 22,000 pamphlets; provides scientific, technical and business management information services to CSIR research staff and to external clients; Man. Dr MARTIE VAN DEVENTER; publs *CSIR Annual Report, Technobrief.*

Department of Agriculture, Information Centre: Private Bag X388, Pretoria 0001; tel. (12) 319-6872; fax (12) 319-7245; e-mail daleenk@nda.agric.za; internet www.nda.agric.za; f. 1910; arranges distribution of departmental publications, and indexing of South African agricultural literature for the AGRIS database of the FAO; 40,000 vols, 200 current periodicals, 140,000 pamphlets; Asst Dir M. M. KOEN.

Department of Arts, Culture, Science and Technology Library: Private Bag X894, Pretoria 0001; tel. (12) 314-6033; fax (12) 323-2720; special collections: library science, science planning, state language services, national terminology services; 42,000 vols; 153 current periodicals; Librarian D.E. MOHLAKWANA.

Department of Education Library: Private Bag X895, Pretoria 0001; tel. (12) 312-5265; fax (12) 325-1475; e-mail bamuza.r@educ.pwv.gov.29; f. 1994; Asst Dir REGINAH BAMUZA.

Gauteng Library Information Policy and Archiving Services: Private Bag X33, Marshalltown 2000; tel. (11) 355-2500; fax (11) 355-2565; e-mail koekie.meyer@gpg.gov.za; internet www.srac.gpg.gov.za; f. 1995; consists of Head Office in Johannesburg, and 4 Regional Libraries; provides library and information service to 324 public and community libraries and depots in Gauteng Province; 3,498,497 vols; Dir J. M. MEYER (acting).

Human Sciences Research Council, Centre for Library and Information Services: 134 Pretorius St, Private Bag X41, Pretoria 0001; tel. (12) 302-2999; fax (12) 302-2933; e-mail library@ludwig.hsrc.ac.za; internet www.hscr.ac.za; f. 1969; 60,000 vols, 700 current periodicals; Pres. Dr F. M. ORKIN.

Mary Gunn Library, South African National Biodiversity Institute: Private Bag X101, Pretoria 0001; tel. (12) 843-5042; fax (12) 804-8740; e-mail potgietere@sanbi.org; internet www.sanbi.org; f. 1916; 12,234 vols; Chief Exec. Prof. B. J. HUNTLEY.

National Archives and Heraldic Services: Private Bag X236, Pretoria 0001; tel. (12) 323-5300; fax (12) 323-5287; e-mail arg02@dacst4.pwv.gov.za; provides a comprehensive archives service to all government offices and local authorities; processes and stores archive material; makes archives and facilities available to researchers; National Archivist for the Republic of South Africa Dr G. A. DOMINY.

State Library: POB 397, Pretoria 0001; tel. (12) 321-8931; fax (12) 325-5984; e-mail statelib@statelib.pwv.gov.za; f. 1887; national and legal depository library, and depository library for US Government and UN publications; 684,000 vols, 9,600 current serials; responsible for compiling the national bibliography; international and national interlending centre; Southern African Book Exchange Centre; ISBN and ISSN centre for South Africa; Dir Dr PETER J. LOR; publs *South African National Bibliography* (quarterly and annual cumulations, paper and machine-readable format), *Index to South African Periodicals* (CD-ROM and machine-readable format), *RSA Government Gazette* (microfiche, quarterly), *South African Newspapers on Microfilm*, *Bibliography of the Xhosa Language*, *Northern Sotho Bibliography*, *Directory of South African Publishers.*

Transvaal Education Department, Education Media Service: 328 Van der Walt St, Private Bag X290, Pretoria 0001; tel. (12) 322-7685; fax (12) 322-7699; f. 1951; 385,000 vols, 600 periodicals, 3,000 videos; Dir J. A. BIERMAN.

University of Pretoria Libraries: Academic Information Service, University of Pretoria, Pretoria 0002; tel. (12) 420-4111; fax (12) 362-5182; e-mail jaboon@up.ac.za; internet www.up.ac.za/asservices/ais/ais.htm; f. 1908; 1,127,237 vols, pamphlets, govt publs, 5,698 periodicals, etc, 8,000 gramophone records, 26,000 items of sheet-music, 2,250 CDs; Dir J. A. BOON.

University of South Africa Library: POB 392, UNISA 0003; tel. (12) 429-3131; fax (12) 429-2925; e-mail hennijc@unisa.ac.za; internet www.unisa.ac.za/library; f. 1947; 1,800,000 vols, 335,000 bound serials; science library and law colln specializing in foreign and comparative law; brs in Cape Town, Durban, Johannesburg and Pietersburg; Exec. Dir J. HENNING (acting); publ. *Mousaion* (irregular).

Sovenga

University of Limpopo Library: Private Bag X1112, Sovenga, Limpopo 0727; tel. (15) 268-2656; fax (15) 268-2198; e-mail matshayap@ul.ac.za; internet www.unorth.ac.za/Library; 80,000 vols, 581 periodicals; University Librarian PATEKA MATSHAYA.

Stellenbosch

University of Stellenbosch Library: University of Stellenbosch, Private Bag XX5036, Stellenbosch 7599; tel. (21) 808-4880; fax (21) 808-4336; e-mail jhvi@maties.sun.ac.za; internet www.sun.ac.za/local/library; f. 1895; 938,000 vols, 5,700 current periodicals; Dir (vacant).

Museums and Art Galleries

Bloemfontein

National Museum: POB 266, Bloemfontein 9300; 36 Aliwal St, Bloemfontein 9301; tel. (51) 447-9609; fax (51) 447-6273; e-mail ornito@nasmus.co.za; internet www.nasmus.co.za; f. 1877; main focus is on natural history (incl. Florisbad human fossil skull); also social and local history; library of 9,000 vols, 1,730 serial titles, 6,200 pamphlets; Dir R. J. NUTTALL; publs *CULNA, Navorsinge van die Nasionale Museum / Researches of the National Museum, Praktikum.*

Cape Town

Iziko Museums of Cape Town: POB 61, Cape Town 8000; tel. (21) 481-3800; fax (21) 481-3993; internet www.iziko.org.za; f. 1999; CEO Prof. H. C. BREDEKAMP.

Art sites:

Iziko–Michaelis Collection: POB 61, Cape Town 8000; The Old Town House, Greenmarket Sq., Cape Town; tel. (21) 481-3933; fax (21) 424-6441; internet www.iziko.org.za/michaelis; f. 1916; Dutch and Flemish paintings, drawings and prints of the 16th century to the early 20th century; Dutch and colonial furniture; library of 1,500 vols; Dir, Art Collns M. H. MARTIN.

Iziko–Natale Labia Museum: POB 61, Cape Town 8000; 192 Main Rd, Muizenberg, Cape Town 7945; tel. (21) 788-4106; fax (21) 788-3908; internet www.iziko.org.za/natale; f. 1988; built 1929 as residence of first Italian Minister Plenipotentiary in SA, Prince Natale Labia; elaborate Italianate furnishings with 18th- and 19th-century British and European art; Dir, Art Collns M. H. MARTIN.

Iziko–South African National Gallery: Government Ave, Cape Town 8001; tel. (21) 467-4660; fax (21) 467-4680; internet www.iziko.org.za/sang; f. 1871; collns of South African, African, British, French, Dutch and Flemish art; also photography, sculpture, beadwork, textiles and architecture; library of 10,000 vols, journals and pamphlets; public access by appointment; Dir, Art Collns M. H. MARTIN.

Natural History sites:

Iziko–Planetarium: 25 Queen Victoria St, Cape Town 8000; tel. (21) 481-3900; fax (21) 481-3990; e-mail tferreira@iziko.org.za; internet www.iziko.org.za/planetarium; Man. THEO FERREIRA.

Iziko–South African Museum: 25 Queen Victoria St, Cape Town 8000; tel. (21) 481-3900; fax (21) 481-3990; internet www.iziko.org.za/sam; f. 1825; collns incl. ethnography, applied arts, philately, transport, weaponry, toys; library of 12,000 vols, 4,000 periodicals; Dir, Natural History Collns Dr H. ROBERTSON; publ. *African Natural History* (annual).

Iziko–West Coast Fossil Park: POB 42, Langebaan 7375; R27 Langebaan Rd, Cape Town 8000; tel. (22) 766-1606; fax (22) 766-1765; internet www.iziko.org.za/wcfp; f. 1998; Dir, Natural History Collns Dr H. ROBERTSON.

Social History sites:

Iziko–Bertram House: Hiddingh Campus, Orange St, Cape Town 8000; tel. (21) 481-3940; fax (21) 481-3941; internet www.iziko.org.za/bertram; f. 1984; Dir, Social History Collns Dr P. J. DAVISON; early 19th-century. Georgian townhouse; displays of Georgian furniture, Chinese and English porcelain, and English silver and kitchenware.

Iziko–Bo-Kaap Museum: 71 Wale St, Cape Town 8000; tel. (21) 481-3939; fax (21) 481-3938; internet www.iziko.org.za/bokaap; f. 1978; focuses on the social history of the local community; Dir, Social History Collns Dr P. J. DAVISON.

Iziko–Groot Constantia: Groot Constantia Estate, Constantia, Cape Town 8000; tel. (21) 795-5140; fax (21) 795-5150; internet www.iziko.org.za/grootcon; f. 1927; 17th-century wine estate and manor house; art colln; wine museum; Dir, Social History Collns Dr P. J. DAVISON.

Iziko–Koopmans-De Wet House: 35 Strand St, Cape Town 8000; tel. (21) 481-3935; fax (21) 424-6441; internet www.iziko.org.za/koopmans; f. 1914; early 18th-century townhouse; colln of Cape furniture, Chinese and Japanese ceramics, Dutch Delft ware, paintings, glass and silverware; Dir, Social History Collns Dr P. J. DAVISON.

Iziko–Rust-en-Vreugd: 78 Buitenkant St, Cape Town 8000; tel. (21) 464-3280; fax (21) 461-9620; internet www.iziko.org.za/rustvreugd; f. 1965; 18th-century Cape Dutch house with colln of Africana watercolours and prints from the William Fehr Colln; Dir, Art Collns M. H. MARTIN.

Iziko–Slave Lodge: 49 Adderley St, Cape Town 8000; tel. (21) 460-8240; fax (21) 460-8202; internet www.iziko.org.za/slavelodge; f. 1966; decorative arts, archaeology, local history, restored houses illustrating life in the 18th and 19th centuries; library of 14,000 vols; Dir, Social History Collns Dr P. J. DAVISON.

Iziko–South African Maritime Museum: Victoria and Albert Waterfront, Table Bay Harbour, Cape Town 8000; tel. (21) 405-2880; fax (21) 405-2882; internet www.iziko.org.za/maritime; f. 1990; focuses on fishing and shipping industry; colln of ships; floating exhibition: SAS *Somerset*, boom defence vessel built in 1942; Dir, Social History Collns Dr P. J. DAVISON.

Iziko–William Fehr Collection: POB 61, Cape Town 8000; The Castle of Good Hope, Buitenkant St, Cape Town 8000; tel. (21) 464-1260; fax (21) 464-1280; internet www.iziko.org.za/castle; f. 1965; colln of paintings and decorative arts of relevance to the Cape region; Dir, Social History Collns P. J. DAVISON.

Museum of Coast and Anti-Aircraft Artillery: Fort Wynyard, POB 14068, Green Point 8051; tel. (21) 419-1765; f. 1987; coast and anti-aircraft guns and relics displayed in a restored coast artillery battery.

Durban

Durban Museums: City Hall, POB 4085, Durban 4000; tel. (31) 300-6911; fax (31) 300-6308; e-mail mnikathib@prcsu.durban.gov.za; internet www.durban.gov.za; f. 1887; South African fauna, flora, ethnography, archaeology, paintings, graphic art, porcelain, sculptures, local history; Dir (Durban Art Gallery) C. BROWN; Dir (Local History Museums) R. OMAR; Dir (Natural Science Museum) Q. B. HENDEY; publ. *Novitates* (annually).

Local History Museums: Old Court House Museum, Aliwal St, Durban; tel. (31) 311-2223; fax (31) 311-2224; f. 1966; local and KwaZulu Natal historical collections, restored Natal colonial public building; Dir R. H. OMAR.

Attached Museums:

Bergtheil Museum: c/o Old Court House Museum, Aliwal St, Durban; e-mail mnikathib@prcsu.durban.gov.za; collections related to local communities, particularly early German settlers.

Cato Manor Heritage Centre: c/o Old Court House Museum, Aliwal St, Durban; e-mail mnikathib@prcsu.durban.gov.za; interpretative centre featuring the history of Cato Manor, including aspects related to forced removals and the Apartheid era.

Kwa Muhle Museum: 130–132 Ordnance Rd, Durban; tel. (31) 311-1111; fax (31) 311-2224; f. 1994; urban life in the Apartheid era, with emphasis on the 'Durban System' of administering the African population 1908–1986.

Old House Museum: c/o Old Court House Museum, Aliwal St, Durban; e-mail mnikathib@prcsu.durban.gov.za; a replica of the Robinson Home, a house belonging to the founder of the city's first morning newspaper; contains displays of early domestic life.

Pinetown Museum: c/o Old Court House Museum, Aliwal St, Durban; e-mail mnikathib@prcsu.durban.gov.za; collections related to the Pinetown area.

Port Natal Maritime Museum: c/o Old Court House Museum, Aliwal St, Durban; f. 1988; Natal and Durban maritime history, two tugs and a minesweeper.

East London

East London Museum: POB 11021, Southernwood, East London 5213; 319 Oxford St, Southernwood, East London 5201; tel. (43) 743-0686; fax (43) 743-3127; e-mail rachel@tsamail.co.za; f. 1931; collns of conchology, ichthyology, ornithology of the Eastern Cape Province, cultural history of the Border region and ethnography of the Southern Nguni peoples; houses specimen of Coelacanth (primitive fish) and world's only dodo egg; administers Victorian house museum; library: library holds books, journals, video cassettes, cartographic material, microfiches, microfilms, photographs, reprints, slides; Museum Dir MCEBISI MAGADLA (acting); Museum Librarian RACHEL WILLIAMS; publs *Annals of the Eastern Cape Museums* (jtly with 4 other museums), *Annual Report*, *Newsletter* (quarterly).

Franschhoek

Huguenot Memorial Museum and Monument: Lambrechts St, POB 37, Franschhoek 7690; tel. (21) 876-2532; fax (21) 876-3649; e-mail hugenoot@museum.co.za; internet www.museum.co.za; f. 1967; research into Cape Huguenot history, exhibition of over 400 Huguenot artefacts and documents; Chair. Prof. P. COERTZEN; Curator L. N. RABIE; publ. *Bulletin of the Huguenot Society of South Africa*.

Grahamstown

Albany Museum: Somerset St, Grahamstown 6139; tel. (46) 622-2312; fax (46) 622-2398; e-mail l.webley@ru.ac.za; internet www.ru.ac.za/albany-museum; f. 1855; archaeology, terrestrial entomology, freshwater ichthyology, freshwater invertebrates, botany, palaeontology, ornithology, history and material cultures of the peoples of the eastern Cape Province; library of 2,000 vols, 1,400 periodicals; Dir Dr L. WEBLEY (acting); publs *Annals of the Eastern Cape Provincial Museums* (jtly with 3 other museums, irreg.), *Southern African Field Archaeology* (annual).

Johannesburg

Apartheid Museum: POB 82283, Southdale 2135 Johannesburg; Northern Parkway and Gold Reef Rd, Ormonde 2001; tel. (11) 309-4700; fax (11) 309-4726; e-mail info@apartheidmuseum.org; internet www.apartheidmuseum.org; f. 2001; film footage, photographs and artefacts illustrating the rise and decline of the apartheid system; Chair. Dr JOHN KANI.

City of Johannesburg Museums and Galleries:; internet www.joburg.org.za/arts/arts_heritage.stm#museums; Dir of Arts, Culture and Heritage Services STEVEN SHACK.

Branch museums:

Adler Museum of Medicine: Univ. of the Witwatersrand, POB 3, Wits 2050; Medical School, 7 York Rd, Parktown, Johannesburg 2193; tel. (11) 717-2081; fax (11) 717-2081; e-mail curator@health.wits.ac.za; internet www.wits.ac.za/museums/adler.html; f. 1962; colln of medical, dental and surgical instruments and equipment; reconstructions of early 20th-century. pharmacy, doctor's and dentist's surgeries, herbalist shop and traditional medicine display; library of 10,000 vols; Curator ROCHELLE KEANE; publ. *Adler Museum Bulletin* (2 a year).

Bensusan Museum of Photography and Library: MuseuMAfricA, 121 Bree St, Newtown, Johannesburg; tel. (11) 833-5624; fax (11) 833-5636; e-mail PhotographicLibrary@joburg.org.za; f. 1968; colln incl. rare and valuable precision-made photographic equipment, incl. early Daguerre camera bought in 1839; Collector's Gallery; colln of pictures from the earliest wet-plate prints to digital images and experiments in 3 dimensions, such as stereoscopic views and holograms; specializes in preserving the work of South African photographers; Curator JONATHAN FROST.

Bernberg Fashion Museum: c/o MuseuMAfricA, POB 517, Newtown 2113, Johannesburg; Duncombe Rd (cnr Jan Smuts Ave), Forest Town, Johannesburg; tel. (11) 646-0716; fax (11) 833-5636; e-mail MuseuMAfrica@joburg.org.za; f. 1973; costume and accessories since the 17th century; temporarily closed for renovation; Fashion Curator (vacant).

Hector Pieterson Museum: 8288 Maseko St, Orlando West 1804; tel. and fax (11) 536-0611; named after one of the first fatalities of the march through Soweto on 16 June 1976, when police were ordered to shoot at a crowd of demonstrating students; commemorates the day's events, incl. television footage of the uprising and coverage of the anti-apartheid struggle generally; museum is next to the Pieterson Memorial, and the area has been declared a nat. heritage site; Curator ALI HLONGWANE.

James Hall Museum of Transport: Pioneers' Park, Rosettenville Rd, La Rochelle 2190, Johannesburg; tel. (11) 435-9485; fax (11) 435-9821; e-mail curator@jhmt.org.za; internet www.jhmt.org.za; f. 1964; largest and most comprehensive land transport museum in South Africa; land transport in all its forms: ox-wagons, coaches and carts, bicycles, motorbikes, tractors, fire engines, buses, trams, trains, and cars from the Model T Ford to electric cars; Curator PETER HALL.

Johannesburg Art Gallery: POB 30951, Braamfontein 2017, Johannesburg; tel. (11) 725-3130; fax (11) 720-6000; e-mail job@joburg.org.za; internet www.joburg.org.za; f. 1910; colln of 9,000 artworks comprising contemporary South African art; traditional southern African art and modern int. art; print colln and historical European paintings and sculptures; extensive public programmes; library of 8,700 vols; Dir CLIVE KELLNER.

MuseuMAfricA: 121 Bree St, Newtown, Johannesburg; tel. (11) 833-5624; fax (11) 833-5636; e-mail museumafrica@joburg.org.za; permanent displays show urban life in Johannesburg and its place in South Africa's history; themes incl. the gold miner, life in a shack and township jazz; coverage of Mahatma Gandhi's and Nelson Mandela's time in the city; displays on early man, stone-age and iron-age communities, San rock art in a reconstructed shelter, lifestyle of the first white settlers in the Johannesburg area; Chief Curator DAWN ROBERTSON.

Roodepoort Museum: Civic Centre, Christiaan de Wet Rd, Florida Park 1709; tel. (11) 761-0225; fax (11) 674-4043; e-mail annes@joburg.org.za; internet www .museums.org.za/roodepoortmuseum; first discovery of payable gold in the area, and the devt of mining into villages and towns; pioneer farmhouse dating from the mid-1800s, a Victorian house from the turn of the 20th century, and 1920s and 1930s lounges; spec. display room houses colln of int. decorative art objects; temporary exhibition gallery has changing displays of local interest.

Kimberley

McGregor Museum: Atlas St, POB 316, Kimberley 8300; tel. (53) 839-2700; fax (53) 842-1433; e-mail cfortune@museumsnc.co.za; internet www.museumsnc.co.za; f. 1907; archaeology and rock art, history (incl. Anglo-Boer War of 1899–1902), geology, zoology and herbarium of N. Cape; ethnological collection housed in Duggan-Cronin Gallery, incorporates Magersfontein Battle-field Museum, Rudd House, Dunluce and Memorial to the Pioneers of Aviation; Dir C. FORTUNE.

King William's Town

Amathole Museum: Cnr Albert Rd and Alexandra Rd, POB 1434, King William's Town 5600; tel. (43) 642-4506; fax (43) 642-1569; e-mail museum@amathole.org.za; internet www.amathole.co.za; f. 1884 as a naturalist society; studies, collects, houses and exhibits southern Africa mammalogy, Xhosa ethnography, local history, Eastern Cape missionary history and Eastern Cape German settler history; library of 8,200 vols, 150 current periodicals; spec. collns incl. Kitton Colln of Africana; Dir LLOYD R. WINGATE; publs *Annual Report*, *Cape Provincial Museums Annals* (jointly with 4 other museums), *Newsletter IMVUBU* (3 a year).

Attached museum:

Missionary Museum: Berkeley St, POB 1434, King William's Town 5600; tel. (43) 642-4506; fax (43) 642-1569; e-mail postmaster@amathole.org.za; f. 1972; missionary history in Eastern Cape; Dir LLOYD WINGATE.

Pietermaritzburg

Natal Museum: Private Bag 9070, Pietermaritzburg 3200; Located at: 237 Loop St, Pietermaritzburg 3201; tel. (33) 345-1404; fax (33) 345-0561; e-mail lib@nmsa.org.za; internet www.nmsa.org.za; f. 1904; collns incl. entomology, mollusca, archaeology, historical anthropology, mammals, arachnology, earthworms, herpetology, palaentology, local history; library of 12,000 books, 2,500 periodicals, 61,000 pamphlets, 8,000 photographs, 900 maps, 8,000 slides; Dir Dr J. LONDT; publs *Annals*, *Natal Museum Journal of Humanities* (annual).

Tatham Art Gallery (Municipal): Commercial Rd, opp. City Hall, Pietermaritzburg; tel. (33) 342-1804; e-mail bell@tatham.org.za; f. 1903; British and French painting since 19th c., sculpture and graphics, Southern African painting, sculpture, ceramics, prints and ethnic objets d'art; library: public reference library of 2,300 vols; Dir BRENDAN BELL.

Port Elizabeth

Bayworld (incorporating Port Elizabeth Museum, Snake Park, Oceanarium and No 7 Castle Hill Historical Museum): POB 13147, Humewood, Port Elizabeth 6013; tel. (41) 584-0650; fax (41) 584-0661; e-mail pr@ bayworld.co.za; internet www.bayworld.co .za; f. 1856; research on marine archaeology, marine biology, marine mammalogy, herpetology, marine ornithology and local history; Museum: marine life, maritime history, birds, dinosaurs, costume and local history; Snake Park: African and worldwide collection of reptiles; Oceanarium; local fish, sharks, sea birds, seals, turtles and dolphins; library of 20,000 vols; Dir SYLVIA VAN ZYL; publs *Annals of the Eastern Cape Museums* (jointly with other EC museums, irregular), *Annual Reports*, *Otolith* (Bayworld newsletter, 4 a year).

Nelson Mandela Metropolitan Art Museum: 1 Park Drive, Port Elizabeth; tel. (41) 586-1030; fax (41) 586-3234; e-mail artmuseum@artmuseum.co.za; internet www.artmuseum.co.za; f. 1956 as King George VI Art Gallery; municipal art museum; collections of South African and British art, Indian miniatures, international graphics, Chinese textiles; library of 5,460 vols; Dir Dr MELANIE HILLEBRAND.

Pretoria

National Cultural History Museum: POB 28088, Sunnyside 0132; tel. (12) 324-6082; fax (12) 328-5173; e-mail nchm@nfi.org.za; internet www.nfi.org.za; f. 1892; exhibitions; research, education and conservation; library; special collns: Jansen, Ethnography, Archaeological, Furniture and Ceramics; library of 17,500 vols, 200 periodicals; Man. NEO MALAO; publ. *Nasko Navorsing* (research by the museum, annually).

Pretoria Art Museum (Municipal Art Gallery): POB 40925, Arcadia Park, Pretoria 0007; Arcadia Park (Cnr Schoeman and Wessels Sts), Arcadia, Pretoria 0083; tel. (12) 344-1807; fax (12) 344-1809; e-mail art .museum@tshwane.gov.za; internet www .pretoriaartmuseum.co.za; f. 1964; South African art, small collection of European graphic art, some 17th c. Dutch art, collection of traditional and contemporary African art; Curator D. OFFRINGA; publ. *Bulletin* (2 a year).

Transvaal Museum: POB 413, Pretoria; tel. (12) 322-7632; fax (12) 322-7939; e-mail malherbe@nfi.co.za; internet www.nfi.org.za/ tmpage.html; f. 1893, from 1964 a Natural History museum only; taxonomy, ecology, zoo-geography and evolutionary studies with main emphasis on Southern Africa; mammals, birds, herpetology, palaeontology (incl. mammal-like reptiles and early hominids), Coleoptera, Lepidoptera, Orthoptera, invertebrates, archaeo-zoology and education; library of 11,000 vols, 2,000 periodicals and 80,000 reprints; rare book collection; Dir. CARINA MALHERBE; publs *Annals of the Transvaal Museum* (annually), *Transvaal Museum Monographs* (irregular).

Stellenbosch

Stellenbosch Museum: Private Bag X5048, Stellenbosch 7599; Erfurthuis, Rynevelstreet 37, Stellenbosch 7600; tel. (21) 887-2948; e-mail stelmus@mweb.co.za; internet www .museums.org.za/stellmus; f. 1962; comprises 18th c. powder magazine (weaponry, Stellenbosch military history), Village Museum (buildings illustrating life from 1690–1890), Toy and Miniature Museum, reference library; Dir E. A. ODENDAAL.

Universities

CAPE PENINSULA UNIVERSITY OF TECHNOLOGY

Founded 2005 by merger of Cape Technikon and Peninsula Technikon.

CONSTITUENT INSTITUTIONS

CAPE TECHNIKON

Tennant St, POB 652, Cape Town 8000

Telephone: (21) 460-3911
Fax: (21) 460-3695
E-mail: rector@ctech.ac.za
Internet: www.ctech.ac.za

Founded 1923, present name 1979
Languages of instruction: English, Afrikaans
Academic year: January to November

Chancellor: GRACE NALEDI MANDISA PANDOR
Vice-Chancellor and Rector: Dr MARCUS BALINTULO
Vice-Rectors: Prof. N. J. KOK, Dr M. A. TSHABALALA
Registrar: ALWYN VAN GENSEN
Director Library Services: J. A. COETZEE
Library of 55,000 books, 1,800 periodicals
Number of teachers: 331
Number of students: 11,842 (9,876 full-time, 1,966 part-time)

Publication: *Rector's Report* (annually)

DEANS

Faculty of Applied Sciences: Prof. LIONEL SLAMMERT
Faculty of the Built Environment and Design: Prof. HAGEN
Faculty of Business Informatics: Prof. G. ERWIN
Faculty of Education: Prof. M. ROBINSON
Faculty of Engineering: Prof. NICO BEUTE
Faculty of Management: Prof. SHAHEED BAYAT

PENINSULA TECHNIKON

POB 1906, Bellville 7535, Cape Province

Telephone: (21) 959-6911
E-mail: jamese@pentech.ac.za
Internet: www.pentech.ac.za

Founded 1967 as Peninsula Technikon
Vice-Chancellor: Prof. BRIAN FIGAJI
Deputy Vice-Chancellor (Academic): Prof. ANTHONY STAAK
Deputy Vice-Chancellor (Student Affairs and Administration): VUYISA MAZWI-TANGA
Library of 88,000 vols
Number of teachers: 221
Number of students: 8,855

DEANS

Faculty of Business: NORMAN JACOBS
Faculty of Engineering: Dr OSWALD FRANKS
Faculty of Science: Dr DHIRO GIHWALA

UNIVERSITY OF CAPE TOWN

Private Bag, Rondebosch 7701, Cape Town

Telephone: (21) 650-9111
Fax: (21) 650-2138
E-mail: dublinc@bremner.uct.ac.za
Internet: www.uct.ac.za

Founded 1829 as South African College; university status 1918
Autonomous, state-subsidized
Language of instruction: English
Academic year: February to December (two semesters)

Chancellor: GRACA SIMBINE MACHEL
Vice-Chancellor: Prof. NJABULO NDEBELE
Deputy Vice-Chancellors: Prof. CHERYL C. DE LA REY, Prof. MARTIN HALL, Prof. JULIA MEKWA, Prof. MARTIN WEST

Registrar: HUGH AMOORE
Librarian: JOAN RAPP
Library: see Libraries and Archives
Number of teachers: 2,000
Number of students: 19,978

Publications: *Contributions from the Bolus Herbarium* (irregular), *Pretexts* (4 a year), *Acta Juridica* (annually), *Social Dynamics* (2 a year), *UCT Research Report* (annually), *Journal of Energy in Southern Africa* (4 a year), *Selected Energy Statistics: Southern Africa* (4 a year), *Sea Changes* (2 a year), *Responsa Meridiana* (annually)

DEANS

Faculty of Commerce: Prof. DOUG PITT
Faculty of Engineering and the Built Environment: Prof. CYRIL T. O'CONNOR
Faculty of Health Sciences: Prof. NICKY PADAYACHEE
Faculty of Humanities: Prof. PAULA ENSOR
Faculty of Law: Prof. HUGH CORDER
Faculty of Science: Prof. DAYA REDDY
Centre for Higher Education Development: Prof. NAN YELD

PROFESSORS

Faculty of Commerce (tel. (21) 650-2694; fax (21) 650-2696; e-mail comsec@commerce.uct.ac.za):

ABEDIAN, I., Economics
BARR, G. D. I., Statistical Sciences
BRADFIELD, D., Statistical Sciences
DORRINGTON, R. E., Management Studies
EVERINGHAM, G. K., Accounting
FAULL, N. H. B., Graduate School of Business
HORWITZ, F., Graduate School of Business
KAHN, S. B., Economics
KANTOR, B. S., Economics
KAPLAN, D., Economics
LICKER, P. S., Information Systems
NATTRASS, N., Economics
SIMPSON, J. D., Business Science
SMITH, D. C., Information Systems
SULCAS, P., Graduate School of Business
TROSKIE, C. G., Statistical Sciences
UNDERHILL, L. G., Statistical Sciences
WILSON, F. A. H., Economics

Faculty of Engineering and the Built Environment (tel. (21) 650-2699; fax (21) 650-3782; e-mail engsec@eng.uct.ac.za):

ABBOTT, J., Civil Engineering
ALEXANDER, M. G., Civil Engineering
ALLEN, C., Mechanical Engineering
BALL, A., Mechanical Engineering
BENNETT, K. F., Mechanical Engineering
BOWEN, P. A., Construction Economics and Management
BRAAE, M., Electrical Engineering
DE JAGER, G., Electrical Engineering
DEWAR, D., School of Architecture and Planning
DOWNING, B. J., Electrical Engineering
EKAMA, G. A., Civil Engineering
GRYZAGORIDAS, T., Mechanical Engineering
HANSFORD, G. S., Chemical Engineering
NURICK, G. N., Mechanical Engineering
O'CONNOR, C. T., Chemical Engineering
REDDY, B. D., Centre for Research in Computational and Applied Mechanics
REINECK, K. M., Electrical Engineering
RÜTHER, H., Geomatics
STEVENS, A. J., Construction Economics and Management

Faculty of Health Sciences (tel. (21) 406-6346; fax (21) 447-8955; e-mail medfac@curie.uct.ac.za):

BAQWA, D., Primary Health Care
BATEMAN, E. D., Medicine
BEATTY, D. W., Paediatrics and Child Health
BENATAR, S. R., Medicine

BENINGFIELD, S. J., Radiology
BONNICI, F., Medicine
BORNMAN, P. C., Surgery
COMMERFORD, P. J., Medicine
CRUSE, J. P., Anatomical Pathology
DAVIDSON, J., Chemical Pathology
DENT, D. M., Surgery
ELS, W. J., Anatomy and Cell Biology
FOLB, P. I., Pharmacology
GEVERS, W., Medical Biochemistry
HALL, P., Anatomical Pathology
HARLEY, E. H., Chemical Pathology
JACOBS, M. E., Paediatrics and Child Health
JAMES, M. F. M., Anaesthetics
KIRSCH, R. E., Medicine
KNOBEL, G. J., Forensic Medicine and Toxicology
LOUW, J., Medicine
MOLTENO, C. D., Psychiatry
MURRAY, A. D. N., Ophthalmology
MYERS, J. E., Community Health
NOAKES, T. D., Physiology
NOVITZKY, N., Haematology
PADAYACHEE, G. N.
PARKER, M. I., Medical Biochemistry
PETER, J. C., Neurosurgery
POWER, D. J., Paediatrics and Child Health
RAMESAR, R., Human Genetics
ROBERTSON, B. A., Psychiatry
RODE, H., Paediatric Surgery
SEGGIE, J., Medicine
SELLARS, S. L., Otorhinolaryngology
STEYN, L. M., Medical Microbiology
VAN DER SPUY, Z. M., Obstetrics and Gynaecology
VAN NIEKERK, J. P., Medicine
VAUGHAN, C. L., Biomedical Engineering
VILJOEN, J. F., Anaesthesia
VON OPPEL, U., Cardiothoracic Surgery
WALTERS, J., Orthopaedic Surgery
WERNER, I. D., Radiation Oncology
WILSON, E. L., Immunology
ZILLA, P., Cardiovascular Research

Faculty of Humanities (tel. (21) 650-4216; fax (21) 686-9840; e-mail artsec@beattie.uct.ac.za).

BRINK, A., English Language and Literature
BUNTING, I., Philosophy
CHIDESTER, D. S., Religious Studies
COCHRANE, J. R., Religious Studies
COETZEE, J. M., English Language and Literature
COOPER, B., Centre for African Studies
CORNILLE, J.-L., French Language and Literature
DE GRUCHY, J., Religious Studies (Graduate School of Humanities)
DU TOIT, A. B., Political Studies
FOSTER, D. H., Psychology
GITAY, Y., Hebrew and Jewish Studies
GODBY, M. A. P., Historical Studies
HAYNES, D. J., Drama
KLATZOW, P., Music
LASS, R. G., Linguistics
LOUW, J., Psychology
MAMA, A., African Gender Institute
MAREE, J., Sociology
MAY, J., South African College of Music
MESTHRIE, R., Linguistics and Southern African Languages
MULLER, J. P., Education
NASSON, W., History
NOYES, J., German Language and Literature
REYNOLDS, P. F., Social Anthropology
SALAZAR, PH.-J., French Language and Literature (Graduate School of Humanities)
SATYO, S. C., African Languages
SAUNDERS, C. C., Historical Studies
SCHRIRE, R. A., Political Studies
SEEGERS, A., Political Studies
SHAIN, M., Hebrew and Jewish Studies

SKOTNES, P., Fine Art
SNYMAN, H. J., Afrikaans and Netherlandic Studies (Graduate School of Humanities)
TAYOB, A. I., Religious Studies
UNDERWOOD, P. G., School of Librarianship
VAN HEERDEN, E. R., Afrikaans and Netherlandic Studies
WEST, M., Social Anthropology
WHITAKER, R. A., Classics
WORDEN, N. A., Historical Studies
YOUNG, D. N., Education
YOUNGE, G., Fine Art

Faculty of Law (tel. (21) 650-3086; fax (21) 686-2577; e-mail lawnv@law.uct.ac.za):

BENNETT, T. W., Public Law
BLACKMAN, M. S., Commercial Law
BURMAN, S. B., Private Law
CHEADLE, M. H., Public Law
CORDER, H. M., Public Law
DEVINE, D. J., Public Law
HUTCHISON, D. B., Private Law
JOOSTE, R. D., Commercial Law
MALUWA, T., Public Law
MURRAY, C. M., Public Law
VAN BUEREN, G., Law
VISSER, D. P., Private Law

Faculty of Science (tel. (21) 650-2712; fax (21) 650-2710; e-mail scifac@psipsy.uct.ac.za):

ASCHMAN, D. G., Physics
BARR, G. D. I., Statistical Sciences
BECKER, R. I., Mathematics and Applied Mathematics
BOND, W., Botany
BRADFIELD, D., Statistical Sciences
BRANCH, G. M., Zoology
BRUNDRIT, G. B., Oceanography
BULL, J., Chemistry
BUTTERWORTH, D. S., Mathematics and Applied Mathematics
CLEYMANS, J. W. A., Physics
DE WIT, M. J., Geological Sciences
DOMINGUEZ, C. A., Physics
DU PLESSIS, M., Zoology
ELLIS, G. F. R., Mathematics and Applied Mathematics
FAIRALL, A. P., Astronomy
FIELD, J. G., Zoology
FUGGLE, R. F., Environmental and Geographical Science
GÄDE, G., Zoology
GURNEY, J. J., Geological Sciences
HALL, M. J., Archaeology
KHAM, M. J., Mathematics, Science and Technology Education
KLUMP, H. H., Biochemistry
KRITZINGER, P. S., Computer Science
KURTZ, D. W., Astronomy
LE ROEX, A. P., Geological Sciences
LUTJEHARMS, J. R. E., Oceanography
MACGREGOR, K. J., Computer Science
MOSS, J. R., Chemistry
NASSIMBENI, L. R., Chemistry
PARKINGTON, J. E., Archaeology
PEREZ, S. M., Physics
REDDY, B. D., Mathematics and Applied Mathematics
SILLEN, A., Archaeology
STEWART, T. J., Statistical Sciences
THOMSON, J. A., Microbiology
TROSKIE, C. G., Statistical Sciences
UNDERHILL, L. G., Statistical Sciences
VAN DER MERWE, N. J., Archaeology
VIOLLIER, R. D., Physics
WARNER, B., Astronomy
WEBB, J. H., Mathematics and Applied Mathematics

RESEARCH CENTRES, INSTITUTES, UNITS AND GROUPS

African Gender Institute: Dir Prof. A. MAMA.

Applied Fiscal Research Centre: Dir Assoc. Prof. I. ABEDIAN.

Avian Demography Unit: Dir Prof. L. G. UNDERHILL.

Cape Heart Centre: Dir Prof. L. H. OPIE.

Cardiovascular Research Unit: Dir Prof. P. ZILLA.

Catalysis Research Group: Dir Assoc. Prof. J. C. Q. FLETCHER.

Centre for Contemporary Islam: Dir Assoc. Prof. E. MOOSA.

Centre for Manufacturing Engineering: Dir Prof. J. GRYZAGORIDIS.

Centre for Marine Studies: Dir Prof. A. C. BROWN.

Centre for Materials Engineering: Dir Dr R. D. KNUTSEN.

Centre for Research in Engineering Education: Dir J. JAWITZ.

Centre for Rhetoric Studies: Dirs Prof. Y. GITAY, Prof. PH.-J. SALAZAR.

Development Policy Research Unit: Dir H. BHORAT.

Electron Microscope Unit: Dir Assoc. Prof. B. T. SEWELL.

Energy and Development Research Centre: Dir Prof. A. A. EBERHARD.

Energy Research Institute: Dir Prof. K. F. BENNETT.

Environmental Evaluation Unit: Dirs Prof. R. F. FUGGLE, Dr M. SOWMAN.

Freshwater Research Unit: Dir Dr J. A. DAY.

Heart Research Unit: Dir Prof. L. H. OPIE.

Housing and Community Development Unit: Dir Prof. B. G. BOADEN.

HSRC/UCT Centre for Gerontology: Dir Dr M. FERREIRA.

Industrial Health Research Group: Dir N. HENWOOD.

Institute for Comparative Religion in Southern Africa: Dir Prof. D. CHIDESTER.

Institute for Plant Conservation: Dir Dr D. M. RICHARDSON.

Institute of Child Health: Chair. of Advisory Cttee Prof. D. BEATTY.

Institute of Criminology: Dir E. VAN DER SPUY.

Institute of Development and Labour Law: Dir Assoc. Prof. E. E. KALULA.

Institute of Theoretical Physics and Astrophysics: Dir Prof. C. A. DOMINGUEZ.

Law, Race and Gender Research Unit: Dir Prof. C. MURRAY.

Lucy Lloyd Archive Resource and Exhibition Centre: Dir Prof. P. SKOTNES.

Marine Biology Research Institute: Dir Prof. C. L. GRIFFITHS.

Minerals Processing Research Unit: Dir Prof. C. T. O'CONNOR.

MRC/UCT Bioenergetics of Exercise Research Unit: Dir Prof. T. D. NOAKES.

MRC/UCT Liver Research Centre: Dir Prof. R. KIRSCH.

MRC/UCT Medical Imaging Research Unit: Dir Prof. C. VAUGHAN.

MRC/UCT Oesophageal Cancer Research Group: Dir Prof. M. I. PARKER.

NRF/UCT Archaeometry Research Unit: Dir Assoc. Prof. J. C. SEALY.

NRF/UCT Centre for Socio-legal Research: Dir Prof. S. BURMAN.

NRF/UCT Religion and Social Change Research Unit: Dir Prof. J. W. DE GRUCHY.

NRF/UCT Research Unit for the Archaeology of Cape Town: Dir Prof. M. J. HALL.

NRF/UCT Science and Technology Policy Research Centre: Dir Assoc. Prof. D. E. KAPLAN.

Occupational Health Research Unit: Dir Prof. J. MYERS.

Percy FitzPatrick Institute of African Ornithology: Dir Prof. M. DU PLESSIS.

Quaternary Research Centre: Dir Dr J. A. LEE-THORP.

Research Institute on Christianity in South Africa: Dirs Prof. J. W. DE GRUCHY, Prof. J. R. COCHRANE.

South African Bird Ringing Unit: Dir Prof. L. G. UNDERHILL.

Southern Africa Labour and Development Research Unit: Dir Prof. F. A. H. WILSON.

Student Learning Research Group: Dir Prof. J. H. F. MEYER.

Supramolecular Chemistry Unit: Dir Prof. L. R. NASSIMBENI.

UCT Drug Surveillance Research Centre: Dir Dr L. WALTERS.

UCT Leukaemia Centre: Dir Prof. N. NOVITZKY.

UCT/University College, London, Hatter Institute: Dirs Dr M. SACK, Prof. D. YELLON (London).

Urban Problems Research Unit: Dir P. WILKINSON.

Women's Health Research Unit: Dirs Dr D. COOPER, Dr M. HOFFMAN.

CENTRAL UNIVERSITY OF TECHNOLOGY, FREE STATE

Pres Brand St 20, Private Bag X20539, Bloemfontein 9300

Telephone: (51) 507-3060

Fax: (51) 507-3019

E-mail: cajvr@cut.ac.za

Internet: www.cut.ac.za

Founded 1981

Academic year: January to December

Principal and Vice-Chancellor: Prof. A. S. KOORTS

Deputy Vice-Chancellor (Academic Affairs): Prof. C. A. J. VAN RENSBURG

Deputy Vice-Chancellor (Advancement and Marketing): Prof. S. M. THULARE

Deputy Vice-Chancellor (Student Services): Prof. M. S. MANDEW

Executive Director (Finance and Operations): R. F. STONE

Executive Director (Human Resources): C. I. GARDNER

Registrar: Dr M. J. DU PLOOY

Welkom Campus Manager: Dr D. SELALEDI

Director of Library and Information Centre: T. VENTER

Library of 65,000 vols

Number of teachers: 432 (182 full-time, 250 part-time)

Number of students: 8,000

DEANS

Faculty of Engineering, Information and Communication Technology: Prof. G. D. JORDAAN

Faculty of Health and Environmental Sciences: Prof. B. J. FREY

Faculty of Management Sciences: Prof. P. G. LE ROUX

WALTER SISULU UNIVERSITY FOR TECHNOLOGY AND SCIENCE, EASTERN CAPE

Founded 2005 by merger of Eastern Cape Technikon, Border Technikon and University of Transkei.

CONSTITUENT INSTITUTIONS

UNIVERSITY OF TRANSKEI

Private Bag X1, Unitra

Telephone: (47) 502-2111

Fax: (47) 532-6820

E-mail: postmaster@getafix.utr.ac.za

Internet: www.utr.ac.za

Founded 1976 as branch of Fort Hare University, independent 1977

State control

Language of instruction: English

Academic year: January to December

Chancellor: (vacant)

Administrator: Prof. N. I. MORGAN

Vice-Principal: Prof. J. M. NORUWANA

Registrar: Prof. P. N. LUSWAZI

Chief Librarian: P. E. OFORI

Number of teachers: 357

Number of students: 4,551

Publications: *Journal of Humanities* (2 a year), *Perspectives in Education* (annually)

DEANS

Faculty of Arts: Prof. N. MIJERE

Faculty of Economic Sciences: Prof. M. MAHABIR

Faculty of Education: Prof. S. V. S. NGUBENTOMBI

Faculty of Law: Prof. V. DLOVA

Faculty of Medicine and Health Sciences: Prof. E. L. MAZWAI

Faculty of Natural Sciences: Prof. B. S. NAKANI

PROFESSORS

Faculty of Arts:

ALABI, G. A., Information Science

COETSER, A., Afrikaans

MIJERE, N., Sociology

Faculty of Economic Sciences:

MAHABIR, M., Business Management

Faculty of Education:

LWANGA-LUKWAGO, J., Social Studies Education

NGUBENTOMBI, S. V. S., Educational Foundations

Faculty of Law:

DLOVA, V., Mercantile Law

Faculty of Medicine and Health Sciences:

ERASMUS, R. T., Chemical Pathology

IPUTO, J. E., Physiology

MAZWAI, E. L., Surgery

MEISSNER, O., Pharmacology

MFENYANA, K., Family and Community Medicine

NGANWA-BAGUMAH, A. B., Anatomy

STEPHEN, A., Pathology

Faculty of Natural Sciences:

EMMERSON, W., Zoology

FANIRAN, J. A., Science Foundation Year Programme

JACOBS, T. V., Botany

MISHRA, S. N., Mathematics

UNIVERSITY OF FORT HARE

Private Bag X1314, Alice 5700

Telephone: (40) 602-22011

Fax: (40) 653-1023

E-mail: dmc@ufh.ac.za

Internet: www.ufh.ac.za

Founded as 'South African Native College' in 1916 by the United Free Church of Scotland; transferred to the Dept of Bantu Education in 1960 to cater specifically for the Xhosa ethnic group; present name 1970; incorporated Medical School of Univ. of Transkei and East London Campus of Rhodes Univ. 2004

Language of instruction: English

Academic year: February to December
Chancellor: Prof. S. M. BHENGU
Vice-Chancellor and Rector: Prof. DERRICK SWARTZ
Deputy Vice-Chancellor (Administration and Finance): R. OLANDER
Dean of Students: N. MORRISON
Librarian: Y. K. SOUL
Library: see Libraries
Number of teachers: 239
Number of students: 2,869
Publications: *Ardrinews, Fort Hare Papers, The Fort Harian*

DEANS

Faculty of Agricultural and Environmental Studies: Prof. J. RAATS
Faculty of Arts: Prof. C. R. BOTHA
Faculty of Economic Sciences: Prof. T. M. JORDAN
Faculty of Education: Prof. P. M. FIHLA
Faculty of Law: Prof. J. ROBBERTSON
Faculty of Medicine and Health Sciences: Prof. E. L. MAZWAI
Faculty of Science and Technology: Dr D. O. OKEYO
Faculty of Social Sciences: Prof. SOBAHLE
Faculty of Theology: Prof. S. P. ABRAHAMS

PROFESSORS

Faculty of Agriculture:
  BESTER, B. J., Agricultural Economics
  IGODAN, C. O., Agricultural Extension and Rural Development
  MNKENI, P. N. S., Crop Science
  MZAMANE, N., Agronomy
  RAATS, J. G., Livestock and Pasture Science
  TROLLOPE, W. S. W., Livestock and Pasture Science
Faculty of Arts:
  AUCAMP, J. C., History
  BOTHA, C. R., African Languages
  BROUWER, P., Political Science and Public Administration
  DE WET, G., Communication
  ELS, J. M., Classical Languages
  ETSIAH, A. K., Political Science and Public Administration
  HALLIER, M. G. T., Fine Arts
  LOSAMBE, L., English
  LOUW, T. J. G., Philosophy
  PRINS, M. J., Afrikaans and Dutch
  SIRAYI, G. T., Centre for Cultural Studies
  VERHAGE, H. M., Psychology
Faculty of Economic Sciences:
  JORDAN, T. M., Accountancy
  SWARTZ, D. I., Intergovernmental Relations
  VAN DAALEN, H. J., Industrial Psychology
Faculty of Education:
  DARGIE, D. J., Music
  DREYER, J. N., Foundations of Education
  FILHA, P. M., Educational Psychology
  JIYA, M. A. Y., Curriculum Studies and Didactics
  LINDEQUE, B. R. G., Curriculum Studies and Didactics
Faculty of Law:
  DU PLESSIS, P. A., Mercantile Law
  IYA, P. F., African and Comparative Law
  LABUSCHAGNE, J., Constitutional and Public International Law
  REMBE, N. S., Oliver Tambo Chair of Human Rights
Faculty of Science:
  BRAND, J. M., Biochemistry and Microbiology
  FATOKI, O. S., Chemistry
  MAKUNGA, O. H. D., Plant Sciences
  SADIMENKO, A., Chemistry
  SANYAL, D. K., Chemistry
  SERETIO, J. R., Physics

TYLER, J. C., Statistics
VAN DYK, T. J., Mathematics
VAN HEERDEN, J. W. A., Zoology
WAGENER, P. C., Applied Mathematics
Faculty of Theology:
  ABRAHAMS, S. P., Old Testament and Hebrew
  THOM, G., Historical and Contextual Theology

ATTACHED INSTITUTES

Academic Development Centre: Dir Dr Z. JIYA.

Agricultural and Rural Development Research Institute: Dir (vacant).

Centre for Cultural Studies: Dir Prof. G. T. SIRAYI.

Fort Hare Institute of Government: Dir Prof. D. SCHWARTZ.

Xhosa Dictionary: Dir Prof. B. M. MINI.

UNIVERSITY OF THE FREE STATE

POB 339, Bloemfontein 9300
Telephone: (51) 401-9111
Fax: (51) 401-2117
E-mail: info@stiq.uovs.ac.za
Internet: www.uovs.ac.za

Founded 1855 (formerly a Constituent College of the University of South Africa); became independent as University of the Orange Free State 1950; present name 2003; incorporated Bloemfontein Campus of Vista University 2004
Languages of instruction: Afrikaans, English
Academic year: February to November
Chancellor: Dr FRANKLIN SONN
Vice-Chancellor and Rector: Prof. FREDERICK FOURIE
Vice-Rector (Academic Operations): Prof. TEUNS VERSCHOOR
Vice-Rector (Academic Planning): Prof. MAGDA FOURIE
Vice-Rector (Student Affairs): Dr RALETSATSI EZEKIEL MORAKA
Dean of Students: Dr NATIE LUYT (acting)
Registrar: Prof. IZAK STEYN
Director, Library and Information Services: CLEMENCE NAMPONYA

Number of teachers: 476
Number of students: 20,000

DEANS

Faculty of Economic and Management Sciences: Prof. TIENIE CROUS
Faculty of Health Sciences: Prof. LETTICIA MOJA
Faculty of Humanities: Prof. GERHARDT DE KLERK
Faculty of Law: Prof. JOHAN HENNING
Faculty of Natural and Agricultural Sciences: Prof. HERMAN VAN SCHALKWYK
Faculty of Theology: Prof. HERMIE VAN ZYL

ATTACHED INSTITUTES

Institute for Contemporary History: Bloemfontein; Dir Prof. J. H. LE ROUX.

Institute for Groundwater Studies: Bloemfontein; Dir Prof. F. D. I. HODGSON.

Research Institute for Education Planning: Bloemfontein; Dir Prof. H. J. VAN DER LINDE.

ATTACHED CAMPUS

University of the Free State, Qwaqwa Campus

Private Bag X13, Phuthaditjhaba 9866
Telephone: (58) 713-0211
Fax: (58) 713-0158
Founded 1982
Chancellor: Dr N. R. MANDELA

Vice-Chancellor and Principal: Prof. N. NDEBELE
Vice-Principal: Prof. Dr W. MÖDINGER
Registrars: A. T. KGABO, T. P. MASIHLEHO, N. T. MOSIA
Librarian: C. J. KOK
Library of 30,000 vols
Number of teachers: 85
Number of students: 2,500

DEANS

Faculty of Arts: Prof. L. J. FERREIRA
Faculty of Education: L. E. MOFOKENG
Faculty of Management Sciences: P. C. MOJET
Faculty of Mathematics and Natural Sciences: Prof. Dr P. C. KEULDER
Faculty of Theology: Dr S. P. BOTHA

PROFESSORS

Faculty of Arts:
  FERREIRA, L. J., Political Science
  JONES, H. J., Afrikaans
  MOOLMAN, J. P. F., History
Faculty of Education:
  MOLETSANE, R. I. M., Comparative Education
Faculty of Management Sciences:
  CLOETE, N., Commercial Law
  JONKER, L. J. G., Business Economics
  VENTER, A. P., Industrial Psychology
  WEBSTER, S. A., Accounting
Faculty of Mathematics and Natural Sciences:
  DE HAAS, W., Physics
  DEN HEYER, J., Zoology
  JORDAAN, D. B., Computer Science
  KEULDER, P. C., Botany
  LUYT, A. S., Chemistry
  MOFFETT, R. O., Botany
  MTHEMBU, T. Z., Mathematics

UNIVERSITY OF JOHANNESBURG

POB 524, Auckland Park, Johannesburg 2092
Telephone: (11) 489-2911
Fax: (11) 489-2191
Internet: www.uj.ac.za

Founded 2005 by merger of Rand Afrikaans University and Technikon Witwatersrand
State control
Languages of instruction: Afrikaans, English
Academic year: January to November
Chancellor (vacant)
Vice-Chancellor and Rector: Prof. T. R. BOTHA
Pro-Vice-Chancellor and Rector: Prof. C. C. MOKADI
Deputy Vice-Chancellor (Academic Administration and External Relations): Prof. E. TYOBOKA
Deputy Vice-Chancellor (Academic Administration and Research): Prof. D. VAN DER MERWE
Deputy Vice-Chancellor (Finance and Information Systems): Prof. D. D. VORSTER
Deputy Vice-Chancellor (Human Resources, Operations and Commercialization): A. HIGGO
Deputy Vice-Chancellor (Strategic and Institutional Planning and Implementation): Prof. A. C. REDLINGHUYS
Library of 452,273 vols
Number of teachers: 350
Number of students: 43,000

DEANS

Faculty of Art, Design and Architecture: E. P. HÖN
Faculty of Economic and Financial Science: Prof. H. KRIEK
Faculty of Education: Prof. M. E. MULLER

Faculty of Engineering: Prof. L. PRETORIUS
Faculty of Health: Prof. H. V. EXNER
Faculty of Humanities: Prof. R. RYAN
Faculty of Law: Prof. J. OTTO
Faculty of Management: Prof. K. K. GOVENDER
Faculty of Natural Science: Prof. K. BURGER

PROFESSORS

ALBERTS, H. L., Physics
ALBERTS, V., Physics
ANKIEWICZ, P. J., Curriculum Studies
BARTON, J. M., Geology
BEUKES, N. J., Geology
BISSCHOFF, T. C., Education
BOESSENKOOL, A. L., Business Economics
BOTHA, W. J., Afrikaans
BURGER, W. D., Afrikaans
BURNETT-LOUW, C., Sport and Movement Studies
CAIRNCROSS, B., Geology
COETSEE, D., Accounting
COETZEE, A. E., Afrikaans
COETZEE, J. H., Biblical Studies
COETZEE, P. P., Chemistry and Biochemistry
CONRADIE, C. J., Afrikaans
CONRADIE, W. M., Business Management
DE BRUIN, G. P., Institute for Child and Adult Guidance
DE BRUYN, H. E. C., Business Management
DE KOKER, L., Law
DEMPSEY, A., Accounting
DE VILLIERS, D. S., Law
DE WET, G. F. D., Communication Studies
DU RAND, J. A., Biblical Studies
DU TOIT, A. S. A., Information Studies
DUBERY, I. A., Chemistry and Biochemistry
EHLERS, E. M., Computer Science
FERREIRA, H. C., Electrical and Electronic Engineering
FERREIRA, J. T., Optometry
FRANGOS, C., Mathematics and Statistics
GELDENHUYS, D. J., Politics and Governance
GRAVETT, S. J., Educational Sciences
GREYLING, L., Economics
GROBLER, B. R., Education Sciences
GRUNDLINGH, L. W. F., Historical Studies
HARRIS, W. F., Optometry
HENDRICKX, B., Greek and Latin Studies
HENNING, E., Curriculum Studies
JANSE VAN RENSBURG, P. A., Geography and Environmental Studies
JANSE VAN VUREN, J. H., Zoology
JOHL, C. S., Linguistics and Literature Science
JOOSTE, C. J., Business Management
KNOBLOCH, H. J., German
KOK, J. C., Education
KRIEK, J. H., Accountancy
KRUGER, G. J., Chemistry and Biochemistry
KRUGER, S., Business Management
LACQUET, B. N., Electrical and Electronic Engineering
LAZARUS, T., Psychology
LESSING, B. C., Human Resource Management
LESSING, N., Business Management
LOMBARD, F., Statistics and Mathematics
LOOTS, A. E., Economics
LOTTER, H. P. P., Philosophy
MALHERBE, E. F. J., Law
MARX, B., Accountancy
MYBURGH, C. P. H., Education
NEELS, J. L., Law
NEL, A. L., Mechanical Engineering
NOLTE, A. G. W., Nursing
O'BRIEN, P. H., Law
OLIVIER, L., Law
OLIVIER, M. P., Law
OTTO, J. M., Law
PATEL, L., Social Work
POGGENPOEL, M., Nursing
POSTHUMUS, L. C., African Languages
PRETORIUS, H. G., Psychology
PRETORIUS, L., Mechanical and Manufacturing Engineering

PRINSLOO, G. C., Transport and Logistics Management
RAUBENHEIMER, H., Statistics and Mathematics
RAUTENBACH, I. M., Law
ROODT, A., Chemistry
ROODT, G., Human Resources Management
ROSSOUW, G. J., Philosophy
RYAN, R. P., English
SADIE, A. Y., Politics and Governance
SCHALING, E., Economics
SCHOEMAN, W. J., Psychology
SLABBERT, J. A., Human Resource Management
SMITH, D. P. J., Education
SMITH, T. H. C., Computer Science
SNYMAN, J. J., Philosophy
SONNEKUS, J. C., Law
STEEB, W.-H., Applied Mathematics
STRAUSS, J., Curriculum Studies
STRYDOM, H. A., Law
STUART, A. D., Psychology
SWART, P. L., Electrical and Electronic Engineering
TRÜMPELMANN, M. H., Curriculum Studies
UYS, J. M., Sociology
UYS, J. S., Industrial Psychology
VAN BRAKEL, P. A., Information Studies
VAN DER WALT, J. G. W., Law
VAN ROOYEN, H. G., Curriculum Studies
VAN WYK, B. E., Botany
VAN ZYL, C., Economics
VENTER, A. J., Political Studies
VERHOEF, G., Historical Studies
VERWEY, S., Communication
VILLET, C. M., Applied Mathematics
VISSER, J. D., Human Resource Management
VON SOLMS, S. H., Computer Science
WALTERS, J., Transport and Logistics Management
WATNEY, M. M., Law
WHITEHEAD, C. S., Botany
WOLMARANS, J. L. P., Greek and Latin Studies

ATTACHED INSTITUTES

Centre for Banking, Business and Taxation Law: Dir Dr S. F. DU TOIT.

Centre for Comparative Tax Law: Dir Prof. L. OLIVIER.

Centre for European Studies in Africa: Dir Prof. G. C. OLIVIER.

Centre for International Labour and Social Security Law: Dir Prof. M. OLIVIER.

Centre for Metropolitan and Local Governance: Dir Prof. W. ZYBRANDS.

Centre for Research in World Wide Web Applications: Dir Prof. P. A. VAN BRAKEL.

Centre for Sociological Research: Dir Prof. P. ALEXANDER.

Centre for Sport Law: Dir Dr S. CORNELIUS.

Centre for the Study of Economic Crime: Dir Prof. L. DE KOKER.

Centre for Teaching, Learning and Assessment: Dir Prof. G. JACOBS.

Centre for Work Performance at RAU: Dir Prof. G. ROODT.

Institute for Child and Adult Guidance: Dir Prof. G. P. DE BRUIN.

Institute for Energy Studies: Chair. Dr C. COOPER.

Institute for Private International Law in Southern Africa: Dir Prof. J. NEELS.

UNIVERSITY OF KWAZULU-NATAL

Westville Campus, Private Bag X54001, Durban 4000

Telephone: (31) 260-7111
Fax: (31) 204-4383
E-mail: enquiries@ukzn.ac.za

Internet: www.ukzn.ac.za
Founded 2004 by merger of Univ. of Natal and Univ. of Durban-Westville
Language of instruction: English
Autonomous control
Academic year: February to December (4 terms)
Chancellor: Judge ZAC M. YACOOB
Vice-Chancellor and Principal: Prof. M. W. MAKGOBA
Deputy Vice-Chancellor for Finance and Admin.: Prof. HILTON STANILAND
Deputy Vice-Chancellor for Research and Devt: Prof. SALIM S. ABDOOL KARIM
Publications: *Calendar* (annual), *Con-text* (irreg.)

DEANS

Faculty of Education: Prof. TUNTUFYE MWAMWENDA
Faculty of Eng.: Prof. DENYS SCHREINER
Faculty of Health Sciences: Prof. LEANA UYS
Faculty of Humanities, Devt and Social Science: (vacant)
Faculty of Law: Prof. L. GERING
Faculty of Management Studies: Prof. KANTILAL BHOWAN (Asst Dean)
Faculty of Nursing: Prof. OLUYINKA ADEJUMO (Head of School)
Faculty of Science and Agriculture: Prof. P. J. K. ZACHARIAS

BRANCH CAMPUSES

Edgewood Campus: cnr Richmond Rd and Marionhill Rd, Pinetown 3605; tel. (31) 260-3414; e-mail connawayn@ukzn.ac.za.

Howard College Campus: University KZN, Durban 4041; tel. (31) 260-2212.

Medical School Campus: Umbilo Rd, Durban 4013; tel. (31) 260-4248; e-mail undergrad@ukzn.ac.za.

Pietermaritzburg Campus: King Edward Ave, Scottsville, Pietermaritzburg 3209; tel. (33) 260-5212; e-mail naidoo@ukzn.ac.za.

UNIVERSITY OF LIMPOPO

Private Bag X1106, Sovenga 0727

Telephone: (15) 268-3061
Fax: (15) 268-3567
Internet: www.ul.ac.za

Founded 2005 by the merger of Medical University of Southern Africa and University of the North
Academic year: January to December
Vice-Chancellor: Prof. MOKGALONG (acting)
Campus Principal: K. NHLANE (acting)
Registrar: Prof. P. FRANKS (acting)
Library: see Libraries and Archives: Sovenga
Number of teachers: 400
Number of students: 12,000.

CONSTITUENT CAMPUSES

Medunsa Campus

POB 189, Medunsa 0204

Telephone: (12) 521-4111

DEANS

Faculty of Dentistry: Prof. T. S. GUGUSHE
Faculty of Medicine: Prof. C. F. VAN DER MERWE (acting)
Faculty of Sciences: Prof. J. V. GROENEWALD
National School of Public Health: Prof. A. A. HERMAN

HEADS OF DEPARTMENTS

Faculty of Dentistry (POB D 12, Medunsa, 0204; tel. (12) 521-4800; fax (12) 521-4102):

Community Dentistry: Prof. J. KROON
Diagnostics and Radiology: Dr C. NOFFKE

Maxillofacial and Oral Surgery: Prof. F. J. JACOBS

Operative Dentistry: Prof. I. C. DU PREEZ

Oral Pathology and Oral Biology: Prof. E. J. RAUBENHEIMER

Orthodontics: Dr M. HARRIS (acting)

Periodontology and Oral Medicine: Prof. L. FELLER

Prosthodontics: Prof. A. R. M. ESSOP

Stomatological Studies: Prof. E. BLIGNAUT, Dr W. P. GROTEPASS

Faculty of Medicine (POB 210, Medunsa 0204; tel. (12) 521-4321; fax (12) 521-5811):

Anaesthesiology: Prof. A. RANTLOANE

Anatomical Pathology: Prof. M. N. MUTHU-PHEL

Anatomy: Prof. M. C. BOSMAN

Cardiology: Dr P. S. MNTLA

Cardio-Thoracic Surgery: Dr P. S. RAMOR-OKO (acting)

Chemical Pathology: Prof. H. F. JOUBERT

Clinical Psychology: Prof. E. M. Q. MOKHUANE

Community Health: Prof. P. W. W. COET-ZER

Dermatology: Prof. C. F. VAN DER MERWE

Diagnostic Radiology and Imaging: Dr TSATSL

Family Medicine: Prof. S. W. P. MHLONGO

Forensic Pathology: Prof. C. G. H. FOSSEUS

Gastroenterology: Prof. C. J. VAN DER MERWE

General Surgery: Prof. C. M. MODIBA

Haematological Pathology: Prof. D. J. WELGEMOED

Hand and Microsurgery: Prof. U. MENNEN

Human Nutrition: Prof. I. I. GLATTHAAR

Intensive Care: Prof. M. J. MPE

Internal Medicine: Prof. O. MZILENI

Medical Physics: Prof. W. J. STRYDOM

Microbiological Pathology: Prof. A. A. HOO-SEN

Neurology: Prof. R. F. GLEDHILL

Neurosurgery: Prof. S. MOKGOKONG

Nuclear Medicine: Dr M. SATHEKGE

Nursing Science: Prof. S. M. MOGOTLANE

Obstetrics and Gynaecology: Dr MOMO-KOANE

Occupational and Environmental Health: Prof. D. J. KOCKS

Occupational Therapy: Prof. E. SHIPHAN

Ophthalmology: Prof. R. C. STEGMANN

Orthopaedics: Prof. R. GOLELE, Prof. M. LUKHELE

Otorhinolaryngology: Prof. TSHISULARO

Paediatric Surgery: Dr. L. MARCISZ

Paediatrics and Child Health: Prof. F. P. R. DE VILLIERS, Dr D. I. S. MANGONGOA

Pharmaceutics: Prof. R. S. SUMMERS

Pharmacology and Therapeutics: Prof. W. J. DU PLOOY

Physiology: Prof. K. A. SMITH

Physiotherapy: N. P. MBAMBO

Plastic and Reconstructive Surgery: Prof. J. F. SCHOLTZ

Psychiatry: Prof. A. E. GANGAT

Radiation Oncology: (vacant)

Radiography: T. S. M. MOALUSI

Urology: Prof. A. M. SEGONE

Virology: Prof. G. LECATSAS

Faculty of Sciences (POB 138, Medunsa 0204; tel. (12) 521-4371; fax (12) 521-3070):

Biology: Prof. F. C. CLARKE, Prof. D. A. ELS

Chemistry and Biochemistry: Prof. M. J. MPHAHLELE, S. NDlOVU

Computer Science: (vacant)

English Language: R. M. MORAKE

Mathematics and Statistics: Prof. J. L. FRESEN, Dr P. R. GOPALRAJ

Physics: Prof. D. M. MAFOKWANE

Psychology: Prof. N. J. S. ELS

National School of Public Health (POB 215, Medunsa 0204; tel. (12) 521-4613; fax (12) 560-0172):

Environmental and Occupational Health: G. SETSWE (acting)

Health Systems Management and Policy: E. PEPRAH (acting)

Social and Behavioural Science: Dr K. MOKWENA (acting)

Turfloop Campus

Private Bag X1106, Sovenga, Limpopo 0727

Telephone: (15) 268-9111

Fax: (15) 267-0152

DEANS

Faculty of Humanities: Prof. L. J. TEFFO

Faculty of Management Sciences and Law: Prof. P. E. FRANKS

Faculty of Sciences, Health and Agriculture: Dr N. M. MOKGALONG

DIRECTORS

Faculty of Humanities:

School of Education: Prof. J. KUIPER

School of Languages and Communication Studies: Prof. S. LOUW

School of Social Sciences: Dr N. C. KIRK

Faculty of Management Sciences and Law:

School of Economics and Management: Prof. A. DE VILLIERS

School of Law: Prof. M. C. OKBPALUBA

Graduate School of Leadership: Prof. L. G. BUBERWA

Faculty of Sciences, Health and Agriculture:

School of Agricultural and Environmental Sciences: Prof. N. M. MOLLEL

School of Computational and Mathematical Sciences: Prof. B. W. BECKER

School of Health Sciences: Prof. P. A. VENTER

School of Physical and Mineral Sciences: Dr W. P. MASHELA (acting)

NELSON MANDELA METROPOLITAN UNIVERSITY

POB 77000 Port Elizabeth 6031

Telephone: (41) 504-3911

Fax: (41) 583-1558

E-mail: info@nmmu.ac.za

Internet: www.nmmu.ac.za

Founded 2005 by merger of University of Port Elizabeth, PE Technikon and the Port Elizabeth Campus of Vista University

Vice-Chancellor and CEO: Dr ROLF STUMPF

Deputy Vice-Chancellors: Prof. IRENE MOU-TLANA, Prof. NTABISENG OGUDE, Prof. EUGENE DU PREEZ

Campus Principals: Prof. N. G. WOOD (Algoa Campus); Prof. E. VAN BILJON (George Campus); Prof. M. STRUWIG (Vista Campus)

Dean of Students: K. MATISO

Library: Library: see Libraries and Archives

Number of teachers: 1,000

Number of students: 20,000

Publication: *Annual Report*

DEANS

Faculty of Arts: Prof. HENRY THIPA

Faculty of Business and Economic Sciences: Prof. NIEKIE DORFLING

Faculty of Education: Prof. ANA NAIDOO

Faculty of Engineering: Prof. THEO VAN NIEKERK

Faculty of Health Sciences: Prof. RAJ NAIDOO

Faculty of Law: Prof. CHRISTO VAN LOGGERN-BURG

Faculty of Science: Prof. EUGEN STREULI

NORTH-WEST UNIVERSITY

Mafikeng Campus, PMB X2046, Mmabatho 2735

Telephone: (18) 389-2111

Fax: (18) 392-5775

E-mail: motabogis@uniwest.ac.za

Internet: www.uniwest.ac.za

Founded 1980 as Univ. of North-West; merged with Potchefstroom Univ. and incorporated Sebokeng Campus of Vista Univ. 2004

Autonomous control

Languages of instruction: Afrikaans, English

Academic year: February to November

Chancellor (vacant)

Vice-Chancellor: Dr THEUNS ELOFF (acting)

Chair. of the Council: L. NYHONYA

Vice-Principal: Dr M. N. TAKALO

Registrar: Prof. C. F. C. VAN DER WALT

Librarian: DUDU NKOSI

Library of 90,000 vols

Number of teachers: 588 (Potchefstroom and Vaal Triangle Campus 226 full-time, 7 part-time (incl. 99 professors); Mafikeng Campus 172 full-time, 183 part-time)

Number of students: 40,702 (Potchefstroom Campus 28,390; Vaal Triangle Campus 2,836; Mafikeng Campus 9,476)

Publications: *Koers* (quarterly), *Literator* (3 a year), *Didaktikom* (quarterly), *Fokus* (quarterly), *Woord en Daad* (quarterly), *In die Skriflig* (quarterly)

DEANS

Mafikeng Campus:

Faculty of Agriculture, Science and Technology: Dr S. H. TAOLE

Faculty of Commerce and Admin.: G. D. STESETSE

Faculty of Education: L. M. E. M. SEHLARE

Faculty of Human and Social Sciences: Dr R. M. MANYANE

Faculty of Law: R. L. KETTLES

Potchefstroom Campus:

Faculty of Arts: Prof. A. L. COMBRINK

Faculty of Economic and Management Sciences: Prof. G. J. DE KLERK

Faculty of Educational Sciences: Prof. H. J. STEYN

Faculty of Eng.: Prof. J. I. J. FICK

Faculty of Health Sciences: Prof. H. A. KOELEMAN

Faculty of Law: Prof. F. VENTER

Faculty of Natural Sciences: Prof. D. J. VAN WYK

Faculty of Theology: Prof. A. LE R. DU PLOOY

Vaal Triangle Campus:

Vaal Triangle Faculty: Prof. A. M. C. THERON

PROFESSORS

Mafikeng Campus (Private Bag X2046, Mmabatho 2735; tel. (18) 389-2111; fax (18) 392-5575; e-mail travisk@uniwest.ac.za; internet www.uniwest.ac.za):

Faculty of Agriculture, Science and Technology:

BEIGHLE, D. E., Animal Health

FUNNAH, S. M., Plant Production

KHALIQUE, C. M., Mathematical Sciences

TAOLO, S. H., Mathematical Sciences

Faculty of Human and Social Sciences:

CHIKULO, B. C., Development Studies

KALULE-SABITI, I., Population Training and Research Unit

MANSON, A., History

MOGEKWU, M., Communication

Faculty of Law:

MBAO, M. L. M., Public Law and Legal Philosophy

Potchefstroom Campus (Private Bag X6001, Potchefstroom 2520; tel. (18) 299-1111; fax (18) 299-2799; internet www.puk.ac.za):

Faculty of Arts:

CARSTENS, W. A. M., School of Languages (Dir)
COMBRINK, A. L., Dean
DE LANGE, A. M., English and Literature
DU PISANI, J. A., History
DU PLESSIS, H. G. W., ATKV Writing School
DU PLOOY, H. J. G., Afrikaans and Dutch
JOOSTE, S. J., Music
MOLLER, P. H., Sociology
SCHUTTE, P. J., Communication Studies
VAN DER WALT, J. L., English and Literature
VAN WYK, W. J., School of Social Studies (Dir)
VENTER, J. J., Philosophy

Faculty of Economic and Management Sciences:

BISSCHOFF, C. A., Potchefstroom Business School
COETSEE, L. D., Potchefstroom Business School
COETZEE, K., Chartered Accountant Training
COETZEE, W. N., Potchefstroom Business School
DE KLERK, G. J., Dean
DU PLESSIS, J. L., Potchefstroom Business School
DU TOIT, A., Chartered Accountant Training
ELOFF, T., School of Accounting Sciences (Dir)
GERICKE, J. S., Chartered Accountant Training
JANSEN VAN RENSBURG, L. R., Entrepreneurship, Marketing and Tourism Management
JORDAAN, K., Chartered Accountant Training
KOTZE, J. G., Potchefstroom Business School
KROON, J., Entrepreneurship, Marketing and Tourism Management
NAUDE, W. A., Decision-making and Management for Economic Development
PRETORIUS, J. P. S., Potchefstroom Business School
RADEMEYER, A., Chartered Accountant Training
ROTHMAN, S., Industrial Psychology
SAAYMAN, M., Tourism
SCHOLTZ, P. E., School of Human Resource Sciences (Dir)
VAN HEERDEN, J. H. P., School of Economics, Risk Management and International Trade (Dir)
VISSER, S. S., Management Accountant Training
VIVIERS, W., Economics, Risk Management and International Trade

Faculty of Educational Sciences:

DREYER, C., Postgraduate School of Education
MENTZ, P. J., Education and Training
MONTEITH, J. L. D. K., Postgraduate School of Education
SPAMER, E. J., Teachers' Centre
STEYN, H. J., Dean
VAN DER WESTHUIZEN, P. C., Postgraduate School of Education

Faculty of Engineering:

DE KOCK, J. A., Electrical and Electronic Engineering
DU TOIT, C. G. D. K., Mechanical and Material Engineering
FICK, J. I. J., Dean
GREYVENSTEIN, G. P., Mechanical and Material Engineering
HELBERG, A. S. J., Electrical and Electronic Engineering
HOFFMAN, A. J., Electrical Electronic Engineering

MATHEWS, E. H., Centre for Research and Commericalisation
ROUSSEAU, P. G., Energy Systems
WAANDERS, F. B., Chemical and Mineral Engineering

Faculty of Health Sciences:

BERGH, J. J., Pharmaceutical Chemistry
BONESCHANS, B., CENQAM
BREYTENBACH, J. C., Pharmaceutical Chemistry
DE RIDDER, J. H., Human Movement Studies
DEKKER, T. G., Industrial Pharmacy
DU PLESSIS, J., Drug Research and Development
GREEF, M., Nursing
HARVEY, B. H., Pharmacy
KOELEMAN, H. A., Dean
KOTZE, G. J., Social Work
KOTZÉ, A. F., Pharmaceutics
LIEBENBERG, W., Institute for Industrial Pharmacy
MALAN, D. D. J., Human Movement Studies
MALAN, N. T., Physiology, Nutrition and Consumer Sciences
OLIVER, D. W., Pharmacy
STRYDOM, H., Social Work
THOMAS, A. J., Pharmacy
VENTER, C. A., Physiology
VENTER, D. P., Pharmacology
WISSING, M. P., Psycho-social Behavioural Science

Faculty of Law:

DU PLESSIS, W., Legal Pluralism and Legal History
FERREIRA, G. M., Public Law and Legal Philosophy
PIENAAR, G. J., Private Law
ROBINSON, J. A., Private Law
STANDER, A. L., Private Law
VENTER, F., Dean

Faculty of Natural Sciences:

BOUWMAN, H., Zoology
BREET, E. L. J., Chemistry
BRUINSMA, O. S. L., Separation Sciences and Technology
BURGER, R. A., Space Physics
DE JAGER, O. C., Physics
DE JONGH, D. C. J., Centre for Business Mathematics and Informatics
DE JONGH, P. J., Centre for Business Mathematics and Informatics
DE KLERK, J. H., Mathematics
DE VILLIERS, A. B., Geography and Environmental Studies
DU TOIT, G. J., Environment Sciences and Management
FOURIE, J. H., Computer, Statistical and Mathematical Sciences
GEYSER, H. S., Town and Regional Planning
GROBLER, J. J., Business Mathematics and Informatics
KOTZÉ, H. F., Biochemistry
MORAAL, H., Physics
PETERSEN, M. A., Mathematics
PIENAAR, J. J., Chemistry and Biochemistry
PIETERSE, A. J. H., Life Sciences
POTGIETER, M. S., Physics
RAUBENHEIMER, B. C., Space Physics
RIEDEL, K. J., Microbiology
STEYN, T., Computer Sciences and Information
STYGER, P., Centre for Business Mathematics and Informatics
SWANEPOEL, J. W. H., Statistics and Operational Research
THERON, P. D., Zoology
VAN DER WALT, D. J., Physics
VAN HAMBURG, H., Environment Sciences and Development
VAN WYK, D. J., Dean

VOSLOO, H. C. M., Chemistry

Faculty of Theology:

DE KLERK, B. J., Practical Theology
DU PLOOY, A. LE R., Dean
JANSE VAN RENSBURG, J. J., New Testament
JORDAAN, G. J. C., New Testament
LOTTER, G. A., Practical Theology
VAN ROOY, H. F., Theology and the Development of the South African Society
VENTER, J. M., Practical Theology
VORSTER, J. M., Ecclesiology

Vaal Triangle Campus (Private Bag X6001, Potchefstroom 2520; tel. (16) 910-3710; fax (16) 910-3103; e-mail dvdamct@puknet.puk .ac.za; internet www.puk.ac.za):

Faculty of the Vaal Triangle:

DE KLERK, P., History
JORDAAN, D. B., Modelling Sciences
LUCOUW, P., Economic Sciences
PRETORIUS, J. B., Business Management
THERON, A. M. C., Dean
VERHOEF, M. M., Languages

ATTACHED INSTITUTES

ATKV Writing School: Prof. H. G. W. DU PLESSIS.

Centre for Business Mathematics and Informatics: Dir Prof. C. M. ERASMUS.

Centre for Education and Traffic Safety: Dir J. F. PIENAAR.

Centre for Research and Commercialisation: Dir Prof. E. H. MATHEWS.

Computational Mechanics Laboratory: Dir Prof. G. J. K. DU TOIT.

Electron Microscopy Laboratory: Dir Dr L. R. TIEDT.

Institute for Tourism, Wildlife Economy and Leisure Studies: Dir Prof. M. SAAYMAN.

UNIVERSITY OF PRETORIA

Pretoria 0002
Telephone: (12) 420-4111
Fax: (12) 362-5168
E-mail: csc@up.ac.za
Internet: www.up.ac.za

Founded 1908 as Transvaal University College; granted Charter as University of Pretoria 1930
Private control
Languages of instruction: Afrikaans, English
Academic year: February to December (two semesters)

Chancellor: Dr C. L. STALS
Vice-Chancellor and Principal: Prof. C. W. I. PISTORIUS
Advisor to the Principal: Prof. A. P. MELCK
Vice-Principals: Prof. C. R. DE BEER, Prof. R. M. CREWE, Prof. N. C. MANGANYI, Prof. R. A. MOGOTLANE
Executive Directors: Prof. A. M. DE KLERK, J. S. J. NEL, Prof. S. VIL-NKOMO
Head of the Secretariat: M. G. VILJOEN
Registrar: Prof. N. J. GROVÉ
Director (Academic Administration): Dr D. D. MARAIS
Director of Academic Information Service: Prof. J. A. BOON (acting)
Director (Client Services Centre): Dr K. LAZENBY
Director (Corporate Communication and Marketing): Dr K. LAZENBY (acting)
Director (Facilities Planning and Services): D. MOKOTEDI
Director (Financial Administration): T. G. KRUGER
Director (Human Resources): Prof. A. VAN ASWEGEN
Director (Department of Information Technology): Dr J. A. PRETORIUS

Director (Institutional Research and Planning): Prof. P. J. VERMEULEN
Director (Mamelodi Campus): E. SMITH
Director (Management Services): Prof. Q. VORSTER
Director (Telematic Learning and Education Innovation): Prof. J. A. BOON
Director (TuksSport): J. K. VAN DER WALT
Dean of Students: Prof. M. T. SPECKMAN

Library: see Libraries and Archives
Number of teachers: 1,385
Number of students: 39,000

Publications: *Jaarverslag* (Annual Review), *Tukkie-Werf* (4 a year), *Publikasies van die Universiteit van Pretoria–Nuwe Reeks* (Publications of the University of Pretoria—New Series (I) Research, annually), *Ad Destinatum: Gedenkboek van die Universiteit van Pretoria, Opvoedkundige Studies* (Educational Studies, 3 or 4 a year), *Openbare Fakulteitslesings* (irregular), *Huldigingsbundels* (irregular)

DEANS

Faculty of Economic and Management Sciences: Prof. C. KOORNHOF
Faculty of Education: Prof. J. D. JANSEN
Faculty of Engineering, Built Environment and Information Technology: Prof. R. F. SANDENBERGH
Faculty of Health Sciences: Prof. T. J. MARIBA
Faculty of Humanities: Prof. M. E. MULLER
Faculty of Law: Prof. D. G. KLEYN
Faculty of Natural and Agricultural Sciences: Prof. A. STRÖH
Faculty of Theology: Prof. C. A. VOS
Faculty of Veterinary Science: Prof. N. P. J. KRIEK
School of Dentistry: Prof. A. J. LIGTHELM (Chair.)

PROFESSORS

Faculty of Economic and Management Sciences:

ALBERTS, N. F., Tourism Management
BASSON, J. S., Human Resources Management
BLIGNAUT, J. N., Economics
BRAND, H. E., Human Resources Management
BRYNARD, P. A., School of Public Management and Administration
DE BEER, J. J., Human Resources Management
DE JAGER, H., Auditing
DE LA REY, J. H., Financial Management
DE VILLIERS, C. J., Financial Management
DE WET, J. M., Marketing and Communication Management
DE WIT, P. W. C., Business Management
DU PLESSIS, P. J., Marketing and Communication Management
FOURIE, D. J., School of Public Management and Administration
GLOECK, J. D., Auditing
GOUWS, D. G., Financial Management
HALL, J. H., Financial Management
HARMSE, C., Economics
HEATH, E. T., Tourism Management
HOOLE, C. R., Human Resources Management
KOORNHOFF, C., Accounting
KUYE, J. O., School of Public Management and Administration
LAMBRECHTS, H. A., Financial Management
MAASDORP, E. F. DE V., Business Management
MARX, A. E., Business Management
OOST, E. J., Financial Management
SCHOEMAN, N. J., Economics
STEYN, F. G., Economics
THORNHILL, C., School of Public Management and Administration
VAN DER SCHYF, D. B., Auditing
VAN HEERDEN, J. H., Economics

VERMEULEN, L. P., Human Resources Management

Faculty of Education:

ALANT, E., Augmentative and Alternative Communication
BECKMANN, J. L., Education Management and Policy Studies
BOUWER, A. C., Educational Psychology
CRONJÉ, J. C., Curriculum Studies
FRASER, W. J., Curriculum Studies
MAREE, J. G., Curriculum Studies
NKOMO, M., Educational Management and Policy Studies
ONWU, G. O. M., Science, Mathematics and Technology Education
VAN ROOYEN, L., Curriculum Studies

Faculty of Engineering, Built Environment and Information Technology (University of Pretoria, Pretoria 0002; tel. (12) 420-2005; fax (12) 362-5173; e-mail dean@eng.up.ac.za; internet www.up.ac.za/ebit):

BOTHMA, T. J. D., Information Science
BRÜMMER, D. G., Construction Economics
CLAASEN, S. J., Industrial and Systems Engineering
CRIMSEHL, U. H. J., Chemical Engineering
DE VILLIERS, C., Informatics
ELOFF, J. H. P., Computer Science
FISHER, R. C., Architecture
GRIMSEHL, U. H. J., Chemical Engineering
HORAK, E., Civil and Biosystems Engineering
LEUSCHNER, F. W., Electrical, Electronic and Computer Engineering
MEYER, J. P., Mechanical and Aeronautical Engineering
ORANJE, M. C., Town and Regional Planning
PISTORIUS, P. C., Materials Science and Metallurgical Engineering
POURIS, A., Institute for Technological Innovation
PRETORIUS, M. W., Engineering and Technology Management
VAN DER MERWE, J. N., Mining Engineering

Faculty of Health Sciences:

ANDERSON, R., Immunology
BARTEL, P. R., Neurology
BECKER, J. H. R., Surgery
BLITZ-LINDEQUE, J. J., Family Medicine
BUCH, E., School of Health Systems and Public Health
DIPPENAAR, N. G., Physiology
DREYER, L., Anatomical Pathology
DU PLESSIS, D. J., Cardiothoracic Surgery
GREY, S. V., Health Sciences General
KER, J. A., Internal Medicine
KRUGER, M., Paediatrics
LEVINSON, I. P., Urology
LINDEQUE, B. G., Obstetrics and Gynaecology
MAFOJANE, N. A., Neurology
MARITZ, N. G. J., Orthopaedics
MATHIVHA, T. M., Cardiology
MEDLEN, C. E., Pharmacology
MEIRING, J. H., Anatomy
MEYER, H. P., Internal Medicine
MOKOENA, T. R., Surgery
MULDER, A. A. H., Ear, Nose and Throat Medicine
MWANTEMBE, O., Internal Medicine
PATTINSON, R. C., Obstetrics and Gynaecology
RANTLOANE, J. L. A., Anaesthesiology
REIF, S., Urology
RHEEDER, P., Clinical Epidemiology
ROOS, J. L., Psychiatry
ROUX, P., Ophthalmology
SAAYMAN, G., Forensic Medicine
SCHOLTZ, M. E., Radiology
SCHUTTE, C.-M., Neurology
SNYMAN, J. R., Pharmacology
STEYN, M., Anatomy
SWART, J. G., Otorhinolaryngology

VAN GELDER, A. L., Internal Medicine
VAN PAPENDORP, D. H., Physiology
VAN WYK, N. C., Nursing Science
VERMAAK, W. J. H., Chemical Pathology
VILJOEN, M., Physiology
WITTENBERG, D. F., Paediatrics

Faculty of Humanities:

ANTONITES, A., Philosophy
BERGH, J. S., Historical and Heritage Studies
BOTHA, P. J., Ancient Languages
CARSTENS, A., Afrikaans
DU PLESSIS, A., Political Sciences
FOURIE, E., Music
GOSLIN, A. E., Biokinetics
GRAY, R. A., English
GROBBELAAR, J., Sociology
HAGEMANN, F. R., Drama
HARRIS, K. L., Historical and Heritage Studies
HOUGH, M., Political Sciences
KRUGER, P. E., Biokinetics, Sport and Leisure Sciences
LOMBARD, A., Social Work
LOUW, B., Communication Pathology
MARCHETTI-MERCER, M. C., Psychology
MAREE, D. J. F., Psychology
MEDALIE, D., English
MITI, K. N., Political Science
MLAMBO, A. S., Historical and Heritage Studies
NEOCOSMOS, M., Sociology
NIEHAUS, I. A., Anthropology and Archaeology
NZEWI, M. E., Music
OHLHOFF, C. H. F., Afrikaans
PEETERS, L. F. H. M. C., Modern European Languages
POTGIETER, J. H., Ancient Languages
PRETORIUS, F., Historical and Heritage Studies
PRETORIUS, R., Criminology
PRINSLOO, D. J., African Languages
PRINSLOO, G. T. M., Ancient Languages
ROODT, P. H., Afrikaans
SAUTHOFF, M. D., Visual Arts
SCHOEMAN, J. B., Psychology
SCHOEMAN, M. M. E., Political Sciences
SHARP, J. S., Anthropology and Archaeology
STANDER, H. F., Ancient Languages
STANFORD, H. J., Music
STEYN, B. J. M., Biokinetics
VAN DER MERWE, A., Communication Pathology
VAN DER MESCHT, H., Music
VAN NIEKERK, C., Music
VAN WYK, G. J., Biokinetics, Sport and Leisure Sciences
VILJOEN, W. D., Music
WALTON, C. R., Music
WEBB, V. N., Afrikaans
WEIDEMAN, A. J., Unit for Language Skills Development
WESSELS, J. A., English
WILLEMSE, H. S. S., Afrikaans

Faculty of Law (tel. (12) 420-2412; fax (12) 362-5184; e-mail duard.kleyn@up.ac.za):

BORAINE, A., Procedural Law
BOTHA, C. J., Public Law
BURDETTE, D. A., Centre for Practical and Continuing Legal Education
CARSTENS, P. A., Public Law
DAVEL, C. J., Private Law and Centre for Child Law
DELPORT, P. A., Mercantile and Labour Law
HANSUNQULE, K. M., Centre for Human Rights
HAUPT, F. S., Law Clinic
HEYNS, C. H., Centre for Human Rights
KLOPPER, H. B., Mercantile and Labour Law
KOTZE, D. J. L., Procedural Law
LOTZ, D. J., Mercantile Law

MAITHUFI, I. P., Private Law
NAGEL, C. J., Mercantile Law
NICHOLSON, C. M. A., Legal History, Comparative Law and Legal Philosophy
SCHOEMAN, M. C., Private Law
SCOTT, T. J., Private Law
THOMAS, P. J., Legal History, Comparative Law and Legal Philosophy
VAN ECK, B. P. S., Mercantile Law
VAN JAARSVELD, S. R., Mercantile Law
VAN MARLE, K., Legal History, Comparative Law and Legal Philosophy
VAN SCHALKWYK, L. N., Private Law
VILJOEN, F. J., Legal History, Comparative Law and Legal Philosophy
VISSER, P. J., Private Law

Faculty of Natural and Agricultural Sciences (Room 2-32, Agricultural Sciences Building, University of Pretoria, Pretoria 0002; tel. (12) 420-3201; fax (12) 420-3890; internet www.up.ac.za/science):

ALBERTS, H. W., Physics
AURET, F. D., Physics
BEAVON, K. S. O., Geography and Geoinformatics
BENNETT, N. C., Zoology and Entomology
BESTER, M. N., Zoology and Entomology
BRAUN, M. W. H., Physics
BREDENKAMP, G. J., Botany
BRINK, D. J., Physics
CASEY, N. H., Animal and Wildlife Sciences
CLOETE, T. E., Microbiology and Plant Pathology
COUTINHO, T. A., Microbiology and Plant Pathology
CROWTHER, N. A. S., Statistics
DE KLERK, H. M., Consumer Science
DE WAAL, S. A., Geology
HUISMANS, H., Genetics
KIRSTEN, J. F., Agricultural Economics, Extension and Rural Development
KUNERT, K. J., Botany
LOTZ, S., Chemistry
LOUW, A. I., Biochemistry
MALHERBE, J. B., Physics
MEYER, J. J. M., Botany
MILLER, H. G., Physics
MINNAAR, A., Food Sciences
NEITZ, A. W. H., Biochemistry
NICOLSON, S. W., Zoology and Entomology
PLASTINO, A. R., Physics
REINHARDT, C. F., Plant Production and Soil Science
ROHWER, E. R., Chemistry
SCHOLTZ, C. H., Zoology and Entomology
STRÖH, A., Mathematics and Applied Mathematics
VAN AARDE, R. J., Zoology and Entomology
VAN ROOYEN, C. J., Agricultural Economics, Extension and Rural Development
VAN WYK, A. E., Botany
VERSCHOOR, J. A., Biochemistry
VLEGGAAR, R., Chemistry

Faculty of Theology:

DE VILLIERS, D. E., Dogmatics and Christian EthicsDREYER, Y., Practical Theology
HOFMEYR, J. W., Church History and Church Policy
HUMAN, D. J., Old Testament Studies
LE ROUX, J. H., Old Testament Studies
MEIRING, P. G. J., Science of Religion and Missiology
MÜLLER, J. C., Practical Theology
VAN AARDE, A. G., New Testament
VAN DER MERWE, P. J., Science of Religion and Missiology
VAN DER WATT, J. G., New Testament Studies
VENTER, P. M., Old Testament Studies
WETHMAR, C. J., Dogmatics and Christian Ethics

Faculty of Veterinary Science (Private Bag X04, Onderstepoort 0110; tel. (12) 529-8000; fax (12) 529-8300; e-mail dean@op.up.ac.za; internet www.up.ac.za/academic/veterinary):

BERTSCHINGER, H. J., Wildlife Unit
BOOMKER, J. D. F., Veterinary Tropical Diseases
BOOTH, K. K., Anatomy and Physiology
COETZER, J. A. W., Veterinary Tropical Diseases
GROENEWALD, H. B., Anatomy and Physiology
GUTHRIE, A. J., Centre for Equine Research
KIRBERGER, R. M., Companion Animal Clinical Studies
LOURENS, D. C., Production Animal Studies
MCCRINDLE, C. M., Paraclinical Sciences
PENZHORN, B. L., Veterinary Tropical Diseases
RAUTENBACH, G. H., Production Animal Studies
STADLER, P., Companion Animal Clinical Studies
SWAN, G. E., Paraclinical Sciences
TERBLANCHE, W. M., Deputy Dean

School of Dentistry:

BOTHA, S. J., Centre for Stomatological Research
BUCH, B., Diagnostics and Röntgenology
BÜTOW, K. W., Maxillo-facial and Oral Surgery
DE WET, F. A., Prosthetics and Dental Mechanics
JACOBS, F. J. (acting), Maxillo-facial and Oral Surgery
KEMP, P. L., Prosthetics and Dental Mechanics
VAN HEERDEN, W. F. P., Oral Pathology and Oral Biology
VAN WYK, P. J., Community Dentistry
VERWAYEN, F. D., Periodontics and Oral Medicine

ATTACHED RESEARCH INSTITUTES

Atomic Energy Institute for Life Sciences: Dir Prof. I. C. DORMEHL.

Carl and Emily Fuchs Institute for Micro-electronics: Dir Prof. M. DU PLESSIS.

Centre for Afrikatourism: Dir Prof. E. T. HEATH.

Centre for Augmentative and Alternative Communication: Dir Prof. E. ALANT.

Centre for Early Intervention in Communication Pathology: Dir Prof. B. LOUW.

Centre for Environmental Biology and Biological Control: Dir Prof. L. KORSTEN.

Centre for Environmental Economics and Policy in Africa: Dir Prof. R. HASSAN.

Centre for Environmental Studies: Dir Prof. J. W. H. FERGUSON.

Centre for Equine Research: Dir Prof. A. J. GUTHRIE.

Centre for Evaluation and Assessment: Dir Prof. S. J. HOWIE.

Centre for Geo Information Services: Dir Prof. P. VAN HELDEN.

Centre for Heritage and History: Dir Prof. K. L. HARRIS.

Centre for Indigenous Knowledge: Dir Prof. C. C. BOONZAAIER (acting).

Centre for Land Related, Regional and Development Policy: Dir Prof. N. J. J. OLIVER.

Centre for Leisure Studies: Dir Prof. A. E. GOSLIN.

Centre for Music Education: Dir Dr H. M. POTGIETER.

Centre for Nutrition: Dir Prof. A. OELOFSE.

Centre for Population Studies: Dir Prof. J. L. VAN TONDER.

Centre for Research on Magmatic Ore Deposits: Dir Prof. S. A. DE WAAL.

Centre for Research in the Politics of Language: Dir Prof. V. N. WEBB.

Centre for Stomatological Research: Dir Prof. W. J. C. COETZEE.

Centre for Theology and Society: Dir Prof. P. R. DU TOIT.

Centre for Wildlife Research: Dir Prof. J. DU P. BOTHMA.

Discovery Centre @ Tuks: Dir Prof. J. VAN STADEN.

Forestry and Agricultural Biotechnology Institute: Dir Prof. M. J. WINGFIELD.

Hans Snyckers Institute (for community-directed health research): Dir Prof. R. J. E. ERASMUS.

Institute of Applied Materials: Dir Prof. W. W. FOCKE.

Institute for Missiological Research: Dir Prof. J. J. KRITZINGER.

Institute for Sports Research: Dir Prof. P. E. KRUGER.

Institute for Strategic Studies: Dir Prof. M. HOUGH.

Institute for Technological Innovation: Dir Prof. A. POURIS.

Joint Centre for Science, Mathematics and Technology Education: Dir Dr L. JITA.

Mammal Research Institute: Dir (vacant).

Postgraduate School of Agriculture and Rural Development: Dir Prof. C. MACHETHE.

South African Institute for Agricultural Extension: Dir Prof. G. H. DÜVEL.

Unit for Language Skills Development (ULSD): Dir Prof. A. J. WEIDEMAN.

Unit for Language and Speech: Dir Prof. V. N. WEBB.

UP Foundation Year Programme: Dir U. SMITH.

RESEARCH BUREAUX

Bureau for Economic Policy and Analysis: Dir Prof. N. J. SCHOEMAN.

Bureau for Financial Analysis: Dir Prof. L. M. BRUMMER.

Bureau for Statistical and Survey Methodology (STATOMET): Dir D. HERBST.

RESEARCH UNITS AND INSTITUTES OF THE MRC

(See under South African Medical Research Council.)

RHODES UNIVERSITY

POB 94, Grahamstown 6140
Telephone: (46) 603-8101
Fax: (46) 603-8127
E-mail: registrar@ru.ac.za
Internet: www.ru.ac.za

Founded 1904; East London Campus incorporated into Univ. of Fort Hare 2004
State control
Language of instruction: English
Academic year: February to November (4 terms)

Chancellor: Prof. G. J. GERWEL
Chairman of the Council: Hon. Mr Justice R. J. W. JONES
Principal and Vice-Chancellor: D. R. WOODS
Vice-Principal and Pro-Vice-Chancellor: C. T. JOHNSON
Dean of Research: J. R. DUNCAN
Dean of Students: M. A. MOTARA
Registrar: S. FOURIE
Librarian: M. A. E. KENYON

Library: see Libraries and Archives
Number of teachers: 305
Number of students: 6,155

Publications: *English in Africa* (annually), *Journal of Contemporary African Studies* (2 a year), *New Coin Poetry* (2 a year), *Philosophical Papers* (2 a year), *Rhodes Journalism Review* (irregular)

DEANS

Faculty of Commerce: A. C. M. WEBB
Faculty of Education: G. J. EUVRARD
Faculty of Humanities: F. T. HENDRICKS
Faculty of Law: J. R. MIDGLEY
Faculty of Pharmacy: I. KANFER
Faculty of Science: P. D. TERRY

PROFESSORS

ADENDORFF, R., English Language and Linguistics
ADESINA, J. O. T., Sociology and Industrial Sociology
ANTROBUS, G. G., Economics
BERGER, G. J. E. G., Journalism and Media Studies
BERNARD, R. T. F., Zoology
BLATCH, G. L., Biochemistry, Microbiology and Biotechnology
BOTHA, C. E. J., Botany
CHARTERIS, J., Human Kinetics and Ergonomics
CLAYTON, P. G., Computer Science
COETZEE, J. K., Sociology and Industrial Sociology
CRAIG, A. T. F., Zoology and Entomology
DAVIES-COLEMAN, M. T., Chemistry
DAYA, S., Pharmacy
DE KLERK, V. A., Linguistics and English Language
DE WET, C. J., Anthropology
DUNCAN, J. R., Biochemistry
EDWARDS, D. J. A., Psychology
EUVRARD, G. J., Education
FABRICIUS, C., Environmental Science
FAURE, P., Economics
FOX, R. C., Geography
GORDON, G. E., Drama
GOUWS, J. S., English
HAIGH, J. M., Pharmacy
HARVEY, N., Management
HENDRICKS, F. T., Sociology and Industrial Sociology
HEPBURN, H. R., Entomology
HODGSON, A. N., Zoology and Entomology
HUGHES, D. A., Water Research
IRWIN, P. R., Education
JACOB, R. E., Geology
JAQUES, F. E., School of Languages
JONAS, J. L., Physics and Electronics
KANFER, I., Pharmaceutics
KAYE, P. T., Organic Chemistry
LEWIS, C. A., Geography
MABIZELA, S. G., Pure and Applied Mathematics
MARSH, J. S., Geology
MAYLAM, P. R., History
McQUAID, C. D., Zoology
MIDGLEY, J. R., Law
MØLLER, V., Social and Economic Research
MOORE, J. M., Exploration Geology
MQEKE, R. B., Law
NEL, E. L., Geography
NEL, H., Economics
NYOKONG, T., Chemistry
RADLOFF, S. E., Statistics
ROSE, P. D., Biotechnology
ROWNTREE, K. M., Geography
SCARR, D. T., Music and Musicology
SCHMAHMANN, B. L., Fine Art
SCOTT, P. A., Human Kinetics and Ergonomics
SEWRY, D. A., Information Systems
SKELTON, P., Aquatic Biodiversity
STACK, E. M., Accounting
STAUDE, G. E., Management
STONES, C. R., Psychology
TERRY, P. D., Computer Science
VALE, P. C. J., Political and International Studies

WALTERS, P. S., English
WEBB, A. C. M., Economics
WENTWORTH, E. P., Computer Science
WRIGHT, L. S., Study of English in Africa

ATTACHED INSTITUTES

Albany Museum: Dir Dr L. WEBLEY (acting).

Dictionary Unit for South African English: Dir J. WOLVAARDT (acting).

Institute of Social and Economic Research (ISER): f. 1954; Dir Prof. V. MØLLER.

Institute for the Study of English in Africa (ISEA): f. 1964; Dir Prof. L. S. WRIGHT.

International Library of African Music: Dir Prof. A. T. N. TRACEY.

National English Literary Museum: f. 1981; Dir M. M. HACKSLEY.

Rhodes Institute for Water Research: f. 1967; Dir Prof. D. A. HUGHES.

South African Institute for Aquatic Biodiversity: f. 1968; Dir Prof. P. H. SKELTON.

UNIVERSITY OF SOUTH AFRICA

POB 392, Unisa 0003
Telephone: (12) 429-3111
Fax: (12) 429-3221
E-mail: artes@unisa.ac.za
Internet: www.unisa.ac.za

Founded 1873, Royal Charter 1877; merged with Technikon Southern Africa and incorporated Vista University 2004
Languages of instruction: Afrikaans, English
Academic year: February to November

Chancellor: Justice BERNARD MAKGABO NGOEPE
Vice-Chancellor: Prof. BARNEY PITYANA
Chairperson of the Council: Dr MATTHEWS PHOSA
Pro-Vice-Chancellor: Prof. NEO MATHABE
Deputy Vice-Chancellor and Vice-Principal (Operations): Prof. D. L. MOSOMA (acting)
Vice-Principal (Academic): Prof. C. F. SWANEPOEL
Vice-Principal (Finance): Prof. G. J. DE J. CRONJE (acting)
Vice-Principal (Learner Support): Prof. A. H. LOUW
Vice-Principal (Research and Planning): Prof. N. BALJNATH
Vice-Principal (Student and Alumni Affairs): Prof. R. C. BODIBE
Registrar: Prof. T. H. LINKS
Registrar (Academic): Prof. L. MOLAMU (acting)
Librarian: Prof. J. WILLEMSE

Number of teachers: 1,074
Number of students: 200,000

Publications: *Africanus* (2 a year), *Ars Nova* (annually), *Codicillus* (2 a year), *Communicatio* (2 a year), *De Arte* (2 a year), *Educare* (annually), *Kleio* (annually), *Language Matters* (annually), *Mousaion* (2 a year), *Musicus* (2 a year), *Politeia* (3 a year), *Scrutiny²* (2 a year), *Unisa Bulletin* (5 a year), *Unisa News* (4 a year), *Unisa Psychologia* (2 a year)

DEANS

College of Agriculture and Environment Sciences: (vacant)
College of Economics and Management Sciences: Prof. MRAD SHAHIA
College of Human Sciences: Prof. M. S. MAKHANYA
College of Law: Prof. RITA MARE'
College of Science, Engineering and Technology: Prof. G. J. SUMMERS
Graduate School of Business Leadership: Prof. H. C. NGAMBI (Executive Director)

PROFESSORS

ABRIE, A., Accounting
ACKERMANN, P. L. S., Graduate School of Business Leadership
ADLEM, W. L. J., Public Administration
AILOLA, D. A., Mercantile Law
BADENHORST, J. A., Business Management
BARROW, J. E., Computer Science
BEATY, D. T., Graduate School of Business Leadership
BECKER, H. M. R., Applied Accountancy
BEGEMANN, E., Business Management
BEKKER, P. M., Criminal and Procedural Law
BESTER, G., Educational Studies
BEYERS, E., Psychology
BISHOP, N. T., Mathematics, Applied Mathematics and Astronomy
BODENSTEIN, H. C. A., Educational Studies
BOOT, G., Accounting
BOOYENS, S. W., Advanced Nursing Sciences
BOOYSE, J. J., Further Teacher Training
BOOYSEN, H., Constitutional and International Law
BORNMAN, C. H., Computer Science
BOTHA, J. E., New Testament
BOTHA, N. J., Constitutional and International Law
BOTHA, P. J. J., New Testament
BRITS, J. P., History
BRYNARD, D. J., Public Administration
BURNS, Y. M., Constitutional and International Law
CALITZ, E., Economics
CANT, M. C., Business Management
CARPENTER, G., Constitutional and International Law
CHURCH, J., Jurisprudence
CILLIERS, C. H., Criminology
CILLIERS, F. VAN N., Industrial Psychology
COETZER, I. A., Educational Studies
CONRADIE, H., Criminology
CRONJE, D. S. P., Private Law
CRONJE, G. J. DE J., Business Management
CRONJE, P. M., Accounting
CROUS, S. F. M., Educational Studies
DADOO, Y., Semitics
DE BEER, C. S., Information Science
DE BEER, F. C., Anthropology and Archaeology
DE BEER, F. C., Development Administration
DE JONGH, M., Anthropology and Archaeology
DEMBETEMBE, N. C., African Languages
DICK, A. L., Information Science
DREECKMEYER, M., Secondary School Education
DREYER, J. M., Advanced Nursing Sciences
DU PISANIE, J. A., Economics
DU PLESSIS, I. J., New Testament
DU PLESSIS, P. J., Graduate School of Business Leadership
DU TOIT, C. W., Research Institute for Theology and Religion
DU TOIT, G. S., Business Management
ENGELBRECHT, J., New Testament
ERASMUS, B. J., Business Management
FARIS, J. A., Criminal and Procedural Law
FAURE, A. M., Political Sciences
FINLAYSON, R., African Languages
FOURIE, D. P., Psychology
FOURIE, L. J., Economics
FOURIE, P. J., Communication
FRANZSEN, R. C. D., Mercantile Law
GELDENHUYS, D. G., Musicology
GHYOOT, V. G., Business Management
GRÄBE, R. C., Theory of Literature
GROBBELAAR, A. F., Accounting
GROBBELAAR, J. I., Sociology
GROBLER, G. M. M., African Languages
GROBLER, P. A., Business Management
GRUNDLINGH, A. M., History
HAVENGA, M. K., Mercantile Law
HAVENGA, P. H., Mercantile Law
HAWTHORNE, L., Private Law
HEIDEMA, J., Mathematics, Applied Mathematics and Astronomy

HENDRIKSE, A. P., Linguistics
HIGGS, P., Educational Studies
HOFMEYR, K. B., Graduate School of Business Leadership
HOUGH, J., Business Management
HUBBARD, E. H., Linguistics
HUGO, P. J., Political Sciences
HUGO, W. M. J., Graduate School of Business Leadership
JANSE VAN RENSBURG, J. B., Applied Accountancy
JORDAAN, W. J., Psychology
JOUBERT, J. J., Criminal and Procedural Law
JULYAN, F. W., Accounting
KATKOVNIK, V., Statistics
KLERCK, W. G., Graduate School of Business Leadership
KRIEK, D. J., Political Science
KRITZINGER, J. N. J., Missiology
KRUGER, E. G., Secondary School Teacher Education
KRÜGER, J. S., Religious Studies
LANDMAN, A. A., Mercantile Law
LEMMER, E. M., Further Teacher Training
LESSING, A. C., Educational Studies
LIEBENBERG, E. C., Geography
LIGTHELM, A. A., Bureau for Market Research
LOMBARD, D. B., Classics
LÖTTER, S., Criminal and Procedural Law
LOUWRENS, L. J., African Languages
LÜBBE, J. C., Semitics
LUCAS, G. H. A., Business Management
MCKAY, V. I., Institute for Adult Basic Education and Training
MCLEARY, F., Graduate School of Business Leadership
MADER, G. J., Classics
MARAIS, A. DE K., Business Management
MARE, E. A., History of Art, Fine Art
MARÉ, M. C., Criminal and Procedural Law
MAREE, M. C., Romance Languages
MARKHAM, R., Statistics
MARTINS, J. A., Bureau for Market Research
MARX, J., Business Management
MISCH, M. K. E., German
MOHR, P. J., Economics
MOTLHABI, M. B. G., Systematic Theology and Theological Ethics
MSIMANG, C. T., African Languages
MYNHARDT, C. M., Mathematics, Applied Mathematics and Astronomy
NAUDE, C. M. B., Criminology
NELL, V., Social and Health Sciences
NESER, J. J., Criminology
NTULI, D. B., African Languages
OBERHOLZER, M. O., Educational Studies
OLIVIER, A., Primary School Education
ORR, M. A., English
PALMER, P. N., Business Management
PAUL, S. O., Chemistry
PAUW, J. C., Public Administration
PELSER, G. P. J., Graduate School of Business Leadership
PIETERSE, H. J. C., Practical Theology
PLUG, C., Psychology
POTGIETER, C., Further Teacher Education
POTGIETER, J. M., Private Law
POTGIETER, T. J. E., Graduate School of Business Leadership
POULOS, G., African Languages
PRETORIUS, E. A. C., New Testament
PRETORIUS, J. T., Mercantile Law
PRETORIUS, L., Sociology
PRINSLOO, E. D., Philosophy
RABINOWITZ, I. A., English
RADEMEYER, G., Psychology
REYNHARDT, E. C., Physics
ROELOFSE, J. J., Communication
ROOS, H. M., Afrikaans
RUTHERFORD, B. R., Mercantile Law
RYAN, P. D., English
SADLER, E., Applied Accountancy
SALBANY, S. DE O., Applied Mathematics, Mathematics and Astronomy
SCHEFFLER, E. H., Old Testament
SCOTT, S. J., Private Law

SEBOTHOMA, W. A., New Testament
SERUDU, S. M., African Languages
SHAHIA, M., Transport Economics and Logistics
SMIT, B. F., Criminology
SMIT, P. J., Business Management
SMITH, J. DU P., Economics
SMITH, K. W., History
SMUTS, C. A., Transport Economics and Logistics
SNYDERS, F. J. A., Psychology
SNYMAN, C. R., Criminal and Procedural Law
SNYMAN, J. W., African Languages
SOFIANOS, S. A., Physics
SÖHNGE, W. F., Educational Studies
STEENEKAMP, T. J., Economics
STEFFENS, F. E., Statistics
STEYN, B. L., Accounting
STRIKE, W. N., Romance Languages
STRYDOM, J. W., Business Management
SUMMERS, G. J., Chemistry
SWANEPOEL, C. F., African Languages
SWANEPOEL, C. H., Institute for Educational Research
SWANEPOEL, C. J., Quantitative Management
SWANEPOEL, F. A., C. B. Powell Bible Centre
SWANEPOEL, P. H., Afrikaans
SWANEVELDER, J. J., Accounting
SWART, G. J., Mercantile Law
SWEMMER, P. N., Auditing
TERBLANCHE, S. S., Criminal and Procedural Law
THOMASHAUSEN, A. E. A. M., Institute for Foreign and Comparative Law
TORR, C. S. W., Economics
TROSKIE, R., Advanced Nursing Sciences
VAKALISA, N. C. G., Secondary School Education
VAN ASWEGEN, A., Private Law
VAN BILJON, R. C. W., Social Work
VAN BLERK, A. E., Jurisprudence
VAN DELFT, W. F., Social Work
VAN DEN BERG, P. H., Graduate School of Business Leadership
VAN DER MERWE, C. A., Quantitative Management
VAN DER MERWE, D. P., Criminal and Procedural Law
VAN DER WALT, A. J., Private Law
VAN DYK, P. J., Old Testament
VAN HEERDEN, B., Auditing
VAN NIEKERK, E., Systematic Theology, Theological Ethics
VAN NIEKERK, J. P., Mercantile Law
VAN ROOY, M. P., Educational Studies
VAN WYK, A. M. A., Private Law
VAN WYK, C. W., Jurisprudence
VAN WYK, D. H., Constitutional and International Law
VAN WYK, H. DE J., Bureau for Market Research
VAN ZYL, A. E., Educational Studies
VILJOEN, H. G., Psychology
VISSER, C. J., Mercantile Law
VISSER, P. S., Educational Studies
VORSTER, H. J. S., Auditing
VORSTER, J. N., New Testament
VORSTER, L. P., Indigenous Law
VORSTER, S. J. R., Mathematics, Applied Mathematics and Astronomy
WATKINS, M. L., Industrial Psychology
WEINBERG, A. M., English
WESSELS, W. J., Old Testament
WHELPTON, F. P. VAN R., Indigenous Law
WIECHERS, E., Educational Studies
WIECHERS, N. J., Private Law
WILLIAMS, G., Applied Accountancy
WOLFAARDT, J. A., Practical Theology
WOLFAARDT, J. B., Industrial Psychology
WOLVAARDT, J. S., Quantitative Management
YADAVALLI, V. S. S., Statistics

ATTACHED INSTITUTES

Centre for African Renaissance Studies: Dir Prof. S. B. O. GUTTO.

Centre for Applied Statistics: Dir Prof. F. E. STEFFENS.

Centre for Business Law: Dir Prof. C. J. VISSER.

Centre for Latin American Studies: Head Z. ROELOFSE-CAMPBELL.

Centre for Women's Studies: Dir Prof. J. R. WILKINSON.

C. B. Powell Bible Centre: Dir Prof. F. A. SWANEPOEL.

Institute for Continuing Education: Head E. P. NONYONGO.

Institute for Criminology: Dir Prof. J. H. PRINSLOO.

Institute for Educational Research: Dir Prof. C. H. SWANEPOEL.

Institute for Foreign and Comparative Law: Dir Prof. A. E. A. M. THOMASHAUSEN.

Institute for Social and Health Sciences: Dir Prof. M. A. SEEDAT.

Research Institute for Theology and Religion: Dir Prof. C. W. DU TOIT.

UNIVERSITY OF STELLENBOSCH

Private Bag X1, Matieland 7602, Cape Province

Telephone: (21) 808-9111
Fax: (21) 808-4499
E-mail: webinfo@maties.sun.ac.za
Internet: www.sun.ac.za

Founded 1918; dental faculty incorporated into University of the Western Cape 2004
Language of instruction: Afrikaans
Academic year: February to December (four terms)

Chancellor: Prof. ELIZE BOTHA
Principal and Vice-Chancellor: Prof. C. H. BRINK
Vice-Principal (Academic): Prof. H. R. BOTMAN
Vice-Principal (Operations): Prof. J. F. SMITH
Vice-Principal (Research): Prof. W. T. CLAASSEN
Registrar: J. A. ASPELING
Director of Library Services (vacant)
Number of teachers: 745
Number of students: 22,000

Publications: *Annals of the University, Calendar, Matieland, Maatskaplike Werk* (Social Work, 4 a year), *Opinion Survey Report* (Bureau of Economic Research, 4 a year), *Survey of Contemporary Economic Conditions and Prospects* (annually), *Research Report* (annually), *Report of the Rector*

DEANS

Faculty of Agriculture and Forestry: Prof. L. VAN HUYSTEEN
Faculty of Arts: Prof. H. J. KOTZÉ
Faculty of Economic and Management Sciences: Prof. J. U. DE VILLIERS
Faculty of Education: Prof. T. PARK
Faculty of Engineering: Prof. A. SCHOONWINKEL
Faculty of Health Sciences: Prof. W. L. VAN DER MERWE
Faculty of Law: (vacant)
Faculty of Military Science: Prof. D. J. MALAN
Faculty of Science: Prof. A. S. VAN JAARSVELD
Faculty of Theology: Prof. A. E. J. MOUTON

PROFESSORS

Faculty of Agriculture and Forestry (tel. (21) 808-4792; fax (21) 808-2001; e-mail lvh@ maties.sun.ac.za; internet www.sun.ac.za/ agric):

AGENBAG, G. A., Agronomy and Pastures
BREDENKAMP, B. V., Forestry Science
BRITZ, T., Food Science
FEY, M. V., Soil Science

GOUSSARD, P. G., Oenology and Viticulture
HOLZ, G., Plant Pathology
MARAIS, G. F., Genetics
SAMWAYS, M. J., Entomology
THERON, K. I., Horticulture
VAN HUYSSTEEN, L., Soil Science
VAN WYK, G., Forestry Science
VINK, N., Agricultural Economics
WARNICH, L., Genetics

Faculty of Arts (tel. (21) 808-2138; fax (21) 808-2123; e-mail hjk@maties.sun.ac.za; internet www.sun.ac.za/arts):

BEKKER, S. B., Sociology
BOTHA, R. P., Linguistics
CILLIERS, F. P., Philosophy
CORNELIUS, I., Ancient Studies
DU TOIT, P. V. D. P., Political Science
GAGIANO, A. H., English
GOUWS, A., Political Science
GOUWS, R. H., Afrikaans and Dutch
GREEN, S., Social Work
GROVÉ, I. J., Music
GRUNDLINGH, A. M., History
HATTINGH, J. P., Philosophy
HAUPTFLEISCH, T., Drama
KAGEE, S. A., Psychology
KINGHORN, J., Biblical Studies
KLOPPER, D. C., English
KLOPPER, S., Fine Arts
KOTZE, H. J., Political Science
KRITZINGER, A. S., Sociology
MOUTON, J., Sociology
NAIDOO, A. V., Psychology
RABE, I., Journalism
ROOSENSCHOON, H., Music
SWARTZ, L. P., Psychology
THOM, J. C., Ancient Studies
VAN DER MERWE, W. L., Philosophy
VAN DER WAAL, C. S., Sociology
VAN NIEKERK, A. A., Philosophy
VILJOEN, L., Afrikaans and Dutch
VON MALTZAN, C. H., Modern Foreign Languages
ZIETSMAN, H. L., Geography and Environmental Studies
ZULU, N. S., African Languages

Faculty of Economic and Management Sciences (tel. (21) 808-2225; fax (21) 808-2409; e-mail calitz@maties.sun.ac.za; internet www.sun.ac.za/economy):

AUGUSTYN, J. C. D., Industrial Psychology
BIEKPE, N. B., Business Administration
BROWN, W., Accounting
BURGER, A. P., Public and Development Management
CLOETE, G. S., Public and Development Management
DE VILLIERS, J. U., Business Management
DE WET, T., Statistics and Actuarial Science
GEVERS, W. R., Business Management and Administration
HOUGH, J., Business Management
LEIBOLD, M., Business Management
MOSTERT, F. J., Business Management
OLIVIER, P., Accounting
OOSTHUIZEN, H., Business Administration
PIENAAR, W. J., Logistics
SCHOOMBEE, G. A., Economics
SCHWELLA, E., Public and Development Management
SLATTERY, P. G., Statistics and Actuarial Science
SMIT, B. W., Economics
SMIT, E. VAN DER M., Business Management and Administration
STEEL, S. J., Statistics and Actuarial Science
SWILLING, M., Public and Development Management
TERBLANCHE, N. S., Business Management
VAN DER BERG, S., Economics
VAN SCHALKWYK, C. J., Accounting

Faculty of Education (tel. (21) 808-2258; fax (21) 808-2269; e-mail tp@maties.sun.ac.za; internet www.sun.ac.za/education):

BERKHOUT, S. J., Educational Policy Studies
BITZER, E. M., Didactics
CARL, A. E., Didactics
KAPP, C. A., Centre for Higher and Adult Education
LE GRANGE, L. L. L., Didactics
PARK, T., Didactics
SCHREUDER, D. R., Didactics
SWART, R. E., Educational Psychology
WAGHID, Y., Educational Policy Studies

Faculty of Engineering (tel. (21) 808-4203; fax (21) 808-4206; e-mail schoonwinkel@maties.sun.ac.za; internet www.sun.ac.za/eng):

ALDRICH, C., Chemical Engineering
BASSON, A. H., Mechanical Engineering
BASSON, G. R., Civil Engineering
BESTER, C. J., Civil Engineering
BRADSHAW, S. M., Chemcial Engineering
BURGER, A. J., Chemical Engineering
CLOETE, J. H., Electrical and Electronic Engineering
DAVIDSON, D. B., Electrical and Electronic Engineering
DUNAISKI, P. E., Civil Engineering
DU PLESSIS, J. P., Applied Mathematics
DU PREEZ, N. D., Industrial Engineering
HERBST, B. M., Applied Mathematics
JENKINS, K. J., Civil Engineering
KAMPER, M. J., Electrical and Electronic Engineering
KNOETZE, J. H., Chemical Engineering
LORENZEN, L., Chemical Engineering
LOURENS, J. G., Electrical and Electronic Engineering
MEYER, P., Electrical and Electronic Engineering
PEROLD, W. J., Electrical and Electronic Engineering
READER, H. C., Electrical and Electronic Engineering
SCHOONWINKEL, A., Electrical and Electronic Engineering
STEYN, W. H., Electrical and Electronic Engineering
VAN NIEKERK, J. L., Mechanical Engineering
VON BACKSTRÖM, T. W., Mechanical Engineering
WEIDEMAN, J. A. C., Applied Mathematics

Faculty of Health Sciences (tel. (21) 938-9200; fax (21) 938-9558; e-mail wvdmerwe@maties.sun.ac.za; internet www.sun.ac.za/med.fac):

BEYERS, N., Paediatrics and Child Health
BRINK, P. A., Internal Medicine
CHIKTE, U. M. E., Associate Dean
COETZEE, A. R., Anaesthesiology
DE VILLIERS, B., Associate Dean
DE VILLIERS, M. R., Family Medicine and Primary Care
DE VILLIERS, P. J. T., Family Medicine and Primary Care
DOUBELL, A. F., Internal Medicine
DU TOIT, D., Anatomy and Histology
EMSLEY, R. A., Psychiatry
ERASMUS, R. T., Chemical Pathology
HEYNS, C. F., Urology
HOUGH, F. S., Internal Medicine
KOESLAG, J. H., Medical Physiology and Biochemistry
KRUGER, T. F., Obstetrics and Gynaecology
LABADARIOS, D., Human Nutrition
LIEBOWITZ, L. D., Medical Microbiology
LOOCK, J. W., Otorhinolaryngology
MANSVELT, E P., Haematology
MEYER, D., Ophthalmology
MOORE, S. W., Surgery
ROSSOUW, G. J., Cardiothoracic Surgery
SCHER, A. T., Radiation Oncology

SCHNEIDER, J. W., Anatomical Pathology
SEEDAT, S., Psychiatry
THERON, G. B., Obstetrics and Gynaecology
VAN DER BIJL, P., Pharmacology
VAN DER MERWE, W. L., Medical Physiology and Biochemistry
VAN HEERDEN, B. B., Head of School of Medicine
VERNIMMEN, F. J. A. I., Radiation Oncology
VLOK, G. J., Orthopaedic Surgery
WARREN, B. L., Surgery
WELMANN, E. B., Nursing Science
WRIGHT, C. A., Anatomical Pathology

Faculty of Law (tel. (21) 808-4853; fax (21) 886-6235; e-mail jsaf@maties.sun.ac.za; internet www.sun.ac.za/law):

BUTLER, D. W., Mercantile Law
DE VOS, W., Private Law and Roman Law
DE WAAL, M. J., Private Law and Roman Law
DU PLESSIS, J. E., Private Law and Roman Law
DU PLESSIS, L. M., Public Law
ERASMUS, M. G., Public Law
HUGO, C. F., Mercantile Law
HUMAN, C. S., Private Law and Roman Law
LIEBENBERG, S., Public Law
LOUBSER, M. M., Private Law and Roman Law
LUBBE, G. F., Private Law and Roman Law
PIENAAR, J. M., Private Law and Roman Law
SUTHERLAND, P. J., Mercantile Law
VAN DER MERWE, S. E., Public Law
VAN DER WALT, A. J., Public Law

Faculty of Science (tel. (21) 808-3072; fax (21) 808-3608; e-mail asvanj@maties.sun.ac.za; internet www.sun.ac.za/science):

CHOWN, S. L., Plant and Animal Science
CROUCH, A. M., Chemistry
DE VILLIERS, J. M., Mathematics
DICKS, L. M. T, Microbiology
DILLEN, J. L. M., Chemistry
EGGERS, H. C., Chemistry
GEYER, H. B., Physics
GREEN, B. W., Mathematics
HAPGOOD, J. P., Biochemistry
HOFMEYR, J. H. S., Biochemistry
KOCH, K. R., Chemistry
KOSSMANN, J. M., Zoology
KRZESINSKI, A. E., Computer Science
LAURIE, D. P., Mathematics
MUCINA, L., Plant and Animal Science
MYBURGH, K. H., Physiological Sciences
PRIOR, B. A., Microbiology
PRODINGER, H., Mathematics
RAUBENHEIMER, H. G., Chemistry
RAWLINGS, D. E., Microbiology
REINECKE, A. J., Plant and Animal Science
RICHARDSON, D. M., Plant and Animal Science
ROBINSON, T. J., Plant and Animal Science
ROZENDAAL, A., Geology
SANDERSON, R. D., Polymer Science
SCHOLTZ, F. G., Physics
SMITH, V. R., Plant and Animal Science
SNOEP, J. L., Biochemistry
STEVENS, G., Geology
SWART, P., Biochemistry
VAN JAARSVELD, A. S., Plant and Animal Science
VAN WYK, L., Mathematics
VAN ZYL, W. H., Microbiology
VON BERGMANN, H. M., Physics

Faculty of Theology (tel. (21) 808-3255; fax (21) 808-3251; e-mail djl@maties.sun.ac.za; internet www.sun.ac.za/theology):

BOSMAN, H. L., Old and New Testament
HENDRIKS, H. J., Practical Theology and Missiology
MOUTON, A. E. J., Old and New Testament
SMIT, D. J., Systematic Theology

ATTACHED RESEARCH INSTITUTES

Advanced Manufacturing Unit: Head C. J. FOURIE.

Centre for Applied Ethics: Head Prof. A. A. VAN NIEKERK.

Centre for Bible Translation in Africa: Head Dr C. H. J. VAN DER MERWE.

Centre for Children's Literature and Media: Head Prof. A. E. CARL.

Centre for Contextual Hermeneutics: Head Prof. J. KINGHORN.

Centre for Disabled Care and Rehabilitation: Head Ms MJI.

Centre for Educational Development: Head Y. WAGHID.

Centre for Electrical and Electronic Engineering: Head Prof. F. S. VAN DER MERWE.

Centre for Entrepreneurship: Head Dr J. VENTER.

Centre for Geographical Analysis: Head Dr J. H. VAN DER MERWE.

Centre for Higher and Adult Education: Head Prof. C. A. KAPP.

Centre for Interdisciplinary Studies: Head Prof. J. MOUTON.

Centre for International and Comparative Politics: Head Prof. H. J. KOTZÉ.

Centre for International Business: Head Prof. M. LEIBOLD.

Centre for Leadership Studies (Southern Africa): Head Prof. H. H. SPANGENBERG.

Centre for Military Studies: Head Col L. DU PLESSIS.

Centre for Molecular and Cellular Biology: Head Prof. P. D. VAN HELDEN.

Centre for Theatre and Performance Studies: Head Prof. T. HAUPTFLEISCH.

Cranio-Facial Unit at Tygerberg Hospital: Head Dr C. S. F. SMIT.

Drug Research Unit: Head Prof. J. R. JOUBERT.

Educational Psychology Unit: Head Dr P. J. NORMAND.

Experimental Phonology Unit: Head Prof. J. C. ROUX.

Institute for Applied Computer Science: Dir Prof. A. E. KRZESINSKI.

Institute for Futures Research: Dir Prof A. ROUX.

Institute for Industrial Engineering: Dir Prof. N. D. DU PREEZ.

Institute for Mathematics and Science Teaching: Dir Dr J. H. SMIT.

Institute for Polymer Science: Dir Prof. R. D. SANDERSON.

Institute for Sport and Movement Studies: Dir Dr J. H. MALAN.

Institute for Structural Engineering: Dir Prof. J. V. RETIEF.

Institute for Theoretical Physics: Dir Prof. H. B. GEYER.

Institute for Thermodynamics and Mechanics: Dir Prof. D. G. KRÖGER.

Institute for Transport Technology: Dir Prof. F. HUGO.

Institute for Wine Biotechnology: Dir Prof. M. VIVIER.

Perinatal Mortality Research Unit: Head Prof. H. J. ODENDAAL.

TSHWANE UNIVERSITY OF TECHNOLOGY

Private Bag X 680, Pretoria 0001
Telephone: (12) 318-5911
Fax: (12) 318-5114

E-mail: general@tut.ac.za
Internet: www.techpta.ac.za
Founded 2004 by merger of Technikon Pretoria, Technikon North Gauteng and Technikon North West
Vice-Chancellor and Rector: Prof. REGGIE NGCOBO
Exec. Managers and Deputy Vice-Chancellors (vacant): Prof. N. P. DU PREEZ, Prof. H. H. DÜRRHEIM, Prof. J. G. PRETORIUS
Registrar: N. J. V. D. M. STOFBERG
Library Director: Dr A. SWANEPOEL
Library of 70,000 vols
Number of students: 40,000

Publications: *Peritus* (4 a year), *School for Chemical Science Newsletter* (quarterly), *Student*

DEANS

Faculty of Agriculture, Horticulture and Nature Conservation: Prof. J. J. BOTHA
Faculty of Arts: E. R. DINKELMANN
Faculty of Economic Sciences: Prof. M. J. VAN DER MERWE
Faculty of Engineering: Prof. F. OTIENO
Faculty of Health Sciences: Prof. M. M. J. LOWES
Faculty of Information and Communication Technology: Dr J. ZAAIMAN
Faculty of Natural Sciences: Prof P. J. J. G. MARAIS
Faculty of Social Development Sciences: Prof. S. N. IMENDA

VAAL UNIVERSITY OF TECHNOLOGY

Private Bag X021, Vanderbijlpark, 1900 Gauteng
Telephone: (16) 950-9000
Fax: (16) 950-9787
E-mail: academic@vut.ac.za
Internet: www.vut.ac.za
Founded 1966, present name 1979
Vice-Chancellor and Rector: Prof. A. T. MOKADI
Vice-Rectors: Prof. ROY DU PRÉ (Academic), Dr PRAKASH NAIDOO (Administration)
Librarian: A. J. GOZO
Library of 42,000 vols, 4,480 periodicals
Number of teachers: 311 full-time
Number of teachers: 551 part-time
Number of students: 12,434
Publications: *Sediba sa Thuto* (academic journal, annually), *Tempo* (communications journal, 2 a year)
Faculties of Applied and Computer Sciences, Engineering and Technology, Humanities and Management Sciences.

UNIVERSITY OF VENDA FOR SCIENCE AND TECHNOLOGY

Private bag X5050, Thohoyandou 0950, Limpopo
Telephone: (15) 962-8000
Fax: (15) 962-4749
E-mail: prd@univen.ac.za
Internet: www.univen.ac.za
Founded 1982 as University of Venda by Venda Parliament; national status as University of Venda 1996; non-statutory name University of Venda for Science and Technology
State control
Schools: agriculture, environmental sciences and engineering; health sciences; human and social sciences; management sciences and law; mathematics and natural sciences; postgraduate and integrated studies; rural development and forestry.
Principal and Vice-Chancellor: Prof. G. M. NKONDO

Library of 90,871 vols, 823 periodicals
Number of teachers: 301
Number of students: 9,500
Publication: *Journal of Educational Studies* (2 a year)

EXECUTIVE DEANS

Faculty of Health, Agriculture and Rural Development: Prof. N. S. MAHOKO
Faculty of Human and Social Sciences, Management Sciences and Law: Prof. M. D. R. RALEBIPI-SIMELA
Faculty of Natural and Applied Sciences: Prof. P. H. OMARA-OJUNGU

PROFESSORS

Faculty of Human and Social Sciences, Management Sciences and Law:

AKINNUSI, D. M.
AYURU, R. N.
BAYONA, E. L. M.
GYEKE, A. B.
LUKHAIMANE, E. K.
MIREKU, O.
SIMUKONDA, H. P. M.
SPENCER, J. P.
STEYN, J. N.

Faculty of Natural and Applied Sciences:

AGBONJINMI, A. P.
AMUSA, L. O.
DU TOIT, P. J.
KHOZA, L. B.
KIRUNDA, E. F.
MAKINDE, M. O.
MBHENYANE, X. G.
OGOLA, J. S.
OLE-MEILUDI, R. E.
OLORUNDA, A. O.
OMARA-OJUNGU, P. H.
ONI, S. A.
SHAI-MAHOKO, N. S.
SIMALENGA, T. E.
VAN DER WAAL, B. C. W.
VAN REE, T.

ATTACHED INSTITUTES

Centre for Youth Studies: Dir Prof. B. C. NINDI.

Es'Kia Mphahlele Centre for African Studies: Dir Prof. T. LO LIYONG.

UNIVERSITY OF THE WESTERN CAPE

Private Bag X17, Bellville 7535
Telephone: (21) 959-2911
Fax: (21) 959-3627
Internet: www.uwc.ac.za
Founded 1960
State-subsidized, but functions under its own charter; incorporated dental faculty of University of Stellenbosch 2004
Languages of instruction: Afrikaans, English
Academic year: February to December
Chancellor: Archbishop DESMOND TUTU
Vice-Chancellor and Rector: Prof. BRIAN O'CONNELL
Vice-Rector (Academic Affairs): Prof. STANLEY RIDGE (acting)
Deputy Vice-Chancellor and Vice-Rector (Student Affairs): Prof. L. TSHIWULA
Registrar: Dr INGRID MILLER
Librarian: E. R. TISE
Library of 278,486 vols, 1,400 journals, 173,000 microfiche items
Number of teachers: 396
Number of students: 14,070
Publications: *Journal of Community Health* (staff research publication, annually), *KRONOS: Journal of Cape History, Law, Democracy and Development* (4 a year)

DEANS

Faculty of Arts: Prof. GEORGE FREDERICKS (acting)
Faculty of Community and Health Sciences: Prof. RATIE MPOFU
Faculty of Dentistry: Prof. M. H. MOOLA
Faculty of Economic and Management Sciences: Prof. CHRIS TAPSCOTT
Faculty of Education: Prof. DIRK MEERKOTTER
Faculty of Law: Prof. N. MOOSA
Faculty of Science: Prof JAN VAN BEVERDONKER

DEPARTMENTAL CHAIRPERSONS

Faculty of Arts (tel. (21) 959-2138; fax (21) 959-2736; e-mail arts@uwc.ac.za; internet www.uwc.ac.za/arts):

Afrikaans and Dutch: Prof. F. S. HENDRICKS
Anthropology and Sociology: Dr A. J. HUMPHREYS
Arabic: Assoc. Prof. Y. MOHAMMED
English: Prof. P. MERRINGTON
French: L. HUET-HAUPT
Geography: Prof. G. PIRIE
German: K. CHUBB
History: Assoc. Prof. U. S. DUPHELIA-MESTHRIE
Latin: Assoc. Prof. B. VAN ZYL SMIT
Linguistics: Assoc. Prof. F. BANDA
Library and Information Sciences: Assoc. Prof. G. FREDERICKS
Philosophy: J. P. ABRAHAMS
Religion and Theology: Prof. W. CLOETE
Women's and Gender Studies: Prof. T. SHEFER
Xhosa: Prof S. J. NEETHLING

Faculty of Community and Health Sciences (tel. (21) 959-2856; fax (21) 959-2755; e-mail chs@uwc.ac.za; internet www.uwc.ac.za/comhealth):

Human Ecology and Dietetics: P. DANIELS
Nursing: T. D. KHANYILE
Occupational Therapy: J. DE JONGH
Physiotherapy: Prof. M. R. MARAIS
Psychology: Prof. C. MALCOM
Public Health: Prof. D. SANDERS
Social Work: Dr V. BOZALEK
Sport Recreation and Exercise Science: Prof. P. AVIS

Faculty of Dentistry (Mitchell's Plain Medical Centre, Town Centre and Tygerberg Hospital; tel. (21) 370-4400; fax (21) 392-3250; internet www.uwc.ac.za/dentistry):

Community Oral Health: A. J. LOUW
Diagnostic Services: Prof. L. X. G. STEPHEN
Maxillofacial and Oral Surgery, Anaesthesiology: Prof. J. A. MORKEL
Oral Hygiene: N. GORDON
Orthodontics and Paediatric Dentistry: Dr A. M. P. HARRIS
Restorative Dentistry: Prof. C. J. DE LA HARPE

Faculty of Economic and Management Sciences (tel. (21) 959-3165; fax (21) 959-2578; internet www.uwc.ac.za/ems):

Accounting: Assoc. Prof. E. ARNOLD
Economics: Assoc. Prof. I. ADAMS
Industrial Psychology: Prof. J. B. VAN LILL
Information Systems: K. SMIT
Management: E. B. H. ISAACS
Political Studies: K. GOTTSHALK
Public Administration: Prof. J. BARDILL

Faculty of Education (tel. (21) 959-2276; fax (21) 959-2960; e-mail ghgamiet@uwc.ac.za; internet www.uwc.ac.za/education):

Centre for Adult Education: Assoc. Prof. Z. GROENER
School of Science and Mathematics Education: Prof. C. JULIE
Teaching Cluster: Advanced Programmes: Prof. M. B. OGUNNIYI

Teaching Cluster: Professional Programmes: Assoc. Prof. J. M. SMIT

Faculty of Law (tel. (21) 959-3292; fax (21) 959-2960; e-mail dsnyders@uwc.ac.za; internet www.uwc.ac.za/law):

Constitutional and Human Rights Law: Prof. P. F. DE VOS
Criminal Justice and Procedure: H. MCCREATH
Jurisprudence: Prof. J. DE VILLE
Labour Law and Social Security Law: Prof. D. DU TOIT
Mercantile Law: G. F. KOTZE
Private Law: Prof. J. J. SARKIN

Faculty of Natural Sciences (tel. (21) 959-3292; fax (21) 959-2960; e-mail science@uwc.ac.za; internet www.science.uwc.ac.za):

Biodiveristy and Conservation Biology (Botany and Zoology): Prof. M. GIBBONS
Biotechnology (Biochemistry and Microbiology): Prof. D. COWAN
Chemistry: Dr D. L. KEY
Computer Science: M. NORMAN
Earth Sciences: M. DOMONEY
Mathematics: Prof. P. WITBOOI
Medical Biosciences (Anatomy and Physiology): Dr I. ISMAIL-WESSO
School of Pharmacy: Prof. J. MYBURGH
Physics: Prof. R. LINDSAY
Statistics: Prof. D. KOTZE

ATTACHED RESEARCH INSTITUTES

Centre for Adult and Continuing Education: Dir Prof. Z. GROENER.

Centre for Southern African Studies: Dir Prof. L. THOMPSON.

Community Law Centre: Dir Prof. N. STEYTLER.

Division of Lifelong Learning: Dir Prof. S. WALTERS.

Entrepreneurship Development Unit: Dir G. SOLOMON.

Environmental Education and Resource Unit: Dir C. KLEIN.

Gender Equity Unit: Dir M. HAMES.

Iilwimi Sentrum for Multilingualism and the Language Professions: Dir Prof. C. DYERS.

Institute for Child and Youth Research and Training: Dir Prof. R. BARNES-SEPTEMBER (acting).

Institute for Historical Research: Dir (vacant).

Institute for Social Development: Dir Prof. P. J. LE ROUX.

International Ocean institute Regional Operational Centre for Southern Africa: Dir Dr K. PROCHAZKA.

Programme for Land and Agrarian Studies: Dir Prof. B. COUSINS.

South African Herbal Science and Medicine Institute: Dir Prof. Q. JOHNSON.

Unit of the Range and forest Institute: Dir Dr N. ALLSOPP.

UNIVERSITY OF THE WITWATERSRAND, JOHANNESBURG

Private Bag 3, Wits 2050
Telephone: (11) 717-1000
Fax: (11) 717-1065
E-mail: studysa@international.wits.ac.za
Internet: www.wits.ac.za
Founded 1922
State-subsidized, but functions under its own charter
Language of instruction: English
Academic year: February to November
Chancellor: Hon. Mr Justice R. GOLDSTONE

Vice-Chancellor and Principal: Prof. LOYISO NONGXA
Vice-Principal and Deputy Vice-Chancellor (Academic): Prof. RICHARD N. PIENAAR
Deputy Vice-Chancellor (Partnerships and Advancement): Prof. THANDWA MTHEMBU
Deputy Vice-Chancellor (Research): Prof. BELINDA BOZZOLI
Registrar: Dr DEREK SWEMMER
Exec. Dir: ANDRÉ DE WET
University Librarian: FELIX OBOGU
Library: see Libraries
Number of teachers: 1,765 (1,120 full-time, 645 part-time)
Number of students: 24,381
Publications: *The Research Report* (annually), *Palaeontologia Africana* (annually), *African Studies* (2 a year), *English Studies in Africa* (2 a year), *Perspectives in Education* (quarterly), *Philosophical Papers* (3 a year), *The Industrial Law Journal* (6 a year)

DEANS

Faculty of Commerce, Law and Management: Prof. DUNCAN REEKIE (acting)
Faculty of Engineering and the Built Environment: Prof. RAYMOND NKADO
Faculty of Health Sciences: Prof. MAX PRICE
Faculty of Humanities: Prof. GERRIT OLIVIER
Faculty of Science: Prof. COLIN WRIGHT

PROFESSORS

Faculty of Arts and Faculty of Science:

ADLER, J., Mathematics Education Development
ALEXANDER, J. J., Microbiology
ANHAEUSSER, C. R., Geology
ASHER, A., Statistics and Actuarial Science
BEICHELT, F., Statistics and Actuarial Science
BONNER, P. L., History
BOZZOLI, B., Sociology
BRADLEY, J. D., Chemistry
BUNN, D., History of Art
CAWTHORN, R. G., Geology
COCK, J., Sociology
COMINS, J. D., Physics
COPLAN, D. B., Social Anthropology
COVILLE, N. J., Organo-Metallic Chemistry
CRUMP, A., Fine Arts
DABBS, E., Genetics
DELIUS, P. S., History
DIRR, H. W., Biochemistry
DRIVER, K., Mathematics
DU PLESSIS, P., Physics
EVERY, A. G., Physics
FABIAN, B. C., Zoology
FATTI, L. P., Statistics
FISHER, J., Psychology
GLASSER, L., Physical Chemistry
HEISS, W. D., Theoretical Physics
HOCH, M. J. R., Solid State Physics
HOFMEYR, I., African Literature
HUFFMAN, T. N., Archaeology
HUNT, J. H. V., Mathematics
LOWTHER, J. E., Physics
LODGE, T., Political Studies
LUBINSKY, D. S., Mathematics
MAAKE, N. P., African Languages
MASON, D. P., Applied Mathematics
MARQUES, H., Chemistry
MCCARTHY, T. S., Geology
MCKENDRICK, B. W., Social Work
MCLACHLAN, D. S., Electronic Properties of Solids
MICHAEL, J. P., Organic Chemistry
MOYS, M., School of Process and Materials Engineering
MURRAY, B. K., Edwardian British History
OLIVIER, G., Afrikaans and Dutch
OWEN-SMITH, N., Zoology
PENDLEBURY, M., Philosophy
PENN, C., Speech Pathology and Audiology
PIENAAR, R. N., Botany

PRODINGER, H., Mathematics
ROBB, L. J., Geology
RODRIGUES, J. A. P., Physics
ROGERS, K. H., Botany
ROGERSON, C. M., Geography
ROLLNICK, M., College of Science
RUBIDGE, B. S., Palaeontology
SCURRELL, M. S., Chemistry
STADLER, A. W., Political Studies
STREMLAU, J. J., International Relations
TAYLOR, J., Dramatic Art
TYSON, P. D., Climatology
VILJOEN, M. J., Mining Geology
VON HOLY, A., Microbiology
WEBSTER, E. C., Sociology
WRIGHT, C., Geophysics
WRIGHT, C. J., Computational and Applied
  Mathematics

Faculty of Commerce:
DAGUT, M., Economics
DE KOKER, A. P., Accounting
NEGASH, M., Accounting
REEKIE, W. D., Business Economics
SIMKINS, C., Economics
VIVIAN, R., Insurance and Risk Manage-
  ment

Faculty of Education:
ENSLIN, P. A.
PENDLEBURY, S. A.
SKUY, M. S.

Faculty of Engineering:
BRYSON, A. W., Chemical Engineering
ERIC, R. H., Metallurgy and Materials
  Engineering
FOURIE, A., Civil Engineering
GLASSER, D., Chemical Engineering
HANRAHAN, H. E., Electrical Engineering
HILDEBRANDT, D., Process and Materials
  Engineering
IWANKIEWICZ, R. M., Applied Mathematics
LANDY, C. F., Electrical Engineering
MACLEOD, I. M., Control Engineering
MCCUTCHEON, R. T., Project and Construc-
  tion Management
ONSONGO, W. M., Undergraduate Engi-
  neering Education
PHILLIPS, H. R., Mining Engineering
REYNDERS, J. P., Electrical Engineering
SHEER, T. J., Mechanical Engineering
SKEWS, B. W., Mechanical Engineering
STEPHENSON, D., Hydraulic Engineering

Faculty of Engineering and the Built Environment:
BREMNER, L., Architecture
MULLER, J. G., Town and Regional Planning
SCHLOSS, R. I., Construction Economics
  and Management

Faculty of Health Sciences:
ALLWOOD, C., Psychiatry
ALTINI, M., Oral Pathology
CARMICHAEL, T., Ophthalmology
CARR, L., Prosthetic Dentistry
CLEATON-JONES, P. E., Experimental Odon-
  tology
COOPER, P. A., Paediatrics
CREWE-BROWN, H., Medical Microbiology
CRONJE, S. L., Cardiothoracic Surgery
DAVIES, M. R. Q., Paediatric Surgery
ERKEN, E. H. W., Orthopaedic Surgery
EVANS, W. G., Orthodontics
FELDMAN, C., Medicine
FRITZ, V. U., Neurology
GEORGE, J. A., Orthopaedic Surgery
GRAY, I. P., Chemical Pathology
HAVLIK, I., Pharmacology
HOFMEYR, G. J., Obstetrics and Gynaecol-
  ogy
HUDDLE, K., Medicine
JOFFE, B. I., Medicine
KALK, W. J., Clinical Endocrinology
KEW, M. C., Medicine
KLUGMAN, K. P., Clinical Microbiology

KRAMER, B., Anatomical Sciences
LABURN, H. P., Physiology
LOWNIE, J. F., Maxillo-Facial and Oral
  Surgery
MACPHAIL, A. P., Medicine
MAINA, J. N., Anatomical Sciences
MANGA, P., Cardiology
MCINTOSH, W., Ear, Nose and Throat
  Surgery
MEYERS, A. M., Nephrology
MILNE, F. J., Medicine
MITCHELL, D., Physiology
MITCHELL, G., Physiology
OWEN, P., Prosthetic Dentistry
PANTANOWITZ, D., Surgery
PATERSON, A. C., Anatomical Pathology
PETIT, J.-C., Oral Medicine and Period-
  ontology
PETTIFOR, J. M., Paediatrics
PICK, W., Community Health
RAMSAY, M., Human Genetics
REES, D., Occupational Health
RUDOLPH, M. J., Community Medicine
SARELI, P., Cardiology
SCHOUB, B. D., Virology
SHIPTON, E. A., Anaesthesia
SPARKS, B. L. W., Family Health
SUR, R., Radiation Oncology
VAN GELDEREN, C. J., Obstetrics and
  Gynaecology
VILJOEN, D., Human Genetics
WADEE, A. A., Immunology

Faculty of Law:
COCKRELL, A. H. P.
HOEXTER, C.
ITZIKOWITZ, A.
LARKIN, M. P.
LEWIS, C. H.
MOSIKATSANA, T.
PAIZES, A. P.
PANTAZIS, A.
SKEEN, A. ST A.

Faculty of Management:
ABRATT, R., Business Administration
AHWIRENG-OBENG, F., Business Adminis-
  tration
CAWTHRA, G., Defence and Security Man-
  agement
DE CONING, C., Development Management
KLEIN, S., International Business
MABIN, A. S., Public and Development
  Management
MHONE, G. C. Z., Public and Development
  Management

ATTACHED RESEARCH INSTITUTES

**Bernard Price Institute of Geophysical
Research:** f. 1936; Dir Prof. C. WRIGHT.

**Bernard Price Institute for Palaeonto-
logical Research:** f. 1949; Dir Prof. B.
RUBIDGE.

Bone Research Laboratory: Dir Prof. U.
RIPAMONTI.

**Centre for Applied Chemistry and Che-
mical Technology:** Dir Prof. N. COVILLE.

Centre for Applied Legal Studies: Dir
Prof. D. UNTERHALTER.

Centre for Continuing Education: Dir
Prof. D. RUSSELL.

**Centre for Control Theory and Optimi-
zation:** Dir Prof. K. WONG.

**Centre for Differential Equations, Con-
tinuing Mechanics and Applications
(DECMA Centre):** Dir Dr F. MAHOMED.

Centre for Health Science Education:
Dir (vacant).

**Centre for Languages and Hearing-
impaired Children:** Dir (vacant).

Centre for Materials Research: Dir Prof.
H. ERIC.

Centre for Non-Linear Studies: Dir Prof.
W. D. HEISS.

Dental Research Institute: Dir Prof. P.
CLEATON-JONES.

**Ernest Oppenheimer Institute for Por-
tuguese Studies:** Dir (vacant).

**John Knopfmacher Centre for Applic-
able Analysis and Number Theory:** Dir
Prof. D. LUBINSKY.

**Palaeoanthropology Research and
Exploration Unit:** Dir Dr L. BERGER.

**Research Centre for Employment Crea-
tion in Construction:** Dir Prof. R.
MCCUTCHEON.

Rock Art Research Institute: Dir Dr B. W.
SMITH.

**Schonland Research Centre for Nuclear
Sciences:** Dir Prof. T. DERRY.

Sterkfontein Research Unit: Dir Prof. P.
V. TOBIAS.

**Wits Institute of Social and Economic
Research:** Dir Prof. D. POSEL.

UNIVERSITY OF ZULULAND

Private Bag X1001, KwaDlangezwa, Kwa-
  Zulu-Natal 3886

Telephone: (35) 902-6000
Fax: (35) 793-3735
Internet: www.uzulu.ac.za

Founded 1960; Umlazi Campus incorporated
  into Durban Institute of Technology 2004
State control
Language of instruction: English
Academic year: February to December

Chancellor: Dr JACOB ZUMA
Vice-Chancellor and Rector: Prof. RACHEL
  GUMBI
Vice-Rector (Academic Affairs and Research):
  Prof. L. M. MAGI
Chief Financial Officer: M. GOUINDSAMY
Dean of Students: M. M. HLONGWANE
Registrar: G. S. MAPHISA
Librarian: L. VAHED

Number of teachers: 293
Number of students: 7,978

Publications: *Journal of Psychology, Paido-
  nomia, Unizul*

DEANS

Faculty of Arts: Prof. L. Z. M. KHUMALO
Faculty of Commerce and Administration:
  Prof. T. R. SABELA
Faculty of Education: Prof. R. V. GABELA
Faculty of Law: Prof. R. SONI
Faculty of Science and Agriculture: Prof. M.
  F. COETSEE
Faculty of Theology and Religious Studies:
  Prof. J. A. LOUBSER

PROFESSORS

Faculty of Arts (tel. (35) 902-6087; e-mail
bbishop@pan.uzulu.ac.za):

BUIJS, G. C. U., Anthropology
DALRYMPLE, L. I., Drama
DE VILLIERS, J., History
EDWARDS, S. D., Psychology
GLASS, H. G. L., Sociology
GUMBI, T. A. P., Social Work
HOOPER, M. J., English
KHUMALO, L. Z. M., African Languages
KLOPPER, R. M., Afrikaans
MAKHANYA, E. M., Geography
MEIHUIZEN, N. C. T., English
MERSHAM, G. M., Communication Science
NZIMAKWE, D. P., Nursing Science
OCHOLLA, D. N., Library and Information
  Science
POTGIETER, P. J., Criminal Justice
WAIT, E. C., Philosophy
ZUNGU, B. M., Nursing Science

Faculty of Commerce and Administration (tel. (35) 902-6173; fax (35) 793-3583; e-mail sbooysen@pan.uzulu.ac.za):

CLOETE, J., Business Management
LIVINGSTONE, M., Accountancy and Auditing
NAIDOO, I. U., Accountancy and Auditing
SABELA, T. R., Public Administration and Political Science
SHRESTHA, B. C., Economics

Faculty of Education (tel. (35) 902-6258; fax (35) 793-3149; e-mail rvgabela@pan.uzulu.ac.za):

COETSEE, M. F., Human Movement Science
DLAMINI, E. T., History of Education and Comparative Education
GABELA, R. V., Educational Planning and Administration
JACOBS, M., Didactics
SIBAYA, P. T., Educational Psychology
URBANI, G., Educational Psychology

Faculty of Law (tel. (35) 902-6212; fax (35) 793-3529; e-mail sjclarke@pan.uzulu.ac.za):

SONI, R., Constitutional Law

Faculty of Science and Agriculture (tel. (35) 902-6649; fax (35) 793-3162; e-mail lorraine@pan.uzulu.ac.za):

BEESHAM, A., Mathematical Sciences
BERMANSEDER, N., Engineering
COETSEE, M. F., Human Movement Science
CYRUS, D. P., Zoology
DAVIDSON, A. T., Physics
DJAVOVA, T., Biochemistry
FERREIRA, D. P., Botany
JURY, M. R., Geography
KELBE, B. E. M.-L., Hydrology
KOLAWOLE, G. A., Chemistry
NDWANDWE, M. O., Physics

Faculty of Theology and Religious Studies (tel. (35) 902-6716; fax (35) 793-3159; e-mail asong@uzulu.ac.za; internet www.uzulu.ac.za/the/the.html):

LOUBSER, J. A., Bibliological Studies
SONG, A., Missiology, Religious Studies and Practical Theology

Institute for Educational and Human Development.

Colleges

DURBAN INSTITUTE OF TECHNOLOGY

41–43 Centenary Rd, Durban 4001
E-mail: webmaster@dit.ac.za
Internet: www.dit.ac.za
Founded 2002 following merger of M. L. Sultan Technikon (f. 1946) and Technikon Natal (f. 1907); incorporated Umlazi Campus of University of Zululand 2004; to incorporate Mangosuthu Technikon 2006
Chancellor: PATRICIA DE LILLE
Vice-Chancellor: Prof. DAN J. NCAYIYANA
Chief Librarian: ROY RAJU.

CAMPUSES

M. L. Sultan Campus

41–43 Centenary Rd, Durban 4001
Telephone: (31) 308-5111
Fax: (31) 308-5194
E-mail: info@mlsultan.ac.za
Internet: www.mlsultan.ac.za
Deputy Vice-Chancellor: UJEN PURMASIR
Library Man.: SIZA RODABE
Library: B. M. Patel Memorial Library of 55,000 books, 900 journals, 4,000 video- and audiotapes
Faculties: Arts, Science, Commerce, Engineering.

Steve Biko Campus
(formerly Technikon Natal)
70 Mansfield Rd, Berea, Durban 4001
Telephone: (31) 204-2111
Fax: (31) 204-2663
E-mail: postmaster@ntech.ac.za
Internet: www.ntech.ac.za

Vice-Chancellor and Principal: Prof. B. KHOAPA
Vice-Principal (Academic): Prof. LOUIS DU PREEZ
Vice-Principal (Administrative): Dr REGINALD THABEDE
Vice-Principal (Student Affairs and Development): Adv. REAGAN JACOBUS
Assistant Vice-Principal (Undergraduate Studies): Prof. NQABOMZI GAWE
Academic Registrar: DAVID HELLINGER
Registrar (Pietermaritzburg): Prof. SAM ZOND
Library of 81,000 vols, 1,001 periodical titles

DEANS

Faculty of Arts: A. R. STARKEY
Faculty of Commerce: T. DAGNALL-QUINN
Faculty of Engineering and Science: M. STEWART
Faculty of Health: A. MILNE

MANGOSUTHU TECHNIKON

POB 12363, Jacobs 4026
Mangosuthu Highway, Umlazi, Durban
Telephone: (31) 907-7111
Fax: (31) 907-2892
E-mail: miken@julian.mantec.ac.za
Internet: www.mantec.ac.za
Founded 1978
Academic year: January to December
Principal and Vice-Chancellor: Prof. A. M. NDLOVU
Vice-Principal (Academic): Prof. E. C. ZINGU
Vice-Principal (Administration): Dr Y. L. MBELE
Academic Registrar: S. NAIDOO
Library of 54,454 vols
Number of teachers: 150
Number of students: 10,000

DEANS

Faculty of Engineering: S. MALINGA
Faculty of Management Sciences: Prof. E. C. ZINGU
Faculty of Natural Sciences: Prof. ALLAN FEMI LANA

SPAIN

The Higher Education System

Institutions of higher education predate the consolidation of the Kingdom of Spain within the Iberian peninsula in the early 16th century, with the oldest being Universidad Pontificia de Slamanca, which was founded in 1134. The Ministry of Education and Science has overall responsibility for higher education, although much of the administration has been devolved to the 17 Autonomous Communities. Universities were granted autonomy under the law of University Reform (1983), which was supplemented by further reforms enacted following the Spanish University law (2001), covering university governance, entrance examinations, quality assurance, accreditation and staff recruitment. Spain participates in the Bologna Process to establish a European Higher Education Area, the first phase of which is to adopt a credit-based system of comparable degrees with two main cycles (undergraduate and graduate). Higher education is provided by public and private universities, higher technical colleges (escuelas técnicas superiores), university colleges (colegios universitarios), university faculties (facultades universitarias) and university schools (escuelas universitarias). Some 1.4m. students were attending university in 2005/06. In that year there were 72 universities, including the open university (UNED), established in 1972.

The main requirements for admission to higher education are the secondary school certificate (Bachillerato) and the university entrance examination (Prueba de Acceso Universidad). University degrees are divided into three cycles. The first cycle lasts three years and is equivalent to a Bachelors; the main qualifications are the Diplomado (offered in the four subject areas of experimental and health science, humanities, social sciences and law, and technical education) and Diplomatura. Professional titles such as Arquitecto Técnico and Ingeniero Técnico are also awarded. The second cycle last two years and is equivalent to the Masters; the main degrees awarded are the Licenciado, Licenciatura or professional title. Finally, the third cycle constistutes the highest level of university degree, namely the Título de Doctorado, which requires three years of classwork and research, culminating with the submission and defence of a thesis.

The main qualification offered in vocational and technical education is the Técnico Superior, awarded after one-and-a-half to two years of study. Occupational training is also available; students are awarded the Certificados de Profesionalidad.

The National Agency for Quality Assessment and Accreditation was founded in 2002 following the Spanish Universities Act and is responsible for accrediting programmes of study, providing quality assurance and acting as the inter-agency coordinating body for Spanish higher education.

Regulatory and Representative Bodies

GOVERNMENT

Ministry of Culture: Plaza del Rey 1, 28071 Madrid; tel. 91-701-70-00; fax 91-701-73-52; e-mail contacte@mcu.es; internet www.mcu.es; Minister CÉSAR ANTONIO MOLINA.

Ministry of Education and Science: Alcalá 36, 28071 Madrid; tel. 91-701-80-00; fax 91-701-86-48; internet www.mec.es; Minister MERCEDES CABRERA CALVO-SOTELO.

ACCREDITATION

Agencia Nacional de Evaluación de la Calidad y Acreditación (National Agency for Quality Assessment and Accreditation): C/ Orense 11, 7a Planta, 28020 Madrid; tel. 91-417-82-30; e-mail informacion@aneca.es; internet www.aneca.es; f. 2002; contributes to the quality improvement of the higher education system through the assessment, certification and accreditation of univ. degrees, programmes, teaching staff and instns; Exec. Dir GEMMA RUARET.

ENIC/NARIC Spain: NARIC Centre of Spain, Subdirección General de Títulos Convalidaciones y Homologaciones, Paseo del Prado 28, 28014 Madrid; tel. 91-506-55-93; fax 91-506-57-06; e-mail nieves.trelles@mec.es; internet www.mec.es; Technical Assessor NIEVES TRELLES.

FUNDING

Fundación Juan March: Castelló 77, 28006 Madrid; tel. 91-435-42-40; fax 91-576-34-20; e-mail webmast@mail.march.es; internet www.march.es; f. 1955; awards scholarships and research grants to Spanish professors and scholars in molecular biology and other fields; organizes cultural, artistic and musical activities; library dealing with modern Spanish theatre and contemporary Spanish music; Pres. JUAN MARCH DELGADO; Dir JAVIER GOMÁ LANZÓN; publs *Boletín Informativo* (monthly), *Anales* (annual report), *Saber Leer* (book review, monthly).

NATIONAL BODIES

Asociación Iberoamericana de Educación Superior a Distancia (Ibero-American Association for Open and Distance Higher Education): UNED, Bravo Murillo 38, 7th Fl., 28015 Madrid; tel. 91-398-74-30; fax 91-398-74-97; e-mail aiesad@adm.uned.es; internet www.uned.es/aiesad; f. 1981; network for the devt of distance education in Spanish-speaking Latin America; biannual int. seminars, joint projects and electronic newsletter; 43 mems; library of 50 vols; bibliography of distance- and open-education in Spanish-speaking Latin America; Pres. Dr JUAN A. GIMENO ULLASTRES; Dir and Sec. Dr MIGUEL ADRIANA; publ. *Revista Iberoamericana de Educación a Distancia (RIED)* (scientific review, available electronically).

Conferencia de Rectores de las Universidades Españolas (CRUE): UNED – Edificio Interfacultativo, Calle Príncipe 1 5a, 28012 Madrid; tel. 91-360-12-00; fax 91-360-12-01; e-mail sgcrue@adm.uned.es; internet www.crue.org; f. 1978; fosters links between the univs, studies and analyses univ. problems, acts as link between the Univ. Council and the state univs; 60 mems; library of 497 vols; Pres. Prof. JUAN ANTONIO VÁZQUEZ GARCÍA; Sec.-Gen. FÉLIX GARCÍA LAUSÍN.

Consejo de Co-ordinación Universitaria: C/ Juan del Rosal 14, 28040 Madrid; tel. 91-453-98-00; fax 91-453-98-86; e-mail carmen.merinero@cuniv.mec.es; internet www.mec.es/educa/ccuniv; f. 1983; advises and assesses in matters concerning higher education policies and promotes co-ordination in the univ. system; Pres. The Min. of Education; mems incl. (among others) the Rectors of the state univs; Sec.-Gen. MARÍA ANTONIA GARCÍA BERNAU.

Consejo General de Colegios Oficiales de Doctores y Licenciados en Filosofía y Letras y en Ciencias (National Council of Official Colleges of Doctors and Licentiates in Philosophy, Letters and Science): Bolsa 11, 2o, 28012 Madrid; tel. 91-522-45-97; fax 91-531-77-78; e-mail secretaria@consejogeneralcdl.org; internet www.consejogeneralcdl.org; f. 1944; 55,800 mems; Dean Dr JOSÉ LUIS NEGRO FERNÁNDEZ; Sec.-Gen. Dr ROBERTO SALMERÓN SANZ; publ. publs information bulletins of the colleges in Barcelona, Bilbao, Madrid, Seville and Valladolid.

Learned Societies

GENERAL

Agencia Española de Co-operación International (Spanish Agency for International Co-operation): Avda de los Reyes Católicos 4, Ciudad Universitaria, 28040 Madrid; tel. 91-583-81-00; fax 91-583-83-10; e-mail infoaeci@aeci.es; internet www.aeci.es; f. 1946; Sec.-Gen. JESÚS GRACIA ALDAZ; publ. *Cooperación Española* (4 a year).

Attached institutes:

Instituto de Cooperación con el Mundo Arabe, Mediterráneo y Países en Desarrollo (Institute for Co-operation with the Arab World, the Mediterranean and Developing Countries): Avda Reyes Católicos 4, 28040 Madrid; tel. 91-583-85-65; fax 91-583-82-19; technical assistance, economic co-operation, cultural activities, research grants, scholarships; library of 65,000 vols, 800 periodicals; Dir SENÉN FLORENSA PALAU; publs *Arabismo* (quarterly), *Awraq* (annually).

Instituto de Cooperación Iberoamericana (Institute for Ibero-American Cooperation): Avda de los Reyes Católicos 4, Ciudad Universitaria, 28040 Madrid; tel. 91-583-81-00; fax 91-583-83-10; f. 1946; promotes cultural understanding between Spain and America by organizing conferences, congresses, cultural exhibitions and university exchanges, scholarships for students; finances programmes of cultural, scientific, economic and technical co-operation; information department; Centre for Advanced Hispanic Studies; organizes programmes to diffuse the Spanish language and culture in the USA; radio, cinema and theatre unit; large library open to students; Spanish Library: see Libraries; Pres. FERNANDO VILLALONGA; Dir-Gen. JESÚS MANUEL GRACIA ALDAZ; Sec.-Gen. LUIS ESPINOSA; publs *Cuadernos Hispanoamericanos* (monthly), *Pensamiento Iberoamericano* (2 a year).

Casa de Velázquez: Ciudad Universitaria, 28040 Madrid; tel. 91-455-15-80; fax 91-544-68-70; e-mail info@casadevelazquez.org; internet www.casadevelazquez.org; f. 1928; French school for research into all aspects of Iberia; grants senior fellowships to French artists or scholars to work in Spain; 34 mems; library of 80,000 vols, 1,000 current periodicals; Dir GÉRARD CHASTAGNARET; publ. *Mélanges*.

Dirección General de Relaciones Culturales y Científicas (Cultural and Scientific Relations Department): Ministerio de Asuntos Exteriores, Calle José Abascal 41, 28003 Madrid; tel. 91-441-16-00; fax 91-441-44-17; f. 1926; promotes Spanish culture and science in foreign countries; international cultural and scientific agreements, exchange of professors and lecturers, scholarships, etc.; Dir-Gen. SANTIAGO CABANAS.

Institut d'Estudis Catalans (Institute of Catalan Studies): Carrer del Carme 47, 08001 Barcelona; tel. 93-270 16 20, fax 93-270-11-80; e-mail informacio@iecat.net; internet www.iecat.net; f. 1907; incorporates sections on History and Archaeology, Science and Technology, Philology, Philosophy and Social Sciences, and Biology; 202 mems (148 ordinary, 54 corresp.), 26 affiliated scientific socs; Pres. JOSEP LAPORTE; Sec.-Gen. SALVADOR ALEGRET; publs *Memòria* (annually), *Anuari de la Societat Catalana de Filosofia*, *Estudis Romànics*, *Biblioteca Litúrgica Catalana*, *Treballs de la Societat Catalana de Biologia*, *Butlletí de la Societat Catalana d'Estudis Històrics*, *Notícies de la Societat Catalana de Matemàtiques*, *Cartografia de Briòfits*, *Butlletí de la Societat Catalana de Musicologia*, *Arxiu de Textos Catalans Antics*, *Lambard*, *Quaderns Agraris*, *Butlletí de la Institució Catalana d'Història Natural*, *Anuari de la Societat Catalana d'Economia*, *Butlletí de la Societat Catalana de Pedagogia*, *Treballs de la Societat Catalana de Geografia*, *Llengua i Literatura*, *Cinematògraf*, *Miscel·lània Litúrgica Catalana*, *Acta Numismàtica*, *Butlletí de les Societats Catalanes de Física, Química, Matemàtiques i Tecnologia. Segona època*, *Gazeta*, *Dossiers Agraris*, *Butlletí de la Societat Catalana de Matemàtiques*, *Periodística*, *Revista Catalan de Dret Privat*, *Revista Catalan de Musicologia*, *Revista Catalan de Pedagogia*, *Revista Catalan de Sociologia*, *Revista de Dret Històrica Català*, *Revista Catalan de Física*, *Revista de la Societat Catalana de Química*, *Sessió Conjunta d'Entomologia*, *Tamid*, *Tecnologia i Ciència dels Aliments (TECA)*, *Treballs de Comunicació*, *Trabades d'Història de la Ciència i la Tècnica*.

Instituto Cervantes: C/ Libreros 23, 28801 Alcalá de Henares, Madrid; tel. 91-885-61-00; fax 91-883-08-14; e-mail informa@cervantes

.es; internet www.cervantes.es; f. 1991; promotes Spanish language and the culture of Spain and Spanish-speaking Latin and Central America globally; operates in 26 countries; maintains teaching centres in Sofia (Bulgaria), Zagreb (Croatia), Belgrade (Serbia and Montenegro) and Hanoi (Vietnam); Dir CÉSAR ANTONIO MOLINA.

Instituto de España (Institute of Spain): San Bernardo 49, 28015 Madrid; tel. 91-522-48-85; fax 91-521-06-54; e-mail Secretaria@Insde.es; internet www.Insde.es; f. 1938; the Institute's constituent academies form a 'Senado de la Cultura Española'; Pres. SALUSTIANO DEL CAMPO URBANO; Sec.-Gen. FRANCISCO J. YNDURÁIN MUÑOZ; publ. *Anuario*.

Constituent academies:

Real Academia Española (Royal Spanish Academy): Calle de Felipe IV 4, 28014 Madrid; tel. 91-420-14-78; fax 91-420-00-79; internet www.rae.es; f. 1713; 41 ordinary mems, 3 elected mems; Dir VICTOR GARCÍA DE LA CONCHA; Sec. GUILLERMO ROJO; publ. *Boletín* (every 6 months).

Real Academia de la Historia (Royal Academy of History): León 21, 28014 Madrid; tel. 91-429-06-11; fax 91-369-46-36; e-mail secretaria.rah@inside.es; f. 1738; 36 mems; library of 350,000 vols, 180,000 MSS; Dir GONZALO ANES Y ÁLVAREZ DE CASTRILLÓN; Sec. ELOY BENITO RUANO; publ. *Boletín* (3 a year).

Real Academia de Bellas Artes de San Fernando (San Fernando Royal Academy of Fine Arts): Alcalá 13, 28014 Madrid; tel. 91-524-08-64; fax 91-524-10-34; f. 1752; 54 mems; library of 40,000 vols; attached museum: see Museums and Art Galleries; Dir RAMÓN GONZÁLEZ DE AMEZÚA; Gen. Sec. ANTONIO IGLESIAS ÁLVAREZ; publ. *Boletín* (2 a year).

Real Academia de Ciencias Exactas, Físicas y Naturales (Royal Academy of Exact, Physical and Natural Sciences): Valverde 22 y 24, 28004 Madrid; tel. 91-701-42-30; fax 91-701-42-32; e-mail secretaria.racefyn@insde.es; f. 1847; sections of Exact Sciences (Pres. DARIO MARAVALL CASENOVES, Sec. MANUEL LOPEZ PELLICER), Physical Sciences (Pres. FRANCISCO YNDURAIN MUÑOZ, Sec. JESUS SANTA MARIA ANTONIO), Natural Sciences (Pres. MANUEL R. LLAMAS MADURGA, Sec. ADRIANO GARCIA LOYGORRI); 54 mems; 90 Spanish corresp. mems; Pres. CARLOS SANCHEZ DEL RIO; Sec.-Gen. JOSÉ J. ETAYO MIQUEO; publs *Memoria*, *Revista*, *Anuario*.

Real Academia de Ciencias Morales y Políticas (Royal Academy of Moral and Political Sciences): Casa de los Lujanes, Plaza de la Villa 2, 28005 Madrid; tel. 91-548-13-30; fax 91-548-19-75; e-mail secretaria@racmyp.es; internet www .racmyp.es; f. 1857; 89 mems (40 ordinary, 14 Spanish corresp., 35 foreign corresp.); library of 115,000 vols, 340 periodicals; Pres. ENRIQUE FUENTES QUINTANA; Sec. JESÚS GONZÁLEZ PÉREZ; publs *Anales* (annually), *Papeles y Memorias* (4 a year).

Real Academia Nacional de Medicina (Royal National Academy of Medicine): Arrieta 12, 28013 Madrid; tel. 91-547-03-18; fax 91-547-03-20; f. 1732; 50 mems; 90 Spanish corresp. mems; 57 foreign corresp. mems; Pres. HIPÓLITO DURÁN SACRISTÁN; Sec. (vacant); publ. *Anales*.

Real Academia de Jurisprudencia y Legislación (Royal Academy of Jurisprudence and Law): Marqués de Cubas 13, 28014 Madrid; tel. 91-522-20-69; fax 91-523-40-21; e-mail secretaria.rajyl@insde.es; internet rajyl.insde.es; f. 1730; 40 mems; library of 35,000 vols; Pres. LAND-

ELINO LAVILLA ALSINA; Sec. RAFAEL NAVARRO-VALLS; publ. *Anales*.

Real Academia Nacional de Farmacia (Royal National Academy of Pharmacy): Farmacia 11, 28004 Madrid; tel. 91-531-03-07; fax 91-531-03-06; e-mail administrador .raf@insde.es; internet www.raf.es; f. 1589; 42 mems; library of 30,000 vols; Pres. JUAN MANUEL REOL TEJADA; Permanent Sec. MARÍA DEL CARMEN FRANCÉS CAUSAPÉ; publ. *Anales* (4 a year).

Instituto de Estudios Norteamericanos (Institute of North American Studies): Vía Augusta 123, 08006 Barcelona; tel. 93-240-51-10; fax 93-202-06-90; e-mail ien@ien.es; internet www.ien.es; f. 1952; cultural exchange programmes, lectures, discussions, musical events, theatre, cinema, art exhibitions, seminars, etc.; courses in English and in American Studies; runs an academic counselling service and is the official centre for examinations for students entering US universities; c. 400 mems; 18,000 students; library of 9,000 vols, 100 periodicals; Pres. ALFREDO SNEYERS; Exec. Dir MARCIA A. GRANT.

Instituto Egipcio de Estudios Islámicos (Egyptian Institute of Islamic Studies): Francisco de Asís Méndez Casariego 1, 28002 Madrid; tel. 91-563-94-68; fax 91-563-86-40; e-mail icgipcio@mundivia.es; internet empresas.mundivia.es/iegipcio/home/html; f. 1950; 14 mems; library of 23,000 vols, 300 periodicals; Dir MOHAMED ABUELATA; publ. *Revista* (annually).

Real Academia de Bellas Artes y Ciencias Históricas de Toledo (Toledo Royal Academy of Fine Arts and Historical Sciences): Calle Esteban Illán 9, Toledo; tel. 925-21-43-22; f. 1916; 25 mems; library of 4,000 vols; Dir Dr FÉLIX DEL VALLE Y DIAZ; Sec. LUIS ALBA GONZÁLEZ; Librarian MARIO ARELLANO GARCÍA; publ. *Toletum*.

Real Academia de Ciencias y Artes de Barcelona (Barcelona Royal Academy of Science and Arts): Rambla de los Estudios 115, 08002 Barcelona; tel. 93-317-05-36; fax 93-304-31-28; e-mail info@racab.es; internet www.racab.es; f. 1764; 130 mems; attached observatory: see Research Institutes; library of 100,000 vols; Pres. Dr RAFAEL FOGUET AMBRÓS; Vice-Pres. Dr RAMON PASCUAL DE SANS; Sec. Dr JOAQUIM AGULLÓ BATLLE; Librarian Dr JAUME CASABÓ GISPERT; publs *Nómina*, *Memorias*.

Real Academia de Ciencias, Bellas Letras y Nobles Artes de Córdoba (Royal Academy of Science, Literature and Fine Arts in Córdoba): Ambrosio de Morales 9, 14003 Córdoba; tel. 957-41-31-68; fax 957-47-66-88; e-mail racordoba@insde.es; f. 1810; 35 mems; 35 corresp. mems; Dir JOAQUÍN CRIADO COSTA; Sec. JOSÉ PORRO HERRERA; publs *Boletín* (2 a year), *Anuario* (annually).

Real Academia de Doctores: Calle de San Bernardo 49, 28015 Madrid; tel. 91-531-95-22; fax 91-524-00-27; e-mail rad@radoctores .es; internet www.radoctores.es; f. 1920; sections of Philosophy and Literature, of Sciences, of Law, of Medicine, of Pharmacy, of Politics, Economics and Commerce, of Engineering, of Architecture, of Theology, of Veterinary Science; 8 hon. mems; 104 mems, 114 national corresp., 86 foreign corresp. mems; Pres. Dr ALBERTO BALLARÍN MARCIAL; Vice-Pres. Dr AMANDO GARRIDO PERTIERRA; Sec.-Gen. Dra BLANCA CASTILLA DE CORTÁZAR; publs *Anuario* (annually), *Anales* (irregular).

Real Academia Gallega (Royal Galician Academy): Tabernas 11, 15001 La Coruña; tel. 981-20-73-08; fax 981-20-73-08; f. 1905; 25 mems; library of 42,000 vols, including valuable collection of books on Galicia; Pres. FRANCISCO FERNANDEZ DEL RIEGO; Sec. CON-

STANTINO GARCÍA; Librarian ANTONIO GIL MERINO; publs *Caderna da Lingua, Diccionario da Lingua Galega*, etc.

Real Academia Hispano-Americana (Royal Spanish-American Academy): Plaza Fragela s/n (Edif. Facultad de Medicina), Apdo 16, 11003 Cádiz; tel. 95-622-88-16; fax 95-622-88-16; f. 1910; 29 mems; Dir JUAN RAFAEL CABRERA AFONSO; Sec.-Gen. FERNANDO SANCHEZ-GARCIA; publ. *Anuario*.

AGRICULTURE, FISHERIES AND VETERINARY SCIENCE

Institut Agrícola (Agricultural Institute): Plaça Sant Josep Oriol 4, 08002 Barcelona; tel. 93-301-17-40; fax 93-317-30-05; e-mail info@institutagricola.org; internet www .institutagricola.org; f. 1851; 2,000 mems; library of 16,000 vols, 200 periodicals; Pres. BALDIRI ROS; Sec.-Gen. FERRAN DE MULLER; publs *La Drecera* (monthly), *Calendari del Pagés* (annually).

Real Academia de Ciencias Veterinarias (Royal Academy of Veterinary Sciences): C/o Prof. Dr Mariano Illera Martín, Maestro Ripoll 8, 28006 Madrid; tel. 91-561-17-99; fax 91-394-38-64; e-mail Academia_Veterinaria@compuserve.com; internet www.ourworld.compuserve.com/ homepages/Academia_Veterinaria; f. 1975; 113 mems; Pres. Prof. Dr MARIANO ILLERA MARTÍN; Sec. Dr JULIO OLIAS PLEITE; publ. *Anales* (annually).

ARCHITECTURE AND TOWN PLANNING

Col·legi d'Arquitectes de Catalunya (Association of Catalan Architects): Plaça Nova 5, 08002 Barcelona; tel. 93-301-50-00; fax 93-412-07-88; e-mail susuari@coac.net; internet www.coac.net; f. 1931; 6,200 mems; library of 80,392 vols; Dean JESÚS ALONSO I SÁINZ; Sec. JORGE OZORES MARCO-GARDOQUI; publs *Quaderns d'Arquitectura i Urbanisma, Informació i debat*.

Subdirección General de Arquitectura: Dirección General de la Vivienda, la Arquitectura y el Urbanismo, Ministerio de Fomento, Paseo de la Castellana 67, 28071 Madrid; tel. 91-597-83-87; fax 91-597-85-10; e-mail jserra@mfom.es; f. 1940; development of technical regulations and recommendations concerning building technology and quality control; test laboratory; technical assistance to the Construction Board of the National Standards Organization; 120 mems; Sub-Dir-Gen. GERARDO MINGO; publs *Normas Tecnológicas de la Edificación, Normas Básicas de la Edificación*.

BIBLIOGRAPHY, LIBRARY SCIENCE AND MUSEOLOGY

Amics dels Museus de Catalunya (Friends of the Catalan Museums): Palau de la Virreina, La Rambla 99, 08002 Barcelona; tel. 93-301-43-79; fax 93-318-94-21; e-mail amics@amicsdelsmuseus.org; internet www .amicsdelsmuseus.org; f. 1933; 800 mems, 6 hon., 81 associates, 52 others; Pres. FAUSTO SERRA DE DALMASES; Vice-Pres. LOLA MITJANS; Sec. MARINA GOMEZ CASAS; publs *Historiales*, monographs.

Asociación Español de Archiveros, Bibliotecarios, Muséologos y Documentalistas: Calle Recoletos 5-3°-izqda, 28001 Madrid; tel. 91-575-17-27; fax 91-575-17-27; f. 1949; 1,616 mems; groups all specialists working in the country's archive services, libraries, museums and documentation services; has regional branches in Galicia, Aragón, Castilla-La Mancha and Murcia; Pres. JULIA M. RODRÍGUEZ BARRERO; Sec. CARMEN CAYETANO MARTIN; publs *Boletín*, many irregular works.

ECONOMICS, LAW AND POLITICS

Centro de Estudios Políticos y Constitucionales (Centre for Political and Constitutional Studies): Plaza de la Marina Española 9, 28071 Madrid; tel. 91-540-19-50; fax 91-541-95-74; e-mail cepc@cepc.es; internet www.cepc.es; f. 1977, having merged with Instituto de Estudios Políticos; organizes courses and seminars on politics and constitutional law; 90 mems; library of 80,000 vols; Dir JOSÉ ALVAREZ JUNCO; Man. JOSÉ ANGEL MANZANO GARCÍA; publs *Anuario Iberoamericano de Justicia Constitucional* (annually), *Revista de Administración Pública* (3 a year), *Revista de Derecho Comunitario Europeo* (3 a year), *Revista de Derecho Privado y Constitución* (annually), *Revista Española de Derecho Constitucional* (3 a year), *Revista de Estudios Políticos* (4 a year).

Col·legi de Notaris de Catalunya (College of Catalan Notaries): Carrer Notariat 4, Barcelona; tel. 93-317-48-00; fax 93-302-63-31; e-mail cnc@colnotcat.es; internet www .colnotcat.es; f. 1932; 501 mems; Dean JOSÉ-FÉLIX BELLOCH JULBE; Sec. ESTEBAN CUYAS HENCHE.

Il·lustre Col·legi d'Advocats de Barcelona (Barcelona Bar Association): C/ Mallorca 283, 08037 Barcelona; tel. 93-496-18-80; fax 93-487-15-89; e-mail icab@icab.es; internet www.icab.es; f. 1832; 17,513 mems; library: see Libraries and Archives; Dean JAUME ALONSO-CUEVILLAS SAYROL; Sec. JOAQUIM DE MIQUEL SAGNIER; publs *Revista Jurídica de Catalunya* (8 a year), *Món Jurídic* (monthly).

Instituto Nacional de Administración Pública (National Institute of Public Administration): Atocha 106, 28012 Madrid; tel. 91-273-92-81; fax 91-273-92-87; e-mail biblioteca@inap.map.es; internet www.inap .map.es; f. 1940; library of 147,790 vols, 3,002 periodicals; Pres. FRANCISCO RAMOS FERNÁNDEZ-TORRECILLA; Dir FERNANDO SAINZ MORENO; Sec.-Gen. JULIÁN ALVAREZ ALVAREZ; publs *Gestión y Análisis de Políticas Públicas* (3 a year), *Cuadernos de Derecho Publico* (3 a year), *Revista Iberoamericana de Administración Pública* (2 a year), *Revista Documentación Administrativa* (3 a year), *Revista de Estudios de Administración Local* (3 a year).

Instituto Nacional de Estadística (National Statistical Office): Paseo de la Castellana 183, 28071 Madrid; tel. 91-583-91-00; fax 91-583-91-58; e-mail info@ine.es; internet www.ine.es; f. 1945; library of 167,000 vols, 127,000 microfiches; Dir CARMEN ALCAIDE; publs *Anuario Estadístico de España* (annually), *Censos de la Población y de la Vivienda* (every 10 years), *Boletín Mensual de Estadística* (data on short-term indicators, monthly), *Nomenclaturas y Metodología*, *Estadística Industrial* (data on production and business turnover, annually), *Boletín Trimestral de Coyuntura* (national accounts and other indicators, 4 a year), *Revista 'Estadística Española'* (statistical theory and methodology), *Epa* (employment), *España en Cifras* (main statistical indicators and data, in Spanish or English), *Dirce* (number of enterprises by sector and breakdown by number of workers and activity).

Real Sociedad Económica de Amigos del País de Tenerife (Royal Economic Society of Friends of Tenerife): La Laguna de Tenerife, Calle San Agustín 23, Tenerife, Canary Is; f. 1777; 490 mems; sections: *Intereses Morales, Intereses Materiales, Intereses Culturales, Intereses Económicos, Prensa y Propaganda*; library of 11,000 vols; museum; Dir Marqués de Villanueva del Prado D. MANUEL DE QUINTANA; publ. publs works relating to the Canary Islands.

EDUCATION

Fundación Ortega y Gasset: Fortuny 53, 28010, Madrid; tel. 91-700-41-00; fax 91-700-35-30; e-mail comunicacion@fog.es; internet www.ortegaygasset.edu; f. 1978; organizes cultural activities and undertakes debate and research in the fields of the social sciences and humanities; Pres. ANTONIO GARRIGUES WALKER; publs *Revista de Occidente* (monthly), *Revista de Estudios Orteguianos* (2 a year).

Attached institutes:

Centro de Estudios Internacionales 'San Juan de la Penitencia' (Centre for International Studies): Callejón de San Justo, s/n , 45001, Toledo; tel. 925-28-43-80; fax 925-22-65-48; e-mail rosa .almoguera@fogtoledo.com; internet www .fogtoledo.com; f. 1982; Offers courses in Hispanic, Latin American and European Studies (incl. anthropology, archaeology, politics, economics, geography, history, art, Spanish language, literature), designed specifically for foreign students; Dir D. MARIO PAOLETTI.

Instituto Universitario de Investigación Ortega y Gasset (Ortega y Gasset University Research Institute): Fortuny 53, 28010, Madrid; tel. 91-700-41-49; fax 91-700-35-30; e-mail jefatura.estudios@fog .es; internet www.ortegaygasset.edu/iuoyg/ principal.htm; f. 1986; affiliated to Universidad Complutense de Madrid; graduate degree programmes and research in social sciences and humanities; library of 50,000 vols, 300 periodicals.

FINE AND PERFORMING ARTS

Asociación Española de Pintores y Escultores (Association of Spanish Artists and Sculptors): Infantas 30, 28004 Madrid; tel. 91-522-49-61; fax 91-522-55-08; e-mail aepe@wanadoo.es; f. 1910; 1,000 mems; Pres. JESÚS CÁMARA; Sec. RAMÓN PÉREZ; publs *Gaceta de las Bellas Artes* (monthly), *Catálogo Salón de Otoño* (annually).

Ateneo Científico, Literario y Artístico (Scientific, Literary and Artistic Athenaeum): Sa Rovellada de Dalt 25, 07703 Mahón, Minorca, Balearic Is; tel. 971-36-05-53; f. 1905; library of 15,000 vols; 630 mems; Pres. JOSÉ ANTONIO FAYAS JANER; Sec. CATALINA SEGUI DE VIDAL; publ. *Revista de Menorca* (quarterly).

Ateneo Científico, Literario y Artístico de Madrid (Scientific, Literary and Artistic Athenaeum in Madrid): Calle del Prado 21, 28014 Madrid; tel. 91-429-62-51; fax 91-429-79-01; e-mail admonateneo@telefonica.net; internet www.ateneodemadrid.com; f. 1820; 6,500 mems; library of 800,000 vols; Pres. JOSÉ LUIS ABELLÁN-GARCÍA GONZÁLEZ; Sec. JOSÉ MANUEL DUARTE.

Ateneu Barcelonès (Barcelona Athenaeum): Carrer Canuda 6, 08002 Barcelona; tel. 93-343-61-21; fax 93-317-15-25; e-mail ateneubarcelones@eresmas.com; internet www.ateneu-bcn.org; f. 1860; library: see Libraries; 3,100 mems; governed by a Directorate; Pres. JORDI SARSANEDAS VIVES; Sec. LLUÍS BUSQUETS I GRABULOSA.

Comité Nacional Español del Consejo Internacional de la Música (National Cttee of the International Music Council): Martín de los Héroes 56, 28001 Madrid; Sec.-Gen. ANTONIO IGLESIAS.

Departamento de Historia del Arte 'Diego Velázquez': Instituto de Historia (CSIC), Duque de Medinaceli 6, 3°, 28014 Madrid; tel. 91-429-06-26; fax 91-369-09-40;

e-mail pazlargacha@ih.csic.es; internet www
.ih.csic.es; f. 1939; attached to the Consejo
Superior de Investigaciones Científicas
(CSIC); history of Spanish art, hispanoamerican art and history of European art in
Spain; 9 mems; library of 50,000 vols, 500
periodicals, 200,000 photographs; Head Dr
MIGUEL CABAÑAS BRAVO; publ. *Archivo Español de Arte* (4 a year).

Institut Amatller d'Art Hispànic (Amatller Institute of Hispanic Art): Passeig de
Gràcia 41, 08007 Barcelona; tel. 93-216-01-
75; fax 93-487-58-27; e-mail amatller@
amatller.org; internet www.amatller.org; f.
1941; library of 25,000 vols; collection of
300,000 photographs; Dir SANTIAGO ALCOLEA
BLANCH.

Institut del Teatre (Theatrical Institute):
Plaça Margarida Xirgu s/n, 08004 Barcelona;
tel. 93-227-39-00; fax 93-227-39-39; e-mail i
.teatre@diba.es; internet www.diba.es/
iteatre; f. 1913; drama and dance school;
documentation and research information
centre; library of 150,000 vols; Dir JORDI
FONT I CARDONA.

**Real Academia de Bellas Artes de la
Purísima Concepción** (Royal Academy of
Fine Arts): Calle del Rastro, Casa de Cer-
vantes, 47001 Valladolid; tel. 983-39 80-04;
fax 983-39-07-03; e-mail bellas-artes@
dirtecdirac.com; f. 1783; 32 mems; Pres.
JAVIER LÓPEZ DE URIBE Y LAYA; Sec. JESUS
URREA FERNANDEZ; publ. *Boletín* (annually).

**Real Academia de Bellas Artes de San
Telmo** (Royal Academy of Fine Arts):
Málaga; f. 1849; 28 mems; Pres. JOSÉ LUIS
ESTRADA SEGALERVA; Secs BALTASAR PEÑA
HINOJOSA, LUIS BONO HERNÁNDEZ DE SANTAO-
LALLA.

**Real Academia de Bellas Artes de Santa
Isabel de Hungría** (Royal Fine Arts Academy): Abades 14, 41004 Seville; tel. and fax
95-422-11-98; e-mail rabasih@insde.es;
internet www.insacan.org/rabasih/
rabasihsede.html; f. 1660; research, courses
and exhibitions; 36 mems; library of 3,800
vols; Pres. ANTONIO DE LA BANDA Y VARGAS;
Sec.-Gen. RAMÓN CORZO SÁNCHEZ; Librarian
IGNACIO OTERO NIETO; publs *Boletín de Bellas
Artes* (annually), *Temas de Estética y Arte*
(annually).

**Real Academia de Nobles y Bellas Artes
de San Luis** (Royal Academy of Fine Arts):
Plaza de Los Sitios 6, 50001 Zaragoza; f.
1792; library of 5,517 vols; composed of 28
Academicians, 84 Spanish and 28 foreign
corresponding members and variable number of delegates; comprises 5 sections (architecture, sculpture, painting, music,
literature) and 3 permanent committees;
Pres. JOSÉ PASQUAL DE QUINTO Y DE LOS RÍOS;
Sec.-Gen. MIGUEL CABALLÚ ALBAIC; publ.
Boletín (irregular).

Real Sociedad Fotográfica (Royal Photographic Society): Apdo 7238, 28080 Madrid;
Calle Tres Peces 2, 28012 Madrid; tel. 91-
539-75-79; e-mail rsf@rsf.es; internet www
.terra.es/personal/realsf; f. 1899; 1,320 mems;
library of 3,780 vols; Pres. JOSÉ MARÍA
MELLADO; Sec.-Gen. EMILIO SÁNCHEZ; publ.
Boletín (4 a year).

**Reial Acadèmia Catalana de Belles Arts
de Sant Jordi** (Royal Catalan Academy of
Fine Arts): Casa Llotja, Passeig d'Isabel II 1
(2°), 08003 Barcelona; tel. 93-319-24-32; fax
93-319-02-16; e-mail racbasj@suport.org;
internet www.ba-stjordi.org; f. 1849; library
of 8,000 vols; Pres. JORDI BONET ARMENGOL;
Sec.-Gen. LEOPOLDO GIL NEBOT; publs
Annuari (every 2 years), *Butlletí* (annually).

**Sociedad de Ciencias, Letras y Artes 'El
Museo Canario'** (Scientific, Literary and
Art Society): Dr Chil 25, 35001 Las Palmas,

Canary Is; f. 1879; incorporated in the
Consejo Superior de Investigaciones Científicas (*q.v.*); museum: see Museums; laboratories; important library (60,000 vols),
archives and periodicals relating to the
history and primitive peoples of the Canary
Islands; Pres. LOTHAR SIEMENS HERNANDEZ;
publ. *El Museo Canario* (annually).

HISTORY, GEOGRAPHY AND ARCHAEOLOGY

**Arxiu Històric de la Ciutat de Barce-
lona:** Casa de l'Ardiaca, Carrer Santa Llúcia
1, 08002 Barcelona; tel. 93-318-11-95; fax 93-
317-83-27; f. 1917; archives of municipal
records and local press; the Archives undertake historical research on Barcelona, organize courses, lectures, exhibitions; library:
see Libraries and Archives; Dir XAVIER
TARRAUBELLA MIRABET; publs *Barcelona Quaderns d'Història* (2 a year), *Història, Antropología, y Fuentes Orales* (2 a year),
*Quaderns del Seminari d'Història de Barce-
lona* (4 a year).

Deutsches Archaeologisches Institut
(German Archaeological Institute): Serrano
159, 28002 Madrid; tel. 91-561-09-04; fax 91-
564-00-54; e-mail sekretariat@madrid.dainst
.org; internet www.dainst.de; f. 1943; library
of 65,000 vols; archive of photographs; Dir Dr
DIRCE MARZOLI; publs *Madrider Mitteilungen*
(annually), *Madrider Forschungen*, *Madrider Beiträge*, *Hispania Antiqua*, *Studien
über frühe Tierknochenfunde von der Iber-
ischen Halbinsel*, *Iberia Archaeologica*.

Instituto de Historia y Cultura Naval
(Institute of Naval History and Culture):
Calle Juan de Mena 1, 28071 Madrid; tel.
91-379-50-50; f. 1942; associated with the
Consejo Superior de Investigaciones Cien-
tíficas; for library see entry under Museo
Naval; Dir Contralmirante TEODORO DE
LESTE CONTRERAS.

Instituto Geográfico Nacional (National
Geographical Institute): Calle del General
Ibáñez de Ibero 3, 28003 Madrid; tel. 91-597-
94-10; fax 91-579-97-53; e-mail ign@mfom.es;
internet www.mfom.es/ign; f. 1870; 1,200
mems; library of 28,000 vols; geodesy and
geophysics, cartography, map printing, seis-
mology, geophysics, astronomy, runs the
National Observatory (see under Research
Institutes); Dir-Gen. JOSÉ ANTONIO CANAS
TORRES; publs *Boletín Astronómico*, *Anuario
del Observatorio Astronómico*, *Anuario de
Geomagnetismo*, *Boletines Sísmicos*, *Boletín
Informativo del IGN*.

Real Sociedad Geográfica (Royal Geographic Society): Calle Pinar 25, 28006
Madrid; tel. 91-561-78-25; fax 91-562-55-67;
internet www.ieg.csic.es/rsg; f. 1876; geography and earth sciences; 433 mems; library of
11,000 vols, 12,700 booklets; Pres. Dr
RODOLFO NÚÑEZ DE LAS CUEVAS; Perm. Sec.
Dr JOAQUÍN BOSQUE MAUREL; publ. *Boletín*
(annually).

**Reial Societat Arqueològica Tarraco-
nense** (Royal Archaeological Society in Tarragona): POB 573, 43080 Tarragona; Carrer
Major 35, 43003 Tarragona; tel. 977-23-37-
89; fax 977-23-93-07; e-mail rsat@tinet.fut
.es; internet www.arqueologica.org; f. 1844;
Iberian, Roman and early Christian archaeology; ancient, medieval, modern and contemporary history of Tarragona; 601 mems;
library of 4,000 vols, 18,000 vols of periodicals; Pres. RAFAEL GABRIEL COSTA; Sec.
MANEL GÜELL JUNKERT; publs *Butlletí
Arqueològic* (quarterly), *Citerior*.

**Servicio de Investigación Prehistórica
de la Excelentísima Diputación Provincial** (Prehistoric Research Society of the
Province of Valencia): Calle de la Corona
36, 46003 Valencia; tel. 96-388-35-87; fax 96-

388-35-36; e-mail helena.bonet@diputacion
.m400.gva.es; internet www.xarxamuseus
.com; f. 1927; palaeolithic, neolithic, Bronze
and Iron Ages, Iberian and colonial exhibits,
prehistoric Americana; 30 mems; library of
47,000 vols; Dir HELENA BONET ROSADO;
publs *Serie de Trabajos Varios*, *Archivo de
Prehistoria Levantina*.

Societat Arqueològica Lul-liana (Archaeological Society): Monti-Sion 9, 07001 Palma
de Mallorca, Balearic Is; tel. 971-21-39-12; f.
1880; 600 mems; library of 20,000 vols;
museum; Pres. MARIA BARCELÓ CRESPÍ; Sec.
GABRIEL ENSENYAT PUJOL; publ. *Boletín*
(annually).

LANGUAGE AND LITERATURE

Alliance Française: Calle Marques de la
Ensenada 10, 28004 Madrid; tel. 917-00-77-
36; fax 917-00-77-07; e-mail dgaf@
alliancefrancaise.es; internet www
.alliancefrancaise.es; offers courses and
exams in French language and culture and
promotes cultural exchange with France;
attached offices in Badajoz, Burgos, Cartagena, Gijon, Girona, Granada, Granollers, La
Coruña, Las Palmas, Leon, Lerida, Llcida,
Malaga, Oviedo, Palma de Mallorca, Sabadell, Sama de Langreo, Santa Cruz de
Tenerife, Santander, Santiago de Compostela, Terrassa, Valladolid, Vigo and Vitoria.

**Asociación de Escritores y Artistas
Españoles** (Writers' and Artists' Association): Calle de Leganitos 10, 28013 Madrid;
tel. 91-559-90-67; fax 91-559-90-67; f. 1872;
1,014 mems; library of 3,000 vols; Pres. JOSÉ
GERARDO MANRIQUE DE LARA; Dir and Gen.
Sec. JOSÉ LÓPEZ MARTÍNEZ.

British Council: Paseo del General Martinez, Campos 31, 28010 Madrid; tel. 91-337-
35-00; fax 91-337-35-73; e-mail general
.enquiries@britishcouncil.es; internet www
.britishcouncil.es; teaching centre; offers
courses and exams in English language and
British culture and promotes cultural
exchange with the UK; six other offices and
adult learners' and young learners' centres in
Madrid; attached teaching centres in Barcelona, Bilbao, Bonanova, Palma de Mallorca,
Segovia and Mallorca; Dir CHRIS HICKEY.

**Euskaltzaindia/Real Academia de la
Lengua Vasca** (Royal Academy of the
Basque Language): Plaza Barria, 15, 48005
Bilbao; tel. 94-415-81-55; fax 94-415-81-44;
e-mail info@euskaltzaindia.net; internet
www.euskaltzaindia.net; f. 1919; research
into and conservation of the Basque language; delegations: Hernani 15, 20004
Donostia/San Sebastián; Conde Oliveto 2,
31002 Iruñea/Pamplona; San Antonio 41,
01005 Vitoria-Gasteiz; rue Thiers 18, 64100
Baiona/Bayonne, France; 24 mems and a
number of honorary and corresponding
mems; library of 70,000 vols specializing in
philology and linguistics, principally of the
Basque language; Pres. ANDRÉS URRUTIA
BADIOLA; Sec. XABIER KINTANA; Librarian
PRUDEN GARTZIA ISASTI; publs *Euskera* (3 a
year), *Iker*, *Jagon*, *Euskararen Lekukoak*,
Onomasticon Vasconiae, *Hiztegiak eta Izen-
degiak/Diccionarios y Nomenclator* (irregu-
lar), *Soziolinguistika Saila/Estudios de
Sociolingüística* (irregular), *Gramatika eta
Metodoak/Gramáticas y Métodos* (irregular),
Euskaltzaindiaren Arauak (3 a year).

Goethe-Institut: c/Zurbarán 21, 28010
Madrid; tel. 91-391-39-44; fax 91-391-39-45;
e-mail schumacher@madrid.goethe.org;
internet www.goethe.de/wm/mad/deindex
.htm; offers courses and exams in German
language and culture and promotes cultural
exchange with Germany; attached centres in
Barcelona, Granada and San Sebastián;

library of 14,000 vols; Dir MARTIN SCHUMA-CHER.

Instituto Aula de 'Mediterráneo': Universidad de Valencia; f. 1942; 545 mems; Dir Dr F. SÁNCHEZ-CASTAÑER; publs *Mediterráneo*, *Unión de Literatura* (quarterly).

Real Academia Sevillana de Buenas Letras (Seville Royal Academy of Belles Lettres): Abades 14, 41004 Seville; tel. 95-422-52-00; f. 1751; 30 mems, 5 honorary, 100 corresponding; library of 10,000 vols; Dir EDUARDO YBARRA HIDALGO; Sec. Dr ROGELIO REYES CANÓ; Librarian ALFREDO JIMÉNEZ NÚÑEZ; publ. *Boletín* (annually); publ. monographs.

Reial Acadèmia de Bones Lletres (Royal Academy of Belles Lettres): Bisbe Cacador 3, 08002 Barcelona; tel. 93-310-23-49; fax 93-310-23-49; e-mail bones-lletres@sct.ictmet.es; f. 1700; 36 mems; Pres. EDUARD RIPOLL; Sec. FREDERIC UDINA; Librarian JOSÉ-ENRIQUE RUIZ DOMÈNEC; publ. *Boletín*.

Seminario de Filología Vasca 'Julio de Urquijo' ('Julio de Urquijo' Seminary of Basque Philology): Palacio de la Diputación Foral de Guipúzcoa, San Sebastián; f. 1953 to encourage the use and scientific study of the Basque language; attached to the University of País Vasco, Vitoria; Dir IBON SARASOLA; publ. *Anuario*.

Sociedad General de Autores y Editores (General Society of Authors and Publishers): Fernando VI 4, 28004 Madrid; tel. 91-349-95-50; internet www.sgae.es; f. 1932; 66,000 mems; library of 22,000 vols, relating to the theatre, music (scores) and cinema only; Dir.-Gen. ENRIQUE LORAS GARCÍA; Sec.-Gen. CARLOS FERNÁNDEZ-LERGA GARRALDA; publ. *Boletín* (quarterly).

MEDICINE

Academia de Ciencias Médicas de Bilbao (Academy of Medicine): Lersundi 9-5°, 48009 Bilbao; tel. 94-423-37-68; fax 94-423-01-11; internet www.icombi.org/academiacm.htm; f. 1895; 1,300 mems; library of 9,070 vols; Pres. Dr CIRIACO AGUIRRE ERRASTI; Sec.-Gen. Dr FRANCISCO JAVIER GARRÓS GARAY; publ. *Gaceta Médica de Bilbao* (quarterly).

Acadèmia de Ciències Mèdiques de Catalunya i de Balears (Catalonian Academy of Medicine): Paseo de la Bonanova 51, 08017 Barcelona; tel. 93-418-87-29; e-mail acm@acmcb.es; tel. www.acmcb.es; f. 1872; 19,000 mems; Pres. JOAQUIM RAMIS I CORIS; Sec. JOSEP REIG VILALLONGA; publs *Annals de Medicina*, *L'informatiu* (monthly).

Academia Española de Dermatología y Venereología (Spanish Academy of Dermatology and Venereology): Calle Ferraz 100, 1° izq, 28008 Madrid; tel. 91-544-62-84; fax 91-549-41-45; e-mail secretaria@aedv.es; internet www.aedv.es; f. 1909; 435 mems, 51 hon., 3 corresp.; library of 900 vols; brs: Andalusia; Asturias, Cantabria and Castille Leon; Canary Islands; Catalonia and the Balearic Islands; Centro; Galicia; Valencia; Euskadi, Navarre, La Rioja and Aragon; Pres Dr JOSÉ LUIS DÍAZ PEREZ; Sec. Dr SALVIO SERRANO ORTEGA; publ. *Actas Dermosifiliográficas*.

Academia Médico-Quirúrgica Española (Spanish Academy of Medicine and Surgery): Villanueva 11, 28001 Madrid; f. 1891; 492 mems; Pres. Prof. EDUARDO ARIAS VALLEJO; Sec. Dr JULIO MÚÑIZ GONZÁLEZ; publ. *Anales*.

Consejo General de Colegios Oficiales de Farmacéuticos (General Council of Official Colleges of Pharmacists): Villanueva 11-4°, 28001 Madrid; f. 1942; 13,500 mems; Pres. ERNESTO MARCO CAÑIZARES; publ. *Boletín de Información*.

Organización Médica Colegial – Consejo General de Colegios Oficiales de Médicos (General Council of Official Medical Colleges): Villanueva 11, 28001 Madrid; tel. 91-431-77-80; fax 91-576-43-88; e-mail administrador@cgcom.org; internet www.cgcom.org; f. 1930; 21 mems; Pres. Dr GUILLERMO SIERRA ARREDONDO; Sec. Dr JUAN JOSÉ RODRÍGUEZ SENDÍN; publs *Europa al Día* (every 2 weeks), *Periódico OMC* (monthly).

Real Academia de Medicina y Cirugía de Palma de Mallorca (Royal Academy of Medicine and Surgery): C/ Morey 8, 07001 Palma de Mallorca; tel. 971-72-12-30; f. 1831; 19 mems; Pres. JOSÉ TOMÁS MONSERRAT; Sec. SANTIAGO FORTEZA FORTEZA.

Sociedad de Pediatría de Madrid y Castilla La Mancha (Paediatrics Society of Madrid and Castilla La Mancha): Villanueva 11, 28001 Madrid; tel. 91-435-80-31; fax 91-435-50-43; e-mail aep@telprof.es; internet www.telprof.es/aep; f. 1913; 750 mems; Pres. CARLOS MARINA; Sec.-Gen. L. A. RUBIO; publ. *MCM – Pediatría* (3 a year).

Sociedad Española de Patología Digestiva y de la Nutrición (Society of Digestive and Nutritional Diseases): Almagro 38, Madrid; f. 1933; 800 mems; Pres. Dr HELIODORO G. MOGENA; publ. *Revista Española de las Enfermedades del Aparato Digestivo y de la Nutrición*.

Sociedad Española de Radiología Médica (Spanish Society of Medical Radiology): Goya 38, 3° izda., 28001 Madrid; tel. 91-575-26-13; fax 91-576-32-79; e-mail secretaria@seram.es; internet www.seram.es; f. 1946; 3,493 mems; 200 founder mems; Pres. Dr LUÍS DONOSO BACH; Sec.-Gen. JAVIER AZPEITIA ARMÁN; publ. *Radiología* (6 a year).

NATURAL SCIENCES
General

Real Academia de Ciencias Exactas, Físicas, Químicas y Naturales de Zaragoza (Royal Academy of Exact, Physical, Chemical and Natural Sciences in Zaragoza): Facultad de Ciencias, C/Pedro Cerbuna 12, 50009 Zaragoza; tel. 976-76-11-28; fax 976-76-11-25; e-mail acz@posta.unizar.es; internet www.unizar.es/acz; f. 1916; comprises sections on Exact Sciences, Physics and Chemistry, and Natural Sciences; Pres. HORACIO MARCO MOLL; Sec. MARIANO GASCA GONZÁLEZ; 40 mems (7 corresponding mems); publ. *Revista* (annually).

Sociedad de Ciencias 'Aranzadi' Zientzi Elkartea: Calle del Alto de Zorroaga 11, 20014 San Sebastián; tel. 943-46-61-42; fax 943-45-58-11; e-mail idazkaritza@aranzadi-zientziak.org; internet www.aranzadi-zientziak.org; f. 1947; to encourage interest in the various branches of natural science, prehistory and ethnology; 1,600 mems; library of 21,000 vols, 1,940 periodicals; Pres. JOSÉ MIGUEL LARRAÑAGA; Sec. JUANTXO AGIRRE; publs *Munibe Antropologia – Arkeologia* (annually), *Munibe Ciencias Naturales – Natur Zientziak* (annually), *Aranzadiana* (annually), *Aranzadi Berriak*, *Boletín de Astronomía* (4 a year).

Biological Sciences

Asociación Española de Entomología (Spanish Entomological Association): Facultad de Ciencias Biológicas, Universidad de Valencia, 46100 Burjasot (Valencia); f. 1977; Pres. Dr EDUARDO GALANTE PATIÑO; Sec. Dr RICARDO JIMÉNEZ PEYDRÓ; publ. *Boletín*.

Institut Botànic de Barcelona (Botanical Institute): Parc de Montjuïc, Avinguda dels Muntanyans, 08038 Barcelona; tel. 93-325-80-50; fax 93-426-93-21; e-mail i.botanic@ibb.csic.es; internet www.institutbotanic.bcn.es;

f. 1917; herbarium of 650,000 specimens; research in systematics, ecology and citology of western Mediterranean vascular plants; library of 11,000 vols, 1,520 periodicals and natural history museum; Dir J. M. MONTSERRAT; publs *Collectanea Botanica*, *Treballs*.

Real Sociedad Española de Historia Natural (Royal Spanish Natural History Society): Facultades de Biología y Geología, Universidad Complutense de Madrid, 28040 Madrid; tel. and fax 91-394-50-00; e-mail rsehno@bio.ucm.es; internet www.ucm.es/info/rsehn; f. 1871; biological and geological sciences; 800 mems; library: c. 10,000 vols, 700 current periodicals; Pres. SANTIAGO CASTROVIEJO BOLIBAR; Sec.-Gen. ANTONIO PEREJÓN RINCÓN; publs *Boletín: Sección Biológica*, *Sección Geológica* (both 4 a year), *Actas* (annually).

Sociedad Española de Etología (Spanish Ethological Society): Museu de Zoologia, Apdo Correos 594, 08080 Barcelona; tel. 93-256-22-17; fax 93-310-49-99; e-mail recercamuseuciencies@mail.bcn.es; internet www.etologia.org; f. 1984; 425 mems; Pres. JUAN CARRANZA; Sec. JUAN CARLOS SENAR; publs *Acta Ethologica* (annually), *Etologuía* (2 a year).

Mathematical Sciences

Real Sociedad Matemática Española (Royal Spanish Mathematical Society): Despacho 525, Facultad de Matemáticas, Universidad Complutense 28040 Madrid; tel. 91-394-49-37; fax 91-394-50-27; e-mail secretaria@rsme.es; internet www.rsme.es; f. 1911; 1,600 mems; Pres. CARLOS ANDRADAS HERANZ; Sec. PATRICIO CIFUENTES MUÑIZ; publs *La Gaceta* (3 a year), *Matemáticas en Breve* (4 a year).

Physical Sciences

Asociación Nacional de Químicos de España (National Association of Chemists): Lagasca 27, 28001 Madrid; tel. 91-431-07-03; fax 91-576-52-79; e-mail anquejg@mail.ddnet.es; internet www.anque.es; f. 1945; 9,000 mems; a member of the international Federation of Mediterranean Associations and of European Federation of Chemical Engineering; Pres. BALDOMERO LÓPEZ PÉREZ; Sec. JOAQUÍN COPADO LÓPEZ; publ. *Química e Industria* (monthly).

Real Sociedad Española de Física (Royal Spanish Society of Physics): Facultad de Ciencias Físicas, Universidad Complutense, 28040 Madrid; tel. 91-394-43-59; fax 91-394-41-62; e-mail rsef@fis.ucm.es; internet www.ucm.es/info/rsef; f. 1903; 800 mems; Pres. Prof. GERARDO DELGADO BARRIO; Sec.-Gen. Prof. ANTONIO DOBADO GONZÁLEZ; publs *Anales de Física* (quarterly), *Revista Española de Física* (quarterly).

Real Sociedad Española de Química (Royal Spanish Society of Chemistry): Facultad de Ciencias Químicas, Universidad Complutense, Ciudad Universitaria s/n, 28040 Madrid; tel. 91-394-43-61; fax 91-543-38-79; e-mail rsequim@rect.ucm.es; internet www.ucm.es/info/rsequim; f. 1903; 2,900 mems; Pres. Prof. LUIS A. ORO GIRAL; Sec.-Gen. JESÚS JIMÉNEZ BARBERO; publ. *Anales* (4 a year).

Sociedad Española de Astronomía (Spanish Astronomical Society): Universidad de Barcelona, Facultad de Física, Avda Martí Franquès 1, 08028 Barcelona; tel. 93-402-11-25; fax 93-402-11-33; e-mail secretaria@sea.am.ub.es; internet sea.am.ub.es/SEAf.html; f. 1911; lectures, courses, etc.; 250 mems; library of 2,800 vols; Pres. EDUARD SALVADOR SOLÉ; Sec. JOSÉ CARLOS DEL TORO INIESTA; publ. *Boletín Informativo* (2 a year).

Sociedad Geológica de España (Geological Society of Spain): Facultad de Ciencias, Universidad de Salamanca, Plaza de la Merced s/n, 37008 Salamanca; tel. 923-29-47-52; e-mail info@geologicas.es; internet www.sociedadgeologica.es; f. 1985; 1,000 mems; Pres. JOSÉ PEDRO CALVO SORANDO; Sec. JOSÉ EUGENIO ORTIZ MENÉNDEZ; publs *Geogaceta* (2 a year), *Revista* (2 a year).

RELIGION, SOCIOLOGY AND ANTHROPOLOGY

Federación Española de Religiosos de Enseñanza (FERE) (Spanish Federation of Religious Centres in Education): Hacienda de Pavones 5 (1°), 28030 Madrid; tel. 91-328-80-00; fax 91-328-80-01; e-mail fere@planalfa.es; internet www.planalfa.es/fere; f. 1957; groups all the centres of elementary, secondary and higher education of the Catholic Church; 2,847 centres; library of 6,200 vols, 156 periodicals; Pres. JOAQUÍN BLANCO RODRÍGUEZ; Sec.-Gen. MANUEL DE CASTRO BARCO; publs *Educadores* (Teachers' Review, 4 a year), *Revista FERE* (6 a year).

Institución 'Fernando el Católico' de la Excma Diputación de Zaragoza: Plaza de España 2, 50071 Zaragoza; tel. 976-28-88-78; fax 976-28-88-69; e-mail ifc@dpz.es; internet ifc.dpz.es; f. 1943; part of CSIC; Sections: Linguistics and Literature, Aragonese Art, History, Geography and Ecology, Economic and Social Studies, Law, Music for Young People, Ancient Music; Council of 12 representing the University and Municipality; library of 83,000 vols; Pres. JAVIER LAMBÁN MONTAÑÉS; Dir GONZALO M. BORRÁS; Sec. ÁLVARO CAPALVO; publs *Archivo de Filología Aragonesa, Caesaraugusta, Ciencia Forense: Revista Aragonesa de Medicina Legal, Cuadernos de Aragón, Emblemata, Estudios de Dialectología Norteafricana y Andalusí, IVS FVGIT: Revista de Estudios Histórico-Jurídicos de la Corona de Aragón, Nassarre* (musicology review), *Palaeohispanica, Revista sobre Lenguas y Culturas de la Hispania Antigua, Revista de Derecho Civil Aragonés, Revista de Historia 'Jerónimo Zurita', Seminario de Arte Aragonés.*

Real Instituto de Estudios Asturianos (Institute of Asturian Studies): 1a Planta, Plaza Porlier 9, 33003 Oviedo; tel. 98-510-64-80; fax 98-510-64-81; e-mail ridea@princast.es; internet tematico.princast.es/cultura/ridea/index.html; f. 1946; 131 mems; library of 24,000 vols, 250 periodicals; Asturian studies (literature, history, folklore, language); historical archive, archive of 3,000 photographs; Dir JOSÉ LUIS PÉREZ DE CASTRO; Sec. OLGA CASARES ABELLA; publs *Boletín de Letras* (2 a year), *Boletín de Ciencias de la Naturaleza* (annually).

Real Sociedad Bascongada de los Amigos del País (Royal Society of Friends of the Basque Country): C/ Peña y Goñi 5 (2° piso), 20002 San Sebastián; internet www.bm30.es/socios/organizaciones/rsbap_eu.html; f. 1764, the first of such societies in Spain; 24 mems; organized Museo de San Telmo and Museo Naval, also Conservatorio Municipal de Música; f. Editorial Guipuzcoana de Ediciones y Publicaciones, Books in Basque and Biblioteca Vascongada de los Amigos del País, collaborated in archaeological exploration of the prehistoric cave dwellings of the district; the Guipuzcoan Office of the Consejo Superior de Investigaciones Científicas, Madrid (see below); Dir IGNACIO M. BARRIOLA IRIGOYEN; publs *Boletín* (4 a year), *Egan* (literary supplement), *Munibe* (natural sciences supplement), *Boletín de la Cofradía Vasca de Gastronomía, Boletín de Estudios Históricos sobre San Sebastián* (annually),

Anuario de Eusko-Folklore Aranzadiana Orria.

TECHNOLOGY

Col·legi Oficial d'Enginyers Industrials de Catalunya: Via Laietana 39, 08003 Barcelona; tel. 93-319-23-00; fax 93-310-06-81; e-mail eic@eic.es; internet www.eic.es; f. 1950; 8,093 mems; is an association of engineering graduates of the Schools of Industrial Engineers of Spain; library of 22,000 vols; Dean ÁNGEL LLOBET I DÍEZ; Sec. JOSEP M. ROVIRA I RAGUÉ; publs *Full Dels Enginyers* (monthly), *Agenda Dels Enginyers* (24 a year).

Instituto de la Ingeniería de España (Spanish Institute of Engineering): General Arrando 38, 28010 Madrid; f. 1905; 20,000 mems; comprises 9 associations of higher engineers and the *Aula de Ingeniería* (training centre), offering courses, seminars, etc. for postgraduate students; Gen. Sec. JAIME TORNOS.

Sociedad Española de Cerámica y Vidrio (Spanish Ceramic and Glass Society): Camino de Valdelatas s/n, Campus de Cantoblanco, 28049 Madrid; tel. 91-735-58-40 ext. 1176; fax 91-735-58-43; e-mail secv@icv.csic.es; internet www.secv.es; f. 1960; promotes technical progress in ceramic and glass work and disseminates information about manufacture and developments within the field; 730 mems; library of 500 vols; Gen. Sec. EMILIO CRIADO; publ. *Boletín* (6 a year).

Research Institutes

GENERAL

Consejo Superior de Investigaciones Científicas (CSIC) (Council for Scientific Research): Serrano 117, 28006 Madrid; tel. 91-585-50-00; fax 91-411-30-77; internet www.csic.es; f. 1940; largest multidisciplinary research body in Spain, to serve culture and technological development; acts as a creative instrument and forum for Spanish science; has 100 research centres distributed throughout Spain, incl. institutes directly governed by CSIC, those operated jointly by CSIC and univs, and others in association with regional govt or other institutions; 7,500 employees, 2,000 scientists, 1,500 trainees, 3,300 researchers and technicians, 700 administrative staff; maintains office for transfer of technology in co-operation with Spanish supervisory agencies for technological development; Library and two centres for documentation and information comprising 100,000 vols, journals published by the institutes, scientific and cultural dissemination, scientific publishing house, technical facilities and installations; Pres. EMILIO LORA TAMAYO D'OCÓN; Vice-Pres. (Scientific and Technological Research) MANUELA JUÁREZ IGLESIAS; Vice-Pres. (Administration and Institutional Relations) MONTSERRAT GOMENDIO KINDELAN; Gen. Sec. EUSEBIO JIMÉNEZ ARROYO; publ. *Arbor* (monthly).

Attached research institutes in the field of Humanities and Social Sciences:

Instituto de Historia: C/ Duque de Medinaceli 6, 28014 Madrid; tel. 91-429-06-26; fax 91-369-09-40; e-mail director .ceh@csic.es; internet www.csic.es; Dir MARÍA PILAR LÓPEZ GARCÍA; publs *Archivo Español de Arqueología* (annual), *Archivo Español de Arte* (quarterly), *Asclepio* (2 a year), *Hispania* (3 a year), *Hispania Sacra* (2 a year), *Revista de Indias* (3 a year), *Trabajos de Prehistoria* (2 a year), *Gladius* (annual).

Centro de Información y Documentación Científica: C/ Joaquín Costa 22, 28002 Madrid; tel. 91-563-54-82; fax 91-564-2644; e-mail director.cindoc@csic.es; internet www.csic.es; Dir CARMEN VIDAL PERUCHO; publ. *Revista Española de Documentación Científica* (quarterly).

Escuela Española de Historia y Arqueología: Via di Torre Argentina 18, 00186 Rome, Italy; tel. Italy 06-6810001; fax Italy 06-68309047; e-mail eeha.csic@giannutri.caspur.it; internet www.csic.es; Dir MANUEL ESPADAS BURGOS.

Escuela de Estudios Árabes: Cta Cuesta del Chapiz 22, 18010, Granada; tel. 958-22-22-90; fax 958-22-47-54; e-mail director .eeh@csic.es; internet www.csic.es; Dir ANTONIO ALMAGRO GORBEA.

Escuela de Estudios Hispano Americanos: C/ Alfonso XII 16, 41002 Seville; tel. 95-450-11-20; fax 95-422-43-31; e-mail director.eeha@csic.es; internet www.csic .es; Dir ENRIQUETA VILA VILAR; publ. *Anuario de Estudios Americanos* (2 a year).

Institución Milá y Fontanals: C/ Egipciaques 15, 08001 Barcelona; tel. 93-442-34-89; fax 93-443-0071; e-mail director .imf@csic.es; internet www.csic.es; Dir LUIS CALVO CALVO; publs *Anuario de Estudios Medievales* (2 a year), *Anuario Musical* (annual).

Instituto de Análisis Económico: Universidad Autónoma, 08193 Bellaterra (Barcelona); tel. 93-580-66-12; fax 93-580-14-52; e-mail director.iae@csic.es; internet www.csic.es; Dir FRANCISCO JAVIER VIVES TORRENTS.

Instituto de Economía y Geografía: C/ Pinar 25, 28006 Madrid; tel. 91-411-10-98; fax 91-562-55-67; e-mail director.ieg@csic .es; internet www.csic.es; Dir ASCENSIÓN CALATRAVA ANDRÉS; publ. *Estudios Geográficos* (quarterly).

Instituto de Estudios Gallegos 'Padre Sarmiento': Rúa do Franco 2, 15702 Santiago de Compostela (La Coruña); tel. 981-58-20-44; fax 981-58-20-49; e-mail director.iegps@csic.es; internet www.csic .es; Dir EDUARDO PARDO DE GUEVARA Y VALDÉS; publ. *Cuadernos de Estudios Gallegos* (annual).

Instituto de Estudios Sociales Avanzados en Andalucía: Campo Santo de los Mártires 7, 14004 Córdoba; tel. 957-76-06-25; fax 957-76-01-53; e-mail director .iesaa@csic.es; internet www.csic.es; Dir MANUEL PÉREZ YRUELA; publ. *Revista Internacional de Sociología* (3 a year).

Instituto de Historia de la Ciencia y Documentación López Piñero: CSIC Universidad de Valencia, C/ Vicente Blasco Ibáñez 17, 46010 Valencia; tel. 96-386-41-64; fax 96-361-39-75; e-mail director.iedh@csic.es; internet www.csic.es; Dir JOSÉ LUIS FRESQUET FEBRER.

Instituto de Filología: C/ Duque de Medinaceli 6, 28014 Madrid; tel. 91-429-06-26; fax 91-369-09-40; e-mail director .ifl@csic.es; internet www.csic.es; Dir MARÍA TERESA ORTEGA MONASTERIO; publs *Al-Qantara* (2 a year), *Emerita* (2 a year), *Sefarad* (2 a year).

Instituto de Filosofía: C/ Pinar 25, 28006 Madrid; tel. 91-411-70-05; fax 91-564-52-52; e-mail director.ifs@csic.es; internet www.csic.es; Dir JOSÉ MARÍA GONZÁLEZ GARCÍA; publ. *Isegoria* (2 a year).

Instituto Histórico Hoffmeyer: Avda de la Constitución 104, 10400 Jaraiz de la Vera (Cáceres); tel. 927-17-06-46; fax 927-17-06-45; internet www.csic.es; Dir MARÍA PILAR LÓPEZ GARCIA.

Instituto de la Lengua Española: Duque de Medinaceli 6, 28014 Madrid; tel. 91-429-06-26; fax 91-369-09-40; e-mail director.ile@csic.es; internet www.csic.es; Dir María Pilar García Mouton; publs *Anales Cervantinos* (annual), *Revista de Dialectología y Tradiciones Populares* (2 a year), *Revista de Filología Española* (2 a year), *Revista de Literatura* (2 a year).

Unidad de Políticas Comparadas: Alfonso XII 18, 5a planta, 28014 Madrid; tel. 91-521-91-60; fax 91-521-81-03; e-mail director.upc@csic.es; internet www.csic.es; Dir Ludolfo Paramio Rodrigo.

Centro de Humanidades: Duque de Medinaceli 6, 28014 Madrid; tel. 91-429-06-26; fax 91-369-09-40; e-mail director .ch@csic.es; internet www.csic.es; Dir (vacant).

Attached research institutes in the field of Biology and Biomedicine:

Instituto de Biología Molecular: Ftad de Ciencias, 28049 Cantoblanco (Madrid); tel. 91-397-50-70; fax 91-397-47-99; e-mail director.ibm@csic.es; internet www.csic.es; Dir Jorge Moscat Guillen.

Centro de Investigaciones Biológicas: C/ Velázquez 144, 28006 Madrid; tel. 91-561-18-00; fax 91-562-75-18; e-mail director.cib@csic.es; internet www.csic.es; Dir Juan Manuel Ramírez de Verger.

Centro de Investigación y Desarrollo: C/ Jordi Girona Salgado 18–26, 08034 Barcelona; tel. 93-400-61-00; fax 93-204-59-04; e-mail director.cid@csic.es; internet www.csic.es; Dir Francisco Camps Diez.

Centro Nacional de Biotecnología: UAM, Campus del Cantoblanco, 28049 Cantoblanco (Madrid); tel. 91-585-45-00; fax 91-585-45-06; e-mail director.cnb@csic .es; internet www.csic.es; Dir Mariano Esteban Rodríguez.

Instituto de Biología Molecular y Celular de Plantas 'Eduardo Primo Yúfera': CSIC-Universidad Politécnica, Camino de Vera s/n, 46022 Valencia; tel. 96-387-78-51; fax 96-377-78-59; e-mail director.ibmcp@csic.es; internet www.csic .es; Dir Vicente Conejero Tomás.

Instituto de Bioquímica: CSIC-Universidad Complutense, Facultad de Farmacia, Ciudad Universitaria, 28040 Madrid; tel. 91-394-17-82; fax 91-394-17-82; e-mail director.ib@csic.es; internet www.csic.es; Dir Lisardo Boscá Gomar.

Instituto de Bioquímica Vegetal y Fotosíntesis: CSIC-Universidad de Sevilla, Americo Vespucio s/n, Isla de la Cartuja, 41092 Seville; tel. 95-448-95-06; fax 95-446-00-65; e-mail director.ibvf@csic .es; internet www.csic.es; Dir Antonia Herrero Moreno.

Instituto de Farmacología y Toxicología: CSIC-Universidad Complutense, Faculted de Medicina, Ciudad Universitaria, 28040 Madrid; tel. 91-394-14-69; fax 91-394-14-70; e-mail director.ift@csic.es; internet www.csic.es; Dir Juan Tamargo Menéndez.

Instituto de Investigaciones Biomédicas 'Alberto Sols': C/ Arturo Duperier 4, 28029 Madrid; tel. 91-585-46-00; fax 91-585-45-87; e-mail director.iib@csic.es; internet www.csic.es; Dir Juan Bernal Carrasco.

Instituto de Microbiología Bioquímica: CSIC-Universidad de Salamanca, Edif. Departmental, Avda Campo Charro s/n, 37007 Salamanca; tel. 923-29-44-62; fax 923-22-48-76; e-mail director .imb@csic.es; internet www.csic.es; Dir María del Pilar Pérez González.

Instituto de Parasitología y Biomedicina 'López Neyra': C/ Ventanilla 11, 18001 Granada; tel. 958-20-38-02; fax 958-20-33-23; e-mail director.ipbln@csic.es; internet www.csic.es; Dir Dolores González Pacanowska.

Instituto Neurobiológica Ramón y Cajal: Doctor Arce 37, 28002 Madrid; tel. 91-585-47-50; fax 91-585-47-54; e-mail director.inrc@csic.es; internet www.csic.es; Dir Ricardo Martínez Murillo.

Instituto de Investigaciones Biomédicas de Barcelona: Rosellón 161, 6 y 7 planta, 08036 Barcelona; tel. 93-363-83-00; fax 93-363-83-01; e-mail director.iibb@csic .es; internet www.csic.es; Dir Emilio Gelpi Monteys.

Centro Biológica Molecular Severo Ochoa: CSIC-Universidad Autonoma de Madrid, Facultad de Ciencias, Cantoblanco U. Auton., 28049 Madrid; tel. 91-397-50-70; fax 91-397-47-99; e-mail director@cbm .uam.es; internet www.csic.es; Dir Federico Mayor Menéndez.

Instituto Biomedicina de Valencia: Jaime Roig 11, 46010 Valencia; tel. 96-339-17-60; fax 96-369-08-00; e-mail director.ibv@csic.es; internet www.ibv.csic .es; f. 1998; research into structural biology (X-ray crystallography), human molecular genetics, molecular/cell biology of cardiovascular disease, inborn errors of the urea cycle, molecular biology, genetics and signalling in type 2 diabetes; Dir Dr Vicente Rubio.

Instituto de Biología Molecular y Celular del Cáncer (CSIC-USAL): Campus Unamuno, Universidad de Salamanca, 37007 Salamanca; tel. 923-29-47-20; fax 923-29-47-43; e-mail cicancer@gugu.usal .es; internet www.cicancer.org; f. 1997; basic, clinical and translational cancer research; Dir Dr Eugenio Santos.

Instituto de Neurociencias: Apdo de Correos 18, 03550 San Juan (Alicante); tel. 96-591-95-45; fax 96-591-95-47; e-mail carlos.belmonte@umh.es; internet www .csic.es; Dir Carlos Belmonte.

Unidad de Biofísica: Apdo 644, 48080 Bilbao; tel. 94-601-26-25; fax 94-464-85-00; e-mail gbpaliza@lg.ehu.es; internet www .csic.es; Dir Alicia Alonso Izquierdo.

Instituto de Biología y Genética Molecular: Facultad de Medicina, Universidad de Valladolid, Ramón y Cajal 7, 47005 Valladolid; tel. 983-42-30-85; fax 983-42-35-88; e-mail director.ibgm@csic.es; internet www.csic.es; Dir Benito Herreros Fernández.

Instituto de Biología Molecular de Barcelona: Jorge Girona Salgado 18–26, 08034 Barcelona; tel. 93-400-61-00; fax 93-204-59-04; e-mail director.cid@csic.es; internet www.csic.es; Dir Pedro Puigdomenech Rosell.

Centro de Investigaciones Científicas Isla de la Cartuja: CSIC-Universidad de Sevilla, Americo Vespucio s/n, Isla de la Cartuja, 41092 Seville; tel. 95-448-95-01; fax 95-446-01-65; e-mail director.cic@csic .es; internet www.csic.es; Dir Antonia Herrero Moreno.

Attached research institutes in the field of Natural Resources:

Centro de Estudios Avanzados de Blanes: Cam. de Santa Bárbara s/n, 17300 Blanes (Gerona); tel. 972-33-61-01; fax 972-33-78-06; e-mail director.ceab@csic .es; internet www.csic.es; Dir Enrique Ballesteros Sagarra.

Estación Biológica de Doñana: Avda Ma. Luisa s/n, Pabellón Peru, 41013 Seville; tel. 95-423-23-40; fax 95-462-11-25; e-mail director.ebd@csic.es; internet www.csic.es; Dir Miguel Ángel Ferrer Baena; publ. *Doñana. Acta Vertebrata* (2 a year).

Estacíon Experimental de Zonas Áridas: C/ General Segura 1, 04001 Almería; tel. 950-27-64-00; fax 950-27-71-00; e-mail director.eeza@csic.es; internet www.csic .es; Dir Eulalia Moreno Mañas.

Instituto de Acuicultura de Torre de la Sal: Planta Pilato de Acuicultura s/n, 12595 C. Torre de la Sal (Castellón); tel. 964-31-95-00; fax 964-31-95-09; e-mail director.iats@csic.es; internet www.csic.es; Dir Francisco Amat Doménech.

Instituto Andaluz de Ciencias de la Tierra: CSIC-Universidad de Granada, Facultad de Ciencias, Avda Fuentenueva s/n, 18002 Granada; tel. 958-24-31-58; fax 958-24-33-84; e-mail director.iact@csic.es; Dir Andrés Maldonado López.

Instituto de Astronomía y Geodesia: CSIC-Universidad Complutense, Facultad de Ciencias Matemáticas, 28040 Madrid; tel. 91-394-45-85; fax 91-394-46-15; e-mail director.iag@csic.es; internet www.csic.es; Dir Ricardo Vieira Díaz.

Instituto Botánico de Barcelona (Institut Botànic de Barcelona): Passeig del Migdia, Parque de Monjuïc, 08038 Barcelona; tel. 93-289-06-11; fax 93-289-06-14; e-mail jmmontserrat@csic.es; internet www.csic.es; f. 1917; affiliated to the Botanic Garden of Barcelona, Montjuïc Park; library of 30,000 vols, 80,000 herbarium sheets; Dir Josep M. Montserrat Martí; publ. *Collectanea Botanica* (irregular).

Instituto de Ciencias del Mar: Paseo Don Juan de Borbón s/n, 08039 Barcelona; tel. 93-221-64-50; fax 93-221-73-40; e-mail director.icm@csic.es; internet www.csic.es; Dir Rosa Flos Bassols; publ. *Scientia Marina* (4 a year).

Instituto de Ciencias de la Tierra 'Jaime Almera': C/ Lluis Solé Sabarís s/n, Apdo 30102, 08028 Barcelona; tel. 93-330-27-16; fax 93-409-54-10; e-mail director.ictja@csic.es; internet www.csic .es; Dir Ángel López Soler.

Centro de Investigaciones sobre Desertificación: Apdo Oficial, 46470 Albal (Valencia); tel. 96-122-05-40; fax 96-127-09-67; e-mail director.cisd@csic.es; internet www.uv.es/cide; f. 1996; Dir Dr Patricio Garcia-Fayos.

Instituto de Ciencias Marinas de Andalucía: C/ República Saharaui 2, Campus Universitario Río San Pedro, 11519 Puerto Real (Cádiz); tel. 956-83-26-12; fax 956-83-47-01; e-mail director .icman@csic.es; internet www.csic.es; f. 1955; Dir Carmen Sarasquete Reiriz.

Instituto de Geología Económica: CSIC-Universidad Complutense, Facultad de Geológicas, Ciudad Universitaria, 28040 Madrid; tel. 91-394-48-13; fax 91-394-48-08; e-mail director.ige@csic.es; internet www.csic.es; Dir José Ramón Peláez Pruneda.

Instituto de Investigaciones Marinas: C/ Eduardo Cabello, 36208 Vigo (Pontevedra); tel. 986-23-19-30; fax 986-29-27-62; e-mail director.iim@csic.es; internet www .csic.es; Dir Ricardo Isaac Pérez Martin.

Instituto Mediterraneo de Estudios Avanzados: CSIC-Universidad de las Islas Baleares, Facultad de Ciencias, Carr. de Valldemossa, km. 7,500, 07071 Palma de Mallorca; tel. 971-17-30-00 ext. 3381; fax 971-17-32-48; e-mail director

.imdea@csic.es; internet www.csic.es; Dir JOAQUÍN TINTORÉ SUBIRANA.

Instituto Pirenaico de Ecología: Avda Montañana 177, Apdo 202, 50080 Zaragoza; tel. 976-57-58-83; fax 976-57-58-84; e-mail director.ipe@csic.es; internet www.csic.es; Dir JUAN PABLO MARTÍNEZ RICA; publ. *Pirineos* (annually).

Museo Nacional de Ciencias Naturales: C/ José Gutiérrez Abascal 2, 28006 Madrid; tel. 91-561-86-00; fax 91-564-50-78; e-mail director.mncn@csic.es; internet www.csic.es; Dir MONTSERRAT GOMENDIO KINDELÁN; publ. *Estudios Geológicos* (6 a year).

Real Jardín Botánico: Pl. de Murillo 2, 28014 Madrid; tel. 91-420-30-17; fax 91-420-01-57; e-mail director.rjb@csic.es; internet www.csic.es; Dir MARÍA TERESA TELLERÍA JORGE; publ. *Anales del Jardín Botánico* (2 a year).

Centro de Ciencias Medioambientales: Serrano 115 bis, 28006 Madrid; tel. 91-562-50-20; fax 91-564-08-00; e-mail director.ccma@csic.es; internet www.csic.es; Dir MARÍA DEL ROSARIO FELIPE ANTON.

Instituto de Recursos Naturales y Agrobiología de Salamanca: Apdo 257, Cordel de Merinas 40–52, 37071 Salamanca; tel. 923-21-96-06; fax 923-21-96-09; e-mail director.irnasa@csic.es; internet www.csic.es; Dir BALBINO GARCÍA CRIADO.

Instituto de Recursos Naturales y Agrobiología de Sevilla: Apdo 1052, Estafeta-Puerto, 41080 Seville; tel. 954-62-47-11; fax 954-62-40-02; e-mail director.irnas@csic.es; internet www.csic.es; Dir JUAN CORNEJO SUERO.

Centro de Edafología y Biología Aplicada del Segura: Avda de la Fama 1, Apdo 195, 30080 Murcia; tel. 968 21-76-42; fax 968-26-66-13; e-mail director.cebas@csic.es; internet www.csic.es; Dir JUAN ALBADALEJO MONTORO.

Instituto Agroquímica y Tecnología Alimentos: Apdo de Correos 73, 46100 Burjassot (Valencia); tel. 96-390-00-22; fax 96-363-63-01; e-mail director.iata@csic.es; internet www.csic.es; Dir JOSÉ LUIS NAVARRO FABRA; publ. *Food Science and Technology International* (6 a year).

Instituto de Investigación en Recursos Cinegéticos: Libertad 7, Apdo 535, 13004 Ciudad Real; tel. 926-22-56-59; fax 926-22-51-84; e-mail irec.csic@uclm.es; internet www.csic.es; Dir RAFAEL VILLAFUERTE FERNÁNDEZ.

Instituto de Productos Naturales y Agrobiología: Astrofísico Francisco Sánchez 3, 38205 La Laguna (Tenerife); tel. 922-25-21-44; fax 922-26-01-35; e-mail director.ipna@csic.es; internet www.csic.es; Dir COSME GARCIA FRANCISCO.

Attached research institutes in the field of Agricultural Sciences:

Estación Experimental de Aula Dei: Avda Montañana 177, Apdo 202, 50080 Zaragoza; tel. 976-57-65-11; fax 976-57-56-20; e-mail director.eead@csic.es; internet www.csic.es; Dir RAFAEL PICOREL CATAÑO.

Estación Experimental del Zaidín: C/ Profesor Albareda 1, 18008 Granada; tel. 958-12-10-11; fax 958-12-96-00; e-mail director.eez@csic.es; internet www.csic.es; Dir JUAN LUIS RAMOS MARTÍN.

Estación Experimental 'La Mayora': Algarrobo-Costa, 29750 Málaga; tel. 952-55-26-56; fax 952-55-26-77; e-mail director.eelm@csic.es; internet www.csic.es; Dir MARÍA LUISA GÓMEZ-GUILLAMÓN ARRABAL.

Instituto de Agricultura Sostenible: Alameda del Obispo s/n, Apdo 4084,

14080 Córdoba; tel. 957-49-92-00; fax 957-49-92-52; e-mail director.ias@csic.es; internet www.csic.es; Dir ELIAS FERERES CASTIEL.

Instituto de Investigaciones Agrobiológicas de Galicia: Avda de Vigo s/n, Apdo 122, 15080 Santiago de Compostela (La Coruña); tel. 981-59-09-58; fax 981-59-25-04; e-mail director.iiag@csic.es; internet www.csic.es; Dir MARIA TARSY CARBALLAS FERNÁNDEZ.

Instituto de Agrobiotecnología y Recursos Naturales: Universidad Publica de Navarra, Campus de Arrosadia, 31006 Pamplona; tel. 948-24-28-34; fax 948-23-21-91; e-mail pmapariciotejo@unavarra.es; internet www.csic.es; Dir PEDRO APARICIO TEJO .

Misión Biológica de Galicia: Apdo 28, 36080 Pontevedra; tel. 986-85-48-00; fax 986-84-13-62; e-mail director.mbg@csic.es; internet www.csic.es; Dir AMANDO ORDÁS PERÉZ.

Estacion Agrícola Experimental de León: Finca Marzanas, Apdo 788, 24080 León; tel. 987-31-70-64; fax 987-31-71-61; e-mail director.eae@csic.es; internet www.csic.es; Dir ANGEL RUIZ MANTECON.

Attached research institutes in the field of the Science and Technology of Physics:

Instituto de Microelectrónica: Universidad Autónoma, 08193 Cerdanyola del Valles (Barcelona); tel. 93-580-26-25; fax 93 580-14-96; e-mail director.imb-cnm@csic.es; internet www.csic.es; Dir FRANCISCO SERRA MESTRES.

Instituto de Acústica: C/ Serrano 144, 28006 Madrid; tel. 91-561-88-06; fax 91-411-76-51; e-mail director.ia@csic.es; internet www.csic.es; Dir CARLOS RANZ GUERRA; publs *IEEE Transactions on Ultrasonics, Ferroelectrics and Frequency Control* (monthly), *Ultrasonics* (monthly), *Ferroelectrics* (monthly).

Instituto de Astrofísica de Andalucía: Camino Bajo de Huetor 24, Apdo 3004, 18008 Granada; tel. 958-12-13-11; fax 958-81-45-30; e-mail director.iaa@csic.es; internet www.csic.es; Dir RAFAEL RODRIGO MONTERO.

Instituto de Automática Industrial: Km. 22.800, Ctra Madrid-Valencia, 28500 Arganda del Rey (Madrid); tel. 91-871-19-00; fax 91-871-50-70; e-mail director.iai@csic.es; internet www.csic.es; Dir SALVADOR ROS TORRECILLAS.

Instituto de Estructura de la Materia: C/ Serrano 113 bis, 28006 Madrid; tel. 91-561-94-00; fax 91-564-24-31; e-mail director.iem@csic.es; internet www.csic.es; Dir FRANCISCO JOSÉ BALTÁ CALLEJA.

Instituto de Física Corpuscular: CSIC-Universidad de Valencia, Avda Doctor Moliner 50, 46100 Burjassot (Valencia); tel. 96-386-45-00; fax 96-386-45-83; e-mail director.ific@csic.es; internet www.csic.es; Dir JORGE VELASCO GONZÁLEZ.

Instituto de Física de Cantabria: CSIC-Universidad de Cantabria, Facultad de Ciencias, 39005 Santander; tel. 942-20-14-61; fax 942-20-14-59; e-mail director.ifc@csic.es; internet www.csic.es; Dir LUIS PESQUERA GONZÁLEZ.

Instituto de Robótica e Informática Industrial: Gran Capitan 2–4, Edificio Nexus, 08034 Barcelona; tel. 93-401-57-51; fax 93-401-57-50; e-mail director.irii@csic.es; internet www.csic.es; Dir RAFAEL MARIA HUBER GARRIDO.

Observatorio Física Cósmica del Ebro: 43520 Roquetas (Tarragona); tel. 977-50-05-11; fax 977-50-46-60; e-mail ebre

.lfalberca@readysoft.es; internet www.csic.es; Dir LUIS FELIPE ALBERCA SILVA.

Instituto de Investigación de Inteligencia Artificial: Universidad Autónoma, 08193 Bellaterra (Barcelona); tel. 93-580-95-70; fax 93-580-96-61; e-mail director.iiia@csic.es; internet www.csic.es; Dir FRANCISCO ESTEVA MASSAGUER.

Instituto de Matemáticas y Física Fundamental: C/ Serrano 113–123, 28006 Madrid; tel. 91-561-68-00; fax 91-585-48-94; e-mail director.imaff@csic.es; internet www.csic.es; Dir ALFREDO TIEMBLO RAMOS.

Instituto de Microelectrónica de Madrid: C/ Isaac Newton 8, Tres Cantos, 28760 Madrid; tel. 91-806-07-00; fax 91-806-07-01; e-mail director.imm-cnm@csic.es; internet www.csic.es; Dir FERNANDO BRIONES FERNÁNDEZ-POLA.

Instituto de Óptica 'Daza de Valdés': Serrano 121, 28006 Madrid; tel. 91-561-68-00; fax 91-564-55-57; e-mail director.io@csic.es; internet www.csic.es; Dir CARMEN NIEVES AFONSO RODRÍGUEZ.

Centro Física 'Miguel A. Catalán': Serrano 121, 28006 Madrid; tel. 91-561-68-00; fax 91-564-55-57; e-mail director.cfmac@csic.es; internet www.csic.es; Dir FRANCISCO JOSE BALTA CALLEJA.

Centro de Tecnologías Físicas 'L. Torres Quevedo': Serrano 144, 28006 Madrid; tel. 91-561-88-06; fax 91-411 76-51; e-mail director.cetef@csic.es; internet www.csic.es; Dir JUAN ANTONIO GALLEGO JUAREZ.

Centro Comunicaciones REDIRIS: Serrano 142, 28006 Madrid; tel. 91-585-51-50; fax 91-585-51-46; e-mail director.rediris@csic.es; internet www.csic.es; Dir VICTOR CASTELO GUTIÉRREZ.

Centro Técnico de Informática: Pinar 25, 28006 Madrid; tel. 91-564-29-63; fax 91-561-61-93; e-mail director.cti@csic.es; internet www.csic.es; Dir JOSÉ CARRERO VIVAS.

Centro Nacional de Microelectrónica: Campus Universidad Autonoma, 08193 Cerdanyola del Valles (Barcelona); tel. 93-594-77-00; fax 93-580-14-96; internet www.cnm.es; f. 1986; research and development of micro- and nanoelectronics; 160 staff; Dir FRANCISCO SERRA MESTRES.

Instituto de Física Aplicada: Serrano 144, 28006 Madrid; tel. 91-561-88-06; fax 91-411-76-51; e-mail director.ifa@csic.es; internet www.csic.es; Dir FRANCISCO JAVIER GUTIÉRREZ MONREAL.

Instituto de Microelectrónica de Sevilla: Avda Reina Mercedes s/n, Edificio Cica, 41012 Seville; tel. 95-423-99-23; fax 95-423-99-40; e-mail director.ims-cnm@csic.es; internet www.csic.es; Dir JOSÉ LUIS HUERTAS DÍAZ.

Attached research institutes in the field of Materials Science and Technology:

Centro Nacional de Investigaciones Metalúrgicas: Avda Gregorio del Amo 8, 28040 Madrid; tel. 91-553-89-00; fax 91-534-74-25; e-mail director.cenim@csic.es; internet www.csic.es; Dir ANTONIO FORMOSO PREGO; publ. *Metalurgia* (6 a year).

Instituto de Cerámica y Vidrio: Km. 24, Ctra Madrid-Valencia 3, 28500 Arganda del Rey (Madrid); tel. 91-871-18-00; fax 91-870-05-50; e-mail director.icv@csic.es; internet www.csic.es; Dir ÁNGEL CABALLERO CUESTA.

Instituto de Ciencia de Materiales de Aragón: CSIC-Universidad de Zaragoza, Pl. de S. Francisco s/n, Facultad de Ciencias, 50009 Zaragoza; tel. 976-55-25-

28; fax 976-76-12-29; e-mail director.icma@csic.es; internet www.csic.es; Dir PABLO JAVIER ALONSO GASCÓN.

Instituto de Ciencia de Materiales de Barcelona: Campus Universidad Autónoma, 08193 Cerdanyola del Valles (Barcelona); tel. 93-580-18-53; fax 93-580-57-29; e-mail director.icmb@csic.es; internet www.csic.es; Dir CARLOS MIRAVITLLES TORRAS.

Instituto de Ciencia de Materiales de Madrid: Cantoblanco, 28049 Madrid; tel. 91-334-90-00; fax 91-372-06-23; e-mail director.icmm@csic.es; internet www.csic.es; Dir FEDERICO JESÚS SORIA GALLEGO.

Instituto de Ciencia de Materiales de Sevilla: CSIC-Universidad de Sevilla, Americo Vespucio s/n, Isla de la Cartuja, 41092 Seville; tel. 95-448-95-27; fax 95-446-06-65; e-mail director.icms@csic.es; internet www.csic.es; Dir AGUSTÍN RODRÍGUEZ GONZÁLEZ-ELIPE.

Instituto de Ciencia y Tecnología de Polímeros: C/ Juan de la Cierva 3, 28006 Madrid; tel. 91-562-29-00; fax 91-564-48-53; e-mail director.ictp@csic.es; internet www.csic.es; Dir MARÍA DEL CARMEN MIJANOS UGARTE.

Instituto de Ciencias de la Construccíon 'Eduardo Torroja': C/ Serrano Galvache s/n, Apdo 19002, 28080 Madrid; tel. 91-302-04-40; fax 91-302-07-00; e-mail director.ietcc@csic.es; internet www.csic.es; Dir MARÍA DEL CARMEN ANDRADE PERDRIX; publs *Informes de la Construcción* (6 a year), *Materiales de la Construcción* (4 a year).

Unidad de Física de Materiales: Facultad de Química, Apdo 1072, 20080 San Sebastián; tel. 943-44-82-06; fax 943-21-22-36; e-mail wapetalap@sq.ehu.es; internet www.csic.es; Dir PEDRO MIGUEL ECHENIQUE LANDIRIBAR.

Attached research institutes in the field of Foodstuff Science and Technology:

Instituto de Fermentaciones Industriales: C/ Juan de la Cierva 3, 28006 Madrid; tel. 91-562-29-00; fax 91-564-48-53; e-mail director.ifi@csic.es; internet www.csic.es; Dir MARÍA DEL CARMEN POLO SÁNCHEZ.

Instituto del Frío: C/ Ramiro de Maeztu s/n, C. Universitaria, 28040 Madrid; tel. 91-549-23-00; fax 91-549-36-27; e-mail director.if@csic.es; internet www.csic.es; Dir MARÍA PILAR CANO DOLADO.

Instituto de la Grasa: Avda Padre García Tejero 4, 41012 Seville; tel. 95-461-15-50; fax 95-461-67-90; e-mail director.ig@csic.es; internet www.csic.es; Dir FRANCISCO JAVIER HIDALGO HUERTAS; publ. *Grasas y Aceites* (6 a year).

Instituto de Nutrición y Bromatología: CSIC-Universidad Complutense, Facultad de Farmacia, Cdad Universitaria, 28040 Madrid; tel. 91-549-00-38; fax 91-549-50-79; e-mail director.inb@csic.es; internet www.csic.es; Dir ASCENSIÓN MARCOS SÁNCHEZ.

Instituto de Productos Lácteos de Asturias: Ctra de Infiesto s/n, Apdo 85, 33300 Villaviciosa (Oviedo); tel. 98-589-21-31; fax 98-589-22-33; e-mail director.ipla@csic.es; internet www.csic.es; Dir JUAN CARLOS BADA GANCEDO.

Attached research institutes in the field of Chemical Science and Technology:

Instituto de Carboquímica: María de Luna 5, 50015 Zaragoza; tel. 976-73-39-77; fax 976-73-33-18; e-mail director.icb@csic.es; internet www.csic.es; Dir RAFAEL MOLINER ALVAREZ.

Instituto de Catálisis y Petroleoquímica: Universidad Autónoma, Camino Valdelatas s/n, 28049 Cantoblanco (Madrid); tel. 91-585-48-00; fax 91-585-47-60; e-mail director.icp@csic.es; internet www.csic.es; Dir JAVIER SORIA RUIZ.

Instituto Nacional del Carbón: C/ La Corredoria s/n, Apdo 73, 33080 Oviedo; tel. 98-528-08-00; fax 98-529-76-62; e-mail director.incar@csic.es; internet www.csic.es; Dir JESÚS A. PAJARES SOMOANO.

Instituto de Química Física Rocasolano: C/ Serrano 119, 28006 Madrid; tel. 91-561-94-00; fax 91-564-24-31; e-mail director.iqfr@csic.es; internet www.csic.es; Dir JOSÉ ANTONIO GARCÍA DOMÍNGUEZ.

Instituto de Química Médica: C/ Juan de la Cierva 3, 28006 Madrid; tel. 91-562-29-00; fax 91-564-48-53; e-mail director.iqm@csic.es; internet www.csic.es; Dir MARÍA TERESA GARCÍA LÓPEZ.

Instituto de Química Orgánica General: C/ Juan de la Cierva 3, 28006 Madrid; tel. 91-561-50-86; fax 91-564-48-53; e-mail director.iqog@csic.es; internet www.iqog.csic.es; f. 1966; rResearch in organic chemistry and related fields, including organic synthesis, inhibitors of proteases, physical organic chemistry, environmental chemistry, analytical chemistry of organic compounds, natural products, bio-organic chemistry, peptides, proteins, computational chemistry, and computational toxicology; library of 3,000 vols; Dir Dr BERNARDO HERRADÓN.

Instituto de Tecnología Química: CSIC-Universidad Politécnica, Avda de los Naranjos s/n, 46022 Valencia; tel. 96-387-78-00; fax 96-387-78-09; e-mail director.itq@csic.es; internet www.csic.es; Dir AVELINO CORMA CANÓS.

Laboratorio de Investigación en Tecnologías de la Combustión (Laboratory for Research in Combustion Technologies): C/ María de Luna 10, 50018 Zaragoza; tel. 976-71-63-03; fax 976-71-64-56; e-mail litec@litec.csic.es; internet www.litec.csic.es; f. 1991; research in combustion and fluid mechanics; Dir Dr ANTONIO LOZANO.

Centro de Química Orgánica Lora Tamayo: Juan de la Cierva 3, 28006 Madrid; tel. 91-562-29-00; fax 91-564-48-53; e-mail director.cenquior@csic.es; internet www.csic.es; Dir MARÍA DEL CARMEN MIJANGOS UGARTE.

Instituto de Investigaciones Químicas y Ambientales Josep Pascual Vila: Jorge Girona Salgado 18-26, 08034 Barcelona; tel. 93-400-61-00; fax 93-204-59-04; e-mail director.cid@csic.es; internet www.csic.es; Dir FRANCISCO CAMPS DIEZ.

Instituto de Investigaciones Químicas: Americo Vespucio s/n, Isla de la Cartuaja, 41092 Seville; tel. 95-448-95-53; fax 95-446-05-65; e-mail director.iiq@csic.es; internet www.csic.es; Dir MANUEL MARTÍN LOMAS.

Fundació Catalana per a la Recerca (Catalan Foundation for Research): Pg Lluís Companys 23, 08010 Barcelona; tel. 93-268-77-00; fax 93-268-37-68; e-mail fcr@fcr.es; internet www.fcr.es; f. 1986; promotes scientific and technological research; Chair. RAFAEL ESPAÑOL I NAVARRO; Man. Dir ENRIC BANDA; publs *Tecno 2000* (6 a year), newsletter (quarterly).

Instituto de Relaciones Europeo-Latinoamericanas (IRELA) (Institute for European-Latin American Relations): Apdo 2600, 28002 Madrid; Pedro de Valdivia 10, 28006 Madrid; tel. 91-561-72-00; fax 91-562-64-99; e-mail info@irela.org; f. 1984; organization of conferences, etc., for European and Latin American officials, diplomats, journalists, politicians, businessmen, trade-unionists and academics on different aspects of European-Latin American relations; collection and systematization of information on relations between the two regions; advisory activities for regional instns in Europe and Latin America; promotion, co-ordination and pursuit of specific research on relations between the two regions; Dir WOLF GRABENDORFF.

AGRICULTURE, FISHERIES AND VETERINARY SCIENCE

Departamento de Protección Vegetal (Plant Protection Department): CIT-INIA, Carretera de la Coruña Km 7.5, Apdo 8.111, 28040 Madrid; tel. 91-2-07-00-40; f. 1888; molecular biology and virology, entomology and plant pathology, weed science; attached to the Instituto Nacional de Investigaciones Agrarias; 60 staff; Head Dr JOSÉ M. GARCÍA-BAUDIN; publ. *Investigación Agraria: Producción y Protección Vegetales* (3 a year).

Instituto Nacional de Investigación y Tecnología Agraria y Alimentaria (INIA) (National Institute for Food and Agricultural Research and Technology): Carretera de la Coruña Km 7.5, 28040 Madrid; tel. 91-347-39-00; fax 91-357-22-93; internet www.inia.es/sapportal/guest/guest; f. 1971; library of 30,000 vols, 5,000 periodicals; Gen. Sec. MARIO GÓMEZ PÉREZ; publs *Spanish Journal of Agricultural Research* (in English, 4 a year), *Sistemas y Recursos Forestales* (3 a year).

ECONOMICS, LAW AND POLITICS

Centro de Investigaciones Sociológicas: Montalbán 8, 28014 Madrid; tel. 91-580-76-00; e-mail cis@cis.es; internet www.cis.es; f. 1977; attached to govt Min. of the Presidency; promotes research in social sciences, arranges courses and seminars, collaborates with similar national and intl orgs, and creates databases for relevant material; library of 15,000 vols; Pres. RICARDO MONTORO ROMERO; Gen. Sec. ANGEL PEDRO MUÑOZ REGIDOR; publs *Revista Española de Investigaciones Sociológicas* (4 a year), *Cuadernos Metodológicos* (4 a year).

Instituto de Estudios Fiscales (Institute of Fiscal Studies): Avda Cardenal Herrera Oria 378, 28035 Madrid; tel. 91-339-89-15; fax 91-339-89-64; internet www.ief.es; f. 1960; public finance; library of 77,000 vols; Dir JUAN JOSÉ RUBIO GUERRERO; publs *Hacienda Pública Española* (4 a year), *Crónica Tributaria* (4 a year), *Presupuesto y Gasto Público* (3 a year).

Instituto Universitario Ortega y Gasset: Calle Fortuny 53, 28010 Madrid; tel. 91-700-41-49; fax 91-700-35-30; e-mail jefatura.estudios@fog.es; internet www.ortegaygasset.edu/iuoyg/principal.htm; f. 1986; affiliated to Univ. Complutense; offers postgraduate courses, doctoral programmes in contemporary Latin America, European studies, linguistics, international relations, and public administration, research and training in social studies and the promotion of scholarship on Ortega y Gasset (Spanish philosopher and essayist) as well as contemporary studies; library of 45,000 vols incl. personal library of Ortega y Gasset, 150 periodicals; archive material concerning Ortega y Gasset; Academic Dir EMILIO LAMO DE ESPINOSA; Sec. CARLOS MALAMUD; publ. *Revista de Occidente* (monthly).

EDUCATION

Centro de Investigación y Documentación Educativa (CIDE): C/ General Oraá 55, 28006 Madrid; tel. 91-745-94-00; fax 91-

745-94-38; e-mail cide@educ.mec.es; internet www.mec.es/cide; f. 1983; conducts and coordinates educational research; manages the library, archive and documentation centre of the Min. of Education and Science; library of 85,000 vols; publ. *Boletín*.

FINE AND PERFORMING ARTS

Instituto del Patrimonio Histórico (Institute of National Heritage): Calle del Greco 4, 28040 Madrid; tel. 91-550-44-36; fax 91-550-44-44; f. 1985; attached to Min. of Education, Culture and Sport; library of 30,000 vols; Gen. Asst Dir ALVARO MARTÍNEZ NOVILLO.

MEDICINE

Instituto Cajal (Santiago Ramón y Cajal Institute of Neurobiological Research): Dr Arce 37, 28002 Madrid; tel. 91-585-47-50; fax 91-585-47-54; f. 1906; 30 mems; library of 35,000 vols; Dir ALBERTO FERRÚS; Sec. M. CARMEN GARCÍA; part of CSIC.

Instituto Español de Hematología y Hemoterapía (Institute of Haematology and Haemotherapy): Gral. Oraá 15, Madrid; f. 1940; Dir Dr CARLOS ELÓSEGUI; publ. *Anales*.

Instituto Nacional de Medicina y Seguridad del Trabajo (National Institute of Medicine and Safety): Pabellón 8, Facultad de Medicina, Ciudad Universitaria, 28003 Madrid; Dir Prof. D. MANUEL DOMINGUEZ CARMONA.

Instituto Nacional de Reeducación de Inválidos (National Institute for Retraining Physically Handicapped): Arnedo 22, 28025 Madrid; tel. 91-462-46-00; fax 91-462-84-44; e-mail dereeduc@centros6.pntic.mec.es; f. 1922; Head of Studies ANA MARÍA MARTÍNEZ ROMERA; publs booklets, films.

NATURAL SCIENCES

General

Instituto Español de Oceanografía (Spanish Institute of Oceanography): Avda de Brasil 31, 28020 Madrid; tel. 91-597-44-43; fax 91-597-47-70; e-mail ieo@md.ieo.es; internet www.ieo.es; f. 1914; comprises Physics, Chemistry, Pollution, Geology, Fishery Biology and Marine Biology sections in Madrid, coastal laboratories at Santander, La Coruña, Vigo, Málaga, San Pedro del Pinatar, Santa Cruz de Tenerife, Palma de Mallorca and Gijón; 6 research vessels; library of 13,987 vols, 3,200 journals; 543 mems; Gen. Dir CONCEPCIÓN SOTO CALVO; publs *Boletín* (4 a year), *Datos y Resúmenes* (irregular), *Informes Técnicos* (4 a year).

Physical Sciences

Centro Meteorológico Territorial de Baleares (Meteorological Station): Muelle de Poniente-Porto Pi, Apdo Oficial, 07015 Palma de Mallorca, Balearic Is; tel. 971-40-35-11; fax 971-40-46-26; f. 1934; library of 600 vols; Dir AGUSTÍN JANSA CLAR; publs *Boletín Mensual Climatológico* (monthly), *Boletín PEMMOC* (2 a year).

Fundación Galileo Galilei: Rambla José Ana Fernández Pérez 7, POB 565, 38712 Breña Baja, La Palma, Canary Islands; tel. 922-43-36-66; fax 922-42-05-08; e-mail oliva@tng.iac.es; internet www.tng.iac.es; f. 1979; attached to Istituto Nazionale di Astrofisica, Italy; promotes astrophysical research by managing and running the Telescopio Nazionale Galileo (TNG), a 3.58-m optical/infrared telescope located on La Palma; Dir of Telescope ERNESTO OLIVA.

Instituto de Astrofísica de Canarias (IAC) (Canaries Institute of Astrophysics): Calle Vía Láctea s/n, 38200 La Laguna, Tenerife, Canary Islands; tel. 922-60-52-00;

fax 922-60-52-10; e-mail postmaster@ll.iac.es; internet www.iac.es; f. 1982; includes international observatories on Tenerife and La Palma; library of 11,000 vols, 360 journals; Dir Prof. FRANCISCO SÁNCHEZ MARTÍNEZ; publs *Annual Report*, *Boletín Noticias* (3 a year), *Annual Report of the International Scientific Committee* (4 a year), *IAC Noticias* (2 a year).

Attached observatories:

Observatorio del Roque de los Muchachos: Apdo 303, 38700 Santa Cruz de La Palma, Canary Islands; tel. 922-40-55-00; fax 922-40-55-01; e-mail adminorm@orm.iac.es; internet www.iac.es; f. 1985; European Northern Observatory; Site Man. Dr JUAN CARLOS PÉREZ ARENCIBIA.

Observatorio del Teide: Calle Vía Láctea s/n, 38200 La Laguna, Tenerife, Canary Islands; tel. 922-32-91-00; fax 922-32-91-17; e-mail teide@ot.iac.es; internet www.iac.es; f. 1985; European Northern Observatory; Site Man. Dr MIQUEL SERRA RICART.

Instituto de Astronomía y Geodesía (Institute of Astronomy and Geodesy): Facultad de Matemáticas, Universidad Complutense, 28040 Madrid; tel. 91-394-45-85; fax 91-394-46-15; internet www.mat.ucm.es/deptos/iag; f. 1983; attached to CSIC (see above); library of 2,069 vols, 675 periodicals; Dir Dr RICARDO VIEIRA DÍAZ.

Instituto Nacional de Meteorología (National Meteorological Institute): Ciudad Universitaria, Apdo 285, Madrid; C/ Leonardo Prieto Castro 8, 28071 Madrid; tel. 91-581-98-10; fax 91-581-98-11; e-mail infomet@inm.es; internet www.inm.es; f. 1887; 15 meteorological centres, 4,500 stations; library of 19,500 vols, 2,000 reports; Dir-Gen. (vacant); publs *Boletín diario*, *Boletín mensual climatológico*, *Resúmenes anuales*, *Calendario Meteorológico*.

Observatorio Astronómico Meteorológico y Sísmico Fabra: Tibidabo, Barcelona; tel. 93-417-57-36; internet www.racab.es/fabra/bnc; f. 1905; attached to Real Academia de Ciencias y Artes de Barcelona; Dir Dr JOSÉ MARÍA CODINA.

Observatorio Astronómico Nacional (National Astronomical Observatory): Calle de Alfonso XII 3, 28014 Madrid; tel. 91-527-01-07; fax 91-527-19-35; e-mail spider@oan.es; internet www.oan.es; f. 1790; attached to Instituto Geográfico Nacional; library: c. 10,000 vols; Dir Dr RAFAEL BACHILLER; publ. *Anuario* (annually).

Observatorio del Ebro (Ebro Observatory): 43520 Roquetes (Tarragona); tel. 977-50-05-11; fax 977-50-46-60; f. 1904; library of 50,000 vols; Dir Rev. L. F. ALBERCA; publ. *Boletín* (in two series: (a) Terrestrial Magnetism; (b) Ionosphere, both irregular).

Observatorio Universitario de Cartuja (Observatory of Cartuja): Apdo Universidad, Granada; f. 1902; 9 mems; library of 6,000 vols; Dir J. BIEL; publ. *Publicaciones* (geophysics).

Real Instituto y Observatorio de la Armada (Royal Naval Institute and Observatory): Cecilio Pujazón s/n, 11110 San Fernando, (Cádiz); tel. 956-59-93-65; fax 956-59-93-66; e-mail secretaria@roa.es; internet www.roa.es; f. 1753; positional astronomy, ephemerides, time, geophysics and satellite geodesy; collaborates with the British and the American Nautical Almanac Offices, Centre National d'Etudes Spatiales, Le Bureau des Longitudes and Das Astronomische Rechen Institut; library of 28,000 vols, 3,500 maps and plans; Dir RAFAEL BOLOIX; publs *Almanaque Náutico* (annual), *Efemérides Astronómicas* (annual), *Anales*, *Observaciones Meteorológicas, Magnéticas y*

Sísmicas, Fenómenos Astronómicos (2 a year).

PHILOSOPHY AND PSYCHOLOGY

Instituto de Filosofía: Pinar 25, 28006 Madrid; tel. 91-411-70-05; fax 91-564-52-52; e-mail gerente.ifs@csic.es; internet www.ifs.csic.es; f. 1986; part of CSIC (q.v.); development of research in philosophy in collaboration with the Spanish universities; main fields of activity: logic and philosophy of science, political philosophy, ethics, philosophy of religion, history of philosophy, science, technology and society; library of 50,000 vols; Dir JOSÉ MARÍA GONZÁLEZ GARCÍA; publs *Isegoría* (2 a year), *SORITES: Electronic Magazine of Analytical Philosophy* (online at: www.sorites.net).

TECHNOLOGY

Centro de Investigaciones Energéticas, Medioambientales y Tecnológicas (Centre for Energy, Environmental and Technological Research): Avda Complutense 22, 28040 Madrid; tel. 91-346-60-00; fax 91-346-60-05; e-mail sisifo@ciemat.es; internet www.ciemat.es; f. 1951; controls and directs research and study of nuclear and new and renewable energies, environmental policy and several advanced technologies; library of 30,500 vols, 300,000 reports, 750,000 microcards, 2,000 periodicals; Pres. ALBERTO LAFUENTE FELEZ; Vice-Pres. and Dir-Gen. JOSÉ ANGEL AZUARA SOLÍS.

Instituto Tecnológico Geominero de España (Geological and Mining Institute). Ministry of the Environment, Ríos Rosas 23, 28003 Madrid; tel. 91-349-57-00; fax 91-442-62-16; f. 1849; library of 42,500 vols; documentation centre of 20,000 items in microfilm; sections: geology, geophysics, mineral resources, subterranean hydrology, laboratories, museum; Dir EMILIO CUSTODIO GIMENA; Sec. FELIPE GARCÍA ORTIZ; publs *Boletín Geológico y Minero* (every 2 months), *Revista Española de Micropaleontología* (3 a year), geological, metallogenic and hydrogeological maps.

Libraries and Archives

Barcelona

Archivo Capitular de la Santa Iglesia Catedral de Barcelona: Catedral de Barcelona, Pla de la Seu s/n, 08002 Barcelona; tel. 93-315-31-56; fax 93-310-07-97; f. 9th c.; documents since 9th c.; treatises on Holy Scripture, ecclesiastical history and law; religious and economic history; 255 MSS, 200 incunabula and various printed books from the original Biblioteca Capitular; 41,000 parchment documents, 20,000 vols; Archives Prefect JOSEP BAUCELLS REIG; Archivist (vacant).

Archivo de la Corona de Aragón (Royal Archives of Aragon): Almogávares 77, 08018 Barcelona; tel. 93-485-42-85; fax 93-300-12-52; e-mail aca@dglab.mcu.es; internet www.cultura.mecd.es/archivos/index.html; f. 14th century; auxiliary 21,000 vols; Dir CARLOS LÓPEZ RODRÍGUEZ.

Archivo Diocesano (Diocesan Archives): Calle Obispo 5, 08002 Barcelona; tel. 93-318-30-31; f. 11th century; registers (1,200) from 1302; Diocesan Archivist Dr JOSÉ Mª MARTI BONET; publ. *El Archivo Diocesano d'Barcelona*.

Biblioteca Balmes (Balmes Library): Durán y Bas 9–11, 08002 Barcelona; f. 1923; specializes in church studies; 40,000 vols, 345 periodicals; Dir RAMÓN CORTS BLAY.

Biblioteca de la Cámara Oficial de Comercio, Industria y Navegación de Barcelona (Library of Chamber of Commerce, Industry and Navigation): Avda Diagonal 454, 08006 Barcelona; tel. 93-415-16-00; fax 93-416-09-84; 108,824 vols; Sec.-Gen. LUIS SOLÁ VILARDELL (acting); Librarian NURIA SAGALÁ; publs *Boletín de la Cámara* (monthly), *Noticiario de Comercio Exterior*, *Boletín Estadístico Coyuntural*.

Biblioteca de la Delegación Territorial de Barcelona, Organización Nacional de Ciegos (Braille Library): Calabria 66–76, 08015 Barcelona; tel. 93-325-92-00; f. 1939; 3,000 vols; loan service; publs 25 monthly magazines.

Biblioteca de la Universitat de Barcelona: Baldiri Reixac 2, 08028 Barcelona; tel. 93-403-57-15; fax 93-403-45-92; e-mail sbib@or.ub.es; internet www.bib.ub.es/bub/bub/htm; f. 1835; general library and 7 special sections; 1,100,000 vols, of which 5,000 date from 16th c., 914 incunabula, 2,039 MSS; Dir DOLORS LAMARCA MORELL; publs *Inventario General de Manuscritos*, *Inventario de Incunables*, *Catàleg Collectiu de la Biblioteca de la Universitat de Barcelona* (CD-ROM), *Catàleg Automatitzat de Publicacions en Sèrie* (CD-ROM).

Biblioteca de l'Arxiu Històric de la Ciutat de Barcelona: Casa de l'Ardiaca, Carrer Santa Llúcia 1, 08002 Barcelona; tel. 93-318-11-95; fax 93-317-83-27; e-mail bibliotecarxiuhistoric@mail.bcn.es; f. 1921; 140,000 vols, divided into several sections; general works, books published in Barcelona since the 15th c.; the Massana Library, containing works on iconography and the history of costume; other libraries donated by private donors, e.g. Eduardo Toda (British and general books); Dir XAVIER TARRAUBELLA MIRABET.

Biblioteca de l'Associació d'Enginyers Industrials de Catalunya (Library of the Association of Industrial Engineers of Catalonia): Via Laietana 39, 08003 Barcelona; tel. 93-319-23-66; fax 93-319-88-11; e-mail biblio@eic.es; internet www.eic.es/biblioteca/biblio.htm; f. 1863; 22,000 vols; Librarian ENRIC BARBERÀ I PELLICER.

Biblioteca del Centre Excursionista de Catalunya (Library of the Catalonia Mountaineering Centre): Paradís 10, 08002 Barcelona; tel. 93-315-23-11; fax 93-315-14-08; e-mail biblioteca@cec-centre.org; internet www.cec-centre.org; f. 1876; 5,500 mems; 32,000 vols, 6,000 maps; Dir FRANCESC OLIVÉ; publs *Muntanya* (every 2 months), *Espeleòleg* (irregular).

Biblioteca del Col·legi de Notaris i Arxiu Històric de Protocols de Barcelona (Library of College of Notaries): Notariat 4, Barcelona; tel. 93-317-48-00; f. 1862; specializes in law and the medieval history of Catalonia; 25,000 vols, 50,000 protocols since 13th c.; Archivist LAUREÀ PAGAROLAS SABATÉ; Librarian MONTSERRAT GÓMEZ; publs *Estudios Històrics i Documents dels Arxius de Protocols*, *La Notaría*.

Biblioteca de l'Il·lustre Col·legi d'Advocats de Barcelona (Barcelona College of Lawyers' Library): Mallorca 283, 08037 Barcelona; tel. 93-496-18-80; fax 93-487-11-28; e-mail biblioteca@icab.es; internet www.icab.es; f. 1832; 250,000 items; Dean JAUME ALONSO-CUEVILLAS SAYROL; publ. *Revista Jurídica de Catalunya* (4 a year).

Biblioteca del Foment del Treball Nacional (Library of Dept of Trade Development): Vía Laietana 32, 08003 Barcelona; tel. 93-484-12-00; fax 93-484-12-30; internet www.foment.com; f. 1889; 90,000 vols, 2,500 periodicals; Librarian NURIA SARDÁ; publ. *Horizonte Empresarial* (monthly).

Bilbao

Biblioteca Universitaria de Deusto: Avda de las Universidades 24, 48007 Bilbao; tel. 94-413-90-32; fax 94-445-23-58; e-mail biblioteca@deusto.es; internet www.biblioteca.deusto.es; f. 1886; 890,000 vols; Dir NIEVES TARANCO.

Granada

Archivo de la Real Chancillería de Granada (Archives of the Royal Chancery of Granada): Plaza del Padre Suárez 1, 18009 Granada; tel. 95-822-23-38; fax 95-822-23-38; f. 1494; 8,810 linear metres of conventional archive material, incl. lawsuits settled by the *Tribunal de la Real Chancillería* from 1490 to 1834; also holds documents issued by the *Audiencia Territorial de Granada* from 1834 to 1970; Dir DAVID TORRES IBÁÑEZ.

Jerez de la Frontera

Biblioteca, Archivo y Colección Arqueológica Municipal (Town Library, Archive and Archaeological Museum): Plaza General Primo de Rivera 7 y 8, Jerez; tel. 956-32-33-00; f. 1873 (library), 1933 (museum); incunabula, important collns from 17th–18th centuries, local collns on horses, bullfighting, flamenco; documents dating back to the reconquest of Jerez by Alfonso El Sabio, documents on the discovery of America; 75,000 vols; Dirs RAMON CLAVIJO PROVENCIO, CRISTOBAL ORELLANA; Librarians CARLA PUERTO CASTRILLON, AMPARO GOMEZ MARTIN.

Biblioteca de la Facultad de Derecho, Universidad de Cádiz: Avda León de Carranza s/n, 11407 Jerez de la Frontera; tel. 95-603-70-15; fax 95-603-70-77; e-mail biblioteca.campusjerez@uca.es; internet biblioteca.uca.es/sbuca/bibcjer.htm; f. 1979; 12,000 vols; Dir ROSA MARÍA TORIBIO RUIZ.

La Coruña

Archivo del Reino de Galicia/Arquivo do Reino de Galicia (Archive of the Kingdom of Galicia): Jardín de San Carlos s/n, 15001 La Coruña; tel. 98-120-03-89; fax 98-120-70-94; e-mail arq.reino.galicia@xunta.es; internet www.xunta.es/conselle/cultura/patrimonio/arquivos/arquivo%20reino/index.html; f. 1775; comprises a total of 143,129 bundles of documents dating back to 867 AD, the most important since 16th c. concerning disputes and lawsuits of the 'Real Audiencia de Galicia' and the 'Audiencia Territorial' relative to the clergy, the nobility, villages and private persons; 18th and 19th c. documents of 'Real Intendencia', concerning government and administration of Galicia; documents 1808–1814 of the 'Junta Superior de Armamento y Defensa' relative to the Peninsular War; documents of Provincial Administration of La Coruña since 19th c., concerning the govt, police, education, economy, tourism, finance, health; records of families, labour unions and churches since 12th c.; collection of parchment 867–1586; 7,200 maps, plans and drawings since 16th c.; 100,032 photographs and postcards, 1,268 microforms; 23,418 vols, 1,831 periodicals (incl. 23 current) and 920 pamphlets closely related to the archives and of special interest for research; Dir GABRIEL QUIROGA BARRO.

Lérida (Lleida)

Arxiu Històric de Lleida: Plaça de Sant Antoni Ma. Claret 5, Casa de Cultura, 25002 Lleida; tel. 973-27-08-67; fax 973-27-31-60; f. 1952; 3,000 vols; Dir PILAR FACI LACASTA.

Madrid

Archivo General de la Administración Civil del Estado: Paseo de Aguadores 2, 28804 Alcalá de Henares, Madrid; tel. 91-889-29-50; f. 1969; preserves and makes available for information or scientific research documents on public administration which are no longer of current administrative relevance; 2,733 vols; Dir MARÍA LUISA CONDE VILLAVERDE.

Archivo Histórico Nacional (National Historical Archives): Calle Serrano 115, 28006 Madrid; tel. (91) 7688500; tel. (91) 5631199; e-mail ahn@dglab.mcu.es; internet www.mcu.es; f. 1866; 400,000 archival items and 30,000 library items, 4,000 ancient monographs and 400 periodical titles; Dir CONCEPCIÓN CONTEL BAREA; publs catalogues, indexes, historical documents.

Biblioteca Alemana Görres (Görres German Library): Calle San Buenaventura 9, 28005 Madrid; tel. 91-366-85-08; fax 91-366-85-09; e-mail bibliotecagoerres@fsandamaso.es; internet www.fsandamaso.es/biblioteca.htm; f. 1929; studies on German-Spanish cultural relations in the 17th, 18th and 19th c.; theology, philosophy, history, cultural history; 25,000 vols; Dir Prof. JUAN JOSÉ PÉREZ-SOBA.

Biblioteca Central de Marina (Central Naval Library): Cuartel General de la Armada, Montalbán 2, Madrid 28014; f. 1856; 65,540 vols; Librarian MERCEDES DORDA SAINZ.

Biblioteca Central del Ministerio de Hacienda (Central Library of the Ministry of Finance): Calle Alcalá 9 – Planta Baja, 28071 Madrid; tel. 91-595-83-42; fax 91-595-84-31; e-mail biblioteca.alcala@minhac.es; f. 1852; 40,000 vols on economics, finance and Government legislation; Librarian ESPERANZA SALÁN PANIAGUA.

Biblioteca Central Militar (Central Military Library): Calle Mártires de Alcalá 9, 28015 Madrid; tel. 91-547-03-00; fax 91-559-43-71; f. 1932; 250,000 vols on military history, civil and military engineering, architecture, science; 1,000 periodicals; rare books, engravings, photographs, maps and plans, microforms; Dir Col. JUAN GARCÍA LEÓN; Head Librarian FERNANDO TORRA.

Biblioteca de la Escuela Técnica Superior de Ingenieros de Caminos, Canales y Puertos (Library of Higher School for Road, Canal and Port Engineers): Ciudad Universitaria, 28040 Madrid; tel. 91-336-67-39; f. 1802; 73,000 vols; Dir VICENTE SÁNCHEZ GALVEZ.

Biblioteca de la Escuela Técnica Superior de Ingenieros Industriales (Library of the Higher School for Industrial Engineers): José Gutiérrez Abascal 2, 28006 Madrid; tel. 91-336-30-75; e-mail biblioteca@etsii.upm.es; f. 1905; 36,000 vols; Librarian MARÍA DOLORES CAMPAÑA.

Biblioteca de la Secretaría de Estado de Cultura (Library of the Office of the Secretary of State for Culture): Plaza del Rey 1, 28004 Madrid; tel. 91-701-70-00 ext. 32500; fax 91-522-93-77; f. 1984; cultural policy, cultural institutions, fine arts, librarianship; 22,000 vols, 500 periodicals; Dir PILAR BLANCO MUÑOZ.

Biblioteca de la Universidad Complutense de Madrid (Complutense University of Madrid Library): Pabellón de Gobierno, C/ Isaac Peral s/n, 28040 Madrid; tel. 91-394-69-25; fax 91-394-69-26; e-mail buc@buc.ucm.es; internet www.ucm.es/bucm; f. 1499; 2,431,198 vols, 81,869 ancient books, 725 incunabula, 132,176 special materials, 43,477 periodicals; Head JOSÉ ANTONIO MAGÁN WALS.

Biblioteca del Ministerio de Asuntos Exteriores (Library of the Ministry of Foreign Affairs): Plaza de la Provincia 1, 28012 Madrid; tel. 91-379-92-19; fax 91-366-60-26; f. 1900; 43,256 vols; works on history, geography, international law, political and civil law, and international relations; Dir MARIA JOSE ALBO ALVAREZ.

Biblioteca del Ministerio de Educación y Cultura (Library of the Ministry of Education and Culture): San Agustín 5, 28014 Madrid; tel. 91-369-30-26; fax 91-429-94-38; e-mail biblioteca@educ.mec.es; internet www.mec.es; f. 1912; 80,000 vols, 1,800 periodicals, 20,000 microforms; Man. ERNESTO CALBET ROSELLÓ; publs *Boletín de Adquisiciones* (monthly), *Boletín de Sumarios* (monthly), *Catálogo de Publicaciones Periódicas* (irregular).

Biblioteca Hispánica (de la Agencia Española de Co-operación Internacional): Avda de los Reyes Católicos 4, Ciudad Universitaria, 28040 Madrid; tel. 91-583-81-75; fax 91-583-85-25; e-mail biblioteca.hispanica@aeci.es; internet www.aeci.es; f. 1947; c. 520,000 vols and 10,200 periodicals; special collection: Latin American incunabula; Dir Dra CARMEN DÍEZ HOYO; publ. *Boletín de Novedades* (online, monthly).

Biblioteca Nacional de España (National Library of Spain): Paseo de Recoletos 20, 28071 Madrid; tel. 91-580-78-00; fax 91-577-56-34; e-mail info@bne.es; internet www.bne.es; f. 1712 as Royal Library; 4,900,000 vols, 3,041,480 pamphlets, 3,000 newspapers, 114,000 periodical publications, 25,000 MSS, 3,000 incunabula, 273,970 rare books, 40,000 drawings and 1,050,000 engravings; deposit library; ISSN national centre; Dir ROSA REGÀS.

Centro de Información y Documentación Científica (CINDOC): Joaquín Costa 22, 28002 Madrid; tel. 91 563 54-82; fax 91-564-26-44; e-mail sdi@cindoc.csic.es; internet www.cindoc.csic.es; f. 1953; Dir CARMEN VIDAL; Sec. M. VILLARREAL; publ. *Revista Española de Documentación Científica* (4 a year).

Hemeroteca Municipal de Madrid (Periodicals Library of the Corporation of Madrid): Calle Conde Duque 9–11, 28015 Madrid; tel. 91-588-57-71; fax 91-588-59-09; e-mail hemeroteca@munimadrid.es; f. 1918; over 20,000 titles; the library maintains a microfilm service; Dir CARLOS DORADO FERNÁNDEZ.

Real Biblioteca (Royal Library): Palacio Real, Calle Bailén s/n, 28071 Madrid; tel. 91-454-87-33; fax 91-454-88-67; e-mail realbiblioteca@patrimonionacional.es; internet www.realbiblioteca.es; f. early 18th century; 250,000 printed vols; fine collections of MSS, incunabula, music, rare editions since 16th century, maps, engravings and drawings; collection of bookbindings; research library; Dir Dr MARÍA LUISA LÓPEZ-VIDRIERO; publ. *Avisos: Noticias de la Real Biblioteca* (quarterly).

Subdirección General de los Archivos Estatales (State Archives Section): Plaza del Rey 1, 28071 Madrid; tel. 91-701-70-00; fax 91-521-05-08; e-mail archivos.estatales@dglabr.mcu.es; f. 1979; Dir ELISA CAROLINA DE SANTOS CANALEJO; publ. *Boletín de Información del Centro de Información Documental de Archivos*.

Subdirección General de Información Administrativa y Publicaciones del Ministerio de Trabajo y Asuntos Sociales (Administrative Information and Publications Section of the Ministry of Labour and Social Affairs): Calle Agustín de Bethencourt 11, 28003 Madrid; tel. 91-363-23-17; fax 91-363-23-49; e-mail sgpublic@mtas.es; internet www.mtas.es; 80,000 vols excluding pamphlets and newspapers; publ. *Revista del Ministerio de Trabajo y Asuntos Sociales* (monthly).

Palma de Mallorca

Arxiu del Regne de Mallorca (Archives of the Kingdom of Mallorca): Calle Ramón Llull 3, 07001 Palma de Mallorca; tel. 971-72-59-99; fax 971-71-87-81; e-mail arm@arxregne.caib.es; internet arxregne.caib.es/web/default.htm; f. 1851; public and private archives since 13th c.; 12,500 vols, 193 periodicals; Dir RICARD URGELL HERNÁNDEZ.

Peralada

Biblioteca del Palacio de Peralada (Palace of Peralada Library): 17491 Peralada; tel. 972-53-81-25; fax 972-53-80-87; f. 1882 by the Count of Peralada; contains 80,000 vols, 200 incunabula, 20,000 pamphlets and parchments on history; Librarian INÉS PADROSA; Archivist JOSEP CLAVAGUERA.

Sabadell

Arxiu Històric de Sabadell (Historical Archives): Indústria 32, 08202 Sabadell; tel. 93-726-87-77; fax 93-727-57-03; e-mail ahs@ajsabadell.es; internet www.sabadell.net/websajsab/arxiu; f. 14th c.; documents since 1111; MS of *Arxius Privats* (Private Records) since 1247, *Fons eclesiàstics* (ecclesiastical archives) since 1334, *Corts Senyorials* (Court of Justice) since 1347, *Escrivania* (Notarial Archives) since 1400, *Actes* (Proceedings of Local Council meetings) since 1449, *Hemeroteca oficial* since 1570, *Fons d'empresa* (Records of 30 Companies) from 19th c.; collection of local journals and reviews since 1855; 9,000 vols, 30,000 photographs and 625 audiovisual records; Dir JOAN COMASÒLIVAS I FONT; publs *Arraona* (annually), *Memòria* (annually).

San Lorenzo de El Escorial

Real Biblioteca del Monasterio de San Lorenzo de El Escorial (Royal Library of the Monastery of San Lorenzo de El Escorial): 28200 San Lorenzo de El Escorial, Madrid; tel. 91-890-38-89; fax 91-890-83-69; e-mail real.biblioteca@ctv.es; f. 1575; 75,000 vols, 650 incunabula, 10,000 engravings and prints; MSS: 2,000 Arabic, 2,090 Latin and vernacular, 72 Hebrew, 580 Greek; many rare and unique edns, incl. complete copy of the *Biblia Poliglota Complutensis* and of the *Biblia Poliglota* of Antwerp on parchment, and the *Epítome de Anatomía*, by Vesalius, also on parchment; Dir P. JOSÉ LUIS DEL VALLE MERINO.

Santander

Biblioteca de Menéndez Pelayo (Menéndez Pelayo Library): Rubio 6, 39007 Santander; tel. 942-23-45-34; e-mail xjagenjo@sarenet.es; the private library of this writer, 45,000 vols, not to be increased in number, left by him to the town; opened to the public 1915; inaugurated 1923 by Alfonso XIII; Dir XAVIER AGENJO BULLÓN; publ. *Boletín* (annually).

Seville

Archivo de la Casa Ducal de Medinaceli (Medinaceli Archives): Plaza de Pilatos 1, Seville; tel. 95-422-50-55; fax 95-422-46-77; e-mail casapilatos@infonegocio.com; archives of 9th to 20th centuries; Archivist JUAN LARIOS DE LA ROSA; publ. *Histórica*.

Archivo General de Indias (Archives of the Indies): Avda de la Constitución 3, 41071 Seville; tel. 95-450-05-30; fax 95-421-94-85; e-mail agi1@cult.mec.es; internet www.cultura.mecd.es/archivos; f. 1785; documents relating to Spanish colonial administration in America and the Philippines; 25,000 vols, 43,000 files; Dir MAGDALENA CANELLAS ANOZ; publs include *Catálogos de Pasajeros a Indias*, *Catálogos de Mapas y Planos*, CD-ROM *Tesoros del Archivo General de Indias*.

Biblioteca Capitular y Colombina: Institución Colombina, C/ Alemanes s/n, 41004 Seville; tel. 95-456-27-21; fax 95-421-18-76; e-mail direccionic@institucioncolombina.org; f. 13th c.; 60,500 vols; includes the 3,500-vol. library of Hernando Colón, son of the explorer, Cristóbal; Man. Dir NURIA CASQUETE DE PRADO SAGRERA.

Simancas

Archivo General de Simancas (Simancas General Archives): C/ Miravete 8, 47130 Simancas (Valladolid); tel. 983-59-00-03; fax 983-59-03-11; e-mail ags@cult.mec.es; internet www.cultura.mecd.es/archivos; f. 1540; 68,242 filed documents and 4,979 vols of documents; 20,000 vols on history; Dir JOSÉ LUIS RODRIGUEZ DE DIEGO.

Toledo

Archivo y Biblioteca Capitulares (Archives and Library of the Cathedral Chapter): Catedral de Toledo, Hombre de Palo 2, 45001 Toledo; tel. 925-21-24-23; fax 925-21-24-23; e-mail archicapto@architoledo.org; internet www.architoledo.org/catedral/archivos; the *Archivo Capitular* contains 11,000 documents (mostly medieval) since 1085; the library (f. 1383) contains 2,521 MSS, 1,200 printed books; Dir Dr ANGEL FERNÁNDEZ COLLADO.

Biblioteca de Castilla–La Mancha: C/ Cuesta Carlos V s/n, 45001 Toledo; tel. 925-25-66-80; fax 925-25-36-42; e-mail biblioclm@jccm.es; internet www.jccm.es/biblioclm; f. 1998; 367,803 vols, 2,300 periodicals; spec. collns incl.: Borbón-Lorenzana (102,519 vols 16th–19th c., 379 incunabula), Fondo Regional; Dirs ALICIA ARELLANO CÓRDOBA, JOAQUÍN SELGAS GUTIÉRREZ.

Valencia

Archivo del Reino de Valencia: Edificio San Miguel de los Reyes, Avda Constitución 284, 46010 Valencia; tel. 96-387-40-00; e-mail areino@cult.gva.es; f. 1419; 71,561 MSS books (13th c. to present), 49,650 files of MSS, 61,483 charters, deeds, etc., since 13th c.; Dir MERCEDES ESCRIG GIMÉNEZ.

Zaragoza

Biblioteca Moncayo: Mayor 62, Jarque, Zaragoza; f. 1972; 15,000 vols by Aragonese authors or on the subject of Aragon; Dir LUIS MARQUINA MARÍN.

Museums and Art Galleries

Barcelona

Museo de Geología (Geology Museum): Parc de la Ciutadella s/n, 08003 Barcelona; tel. 93-256-22-22; fax 93-256-21-90; e-mail museuciencies@mail.bcn.es; f. 1882; library: geology library; Dir Dra ALICIA MASRIERA; publ. *Treballs del Museu de Geologia de Barcelona* (annually).

Museo de la Música: Zona Franca, Carrer F 22, 08040 Barcelona; tel. 93-263-13-49; fax 93-336-46-51; internet www.museumusica.bcn.es; f. 1946; valuable collections of antique instruments; phonographs and gramophones, historical early recordings; archives of Albéniz, Granados and other Catalan composers; Dir ROMÀ ESCALAS.

Museu Etnològic: Passeig Sta Madrona s/n, Parc de Montjuïc, 08038 Barcelona; tel. 93-424-64-02; fax 93-423-73-64; e-mail metno@intercom.es; f. 1948; African, Asiatic, American, Oceanic, and Spanish ethnography and

American archaeology; library of 40,000 vols, 1,046 periodicals; Dir CARMEN FAURIA ROMA.

Museu Geològic del Seminari de Barcelona (Geological Museum of Barcelona Seminary): Diputació 231, 08007 Barcelona; tel. 93-454-16-00; fax 93-452-55-38; e-mail mgsb@paleontologia.e.telefonica.net; internet www.bcn.es/medciencies/mgsb; f. 1874; palaeontology of invertebrates, collection of 70,000 fossils; library of 13,000 vols; Dir Dr S. CALZADA; publs *Batalleria* (annually), *Scripta Musei Geologici Seminarii* (irregular), *Pagurus* (online, 4 a year), *Butlletí de l'Associació d'Amics de l'MGSB* (4 a year).

Museu d'Art Contemporani de Barcelona (Barcelona Museum of Contemporary Art): Plaça dels Angels 1, 08001 Barcelona; tel. 93-412-08-10; fax 93-412-46-02; e-mail administracio@macba.es; internet www.macba.es; f. 1995; modern Catalan and international art; Dir MANUEL J. BORJA-VILLEL.

Museu d'Arqueologia de Catalunya (Archaeological Museum of Catalonia): Passeig de Santa Madrona 39–41, Parc de Montjuïc, 08038 Barcelona; tel. 93-424-65-77; fax 93-424-56-30; e-mail difusiomac.cultura@gencat.net; internet www.mac.es; f. 1935; collections of pre-historic, Greek, Phoenician, Visigothic and Roman art; library of 40,000 vols; Dir FRANCESC TARRATS-BOU; publ. *Empúries* (annually).

Museu de Ciències Naturals de la Ciutadella: Passeig Picasso s/n, 08003 Barcelona; tel. 93-256-21-83; fax 93-310-49-99; e-mail museuciencies@mail.bcn.es; internet www.bcn.es/museuciencies; f. 1878; permanent exhibitions on classification of the animal kingdom; honey bees; urban birds; minerals, rocks and fossils; large collns of coleptera, mollusca, fossils and minerals; 2–4 temporary exhibitions annually; research areas include evolutionary ecology, bioespeleology, paleontology, petrology and the history of science; library of 12,000 vols, 1,700 periodicals, 3,200 maps; Dir ANNA OMEDES; publs *Animal Biodiversity and Conservation* (2 a year), *Arxius de Miscelolània Zoològica* (online), *Monografies del Museu de Ciències Naturals* (annually), *Treballs del Museu de Geologia* (annually).

Museu d'Història de la Ciutat: Plaça del Rei s/n, 08002 Barcelona; tel. 93-315-11-11; fax 93-315-09-57; e-mail museuhistoria@mail.bcn.es; internet www.museuhistoria.bcn.es; f. 1943; 15th-c. mansion containing Roman remains *in situ* (1st–4th-c. Roman wall), 11th–15th c. Royal Palace; documentation centre, information service; Dir ANTONI NICOLAU MARTÍ.

Subordinate institutions:

Centre d'Interpretació del Park Güell: Pavelló de Consergia, Park Güell, Carrer Olot s/n, 08024 Barcelona; tel. 93-285-68-99; fax 93-285-69-00; information centre.

Conjunt Monumental de la Plaça del Rei: Plaça del Rei s/n, 08002 Barcelona; tel. 93-315-11-11; fax 93-315-09-57; e-mail museuhistoria@mail.bcn.es; 11th c. Count's Palace, later the residence of the kings of Catalonia and Aragón; Padellàs House, a Gothic palace; Roman remains *in situ* (1st c. BC–8th c. AD); Chief Curator JULIA BELTRÁN DE HEREDIA.

Museu-Casa Verdaguer: Vil·la Joana, Vallvidrera, 08017 Barcelona; tel. 93-204-78-05; fax 93-204-11-85; e-mail museuverdaguer@mail.bcn.es; 18th c. farmhouse, former home of the poet Jacint Verdaguer; Chief Curator MARI CRUZ MARTÍN AGUILERA.

Museu-Monestir de Pedralbes: Baixada del Monestir 9, 08034 Barcelona; tel. 93-203-92-82; fax 93-203-94-08; e-mail monestirpedralbes@mail.bcn.es; f. 1327; Gothic church and monastery; Chief Curator ANNA CASTELLANO I TRESSERRA.

Museu Marítim de Barcelona (Barcelona Maritime Museum): Avda de les Drassanes s/n, 08001 Barcelona; tel. 93-342-99-20; fax 93-318-78-76; e-mail m.maritim@diba.es; internet www.diba.es/mmaritim; f. 1941; library of 15,000 vols; photographic, cartographic and documental archives, restoration workshop; Dir ELVIRA MATA ENRICH; publ. *El Pirata* (4 a year).

Museu Nacional d'Art de Catalunya (National Art Museum of Catalonia): Palau Nacional, Parc de Montjuïc, 08038 Barcelona; tel. 93-622-03-60; fax 93-622-03-74; e-mail mnac@mnac.es; internet www.mnac.es; f. 1934; incl., on various sites, National Art Museum of Catalonia (Curators: JORDI CAMPS, MONTSERRAT PAGÈS (Romanesque), ROSA MARIA MANOTE (Gothic), MARGARITA CUYÁS (Renaissance and Baroque), CECÍLIA VIDAL (Drawings and Engravings), DAVID BALSELLS (Photographs), Museum of Modern Art (art since 19th c., Curator: CRISTINA MENDOZA), Numismatic Division (Curator: MARTA CAMPO); library of 120,000 vols, 2,300 periodicals; Dir-Gen. EDUARD CARBONELL I ESTELLER; publ. *Butlletí*.

Museu Picasso: Montcada 15–23, 08003 Barcelona; tel. 93-319-63-10; fax 93-315-01-02; e-mail museupicasso@mail.bcn.es; internet www.museupicasso.bcn.es; f. 1963; paintings, pottery, drawings and engravings by Pablo Picasso, 1881–1973, including the series 'Las Meninas' and the artist's donation, in 1970, of 940 works of art; library of 4,000 vols; Dir JOSEP SERRA.

Bilbao

Guggenheim Bilbao Museoa: Abandoibarra 2, 48001 Bilbao; tel. 94-435-90-08; fax 94-435-90-10; internet www.guggenheim-bilbao.es; f. 1997; modern American and European art; Dir-Gen. JUAN IGNACIO VIDARTE.

Museo de Bellas Artes de Bilbao: Plaza del Museo 2, 48011 Bilbao; tel. 94-439-60-60; fax 94-439-61-45; e-mail info@museobilbao.com; internet www.museobilbao.com; f. 1908; collection includes major works by El Greco, Moro, Murillo, Zurbarán, Ribera, Goya, Meléndez, Arellano, Paret, Benson, Mandjin, De Vos, Van Dyck, Gentileschi, Bellotto, Ribot, Guiard, Regoyos, Zuloaga, Arteta, Gauguin, Cassatt, Ensor, Sorolla, Solana, Tàpies, Oteiza, Chillida, Caro, Saura, Bacon, Barceló, Kitaj, Blake, Lüpertz; library of 23,000 vols, 290 periodicals; Dir JAVIER VIAR.

Burgos

Museo de Burgos: Casa Miranda – Casa Angulo, Calle Calera 25, 09002 Burgos; tel. 947-26-58-75; fax 947-27-67-92; f. 1871; Casa Miranda: archaeological collections (from Palaeolithic to Visigothic); Casa Angulo: fine arts collections (from Mozarabic to contemporary painting), enamels, ivories, tomb of Juan de Padilla, Tablas Flamencas (Ecce Homo) and 15th- to 20th-century painting, sculpture, altarpieces; library of 2,000 vols, specializing in archaeology and art; Dir Dr J. C. ELORZA Y GUINEA; publ. *Anales*.

Cartagena

Museo Arqueológico Municipal: Calle Ramón y Cajal 45, 30205 Cartagena; tel. 968-53-90-27; fax 96851-54-49; e-mail museoarqueologico@ayto-cartagena.es; internet www.ayto-cartagena.es; f. 1943; important collections of Roman remains found in the area, including mining, architecture, sculpture, industrial arts exhibits; model sites; Dir Dra ELENA RUIZ VALDERAS.

Chipiona

Museo Misional de Nuestra Señora de Regla: Colegio de Misioneros Franciscanos, Chipiona; f. 1939; about 600 exhibits of early Roman Christian relics, ancient Egyptian and other North African objects, antique coins, etc.; Dir R. P. Rector del Colegio.

Córdoba

Museo Arqueológico Provincial de Córdoba: Plaza de Jerónimo Páez 7, 14003 Córdoba; tel. 95-747-40-11; fax 95-748-19-87; f. 1867; 30,200 exhibits; archaeological, prehistoric and local finds, Roman and medieval collections; library of 12,000 vols; Dir MARÍA DOLORES BAENA ALCANTARA.

Figueres

Teatre-Museu Dalí: Plaça Gala–Salvador Dalí 5, 17600 Figueres; tel. 972-51-18-00; fax 972-50-16-66; e-mail t-mgrups@dali-estate.org; internet www.salvador-dali.org; f. 1974; paintings, sculpture and other works by Salvador Dalí and his private colln of works by other artists; Dir ANTONI PITXOT I SOLER.

Granada

Museo de Bellas Artes: Palacio de Carlos V, 18009 Granada; tel. 958-22-48-43; f. 1958 (present site); paintings and sculpture by local artists from 16th century to mid-20th century; library of 4,000 vols; Dir ANTONIO GARCÍA BASCÓN; publ. *Guide*.

Ibiza

Museo Arqueológico de Ibiza y Formentera: Plaza de la Catedral 3, 07800 Ibiza; tel. 97-130-12-31; fax 97-130-32-63; e-mail maef@telefonica.net; f. 1907; Phoenician, Carthaginian and Roman remains from the necropolis of Puig des Molins (national monument and World Heritage Property); Dir JORGE H. FERNÁNDEZ GÓMEZ; publ. *Treballs del Museu Arqueológic d'Eivissa I Formentera* (2 a year).

Attached museum:

Museo y Necrópolis del Puig des Molins: Via Romana 31, Ibiza; tel. 97-130-17-71; fax 97-130-32-63; e-mail mmpm@telefonica.net; f. 1966; Carthaginian and Roman remains from the national monument of Puig des Molins; excavations in Ibiza and Formentera; library of 16,300 vols; Dir JORGE H. FERNÁNDEZ GÓMEZ; publ. *Treballs del Museu Arqueológic d'Eivissa I Formentera*.

La Escala

Museu d'Arqueologia de Cataluyna – Empúries: Apdo Correos 21, 17130 L'Escala; tel. 97-277-02-08; fax 97-277-42-60; e-mail macempuries.cultura@gencat.es; internet cultura.gencat.net/mac/empuries; f. 1908; collection of excavations of the Greco-Roman city; library of 3,000 vols; Dir XAVIER AQUILUÉ.

Las Palmas

Museo Canario: Dr Verneu 2, Vegueta, 35001 Las Palmas; tel. 928-33-68-00; fax 928-33-68-01; e-mail info@elmuseocanario.com; internet www.elmuseocanario.com; f. 1879; local archaeology and anthropology, ethnography and natural sciences; library of 60,000 vols; Man. Dir DIEGO LÓPEZ DÍAZ; publ. *El Museo Canario* (annually).

Lérida (Lleida)

Gabinet Numismàtic: Institut d'Estudis Ilerdencs, Plaça de la Catedral s/n, 25002 Lérida; tel. 973-27-15-00; e-mail iei@fpiei.es;

Roman, Iberian, Ibero-Roman, Medieval and Modern exhibits; local collections.

Museo Diocesano: Jaume el Conqueridor 67, 25002 Lérida; tel. 973-27-32-30; fax 973-26-57-03; f.1893; medieval sculptures; also sub-section at Rambla de Aragón containing religious paintings, metal work and vestments; Dir JESÚS TARRAGONA MURAY; publ. *Catàlog del Museu*.

Museu d'Art Modern 'Jaume Morera': Edificio El Roser, Caballers 15, 25002 Lérida; tel. 973-27-36-65; fax 973-26-01-61; e-mail mmorera@paeria.es; internet www.paeria.es/mmorera; f. 1917; museum of modern paintings mainly by Catalan artists, including works by Morera, C. Haes and others; Dir JESÚS NAVARRO GUITART.

Restes Monumentals-Museo de la Paeria: Plaça Paeria 1; 25007 Lérida; tel. 902-25-00-50; fax 973-23-89-53; f. 1963; historical documents and objects belonging to the municipality; archaeological finds of Lérida.

Sala d'Arqueologia de la Fundació Pública: Institut d'Estudis Ilerdencs, Plaça Catedral s/n, 25002 Lérida; tel. 973-27-15-00; fax 973-27-45-38; f. 1954; archaeology (Bronze Age, Iberian, Roman, Visigoth); Dir JOSEP BORRELL I FIGUERA.

Madrid

Fundación Lázaro Galdiano: Calle Serrano 122, 28006 Madrid; tel. 91-561-60-84; fax 91-561-77-93; e-mail goya@flg.es; internet www.flg.es; f. 1951; 12,600 items: Italian, Spanish and Flemish Renaissance paintings; Primitives; Golden Age, 18th c. and 19th c. Spanish paintings; 16th c. and 17th c. Dutch paintings; English 18th c. and 19th c. collection; Golden Age MSS and incunabula; collections of ivory, enamels, watches, jewellery, furniture, weapons and armour, oriental and Spanish tapestries and cloth; library of 40,000 vols, 1,100 periodicals; Dir LETIZIA ARBETETA MIRA; publ. *'Goya' Revista de Arte* (6 a year).

Instituto de Valencia de Don Juan (Don Juan Institute of Valencia): Fortuny 43, 28010 Madrid; tel. 91-308-18-48; f. 1916; historical archives; library of 10,024 historical and art vols; illuminated MS *Les Statuts de la Toison d'Or* with miniatures; museum of ancient Spanish industrial arts; Pres. CARLOS MARTÍNEZ DE IRUJO; Dir BALBINA MARTÍNEZ CAVIRO.

Museo Arqueológico Nacional (National Archaeological Museum): Serrano 13, 28001 Madrid; tel. 91-577-79-12; fax 91-431-68-40; e-mail sec@man.es; internet www.man.es; f. 1867; 16th c. miniatures; collections relating to Egyptian, Cypriot, Greek and Etruscan Antiquities and to national prehistory, Iron Age, Iberian and Hispano-Roman Art; from medieval and modern times: ivory carvings, Spanish pottery, Islamic pottery, brocades, tapestries, porcelain, furniture, textiles and a numismatic collection; library of 70,000 vols, 2,700 periodicals; medieval MSS include Huesca Bible of 12th c., *Beato de Liébana*, *Comentarios al Apocalipsis* (12th–13th c.), *Martirologio y Regla de S. Benito* (13th c.), *Cantorales* (15th c.),; Dir MIGUEL ANGEL ELVIRA BARBA; publ. *Boletín* (annually).

Museo Cerralbo: Ventura Rodríguez 17, 28008 Madrid; tel. 91-547-36-46; fax 91-559-11-71; e-mail mudeo@mcerralbo.mcu.es; internet museocerralbo.mcu.es; f. 1924; the 17th Marquis of Cerralbo left his house to the nation as a museum, together with his collection of paintings, drawings, engravings, porcelain, arms, carpets, coins, furniture; includes paintings by El Greco, Ribera, Titian, Van Dyck, Tintoretto; library of 12,000 vols; Dir LURDES VAQUERO ARGÜELLES.

Museo de la Farmacia Hispana: Facultad de Farmacia, Universidad Complutense, Ciudad Universitaria, 28040 Madrid; tel. 91-394-17-97; fax 91-394-17-97; f. 1951; library: *c.* 10,000 vols; Dir FRANCISCO JAVIER PUERTO SARMIENTO.

Museo de la Real Academia de Bellas Artes de San Fernando: Alcalá 13, 28014 Madrid; tel. 91-524-08-64; fax 91-524-10-34; e-mail scria_museo@terra.es; internet rabasf.insde.es; f. 1744; Spanish paintings since 16th c. (incl. works by Goya, Zurbarán, Murillo, Ribera and Pereda), 16th–18th c. European paintings, Spanish sculpture since 17th c.; Dir D. VICTOR NIETO ALCAIDE; publ. *Academia* (2 a year).

Museo del Ejército (Army Museum): Méndez Núñez 1, 28071 Madrid; tel. 91-522-89-77; fax 91-531-46-24; e-mail joseavitas@et.mde.es; internet www.mde.es/mde/cultura/patrim/museo1.htm; f. 1803; some 30,000 exhibits; collections of arms, war trophies, flags and tin soldiers; br. museum in Toledo; library of 8,669 vols; Dir Gen. JOSÉ A. RIVAS OCTAVIO.

Museo del Ferrocarril (Railway Museum): Paseo de las Delicias 61, 28045 Madrid; tel. 90-222-88-22; fax 91-506-80-24; e-mail museoffcc@ffe.es; internet www.museodelferrocarril.org; f. 1984; steam, diesel and electric trains, models, exhibitions; photographic archive.

Museo Municipal de Madrid (City Museum of Madrid): Calle Fuencarral 78, 28004 Madrid; tel. 91-701-18-63; fax 91-701-16-86; e-mail smuseosm@munimadrid.es; internet www.munimadrid.es/museomunicipal; f. 1929; historical and artistic evolution of Madrid since 16th century; portraits, paintings, designs, engravings, sculptures, plans, silversmiths' work, coins, ceramics, porcelain, paintings by Berruguete, Maella, Luca Giordano, Bayeu, Castillo, Goya and other contemporary artists, 1830 Madrid scale-model, Ramón de Mesonero Romanos and Ramón Gómez de la Serna studios; currently undergoing restoration—exhibition depicting the historical evolution of Madrid and a selection of items representing each of the museum's collns housed in Chapel; Dir CARMEN PRIEGO FERNÁNDEZ DEL CAMPO.

Museo Nacional Centro de Arte Reina Sofía: Plaza Santa Isabel 52, 28012 Madrid; tel. 91-774-10-00; fax 91-774-10-56; internet museoreinasofia.mcu.es; internet www.museoreinasofia.es; f. 1986 in a refurbished 18th c. building; contemporary art; library of 100,000 vols, 1,000 periodicals; Dir ANA MARTINEZ DE AGUILAR.

Museo Nacional de Antropología (National Anthropological Museum): Alfonso XII 68, 28014 Madrid; tel. 91-539-59-95; fax 91-467-70-98; e-mail antropologico@mna.mcu.es; internet www.mnantropologia.mcu.es; f. 1910, present name 1993 through the merger of Museo Nacional de Etnología and Museo Nacional del Pueblo Español; 30,000 exhibits and about 1,500 skulls; famous collections from Europe, the former Spanish Guinea, the Philippines, South America, Micronesia, Melanesia, the Sahara, Morocco, Asia and West and Central Africa; Inuit and Mesoamerican exhibits; library of 14,000 vols and anthropological periodicals; Dir PILAR ROMERO DE TEJADA PICATOSTE; publs *Catalogues, Anales* (annually).

Museo Nacional de Artes Decorativas: Calle Montalbán 12, 28014 Madrid; tel. 91-532-64-99; fax 91-523-20-86; e-mail mnad@mnad.mcu.es; internet mnartesdecorativas.mcu.es/; f. 1912; contains collections of interior decorative arts, especially Spanish from 15th–19th c., including carpets, furniture, leatherwork, jewellery, tapestries, ceramics, glass, porcelain, textiles, etc.; library of 12,000 vols; Dir Dr ALBERTO BARTOLOMÉ ARRAIZA.

Museo Nacional de Ciencia y Tecnología (National Museum of Science and Technology): Paseo de las Delicias 61, 28045 Madrid; tel. 91-530-30-01; fax 91-467-51-19; e-mail museo.mnct@mcyt.es; internet mnct.mcyt.es; f. 1980; library of 8,000 vols, 800 periodicals; Dir Dra AMPARO SEBASTIÁN CAUDET.

Museo Nacional de Ciencias Naturales (Natural Science Museum): José Gutiérrez Abascal 2, 28006 Madrid; tel. 91-411-13-28; fax 91-564-50-78; internet www.mncn.csic.es; f. 1771 as Gabinete de Historia Natural by Carlos III; attached to CSIC; valuable natural history and scientific collections, mainly from Iberia, Central and South America, Philippines and North Africa; library of 62,300 vols, incl. over 2,000 volumes from 15th–18th c. and 1 incunabulum; 4,300 periodicals, since 1790; Dir ALFONSO GABRIEL NAVAS SÁNCHEZ; publs *Graellsia* (annually), *Estudios Geológicos* (3 a year).

Museo Nacional de Reproducciones Artísticas (Reproductions of Works of Art): Avda Juan de Herrera 2, 28040 Madrid; tel. 91-549-66-18; fax 91-544-80-04; internet mnreproduccionesartisticas.mcu.es; f. 1878; library of 10,000 vols; 3,287 reproductions of Oriental, Greek, Roman and Hispano-Roman statuary, medieval and Renaissance art, classical and medieval sculpture and decorative arts; Dir Ma JOSÉ ALMAGRO GORBEA.

Musco Nacional dcl Prado (National Prado Museum): Paseo del Prado s/n, 28014 Madrid; tel. 91-330-28-00; fax 91-330-28-56; e-mail museo.nacional@prado.mcu.es; internet www.museoprado.es; f. 1819; paintings by Botticelli, Rembrandt, Velázquez, El Greco, Goya, Murillo, Raphael, Bosch, Van der Weyden, Zurbarán, Van Dyck, Tiepolo, Ribalta, Rubens, Titian, Veronese, Tintoretto, Moro, Juanes, Meléndez, Poussin, Ribera; Classical and Renaissance sculpture; jewels and medals; library of 45,196 vols, 616 periodicals; Dir MIGUEL ZUGAZA; publ. *Boletín* (annually).

Museo Naval (Naval Museum): Paseo del Prado 5, 28014 Madrid; tel. 91-379-52-99; fax 91-379-50-56; e-mail www.direccion@museonavalmadrid.com; internet www.museonavalmadrid.com; f. 1843; engravings of sea battles, portraits, nautical instruments and armaments; models of ships since 14th c.; some 6,000 original maps, charts, prints and drawings of many countries since 1600; files containing more than 17,800 photographs; library of 20,000 vols, 3,500 vols of MSS; Dir FERNANDO RIAÑO LOZANO; publ. *Revista de Historia Naval* (4 a year).

Museo Romántico (Museum of the Romantic Period): San Mateo 13, 28004 Madrid; tel. 91-448-10-45; fax 91-594-28-93; e-mail museo@mromantico.mcu.es; internet museoromantico.mcu.es; f. 1924; paintings, furniture, books and decorations of the Spanish romantic period; Dir Dra BEGOÑA TORRES GONZÁLEZ.

Museo San Isidro (San Isidro Museum): Plaza San Andrés 2, 28005 Madrid; tel. 91-366-74-15; fax 91-364-51-49; e-mail museosanisidro@munimadrid.es; internet www.munimadrid.es/museosanisidro; f. 2000; archaeology and history of Madrid and environs; library of 11,044 vols; Dir EDUARDO SALAS VÁZQUEZ; publ. *Estudios de Prehistoria y Arqueología Madrileñas* (annually).

Museo Sorolla (Sorolla Museum): General Martínez Campos 37, 28010 Madrid; tel. 91-310-15-84; fax 91-308-59-25; e-mail museo@msorolla.mcu.es; internet museosorolla.mcu

.es; f. 1931; permanent exhibition of some 350 of the artist's works, including drawings, water-colours, portraits, and his own art collections; library of 6,997 vols; Dir FLORENCIO DE SANTA-ANA Y ALVAREZ OSSORIO.

Museo Thyssen-Bornemisza: Paseo del Prado 8, 28014 Madrid; tel. 91-420-39-44; fax 91-420-27-80; e-mail urts@museothyssen .org; internet www.museothyssen.org; f. 1992; paintings and sculpture since 13th c.; Dir TOMAS LLORENS.

Patrimonio Nacional: Palacio Real, Calle Bailen s/n, 28071 Madrid; tel. 91-454-87-00; fax 91-542-69-47; e-mail info@ patrimonionacional.es; internet www .patrimonionacional.es; f. 1940; responsible for all the museums situated in royal palaces and properties; governed by Admin. Council; Dir MIGUEL ANGEL RECIO CRESPO; publ. *Reales Sitios* (quarterly).

Subordinate institutions:

Monasterio de las Descalzas Reales: Plaza de las Descalzas s/n, 28013 Madrid; tel. 91-454-88-00; fax 91-542-69-47; internet www.patrimonionacional.es; f. 16th century; combined museum and enclosed convent; 16th- and 17th-century. paintings and artefacts.

Monasterio de la Encarnación: Plaza de la Encarnación 1, 28013 Madrid; tel. 91-454-88-00; fax 91-542-69-47; internet www .patrimonionacional.es; f. 17th century; combined museum and enclosed convent; 17th-century art.

Monasterio de las Huelgas: Calle Los Compases s/n, 09001 Burgos; tel. 947-20-16-30; fax 947-27-97-29; internet www .patrimonionacional.es; f. by Alfonso VIII in the 12th century.

Monasterio Valle de Los Caídos: 28209 Valle de Cuelgamuros, (Madrid); tel. 91-890-56-11; fax 91-890-55-44; internet www .patrimonionacional.es; monument to the fallen, commissioned by General Franco, begun in 1940 and finished in 1958.

Monasterio de San Lorenzo de El Escorial: C/ Juan de Borbón y Battemberg s/n, 28200 San Lorenzo de El Escorial; tel. 91-890-59-03; fax 91-890-78-18; internet www.patrimonionacional.es; built in the 16th century by Philip II; 16th-century frescoes and canvases.

Monasterio de Santa Clara: 47100 Tordesillas (Valladolid); tel. 983-77-00-71; fax 983-77-04-63; internet www .patrimonionacional.es; f. 14th century.

Palacio de la Almudaina: Calle Palau Reial s/n, 07001 Palma de Mallorca, Balearic Is; tel. 971-21-41-34; fax 971-71-91-45; internet www.patrimonionacional.es; f. built in the Middle Ages; Royal Palace; Gothic chapel of St Anne; Arab baths.

Palacio Real de Aranjuez: Plaza de Parejas, 28300 Aranjuez; tel. 91-892-43-32; fax 91-892-15-32; internet www .patrimonionacional.es; former royal palace rich in 18th-century art.

Palacio Real de El Pardo: C/ Manuel Alonso s/n, 24048 El Pardo (Madrid); tel. 91-376-15-00; fax 91-376-04-52; internet www.patrimonionacional.es; f. built for Carlos V in 1547 and enlarged in the 18th century by Sabatini; 18th-century tapestries, some by Goya.

Palacio de La Granja: Plaza de España 17, 40100 La Granja de San Ildefonso (Segovia); tel. 921-47-00-19; fax 921-47-18-95; internet www.patrimonionacional .es; f. 18th century; built for Philip V; gardens and fountains, tapestry museum.

Palacio Real de Madrid: Calle Bailen s/ n, 28071 Madrid; tel. 91-454-88-00; fax 91-

542-69-47; e-mail antonio.rubio@ patrimonionacional.es; internet www .patrimonionacional.es; f. 18th century; rooms devoted to 16th- to 18th-century tapestries, clocks, painting and porcelain from the royal palaces and pharmacy; Royal Armoury; rooms with original 18th-century decor; colln of furniture, paintings and porcelain from the 18th and 19th centuries; library: see Libraries and Archives; archives since the 12th century.

Palacio de Riofrío: Bosque de Riofrío, 40420 Navas de Riofrío (Segovia); tel. 921-47-00-19; fax 921-47-18-95; internet www .patrimonionacional.es; f. 1752.

Planetario de Madrid: Parque Tierno Galván, 28045 Madrid; tel. 91-467-34-61; fax 91-468-11-54; e-mail buzon@planetmad .es; internet www.planetmad.es; f. 1986; exhibition and projection room seating 250 people; Dir ASUNCIÓN SÁNCHEZ JUSTEL.

Real Jardín Botánico (Royal Botanical Garden): Plaza de Murillo 2, 28014 Madrid; tel. 91-420-30-17; fax 91-420-01-57; internet www.rjb.csic.es; part of CSIC (*q.v.*); f. 1755; botanical research; herbarium with 1,000,000 specimens; library of 21,533 vols, 1,970 periodicals, 22,000 reprints, 3,927 microfiches, MSS, 13,000 botanical drawings, 6,900 slides; Dir GONZALO NIETO FELINER; Man. JAVIER GIL ORTIZ; publ. *Anales* (2 a year).

Mérida

Museo Nacional de Arte Romano: José Ramón Mélida s/n, 06800 Mérida; tel. 924-31-19-12; fax 924-30-20-06; e-mail mnar@mnar .es; internet www.mnar.es; f. 1838; Roman archaeology; library of 24,800 specialized vols, periodicals; Dir Dr JOSÉ M. ALVAREZ MARTÍNEZ; publs *Mongrafías Emeritenses*, *Anas* (irregular), *Cuadernos Emeritenses*, *Studia Lusitana*.

Palma de Mallorca

Museo de Mallorca: Calle Portella 5, 07001 Palma; tel. 971-71-75-40; fax 971-71-04-83; f. 1961; history, ethnology, fine arts, prehistory; Dir GUILLERMO ROSSELLÓ BORDOY.

Pontevedra

Museo de Pontevedra: Calle Pasantería 10, 36002 Pontevedra; tel. 98-685-14-55; fax 98-684-06-93; e-mail secretaria@muspontev .es; f. 1927; pottery and ancient industrial and naval history of Galicia; prehistoric jewellery and jet ornaments; Spanish paintings since 15th c.; library of 100,000 vols on literature, art and archaeology of Galicia; Dir Dr JOSÉ CARLOS VALLE PÉREZ; publ. *El Museo de Pontevedra* (annually).

Sabadell

Museu d'Art de Sabadell: Carrer Dr Puig 16, 08202 Sabadell; tel. 93-725-77-47; fax 93-727-55-07; e-mail m.sabadell.art@diba.es; f. 1978; painting, ceramics, photography; Dir JOSEP SERRANO; Curator ENGRÀCIA TORRELLA; publ. *Arraona*.

Museu d'Història de Sabadell: Carrer Sant Antoni 13, 08201 Sabadell; tel. 93-727-85-55; fax 93-726-60-42; e-mail mhs@ ajsabadell.es; f. 1931; prehistoric archaeological, numismatic collections, native handicrafts; Iberico-Roman section, and sections on textiles and mineralogy; Dir GENÍS RIBÉ MONGÉ; publ. *Arraona* (annually).

Sabiñánigo

Museo de Dibujo 'Castillo de Larrés': Apdo 25, 22600 Sabiñánigo (Huesca); tel. 974-48-29-81; e-mail serrablo@serrablo.org; f. 1986 by 'Amigos de Serrablo', a cultural asscn specializing entirely in contemporary

Spanish and Spanish-American design; Pres. JULIO GAVÍN MOYA.

San Roque

Museo Histórico de San Roque: Ayuntamiento, San Roque, Prov. Cádiz; f. 1956; documents of Gibraltar and museum of Carteyan excavations; Dir RAFAEL CALDELA LÓPEZ; Chief of Archaeological Section FRANCISCO PRESCEDO.

San Sebastián

Museo Municipal de San Telmo: Plaza Ignacio Zuloaga 1, 20003 Donostia-San Sebastián; tel. 943-48-15-80; fax 943-48-15-81; e-mail santelmo@donostia.org; internet www.santelmomuseoa.com; f. 1902; housed in the former Dominican convent of San Telmo built in the reign of Emperor Charles V (1500–1558); inaugurated 1932 by Alfonso XIII; sections on archaeology, fine arts, ethnography and history; Dir SUSANA SOTO.

Palacio del Mar – Aquarium (Sea Museum and Aquarium): Sociedad de Oceanografía de Guipúzcoa, Plaza Carlos Blasco de Imaz s/n, 20003 Donostia- San Sebastián; tel. 943-44-00-99; fax 943-43-00-92; e-mail sog@ aquariumss.com; internet www.aquariumss .com; f. 1908; history of seafaring since 13th c., models of historical ships, portraits of navigators and local fishing tackle; oceanographic museum and marine laboratory; aquarium with Atlantic and tropical fishes; Dir CARMEN ARRAZOLA.

Santander

Museo de Prehistoria y Arqueología (Prehistoric and Archaeological Museum): Casimiro Sainz 4, 39003 Santander; tel. 942-20-71-09; fax 942-20-71-06; f. 1941; palaeolithic to Middle Ages in Cantabria; library of 60,000 vols; Curator AMPARO LÓPEZ ORTIZ.

Santiago de Compostela

Museo das Peregrinacións (Pilgrimage Museum): San Miguel 4, 'Casa Gotica', 15704 Santiago de Compostela; tel. 98-158-15-58; fax 98-158-19-55; e-mail informacion@ mdperegrinacions.com; internet www .mdperegrinacions.com; f. 1951, inaugurated 1965; relics and items related to St James and the Pilgrimages; medieval art and history of the 'Camino de Santiago'; library of 5,446 vols, 224 periodicals; Dir BIEITO PÉREZ OUTEIRIÑO; Curator Mª. ISABEL PESQUERA VAQUERO.

Seville

Museo Arqueológico de Sevilla: Plaza de América (Parque de María Luisa), 41013 Seville; tel. 95-423-24-01; fax 95-462-95-42; e-mail museoarqueologicosevilla.ccul@ juntadeandalucia.es; internet www .juntadeandalucia.es/cultura/museos; f. 1880; 10,000 exhibits; Roman statues, mosaics; incorporates the municipal collections; treasures of Tarshish; Dir CONCEPCIÓN SAN MARTÍN MONTILLA.

Museo de Bellas Artes de Sevilla: Plaza del Museo 9, 41001 Seville; tel. 95-422-18-29; fax 95-422-43-24; f. 1835; paintings by local artists from 15th to 20th centuries; Baroque art (esp. Murillo, Zurbarán and Valdés Leal); library of 11,000 vols, 400 periodicals; Dir IGNACIO CANO RIVERO.

Sitges

Museu Cau Ferrat: Calle Fonollar s/n, 08870 Sitges; tel. 93-894-03-64; fax 93-894-85-29; e-mail m.sitges@diba.es; internet www.diba.es/museus/sitges/asp; f. 1933; house and studio of the painter and writer Santiago Rusiñol; contains drawings and paintings by Rusiñol and his friends and contemporaries; (Casas, Picasso, Utrillo); also woodcarving, sculpture, ancient painting (El Greco), ceramics (since 14th c.), furniture, ironwork (13th–19th c.), glass (16th–19th c.); Dir MARIA-NADAL SAU I GIRALT.

Soria

Museo Numantino: Paseo del Espolón 8, 42001 Soria; tel. 975-22-13-97; fax 975-22-98-72; e-mail cultura@dipsoria.com; internet www.dipsoria.com; f. 1916; prehistoric, ethnological, Roman and medieval archaeological collections, comprising 180,000 objects; library of 10,000 vols; Dir ELÍAS TERÉS NAVARRO.

Tarragona

Museu i Necròpolis Paleocristians: Avda de Ramon y Cajal 84, 43005 Tarragona; tel. 977-25-15-15; fax 977-25-22-86; e-mail mnat@mnat.es; internet www.mnat.es/cat/mnat/necr/index.html; f. 1930; objects discovered during excavation of the Roman-Christian necropolis; Dir PILAR SADA CASTILLO.

Museu Nacional Arqueològic de Tarragona (Archaeological Museum): Plaça del Rei 5, 43003 Tarragona; tel. 977-25-15-15; fax 977-25-22-86; e-mail mnat@mnat.es; internet www.mnat.es; f. 1834; archaeological, historical, local Roman exhibits; library of 12,000 vols; Dir PILAR SADA CASTILLO; publ. *Forum.*

Toledo

Museo del Greco (El Greco Museum): Calle Samuel Leví s/n, 45002 Toledo; tel. 925-22-44-05; fax 925-22-45-59; e-mail secretaria .greco@telefonica.net; f. 1911; the artist's house; contains important later works by El Greco; works from the Spanish schools of the 17th c.; furniture of the 16th–17th c. and ceramics from the Talaverana factory; Dir ANA CARMEN LAVÍN BERDONCES; Curator LUIS CABALLERO GARCÍA.

Museo de Santa Cruz: Calle Cervantes 3, 45001 Toledo; tel. 925-22-10-36; fax 925-22-58-62; f. 1958; archaeology, fine arts, industrial and decorative arts; library of 12,000 vols; Dir RAFAEL GARCÍA SERRANO; publ. *Memoria del Museo de Santa Cruz* (irregular).

Affiliated museums:

Museo de Arte Contemporáneo (Museum of Contemporary Art): Calle de las Bulas, 45002 Toledo; tel. 925-22-78-71; f. 1973; closed for renovation until further notice.

Museo Casa de Dulcinea en El Toboso: 45820 El Toboso; tel. 925-19-72-88; f. 1967; ethnography of La Mancha area and period reconstruction in the 17th-c. Casa Solariega.

Museo de Cerámica 'Ruíz de Luna': Calle San Agustín, 45600 Talavera de la Reina; tel. 925-80-01-49; f. 1963; local ceramics.

Museo de los Concilios y de la Cultura Visigoda: Calle San Román s/n, 45002 Toledo; tel. 925-22-78-72; f. 1969; Visigothic art and archaeology.

Museo Taller del Moro: Calle Taller del Moro 4, 45002 Toledo; tel. 925-22-45-00; f. 1961; Mudejar art and archaeology.

Sinagoga del Tránsito: Calle Samuel Leví s/n, 45002 Toledo; tel. 92-522-36-65; fax 92-521-58-31; e-mail transito@mail.ddnet.es; f. 1964; Jewish synagogue built in the 14th c. by Samuel Ha-Levi, treasurer to King Don Pedro I, 'The Cruel'; given to the Military Order of Calatrava in 1494 by Ferdinand and Isabella; in 18th c. became church of Sta María del Tránsito; national monument;

created Sephardic Museum 1964; archaeology, life and costumes of Sephardic Jews; library of 12,000 vols on Judaism, Hebraism, Sephardism etc.; Dir ANA MARÍA LÓPEZ ALVAREZ.

Valencia

Museo de Bellas Artes (Museum of Fine Arts): Calle de San Pío V 9, 46010 Valencia; tel. 96-360-57-93; fax 96-369-71-25; internet www.cult.gva.es/mbav; housed in an fmr palace; f. 1839; more than 3,000 paintings, also sculpture, archaeology, drawing and print sections; library of 22,764 vols on art, 771 periodicals, 7,892 photographs; Dir FERNANDO BENITO DOMÉNECH.

Museo Nacional de Cerámica 'González Marti': Poeta Querol 2, 46002 Valencia; tel. 96-351-63-92; fax 96-351-35-12; e-mail ceramica@museo.mec.es; internet mnceramica.mcu.es; f. 1947; a national museum of ceramics and decorative arts, set in the Palace of the Marquis of Dos Aguas; library of 20,000 vols; Dir Dr JAUME COLL CONESA.

Museu de Prehisòria i de les Cultures de València: Valencia; tel. 96-388-36-19; e-mail joan.gregori@diputacion.m400.gva.es; internet www.xarxamuseus.com/prehistoria; prehistoric art and culture; Roman era; Iberian culture and coin collections; Valencian archaeology, history, culture and ethnology; library of 42,700 vols; Dir JOAN GREGORI BERENGUER.

Valladolid

Casa de Cervantes (Cervantes' House): Calle del Rastro 7, 47001 Valladolid; tel. 983-30-88-10; fax 983-39-07-03; f. 1948; furniture and possessions of the writer; Pres. JESÚS URREA FERNANDEZ; Dirs NICOMEDES SANZ Y RUIZ DE LA PEÑA, AMPARO MAGDALENO DE LA CRUZ.

Museo de Valladolid: Palacio de Fabio Nelli, Plaza de Fabio Nelli s/n, 47003 Valladolid; tel. 98-335-13-89; fax 98-335-04-22; e-mail museo.valladolid@jcyl.es; f. 1879; archaeology and fine art, articles from palaeolithic times to the 18th c.; library: specialized library of 12,000 vols with restricted access; Dir ELOISA WATTENBERG GARCÍA.

Museo Nacional de Escultura: Cadenas de San Gregorio 1, 2 y 3, 47011 Valladolid; tel. 983-25-03-75; fax 983-25-93-00; e-mail mne@mne.es; internet www.mne.es; f. 1933; housed in the old Colegio de San Gregorio, since late 15th c.; works by Alonso Berruguete, Juan de Juni, Gregorio Fernández, and others; library of 7,277 vols; Dir JESÚS URREA FERNÁNDEZ.

Vic

Museu Episcopal de Vic (Vic Episcopal Museum): Pl. Bisbe Oliba 3, 08500 Vic; tel. 93-886-93-60; fax 93-889-44-17; e-mail difusio@museuepiscopalvic.com; f. 1891; medieval arts, provincial Romanesque, Gothic precious metalwork, textiles, embroideries, liturgical vestments, forged iron, etc.; Dir MIQUEL TRESSERRAS.

Zamora

Museo de Zamora: Palacio del Cordón, Plaza de Sta Lucía 2, 49002 Zamora; tel. 980-51-61-50; fax 980-53-50-64; e-mail museo .zamora@jcyl.es; f. 1877; housed in 16th c. palace; collections (300,000 items): palaeontology, prehistory and archaeology, fine arts, ethnography; library of 6,246 vols; Dir ROSARIO GARCÍA ROZAS.

Zaragoza

Museo de Zaragoza: Plaza de los Sitios 6, 50001 Zaragoza; tel. 97-622-21-81; fax 97-

622-23-78; e-mail museoza@aragon.es; internet www.aragon.es/edycul/patrimo/museos/zaragoza.htm; f. 1848; archaeological; prehistory, Roman, Arab, Gothic, Moorish, Romanesque and Renaissance exhibits; primitive arts and crafts, paintings from 14th–19th c., contemporary Aragonese artists; ethnology and ceramics sections are Located at Parque Primo de Rivera; library of 31,000 vols; Dir Dr MIGUEL BELTRÁN LLORIS; Curators SILVIA FAYANAS BUEY, JUAN PAZ PERALTA; publs *Boletín* (annually), *Guías Didácticas* (2 or 3 a year), *Catálogos Exposiciones.*

Museo Pablo Gargallo: Plaza de San Felipe 3, 50003 Zaragoza; tel. 976-72-49-22; fax 976-39-20-76; e-mail museogargallo-oficinas@ayto-zaragoza.es; internet www.zaragoza.es/museos; f. 1982; important collection of sculpture, designs and cartoons by Gargallo; research on his life and works, and modern art in general; documentation centre of 15,000 vols on Gargallo and sculpture in general; Dir MARÍA CRISTINA GIL IMAZ.

Universities

UNIVERSIDAD NACIONAL DE EDUCACIÓN A DISTANCIA
(Open University)

Ciudad Universitaria s/n, 28040 Madrid
Telephone: 91-398-60-16
Fax: 91-398-60-37
E-mail: infouned@adm.uned.es
Internet: www.uned.es

Founded 1972
State control
Language of instruction: Spanish
Academic year: October to July

Rector: MÁ ARACELI MACIÁ ANTÓN
Vice-Rector (Academic Affairs): MIGUEL ÁNGEL SEBASTIÁN PÉREZ
Vice-Rector (Associated Centres): JUAN JOSÉ DE BENITO MUÑOZ
Vice-Rector (New Technology): MANUEL CASTRO GIL
Vice-Rector (Institutional Relations and University Extension): JOSÉ LUIS FERNÁNDEZ MARRÓN
Vice-Rector (Evaluation and Quality) (vacant)
Vice-Rector (Research): JOSÉ FRANCISCO ÁLVAREZ ÁLVAREZ
Vice-Rector (Alumni): JORGE J. MONTES SALGUERO
Vice-Rector (International Relations): FANNY CASTRO-RIAL GARRONE
Vice-Rector (Continuing Education): MARÍA JOSÉ LORENZO SEGOVIA
Vice-Rector (Print and Audiovisual Media): ANA MARÍA PÉREZ GARCÍA
Registrar: PEDRO ANTONIO TAMAYO LORENZO
Chief of Administration: JUAN JOSÉ DE LA VEGA Y VIÑAMBRES
Librarian: ISABEL BELMONTE MARTÍNEZ

Number of teachers: 879
Number of students: 143,324 (109,653 in faculties, 33,671 foundation and courses)

DEANS

Faculty of Law: CONCEPCIÓN ESCOBAR HERNÁNDEZ
Faculty of Psychology: ENCARNACIÓN SARRIÁ SÁNCHEZ
Faculty of Philosophy: MANUEL FRAIJÓ NIETO
Faculty of Education: LORENZO GARCÍA ARETIO
Faculty of Economics and Business Studies: RAFAEL CASTEJÓN MONTIJANO
Faculty of Philology: FRANCISCO GUTIÉRREZ CARBAJO

Faculty of Geography and History: ENRIQUE CANTERA MONTENEGRO

Faculty of Politics and Sociology: JOSÉ MARÍA ARRIBAS MACHO

Faculty of Sciences: AGUSTÍN ESPINOSA BOISSIER

Technical School of Computer Science: JOAQUÍN ARANDA ALMANSA (Dir)

School of Industrial Engineering: SANTIAGO AROCA LASTRA (Dir)

HEADS OF DEPARTMENTS

Economic Analysis I: Profa MA. ISABEL ESCOBEDO

Economic Analysis II: Prof. FRANCISCO MOCHÓN MORCILLO

Social and Cultural Anthropology: Dr HONORIO MANUEL VELASCO MAÍLLO

Politics and Administration: ANDRÉS DE BLAS GUERRERO

Analytical Sciences: Prof. Dr JESÚS SENÉN DURAND ALEGRÍA

Physical Chemistry: Prof. Dr ARTURO HORTA ZUBIAGA

Administrative Law: Dr JOSÉ RAMÓN PARADA VÁZQUEZ

Civil Law: Dr CARLOS LASARTE ÁLVAREZ

Constitutional Law: Dr ANTONIO TORRES DEL MORAL

Public Law: Dra PALOMA GARCÍA PICAZO (Private International Law: Dra MA. TERESA REGUEIRO GARCÍA (State Canon Law)

Company Law: Dra ANA PALOMA ABARCA JUNCO

Penal Law: Dr ALFONSO SERRANO MAÍLLO

Political Law: Prof. Dr OSCAR ALZAGA VILLAMIL

Procedural Law: Prof. VICENTE GIMENO SENDRA

Education, School Organization and Special Education: Dr ANTONIO MEDINA RIVILLA

Quantitative Applied Economics I: NELSON ÁLVAREZ VÁZQUEZ

Quantitative Applied Economics II: EMILIO PRIETO SÁEZ

Applied Economics and Statistics: JULIÁN SANTOS PEÑAS

Applied Economics and Economic History: MANUEL JESÚS GONZÁLEZ GONZÁLEZ

Applied Economics and Public Administration: Prof. Dr JUAN ANTONIO GIMENO ULLASTRES

Business Finance and Accounting: ÁNGEL MUÑOZ MERCHANTE

Statistics, Operational Research and Calculus: Dr ILDEFONSO YÁÑEZ DE DIEGO

Classical Philology: Prof. Dr JOSÉ MARÍA LUCAS DE DIOS

French Philology: Profa Dra ALICIA YLLERA FERNÁNDEZ

Foreign Languages and Linguistics: Profa Dra MARÍA TERESA GIBERT MACEDA

Philosophy: Dr DIEGO SÁNCHEZ MECA

Philosophy of Law: Dr BENITO DE CASTRO CID

Philosophy and Political and Moral Philosophy: Dr JAVIER SÁNCHEZ MARTÍN SALA

Physics of Materials: Prof. Dr MANUEL YUSTE LLANDRES

Basic Physics: JAVIER DE LA RUBIA SÁNCHEZ

Mathematical Physics and Fluidics: Dr JOSÉ CARLOS ANTORANZ CALLEJO

Geography: Dr JULIÁN ALONSO FERNÁNDEZ

Contemporary History: Prof. Dr JAVIER TUSELL GÓMEZ

History of Education and Comparative Education: Prof. Dr FEDERICO GÓMEZ RODRÍGUEZ DE CASTRO

History of Art: Prof. Dr VÍCTOR MANUEL NIETO ALCAIDE

History of Law and Institutions: Prof. Dr JAVIER ALVARADO PLANAS

Modern and Medieval History and Historiography: Prof. Dr CARLOS MARTÍNEZ SHAW

Comparative Science and Automation: SEBASTIÁN DORMIDO BENCOMO

Construction and Manufacturing Engineering: Prof. Dr MARIANO RODRÍGUEZ-AVIAL LLARDENT

Power Engineering: Prof. Dr FRANCISCO CASTRO DELGADO

Artificial Intelligence: Prof. JOSÉ MIRA

Spanish Language and General Linguistics: Dra JUANA GIL FERNÁNDEZ

Computer Languages and Systems: Profa Dra MA. FELISA VERDEJO MAILLO

Spanish Literature and Theory of Literature: Prof. Dr MIGUEL ÁNGEL PÉREZ PRIEGO

Logic, History and Philosophy of Science: Dr MANUEL SELLÉS GARCÍA

Applied Mathematics I: LUIS RODRÍGUEZ MARÍN

Basic Mathematics: Prof. Dr ANTONIO F. COSTA GONZÁLEZ

Mechanics: Prof. MARIANO ARTÉS GÓMEZ

Methodology of Behavioural Sciences: CARMEN PÉREZ-LLANTADA RUEDA

Research Methods and Diagnosis in Education: Profa Dra ELVIRA REPETTO TALAVERA

Business Organization: Prof. SANTIAGO GARRIDO BUJ

Prehistory and Ancient History: Prof. Dr SERGIO RIPOLL LÓPEZ

Psychobiology: Dra ÁGUEDA DEL ABRIL ALONSO

Basic Psychology I: Dra PILAR SÁNCHEZ BALMASEDA

Basic Psychology II: Dr ANTONIO CRESPO

Psychology of Personality, Psychological Assessment and Treatment: Dr BONIFACIO SANDÍN FERRERO

Evolutionary Psychology and Psychology of Education: Dr JUAN ANTONIO GARCÍA MADRUGA

Social and Organizational Psychology: Profa ELENA GAVIRIA STEWART

Chemistry Applied to Engineering: Prof. Dr ALFONSO CONTRERAS LÓPEZ

Inorganic and Technical Chemistry: Prof. Dr ANTONIO JEREZ MÉNDEZ

Organic Chemistry and Biology: Profa Dra ROSA MA. CLARAMUNT VALLESPÍ

Sociology I, Theory, Methodology and Social Change: Profa CONSUELO DEL VAL CID

Sociology II: Dr LUIS GARRIDO MEDINA

Sociology III: JOSÉ FÉLIX TEZANOS TORTAJADA

The University has 60 associated centres in Spain, and 19 abroad in Berlin, Cologne, Munich, Brussels, Bern, Geneva, Paris, London, Lisbon, Miami, Mexico City, Caracas, Buenos Aires, Rosario, São Paulo, Lima, Tangier and Equatorial Guinea (two)

UNIVERSITAT ABAT OLIBA-C.E.U.

Bellesguard 30, 08022 Barcelona

Telephone: 93-254-09-00

Fax: 93-418-93-80

E-mail: info@abatoliba.edu

Internet: www.abatoliba.edu

Founded 2003

Private control

Languages of instruction: Spanish, English, Catalan

Rector: Dr JUAN F. CORONA

Vice-Rectors: Dr FERRAN PORTA, Dr MARCIN KAZMIERCZAK

General Secretary: Dr MARC B. ESCOLÀ

Library of 20,000 vols, 100 periodicals

Courses in law, business administration and management economics, politics, public management, advertising, publicity, public relations, higher education management, journalism, psychology and computer engineering.

ATTACHED CENTRE

Centre for Research and Development and Business Services: Monestir 10, 08034 Barcelona; tel. 93-254-09-00; fax 93-418-93-80; e-mail cide@abatoliba.edu; internet www.abatoliba.edu/cide; Dir JOSEP MISÓ.

UNIVERSIDAD DE ALCALÁ

Colegio de San Ildefonso, Plaza de San Diego s/n, 28801 Alcalá de Henares (Madrid)

Telephone: 91-885-40-00

Fax: 91-885-40-95

E-mail: ciu@uah.es

Internet: www.uah.es

Founded 1977

State control

Language of instruction: Spanish

Academic year: September to June

Rector: VIRGILIO ZAPATERO GÓMEZ

Vice-Rector (European Harmonization and Planning): PURIFICACIÓN MOSCOSO CASTRO

Vice-Rector (Alcalá Campus and Environmental Quality: ANTONIO GÓMEZ SAL

Vice-Rector (Academic Organization): FERNANDO GALVÁN REULA

Vice-Rector (Academic Staff): FILOMENA RODRÍGUEZ CAABEIRO

Vice-Rector (Research): ELOY GARCÍA CALVO

Vice-Rector (International Relations): JUAN SOLOZÁBAL PASTOR

Vice-Rector (Guadalajara Campus): MICHEL HEYKOOP FUNG-A-YOU

Vice-Rector (Students and Promotion): JOSÉ LUIS LÁZARO GALILEA

Vice-Rector (Extramural Activities): DOLORES CABAÑAS GONZÁLEZ

Vice-Rector (Postgraduate Studies, Unregulated Teaching and Continuing Education): JAIME CONTRERAS CONTRERAS

Registrar: JOSÉ MARÍA ESPINAR VICENTE

General Manager: DANIEL SOTELSEK SALEM

Library Director: CARMEN FERNÁNDEZ-GALIANO PEYROLÓN

Number of teachers: 1,625

Number of students: 23,000

Publications: *Paraninfo, Encuentro, Estudios de Historia Económica y Social de América, Henares, Teatro, Polis, Reale, Reden, Las Comarcas Agrarias de España, Signo, Barataria, Idagación, Quodlibet, Cairón, Quórum. Revista de Pensamiento Iberoamericano, Revista*

DEANS

Faculty of Philosophy and Arts: MERCEDES BENGOECHEA BARTOLOMÉ

Faculty of Chemistry: JUAN JOSÉ VAQUERO LÓPEZ

Faculty of Pharmacy: FIDEL ORTEGA ORTIZ DE APODACA

Faculty of Law: DIEGO MANUEL LUZÓN PEÑA

Faculty of Economics and Business: TOMÁS MANCHA NAVARRO

Faculty of Medicine: ANTONIO LÓPEZ ALONSO

Faculty of Biology: JOSÉ MANUEL VIÉITEZ MARTÍN

Faculty of the Environmental Sciences: ANTONIO SASTRE MERLÍN

Faculty of Library Science: VIRGINIA ORTIZ-REPISO JIMÉNEZ

DIRECTORS

School of Architecture and Geodesy: MARÍA ROSA CERVERÁ SARDÁ

School of Computer Engineering: (vacant)

School of Engineering: JOSÉ ANTONIO PAMIES GUERRERO

School of Nursing and Physiotherapy: ÁNGEL LUIS ASENJO ESTÉVEZ

School of Business Studies: JOSÉ MELCHOR MARTÍN BUENO

School of Technical Architecture: MIGUEL TRALLERO SANZ

School of Tourism: CAROLINA JIMÉNEZ GONZÁLEZ

HEADS OF DEPARTMENTS

Anatomy and Human Embryology: (vacant)
Architecture: FLAVIO CELIS D'AMICO
Automation: DANIEL MEZIAT LUNA
Ecology: JOSÉ MARÍA REY BENAYAS
Cellular Biology and Genetics: NICOLÁS JOUVE DE LA BARREDA
Botanical Biology: MERCEDES MARTÍN MARQUÍNEZ
Biochemistry and Molecular Biology: MARÍA NATIVIDAD RECIO CANO
Computer Sciences: LUIS LÓPEZ CORRAL
Business: ALEJANDRO LARRIBA DÍAZ-ZORITA
Sanitary Sciences and Social Medicine: MARÍA TERESA ALFONSO GALÁN
Surgery: PEDRO CARDA ABELLA
Private Law: JOSÉ MARÍA DE SOLAS RAFECAS
Public Law: ALFONSO MARTÍNEZ GARCÍA-MONCÓ
Applied Economics: ISABEL ENCABO RODRÍGUEZ
Education: PEDRO M. ALONSO MARAÑÓN
Electronics: FRANCISCO JAVIER RODRÍGUEZ SÁNCHEZ
Nursing: FRANCISCA CASAS MARTÍNEZ
Physiotherapy: TOMÁS GALLEGO IZQUIERDO
Specialized Medical Fields: JOSÉ LUIS BARDASANO RUBIO
Statistics, Economic Structure and International Economic Organization: FÉLIX VARELA PARACHE
Pharmacy and Pharmaceutical Technology: BEGOÑA ESCALERA IZQUIERDO
Pharmacology: EDUARDO CUENCA FERNÁNDEZ
Philology: ÁNGEL BERENGUER CASTELLARY
Modern Philology: ALBERTO LÁZARO
Physics: JUAN SEQUEIROS UGARTE
Physiology: MANUEL RODRÍGUEZ PUYOL
Principles of Economics and Economic History: INMACULADA CEBRIÁN LÓPEZ
Principles of Law and Penal Law: CARLOS GARCÍA VALDÉS
Geography: JOSÉ SANCHO COMINS
Geology: ROSA VICENTE LAPUENTE
History I and Philosophy: SERAFÍN VEGAS GONZÁLEZ
History II: MANUEL MARTÍNEZ RIPOLL
Mathematics: JUAN LLOVET VERDUGO
Medicine: MELCHOR ÁLVAREZ DE MON SOTO
Microbiology and Parasitology: JUAN SOLIVERI DE CARRANZA
Nutrition, Bromatology and Toxicology: MARÍA DEL CARMEN MARTÍNEZ PARA
Analytical Chemistry and Chemical Engineering: SOLEDAD VERA LÓPEZ
Physical Chemistry: MARÍA DOLORES MARÍN NOARBE
Inorganic Chemistry: AMELIO VÁZQUEZ DE MIGUEL (acting)
Organic Chemistry: MARÍA LUISA IZQUIERDO CEINOS (acting)
Signalling and Communications Theory: FRANCISCO LÓPEZ FERRERAS
Zoology and Physical Anthropology: GONZALO PÉREZ SUÁREZ

ATTACHED INSTITUTES

Luis Vives Centre of Advanced Teacher Training: Dir CLEMENTE DEL RÍO GÓMEZ.

Institute of Management and Business Organization (IDOE): Dir SANTIAGO GARCÍA ECHEVARRÍA.

Institute of Education: Dir ISABEL BRINCONES CALVO.

Foreign Languages Centre: Dir GEORG PICHLER.

Cardinal Cisneros School of Teacher Training: Dir LUIS F. REBOLLO FERREIRO.

School of Nursing (Guadalajara): Dir HELENA HERNÁNDEZ MARTÍNEZ.

Institute of Sephardic and Andalusian Studies: Dir JAIME CONTRERAS CONTRERAS.

Centre for Initiatives in Co-operation for Development: Dir MANUEL GUEDÁN MENÉNDEZ.

Corpus Inscriptionum Latinarum: Dirs LUIS A. GARCÍA MORENO, JOSÉ LUIS MORALEJO ÁLVAREZ, ARMIN U. STYLOW.

Centre of Cervantes Studies: Dir CARLOS ALVAR EZQUERRA.

Cisneros International Centre of Historical Studies: Dir SANTIAGO AGUADÉ NIETO.

Institute of North-American Studies: Dir SATURNINO AGUADO SEBASTIÁN.

Juan Carlos I Royal Botanical Garden: Dir ROSENDO ELVIRA.

Servilab. Services Sector Research Laboratory: Dir JUAN R. CUADRADO ROURA.

UNIVERSIDAD ALFONSO X EL SABIO

Avda Universidad 1, 28691 Villanueva de la Cañada, Madrid

Telephone: 91-810-92-00
Fax: 91-810-91-02
E-mail: rectorado@uax.es
Internet: www.uax.es

Founded 1993

Academic year: October to June

President: JESÚS NÚÑEZ VELÁZQUEZ

Library of 15,000 vols
Number of teachers: 900
Number of students: 10,000

Publications: *Saberes* (law, economics and social sciences, online), *Linguax* (applied languages, online), *Revista Electrónica Biociencias* (life sciences, online), *Tecnología y Desarrollo* (science, technology and environment, online)

DEANS

Faculty of Applied Languages: Dr JOAQUÍN GONZÁLEZ IBÁÑEZ
Faculty of Health Sciences: Dr ALFREDO ENTRALA BUENO
Faculty of Social Studies: Dr ANDRÉS TAGLIAVIA LÓPEZ
Polytechnic School: Dr JUAN HERRANZ ARRIBAS

UNIVERSIDAD DE ALICANTE

San Vicente del Raspeig, 03690 Alicante

Telephone: 96-590-34-00
Fax: 96-590-36-72
E-mail: sri@sri.ua.es
Internet: www.ua.es

Founded 1979

State control

Languages of instruction: Spanish, Valenciano

Academic year: October to July

President: Dr SALVADOR ORDÓÑEZ DELGADO
Vice-President (Academic Affairs): Dr MIGUEL LOUIS CERECEDA
Vice-President (European Convergence and Quality Standards): Dr GUILLERMO BERNABEU PASTOR
Vice-President (Development of Regulations): Dr JUAN ROSA MORENO
Vice-President (Economic Affairs, Infrastructure and Services): Dr IGNACIO JIMÉNEZ RANEDA
Vice-President (Research): Dr ANTONIO MARCILLA GOMIS
Vice-President (Students): Dr Ma. JOSÉ FRAU LLINARES
Vice-President (Extracurricular Activities): Dr JOSÉ CARLOS ROVIRA SOLER
Vice-President (Co-ordination and Communication): Dr ROQUE MORENO FONSERET
Vice-President (Corporations and Foundations): Dra OLGA FUENTES SORIANO
Registrar: ISABEL LIFANTE VIDAL

Number of teachers: 1,600
Number of students: 30,000
Publications: *Anales* (all faculties)

DEANS

Faculty of Arts: JOSÉ LUÍS CIFUENTES HONRUBIA
Faculty of Sciences: FRANCISCO LLORCA ALCARAZ
Faculty of Law: JUAN JOSÉ DÍEZ
Faculty of Economics and Business Administration: JOAQUÍN MARHUENDA FRUCTUOSO
Faculty of Education: ANTONIO MULA FRANCO

DIRECTORS

University Collegel of Business Studies: CARMEN MARTÍNEZ MORA
University College of Labour Relations: JUAN RAMÓN RIVERA SÁNCHEZ
University College of Social Work: JOSEFA LORENZO GARCÍA
University College of Optics and Optometry: VALENTÍN VIQUEIRA PÉREZ
University College of Nursing: MARÍA LORETO MACIÁ SOLER
Polytechnic University College: FARAÓN LLORENS LARGO

HEADS OF DEPARTMENTS

Agrochemistry and Biochemistry: JUAN SÁNCHEZ ANDREU
Applied Economic Analysis: INMACULADA LÓPEZ ORTIZ
Regional Geographical Analysis: ALFREDO MORALES GIL
Mathematical Analysis: GASPAR MORA MARTÍNEZ
Biotechnology: JOAQUIN DE JUAN HERRERO
Artificial Intelligence and Computation: RAMÓN RIZO ALDEGUER
Environmental Science and Natural Resources: M. BENITO CRESPO
Environmental and Earth Sciences: ANTONIO ESTÉVEZ RUBIO
Historico-Juridical Sciences: MARÍA ARANZAZU CALZADA GONZÁLEZ
Architectural Construction: ROBERTO VERA SORIANO
Civil Law: JUAN ANTONIO MORENO MARTÍNEZ
Labour and Social Security Law: FRANCISCO LÓPEZ-TARRUELLA MARTÍNEZ
Mercantile and Procedural Law: JOSÉ MARÍA ASCENCIO MELLADO
General and Specialized Education: NARCISO SAULEDA PARES
Economic and Financial Studies: MARÍA TERESA SOLER ROCH
Ecology: JUAN FRANCISCO BELLOT ABAD
Applied Economics and Economic Policy: DIEGO SUCH PÉREZ
Finance, Accounting and Marketing: JOSÉ CARLOS GÓMEZ SALA
Nursing: LUIS CIBANAL JUAN
Statistics and Operational Research: MARGARITA RODRÍGUEZ ÁLVAREZ
Technical Drawing and Cartography: ANTONIO GONZÁLEZ CABEZAS
Catalan: ENRIC BALAGUER PASCUAL
Spanish Language, General Linguistics and Theory of Literature: MARÍA ANTONIA MARTÍNEZ LINARES
English: VICTORIA GUILLÉN NIETO
Integrated Philologies: MARIA ÁNGELES SIRVENT RAMOS
Philosophy of Law and Private International Law: JOSEP AGUILÓ REGLA
Applied Physics: JUAN ANTONIO MIRALLES TORRES
Physics, Systems Engineering and Signal Theory: AUGUSTO BELÉNDEZ VÁZQUEZ
Physiology, Genetics and Microbiology: ANDRÉS MORALES CALDERÓN
Principles of Economic Analysis: ANTONIO VILLAR
Human Geography: VICENTE GOZÁLVEZ PÉREZ

Medieval and Modern History: ARMANDO ALBEROLA ROMA
Contemporary Humanities: GLICERIO SÁNCHEZ RECIO
Construction Engineering, Public Works and Urban Infrastructure: JOSÉ MIGUEL SAVAL PÉREZ
Chemical Engineering: FRANCISCO RUIZ BEVIA
Innovation and Teacher Training: SALVADOR LLINARES CISCAR
Optics: CARLOS ILLUECA CONTRI
Computer Languages and Systems: MANUEL PALOMAR SANZ
Applied Mathematics: JOSÉ MANUEL FERRANDIZ LEAL (acting)
Business Organization: ENRIQUE CLAVER CORTES
Prehistory, Archaeology, Ancient History, Greek and Latin: LORENZO ABAD CASAL
Psychology of Health: ABILIO REIG FERRER
Analytical Chemistry: JOSÉ MARÍA SANTIAGO PÉREZ
Inorganic Chemistry: DIEGO CAZORLA AMORÓS
Organic Chemistry: CARMEN NÁJERA DOMINGO
Physical Chemistry: ANTONIO ALDAZ RIERA
Public Health: JUAN ANDRÉS NOLASCO BONMATÍ
Sociology I and Theory of Education: MARÍA TERESA ALGADO FERRER
Sociology II, Psychology, Communication and Education: JUAN LUIS CASTEJÓN COSTA
Information Technology and Computation: JUAN MANUEL GARCÍA CHAMIZO
Social Work and Social Services: MARÍA ASUNCIÓN MARTÍNEZ ROMÁN

ATTACHED INSTITUTES

University Institute of Geography: e-mail inst.geografia@ua.es; internet www.ua.es/institutos/inst.geografia/iug.htm; Dir ANTONIO GIL OLCINA.

University Institute of Water and Environmental Sciences: e-mail sti@ua.es; internet www.ua.es/iuaca/inicio.htm; Dir DANIEL PRATS RICO.

Inter-university Institute of Valencian Philology: e-mail inst.filovalen@ua.es; internet www.ua.es/institutos/inst/filovalen/iifv.htm; Dir Dr JOAN J. PONSODA.

Inter-university Institute of International Economics: Edificio de Institutos Universitarios, Campus de San Vicente del Raspeig, Apdo Correos 99, 03080 Alicante; tel. 965-90-35-82; fax 965-90-38-16; e-mail iei@ua.es; internet iei.ua.es; Dir GLORIA PARDO ALÉS.

Women's Studies Centre: tel. 965-90-94-15; fax 965-90-98-03; e-mail cem@ua.es; internet www.ua.es/cem; Dir Prof. SILVIA CAPORALE BIZZINI.

Latin American Centre for Biodiversity: CIBIO, Apdo Correos 99, 03080 Alicante; tel. 965-90-96-07; fax 965-90-38-15; e-mail cibio@ua.es; internet carn.ua.es/CIBIO/cibiocast.html; Dir Dr EDUARDO GALANTE.

Education Sciences Institute: Universidad de Alicante, Apdo Correos 99, 03080 Alicante; tel. 965-90-35-20; fax 965-90-36-84; e-mail ice@ua.es; internet www.ua.es/ice; Dir MARÍA DE LOS ÁNGELES MARTÍNEZ RUIZ.

International Maritime Institute of Alicante: Centro de Simulación de Maniobra y Navegación, Avda Ramón y Cajal 4, 03001 Alicante; tel. 965-14-59-59; fax 965-14-59-58; e-mail imia@ua.es; internet www.ua.es/imia; Dir (vacant).

Group for Studies on Peace and Development: Departamento de Sociología II, Universidad de Alicante, Apdo Correos 99, 03080 Alicante; internet www.ua.es/es/cultura/gepyd; Co-ordinator Prof. CLEMENTE PENALVA.

University Institute of Criminology: Campus San Vicente del Raspeig, Apdo 99, 03080 Alicante; tel. 965-90-35-68; fax 965-90-94-69; e-mail inst.criminologia@ua.es; internet www.ua.es/criminologia; Dir Prof. Dr CARMEN JUANATEY DORADO.

Valencian Institute of Economic Research: C/ Guardia Civil 22 esc. 2 1°, 46020 Valencia; tel. 96-319-00-50; fax 96-319-00-55; e-mail ivie@ivie.es; internet www.ivie.es; Dir of Research Prof. Dr FRANCISCO PÉREZ GARCÍA; Man. Dir DANIEL ROMERO MOLINS.

UNIVERSIDAD DE ALMERÍA

Ctra Sacramento s/n, La Cañada de San Urbano, 04120 Almería

Telephone: 950-01-50-00
E-mail: aagg@ual.es
Internet: www.ual.es

Founded 1993
State control

Rector (vacant)
Vice-Rector (Students): JUAN JOSÉ GIMÉNEZ MARTÍNEZ
Vice-Rector (University Extension): CARLOS ASENSIO GRIMA
Vice-Rector (Planning and Infrastructure): JOAQUÍN A. URDA CARDONA
Vice-Rector (International Relations): MANUEL JAÉN GARCÍA
Registrar: RAMÓN HERRERA CAMPOS
Manager: FERNANDO CONTRERAS IBÁÑEZ

Publications: *Nimbus* (climatology and meteorology, 2 a year), *Odisea* (English studies, annually)

DEANS

Faculty of Experimental Sciences: CARMEN FRANCISCA BARÓN BRAVO
Faculty of Humanities and Education: ANTONIO DANIEL FUENTES GONZÁLEZ
Faculty of Law: JOSÉ MARÍA VÁZQUEZ GARCÍA-PEÑUELA
Faculty of Economics and Business: FRANCISCO DE ASÍS LÓPEZ CRUCES
Polytechnic University College: JOSÉ LUIS CALLEJÓN BAENA (Dir)
University School of Nursing: JOSEFA MÁRQUEZ MEMBRIVE (Dir)

HEADS OF DEPARTMENTS

Algebra and Mathematical Analysis: ANTONIO JIMÉNEZ VARGAS
Applied Biology: RAFAEL LOZANO RUIZ
Vegetal Biology and Ecology: MIGUEL CUETO ROMERO
Human and Social Sciences: FRANCISCO CHECA OLMOS
Law I (Private Law): PEDRO RESINA SOLA
Law III (Public Law): JAVIER ROLDÁN BARBERO
Teaching Language, Literature and Social Sciences: JOSÉ MIGUEL MARTÍNEZ LÓPEZ
Teaching Mathematics and Experimental Sciences: MA. FRANCISCA MORENO CARRETERO
Teaching and School Organization: JUAN FERNÁNDEZ SIERRA
Applied Economics: AGUSTÍN MOLINA MORALES
Soil Science and Agricultural Chemistry: JUAN A. SÁNCHEZ GARRIDO
Nursing: CARMEN GONZÁLEZ CANALEJO
Statistics and Applied Mathematics: RAMÓN CARREÑO CARREÑO
Spanish and Latin: LUIS CORTÉS RODRÍGUEZ
French, General Linguistics and Teaching Expression: FRANCISCO J. GARCÍA MARCOS
English and German: JUAN JOSÉ TORRES NÚÑEZ
Applied Physics: FRANCISCO JAVIER DE LAS NIEVES LÓPEZ

Geometry, Topology and Organic Chemistry: FERNANDO LÓPEZ ORTIZ
Hydrogeology and Analytical Chemistry: JOSÉ LUIS MARTÍNEZ VIDAL
History, Geography and History of Art: FRANCISCO ANDÚJAR CASTILLO
Chemical Engineering: EMILIO MOLINA GRIMA
Rural Engineering: JOSÉ ANTONIO SALINAS ANDÚJAR
Languages and Computation: SAMUEL TÚNEZ RODRÍGUEZ
Personality, Evaluation and Psychological Treatment: JESÚS GIL ROALES-NIETO
Vegetal Production: JULIO CESAR TELLO MARQUINA
Evolutionary and Educational Psychology: FRANCISCO MIRAS MART
Physical Chemistry, Biochemistry and Inorganic Chemistry: EMILIO GONZÁLEZ PRADAS

UNIVERSIDAD INTERNACIONAL DE ANDALUCÍA

Rectorado de la Universidad, Sede de la Cartuja, Monasterio Santa María de las Cuevas, C/ Americo Vespucio 2, Isla de la Cartuja, 41092 Seville

Telephone: 954-46-22-99
Fax: 954-46-22-88
E-mail: cartuja@unia.es
Internet: www.unia.es

Founded 1994

Rector: JOSÉ MARÍA MARTÍN DELGADO
Vice-Rector (Academic Organization and Teaching Staff): SEBASTIÁN CHAVEZ DE DIEGO
Vice-Rector (Institutional Relations): ANTONIO J. DURÁN GUARDEÑO
Vice-Rector (International Relations): SALVADOR MONTESA PEYDRO
Vice-Rector (Research and New Technologies): ANGEL PÉREZ GÓMEZ
Registrar: ESTEBAN MORENO TORAL
Manager: LUISA MARGARITA RANCAÑO MARTÍN.

CAMPUSES OF THE UNIVERSITY

Sede Antonio Machado

Plaza de Santa María s/n, 34440 Baeza (Jaén)

Telephone: 953-74-27-75
Fax: 953-74-29-75
E-mail: machado@unia.es

Dir: SALVADOR CRUZ ARTACHO.

Sede Iberoamericano Santa María de La Rábida

Paraje La Rábida s/n, 21819 Palos de la Frontera (Huelva)

Telephone: 959-35-04-52
Fax: 959-35-01-58
E-mail: larabida@unia.es

Dir: MARÍA ANTONIA PEÑA GUERRERO.

Sede de Málaga

Severo Ochoa 10, Parque Tecnológico de Andalucía, 20590 Málaga

Telephone: 952-02-84-11
Fax: 952-02-84-19
E-mail: cintaf.pta@unia.es.

UNIVERSIDAD ANTONIO DE NEBRIJA

Campus de la Berzosa, Hoyo de Manzanares, 28240 Madrid

Telephone: 90-232-13-22
E-mail: informa@nebrija.es
Internet: www.nebrija.com

Founded 1995
Private control

Rector: MANUEL VILLA CELLINO
Director of Academic Affairs: LUIS DÍAZ MARCOS
Chief of External Relations and Publications: JAVIER ESPINIELLA TENDERO
Director of Administration: JESÚS ROBLEDO MONASTERIO
Number of students: 2,356

DEANS

Faculty of Law, Economics and Business: EMILIO FONTELA
Faculty of Communications Science: MANUEL ROGLÁN LOMBARTE
Faculty of Applied Languages and Humanities: BRUNO PUJOL BENGOECHEA (Dir)
Polytechnic University College: ALBERTO LÓPEZ ROSADO (Dir)

UNIVERSITAT DE BARCELONA

Gran Via de les Corts Catalanes 585, 08007 Barcelona
Telephone: 93-402-11-00
Fax: 93-302-59-47
Internet: www.ub.es

Founded 1450
State control
Languages of instruction: Catalan, Castilian
Academic year: October to September

Rector: Dr JOAN TUGORES I QUES
Vice-Rector (Assistant to the Rector): Dr RAMON ALEMANY
Vice-Rector (Academic Policy): Dra NURIA CASAMITJANA
Vice-Rector (Research): Dr JORDI SURIÑACH
Vice-Rector (Scientific Policy): Dr ALBERT CASAS
Vice-Rector (Institutional Relations and Linguistic Policy): Dr JORDI MATAS
Vice-Rector (Information and Documentation Systems): Dr ANTONI SANS
Vice-Rector (Students): Dr JOAN GUARDIA
Vice-Rector (International Relations): Dr JORDI MARTINELL
Vice-Rector (Cultural Activities and Heritage): Dr SALVADOR CLARAMUNT
Vice-Rector (Institutional Projects): Dr AGUSTÍN GONZÁLEZ
Vice-Rector (Publishing): Dr GABRIEL OLIVER
Registrar: Dra ELENA LAUROBA
Manager: OLGA LANAU
Library Director: DOLORS LAMARCA MARGALEF
Number of teachers: 4,149
Number of students: 76,000

DEANS

Faculty of Dentistry: LEONARDO BERINI AYTÉS (acting)
Faculty of Fine Arts: JOSEP CERDÀ FERRE
Faculty of Library Science and Documentation: ASSUMPCIÓ ESTIVILL RIUS
Faculty of Biology: JOSEP SANCHEZ CARRALERO
Faculty of Economics and Business: MANUEL ARTÍS ORTUÑO
Faculty of Law: MIGUEL ÁNGEL APARICIO PÉREZ
Faculty of Pharmacy: VICTÒRIA GIRONA BRUMÓS
Faculty of Philology: COLOMA LLEAL GALCERAN
Faculty of Philosophy: SALVI TURRÓ I TOMÁS
Faculty of Teacher Training: GEMMA TRIBÓ TRAVERIA
Faculty of Physics: BLAI SANAHUJA PARERA
Faculty of Geography and History: PEDRO CLAVERO PARICIO
Faculty of Geology: PERE FRANCISCO SANTANACH PRAT
Faculty of Mathematics: JOAQUIN M. ORTEGA ARAMBURU
Faculty of Medicine: M. TERESA ESTRACH PANELLA

Faculty of Educational Sciences: JOAN MATEO ANDRES
Faculty of Psychology: MONTSERRAT FREIXA BLANXART
Faculty of Chemistry: FIDEL CUNILL GARCÍA

CHAIRMEN

Division of Human and Social Sciences: JESÚS CONTRERAS HERNANDEZ
Division of Legal, Economic and Social Studies: RICARD PANERO GUTIÉRREZ
Division of Experimental Sciences and Mathematics: CLAUDI MANS TEIXIDÓ
Division of Health Sciences: GASPAR LOREN EGEA
Division of Educational Sciences: GLORIA BORDONS DE PORRATA-DORIA

DIRECTORS OF UNIVERSITY SCHOOLS

School of Business Administration: JOAN FRANCESC PONT CLEMENTE
School of Nursing: MARGARITA PEYA GASCONS

DIRECTORS OF ATTACHED CENTRES

University School 'Abat Oliba' (Barcelona): FRANCISCO TARRAGÓ
Centre of Nursing 'Nuestra Señora del Mar' (Barcelona): NATIVITAT ESTEVE RIOS
Centre of Nursing 'Sant Joan de Deu' (Barcelona): ROSA MATA ROCH
Centre of Nursing 'Santa Madrona' (Barcelona): MONSERRAT TEIXIDOR FREIXA
University School of Business Administration 'Osona' (Vic): JOAN CARLES SUARI ANIORTE
Faculty of Translation and Interpreting of Osona (Vic): MARTHA TENNENT HAMILTON
Centre of Education 'Jaume Balmes' (Vic): ANTONI TORT BARDOLET
Centre of Social Work: MARTA LLOBET
School of Social Work (Barcelona): JOSEP RIDAO SEIX
Catalan National Institute for Physical Education: AUGUSTÍ BOIXEDA DE MIQUEL
University College of Higher Education in Hotel Management (Cett): XAVIER TRIADO
Centre of Higher Education in Nutrition and Dietetics: PILAR CERVERA RAL
Catalan College of Higher Education in Cinema and Audiovisual Techniques: LLUÍS TORT RAVENTÓS
Faculty of Legal and Economic Sciences of Osona: JOSEP BURGAYA

ATTACHED INSTITUTE

Institute of Educational Sciences (ICE): Dir JESÚS GARANTO ALÓS.

UNIVERSITAT AUTÒNOMA DE BARCELONA

Campus Universitari, 08193 Bellaterra (Barcelona)
Telephone: 93-581-11-11
Fax: 93-581-20-00
E-mail: informacio@uab.es
Internet: www.uab.es

Founded 1968
Regional government control
Languages of instruction: Spanish, Catalan
Academic year: September to June

Rector: LLUÍS FERRER CAUBET
Vice-Rector (Institutional Relations) and General Secretary: RAFAEL GRASA HERNÁNDEZ
Vice-Rector (Academic Affairs): DOLORS RIBA LLORET
Vice-Rector (Students and Cultural Promotion): JOAN CARBONELL MANILS
Vice-Rector (Academic, Administrative and Services Staff): JORDI MARQUET CORTÉS
Vice-Rector (Financial Affairs): SANTIAGO GUERRERO BONED
Vice-Rector (Research): JOSEP SANTALÓ PEDRO

Vice-Rector (Doctorate Studies and Continuing Education): JOAN GÓMEZ PALLARÈS
Vice-Rector (Strategic Projects): FRANCESC GÒDIA CASABLANCAS
Vice-Rector (External Relations and Inter-university Co-operation): MURIEL CASALS COUTURIER
Vice-Rector (Relations with Health Institutions): MIQUEL VILARDELL TARRÉS
Manager: MIQUEL ESPINOSA SÁENZ
Librarian: JOAN RAMÓN GÓMEZ ESCOFET

Library of 725,000 , 39,000 periodicals
Number of teachers: 2,900
Number of students: 51,650, (40,360 undergraduate, 11,290 graduate)

Publications: *Memòria de la Recerca, Anàlisi: Quaderns de Comunicació i Cultura, Anuari d'Anglès, Cuadernos de Psicología, Cuadernos de Traducción e Interpretación, Documents d'Anàlisi Geogràfica, Educar, Enrahonar: Quaderns de Filosofia, Estudios de la Antigüedad, Faventia, Medievalia, Orsis: Organismes i Sistemes, Papers: Revista de Sociologia, Quaderns de Treball, Recerca Musicològica, Quaderns de Música Històrica Catalana*

DEANS

Faculty of Letters: ELISEO SÁNCHEZ LANCIS
Faculty of Medicine: ALVAR NET CASTEL
Faculty of Educational Sciences: ANNA CROS ALAVEDRA
Faculty of Economics and Business: JORDI CABALLÉ VILELLA
Faculty of Science: ANTONI MÉNDEZ I VILA-SECA
Faculty of Law: FRANCESCA PUIGPELAT MARTÍ
Faculty of Communication Science: MARCIAL MURCIANO MARTÍNEZ
Faculty of Political Sciences and Sociology: FAUSTINO MIGUÉLEZ LOBO
Faculty of Veterinary Medicine: JOSEP GASA GASÓ
Faculty of Psychology: JORDI FERNÁNDEZ CASTRO
Faculty of Translation and Interpretation: LAURA BERENGUER ESTELLES

DIRECTORS

Engineering School: JOAN SORRIBES GOMIS
School of Business Administration of Sabadell: MANUEL ÁLVAREZ GÓMEZ
School of Computer Studies of Sabadell: REMO LUCIO SUPPI BOLDRITO
Graduate School: MARIA YSÀS SOLANES

HEADS OF DEPARTMENTS

Anglo-Germanic Philology: ALAN DAVIDSON REEVES
Animal and Plant Biology and Ecology: JORDINA BELMONTE I SOLER
Animal Health and Anatomy: FRANCISCO JAVIER CABAÑES SÁENZ
Animal Science and Food: MARÍA TERESA REYES PLA SOLER
Antiquity and Middle Ages: JOSÉ ENRIQUE RUIZ DOMÈNEC
Applied Economics: JORDI ROSELL FOXA
Applied Education: JOSEP MONTANÉ I CAPDEVILA
Art: FRANCESC DE ASSÍS CORTÉS MIR
Audiovisual Communication and Publicity: ANGEL RODRÍGUEZ BRAVO
Basic and Evolutionary Psychology and Educational Psychology: CONRADO IZQUIERDO RODRÍGUEZ
Biochemistry and Molecular Biology: JOSÉ AGUILERA ÁVILA
Business Economics: DIEGO PRIOR JIMÉNEZ
Catalan Philology: DANIEL RECASENS VIVES
Cell Biology, Physiology and Immunology: CRISTINA TEMPLADO MESEGUER
Chemical Engineering: JOSEP LÓPEZ SANTÍN
Chemistry: JOSEP ROS I BADOSA
Computing: EMILIO LUQUE FADÓN

Economics and Economic History: ISABEL
FRADERA GARRIGA
Electronic Engineering: XAVIER AYMERICH I
HUMET
French and Romance Philology: JAVIER
BLANCO ESCODA
Genetics and Microbiology: RICARDO MARCOS
DAUDER
Geography: GEMMA CANOVÉS VALIENTE
Geology: ESMERALDA CAUS GRACIA
Journalism and Communication Science:
EUGENI GIRAL QUINTANA
Mathematics: FREDERIC UTZET CIVIT
Medicine: JOAN RÚBIES I PRAT
Modern and Contemporary History: FRAN-
CESC ESPINET BURUNAT
Morphological Sciences: JOSEP DOMÈNECH
MATEU
Paediatrics, Obstetrics and Gynaecology, and
Preventive Medicine: RAMÓN CARRERAS I
COLLADO
Pathology and Animal Production: JORDI
CASAL I FÀBREGA
Pharmacology, Therapeutics and Toxicology:
ALBERT BADÍA SANCHO
Philosophy: ANNA ESTANY PROFITÓS
Physics: JOSEP ANTONI GRIFOLS GRAS
Political Science and Public Law: FRANCESC
DE ASSÍS DE CARRERAS SERRA
Private Law: MARIA ISABEL MARTÍNEZ JIMÉ-
NEZ
Psychiatry and Legal Medicine: ADOLFO
TOBEÑA PALLARÉS
Psychobiology and Methodology of Health
Sciences: MARGARITA MARTÍ NICOLOVIUS
Psychology of Health and Social Psychology:
ROSA MARIA RAICH ESCURSELL
Public Law and Historical-Juridical Sciences:
JOAN LLUÍS PIÑOL RULL
Social Anthropology and Prehistory: VICENÇ
LULL SANTIAGO
Sociology: JOSEP MARIA MASJUAN CODINA
Spanish Philology: GUILLERMO SERÉS GUIL-
LÉN
Surgery: MANUEL ARMENGOL CARRASCO
Systematic and Social Education: XAVIER
ÚCAR MARTÍNEZ
Teaching of Language, Literature and Social
Sciences: ORIOL GUASCH BOYÉ
Teaching of Mathematics and Experimental
Sciences: MARIA ESPINET BLANCH
Teaching of Musical, Plastic and Corporal
Expression: MARIA PRAT GRAU
Telecommunications and Systems Engineer-
ing: ROMUALDO MORENO ORTIZ
Translation and Interpretation: ALLISON
BEEBY LONSDALE
Veterinary Medicine and Surgery: YVONNE
ESPADA GERLACH

ATTACHED INSTITUTES

'Vincent Villar i Palasí' Institute of
Biotechnology and Biomedicine: Edifici
IBB, 08193 Bellaterra; tel. 93-581-12-33; fax
93-581-20-11; internet www.uab.es/ibb; Dir
ENRIQUE QUEROL MURILLO.

Institute of Education: Edifici del Rectorat, 08193 Bellaterra; tel. 93-581-17-08; fax
93-581-20-00; e-mail ga.ice@uab.es; internet
www.uab.es/ice; Dir NEUS SANMARTÍ PUIG.

Institute of Ocular Microsurgery: C/
Munner 10, 08022 Barcelona; tel. 93-253-
15-00; fax 93-417-13-01; e-mail imo@tising
.es; Medical Dir BORJA CORCÓSTEGUI.

Medieval Studies Institute: Edifici B,
08193 Bellaterra; tel. and fax 93-581-11-44;
e-mail i.est.medievals@uab.es; Dir JOSÉ ENRI-
QUE RUIZ DOMÈNEC.

Barraquer Institute: C/ Laforja 88, 08021
Barcelona; tel. 93-414-67-98; fax 93-414-12-
28; e-mail info@co-barraquer.es; internet
www.co-barraquer.es; Dir JOAQUÍM BARRA-
QUER.

Social and Political Sciences Institute:
C/ Mallorca 244 pral., 08008 Barcelona; tel.
93-487-10-76; fax 93-487-11-49; e-mail con
.icps@diba.es; internet www.icps.es; Manager MONTSERRAT SOLER I BORRÀS.

Dexeus Institute: Pg. Bonanova 67, 08017
Barcelona; tel. 93-227-47-46; fax 93-211-16-
54; Medical Dir BARTOLOMÉ MARTÍNEZ JOVER.

European Studies Institute: Edifici E,
08193 Bellaterra; tel. 93-581-20-16; fax 93-
581-30-63; e-mail iuee@cc.uab.es; internet
www.uab.es/iuee; Dir ESTHER BARBÉ IZUEL.

High-Energy Physics Institute: Edifici
Cn, 08193 Bellaterra; tel. 93-581-19-84; fax
93-581-19-38; e-mail secretaria@ifae.es;
internet www.uab.es/ifae; Dir ENRIQUE FER-
NÁNDEZ SÁNCHEZ.

Santa Creu and Sant Pau Hospital
Research Institute: Sant Antoni Maria
Claret 167, 08025 Barcelona; tel. 93-291-91-
04; fax 93-455-23-31; e-mail ir@santpau.es;
Dir MANUEL JOSEP BARBANOJ RODRÍGUEZ
(acting).

Inter-University Institute of Ancient
Middle Eastern Studies: Departament de
Ciències de l'Antiguitat i de l'Edat Mitjana,
Edifici B, 08193 Bellaterra; tel. 93-581-23-84;
fax 93-581-31-14; UAB Dir JORDI CORS MEYA.

Ecological Research and Forestry Centre: Edifici Cc. Àrea 9, 08193 Bellaterra; tel.
93-581-13-12; fax 93-581-13-21; e-mail
ibec0@uab.es; internet www.creaf.uab.es/
creaf/index.htm; Dir FERRAN RODÀ.

Centre for Mathematical Research: Edifici Cc, 08193 Bellaterra; tel. 93-581-10-81;
fax 93-581-22-02; e-mail crm@crm.es;
internet crm.es; Dir MANUEL CASTELLET
SOLANAS.

Centre for Demographic Studies: Edifici
E, 08193 Bellaterra; tel. 93-581-30-60; fax 93-
581-30-61; e-mail demog@cedserver.uab.es;
internet www.uab.es/ced; Dir ANNA CABRÉ.

Centre for Olympic Studies and Sports
Studies: Edifici N, 08193 Bellaterra; tel. 93-
581-19-92; fax 93-581-21-39; e-mail iceo2@cc
.uab.es; internet www.uab.es/ceoe; Dir
MIQUEL DE MORAGAS SPÀ.

Supercomputing Centre of Catalonia:
Gran Capità 2–4 (Edifici Nexus), 08034
Barcelona; tel. 93-205-64-64; fax 93-205-69-
79; internet www.cesca.es; Dir MIQUEL
HUGUET.

Computer Imaging Centre: Edifici O,
08193 Bellaterra; tel. 93-581-18-28; fax 93-
581-16-70; e-mail www@cvc.uab.es; internet
www.uab.es/cvc; Dir JUAN JOSÉ VILLANUEVA
PIPAÓN.

Institute of Metropolitan Studies of
Barcelona: Campus de Bellaterra, 08193
Bellaterra; tel. 93-961-83-61; fax 93-580-65-
72; e-mail iermb@uab.es; internet www.uab
.es/iermb; Dir JOSEP MARIA VEGARA I CARRIÓ.

Guttmann Neurorehabilitation Institute: Camí de Can Ruti s/n, 08916 Badalona;
tel. 93-497-77-00; fax 93-497-77-10; e-mail
institut@guttmann.com; internet www
.guttmann.com; Man. Dir JOSEP M. RAMÍREZ
RIBAS.

Human Rights Studies Centre: Edifici B,
08193 Bellaterra; tel. 93-581-22-43; fax 93-
581-29-88; e-mail ce.drets.humans@uab.es;
Dir TERESA FREIXES SANJUÁN.

Centre for Studies in Peace and Disar-
mament: Edifici B, Despatx B3-115, 08193
Bellaterra; tel. 93-581-24-24; fax 93-581-20-
02; e-mail ce.pau@uab.es; Dir ESTHER BARBÉ
IZUEL.

Centre for the Study of Organizations
and Economic Decisions: Edifici B, 08193
Bellaterra; tel. 93-581-17-97; fax 93-581-20-
12; e-mail code@uab.es; Dir SALVADOR BAR-
BERÀ SÀNDEZ.

Institute of Communication: Edifici N,
08193 Bellaterra; tel. 93-581-29-07; fax 93-
581-26-96; e-mail incom@blues.uab.es;
internet www.uab.es/incom; Dirs MIQUEL DE
MORAGAS I SPÀ.

Food Technology Plant: Edifici V, 08193
Bellaterra; tel. 93-581-19-56; e-mail tecn
.aliments@uab.es; internet www.uab.es/
cer-planta-tecnologia-aliments; Dir BUENA-
VENTURA GUAMIS LÓPEZ.

CSIC National Microelectronics Centre:
Campus de Bellaterra, 08193 Bellaterra; tel.
93-594-77-00; fax 93-580-14-96; e-mail info@
cnm.es; internet www.cnm.es; Dir FRANCESC
SERRA MESTRES.

CSIC Institute of Economic Analysis:
Campus de Bellaterra, 08193 Bellaterra; tel.
93-580-66-12; fax 93-580-14-52; e-mail iae@cc
.uab.es; internet www.iae-csic.uab.es; Dir
JOAN MARIA ESTEBAN MARQUILLAS.

CSIC Institute for Research into Artificial Intelligence: Campus de Bellaterra,
08193 Bellaterra; tel. 93-580-95-70; fax 93-
580-96-71; e-mail www@iiia.csic.es; internet
www.iiia.csic.es; Dir FRANCESC ESTEVA MAS-
SAGUER.

CSIC Materials Science Institute of
Barcelona: Campus de Bellaterra, 08193
Bellaterra; tel. 93-580-18-53; fax 93-580-57-
29; e-mail joan@icmab.es; internet www
.icmab.es; Dir CARLES MIRAVITLLES TORRES.

Institute of Environmental Science and
Technology: Edifici Cn, Torre C5, 4a planta
(parells), 08193 Bellaterra; tel. 93-581-29-74;
fax 93-581-33-31; e-mail icta@uab.es;
internet www.uab.es/cea; Dir XAVIER GABAR-
RELL DURANY.

Neurosciences Institute: Edifici M, 08193
Bellaterra; tel. and fax 93-581-38-61; e-mail i
.neurociencies@uab.es; Dir JOSÉ RODRÍGUEZ
ÁLVAREZ.

Parc Taulí Institute: Edifici Victòria Eugè-
nia, Parc Taulí s/n, 08208 Sabadell; tel. 93-
723-66-73; fax 93-723-49-15; e-mail ftp@cspt
.es; internet www.cspt.es; Dir JULI DE NADAL I
CAPARA.

Synchrotron Laboratory: Edifici C, 08193
Bellaterra; tel. 93-581-28-41; fax 93-581-32-
13; internet www.lls.ifae.es/indexCATALAN
.html; Dir JOAN BORDAS ORPINELL.

Centre for Studies on the Archaeological Heritage of Prehistory: Edifici B,
08193 Bellaterra; tel. 93-402-07-20; fax 93-
402-07-04; e-mail rafael.mora@uab.es;
internet www.uab.es/cepap; Dir RAFAEL
MORA TORCAL.

Centre for Studies on the Francoist and
Democratic Eras: Edifici B, 08193 Bellaterra; tel. 93-581-32-53; fax 93-581-20-01;
e-mail ce.efid@uab.es; internet www.uab.es/
cefid; Dir CARME MOLINERO RUIZ.

Animal Biotechnology and Gene Therapy Centre: tel. 93-581-10-43; fax 93-581-
20-06; Contacts FÀTIMA BOSCH, ANNA PUJOL,
PEDRO OTAEGUI, MIGUEL CHILLÓN.

Group for Sociological Studies on Daily
Life and Work: Edifici B, despatx B3/057,
08193 Bellaterra; tel. 93-581-24-05; fax 93-
581-28-27; e-mail quit@uab.es; Dir FAUSTINO
MIGUÉLEZ LOBO.

Institute of Government and Public
Policy: Edifici B, despatx B3-115, 08193
Bellaterra; tel. 93-581-34-48; fax 93-581-34-
48; e-mail gr.igop@uab.es; Dir JOAN SUBIRATS
HUMET.

PROLOPE (Proyecto Edición Lope de
Vega): Edifici B, despatx B9/122, 08193
Bellaterra; tel. 93-581-10-34; e-mail
prolope@uab.es; internet www.uab.es/
prolope; Dirs ALBERTO BLECUA, GUILLERMO
SERÉS.

Centre for Studies on the History of Science: Edifici Cc, 08193 Bellaterra; tel. 93-581-13-08; fax 93-581-20-03; e-mail cehic@uab.es; internet www.uab.es/cehic; Dir XAVIER ROQUÉ RODRÍGUEZ.

Centre for International and Intercultural Studies: Edifici E-1, 08193 Bellaterra; tel. 93-581-21-11; fax 93-581-32-66; e-mail ce.internacionals@uab.es; internet www.uab.es/ceii; Dir SEÁN GOLDEN.

Animal Health Research Centre: Facultat de Veterinària, Edifici V, 08193 Bellaterra; tel. 93-581-15-99; fax 93-581-31-42; e-mail mariano.domingo@uab.es; Dir MARIANO DOMINGO.

UNIVERSIDAD DE BURGOS

Hospital del Rey s/n, 09001 Burgos
Telephone: 947-25-87-00
Fax: 947-25-87-44
E-mail: intl@ubu.es
Internet: www.ubu.es

Founded 1994

Rector: Prof. JOSÉ MARÍA LEAL VILLALBA
Vice-Rector (Academic Organization and Teaching Staff): JUAN ALFREDO JIMÉNEZ Y EGUIZÁBAL
Vice-Rector (Students and University Extension): MARÍA TERESA DE VICO CARRANCHO HERRERO
Vice-Rector (Research and International Relations): JULIA ARCOS MARTÍNEZ
Vice-Rector (Innovation and Quality): MIGUEL ÁNGEL MANZANEDO DEL CAMPO
Vice-Rector (Management and Resources): JOSÉ ANTONIO MARTÍNEZ MARTÍNEZ
Vice-Rector (Finance): JOSÉ MANUEL VILLANUEVA SAIZ
Registrar: JOSÉ MARÍA DE LA CUESTA SÁENZ
Man.: CARLOS VILLACE FERNÁNDEZ
Library Dir: FERNANDO MARTÍN RODRÍGUEZ

Library of 100,000 vols, 1,500 periodicals
Number of students: 11,000

DEANS

Faculty of Economics and Business: JUAN MANUEL DE LA FUENTE SABATÉ
Faculty of Humanities and Education: FEDERICO SANZ DÍAZ
Faculty of Law: ALFONSO MURILLO VILLAR
Faculty of Sciences: TOMÁS TORROBA PÉREZ

DIRECTORS

School of Engineering: RICARDO RENUNCIO ANGULO
School of Labour Relations: JOSÉ ANTONIO DÍEZ VILLANUEVA
School of Nursing: MA. VICTORIA CANTÓN NOGAL

UNIVERSIDAD DE CÁDIZ

C/ Ancha 16, 11001 Cádiz
Telephone: 956-01-50-00
E-mail: jose.palao@uca.es
Internet: www.uca.es
Founded 1979
Academic year: October to July
Rector: DIEGO SALES MÁRQUEZ
Vice-Rector (Academic Staff): JOSÉ MARÍA TERRADILLOS BASOCO
Vice-Rector (Alumni): DAVID ALMORZA GOMAR
Vice-Rector (Bahía de Algeciras Campus): FRANCISCO TRUJILLO ESPINOSA
Vice-Rector (Economic Planning and Infrastructure): MANUEL LARRÁN JORGE
Vice-Rector (Research, Technological Development and Innovation): RAFAEL GARCÍA ROJAS
Vice-Rector (University Extension): VIRTUDES ATERO BURGOS
Secretary-General: MARÍA ZAMBONINO PULITO
Manager: ANTONIO VADILLO IGLESIAS (acting)

Administration Officer: JOSÉ RAMÓN REPETO GUTIÉRREZ
Library Director: MIGUEL DUARTE BARRIONUEVO (acting)

Number of teachers: 1,585
Number of students: 23,990

DEANS

Faculty of Economics and Business: HÉCTOR RAMOS ROMERO
Faculty of Educational Science: ANTONIO MORENO VERDILLA
Faculty of Labour Sciences: SEVERIANO FERNÁNDEZ RAMOS
Faculty of Law: ROCÍO DOMÍNGUEZ BARTOLOMÉ
Faculty of Marine and Environmental Sciences: MARÍA LUISA GONZÁLEZ DE CANALES GARCÍA
Faculty of Medicine: JUAN GIBERT RAHOLA
Faculty of Nautical Science: JUAN MORENO GUTIÉRREZ
Faculty of Philosophy and Letters: FRANCISCO VÁZQUEZ GARCÍA
Faculty of Sciences: FRANCISCO ANTONIO MACIAS DOMÍNGUEZ

DIRECTORS

School of Engineering: MARIANO MARCOS BARCENA
School of Naval Engineering: ALFREDO CASO GÓMEZ
School of Business Studies and Public Administration: ENRIQUE MONTAÑÉS PRIMICIA
School of Nursing and Physiotherapy of Jerez: ALBERTO PÉREZ MORENO
Higher Polytechnic School: IGNACIO TURIAS DOMÍNGUEZ
School of Nursing of Algeciras: ÁNGELES MARTELO BARO

AFFILIATED CENTRES

Centre for Higher Studies: Academic Dir ARTURO ÁLVAREZ ALARCÓN.
'Francisco Tomás y Valiente' School of Legal and Economic Studies of Algeciras: Academic Dir OCTAVIO ARIZA SÁNCHEZ.
'Salus Infirmorum' School of Nursing: Academic Dir MIGUEL ÁNGEL VELASCO GARCÍA.
School of Labour Relations, Social Work and Tourism of Jerez: Academic Dir JUAN RODRÍGUEZ GARCÍA.
'Virgen de Europa' School of Teacher Training: Academic Dir MANUEL BUSTOS RODRÍGUEZ.

UNIVERSIDAD CAMILO JOSÉ CELA

C/ Castillo de Alarcón 49, Villafranca del Castillo, 28692 Madrid
Telephone: 91-815-31-31
Fax: 91-815-31-30
E-mail: ucjc@ucjc.edu
Internet: www.ucjc.edu
Founded 1999
Private control
Rector: Dr RAFAEL CORTÉS ELVIRA
Vice-Rector (University Extension): MARÍA EUGENIA DELSO MARTÍNEZ-TREVIJANO
Library Director: BELÉN PALOMERO

HEADS OF DEPARTMENTS

Architecture: ALICIA OZAMIZ FORTIS
Technical Architecture: ALICIA OZAMIZ FORTIS
Computer Engineering: JESÚS VICENTE GUERRA
Communication: PILAR ANTOLINEZ
Psychology and Education: Dr ADOLFO SÁNCHEZ BURÓN

UNIVERSIDAD DE CANTABRIA

Avda de los Castros s/n, 39005 Santander
Telephone: 942-20-15-00
Fax: 942-20-11-03
E-mail: morenof@gestion.unican.es
Internet: www.unican.es

Founded 1972 as Universidad de Santander
State control
Language of instruction: Spanish
Academic year: October to June

Rector: FEDERICO GUTIÉRREZ-SOLANA SALCEDO
Vice-Rector (Campus, Organization and Communication): JORGE TOMILLA URBINA
Vice-Rector (Academic Organization and Teaching Staff): FRANCISCO JAVIER MARTÍNEZ GARCÍA
Vice-Rector (Student Affairs): EMILIO EGUÍA LÓPEZ
Vice-Rector (International Relations): JOSÉ MANUEL REVUELTA SOBA
Vice-Rector (Quality and Educational Innovation): BEATRIZ ARÍZAGA BOLUMBURU
Vice-Rector (University Extension): EDUARDO CASAS RENTERÍA
Vice-Rector (Research and Development): JOSÉ CARLOS GÓMEZ SAL
Registrar: LUIS GASPAR VEGA ARGÜELLES
Manager: ENRIQUE ALONSO DÍAZ
Library Director: MARÍA JESÚS SÁIZ

Number of teachers: 965
Number of students: 15,000

DEANS

Faculty of Sciences: LAUREANO GONZÁLEZ VEGA
Faculty of Medicine: JOSÉ A. AMADO SEÑARIS
Faculty of Arts: MANUEL GONZÁLEZ MORALES
Faculty of Law: JESÚS IGNACIO MARTÍNEZ GARCÍA
Faculty of Economics and Business Studies: CONCEPCIÓN LÓPEZ FERNANDEZ
Faculty of Education: TOMÁS RODRÍGUEZ FERNÁNDEZ

DIRECTORS

School of Civil Engineering: FERNANDO CAÑIZAL BERINI
School of Industrial Engineering and Telecommunications: EDUARDO MORA MONTE
School of Nautical Studies: JUAN JOSÉ ACHÚTEGUI RODRÍGUEZ
School of Teacher Training: DEMETRIO CASCÓN MARTÍNEZ
School of Mining Engineering: EDUARDO PARDO DE SANTAYANA DE LA HIDALGA
School of Nursing: CELIA NESPRAL GAZTELUMENDI
School of Labour Relations: JESÚS RAFAEL MERCADER

HEADS OF DEPARTMENTS

Anatomy and Cell Biology: JUAN MARIO HURLE GONZÁLEZ
Applied Mathematics and Computation Science: JOSÉ MANUEL GUTIÉRREZ
Applied Physics: JAIME AMORÒS ARNAU
Business Administration: BEGOÑA TORRE OLMO (acting)
Chemical Engineering and Inorganic Chemistry: IÑAKI FERNÁNDEZ OLMO
Communications Engineering: JOSE LUIS GARCÍA GARCÍA
Earth Science and Condensed Matter Physics: JOSÉ CARLOS GÓMEZ SAL
Economics: BLANCA SÁNCHEZ-ROBLES RUTE
Education: JOSÉ MANUEL OSORO SIERRA
Electrical and Energy Engineering: LUIS IGNACIO EGUÍLUZ MORÁN
Electronic Technology, Systems Engineering and Automation: SALVADOR BRACHO DEL PINO
Electronics and Computers: JOSÉ MA. DRAKE MOYANO

Geographical Engineering and Technical Drawing: FERNANDO FADÓN SALAZAR

Geography and Regional and Town Planning: PEDRO REQUES VELASCO

History: RAMÓN TEJA CASUSO

Mathematics, Statistics and Computation: LUIS ALBERTO FERNANDO

Medical and Surgical Sciences: JOSÉ MANUEL REVUELTA SOBA

Medicine and Psychiatry: JESÚS GONZÁLEZ MACÍAS

Modern and Contemporary History: JULIO POLO SÁNCHEZ

Modern Physics: MA. TERESA BARRIUSO PÉREZ

Molecular Biology: JESÚS MERINO PÉREZ

Nursing: MA. DEL PILAR SANTOS ABAUNZA

Philology: ROSARIO PORTILLO MAYORGA

Physiology and Pharmacology: ANGEL PAZOS CARRO

Private Law: JUAN BARÓ PAZOS

Public Law: CONCEPCIÓN ESCOBAR HERNÁNDEZ

Science and Technique of Navigation and Ship Construction: MARCELINO SOBRÓN IRURETAGOYENA

Soil and Materials Science and Engineering: CESAR SAGASETA MILLÁN

Structural and Mechanical Engineering: LUIS VILLEGAS CABREDO

Transport and Project and Process Engineering: MIGUEL ÁNGEL CALZADA PÉREZ (acting)

Water and Environmental Sciences: JOAQUÍN DÍEZ-CASCÓN SAGRADO

ATTACHED INSTITUTES

Institute of Education: Dir LAURENTINO SALVADOR BLANCO.

Cantabria Physics Institute: Dir JESÚS MARCO.

Leonardo Torres Quevedo Foundation: Man. JORGE MEDINA LÓPEZ.

UNIVERSIDAD CARDENAL HERRERA-C.E.U.

Edificio Seminario s/n, 46113 Moncada (Valencia)

Telephone: 96-136-90-00

Fax: 96-139-52-72

E-mail: informa@uch.ceu.es

Internet: www.uch.ceu.es

Founded 1999

Private control

Rector: ALFONSO BULLÓN DE MENDOZA Y GÓMEZ DE VALUGERA

Vice-Rector (University Extension and Student Affairs): MA. ISABEL DE SALAS NESTARES

Vice-Rector (Academic Affairs and Teaching Staff): JOSÉ VICENTE PREDRAZA BOCHONS

Vice-Rector (Research and Development): JAVIER ROMERO GÓMEZ

Registrar: FEDERICO MARTÍNEZ RODA

Manager: BARTOLOMÉ SERRA MARQUÉS

Library Director: ELENA SAURÍ RODRIGO

Library of 52,973 vols, 1,266 periodicals

DEANS

Faculty of Social Sciences and Law: ROSA VISIEDO CLAVEROL

Faculty of Experimental Sciences and Health: SANTIAGO VEGA GARCÍA

DIRECTORS

Higher School of Technical Tuition: JOSÉ LUIS FERRER MUÑOZ

Centre at Elche: FRANCISCO SÁNCHEZ MARTÍNEZ

HEADS OF DEPARTMENTS

Faculty of Social Sciences and Law:

Journalism: BEGOÑA ECHEVARRIA LLOMBART

Law: JAVIER GARCÍA GONZÁLEZ

Advertising and Public Relations: MA. JOSÉ GONZÁLEZ SOLAZ

Audiovisual Communication: SANTIAGO MAESTRO CANO

Politics and Administration: IGNACIO SEVILLA MERINO

Faculty of Experimental Sciences and Health:

Pharmacy: NURIA DE LA MUELA GIL

Dentistry: MA. CARMEN LLENA PUY

Nursing: LORETO PEYRO GREGORI

Physiotherapy: PEDRO ROSADO CALATALUD

Veterinary Science: JOAQUÍN SOPENA JUNCOSA

Higher School of Technical Tuition:

Technical Engineering in Industrial Design: FERNANDO SÁNCHEZ LÓPEZ

Technical Engineering in Management Information Science: GUSTAVO SALVADOR HERRANZ

Arquitecture: SALVADOR LÓPEZ ALFONSO

Centre at Elche:

Law: EMILIA IÑESTA PASTOR (Co-ordinator)

Journalism: JORDI PÉREZ LLAVADOR (Co-ordinator)

Nursing: MODESTA SALAZAR AGULLÓ (Co-ordinator)

ATTACHED SCHOOL

San Pablo Business School: Palacio de Colomina, Almudín 1, 46003 Valencia; tel. 96-315-63-06; fax 96-391-86-84; e-mail env@env.ceu.es; internet www.env.ceu.es; Dir RAFAEL OLCINA REIG.

UNIVERSIDAD CARLOS III DE MADRID

Calle Madrid 126, 28903 Getafe, Madrid

Telephone: 91-624-95-00

Fax: 91-624-97-57

Internet: www.uc3m.es

Founded 1989

State control

Language of instruction: Spanish, English

Academic year: September to June

Rector: DANIEL PEÑA SANCHEZ

Vice-Rector (Teaching Staff, Graduate Affairs and Depts): JUAN JOSÉ ROMO URROZ

Vice-Rector (Academic Organization): ZULIMA FERNÁNDEZ RODRÍGUEZ

Vice-Rector (Co-ordination): LUCIANO PAREJO ALFONSO

Vice-Rector (Research and Innovation): FRANCISCO JOSÉ MARCELLÁN ESPAÑOL

Vice-Rector (Academic Infrastructures): JOSÉ MANUEL TORRALBA CASTELLÓ

Vice-Rector (University Extension): MERCEDES CARIDAD SEBASTIÁN

Vice-Rector (Cultural Activities, Sport and Residences): SANTIAGO AREAL LUDEÑA

Vice-Rector (International and Institutional Relations and Communication): ANGEL LLAMAS CASCÓN

Vice-Rector (Student Affairs): CARLOS R. FERNÁNDEZ LIESA

Vice-Rector (Director of Specific Programmes and Humanities Courses): JOSÉ ANTONIO PASCUAL RODRÍGUEZ

Vice-Rector (Colmenarejo Campus): AGUSTÍN EUGENIO ASÍS ROIG

Registrar: LUCIANO JOSÉ PAREJO ALFONSO

Manager: RAFAEL ZORRILLA TORRÁS

Librarian: MARGARITA TALADRIZ MÁS

Number of teachers: 1,226

Number of students: 16,000

Publications: *Cuadernos del Instituto Antonio de Nebrija, Derechos y Libertades* (published by 'Bartolomé de las Casas' Institute of Human Rights), *Cuadernos Bartolomé de las Casas* (published by 'Bartolomé de las Casas' Institute of Human Rights), *Revista española de derecho internacional* (published by 'Francisco de Vitoria Institute of International and

European Studies'), *Diagnóstico de la economía española* (published by 'Flores de Lemus Institute of Advance Studies in Economics'), *Safo* (published by 'Safo Cultural Association and Service of Young Information of the University'), *Semiosfera* (published by 'Miguel de Unamuno Institute of Culture and Technology'), *Boletín*, *Revista Carlos III*

DEANS

Faculty of Social and Juridical Sciences: Prof. Dr ALVARO ESCRIBANO SÁEZ

Faculty of Humanities and Communications: Prof. Dr ANTONIO RODRÍGUEZ DE LAS HERAS

Higher Polytechnical School: Prof. Dr CARLOS NAVARRO UGENA

ATTACHED INSTITUTES

'Bartolomé de las Casas' Institute of Human Rights: Dir Prof Dr RAFAEL DE ASIS ROIG.

'Miguel de Unamuno' Institute of Culture and Technology: Dir Prof. Dr ANTONIO RODRÍGUEZ DE LAS HERAS.

'Pascual Madoz' Institute of Territorial, Urban and Environmental Studies: Dir Prof. Dr LUCIANO PAREJO ALFONSO.

University Institute of Law and Economics: Dir (vacant).

'Flores de Lemus' Institute of Advanced Studies in Economics: Dir Prof. Dr ANTONI ESPASA TERRADES.

'Francisco de Vitoria' Institute of International and European Studies: Dir Prof. Dr FERNANDO MARIÑO MENÉNDEZ.

'Augustín Millares' Institute of Documentation and Information Management: Dir Profa. Dra MERCEDES CARIDAD SEBASTIÁN.

'Antonio de Nebrija' Institute of University Studies: Dir Profa. Dra ADELA MORA CAÑADA.

'Manuel García Pelayo' Institute of Comparative Public Law: Dir Prof. Dr PABLO PÉREZ TREMPS.

'Pedro Juan de Lastanosa' Institute of Technological Development and the Promotion of Innovation: Dir Prof. Dr FERNANDO LÓPEZ MARTÍNEZ.

'Juan Luis Vives' Institute of Social Security: Dir Prof. Dr SANTIAGO GONZÁLEZ ORTEGA.

Institute of Automotive Vehicle Safety: Dir Prof. Dr VICENTE DÍAZ.

'Álvaro Alonso Barba' Technological Institute of Chemistry and Materials: Dir Prof. Dr JUAN BASELGA LLIDÓ.

Interuniversity Institute for Cultural Communication: Dirs Prof. Dr LUCIANO PAREJO ALFONSO, Prof. Dr JESÚS PRIETO DE PEDRO, Prof. Dr MARCOS VAQUER CABALLERÍA, Prof. Dr HONORIO VELASCO MAILLO.

'Duque de Ahumada' University Institute for Studies in Safety: Dir Prof. Dr MANUEL ABELLÁN VELASCO.

UNIVERSIDAD DE CASTILLA–LA MANCHA

C/ Altagracia 50, 13071 Ciudad Real

Telephone: 902-20-41-00

Fax: 902-20-41-30

E-mail: informacion@uclm.es

Internet: www.uclm.es

Founded 1982

State control

Language of instruction: Spanish

Academic year: October to June

Rector: Prof Dr ERNESTO MARTÍNEZ ATAZ

Vice-Rector (Co-ordination, Economic Affairs and Communication): Prof. Dr JESÚS FERNANDO SANTOS PEÑALVER

Vice-Rector (Infrastructure and Business Development): Prof. Dr ANTONIO DE LUCAS MARTÍNEZ

Vice-Rector (Studies and Programmes): Prof. Dr MIGUEL ÁNGEL COLLADO YURRITA

Vice-Rector (European Convergence and Academic Organization): Profa Dra CARMEN FENOLL COMES

Vice-Rector (Teaching Staff): Prof. Dr PABLO CAÑIZARES CAÑIZARES

Vice-Rector (Research): Prof. Dr FRANCISCO JOSÉ QUILES FLOR

Vice-Rector (Students): Profa Dra MA. ÁNGELES ALCALÁ DÍAZ

Vice-Rector (Entrepreneurial Projects and Albacete Campus): Prof. Dr ANTONIO RONCERO SÁNCHEZ

Vice Rector (Cultural Co-operation and Ciudad Real Campus): Prof. Dr FRANCISCO ALIA MIRANDA

Vice-Rector (University Extension and Cuenca Campus): Prof. Dr JOSÉ IGNACIO ALBENTOSA HERNÁNDEZ

Vice-Rector (Institutional Relations and Toledo Campus): Profa Dra EVANGELINA ARANDA GARCÍA

Vice-Rector (International Relations): Prof. Dr PUBLIO PINTADO SANJUÁN

Registrar: Prof. Dr JUAN RAMÓN DE PÁRAMO ARGÜELLES

Chief Administrative Officer: JOSÉ LUIS GONZÁLEZ QUEJIGO

Librarian: FRANCISCO ALIA MIRANDA

Number of teachers: 2,101
Number of students: 28,713

Publication: *Info-Campus* (monthly)

DEANS

Faculty of Economics and Business Sciences (Albacete): MIGUEL RAMÓN PARDO PARDO

Faculty of Law (Albacete): MARINA GASCÓN ABELLÁN

Faculty of Humanities (Albacete): MIGUEL PANADERO MOYA

Faculty of Medicine (Albacete): JORGE LABORDA FERNÁNDEZ

Faculty of Chemical Sciences (Ciudad Real): ANTONIO ANTIÑOLO GARCÍA

Faculty of Law and Social Sciences: ENRIQUE VIAÑA REMIS

Faculty of Arts (Ciudad Real): ELENA GONZÁLEZ CÁRDENAS

Faculty of Fine Arts (Cuenca): VICENTE JARQUE SORIANO

Faculty of Education Sciences and Humanities (Cuenca): MA. DEL CARMEN POYATO HOLGADO

Faculty of Social Sciences (Cuenca): MARÍA ÁNGELES ZURILLA CARIÑANA

Faculty of Sport Sciences (Toledo): FERNANDO SÁNCHEZ BAÑUELOS

Faculty of Environmental Sciences (Toledo): FEDERICO FERNÁNDEZ GONZÁLEZ

Faculty of Juridical and Social Sciences (Toledo): TIMOTEO MARTÍNEZ AGUADO

Faculty of Humanities (Toledo): RICARDO IZQUIERDO BENITO

DIRECTORS

Higher Polytechnic University College (Albacete): ANTONIO GARRIDO DEL SOLO

Higher Technical College of Agronomist Engineering (Albacete): FRANCISCO MONTERO RIQUELME

University College of Nursing (Albacete): CARMEN ORTEGA MARTÍNEZ

University College of Teacher Training (Albacete): PEDRO LOSA SERRANO

University College of Labour Relations (Albacete): JOAQUÍN APARICIO TOVAR

Higher Technical College of Industrial Engineers (Ciudad Real): VICENTE FELIU BATLLE

Higher University College of Computer Science (Ciudad Real): JUAN CARLOS LÓPEZ LÓPEZ

Higher Technical College of Civil Engineering (Ciudad Real): JOSÉ MARÍA UREÑA FRANCÉS

Polytechnic University College of Almadén (Ciudad Real): LUIS MANSILLA PLAZA

University College of Nursing (Ciudad Real): CARMEN PRADO LAGUNA

University College of Teacher Training (Ciudad Real): ANGEL GREGORIO CANOVELA

University College of Technical Agricultural Engineering (Ciudad Real): ROCÍO GÓMEZ GÓMEZ

University College of Nursing (Cuenca): VICENTE MARTÍNEZ VIZCAÍNO

University College of Teacher Training (Cuenca): MARTÍN MUELAS HERRAÍZ

University College of Social Work (Cuenca): FERNANDO CASAS MÍNGUEZ

Polytechnic University College (Cuenca): MIGUEL ÁNGEL LÓPEZ GUERRERO

Centre of University Studies of Talavera de la Reina (Toledo): PEDRO JIMÉNEZ ESTÉVEZ

University College of Nursing and Physiotherapy (Toledo): CARMEN LÓPEZ BALBOA

University College of Teacher Training (Toledo): RAMÓN SÁNCHEZ GONZÁLEZ

University College of Industrial Technical Engineering: ANTONIO CLAMAGIRAND SÁNCHEZ

DIRECTORS OF DEPARTMENTS

Agroforestry Science and Technology: LAUREANO GALLEGO MARTÍNEZ

Analytical Chemistry and Food Technology: MARÍA DOLORES CABEZUDO IBÁÑEZ

Applied Mechanics and Project Engineering: MAGÍN LAPUERTA AMIGO

Applied Physics: JOSÉ MANUEL RIVEIRO CORONA

Arts: JOSÉ MARÍA LILLO PÉREZ

Chemical Engineering: JOSE LUIS VALVERDE PALOMINO

Computer Science: FERNANDO CUARTERO GÓMEZ

Crop Production and Agricultural Technology: JOSÉ MARÍA HERRANZ SANZ

Economics and Business: JOSÉ VICTOR GUARNIZO GARCÍA

Electric and Electronic Engineering: BALDOMERO GONZÁLEZ SÁNCHEZ

Environmental Sciences: JOSÉ MANUEL MORENO RODRÍGUEZ

Geography and Territory Ordination: MIGUEL PANADERO MOYA

Geological and Mining Engineering: JOSÉ MARÍA IRAIZOZ FERNÁNDEZ

Hispanic and Classical Philology: ANGELES CARRASCO GUTIERREZ

History: JUAN SISINIO PÉREZ GARZÓN

History of Art: MIGUEL CORTES ARRESE

Inorganic and Organic Chemistry and Biochemistry: ANTONIO DE LA HOZ AYUSO

Juridical Science: ANTONIO BAYLOS GRAU

Mathematics: VÍCTOR MANUEL PÉREZ GARCÍA

Medical Sciences: CARMEN DÍAZ DELGADO

Modern Philology: SILVIA MOLINA PLAZA

Nursing and Physiotherapy: VICTORIA DELICADO USEROS

Pedagogy: ANTONIO MATEOS JIMÉNEZ

Philosophy: JULIÁN CARVAJAL CORDÓN

Physical Chemistry: JOSÉ ALBADALEJO PÉREZ

Psychology: JUAN MONTAÑÉS RODRÍGUEZ

Teaching of Music, Plastic and Body Expression: ONOFRE RICARDO CONTRERAS

UNIVERSITAT OBERTA DE CATALUNYA

Avda Tibidabo 39–43, 08035 Barcelona
Telephone: 93-253-23-00
Fax: 93-471-64-95
Internet: www.uoc.edu

Founded 1995

Rector: GABRIEL FERRATÉ

Vice-Rector (Academic Policy and Teaching Staff): CARLES SIGALÉS

Vice-Rector (Research, Innovation and Educational Methodology): FRANCESC VALLVERDÚ

Vice-Rector (Institutional Relations and Cultural Politics): JOAN FUSTER

Vice-Rector (International Relations): FRANCISCO RUBIO

General Manager: XAVIER ARAGAY

Librarian: ADORACIÓ PEREZ

Library of 17,900 vols
Number of teachers: 120
Number of students: 25,000

DIRECTORS

Business Administration and Economics: JORDI VILASECA REQUENA

Humanities: ISIDOR MARÍ

Law: JOAN PRATS

Documentation: AGUSTÍNO CANALS PARERA

Educational Psychology: CARLES SIGALÉS CONDE

Psychology: JORDI MENÉNDEZ PABLO

Software Engineering: RAFAEL MACAU

UNIVERSIDAD PONTIFICIA 'COMILLAS'

Calle Alberto Aguilera 23, 28015 Madrid
Telephone: 91-542-28-00
Fax: 91-559-65-69
E-mail: oia@oia.upco.es
Internet: www.upco.es

Founded by Pope Leo XIII; classes commencing at Comillas, Santander, in 1890; the right to confer degrees was granted in 1904; moved to Madrid in 1960

Private control (Society of Jesus)
Language of instruction: Spanish
Academic year: October to June

Grand Chancellor: R. P. PETER-HANS KOLVENBACH

Rector: Dr JOSÉ RAMÓN BUSTO SAIZ

Vice-Rector (Academic Organization and Teaching Staff): Dra BELÉN UROSA SANZ

Vice-Rector (Economic Affairs): Dr CECILIO MORAL BELLO

Vice-Rector (Extension and Services to the University Community): Dra CRISTINA GORTÁZAR ROTAECHE

Vice-Rector (Research, Development and Innovation): Dra ANGELA JIMÉNEZ CASAS

Registrar: Dra ANA SOLER PRESAS

Librarian: EUSEBIO GIL CORIA

Number of teachers: 1,787
Number of students: 10,223

Library of 550,000 vols

Publications: *Estudios Eclesiásticos* (4 a year), *ICADE* (4 a year), *Migraciones* (2 a year), *Miscelánea Comillas* (3 a year), *Pensamiento* (3 a year)

DEANS

Faculty of Canon Law: Dr JESÚS SANTIAGO MADRIGAL TERRAZAS

Faculty of Economics and Business: Dra MA. JOSEFA PERALTA ASTUDILLO

Faculty of Human and Social Sciences: Dr MIGUEL JUÁREZ GALLEGO

Faculty of Law: Dr ANTONIO OBREGÓN GARCÍA

Faculty of Theology: Dr JESÚS SANTIAGO MADRIGAL TERRAZAS

DIRECTORS

Higher Technical School of Engineering: Dr Ing. FERNANDO DE CUADRA GARCÍA

San Juan de Dios University School of Nursing and Physiotherapy: Dr JULIO VIELVA ASEJO, ROSA FERNÁNDEZ AYUSO (Technical Director in Ciempozuelos)

School of Legal Practice: EDUARDO MOLINA ESTEBAN

Institute of Technological Research: Dr MICHEL RIVIER ABBAD

Institute of Computing in Law: Dr MIGUEL ANGEL DAVARA RODRÍGUEZ

Institute for Research into Liberalism, Krausism and Freemasonry: Dr ENRIQUE MENÉNDEZ UREÑA

Institute of Postgraduate Studies and Continuing Education: Dr CECILIO MORAL BELLO

Institute of Education: Dra ROSA SALAS LABAYEN

University Institute of Migration Studies: Dr JULIO LUIS MARTÍNEZ MARTÍNEZ

Institute of Modern Languages: MARCELLA C. CHARTRAND TUOHY

University Institute of the Family: Dra MARÍA ISABEL ALVAREZ VÉLEZ

University Institute of Spirituality: Dr PASCUAL CEBOLLADA SILVESTRE

ATTACHED INSTITUTES

Instituto Superior de Ciencias Morales: Calle Félix Boix 13, 28016 Madrid.

Estudio Teológico Agustiniano: Paseo de Filipinos 7, 47007 Valladolid.

Estudio Teológico del Seminario Mayor Diocesano: Carretera de Porzuna s/n, 13002 Ciudad Real.

Estudio Teológico Claretiano: Juan Alvarez Mendizal 65 Duplicado, 1° 28008 Madrid.

Centro Teológico de Las Palmas de Gran Canaria: Seminario Mayor, 35001 Las Palmas de Gran Canaria.

Estudio Teológico Monseñor Romero: Apdo Postal (01) 168, San Salvador El Salvador (Central America).

Estudio Teológico del Seminario Mayor de Logroño: Seminario Mayor, Apdo de Correos 150, 26080 Logroño.

Estudio Teológico del Seminario Mayor de Córdoba: Amador de los Ríos 1, 14004 Córdoba.

Estudio Teológico del Seminario Mayor 'Tagaste': Padres Agustinos, Santa Emilia 10, 28409 Los Negrales (Madrid).

Instituto Fe y Secularidad: Diego de León 33, 28006 Madrid.

Instituto Internacional de Teología a Distancia: José Ortega y Gasset 62, 1°, 28006 Madrid.

Instituto Superior de Ciencias Religiosas 'San Agustin': José Ortega y Gasset 62, 1°, 28006 Madrid.

ASSOCIATED INSTITUTIONS; THERE ARE OTHER THEOLOGICAL AND PHILOSOPHICAL FACULTIES IN SPAIN CONFERRING DEGREES, WHICH ARE PARTLY ASSOCIATED WITH THE PONTIFICAL UNIVERSITIES, AS FOLLOWS:

Facultad de Teología

Apdo 2002, 18080 Granada

Telephone: 958-18-52-52

Fax: 958-16-25-59

E-mail: info@teol-granada.com

Internet: www.teol-granada.com

Founded 1939

Academic year: October to July

Grand Chancellor: R. P. PETER-HANS KOLVENBACH

Vice-Grand Chancellor: R. P. FRANCISCO JOSÉ RUIZ PÉREZ

Rector: Prof. ILDEFONSO CAMACHO LARAÑA

Vice-Rector (Academic): Prof. JOSÉ LUIS SÁNCHEZ NOGALES

Vice-Rector (Institutional Relations): Prof. JOSÉ LUIS SÁNCHEZ NOGALES

Registrar: CARLOS JAVIER PALOMEQUE BAENA

Librarian: GABRIEL VERD CONRADI

Library of 350,000 vols

Number of teachers: 36

Number of students: 551

Publications: *Archivo Teológico Granadino* (Post-Tridentine theology, 4 a year), *Proyección* (4 a year)

PROFESSORS

ALARCOS MARTÍNEZ, F., Moral Theology

BERDUGO VILLENA, T., Latin

BORREGO PIMENTEL, E., Philosophy

CAMACHO LARAÑA, I., Moral Theology

CARNERERO LARAÑA, I., Canon Law

CASTÓN BOYER, P., Sociology

CONTRERAS MOLINA, F., Scripture

DOMÍNGUEZ MORANO, C., Psychology

GARCÍA GÓMEZ, M., Moral Theology

GERVILLA CASTILLO, E., Pedagogy

GRANADO BELLIDO, C., Patrology and Dogmatic Theology

HERNÁNDEZ MARTÍNEZ, J., Dogmatic Theology

JIMÉNEZ ORTIZ, A., Fundamental Theology

LEÓN, T., Theology

LÓPEZ AZPITARTE, E., Moral Theology

LÓPEZ CUERVO, T., Greek

MARTÍNEZ MEDINA, J., Ecclesiastical Art

MOLINA MOLINA, D., Dogmatic Theology

NAVAS GUTIÉRREZ, A., Ecclesiastical History

NUÑEZ DE CASTRO GARCÍA, I., Philosophy

PEINADO MUÑOZ, M., Scripture

PÉREZ NIETO, J., Philosophy

POZO, C., Dogmatic Theology

RODRÍGUEZ CARMONA, A., Scripture

RODRÍGUEZ IZQUIERDO, J. M., Liturgy

ROJAS GÁLVEZ, I., Scripture

ROMÁN MARTÍNEZ, M. C., Scripture

SÁNCHEZ NOGALES, J. M., Liturgy

SEQUEIROS SANROMÁN, L., Philosophy

SICRE DÍAZ, J. L., Scripture

SOTOMAYOR MURO, M., Ecclesiastical History, Christian Archaeology

VÍCHEZ LÍNDEZ, J., Dogmatic Theology, Scripture

VOLO PÉREZ, R., Scripture

ATTACHED INSTITUTES

Instituto Superior de Ciencias Religiosas 'Tomás Sánchez': Apdo 2002, 18080 Granada; Rector ANTONIO M. NAVAS GUTIÉRREZ.

Instituto Superior de Ciencias Religiosas 'San Pablo': Santa María 20, 29015 Málaga; Rector ILDEFONSO CAMACHO LARAÑA.

Centro Diocesano de Teología de Málaga: Calle Toquero 20, 29013 Málaga; Rector (vacant).

Centro de Estudios Teológicos: Avda Cardenal Buenomonreal 43, 41012 Seville; Rector LUIS F. ALVAREZ.

Centro de Estudios Teológicos: Juan Montilla 1, 23002 Jaén; Rector MANUEL RUIZ CARRERO.

Centro de Estudios Teológicos: Compañía s/n, 11005 Cádiz; Rector JESÚS J. GARCÍA CORNEJO.

Centro de Estudios Teológicos: Carretera de Nijar 61, 04009 Almería; Rector JUAN A. MOYA SÁNCHEZ.

Institut de Teologia Fonamental

Sant Cugat del Vallés, Llaceres 30, Barcelona

Telephone: 93-674-11-50

Fax: 93-590-81-11

E-mail: itf@jesuites.net

Founded 1864

Jesuit College forming part of the Faculty of Theology of Barcelona, and is open to non-Jesuit students

Chancellor: Dr LLUÍS MARTÍNEZ SISTACH (Archbishop of Barcelona)

General Moderator: R. P. PERE BORRÁS

Director: R.P. JOSEP BOADA

Registrar: P. JOSEP SUGRAÑES

Librarian: P. JAUME FILELLA

Number of teachers: 19

Number of students: 200

Publications: *Actualidad Bibliográfica, Cuadernos de Teología Fundamental, Estudios Eclesiásticos, Manresa, Pensamiento, Selecciones de Teología*

PROFESSORS

ALEGRE, X., New Testament Scripture

BADIA, A., Fundamental Theology

BOADA, J., Fundamental Theology

CARRERA,, J., Fundamental Moral Theology

COLL, J. MA., Fundamental Theology

ESCUDÉ, J., Fundamental Moral Theology

FILELLA, J., Psychology of Religion

GARCÍA DONCEL, M., Philosophy of Sciences

GIMÉNEZ,, J., Fundamental Theology

GONZÁLEZ FAUS, J. I., Systematic Theology

MANRESA, F., Fundamental Theology

MELLONI, X., Fundamental Theology

MUÑOZ, M., Fundamental Theology

RAMBLA, J. MA., Spiritual Theology

SALVAT, I., Fundamental Social Morality

TUÑÍ, O., New Testament Scripture

VIVES, J., Systematic Theology

UNIVERSIDAD DE CÓRDOBA

Alfonso XIII 13, 14071 Córdoba

Telephone: 957-21-80-00

Fax: 957-21-80-30

E-mail: secretaria.rector@uco.es

Internet: www.uco.es

Founded 1972

Language of instruction: Spanish

Academic year: October to June

Rector: EUGENIO DOMÍNGUEZ VILCHES

Vice-Rector (Research and New Technology): ENRIQUE AGUILAR BENÍTEZ DE LUGO

Vice-Rector (Academic Staff): JOSÉ MANUEL ROLDÁN NOGUERAS

Vice-Rector (Students): MANUEL TORRES AGUILAR

Vice-Rector (Computing Services): JUAN ANTONIO CABALLERO MOLINA

Vice-Rector (Management and Resources): JOSÉ ROLDÁN CAÑAS

Vice-Rector (Infrastructure): JOSÉ MANUEL MUÑOZ MUÑOZ

Vice-Rector (International and Institutional Relations): MARGARITA CLEMENTE MUÑOZ

Vice-Rector (Development of Regulations): PEDRO GÓMEZ CABALLERO

Vice-Rector (Co-ordination and Communication): MANUEL TORRALBO RODRIGUEZ

Registrar: ENRIQUE AGUILAR GAVILÁN

Librarian: MARÍA DEL CARMEN LIÑÁN MAZA

Library of 427,832 , 10,220 periodicals

Number of teachers: 1,193

Number of students: 19,314

DEANS

Faculty of Education: Profa Dra JULIA ANGULO ROMERO

Faculty of Labour Relations: Prof. Dr FEDERICO NAVARRO NIETO

Faculty of Law: Prof. Dr RAFAEL CASADO RAIGÓN

Faculty of Medicine: Prof. Dr RAFAEL SOLANA LARA

Faculty of Philosophy and Letters: Prof. Dr JOAQUÍN MELLADO RODRÍGUEZ

Faculty of Science: Prof. Dr LUIS CORRAL MORA

Faculty of Veterinary Science: Prof. Dr JUAN ANSELMO PEREA REMUJO

DIRECTORS

Higher Technical School for Agricultural and Forestry Engineers: Prof. Dr MIGUEL ALCAIDE GARCÍA

School of Nursing: Profa Dra CARIDAD ALBACETE CARREIRA

Higher Polytechnic School: Prof. Dr LORENZO SALAS MORERA

University School of Technical Engineering: Dr JOSÉ MARÍA FERNÁNDEZ RODRÍGUEZ

Centre for Personal Studies: Prof. Dr ANTONIO CUBERO ATIENZA

HEADS OF DEPARTMENTS

Agricultural and Forestry Science and Resources: LUIS LÓPEZ BELLIDO

Agro-chemistry and Pedology: MANUEL MEDINA CARNICER

Agronomy: LUIS RALLO ROMERO

Comparative Anatomy and Comparative Pathological Anatomy: JOSÉ GARCÍA MONTERDE

Animal Biology: MANUEL BUSTOS RUIZ

Animal Health: SANTIAGO HERNÁNDEZ RODRÍGUEZ

Animal Production: ANTONIO GUSTAVO GÓMEZ CASTRO

Mathematics: MA. HUMILDAD CAMACHO SÁNCHEZ

Physics: VICENTE COLOMER VIADEL

History of Art, Archaeology and Music: ALBERTO VILLAR MOVELLÁN

Bromatology and Food Technology: FRANCISCO LEÓN CRESPO

Cellular Biology, Physiology, Immunology: JOSÉ EUGENIO SÁNCHEZ CRIADO

Analytical Chemistry and Ecology: MANUEL SILVA RODRIGUEZ

Inorganic Chemistry and Chemical Engineering: LUIS JIMÉNEZ ALCAIDE

Animal Medicine and Surgery: RAFAEL MAYER VALOR

Teaching of Social and Experimental Sciences: FRANCISCO VALVERDE FERNÁNDEZ

Education: ROSARIO ORTEGA RUIZ

English and German Philology: BERNHARD DIETZ GUERRERO

Genetics: LUIS MIGUEL MARTÍN MARTÍN

Graphic Engineering, Engineering and Systems of Cartographic Information: FRANCISCOL MONTES TUBÍO

Juridical, International and Historical Sciences, Philosophy of Law: DIEGO MEDINA MORALES

Geography and Territorial Sciences: JOSÉ LUIS SANCHIDRIÁN TORTI

Labour Law, Social Security and Applied Economics: CARMEN SAEZ LARA

Mechanics: JOSÉ MIGUEL MARTÍNEZ JIMÉNEZ

Medical and Surgical Specializations: PEDRO CARPINTERO BENÍTEZ

Medicine (Dermatology, Otorhinolaryngology): JOSÉ CARLOS MORENO GIMÉNEZ

Microbiology: MANUEL CASAL ROMÁN

Modern and Contemporary History and American History: JOSÉ MANUEL CUENCA TORIBIO

Organic Chemistry: JUAN MANUEL CAMPELLO PÉREZ

Philology and Teaching of Spanish: FERNANDO RIVERA CÁRDENAS

Social Sciences and Humanities: RAMÓN ROMÁN ALCALÁ

Physical Chemistry and Applied Thermodynamics: JUAN JOSÉ RUIZ SÁNCHEZ

Plant Biology: CARMEN GALÁN SOLDEVILLA

Civil, Criminal and Procedural Law: JUAN JOSÉ GONZÁLEZ RUS

Rural Engineering: RAFAEL AYUSO MUÑOZ

Science of Antiquity and Middle Ages: JUAN FCO. RODRÍGUEZ NEILA

Public and Economic Law: JUAN IGNACIO FONT GALÁN

Biochemistry and Molecular Biology: MANUEL TENA ADAVE

Morphological Sciences: JOSÉ LUIS LANCHO ALONSO

Agrarian Economy, Sociology and Policy: FELISA CEÑA DELGADO

Nursing: FRANCISCA SERRANO PRIETO

Pharmacology and Toxicology: DIEGO SANTIAGO LAGUNA

Electrotechnics and Electronics: VICENTE BARRANCO LÓPEZ

Artistic and Physical Education: MANUEL GUILLÉN DEL CASTILLO

Statistics, Econometrics, Operational Research and Company Organization: JOSÉ MA. CARIDAD Y OCERÍN

Spanish Literature: ANGELINA COSTA PALACIOS

Informatics and Numerical Analysis: SEBASTIÁN VENTURA SOTO

Public Health Sciences, Radiology and Physical Medicine: MARÍA FELISA MARTÍNEZ PAREDES

Romance Languages and Semitic Studies: MIGUEL ANGEL GARCÍA PEINADO

Forestry Engineering: SIMÓN CUADROS TAVIRA

Applied Physics: PILAR MARTÍNEZ JIMÉNEZ

UNIVERSIDADE DA CORUÑA

A Maestranza s/n, 15001 A Coruña

Telephone: 981-16-70-00

Fax: 981-16-70-11

E-mail: rcdc@udc.es

Internet: www.udc.es

Founded 1989

Languages of instruction: Spanish, Galician

Rector: JOSÉ MARÍA BARJA PÉREZ

Vice-Rector (Quality and European Harmonization): MANUEL PERALBO UZQUIANO

Vice-Rector (Strategy and Economic Planning): ANXO RAMÓN CALVO SILVOSA

Vice-Rector (Student Affairs): MIGUEL ÁNGEL SIMÓN LÓPEZ

Vice-Rector (University Extension and Communication): LUIS CAPARRÓS ESPERANTE

Vice-Rector (Campus at Ferrol and University-Business Relations: LUIS FERNANDO BARRAL LOSADA

Vice-Rector (Research): MARÍA CONCEPCIÓN HERRERO LÓPEZ

Vice-Rector (Academic Organization): PILAR URIZ TOME

Vice-Rector (Teaching Staff): XOSE LUIS ARMESTO BARBEITO

Vice-Rector (Infrastructure and Environmental Management): JOSÉ LUIS MARTÍNEZ SUÁREZ

Registrar: PATRICIA FARALDO CABANA

Manager: RAFAEL COUTO LESTAO

Number of teachers: 1,215

Number of students: 24,973

DEANS

Faculty of Law: JOSÉ MARÍA PENA LÓPEZ

Faculty of Sciences: (vacant)

Faculty of Communication Science: ANTONIO SANJUAN PÉREZ

Faculty of Education: MARÍA DOLORES CANDEDO GUNTURIZ

Faculty of Health Sciences: JORGE TEIJEIRO VIDAL

Faculty of Computing: ALBERTO VALDERRUTEN VIDAL

Faculty of Business and Economics: LUIS PEDRO PEDREIRA ANDRADE

Faculty of Philology: MARÍA JOSÉ MARTÍNEZ LÓPEZ

Faculty of Humanities: CARMEN FERNÁNDEZ CASANOVA

DIRECTORS

Higher Technical School of Architecture: JOSÉ JUAN GONZALEZ-CEBRIAN TELLO

University School of Nursing and Chiropody (Ferrol): MANUEL ROMERO MARTÍN

University School of Nursing (Coruña): MA. CARMEN MENDEZ PAZOS

Higher School of the Civil Marine: FRANCISCO BLANCO FILGUEIRA

University School of Technical Architecture: JAIME NÚÑEZ SAL

University School of Business Studies: AURELIA BLANCO GONZÁLEZ

University Polytechnical School: JESÚS MANUEL CASTRO ROMERO

University School of Physiotherapy: RAMON FERNANDEZ CERVANTES

Higher Technical School of Roads, Canals and Ports: FERNANDO MARTÍNEZ ABELLA

Higher Polytechnical School: ANGEL EDUARDO VARELA LAFUENTE

University School of Industrial Design: JOSÉ RAMÓN MÉNDEZ SALGUEIRO

University School of Labour Relations: CIPRIANO ANGEL DOBARRO MONTERO

National Institute of Physical Education: RAFAEL MARTÍN ACERO

HEADS OF DEPARTMENTS

Animal and Vegetable Biology and Ecology: EDUARDO GONZÁLEZ GURRIARAN

Molecular and Cell Biology: JOSEFINA MÉNDEZ FELPETO

Health Sciences: MARÍA JOSEFA PILCHE GUERRERO

Physics: EULOGIO JIMÉNEZ CUESTA

Physiotherapy: LUZ GONZÁLEZ DONIZ

Mathematics: JUAN MANUEL VILAR FERNÁNDEZ

Medicine: ROSA MEIJIDE FAILDE

Analytical Chemistry: SOLEDAD MUNIATEGUI LORENZO

Physical Chemistry and Chemical Engineering I: MANUEL ESTEBAN SASTRE DE VICENTE

Basic Chemistry: JOSÉ MARÍA QUINTELA LÓPEZ

Specialized Teaching: ALFREDO RODRÍGUEZ LÓPEZ-VÁZQUEZ

Spanish and Latin Philology: CARMEN PARRILLA GARCÍA

English Philology: MARÍA JESÚS LORENZO MODIA

Philosophy and Research Methods in Education: EDUARDO ABALDE PAZ

Galician-Portuguese, French and Linguistics: CARLOS PAULO MARTÍNEZ PEREIRO

Humanities: JOSE ANTONIO FERNÁNDEZ DE ROTA Y MONTER

Education and Teaching Experimental Sciences: NARCISO DE GABRIEL FERNÁNDEZ

Psychology: MIGUEL CLEMENTE DIAZ

Evolutionary Psychology and Educational Psychology: RAMÓN GONZÁLEZ CABANACH

Navigation and Earth Sciences: ANTONIO PAZ GONZÁLEZ

Composition: CELESTINO GARCÍA BRAÑA

Computation: JOSÉ LUIS FREIRE NISTAL

Architectural Construction: JOAQUÍN FERNÁNDEZ MADRID

Naval Construction: JOSÉ LUIS BOUZA COLLADO

Electronics and Systems: LUIS CASTEDO RIBAS

Energy and Marine Propulsion: RAFAEL RODRÍGUEZ VALERO

Industrial Engineering: MANUEL LUACES RODRÍGUEZ

Industrial Engineering II: ARMANDO JOSÉ YÁÑEZ CASAL

Naval and Oceanic Engineering: ENRIQUE CASANOVA RIVAS

Mathematical Methods and Representation: RAMÓN MARTUL ALVAREZ DE NEYRA

Architectural Projects and Town Planning: JOSÉ MANUEL CASABELLA LÓPEZ

Representation and Architectural Theory: JOSÉ ANTONIO FRANCO TABOADA

Construction Technology: JUAN BAUTISTA PÉREZ VALCARCEL

Architectural Drawing: RAFAEL PÉREZ ROEL

Information and Communication Technology: JUAN MANUEL ARES CASAL

Economic Analysis and Business Adminis-
tration: LAURENTINO BELLO ACEBRÓN
Private Law: JOSÉ LUIS GARCÍA-PITA Y LAS-
TRES
Public Law: JOSÉ RAMÓN RUIZ GARCÍA
Special Public Law: JAVIER SANZ LARRUGA
Applied Economics 1: JOSÉ MANUEL SÁNCHEZ
SANTOS
Applied Economics 2: FERNANDO REY MÍGUEZ
Finance and Accounting: FÉLIX RAMÓN DOL-
DAN TIE
Sociology and Politics of Administration:
VICENTE GONZÁLEZ ROLDÁN

ATTACHED INSTITUTES

Institute of European Studies: Casa de
Galería, Campus de Elviña s/n, 15071 A
Coruña; tel. 981-16-70-00 ext. 1966; fax 981-
16-70-13; e-mail iuee@udc.es; internet www
.udc.es/iuee; Dir JOSÉ MANUEL SOBRINO HER-
EDIA.

Institute of Geology: Edificio de Servicios
Centrales de Investigación, Campus de
Elviña, 15071 A Coruña; tel. 981-16-70-00
ext. 2910; fax 981-16-71-72; e-mail xeoloxia@
udc.es; internet www.udc.es/dep/geda; Dir
JUAN RAMÓN VIDAL ROMANI.

Institute of Health Sciences: Hospital
Marítimo de Oza, Area Jubias de Arriba, A
Coruña; tel. 981-17-13-60; fax 981-13-87-14;
internet   www.udc.es/cisaude/homepage
.html; Dir Dr ALFONSO CASTRO BEIRAS.

Institute of the Environment: Pazo de
Lóngora 29, Santa Eulalia de Liáns, 15179
Oleiros; tel. 981-64-85-69; fax 981-64-85-68;
e-mail iuma@udc.es; internet www.udc.es/
iuma; Dir Prof. Dr DARÍO PRADA RODRÍGUEZ.

Institute of Maritime Studies: Universidade da Coruña, Campus de Elviña, 15071 A
Coruña; tel. 981-16-70-00 ext. 2463; fax 981-
16-71-25; e-mail iuem@udc.es; internet www
.udc.es/iuem; Dir FERNANDO GONZÁLEZ LAXE.

Institute of Irish Studies: Edificio Servicios Centrais de Investigación, Campus de
Elviña s/n, 15071 A Coruña; tel. 981-16-70-00
ext. 2686; fax 981-16-71-72; e-mail amergin@
udc.es; internet www.udc.es/amergin; Dir
ANTONIO RAÚL DE TORO SANTOS.

**Technological Institute of Communica-
tion:** Paseo de Ronda 47, 15011 A Coruña;
tel. 981-15-01-00; e-mail info@telematica.org;
internet www.telematica.org; Dir Dr ANGEL
VIÑA.

**Centre of Educational Training and
Innovation:** Edificio Facultade de Socio-
loxía, 1° andar, Campus de Elviña s/n,
15071 A Coruña; tel. 981-16-71-89; fax 981-
16-71-88; e-mail cufie@six.udc.es; internet
www.udc.es/cufie; Dir JUAN JOSÉ BUENO
AGUILAR.

UNIVERSIDAD DE DEUSTO

Apdo 1, 48080 Bilbao
Located at: Avda de las Universidades 24,
48007 Bilbao
Telephone: 94-413-90-00
Fax: 94-413-90-98
E-mail: rectorado@deusto.es
Internet: www.deusto.es
Founded 1886
Private control, directed by the Jesuits
Languages of instruction: Spanish, Basque
Academic year: October to June

Chancellor: R. P. PETER-HANS KOLVENBACH
Vice-Chancellor: R. P. JUAN MIGUEL ARREGUI
ECHEVERRÍA
Rector: R. P. JAIME ORAÁ ORAÁ
Vice-Rector (Academic Organization): LUIS
MIGUEL VILLAR GARCÍA
Vice-Rector (Research): JOSÉ LUIS AVILA
ORIVE

Vice-Rector (Innovation and Quality): AURE-
LIO VILLA SÁNCHEZ
Vice-Rector (Student Affairs and Language
Policy): ROSA MIREN PAGOLA PETRIRENA
Vice-Rector (San Sebastián Campus): R. P.
JOSÉ MARÍA GUIBERT UCIN
Vice-Rector (International Relations): JULIA
GONZÁLEZ FERRERAS
Registrar: JOSÉ LUIS AVILA ORIVE
Librarian: NIEVES TARANCO
Library: see Libraries and Archives
Number of teachers: 1,682
Number of students: 10,040

Publications: *Estudios de Deusto* (2 a year),
Boletín de Estudios Económicos (3 a year),
Letras de Deusto (4 a year), *Cuadernos
Europeos de Deusto* (2 a year), *Revista de
Derecho y Genoma Humano* (2 a year),
Revista Noticias UD Berriak (4 a year),
Mundaiz (2 a year), *Estudios Empresar-
iales* (3 a year), *Anuario de Estudios
Cooperativos* (annually), *Enseiukarrean*
(annually), *Anuario del Instituto Ignacio
de Loyola* (annually), *ADOZ Boletín del
Centro de Documentación en Ocio* (4 a
year), *RAS* (2 a year), *ESIDE* (annually),
*Boletín Asociación Internacional de Dere-
cho Cooperativo* (6 a year)

DEANS

Faculty of Law: JUAN IGNACIO ECHANO BASAL-
DUA
Faculty of Philosophy and Letters: ANGEL
MA. ORMAECHEA HERNÁIZ
Faculty of Arts (San Sebastián): JOSÉ ANGEL
ACHÓN INSAUSTI
Faculty of Theology: JOSÉ JAVIER PARDO IZAL
Faculty of Political Sciences and Sociology:
MARÍA SILVESTRE CABRERA
Faculty of Philosophy and Education: SUSANA
GORBEÑA ETXEBARRIA
Faculty of Economics and Business Studies
(Bilbao): SUSANA RODRÍGUEZ VIDARTE
Faculty of Economics and Business Studies
(San Sebastián): VÍCTOR URCELAY YARZA
Faculty of Computer Science: JOSÉ LUIS DEL
VAL ROMÁN

DIRECTORS

School of Tourism (Bilbao): ALEJANDRO MAR-
TÍNEZ CHARTERINA
School of Tourism (San Sebastián): IÑAKI
ABAUNZ GÁRATE
Institute of Educational Sciences (ICE):
ITZIAR ELÉXPURU ALBIZURI
School of Secretarial Studies: GEMA TOMÁS
MARTÍNEZ
School of Legal Practice: ANTÓN HERNÁNDEZ
ZUBIZARRETA
International Institute of Business Manage-
ment: SUSANA RODRÍGUEZ VIDARTE
Institute of Basque Studies: SANTIAGO LARRA-
ZÁBAL BASÁÑEZ
Higher Institute of Religious Science: VICE-
NTE VIDE RODRÍGUEZ
Institute of European Studies: BEATRIZ PÉREZ
DE LAS HERAS
Institute of Co-operative Studies: AITZIBER
MUGARRA ELORRIAGA
Institute of Drug Addiction: LUIS PANTOJA
VARGAS
Institute of Leisure Studies: ROBERTO SAN
SALVADOR DEL VALLE DOISTUA
Institute 'Ignacio de Loyola': R. P. JUAN
PLAZAOLA ARTOLA
Pedro Arrupe Institute of Human Rights:
EDUARDO J. RUIZ VIEYTEZ
Research Management and Support Agency–
DEIKER: FERNANDO DÍEZ RUIZ
Institute for Postgraduate Studies and Con-
tinuing Education: MIGUEL ANGEL ESCOTET
ÁLVAREZ
Euskal Irakaslegoa (Basque Teacher Train-
ing): MERCEDES LUZURIAGA GABIÑA

Modern   Languages   Centre: WINFRIED
ARNOLD

UNIVERSIDAD EUROPEA DE MADRID
(CEES)

C/ Tajo s/n, Urbanización el Bosque, 28670
Villaviciosa de Odón, Madrid
Telephone: 91-211-52-00
E-mail: uem@uem.es
Internet: www.uem.es
Founded 1995

Rector: FERNANDO FERNÁNDEZ MÉNDEZ DE
ANDÉS
Vice-Rector (Institutional Relations): JUAN
CAYÓN
Vice-Rector (Research and Third-Year Stu-
dies): YOLANDA MARTÍN
Vice-Rector (Academic Organization and
University Extension): ÁGUEDA BENITO
Registrar: FRANCISCO MANUEL EDO
Librarian: ISABEL RICO RODRÍGUEZ

DEANS AND DIRECTORS

Faculty of Communication and Humanities:
Dra INMACULADA CHACÓN GUTIÉRREZ
Faculty of Economics, Law and Business: Dr
FERNANDO F. CARMENA
Faculty of Health Sciences: Dr ANTONIO
BAÑARES CAÑIZARES
Faculty of Physical Education and Sport: Dr
JUAN MAYORGA GARCÍA
Higher School of Art and Architecture: Dr
JUAN FERNANDO ESPUELAS CID
Higher Polytechnic School: Dr JOSÉ MANUEL
CAMPOS HERNÁNDEZ

UNIVERSIDAD DE EXTREMADURA

Avda de Elvas s/n, 06071 Badajoz; and Plaza
de los Caldereros 1, 10071 Cáceres
Telephone: 924-28-93-00 (Badajoz); 927-25-
700-00 (Cáceres)
Fax: 924-27-29-83 (Badajoz); 927-25-70-02
(Cáceres)
E-mail: rector@unex.es
Internet: www.unex.es
Founded 1973
State control
Language of instruction: Spanish
Academic year: October to June

Rector: Prof. Dr JUAN FRANCISCO DUQUE
CARRILLO
Vice-Rector (Co-ordination and Institutional
Relations): Prof. SEGUNDO PÍRIZ DURÁN
Vice-Rector (Research, Development and
Innovation): Prof. FERNANDO GUIBERTAU
CABANILLAS
Vice-Rector (Student Affairs): ANTONIO
JAVIER FRANCO RUBIO
Vice-Rector (Teaching Staff and Depart-
ments): ANTONIO HIDALGO GARCÍA
Vice-Rector (Teaching and European Inte-
gration): MARÍA JOSÉ MARTÍN DELGADO
Vice-Rector (Planning and Economics): AGUS-
TÍN GARCÍA GARCÍA
Vice-Rector (University Extension): PILAR
MOGOLLÓN CANO-CORTÉS
Vice-Rector (New Technology and Computing
Affairs): FERNANDO SÁNCHEZ FIGUEROA
Registrar: Prof. FRANCISCO ÁLVAREZ ARROYO
Manager: FRANCISCO JAVIER BLANCO NEVADO
Number of teachers: 1,057
Number of students: 19,179

Publication: *Boletín*

DEANS

Faculty of Science (Badajoz): MANUEL GONZÁ-
LEZ LENA
Faculty of Medicine (Badajoz): PEDRO BUREO
DACAL
Faculty of Philosophy and Letters (Cáceres):
LUIS MERINO JEREZ

Faculty of Economics and Business (Badajoz): ANTONIO FERNÁNDEZ FERNÁNDEZ

Faculty of Veterinary Science (Cáceres): PEDRO LUIS RODRÍGUEZ MEDINA

Faculty of Library Science (Badajoz): ANTONIO PULGARÍN GUERRERO

Faculty of Sports Science (Cáceres): FERNANDO DEL VILLAR ÁLVAREZ

Faculty of Education (Badajoz): MA. ROSA LUENGO GONZÁLEZ

Faculty of Law (Cáceres): EMILIO CORTÉS BECHIARELLI

Faculty of Teacher Training (Cáceres): BEATRIZ MARTÍN MARÍN

Faculty of Business Studies and Tourism (Cáceres): JOSÉ ANTONIO PÉREZ RUBIO

DIRECTORS

School of Agricultural Engineering (Badajoz): JOSÉ MIGUEL COLETO MARTÍNEZ

University School of Industrial Engineering (Badajoz): FRANCISCO QUINTANA GRAGERA

University School of Nursing and Occupational Therapy (Cáceres): BLANCA FAJARDO UTRILLA

Polytechnic School (Cáceres): VICENTE RAMOS ESTRADA

University Centre at Plasencia: JOSÉ ANTONIO VEGA VEGA

University Centre at Mérida: ANTONIO CASTILLO MARTÍNEZ

HEADS OF DEPARTMENTS

Vegetable Biology and Production: LEOPOLDO OLEA MÁRQUEZ DE PRADO

Molecular Biology and Biochemistry and Genetics: JOSÉ CARLOS CAMESELLE VIÑA

Antiquity Studies: EUSTAQUIO SÁNCHEZ SALOR

Education: FELICIDAD SÁNCHEZ PASCUA

Morphology and Cell Biology: MANUEL BLASCO RUIZ

Surgery and Medico-Surgical Specialisms: LUIS MARÍA VINAGRE VELASCO

Private Law: ANTONIO MANUEL ROMÁN GARCÍA

Public Law: CLEMENTE CHECA GONZÁLEZ

Teaching Language and Literature: ENRIQUE GARCÍA MENDO

Teaching Experimental Sciences and Mathematics: TEODORO GONZÁLEZ BRAVO

Teaching Social Sciences: FRANCISCO ESPAÑA FUENTES

Teaching Music, Plastic Arts and Movement: ZACARIAS CALZADO ALMODÓVAR

Applied Economics and Business Organization: JULIÁN RAMAJO HERNÁNDEZ

Finance and Accounting: JUAN MONTERREY MAYORAL

Electronics and Electromechanical Engineering: JUAN FRANCISCO DUQUE CARRILLO

Nursing: DIEGO PEDRERA ZAMORANO

Technical Graphic Expression: CÁNDIDO PRECIADO BARRERA

Pharmacology and Psychiatry: JULIO BENÍTEZ RODRÍGUEZ

Hispanic Philology: JOSÉ MANUEL GONZÁLEZ CALVO

Romance Philology: JUAN MARÍA CARRASCO GONZÁLEZ

English and German Philology: JOSÉ ANTONIO HOYAS SOLÍS

Physics: ALEJANDRO MARTÍN SÁNCHEZ

Physiology: JOSÉ ENRIQUE CAMPILLO ÁLVAREZ

Geography and Town and Country Planning: JOSÉ LUIS GURRÍA GASCÓN

History: MARIO PEDRO DÍAZ BARRADO

Art History: PILAR MOGOLLÓN CANO-CORTÉS

Computer Science: JUAN HERNÁNDEZ NÚÑEZ

Chemical and Fuel Engineering: FERNANDO JUAN BELTRÁN NOVILLO

Institute of Education: FLORENTINO BLÁZQUEZ ENTONADO

English Language: RAFAEL ALEJO GONZÁLEZ

Mathematics: GERMÁN GIRÁLDEZ TIEBO

Animal Health and Medicine: SANTIAGO VADILLO MACHOTA

Microbiology: GERMÁN LARRIBA CALLE

Pathology and Human Clinics: GUILLERMO SÁNCHEZ SALGADO

Educational Sociology and Psychology: FLORENCIO VICENTE CASTRO

Analytical Chemistry: FRANCISCO SALINAS LÓPEZ

Analytical Chemistry and Electrochemistry: FRANCISCO VINAGRE JARA

Physical Chemistry: SANTIAGO TOLOSA ARROYO

Inorganic Chemistry: ÁLVARO BERNALTE GARCÍA

Organic Chemistry: JOSÉ LUIS JIMÉNEZ REQUEJO

Building Techniques, Methods and Principles: ELEUTERIO SÁNCHEZ VACA

Zootechnics: JESÚS VENTANAS BARROSO

UNIVERSITAT DE GIRONA

Pl. Sant Domènec 3, 17071 Gerona

Telephone: 972-41-80-28

Fax: 972-41-80-31

E-mail: informacio@udg.es

Internet: www.udg.es

Founded 1992

State control

Academic year: September to June

Rector: Dr JOAN BATLLE GRABULOSA

First Vice-Rector (Organization and Quality Management): Dr RAMON MORENO AMICH

Vice-Rector (Campus): Dr JOAQUIM SALVI MAS

Vice-Rector (Research): Dra VICTÒRIA SALVADÓ

Vice-Rector (Teaching Staff): Dra BLANCA PALMADA

Vice-Rector (Student Affairs and External Relations): Dr DAVID BRUSI

Vice-Rector (Regulation Development): Dr JOSEP ORIOL LLEBOT MAJÓ

Vice-Rector (Staff): Dr JOAN MARTÍ BONMATÍ

Registrar: Dr JOSEP ORIOL LLEBOT MAJÓ

Manager: MIQUEL AMORÓS

Librarian: ANTÒNIA BOIX

Library of 272,973 books, 10,692 periodicals

Number of teachers: 804

Number of students: 15,783

DEANS

Faculty of Sciences: DAVID BRUSI

Faculty of Education and Psychology: ANNA M. GELI

Faculty of Arts: ROSA CONGOST COLOMER

Faculty of Economics and Business Studies: ROSA ROS MASSANA

Faculty of Law: JOSÉ LUIS LINARES PINEDA

DIRECTORS

Higher Polytechnic School: JOAQUIM VELAYOS SOLÉ

University School of Nursing: JORDI DOLTRA CENTELLAS

University School of Tourism: JOAQUIM MAJÓ FERNÀNDEZ

HEADS OF DEPARTMENTS

Architecture and Construction Engineering: EMILI SAGRERA BUSQUETS

Biology: Dr L. JESÚS GARCIA-GIL

Environmental Sciences: Dr LLUÍS PALLÍ I BUXÓ

Specialized Teaching: Dra ROSER JUANOLA I TERRADELLAS

Private Law: Dr MIQUEL MARTÍN CASALS

Public Law: Dr RAMÓN PANIAGUA REDONDO

Economics: MODEST FLUVIÀ FONT

Electronics, Computer Science and Automation: XAVIER CUFÍ

Business: Dr JOAN CARLES FERRER I COMALAT

Mechanical Engineering and Industrial Construction: LLUÍS TORRES LLINÀS

Chemical Engineering, Agriculture and Food Technology: JAUME PUIG I BARGUÉS (acting)

Philology and Philosophy: FRANCESC FELIU TORRENT

Physics: ELENA ROGET I ARMENGOL

Geography, History and Art History: ANNA MARIA GARCIA ROVIRA

Nursing: DAVID BALLESTER FERRANDO

Computer Science and Applied Mathematics: ÁNGEL CALSINA

Business Administration, Management and Product Design: RUDI DE CASTRO VILA

Education: SALOMÓ MARQUÉS

Psychology: ESPERANZA VILLAR HOZ

Chemistry: Dr MIQUEL DURAN

ATTACHED SCHOOLS AND INSTITUTES

University School of Communication Sciences: Campus de Montilivi s/n, 17071 Gerona; tel. 972-41-89-04; fax 972-41-87-32; e-mail iolanda.vila@pas.udg.es; internet www.eucc-udg.org; Dir Dra CARMEN ECHAZARRETA SOLER.

CETA University School of Tourism: C/ Pàdua 11–13, 08023 Barcelona; tel. 93-211-80-74; e-mail informacio@cetaturisme.com; internet www.cetaturismo.com; Dir Dr RAMÓN BOSCH.

ESMA University School of Tourism: Consell de Cent 42, 08014 Barcelona; tel. 93-426-99-88; fax 93-426-76-21; e-mail esma@esma.es; internet www.esma.es; Man. Dir JOAN B. RENART I MONTALAT.

Euroaula University School of Tourism: C/ Aragó 208–210, 08011 Barcelona; tel. 93-451-03-06; e-mail turisme@euroaula.com; internet www.euroaula.com.

Sant Pol de Mar University School of Hotel Business and Tourism: Carretera N-II s/n, 08395 Sant Pol de Mar, Barcelona; tel. 93-760-02-12; fax 93-760-09-85; e-mail %20mail@euht-santpol.org; internet www.euht-santpol.org; President RAMON SERRA.

Terrassa University School of Tourism: Vapor Universitari, Colom 114, 08222 Terrassa; tel. 93-731-18-69; fax 93-784-37-06; e-mail info-turisme@fundaciofiac.com; internet www.fundaciofiac.com.

School of Audiovisual and Multimedia Production: Crta Santa Coloma 115, 17005 Gerona; tel. 972-40-13-00; e-mail escola@ege.es; internet www.ege.es/eram.

Garbí University School of Physiotherapy: C/ Ángel Guimerà 108, 17190 Salt, Gerona; tel. 972-40-51-30; e-mail garbi.girona@udg.es; internet www.fisiogarbi.org; Dir ANTONIO NARBONA JIMÉNEZ.

Josep Pallach Institute of Education: Plaça de Sant Domènec 9, 17071 Gerona; tel. 972-41-87-02; fax 972-41-82-47; e-mail ice@udg.es; internet www.udg.edu/ice; Dir M. CARME SAURINA CANALS.

Institute of Aquatic Ecology: Campus Montilivi, 17071 Gerona; tel. 972-41-81-77; fax 972-41-81-50; e-mail teresa.roura@pas.udg.es; internet ciencies.udg.es/iea; Dir XAVIER QUINTANA.

Institute of Computer Science and Its Applications: Campus de Montilivi, 17071 Gerona; tel. 972-41-89-56; fax 972-41-82-59; e-mail techsec@iiia.udg.es; internet iiia.udg.es; Dir MATEU SBERT.

Institute of Catalan Language and Culture: Plaça Ferrater Mora 1, 17071 Gerona; tel. 972-41-89-45; fax 972-41-82-30; e-mail ilcc@udg.es; internet www.udg.edu/ilcc; Dir ALBERT ROSSICH ESTRAGÓ.

Institute of the Environment: Campus Montilivi M24, 17071 Gerona; tel. 972-41-98-48; fax 972-41-98-49; e-mail imaudg@xamba.udg.es; internet insma.udg.es; Dir MIQUEL RIGOLA LAPEÑA.

Institute of Cultural Heritage: Pl. Ferrater Mora 1, 17071 Gerona; tel. 972-41-98-04;

fax 972-41-82-30; e-mail dir.ipac@udg.es;
internet www.udg.edu/ipac; Dir GABRIEL
ALCALDE GURT.

Institute of Computational Chemistry:
Campus de Montilivi, Facultat de Ciènces,
despatx 164, 17071 Gerona; tel. 972-41-83-
57; fax 972-41-83-56; e-mail secretaria@iqc
.edg.es; internet iqc.udg.es; Dir Prof. EMILI
BESALÚ.

**Institute of Research on the Quality of
Life:** Edifici Seminari, Pl. Sant Domènec 9,
17071 Gerona; tel. 972-41-89-80; fax 972-41-
83-45; e-mail isabel.moradell@pas.udg.es;
internet www.udg.edu/irqv; Dir FERRAN
CASAS.

**Institute of Agricultural and Food Tech-
nology:** Escola Politècnica Superior, Avda.
Lluís Santaló s/n, 17071 Gerona; tel. 972-41-
84-76; fax 972-41-83-99; e-mail intea@intea
.udg.es; internet intea.udg.es; Dir Dr EMILI
MONTESINOS SEGUÍ.

UNIVERSIDAD DE GRANADA

Hospital Real, Calle Cuesta del Hospicio s/n,
18071 Granada

Telephone: 958-243063
Fax: 958-243066
Internet: www.ugr.es
Founded 1526, charter granted 1531, estab-
lished 1536
State control
Language of instruction: Spanish
Academic year: October to May

Rector: DAVID AGUILAR PEÑA
Pro-Vice-Chancellor (Academic Organiza-
tion): GABRIEL CARDENETE HERNÁNDEZ
Pro-Vice-Chancellor (Heritage, Infrastruc-
ture and Equipment): ELENA DÍEZ JORGE
Pro-Vice-Chancellor (International and Insti-
tutional Relations): MANUEL DÍAZ CARRILLO
Pro-Vice-Chancellor (Planning, Quality and
Evaluation): LUIS RICO ROMERO
Pro-Vice-Chancellor (Research and Third-
Year Studies): RAFAEL PAYÁ ALBERT
Pro-Vice-Chancellor (Student Affairs):
RAFAEL DÍAZ DE LA GUARDIA GUERRERO
Pro-Vice-Chancellor (University Extension
and Co-operation): MARÍA JOSÉ OSORIO
PÉREZ
Pro-Vice-Chancellor (New Technologies):
FÉLIX DE MOYA ANEGÓN
Pro-Vice-Chancellor (Postgraduate Affairs
and Continuing Education): FRANCISCO
JAVIER MARTOS PERALES
Pro-Vice-Chancellor (Relations with the
Business World and Strategic Planning):
TEODORO LUQUE MARTÍN
Registrar: ESTEBAN PÉREZ ALONSO
Manager: JOSÉ JIMÉNEZ BENAVIDES
Librarian: FRANCISCO HERRANZ NAVARRA
Library of 686,300 vols, 15,338 periodicals,
35 incunabula; faculty libraries: 408,000
vols
Number of teachers: 3,423
Number of students: 82,596
Publications: *Miscelánea de Estudios Árabes
y Hebraicos, Anales de la Cátedra Fran-
cisco Suarez, Arenal: Revista de Historia
de Mujeres, Chronica Nova: Revista de
Historia Moderna, Cuadernos de Arte,
Cuadernos de Estudios Medievales, Cua-
dernos de Estudios Medievales y Ciencias y
Técnicas Historiográficas, Cuadernos de
Prehistoria, Cuadernos Geográficos, Dyna-
mis: Acta Hispanica ad Medicinae: Scien-
tiarumque Historiam Ilustrandam,
Florentia Iliberritana, Revista de Educación, Revista de la Facultad de Derecho de
la Universidad de Granada, Sendebar:
Boletín de la Facultad de Traducción e
Interpretación, Zoologica Baetica*

DEANS

Faculty of Dentistry: ANTONIO CEBALLOS
SALOBREÑA
Faculty of Education and Humanities
(Ceuta): FRANCISCO JAVIER GONZÁLEZ VÁZ-
QUEZ
Faculty of Education and Humanities
(Melilla): LUÍS SERRANO ROMERO
Faculty of Fine Arts: JUAN JOSÉ CABRERA
CONTRERAS
Faculty of Economic and Business Adminis-
tration: LÁZARO RODRÍGUEZ ARIZA
Faculty of Education: FRANCISCO FERNANDEZ
PALOMARES
Faculty of Law: Prof. Dr JUAN LÓPEZ MAR-
TÍNEZ
Faculty of Library Science and Documenta-
tion: JOSEFINA VILCHEZ PARDO
Faculty of Medicine: Prof. JOSÉ MARÍA PEI-
NADO HERREROS
Faculty of Pharmacy: FERNANDO MARTÍNEZ
MARTÍNEZ
Faculty of Philosophy and Letters: MARIA
ELENA MARTIN-VIVALDI CABALLERO
Faculty of Physical Sciences and Sports:
PAULINO PADIAL PUCHE
Faculty of Political Science and Sociology:
MARGARITA LATIESA RODRÍGUEZ
Faculty of Psychology: MIGUEL CARLOS MOYA
MORALES
Faculty of Sciences: Prof. Dr ENRIQUE HITA
VILLAVERDE
Faculty of Translation and Interpretation:
EVA MUÑOZ RAYA
Faculty of Work Sciences: ANTONIO DELGADO
PADIAL

DIRECTORS

University School of Architecture: JOAQUÍN
PASSOLAS COLMENERO
University School of Business Studies
(Melilla): ISABEL QUESADA VÁZQUEZ
University School of Health Sciences: MAN-
UEL PEÑAS MALDONADO
University School of Social Work: BLANCA A.
GIRELA REJÓN
Higher Technical School of Architecture:
JUAN CALATRAVA ESCOBAR
Higher Technical School of Computer Engi-
neering: CARLOS UREÑA ALMAGRO
Higher Technical School of Road, Canal and
Port Engineers: ANTONIO MENÉNDEZ
ONDINA

HEADS OF DEPARTMENTS

Algebra: Dr JOSÉ GÓMEZ TORRECILLAS
Regional Geographical Analysis and Physical
Geography: Prof. RAFAEL MACHADO SAN-
TIAGO
Mathematical Analysis: JUAN CARLOS
CABELLO PIÑAR
Pathological Anatomy and History of
Science: (vacant)
Human Embryology and Anatomy: Prof. Dr
MIGUEL LÓPEZ SOLER
Anthropology and Social Work: (vacant)
Architecture and Computer Technology:
ALBERTO PRIETO ESPINOSA
Animal Biology and Ecology: Prof. Dr MAN-
UEL GARCÍA GALLEGO
Cell Biology: Prof. JULIO NAVASCUÉS MAR-
TÍNEZ
Biochemistry and Molecular Biology: Prof.
Dr JOSÉ ANTONIO GÓMEZ-CAPILLA
Botany: MANUEL CASARES PORCEL
Politics and Administration: Prof. Dr JUAN
NÚÑEZ PÉREZ
Computer Science and Artificial Intelligence:
AMPARO VILA MIRANDA
Marketing and Market Research: Dr TEO-
DORO LUQUE MARTÍNEZ
Architectural Construction: Prof. EMILIO
HERRERA CARDENETE
Administrative Law: RAFAEL BARRANCO VELA
Civil Law: JUAN MIGUEL OSSORIO SERRANO

Constitutional Law: Prof. Dr FRANCISCO
BALAGUER CALLEJÓN
Labour Law and Social Security Law: JOSÉ
LUIS MONEREO PÉREZ
Private International Law and History of
Law: Dr SIXTO SÁNCHEZ LORENZO
Public International Law and International
Relations: Prof. Dr DIEGO J. LIÑÁN
NOGUERAS
Mercantile Law and Roman Law: Prof. Dr
JOSÉ LUIS PÉREZ-SERRABONA GONZÁLEZ
Penal Law: Prof. Dr LORENZO MORILLAS
CUEVA
Procedural Law: FERNANDO GONZÁLEZ MON-
TES
Ecclesiastical Law: Prof. Dr MARÍA ÁLVAREZ-
MANZANEDA ROLDÁN
Teaching of Music, Plastic Arts and Move-
ment: Dr DANIEL LINARES GIRELA
Teaching of Mathematics: Dra ENCARNACIÓN
CASTRO MARTÍNEZ
Teaching of Experimental Sciences: JOSÉ
ANTONIO NARANJO RODRÍGUEZ
Teaching and School Organization: Dr MAN-
UEL LORENZO DELGADO
Finance and Accounting: ANTONIO M. LÓPEZ
HERNÁNDEZ
Electromagnetism and Physics of Materials:
Dr J. MARRO BORAU
Electronics and Computer Technology: Dr
PEDRO CARTUJO ESTÉBANEZ
Nursing: ADOLFO GÁZQUEZ CAZORLA
Stomatology: MANUEL BRAVO PÉREZ
Stratigraphy and Paleontology: PASCUAL
RIVAS CARRERA
Semitic Studies: Dra CONCEPCIÓN CASTILLO
CASTILLO
Architectural and Engineering Drawing:
FRANCISCO GIMÉNEZ YANGUAS
Pharmacology: JOSÉ JIMÉNEZ MARTÍN
Greek Philology: MIGUEL VILLLENA PONSODA
English and German Philology: Dr LUIS
QUEREDA RODRÍGUEZ-NAVARRO
Romance Philology: MARÍA DOLORES VALEN-
CIA MIRÓN
Philosophy: PEDRO GÓMEZ GARCÍA
Philosophy of Law: Prof. Dr NICOLÁS MARÍA
LÓPEZ CALERA
Applied Physics: ANTONIO MOLINA CUEVAS
Modern Physics: ANTONIO M. LALLENA ROJO
Theoretical Physics and Astrophysics:
(vacant)
Vegetal Physiology: JOSÉ MARÍA RAMOS CLA-
VERO
Genetics: Prof. Dr JUAN PEDRO MARTÍNEZ
CAMACHO
Geodynamics: FRANCISCO GONZÁLEZ LODEIRO
Human Geography: MANUEL SÁENZ LORITE
Geometry and Topology: JUAN DE DIOS PÉREZ
JIMÉNEZ
Histology: PASCUAL VICENTE CRESPO FERRER
Ancient History: Prof. CRISTÓBAL GONZÁLEZ
ROMÁN
Contemporary History: Prof. Dr JUAN GAY
ARMENTEROS
History of Art: IGNACIO HENARES CUÉLLAR
Medieval History and Historiography: MARÍA
CARMEN CALERO PALACIOS
Modern and American History: Prof. MIGUEL
MOLINA MARTÍNEZ
Civil Engineering: JOSÉ CHACON MONTERO
Spanish Language: JUAN ANTONIO MOYA
CORRAL
Applied Mathematics: MIGUEL PASADAS FER-
NÁNDEZ
Medicine: Prof. BLAS GIL EXTREMERA
Legal Medicine and Psychiatry: Prof. Dr
ENRIQUE VILLANUEVA CAÑADAS
Preventive Medicine and Public Health: Prof.
Dr RAMÓN GÁLVEZ VARGAS
Continuum Mechanics and Theory of Struc-
tures: Prof. RAFAEL GALLEGO SEVILLA
Quantitative Methods for Economics and
Business: RAFAEL HERRERÍAS PLEGUEZUELO
Research and Diagnostic Methods in Educa-
tion: (vacant)

Microbiology: FERNANDO MARTÍNEZ MARTÍNEZ

Mineralogy and Petrology: Prof. Dr MIGUEL ORTEGA HUERTAS

Nutrition and Bromatology: Dra FATIMA OLEA SERRANO

Obstetrics and Gynaecology: Prof. LUIS NAVARRETE LÓPEZ-CÓZAR

Optics: LUIS MIGUEL JIMÉNEZ DEL BARCO JALDO

Business Organization: JUAN ALBERTO ARAGÓN CORREA

Parasitology: Profa ROCÍO BENÍTEZ RODRÍGUEZ

Education: DIEGO SEVILLA MERINO

Evolutionary Psychology and Psychology of Education: FERNANDO JUSTICIA JUSTICIA

Analytical Chemistry: Dr JOSÉ LUIS VILCHEZ QUERO

Physical Chemistry: Prof. PEDRO LUIS MATEO ALARCÓN

Inorganic Chemistry: JUAN MANUEL SALAS PEREGRÍN

Organic Chemistry: ANDRÉS GARCÍA GRANADOS LÓPEZ DEL HIERRO

Radiology and Physical Medicine: VICENTE PEDRAZA MURIEL

Sociology: Dr PEDRO CASTÓN BOYER

Translation and Interpretation: PAMELA FABER

AFFILIATED INSTITUTIONS

'Federico Oloriz' Institute of Neurosciences: C/ Avda de Madrid s/n, Facultad de Medicina, Universidad de Granada, Granada; tel. 958-24-40-33; fax 958-24-61-87; e-mail ifeolo@andalusi.ugr.es; internet www.ugr.es/%7Einsneuro; Dir Dr JOSÉ MANUEL BAEYENS CABRERA.

Water Institute: Edif. Fray Luis de Granada, C/ Ramon y Cajal 4, 18071 Granada; tel. 958-24-30-93; fax 958-24-30-94; e-mail javicruz@instagua.ugr.es; internet www.ugr.es/%7Ejjcruz/instagua.htm; Dir LUIS CRUZ PIZARRO.

Biotechnology Institute: Facultad de Ciencias, Universidad de Granada, Campus Fuentenueva s/n, 18002 Granada; tel. 958-20-06-86; e-mail info@biotec.ugr.es; internet biotec.conzepto.com/index.asp; Dir Dr ANTONIO OSUNA CARRILLO DE ALBORNOZ.

Andalusian Institute of Earth Sciences: Facultad de Ciencias, Universidad de Granada, Campus Fuentenueva s/n, 18002 Granada; tel. 958-24-31-58; fax 958-24-33-84; e-mail offiact@ugr.es; internet www.iact.csic.es; Dir ANDRES MALDONALDO LOPEZ.

Andalusian Institute of Geophysics and Prevention of Seismic Disasters: Campus Universitario de Cartuja s/n, 18071 Granada; tel. 958-24-35-57; fax 958-16-09-07; e-mail morales@iag.ugr.es; internet www.ugr.es/%7Eiag; Dir JOSÉ MORALES SOTO.

Regional Development Institute: Universidad de Granada, Edificio Centro de Documentación Científica, C/ Rector López Argüeta s/n, 18071 Granada; tel. 958-24-30-83; fax 958-24-89-67; e-mail idesareg@azahar.ugr.es; internet www.ugr.es/%7Eidr; Dir Dr FRANCISCO RODRÍGUEZ MARTÍNEZ.

'Carlos I' Institute of Theoretical and Computational Physics: Facultad de Ciencias, Universidad de Granada, Campus de Fuentenueva, 18071 Granada, tel. 958-24-28-60; fax 958-24-28-62; e-mail carlos1@ugr.es; internet www.ugr.es/%7Ecarlos1; Dir PEDRO L. GARRIDO GALERA.

Interuniversity Andalusian Institute of Criminology: Sección Universidad de Granada, Edificio Centro de Documentación Científica, C/ Rector López Argüeta s/n, 18071 Granada; tel. 958-24-31-50; fax 958-24-30-95; e-mail criminol@ugr.es; internet www.ugr.es/%7Ecriminol; Dir Prof. Dr JESÚS BARQUÍN SANZ.

Institute of Nutrition and Food Technology: Edif. Fray Luís de Granada C/ Ramón y Cajal 4, 18071 Granada; tel. 958-24-41-74; fax 958-24-83-26; internet www.ugr.es/%7Ewinyta; Dir EMILIO MARTÍNEZ DE VICTORIA MUÑOZ.

University Institute of Studies on Women: Edificio de Documentación Científica, C/ Rector López Argüeta s/n, 18071 Granada; tel. 958-24-83-66; fax 958-24-28-28; e-mail insmujer@azahar.ugr.es; internet www.ugr.es/%7Eiem; Dir Dra MARIA EUGENIA FERNÁNDEZ FRAILE.

University Institute of Peace and Conflict: Edificio de Documentación Científica, C/ Rector López Argüeta s/n, 18071 Granada; tel. 958-24-41-42; fax 958-24-89-74; e-mail eirene@ugr.es; internet www.ugr.es/%7Eeirene; Dir Prof. MARIO LÓPEZ MARTÍNEZ.

'La Inmaculada' University College of Teacher Training: Carretera de Murcia s/n, 18010 Granada; tel. 958-20-58-61; fax 958-28-74-69; internet www.lainmaculada.com; Pres. and Dir ANTONIO ALMENDROS GALLEGO.

UNIVERSIDAD DE HUELVA

C/ Dr Cantero Cuadrado 6, 21071 Huelva

Telephone: 959-01-80-00

Fax: 959-01-80-80

Internet: www.uhu.es

Founded 1993

State control

Rector: Prof. Dr ANTONIO RAMÍREZ DE VERGER JAÉN

Vice-Rector (Research): Prof. Dr EMILIO PASCUAL MARTÍNEZ

Vice-Rector (Infrastructure and Equipment): Prof. Dr ENRIQUE BONSÓN PONTE

Vice-Rector (Student Affairs and Institutional Relations): Profa Dra MA. ANGELES FERNÁNDEZ RECAMALES

Vice-Rector (International Relations and European Convergence): Prof. Dr LUIS RIVERO GARCÍA

Vice-Rector (Academic Organization and Teaching Staff): Prof. Dr RAFAEL TORRONTERAS SANTIAGO

Vice-Rector (Studies, Doctorate Affairs and Educational Innovation): Prof. Dr LUIS CARLOS CONTRERAS GONZÁLEZ

Vice-Rector (Computing Affairs and Communications): Prof. Dr JOSÉ MA. MADIEDO GIL

Vice-Rector (Quality and Strategic Planning): Profa Dra MA. ÁNGELES PLAZA MEJÍA

Registrar: Prof. Dr CARLOS PETIT CALVO

Manager: RAFAEL SERRANO AGUILAR

Librarian: MA. ANTONIA ÁLVAREZ ÁLVAREZ

Library of 120,000 vols, 4,280 periodicals

Number of teachers: 643

Number of students: 13,600

DEANS

Faculty of Experimental Sciences: GABRIEL RUIZ DE ALMODÓVAR

Faculty of Business Studies: Prof. Dr JOSÉ DOMÍNGUEZ CASADO

Faculty of Law: Prof. Dr SALVADOR RAMÍREZ GÓMEZ

Faculty of Humanities: Prof. Dr FERNANDO NAVARRO ANTOLÍN

Faculty of Education: JOSÉ MANUEL CORONEL LLAMAS

Faculty of Labour Relations: AGUSTÍN GALÁN GARCÍA

DIRECTORS

Higher Polytechnic School: FULGENCIO PRAT HURTADO

University School of Nursing: Profa Dra MA. ISABEL MARISCAL CRESPO

University School of Social Work: OCTAVIO VÁZQUEZ AGUADO

HEADS OF DEPARTMENTS

Anton Menger: Prof. Dr MIGUEL RODRÍGUEZ-PIÑERO ROYO

Environmental Biology and Public Health: Prof. Dr CARLOS RUIZ FRUTOS

Agriculture and Forestry: Prof. Dr MANUEL FERNÁNDEZ MARTÍNEZ

Public Law: Prof. Dr JOSÉ MA. MORALES ARROYO

Teaching of Sciences: Prof. Dr JESÚS ESTEPA GIMÉNEZ

Business Management and Marketing: Dr JUAN MANUEL CEPEDA PÉREZ

General Economics and Statistics: Dra MANUELA DE PAZ BÁÑEZ

Finance, Accounting and Direction of Operations: Dr JUAN JOSÉ GARCÍA MACHADO

Nursing: Prof. JOSÉ LUIS SÁNCHEZ RAMOS

Self-Expression through Music, Plastic Arts and Movement, and Their Teaching: Prof. MANUEL DÍAZ TRILLO

Spanish Philology and Its Teaching: Prof. Dr LUIS GÓMEZ CANSECO

English Philology: Dra PILAR CUDER DOMÍNGUEZ

Integrated Philologies: Dra MA. REGLA FERNÁNDEZ GARRIDO

Applied Physics: JUAN PEDRO BOLÍVAR RAYA

Geology: Dr JOSÉ BORREGO FLORES

Geodynamics and Paleontology: Dr FRANCISCO RUIZ MUÑOZ

History I: Prof. Dr JUAN MANUEL CAMPOS CARRASCO

History II: Prof. Dr JUAN ANTONIO MÁRQUEZ DOMÍNGUEZ

Design Engineering and Project Engineering: Prof. MANUEL IGNACIO BAHAMONDE GARCÍA

Electrical and Heat Engineering: Prof. Dr PATRICIO SALMERÓN REVUELTA

Electronic and Computer Engineering and Automation: Dr JOSÉ MANUEL ANDÚJAR MÁRQUEZ

Chemical Engineering, Physical Chemistry and Organic Chemistry: Dr JOSÉ ARIZA CARMONA

Mining Engineering and Mechanical and Fuel Engineering: Dr EMILIO M. ROMERO MACÍAS

Mathematics: Prof. Dr ANTONIO ALGABA DURÁN

Psychology: Prof. Dr FRANCISCO REVUELTA PÉREZ

Chemistry and Materials Science: Prof. Dr PEDRO PÉREZ ROMERO

Sociology and Social Work: Profa Dra ANDREA F. CAPILLA PÉREZ

Theodor Mommsen Law Centre: Prof. Dr MANUEL GÓMEZ DEL CASTILLO

ASOCIACIÓN UNIVERSITARIA IBEROAMERICANA DE POSTGRADO

C/ Consuelo 32, Torre del Clavero, 37001 Salamanca

Telephone: 923-21-00-39

Fax: 923-21-49-49

Director-General: VICTOR CRUZ CARDONA

Deputy Director-General: ANGEL ESPINA BARRIO

Publications: *Catálogo General AUIP*, *Boletín Informativo AUIP*, *Estudios Monográficos sobre Educación Superior*

One hundred universities offer 1,500 postgraduate courses under the aegis of the AUIP.

UNIVERSIDAD DE JAÉN

Campus Las Lagunillas, 23071 Jaén

Telephone: 953-01-21-21

Fax: 953-01-22-39

E-mail: rectorado@ujaen.es

Internet: www.ujaen.es

Founded 1993
State control

Rector: LUIS PARRAS GUIJOSA
Vice-Rector (Academic Organization and Teaching Staff): RAFAEL PEREA CARPIO
Vice-Rector (Research): REYES PEÑA SANTIAGO
Vice-Rector (Student Affairs): JOSÉ GONZÁLEZ GARCÍA
Vice-Rector (University Extension): CARMEN RÍSQUEZ CUENCA
Vice-Rector (Infrastructure and Teaching Equipment): JOSÉ ANTONIO TORRES GONZÁLEZ
Vice-Rector (Quality and Strategic Direction): EMILIO LOZANO AGUILERA
Vice-Rector (Co-ordination and Communication): ADOLFO SÁNCHEZ RODRIGO
Registrar: PILAR FERNÁNDEZ PANTOJA
Manager: JUAN HERNÁNDEZ ARMENTEROS
Library Director: SEBASTIÁN JARILLO CALVARRO

Library of 205,000 vols, 4,356 periodicals
Number of teachers: 673
Number of students: 15,523

DEANS

Faculty of Experimental Sciences: Dra AMELIA ARÁNEGA JIMÉNEZ
Faculty of Social Sciences and Law: Prof. JOSÉ CUESTA REVILLA
Faculty of Humanities and Education: Dr GABRIEL TEJADA MOLINA

DIRECTORS

Higher Polytechnic School: PEDRO GÓMEZ VIDAL
University Polytechnic School in Linares: FRANCISCO JAVIER REY ARRANS
University School of Social Work in Linares: YOLANDA MARÍA DE LA FUENTE ROBLES

HEADS OF DEPARTMENTS

Business Administration, Accounting and Sociology: MARÍA JESÚS HERNÁNDEZ ORTIZ
Vegetal and Animal Biology and Ecology: CARLOS SALAZAR MENDIAS
Experimental Biology: FERMÍN ARANDA HARO
Health Science: JESÚS LÓPEZ ORTEGA
Civil Law, Finance Law and Tax Law: Dr ELADIO JOSÉ APARICIO CARRILLO
Roman Law, Procedural Law, Public International Law and Canon Law: DANIEL MA. TIRAPU MARTÍNEZ
Penal Law, Philosophy of Law, Moral Philosophy and Philosophy: GUILLERMO PORTILLA CONTRERAS
Public Law and Special Private Law: (vacant)
Teaching of Self-expression in Music, Plastic Arts and Movement: MA. LUISA ZAGALAZ SÁNCHEZ
Teaching of Sciences: ALCÁZAR CRUZ RODRÍGUEZ
Applied Economics: Prof. Dr ANTONIO MARTÍN MESA
Electronics: NICOLÁS RUIZ REYES
Statistics and Operational Research: JUAN CARLOS RUIZ MOLINA
Spanish Philology: Prof. Dr RAFAEL ALARCÓN SIERRA
English Philology: Prof. Dr LUCIANO GARCÍA GARCÍA
Physics: JOAQUÍN TOVAR PESCADOR
Geology: JOSÉ MIGUEL MOLINA CÁMARA
Computer Science: FRANCISCO FEITO HIGUERUELA
Cartographic and Geodesic Engineering and Photogrammetry: Prof. Dr JORGE DELGADO GARCÍA
Electrical Engineering: FRANCISCO JURADO MELGUIZO
Project, Design and Graphic Engineering: (vacant)

Mining and Mechanical Engineering: JOSÉ MANUEL PALOMAR CARNICERO
Materials, Environmental and Chemical Engineering: Dr EULOGIO CASTRO GALIANO
Mediterranean Cultures and Languages: Dra GUADALUPE SAIZ MUÑOZ
Mathematics: DANIEL CÁRDENAS MORALES
Education: LORENZO ALMAZÁN MORENO
Psychology: Dra ENCARNACIÓN RAMÍREZ FERNÁNDEZ
Analytical and Physical Chemistry: ANTONIO MOLINA DÍAZ
Organic and Inorganic Chemistry: MIGUEL MORENO CARRETERO

ATTACHED INSTITUTIONS

Andalusian Centre of Iberian Archaeology: Paraje las Lagunillas s/n, 23071 Jaén; tel. 953-01-21-32; fax 953-01-22-87; e-mail caai@ujaen.es; internet www.ujaen.es/centros/caai; Dir Dr ARTURO CARLOS RUIZ RODRÍGUEZ.

University School of Teacher Training in Ubeda: Avda Cristo Rey 25, 23400 Ubeda (Jaén); tel. 953-79-61-02; e-mail magisterio@safa.edu; internet www.eumsafa.org; Dir FRANCISCO JAVIER MUÑOZ DELGADO.

UNIVERSIDAD JAUME I DE CASTELLÓN

Campus de Riu Sec, Avda de Vicent Sos Baynat s/n, 12071 Castellón
Telephone: 964-72-80-00
Fax: 964-72-90-16
E-mail: info@uji.es
Internet: www.uji.es

Founded 1991
State control

Rector: FRANCISCO TOLEDO LOBO
Vice-Rector assisting the Rector: AGUSTÍN ESCARDINO BENLLOCH
Vice-Rector (Economic Affairs and University Planning: VICENT PALMER ANDREU
Vice-Rector (International Co-operation and Solidarity): ANA FUERTES EUGENIO
Vice-Rector (Infrastructure and Services): VICENT CERVERA MATEU
Vice-Rector (Research and Graduate Affairs): VICENT ORTS RIOS
Vice-Rector (Academic Organization and Students): EVA ALCÓN SOLER
Vice-Rector (Teaching Staff and Social Welfare): MANUEL CHUST CALERO
Vice-Rector (Scientific Promotion and Technology): JUAN ANDRÉS BORT
Vice-Rector (Linguistic, Sociocultural and University Promotion): MARGARITA PORCAR MIRALLES
Vice-Rector (Educational Quality and European Harmonization): ROSA MARÍA GRAU GUMBAU
Registrar: MODESTO FABRA VALLS
Library Dir: VICENT FALOMIR DEL CAMPO

Library of 224,647 vols
Number of teachers: 970
Number of students: 13,374

DEANS

Faculty of Human and Social Sciences: Prof. MANUEL ROSAS ARTOLA
Faculty of Law and Economics: Prof. GERMÁN ORÓN MORATAL
Higher School of Technology and Experimental Sciences: Prof. FERNANDO RAJADELL VICIANO (Dir)

HEADS OF DEPARTMENTS

Experimental Sciences: Prof. FRANCISCO LÓPEZ BENET
Chemical Engineering: Prof. ANTONIO BARBA JUAN
Computer Systems and Languages: Prof. PABLO AIBAR AUSINA

Computer Science and Engineering: Prof. JOSÉ IGNACIO ALIAGA ESTELLÉS
Mathematics: Profa PILAR ORÚS BÀGUENA
Organic and Inorganic Chemistry: Prof. SANTIAGO V. LUIS LAFUENTE
Technology: Prof. PEDRO P. COMPANY CALLEJA
Business Administration and Marketing: RAFAEL LAPIEDRA ALCAMÍ
Private Law: Prof. FRANCISCO J. ZAMORA CABOT
Public Law: Prof. JOSÉ LUIS GONZÁLEZ CUSSAC
Economics: Prof. JOAN SERAFÍ BERNAT MARTÍ
Finance and Accounting: Prof. JOSÉ J. ALCARRIA JAIME
Education: Prof. MIGUEL SALVADOR BAUZÁ
English: JOSÉ LUIS OTAL CAMPO (acting)
Philology and European Cultures: JESÚS BERMÚDEZ RAMIRO (acting)
Philosophy, Sociology, Audiovisual Communication and Advertising: Prof. SALVADOR CABEDO MANUEL
History, Geography and Art: Prof. VÍCTOR MÍNGUEZ CORNELLES
Basic Psychology, Clinical Training and Psychobiology: Prof. CARLOS M. GONZÁLEZ ARAGÓN
Social, Educational and Evolutionary Psychology and Methodology: Profa PILAR JARA JIMÉNEZ (acting)
Translation and Communication: Prof. JUAN CARLOS RUÍZ ANTÓN

ATTACHED INSTITUTE

Institute of Ceramic Technology: Campus Universitario Riu Sec, 12006 Castellón; tel. 964-34-24-24; fax 964-34-24-25; e-mail itc@itc.uji.es; internet www.itc.uji.es; Dir Dr AGUSTÍN ESCARDINO.

UNIVERSIDAD DE LA LAGUNA

Molinos de Agua s/n, 38207 La Laguna, Tenerife, Canary Islands
Telephone: 922-31-90-00
Fax: 922-25-96-28
E-mail: ccti@ull.es
Internet: www.ull.es

Founded 1792
State control
Language of instruction: Spanish
Academic year: October to June

Rector: ÁNGEL M. GUTIÉRREZ NAVARRO
Vice-Rector (Academic Organization and Teaching Staff): ADRIANA FABIOLA MARTÍN CÁCERES
Vice-Rector (Cultural Affairs and Institutional Relations): CÁNDIDO ROMÁN CERVANTES
Vice-Rector (Information and Communication Technologies): LEOPOLDO ACOSTA SANCHEZ
Vice-Rector (Programming and Infrastructure): MARÍA DEL ROSARIO ALONSO ALONSO
Vice-Rector (Research and Technological Development): CARMEN MARÍA ÉVORA GARCÍA
Vice-Rector (Students): ROBERTO RODRÍGUEZ GUERRA
Vice-Rector (Study Programmes and Specific Degrees): MARTA JIMÉNEZ JAÉN
Manager (vacant)
Registrar: FÁTIMA FLORES MENDOZA
Librarian: FERNANDO RODRIGUEZ JUNCO

Number of teachers: 1,826
Number of students: 26,111

Publications: *Revista de Historia Canaria* (annually), *Anales de la Facultad de Derecho* (annually), *Revista Canaria de Estudios Ingleses* (2 a year), *Revista Fortunatae* (annually), *Revista de Filología* (annually), *Cuadernos de Cemyr* (annually), *Revista Laguna* (2 a year), *Tempora* (annually), *Qurriculum* (annually), *Clepsidra* (annually), *Revista de Bellas Artes* (annually), *Latente* (annually)

DEANS

Faculty of Biology: PILAR BADÍA CUBAS
Faculty of Chemistry: ANDREA BRITO ALAYÓN
Faculty of Economics and Business Administration: JOSÉ MARCOS AFONSO CASADO
Faculty of Education: AMADOR GUARRO PALLÁS
Faculty of Fine Arts: MARÍA PILAR BLANCO ALTOZANO
Faculty of Geography and History: RAMON PEREZ GONZALEZ
Faculty of Information Science: HUMBERTO HERNÁNDEZ HERNÁNDEZ
Faculty of Law: ANDRÉS MANUEL GONZÁLEZ SANFIEL
Faculty of Mathematics: FERNANDO PÉREZ GONZÁLEZ
Faculty of Medicine: EDUARDO DOMENECH MARTINEZ
Faculty of Pharmacy: JOSÉ BRUNO FARIÑA ESPINOSA
Faculty of Philology: FÉLIX RÍOS TORRES
Faculty of Philosophy: AGUSTÍN SANTANA TALAVERA
Faculty of Physics: FRANCISCO MAURICIO DOMÍNGUEZ
Faculty of Psychology: CARMELO MILITELLO
Higher Technical College of Agricultural Engineering: JUAN FELIPE PÉREZ FRANCÉS
Higher Technical College of Civil and Industrial Engineering: (vacant)
Higher Technical College of Computer Engineering: LEOPOLDO ACOSTA SÁNCHEZ
Centre of Nautical and Marine Studies: ISIDRO PADRÓN ARMAS
Centre of Political and Social Sciences: LEOPOLDO CABRERA RODRÍGUEZ

DIRECTORS

University School of Business Studies: FRANCISCO CALERO GARCÍA
University School of Nursing and Physiotherapy: MIGUEL ANGEL ACOSTA HERRERA
University School of Technical Architecture: FELIPE AGUSTÍN MONZÓN PEÑATE
Nuestra Señora de la Candelaria School of Nursing: MA. MERCEDES ABELLA SOCORRO

ATTACHED INSTITUTES

Andrés Bello Institute of Linguistics: C/ Juan de Vera 13, La Laguna; Dir MANUEL ALMEIDA SUÁREZ.

Antonio González University Institute of Bio-Organics: Avda Astrofísico Fco. Sánchez 2, La Laguna; tel. 922-31-85-70; fax 922-31-85-71; e-mail iubo@ull.es; internet www.iubo.ull.es; Dir VÍCTOR SOTERO MARTÍN GARCÍA.

Astrophysics Institute of the Canary Islands: Avda Astrofísico Francisco Sánchez s/n, 38206 La Laguna; tel. 922-31-81-21; fax 922-31-81-23; e-mail mcv@ll.iac.es; internet www.ull.es/departamento; Dirs MANUEL MAS GARCÍA, ANTONIO APARICIO JUAN.

University Business Institute: Avda 25 de Julio 9, 38004 Santa Cruz de Tenerife; tel. 922-31-97-08; fax 922-31-97-09; e-mail iude@ull.es; Dir Dr JOSÉ ANTONIO LASTRES SEGRET.

University Institute of Political and Social Sciences: Facultad de Derecho, módulo D-02, Campus de Guajara, 38071 La Laguna; tel. 922-31-73-06; fax 922-31-73-08; e-mail inucps@ull.es; Dir MA. TERESA GONZÁLEZ DE LA FE.

University Institute of Regional Development: Facultad de Económicas, Campus de Guajara s/n, 38071 La Laguna; tel. 922-31-71-12; Dir ROSA MARINA GONZÁLEZ MARRERO.

University Institute of Tropical Diseases and Public Health of the Canaries: Unidad de Parasitología. Facultad de Farmacia, Avda Astrofísico Fco. Sánchez s/n, 38071 La Laguna; tel. 922-31-84-86; e-mail jcastilo@ull.es; Dir JOSÉ ANTONIO DEL CASTILLO REMIRO.

UNIVERSIDAD DE LA RIOJA

C/ Avda de La Paz, 93–103, 26006 Logroño
Telephone: 941-29-91-00
Fax: 941-29-91-20
E-mail: informacion@unirioja.es
Internet: www.unirioja.es
Founded 1992
State control
Academic year: September to July
Rector: CARMEN ORTIZ LALLANA
Vice-Rector (Planning and Academic Organization): JOSÉ IGNACIO CASTRESANA RUIZ-CARRILLO
Vice-Rector (Academic Staff): FRANCISCO JAVIER MARTÍN ARISTA
Vice-Rector (Research): MIGUEL ANGEL RODRÍGUEZ BARRANCO
Vice-Rector (Innovation in Teaching): ANA MARÍA PONCE DE LEÓN ELIZONDO
Vice-Rector (Student Affairs): JOSÉ MANUEL GUTIÉRREZ JIMÉNEZ
Vice-Rector (New Technology and Computer Equipment): MIGUEL ANGEL MARÍN LÓPEZ
Registrar: ALFONSO AGUDO RUIZ
Manager: JOSÉ MIGUEL ROS VÁZQUEZ
Librarian: MARTA MAGRIÑÁ CONTRERAS

Library of 160,515 vols, 3,625 periodicals
Number of teachers: 366
Number of students: 7,450

Publications: *Cuadernos de Investigación Geográfica* (annually), *Brocar – Cuadernos de Investigación Histórica* (annually), *Cuadernos de Investigación Filológica* (annually), *Journal of English Studies* (annually), *Contextos Educativos* (education review, annually), *Boletín Europeo de la Universidad de La Rioja* (2 a year), *Anuario Jurídico de La Rioja* (annually), *Iberia: Revista de la Antigüedad* (annually), *Cuadernos de Gestión* (2 a year)

DIRECTORS

Centre for Humanities, Law and Social Sciences: MA. JESÚS SALINERO CASCANTE
Teaching Centre for Science and Technology: IRENE BAÑOS ARRIBAS

HEADS OF DEPARTMENTS

Agriculture and Food: MARÍA CARMEN DE LEMUS VARELA
Human and Social Sciences: SYLVIA SASTRE I RIBA
Law: JOSÉ MARÍA MARTÍNEZ DE PISÓN CAVERO
Economics and Business: JUAN CARLOS AYALA CALVO
Artistic Expression: ROMÁN EGÜEN GARCÍA
Hispanic and Classical Languages: FRANCISCO DOMÍNGUEZ MATITO
Modern Languages: FRANCISCO RUIZ DE MENDOZA IBÁNEZ
Electrical Engineering: CARLOS ALBERTO RODRÍGUEZ GONZÁLEZ
Mechanical Engineering: JOAQUÍN B. ORDIERES MERE
Mathematics and Computation: JOSÉ IGNACIO EXTREMIANA ALDANA
Chemistry: PEDRO JOSÉ CAMPOS GARCÍA

ATTACHED INSTITUTIONS

University School of Labour Relations: Edificio Quintiliano, La Cigüeña 60, 26004 Logroño; tel. 941-29-92-45; fax 941-29-92-44; internet www.unirioja.es/dptos/rellab; Dir ANTONIO SALVADO RUIZ.

University School of Nursing: C/ Donantes de Sangre s/n, 26004 Logroño; tel. 941-26-14-43; fax 941-26-14-43; Dir ROSARIO ARÉJULA BENITO.

University School of Tourism: C/ Quintiliano 5–7, 26005 Logroño; tel. 941-25-73-72; fax 941-24-85-06; General Dir YOLANDA MONFORTE MORÚA; Academic Dir MERCEDES GONZÁLEZ MARIJUÁN.

UNIVERSIDAD DE LAS PALMAS DE GRAN CANARIA

Calle Juan de Quesada 30, 35001, Las Palmas de Gran Canaria, Canary Islands
Telephone: 928-45-10-00
Fax: 928-45-10-22
E-mail: universidad@ulpgc.es
Internet: www.ulpgc.es
Founded 1980
State control
Language of instruction: Spanish
Academic year: October to September
Rector: MANUEL LOBO CABRERA
Vice-Rector (Research, Development and Innovation): Dr ANTONIO FERNÁNDEZ RODRÍGUEZ
Vice-Rector (Academic Organization and Teaching Staff): Dr ROBERTO SARMIENTO RODRÍGUEZ
Vice-Rector (Planning and Quality): Dr GONZALO MARRERO RODRÍGUEZ
Vice-Rector (International Relations and Communication): Dr PABLO MARTEL ESCOBAR
Vice-Rector (Culture and Sport): Dra ALEJANDRA SANJUÁN HERNÁN-PÉREZ
Vice-Rector (Institutional Development and New Technology): Dr JORGE RODRÍGUEZ DÍAZ
Vice-Rector (Student Affairs): Dra DOLORES CABRERA SUÁREZ
Registrar: Dr EDUARDO GALVÁN RODRÍGUEZ
Manager: Dr FRANCISCO QUINTANA NAVARRO
Library Dir: ALICIA GIRÓN GARCÍA

Library of 477,251 vols, 9,634 periodicals
Number of teachers: 1,548
Number of students: 24,551

DEANS

Faculty of Computer Science: MANUEL GONZÁLEZ RODRÍGUEZ
Faculty of Health Sciences: JUAN CABRERA CABRERA
Faculty of Marine Sciences: JOSÉ MIGUEL PACHECO CASTELAO
Faculty of Veterinary Science: ANSELMO GRACIA MOLINA
Faculty of Philology: EUGENIO PADORAO NAVARRO
Faculty of Geography and History: JOSEFA DOMÍNGUEZ MUJICA
Faculty of Translating and Interpreting: MA. JESÚS GARCÍA DOMÍNGUEZ
Faculty of Physical Activity Science and Sport: FERNANDO AMADOR RAMÍREZ
Faculty of Economics and Business: SERGIO J. MARTÍN MACHÍN
Faculty of Law and Social Sciences: IGNACIO DÍAZ DE LEZCANO SEVILLANO
Faculty of Teacher Training: GERMÁN HERNÁNDEZ RODRÍGUEZ

DIRECTORS

Higher Technical School of Industrial Engineering: LUIS ÁLVAREZ ÁLVAREZ
Higher Technical School of Architecture: FLORA PESCADOR MONAGAS
Higher Technical School of Telecommunications Engineering: JUAN ANTONIO MONTIEL NELSON
University School of Technical Engineering in Telecommunications: EDUARDO ROVARIS ROMERO

University School of Computer Science: BEA-TRIZ CORREAS SUÁREZ
University Polytechnic School

HEADS OF DEPARTMENTS

Applied Economic Analysis: LOURDES TRU-JILLO CASTELLANO
Art, City and Territory: VICENTE MIRALLAVE IZQUIERDO
Biology: PEDRO ANTONIO SOSA HENRÍQUEZ
Biochemistry, Molecular Biology, Physiology, Genetics and Immunology: LUISA FANJUL RODRÍGUEZ
Cartography and Engineering Drawing: MELCHOR GARCÍA DOMÍNGUEZ
Clinical Science: LUIS SERRA MAJEN
History: JUAN MANUEL SANTANA PÉREZ
Basic Law: PABLO SAAVEDRA GALLO
Medical Science and Surgery: SERGIO RUIZ SANTANA
Architecture and Construction: CARMELO PADRÓN DÍAZ
Public Law: JOSÉ SUAY RINCÓN
Teaching Specialist Subjects: ISABEL RUIZ DE FRANCISCO
Finance and Accountancy: JUAN GARCÍA BOZA
Economics and Business Management: ÁNGEL GUTIÉRREZ PADRÓN
Education: JOSEFA RODRÍGUEZ PULIDO
Physical Education: JUAN MANUEL GARCÍA MANSO
Nursing: CARMEN DELIA MEDINA CASTELLANO
Draughtsmanship and Architectural Pro-jects: ENRIQUE SOLANA SUÁREZ
Spanish, Classical and Arabic Philology: JOSÉ ANTONIO SAMPER PADILLA
Modern Philology: SANTIAGO HENRÍQUEZ JIMÉ-NEZ
Physics: PEDRO SANCHO DÍAZ
Geography: MA. EMMA PÉREZ-CHACÓN ESPINO
Computer Science and Systems: SANTIAGO CANDELA SOLÁ
Civil Engineering: EDUARDO MURILLO TORO
Process Engineering: SEBASTIÁN PÉREZ BÁEZ
Electrical Engineering: MIGUEL J. MARTÍNEZ MELGAREJO
Electronic Engineering and Automation: AURELIO VEGA MARTÍNEZ
Mechanical Engineering: JOSÉ CARTA GONZÁ-LEZ
Data Transmission Engineering: ÁLVARO SUÁREZ SARMIENTO
Mathematics: ANGELO SANTANA DEL PINO
Quantitative Methods in Economics and Management: FERNANDO FERNÁNDEZ RODRÍGUEZ
Morphology: JOSÉ REGIDOR GAR
Animal Pathology, Animal Production, Bro-matology, Food Science and Technology: JOSÉ ALBERTO MONTOYA ALONSO
Psychology and Sociology: OLGA ESCANDELL BERMÚDEZ
Chemistry: MIGUEL ÁNGEL SUÁREZ DE TANGIL NAVARRO
Signals and Communications: RAFAEL PÉREZ JIMÉNEZ

ATTACHED INSTITUTES

Institute of Applied Microelectronics: Edificio de Electrónica y Telecomunicación, Campus Universitario de Tafira, 35017 Las Palmas de G.C.; tel. 928-45-12-33; fax 928-45-12-43; e-mail carballo@iuma.ulpgc.es; internet www.iuma.ulpgc.es; Dir ANTONIO HERNÁNDEZ BALLESTER.

Marine Biotechnology Centre: Muelle de Taliarte s/n, 35214 Telde, Las Palmas de G.C.; tel. 928-13-32-90; fax 928-13-28-30; e-mail ggarcia@dbio.ulpgc.es; internet www.ulpgc.es/webs/cbm; Dir Prof. GUILLERMO GARCÍA REINA.

Innovation Centre for the Information Society: Edificio Central del Parque Cien-tífico y Tecnológico, Campus Universitario de Tafira, 35017 Las Palmas de G.C.; tel. 928-

45-18-64; fax 928-45-14-92; e-mail info@cicei.com; internet www.cicei.com; Dir Prof. Dr ENRIQUE RUBIO ROYO.

Institute for Cybernetic Science and Technology: Campus Universitario de Tafira, 35017 Las Palmas de G.C.; tel. 928-45-71-00; e-mail mperez@ciber.ulpgc.es; internet www.iuctc.ulpgc.es.

UNIVERSIDAD DE LEÓN

Rectorado, Pabellón de Gobierno, Avda de la Facultad 25, 24071 León
Telephone: 987-29-10-00
Fax: 987-29-16-14
E-mail: rectorado@unileon.es
Internet: www.unileon.es

Founded 1979
State control
Language of instruction: Spanish
Academic year: October to September

Rector: ÁNGEL PENAS MERINO
Vice-Rector (Research): MARCELINO PÉREZ DE LA VEGA
Vice-Rector (Academic Organization): JUAN RAMÓN ALVAREZ BAUTISTA
Vice-Rector (Planning and Evaluation): JAVIER VIDAL GARCÍA
Vice-Rector (International Relations): JESÚS SALVADOR GONZÁLEZ ÁLVAREZ
Vice-Rector (Students and Social Affairs): ANA BERNARDO ÁLVAREZ
Vice-Rector (Institutional Relations and Uni-versity Extension): FRANCISCO FLECHA ANDRÉS
Vice-Rector (Technological Innovation): CAR-LOS REDONDO GIL
Vice-Rector (Teaching Staff): JOSÉ MIGUEL FERNÁNDEZ FERNÁNDEZ
Vice-Rector (Economic Affairs): JOSÉ LUIS PLACEE GALÁN
Vice-Rector (Ponferrada Campus): LUIS HER-RÁEZ ORTEGA
Manager: LORENZO MARTÍNEZ RODRÍGUEZ
Library Director: MARÍA MARSÁ VILA
Library of 290,000 vols, 8,000 periodicals
Number of teachers: 898
Number of students: 15,072

Publications: *Estudios Humanísticos—Filo-logía*, *Estudios Humanísticos—Historia*, *Contextos*, *Polígonos*, *De Arte*, *Silva: Estu-dios de Humanismo y Tradición Clásica*, *Lancia: Revista de Arqueología, Prehis-toria e Historia Antigua*

DEANS

Faculty of Veterinary Science: JUAN FRAN-CISCO GARCÍA MARÍN
Faculty of Biology and Environmental Sciences: JOSÉ CARLOS PENA ALVAREZ
Faculty of Law: Dr MIGUEL DÍAZ Y GARCÍA CONLLEDO
Faculty of Philosophy and Letters: FRANCISCO CARANTOÑA ÁLVAREZ
Faculty of Economics and Business: MA. JESÚS MURES QUINTANA
Faculty of Labour Studies: GERMÁN BARREIRO GONZÁLEZ
Faculty of Education: JUSTO FERNÁNDEZ OBLANCA
Faculty of Physical Education and Sport: JUAN CARLOS REDONDO CASTÁN

DIRECTORS

School of Industrial and Computer Engineer-ing: ÁNGEL ALONSO ALVAREZ
Higher School of Mining Engineering: JAIME CIFUENTES GONZÁLEZ
Higher School of Agricultural Engineering: JUAN ANTONIO BOTO FIDALGO
University School of Health Sciences: LEAN-DRO B. RODRÍGUEZ APARICIO
University School of Social Work: VICENTE GARCÍA LOBO

HEADS OF DEPARTMENTS

Animal Biology: Dr ANTONIO JOSÉ LABORDA NAVIA
Cell Biology and Anatomy: Dr JOSÉ MARÍA VILLAR LACILLA
Vegetal Biology: FÉLIX LLAMAS GARCÍA
Biochemistry and Molecular Biology: Dr ÁNGEL REGLERO CHILLÓN
Basic Law: Dra PIEDAD GONZÁLEZ GRANDA
Administrative Law and International Rela-tions: Dra MANUELA VEGA HERRERO
Private Law: Dra ETELVINA VALLADARES RASCÓN
Basic Public Law: Dr JUAN ANTONIO GARCÍA AMADO
Teaching Self-expression through Music, Plastic Arts, Movement, Drawing and Physical Education and Sport: RAMIRO JOVER RUIZ
Business Management and Finance: MAR-IANO NIETO ANTOLIN
Ecology, Genetics and Microbiology: PALOMA LIRAS PADÍN
Economics: JOSÉ MANUEL DÍEZ MODINO
Classical Studies: MAURILIO PÉREZ GONZÁLEZ
Nursing and Physiotherapy: ANA I. LÓPEZ ALONSO
Pharmacology and Toxicology: Dr RAFAEL BALAÑA FOUCE
Spanish: Dr JOSÉ RAMÓN MORALA RODRÍGUEZ
Modern Languages: Dr MANUEL BRONCANO RODRÍGUEZ
Philosophy and Education: Dra MA. ISABEL LAFUENTE GUANTES
Physics, Chemistry and Engineering Draw-ing: Dr JAVIER MARTIN VILLACOSTA
Physiology: Dr JAVIER GONZÁLEZ GALLEGO
Geography: JOSÉ SOMOZA MEDINA
Hygiene and Food Technology: JESÚS ÁNGEL SANTOS BUELGA
History: CESAR ÁLVAREZ ÁLVAREZ
Agricultural Engineering: TELESFORO DE LA PUENTE Y PUENTE
Electrical and Electronic Engineering: JORGE BLANES PEIRÓ
Mining Engineering: Dr SANTIAGO ALFAGEME DÍEZ
Mathematics: Dr JOSÉ ÁNGEL HERMIDA ALONSO
Animal Pathology (Animal Medicine): Dr JOSÉ MANUEL GONZALO CORDERO
Animal Pathology (Veterinary Medicine): FELIPE PRIETO MONTAÑA
Animal Pathology (Animal Health): Dr ELÍAS FERNÁNDEZ RODRÍGUEZ FERRI
Built, Artistic and Written Heritage: Dra MA. VICTORIA HERRÁEZ ORTEGA
Animal Breeding I: LUIS FERNANDO DE LA FUENTE CRESPO
Animal Breeding II: Dr VICENTE GAUDIOSO LACASA

ATTACHED INSTITUTES

Advanced Training and Educational Innovation Centre: Campus de Veganaza, Facultad de CC. del Trabajo, 24071 León; tel. 987-29-14-43; fax 987-29-14-71; e-mail cfaie@unileon.es; Dir Dr DELIO DEL RINCÓN IGEA.

Institute of Food Science and Technol-ogy: C/ La Serna 56, 24007 León; tel. 987-24-31-23; e-mail dhtjfb@unileon.es; Dir Dr JOSÉ MARÍA FRESNO BARO.

Institute of the Environment: C/ La Serna 56, 24007 León; tel. 987-29-15-68; e-mail degelc@unileon.es; Dir Dr ESTANISLAO LUIS CALABUIG.

Institute of Biomedical Research: Depar-tamento de Fisiología, Campus de Veganaza, 24071 León; tel. 987-29-12-58; fax 987-29-12-67; e-mail dfijgg@unileon.es; Dir Dr JAVIER GONZÁLEZ GALLEGO.

Institute of Cattle Development: Campus de Veganaza, 24071 León; tel. 987-29-19-28;

fax 987-29-16-38; e-mail dbbmfg@unileon.es; Dir (vacant).

Institute of Natural Resources: Campus de la Escuela T y S de Agrónomos, Avda. de Portugal 42, 24071 León; tel. 987-29-18-44; fax 987-29-18-39; e-mail dfqamp@unileon.es; Dir Dr ANTONIO MORÁN PALAO.

Institute of Automation and Manufacturing: Dirs DAVID MARCOS MARTÍNEZ (Automation Section MANUEL DOMÍNGUEZ GONZÁLEZ (Automation Section ÁNGEL ALONSO ÁLVAREZ (Imaging Section JULIO LABARGA (Manufacturing Engineering Section.

Energy and Mining Research Society: Avda Real 1, 24006 León; tel. 987-21-01-98; fax 987-21-00-70; e-mail dimblg@unileon.es; internet www3.unileon.es/ins/insaiem/indice .htm; Dir Dr BERNARDO LLAMAS GARCÍA.

Institute of Biotechnology: Avda Real 1, 24006 León; tel. 987-21-03-08; fax 987-21-03-88; e-mail degjmm@unileon.es; internet www .inbiotec.es; Dir Dr JUAN FRANCISCO MARTÍN MARTÍN.

Institute of Toxicology: Avda Real 1, 24006 León; tel. 987-21-00-83; fax 987-21-00-91; e-mail dftdoe@unileon.es; Dir Dr DAVID ORDÓÑEZ ESCUDERO.

UNIVERSITAT DE LLEIDA

Plaça de Víctor Siurana 1, 25003 Lleida
Telephone: 973-70-20-00
Fax: 973-70-20-62
E-mail: pdi@seu.udl.es
Internet: www.udl.es

Founded 1991
State control
Language of instruction: Catalan, Spanish, English
Academic year: September to July
Rector: Dr JOAN VIÑAS SALAS
Vice-Rector (Cultural Activities and University Promotion): Dr JAUME BARULL PELEGRÍ
Vice-Rector (Economic Affairs): Dra MARIONA FABRÉ PERDIGUER
Vice-Rector (Finance): JOSEP M. SENTÍS SUÑÉ
Vice-Rector (Infrastructure and Information Technology): Dr CÈSAR FERNÁNDEZ CAMON
Vice-Rector (International Relations): Dra CARMEN FIGUEROLA CABROL
Vice-Rector (Quality and Strategic Planning): Dr JOAN PRAT COROMINAS
Vice-Rector (Rectorate): Dr XAVIER GÓMEZ ARBONÉS
Vice-Rector (Research and Innovation): Dr RAMON CANELA GARAYOA
Vice-Rector (Secretary-General): Dra ANA M. ROMERO BURILLO
Vice-Rector (Teaching Personnel): Dr JOAN RAMON ROSELL POLO
Vice-Rector (Teaching and Student Affairs): Dr CARLES ALSINET MORA
Registrar: Dra ANA ROMERO BURILLO
Manager: JOSEP M. SENTÍS SUÑÉ
Library Director: LOLI MANCIÑEIRAS VAZ-ROMERO
Library of 240,697 vols, 4,228 periodicals, 6,266 e-journals, 5,305 e-books
Number of teachers: 780
Number of students: 9,835

Publications: *Arrabal* (annually), *Bulletin Oficial* (11 a year), *Qualitative Theory of Dynamic Systems* (2 a year), *Revista d'Arqueologia de Ponent* (annually), *Sintagma* (annually), *Ull Crític* (annually)

DEANS

Faculty of Arts: Dr EMILI JUNYENT SÁNCHEZ
Faculty of Education: Dra M. ÀNGELS BALSELLS BAILÓN
Faculty of Law and Economics: Dra AGNÈS PARDELL VEÀ

Faculty of Medicine: Dr ÀNGEL RODRÍGUEZ POZO

DIRECTORS

Higher Technical School of Agricultural Engineering: Dr ANTONIO MICHELENA BÁRCENA
Institute of Education: ISABEL DEL ARCO BRAVO
University Polytechnic School: JAVIER CHAVARRIGA SORIANO
University School of Nursing: CARME NUIN ORRIO

HEADS OF DEPARTMENTS

Agroforestry Engineering: Dr MIQUEL LLORCA MARQUÉS
Agronomy and Forest Science: XAVIER PONS DOMÈNECH
Animal Production: EDUARDO ANGULO ASENSIO
Applied Economics: JOAN BARÓ LLINÀS
Basic Medical Sciences: Dr ALBERT SORRIBAS TELLO
Business Administration and Economic Management of Natural Resources: JOSÉ LUIS GALLIZO LARRAZ
Catalan Philology: Dr XAVIER MACIÀ COSTA
Chemistry: JAUME PUY LAURENS
Classical, French and Hispanic Philology: PERE SOLÀ SOLÉ
Education and Psychology: JAUME SANUY BURGUÉS
English and Linguistics: ENRIC LLURDA GIMENEZ
Environmental and Soil Science: Dr PEDRO J. PÉREZ GARCÍA
Food Technology: OLGA MARTÍN BELLOSO
Geology and Sociology: Dr JOAN GANAU i CASAS
History: ENRIC VICEDO RIUS
History of Art and Social History: ROBERTO FERNÁNDEZ DÍAZ
Mathematics: JOAN CECILIA AVEROS
Nursing: RAMON COLELL BRUNET
Private Law: Prof. Dr ANTONI VAQUER ALOY
Surgery: Prof. LUIS PÉREZ RUIZ
Teaching Specialized Subjects: PILAR VINUESA VILELLA
Vegetable- and Fruit-Growing, Botany and Garden Maintenance: ANA MARÍA PELACHO AJA

ATTACHED CENTRES

National Institute of Physical Education of Catalonia: Pda. de la Caparrella s/n, 25192 Lleida; tel. 973-27-20-22; fax 973-27-59-41; e-mail webmaster@inefc.es; internet www.inefc.es/lleida; Dir Dr JOAN PALMI GUERRERO.

'Terres de Lleida' University School of Tourism: Henri Dunant 3, 25003 Lleida; tel. 973-21-33-33; fax 973-20-86-24; e-mail informacio@eutl.org; internet www.eutl.org; Dir JOSEP M. BALSELLS SESPLUGUES.

University School of Labour Relations: Henri Dunant 3, 25003 Lleida; tel. 973-24-89-93; fax 973-22-18-18; e-mail inforl@eurl .es; internet www.eurl.es; Dir Dra MARIA JOSÉ PUYALTO FRANCO.

University School of Tourism at Manresa: Folch i Torres 5–13, 08241 Manresa (Barcelona); tel. 938-72-69-88; fax 938-72-85-81; e-mail secretaria@joviat.com; internet www.joviat.com/catala/Joviat1/tur.htm; Dir JOSEP CODINA i CONTRERAS.

UNIVERSIDAD COMPLUTENSE DE MADRID

Ciudad Universitaria, Avda Seneca 2, 28040 Madrid
Telephone: 91-394-35-21
Fax: 91-394-34-00
E-mail: infocom@ucm.es

Internet: www.ucm.es
Founded 1508
Rector: Prof. CARLOS BERZOSA ALONSO-MARTÍNEZ
Vice-Rector (Economic Affairs): CARMEN NOVERTO LABORDA
Vice-Rector (Departments and Centres): MARÍA JESÚS SUÁREZ GARCÍA
Vice-Rector (Student Affairs): MARGARITA BARÁNANO CID
Vice-Rector (Studies): MANUEL RODRÍGUEZ SÁNCHEZ
Vice-Rector (Extension and Cultural Relations): ISABEL TAJAHUERCE ÁNGEL
Vice-Rector (Innovation, Organization and Quality): JOSÉ CARRILLO MENÉNDEZ
Vice-Rector (Research): CARLOS ANDRADAS HERANZ
Vice-Rector (Academic Organization): ELENA HERNÁNDEZ SANDOICA
Vice-Rector (Graduate Studies and Continuing Education): MARÍA LUZ MORÁN CALVO-SOTELO
Vice-Rector (Institutional Relations and Assistance in Development): RAFAEL HERNÁNDEZ TRISTÁN
Vice-Rector (International Relations): ROSARIO OTEGUI PASCUAL
Registrar: JULIO GONZÁLEZ GARCÍA
Manager: ISIDRO LÓPEZ CUADRA
Librarian: JOSÉ ANTONIO MAGÁN WALS
Library of 2,000,000 vols, 40,000 periodicals
Number of teachers: 5,915
Number of students: 98,142
Publications: *Memoria de la UCM, Gaceta Complutense*, various faculty publications

DEANS

Faculty of Fine Arts: MANUEL PARRALDO DORADO
Faculty of Biological Sciences: JOSÉ LUIS TELLERÍA JORGE
Faculty of Economics and Business: JAVIER ZORNOZA BOY
Faculty of Physics: JOSÉ MARÍA GÓMEZ GÓMEZ
Faculty of Geological Sciences: EUMENIO ANCOCHEA SOTO
Faculty of Information Science: FRANCISCO JAVIER DAVARA RODRÍGUEZ
Faculty of Mathematics: JUAN ANTONIO TEJADA CAZORLA
Faculty of Politics and Sociology: FRANCISCO ALDECOA LUZÁRRAGA
Faculty of Chemical Sciences: JESÚS SANTAMARÍA ANTONIO
Faculty of Law: JOSÉ ITURMENDI MORALES
Faculty of Education: LUIS ARRANZ MARTÍNEZ
Faculty of Pharmacy: BENITO DEL CASTILLO GARCÍA
Faculty of Philology: PILAR SAQUERO SUÁREZ-SOMONTE
Faculty of Philosophy: JUAN MANUEL NAVARRO CORDÓN
Faculty of Geography and History: MERCEDES MOLINA IBÁÑEZ
Faculty of Computer Science: CARMEN FERNÁNDEZ CHAMIZO
Faculty of Medicine: ÁNGEL NOGALES ESPERT
Faculty of Odontology: JOSÉ FRANCISCO LÓPEZ LOZANO
Faculty of Psychology: ANGELA CONCHILLO JIMÉNEZ
Faculty of Veterinary Science: JOAQUÍN GOYACHE GOÑI

DIRECTORS

University School of Librarianship and Documentation: PEDRO LÓPEZ LÓPEZ
University School of Nursing, Physiotherapy and Paedology: JUAN VICENTE BENEIT MONTESINOS
University School of Statistics: EDUARDO ORTEGA CASTELLÓ
University School of Business Studies: JOSÉ LUIS MARTÍN SIMÓN

University School of Optics: MIGUEL ÁNGEL MUÑOZ SANZ
University School of Social Work: MANUEL SERRANO RUIZ-CALDERÓN
University College of Financial Studies: JAIME REQUEIJO GONZÁLEZ
School of Clinical Analysis: ANTONIO MARTÍNEZ FERNÁNDEZ
School of Specialization in Health Sciences: PILAR FERNÁNDEZ FERNÁNDEZ
School of Co-operative Studies: GUSTAVO LEJARRIAGA PÉREZ DE LAS VACAS
School of Medical Hydrology and Hydrotherapy: FRANCISCO MARAVER EYZAGUIRRE
School of Medical Care in Physical Education and Sport: JULIO CÉSAR LEGIDO ARCE
School of Medical Care in the Workplace: CÉSAR BOROBIA FERNÁNDEZ
School of Forensic Medicine: JOSÉ MARÍA DE LA CUESTA
School of Legal Practice: JOSÉ LEANDRO MARTÍNEZ-CARDO RUIZ
School of Labour Relations: JULIO FERNÁNDEZ GARRIDO

HEADS OF DEPARTMENTS

Faculty of Fine Arts:

Drawing I (Drawing and Engraving): RAMÓN DÍAZ PADILLA
Drawing II (Design and Image): MIGUEL RUIZ MASSIP
Teaching Self-Expression in the Plastic Arts: MANUEL HERNÁNDEZ BELVER
Sculpture: JOSÉ LUIS GUTIÉRREZ MUÑOZ
Painting (Painting and Restoration): JESÚS LARRAÑAGA ALTUNA

Faculty of Biological Sciences:

Cell Biology: JOAQUÍN FERNÁNDEZ PÉREZ
Vegetal Biology I: ROSALÍA RAMÍREZ VERA
Ecology: FRANCISCO DÍAZ PINEDA
Physiology (Animal Physiology II): MARISA PUERTA LÓPEZ
Genetics: JUAN RAMÓN LACADENA CALERO
Applied Mathematics (Biomathematics): CRISTINA MARTÍNEZ CALVO
Microbiology III: COVADONGA VÁZQUEZ ESTÉVEZ
Zoology and Physical Anthropology: JACINTO BERZOSA DURÁN

Faculty of Economics and Business:

Applied Economics I (International Economics and Development): LUIS HERNÁNDEZ MENDOZA (acting)
Applied Economics II (Economic Structure and Industrial Economics): RAFAEL MYRO SÁNCHEZ
Applied Economics III (Economic Policy): JAVIER CASARES RIPOL
Applied Economics VI (Public Finance and Fiscal System): LAURA DE PABLOS ESCOBAR
Financial Economics and Accountancy I (Financial and Actuarial Economics): JOSÉ ANTONIO GIL FANA
Financial Economics and Accountancy II (Accountancy): ESTHER FIDALGO CERVIÑO
Principles of Economic Analysis I (Economic Analysis): EMILIO CERDÁ TENA
Principles of Economic Analysis II (Quantitative Economics): MIGUEL JEREZ MÉNDEZ
History and Economic Institutions I: JUAN HERNÁNDEZ ANDRÉU
History and Economic Institutions II (Economic History): ENRIQUE LLOPIS AGELÁN
Business Organization: JOSÉ EMILIO NAVAS LÓPEZ
Financial Economics and Accountancy III (Business Economics and Financial Administration): JUAN ANTONIO MAROTO ACÍN
Statistics and Operational Research II (Decision-Making: ROQUE PIÑOLE VILLAR

Marketing and Market Research: JOSÉ MARÍA SANTIAGO MERINO

Faculty of Physics:

Applied Physics I (Thermology): JUAN IGNACIO MENGUAL CABEZÓN
Applied Physics III (Electricity and Electronics): GERMÁN GONZÁLEZ DÍAZ
Atomic, Molecular and Nuclear Physics (Atomic Physics and Astrophysics): CARLOS ARMENTA DÉU
Geophysics, Astronomy and Astrophysics I (Geophysics, Meteorology, Astronomy and Geodesy): AGUSTÍN UDÍAS VALLINA
Geophysics, Astronomy and Astrophysics II (Astrophysics and Atmospherical Science): MANUEL EDUARDO REGO FERNÁNDEZ
Physics of Materials: JAVIER PIQUERAS DE NORIEGA
Theoretical Physics I: RAMÓN FERNÁNDEZ ÁLVAREZ-ESTRADA
Theoretical Physics II (Mathematical Methods of Physics): ARTEMIO GONZÁLEZ TIXAIRE
Optics: JOSÉ MANUEL GUERRA PÉREZ
Computer Architecture and Automation (Computer Architecture and Technology, Systems Engineering and Automation): MILAGROS FERNÁNDEZ CENTENO

Faculty of Geological Sciences:

Crystallography and Mineralogy: JUAN LUIS MARTÍN-VIVALDI CABALLERO
Stratigraphy: ÁLVARO GARCÍA QUINTANA
Geodynamics: ANDRÉS CARBÓ GOROSABEL
Palaeontology: MARÍA DOLORES GIL CID
Petrology and Geochemistry: MANUEL BUSTILLO REVUELTA

Faculty of Information Science:

Audiovisual Communication and Advertising I: EMILIO C. GARCÍA FERNÁNDEZ
Audiovisual Communication and Advertising II: UBALDO CUESTA CAMBRA
Spanish Philology III (Language and Literature): MILAGROS ARIZMENDI MARTÍNEZ
History of Social Communication: INGRID SCHULZE SCHNEIDER
Journalism I (Analysis of the News Article): MARÍA JESÚS CASALS CARRO
Journalism II (Structure and Information Technology): MARIANO CEBRIÁN HERREROS
Journalism III (General Theory of Information): JORGE LUIS LOZANO HERNÁNDEZ
Journalism IV (News Publishing): JOSÉ IGNACIO POBLACIÓN BERNARDO
Librarianship and Documentation: ALFONSO LÓPEZ YEPES
Sociology VI (Public Opinion and Mass Culture): FERMÍN BOUZA ÁLVAREZ

Faculty of Mathematics:

Algebra: IGNACIO LUENGO VELASCO
Mathematical Analysis: JOSÉ MENDOZA CASAS
Statistics and Operational Research I: TEÓFILO VALDÉS SÁNCHEZ
Geometry and Topology: JUAN TARRÉS FREIXENET
Applied Mathematics: SIXTO JESÚS ÁLVAREZ CONTRERAS

Faculty of Politics and Sociology:

Social Anthropology: JOSÉ LUIS GARCÍA GARCÍA
Political and Administrative Science I: JULIÁN SANTAMARÍA OSORIO
Political and Administrative Science II: FRANCISCO JAVIER ROIZ PARRA
Public International Law and International Relations (International Studies): EDUARDO VILARIÑO PINTOS
Applied Economics V: JUAN MUÑOZ GARCÍA
Political Science of Administration III (Political Theories and Methods and

Human Geography): ANTONIO ELORZA DOMÍNGUEZ
Sociology I (Social Change): RAMÓN RAMOS TORRE
Sociology II (Human Ecology and Population): DAVID-SEVEN REHER SULLIVAN
Sociology III (Social Structure and Sociology of Education): RAFEL FEITO ALONSO
Sociology IV (Research Methodology and Theory of Communication): FRANCISCO ALVIRA MARTÍN
Sociology V (Social Theory): FERNANDO J. GARCÍA SELGAS
History of Thought and of Social and Political Movements: RAFAEL CRUZ MARTÍNEZ
Social Psychology: MARÍA ROS GARCÍA

Faculty of Chemical Sciences:

Biochemistry and Molecular Biology I: JOSÉ G. GAVILANES FRANCO
Materials Science and Metallurgical Engineering: CONCEPCIÓN MERINO CASALS
Chemical Engineering: JOSÉ LUIS SOTELO SANCHO
Analytical Chemistry: JOSÉ MANUEL PINGARRÓN CARRAZÓN
Physical Chemistry I: EMILIO AICART SOSPEDRA
Inorganic Chemistry I: JOSÉ MARÍA GARCÍA CALBET
Organic Chemistry I: JOAQUÍN PLUMET ORTEGA

Faculty of Law:

Administrative Law: LORENZO MARTÍN-RETORTILLO BAQUER
Civil Law: JOAQUÍN RAMS ALBESA
Constitutional Law: JORGE DE ESTEBAN ALONSO
Labour and Social Security Law: ALFREDO MONTOYA MELGAR
State Ecclesiastical Law: JOSÉ ANTONIO SOUTO PAZ
Financial and Tax Law: LEONARDO GARCÍA DE LA MORA
Public International Law and Private International Law: LUIS IGNACIO SÁNCHEZ RODRÍGUEZ
Mercantile Law: CARMEN ALONSO LEDESMA
Penal Law: EMILIO OCTAVIO DE TOLEDO Y UBIETO
Procedural Law: ANDRÉS DE LA OLIVA SANTOS
Roman Law: FRANCISCO JAVIER PARICIO SERRANO
Applied Economics IV (Political Economy and Public Finance): FRANCISCO CABRILLO RODRÍGUEZ
Philosophy of Moral Law and Politics I: MARCELINO RODRÍGUEZ MOLINERO
History of Law and of Institutions: JOSÉ SÁNCHEZ ARCILLA BERNAL

Faculty of Education:

Teaching and School Organization: ANTONIO MONCLÚS ESTELLA
Research Methods and Diagnostics in Education: NARCISO GARCÍA NIETO
Evolutionary and Educational Psychology: JESÚS BELTRÁN LLERA
Theory and History of Education: JOSÉ VICENTE MERINO FERNÁNDEZ
Teaching Self-Expression Through Music and Movement: NICOLÁS ORIOL DE ALARCÓN
Teaching Language and Literature (Spanish, French, English): JAIME GARCÍA PADRINO
Teaching Experimental Science (Physics, Chemistry, Biology and Geology): MANUELA MARTÍN SÁNCHEZ
Teaching Social Sciences (Geography, History and History of Art): MARÍA JESÚS MARRÓN GAITE
Teaching Mathematics: MARTÍN MANUEL GARBAYO MORENO

Faculty of Pharmacy:

Vegetal Biology II: SALVADOR RIVAS MAR-
TÍNEZ
Biochemistry and Molecular Biology II:
MANUEL ROMÁN BENITO DE LAS HERAS
Soil Science: JUANA GONZÁLEZ PARRA
Pharmacy and Pharmaceutical Technol-
ogy: IRENE TERESA MOLINA MARTÍNEZ
Pharmacology (Pharmacognosy and
Experimental Pharmacology: ÁNGEL
MARÍA VILLAR DEL FRESNO
Microbiology II: MARÍA MOLINA MARTÍN
Nutrition and Bromatology I (Nutrition):
ANA MARÍA REQUEJO MARCOS
Nutrition and Bromatology II (Bromatol-
ogy): MARÍA AURORA ZAPATA REVILLA
Parasitology: ANTONIO RAMÓN MARTÍNEZ
RAMÍREZ
Inorganic and Bioinorganic Chemistry:
MARÍA VALLET REGI
Organic and Pharmaceutical Chemisty:
ELENA DE LA CUESTA ELÓSEGUI
Physical Chemistry II (Pharmaceutical
Physical Chemistry): FRANCISCO GARCÍA
BLANCO

Faculty of Philosophy:

Philosophy of Moral Law and Politics II
(Ethics and Sociology): LUIS MÉNDEZ
FRANCISCO
Philosophy II (Metaphysics and Theory of
Knowledge): MARÍA JOSÉ CALLEJO HER-
NANZ
Philosophy III (Hermeneutics and Philoso-
phy of History): ANTONIO GIMÉNEZ GAR-
CÍA
Logic and Philosophy of Science: LUCILA
GONZÁLEZ PAZOS
Philosophy IV (Theory of Knowledge and
History of Thought): ANTONIO MIGUEL
LÓPEZ MOLINA

Faculty of Geography and History:

Regional Geographical Analysis and Phy-
sical Geography: JUAN ANTONIO CÓRDOBA
Y ORDÓNEZ
Historiographical and Archaeological
Sciences and Methods: JUAN CARLOS
GALENDE DÍAZ
Human Geography: MIGUEL ÁNGEL TROI-
TIÑO VINUESA
Ancient History: JOSÉ MANUEL ROLDÁN
HERVÁS
Contemporary History: GUADALUPE GÓMEZ-
FERRER MORANT
American History I: SILVIA LYN HILTON
STOW
American History II (Anthropology of
America): JOSÉ LUIS DE ROJAS Y GUTIÉR-
REZ DE GANDARILLA
History of Art I (Medieval): FERNANDO
OLAGUER-FELIU ALONSO
History of Art II (Modern): FRANCISCO
PORTELA SANDOVAL
History of Art III (Contemporary): ANA
MARÍA ARIAS DE COSSÍO
Medieval History: JOSÉ MANUEL NIETO
SORIA
Modern History: MARÍA VICTORIA LÓPEZ-
CORDÓN CORTEZO
Prehistory: TERESA CHAPA BRUNET

Faculty of Computer Science:

Computer Systems and Programming
(Computer Languages and Systems,
Computation Science and Artificial Engi-
neering): MARIO RODRÍGUEZ ARTALEJO

Faculty of Medicine:

Anatomy and Human Embryology I: FER-
MÍN VIEJO TIRADO
Anatomy and Human Embryology II: JOSÉ
FRANCISCO RODRÍGUEZ VÁZQUEZ
Pathological Anatomy: JULIÁN SANZ ESPO-
NERA
Cell Biology: JESÚS BOYA VEGUE

Biochemistry and Molecular Biology III:
JORGE TAMARIT RODRÍGUEZ
Surgery I: JOSÉ LUIS BALIBREA CANTERO
Pharmacology: PEDRO LORENZO FERNÁNDEZ
Physiology: FRANCISCO MORA TERUEL
Medicine I: JOSÉ LUIS ÁLVAREZ-SALA
WALTHER
Medicine II (Dermatology): EVARISTO SÁN-
CHEZ YUS
Preventive Medicine, Public Health and
History of Science: VICTORIA DOMÍNGUEZ
ROJAS
Obstetrics and Gynaecology: MANUEL
ESCUDERO FERNÁNDEZ
Ophthalmology and Otorhinolaryngology:
JOSÉ MANUEL RAMÍREZ SEBASTIÁN
Paediatrics: MANUEL MORO SERRANO
Psychiatry: TOMÁS ORTIZ ALONSO
Radiology and Physical Medicine (Radiol-
ogy): LUCIANO GONZÁLEZ GARCÍA
Toxicology and Health Legislation: JOSÉ
ANTONIO SÁNCHEZ SÁNCHEZ
Microbiology I: JUAN JOSÉ PICAZO DE LA
GARZA
Physical Medicine and Rehabilitation,
Medical Hydrology: LUIS PABLO
RODRÍGUEZ RODRÍGUEZ

Faculty of Odontology:

Stomatology I (Buccofacial Prosthesis):
FERNANDO DEL RÍO DE LAS HERAS
Stomatology II (Conservation Odontology):
JUAN ANTONIO LÓPEZ CALVO
Stomatology III (Medicine and Buccofacial
Surgery: VICTORIANO SERRANO CUENCA
Stomatology IV (Prophylaxis, Odontopae-
diatrics and Orthodontics): JUAN CARLOS
PALMA FERNÁNDEZ

Faculty of Psychology:

Methology of the Behavioural Sciences:
JOSÉ MARÍA ARREDONDO RODRÍGUEZ
Personality, Evaluation and Psychological
Treatment I (Personality, Evaluation
and Clinical Psychology): CRISTINA LAR-
ROY GARCÍA
Personality, Evaluation and Psychological
Treatment II (Differential Psychology
and Psychology of Work): SANTIAGO PER-
EDA MARTÍN
Psychobiology: JESÚS MARTÍN RAMÍREZ
Basic Psychology I (Basic Processes): FRAN-
CISCO DE VICENTE PÉREZ
Basic Psychology II (Cognitive Processes):
JAVIER GONZÁLEZ MARQUÉS

Faculty of Veterinary Science:

Anatomy and Comparative Pathological
Anatomy (Anatomy and Embryology):
RAFAEL MARTÍN ORTI
Biochemistry and Molecular Biology IV:
MARÍA TERESA MIRAS PORTUGAL
Physiology (Animal Physiology): JUAN CAR-
LOS ILLERAS DEL PORTAL
Medicine and Animal Surgery: JUANA
MARÍA FLORES LANDEIRA
Nutrition, Bromatology and Food Technol-
ogy: LORENZO DE LA HOZ PERALES
Animal Production: PEDRO FERNANDO
ROUCO PÉREZ
Animal Health: RICARDO DE LA FUENTE
LÓPEZ
Toxicology and Pharmacology: ARTURO
ANADÓN NAVARRO

ATTACHED INSTITUTES

**Instituto Universitario de Investigación
Ortega y Gasset** (Ortega y Gasset Univer-
sity Research Institute): see under Learned
Societies—Education.

**Higher Centre for Studies on Manage-
ment, Analysis and Evaluation:** Finca
Mas Ferré, Edificio B, Campus de Somosaguas, 28223 Pozuelo de Alarcón (Madrid); tel.
91-394-29-58; fax 91-394-29-56; e-mail
csegae05@cseg.ucm.es; internet www.ucm
.es/info/csegae; Dir JUAN GÓMEZ CASTAÑEDA.

Institute of Bromatology and Nutrition:
Facultad de Farmacia, Planta 2a, Ciudad
Universitaria, 28040 Madrid; tel. 91-394-17-
99; fax 91-394-17-32; Dir ESPERANZA TORIJA
ISASA.

**Institute of Meat Science and Technol-
ogy:** Facultad de Veterinaria, Planta 2a,
Ciudad Universitaria, 28040 Madrid; tel.
91-394-37-49; fax 91-394-37-43; e-mail
icamber@vet.ucm.es; Dir ISABEL CAMBERO
RODRÍGUEZ.

Institute of Environmental Science:
Manuel Bartolomé Cossio s/n, Planta 1a,
28040 Madrid; tel. and fax 91-549-10-75;
e-mail lopezal@pdi.ucm.es; internet www
.ucm.es/info/iuca; Dir ALEJANDRO LÓPEZ
LÓPEZ.

Institute of Education: C/ Santísima Trinidad 37, 28010 Madrid; tel. 91-394-67-07;
fax 91-394-66-95; e-mail captutor@edu.ucm
.es; internet www.ice.ucm.es; Dir MARÍA DEL
CARMEN CHAMORRO PLAZA.

**Complutense Institute of Economic
Analysis:** Facultad de Ciencias Económicas
y Empresariales. Pabellón prefabricado, 1a
Planta, ala Norte, Campus de Somosaguas,
28223 Pozuelo de Alarcón (Madrid); tel. 91-
394-26-11; fax 91-394-26-13; e-mail icaesec@
ccee.ucm.es; internet www.ucm.es/icae; Dir
ANTONIO ABADÍA CASELLES.

**Complutense Institute of Industrial and
Financial Analysis:** Facultad de Ciencias
Económicas y Empresariales. Pabellón Central, 1a Planta, Campus de Somosaguas,
28223 Pozuelo de Alarcón (Madrid); tel. and
fax 91-394-24-56; e-mail joost@ccee.ucm.es;
internet www.ucm.es/BUCM/cee/iaif; Dir
MIKEL BUESA BLANCO.

**Complutense Institute of Administra-
tive Science:** Facultad de Ciencias Políticas
y Sociología, Departamento de Derecho Ami-
nistrativo II, Planta 3a, Martillo 5°, Campus
de Somosaguas, 28223 Pozuelo de Alarcón
(Madrid); tel. 91-394-28-93; fax 91-394-26-20;
Dir JOSÉ VICENTE GÓMEZ RIVAS.

**Complutense Institute of Morphofunc-
tional and Sport Sciences:** Facultad de
Medicina, Pabellón 6, Plantas baja, Ciudad
Universitaria, 28040 Madrid; tel. 91-394-13-
39; fax 91-394-13-42; Dir JOSÉ RAMÓN MÉRIDA
VELASCO.

UNIVERSIDAD AUTÓNOMA DE MADRID

Ciudad Universitaria de Cantoblanco, Carretera de Colmenar Km. 15, 28049 Madrid

Telephone: 91-397-50-00
Fax: 91-397-41-23
E-mail: informacion.general@uam.es
Internet: www.uam.es

Founded 1968
State control
Language of instruction: Spanish
Academic year: October to June

Rector: ÁNGEL GABILONDO PUJOL
Vice-Rector (Campus and Environmental
Quality): JAVIER BENAYAS DEL ALAMO
Vice-Rector (Information and Labour Inte-
gration): JUAN ALBERTO SIGÜENZA PIZARRO
Vice-Rector (University Extension and Co-
operation): PEDRO ANTONIO MARTÍNEZ LILLO
Vice-Rector (Infrastructure and Technologi-
cal Development): JOSÉ MARÍA SANZ MAR-
TÍNEZ
Vice-Rector (Teaching Staff): JOSÉ MANUEL
LÓPEZ POYATO
Vice-Rector (International Relations): PILAR
RODRÍGUEZ
Vice-Rector (Co-ordination, Communication
and Information): ÁNGELA LOECHES
Vice-Rector (Students): PALOMA CALLE DIEZ

Vice-Rector (Studies and Educational Innovation): AMELIA CABALLERO BORDA
Vice-Rector (Research): MA. JESÚS MATILLA QUIZA
Vice-Rector (Planning and Quality): FLOR SÁNCHEZ FERNÁNDEZ
Registrar: PILAR BENAVENTE MOREDA
Manager: FERNANDO CASANI
Librarian: MIGUEL JIMÉNEZ ALEIXANDRE

Library of 500,000 vols, 4,500 periodicals
Number of teachers: 2,157
Number of students: 33,077

Publications: *Edad de Oro* (annually), *Narria* (4 a year), *Cuadernos de Prehistoria y Arqueología* (annually), *Manuscrit. CAO* (annually), *Al Sur* (4 a year), *Anuario del Departamento de Filosofía* (annually), *Anuario del Departamento de Historia de la Filosofía* (annually), *Anuario del Departamento de Historia y Teoría del Arte* (annually), *Apuntes de la Autónoma* (irregular), *Boletín del Instituto de Ciencias de la Educación* (irregular), *Boletín Geográfico* (3 a year), *Cantoblanco: Noticias de la Universidad Autónoma de Madrid* (4 a year), *Coyuntura Trimestral* (journal of the Laurence R. Klein Institute of Economic Forecasting, 4 a year), *Cuaderno Gris* (3 a year), *La Ecoalternativa* (4 a year), *Encuentros Multidisciplinares* (multidisciplinary research and debate, 3 a year), *Journal of Human Ecology* (irregular), *Revista de Cantoblanco* (12 a year), *Revista de Lengua y Literatura Catalana, Gallega y Vasca* (annually), *Tarbiya* (educational research and innovation, 3 a year)

DEANS

Faculty of Medicine: VALENTÍN CUERVAS-MONS MARTÍNEZ
Faculty of Economics and Business Studies: JOSÉ ANTONIO ÁLVAREZ VÁZQUEZ
Faculty of Philosophy and Letters: HUBERTO MARRAUD GONZÁLEZ
Faculty of Science: JOSÉ ANTONIO PÉREZ LÓPEZ
Faculty of Law: CARLOS PALAO TABOADA
Faculty of Psychology: JUAN MANUEL SERRANO RODRÍGUEZ
Faculty of Teacher Training and Education: ANTONIO MALDONADO RICO

DIRECTOR

Higher Polytechnic School: MANUEL ALFONSECA MORENO

HEADS OF DEPARTMENTS

Biology: CARLOS GARCÍA DE LA VEGA
Molecular Biology: MANUEL FRESNO ESCUDERO
Ecology: CARMEN CASADO SANCHO
Mathematics: ANTONIO CÓRDOBA
Applied Physics: MÁXIMO LEÓN MACARRÓN
Physics of Materials: JOSÉ GARCÍA SOLÉ
Condensed Matter Physics: SEBASTIÁN VIEIRA DÍAZ
Theoretical Condensed Matter Physics: FERNANDO FLORES SINTAS
Theoretical Physics: ALFREDO POVES PAREDES
Chemistry: LUIS F. ERREA RUIZ
Agricultural Chemistry, Geology and Geochemistry: MANUEL POZO RODRÍGUEZ
Analytical Chemistry, Instrumental Analysis: JOSÉ MARÍA PINILLA MACÍAS
Applied Physical Chemistry: JESÚS TORNERO GÓMEZ
Inorganic Chemistry: CARMEN NAVARRO RANNINGER
Organic Chemistry: TOMÁS TORRES CEBADA
Computer Engineering: MANUEL ALFONSECA MORENO
Public Law, Legal Philosophy: ANTONIO ROVIRA VIÑAS
Private, Social and Economic Law: JUAN DAMIÁN MORENO

Politics and International Relations: JOSÉ RAMÓN MONTERO GIBERT
Social Anthropology and Philosophical Thought: ENRIQUE LUQUE BAENA
Arabic and Islamic Studies, Oriental Studies: WALEED SALEH AL-KHALIFA
Classical Philology: HELENA MAQUIEIRA RODRÍGUEZ
Spanish Philology: FLORENCIO SEVILLA ARROYO
French Philology: ARLETTE VÉGLIA ANDREA
Philosophy: ENRIQUE LÓPEZ CASTELLÓN
Geography: FERNANDO ARROYO ILERA
Ancient and Medieval History, Palaeography, Diplomacy: VICENTE A. ALVAREZ PALENZUELA
Contemporary History: JAVIER MA. DONEZAR Y DÍEZ DE ULZURRUN
Modern History: MARGARITA ORTEGA LÓPEZ
History and Theory of Art: SILVIA CUBILES FERNÁNDEZ
Linguistics, Modern Languages, Logic, Philosophy of Science, Theory of Literature and Comparative Literature: JAVIER RODRÍGUEZ PEQUEÑO
Prehistory and Archaeology: MA. CARMEN FERNÁNDEZ OCHOA
Basic Psychology: JUAN IGNACIO POZO MUNICIO
Biological Psychology and Psychology of Health: JOSÉ ANTONIO CARROBLES ISABEL
Evolutionary Psychology and Psychology of Education: JOSÉ LUIS LINAZA IGLESIAS
Social Psychology and Methodology: PILAR CARRERA LEVILLAIN
Biochemistry: RAFAEL GARESSE ALARCÓN
Pharmacology and Therapeutics: ANTONIO GARCÍA GARCÍA
Physiology: LUIS MONGE SÁNCHEZ
Preventive Medicine and Public Health: RAFAEL HERRUZO CABRERA
Morphology: CARLOS AVENDAÑO TRUEBA
Pathological Anatomy: JAVIER LARRAURI MARTÍNEZ
Surgery: JOSÉ ANTONIO RODRÍGUEZ MONTES
Obstetrics and Gynaecology: ANTONIO GONZÁLEZ GONZÁLEZ
Paediatrics: JOSÉ QUERO JIMÉNEZ
Medicine: LUIS FELIPE PALLARDO SÁNCHEZ
Psychiatry: ENRIQUE BACA BALDOMERO
Economic Analysis (Economic Theory and Economic History): FELIPE SÁEZ FERNÁNDEZ
Economic Analysis (Quantitative Economics): PALOMA SANZ ALVARO
Accounting and Company Organization: JORGE TUA PEREDA
Applied Economics: ISABEL TOLEDO MUÑOZ
Economics and Public Finance: DOLORES DIZY MENÉNDEZ
Economic Structure, Economics of Development: JOSÉ SERRANO PÉREZ
Commercial Financing and Research: IGNACIO CRUZ ROCHE
Sociology: LUIS ENRIQUE ALONSO
Education and Theory of Education: INMACULADA EGIDO GÁLVEZ
Music, Sculpture and Self-Expression through Movement: JUAN LUIS HERNÁNDEZ ÁLVAREZ
Specific Education: MA. CARMEN GARCÍA GÓMEZ

ATTACHED INSTITUTES

CSIC National Biotechnology Centre: Campus Universidad Autónoma, Cantoblanco, 28049 Madrid; tel. 91-585-45-00; fax 91-585-45-06; e-mail cnb@cnb.uam.es; internet www.cnb.uam.es; Dir MARIANO ESTEBAN RODRÍGUEZ.

CSIC Institute of Catalysis and Petrochemistry: C/ Marie Curie s/n, Campus de Cantoblanco, 28049 Madrid; tel. 91-585-48-00; fax 91-585-47-60; internet www.icp.csic.es; Dir Dra SAGRARIO MENDIÓROZ ECHEVERRÍA.

CSIC Madrid Institute of Materials Science: Campus Universidad Autónoma, Cantoblanco, 28049 Madrid; tel. 91-372-14-20; fax 91-372-06-23; internet www.icmm.csic.es; Dir Prof. FEDERICO SORIA GALLEGO.

CSIC 'Alberto Sols' Institute of Biomedical Research: C/ Arturo Duperier 4, 28029 Madrid; tel. 91-585-44-00; fax 91-585-44-01; e-mail director@iib.uam.es; internet www.iib.uam.es; Dir SEBASTIÁN CERDÁN.

Institute of Molecular Biology: Facultad de Ciencias, Campus de Cantoblanco, 28049 Madrid; tel. 91-397-48-66; fax 91-397-48-70; internet www.uam.es/institutos/BMolecular; Dir JOSÉ M. CUEZVA.

Institute of Education: Ctra Colmenar Viejo, Km 15, Cantoblanco, 28049 Madrid; tel. 91-397-43-97; fax 91-397-50-20; e-mail cesar.saenz@uam.es; internet www.uam.es/servicios/apoyodocencia/ice/default.html; Dir CÉSAR SAÉNZ DE CASTRO.

Research Institute of Ageing and Metabolism: C/ Diego de León 62 (Hospital de la Princesa), 28006 Madrid; tel. 91-402-63-48; e-mail aruiz/princesa@hup.es; internet www.hup.es/ecl/end/luigm.html; Dir Prof. Dr A. RUIZ-TORRES.

Business Administration Institute: Facultad de Ciencias Económicas y Empresariales, Módulo E-VIII, Crta Colmenar Viejo, Km 15, 28049 Madrid; tel. 91-397-42-75; fax 91-397-42-18; e-mail iade@uam.es; internet www.iade.org; Dir PATRICIO MORCILLO ORTEGA.

'Nicolás Cabrera' Materials Science Institute: Facultad de Ciencias Campus de Cantoblanco, Módulo C-XVI. Pta 4, 28049 Madrid; tel. 91-497-46-89; fax 91-497-87-34; e-mail inc@uam.es; internet www.uam.es/otroscentros/inc; Dir FERNANDO SOLS LUCIA.

Institute of Studies on Women: Edificio Rectorado, 3a Entreplanta, Universidad Autónoma de Madrid-Cantoblanco, 28049 Madrid; tel. 91-497-45-95; fax 91-497-55-53; e-mail iuem@uam.es; internet www.uam.es/otroscentros/institutomujer/default.html; Dir VIRGINIA MAQUIEIRA D'ANGELO.

Institute of Sociology of New Technologies: Departamento de Ciencia Política, Edificio de la Facultad de Formación de Profesorado y Educación, Campus de Cantoblanco, 28049 Madrid; tel. 91-397-51-32; fax 91-397-51-27; internet www.uam.es/otroscentros/nuevastecnologias/default.html; Dir UBALDO MARTÍNEZ VEIGA.

L. R. Klein Institute of Economic Forecasting: Facultad de CC. EE. y EE., Módulo E-XIV, 28049 Madrid; tel. 91-397-86-70; fax 91-397-86-70; internet www.uam.es/otroscentros/klein; Dirs JOSÉ VICÉNS, ANTONIO PULIDO.

'Severo Ochoa' Molecular Biology Centre: Campus de Cantoblanco, 28049 Madrid; tel. 91-497-50-70; fax 91-497-47-99; e-mail institucional@cbm.uam.es; internet www2.cbm.uam.es/cbm2001; Dir CECILIO GIMÉNEZ MARTÍN.

Centre of Documentation and Studies on the History of Madrid: Edificio del Rectorado, Planta Baja, Campus de Cantoblanco, 28049 Madrid; tel. 91-397-42-01; fax 91-397-41-23; e-mail director.cdhm@uam.es; internet www.uam.es/otroscentros/historiamadrid/default.html; Dir VIRGILIO PINTO CRESPO.

East Asian Studies Centre: Edificio Rectorado, 5a Planta, Campus de Cantoblanco, 28049 Madrid; tel. 91-397-46-95; fax 91-397-52-78; e-mail ceao@uam.es; internet www.uam.es/otroscentros/asiaoriental; Dir TACIANA FISAC BADELL.

'Pablo Olavide' Urban Studies Centre: Área de Derecho Administrativo, Facultad de Derecho, Campus de Cantoblanco, 28049 Madrid; tel. 91-397-81-52; fax 91-397-82-16; internet www.uam.es/otroscentros/ pablolavide/default.html; Dir ALFREDO GALLEGO ANABITARTE.

Materials Microanalysis Centre: Campus Universidad Autónoma, Cantoblanco, 28049 Madrid; tel. 91-497-36-21; fax 91-497-36-23; e-mail cmam@uam.es; internet www.uam.es/ otroscentros/cmam; Dir AURELIO CLIMENT FONT.

Applied Psychology Centre: Facultad de Psicología (planta sótano), Campus de Cantoblanco, 28049 Madrid; tel. 91-397-86-87; fax 91-397-52-15; e-mail cpa@uam.es; internet www.uam.es/otroscentros/ psicologiaplicada/default.html; Dir MERCEDES BELINCHÓN CARMONA.

Political Theory Centre: Departamento de Ciencia Política, Ciudad Universitaria de Cantoblanco, 28049 Madrid; tel. 91-397-41-66; e-mail ctp@uam.es; internet www.uam .es/otroscentros/teoriapolitica/default.html; Dir FERNANDO VALLESPÍN OÑA.

'Carlos V' International Centre: Campus de Cantoblanco, 28049 Madrid; tel. 91-497-39-17; e-mail centro.carlosv@uam.es; internet www.carlosvuam.com; Dir MAXIMINO CARPIO.

Higher Centre of Studies on Assyriology and Egyptology: Facultad de Filosofía y Letras, Cantoblanco, 28049 Madrid; tel. 91-497-76-70; fax 91-497-39-30; e-mail ceae@ uam.es; internet www.uam.es/otroscentros/ asiriologiayegipto/default.html.

Higher Centre to Research and Promote Music: Pabellón A, Campus de Cantoblanco, 28049 Madrid; tel. 91-397-49-78; fax 91-397-46-70; internet www.uam.es/otroscentros/ centromusica/default.html; Dir JOSÉ PERIS LACASA.

Business Training and Research Centre: C/ Pedro Salinas 11, 28043 Madrid; tel. 91-538-38-38; fax 91-538-38-03; e-mail administracion.cuife@uam.es; internet www .uam.es/otroscentros/cuife/default.html; Man. FERNANDO RÍOS.

Public Health Centre: C/ Gran Vía 27, 28013 Madrid; tel. 91-308-95-68; fax 91-308-95-89; e-mail administracion.cusp@uam.es; internet www.uam.es/otroscentros/ saludpublica/cusp/principal.htm.

Clinical Pharmacology Centre: Avda del Arzobispo Morcillo s/n, 28029 Madrid; tel. 91-397-53-34; fax 91-397-53-74; e-mail cfc@uam .es; internet www.uam.es/departamentos/ medicina/farmacologia/especifica/cfc; Dir ANTONIO GARCÍA GARCÍA.

School of Gemology: Facultad de Ciencias, Módulo C-VI, 3a Planta, Campus de Cantoblanco, 28049 Madrid; tel. 91-397-48-06; fax 91-397-49-00; internet www.uam.es/ otroscentros/gemologia/especifica/default .html; Dir MIGUEL ÁNGEL HOYOS GUERRERO.

U.A.M./El País School of Journalism: C/ Miguel Yuste 40, 28037 Madrid; tel. 91-337-77-60; fax 91-337-83-48; internet www.elpais .es/corporativos/elpais/escuela; Dir JOAQUÍN ESTEFANÍA.

Fernando González Bernáldez Interuniversity Foundation: Facultad de Ciencias, Módulo C-XVI, Despacho 206, Campus de Cantoblanco, 28049 Madrid; tel. 91-497-76-76; fax 91-497-35-58; e-mail fundacion .gbernaldez@uam.es; internet www.uam.es/ otros/fungobe.

Institute of Theoretical Physics: Facultad de Ciencias, Módulo C-XVI, 3a Planta, Campus de Cantoblanco, 28049 Madrid; tel. 91-497-85-43; fax 91-497-85-57; e-mail cesar

.gomez@uam.es; internet gesalerico.ft.uam .es; Dir CÉSAR GÓMEZ LÓPEZ.

Institute of Knowledge Engineering: UAM - Cantoblanco, Escuela Política Superior, Edificio B, 5a Planta, 28049 Madrid; tel. 91-497-23-23; fax 91-497-23-34; e-mail iic@iic .uam.es; internet www.iic.uam.es; Dir JOSÉ MIGUEL MATA.

Institute of Infants' and Adolescents' Needs and Rights: Facultad de Ciencias, Módulo CXVI, Ciudad Universitaria de Cantoblanco, 28049 Madrid; tel. 91-497-76-04; fax 91-497-24-37; e-mail iundia@uam.es; internet www.uam.es/otroscentros/iundia/ default.html; Dir ESPERANZA OCHAÍTA ALDERETE.

Cartographic Service: tel. 91-497-55-34; fax 91-497-85-99; e-mail servicio .cartografia@uam.es; internet www.uam.es/ otroscentros/cartografia/equipo.htm; Dir JAVIER ESPIAGO.

Microelectronics Laboratory: Facultad de Ciencias, Módulo C-XI 100, 1a Planta, Carretera de Colmenar Viejo, Km 15 (Cantoblanco), 28049 Madrid; tel. 91-497-49-21; fax 91-497-48-95; e-mail juan.piqueras@uam.es; internet micro.fa.uam.es; Dirs JUAN PIQUERAS, JAVIER GARRIDO.

UNIVERSIDAD DE MÁLAGA

El Ejido s/n, 29071 Málaga

Telephone: 95-213-10-00
Fax: 95-226-38-58
E-mail: relint@uma.es
Internet: www.uma.es

Founded 1972
State control
Language of instruction: Spanish
Academic year: October to July

Rector: ADELAIDA DE LA CALLE MARTÍN
Vice-Rector (Academic Organization): ANA CAÑIZARES LASO
Vice-Rector (Culture and International Relations): MERCEDES VICO MONTEOLIVA
Vice-Rector (Teaching Staff): ANA MARÍA SÁNCHEZ TEJEDA
Vice-Rector (Research and Graduate Studies): JOSÉ ÁNGEL NARVÁEZ BUENO
Vice-Rector (University Co-ordination): ENRIQUE CARO GUERRA
Vice-Rector (Student Affairs): JUAN ANTONIO PERLES ROCHEL
Vice-Rector (Technological Development and Innovation): JOSÉ ANTONIO FERNÁNDEZ GARCÍA
Vice-Rector (Business Co-operation): JUAN JOSÉ BORREGO GARCÍA
Vice-Rector (Infrastructure and Planning): RAFAEL MORALES BUENO
Vice-Rector (Services to the University Community): JUAN SANZ SAMPELAYO
Registrar: MIGUEL PORRAS FERNÁNDEZ
Manager: JOSÉ ANTONIO MOLINA RUIZ
Library Co-ordinator: GREGORIO GARCÍA RECHE

Library of 202,367 vols, 4,300 periodicals
Number of teachers: 1,600
Number of students: 33,000

Publications: *Filosofía Malacitana* (annually), *Boletín de Arte* (annually), *Histología Médica* (2 a year)

DEANS

Faculty of Industrial Relations: Dr MANUEL MONTALBÁN PEREGRÍN
Faculty of Science: JOSÉ JOAQUÍN QUIRANTE SÁNCHEZ
Faculty of Education: PILAR PÉREZ MIRANDA
Faculty of Communication: JUAN ANTONIO GARCÍA GALINDO
Faculty of Economic and Business Sciences: Dr EUGENIO JOSÉ LUQUE DOMÍNGUEZ

Faculty of Law: Dr JOSÉ MANUEL RUIZ-RICO RUIZ
Faculty of Philosophy and Letters: RAFAEL DOMÍNGUEZ RODRÍGUEZ
Faculty of Medicine: Prof. SALVADOR GONZÁLEZ BARÓN
Faculty of Psychology: ALFREDO FIERRO BARDAJÍ

DIRECTORS

Higher Technical School of Telecommunications Engineering: ANTONIO PUERTA NOTARIO
Higher Technical School of Industrial Engineering: RAMÓN FERNÁNDEZ FERIA
Higher Technical School of Computer Engineering: JOSÉ MARÍA TROYA LINERO
University School of Health Sciences: (vacant)
University School of Business Studies: FRANCISCO CANTALEJO GARCÍA
University School of Tourism: LUIS GONZÁLEZ GARCÍA
University Polytechnic School: FRANCISCO J. MUÑOZ GUTIÉRREZ

HEADS OF DEPARTMENTS

Algebra, Geometry and Topology: ANTONIO SÁNCHEZ SÁNCHEZ
Mathematical Analysis: DANIEL GIRELA ÁLVAREZ
Anatomy and Forensic Medicine: INÉS FERNÁNDEZ ORTEGA
Archaeology and Medieval History: MANUEL ACIÉN ALMANSA
Computer Architecture: EMILIO LÓPEZ-ZAPATA
Animal Biology: VALENTÍN SANS COMA
Cell Biology and Genetics: JOSÉ BECERRA RATIA
Molecular Biology and Biochemistry: FRANCISCO ALONSO CARRIÓN
Vegetal Biology: BALTASAR CABEZUDO ARTERO
Biochemistry, Molecular Biology and Organic Chemistry: MIGUEL MORELL OCAÑA (Faculty of Medicine: R. GARCÍA SEGURA (Faculty of Science)
Historiography, Ancient History and Prehistory: GONZALO CRUZ ANDREOTTI
Surgery, Obstetrics and Gynaecology: Ma. PILAR SÁNCHEZ GALLEGOS
Accountancy and Management: DANIEL CARRASCO DÍAZ
Civil Law, Ecclesiastical State Law and Roman Law: ANTONIO ORTEGA CARRILLO DE ALBORNOZ
State Law and Sociology: JUAN DEL PINO ARTACHO
Financial Law, Political Economy and Philosophy of Law: JUAN CARLOS MARTÍNEZ COLL
Special Private Law: ADOLFO AURIOLES MARTÍN
Public Law: ÁNGEL SÁNCHEZ BLANCO
Teaching Self-Expression through Music, Plastic Arts and Movement: RAFAEL BRAVO BERROCAL
Teaching Language and Literature: CRISTÓBAL GONZÁLEZ ÁLVAREZ
Teaching Mathematics, Social Sciences and Experimental Sciences: MARÍA ÁNGELES JIMÉNEZ LÓPEZ
Education and School Organization: JOSÉ IGNACIO RIVAS FLORES
Ecology and Geology: JUAN LUCENA RODRÍGUEZ
Applied Economics (Statistics and Econometrics 15): ANTONIO MORILLAS RAYA
Applied Economics (Statistics and Econometrics 68): JOSÉ MARÍA OTERO
Applied Economics (Economic Structure): ANDRÉS MARCHANTE MENA
Applied Economics (Public Finance): JOSÉ SÁNCHEZ MALDONADO
Applied Economics (Mathematics): ALFONSO C. GONZÁLEZ PAREJA
Applied Economics (Economic Policy): JOSÉ EMILIO VILLENA PEÑA

Business Economics and Administration: FRANCISCA PARRA GUERRERO

Electronics: ALFREDO GAGO BOHÓRQUEZ

Graphics, Design and Plans: ISIDRO LADRÓN DE GUEVARA LÓPEZ

Pharmacology and Paediatrics: FELIPE SÁNCHEZ DE LA CUESTA Y ALARCÓN

Spanish and Romance Philology: ASUNCIÓN RALLO GRUSS

Spanish Philology II, Theory of Literature and Journalism: ANTONIO A. GÓMEZ YEBRA

Greek Philology, Arabic Studies and Translation and Interpreting: AURELIO PÉREZ JIMÉNEZ

English, French and German Philology: RICARDO REDOLI MORALES

Latin Philology: ANTONIO ALBERTE GONZÁLEZ

Philosophy: JOSÉ MARÍA ROSALES JAIME

Finance and Accounting: VICENTE GARCÍA MARTÍN

Applied Physics I: JOSÉ RAMÓN RAMOS BARRADO

Human Physiology and Physical and Sport Education: SALVADOR GONZÁLEZ BARÓN

Geography: CARMEN OCAÑA OCAÑA

Histology and Pathological Anatomy: ALFREDO MATILLA VICENTE

History of Art: JUAN MARÍA MONTIJANO GARCÍA

Modern and Contemporary History: ANTONIO NADAL SÁNCHEZ

Communications Engineering: CARLOS CAMACHO PEÑALOSA

Systems Engineering and Automation: JORGE LUIS MARTÍNEZ RODRÍGUEZ (acting)

Electrical Engineering: MANUEL MEDINA TEXEIRA

Chemical Engineering: PEDRO MARTÍNEZ DE LA CUESTA

Computer Languages and Science: JOSÉ LUIS PÉREZ DE LA CRUZ MOLINA

Applied Mathematics: JUAN JOSÉ SAAMEÑO RODRÍGUEZ

Thermic Machines and Motors: FRANCISCO SERRANO CASARES

Medicine and Dermatology: (vacant)

Preventive Medicine and History of Medicine (Biostatistics): JOAQUÍN FERNÁNDEZ-CREHUET NAVAJAS

Research Methods and Educational Innovation: ÁNGELES GERVILLA CASTILLO

Microbiology: ANTONIO DE VICENTE MORENO

Personality, Assessment and Psychological Treatment: ROSA ESTEVE ZARAZAGA

Social Psychology and Anthropology, Social Work and Social Services: MA. ISABEL HOMBRADOS MENDIETA

Basic Psychology: JOSÉ MIGUEL RODRÍGUEZ SANTOS

Psychobiology and Methodology of Behavioural Sciences: MA. JOSÉ BLANCA MENA

Evolutionary and Educational Psychology: JUAN F. ROMERO PÉREZ

Psychiatry and Physiotherapy: M. TERESA LABAJOS MANZANARES

Analytical Chemistry: FRANCISCO GARCÍA SÁNCHEZ

Physical Chemistry: JUAN FRANCISCO ARENAS ROSADO

Inorganic Chemistry, Crystallography and Mineralogy: ANTONIO JIMÉNEZ LÓPEZ

Radiology and Physical Medicine, Ophthalmology and Otorhinolaryngology: MANUEL MARTÍNEZ MORILLO

Electrical Technology: ANTONIO DÍAZ ESTRELLA

Theory and History of Education: MA. CARMEN SANCHIDRIÁN BLANCO

Economic Theory and History: JUAN PÁEZ PÁEZ-CAMINO

PROFESSORS

Faculty of Economic and Business Studies:

AGUIRRE SADABA, A., Economics and Business Administration

GARCÍA LIZANA, A., Applied Economics (Political)

GONZÁLEZ PAREJA, A., Applied Economics (Mathematics)

MOCHON MORCILLO, F., Economic Analysis

OTERO MORENO, J. M., Applied Economics (Statistics and Econometrics)

PINO ARTACHO, J. DEL, State Law and Sociology

REQUENA RODRÍGUEZ, J. M., Financial Economics and Accountancy

SANCHEZ MALDONADO, J., Applied Economics (Structure and Public Finance)

Faculty of Medicine:

BROTAT ESTER, M., Radiology, Physical and Psychiatric Medicine

CASTILLA GONZALO, J., Normal and Pathological Morphology

FERNÁNDEZ-CREHUET NAVAJAS, J., Preventative Medicine and Public Health

OCAÑA SIERRA, J., Medicine

SÁNCHEZ DE LA CUESTA Y ALARCÓN, F., Physiology, Pharmacology and Paediatrics

SÁNCHEZ DEL CURA, G., Surgery, Obstetrics and Gynaecology

Faculty of Philosophy and Letters:

ALVAR EZQUERRA, M., Spanish and Romance Philology

CUEVAS GARCÍA, C., Spanish Philology and Theory of Literature

ESTEVE ZARAZAGA, J. M., Theory and History of Education

GARCÍA DE LA FUENTE, O., Classical Philology and Arabic and Islamic Studies

LAVIN CAMACHO, E., English and French Philology

MARTÍNEZ FREIRE, P., Philosophy

MORALES FOLGUERAS, J. M., History of Art

NADAL SANCHEZ, A., Modern History

OCANA OCANA, M. C., Geography

PEREZ GOMEZ, A., Didactics

RODRIGUEZ OLIVA, P., Prehistory and Science of Antiquity and Middle Ages

TRAINES TORRES, M. V., Psychology

Faculty of Sciences:

ARENAS ROSADO, J. F., Physical Chemistry

CABEZUDO ARTERO, B., Plant Biology

CANO PAVÓN, J. M., Analytical Chemistry

CUENCA MIRA, J. A., Algebra, Geometry and Topology

FERNÁNDEZ-FIGARES PEREZ, J. M., Cellular and Genetic Biology

FERNÁNDEZ JIMENEZ, C., Applied Physics

GARCÍA RASO, E., Animal Biology

JIMÉNEZ LÓPEZ, A., Inorganic Chemistry, Crystalography and Mineralogy

RODRÍGUEZ JIMENEZ, J. J., Chemical Engineering

RODRÍGUEZ ORTIZ, C., Applied Mathematics and Statistics

SERRANO LOZANO, L., Ecology and Geology

SUAU SUÁREZ, R., Biochemistry, Molecular Biology and Organic Chemistry

Faculty of Law:

AURIOLES MARTIN, A., Private Law

CARRETERO LESTON, J. L., Public Law

ORTEGA CARILLO DE ALBÓRNOZ, A., Civil, Ecclesiastical and State Law

ROBLES GARZON, J. A., Political Science, International Law

University School of Teacher Training:

DEL CAMPO Y DEL CAMPO, M., Didactics of Expression, Music

GARCÍA ESPAÑA, J., Didactics, Social Science, Experimental Science

MANTECON RAMIREZ, B., Didactics of Language and Literature

University Polytechnic:

OLLERO BATURONE, A., Systems Engineering, Information Science, Electronics

RUIZ MUÑOZ, J. M., Electrical Engineering, Electronic Technology

SIMON MATA, A., Mechanical Engineering, Engineering Graphics

TROYA LINERO, J. M., Language and Science of Computing

AFFILIATED INSTITUTES

Institute of Education Sciences: Dir MIGUEL ANGEL SANTOS GUERRA.

University Institute of Technological Research and Control: Dir FRANCISCO SERRANO CASARES.

UNIVERSIDAD MIGUEL HERNÁNDEZ DE ELCHE

Edificio Torrevaillo, Avda de la Universidad s/n, 03202 Elche (Alicante)

Telephone: 96-665-86-04

Fax: 96-665-86-02

E-mail: gerente@umh.es

Internet: www.umh.es

State control

Rector: JESÚS RODRÍGUEZ MARÍN

Vice-Rector (Economic Affairs, Employment and Relations with Business): JOSÉ MARÍA GÓMEZ GRAS

Vice-Rector (Co-ordination and Scheduling): CARMEN VICTORIA ESCOLANO ASENSI

Vice-Rector (Student Affairs): FERNANDO BORRÁS ROCHER

Vice-Rector (Research and Technological Development): SALVADOR VINIEGRA BOVER

Vice-Rector (Academic Planning and Studies): JOSÉ NAVARRO PEDREÑO

Vice-Rector (Personnel): JOSÉ FRANCISCO GONZÁLEZ CARBONELL

Vice-Rector (University Planning and Continuing Education): JUANA GALLAR MARTÍNEZ

Vice-Rector (Material Resources and Equipment): JOAQUÍN JULIÁN PASTOR PÉREZ

Vice-Rector (International Relations): JUSTO MEDRANO HEREDIA

Registrar: FERMÍN CAMACHO DE LOS RÍOS

Manager: RAFAEL GANDÍA BALAGUER

DEANS

Faculty of Fine Arts: RAMÓN DE SOTO ARANDIGA

Faculty of Experimental Sciences: MARÍA DOLORES ESTEBAN LEFLER

Faculty of Social and Juridical Sciences at Elche: JOSÉ ANTONIO TRIGUEROS PINA

Faculty of Social and Juridical Sciences at Orihuela: JAVIER REIG MULLOR

Faculty of Pharmacy: MARÍA DEL CARMEN DE FELIPE FERNÁNDEZ

Faculty of Medicine: JUAN MANUEL CATURLA SUCH

DIRECTORS

Higher Technical School at Elche: EMILIO VELASCO SÁNCHEZ

Higher Technical School at Orihuela: JUAN JOSÉ RUIZ MARTÍNEZ

HEADS OF DEPARTMENTS

Agrochemistry and Environment: IGNACIO GÓMEZ LUCAS

Art, Humanities and Social and Juridical Sciences: RICARDO GÓMEZ RIVERO

Applied Biology: JOSÉ LUIS MICOL MOLINA

Biochemistry and Molecular Biology: JOSÉ ANTONIO FERRAGUT RODRÍGUEZ

Materials Science and Technology: ANTONIO FIMIA GIL

Agroenvironmental Economy, Cartography and Engineering Drawing: FRANCISCO JOSÉ DEL CAMPO GOMIS

Statistics and Applied Mathematics: JOSÉ LUIS RUIZ GÓMEZ

Economic and Financial Studies: EVA ALIAGA AGULLO

Pharmacology, Paediatrics and Organic Chemistry: MANUEL MOYA BENAVENT

...ERSITIES

...s and Computer Architecture: GABRIEL
...RUIZ
...ology: MIGUEL ÁNGEL VALDEOLMILLOS
...EZ
...logy and Anatomy: EDUARDO FERNÁNDEZ
...VER
...neering: TERESA GARCÍA ORTUÑO
...strial Systems Engineering: OSCAR REIN-
...SO GARCÍA
...ical Medicine: JAIME MERINO SÁNCHEZ
...thology and Surgery: MARÍA TERESA PÉREZ
...VÁZQUEZ
...getal Production and Microbiology: PABLO
...MELGAREJO MORENO
...ealth Psychology: SOFÍA LÓPEZ ROIG
...ublic Health, History of Science and Gynae-
...cology: ENRIQUE PERDIGUERO GIL
...Agricultural Food Technology: SALVADOR
...CASTILLO GARCÍA

ATTACHED INSTITUTES

Operational Research Centre: Campus de
Elche, Edificio Torretamarit, Avda del Ferrocarril s/n, 03202 Elche; tel. 96-665-87-52; fax
96-665-87-15; e-mail cio@umh.es; internet cio
.umh.es; Dir JESÚS TADEO PASTOR CIURANA.

Institute of Bioengineering: Edificio
Vinalopó, Avda del Ferrocarril s/n, 03202
Elche; tel. 96-665-85-10; fax 96-665-85-11;
internet bioengenieria.umh.es; Dir BERNAT
SORIA ESCOMS.

Institute of Molecular and Cell Biology:
Edificio Torregaitán, Avda de la Universidad
s/n, 03202 Elche; tel. 96-665-87-59; fax 96-
665-87-58; e-mail biomolcel@umh.es;
internet ibmc.umh.es; Dir JOSÉ MANUEL
GONZÁLEZ ROS.

**Institute of Research into Drug Addic-
tion:** Facultad de Medicina, Campus de San
Juan, Ctra Alicante-Valencia, Km 87, Apdo
no. 18, 03550 San Juan de Alicante; tel. 96-
591-93-19; fax 96-591-95-66; e-mail inid@
umh.es; internet inid.umh.es; Dir JOSÉ ANTO-
NIO GARCÍA DEL CASTILLO RODRÍGUEZ.

Neurosciences Institute: Apdo 18, 03550
San Joan d'Alacant; tel. 96-591-94-87; fax 96-
591-95-61; e-mail in@umh.es; internet in
.umh.es/index2.htm; Dir CARLOS BELMONTE
MARTÍNEZ.

MONDRAGON UNIBERTSITATEA

...oramendi 4, Apdo 23, 20500 Mondragón
Telephone: 943-71-21-85
...ax: 943-71-21-93
...mail: info@mondragon.edu
...ternet: www.mondragon.edu
...unded 1997
...vate control
...guages of instruction: Basque, Spanish,
...nglish
...demic year: September to July
...or: INAXIO OLIVERI ALBISU
...emic Vice-Rector: JOSE MARI AIZEAGA
...LLAGA
...OR... of Research: SABIN FERNÁNDEZ
...RTE
...r: IDOIA PEÑACOBA ETXEBARRIA
...istrative Director: MILAGROS BELATE-
...OJAOLA
...: OBDULIA VELEZ
...of teachers: 240
...of students: 3,995

...f Business: JOSÉ LUIS ABAUNZ ZUBIA
...f Humanities and Education: JOSE
...MENDIKUTE BADIOLA
...lytechnic School: JAVIER RETEGUI
(Director)

UNIVERSIDAD DE MURCIA

Avda Teniente Flomesta 5, 30003 Murcia
Telephone: 968-36-30-00
Fax: 968-36-36-03
E-mail: siu@um.es
Internet: www.um.es
Founded 1915
State control
Language of instruction: Spanish
Academic year: September to June
Rector: JOSÉ BALLESTA GERMÁN
Vice-Rector (Quality and European Integra-
tion): EDUARDO JAVIER OSUNA CARRILLO DE
ALBORNOZ
Vice-Rector (Planning and Infrastructure):
JOSÉ MARÍA GÓMEZ ESPÍN
Vice-Rector (Student and Post-graduate Stu-
dies): JUANA CASTAÑO RUIZ
Vice-Rector (Academic Staff and Training):
FRANCISCO DE ASÍS MARTÍNEZ ORTIZ
Vice-Rector (Students and Employment):
NORBERTO NAVARRO ADELANTADO
Vice-Rector (Research and New Technolo-
gies): SANTIAGO TORRES MARTÍNEZ
Vice Rector (Cultural and University Projec-
tion): CONRADO NAVALÓN VILA
Registrar: NATALIA EGEA DÍAZ
Manager: JORGE NAVARRO OLIVARES
Library Director: LOURDES COBACHO GÓMEZ
Library of 629,000 vols, 12,345 periodicals
(incl. 3,200 online)
Number of teachers: 1,832
Number of students: 31,313

Publications: *Historia Agraria* (4 a year),
Myrtia (classical philology, 2 a year),
Daimon (philosophy, 2 a year), *Antigüedad
y Cristianismo* (annually), *Anales de Biología* (annually), *Papeles de Geografía* (2 a
year)

DEANS

Faculty of Arts: JOSÉ MARÍA JIMÉNEZ CANO
Faculty of Law: JOSÉ ANTONIO COBACHO
GÓMEZ
Faculty of Chemistry: M. GLORIA VILLORA
CANO
Faculty of Mathematics: JOSÉ MA. RUÍZ
GÓMEZ
Faculty of Medicine: FERNANDO SÁNCHEZ
GASCÓN
Faculty of Psychology: JESÚS GÓMEZ AMOR
Faculty of Economics and Business Studies:
JOSÉ DANIEL BUENDÍA AZORÍN
Faculty of Communication and Documenta-
tion: JOSÉ VICENTE RODRÍGUEZ MUÑOZ
Faculty of Veterinary Studies: ANTONIO BER-
NABÉ SALAZAR
Faculty of Philosophy: JOSÉ LORITE MENA
Faculty of Biology: JOSÉ MARÍA EGEA FER-
NÁNDEZ
Faculty of Education: DIEGO GUZMÁN MAR-
TÍNEZ-VALLS
Faculty of Computer Sciences: LEANDRO
MARÍN MUÑOZ
Faculty of Fine Arts: JUAN ROMERA AGULLÓ
Faculty of Industrial Relations: MARÍA ISABEL
SÁNCHEZ-MORA MOLINA

DIRECTORS

University School of Nursing (in Murcia):
CARMEN ISABEL GÓMEZ GARCÍA
University School of Social Work: REMEDIOS
MAURANDI GUIRADO
Nursing Training School: MERCEDES SANTES-
TEBAN DE MINGO
Law Training School: FERNANDO JIMÉNEZ
CONDE
Labour Affairs Training School: GUILLERMO
RODRÍGUEZ INIESTA
Psychology Training School: FRANCISCO
JAVIER CORBALÁN BERNA
Social Work Training School: ENRIQUE PAS-
TOR SELLER

Technology Training School: LUIS DANIEL
HERNÁNDEZ MOLINERO
University School of Tourism: FRANCISCO
CREMARES BAÑÓN

HEADS OF DEPARTMENTS

Human Anatomy and Psychobiology: LUIS
PUELLES LÓPEZ
Cell Biology: MA. CONCEPCIÓN FERRER
CAZORLA
Biochemistry and Molecular Biology: ENCAR-
NACIÓN MUÑOZ DELGADO
Biochemistry, Molecular Biology and Immu-
nology: ARTURO MANJÓN RUBIO
Marketing and Market Research: JOSÉ LUIS
MUNUERA ALEMÁN
Politics and Administration: MÓNICA MÉNDEZ
LAGO, MIREIA GRAU I CREUS
Administrative Law: ANTONIO GUTIERREZ
LLAMAS
Financial, International and Procedural
Law: GEMMA GARCÍA-ROSTAN CALVIN
Private Law: ROSALÍA ALFONSO SANCHEZ
Dermatology, Stomatology, Radiology and
Physical Medicine: MIGUEL ALCARAZ BAÑOS
Teaching Literature and Languages: AMANDO
LÓPEZ VALERO
Teaching Experimental Sciences: ANTONIO
JOSÉ DE PRO BUENO
Teaching Mathematics and Social Sciences:
ANDRÉS NORTES CHECA
Education and School Organization: PILAR
ARNAIZ SÁNCHEZ
Ecology and Hydrology: ROSARIO VIDAL-
ABARCA GUTIÉRREZ
Applied Economics: FERNANDO IGNACIO SÁN-
CHEZ MARTÍNEZ
Finance and Accounting: PEDRO LUENGO
MULET
Statistics and Operational Research: LÁZARO
CÁNOVAS MARTÍNEZ
Politics and Administration: MÓNICA MÉNDEZ
LAGO, MIREÍRA GRAU I CREUS
Pharmacology: ELISA ESCUDERO PASTOR
Classical Philology: FRANCISCO MOYA DEL
BAÑO
French, Romance, Italian and Arabic Philol-
ogy: CONCEPCIÓN PALACIOS BERNAL
English Philology: PASCUAL CANTOS GÓMEZ
Philosophy: ANTONIO CAMPILLO MESEGUER
Physiotherapy: ANTONIA GÓMEZ CONESA
Principles of Economic Analysis: FRANCISCO
ALCALÁ AGULLÓ
Principles of Juridical and Constitutional
Order: RAFAEL HERNÁNDEZ MARÍN
Physical and Human Geography and Regio-
nal Analysis: FRANCISCO CALVO CONESA
GARCÍA
Public Finance and Public Sector Economics:
AMBROSIO GARCÍA-TORNEL
Modern, Contemporary and American His-
tory: JUAN B. VILAR RAMÍREZ
Information and Documentation: VIVINA
ASENSI ARTIGA
Computer Science and Systems: ISIDRO
VERDÚ CONESA
Information and Communications Engineer-
ing: ANTONIO F. GÓMEZ SKARMETA
Chemical Engineering: ANTONIO BÓDALO SAN-
TOYO
Computer Engineering and Technology:
PEDRO ENRIQUE LÓPEZ DE TERUEL ALCOLEA
Spanish Language and General Linguistics:
RICARDO ESCAVY ZAMORA
Spanish Literature, Theory of Literature and
Comparative Literature: FRANCISCO JAVIER
DÍEZ DE REVENGA TORRES
Applied Mathematics: FRANCISCO JOSÉ VERA
LÓPEZ
Mathematics: PASCUAL LUCAS SAORÍN
Internal Medicine: MARIANO VALDÉS CHÁ-
VARRI
Animal Medicine and Surgery: ANA MA.
MONTES CEPEDA
Quantitative Methods for Economics: ANTO-
NIO CALVO-FLORES SEGURA

Research Methods and Diagnostics in Education: FUENSANTA HERNÁNDEZ PINA
Ophthalmology, Otorhinolaryngology and Pathological Anatomy: MANUEL VIDAL SANZ
Business and Financial Organization: RAMÓN SABATER SÁNCHEZ
Prehistory, Archaeology, Ancient and Medieval History and Historiographical Sciences and Methods: JOAQUÍN LOMBA MAURANDI
Basic Psychology and Methodology: JUAN ANTONIO VERA FERRÁNDIZ
Evolutionary Psychology and Educational Psychology: JOSÉ ANTONIO CARRANZA CARNICERO
Psychiatry and Social Psychology: JOAQUÍN NIETO MUNUERA
Agrochemistry, Geology and Soil Science: ROQUE ORTIZ SILLA
Inorganic Chemistry: GREGORIO LÓPEZ LÓPEZ
Organic Chemistry: ARTURO ESPINOSA FERAO
Religion: JUAN CARLOS GARCÍA DOMENE
Sociology and Social Policy: JUAN JOSÉ GARCÍA ESCRIBANO
Food Technology, Nutrition and Bromatology: GASPAR ROS BERRUEZO
Theory and History of Education: PEDRO LUIS MORENO MARTÍNEZ
Zoology and Physical Anthropology: JUAN JOSÉ PRESA ASENSIO

ATTACHED INSTITUTIONS

University School of Tourism: Paseo de Malecón 5, 30004 Murcia; tel. 968-29-36-24; fax 968-29-10-96; e-mail eutm@um.es; Academic Dir FRANCISCO CREMADES BAÑÓN.

University School of Nursing in Cartagena: Plaza San Agustín 3, 30201 Cartagena (Murcia); tel. 968-32-66-96; fax 968-32-66-95; internet www.um.es/eu-enfermeria-ct/; Dir (vacant) J. M. HERNÁNDEZ CONESA.

Pérez de Lema Centre of University Teaching: C/ Real 80, Cartagena (Murcia); tel. 968-50-53-13; internet www.um.es/perezdelema/; Dir Mª. DOLORES FONTES BASTOS.

Institute of Education: Edificio D, 3a Planta, Campus de Espinardo, 30100 Murcia; tel. 968-36-39-26; fax 968-36-39-25; e-mail ice@um.es; internet www.um.es/ice; Dir JUAN MANUEL ESCUDERO MUÑOZ.

Institute of Water and the Environment: Edificio D, Campus de Espinardo, 30100 Murcia; tel. 968-36-49-10; fax 968-36-33-89; e-mail inuama@um.es; internet www.um.es/inuama; Dir ALBERTO BARBA NAVARRO.

Inter-university Institute of the Ancient Near East: Antigua Escuela de Empresariales, C/ Actor Isidoro Máiquez 8, Vistalegre, 30007 Murcia; tel. 968-36-38-90; fax 968-36-38-90; e-mail ipoa@um.es; internet www.um.es/ipoa.

Institute of Sport Science: Facultad de Educación, Campus Universitario de Espinardo, 30100 Espinardo (Murcia); tel. 968-36-40-52; fax 968-36-41-46; e-mail icd@um.es; internet www.um.es/icd; Dir ARTURO DÍAZ SUÁREZ.

Institute of Ageing: Campus Universitario de Espinardo, 30100 Espinardo (Murcia); tel. 968-36-34-99; e-mail maemedina@um.es; internet www.um.es/estructura/institutos/iupe; Dir MANUEL E. MEDINA TORNERO.

Institute of Financial and Fiscal Studies: Dpto Hacienda y Economía del Sector Público, Despacho B109, Campus de Espinardo, 30100 Murcia; tel. 968-36-77-98; e-mail inueff@um.es; internet www.um.es/inueff; Dir GLORIA ALARCÓN GARCÍA.

UNIVERSIDAD DE NAVARRA

Campus Universitario, 31080 Pamplona
Telephone: 948-42 56 00
Fax: 948-42-56-19
E-mail: relint@unav.es
Internet: www.unav.es

Founded 1952
State control
Language of instruction: Spanish
Academic year: September to June

Chancellor: JAVIER ECHEVARRÍA
Vice-Chancellor: RAMÓN HERRANDO
Rector: JOSÉ Mª. BASTERO ELEIZALDE
Vice-Rector (Academic Staff): MA... CASADO-VELARDE
Vice-Rector (External Relations): JA... NUBIOLA
Vice-Rector (Quality, Innovation and Information Technology): CONCEPCIÓN NAVAL
Vice-Rector (Research): PILAR FERNÁND... OTERO
Vice-Rector (Student Affairs and Academic Organization): ÁNGEL JOSÉ GÓMEZ MO... TORO
Secretary-General: GONZALO ROBLES
Librarian: VÍCTOR SANZ-SANTACRUZ

Library of 800,988 vols, 24,908 periodicals (incl. 6,515 online)
Number of teachers: 2,047
Number of students: 15,471

Publications: *Revista de Medicina* (4 a year), *Ius Canonicum* (2 a year), *Nuestro Tiempo* (12 a year), *Scripta Theologica* (4 a year), *Redacción* (4 a year), *Anuario Filosófico* (3 a year), *Anuario de Derecho Internacional* (annually), *Persona y Derecho* (2 a year), *Revista de Edificación* (4 a year), *Comunicación y Sociedad* (2 a year), *RILCE* (2 a year)

DEANS

Faculty of Law: JULIO JAVIER MUERZA ESPARZA
Faculty of Communication: ALFONSO SÁNCHEZ-TABERNERO
Faculty of Medicine: MARÍA PILAR CIVEIRA MURILLO
Faculty of Canon Law: RAFAEL RODRÍGUEZ-OCAÑA
Faculty of Pharmacy: ICIAR ASTIASARAN
Faculty of Sciences: MARIA PILAR SESMA
Faculty of Theology: FRANCISCO VARO
Faculty of Economics: LUIS RAVINA BOHÓRQUEZ
Faculty of Humanities and Social Sciences: CARMEN SARALEGUI PLATERO
Faculty of Engineering: CARLOS BASTERO DE ELEIZALDE
Faculty of Architecture: JUAN-MIGUEL OTXO... TORENA
Faculty of Nursing: MARIA-ISABEL SARACIBA...

DIRECTORS OF AFFILIATED COLLEGES, SCHOOLS AND INSTITUTES

School of Engineering: CARLOS BASTERO ELEIZALDE
School of Architecture: JUAN MIGUEL OT... TORENA
Institute of Liberal Arts: JAVIER DE NA... CUÉS
Institute of Church History: MARCELO ... INO RODRÍGUEZ
Institute of Modern Languages: RUTH BR...
Higher Institute of Secretarial and Administrative Studies: MARÍA DEL MAR ARA... LETAMENDÍA
Institute of Spanish Language and Cu... CONCHA MARTÍNEZ PASAMAR
School of Nursing: ISABEL SARACÍBAR ...

HEADS OF DEPARTMENTS

Human, Legal and Social Sciences:
Public Communication: ALEJANDRO ...
Culture and Audiovisual Communi... ALEJANDRO PARDO FERNÁNDEZ
Canon Law and Ecclesiastical La... State: JUAN FORNÉS

Haematology: EDUARDO ROCHA

Histology and Pathological Anatomy: LUIS MONTUENGA BADÍA

Biomedical Humanities: MA. PILAR LEÓN SANZ

Nuclear Medicine: JOSÉ ÁNGEL RICHTER ECHEVARRÍA

Microbiology and Parasitology: IGNACIO MORIYÓN

Neurology and Neurosurgery: JOSÉ MASDEU (Neurology: JULIO ARTIEDA GONZÁLEZ-GRANDA (Neurophysiology: MIGUEL MANRIQUE SMELA (Neurosurgery)

Nephrology: ANDRÉS PURROY UNANUA

Obstetrics and Gynaecology: GUILLERMO LÓPEZ GARCÍA

Ophthalmology: JAVIER MORENO MONTAÑÉS

Oncology: SALVADOR MARTÍN ALGARRA

Otorhinolaryngology: NICOLÁS PÉREZ FERNÁNDEZ

Paediatrics: LUIS SIERRASESÚMAGA

Architectural Projects: JUAN MIGUEL OTXOTORENA ELIZEGI

Psychiatry and Medical Psychology: SALVADOR CERVERA ENGUIX

Chemistry and Soil Science: JOSÉ MARÍA FERNÁNDEZ ALVAREZ

Radiology: JOSÉ IGNACIO BILBAO

Theory and History of Architecture: MA. ANTONIA FRÍAS SAGARDOY

Town Planning: EDUARDO ROJO FRAILE

Urology: JOSÉ MARÍA BERIÁN POLO

Zoology and Ecology: CARMEN ESCALA URDAPILLETA

Institute of Advanced Business Studies:

Decision Analysis: MIGUEL ÁNGEL ARIÑO

Accounting and Control: FERNANDO PEÑALVA

Business Management: JULIÁN VILLANUEVA

Human Resources Management: JOSÉ R. PIN

Production Technology and Operational Management: FREDERIC SABRIÀ

Financial Management: JAVIER SANTOMÁ

General Management: JOAN ENRIC RICART

Economics: JORDI GUAL

Business Ethics: DOMÈNEC MELÉ

Entrepreneurial Initiative: PEDRO NUENO

Information Systems: JOSEP VALOR

PROFESSORS

Faculty of Law:

APARISI, A., Philosophy of Law
ARECHEDERRA, L., Civil Law
BLANCO, M., Canon Law
CORDÓN, F., Procedural Law
DE LA IGLESIA, A., Constitutional Law
DOMINGO, R., Roman Law
FAJARDO, J., Civil Law
FORNÉS DE LA ROSA, J., Canon Law
GALÁN, M., History of Law
GARCÍA, R., History of Law
GÓMEZ, A., Constitutional Law
GUTIÉRREZ DE CAVIEDES, P., Procedural Law
IÑIGO, E., Penal Law
LÓPEZ SÁNCHEZ, M. A., Commercial Law
LÓPEZ-JURADO, B., Administrative Law
MUERZA, J., Procedural Law
NANCLARES, J., Civil Law
PÉREZ, F., Canon Law
ROSENDE, C., Procedural Law
RUIZ DE APODACA, A., Administrative Law
SALCEDO, J., History of Law
SALVADOR, Á., Administrative Law
SAN JULIÁN, V., Civil Law
SIMÓN, E., Financial Law
VALPUESTA, E., Commercial Law
VÁZQUEZ DEL REY, A., Financial and Tax Law

Faculty of Humanities and Social Sciences:

AGUADO ALONSO, G., Education
ALARCÓN MORENO, E., Philosophy

ALONSO DEL REAL MONTES, C., Classical Philology
ALTAREJOS MASOTA, F., Education
ALVIRA DOMÍNGUEZ, R., Philosophy
ARANGUREN ARAMENDIA, J. A., Philosophy
ARELLANO AYUSO, I., Spanish Literature
ARTIGAS MAYAYO, M., Philosophy
AURELL CARDONA, S., History
AZANZA LÓPEZ, J., Art
BAENA MOLINA, R., General Linguistics and Spanish Language
BAÑALES LEOZ, J. M., Classical Philology
BANÚS IRUSTA, E., Spanish Literature
BEGUIRISTAIN GÚRPIDE, M. A., History
BERIAIN LURI, I., Geography and Town and Country Planning
BERNAL MARTÍNEZ-SORIA, A., Education
BLANCO SARALEGUI, C., General Linguistics and Spanish Language
BREEZE, A., General Linguistics and Spanish Language
CÁRCELES LABORDE, C., Education
CASADO VELARDE, M., General Linguistics and Spanish Language
CASPISTEGUI GORASURRETA, F. J., History
CASTIELLA RODRÍGUEZ, A., History
CASTILLO CEBALLOS, G., Education
CEREZO LALLANA, M., Philosophy
CROSAS LÓPEZ, F., Spanish Literature
CRUZ CRUZ, J., Philosophy
CRUZ PRADOS, A., Philosophy
D'ENTREMONT, A., Geography and Town and Country Planning
DAVIS, R., General Linguistics and Spanish Language
DE MEER LECHÁ-MARZO, F., History
DE NAVASCUÉS Y MARTÍN, J., Spanish Literature
DIZ-LOIS MARTÍNEZ, C., History
DOMEÑO MARTÍNEZ DE MORENTÍN, A., Art
ESCUDERO BAZTÁN, J. M., Spanish Literature
FERNÁNDEZ GONZÁLEZ, A. R., Spanish Literature
FERNÁNDEZ GRACIA, R., Art
FERNÁNDEZ RODRÍGUEZ, J. L., Philosophy
FERNÁNDEZ URTASUN, R., Spanish Literature
FERNÁNDEZ-LADREDA AGUADÉ, C., Art
FERRARY OJEDA, A., History
FLAMARIQUE ZARATIEGUI, L., Philosophy
FREIRE, J. B., Education
GALVÁN MORENO, L., Spanish Literature
GARCÍA ARANCÓN, R., History
GARCÍA BOURELLIER, R., History
GARCÍA DE LA BORBOLLA, A., History
GARCIA GAINZA, C., Art
GARCÍA RUIZ, V., Spanish Literature
GONZÁLEZ, A. L., Philosophy
GONZÁLEZ ENCISO, A., History
GONZÁLEZ GONZÁLEZ, A. M., Philosophy
GONZÁLEZ RUIZ, R., General Linguistics and Spanish Language
GONZÁLEZ TORRES, M. DEL C., Education
HERRERO LÓPEZ, M., Philosophy
INSAUSTI HERRERO-VELARDE, G., General Linguistics and Spanish Language
IRIARTE REDÍN, C., Education
ISAACS, D., Education
LABRADA RUBIO, M. A., Philosophy
LARA ROS, S., Education
LARRAZA MICHELTORENA, M. DEL M., History
LASPALAS PÉREZ, J., Education
LATASA VASSALLO, P., History
LÁZARO CANTERO, R., Philosophy
LIZARRAGA GUTIÉRREZ, P, Philosophy
LIZARRAGA LEZAUN, M. A., Geography and Town and Country Planning
LIZASOAIN RUMEU, O., Education
LLANO CIFUENTES, A., Philosophy
LONGARES ALONSO, J., History
LÓPEZ HERNÁNDEZ, M. D., Geography and Town and Country Planning
MARTÍNEZ FERNÁNDEZ, R., Classical Philology

MARTÍNEZ PASAMAR, C., General Linguistics and Spanish Language
MOLINOS TEJADA, M. DEL C., Education
MONTORO GURICH, C., Geography and Town and Country Planning
MÚGICA MARTINENA, F., Philosophy
MURILLO GÓMEZ, J. I., Philosophy
NARBONA GARCÍA, J., Education
NAVAL DURÁN, C., Education
NAVAS GARCÍA, A., Philosophy
NAVARRO SANTANA, J., History
NAVAS GARCÍA, A., Philosophy
NUBIOLA, J., Philosophy
OCHOA LINACERO, B., Education
OLÁBARRI GORTÁZAR, I., History
PAVÓN BENITO, J., History
PERALTA LÓPEZ, F., Education
PÉREZ-ILZARBE SERRANO, P., Philosophy
PÉREZ-SALAZAR RESANO, C., General Linguistics and Spanish Language
PINILLOS SALVADOR, M. C., Spanish Literature
PONS IZQUIERDO, J. J., Geography Town and Country Planning
REDONDO GALVEZ, G., History
REPÁRAZ ABAITUA, R., Education
RODRÍGUEZ SEDANO, A., Education
ROMERO GUALDA, M. V., General Linguistics and Spanish Language
SÁNCHEZ-OSTIZ GUTIÉRREZ, Á., Classical Philology
SANTOS CAMACHO, M., Philosophy
SANZ SANTACRUZ, V., Philosophy
SARALEGUI PLATERO, M. C., General Linguistics and Spanish Language
SARRAIS OTEO, F., Education
SELLÉS DAUDER, J. F., Philosophy
SISON GALSIM, A. J., Philosophy
SOBRINO MORRÁS, A., Education
SOTO BRUNA, M. J., Philosophy
SPANG, K., Spanish Literature
TABERNERO SALA, C., General Linguistics and Spanish Language
TORRES GUERRA, J., Classical Philology
TOURON FIGUEROA, J., Education
URABAYEN PÉREZ, J., Philosophy
URPI GUERCIA, C., Education
USUNÁRIZ GARAYOA, J. M., History
VÁZQUEZ DE PRADA TIFFÉ, M., History
VERGARA, J., History of Education
ZABALZA SEGUÍN, A., History
ZUGASTI ZUGASTI, M., Spanish Literature

Faculty of Medicine:

ALBEROLA GÓMEZ-ESCOLAR, I., Internal Medicine
ALCÁZAR ZAMBRANO, J. L., Obstetrics and Gynaecology
ALEGRÍA EZQUERRA, E., Cardiology
ÁLVAREZ-CIENFUEGOS SUÁREZ, J., General Surgery
ALZINA DE AGUILAR, V., Paediatrics
AMILLO GARAYOA, S., Orthopaedics Surgery
AQUERRETA BEOLA, A., Radiology
ARTIEDA GONZÁLEZ-GRANDA, J., Neurology
AYMERICH SOLER, M. S., Neurology
AZANZA PEREA, J. R., Pharmacology
AZCONA SAN JULIÁN, C., Paediatrics
BARBA COSIALS, J., Cardiology
BAZÁN ÁLVAREZ, A., Plastic Surgery
BEGUIRISTAIN GÚRPIDE, J. L., Orthopaedics Surgery
BELOQUI RUIZ, Ó., Internal Medicine
BERIÁN POLO, J. M., Urology
BILBAO JAUREGUIZAR, I., Radiology
BODEGAS FRÍAS, M. E., Histology
BORRÁS CUESTA, F., Biochemistry
BURRELL BUSTOS, M. A., Pathological Anatomy
CALABUIG NOGUÉS, J., Cardiology
CALVO GONZÁLEZ, A., Histology
CARRASCOSA MORENO, F., Anaesthesiology and Resuscitation
CASADO CASADO, M., Radiology
CENARRUZBEITIA SAGARMINAGA, E., Physiology

CERVERA ENGUIX, S., Psychiatry
CIVEIRA MURILLO, M. P., Medical Secretary-ship
COLINA LORDA, I., Internal Medicine
COMA CANELLA, I., Cardiology
CORRALES IZQUIERDO, J., Internal Medicine
CUESTA PALOMERA, B., Haematology
DE CASTRO, P., Neurology
DE MIGUEL VÁZQUEZ, C., Biochemistry
DEL POZO LEÓN, J. L., Microbiology
DÍAZ GARCÍA, R., Microbiology
DIÉGUEZ LÓPEZ, I., Allergology
DIEZ GOÑI, N., Physiology
DÍEZ MARTÍNEZ, J., Internal Medicine
ECHARTE ALONSO, L., Biomedicine
FERNÁNDEZ ALONSO, M., Microbiology
FORRIOL CAMPOS, F., Laboratory Medicine
FRECHILLA MANSO, D., Pharmacology
GARCÍA-MORATO, J. R., Anthropology
GIL SOTRES, P., Biomedicine
HONORATO PÉREZ, J., Pharmacology
HONTANILLA CATALAY, B., Plastic Surgery
IDOATE GASTEARENA, M., Pathological Anatomy
IRABURU ELIZALDE, M., Biochemistry
IRALA ESTEVEZ, J. DE, Preventive Medicine
LAHORTIGA RAMOS, F., Psychiatry
LASHERAS ALDAZ, B., Pharmacology
LÁZARO CANTERO, R., Anthropology
LEÓN SANZ, M. P., Biomedicine
LÓPEZ GARACÍA, M. P., Psychiatry
LOZANO ESCARIO, M. D., Pathological Anatomy
LUCAS ROS, I., Internal Medicine
LUQUIN PULIDO, M. R., Neurology
MALDONADO LÓPEZ, M., Ophthalmology
MANRIQUE RODRÍGUEZ, M., Otolaryngology
MANRIQUE SMELA, M., Neurology
MARTÍN ALGARRA, S., Oncology
MARTÍN TRENOR, A., General Surgery
MARTÍNEZ DE TEJADA DE GARAIZABAL, G., Microbiology
MARTÍNEZ GONZÁLEZ, M. A., Epidemiology and Public Health
MARTÍNEZ IRUJO, J. J., Biochemistry
MARTÍNEZ LAGE, M., Neurology
MARTÍNEZ MONGE, R., Radiology
MARTÍNEZ REGUEIRA, F., General Surgery
MARTÍNEZ VILA, E., Neurology
MASDEU PUCHE, J., Neurology
MEDINA CABRERA, J. F., Internal Medicine
MELERO BERMEJO, I., Immunology
MENGUAL POZA, E., Anatomy
MERINO RONCAL, J., Immunology
MONEDERO RODRÍGUEZ, P., Anaesthesiology and Resuscitation
MORENO MONTAÑÉS, J., Ophthalmology
MONTUENGA BADIA, L., Histology
MORIYÓN URÍA, I., Microbiology
MUÑOZ NAVAS, M. A., General Surgery
NARBONA GARCÍA, J., Paediatrics
NOVO VILLAVERDE, J., Genetics
OBESO INCHAUSTI, J., Neurology
ODERO DE DIOS, L., Genetics
OLAVIDE GOYA, I., Anaesthesiology
PÁRAMO FERNÁNDEZ, J. A., Haematology
PARDO CABALLOS, A., Biomedicine
PARDO MINDÁN, J., Pathological Anatomy
PASTOR MUÑOZ, M. A., Neurology
PEÑUELAS SÁNCHEZ, I., Biochemistry
PÉREZ FERNÁNDEZ, N., Otolaryngology
PÉREZ MEDIAVILLA, L. A., Biochemistry
PRENSA SEPÚLVEDA, L., Anatomy
PRIETO VALTUEÑA, J., Internal Medicine
PRÓSPER, F., Haematology
PURROY UNANUA, A., Nephrology
QIAN, C., Internal Medicine
QUIROGA VILAS, J., Internal Medicine
REDONDO, P., Dermatology
RICHTER ECHEVARRÍA, J. A., Nuclear Medicine
RIO ZAMBRANA, J., Pharmacology
ROBLES GARCÍA, J. E., Urology
ROCHA HERNANDO, E., Haematology
RODRÍGUEZ ORTIGOSA, C., Biochemistry
ROSELL COSTA, D., Urology

ROUZAUT SUBIRÁ, A., Biochemistry
RUBIO VALLEJO, M., Microbiology
RUIZ-CANELA LÓPEZ, M., Biomedicine
SALVADOR RODRÍGUEZ, F. J., Endocrinology
SÁNCHEZ IBARROLA, A., Immunology
SANGRO GÓMEZ-ACEBO, B., Internal Medicine
SANTIDRIAN ALEGRE, S., Physiology
SANZ LARRUGA, M. L., Allergology
SEGUÍ GÓMEZ, M., Internal Medicine
SERRANO MARTÍNEZ, J., Internal Medicine
SESMA EGOZCUE, P., Pathological Anatomy
SIERRASESÚMAGA ARIZNAVARRETA, L., Paediatrics
SOLA GALLEGO, J. J., Pathological Anatomy
TORRE BUXALLEU, W., General Surgery
ULLÁN SERRANO, J., Anatomy
VALENTÍ NIN, J. R., Orthopaedic Surgery
VELAYOS JORGE, J. L., Anatomy
VILLARO GUMPERT, A. C., Histology
VILLAS TOMÉ, C., Orthopaedic Surgery
VITERI TORRES, C., Neurology
ZAPATA GARCÍA, R., Psychiatry
ZORNOZA CELAYA, G., General Surgery
ZUBIETA ZARRAGA, J. L., Radiology
ZUDAIRE BERGARA, J. J., Urology

Faculty of Pharmacy

(Some professors also serve in the Faculty of Sciences)

AGUIRRE GARCÍA, N., Pharmacology
ALDANA MORAZA, I., Organic Chemistry
ALDAZ PASTOR, A., Pharmacy and Pharmaceutical Technology
ANSORENA, D., Bromatology and Toxicology
AQUERRETA GONZÁLEZ, I., Pharmacy and Pharmaceutical Technology
ASTIASARÁN ANCHÍA, I., Bromatology and Toxicology
BARBER CÁRCAMO, A., Physiology and Nutrition
BEITIA BERROTARÁN, G.
BERJÓN SAN JUAN, A., Physiology and Nutrition
BLANCO, M. J., Pharmacy and Pharmaceutical Technology
CALVO, I., Pharmacy and Pharmaceutical Technology
CID CANDA, C., Bromatology and Toxicology
DE PEÑA FARIZA, M. P., Bromatology
DÍAZ GARCÍA, J. M., Pharmacy and Pharmaceutical Technology
DIOS VIÉITEZ, C., Pharmacy and Pharmaceutical Technology
ESPUELAS, S., Pharmacy and Pharmaceutical Technology
IDOATE GARCÍA, A., Pharmacy and Pharmaceutical Technology
FERNÁNDEZ DE TROCÓNIZ, I., Pharmacy and Pharmaceutical Technology
FONT ARELLANO, M., Organic Chemistry
GARCÍA DEL BARRIO, G., Pharmacy and Pharmaceutical Technology
GARRIDO, M. J., Pharmacy and Pharmaceutical Technology
GIL ROYO, A. G., Bromatology and Toxicology
GIRÁLDEZ DEIRÓ, J., Pharmacy and Pharmaceutical Technology
GOÑI LEZA, M. DEL M., Pharmacy and Pharmaceutical Technology
LACASA ARREGUI, C., Pharmacy and Pharmaceutical Technology
LASHERAS ALDAZ, B., Pharmacology
LIZARRAGA PÉREZ, E., Organic Chemistry
LOBO, J. M., Pharmacy and Pharmaceutical Technology
LÓPEZ DE CERÁIN, A., Bromatology and Toxicology
LÓPEZ GUZMÁN, J., Biomedicine
LOSTAO CRESPO, P., Physiology and Nutrition

Physics and Computer Architecture: GABRIEL RUIZ RUIZ

Physiology: MIGUEL ÁNGEL VALDEOLMILLOS LÓPEZ

Histology and Anatomy: EDUARDO FERNÁNDEZ JOVER

Engineering: TERESA GARCÍA ORTUÑO

Industrial Systems Engineering: OSCAR REINOSO GARCÍA

Clinical Medicine: JAIME MERINO SÁNCHEZ

Pathology and Surgery: MARÍA TERESA PÉREZ VÁZQUEZ

Vegetal Production and Microbiology: PABLO MELGAREJO MORENO

Health Psychology: SOFÍA LÓPEZ ROIG

Public Health, History of Science and Gynaecology: ENRIQUE PERDIGUERO GIL

Agricultural Food Technology: SALVADOR CASTILLO GARCÍA

ATTACHED INSTITUTES

Operational Research Centre: Campus de Elche, Edificio Torretamarit, Avda del Ferrocarril s/n, 03202 Elche; tel. 96-665-87-52; fax 96-665-87-15; e-mail cio@umh.es; internet cio .umh.es; Dir JESÚS TADEO PASTOR CIURANA.

Institute of Bioengineering: Edificio Vinalopó, Avda del Ferrocarril s/n, 03202 Elche; tel. 96-665-85-10; fax 96-665-85-11; internet bioengenieria.umh.es; Dir BERNAT SORIA ESCOMS.

Institute of Molecular and Cell Biology: Edificio Torregaitán, Avda de la Universidad s/n, 03202 Elche; tel. 96-665-87-59; fax 96-665-87-58; e-mail biomolccl@umh.es; internet ibmc.umh.es; Dir JOSÉ MANUEL GONZÁLEZ ROS.

Institute of Research into Drug Addiction: Facultad de Medicina, Campus de San Juan, Ctra Alicante-Valencia, Km 87, Apdo no. 18, 03550 San Juan de Alicante; tel. 96-591-93-19; fax 96-591-95-66; e-mail inid@umh.es; internet inid.umh.es; Dir JOSÉ ANTONIO GARCÍA DEL CASTILLO RODRÍGUEZ.

Neurosciences Institute: Apdo 18, 03550 San Joan d'Alacant; tel. 96-591-94-87; fax 96-591-95-61; e-mail in@umh.es; internet in .umh.es/index2.htm; Dir CARLOS BELMONTE MARTÍNEZ.

MONDRAGON UNIBERTSITATEA

Loramendi 4, Apdo 23, 20500 Mondragón

Telephone: 943-71-21-85

Fax: 943-71-21-93

E-mail: info@mondragon.edu

Internet: www.mondragon.edu

Founded 1997

Private control

Languages of instruction: Basque, Spanish, English

Academic year: September to July

Rector: INAXIO OLIVERI ALBISU

Academic Vice-Rector: JOSE MARI AIZEAGA ZUBILLAGA

Director of Research: SABIN FERNÁNDEZ UGARTE

Registrar: IDOIA PEÑACOBA ETXEBARRIA

Administrative Director: MILAGROS BELATEGUI TROJAOLA

Librarian: OBDULIA VELEZ

Number of teachers: 240

Number of students: 3,995

DEANS

Faculty of Business: JOSÉ LUIS ABAUNZ ZUBIA

Faculty of Humanities and Education: JOSE ANTONIO MENDIKUTE BADIOLA

Higher Polytechnic School: JAVIER RETEGUI ALBISUA (Director)

UNIVERSIDAD DE MURCIA

Avda Teniente Flomesta 5, 30003 Murcia

Telephone: 968-36-30-00

Fax: 968-36-36-03

E-mail: siu@um.es

Internet: www.um.es

Founded 1915

State control

Language of instruction: Spanish

Academic year: September to June

Rector: JOSÉ BALLESTA GERMÁN

Vice-Rector (Quality and European Integration): EDUARDO JAVIER OSUNA CARRILLO DE ALBORNOZ

Vice-Rector (Planning and Infrastructure): JOSÉ MARÍA GÓMEZ ESPÍN

Vice-Rector (Student and Post-graduate Studies): JUANA CASTAÑO RUIZ

Vice-Rector (Academic Staff and Training): FRANCISCO DE ASÍS MARTÍNEZ ORTIZ

Vice-Rector (Students and Employment): NORBERTO NAVARRO ADELANTADO

Vice-Rector (Research and New Technologies): SANTIAGO TORRES MARTÍNEZ

Vice Rector (Cultural and University Projection): CONRADO NAVALÓN VILA

Registrar: NATALIA EGEA DÍAZ

Manager: JORGE NAVARRO OLIVARES

Library Director: LOURDES COBACHO GÓMEZ

Library of 629,000 vols, 12,345 periodicals (incl. 3,200 online)

Number of teachers: 1,832

Number of students: 31,313

Publications: *Historia Agraria* (4 a year), *Myrtia* (classical philology, 2 a year), *Daimon* (philosophy, 2 a year), *Antigüedad y Cristianismo* (annually), *Anales de Biología* (annually), *Papeles de Geografía* (2 a year)

DEANS

Faculty of Arts: JOSÉ MARÍA JIMÉNEZ CANO

Faculty of Law: JOSÉ ANTONIO COBACHO GÓMEZ

Faculty of Chemistry: M. GLORIA VILLORA CANO

Faculty of Mathematics: JOSÉ MA. RUIZ GOMEZ

Faculty of Medicine: FERNANDO SÁNCHEZ GASCÓN

Faculty of Psychology: JESÚS GÓMEZ AMOR

Faculty of Economics and Business Studies: JOSÉ DANIEL BUENDÍA AZORÍN

Faculty of Communication and Documentation: JOSÉ VICENTE RODRÍGUEZ MUÑOZ

Faculty of Veterinary Studies: ANTONIO BERNABÉ SALAZAR

Faculty of Philosophy: JOSÉ LORITE MENA

Faculty of Biology: JOSÉ MARÍA EGEA FERNÁNDEZ

Faculty of Education: DIEGO GUZMÁN MARTÍNEZ-VALLS

Faculty of Computer Sciences: LEANDRO MARÍN MUÑOZ

Faculty of Fine Arts: JUAN ROMERA AGULLÓ

Faculty of Industrial Relations: MARÍA ISABEL SÁNCHEZ-MORA MOLINA

DIRECTORS

University School of Nursing (in Murcia): CARMEN ISABEL GÓMEZ GARCÍA

University School of Social Work: REMEDIOS MAURANDI GUIRADO

Nursing Training School: MERCEDES SANTESTEBAN DE MINGO

Law Training School: FERNANDO JIMÉNEZ CONDE

Labour Affairs Training School: GUILLERMO RODRÍGUEZ INIESTA

Psychology Training School: FRANCISCO JAVIER CORBALÁN BERNA

Social Work Training School: ENRIQUE PASTOR SELLER

Technology Training School: LUIS DANIEL HERNÁNDEZ MOLINERO

University School of Tourism: FRANCISCO CREMARES BAÑÓN

HEADS OF DEPARTMENTS

Human Anatomy and Psychobiology: LUIS PUELLES LÓPEZ

Cell Biology: MA. CONCEPCIÓN FERRER CAZORLA

Biochemistry and Molecular Biology: ENCARNACIÓN MUÑOZ DELGADO

Biochemistry, Molecular Biology and Immunology: ARTURO MANJÓN RUBIO

Marketing and Market Research: JOSÉ LUIS MUNUERA ALEMÁN

Politics and Administration: MÓNICA MÉNDEZ LAGO, MIREIA GRAU I CREUS

Administrative Law: ANTONIO GUTIERREZ LLAMAS

Financial, International and Procedural Law: GEMMA GARCÍA-ROSTAN CALVIN

Private Law: ROSALÍA ALFONSO RODRÍGUEZ

Dermatology, Stomatology, Radiology and Physical Medicine: MIGUEL ALCARAZ BAÑOS

Teaching Literature and Languages: AMANDO LÓPEZ VALERO

Teaching Experimental Sciences: ANTONIO JOSÉ DE PRO BUENO

Teaching Mathematics and Social Sciences: ANDRÉS NORTES CHECA

Education and School Organization: PILAR ARNAIZ SÁNCHEZ

Ecology and Hydrology: ROSARIO VIDAL-ABARCA GUTIÉRREZ

Applied Economics: FERNANDO IGNACIO SÁNCHEZ MARTÍNEZ

Finance and Accounting: PEDRO LUENGO MULET

Statistics and Operational Research: LÁZARO CÁNOVAS MARTÍNEZ

Politics and Administration: MÓNICA MÉNDEZ LAGO, MIREÍA GRAU I CREUS

Pharmacology: ELISA ESCUDERO PASTOR

Classical Philology: FRANCISCO MOYA DEL BAÑO

French, Romance, Italian and Arabic Philology: CONCEPCIÓN PALACIOS BERNAL

English Philology: PASCUAL CANTOS GÓMEZ

Philosophy: ANTONIO CAMPILLO MESEGUER

Physiotherapy: ANTONIA GÓMEZ CONESA

Principles of Economic Analysis: FRANCISCO ALCALÁ AGULLÓ

Principles of Juridical and Constitutional Order: RAFAEL HERNÁNDEZ MARÍN

Physical and Human Geography and Regional Analysis: FRANCISCO CALVO CONESA GARCÍA

Public Finance and Public Sector Economics: AMBROSIO GARCÍA-TORNEL

Modern, Contemporary and American History: JUAN B. VILAR RAMÍREZ

Information and Documentation: VIVINA ASENSI ARTIGA

Computer Science and Systems: ISIDRO VERDÚ CONESA

Information and Communications Engineering: ANTONIO F. GÓMEZ SKARMETA

Chemical Engineering: ANTONIO BÓDALO SANTOYO

Computer Engineering and Technology: PEDRO ENRIQUE LÓPEZ DE TERUEL ALCOLEA

Spanish Language and General Linguistics: RICARDO ESCAVY ZAMORA

Spanish Literature, Theory of Literature and Comparative Literature: FRANCISCO JAVIER DÍEZ DE REVENGA TORRES

Applied Mathematics: FRANCISCO JOSÉ VERA LÓPEZ

Mathematics: PASCUAL LUCAS SAORÍN

Internal Medicine: MARIANO VALDÉS CHÁVARRI

Animal Medicine and Surgery: ANA MA. MONTES CEPEDA

Quantitative Methods for Economics: ANTONIO CALVO-FLORES SEGURA

Research Methods and Diagnostics in Education: FUENSANTA HERNÁNDEZ PINA

Ophthalmology, Otorhinolaryngology and Pathological Anatomy: MANUEL VIDAL SANZ

Business and Financial Organization: RAMÓN SABATER SÁNCHEZ

Prehistory, Archaeology, Ancient and Medieval History and Historiographical Sciences and Methods: JOAQUÍN LOMBA MAURANDI

Basic Psychology and Methodology: JUAN ANTONIO VERA FERRÁNDIZ

Evolutionary Psychology and Educational Psychology: JOSÉ ANTONIO CARRANZA CARNICERO

Psychiatry and Social Psychology: JOAQUÍN NIETO MUNUERA

Agrochemistry, Geology and Soil Science: ROQUE ORTIZ SILLA

Inorganic Chemistry: GREGORIO LÓPEZ LÓPEZ

Organic Chemistry: ARTURO ESPINOSA FERAO

Religion: JUAN CARLOS GARCÍA DOMENE

Sociology and Social Policy: JUAN JOSÉ GARCÍA ESCRIBANO

Food Technology, Nutrition and Bromatology: GASPAR ROS BERRUEZO

Theory and History of Education: PEDRO LUIS MORENO MARTÍNEZ

Zoology and Physical Anthropology: JUAN JOSÉ PRESA ASENSIO

ATTACHED INSTITUTIONS

University School of Tourism: Paseo de Malecón 5, 30004 Murcia; tel. 968-29-36-24; fax 968-29-10-96; e-mail eutm@um.es; Academic Dir FRANCISCO CREMADES BAÑÓN.

University School of Nursing in Cartagena: Plaza San Agustín 3, 30201 Cartagena (Murcia); tel. 968-32-66-96; fax 968-32-66-95; internet www.um.es/eu-enfermeria-ct/; Dir (vacant) J. M. HERNÁNDEZ CONESA.

Pérez de Lema Centre of University Teaching: C/ Real 80, Cartagena (Murcia); tel. 968-50-53-13; internet www.um.es/perezdelema/; Dir MA. DOLORES FONTES BASTOS.

Institute of Education: Edificio D, 3a Planta, Campus de Espinardo, 30100 Murcia; tel. 968-36-39-26; fax 968-36-39-25; e-mail ice@um.es; internet www.um.es/ice; Dir JUAN MANUEL ESCUDERO MUÑOZ.

Institute of Water and the Environment: Edificio D, Campus de Espinardo, 30100 Murcia; tel. 968-36-49-10; fax 968-36-33-89; e-mail inuama@um.es; internet www.um.es/inuama; Dir ALBERTO BARBA NAVARRO.

Inter-university Institute of the Ancient Near East: Antigua Escuela de Empresariales, C/ Actor Isidoro Máiquez 8, Vistalegre, 30007 Murcia; tel. 968-36-38-90; fax 968-36-38-90; e-mail ipoa@um.es; internet www.um.es/ipoa.

Institute of Sport Science: Facultad de Educación, Campus Universitario de Espinardo, 30100 Espinardo (Murcia); tel. 968-36-40-52; fax 968-36-41-46; e-mail icd@um.es; internet www.um.es/icd; Dir ARTURO DÍAZ SUÁREZ.

Institute of Ageing: Campus Universitario de Espinardo, 30100 Espinardo (Murcia); tel. 968-36-34-99; e-mail maemedina@um.es; internet www.um.es/estructura/institutos/iupe; Dir MANUEL E. MEDINA TORNERO.

Institute of Financial and Fiscal Studies: Dpto Hacienda y Economía del Sector Público, Despacho B109, Campus de Espinardo, 30100 Murcia; tel. 968-36-77-98; e-mail inueff@um.es; internet www.um.es/inueff; Dir GLORIA ALARCÓN GARCÍA.

UNIVERSIDAD DE NAVARRA

Campus Universitario, 31080 Pamplona
Telephone: 948-42-56-00

Fax: 948-42-56-19
E-mail: relint@unav.es
Internet: www.unav.es
Founded 1952
State control
Language of instruction: Spanish
Academic year: September to June

Chancellor: JAVIER ECHEVARRÍA
Vice-Chancellor: RAMÓN HERRANDO
Rector: JOSÉ MA. BASTERO ELEIZALDE
Vice-Rector (Academic Staff): MANUEL CASADO-VELARDE
Vice-Rector (External Relations): JAIME NUBIOLA
Vice-Rector (Quality, Innovation and Information Technology): CONCEPCIÓN NAVAL
Vice-Rector (Research): PILAR FERNÁNDEZ OTERO
Vice-Rector (Student Affairs and Academic Organization): ANGEL JOSÉ GÓMEZ MONTORO
Secretary-General: GONZALO ROBLES
Librarian: VÍCTOR SANZ-SANTACRUZ

Library of 800,988 vols, 24,908 periodicals (incl. 6,515 online)
Number of teachers: 2,047
Number of students: 15,471

Publications: *Revista de Medicina* (4 a year), *Ius Canonicum* (2 a year), *Nuestro Tiempo* (12 a year), *Scripta Theologica* (4 a year), *Redacción* (4 a year), *Anuario Filosófico* (3 a year), *Anuario de Derecho Internacional* (annually), *Persona y Derecho* (2 a year), *Revista de Edificación* (4 a year), *Comunicación y Sociedad* (2 a year), *RILCE* (2 a year)

DEANS

Faculty of Law: JULIO JAVIER MUERZA ESPARZA
Faculty of Communication: ALFONSO SÁNCHEZ-TABERNERO
Faculty of Medicine: MARÍA PILAR CIVEIRA MURILLO
Faculty of Canon Law: RAFAEL RODRÍGUEZ-OCAÑA
Faculty of Pharmacy: ICIAR ASTIASARAN
Faculty of Sciences: MARIA PILAR SESMA
Faculty of Theology: FRANCISCO VARO
Faculty of Economics: LUIS RAVINA BOHÓRQUEZ
Faculty of Humanities and Social Sciences: CARMEN SARALEGUI PLATERO
Faculty of Engineering: CARLOS BASTERO DE ELEIZALDE
Faculty of Architecture: JUAN-MIGUEL OTXOTORENA
Faculty of Nursing: MARIA-ISABEL SARACIBAR

DIRECTORS OF AFFILIATED COLLEGES, SCHOOLS AND INSTITUTES

School of Engineering: CARLOS BASTERO DE ELEIZALDE
School of Architecture: JUAN MIGUEL OTXOTORENA
Institute of Liberal Arts: JAVIER DE NAVASCUÉS
Institute of Church History: MARCELO MERINO RODRÍGUEZ
Institute of Modern Languages: RUTH BREEZE
Higher Institute of Secretarial and Administrative Studies: MARÍA DEL MAR ARALUCE LETAMENDÍA
Institute of Spanish Language and Culture: CONCHA MARTÍNEZ PASAMAR
School of Nursing: ISABEL SARACÍBAR RAZQUIN

HEADS OF DEPARTMENTS

Human, Legal and Social Sciences:
Public Communication: ALEJANDRO NAVAS
Culture and Audiovisual Communication: ALEJANDRO PARDO FERNÁNDEZ
Canon Law and Ecclesiastical Law of the State: JUAN FORNÉS

Civil Law: (vacant)
Constitutional Law: ÁNGEL J. GONZÁLEZ MONTORO
Financial and Tax Law: EUGENIO SIMÓN ACOSTA
Private International Law: JOSÉ JAVIER PÉREZ MILLA
Public International Law: EUGENIA LÓPEZ-JACOISTE DÍAZ
Penal Law: PABLO SÁNCHEZ-OSTIZ GUTIÉRREZ
Procedural Law: FAUSTINO CORDÓN MORENO
Roman Law: RAFAEL DOMINGO
Economics: FERNANDO PÉREZ DE GRACIA HIDALGO
Education: ALFREDO RODRÍGUEZ SEDANO
Business Studies: JAVIER GÓMEZ BISCARRI
Information Industry: MERCEDES MEDINA LAVERÓN
Classical Philology: JOSÉ B. TORRES GUERRA
Philosophy: FERNANDO MÚGICA
Philosophy of Law: ÁNGELA APARISI MIRALLES
Geography and Town and Country Planning: ALBÁN D'ENTREMONT
History: ALVARO FERRARY
History of the Church: MARCELO MERINO RODRÍGUEZ
History of Art: CONCEPCIÓN GARCÍA GAINZA
Humanities: MA. AMOR BEGUIRISTAIN
Modern Languages: MANUEL CASADO VELARDE
General Linguistics and Spanish Language: MANUEL CASADO VELARDE
Hispanic Literature and Theory of Literature: IGNACIO ARELLANO AYUSO
Quantitative Methods: JUNCAL CUÑADO EIZAGUIRRE
Pastoral Letters and Sunday School: JAIME PUJOL
Journalistic Projects: FERNANDO LÓPEZ PAN
Holy Scripture: SANTIAGO AUSÍN OLMOS
Dogmatic Theology: CÉSAR IZQUIERDO
Moral and Spiritual Theology: AUGUSTO SARMIENTO

Experimental and Technical Sciences:
Allergology and Clinical Immunology: ISAURO DIEGUEZ LÓPEZ
Anatomy: JOSÉ LUIS VELAYOS
Anaesthesiology and Resuscitation: PABLO MONEDERO RODRÍGUEZ
Biochemistry and Molecular Biology: MARÍA JESÚS LÓPEZ ZABALZA
Botany: ANA MA. DE MIGUEL VELASCO
Bromatology, Food Technology and Toxicology: MA. DE LA CONCEPCIÓN CID CANDA
Cardiology and Cardiovascular Surgery: JOAQUÍN BARBA COSIALS, JESÚS HERREROS GONZÁLEZ
General and Digestive Surgery: FRANCISCO JAVIER ALVAREZ-CIENFUEGOS
Orthopaedic Surgery and Traumatology: JUAN RAMÍREZ VALENTÍ
Plastic and Reconstructional Surgery: ANTONIO BAZÁN ALVAREZ
Dermatology: PEDRO REDONDO
Construction: MIGUEL ÁNGEL GUTIÉRREZ FERNÁNDEZ
Endocrinology: JAVIER SALVADOR RODRÍGUEZ
Structures: EDUARDO BAYO PÉREZ
Pharmacy and Pharmaceutical Technology: MA. JESÚS RENEDO OMAECIIEVARRÍA
Pharmacology: JOAQUÍN DEL RÍO
Clinical Pharmacology: JESÚS HONORATO
Physics and Applied Mathematics: HÉCTOR L. MANCINI
Human Physiology: SANTIAGO SANTIDRIÁN ALEGRE
Vegetal Physiology: MANUEL SÁNCHEZ-DÍAZ
Physiology and Nutrition: J. ALFREDO MARTÍNEZ HERNÁNDEZ
Genetics: (vacant)

Haematology: EDUARDO ROCHA
Histology and Pathological Anatomy: LUIS MONTUENGA BADÍA
Biomedical Humanities: MA. PILAR LEÓN SANZ
Nuclear Medicine: JOSÉ ÁNGEL RICHTER ECHEVARRÍA
Microbiology and Parasitology: IGNACIO MORIYÓN
Neurology and Neurosurgery: JOSÉ MASDEU (Neurology: JULIO ARTIEDA GONZÁLEZ-GRANDA (Neurophysiology: MIGUEL MANRIQUE SMELA (Neurosurgery)
Nephrology: ANDRÉS PURROY UNANUA
Obstetrics and Gynaecology: GUILLERMO LÓPEZ GARCÍA
Ophthalmology: JAVIER MORENO MONTAÑÉS
Oncology: SALVADOR MARTÍN ALGARRA
Otorhinolaryngology: NICOLÁS PÉREZ FERNÁNDEZ
Paediatrics: LUIS SIERRASESÚMAGA
Architectural Projects: JUAN MIGUEL OTXOTORENA ELIZEGI
Psychiatry and Medical Psychology: SALVADOR CERVERA ENGUIX
Chemistry and Soil Science: JOSÉ MARÍA FERNÁNDEZ ÁLVAREZ
Radiology: JOSÉ IGNACIO BILBAO
Theory and History of Architecture: MA. ANTONIA FRÍAS SAGARDOY
Town Planning: EDUARDO ROJO FRAILE
Urology: JOSÉ MARÍA BERIÁN POLO
Zoology and Ecology: CARMEN ESCALA URDAPILLETA

Institute of Advanced Business Studies:

Decision Analysis: MIGUEL ÁNGEL ARIÑO
Accounting and Control: FERNANDO PEÑALVA
Business Management: JULIÁN VILLANUEVA
Human Resources Management: JOSÉ R. PIN
Production Technology and Operational Management: FREDERIC SABRIÀ
Financial Management: JAVIER SANTOMÁ
General Management: JOAN ENRIC RICART
Economics: JORDI GUAL
Business Ethics: DOMÈNEC MELÉ
Entrepreneurial Initiative: PEDRO NUENO
Information Systems: JOSEP VALOR

PROFESSORS

Faculty of Law:

APARISI, A., Philosophy of Law
ARECHEDERRA, L., Civil Law
BLANCO, M., Canon Law
CORDÓN, F., Procedural Law
DE LA IGLESIA, A., Constitutional Law
DOMINGO, R., Roman Law
FAJARDO, J., Civil Law
FORNÉS DE LA ROSA, J., Canon Law
GALÁN, M., History of Law
GARCÍA, R., History of Law
GÓMEZ, A., Constitutional Law
GUTIÉRREZ DE CAVIEDES, P., Procedural Law
IÑIGO, E., Penal Law
LÓPEZ SÁNCHEZ, M. A., Commercial Law
LÓPEZ-JURADO, B., Administrative Law
MUERZA, J., Procedural Law
NANCLARES, J., Civil Law
PÉREZ, F., Canon Law
ROSENDE, C., Procedural Law
RUIZ DE APODACA, A., Administrative Law
SALCEDO, J., History of Law
SALVADOR, A., Administrative Law
SAN JULIÁN, V., Civil Law
SIMÓN, E., Financial Law
VALPUESTA, E., Commercial Law
VÁZQUEZ DEL REY, A., Financial and Tax Law

Faculty of Humanities and Social Sciences:

AGUADO ALONSO, G., Education
ALARCÓN MORENO, E., Philosophy

ALONSO DEL REAL MONTES, C., Classical Philology
ALTAREJOS MASOTA, F., Education
ALVIRA DOMÍNGUEZ, R., Philosophy
ARANGUREN ARAMENDIA, J. A., Philosophy
ARELLANO AYUSO, I., Spanish Literature
ARTIGAS MAYAYO, M., Philosophy
AURELL CARDONA, S., History
AZANZA LÓPEZ, J., Art
BAENA MOLINA, R., General Linguistics and Spanish Language
BAÑALES LEOZ, J. M., Classical Philology
BANÚS IRUSTA, E., Spanish Literature
BEGUIRISTAIN GÚRPIDE, M. A., History
BERIAIN LURI, I., Geography and Town and Country Planning
BERNAL MARTÍNEZ-SORIA, A., Education
BLANCO SARALEGUI, C., General Linguistics and Spanish Language
BREEZE, A., General Linguistics and Spanish Language
CÁRCELES LABORDE, C., Education
CASADO VELARDE, M., General Linguistics and Spanish Language
CASPISTEGUI GORASURRETA, F. J., History
CASTIELLA RODRÍGUEZ, A., History
CASTILLO CEBALLOS, G., Education
CEREZO LALLANA, M., Philosophy
CROSAS LÓPEZ, F., Spanish Literature
CRUZ CRUZ, J., Philosophy
CRUZ PRADOS, A., Philosophy
D'ENTREMONT, A., Geography and Town and Country Planning
DAVIS, R., General Linguistics and Spanish Language
DE MEER LECHÁ-MARZO, F., History
DE NAVASCUÉS Y MARTÍN, J., Spanish Literature
DIZ-LOIS MARTÍNEZ, C., History
DOMEÑO MARTÍNEZ DE MORENTÍN, A., Art
ESCUDERO BAZTÁN, J. M., Spanish Literature
FERNÁNDEZ GONZÁLEZ, A. R., Spanish Literature
FERNÁNDEZ GRACIA, R., Art
FERNÁNDEZ RODRÍGUEZ, J. L., Philosophy
FERNÁNDEZ URTASUN, R., Spanish Literature
FERNÁNDEZ-LADREDA AGUADÉ, C., Art
FERRARY OJEDA, A., History
FLAMARIQUE ZARATIEGUI, L., Philosophy
FREIRE, J. B., Education
GALVÁN MORENO, L., Spanish Literature
GARCÍA ARANCÓN, R., History
GARCÍA BOURELLIER, R., History
GARCÍA DE LA BORBOLLA, A., History
GARCÍA GAINZA, C., Art
GARCÍA RUIZ, V., Spanish Literature
GONZÁLEZ, A. L., Philosophy
GONZÁLEZ ENCISO, A., History
GONZÁLEZ GONZÁLEZ, A. M., Philosophy
GONZÁLEZ RUIZ, R., General Linguistics and Spanish Language
GONZÁLEZ TORRES, M. DEL C., Education
HERRERO LÓPEZ, M., Philosophy
INSAUSTI HERRERO-VELARDE, G., General Linguistics and Spanish Language
IRIARTE REDÍN, C., Education
ISAACS, D., Education
LABRADA RUBIO, M. A., Philosophy
LARA ROS, S., Education
LARRAZA MICHELTORENA, M DEL M., History
LASPALAS PÉREZ, J., Education
LATASA VASSALLO, P., History
LÁZARO CANTERO, R., Philosophy
LIZARRAGA GUTIÉRREZ, P, Philosophy
LIZARRAGA LEZAUN, M. A., Geography and Town and Country Planning
LIZASOAIN RUMEU, O., Education
LLANO CIFUENTES, A., Philosophy
LONGARES ALONSO, J., History
LÓPEZ HERNÁNDEZ, M. D., Geography and Town and Country Planning
MARTÍNEZ FERNÁNDEZ, R., Classical Philology

MARTÍNEZ PASAMAR, C., General Linguistics and Spanish Language
MOLINOS TEJADA, M. DEL C., Education
MONTORO GURICH, C., Geography and Town and Country Planning
MÚGICA MARTINENA, F., Philosophy
MURILLO GÓMEZ, J. I., Philosophy
NARBONA GARCÍA, J., Education
NAVAL DURÁN, C., Education
NAVAS GARCÍA, A., Philosophy
NAVARRO SANTANA, J., History
NAVAS GARCÍA, A., Philosophy
NUBIOLA, J., Philosophy
OCHOA LINACERO, B., Education
OLÁBARRI GORTÁZAR, I., History
PAVÓN BENITO, J., History
PERALTA LÓPEZ, F., Education
PÉREZ-ILZARBE SERRANO, P., Philosophy
PÉREZ-SALAZAR RESANO, C., General Linguistics and Spanish Language
PINILLOS SALVADOR, M. C., Spanish Literature
PONS IZQUIERDO, J. J., Geography Town and Country Planning
REDONDO GALVEZ, G., History
REPÁRAZ ABAITUA, R., Education
RODRÍGUEZ SEDANO, A., Education
ROMERO GUALDA, M. V., General Linguistics and Spanish Language
SÁNCHEZ-OSTIZ GUTIÉRREZ, Á., Classical Philology
SANTOS CAMACHO, M., Philosophy
SANZ SANTACRUZ, V., Philosophy
SARALEGUI PLATERO, M. C., General Linguistics and Spanish Language
SARRAIS OTEO, F., Education
SELLÉS DAUDER, J. F., Philosophy
SISON GALSIM, A. J., Philosophy
SOBRINO MORRÁS, A., Education
SOTO BRUNA, M. J., Philosophy
SPANG, K., Spanish Literature
TABERNERO SALA, C., General Linguistics and Spanish Language
TORRES GUERRA, J., Classical Philology
TOURON FIGUEROA, J., Education
URABAYEN PÉREZ, J., Philosophy
URPI GUERCIA, C., Education
USUNÁRIZ GARAYOA, J. M., History
VÁZQUEZ DE PRADA TIFFÉ, M., History
VERGARA, J., History of Education
ZABALZA SEGUÍN, A., History
ZUGASTI ZUGASTI, M., Spanish Literature

Faculty of Medicine:

ALBEROLA GÓMEZ-ESCOLAR, I., Internal Medicine
ALCÁZAR ZAMBRANO, J. L., Obstetrics and Gynaecology
ALEGRÍA EZQUERRA, E., Cardiology
ÁLVAREZ-CIENFUEGOS SUÁREZ, J., General Surgery
ALZINA DE AGUILAR, V., Paediatrics
AMILLO GARAYOA, S., Orthopaedics Surgery
AQUERRETA BEOLA, A., Radiology
ARTIEDA GONZÁLEZ-GRANDA, J., Neurology
AYMERICH SOLER, M. S., Neurology
AZANZA PEREA, J. R., Pharmacology
AZCONA SAN JULIÁN, C., Paediatrics
BARBA COSIALS, J., Cardiology
BAZÁN ÁLVAREZ, A., Plastic Surgery
BEGUIRISTAIN GÚRPIDE, J. L., Orthopaedics Surgery
BELOQUI RUIZ, Ó., Internal Medicine
BERIÁN POLO, J. M., Urology
BILBAO JAUREGUIZAR, I., Radiology
BODEGAS FRÍAS, M. E., Histology
BORRÁS CUESTA, F., Biochemistry
BURRELL BUSTOS, M. A., Pathological Anatomy
CALABUIG NOGUÉS, J., Cardiology
CALVO GONZÁLEZ, A., Histology
CARRASCOSA MORENO, F., Anaesthesiology and Resuscitation
CASADO CASADO, M., Radiology
CENARRUZBEITIA SAGARMINAGA, E., Physiology

CERVERA ENGUIX, S., Psychiatry
CIVIERA MURILLO, M. P., Medical Secretary-
ship
COLINA LORDA, I., Internal Medicine
COMA CANELLA, I., Cardiology
CORRALES IZQUIERDO, J., Internal Medicine
CUESTA PALOMERA, B., Haematology
DE CASTRO, P., Neurology
DE MIGUEL VÁZQUEZ, C., Biochemistry
DEL POZO LEÓN, J. L., Microbiology
DÍAZ GARCÍA, R., Microbiology
DIÉGUEZ LÓPEZ, I., Allergology
DIEZ GOÑI, N., Physiology
DÍEZ MARTÍNEZ, J., Internal Medicine
ECHARTE ALONSO, L., Biomedicine
FERNÁNDEZ ALONSO, M., Microbiology
FORRIOL CAMPOS, F., Laboratory Medicine
FRECHILLA MANSO, D., Pharmacology
GARCÍA-MORATO, J. R., Anthropology
GIL SOTRES, P., Biomedicine
HONORATO PÉREZ, J., Pharmacology
HONTANILLA CATALAY, B., Plastic Surgery
IDOATE GASTEARENA, M., Pathological Anat-
omy
IRABURU ELIZALDE, M., Biochemistry
IRALA ESTEVEZ, J. DE, Preventive Medicine
LAHORTIGA RAMOS, F., Psychiatry
LASHERAS ALDAZ, B., Pharmacology
LÁZARO CANTERO, R., Anthropology
LEÓN SANZ, M. P., Biomedicine
LÓPEZ GARACÍA, M. P., Psychiatry
LOZANO ESCARIO, M. D., Pathological Anat-
omy
LUCAS ROS, I., Internal Medicine
LUQUIN PULIDO, M. R., Neurology
MALDONADO LÓPEZ, M., Ophthalmology
MANRIQUE RODRÍGUEZ, M., Otolaryngology
MANRIQUE SMELA, M., Neurology
MARTÍN ALGARRA, S., Oncology
MARTÍN TRENOR, A., General Surgery
MARTÍNEZ DE TEJADA DE GARAIZABAL, G.,
Microbiology
MARTÍNEZ GONZÁLEZ, M. A., Epidemiology
and Public Health
MARTÍNEZ IRUJO, J. J., Biochemistry
MARTÍNEZ LAGE, M., Neurology
MARTÍNEZ MONGE, R., Radiology
MARTÍNEZ REGUEIRA, F., General Surgery
MARTÍNEZ VILA, E., Neurology
MASDEU PUCHE, J., Neurology
MEDINA CABRERA, J. F., Internal Medicine
MELERO BERMEJO, I., Immunology
MENGUAL POZA, E., Anatomy
MERINO RONCAL, J., Immunology
MONEDERO RODRÍGUEZ, P., Anaesthesiology
and Resuscitation
MORENO MONTAÑÉS, J., Ophthalmology
MONTUENGA BADIA, L., Histology
MORIYÓN URÍA, I., Microbiology
MUÑOZ NAVAS, M. A., General Surgery
NARBONA GARCÍA, J., Paediatrics
NOVO VILLAVERDE, J., Genetics
OBESO INCHAUSTI, J., Neurology
ODERO DE DIOS, L., Genetics
OLAVIDE GOYA, I., Anaesthesiology
PÁRAMO FERNÁNDEZ, J. A., Haematology
PARDO CABALLOS, A., Biomedicine
PARDO MINDÁN, J., Pathological Anatomy
PASTOR MUÑOZ, M. A., Neurology
PEÑUELAS SÁNCHEZ, I., Biochemistry
PÉREZ FERNÁNDEZ, N., Otolaryngology
PÉREZ MEDIAVILLA, L. A., Biochemistry
PRENSA SEPÚLVEDA, L., Anatomy
PRIETO VALTUEÑA, J., Internal Medicine
PRÓSPER, F., Haematology
PURROY UNANUA, A., Nephrology
QIAN, C., Internal Medicine
QUIROGA VILAS, J., Internal Medicine
REDONDO, P., Dermatology
RICHTER ECHEVARRÍA, J. A., Nuclear Medi-
cine
RIO ZAMBRANA, J., Pharmacology
ROBLES GARCÍA, J. E., Urology
ROCHA HERNANDO, E., Haematology
RODRÍGUEZ ORTIGOSA, C., Biochemistry
ROSELL COSTA, D., Urology

ROUZAUT SUBIRÁ, A., Biochemistry
RUBIO VALLEJO, M., Microbiology
RUIZ-CANELA LÓPEZ, M., Biomedicine
SALVADOR RODRÍGUEZ, F. J., Endocrinology
SÁNCHEZ IBARROLA, A., Immunology
SANGRO GÓMEZ-ACEBO, B., Internal Medi-
cine
SANTIDRIAN ALEGRE, S., Physiology
SANZ LARRUGA, M. L., Allergology
SEGUÍ GÓMEZ, M., Internal Medicine
SERRANO MARTÍNEZ, M., Internal Medicine
SESMA EGOZCUE, P., Pathological Anatomy
SIERRASESÚMAGA ARIZNAVARRETA, L., Pae-
diatrics
SOLA GALLEGO, J. J., Pathological Anatomy
TORRE BUXALLEU, W., General Surgery
ULLÁN SERRANO, J., Anatomy
VALENTÍ NIN, J. R., Orthopaedic Surgery
VELAYOS JORGE, J. L., Anatomy
VILLARO GUMPERT, A. C., Histology
VILLAS TOMÉ, C., Orthopaedic Surgery
VITERI TORRES, C., Neurology
ZAPATA GARCÍA, R., Psychiatry
ZORNOZA CELAYA, G., General Surgery
ZUBIETA ZARRAGA, J. L., Radiology
ZUDAIRE BERGARA, J. J., Urology

Faculty of Pharmacy
(Some professors also serve in the Faculty of
Sciences)

AGUIRRE GARCÍA, N., Pharmacology
ALDANA MORAZA, I., Organic Chemistry
ALDAZ PASTOR, A., Pharmacy and Pharma-
ceutical Technology
ANSORENA, D., Bromatology and Toxicology
AQUERRETA GONZÁLEZ, I., Pharmacy and
Pharmaceutical Technology
ASTIASARÁN ANCHÍA, I., Bromatology and
Toxicology
BARBER CÁRCAMO, A., Physiology and
Nutrition
BEITIA BERROTARÁN, G.
BERJÓN SAN JUAN, A., Physiology and
Nutrition
BLANCO, M. J., Pharmacy and Pharmaceu-
tical Technology
CALVO, I., Pharmacy and Pharmaceutical
Technology
CID CANDA, C., Bromatology and Toxicol-
ogy
DE PEÑA FARIZA, M. P., Bromatology
DÍAZ GARCÍA, J. M., Pharmacy and Phar-
maceutical Technology
DIOS VIÉITEZ, C., Pharmacy and Pharma-
ceutical Technology
ESPUELAS, S., Pharmacy and Pharmaceu-
tical Technology
IDOATE GARCÍA, A., Pharmacy and Pharma-
ceutical Technology
FERNÁNDEZ DE TROCÓNIZ, I., Pharmacy and
Pharmaceutical Technology
FONT ARELLANO, M., Organic Chemistry
GARCÍA DEL BARRIO, G., Pharmacy and
Pharmaceutical Technology
GARRIDO, M. J., Pharmacy and Pharma-
ceutical Technology
GIL ROYO, A. G., Bromatology and Toxicol-
ogy
GIRÁLDEZ DEIRÓ, J., Pharmacy and Phar-
maceutical Technology
GOÑI LEZA, M. DEL M., Pharmacy and
Pharmaceutical Technology
LACASA ARREGUI, C., Pharmacy and Phar-
maceutical Technology
LASHERAS ALDAZ, B., Pharmacology
LIZARRAGA PÉREZ, E., Organic Chemistry
LOBO, J. M., Pharmacy and Pharmaceuti-
cal Technology
LÓPEZ DE CERÁIN, A., Bromatology and
Toxicology
LÓPEZ GUZMÁN, J., Biomedicine
LOSTAO CRESPO, P., Physiology and Nutri-
tion

MANUEL IRACHE GARRETA, J. M., Pharmacy
and Pharmaceutical Technology
MARTÍ DEL MORAL, A., Physiology and
Nutrition
MARTÍNEZ HERNÁNDEZ, A., Physiology and
Nutrition
MOHINO SÁNCHEZ, A., Bromatology and
Toxicology
MONGE VEGA, A., Organic Chemistry
MORENO ALIAGA, M. J., Physiology and
Nutrition
MUÑOZ HORNILLOS, M., Physiology and
Nutrition
ORTEGA ESLAVA, A., Pharmacy and Phar-
maceutical Technology
PALOP CUBILLO, J. A., Organic Chemistry
RAMÍREZ GIL, M. J., Pharmacology
RECARTE FLAMARIQUE, F., Pharmacy and
Pharmaceutical Technology
RENEDO OMAECHEVARRÍA, M. J., Pharmacy
and Pharmaceutical Technology
ROMERO CUEVAS, M., Organic Chemistry
RUIZ DE LA HERAS, A., Bromatology and
Toxicology
SANMARTÍN GRIJALBA, C., Organic Chemis-
try
TROS DE ILARDUYA, C., Pharmacy and
Pharmaceutical Technology
YGARTUA AYERRA, P., Pharmacy and Phar-
maceutical Technology
ZAMARREÑO ARREGUI, A. M., Pharmacy and
Pharmaceutical Technology
ZAPELENA IÑIGUEZ, M. J., Bromatology and
Toxicology
ZULET ALZÓRRIZ, M. A., Physiology

Faculty of Sciences:

AGUIRREOLA MORALES, J., Plant Physiology
ALVAREZ CALVIÑO, R., Botany
ALVAREZ GALINDO, J. I., Chemistry and
Pedology
ÁLVAREZ JAURRIETA, M. L., Chemistry and
Edaphology
ANTOLÍN BELLVER, C., Plant Physiology
AQUERRETA MOLINA, S., Botany
ARDANZA-TREVIJANO, S., Physics and
Applied Mathematics
ARIÑO PLANA, A., Zoology and Ecology
AZCÁRATE IRIARTE, R., Chemistry and Eda-
phology
BAQUERO MARTÍN, E., Zoology and Ecology
BRAGARD, J., Physics and Applied Mathe-
matics
BURGUETE MÁS, F. J., Physics and Applied
Mathematics
CALASANZ ABINZANO, M. J., Genetics
CAVERO, Y., Chemistry and Pedology
CHASCO UGARTE, M. J., Physics and Applied
Mathematics
CLAVERÍA IRACHETA, V., Botany
DE MIGUEL VELASCO, A., Botany
DÍAZ CALAVIA, E. J., Physics
EDERRA INDURAIN, A., Botany
ESCALA URDAPILLETA, C., Zoology and Ecol-
ogy
FERNÁNDEZ ALVAREZ, J. M., Chemistry and
Pedology
FERNÁNDEZ ASENJO, L., Chemistry and
Pedology
GARAYOA POYO, R., Economy
GARCÍA CASADO, P., Chemistry and Pedol-
ogy
GARCÍA DELGADO, M., Genetics
GARCÍA UNCITI, M. S., Dietetics
GARCÍA ZAMORA, J. M., Chemistry and
Pedology
GARCÍA-MINA FREIRE, J. M., Chemistry and
Pedology
GARCIMARTÍN, A., Physics and Applied
Mathematics
GARDE GARDE, J. M., Zoology and Ecology
GARRIGÓ I REIXACH, J., Chemistry and
Pedology
GOICOECHEA PREBOSTE, N., Plant Physiol-
ogy

GONZÁLEZ, W., Physics and Applied Mathematics
GONZÁLEZ GAITANO, G., Chemistry and Pedology
GUERRERO SETAS, D., Edaphology
HERNÁNDEZ MINGUILLÓN, M. A., Zoology and Ecology
HERRERA MESA, L., Zoology and Ecology
IBÁÑEZ GASTÓN, R., Botany
IRIGOYEN IPARREA, J. J., Plant Physiology
ISASI ALLICA, J. R., Chemistry and Pedology
JORDANA BUTTICAZ, R., Zooology and Ecology
JUARISTI IRANZU, R., Botany
LABAT AYERRA, A., Chemistry and Pedology
LARRAZ AZCÁRATE, M., Zooology and Ecology
LÓPEZ FERNÁNDEZ, M. L., Botany
LÓPEZ GOÑI, I., Microbiology
LÓPEZ MORATALLA, N., Biochemistry
LÓPEZ ZABALZA, M. J., Biochemistry
MANCINI, H., Physics and Applied Mathematics
MARTÍN BACHILLER, C., Chemistry and Pedology
MARTÍNEZ OHARRIZ, C., Chemistry and Pedology
MARTÍNEZ REMÍREZ, M., Physiology
MAZA OZCOIDI, D., Physics and Applied Mathematics
MIRANDA FERREIRO, R., Zooology and Ecology
MORAZA ZORRILLA, L., Zoology and Ecology
NAVARRO BLASCO, I., Chemistry and Pedology
NOVO VILLAVERDE, J., Genetics
ODERO DE DIOS, M. D., Genetics
PALACIOS, C., Physics and Applied Mathematics
PELAEZ LÓPEZ, A., Physics and Applied Mathematics
PEÑAS, F. J., Chemistry and Pedology
PÉREZ GARCÍA, C., Physics and Applied Mathematics
PIUDO AINZINENA, M. J., Botany
PUIG BAGUER, J., Zoology and Ecology
RODÉS NAVARRO, D., Zoology and Ecology
RODRÍGUEZ GARCÍA, J. A., Genetics
RUILOPE PINEDA, R., Chemistry and Pedology
SÁNCHEZ CARPINTERO, I., Chemistry and Pedology
SÁNCHEZ DÍAZ, M., Plant Physiology
SÁNCHEZ GONZÁLEZ, M., Chemistry and Pedology
SÁNCHEZ MONGE, J. M., Chemistry and Pedology
SANTAMARÍA ELOLA, C., Chemistry and Pedology
SANTAMARÍA ULECIA, J. M., Chemistry and Pedology
SERRANO MARTÍNEZ, M., Zoology and Ecology
SIRERA BEJARANO, R., Chemistry and Pedology
VELAZ RIVAS, I., Chemistry and Pedology
VIZMANOS, J. L., Genetics
ZORNOZA CEBEIRO, A., Chemistry and Pedology
ZUDAIRE RIPA, I., Genetics

Faculty of Communication:

AMOEDO CASAIS, A., Journalistic Projects
ARRESE RECA, A., Media Business
ARTÁZCOZ LÓPEZ, M. A., Journalistic Projects
AZURMENDI ADARRAGA, A., Public Communication
BARRERA DEL BARRIO, C., Public Communication
BRINGUÉ SALA, J., Media Business
CODINA BLASCO, M., Public Communication
CUEVAS ÁLVAREZ, E., Audiovisual Communication

DE LA RICA ARANGUREN, A., Audiovisual Communication
DE LOS ÁNGELES VILLENA, J., Media Business
ECHART ORÚS, P., Audiovisual Communication
ETAYO PÉREZ, C., Media Business
FAUS BELAU, A., Audiovisual Communication
GARCÍA AVILÉS, J. A., Journalistic Projects
GARCÍA-NOBLEJAS LINIERS, J. J., Audiovisual Communication
JIMENO LÓPEZ, M. A., Journalistic Projects
LA PORTE FERNÁNDEZ-ALFARO, M. T., Public Communication
LATORRE IZQUIERDO, J., Audiovisual Communication
LEÓN ANGUIANO, B., Journalistic Projects
LÓPEZ PAN, F., Jounalistic Projects
LÓPEZ-ESCOBAR FERNÁNDEZ, E., Public Communication
LOZANO BARTOLOZZI, P., Public Communication
MARTÍNEZ COSTA, M. P., Jounalistic Projects
MEDINA, M., Media Business
MONTERO DÍAZ, M., Public Communication
MORENO MORENO, E., Jounalistic Projects
NAVAS GARCÍA, A., Public Communication
ORIHUELA COLLIVA, J. L., Audiovisual Communication
PARDO FERNÁNDEZ, A., Audiovisual Communication
PÉREZ LATRE, F. J., Media Business
PIQUE I FERNÁNDEZ, A. M., Journalistic Projects
PORTILLA MANJÓN, I., Media Business
REDONDO GÁLVEZ, G., History
SÁDABA CHALEZQUER, R., Media Business
SÁDABA GARRAZA, M T., Public Communication
SALAVERRÍA ALIAGA, R., Jounalistic Projects
SÁNCHEZ ARANDA, J. J., Public Communication
SÁNCHEZ-TABERNERO SÁNCHEZ, A., Media Business
VARA MIGUEL, A., Media Business
VERDERA ALBIÑANA, F., Public Communication
ZORRILLA RUIZ, J., Jounalistic Projects

School of Architecture:

ADARRAGA ELIZARAN, R., Structures
ALONSO DEL VAL, M. A., Projects
AYUCAR RUIZ DE GALARRETA, J. J., Projects
BARRIO SUÁREZ, A., Structures
BAYO PÉREZ, E., Structures
BAZAL CORRALES, J. J., Projects
BERGARA SERRANO, J. I., Projects
CAPILLA FRÍAS, C., Town Planning
CHOCARRO BUJANDA, C., Theory and History
DOCAL ORTEGA, C., Projects
FERNÁNDEZ NÚÑEZ, R., Construction
FRÍAS SAGARDOY, M. A., Theory and History
FUERTES MARTÍNEZ, A. F., Structures
GARCÍA DURÁN, L., Structures
GIL CORNET, L., Theory and History
GOÑI LASHERAS, R., Structures
GONZÁLEZ MARTÍNEZ, M. P., Construction
GONZÁLEZ PRESENCIO, M., Projects
GUTIÉRREZ FERNÁNDEZ, M. A., Construction
HERNÁNDEZ MINGUILLÓN, R. J., Construction
IRIGOYEN DE LA RASILLA, D., Construction
JIMÉNEZ CABALLERO, M. I., Projects
LABARTA AIZPUN, C., Projects
LIZARRAGA MICHEL, J., Structures
LORDA IÑARRA, J. M., Theory and History
LUQUE VALDIVIA, J., Town Planning
MANGADO BELOQUI, F. J., Projects
MAYA MIRANDA, E., Construction
MUÑOZ CASTIEL, M., Structures
MUÑOZ MUÑOZ, F., Construction
NAYA VILLAVERDE, C. J., Projects
OCHOTORENA ELICEGUI, J. M., Projects

OLIVER FERRER, M., Projects
ORDEIG CORSINI, J. M., Town Planning
PELLICER DAVIÑA, D., Construction
POZO MUNICIO, J. M., Projects
ROJO FRAILE, E., Town Planning
SACRISTÁN FERNÁNDEZ, J. A., Construction
SÁNCHEZ-OSTIZ GUTIÉRREZ, A., Construction
SANZ LARREA, C., Construction
TENA NÚÑEZ, L., Town Planning
VISIERS GUIXOT, J. I., Projects

Faculty of Canon Law:

BAÑARES, J. I., Family Law
BERNAL PASCUAL, J., Ecclesiastical Law
CALVO, J., Administrative Canon Law
CENALMOR PALANCA, D., Ecclesiastical Law
FUENTES, J. A., Administrative Canon Law
MARZOA, A., Penal Canon Law
MIRAS POUSO, J. M., Ecclesiastical Law
MOLANO, E., Constitutional Canon Law
OTADUY, J., General and Personal Law
OTADUY, J., Ecclesiastical Law
RINCÓN, T., Administrative Canon Law
RODRIGUEZ, R., Procedural Canon Law
TEJERO, E., History of Canon Law
VIANA, A., Ecclesiastical Organization
VILADRICH, P. J., Canon Law

Faculty of Theology:

ADEVA, I., Latin Language
ALONSO GARCÍA, J., Dogmatic Theology
ALVIAR, J. J., Dogmatic Theology
ARANDA, A., Dogmatic Theology
ARANDA, G., Sacred Scripture: New Testament
AROCENA, F. M., Dogmatic Theology
AUSIN, S., Sacred Scripture: Old Testament
BALAGUER BELTRÁN, V., Sacred Scripture
BASEVI, C., Fundamental Dogmatic Theology
BASTERO, J. L., Dogmatic Theology
BURGGRAF, J., Philosophy
CABALLERO, J. L., Sacred Scripture
CASAS, P., Moral and Spiritual Theology
CHAPA, J., Sacred Scripture (New Testament)
DE LA LAMA CERECEDA, E., History of Theology
DE MIGUEL SICILIA, J. J., Moral and Spiritual Theology
DOMINGO, F. J., Dogmatic Theology
GUTIÉRREZ MARTÍN, J. L., Dogmatic Theology
ILLANES, J. L., Fundamental Dogmatic Theology
IZQUIERDO, C., Fundamental Theology
LABARGA GARCÍA, F., History of Theology
LOPEZ, T., History of Theology: Middle Ages
LORDA, J. L., Dogmatic Theology
LUQUE ALCAIDE, E., History of Theology
MATEO-SECO, L. F., Dogmatic Theology
MERINO, M., Patristics
MOLINA DÍEZ, E., Moral and Spiritual Theology
MORALES, J., Dogmatic Theology
MUÑOZ DE JUANA, R., Moral and Spiritual Theology
ODERO, J. M., Fundamental Theology
PELLITERO IGLESIAS, R., Dogmatic Theology
POZO SERRANO, J. F., Moral and Spiritual Theology
PUJOL, J., Theological Methodology
REINHARDT AMANN, E., History of Theology
RODRÍGUEZ, P., Dogmatic Theology
SARANYANA, J. I., History of Theology
SARMIENTO, A., Moral Theology
SESE, F. J., Spiritual Theology
TINEO, P., History of the Early Church
TRIGO OUBIÑA, T. A., Moral and Spiritual Theology
VARO, F., Sacred Scripture (New Testament)
VILAR SALDAÑA, J. R., Dogmatic Theology

Graduate School of Business Administration:

ABADIA, L., Business Policy
AGELL, P., Managerial Economics
AGUIRRE, J., Finance
ALVAREZ, J. L., Human Behaviour
ALVAREZ DE MON, S., Human Behaviour
ANDREU, R., Managerial Economics
ANZIZU, J. M., Business Policy
ARGANDOÑA, A., Business Policy
ARIÑO, M. A., Decision Analysis
BALLARÍN, E., Control
BLANC, M., Organizational Behaviour
CANALS, J., Social and Economic Analysis
CARRASCO, R., Financial Management
CAVALLE, C., Production Management
CHIESA, C., Marketing
CHINCHILLA, M. N., Human Behaviour
CORTES, L. J., Social and Economic Analysis
DIONIS, L., Production Management
ELORDUY, J. M., Business Policy
FARRAN, J., Marketing
FATIMA, A. DE, Finance
FAUS, J., Managerial Economics
FERNÁNDEZ LÓPEZ, P., Finance
FERRAZ, R., Control
FONT, V., Marketing
GALLO, M. A., Business Policy
GARCIA, C., Business Policy
GINEBRA, J., Marketing
GOMEZ, P. S., Human Behaviour
GÓMEZ-LLERA, G., Environmental Analysis for Management
GRANDES, M. J., Control
GUAL, J., Social and Economic Analysis
GUILLÉN, F. J., Marketing
HUERTA, F., Financial Management
HUETE, L. M., Production Management
JORDAN, P., Financial Management
KASE, K., Marketing
LACUEVA, F., Business Policy
LEGETT, B., Managerial Communications
LÓPEZ, J., Financial Management
LUCAS, J. L., Business Policy
MARTINEZ, E., Finance
MASIFERN, E., Business Policy
MELE, D., Business Ethics
MONS, J., Finance
NEGRE, A., Financial Management
NUENO, J. L., Marketing
NUENO, P., Production Management
O'CALLAGHAN, R., Information Systems
OCARIZ, J., Environmental Analysis for Management
PALACIOS, J. A., Financial Management
PARES, F., Marketing
PEREIRA, F., Control
PIN, J. R., Human Behaviour
PONS, J. M., Marketing
POU, V., Environmental Analysis for Management
PREGEL, G., Finance
RABADAN, M., Finance
RENART, L. G., Marketing
RIBERA, J., Production Management
RICART, J. E., Managerial Economics
RIVEROLA, J., Managerial Economics
RODRÍGUEZ, J. M., Organizational Behaviour
ROIG, B., Business Policy
ROSANAS, J. M., Control
ROURE, J., Production Management
SABRIA, F., Production
SANTOMA, J., Financial Management
SCHERK, W., Finance
SEGARRA, J. A., Marketing
SUÁREZ, J. L., Financial Management
SUBIRA, A., Managerial Economics
TAPIES, J., Financial Management
TERMES, R., Financial Management
TORIBIO, J. J., Social and Economic Analysis
TORRES, J., Control
TREVILLE, S., Production
VALERO, A., Business Policy

VALOR, J., Managerial Economics
VÁZQUEZ-DODERO, J. C., Control
VELILLA, M., Control
VILLAMARIN, B., Managerial Economics
WEBER, E., Control
ZANTINGA, J., Production

School of Engineering:

ALVAREZ SÁNCHEZ-ARJONA, M. J., Industrial Organization
ARCELUS ALONSO, M., Organization
ARIZTI URQUIJO, F., Fundamental Electronics
AVELLO ITURRIAGAGOITIA, A., Theory of Machines
BAGUER ALCALÁ, A., Organization of Work
BASTERO DE ELEIZALDE, C., Mathematical Methods
BASTERO DE ELEIZALDE, J. M., Mechanics
BERENGUER PÉREZ, R., Electronics
BISTUÉ GARCÍA, G., Electricity
BLANCO DEL PRADO, C., Calculus
BUSTAMENTE MERINO, P., Informatics
CAMPOS CAPELASTEGUI, J., Mechanics
CELIGÜETA LIZARZA, J. T., Computational Mechanics
DE LOS MOZOS VILLAR, L., Mechanics
DE MIGUEL SICILIA, J. J., Anthropology
DE NO LENGARÁN, J., Electricity
FERNÁNDEZ DÍEZ, J., Mechanical Technology
FLAQUER FUSTER, J., Linear Algebra
FLÓREZ ESNAL, J., Robotics
FONTAN AGORRETA, L., Fundamentals of Electronics
FUENTES PÉREZ, M., Metallurgy
GARCÍA RICO, A., Electrical Machines
GARCÍA-ALONSO MONTOYA, A, Electrical Engineering
GARCÍA-ROSALES VÁZQUEZ, C., Materials
GIL NOBAJAS, J. J., Electricity and Electronics
GIL SEVILLANO, J., Metallurgy
GIMÉNEZ ORTIZ, G., Mechanical Technology
GÓMEZ-ACEBO TEMES, T., Thermodynamics
GRACIA GAUDÓ, J., Electronics
GURRUCHAGA VÁZQUEZ, J. M., Technical Drawing
IZU BELLOSO, P., Materials
JIMÉNEZ CONDE, M., General Physics
LÓPEZ DE ARANCIBIA, A., Mechanics
LÓPEZ SORIA, B., Materials
MARTÍN ABREU, F., Mechanics
MARTÍNEZ ESNAOLA, J. M., Mechanics of Continua
MUÑOZ EMPARAN, A., Telecommunications
PARGADA GIL, M., Advanced Mathematics
PÉREZ TOCA, M., Electricity
PUENTE URRUZMENDI, I., Mechanics
RAMOS GONZÁLEZ, J. C., Mechanics
RIVAS NIETO, A., Fluids
RODRÍGUEZ IBABE, J. M., Materials
RUBIO DÍAZ-CORDOVÉS, A. R., Electricity
SANCHO SEUMA, J. I., Electricity
SANTOS GARCÍA, J., Organization
SARRIEGUI DOMÍNGUEZ, J. M., Organization
SERNA OLIVEIRA, M. A., Mechanics
SERRANO BÁRCENA, N., Organization
VERA RODRÍGUEZ, E., Steel Structures
VILES DÍEZ, E., Statistics
VIÑOLAS PRAT, J., Mechanics

Faculty of Economics and Management:

ALVAREZ ARCE, J. L., Economics
ARANDA LEÓN, C., Business
ARELLANO GIL, J., Business
BERENGUER PEÑA, J. M., Business
CALDERÓN CUADRADO, R., Business
CUÑADO EIZAGUIRRE, J., Quantitative Methods
GALERA PERAL, F., Economics
GARCÍA DEL BARRIO, P., Economics
GARCÍA RUIZ, P., Business
GIL ALAÑA, L., Quantitative Methods
GÓMEZ BISCARRI, J., Economics
GONZALEZ ENCISO, A., Economics
MARTINEZ CHACÓN, E., Economics

MARTÍNEZ-ECHEVARRÍA, M. A., Economics
MATEO DUEÑAS, R., Business
MENDI GÜEMES, P., Economics
MOLERO GARCÍA, J. C., Economics
MORENO AMÁRCEGUI, A., Economics
PÉREZ DE GRACIA, F., Economics
PUJOL TORRAS, F., Economics
RÁBADE Y HERRERO, A., Business
RAVINA BOHORQUEZ, L., Economics
SALVATIERRA, S. M., Quantitative Methods
SANJURJO SAN MARTÍN, E., Quantitative Methods
SAN MARTÍN ECHAURI, C., Quantitative Methods
TOLSA MAJÓS, A., Quantitative Methods
TORRES SÁNCHEZ, R., Economics
UGALDE BARBERÍA, M. J., Business
VEGA GORDILLO, M., Quantitative Methods
ZARATIEGUI LAVIANO, J. M., Economics

ATTACHED INSTITUTES

Institute of Advanced Business Studies (IESE): Avda Pearson 21, 08034 Barcelona; tel. 93-253-42-00; fax 93-253-43-43; e-mail info@iese.edu; internet www.iese.edu/en/home.asp; *also at:* Camino del Cerro del Águila 3 (Ctra. de Castilla km 5.180), 28023 Madrid; tel. (91) 357-08-09; fax (91) 357-29-13; e-mail info@iese.edu; internet www.iese.edu/en/home.asp; f. 1958; business administration; 86 full-time teachers; 1,200 students; library of 32,000 vols, 370 periodicals; Dean Prof. Dr JORDI CANALS.

Martín Azpilcueta Institute: Edificio de Bibliotecas, Campus Universitario s/n, 31080 Pamplona; tel. 948-42-56-00; fax 948-42-56-36; e-mail ima@unav.es; internet www.unav.es/ima; Dir JORGE OTADUY.

Enterprise and Humanism Institute: Edificio de Bibliotecas, Campus Universitario s/n, 31080 Pamplona; tel. 948-42-56-00; e-mail cosinaga@unav.es; internet www.unav.es/empresayhumanismo; Dir RAFAEL ALVIRA.

Institute of Human Rights: Despacho 1731, Edificio de Bibliotecas, Campus Universitario s/n, 31080 Pamplona; tel. 948-42-56-00; fax 948-42-56-21; e-mail idh@unav.es; internet www.unav.es/idh/default.html; Dir ÁNGELA APARISI MIRALLES.

Centre for Technical Studies and Research in Gipuzkoa: Paseo de Manuel Lardizabal 15, 20018 San Sebastián; tel. 943-21-28-00; fax 943-21-30-76; e-mail agonzalez@ceit.es; internet www.ceit.es/index.htm; Gen. Dir ALEJO AVELLO ITURRIAGAGOITIA.

Professional School of Internal Medicine: Facultad de Medicina; Dir JESÚS PRIETO.

University Clinic: Avda Pío XII 36, 31008 Pamplona; tel. 948-25-54-00; fax 948-29-65-00; internet www.cun.es; Gen. Dir AMADOR SOSA LORA; Medical Dir Dr JAVIER ÁLVAREZ-CIENFUEGOS SUÁREZ.

Urban Ecology Studies Centre: Dir MANUEL FERRER.

European Studies Centre: Edificio de Derecho, Universidad de Navarra, 31080 Pamplona; tel. 948-42-56-34; fax 948-42-56-22; e-mail ebanus@unav.es; internet www.unav.es/cee; Dir ENRIQUE BANÚS IRUSTA.

School of Legal Practice: Dir FAUSTINO CORDON.

Institute of Family Studies: Edificio Los Nogales, Universidad de Navarra, 31080 Pamplona; tel. 948-42-56-00; fax 948-42-56-40; e-mail icf@unav.es; internet www.unav.es/icf; Dir PEDRO-JUAN VILADRICH BATALLER.

Applied Medicine Research Centre: Dir FERNANDO DE LA PUENTE.

Computer Technology Centre: Dir IGNACIO COUPEAU.

Applied Pharmacobiology Research Centre: Dir ANTONIO MONGE.

Professional School of Medical-Surgical Dermatology and Venereology: Dir (vacant).

Professional School of Clinical Biochemistry: Dir (vacant).

Professional School of Psychiatry: Dir SALVADOR CERVERA.

Professional School of the Digestive Apparatus: Dir FEDERICO CONCHILLO.

Institute of Physics: Universidad de Navarra, Irunlarrea s/n, 31080 Pamplona; e-mail hmancini@fisica.unav.es; internet instituto.fisica.unav.es; Dir HÉCTOR L. MANCINI.

Institute of Anthropology and Ethics: Universidad de Navarra, Edificio Central, 31009 Pamplona; tel. 948-42-56-00 ext. 2047; e-mail iae@unav.es; internet www.unav.es/iae; Dir MIGUEL LLUCH BAIXAULI.

Higher Institute of Religious Studies: Universidad de Navarra, Edificio de Facultades Eclesiásticas, 31009 Pamplona; tel. 948-42-57-16; fax 948-42-56-33; e-mail iscr@unav.es; internet www.unav.es/iscr; Dir JAIME PUJOL.

Institute of Medieval Studies: e-mail saurell@unav.es; internet www.unav.es/iestmedie; Dir JAUME AURELL.

Science and Technology Institute of Navarre: Avda Pío XII 53, 31008 Pamplona; tel. 948-17-67-48; fax 948-42-52-23; e-mail ict@unav.es; internet www.unav.es/ict.

Institute of Food Sciences: Edificio de Ciencias, Universidad de Navarra, C/ Irunlarrea 1, 31008 Pamplona; tel. 948-42-56-00; fax 948-42-56-49; e-mail icaun@unav.es; internet www.unav.es/icaun.

Josemaría Escrivá de Balaguer Documentation and Study Centre: Edificio de Bibliotecas, Campus Universitario s/n, 31080 Pamplona; tel. 948-42-56-00; fax 948-42-56-36; e-mail codoj@unav.es; internet www.unav.es/centrojcscriva; Dir JOSÉ LUIS ILLANES.

UNIVERSIDAD PÚBLICA DE NAVARRA / PUBLIC UNIVERSITY OF NAVARRE

Campus de Arrosadía, 31006 Pamplona (Navarre)

Telephone: 34-948-16-90-00
Fax: 34-948-16-90-04
E-mail: infoweb@unavarra.es
Internet: www.unavarra.es

Founded 1987
State control ended September 1993
Languages of instruction: Spanish, Basque, English
Academic year: September to June

Rector: PEDRO BURILLO LÓPEZ
Vice-Rector (European Convergence and Institutional Relations): JOSÉ LUIS IRIARTE ÁNGEL
Vice-Rector (Normative Development): PATRICIA PLAZA VENTURA
Vice-Rector (Planning): JUAN MANUEL CABASÉS HITA
Vice-Rector (Research): CÉSAR ARRESE-IGOR SÁNCHEZ
Vice-Rector (Student Affairs and University Extension): JULIAN JOSÉ GARRIDO SEGOVIA
Vice-Rector (Teaching): JUAN CARRASCO PÉREZ
Vice-Rector (Teaching Staff): LUIS EZQUERRO MARÍN
Registrar: GABRIEL LERA CARRERAS
Manager: LUIS CRUCHAGA EQUIZA
Library Dir: GUILLERMO SÁNCHEZ MARTÍNEZ

Communication Director: JESÚS MARTÍNEZ TORRES
Library of 339,160 vols, 9,309 periodicals
Number of teachers: 801
Number of students: 9,000
Publications: *Anales de Derecho* (annually), *Filología y Didáctica de la Lengua, Geografía e Historia* (annually), *Psicología y Pedagogía* (annually)

DEANS

Faculty of Economics and Business: JUAN FRANCO PUEYO
Faculty of Humanities and Social Sciences: IGNACIO SÁNCHEZ DE LA YNCERA

DIRECTORS OF UNIVERSITY SCHOOLS

Agricultural Engineering: RAFAEL GARCÍA SANTOS
Health Studies: BLANCA MARÍN FERNÁNDEZ
Industrial and Telecommunications Engineering: PAULINO MARTÍNEZ LANDA

HEADS OF DEPARTMENTS

Agrarian Production: PRIMITIVO CABALLERO MURILLO
Applied Chemistry: PALOMA VÍRSEDA CHAMORRO
Automation and Computation: ANA BURUSCO JUANDEABURRE
Business Management: KATRÍN SIMÓN ELORZ
Economics: JUAN CARLOS LONGÁS GARCÍA
Electrical and Electronic Engineering: BLAS HERMOSO ALAMEDA
Environmental Sciences: PALOMA TORRE HERNÁNDEZ
Geography and History: ELOISA RAMÍREZ VAQUERO
Health Sciences: IGNACIO JOSÉ ENCÍO MARTÍNEZ
Mathematics and Computer Science: MARÍA JOSÉ ASIÁIN OLLO
Mechanical, Energy and Materials Engineering: CARMELO JAVIER LUIS PÉREZ
Philology and Language Teaching: MARÍA JESÚS GOIKOETXEA TABAR
Physics: CARLOS SÁENZ GAMASA
Private Law: JOSÉ LUIS GOÑI SEIN
Projects and Rural Engineering: PAULINO MARTÍNEZ LANDA
Psychology and Pedagogy: BENJAMÍN ZUFIAURRE GOIKOETXEA
Public Law: FERNANDO DE LA HUCHA CELADOR
Social Work: CAMINO OSLÉ GUERENDIÁIN
Sociology: JOSÉ MIGUEL BERIÁIN RAZQUIN
Statistics and Operational Research: CARMEN GARCÍA OLAVERRI

ATTACHED INSTITUTIONS

'Estanislao de Aranzadi' School of Practice in Law: Edificio de El Sario, Módulo 2, 2a planta, Campus de Arrosadía, 31006 Pamplona; tel. 948-16-98-14; e-mail escuela.practica.juridica@unavarra.es; Dir PEDRO CHARRO AYESTARÁN.

Institute of Agrobiotechnology and Natural Resources: Campus de Arrosadía, 31192 Mutilva Baja (Navarra); tel. 948-24-28-34; fax 948-23-21-91; Dir JAVIER POZUETA ROMERO.

UNIVERSIDAD DE OVIEDO

Calle San Francisco 3, 33003 Oviedo
Telephone: 985-510-40-58
Fax: 985-522-71-26
E-mail: rector@rectorado.uniovi.es
Internet: www.uniovi.es

Founded 1608
Language of instruction: Spanish
State control
Academic year: October to June

Rector: Prof. JUAN A. VAZQUEZ

Vice-Rector (Academic Organization and Teaching Staff): ANTONIO CUETO ESPINAR
Vice-Rector (University Extension): PAZ ANDRÉS SÁENZ DE SANTA MARÍA
Vice-Rector (Research and Relations with the Business World): ANA ISABEL FERNÁNDEZ ÁLVAREZ
Vice-Rector (Student Affairs and Co-operation): SANTOS GONZÁLEZ JIMÉNEZ
Vice-Rector (Campus and Infrastructure): MARÍA ISABEL VIÑA OLAY
Vice-Rector (European Convergence, Graduate Studies and Special Courses): MIGUEL ANGEL COMENDADOR
Vice-Rector (Quality, Planning and Innovation): J. ESTEBAN FERNÁNDEZ RICO
Vice-Rector (Institutional Relations, Co-ordination and Communication): SANTIAGO MARTÍNEZ ARGÜELLES
Registrar: IGNACIO VILLAVERDE MENÉNDEZ
Manager: JOSÉ ANTONIO DÍAZ LAGO
Librarian: RAMÓN RODRÍGUEZ ALVAREZ
Library of 700,000 vols, 14,000 periodicals
Number of teachers: 1,739
Number of students: 41,070
Publications: *Revista de Ciencias, Archivos de la Facultad de Medicina, Memorias de Historia Antigua, Asturiensía Medievalía, Revista de Minas, Trabajos de Geología, Revista de Biología, Brevoria Geológica Astúrica*

DEANS

Faculty of Biology: MANUEL MARTÍNEZ ESTEBAN
Faculty of Chemistry: JOSÉ MANUEL CONCELLÓN GRACIA
Faculty of Economics and Business Studies: JAVIER SUÁREZ PANDIELLO
Faculty of Education: AQUILINA FUEYO GUTIÉRREZ
Faculty of Geography and History: JOSÉ PASCUAL GIRÓN GARROTE
Faculty of Geology: DANIEL MANUEL ARIAS PRIETO
Faculty of Law: ANDRÉS CORSINO ÁLVAREZ CORTINA
Faculty of Medicine: ENRIQUE MARTÍNEZ RODRÍGUEZ
Faculty of Philology: ANA MARÍA CANO GONZÁLEZ
Faculty of Philosophy: ALFONSO GARCÍA SUÁREZ
Faculty of Psychology: JOSÉ MUÑIZ FERNÁNDEZ
Faculty of Science: CONCEPCIÓN MASA NOCEDA

DIRECTORS OF UNIVERSITY SCHOOLS

Business Studies (Oviedo): MANUEL LAFUENTE ROBLEDO
Computer Engineering (Oviedo): JUAN MANUEL CUEVA LOVELLE
Computer Engineering (Gijón): PEDRO HERNÁNDEZ ARAUZO
'Guillermo Schulz' Polytechnic: CELESTINO GONZÁLEZ NICIEZA
Industrial Engineering: JOAQUÍN MATEOS PALACIO
Industrial Relations: OSCAR RODRÍGUEZ BUZNEGO
Jovellanos (Gijón): ROSA ISABEL AZA CONEJO
Nursing and Physiotherapy: MA. DEL PILAR MOSTEIRO DÍAZ
Teacher Training: DARIO DANIEL HIGINIO RODRÍGUEZ DEL AMO
Technical Engineering (Mieres): ANTONIO BERNARDO SÁNCHEZ

DIRECTORS OF HIGHER TECHNICAL SCHOOLS

Civil Marine: RAFAEL GARCÍA MÉNDEZ
Engineering Polytechnic (Gijón): RICARDO TUCHO NAVARRO
Mining Engineering: MARIO MENÉNDEZ ALVAREZ

DIRECTOR OF POSTGRADUATE SCHOOL

Stomatology: JUAN SEBASTIÁN LOPEZ-ARRANZ ARRANZ

HEADS OF DEPARTMENTS

Anglo-Germanic and French Philology: MA. SOCORRO SUÁREZ LAFUENTE

Applied Economics: CÁNDIDO PAÑEDA FERNÁNDEZ

Basic Law: JOSÉ MA. GONZÁLEZ DEL VALLE

Biochemistry and Molecular Biology: MA. PAZ SUÁREZ RENDUELES

Biology of Organisms and Systems: TOMÁS EMILIO DÍAZ GONZÁLEZ

Business Studies and Accounting: JUAN A. TRESPALACIOS GUTIÉRREZ

Chemical Engineering and Environmental Engineering: JOSÉ COCA PRADOS

Classical and Romance Philology: FAUSTO DÍAZ PADILLA

Computer Science: (vacant)

Construction and Production Engineering: GONZALO MORIS MENÉNDEZ-VALDES

Economics: JOAQUÍN LORENCES RODRÍGUEZ

Education: JOSÉ VICENTE PEÑA CALVO

Electrical, Electronic, Computer and Systems Engineering: JOSÉ GÓMEZ CAMPOMANES

Energy: JORGE XIBERTA BERNAT

Functional Biology: RAMÓN GIRÁLDEZ CEBALLOS-ESCALERA

Geography: TOMÁS CORTIZO ÁLVAREZ

Geology: LUIS C. SÁNCHEZ POSADA

History: MA. JOSEFA SANZ FUENTES

History of Art and Musicology: MA. SOLEDAD ÁLVAREZ MARTÍNEZ

Materials Science and Metallurgical Engineering: F. JAVIER BELZUNCE VARELA

Mathematics: BENJAMÍN DUGNOL ÁLVAREZ

Medicine: ANTONIO CUETO ESPINAS

Mining: JESÚS GARCÍA IGLESIAS

Morphology and Cell Biology: ALFONSO LÓPEZ MUÑIZ

Organic and Inorganic Chemistry: VICENTE GOTOR SANTAMARÍA

Philosophy: JULIÁN VELARDE LOMBRAÑA

Physical and Analytical Chemistry: PAULINO TUÑÓN BLANCO

Physics: MARCOS TEJEDOR GANCEDO

Private Law and Company Law: RAMÓN DURÁN RIVACOBA

Psychology: JULIO ANTONIO GONZÁLEZ GARCÍA

Public Law: PAZ ANDRÉS SÁENZ DE SANTA MARIA

Quantitative Economics: EMILIO COSTA REPARAZ

Spanish Philology: JOSÉ ANTONIO MARTÍNEZ GARCÍA

Surgery: JUAN SEBASTIÁN LÓPEZ-ARRANZ

ATTACHED SCHOOLS AND CENTRES

University School of Nursing: Calle Hospital de Cabueñes s/n, 33294 Gijón; e-mail eue@hcabuenes.es; Dir CARMEN BURZACO BLANCO.

'Padre Enrique de Ossó' University School of Teacher Training: Calle Prau Picon s/n, 33008 Oviedo; e-mail eumpeosso@planalfa.es; internet www.padre-osso.org; Dir FERNANDO PENDAS FERNÁNDEZ.

University School of Industrial Relations: Avda Manuel Llaneza 75, 33208 Gijón; e-mail eurlgijo@correo.uniovi.es; internet www.iespana.es/eurelacioneslaboralesgijon; Dir JOSÉ TOURIÑO ALBAÑIL.

University School of Social Work (Gijón): Calle Fortuna Balnearia 1, 33207 Gijón; e-mail eutsgij@correo.uniovi.es; internet web.uniovi.es/eutsg; Dir MA. JOSÉ CAPELLÍN CORRADA.

University School of Social Work (Oviedo): Calle Jovellanos 6, 33003 Oviedo; e-mail eutsovi@correo.uniovi.es; Dir (vacant).

University School of Tourism in Asturias: Avda de los Monumentos 11, 33012 Oviedo; e-mail escuastur@fade.es; internet www.fade.es/inas; Dir COVADONGA VIGIL ÁLVAREZ.

Co-operation and Territorial Development Centre: Chalet de Figaredo s/n, 33683 Figaredo (Asturias); tel. 985-42-68-88; fax 985-42-70-46; e-mail cecodet@correo.uniovi.es; internet www.uniovi.es/cecodet; Dir FERMÍN RODRÍGUEZ GUTIÉRREZ.

Artificial Intelligence Centre: Campus de Viesques, Universidad de Oviedo en Gijón, 33271 Gijón; tel. 985-18-20-32; fax 985-18-21-25; e-mail centroia@aic.uniovi.es; internet www.aic.uniovi.es; Dir ANTONIO BAHAMONDE RIONDA.

Institute of Education: Universidad de Oviedo, C/ Quintana 30-1°, 33009 Oviedo; tel. 985-22-75-38; fax 985-22-86-73; e-mail ice@correo.uniovi.es; internet www.uniovi.es/ICE; Dir RAQUEL RODRÍGUEZ GONZÁLEZ.

'Enrique Moles' Institute of Organometallic Chemistry: Facultad de Química, Julián Clavería 8, 33006 Oviedo; tel. and fax 985-10-34-50; e-mail erubio@sauron.quimica.uniovi.es; internet www.uniovi.es/emoles; Dir JOSÉ BARLUENGA MUR.

Institute of Natural Resources and Country Planning: Universidad de Oviedo, Campus de Mieres, 33600 Mieres; tel. 985-45-81-18; fax 985-45-81-10; e-mail indurot@indurot.uniovi.es; internet 156.35.47.1; Dir MIGUEL A. ÁLVAREZ GARCÍA (acting).

Feijoo Institute of Eighteenth-Century Studies: Facultad de Filología, Universidad de Oviedo, Campus de Humanidades s/n, 33011 Oviedo; tel. 985-10-46-52; fax 985-10-46-70; e-mail inurz@sci.cpd.uniovi.es; internet www.uniovi.es/feijoo; Dir (vacant).

University Institute of Business: C/ González Besada 13, 4a planta, 33007 Oviedo; tel. 985-10-30-19; fax 985-10-30-45; e-mail iude@sci.cpd.uniovi.es; internet www.uniovi.es/iude; Dir JUAN VENTURA VICTORIA.

University Institute of Oncology: C/ Fernando Bongera s/n, Edificio 'Santiago Gascón', 2a planta, despacho 2.3, Campus El Cristo B, 33006 Oviedo; tel. 985-10-62-71; e-mail carlos.suarez@sespa.princast.es; internet www.uniovi.es/Oncologia; Dir CARLOS SUÁREZ NIETO.

University Institute of Industrial Technology of Asturias: Campus de Gijón, Universidad de Oviedo, 33204 Gijón; tel. 985-18-23-83; fax 985-18-20-89; e-mail iuta@epsig.uniovi.es; internet www.uniovi.es/IUTA; Dir ELENA MARAÑÓN MAISON.

UNIVERSIDAD PABLO DE OLAVIDE

Carretera de Utrera Km. 1, 41013 Seville

Telephone: 954-34-92-00

Fax: 954-34-92-04

Internet: www.upo.es

Founded 1997

State control

Language of instruction: Spanish

Academic year: September to July

Rector: AGUSTÍN MADRID PARRA

Vice-Rector (Academic Organization and Graduate Studies): JUAN FERNÁNDEZ VALVERDE

Vice-Rector (Teaching Staff): ESTEBAN RUIZ BALLESTEROS

Vice-Rector (Research and New Technology): EDUARDO SANTERO SANTURINO

Vice-Rector (Student Affairs): BRUNO MARTÍNEZ HAYA

Vice-Rector (Social Promotion and University Extension): LUIS VICENTE AMADOR MUÑOZ

Vice-Rector (Services and Planning): FLOR MARÍA GUERRERO CASAS

Vice-Rector (Institutional and International Relations): ANDRÉS RODRÍGUEZ BENOT

Registrar: VICENTE CARLOS GUZMÁN FLUJA

Manager: FELIPE TUDELA GARCÍA

Library of 46,000 vols, 5,790 periodicals (incl. 5,000 online)

DEANS

Faculty of Business: FRANCISCO CARRASCO FENECH

Faculty of Experimental Sciences: MODESTO LUCEÑO GARCÉS

Faculty of Humanities: JUAN MANUEL CORTÉS COPETE

Faculty of Law: MA. CARMEN VELASCO GARCÍA

School of Social Work: JOSÉ LUIS MALAGÓN BERNAL (Dir)

HEADS OF DEPARTMENTS

Economics and Business: JOSÉ LUIS MARTÍN MARÍN

Environmental Sciences: AGUSTÍN GONZÁLEZ FONTES

Humanities: STEFAN RUHSTALLER KÜHNE

Private Law: FERNANDO ELORZA GUERRERO

Public Law: CARLOS ALARCÓN CABRERA

Social Work and Social Sciences: JOSÉ ANTONIO SÁNCHEZ MEDINA

ATTACHED CENTRES

Andalusian Centre of Developmental Biology: Universidad Pablo de Olavide, Carretera de Utrera Km. 1, 41013 Seville; e-mail jjimenez@dex.upo.es; fax 954-34-93-76; internet www.upo.es/CABD; Dir JUAN JIMÉNEZ.

Centre for Research in Social and Environmental Accounting: Edificio no. 10, planta 2a, despacho 24, Universidad Pablo de Olavide, Ctra de Utrera Km. 1, 41013 Seville; tel. 954-34-92-78; fax 954-34-93-39; e-mail fcarfen@dee.upo.es; internet www.upo.es/depa/cicsma/indcicsma.htm; Dir FRANCISCO CARRASCO FENECH.

UNIVERSIDAD DEL PAÍS VASCO/ EUSKAL HERRIKO UNIBERTSITATEA (University of the Basque Country)

Apdo 1397, 48080 Bilbao

Telephone: 94-601-20-00

Fax: 94-480-15-90

E-mail: relaciones-internacionales@ehu.es

Internet: www.ehu.es

Founded 1968, reorganized 1980

Located on three campuses: Bizkaia Campus, Araba Campus, Gipuzkoa Campus

Basque Regional Government control

Languages of instruction: Spanish, Basque

Academic year: October to June

Rector: JUAN IGNACIO PÉREZ IGLESIAS

Vice-Rector (Araba Campus): JOAN SALLÉS ALVIRA

Vice-Rector (Bizkaia Campus): ANTON ERKOREKA BARRENA

Vice-Rector (Gipuzkoa Campus): CRISTINA URIARTE TOLEDO

Vice-Rector (Co-ordination and Planning): ITSASO IBÁÑEZ FERNÁNDEZ

Vice-Rector (Student Affairs): MAITE ERRO JAUREGI

Vice-Rector (Economic Affairs): EVA FERREIRA GARCÍA

Vice-Rector (Basque Language): LUDGER MEES

Vice-Rector (Graduate Studies): CARMEN GONZÁLEZ MURUA

Vice-Rector (University Extension): ANDER GONZÁLEZ ANTONA

Vice-Rector (Innovation in Teaching): XABIER ETXAGUE ALCALDE

Vice-Rector (Research): MIGUEL ÁNGEL GUTIÉRREZ ORTIZ
Vice-Rector (Academic Organization): IÑAKI GOIRIZELAIA ORDORIKA
Vice-Rector (Teaching Staff): JUAN JOSÉ UNCILLA GALÁN
Vice-Rector (International Relations): JASONE CENOZ IRAGUI
Registrar: IÑAKI ESPARZA LEIBAR
Administrative Director: MOISES GURIDI
Librarian: CARMEN GUERRA

Library of 873,116 vols, 17,008 periodicals
Number of teachers: 3,537
Number of students: 50,220

Publications: *Lección Inaugural, Memoria Estadística, Catálogo de Biblioteca, Recursos Científicos y Líneas de Investigación, Nomenclator, Memoria de Actividades, Cursos Monográficos de Doctorado, Resúmenes de Tesis Doctorales, Acto de Investidura* (all annually)

DEANS

(The letters A, B, G refer to the Araba, Bizkaia and Gipuzkoa campuses)

Faculty of Chemistry (G): ANA ARRIETA AYESTARÁN
Faculty of Computer Science (G): JULIÁN GUTIÉRREZ SERRANO
Faculty of Economics and Business Administration (B): CARMEN MUÑOZ BERGER
Faculty of Fine Arts (B): AGUSTÍN RAMOS IRIZAR
Faculty of Law (G): FRANCISCO JAVIER EZQUIAGA GANUZAS
Faculty of Medicine and Dentistry (B): LUISA UGEDO URRUELA
Faculty of Pharmacy (A): JOAN SALLÉS ALVIRA
Faculty of Philology, Geography and History (A): JOSEBA A. LAKARRA
Faculty of Philosophy and Education (G): LUIS LIZASOAIN HERNÁNDEZ
Faculty of Psychology (G): JOAQUÍN DE PAUL OCHOTORENA
Faculty of Sciences (B): JUAN RAMÓN GONZÁLEZ VELASCO
Faculty of Social and Communication Sciences (B): JOSÉ MANUEL MATA LÓPEZ

DIRECTORS

(The letters A, B, G refer to the Araba, Bizkaia and Gipuzkoa campuses)

Higher Technical School of Architecture (G): RAMÓN ALUSTIZA GARCÍA
Higher Technical School of Industrial Engineering and Telecommunications (B): JAVIER MUNIOZGUREN COLINDRES
Higher Technical School of Navigation and Naval Engineering (B): FERNANDO CAYUELA CAMARERO
College of Business Studies (A): ANDRÉS ARAUJO DE LA MATA
College of Business Studies (B): LAMBERTO BENITO DEL VALLE ESKAURIAZA
College of Business Studies (G): ALBERTO DÍAZ DE JUNGUITU GONZÁLEZ DE DURANA
College of Industrial and Topographical Engineering (A): LUIS MIGUEL CAMARERO ESTELA
College of Industrial Engineering (B): FRANCISCO JOSÉ SAINZ ALVES
College of Industrial Engineering (G): IGNACIO BORINAGA LÓPEZ
College of Industrial Relations (B): (vacant)
College of Mining Engineering (B): CRISTINA AVILÉS GONZÁLEZ
College of Nursing (B): CONCEPCIÓN FERNÁNDEZ CAMINOS
College of Nursing (G): PILAR TAZON ANSOLA
College of Social Work (A): ELENA PECIÑA ANÍTUA
Teacher Training College (A): (vacant)
Teacher Training College (B): CARLOS CASTAÑO GARRIDO

Teacher Training College (G): TOMÁS ZUBIMENDI
Polytechnic College (G): ARANTXA TAPIA ÓTAEGI

HEADS OF DEPARTMENTS

Computer Architecture and Engineering: JOSÉ MARÍA RIVADENEYRA SICILIA
Cell Biology and Histology: JUAN ARÉCHAGA MARTÍNEZ
Vegetal Biology and Ecology: (vacant)
Biochemistry and Molecular Biology: JUAN MANUEL GONZÁLEZ MAÑAS
Computation and Artificial Intelligence: BASILIO SIERRA
Politics and Administration: FRANCISCO JOSÉ LLERA RAMO
Polymer Science and Technology: PEDRO A. SANTAMARÍA
Surgery, Radiology and Physical Medicine: JAIME J. MÉNDEZ MARTÍN
Company Law: ALBERTO EMPARANZA SOBEJANO
Public International Law, International Relations, History of Law and History of Institutions: FRANCISCO JAVIER QUEL LÓPEZ
Teaching Language and Literature: LAURA MINTEGI LAKARRA
Applied Economics III: KARMELE FERNÁNDEZ AGUIRRE
Applied Economics IV: CASILDA LASSO DE LA VEGA MARTÍNEZ
Applied Economics V: FELIPE SERRANO
Financial Economics II (Financial Economics and Accounting, Marketing and Market Research): ARTURO RODRÍGUEZ CASTELLANOS
Electricity and Electronics: JOSÉ MANUEL BARANDIARÁN GARCÍA
Electronics and Telecommunications: AMAIA ARRINDA SANZBERRO
Nursing II: ENCARNA ENCINAS PRIETO
Technical Drawing and Engineering Projects: AGUSTÍN ARIAS COTERILLO
English and German Philology: MARIO SAALBACH
Philosophy: (vacant)
Applied Physics I: JOAQUÍN FERNÁNDEZ RODRÍGUEZ
Theoretical Physics and History of Science: (vacant)
Principles of Economic Analysis I: JOSÉ RAMÓN URIARTE AYO
Principles of Economic Analysis II: (vacant)
Genetics, Physical Anthropology and Animal Physiology: (vacant)
Contemporary History: FÉLIX LUENGO TEIXIDOR
Economic History and Institutions: EMILIANO FERNÁNDEZ DE PINEDO FERNÁNDEZ
Systems Engineering and Automation: (vacant)
Electrical Engineering: INMACULADA ZAMORA BELVER
Mechanical Engineering: ERNESTO GARCÍA VADILLO
Nuclear Engineering and Fluid Mechanics: MARGARITA HERRANZ SOLER
Immunology, Microbiology and Parasitology: RAMÓN CISTERNA CANCER
Computer Languages and Systems: (vacant)
Thermic Machines and Motors: JOSÉ MARÍA SALA LIZARRAGA
Applied Mathematics, Statistics and Operational Research: (vacant)
Mathematics: MA. ÁNGELES DE PRADA VICENTE
Preventive Medicine and Public Health: JOSÉ RAMÓN SÁENZ DOMÍNGUEZ
Research Methods and Diagnostics in Education: (vacant)
Mineralogy and Petrology: PEDRO PABLO GIL CRESPO
Business Organization: PABLO DÍAZ DE BASURTO URAGA
Journalism: CARMEN PEÑAFIEL

Journalism II: JESÚS CANGA LAREQUI
Analytical Chemistry: (vacant)
Physical Chemistry: (vacant)
Inorganic Chemistry: (vacant)
Organic Chemistry I: FRANCISCO PALACIOS GAMBRA
Organic Chemistry II: (vacant)
Sociology: BEATRIZ MIRANDA DE BENITO
Sociology II: ANDER GURRUTXAGA

ATTACHED INSTITUTES

Basque Institute of Criminology/Kriminologiaren Euskal Institutua: Villa Soroa, Ategorrieta 22, 20013 San Sebastián; tel. 94-301-74-84; fax 94-332-12-72; e-mail szoivac@sc.ehu.es; internet www.ehu.es/scrwwwiv/ivac.html; Dir Prof. Dr JOSÉ LUIS DE LA CUESTA ARZAMENDI.

Institute of Public-Sector Economics/Ekonomia Publikorako Institutua: Facultad de Ciencias Económicas y Empresariales, Lehendakari Agirre 83, 48015 Bilbao; tel. 94-601-36-55; fax 94-447-51-54; e-mail iep@bs.ehu.es; internet www.bl.ehu.es; Dirs of Doctorate Programme JUAN CARLOS BÁRCENA RUIZ, JOSU ARTECHE GONZÁLEZ.

Institute of Epidemiology and Prevention of Cardiovascular Diseases: Hospital Civil de Bilbao, Gurtubay s/n, 48012 Bilbao; Dir MIGUEL M. IRIARTE.

Institute of Co-operative Law and Social Economy/Gizarte-Ekonomia eta Zuzenbide Kooperatiboaren Institutua: Villa Soroa, Avda Ategorrieta 22, 20013 San Sebastián; tel. 94-301-74-98; fax 94-329-28-25; e-mail szzmacom@sc.ehu.es; internet www.sc.ehu.es/szwgezki/gezki.html; Dir Dr BALEREN BAKAIKOA AZURMENDI.

Institute of Applied Business Economics/Enpresari Aplikaturiko Ekonomi Institutua: Facultad de Ciencias Económicas y Empresariales, Lehendakari Agirre 83, 48015 Bilbao; tel. 94-601-37-05; fax 94-601-37-10; e-mail egplaroj@bs.ehu.es; internet www.ehu.es/ieae; Dir JON LANDETA RODRÍGUEZ.

Institute of Research and Development of Processes: Facultad de Ciencias, Bº Sarriena s/n, 48940 Leioa (Vizcaya); e-mail msen@we.lc.ehu.es; internet www.ehu.es/IIDP; Dir Prof. Dr MANUEL DE LA SEN PARTE.

'Valentín de Foronda' Institute of Social History/Gizarte Historiako Unibertsitate Institutua: C/ Nieves Cano K. 33, 01006 Vitoria; tel. 94-501-43-11; fax 94-523-49-56; e-mail ih@vv.ehu.es; internet www.vc.ehu.es/ih; Dir Dr JAVIER UGARTE TELLERÍA.

Institute of Financial and Actuarial Studies: Avda Lehendakari Aguirre 83, 48015 Bilbao; Dir AMANCIO BETZUEN.

Medical Institute in Basurto: Facultad de Medicina y Odontología, 48940 Leioa (Vizcaya).

Centre for Studies on Collective Identity: Departamento de Sociología 2, Facultad de Ciencias Sociales, Universidad del País Vasco, Campus de Leioa, 48940 Leioa (Vizcaya); tel. 94-601-50-93; fax 94-464-82-99; e-mail cjxssceic@lg.ehu.es; internet www.ehu.es/CEIC; Dir Dr BENJAMÍN TEJERINA.

Institute for Studies on Development and International Co-operation (HEGOA)/Nazioarteko Lankidetza eta Garapenari Buruzko Ikasketa Institutua: Facultad de Ciencias Económicas y Empresariales, Lehendakari Agirre 83, 48015 Bilbao; tel. 94-601-70-91; fax 94-601-70-40; e-mail hegoa@bs.ehu.es; internet www.hegoa.ehu.es; Dir PEDRO IBARRA.

Institute of Polymeric Materials/Material Polimerikoen Institutua: Manuel de Lardizábal 3, 20018 San Sebastián; tel. 94-

301-53-47; fax 94-321-22-36; e-mail polymat@sq.ehu.es; internet www.sc.ehu.es/powgep99/polymat/homepage.html; Dir Dr José M. Asua.

Institute for Logic, Cognition, Language and Information/Logika, Kognizio, Hizkuntza eta Informaziorako Instituta: Avda Alcalde J. Elosegi 275, 20015 San Sebastián; tel. 94-301-74-51; fax 94-301-74-30; e-mail ilcli@sf.ehu.es; internet www.sc.ehu.es/ilwlaanj/ilcli.html; Dir Dr Kepa Korta.

Institute of Microelectronic Technology: internet tim.ehu.es.

UNIVERSITAT DE LES ILLES BALEARS

Campus Universitari, Cra. de Valldemossa km 7.5, 07122 Palma de Mallorca

Telephone: 971-17-30-00

Fax: 971-17-28-52

E-mail: informacio@uib.es

Internet: www.uib.es

Founded 1978
State control
Languages of instruction: Catalan, Spanish
Academic year: October to September

Rector: Avel·lí Blasco Esteve
Vice-Rector (Student Affairs): Joan Antoi Mesquida Cantallops
Vice-Rector (Infrastructure and Environment): Gabriel Moyà Niell
Vice-Rector (Graduate Affairs and Rector's Office): Mercè Gambús Saiz
Vice-Rector (Research and Science Policy): Francisco Muñoz Izquierdo
Vice-Rector (Academic Affairs): Sergio Alonso Oroza
Vice-Rector (Economic and Administrative Planning): Josep Ignasi Aguiló Fuster
Vice-Rector (Teaching Staff): Esperança Munar Muntaner
Vice-Rector (External Relations): Francesca Salvà Mut
Vice-Rector (Cultural Projection): Francesca Lladó Pol
Registrar: Lluís Garau Juaneda
Manager: Andreu Alcover Ordinas
Librarian: Miquel Pastor Tous

Number of teachers: 1,067 (594 full-time, 461 part-time)
Number of students: 15,000

Publications: *Grama i Cal*, *Educació i Cultura*, *Mayurqa*, *Taula*, *Treballs de Geografia*, *Psicología del Deporte*

DEANS

Faculty of Philosophy and Arts: Nicolau Dols Salas
Faculty of Economics and Business Sciences: Eugeni Aguiló Pérez
Faculty of Education: M. Dolors Forteza Forteza
Faculty of Law: Pedro A. Munar Bernat
Faculty of Psychology: Miquel Tortella Feliu
Faculty of Sciences: Francesca Garcias Gomila

HEADS OF SCHOOLS

Higher Polytechnic School: Gabriel Oliver Codina
University School of Business Studies: Margalida Payeras Llodrà
University School of Nursing and Physiotherapy: Joan Ernest de Pedro Gómez
University School of Tourism: Francesc Sastre Albertí
School of Labour Relations: Remedios Roqueta Buj

HEADS OF DEPARTMENTS

Biology: Hipólito Medrano Gil

Fundamental Biology and Health Sciences: María Pilar Roca Salom
Education: Josep A. Pérez Castelló
Earth Sciences: Lluís Pomar Gomà
History and Theory of the Arts: Catalina Cantarellas Camps
Mathematics and Computer Science: Arnau Mir Torres
Private Law: Irene Nadal Gómez
Public Law: Román Piña Homs
Applied Economics: Andreu Sansó Rosselló
Economics and Enterprise: Antoni Socias Salvà
Catalan Philology and General Linguistics: Joan Mas i Vives
Spanish, Modern and Latin Philology: Josep Servera Baño
Philosophy and Social Work: Camilo J. Cela Conde
Physics: Lluís Mas Franch
Nursing and Physiotherapy: M. Pilar Sánchez-Cuenca López
Psychology: Mateu Servera Barceló
Chemistry: Josefa L. Donoso Pardo

ATTACHED INSTITUTES

Institute of Education: Miquel dels Sants Oliver 2, 07122 Palma; tel. 971-17-31-32; fax 971-17-24-35; e-mail icecms@uib.es; internet www.uib.es/ICE; support and extracurricular courses; Dir Joan Jordi Muntaner Guasp.

Mediterranean Institute of Advanced Studies: Edifici Mateu Orfila i Rotger, Campus UIB, Ctra. de Valldemossa km 7.5, 07071 Palma; fax 971-17-32-48; internet www.imedea.uib.es; natural resources, interdisciplinary physics, psycholinguistics; Dir Joaquín Tintoré Subirana.

Institute for Research in Health Sciences: internet www.uib.es/recerca/iunics/index.html.

Alberta Giménez University College: C/ de Saragossa 16, Palma; tel. 971-79-28-18; fax 971-79-80-78; internet www.eualbertagimenez.com; Dir Jaume Oliver Jaume.

College of Industrial Relations: Via Alemanya 7, 2n dreta, 07003 Palma; tel. 971-72-32-68; Dir Remedios Roqueta Buj.

College of Tourism of the Island Council of Ibiza-Formentera: Edifici Polivalent, Cas Serres s/n, 07800 Ibiza; tel. 971-39-27-62; fax 971-30-72-55; Dir Vicente A. Barros Bonnín.

Felipe Moreno College of Tourism (Palma): C/ Sol 1, 07001 Palma; tel. 971-72-14-73; fax 971-71-49-88; e-mail info@escoladeturisme.com; internet www.escoladeturisme.com; Dir Felipe Moreno Rodríguez.

Felipe Moreno College of Tourism (Mahón): Avda Sant Ferran 17, 07702 Mahón, Menorca, Islas Baleares; tel. and fax 971-35-05-08; internet www.uib.es; Dir Felipe Moreno Rodríguez.

Balearic Islands College of Hotel Management: Edifici Arxiduc Lluís Salvador, Campus Universitari, Cra. de Valldemossa km 7.5, 07071 Palma; tel. 971-17-26-08; fax 971-17-26-17; e-mail escola.hoteleria@uib.es; internet euht.uib.es; Dir Maria Antònia Garcia Sastre.

UNIVERSITAT POMPEU FABRA

Plaça de la Mercè 10–12, 08002 Barcelona

Telephone: 93-542-20-00

Fax: 93-542-20-02

E-mail: webmaster@upf.es

Internet: www.upf.edu

Founded 1990
Regional govt control

Languages of instruction: Catalan, Spanish
Academic year: September to June

Rector: Dra M. Rosa Virós
Vice-Rector (Economy, Promotion and Services): Dr Daniel Serra
Vice-Rector (Academic Affairs and Teaching Staff): Dr José Juan Moreso
Vice-Rector (Science Policy): Dr Ferran Sanz
Vice-Rector (Postgraduate and Doctoral Studies): Dr Jaume Casals
Vice-Rector (Programming, Teaching and Evaluation): Dr Jacint Jordana
Vice-Rector (Institutional Relations) and Secretary: Dr Tomàs de Montagut
Vice-Rector (University Community): Josep M. Vilajosana
Manager: Pere Fons Vilardell
Librarian: Mercè Cabo

Library of 500,000 vols, 8,600 periodicals
Number of teachers: 875
Number of students: 9,500

Publications: *Línia 14* (4 a year), *e-Noticies* (online journal)

DEANS

Faculty of Economics and Business: Dr Xavier Freixas
Faculty of Law: Dra Antonia Agulló
Faculty of Humanities: Dr Miquel Berga
Faculty of Journalism: Dr Jaume Guillamet
Faculty of Translation and Interpreting: Dr Lluis Pegenaute
Faculty of Audiovisual Communication: Dr Domenec Font
Faculty of Political Sciences and Public Administration: Dr Jordi Guiu
University School of Business Studies: Dr Joaquín Tena
University School of Labour Relations: Dr Josep Fargas
Faculty of Health and Life Sciences: Dr Jordi Pérez
Polytechnic College: Josep Blat

HEADS OF DEPARTMENTS

Economics and Business: Oriol Amat
Experimental and Health Sciences: Fernando Giráldez Orgaz
Humanities: María Morrás Ruíz-Falcó
Journalism and Audiovisual Communication: Josep M. Casasús i Guri
Law: Montserrat Cuchillo Foix
Politics and Social Sciences: Francesc Pallarés Porta
Technology: Xavier Serra Casals
Translation and Philology: Toni Badia

ATTACHED INSTITUTES

Institut Universitari d'Història Jaume Vicens i Vives: Dir Dr Jaume Torras.

Institut Universitari de Lingüística Aplicada: Dir Dra M. Teresa Turell.

Centre d'Economia Internacional: Dir Dr Jordi Galí.

Institut Universitari de l'Audiovisual: Dir Xavier Serra.

Institut d'Estudis Territorials: Dir Dr Daniel Serra.

Institut Universitari de Cultura: Dir Dr Rafael Argullol.

Institut Municipal d'Investigació Mèdica: Dir Dr Jordi Camí.

UNIVERSITAT RAMÓN LLULL

Claravall 1–3, 08022 Barcelona

Telephone: 93-602-22-00

Fax: 93-602-22-49

E-mail: urlsc@sec.url.es

Internet: www.url.es

Founded 1990
Private control
Academic year: September to June

Rector: Dra ESTHER GIMÉNEZ-SALINAS COLOMER
Vice-Rector (Academic Affairs): Dr JOSEP GALLIFFA I ROCA
Vice-Rector (Research and Technology): Dr JOSEP MA. GARRELL GUIU
Vice-Rector (International Relations): Dra ROSA NOMEN RIBÉ
Registrar: Dr JOSEP GALLIFFA I ROCA
Library of 1,165,732 vols, 4,000 periodicals
Number of teachers: 1,297
Number of students: 16,898
Publications: *La URL Informa, Signes*

DEANS

Sarrià Chemical Institute: Dr LLUÍS VICTORI COMPANYS
Faculty of Economics: Dr JESÚS TRICÀS PRECKLER
Blanquerna Faculty of Psychology and Educational Sciences: Dr CLIMENT GINÉ I GINÉ
Blanquerna Faculty of Communication Sciences: Dr MIQUEL TRESSERRAS I MAJÓ
Faculty of Philosophy of Catalonia: Dr JAUME AYMAR RAGOLTA
Higher School of Business Administration and Management (ESADE): Dr XAVIER MENDOZA MAYORDOMO
Faculty of Law at the Higher School of Business Administration and Management (ESADE): Dr PERE MIROSA MARTÍNEZ

DIRECTORS

Blanquerna University School of Nursing and Physiotherapy: MÀRIUS DURAN I HORTOLÀ
Blanquerna University School of Industrial Relations: MARCEL GABARRÓ PALLARÈS
La Salle University School of Telecommunications Engineering Technology: MIQUEL A. BARRABEIG DOLS
La Salle Higher Technical School of Electronic Engineering and Computing: Dra ELISABET GOLOBARDES RIBÉ
La Salle Higher Technical School of Architecture: ROBERT TERRADAS MUNTAÑOLA
Sant Ignasi School of Tourism at the Higher School of Business Administration and Management (ESADE): ENRIC LÓPEZ VIGURIA
Pere Tarrés University School of Social Work and Social Education: Dr JOSEP MONTSERRAT
University Observatory Institute: Dr JOAN MIQUEL TORTA MARGALEF
Vidal i Barraquer Mental Health Institute: Dr CARLES PÉREZ TESTOR
Borja Bioethics Institute: NURIA TERRIBAS SALA
Higher School of Design (ESDI): Dra ANA PUJOL

UNIVERSIDAD REY JUAN CARLOS

C/ Tulipán s/n, 28933 Móstoles (Madrid)
Telephone: 916-65-50-60
Fax: 916-14-71-20
E-mail: info@urjc.es
Internet: www.urjc.es
Founded 1997
State control
Academic year: October to June
Rector: PEDRO GONZÁLEZ-TREVIJANO SÁNCHEZ
Vice-Rector (Academic Affairs and Teaching Staff): EDUARDO GARCÍA POBLETE
Vice-Rector (International Relations and New Technology): DAVID RÍOS INSUA
Vice-Rector (Student Affairs): JOSÉ MANUEL VERA SANTOS
Vice-Rector (Research and Development): RAFAEL VAN GRIEKEN SALVADOR
Vice-Rector (Institutional Relations and University Extension): DAVID ORTEGA GUTIÉRREZ

Vice-Rector (Special Courses and Graduate Affairs): PILAR LAGUNA SÁNCHEZ
Vice-Rector (Co-ordination and Campus): FERNANDO SUÁREZ BILBAO
Registrar: ANDRÉS GAMBRA GUTIÉRREZ
General Manager: JOSÉ JAVIER FERNÁNDEZ SANTAMARÍA
Library Director: RICARDO GONZÁLEZ CASTRILLO
Number of teachers: 840
Number of students: 13,021

DEANS

Faculty of Health Sciences: RAFAEL LINARES GARCÍA-VALDECASAS
Faculty of Communication Science and Tourism: ALFONSO DE ESTEBAN ALONSO
Faculty of Law and Social Sciences: CARLOS FERNANDO DE CASADEVANTE ROMANÍ
Higher School of Experimental Sciences and Technology: JOSÉ AGUADO ALONSO (Dir)

HEADS OF DEPARTMENTS

Private Law: ARMANDO TORRENT RUIZ (acting)
Labour and Social Security Law: ANTONIO VICENTE SEMPERE NAVARRO (acting)
Public Law I and Politics: JESÚS GONZÁLEZ SALINAS (acting)
Public Law II: ANTONIO CUERDA RIEZU (acting)
History, History of Law and Classical Studies: FRANCISCO REYES TÉLLEZ (acting)
History and Economic Institutions: PILAR GRAU CARLES (acting)
Applied Economics I: PILAR GRAU CARLES (acting)
Applied Economics II and Principles of Economic Analysis: PILAR GRAU CARLES (acting)
Financial Economics, Accounting and Marketing: CATALINA VACAS GUERRERO
Business Organization: LUIS ÁNGEL GUERRAS MARTÍN (acting)
Communication Science: CARMEN CAFFAREL SERRA
Social Sciences: OCTAVIO UÑA JUÁREZ
Philology: RAMÓN SARMIENTO GONZÁLEZ
Health Sciences: MANUEL ROS PÉREZ
Computer Science, Statistics and Telematics: LUIS PASTOR PÉREZ
Chemical, Environmental and Materials Technology: DAVID SERRANO GRANADOS
Applied Mathematics and Physics and Natural Sciences: ADRIÁN ESCUDERO ALCÁNTARA

ATTACHED INSTITUTES AND CENTRES

Humanities Institute: internet www.urjc .es/z_files/ad_centros/ihumanidades/humanidades.html; Dir LUIS PALACIOS BAÑUELOS.
'Emile Noël' Centre of European Union Documentation and Studies: Facultad de Ciencias Jurídicas y Sociales, Campus de Vicálvaro, Edificio Jovellanos, 28032 Vicálvaro (Madrid); tel. 91-301-99-59; fax 91-371-85-99; e-mail centroeuropeo@fcjs.urjc .es; internet www.urjc.es/z_files/ad_centros/ ad03/emil.html; Dir ROGELIO PÉREZ BUSTAMANTE.
Co-operation and Voluntary Work Centre: Campus de Alcorcón, Avda de Atenas s/ n, 28922 Alcorcón (Madrid); tel. 91-488-88-49; e-mail ccv@urjc.es; internet www.urjc.es/ z_files/ad_centros/ad03/cooperacion.html; Dir ÁNGEL GIL DE MIGUEL.
'Alicia Alonso' Higher Institute of Dance: Plaza de la Cultura 1, 3a planta, 28931 Móstoles (Madrid); tel. 91-664-54-57; e-mail fundacion_danza@hotmail.com; internet www.urjc.es/z_files/ad_centros/ ad03/danza/index.html; Dir ALBERTO GARCÍA CASTAÑO.
International Legal Studies Institute: Facultad de Ciencias Jurídicas y Sociales,

Campus de Vicálvaro, 28032 Vicálvaro (Madrid); tel. 91-301-99-54; internet www .urjc.es/z_files/ad_centros/ad03/estudios .html; Dir BRUNO AGUILERA BARCHET.
Institute of Public Law: Facultad de Ciencias Jurídicas y Sociales, Despacho 2, Campus de Vicálvaro, Paseo de Artilleros s/n, 28032 Vicálvaro (Madrid); tel. 91-488-77-92; fax 91-371-88-85; e-mail idp@fcjs.urjc.es; internet www.fcjs.urjc.es/DerPubli/Principal .html; Dir Prof. Dr ENRIQUE ALVAREZ CONDE.
Higher College of Business Management and Marketing (ESIC): Avda Valdenigrales s/n, 28223 Pozuelo de Alarcón (Madrid); tel. 91-452-41-00; fax 91-352-85-34; internet www.esic.es; Gen. Dir SIMÓN REYES MARTÍNEZ CÓRDOVA; Dir of Management CARLOS LARREA PASCAL.

UNIVERSITAT ROVIRA I VIRGILI

Calle de l'Escorxador s/n, 43003 Tarragona
Telephone: 902-33-78-78
Fax: 977-55-82-58
E-mail: secgc@urv.net
Internet: www.urv.net
Founded 1991
State control
Academic year: September to July
Rector: LLUÍS ARÓLA FERRER
Vice-Rector (Academic Planning and Research): Dr FRANCESC XAVIER GRAU VIDAL
Vice-Rector (Campus and Institutional Relations): Dr ANTONI GONZÁLEZ SENMARTÍ
Vice-Rector (Innovation, Transfer and Society): Dr XAVIER CORREIG BLANCHAR
Vice-Rector (Research and Health Institutions): Dra ROSA SOLÀ I ALBERICH
Vice-Rector (Teaching and Research Staff): Dr JOSEP ANTON FERRER VIDAL
Vice-Rector (Teaching Staff): Dra MERCÈ GISBERT CERVERA
Vice-Rector (University Community): Dra JOANA ZARAGOZA I GRAS
Registrar: Dr ANTONI PIGRAU SOLÉ
Manager: MANUEL MOLINA CLAVERO
Library of 255,000 vols
Number of teachers: 1,286
Number of students: 22,136
Publications: *Indicador Universitari* (monthly), *Rovira i Virgili* (quarterly)

DEANS

Faculty of Arts: Dra MERCÈ JORDÀ OLIVES
Faculty of Chemistry: Dr JOSEP MANEL RICART PLA
Faculty of Economics and Business Studies: Dr MIQUEL ÁNGEL BOVÉ SANS
Faculty of Education and Psychology: Dra MISERICÒRDIA CAMPS LLAURADÓ
Faculty of Law: Dr SANTIAGO JOSÉ CASTELLÀ SURRIBAS
Faculty of Medicine and Health Sciences: Dr RODRIGO C. MIRALLES MARRERO
Faculty of Oenology: Dr FERNANDO ZAMORA MARÍN

DIRECTORS

School of Chemical Engineering: Dr XAVIER FARRIOL ROIGES
School of Engineering: Dr XAVIER MAIXÉ ALTÉS
School of Nursing: ROSER RICOMÀ MUNTANÉ
School of Tourism and Leisure: Dr SALVADOR ANTON CLAVÉ (President)

HEADS OF DEPARTMENTS

Faculty of Arts (Plaça Imperial Tárraco 1, 43005 Tarragona; tel. 977-55-95-98; fax 977-55-95-97; e-mail secllet1@urv.net; internet www.urv.net/centres/lletres):
Department of Anglo-Germanic Philology: PERE GALLARDO TORRADO

Department of Catalan Philology: Dr
MIQUEL ANGEL PRADILLA CARDONA
Department of History and Geography: Dr
JOSEP OLIVERAS SAMITIER
Department of Romance Philology: Dr
CARLOS MARTÍN VIDE
Department of Social Anthropology, Philo-
sophy and Social Work: Dr JOSEP OLI-
VERAS SAMITIER
Preparatory Department of Communica-
tion: Dr BERNAT LÓPEZ LÓPEZ

School of Chemical Engineering (Avda Països
Catalans 26, 43006 Tarragona; tel. 977-55-
97-00; fax 977-55-96-99; e-mail secetseq@urv
.net; internet www.etseq.urv.net):

Department of Chemical Engineering: Dr
IOANIS KATAKIS
Department of Mechanical Engineering:
Dr ILDEFONSO CUESTA ROMERO

Faculty of Chemistry (Marcel·lí Domingo s/n,
43007 Tarragona; tel. 977-55-86-00; fax 977-
55-95-28; e-mail secquim@urv.net; internet
www.quimica.urv.net):

Department of Analytical and Organic
Chemistry: Dra MARISOL LARRECHI GAR-
CÍA
Department of Biochemistry and Biotech-
nology: Dr ANTONI ROMEU FIGUEROLA
Department of Physical and Inorganic
Chemistry: Dra PILAR SALAGRE CARNERO

Faculty of Economics and Business Studies
(Avda de la Universitat 1, 43204 Reus; tel.
977-75-98-01; fax 977-75-98-10; e-mail
secemp@urv.net; internet www.fcee.urv.net):

Department of Business Administration:
Dr ANTONI TERCEÑO GÓMEZ
Department of Economics: Dr MARTÍ OLIVA
I FURÉS

Faculty of Education and Psychology (Crta
de Valls s/n, 43007 Tarragona; tel. 977-55-80-
98; fax 977-55-80-55; e-mail secedu1@urv
.net; internet www.fcep.urv.net):

Department of Education: Dra ROSARIO
BARRIOS ARÓS
Department of Psychology: Dr ANDREU
VIGIL COLET

School of Engineering (Avda dels Països
Catalans 17, 43005 Tarragona; tel. 977-55-
97-00; fax 977-55-96-99; e-mail secetse@urv
.net; internet www.etse.urv.net):

Department of Electronics, Electrical Engi-
neering and Automation: Dr JOSEP PAL-
LARES MARZAL
Department of Mathematics and Computer
Engineering: Dr JOAN FERRER GENER

Faculty of Law (Avda Catalunya 35, 43002
Tarragona; tel. 977-55-83-82; fax 977-55-83-
86; e-mail secfcj@urv.net; internet www.fcj
.urv.net):

Department of Private Law: Dra ENCARNA-
CIÓ RICART MARTÍ
Department of Public Law: Dr MARIO RUIZ
SANZ

Faculty of Medicine and Health Sciences
(Sant Llorenç 21, 43201 Reus; tel. 977-75-
93-45; fax 977-75-93-55; e-mail secmed@urv
.net; internet www.urv.net/centres/fmcs):

Department of Basic Medicine: Dra VER-
ÒNICA PIERA LLUCH
Department of Medicine and Surgery: Dr
RICARDO CLOSA MONASTEROLO

School of Nursing (Avda de Roma 17, 43005
Tarragona; tel. 977-25-01-25; fax 977-25-14-
24; e-mail secinf@urv.net; internet www.urv
.net/centres/infermeria):

Department of Nursing: MARIA ANTONIA
MARTORELL POVEDA

ATTACHED INSTITUTIONS

**Centre for Advanced Studies in Avia-
tion (CESDA):** Campus Aeronáutico, Reus
(Tarragona); tel. 977-30-00-27; fax 977-30-00-

28; e-mail cesda@cesda.com; internet www
.cesda.com; Dir FRANCESC DÍAZ GONZÁLEZ.

Institute of Advanced Studies: e-mail
iea@astor.urv.es; Areas of study: quaternary,
mycology, applied medicine, anthropology,
chemometrics, quantum chemistry; Dir
ROSA CABALLOL LORENZO.

Institute of Education: Edifici Ventura i
Gassol, Carretera de Valls s/n, 43007 Tarragona; tel. 977-55-80-71; fax 977-55-80-73;
e-mail gesice@ice.urv.es; internet www.ice
.urv.es; Dir ANGEL-PÍO GONZÁLEZ SOTO.

UNIVERSIDAD PONTIFICIA DE SALAMANCA

Calle Compañía 5, Apdo 541, 37002 Sala-
manca
Telephone: 923-27-71-00
Fax: 923-26-24-56
Internet: www.upsa.es
Founded 1134 as the Ecclesiastical School of
Salamanca Cathedral; named a University
by Alfonso IX of León in 1219. The
University had ceased to function by the
end of the 18th century, but was restored
in 1940 by Pope Pius XII
Private control
Language of instruction: Spanish
Academic year: October to June
Grand Chancellor: Dr RICARDO BLÁZQUEZ
PÉREZ
Rector: Dr MARCELIANO ARRANZ RODRIGO
Vice-Rector (Academic Organization and
Economy): Dra MA. FRANCISCA MARTÍN
TABERNERO
Vice-Rector (Pastoral Affairs, Research and
Quality): Dr SANTIAGO GUIJARRO OPORTO
Vice-Rector (Teaching Staff, Student Affairs,
Communication and Services): Dra ROSA
PINTO LOBO
Registrar: Dr LUIS MIGUEL PEDRERO ESTEBAN
Administrative Co-ordinator: Lic. MA. TERESA
GÓMEZ MARCOS
Director of Library: Dr ANTONIO GARCÍA
MADRID
Library of 500,000 vols and numerous MSS
Number of teachers: 351
Number of students: 8,500
Publications: *Salmanticensis, Helmántica,
Crónica* (bulletin), *Cuadernos Salmantinos
de Filosofía, Diálogo Ecuménico, Revista
Española de Derecho Canónico, Sociedad y
Utopía, Comunicación y Pluralismo, Mis-
celánea Pedagógica, Revista de Ciencias y
Orientación Familiar*

DEANS

Faculty of Theology: Dr JOSÉ-RAMÓN FLECHA
ANDRÉS
Faculty of Canon Law: Dr FEDERICO RAFAEL
AZNAR GIL
Faculty of Philosophy: Dr LEONARDO
RODRÍGUEZ DUPLÁ
Faculty of Education: Dr ANTONIO GARCÍA
MADRID
Faculty of Psychology: Dr MA. PAZ QUEVEDO
AGUADO
Faculty of Communication: Dr ÁNGEL LOSADA
VÁZQUEZ
Faculty of Political and Social Sciences
(Madrid): Dr JUAN MANUEL DÍAZ SÁNCHEZ
Faculty of Computer Sciences (Madrid): Dr
LUIS JOYANES AGUILAR
Faculty of Insurance, Law and Management
(Madrid): Dr ANTONIO GUARDIOLA LOZANO

DIRECTORS

University School of Computer Science (Sal-
amanca): Dr VIDAL ALONSO SECADES
University School of Computer Science
(Madrid): Dr LUIS JOYANES AGUILAR

'Salus Infirmorum' University School of
Nursing (Salamanca): Dr JULIÁN BENA-
VENTE HERRERO
University School of Nursing (Madrid): Dr
CARLOS CHAMORRO JAMBRINA
'Luis Vives' University Teacher Training
School (Salamanca): Dr JOSÉ SARRIÓN
CAYUELA
University School of Physiotherapy (Madrid):
Dr FRANCISCO DE GALA SÁNCHEZ

PROFESSORS

Faculty of Theology (tel. 923-27-71-06; fax
923-27-71-01; e-mail teologia@upsa.es;
internet www.teologia.upsa.es):

BOROBIO GARCÍA, D., Liturgy and Sacra-
ments
FLECHA ANDRÉS, J., Fundamental Moral
Theology
GARCÍA LOPEZ, F., Old Testament Exegesis
GONZÁLEZ HERNÁNDEZ, O., Christology
PIKAZA IBARRONDO, J., Phenomenology of
Religion
RAMOS GUERREIRA, J., Pastoral Theology
SANCHEZ CARO, J. M., Introduction to the
Scriptures
TELLECHEA IDÍGORAS, J. I., Church History
TREVIJANO ECHEVERRIA, R., Patrology

Faculty of Canon Law (tel. 923-27-71-07; fax
923-27-71-01; e-mail canon@upsa.es; internet
www.canonico.upsa.es):

AZNAR GIL, F., Matrimonial, Hereditary
and Penal Law
CORTÉS DIÉGUEZ, M., Ecclesiastical Public
Law
GARCÍA Y GARCÍA, A., Canon Law
MANZANARES MARIJUÁN, J., Constitutional
Law

Faculty of Philosophy (tel. 923-27-71-08; fax
923-27-71-01; e-mail info.alumno@upsa.es;
internet www.filosofia.upsa.es):

ANDALUZ ROMANILLOS, A. M., Metaphysics
ARRANZ RODRIGO, M., Natural Philosophy
CASTILLO CABELLERO, D., Theodicy
MURILLO MURILLO, I., Logic
PINTOR RAMOS, A., History of Modern
Philosophy
RODRÍGUEZ DUPLÁ, L., Ethics and Political
Philosophy

Faculty of Education (tel. 923-27-71-09; fax
923-27-71-01; e-mail decanato@upsa.es;
internet www.educacion.upsa.es):

CASTRO POSADA, J. A., Child Psychology
FERNÁNDEZ FALAGÁN, P., Curriculum Eva-
luation
GARCÍA ARROYO, M. J., Educational Psy-
chology
HOLGADO SÁNCHEZ, A., General Didactics

Faculty of Psychology (tel. 923-27-71-13; fax
923-27-71-14; e-mail psi.secretaria@upsa.es;
internet www.psicologia.upsa.es):

CASTRO POSADA, J. A., Experimental Psy-
chology
GONZÁLEZ GONZÁLEZ, J. A., Psychophysiol-
ogy
MÁLAGA GUERRERO, J., Psychopathology of
Human Communications
MARTÍN TABERNERO, M. F., Statistics
Applied to Human Sciences
PASTOR RAMOS, G., Social Psychology
QUEVEDO AQUADO, M. P., Psychology of the
Personality

Faculty of Political and Social Sciences
(Paseo Juan XXIII 3, 28040 Madrid; tel. 91-
514-17-09; e-mail informacion@fpablovi.org;
internet www.upsam.com):

ALVAREZ RICO, M., Administration
BUCETA FACORRO, L., Social Psychology
CAPELO MARTÍNEZ, M., Economic Policy
GONZÁLEZ-ANLEO, J., Sociology
SÁNCHEZ JIMÉNEZ, J., Economic and Social
History

VALVERDE MUCIENTES, C., Theology of Social Reality

Faculty of Information Science (Avda de Champagnat 121, 37007 Salamanca; tel. 923-28-23-57):

ECHEVERRI GONZÁLEZ, A. L., Media Company Management
LOSADA VÁZQUEZ, A., Institutional Communication
MARTÍNEZ VALWEY, F., Newspaper Editing
MERAYO PÉREZ, A., Communication, Audiovisual Information
NÓ SÁNCHEZ, J., Information Technology
PINTO LOBO, MA. R., Theory of Communication and Information

AFFILIATED INSTITUTES AND CENTRES

College of Christian Education: Co-ordinator Dra ASUNCIÓN ESCRIBANO HERNÁNDEZ.

Higher Institute of Pastoral Studies: Paseo Juan XXIII 3, 28040 Madrid; tel. 91-514-17-00; fax 91-534-09-83; e-mail instpast@teleline.es; internet www.upsa.es/w3/sitios/Facultades/pastoralm/indexisp.htm; Dir Dr JOSÉ LUIS CORZO TORAL.

Institute of Education Science: tel. 923-27-71-40; fax 923-27-71-01; e-mail ice@upsa.es; internet www.ice.upsa.es; Dir Dra MARÍA JESÚS GARCÍA ARROYO.

Institute of European Studies and Human Rights: tel. 923-27-71-42; fax 923-27-71-01; e-mail europa@upsa.es; internet www.europa.upsa.es; Dir Dr JOSÉ-ROMÁN FLECHA ANDRÉS.

Institute of Clinical Child Psychology: Dir (vacant).

Institute of Iberoamerican Thought: tel. 923-27-71-43; fax 923-27-71-01; e-mail ipi@upsa.es; internet www.ipi.upsa.es; Dir Prof. Dr ILDEFONSO MURILLO MURILLO.

I.S.E.F.A.: tel. 923-27-71-39; fax 923-27-71-01; internet www.isefa.upsa.es; Dir Dra ADORACIÓN HOLGADO SÁNCHEZ.

Logopedia: tel. 923-27-71-16; fax 923-27-71-01; e-mail logopedia@upsa.es; internet www.logopedia.upsa.es; Dean Dra MA. PAZ QUEVEDO AGUADO.

Psychology of Language: Dir Dr JESÚS MÁLAGA GUERRERO.

Higher Institute of Family Studies: tel. 923-27-71-41; fax 923-27-71-01; e-mail cc.familia@upsa.es; internet www.ccfamilia.upsa.es; Dir Dr JORGE JUAN FERNÁNDEZ SANGRADOR.

Spanish Language and Culture: Dir Dra MARÍA MERCEDES SANDE BUSTAMANTE.

Oriental and Ecumenical Studies: Dir Dr FERNANDO RODRÍGUEZ GARRAPUCHO.

Institute of History of Theology: Dir Dr ANTONIO GARCÍA Y GARCÍA.

Higher Institute of Philosophy (Valladolid): Dir (vacant).

'Pius X' Institute of Catechetical Studies (Madrid): Dir Dr EDUARDO MALVIDO MIGUEL.

Theological Institute of Religious Life: Dir Dr BONIFACIO FERNÁNDEZ GARCÍA.

Theological Institute of Santiago de Compostela: Dir Dr SEGUNDO PÉREZ LÓPEZ.

Theological Institute of Murcia: Dir PEDRO RIQUELME OLIVA.

Theological Institute of Oviedo: Dir Dr MANUEL ANGEL ACEBES.

Theological Institute of León: Dir Lic. ANTONIO TROBAJO DIAZ.

Theological Institute of Aragón: Dir Lic. JULIÁN RUIZ MARTORELL.

Theological Institute of El Escorial: Dir Dr FERMIN FERNANDEZ BIENZOBAS.

Theological Institute of Pamplona: Dir Dr ANGEL IRIARTE ARRIAZU.

Theological Institute of Badajoz: Dir Rvdo PEDRO RODRÍGUEZ GALLEGO.

Theological Institute of San Fulgencio (Murcia): Dir Lic. GINÉS PAGÁN LAJARA.

University School of Family Science (Valladolid): Dir Dr JESUS MA. GALDEANO ARAMENDIA.

University School of Family Science (Murcia): Dir Dr JOSÉ LUIS PARADA NAVAS.

University School of Family Science (Sevilla): Dir Dr ANTONIO LARIOS RAMOS.

Spanish Biblico-Archaeological Institute: fax 923-26-24-56; e-mail viceinvestigacion@upsa.es; internet www.ieba.upsa.es; Dir Lic. ÁNGEL TABARÉS GOLDAR.

UNIVERSIDAD DE SALAMANCA

Patio de Escuelas 1, Apdo 20, 37008 Salamanca

Telephone: 923-29-44-00
Fax: 923-29-45-02
E-mail: gabinete@gugu.usal.es
Internet: www.usal.es

Founded 1218 by Alfonso IX of León and reorganized 1254 by Alfonso X of Castile
State control
Language of instruction: Spanish
Academic year: October to July

Rector: ENRIQUE BATTANER ARIAS
Vice-Rector (Academic Organization): JOSÉ MARÍA MUÑOZ PORRAS
Vice-Rector (Planning and Innovation in Teaching): JOSÉ MARÍA HERNÁNDEZ DÍAZ
Vice-Rector (Research): ARTURO PEREZ ESLAVA
Vice-Rector (Programming and Development): SANTIAGO LÓPEZ GARCÍA
Vice-Rector (Infrastructure): LIBIA SANTOS REQUEJO
Vice-Rector (Institutional Relations): JOSÉ MANUEL LLORENTE PINTO
Vice-Rector (Student Affairs and University Extension): ANGEL INFESTAS GIL
Registrar: ELISA MUÑOZ TORRES
Manager: FELISA CHINCHETRU PÉREZ
Library of 885,066 vols, 20,338 periodicals
Number of teachers: 2,171
Number of students: 32,338

DEANS

Faculty of Philology: ROMÁN ÁLVAREZ RODRÍGUEZ
Faculty of Geography and History: VALENTÍN CABERO DIÉGUEZ
Faculty of Philosophy: PABLO GARCÍA CASTILLO
Faculty of Psychology: JOSÉ LUIS VEGA VEGA
Faculty of Chemistry: ELADIO JAVIER MARTÍN MATEOS
Faculty of Biology: JOSÉ RAMÓN ALONSO PEÑA
Faculty of Law: RAFAEL DE AGAPITO SERRANO
Faculty of Medicine: JOSÉ IGNACIO PAZ BOUZA
Faculty of Pharmacy: JULIÁN C. RIVAS GONZALO
Faculty of Fine Arts: RAFAEL SÁNCHEZ-CARRALERO LÓPEZ
Faculty of Sciences: FRANCISCO FERNÁNDEZ GONZÁLEZ
Faculty of Economics and Business: ALBERTO DE MIGUEL HIDALGO
Faculty of Social Sciences: PEDRO LUIS IRISO NAPAL
Faculty of Education: FERNANDO GÓMEZ MARTÍN
Faculty of Translation and Documentation: CARLOS FORTEA GIL
Faculty of Agricultural and Environmental Sciences: FERNANDO SANTOS FRANCÉS

DIRECTORS

Higher Polytechnic College at Ávila: MANUEL ALVAREZ-CLARO IRISARRI
Higher Polytechnic College at Zamora: MARGARITA MORÁN MARTÍN
Teacher Training College at Zamora: FRANCISCO JOSÉ CUADRADO SANTOS
College of Education at Ávila: JUSTO BOLEKIA BOLEKÁ
School of Nursing and Physiotherapy: FERNANDO SÁNCHEZ HERNÁNDEZ
Higher Technical School of Industrial Engineering at Béjar: FRANCISCO MARTÍN LABAJOS

HEADS OF DEPARTMENTS

Business Administration and Economics: PABLO ANTONIO MUÑOZ GALLEGO
Human Anatomy and Histology: FRANCISCO COLLÍA FERNÁNDEZ (acting)
Library Science and Documentation: JOSÉ ANTONIO FRÍAS MONTOYA
Animal Biology, Parasitology, Ecology, Soil Science and Chemistry: SEVERIANO FERNÁNDEZ GAYUBO
Cell Biology and Pathology: JOSÉ AIJÓN NOGUERA
Biochemistry and Molecular Biology: ENRIQUE BATTANER ARIAS
Botany: CIPRIANO JESÚS VALLE GUTIÉRREZ
Surgery: ALBERTO GÓMEZ ALONSO
Construction and Agronomy: ANA MARÍA VIVAR QUINTANA (Deputy Director)
Administrative, Financial and Procedural Law: NICOLÁS RODRÍGUEZ GARCÍA
Private Law: MARÍA JOSÉ HERRERO GARCÍA
General Public Law: JOSÉ LUIS CASCAJO CASTRO
Labour Law and Social Work: MANUEL CARLOS PALOMEQUE LÓPEZ
Teaching Self-Expression through Music, Plastic Arts and Movement: DÁMASO GARCÍA FRAILE
Teaching Mathematics and Experimental Sciences: MIGUEL CLAUDIO SÁNCHEZ-BARBUDO RUIZ-TAPIADOR
Teaching, Organization and Research Methods: MARÍA DEL PINO LECUONA NARANJO
Applied Economics: RAFAEL MUÑOZ DE BUSTILLO LLORENTE
Economics and Economic History: JOSÉ MANUEL GUTIÉRREZ DÍEZ
Nursing: JOSÉ MARÍA MARTÍN GARCÍA
Statistics: MARÍA PURIFICACIÓN GALINDO VILLARDÓN
Pharmacy and Pharmaceutical Technology: JOSÉ MARTÍNEZ LANAO
Classical and Indoeuropean Philology: AGUSTÍN RAMOS GUERREIRA
French Philology: TOMÁS GONZALO SANTOS
English Philology: ANTONIO RODRÍGUEZ CELADA
Modern Philology: VICENTE GONZÁLEZ MARTÍN
Philosophy, Logic and Philosophy of Science: MARÍA CARMEN PAREDES MARTÍN
Applied Physics: DANIEL PARDO COLLANTES
General Physics and Atmospheric Physics: MOISÉS EGIDO MANZANO
Physics, Engineering and Medical Radiology: JOSÉ JULIO SOLER RIPOLL
Vegetal Physiology: GREGORIO NICOLÁS RODRIGO
Physiology and Pharmacology: JOSÉ JUAN GARCÍA MARÍN
Geography: VALENTÍN CABERO DIÉGUEZ
Geology: ANGEL CORROCHANO SÁNCHEZ
Medieval, Modern and Contemporary History: ANGEL VACA LORENZO
History of Art and Fine Art: ARTURO MARTÍNEZ RODRÍGUEZ
History of Law and Legal, Moral and Political Philosophy: MIGUEL ÁNGEL RODILLA GONZÁLEZ
Computer Science and Automation: LUIS ALONSO ROMERO

Cartographic Engineering and Land Engineering: MIGUEL HERRERO MATÍAS

Mechanical Engineering: JOSÉ ANTONIO CABEZAS FLORES

Chemical and Textile Engineering: JORGE CUELLAR ANTEQUERA

Spanish Language: LUIS SANTOS RÍO

Spanish and Hispanoamerican Literature: MANUEL MARÍA PÉREZ LÓPEZ

Applied Mathematics: LUIS FERRAGUT CANALS

Mathematics: JOSÉ MARÍA MUÑOZ PORRAS

Medicine: JOSÉ MANUEL MIRALLES GARCÍA

Preventive Medicine, Public Health and Medical Microbiology: MARÍA DEL CARMEN SÁENZ GONZÁLEZ

Microbiology and Genetics: ANDRÉS CHORDI CORBO

Obstetrics, Gynaecology and Paediatrics: ANGEL AGUSTÍN GARCÍA IGLESIAS

Personality, Assessment and Psychological Treatment: FERNANDO JIMÉNEZ GÓMEZ

Prehistory, Ancient History and Archaeology: MARÍA SOLEDAD CORCHÓN RODRÍGUEZ

Basic Psychology, Psychobiology and Methodology of the Behavioural Sciences: RAMÓN FERNÁNDEZ PULIDO

Evolutionary Psychology of Education: JOSÉ ANTONIO FUERTES MARTÍN

Social Psychology and Anthropology: EUGENIO GARRIDO MARTÍN

Psychiatry, Medical Psychology, Forensic Medicine and History of Science: RAFAEL MUÑOZ GARRIDO

Analytical Chemistry, Nutrition and Bromatology: RITA CARABIAS MARTÍNEZ

Pharmaceutical Chemistry: ARTURO SAN FELICIANO MARTÍN

Physical Chemistry: FERNANDO GONZÁLEZ VELASCO

Inorganic Chemistry: JOSÉ MANUEL MARTÍN LLORENTE

Organic Chemistry: MANUEL GRANDE BENITO

Sociology and Communication: RAFAEL ESCOBAR MERCADO

Theory and History of Education: LEONCIO VEGA GIL

Translation and Interpretation: JOAQUÍN GARCÍA PALACIOS

ATTACHED INSTITUTES AND CENTRES

College of Nursing at Ávila: C/ Canteros s/n, 05005 Avila; tel. 920-25-38-89; fax 920-20-01-64; Dir MARÍA DEL PILAR GONZÁLEZ ARRIETA.

College of Nursing at Zamora: Avda de Requejo 21-1°, 49014 Zamora; tel. 980-51-93-43; fax 980-51-94-62; Dir MARÍA SOLEDAD SÁNCHEZ ARNOSI.

College of Industrial Relations: C/ San Torcuato 43, 49014 Zamora; tel. 980-53-15-49; fax 980-53-36-23; Dir JULIÁN CALVO ANDRÉS.

Institute of Education: internet iuce.usal.es; Dir JOSÉ ORTEGA ESTEBAN.

Interuniversity Institute of Iberoamerican and Portuguese Studies: C/ San Pablo 26, 37001 Salamanca; tel. 923-29-46-36; fax 923-29-46-37; e-mail ieiyp@usal.es; internet iberoame.usal.es; Dir MANUEL ALCÁNTARA SÁEZ.

Institute of Integration into the Community: Avda de la Merced 109–131, 37005 Salamanca; tel. 923-29-46-95; fax 923-29-46-85; e-mail inico@usal.es; internet www3.usal.es/~inico; Dir MIGUEL ANGEL VERDUGO.

Cancer Research Centre: Campus Miguel de Unamuno, 37007 Salamanca; tel. 923-29-47-20; fax 923-29-47-95; e-mail cicancer@usal.es; internet www.cicancer.es; Dir EUGENIO SANTOS.

Neurosciences Institute of Castilla y León: Facultad de Medicina, Campus Unamuno, Avda Alfonso X El Sabio s/n, 37007 Salamanca; tel. 923-29-47-30; e-mail incyl@usal.es; internet www-incyl.usal.es; Dir MIGUEL MERCHÁN CIFUENTES.

European Documentation Centre: Biblioteca Francisco de Vitoria, 2a Planta, Campus Miguel de Unamuno, 37007 Salamanca; tel. 923-29-44-00 ext. 3545; fax 923-29-47-38; e-mail cde@usal.es; internet cde.usal.es; Dir ARACELI MANGAS MARTÍN.

Alfonso IX University History Centre: Colegio Mayor San Bartolomé, Plaza de Fray Luis de León 1–8, 37008 Salamanca; tel. 923-29-45-00; fax 923-29-47-79; e-mail chuaix@usal.es; internet www3.usal.es/alfonsoix; Dir LUIS E. RODRÍGUEZ-SAN PEDRO BEZARES.

Centre for Research and the Technological Development of Water: Campus Miguel de Unamuno, 37007 Salamanca; tel. 923-29-46-70; fax 923-29-47-44; e-mail cidta@usal.es; internet cidta.usal.es; Administrator JUAN MANUEL CACHAZA GIANZO.

Linguistics Research Centre: Casa Dorado Montero, Paseo del Rector Esperabé 47, 37008 Salamanca; tel. 923-29-44-00; fax 923-29-46-55; e-mail cil@gugu.usal.es; internet www3.usal.es/~cilus; Dir JOSÉ LUIS HERRERO INGELMO.

Behavioural Sciences Research Centre: Facultad de Psicología, Avda La Merced 109–131, 37005 Salamanca; tel. 923-29-44-00 ext. 3257; e-mail cicco@usal.es; internet www3.usal.es/~cicco; Contact MAIKA DÍAZ AGUILAR.

Hispano-Japanese Cultural Centre: Plaza San Boal 11–13, 37002 Salamanca; tel. 923-29-45-60; fax 923-29-47-59; e-mail nipocent@usal.es; internet www3.usal.es/~nipocent; Dir ANTONIO LÓPEZ SANTOS.

Brazilian Studies Centre: Colegio Arzobispo Fonseca, C/ Fonseca 4, 37002 Salamanca; tel. 923-29-48-25; fax 923-29-45-87; internet www3.usal.es/~cebusal; Dir JOSÉ MANUEL SANTOS.

UNIVERSIDAD SAN PABLO-C.E.U.

C/ Julián Romea 23, 28003 Madrid

Telephone: 91-536-27-27

E-mail: international.office@ceu.es

Internet: www.uspceu.com

Founded 1993

Private control

Languages of instruction: Spanish, English

Academic year: September to June

Rector: Dr JOSÉ ALBERTO PAREJO GÁMIR

Vice-Rector (Academic Affairs and Teaching Staff): Dr ANTONIO CALVO BERNARDINO

Vice-Rector (Organization): Dr JAVIER ITURRIOZ DEL CAMPO

Vice-Rector (Research): Dr ELIO GALLEGO GARCÍA

Vice-Rector (Student Affairs): Dr LUIS EUGENIO TOGORES SÁNCHEZ

Registrar: Dr JUAN CARLOS DOMÍNGUEZ NAFRÍA

Library Director: JOSÉ MORILLO-VELARDE SERRANO

Library of 42,000 vols

Number of teachers: 752

Number of students: 8,538

DEANS

Faculty of Business and Economics: Dr ANDRÉS M. GUTIÉRREZ GÓMEZ

Faculty of Humanities and Communication Sciences: Dra M. CONSOLACIÓN ISART HERNÁNDEZ

Faculty of Law: Dr JUAN MANUEL BLANCH NOUGUÉS (acting)

Faculty of Pharmacy: Dr AUGUSTÍN PROBANZA LOBO

Higher Polytechnic School: Dr FELIX HERNANDO MANSILLA (Dir)

HEADS OF DEPARTMENTS

Advertising and Institutional Communication: ELSA MARTÍNEZ CABALLERO

Applied Physics, Physical Chemistry and Optics: CRISTINA ABRADELO DE USERA

Audiovisual Communication and New Technology: PEDRO PÉREZ CUADRADO

Basic Law Disciplines: JUAN IGLESIAS REDONDO

Biochemistry, Cell Biology and Molecular Biology: EMILIO HERRERA CASTILLÓN

Business: ANTONIO SÁINZ FUERTES

Chemistry: BEATRIZ DE PASCUAL TERESA

Computer Science Applied to Social Sciences: ELENA GARCÍA CUEVAS

Construction Procedures: JUAN TEJELA JUEZ

Electronic Systems Engineering and Telecommunications: GIANLUCA CORNETTA

Environmental Sciences and Natural Resources: JAVIER GUTIERREZ MAÑERO

Finance and Accountancy: ENRIQUETA GALLEGO DÍEZ

General Economics: BEGOÑA BLASCO TORREJÓN

History and Thought: JOSÉ LUIS ORELLA MARTÍNEZ

Journalism: SALOMÉ BERROCAL GONZALO

Medical Sciences: JOSÉ ANTONIO VEGA ALVAREZ

Modern Languages: MILAGROS BELTRÁN GANDULLO

Nursing: FRANCISCO JAVIER SANTOS HEREDERO

Nutrition, Bromatology and Food Science: GREGORIO VARELA MOREIRAS

Pharmacology, Technology and Pharmaceutical Development: LUIS FERNANDO ALGUACIL MERINO

Physiotherapy: LUIS FERNÁNDEZ ROSA

Private Law: IVÁN MILANS DEL BOSCH PORTOLÉS

Psychology: AQUILINO POLAINO LORENTE

Public Law I: ERNESTO LEJEUNE VALCÁRCEL

Public Law II: ALFREDO GARCÍA GÁRATE

Quantitative Methods: ANTONIO FRANCO RODRÍGUEZ LÁZARO

Software Engineering and Knowledge Engineering: MARIANO FERNÁNDEZ LÓPEZ

Theory and Design in Architecture and Town Planning: FEDERICO DE ISIDRO GORDEJUELA

ATTACHED INSTITUTIONS

Ángel Ayala Institute of Humanities: Julián Romea 20, 28003 Madrid; tel. 91-514-04-43; fax 91-554-10-92; e-mail ihuman@ceu.es; internet www.ceu.es/angelayala/IHAA/home.htm; Dir JOSÉ LUIS GUTIÉRREZ GARCÍA.

European Documentation Centre: Campus Moncloa, Julián Romea 22 (planta baja), 28003 Madrid; tel. 91-514-04-00; fax 91-535-09-91; e-mail europa@ceu.es; Librarian ASCENSIÓN GIL.

Institute of Democracy Studies: Julián Romea 23, 28003 Madrid; tel. 91-456-63-11; fax 91-514-01-41; e-mail id@ceu.es; Dir LUIS NÚÑEZ LADEVÉZE.

Institute of European Studies: Julián Romea 22, 28003 Madrid; tel. 91-514-04-22; fax 91-514-04-28; e-mail idee@ceu.es; internet www.ceu.es/idee; Dir Dr JOSÉ MARÍA BENEYTO PÉREZ.

Institute of Family Studies: Julián Romea 23, 28003 Madrid; tel. 91-456-63-11; fax 91-514-01-41; e-mail if@ceu.es; Dir ENRIQUE MARTÍN LÓPEZ.

UNIVERSIDADE DE SANTIAGO DE COMPOSTELA

Praza do Obradoiro s/n, 15705 Santiago de Compostela

Telephone: 981-56-31-00

Fax: 981-58-85-22

Internet: www.usc.es

Founded 1495

State control

Languages of instruction: Spanish, Galician

Rector: SENÉN BARRO

Vice-Rectors: JOSÉ RAMÓN LEIS FIDALGO, CELSO RODRÍGUEZ FERNÁNDEZ, CASTOR MÉNDEZ PAZ, FERNANDO DOMÍNGUEZ PUENTE, FRANCISCO MASEDA EIMIL, ANTONIO LÓPEZ DÍAZ, MANUEL CASTRO COTÓN, BLANCA-ANA ROIG RECHOU, JOSÉ M. RIVERA OTERO

Secretary-General: GUMERSINDO GUINARTE CABADA

Administrator: ANA FERNÁNDEZ PULPEIRO

Librarian: CONCEPCIÓN VARELA OROL

General Library of 1,500,000 volumes, more than 140 incunabula, prayer book of Fernando I of Castile (11th c.); other special libraries in the faculties

Number of teachers: 1,536

Number of students: 35,000

Publications: *Trabajos Compostelanos de Biología, Memoria, Verba, Anuario Gallego de Filología, Anejos de la revista Verba, Cursos y Congresos de la Universidad de Santiago de Compostela, Monografías, Acta Científica Compostelana*

DEANS

Faculty of Philosophy and Education: JUAN VÁZQUEZ SÁNCHEZ

Faculty of Law: JAVIER GÁRATE CASTRO

Faculty of Medicine and Dentistry: ANDRÉS BEIRAS IGLESIAS

Faculty of Pharmacy: ISABEL SUÁREZ GIMENO

Faculty of Economic and Business Science: XAVIER ROJO SÁNCHEZ

Faculty of Philology: EMILIO MONTERO CARTELLE

Faculty of Geography and History: JOSÉ CARLOS BERMEJO BARRERA

Faculty of Sciences (in Lugo): EUGENIO RODRÍGUEZ NÚÑEZ

Faculty of Political and Social Sciences: JOSÉ VILAS NOGUEIRA

Faculty of Information Science: MARGARITA LEDO ANDIÓN

Faculty of Psychology: JOSÉ M. SABUCEDO CAMESELLE

Faculty of Humanities: CONCEPCIÓN DEL BURGO LÓPEZ

Faculty of Chemistry: JUAN M. NAVAZA DAFONTE

Faculty of Physics: JOSÉ M. FDEZ. DE LABASTIDA Y DEL OLMO

Faculty of Mathematics: ENRIQUE MACÍAS VIRGÓS

Faculty of Veterinary Science: ENRIQUE ANTONIO GONZÁLEZ GARCÍA

Faculty of Biology: JOSÉ C. OTERO GONZÁLEZ

DIRECTORS

Higher Polytechnic School: EDUARDO ZURITA DE LA VEGA

University School of Nursing: PILAR SÁNCHEZ SEBIO

University School of Business Studies: Mª ROSA VARELA PUGA

University School of Optics: VICENTE MORENO DE LAS CUEVAS

UNIVERSIDAD S. E. K. DE SEGOVIA

Campus de Santa Cruz la Real, 40003 Segovia

Telephone: 921-41-24-10

Fax: 921-44-55-93

E-mail: usek@usek.edu

Internet: www.usek.es

Founded 1992

Private control

Academic year: September to June

Rector: Dr ARTURO COLORADO CASTELLARY

Vice-Rector (Research and Graduate Affairs): CESÁREO PÉREZ GONZÁLEZ

Vice-Rector (Academic Affairs and Studies): SAMUEL GONZÁLEZ MANCEBO

Registrar: GUILLERMO RUIZ ARNÁIZ

Director of University Extension and Student Affairs: ROBERTO RUIZ SALCES

Manager: IGNACIO SOTOMAYOR SAEZ

Library Director: MARTA MUÑOZ CASADO

DEANS

Faculty of Experimental Sciences: JESÚS A. GÓMEZ OCHOA DE ALDA

Faculty of Human, Social and Communication Sciences: SANTIAGO LÓPEZ NAVIA

DIRECTORS

Higher Technical School of Integrated Architectural Studies: JOSÉ JAVIER SARRÍA ODIAGA

Higher Polytechnic School: ÁNGEL MÉNDEZ

HEADS OF DEPARTMENTS

Molecular and Cell Biology and Environmental Sciences: JESÚS A. GÓMEZ OCHOA DE ALDA

Social Sciences, Law and Economics: LUIS A. ANGUITA VILLANUEVA

History and Heritage: MIGUEL LARRAÑAGA ZULUETA

Audiovisual Communication and Advertising: ANA MARTÍN LÓPEZ

Architectural Construction: FRANCISCO JAVIER ESPEJO GUTIÉRREZ

Philology: SANTIAGO LÓPEZ NAVIA

Journalism: FERNANDA SANTANA CRUZ

Architectural Projects: JOSÉ JAVIER SARRÍA ODIAGA

Psychology and Sociology: MIGUEL A. GANDARILLAS SOLINÍS

UNIVERSIDAD DE SEVILLA

Calle de San Fernando 4, 41004 Seville

Telephone: 95-455-10-00

Fax: 95-421-28-03

E-mail: relint6@us.es

Internet: www.us.es

Founded 1505

State control

Language of instruction: Spanish

Academic year: October to July

Rector: Dr MIGUEL FLORENCIO LORA

Vice-Rector (Research): Dr SATURIO RAMOS VICENTE

Vice-Rector (Academic Affairs): Dr JUAN JOSÉ IGLESIAS RODRÍGUEZ

Vice-Rector (Organization of Teaching): Dr PEDRO JOSÉ PAÚL ESCOLANO

Vice-Rector (Institutional Relations, International Relations and Cultural Extension): Dra MARYCRUZ ARCOS VARGAS

Vice-Rector (Graduate and Doctorate Affairs): Dr ANTONIO VENTOSA UCERO

Vice-Rector (Student Affairs): Dr PEDRO NÚÑEZ ABADES

Vice-Rector (Infrastructure and New Technology): Dr JOAQUÍN LUQUE RODRÍGUEZ

Vice-Rector (Technical Transfer): Dr LUIS GERARDO ONIEVA GIMÉNEZ

Vice-Rector (Teaching): Dr CARLOS ARIAS MARTÍN

Registrar: Dr JUAN MANUEL CALERO GALLEGO

Manager: JUAN IGNACIO FERRARO GARCÍA

Library Director: SONSOLES CELESTINO ANGULO

Number of teachers: 3,500

Number of students: 75,000

Publication: *Anales de la Universidad Hispalense* (annually)

DEANS

Faculty of Biology: FRANCISCO GIL MARTÍNEZ

Faculty of Chemistry: MARÍA ÁNGELES ÁLVAREZ RODRÍGUEZ

Faculty of Communication: MIGUEL NIETO NUÑO

Faculty of Economics and Business: FRANCISCO JAVIER LANDA BERCEBAL

Faculty of Education: SANTIAGO ROMERO GRANADOS

Faculty of Fine Arts: MILLÁN GARCÍA TORAL

Faculty of Geography and History: JOSÉ FERNÁNDEZ LÓPEZ

Faculty of Labour Science: CARLOS ARENAS POSADAS (acting)

Faculty of Law: MANUEL RAMÓN ALARCÓN CARACUEL

Faculty of Mathematics: JUAN MANUEL MUÑOZ PICHARDO

Faculty of Medicine: MARÍA DEL CARMEN OSUNA FERNÁNDEZ

Faculty of Odontology: RAFAEL LLAMAS CADAVAL

Faculty of Pharmacy: AGUSTÍN GARCÍA ASUERO

Faculty of Philology: JESÚS DÍAZ GARCÍA

Faculty of Philosophy: JOSÉ LUIS LÓPEZ LÓPEZ

Faculty of Physics: MANUEL GARCÍA LEÓN

Faculty of Psychology: FRANCISCO FERNÁNDEZ SERRA

DIRECTORS

Higher Technical School of Architecture: JOSÉ ORAD ARAGÓN

Higher Technical School of Computer Engineering: FRANCISCO PÉREZ GARCÍA

Higher Technical School of Industrial Engineering: FEDERICO PARÍS CARBALLO

University School of Architecture: ANTONIO RAMÍREZ DE ARELLANO AGUDO

University School of Business Studies: MANUEL REY MORENO

University School of Health Sciences: JESÚS REBOLLO ROLDÁN

University School of Technical Agricultural Engineering: JOSÉ MARÍA ABRIL HERNÁNDEZ

University Polytechnic School: JUAN ANTONIO PEDRAZ ANTÚNEZ

HEADS OF DEPARTMENTS

Business Administration, Marketing and Market Research: JOSÉ LUIS GALÁN GONZÁLEZ

Algebra: EMILIO BRIALES MORALES

Mathematical Analysis: GENARO LÓPEZ ACEDO

Human Anatomy and Embryology: JUAN JIMÉNEZ-CASTELLANOS BALLESTEROS

Social Anthropology: ELIAS ZAMORA ACOSTA

Computer Architecture and Technology: ANTONIO ABAD CIVIT BALCELLS

Cell Biology: JOSÉ TORREBLANCA LÓPEZ

Vegetal Biology and Ecology: CARLOS GRANADO LORENCIO

Medical Biochemistry and Molecular Biology: JUAN MIGUEL GUERRERO MONTAVEZ

Vegetal Biochemistry and Molecular Biology: FRANCISCO JAVIER FLORENCIO BELLIDO

Biochemistry, Bromatology, Toxicology and Forensic Medicine: ALBERTO MACHADO DE LA QUINTANA

Agroforestry: JOSÉ ORDOVAS ASCASO

Computation Science and Artificial Intelligence: JOSÉ ANTONIO ALONSO JIMÉNEZ

Basic Law (Roman Law, History of Law and Ecclesiastical Law of the State): ANTONIO MERCHAN ÁLVAREZ

Public Health: MANUEL CONDE HERRERA

Surgery: JOSÉ MARÍA ORTEGA BEVIA

Cytology and Normal and Pathological Histology: MARÍA VICTORIA SAN MARTÍN DIEZ

Audiovisual Communication, Publicity and Literature: MANUEL ÁNGEL VÁZQUEZ MEDEL

Architectural Construction I: MANUEL OLIVARES SANTIAGO

Architectural Construction II: JOSÉ MARÍA CALAMA RODRÍGUEZ

Accountancy and Finance: GUILLERMO JUAN SIERRA MOLINA

Crystallography, Mineralogy and Agricultural Chemistry: NICOLÁS BELLINFANTE CROCCI

Administrative Law and International Public Law: CONCEPCIÓN BARRERO RODRÍGUEZ

Civil Law and Private International Law: ÁNGEL MANUEL LÓPEZ Y LÓPEZ

Constitutional Law: JAVIER PÉREZ ROYO

Labour and Social Security Law: JAIME CASTIÑEIRA FERNÁNDEZ

Financial and Tax Law: ANTONIO MANUEL CUBERO TRUYO

Mercantile Law: ALBERTO DÍAZ MORENO

Penal and Procedural Law: JULIO GARCÍA CASAS

Drawing: JAIME GIL ARÉVALO

Teaching Self-Expression through Music, Plastic Arts and Movement: MARÍA JOSÉ PACHECO MORENO

Teaching Language, Literature and Integrated Philology: JOSÉ LUIS NAVARRO GARCÍA

Teaching Experimental and Social Sciences: ROSA DEL CID FERNÁNDEZ-MENSAQUE (acting)

Teaching Mathematics: MARÍA VICTORIA SÁNCHEZ GARCÍA

Teaching and Educational Organization: JUAN ANTONIO MORALES LOZANO

Applied Economics I: ANTONIO RALLO ROMERO

Applied Economics II: JOSÉ LUIS OSUNA LLANEZA

Applied Economics III: MARÍA JOSÉ VÁZQUEZ CUETO

Finance and Operational Management: ANTONIO RUIZ JIMÉNEZ

Differential Equations and Numerical Analysis: JOSÉ DOMINGO MARTÍN GÓMEZ (acting)

Electronics and Electromagnetism: ADORACIÓN RUEDA RUEDA

Nursing: CONCEPCIÓN GARCÍA GONZÁLEZ

Sculpture and History of the Plastic Arts: JUAN MANUEL MIÑARRO LÓPEZ

Statistics and Operational Research: JOAQUÍN MUÑOZ GARCÍA

Aesthetics and History of Philosophy: JOSÉ ANTONIO ANTÓN PACHECO

Stomatology: EMILIO JIMÉNEZ-CASTELLANOS BALLESTEROS

Graphic Expression in Building: DAVID MARÍN GARCÍA

Graphic and Architectural Expression: JOSÉ ANTONIO RUIZ DE LA ROSA

Pharmacy and Pharmaceutical Technology: ANTONIO MARÍA RABASCO ÁLVAREZ

Pharmacology: MARÍA TERESA SAENZ RODRÍGUEZ

Pharmacology, Paediatrics and Radiology: ANTONIO HEVIA ALONSO

German Philology: ASUNCIÓN SAINZ LERCHUNDI

French Philology: ELENA SUÁREZ SÁNCHEZ

Greek and Latin Philology: ANTONIO SANCHO ROYO

English Philology (English Language): JANE ARNOLD MORGAN

English Philology (English and North American Literature): JOSÉ CARNERO GONZÁLEZ

Integrated Philologies: MANUEL CARRERA DÍAZ

Philosophy of Law: ANTONIO ENRIQUE PÉREZ LUÑO

Philosophy, Logic and Philosophy of Science: JOSÉ MARÍA PRIETO SOLER

Applied Physics I: FABIÁN FRUTOS RAYEGO

Applied Physics II: FRANCISCO GASCÓN LATASA

Applied Physics III: MARCELO RODRÍGUEZ DANTA

Atomic, Molecular and Nuclear Physics: MANUEL LOZANO LEYVA

Condensed Matter Physics: MANUEL JIMÉNEZ MELENDO

Medical and Biophysical Physiology: JUAN RIBAS SERNA

Physiology and Zoology: MARÍA ELVIRA OCETE RUBIO

Physiotherapy: JULIÁN MAYA MARTÍN

Genetics: JOSEP CASADESUS PURSALS

Physical Geography and Regional Geographical Analysis: MARÍA FERNANDA PITA LÓPEZ

Human Geography: JUAN LUIS SUÁREZ DE VIVERO

Geometry and Topology: JOSÉ LUIS CABRERIZO JARÁIZ

Ancient History: PEDRO SAEZ FERNÁNDEZ

Contemporary History: JOSÉ MANUEL MACARRO VERA

American History: ANTONIO ACOSTA RODRÍGUEZ

History of Art: MARÍA JESÚS SANZ SERRANO

Medieval History and Historiography: MANUEL GONZÁLEZ JIMÉNEZ

Modern History: ANTONIO GARCÍA-BAQUERO GONZÁLEZ

Architectural History, Theory and Composition: VICTORIA PÉREZ ESCOLANO

Systems Engineering and Automation: FRANCISCO RODRÍGUEZ RUBIO

Design Engineering: ANTONIO MARTÍN NAVARRO

Electrical Engineering: ANTONIO GÓMEZ EXPOSITO

Electronic Engineering: LEOPOLDO GARCÍA FRANQUELO

Power Engineering and Fluid Mechanics: TOMÁS SÁNCHEZ LENCERO

Graphical Engineering: MIGUEL BERMEJO HERRERO

Mechanical and Materials Engineering: ENRIQUE J. HERRERA LUQUE

Chemical Engineering: VICENTE FLORES LUQUE

Chemical and Environmental Engineering: JOSÉ VALE PARAPAR

Spanish Language, Linguistics and Theory of Literature: RAFAEL CANO AGUILAR

Computer Languages and Systems: JOSÉ CRISTÓBAL RIQUELME SANTOS

Spanish Literature: PEDRO M. PIÑERO RAMÍREZ

Applied Mathematics I: FELIPE MATEOS MATEOS

Applied Mathematics II: ANTONIO FERNÁNDEZ CARRIÓN

Continuum Mechanics, Theory of Structures and Land Engineering: JOSÉ FÉLIX ESCRIG PALLARES

Medicine: RAMÓN PÉREZ CANO

Metaphysics and Current Developments in Philosophy, Ethics and Political Philosophy: JOSÉ MANUEL SEVILLA FERNÁNDEZ

Research Methods and Diagnosis in Education: EDUARDO GARCÍA JIMÉNEZ

Microbiology: EVILIO JOSÉ PEREA PÉREZ

Microbiology and Parasitology: MANUEL MEGIAS GUIJO

Industrial Organization and Business Management: FRANCISCO DE LAS CUEVAS GIL

Journalism I: ANTONIO LUIS GARCÍA GUTIÉRREZ

Journalism II: JOSÉ MANUEL GÓMEZ Y MÉNDEZ

Personality, Psychological Assessment and Treatment: MERCEDES BORDA MAS

Painting: FRANCISCO ARQUILLO TORRES

Chiropody: LUIS MARTÍNEZ CAMUÑA

Prehistory and Archaeology: OSWALDO ARTEAGA MATUTE

Architectural Projects: JOSÉ ENRIQUE LÓPEZ-CANTI MORALES

Evolutionary and Educational Psychology: MARÍA VICTORIA HIDALGO GARCÍA

Experimental Psychology: JOSÉ CARLOS CARACUEL TUBIO

Social Psychology: SILVERIO BARRIGA JIMÉNEZ

Psychiatry: JOSÉ GINER UBAGO

Analytical Chemistry: ALFONSO GUIRAUM PÉREZ

Physical Chemistry: ALFREDO MAESTRE ÁLVAREZ

Inorganic Chemistry: ALFONSO CABALLERO MARTÍNEZ

Organic Chemistry: JOSÉ FUENTES MOTA

Organic and Pharmaceutical Chemistry: FELIPE ALCUDIA GONZÁLEZ

Sociology: CUSTODIO DELGADO VALBUENA

Electronic Technology: MANUEL VALENCIA BARRERO

Theory and History of Education and Social Education: JUAN AGUSTÍN MORÓN MARCHENA

Economic Theory and Political Economy: CAMILO LEBON FERNÁNDEZ

Town Planning: RAMÓN QUEIRO FILGUEIRA

ATTACHED CENTRES AND INSTITUTES

'Cardenal Spinola' Centre for Advanced Studies: Campus Universitário, 41930 Bormujos (Sevilla); tel. 95-448-80-00; fax 95-448-80-10; e-mail info@ceuandalucia.com; internet www.ceuandalucia.com/indice.html; education and educational psychology; Dir MANUEL GÓMEZ GUILLÉN.

'Francisco Maldonado' University College: Campo de Cipreses 1, (Edif. Antigua Universidad), 41640 Osuna; tel. 95-582-02-92; fax 95-582-02-89; internet www.euosuna.org; Dir JAVIER MUÑOZ RANGEL.

'Cruz Roja Española' University College of Nursing: Avda de la Cruz Roja 1, 41009 Seville; tel. and fax 95-435-09-97; e-mail creseue@creseue.infonegocio.com; internet www.infonegocio.com/creseue; Dir FÉLIX JULIO JARA FERNÁNDEZ.

'Virgen del Rocío' University College of Nursing: Avda Manuel Siurot s/n, Edificio de Gobierno, 41013 Seville; tel. 95-501-34-34; fax 95-501-34-73; e-mail eu.hvr.sspa@juntadeandalucia.es; Dir MERCEDES BUENO FERRÁN.

University College of Tourism: C/ Isabela 1, 41013 Seville; tel. 95-423-87-97; fax 95-423-89-42; e-mail cpino@eusa.cenp.es; internet www.eusa.cenp.es/turismo.htm; Dir FRANCISCO GUERRERO DÍAZ.

National Accelerators Centre: Parque Tecnológico Cartuja 93, Avda Thomas A. Edison s/n, 41092 Seville; tel. 95-446-05-53; fax 95-446-01-45; e-mail respaldiza@us.es; internet www.us.es/cna; Dir MIGUEL ÁNGEL RESPALDIZA GALISTEO.

Institute of Education: Facultad de Ciencias Económicas y Empresariales, Avda Ramón y Cajal s/n, 41018 Seville; tel. 95-455-67-91; e-mail colmenar@us.es; internet www.ice.us.es; Dir JOSÉ MARÍA MESA LÓPEZ-COLMENAR.

Institute of Regional Development: Avda S. Francisco Javier 24, Edif. Sevilla 1, 41018 Seville; tel. 95-493-40-40; fax 95-493-25-65; e-mail idr@idr.es; Dir CARLOS ROMÁN DEL RÍO.

Institute of Languages: Avda Reina Mercedes s/n, 41012 Seville; tel. 95-455-11-55; fax 95-455-14-50; e-mail idijsec@us.es; internet www.us.es/idi; Dir MARÍA ISABEL ROMÁN GUTIÉRREZ.

Institute of Developmental Biology: Facultad de Medicina, Avda Sánchez Pizjuán 4, 1a planta, 41009 Seville; tel. 95-455-28-65; fax 95-438-16-62; e-mail secanatomia@us.es; Dir ADELA QUESADA RUÍZ.

Institute of Construction Sciences: Escuela Técnica Superior de Arquitectura, Avda Reina Mercedes 2, 41012 Seville; tel. 95-455-65-95; e-mail mjose@arqui4.us.es; internet www.iucc.us.es; Dir JUAN JOSÉ SENDRA SALAS.

Institute of Legal Medicine and Forensic Science: Facultad de Medicina, Avda

Sánchez Pizjuán 4, 41009 Seville; tel. 95-455-98-39; fax 95-437-26-76; Dir LUIS FRONTELA CARRERA.

Andalusian Inter-university Institute of Criminology (Seville Branch): Escuela Técnica Superior de Ingeniería Informática, Avda Reina Mercedes s/n, 41012 Seville; tel. 95-455-13-96; fax 95-455-13-97; e-mail iaic@us.es; internet www.iaic.us.es; Dir BORJA MAPELLI CAFFARENA.

García Oviedo Institute: Facultad de Derecho, Avda del Cid s/n, 41004 Seville; tel. 95-455-12-26; fax 95-455-78-99; e-mail instgarciaov@us.es; internet www.us.es/iugo; administrative law; Dir FRANCISCO LÓPEZ MENUDO.

UNIVERSITAT DE VALÈNCIA
(University of Valencia)

Avda Blasco Ibáñez 13, 46071 Valencia

Telephone: 96-386-41-00

Fax: 96-386-48-85

E-mail: rectorado@uv.es

Internet: www.uv.es

Founded 1502

State control

Languages of instruction: Valencian, Spanish

Academic year: October to September

Rector: FRANCISCO TOMÁS VERT

Vice-Rector (Scientific Policy and International Co-operation): MANUEL COSTA TALENS

Vice-Rector (Economics and Administration): MATILDE FERNÁNDEZ BLANCO

Vice-Rector (Statutes and Normative Rules): JUAN CARLOS CARBONELL MATEU

Vice-Rector (University Extension and Society Relations): FRANCISCO TORTOSA GIL

Vice-Rector (Academic): JOSE MARÍA GOERLICH PESET

Vice-Rector (Institutional Relations): JOSE MANUEL RODRIGO GÓMEZ

Vice-Rector (Studies and Academic Organization): ANTONIO ARIÑO VILLARROYA

Vice-Rector (Infrastructure and Planning): AURELIO BELTRÁN PORTER

Vice-Rector (Research): MARIA JOSEP CUENCA ORDINYANA

Vice-Rector (Information and Communication Technologies): VICENTE CERVERÓN LLEÓ

Vice-Rector (Culture): RAFAEL GIL SALINAS

Registrar: MARIA LUISA CONTRI SEMPERE

Manager: JOAN OLTRA VIDAL

Library Director: JOSEP LLUÍS SIRERA TURÓ

Library of 227,453 vols and 2,720 MSS; libraries are also attached to each faculty

Number of teachers: 3,159

Number of students: 49,858

Publication: *Memoria Anual*

DEANS

Faculty of Biology: JUAN JAVIER DÍAZ MAYANS

Faculty of Chemistry: JOSÉ MARÍA MORATAL MASCARELL

Faculty of Economics: ENRIQUE VILLARREAL RODRÍGUEZ

Faculty of Geography and History: JORGE HERMOSILLA PLA

Faculty of Law: CARLOS LUIS ALFONSO MELLADO

Faculty of Mathematics: JUAN JOSÉ NUÑO BALLESTEROS

Faculty of Medicine and Odontology: ESTEBAN MORCILLO SÁNCHEZ

Faculty of Pharmacy: ANTONIO SIMÓN FUENTES

Faculty of Philology: JOSEP LLUÍS CANET VALLÉS

Faculty of Philosophy and Education: MANUEL ENRIQUE VÁZQUEZ GARCÍA

Faculty of Physical Activity and Sport: VICENTE CARRATALÁ DEVAL

Faculty of Physics: CARLOS FERREIRA GARCÍA

Faculty of Psychology: MA. VICENTA MESTRE ESCRIVÁ

Faculty of Social Sciences: ERNEST GARCÍA I GARCÍA

DIRECTORS

Higher Technical School of Engineering: JOAN V. PELECHANO FABREGAT

'Ausiàs March' Teacher Training College: BERNARDO GÓMEZ ALFONSO

School of Nursing: LLUÍS FRANCESC SANJUAN I NEBOT

School of Physiotherapy: CELEDONIA IGUAL CAMACHO

HEADS OF DEPARTMENTS

Faculty of Biological Sciences:

Functional Biology and Physical Anthropology: MARÍA DOLORES GARCERÁ ZAMORANO

Vegetal Biology: JUAN BAUTISTA DEL AMO MARCO

Biochemistry and Molecular Biology: PEDRO CARRASCO SORLÍ

Botany: GERARDO STÜBING MARTÍNEZ

Genetics: JOAN FERRÉ MANZANERO

Geology: JUAN USERA MATA

Microbiology and Ecology: ROSA MA. MIRACLE SOLÉ

Zoology: VICENTE ROCA VELASCO

Faculty of Mathematics:

Algebra: JOSE RAMÓN MARTÍNEZ VERDUCH

Mathematical Analysis: OSCAR FRANCISCO BLASCO DE LA CRUZ

Astronomy and Astrophysics: JOSE MARÍA IBÁÑEZ CABANELL

Statistics and Operational Research: RAMÓN ÁLVAREZ-VALDÉS

Geometry and Topology: MA. CARMEN ROMERO FUSTER

Applied Mathematics: FRANCESC ARANDIGA LLAUDES

Faculty of Social Sciences:

Sociology and Social Anthropology: RAFAEL VICENT XAMBO OLMOS

Social Work and Social Services: MARÍA JOSE HERVAS GUANTER

Faculty of Economics:

Economic Analysis: JAVIER ANDRÉS DOMINGO

Accountancy: VICENTE RIPOLL FELIU

Business Management: JOSÉ PLÁ BARBER

Applied Economics: ROBERTO ESCUDER VALLÉS

Financial Economics: MA. PAZ JORDÁ DURÁ

Economic Structure: VICENT SOLER I MARCO

Business Finance: C. JOSÉ GARCÍA MARTÍN

Mathematics in Economics and Business: RAMÓN SALA GARRIDO

Marketing and Market Research: ENRIQUE BIGNÉ ALCAÑIZ

Faculty of Law:

Administrative and Procedural Law: (vacant)

Civil Law: MARIO E. CLEMENTE MEORO

Constitutional Law, Political Science and Administrative Law: VICENT FRANCH FERRER

Philosophy of Law, Ethical and Political Philosophy: ERNESTO VIDAL GIL

Financial Law and History of Law: JORGE CORREA BALLESTER

International Law: CARLOS AURELIO ESPLUGUES MOTA

Mercantile Law: VICENTE ANTONIO SOTILLO MARTÍ

Penal Law: ENRIQUE ORTS BERENGUER

Roman and Ecclesiastical State Law: MA. LUISA JORDAN VILLACAMPA

Labour and Social Security Law: JUAN MANUEL RAMÍREZ MARTÍNEZ

Faculty of Pharmacy:

Pharmacy and Pharmaceutical Technology: MARINA HERRAEZ DOMÍNGUEZ

Pharmacology: MA. CARMEN ZAFRA-POLO CARRERAS

Preventive Medicine and Public Health, Bromatology, Toxicology and Forensic Medicine: GUILLERMINA FONT PÉREZ

Parasitology and Cell Biology: SANTIAGO MAS COMA

Faculty of Philology:

English and German Philology: BARRY PENNOCK SPECK

Catalan Philology: J. RAFAEL RAMOS ALFAJARÍN

Classical Philology: JAIME SILES RUIZ

Spanish Philology: MA. TERESA ECHENIQUE ELIZONDO

French and Italian Philology: ANA MONLEÓN DOMÍNGUEZ

Theory of Languages: CARLOS HERNÁNDEZ SACRISTÁN

Faculty of Philosophy and Education:

Philosophy: SERGIO SEVILLA SEGURA

Metaphysics and Theory of Knowledge: JOSEP LLUÍS BLASCO ESTELLÉS

Logic and Philosophy of Science: RAFAEL BENEYTO TORRES

Research Methods and Diagnostics in Education: JOSÉ GONZÁLEZ SUCH

Theory of Education: BERNARDO GARGALLO LÓPEZ

Comparative Education and History of Education: LUIS MIGUEL LÁZARO LORENTE

Teaching and School Organization: MA. LUISA MONERA OLMOS

Faculty of Physics:

Applied Physics: ALFREDO SEGURA GARCÍA DEL RÍO

Atomic, Molecular and Nuclear Physics: MANUEL RAMÓN CASES RUIZ

Theoretical Physics: JORDI VIDAL PERONA

Optics: PEDRO ANDRÉS BOU

Thermodynamics: JOAQUÍN MELIÁ MIRALLES

Faculty of Geography and History:

Prehistory and Archaeology: EMILIO AURA TORTOSA

History of Antiquity and Written Culture: FRANCISCO GIMENO BLAY

Medieval History: PAULINO IRADIEL MURUGARREN

Modern History: RAFAEL BENÍTEZ SÁNCHEZ-BLANCO

Contemporary History: TERESA CARNERO ARBAT

Geography: EUGENIO LUIS BURRIEL DE ORUETA

History of Art: JOSEP MONTESINOS I MARTÍNEZ

Faculty of Medicine and Odontology:

Anatomy and Embryology: (vacant)

Surgery: FRANCISCO GOMAR SANCHO

Stomatology: ANTONIO FONS FONT

Physiology: ANTONIO M. ALBEROLA AGUILAR

History of Science and Documentation: MA. FRANCISCA ABAD GARCÍA

Medicine: JUAN FRANCISCO ASCASO GIMILIO

Pathology: AMANDO PEYDRO OLAYA

Paediatrics, Obstetrics and Gynaecology: ROBERTO HERNÁNDEZ MARCO

Faculty of Psychology:

Basic Psychology: ESTHER BARBERÁ HEREDIA

Social Psychology: ROSARIO ZURRIAGA LLORENS

Methodology in Behavioural Sciences: MA. DOLORES SANCERNI BEITIA

Personality, Assessment and Psychological Treatment: M. CARMEN MARTORELL PALLÁS

Evolutionary and Educational Psychology: EDUARDO VIDAL ABARCA

Psychobiology: VICENTE SIMÓN PÉREZ

Faculty of Chemistry:

Analytical Chemistry: CARLOS MONGAY FERNÁNDEZ

Physical Chemistry: ISIDRO SALVADOR MONZÓ MANZANET

Inorganic Chemistry: FRANCISCO ESTEVAN ESTEVAN

Organic Chemistry: DESAMPARADOS TORTAJADA LÓPEZ

Higher Technical School of Engineering:

Computer Science: JESÚS ALBERT BLANCO

Electronic Engineering: JAVIER CALPE MARAVILLA

Chemical Engineering: ANTONI MARTÍNEZ ANDREU

Teacher Training College:

Teaching of Mathematics: ALEJANDRO FERNÁNDEZ LAJUSTICIA

Teaching of Language and Literature: MATEO DEL POZO DE LA VIUDA

Teaching of Experimental and Social Sciences: VALENTÍN GAVIDIA CATALÁN

Teaching of Self-Expression through Music, Plastic Arts and Movement: CARMINA PASCUAL BAÑOS

School of Nursing:

Nursing: ANTONIO MERELLES TORMO

School of Physiotherapy:

Physiotherapy: JOSÉ SANTOS FRUTOS

Other Departments:

Physical and Sports Education: VÍCTOR JOSÉ TELLA MUÑOZ

ATTACHED INSTITUTES

Institute of Studies of Women: Blasco Ibáñez 21, Valencia; tel. 96-398-31-35; e-mail iu.estudis.dona@uv.es; internet www.uv.es/%7Eiued.

Institute of Materials Science: Apdo de Correos 22085, 46071 Valencia; tel. 96-354-48-58; fax 96-354-36-33; e-mail icmuv@uv.es; internet www.uv.es/icmuv; Dir RAFAEL IBÁÑEZ PUCHADES.

Institute of Molecular Science: Departamento Química Inorganica, Universidad de Valencia, Dr. Moliner 50, 46100 Burjassot; tel. and fax 96-354-44-15; e-mail eugenio.coronado@uv.es; internet www.uv.es/%7Eicmol/index.htm; Dir EUGENIO CORONADO.

Cavanilles Institute of Biodiversity and Evolutionary Biology: Polígono La Coma s/n, 46980 Paterna (Valencia); internet www.uv.es/cavanilles/index.htm.

Institute of Creativity and Educational Innovation: Universidad de Valencia, Avda Blasco Ibáñez 21, 1a Planta, 46010 Valencia; tel. 96-386-41-32; fax 96-369-60-23; internet www.uv.es/icie/index.html.

Institute of Corpuscular Physics: Edificio Institutos de Investigación, Apdo de Correos 22085, 46071 Valencia; tel. 96-354-34-73; fax 96-354-34-88; e-mail juan.fuster@ific.uv.es; internet ific.uv.es; Dir JUAN A. FUSTER VERDÚ.

Institute of International Economics: Campus dels Tarongers, 46002 Valencia; tel. 96-382-84-37; fax 96-382-84-34; e-mail secretaria@iei.uv.es; internet iei.uv.es; Dir J. ISMAEL FERNÁNDEZ GUERRERO.

Interuniversity Institute of Valencian Philology: Facultat de Filologia, Blasco Ibáñez 32, 46010 Valencia; tel. 96-386-40-90; fax 96-386-44-93; e-mail francesc.perez@uv.es; internet www.uv.es/~iifv.

Institute of Robotics: e-mail juan.domingo@uv.es; internet robotica.uv.es; Dir JUAN DE MATA DOMINGO ESTEVE.

'López Piñero' Institute of the History of Science and Documentation: Facultad de Medicina, Blasco Ibáñez 15, 46010 Valencia; tel. 96-386-41-64; fax 96-361-39-75; e-mail iu.historia.ciencia.doc@uv.es; internet www.uv.es/~fresquet/TEXTOS; Dir Prof. Dr JOSÉ LUIS FRESQUET FEBRER.

Botanical Garden: C/ Quart 80. 46008 Valencia; tel. 96-315-68-00; e-mail info@botanic.org; internet www.jardibotanic.org; Dir ANTONI AGUILELLA PALASÍ.

Astronomical Observatory: Edifici Instituts d'Investigació, Polígon La Coma, 46980 Paterna (Valencia); tel. 96-354-34-83; fax 96-354-37-44; e-mail observatori.astronomic@uv.es; internet www.uv.es/obsast; Dir VICENT J. MARTÍNEZ.

UNIVERSIDAD DE VALLADOLID

Plaza de Santa Cruz 8, 47002 Valladolid

Telephone: 983-29-14-67

Fax: 983-42-32-34

E-mail: relint@uva.es

Internet: www.uva.es

Founded 13th c.

Academic year: October to June

Rector: JOSÉ MARÍA SANZ SERNA

Vice-Rector (Research): EMILIO SUÁREZ DE LA TORRE

Vice-Rector (Academic Affairs): ÁNGEL MARÍA CARTÓN LÓPEZ

Vice-Rector (Economy): PEDRO ANTONIO FUERTES OLIVERA

Vice-Rector (Students and Social Affairs): ALFONSO CARVAJAL GARCÍA-PANDO

Vice-Rector (Academic Organization): MARÍA ISABEL DEL VAL VALDIVIESO

Vice-Rector (International Relations): MARÍA JOSÉ SÁEZ BREZMES

Vice-Rector (University Extension): MARÍA TERESA ALARIO TRIGUEROS

Vice-Rector (Facilities): DARIO ÁLVAREZ ÁLVAREZ

Vice-Rector (Palencia Campus): ELENA HIDALGO RODRÍGUEZ

Vice-Rector (Soria Campus): EMILIA LATORRE MACARRÓN

Vice-Rector (Segovia Campus): SANTIAGO HIDALGO ALONSO

Registrar: JUAN ANTONIO BONACHÍA HERNANDO

Manager: MONTSERRAT BOTAYA SINDREU

Library Director: MARÍA SOLEDAD CARNICER ARRIBAS

Library of 581,920 vols, 13,066 periodicals and 5,050 audiovisual items

Number of teachers: 2,427

Number of students: 33,100, (incl. 1,320 graduates)

DEANS

Faculty of Arts: LUIS ANTONIO SANTOS DOMÍNGUEZ

Faculty of Economics and Business: JOSEFA EUGENIA FERNÁNDEZ ARUFE

Faculty of Education and Social Work: JOSÉ MARÍA ROMÁN SÁNCHEZ

Faculty of Law: PALOMA BIGLINO CAMPOS

Faculty of Medicine: SANTIAGO RODRÍGUEZ GARCÍA

Faculty of Science: GERARDO GONZÁLEZ BENITO

Faculty of Labour Science (Palencia): ANTONIO JOSÉ PIÑEYROA DE LA FUENTE

Faculty of Translation and Interpretation (Soria): MIGUEL IBÁÑEZ RODRÍGUEZ

Faculty of Social, Legal and Communication Sciences (Segovia): FRANCISCO JAVIER GARCÍA ROCA

DIRECTORS

Higher Technical School of Architecture: LEOPOLDO URIA IGLESIAS

Higher Technical School of Computer Engineering: VALENTÍN CARDEÑOSO PAYO

Higher Technical School of Industrial Engineering: JOSÉ ANTONIO GARRIDO GARCÍA

Higher Technical School of Telecommunications Engineering: EVARISTO JOSÉ ABRIL DOMINGO

Higher Technical School of Agricultural Engineering (Palencia): FELIPE BRAVO OVIEDO

School of Nursing: ISABEL GUERRA CUESTA

School of Business Studies: MANUEL DE PRADA MORAGA

University Polytechnic School: MARÍA ÁNGELES MARTÍN BRAVO

School of Education (Palencia): MARÍA CARMEN ALARIO TRIGUEROS

School of Computer Science (Segovia): JOSÉ IGNACIO FARRÁN MARTÍN

School of Teacher Training (Segovia): JESÚS NIETO DÍEZ

School of Education (Soria): JOSÉ MARÍA MARBÁN PRIETO

School of Business Studies (Soria): FERNANDO JAVIER DÍAZ MARTÍNEZ

School of Physiotherapy (Soria): MANUEL CUERVAS-MONS FINAT

School of Agricultural Engineering (Soria): JESÚS CIRIA CIRIA

'Doctor Sala de Pablo' School of Nursing (Soria): PILAR GONZALO VICENTE

HEADS OF DEPARTMENTS

Algebra, Geometry and Topology: FÉLIX DELGADO DE LA MATA

Mathematical Analysis and Teaching of Mathematics: FERNANDO SÁIZ ZALDO

Pathological Anatomy, Microbiology, Preventive Medicine and Public Health, Legal and Forensic Medicine: ANTONIO RODRÍGUEZ TORRES

Anatomy and Radiology: ENRIQUE BARBOSA AYUCAR

Cell Biology, Histology and Pharmacology: MANUEL JOSÉ GAYOSO RODRÍGUEZ

Biochemistry, Molecular Biology and Physiology: CONSTANCIO GONZÁLEZ MARTÍNEZ

Materials Science and Metallurgical Engineering, Engineering Draughtsmanship, Cartography, Geodesy and Photogrammetry, Mechanical and Process Engineering: MANUEL FEDERICO LÓPEZ APARICIO

Agroforestry: JOSÉ MARÍA DEL ARCO MONTERO

Surgery, Ophthalmology. Otorhinolaryngology and Physiotherapy: GUILLERMO RAMOS SEISDEDOS

Civil Law: IGNACIO SERRANO GARCÍA

Constitutional, Procedural and Ecclesiastical State Law: ERNESTO PEDRAZ PENALVA

Mercantile, Labour and Private International Law: ANTONIO JAVIER ADRIÁN ARNAIZ

Penal Law, History of Law and of Institutions, Philosophy of Law and Roman Law: DAVID TORRES SANZ

Public Law: JOSÉ LUIS MARTÍNEZ LÓPEZ-MUÑIZ

Teaching of Self-Expression through Music, Plastic Arts and Movement: MARÍA ANTONIA VIRGILI BLANQUET

Teaching of Language and Literature: JOSÉ LINO BARRIO VALENCIA

Teaching of Social and Experimental Sciences: ISIDORO GONZÁLEZ GALLEGO

Applied Economics: AVELINO GARCÍA VILLAREJO

Financial Economics and Accountancy: BEGOÑA BUSTO MARROQUÍN

Electricity and Electronics: JUAN JOSÉ BARBOLLA SANCHO

Nursing: PEDRO MARTÍN VILLAMOR

Statistics and Operational Research: JOSÉ ANTONIO MENÉNDEZ FERNÁNDEZ

Classical Philology: JOSÉ IGNACIO BLANCO PÉREZ

French and German Philology: FRANCISCA ARAMBURU RIERA

English Philology: MARÍA JOSÉ CRESPO ALLUE

Philosophy, Logic, Philosophy of Science, Theory and History of Education: ALFREDO FAUSTINO MARCOS MARTÍNEZ

Applied Physics and External Geodynamics: JOSÉ LUIS CASANOVA ROQUE

Condensed Matter Physics, Crystallography and Mineralogy: JOSÉ ANTONIO SAJA SÁEZ

Theoretical, Atomic, Molecular, and Nuclear Physics and Optics: SANTIAGO MAR SARDAÑA

Principles of Economic Analysis and Economic History and Institutions: ÁNGEL GARCÍA SANZ

Geography: PEDRO CABALLERO FERNÁNDEZ-RUFETE

Ancient and Medieval History: TOMÁS GARABITO GÓMEZ

History of Art: FRANCISCO J. DE LA PLAZA SANTIAGO

Modern, Contemporary and American History, Journalism, Audiovisual Communication and Advertising: CELSO JESÚS ALMUIÑA FERNÁNDEZ

Information Science (Computer Architecture and Technology, Computation Sciences and Artificial Intelligence, Computer Languages and Systems): CARLOS JAVIER ALONSO GONZÁLEZ

Agricultural and Forestry Engineering: LUIS MANUEL NAVAS GRACIA

Structural Engineering, Land Engineering and Construction: JESÚS FEIJO MUÑOZ

Systems Engineering and Automation: JOSÉ RAMÓN PERÁN GONZÁLEZ

Electrical Engineering: MANUEL VICENTE RIESCO SANZ

Power Engineering and Fluid Mechanics: MARÍA DEL CARMEN MARTÍNEZ GONZÁLEZ

Chemical Engineering: PEDRO ANTONIO GARCÍA ENCINA

Spanish Language: MARÍA ISABEL ACERO DURÁNTEZ

Spanish Literature, Theory of Literature and Comparative Literature: MARÍA DEL PILAR CELMA VALERO

Applied Mathematics: CÉSAR PALENCIA DE LARA

Medicine: JESÚS BUSTAMANTE BUSTAMANTE

Business Organization, Marketing and Market Research: CESAREO HERNÁNDEZ IGLESIAS

Education: MARÍA DEL CARMEN GÓMEZ NIETO

Paediatrics and Immunology, Obstetrics and Gynaecology, Nutrition and Bromatology, Psychiatry and History of Science: ALFREDO BLANCO QUIRÓS

Prehistory, Archaeology, Social Anthropology and Historiography: CARLOS SANZ MINGUEZ

Vegetal Production and Forest Resources: JOSÉ LUIS VILLARÍAS MORADILLO

Psychology: ANASTASIO OVEJERO BERNAL

Analytical Chemistry: JOSÉ LUIS BERNAL YAGUE

Physical Chemistry and Inorganic Chemistry: DANIEL MIGUEL SAN JOSÉ

Organic Chemistry: ALFONSO GONZÁLEZ ORTEGA

Sociology and Social Work: FLORENTINA MORENO PELÁEZ

Electronic Technology: SANTIAGO LORENZO MATILLA

Architectural Theory and Architectural Projects: JUAN CARLOS ARNUNCIO PASTOR

Signal and Communications Theory and Telemetry: MIGUEL LÓPEZ CORONADO

Town Planning and Architectural Display: CARLOS FRANCISCO MONTES SERRANO

ATTACHED INSTITUTES AND CENTRES

Institute of Biology and Molecular Genetics: C/ Ramón y Cajal 7, 47005 Valladolid; tel. 983-42-30-85; fax 983-42-35-88; e-mail ibgm@bio.uva.es; Dir MARÍA CARMEN DOMÍNGUEZ LOBATON.

Institute of European Studies: Plaza Universidad s/n, 47002 Valladolid; tel. and fax 983-42-36-52; e-mail seciee@uva.es; internet www.der.uva.es/iee; Dir MARCOS SACRISTÁN REPRESA.

Simancas Institute of History: C/ Real de Burgos s/n, 47011 Valladolid; tel. and fax 983-42-35-27; e-mail iushima@uva.es; internet www3.uva.es/simancas; Dir JULIO VALDEÓN BARUQUE.

Castilla y León Neurosciences Institute: C/ Ramón y Cajal 7, 47005 Valladolid; tel. 983-42-30-79; internet www-incyl.usal.es.

Institute of Applied Ophthalmobiology: C/ Ramón y Cajal 7, 47005 Valladolid; tel. 983-42-32-74; fax 983-42-32-35; e-mail ioba@ioba.med.uva.es; internet www.ioba.med.uva.es; Dir JOSÉ CARLOS PASTOR JIMENO.

Inter-University Institute of Latin American and Portuguese Studies: Casa del Tratado, Tordesillas; tel. 983-77-18-06; fax 983-79-63-38; internet www3.uva.es/ieip; Dir CÉSAR HERNÁNDEZ ALONSO.

Institute of Town Planning: Avda Salamanca s/n, 47014 Valladolid; tel. 983-42-34-65; fax 983-42-34-39; e-mail insur@uva.es; internet www3.uva.es/iuu; Dir JUAN LUIS DE LAS RIVAS SANZ.

Asian Studies Centre: Po Prado de la Magdalena s/n 47011 Valladolid; tel. 983-18-38-15; fax 983-42-30-56; e-mail cea@uva.es; internet www3.uva.es/cea; Dir (vacant).

Centre for Lower Atmosphere Research: Po Prado de la Magdalena s/n 47011 Valladolid; tel. and fax 983-42-31-30; e-mail jois@latuv.uva.es; Dir JOSÉ LUIS CASANOVA ROQUE.

Sugar Technology Centre: C/ Real de Burgos s/n, 47011 Valladolid; tel. 983-42-35-63; fax 983-42-36-16; e-mail transi@cta.uva.es; internet www.cta.uva.es; Dir MARÍA TERESA GARCÍA CUBERO.

Geographical Information Systems and Teledetection Technological Centre: Po. Prado de la Magdalena s/n, 47011 Valladolid; tel. 983-42-31-50; fax 983-42-31-49; e-mail csig@fyl.uva.es; Dir (vacant).

Institute of Medical Sciences: C/ Ramón y Cajal 7, 47005 Valladolid; tel. 983-42-34-76; Dir JAVIER CASTAÑEDA CASADO.

Institute of Business Mathematics and Regional Development Studies: Avda Valle Esgueva 6, 47011 Valladolid; Dir JULIO GARCÍA VILLALON.

Institute of Pharmacoepidemiology: C/ Ramón y Cajal 7, 47005 Valladolid; tel. 983-26-30-21; fax 983-42-30-22; e-mail ife@ife.uva.es; internet www.ife.uva.es; Dir ALFONSO CARVAJAL GARCÍA-PANDO.

History of Science and Technology Institute: Po. Prado de la Magdalena s/n, 47011 Valladolid; tel. and fax 983-42-31-79; e-mail esteban@maf.uva.es; Dir MARIANO ESTEBAN PIÑEIRO.

Institute of Educational Research: Po. de Belén 1, Campus Miguel Delibes, 47011 Valladolid; tel. 983-18-38-39; fax 983-42-34-36; e-mail iice@iice.uva.es; internet www3.uva.es/iice; Dir CARLOS HERMINIO MORIYÓN MOJICA.

Institute of Research and Industrial Technological Development: Po. del Cauce s/n, 47011 Valladolid; tel. 983-42-33-64; fax 983-42-33-63; e-mail miguel.villamanan@eis.uva.es; Dir MIGUEL ÁNGEL VILLAMAÑAN OLFOS.

Institute of Neurotechnology and Related Techniques: Co. Cementerio s/n, Campus Miguel Delibes, 47011 Valladolid; tel. 983-42-36-65; fax 983-42-36-67; e-mail ejabril@tel.uva.es; Dir EVARISTO JOSÉ ABRIL DOMINGO.

Institute of Quality in Public Health: Plaza Santa Cruz 5, 47002 Valladolid; tel. 983-42-35-49; fax 983-42-35-48; e-mail icas@uva.es; internet www3.uva.es/icas; Dir JOSÉ LUIS GARCÍA ROLDÁN.

'Juan de Villanueva' Construction Institute: Avda Salamanca s/n, 47014 Valladolid; tel. and fax 983-42-34-42; e-mail edifica@modulor.arq.uva.es; Dir JESÚS FEIJO MUÑOZ.

Environmental Technology and Mangement Institute: Po. Prado de la Magdalena s/n, 47011 Valladolid; tel. and fax 983-42-31-66; e-mail pedro@ig.cie.uva.es; Dir PEDRO GARCÍA ENCINA.

Institute of Advanced Technology in Production: Po. del Cauce s/n, 47011 Valladolid; tel. 983-42-33-68; fax 983-42-33-10; e-mail lara@marte.eis.uva.es; Dir ANTONIO LARA FERIA.

Institute of Bilingual Terminology and Specialized Translation: Co. Cementerio s/n, Campus Miguel Delibes, 47011 Valladolid; tel. 983-26-64-20; fax 983-26-64-76; e-mail purifer@itbyte.uva.es; internet www3.uva.es/itbyte/itbyte_main.htm; Dir PURIFICACIÓN FERNÁNDEZ NISTAL.

Spanish Institute of Architecture: Avda Salamanca s/n, 47014 Valladolid; tel. 983-42-36-92; fax 983-42-34-25; e-mail iea@modulor.arq.uva.es; internet www.iea.uva.es; Dir JAVIER RIVERA BLANCO.

Agricultural and Food Technology Institute: Avda Madrid 57, 34004 Palencia; tel. 979-10-83-03; fax 979-10-83-01; e-mail itagra@uva.es; Dir FERNANDO GONZÁLEZ HERRERO.

Institute of Forensic Computer Science: Co. Cementerio s/n, Campus Miguel Delibes, 47011 Valladolid; tel. 983-42-30-98; e-mail nicabe@der.uva.es; Dir ERNESTO PEDRAZ PENALVA.

Institute of Sport: Plaza Universidad s/n, 47002 Valladolid; Dir ABELARDO RODRÍGUEZ MERINO.

Institute of Studies on Alcohol and Drugs: C/ Ramón y Cajal 7, 47005 Valladolid; tel. 983-42-30-77; fax 983-42-30-22; e-mail alvarez@med.uva.es; Dir FRANCISCO JAVIER ÁLVAREZ GONZÁLEZ.

Institute of Endocrinology and Nutrition: C/ Ramón y Cajal 7, 47005 Valladolid; tel. 983-18-38-11; internet www.ienva.org; Dir ENRIQUE ROMERO BOBILLO.

UNIVERSIDAD VIC

C/ Sagrada Família 7, 08500 Vic, (Barcelona)

Telephone: 938-86-12-22

Fax: 938-89-10-63

E-mail: relin@uvic.es

Internet: www.uvic.es

Founded 1977, present status since 1997

President: JACINT CODINA

Rector: DAVID SERRAT I CONGOST

Vice-Rector (Academic Affairs): PERE QUER

Vice-Rector (Research): JOSEP M. SERRAT

Registrar: MONTSERRAT VILALTA

General Manager: ANTONI UIX

Library Director: ANNA ANDREU MOLINA

Library of 64,000 vols, 68,000 docs, 2,763 periodicals, 646 cassettes, 723 CD-ROMs, 418 discs, 256 maps, 1,463 videos, 116 DVDs

DEANS

Faculty of Education: ASSUMPTA FARGAS I RIERA

Faculty of Humanities, Translation and Documentation: JOAN SOLÀ

Faculty of Business and Communication: Dra MANUELA BOSCH

DIRECTORS

University School of Health Sciences: MON-
TSERRAT VALL
Higher Polytechnic School: CARLES TORRES I
FEIXAS
Language School: SERGI DOMÍNGUEZ

HEADS OF DEPARTMENTS

Faculty of Education:

Sciences and Social Sciences: JOSEP CASA-
NOVAS I PRAT
Psychology: ANGEL ALSINA I PASTELLS
Education: ESTHER FATSINI I MATHEU
Philology: FRANCESC CODINA I VALLS
Artistic Expression, Movement and Sport:
MIQUEL PÉREZ I MAS

Faculty of Business and Communication:

Business: RAMON FABRE VERNEDAS
Economics, Mathematics and Computer
Science: Dr SANTI PONCE
Corporate Communcation: Dr PAUL
CAPRIOTTI
Digital Communication: Dr CARLOS SCO-
LARI

Faculty of Humanities, Translation and
Documentation:

Information and Documentation: JOAN-
ISIDRE BADELL
Catalan and Spanish Philology: (vacant)
Foreign Languages: Dra LUCRECIA KEIM
Translation and Interpretation: Dra XUS
UGARTE I BALLESTER

University School of Health Sciences:

Nursing: MONTSERRAT FARO I BASCO
Public Health and Mental Health: ÀNGEL
TORRES I SANCHO
Physiotherapy: SEBASTIÀ CANAMASAS I IBÁ-
ÑEZ
Occupational Therapy: NILDA ESTRELLA I
SAYAG
Human Nutrition and Dietetics: EVA
ROVIRA I PALAU

Higher Polytechnic School:

Electronics and Telecommunications: JULI
ORDEIX I RIGO
Agroalimentary Industry and Environ-
mental Sciences: CARME CASAS I ARCAR-
ONS
Computer Science and Mathematics: JOAN
VANCELLS I FLOTATS
Industrial Organization: FRANCESC CASTEL-
LANA I MÉNDEZ

ATTACHED INSTITUTES

ESERP College of Tourism (Barcelona):
internet www.eserp.com; Gen. Dir JOSÉ
DANIEL BARQUERO CABRERO.

BAU College of Design: C/ Pujades 118,
08005 Barcelona; tel. 93-415-34-74; fax 93-
300-15-52; e-mail info@baued.es; internet
www.baued.es; Academic Dir HUMBERT PLAN-
TADA.

**Tenerife Technical Institute of Tourism
Studies:** C/ Murillo 5, 38007 Santa Cruz de
Tenerife, Canary Isles; tel. 922-22-50-06; fax
922-22-51-05; e-mail instetur@cece.es;
internet www.cece.es/tenerife/index.htm.

Institute of Science and Technology: C/
Álvarez de Castro 63, 08100 Mollet del Vallés
(Barcelona); tel. 93-579-34-32; fax 93-570-57-
45; e-mail labquim@iuct.com; internet www
.iuct.com; Gen. Dir JOSEP CASTELLS I BOLIART.

**Institute of Marketing of the Basque
Country:** Larrauri 1, Edificio A (Antiguo
Seminario), 48160 Derio (Vizcaya); tel. 94-
454-16-03; fax 94-454-15-89; e-mail
secretaria@impv.com; internet www.impv
.com.

UNIVERSIDADE DE VIGO

Campus As Lagoas, Marcosende, 36310 Vigo
Telephone: 986-81-20-00
Fax: 986-81-35-54
E-mail: informacion@uvigo.es
Internet: www.uvigo.es

Founded 1990
State control
Academic year: October to July
Rector: Prof. DOMINGO DOCAMPO AMOEDO
Vice-Rector (Research): Prof. SALUSTIANO
MATO DE LA IGLESIA
Vice-Rector (Institutional Relations): Prof.
XAVIER MARTÍNEZ COBAS
Vice-Rector (Academic Affairs and Teaching
Staff): Prof. MARGARITA ESTÉVEZ TORANZO
Vice-Rector (Degrees, Graduate Affairs and
Continuing Education): Prof. ANTÓN FER-
NÁNDEZ ÁLVAREZ
Vice-Rector (Planning): Prof. ALBERTO GAGO
RODRÍGUEZ
Vice-Rector (University Extension and Stu-
dent Affairs): Prof. OSCAR RUBIÑOS LÓPEZ
Vice-Rector (Innovation and Quality): Prof.
JOSÉ CIDRÁS PIDRE
Vice-Rector (Planning and Development of
the Orense Campus): Prof. ANDRÉS
MAZAIRA CASTRO
Registrar: Profa MA. TERESA IGLESIAS RAN-
DULFE
Manager: AUGUSTO VISO ALONSO
Librarian: MA. DEL CARMEN PÉREZ PAIS
Library of 170,000 vols
Number of teachers: 1,200
Number of students: 30,000
Publication: *DUVI* (online newspaper, daily)

DEANS

Vigo Campus (Lagoas-Marcosende) (Campus
As Lagoas, Marcosende, 36310 Vigo; tel. 986-
81-20-00; fax 986-81-35-59; e-mail secxeral@
uvigo.es; internet www.uvigo.es):

Faculty of Humanities: Prof. LUIS DOM-
ÍNGUEZ CASTRO
Faculty of Science: Prof. MIGUEL ÁNGEL
NOMBELA CASTAÑO
Faculty of Economics and Management:
Prof. JOSÉ MARÍA MARTÍN MORENO
Faculty of Law and Labour Science: FER-
NANDO LORENZO MERINO
Faculty of Biology: PEDRO PABLO GALLEGO
VEIGAS
Faculty of Chemistry: EDUARDO FREIJANES
RIVAS
Faculty of Philology and Translation: LUIS
DOMÍNGUEZ CASTRO
Higher Technical School of Industrial
Engineering: Prof. LUIS GONZÁLEZ PIÑE-
IRO (Dir)
Higher Technical School of Telecommuni-
cations Engineering: Prof. XOSÉ MARÍA
POUSADA CARBALLO (Dir)
Higher Technical School of Mining Engi-
neering: Prof. JOSÉ MA. LANAJA DEL
BUSTO (Dir)

Vigo City Campus (Campus As Lagoas,
Marcosende, 36310 Vigo; tel. 986-81-20-00;
fax 986-81-35-59; e-mail secxeral@uvigo.es;
internet www.uvigo.es):

University Business School: Prof. PATRICIO
SÁNCHEZ BELLO (Dir)
University School of Nursing (Meixoeiro):
LUIS MORANO AMADO (Dir)
University School of Nursing (Povisa):
FERNANDO REY FERRO (Dir)
University School of Technical Industrial
Engineering: Prof. CARLOS VIVAS MAR-
TÍNEZ (Dir)
University Teacher Training School: ANTO-
NIO RODRÍGUEZ SUÁREZ (Dir)

Orense Campus (Campus As Lagoas, Marcosende, 36310 Vigo; tel. 986-81-20-00; fax 986-

81-35-59; e-mail secxeral@uvigo.es; internet
www.uvigo.es):

Faculty of Humanities: Profa SUSANA
REBOREDA MORILLO
Faculty of Science: Prof. JUAN CARLOS
MEJUTO FERNÁNDEZ
Faculty of Law: Prof. PEDRO FRANCISCO
RABANAL CARBAJO
Faculty of Business: Profa JOSÉ ANTONIO
FRAIZ BREA
Faculty of Education: Profa XOSÉ MANUEL
CID FERNÁNDEZ
Higher School of Computer Engineering:
Prof. JUAN FRANCISCO GÁLVEZ GÁLVEZ
(Dir)
University School of Nursing: CLARA RIV-
ERO MARTÍNEZ (Dir)

Pontevedra Campus (Campus A Xunqueira;
tel. 986-81-20-00; fax 986-81-35-59; e-mail
secxeral@uvigo.es; internet www.uvigo.es):

Faculty of Fine Arts: Prof. JESÚS HERNÁN-
DEZ SÁNCHEZ
Faculty of Social Sciences and Communi-
cation: Prof. XAIME FANDIÑO ALONSO
Faculty of Education: Profa MA. LUISA
ALONSO ESCONTRELA
University School of Nursing: JOSÉ LUIS
VÁZQUEZ REY (Dir)
University School of Forestry Engineering:
Prof. ENRIQUE VALERO GUTIÉRREZ DEL
OLMO (Dir)
University School of Physiotherapy: GUS-
TAVO RODRÍGUEZ FUENTES (Dir)

HEADS OF DEPARTMENTS

Science:

Functional Biology and Health Sciences:
CRISTINA ARIAS FERNÁNDEZ
Vegetal Biology and Soil Science: MANUEL
JOAQUÍN REIGOSA ROGER
Biochemistry, Genetics and Immunology:
FRANCISCO JAVIER RODRÍGUEZ BERROCAL
Ecology and Animal Biology: JESÚS SOUZA
TRONCOSO
Statistics and Operational Research: ANTO-
NIO VAAMONDE LISTE (acting)
Mathematics: MANUEL BESADA MORAIS
Analytical and Food Chemistry: JOSÉ
ANTONIO RODRÍGUEZ VÁZQUEZ
Inorganic Chemistry: JORGE BRAVO BER-
NÁNDEZ
Marine Geosciences: SOLEDAD GARCÍA GIL
Physical Chemistry: LUIS MANUEL LIZ
MARZÁN
Organic Chemistry: LUIS MUÑOZ LÓPEZ

Technology:

Design Engineering: JOSÉ POSE BLANCO
Electrical Engineering: CARLOS GARRIDO
SUÁREZ
Mechanical Engineering, Thermic
Machines and Motors, Fluids: JOSÉ
ANTONIO FERNÁNDEZ VILÁN
Chemical Engineering: JOSÉ MA. CORREA
OTERO
Materials Engineering, Applied Mechanics
and Construction: SALVADOR VILLAGRASA
MARÍN
Natural Resources Engineering and Envir-
onment: JAVIER TABOADA CASTRO
Systems Engineering and Automation:
RAFAEL SANZ DOMÍNGUEZ
Applied Physics: JOSÉ LUIS LEGIDO SOTO
Electronic Technology: JESÚS DOVAL GAN-
DOY
Telematic Engineering: CÁNDIDO ANTONIO
LÓPEZ GARCÍA
Signal and Communications Theory: MAN-
UEL GARCÍA SÁNCHEZ
Computer Science: PEDRO VILLAR CASTRO
Applied Mathematics I: RICARDO VIDAL
VÁZQUEZ
Applied Mathematics II: JOSÉ DURANY
CASTRILLO

Law and Social Sciences:

Psychosocioeducational Analysis and Control: ANTONIO LÓPEZ CASTEDO
Private Law: ANXO TATO PLAZA
Public Law: PABLO MENÉNDEZ GARCÍA
Teaching, School Organization and Research Methods: ALFONSO CID SABUCEDO
Special Education: AURORA MARTÍNEZ VIDAL
Applied Economics: CARLOS SURIS REQUEIRO
Financial Economics and Accountancy: BELÉN FERNÁNDEZ-FEIJÓO SOUTO
Principles of Economic Analysis, and Economic History and Institutions: ABEL CABALLERO ÁLVAREZ
Business Management and Marketing: ENCARNACIÓN GONZÁLEZ VÁZQUEZ
Evolutionary Psychology and Communication: JORGE JUAN GÓMEZ GUDE
Sociology, Political and Administrative Science, and Philosophy: XAN BOUZADA FERNÁNDEZ
Special Public Law, Audiovisual Communication and Advertising: ANA MA. PITA GRANDAL

Humanities:

Galician and Latin Philology: XOSÉ HENRIQUE COSTAS GONZÁLEZ
English, French and German Philology: MARTA DAHLGREN THORSELL
History, Art and Geography: MA. VICTORIA CARBALLO-CALERO RAMOS (acting)
Sculpture: JUAN FERNANDO DE LAIGLESIA
Painting: JOSÉ CHAVETE RODRÍGUEZ
Drawing: JOSÉ RAMÓN RÚA RODRÍGUEZ
Spanish Language: ROSA PÉREZ RODRÍGUEZ
Spanish Literature and Theory of Literature: MA. DOLORES TRONCOSO DURÁN
Translation and Linguistics: ARTURO PARADA DIÉGUEZ

UNIVERSIDAD DE ZARAGOZA

C/ Pedro Cerbuna 12, 50009 Zaragoza
Telephone: 976-76-10-01
Fax: 976-76-10-09
Internet: www.unizar.es
Founded in 1542 by the Emperor Charles V
State control
Language of instruction: Spanish
Academic year: October to June

Rector: FELIPE PÉTRIZ CALVO
Vice-Rector (Academic Staff): JUAN JOSÉ AGUILAR MARTÍN
Vice-Rector (Academic Affairs): ANTONIO HERRERA MARTEACHE
Vice-Rector (Huesca Campus): PILAR BOLEA CATALÁN
Vice-Rector (International Relations): NATIVIDAD FERNÁNDEZ SOLA
Vice-Rector (Planning, Quality and Resources): NATIVIDAD BLASCO DE LAS HERAS
Vice-Rector (Research, Development and Innovation): JOSÉ ÁNGEL VILLAR RIVACOBA
Vice-Rector (Social and Cultural Affairs and Institutional Relations): JOSÉ MARÍA RODANÉS VICENTE
Vice-Rector (Student Affairs): JULIÁN MUELA EZQUERRA
Vice-Rector (Teruel Campus): RAFAEL BLASCO JIMÉNEZ
Registrar: ANDRÉS GARCÍA INDA
Manager: ROGELIO CUAIRÁN BENITO
Librarian: REMEDIOS MORALEJO

Library of 839,375 vols
Number of teachers: 3,006
Number of students: 35,886
Publications: *Temas, Archivos de la Facultad de Medicina, Anales de la Facultad de Veterinaria, Guía, Boletín Informativo, Revista Universidad, Resúmenes de Tesis*

Doctorales, Ager. Revista de Estudios sobre Despoblación Rural (rural depopulation, annually), *Anuario de pedagogía* (annually), *Antigrama. Revista del Departamento de Historia del Arte* (annually), *Boletín de la Asociación de Demografía Histórica* (2 a year), *Cuadernos Aragoneses de Economía* (2 a year), *Cuadernos de Bioestadística y sus Aplicaciones Informáticas* (2 a year), *Kalathos. Revista del Seminario de Arqueología y Etnología Turolense* (annually), *Llull. Revista de la Sociedad Española de Historia de la Ciencia y de las Técnicas* (3 a year), *Medicina Naturista. Revista Internacional de Difusión Biomédica* (4 a year), *Miscelánea* (annually), *Naturaleza Aragonesa. Revista de la Sociedad de Amigos del Museo Paleontológico* (2 a year), *Organización del Conocimiento en Sistemas de Información y Documentación* (2 a year), *Revista de Demografía Histórica* (2 a year), *Revista de Gestión Pública y Privada* (annually), *Revista Española de Filosofía Medieval* (annually), *Revista Interuniversitaria de Formación del Profesorado* (3 a year), *Riff-Raff. Revista de Pensamiento y Cultura* (3 a year), *Saldvie. Estudios de Prehistoria y Archeología* (annually), *Scire. Representación y Organización del Conocimiento* (2 a year), *Stvdivm. Revista de Humanidades* (2 a year), *Tropelías. Revista de Teoría de la Literatura y Literatura Comparada* (annually), *Arqueología Espacial. Revista del Seminario de Arqueología y Etnología Turolense, Geórgica, Revista de Desarrollo Rural y Cooperativismo Agrario, Revista Áquatic, European Journal of Psychiatry, Monografías de Filología Griega, Geographicalia, Aragón en la Edad Media, El Gnomo. Boletín de Estudios Becquerianos*

DEANS

Faculty of Arts: Dr MIGUEL ÁNGEL RUIZ CARNICER
Faculty of Economics and Business Studies: Dr MARCOS SANSO FRAGO
Faculty of Education: Dra MA. CARMEN MOLINA ORTÍN
Faculty of Health Sciences and Sport, Huesca: Dr FERNANDO SOTERAS ABRIL
Faculty of Humanities and Education, Huesca: JOSÉ MARÍA NASARRE LÓPEZ
Faculty of Humanities and Social Sciences, Teruel: PASCUAL RUBIO TERRADO
Faculty of Law: JOSÉ MO. GIMENO FELIU
Faculty of Medicine: ARTURO VERA GIL
Faculty of Sciences: ANTONIO ELIPE SÁNCHEZ
Faculty of Veterinary Science: F. MANUEL GASCÓN PÉREZ

DIRECTORS

Higher Polytechnic Centre: RAFAEL NAVARRO LINARES
Polytechnic University School, Huesca: JOSÉ MANUEL MUNIOZGUREN ETCHEVERRY
Polytechnic University School, Teruel: ALFONSO BLESA GASCÓN
University School of Economics and Business Administration, Huesca: MARIA VICTORIA SANAGUSTÍN FONS
University School of Economics and Business Administration, Zaragoza: PILAR URQUIZA SAMPER
University School of Health Sciences, Zaragoza: LUIS BERNUÉS VÁZQUEZ
University School of Industrial Engineering, Zaragoza: FRANCISCO JAVIER ARCEGA SOLSONA
University School of Social Studies, Zaragoza: JOSÉ MANUEL LASIERRA ESTEBAN

HEADS OF DEPARTMENTS

Faculty of Arts:

Documentation Science and History of Science: MIGUEL ÁNGEL ESTEBAN NAVARRO
English and German Philology: FRANCISCO COLLADO RODRÍGUEZ
Medieval History, Historiography and Arabian and Islamic Studies: J. F. UTRILLA UTRILLA
Modern and Contemporary History: CARLOS FORCADELL ÁLVAREZ
Spanish Philology (Spanish and Hispanic Literature): GONZALO CORONA

Faculty of Economics and Business Studies:

Accounting and Finance: JOSÉ ANTONIO LAÍNEZ GADEA
Economic Analysis: FERNANDO SANZ GRACIA
Economy and Business Management: YOLANDA POLO REDONDO
Psychology and Sociology: CARLOS GÓMEZ BAHILLO
Structure, Economic History and Public Economy: JOSÉ AIXALÁ PASTÓ

Faculty of Law:

Business Law: ANTONIO CAYÓN GALIARDO
Penal Law, Philosophy of Law and History of Law: MIGUEL ÁNGEL BOLDOVA PASAMAR
Private Law: CARLOS MARTÍNEZ DE AGUIRRE Y ALDAZ
Public Law: ZOILA COMBALÍA SOLÍS

Faculty of Medicine:

Human Anatomy and Histology: RENÉ SARRAT TORREGUITART
Medicine, Psychiatry and Dermatology: IGNACIO FERREIRA MONTERO
Microbiology, Preventive Medicine and Public Health: CARMEN RUBIO CALVO
Paediatrics, Radiology and Physical Medicine: JOSÉ MARÍA PÉREZ GONZÁLEZ
Pathological Anatomy, Legal and Forensic Medicine and Toxicology: FRANCISCO JAVIER ORTEGO Y FERNÁNDEZ DE RETANA
Pharmacology and Physiology: MÁXIMO BARTOLOMÉ RODRÍGUEZ
Surgery, Gynaecology and Obstetrics: VICENTE CALATAYUD MALDONADO

Faculty of Sciences:

Analytical Chemistry: JUAN RAMÓN CASTILLO SUÁREZ
Applied Mathematics: MARIANO GASCA GONZÁLEZ
Applied Physics: JOSÉ MIGUEL ÁLVAREZ ABENIA
Biochemistry, Molecular and Cell Biology: ACISCLO PÉREZ MARTOS
Chemical and Environmental Engineering: RAFAEL BILBAO DUÑABEITIA
Computer Science and Systems Engineering: CARLOS SAGÜÉS BLÁZQUIZ
Earth Sciences: ALFONSO MELÉNDEZ HEVIA
Electronic Engineering and Communications: ENRIQUE MASGRAU GÓMEZ
Inorganic Chemistry: LUIS A. ORO GIRAL
Mathematics: JESÚS BASTERO ELEIZALDE
Organic Chemistry and Physical Chemistry: JOSÉ L. SERRANO OSTARIZ
Statistical Methods: JOSÉ ANTONIO CRISTÓBAL CRISTÓBAL

PROFESSORS

Faculty of Arts:

ÁLVARO ZAMORA, M. I., History of Art
ANDRÉS RUPÉREZ, M. T., Ancient History
BIELZA DE ORY, V., Land Regulation
BORRÁS GUALIS, G. M., History of Art
CABANÉS PECOURT, M. D., Medieval History
CALVO PALACIOS, J. L., Land Regulation
CORCUERA MANSO, J. F., French Philology
CORRIENTE CÓRDOBA, F., Medieval History
EGIDO MARTÍNEZ, A. G., Spanish Philology
FATÁS CABEZA, G., Ancient History

FLORÉN SERRANO, C., English and German Philology

FORCADELL ÁLVAREZ, C., Modern and Contemporary History

FRAGO GRACIA, J. A., General and Hispanic Linguistics

FRUTOS MEJÍAS, L. M., Land Regulation

GUILLÉN SELFA, L, Ancient History

ISO ECHEGOYEN, J. J., Ancient History

LACARRA DUCAY, M. C., History of Art

LOMBA FUENTES, J., Philosophy and History of Science

MAINER BAQUÉ, J. C., Spanish Philology

MARCO SIMÓN, F., Ancient History

MARTÍN BUENO, M., Ancient History

MARTÍN ZORRAQUINO, M. A., General and Hispanic Linguistics

ONEGA JAÉN, S., English and German Philology

PEÑA MONNÉ, J. L., Land Regulation

ROMERO TOBAR, L., Spanish Philology

SÁNCHEZ VIDAL, A., History of Art

SESMA MUÑOZ, J. A., Medieval History

UTRILLA MIRANDA, P., Ancient History

VAL ALVARO, J. F., General and Hispanic Linguistics

Faculty of Economics and Business Studies:

AZNAR GRASA, A., Economic Analysis

BANDRÉS MOLINÉ, E. M., Economic Structure and History, Public Economy

BIESCAS FERRER, J. A., Economic Structure and History, Public Economy

BROTO RUBIO, J., Accounting and Finance

CÓNDOR LÓPEZ, V., Accounting and Finance

ESPITIA ESCUER, M. A., Economy and Business Management

FERNÁNDEZ CLEMENTE, E., Economic Structure and History, Public Economy

GABÁS TRIGO, E. F., Accounting and Finance

LAFUENTE FÉLEZ, A., Economics and Business Management

LAÍNEZ GADEA, J. A., Accounting and Finance

OLAVE RUBIO, M. P., Statistical Methods

OLIVER PÉREZ-SANTACRUZ, E., Economic Analysis

POLO REDONDO, J. M. Y., Economics and Business Management

SALAS FUMAS, V., Economics and Business Management

SÁNCHEZ CHÓLIZ, J., Economic Analysis

SANSO FRAGO, M. B., Economic Analysis

SERRANO SANZ, J. M., Economic Structure and History, Public Economy

Faculty of Law:

ARNAL MONREAL, M., Economic Structure and History, Public Economy

BERMEJO VERA, J., Public Law

BERNAD ÁLVAREZ DE EULATE, M., Public Law

BONET NAVARRO, A., Private Law

CAYÓN GALIARDO, A., Company Law

CONTRERAS CASADO, M., Public Law

CRISTÓBAL MONTES, A., Private Law

DELGADO ECHEVERRÍA, J., Private Law

EMBID IRUJO, A., Public Law

FERRER ORTIZ, F. J., Public Law

GARCÍA BLASCO, J., Company Law

GARCÍA-CRUCES GONZÁLEZ, J. A., Company Law

GIL CREMADES, J. J., Public Law

GONZÁLEZ DE SAN SEGUNDO, M., Public Law

GRACIA MARTÍN, L., Public Law

HIGUERA GUIMERA, J. F., Public Law

LACASTA ZABALZA, J. I., Public Law

LÓPEZ RAMÓN, F., Public Law

LOZANO CORBI, E. A., Private Law

MARTÍNEZ DE AGUIRRE ALDAZ, C., Private Law

MOREU BALLONGA, J. L., Private Law

QUINTANA CARLO, I., Company Law

RAMÍREZ JIMÉNEZ, M., Public Law

RIVERO LAMAS, J., Company Law

ZABALO ESCUDERO, M. E., Private Law

Faculty of Medicine:

AZANZA RUIZ, M. J., Morphology

BARTOLOMÉ RODRÍGUEZ, M., Pharmacology and Physiology

BUENO GÓMEZ, J.

BUENO SÁNCHEZ, M., Paediatrics, Radiology and Physical Medicine

CALATAYUD MALDONADO, V., Surgery, Gynaecology and Obstetrics

CARAPETO MÁRQUEZ PRADO, F. J., Medicine and Psychiatry

CÍA GÓMEZ, P., Medicine and Psychiatry

CONDE GUERRI, M. B., Morphology

ESCANERO MARCÉN, J. F., Pharmacology and Physiology

FABRE GONZÁLEZ, E., Surgery, Obstetrics and Gynaecology

FERREIRA MONTERO, I. J., Medicine and Psychiatry

GÓMEZ LÓPEZ, L. I., Microbiology, Preventive Medicine and Public Health

GÓMEZ-LUS LAFITA, R., Microbiology, Preventive Medicine and Public Health

GUILLÉN MARTÍNEZ, G., Medicine and Psychiatry

GUTIÉRREZ MARTÍN, M., Medicine and Psychiatry

LOZANO MANTECÓN, R., Surgery, Gynaecology and Obstetrics

MARTÍNEZ DÍEZ, M., Surgery, Gynaecology and Obstetrics

MARTÍNEZ HERNÁNDEZ, H., Surgery, Obstetrics and Gynaecology

ORTEGO FERNÁNDEZ DE RETANA, F. J., General Pathology, Forensic Medicine and Toxicology

PÉREZ CASTEJÓN, M. C. N., Morphology

PÉREZ GONZÁLEZ, J. M., Paediatrics, Radiology and Physical Medicine

RAMÓN Y CAJAL JUNQUERA, S., General Pathology, Forensic Medicine and Toxicology

RIOJA SANZ, L. A., Surgery, Gynaecology and Obstetrics

RUBIO CALVO, E., Microbiology, Preventive Medicine and Public Health

RUBIO CALVO, M. C., Microbiology, Preventive Medicine and Public Health

SARRAT TORREGUITART, R., Morphology

SERAL IÑIGO, F., Surgery, Gynaecology and Obstetrics

SEVA DÍAZ, A., Medicine and Psychiatry

TRES SÁNCHEZ, A., Medicine and Psychiatry

VERA GIL, A., Morphology

Faculty of Science:

ALCALÁ ARANDA, R., Condensed Matter Physics

ALFARO GARCÍA, M. P., Mathematics

ALONSO BUJ, J. L., Theoretical Physics

ÁLVAREZ ABENIA, J. M., Applied Physics

BASTERO ELEIZALDE, J., Mathematics

BILBAO DUÑABEITIA, R., Chemical Engineering and Environmental Technology

BOYA BALET, L. J., Theoretical Physics

CACHO PALOMAR, J. F., Analytical Chemistry

CALVO PINILLA, M., Applied Mathematics

CARIÑENA MARZO, J. F., Theoretical Physics

CASTILLO SUÁREZ, J. R., Analytical Chemistry

CATVIELA MARÍN, C., Organic and Physical Chemistry

CRISTÓBAL CRISTÓBAL, J. A., Statistical Methods

CRUZ FLOR, A., Theoretical Physics

CUARTERO RUIZ, B., Mathematics

DOMÍNGUEZ MURILLO, E., Computer Science and Systems Engineering

ELDUQUE PALOMO, A. C., Mathematics

ESCUDERO ESCORZA, T., Education

FERNÁNDEZ-PACHECO PÉREZ, A., Theoretical Physics

FORNIÉS GRACIA, J. O., Inorganic Chemistry

GARAY DE PABLO, J., Mathematics

GASCA GONZÁLEZ, M., Applied Mathematics

GIL PÉREZ, J. J., Institute of Education

GÓMEZ-MORENO CALERA, C., Biochemistry, Molecular and Cellular Biology

GONZÁLEZ ÁLVAREZ, D., Condensed Matter Physics

GONZÁLEZ LÓPEZ, J. M., Earth Sciences

GRACIA TORRECILLA, M., Organic and Physical Chemistry

GUTIÉRREZ ELORZA, M., Earth Sciences

IBARRA GARCÍA, M. R., Condensed Matter Physics

LAGUNA CASTRILLO, A., Inorganic Chemistry

LEÓN PUY, J. F., Psychiatry and Nursing

LIÑAN GUIJARRO, E., Earth Sciences

LISBONA CORTÉS, F. J., Applied Mathematics

LOZANO IMIZCOZ, M. T., Mathematics

MARTÍNEZ GIL, F. J., Earth Sciences

MARTÍNEZ MARTÍNEZ, P. A., Electronic Engineering and Communications

MELÉNDEZ ANDREU, E., Organic and Physical Chemistry

MORAL GÁMIZ, A. DEL, Condensed Matter Physics

MORALES VILLASEVIL, A., Theoretical Physics

NAVARRO MARTÍN, R., Inorganic Chemistry

NÚÑEZ-LAGOS ROGLA, R., Theoretical Physics

ORO GIRAL, L. A., Inorganic Chemistry

OTAL CINCA, J., Mathematics

OTÍN LACARRA, S. F., Organic and Physical Chemistry

PIÑEIRO ANTÓN, A. A., Biochemistry, Molecular and Cellular Biology

QUINTANILLA MONTÓN, M., Applied Physics

REBOLLEDO SANZ, M. A., Applied Physics

SAN MIGUEL MARCO, M., Statistical Methods

SÁNCHEZ CELA, V. E., Earth Sciences

SANTAMARÍA RAMIRO, J. M., Chemical Engineering and Environmental Technology

SERRANO OSTÁRIZ, L., Organic and Physical Chemistry

SESMA BIENZOBAS, J., Theoretical Physics

TORRES IGLESIAS, M., Mathematics

URIETA NAVARRO, J. S., Organic and Physical Chemistry

VAREA AGUDO, V. R., Mathematics

VILLENA MORALES, J., Earth Sciences

Faculty of Veterinary Science:

BADIOLA DÍEZ, J. J., Animal Pathology

BASCUAS ASTA, J. A., Animal Pathology

BONAFONTE ZARAGOZANO, J. I., Animal Pathology

BURGOS GONZÁLEZ, J., Animal Production and Food Technology

CLIMENT PERIS, S., Anatomy, Embryology and Genetics

DUCHA SARDAÑA, J. J., Animal Pathology

ESPINOSA VELÁZQUEZ, E., Animal Pathology

GÓMEZ PIQUER, J., Animal Pathology

GUADA VALLEPUGA, J. A., Animal Production and Food Technology

HERRERA MARTEACHE, A., Animal Production and Food Technology

JOSA SERRANO, A., Animal Pathology

LÓPEZ PÉREZ, M. J., Biochemistry, Molecular and Cellular Biology

RODRÍGUEZ MOURE, A. A., Animal Pathology

SALA TREPAT, F. J., Animal Production and Food Technology

SÁNCHEZ ACEDO, M. C., Animal Pathology

SIERRA ALFRANCA, I., Animal Production and Food Technology

ZARAGOZA FERNÁNDEZ, M. P., Anatomy, Embryology and Genetics

Faculty of Veterinary Science:

Agriculture and Agricultural Economics: CARLOS FERRER BENIMELI

Animal Anatomy, Embryology and Genetics: SALVADOR CLIMENT PERIS

Animal Pathology: EMILIO ESPINOSA VELÁZ-
QUEZ

Animal Production and Food Science: JOSÉ
ANTONIO GUADA VALLEPUGA

Faculty at Huesca:

TRESACO BELÍO, S. M. P., French Philology

Higher Polytechnic Centre:

Design Engineering and Manufacturing:
LUIS BERGES MURO

Higher School of Industrial Engineering:

CAMARENA BADÍA, V., Applied Mathematics
CANO FERNÁNDEZ, J. L., Product Design
and Engineering
CASTANY VALERI, F. J., Mechanical Engi-
neering
CORREAS DOBATO, J. M., Applied Mathe-
matics
DOBLARÉ CASTELLANO, M., Mechanical
Engineering
DOPAZO GARCÍA, C., Science and Technol-
ogy of Materials and Fluids
MARTÍNEZ RODRÍGUEZ, F. J., Computer
Science and Systems Engineering
MASGRAU GÓMEZ, E. J., Electronic Engi-
neering and Communications
MIRAVETE DE MARCO, A., Mechanical Engi-
neering
NAVARRO ARTIGAS, J., Electronic Engineer-
ing and Communications
NAVARRO LINARES, R., Science and Technol-
ogy of Materials and Fluids
NERÍN DE LA PUERTA, M. C. C., Analytical
Chemistry
PASTOR FRANCO, J., Electronic Engineering
and Communications
PÉTRIZ CALVO, F., Applied Mathematics
PUERTOLAS RAFALES, J. A., Science and
Technology of Materials and Fluids
ROY YARZA, A., Electronic Engineering and
Communications
SILVA SUÁREZ, M., Computer Science and
Systems Engineering
TORRES LEZA, F., Product Design and
Engineering
VALERO CAPILLA, A., Mechanical Engineer-
ing

School of Business Studies at Zaragoza:

FÉRRIZ MARCÉN, M. R., Economics and
Business Management
INFANTE DÍAZ, J., Economic Structure and
History, Public Economy
VALERO GANCEDO, A., French Philology
ZABAL CORTÉS, T., Economic Analysis

School of Industrial Engineering at Zaragoza:

ANTOLÍN COMÁ, J. A., Applied Physics
ARCEGA SOLSONA, F. J., Electrical Engi-
neering
ESTEBAN PÉREZ, M. M., Inorganic Chemis-
try
FERNÁNDEZ SORA, A., Product Design and
Engineering
GUTIÉRREZ GIMÉNEZ, C., Mechanical Engi-
neering
IRANZO VILLACAMPA, C., Chemical Engi-
neering and Environmental Technology
LERIS LÓPEZ, M. D., Applied Mathematics
PARRA GONZÁLEZ, R., Applied Mathematics
REVUELTA BLANCO, G., Chemical Engineer-
ing and Environmental Technology

School of Social Studies at Zaragoza:

GUTIÉRREZ RESA, A., Psychology and Sociology

Teacher Training College at Huesca:

MEDRANO MIR, G., Psychology and Sociology

Teacher Training College at Zaragoza:

BERNAT MONTESINOS, A., Education
BOLOQUI LARRAYA, M. B., History of Art
DOMÍNGUEZ CABREJAS, M. R., Education
GÓMEZ MORENO, A., Education

GOMIS VAN HETEREN, A., English and Ger-
man Philology
MOLINA GARCÍA, S., Education
SÁNCHEZ GONZÁLEZ, M. D., Teaching of
Experimental Sciences

ATTACHED INSTITUTIONS

Aragón Institute of Nanoscience: Edificio
Interfacultativo II, C/ Pedro Cerbuna 12,
50009 Zaragoza; tel. 976-76-27-77; fax 976-
76-27-76; e-mail ina@unizar.es; internet ina
.unizar.es; Dir M. RICARDO IBARRA GARCÍA.

**Engineering Research Institute of Ara-
gón:** I3A Ed. Torres Quevedo, C/ María de
Luna 3, 50018 Zaragoza; tel. 976-76-27-60;
fax 976-76-20-43; e-mail i3a@unizar.es;
internet i3a.unizar.es; Dir MANUEL DOBLARÉ.

**Institute of Biocomputation and Phy-
sics of Compex Systems:** C/ Corona de
Aragón 42, 50009 Zaragoza; tel. 976-56-22-
13; e-mail bifi@unizar.es; internet bifi.unizar
.es; Dir JOSÉ FÉLIX SÁENZ LORENZO.

Institute of Education: C/ Pedro Cerbuna
12, 50009 Zaragoza; tel. 976-76-14-94; fax
976-76-13-45; e-mail secice@posta.unizar.es;
internet www.unizar.es/ice.

**Polytechnic University School, La
Almunia:** C/ Mayor s/n, 50100 La Almunia
de Doña Godina (Zaragoza); tel. 976-60-08-
13; internet www.eupla.unizar.es/
universidad/index.html; engineering, architecture; Dir ANTONIO ORZEGA TELLO.

University College of Nursing, Teruel:
Avda América 15, 44002 Teruel; tel. 978-62-
06-48; fax 978-62-09-54; internet teruel
.unizar.es/enfermeria/enfermeria.html; Dir
MA. CARMEN GÓRRIZ GONZÁLEZ.

Polytechnics

UNIVERSIDAD POLITÉCNICA DE CARTAGENA

Plaza del Cronista Isidoro Valverde, Edif. La
Milagrosa, 30202 Cartagena (Murcia)

Telephone: 968-32-54-00
Fax: 968-32-59-72
E-mail: relint@upct.es
Internet: www.upct.es
Founded 1998
State control
Language of instruction: Spanish
Academic year: October to July

Rector: FÉLIX FAURA MATEU
Vice-Rector (Academic Staff and Teaching):
CARLOS F. GONZÁLEZ FERNÁNDEZ
Vice-Rector (Research and Innovation): JOSÉ
ANTONIO FRANCO LEEMHUIS
Vice-Rector (Doctorate and Graduate Affairs
and International Relations): ANTONIO
VIEDMA ROBLES
Vice-Rector (Infrastructure): BLAS ZAMORA
PARRA
Vice-Rector (Academic Affairs): JOSÉ ANTO-
NIO CASCALES PUJALTE
Vice-Rector (Student Affairs and University
Extension): FRANCISCO MARTÍNEZ GONZÁLEZ
Vice-Rector (Planning and Economic Affairs):
IGNACIO SEGADO SEGADO
Registrar: MARÍA DEL MAR ANDREU MARTÍ
Manager: JUAN MADRIGAL DE TORRES
Librarian: MA. ÁNGELES GARCÍA DEL TORO

Library of 47,754 books, 2,528 periodicals
Number of teachers: 501
Number of students: 6,446.

CONSTITUENT SCHOOLS

**Higher Technical School of Agricultural
Engineering:** Paseo Alfonso XIII, 30203
Cartagena; tel. 968-32-54-19; fax 968-32-57-
93; e-mail direccion@etsia.upct.es; internet

www.upct.es/~etsia; Dir MA. DOLORES DE
MIGUEL GÓMEZ.

**Higher Technical School of Industrial
Engineering:** Campus Muralla del Mar, C/
Doctor Fleming s/n, 30202 Cartagena; tel.
968-32-54-17; fax 968-32-54-20; e-mail etsii@
etsii.upct.es; internet www.upct.es/~etsii;
Dir ANTONIO GABALDÓN MARÍN.

**Higher Technical School of Telecommu-
nications Engineering:** Campus Muralla
del Mar, C/ Doctor Fleming s/n, 30202
Cartagena; tel. 968-32-53-13; fax 968-32-53-
38; e-mail etsit@etsit.upct.es; internet www
.teleco.upct.es; Dir JUAN GARCÍA HARO.

**Higher Technical School of Naval Engi-
neering:** Paseo Alfonso XIII, 30203 Cartagena; tel. 968-32-54-21; fax 968-32-54-22;
e-mail secretaria@etsino.upct.es; internet
www.upct.es/~etsino; Dir JOSÉ ALFONSO MAR-
TÍNEZ GARCÍA.

University School of Civil Engineering:
Paseo Alfonso XIII, 30203 Cartagena; tel.
and fax 968-32-54-25; internet www.upct.es/
~euitc; Dir ANTONIO GARCÍA MARTÍN.

Faculty of Business Studies: Paseo
Alfonso XIII, 30203 Cartagena; tel. 968-32-
55-76; fax 968-32-55-77; e-mail decanato@fce
.upct.es; internet www.upct.es/~fcee; Dean
JUAN PATRICIO CASTRO VALDIVIA

HEADS OF DEPARTMENTS

Architecture and Building Technology: VICE-
NTE MIGUEL FERRÁNDIZ ARAUJO
Agricultural Science and Technology: ANTO-
NIO CALDERÓN GARCÍA
Law: JOSÉ LUJÁN ALCARAZ
Economics: ANTONIO GARCÍA SÁNCHEZ
Business Economics: ANGEL RAFAEL MAR-
TÍNEZ LORENTE
Financial Economics and Accountancy. DOM-
INGO GARCÍA PÉREZ DE LEMA
Electronics, Computer Technology and Pro-
jects: VICENTE GARCERÁN HERNÁNDEZ
Structures and Building: PASCUAL MARTÍ
MONTRULL
Technical Drawing: JOSÉ NIETO MARTÍNEZ
Applied Physics: FRANCISCO ALHAMA LÓPEZ
Food Technology and Agricultural Equip-
ment Engineering: ANTONIO LÓPEZ GÓMEZ
Electrical Engineering: JUAN JOSÉ PORTERO
RODRÍGUEZ
Materials Engineering and Manufacturing
Engineering: GINÉS MARTÍNEZ NICOLÁS
Mechanical Engineering: ANICETO VALVERDE
MARTÍNEZ
Mining, Geological and Cartographic Engi-
neering: EDUARDO PÉREZ PARDO
Chemical and Environmental Engineering:
ENRIQUE SOLANO ORIA
Systems Engineering and Automation: JUAN
ANTONIO LÓPEZ CORONADO
Heat Engineering and Fluid Mechanics: JOSÉ
RAMÓN GARCÍA CASCALES
Applied Mathematics and Statistics: ANTONIO
GUILLAMÓN FRUTOS
Quantitative and Computing Methods: JUAN
JESÚS BERNAL GARCÍA
Vegetal Production: PABLO BIELZA LINO
Electronic Technology: ANDRÉS IBORRA GAR-
CÍA
Information and Communications Technol-
ogy: BÁRBARA ÁLVAREZ TORRES
Naval Technology: TOMÁS LÓPEZ MAESTRE

ATTACHED INSTITUTES

**University School of Industrial Rela-
tions:** C/ Real 80, 30201 Cartagena; tel.
968-50-52-03; fax 968-50-36-05; e-mail
relaciones.laborales@upct.es; internet www
.upct.es/eurl/Indice.html.

University School of Tourism: C/ Ingeniero de la Cierva s/n, Edificio UNED 4a
planta, 30203 Cartagena; tel. 968-52-80-27;
fax 968-52-80-27; e-mail escuela.turismo@

upct.es; internet www.eutcartagena.com; Dir
MARÍA DEL CARMEN PASTOR ÁLVAREZ.

UNIVERSITAT POLITÈCNICA DE CATALUNYA

C. Jordi Girona 31, 08034 Barcelona
Telephone: 93-401-62-00
Fax: 93-401-62-10
E-mail: area.relacions.internacionals@upc
  .edu
Internet: www.upc.es
Founded 1971
Regional government control
Languages of instruction: Spanish, Catalan
Academic year: September to June

Rector: JOSEP FERRER LLOP
Vice-Rector (Academic Affairs): ALBERT COR-
  OMINAS SUBÍAS
Vice-Rector (Continuing Education): JOSEP
  MARIA MONGUET FIERRO
Vice-Rector (Doctorate Affairs, Research and
  International Relations): JUAN JESÚS PÉREZ
  GONZÁLEZ
Vice-Rector (Personnel): VERA SACRISTÁN ADI-
  NOLFI
Vice-Rector (Promotion and Territorial Inte-
  gration): RAMON SANS FONFRÍA
Vice-Rector (Science Policy): FRANCESC FAYOS
  VALLÈS
Vice-Rector (Strategic Planning, Library and
  Language Policy): RAMON CARRERAS PLA-
  NELLS
Vice-Rector (Teaching and University Exten-
  sion): JOAN MARIA MIRÓ SANS
Registrar: CARME PEÑAS ZAPATA
Administrative Director: ANTONI BARÓN PLA-
  DEVALL
Library: each constituent school has an
  attached library
Number of teachers: 2,531
Number of students: 28,362

Publications: Butlletí UPC, Informations.

CONSTITUENT SCHOOLS
Faculty of Mathematics and Statistics:
C. Pau Gargallo 5, 08028 Barcelona; tel. 93-
401-72-98; fax 93-401-58-81; internet
www-fme.upc.es; Dean SEBASTIÀ XAMBÓ DES-
CAMPS.

Faculty of Nautical Studies, Barcelona:
Pl. de Palau 18, 08003 Barcelona; tel. 93-401-
79-36; fax 93-401-79-10; internet www.fnb
.upc.es; Dean ALEXANDRE MONFERRER DE LA
PEÑA.

**Higher Polytechnic School of Building,
Barcelona:** Avda Doctor Marañon 44–50,
08028 Barcelona; tel. 93-401-63-00; fax 93-
401-77-00; internet www.epseb.upc.edu; Dir
FRANCISCO JAVIER LLOVERA SÁEZ.

**Higher Polytechnic School, Castellde-
fels:** Avda del Canal Olímpic s/n, 08860
Castelldefels; tel. 93-413-70-00; fax 93-413-
70-07; e-mail info@epsc.upc.es; internet
www-epsc.upc.es; Dir MIGUEL VALERO GAR-
CIA.

**Higher Polytechnic School of Engineer-
ing, Vilanova i la Geltrú:** Avda Víctor
Balaguer s/n, 08800 Vilanova i la Geltrú; tel.
93-896-77-01; fax 93-896-77-00; internet
www.upc.edu/epsevg; Dir ANDREU CATALÀ
MALLOFRÉ.

**Higher Technical School of Architec-
ture, Barcelona:** Avda Diagonal 649,
08028 Barcelona; tel. 93-401-63-59; fax 93-
401-58-71; internet www.upc.es/etsab; Dir
JAUME SANMARTÍ VERDAGUER.

**Higher Technical School of Architec-
ture, Vallès:** C. Pere Serra 1–15, 08190 St
Cugat del Vallès; tel. 93-401-79-00; fax 93-
401-79-01; e-mail pilar@etsAvdaupc.es;
internet www.etsAvdaupc.es; Dir RAMON
SASTRE SASTRE.

**Higher Technical School of Civil Engi-
neering, Barcelona:** C. Jordi Girona 1–3,
Campus Norte, Ed. C2, 08034 Barcelona; tel.
93-401-69-00; fax 93-401-65-04; internet
www-camins.upc.es; Dir FRANCESC ROBUSTÉ I
ANTON.

**Higher Technical School of Industrial
Engineering, Barcelona:** Avda Diagonal
647, 08028 Barcelona; tel. 93-401-67-00; fax
93-401-66-00; e-mail punt_inf@etseib.upc.es;
internet www.etseib.upc.es; Dir FERRAN
PUERTA SALES.

**Higher Technical School of Industrial
Engineering, Terrassa:** C. Colom 11,
08222 Terrassa; tel. 93-739-81-02; fax 93-
739-81-01; internet etseit-ct.upc.es; Dir
JAUME GIBERT PEDROSA.

**Higher Technical School of Telecommu-
nications Engineering, Barcelona:** C.
Jordi Girona 1–3, Campus Norte, Ed. B3,
08034 Barcelona; tel. 93-401-68-00; fax 93-
401-68-01; e-mail infoteleco@etsetb.upc.es;
internet www.etsetb.upc.es; Dir JUAN ANTO-
NIO FERNÁNDEZ RUBIO.

School of Informatics, Barcelona: C.
Jordi Girona 1–3, Campus Norte, Ed. B6,
08034 Barcelona; tel. 93-401-70-00; fax 93-
401-71-13; e-mail informacio@fib.upc.es;
internet www.fib.upc.es; Dean MARIA RIBERA
SANCHO.

**University Polytechnic School, Man-
resa:** Avda de les Bases de Manresa 61–73,
08240 Manresa; tel. 93-877-72-00; fax 93-
877-72-02; e-mail eupm@eupm.upc.es;
internet www.eupm.upc.es; Dir JUAN JORGE
SÁNCHEZ.

**University School of Industrial Engi-
neering, Terrassa:** C. Colom 1, 08222
Terrassa; tel. 93-739-81-32; fax 93-739-82-
25; internet euetit-ct.upc.es; Dir JUAN ANTO-
NIO GALLARDO LEÓN.

**University School of Optics and Opto-
metry, Terrassa:** C. Violinista Vellsolà 37,
08222 Terrassa; tel. 93-739-83-00; fax 93-
739-83-01; internet euoot-ct.upc.es; Dir
NÚRIA LUPÓN BAS

HEADS OF DEPARTMENTS
Applied Mathematics I: JOAN SOLÀ-MORALES
Applied Mathematics II: MARC NOY SERRANO
Applied Mathematics III: EUSEBI JARAUTA
  BRAGULAT
Applied Mathematics IV: JOSEP FÀBREGA
  CANUDAS
Applied Physics: ALFONSO ALBAREDA TIANA
Architectural Design: FÉLIX SOLAGUREN-
  BEASCOA DE CORRAL
Architectural Presentation I: LLUÍS VILLA-
  NUEVA BARTRINA
Architectural Presentation II: JULIO ÁNGEL
  IGLESIAS
Architectural Technology I: JAUME AVELLA-
  NEDA DÍAZ-GRANDE
Architectural Technology II: FRANCESC DE
  PAULA JORDANA RIBA
Automatic Control: ALBERTO SANFELIU
  CORTÉS
Building Engineering: LLUÍS AGULLÓ FITÉ
Chemical Engineering: ANA MARÍA SASTRE
  REQUENA
Electrical Engineering: ORIOL BOIX ARAGONÉS
Electronic Engineering: JOAN CABESTANY
  MONCUSÍ
Engineering Design: JOSÉ M. BALDASANO
  RECIO
Engineering Presentation: FRANCISCO HER-
  NÁNDEZ ABAD
Fluid Mechanics: ENRIC TRILLAS
Food Engineering and Biotechnology: ROSA
  FLOS
Geotechnical Engineering and Geosciences:
  ANTONIO GENS SOLE
Heat Engines: JOSEP MONTSERRAT JORDÀ

History and Theory of Architecture: PERE
  HEREU PAYET
Hydraulic, Maritime and Environmental
  Engineering: JOAN PAU SIERRA
Management: LLUÍS CUATRECASAS
Materials Science and Metallurgy: MARC J.
  ANGLADA GOMILA
Mechanical Engineering: RAMON CAPDEVILA
  PAGÈS
Mining Engineering and Natural Resources:
  XAVIER DE LAS HERAS
Nautical Sciences and Engineering: JOAN
  OLIVELLA
Optics and Optemetry: JOSEP PLADELLORENS
Physics and Nuclear Engineering: ANTONI
  GIRÓ ROCA
Signal Theory and Communications: ANTONI
  BROQUETAR IBARS
Software: CONRADO MARTINEZ PARRA
Statistics and Operational Research: MANUEL
  MARTÍ RECOBER
Strength of Materials and Structural Engi-
  neering: ANTONIO VIEDMA MARTÍNEZ
Structural Architecture: JOAN JACAS MORAL
Telematic Engineering: JORDI CASADEMONT
Textile and Paper Engineering: FRANCESC
  XAVIER CARRIÓN
Transport and Highway Engineering: MAN-
  UEL HERCE VALLEJO
Town and Country Planning: MIGUEL DOM-
  INGO I CLOTA

ATTACHED INSTITUTES
Caixa Terrassa Business College: Ctra.
de Terrassa Km. 3, 08227 Terrassa; tel. 93-
730-19-00; fax 93-730-19-01; internet www
.euncet.com; Dir JORDI BALCELLS GENÉ.

**Catalan Technical Foundation School of
Photography:** C/ de la Igualtat 33, 08222
Terrassa; tel. 93-739-83-12; fax 93-739-83-65;
internet www.citm.upc.es; Dir of Centre of
the Image and Multimedia Technology
MIQUEL MORÓN TARIFA.

College of Agricultural Engineering:
Comte d'Urgell 187, 08036 Barcelona; tel.
93-413-75-00; fax 93-413-75-01; internet
www.esab.upc.es; Dir F. XAVIER MARTÍNEZ
FARRÉ.

**College of Industrial Engineering, Bar-
celona:** Comte d'Urgell 187, 08036 Barcelona; tel. 93-413-74-00; fax 93-413-74-01;
internet www.euetib.upc.es; Dir MARTÍ LLO-
RENS MORRAJA.

**College of Industrial Engineering, Igua-
lada:** Plaça del Rei 15, 08700 Igualada; tel.
93-803-53-00; fax 93-803-15-89; internet
www.euetii.upc.es; Deputy Dir RITA PUIG I
VIDAL.

College of Knitted Fabric Engineering:
Plaça de la Indústria 1, 08360 Canet de Mar;
tel. 93-794-01-50; fax 93-795-48-17; internet
www.diba.es/canet; Dir MIQUEL SOLER
LUQUE.

Institute of Education: C. Jordi Girona 29,
Edifici Nexus II, Despatx OD, 08034 Barcelona; tel. 93-413-76-43; e-mail info.ice@upc
.es; internet www-ice.upc.es; Dir RAFAEL
PINDADO RICO.

**Institute of Industrial Systems Organi-
zation and Control:** Avda Diagonal 647,
planta 11, edifici.H, 08028 Barcelona; tel. 93-
401-66-53; fax 93-401-66-05; e-mail enric
.fossas@upc.es; internet www.ioc.upc.es; Dir
ENRIC FOSSAS COLET.

Institute of Power Engineering: Avda
Diagonal 647, 08028 Barcelona; tel. 93-401-
66-92; fax 93-401-71-49; e-mail ortega@inte
.upc.es; internet www.upc.es/inte/index
.html; Dir XAVIER ORTEGA ARAMBURU.

**Institute of Textile Research and Indus-
trial Co-operation, Terrassa:** C. Colom 15,
08222 Terrasa; tel. 93-739-82-70; fax 93-739-
82-72; e-mail director-ins@intexter.upc.es;

internet www.ct.upc.es/intexter; Dir LLIBERT COLL TORTOSA.

Mataró Technical College: Avda Puig i Cadafalch 101–111, 08303 Mataró; tel. 93-757-44-04; fax 93-757-05-24; internet www .eupmt.es; Dir JOAN GIL LÓPEZ.

School of Business Administration: Aragó 55, 08015 Barcelona; tel. 93-227-80-90; fax 93-319-44-36; e-mail eae@eae.es; internet www.eae.es; Dir FERNANDO CASADO JUAN.

School of Multimedia of the UPC Foundation: C/ de la Igualtat 33, 08222 Terrassa.

School of Occupational Hazard Prevention: C/ Dulcet 2–10, 08034 Barcelona; tel. 93-280-45-42; fax 93-280-36-42; e-mail neus .guardiola@fpc.upc.es; internet www .escuela-prevencion.com.

UNIVERSIDAD POLITÉCNICA DE MADRID

C/ Ramiro de Maeztu 7, 28040 Madrid
Telephone: 91-336-60-00
Fax: 91-336-61-73
Internet: www.upm.es
Founded 1971
State control
Language of instruction: Spanish
Academic year: October to July

Rector: JAVIER UCEDA ANTOLÍN
Vice-Rector (Academic Affairs and Strategic Planning): CARLOS CONDE LÁZARO
Vice-Rector (Academic Management and Teaching Staff): EMILIO MÍNGUEZ TORRES
Vice-Rector (Doctorate and Postgraduate Studies): LUIS DE VILLANUEVA DOMÍNGUEZ
Vice-Rector (Economic Planning): VICENTE SÁNCHEZ GÁLVEZ
Vice-Rector (International Relations): JOSÉ MANUEL PÁEZ BORRALLO
Vice-Rector (New Technology and Network Services): JOSÉ MANUEL PERALES PERALES
Vice-Rector (Research): GONZALO LEÓN SERRANO
Vice-Rector (Student Affairs): LUIS GARCÍA ESTEBAN
Registrar: ADOLFO CAZORLA MONTERO
Chief Administrative Officer: FERNANDO LANZACO BONILLA

Library: There is a library attached to each constituent school of the University
Number of teachers: 3,300
Number of students: 40,697.

CONSTITUENT SCHOOLS

Faculty of Computer Science: Campus Montegancedo, Boadilla del Monte, 28660 Madrid; tel. 91-336-73-99; fax 91-336-74-12; internet www.fi.upm.es; Dean FRANCISCO JAVIER SEGOVIA PÉREZ.

Faculty of Physical Activity and Sport: C/ Martín Fierro s/n, Ciudad Universitaria, 28040 Madrid; tel. 91-336-40-00; fax 91-544-13-31; internet www.inef.upm.es; Dir JESÚS JAVIER ROJO GONZÁLEZ.

Higher Technical School of Aeronautical Engineering: Pza Cardenal Cisneros 3, Ciudad Universitaria, 28040 Madrid; tel. 91-336-63-00; fax 91-543-98-59; internet www .aero.upm.es; Dir JOSÉ LUIS MONTAÑÉS GARCÍA.

Higher Technical School of Agronomy: Avda Complutense s/n, Ciudad Universitaria, 28040 Madrid; tel. 91-336-56-00; fax 91-543-48-79; internet www.etsia.upm.es; Dir JESÚS VÁZQUEZ MINGUELA.

Higher Technical School of Architecture: Avda Juan de Herrera 4, Ciudad Universitaria, 28040 Madrid; tel. 91-336-65-24; fax 91-544-24-81; internet www.aq.upm .es; Dir JUAN MIGUEL HERNÁNDEZ LÉON.

Higher Technical School of Civil Engineering: Ciudad Universitaria, 28040 Madrid; tel. 91-336-68-00; fax 91-549-22-89; internet www.caminos.upm.es; Dir EDELMIRO RÚA ÁLVAREZ.

Higher Technical School of Forestry: Ciudad Universitaria, 28040 Madrid; tel. 91-336-70-73; fax 91-543-95-57; internet www.montes.upm.es; Dir ARTURO DÍAZ DE BARRIONUEVO.

Higher Technical School of Industrial Engineering: Calle José Gutiérrez Abascal 2, 28006 Madrid; tel. 91-336-30-60; internet www.etsii.upm.es; Dir CARLOS VERA ÁLVAREZ.

Higher Technical School of Mining Engineering: Ríos Rosas 21, 28003 Madrid; tel. 91-336-70-71; internet www.minas.upm .es; Dir ALFONSO MALDONADO ZAMORA.

Higher Technical School of Shipbuilding: Avda Arco de la Victoria s/n, Ciudad Universitaria, 28020 Madrid; tel. 91-336-71-40; fax 91-336-75-11; internet www.etsin .upm.es; Dir LUIS RAMÓN NUÑEZ RIVAS.

Higher Technical School of Telecommunications Engineering: Ciudad Universitaria, 28040 Madrid; tel. 91-336-72-34; fax 91-543-96-52; internet www.etsit.upm.es; Dir JOSÉ MANUEL PÁEZ BORRALLO.

Polytechnic School of Higher Education: C/ Ramiro de Maeztu 7, 28040 Madrid; tel. 91-336-59-12; fax 91-336-59-12; Dir JOSÉ LUIS ENRÍQUEZ ESCUDERO.

University School of Aeronautical Engineering: Pza Cardenal Cisneros s/n, Ciudad Universitaria, 28040 Madrid; tel. 91-336-41-66; fax 91-336-75-11; internet www.euita .upm.es; Dir MIGUEL MERCÉ BERMEJO.

University School of Agricultural Engineering: Ciudad Universitaria, 28040 Madrid; tel. 91-336-54-00; internet www .agricolas.upm.es; Dir JOAQUÍN GARCÍA DE MARTITEGUI.

University School of Architecture: Avda Juan de Herrera 6, Ciudad Universitaria, 28040 Madrid; tel. 91-336-76-36; fax 91-336-76-44; internet ww.euatm.upm.es; Dir MIGUEL OLIVER ALEMANY.

University School of Computer Science: Camino de la Arboleda s/n, Complejo Politécnico de Vallecas, 28031 Madrid; tel. 91-336-79-03; internet www.eui.upm.es; Dir JOSÉ GABRIEL ZATO RECELLADO.

University School of Forestry: Avda Ramiro de Maeztu s/n, Ciudad Universitaria, 28040 Madrid; tel. 91-336-76-52; internet www.forestales.upm.es; Dir JAVIER ZAZO MUNCHARAZ.

University School of Industrial Engineering: Ronda de Valencia 3, 28012 Madrid; tel. 91-336-76-99; internet www .euiti.upm.es; Dir ÁLVARO GUSTAVO VITORES GONZÁLEZ.

University School of Public Works: Alfonso XII 3, 28014 Madrid; tel. 91-336-77-43; fax 91-336-79-58; internet www.op.upm .es; Dir DIEGO RAMOS LÓPEZ-ARNO.

University School of Telecommunications Engineering: Camino de la Arboleda s/n, Complejo Politécnico de Vallecas, 28031 Madrid; tel. 91-336-77-80; fax 91-331-92-29; internet www.euitt.upm.es; Dir JOSÉ ANTONIO SÁNCHEZ FERNÁNDEZ (acting).

University School of Topographic Engineering: Camino de la Arboleda s/n, Complejo Politécnico de Vallecas, 28031 Madrid; tel. 91-336-79-15; internet www.euitto.upm .es; Dir NICOLÁS SERRANO COLMENAREJO

HEADS OF DEPARTMENTS

Agricultural Chemistry and Analysis: MARÍA CARMEN CARTAGENA CAUSAPÉ

Applied Computer Science: FRANCISCO AYLAGAS ROMERO
Applied Intelligent Systems: EDUARDO MARTÍNEZ MURCIANO
Applied Mathematics: JESÚS GARCÍA LÓPEZ DE LACALLE
Applied Mathematics and Computing Methods: JULIÁN ALONSO MARTÍNEZ
Applied Mathematics and Statistics: MANUEL ABEJÓN ADÁMEZ
Applied Physics: RAFAEL RAMIS ABRIL
Architectural Composition: MIGUEL ÁNGEL BALDELLOU SANTOLARIA
Architectural Concepts: JAVIER SEGUI DE LA RIVA
Architectural Projects: GABRIEL RUIZ CABRERO
Architecture and Technology of Information Systems: FERNANDO PÉREZ COSTOYA
Artificial Intelligence: ANA MARÍA GARCÍA SERRANO
Basic Mechanics and Physics and Their Application to Agroforestry Engineering: JOSÉ MANUEL AMAYA GARCÍA DE LA ESPOSURA
Biotechnology: TOMÁS RUIZ ARGÜESO
Building and Country Roads: JOSÉ RAMÓN MARCET ROIG
Chemical Engineering and Combustibles: EMILIO LLORENTE GÓMEZ
Civil Engineering: Hydraulics and Energetics: JOSÉ JESÚS FRAILE MORA
Civil Engineering: Town and Country Planning and the Environment: J. JAVIER DÍEZ GONZÁLEZ
Civil Engineering: Transport: MIGUEL ÁNGEL DEL VAL (acting)
Computer Architecture and Technology: ANTONIO DÍAZ LAVADORES
Continuum Mechanics and Theory of Structures: JOSÉ MARÍA GOICOLEA RUIGOMEZ
Economics and Forest Management: ANTONIO PRIETO RODRÍGUEZ
Electrical Engineering: JORGE MORENO MOHINO
Electromagnetism and Theory of Circuits: JESÚS GARCÍA JIMÉNEZ
Electronic Technology: JESÚS SANGRADOR GARCÍA
Engineering and Materials Science: CARLOS RANNINGER RODRÍGUEZ
Forest Engineering: JOSÉ REINERIO BARAGAÑO GALÁN
Geological Engineering: FERNANDO VÁZQUEZ GUZMÁN
Industrial Chemistry and Polymers: JAVIER ALBÉNIZ MONTES MARTÍN
Industrial Mechanics: JULIÁN PLÁCIDO PECHARROMÁN SACRISTÁN
Industrial Technical Drawing: JOSÉ MANUEL ARENAS REINA
Infrastructure, Aerospace Systems and Airports: RAFAEL SANJURJO NAVARRO
Languages Applied to Science and Technology: PILAR DURÁN ESCRIBANO
Languages, Projects and Information Systems: JESÚS LÓPEZ SÁNCHEZ
Materials and Aerospace Production: ALFREDO GÜEMES
Mathematics Applied to Information Technology: LORENZO JAVIER MARTÍN GARCÍA
Mathematics Applied to Natural Resources: LUIS GAVETE CORVINOS
Mathematics Applied to Town Planning, Building and the Environment: JOSÉ LUIS PINILLA FERRANDO
Organization and Structure of Information: CARLOS DEL CUVILLO MARTÍNEZ-RIDRUEJO
Organization, Business Administration and Statistics: FELIPE RUIZ LÓPEZ
Photonic Technology: JULIO GUTIÉRREZ RÍOS
Physics Applied to Information Technology: PEDRO SÁNCHEZ SÁNCHEZ
Physics Applied to Natural Resources: MIGUEL BALBÁS ANTÓN

Projects and Rural Planning: GABRIEL DOR-
ADO MARTÍN
Signals, Systems and Radio Communication:
FÉLIX PÉREZ MARTÍNEZ
Soil Science: JOSÉ M. GASCO
Special Technology Applied to Telecommuni-
cations: ERNESTO CASTAÑEDA MARTÍN
Structural Mechanics and Industrial Struc-
tures: SAGRARIO GÓMEZ LERA
Topographic Engineering and Cartography:
MIGUEL ÁNGEL BERNABÉ POVEDA
Vegetal Biology: JOSÉ MARÍA IRIONDO ALEGRÍA

ATTACHED INSTITUTES

Higher Centre of Fashion Design:
Camino de la Arboleda s/n, Complejo Politécnico de Vallecas, 28031 Madrid; tel. 91-
331-01-26; fax 91-332-17-67; internet www
.upm.es/centros/csdm.html; Dir MIGUEL
ÁNGEL PASCUAL.

Higher School of Brewing: E. T. S. de
Ingenieros Industriales, Laboratorio de tecnología química, Calle José Gutiérrez Abascal 2, 28006 Madrid; tel. 91-336-31-90; fax
91-336-30-09; e-mail eroche@etsii.upm.es;
internet www.aetcm.es/escuela/escuela
.htm#inicio.

Institute of Automobile Research: Ctra
de Valencia Km 7, Campus Sur UPM, 28031
Madrid; tel. 91-336-53-00; fax 91-336-53-02;
e-mail insia@insia.upm.es; internet www
.insia.upm.es.

Institute of Education: C/ Profesor Aranguren s/n, Ciudad Universitaria, 28040
Madrid; tel. 91-336-68-15; fax 91-336-68-12;
e-mail ice@ice.upm.es; internet www.ice.upm
.es; Dir ROSA Mª. GONZÁLEZ TIRADOS.

**Institute of Microgravity 'Ignacio Da
Riva':** UPM, ETSI Aeronáuticos, 28040
Madrid; tel. 91-336-63-53; fax 91-336-63-63;
e-mail idr@idr.upm.es; internet www.idr
.upm.es.

Institute of Nuclear Fusion: E. T. S. de
Ingenieros Industriales, Calle José Gutiérrez
Abascal 2, 28006 Madrid; tel. 91-336-31-08.

**Institute of Optoelectronic Systems and
Microtechnology:** ETSI Telecomunicación
(UPM), Ciudad Universitaria, 28040 Madrid;
tel. 91-336-73-21; fax 91-549-09-09; e-mail
montse.isom@die.upm.es; internet www.isom
.upm.es; Dir ELÍAS MUÑOZ MERINO.

Institute of Solar Engergy: E. T. S. de
Ingenieros de Telecomunicación, Ciudad
Universitaria, 28040 Madrid; tel. 91-544-10-
60; fax 91-544-63-41; e-mail info@ies-def.upm
.es; internet www.ies.upm.es; Dir ANTONIO
LUQUE.

Laser Centre: Edificio Tecnológico 'La
Arboleda', Campus Sur UPM, Carretera de
Valencia Km 7,300, 28031 Madrid; tel. 91-
332-42-80; fax 91-331-69-06; e-mail jlocana@
faii.etsii.upm.es; internet www.upmlaser
.upm.es; Dir JOSÉ LUIS OCAÑA MORENO.

UNIVERSIDAD POLITÉCNICA DE VALENCIA

Camino de Vera s/n, 46022 Valencia
Telephone: 96-387-70-00
Fax: 96-387-90-09
E-mail: informacion@upvnet.upv.es
Internet: www.upv.es
Founded 1968
State control
Languages of instruction: Spanish, Valen-
cian
Academic year: October to June
Rector: JUSTO NIETO NIETO
Vice-Rector (Academic and Research Staff):
JAIME GÓMEZ HERNÁNDEZ
Vice-Rector (Higher Education in Europe):
JOSÉ E. CAPILLA ROMÁ

Vice-Rector (Student Affairs): MARÍA CONCEP-
CIÓN MAROTO ÁLVAREZ
Vice-Rector (Employment Policy): J. CARLOS
AYATS SALT
Vice-Rector (Language Promotion): BERNABÉ
MARÍ SOUCASE
Vice-Rector (Research, Development and
Innovation): VICENTE HERNÁNDEZ GARCÍA
Vice-Rector (New Technology): LUIS VERGARA
DOMÍNGUEZ
Vice-Rector (Co-operation and International
Projects): SALVADOR FERNANDO CAPUZ RIZO
Vice-Rector (Doctorate and Graduate
Affairs): MARÍA AMPARO CHIRALT BOIX
Vice-Rector (Polytechnic Campus of Innova-
tion): FRANCISCO JOSÉ MORA MÁS
Vice-Rector (Culture): ÁNGELA GARCÍA
CODOÑER
Vice-Rector (Sport): ÁNGEL FRANCISCO BENITO
BEORLEGUI
Vice-Rector (Infrastructure and Mainte-
nance): ARTURO MARTÍNEZ BOQUERA
Vice-Rector (Institutional Relations): ANTO-
NIO HERVÁS JORGE
Vice-Rector (Planning, Quality and Economic
Affairs): FRANCISCO JAVIER SANZ FERNÁNDEZ
Vice-Rector (Support Staff Training Policy):
PATRICIO MONTESINOS SANCHÍS
Registrar: VICENT CASTELLANO I CERVERA
Librarian: JOSÉ LLORENS SÁNCHEZ

Number of teachers: 2,401
Number of students: 35,840.

CONSTITUENT SCHOOLS

Higher Technical School of Agronomy:
Edificio 3H, Camino de Vera s/n, 46022
Valencia; tel. 96-387-71-30; fax 96-387-71-
39; e-mail etsia@etsia.upvnet.upv.es;
internet www.etsia.upv.es; Dir NEMESIO FER-
NÁNDEZ MARTÍNEZ.

**Higher Technical School of Architec-
ture:** Edificio 2F, Camino de Vera s/n,
46022 Valencia; tel. 96-387-71-10; fax 96-
387-71-19; e-mail etsa@upvnet.upv.es;
internet www.arq.upv.es; Dir IGNACIO BOSCH
REIG.

**Higher Technical School of Civil Engi-
neering:** Edificio 4H, Camino de Vera s/n,
46022 Valencia; tel. 96-387-71-50; fax 96-387-
71-59; e-mail etsiccp@upvnet.upv.es;
internet www.iccp.upv.es; Dir JOSÉ AGUILAR
HERRANDO.

**Higher Technical School of Industrial
Engineering:** Edificio 5F, Camino de Vera s/
n, 46022 Valencia; tel. 96-387-71-70; fax 96-
387-71-79; e-mail etsii@upvnet.upv.es;
internet www.etsii.upv.es; Dir JUAN JAIME
CANO HURTADO.

**Higher Technical School of Telecommu-
nications Engineering:** Edificio 4D,
Camino de Vera s/n, 46022 Valencia; tel.
96-387-71-90; fax 96-387-71-99; e-mail
etsitv@upvnet.upv.es; internet www.etsit
.upv.es; Dir ELÍAS DE LOS REYES DAVÓ.

**Higher Technical School of the Rural
Environment and Oenology:** Avda Blasco
Ibáñez, 21, 46010 Valencia; tel. 96-387-71-40;
fax 96-387-71-49; e-mail euita@upvnet.upv
.es; internet www.euita.upv.es; Dir SANTIAGO
GUILLEM PICÓ.

**Higher Technical School of Design Engi-
neering:** Edificio 7B, Camino de Vera s/n,
46022 Valencia; tel. 96-387-71-80; fax 96-387-
71-89; e-mail info@etsid.upv.es; internet
www.etsid.upv.es; Dir ENRIQUE BALLESTER
SARRIAS.

**Higher Technical School of Geodesic,
Cartographic and Topographic Engineering:** Edificio 7E, Camino de Vera s/n,
46022 Valencia; tel. 96-387-71-60; fax 96-387-
71-69; e-mail etsigct@upvnet.upv.es; internet
www.top.upv.es; Dir MANUEL CHUECA PAZOS.

**Higher Technical School of Building
Management:** Edificio 1B, Camino de Vera
s/n, 46022 Valencia; tel. 96-387-71-20; fax 96-
387-79-43; e-mail euat@upvnet.upv.es;
internet www.arq.upv.es; Dir RAFAEL CAPUZ
LLADRÓ.

**Higher Technical School of Applied
Computer Science:** Edificio 1G, Camino
de Vera s/n, 46022 Valencia; tel. 96-387-72-
10; fax 96-387-72-19; e-mail einf_ei@upvnet
.upv.es; internet www.eui.upv.es; Dir ANTO-
NIO ROBLES MARTÍNEZ.

**Faculty of Business Administration and
Management:** Edificio 8H, Camino de Vera
s/n, 46022 Valencia; tel. 96-387-92-70; fax 96-
387-92-79; e-mail ade@upv.es; internet www
.upv.es/ade; Dean ENRIQUE DE MIGUEL FER-
NÁNDEZ.

Faculty of Fine Arts: Edificio 3L, Camino
de Vera s/n, 46022 Valencia; tel. 96-387-72-
20; fax 96-387-92-29; e-mail fbbaa@upvnet
.upv.es; internet www.bbaa.upv.es; Dean
ELÍAS MIGUEL PÉREZ GARCÍA.

Faculty of Computer Science: Edificio 1E,
Camino de Vera s/n, 46022 Valencia; tel. 96-
387-72-00; fax 96-387-79-24; e-mail finfv@
upvnet.upv.es; internet www.fiv.upv.es;
Dean EMILIO SANCHÍS ARNAL.

Higher Polytechnic School, Gandía: Carretera Nazaret-Oliva s/n, 46730 Gandía
(Valencia); tel. 96-284-93-00; fax 96-284-93-
09; e-mail epsg@upvnet.upv.es; internet
www.epsg.upv.es; Dir MARÍA MANUELA FER-
NÁNDEZ MÉNDEZ.

Higher Polytechnic School, Alcoy: Pl.
Ferrándiz Carbonell s/n, 08301 Alcoy (Alicante); tel. 96-652-84-00; fax 96-652-84-09;
e-mail epsa@upvnet.upv.es; internet www
.epsa.upv.es; Dir ENRIQUE JUAN MASIÁ
BUADES

HEADS OF DEPARTMENTS

Agricultural Mechanization and Technology:
CARLOS GRACIA LÓPEZ
Agroforestry Ecosystems: HERMINIO BOIRA
TORTAJADA
Animal Science: MARCIAL PLA TORRES
Applied Mathematics: ALFREDO PERIS MAN-
GUILLOT
Applied Physics: MARÍA DEL CARMEN MILLÁN
GONZÁLEZ
Applied Statistics and Operational Research
and Quality: ANDRÉS CARRIÓN GARCÍA
Applied Thermodynamics: JOSÉ MANUEL
PINAZO OJER
Architectural Composition: JUAN FRANCISCO
NOGUERA GIMÉNEZ
Architectural Drawing: JUAN JOSÉ CISNEROS
VIVÓ
Architectural Projects: VICENTE MAS LLORENS
Architectural Structures: JAVIER BENLLOCH
MARCO
Audiovisual Communication, Documentation
and History of Art: JOAN IGNACI ALIAGA
MORELL
Biotechnology: LUIS ANTONIO ROIG PICAZO
Business Organization, Financial Economics
and Accountancy: IGNACIO GIL PECHUÁN
Cartographic Engineering, Geodesy and
Photogrammetry: JOSÉ LUIS BERNE VALERO
Chemical and Nuclear Engineering: JAIME
LORA GARCÍA
Chemistry: MARÍA DOLORES CLIMENT MORATO
Communications: ALBERTO GONZÁLEZ SALVA-
DOR
Conservation and Restoration of Items of
Cultural Merit: M. PILAR ROIG PICAZO
Construction Engineering and Civil Engi-
neering Projects: PEDRO MIGUEL SOSA
Continuum Mechanics and Theory of Struc-
tures: JUAN ANTONIO ROVIRA SOLER
Drawing: MIGUEL ÁNGEL GUILLEM ROMEU
Economics and Social Sciences: RICARDO JOSÉ
SERVER IZQUIERDO

Electrical Engineering: JOSÉ ROGER FOLCH

Electronic Engineering: ANTONIO MOCHOLÍ SALCEDO

Engineering Drawing: FRANCISCO DE ASÍS GOZALVEZ BENAVENTE

Engineering Projects: ELISEO GÓMEZ-SENENT MARTÍNEZ

Food Technology: PEDRO FITO MAUPOEY

Hydraulic Engineering and Environment: JUAN BAUTISTA MARCO SEGURA

Information Systems and Computation: OSCAR PASTOR LÓPEZ

Land Engineering: FRANCISCO ÁNGEL IZQUIERDO SILVESTRE

Languages: MA. CRISTINA PÉREZ GUILLOT

Mechanical and Materials Engineering: CARLOS FERRER GIMÉNEZ

Painting: JUAN BAUTISTA PEIRÓ LÓPEZ

Rural and Agroalimentary Engineering: JOSÉ LUIS GUTIÉRREZ MONTES

Sculpture: EMILIO JOSÉ MARTÍNEZ ARROYO

Systems and Computer Information Science: PEDRO JOAQUÍN GIL VICENTE

Systems Engineering and Automation: JULIÁN JOSÉ SALT LLOBREGAT

Textile and Paper Engineering: FRANCISCO JAVIER CASES IBORRA

Thermic Machines and Motors: FRANCISCO PAYRI GONZÁLEZ

Town Planning: JOSÉ VICENTE FERRANDO CORELL

Transport Engineering and Infrastructure: JOSÉ VICENTE COLOMER FERRANDIZ

Vegetal Biology: JOSÉ LUIS GUARDIOLA BARCENA

Vegetal Production: MANUEL AGUSTÍ FONFRÍA

ATTACHED INSTITUTIONS

Faculty of Business Studies: Guillem de Castro 175, 46008 Valencia; tel. 96-392-48-84; fax 96-391-98-27; e-mail fee@fee.edu; internet www.fee.edu; Dir, International Area FRANCISCO JAVIER LARA.

Florida Training Centre: C/ Rei En Jaume I No. 2, Ap. Correos 15, 46470 Catarroja (Valencia); tel. 96-122-03-80; fax 96-126-99-33; e-mail info.general@florida-uni.es; internet www.florida-uni.es; Areas of study: mechanics, industrial electronics; Gen. Dir EMPAR MARTÍNEZ BONAFÉ.

Mediterranean University of Science and Technology: Edificio Galileo Galilei, Avda de los Naranjos s/n, 46022 Valencia; tel. 96-372-27-55; fax 96-355-26-18; e-mail secretary@must-es.com; internet www .must-es.com; Dir Dr MEIAD THANOON YOUNIS.

Pax University College of Tourism: Espinosa 5, 46008 Valencia; tel. 96-391-33-94; fax 96-391-98-63; e-mail pax@cece.es; internet www.paxcentroestudios.com.

UPV Xàtiva: C/ San Agustín 9, 46800 Xàtiva (Valencia); tel. 96-228-34-06; fax 96-228-39-83; Areas of study: automatic systems, computer applications.

Colleges

GENERAL

Schiller International University – Spain: (For general information, see entry for Schiller International University in Germany chapter)

San Bernardo 97–99, Edif. Colomina, 28015 Madrid; tel. 91-448-24-88; fax 91-445-21-10; e-mail admissions@schillermadrid.edu; internet www.schillermadrid.edu; f. 1967; Dir L. BURGUNDE.

Universidad Internacional Menéndez Pelayo: Palacio de la Magdalena, 39005 Santander; tel. 942-29-88-00; fax 942-29-88-

20; internet www.uimp.es; f. 1932; offers long-vacation courses to Spanish and foreign students and grants fellowships for scientific research; library: 15,200 vols; 700 teachers; 15,000 students; there are campuses in Santander, Barcelona, Cuenca, Santa Cruz de Tenerife, La Coruña, Seville, Valencia, Formigal (Huesca); Rector JOSÉ LUIS GARCÍA DELGADO; Vice-Rector (Academic Affairs) ROSARIO GANDOY JUSTE; Vice-Rector (Economic Affairs) MONTSERRAT CASADO FRANCISCO; Vice-Rector (Courses for Foreign Students) ANTONIO SÁNCHEZ TRIGUEROS; Vice-Rector (Institutional Relations) SANTOS MIGUEL RUESGA BENITO; Registrar MIGUEL CARRERA TROYANO; Manager JESÚS GÜEMES MUTILBA.

ECONOMICS AND LAW

ESADE (Escuela Superior de Administración y Dirección de Empresas) (Higher School of Administration and Business Management): Avda Pedralbes 60–62, 08034 Barcelona; tel. 93-280-61-62; fax 93-204-81-05; e-mail info@esade.edu; internet www.esade.es; f. 1958; schools of business, law, languages, tourism; Dir-Gen. CARLOS LOSADA MARRODÁN; Registrar ANTONI M. GÜELL; Chief Administrator JOSEP MARÍA BRIL COMBALÍA; Madrid Campus at: C/ Mateo Inurria 27, 28036 Madrid; tel. 91-359-77-14; fax 91-703-00-62; e-mail esade.madrid@esade.edu.

EuroArab Management School (EAMS): Calle Cárcel Baja 3, 18001 Granada; tel. 958-80-50-50; fax 958-80-01-52; e-mail info@eams .fundea.es; internet www.eams.fundea.es; f. 1995 jtly by the EU and the League of Arab States, with support of Spanish Govt; management development; Dir-Gen. JOAQUÍN ABÓS.

Institut Universitari d'Estudis Europeus: Universitat Autonoma de Barcelona Edifici E1, 08193 Bellaterra (Barcelona); tel. 93-581-70-16; fax 93-581-30-63; internet selene.uab.es/_cs_ivee/; studies in political, economic, cultural, scientific and judicial aspects of modern Europe; participates in conferences on European issues throughout Spain; Jt Presidents ANNA TERRON, LLUÍS FERRER; Dir FRANCESC MORATA.

Instituto de Empresa: María de Molina 11, 28006 Madrid; tel. 91-568-96-00; fax 91-411-55-03; e-mail admissions@ie.edu; internet www.ie.edu; f. 1973; MBA and other management-related postgraduate programmes; Dean ANGEL CABRERA.

Real Colegio Universitario 'Escorial-María Cristina': Paseo de los Alamillos 2, 28200 San Lorenzo del Escorial, (Madrid); tel. 91-890-45-45; fax 91-890-66-09; e-mail secretaria@rcumariacristina.com; internet www.rcumariacristina.com/esp/index.php; f. 1892; private college of the Augustinian Fathers accredited by Universidad Complutense de Madrid; library: 57,000 vols, 500 periodicals; 60 teachers; 1,200 students; Rector EDELMIRO MATEOS MATEOS; Vice-Rector JESÚS MIGUEL BENÍTEZ SÁNCHEZ; Secretary JOSE RODRÍGUEZ DÍEZ; Dean of the Faculty of Law PROMETEO CEREZO DE DIEGO; Dean of the Faculty of Economics AGUSTÍN ALONSO RODRÍGUEZ; Librarian FLORENTINO DÍEZ FERNÁNDEZ; publs *Anuario jurídico y económico escurialense* (annually), *La Ciudad de Dios* (quarterly), *Nueva Etapa* (annually).

MEDICINE

Escuela Andaluza de Salud Pública: Campus Universitario de Cartuja, Apdo 2070, 18080 Granada; tel. 958-02-74-00; fax 958-02-75-03; e-mail comunicacion@easp.es;

internet www.easp.es; f. 1985; master's degree and other courses in public health management and services; drug information centre; cancer registry; library: 28,000 vols, 842 current periodicals; 45 teachers; 1,900 students; Dir HERMINIA MUÑOZ.

MILITARY SCIENCE

Escuela de Guerra del Ejército (Army War College): Santa Cruz de Marcenado 25, 28015 Madrid; tel. 91-547-96-01; fax 91-542-55-09; f. 1842; 60 teachers; 180 students; library: 135,202 vols; Dir Brig.-Gen. RICARDO MARTÍNEZ ISIDORO.

TECHNOLOGY

Escuela Técnica Superior de Ingenieros Industriales (School of Industrial Engineering): José Gutiérrez Abascal 2, 28006 Madrid; tel. 91-261-58-91; fax 91-261-86-18; internet www.etsii.upm.es; f. 1850; 350 teachers; 3,500 students; library: see Libraries; Dir CARLOS VERA ÁLVAREZ.

ETEA: Escritor Castilla Aguayo 4, Apdo 439, 14004 Córdoba; tel. 957-22-21-00; fax 957-22-21-01; e-mail comunica@etea.com; internet www.etea.com; f. 1963; undergraduate and postgraduate courses in business administration; research institute; extension courses in management; management consultancy services; 150 teachers; library: 40,000 vols, 400 periodicals; Dir JESÚS RAMÍREZ SOBRINO.

Institut Químic de Sarrià (Sarrià Institute of Chemistry): Universitat Ramon Llull, Calle Via Augusta 390, 08017 Barcelona; tel. 93-267-20-00; fax 93-205-62-66; e-mail secre@iqs.url.edu; internet www.iqs.edu; f. 1916; library: 55,000 vols, 780 periodicals; 125 teachers; 1,120 students; Pres. Dr LLUÍS VICTORI COMPANYS; Sec. Dr XAVIER TOMÀS MORER; Librarian ROSER ÉSCUDÉ; publs *Afinidad* (6 a year), *IQS* (annually)

DIRECTORS

Analytical Chemistry: Dr LLUÍS VICTORI COMPANYS

Applied Statistics: Dr XAVIER TOMÀS MORER

Business Management: Dr JESÚS TRICÀS PRECKLER

Chemical Engineering: Dr MIQUEL GASSIOT MATAS

Economics and Finance: Dr CARLOS MOSLARES GARCÍA

Industrial Engineering: EMILIO LÓPEZ TORIBIO

Organic Chemistry: Dr JOSÉ I. BORRELL BILBAO

Schools of Art, Architecture and Music

Conservatorio Profesional de Música y Escuela de Arte Dramático: Málaga; 450 students; Dir JOSÉ ANDREU NAVARRO.

Conservatorio Superior de Música: Angel de Saavedra 1, 14003 Córdoba; tel. 957-47-66-61; fax 957-48-77-52; f. 1862; 2,300 students; library: 15,000 vols; Dir MA SOLEDAD NIETO GARCÍA; Sub-Dir CASIMIRO TIRADO ROJAS; Sec. JOAQUÍN CASTELLS CANET.

Conservatorio Superior de Música: Calle Jesús del Gran Poder 49, 41002 Seville; tel. 95-438-10-09; fax 95-438-33-57; f. 1935; teaching and training in music; 117 teachers; 2,400 students; library: 8,000 vols, 20,000 scores; Dir FERNANDO PÉREZ HERRERA; Vice-Dir FRANCISCO JAVIER LÓPEZ; Sec. BEGOÑA SÁNCHEZ PEÑA; publ. *Diferencias*.

Conservatorio Superior de Música de San Sebastián: Easo 45, 20006 San Sebastián; tel. 943-46-64-88; fax 943-45-18-92; 45

teachers; library of 3,000 books, 2,500 records, 16,500 scores; Dir ROBERTO NUÑO.

Conservatorio Superior de Música y Escuela de Arte Dramático: Paseo del Malecón s/n, 30009 Murcia; tel. 968-29-47-58; f. 1916; 100 teachers; 3,000 students; library: c. 5,000 vols; 1,200 audio materials; Dir CELIA GUIRADO CID; publ. *Cadencia* (3 a year).

Conservatorio Superior de Música de Valencia: Camino de Vera 29, 46022 Valencia; tel. 96-369-67-32; fax 96-393-37-98; e-mail 46013129@centres.cult.gua.es; f. 1879; 40 teachers; 900 students; library: 10,820 vols; Dir JOSÉ VICENTE CERVERA; Sec. GREGORIO JIMÉNEZ; publ. *Memoria* (annually).

Conservatorio Superior Municipal de Música de Barcelona: Calle Bruc 112, 08009 Barcelona; tel. 93-458-43-02; fax 93-459-31-04; f. 1886; 102 teachers; 1,815 students; library: 27,400 vols and scores; 7,250 items of audio material; Dir ESTHER VILAR TORRENS.

Escuela Superior de Bellas Artes de San Carlos (Valencia School of Fine Arts): San

Pio 9, 46010 Valencia; f. 1756; library: 5,105 vols; 26 teachers; 300 students; Dir DANIEL DE NUEDA LLISIONA; Sec. AMANDO BLANQUER PONSODA.

Escuela Superior de Musica Reina Sofía (Reina Sofía Higher School of Music): Mártires Oblatos 25, Pozuelo de Alarcón (Estación), 28224 Madrid; tel. 91-351-10-60; fax 91-351-07-88; internet www .fundacionalbeniz.com/flash/fia.html; f. 1991; depts of performance, academic studies, artististic studies, and complementary training; library: 1,200 books, 3,600 musical scores, 2,400 CDs, 2,500 LPs, 2,500 video and audio cassettes; Pres. PALOMA O'SHEA; Acad. Dir FABIÁN PANISELLO.

Escuela Técnica Superior de Arquitectura de Sevilla (School of Architecture): Avda Reina Mercedes 2, 41012 Seville; tel. 95-455-65-00; fax 95-455-65-34; internet www.arquitectura.us.es; f. 1964; 2,200 students; 153 teachers; library: 17,000 vols; Dir Dr JOSÉ ORAD ARAGÓN.

Instituto Formación Profesional 'Islas Filipinas': Calle Jesús Maestro, 28003 Madrid; tel. 91-534-37-08; f. 1985; library:

15,000 vols; 109 teachers; 1,900 students; delineation and graphics; Dir FIDEL HIGUERA GORRIDO.

Real Conservatorio Profesional de Música 'Manuel de Falla': Calle Marquez del Real Tesoro s/n, 11001 Cádiz; tel. 956-21-22-82; fax 956-22-39-18; 1,000 students.

Real Conservatorio Superior de Música de Madrid (Royal Academy of Music): Calle Doctor Mata 2, 28012 Madrid; tel. 91-539-29-01; fax 91-468-44-25; e-mail direccion@ real-conserv-madrid.es; internet www .real-conserv-madrid.es; f. 1830; 150 teachers; 700 students; library: 175,000 vols; Dir MIGUEL DEL BARCO; Deputy Dir DANIEL VEGA; Sec. JOSE M. MUÑOZ; publ. *Musica* (annually).

Real Escuela Superior de Arte Dramático (Royal School of Dramatic Art): Avda de Nazaret 2, Madrid 28009; tel. 91-504-21-51; fax 91-574-11-38; e-mail resad@resad.es; internet www.resad.es; f. 1831; 50 teachers; 325 students; library: 22,300 vols; Dir IGNACIO GARCÍA MAY.

SRI LANKA

The Higher Education System

Institutions of higher education predate the independence of Sri Lanka (formerly Ceylon) from the United Kingdom in 1948, with the oldest being University of Colombo, which was founded in 1921 (present name 1979). In 1978 an Act of Parliament created the current university system, following which several existing colleges were promoted to university status. There are 26 teacher-training colleges, 12 universities, 13 polytechnic institutes, eight junior technical colleges and an open university. In 2003 there were 59,734 students enrolled at the 12 universities. The governing body of the universities is the University Grants Commission. The universities are mostly government funded, and although students do not pay tuition fees they are required to pay registration and examination fees.

A minimum of three GCE A-level passes are required for admission to higher education. The undergraduate Bachelors degree is classified as either 'General' or 'Special': the former last three years and covers three subjects in equal depth, while the latter lasts four years and is a subject-specific programme of study, culminating with a dissertation. Professional degrees last four years and are offered in technical or practical disciplines such as medicine, engineering and architecture. Graduates with the Bachelors degree are eligible for the one-year Postgraduate Diploma or the two-year Masters degree. Finally, the Doctorate (mostly PhD) is awarded after a two- or three-year period of research following the award of the Masters.

Post-secondary technical and vocational education comprises: short-term training courses of up to six months offered to all school-leavers by the Ministry of Vocational and Technical Training and the National Apprenticeship Board; and courses of two to four years leading to the award of, variously, the National Certificate, National Diploma and Higher National Diploma.

Learned Societies

GENERAL

Institute of Sinhala Culture: 375 Bauddhaloka Mawatha, Colombo 7; tel. (11) 4687979; f. 1954 for the preservation and development of Sinhala culture: art and architecture, drama, dance, music, folklore, arts and crafts, film, research, traditional embroidery, puppetry; presents cultural programmes; holds seminars and workshops; 680 mems; Pres. L. STANLEY JAYEWARDANE; Hon. Sec. Mrs R. G. SENANAYAKE.

National Academy of Sciences of Sri Lanka: 120/10 Wijerama Mawatha, Colombo 7; f. 1976; 104 mems; Pres. Prof. M. U. S. SULTANBAWA; Gen. Sec. Prof. ERIC H. KARUNANAYAKE; Sec. for Foreign Relations Dr U. PETHIYAGODA.

Royal Asiatic Society of Sri Lanka: Royal Asiatic Society Bldg, 96 Ananda Coomaraswamy Mawatha, Colombo 7; tel. and fax (11) 2699249; e-mail rassl@col7.metta.lk; internet www.rassrilanka.org; f. 1845; promotes inquiries into the history, religions, languages, literature, arts, sciences and social conditions of the present and former inhabitants of Sri Lanka, and connected cultures; library contains one of the largest collections of books on Sri Lanka, and others on Indian and Eastern culture in general; 500 mems; Pres. Dr K. D. PARANAVITANA; Hon. Secs K. ARUNASIRI, M. G. SAMARAWEERA; Admin. Sec. B. E. WIJESURIYA; publ. *Journal* (annually).

BIBLIOGRAPHY, LIBRARY SCIENCE AND MUSEOLOGY

Sri Lanka Library Association: The Professional Centre, 275/75 Bauddhaloka Mawatha, Colombo 7; tel. (11) 4589103; f. 1960; 415 mems; Pres. H. U. YAPA; Gen. Sec. DEEPDI TALAGALA; publs *Sri Lanka Library Review* (annually), *SLLA Newsletter* (quarterly).

ECONOMICS, LAW AND POLITICS

Ceylon Institute of World Affairs: c/o Mervyn de Silva, 82B Ward Place, Colombo 7; f. 1957; Pres. Maj.-Gen. ANTON MUTTUKUMARU.

EDUCATION

National Education Society of Sri Lanka: Faculty of Education, University of Colombo, Colombo 3; 75 mems; publ. *Education*.

FINE AND PERFORMING ARTS

Arts Council of Sri Lanka: 8th Fl., Sethsiripaya, Battaramulla; tel. (11) 4872031; fax (11) 4872035; f. 1952 to promote art projects in Sri Lanka; the Council carries out projects in all fields of arts, incl. painting, drama, music, literature, ballet, dancing, folk song, folklore; Pres. K. JAYATILAKA; Sec. RAJENDRA BANDARA; publ. *Kala Magazine* (4 a year).

Ceylon Society of Arts: Art Gallery, Ananda Coomarassamy Mawatha, Colombo 7; tel. (11) 4693067; f. 1887; Pres. KALAPATHI P. SUNIL; Hon. Gen. Sec. M. D. S. GUNATHILAKE.

HISTORY, GEOGRAPHY AND ARCHAEOLOGY

Archaeological Society of Sri Lanka: c/o Dept of Archaeology, Sir Marcus Fernando Mawata, Colombo 7; f. 1966; Pres. Prof. CHANDRA WIKKRAMAGAMAGE; Co-Secs S. LAKDUSINGHE, W. H. WIJAYAPALA.

Ceylon Geographical Society: 61 Abdul Caffoor Mawatha, Colombo 3; f. 1938; 100 mems; Pres. Prof. K. KULARATNAM; Secs Dr W. P. T. SILVA, Dr K. U. SIRINANDA; publ. *The Ceylon Geographer* (annually).

LANGUAGE AND LITERATURE

Alliance Française: 11 Barnes Pl., Colombo 7; tel. (11) 2693467; fax (11) 2688735; e-mail info@alliancefr.lk; internet www.alliancefr.lk; f. 1955; offers courses and exams in French language and culture and promotes cultural exchange with France; attached teaching centres in Kandy and Matara; 600 mems; Dir JEAN-PAUL FAURE; publ. *Rendezvous* (monthly).

British Council: 49 Alfred House Gardens, POB 753, Colombo 3; tel. (11) 2581171; fax (11) 2587079; e-mail enquiries@britishcouncil.lk; internet www.britishcouncil.lk; teaching centre; offers courses and exams in English language and British culture and promotes cultural exchange with the UK; responsible for British Council work in the Maldives; attached teaching centre in Kandy; Dir TONY O'BRIEN; Teaching Centre Man. RICHARD LUNT.

English Speaking Union of Sri Lanka: 14A, 16k Lane Galle Rd, Colombo 3; tel. (11) 4575843; f. 1981; library of 3,000 vols; includes an English Language School; Pres. Dr TERENCE AMERASINGHE; publ. *Open Mind* (quarterly).

Goethe-Institut: 39, Gregory's Rd, Colombo; tel. (11) 2694562; fax (11) 2693351; e-mail vt@colombo.goethe.org; internet www.goethe.de/colombo; f. 1957; offers courses and exams in German language and culture and promotes cultural exchange with Germany; library of 6,000 vols; Dir RICHARD LANG.

MEDICINE

Sri Lanka Medical Association: Wijerama House, 6 Wijerama Mawatha, Colombo 7; tel. (11) 4693324; fax (11) 4698802; e-mail slma@eureka.lk; f. 1887; 1,200 mems; Pres. Prof. RAVINDRA FERNANDO; Hon. Sec. Dr CHANDRIKA N. WIJEYARATNE; publs *Newsletter* (monthly), *Ceylon Medical Journal* (4 a year), *Abstracts of Anniversary Academic Sessions* (annually).

NATURAL SCIENCES

General

Sri Lanka Association for the Advancement of Science: 120/10 Vidya Mandiraya, Vidya Mawatha, Colombo 7; tel. and fax (11) 2691681; e-mail slaas@ltmin.com; internet www.nsf.ac.lk/slaas; f. 1944 to provide for systematic direction of scientific enquiry in the interests of the country, to promote contact among scientific workers, and to disseminate scientific knowledge, etc.; holds annual session; seven sections; 6,000 mems; Gen. Pres. Dr T. SOMASERKARAM; Gen. Secs Prof. JAYANTHA WELIHINDA, Dr SUDARSHINI WASALATANTHRI; publs *Proceedings*, *Vidya Viyapthi*, *Vingnana Murusu*.

PHILOSOPHY AND PSYCHOLOGY

Ceylon Humanist Society: Rutnam Inst. Bldg, University Lane, Jaffna; Pres. J. T. RUTNAM; Sec. O. M. DE ALWIS.

RELIGION, SOCIOLOGY AND ANTHROPOLOGY

Buddhist Academy of Ceylon: 109 Rosmead Place, Colombo.

Maha Bodhi Society of Sri Lanka: 130 Rev. Hikkaduwe Sri Sumangala Na Himi Mawatha, Colombo 10; tel. and fax (11) 2677626; f. 1891 for propagation of Buddhism throughout the world; 892 mems; Pres. BANAGALA UPATISSA NAYAKA THERO; Hon. Sec. DAYANANDA TISSERA; publ. *Sinhala Bauddhaya* (monthly).

TECHNOLOGY

Institution of Engineers, Sri Lanka: 120/15 Wijerama Mawatha, Colombo 7; tel. (11) 4698426; fax (11) 4699202; e-mail iesl@slt.lk; internet www.iesl.slt.lk; f. 1906; 7,273 mems; library of 12,000 vols; Pres. Eng. Prof. L. RATNAYAKE; Exec. Sec. Eng. RUSSEL DE ZILVA; publs *Engineer* (every 4 months), *Sri Lanka Engineering News* (monthly), *Transactions* (annually).

Research Institutes

AGRICULTURE, FISHERIES AND VETERINARY SCIENCE

Coconut Research Institute: Bandirippuwa Estate, Lunuwila 61150; tel. (31) 2255300; fax (31) 2257391; e-mail director@cri.lkt; internet www.cri.lk; f. 1929; quasi-governmental research institute serving coconut industry of Sri Lanka; library: see Libraries and Archives; Chair. Dr D. B. T. WIJERATNE; Dir Dr C. JAYASEKEARE; publs *COCOS, Coconut Bulletin, Annual Report, Coco News* (4 a year).

Hector Kobbekaduwa Agrarian Research and Training Institute: POB 1522, 114 Wijerama Mawatha, Colombo 7; tel. (11) 4696981; fax (11) 4692423; e-mail harti@slt.lk; internet www.harti.slt.lk; f. 1972; research into and policy analysis on agrarian structures and the economic, social and institutional aspects of agricultural development; operates training programmes; library: see Libraries; Dir Dr S. G. SAMARASINGHE; publ. *Sri Lanka Journal of Agrarian Studies* (in English and Sinhala, 2 a year).

Horticultural Research and Development Institute: Gannoruwa, Peradeniya; tel. (81) 2288011; f. 1965; research on fruit, vegetables, roots and tubers and other horticultural crops, and soya processing; library of 16,500 vols; Dir Dr S. D. B. G. JAYAWARDANE; publ. *Tropical Agriculturist* (annually).

National Aquatic Resources Research and Development Agency: Crow Island, Colombo 15; tel. (11) 4522000; fax (11) 4522932; e-mail postmast@nara.ac.lk; internet www.nara.ac.lk; f. 1982; Dir-Gen. D. S. JAYAKODY; publ. *Journal* (annually).

Rice Research and Development Institute: Batalagoda, Ibbagamuwa; tel. (37) 2222681; fax (37) 2222681; e-mail rice@rrdi.ac.lk; f. 1994; Dir S. ABEYSIRIWARDENE.

Rubber Research Institute of Sri Lanka: Dartonfield, Agalawatta; tel. (34) 2247426; fax (34) 2247427; e-mail director@rri.ac.lk; f. 1910; Colombo office and laboratories: Telawala Rd, Ratmalana, Mt Lavinia; research and advisory services on rubber planting and manufacture; comprises five research depts, extension dept and economic research unit, specification unit and estate dept; about 500 staff; Dir Dr L. M. K. TILLEKERATNE; publs *Annual Report, Annual Review*, journals, bulletins and advisory circulars.

Tea Research Institute of Sri Lanka: St Coombs, Talawakelle; tel. (52) 2258385; fax (52) 2258311; e-mail postmaster@tri.ac.lk; internet www.tri.gov.lk; f. 1925; library: see Libraries; Dir M. T. ZIYAD MOHAMED; publs *Annual Report, Sri Lanka Journal of Tea Science* (2 a year), *Tea Bulletin* (2 a year), *TRI Update* (2 a year).

Veterinary Research Institute: POB 28, Gannoruwa, Peradeniya; tel. (81) 2288311; fax (81) 2288125; e-mail ddvri@slk.lk; f. 1967; concerned with research and investigations into health and production problems of livestock and poultry; veterinary vaccine production; Head Dr RANJITH WICKRAMASINGHE; publ. *Sri Lanka Veterinary Journal* (4 a year).

ECONOMICS, LAW AND POLITICS

Economic Research Unit: Business Intelligence Dept, Bank of Ceylon, Colombo; Business Intelligence Officer S. E. A. JAYAWICKREMA.

Marga Institute: POB 601, 93/10 Dutugemunu St, Kirullapone, Colombo 6; tel. (11) 4829051; fax (11) 4828597; e-mail marga@sri.lanka.net; internet www.margasrilanka.org; f. 1972; non-profit multi-disciplinary research org. undertaking critical, non-partisan study of devt issues in Sri Lanka and the wider Asian region; library of 25,000 vols, 37 periodicals; Chair. Dr LLOYD FERNANDO; Exec. Gov. BASIL ILANGAKOON; publ. *The Marga Quarterly Journal*.

Wiros Lokh Institute: 81-1A Isipatana Mawatha, Colombo 5; tel. and fax (11) 2580817; e-mail wiroshermes@yahoo.com; internet saarcwb.1accesshost.com; f. 1981; private research and training foundation; promotes awareness of globalization in the region; special projects: innovation in social housing and financing, urban regeneration and sports recreation for urban areas; library of 17,000 vols; Dir (Child Div.) CHANDRIKA GUNESEKERA.

HISTORY, GEOGRAPHY AND ARCHAEOLOGY

Archaeological Survey Department of Sri Lanka: Sir Marcus Fernando Rd, Colombo 7; tel. (11) 4694727; fax (11) 4696250; e-mail arch@diamond.lanka.net; f. 1890; library of 15,000 vols; Dir-Gen. S. U. DERANIYAGALA; publs *Administration Report* (annually), *Ancient Ceylon* (annually), *Memoirs*.

MEDICINE

Medical Research Institute: Baseline Rd, Colombo 8; tel. (11) 4677715; e-mail medrisit@slt.lk; f. 1900; comprising departments of Bacteriology, Biochemistry, Chemistry of Natural Products, Entomology, Food and Water Bacteriology, Leptospira, Media, Mycology, Clinical Pathology, Parasitology, Nutrition, Pharmacology, Salmonella, Serology, Vaccines, Virology, Animal Centre, School of Medical Laboratory Technology; Dir Dr G. S. S. K. COLOMBAGE.

NATURAL SCIENCES

Biological Sciences

Department of Wild Life Conservation: 18 Gregory's Rd, Colombo 7; tel. (11) 4698086; fax (11) 4698556; f. 1950; library of 1,962 vols; Dir N. W. DISSANAYAKE; publs *Sri Lanka Wild Life, Vana Divi* (annually), *National Parks of Sri Lanka*.

Physical Sciences

Colombo Observatory: Dept of Meteorology, Bauddhaloka Mawatha, Colombo 7; tel. (11) 4684746; fax (11) 4691443; e-mail meteo@slt.lk; f. 1907; climatological data for Sri Lanka; time service; astronomical service; weather forecasting; agrometeorological service; library of 18,000 vols; Dir Dr A. W. MOHOTTALA; publs *Report of the Department of Meteorology* (annually), *Agrometeorological Bulletin* (4 a year).

TECHNOLOGY

Geological Survey and Mines Bureau: Senanayake Bldg, 4 Galle Rd, Dehiwala; tel. (11) 2725745; fax (11) 2735752; e-mail gsmb@slt.lk; internet www.gsmb.sit.lk; f. 1903; systematic geological mapping of Sri Lanka; identification and assessment of its mineral resources; issues licences to regulate exploration, mining, processing, transport, trading in and export of minerals; Chair. Prof. P. G. R. DHARMARATNE (acting); Dir S. WEERAWARNAKULA; publs *Annual Report, Memoirs, Mineral Year Book*.

Industrial Technology Institute: 363 Bauddhaloka Mawatha, Colombo 7; tel. (11) 4693807; fax (11) 4686567; e-mail info@iti.lk; internet www.iti.lk; f. 1955 as Ceylon Institute of Scientific and Industrial Research; present name 1998; applied technical research in several industrial sectors for government agencies and the public; process research, resource studies, waste material utilization, product testing, standards, calibration and repair of instruments, technical consultation; industrial devt; information services centre: see Libraries and Archives; Chair Prof. VIJAYA KUMAR; publs *Annual Report, Bulletin* (4 a year).

National Science Foundation: 47/5 Maitland Pl., Colombo 7; tel. (11) 2696771; fax (11) 2691691; e-mail info@nsf.ac.lk; internet www.nsf.ac.lk; f. 1968 as Nat. Science Council; initiates, facilitates and supports basic and applied scientific research by universities, scientific and technological institutions and scientists; fosters the interchange of scientific information among scientists in Sri Lanka and foreign countries; awards scholarships and fellowships for scientific study or work at appropriate institutions; provides a central clearing house for the collection and analysis of data on the scientific and technical resources in Sri Lanka; provides information for policy formulation on science and technology; promotes the popularization of science; documentation and publications unit; acts as National Research Reports Depository on science and technology; library of 6,518 vols; Dir M. WATSON; publs *Journal* (4 a year), *Sri Lanka Journal of Social Sciences* (2 a year).

Sri Lanka Water Resources Board: 2A Gregory's Ave, Colombo 7; established 1966; advises the Government on all matters concerning the conservation and utilization of water resources; library of 4,620 vols, 60 periodicals; Chair. K. YOGANATHAN.

Libraries and Archives

Agalawatta

Rubber Research Institute of Sri Lanka Library: Dartonfield, Agalawatta; branch library: Telawala Rd, Ratmalana; tel. (34) 2247426; fax (34) 2247427; e-mail dir_rri@edb.tradesitsl.lk; f. 1953; 8,000 vols, 236 periodical titles; Dir Dr L. M. K. TILLEKERATNE; publs *Annual Review, Journal* (2 a year), *Bulletin* (2 a year), *Rubber Puwath* (annually).

Colombo

Centre for Development Information: National Planning Dept, Ministry of Finance and Planning, POB 1547, Galleface Secretariat, Colombo 1; tel. (11) 4449378; fax (11) 4448063; e-mail cdinp@sltnet.lk; f. 1979 to co-ordinate and collate socio-economic information; participates in regional information networks, and maintains an int. exchange programme; national focal point for the SAARC Documentation Centre, New Delhi, India; 15,000 vols, unpublished reports collection; Deputy Dir ANNE PERERA; publs *Bibliography of Economic and Social Development in Sri Lanka, Register of Development Research in Sri Lanka, Press Index* (quarterly), *Guide to current periodical literature in economic and social development* (quarterly), *Current Acquisitions* (quarterly).

Colombo National Museum Library: POB 854, Colombo 7; f. 1877 (incorporating collection of Government Oriental Library, f. 1870); depository for Sri Lanka publications since 1885; 618,221 items (including 141,703 monographs, 4,500 periodical titles, 3,772 palm leaf MSS in Sinhala and Sanskrit, Pali, Burmese and Cambodian); publs *Sri Lanka Periodicals Index, NML Acquisitions Bulletin, Sri Lanka Periodicals Directory, Bibliographical Series.*

Department of National Archives: POB 1414, 7 Reid Ave, Colombo 7; tel. (11) 4694523; f. 1902; contains official records of the Dutch Administration from 1640 to 1796, British Administration from 1796 to 1948; official records of Independent Sri Lanka since 1948; a few codices of Portuguese Administration prior to 1656 and some documents in French, Sinhalese and Tamil; operates a Presidential Archival Depository and a Reference Service; operates Hon. J. R. Jayewardene Research Centre; deals with documents in private possession; is the legal depository for all printed material in the country, effects the registration of printing presses, printed publications, and newspapers; holds copies of books printed since 1885 and newspapers since 1832; Dir Dr K. D. G. WIMALARATNE; publs *Administration Report of The National Archives, Quarterly Statement of Books printed in Sri Lanka* (quarterly), *Catalogue of Newspapers* (annually), *Sri Lanka Archives* (annually).

Hector Kobbekadwa Agrarian Research and Training Institute Library: POB 1522, 114 Wijerama Mawatha, Colombo 7; tel. (11) 4696981; fax (11) 4692423; e-mail harti@slt.lk; internet www.harti.slt.lk; f. 1972; 18,000 vols and 62 periodicals; several hundred reports and reprints; special collection on Sri Lanka; part of Nat. Centre for Information on Agrarian Development; Librarian G. H. KARUNARATNE.

Industrial Technology Institute Information Services Centre: 363 Bauddhaloka Mawatha, Colombo 7; tel. (11) 4698624; f. 1955; 35,000 vols, 300 journals; several thousand reports, reprints, standards; information service to scientists, industrialists and engineers; computer database of books and articles in periodicals; national centre of Asian and Pacific Information Network on Medicinal and Aromatic Plants; Man. Information Services Centre D. S. T. WARNASURIYA; publs *Bibliographical Series, State of the Art surveys on spices and essential oilbearing plants, News Digest, Food Digest, CISIR News Bulletin, S & T News, Management Thought.*

Law Library: Hultsdorp, Colombo 12; tel. (11) 4324676; f. 1855; Dir A. COOREY.

Municipal Council Public Library: 15 Sir Marcus Fernando Mawatha, Colombo 7; tel. (11) 4691968; f. 1925; 15 brs; five mobile libraries; 794,088 vols, 2,000 periodical titles; special collections: Sri Lanka, Buddhism, FAO Depository, fine arts, Braille, Japan, Theo Auer collection; Chief Librarian M. D.

H. JAYAWARDHANA; publ. *Administration Report* (annually).

National Library and Documentation Centre: 14 Independence Ave, Colombo 7; tel. (11) 2687581; fax (11) 2685201; e-mail nldc@mail.natlib.lk; internet www.natlib.lk; f. 1990; 257,000 vols (incl. govt publs), 500 periodical titles, 6,000 microforms, 1,800 maps, audio-visual items, electronic media; special collections: Ola Leaf collection, drama MS collection, library and information science collection, Martin Wickramasinghe collection, folklore collection; ISBN, ISMN and ISSN national centres; compiles National Union Catalogue and Online Public Access Catalogue (OPAC); Dir M. S. UPALI AMARASIRI; publs *Sri Lanka National Bibliography* (monthly), *Library News* (quarterly), *Sri Lanka Newspaper Index, Periodical Article Index* (quarterly), *ISBN Publishers Directory, Natnet Lanka Newsletter, Directory of Government Publications, Index to Postgraduate Theses, Devolution of Power and Ethnic Problems* (database).

University of Colombo Library: Colombo 3; tel. and fax (11) 4583043; e-mail scj@cmb .ac.lk; f. 1967; 240,000 vols; Librarian S. C. JAYASURIYA; publs *University of Colombo Review* (annually), *Ceylon Journal of Medical Science* (2 a year), *Colombo Law Review* (annually), *Sri Lanka Journal of International Law* (annually).

Lunuwila

Coconut Research Institute Library: Lunuwila; tel. (31) 2253795; fax (31) 2257391; e-mail library@cri.lk; internet www.cri.lk; f. 1929; 9,000 vols; houses the Intl Coconut Information Centre; special collection of world literature on coconut available in hard copy; microfiches, diskettes; Librarian P. D. U. C. DHARMAPALA (acting).

Moratuwa

Centre for Industrial Technology Information Services: I. D. B., 615 Galle Rd, Katubedda, Moratuwa; tel. (11) 4605372; fax (11) 4607002; e-mail citis@slt.lk; internet www.idb.lk; f. 1988; acquisition, processing and dissemination of technology information, reference and enquiry services, networking; 13,100 vols, 42 current periodicals; Dir NALINI DE SILVA; publs *Current Awareness Bulletin, Current Contents, Karmantha Bulletin* (2 a year), *Industrial Newsletter* (4 a year).

Peradeniya

University of Peradeniya Library: POB 35, Peradeniya; tel. and fax (81) 2388678; e-mail librarian@pdn.ac.lk; internet www .pdn.ac.lk; f. 1921; 670,062 vols; collns incl. deposit materials obtained under printers' and publishers' ordinance since 1955, reference colln on Sri Lanka, palm-leaf manuscripts and rare materials on Sri Lanka, and collns on environmental and religious studies; Librarian P. E. HARRISON PERERA; publs *Ceylon Journal of Science–Biological Sciences, Ceylon Journal of Science – Physical Sciences, Sri Lanka Journal of the Humanities, Modern Sri Lanka Studies.*

Talawakele

Tea Research Institute Library: St Coombs, Talawakele; tel. (51) 2223082; fax (52) 2258229; f. 1925; 15,500 vols and 250 periodicals for reference and loan, including a specialist reference section dealing with tea and allied subjects; Librarian (vacant).

Museums and Art Galleries

Anuradhapura

Anuradhapura Folk Museum: Anuradhapura; tel. (25) 2252589; f. 1971; regional museum for North Central Province.

Colombo

Colombo Dutch Period Museum: Pettah, Colombo; tel. (11) 4448466; f. 1982; period museum depicting life and times during the Dutch rule 1656–1796.

National Museum (Cultural): Sir Marcus Fernando Mawatha, Colombo 7; tel. (11) 2697467; e-mail nmdep@slt.lk; f. 1877; national collection of art, antiquities and folk culture; research centre; Dir YASANTHA MAPATUNA.

National Museum (Natural History): Ananda Coomaraswamy Mawatha, Colombo 7; tel. (11) 2694767; f. 1985; national collection of natural sciences.

Galle

Galle National Museum: Church St, Galle; tel. (91) 2232051; f. 1986; regional museum for Galle District.

Kandy

Kandy National Museum: Dharmapala Mawatha, Kandy; tel. (81) 2223867; f. 1942; regional museum for the Central Province; 17th-18th c. Kandyan history.

Peradeniya

Royal Botanic Gardens: Peradeniya; tel. and fax (81) 2388238; e-mail dirnbg@sltnet .lk; f. 1821; 62 ha. of gardens; botanical survey of Sri Lanka, floriculture research and development; education, training and extension; Supt Dr D. S. A. WIJESUNDARA.

Ratnapura

Ratnapura National Museum: Ehelapola Walauwa, Colombo Rd, Ratnapura; tel. (45) 2252451; f. 1942; regional museum for the Sabaragamuwa Province; prehistory of the region and exhibits on gem-mining.

Universities

UNIVERSITY OF COLOMBO

94 Cumaratunga Munidasa Mawatha, Colombo 3

Telephone: (11) 2581835
Fax: (11) 2583810
Internet: www.cmb.ac.lk

Founded 1921, present name 1979
State control
Languages of instruction: Sinhala, Tamil, English
Academic year: October to September

Chancellor: Rev. Bishop OSWALD GOMIS
Vice-Chancellor: Prof. T. HETHARACHCHY
Registrar: V. S. SIVALINGAM (acting)
Rector of Sripalee Campus: W. N. WILSON
Librarian: S. C. JAYASURIYA

Number of teachers: 448
Number of students: 9,158

Publications: *The Ceylon Journal of Medical Science* (2 a year), *University of Colombo Review* (annually), *Annual Report, University Calendar* (every 3 years)

DEANS

Faculty of Arts: Prof. S. M. P. SENANAYAKE
Faculty of Education: Prof. L. S. PERERA
Faculty of Law: N. SELVAKKUMARAN

Faculty of Management and Finance: M. G.
S. P. RANDIWELA
Faculty of Medicine: Prof. S. P. LAMABADU-
SURIYA
Faculty of Science: Prof. R. L. C. WIJESUN-
DERA
Faculty of Graduate Studies: Prof. D. M. S. S.
L. DISSANAYAKE

HEADS OF DEPARTMENTS

Faculty of Arts (Reid Ave, Colombo 7; tel. (11)
2500457; fax (11) 2505758; e-mail dean@arts
.cmb.ac.lk):

Demography: W. P. AMARABANDU
Economics: Prof. A. M. G. N. K. ATTA-
NAYAKE
English: Prof. S. FERNANDO
Geography: Prof. D. H. R. JAYANTHI DE
SILVA
History and International Relations: Prof.
A. JAYAWARDENA
Political Science and Public Policy: Prof. J.
UYANGODA
Sinhala: Prof. R. PARANAVITHANA
Sociology: I. V. EDIRISINGHE

Faculty of Education (Bauddhaloka
Mawatha, Colombo 7; tel. (11) 2588812; fax
(11) 2596888; e-mail lalp@isplanka.lk):

Educational Psychology: R. ABEYPALA
Humanities Education: Dr M. E. S. PERERA
Science and Technical Education: Prof. W.
G. KARUNARATNE
Social Science Education: H. M. SENEVIR-
ATNE

Faculty of Law (Reid Ave, Colombo 7; tel. (11)
2500942; fax (11) 2502001; e-mail selvak@
lawcmb.ac.lk):

Law: Dr DEEPIKA UDAGAMA

Faculty of Management and Finance (Bauddhaloka Mawatha, Colombo 7; tel. (11)
2501295; fax (11) 2598324; e-mail office@
mgmt.cmb.ac.lk):

Commerce: D. T. D. KODAGODA
Management Studies: G. RANAWEERAGE

Faculty of Medicine (Kynsey Rd, Colombo 8;
tel. (11) 2698449; fax (11) 2691581; e-mail
dean@medifac.cmb.ac.lk):

Anatomy: B. J. J. F. PERERA
Biochemistry and Molecular Biology: Prof.
SUNETHRA ATHUKORALA
Clinical Medicine: Prof. M. H. R. SHERIFF
Community Medicine: Prof. DULITHA FER-
NANDO
Forensic Medicine and Toxicology: Dr J.
PERERA
Microbiology: Prof. JENNIFER PERERA
Obstetrics and Gynaecology: Prof. H. R.
SENEVIRATNE
Paediatrics: Prof. MANOURI SANANAYAKE
Parasitology: Prof. N. D. KARUNAWEERA
Pathology: Prof. M. V. C. DE SILVA
Pharmacology: Prof. L. JAYAKODY
Physiology: Prof. K. TENNAKOON
Psychological Medicine: Prof. N. MENDIS
Surgery: Prof. G. J. B. W. JAYASEKERA

Faculty of Science (Cumaratunga Munidasa
Mawatha, Colombo 3; tel. (11) 2503148; fax
(11) 2503148; e-mail dean@science.cmb.ac
.lk):

Botany: Prof. S. S. M. K. KSHANIKA HIR-
IMBUREGAMA
Chemistry: Dr M. D. P. DE COSTA
Mathematics: Dr A. K. K. PREMADASA
Nuclear Science: Prof. R. HEWAMANNE
Physics: Dr J. K. D. S. JAYANETTI
Plant Sciences: Prof. S. S. M. K. HIRIMBUR-
EGANA
Statistics: Dr D. R. WEERASEKERA
Zoology: D. N. DE SILVA

ATTACHED INSTITUTES

**Institute of Biochemistry, Molecular
Biology and Biotechnology:** Dir Prof. U.
P. E. H. KARUNANAYAKE.
Institute of Indigenous Medicine:
Nawala, Rajagiriya; Dir Dr H. JAYAWARDENA.
Institute of Workers' Education: 275
Bauddhaloka Mawatha, Colombo 7; Dir
Prof. H. P. R. GUNAWARDENA.
**National Institute of Library and Infor-
mation Science:** Dir PRADEEPA WIJETUNGA.
Postgraduate Institute of Medicine: 160
Norris Canal Rd, Colombo 8; Dir Prof.
LALITHA MENDIS.
**University of Colombo School of Com-
puting:** UCSC Building Complex No. 35,
Reid Ave, Colombo 7; Dir Dr A. R. WEER-
ASINGHE.

EASTERN UNIVERSITY

Vantharumoolai, Chenkaladi
Telephone: (65) 2240490
Fax: (65) 2240585
E-mail: euslreg@sltnet.lk
Internet: www.esn.ac.lk
Founded 1981 as Batticaloa University Col-
lege, present name 1986
State control
Languages of instruction: English, Tamil
Academic year: January to December
Chancellor: Dr T. VARAGUNAM
Vice-Chancellor: Prof. M. S. MOOKIAH
Registrar: A. D. HARRIS (acting)
Senior Assistant Librarian: T. ARULNANDHY
Library of 60,000 vols
Number of teachers: 105
Number of students: 2,423 (1,514 internal,
909 external)

DEANS

Faculty of Agriculture: S. RAVEENDRANATH
Faculty of Arts and Culture: A. MURUGATHAS
(acting)
Faculty of Commerce and Management: S.
SENTHILNATHAN
Faculty of Science: Dr J. C. N. RAJENDRA

HEADS OF DEPARTMENTS

Faculty of Agriculture (tel. (65) 2240530; fax
(65) 2240570; e-mail deanagri@esn.ac.lk):

Agricultural Economics: P. SIVARAJAH
Agronomy: Dr T. THIRUCHELVAM
Animal Science: J. SINNIAH

Faculty of Arts and Culture (tel. (65)
2240165; fax (65) 2240971; e-mail
deanarts@esn.ac.lk):

Arabic: Dr S. SAMINATHAN (acting)
Fine Arts: Prof. S. MAUNAGURU
Geography: S. PONNIAH
Islamic Studies: M. SELVARAJAH (acting)
Languages: Dr S. YOGARAJAH
Social Sciences: (vacant)

Faculty of Commerce and Management (tel.
(65) 2240214; fax (65) 2240591; e-mail
deanfcm@esn.ac.lk):

Commerce: N. LOGESWARAN
Economics: K. THAMBIAH
Management: Dr G. RAGURAGAVAN

Faculty of Science (tel. (65) 2240758; fax (65)
2240583; e-mail deansci@esn.ac.lk):

Botany: Dr S. KANESANATHAN (acting)
Chemistry: Dr R. VINOBABA (acting)
Mathematics: Dr R. VIGNESWARAN
Physics: Dr N. PATHMANATHAN
Zoology: Dr P. VINOBABA

UNIVERSITY OF JAFFNA

Thirunelvely, Jaffna
Telephone: (21) 2222483

Fax: (21) 2222006
E-mail: ujvc@mail.ewisl.net
Founded 1974, present name 1978
State control
Languages of instruction: Tamil, English
Academic year: October to July
Chancellor: Prof. M. SIVASURIYA
Vice-Chancellor: Prof. S. MOHANADAS
Registrar (vacant)
Librarian: R. PARARAJASINGAM
Library of 156,108 vols
Number of teachers: 225
Number of students: 6,107

Publications: *Cintanai* (4 a year), *Journal of
Science* (2 a year), *Sri Lanka Journal of
South Asian Studies* (annually), *Vingna-
nam*

DEANS

Faculty of Agriculture: S. RAJADURAI
Faculty of Arts: Prof. S. SIVACHANDRAN
Faculty of Management Studies and Com-
merce: Prof. S. RAJADURAI
Faculty of Medicine: Dr K. SIVAPALAN
Faculty of Science: Prof. R. KUMARAVADIVEL
Faculty of Graduate Studies: Prof. S. K.
SITRAMPALAM

HEADS OF DEPARTMENTS

Faculty of Agriculture (tel. (21) 2222973; fax
(21) 2222973; e-mail deanagriuj@yahoo.com):

Agricultural Biology: G. MIKUNTHAN (act-
ing)
Agricultural Chemistry: T. MIKUNTHAN
Agricultural Economics: K. SOORIYAKUMAR
(acting)
Agricultural Engineering: P. ALVAPPILLAI
(acting)
Agronomy: Dr S. SIVACHANDRAN
Animal Science: S. UTHAYATHAS

Faculty of Arts (tel. (21) 2223091; fax (21)
2223091; e-mail deanarts@sltnet.lk):

Christian and Islamic Civilization: Rev. Dr
RAJ. MATHTHIAS
Dance: K. RAVEENDRA
Economics: Prof. V. NITHIYANANDAM
Education: M. SINNATHAMBY
English Language Teaching Centre: S.
RAVEENDRAN
Fine Arts: Dr K. SITHAMPARANATHAN
Geography: Prof. K. KUGABALAN
Hindu Civilization: N. SELVANAYAGAM
History: Prof. S. SATHIASEELAN
Linguistics and English: Dr S. RAMESH
Music: P. NADARAJAH
Philosophy: Prof. S. KRISHNARAJAH
Political Science and Sociology: Prof. N.
SHANMUGALINGAM
Sanskrit: V. SIVACHANDRAN
Tamil: Dr S. SIVALINGARAJAH

Faculty of Management Studies and Commerce (tel. (21) 2223610; fax (21) 2223610;
e-mail ujmaco@sltnet.lk):

Commerce: K. THEVARAJAH
Management Studies: T. SIVASKARAN

Faculty of Medicine (tel. (21) 2222073; fax
(21) 2222073; e-mail msuj@sltnet.lk):

Anatomy: Dr R. RAJENDRAPRASAD
Biochemistry: Dr A. SENTHURAN
Community Medicine: (vacant)
Forensic Medicine: (vacant)
Medicine: Dr K. GANESHAMOORTHY
Obstetrics and Gynaecology: Dr G. BHA-
VANI
Paediatrics: (vacant)
Pathology: (vacant)
Pharmacology: Prof. V. ARASARATNAM
Physiology: Prof. S. V. PARAMESWARAN
Psychiatry: Prof. D. J. SOMASUNDARAM
Siddha Medicine: Dr S. PANCHARAJAH
Surgery: (vacant)

Faculty of Science (tel. (21) 2222685; fax (21) 2222685):

Botany: N. RAVIMANNAN
Chemistry: Dr M. SENTHINANTHANAN
Computer Science: Dr S. MAHESAN
Computer Unit: Prof. K. KANADASAMY
Mathematics and Statistics: Dr S. SRISAT-KUNARAJAH
Physics: Prof. K. KANDASAMY (acting)
Zoology: J. NANTHAKUMAR (acting)

UNIVERSITY OF KELANIYA

Dalugama, Kelaniya
Telephone: (11) 4911391
Fax: (11) 4911485
Formerly Vidayalankara Pirivena; University status 1959; reorganized 1972 as a campus of University of Sri Lanka; present name 1978
State control
Languages of instruction: English, Sinhala
Chancellor: Rev. KUSALADHAMMA DHARMA-KEERTHI
Vice-Chancellor: Prof. K. THILAKARATHNE
Deputy Vice-Chancellor: (vacant)
Registrar: N. B. AMARASINGHE
Librarian: Dr JAYASIRI LANKAGE
Number of teachers: 325
Number of students: 6,392
Publications: *Journal of the Faculty of Humanities* (annually), *Journal of the Faculty of Social Science* (annually), *Kalyani* (annually)

DEANS

Faculty of Commerce and Management Studies: A. PATABENDIGE
Faculty of Humanities: Prof. C. PALLIYAGURU
Faculty of Medicine: Prof. H. J. DE SILVA
Faculty of Science: Prof. M. J. S. WIJAYAR-ATNE
Faculty of Social Science: A. A. D. AMARASE-KERA

PROFESSORS

ARIYARATNE, J. K. P., Chemistry
CHANDRASENA, L. G., Biochemistry
DANGALLA, N. K., Geography
DHARMASENA, K., Economics
EDIRISINGHE, D., Philosophy
GUNASEKERA, S. A., Botany
GUNATHILAKE, D. C. R. A., English
ILANGASINGHE, H. B. M., History
KARUNADASA, Y., Pali and Buddhist Studies
KARUNANAYAKE, K., Economics
KARUNATHILAKE, W. S., Linguistics
LIYANAGAMAGA, A., History
SIRISENA, J. L. G. J., Obstetrics and Gynaecology
THILAK KARIYAWASAM, Pali and Buddhist Studies
VIDANAPATHIRENA, S., Microbiology

ATTACHED INSTITUTES

Institute of Aesthetic Studies: Dir Prof. ANANDA ABEYSIRIWARDENA.
Postgraduate Institute of Archaeology: Dir S. LAKDUSINGHE.
Postgraduate Institute of Pali and Buddhist Studies: Dir Prof. THILAK KARIYAWASAM.
Wickramaarachchi Ayurvedic Institute: Dir Prof. A. S. DISSANAYAKE.

UNIVERSITY OF MORATUWA

Katubedda, Moratuwa
Telephone: (11) 4650441
Fax: (11) 4650722
E-mail: enquire@mail.ac.lk
Internet: www.mrt.ac.lk

Founded 1966 as Ceylon College of Technology; present name 1978
State control
Language of instruction: English
Academic year: October to September
Chancellor: Dr ARTHUR C. CLARKE
Vice-Chancellor: Prof. DAYANTHA S. WIJEYE-SEKERA
Registrar: D. C. DE SILVA
Librarian: R. C. KODIKARA
Number of teachers: 222
Number of students: 2,723
Publications: *Development Planning Review* (4 a year), *Ambalama*, *Tampitavihara*

DEANS

Faculty of Architecture: Prof. L. BALASURIYA
Faculty of Engineering: Prof. K. A. M. K. RANASINGHE
Faculty of Information Technology: Dr R. L. M. P. D. C. WIJETUNGA (acting)
Institute of Technology: Dr T. A. PIYASIRI (Dir, acting)

HEADS OF DEPARTMENTS

Faculty of Architecture (tel. (11) 4650216; fax (11) 4650216; e-mail kithsiri@archi.mrt.ac.lk):

Architecture: Prof. T. K. N. P. DE SILVA
Building Economics: M. L. DE SILVA
Town and Country Planning: K. D. FERNANDO

Faculty of Engineering (tel. (11) 4650184; fax (11) 4651786; e-mail jayanthi@mrt.ac.lk):

Chemical and Process Engineering: Dr B. M. W. P. K. S. AMARSINGHE
Civil Engineering: Dr G. W. KODIKARA
Computer Science and Engineering: Dr N. K. WICKRAMARACHCHI
Earth Resources Engineering: S. WEERA-WARNAKULA
Electrical Engineering: Prof. J. R. LUCAS
Electronic and Telecommunications Engineering: Dr S. A. D. DIAS
Management of Technology: Prof. A. K. W. JAYAWARDENE
Materials Engineering: Dr N. MUNASINGHE
Mathematics: Dr M. INDRALINGAM
Mechanical Engineering: Dr S. R. TITTA-GALA
Physics Unit: L. P. J. P. PREMARATNE
Textile Technology: Dr N. DE SILVA

Faculty of Information Technology:

Computational Mathematics: Prof. I. J. DAYAWANSA (acting)
Information Technology: Dr T. A. PERIES (acting)
Multidisciplinary Studies: Dr N. D. GUNA-WARDENA

Institute of Technology (tel. (11) 4650064; fax (11) 4650064):

Civil Engineering: Dr C. JAYASINGHE
Electrical and Electronic Engineering: D. G. U. SOLANGAARACHCHI
Interdisciplinary Studies: Dr W. K. WIMAL-SIRI
Mechanical Engineering and Maritime Studies: Dr P. A. B. A. R. PERERA
Polymer, Textile and Chemical Engineering: K. SUBRAMANIAN

OPEN UNIVERSITY OF SRI LANKA

POB 21, Nawala, Nugegoda
Telephone: (11) 2822712
Founded 1980
State control
Languages of instruction: Sinhala, Tamil, English
Chancellor: Dr GAMINI COREA
Vice-Chancellor: Prof. U. COOMARASWAMY
Registrar: S. J. JAYASOORIYA

Librarian: S. R. KORALE
Number of teachers: 306
Number of students: 19,287
Publication: *Open University Review of Engineering Technology*

DEANS

Faculty of Engineering Technology: Dr H. D. GOONETILLEKE
Faculty of Humanities and Social Sciences: Prof. G. I. C. GUNAWARDENA
Faculty of Natural Sciences: Prof. E. M. JAYASINGHE

HEADS OF ACADEMIC DIVISIONS

Agricultural and Plantation Engineering: Dr S. A. M. A. N. S. SENANAYAKE
Botany: Dr A. C. I. SAMARANAYAKE
Chemistry: Dr G. BANDARAGE
Civil Engineering: Dr H. G. P. A. RATNA-WEERA
Early Childhood Education: Dr D. W. PALI-HAKKARA
Education: Dr V. WICKRAMARATNE
Electrical and Electronics Engineering: Dr L. S. K. UDUGAMA
Language Studies: Dr H. V. M. RATWATTE
Legal Studies: N. G. T. RAJAPAKSE
Management Studies: A. W. SILVA
Mathematics: Dr A. S. KARUNANANDA
Mathematics and Philosophy of Engineering: M. P. W. S. FERNANDO
Mechanical Engineering: P. D. SARATH CHAN-DRA
Physics: Dr L. S. G. LIYANAGE
Social Studies: U. VIDANAPATHIRANA
Textile Technology: G. Y. A. R. JAYANANDA
Zoology: Dr H. T. R. JAYASOORIYA

UNIVERSITY OF PERADENIYA

University Park, Peradeniya
Telephone: (81) 2388151
Fax: (81) 2389164
E-mail: vc@pdn.ac.lk
Internet: www.pdn.ac.lk

Founded 1942 by the incorporation of the Ceylon Medical College (f. 1870) and the Ceylon University College (f. 1921); reorganized 1972, present name 1978
State control
Languages of instruction: Sinhala, Tamil, English
Academic year: October to September
Chancellor: Deshamanya. R. K. W. GOONESE-KERA
Vice-Chancellor: Prof. K. G. A. GOONESEKERE
Registrar: M. S. M. MUSTHAFA (acting)
Librarian: P. E. HARRISON PERERA
Number of teachers: 745
Number of students: 9,500
Publications: *Modern Sri Lanka Studies, Sri Lanka Journal of Biological Science, Sri Lanka Journal of Humanities, Sri Lanka Journal of Physical Science*

DEANS

Faculty of Agriculture: Prof. P. W. M. B. B. MARAMBE
Faculty of Arts: Prof. Y. R. AMARASINGHE
Faculty of Dental Sciences: Prof. R. L. WIJEYEWEERA
Faculty of Engineering: Dr S. D. PATHIRANA
Faculty of Medicine: Dr A. S. B. WIJEKOON
Faculty of Science: Prof. V. KUMAR
Faculty of Veterinary Medicine and Animal Science: Dr H. ABEYGUNAWARDENA

PROFESSORS

Faculty of Agriculture (tel. (81) 2388041; fax (81) 2388041; e-mail nimalgun@mail.pdn.ac.lk; internet www.pdn.ac.lk/agri/home/homepage/agricindex.html):

BANDARA, J. M. R. S., Agricultural Biology

BOGAHAWATTA, C., Agricultural Economics
CYRIL, H. W., Animal Science
DE COSTA, W. A. J. M., Crop Science
GOONASEKERE, K. G. A., Agricultural Engineering
GUNATHILAKA, H. M., Agricultural Economics
GUNAWARDENA, E. R. N., Agricultural Engineering
IBRAHIM, M. N. M., Animal Science
ILLEPERUMA, D. C. K., Food Science and Technology
JAYAKODY, A. N., Agricultural Soil Science
KUMARAGAMAGE, D., Agricultural Soil Science
MAPA, R. B., Soil Science
PEIRIS, B. C. N., Agricultural Crop Science
PERERA, A. L. T., Agricultural Biology
PERERA, A. N. F., Animal Science
PERERA, E. R. K., Animal Science
SAMARAJEEWA, U., Food Science and Technology
SANGAKKARA, U. R., Agricultural Crop Science
SIVAYOGANATHAN, C., Agricultural Extension
THATTIL, R. O., Crop Science

Faculty of Arts (tel. (81) 2388345; fax (81) 2388933; e-mail dean@arts.pdn.ac.lk; internet www.pdn.ac.lk/arts):

AMARASINGHE, Y. R., Political Science
DE SILVA, M. W. A., Sociology
GUNATHILAKE, W. M., Sinhala
HENNAYAKE, H. M. S. K., Geography
KARUNATILAKE, P. V. B., History
LIYANAGE, K., Political Science
MADDEGAMA, U. P., Sinhala
MADDUMA BANDARA, C. M., Geography
NUHUMAN, M. A. M., Tamil
PATHMANATHAN, S., History
PERERA, S. W., English
PREMASIRI, P. D., Pali and Buddhist Studies
SAMARANAYAKE, S. V. D. G., Political Science
SENADHEERA, S., Education
SENEVIRATNE, S. D. S., Archaeology
SILVA, K. T., Sociology
SIRISENA, W. M., Sociology
SIRIWEERA, W. S., History
SIVARAJAH, A., Political Science
WEERAKKODY, D. P. M., Classical Languages
WICKRAMASINGHE, A., Geography

Faculty of Dental Sciences (tel. (81) 2388948; fax (81) 2388948; e-mail deandental@pdn.ac.lk; internet www.pdn.ac.lk/dental):

AMARATUNGE, N. A. DE S., Oral Surgery
EKANAYAKE, A. N. I., Community Dentistry
EKANAYAKE, S. L., Community Dentistry
MENDIS, B. R. R. N., Oral Pathology
NANAYAKKARA, C. D., Basic Science
WIJEYEWEERA, R. L., Community Dentistry

Faculty of Engineering (tel. (81) 2388322; fax (81) 2388158; e-mail deaneng@pdn.ac.lk; internet www.pdn.ac.lk/eng):

AMIRTHANATHAM, G. E., Chemical Engineering
EKANAYAKE, E. M. N., Electrical and Electronic Engineering
Computer Science
HOOLE, S. R. H., Electrical and Electronic Engineering
RANAWEERA, M. P., Civil Engineering
SAMUEL, T. D. M. A., Engineering Mathematics
SENEVIRATNE, K. G. H. C. N., Civil Engineering
SIVASEGARAM, S., Mechanical Engineering

Faculty of Medicine (tel. (81) 2388315; fax (81) 2389106; e-mail dean@med.pdn.ac.lk; internet www.pdn.ac.lk/med):

AMARASINGHE, W. I., Obstetrics and Gynaecology

CHANDRASEKERA, M. S., Anatomy
EDIRISINGHE, J. S., Parasitology
NUGEGODA, D. B., Community Medicine
PERERA, P. A. J., Biochemistry
RATNATUNGE, N. V. I., Pathology
RATNARUNGE, P. C. A., Surgery
SENANAYAKE, N., Medicine
THEVANESAN, V., Microbiology
UDUPIHILLE, M., Physiology
WELGAMA, D. J., Parasitology
WIJESUNDARA, M. K. DE S., Parasitology

Faculty of Science (tel. (81) 2389126; fax (81) 2388018; e-mail dean@sci.pdn.ac.lk; internet www.pdn.ac.lk/sci):

ADIKARAM, N. K. B., Botany
BANDARA, B. M. R., Chemistry
BANDARA, H. M. N., Chemistry
CAREEM, M. A., Physics
DAHANAYAKE, K. G. A., Geology
DE SILVA, K. H. G. M., Zoology
DE SILVA, P. K., Chemistry
DISSANAYAKE, C. B., Geology
DISSANAYAKE, M. A. K. L., Physics
EDIRISINGHE, J. P., Zoology
GUNATILLAKE, C. V. S., Botany
GUNATILLAKE, I. A. U. N., Botany
GUNAWARDANA, R. P., Chemistry
ILLEPERUMA, O. A., Chemistry
KARUNARATHNA, N. L. V. V., Chemistry
KARUNARATNE, B. S. B., Physics
KARUNARATNE, S. H. P. P., Zoology
KULASOORIYA, S. A., Botany
KUMAR, N. S., Chemistry
KUMAR, V., Chemistry
NAMAL PRIYANTHA, Chemistry
RAJAPAKSHE, R. M. G., Chemistry
SENEVIRATNE, H. H. G., Mathematics
TENNAKOON, D. T. B., Chemistry

Faculty of Veterinary Medicine and Animal Science (tel. (81) 2388205; fax (81) 2388205; e-mail dean@vet.pdn.ac.lk; internet www.pdn.ac.lk/vet):

ABEYGUNAWARDENA, H., Farm Animal Production and Health
ABEYNAYAKE, P., Veterinary Pathological Biology
GUNAWARDENA, V. K., Veterinary Basic Science
KURUWITA, V. Y., Veterinary Clinical Science
SILVA, I. D., Veterinary Clinical Science

Postgraduate Institute of Agriculture (tel. (81) 2389205; fax (81) 2388318; e-mail congress@pgia.pdn.ac.lk; internet www.pgia.ac.lk):

THATTIL, R. O. (Dir)

Postgraduate Institute of Science (tel. (81) 2387218; fax (81) 2389029; e-mail director@pgis.lk; internet www.pgis.lk):

DISSANAYAKE, M. (Dir)

RAJARATA UNIVERSITY OF SRI LANKA

Mihintale, Anuradhapura
Telephone: (25) 2266650
Fax: (25) 2266511
E-mail: rajalib@sltnet.lk
Founded 1996
State control
Languages of instruction: Sinhala, English
Chancellor: Dr J. B. KELEGAMA
Vice-Chancellor: Prof. W. I. SIRIWEERA
Registrar: A. G. KARUNARATNE
Librarian: K. J. SIRISENA
Library of 43,000 vols
Number of teachers: 60
Number of students: 418

DEANS

Faculty of Applied Sciences: Dr J. L. RATNASEKARA

Faculty of Management Studies: T. B. ANDARAWEWA
Faculty of Social Sciences and Humanities: Prof. K. WIJERATNE

UNIVERSITY OF RUHUNA

Matara
Telephone: (41) 2222681
Fax: (41) 2222683
E-mail: vc@ruh.ac.lk
Internet: www.ruh.ac.lk
Founded 1978 as Ruhuna University College, present name 1984
State control
Languages of instruction: Sinhala, English
Academic year: October to September
Chancellor: Ven. Dr Sri ATHTHUDAWE RAHULA THERO
Vice-Chancellor: Prof. R. SENARATNE
Registrar: K. D. DUMINDUSENA
Librarian: K. J. SIRISENA
Library of 140,000 vols
Number of teachers: 550
Number of students: 5,500

DEANS

Faculty of Agriculture: Prof. K. D. N. WEERASINGHE
Faculty of Engineering: Prof. C. L. V. JAYATHILLAKE
Faculty of Humanities and Social Sciences: S. WAWWAGE
Faculty of Medicine: Prof. A. L. S. MENDIS
Faculty of Science: Prof. R. N. PATHIRANA

HEADS OF DEPARTMENTS

Faculty of Agriculture:

Animal Science: Prof. R. T. SERASINGHE
Agricultural Biology: Dr R. W. K. PUNCHIHEWA
Crop Science: Dr S. SUBSINGHE
Agricultural Engineering: Dr P. L. A. G. ALWIS
Agricultural Chemistry: Dr S. P. WANNIARACHCHI
Agricultural Economics: Dr M. DE SOYZA

Faculty of Engineering:

Civil and Environmental Engineering: Dr A. K. SOMASUNDARASWARAN
Electrical and Information Engineering: Dr L. WICKRAMARATNE
Interdisciplinary Engineering: Dr A. M. N. ALAGIYAWANNA
Mechanical and Manufacturing Engineering: Dr N. WIJAYARATNE

Faculty of Humanities and Social Sciences:

Business Administration: H. S. C. PERERA
Economics: Prof. D. ATAPATTU
Geography: Prof. L. K. RATHNAYAKA
History: S. A. PIYASENA
Pali: Rev. M. SORATHA
Sinhala: Dr Rev. K. ANANDA
Sociology: Prof. S. W. AMARASINGHE

Faculty of Medicine:

Medicine: Dr P. L. ARIYANANDA
Surgery: Dr M. M. A. J. KUMARA
Community Medicine: Prof. P. H. G. FONSEKA
Anatomy: Dr T. R. WEERASOORIYA
Biochemistry: Prof. C. PATHIRANA
Microbiology: N. DE SILVA
Nuclear Medicine: Dr K. W. C. E. LIYANGE
Obstetrics and Gynaecology: Prof. I. M. R. GUNAWARDENA
Paediatrics: T. S. W. AMARASENA
Parasitology: Prof. M. V. WEERASOORIYA
Pathology: L. K. B. MUDDUWA
Pharmacology: Prof. A. I. FERNANDO
Physiology: Dr K. G. SOMASIRI
Psychiatry: M. K. G. R. DE S. JAYAWARDENA

Colleges

Faculty of Science:

Botany: Prof. S. P. SAMARAKOON
Chemistry: Dr H. M. K. K. PATHIRANA
Computer Science: S. C. JAYAWARDENA
Fisheries Biology: P. R. T. CUMARANATUNGA
Mathematics: Dr L. A. L. W. JAYASEKARA
Physics: W. G. D. DHARMARATNE
Zoology: Dr C. N. L. BOGAHAWATTA

SABARAGAMUWA UNIVERSITY OF SRI LANKA

POB 02 Belihuloya, Ratnapura

Founded 1991 as Sabaragamuwa Affiliated University; present name and status 1995

State Control

Chancellor: Dr C. R. PANABOKKE
Vice-Chancellor: Prof. DAYANANDA SOMASUNDARA.

SOUTH EASTERN UNIVERSITY OF SRI LANKA

University Park, Oluvil 32360

Telephone: and fax (67) 2255168

E-mail: seusl@seu.ac.lk

Internet: www.seu.ac.lk

Founded 1995 at Addalaichenai as South Eastern University College; present name, status and location 1996

State control

Languages of instruction: English, Tamil

Vice-Chancellor: Dr A. G. HUSAIN ISMAIL
Registrar: M. F. HIBATHUL CAREEM (acting)
Bursar: A. GULAM RASHEED
Librarian: M. M. RIFAUDEEN (acting)

Library of 45,000 books, 20 periodicals
Number of teachers: 118
Number of students: 1,270

Publication: *Journal of Management* (annually)

DEANS

Faculty of Applied Sciences: A. N. AHMED (acting)
Faculty of Arts and Culture: M. I. M. KALEEL
Faculty of Islamic Studies and Arabic Language: M. S. M. JALALDEEN
Faculty of Management and Commerce: HANSIYA RAUFF

ATTACHED RESEARCH INSTITUTE

Centre for Extension Studies

UNIVERSITY OF SRI JAYEWARDENEPURA

Gangodawila, Nugegoda

Telephone: (11) 2802695

Fax: (11) 2801604

E-mail: unisjay@sjp.ac.lk

Internet: www.sjp.ac.lk

Founded 1959 as Vidyodaya University of Ceylon; reorganized 1972 as campus of University of Sri Lanka; present name and status 1978

Languages of instruction: Sinhala, English

Chancellor: Rev. Dr MEDAGODA SUMANATISSA THERO
Vice-Chancellor (vacant): Prof. NARADA WARNASURIYA
Registrar: D. P. ATHULATHMUDALI
Librarian: P. VIDANAPATHIRANA

Number of teachers: 410
Number of students: 8,400

Publications: *Vidyodaya Journal of Sciences, Vidyodaya Journal of Social Sciences*

DEANS

Faculty of Applied Sciences: Prof. W. S. FERNANDO
Faculty of Arts: Prof. CHANDIMA WIJEBANDARA
Faculty of Management Studies and Commerce: W. H. E. SILVA
Faculty of Medical Sciences: Prof. D. P. A. FERNANDO
Faculty of Graduate Studies: Prof. D. A. THANTHIRIGODA

PROFESSORS

ABEYSEKARA, A. M., Chemistry
ARIYARATNE, S., Sinhala
BAMUNUARACHCHI, A., Chemistry
DAYANANDA, R. A., Statistics
DE SILVA, W. M. M., Surgery
DERANIYAGALA, S. P., Chemistry
ENDAGAMA, M., History and Archaeology
FERNANDO, D. J. S., Medicine
FERNANDO, D. P. A., Surgery
FERNANDO, G. H., Pharmacology
FERNANDO, S., Microbiology
FERNANDO, W. S., Chemistry
HETTIARATCHI, S. B., History and Archaeology
JANSZ, E. R., Biochemistry
JAYATISSA, W. A., Social Statistics
JAYAWARDENA, M. A. J., Obstetrics and Gynaecology
JIFFRY, M. T. M., Physiology
JINADASA, J., Zoology
KARIYAWASAM, T., Sinhala
KARUNANAYAKE, M. M., Geography
NANDADASA, H. G., Botany
PERERA, B. A. T., Sociology and Anthropology
PERERA, G. A., Pali and Buddhist Studies
PIYASIRI, S., Zoology
RANASINGHE, D. M. S. H. K., Forestry and Environmental Science
TANTRIGODA, D. A., Physics
WARNASOORIYA, N. D., Paediatrics
WEERAKOON, S., Mathematics
WEERASEKARA, D. S., Obstetrics and Gynaecology
WICKRAMASINGHE, S. M. D. N., Biochemistry
WIJAYARATNE, M. W. W., Sinhala
WIJEBANDARA, W. D. C., Pali and Buddhist Studies
WIJEWARDENA, K. A. K. K., Community Medicine and Family Medicine
WITHANA, R. J., Pathology
YAPA, P. A. J., Botany

AFFILIATED INSTITUTE

Post-Graduate Institute of Management: Dir Prof. G. NANAYAKKARA.

WAYAMBA UNIVERSITY OF SRI LANKA

Kuliyapitiya

Telephone: (37) 81392

Fax: (37) 81392

E-mail: appliedadd@slt.lk

Founded 1999

Chancellor: W. D. AMARADEVA
Vice-Chancellor: Prof. V. Y. KURUWITA
Registrar: R. M. B. MUTHUBANDA (acting)
Librarian: K. J. SIRISENA
Number of students: 1,309

DEANS

Faculty of Agriculture and Plantation Management: S. J. JAYASEKERA
Faculty of Applied Sciences: Dr E. M. P. EKANAVAKE
Faculty of Business Studies and Finance: E. S. WICKRAMASINGHE
Faculty of Livestock, Fisheries and Nutrition: Prof. T. S. G. FONSEKA

Aquinas College of Higher Studies: Colombo 8; tel. (11) 2694014; fax (11) 2678463; e-mail aqrector@pan.lanka.net; internet www.webstation.lk/aquinas; f. 1954; courses for the external examinations of Universities in Sri Lanka and abroad, for the Aquinas Diplomas and Certificates, and for examinations conducted by professional institutions in Sri Lanka and abroad; faculties of arts and science; institute of technology; school of agriculture; school of English; school of computer studies; school of psychology and counselling; experimental farm at Ragama; library: 43,000 vols; 150 teachers; 7,500 students; Rector Rev. Fr W. D. G. CHRISPIN LEO; Vice-Rector Rev. Fr NAMAL FERNANDO; Registrar M. L. FERNANDO; publ. *Aquinas Journal* (annually).

Ceylon College of Physicians: 6 Wijerama Mawatha, Colombo 7; tel. (11) 671842; fax (11) 695418; e-mail ccp@eureka.lk; f. 1967; 360 mems; Pres. Prof. SAMAN GUNATILAKE; Joint Secs Dr UDAYA RANAWAKA, Dr NAOMALI AMAVASENA; publ. *Ceylon College of Physicians Journal* (annually).

In-Service Training Institute: Gannoruwa, POB 21, Peradeniya; tel. (81) 2288146; f. 1965; agricultural education and training; 22 staff; Dir HENRY GAMAGE.

Institute of Aesthetic Studies: 21 Albert Crescent, Colombo 7; tel. and fax (11) 2686071; f. 1974; attached to University of Kelaniya; dancing, music, art and sculpture; 78 teachers; 8,057 students; library: 23,000 vols; Dir H. M. K. HERATH.

Jaffna College: Vaddukoddai; tel. (70) 2212531; f. 1823, renamed 1872; provides primary, secondary, tertiary and technical education; library: 60,000 vols; 55 teachers; 1,172 students; Principal Rev. ANTHONY A. PAUL; publ. *Jaffna College Miscellany.*

Attached institutes:

Christian Institute for the Study of Religion and Society: c/o Christian Theological Seminary, Maruthanarmadam, Chunnakam; Dir C. V. SELLIAH.

Evelyn Rutnam Institute for Inter-Cultural Studies: University Lane, Thirunelvely, Jaffna; Dir Rev. ANTHONY A. PAUL.

Institute of Agriculture: Maruthanamadam; 5 teachers; 40 students; Principal T. KUGATHASAN.

Institute of Technology: Vaddukoddai; 11 teachers; 150 students; Dir H. R. G. HOOLE (acting).

School of Agriculture: Kundasale; tel. and fax (81) 2420485; f. 1916; library: 5,500 vols; 20 teachers; 253 students; Principal P. K. K. R. PERERA; publ. *Progress Report* (annual).

Sri Lanka Law College: 244 Hulftsdorp St, Colombo 12; tel. (11) 4323759; fax (11) 4436040; f. 1900; run by Council of Legal Education; prepares students for admission to the Bar, and conducts the examinations; 1,500 students; library: 11,462 vols; Principal Dr H. J. F. SILVA.

Sri Lanka Technical College: Colombo 10; f. 1893; courses in trades and commerce; 4,525 students; Principal B. P. H. S. MENDIS; Registrar H. V. S. BREMADASA; Librarian A. A. WIJERATNE.

SUDAN

The Higher Education System

Higher education institutions predate the independence of Sudan (formerly The Sudan) from the United Kingdom in 1956, with the oldest being Omdurman Islamic University, which was founded in 1912. Gordon Memorial College (founded 1902) has offered degrees since 1945, under the supervision of University of London (United Kingdom), and from 1956 became known as University of Khartoum. In 2000 there were an estimated 200,538 students enrolled in universities (of which 26 were public) and other institutions of higher education.

There is a Ministry of Higher Education and Scientific Research, and higher education is governed by the Higher Education Act (1990) and the Higher Education Regulatory Act (2005). The National Council of Higher Education, which consists of the Minister of Education, university vice-chancellors and prominent academic figures, is responsible for implementing government policies on higher education; this body is also responsible for quality assurance. The President of Sudan is the Chancellor of every university and is also responsible for appointing most of the other senior officers. Each university is operated by a University Council.

Results in the Sudan School Certificate are the main criteria for admission to higher education: students are required to achieve a pass-mark of 50% or higher in seven subjects to be admitted to university, and 50% or higher in five subjects to be admitted to non-university courses. Non-university courses consist principally of Intermediate or General Diplomas and are offered by several public and private institutions. Courses last for three years. The Bachelors is the undergraduate qualification, and may be either awarded as either a 'General' (four-years) or 'Honours' (five-years) degree. Professional areas of study, such as medicine, dentistry and engineering, may last longer (up to six years). Graduates with either of the Bachelors degrees may be admitted to programmes of study leading to the award of the Postgraduate Diploma, a one-year course, but only graduates with the Bachelors (Honours) degree may be admitted to the postgraduate Masters degree, a two- to three-year programme of study. The highest university-level degree is the Doctor of Philosophy, a three-year research degree.

Technical and vocational education is principally offered at secondary level, but the Sudan University of Science and Technology and the Sudan Open University (founded 2002) provide correspondence courses and continuing education.

Learned Societies

LANGUAGE AND LITERATURE

Alliance Française: POB 465, El Obeid; tel. (183) 23617; e-mail haidaro2000@yahoo.fr; offers courses and exams in French language and culture and promotes cultural exchange with France; attached teaching centre in Wad Medani.

British Council: 14 Abu Sin St, POB 1253, Central Khartoum; tel. (183) 780817; fax (183) 774935; e-mail info@sd.britishcouncil .org; internet www.britishcouncil.org/sudan; offers courses and exams in English language and British culture and promotes cultural exchange with the UK; library of 10,000 vols, 90 periodicals; Dir DAVID CODLING.

Research Institutes

GENERAL

National Centre for Research: POB 2404, Khartoum; tel. (183) 779040; fax (183) 770701; e-mail profsalih@hotmail.com; f. 1991; conducts pure and applied scientific research for the realization of Sudan's economic and social development; incorporates research institutes in renewable energy, environment and natural resources, technology, tropical medicine, medicinal and aromatic plants, economic and social studies, remote sensing, biotechnology and biological engineering; Dir Prof. ABDEL KARIM MOHAMED SALIH.

AGRICULTURE, FISHERIES AND VETERINARY SCIENCE

Agricultural Research Corporation: POB 126, Wad Medani; tel. (511) 42226; fax (511) 43213; e-mail arcdg@sudanmail.net; internet www.arcsudan.org; f. 1904; part of Ministry of Science and Technology; research centres: Food Research Centre, Land and Water Research Centre, Crop Protection Research Centre, Forestry Research Centre, Date Palm Research Centre; 16 research stations; library: see Libraries; Dir-Gen. Prof. AZHARI ABDELAZIM HAMADA; publ. *Sudan Journal of Agricultural Research* (2 a year).

Animal Production Corporation, Research Division: POB 624, Khartoum; Dir of Research Dr MUHAMMAD EL TAHIR ABDEL RAZIG; Senior Veterinary Research Officer Dr AMIN MAHMOUD EISA.

Forestry Research Centre: POB 7089, Khartoum; f. 1962; Dir Prof. HASSAN A. MUSNAD.

ECONOMICS, LAW AND POLITICS

Sudan Academy for Administrative Sciences: POB 2003, Khartoum; f. 1980; provides post-service training for government officials; conducts studies on current administrative problems; Dir-Gen. Dr OSMAN ELZUBERI AHMED; publ. *Journal of Administration and Development*.

MEDICINE

Sudan Medical Research Laboratories: POB 287, Khartoum; f. 1935; Dir MAHMOUD ABDEL RAHMAN ZIADA.

NATURAL SCIENCES

Physical Sciences

Geological Research Authority: POB 410, Khartoum; tel. (183) 777939; fax (183) 776681; e-mail gras@sudanmail.net; internet www.gras-sd.com; f. 1905; attached to Min. of Energy and Mining; applied research and surveys; library: see Libraries and Archives; Dir-Gen. Dr ABDELRAZIG O. M. AHMED.

TECHNOLOGY

Industrial Research and Consultancy Centre: POB 268, Khartoum; tel. (183) 613225; f. 1965 by the Government with assistance from the UN Development Programme; performs tests, investigations, analysis, research and surveys; offers advice and consultation services to industry; General Dir Dr IBRAHIM HASSAN M. EL AMIN.

Libraries and Archives

Juba

University of Juba Library: POB 82, Juba; f. 1977; 38,700 vols, 664 periodicals; acts as a depository library for UN, UNESCO, WHO, FAO and World Bank; Librarian OKENY A. ADALA (acting).

Khartoum

Antiquities Service Library: POB 178, Khartoum; tel. (183) 780935; fax (183) 786784; f. 1946; 7,200 vols excluding periodicals; Librarian AWATIF AMIN BEDAWI.

Educational Documentation Centre: POB 2490, Khartoum; tel. (183) 71898; f. 1967; 7 mems; 20,000 vols; Dir IBRAHIM M. S. SHATIR; publs *Al-Tawitheq El Tarbawi* (Educational Documentation, 2 a year), annual reports and educational researches.

Flinders Petrie Library: Sudan Antiquities Service, POB 178, Khartoum; tel. (183) 780935; fax (183) 786784; f. 1946; 6,000 vols.

Geological Research Authority of the Sudan Library: POB 410, Khartoum; tel. (183) 770934; f. 1904; 2,200 vols, 63 periodicals; special collection: geology of the Sudan; Chief Librarian SALAH ABDEL GADIR MOHMED; publs *Annual Report, Bulletin*.

Library of the Sudan University of Science and Technology: POB 407, Khartoum; tel. (183) 778922; fax (183) 774559; e-mail sudan_library@hotmail.com; f. 1950; 14 libraries on 9 sites; 55,000 vols; Chief Librarian GAWAHIR SIDAHMED EL HASSAN.

National Chemical Laboratories Library: National Chemical Laboratories, Ministry of Health, POB 287, Khartoum; f. 1904; 2,500 vols, 1,600 pamphlets.

National Records Office: POB 1914, Khartoum; f. 1953; 20,000,000 documents covering

Sudanese history since 1870; 12,820 vols; Sec.-Gen. Dr M. I. ABU SALEEM; publ. *Majallatal Wathaiq* (Archives Magazine).

Sudan Medical Research Laboratories Library: POB 287, Khartoum; f. 1904 (as part of Wellcome Tropical Research Laboratories); 7,000 pamphlets, 6,000 vols.

University of Khartoum Library: POB 321, Khartoum; f. 1945; 333,000 vols, 4,200 periodicals; includes a special Sudan and African collection; acts as a depository library for UN, FAO, ILO, WHO and UNESCO publications; both are under the general charge of the University Librarian Dr EL-HIBIR YOUSIF.

Omdurman

Omdurman Central Public Library: Omdurman; f. 1951; 17,650 vols.

Wad Medani

Agricultural Research Corporation Central Library: POB 126, Wad Medani; tel. (511) 42226; fax (511) 43213; e-mail libraryarc@yahoo.com; internet www.arcsudan.org; f. 1930; 15,000 books, 20,000 pamphlets, 250 periodicals; Librarian AHLAM ISMAIL MUSA.

Gezira Research Station Library: Wadi Medani; 6,500 vols on agricultural topics.

Museums and Art Galleries

Khartoum

Sudan National Museum: POB 178, Khartoum; tel. (183) 70680; f. 1971; Departments of Antiquities, Ethnology and Sudan Modern History; Dir HASSAN HUSSEIN IDRIS; Curator SIDDIG M. GASM AL-SID; publ. *Report on the Antiquities Service and Museums, Kush* (annually).

Attached museums:

Ethnographical Museum: POB 178, Khartoum; tel. (183) 77052; f. 1956; collection and preservation of ethnographical objects; Curator MOHAMMED HAMED.

Khalifa's House: Omdurman.

Merowe Museum: Merowe, Northern Province; antiquities and general.

Sheikan Museum: El Obeid; archaeological and ethnographic museum.

Sultan Ali Dinar Museum: El Fasher.

Sudan Natural History Museum: University of Khartoum, POB 321, Khartoum; tel. (183) 81873; f. 1920; library of 801 vols; Dir Dr DAWI MUSA HAMED.

Universities

AL-FASHIR UNIVERSITY

POB 125, Al-Fashir, North Darfur
Telephone: (527) 43394
Fax: (527) 52111
Founded 1975
Vice-Chancellor: ABD ELBAGI MOHAMMED KABIR
Faculties of Education, Environmental Studies and Natural Resources and Medicine and Health Sciences; Centres of Scientific Research and Documentation and Societal Development and Extramural Studies.

AL-NEELAIN UNIVERSITY

POB 12702, Khartoum 12702
Founded 1955 as Khartoum branch of Cairo University; independent status and present name 1993
State Control
Language of instruction: Arabic
Vice-Chancellor: AWAD HAJ ALI AHMED
Number of teachers: 270
Number of students: 36,000
Faculties of Agriculture, Animal Production and Fisheries, Arts, Commerce and Socio-Economic Studies, Engineering, Graduate Studies, Law, Medicine, Optometry and Visual Sciences, Science and Technology and Statistics, Population Studies and Information Technology; Nile Basin Studies Research Centre.

AL-ZAIEM AL-AZHARI UNIVERSITY

POB 1933, Omdurman
Telephone: (15) 560501
Fax: (15) 562536
E-mail: qurashi@sudanmail.net
Founded 1993
State control
Number of teachers: 350
Number of students: 5,109.

BAHR AL-GHAZAL UNIVERSITY

POB 10739, Khartoum, West Bahr Al-Ghazal
Telephone: (183) 224629
Fax: (183) 223015
E-mail: ubgzal@sudanmail.net
Founded 1991
State Control
Languages of instruction: Arabic, English
Vice-Chancellor: ADUOL MATHEW ATEM
Number of teachers: 273
Number of students: 1,513
Publication: *The Pioneer* (2 a year)

DEANS

College of Economics and Rural Studies: MADUT ABALLIAAK THEM
College of Education: ALAMIN ALFATEH MUSTAFA
College of Medicine and Health Sciences: ABDEL LATIF JUBARA MAHMOUD
College of Veterinary Science: ALI HASSAN AHMED

ATTACHED RESEARCH INSTITUTE

Institute of Public and Environmental Health Studies: Dir BOL ANYUAT ANGUI.

BAKHET EL-RUDDA UNIVERSITY

POB 1311, Khartoum, Eldewaym
Telephone: (531) 22440
Fax: (531) 20548
Founded 1997
State Control
Languages of instruction: Arabic, English
Vice-Chancellor: ANAAS A. EL-HAFEEZ
Number of teachers: 198
Number of students: 4,035

DEANS

Faculty of Agriculture and Natural Resources: GHANIM SABIH
Faculty of Economics and Administration: ILHAM SAADALLAH
Faculty of Education: SALIH NOURIN
Faculty of Medicine: YOUSIF SULTAN
Faculty of Postgraduate Studies: MAHMOUD HASSAN

BLUE NILE UNIVERSITY

POB 143, Damazeen, Blue Nile
Telephone: (183) 785614
Vice-Chancellor: MOHAMMED EL-HASSAN ABDUL EL-RAHMAN
Founded 1995
Faculties of Education and Engineering; Centres of Extramural Studies and Continuing Education.

UNIVERSITY OF DONGOLA

POB 47, Dongola
Telephone: (241) 21515
Fax: (241) 21514
Founded 1994
State Control
Vice-Chancellor: MOHAMMED OSMAN AHMED
Faculties of Agriculture, Arts, Education, Law and Islamic Law, Medicine and Mining and Earth Sciences.

EL-DALANG UNIVERSITY

El-Dalang, South Kordofan
Telephone: (183) 785614
Founded 1990
State Control
Vice-Chancellor: KAMESS KAGO KUNDA
Faculties of Agriculture, Education, Social Development and Teacher Training; Centres of Computer Science and Peace Studies.

EL-GADARIF UNIVERSITY

POB 449, El-Gadarif 32211
Telephone: (441) 43668
Fax: (441) 43120
E-mail: unged@sudanmail.net
Founded 1990; university status 1994
State Control
Languages of instruction: Arabic, English
Vice-Chancellor: OMER KURDI
Number of teachers: 154
Number of students: 3,845

DEANS

Faculty of Agricultural and Environmental Sciences: ABDEL-AZIZA TAHA
Faculty of Economics and Administrative Science: EL-GUZOLI MOHAMAD
Faculty of Education: SULTAN NOUR
Faculty of Medicine and Medical Sciences: EL-DIRDIRY SALAH

ATTACHED RESEARCH INSTITUTES

Centre for Computer and Information Technology.
Centre for Continuing Education.
Centre for the Languages of the Horn of Africa.
Centre for Women's Studies.

EL-IMAM EL-MAHDI UNIVERSITY

POB 209, Kosti 11588
Telephone: (571) 22545
Fax: (571) 22222
E-mail: abdosm@sudanmail.net
Founded 1993
State Control
Vice-Chancellor: ABDELRAHIM OSMAN MOHAMED
Faculties of Arabic and Islamic Sciences, Arts, Engineering and Technical Studies, Law and Islamic Law and Medicine and Health Sciences; Centres for Computer Studies and Extramural Studies.

UNIVERSITY OF GEZIRA

POB 20, Wad Medani, 2667 Khartoum

Founded 1975

Language of instruction: English

Vice-Chancellor (vacant)

Secretary-General: Dr MAHMOUD ABDALLA IBRAHIM

Librarian: ABUEL GAITH SANHOURI

Number of teachers: 140

Number of students: 1,000

DEANS

Faculty of Agriculture: Dr OSMAN ALI SID AHMED

Faculty of Economics and Rural Development: Dr EL TAHIR MOHAMED NUR

Faculty of Education: Prof. ABDEL SALAM MAHMOUD ABDALLA

Faculty of Medicine: Prof. SALAH ELDIN TAHA SALIH

Faculty of Science and Technology: Dr ELNUR KAMAL EL DIN ABU SABAH

Graduate Studies and Academic Affairs: ISAM ABDEL RAHMAN AHMED

Preparatory College: Prof. FAYSAL AWAD

Students: Dr ABD EL-MUTAAL GIRSHAB

UNIVERSITY OF HOLY QU'RAN AND ISLAMIC SCIENCES

POB 1459, Omdurman

Telephone: (15) 559594

Fax: (15) 559175

Founded 1990 by merger of Holy Qu'ran College and Omdurman Higher Institute

State Control

Vice-Chancellor: AHMED KHALID BABIKER

Faculties of Arabic Language, Community Development, Media Studies, Education, Educational Sciences, the Holy Qu-ran and Islamic Law and Law; Centre for Women's Studies.

UNIVERSITY OF JUBA

POB 82, Juba

Telephone: 2113

Founded 1975 with financial help from the EEC; first student admission 1977

Language of instruction: English

Academic year: March to December (two semesters)

Chancellor (vacant)

Vice-Chancellor: Prof. MAHMOUD MUSA MAHMOUD

Secretary-General: Prof. MOSES MACAR KACUOL

Librarian: ALFRED D. LADO (acting)

Number of teachers: 220

Number of students: 1,200

Publications: *Juvarsity* (monthly), *Library News* (monthly)

DEANS

College of Adult Education and Training: GEORGE ISMAIL GABRA

College of Education: Dr ABDEL MONIEM MOHAMED OSMAN

College of Medicine: Dr MATHEW ATEM ADUOL

College of Natural Resources and Environmental Studies: Prof. JOSEPH AWAD MORGAN

College of Social and Economic Studies: Dr VENANSIO TOMBE MULUDIANG

Dean of Students: AJANG BIOR DUOT

PROFESSORS

College of Medicine:

SUBBARAO, V. V., Physiology

College of Natural Resources and Environmental Studies:

ASHRAF, M., Crop Breeding

MORGAN, J. A., Animal Production

TINGWA, P. O., Horticulture

KASSALA UNIVERSITY

Kassala 266

Telephone: (411) 22095

Fax: (411) 23501

Founded 1990

State Control

Vice-Chancellor: MUSTAFA ALI ABASHER

Faculties of Agriculture and Natural Resources, Economics and Administration, Education and Medicine and Health Sciences.

UNIVERSITY OF KHARTOUM

POB 321, 11115 Khartoum

Telephone: (83) 772601

Fax: (83) 780295

E-mail: vc@uofk.edu

Internet: www.uofk.edu

Founded 1956; formerly University College of Khartoum

State control

Languages of instruction: Arabic, English

Academic year: July to April

Chancellor: THE PRESIDENT OF THE REPUBLIC

Vice-Chancellor: Prof. MOHAMED AHMED ALI EL SHEIKH

Deputy Vice-Chancellor: Prof. EL SIDDIG AHMED EL MUSTAFA EL SHEIKH

Principal: Prof. MOHAMED NOURI EL AMIN

Academic Secretary: Dr MUSTAFA MOHAMED ALI EL BALLA

Personnel Secretary: Ustaz EL TAHIR OMER KHALID

Librarian: Prof. MONA MAHJOUB MOHAMED AHMED

Library: see Libraries and Archives

Number of teachers: 1,560

Number of students: 19,814

DEANS

Faculty of Agriculture: Dr SIDDIG MOHAMED EL HASSAN

Faculty of Animal Production: Dr OSMAN ALI OSMAN ELOUMIE

Faculty of Arts: Dr MOHAMED A. HALIM MOHAMED

Faculty of Dentistry: Dr AHMED MOHAMED SULEIMAN

Faculty of Economic and Social Studies: Dr AHMED EL SHEIKH MOHAMED AHMED

Faculty of Education: Dr ABDALLA EL KHIDIER MADANI

Faculty of Engineering and Architecture: Dr ABDALLA KHOJALI AHMED

Faculty of Forestry: Dr ABDEL AZIM YASSIN ABDEL GADIR

Faculty of Law: Dr MOHAMED IBRAHIM EL TAHER

School of Management Studies: Dr AHMED OSMAN HAMZA

Faculty of Mathematical Sciences: Dr MOHSIN HASSAN ABDALLA HASHIM

Faculty of Medical Laboratory Sciences: Dr SAYDA HASSAN EL-SAFI

Faculty of Medicine: Prof. ABDEL GADIR MOHAMED YOUSIF EL KADAROU

Faculty of Nursing Sciences: Dr NIEMA MIRGHANI IBRAHIM

Faculty of Pharmacy: Prof. KAMAL EL DIN EL TAYIB IBRAHIM

Faculty of Public Health and Environmental Hygiene: Dr ABDEL WAHAB MOHAMED EL MAKIE

Faculty of Science: Dr OSMAN IBRAHIM OSMAN ABDEL KARIM

Faculty of Technological and Developmental Studies: Dr ABDALLA GUMAA FRWA

Faculty of Veterinary Medicine: Prof. SULIMAN MOHAMED ELSONOSI

Graduate College: Prof. ZEN EL ABDEEN A. RAHEEM KARAR

ATTACHED RESEARCH INSTITUTES

Centre for Camel Research.

Centre for Diplomatic Studies: Dean Dr ZAKARIA ALI AHMED.

Centre for Educational Development of Health Professions: Dean Prof. AHMED HASSAN FAHAL.

Centre for Health Economics: Dean Dr ELTAYEB AHMED SHUMU.

Centre for Information Technology and Communication: Dean Dr NUHA MUDATHER BEHARY.

Centre of Staff Member Skills Development: Dean Dr KABASHOUR KUKU GAMBIL.

Institute of African and Asian Studies: Dean Prof. AL-AMIN ABU-MANGA MOHAMED.

Institute for Animal Exports Development: Dean Prof. SALIN AHMED BABIKER.

Institute of Building and Road Research: Dean Dr ABDEL KARIM MOHAMED ZEIN.

Institute of Desertification and Desert Cultivation Studies: Dean Prof. MUKHTAR AHMED MUSTAFA.

Institute of Developmental Studies and Research: Dean Dr MUSTAFA BABIKIR ABUSH-AIBA.

Institute of Endemic Disease: Dean Prof. MAOWIA M. MUKHTAR.

Institute of Environmental Studies: Dean Dr MIRGHANI TAG EL SAYID AHMED.

Institute of Peace Research: Dean Dr ELTYEB HAG ATTIA.

Institute for the Study of Public Administration and Federalism: Dean Dr ADAM AZZAIN MOHAMED.

Institute of Urban Studies: Dean Dr BUSHRA ELTAYEB BABIKER.

Prof. Abdalla El Tayib Institute for Arabic Language Studies: Dean Prof. MUHAMMAD YUSUF MUSTAFA AL-WATHIQ.

UNIVERSITY OF KORDOFAN

POB 160, El Obeid, North Kordofan 517

Telephone: (611) 23119

Fax: (611) 23108

E-mail: info@uni-kordofan.com

Internet: www.uni-kordofan.com

Founded 1990

State Control

Vice-Chancellor: OSMAN ADAM OSMAN

Faculties of Education, Engineering and Technical Science, Medicine and Health Sciences, Natural Resources, Science and Humanities and Commercial Studies and Business Administration; Gum Arabic Research Centre; Institute of Accounting, Banking and Information Systems; Centre for Intermediate Technology in Agriculture.

NILE VALLEY UNIVERSITY

POB 52, Addamer

Telephone: (216) 24433

Fax: (216) 24106

Internet: www.nile-vunv.net

Founded 1990

State control

Language of instruction: Arabic

Academic year: October to June

Vice-Chancellor: Prof. FASIAL A. EL-HAG

Principal: Dr ATTA A. FADLALLA

Academic Secretary: Prof. MAHMOUD Y. OSMAN

Library of 31,143 books, 76 periodicals

Number of teachers: 240
Number of students: 6,886 (6,796 undergraduate, 90 postgraduate)

DEANS

Faculty of Agriculture: Dr SAIFELDIN M. AL-
AMIN
Faculty of Commerce and Business Admin-
istration: HAMZA A. HAMZA
Faculty of Education: Dr MOHMED A.
MOHAMED
Faculty of Engineering and Technology:
IZZELDIN A. ABDALLA
Faculty of Islamic and Arabic Studies:
ABDELNABI A. EL-TAYEB
Faculty of Medicine: (vacant)
Teaching-Training College: ABDELGADIR S.
HAMAD

NYALA UNIVERSITY

POB 155, Nyala, South Darfur
Telephone: (711) 33122
Fax: (711) 33123
E-mail: nyalauni@yahoo.com
Internet: www.nyalauniversity.net
Founded 1994
State control
Academic year: April to December

Vice-Chancellor

Number of teachers: 151
Number of students: 6,301

Faculties of Community Development, Economics and Commerce, Education, Engineering, Law, Nursing, Technology and
Veterinary Science; Centre for Peace Studies.

OMDURMAN ISLAMIC UNIVERSITY

POB 382, Omdurman
Telephone: (187) 511525
Fax: (187) 511525
Internet: www.oiu.edu
Founded 1912; university status 1965
State control
Language of instruction: Arabic
Academic year: October to June
Chairman of University Council: Sheikh M.
M. SADIQ AL-KAMMOURI
Vice-Chancellor: Prof. MOHAMMED OSMAN
SALIH
Secretary-General: Dr HASSAN AHMED HAS-
SAN
Academy Secretary: Prof. HASSAN AHMED EL-
HASSAN
Librarian: ABDUL SEED OSMAN
Library of 172,858 vols
Number of teachers: 854
Number of students: 51,636 (47636 under-
graduate, 4,000 postgraduate)
Publications: *Faculty of Arts Magazine,
Faculty of Islamic Studies Magazine*

DEANS

Faculty of Agriculture: Dr M. AL-H. SIDDEEG
Faculty of Arabic Language: Prof. BABEKIR
AL-ZACOULT
Faculty of Arts: Prof. H. ABDUL-RAHMAN
Faculty of Basic Medical Sciences: Dr M.
SALAH ELDIN
Faculty of Computer Sciences: M. S.
MOHAMMED
Faculty of Economics: Dr S. M. MOHAMED
Faculty of Education: Prof. AL-H. OMER HAJ
Faculty of Engineering: Dr H. AL-TAYEB
Faculty of Higher Studies: Dr H. AL-ABBASSI
Faculty of Human Development: Dr IBRA-
HEEM A. M. AHMED
Faculty of Management Science: Dr A.
ABDELRAIID
Faculty of Medicine: Prof. A. I. YOUSSIF
Faculty of Pharmacy: Dr M. AL-H. ABDULLAH

Faculty of Sharia and Law: Dr A. IBRAHEEM

RED SEA UNIVERSITY

POB 24, Port Sudan
Telephone: (311) 27878
Fax: (311) 27778
Founded 1994
State Control
Vice-Chancellor: ABDEL GADIR DAFALLA
ELHAG
Number of teachers: 80
Number of students: 800
Faculties of Applied Sciences, Earth
Sciences, Economics and Administration,
Education, Engineering, Marine Science
and Fisheries, Maritime Transport Eco-
nomics, Medicine and Health Sciences and
Teacher Training; Institute of Oceanogra-
phy.

SHENDI UNIVERSITY

POB 142, Shendi
Telephone: (261) 72184
Fax: (261) 72509
Founded 1990 as Faculty of Nile Valley
University; present status and title 1994
State Control
Vice-Chancellor and President: ALI ABDEL
ABDEL RAHMAN BARRI
Number of teachers: 215
Number of students: 3,700
Publication: *Journal if Shendi University*
(Scientific, cultural and social topics, 2 a
year)
Faculties of Arts, Community Development,
Economics, Commerce and Business
Administration, Law (incl. Sharia Law),
Medicine and Health Sciences and Pri-
mary School Teacher Training; Centres for
Adult Education and Extramural Studies,
Agricultural Irrigation, Animal Production
and Crop Research and Educational Devel-
opment and Continuing Education; Al-
Faith Islamic Studies Centre.

SINAR UNIVERSITY

Sinar
Telephone: (561) 785614
Fax: (561) 730697
Founded 1977; present status 1995
Principal: MOHAMMED AWAD SALIH
Faculties of Agriculture, Arabic and Islamic
Studies, Education, Engineering, Medicine
and Natural Resources and Environment;
Centre for Extramural Studies; Da'wah
Centre.

SUDAN UNIVERSITY OF SCIENCE AND TECHNOLOGY

POB 407, Khartoum
Telephone: (183) 772508
Fax: (183) 774559
E-mail: sust@sudanet.net
Internet: www.sustech.edu
Founded 1950
State control
Academic year: September to May
Vice-Chancellor: Prof. Dr IZZELDIN MOHAMED
OSMAN
Deputy-Vice-Chancellor: Prof. Dr SADIG HAS-
SAN EL SADIG
Secretary-General: ALI EL RAHMAN ALI EL
HAG
Number of teachers: 750
Number of students: 21,500 (14,000 full-time,
7,500 part-time)

Publication: *Science and Technology* (2 a
year)

DEANS

College of Agriculture: Dr ABDULAZIZ MAKAWI
College of Business: ALI ABDALLA ADAM
College of Earth Sciences at Wad-al-Mag-
boul: Al RAHMAN GURASHI
College of Education: Dr AHMED SAAD
MASOUD
College of Engineering: Prof. Dr AHMED EL
TAYEB
College of Fine and Applied Arts: Dr ALI
MOHAMED OSMAN
College of Forestry and Pastures: SALIH
SULIMAN
College of Music and Drama: Dr AHMAD
ABDUAAL
College of Physical Education: SHARAFELIN
AL DAROUTI
College of Radiography and Radiotherapy:
Dr BUSHRA HUSSEIN AHMED
College of Sciences: HAGO AHMAD MOHAMED
College of Technology and Human Develop-
ment: Dr ABDUL RAHIM MOHAMED EL AMIN
College of Veterinary and Animal Science:
Prof. Dr OSMAN SAAD
College of Graduate Studies: Prof. Dr SABIR
MOHAMED SALIH

UPPER NILE UNIVERSITY

POB 1660, Khartoum
Telephone: (183) 220825
Founded 1991
State control
Language of instruction: Arabic
Academic year: November to June
Vice-Chancellor: Prof. MOSES MACAR KACUOL
Deputy Vice-Chancellor (Academic): Dr
JOSHUA OTOR AKOL
Principal (Administration): NATHANIEL GANY
GAI
Librarian: ABDEL BAGI MOHAMED EL-FAHAL
(acting)
Library of 23,000 vols
Number of teachers: 92
Number of students: 1,167

DEANS

College of Agriculture: SAYED BUNDUKI BOLLO
College of Animal Production: ZEINAB
MOHAMED TOM
College of Education: AKOY DUAL AKOY
College of Forestry: MASIMO KALISTO MOI-
LINGA
College of Medicine: Dr OSMAN AHMED EL-
BAKHIT
School of Nursing: NAHID KHALIL EL-FAKI
(Director)
School of Public and Environmental Health:
HATIM RAHAMTALLA ALALAWI (Director)

UNIVERSITY OF WEST KORDOFAN

POB 16722, Khartoum, El-Foula, West Kor-
dofan
Telephone: (183) 785614
Founded 1997
State Control
Vice-Chancellor: IBRAHIM MUSA TIBIN
Faculties of Economics and Community
Development, Education, Islamic and Ara-
bic Sciences and Natural Resources and
Environmental Studies.

UNIVERSITY OF ZALENGEI

Zalengei, West Darfur 6
Telephone: (713) 22013
Fax: (713) 22013
E-mail: uzal@student.net
Founded 1994

State Control
Language of instruction: Arabic
Vice-Chancellor: AHMED MOHAMED ABAKER
Number of teachers: 105
Number of students: 1,249

DEANS

Faculty of Agriculture: KUMAL IBRAHIM ADAM
Faculty of Education: ABDUL MUTALIB MOHAMED KHATIR
Holy Koran and Islamic Studies Institute: ABDOUL MUTALIB MOHAMED KHATIR

Computer and Information Science Centre: Dir MOHAMED EL AMIN IBRAHIM.

Peace and Development Centre: Dir MUSA ADAM ISMALI.

Colleges and Institutes

Faculty of Hygiene and Environmental Studies: POB 205, Khartoum; tel. 72690; f. 1933; 26 staff; 4 depts; awards BSc and MSc in Environmental Health; Librarian M. MOHD. SALIH; Dean B. M. EL-HASSAN

Environmental Health: Dr M. A. H. ALLOBA
Epidemiology and Bio-statistics: Dr A. TIGANI
Field Training Unit: AHMED ABDALLA
Health Education: MAHMOUD A. RAHMAN
Nutrition and Food Hygiene: ALI NASIR

Khartoum Nursing College: POB 1063, Khartoum; 3-year diploma course; Principal A. M. OSMAN.

Yambio Institute of Agriculture: Sud 82/002, c/o UNDP POB 913, Khartoum; f. 1972; library: 5,000 vols; 15 staff; 130 students; two-year diploma courses; Principal CHRISTOPHER LADO GALE.

SURINAME

The Higher Education System

Higher education institutions predate the independence of Suriname (formerly Dutch Guiana) from the Netherlands in 1975, with the oldest being Anton de Kom Universiteit van Suriname (Anton de Kom University of Suriname), which was founded in 1968. In addition to the university, higher education is offered by technical and vocational schools. The Ministry of Education and National Development is the government agency responsible for higher education. In 2001/02 there

were 3,250 students enrolled at the university, with a further 1,936 students enrolled in other institutions of higher education in 2000/01.

The Dutch-style secondary school certificate (VWO) is the main criteria for admission to higher education. The Bachelors is the undergraduate degree at the University and last four years, including a practicum. Bachelors degrees are also offered by the Academie voor Hoger Kunst en Cultuuronderwijs, and last four years. The University does not offer Masters degrees.

Learned Society

LANGUAGE AND LITERATURE

Alliance Française: Prins Hendrikstraat 8, POB 9209, Paramaribo; e-mail afsuriname@surimail.sr; tel. 4211305; offers courses and exams in French language and culture and promotes cultural exchange with France.

Research Institutes

AGRICULTURE, FISHERIES AND VETERINARY SCIENCE

Centre for Agricultural Research in Suriname: POB 1914, Paramaribo; tel. 490128; fax 498069; e-mail celos@sr.net; internet www.celos.sr.org; f. 1965; a branch of the University of Suriname; research in tropical agriculture; Dir R. O. RAVENSWAAY; publ. *Celos Bulletins.*

Landbouwproefstation (Agricultural Experiment Station): POB 160, Paramaribo; tel. 472442; fax 478986; f. 1903; attached to the Min. of Agriculture, Animal Husbandry and Fisheries; library of 28,502 vols, including bound periodicals and pamphlets; Dir Drs ELVIS GOEDHART (acting); publs *Annual Report, Suriname Agriculture* (2 to 3 a year), *Bulletins* (irregular).

TECHNOLOGY

Geologisch Mijnbouwkundige Dienst (Geological Mining Service): 2–6 Kleine Waterstraat, Paramaribo; tel. 476215; f. 1943; library of 20,000 vols; Dir Dr R. L. VERWEY; publs contributions in *Mededelingen*, geological maps.

Library

Paramaribo

Bibliotheek van het Cultureel Centrum Suriname (Library of the Suriname Cultural Centre): POB 1241, Paramaribo; tel. 472369; fax 473903; f. 1947; 500,000 vols; 7 branches, 1 book-mobile; Librarian G. R. KOORNAAR.

Museum

Paramaribo

Stichting Surinaams Museum: POB 2306, Abraham Crijnssenweg 1, Paramaribo; tel. 425871; fax 425881; e-mail museum@cq-link.sr; internet www.surinaamsmuseum.net; f. 1947; library of 35,000 vols; archaeology, art, history, ethnology; Dir Drs J. H. J. VAN PUTTEN.

University

ANTON DE KOM UNIVERSITEIT VAN SURINAME
(Anton de Kom University of Suriname)

Universiteitscomplex Leysweg 73, POB 9212, Paramaribo

Telephone: 465558
Fax: 462291
E-mail: adek.bestuur@sr.net
Internet: www.uvs.edu

Founded 1968
Language of instruction: Dutch
Academic year: October to September

President: Dr G. A. RUSLAND
Vice-President: Drs A. LIFOSJOE
Secretary: Drs J. C. PAWIROREDJO

Number of teachers: 286
Number of students: 3,400

Publications: *Journal of Social Sciences* (2 a year), *Suriname Medical Bulletin* (4 a year)

DEANS

Faculty of Medicine: Drs G. OEHLERS
Faculty of Social Sciences: URLIE LEMEN
Faculty of Technology: Ir J. MARTINUS

SWAZILAND

The Higher Education Sytem

Higher education institutions predate the independence of Swaziland from the United Kingdom in 1968, with the oldest being University of Swaziland (formerly University of Botswana, Lesotho and Swaziland), which was founded in 1964. In 2003/04 4,198 students were enrolled at the University of Swaziland, which has campuses at Luyengo and Kwaluseni; there are also a number of other institutions of higher education.

The GCE A-Levels, the Cambridge Overseas School Certificate or Cambridge Overseas Higher School Certificate are the main criteria for admission to undergraduate courses at the University. The undergraduate Bachelors degree is divided into Part 1 and Part 2, lasting four years overall. Postgraduate Masters degrees are awarded in a restricted number of fields, including arts, sciences and education. Masters degrees are usually one-year programmes of full-time study (or two-years part-time).

Post-secondary technical and vocational education is offered by a number of institutions, including Swaziland College of Technology, Institute of Health Sciences and Swaziland Institute of Management and Public Administration.

Learned Societies

GENERAL

Royal Swaziland Society of Science and Technology: c/o The University, Private Bag, Kwaluseni; tel. 5284011; fax 5285276; f. 1977 to promote science and technology and relevant research; organizes meetings, seminars, etc.; 100 mems; Pres. Prof. L. P. MAKHUBU; Sec. R. MARTIN; publ. *Swaziland Journal of Science and Technology* (2 a year).

BIBLIOGRAPHY, LIBRARY SCIENCE AND MUSEOLOGY

Swaziland Library Association: POB 2309, Mbabane; tel. (c/o Swaziland National Library) 4042633; fax 4043863; e-mail nomkhwa@realnet.co.sz; internet www .uniswa.sz; f. 1984; 120 mems; Chair. NOMSA V. MKHWANAZI; Sec. SIBONGILE NXUMALO; publs *SWALA Journal* (2 a year), *SWALA Newsletter* (4 a year).

FINE AND PERFORMING ARTS

Swaziland Art Society: POB 812, Mbabane; tel. 4044136; e-mail artsociety@mailfly .com; internet www.swazilandartsociety.org .sz; f. 1970; classes, workshops, exhibitions, films, discussions, etc.; 60 mems; Chairs HELEN MOIR, ANS VRIEND.

LANGUAGE AND LITERATURE

Alliance Française: Swazi Plaza, POB A266, Mbabane; tel. 4043667; fax 4048340; e-mail mbabane@alliance.org.za; internet www.swaziplace.com/alliancefrancaise/index .html; offers courses and exams in French language and culture and promotes cultural exchange with France.

Research Institutes

AGRICULTURE, FISHERIES AND VETERINARY SCIENCE

Lowveld Experiment Station: POB 11, L312 Matata; tel. 3636311; fax 5283360; e-mail les@iafrica.sz; f. 1964; agricultural research, cotton breeding, cotton entomology; Chief Research Officer P. MKHATSHWA.

Malkerns Research Station: POB 4, Malkerns; tel. 5283306; fax 5283306; e-mail malkernsresearch@africaonline.co.sz; f. 1959; general research on crops, vegetables, fruits and farming systems; 14 research sections; library of 5,000 vols; Chief Research Officer P. D. MKHATSHWA.

Mpisi Cattle Breeding Experimental Station: Mpisi; to improve indigenous Nguni cattle; to provide multiplication studs of Brahman, Simmentaler and Friesland cattle for beef, milk and cross breeding; Dir R. A. JOHN; Man. I. A. MORLEY HEWITT.

TECHNOLOGY

Geological Survey and Mines Department: POB 9, Mbabane; tel. 4042411; fax 4045215; e-mail geo.director@swazi.net; f. 1944; activities: mapping of the territory (published at a scale of 1:25,000 and 1:50,000), the investigation of mineral occurrences by prospecting, detailed mapping and diamond drilling, mine and quarry inspections, control of explosives and prospecting; 18 mems; small library; Dir Dr M. MAPHALALA; publs *Annual Reports*, *Bulletins*.

Libraries and Archives

Mbabane

Swaziland National Archives: POB 946, Mbabane; tel. 4161278; fax 4161241; e-mail sdnationalarchives@realnet.co.sz; f. 1970; 5,600 vols; govt records since 1880s; collection of historical photographs, newspapers, maps, reports; oral history and biographies of prominent Swazis; Dir D. F. K. MTHETHWA (acting).

Swaziland National Library Service: POB 1461, Mbabane; tel. 4042633; fax 4043863; e-mail snlssz@realnet.co.sz; f. 1971; operates a public library service throughout the country with branch libraries at Manzini, Mpaka, Lomahasha, Nhlangano, Siteki, Pigg's Peak, Big Bend, Bhunya, Tshaneni, Mankayana, Lavumisa, Hlatikulu and Mhlume; mobile library visits; libraries at secondary schools; 80,000 vols, 150 periodicals; a national library was est. in 1986 which will eventually function as the focal point in Swaziland's documentation and information system; Dir D. J. KUNENE; publs *Annual Report*, *Index to Swaziland Collection* (irregular), *Accessions List* (irregular).

Museum

Lobamba

Swaziland National Museum: POB 100, Lobamba; tel. 4161178; fax 4161875; f. 1972, under the patronage of the Swaziland National Trust Commission; museum with extra-mural functions, giving information about Swazi culture as well as other Southern African Bantu groups; reference library; Curator ROSEMARY ANDRADE; publs *Annual Report*, *Museum Occasional Paper*.

University

UNIVERSITY OF SWAZILAND

Private Bag 4, M201 Kwaluseni
Telephone: 5184011
Fax: 5185276
E-mail: registrar@admin.uniswa.sz
Internet: www.uniswa.sz

Founded 1964 as part of University of Botswana, Lesotho and Swaziland, present name 1982
Language of instruction: English
Academic year: August to May
Chancellor: HM KING MSWATI III
Vice-Chancellor: (vacant)
Pro-Vice-Chancellor: Prof. C. M. MAGAGULA
Registrar: S. S. VILAKATI
Librarian: M. R. MAVUSO

Library of 178,000 vols, 1,500 periodicals
Number of teachers: 303
Number of students: 4,198

Publications: *UNISWA Journal of Agriculture, Science and Health Sciences* (2 a year), *UNISWA Journal of Social Science, Humanities and Education* (2 a year)

DEANS

Faculty of Agriculture: Dr G. N. SHONGWE
Faculty of Commerce: Prof. M. A. KHAN
Faculty of Education: Prof. J. C. B. BIGALA
Faculty of Health Sciences: Dr P. S. DLAMINI
Faculty of Humanities: Dr H. L. NDLOVU
Faculty of Social Sciences: Prof. A. A. AL-TERAIFI
Faculty of Science: Prof. V. S. B. MTETWA
Faculty of Postgraduate Studies: Prof. E. C. L. KUNENE

There is also an Institute of Distance Education

HEADS OF DEPARTMENTS

Faculty of Agriculture (tel. 5283021; fax 5283021):

Agricultural Economics and Management: Dr P. M. DLAMINI
Agricultural Extension and Education: Dr M. P. DLAMINI

Animal Production and Health: Dr A. M. DLAMINI
Crop Production: Dr G. T. MASINA
Home Economics: Dr P. J. MUSI
Land Use and Mechanization: Dr A. M. MAMYATSI

Faculty of Commerce:

Accountancy: M. T. NTENTESA
Business Administration: N. M. MNDZEBELE

Faculty of Education:

Adult Education: Dr J. P. B. MUTANGIRA
Curriculum and Teaching: Dr E. Z. MAZIBUKO
Educational Foundations and Management: Dr A. M. NXUMALO
In-Service Education: Dr S. E. MAMYATSI
Primary Education: Dr B. E. M. DLAMINI

Faculty of Health Sciences (tel. 4040171; fax 4046241):

Community Health Nursing: E. M. MABUZA
Environmental Health Science: J. D. NXUMALO
General Nursing: R. L. L. MANANA
Midwifery Science: P. P. MAMBA

Faculty of Humanities:

Academic Communication Skills: G. S. MKHWANAZI
African Languages and Literature: E. S. SIBANDA
English Language and Literature: Dr C. TSABEDZE
History: Prof. K. M. KANDUZA
Modern Languages (French): K. A. F. FERREIRA-MEYERS
Theology and Religious Studies: Dr H. L. NDLOVU

Faculty of Science:

Biological Sciences: Dr B. S. NKOSI
Chemistry: Dr J. THWALA
Computer Studies: Dr P. M. MASHWAMA
Geography and Environmental Planning: Dr N. O. SIMELANE
Mathematics: Dr M. KHUMALO
Physics and Electronic Engineering: Prof. M. D. DLAMINI

Faculty of Social Sciences:

Economics: Dr D. F. DLAMINI
Law: G. N. K. VUKOR-QUARSHIE
Political and Administrative Studies: T. M. SHIMBIRA
Sociology: Prof. J. K. NGWISHA

Statistics and Demography: C. M. MKHWANAZI

Colleges

Swaziland College of Technology: POB 69, H100 Mbabane; tel. 4042681; fax 4044521; e-mail scot@africaonline.co.sz; f. 1946 as Trade School, present name 1968; diploma courses in mechanical engineering, electrical and electronics engineering, telecommunications engineering, building and civil engineering, hotel and catering, secretarial studies, commercial and technical teaching; certificate courses in accounting, plumbing, block- and bricklaying, and carpentry; library: 18,000 vols; 60 teachers; 700 students; Prin. HEBRON T. SUKATI; Registrar ATWELL GULE.

Swaziland Institute of Management and Public Administration: POB 495, Mbabane; tel. 4220740; fax 4220742; e-mail simpa@realnet.co.sz; f. 1965; 21 teachers (15 full-time, 6 part-time); 900 students; Principal M. N. KHOZA.

SWEDEN

The Higher Education System

The oldest institution of higher education is Uppsala Universitet (Uppsala University), which was founded in 1477; the next oldest is Lunds Universitet (Lunds University), which was founded in 1666. Several institutions date from the 19th century, among them Kungliga Tekniska Högskolan (Royal Institute of Technology—founded 1827), Stockholms Universitet (Stockholm University—founded 1878) and Göteborgs Universitet (Gothenburg University—founded 1891).

In 1977 the Higher Education Act classified 100 programmes of undergraduate education by five subject areas (administrative, economic and social science; health; information, communication and fine arts; teacher training; and technical); however, in 1989 responsibility for curriculum planning was handed over to the universities, and further reforms in 1993 delineated undergraduate programmes into general or professional fields of study. Also in that year higher education was decentralized and a new degree system was introduced. Sweden participates in the Bologna Process to establish a European Higher Education Area, the first phase of which is to adopt a credit-based system of comparable degrees with two main cycles (undergraduate and graduate). In 2002 the Ministry of Education and Research established a working group to assess the feasibility of introducing a new degree system to correspond with the criteria of the Bologna Process, and subsequently a new system (see below) was fully implemented in 2007. Higher education is offered by universities (universitet), university colleges or institutes of higher education (högskola). In 2003/04 there were 397,679 students enrolled in higher education.

The main requirement for admission to higher education is completion of secondary education and award of the Upper Secondary School Leaving certificate (Avgångsbetyg or Slutbetyg från Gymnasieskola). Alternatively, applicants can be admitted upon completion of adult secondary school (komvux), completion of folk high school (folkhögskola) or at least four years of professional experience before the age of 25. Specialist programmes of study may have additional criteria. Furthermore, applicants sit either a special aptitude test (Högskoleprov) or National University Aptitude Test (Högskoleprovet). The newly-established university degree system comprises three cycles, each sub-divided into two parts; degrees are awarded on a 'credit' basis, and Sweden has adopted the European Credit Transfer System (ECTS). The undergraduate Bachelors degrees are the Högskoleexamen, which requires 80 credits over two years, and the Kandidatexamen, which requires 120 credits over three years. Professional degrees (Yrkesexamen) may last longer. The Masters-equivalent degrees are the Magisterexamen, lasting one year, and the Masterexamen, which lasts two years. Finally, doctoral-level studies consist of the Licentiatexamen, a two-year research degree, and the Doktorsexamen, a research degree culminating with submission and defence of a thesis; the Doktorsexamen requires a minimum of 160 credits in at least four years.

In 2002 legislation was enacted establishing a new form of post-secondary technical and vocational education called Advanced Vocational Education (Kvalificerad Yrkesutbildning). This primarily consists of programmes of study jointly-organized by employers and institutions of tertiary education; the main Government provider is the Swedish Agency for Advanced Vocational Education (Myndigheten för Kvalificerad Yrkesutbildning).

Regulatory and Representative Bodies

GOVERNMENT

Ministry of Culture: Drottninggt. 16, 103 33 Stockholm; tel. (8) 405-10-00; fax (8) 21-68-13; e-mail registrator@culture.ministry.se; internet kultur.regeringen.se; Minister LENA ADELSOHN LILJEROTH.

Ministry of Education and Research: Drottninggt. 16, 103 33 Stockholm; tel. (8) 405-10-00; fax (8) 723-11-92; e-mail registrator@educcult.ministry.se; internet utbildning.regeringen.se; Minister LARS LEIJONBORG.

ACCREDITATION

ENIC/NARIC Sweden: Swedish Nat. Agency for Higher Education, POB 7851, 103 99 Stockholm; tel. (8) 563-085-00; fax (8) 563-086-50; e-mail hsv@hsv.se; internet www.hsv.se; Head LARS PETERSSON.

NATIONAL BODIES

Folkhögskolornas informationstjänst (Information Service of the Swedish Folk High Schools): Box 740, 101 35 Stockholm; Västmannagatan 1, Stockholm; tel. (8) 796-00-50; fax (8) 21-88-26; e-mail info@folkhogskola.nu; internet www.folkhogskola.nu; provides information on liberal adult education that is also non-formal and voluntary.

Högskoleverket (National Agency for Higher Education): Luntmakargatan 13, Box 7851, 103 99 Stockholm; tel. (8) 563-085-00; fax (8) 563-085-50; e-mail hsv@hsv.se; internet www.hsv.se; f. 1995; central agency responsible for matters relating to higher education institutions; Dir-Gen. SIGBRIT FRANKE; Head of Information EVA FERNDAHL.

Myndigheten för kvalificerad yrkesutbildning (Swedish Agency for Advanced Vocational Education): Norra Stationsgatan 2B, 281 48 Hässleholm; tel. (451) 45-480; fax (451) 45-499; e-mail ky@ky.se; internet www.ky.se; f. 2002; draws up guidelines for advanced vocational education courses and contributes to their devt, approves applications, awards grants and supervises and follows up the courses; Gen. Dir SONJA ERIKSSON.

Myndigheten för nätverk och samarbete inom högre utbildning (Swedish Agency for Networks and Co-operation in Higher Education): POB 194, 871 24 Härnösand; Brunnshusgatan 6, 871 33 Härnösand; tel. (611) 34-95-00; fax (611) 34-95-05; e-mail info@nshu.se; internet www.nshu.se; supports and promotes the devt of higher education and the new structure of higher education and degrees (the Bologna Process); has a searchable database of 2,700 IT-supported distance education courses and study programmes; 35 mems (univs and colleges); Chair. INGEGERD PALMÉR (acting); Dir-Gen. HÅKAN LARSSON (acting).

Rådet för högre utbildning (Council for the Renewal of Higher Education): POB 7285, 103 89 Stockholm; tel. (8) 56-30-88-61; fax (8) 56-30-88-50; e-mail rhu@rhu.se; internet www.rhu.se; f. 1990; dept of Nat. Agency for Higher Education; promotes and supports efforts to develop the quality and pedagogical renewal of undergraduate and postgraduate education, and administers funds provided by the Swedish Parliament for experiments in undergraduate and postgraduate education; 9 mems; Chair. Prof. LARS HAIKOLA.

Skolverket (Swedish National Agency for Education): 106 20 Stockholm; Alströmergatan 12, Stockholm; tel. (8) 52-73-32-00; fax (8) 24-44-20; e-mail skolverket@skolverket.se; internet www.skolverket.se; central admin. authority for the Swedish public school system for children, young people and adults; audits preschool activities, care for school children, schools and adult education; has regional offices in Göteborg, Linköping, Lund, Stockholm and Umeå; Head PER THULLBERG.

Styrelsen för internationellt utvecklingssamarbete (Swedish Agency for International Development Co-operation): Valhallavägen 199, 105 25 Stockholm; tel. (8) 698-50-00; fax (8) 20-88-64; e-mail sida@sida.se; internet www.sida.se; attached to Min. for Foreign Affairs; helps poor people in foreign countries to improve their living conditions; has offices in 50 countries; Dir-Gen. and Chair. GÖRAN HOLMQVIST (acting).

Svenska institutet (Swedish Institute): Skeppsbron 2, Box 7434, 103 91 Stockholm; Slottsbacken 10, Stockholm; tel. (8) 453-78-00; fax (8) 20-72-48; e-mail si@si.se; internet www.si.se; public agency that promotes interest in Sweden abroad; seeks to establish co-operation and lasting relations with other countries through active communication and cultural, educational and scientific exchanges; Dir-Gen. OLLE WÄSTBERG.

Sveriges universitets- och högskoleförbund (Association of Swedish Higher Education): Rådmansgatan 72, 113 60 Stockholm; tel. (8) 32-13-88; fax (8) 32-93-70; e-mail kerstin.reithner@suhf.ki.se; internet www .suhf.se; f. 1995; 40 mems; Chair. Prof. BO SUNDQVIST; Sec.-Gen. BENGT KARLSSON.

Learned Societies

GENERAL

Kungl. Humanistiska Vetenskaps-Samfundet i Uppsala (Royal Society of Humanities at Uppsala): c/o Prof. Staffan Fridell, Dept of Scandinavian Languages, POB 526, 751 20 Uppsala; tel. (18) 471-12-79; fax (18) 471-12-72; e-mail staffan.fridell@nordiska.uu .se; f. 1889 to promote the study of humanities; 5 meetings a year, with lectures and discussion; distributes awards and scholarships; 120 mems (100 Swedish, 20 foreign); Pres. Prof. ANNA SÅGVALL HEIN; Sec. Prof. STAFFAN FRIDELL; publs Arsbok (Yearbook), Skrifter (Proceedings, irreg.).

Kungl. Vetenskaps- och Vitterhets-Samhället i Göteborg (Gothenburg Royal Society of Arts and Sciences): c/o Klassiska institutionen, Gothenburg University, Box 200, 405 30 Göteborg; tel. (31) 772-12-42; fax (31) 772-12-62; e-mail birger.karlsson@me .chalmers.sc; f. 1778; 264 mems (218 Swedish, 46 foreign); Sec. Prof. BIRGER KARLSSON; publs Acta Regiae Societatis Scientiarum et Litterarum Gothoburgensis (monographs), Arsbok.

Kungl. Vetenskaps-Societeten i Uppsala (Royal Society of Sciences of Uppsala): St Larsgatan 1, 753 10 Uppsala; f. 1710, charter 1728; to promote research principally in mathematics, natural sciences, medicine, Swedish antiquities and topography, by (a) publishing works of scholarship, (b) awarding grants, (c) collecting and making available relevant publications, (d) lectures; mems in four sections: physics and mathematics (40 national, 40 foreign), natural history and medicine (50 national, 40 foreign), history and archaeology (20 national, 10 foreign), technology and economics (20 national, 10 foreign); library of 600 periodicals; Pres. Prof. KERSTIN OLSSON; Sec. Prof. LARS-OLOF SUNDELÖF; publs Arsbok (annually), Matrikel (annually), Nova Acta (irregular).

Kungl. Vetenskapsakademien (Royal Swedish Academy of Sciences): Box 50005, 104 05 Stockholm; tel. (8) 673-95-00; fax (8) 15-56-70; e-mail rsas@kva.se; internet www .kva.se; f. 1739; sections of Mathematics (Chair. J.-E. ROOS), Astronomy and Space Sciences (Chair. H. RICKMAN), Physics (Chair. J. NORDGREN), Chemistry (Chair. B. NORDÉN), Geosciences (Chair. S. CLAESSON), Biosciences (Chair. S. GRILLNER), Medical Sciences (Chair. A. APERIA), Engineering Sciences (Chair. H. FRANK), Economics and Social Sciences (Chair. L. ENGWALL), Humanities and Other Sciences and for Distinguished Services to Scientific Research (Chair. G. CAVALLI-BJÖRKMAN); 520 mems (356 Swedish, 164 foreign); attached research institutes: see Research Institutes; library: see Libraries and Archives; Pres.

Prof. BO SUNDQVIST; Sec.-Gen. Prof. GUNNAR ÖQUIST; publs Acta Mathematica, Acta Zoologica, Ambio, Arkiv för Matematik, Documenta, Physica Scripta, Zoologica Scripta.

Kungl. Vitterhets Historie och Antikvitets Akademien (Royal Academy of Letters, History and Antiquities): Box 5622, 114 86 Stockholm; tel. (8) 440-42-80; fax (8) 440-42-90; e-mail kansli@vitterhetsakad.se; internet www.vitterhetsakad.se; f. 1753; humanities, social sciences, religion, law; 176 mems (131 Swedish, 45 foreign); library: see Libraries and Archives; Pres. Prof. ANDERS JEFFNER; Sec.-Gen. Prof. ULF SPORRONG; publs Fornvännen (journal), Handlingar (proceedings), Arkiv (archives).

Svenska institutet (The Swedish Institute): Box 7434, 103 91 Stockholm; tel. (8) 453-78-00; fax (8) 20-72-48; e-mail si@si.se; internet www.si.se; f. 1945; disseminates knowledge about Sweden abroad and arrange exchanges with other countries in the fields of culture, education, scientific research and public life in general; 90 staff; Dir-Gen. OLLE WÄSTBERG.

AGRICULTURE, FISHERIES AND VETERINARY SCIENCE

Kungl. Skogs- och Lantbruksakademien (Royal Swedish Academy of Agriculture and Forestry): Drottninggatan 95B, Box 6806, 113 86 Stockholm; tel. (8) 545-477-00; fax (8) 545-477-10; e-mail akademien@ksla.se; internet www.ksla.se; f. 1811 to apply science to the development and improvement of agriculture and forestry; 540 mems (15 hon., 400 working, 125 foreign); library: see Libraries and Archives; Pres. MÅRTEN CARLSSON; Deputy Perm. Sec. Prof. BRUNO NILSSON; publ. Kungl. Skogs och Lantbruksakademiens Tidskrift (quarterly).

ARCHITECTURE AND TOWN PLANNING

Svensk Teknik och Design (STD) (Swedish Federation of Consulting Engineers and Architects): Blasieholmsgatan 5, POB 16105, 103 22 Stockholm; tel. (8) 762-67-00; fax (8) 762-67-10; e-mail std@std.se; internet www .std.se; f. 2001; mems: 800 companies; Exec. Man. LISE LANGSETH; publ. Sector Review (annually).

ECONOMICS, LAW AND POLITICS

Centre for the Study of International Relations: Hagtornsvägen 9, Enebyberg 182 47 Stockholm; tel. (8) 612-33-62; fax (8) 758-30-39; e-mail info@cintrel.org; f. 1971; studies social sciences, international politics, law and economy; independent of any political party; organizes lectures and conferences, research seminars; library; Pres. CLÄES PALME; Vice-Pres. and Dir Prof. Dr RICHARD K. T. HSIEH; Secs Prof. Dr LARS HJERNER, Prof. Dr JACOB W. F. SUNDBERG; publ. Review.

International Law Association, Swedish Branch: c/o Andersson Gustafsson Advokatbyrå, POB 3124, 103 62 Stockholm; tel. (8) 677-17-00; fax (8)677-17-10; e-mail info@ ilasweden.se; internet www.ilasweden.se; f. 1922; Pres. Prof. OVE BRING; Sec. JOHN KADELBURGER.

Kungl. Krigsvetenskapsakademien (Royal Swedish Academy of War Sciences): Teatergatan 3, 5 tr, 111 48 Stockholm; tel. (8) 611-14-00; fax (8) 667-22-53; e-mail info@ kkrva.se; internet www.kkrva.se; f. 1796 to promote military sciences, including civil defence, economic defence and psychological defence, security and defence policy; 380 mems; Pres. ERIK NORBERG; Sec. Brig. KIM ÅKERMAN; publ. Handlingar och Tidskrift (every 2 months).

Nationalekonomiska Föreningen (Swedish Economic Association): c/o IUI, POB 5501, 114 85 Stockholm; tel. (8) 665-45-24; fax (8) 665-45-99; e-mail mattias.gansland@ iui.se; internet www.ne.su.se/ed; f. 1877; study of economics; 1,200 mems; Chair. TOMAS BRUCE; Sec. MATTIAS GANSLANDT; publ. Ekonomisk Debatt (8 a year).

Utrikespolitiska Institutet (Swedish Institute of International Affairs): Box 1253, 111 82 Stockholm; tel. (8) 696-05-00; fax (8) 20-10-49; e-mail siia@ui.se; internet www.ui .se; f. 1938; research on international affairs, enhancing public understanding of current international affairs; conferences, seminars and other events; library of 40,000 vols, 400 periodicals; Pres. ERIK BELFRAGE; Man. Dir Dr TOMAS RIES; publs Conference Papers, Internationella studier, Länder i fickformat, Research Report, Världens Fakta, Världspolitikens dagsfrågor.

FINE AND PERFORMING ARTS

Föreningen Svenska Tonsättare (Society of Swedish Composers): POB 27327, 102 54 Stockholm; tel. (8) 783-95-90; fax (8) 783-95-40; e-mail kansli@fst.se; internet www.fst.se; f. 1918; 270 mems; Pres. STEN MELIN.

Fylkingen (Society of Contemporary Music and Intermedia Art): POB 17044, 104 62 Stockholm; Torkel Knutssonsgatan 2, Münchenbryggeriet, Stockholm; tel. (8) 84-54-43; fax (8) 669-38-68; e-mail intermedia@ fylkingen.se; internet www.fylkingen.se; f. 1933; new music and intermedia art; 188 mems; Chair. LISE-LOTTE NORELIUS.

Kungl. Akademien för de fria Konsterna (Konstakademien) (Royal Academy of Fine Arts): Fredsgatan 12/Jakobsgatan 27, Box 16317, 103 26 Stockholm; tel. (8) 23-29-45; fax (8) 790-59-24; internet www .konstakademien.se; f. 1735 to promote the development of painting, sculpture, architecture and allied arts; 172 mems (123 Swedish, 29 foreign, 20 hon.); library of 40,000 vols; Sec.-Gen. OLLE GRANATH; publ. Meddelanden.

Kungl. Musikaliska Akademien (Royal Swedish Academy of Music): Blasieholmstorg 8, 111 48 Stockholm; tel. (8) 407-18-00; fax (8) 611-87-18; e-mail adm@musakad.se; internet www.musakad.se; f. 1771 for the promotion and protection of the art and science of music; awards the Polar Music Prize, Rolf Schock Prize, Christ Johnson Prize and Royal Swedish Academy of Music Jazz Prize; 175 Swedish mems; 65 foreign mems; Pres. Dr GUNNAR PETRI; Sec.-Gen. Dr ÅKE HOLMQUIST; publs Arsskrift (year book), Musica Sveciae (record anthology), etc.

Musikaliska Konstföreningen (Musical Art Association): Blasieholmstorg 8, 111 48 Stockholm; e-mail mk@westelius.com; internet www.musikaliskakonstforeningen .org.se; f. 1859 for the publication of Swedish music; Chair. ERIK LUNDKVIST; Sec. HANS ENFLO.

Statens Kulturråd (Kulturrådet) (Swedish National Council for Cultural Affairs): Box 7843, 103 98 Stockholm; tel. (8) 519-264-00; fax (8) 519-264-99; e-mail kulturradet@ kulturradet.se; internet www.kulturradet.se; f. 1974 as funding, advisory and investigatory body responsible for implementing national cultural policy; covers theatre, dance, music, literature, cultural journals, public libraries, art, museums and exhibitions; Chair. ANNA HEDBORG; Dir-Gen. KRISTINA RENNERSTEDT; publ. Kulturrådet.

Svensk Form (Swedish Society of Crafts and Design): Holmamiralens väg 2, 111 49 Stockholm; tel. (8) 463-31-30; fax (8) 644-22-85; e-mail info@svenskform.se; internet www

.svenskform.se; f. 1845; 8,000 mems; Chair. ERIKA LAGERBIELKE; publ. *Form* (every 2 months).

Svenska samfundet för musikforskning (Swedish Society for Musicology): Box 7448, 103 91 Stockholm; e-mail samfundet@ mbox301.swipnet.se; internet www.musik.uu .se/ssm; f. 1919; 325 mems; Pres. GUNNAR TERNHAG; Sec. CHRISTINA TOBECK; publs *Monumenta Musicae Sveciae, Svensk Tidskrift för Musikforskning* (Swedish Journal of Musicology, annually).

Sveriges Allmänna Konstförening (Swedish General Art Association): POB 5343, 102 47 Stockholm; Located at: Linnégatan 19, 102 47 Stockholm; tel. (8) 10-46-77; fax (8) 20-14-57; e-mail info@konstforeningen .se; internet www.konstforeningen.com; f. 1832; 13,000 mems; Pres. MÅRTEN LINDSTÅHL; publ. *Sveriges Allmänna Konstförenings årspublikation* (Swedish General Art Association's annual publication).

HISTORY, GEOGRAPHY AND ARCHAEOLOGY

Kartografiska Sällskapet (Swedish Cartographic Society): c/o Lantmäteriverket, 801 82 Gävle; e-mail kartografiska@geoforum.se; internet www.kartografiska.com; f. 1908; 2,800 mems; Pres. PETER NYHLÉN; Sec. PATRIK OTTOSON; publs *Kart & Bildteknik* (4 a year), *National Report* (mapping activities, in English, every 4 years), *Sveriges Kartläggning* (mapping of Sweden, every 10 years).

Svenska Museiföreningen (Swedish Museums Association): Fridhemsgaten 68, 112 46 Stockholm; tel. (8) 653-60-34; fax (8) 653-01-70; e-mail info@museiforeningen.se; internet www.museiforeningen.se; f. 1906; association of Swedish museums and members of staff; debates, etc., concerning practical development and museum policy issues; 1,000 individual mems, 200 institutional mems; Pres. ERIKA ARONOWITCH; publ. *Svenska Museer* (5 a year).

Svenska Sällskapet för Antropologi och Geografi (Swedish Society for Anthropology and Geography): Naturgeografiska Institutionen, Stockholms Universitet, 106 91 Stockholm; internet www.ssag.se; f. 1880; aims: to forward the development of anthropology and geography in Sweden, to communicate with foreign societies with the same objectives, and to support investigations into anthropology and geography; 900 mems; library of 10,000 vols; Pres. GUNHILD ROSQVIST; Sec. MONA PETERSSON; publs *Årsboken Ymer, Geografiska Annaler* (series A and B), *Human Geography, Physical Geography*.

LANGUAGE AND LITERATURE

Alliance Française: c/o Bratt Karlaplan 3A, 11460 Stockholm; tel. (8) 663-03-80; e-mail info@alliancefrancaisesthlm.com; internet www.alliancefrancaisesthlm.com; offers courses and exams in French language and culture and promotes cultural exchange with France; attached offices in Borås, Falun, Gothenburg, Halmstad, Helsingborg, Höglandet, Jönköping, Kalmar, Kristianstad, Linköping, Lund, Norrköping, Nyköping, Örebro, Ornskoldsvik, Östersund, Skaraborg, Skelleftea and Uppsala; Pres. JOHAN STENBERG.

British Council: c/o British Embassy, Skarpögatan 6–8, POB 27819, 115 93 Stockholm; tel. (8) 671-31-10; fax (8) 663-72-71; e-mail info@britishcouncil.se; internet www .britishcouncil.org/sweden; offers courses and exams in English language and British culture and promotes cultural exchange with the UK; Country Man. ROGER BUDD.

Goethe-Institut: Bryggargatan 12A, 111 21 Stockholm; tel. (8) 459-12-00; fax (8) 459-12-15; e-mail info@stockholm.goethe.org; internet www.goethe.de/ne/sto/deindex.htm; offers courses and exams in German language and culture and promotes cultural exchange with Germany; attached teaching centre in Gothenburg; library of 3,500 vols, 45 periodicals; Dir BERTHOLD FRANKE.

Instituto Cervantes: Bryggargatan 12A, 111 21 Stockholm; tel. (8) 440-17-60; fax (8) 21-04-31; e-mail info.stockholm@cervantes .es; internet www.cervantes.se; offers courses and exams in Spanish language and culture and promotes cultural exchange with Spain and Spanish-speaking Latin and Central America; library of 6,500 vols; Dir GASPAR CANO PERAL.

Samfundet de Nio (Academy of the Nine): Villagatan 14, Box 1703, 114 32 Stockholm; tel. (8) 411-15-42; internet www .samfundetdenio.se; f. 1913; Pres. INGE JONSSON (professor); Sec. ANDERS R. ÖHMAN (lawyer).

Svenska Akademien (Swedish Academy): Box 2118, 103 13 Stockholm; tel. (8) 555-125-00; fax (8) 555-125-49; e-mail sekretariat@ svenskaakademien.se; internet www .svenskaakademien.se; f. 1786; Swedish language and literature; awards Nobel Prize for Literature; 18 mems; library: see Libraries and Archives; Permanent Sec. Prof. HORACE ENGDAHL; publ. *Svenska Akademiens Handlingar* (annually).

Svenska PEN (Swedish PEN): Kristina Ahlinder, c/o Svenska Förläggareföreningen, Drottninggatan 97, 113 60 Stockholm; tel. (8) 736-19-40; e-mail info@pensweden.org; internet www.pensweden.org; f. 1922; 500 mems; Pres. LJILJANA DUFGRAN.

Sveriges Författarförbund (The Swedish Writers' Union): Box 3157, Drottninggatan 88B, 103 63 Stockholm; tel. (8) 545-132-00; fax (8) 545-132-10; e-mail sff@ forfattarforbundet.se; internet www .forfattarforbundet.se; f. 1893 to protect the intellectual and economic interests of writers and translators; 2,300 mems; Pres. BUNNY RAGNERSTAM; Dir HELENA NELSON-BÜLOW; publ. *Författaren* (6 a year).

MEDICINE

Socialstyrelsen (National Board of Health and Welfare): 106 30 Stockholm; tel. (8) 783-30-00; fax (8) 783-32-52; e-mail socialstyrelsen@socialstyrelsen.se; internet www.socialstyrelsen.se; public health, medical and social services administration; f. 1663; Dir-Gen. KJELL ASPLUND; publs *Cancer Incidence in Sweden* (Report of the Board's Cancer Registry), *Nytt fran Socialstyrelsen* (bulletins).

Svenska Läkaresällskapet (Swedish Society of Medicine): Box 738, 101 35 Stockholm; tel. (8) 440-88-60; fax (8) 440-88-99; e-mail sls@svls.se; internet www.svls.se; f. 1807; 20,000 mems; Exec. Dir CHRISTER EDLING; publ. *Svenska Läkaresällskapets Handlingar Hygiea*.

NATURAL SCIENCES

General

Wenner-Gren Stiftelserna (Wenner-Gren Foundations): Sveavägen 166, 23rd fl., 113 46 Stockholm; tel. (8) 7369800; fax (8) 318632; internet www.swgc.org; f. 1962; residence and meeting place for foreign and visiting scientists; Pres. of the Board Prof. INGE JONSSON; Scientific Sec. Prof. BERTIL DANEHOLT.

Biological Sciences

Kungl. Fysiografiska Sällskapet i Lund (Royal Physiographic Society of Lund): Stortorget 6, 222 23 Lund; tel. (46) 13-25-28; fax (46) 13-19-44; e-mail kansli@fysiografen.se; internet www.fysiografen.se; f. 1772; science, medicine and technology; 500 mems, 100 foreign corresps; Pres. Prof. BÄRBEL HAHN-HÄGERDAL; Sec. Prof. ROLF ELOFSSON; publ. *Årsbok* (every 2 years).

Svenska Naturskyddsföreningen (Swedish Society for Nature Conservation): Box 4625, Asögatan 115, 116 91 Stockholm; tel. (8) 702-65-00; fax (8) 702-08-55; e-mail info@ snf.se; internet www.snf.se; f. 1909; mem of IUCN; 176,000 mems; Sec. Gen. SVANTE AXELSSON; publs *Sveriges Natur* (every 2 months), a yearbook.

Mathematical Sciences

Lunds Matematiska Sällskap (Lund Mathematical Society): c/o Matematiska Institutionen, Box 118, 221 00 Lund; fax (46) 222-40-10; internet www.matematik.lu .se/LMS; f. 1923; 150 mems; Pres. Prof. NILS DENCKER; Sec. and Treas. MARCUS CARLSSON.

Matematiska Föreningen i Uppsala (Mathematical Society): Department of Mathematics, Uppsala Univ., POB 480, 751 06 Uppsala; tel. (18) 471-3200; fax (18) 471-3201; e-mail cecilia.holmgren@math.uu.se; internet www.math.uu.se/~renlund/mf/mf .html; f. 1853; 50 mems; Pres. CECILIA HOLMGREN; Sec. ANDERS FRISK.

Statistiska Föreningen (Statistical Society): Statistiska Centralbyrån, POB 24300, 104 51 Stockholm; internet www .statistiskaforeningen.se; f. 1901; provides a forum for statisticians and laymen interested in statistics, and by means of lectures, discussions and reports contributes to the analysis of problems in this field of science; 530 mems; Pres. MATS FORSBERG; Sec. ÅSA GREIJER.

Svenska Matematikersamfundet (Swedish Mathematical Society): c/o Ulf Persson, Matematiska Institutionen, Chalmers Tekniska Högskola, 412 96 Göteborg; e-mail ulfp@math.chalmers.se; internet www .matematikersamfundet.org.se; f. 1950; 540 mems; Chair. Prof. OLLE HÄGGSTRÖM; Sec. JOHAN JONASSON; publs *Mathematica Scandinavia* (with other Scandinavian Mathematical Societies), *Nordisk Matematisk Tidskrift*.

Physical Sciences

Geologiska Föreningen (Geological Society of Sweden): c/o Department of Geology and Geochemistry, Stockholm University, 106 91 Stockholm; tel. (8) 674-77-27; fax (8) 674-78-97; e-mail gff@geo.su.se; internet www.geologiskaforeningen.nu; f. 1871; 566 mems; Pres. Prof. BARBARA WOHLFAHRT; Sec. Assoc. Prof. MIKAEL CALNER; publs *Geologiskt forum* (in Swedish, 4 a year), *GFF* (in English, 4 a year).

Svenska Fysikersamfundet (Swedish Physical Society): Manne Siegbahnlaboratoriet, Frescativägen 24, 104 05 Stockholm; tel. (8) 553-786-79; e-mail kansliet@ fysikersamfundet.se; internet www .fysikersamfundet.se; f. 1920; 900 mems; Chair. Prof. BJÖRN JONSON; Sec. HÅKAN DANARED; publs *Fysikaktuellt* (quarterly), *Kosmos* (annually).

RELIGION, SOCIOLOGY AND ANTHROPOLOGY

Kungl. Gustav Adolfs Akademien för svensk folkkultur (Royal Gustavus Adolphus Academy for Swedish Folk Culture): Klostergatan 2, 753 21 Uppsala; tel. (18) 71-16-38; fax (18) 54-87-83; e-mail info@kgaa

.nu; internet www.kgaa.nu; f. 1932; 220 mems (incl. honorary); Pres. Prof. LENNART ELMEVIK; Vice-Pres. Prof. BIRGITTA SKARIN FRYKMAN; Sec. Prof. MATS HELLESPONG; publs *Acta Academiae Regiae Gustavi Adolphi*, *Arv. Nordic Yearbook of Folklore* (annual), *Ethnologia Scandinavica* (annual), *Namn och bygd* (annual), *Saga och Sed* (annual), *Svenska landsmål och svenskt folkliv* (annual).

TECHNOLOGY

Kungl. Ingenjörsvetenskapsakademien (Royal Swedish Academy of Engineering Sciences): Box 5073, 102 42 Stockholm; Located at Grev Turegatan 14, 102 42 Stockholm; tel. (8) 791-29-00; fax (8) 611-56-23; e-mail info@iva.se; internet www.iva.se; f. 1919 to promote engineering and economic science; acts as a clearing house for scientific information; establishes contacts with foreign research organizations by means of lectures and conferences, trade research organizations and research agreements with East European countries, China and the Republic of Korea; 720 Swedish mems, 240 foreign or corresponding mems; Dir Prof. LENA TRESCHOW TORELL; publs *IVA-Aktuellt*, *Meddelanden*, *Rapporter*.

Svenska Geotekniska Föreningen (Swedish Geotechnical Society): c/o Swedish Geotechnical Institute, 581 93 Linköping; tel. (13) 20-18-16; fax (13) 20-19-09; e-mail info@sgf.net; internet www.sgf.net; f. 1950; soil mechanics and foundation engineering; 700 indiv. mems, 30 corporate mems; Chair. HÅKAN GARIN; Sec. and Treas. GUNNAR WESTBERG.

Sveriges Ingenjörer (Swedish Engineers): Malmskillnadsgatan 48, POB 1419, 111 84 Stockholm; tel. (8) 613-80-00; e-mail info@cf .se; internet www.cf.se; f. 1861, present name 2007; 74,000 mems; Pres. ULF BENGTSSON; Man. Dir RICHARD MALMBORG; publs *Civilingenjören* (9 a year), *Ny Teknik-Teknisk Tidskrift* (weekly).

Research Institutes

GENERAL

Forskningsrådet Formas (Swedish Research Council Formas): Kungsbron 21, POB 1206, 111 82 Stockholm; tel. (8) 775-40-00; fax (8) 775-40-10; e-mail info@formas.se; internet www.formas.se; f. 2001; govt research funding agency; encourages and supports research related to sustainable devt; programme areas: environment, agriculture (incl. horticulture, fisheries and reindeer husbandry), forestry and the natural environment, the built environment, urban and regional planning; Dir-Gen. ROLF ANNERBERG; publs *Miljöforskning* (6 a year, also online), *Sustainability* (in English, quarterly).

Vetenskapsrådet (Swedish Research Council): Regeringsgatan 56, 103 78 Stockholm; tel. (8) 546-440-00; fax (8) 546-441-80; e-mail vetenskapsradet@vr.se; internet www.vr.se; f. 2001; took over duties of former Swedish Council for Planning and Co-ordination of Research, Swedish Council for Research in the Humanities and Social Sciences, Swedish Medical Research Council, Swedish Natural Science Research Council, and Swedish Research Council for Engineering Sciences; cttees for Culture and the Social Sciences (First Sec. BENGT HANSSON), Medicine (First Sec. OLLE STENDAHL), Natural and Engineering Sciences (First Sec. KÅRE BREMER); Dir-Gen. PÄR OMLING.

AGRICULTURE, FISHERIES AND VETERINARY SCIENCE

JTI – Institutet för jordbruks- och miljöteknik (Swedish Institute of Agricultural and Environmental Engineering): POB 7033, 750 07 Uppsala; tel. (18) 30-33-00; fax (18) 30-09-56; internet www.jti.slu.se; f. 1945; Dir LENNART NELSON; publs *JTI Informerar* (8 a year), *JTI Reports* (two series, in Swedish with English summary).

Statens Veterinärmedicinska Anstalt (National Veterinary Institute): Ulls Väg 2B, 751 89 Uppsala; tel. (18) 67-40-00; fax (18) 30-91-62; e-mail sva@sva.se; internet www.sva.se; f. 1911; research, diagnostic work, consultative work concerning control and prophylaxis of animal diseases; national veterinary laboratory; organization: central laboratory, epizootiology unit, animal diseases specialists unit, administration; library of 27,000 vols; Dir-Gen. L.-E. EDQVIST; Admin. Dir C. HOEL; publ. *SVA Vet* (Irregular).

STFI-Packforsk AB: POB 5604, 114 86 Stockholm; tel. (8) 676-70-00; fax (8) 411-55-18; e-mail info@stfi.se; internet www .stfi-packforsk.se; f. 1942; research into pulp, paper, graphic media, packaging and logistics; activities range from basic research to projects into packaging, graphic media and environmentally-friendly energy and chemicals; library of 15,000 vols, 500 periodicals; Pres. Prof. GUNNAR SVEDBERG; publ. *Beyond* (6 a year).

ARCHITECTURE AND TOWN PLANNING

Nordregio (Nordic Centre for Spatial Development): Box 1658, 111 86 Stockholm; tel. (8) 463-54-00; fax (8) 463-54-01; e-mail nordregio@nordregio.se; internet www .nordregio.se; f. 1997; administered by Nordic Council of Ministers; urban and regional studies, spatial planning, and regional economic development and policy; Dir OLE DAMSGAARD; publs *Journal of Nordregio* (4 a year), *European Journal of Spatial Development* (online at www.nordregio.se/EJSD).

ECONOMICS, LAW AND POLITICS

Humanistisk-samhällsvetenskapliga (Swedish Council for Humanities and Social Sciences): POB 7120, 103 78 Stockholm; tel. (8) 454-43-10; fax (8) 454-43-20; internet www.vr.se; f. 1977; 11 mems; Chair. Dr JANE CEDERQVIST; Sec.-Gen. Prof. ANDERS JEFFNER; Dir BJÖRN THOMASSON.

Institutet för Näringslivsforskning (Research Institute of Industrial Economics): POB 55665, 102 15 Stockholm; Located at: Grevgatan 34, 2nd Fl., 102 15 Stockholm; tel. (8) 665-45-00; fax (8) 665-45-99; e-mail info@ industrialeconomics.se; internet www .industrialeconomics.se; f. 1939; industrial economics; 20 research fellows; Dir MAGNUS HENREKSON.

Latinamerika-institutet i Stockholm (Institute of Latin American Studies, University of Stockholm): 106 91 Stockholm; tel. (8) 16-28-82; fax (8) 15-65-82; e-mail lai@lai .su.se; internet lai.su.se; f. 1951; library of 40,000 vols; research on Latin American economic, social and political development; information, seminars, courses; Dir Prof. MONA ROSENDAHL; Librarian MARGARETA BJÖRLING; publ. *Ibero-Americana: Nordic Journal of Latin American Studies*.

Nordiska Afrikainstitutet (Nordic Africa Institute): POB 1703, 751 47 Uppsala; tel. (18) 56-22-00; fax (18) 56-22-90; e-mail nai@ nai.uu.se; internet www.nai.uu.se; f. 1962; documentation and research centre for current African affairs, publication work, lectures and seminars; library of 60,000 vols,

500 periodicals; Dir CARIN NORBERG; Chief Librarian ÅSA LUND MOBERG; publs *Annual Report*, *Current African Issues*, *Discussion Paper*, *News from Nordiska Afrikainstitutet*, *Research Reports*, *Seminar Proceedings*.

Statistiska Centralbyrån (Statistics Sweden): Karlavägen 100, POB 24300, 104 51 Stockholm; tel. (8) 506-940-00; fax (8) 661-52-61; e-mail information@scb.se; internet www .scb.se and at: Klostergatan 23, 701 89 Örebro; tel. (19) 17-60-00; fax (19) 17-70-80; f. 1858; library: see Libraries and Archives; Dir.-Gen. KJELL JANSSON; publs include *Journal of Official Statistics, Statistical Abstract of Sweden, Statistical Reports, Survey of Living Conditions*.

Swedish Collegium for Advanced Study (SCAS): Götavägen 4, 752 36 Uppsala; tel. (18) 55-70-85; fax (18) 52-11-09; internet www.swedishcollegium.se; f. 1985; offers 14 fellowships for study at the Collegium each semester; Admin. Dir Prof. BJÖRN WITTROCK.

MEDICINE

Livsmedelsverket (National Food Administration): POB 622, 751 26 Uppsala; fax (18) 10-58-48; e-mail livsmedelsverket@slv.se; internet www.slv.se; f. 1972; central administrative agency in Sweden for foodstuffs and handling of foodstuffs in accordance with the Food Act; library of 11,000 vols; Dir-Gen. INGER ANDERSSON; publs *Livsmedelsverkets författningar* (The National Food Administration's Regulations), *Livstecknet* (Newsletter), *Vår Föda* (popular scientific).

NATURAL SCIENCES

General

Abisko naturvetenskapliga station (Abisko Scientific Research Station): 981 07 Abisko; tel. (980) 400-21; fax (980) 401-71; e-mail ans@ans.kiruna.se; internet www.ans .kiruna.se; f. 1913; belongs to the Royal Swedish Academy of Sciences; research mainly on sub-arctic biology and earth sciences; hosts the Climate Impacts Research Centre (CIRC); Dir Prof. TERENCE CALLAGHAN.

Kristinebergs Marina Forskningsstation (Kristineberg Marine Research Station): S-450 34 Fiskebäckskil; tel. (523) 185-00; fax (523) 185-02; internet www.kmf.gu .se; f. 1877; belongs to the Royal Swedish Academy of Sciences and Gothenburg University; marine ecology, taxonomic, morphological and physiological research on marine animals and plants; Dir Prof. MIKE THORNDYKE.

Stockholm Environment Institute: Box 2142, 103 14 Stockholm; tel. (8) 412-14-00; fax (8) 723-03-48; e-mail postmaster@sei.se; internet www.sei.se; f. 1989; partially core-funded by Swedish Government, but independently governed by an international Board; policy-related research on international environmental technology and management issues, including acidic deposition co-ordinated abatement strategies, climatic change assessment, energy futures, economics and environmental value, water, sanitation and integrated waste-management, urban environment, common property, energy and development, biotechnology, risk assessment, atmospheric environment, cleaner production, sustainable development planning and computer tools for integrated management risk and vulnerability; centres in Stockholm, Tallinn (Estonia), Bangkok (Thailand) York (UK) and Boston (USA); Exec. Dir JOHAN ROCKSTRÖM; publ. *Renewable Energy for Development* (4 a year).

Biological Sciences

Bergianska stiftelsen (Bergius Foundation): Box 50017, 104 05 Stockholm; tel. (8) 15-68-96; fax (8) 612-90-05; e-mail birgitta .bremer@bergianska.se; internet www .bergianska.se/forskning.html; f. 1791; attached to the Royal Swedish Academy of Sciences; botanical and horticultural research; biodiversity projects: Rubiaceae, Rosaleae; Dir Prof. Bergianus BIRGITTA BREMER.

Mathematical Sciences

Institut Mittag-Leffler (Mittag-Leffler Institute): Auravägen 17, 182 62 Djursholm; tel. (8) 622-05-60; fax (8) 622-05-89; e-mail info@mittag-leffler.se; internet www .mittag-leffler.se; f. 1916; research institute to promote pure mathematics; belongs to the Royal Swedish Academy of Sciences; library of 60,000 vols; Dir Prof. ANDERS BJÖRNER; publs *Acta Mathematica* (quarterly), *Arkiv för matematik* (2 a year).

Physical Sciences

Kungl. Vetenskapsakademiens Institut för Solfysik (Institute for Solar Physics of the Royal Swedish Academy of Sciences): AlbaNova University Centre, Roslagstullsbacken 21 106 91 Stockholm; tel. (8) 553-785-03; fax (8) 553-785-20; internet www .solarphysics.kva.se; f. 1951, reorganized 1978; belongs to Royal Swedish Academy of Sciences; solar research; Dir Prof. GÖRAN SCHARMER.

Manne Siegbahn Laboratory (MSL): Stockholm University, Frescativ 24, 104 05 Stockholm; tel. (8) 16-20-00; fax (8) 15-86-74; internet www.msi.se; f. 1937 as Nobel Institute of Physics, present name 1993; research in atomic, molecular and surface physics; low-energy ion accelerators (ion sources), accelerator-storage ring for highly charged ions; computer, electronics, and mechanical workshop divisions; library of 10,000 vols; Dir HÅKAN DANARED; publ. *Annual Report*.

Stockholms Observatorium (Stockholm Observatory): 106 91 Stockholm; tel. (8) 553-485-00; fax (8) 553-485-10; internet www.astro.su.se; f. 1753; Dir Assoc. Prof. CLAES-INGVAR BJÖRNSSON.

Sveriges Geologiska Undersökning (Geological Survey of Sweden): POB 670, 751 28 Uppsala; tel. (18) 17-90-00; fax (18) 17-92-10; e-mail sgu@sgu.se; internet www.sgu.se; f. 1858; library of 100,000 vols; Dir.-Gen. LARS LJUNG.

Swedish Institute of Space Physics: POB 812, 981 28 Kiruna; tel. (980) 790-00; fax (980) 790-50; e-mail irf@irf.se; internet www .irf.se; f. 1957 as an institute of the Swedish Acad. of Sciences; govt research institute since 1973; research and graduate education in space physics, space technology, atmospheric physics and related fields; library of 7,000 vols; Dir Dr LARS ELIASSON; publs *IRF Scientific Report*, *Kiruna Geophysical Data*.

TECHNOLOGY

Cement och Betong Institutet (Swedish Cement and Concrete Research Institute): 100 44 Stockholm; tel. (8) 696-11-00; fax (8) 24-31-37; e-mail cbi@cbi.se; internet www.cbi .se; f. 1942; conducts research into and acts as a consultancy for engineering materials based on cement and concrete and allied materials; library of 10,000 vols; Dir Prof. JOHAN SILFWERBRAND; Librarian TUULA OJALA; publ. *CBI rapporter / report*.

IFP Research AB: POB 104, 431 22 Mölndal; tel. (31) 706-63-00; fax (31) 706-63-63; e-mail info@ifp.se; internet www.ifp.se; f. 1943; research and development into chemical, physical and mechanical properties of fibrous and polymeric material; production technologies of textiles, plastics, non-wovens and rubber products and their waste management; library of 6,000 vols; Man. Dir RONALD PEDERSEN; publ. *Struktur* (6 a year).

Korrosions- och Metallforskningsinstitutet AB (KIMAB) (Corrosion and Metals Research Institute AB): Drottning Kristinas väg 48, 114 28 Stockholm; tel. (8) 440-48-00; fax (8) 440-45-35; e-mail info@kimab.com; internet www.kimab.com; f. 1921; areas of research include: application of instrumental methods for chemical analysis, welding, brazing and soldering; hot working, cold forming and microscopy; the relationship between microstructure and properties; solidification processes and their industrial applications; continuous casting; powder metallurgy; corrosion problems in connection with microstructure with a special interest in stainless steels; library of 2,000 books, 50 periodicals; Pres. Prof. STAFFAN EKELUND; publ. *Annual Report*.

SIK, Institutet för Livsmedel och Bioteknik (Swedish Institute for Food and Biotechnology): Box 5401, 402 29 Gothenburg; tel. (31) 335-56-00; fax (31) 83-37-82; e-mail info@sik.se; internet www.sik.se; f. 1946; research and development, documentation and education on production, preservation, food safety, biotechnology, structure and rheology, packaging, information and marketing; library of 7,000 vols; Dir Prof. KAJ MÅRTENSSON; publs *SIK Annual Report* (in English), *SIK-Dokument*, *SIK-Infood* (in English), *SIK-Publikation*, *SIK-Rapport*.

Statens Geotekniska Institut (Swedish Geotechnical Institute): Olaus Magnus Väg 35, 581 93 Linköping; tel. (13) 20-18-00; fax (13) 20-19-14; e-mail info@swedgeo.se; internet www.swedgeo.se; f. 1944; research, information and consulting work in soil mechanics and foundation engineering, environment and energy geotechnology; computerized library retrieval system; Dir-Gen. BIRGITTA BOSTRÖM; publs *Information*, *Report*, *SGI Varia*.

Sveriges Provnings- och Forskningsinstitut (Swedish National Testing and Research Institute): POB 857, 501 15 Borås; Located at Brinellgatan 4, 501 15 Borås; tel. (33) 16-50-00; fax (33) 13-55-02; e-mail info@ sp.se; internet www.sp.se; f. 1920; fmrly Testing Institute of the Royal Institute of Technology, f. 1896; focuses on calibration, testing, inspection and certification of products and management systems; undertakes applied research and services in technical evaluation and metrology; library: *c.* 17,000 vols; Dir-Gen. Prof. Dr CLAES BANKVALL; publs *Kontrollbestämmelser*, *SP Rapport* (technical reports).

Totalförsvarets Forskningsinstitut (FOI) (Swedish Defence Research Agency): 172 90 Stockholm; tel. (8) 555-030-00; fax (8) 555-031-00; e-mail registrator@foi.se; internet www.foi.se; f. 2001; conducts research into security-policy studies and analyses of defence and security; systems for control and management of crises; protection against and management of hazardous substances, IT security; Dir-Gen. MADELENE SANDSTRÖM; publ. *Framsyn*.

Libraries and Archives

Borås

Borås stadsbibliotek (Borås City Library): Box 856, 501 15 Borås; tel. (33) 35-70-00; fax (33) 35-76-75; e-mail boras.stadsbibliotek@ boras.se; internet www.boras.se/kultur/ stadsbiblioteket; f. 1860; 695,000 vols; Chief Librarian BRITT-INGER LINDQVIST.

Eskilstuna

Eskilstuna stads- och länsbibliotek (Eskilstuna Municipal and County Library): Kriebsensgatan 4, 632 20 Eskilstuna; tel. (16) 10-13-51; fax (16) 13-29-49; internet www.eskilstuna.se/biblioteket/; f. 1925; 550,000 vols; Chief Librarian ANN WIKLUND.

Gävle

Gävle stadsbibliotek (Gävle City Library): POB 801, 801 30 Gävle; tel. (26) 17-80-00; fax (26) 68-85-62; e-mail info@gavlebibliotek.se; f. 1907; 700,000 vols; Dir of Libraries LISBETH FORSLUND.

Gothenburg

Chalmers Tekniska Högskolas Bibliotek (Chalmers University of Technology Library): Chalmers Tvärgata 1, 412 96 Gothenburg; tel. (31) 772-10-00; fax (31) 16-84-94; e-mail request@lib.chalmers.se; internet www.lib.chalmers.se; f. 1829; 540,000 vols; Dir ANNIKA SVERRUNG.

Göteborgs stadsbibliotek (Gothenburg City Library): Götaplatsen, Box 5404, 402 29 Gothenburg; tel. (31) 61-65-00; fax (31) 61-66-93; e-mail info@stadsbiblioteket.goteborg .se; internet www.stadsbiblioteket.goteborg .se; f. 1861; 700,000 vols; Chief Librarian ANITA SINDLER.

Göteborgs universitetsbibliotek (Gothenburg University Library): POB 222, 405 30 Gothenburg; Located at: Renströmsgatan 4, Gothenburg; tel. (31) 773-10-00; fax (31) 16-37-97; e-mail universitetsbiblioteket@ub.gu.se; internet www.ub.gu.se; f. 1861; 2,800,000 vols; legal deposit library for Swedish publications; special collections include MSS collection, Women's History Collection, Snoilsky Collection (early Swedish literature), Sound and Video Archives; Chief Librarian AGNETA OLSSON; publ. *Acta*.

Halmstad

Halmstads Stadsbibliotek (Halmstad City Library): Axel Olsons Gata 1, 302 27 Halmstad; tel. (35) 13-71-81; fax (35) 13-71-82; e-mail stadsbiblioteket@halmstad.se; internet www.halmstad.se; f. 1922; 209,000 vols; Chief Librarian ANETTE HAGBERG.

Jönköping

Jönköpings stadsbibliotek (City Library and County Library of Jönköpings län): Box 1029, 551 11 Jönköping; tel. (36) 10-50-00; fax (36) 10-70-44; e-mail stadsbibl@kn .jonkoping.se; internet lingonline.jonkoping .se; f. 1916; 600,000 vols; Head of City Library ERIK LINDFELT; Head of County Library KATINKA BORG.

Kalmar

Kalmar Stadsbibliotek (Kalmar City Library): Huvudbiblioteket, POB 610, 391 26 Kalmar; tel. (480) 45-06-30; fax (480) 45-06-32; e-mail kalmarsb.info@kalmar.se; internet www.kalmar.se/bibliotek; f. 1922; 407,000 vols; Chief Librarian PIA AXEHEIM.

Linköping

Linköpings stadsbibliotek (Linköping City Library): Box 1984, 581 19 Linköping 3; tel. (13) 20-60-00; fax (13) 20-66-50; e-mail stadsbiblioteket@linkoping.se; internet www .linkoping.se/bibliotek; f. 1926; 666,000 vols; Chief Librarian HELENA SELBING.

Linköpings universitetsbibliotek (Linköping University Library): S-581 83 Linköping; tel. (13) 28-10-00; fax (13) 28-44-24; e-mail liub@bibl.liu.se; internet www.bibl

.liu.se; f. 1969; 694,000 vols; Chief Librarian MARIANNE NORDLANDER; publ. *Publikation.*

Luleå
Luleå Stadsbiblioteket (Luleå City Library): Kyrkogatan 15, POB 50065, 951 05 Luleå; tel. (920) 29-48-40; fax (920) 43-50-44; e-mail biblioteket@kulturen.lulea.se; internet www.lulea.se/bibliotek; Librarian BRITT-INGER RÖNNQVIST.

Lund
Landsarkivet i Lund (Lund Regional Archives): Dalbyvägen 4, POB 2016, 220 02 Lund; tel. (46) 19-70-00; fax (46) 19-70-70; e-mail landsarkivet@landsarkivet-lund.ra .se; internet www.ra.se/lla; f. 1903; holds records of government bodies in the south of Sweden (counties of Halland, Skåne, Blekinge); 38,000 shelf metres of records; special collections: estate archives; library: 500 shelf metres, mainly genealogy and topography; Chief Archivist JAN DAHLIN.

Universitetsbiblioteket, Lunds Universitet (Lund University Library): POB 134, 221 00 Lund; tel. (46) 222-00-00; fax (46) 222-42-43; internet www.lub.lu.se/ub; f. 1671; legal deposit library and national lending library; 5,000,000 vols, 129,000 MSS, 120,000 items of microforms; MSS include *Necrologium Lundense*, the oldest Scandinavian MS; special collections: *Bibliotheca Gripenhielmiana* (6,000 vols 16th- and 17th c. prints), Taussig collection of Schubert MSS, Broman collection of Elsevier prints, De La Gardie collection of prints and MSS; Dir CHRISTINA FRISTRÖM.

Malmö
Malmö Stadsbibliotek (Malmö City Library): 205 81 Malmö; Kung Oscars v. 11, 211 33 Malmö; tel (40) 660 85 00; fax (40) 660-86-81; e-mail info.stadsbibliotek@malmo .se; internet malmo.stadsbibliotek.org; f. 1905; 1,003,469 vols; Chief Librarian GUNILLA KONRADSSON.

Norrköping
Norrköpings Stadsbibliotek (Norrköping City Library): Södra Promenaden 105, POB 2113, 600 02 Norrköping; tel. (11) 15-26-65; e-mail stadsbiblioteket@norrkoping.se; internet www.nsb.norrkoping.se; f. 1913; 8 branch libraries, 3 bookmobiles; 472,785 vols; Chief Librarian BIRGITTA BENGTSSON.

Nyköping
Studsvikbiblioteket Kungl. Tekniska Högskolans Bibliotek (Royal Institute of Technology): Studsvik Library, Royal Institute of Technology, 611 82 Nyköping; tel. (155) 22-10-00; fax (155) 26-30-44; e-mail stubib@lib.kth.se; internet www.lib.kth.se/ main/studsvikbiblioteket.asp; f. 1947; energy research, technology and safety, environmental research; NTIS (USA) co-operating organization for sale in Nordic countries; 80,000 vols, 2m. reports (c. 1.5m. as microfiche), 150 printed and 4,000 electronic periodicals; Chief Librarian GUNNAR LAGER.

Örebro
Örebro stadsbibliotek (City Library and County Library of Örebro län): Näbbtorgsgatan 12, POB 325 10, 701 35 Örebro; tel. (19) 21-10-00; fax (19) 21-61-62; e-mail biblinfo@ orebro.se; internet www.orebro.se; f. 1862; 780,000 vols; Chief Librarian CHRISTER KLINGBERG; publ. *Samfundet Örebro Stadsoch Länsbiblioteks vänner. Meddelande 1929–.*

Östersund
Jämtlands Läns Bibliotek (City Library of Östersund and County Library of Jämtlands

län): Rådhusgatan 25 27, 831 80 Östersund; tel. (63) 14-30-00; fax (63) 10-98-40; e-mail lansbiblioteket@ostersund.se; internet www .z.lanbib.se; f. 1833; 550,000 vols; Chief Librarian BODIL KOPSEN.

Skara
Stifts- och Landsbiblioteket i Skara (State County and City Library of Skaraborgs Län): Prubbatorget 1, POB 194, 532 23 Skara; tel. (511) 32-060; fax (511) 32-069; e-mail skarabibliotek@skara.se; internet www.skara.se/bibliotek; f. 1938; 400,000 vols, 200 running metres MSS; Chief Librarian KERSTIN ANDERSSON; publ. *Acta.*

Stockholm
Antikvarisk-topografiska arkivet (Antiquarian Topographical Archives): Box 5405, 114 84 Stockholm; tel. (8) 519-180-00; fax (8) 519-180-88; e-mail ata@raa.se; internet www .raa.se/ata; f. 1786; archives of the Collegium Antiquitatum and the Royal Archives of Antiquities (1666–1786), archives and collections of the Royal Academy of Letters, History and Antiquities (1786–1975) and of the Central Board of Antiquities and National Historical Museums, archives of the office of monuments (1918–67) of the National Board of Public Buildings; 300 private archives; 120,000 maps and drawings; 1,100,000 negatives and photographs; open to the public; Dir Dr ANN HÖRSELL.

Handelshögskolans i Stockholm - Bibliotek (Library of the Stockholm School of Economics): POB 6501, 113 83 Stockholm; tel. (8) 736-97-00; e-mail library@hhs.se; internet www.hhs.se/library; f. 1909; 160,000 vols, 1,800 e-journals, 460 printed periodicals; Dir MARIE-LOUISE FENDIN.

Karolinska Institutet, Universitetsbiblioteket (Karolinska Institute University Library): Stockholm branch: POB 200, 171 77 Stockholm; Huddinge branch: Alfred Nobels allé 8, 141 83 Huddinge; tel. (8) 524-840-00; fax (8) 524-843-10; e-mail ub@ki.se; internet ki.se/ub; f. 1810; Chief Librarian CHRISTER BJÖRKLUND.

Konstbiblioteket, Nationalmuseum och Moderna Museet (Joint Art Library of the National Museum of Fine Arts and the Museum of Modern Art): Box 16176, 103 24 Stockholm; Riddargatan 13, Port C, Stockholm; tel. (8) 519-543-52; fax (8) 519-543-76; e-mail konstbiblioteket@nationalmuseum.se; f. late 19th c.; 330,000 vols, 247 serials, 2,390,000 cuttings; literature on Western art since the Renaissance; jt library of the Nationalmuseum and Moderna Museet; Librarian MARIA SYLVÉN.

Kungl. biblioteket (National Library): POB 5039, 102 41 Stockholm; tel. (8) 463-40-00; fax (8) 463-40-04; e-mail kungl.biblioteket@ kb.se; internet www.kb.se; f. early 16th century; 4,000,000 vols; Nat. Library of Sweden with the most complete colln of Swedish printed books in the world; foreign holdings in humanities; important collns of Old Swedish and Icelandic MSS; spec. collns incl. incunabula, elzeviers, maps, portraits, heraldry; responsible for the union catalogue *LIBRIS* and for co-operation among scientific libraries (Nat. Co-operation Dept); Nat. Librarian Dr GUNNAR SAHLIN; publ. *Acta Bibliothecæ regiæ Stockholmiensis.*

Kungl. Skogs- och Lantbruksakademiens Bibliotek (Royal Swedish Academy of Agriculture and Forestry Library): Box 6806, S-113 86 Stockholm; tel. (8) 545-477-20; fax (8) 545-477-30; e-mail kslab@ksla.se; internet www.kslab.ksla.se; f. 1811; 80,000 vols, 400 periodicals; collection of books on rural and agricultural history, horticulture, forestry and related fields; Chief Librarian

LARS LJUNGGREN; publ. *Skogs- och Lantbrukshistoriska Meddelanden* (irregular).

Kungl. Tekniska Högskolans Bibliotek (Royal Institute of Technology Library): Osquars Backe 31, 100 44 Stockholm; tel. (8) 790-60-00; fax (8) 790-96-70; e-mail sekr@ lib.kth.se; internet www.lib.kth.se; f. 1826; centre for computerized information and documentation services in science and technology; 855,000 vols, 1,000 print periodicals, 4,600 e-journals (incl. br. libraries), 2,000,000 microforms; Chief Librarian GUNNAR LAGER; publ. *Stockholm Papers in History and Philosophy of Science and Technology.*

Östasiatiska Biblioteket (Far Eastern Library — Library of the Museum of Far Eastern Antiquities): Box 16381, 103 27 Stockholm; tel. (8) 519-557-78; fax (8) 519-557-55; e-mail biblioteket@ostasiatiska.se; internet www.ostasiatiska.se; f. 1986; 120,000 vols, 1,150 current periodicals; collection of Chinese periodicals, Japanese collection of A.E. Nordenskiöld, collection of Chinese congshu, collection of western-language books on Asia; library is administered within the MFEA Unit for Research and Development (Head: Dr EVA MYRDAL); Museum Dir MAGNUS FISKESJÖ; Librarians LARS FREDRIKSSON YUYING JIN, AKIKO NAKAGAKI.

Regeringskansliet Utrikesdepartementets Bibliotek (Library of the Swedish Ministry for Foreign Affairs): 103 33 Stockholm; tel. (8) 405-10-00; internet www .regeringen.se; not open to the public.

Riksarkivet (National Archives): Fyrverkarbacken 13, POB 12541, 102 29 Stockholm; tel. (8) 737-63-50; fax (8) 737-64-74; e-mail riksarkivet@riksarkivet.ra.se; internet www .statensarkiv.se; f. 1618; 130,000 linear m of archival holdings, 120,000 vols, spec. collns on archival science and Swedish history; Dir-Gen. Dr TOMAS LIDMAN; publs *Arsbok för Riksarkivet och landsarkiven* (annual), *Glossarium till medeltidslatinet i Sverige, Rapport* (1 or 2 a year), *Skrifter utgivna av Riksarkivet, Svenskt diplomatarium.*

Riksdagsbiblioteket (Parliamentary Library): 100 12 Stockholm; tel. (8) 786-40-00; fax (8) 786-58-70; e-mail biblioteket@ riksdagen.se; internet www.riksdagen.se; f. 1851; serves the Riksdag, the administrative services and research; open to the public; 700,000 vols; chiefly devoted to political science, administration, social science and law; Chief Librarian GUNILLA LILIE BAUER; publs *Fakta om folkvalda: Riksdagen 1985–* (biographical handbook, every 4 years), *Statliga publikationer* (government publications, database only).

Stadsarkivet i Stockholm (Stockholm City Archives): Kungsklippan 6, Box 22063, 104 22 Stockholm; tel. (8) 508-283-00; fax (8) 508-283-01; e-mail stadsarkivet@ssa.stockholm .se; internet www.ssa.stockholm.se; f. 1930; documents from regional authorities and the municipal government of Stockholm; archives on urban history of Stockholm; 120,000 vols; archives: 68,000 shelf-metres; City Archivist BJÖRN JORDELL; publs *Stadsarkivets småtryck* (irregular), *Stockholms stadsarkiv. Arsberättelse* (annually), *Stockholms tänkeböcker från år 1592* (irregular).

Statens musikbibliotek (Music Library of Sweden): Box 16326, 103 26 Stockholm; Torsgatan 21, Stockholm; tel. (8) 519-554-12; fax (8) 519-554-45; e-mail exp@muslib.se; internet www.muslib.se; f. 1771; 50,000 books on music, 400,000 scores of music, 28,000 MSS and about 15,000 letters; large collection of 18th c. music and includes a documentation centre for Swedish music; Chief Librarian ANDERS LÖNN.

Statistiska Centralbyråns Information och Bibliotek (Statistics Sweden Information Centre and Library): POB 24300, 104 51 Stockholm; tel. (8) 506-950-66; fax (8) 506-940-45; e-mail library@scb.se; internet www .scb.se; f. 1858; 230,000 vols, 1,400 periodicals; Chief Librarian LENA GUSTAFSSON; publ. *Statistics from International Organizations and other Issuing Bodies* (annually).

Stockholms stadsbibliotek (City Library of Stockholm): Odengatan 63, Spelbomskan, 113 80 Stockholm; tel. (8) 508-311-00; fax (8) 508-310-07; e-mail stadsbiblioteket@kultur .stockholm.se; internet www.ssb.stockholm .se; f. 1927; 2,225,000 vols; Chief Librarian KIA GUMBEL.

Stockholms universitetsbibliotek (Stockholm University Library): 106 91 Stockholm; tel. (8) 16-20-00; fax (8) 15-77-76; internet www.sub.su.se; 2,500,000 vols; Librarian Dr CATARINA ERICSON-ROOS.

Svenska Akademiens Nobelbibliotek (Nobel Library of the Swedish Academy): Källargränd 4, Box 2118, 103 13 Stockholm; tel. (8) 555-125-50; fax (8) 555-125-99; e-mail info@nobelbiblioteket.se; internet www .nobelbiblioteket.se; f. 1901; 200,000 vols; Librarian LARS RYDQUIST.

Sveriges Radio Förvaltings AB (Resources of the Swedish Broadcasting Corporation): 105 10 Stockholm; tel. (8) 784-14-47; fax (8) 660-45-93; internet www.srf.se; f. 1925; documents relating to Swedish public service broadcasting and television; Chief Archivist CARINA SJÖGREN.

Vitterhetsakademiens Bibliotek (Library of the Royal Academy of Letters, History and Antiquities): POB 5405, Storgatan 41, 114 84 Stockholm; tel. (8) 519-180-00; fax (8) 663-35-28; e-mail bibl@raa.se; internet www.raa.se/ bibliotek; f. 1786; 400,000 vols; special collections on archaeology, medieval art and architecture, numismatics, preservation of cultural heritage; open to the public; Chief Librarian KERSTIN ASSARSSON-RIZZI; publ. *Fornvännen*.

Umeå

Umeå stadsbibliotek (Umeå City Library): 901 78 Umeå; tel. (90) 16-33-04; fax (90) 16-33-16; e-mail stadsbiblioteket@umea.se; internet www.bibliotek.umea.se; f. 1903; 770,000 vols; Chief Librarian INGER EDEBRO SIKSTRÖM.

Umeå Universitetsbibliotek (University of Umeå Library): 901 74 Umeå; tel. (90) 786-56-93; fax (90) 786-74-74; e-mail laneexp@ub.umu.se; internet www.ub.umu .se; f. 1964; 1,000,000 vols; Senior Librarian KJELL JONSSON.

Uppsala

Sveriges lantbruksuniversitets bibliotek (Library of the Swedish University of Agricultural Sciences): Box 7071, 750 07 Uppsala; tel. (18) 67-10-00; fax (18) 67-28-53; e-mail infosok@bibul.slu.se; internet www.bib.slu.se; f. 1977; consists of Ultunabiblioteket (main library, in Uppsala) and branch libraries: Alnarp Library and Forest Library (Umeå), Herquist Library (Skara); Chief Librarian SNORRE RUFELT.

Uppsala stadsbibliotek (Uppsala City Library): Svartbäcksgatan 17, 753 75 Uppsala; tel. (18) 727-17-00; fax (18) 727-06-40; e-mail stadsbiblioteket.information@ uppsala.se; internet www.uppsala.se/ stadsbiblioteket; f. 1906; 791,000 vols; Chief Librarian MARIE-LOUISE RITON.

Uppsala universitetsbibliotek (Uppsala University Library): POB 510, 751 20 Uppsala; tel. (18) 471-39-00; fax (18) 471-39-13; e-mail info@ub.uu.se; internet www.ub .uu.se; f. 1620; consists of 15 library units

and extensive cultural heritage collns; 5,300,000 vols, 14,000 electronic periodicals, 40,000 e-books, 150 databases, 30 encyclo-paedias and 62,000 MSS, including the famous *Codex argenteus*, the 'Silver Bible' from the 6th century, a translation of the Gospels into the Gothic language, Swedish and Icelandic medieval MSS, the Bibliotheca Walleriana (medical books), a colln of old music books and MSS, a colln of old maps, engravings and drawings, incl. the *Carta Marina* of 1539 by Olaus Magnus (earliest accurate map of Scandinavia); Dir Prof. ULF GÖRANSON; publs incl. *Acta Bibliothecae R. Universitatis Upsaliensis, Acta Universitatis Upsaliensis, Scripta Minora Bibliothecae R. Universitatis Upsaliensis, Uppsala universitetsbiblioteks utställnings-kataloger* (exhibition catalogues), etc.

Västerås

Västerås stadsbibliotek (Västerås City Library): 721 87 Västerås; tel. (21) 39-46-00; fax (21) 39-46-80; e-mail stadsbibliotek@ vasteras.se; internet www.bibliotek.vasteras .se; f. 1952; 571,000 vols; Chief Librarian STAFFAN RUNEEVA MATSSON.

Växjö

Växjö Bibliotek (City and County Library, Kronobergs län): Västra Esplanaden 7, 351 12 Växjö; tel. (470) 4-14-44; fax (470) 79-69-92; e-mail stadsbiblioteket@kommun.vaxjo .se; internet www.vaxjo.se/bibliotek/; f. 1954; 460,000 vols; Chief Librarians IRENE KARLSSON, ANNA-KARIN AXELSSON.

Visby

Almedalsbiblioteket (Almedals Library): Cramergatan 3-5, 621 81 Visby; tel. (498) 29-90-00; fax (498) 29-90-11; e-mail almedalsbiblioteket@hgo.se; internet bibliotek.gotland.se; f. 1865; 502,000 vols; Chief Librarian ANNA SÄVE-SÖDERBERGH (on leave until 2007).

Museums and Art Galleries

Gothenburg

Göteborgs Naturhistoriska Museet (Gothenburg Natural History Museum): POB 7283, 402 35 Göteborg; Slottsskogen vid Linnéplatsen, 402 35 Göteborg; tel. (31) 775-24-00; fax (31) 12-98-07; e-mail info@ gnm.se; internet www.gnm.se; f. 1833; Dir GÖRAN ANDERSSON.

Göteborgs stads kulturförvaltning (Gothenburg Arts and Culture): Norra Hamngatan 8, 411 14 Gothenburg; tel. (31) 61-50-10; fax (31) 61-50-11; e-mail info@ kultur.goteborg.se; internet www.kultur .goteborg.se; f. 1861; Chair. of Trustees VIVI-ANN NILSSON; Man. Dir CHRISTINA HJORTH; publ. *Annual Report*.

Attached museums:

> **Göteborgs Konstmuseum** (Gothenburg Museum of Art): Götaplatsen, 412 56 Gothenburg; tel. (31) 61-29-80; fax (31) 18-41-19; e-mail information@ konstmuseum.goteborg.se; internet www .konstmuseum.goteborg.se; f. 1923; European paintings, sculpture, prints and drawings from 1500, special collections of French art since 1820 and Scandinavian art; art library; Dir BIRGITTA FLENSBURG.

> **Göteborgs Sjöfartsmuseum** (Maritime Museum and Aquarium): Karl Johansgatan 1-3, 414 59 Gothenburg; tel. (31) 61-29-00; fax (31) 24-61-82; e-mail info@ sjofartsmuseum.goteborg.se; internet www .sjofartsmuseum.goteborg.se; f. 1913;

Swedish maritime history; library of 14,000 vols; Dir ANNA ROSENGREN; publ. *Unda Maris*.

Göteborgs Stadsmuseum (Gothenburg City Museum): Norra Hamngatan 12, 411 14 Gothenburg; tel. (31) 61-27-70; fax (31) 774-03-58; e-mail adm@stadsmuseum .goteborg.se; internet www.stadsmuseum .goteborg.se; f. 1861; archaeology since prehistoric times, industrial heritage; Dir INGRID LOMFORS.

Röhsske Museet (Röhss Museum of Applied Art and Design): Vasagatan 37-39, 400 15 Gothenburg; tel. (31) 61-38-50; fax (31) 18-46-92; e-mail info@ designmuseum.se; internet www .designmuseum.se; f. 1916; Dir ELSEBETH WELANDER-BERGGREN.

Linköping

Flygvapenmuseum (Swedish Air Force Museum): Carl Cederströms Gata, 581 98 Linköping; tel. (13) 28-35-67; fax (13) 29-93-04; e-mail info@flygvapenmuseum.se; internet www.flygvapenmuseum.se; f. 1984; library of 10,000 vols; Dir MIKAEL PARR; publs *Ikaros* (annually), *ÖFS-meddelande* (4 a year).

Lund

Kulturhistoriska Museet (Cultural History Museum): POB 1095, Tegnérsplatsen, 221 04 Lund; tel. (46) 35-04-00; fax (46) 35-04-70; e-mail kulturen@kulturen.com; internet www.kulturen.com; f. 1882; ethnography, cultural history, medieval archaeology; open-air museum, town and country houses; applied arts (ceramics, textiles, silver, glass); weapons and uniforms; musical instruments; furniture and fittings; trades; commerce and crafts; fishery; farming; folk art; archaeological finds from medieval Lund; Östarp, old farm with inn, 30 km from Lund; library of 35,000 vols; Dir MARGARETA ALIN; publ. *Kulturen* (yearbook).

Mariefred

Swedish National Portrait Gallery: c/o Royal Castle Collections, Nationalmuseum, POB 16176, 103 24 Stockholm; Located at: Gripsholm Castle, Mariefred; tel. (8) 519-543-00; fax (8) 519-544-56; internet www .nationalmuseum.se; f. c.1550; Dir Dr MAGNUS OLAUSSON.

Stockholm

Armémuseum (Army Museum): Riddargatan 13, POB 14095, 104 41 Stockholm; tel. (8) 788-95-60; fax (8) 662-68-31; e-mail info@ armemuseum.se; internet www .armemuseum.se; f. 1879; library of 60,000 vols; Dir STAFFAN FORSSELL; publs *Meddelanden, Skrifter, Småskrifter*.

Dance Museum: Gustav Adolfs torg 22-24, 111 52 Stockholm; tel. (8) 441-76-50; fax (8) 20-06-02; e-mail info@dansmuseet.se; internet www.dansmuseet.se; f. 1932 in Paris as Archives Internationales de la Danse, 1950 in Sweden; performing arts museum; exhibitions of dance, theatre, visual art and photography; material from all over the world, notably Ballets Suédois; videotheque, folk dance dept, Rolf de Maré archive; Dir Dr ERIK NÄSLUND.

Etnografiska Museet (Museum of Ethnography): POB 27140, Djurgårdsbrunnsvägen 34, 102 52 Stockholm; tel. (8) 519-550-00; e-mail info@etnografiska.se; internet www .etnografiska.se; f. 1880; colln of 150,000 artefacts from Africa, America, Asia, Australia and the Pacific; also houses the Sven Hedin Foundation; Dir ANDERS BJÖRKLUND; publs *Ethnos* (2 a year), Monograph Series.

Historiska Museet (Museum of National Antiquities): POB 5428, Narvavägen 13-17, 114 84 Stockholm; tel. (8) 519-55-60; fax (8) 519-556-40; e-mail info@historiska.se; internet www.historiska.se; comprises Museum of National Antiquities and Royal Cabinet of Coins and Medals; Dir.-Gen. LARS AMRÉUS.

Livrustkammaren, Skoklosters Slott och Hallwylska Museet (Royal Armoury, Skokloster Castle and Hallwyl Museum): Slottsbacken 3, 111 30 Stockholm; tel. (8) 519-555-00; fax (8) 519-555-11; e-mail livrustkammaren@lsh.se; internet www.lsh.se; f. 1628; Dir BARBRO BURSELL.

Component sites:

Hallwylska Museet: Hamngatan 4, 111 47 Stockholm; tel. (8) 519-555-00; fax (8) 519-555-85; e-mail hallwyl@lsh.se; internet www.lsh.se; f. c.1900; private residence of Hallwyl family; colln of furniture, paintings, applied art, etc.; Dir MAGNUS HAGBERG; publ. *Hallwyliana*.

Livrustkammaren: Slottsbacken 3, 111 30 Stockholm; tel. (8) 519-555-00; fax (8) 519-555-11; e-mail livrustkammaren@lsh.se; internet www.lsh.se; f. 1628; housed in south-east wing of Royal Palace; historical collns dating from mid-16th century; Swedish royal arms, costumes, jewels, coaches, etc.; library of 45,000 vols; Dir BARBRO BURSELL; Curators NILS DREJHOLT, LENA RANGSTRÖM, HENRIK ANDERSSON; publ. *Livrustkammaren* (Journal of Royal Armour, annual).

Skoklosters Slott: 746 95 Bålsta; tel. (18) 38-60-77; fax (18) 38-64-46; e-mail skoklaster@lsh.se; internet www.lsh.se; baroque castle built 1654 by Count C. G. Wrangel; contains mainly 17th-century furniture, paintings, applied art and armour; library; Dir CARIN BERGSTRÖM; publ. *Skokloster Studies*.

Moderna Museet (Museum of Modern Art): Skeppsholmen, Box 16382, 103 27 Stockholm; tel. (8) 519-552-00; fax (8) 519-552-10; e-mail info@modernamuseet.se; internet www.modernamuseet.se; f. 1958; contemporary paintings and sculptures by Swedish and foreign artists, also photographs and drawings; Dir LARS NITTVE.

Musikmuseet: Box 16326, 103 26 Stockholm; tel. (8) 519-554-90; fax (8) 663-91-81; e-mail museum@musikmuseet.se; f. 1899; more than 6,000 art and folk music instruments; exhibitions, archives and library; Dir STEFAN BOHMAN.

Nationalmuseum: Södra Blasieholmshamnen, Box 16176, 103 24 Stockholm; tel. (8) 519-543-00; fax (8) 519-544-50; e-mail info@nationalmuseum.se; internet www.nationalmuseum.se; f. 1792; 16,000 paintings, sculptures and other objects, 500,000 drawings and prints, 30,000 items of applied art; also administers collections of several royal castles with 23,000 works of art; library: see Libraries and Archives; Dir Prof. SOLFRID SÖDERLIND; publs *Art Bulletin of Nationalmuseum Stockholm* (annually), *Nationalmuseums skriftserie. N. S.*

Naturhistoriska Riksmuseet (Swedish Museum of Natural History): Box 50007, 104 05 Stockholm; tel. (8) 519-540-00; fax (8) 519-540-85; e-mail myndigheten@nrm.se; internet www.nrm.se; f. 1739; collns and research units: vertebrates, entomology, invertebrates, palaeozoology, phanerogamic botany, cryptogamic botany, palaeobotany, mineralogy, isotope geology, DNA laboratory, contaminants; Dir CHRISTINA HALLMAN.

Nordiska museet: Djurgårdsvägen 6–16, Box 27820, 115 93 Stockholm; tel. (8) 519-546-00; fax (8) 519-545-80; e-mail nordiska@

nordiskamuseet.se; internet www.nordiskamuseet.se; f. 1873; national museum of cultural history since 16th c. ethnological and industrial art collections; 10m. archive and photographic items; library of 300,000 vols; Dir CHRISTINA MATTSSON.

Östasiatiska Museet (Museum of Far Eastern Antiquities): Skeppsholmen, POB 16381, 103 27 Stockholm; tel. (8) 519-557-50; fax (8) 519-557-55; e-mail info@ostasiatiska.se; internet www.ostasiatiska.se; f. 1926; Chinese paintings, sculptures and ceramics; Chinese pottery and bronze objects; Japanese, Korean, Southeast Asian and Indian collections; Far Eastern Library; Dir SANNE HOUBY-NIELSEN; publ. *Bulletin* (annually).

Skansen: POB 27807, 115 93 Stockholm; tel. (8) 442-80-00; fax (8) 442-82-80; e-mail info@skansen.se; internet www.skansen.se; f. 1891; open-air museum and zoological garden; Dir JOHN BRATTMYHR; Keeper of Buildings BO NILSSON; Keeper of Natural History BENGT ROSÉN; publs daily programmes, guides, etc.

Statens försvarshistoriska museer (National Swedish Museums of Military History): Riddargatan 13, POB 14095, 104 41 Stockholm; tel. (8) 519-563-10; e-mail info@sfhm.se; internet www.sfhm.se; f. 1976; administers Armémuseum, Flygvapenmuseum (qq.v.), Försvarets Traditions nämnd (Board of Military Traditions), Marinenheten (Maritime Department); Dir-Gen. CHRISTINA VON ARBIN.

Statens maritima museer (National Maritime Museums): POB 27131, 102 52 Stockholm; tel. (8) 519-549-00; fax (8) 519-549-89; e-mail registrator@maritima.se; internet www.maritima.se; Pres. INGRID HALL ROTH.

Component museums:

Marinmuseum (Naval Museum): Stumholmen, 371 32 Karlskrona; tel. (455) 539-00; fax (455) 539-49; e-mail marinmuseum@maritima.se; internet www.marinmuseum.se; f. 1752; 30,000 exhibits since 17th c.; library of 22,000 vols, 4,000 maps and blueprints, 200,000 negatives and photographs; Dir (vacant); publ. *Aktuellt-Marinmuseum* (yearbook).

Sjöhistoriska museet (Maritime Museum): POB 27131, 102 52 Stockholm; tel. (8) 519-549-00; fax (8) 519-549-49; e-mail smm@maritima.se; internet www.sjohistoriska.se; f. 1938; collections give a view of Swedish naval and merchant history, vessels of the past and of today as well as the history of Swedish shipbuilding; archive of drawings and photographs; library of 60,000 vols; Dir KLAS HELMERSON; publ. *Sjöhistorisk årsbok*.

Vasamuseet (Vasa Museum): POB 27131, 102 52 Stockholm; tel. (8) 519-548-00; fax (8) 519-548-88; e-mail vasamuseet@maritima.se; internet www.vasamuseet.se; f. 1961; the Swedish warship *Vasa*, lost in 1628 and raised in 1961, and associated exhibits; also steam icebreaker *Sankt Erik* and lightship *Finngrundet*; Dir KLAS HELMERSON.

Stockholms Stadsmuseum (Stockholm City Museum): POB 15025, 104 65 Stockholm; premises at: Ryssgården, Slussen; tel. (8) 508-316-00; fax (8) 508-316-99; e-mail info@stadsmuseum.stockholm.se; internet www.stadsmuseum.stockholm.se; f. 1937; history and development of Stockholm; archaeology and cultural heritage; collection of photographs, maps, art and artefacts; incl. a library and archives; Dir BERIT SVEDBERG; publs *Annual Report*, *Blick* (articles covering the activity of the administration), *Sankt Eriks årsbok* (year book).

Affiliated museum:

Stockholms Medeltidsmuseum (Museum of Medieval Stockholm): Strömparterren, Norrbro, 100 12 Stockholm; tel. (8) 508-317-08; fax (8) 508-317-99; e-mail info@medeltidsmuseet.stockholm.se; internet www.medeltidsmuseet.stockholm.se; f. 1986; archaeological remains of Stockholm, reflecting its foundation and history from c. 1250–1550; Dir SOLBRITT BENNETH.

Tekniska Museet (National Museum of Science and Technology): POB 27842, 115 93 Stockholm; Located at: Museivägen 7, 115 93 Stockholm; tel. (8) 450-56-00; fax (8) 450-56-01; e-mail info@tekniskamuseet.se; internet www.tekniskamuseet.se; f. 1924; history of science and technology; devt of Swedish industry and engineering; mining, iron and steel, steam power and machines, cars and aircraft, history of electricity, chemistry, computers, Polhem's colln of engineering models, mechanical workshop and model railway; Teknorama science centre; archives of drawings and photographs; library of 50,000 vols; Dir ANNE-LOUISE KEMDAL; publ. *Daedalus* (annual).

Uppsala

Upplandsmuseet (Upplands Museum): St Eriksgränd 6, 753 10 Uppsala; tel. (18) 16-91-00; fax (18) 69-25-09; e-mail info@upplandsmuseet.se; internet www.upplandsmuseet.se; f. 1959; provincial cultural history, Dir HÅKAN LIBY; publ. *Uppland*.

Universities

GÖTEBORGS UNIVERSITET
(Gothenburg University)

POB 100, 405 30 Gothenburg

Telephone: (31) 773-10-00
Fax: (31) 773-10-66
E-mail: registrator@gu.se
Internet: www.gu.se

Founded 1891, became state university 1954
Academic year: September to June

Rector: Prof. G. SVEDBERG
Vice-Rectors: Asst Prof. K. NORÉN, Prof. M. WALLIN PETERSON
Head of Administration: P.-O. REHNQUIST
Librarian: A. OLSSON

Library: see Libraries and Archives
Number of students: 51,000

Publication: *Acta Universitatis Gothoburgensis*

DEANS

Faculty of Arts: Prof. C. AHLBERGER
School of Economics and Commercial Law: Prof. R. WOLFF
Faculty of Education: Prof. P.- O. THÄNG
Faculty of Fine and Applied Arts: Prof. H. HEDBERG
Faculty of Science: Prof. D. TURNER
Faculty of Social Sciences: Prof. L. WEIBULL
IT University: Prof. P. BRENNER
Sahl Grenska Academy: Prof. P. FREDMAN

PROFESSORS

Faculty of Arts (POB 200, 405 30 Gothenburg; fax (31) 773-11-44; internet www.hum.gu.se):

AGRELL, B., Comparative Literature
AHLBERGER, C., History
AHLSÉN, E., Neurolinguistics
AIJMER, K., English
ALLWOOD, J., General Linguistics
ANDERSSON, L.-G., Modern Swedish
ANDERSSON, S.-G., German
BENSON, K., Spanish

BERGH, G., English
BJÖRNBERG, A., Musicology
BORIN, L., Natural Language Processing
BOYD, S., General Linguistics
BYRSKOG, S., New Testament Exegesis
BÄRMARK, J., Theory of Science
COOPER, R., Computational Linguistics
DAHL, E.-L., History of Science and Ideas
EDSTRÖM, K.-O., Musicology
ENGDAHL, E., Swedish
EKLUND, B.-L., Modern Greek
ERIKSSON, A., Phonetics
FLORBY, G., English Literature
FORSER, T., Comparative Literature
HAGLUND, D., Religious Studies
HALLBERG, M., Theory of Science
HANSSON, S., Comparative Literature
HELDNER, C., French
HOLMQUIST, I., Women Studies
JOHANNESSON, L., History of Art
KRISTIANSEN, K., Archaeology
LAGER, T., Computational Linguistics
LARSSON, L., Comparative Literature
LEGÈRE, K., African Languages
LIEDMAN, S.-E., History of Science and Ideas
LILJA, E., Comparative Literature
LILLIESTAM, L., Musicology
LINDBERG, B., History of Science and Ideas
LINDBERG, I., Swedish as a Second Language
LINDKVIST, T., Medieval History
LJUNGGREN, M., Russian Literature
MALM, M., Comparative Literature
MALMGREN, H., Theoretical Philosophy
MALMGREN, S.-G., Swedish
MALMSTEDT, G., History
MUNTHE, C., Practical Philosophy
NILSSON, B., History of Christianity
NILSSON, I., History of Science and Ideas
NORDBLADH, J., Archaeology
NÄSSTRÖM, B.-M., History of Religion
OHLANDER, S., English
OLAUSSON, L., Conditions in Science and Humanities
OLOFSSON, A., English
OLOFSSON, S., Old Testament Exegesis
PANKOW, C., German
PERSSON, I., Practical Philosophy
PERSSON, L., History
PLATEN, E., German Literature
RALPH, B., Northern Languages
RETSÖ, J., Arabic
SANDBERG, B., German
SJÖGREN, O., Film Studies
SKARIN-FRYKMAN, B., Ethnology
STÅLHAMMAR, M., English Terminology
STRANDBERG-OLOFSSON, M., Classical Archaeology and Ancient History
THUNMAN, N., Japanese
WESTERSTÅHL, D., Theoretical Philosophy
WINBERG, C., History
WISTRAND, M., Latin

School of Economics and Commercial Law (POB 605, 405 30 Gothenburg; fax (31) 773-55-20; internet www.handels.gu.se):

ALVSTAM, C.-G., International Economic Geography
ANDERSSON, D. T., Marketing
BERGENDAHL, G., Managerial Economics
BIGSTEN, A., Economics
CRAMÉR, P., International Law, European Integration Law
CZARNIAWSKA, B., Business Administration
DOTEVALL, R., Commercial Law
FLOOD, L., Econometrics
FRISÉN, M., Statistics
GADD, C.-J., Economic History
HIBBS, D., Economics
HJALMARSSON, L., Economics
JENSEN, A., Transport Management
JOHANSSON STENMAN, O., Economics
JONSSON, S., Economic History
JÖNSSON, S., Business Administration
LINDBLOM, T., Business Administration

MÅRTENSSON, R., Business Administration
NORBÄCK, L.-E., Business Administration
NORDSTRÖM, L., Human Geography
OLSON, O., Accounting and Finance
OLSSON, U., Economic History
POLESIE, T., Accounting and Finance
PÅHLSSON, R., Tax Law
RAMBERG, C., Commercial Law
SANDELIN, B., Economics
SOLLI, R., Business Administration
STERNER, T., Environmental Economics
STJERNBERG, T., Management and Organization
TÖLLBORG, D., Legal Science
TÖRNQVIST, U., Business Administration
VILHELMSON, B., Human Geography
WESTERHÄLL, V. L., Public Law

Faculty of Education (POB 300, 405 30 Gothenburg; fax (31) 773-22-42; e-mail mailer@ped.gu.se; internet www.ped.gu.se):

AHLBERG, A., Special Education and Educational Research
ALEXANDERSSON, M., Education and Educational Research (Didactics)
ANDERSSON, B., Education and Educational Research (Didactics)
BENGTSSON, J., Philosophy of Education
GUNNARSSON, L., Education and Educational Research
GUSTAFSSON, J.-E., Education and Educational Research
HOLMER, J., Work Science
LANDER, R., Education and Educational Research
LASSBO, G., Education and Educational Research
LINDBLAD, S., Education and Educational Research
LINDSTRÖM, B., Education and Educational Research
MARTON, F., Education and Educational Research
MUNCK, J., Education and Educational Research
NILSSON, L., Education and Educational Research
OHLANDER, S., English
OSCARSON, M., Education and Educational Research
OTT, A., Science Education
PATRIKSSON, G., Education and Educational Research
PRAMLING-SAMUELSSON, I., Education and Educational Research
SÄLJÖ, R., Education and Educational Science
SHANAHAN, H., Home Economics
SIMONSON, B., History
THÅNG, P.-O., Education and Educational Research
WENESTAM, C.-G., Education and Educational Research
WERNERSSON, I., Education and Educational Research

Faculty of Fine and Applied Arts (POB 210, 405 30 Gothenburg; fax (31) 773-13-18; internet www.gu.se/konst):

DU RÉES, G., Film Directing
DAVIDSSON, H., Organ
EKLUND, B., Trumpet
ELDENIUS, M., Music Theory
FOLKESTAD, G., Research in Music Education
GÅRDFELDT, G., Communication and Performance Skills, Drama
HYBBINETTE, P., Fine Arts in Design
JORMIN, A., Contrabass and Improvisation
LÜTZOW-HOLM, O., Composition
NÄSSEN, E., Voice
NIELSEN, E., Percussion and Contemporary Music
OLSSON, B., Research in Music Education
THORSÉN, S.-M., Music and Society
WASKO, R., Fine Arts
WIKLUND, A., Music Drama

Faculty of Science (POB 460, 405 30 Gothenburg; fax (31) 773-48-39; internet www.science.gu.se):

ABRAMOWICZ, M., Astrophysics
ADLER, L., Marine Microbiology
AHLBERG, E., Inorganic Chemistry
AHLBERG, P., Organic Chemistry
ANDERSSON, L., Hydrosphere Science
ANDERSSON, M., Zooecology
ANDERSSON, S., Animal Ecology
ANDERSSON, S., Physics
ANDREASSON, L.-E., Molecular Bophysics
ARKERYD, L., Applied Mathematics
AXELSSON, M., Comparative Integrative Zoology
BADEN, S. P., Marine Ecology
BILLETER, M., Molecular Biophysics
BJURSELL, G., Molecular Biology
BJÖRNSSON, B. T., Zoophysiology
BJÖRK, G., Polar Oceanography
BLANCK, H., Plant Physiology
BLOMBERG, A., Functional Genomics
BOHLIN, T., Animal Ecology
BRZEZINSKI, J., Mathematics
CAMPBELL, E., Atomic and Molecular Physics
CARLSSON, P., Genetics
CEDERWALL, M., Theoretical Physics
CHEN, D., Physical Meteorology
CLARKE, A., Plant Molecular Biology
CORNELL, D., Geochemistry
DAVE, G., Environmental Protection
ELWING, H., Surface Biophysics
ERSÉUS, C., Evolutionary Morphology and Systematics
FÖRLIN, L., Zoophysiology
FRANZÉN, L., Physical Geography
GÖTMARK, F., Zooecology
HALL, P., Marine Sediment Diagenesis
HALLENBERG, N., Systematic Biology
HANSTORP, D., Experimental Physics
HELLSING, B., Physics
HERMANSSON, M., Marine Microbiology
HOHMANN, S., Molecular Microbial Physiology
HOLMGREN, S., Zoophysiology
HOLMLID, L., Physical Chemistry, especially Energy-related Basic Research
HÅKANSSON, M., Organometallic Chemistry
JAGNER, D., Analytical Chemistry
JOHANNESSON, H., Theoretical Physics
JOHANNESSON, K., Biology, Marine Ecology
JONSON, M., Condensed Matter Physics
JONSSON, P., Marine Ecology
KARLBERG, A.-T., Dermatochemistry and Skin Allergy
KJELLANDER, R., Physical Chemistry
KOMITOV, L., Physics
LARSON, S. A., Geology
LARSSON, Å., Environmental Protection
LEVAN, G., Genetics
LINDHE, U., Zoology (Structural and Animal)
LINDQVIST, O., Inorganic Chemistry
LINDQVIST, S., Physical Geography
LINDVALL, T., Mathematical Statistics
LJUNGSTRÖM, E., Atmospheric Science
LUTHMAN, K., Medicinal Chemistry
MALMGREN, B., Marine Geology
MEHLIG, B., Physics
MOLAU, U., Plant Ecology
NILSSON, S., Zoophysiology
NORDBERG, K., Paleoceanography
NORDHOLM, S., Physical Chemistry
NYMAN, G., Physical Chemistry
NYSTRÖM, T., Scientific Microbiology
OLSSON, O., Developmental Biology of Plants
OMSTEDT, A., Geosphere Dynamics
PEDERSEN, K., Biology, Microbiology
PENDRILL, A.-M., Physics
PETTERSSON, J., Environmental Atmospheric Sciences
PIHL, L., Marine Fish Ecology
PLEIJEL, H., Environmental Protection

RODHE, J., Oceanography
ROSEN, A., Molecular Physics
ROSENBERG, R., Marine Ecology
RYDBERG, L., Oceanography
RYDSTRÖM, J., Biochemistry
SANDELIUS, A.-S., Plant Physiology
SELLDÉN, G., Tree Physiology, Influence of Air Pollution
SHCHERBINA, N., Mathematics
SHEKTER, R., Theoretical Physics
SILVERIN, B., Zoology (Structural and Animal)
SJÖGREN, P., Mathematics
SJÖLIN, L., Inorganic Chemistry
STENSON, J., Biology, Aquatic Ecology
STEVENS, R., Environmental and Quaternary Geology
STIGEBRANDT, A., Oceanography
STIGH, J., Bedrock Geology
STOLIN, A., Mathematics
SUNDBÄCK, K., Biology, Marine Botany
SUNDBERG, P., Zoomorphology
SUNDELL, K., Animal Zoophysiology
SUNDQVIST, CH., Plant Physiology
SUNNERHAGEN, P., Eucaryotic Molecular Biology
SVANSTEDT, N., Mathematics
TISELIUS, P., Marine Ecology
TURNER, D. R., Marine Chemistry
WALLENTINUS, I., Marine Botany
WALLIN PETERSSON, M., Zoophysiology
WEDBORG, M., Marine Analytical Chemistry
WERMUTH, N. E., Biostatistics
WETTERBERG, O., Conservation, specializing in integrated conservation of the built environment
WILLANDER, M., Experimental Physics
ZHUKOV, M., Theoretical Physics
ÅBERG, P., Marine Ecology
ÖSTLUND, S., Solid State Physics

Faculty of Social Sciences (POB 720, 405 30 Gothenburg; fax (31) 773-19-40; internet www.samfak.gu.se):

ARCHER, T., Psychology
ASP, K., Journalism
BJERELD, U., Political Science
BJÖRNBERG, U., Sociology
BOHOLM, A., Social Anthropology
BROBERG, A., Psychology
BRORSTRÖM, B., Management Economics
BÄCK, H., Public Administration
BÄCK-WIKLUND, M., Social Work
DEMKER, M., Political Science
ESAIASSON, P., Political Science
FURÅKER, B., Sociology
GILLJAM, M., Political Science
GLIMELL, H., Science and Technology Studies
GUSTAFSSON, B., Social Work
GÄRLING, T., Psychology
HANSEN, S., Psychology
HETTNE, B., Peace and Conflict Research
HJELMQUIST, E., Behavioural Studies of Disabilities and Handicap
HOLMBERG, S., Political Science
HWANG, P., Psychology
HÖGLUND, L., Library and Information Science
JOHANSSON, B., Psychology
JONSSON, D., Sociology
LINDAHL, R., Political Science
LUNDQVIST, L. J., Political Science
OLSSON, S., Social Work
PETERSON, A., Sociology
PIERRE, J., Political Science
ROMBACH, B., Management Economics
ROTHSTEIN, B., Political Science
SVENSSON, L. G., Sociology
WEIBULL, L., Mass Communication
ÅRHEM, K., Social Anthropology

IT-University (POB 8718, 402 75 Gothenburg; tel. (31) 772-48-95; fax (31) 772-48-99; e-mail info@ituniv.se; internet www.ituniv.se):

BRENNER, P., Mathematics
COQUAND, T., Computer Science
DAHLBOM, B., Informatics

Sahlgrenska Academy (POB 400, 405 30 Gothenburg; fax (31) 773-33-99; e-mail registrator@sahlgrenska.gu.se; internet www.sahlgrenska.gu.se):

AHLMAN, H., Endocrine Surgery
ALBERTSSON-WIKLAND, K., Paediatric Growth Research
ALBREKTSSON, T., Handicap Research
ALLEBECK, P., Social and Preventive Medicine
ANDERSSON, O., Medicine
ASHTON, M., Biopharmacy
AXELSSON, G., Hygiene
AXELSSON, R., Psychiatry
BAGGE, U., Anatomy
BARREGÅRD, L., Clinical Environmental Medicine
BENGTSSON, B.-Å, Clinical Endocrinology
BERGBOM, I., Nursing
BERGFELDT, L., Cardiology
BERGGREN, U., Odontological Psychology
BERGLUNDH, T., Parodontology
BERGSTRÖM, T., Clinical Microbiology
BETSHOLTZ, CH., Medical Biochemistry
BIBER, B., Anaesthesiology and Intensive Care
BILLIG, B., Cellular Aging and Apoptosis
BIRKHED, D., Cariology
BJÖRKELUND, C., General Medicine
BLENNOW, K., Clinical Neurochemistry
BLOMSTRAND, C., Neurology
BONDJERS, G., Cardiological Research
BORÉN, J., Cardiovascular Research
BRAIDE, M., Anatomy
BREIMER, M., Clinical Molecular Genetics
BRY, K., Paediatrics, especially Neonatology
BRÄNNSTRÖM, M., Obstetrics and Gynaecology
CARLSSON, J., Physiotherapy
CARLSSON, L., Clinical Metabolic Research
CARLSTEN, H., Rheumatology
DAHLÉN, G., Oral Microbiology
DAHLGREN, C., Medical Microbiology
DAHLGREN, U., Oral Immunology
DAHLSTRÖM, A., Histology
DAMBER, J.-E., Urology
DICKSON, S., Psychology, especially Neuro Endocrinology
EDÉN, S., Physiology, especially Endocrinology
EDENBRANDT, L., Clinical Physiology, especially Nuclear Medicine
EKROTH, R., Thoracic Surgery
EKSTRÖM, J., Pharmacology
ELAM, M., Clinical Neurophysiology
ELIAS, P., Medicinal Biochemistry
EMILSON, C.-G., Cardiology
ENERBÄCK, S., Medical Genetics
ENGEL, J., Pharmacology
ERICSON, L., Anatomy
ERIKSSON, E., Pharmacology
ERIKSSON, P., Neurobiology, especially Stem Cell Research
FÄNDRIKS, L., Integrative Physiology and Pharmacology
FASTH, A., Paediatric Immunology and Rheumatology
FOSSELL-ARONSSON, E., Radiophysics
FREDMAN, P., Neurochemistry
FRIBERG, P., Clinical Physiology
FUNA, K., Medical Cell Biology
GASTON-JOHANSSON, F., Nursing Sciences
GILLBERG, C., Child and Youth Psychiatry and Handicap Research
GRANSTRÖM, G., Oto-rhino-laryngology
GRÖNDAHL, H.-G., Oral Diagnostic Radiology
GRÖNDAHL, K., Oral Diagnostic Radiology
GUSTAFSSON, B., Neurophysiology
HAGBERG, H., Obstetrics and Gynaecology, especially Peridontology

HAGBERG, M., Occupational Medicine
HAGLID, K., Histology
HAMBERGER, L., Obstetrics and Gynaecology
HANSSON, G., Biochemistry, especially Gastrointestinal Glycobiology
HANSSON, H.-A., Histology
HANSSON, T., Occupational Orthopaedics
HANSSON RÖNNBÄCK, E., Glia Cell Research
HÄRD, T., Structural Biology, especially Protein Chemistry
HARALDSSON, B., Kidney Medicine with Experimental Alignment
HEDNER, T., Clinical Pharmacology
HELLSTRAND, K., Immune Therapy
HELLSTRÖM, A., Paediatric Ophtalmology, especially Growth Factors
HELLSTRÖM, M., Diagnostic Radiology
HJALMARSSON, O., Paediatrics
HOLM, S., Experimental Surgery
HOLMGREN, J., Medical Microbiology
HOLMSTRÖM, H., Plastic Surgery
HOLMÄNG, A., Laboratory Medicine
HULTBORN, R., Oncology
HULTHÉN, L., Clinical Nutrition, especially Human Trace Element Research
ISAKSSON, O., Endocrinology
ISGAARD, J., Hormonal Regulation of the Heart, especially Growth and Repair Processes
IWARSON, S., Infectious Diseases
JACOBSSON, L., Medical Radiophysics
JANSON, P.-O., Obstetrics and Gynaecology
JANSSON, J.-O., Tissue Regeneration
JANSSON, T., Physiology, especially Perinatal Physiology
JERN, C., Neurology, especially Vascular Diseases and Vascular Genetics
JERN, S., Cardiovascular Physiology
JOHANSSON, B. R., Anatomy
JONASON, J., Pharmacology
JONTELL, M., Endocrinology with Oral Diagnostics
KAHNBERG, K.-E., Dental Surgery
KARLSSON, A., Experimental Rheumatology
KARLSSON, J.-O., Histology
KARLSSON, S., Prosthetic Dentistry
KINDBLOM, L.-G., Pathology
KÄRRHOLM, J., Orthopaedic Surgery
LAGERGÅRD, T., Vaccine Research
LARKÖ, O., Dermatology and Venereal Disease
LARSON, G., Laboratory Medicine, especially Glycobiology
LARSSON, S., Pneumology
LEKHOLM, U., Oral Implant Surgery
LINDAHL, A., Cartilage Tissue Regeneration
LINDBLOM, B., Eye Diseases
LINDE, A., Oral Biochemistry
LISSNER, L., Epidemiology
LUNDHOLM, K., Surgery
LYCKE, N., Clinical Immunology
LÖTVALL, J., Clinical Allergology
MAGNUSSON, B., Oral Pathology
MATTSSON, B., General Medicine
MEIS-KINDBLOM, J., Pathology
MELLANDER, L., International Medicine
MILSOM, I., Gynaecology and Obstetrics
MÖLLER, C., Audiology
MOHLIN, B., Orthodontics
NILSSON, O., Pathology
NILSSON, T., Functional Morphology
NISSBRANDT, H., Pharmacology
NORDGREN, S., Surgery
NORÉN, J., Paedodontics
NYGREN, H., Histology
NYSTRÖM, E., Medicine
OHLSSON, C., Hormonal Regulation of Bone Metabolism and Growth
OLAUSSON, M., Clinical Transplantation Surgery
OLDFORS, A., Pathology
OLMARKER, K., Experimental Spinal Pain Research, especially Neuropathic Pain Mechanism

OLOFSSON, S.-O., Medical Biochemistry
OLSSON, J., Odontological Technology
PILHAMMAR-ANDERSSON, E., Nursing Pedagogics
REIT, C., Endodontology
RIDELL, M., Medical Microbiology
RISBERG, B., Surgery
ROSENGREN, A., Epidemiology
ROUPE, G., Dermatology and Venereal Diseases
RYDEVIK, B., Orthopaedic Surgery
RYMO, L., Clinical Chemistry
RÖNNBÄCK, L., Neurology
SAMUELSSON, B., Transfusion Medicine
SANDBERG, M., Biochemistry
SEMB, H., Evolutionary Biology
SENNERBY, L., Handicap Research, especially Experimental and Clinical
SILLÉN, U., Paediatric Surgery
SJÖBERG, B., Medical Biochemistry
SJÖSTRÖM, L., Clinical Research
SJÖVALL, H., Physiology and Pathophysiology of the Digestive and Intestinal Channel
SKOOG, I., Psychiatry, especially Social Psychiatry and Epidemology
SMITH, U., Medicine
SOUSSI, B., Experimental Medicine, especially NMR Spectroscopy
STEINECK, G., Cancer Epidemiology
STENEVI, U., Ophthalmology
STENMAN, G., Pathology
STRANDVIK, B., Paediatrics
SULLIVAN, M., Psychology
SVENNERHOLM, A.-M., Infectious Diseases and Immunology
SWEDBERG, K., Medicine
TARKOWSKI, A., Rheumatology
THELLE, D., Cardiovascular Epidemiology and Prevention
THOMSEN, P., Medical Biomaterials Research
TYLÉN, U., X-Ray Diagnostics
WAHLSTRÖM, J., Clinical Genetics
WALLERSTEDT, S., Medicine
WALLGREN, A., Radio Therapeutics
WALLIN, A., Geriatric Neuropsychiatry
WENNERBERG, A., Oral Prosthetics
WENNERGREN, G., Paediatrics
WENNSTRÖM, J., Parodontology
WICK, M. J., Clinical and Experimental Immunology
WIGSTRÖM, H., Medical Physics
WIKKELSÖ, C., Neurology
WIKLUND, O., Medicine
WIKSTRÖM, M., Oral Microbiology
ÅMAN, P., Tumour Biology
ÖSTMAN-SMITH, I., Paediatric Cardiology

KARLSTADS UNIVERSITET
(Karlstad University)

651 88 Karlstad
Telephone: (54) 700-10-00
Fax: (54) 700-14-60
E-mail: information@kau.se
Internet: www.kau.se

Founded 1967 as Universitetsfilialen; became Högskolan i Karlstad 1977; present name 1999
State control
Academic year: August to June

Rector: CHRISTINA ULLENIUS
Pro-Rector: LARS HAGLUND
Vice-Rector: BOEL HENCKEL
Head of Administration: LENA LARSSON
Chief Librarian: EWA HESSELGREN

Library of 150,000 vols
Number of teachers: 900
Number of students: 11,000

Publications: *Anslaget* (every 2 weeks), *Utbilder* (6 a year)

DEANS

Educational Sciences: ANDERS ARNQVIST
Humanities, Social and Natural Sciences: STEPHEN HWANG

HEADS OF DIVISIONS

BLOMQUIST, L., Division for Social Sciences
BORGSTEN, T., Division for Culture and Communication
Division for Information Technology: (vacant)
HÅKANGÅRD, S., Division for Environmental Sciences
JOHANSSON, K., Division for Health and Caring Sciences
KARDEMARK, G., Division for Business and Economics
KARLSSON, P., Division for Educational Sciences
SCHAGERHOLM, M., Division for Chemistry
SUNDQVIST, M., Division for Engineering Sciences, Physics and Mathematics

LINKÖPINGS UNIVERSITET
(Linköping University)

581 83 Linköping
Telephone: (13) 28-10-00
E-mail: info@liu.se
Internet: www.liu.se

Founded 1970
Academic year: September to June
Rector: Prof. B. ANDERSSON
Registrar: C. KARLSSON

Library: see Libraries and Archives
Number of teachers: 1,800
Number of students: 22,000

DEANS

Faculty of Arts and Sciences: Prof. B. SANDIN
Faculty of Medicine: Prof. R. ANDERSSON
Faculty of Technology: Prof. M. MILLNERT

PROFESSORS

Faculty of Arts and Sciences:

ADELSWÄRD, V., Communication Studies
ALLARD, B., Water and Environmental Studies
ANSELM, J., Technology and Social Change
ANWARD, J., Language and Culture Studies
ARNESDOTTER, I., Business Law
ARONSSON OTTOSSON, K., Child Studies
BECKMAN, S., Technology and Social Change
BERNER, B., Technology and Social Change
BORGQUIST, L., Health and Society
CARLGREN, I., Education
CARSTENSEN, J., Health and Society
COLLSTE, G., Applied Ethics
DAHLGREN, L.-O., Education
EDQUIST, C., Technology and Social Change
ELLEGÅRD, K., Technology and Social Change
ELLSTÖM, P.-E., Education
ERIKSSON, B. E., Health and Society
FRODI, A., Psychology
GOLDKUHL, G., Information Systems
GRANSTÖM, K., Education
GRIMWALL, A., Statistics
HALLDÉN, G., Child Studies
HELLGREN, B., Management
HJORT AF ORNÄS, A., Water and Environmental Studies
HULTMAN, G., Education
HYDÉN, L.-C., Communication Studies
INGELSTAM, L., Technology and Social Change
JANSSON, J., Transport Economics
JOHANSSON, R., Ethnicity Studies
KYLHAMMER, J., Communication Studies
LINDKVIST, L., Management
LINELL, P., Communication Studies
LOHM, U., Water and Environmental Studies

LUNDQVIST, J., Water and Environmental Studies
LYKKE, N., Gender Studies
LYXELL, B., Psychology
MYRBERG, M., Education
NÄSMAN, E., Society and Cultural Studies
NELSON, M. C., History
NILSSON, G. B., Technology and Social Change
NORDENFELT, L., Health and Society
NORDIN, I., Health and Society
PETERSON, B., Philosophy
QVARSELL, R., Health and Society
RAHM, L., Water and Environmental Studies
RÖNNBERG, J., Psychology
SANDELL, R., Clinical Psychology
SANDIN, B., Child Studies
SJÖGREN, H., Technology and Social Change
SKOGH, G., Economics
SUNDIN, E., Technology and Social Change
SUNDIN, J., Health and Society
SVENSSON, B., Water and Environmental Studies
ÅHLUND, A, Ethnicity Studies
ÖBERG, G., Water and Environmental Studies

Faculty of Medicine:

ALM-CARLSSON, G., Medical Radiation Physics
ANDERSSON, R., Pharmacology
ARNQVIST, H., Medical Cell Biology
ASPENBERG, P., Orthopaedic Surgery
AXELSON, O., Occupational and Environmental Medicine
BERGDAHL, B., Medicine
BLOMQUIST, A., Pain Research
BORCH, K., Surgery
BRUNK, U., Pathology
CARLSSON, P., Health Technology Assessment
EK, A.-C., Caring Science
EKBERG, K., Work and Rehabilitation
FAGERHOLM, P., Ophthalmology
FORSBERG, P., Infectious Diseases
FORSUM, U., Clinical Microbiology
GERDLE, B., Rehabilitation Medicine
GRANERUS, A.-K., Geriatric Medicine
HAMMAR, M., Obstetrics and Gynaecology
HAMMARSTRÖM, S., Medical Cell Biology
HILDEBRAND, C., Medical Cell Biology
HULTMAN, P., Pathology
KÅGEDAL, B., Clinical Chemistry
KARLBERG, B., Medicine
KINLSTRÖM, E., Clinical Microbiology
LARSSON, S.-E., Orthopaedic Surgery
LENNQUIST, S., Disaster Medicine and Traumatology
LINDSTRÖM, S., Medical Cell Biology
LISANDER, B., Anaesthesiology
LUDVIGSSON, J., Paediatrics
LUNDBLAD, A., Clinical Chemistry
LUNDQUIST, P.-G., Oto-Rhino-Laryngology
MAGNUSSON, K.-E., Medical Microbiology
MARAISSON, J., Geriatrics
MESSNER, K., Skeletal Biology
MÄRDH, S., Cell Biology
NILSSON, L., Microbiology
NORDENSKJÖLD, B., Oncology
NORDIN, C., Psychiatry
ÖBERG, B., Physiotherapy
OLIN, C., Cardiothoracic Surgery
OLSSON, A. G., Internal Medicine
OLSSON, J.-E., Neurology
PAULETTE-HULTCRANTZ, E., Oto-Rhino-Laryngology
PETERSSON, C., Clinical Pharmacology
RAMMER, L., Forensic Science and Medicine
ROSDAHL, I., Dermatology and Venerology
ROSÉN, A., Inflammation and Tumour Biology
SERUP, J., Dermatology and Venereology
SJÖBERG, F., Critical Care, especially Burn Intensive Care

SMEDBY, Ö., Diagnostic Radiology
SMEDS, S., Surgery
STENDAHL, O., Medical Microbiology
STENMAN, G., Medical Genetics
STRANG, P., Palliative Medicine
STRÅLFORS, P., Medical Cell Biology
SUNDQUIST, T., Medical Microbiology, especially Inflammation
SVANBORG, E., Clinical Neuropsychology
SVANVIK, J., Surgery
SÖDERFELT, B., Neurology
SÖDERKVIST, P., Cell Biology, especially Medical Genetics
TAGESSON, C., Experimental Medicine
THEODORSSON, E., Neurochemistry
TIMPKA, T., Social Medicine and Public Health Sciences
TRELL, E., Primary Health Care and General Practice
WASTESON, Å., Medical Cell Biology
WIGERTZ, O., Medical Engineering (Medical Information Processing)
WIJMA, B., Women's Health
WRANNE, B., Clinical Physiology
WÅLINDER, J., Psychiatry
ÖBERG, A., Medical Engineering (Instrumentation)
ÖSTRUP, L., Plastic Surgery

Faculty of Technology:

ABRAHAMSSON, M., Logistics Management
AHRENBERG, L., Computational Linguistics
ANDERSSON, L.-E., Applied Mathematics
ARONSSON, G., Applied Mathematics
ARWIN, H., Applied Optics
ASK, P., Biomedical Engineering
BALTZER, L., Organic Chemistry
BERGGREN, C., Production Management
BERGGREN, K.-F., Theoretical Physics
BORÉN, H., Organic Chemistry
BRANDES, O., Industrial Marketing
BREGE, S., Industrial Marketing
CARLSSON, U., Biochemistry
CHEN, W., Materials Science
DADFAR, H., International Marketing
DAHLBERG, T., Solid Mechanics and Strength of Materials
DAHLGAARD, J. J., Quality Technology and Management
DOHERTY, P., Computer Science
EDGAR, B., Applied Mathematics
EKEDAHL, L.-G., Applied Physics, Catalytic Reactions
EKLUND, J., Industrial Ergonomics
ELDÉN, L., Numerical Analysis
ERICSSON, T., Data Transmission
ERICSSON, T., Engineering Materials
FAHLMAN, A., Physics
FRITZSON, P., Computer Science
GLAD, T., Automatic Control
GRANLUND, G., Computer Vision
GRUBBSTRÖM, R. W., Production Economics
GUSTAFSSON, F., Communication Systems
HANSSON, G., Experimental Semiconductor Physics
HELMERSSON, U., Thin Film Physics
HOLLNAGEL, E., Industrial Ergonomics
HOLMBERG, K., Optimization
HOLTZ, P.-O., Materials Science
HULTMAN, L., Thin Film Physics
HÄGGLUND, S., Computer Science
INGANÄS, O., Biomolecular and Organic Electronics
INGEMARSSON, I., Information Theory
JANZÉN, E., Semiconductor Physics
JOHANSSON, L., Materials Science
JONSSON, B. H., Biochemistry
KAMKAR, M., Software Engineering
KARLSSON, B., Energy Systems
KARLSSON, J. M., Telecommunications
KLARBRING, A., Optimization Models in Structural Mechanics
KNUTSSON, H., Medical Informatics
KOSKI, T., Mathematical Statistics
KRUS, P., Fluid Power Technology

KRUSE, B., Digital Images and Media Technology
KVARNSTRÖM, I., Organic Chemistry
LIEDBERG, B., Sensor Science
LINDBERG, P.-O., Optimization
LINUSSON, S., Applied Mathematics
LIU, D., Computer Engineering
LJUNG, L., Automatic Control
LOYD, D., Applied Thermodynamics and Fluid Mechanics
LUND, A., Chemical Physics
LUNDGREN, J., Traffic Systems
LUNDSTRÖM, I., Applied Physics
MALUSZYNSKI, J., Programming Theory
MANDENIUS, C.-F., Biotechnology
MAZ'YA, V., Applied Mathematics
MILLNERT, M., Automatic Control
MONEMAR, B., Condensed Matter Physics
MOSFEGH, B., Energy Systems
MUKHERJEE, S. D., Electronic Production
NIELSEN, L., Vehicle Systems
NILSSON, G., Biomedical Instrumentation
NILSSON, L., Solid Mechanics
NOVAK, A., Production Engineering
OHLSSON, K., Industrial Ergonomics
PALMBERG, J.-O., Fluid Power Technology
PENG, Z., Computer Systems
PERSSON, J., Medical Technology Assessment
RAPP, B., Economic Information Systems
RAUCH, S., Applied Mathematics
RIKLUND, R., Theoretical Physics
RYDBERG, K.-E., Fluid Power Technology
RÖNNQVIST, M., Optimization
SALANECK, W., Surface Physics and Chemistry
SANDAHL, K., Software Engineering
SANDEWALL, E., Computer Science
SANDKULL, B., Industrial Organization
SERNELIUS, B., Theoretical Physics
SHAHMEHRI, N., Computer Science
SJÖLANDER, S., Zoology
STAFSTRÖM, S., Computational Physics
STRANDBERG, L., Traffic Safety and Environment
SVENSSON, C., Electronic Devices
TENGVALL, P., Applied Physics
UHRBERG, R., Surface and Semiconductor Physics
VÄRBRAND, P., Optimization
WANHAMMAR, L., Electronic Systems
WIGERTZ, O., Medical Informatics
ÖBERG, A., Biomedical Engineering

LULEÅ TEKNISKA UNIVERSITET
(Luleå University of Technology)

971 87 Luleå
Telephone: (920) 49-10-00
Fax: (920) 49-13-99
E-mail: universitet@luth.se
Internet: www.luth.se

Founded 1971
State control
Language of instruction: Swedish

President: INGEGERD PALMÉR
Vice-President: JOHAN STERTE
Chief Administrative Officer: STAFFAN SARBÄCK
University Librarian: TERJE HÖISETH

Number of teachers: 970 (incl. researchers)
Number of students: 12,000

DEANS

Faculty of Humanities and Natural Sciences: STURE BRÄNDSTRÖM
Faculty of Technology: ERIK HÖGLUND

PROFESSORS

Faculty of Humanities and Natural Sciences
Department of Business Administration and Social Sciences:
BERGSTRÖM, I., Management Control

DE RAADT, D., Informatics and Systems Sciences
HANSSON, S., Political Science, History and Geography
LUNDGREN, N.-G., Political Science, History and Geography
MICHANEK, G., Jurisprudence
RADETZKI, M., Economics
SALEHI-SANGARI, E., Industrial Marketing

Department of Communication and Languages:
MAGNUSSON, U., English
PERSSON, G., English

School of Music:
BRÄNDSTRÖM, S., Education and Teaching Methods in Music
ERICSSON, H.-O., Organ
SANDSTRÖM, J., Composition
WESTBERG, E., Choir Singing and Choir Conducting

Faculty of Technology

Department of Applied Physics and Mechanical Engineering:
FREDRIKSSON, S., Physics
GUSTAVSSON, H., Fluid Mechanics
HÖGLUND, E., Machine Elements
JINYUE, Y., Energy Engineering
KAPLAN, A., Systems Engineering
KARLSSON, L., Computer Aided Design
MOLIN, N. E., Experimental Mechanics
ODÉN, M., Engineering Materials
OLDENBURG, M., Solid Mechanics
VARNA, J., Polymer Engineering

Department of Business Administration and Social Sciences:
HÄGERFORS, A., Computer and Systems Sciences
HÖRTE, S.-Å., Industrial Organization
KLEFSJÖ, B.
WIKLUND, H., Quality and Environmental Management

Department of Chemical and Metallurgical Engineering:
BERGLUND, K. A., Biochemical and Chemical Process Engineering
BJÖRKMAN, B., Process Metallurgy
FORSSBERG, E., Mineral Processing
FORSLING, W., Chemistry
STERTE, J., Chemical Technology

Department of Civil and Mining Engineering:
BORGBRANT, J., Construction Management
ELFGREN, L., Structural Engineering
JOHANSSON, B., Steel Structures
KLISINSKI, M., Structural Mechanics
KNUTSSON, S., Soil Mechanics and Foundation Engineering
KUMAR, U., Operation and Maintenance Engineering
LAGERQVIST, O., Steel Structures
LINDQVIST, P.-A., Rock Engineering
NORDLUND, E., Rock Mechanics
OLOFSSON, T., Structural Engineering

Department of Computer Science and Electrical Engineering:
DELSING, J., Embedded Internet Systems Laboratory (EISLAB)
MEDVEDEV, A., Automatic Control
WERNERSSON, A., Embedded Internet Systems Laboratory (EISLAB)

School of Education:
ALEXANDERSSON, M., Pedagogics

Department of Environmental Engineering:
ELMING, S.-Å., Applied Geophysics
HANAEUS, J., Sanitary Engineering
LAGERKVIST, A., Water Science and Technology
NORDELL, B., Renewable Energy
ÖHLANDER, B., Applied Geology
ÖSTMAN, A., Geographical Information Technology

SELLGREN, A., Water Resources Engineering
Department of Human Work Sciences:
ALM, H., Engineering Psychology
JOHANSSON, J., Industrial Work Environment
PETTERSSON, D., Industrial Design
ÅGREN, A., Sound and Vibration
Department of Mathematics:
EULER, M., Applied Mathematics
HEABERG, T., Applied Mathematics
PERSSON, L.-E., Applied Mathematics
STRAESSER, R., Applied Mathematics
Department of Wood Technology:
GRÖNLUND, A., Wood Technology
MORÉN, T., Wood Physics
WESTERMARK, U., Wood Material Science

LUNDS UNIVERSITET

POB 117, 221 00 Lund
Telephone: (46) 222-00-00
Fax: (46) 222-47-20
E-mail: luniver@luniver.lu.se
Internet: www.lu.se
Founded 1666
State control
Languages of instruction: Swedish, English
Academic year: September to June (two semesters)

Rector: GÖRAN BEXELL
Deputy-Rector: ANN NUMHAUSER-HENNING
Head of Administration: HANS MODIG

Library: see Libraries and Archives
Number of teachers: 2,000
Number of students: 35,000

Publication: *LUM* (11 a year)

DEANS

Faculty of Humanities: Prof. G. BEXELL
Faculty of Law: Prof. P. O. TRÄSKMAN
Faculty of Medicine: Prof. J. NILSSON
Faculty of Political and Social Sciences: Prof. G. HANSSON
Faculty of Science: Prof. B. SÖDERSTRÖM
Faculty of Technology: Prof. G. JÖNSSON
Faculty of Theology: Prof. S. HIDAL

PROFESSORS

Faculty of Humanities:
ANDERSSON, G., Musicology
ANDRÉN, A., Medieval Archaeology
BJÖRLING, F., Slavic Languages
BLOMQVIST, J., Greek Language and Literature
BROBERG, G., History of Ideas and Sciences
BRUCE, G., Phonetics
EDLUND, B., Musicology
EINARSSON, J., Scandinavian Languages
ENÉVIST, I., Spanish
FLORBY, G., English Literature
FRYKMAN, J., European Ethnology
GREATREX, R., Chinese
GÄRDENFORS, P., Cognitive Science
GUSTAFSSON, H., History
HAETTNER-AURELIUS, E., Literature
HÅKANSSON, G., General Linguistics
HANSSON, B., Theoretical Philosophy
HEDLING, E., Film
HOADLEY, M., Southeast Asian History and Bahasa Indonesia
HOLMBERG, B., Semitic Languages
HORNBORG, A., Human Ecology
HÅRDH, B., Archaeology
IREGREN, E., Historical Osteology
KARLSSON, K.-G., History
LARSSON, B., French
LARSSON, L., Archaeology
LARSSON, L., Literature
LÖFGREN, O., European Ethnology
LÖVKRONA, I., European Ethnology
MOLNÁR, V., German
NORDIN, S., History of Ideas and Science

OLAUSSON, D., Archaeology
OREDSSON, S., History
PALM, A., Literature
PERSSON, I., Practical Philosophy
PILTZ, A., Latin
PLATZACK, C., Scandinavian Languages
RABINOWICZ, W., Practical Philosophy
RAGVALD, L., Chinese
RIDDERSTAD, P. S., Book and Library History
RYDÉN, P., Literature
RYSTEDT, E., Classical Archaeology and Ancient History
SAHLIN, N.-E., Theoretical Philosophy
SALOMON, K., International History
SALOMOUSSON, A., European Ethnology
SANDQVIST, S., French
SCHLYTER, S., Romance Languages
SJÖBLAD, C., Literature
SJÖLIN, J.-G., History of Contemporary Art
SONESSON, G., Cultural Semiotics
STEENSLAND, L., Slavic Languages
STRÖMQVIST, S., Language Acquisition
SVANTESSON, J.-O., General Linguistics
SVENSSON, J., Swedish
SVENSSON, L.-H., English Literature
THORMÄHLEN, M., English Literature
VIBERG, Å., General Linguistics
WARREN, B., English
WEIMARCK, T., History of Contemporary Art
WIÉANDER, Ö., Classical Archaeology
WIENBERG, J., Medieval Archaeology
ÖSTERBERG, E., History

Faculty of Law:
BERGHOLTZ, G., Legal Procedure
BERGSTRÖM, S., Tax Law
BOGDAN, M., Comparative and Private International Law
FAHLBECK, R., Labour Law
GORTON, L., Banking Law
MELANDER, G., Public International Law
MODÉER, K. Å., Legal History
NUMHAUSER-HENNING, A., Private Law
NYSTRÖM, B., Private Law
PECZENIK, A., Jurisprudence
TRÄSKMAN, P. O., Criminal Law
VOGEL, H.-H., Public Law
WESTBERG, P., Legal Procedure

Faculty of Medicine:
ABRAHAMSSON, P.-A., Oncological Urology
AHRÉN, B., Clinical Metabolic Research
ALLING, CH., Medical Neurochemistry
ALM, P., Pathology
ANDERSSON, K.-E., Clinical Pharmacology
ANDERSSON, R., Surgery
ANDERSSON, T., Experimental Pathology
ARNER, A., Physiology
BELFRAGE, P., Medical Biochemistry
BERGLUND, G., Internal Medicine
BERGLUND, M., Clinical Alcohol Research
BJURSTEN, L.-M., Bio-implant Research
BJÖRCK, L., Medical Biochemistry
BJÖRKLUND, A., Histology
BORGSTRÖM, A., Surgery
BRUNDIN, P., Neuroscience
BÄCK, O., Dermatology
CARLSTEDT, I., Mucosal Biology
DAHLBÄCK, B., Coagulation Research
DEGERMAN, E., Experimental Diabetes Research
DEHLIN, O., Geriatric Medicine
DILLNER, J., Virology
EHINGER, B., Ophthalmology
EKBLOM, P., Molecular Cell Biology
EKDAHL, C., Physiotherapy
EKHBERG, O., Diagnostic Radiology
ELMESTÅHL, S., Geriatrics
ERLANSON-ALBERTSSON, C.
FENYÖ, E.-M., Virology
FORSGREN, A., Clinical Bacteriology
FRANSSON, L.-Å., Cell Biology
FÄSSLER, R., Experimental Pathology
GERDTHAM, U., Public Health Science
GROOP, L., Endocrinology

GRUBB, A., Clinical Biochemistry
GRÄNDE, P.-O., Anaesthesia and Intensive Care
GULLBERG, U., Haematology
GUSTAFSON, L., Geriatric Psychiatry
HAGANDER, B., Medicine
HAGMAR, L., Environmental Medicine
HEIJL, A., Ophthalmology
HEINEGÅRD, D., Medical Biochemistry
HELLSTRAND, P., Muscle Research
HERMERÉN, G., Medical Ethics
HESSLOW, G., Neuroscience
HOLMBERG, L., Paediatrics
HOLMDAHL, R., Medical Inflammation Research
HOLMER, N.-G., Biomedical Engineering
HOLM WALLENBERG, C., Molecular Cell Biology
HOLTÅS, S., Neuroradiology
HOVELIUS, B., General Practice
HÅKANSSON, R., Experimental Endocrinology
HÖGESTÄTT, E., Clinical Pharmacology
IHSE, I., Surgery
JACOBSEN, S. E., Stem Cell Biology
JANZON, L., Epidemiology
JEPPSSON, B., Surgery
JOHNELL, O., Orthopaedic Surgery
JONSON, B., Clinical Physiology
KARLSSON, S., Gene Therapy in Molecular Medicine
KILLANDER, D., Oncology
LANDBERG, G., Pathology
LEANDERSON, T., Immunology
LEED-LUNDBERG, F., Cellular and Molecular Physiology
LERNMARK, A., Experimental Diabetes Research
LEVANDER, S., Psychiatry
LIDGREN, L., Orthopaedics
LINDAHL, G., Medical Microbiology and Immunology
LINDGREN, B., Health Economics
LINDGREN, S., Medicine
LINDVALL, O., Restorative Neurology
LJUNGGREN, B., Dermatology and Venereology
LOHMANDER, S., Orthopaedics
LUNDBERG, D., Anaesthesiology
LUNDBORG, G., Hand Surgery
LUNDQUIST, I., Pharmacology
LUTHMAN, H., Genetic Epidemiology
LÖFDAHL, C.-G., Lung Disease
LÖFQVIST, A., Logopaedic Phonetics
LÖWENHIELM, P., Forensic Medicine
McNEIL, T., Medical Behavioural Research
MAGNUSSON, M., Otorhinolaryngology
MALMSTRÖM, A., Medical and Physiological Chemistry
MARSAL, K., Obstetrics and Gynaecology
MATTIASSON, A., Urology
MATTSON, R., Reproduction Immunology
MATTSSON, S., Medical Radiation Physics
MITELMAN, F., Clinical Genetics
NETTELBLADT, U., Logopaedics
NILSSON, Å., Internal Medicine
NILSSON, J., Experimental Cardiovascular Research
NILSSON-EHLE, P., Clinical Chemistry
NORRBY, R., Infectious Diseases
NORRVING, B., Neurology
OLBRANT, K., Cell Biology
OLOFSSON, T., Haematology
OLSSON, B., Cardiology
OLSSON, H., Oncology
OLSSON, I., Haematology
OWMAN, CH., Histology
PERSSON, B., Medical Radiation Physics
PERSSON, C. G. A., Experimental Clinical Pharmacology
PESONEN, E., Child Cardiology
PETTERSSON, H., Diagnostic Radiology
PRELLNER, K., Otorhinolaryngology
PÅHLMAN, S., Molecular Medicine
RAHM-HALLBERG, I., Caring Sciences
RENCK, H., Anaesthesiology

AXELSSON, A., Chemical Engineering
AXSÄTER, S., Production Management
BARUP, K., Architectural Conservation and Restoration
BENGTSSON, L., Water Resources Engineering
BENGTSSON, P.-E., Laser-Based Combustion Diagnostics
BENGTSSON, R., Mathematical Physics
BERGENSTÅHL, B., Food Technology
BERNDTSSON, R., Water Resources Engineering
BERNHARDSSON, B., Automatic Control
BJELM, L., Engineering Geology
BJÖRK, I., Applied Nutrition and Food Chemistry
BOHGARD, M., Ergonomics and Aerosol Technology
BOLMSJÖ, G., Robotics
BORREBAECK, C., Immunotechnology
BOVIN, J.-O., Materials Chemistry and High-Resolution Electron Microscopy
BÜLOW, L., Biochemistry
BÖRJESSON, P.-O., Signal Processing
DAHLBLOM, O., Structural Mechanics
DAMS, M., Computer Science
DEJMEK, P., Food Engineering
ECKHARDT, C.-C., Industrial Design
EDFORS, O., Radio Communications
EDSTRÖM, M., Architectural Conservation and Restoration
EKHOLM, A., Computer Aided Architectural Design
ELIASSON, A.-C., Cereal Technology
ELMROTH, A., Building Physics
ENGSTRÖM, L., Experimental Physics, especially Atomic Physics and Optics
FAGERLUND, G., Building Materials
FREDLUND, B., Building Science
FUCHS, L., Fluid Mechanics
GONZALEZ, A., Theoretical and Applied Aesthetics
GUSTAFSSON, P. J., Structural Mechanics
HAGANDER, P., Automatic Control
HAHN-HÄGERDAL, B., Applied Microbiology
HALLE, B., Physical Chemistry
HANSON, H., Water Resources Engineering
HANSSON, B., Construction Management
HELSING, J., Scientific Computing
HEYDEN, A., Mathematics
HOLMBERG, B., Traffic Planning
HOLMSTEDT, G., Fire Safety Engineering
HOLST, J., Mathematical Statistics
HOLST, O., Biotechnology
HOLST, U., Mathematical Statistics
HYDÉN, C., Traffic Engineering
HÄGGLUND, T., Automatic Control
JACOBSON, B., Machine Elements
JAMES, P., Proteomics
JARLSKOG, C., Theoretical Particle Physics
JENSEN, L. H., Building Services
JENSEN, U., Real Estate Management
JOHANNESSON, R., Information Theory
JOHANNESSON, T., Materials Engineering
JOHANSSON, B., Combustion Engines
JOHANSSON, G., Ergonomics and Aerosol Technology
JOHANSSON, R., Automatic Control
JOHANSSON, T., Information Theory
JOHANSSON, T.-B., Energy Systems Analysis
JÖNSON, G., Packaging Logistics
JÖNSSON, A. S., Chemical Engineering
JÖNSSON, B., Physical Chemistry
JÖNSSON, B., Rehabilitation Engineering
KARLSSON, A., Electromagnetic Theory
KARLSSON, H., Chemical Engineering, Process Chemistry and Catalysis
KARLSSON, J. M., Communication Systems
KRISTENSSON, G., Electromagnetic Theory
KRÖLL, S., Atomic Physics
KUCHINSKI, K., Computer Science
KÜLLER, R., Environmental Psychology
KÖRNER, U., Communication Systems
L'HUILLIER, A., Atomic Physics

LA COUR JANSEN, J., Water and Waste Water Engineering
LARSON, M., Water Resources Engineering
LARSSON, P.-O., Applied Biochemistry
LAURELL, T., Electrical Measurements
LIDÉN, G., Chemical Reaction Engineering
LIDGREN, K., Environmental Economics
LINDGREN, G., Mathematical Statistics
LINDSTRÖM, K., Electrical Measurements
LUNDHOLM, G., Combustion Engines
MAGNUSSON, B., Software Technology
MAGNUSSON, S.-E., Fire Safety Engineering
MALMQVIST, K., Nuclear Physics
MARTINSSON, B., Aerosol Physics
MATTIASSON, B., Biotechnology
MAURER, F., Polymer Technology
MOLIN, G., Food Hygiene
MOLISCH, A., Radio Communications
MONTELIUS, L., Solid State Physics
NILSSON, S., Technical Analysis Chemistry, especially Microanalytical Chemistry
NYMAN, M., Food Chemistry
ODENBRAND, I., Chemical Engineering, especially Environmental Catalysis
OLSSON, G., Industrial Automation
OMLING, P., Solid State Physics
PAULSSON, M., Dairy Technology
PERSSON, H. W., Electrical Measurements
PETERSON, H., Structural Mechanics
PHILIPSON, L., Computer Systems
PIÓRO, M., Communication Systems
PISTOL, M.-E., Solid State Physics
RAGNARSSON, I., Mathematical Physics
RANTZER, A., Automatic Control
REUTERSWÄRD, L., Architecture and Development Studies
RISTINMAA, M., Solid Mechanics
RYCHLIK, I., Mathematical Statistics
RYDÉN, T., Mathematical Statistics
RÅDBERG, J., Urban Planning
RÅDSTRÖM, P., Applied Microbiology, especially Genetic Applications
SAABYE OTTOSEN, N., Solid Mechanics
SAMUELSSON, L., Solid State Physics
SANDBERG, G., Structural Mechanics
SCHMELING, J., Mathematics
SEIFERT, W., Solid State Physics
SENTLER, L., Structural Engineering
SMEETS, B., Information Theory
SPARR, G., Mathematics
STENSTRÖM, S., Chemical Engineering
STERNER, O., Bio-organic Chemistry
STÅHL, A., Traffic Planning
STÅHL, J.-E., Production and Materials Engineering
SUNDÉN, B., Heat Transfer
SVANBERG, S., Atomic Physics
SVERDRUP, H., Biogeochemistry
SÄRNER, E., Water and Environmental Engineering
SÖDERBERG, J., Construction Management
SÖRNMO, L., Biomedical Signals Processing
THAM, K., Architecture
THELANDERSSON, S., Structural Engineering
THÖRNQVIST, L., Energy Economics and Planning
TORISSON, T., Thermal Power Engineering
TORNBERG, E., Food Engineering
TRÄGÅRDH, C., Food Engineering
TRÄGÅRDH, G., Food Engineering, especially Membrane Technology
WAHSTRÖM, C.-G., Experimental Physics
WAHLUND, K.-G., Technical Analytical Chemistry
WALLENBERG, R., Solid State Chemistry
WANDEL, S., Engineering Logistics
WARFVINGE, P., Biogeochemistry
WERNE, F., Building Functions Analysis
WHITLOW, H. J., Nuclear Physics, especially Ion Physics
WIMMERSTEDT, R., Chemical Engineering
WITTENMARK, B., Automatic Control
WOHLIN, C., Software Systems Engineering
YUAN, J., Circuit Design
ZACCHI, G., Chemical Engineering

ZIGANGIROW, K. S., Telecommunications Theory
ÅBERG, S., Mathematical Physics
ÅKESSON, B., Applied Nutrition
ÅRZÉN, K.-E., Automatic Control
ÅSTRÖM, K. J., Mathematics

Faculty of Theology:
BEXELL, G., Ethics
DAHLGREN, C., Sociology of Religion
GEELS, A., Psychology of Religion
GUSTAFSSON, G., Sociology of Religion
HALLONSTEN, G., Systematic Theology
HAMBERG, E., Immigration Studies
HIDAL, S., Old Testament Exegesis
HJÄRPE, J., Islamic Studies
HOFMANN, M., Systematic Theology
HOLMBERG, B., New Testament Exegesis
JARLERT, A., Church History
JEANROND, W., Systematic Theology
LANDE, A., Missiology with Ecumenical Theology
LINDSTRÖM, F., Old Testament Exegesis
OLSSON, B., New Testament Exegesis
OLSSON, T., History and Phenomenology of Religions
METTINGER, T., Old Testament Exegesis
RUBENSON, S., Church History
STENQVIST, C., Philosophy of Religion
TRAUTNER-KROMANN, H., Jewish Studies

Malmö Academy of Music:
FOLKESTAD, G., Music Education
HARDENBERGER, H., Trumpet
HELLSTEN, H., Organ
INGELF, S., Music Theory with Arranging
LINDROOS, P., Singing
PÅLSSON, H., Piano
SÖLLSCHER, G., Guitar
WESOLOWSKI, M., Piano

Malmö Art Academy:
NILSSON, L., Fine Arts
TOTTI, S., Fine Arts

MITTUNIVERSITETET
(Mid-Sweden University)

851 70 Sundsvall

Telephone: (771) 97-50-00
E-mail: info@miun.se
Internet: www.miun.se

Campuses in Härnösand, Örnsköldsvik, Östersund, and Sundsvall

Founded 1993

Rector: THOMAS LINDSTEIN
Director of Libraries: ROLAND HJERPPE

Library of 100,000 vols
Number of teachers: 500
Number of students: 13,000

Faculties of Educational Science, Human Sciences and Science, Technology and Media.

ÖREBRO UNIVERSITET
(University of Örebro)

701 82 Örebro

Telephone: (19) 30-30-00
Fax: (19) 33-02-38
E-mail: info@oru.se
Internet: www.oru.se

Founded 1967 as Högskolan i Örebro; present name and status 1999

State control

Academic year: September to June

Vice-Chancellor: JANERIK GIDLUND
Deputy Vice-Chancellor: JENS SCHOLLIN
Registrar: CHRISTINA NILSON
Information Officer: ULLA FOGELSTRÖM
Librarian: ELISABET ANDERSSON

Library of 230,000 vols
Number of teachers: 1,000
Number of students: 15,000

Publication: *Oru.magasinet* (irregular)

DEANS

Behavioural, Social and Legal Sciences: KERSTIN HOLLERTZ
Caring Sciences: EVA SAHLBERG-BLOM
Clinical Medicine: ULF TIDEFELT
Domestic Science: THOMAS BLOM
Economics, Statistics and Computer Science: KERSTIN NILSSON
Humanities: SÖREN KLINGNÉUS
Natural Sciences: ÅKE STRID
Social Sciences: MATS LINDBERG
Sports and Physical Training: ANITA NILSSON
Teacher-Training: NINNI WAHLSTRÖM
Technology: JOHAN KJELLANDER
Training of Music Teachers: SVEN LANDH

STOCKHOLMS UNIVERSITET

106 91 Stockholm
Telephone: (8) 16-20-00
Fax: (8) 15-36-93
E-mail: info@su.se
Internet: www.su.se

Founded 1878, became State University 1960
State control
Language of instruction: Swedish
Academic year: August to June

Vice-Chancellor: Prof. KÅRE BREMER
Pro-Vice-Chancellor: Prof. LENA GERHOLM
Head of Administration: LEIF LINDFORS
Library: see Libraries and Archives
Number of teachers: 4,240 (2,480 full-time,
    1,800 part time and temporary)
Number of students: 37,000

Publication: *Acta Universitatis Stockhol-
    miensis*

DEANS

Faculty of Humanities: Prof. K. DAHLBÄCK
Faculty of Law: Prof. P. SEIPEL
Faculty of Natural Sciences: Prof. H. ROHDE
Faculty of Social Sciences: Prof. E. WADENSJÖ

PROFESSORS

Faculty of Humanities
    History-Philosophy Section:
AILI, H., Latin
ALBERG-JENSEN, P., Slavic Languages
ANDRÉN, A., Archaeology
BARTNING, I., French
BECKER, K., Journalism
BERGLIE, Q., Religion
BERGMAN, B., Sign Language
BILY, M., Slavic Languages
BODIN, P.-A., Slavic Languages
BOLTON, K., English
CARLSHAMRE, S., Theoretical Philosophy
CULLHED, A., Literary History
DAHL, Ö., General Linguistics
DAHLBÄCK, G., History of the Middle Ages
EKECRANTZ, J., Media and Communication
ENGSTRAND, O., Phonetics
FALK, C., Swedish Language
FALK, J., Spanish
FANT, L., Ibero-Romance Languages
FAWKNER, H., English
FERM, O., History
FORSGREN, M., French
GERHOLM, L., Ethnology
GERÖ, E.-C., Greek
GLETE, J., History
HALL, T., Scandinavian and Comparative
    Art History
HEED, S.-A., Theatre Studies
HELANDER, K., Theatre Studies
HELLBERG, S., Scandinavian Languages
HVITFELT, H., Journalism
HYLTENSTAM, K., Bilingualism
INGDAHL KAZMIERA, A., Slavic Languages
IVERSEN, H., Latin
JARRICK, A., History
JOHANNESSON, N.-L., English
KANGERE, B., Baltic Languages

KOPTJEVSKAJA TAMM, M., General Linguis-
    tics
KÖLL, A. M., Baltic Studies
KOSKINEN, M., Film Studies
LACERDA, F., Phonetics
LANGE, S., Scandinavian Languages
LARSEN, H., Musicology
LEANDER-TOUATI, A.-M., Ancient Culture
LIDÉN, K., Archaeology
LILJA, S., History
LINDBERG-WADA, G., Japanology
LINDROTH, J., History of Athletics
LJUNGGREN, A., Russian
LODÉN, T., Language and Culture of China
LYSELL, R., History of Literature
MALMNÄS, P.-E., Theoretical Philosophy
MOLIN, K., History
MURDOCH, D., Theoretical Philosophy
NEEDHAM, P., Theoretical Philosophy
NEUGER, L., Polish
NIKOLAJEVA, M., History of Literature
NILSSON, L., History of Municipality
NYSTEDT, J., Italian
OETKE, C., Language and Culture of India
OHLSSON, R., Practical Philosophy
OLSSON, J., Film Studies
PAGIN, P., Theoretical Philosophy
RIAD, T., Scandinavian Languages
ROSÉN, S., Language and Culture of Korea
ROSENBERG, T., Gender Studies
ROSENDAHL, M., Latin American Studies
ROSSHOLM, G., History of Literature
ROSSHOLM LAGERLÖF, M., Art History
RÖHL, M., History of Literature
SAUTER, W., Theatre Studies
SCHEFFER, C., Ancient Culture
SJØVOLD, T., Historical Osteology
SMITH, W., Indology
STRAND, H., Swedish
STROUD, C., Bilingualism
SVARTHOLM, K., Swedish as a Second
    Language for the Deaf
SVENSSON, G., Theoretical Philosophy
SÖDERBERGH WIDDING, A., Film Studies
TEODOROWICZ-HELLMAN, E., Polish
TERSMAN, F., Practical Philosophy
TRAUNMÜLLER, H., Auditative Phonetics
TÄNNSJÖ, T., Practical Philosophy
VOLK, M., Computer Linguistics
WANDE, E., Finnish
WARDINI, E., Arabic
WESTIN, B., History of Literature
WÅGHÄLL NIVRE, E., German
AMARK, K., History

Faculty of Law:
BJARUP, J., Jurisprudence
BOHLIN, A., Public Law
BRING, O., International Law
DIESEN, C., Procedure
EBBESSON, J., Environmental Law
EDELSTAM, H., Procedure
EKLUND, R., Private Law, Labour Law
HEUMAN, L., Procedure
KLEINEMAN, J., Civil Law
KÄLLSTRÖM, K., Private Law
LEIJONHUFVUD, M., Penal Law
LEVIN, M., Private Law
MAGNUSSON SJÖBERG, C., Law and Infor-
    matics
MAHMOUDI, S., International Law
MELZ, P., Financial Law
PEHRSON, L., Economics and Economic Law
PETERSON, C., Legal History
ROSÉN, J., Civil Law
SANDGREN, C., Civil Law
SANDSTRÖM, M., History of Law
SCHIRATSKY, D., Theoretical Philosophy
SEIPEL, P., Law and Informatics
SILFVERBERG, C., Financial Law
VOGEL, H.-H., Public Law
WAHL, N., European Law
WAHLGREN, P., Law and Informatics
WARNLING-NEREP, W., Public Law
WENNBERG, S., Penal Law

Faculty of Natural Sciences
    Biology Section:
BERGMAN, B., Physiological Botany
BORG, H., Aquatic Environmental Chemis-
    try
BROMAN, D., Aquatic Ecotoxicology
CANNON, B., Animal Physiology
ELMGREN, R., Marine Ecology
ERIKSSON, O., Plant Ecology
FOLKE, C., Management of Natural
    Resources
GRÄSLUND, A., Biophysics
HAGGÅRD, E., Genetics
ISAKSSON, L., Microbiology
KAUTSKY, N., Marine Ecotoxicology
LINDBERG, U., Zoological Cell Biology
MÖLLER, G., Immunology
NÄSSEL, D., Functional Zoomorphology
RADESÄTER, T., Ethology
RANNUG, U., Toxicological Genetics
SJÖBERG, B.-M., Molecular Biology
WALLES, B., Morphological Botany
WIESLANDER, L., Molecular Genome
    Research
WIKLUND, C., Ecological Zoology
WULFF, F., Marine Systems Ecology
    Chemistry Section:
ANDERSSON, B., Biochemistry
BARTFAI, T., Neurochemistry
BERGMAN, A., Environmental Chemistry
BRZEZINSKI, P., Biochemistry, esp. Molecu-
    lar Energy Research
BÄCKVALL, J.-E., Organic Chemistry
DEPIERRE, J., Biochemistry, especially
    Enzymological Toxicology
HULTH, P.-O., Experimental Physics
JANSSON, B., Chemical Environmental
    Analysis
JOSEFSSON, B., Analytical Chemistry
KOWALEWSKI, J., Physical Chemistry
LEVITT, M., Chemical Spectroscopy
LIDIN, S., Inorganic Chemistry
NELSON, D., Biochemistry
NORDLUND, P., Structural Biochemistry
NORRESTAM, R., Structural Chemistry
NYGREN, M., Material Chemistry, Electro-
    ceramics
ODHAM, G., Analytical Environmental
    Chemistry
SONNHAMMER, E., Bioinformatics
VON HEIJNE, G., Theoretical Chemistry
Earth and Environmental Studies Section:
BACKMAN, J., General and Historical Geol-
    ogy
HALLBERG, R., Microbial Chemistry
HOLMGREN, K., Physical Geography
IHSE, M., Ecological Geography
INGRI, J., Geochemistry and Petrology
KARLÉN, W., Physical Geography
LUNDÉN, B., Remote Sensing
RINGBERG, B., Quaternary Geology
ROSSWALL, T., Water and Environmental
    Studies
WASTENSON, L., Remote Sensing
    Mathematics-Physics Section:
BARGHOLTZ, C., Nuclear Physics
BJÖRK, J.-E., Mathematics
BOHM, C., Technology of Physical Systems
EKEDAHL, T., Mathematics
FRANSSON, C., Astrophysics
HANSSON, H., Theoretical Physics
HANSSON, H.-C., Air Pollution
HOLMGREN, S.-O., High-Energy Physics
KÄLLEN, E., Dynamic Meteorology
LARSSON, M., Experimental Molecular Phy-
    sics
MARTIN-LÖF, A., Actuarial Mathematics
    and Mathematical Statistics
OLOFSSON, H., Astronomy
PALMGREN, J., Biostatistics
PASSARE, M., Mathematics
RODHE, H., Chemical Meteorology
ROOS, J. E., Mathematics
SCHUCH, R., Atomic Physics

SIEGBAHN, P., Theoretical Physics
SUNDQVIST, H., Meteorology
SVENSSON, R., Astrophysics with Cosmology

Faculty of Social Sciences:

AGELL, J., Economics
AHRNE, G., Sociology
ALMKVIST, O., Psychology
ARAI, M., Economics
BACKENROTH-OHSAKO, G., Psychology
BERG, P.-O., Business Administration
BERGLUND, B., Perception and Psychophysics
BERGMARK, A., Social Work
BERNHARDT, E., Demography
BJÖRKUND, A., Economics
CALMFORS, L., International Economics
CHINAPAH, V., International Education
CHRISTIANSSON, S.-Å., Psychology
DAHL, G., Social Anthropology, Development Research
DAHLERUP, O., Political Science
DAUN, H., International Education
EDWARDS, M., Political Science
EKBERG, J., Economics
EKENBERG, L., Computer and Systems Science
ERIKSON, R., Sociology
FLAM, H., International Economics
FLYGHED, J., Criminology
FORSBERG, G., Human Geography
FRANK, O., Statistics
FÄGERLIND, I., International and Comparative Education
GOLDMANN, K., Political Science
GUILLET DE MONTHOUX, P., Business Administration
GUMMESSON, E., Business Administration
HANNERZ, U., Social Anthropology
HART, T., Pacific Asia Studies
HEDBERG, B., Business Administration
HEDSTRÖM, P., Sociology, Population Processes
HESSLE, S., Social Work
HOEM, J., Demography
HORN AF RANTZIEN, H., International Economics
JOHANSSON, G., Working Life Psychology
JONSSON, E., Business Administration, Administrative Economics
KORPI, W., Social Politics
KÜHLHORN, E., Sociological Alcoholic Research
LENNTORP, B., Human and Economic Geography
LUNDBERG, B., Information Administration
LUNDBERG, U., Human Biological Psychology
MONTGOMERY, H., Cognitive Psychology
NILSSON, L.-G., Psychology
NORSTRÖM, T., Sociology, Social Politics
NYSTEDT, L., Psychology, Social Perception
OVARSELL, B., Education
PALME, J., Computer and Systems Sciences
PALME, M., Social Security
PERSSON, M., International Economics
PERSSON, T., International Economics
PREMFORS, R., Political Science
SAHLIN-ANDERSON, K., Public Organization
SARNECKI, J., Criminology
SIVEN, C.-H., Economics, especially Economic Politics
SKÖLDBERG, K., Business Administration
SPORRONG, U., Geography, especially Human Geography
SVEDBERG, P., Development Economics
SVENSON, O., Nuclear Power Safety (Psychology)
SVENSSON, L., International Economics
SWEDBERG, R., Economic Sociology
SÖDERBERG, J., Economic History
TARSCHYS, D., Political Science, especially Planning and Administration
THAM, H., Criminology
THORBURN, D., Statistics

THORSLUND, M., Social Work
TÅHLIN, M., Sociology
VÅGERÖ, D., Medical Sociology
WADENSJÖ, E., Employment Policy
WESTIN, C., Immigration Research
WIJKANDER, H., International Economics
WIKANDER, U., Economic History
WITTROCK, B., Political Science
ÖST, L.-G., Clinical Psychology

AFFILIATED INSTITUTES

Bergianska trädgården (Bergius Garden): Dir Prof. B. BREMER.

Centrum för naturresurs- och miljöforskning (Centre for Natural Resources and Environmental Research): Dir Prof. ANNMARI JANSSON.

Latinamerika-institutet (Institute of Latin American Studies): Dir WEINE KARLSSON; see under Research Institutes.

Manne Siegbahn-laboratoriet: Dir K.-G. RENSFELT.

Tolk- och översättarinstitutet (Institution for Interpretation and Translation Studies): Dir GUNNAR LEMHAGEN.

SVERIGES LANTBRUKSUNIVERSITET (Swedish University of Agricultural Sciences)

Box 7070, 750 07 Uppsala

Telephone: (18) 67-10-00
Fax: (18) 67-20-00
E-mail: registrator@slu.se
Internet: www.slu.se

Founded 1977 by amalgamation of the former *Lantbrukshögskolan, Skogshögskolan*, and *Veterinärhögskolan*
Academic year: September to May

Rector: Prof. A.-C. BYLUND
Pro-Rector: Prof. T. FAGERSTRÖM
Vice-Rector (External Contacts): CHRISTER HEINEGÅRD
Vice-Rector (Undergraduate Education): Dr K. ÖSTENSSON
Deputy Rector (Alnarp): Prof. R. VON BOTHMER
Deputy Rector (Skara): Dr S. JOHNSSON
Deputy Rector (Umeå) (vacant)
Head of Administration: K.-J. JOHANSSON
Director of Library (vacant)

Library: see Libraries and Archives
Number of teachers: 500
Number of students: 3,800

DEANS

Faculty of Agriculture, Landscape Planning and Horticulture: Dr B. FAGERBERG
Faculty of Forestry: Prof. J.-E. HÄLLGREN
Faculty of Veterinary Medicine: G. DALIN

PROFESSORS

(Some professors serve in more than one faculty)

Faculty of Agriculture, Landscape Planning and Horticulture:

ANDERSSON, G., Molecular Genetics
ANDERSSON, H., Agricultural Economics
ANDERSSON, I., Plant Biochemistry
ANDRÉN, O., Soil Biology and Agriculture
BENGTSSON, B., International Crop Production Science
BENGTSSON, J., Environmental Science and Conservation
BERGSTRÖM, L., Water Quality Management
BJÖRCK, L., Dairy Products Science
BJÖRNHAG, G., Animal Physiology
BOLIN, O., Economics of Agriculture, International Trade
BOTHMER, R. VON, Genetics and Breeding of Cultivated Plants
BRYNGELSSON, T., Molecular Plant Biology

BUCHT, E., Landscape Planning
BYLUND, A.-C., Meat Science
DANELL, B., Animal Breeding
DANELL, Ö., Reindeer Husbandry
EBBERSTEN, S., Organic Farming/Ecological Farming
EKBOM, B., Entomology
EKLUND, H., Structural Molecular Biology
EMMELIN, L., Environmental Impact Assessment
FLORGÅRD, C., Landscape Architecture
GEBRESENBET, G., Agricultural Engineering
GERHARDSON, B., Plant Pathology
GLIMELIUS, K., Genetics and Plant Breeding
GREN, J.-M., Natural Resource and Environmental Economics
GULLBERG, U., Plant Breeding
GUSTAFSON, A., Water Quality Management
GUSTAFSSON, L., Systems Analysis
GUSTAFSSON, M., Plant Disease Resistance
GUSTAFSSON, P., Landscape Architecture
GUSTAVSSON, R., Planting Design and Management
HANSSON, B. S., Plant Protection Sciences
HAVNEVIK, K., Rural Development
HUSS-DANELL, K., Crop Science
JANSSON, C., Molecular Cell Biology
JARVIS, N., Biogeophysics
JENSÉN, P., Horticultural Science
JILAR, T., Horticultural Building and Climate Technology
JÄGERSTAD, M., Food Chemistry
KENNE, L., Organic Chemistry
KIRCHMANN, H., Soil Fertility
KNIGHT, S., Biochemistry
LARSEN, R., Greenhouse Production, Horticultural Crops
LARSSON, L.-G., Molecular Genetics
LILJENSTRÖM, H., Biometry
LINDBERG, J.-E., Animal Nutrition and Management
LUNDQVIST, P., Work Science
LUNDSTRÖM, K., Meat Science
MEIJER, J., Molecular Cell Biology
MERKER, A., Plant Breeding
MOWBRAY, S., Biochemistry
MYRDAL, J., History of Agriculture
MÅRTENSSON, A., Soil Fertility
NILSSON, C., Building Science
NILSSON, I., Soil Chemistry and Pedology
NILSSON, J., Co-operation
NITSCH, U., Agricultural Communication
NORBERG, T., Inorganic Chemistry
NYBOM, H., Horticultural Genetics and Plant Breeding
NYBRANT, T., Agricultural Control Engineering
OLOFSSON, C., Entrepreneurial Studies
OLSSON, K., Animal Physiology
OLWIG, K. R., Landscape Planning
PERSSON, I., Inorganic and Physical Chemistry
PETTERSSON, J., Applied Entomology
RABINOWICZ, E., Economic Analysis of Food and Agricultural Systems
RIDDERSTRÅLE, Y., Animal Physiology
RONNE, H., Molecular Genetics
ROSSWALL, T., Water and Environmental Studies
SCHNÜRER, J., Food Microbiology
SKÄRBÄCK, E., Comprehensive Landscape Planning
SORTE, G., Landscape Architecture
STYMNE, S., Plant Breeding, Biochemistry
SÄLLVIK, K., Agricultural Building Functions Analysis
TORSTENSSON, L., Soil Microbiology
UVNÄS-MOBERG, K., Animal Physiology
VALKONEN, J., Virology comprising Plant Viruses
VON ROSEN, D., Statistics
WELANDER, M., Horticultural Science

WIKTORSSON, H., Animal Nutrition and Management
YUEN, J., Plant Pathology
ÅMAN, P., Plant Products
ÖBERG, K., Ergonomics
ÖHLMER, B., Agricultural Business Administration

Faculty of Forestry:

ANDRÉN, H., Conservation Biology
ARNOLD, S. VON, Forest Cell Biology
BERGSTEN, U., Reforestation
BISHOP, K., Environmental Assessment
BORGEFORS, G., Remote Sensing and Image Analysis
CLARHOLM, M., Soil Ecology
DANELL, K., Wildlife Ecology
DANIEL, G., Wood Products
ELFVING, B., Forest Yield Research
ELOWSON, T., Wood Technology
ERICSSON, A., Forest Plant Physiology
ERIKSSON, L.-O., Aquaculture
ERIKSSON, L. O., Forest Planning
FINLAY, R., Forest Microbiology
GEMMEL, P., Forestry
GOBRAN, G., Ecology, Soil Science
GUSTAVSSON, L., Conservation Biology
HANSSON, L., Population Ecology
HÅNELL, B., Silviculture
HÄLLGREN, J.-E., Forest Plant Physiology
HÖGBERG, P., Soil Science
JEGLUM, J., Forest Peatland Science
JOHANSSON, M.-B., Forest Soil Science
JOHANSSON, T., Forest Management
JOHNSSON, R., Aquatic Ecology
KRISTRÖM, B., Natural Resources Economics
LARSSON, S., Forest Entomology
LINDER, S., Forest Ecology
LINDGREN, D., Forest Genetics
LOHMANDER, P., Forest Management
LUNDKVIST, H., Soil Ecology
LUNDQVIST, H., Fish Biology
LÅNGSTROM, B., Forest Protection from Insects
LÖNNSTEDT, L., Business Economics
MAGNHAGEN, C., Aquaculture
MORITZ, T., Forest Plant Physiology
NILSSON, M.-C., Forest Vegetation Ecology
NILSSON, P.-O., Energy System in Forestry
NILSSON, T., Ultrastructure and Disintegration of Wood
NILSSON, U., Reforestation
NYLINDER, M., Wood Measurement and Cross-Cutting
NYLUND, J.-E., Forest Microbiology
NÄSHOLM, T., Forest Plant Physiology
ODÉN, P. C., Forestry Seed Research
OLSSON, H., Remote Sensing applied to Forestry
OLSSON, M., Forest Soil Chemistry
PERSSON, H., Root Ecology
PERSSON, T., Biology of Forest Soils
RANNEBY, B., Forest Survey
ROSEN, K., Forest Soils
SALLNÄS, O., Forest Operations
SANDBERG, G., Morphogenesis of Trees
STENLID, J., Pathology of Forest Trees
STÅHL, G., Forest Survey
SUNDBERG, B., Forest Plant Physiology
VERWIJST, T., Forestry
WIBE, S., Forest Economics
WINGSLE, G., Forest Plant Physiology
WÄSTERLUND, I., Forestry Technology
ZACKRISSON, O., Forest Vegetation Ecology
ÅGREN, G., Systems Ecology

Faculty of Veterinary Medicine (tel. (18) 67-35-70):

ALENIUS, S., Medicine for Ruminants
ALGERS, B., Animal Hygiene
ALM, G., Immunology
ANDERSSON, L., Genetics
BELAK, S., Virology
BJÖRK, I., Medical and Physiological Chemistry
DANIELSSON-THAM, M.-L., Food Hygiene

DREVEMO, S., Anatomy and Histology
EINARSSON, S., Obstetrics and Gynaecology
ENGSTRÖM, W., Pathology
ERIKSSON, S., Medical and Physiological Chemistry
FELLSTRÖM, C., Swine Diseases
FORSBERG, M., Veterinary Diagnostic Endocrinology
GUSTAVSSON, I., Genetics
HEDHAMMER, H., Small Animal Medicine
JENSEN, P., Ethology
JENSEN-WAERN, M., Comparative Medicine
JONES, B., Clinical Chemistry
JÖNSSON, L., Pathology
KINDAHL, H., Obstetrics and Gynaecology
KVART, C., Clinical Physiology
LINDE-FORSBERG, C., Small Animal Reproduction
LINNÉ, T., Virology
LORD, P., Clinical Radiology
LUTHMAN, J., Medicine for Ruminants
MORENO-LOPEZ, J., Virology
NORRGREN, L., Aquatic Ecotoxicology
OSKARSSON, A., Food Hygiene
PLÖEN, L., Anatomy and Histology
PRINGLE, J., Equine Medicine
RODRÍGUEZ-MARTÍNEZ, H., Reproduction Biotechnology
SVENSSON, C., Production Diseases of Farm Animals
SVENSSON, S., Bacteriology
TJÄLVE, H., Toxicology
UGGLA, A., Parasitology

UMEÅ UNIVERSITET

901 87 Umeå
Telephone: (90) 786-50-00
Fax: (90) 786-99-95
E-mail: umea.universitet@umu.se
Internet: www.umu.se

Founded 1965
State control
Academic year: September to May
Vice-Chancellor: Prof. INGE-BERT TÄLJEDAL
Pro-Vice-Chancellor: Prof. ULF EDLUND
Vice-Rectors: ULF EDLUND, LISBETH LUNDAHL
University Director: JAN-ERIK OGREN
Head of the Information Office (vacant)
Library: see Libraries and Archives
Number of teachers: 1,600
Number of students: 28,000

DEANS

Faculty of Humanities: (vacant)
Faculty of Medicine: (vacant)
Faculty of Science and Technology: STAFFAN UVELL
Faculty of Social Sciences: Prof. ULF WIBERG
Faculty of Teacher Education and Research: (vacant)

PROFESSORS

Faculty of Humanities (fax (90) 786-97-96; e-mail humfak@adm.umu.se; internet www.umu.se/humfak):

ANDERSSON, G., Science of Science
BANNERT, R., Phonetics
BRÄNDSTRÖM, A., Historical Demography
EDLUND, L.-E., Scandinavian Languages
EDMAN, M., Philosophy and Science of Humanities
EHN, B., Ethnology
ERICSSON, T., History
FORSGREN, K.-Å., German Language
GENRUP, K., Ethnology
GRANQVIST, R., English Language
GROUNDSTROEM, A., Finnish Language
HATJE, A.-K., History
HENE, B., Swedish Language
JOHANSSON, I., Theoretical Philosophy
JONSSON, K., History of Science and Ideas
LARSSON, T., Archaeology
LILIEQUIST, M., Ethnology

LINDBLAD, I.-B., Media and Communications
LINDSTRÖM, S., Theoretical Philosophy
LUNDGREN, B., Ethnology
PETTERSSON, A., Comparative Literature
POUSSA, P., English Language
RAMQVIST, P., Archaeology
RINGBY, P., Comparative Literature
SJÖBERG TAUSSI, M., History in a Social Historic Perspective
SKÖLD, P., History, Lapp Culture
SMEDS, K., Museology
SPOLANDER, R., History of Art
STRAARUP, J., Religious Studies
STRANGERT, E., Phonetics
SUNDIN, B., History of Science and Ideas
SVONNI, M., Lapp Language and Culture
SÖRLIN, S., Environmental History
WERBART, B., Archaeology
WIKSTRÖM, E., Fine Arts

Faculty of Medicine (fax (90) 786-76-60; internet www.umu.se/medfak):

ADOLFSSON, R., Psychiatry
ALFREDSSON, H., Sports Medicine
ALSTERMARK, B., Physiology, especially Neurology
ASIKAINEN, S., Oral Microbiology
BERGENHEIM, T., Neurosurgery
BERGH, A., Pathology
BERGSTRÖM, S., Microbiology
BERNSPÅNG, B., Occupational Therapy
BJÖRNSTIG, U., Surgery, especially Trauma and Civil Defence Medicine
BOMAN, K., Medicine
BORÉN, T., Medical Chemistry
BROSTRÖM, L.-A., Orthopaedics
BUCHT, G., Geriatrics
BÄCKSTRÖM, T., Obstetrics and Gynaecology
DAHLQUIST, G., Paediatrics, especially Diabetes
DAHLQVIST, S., Rheumatology
DANIELSSON, Å., Gastroenterology
DIJKEN, J. VAN, Cariology
DOORN, J. VAN, Logopedics
EDLUND, H., Molecular Development Biology
EDLUND, T., Molecular Genetics
EGELRUD, T., Dermatology and Venereology
EMDIN, S., Surgery
ERIKSSON, A., Forensic Medicine
ERIKSSON, J., Medicine
ERIKSSON, P.-O., Clinical Oral Physiology
FÄLLMAN, M., Medical Microbiology
FISHER, A., Occupational Therapy
FORSGREN, L., Neurology
FOWLER, C., Pharmacology
GOTHEFORS, L., Paediatrics
GRANKVIST, K., Clinical Chemistry, especially Experimental Toxicology
GROTH, S., Clinical Physiology
GRUNDSTRÖM, T., Tumour Biology
GRÖNBERG, H., Oncology
GUNNE, J., Prosthetic Dentistry
GUSTAFSON, Y., Geriatric Medicine
HALLMANS, G., Nutrition Research
HAMMARSTRÖM, A., Public Health (Gender Perspective)
HAMMARSTRÖM, M.-L., Immunology
HAMMARSTRÖM, S., Immunology
HENRIKSSON, R., Experimental Oncology
HERNELL, O., Paediatrics, especially Nutrition Research
HOLMBERG, D., Molecular Genetics
HULTMARK, D., Medical Molecular Biology
HÄGGLÖF, B., Child and Youth Psychiatry
HÖGBERG, U., Obstetrics and Gynaecology
JACOBSSON, L., Psychiatry
JANLERT, U., Public Health
JOHANSSON, I., Cariology
JOHANSSON, R., Physiology
JOHANSSON, S., Physiology
JÄRVHOLM, B., Occupational and Environmental Medicine

KARLSSON, M., Medical Radiation Physics
KELLERTH, J.-O., Anatomy
KULLGREN, G., Psychiatric Epidemiology
LALOS, A., Public Health (Gender Perspective)
LARSÉN, K., Sports Medicine
LERNER, U., Oral Cell Biology
LIBELIUS, R., Clinical Neurophysiology
LINDHOLM, L., Family Medicine
LINDSTRÖM, P., Histology and Cell Biology
LJUNGBERG, B., Urology
LORENTZON, R., Sports Medicine
LUNDGREN, E., Applied Cell Biology
LUNDGREN, S., Oral and Maxillofacial Surgery
LUNDMAN, B., Nursing
MARKLUND, S., Clinical Chemistry
MOLIN, M., Prosthetic Dentistry
NAREDI, P., Surgery
NILSSON, E., Surgery
NORBERG, A., Advanced Nursing
NORDBERG, G., Health and Hygiene
NORGREN, M., Biomedical Laboratory Sciences
NY, T., Medical and Physiological Chemistry
OLIVECRONA, G., Medical Chemistry
OLOFSSON, B.-O., Medicine
OLSSON, K., Physiology
OLSSON, T., Medicine
ROOS, G., Pathology
SANDMAN, P.-O., Advanced Nursing
SANDSTRÖM, T., Pulmonary Medicine
SCHLEUCHER, J., Medical Biophysics
SEHLIN, J., Histology and Cell Biology
SELSTAM, G., Physiology
SJÖLUND, B. H., Rehabilitation Medicine
SJÖSTEDT, A., Clinical Bacteriology
STENLING, R., Pathology
STIGBRAND, T., Immunochemistry
STRÖMBERG, I., Histology and Cell Biology
STRÖMBERG, N., Cardiology
SUNDELIN, G., Advanced Nursing
SUNDVIST, K. G., Clinical Immunology
SVENSSON, O., Orthopaedics
THELANDER, L., Medical and Physiological Chemistry
THORNELL, L.-E., Anatomy
TWETMAN, S., Paedodontics
TÄLJEDAL, I.-B., Histology
TÄRNVIK, A., Infectious Diseases
UHLIN, B. E., Medical Microbiology
WACHTMEISTER, L., Ophthalmology
WADELL, G., Virology
WALDENSTRÖM, A., Cardiology
WALL, S., Epidemiology and Public Health
WESTER, P., Medicine
WESTMAN, K., Family Medicine
WIBERG, M., Anatomy
WIDMARK, A., Oncology
WINKVIST, A., Epidemiology
AHLSTRÖM, K., X-Ray and Diagnostics

Faculty of Science and Technology (fax (90) 786-97-96; e-mail teknat@adm.umu.se; internet www.teknat.umu.se):

ANDERSSON, B., Environmental Chemistry
AVONDOGLIO, P., Industrial Design
AXNER, O., Physics
BJÖRK, G., Microbiology
BONDESSON, L., Mathematical Statistics
BYSTRÖM, A., Microbiology
BÅMSTEDT, U., Marine Sciences
BRODIN, G., Physics
CEDERGREN, A., Analytical Chemistry
CEGRELL, U., Mathematics (Complete Analysis)
EDLUND, U., Organic Chemistry
EKLUND, P., Computer Science
ERICSON, L., Plant Ecology
ERIKSSON, E. S., Structural Biology
FRECH, W., Analytical Chemistry
GARDESTRÖM, P., Plant Physiology
GILLBRO, T., Biophysical Chemistry
GUSTAFSSON, P., Plant Molecular Biology

HEBY, O., Cellular and Developmental Biology
HÄGGKVIST, R., Discrete Mathematics
IRGUM, K., Analytical Chemistry
JANLERT, L.-E., Computing Science
JANSSON, M., Physical Geography
JANSSON, S., Plant Biology
JOHANSSON, L., Physical Chemistry
JOHNELS, D., Organic Chemistry
KASTBERG, A., Experimental Optical Physics
KIHLBERG, J., Organic Chemistry
KIRKWOOD, S., Atmospheric Physics
KLECZKOWSKI, L., Plant Physiology
KULLMAN, L., Physical Geography
KÅGSTRÖM, B., Numerical Analysis and Parallel Computing
LARSON, M., Applied Mathematics
LARSSON, J., Plasma Physics
LESTANDER, Å., Genetics
LI, H., Signal Processing
LINDAHL, O., Medical Technology
LINDBLOM, G., Physical Chemistry
LUNDIN, R., Space Physics
MALMQVIST, B., Ecology
MARKLUND, S., Environmental Chemistry
MINNHAGEN, P., Theoretical Physics
NILSSON, C., Landscape Ecology, especially Running Waters
NORDIN, A., Energy Technology
OKSANEN, L., Ecology
OLIVEBERG, M., Biochemistry
OTTO, CH., Animal Ecology
PALMGREN, B., Design
PERSSON, L., Aquatic Ecology
PERSSON, P., Chemistry, Molecular Chemistry
PETTERSSON, L., Inorganic Chemistry
RAMMER, J., Condensed Matter Theory
RENBERG, I., Ecological and Environmental Impact Assessment
RÖNNMARK, K., Theoretical Space Physics
SAMUELSSON, G., Plant Physiology
SANDAHL, I., Space Physics
SAURA, A., Genetics
SCHRÖDER, W., Biochemistry
SELLSTEDT, A., Plant Physiology
SHELANKOV, A., Condensed Matter Physics
SHINGLER, V., Microbiology
SHIRIAEV, A., Automatic Control Engineering
SJÖBERG, S., Inorganic Chemistry
SJÖSTRÖM, M., Inorganic Chemistry
STENFLO, L., Theoretical Plasma Physics
STOTT, M., Interaction Design
SUNDQVIST, B., Condensed Matter Physics
TYSKLIND, M., Environmental Chemistry
WEDIN, P.-Å., Numerical Analysis
WESTLUND, P.-O., Theoretical Chemistry
WOLD, S., Chemometrics
WOLF-WATZ, H., Applied Molecular Biology
ÖHMAN, L.-O., Inorganic Chemistry
ÖQUIST, G., Plant Physiology

Faculty of Social Sciences (fax (90) 786-66-75; internet www.umu.se/samfak):

ARMELIUS, B.-Å., Clinical Psychology
ARMELIUS, K., Clinical Psychology
ARONSSON, T., Environmental and Natural Resources Economics
BACKMAN, J., Pedagogics and Educational Psychology
BENGTSSON, M., Business Administration and Economics
BOTER, H., Business Administration and Economics
BROSTRÖM, G., Statistics
BRÄNNLUND, R., Economics
BRÄNNÄS, K., Econometrics
DAHLGREN, L., Medical Sociology
ECKERBERG, K., Political Science
EDSTRÖM, Ö., Legal Science
FRANKE, S., Pedagogics
GUNNARSSON, Å, Legal Science
GUSTAFSSON, G., Political Science
HALLERÖD, B., Sociology

HALLSTRÖM, P., Legal Science
HAMILTON, D., Pedagogics
HENRIKSSON, W., Pedagogics
HOLM, E., Social and Economic Geography, especially Social Community Planning and Financial Control
JOHANSSON, G., Nutritional Studies
JOHANSSON, M., Pedagogics (Sports)
JOHANSSON, O., Political Science
JOHANSSON, S., Social Work
JOHANSSON, U., Pedagogics
KAPTELININ, V., Informatics
LINDQVIST, R., Social Work
LÖFGREN, K.-G., Economics, especially Evaluating Labour Market Research
MALMBERG, G., Social and Economic Geography
MOLANDER, B., Psychology
MÄNTYLÄ, T., Psychology (Cognitive Science)
NIEMI-KIESILÄINEN, J., Legal Science
NILSSON, I., Pedagogics
NYBERG, L., Psychology
NYGREN, L., Social Work
PERSSON, O., Library and Information Science
RÄTHZEL, N., Sociology
SÖDERHOLM, A., Informatics
SKÖG, L. A., Busin
STAGE, C., Pedagogics
STOLTERMAN, E., Informatics
SUNDBOM, E., Clinical Psychology
SVALLFORS, S., Sociology
TESAR, G., Business Administration and Economics (Marketing and International Business Administration)
WATERWORTH, J., Informatics
WIBERG, U., Economic Geography, especially the Structural Issues of Sparsely Populated Areas
ÅBERG, R., Sociology

Faculty of Teacher Education and Research (fax (90) 786-77-95; internet www.educ.umu.se):

LINDMARK, D., History (Teacher Education and Teaching Profession)
LUNDAHL, L., Mathematics (Teacher Education and Teaching Profession)
LUNDAHL, L.
WEINER, G., Teacher Education and Teaching Profession (from a Gender Perspective)

UPPSALA UNIVERSITET

POB 256, 751 05 Uppsala
Telephone: (18) 471-00-00
Fax: (18) 471-20-00
E-mail: info@uadm.uu.se
Internet: www.uu.se

Founded 1477
Academic year: September to June

Rector: Prof. B. SUNDQVIST
Vice-Rector: Prof. L. MARCUSSON
Head of Administration: M. O. OTTOSSON
Chief Librarian: U. GÖRANSSON

Library: see Libraries and Archives
Number of teachers: 3,000
Number of students: 36,000 (incl. 2,500 postgraduates)
Publications: *Acta Universitatis Upsaliensis*, *Multiethnica*, *Universen* (monthly), *Uppsala Accelerator News*, *Uppsala Newsletter in History of Science*

DEANS

Faculty of Law: Prof. Å. SALDEEN
Faculty of Medicine: Prof. B. WESTERMARK
Faculty of Pharmacy: Prof. L. DENCKER
Faculty of Science and Technology: Prof. J.-O. CARLSSON
Faculty of Social Science: Prof. O. LUNDÉN
Faculty of Theology: Prof. S.-E. BRODD

Historical-Philosophical Division: Prof. M. FAHLGREN

Linguistic Division: Prof. R. LUNDÉN

PROFESSORS

Faculty of Arts

I. Historical-Philosophical Division:

ALANEN, L., History of Philosophy
ARVASTSON, G., Ethnology
BEACH, H., Cultural Anthropology
BURMAN, L., Rhetoric
DANIELSSON, S. O., Practical Philosophy
FAHLGREN, M., Literature
FRÄNGSMYR, T., History of Science
HERSCHEND, F., Archaeology
IVARSDOTTER, A., Musicology
JANSSON, T., History
JOHANNISSON, K. M., History of Science and Ideas
KJELLBERG, E., Musicology
KYHLBERG, O., Archaeology
LANDGREN, B., Literature
LINDEGREN, J., History
PARKMAN, S., Musicology
PETTERSSON, T., Literature
RUNBLOM, H., History
SANTILLO FRIZELL, B., Archaeology
SINCLAIR, P., African Archaeology
SKUNCKE, M.-C., Literature
SVEDJEDAL, J. O., Literature
SÖDERLIND, S., Art History
TROY, L., Archaeology
ÅHLBERG, L.-O., Aesthetics and Cultural Studies

II. Linguistic Division:

EKLUND, S. I., Latin
FRYCKSTEDT, M., English Literature
GREN-EKLUND, G., Indology
GUSTAVSSON, S. R., Slavic Languages
HELANDER, H. O., Latin
ISAKSSON, B., Semitic Languages
JONASSON, K., French Language
KINDSTRAND, J. F., Greek Language and Literature
KROHN, D., German Language
KRONNING, H., French Language
KYTÖ, M., English Language
LARSSON, L.-G., Finno-Ugrian Languages
LUNDÉN, R., American Literature
MAIER, I., Russian Language
MELANDER, B., Swedish Language
MULLER, G., German Language and Literature
NORDBERG, B., Sociolinguistics
PACKALEN, A. M., Polish Language
PALM MEISTER, C., German Language
PEDERSEN, O., Assyriology
PETERSON, L., Scandinavian Languages
RAAG, R., Finno-Ugric Languages
ROSENQVIST, J.-O., Byzantine Studies
STRANDBERG, S., Scandinavian Onomastics
SUNDELL, L.-G., French Language
SVANE, B., French Literature
SÅGVALL-HEIN, A., Computational Linguistics
THELANDER, M., Swedish Language
UTAS, B., Iranian Studies
VIBERG, A, Linguistics
WILLIAMS, H., Swedish Language
WOLLIN, L., Scandinavian Languages

Faculty of Law:

ANDERSSON, H., Private Law
ANDERSSON, T., Private Law
CAMERON, I., International Law
ERIKSSON, M., International Law
FRÄNDBERG, A., History of Law
JAREBORG, N., Penal Law
JÄNTERÄ-JAREBORG, M., International Law
LEHRBERG, B., Penal Law
LINDBLOM, P. H., Judicial Procedure
LINDELL, B., Judicial Procedure
LYSEN, G., International Law
MARCUSSON, L. M., Administrative Law
MATTSSON, N. G., Taxation

MÖLLER, M., Private Law
NYGREN, R. O., History of Law
SALDEEN, A., Private Law
THORELL, P. H., Business Law
WESTERLUND, S., Environmental Law
ÖSTERDAHL, I., International Law

Faculty of Medicine:

AKUSJÄRVI, G., Microbiology
ALDSKOGIUS, H., Medical Structural Biology
ALM, A., Ophthalmology
ANDERSSON, A. E. V., Diabetes Research
ANDERSSON, J. H., Immunology
ANNIKO, M., Otorhinolaryngology
AQUILONIUS, S.-M., Neurology
ARNETZ, B., Social Medicine
AXELSSON, O. L., Women's and Children's Health
BERGQVIST, D., Vascular Surgery
BERNE, CH., Medicine
BLOMBERG, J., Clinical Virology
BOBERG, M., Social Medicine
BOMAN, G., Pulmonary Medicine
CARLSSON, J., Biomedical Radiation Science
CLAESSON-WELSH, L., Genetics and Pathology
DAHL, M.-L., Medicine
DAHL, N., Clinical Genetics
DUMANSKI, J., Genetics and Pathology
EBENDAL, T., Developmental Biology
EDLING, C., Occupational Medicine
ERIKSSON, U., Histology
FLEMSTRÖM, G. F., Physiology
FRIES, E., Cell Biology
FRIMAN, G., Infectious Diseases
GEBRE-MEDHIN, M., International Child Care
GERDIN, B., Intensive and Burns Care
GLIMELIUS, B., Oncology
GUSTAFSSON, J., Women's and Children's Health
GYLFE, E., Secretion Research
GYLLENSTEN, U., Medical Molecular Genetics
HAGLUND, U., Surgery
HÄLLGREN, R., Medicine
HAU, J., Comparative Medicine
HEDENSTIERNA, G., Medicine
HEYMAN, B., Genetics and Pathology
HILLERED, L., Clinical Neurochemistry
HOLMBERG, L., Surgery
JOHANSSON, S., Cell Biology
KARLSSON, A., Experimental Endocrinology
KJELLEN, L., Medical Biochemistry and Microbiology
KÄMPE, O., Molecular Medicine
LANDEGREN, U., Molecular Medicine
LARHAMMAR, D. S., Molecular Cell Biology
LARSSON, R., Medicine
LINDAHL, U., Medical Chemistry
LINDGREN, P. G., X-ray Diagnosis
LINDHOLM, D., Neurobiology
LINDMARK, G., International Mother and Child Health
LITHELL, H., Geriatrics
LJUNGHALL, S., Medicine
LUNDQVIST, H., Oncology
LÖNNERHOLM, G., Women's and Children's Health
MAGNUSSON, A., Oncology
MAGNUSSON, G., Molecular Virology
MÅRDH, P.-A., Medicine
NILSSON, K., Cell Pathology
NILSSON, O., Orthopaedics
NISTÉR, M., Experimental Pathology
NORLÉN, B. J., Urology
ORELAND, L. A. M., Pharmacology
PERSSON, E., Physiology
PERSSON, L., Physiology
PETTERSSON, U. G., Medical Genetics
PÅHLMAN, L., Surgery
RAININKO, R., Neuroradiology
RASK, L., Medical Biochemistry
RASK-ANDERSEN, H., Surgery

RASTAD, J., Surgery
RAUSCHNING, W., Surgery
ROOMANS, G. M., Medical Ultrastructure
ROSENQVIST, U., Health Services Research
RUBIN, K., Connective Tissue Biochemistry
SALDEEN, T., Forensic Medicine
SANDLER, S., Medical Cell Biology
SCHWARTZ, S., Medical Biochemistry and Microbiology
SEDIN, G., Perinatal Medicine
SIEGBAHN, A., Medicine
SJÖDÉN, P.-O., Nursing and Health Care
SJÖQVIST, M. I. J., Physiology
STJERNSCHANTZ, J., Pharmacology
SVÄRDSUDD, K., Family Medicine
SYVÄNEN, A.-C., Medicine
TOREBJÖRK, E., Pain Research
TURESSON, I., Oncology
TUVEMO, T., Paediatrics
TÖTTERMAN, T., Clinical Immunology
ULMSTEN, U., Obstetrics and Gynaecology
VAHLQUIST, A., Dermatology and Venereology
VENGE, P., Clinical Chemistry
VON KNORRING, A.-L., Child Psychiatry
VON KNORRING, L., Psychiatry
WADELIUS, C., Genetics and Pathology
WALLENTIN, L., Cardiology
WESTERMARK, B. A., Tumour Biology
WESTERMARK, P., Pathology
WESTMAN, J. O., Anatomy
WIESEL, F.-A., Psychiatry
WIKLUND, L., Anaesthesiology
ÅKERMAN, K., Cell Physiology
ÅKERSTRÖM, G., Endocrinological Surgery
ÖBERG, K., Oncological Endocrinology

Faculty of Pharmacy:

ALDERBORN, G., Pharmacy
ARTURSSON, P., Pharmacy
BOHLIN, L., Pharmacognosy
BRITTEBO, E. B., Toxicology
DENCKER, L., Toxicology
ENGSTRÖM, S. O. A., Pharmacy
HALLBERG, A., Organic Pharmaceutical Chemistry
HAMMARLUND-UDENAES, M., Pharmacokinetics
ISACSON, D., Pharmacy
KARLSSON, M., Pharmacokinetics
LANG, M., Biochemistry
LENNERNÄS, H., Pharmacy
NYBERG, F., Pharmacological and Biological Research on Drug Dependence
NYSTRÖM, L.-CHR., Pharmacy
OLIW, E., Pharmacological and Biological Research on Drug Dependence
PETTERSSON, C., Analytical Pharmaceutical Chemistry
WESTERLUND, D., Analytical Pharmaceutical Chemistry
WIKBERG, J., Pharmacological and Biological Research on Drug Dependence
WIKVALL, K., Biochemistry

Faculty of Science and Technology:

AHLÉN, A., Signal Processing
ALEKLETT, K., Nuclear Physics
ALEXEEV, A., Theoretical Physics
ALMGREN, M., Biochemistry
ANDERSSON, A., Computer Science
ANDERSSON, P., Organic Chemistry
ANDERSSON, S., Evolutionary Biology
ANNERSTEN, H. S., Mineral Chemistry and Petrology
ARNESEN, A., Physics
BADELEK, B., Experimental Physics
BENGTSSON, E., Computerized Image Analysis
BENNETT, K. D., Quaternary Geology
BERG, O., Molecular Evolution
BERG, S., Solid State Electronics
BERGER, R., Inorganic Chemistry
BERGLUND, A., Animal Ecology
BERGSTRÖM, Y., Materials Science
BJÖRKLUND, M., Animal Ecology
BOHMAN, O., Organic Chemistry

BOTNER, O., High Energy Physics
BRANDT, I., Ecotoxicology
BRANDT ANDERSSON, Y., Inorganic Chemistry
BREMER, B., Systematic Botany
BREMER, K., Systematic Botany
BRUNSTRÖM, B. O., Ecotoxicology
BRÄNDAS, E., Quantum Chemistry
CARLSSON, B., Systems and Control
CARLSSON, J.-O., Inorganic Chemistry
CHATTOPADHYAYA, J., Bio-organic Chemistry
COORAY, V., Electricity and Lightning
DAHLGREN CALDWELL, K., Surface Biotechnology
DANIELSSON, U., Theoretical Physics
EDWARDS, K., Physical Chemistry
EHRENBERG, M., Molecular Biology with Kinetics
EKELÖF, T., Experimental Elementary Particle Physics
EKMAN, J., Population Biology
ELLEGREN, H., Evolutionary Biology
ENGMAN, L., Organic Chemistry
ENGSTRÖM, P., Physiological Botany
ERICSSON, T., Materials Physics
ERIKSSON, O., Condensed Matter Physics
FROELICH, P., Quantum Chemistry
FÄLDT, G. L., Theoretical Physics
GEE, D. G., Orogenic Dynamics
GELIUS, U., Physics
GESTBLOM, B., Physics
GOSCINSKI, O., Quantum Chemistry
GRANQVIST, C.-G., Solid State Physics
GUNNINGBERG, P., Computer Communication
GUSTAFSSON, B., Numerical Analysis
GUSTAFSSON, B., Theoretical Astrophysics
GUSTAFSSON, L., Animal Ecology
GUT, A., Mathematical Statistics
HAGERSTEN, E., Computer Architecture
HAJDU, J., Biochemistry
HALLDIN, S., Hydrology
HALLGREN, A., Experimental Physics
HEJHAL, D. A., Mathematics
HELLMAN, L., Molecular and Comparative Immunology
HERMANSSON, K. G., Inorganic Chemistry
HILBORN, J., Polymer Chemistry
HOGMARK, S., Materials Science
HOLMER, L., Historical Geology and Palaeontology
HUGHES, D., Evolutionary Biology
HÅKANSSON, L., Sedimentology
HÅKANSSON, P., Ion Physics
HÖGLUND, J., Population Biology
HÖISTAD, B., Nuclear Physics
INGELMANN, G., High Energy Physics
ISRAELSSON, S. O., Meteorology
JACOBSON, S., Materials Science
JANSON, S., Mathematics
JANSSON, U., Inorganic Chemistry
JOHANSSON, B., Condensed Matter Theory
JOHANSSON, S., Materials Science
JOHANSSON, T., Nuclear Physics
JONES, A., Structural Molecular Biology
JONSSON, B., Computer Systems
JUHL-JÖRICKE, B., Mathematics
KAISER, S. G., Mathematics
KARLSSON, L., Experimental Physics
KIRSEBOM, L., Evolutionary Biology
KISELMAN, C. O., Mathematics
KOLSTRUP, E., Physical Geography
KÄLLNE, J., Neutron Physics
LANSHAMMER, H., Systems and Control
LEIJON, M., Electricity
LIBERMAN, M., Theoretical Statistical Physics
LILJAS, L., Evolutionary Biology
LINDBLAD, P., Evolutionary Biology
LINDER, C., Physical Didactics
LINDGREN, J. B. R., Inorganic Chemistry
LUNDAHL, P., Biochemistry
LUNDBERG, A., Evolutionary Biology
LUNDBERG, B., Solid Mechanics

LUNELL, S. G., Applied Quantum Chemistry
LÅNGSTROM, B., Radiopharmaceutical Organic Chemistry
LÖTSTEDT, P., Numerical Analysis
MANNERVIK, B., Biochemistry
MARKIDES, K., Analytical Chemistry
MATTSSON, O. L., Organic Chemistry
McGREEVY, R. L., Neutron Research
MILBRINK, G., Animal Ecology
MOLLER, F., Computing Science
MÅRTENSSON, N., Physics of Metals and Metal Surfaces
NIEMI, A., Theoretical Physics
NIKLASSON, G., Materials Science and Solar Energy
NILSSON, A., Chemical Physics
NILSSON, A., Systematic Botany
NORDBLAD, P., Solid State Physics
NORDGREN, J., Soft X-ray Physics
NYHOLM, L., Analytical Chemistry
OHLSSON, R., Developmental Zoology
OLSSON, E., Experimental Physics
PAMILO, P., Conservation Biology
PAROSH, A., Computer Systems
PAVLENKO, V. P., Astronomy
PEDERSEN, L. B., Solid Earth Physics
PEEL, J. S., Historical Geology and Palaeontology
PETTERSSON, K. I., Evolutionary Biology
PILSTRÖM, L. H., Immunology
PISKOUNOV, N., Astronomy
POSSNERT, G., Accelerator Mass Spectrometry
RIBBING, C.-G., Solid State Physics
RICKMAN, H., Astronomy
ROBERTS, R., Solid Earth Physics
RODHE, A., Hydrology
RONQUIST, F., Systematic Zoology
ROOS, A., Solid State Physics
RYDIN, H., Plant Ecology
SAXENA, S., Theoretical Geochemistry
SCHWEITZ, J.-A., Materials Science
SIEGBAHN, H., Atomic and Molecular Physics
SJÖBERG, S., Organic Chemistry
SKÖLD, K., Neutron Research
SMEDMAN, A.-S., Meteorology
STERNAD, M., Signals and Systems
STOICA, P., Systems Modelling
STOLTENBERG-HANSEN, V., Logic of Mathematics
STRÖMQUIST, L., Applied Environmental Impact Analysis
SUNDQVIST, B. U. R., Ion Physics
SVEDLINDH, P., Solid State Physics
SVENSSON, B. W., Animal Ecology
SVENSSON, S., Physics
SÖDERHÄLL, K. T., Physiological Mycology
SÖDERSTRÖM, T., Automatic Control
TALBOT, C. J., Geodynamics and Tectonics
TAPIA-OLIVARES, O., Physical Chemistry
TEGELSTRÖM, H., Conservation Biology and Genetics
TEGENFELT, J. S., Inorganic Chemistry
THOMAS, J. O., Solid State Electro-chemistry
THOTTAPPILLIL, R., Electricity
THULIN, M., Systematic Botany
THUNE, M., Scientific Computing
TIBELL, L. B., Systematic Botany
TINTAREV, K., Mathematics
TOTTMAR, O., Comparative Physiology
TRANVIK, L., Limnology
TÄRNLUND, S. A., Computer Science
VIRO, O., Mathematics
VIRTANEN, A., Molecular Cell Biology
WAGNER, G., Microbiology
WAHLBERG, C., Astronomy
WANG, Y., Computer Systems
WÄPPLING, R., Physics
ZILITINKEVICH, S., Meteorology
ÅGREN, J., Ecological Botany
ÅQVIST, J., Evolutionary Biology

Faculty of Social Sciences:
AGELL, J., Economics
ANDERSSON, R. K. G., Housing and Urban Research
BLOMQUIST, S., Local Public Economics
BOHLIN, G., Developmental Psychology
BORGEGÅRD, L.-E., Urban Geography
BROADY, D., Education
BURNS, T., Sociology
BÄCK, L., Urban Geography
BÄCKMAN, L., Cognitive Psychology
BÖRJESSON, E. A., Psychology
CARLSNAES, W., Political Science
CHRISTOFFERSSON, A. L., Statistics
DIMBERG, U., Psychology
EDIN, P.-A., Labour Market Relations
EKEHAMMAR, B., Psychology
ENGWALL, L., Business Studies
EYERMAN, R., Sociology
FOGELKLOU, A., East European Studies
FORSGREN, M. O., International Business Studies
FREDRIKSON, M., Clinical Psychology
GERNER, K., East European Studies
GOTTFRIES, N., Economics
GUSTAFSSON, C., Education
HADENIUS, A., Political Science
HAGEKULL, B., Developmental Psychology
HALLEN, L., Business Studies
HAMFELT, A., Computer Science
HAMMARSTRÖM, G., Sociology
HANSSON, A., Computer Science
HEDLUND, S., East European Studies
HEDMAN, L., Media and Communication
HERMANSSON, B. J., Political Science
HOLMLUND, B., Economics
HOPPE, G., Economic Geography
HÅKANSSON, K. G., Sociology
ISACSON, M., Economic History
KEMENY, P. J., Urban Sociology
KLEVMARKEN, A., Econometrics
LEWIN, L., Political Science
LINDBLAD, S., Education
LINDH, T., Economics
LUNDGREN, E., Sociology
LUNDGREN, U. P., Education
MAGNUSSON, L., Economic History
MALMBERG, A., Economic Geography
MELIN, L. G., Clinical Psychology
OHLSSON, H., Economics
PETERSSOHN, E., Business Administration
RIIS, U., Education
RISCH, T., Computer Science
SAHLIN-ANDERSSON, K., Business Studies
SOMMESTAD, L., Economic History
SÖDER, M., Sociology
SÖDERSTEN, J., Economics
TORNSTAM, L., Sociology
TURNER, B., Housing Economics
VEDUNG, E., Housing Policy
VON HOFSTEN, C., Perceptual Psychology
WALLENSTEEN, P. N., Peace and Conflict
WIGREN, R., Economics
WITTROCK, B., Advanced Study in the Social Sciences
ÖBERG, S., Social and Economic Geography

Faculty of Theology:
BEXELL, O., Ecclesiology
BRODD, S.-E., Studies of Churches and Religious Denominations
BRÅKENHIELM, C.-R., Studies of Faiths and Ideologies
BÄCKSTRÖM, A., Sociology of Religion
DE MARINIES, VALERIE, Psychology of Religion
FRANZÉN, R., Church History
GRENHOLM, C.-H., Ethics
HERRMANN, E., Philosophy of Religions
HULTGÅRD, A., History of Religions
NORIN, S., Old Testament Exegesis
PETTERSSON, T., Sociology of Religion
SCHALK, P., History of Religions
SYREENI, K., New Testament Exegesis
WIKSTRÖM, O., Psychology of Religion

ATTACHED INSTITUTES

Centre for Image Analysis: Lägerhyddsvägen 17, 752 37 Uppsala; Dir Prof. G. BORGEFORS.

Ludwig Institute for Cancer Research: Uppsala Biomedical Centre BMC, POB 595, 751 23 Uppsala; br. of International Ludwig Institute; Dir Prof. C.-H. HELDIN.

VÄXJÖ UNIVERSITET
(Växjö University)

351 95 Växjö
Telephone: (470) 70-80-00
Fax: (470) 832-17
Internet: www.vxu.se

Founded 1967 as a branch of Lund University; independent status 1977; fmr name Högskolan i Växjo; present name and status 1999
State control
Languages of instruction: Swedish, English
Academic year: September to June
Rector: Asst Prof. MAGNUS SÖDERSTRÖM
Registrar: ELISABETH YDERBORG
Chief Librarian: BRIGITTE KÜHNE
Library of 160,000 vols
Number of teachers: 300
Number of students: 10,000
Publications: *Acta Wexionensia* series including: *Växjö Social Studies, Behavioural Science, Economics and Politics, Economy and Labour Market, Language and Literature, Växjö Migration Studies*

HEADS OF SCHOOL

Bioscience and Process Technology: HÅKAN ANNEHED
Education: LENA FRITZÉN
Health Science and Social Work: BIRGITTA BERGSTEN
Humanities: HANS LINDQUIST
Industrial Engineering: LARS-OLOF RASK
Management and Economics: ROLF G. LARSSON
Mathematics and Systems Engineering: MATHIAS HEDENBORG
Social Sciences: BETTY RHODIN

PROFESSORS

ABRAHAMSSON, B., Sociology (esp. Organizational Theory)
ARONSSON, P., History
BAUDIN, A., Forestry Marketing
BJÖRHEDEN, R., Forestry Technology
EKBERG, J., National Economy (esp. Study of Migration)
ERIKSSON, O., French (esp. Linguistics)
FLENSBURG, P., Computer Science
FRITZELL, C., Education
GAILLARD-LEMDAHL, M.-J., Botany
JENNER, H., Education
JOHANNISSON, B., Enrepreneurship and Business Administration
JOHNSSON-SMARAGDI, U., Media and Communications Studies
JONNERGÅRD, K., Business Economics
KHRENNIKOV, A., Applied Mathematics
LARSSON RINGQVIST, E., French
LINDKVIST, L., Business Economics
LÖWE, W., Computer Science
NIKLASSON, H., Economics
NODEBO, S., Signals Processing
OLOFSSON, G., Sociology
OLSSON, L., History
PEHRSSON, A., Business Economics
PERSSON, B., Biochemistry
ROSLING, K., Economics of Industrial Production
SALONEN, T., Social Work
SANATI, M., Process Chemistry
SHERWIN, D., Terotechnology
STENBERG, G., Psychology
SWÄRD, H., Social Work

THÖRNQVIST, T., Wood Science
TRONDMAN, M., Sociocultural Studies
VIRTANEN-ULFHIELM, T., English (esp. Linguistics)
ZANDERIN, L., Sociology
ZETHRAEUS, B., Bioenergetics

ATTACHED INSTITUTES

Centre for the Humanities: 351 95 Växjö; tel. (470) 685-00; Dir (vacant).
Centre for Labour Market Research: 351 95 Växjö; tel. (470) 685-00; Dir LENNART DELANDER.
Centre for Small Business Development: 351 95 Växjö; tel. (470) 685-00; Dir STIG MALM.
Communication Centre: 351 95 Växjö; tel. (470) 685-00; Dir BETTY ROHDIN.
Computer Science Unit: 351 95 Växjö; tel. (470) 685-00; Dir MATHIAS HEDENBORG.
Transportation Centre: 351 95 Växjö; tel. (470) 685-00; Dir JONAS MÅNSSON.

Other Institutes of University Standing
UNIVERSITY COLLEGES

Högskolan i Borås (University College of Borås): Allégatan 1, 501 90 Borås; tel. (33) 435-40-00; fax (33) 435-40-03; e-mail registrator@hb.se; internet www.hb.se; f. 1977; library: 150,060 vols; 330 teachers; 11,347 students; Rector Prof. LENA NORDHOLM; Pro-Vice-Rector Prof. KAJ LINDECRANTZ; Vice-Rector for Education JÜRGEN THOLIN; Vice-Rector for External Contacts STAFFAN LÖÖF; Vice-Rector for Research Prof. LARS HÖGLUND; Library Director JON ERIK NORDSTRAND

DEANS

School of Business and Informatics: ROLF APPELQVIST
School of Education and Behavioural Sciences: ULRIC BJÖRCK
School of Engineering: CHARLOTTE BENGTSSON
School of Health Sciences: CAROLINE AHL
School of Textiles: KENNETH TINGSVIK
Swedish School of Library and Information Studies: KATRIINA BYSTRÖM

Högskolan Dalarna (Dalarna University College): Selma Lagerlöfsplatsen, 791 88 Falun; tel. (23) 77-80-00; fax (23) 77-80-80; e-mail ioffice@du.se; internet www.du.se; f. 1977; departments of economics, social sciences, arts and languages, health and social sciences, culture, media, computer sciences, mathematics, natural sciences and engineering; 10,000 students; Rector AGNETA STARK; Librarian DANELID HANS.

Högskolan i Gävle (Gävle University College): 801 76 Gävle; tel. (26) 64-85-00; fax (26) 64-86-86; e-mail registrator@hig.se; internet www.hig.se; f. 1977; mathematics, natural sciences, and computer science, technology, humanities and social sciences, teacher training and healthcare; library: 85,000 vols, 550 periodicals; 430 (including 30 professors, 150 senior lecturers); 13,000 students; Rector LEIF SVENSSON.

Högskolan på Gotland (Gotland University): Cramérgatan 3, 621 57 Visby; tel. (498) 29-99-00; fax (498) 29-99-62; e-mail info@hgo .se; internet www.hgo.se; f. 1998; primarily business administration and international management and coastal zone management, secondary subjects include archaeology, osteology, information technology and business administration, international business

relations, technology, art and new media, building restoration, Russian, history, human geography, ethnology, ecology, art history and cross-cultural communication; 150 teachers; 4,000 students; Rector LEIF BORGERT.

Högskolan Halmstad: Box 823, S-30118 Halmstad; tel. (35) 16-71-00; fax (35) 14-85-33; e-mail registrator@hh.se; internet www .hh.se; f. 1983; academic year September to June; library: 74,000 vols; 400 teachers; 7,000 students; Vice-Chancellor ROMULO ENMARK; Pro-Vice-Chancellor ALBERT-JAN BAERVELDT; Administrative Officer MAJ-BRITT BÄCK; Librarian GÖRAN ERICSSON

HEADS OF DEPARTMENTS

Business and Engineering: PER-OLA ULVENBLAD
Humanities: HUGO PALMSKÖLD
Information Science, Computer and Electrical Engineering: MAGNUS LARSSON
Social and Health Sciences: OLE OLSSON
Teacher Education Unit: GUNILLA LUNDKVIST

Högskolan i Jönköping: POB 1026, 551 11 Jönköping; tel. (36) 15-77-00; fax (36) 15-77-18; e-mail hj@hj.se; internet www.hj.se; f. 1977; library: 200,000 vols; 470 teachers; 8,500 students; Pres. CLAS WAHLBIN; Librarian INGER MELIN

DEANS

Jönköping International Business School: ROLF A. LUNDIN
Jönköping School of Education and Communication: HENNING JOHANSSON
Jönköping School of Engineering: ROY HOLMBERG
Jönköping School of Health Sciences: BIRGITTA LUNDGREN LINDQUIST

Högskolan i Kalmar (University of Kalmar): 391 82 Kalmar; tel. (480) 44-60-00; fax (480) 44-60-32; e-mail info@hik.se; internet www.hik.se; f. 1977, fmrly teacher training college (f. 1876); library: 99,000 vols; 530 teachers; 9,800 students; Vice-Chancellor AGNETA BLADH; Administrative Officer ANN FUST; Librarian BERTIL JANSSON

HEADS OF DEPARTMENTS

Biology and Environmental Science: IRENE BOHMAN
Chemistry and Biomedical Sciences: HÅKAN HALLMER
Health and Behavioural Sciences: GÖRAN JOHANSSON
Humanities and Social Sciences: EVA ÖRTENGREN
In-service Training of Journalists: ANNELIE EWERS
Management and Economics: NILS NILSSON
Maritime Academy: TOR CARLSEN
Media Science and Journalism: MATS LINDE
Technology: GÖRAN BORGÖ

Högskolan Kristianstad (Kristianstad University College): Elmetorpsvägen 15, 291 88 Kristianstad; tel. (44) 20-30-00; fax (44) 12-96-51; e-mail info@hkr.se; internet www.hkr.se; f. 1977; languages of instruction: Swedish, English; departments of behavioural sciences, business studies, humanities and social sciences, health sciences and mathematics and science; school of engineering; Vice-Pres. MALIN IRHAMMAR.

Högskola Malmö (Malmo University College): 205 06 Malmö; tel. (40) 665-70-00; fax (40) 665-60-10; e-mail info@mah.se; internet www.mah.se; f. 1998; faculties of health and society and odontology; schools of arts and communication, international migration and ethnic relations; teacher education school of technology and society; 50 professors; 21,000 students; Vice-Chancellor LENNART OLAUSSON.

Högskolan i Skövde: Box 408, 541 28 Skövde; tel. (500) 44-80-00; fax (500) 41-63-25; e-mail info@his.se; internet www.his.se; f. 1983; business administration, economics, engineering science, biosciences, computer science, languages, art, social science, nursing; library: 106,000 vols; 290 teachers; 8,000 students; Rector LEIF LARSSON; Librarian LENA OLSSON.

Högskolan Väst (University West): POB 936, 461 29 Trollhättan; tel. (520) 47-50-00; fax (520) 47-51-99; internet www.htu.se; f. 1990 as Högskolan Trollhättan/Uddevalla; present name 2006; science and technology, nursing and health sciences, social and behavioural sciences, information technology and computer science, language studies and teacher training; 500 teachers; 10,000 students; Rector LARS EKEDAHL.

Mälardalens Högskola (Mälardalen University College): POB 883, 721 23 Västerås; tel. (21) 10-13-00; fax (21) 10-15-44; e-mail info@mdh.se; internet www.mdh.se; f. 1977; library: 81,000 vols; 650 teachers; 15,000 students; Rector MAGNUS SÖDERSTRÖM

HEADS OF DEPARTMENTS

Biology and Chemical Engineering: PER KÅRSNÄS
Business Studies and Informatics: GÖRAN BRYDING
Caring Sciences: ROLAND SVENSSON
Computer Engineering: JAN GUSTAFSSON
Electrical Engineering: HANS BERGGREN
Energy: LARS WESTER
Humanities: IRÉNE ARTÆUS
Information Design and Product Development: STEN EKMAN
Mathematics and Physics: PETER GUSTAFSSON
Social Sciences: TOLA JONSSON

Södertörns Högskola (Sodertorn University College): Alfred Nobels allé 7, Flemingsberg, 141 89 Huddinge; tel. (8) 608-40-00; fax (8) 608-40-10; e-mail info@sh.se; internet www.sh.se; f. 1996; faculties of humanities, social sciences and technology, science and teacher training and education studies; library: 88,400 vols (77,000 at the main Campus, 11,400 at Haninge Campus); 19,500 books accessible electronically; 453 teachers; 12,000 students; Vice-Chancellor Prof. INGELA JOSEFSON.

ART

Högskolan för Design och Konsthantverk (School of Design and Crafts): Box 131, 405 30, Gothenburg; tel. (31) 773-48-71; fax (31) 773-48-88; internet www.hdk.gu.se; f. 1848; affiliated to Gothenburg University; product design, interior and graphic design, ceramic art, textile art, jewellery design, film scenography; library: 20,000 vols; 40 teachers; 250 students; Dean KARL-OLA WARN-HAMMAR.

Konstfack (University College of Arts, Crafts and Design): POB 24115, Valhallavägen 191, 104 51 Stockholm; tel. (8) 450-41-00; fax (8) 450-41-90; e-mail info@konstfack.se; internet www.konstfack.se; f. 1844; graphic design and illustration, industrial design, interior architecture, furniture design, textile design, ceramics and glass, metalwork design, fine art, art education; library: 110,000 vols; 135 teachers; 550 students; Rector Prof. LARS LALLERSTEDT.

Konsthögskolan Valand: Box 132, Vasagatan 50, 405 30 Gothenburg; tel. (31) 773-51-00; fax (31) 773-51-19; e-mail info@valand.gu.se; internet www.valand.gu.se; f. 1865; affiliated to Gothenburg University; 15 teachers; 100 students; Dir LESLIE JOHNSON.

Kungl. Konsthögskolan (Royal University College of Fine Arts): Flaggmansv. 1, Box 16

315, 103 26 Stockholm; tel. (8) 614-40-00; fax (8) 679-86-26; e-mail info@kkh.se; internet www.kkh.se; f. 1735; 38 teachers; 215 students; Principal MARIE-LOUISE EKMAN; Admin. Man. EVA BORGSTRÖM; Librarian A. EKSTRÖM; publs *Konsthögskolans Broschyr*, *Konsthögskolan Elevkatalog*

PROFESSORS

BEDOIRE, F., History of Swedish Architecture, Comparative Architectural History
HAGDAHL, B.
SCHULMAN, S., Restoration
RANTANEN, M.
SCOTT, J.
ŞENNEBY, A.
SUŠTERŠIČ, A.
WIDÉN, J.
PALMER, H., Architecture

ECONOMICS AND ADMINISTRATION

Handelshögskolan i Stockholm (Stockholm School of Economics): Box 6501, 113 83 Stockholm; tel. (8) 736-90-00; fax (8) 31-81-86; e-mail info@hhs.se; internet www.sse.edu; f. 1909; private; library: see Libraries; 200 teachers; 1,700 students; Pres. Prof. LEIF LINDMARK; Admin. Dir LARS BURSTEDT; Librarian E. THOMSON-ROOS

PROFESSORS

AXELSSON, B., Marketing
BERGMAN, L., Environmental and Energy Economics
BERGSTRÖM, C., Finance and Law
BJÖRK, T., Mathematical Finance
BLOMSTRÖM, M., International Business
BRUNSSON, N., Public Administration
DEO SHARMA, D., International Marketing
ELIAESON, P.-J.
ELLINGSEN, T., Microeconomics
ENGLUND, P., Banking and Insurance
HENREKSON, M., Economics
HERRE, J., Law
HOLMQUIST, C., Entrepreneurship and Business
JENNERGREN, P., Management
JOHANSSON, P.-O., Health Economics
JULANDER, C.-R., Marketing and Consumer Behaviour
JÖNSSON, B., Health Economics
KARLSSON, C., Industrial Production
LINDGREN, H., Banking and Finance History
LINDMARK, L.
LJUNGQVIST, L., Economics
LUNDAHL, M., Development Economics
LUNDEBERG, M., Information Management
NEREP, E., Swedish and International Commercial Law
SAMUELSON, L., Management Control Systems
SEGERSTROM, P. S., International Economics
SEVÒN, G., Organizational Psychology
SJÖBERG, L., Economic Psychology
SJÖBERG, Ö., Economic Geography
SJÖSTRAND, S.-E., Management
SKOGSVIK, K., Financial Accounting and Finance
STYMNE, B., Organization Theory
STÅHL, I., Computer Based Applications of Economic Theory
SÖLVELL, Ö, International Business
TERÄSVIRTA, T., Economic Statistics
WEIBULL, J. W., Economics
WESTLUND, A., Economic Statistics
WIMAN, B., Tax Law
ZANDER, U., International Business
ÖSTMAN, L., Accountancy and Finance.

Affiliated institutes:

Ekonomiska Forskningsinstitutet vid Handelshögskolan i Stockholm (Economic Research Institute at the Stockholm School of Economics): Sveavägen 65, Stockholm; f. 1929; scientific research in man-

agement science and economics; 300 research fellows; Dir Assoc. Prof. BO SELLSTEDT; publ. *EFI News*.

Japaninstitutet (European Institute of Japanese Studies at the Stockholm School of Economics): POB 6501, 113 83 Stockholm; f. 1992; research and educational programmes concerning Japanese and East-Asian economies and business in relation to Europe; 12 research fellows; Dir Prof. MAGNUS BLOMSTRÖM.

Institutet för Internationellt Företagande (Institute of International Business): Box 6501, 113 83 Stockholm; f. 1975; centre for research and education in international business, particularly the strategy and management of multinational corporations; 20 researchers; Dir Assoc. Prof. PETER HAGSTRÖM.

Stockholm Institute of Transition Economics and East European Economies (SITE): Box 6501, 113 83 Stockholm; f. 1989; research into the economic development of Eastern Europe; 12 research fellows; Dir Assoc. Prof. ERIC BERGLÖF; publ. *Newsletter*.

Internationella Handelshögskolan (Jönköping International Business School): POB 1026, 551 11 Jönköping; tel. (36) 15-77-00; fax (36) 16-50-69; e-mail info@ihh.hj.se; internet www.ihh.hj.se; f. 1994; business administration, economics, political science, business informatics and commercial law; 79 staff (25 full professors, 8 assoc. professors, 26 asst professors, 20 lecturers); 2,000 students; Dean ROLF A. LUNDIN.

EDUCATION

Lärarhögskolan i Stockholm (Stockholm Institute of Education): Konradsbergsgatan 5A, POB 34103, 100 26 Stockholm; tel. (8) 737-55-00; fax (8) 737-55-01; e-mail info@lhs.se; internet www.lhs.se; pedagogy, curriculum studies, special education and childhood and youth studies; library: 67,689 vols, 20,000 electronic titles, 660 periodicals; 630 teachers; 15,000 students; Rector ESKIL FRANCK.

MEDICINE

Karolinska Institutet: 171 77 Stockholm; tel. (8) 728-64-00; fax (8) 31-11-01; internet www.ki.se; f. 1810; library: see Libraries and Archives; 400 teachers; 2,600 students; Vice-Chancellor HARRIET WALLBERG-HENRIKSSON; Dir RUNE FRANSSON; Librarian PER OLSSON; publs *Computerized Publication Register* (information on all publs issued by the Institute), *Curriculum*, *Students' Handbook*

DEANS

Faculty of Medicine: Prof. JAN CARLSTEDT-DUKE

PROFESSORS

Faculty of Medicine:

AHLBOM, N. A., Epidemiology
AHLBORG, U. G., General Toxicology
AKUSJÄRVI, K. G. O., Microbial Genetics
ALLANDER, E., Social Medicine
ALVESTRAND, A., Renal Medicine
ANGELIN, B., Metabolism
APERIA, A. CH., Paediatrics
ASPELIN, P., Diagnostic Radiology
BERGLUND, B., Environmental Psychology
BERGMAN, H. O. M., Psychology of Alcoholism
BIBERFELD, G., Clinical Immunology
BJÖRKHEM, J. I., Biochemical Research on Atherosclerosis
BRITTON, S. F. F., Infectious Diseases
BYGDEMAN, M. A., Obstetrics and Gynaecology

CAMNER, P. J. H., Pulmonary Medicine
CARLSÖÖ, B., Otorhinolaryngology
COLLINS, P., Tumour Pathology
DALLNER, G., Pathology
DANEHOLT, P. B. E., Molecular Genetics
DE FAIRE, U., Tumour Pathology
EDSTRÖM, L., Neurology
EFENDIĆ, S., Clinical Diabetes Research
EINARSSON, K., Gastroenterology
EKBLOM, B. T., Exercise Physiology
EKHOLM, J. T., Physical Medicine and Rehabilitation
EKMAN, P., Urology
ELMQVIST, H., Medical Technology
ENEROTH, H. E. P., Hormone Research
ERICSON, K. L., Neuroradiology
ERICSSON, H., Clinical Bacteriology
ERIKSSON, H. A., Reproductive Endocrinology
ERIKSSON, L. A., Neurophysics
FLOCK, K. A. I., Physiology
FREDHOLM, B., Pharmacology
FUXE, K. G., Histology
GAHRTON, C. A. G., Medicine
GAROFF, P. H., Molecular Biology
GOLDIE, I. R. V. G. F., Orthopaedic Surgery
GRANT, N. G., Anatomy
GRILLNER, S. E., Exercise Physiology
GROTH, C.-G., Transplantation Surgery
GUSTAFSSON, J.-A., Medical Nutrition
HAGENFELDT, L., Clinical Chemistry
HAKULINEN, T., Epidemiology and Biostatistics
HAMBERGER, K. B., Surgery
HANSSON, G., Experimental Cardiovascular Research
HEDQVIST, P. O., Physiology
HEMMINKI, K. J., Epidemiology
HENRIKSSON, J., Physiology
HOLMGREN, K. A., Medical Protein Chemistry and Enzymology
HÄLLSTRÖM, T., Psychiatry
HÖGLUND, G., Neuromedicine
HÖKFELT, T. G. M., Histology with Cell Biology
JANSSON, B. I., Psychiatry
JANSSON, P. E., Bioanalysis, Analytical Biochemistry
JOHANSSON, S. G. O., Clinical Immunology
JÖRNVALL, H. E., Medical and Physiological Chemistry
KAIJSER, L., Clinical Physiology
KIESSLING, R., Oncology
KLARESKOG, L., Rheumatology
KNUTSSON, E., Clinical Neurophysiology
KOLMODIN-HEDMAN, B., Occupational Medicine
KRISTENSSON, S. K., Pathology (Neuropathology)
KRONVALL, H. C. G., Clinical Bacteriology
KÄRRE, K., Molecular Immunology
LADENSTEIN, R., Structural Biochemistry
LAGERCRANTZ, H., Paediatrics, Neonatology
LAGERLÖF, B. A. M., Pathology
LAMBERT, B. B., Genetic Toxicology
LARSSON, A., Paediatrics
LARSSON, J., Anaesthesiology, Radiology, Orthopaedics
LENNERSTRAND, Å. G., Ophthalmology
LENNERSTRAND, G., Ophthalmology
LERNMARK, Å., Experimental Endocrinology
LIDBERG, L. G., Social and Forensic Psychiatry
LIDÉN, S. S., Dermatology and Venereology
LINDAHL, S. G. E., Anaesthesiology
LINDBERG, A. E. A., Clinical Bacteriology
LINDGREN, J. U., Orthopaedic Surgery
LINDSTEN, J. E., Medical Genetics
LINDVALL, S. T. I., General Hygiene
LINK, H. G., Neurology
LINNARSSON, D., Baromedicine
LJUNGQVIST, A. G., Pathology

LUNDBERG, J., Neurotransmission Research
LUNELL, N.-O., Obstetrics and Gynaecology
MIDTVEDT, T., Medical Microbial Ecology
MOLDÉUS, P. W., Biochemical Toxicology
MÖLLBY, N. R., Bacteriology
MÖLLER, E. B., Transplantation Immunology
NORD, C.-E., Oral Microbiology
NORDBERG, A., Medical Tobacco Research
NORDENSKJÖLD, M., Clinical Genetics
NORMARK, S., Medical Microbiology
NORRBY, E. C. J., Virus Research
OLSON, O. L., Neurobiology
OLSSON, P. I., Experimental Surgery
ORLOVSKI, G., Physiology
ORRENIUS, S. G., Toxicology
OTTING, G., Molecular Biophysics
PERSHAGEN, B. G., Environmental Epidemiology
PHILIPSON, B. T., Ophthalmology
PISCATOR, E. M., Hygiene
RAJS, J., Forensic Medicine
RIGLER, R. H. A., Medical Physics
RINGBORG, U., Oncology
RINGDEN, O., Transplantation Immunology
RINGERTZ, H. G., Diagnostic Radiology
RINGERTZ, N. R., Medical Cell Genetics
RITZÉN, E. M., Paediatric Endocrinology
ROLAND, P. E., Positron Emission Tomography
ROSENHALL, U., Clinical Audiology
RYDBERG, U. S., Clinical Alcohol and Drug Addiction Research
RYDELIUS, P.-A., Child and Adolescent Psychiatry
RYDÉN, L. E., Cardiology
RÅDEGRAN, K., Thoracic Surgery
RÖSNER, S., Health Behaviour Research
SALTIN, B., Physiology
SAMUELSSON, B. I., Medical and Physiological Chemistry
SCHNEIDER, G., Molecular Structural Biology
SEDVALL, C. G., Psychiatry
SEIGER, A. B., Geriatric Medicine
SJÖQVIST, F. G. F., Clinical Pharmacology
STONE-ELANDER, S., Medical Radiochemistry
SVANSTRÖM, L. O. E., Social Medicine
SVENDGAARD, N.-A., Neurosurgery
SVENSSON, H. T., Pharmacology
TENGROTH, B. M., Ophthalmology
TERENIUS, L., Experimental Alcohol and Drug Addiction Research
THOMASSON, B. H., Paediatric Surgery
THORÉN, P., Physiology
TOFTGÅRD, R., Environmental Toxicology
TRYGGVASON, K., Medical Chemistry
UNGERSTEDT, C. U., Neuropsychopharmacology
VAHLNE, A., Clinical Virology
VAHTER, M. E., Metal Toxicology
VENNSTRÖM, B. R., Molecular Biology
VON SCHOULTZ, B., Obstetrics and Gynaecology
WAHLGREN, M., Parasitology
WAHREN, B., Clinical Virology
WETTERBERG, C. L. E., Psychiatry
WIGZELL, H. L. R., Immunology
WIMAN, B., Clinical Coagulation Research
WINBLAD, B. G., Geriatric Medicine
WRETLIND, B., Clinical Bacteriology
ZETTERBERG, A. H. D., Pathology, Tumour Cytology
ÅBERG, H. E., Family Medicine
ÅSBERG, M., Psychiatry
ÖBRINK, B. J., Medical Cell Biology
ÖHMAN, A., Psychology

MUSIC AND DRAMA

Dramatiska Institutet (University College of Film, Radio, Television and Theatre): Filmhuset, Borgvägen 5, Box 27090, 102 51 Stockholm; tel. (8) 665-13-00; fax (8) 662-14-84; e-mail kansli@draminst.se; internet www.draminst.se; f. 1970; Pres. PER LYSANDER.

Konstnärliga högskolorna i Malmö (Malmö Academies of Performing Arts): Ystadvägen 25, Box 8203, 200 41 Malmö; tel. (40) 32-54-50; fax (40) 22-54-80; f. 1907; comprises Malmö Academy of Music, Malmö Theatre Academy, Malmö Academy of Art; 230 teachers; 650 students; Dean HÅKAN LUNDSTRÖM.

Kungl. Musikhögskolan i Stockholm (Royal College of Music in Stockholm): Valhallavägen 105, Box 27711, 115 31 Stockholm; tel. (8) 16-18-00; fax (8) 664-14-24; e-mail international@kmh.se; internet www.kmh.se; f. 1771; 30 teachers; 1,000 students; Principal GUNILLA VON BAHR.

Musikhögskolan vid Göteborgs Universitet: POB 210, 405 30 Gothenburg; Located at: Fågelsången 1, Gothenburg; tel. (31) 773-40-20; fax (31) 773-40-30; e-mail GMH@musik.gu.se; internet www.musik.gu.se; f. 1916; music education, performing, church music, composition, world music, jazz, electri-acoustic composition, music technology; affiliated to Göteborg University; 200 teachers; 600 students; Pres. (vacant); Principal INGEMAR HENNINGSSON; Librarian PIA SHEKHTER.

Teater- och operahögskolan: POB 210, 405 30 Gothenburg; f. 1964; 50 students; affiliated to Gothenburg University; Head HARALD EK; Admin. MARGARETA HANNING.

PHYSICAL EDUCATION

Idrottshögskolan (Stockholm University College of Physical Education and Sports): POB 5626, 114 86 Stockholm; tel. (8) 402-22-00; internet www.ihs.se; f. 1813; library: 50,000 vols; 60 teachers; 700 students; Rector Prof. BJÖRN EKBLOM.

TECHNOLOGY

Blekinge Tekniska Högskola (Blekinge Institute of Technology): 371 79 Karlskrona; tel. (455) 38-50-00; fax (455) 38-50-57; e-mail info@bth.se; internet www.bth.se; f. 1989; applied information technology and sustainable development of industry and society; 480 teachers; 6,100 students; Vice-Chancellor LARS HAIKOLA.

Chalmers Tekniska Högskola (Chalmers University of Technology): 412 96 Gothenburg; tel. (31) 772-10-00; fax (31) 772-38-72; e-mail info@adm.chalmers.se; internet www.chalmers.se; f. 1829; Private control; language of instruction: Swedish; academic year September to June; library: see Libraries and Archives; 1,600 teachers; 6,850 students; Pres. Prof. J.-E. SUNDGREN; Vice-Pres. Prof. LENA GUSTAFSSON; Libraries Director L. NELLDE

DEANS

School of Architecture: Prof. HANS LINDGREN
School of Chemical Engineering: Prof. J. ALBERTSSON
School of Civil Engineering: Prof. G. GUSTAFSON
School of Computer Science and Engineering: Prof. J. SMITH
School of Electrical Engineering: Assoc. Prof. H. BROMAN
School of Environmental Sciences: Prof. O. LINDQVIST
School of Mathematical Sciences: Prof. B. BERNDTSSON
School of Mechanical Engineering: Prof. L. JOSEFSON
School of Physics and Engineering Physics: (vacant)

School of Technology Management and Economics: Prof. H. JOHANSSON
Department of Microtechnology and Nanoscience: Prof. STEFAN BENGTSSON

PROFESSORS

School of Architecture (tel. (31) 772-2400; fax (31) 772-2485; e-mail info@arch.chalmers.se; internet www.arch.chalmers.se):

BJUR, H., Urban Design and Planning
CALDENBY, C., Theory and History of Architecture
EDÉN, M., Design for Sustainable Urban Development
HOLMDAHL, B., Housing Design
JANSON, U., Building Design
MALBERT, B., Design for Sustainable Urban Development
ULLMARK, P., Workspace Design

School of Chemical Engineering (tel. (31) 772-2750; fax (31) 772-2981; internet www.che.chalmers.se):

ALBERTSSON, J., Inorganic Chemistry
ANDERSSON, B., Chemical Reaction Engineering
BERNTSSON, T., Heat and Power Technology
ENGSTRÖM, S., Pharmaceutical Technology
FREDERICK, Jr, W. J., Green Chemistry
GATENHOLM, P., Biopolymer Technology
GUSTAFSSON, L., Biotechnology
HJERTBERG, TH., Polymer Technology
HOLMBERG, K., Applied Surface Chemistry
IRANDOUST, S., Chemical Engineering
JAGNER, S., Co-ordination Chemistry
LARSSON, S., Theoretical Chemistry
NIKLASSON, C., Chemical Reaction Engineering
NORDÉN, B., Physical Chemistry
ORWAR, O., Biophysical Chemistry
RASMUSON, A., Chemical Engineering Design
SANDBERG, A.-S., Food Chemistry
SIHVER, L., Nuclear Chemistry
SKARNEMARK, G., Nuclear Chemistry
THELIANDER, H., Forest Products and Chemical Engineering

School of Civil Engineering (tel. (31) 772-19-30; fax (31) 18-97-05; internet www.vsect.chalmers.se):

BERGDAHL, L., Hydraulics
CLAESSON, J., Building Physics
FAHLÉN, P., Building Services Engineering
GUSTAFSON, G., Engineering Geology
GYLLTOFT, K., Concrete Structures
HAGENTOFT, C.-E., Building Physics
KLEINER, M., Applied Acoustics
KLIGER, R., Steel and Timber Structures
KROPP, W., Applied Acoustics
MORRISON, G., Sustainable Aquatic Systems
NILSSON, L.-O., Building Materials
SÄLLFORS, G., Geotechnical Engineering
TILLMAN, A.-M., Environmental Systems Technology
WIBERG, N.-E., Structural Mechanics
WOLFF, R., Environmental Management

School of Computer Science and Engineering (tel. (31) 772-10-00; fax (31) 16-56-55; internet www.cse.chalmers.se):

AULIN, T., Computer Engineering
COQUAND, T., Computer Science
DYBJER, P., Computer Science
HUGHES, J., Computer Science
JONSSON, E., Computer Engineering
LARSSON-EDEFORS, P., Computer Engineering
NORDSTRÖM, B., Computer Science
SANDS, D., Computer Science
SHEERAN, M., Computer Science
SMITH, J., Computer Science
STENSTRÖM, P., Computer Engineering
SURI, N., Computer Engineering
TAFVELIN, S., Computer Engineering

School of Electrical Engineering (tel. (31) 772-1550; fax (31) 772-1561; internet www.ee.chalmers.se):

ANDERSON, D., Electromagnetics
BOLLEN, M/, Electric Power Systems
BONDESON, A., Electromagnetic Field Theory
DAALDER, J., Electrical Power Systems
EGERT, B., Control Engineering
ELGERED, G., Electrical Measurements
GUBANSKI, S., Electric Power Systems
GUSTAVSSON, T., Imaging and Image Analysis
HAMDI, E., Electrical Machines
HEDELIN, P., Information Theory
KILDAL, P.-S., Microwave Antennae
LENNARTSSON, B., Automation
LISAK, M., Electromagnetics
MURTAGH, D., Global Environmental Measurements
SVENSON, A., Communication Systems
VIBERG, M., Applied Electronics
WEILAND, J., Plasma Physics

School of Mathematical Sciences (tel. (31) 772-10-00; fax (31) 16-19-73; internet www.math.chalmers.se):

ANDERSSON, M., Mathematics
ARKERYD, L., Mathematics
BERNDTSSON, B., Mathematics
BORELL, C., Mathematics
BRENNER, P., Mathematics
BRZEZINSKI, J., Mathematics
DE MARÉ, J., Mathematical Statistics
HÄGGSTRÖM, O., Mathematical Statistics
JAGERS, P., Mathematical Statistics
JOHNSON, C., Applied Mathematics
LINDVALL, T., Mathematical Statistics
NERMAN, O., Mathematical Statistics
PERSSON, U., Mathematics
ROOTZÉN, H., Mathematical Statistics
ROZENBLIOUM, G., Mathematics
RUDEMO, M., Mathematical Statistics
SHCHERBINA, N., Mathematics
SJÖGREN, P., Mathematics
STEIF, J., Mathematics
SVANSTEDT, N., Applied Mathematics

School of Mechanical Engineering (tel. (31) 772-1190; fax (31) 772-1192; internet www.me.chalmers.se):

ABRAHAMSSON, T., Structural Dynamics
ALMSTEDT, A.-E., Multiphase Flow
BERBYUK, V., Mechanical Systems
BOSTRÖM, A., Mechanics
DAVIDSSON, L., Heat Transfer
DENBRATT, I., Combustion Engine Technology
ERIKSSON, L.-E., Compressible Flow
GEORGE, W. K., Turbulence
HÅLL, U., Turbo Machinery
JOHANNESSON, H., Machine Design
JOHNSSON, F., Sustainable Energy Systems
JOSEFSON, L., Solid Mechanics
KARLSSON, B., Engineering Materials
KINNANDER, A., Manufacturing Systems
KLEMENT, U., Materials Science (with emphasis on Electron Microscopy)
LARSSON, L., Hydromechanics
LIU, J., Electronics Production
LYNGFELT, A., Energy Conversion Technology
LÖFDAHL, L., Fluid Mechanics
LÖVSUND, P., Traffic Safety
NYBORG, L., Surface Technology
OLSSON, P., Mechanics
RIGDAHL, M., Polymer Materials
ROSENBLAD, E., Human-Centred Technology
RUNESSON, K., Material Mechanics
SJÖBERG, J., Mechatronics
TOLL, S., Micromechanics
ULFVARSSON, A., Marine Structural Engineering
ÖRTENGREN, R., Ergonomics

School of Physics and Engineering Physics (tel. (31) 772-3205; fax (31) 772-3202; internet fyservi.fy.chalmers.se):; Several Professors at Gothenburg University also serve in this School

ANDERSSON, S., Surface Physics
AZAR, C., Sustainable Industrial Metabolism
BRINK, L., Elementary Particle Physics
BÖRJESSON, L., Condensed Matter Physics
JONSON, B., Subatomic Physics
JONSON, M., Condensed Matter Theory
KASEMO, B., Chemical Physics
NILSSON, B., Mathematical Physics
NILSSON, P.-O., Electronic Structure of Condensed Matter
PÁZSIT, I., Reactor Physics
WALLDÉN, L., Social State Physics
ÖSTLUND, S., Solid State Theory

School of Technology Management and Economics (tel. (31) 772-1210; fax (31) 772-3485; e-mail infomaster@mot.chalmers.se; internet www.mot.chalmers.se):

BERGLUND, B., Technology and History
BERGMAN, B., Quality Sciences
BJÖRNSSON, H., Systems Management
BRÖCHNER, J., Service Management
GADDE, L.-E., Industrial Marketing
GRANSTRAND, O., Industrial Management and Economics
GUSTAVSSON, S.-O., Operation Management and Work Organization
JACOBSSON, S., Industrial Dynamics
JOHANSSON, M., Logistics and Transportation
LUMSDEN, K., Logistics and Transportation
McKELVEY, M., Industrial Dynamics
NORRGREN, F., Project Management
SJÖLANDER, S., Innovation Engineering and Management
VEDIN, A., Centre for Intellectual Property Studies (CIP)
WOLF, R., Sustainable Business Studies
ÅHLSTRÖM, P., Operation Management and Work Organization

Department of Microtechnology and Nanoscience (tel. (31) 772-1000; fax (31) 772-8498; e-mail info@mc2.chalmers.se; internet www.mc2.chalmers.se):

ANDREKSSON, P., Photonics
BENGTSSON, S., Solid State Electronics
CLAESON, T., Applied Sold State Physics
DELSING, P., Experimental Mesoscopic Physics
ENGSTRÖM, O., Solid State Electronics
ENOKSSON, P., Micro-Opto-Electro-Mechanical Systems
GEVORGIAN, S., Microwave Electronics
HÅRD, S.
LARSSON, A., Optoelectronics
WENDIN, G., Theoretical Physics
WINKLER, D., Physics
ZIRATH, H., High Speed Electronics.

ATTACHED RESEARCH INSTITUTES:

Centre for the Built Environment in Western Sweden: tel. (31) 772-20-31.

Chalmers Lindholmen högskola (Chalmers Lindholmen University College): POB 8873, 402 72 Gothenburg; tel. (31) 772-10-00; fax (31) 772-57-67; f. 1841 as Nautical College; 2,200 students; Dir Prof. B. RÖNNÄNG; Man. of Admin. B. CARLSSON

HEADS OF DEPARTMENTS

Applied Buildings and Civil Engineering: LYNGFELT, S.
Chemical Engineering: STRÖM, K.
Continuing and Professional Studies: OSKARSON, H.-B.
Electrical and Computer Engineering: MILTHON, E.
Language and Communication: HOOD, E.

Maritime Studies: RUTGERSSON, O.
Mathematics: BLOMQVIST, H.
Mechanical Engineering: CARLSSON, D.

Chalmers Science Park: Sven Hultins
gata 9, 412 88 Gothenburg; tel. (31) 772-40-
00; fax (31) 772-42-40; Man. L. JACOBSON.

Onsala Space Observatory: 439 00
Onsala; tel. (31) 772-55-00; fax (31) 772-
55-90; national facility for radio astronomy; Dir Prof. R. S. BOOTH.

Kungliga Tekniska Högskolan (Royal
Institute of Technology): S-100 44 Stockholm;
tel. (8) 790-60-00; fax (8) 790-65-00; e-mail
tele@admin.kth.se; internet www.kth.se; f.
1827; State control; academic year September to June; library: see Libraries and
Archives; 1,900 teachers; 10,500 students;
President Prof. A. FLODSTRÖM; Vice-Presidents Prof. A. ERIKSSON, Prof. M. UHLÉN,
Prof. B. WAHLBERG; Chief Administrative
Officer A. LUNDGREN; Chief Librarian G.
LAGER; publs *Catalogue*, *Study Handbook*
(annually)

DEANS

School of Architecture, Surveying and Civil
Engineering: Prof. K. ÖDEÉN
School of Chemistry and Chemical Engineer-
ing: Prof. A. HULT
School of Electrical Engineering and Infor-
mation Technology: Prof. G. LANDGREN
School of Engineering Physics: Prof. A.
JOHNSON
School of Mechanical and Materials Engi-
neering: Prof. M. HANSON

PROFESSORS

School of Architecture, Surveying and Civil
Engineering:

ANDERSSON, R., Real Estate Economics
ATKIN, B., Construction Management
BÅNG, K.-L., Transport and Traffic Plan-
ning
BJÖRK, B.-C., Construction Management
CARLSSON, K., Photogrammetry and Image
Physics
CEDERWALL, K., Hydraulic Engineering
CVETKOVIC, V., Water Resources Engineer-
ing
DESTOUNI, G., Water Resources Engineer-
ing
ERIKSSON, A., Structural Mechanics and
Engineering
HOLMGREN, J., Concrete Structures
HÖGLUND, T., Steel Structures
ISACSSON, U., Highway Engineering
JACKS, G., Land and Water Resources
JANSSON, P.-E., Land and Water Resources
JOHANNESSON, G. A., Building Technology
KRUPINSKA, J., Architecture
LILJEFORS, A., Architecture
LJUNG, B., Business Administration
LJUNGGREN, S., Building Acoustics
LJUNGQVIST, B., Building Technology
LUNDEQUIST, J., Design Methodology
MALMSTRÖM, T.-G., Building Services
Engineering
MATTSSON, H., Real Estate Planning
MÅRTELIUS, J., History of Architecture
NORLÉN, U., Building Analysis and Hous-
ing Quality
QUIEL, F., Environmental and Natural
Resources Information Systems
SAMUELSSON, S., Building Engineering
SANDBERG, M., Indoor Environment and
Ventilation
SJÖBERG, L. E., Geodesy
SJÖSTRÖM, C., Materials Technology
SNICKARS, F., Regional Planning
STEPHANSSON, O., Engineering Geology
STILLE, H., Rock Mechanics
SUNDQUIST, H., Structural Design and
Bridges
TORLEGÅRD, K., Photogrammetry

WARTIANEN, K., Town Planning and Urban
Design
VESTBRO, D. U., Building Function Analy-
sis
VICTORIN, A., Law of Real Estate Buildings
Valuation
ÖDEÉN, K., Buildings Materials

School of Chemistry and Chemical Engineering:

ALBERTSSON, A.-C., Polymer Technology
BJÖRNBOM, P., Chemical Technology
CLAESSON, P., Surface Chemistry
ENFORS, S.-O., Biotechnology
ERIKSEN, T., Nuclear Chemistry
GELLERSTEDT, G., Wood Chemistry
GLASER, J., Inorganic Chemistry
HENRIKSSON, U., Physical Chemistry
HULT, A., Surface Treatment Technology
HULT, K.-A., Biochemistry
HÄRD, T., Structural Biochemistry
JÄRÅS, S., Chemical Technology
KARLSSON, S., Polymer Technology
MOBERG, C., Organic Chemistry
MÅNSSON, J.-A. E., Polymer Technology
NERETNIEKS, I., Chemical Engineering
NORMAN, B., Paper Technology
NYGREN, P.-Å., Biotechnology
NYRÉN, P., Biochemistry
RASMUSON, A., Chemical Engineering
SANDSTRÖM, M., Inorganic Chemistry
STENBERG, B., Polymer Technology
STILBS, P., Physical Chemistry
STÅHL, S., Biotechnology
TEDER, A., Pulp Technology
TEERI, T., Biochemistry
UHLEN, M., Biochemistry and Microbiol-
ogy
ZETHRACUS, B., Bioenergy Technology
ÅGREN, H., Theoretical Chemistry

School of Electrical Engineering and Information Technology:

ANDERSSON, G., Electric Power Systems
ARNBORG, S., Computing Science
AYANI, R., Computer Systems Laboratory
BJÖRK, G., Photonics and Microwave Engi-
neering
BRENNING, N., Plasma Physics
BUBENKO, J., Information Processing, esp.
Automatic Data Processing
CARLSON, R., Speech Technique
CEGRELL, T., Industrial Control Systems
CHRISTENSON, H., Computer Science
DRAKE, J. R., Fusion Plasma Physics
EKLUNDH, J.-O., Computer Vision
EKSTRÖM, A., High-power Electronics
ENGQUIST, B., Numerical Analysis
ERIKSSON, R., Electrical Plant Engineering
GRANSTRÖM, B., Speech Technique
HARIDI, S., Computer Systems
HELLSTEN, T., Fusion Plasma Physics
KARLSSON, G., Teletraffic Systems
KLEIJN, B., Speech Technology
LANDGREN, G., Semiconductor Materials
LANSNER, A., Computing Science
LEIJON, A., Hearing Technique
MAGUIRE, G., Computer Systems
MARKLUND, G., Plasma Physics
NEE, H.-P., Electrical Machines and
Drives
OLSSON, H., Radio Electronics
OTTERSTEN, B., Signal Processing
PARROW, J., Distribution Systems
PEHRSON, B., Telecommunication
PETERSSON, S., Solid State Electronics
SADARANGANI, C., Electrical Machines and
Drives
SEVERINSON-EKLUNDH, K., Interaction and
Presentation
STEMME, G., Electrical Measurement
SUNDBERG, J., Music Acoustics
SUNDBLAD, Y., Computing Science
SVENSSON, B., Solid State Electronics
SÖDER, L., Electronic Power Systems
TENHUNEN, H., Electronics
THYLEN, L., Photonics and Microwave

TORVEN, S., Plasma Physics
TYUGU, E., Teleinformatics
WAHLBERG, B., Automatic Control
ZANDER, J., Radio Communication
ÖSTLING, M., Solid State Electronics

School of Engineering Physics:

ALFREDSSON, H., Fluid Physics
AMBERG, G., Mechanics
BARK, F., Hydromechanics
BENEDICKS, M., Mathematics
BIEDERMANN, K., Optics
BJÖRNER, A., Mathematics
BLOMBERG, C.-O., Theoretical Physics
CARLSON, P., Particle Physics
ELIASSON, H., Mathematics
ERMAN, P., Physics
FLODSTRÖM, A., Materials Physics
FRIBERG, A., Optics
GRIMVALL, G., Theoretical Physics
GRISHIN, A., Materials Physics
HAVILAND, D., Physics of Nanostructures
HENNINGSSON, D., Mechanics
HERTZ, H., Materials Physics
HOLST, L., Mathematical Statistics
HÅSTAD, J., Theoretical Computer Science
JOHANSSON, A., Mechanics
JOHNSON, A., School of Engineering Phy-
sics
KARLSSON, U. H., Material Physics
LAKSOV, D., Applied Mathematics
LESSER, M., Mechanics
LINDQUIST, A., Optimization Theory and
Systems Theory
MICKELSSON, J., Mathematical Physics
RACHLEW-KÄLLNE, Atomic and Molecular
Physics
RAO, V., Condensed Matter Physics
RAPP, Ö, Condensed Matter Physics
ROSENGREN, A., Condensed Matter Theory
SJÖLIN, P., Mathematical Analysis
SNELLMAN, H., Theoretical Physics
STENHOLM, S., Laser Physics and Quan-
tum Optics
STRÖMBERG, J.-O., Computational Harmo-
nics Analysis

School of Mechanical and Materials Engineering:

ANDERSSON, S., Machine Elements
ARNSTRÖM, A., Assembly Systems
BLOMSTRAND, J., Nuclear Reactor Engi-
neering
BÄCKLUND, J., Lightweight Structures
ELIASSON, G., Industrial Competence Edu-
cation
ENLUND, N., Graphic Art Technology
ERICSON, M., Industrial Economics and
Management
FORSLIN, J., Industrial Management
FRANSSON, T., Heat and Power Technology
FREDRIKSSON, H., Metal Casting
GUDMUNDSON, P., Materials Mechanics
GUSTAFSSON, C., Industrial Economics and
Management
HANNERZ, N. E., Welding Technology
HUML, P., Metal Forming
JÖNSSON, P., Process Metallurgy
KAIJSER, A., History of Science and Tech-
nology
LEYGRAF, C., Corrosion Science
LINDSTRÖM, B., Production Engineering
MATTSSON, L., Industrial Metrology
MUHAMMED, M., Inorganic Materials
Chemistry
NILSSON, A., Technical Acoustics
NILSSON, F., Solid Mechanics
NISSER, M., History of Science and Tech-
nology
NORELL-BERGENDAHL, M., Integrated Pro-
duct Development
OLSSON, K.-A., Aeronautics
PERSSON, J.-G., Machine Design
PETERSON, F., Heating and Ventilation
Technology
PETTERSSON, K., Metallography
RINGERTZ, U., Aeronautics

RIZZI, A., Aeronautical Engineering
ROWCLIFFE, D., Ceramic Technology
RUTGERSSON, O., Vehicle Engineering
SANDSTRÖM, R., Applied Materials Technology

SEETHARAMAN, S., Theoretical Metallurgy
SOHLENIUS, G., Manufacturing Systems
STORÅKERS, B., Solid Mechanics
STÅHLBERG, U., Metal Forming
WENNERSTRÖM, E., Vehicle Engineering

WIKANDER, J., Mechatronics
WIKLUND, M., Carpentry
ÅGREN, J., Metallography
ÅNGSTRÖM, H.-E., Internal Combustion
Engineering

SWITZERLAND

The Higher Education System

Higher education institutions predate the proclamation of the Helvetic Republic in 1798, with the oldest being the Universität Basel, which was founded in 1460. Other long-standing institutions include the Université de Lausanne (founded in 1537), the Université de Geneve (founded in 1559) and the Universität Luzern (founded in 1574; current status since 2000). There is no Federal agency for higher education, which is instead governed by the individual Cantons. There are ten Cantonal universities, and the main languages of instruction are French, German or Italian, depending on the Canton. Other institutions of higher education include two Federal Institutes of Technology and universities of applied sciences (known as Fachhochoshulen, Hautes Ecoles Spécialisées or Scuole Universitarie Professionale). Switzerland participates in the Bologna Process to establish a European Higher Education Area, the first phase of which is to adopt a credit-based system of comparable degrees with two main cycles (undergraduate and graduate). In 2004 there were 200,777 students enrolled in higher education.

Either the Federal Maturity Certificate (Maturitätszeugnis, Certificat de Maturité, Baccalauréat or Attestato di Maturità) or the Federally-recognized Cantonal Maturity Certificate (Eidgenössisch anerkanntes kantonales Maturitätszeugnis, Certificat de Maturité cantonal reconnu par la Confédération or Attestato di Maturità cantonale riconosciuto dalla Confed-

erazione) is the main requirement for admission to university. The Cantonal Maturity Certificate (Kantonale Maturität, Maturité Cantonale or Maturità Cantonale) gives limited access to higher education, while the Certificate of Professional Maturity (Berufsmaturität, Maturité Professionelle or Maturità Professionale) is required for admission to the Fachhochoshulen, Hautes Ecoles Spécialisées or Scuole Universitarie Professionale. The two-tier Masters and Bachelors degree system is due to be fully implemented by 2010; meanwhile, old-style university degrees are still available from many institutions. The Bachelors is a three-year degree, equivalent to the old four-year Diplom, Diplôme, Licence or Lizentiat. The first postgraduate degree is the Masters, a one- to two-year programme following the Bachelors. Finally, the highest university degree is the Doctorate (Doktorat, Doctorat), which is awarded after between two to five years of research, culminating with defence of a thesis.

Technical and vocational education is regulated by Federal law and implemented by Cantonal authorities. Students split their time between the workplace and the classroom and the primary qualification is the Federal Apprenticeship Certificate or Certificate of Proficiency (Fahigkeitszeugnis, Certificate de Capacité or Attestato di Capacità). There are also Advanced Vocational Schools (Ecoles Professionnelles Supérieures or Scuole Medie Professionale) offering advanced programmes in technical and vocational education.

Regulatory and Representative Bodies

GOVERNMENT

Staatssekretariat für Bildung und Forschung/Secrétariat d'Etat à l'éducation et à la recherche (State Secretariat for Education and Research): Hallwylstr. 4, 3003 Bern; tel. 313229691; fax 313227854; e-mail info@sbf.admin.ch; internet www.sbf.admin .ch; State Sec. CHARLES KLEIBER.

ACCREDITATION

ENIC/NARIC Switzerland: Recognition Information Centre, Rectors' Conference of the Swiss Universities, Postfach 607, 3000 Bern 9; tel. 313066032; fax 313066020; e-mail christine.gehrig@crus.ch; internet www.crus.ch/engl/enic; Head CHRISTINE GEHRIG.

Organ für Akkreditierung und Qualitätssicherung der Schweizerischen Hochschulen/Organe d'accréditation et d'assurance qualité des hautes écoles suisses (Centre of Accreditation and Quality Assurance of the Swiss Universities): Falkenplatz 9, POB, 3001 Bern; tel. 313801150; fax 313801155; e-mail info@oaq.ch; internet www.oaq.ch; f. 2001; ind. body assuring and promoting the quality of teaching and research at Swiss academic instns; Dir Dr ROLF HEUSSER; publ. *Newsletter* (in German or French, 2 a year).

FUNDING

Schweizerischer Nationalfonds zur Förderung der wissenschaftlichen Forschung/Fonds national suisse de la Recherche scientifique (Swiss National Science Foundation): Wildhainweg 3, POB 8232, 3001 Bern; tel. 313082222; fax

313013009; e-mail pri@snf.ch; internet www .snf.ch; f. 1952; promotes ind. scientific research and is Switzerland's leading provider of scientific research funding, supports basic research in all disciplines; encourages dialogue between scientists and reps in society, politics and the economy; Pres., Foundation Council Dr FRITZ SCHIESSER; Dir DANIEL HÖCHLI.

NATIONAL BODIES

EDK/IDES (Information, Documentation, Education in Switzerland): Zähringerstr. 25, 3001 Bern; tel. 313095100; fax 313095110; e-mail ides@edk.unibe.ch; internet www.edk .ch; f. 1962 (with partial integration of CESDOC 1994) to inform Swiss and foreign services on questions concerning teaching and education in Switzerland; library of 8,000 vols, 400 periodicals, 6,000 documents; Dir ANNEMARIE STREIT.

Rat der Eidgenössischen Technischen Hochschulen/Conseil des Ecoles polytechniques fédérales (Board of the Swiss Federal Institutes of Technology): Häldeliweg 15, 8092 Zürich; tel. 446322367; fax 446321190; internet www.ethrat.ch; Pres. Prof. Dr ALEXANDER J. B. ZEHNDER.

Rektorenkonferenz der Schweizer Universitäten/Conférence des Recteurs des Universités Suisses (CRUS) (Rectors' Conference of the Swiss Universities): Sennweg 2, 3012 Bern; tel. 313066036; fax 313066050; e-mail crus@crus.ch; internet www.crus.ch; f. 1904; represents Swiss univs in relations with govt and other bodies; is responsible for strategic planning and co-operation between the Swiss univs; provides information service on Swiss and foreign univs; administers bilateral govt scholarships for Swiss students; nat. agency for the admin. and co-ordination of the European univ. co-opera-

tion programme Socrates/ERASMUS (Information and Co-ordination ERASMUS Switzerland, ICES); nat. information service on questions of academic recognition (Swiss ENIC); 12 mems; library of 4,000 vols; Pres. Prof. Dr HANS WEDER; Sec.-Gen. Dr MATHIAS STAUFFACHER; publs *proff.ch* (print and online), *Studying in Switzerland: Universities*.

Schweizerische Konferenz der kantonalen Erziehungsdirektoren/Conférence suisse des directeurs cantonaux de l'instruction publique (Swiss Conference of Cantonal Ministers of Education): Zähringerstr. 25, Postfach 5975, 3001 Bern; tel. 313095111; fax 313095150; e-mail edk@edk .ch; internet www.edk.ch; assembly of the 26 cantonal govt ministers who are responsible for education, training, culture and sport; responsible for nat. co-ordination in all areas of educational and cultural policy; Pres. ISABELLE CHASSOT; Sec.-Gen. HANS AMBÜHL.

Schweizerische Universitätskonferenz/Conférence Universitaire Suisse: Sennweg 2, 3012 Bern; tel. 313066060; fax 313021792; e-mail cus@cus.ch; internet www.cus.ch; f. 1969; co-ordination of Swiss univs and institutes of higher education; 18 mems, representing cantons, univs, Nat. Union of Students, etc.; Pres. AUGUSTIN MACHERET; Sec.-Gen. N. ISCHI; publ. *Info CUS* (6 a year).

Schweizerischer Wissenschafts- und Technologierat/Conseil suisse de la science et de la technologie (Swiss Science and Technology Council): Inselgasse 1, 3003 Bern; tel. 313230048; fax 313239547; e-mail swtr@swtr.admin.ch; internet www .swtr.ch; advisory body to govt on all matters relating to science policy; provides and evaluates the fundamentals of a nat. policy on education, research and technology; Pres.

Prof. Dr SUSANNE SUTER; Head of Secretariat BERNHARD NIEVERGELT.

Vereinigung Schweizerischer Hochschuldozenten/Association Suisse des Professeurs d'Université: Hohstalenweg 30, 3047 Bremgarten; tel. 313020395; fax 313020395; e-mail dwegenast@freesurf .ch; internet www.unine.ch/apu; f. 1917; 1,180 mems; Pres. Prof. Dr ALEXANDER VON ZELEWSKY; Sec. Prof. Dr KLAUS WEGENAST; publ. *Bulletin VSH* (4 a year).

Learned Societies

GENERAL

Institut National Genevois: Promenade du Pin 1, 1204 Geneva; tel. 223104188; fax 223103453; e-mail ing@cortex.ch; internet www.inge.ch; f. 1853; 750 mems; Pres. PIERRE KUNZ; Sec.-Gen. MONIQUE TANNER; consists of Moral and Political Sciences Section (Pres. GIORGIO QUADRANTI), Economy Section (Pres. OLIVIER TERRETTAZ), Fine Arts Section (Pres. GIORGIO QUADRANTI); publs *Mémoires, Bulletin*.

Schweizerische Akademie der Geistes- und Sozialwissenschaften/Académie Suisse des Sciences Humaines et Sociales (Swiss Academy of Humanities and Social Sciences): Postfach 8160, Hirschengraben 11, 3001 Bern; tel. 313131440; fax 313131450; e-mail sagw@ sagw.unibe.ch; internet www.sagw.ch; f. 1946; 50 mem. socs; Pres. Prof. Dr ANNE-CLAUDE BERTHOUD; Sec.-Gen. Dr MARKUS ZÜRCHER; publs *Bulletin der SAGW, SAGW-Kolloquien.*

Schweizerische Akademie der Naturwissenschaften/Académie suisse des sciences naturelles (Swiss Academy of Sciences): Schwarztorstrasse 9/11, 3007 Bern; tel. 313104020; fax 313104029; e-mail sanw@sanw.unibe.ch; internet www.sanw .ch; f. 1815; promotion of research, international relations; 74 mem. orgs, 27 commissions, 38 nat. committees, 4 fora; library: see Stadtbibliothek, Bern; Pres. Prof. Dr P. BACCINI; Sec.-Gen. Dr INGRID KISSLING-NÄF; publs *Jahrbuch* (annually), *Denkschriften, Info* (bulletin, 4 a year).

Schweizerische Akademie der Technischen Wissenschaften/Académie Suisse des Sciences Techniques (Swiss Academy of Engineering Sciences): Postfach, 8023 Zürich; Seidengasse 16, 8001 Zürich; tel. 442265011; fax 442265020; e-mail info@ satw.ch; internet www.satw.ch; f. 1981; 200 individual mems, 60 constituent societies with 74,000 mems; co-operation with similar societies and acts in advisory capacity to the govt; Pres. Prof. em. Dr RENÉ DÄNDLIKER; Sec.-Gen. Dr HANS HÄNNI.

Schweizerischer Nationalfonds zur Förderung der Wissenschaftlichen Forschung/Fonds National Suisse de la Recherche Scientifique (Swiss National Science Foundation): Wildhainweg 3, 3001 Bern; tel. 313082222; fax 313013009; e-mail pri@snf.ch; internet www.snf.ch; f. 1952 for the promotion of basic non-commercial scientific research at Swiss universities and other scientific institutions in all branches of science; furthers independent basic research with project grants, conducts research programmes and administers National Centres of Competence in Research, awards fellowships to young researchers, promotes international co-operation in research and facilitates publication in the sciences; 120 mems; Pres. Council of Foundation Dr FRITZ SCHIESSER; Pres. National Research Council

Prof. DIETER IMBODEN; Dir Dr DANIEL HÖCHLI; publs *Annual Report, Horizonte*.

Schweizerischer Wissenschafts- und Technologierat/Conseil Suisse de la Science et de la Technologie (Swiss Science and Technology Council): Inselgasse 1, 3003 Bern; tel. 313230048; fax 313239547; e-mail swtr@swtr.admin.ch; internet www .swtr.ch; f. 1965 to co-ordinate and examine national policy on science and research and aid its implementation; 12 mems; Pres. Prof. SUSANNE SUTER.

AGRICULTURE, FISHERIES AND VETERINARY SCIENCE

Association des Groupements et Organisations Romands de l'Agriculture—AGORA: Ave des Jordils 3, CP, 1000 Lausanne 6; tel. 216177477; fax 216177618; f. 1881; 28,000 mems; library of 200 vols; Dir CHRISTOPHE DARBELLAY; publs *Revue suisse de viticulture, d'arboriculture et d'horticulture* (every 2 months), *Revue suisse d'agriculture* (every 2 months).

Gesellschaft Schweizerischer Tierärzte/Société des Vétérinaires Suisses: POB 6324, 3001 Bern; tel. 313073535; fax 313073539; e-mail info@gstsvs.ch; internet www.gstsvs.ch; f. 1813; 2,546 mems; Pres. Dr A. MEISSER; Secs-Gen. S. SCHLÄPPI J. RÖTHLISBERGER, B. GSTEIGER O. FLECHTNER; publ. *Schweizer Archiv für Tierheilkunde* (monthly).

ARCHITECTURE AND TOWN PLANNING

Bund Schweizer Architekten (BSA)/Fédération des Architectes Suisses (FAS): Pfluggässlein 3, 4001 Basle; tel. 612621010; fax 612621009; e-mail bsa@bluewin.ch; internet www.architects-fsa.ch; f. 1908; 790 mems; Pres. PATRICK DEVANTHÉRY; publ. *Werk, Bauen und Wohnen* (monthly).

Schweizer Heimatschutz (Swiss National Trust): Seefeldstr. 5A, Postfach, 8032 Zürich; tel. 442545700; fax 442522870; e-mail info@ heimatschutz.ch; internet www .heimatschutz.ch; f. 1905; 20,000 mems; Pres. Councillor CASPAR HÜRLIMANN; Sec.-Gen. PHILIPP MAURER; publ. *Heimatschutz* (French and German, quarterly).

Société Suisse des Ingénieurs et des Architectes: Selnaustr. 16, 8039 Zürich; tel. 442831515; fax 442016335; e-mail gs@ sia.ch; internet www.sia.ch; f. 1837; 12,000 mems; Pres. DANIEL KÜNDIG; Gen. Sec. E. MOSIMANN; publs *Schweizer Ingenieur und Architekt* (Schweizerische Bauzeitung), *Ingénieurs et architectes suisses* (Bulletin technique de la Suisse romande), *Rivista tecnica della Svizzera italiana*.

BIBLIOGRAPHY, LIBRARY SCIENCE AND MUSEOLOGY

Schweizer Diplombibliothekare, -innen (SDB)/Bibliothécaires diplômé(e)s suisses (BDS) (Association of Swiss Graduate Librarians): Postfach 607, CH-3000 Bern 7; e-mail info@sdb-bds.ch; internet www .sdb-bds.ch; f. 1988; promotes the professional interests of qualified librarians; 500 mems; publ. *SDB/BDS News* (3 a year).

Schweizerische Bibliophilen Gesellschaft/Société Suisse des Bibliophiles: Voltastr. 43, 8044 Zürich; f. 1921; 600 mems; Pres. Dr CONRAD ULRICH; publs *Stultifera Navis 44–57, Librarium 58* (3 a year).

Schweizerische Gesellschaft für die Rechte der Urheber musikalischer Werke (SUISA) (Swiss Society for Rights of Authors of Musical Works): Bellariastr. 82, 8038 Zürich; tel. 444856666; fax 444824333; e-mail suisa@suisa.ch; internet www.suisa

.ch; f. 1923; 19,500 mems; Pres. HANS ULRICH LEHMANN; Gen. Dir ALFRED MEYER.

Schweizerische Vereinigung für Dokumentation (SVD)/Association Suisse de Documentation (ASD) (Swiss Association for Documentation): POB 601, Schmidgasse 4, 6301 Zug; tel. 417264505; e-mail svd-asd@ hispeed.ch; internet www-svd-asd.org; f. 1939; collaboration and representation of Swiss documentation in nat. and int. spheres; consultation on documental problems; training of documentalists; 500 mems (individual and collective); Pres. Prof. Dr URS NAEGELI; Sec. HARALD SCHWENK; publ. *ARBIDO* (newsletter).

Verband der Bibliotheken und der Bibliothekareinnen/Bibliothekare der Schweiz (BBS)/Association des Bibliothèques et Bibliothécaires Suisses (Swiss Association of Libraries and Librarians): Hallerstr. 58, 3012 Bern; tel. 313824240; fax 313824648; e-mail bbs@bbs .ch; internet www.bbs.ch; f. 1894; 1,950 mems; Pres. Dr PETER WILLE; Sec. BARBARA KRÄUCHI; publ. *ARBIDO* (monthly).

Verband der Museen der Schweiz/Association des Musées Suisses: c/o Schweiz Landesmuseum, Postfach 6789, 8023 Zürich; tel. 442186588; fax 442186589; e-mail contact@vms-ams.ch; internet www.vms-ams .ch; f. 1966; asscn of Swiss museums and zoological and botanical gardens, to represent their interests; forms a link between Swiss museums and International Council of Museums (see International chapter); organizes annual conference and work sessions on museology, conservation, restoration and other related topics; 670 mems; Pres. BERNARD A. SCHÜLE; Sec. JOSEF BRÜLISAUER; publs *Revue museums.ch* (annually), *Schweizer Museums Führer/Guide des musées suisses* (every 2 to 4 years).

Verein Schweizerischer Archivarinnen und Archivare/Association des archivistes suisses (Association of Swiss Archivists): Archives fédérales suisses, Archivstr. 24, 3003 Berne; tel. 313228992; fax 313227823; e-mail andreas .kellerhals-maeder@bar.admin.ch; internet www.staluzern.ch/vsa; f. 1922; lectures, discussions, etc., concerning archive work; 502 mems; Pres. ANDREAS KELLERHALS-MAEDER; publ. *ARBIDO* (11 a year).

ECONOMICS, LAW AND POLITICS

Bundesamt für Statistik/Office Fédéral de la Statistique (Federal Statistical Office): Espace de l'Europe 10, 2010 Neuchâtel; tel. 327136011; fax 327136012; e-mail info@bfs.admin.ch; internet www.statistik .admin.ch; f. 1860; for production and publication of statistics; Dir Dr CARLO MALAGUERRA; publs *Statistical Yearbook*, other statistical and economics publications.

Gottlieb Duttweiler Institute for Economic and Social Studies: Langhaldenstr. 21, 8803 Rüschlikon/Zürich; tel. 447246111; fax 447246262; e-mail info@gdi.ch; internet www.gdi.ch; f. 1963; monitoring of societal change; symposia; management development; 35 mems; Pres. Dr ANTON SCHERRER; Dir Dr DAVID BOSSHART; publ. *gdi-impuls*.

Schweizerische Gesellschaft für Aussenpolitik/Association Suisse de Politique Etrangère: Stapferhaus, Bleicherain 7, 5600 Lenzburg; tel. 628911469; fax 628918025; f. 1968; 800 mems; Pres. THOMAS WAGNER; Sec. GABRIELA WINKLER.

Schweizerische Gesellschaft für Statistik und Volkswirtschaft/Société Suisse de Statistique et d'Economie Politique: Espace de l'Europe 10, 2010 Neuchâtel; tel. 327136053; f. 1864; aims to encourage research, familiarize practicians in the field with recent developments, develop personal contacts, encourage students of economics; 1,290 mems; library: library: see entry for Schweiz. Wirtschaftsarchiv; Pres. E. BALTENSPERGER; Sec. GABRIEL GAMEZ; publ. *Zeitschrift für Volkswirtschaft und Statistik/Revue suisse d'économie politique et de statistique* (quarterly).

Schweizerische Vereinigung für Internationales Recht/Société Suisse de Droit International: Postfach 690, 8027 Zürich; f. 1914; 990 mems; Pres. Prof. Dr W. KÄLIN; Sec. Dr STEFAN BREITENSTEIN; publs *Schweizerische Zeitschrift für internationales und europäisches Recht, Swiss Studies in International Law.*

Schweizerischer Anwaltsverband/Fédération Suisse des Avocats/Federazione Svizzera degli Avvocati (Swiss Bar Association): Marktgasse 4, Postfach 8321, 3011 Bern; tel. 313130606; fax 313130616; e-mail info@swisslawyers.com; internet www.swisslawyers.com; f. 1898; 6,300 mems; Pres. EVA SALUZ; publ. *Anwaltsrevue/Revue de l'Avocat* (monthly); publ. *Schriftenreihe.*

Schweizerischer Notarenverband/Fédération Suisse des Notaires/Federazione Svizzera dei Notai: Gerechtigkeitsgasse 52, 3000 Bern 8; tel. 313105840; fax 313105850; e-mail info@schweizernotare.ch; internet www.schweizernotare.ch; f. 1920; 1,500 mems; Pres. Me PHILIPPE BOSSET; Sec. Me ANDREAS B. NOTTER.

EDUCATION

Institut de Recherche et de Documentation Pédagogique: Faubourg de l'Hôpital 43–45, CP 54, 2007 Neuchâtel 7; tel. 328896970; fax 328896971; e-mail irdp@ne.ch; internet www.unine.ch/irdp; f. 1969; research in French-speaking Switzerland, into educational methods, organization and administration; creation and analysis of teaching aids; documentation; 22 mems; library of 10,000 vols; Pres. (vacant); Dir MATTHIS BEHRENS; publ. *Le point sur la recherche* (2 a year).

FINE AND PERFORMING ARTS

Fondation Hindemith: Champ Belluet 41, 1807 Blonay; tel. 219430528; fax 219430529; internet www.hindemith.org; f. 1968 to promote and cultivate music, in particular contemporary music; maintains the musical and literary heritage of Paul Hindemith, and encourages research in the field of music and diffusion of research results; Pres. Prof. Dr A. ECKHARDT (Germany); Exec. Vice-Pres. FRANÇOIS MARGOT (Switzerland); publs *Frankfurter Studien, Hindemith-Forum* (1 or 2 a year), *Hindemith General Original Edition, Les Annales Hindemith* (annually).

Attached institutions:

Hindemith Institute Frankfurt: Eschersheimer Landstrasse 29–39, 60322 Frankfurt-am-Main, Germany; tel. (69) 5970362; fax (69) 5963104; internet www.hindemith.org; archives.

Hindemith Music Center Blonay: Blonay; tel. 219430520; fax 219430521; internet www.hindemith.org; chamber music master classes.

Gesellschaft für Schweizerische Kunstgeschichte: Pavillonweg 2, 3012 Bern; tel. 313083838; fax 313016991; e-mail gsk@gsk.ch; internet www.gsk.ch; f. 1880; 9,500 mems; Pres. CHRISTOPH J. JOLLER; publs *Die Kunstdenkmäler der Schweiz, Inventar der neueren Schweizer Architektur 1850–1920, Schweiz. Kunstführer* (20 a year), *Kunst Architektur in der Schweiz* (quarterly), *Beit-*

räge zur Kunstgeschichte der Schweiz, Kunstführer durch die Schweiz.

Gesellschaft Schweizerischer Maler, Bildhauer und Architekten/Société des Peintres, Sculpteurs et Architectes Suisses: Räffelstrasse 32, 8045 Zürich; tel. 444621030; fax 444621610; internet www.visarte.ch; f. 1865; 2,000 active mems; Pres. JEAN-PIERRE GERBER; Dir ROBERTA WEISSMARIANI; publs *Schweizer Kunst, Art Suisse, Arte Svizzera.*

Kunstverein St Gallen: Museumstr. 32, 9000 St Gallen; tel. 712420674; tel. 712420672; e-mail kunstverein@kunstmuseumsg.ch; internet www.kunstmuseumsg.ch; f. 1827; organizes exhibitions; 2,400 mems; Pres. Dr BENNO GROSSMANN; Man. Dir CHRISTINE KALTHOFF.

Pro Helvetia (Swiss Arts Council): Hirschengraben 22, 8024 Zürich; tel. 442677171; fax 442677106; e-mail info@prohelvetia.ch; internet www.prohelvetia.ch; f. 1939; public foundation funded by the Swiss Confederation; provides Swiss cultural practitioners with the optimum conditions for the creation and dissemination of their works at home and abroad; fosters co-operation with foreign artists; Pres. MARIO ANNONI; Dir PIUS KNÜSEL; publ. *Passages* (3 a year).

Schweizer Blasmusikverband/Association Suisse des Musiques: Geschäftsstelle, Postfach, 5001 Aarau; tel. 648228111; fax 648228110; e-mail info@windband.ch; internet www.windband.ch; f. 1862; 88,000 mem. musicians in 2,136 local bands, which play concert and marching music; Pres. HANS LUTERNAUER; publ. *Unisono* (every 2 weeks).

Schweizer Musikrat (SMR)/Conseil Suisse de la Musique (CSM) (Swiss Music Council): Haus der Musik, Gönhardweg 32, 5000 Aarau; tel. 628229423; fax 628229407; e-mail info@musikrat.ch; internet www.musikrat.ch; f. 1964; mem. of the CIM (UNESCO); mem. of various musical orgs; 60 mem. orgs; Pres. Prof. Dr ALOIS KOCH; Exec. Officer PATRICK LINDER; publs *Guide for Musical Studies in Switzerland, Schweizer Muzikzeitung* (irreg.).

Schweizerische Musikforschende Gesellschaft (SMG): Schönaustr. 15, 3600 Thun; tel. and fax 332225232; e-mail therese.bruggisser@bluewin.ch; f. 1916; 700 mems; Pres. Dr THERESE BRUGGISSER-LANKER; Sec. PIO PELLIZZARI; publs *Schweiz. Musikdenkmäler, Publikationen der SMG: Serie II, Schweizer Jahrbuch für Musikwissenschaft* (annually).

Schweizerischer Kunstverein/Société Suisse des Beaux-Arts/Società Svizzera di Belle Arti: Zeughausstrasse 55, 8026 Zürich; tel. 442416301; fax 442416373; e-mail info@kunstverein.ch; internet www.kunstverein.ch; f. 1806; aims to promote and protect the interests of art assocs and art lovers on a federal level; acts as the umbrella org. for 33 mem. sections; Pres. REINER PEIKERT (acting); publ. *Kunst-Bulletin* (10 a year).

Schweizerischer Tonkünstlerverein/Association Suisse des Musiciens: Ave du Grammont 11 bis, 1000 Lausanne 13; tel. 216143290; fax 216143299; e-mail asm-stv@span.ch; internet www.asm-stv.ch; f. 1900; 950 mems; Pres. ROMAN BROTBECK; Sec. CLAUDINE WYSSA; publ. *Dissonanz/Dissonance* (6 a year).

Schweizerischer Werkbund (SWB): Limmatstr. 118, 8031 Zürich; tel. 442727176; fax 442727506; e-mail swb@werkbund.ch; internet www.werkbund.ch; f. 1913; 1,000 mems; Dir IRMA NOSEDA; publs *SWB-Dokumente, SWB-Information* (quarterly).

Schweizerisches Institut für Kunstwissenschaft/Institut Suisse pour l'Étude de l'Art: Zollikerstr. 32, 8032 Zürich; tel. 443885151; fax 443815250; e-mail sik@sikart.ch; internet www.unil.ch/isea; f. 1951; registration of Swiss works of art and Swiss artists; studies in art and technology; 1,700 mems; library of 100,000 books, 78,000 reproductions; Pres. HEINZ A. HERTACH; Dir Dr HANS-JÖRG HEUSSER; publs *Jahresbericht* (annual report), *Bulletin* (2 a year).

SGD Swiss Graphic Designers: Limmatstr. 63, 8005 Zürich; tel. 442724555; fax 442725282; f. 1972; 600 mems; Pres. ERIKA REMUND; publ. *SGD Information* (4 a year).

Société Suisse de Pédagogie Musicale/Società Svizzera di Pedagogia Musicale/Schweizerische Musikpädagogische Verband: Korneliusstr. 2, 8008 Zürich; tel. 443820527; fax 443820528; e-mail smpv@bluewin.ch; internet www.smpv.ch; f. 1893; 5,000 mems; Pres. JAKOB STAEMPFLI; Sec. HELENE KERN; publ. *Agenda du musicien.*

HISTORY, GEOGRAPHY AND ARCHAEOLOGY

Antiquarische Gesellschaft in Zürich: Staatsarchiv, Postfach, 8057 Zürich; tel. 446356911; fax 446356905; e-mail staatsarchivzh@ji.zh.ch; internet www.antiquarische.ch; f. 1832; concerned with history of Zürich and Swiss history in general; 500 mems; Pres. Dr JÜRG E. SCHNEIDER; publ. *Mitteilungen der Antiquarischen Gesellschaft in Zürich* (annually).

Archäologie Schweiz/Archéologie Suisse/Archeologia Svizzera: Petersgraben 9–11, 4001 Basel; tel. 612613078; fax 612613076; internet www.archaeologie-schweiz.ch; e-mail info@archaeologie-schweiz.ch; f. 1907; 2,200 mems; Pres. HANSJÖRG BREM; publs *Archäologie der Schweiz/Archéologie Suisse* (quarterly), *Jahrbuch/annuaire* (annually).

Geographisch-Ethnographische Gesellschaft Zürich: Geographisches Institut, Universität Zürich-Irchel, Winterthurerstr. 190, 8057 Zürich; tel. 446355142; fax 446356848; e-mail gegz@geo.unizh.ch; internet www.geo.unizh.ch/gegz; f. 1889; 450 mems; Pres. Prof. Dr MAX MAISCH; Vice-Pres. Prof. Dr ULRIKE MÜLLER-BÖKER; Sec. Dr C. DEFILA; publ. *Geographica Helvetica* (4 a year).

Geographisch-Ethnologische Gesellschaft Basel: c/o Geographisches Institut, Klingelbergstr. 27, 4056 Basel; tel. 612673660; fax 612673651; e-mail info@gegbasel.ch; internet www.gegbasel.ch; f. 1923; 428 mems; Pres. Dr JUSTIN WINKLER; Sec. DIETER OPFERKUCH; publs *Regio Basiliensis* (3 a year), *Basler Beiträge zur Geographie* (irregular), *Basler Beiträge zur Physiogeographie* (irregular), *Basler Beiträge zur Physiogeographie* (irregular).

Geographische Gesellschaft Bern: Hallerstr. 12, 3012 Bern; tel. 316318869; fax 316318544; e-mail wiesmann@giub.unibe.ch; internet www.swissgeography.ch/regional.html; f. 1873; 650 mems; Pres. Dr U. WIESMANN; Sec. M. WAELTI; publs *Berner Geographische Mitteilungen* (annually), *Jahrbuch* (every 2 to 3 years).

Historische und Antiquarische Gesellschaft zu Basel: Staatsarchiv Basel-Stadt, Martinsgasse 2, 4001 Basel; tel. 612673111; fax 612673103; internet www.unibas.ch/hag; f. 1836; 500 mems; library of 30,000 vols; Pres. Dr UELI DILL; publ. *Basler Zeitschrift für Geschichte und Altertumskunde* (annually).

Historischer Verein des Kantons Bern: c/o Burgerbibliothek, Münstergasse 63, 3000

Bern 8; tel. 313203333; internet www.stub
.unibe.ch/extern/hv; f. 1847; 1,100 mems;
Pres. Dr J. SEGESSER; publs *Archiv des
Historischen Vereins* (annually), *Berner
Zeitschrift für Geschichte und Heimatkunde*
(4 a year).

**Historischer Verein des Kantons St
Gallen:** c/o Stiftsarchiv St Gallen, Klosterhof
1, 9001 St Gallen; internet www.hvsg.ch; f.
1859; 800 mems; Pres. Dr FRANZ XAVIER
BISHOF.

**Schweizerische Gesellschaft für
Geschichte/Société Suisse d'Histoire/
Società Svizzera di Storia:** Hirschengraben 11, Postfach 6576, 3001 Bern; tel.
313131338; fax 313131339; e-mail
generalsekretariat@sgg-ssh.ch; internet
www.sgg-ssh.ch; f. 1841; 1,400 mems; Pres.
Prof. Dr REGINA WECKER; publs *Schweizerische Zeitschrift für Geschichte*, *Bulletin*,
Quellen zur Schweizergeschichte.

**Schweizerische Gesellschaft für Karto-
graphie:** c/o Hans-Uli Feldmann, Bundesamt für Landestopografie, Seftigenstr. 264,
3084 Wabern; tel. 319632327; fax 319632459;
e-mail hans-uli.feldmann@swisstopo.ch;
internet www.kartographie.ch; f. 1969; educational publications and courses; 310 mems;
Pres. HANS-ULI FELDMANN; Sec. STEFAN
RÄBER; publs *Cartographica Helvetica* (2 a
year), *Topographic Maps: Map Graphics ad
Generalisation*.

**Schweizerische Numismatische
Gesellschaft/Société Suisse de Numismatique:** c/o J.-P. Righetti, 24 rue de
Romont, 1700 Fribourg; tel. 263214161; fax
263228301; internet www.numisuisse.ch; f.
1879; 650 mems; Pres. HORTENSIA VON ROTEN;
publs *Revue Suisse de Numismatique*,
Schweizer Münzkatalog, *Schweizer Münz-
blätter / Gazette numismatique suisse* (4 a
year), *Schweizerische Numismatische
Rundschau* (annually).

**Schweizerische Vereinigung für Alter-
tumswissenschaft/Association Suisse
pour l'Étude de l'Antiquité:** Institut für
Klassische Philologie, Länggass-Str. 49, 3000
Bern 9; tel. 316318013; fax 316314486;
e-mail heinz-guenther.nesselrath@kps.unibe
.ch; f. 1943; 150 mems; Pres. Prof. HEINZ-
GÜNTHER NESSELRATH; publ. *Museum Helve-
ticum* (4 a year).

Società Storica Locarnese: c/o Archivio
Comunale, Pza de' Capitani, 6600 Locarno; f.
1955; collection and conservation of documents relating to the history of the Locarno
area, organizes exhibitions and lectures; 150
mems; Pres. Dr UGO ROMERIO.

Société de Géographie de Genève: rue de
l'Athénée 2, 1205 Geneva; tel. 316318561; fax
316318511; e-mail veit@giub.unibe.ch;
internet www.swissgeography.ch; f. 1858;
250 mems; Pres. HEINZ VEIT; publ. *Le Globe*
(annually).

Société d'Egyptologie, Genève: Case postale 26, 1218 Grand-Saconnex; tel.
227910974; e-mail info@segweb.ch; internet
www.segweb.ch; f. 1978; 450 mems; library of
2,000 vols; Pres. PHILIPPE GERMOND; Sec.
SANDRA GUARNORI NICOLLIN; publs *Bulletin*
(annually), *Cahiers* (irregular).

**Société d'Histoire de la Suisse
Romande:** Bibliothèque Cantonale et Universitaire, Dorigny, 1015 Lausanne; e-mail
mail@shsr.ch; internet www.shsr.ch; f. 1837;
530 mems; library: see Bibliothèque Cantonale et Universitaire de Lausanne; Pres.
FRANÇOISE VANNOTTI.

Société d'Histoire et d'Archéologie: c/o
Bibliothèque publique et universitaire, Les
Bastions, 1211 Geneva 4; f. 1838; 550 mems;
library of 10,000 vols, 1,000 MSS (contact: c/o
Archives de la Ville de Genève, Palais

Eynard, 4 rue de la Croix-Rouge, 1211
Geneva 3); Pres. MICHEL GRANDJEAN; Sec.
FABIA CHRISTEN KOCH; publs *Bulletin*
(annually), *Mémoires et Documents*, *Bibliographie genevoise* (annually).

**Société Vaudoise d'Histoire et d'Arché-
ologie:** 32 rue de la Mouline, 1022 Cha-
vannes-près-Renens; tel. 213163711; fax
213163755; e-mail info@svha-vd.ch; internet
www.svha-vd.ch; f. 1902; 850 mems; publ.
Revue historique vaudoise (annually).

**Verband der Schweize Geographen/
Association Suisse de Géographie** (Association of Swiss Geographers): Geographisches Institut der Universität Basel,
Spalenring 145, 4055 Basel; tel. 612726480;
fax 612726923; f. 1990; co-ordinates six
regional and five thematic socs, and nine
university institutes; no individual mems;
Central Cttee acts as nat. cttee of IGU; Pres.
Dr DANIEL SCHAUB; Sec. HELLA MARTI; publ.
GeoAgenda (Mitteilungsblatt der ASG)
(every 2 months).

**Vereinigung der Freunde Antiker
Kunst/Association des Amis de l'Art
Antique** (Association of Friends of Classical
Art): c/o Archäologisches Seminar der Universität, Schönbeinstr. 20, 4056 Basel; fax
613038676; e-mail publisher@antikekunst
.ch; internet www.antikekunst.ch; f. 1956;
1,050 mems; Pres. Dr JEAN-ROBERT GISLER;
publ. *Antike Kunst* (annually).

LANGUAGE AND LITERATURE

Alliance Française: Merkurstr. 34, 8032
Zürich; tel. 442619306; fax 442619330; e-mail
info@afz.ch; internet www.afz.ch; offers
courses and exams in French language and
culture and promotes cultural exchange with
France; attached offices in Basel, Berne,
Fribourg, Hermance, Locarno, Lucerne,
Lugano, Lugnasco and St-Gallen.

British Council: Sennweg 2, POB 532, 3000
Berne 9; tel. 313011473; fax 313011459;
e-mail britishcouncil@britishcouncil.ch;
internet www.britishcouncil.ch; offers
courses and exams in English language and
British culture and promotes cultural
exchange with the UK; Dir CAROLINE MOR-
RISSEY.

Collegium Romanicum: c/o G. Eckard,
Université de Neuchâtel, Institut de Philologie Romane et Linguistique Française,
Espace Louis-Agassiz 1, 2000 Neuchâtel;
tel. 327181773; e-mail gilles.eckard@unine
.ch; internet www.sagw.ch; f. 1947; study of
Romance languages and literature; 200
mems; Pres. Dr GILLES ECKARD; publs *Romanica Helvetica*, *Versants* (2 a year), *Vox
Romanica* (annual).

Deutschschweizer PEN-Zentrum:
Zypressenstr. 76, 8004 Zurich; tel.
442422111; fax 442416032; e-mail infopen@
tiscalinet.ch; internet www.pen-dschweiz.ch
.vu; f. 1932; 80 mems; Pres. KRISTIN T.
SCHNIDER; Sec. SEBASTIAN HEFTI; publ. *Brief-
zeitung* (2 a year).

**Gesellschaft für Deutsche Sprache und
Literatur in Zürich:** Deutsches Seminar
der Universität Zürich, Schönberggasse 9,
8001 Zürich; tel. 446342571; e-mail
uguenthe@ds.unizh.ch; f. 1894; 210 mems;
Pres. Dr ULLA KLEINBERGER GÜNTHER.

**Institut dal Dicziunari Rumantsch
Grischun:** Ringstr. 34, 7000 Chur; tel.
812846642; fax 812840204; e-mail info@drg
.ch; internet www.drg.ch; f. 1885; conservation and research into the Romansch language; 1,000 mems; library of 18,000 vols;
Pres. Dr CHRISTIAN COLLENBERG; publs
Annalas (annually), *Dicziunari Rumantsch
Grischun* (2 a year).

Institut et Musée Voltaire: 25 rue des
Délices, 1203 Geneva; tel. 223447133; fax
223451984; e-mail institut.voltaire@ville-ge
.ch; internet www.ville-ge.ch/imv; f. 1954;
library of 28,000 vols and MSS; Curator
FRANÇOIS JACOB; publ. *La Gazette des Délices*
(quarterly).

PEN Club de Suisse Romande: 14 rue
Crespin, 1206 Geneva; e-mail
jakoutchoumow@bluewin.ch; f. 1949; defends
freedom of expression and promotes international cultural exchanges; 70 mems; Pres.
ALEXIS KOUTCHOUMOW; publ. *Newsletter*.

**Schweizerische Sprachwissenschaf-
tliche Gesellschaft/Société Suisse de
Linguistique/Società Svizzera di Linguistica:** Institut de linguistique et des
sciences du langage, BFSH 2, 1015 Lausanne; f. 1947; 207 mems; Pres. Prof. Dr
ANNE-CLAUDE BERTHOUD; Sec. Dr PASCAL
SINGY; publs *Bulletin CILA* (2 a year),
Cahiers Ferdinand de Saussure (annually).

**Schweizerischer Schriftstellerinnen-
und Schriftsteller-Verband** (Swiss Society
of Writers): Nordstr. 9, 8035 Zürich; tel.
443500460; fax 443500461; e-mail letter@
ch-s.ch; f. 1912; 670 mems; Pres. EDITH
GLOOR; Sec. LOU PFLÜGER.

MEDICINE

**Académie Suisse des Sciences Médi-
cales/Schweizerische Akademie der
Medizinischen Wissenschaften** (Swiss
Academy of Medicine): Petersplatz 13, 4051
Basel; tel. 612699030; fax 612699039;
internet www.samw.ch; f. 1943; 56 mems;
Pres. Prof. PETER M. SUTER; Sec.-Gen. Dr
MARGRIT LEUTHOLD; publ. *Bulletin*.

**Schweizerische Gesellschaft für Balneo-
logie und Bioklimatologie/Société
Suisse de Médecine Thermale et Climatique:** c/o Dr R. Eberhard, Heilbadzentrum,
7500 St Moritz; tel. 818337171; f. 1902; aims
to develop thermal and climate medicine,
physical and dietary therapy, and to improve
scientific, professional and social links with
the medical profession; 126 mems; library of
3,000 vols; Pres. Dr O. KNÜSEL; Sec. Dr R.
EBERHARD; publ. Congress report.

**Schweizerische Gesellschaft für Chirur-
gie/Société Suisse de Chirurgie:** Service
de chirurgie, CHUV, 1011 Lausanne; f. 1913;
1,106 mems; Pres. Prof. Dr T. RÜEDI; Sec.
(vacant); publ. *Swiss Surgery*.

**Schweizerische Gesellschaft für
Geschichte der Medizin und der Natur-
wissenschaften/Société Suisse d'Histoire de la Médecine et des Sciences
Naturelles:** c/o Prof. Hans Konrad Schmutz,
Naturmuseum Winterthur, Museumstr. 52,
8400 Winterthur; e-mail hanskonrad
.schmutz@win.ch; internet www.sggmn.ch; f.
1921; 350 mems; Pres. Prof. Dr. phil. HANS
KONRAD SCHMUTZ; publ. *Gesnerus* (quarterly).

**Schweizerische Gesellschaft für Innere
Medizin/Société Suisse de Médecine
Interne:** c/o Dr V. Briner, Med. Klinik,
Kantonsspital, 6004 Luzern; internet www
.sgim.ch; f. 1932; 2,100 mems; Pres. Prof.
VERENA BRINER; publs reports of meetings,
etc.

**Schweizerische Gesellschaft für Neuro-
logie:** c/o Prof. P. A. Despland, CHUV
Neurologie, 11 rue du Bugnon, 1011 Lau-
sanne; f. 1908; 368 mems; Pres. Prof. K.
HESS; Sec. Dr H. STÖCKLI; publ. *Schweizer
Archiv für Neurologie und Psychiatrie*.

**Schweizerische Gesellschaft für Ortho-
pädie/Société Suisse d'Orthopédie:** 15,
Ave des Planches, 1820 Montreux; tel.
219632139; fax 219632149; e-mail sgo-sso@
bluewin.ch; internet www.sgosso.ch; f. 1942;
professional organization for orthopaedic

surgeons which promotes specialization in orthopaedics and safeguards professional interests; 526 mems; Pres. Dr MICHEL DUTOIT; Sec. Dr THOMAS KEHL; publs *Bulletin d'information* (3 a year), report of annual congress.

Schweizerischer Apothekerverband/ Société Suisse des Pharmaciens: Stationsstr. 12, 3097 Bern-Liebefeld; tel. 319785858; fax 319785859; e-mail sav@sphin.ch; internet www.pharmagate.ch; f. 1843; 5,373 mems; publs *Schweizer Apothekerzeitung* (24 a year), *Index Nominum*, *Pharmactuel* (6 a year), *Apotheken-Handbuch* (annually).

NATURAL SCIENCES

General

Naturforschende Gesellschaft in Basel: Universitätsbibliothek, CH-4056 Basel; internet www.ngib.ch; f. 1817; 600 mems; library of 74,000 vols; Pres. Prof. Dr DOLF VAN LOON; Sec. Dr SABINE ROSTA; publ. *Verhandlungen* (annually).

Naturforschende Gesellschaft in Bern: Universitätsbibliothek, Muenstergasse 61, Postfach, 3000 Bern 8; tel. 313203231; fax 313203299; e-mail info@ngb.ch; internet www.ngbe.ch; f. 1786; 350 mems; Pres. Prof. ERWIN FLÜCKIGER; Sec. Dr KURT GROSSENBACHER; publ. *Mitteilungen der Naturforschenden Gesellschaft in Bern* (annual).

Naturwissenschaftliche Gesellschaft Winterthur (NGW): Stadtbibliothek Winterthur, Museumstr. 52, 8401 Winterthur; internet www.ngw.ch; f. 1884; lectures, field trips, publications; 340 mems; Pres. Dr K. F. KAISER; publ. *Mitteilungen* (every 3 years).

Schweizerische Energie-Stiftung/Fondation Suisse pour l'Energie: Sihlquai 67, 8005 Zürich; tel. 442715464; fax 442730369; e-mail info@energiestiftung.ch; internet www.energiestiftung.ch; f. 1976; 3,000 ; aims to promote an energy policy suitable for human beings and the environment; and the control of energy consumption; promotes alternative sources of energy and the practice of conservation; Pres. GERI MÜLLER; publs *Energie Umwelt*, *SES-Reports* (irregular).

Schweizerische Stiftung für Alpine Forschungen (Swiss Foundation for Alpine Research): Binzstr. 23, 8045 Zürich; tel. 444610147; fax 442871368; e-mail mail@alpinfo.ch; internet www.alpineresearch.ch; f. 1939; 11 mems; Pres. Dr JÜRG MARMET; Sec. Dr F. H. SCHWARZENBACH.

Società Ticinese di Scienze Naturali: c/o Museo cantonale di Storia naturale, viale Cattaneo 4, 6900 Lugano; tel. 919115380; fax 919115389; e-mail stsn-info@sanwnet.ch; internet stsn-sanwnet.ch; f. 1903; promotion and advancement of natural sciences; 450 mems; Pres. Dr F. RAMPAZZI; publs *Bollettino* (annually), *Memorie*.

Société de Physique et d'Histoire Naturelle de Genève: POB 6434, 1211 Geneva 6; tel. 224186300; fax 224186301; internet www.unige.ch/sphn; f. 1790; natural and exact sciences; 209 mems; Pres. Dr MICHEL GRENON; Sec. CATHERINE DE JONG; publ. *Archives des sciences* (3 a year).

Société Vaudoise des Sciences Naturelles: Palais de Rumine, 1005 Lausanne; tel. and fax 213124334; e-mail svsn@unil.ch; internet www2.unil.ch/svsn; f. 1815; 600 mems; library: 1,000 periodicals in the library reading-room: see also Bibliothèque Cantonale et Universitaire de Lausanne; Pres. CLAUDE-ALAIN ROTEN; publs *Bulletin* (2 a year), *Mémoires* (irregular).

Biological Sciences

Bernische Botanische Gesellschaft: Altenbergrain 21, 3013 Bern; tel. 316314911; fax 313322059; internet homepage.hispeed.ch/bebcge; f. 1918; 380 mems; Pres. ANDREAS STAMPFLI; Sec. RITA GERBER; publ. *Sitzungsberichte* (annually).

Schweizerische Botanische Gesellschaft: c/o Institut de Botanique Systématique et de Géobotanique, Université, 1015 Lausanne; internet www.botanica-helvetica.ch; f. 1890; 700 mems; Pres. GREGOR KOZLOWSKI; publ. *Botanica Helvetica*.

Schweizerische Entomologische Gesellschaft: c/o CSCF, Terreaux 14, 2000 Neuchâtel; tel. 327257257; internet www.senateweb.ch; f. 1858; 293 mems; library of 18,000 vols; Pres. Dr DANIEL BURCKHARDT; Sec. HANNES BAUR; publ. *Mitteilungen* (annually).

Mathematical Sciences

Schweizerische Mathematische Gesellschaft/Société Mathématique Suisse: Mathematisches Institut, Universität Bern, Sidlerstr. 5, 3012 Bern; internet www.math.ch; f. 1910; 480 mems; Pres. Prof. URS WÜRGLER; Sec. Prof. PETER BUSER; publs *Commentarii Mathematici Helvetici* (quarterly), *Elemente der Mathematik* (quarterly).

Physical Sciences

Bundesamt für Meteorologie und Klimatologie (MeteoSchweiz) (Federal Office for Meteorology and Climatology): Krähbühlstr. 58, 8044 Zürich; tel. 442569211; fax 442569278; internet www.meteoschweiz.ch; f. 1880; 280 mems; meteorological and climatological services; library of 40,000 vols; Dir DANIEL K. KEUERLEBE; Librarian GREGOR STORK; publs *Annalen*, *Arbeitsberichte der MeteoSchweiz*, *Veröffentlichung der MeteoSchweiz*.

Neue Schweizerische Chemische Gesellschaft/Nouvelle Société Suisse de Chimie: c/o SANW, Bärenplatz 2, 3001 Bern; tel. 616966626; fax 616966985; e-mail info@swiss-chem-soc.ch; internet www.swiss-chem-soc.ch; f. 1992; 2,200 mems; Pres. Prof GEORG FRÁTER; Sec.-Gen. Dr MARKUS STRAUB; publs *Chimia* (online, at www.chimia.ch), *Helvetica Chimica Acta*.

Schweizerische Astronomische Gesellschaft/Société Astronomique Suisse (Swiss Astronomical Society): c/o Dr Max Hubmann, Waldweg 1, 3072 Ostermundigen; tel. 319311446; e-mail hubmann_ulmer@freesurf.ch; internet www.astroinfo.ch; f. 1938; 2,000 mems; Pres. Dr MAX HUBMANN; publ. *Orion* (6 a year).

Schweizerische Geologische Gesellschaft/Société Géologique Suisse (Swiss Geological Society): c/o Dr M. Sartori, Dept de géologie, Université de Genève, 13 rue des Maraîchers, 1211 Geneva 4; tel. 227026611; fax 223205732; f. 1882; 1,000 mems; promotes geology from a general viewpoint; regular annual meetings; Pres. Dr P. JORDAN; Sec. Dr M. SARTORI; publ. *Eclogae geologicae Helvetiae* (Swiss Journal of Geosciences, 3 a year).

Schweizerische Paläontologische Gesellschaft (SPG)/Société Paléontologique Suisse (SPS): Institut de Géologie et Paléontologie, Université de Lausanne, Dorigny–Anthropole, 1015 Lausanne; internet spg.scnatweb.ch; f. 1921; 260 mems; Pres. Dr URSULA MENKVELD-GFELLER; publ. *Bericht*.

Schweizerische Physikalische Gesellschaft/Société Suisse de Physique (Swiss Physical Society): Institut für Physik, Klingelbergstr. 82, 4056 Basel; fax 612673784; e-mail sps@unibas.ch; internet www.sps.ch; f. 1908; 1,200 mems; Pres. Dr TIBOR GYALOG.

PHILOSOPHY AND PSYCHOLOGY

Schweizerische Gesellschaft für Psychologie/Société Suisse de Psychologie: Institut für Psychologie, Universität Bern, Muesmattstr. 45, 3000 Bern 9; tel. 316313121; fax 316318212; e-mail sgp-ssp@unifr.ch; internet www.unifr.ch/psycho/sgp-ssp; f. 1943; 360 mems; Pres. Prof. Dr JEAN RETSCHITZKI; publ. *Swiss Journal of Psychology*.

Schweizerische Philosophische Gesellschaft/Société Suisse de Philosophie: c/o Hans Hirschi, Winkelbüelrain 1, 6043 Adligenswil; internet www.sagw.ch/philosophie; f. 1940; 800 mems; Pres. HANS HIRSCHI; publs *Studia philosophica* (annually), *Supplementa* (irregular).

Schweizerischer Berufsverband für Angewandte Psychologie/Association Professionnelle Suisse de Psychologie Appliquée/Associazone Professionale Svizzera della Psicologia Applicata: Merkurstr. 36, 8032 Zürich; tel. 432680405; fax 432680406; e-mail info@sbap.ch; internet www.sbap.ch; f. 1952; 580 mems; Pres. HEIDI AESCHLIMANN; Sec. SYBILLE SCHENKER; publ. *Punktum* (4 a year).

RELIGION, SOCIOLOGY AND ANTHROPOLOGY

Schweizerische Afrika-Gesellschaft/Société Suisse d'Etudes Africaines: Universität Basel, Rheinsprung 9, 4051 Basel; tel. 612672742; internet www.sagw.ch/africa; f. 1974; co-ordinates multidisciplinary research on Africa; 200 mems; Pres. Dr LILO ROOST VISCHER; publs *Newsletter* (quarterly), *Swiss Bibliography of Africa* (annually).

Schweizerische Gesellschaft für Soziologie/Société Suisse de Sociologie: c/o PHTG Nationalstr. 19, 8280 Kreuzlingen; tel. 716785645; fax 716785657; e-mail sgs@phtg.ch; internet www.sagw.ch/soziologie; f. 1955; 600 mems; Pres. Prof. Dr CHRISTOPH MAEDER; publs *Bulletin* (2 a year), *Schweizerische Zeitschrift für Soziologie/Revue suisse de sociologie/Swiss Journal of Sociology* (3 a year), *Newsletter* (online, 10 a year).

Schweizerische Gesellschaft für Volkskunde/Société Suisse des Traditions Populaires: Spalenvorstadt 2, 4001 Basel; tel. 612671163; fax 612671163; e-mail sgv-sstp@volkskunde.ch; internet www.volkskunde.ch; f. 1896; 1,300 mems; Pres. Prof. Dr WALTER LEIMGRUBER; Sec. Dr R. ANZENBERGER; publs *Schweizerisches Archiv für Volkskunde* (2 a year), *Schweizer Volkskunde* (quarterly).

Schweizerische Theologische Gesellschaft/Société Suisse de Théologie: Postfach 8204, 3001 Bern; internet www.sagw.ch/dt/mitglieder/outer.asp?id=28; f. 1965; 280 mems; Pres. Prof. Dr WOLFGANG W. MULLER; Sec. KATHERINE SIEGENTHALER; publ. *Bulletin* (2 a year).

Schweizerische Trachtenvereinigung/Fédération Nationale des Costumes Suisses: Rosswiesstr. 29, Postfach 8608 Bubikon; tel. 552631563; fax 552631561; e-mail info@trachtenvereinigung.ch; internet www.trachtenvereinigung.ch; f. 1926; folk dance records and descriptions; 22,866 mems; Dir JOHANNES SCHMID-KUNZ; publ. *Tracht und Brauch/Costumes et Coutumes* (4 a year).

Verband Jüdischer Lehrer und Kantoren der Schweiz (Society of Jewish teachers and cantors in Switzerland):

Brandschenksteig 12, 8002 Zürich; f. 1926; 62 mems; Pres. ERICH HAUSMANN; Sec. MICHEL BOLLAG; publ. *Bulletin*.

TECHNOLOGY

Fachleute Geomatik Schweiz (Swiss Association of Surveyors): c/o Franziska André, Flühlistr. 30B, 3612 Steffisburg; tel. 334381462; fax 334381464; e-mail admin@ pro-geo.ch; internet www.pro-geo.ch; f. 1929 as Verband Schweizerische Vermessungsfachleute; 1,500 mems; Pres. LAURENT BERSET; Sec. FRANZISKA ANDRÉ; publ. *Geomatik Schweiz* (12 a year).

Schweizerische Gesellschaft für Automatik/Association Suisse pour l'Automatique (Swiss Federation of Automatic Control): c/o Hörrmann Secretarial Services, Postfach, 5442 Fislisbach; tel. 564703666; fax 564703668; e-mail hoerrmann@lcc.ch; internet www.sga.ee.ethz.ch; f. 1956; promotes and develops knowledge of techniques of measurement, control and calculation, and their application in the field of automation; 200 individual mems, 17 corporate mems; Pres. Prof. HEINZ DOMEISEN; Sec. J. HOERRMANN-CLARKE; publs *SGA-ASSPA-Bulletin* (quarterly), *Lernmodule* (4 a year).

Schweizerische Gesellschaft für Mikrotechnik/Association Suisse de Microtechnique: c/o FRSM, Ruelle DuPeyrou 4, Case postale 2353, 2001 Neuchâtel; tel. 327200900; fax 327200990; e-mail fsrm@ fsrm.ch; internet www.fsrm.ch; f. 1962; 73 mems; Pres. P. STAUBER; Sec. S. SCHWEND-ENER; publ. *Bulletin* (annually).

Schweizerischer Verband der Ingenieur-Agronomen und der Lebensmittel-Ingenieure/Association suisse des ingénieurs agronomes et des ingénieurs en technologie alimentaire: Länggasse 79, 3052 Zollikofen; tel. 319110668; fax 319114925; e-mail svial@svial.ch; internet www.svial.ch; f. 1901; 2,350 mems; Pres. ROLAND GRUNDER; Vice-Pres. Prof. Dr JACQUES MOREL; publ. *Journal* (4 a year).

Swiss Engineering–STV (Association of Engineers and Architects): Weinbergstr. 41, STV-Haus, 8023 Zürich; tel. 442683311; fax 442683700; e-mail info@swissengineering.ch; internet www.swissengineering.ch; f. 1905; 17,000 mems; Pres. RUEDI NOSER; Sec.-Gen. ANDREAS HUGI; publs *Schweizerische Technische Zeitschrift*, *Revue Technique Suisse*.

Verband Schweizer Abwasser- und Gewässerschutzfachleute (Swiss Water Pollution Control Association): Strassburgstr. 10, Postfach 2443, 8026 Zürich; tel. 433437070; fax 433437071; e-mail sekretariat@vsa.ch; internet www.vsa.ch; f. 1944; 1,350 mems, 2,400 reps; Pres. JÜRG MEYER.

Research Institutes

AGRICULTURE, FISHERIES AND VETERINARY SCIENCE

Office Fédéral de l'Agriculture (Federal Office of Agriculture): Ministry of Public Economy, Mattenhofstr. 5, 3003 Bern; tel. 313222511; fax 313222634; e-mail info@blw .admin.ch; internet www.blw.admin.ch; the centre for federal agricultural research; Dir Dr MANFRED BÖTSCH; Deputy Dir Dr JACQUES CHAVAZ; Head of Agricultural Research Prof. Dr JACQUES MOREL; publs *Agrarforschung* (monthly), *Revue suisse d'agriculture* (monthly).

Federal agricultural research stations:

Agroscope FAL Reckenholz: Station Fédérale de Recherches en Ecologie et Agriculture (Federal Research Station for Agroecology and Agriculture): Reckenholzstrasse 191, Postfach, 8046 Zürich-Reckenholz; tel. 443777111; fax 443777201; e-mail info@fal.admin.ch; internet www.reckenholz.ch; Dir PAUL STEFFEN; publ. *Agrarforschung* (monthly).

Agroscope FAT Tänikon: Recherches d'Economie d'Entreprise et de Génie rural (Federal Research Station for Agricultural Economics and Engineering at Tänikon): 8356 Ettenhausen; tel. 523683131; fax 523651190; e-mail info@ fat.admin.ch; Dir Prof. Dr WALTER MEIER; publ. *FAT-Berichte* (2 a month).

Agroscope FAW: Recherches en Arboriculture, Viticulture et Horticulture de Wädenswil (Federal Research Station for Fruit-Growing, Viticulture and Horticulture): Postfach 185, 8820 Wädenswil; tel. 447836111; fax 447806341; e-mail info@faw.admin.ch; internet www.faw.ch; Dir Dr URS HILBER; publ. *Obst- und Weinbau* (monthly).

Agroscope Liebefeld-Posieux (Federal Dairy Research Station): Tioleyre 4, 1725 Posieux, Bern; tel. 264077111; fax 264077300; e-mail info@alp.admin.ch; Dir Dr DANIELLE GAGNAUX; publ. *Agrarforschung* (monthly).

Agroscope RAC Changins: Station Fédérale de Recherches Agronomique (Federal Research Station for Plant Production): Château de Changins, 1260 Nyon; tel. 223634444; fax 223621325; e-mail info@rac.admin.ch; internet www .racchangins.ch; Dir Dr ANDRÉ STÄUBLI; publ. *Revue suisse d'agriculture* (monthly).

ECONOMICS, LAW AND POLITICS

Center for Comparative and International Studies (CIS) Zürich: Rämistr. 71, 8006 Zürich; tel. 446327968; fax 446321942; internet www.uzh.ch; f. 1997; research centre for comparative politics and int. relations, created jtly by the Eidgenössische Technische Hochschule Zürich and the Universität Zürich; Dir Prof. HANSPETER KRIESI.

Institut Suisse de Droit Comparé/ Schweizerisches Institut für Rechtsvergleichung/Istituto Svizzero di Diritto Comparato (Swiss Institute of Comparative Law): 1015 Lausanne-Dorigny; tel. 216924911; fax 216924949; e-mail secretariat.isdc-dfjp@unil.ch; internet www .isdc.ch; f. 1978; provides the Federal Government with the documents and studies necessary for legislation and for the conclusion of international conventions; participates in international efforts towards approximation and unification of law; gives information and consultations to courts, administrations, attorneys and interested persons; conducts its own scientific research, promotes and co-ordinates studies in Swiss universities and provides researchers in Switzerland with an appropriate centre for study; library: see Libraries and Archives; Dir Prof. BERTIL COTTIER.

Schweizerisches Institut für Auslandforschung (Swiss Institute of International Studies): Seilergraben 49, 8001 Zürich; tel. 446363362; fax 446321947; Dir Prof. Dr DIETER RULOFF; publ. *Sozialwissenschaftliche Studien* (annually).

MEDICINE

Institut für Geschichte und Epistemologie der Medizin (Institute for the History and Epistemology of Medicine): Schönbeinstr. 18/20, 4056 Basel; tel. 612601132; fax 612601133; f. 1964; library of 10,000 vols; Dir Prof. U. TROEHLER.

Institut Suisse de Recherche Expérimentale sur le Cancer/Schweizerisches Institut für Experimentelle Krebsforschung (Swiss Institute for Experimental Cancer Research): Ch. des Boveresses 155, 1066 Epalinges s. Lausanne; tel. 216925858; fax 216526933; e-mail relations .publiques@isrec.ch; internet www.isrec.ch; f. 1964; 180 mems; library of 2,000 vols, 100 periodicals, 5,000 online periodicals; Pres. Y. J. PATERNOT; Dir Prof. M. AGUET.

Schweizerisches Tropeninstitut (STI)/ Institut Tropical Suisse: Socinstrasse 57, 4002 Basel; tel. 612848111; fax 612718654; e-mail sticourses@ubaclu.unibas.ch; internet www.sti.ch; f. 1943; library of 7,000 vols; Dir Prof. Dr MARCEL TANNER.

NATURAL SCIENCES

General

Bundesamt für Bildung und Wissenschaft/Office Fédéral de l'Education et de la Science (Federal Office for Education and Science): Hallwylstr. 4, 3003 Bern; tel. 313229691; fax 313227854; e-mail martin .fischer@bbw.admin.ch; f. 1969; prepares policy decisions for education and science and executes scientific policy; co-ordinates activities of Federal bodies concerned with research and education; supports universities and other institutes of higher education and contributes to grants; is responsible for encouragement and general co-ordination of research and higher education; with other Departments deals with international scientific affairs; Dir GERHARD M. SCHUWEY.

Collegium Basilea (Institute of Advanced Study): Hochstr. 51, 4053 Basel; tel. 613619523; fax 613619524; e-mail cb@ unibas.ch; internet pages.unibas.ch/colbas; f. 1999; Institute of Advanced Study supporting interdisciplinary postdoctoral research, mainly in the biological, physical and chemical sciences, with an emphasis on the physico-chemical foundations of living systems; 45 mems (5 full, 40 assoc.); library of 7,000 vols; Pres. Prof. Dr JEREMY J. RAMSDEN; publs *Journal of Biological Physics and Chemistry* (quarterly), *Nanotechnology Perceptions* (review of ultraprecision engineering and nanotechnology, 3 a year).

Jungfraujoch and Gornergrat Scientific Stations: Secretariat, Sidlerstr. 5, 3012 Bern; tel. 316314052; fax 316314405; e-mail louise.wilson@phim.unibe.ch; internet www .ifjungo.ch; f. 1930; high-altitude research in solar astronomy, astrophysics, environmental sciences, atmospheric physics, atmospheric chemistry, glaciology, meteorology, physics and biology; international foundation run by scientific organizations of Austria, Belgium, Germany, Great Britain, Italy, Switzerland; Dir Prof. E. FLÜCKIGER; publ. *Review on Activity*.

Stiftung für Humanwissenschaftliche Grundlagenforschung/Fondation pour la Recherche de Base dans les Sciences de l'Homme: Postfach 112, 8030 Zürich; tel. 443830922; f. 1970; basic research in human sciences; Pres. Prof. JULES ANGST; Dir Dr WALTER BODMER.

Biological Sciences

Conservatoire et Jardin botaniques de la Ville de Genève: CP 60, 1292 Chambésy; tel. 224185100; fax 224185101; e-mail periodiques.cjb@ville-ge.ch; internet www .ville-ge.ch/cjb; f. 1817; systematic botany, taxonomy, floristics, ecology, phytogeography; 95 mems, including 21 scientific mems; library of 220,000 vols, 4,007 periodicals; Dir Prof. RODOLPHE SPICHIGER; publs *Candollea*, *Boissiera*.

Institut für Pflanzenwissenschaften (Institute of Plant Sciences): Altenbergrain 21, 3013 Bern; tel. 316314911; fax 313222059; f. 1862; Dir Prof. Dr U. FELLER.

Botanic garden:

Botanischer Garten: Altenbergrain 21, 3013 Bern; tel. 316314937; fax 316314993; e-mail info@botanischergarten.ch; internet www.botanischergarten.ch; Dir Dr K. AMMANN.

Physical Sciences

Eidgenössisches Institut für Schnee- und Lawinenforschung (SLF) (Federal Institute for Snow and Avalanche Research): Flüelastrasse 11, 7260 Davos Dorf; tel. 814170111; fax 814170110; e-mail info@slf.ch; internet www.slf.ch; f. 1936; physics and mechanics of snow and snow pack, avalanche formation and mechanics, protective structure, snow and avalanche interaction with forests, and an avalanche warning service; 150 mems; library of 20,000 titles; Dir Dr WALTER AMMANN; publs *Winterbericht* (annually), *Mitteilungen*, *Unfallberichte*.

Institut für Astronomie: ETH-Zentrum, 8092 Zürich; tel. 446323813; fax 446321205; internet www.astro.phys.ethz.ch; f. 1864; 35 mems; astrophysics; Dir Prof. Dr J. O. STENFLO.

Observatoire Cantonal: 2000 Neuchâtel; tel. 328896870; fax 328896281; e-mail secretariat.on@on.unine.ch; f. 1858; research in atomic frequency standards, space clocks and lidar geophysics; dissemination of official time in Switzerland; library of 1,000 vols; Dir G. BUSCH; publ. annual report.

Observatoire de Genève: 51 Ch. des Maillettes, 1290 Sauverny–Geneva; tel. 227552611; fax 227553983; e-mail michel.mayor@obs.unige.ch; internet www.unige.ch/sciences/astro; f. 1772; astrophysics, galactic structure, extra-solar planets, space research; library of 6,000 vols, 500 periodicals; Dir Dr Prof. MICHEL MAYOR.

Schweizerische Gesellschaft für Astrophysik und Astronomie/Société Suisse d'Astrophysique et d'Astronomie: Astronomisches Institut der Universität Basel, Venusstr. 7 4102 Binningen; e-mail binggeli@astro.unibas.ch; internet obswww.unige.ch/ssaa; f. 1968; research in astrophysics; 175 mems; Pres. Prof. GERHARD BEUTLER; Sec. Dr BRUNO BINGGELI.

Specola Solare Ticinese: Via ai Monti 146, 6600 Locarno; tel. 917562376; fax 917562375; internet www.specola.ch; f. 1957; solar observation; library of 600 vols; Dir Prof. Dr PHILIPPE JETZER.

Libraries and Archives

Aarau

Aargauer Kantonsbibliothek: Aargauerplatz, 5000 Aarau; tel. 628352360; fax 628352369; e-mail kantonsbibliothek@ag.ch; internet www.ag.ch/kantonsbibliothek; f. 1803; 600,000 vols, 2,000 periodicals; 850 incunabula, 1,500 MSS; special collections: Zurlaubiana (history of Switzerland and Europe), Frank Wedekind archive; Dir Dr RUTH WÜST.

Staatsarchiv des Kantons Aargau: Entfelderstr. 22, 5001 Aarau; tel. 628351290; fax 628351299; e-mail staatsarchiv@ag.ch; internet www.ag.ch/staatsarchiv; f. 1803; State Archivist Lic. phil. ANDREA VOELLMIN.

Basel

Allgemeine Bibliotheken der Gesellschaft für das Gute und Gemein-nützige: Rümelinsplatz 6, 4001 Basel; tel. 612641111; fax 612641190; e-mail abg@ubaclu.unibas.ch; f. 1807; 290,000 vols; central library and 8 br. libraries; Dir KURT WALDNER; publ. *Jahresbericht*.

Archiv für Schweizerische Kunstgeschichte: Münzgasse 16, 4051 Basel; tel. 612672943; 6,000 vols; Dir NIKLAUS MEIER.

Bibliothek des Museums der Kulturen Basel: Augustinergasse 2, 4001 Basel; tel. 612665630; fax 612665605; e-mail elisabeth.idris@bs.ch; internet www.mkb.ch; f. 1901; 80,000 vols on ethnography of the world; Librarian ELISABETH IDRIS-HÖHENER.

Öffentliche Bibliothek der Universität Basel (Public University Library): Schönbeinstr. 18–20, 4056 Basel; tel. 612673111; fax 612673103; e-mail sekretariat-ub@unibas.ch; internet www.ub.unibas.ch; f. 1460; 3,000,000 vols; scientific works, special collections of MSS, incunabula, maps, portraits; Chief Librarian H. HUG; publs *Bericht über die Verwaltung der Öffentlichen Bibliothek der Universität Basel* (annually), *Jahresverzeichnis der Schweizerischen Hochschulschriften*, *Die mittelalterlichen Handschriften der Universitätsbibliothek Basel*, *Die Matrikel der Universität Basel*, *Die Amerbachkorrespondenz*.

Schweizerisches Wirtschaftsarchiv/Archives Economiques Suisses (Swiss Economic Archive): Petersgraben 51, Postfach 4003 Basel; tel. 612673219; fax 612673208; e-mail info-wwzb@unibas.ch; internet www.ub.unibas.ch/wwz; f. 1910; 650,000 vols, including business reports, periodicals, statistical publications, reports on social institutions and professional societies; 2,000,000 newspaper cuttings; open to the general public; Dir JOHANNA GISLER.

Staatsarchiv Basel Stadt: Martinsgasse 2, 4001 Basel; tel. 612678601; fax 612676571; e-mail stabs@bs.ch; internet www.bs.ch/stabs; Dir Dr J. ZWICKER; publs *Jahresberichte*, *Quellen und Forschungen zur Basler Geschichte*.

Bern

Bibliothek des Konservatoriums für Musik und Theater: Kramgasse 36, 3011 Bern; f. 1917; 50,000 vols; Pres. ANNAMARIE ZINSLI.

Burgerbibliothek Bern/Bibliothèque de la Bourgeoisie de Berne: Münstergasse 63, 3000 Bern 8; tel. 313203333; fax 313203370; e-mail bbb@burgerbib.unibe.ch; internet www.cx.unibe.ch/burgerbib; f. 1951; 15,000 vols, 50 periodicals, 2,700 metres of historical MSS, of which 50 metres medieval MSS; Dir J. H. WÄBER.

Centre de Documentation de Politique de la Science/Dokumentationsstelle für Wissenschaftspolitik (Documentation Centre for Political Science): Effingerstr. 43, 3003 Bern; tel. 313229655; fax 313228070; e-mail edith.imhof@cest.admin.ch; internet www.cest.ch; f. 1972; 15,000 vols, 86 periodicals; Head EDITH IMHOF.

Eidgenössische Parlaments- und Zentralbibliothek (Central Library of Parliament and Federal Administration): Bundeshaus West, 3003 Bern; tel. 313223789; fax 313227807; e-mail info-epzb@bk.admin.ch; f. 1848; 110,000 vols; open to the public for reference only; Dir CHARLES R. PFERSICH.

Schweizerische Nationalbibliothek/Bibliothèque nationale suisse / Biblioteca nazionale svizzera (Swiss National Library): Hallwylstr. 15, 3003 Bern; tel. 313228911; fax 313228463; e-mail info@nb.admin.ch; internet www.nb.admin.ch; f. 1895; contains all publs issued in Switzerland and foreign publs by Swiss authors or concerning Switzerland; Swiss union catalogue, SwissInfoDesk, Swiss Literary Archives, Prints and Drawings Dept, Swiss ISSN Centre, Centre Dürrenmatt Neuchâtel; 3,853,533 vols, 686,002 bound vols of periodicals, 368,450 engravings, photos and maps, 61,984 musical publs, 13,076 microforms and CD-ROMs, 15,115 audiovisual items; 215 collns in the Swiss Literary Archives; Dir MARIE-CHRISTINE DOFFEY; publs *The Swiss Book / Le Livre suisse / Das Schweizer Buch / Il libro svizzero* (24 a year), *Bibliographie der Schweizergeschichte / Bibliographie de l'histoire suisse*.

Schweizerisches Bundesarchiv: Archivstr. 24, 3003 Bern; tel. 313228989; fax 313227823; f. 1798; Dir Prof. CHRISTOPH GRAF.

Staatsarchiv des Kantons Bern: Falkenplatz 4, 3012 Bern; tel. 316335101; fax 316335102; internet www.sta.be.ch/staatsarchiv; archives of the Canton of Bern; Archivist Dr KARL F. WÄLCHLI; publ. *Das Staatsarchiv des Kantons Bern*.

Universitätsbibliothek Bern: Münstergasse 61, 3000 Bern 8; tel. 316319211; fax 316319299; e-mail info@ub.unibe.ch; internet www.ub.unibe.ch; f. 1528; 2,300,000 vols; Chief Librarian Dr SUSANNA BLIGGENSTORFER.

Bubendorf

Fondation Bibliotheca Afghanica/Swiss Afghanistan Institute: Hauptstrasse 34, 4416 Bubendorf; tel. 619339877; fax 619339878; e-mail sai@tiscali.ch; internet www.afghanistan-institut.ch; f. 1975; research institute and archive; Afghanistan Museum-in-Exile; 14,000 vols, 10,000 photographs; material on Afghan history, geography, ethnography, religion and politics; German newspaper clippings; Mujahideen and Communist government publications; Dir PAUL BUCHERER-DIETSCHI.

Chur

Staatsarchiv Graubünden: Karlihofplatz, 7001 Chur; tel. 812572803; fax 812572001; e-mail info@sag.gr.ch; internet www.staatsarchiv.gr.ch; f. 1803; Dir Dr S. MARGADANT.

Cologny

Bibliotheca Bodmeriana (Fondation Martin Bodmer): 19–21 route du Guignard, 1223 Cologny; tel. 227074433; fax 227074430; e-mail info@fondationbodmer.ch; internet www.fondationbodmer.org; f. 1972; 160,000 vols; special collections of papyrus, MSS, autographs, incunabula, music manuscripts, drawings; Dir Dr M. BIRCHER.

Fribourg

Bibliothèque Cantonale et Universitaire/Kantons- und Universitätsbibliothek: rue Joseph-Piller 2, 1701 Fribourg; tel. 263051333; fax 263051377; e-mail bcu@fr.ch; internet www.fr.ch/bcu; f. 1848; 2,000,000 vols; Dir Dr MARTIN GOOD.

Geneva

Archives d'Etat: 1 rue de l'Hôtel de Ville, 1211 Geneva 3; tel. 223273395; fax 223273365; e-mail archives@etat.ge.ch; internet www.geneve.ch/archives; material on history of Geneva; Archivist C. SANTSCHI.

Bibliothèque d'Art et d'Archéologie: 5 Promenade du Pin, 1204 Geneva; tel. 224182700; fax 224182701; e-mail info.baa@ville-ge.ch; internet mah-ville-ge.ch/musee/baa/baa.html; f. 1911; subsidiary of Musées d'Art et d'Histoire; 200,000 vols, 150,000 slides, 5,600 periodicals, 140,000 exhibition and auction catalogues, CD-ROMs, databases; Head Librarian VÉRONIQUE GONCERUT ESTÈBE.

Bibliothèque des Nations Unies/United Nations Library: Palais des Nations, 1211 Geneva 10; tel. 229174181; fax 229170028; e-mail library@unog.ch; internet www.unog.ch/library; f. 1919; 1,100,000 vols, 4m. documents and publications of the United Nations and its specialized agencies, 500,000 govt documents, 9,000 periodicals; archives of the League of Nations; Chief Librarian PIERRE LE LOARER; publs *Bibliographie Mensuelle* (monthly), *Catalogue des Publications en Série* (serials catalogue).

Bibliothèque Publique et Universitaire de Genève: Promenade des Bastions, 1211 Geneva 4; tel. 224182800; fax 224182801; e-mail info.bpu@ville-ge.ch; internet www.ville-ge.ch/bpu; f. 1562; 2,000,000 vols and pamphlets, 70,000 posters, 23,000 maps, 45,000 engravings, 400 painted portraits, 15,000 MSS; Dir ALAIN JACQUESSON.

Bibliothèques Municipales: 10 rue de la Tour-de-Boël, CP 3930 1211 Geneva; tel. 224183250; fax 224183251; internet www.ville-ge.ch/bmu; f. 1931; adult libraries (7 brs, 400,000 vols); children's libraries (7 brs, 175,000 vols); 5 bookmobiles, 60,000 vols; 2 sound-recording libraries, 80,000 records; Dir ISABELLE RUEPP.

International Labour Office Library: 1211 Geneva 22; tel. 227998675; fax 227996516; internet www.ilo.org/public/english/support/lib/index.htm; f. 1919; 1,000,000 vols and pamphlets, 5,500 current periodicals (including annuals and official gazettes); computerized data base (LABORDOC), containing 210,000 abstracts, available for on-line searching world-wide through the facilities of ESA-IRS and Questel-ORBIT and on CD-ROM; open to the public on request; Dir E. FRIERSON; publs *International Labour Documentation* (10 a year), *ILO Thesaurus: labour, employment and training terminology.*

World Health Organization Library and Information Networks for Knowledge: 20 ave Appia, 1211 Geneva 27; tel. 227912062; fax 227914150; e-mail library@who.int; internet www.who.int/library; f. 1948; WHO permanent collection, international public health literature, journals and databases, historical collection, government statistical reports, WHOLIS database; Co-ordinator YVONNE GRANDBOIS.

Grand Saint-Bernard

Bibliothèque de l'Hospice du Grand Saint-Bernard: 1931 Bourg-Saint-Pierre, Canton de Valais; library of Austin Canons monastery (f. 1050); works on botany and numismatics, ancient MSS and maps; over 30,000 vols and many thousands of brochures.

Lausanne

Bibliothèque Cantonale et Universitaire de Lausanne: Palais de Rumine, 1005 Lausanne; tel. 213167880; fax 213167870; internet www2.unil.ch/BCU (Dorigny br.: 1015 Lausanne; tel. 216921111; fax 216924845); f. 1537; legal deposit library of Vaud Canton; regional documentation; 1,400,000 vols, 150 incunabula; 8,500 CD and 2,500 LP records; the library is open to the public; Dir HUBERT VILLARD; publs *Catalogues des fonds de manuscrits, Catalogues des manuscrits musicaux, Rapport annuel.*

Bibliothèque centrale de l'École Polytechnique Fédérale de Lausanne: 1015 Lausanne; tel. 216932156; fax 216935100; e-mail info.bc@epfl.ch; internet library.epfl.ch; f. 1945; science and technology; 550,000

vols, 5,000 electronic journals, 100 databases; open to the public; Dir DAVID AYMONIN.

Bibliothèque de l'Institut Suisse de Droit Comparé/Bibliothek des Schweizerischen Instituts für Rechtsvergleichung: 1015 Lausanne-Dorigny; tel. 216924911; fax 216924949; e-mail jarka.looks@isdc-dfjp.unil.ch; internet www.isdc.ch; f. 1982; collects legal material from all countries in all fields of law, incl. international law, 250,000 vols, 2,000 periodicals, 700 electronic resources; also European documentation centre; Librarian JARMILA LOOKS.

Bibliothèque et Centre de Documentation de la Faculté de Médecine: Centre Hospitalier Universitaire Vaudois, 1011 Lausanne; tel. 213145082; fax 213145070; e-mail bdfm@chuv.hospvd.ch; internet www.hospvd.ch/chuv/bdfm; f. 1968; 60,000 vols, 2,000 periodicals; microcomputer facilities, videodiscs, audiovisual library; Librarian ISABELLE DE KAENEL.

Bibliothèque Municipale de la Ville de Lausanne: 11 place Chauderon, 1003 Lausanne; tel. 213156911; fax 213156007; e-mail bml@lausanne.ch; internet www.lausanne.ch/bibliotheque; f. 1934; 428,000 vols; Dir PIERRE-YVES LADOR.

Lucerne

Staatsarchiv des Kantons Luzern: Schützenstr. 9, 6000 Lucerne 7; tel. 412285365; fax 412286663; e-mail staatsarchiv@lu.ch; internet www.staluzern.ch; f. 1803; local history, 25,000 vols; Archivist Dr A. GÖSSI; publs *Jahresbericht des Staatsarchivs Luzern, Luzerner Historische Veröffentlichungen* (irregular).

Zentral- und Hochschulbibliothek Luzern: Sempacherstr. 10, 6002 Lucerne; tel. 412285310; fax 412108255; e-mail info@zhbluzern.ch; internet www.zhbluzern.ch; f. 1951; 950,000 vols, 2,680 MSS, 130,000 engravings, photos and maps, 35,000 microforms; incl. Burghers' library, canton library and library of the Univ. of Lucerne; collection of Swiss publs up to 1848; Lucerne Documentary Heritage Collection; Dir Dr ULRICH NIEDERER.

Lugano

Biblioteca Cantonale: Lugano, Ticino: Viale C. Cattaneo 6, 6901 Lugano; tel. 918154611; fax 918154619; internet www.sbt.ti.ch/bclugano; f. 1852; 270,000 vols; only public library of Italian culture in Switzerland; incorporates *Libreria Patria*, special collection of 'Ticinensia', 40,000 vols, also Archivio Prezzolini and collections on contemporary culture; Dir Prof. GERARDO RIGOZZI.

Neuchâtel

Archives de l'Etat: Le Château, 12 rue de la Collégiale, 2001 Neuchâtel; tel. 328896040; fax 328896088; e-mail service.archivesEtat@ne.ch; internet www.ne.ch/archives; f. 1898; maintains a historical library and an administrative library; State Archivist ALEXANDRE DAFFLON.

Bibliothèque des Pasteurs: Fbg de l'Hôpital 41, 2000 Neuchâtel; tel. 327254666; f. 1538; theological library of 70,000 vols, 20,000 pamphlets; Librarian RENÉ PÉTER-CONTESSE.

Bibliothèque Publique et Universitaire: 3 place Numa-Droz, Neuchâtel; tel. 327177300; fax 327177309; e-mail secretariat.bpu@bpu.unine.ch; internet bpun.unine.ch; f. 1788; 500,000 vols, including vols of periodicals, an Encyclopaedia Library, Swiss theses, many reviews received mostly by exchange; MSS of J.-J. Rousseau (works and correspondence) and Mme de Charrière;

archives of Société typographique de Neuchâtel; Dir M. SCHLUP; publs *Bibliothèques et musées, Revue historique neuchâteloise*, and bulletins of chronometry, geography, and natural sciences.

St Gallen

Kantonsbibliothek Vadiana St Gallen: Notkerstr. 22, 9000 St Gallen; tel. 712292321; fax 712292345; e-mail kb.vadiana@sg.ch; internet www.kb.sg.ch; f. 1551; 800,000 vols; open to the public; Dir Dr CORNEL DORA.

Stiftsbibliothek St Gallen: Klosterhof 6D, Postfach, 9004 St Gallen; tel. 712273416; fax 712273418; e-mail stibi@stibi.ch; internet www.stiftsbibliothek.ch; f. 719; library of former Benedictine Abbey of St Gall; 150,000 vols; important collection of manuscripts from Carolingian and Ottonian periods (8th–11th c.); Dir Prof. Dr ERNST TREMP.

Sion

Médiathèque Valais (Bibliothèque Cantonale)/Mediathek Wallis (Kantonsbibliothek): 9 rue des Vergers, CP 182, 1951 Sion; tel. 276064550; fax 276064554; e-mail mv.sion@mediatheque.ch; internet www.mediatheque.ch; f. 1853; 500,000 vols; 4 brs; spec. collns on the Alps; Dir JACQUES CORDONIER.

Solothurn

Bibliomedia Suisse/Bibliothèque pour tous: Rosenweg 2, 4500 Solothurn; tel. 326233231; fax 326233380; e-mail solothurn@bibliomedia.ch; internet www.svbbpt.ch; f. 1920; 500,000 vols, 3 brs; Dir Dr P. WILLE.

Zentralbibliothek: Bielstr. 39, 4502 Solothurn; tel. 326241141; fax 326241145; internet www.zbsolothurn.ch; f. 1930; 800,000 vols, 900 incunabula, 13,200 MSS, 7,000 illustrations and graphics, 18,000 music scores, 42,000 records and cassettes, 550 current periodicals and series, 30,000 children's books; Dirs VERENA BIDER, PETER PROBST; publs *Jahresbericht, Veröffentlichungen.*

Winterthur

Stadtbibliothek: Museumstr. 52, 8401 Winterthur; tel. 522675145; fax 522675140; e-mail stadtbibliothek@win.ch; internet www.winbib.ch; f. 1660; 870,000 items; special collections of local history, numismatics, music, African languages and literature; open to the public; Dir Dr HERMANN ROMER; publ. *Neujahrsblatt* (annually).

Zürich

ETH-Bibliothek (Library of the Swiss Federal Institute of Technology): Rämistr. 101, 8092 Zürich; tel. 446322549; fax 446321357; e-mail library@library.ethz.ch; internet www.ethbib.ethz.ch; f. 1855; university library specializing in science and technology; 5,700,000 vols and documents incl. 6,000 current periodicals, 10,000 current serials, 2,000,000 reports, 300,000 maps, 350,000 documents on history of science; affiliated libraries: Earth Sciences Library, Architecture and Civil Engineering Library, Industrial Engineering and Management Library, Forestry Library; Dir Prof. Dr W. NEUBAUER; publs *Schriftenreihe A: History of Science* (irregular), *Schriftenreihe B: Library Science* (irregular).

Schweizerisches Sozialarchiv/Archives sociales suisses: Stadelhoferstr. 12, 8001 Zürich; tel. 432688740; fax 432688759; e-mail sozarch@sozarch.unizh.ch; internet www.sozialarchiv.ch; f. 1906; Swiss centre of social documentation; 100,000 vols, 300,000 brochures, pamphlets, etc.; 1,300 current newspapers and reviews in the lecture hall; newspaper cuttings; the library is open to the public; Librarian Dr ANITA ULRICH.

Staatsarchiv des Kantons Zürich: Winterthurerstr. 170, Postfach, 8057 Zürich; tel. 446356911; fax 446356905; e-mail staatsarchivzh@ji.zh.ch; internet www .staatsarchiv.zh.ch; f. 1837; contains the archives of the canton of Zürich since 853 and a specialized library (local publications and collections of statutes, 30,000 vols and numerous pamphlets); Dir Dr OTTO SIGG.

Zentralbibliothek Zürich: Zähringerplatz 6, 8001 Zürich; tel. 442683100; fax 442683290; e-mail zb@zb.unizh.ch; internet www.zb.unizh.ch; f. 1914; city, cantonal and university library, incorporating also the libraries of Naturforschende Gesellschaft in Zürich, Antiquarische Gesellschaft in Zürich, Geographisch-Ethnographische Gesellschaft Zürich, Schweizerischer Alpenclub, Allgemeine MusikGesellschaft Zürich, Bibliotheca Fennica, etc.; 4,700,000 vols, 106,000 MSS and autographs, 1,600 incunabula, 212,000 maps, and special collections of graphic arts (210,000 items), 35,000 records and cassettes; 9,200 current print periodicals, 16,000 electronic periodicals, 190 newspapers; Dir Dr HERMANN KÖSTLER.

Zentrale für Wirtschaftsdokumentation, Universität Zürich (Economic Documentation Centre, University of Zurich): Plattenstr. 14, 8032 Zürich; tel. 446343911; fax 446344995; e-mail bfb@irc.unizh.ch; internet www.irc.unizh.ch/bfb; f. 1910; attached to the University of Zurich; large world-wide collection of annual reports of major companies; periodicals, OECD collection, online library catalogues in fields of business studies and economics, daily newspapers, magazines and statistical material available; 29,250 vols, 172 periodicals; Dir KATHARINA HERTZBERG-SCHILLING.

Museums and Art Galleries

Aarau

Aargauer Kunsthaus: Aargauer-Platz, 5001 Aarau; tel. 628352330; fax 628352329; e-mail kunsthaus@ag.ch; internet www .aargauerkunsthaus.ch; f. 1960; Swiss painting and sculpture since 1750; collection of paintings by Caspar Wolf (1735–1783), painter of the Alps, and by the landscape painter, Adolf Staebli, and by Auberjonois, Brühlmann, Amiet, G. Giacometti, Hodler, Meyer-Amden, Louis Soutter, Vallotton; Dir BEAT WISMER.

Avenches

Musée Romain Avenches: 1580 Avenches; tel. 266751727; fax 266764215; e-mail musee .romain@vd.ch; internet www.avenches.ch/ aventicum; f. 1824; situated at a 2th c. Roman amphitheatre; mosaics, funerary stelae and sculptures; excavations of Aventicum; library of 15,000 vols; Pres. Prof. P. DUCREY; Dir Dr A. HOCHULI-GYSEL; publs *Aventicum* (2 a year), *Bulletin de l'Association Pro Aventico* (annually).

Basel

Antikenmuseum Basel und Sammlung Ludwig: St Albangraben 5, 4052 Basel; tel. 612011212; fax 612011210; e-mail office@ antikenmuseumbasel.ch; internet www .antikenmuseumbasel.ch; f. 1961; collections of Greek art (2500–100 BC), Roman art (100 BC–AD 300), Etruscan art and Egyptian art; Dir Prof. Dr P. BLOME.

Historisches Museum Basel: Verwaltung, Steinenberg 4, 4051 Basel; tel. 612058600; fax 612058601; e-mail historisches.museum@ bs.ch; internet www .historischesmuseumbasel.ch; f. 1856; 4 brs containing collection of objects from Middle Ages to 20th c., civic culture of Basel in 18th and 19th c. and collection of old musical instruments, coaches and sleighs; Dir Dr BURKARD VON RODA; publs *Jahresberichte* (annually), *Basler Kostbarkeiten* (annually).

Kunstmuseum der Öffentlichen Kunstsammlung Basel: St Albangraben 16, 4010 Basel; tel. 612066262; fax 612066252; internet www.kunstmuseumbasel.ch; f. 1662; pictures from 15th c. to present day, notably by Witz, Holbein and contemporary painters; collection includes Grünewald, Rembrandt, 16th and 17th c. Dutch painting, Cézanne, Gauguin and Van Gogh; large collection of cubist art; sculptures by Rodin and 20th c. artists; American art since 1945; Dept of prints and drawings with old Upper Rhine, German and Swiss masters and 20th c. works; library of 135,000 vols, 200 periodicals; Dir Dr KATHARINA SCHMIDT; Curators Dr THEODORA VISCHER, Dr CHRISTIAN MÜLLER, Dr BERND W. LINDEMANN; Librarian NIKOLAUS MEIER.

Attached museum:

Museum für Gegenwartskunst der Öffentlichen Kunstsammlung Basel: St Alban-Rheinweg 60, 4010 Basel; tel. 612066262; fax 612066253; internet www .mgkbasel.ch; f. 1910; modern art from 1960 to the present; Dir Dr KATHARINA SCHMIDT; Curator Dr THEODORA VISCHER.

Museum der Kulturen Basel: Augustinergasse 2, Postfach, 4001 Basel; tel. 612665500; fax 612665605; e-mail info@mkb.ch; internet www.mkb.ch; f. 1849; ethnographical collections from all parts of the world, especially from Oceania, Indonesia, South America and Europe; textiles; library of 66,000 vols; Dir Dr C. B. WILPERT; publs *Annual Report, Basler Beiträge zur Ethnologie*, guides.

Bern

Bernisches Historisches Museum: Helvetiaplatz 5, 3005 Bern; tel. 313507711; fax 313507799; e-mail info@bhm.ch; internet www.bhm.ch; f. 1881; pre- and early history, history, applied arts, 15th c. tapestries, coin collections, ethnology, folklore; Dir PETER JEZLER.

Kunstmuseum: Hodlerstr. 8–12, 3000 Bern 7; tel. 313280944; fax 313280955; e-mail kmbadmin@kmb.unibe.ch; internet www .kunstmuseumbern.ch; f. 1879; colln of 3,000 paintings and sculptures incl. Italian paintings from 14th–16th c., works by Swiss masters from 15th–19th c., works illustrating the development of art since 19th c. by Manet, Cézanne, Monet, Pissaro, Renoir, van Gogh, members of the 'Blaue Ritter', 'Brücke', and Bauhaus movements, Rothko and Pollock, and other modern works by Hodler and other Swiss, French and German artists; Hermann and Margrit Rupf foundation, incl. paintings by Picasso, Braque, Léger, Gris and Kandinsky; Adolf Wölfli Foundation;graphic colln of more than 48,000 drawings, engravings, photographs, video cassettes and films; library of 110,000 vols; Dir Dr MATTHIAS FREHNER; publ. *Berner Kunstmitteilungen* (4 a year).

Naturhistorisches Museum: Bernastr. 15, 3005 Bern; tel. 313507111; fax 313507499; e-mail contact@nmbe.unibe.ch; internet www.nmbe.ch; f. 1832; collection includes 220 dioramas of Swiss mammals and birds, big game (especially African), Swiss fish, amphibians and reptiles, minerals of the Swiss Alps, invertebrates, hall of skeletons;

Dir Prof. Dr M. GÜNTERT; publs *Jahrbuch* (every 3 years), *Contributions to Natural History* (2 a year).

Zentrum Paul Klee: Monument im Fruchtland 3, Postfach 3000, Bern 31; tel. 313590101; fax 313590102; e-mail kontakt@ zpk.org; internet www.zpk.org; f. 2005; 4,000 works of art by Paul Klee (1879–1940) and a large collection of biographical material; exhibition space for contemporary artists; children's museum 'Creaviva'; Dir ANDREAS MARTI; publ. *Newsletter* (online).

Biel

Museum Schwab: Seevorstadt 50, 2502 Biel; tel. 323227603; fax 323233768; e-mail muschwab@bielsta.ch; f. 1872; contains prehistoric exhibits, especially of the lake-dwelling culture, the New Stone Age, the Bronze Age, and the second Iron Age; also a collection of the Roman period (Petinesca); Dir (vacant).

Chur

Bündner Kunstmuseum: Postfach 7002 Chur; tel. 812572868; fax 812572172; e-mail info@bkm.gr.ch; internet www .buendner-kunstmuseum.ch; f. 1900; contains works by Swiss artists, principally Segantini, Hodler, Alberto, Augusto and G. Giacometti, E. L. Kirchner and Angelica Kauffmann; exhibitions of Swiss and foreign art; Dir Dr BEAT STUTZER.

Fribourg

Musée d'Art et d'Histoire: 12 rue de Morat, 1700 Fribourg; tel. 263055140; fax 263055141; e-mail mahf@fr.ch; internet www .fr.ch/mahf; f. 1823; housed in Hotel Ratzé (16th c.); collections of prehistoric, Roman and medieval exhibits; important collections of Swiss sculpture and painting since 11th c.; works from the Marcello Foundation; monumental pieces by Jean Tinguely; Curator YVONNE LEHNHERR; publs *Annual Report*, exhibition catalogues.

Geneva

Collections Baur: 8 rue Munier Romilly, 1206 Geneva; tel. 227043282; fax 227891845; e-mail info@collections-baur.ch; internet www.collections-baur.ch; f. 1944, opened to public 1964; ceramics and works of art from China and Japan; library of 5,500 vols; Pres. CHARLES MÜLLER; Curator MONIQUE CRICK; publ. *Bulletin des Collections Baur* (annually).

Musée d'Art et d'Histoire: 2 rue Charles Galland, CP 3432, 1211 Geneva 3; tel. 224182600; fax 224182601; e-mail mah@ ville-ge.ch; internet mah.ville-ge.ch; f. 1910; contains local prehistory section; Mediterranean, Egyptian, Near Eastern, Byzantine and Coptic archaeology; Italian, Dutch, Flemish, German, French, English and Swiss (especially Genevese) paintings, paintings since beginning of 20th c., European sculpture, applied art and numismatic collection; library of 95,000 vols; Dir CÄSAR MENZ; publs *Genava* (annually), *Journal des Musées d'Art et d'Histoire* (quarterly).

Attached museums:

Cabinet des Estampes: 5 promenade du Pin, 1204 Geneva; tel. 224182770; fax 224182771; f. 1952; ancient and modern prints and twentieth-century books; Curator RAINER M. MASON.

Maison Tavel: 6 rue du Puits Saint-Pierre, 1204 Geneva; tel. 224183700; fax 224183701; f. 1985; history of the city; Curator LIVIO FORNARA.

Musée Ariana: 10 ave de la Paix, 1202 Geneva; tel. 224185450; fax 224185451; f.

1884; European and Eastern ceramics and glass; Curator ROLAND BLAETTLER.

Musée d'Histoire des Sciences: 128 rue de Lausanne, 1202 Geneva; tel. 224815060; fax 224815061; f. 1964; scientific instruments; library of 10,000 vols; Curator NINIAN HUBERT VAN BLYENBURGH.

Musée de l'Horlogerie: 15 route de Malagnou, 1208 Geneva; tel. 224186470; fax 224186471; f. 1972; European clock and watchmaking; enamels, jewellery and miniatures, 1600–1900; Curator ESTELLE FALLET.

Musée Rath: Place Neuve, 1204 Geneva; tel. 224183340; fax 224183341; f. 1828; temporary exhibitions; Dir CÄSAR MENZ.

Musée d'Art Moderne et Contemporain (MAMCO) (Museum of Modern and Contemporary Art): 10 rue des Vieux-Grenadiers, 1205 Geneva; tel. 223206122; fax 227815681; internet www.mamco.ch; f. 1994; specialises in works since 1960; Dir CHRISTIAN BERNARD.

Musée d'Ethnographie de la Ville de Genève: 65–67 blvd Carl-Vogt, 1205 Geneva; tel. 224184550; fax 224184551; e-mail musee.ethno@ville-ge.ch; internet www .ville-ge.ch/eth; f. 1901; collections of ethnographic artefacts from all continents; collection of musical instruments and of popular pottery; library of 20,000 vols; also houses the Société Suisse des Américanistes and the Archives Internationales de Musique Populaire; Dir Dr NINIAN HUBERT VAN BLYENBURGH; Curators MARC COULIBALY (Africa), LEONID VELARDE (Americas), Dr JERÔME DUCOR (Asia), LAURENT AUBERT (Ethnomusic), CHRISTOPHE GROS (Europe), ROBERTA COLOMBO DOUGOUD (Oceania), MAJAN GARLINSKI (Visual Anthropology); publs *Bulletin du Centre Genevois d'Anthropologie* (annually), *Bulletin de la Société suisse des Américanistes* (annually), *Totem* (6 a year).

Muséum d'Histoire Naturelle: Route de Malagnou, CP 6434, 1211 Geneva 6; tel. 224186300; fax 224186301; e-mail volker .mahnert@mhn.ville-ge.ch; internet www .ville-ge.ch/mhng; f. 1820; departments of mammalogy and ornithology, herpetology and ichthyology, invertebrates, arthropods and insects, entomology, archaeozoology, geology and palaeontology, mineralogy; library of 125,000 vols; 120 mems; Dir Dr DANIELLE DECROUEZ; Librarian CHRISTELLE MOUGIN; publs *Catalogue des Invertébrés de la Suisse*, *Revue suisse de Zoologie* (quarterly), *Revue de Paléobiologie* (2 a year), *Le Rhinolophe* (annually).

Glarus

Kunsthaus Glarus: Im Volksgarten, 8750 Glarus; tel. 556402535; fax 556402519; e-mail office@kunsthausglarus.ch; internet www.kunsthausglarus.ch; f. 1870; 19th and 20th c. Swiss art, Swiss and foreign contemporary art; Pres. ENGI KASPAR MARTI.

La Chaux-de-Fonds

Musée des Beaux-Arts: 33 rue des Musées, 2300 La Chaux-de-Fonds; tel. 329130444; fax 329136193; e-mail mba.vch@ne.ch; internet www.chaux-de-fonds.ch; f. 1864; comprises paintings and sculpture by Swiss artists, particularly of the Neuchâtel district, European paintings and sculpture, and prints and drawings since 19th c.; Dir EDMOND CHARRIÈRE.

Musée International d'Horlogerie: 29 rue des Musées, CP 952, 2301 La Chaux-de-Fonds; tel. 329676861; fax 329676889; e-mail mih.vch@ne.ch; internet www.mih.ch; f. 1902; artistic and technical collections of watches, clocks, instruments and objects connected with the measurement of time;

time research department; a modern carillon; library: specialist library of 3,000 vols; Curator LUDWIG OECHSLIN.

Lausanne

Musée Cantonal des Beaux-Arts: Palais de Rumine, Pl. Riponne 6, 1014 Lausanne; tel. 213163445; fax 213163446; e-mail info@ beaux-arts.vd.ch; internet www.beaux-arts .vd.ch; f. 1841 by the painter Marc-Louis Arlaud; collection of works since 18th c., mainly by Swiss artists; international exhibitions of classical, modern and contemporary art; Dir Y. AUPETITALLOT.

Musée Historique de Lausanne: 4 Place de la Cathédrale, 1005 Lausanne; tel. 213154101; fax 213154102; e-mail musee .historique@lausanne.ch; internet www .lausanne.ch/mhl; f. 1918; permanent and temporary exhibitions; model of 17th c. Lausanne, collections of antique silver and antique musical instruments; library; Dir LAURENT GOLAY; publ. *Mémoire vive* (annually).

Olympic Museum and Olympic Studies Centre/Musée Olympique et Centre d'Etudes Olympiques: Quai d'Ouchy 1, CP 1001, Lausanne; tel. 216216511; fax 216216512; e-mail studies.centre@olympic .org; internet www.olympic.org; f. 1993; attached to International Olympic Committee; library of 24,000 vols, 250 current periodicals, 100 CD-Roms, 2,500 linear m of historic archives, 18,200 hours of film footage, 450,000 photographic documents; Dir of the IOC Information Management Dept PHILIPPE BLANCHARD; publ. *Symposium on Olympism – Proceedings* (annually).

Ligornetto

Museo Vela: 6853 Ligornetto, Largo Vincenzo Vela; tel. 916407044; fax 916473241; e-mail museo.vela@bak.admin.ch; internet www.museo-vela.ch; f. 1897 by the Vela family; the works of Vincenzo, Lorenzo and Spartaco Vela comprise the basis of the collection, which also includes paintings from Lombard schools (17th–19th c.), sketches, drawings and photographs; Curator Dr GIANNA A. MINA.

Locarno

Museo Civico e Archeologico, Servizi Culturali: Via B. Rusca 5, 6600 Locarno; tel. 917563180; fax 917519871; e-mail servizi .culturali@locarno.ch; internet www.locarno .ch/servizi.culturali; f. 1970; 14th c. fortress housing an archaeological collection and historical museum; Dir Prof. RICCARDO CARAZZETTI.

Pinacoteca Casa Rusca: Servizi Culturali, Via B. Rusca 5, 6600 Locarno; tel. 917563185; fax 917519871; e-mail servizi.culturali@ locarno.ch; internet www.locarno.ch/servizi .culturali; f. 1987; restored 17th c. building housing the municipal art gallery; includes Jean Arp collection, and works by Calder, Hans Richter, Van Doesburg, etc.; Dir Prof RICCARDO CARAZZETTI.

Lucerne

Historisches Museum: Altes Zeughaus, Pfistergasse 24, POB 7437, 6000 Lucerne 7; tel. 412285424; fax 412285418; e-mail historischesmuseum@lu.ch; internet www .hmluzern.ch; f. 1878; Dir Dr HEINZ HORAT; publs *Jahrbuch der Historischen Gesellschaft Luzern*, *Jahresbericht des Historischen Museums*.

Kunstmuseum Luzern: Europaplatz, 6002 Lucerne; tel. 412267800; fax 412267801; e-mail kml@kunstmuseumluzern.ch; internet www.kunstmuseumluzern.ch; f. 1925; 18th- to 20th-century Swiss landscape painting and portraiture, Swiss art after

1945, foreign contemporary art; Dir PETER FISCHER.

Richard Wagner-Museum: Richard Wagner-Weg 27, 6005 Lucerne-Tribschen; tel. 413602370; fax 413602379; e-mail info@ richard-wagner-museum.ch; internet www .richard-wagner-museum.ch; f. 1933; home of Richard Wagner from 1866–1872; contains original scores of *Siegfried-Idyll*, *Schusterlied (Meistersinger)*, etchings, paintings, busts and the Erard grand piano which accompanied Wagner throughout Europe; also collection of 17th–19th c. musical instruments from around the world; Dir Dr UELI HABEGGER.

Verkehrshaus der Schweiz (Swiss Transport Museum): Lidostr. 5, 6006 Lucerne; tel. 413704444; fax 413706168; e-mail mail@ verkehrshaus.org; internet www .verkehrshaus.org; f. association founded 1942, museum opened 1959; transport by land, water and air, communication and tourism; transportation archives; IMAX Theatre; planetarium; Dir DANIEL SUTER.

Lugano

Museo Civico di Belle Arti: Villa Ciani, 6900 Lugano; f. 1903 by Antonio Caccia; works by artists of the Ticino since 17th c., and by French and Italian artists.

Neuchâtel

Musée d'Art et d'Histoire: Esplanade Léopold Robert 1, 2000 Neuchâtel; tel. 327177920; fax 327177929; e-mail mahn@ne .ch; internet www.mahn.ch; f. 1885; pictures, drawings, prints and sculptures by local and other Swiss artists; French 18th and 19th c. works (Courbet, Corot, and others); French Impressionists; furniture, coins and medals; an exceptional collection of 18th c. automata by Jaquet-Droz; Dir CHANTAL LAFONTANT VALLOTTON.

Attached Gallery:

Galeries de l'Histoire: Ave DuPeyrou 7, 2000 Neuchâtel; tel. 327177920; fax 327177959; e-mail mahn@ne.ch; internet www.mahn.ch; f. 2003; Curator CHANTAL LAFONTANT VALLOTTON.

Musée d'Ethnographie: 4 rue Saint-Nicolas, 2000 Neuchâtel; tel. 327181960; fax 327181969; e-mail secretariat.men@ne.ch; internet www.men.ch; f. 1795; collns incl. Africa, America, Asia, Ancient Egypt, Europe, South Sea Islands; library of 17,000 vols, 250 periodicals; music archives of original recordings; Curator JACQUES HAINARD.

Muséum d'Histoire Naturelle: Terreaux 14, 2000 Neuchâtel; tel. 327177960; fax 327177969; e-mail info.museum@unine.ch; internet www.museum-neuchatel.ch; f. 1835; Curator CHRISTOPHE DUFOUR; publ. *Ville de Neuchâtel, Bibliothèques et Musées* (annual).

Olten

Kunstmuseum Olten: Kirchgasse 8, 4603 Olten; tel. 622128676; fax 622123466; e-mail kunstmuseum.olten@bluewin.ch; internet www.kunstmuseum-olten.ch; f. 1845; drawings and paintings by Martin Disteli (1802–1844); paintings, drawings and sculptures by Swiss artists; library of 500 vols; Curator PATRICIA NUSSBAUM.

St Gallen

Historisches und Völkerkundemuseum: Museumstr. 50, 9000 St Gallen; tel. 712420642; fax 712420644; e-mail info@ hmsg.ch; internet www.hmsg.ch; f. 1877 as Historisches Museum; present name 2004 following merger with Völkerkundemuseum; collection of arms, banners, porcelain, painted glass, ancient chambers, ancient stoves; ethnological objects from Africa, America, Asia, Oceania and pre-Roman Italy; Dir Dr DANIEL STUDER.

Kunstmuseum: Museumstr. 32, 9000 St Gallen; tel. 712420671; fax 712420672; e-mail info@kunstmuseumsg.ch; internet www.kunstmuseumsg.ch; f. 1877; works by 19th and 20th c. masters, post-war sculpture, contemporary art; Dir ROLAND WÄSPE.

Museum Kirchhoferhaus: Museumstr. 27, St Gallen; tel. 712447521; fax 712420644; e-mail info@hmsg.ch; prehistoric and historic exhibits; 17th–19th c. paintings by Graff, Diogg, Stäbli, Hodler, Corot, Renoir and others; peasant art of eastern Switzerland; furniture, silverware; Dir Dr DANIEL STUDER.

Naturmuseum St Gallen: Museumstr. 32, 9000 St Gallen; tel. 712420670; fax 712420672; e-mail info@naturmuseumsg.ch; internet www.naturmuseumsg.ch; f. 1846; library of 2,000 vols; 19th c. exhibits incl. birds, plants and insects; Nile crocodile from 1623; Curator Dr T. BÜRGIN; publs *Museumsbriefe, Jahresberichte*.

Textilmuseum mit Textilbibliothek: Vadianstr. 2, 9000 St Gallen; tel. 712221744; fax 712234239; e-mail info@textilmuseum.ch; internet www.textilmuseum.ch; f. 1886; lace, embroideries, woven and printed fabrics; Coptic fabrics; period and modern textiles; library of 20,000 vols; special collection of 2m. textile samples; Curators Dr A. WANNER, JEAN RICHARD, M. GÄCHTER-WEBER; Head Librarian MONICA STRÄSSLE.

Schaffhausen

Museum zu Allerheiligen: Baumgartenstr. 6, 8200 Schaffhausen; tel. 526330777; fax 526330788; e-mail admin.allerheiligen@stsh.ch; internet www.allerheiligen.ch; f. 1938; archaeology, history, natural history and art of the City and Canton of Schaffhausen and of Switzerland; Dir ROGER FAYET.

Solothurn

Kunstmuseum Solothurn: Werkhofstr. 30, 4500 Solothurn; tel. 326222307; fax 326225001; e-mail kunstmuseum@egs.so.ch; internet www.kunstmuseum-so.ch; f. 1902; small old master collection including works by Hans Holbein the younger; small international colln, incl. works by Van Gogh, Klimt, Matisse, Picasso and Braque; Swiss art collection from 1850 to 1990, incl. works by Hodler; paintings, drawings, water-colours; primitive art section; Curator Dr CHRISTOPH VÖGELE.

Vevey

Jenisch Museum: 2 ave de la Gare, 1800 Vevey; tel. 219212950; fax 219216292; e-mail info@museejenisch.ch; internet www.museejenisch.ch; f. 1898; comprises Fine Arts Museum (19th c. and 20th c. Swiss and foreign artists, old master drawings, Oskar Kokoschka Foundation, Balthus Foundation) and Cantonal Museum of Prints (16th–20th c. prints); Dir DOMINIQUE RODRIZ-ZANI.

Winterthur

Kunstmuseum Winterthur: Museumstr. 52, POB 378, 8402 Winterthur; tel. 522675162; fax 522675317; e-mail info@kmw.ch; internet www.kmw.ch; f. 1848; painting and sculpture from late 19th c. to the present, including works by Monet, Degas, Picasso, Gris, Léger, Klee, Schlemmer, Magritte, Arp, Kandinsky, Bonnard, Maillol, Van Gogh, Rodin, M. Rosso, Lehmbruck, Brancusi, Morandi, Giacometti, de Staël, Guston, Bishop, Marden, D. Rabinowitch, Richter, Fontana, Manzoni, Merz, Kounellis, Fabro, Paolini; drawings and prints; administered by Kunstverein Winterthur; 2,700 mems; Pres. ALFRED R. SULZER; Dir Dr DIETER SCHWARZ; Sec. CAROLINE JAEGGLI; publs *Jahresbericht des Kunstvereins Winterthur*, collection and exhibition catalogues.

Museum Oskar Reinhart am Stadtgarten: Stadthausstr. 6, 8400 Winterthur; tel. 522675172; fax 522676228; e-mail museum.oskarreinhart@win.ch; internet www.museumoskarreinhart.ch; f. 1951; public art gallery; Pres. ERNST WOHLWEND; Curator PETER WEGMANN.

Zürich

Botanischer Garten und Museum der Universität Zürich: Zollikerstr. 107, 8008 Zürich; tel. 446348461; fax 446348404; e-mail enz@systbot.unizh.ch; internet www.bguz.unizh.ch; f. 1836; world-wide herbarium, especially of African and New Caledonian flora; library of 100,000 vols; Dir Prof. Dr H. P. LINDER; Curator PETER ENZ.

Graphische Sammlung der Eidgenössischen Technischen Hochschule: Rämistr. 101, 8092 Zürich; tel. 446324046; f. 1867; 150,000 examples of the graphic art of all periods and schools, with special reference to the development of graphic art in Switzerland; Curator PAUL TANNER; publ. publs catalogues covering the work of individual artists and the exhibitions.

Kunsthaus Zürich: Heimplatz 1, 8001 Zürich; tel. 442538484; fax 442538433; e-mail info@kunsthaus.ch; internet www.kunsthaus.ch; f. 1787; chiefly paintings and sculptures since 19th c. by Swiss and foreign artists; small selection of old masters; extensive collection covering all branches of graphic art since 16th c.; library of 169,445 vols; Dir CHRISTOPH BECKER.

Musée Suisse/Schweizerisches Landesmuseum (Swiss National Museum): Museumstr. 2, 8023 Zürich; tel. 442186511; fax 442112949; e-mail kanzlei@slm.admin.ch; internet www.musee-suisse.ch; f. 1898; history and development of culture in Switzerland since prehistoric times; library of 90,000 vols, 2,000 periodicals; Dir Dr ANDRES FURGER; publs *Zeitschrift für Schweizerische Archäologie und Kunstgeschichte* (quarterly), *Jahresbericht* (annually), *Kulturagenda* (monthly).

Museum für Gestaltung Zürich (Museum of Design Zürich): Ausstellungsstr. 60, Postfach, 8031 Zürich; tel. 434466767; fax 434464567; e-mail welcome@museum-gestaltung.ch; internet www.museum-gestaltung.ch; f. 1875; design collection, graphic art collection, poster collection; library: public library of 90,000 vols; Dir CHRISTIAN BRÄNDLE.

Affiliated museum:

Museum Bellerive: Höschgasse 3, 8008 Zürich; tel. 434464469; fax 434464503; e-mail welcome@museum-gestaltung.ch; internet www.museum-bellerive.ch; f. 1968; collection of applied and fine arts in glass, ceramics, textiles, marionettes, musical instruments, etc.; Dir EVA AFUHS.

Museum Rietberg: Gablerstr. 15, 8002 Zürich; tel. 442063131; fax 442063132; e-mail museum@rietb.stzh.ch; internet www.rietberg.ch; f. 1952; works of art from Asia, Africa, Oceania and the Americas; E. von der Heydt collection and others; Dir Dr ALBERT LUTZ.

Paläontologisches Institut und Museum der Universität: Karl Schmid-Str. 4, 8006 Zürich; tel. 446342339; fax 446344923; internet www.palinst.unizh.ch; f. 1956; Triassic reptiles and fishes, Triassic and Jurassic invertebrates, Tertiary mammals; library of 5,500 vols, 30,000 publs; Dir Prof. Dr H. BUCHER.

Zoologisches Museum der Universität: Karl Schmid-Str. 4, 8006 Zürich; tel. 446343838; fax 446343839; e-mail zmdirektion@zoolmus.unizh.ch; internet www.unizh.ch/zoolmus; f. 1837; research in systematics, taxonomy, and population biology; exhibitions of birds, molluscs and mammals of the world and Swiss fauna; public slide shows and films; library of 7,000 vols; Dir PAUL I. WARD; publ. *Jahresbericht*.

Universities

UNIVERSITÄT BASEL

Petersplatz 1, 4003 Basel
Telephone: 612673011
Fax: 612673035
E-mail: studsek@unibas.ch
Internet: www.unibas.ch

Founded 1460
Language of instruction: German
Academic year: October to July

Rector: Prof. Dr theol. U. GÄBLER
Vice-Rectors: Prof. Dr phil. U. DRUWE-MIKUSIN, Prof. Dr P. J. MEIER-ABT
Registrar: Dr HANS-PETER MEISTER
Librarian: H. HUG

Number of teachers: 1,344
Number of students: 7,612

DEANS

Faculty of Economics: Prof. Dr rer. pol. H. ZIMMERMANN
Faculty of Jurisprudence: Prof. Dr iur. A. PETERS
Faculty of Medicine: Prof. Dr med. A. P. PERRUCHOUD
Faculty of Philosophy and History: Prof. Dr phil. E. ANGEHRN
Faculty of Psychology: Prof. Dr phil. K. OPWIS
Faculty of Science: Prof. Dr sc. techn H.-J. WIRZ
Faculty of Theology: Prof. Dr theol. G. PFLEIDERER

PROFESSORS

Faculty of Economics (Wirtschaftswissenschaftliches Zentrum (WWZ), Petersgraben 51, 4003 Basel):

BORNER, S., Political Economics
BRUHN, M., Marketing and Management
KUGLER, P., Monetary Macroeconomics
MÜLLER, W. R., Business Administration
SCHIERENBECK, H., Business Administration
WEDER, R., Economics
ZIMMERMANN, H., Finance Theory

Faculty of Law (Maiengasse 51, 4056 Basel; tel. 612672531; fax 612672508; e-mail dekanat-ius@unibas.ch; internet www.ius.unibas.ch):

BREITENMOSER, S., Public Law
HAFNER, F., Public Law
JUNG, P., Private Law
KRAMER, E. A., Civil Law
PETERS, A., Public Law, Swiss National Law
PIETH, M., Penal Law
RHINOW, R. A., Public Law
RIVA, E., Public Law
SCHEFER, G., Swiss National Law
SCHWENZER, I., Civil Law
SEELMANN, K., Penal Law, Philosophy of Law
STÖCKLI, F., Private Law
SUTTER-SOMM, T., Civil Law and Civil Procedural Law

Faculty of Medicine (Kantonsspital, Klingelbergstr. 23, 4031 Basel; tel. 612652050; fax

612652230; internet www.medizin.unibas
.ch):

ACKERMANN-LIEBRICH, U., Social and Pro-
phylactic Medicine
BETTLER, B., Physiology
BÜHLER, F. R., Pharmaceutical Medicine
CHRISTOFORI, G., Biochemistry and Genet-
ics
DE GEEST, S., Nursing
DICK, W., Orthopaedics
DITTMANN, V., Legal Medicine
FLAMMER, J., Ophthalmology
GASSER, TH., Urology
GRATWOHL, A., Internal Medicine
HOLLÄNDER, G., Paediatric Molecular Med-
icine
HOLZGREVE, W., Gynaecology and Obste-
trics
KRAPF, R., Internal Medicine
LAMBRECHT, J. TH., Dentistry
MARINELLO, C. P., Dentistry
MEYER, U., Pharmacology
MIHATSCH, M. J., General and Special
Pathology
MORONI, CHR., Medical Microbiology
MÜLLER-SPAHN, F. S., Adult Psychiatry
OERTLI, D., General Surgery
PALMER, E., Experimental Transplantation
Immunology and Nephrology
PERRUCHOUD, A., Pneumology
PFISTERER, M., Cardiology
PROBST, R., Otorhinolaryngology
RIECHER-RÖSSLER, Adult Psychiatry
ROLINK, A., Immunology
SCHAAD, U. B., Paediatrics
SCHEIDEGGER, D. H., Anaesthetics
SCHIFFERLI, J., Internal Medicine
SKODA, R., Molecular Medicine
STECK, A., Neurology
STEIGER, J., Internal Medicine
STEINBRICH, W., Medical Radiology
TYNDALL, L. A., Rheumatology
WEIGER, R., Dentistry
WICHELHAUS, A., Dentistry
ZEILHOFER, H.-F., Reconstructive Surgery
ZERKOWSKI, H.-R., Heart and Thorax Sur-
gery
ZELLER, R., Anatomy and Embryology
ZIMMERLI, W., Internal Medicine

Faculty of Philosophy and History (Bernou-
listr. 28, 4056 Basel):

ANGEHRN, E., Philosophy
ARLT, W., Musicology
BERGMAN, M., Sociology
BEYER, A., Modern History of Art
BIERL, A., General Philology
BOEHM, G., History of Art
BURGHARTZ, S., History of the 14th–16th
Centuries
ENGLER, B., English Philology
FÖRSTER, T., Ethnology
GLAUSER, J., Nordic Philology
GUSKI, A., Slavonic Philology
HÄCKI BUHOFER, A., German Philology
HARICH-SCHWARZBAUER, H., Latin Philology
HAUMANN, H., History of Eastern Europe
HONOLD, A., Modern German Literature
KOPP, R., Romance Philology
KREBS, A., Philosophy
KREIS, G., Modern General History and
Swiss History
LEIMGRUBER, W., Folklore, European Eth-
nology
LOPRIENO, A., Egyptology
LÜDI, G., Romance Philology
MÄDER, U., Sociology
MILLET, O., French Philology
MOOSER, J., History of the 20th century
MÜLLER, A. VON, Medieval History
OPITZ-BELAKHAL, C., History of the 17th
and 18th centuries
PILLER, I., Sociolinguistics and Sociology of
English as a Global Language
SCHAFFNER, M., Swiss History and Recent
General History

SCHELLEWALD, B., History of Art
SCHNELL, R., German Philology
SCHOELER, G., Islamic Studies
SCHMID, B., Ibero-Romance Philology
SIEGMUND, F., Prehistory and Early His-
tory
SIMON, R., German Literary Studies
STÄHELI, U., Sociology
STUCKY, R., Classical Archaeology
TERZOLI, M. A., Romance Philology
THOLEN, G. C., Media Science
UNGERN-STERNBERG, J. VON, Ancient His-
tory
VON GREYERZ, K., Recent General History
and Swiss History

Faculty of Psychology (Missionsstr. 60–62,
4055 Basel; tel. 612673528; fax 612673526;
e-mail info-psycho@unibas.ch; internet www
.unibas.ch/psycho):

GROB, A., Developmental Psychology
MARGRAF, J., Clinical Psychology
OPWIS, K., General Psychology and Meth-
odology
WÄNKE, M., Social and Business Psychol-
ogy

Faculty of Science (Pharmazentrum, Klingelbergstr. 50, 4056 Basel; tel. 612673053;
fax 612671434; internet www.unibas.ch/
philnat):

A'CAMPO, N., Mathematics
AEBI, U., Structural Biology
AFFOLTER, M., Neurobiology and Develop-
mental Biology
ALEWELL, CH., Enivronmental Earth
Sciences
BARDE, Y. A., Neurobiology
BICKLE, T. A., Microbiology
BOLLER, TH., Botany
BRUDER, C., Theoretical Physics
CONSTABLE, E., Inorganic Chemistry
CORNELIS, G., Microbiology
EBERT, D., Zoology
ENGEL, A., Structural Biology
ERNST, B., Molecular Pharmaceutics
FOLKERS, G., Pharmaceutical Chemistry
GASSER, S., Molecular Biology
GEHRING, W. J., Physiology of Development
and Genetics
GIESE, B., Organic Chemistry
GROTE, M. S., Mathematics
GRZESIEK, S., Structural Biology
GÜNTHERODT, H.-J., Experimental Physics
HALL, M., Biochemistry
HAMBURGER, M. O., Pharmacy
HAURI, H., Cell Biology
IM HOF, H.-CHR., Mathematics
KELLER, W., Cell Biology
KÖRNER, CHR., Botany
KRAFT, H., Mathematics
LESER, H., Physical Geography
LE TENSORER, J.-M., Pre- and Early History
LEUENBERGER, H., Pharmaceutical Tech-
nology
LOSS, D., Theoretical Physics
MAIER, J. P., Physical Chemistry
MASSER, D., Mathematics
MEIER, W., Chemistry
PARLOW, E., Meteorology and Climatology
PFALTZ, A., Organic Chemistry
PHILIPPSEN, P., Applied Microbiology
REICHERT, H., Zoology
RÜEGG, M., Neurobiology
SCHMID, S. M., Geology and Palaeontology
SCHNEIDER-SLIWA, R., Human Geography
SCHÖNENBERGER, CH., Experimental Phy-
sics
SEELIG, J., Structural Biology
SPIESS, M., Biochemistry
TANNES, M., Epidemiology and Medical
Parasitology
THIELEMANN, F. K., Theoretical Physics
TSCHUDIN, CH., Applied Information Tech-
nology
VETTER, T., Applied Information Technol-
ogy

WIEMKEN, A. M., Botany
ZUBERBÜHLER, A., Inorganic Chemistry

Faculty of Theology (Nadelberg 10, 4051
Basel; tel. 612672901; fax 612672902;
internet www.unibas.ch/theologie):

BERNHARDT, R., Systematic Theology, Dog-
matics
BRÄNDLE, R., New Testament, History of
the Early Church
GÄBLER, U., Ecclesiastical and Dogmatic
History
GRÖZINGER, A., Practical Theology
LIENEMANN, CH., Ecumenical Movement
and Mission
MATHYS, H.-P., Old Testament and Semitic
Languages
PFLEIDERER, G., Systematic Theology,
Ethics
STEGEMANN, E., New Testament

Institute for Jewish Studies (Leimenstr. 48,
4051 Basel; tel. 612051636; fax 612051640;
e-mail institut-judaistik@unibas.ch; internet
www.jewishstudies.unibas.ch):

BODENHEIMER, A., Jewish Literature and
History
PICARD, J., Modern Jewish History and
Culture

UNIVERSITÄT BERN

Hochschulstr. 4, 3012 Bern
Telephone: 316318111
Fax: 316313939
E-mail: kommunikation@unibe.ch
Internet: www.unibe.ch

Founded 1834 (incorporating the Theological
School, founded 1528)
State control
Language of instruction: German
Academic year: September to August

Rector: Prof. ULRICH GÄBLER
Vice-Rectors: Prof. ULRICH DRUWE, Prof.
GIAN-RETO PLATTNER
Administrator: KURT ALTERMATT
Chief Librarian: Prof. Dr ROBERT BARTH
Number of teachers: 1,200, including 500
professors
Number of students: 10,000

DEANS

Faculty of Economic Sciences: Prof. Dr
WERNER R. MÜLLER
Faculty of Jurisprudence: Prof. Dr MARKUS
SCHEFER
Faculty of Medicine: Prof. Dr ANDRÉ PERRU-
CHOUD
Faculty of Natural Sciences: Prof. Dr MARCEL
TANNER
Faculty of Philosophy and History: Prof. Dr
ANNELIES HÄCKI BUHOFER
Faculty of Psychology: Prof. Dr KLAUS OPWIS
Faculty of Theology: Prof. Dr EKKEHARD
STEGEMANN

UNIVERSITÉ DE FRIBOURG

1700 Fribourg
Telephone: 263007111
Fax: 263009700
E-mail: rectorat@unifr.ch
Internet: www.unifr.ch

Founded 1889
State control
Languages of instruction: French, German
Academic year: October to June

Rector: Prof. U. ALTERMATT
Vice-Rectors: Prof. R. GRUENIG, Prof. M.
MONBARON, Prof. E. MURER, Prof. G. VER-
GAUVEN
Librarian: M. GOOD

Library of 2,000,000 vols
Number of teachers: 700
Number of students: 9,600

Publications: *Uni Reflets* (10 a year), *Universitas Friburgensis* (4 a year)

DEANS

Faculty of Economics and Social Sciences: Prof. J. PASQUIER-ROCHA
Faculty of Law: Prof. J.-B. ZUFFEREY
Faculty of Letters: Prof. R. FRIEDLI
Faculty of Sciences: Prof. D. BAERISWYL
Faculty of Theology: Prof. A. SCHENKER

PROFESSORS

Faculty of Economics and Social Sciences (Ave Beauregard 13, 1700 Fribourg; tel. 263008200; fax 263009725; e-mail decanat-ses@unifr.ch; internet www.unifr.ch/economics):

BORTIS, H., History of Economic Theory
BOSSHART, L., Media and Communication
BRACHINGER, H.-W., Statistics
DAFFLON, B., Public Finance
DESCHAMPS, P., Econometrics
EICHENBERGER, R., Public Finance
FRIBOULET, J.-J., Economic History
GROEFLIN, H., Information Systems
GRUENIG, R., Management
GÖX, R., Finance and Controlling
GUGLER, P., Social and Political Economy
HELMIG, B., NPO-Management and Marketing
KIRSCH, G., Public Finance
KOHLAS, J., Operations Research
KLEINEWEFLERS, H., Political Economy
LUCCHINI, R., Sociology
MEIER, A., Informatics
PASQUIER-DORTHE, J., Advertising Techniques
PASQUIER-ROCHA, J., Operations Research
PURTSCHERT, R., Management for Non-Profit Organizations
TEUFEL, S., International Telecommunications Management
VANETTI, M., Marketing
VILLET, M., Economic Theory
WALLMEIER, M., Financial Management
WIDMER, J., Media and Communication
WIDMER, M., Decision Support Systems
WOLFF, R., Economic Theory and Empirical Research

Faculty of Law (Ave Beauregard 13, 1700 Fribourg; tel. 263008000; fax 263009719; e-mail decanat-droit@unifr.ch; internet www.unifr.ch/droit/fr):

AMSTUTZ, M., Private Law
BORGHI, M., Public Law
EPINEY, A., Constitutional Law, International Public Law, European Law
FLEINER, T., General and Swiss Public Law
GAUCH, P., Private Law
HAENNI, P., Constitutional and Administrative Law
HURTADO POZO, J., Criminal Law
LE ROY, Y., History of Law, Canon Law
MURER, E., Labour and Social Insurance Law
NIGGLI, M., Criminal Law
PICHONNAZ, P., Private Law
PAHUD DE MORTANGES, R., History of Law
QUELOZ, N., Criminal Law
RIKLIN, F., Criminal Law
RUMO, A., Private Law
STEINAUER, P.-H., Civil Law
STOFFEL, W., International Private Law, Trade Law
TERCIER, P., Private Law
TORRIONE, H., Fiscal Law
VOLKEN, P., Private International Law, Trade Law, Bankruptcy Law
WERRO, F., Private Law
ZUFFEREY, J. B., Administrative Law

Faculty of Letters (Ave Beauregard 13, 1700 Fribourg; tel. 263007500; fax 263009709; e-mail de-lettres@unifr.ch; internet www.unifr.ch/de-lettres):

ALTERMATT, U., General and Swiss Contemporary History
BERRENDONNER, A., French Linguistics
BILLERBECK, M., Classical Philology
BLESS, G., Therapeutic Pedagogy
DAPHINOFF, D., English Literature
DARMS, G., Rhaeto-Romance Language and Culture
FAUDEMAY, A., French Language and Literature
FIEGUTH, R., Slavonic Studies
FRICKE, H., Modern German Literature
FRIEDLI, R., Science of Religions
GIORDANO, C., Ethnology
GIRAUD, Y., French Literature
GURTNER, J. L., General Pedagogy
HAAS, W., German Philology
HAEBERLIN, U., Therapeutic Pedagogy
HUBER, O., General Psychology
KURMANN, P., History of Art
LAMBERT, J.-L., Therapeutic Pedagogy
LUTZ, E. C., German Philology
MARSCH, E., German Literature
MARTINI, A., Italian Literature
MENICHETTI, A., Romance Philology
MORTIMER, A., English Literature
NIDA-RUMELIN, M., Philosophy
OSER, F., General Pedagogy
PENATE, J., Spanish Literature
PERREZ, M., Clinical Psychology
PIÉRART, M., Ancient History
PYTHON, F., General and Swiss Contemporary History
REHDER, R., English and American Literature
REICHERTS, M., Clinical Pyschology
REINHARDT, V., Early Modern History of Europe and Switzerland
RETSCHITZKI, J., General Psychology
RIGOLI, J., French Literature
SCHAMP, J., Classical Philology
SCHMIDT, H. J., Medieval History of Europe and Switzerland
SOLDATI, G., Philosophy
SOULET, M.-H., Social Work
SPIESER, J.-M., Early Christian Archaeology
STOICHITA, V., History of Art
TRUDGILL, P., English Linguistics
TURCHETTI, M., Early Modern History of Europe and Switzerland
WOLF, J.-U., Ethical and Political Philosophy
WÜRFFEL, S. B., German Literature
ZOPPELLI, L., History of Music

Faculty of Sciences (Ch. du Musée 6, Pérolles, 1700 Fribourg; tel. 263008450; fax 263009729; internet www.unifr.ch/sciences):

ANTILLE, A., Mathematics
BAERISWYL, D., Theoretical Physics
BENISTON, M., Geography
BERRUT, J.-P., Mathematics
CARON, C., Geology
CELIO, M., Histology
CONZELMANN, A., Biochemistry
DOUSSE, J.C., Experimental Physics
EBERT, D., Ecology
GOSSAUER, A., Organic Chemistry
HIRSBRUNNER, B., Computer Science
HUNGERBUEHLER, N., Mathematics
INGOLD, R., Computer Science
KELLERHALS, R., Mathematics
LEIMGRUBER, W., Geography
MAGGETTI, M., Mineralogy and Petrography
MÉTRAUX, J.-P., Plant Biology
MONBARON, M., Geography
MONTANI, J.-P., Physiology
MÜLLER, F., Zoology
RAGER, G., Anatomy
RUH, E., Mathematics
RUSCONI, A., Biochemistry
SCHLAPBACH, L., Experimental Physics
SCHURTENBERGER, P., Experimental Physics

STREBEL, R., Mathematics
TOBLER, H., Zoology
WEIS, A., Experimental Physics
VON ZELEWSKY, A., Inorganic Chemistry
ZHANG, Y.-C., Theoretical Physics

Faculty of Theology (Ave Beauregard 13, 1700 Fribourg; tel. 263007370; fax 263009708; e-mail decanat-theol@unifr.ch; internet www.unifr.ch/de-theo):

AIMONE, P.-V., Ecclesiastical Law
BEDOUELLE, G.-T., Ecclesiastical History
BERTHOUZOZ, R., Moral Theology
BUJO, B., Moral Theology
EMERY, G., Dogmatic Theology
HALLENSLEBEN, B., Dogmatic Theology
HOLDEREGGER, A., Moral Theology
KARRER, L., Pastoral Theology
KLÖCKENER, M., Liturgy
O'MEARA, D., Philosophy
SCHENKER, A., Old Testament Exegesis
VERGAUWEN, G., Fundamental Theology
VIVIANO, B. T., New Testament
WERMELINGER, O., Patristics

ASSOCIATED INSTITUTES

Institute of Canon and Ecclesiastical Law: Dir R. PAHUD DE MORTANGES.

Institute for Ecumenical Studies: Dir G. VERGAUWEN.

Institute for European Law: Dir A. EPINEY.

Institute of Federalism: Dir T. FLEINER.

Institute of General and Comparative Literature: Dir R. FIEGUTH.

Institute for Management of Non-Profit Organizations: Dir R. PURTSCHERT.

Institute of Medieval Studies: Dir J.-M. SPIESER.

Institute for Missiology and Religions: Dir A. NAYAK (acting).

Institute of Physical Education and Sport: Dir F. SOTTAS.

Institute for Swiss and International Construction Law: Dir J. B. ZUFFEREY.

Institute of Therapeutic Pedagogy: Dir U. HAEBERLIN.

Interdisciplinary Institute of Eastern and Central Europe: Dir N. HAYOZ.

Interdisciplinary Institute of Ethics and Human Rights: Dir J.-J. FRIBOULET.

Interdisciplinary Institute of Family Research and Counselling: Dir G. BODENMANN.

International Institute of Management in Telecommunications: Dir S. TEUFEL.

UNIVERSITÉ DE GENÈVE

24 rue Général-Dufour, 1211 Geneva 4
Telephone: 223797111
Fax: 223791134
E-mail: webmaster@unige.ch
Internet: www.unige.ch

Founded 1559
Language of instruction: French
Academic year: October to July

Rector: Prof. ANDRÉ HURST
Administrative Director: L. PALLY
Secretary-General: Dr S. BERTHET
Library: see Libraries and Archives
Number of teachers: 3,318
Number of students: 14,685

DEANS

Faculty of Arts and Humanities: Prof. C. GENEQUAND
Faculty of Economics and Social Science: Prof. P. ALLAN
Faculty of Law: Prof. R. ROTH
Faculty of Medicine: Prof. J.-L. CARPENTIER
Faculty of Protestant Theology: (vacant)

Faculty of Psychology and Educational Sciences: Prof. A. DE RIBAUPIERRE
Faculty of Science: Prof. P. SPIERER
Institute of Architecture: Prof. J.-P. CÊTRE
School of Translation and Interpretation: (vacant)

PROFESSORS

Faculty of Arts and Humanities (3 rue de Candolle, 1211 Geneva 4; tel. 223797111; fax 223791029; internet www.unige.ch/lettres):

ADAMZIK-BEVAND, K., German Literature and Civilization
ALVAR, C., Spanish Language and Literature
BARDAZZI, G., Romance Literature
BERELOWITCH, W., History
BOCCADORO, B., Musicology
BOLENS-JEANNERET, G., English Language and Literature
BORGEAUD, P., History of Ancient Religions
CAVIGNEAUX, A., Oriental Languages
CERUTTI, M., General History
CONRAD, C., History
DARBELLAY, E., Musicology
DE LIBERA, A., Philosophy
DESCOEUDRES, J.-P., Archaeology
FOEHR-JANSSENS, Y., Medieval French Literature
GAJO, G., Romance Literature
GAMBONI, L., Linguistics
GENEQUAND, C., Muslim and Arab Civilization
GROSRICHARD, A., French Literature
HAEBERLI, E., English Literature
HELG, A., General History
HURST, A., Classical Greek
JACCARD, J.-P., Russian Language
JENNY, L., French Literature
KOT, S., General History
LASSITHIOTAKIS, M., Modern Greek
LOMBARDO, P., French Literature
MADSEN, D., English Language and Literature
MANZOTTI, E., Italian Linguistics
MÉLA, CH., Medieval Romance Languages and Literature
MOESCHLER, J., General Linguistics
MORENZONI, F., History
MULLIGAN, K., Philosophy
NAEF, S., Arabic Language
NATALE, M., History of Art
NELIS, D., Latin Literature
PERUGI, M., Medieval Latin Language and Literature
PONT, J.-C., History of Sciences
PORRET, M., Modern History
POT, O., French Literature
RIGOLI, J., French Literature
SCHRADER, H. J., German Literature and Civilization
SCHUBERT, P., Modern Greek
SHLONSKY, UR., Linguistics
SOUYRI, P.-F., Japanese
SPURR, D. A., Modern English Literature
TALENS, C. J., Spanish Language and Literature
TILLIETTE, J.-Y., Medieval Latin Language and Literature
VALLOGGIA, M., Egyptology
WALTER, F., General History
WEHRLI, E., French Linguistics and Computer Science
WETZEL, R., German Literature and Civilization
WINKLER, M., German Literature and Civilization
WIRTH, J., History of Art in the Middle Ages
ZUFFEREY, Chinese Studies

Faculty of Economics and Social Science (40 blvd du Pont-d'Arve, 1211 Geneva 4; tel. 223797111; fax 223799919; internet www .unige.ch/ses):

ALLAN, P., Political Science

ANTILLE GAILLARD, G., Economics and Social Science
BALLMER-CAO, T.-H., Political Science
BENDER, A., Industrial Organization
BERGADAA DELMAS, M., Marketing
BRAILLARD, P., European Globalization
BURGENMEIER, B., Political Economy
CARLEVARO, F., Econometrics
CASSIS, Y., Economic History
CATTACIN, S., Sociology
CURZON-PRICE, V., Economics
DE BLASIS, J. P., Industrial Organization
DE LA GRANDVILLE, O., Political Economy
DE MELO, J., Political Economy
DEBARBIEUX, B., Geography
DENIS, J. E., Industrial Organization
DUMONT, P.-A., Industrial Organization
DUMONTIER, P., Accountancy
FLUECKIGER, Y., Political Economy
GILLI, M., Computer Science, Econometrics
HOESLI, M. E. R., Real Estate Financing
HORBER, E., Sociology
HUSSY, C., Geography
JARILLO, J.-C., Economic Strategy
KELLERHALS, J., Sociology
KONSTANTAS, D., Information Systems
KRISHNAKUMAR, J., Econometrics
LANE, J. E., Political Science
LAWRENCE, R. J., Human Ecology
LEFOLL, J., Industrial Organization
LEONARD, M., Computer Science applied to Business
LOUBERGÉ, H., Political Economy
MAGNENAT THALMANN, N., Information Systems
MIRONESCO, C., Political Science
MORARD, B., Accountancy
MÜLLER, T., Econometrics
ORIS, M., Economic History
OSSIPOW, W., Political Science
PROBST, G., Industrial Organization
RAFFOURNIER, B., Accountancy
RECORDON, P. A., Contracts
RITSCHARD, G., Econometrics
RONCHETTI, E., Industrial Organization
ROYER, D., Statistics
SAUVAIN, C., Demography
SCAILLET, O., Statistics and Probability
SCHMITT, N., Political Economy
SCIARINI, P., Political Science
SCHNEIDER, S. C., Industrial Organization
SCHULTHEISS, F., Sociology
THOENIG, M., Political Economy
VERLEY, P., Economic History
VERNEX, J. C., Geography
VIAL, J.-PH., Industrial Organization
VIALLON, P., Sociology
VICTORIA FESER, M.-P., Statistics and Probability
WEBER, L., Political Economy
WINDISCH, U., Sociology

Faculty of Law (40 blvd du Pont-d'Arve, 1211 Geneva 4; tel. 223797111; fax 223799916; internet www.unige.ch/droit):

AUBERT, G., Administrative Law
AUER, A., Constitutional Law
BADDELEY, M., Civil Law
BELLANGER, F., Fiscal Law
BOISSON DE CHAZOURNES, L., Public International Law
BOVET, C., Fiscal Law
BUCHER, A., Civil Law
CASSANI, U., Penal Law
CHAPPUIS, C., Business Law
DELLEY, J.-D., Constitutional Law
FLUECKIGER, A., Constitutional Law
FOEX, B., Civil Law
GREBER, P. Y., Administrative Law
HOTTELIER, M., Constitutional Law
JEANDIN, N., Civil Law
KADDOUS, C., Public International Law
KADNER, T., Civil Law
KELLER, A., History of Institutions and Law

KAUFMANN-KOHLER, G., Private International Law
LEVRAT, N., Public International Law
MALINVERNI, G., Constitutional Law, Introduction to the Science of Law
MANAÏ-WEHRLI, D., Civil Law
MONNIER, V., History of Institutions and Law
OBERSON, X. B., Fiscal Law
PETER, H., Civil Law
PETITPIERRE-SAUVAIN, A., Commercial Law
ROBERT, C. N., Penal Law, Criminology
ROTH, R., Penal Law
SASSOLI, M., Public International Law
STAUDER, B., German Commercial Law
STETTLER, M., Civil Law
TANQUEREL, T., Constitutional Law
THÉVENOZ, L., Civil Law
TRIGO TRINDADE, R. M., Business and Commercial Law
WINIGER, B., European and Civil Law

Faculty of Medicine (C.M.U., 1 rue Michel-Servet, 1211 Geneva 4; tel. 223795111; fax 223473334; internet www.unige.ch/medecine):

ANTONORAKIS, S., Genetics and Microbiology
ASSIMACOPOULOS, F., Medical Biochemistry
BADER, C., Oto-neuro-ophthalmology
BAEHNI, P., Dentistry
BAERTSCHI, A. J., Physiology
BAIROCH, A., Medical Biochemistry
BARRAZZONE, C., Paediatrics
BECKER, C., Radiology
BEGHETTI, M., Paediatrics
BELIN, D., Pathology
BELLI, D. C., Paediatrics
BELSER, U., Dentistry
BERNER, M., Paediatrics
BERNHEIM, L., Physiology
BERTRAND, D., Physiology
BERTSCHY, G., Psychiatry
BISCHOF, P. A., Gynaecology and Obstetrics
BORISCH, B., Pathology
BOUNAMEAUX, H., Medicine
CAPPONI, A., Endocrinology
CARPENTIER, J.-L., Morphology
CAVERZASIO, J., Medicine
CHARDOT, C., Paediatrics
CHEVROLET, J.-C., Medicine
CLERGUE, F., Cardiology
COLLART BUCKHARD, M., Medical Biochemistry
COSSON, P., Morphology
DAYER, J.-M., Medicine
DAYER, P., Pharmacology
DE TRIBOLET, N., Oto-neuro-ophthalmology
DEMAUREX, N., Physiology
DUBUISSON, J.-S., Gynaecology and Obstetrics
FANTINI, B., Medicine
FASEL, J., Morphology
FERRERO, F., Pharmacology
FRENCH, L., Oto-Neuro-Ophthalmology
GABAY, C., Medicine
GEISSBUHLER, A., Radiology
GENTA, R., Pathology
GEORGOPOULOS, C. P., Medical Biochemistry
GIANNAKOPOULOS, P., Psychiatry
GIRARDIN, E., Paediatrics
GOLAY, A., Medicine
GUYOT, J., Oto-Neuro-Ophthalmology
HADENGUE, A., Medicine
HALBAN, PH., Medicine
HARDING, T., Legal Medicine
HOCHSTRASSER, D., Medical Biochemistry
HOESSLI, D., Pathology
HOFFMEYER, P., Surgery
HUEPPI, P., Paediatrics
IMHOF, B., Pathology
ISELIN, C., Surgery
IZUI, S., Pathology
KATO, A. C., Oto-neuro-ophthalmology
KAYSER BENGT, E. J., Sports Medicine

KILIARIDIS, S., Orthodontics
KISS, J. Z., Morphology
KOLAKOFSKY, D., Microbiology
KRAUSE, K. H., Medicine
KREJCI, I., Dentistry
LANDIS, T., Oto-neuro-ophthalmology
LE COULTRE, C., Surgery
LERCH, R., Medicine
LEW, D. P., Microbiology
LINDER, P., Medical Biochemistry
LÜSCHER, C., Oto-neuro-ophthalmology
MAGISTRETTI, P., Psychiatry
MALAFOSSE, A., Psychiatry
MARTIN, P.-Y., Nephrology
MAURON, A., Clinical Ethics
MEDA, P., Morphology
MENTHA, G., Surgery
MICHEL, C., Oto-neuro-ophthalmology
MICHEL, J.-P., Geriatrics
MOMBELLI, A., Orthodontics
MONTESANO, R., Morphology
MORABIA, A., Social Medicine
MOREL, D., Cardiology
MOREL, PH., Surgery
MUHLETHALER, M., Neurophysiology
MÜLLER, D., Pharmacology
MÜLLER, F., Dental Prosthesis
PALACIO-ESPASA, F., Psychiatry
PANIZZON, R., Oto-neuro-ophthalmology
PELIZZONE, M., Oto-neuro-ophthalmology
PERNEGER, T., Social Medicine
PERRIER, A., Medicine
PETER, R., Surgery
PHILIPPE, J., Medicine
PITTET, D., Medicine
PITTET-CUENOD, B., Surgery
PRALONG, F., Medicine
RAPIN, CH.-H., Gerontology
RATIB, O., Radiology
REITH, W., Genetics, Microbiology
RICHTER, M. W., Surgery
ROCHAT, T., Medicine
ROSE, K., Medical Biochemistry
ROUGEMONT, A., Social Medicine
ROUX, L., Genetics, Microbiology
RUEFENACHT, D., Radiology
RUIZ-ALTABA, A., Stem Cells
SAFRAN, A.-B., Oto-neuro-ophthalmology
SAMSON, J., Dentistry
SAPPINO, P., Oncology
SAURAT, J.-H., Dermatology
SCHLEGEL, W., Medicine
SCHNIDER, A., Oto-neuro-ophthalmology
SIEGRIST, C.-A., Paediatrics
SIGWART, U., Medicine
SOLDATI-FAVRE, D., Genetics, Microbiology
STALDER, J., Medicine
STRUBIN, M., Genetics, Microbiology
SUTER, P., Surgery
SUTER, S., Paediatrics
VAN DER GOOT GRUNBERG, F., Genetics, Microbiology
VASSALLI, J.-D., Morphology
VILLEMURE, J.-G., Oto-neuro-ophthalmology
VU, NU. V., Medicine
WOLLHEIM, C., Medicine
ZUBLER, R., Medicine

Faculty of Protestant Theology (3 rue de Candolle, 1211 Geneva 4; tel. 223797111; fax 223797430; e-mail info@theologie.unige.ch; internet www.unige.ch/theologie):

BACKUS, I., History of the Reformation
BENEDICT, J., History of the Reformation
DERMANGE, F., Ethics
DETTWILER, A., New Testament Exegesis
GRANDJEAN, M., History of Christianity
NORELLI, E., New Testament Exegesis
PITASSI, M. C., History of the Reformation

Faculty of Psychology and Educational Sciences (40 blvd du Pont-d'Arve, 1211 Geneva 4; tel. 223797111; fax 223799020; internet www.unige.ch/fapse):

Section of Psychology:
BARISUKOV, K., Psychology of Mental Deficiency
BETRANCOURT, M., Training Technologies
CASPAR, F., Psychology
DE RIBAUPIERRE, A., Differential Psychology
EID, M., Data Analysis
FRAUENFELDER, U. H., Psycholinguistics
GENDOLLA, G., Psychology
GILLIÈRON-PALÉOLOGUE, C., Psychology, Epistemology
HAUERT, C.-A., Psychology of Development
KERZEL, D., Cognitive Psychology
KAISER, S., Verbal and Non-Verbal Communication
LORENZI-CIOLDI, F., Social Psychology
MOUNOUD, P., Psychology of Personality Development
MUGNY, G., Social Psychology
ROBERT-TISSOT, C., Child Psychotherapy
SCHERER, K., Social Psychology
VAN DER LINDEN, M., Psychopathology
VIVIANI, P., Statistics and Modelling in Psychology
VANHULLE, S., Psychology
ZESIGER, P. E., Language Disorders

Section of Educational Sciences:
ALLAL, L., Pedagogical Evaluation
AUDIGIER, F., Teaching of Social Science and Humanities
BAYER, E., Research Techniques in Education
BELLIER, S., Educational Sciences
BRONCKART, J.-P., Introduction to Language Theories
BUCHEL, F., Cognitive Education
CHATELANAT, G., Educational Sciences
CIFALI, M., Psycho-pedagogy
CRAHAY, M., Educational Sciences
DASEN, P., Introduction to Educational Sciences
DOLZ-MESTRE, J., Educational Sciences
DURAND, M., Adult Education
GIORDAN, A., Psycho-pedagogy in Sciences
HANHART, S., Education
HOFSTETTER-ROSET, R., Educational Sciences
JOBERT, G., Adult Education
MAGNIN, C. F., History of Education
PAYET, J. P., Sociology of Education
PERAYA, D., Educational Sciences
PERREGAUX, C., Cultural and Linguistic Diversity at School
PERRENOUD, P., General Pedagogy
SAADA-ROBERT, M., Learning Process
SCHNEUWLY, B., Introduction to Language Theories
SCHUBAUER, M.-L., Social Psychology
SCHURMANS BRONCKART, M. N., Social Construction of Knowledge

Faculty of Science (30 quai Ernest-Ansermet, 1211 Geneva 4; tel. 223796111; fax 223796698; internet www.unige.ch/sciences):

ALEXAKIS, A, Organic Chemistry
ALEXEEV, A., Mathematics
AUGUSTYNSKI, J., Applied Mineral Chemistry
BALLIVET, M., Biochemistry
BENY, J.-L., Animal Biology
BESSE, M., Anthropology, Ecology
BLECHA, A., Astronomy
BLONDEL, J., Nuclear Physics
BORKOVEC, M., Applied Mineral Chemistry
BOURQUIN, M., Nuclear Physics
BROUGHTON, W. J., Botany
BUCHS, D., Electronic Computing
BUETTIKER, M., Theoretical Physics
BUFFLE, J., Mineral Chemistry
BURKI, G., Astronomy
CARRUPT, P. A., Pharmacy
CHOPARD, B., Electronic Computing
CLARK, A. G., Nuclear Physics
CORAY, D., Mathematics

COURVOISIER, TH., Astronomy
DAVAUD, E. J., Geology
DE LA HARPE, P., Mathematics
DOELKER, E., Pharmacy
DOMINIK, J., History and Philosophy of Science
DROZ, M., Theoretical Physics
DUBOULE, D., Animal Biology
DUNGAN, M., Mineralogy
DURRER, R., Theoretical Physics
ECKMANN, J. P., Theoretical Physics and Mathematics
EDELSTEIN, S., Biochemistry
FISCHER, Ø., Physics
FONTBOTÉ, L., Mineralogy
GANDER, M.-J., Mathematics
GEOFFROY, M., Physical Chemistry
GIAMARCHI, T., Solid State Physics
GISIN, N., Theoretical Physics
GORIN, G. E., Geology
GRENON, M., Astronomy
GRUENBERG, J., Biochemistry
GULAÇAR, F., Physical Chemistry
GURNY, R., Pharmacy
HAIRER, E., Mathematics
HAUSER, A., Physical Chemistry
HOCHSTRASSER, D., Pharmacy
HOPFGARTNER, G., Pharmacy
HOSTETTMANN, K., Pharmacy
IZZAURRALDE, E., Molecular Biology
JEAN-PETIT-MATILE, S., Organic Chemistry
KIENZLE, M.-N., Solid State Physics
KINDLER, P., Geology and Palaeontology
KRAEMER BILBE, A., Cell Biology
KUNDIG, E. P., Organic Chemistry
LACHAL, B. M., Problems of Energy
LACHAVANNE, J.-B., Anthropology
LACOUR, J., Organic Chemistry
LANGANEY, A., Anthropology
LELUC, C., Nuclear Physics
MAEDER, A., Astronomy
MAGGIORE, M., Theoretical Physics
MARTINOU, J.-C., Cell Biology
MAYOR, M., Astronomy
MONOD, N., Mathematics
PALAZZO ROLIM, J., Electronic Computing
PASZKOWSKI, J., Vegetal Biology
PELLEGRINI, CH., Computer Science
PENEL, C., Botany
PFENNIGER, D., Astronomy
PICARD, D., Biology
PIGUET, C., Mineral Chemistry
POHL, M., Nuclear Physics
PONT, J.-C., History and Philosophy of Science
PUN, T., Computer Science
RAPIN, D., Nuclear Physics
RIEZMAN, H., Biochemistry
ROCHAIX, J.-D., Biology
RODRIGUEZ, I., Animal Biology
RONGA, F., Mathematics
RUEGG, U.-T., Pharmacy
SANCHEZ-MAZAS DE ABREU, A., Anthropology
SCAPPOZZA, L., Pharmacy
SCHALTEGGER, U., Mineralogy
SCHIBLER, U., Molecular Biology
SHORE, D., Molecular Biology
SMIRNOV, S., Mathematics
SPIERER, P., Animal Biology
STRASSER, R., Botany
STREIT, F., Mathematics
TRISCONE, J.-M., Solid State Physics
VAN DER MAREL, D., Solid State Physics
VAUTHEY, E., Physical Chemistry
VEUTHEY, J.-L., Pharmaceutical Chemistry
WANNER, G., Mathematics
WERNLI, R., Micropalaeontology
WILDI, W., Geology
WILLIAMS, A. F., Applied Mineral Chemistry
WITTWER, P., Theoretical Physics
WOLF, J.-P., Physics
WOLFENDER, J. L., Pharmacy
YVON, K., Structural Crystallography
ZANINETTI, L., Zoology and Palaeontology

Institute of Architecture (7 route de Drize, 1227 Carouge; tel. 223790799; fax 223799789; e-mail info@archi.unige.ch; internet www.unige.ch/ia):

CÊTRE, J.-P., Materials and Structures
MARIANI, R., Urban History
REICHLIN, B., Theory of Architecture
SCHEIWILLER, A., Architectural Design and Arts and Crafts
SIMONNET, C., Culture and History of Architecture and Arts and Crafts
WEBER, W., Architecture

School of Translation and Interpretation (40 blvd du Pont-d'Arve, 1211 Geneva 4; tel. 223797111; fax 223798750; internet www .unige.ch/eti):

ABDEL HADI, M., Arabic
ARMSTRONG, S., Use of Computers
BOCQUET, C.-Y., French
DANIEL, M., Translation with Computer Assistance
DE BESSÉ, B., Terminology
FANTUZZI, M., Italian
GEMAR, J.-C., French
GRIN, F., French
HEWSON LANCE, S. F., English
LEE-JAHNKE, H., German
MARCHESINI, G., Italian
MOSER-MERCER, B., German
SETTON, R. A. M., Interpretation
WEIBEL, L., French

INTER-FACULTY CENTRES

Centre Interfacultaire de Gérontologie (Interfaculty Centre for Gerontology): 59 route de Mon-Idée, 1226 Thônex; tel. 223056601; fax 223489077; internet www .unige.ch/cig; Dir A. DE RIBAUPIERRE.

Centre Universitaire d'Ecologie Humaine et des Sciences de l'Environnement (University Centre for Human Ecology and Environmental Sciences): 40 blvd du Pont-d'Arve, 1211 Genève 4; tel. 223798172; fax 223798173; internet ecolu-info.unige.ch; Dir B. BÜRGENMEIER.

Centre Universitaire d'Etude des Problèmes de l'Energie (University Centre for the Study of Energy Problems): Battelle, Bâtiment A, 7 route de Drize, 1277 Carouge; tel. 223790661; fax 223799639; internet www .unige.ch/cuepe; Dir W. WEBER.

Centre Universitaire d'Informatique (Computer Science Department): 24 rue Général-Dufour, 1211 Genève 4; tel. 223797770; fax 223797780; internet cui .unige.ch; Dir N. MAGNENAT THALMANN.

Institut Européen de l'Université de Genève (Europe Institute of the University of Geneva): 2 rue Jean-Daniel Colladon, 1204 Genève; tel. 223797850; fax 223797852; internet www.unige.ch/ieug; Dir P. BRAILLARD.

Institut d'Histoire de la Réformation: 3 place de l'Université, 1211 Geneva 4; tel. 223797128; fax 223797133; internet www .unige.ch/ihr; Dir M. C. PITASSI.

ATTACHED SCHOOLS

École d'Education Physique et de Sport (School of Physical Education and Sport): tel. 223797722; attached to Faculty of Medicine; Dir P. HOLENSTEIN.

École de Langue et de Civilisation Françaises (School of French Language and Culture): tel. 223797111; fax 223797681; internet www.unige.ch/lettres/ elcf; attached to Faculty of Arts and Humanities; Dirs J. M. LUSCHER, M. POULIOT, F. PRICAM DJEGUIME.

ASSOCIATED INSTITUTES

Institut Oecuménique de Bossey (Graduate Institute of Ecumenical Studies): Château de Bossey, 1298 Céligny; tel. 229607300; fax 229607310; internet www.wcc-coe.org/ bossey; Dir IOAN SAUCA.

Institut Universitaire d'Etudes du Développement (Graduate Institute of Development Studies): 24 rue Rothschild, 1211 Geneva 21; tel. 229065940; fax 229065947; e-mail iued@unige.ch; internet www.unige.ch/iued; f. 1961; African history, Middle Eastern and Latin American studies, international relations, Switzerland–Third World economic relations; Dir J.-L. MAURER.

Institut Universitaire de Hautes Etudes Internationales (Graduate Institute of International Studies): 132 rue de Lausanne, 1211 Geneva 21; tel. 229085700; fax 229085710; e-mail info@hei.unige.ch; internet heiwww.unige.ch; f. 1927; a research and teaching institution studying international questions from the juridical, political and economic viewpoints; Dir J.-M. JACQUET.

UNIVERSITÉ DE LAUSANNE

Bâtiment du Rectorat et de l'Administration Centrale, 1015 Lausanne
Telephone: 216921111
Fax: 216922015
E-mail: info@sg.unil.ch
Internet: www.unil.ch

Founded 1537
Language of instruction: French
Academic year: October to July

Rector: Prof. JEAN-MARC RAPP
Vice-Rectors: DOMINIQUE ARLETTAZ, JACQUES BESSON, MAIA WENTLAND-FORTE
President: Prof. SAMUEL BENDAHAN
Administrative Director: JEAN-PAUL DÉPRAZ
Librarian: H. VILLARD

Library: see Libraries and Archives
Number of teachers: 950
Number of students: 10,000

Publications: *Allez Savoir!*, *L'Enseignement*, *La Recherche*, *Uniscope*

DEANS

Faculty of Biology and Medicine: Prof. PATRICE MANGIN
Faculty of Earth Sciences and Environment: Prof. JEAN HERNANDEZ
Faculty of Law: Prof. DENIS TAPPY
Faculty of Letters: Prof. ANDRÉ WYSS
Faculty of Social and Political Science: Prof. NICOLAS DURUZ
Faculty of Theology: Prof. DANIEL MARGUERAT
School of Higher Business Studies: Prof. FRANÇOIS GRICE

PROFESSORS

Faculty of Biology and Medicine (Rue du Bugnon 21, 1005 Lausanne; tel. 216925000; fax 216925005; e-mail info.fbm@unil.ch; internet www.unil.ch/fbm):

AGUET, M., Molecular Oncology
ANSERMET, F., Child Psychiatry
BACHMANN, C., Clinical Chemistry
BARRANDON, Y., Experimental Surgery
BARRAS, V., History of Medicine
BAUMANN, P., Psychopharmacology
BECKMANN, J., Genetics
BILLE, J., Microbiology
BIOLLAZ, J., Clinical Pharmacology
BISCHOF-DELALOYE, A., Nuclear Medicine
BOGOUSSLAVSKY, J., Neurology
BOILLAT, M.-A., Occupational Medicine
BORGEAT, F., Psychiatry
BOSMAN, F. T., Pathology
BURNIER, M., Hypertension
CHIOLERO, R. L., Intensive Surgical Care
CLARKE, S., Neuropsychology
COTECCHIA, S., Pharmacology
DANUSER, B., Work Health
DE GRANDI, P., Gynaecology and Obstetrics

DE TRIBOLET, N., Neurosurgery
DESPLAND, P.-A., Neurological Electrophysiology
DIEZI, J., Toxicology
DOTTO, G.-P., Biochemistry
DUBOCHET, J., Microscopy
EGLOFF, D. V., Plastic and Reconstructive Surgery
FANCONI, S., Paediatrics
FARMER, E., Molecular Biology
FRANCIOLI, P., Epidemiology of Infectious Diseases
GAILLARD, R., Endocrinology
GEERING, K., Pharmacology, Toxicology
GIANNAKOPOULOS, P., Psychogeriatrics
GLAUSER, M.P., Internal Medicine, Infectious Diseases
GONVERS, J.-J., Gastroenterology
GUEX, P., Psychological and Social Medicine
GUILLOU, L., Pathology
HAAS, D., Microbiology
HAYOZ, D., Angiology
HERR, W., Genomics
HOHLFELD, P., Obstetrics
HORISBERGER, J.-D., Pharmacology
KAPPENBERGER, L., Cardiology
KELLER, L., Ecology and Evolution
KUCERA, P., Physiology
LAUNOIS, P., Immunology
LEHR, H.-A., Pathology
LEISINGER, H. J., Urology
LEUENBERGER, P., Pneumology
LEVI, F. G., Non-Infectious Epidemiology
LEYVRAZ, P.-F., Orthopaedics
MAGISTRETTI, P., Physiology
MANGIN, P., Forensic Medicine
MAYER, A., Biochemistry
MERMOD, N., Biotechnology
MICHAUD, P.-A., Adolescent Health
MICHETTI, P., Gastroenterology
MIRIMANOFF, R.-O., Radiotherapy
MOESSINGER, A. C., Neonatology
MONNIER, P., Otorhinolaryngology
MOREILLON, P., Internal Medicine, Infectious Diseases
NICOD, P., Internal Medicine
PACCAUD, F. M., Social and Preventive Medicine
PANIZZON, R., Dermatology
PANTALEO, G., AIDS Immunopathology
PASCUAL, M., Transplantation
PÉCOUD, A., General Medicine
PERRIN, N., Ecology and Evolution
RIS, H.-B. F., Thoracic Surgery
ROSSIER, B., Pharmacology
SAURAT, J. H., Dermatology, Venereology
SCHAPIRA, M., Haematology
SCHNYDER, P.-A., Radiology
SO, A., Rheumatology
SPAHN, D., Anaesthesiology
STAMENKOVIC, I., Experimental Pathology
SUPERTI-FURGA, A., Pediatry
TAPPY, L., Physiology
TELENTI, A., Microbiology
THORENS, B., Pharmacology, Toxicology
TISSOT, J.-D., Haematology
TSCHOPP, J., Biochemistry
VILLEMURE, J.-G., Neurosurgery
VOGEL, P., ecology and Evolution
VOLTERRA, A., Cellular Biology, Morphology
VON SEGESSER, L.-K., Cardiovascular Surgery
WAEBER, B., Hypertension
WAEBER, G., Internal Medicine
WAHLI, W., Genomics
WIDMER, F., Ecology and Evolution
ZOGRAFOS, L., Ophthalmology

Faculty of Earth Sciences and Environment (tel. 216923500; fax 216923505; internet www.unil.ch/gse):

BAUMGARTNER, P. O., Institute of Geology and Palaentology

BAUMGARTNER, L., Institute of Mineralogy and Geochemistry
KANEVSKI, M., Institute of Geomatics and Risk Analysis
MARILLIER, F., Institute of Geophysics
RACINE, J. B., Institute of Geography
RUEGG, J., Institute of Territorial Politics and Human Ecology

Faculty of Law (tel. 216922740; fax 21692745; internet www.unil.ch/droit):

BONOMI, A., Comparative Civil Law and International Private Law
BRIDEL, P., Political Economics
CHERPILLOD, I., Intellectual Property
DESSEMONTET, F., Law of Obligation
DUTOIT, B., International Private Law, Comparative Civil Law
GRISEL, E., Constitutional Law
HEINEMANN, A., German Law
KAHIL-WOLFF, B., Social Security
KILLIAS, M., Penal Law
KUHN, M., FCriminology
MARGOT, P., Criminal Investigation, IPSC
MOREILLON, L., Penal Law
MORIN, A., Law of Obligation
NOËL, Y., Tax Law
OYON, D., Accounting
PETER, H., Roman Law, Bankruptcy Law
PIOTET, D., Civil Law
POLTIER, E., Administrative Law
SANDOZ, S., Civil Law
TAPPY, D., Private Law, History of Public Institutions and Sources, Civil Procedure
ZIEGLER, A., Foreign Trade Law and International Public Law

Faculty of Letters (BFSH2, 1015 Lausanne; tel. 216922978; fax 216922905; internet www.unil.ch/lettres):

ADAM, J.-M., French Linguistics
ALBERA, F., History of Cinema
BÉRARD, C., Classical Archaeology
BERTHOUD, A.-C., Applied Linguistics
BRONKHORST, J., Sanskrit, Indian Studies
BOUVIER, D., Greek Language and Literature
CÉLIS, R., Philosophy
DUCREY, P., Ancient History
EBERENZ, R., Spanish Linguistics and Philology
ESFELD, M. A., Philosophy
FORSYTH, N., English Literature
HALTER, P., American Literature
HART-NIBBRIG, C., German Language and Literature
HELLER, L., Modern Russian Literature
HOFMANN, E., History
JEQUIER, F., Modern History
JOLIVET, R., Theoretical Linguistics, Sociolinguistics
JOST, H.-U., Modern Swiss History
KAEMPFER, J., French Literature
KELLER, E., Computing for the Humanities
LARA POZUELO, A., Spanish Language and Literature
MAGGETTI, D., French Literature
MARCHAND, J.-J., Italian Language and Literature
MICHEL, C., History of Art
MÜHLETHALER, J.-C., Medieval French
NESCHKE HENTSCHKE, A., Philosophy
PARAVICINI, A., Medieval History
PRALORAN, M., Italian Linguistics
REICHLER, C., French Language and Literature
ROMANO G. DI STURMECK, S., History of Art
SCHWARZ, A., German Linguistics
SCHWYTER, J., English Linguistics
SERIOT, P., Russian Linguistics and Philology
TILLEMANS, T., Oriental Languages and Civilizations
TOSCATO-RIGO, D., Modern History
UTZ, P., German Language and Literature

VAN MAL-MAEDER, D., German Language and Literature
WYSS, A., Modern French Language and Literature

Faculty of Social and Political Science (BFSH2, 1015 Lausanne; tel. 216923100; fax 216923115; internet www.unil.ch/wwp):

BATOU, J., European Political and Social History
BEAUD, P., Sociology
BERTHOUD, G., Cultural and Social Anthropology
BRAUN, D., Political Science
BUTERA, F., Social Psychology
DAUWALDER, J.-P., Psychology
DE SENARCLENS, P, International Relations
DROZ, R., Psychology
DURUZ, N., Introduction to Psychopathology
FILLIEULE, B., Study of Social and Political Movements
FONTANA, B., History of Political Theory
GAILLARD, F., Applied Psychology
GROSSEN, M., Clinical Psychosociology
HOFMANN, E., History and Social Sciences
KILANI, M., Cultural and Social Anthropology
KNUSEL, R., Social Policies
LEVY, R., Sociology
MAST, F., Cognitive Psychology
MERRIEN, F., Sociology, Social Policy
PAPADOPOULOS, I., Public Policies
PETITAT, A., Sociology, Education
SANTIAGO, M., Health Psychology
VUELIN, C., Child and General Psychology
VOLKEN, H., Mathematics

Faculty of Theology (BFSH2, 1015 Lausanne; tel. 216922700; fax 216922700; e-mail secretariattheologie@unil.ch; internet www.unil.ch/theol):

BURGER, M., Science of Religions
EHRENFREUND, J., History of Jews and Judaism
GISEL, P., Dogmatics and Fundamental Theology
JUNOD, E., History of Christianity
MARGUERAT, D., New Testament
MÜLLER, D., Ethics
RÖMER, T., Old Testament
STOLZ, J., Religious Sociology

Business School (BFSH1, 1015 Lausanne; tel. 216923300; fax 216933005; internet www.hec.unil.ch):

ANTONAKIS, J., Organizational Behaviour
AUTIO, E., Strategic Technology Management
BERGMANN, A., Organizational Behaviour
BRÜLHART, M., International Economics, Applied Econometrics
BÜTLER, M., Economics, Public Finance
CADOT, O., International Economy
CATRY, B., Business Policy
CESTRE, G., Marketing
DANTHINE, J.-P., Monetary Theory and Policy, Macroeconomics, Quantitative Methods
DE TREVILLE, S., Productivity in Operations Management
DUBEY, A., Actuarial Mathematics
DUFRESNE, F., Economic and Actuarial Mathematics
DUPARC, J., Theoretical Computer Science
GARBINATO, B., Programming
GERBER, H.-U., Economic and Actuarial Mathematics
GHERNAOUTI HÉLIE, S., Information Systems
HAMERI, A., Operations Management
HOFFRAGE, U., Risk Theory
HOLLY, A., Econometrics
IMBS, J., Macroeconomics
BURGER, M., Science of Religions
JONDEAU, E., Finance
LIMAYEM, M., Information Technology

MATTEI, A., Microeconomics and Statistics
MORELLEC, E., Finance
MUNARI, S., System Management
OYON, D., Accounting
PIGNEUR, Y., Information Systems
RACINE, J.-B., Geographical Structures
ROCKINGER, M., Finance
ST-AMOUR, P., Macroeconomics
STETTLER, A., Financial Accounting
USUNIER, J.-C., International Marketing
VAN ACKERE, A., Decision Science
VON UNGERN, T., Analysis of Industrial Structures, Macroeconomics
WEISS, L., Financial Accounting
WENTLAND FORTE, M., Knowledge Management

ATTACHED SCHOOLS

School of Criminal Sciences

Telephone: 216924600
Fax: 216924605
E-mail: esc@unil.ch
Internet: www.unil.ch/esc

School of Modern French

Telephone: 216923080
Fax: 216923085
E-mail: msecr@cfm.unil.ch
Internet: www.unil.ch/efm

UNIVERSITÄT LUZERN

Pfistergasse 20, Postfach 7979, 6000 Lucerne 7

Telephone: 412285510
Fax: 412285505
E-mail: rektorat@unilu.ch
Internet: www.unilu.ch

Founded 1574; university status 2000
Language of instruction: German
Academic year: October to July
Rector: Prof. Dr MARKUS RIES
Vice-Rector: Prof. Dr PAUL RICHLI

Number of teachers: 40
Number of students: 1,200

DEANS

Faculty of Humanities: Prof. Dr GAETANO ROMANO
Faculty of Law: Prof. Dr PAUL RICHLI
Faculty of Theology: Prof. Dr MONIKA JAKOBS

UNIVERSITÉ DE NEUCHÂTEL

26 ave du 1er Mars, 2000 Neuchâtel
Telephone: 327181000
Fax: 327181001
E-mail: service.academique@unine.ch
Internet: www.unine.ch

Founded 1909
Language of instruction: French
Academic year: October to July
Rector: Prof. A. STROHMEIER
Vice-Rectors: Prof. D. HAAG, Prof. R. NEIER, Prof. D. SCHULTHESS
Secretary-General: P. BARRAUD
Administrative Director: S. DUINA
Librarian: L. REGAMEY

Number of teachers: 340
Number of students: 3,305

Publications: *Guide des Études* (annually), *Programme de Cours* (annually), *Rapport d'activité de l'Université, Recueils, Unicité* (5 a year)

DEANS

Faculty of Economics: Prof. M. DUBOIS
Faculty of Law: Prof. O. GUILLOD
Faculty of Letters: Prof. R. GLAUSER

Faculty of Science: Prof. M. RAHIER
Faculty of Theology: Prof. P.-L. DUBIED

PROFESSORS

Faculty of Economics (26 ave du 1er Mars, 2000 Neuchâtel; tel. 327181500; fax 327181501; e-mail secretariat.seco@unine.ch; internet www.unine.ch):

BANGERTER, A., Psychology
BÉGUIN, F., Financial Strategy
BLILI, S., e-business
DUBOIS, M., Finance
GRETHER, J.-M., International Economics
HAAG, D., Financial Accounting
HAINARD, F., Sociology
JEANRENAUD, C., Public Economics
KOSTECKI, M., Marketing
MAILLAT, D., Political Economics
SAVOY, J., Informatics in Economics
STOFFEL, K., Computer Science
SUTER, C., Sociology
TILLÉ, Y., Applied Statistics
TSCHAN SEMMER, F., Psychology
ZARIN-NEJADAN, M., Political Economics

Faculty of Law (26 ave du 1er Mars, 2000 Neuchâtel; tel. 327181200; fax 327181201; e-mail secretariat.droit@unine.ch; internet www.unine.ch/droit):

BOLLE, P.-H., Criminal Law and Procedure
DUNAND, J.-P., Legal History, Roman Law
GUILLOD, O., Family Law, Medical Law
KNOEPFLER, F., Private International Law
KOLB, R., Public International Law
MAHON, P., Constitutional Law
MARCHAND, S., Property Law, Bankruptcy Law
MAVROIDIS, P., European and WTO Law
PROBST, T., Contract Law
RUEDIN, R., Commercial Law
TISSOT, N., Intellectual Property Law
WESSNER, P., Law of Obligations, Torts
ZEN-RUFFINEN, P., Administrative Law

Faculty of Letters (Espace Louis-Agassiz 1, 2000 Neuchâtel; tel. 327181700; fax 327181771; e-mail secretariat.lettres@unine.ch; internet www.unine.ch/lettres):

ANDRÉS-SUÁREZ, I., Spanish Language and Literature
AUBERT, J. J., Latin Literature
BÉGUELIN, M.-J., French Linguistics
DE WECK, G., Language Ontogenesis
ECKARD, G., Medieval French Language and Literature
EGLOFF, M., Archaeology
EIGELDINGER, F., Modern French
GHASARIAN, C., French Literature
GLAUSER, R., General Philosophy
GRIENER, P., History of Art
GROSJEAN, F., Linguistics
HENRY, P., Swiss History
HERTZ, E., Archaeology
JAQUIER, C., French Literature
KAMBER, A., Modern French
KNÖPFLER, D., Archaeology and Ancient History
KRISTOL, A. M., Gallo-Roman Dialectology
MARGUERAT, P., Modern History
MAURICE, A., Journalism
MIEVILLE, D., Logic, History and Philosophy of Science
MOREROD, J. D., History
NAEF, A., German Language
PEKAREK-DOEHLER, S., Applied Linguistics
PERRET-CLERMONT, A.-N., Psychology
PETRIS, L., Modern French
PIQUET, E., Geography
RYTZ, F., French Language
SANDOZ, C., Linguistics
SANGSUE, D., French Literature
SCHULTHESS, D., Philosophy
SKUPIEN, C., Modern French
SÖDERSTRÖM, O., Geography
SÖRING, J., German Literature

TERRIER, PH., French Language and Literature
VAN ELSLANDE, J. P., Modern French Literature
VINCENT, P., English Literature

Faculty of Science (rue Emile-Argand 11, 2000 Neuchâtel; tel. 327182100; fax 327182103; e-mail secretariat.sciences@unine.ch; internet www.unine.ch/sciences):

AEBI, PH., Physics
ARAGNO, M., Bacteriology
BALLIF, C., Electronics
BSHARY, R., Ethology
BENAIM, M., Mathematics
BESSON, O., Mathematics
BETSCHART, B., Parasitology
BLAU, M., Physics
BURKHARD, M., Structural Geology
COLBOIS, B., Mathematics
DERENDINGER, J.-P., Theoretical Physics
DE ROOIJ, N., Microelectronics
DESCHENAUX, R., Organic Chemistry
DIEHL, P.-A., Zoology
FAIST, J., Physics
FARINE, P. A., Electronics
FELBER, P., Electronics
FÖLLMI, K., Geology
GOBAT, J.-M., Vegetal Ecology
HERZIG, H. P., Optics
KALT, A., Geology
KESSLER, F., Vegetal Physiology
KROPF, P., Computer Science
KÜPFER, PH., Systematic Botany
MARTINOLI, P., Physics
NEIER, R., Organic Chemistry
NEUHAUS, J.-M., Biochemistry
PERROCHET, P., Hydrogeology
RAHIER, M., Entomology
SEITZ, P., Microtechnology
SHAH, A., Electronics
SIGRIST, F., Mathematics
STOECKLI, F., Physical Chemistry
STÖCKLI-EVANS, H.-H., Chemistry
SUSS-FINK, G., Chemistry
TABACCHI, R., Organic Chemistry
VALETTE, A., Mathematics
VERRECCHIA, E., Geology
VUILLEUMIER, J. L., Physics
WARD, T., Chemistry
ZWAHLEN, F., Hydrogeology

Faculty of Theology (Fbg de l'Hôpital 41, 2000 Neuchâtel; tel. 327181900; fax 327181901; e-mail secretariat.factheol@unine.ch; internet www.unine.ch/theol):

BASSET, L., Practical Theology
DUBIED, P.-L., Practical Theology
MOSES, F., Practical Theology
ROSE, M., Old Testament

ASSOCIATE INSTITUTE

Institute of French Language and Civilisation: 10 professors; 150 students; Dir PH. TERRIER.

UNIVERSITÄT ST GALLEN – HOCHSCHULE FÜR WIRTSCHAFTS-, RECHTS- UND SOZIALWISSENSCHAFTEN (University of St Gallen – Graduate School of Business Administration, Economics, Law and Social Sciences)

Dufourstr. 50, 9000 St Gallen
Telephone: 712242111
Fax: 712242816
E-mail: unihsg@unisg.ch
Internet: www.unisg.ch

Founded 1898
State control
Languages of instruction: German, English
Academic year: April to March

Rector: Prof. Dr PETER GOMEZ

Vice-Rectors: Prof. Dr THOMAS DYLLICK, Prof. Dr BERNHARD EHRENZELLER, Prof. Dr ERNST MOHR
Administrative Director: Dr MARKUS FRANK
Secretary-General: Dr DANIEL CANDRIAN
Librarian: Dr X. BAUMGARTNER

Number of teachers: 320 (120 full-time, 200 part-time)
Number of students: 4,500

Publications: *Aussenwirtschaft* (6 a year), *Electronic Markets* (4 a year), *Thexis* (6 a year)

DEANS

Faculty of Business Administration: Prof. Dr THOMAS BIEGER
Faculty of Cultural Sciences: Prof. Dr DIETER THOMÄ
Faculty of Economics: Prof. Dr HEINZ MUELLER
Faculty of Law: Prof. Dr PHILIPPE MASTRONARDI

PROFESSORS

ANDEREGG, J., German Language and Literature
BACK, A., Information Processing
BAUDENBACHER, C., Private, Commercial and Economic Law
BAUMER, J.-M., Development Policy
BEHR, G., Business Administration
BELZ, C., Marketing
BERNET, B., Business Administration, Banking
BIEGER, T., Business Administration, Tourism
BOURQUI, C., Business Administration
BURMEISTER, K. H., History of Law
CHONG, L., Business Administration
DACHLER, P., Psychology
DOPFER, K., Foreign Trade and Development Theory
DRUEY, J. N., Civil and Commercial Law
DUBS, R., Business Pedagogy
DYLLICK, T., Business Administration
EHRENZELLER, B., Public Law
FICKERT, R., Business Administration
FISCHER, G., Economics
FRAUENDORFER, K., Operations Research
GÄRTNER, M., Economics
GEISER, T., Civil and Commercial Law
GOMEZ, P., Business Administration
GROSS, P., Sociology
GRÜNBICHLER, A., Finance
HALLER, M., Insurance and Business Administration, Risk Management
HAUSER, H., Foreign Trade Theory and Policy
HILB, M., Business Administration
INGOLD, F. P., Russian Language and Literature
JAEGER, F., Economic Policy
KAUFMANN, V., French Language and Literature
KEEL, A., Statistics
KIRCHGÄSSNER, G., Economics
KLEY, R., Political Science
KOLLER, A., Civil and Commercial Law
LECHNER, M., Empirical Economic Research and Econometrics
LEUENBERGER, T., Modern History
MANELLA, J., Business Administration
MARTINONI, R., Italian Language and Literature
MASTRONARDI, P., Public Law
MEIER, A., Economics
MEIER-SCHATZ, C., Civil and Commercial Law
METZGER, CH., Business Administration
MOHR, E., Economics
MÜLLER, H., Mathematics
MÜLLER-STEWENS, G., Business Administration
NOBEL, P., Private, Commercial and Economic Law
OESTERLE, H., Information Processing
PLEITNER, H. J., Business Administration

REETZ, N., Economics
RIKLIN, A., Political Science
ROBERTO, V., Private, Commercial and Economic Law
ROBINSON, A. D., English Language and Literature
RUIGROK, W., International Management
RUUD, F., Accounting
SCHEDLER, K., Public Management
SCHMID, B., Information Processing
SCHMID, H., Economics
SCHUH, G., Technology
SCHWANDER, I., Civil Law
SCHWEIZER, R., Public Law
SILES, J. R., Spanish Language and Literature
SPREMANN, K., Business Administration
STÄHLY, P., Operations Research
STIER, W., Empirical Social Research and Applied Statistics
TOMCZAK, T., Business Administration
TRECHSEL, ST., Criminal Law and Criminal Case Law
ULRICH, P., Economic Ethics
VALLENDER, C., Public Law and Law of Taxation
VON KROGH, F., Business Administration
WALDBURGER, R., Taxation Law
WINTER, R., Information Processing
WUNDERER, R., Business Administration
ZIMMERMANN, H., Financial Market Analysis

ATTACHED INSTITUTES

Institute for Accounting, Controlling and Auditing: tel. 712247400; fax 712247423; e-mail aca-admin@unisg.ch.

Institute for Business Ethics: tel. 712242644; fax 71222881.

Institute of Business Management: tel. 712242360; fax 71222355.

Institute for Economy and Ecology: tel. 712242584; fax 71222722.

Institute for Empirical Economic Research: tel. 712242320; fax 71222302; e-mail few-hsg@unisg.ch.

Institute of European, and International Law: tel. 712242616; fax 712242611; e-mail europarecht@unisg.ch.

Institute for Information Management: tel. 712243800; fax 71222189; e-mail iwi-info@unisg.ch.

Institute of Insurance Economics (with European Centre for Insurance Education and Training): tel. 712434043; fax 712434040.

Institute for Leadership and Human Resources Management: tel. 712242370; fax 71222374; e-mail contactifpm@unisg.ch.

Institute for Legal Sciences and Practice: tel. 712242424; fax 712242883.

Institute of Marketing and Distribution: tel. 712242820; fax 712242857; e-mail imhhsg@unisg.ch.

Institute for Media and Communications Management: tel. 712242297; fax 712242771.

Institute for Operations Research and Computational Finance: tel. 712242101; fax 71222102.

Institute of Political Science: tel. 712242600; fax 712242974.

Institute of Public Finance and Fiscal Law: tel. 712242520; fax 712242670.

Institute for Public Services and Tourism: tel. 712242525; fax 71222563.

Institute for the Teaching of Economics: tel. 712242630; fax 712242619; e-mail iwphsg@unisg.ch.

Institute for Technology Management: tel. 712247320; fax 712247301.

Kühne Institute for Logistics: tel. 712247280; fax 712247315; e-mail KLOG-HSG@unisg.ch.

Research Centre for Information Rights: tel. 712247774; fax 712242771.

Research Institute of Economic Geography and Regional Policy: tel. 712242111; fax 712242816.

Research Institute for International Management: tel. 712242448; fax 712242447.

Research Institute for Labour Economics and Labour Law: tel. 712242800; fax 712242807.

Sociology Seminar: tel. 712242817; fax 712242928.

Swiss Institute of Banking and Finance: tel. 712247090; fax 712247088.

Swiss Institute for International Economics and Applied Economic Research: tel. 712242350; fax 712242298.

Swiss Research Institute of Small Business and Entrepreneurship: tel. 712247100; fax 712247101.

UNIVERSITÀ DELLA SVIZZERA ITALIANA

Via Lambertenghi 10, 6904 Lugano

Telephone: 919238162
Fax: 919238163
E-mail: admin@unisi.ch
Internet: www.unisi.ch

Founded 1995
State control
Language of instruction: Italian
Academic year: October to June
President: Prof. MARCO BAGGIOLINI
Secretary-General: Lic. phil. ALDINO ZGRAGGEN
Head Librarians: Dr GIUSEPPE ORIGGI (Lugano): SERGIO STEFFEN (Mendrisio)
Library of 70,000 vols
Number of teachers: 300
Number of students: 1,500
2 Campuses at Lugano and Mendrisio

DEANS

Faculty of Communication Sciences: Prof. EDO POGLIA
Faculty of Economics: Prof. GIOVANNI BARONE ADESI
Academy of Architecture: Prof. AURELIO GALFETTI

ATTACHED INSTITUTES

Advanced Learning and Research Institute: tel. 919124706; fax 919124647; e-mail master@alari.ch; internet www.alari.ch; Pres. LUIGI DADDA.

Finance Institute: Via G. Buffi 13, 6900 Lugano; tel. 919124753; fax 919124629; internet www.istfin.eco.unisi.ch; Dir GIOVANNI BARONE-ADESI.

Institute for Business Administration: 13 via Giuseppe Buffi, 6900 Lugano; internet www.idea.eco.unisi.ch.

Institute for Communication and Education: 13 via Giuseppe Buffi, 6900 Lugano; tel. 919138516; fax 919124647; e-mail icef@lu.unisi.ch; internet www.icef.com.unisi.ch; Dir GIANNI GHISLA.

Institute for Communication Technologies: Via Giuseppe Buffi 13, 6904 Lugano; tel. 919138513; fax 919124647; internet www.itc.com.unisi.ch; Dir MARCO COLOMBETTI.

Institute for Corporate Communication: 13 via Giuseppe Buffi, 6900 Lugano; tel. 919124646; fax 919124647; internet www.ica.com.unisi.ch; Dir RENATO FIOCCA.

Institute for Economic Research: Via Maderno 24, 6900 Lugano; tel. 919124661; fax 919124662; e-mail info.ire@lu.unisi.ch; internet www.ire.eco.unisi.ch; Dir RICO MAGGI.

Institute for the History of the Alps: tel. 919124705; fax 919124740; e-mail info@isalp.unisi.ch; internet www.isalp.unisi.ch; Pres. JEAN-FRANÇOIS BERGIER.

Institute for Linguistics and Semiotics: 13 via Giuseppe Buffi, 6900 Lugano; e-mail ils@lu.unisi.ch; internet www.ils.com.unisi.ch; Dir EDDO RIGOTTI.

Institute for Media and Journalism: Via G. Buffi 13, 6900 Lugano; tel. 919124738; fax 919124647; e-mail imeg@lu.unisi.ch; internet www.imeg.com.unisi.ch; Dir GIUSEPPE RICHERI.

Institute for Mediterranean Studies: tel. 919124705; fax 919124771; e-mail info@ism.unisi.ch; internet www.ism.unisi.ch; Dir ATHANASIOS MOULAKIS.

Institute for Microeconomics and Public Economics: Via Maderno 24, 6900 Lugano; tel. 919124783; fax 919124733; internet www.mecop.eco.unisi.ch; Dir MASSIMO FILIPPINI.

UNIVERSITÄT ZÜRICH

Rämistr. 71, 8006 Zürich

Telephone: 446341111
Fax: 446342304
Internet: www.uzh.ch

Founded 1833
State control
Language of instruction: German
Academic year: October to July (2 semesters)

Rector: Prof. H. WEDER
Vice-Rector for Planning: Prof. Dr H. C. VON DER CRONE
Vice-Rector for Research: Prof. H. MURER
Vice-Rector for Teaching: Prof. A. FISCHER
Dir of Admin.: P. BLESS
Sec.: Dr K. REIMANN
Librarian: Dr H. KÖSTLER

Number of teachers: 2,622
Number of students: 23,492

Publications: *unijournal* (6 a year), *unimagazin* (quarterly), *unireport* (annual)

DEANS

Faculty of Econ.: Prof. Dr H. P. WEHRLI
Faculty of Law: Prof. Dr T. JAAG
Faculty of Medicine: Prof. W. BÄR
Faculty of Philosophy: Prof. Dr R. FATKE
Faculty of Science: Prof. D. WYLER
Faculty of Theology: Prof. Dr S. VOLLENWEIDER
Faculty of Veterinary Medicine: Prof. F. ALTHAUS

PROFESSORS

Centre for Dentistry, Oral and Maxillary Medicine (Plattenstr. 11, Postfach, 8028 Zürich; tel. 446343203):

GRÄTZ, K., Oral Surgery
HÄMMERLE, C., Crowns and Bridges
IMFELD, T., Preventive Dentistry, Periodontology, Cardiology
PALLA, S., Dental Prosthesis
PELTOMÄKI, T., Children's Dentistry

Faculty of Economics (tel. 446342314; e-mail dekanatww@zuv.uzh.ch; internet www.oec.uzh.ch):

BACKES-GELLNER, U., Business Admin.
BERNSTEIN, A., Dynamic and Distributed Application Systems
CHESNEY, M., Quantitative Finance
DIETL, H., Service and Operation Management
DITTRICH, K. R., Computer Science

EWERHART, C., Information Economy

FALKINGER, J., Finance and Macroeconomics

FEHR, E., Econ.

FRANCK, E., Business Admin.

GALL, H. C., Software Eng.

GEIGER, H., Banking and Finance

GIBSON-ASNER, R., Financial Econ.

GLINZ, M., Informatics

HABIB, M., Corporate Finance Theory

HENS, T., Financial Econ.

HOFFMANN, M., Int. Trade and Finance

HOTZ-HART, B., Econ.

JANSSEN, M., Financial Econ.

KLATTE, D., Mathematics and Econ.

MEYER, C., Accountancy and Financial Control

OSTERLOH, M., Business Admin.

PAJAROLA, R., Multimedia

PAOLELLA, M., Empirical Finance

PFAFF, D., Accountancy and Financial Control

PFEIFER, R., Computer Science

RUUD, F., Accountancy and Financial Control

SAEZ-MARTI, F., Microeconomics

SCHAUER, H., Computer Science

SCHENKER-WICKI, A., Business Management

SCHERER, A. G., Business Admin.

SCHMUTZLER, A., Econ.

SCHWABE, G., Information Management

STAFFELBACH, B., Business Admin.

STILLER, B., System and Communication

VOLKART, R., Banking and Finance

WEHRLI, H. P., Business Admin.

WINKELMANN, R., Empirical Econ.

WOITEK, U., History of Econ. and National Economy

ZILIBOTTI, F., National Econ.

ZWEIFEL, P., Political Economy

ZWEIMÜLLER, J., Macroeconomics

Faculty of Law (tel. 446342233; e-mail dekrwf@ius.uzh.ch; internet www.jur.uzh.ch):

BIAGGINI, G., State, Administrative and European Law

BREITSCHMID, P., Private Law

BÜCHLER, A., Private Law

DONATSCH, A., Criminal Law

ERNST, W., Roman Law

FÖGEN, M. T., Roman Law and Comparative Law

FORSTMOSER, P., Trade Law

GÄCHTER, TH., State, Administrative and Securities Law

GRIFFEL, A., State and Administrative Law

HEINEMANN, A., Economic Law

HILTY, R., Private Law

HONSELL, H., Swiss and European Civil Law, Roman Law

HUGUENIN, C., Private Economic Law and European Law

JAAG, T., State and Administrative Law

JOSITSCH, D., Criminal Law

KAUFMANN, C., State and Administrative Law, Law of Nations

KELLER, H., State Law

KILLIAS, M., Criminal Law

KLEY, A., State Law

MEIER, I., Civil Case Law, Bankruptcy Law

NOBEL, P. J., Swiss and European Trading and Economic Law

OBERHAMMER, P., Civil Case Law

OTT, W., Philosophical and Swiss Civil Law

PORTMANN, W., Private and Industrial Law

RAUSCH, H., Environmental and Administrative Law

REICH, M., Tax, Fiscal and Administrative Law

REY, H., Swiss Civil Law

SCHNYDER, A., Private Economic Law

SENN, M., Philosophical Law

TAG, B., Criminal Law

THIER, A., History of Law

THÜRER, D., Law of Nations, State and Administrative Law

UHLMANN, F., State and Administrative Law

VON DER CRONE, H. C., Private and Business Law

WEBER, R., European Law

WEBER-DÜRLER, B., State and Administrative Law

WOHLERS, P., Private, Economic and European Law

ZOBL, D., Civil Law, Banking and Securities Law

Faculty of Medicine (Zürichbergstr. 14, 8091 Zürich; tel. 446341071; e-mail renate.gay@usz.ch; internet www.med.uzh.ch):

AGUZZI, A., Neuropathology

AKDIS, C., Immunology

ARAND, M., Pharmacology

ATTIN, TH., Preventive Dentistry

BÄR, W., Forensic Medicine

BASSETTI, C., Neurology

BERGER, E. G., Physiology

BERGER, W., Medical Molecular Genetics

BILLER-ANDORNO, N., Biomedical Ethics

BOLTSHAUSER, E., Paediatrics

BORGEAT, A., Anaesthesiology

BÖSIGER, P., Biomedical Technology

BÖTTGER, E. C., Medical Microbiology

BOUTELLIER, U., Physiology

BUCHER, H. U., Neonatology

BUCK, A., Nuclear Medicine

BUDDEBERG, C., Social Psychology

CLAVIEN, P. A., Abdominal Surgery

DIETZ, V., Paraplegology

FEHR, J., Haematology

FINK, D. A., Gynaecology

FONTANA, A., Clinical Immunology

FRENCH, L., Dermatology

FRIED, M., Gastroenterology

FRITSCHY, J. M., Neuropharmacology

GAY, S., Experimental Rheumatology

GENONI, M., Heart Surgery

GERBER, C., Orthopaedics

GIOVANOLI, P., Surgery

GRÄTZ, K., Pathology

GROSCURTH, P., Anatomy

GRÜTTER, M. G., Biochemistry, Macromolecular Crystallography

GUTZWILLER, F., Social and Preventive Medicine

HÄMMERLE, CH., Dentistry

HELD, L., Biostatics

HELL, D., Clinical Psychiatry

HELMCHEN, F., Neurology

HENGARTNER, H., Experimental Pathology

HENNET, TH., Human Biology

HOCK, C., Biological Pharmacology

HODLER, J., Radiology

HUG, E., Radiology

IMFELD, TH., Preventive Dentistry

IMTHURN, B., Gynaecological Endocrinology

JENNI, R., Cardiology

JIRICNY, J., Molecular Radiology

KAISSLING, B., Anatomy

KNUTH, A., Oncology

KOLLIAS, S., Radiology

KULLAK-UBLICK, G. A., Clinical Pharmacology

LANDAU, K., Ophthalmology

LIPP, H. P., Anatomy

LOFFING, J., Anatomy

LÜSCHER, T. F., Cardiology

LÜTOLF, U. M., Radiotherapy

MANSUY, I., Neurology

MARINCEK, B., Diagnostic Radiology

MEULI, M., Surgery

MICHEL, B., Rheumatology

MITSIADIS, TH., Oral Biology

MOCH, H., Pathology

MODESTIN, J., Clinical Psychiatry

MÖLLING, K., Virology

MURER, H., Physiology

NADAL, D., Paediatrics

NEUHASS, S., Neurobiology

NITSCH, R. M., Psychiatry

NOLL, G., Molecular Biology

PALLA, S., Prosthetics

PELTOMÄKI, T., Maxillary Orthopaedics

PLÜCKTHUN, A., Biochemistry

PRÊTRE, R., Children's Cardiac Surgery

PROBST, R. R., Otorhinolaryngology

PRUSCHY, M., Molecular Biology

REINECKE, M., Anatomy

ROGLER, G., Internal Medicine

RÖSSLER, W., Clinical Psychiatry

ROTH, J., Cell Molecular Pathology

RUDIN, M., Pharmacology

RUSSI, E., Internal Medicine

RÜTTIMANN, B., History of Medicine

SALLER, R., Naturopathy

SCHINZEL, A., Medical Genetics

SCHMID, E., Anaesthesia

SCHMID, S., Otorhinolaryngology

SCHNYDER, U., Psychiatry

SCHÖNLE, E., Paediatrics

SCHWAB, M. E., Neurology and Anatomy

SEGER, R., Children's Medicine, Immunology and Haematology

SENNHAUSER, F. H., Paediatrics

SONDEREGGER, P., Biochemistry

SPAHN, D. R., Anaesthesiology

SPINAS, G. A., Endocrinology, Diabetology and Pathophysiology

STEINHAUSEN, H.-C., Child and Youth Psychiatry

STEINMANN, B. U., Paediatrics

STEURER, J., Internal Medicine

SULSER, T., Urology

TRENTZ, O., Accident Surgery

VALAVANIS, A., Neuroradiology

VERREY, F., Physiology

VETTER, W., Internal Medicine

VON ECKARDSTEIN, A., Clinical Chemistry

VON SCHULTHESS, G. K., Nuclear Medicine

WAGNER, A., Bioinformatics

WEBER, R., Clinical Infectology

WEDER, W., Thorax Surgery

WENGER, R. H., Physiology

WIESER, H.-G., Neurology, Special Epileptology

WOGGON, B., Pharmacotherapy

WOLFER, D., Anatomy

WÜTHRICH, B., Dermatology and Venereology

ZEILHOFER, H. U., Pharmacology

ZIMMERMANN, R., Obstetrics and Gynaecology

ZINKERNAGEL, R. M., Experimental Pathology

ZÜND, G., Surgery

Faculty of Philosophy (tel. 446342234; fax 446344966; e-mail heidi.moor@access.unizh.ch; internet www.uzh.ch/fakultaet/phil):

BONFADELLI, H., Journalism

BOOTHE, B., Clinical Psychology

BORNSCHIER, V., Economic Sociology

BOSKOVSKA, N., History of Eastern Europe

BOSSONG, G., Romance Philology

BRANDSTÄTTER, V., General Psychology

BRONFEN, E., English and American Literature

BUCHMANN, M., Sociology

CLAUSSEN, P. C., Art History of the Middle Ages

CRIVELLI, T., Special Romance Literature

DELLA CASA, PH., History of Medieval Art

DESCOEDRES, G., History of Medieval Art

DUNKEL, G. E., Comparative Indo-German Linguistics

DURSCHEID, CH., German Language

EBERLE, F., Pedagogy

EBERT, K. H., General German Philology

EHLERT, U., Psychology

EIGLER, U., Classical Philology

ESSER, F., Journalism

ESTERHAMMER, A., English Literature

FATKE, R., Pedagogy, Special Social Pedagogics

FINKE, P., Ethnology

FISCH, J., General Modern History
FISCHER, A., English Philology
FREUD, A., Applied Psychology
FRIES, U., English Philology
FRÖHLICHER, P., History of French Literature
GASSMANN, R. H., Sinology
GESER, H., Sociology
GILOMEN, H. J., General Economic and Social History, Swiss History
GLASER, E., German Philology
GLAUSER, J., Nordic Philology
GLESSGEN, M.-D., Romance Philology
GLOCK, H.-J., Philosophy
GONON, P., Pedagogy
GRODDECK, W., New German Literature
GÜNTHER, H., History of Modern Art
GUTSCHER, H., Social Psychology
GYR, U., Folklore
HAUG, H.-J., Psychiatry
HAUSENDORF, H., German Language
HELBLING, J., Ethnology
HESS, M., Computer Linguistics
HEUSSER, M., English Literature
HINRICHSEN, H.-J., Musicology
HIRSIG, R., Psychological Methods
HORNUNG, R., Social Psychology
HUG, S., Political Science
IMHOF, K., Journalism
JÄNCKE, L., Neuropsychology
JARREN, O., Publicity Science
JONAS, K., Social Psychology
JUCKER, A., English Philology
KELLNER, B., Old German Literature
KIENING, C., German Literature
KLEINMANN, M., Psychology
KOHLER, G., Philosophy, Political Philosophy
KOLB, G., Ancient History
KRIESI, H., Political Science
KRÜGER, G., Modern History
KYBURZ-GRABER, R., Pedagogy
LA FAUCI, N., Romance Philology, Italian Linguistics
LABARTHE, P., Romance Literature
LEIST, A., Ethics
LIENHARD, M., Spanish
LINKE, W. A., German Literature
LOETZ, F., History
LOPEZ GUIL, I., Iberoromanic Literature
LUPORCARO, M., Romance Philology, History of Italian
LÜTTEKEN, L., Musicology
MAERCKER, A., Psychopathology
MAREK, CH., Ancient History
MARTIN, M., Gerontology
MARX, W., General Psychology
MICHAELOWA, K., Politology
MICHEL, P., Ancient German Literature
MOOS, C., General and Swiss Modern History
MÜLLER NIELABA, D., German Literature
NÄF, B., Ancient History
NAUMANN, B., German Literature
OELKERS, J., Pedagogy
OPPITZ, M., Ethnology
PETERS, J.-U., Slavic Philology
PICONE, M., Italian Literature
RANDERIA, S., Ethnology
REDDICK, A., English Literature
REUSSER, K., Pedagogy
RIATSCH, C., Romance Literature
RIEDWEG, C., Classical Philology, Ancient Greek Studies
RIEMENSCHNITTER, A., Chinese Philology
ROECK, B., General and Swiss History
ROSSI, L., Romance Literature
RUCH, W., Psychology
RUDOLPH, U., Islamic Sciences
RUF, U., Pedagogy
RULOFF, D., Political Science
SAPORITI, K., Philosophy
SARASIN, P., General and Swiss Modern History
SCHABER, P., Philosophy
SCHNEIDER, S., German Literature

SCHREIER, D., English Language
SCHREINER, P., Indology
SCHULTHESS, P., Philosophical Theory
SIEGERT, G., Journalism
STOTZ, P., Middle Latin Philology
SZYDLIK, M., Sociology
TANNER, J., General and Swiss Modern History
TEUSCHER, S., Medieval Studies
TRÖHLER, M., Cinema Studies
URSPRUNG, PH., Modern Art
WAGNER, K., German Literature
WEISS, D., Slavonic Languages
WILKENING, F., General Psychology
WIRTH, W., Publicity Science
ZEY, C., History

Faculty of Science (Winterthurerstr. 190, 8057 Zürich; tel. 446344002; fax 446346806; e-mail dekanat@mnf.uzh.ch; internet www .mnf.uzh.ch):

ACBERSOLD, R., Functional Genomics
ALBERTO, R., Inorganic Chemistry
AMSLER, C., Experimental Physics
BALDRIDGE, K., Computer-supported Chemistry
BARBOUR, A. D., Biomathematics
BASLER, K., Zoology, Molecular Development Genetics
BERKE, H. G. H., Inorganic Chemistry
BOLTHAUSEN, E., Mathematics, esp. Applied Mathematics
BRODMANN, M., Mathematics
BUCHER, H. F. R., Palaeontology
BURG, J.-P., Geology
CAFLISCH, A., Computer-supported Structural Biology
CATTANEO, A. S., Mathematics
CHIPOT, M. M., Mathematics
CONTI, E., Systematic Biology
DE LELLIS, C., Pure Mathematics
DOUGLAS, R., Neuroinformatics
EBERL, L., Microbiology
ELSASSER, H., Geography
ENDRESS, P. K., Systematic Botany
FABRIKANT, S. I., Geography, esp. Geographical Information Science
FINK, H.-W., Experimental Physics
GEHRMANN, T., Theoretical Physics
GREBER, U., Zoology
GROSSNIKLAUS, U., Biology
HAEBERLI, W., Geography
HAHNLOSER, R., Neuroinformatics
HAMM, P., Physical Chemistry
HEINRICH, C. A., Crystallography and Petrography
HENGARTNER, M. O., Molecular Biology
HUTTER, J., Physical Chemistry
ITTEN, K. I., Geography
KAPPELER, T., Mathematics
KELLER, B., Plant Molecular Biology
KELLER, H., Physics of Condensed Matter
KÖNIG, B., Zoology, Behavioural Biology
KRESCH, A., Pure Mathematics
LAKE, G., Theoretical Physics
LEHNER, C. F., Developmental Biology
LINDER, H. P., Systematic Biology
MARTIN, K. A., Neurophysiology Systems
MARTINOIA, E., Plant Biology
MOORE, B., Theoretical Physics
MÜLLER-BÖKER, U., Anthropogeography
NOLL, M., Molecular Biology
OKONEK, CH., Mathematics
OSTERWALDER, J., Experimental Physics
REYER, H.-U., Zoology
ROBINSON, J. A., Organic Chemistry
ROSENTHAL, J. J., Mathematics
SAUTER, S. A., Mathematics
SCHAFFNER, W., Molecular Biology
SCHILLING, A., Experimental Physics
SCHMID, B., Environmental Science
SCHMIDT, M., Physical Geography
SCHMIDT, M. W., Crystalline Geology
SCHROEDER, V., Mathematics
SEEGER, S., Physical Chemistry
SELJAK, U., Theoretical Physics

SIEGEL, J. S., Organic Chemistry
STEINMANN-ZWICKY, M., Zoology
STENFLO, J. O., Astronomy
STEURER, W., Crystallography
STOECKLI, E., Neurobiology
STRAUMANN, U., Physics
THIERSTEIN, H. R., Micro-Palaeontology
THOMPSON, A. B., Petrology
VAN SCHAIK, C. P., Anthropology
VON MERING, CH., Bioinformatics
WARD, P., Zoology, Ecology
WEIBEL, R., Geography
WYLER, D., Theoretical Physics
ZOLLIKOFER, CH., Zoology

Faculty of Theology (Kirchgasse 9, 8001 Zürich; tel. 446344721; e-mail dekanat@ theol.uzh.ch):

BERGIAN, S., History of Church and Dogma
BÜHLER, P., Systematic Theology
CAMPI, E., History of Church and Dogma
DALFERTH, I. U., Systematic Theology
FISCHER, J., Theological Ethics
KRÜGER, T., Old Testament
KUNZ, R., Practical Theology
SCHMID, K., Old Testament
UEHLINGER, C., History and Science of Religions
VOLLENWEIDER, S., New Testament
ZUMSTEIN, J., New Testament

Faculty of Veterinary Medicine (Winterthurerstr. 252, 8057 Zürich; tel. 446358121; fax 446358902; e-mail dekanat@vetadm.uzh.ch; internet www.vet.uzh.ch):

ACKERMANN, M., Virology
ALTHAUS, F., Pharmacology and Toxicology
AUER, J. A., Veterinary Surgery
BRAUN, U., Internal Medicine of Ruminants
BÜRKI, K., Laboratory Animal Science
DEPLAZES, P., Parasitology
EHRENSPERGER, F., Immunopathology
GASSMAN, M., Veterinary Physiology
HATT, J. M., Small Animals
HOTTIGER, M., Molecular Biology
HÜBSCHER, U., Biochemistry
KÄHN, W., Reproductive Medicine
LUTZ, H., Internal Medicine
LUTZ, TH., Physiology
MONTAVON, P. M., Surgery of Small Domestic Animals
NAEGELI, H. P., Toxicology
POSPISCHIL, A., Pathology
REUSCH, C., Internal Medicine (Small Animals)
SPIESS, B., Veterinary Ophthalmology
STEPHAN, R., Foodstuff Security
WANNER, M., Animal Nutrition
WITTENBRINK, M. M., Veterinary Bacteriology

AFFILIATED INSTITUTES

Center for Comparative and International Studies (CIS) Zürich: see Research Institutes (Economics, Law and Politics).

Institut für Suchtforschung: Konradstr. 32, 8005 Zürich; drug dependence research; Dir Prof. A. UCHTENHAGEN.

Polyphor AG: Winterthurerstr. 190, 8057 Zürich; tel. 443504646; fax 443504645; e-mail info@polyphor.com; internet www.polyphor .com; Man. Dr J.-P. OBRECHT.

Prionics AG: Wagistr. 27A, 8952 Schlieren; tel. 442002000; fax 442002010; e-mail markus.moser@prionics.ch; internet www .prionics.ch; Co-Chairs Dr M. MOSER, Dr B. OESCH.

Schweizerisches Institut für Allergie- und Asthmaforschung (SIAF): Obere Str. 22, 7270 Davos Platz; tel. 814100848; fax 814100840; e-mail siaf@siaf.uzh.ch; internet www.siaf.uzh.ch; Dir Prof. Dr C. A. AKDIS.

Schweizerisches Institut für Ausland-forschung: Seilergraben 49, 8001 Zürich;

tel. 446326362; fax 446321947; e-mail siafcd@pw.uzh.ch; internet www.siaf.ch; Man. Prof. Dr D. RULOFF.

Technical Universities

ÉCOLE POLYTECHNIQUE FÉDÉRALE DE LAUSANNE

Ecublens, 1015 Lausanne
Telephone: 216931111
Fax: 216934380
Internet: www.epfl.ch

Founded 1853; present status 1969
Language of instruction: French
Federal government control
Academic year: October to July

President: Prof. PATRICK AEBISCHER
Vice-President (Academic Affairs): Prof. GIORGIO MARGARITANDO
Vice-President (Innovation and Technology Transfer): Prof. JAN-ANDERS MANSON
Vice-President (International Relations): Prof. MARTIN VETTERLI
Vice-President (Planning and Logistics): Prof. FRANCIS-LUC PERRET
Secretary-General: SUSAN KILLIAS
Planning and Research Director: J.-J. PALTENGHI
Library Director: J. NOENINGER
Library: see Libraries and Archives
Number of teachers: 240
Number of students: 6,300

Publications: *Annual Report, General Prospectus*

DEANS

Faculty of Information and Communications: Prof. WILLY ZWAENEPOEL
Faculty of Life Sciences: DIDIER TRONO
Faculty of Materials and Engineering Science: Prof. MICHEL DECLERCQ
Faculty of the Natural and Built Environment: Prof. LAURENT VULLIET
School of Basic Sciences: Prof. THOMAS RIZZO

HEADS OF DEPARTMENTS

Department of Architecture: Prof. LUCA ORTELLI
Department of Chemistry and Chemical Engineering: Prof. URSULA ROETHLISBERGER
Department of Civil Engineering: Prof. AURÈLE PARRIAUX
Department of Communication Systems: Prof. BIXIO RIMOLDI
Department of Computer Sciences: Prof. MARTIN ODERSKY
Department of Electrical and Electronics Engineering: Prof. MAHER KAYAL
Department of Environmental Sciences and Engineering: Prof. JEOSEPH TARRADELLAS
Department of Life Sciences: WILLIAM PRALONG
Department of Mathematics: Prof. ANTHONY C. DAVISON
Department of Materials Science and Engineering: Prof. HEINRICH HOFMANN
Department of Mechanical Engineering: Prof. MICHEL DEVILLE
Department of Microengineering: Prof. PETER RYSER
Department of Physics: Prof. JEAN-JACQUES MEISTER

PROFESSORS

Department of Architecture:
ABOU-JAOUDÉ, G., Computer-Aided Design
BERGER, P., Architecture
CANTAFORA, A., Architecture
CHUARD, P., Building Techniques
DUTRY, G.

LAMUNIÈRE, I., History and Theory of Architecture
LUCAN, J., Architectural Theory
MANGEAT, V., Architecture
MARCHAND, B., History and Theory of Architecture
MESTELAN, P., Architecture
MOREL, C., Building Techniques
ORTELLI, L., Architectural Theory
SCARTEZZINI, J.-L., Solar Energy Research Building
STEINMANN, M., Architecture
THALMANN, P., Economics

Department of Biomedical Engineering:
EBRAHIMI, T., Visual Information Processing
LASSER, T., Biomedical Optics
SALATHE, R., Applied Optics
STERGIOPULOS, N., Cardiovascular Technology
UNSER, M., Biomedical Imaging
ZUPPIROLI, L., Optoelectronics

Department of Chemistry and Chemical Engineering:
BODENHAUSEN, G.
BÜNZLI, J.-C.
DYSON, P.
FREITAG, R., Laboratory of Cellular Biotechnology
GIRAULT, H., Institute of Physical Chemistry
GRAETZEL, M., Institute of Physical Chemistry
JOHNSSON, K.
KROSSING, I.
MERBACH, A.
MUTTER, M.
PITSCH, S.
RENKEN, A., Institute of Chemical Engineering III
RIZZO, T., Institute of Physical Chemistry
RÖTHLISBERGER, U.
ROULET, R.
SEVERIN, K.
VOGEL, H., Laboratory of Polymer Chemistry
VOGEL, P.
VON STOCKAR, U.

Department of Civil Engineering:
BADOUX, M., Institute of Reinforced and Prestressed Concrete
BOVY, P., Institute of Transportation and Planning
BRUEHWILER, E., Maintenance, Construction and Safety of Structures
DESCOEUDRES, F., Road Mechanics
DUMONT, A.-G., Institute of Soils, Rocks and Foundations
FAVRE, R., Institute of Structural Engineering
FREY, FR., Laboratory of Structural and Continuum Mechanics
GRAF, W.-H., Hydraulic Research
HIRT, M., Institute of Steel Structures
JACQUOT, P., Stress Analysis and Measurement
LAFITTE, R., Institute of Hydraulics and Energy
MARCHAND, J.-D., Economics of Infrastructure
NATTERER, J., Timber Construction
PARRIAUX, A., Geology
PERRET, F.-L., Construction Management
PFLUG, L., Optical Stress Analysis Laboratory
RIVIER, R., Institute of Transportation and Planning
SANDOZ, J.-L., Timber Construction
SARLOS, G., Institute of Hydraulics and Energy
SCHLEISS, A., Institute of Hydraulics and Energy
SMITH, I., Institute of Reinforced and Prestressed Concrete

VULLIET, L., Soil Mechanics

Department of Communications Systems:
HUBAUX, J.-P.
KUNT, M.
LE BOUDEC, J.-Y.
NUSSBAUMER, H.
PETITPIERRE, C.
VETTERLI, M.

Department of Computer Science:
BOURLARD, H., Artificial Intelligence Laboratory
CORAY, G., Dir, Theoretical Computer Science Laboratory
COULON, F. DE, Dir, Computer-Aided-Learning Laboratory
FALTINGS, B., Dir, Artificial Intelligence Laboratory
GERSTNER, W., Mini- and Micro-Computer Laboratory
HERSCH, R.-D., Dir, Peripheral Systems Laboratory
LE BOUDEC, J.-Y., Dir, Communication Network Laboratory
MANGE, D., Dir, Logic Systems Laboratory
NICOUD, J.-D., Dir, Mini- and Micro-Computer Laboratory
PETITPIERRE, C., Dir, Data Communication Laboratory
SANCHEZ, E., Logic Systems Laboratory
SCHIPER, A., Dir, Operating Systems Laboratory
SPACCAPIETRA, S., Dir, Databases Laboratory
STROHMEIER, A., Dir, Software Engineering Laboratory
THALMANN, D., Dir, Computer Graphics Laboratory
THIRAN, P., Institute of Data Communication
WEGMANN, A., Industrial Computer Engineering Laboratory
ZAHND, J., Dir, Logic Systems Laboratory

Department of Electrical Engineering:
DECLERCQ, M., Electronics Laboratory
ENZ, C., General Electronics
FAZAN, P., Electronics Laboratory
GERMOND, A., Electrical Installations Laboratory
IONESCU, M.-A., General Engineering
JUFER, M., Electromechanics Laboratory
KAYAL, M., General Electronics
KUNT, M., Signal Processing Laboratory
MLYNEK, D., Electronics Laboratory
MOSIG, J., Electromagnetism and Acoustics
ROBERT, PH., Metrology Laboratory
ROSSI, M., Electromagnetism and Microwaves Laboratory
RUFER, A.-C., Electronics Laboratory
SIMOND, J.-J., Electromechanics and Electrical Machines Laboratory
SKRIVERVIK, A., Electromagnetism and Acoustics
WAVRE, N., Electromechanics and Electrical Machines Laboratory

Department of Environmental Engineering:
BEY, I., Atmospheric Chemistry Modelling
HARMS, H., Pedology
HOLLIGER, C., Environmental Biotechnology
MERMOUD, A., Institute of Development of Earth and Water
JOLLIET, O., Ecosystem Management
MUSY, A., Institute of Agricultural Engineering
PÉRINGER, P., Institute of Environmental Engineering
SCHLAEPFER, R., Soils and Water
TARRADELLAS, J., Institute of Environmental Engineering
VAN DEN BERGH, H., Institute of Environmental Engineering
VÉDY, J.-C., Institute of Agricultural Engineering

Department of Mathematics:

BARTHOLDI, L.
BAYER-FLUCKIGER, E.
BEN AROUS, G., Probability Theory
BUSER, P., Geometry
DACAROGNA, B., Analysis
DALANG, R., Probability Theory
DAVISON, A.
DERIGHETTI, A.
JORIS, H.
LIEBLING, T., Operational Research
MADDOCKS, J., Analysis
MORGENTHALER, S., Statistics
MOUNTFORD, T.
OJANGUREN, M., Mathematical Methodology
QUARTERONI, A.
RAPPAZ, J.
RATIU, T. S.
SHOKROLLAHI, A.
STUART, C., Numerical Analysis and Simulation
THÉVENAZ, J.
WERRA, D. DE, Operational Research

Department of Materials Science and Engineering:

HOFMANN, H., Powder Technology Laboratory
JACQUOT, P., Meteorology and Photonics
KURZ, W., Metallurgy
LANDOLT, D., Chemical Metallurgy
MÅNSON, J.-A., Polymer Composite Technology
MATHIEU, H. J., Chemical Metallurgy Laboratory
MORTENSEN, A., Mechanical Metallurgy Laboratory
RAPPAZ, M., Physical Metallurgy Laboratory
SCRIVENER, K., Construction Materials
SETTER, N., Ceramics Laboratory

Department of Mechanical Engineering:

AVELLAN, F., Institute of Hydraulic Machinery and Fluid Mechanics
BÖLCS, A., Institute of Thermal Engineering
BONVIN, D., Institute of Automatic Control
BOTSIS, J., Applied Mechanics
CURNIER, A., Laboratory of Applied Mechanics
DEVILLE, M., Institute of Hydraulic Machinery and Fluid Mechanics
FAVRAT, D., Laboratory of Industrial Energy Systems
GIOVANOLA, J., Laboratory of Mechanical Systems Design
GLARDON, R., Applied Mechanics and Institute of Machine Design
LONGCHAMP, R., Institute of Automatics
MONKEWITZ, P., Institute of Hydraulic Machinery and Fluid Mechanics
OWEN, R., Fluid Mechanics
THOME, J., Laboratory of Applied Thermodynamics
XIROUCHAKIS, P., Applied Mechanics and Institute of Machine Design
ZYSSET, P., Laboratory of Applied Mechanics

Department of Microengineering:

BLEULER, H., Institute of Microtechnology
CLAVEL, R., Institute of Microtechnology
GIJS, M., Microsystems
HONGLER, M.-O., Microtechnology
JACOT-DESCOMBES, J., Institute of Microtechnology
LEBLEBICI, Y., Microelectronics
NICOLLIER, C., Institute of Microtechnology
PFLUGER, P., Institute of Microtechnology
POPOVIC, R., Institute of Microtechnology
RENAUD, P., Institute of Microtechnology
RYSER, P., Microtechnology
SIEGWART, R., Institute of Microtechnology

Department of Physics:

ANSERMET, J.-P., Experimental Physics Institute
BALDERESCHI, A., Applied Physics Institute
BARÈS, P.-A., Theoretical Physics
BENOIT, W., Nuclear Engineering Institute
BRÜESCH, P., General Physics of Solids
BUTTET, J., Experimental Physics Institute
CHÂTELAIN, A., Experimental Physics Institute
CHAWLA, R., Nuclear Engineering Institute
DEVEAUD-PLEDRAN, B., Micro- and Opto-electronics Institute
FIVAZ, R., Dir, Applied Physics Institute
GRUBER, C., Theoretical Physics Institute
ILEGEMS, M., Dir, Micro- and Opto-electronics Institute
KAPON, E., Micro- and Opto-electronics Institute
KERN, K., Experimental Physics Institute
KUNZ, H., Theoretical Physics Institute
LÉVY, F., Applied Physics Institute
MARGARITONDO, G., Applied Physics Institute
MARTIN, J.-L., Dir, Nuclear Engineering Institute
MARTIN, PH., Theoretical Physics Institute
MEISTER, J.-J., Applied Physics Institute
MONOT, R., Experimental Physics Institute
QUATTROPANI, A., Theoretical Physics Institute
REINHART, F. K., Micro- and Opto-electronics Institute
STERGIOPOULOS, N., Medical Engineering
ZUPPIROLI, L., Nuclear Engineering Institute

INTERDISCIPLINARY UNITS

Bernoulli Interfaculty Centre of Mathematics: Dir TUDOR RATIU.

Centre for Biomedical Engineering and Biotechnology: Dir ALAN HUBBEL JEFFREY.

Centre for Biomedical Imaging: Dir ROLF GRUTTER.

Centre for Electron Microscopy: Dir Prof. P. BUFFAT.

Centre for Space Technology: Dir ROLAND SIEGWART.

Institute of Computational Condensed Matter: Gen. Sec. ALFONSO BALDERESCHI.

Integrated Systems Centre: Head GIOVANNI DE MICHELI.

Micro-Nanotechnology Centre: Dir PHILIPPE FLÜCKIGER.

Plasma Physics Research Centre: Dir Prof. MINH QUANG TRAN.

EIDGENÖSSISCHE TECHNISCHE HOCHSCHULE ZÜRICH
(Swiss Federal Institute of Technology)

Rämistr. 101, ETH-Zentrum, 8092 Zürich
Telephone: 446321111
Fax: 446321001
E-mail: praesidium@sl.ethz.ch
Internet: www.ethz.ch

Founded 1855
Language of instruction: German (some basic lectures are given in French)
Federal State control
Academic year: October to July (two semesters)
President: Prof. OLAF KÜBLER
Rector: Prof. KONRAD OSTERWALDER
Vice-President for Planning and Logistics: Prof. GERHARD SCHMITT
Vice-President for Research and Business Relations: Prof. ULRICH W. SUTER
Secretary-General: Dr PETER KOTTUSCH
Library: see Libraries and Archives
Number of teachers: 356
Number of students: 12,626

Publications: *Academic Guide* (1 each semester), *Annual Report*, *ETH Bulletin* (quarterly), *ETH Life Print* (every 2 months)

HEADS OF DEPARTMENTS (RESEARCH AND TEACHING)

Agriculture and Food Science: Prof. F. ESCHER
Applied Biosciences: Prof. H. WUNDERLI-ALLENSBACH
Architecture: Prof. V. MAGNAGO LAMPUGNANI
Biology: Prof. H. HENGARTNER
Chemistry: Prof. W. VAN GUNSTEREN
Civil, Environmental and Geomatics Engineering: Prof. H.-R. SCHALCHER
Computer Science: Prof. W. GANDER
Earth Sciences: Prof. H. R. THIERSTEIN
Electrical Engineering: Prof. W. FICHTNER
Environmental Sciences: Prof. P. EDWARDS
Forest Sciences: Prof. O. HOLDENRIEDER
Humanities, Social and Political Sciences: Prof. M. BUCHMANN
Industrial Management and Manufacturing: Prof. U. MEYER
Materials Sciences: Prof. H. C. ÖTTINGER
Mathematics: Prof. G. MISLIN
Mechanical and Process Engineering: Prof. PH. RUDOLF VON ROHR
Physics: Prof. J. FRÖHLICH

PROFESSORS

Agriculture and Food Science (D-Agrl, ETH Zentrum, 8092 Zürich; tel. 446323887; fax 446321161; e-mail rutz@agrl.ethz.ch; internet www.agrl.cthz.ch/index-en.html):

ABDULAI, A., Economics of Nutrition
AMADÒ, R., Food Chemistry
AMRHEIN, N., Plant Science
APEL, K., Plant Science
DORN, S., Applied Entomology
ESCHER, F., Food Technology
FROSSARD, E., Plant Nutrition
GRUISSEM, W., Plant Biotechnology
HURRELL, R. F., Human Nutrition
KREUZER, M., Animal Nutrition
KÜNZI, N., Animal Breeding
LANGHANS, W., Physiology and Animal Husbandry
LEHMANN, B., Farm and Agrobusiness Management
MCDONALD, B., Phytopathology
PUHAN, Z., Dairy Science
RIEDER, P., Agricultural Market and Policy
STAMP, P., Agronomy and Plant Breeding
STRANZINGER, G., Breeding Biology
TEUBER, M., Food Microbiology
WENK, C., Biology of Nutrition
WINDHAB, E., Food Engineering

Applied Biosciences (D-Anbi, Uni Irchel, Winterthurerstr. 110, 8057 Zürich; tel. 446356042; fax 446356883; e-mail wyrsck@anbi.ethz.ch; internet www.pharma.ethz.ch):

BOUTELLIER, U., Exercise Physiology
FOLKERS, G., Pharmaceutical Chemistry
MERKLE, H. P., Galenic Pharmacy
MÖHLER, H., Pharmacology
MÜNTENER, M., Anatomy
MURER, K.
NERI, D., Protein Engineering
SCHUBIGER, P. A., Radiopharmacy
STICHER, O., Pharmacognosy and Phytochemistry
WUNDERLI-ALLENSPACH, H., Biopharmacy

Architecture (D-Arch, ETH Honggerberg, 8093 Zürich; tel. 446332885; fax 446331053; e-mail michel@arch.ethz.ch; internet www.arch.ethz.ch/welcome_f.html):

ANGÉLIL, M., Architecture and Design
CAMINADA, G. A., Architecture and Design
CAMPI, M., Architecture and Design
DANIELS, K., Building Systems
DE MEURON, P., Architecture and Design
DEPLAZES, A., Architecture and Technology
DIENER, R., Architecture and Design

EBERLE, D., Architecture and Design
ENGELI, M., Architecture and Computer-Aided Architectural Design
FLÜCKIGER, H., Spatial Development
HERZOG, J., Architecture and Design
HOVESTADT, L., Computer-Aided Architectural Design
JENNY, P., Visual Design
KELLER, B., Building Physics
KÖHLER, B., History and Theory of Architecture
KOLLHOFF, H., Architecture and Technology
KRAMEL, H. E., Architecture and Technology
KRUCKER, B., Architecture and Design
KÜNZLE, O., Building Structures
LYNN, G., Spatial Conception and Exploration
MAGNAGO LAMPUGNANI, V., History of Urbanism
MEILI, M., Architecture and Design
MEYER, A., Architecture and Design
MEYER, P., Architecture and Building Realization
MÖRSCH, G., Preservation of Historical Monuments and Sites
OECHSLIN, W., History of Art and Architecture
OSWALD, F., Architecture and Urbanism
RUCHAT-RONCATI, F., Architecture and Design
RÜEGG, A., Architecture and Design
SCHETT, W., Architecture and Design
SCHMID, W. A., Regional Planning and Methodology
SCHMITT, G., Computer-aided Architectural Design
SIK, M., Architecture and Design
THIERSTEIN, A., Spatial Development

Biology (D-Biol, ETH Zentrum, 8092 Zürich; tel. 446325942; fax 446321151; e-mail ulrich@biol.ethz.ch; internet www.biol.ethz.ch):

AEBI, M., Microbiology
BAILEY, J. E., Biotechnology
BARRAL, Y., Biochemistry
DIMROTH, P., Microbiology
EPPENBERGER, H. M., Cell Biology
FELDON, J., Behavioural Neurobiology
GLOCKSHUBER, R., Molecular Biology and Biophysics
HELENIUS, A., Biochemistry
HENGARTNER, H., Experimental Immunology
HENNECKE, H., Microbiology
KUTAY, U., Biochemistry
LEISINGER, TH., Microbiology
MANSUY, I., Neurobiology
MARTIN, K. A. C., Systematic Neurophysiology
RICHMOND, T. J., Molecular Biology and Biophysics
SCHWAB, M. E., Neuroscience
SUTER, U., Cell Biology
THÖNY-MEYER, L., Molecular Microbiology
WERNER, S., Cell Biology
WINKLER, F. K., Structural Biology
WITHOLT, B., Biotechnology
WÜRGLER, F. E., Genetics
WÜTHRICH, K., Molecular Biology and Biophysics

Chemistry (D-Chem, ETH Zentrum, 8093 Zürich; tel. 446323055; fax 446321058; e-mail hauser@chem.ethz.ch; internet www.chem.ethz.ch):

BAIKER, A., Chemical Engineering and Catalysis
CARREIRA, E. M., Organic Chemistry
CHEN, P., Physical-organic Chemistry
DIEDERICH, F., Organic Chemistry
GRÜTZMACHER, H., Inorganic Chemistry
GÜNTHER, D., Analytical Chemistry
HILVERT, D., Organic Chemistry
HÜNENBERGER, PH. H., Physical Chemistry

HUNGERBÜHLER, K., Safety and Environmental Protection
KOPPENOL, W. H., Bioinorganic Chemistry
MEIER, B. H., Physical Chemistry
MERKT, F., Physical Chemistry
MORBIDELLI, M., Chemical Reaction Engineering
NESPER, R., Inorganic Chemistry
PRINS, R., Industrial Chemistry
QUACK, M., Physical Chemistry
RÖTHLISBERGER, U., Computer-aided Inorganic Chemistry
RYS, P., Technical Chemistry
SCHWEIGER, A., Physical Chemistry
SEEBACH, D., Organic Chemistry
TOGNI, A., Organometallic Chemistry
VAN GUNSTEREN, W. F., Computer-aided Chemistry
VASELLA, A. T., Organic Chemistry
WILD, U. P., Physical Chemistry
WOKAUN, A., Chemistry
ZENOBI, R., Analytical Chemistry

Civil, Environmental and Geomatics Engineering (D-Baug, ETH Honggerberg, 8093 Zürich; tel. 446332691; fax 446331088; e-mail altenburger@baug.ethz.ch; internet www.baum.ethz.ch/welcome_en.html):

AMANN, P., Soil Engineering and Soil Mechanics
ANDERHEGGEN, E., Applied Computer Science
AXHAUSEN, K. W., Traffic Engineering
BACCINI, P., Material Flux and Waste Management
BÖHNI, H., Materials Science
BRÄNDLI, H., Traffic Engineering
BURLANDO, P., Hydrology and Water Resource Management
CAROSIO, A., Geodesy
FABER, M., Structural Engineering
FONTANA, M., Structural Engineering
GIGER, CH., Geographic Information Systems
GIRMSCHEID, G., Construction Management and Process Technology
GRÜN, A., Photogrammetry
GUJER, W., Sanitary Engineering
HERMANNS STENGELE, R., Geotechnics
HURNI, L., Cartography
INGENSAND, H., Geodesy
KAHLE, H.-G., Geodesy
KINZELBACH, W., Hydromechanics
KOVARI, K., Tunnelling
MARTI, P., Structural Engineering
MINOR, H.-E., Hydraulic Structures
SCHALCHER, H.-R., Planning and Construction Management
SCHMID, W. A., Rural Engineering and Planning
SPRINGMAN, S., Geotechnical Engineering
VIRTANEN, S., Metallic High-Performance Materials
VOGEL, TH., Structural Engineering
WITTMANN, F. H., Materials Science

Computer Science (D-Infk, ETH Zentrum, 8092 Zürich; tel. 446327220; fax 446321620; e-mail haeni@inf.ethz.ch; internet www.inf.ethz.ch):

ALONSO, G., Information Systems
BIERE, A., Computer Systems
GANDER, W., Scientific Computing
GONNET, G. H., Scientific Computing
GROSS, M., Computer Graphics
GROSS, TH., Computer Systems
GUTKNECHT, J., Computer Systems
MATTERN, F., Information Systems
MAURER, U., Theoretical Computer Science
NAGEL, K., Scientific Computing
NIEVERGELT, J., Theoretical Computer Science
NORRIE, M., Information Systems
RICHTER-GEBERT, J., Theoretical Computer Science
SCHEK, H.-J., Information Systems
SCHIELE, B., Scientific Computing

STÄRK, R., Theoretical Computer Science
STRICKER, TH. M., Computer Systems
WELZL, E., Theoretical Computer Science
WIDMAYER, P., Theoretical Computer Science
ZEHNDER, C. A., Information Systems

Earth Sciences (D-Erdw, ETH Zentrum, 8092 Zürich; tel. 446325647; fax 446321112; e-mail bonadurer@erdw.ethz.ch; internet www.erdw.ethz.ch):

BURG, J.-P., Structural Geology
GIARDINI, D., Seismology and Geodynamics
GREEN, A. G., Applied Geophysics
HALLIDAY, A. N., Isotope Geochemistry
HEINRICH, CH. A., Mineral Resources and Processes of the Earth's Interior
KUNZ, M., Crystallography
LÖW, S., Engineering Geology
LOWRIE, W., Geophysics
MCKENZIE, J., Earth System Sciences
SEWARD, T. M., Geochemistry
STEURER, W., Crystallography
THIERSTEIN, H. R., Micropalaeontology
THOMPSON, A. B., Petrology
TROMMSDORFF, V., Petrography

Electrical Engineering (D-Elek, ETH Zentrum, 8092 Zürich; tel. 446325002; fax 446321492; e-mail marcel.kreuzer@ee.ethz.ch; internet www.ee.ethz.ch/index.en.html):

ANDERSSON, G., Electrical Energy Systems and Processes
BÄCHTOLD, W., Electromagnetic Fields and Microwaves
DAHLHAUS, D., Mobile Radio Communication
EGGIMANN, F., Signal and Information Processing
ERLEBACH, TH., Theory of Communication Networks
FICHTNER, W., Integrated Systems
FRÖHLICH, K., Electric Power Transmission and High Voltage Technology
GUT, J., Military Security Technology
HUANG, Q., Integrated Systems
HUBBELL, J. A., Biomedical Engineering and Medical Informatics
HUGEL, J., Electrical Engineering Design
JÄCKEL, H., Electronics
KÜNDIG, A., Computer Engineering and Communication Networks
LAPIDOTH, A., Information Theory
LEUTHOLD, P., Communication Technology
LOELIGER, H.-A., Signals Processing
MORARI, M., Automatic Control
NIEDERER, P., Biomedical Engineering and Medical Informatics
PLATTNER, B., Computer Engineering and Communications Networks
SCHAUFELBERGER, W., Automatic Control
STILLER, B., Communication Systems
THIELE, L., Computer Engineering
TRÖSTER, G., Electronics
VAHLDIECK, R., Field Theory
VAN GOOL, L., Computer Vision

Environmental Sciences (D-Umnw, ETH Zentrum, 8092 Zürich; tel. 446322523; fax 446321309; e-mail secretariat@umnw.ethz.ch; internet www.umnw.ethz.ch/umnw_e.html):

DAVIES, H. C., Atmospheric Physics, Dynamic Meteorology
EDWARDS, P., Plant Ecology
EWALD, K., Nature and Landscape Protection
FLÜHLER, H., Soil Physics
IMBODEN, D., Environmental Physics
KAISER, F. G., Human–Environmental Relations
KRETZSCHMAR, R., Soil Chemistry
MIEG, H. A., Human–Environmental Relations
OHMURA, A., Climatology
PETER, TH., Atmospheric Chemistry
ROY, B. A., Plant Biodiversity

SCHÄR, C., Hydrology and Climatology
SCHMID-HEMPEL, P., Experimental Ecology
SCHOLZ, R. W., Environmental Sciences
SCHULIN, R., Soil Protection
SCHWARZENBACH, R., Organic Environmental Chemistry
WALDVOGEL, A., Atmospheric Physics
WARD, J. V., Aquatic Ecology
WEHRLI, B., Aquatic Chemistry
ZEHNDER, A. J. B, Environmental Biotechnology
ZEYER, J., Soil Biology

Forest Sciences (D-Fowi, ETH Zentrum, 8092 Zürich; tel. 446326194; fax 446321575; e-mail benz@fowi.ethz.ch; internet www.fowi.ethz .ch):

BACHMANN, P., Forest Inventory and Planning
BUGMANN, H., Mountain Forest Ecology
HEINIMANN, H. R., Forestry Engineering
HOLDENRIEDER, O., Forest Pathology and Dendrology
KISSLING-NÄF, I., Forest Resource Economics
SCHMITHÜSEN, F., Forestry Policy and Economics
SCHÜTZ, J.-PH., Silviculture

Humanities, Social and Political Sciences (D-Gess, ETH Zentrum, 8092 Zürich; tel. 446322308; fax 446321027; e-mail margelisch@gess.ethz.ch; internet www.gess .ethz.ch):

BERNAUER, T., International Relations
BESOMI, O., Italian Language and Literature
BUCHMANN, M., Sociology
DÄLLENBACH, L., French Language and Literature
EISNER, M., Sociology
FREY, K., Education
GABRIEL, J. M., International Relations
GUGERLI, D., History of Technology
HERTIG, G., Law
HOLENSTEIN, E., Philosophy
KAPPEL, R., Problems of Developing Countries
NEF, U. CH., Law
NOWOTNY, H., Philosophy and Social Studies
RIS, R., German Language and Literature
RUCH, A., Law
SCHIPS, B., Economics
SCHUBERT, R., Economics
SPILLMAN, K. R., Security Studies and Conflict Research
SUTER, CH., Sociology
TOBLER, H. W., General History
VICKERS, B., English Language and Literature
WENGER, A., Swiss and International Security Policy

Industrial Management and Manufacturing Engineering (D-Bepr, ETH Zentrum, 8092 Zürich; tel. 446325718; fax 446321047; e-mail wismer@bepr.ethz.ch; internet www.bepr .ethz.ch/main.htm):

ABELL, D. F., Technology and Management
FAHRNI, F., Technology Management
GROTE, G., Work Psychology
HUBER, F., Industrial Engineering and Management
KOLLER, TH., Hygiene and Applied Physiology
KRUEGER, H., Ergonomics
MEYER, U., Textile Machinery
REISSNER, J., Forming Technology
SCHÖNSLEBEN, P., Industrial Engineering and Management
TSCHIRKY, H., Industrial Engineering and Management
WEHNER, T., Work and Organizational Psychology

Materials Sciences (D-Werk, ETH Zentrum, 8092 Zürich; tel. 446322520; fax 446321028; e-mail krombach@ifp.mat.ethz.ch; internet www.mat.ethz.ch/d-werk/welcome.html):

GAUCKLER, L. J., Non-metallic Materials
LUISI, P. L., Macromolecular Chemistry
ÖTTINGER, H. CH., Polymer Physics
SMITH, P., Polymer Technology
SPEIDEL, M. O., Metals and Metallurgy
SPENCER, N. D., Surface Technology
STÜSSI, E., Biomechanics
SUTER, U. W., Macromolecular Chemistry
WINTERMANTEL, E., Biocompatible Materials

Mathematics (D-Math, ETH Zentrum, 8092 Zürich; tel. 446325615; fax 446321085; e-mail mathdept@math.ethz.ch; internet www .math.ethz.ch):

BÜHLMANN, P. L., Mathematics
BURGER, M., Mathematics
DELBAEN, F., Financial Mathematics
EMBRECHTS, P., Mathematics
FEICHTNER, E. M., Mathematics
FELDER, G., Mathematics
GROTE, M. J., Mathematics
HAMPEL, F., Statistics
ILMANEN, T., Mathematics
JELTSCH, R., Applied Mathematics
KIRCHGRABER, U., Mathematics
KNÖRRER, H., Mathematics
KNUS, M. A., Mathematics
KÜNSCH, H. R., Mathematics
LANFORD, O. E., III, Mathematics
LANG, U., Mathematics
LÜTHI, H.-J., Operations Research
MISLIN, G., Mathematics
NUCINKIS, B. E. A., Mathematics
OSTERWALDER, K., Mathematics
PINK, R., Mathematics
SALAMON, D. A., Mathematics
SALMHOFER, M., Mathematics
SCHWAB, CH., Applied Mathematics
STAMMBACH, U., Mathematics
STRUWE, M., Mathematics
SZNITMAN, A.-S., Mathematics
TRUBOWITZ, E., Mathematics
WÜSTHOLZ, G., Mathematics
ZEHNDER, E., Mathematics

Mechanical and Process Engineering (D-Mavt, ETH Zentrum, 8092 Zürich; tel. 446322596; fax 446321483; e-mail vonrohr@ mavt.ethz.ch; internet www.mavt.ethz.ch/ index-en.html):

ABHARI, R., Turbomachinery
DUAL, J., Mechanics
EBERLE, M., Internal Combustion Engines and Combustion Technology
ERMANNI, P., Composites and Structures
FILIPPINI, M., Economics and Energy Policy
GEERING, H. P., Measurement and Control
GUZZELLA, L., Internal Combustion Engines
JOCHEM, E., Economics and Energy Policy
KLEISER, L., Fluid Dynamics
KOUMOUTSAKOS, P., Fluid Dynamics
KRÖGER, W., Safety Technology
MAZZOTTI, M., Process Engineering
MEIER, M., Product Development
MEYER-PIENING, H.-R., Lightweight Structures and Ropeways
POULIKAKOS, D., Thermodynamics in Emerging Technology
PRATSINIS, S. E., Process Engineering
RÖSGEN, TH., Fluid Dynamics
RUDOLF VON ROHR, PH., Process Engineering
SAYIR, M., Mechanics
SCHWEITZER, G., Robotics
SEILER, A., Engineering and Management
STEINER, M., Control Systems
STEINFELD, Renewable Energy Carriers
STEMMER, A., Nanotechnology
YADIGAROGLU, G., Nuclear Engineering

Physics (D-Phys, ETH Hönggerberg, 8093 Zürich; tel. 446332585; fax 446331106; e-mail rafailidis@phys.ethz.ch; internet www.phys .ethz.ch):

BALTES, H., Quantum Electronics
BATLOGG, B., Solid State Physics
BLATTER, J. W., Theoretical Physics
DEGIORGI, L., Solid State Physics
DOUGLAS, R. J., Theoretical Neuroinformatics
EICHLER, R., Experimental Particle Physics
ENSSLIN, K., Solid State Physics
FRÖHLICH, J., Theoretical and Mathematical Physics
GRAF, G. M., Theoretical Physics
GÜNTER, P., Quantum Electronics
HEPP, K., Theoretical Physics
HOFER, H., Experimental Particle Physics
HUNZIKER, W., Theroretical Physics
KELLER, U., Quantum Electronics
KOSTORZ, G., Applied Physics
LANDOLT, M., Solid State Physics
LANG, J., Experimental Particle Physics
MARTIN, K. A. C., Systematic Neurophysiology
OTT, H. R., Solid State Physics
PAUSS, F., Experimental Particle Physics
PESCIA, D., Solid State Physics
RICE, TH. M., Theoretical Physics
RUBBIA, A., Experimental Particle Physics
SCHMID, CH., Theoretical Physics
STENFLO, J. O., Astrophysics
VAN DER VEEN, J. F., Experimental Particle Physics

ASSOCIATED INSTITUTES

Center for Comparative and International Studies (CIS) Zürich: see Research Institutes (Economics, Law and Politics)

INSTITUTES IN THE DOMAIN OF THE BOARD OF SWISS FEDERAL INSTITUTES OF TECHNOLOGY

Eidgenössische Anstalt für Wasserversorgung, Abwasserreinigung und Gewässerschutz (EAWAG) (Federal Institute for Water Resources and Water Pollution Control): Überlandstr. 133, 8600 Dübendorf; tel. 448235511; fax 448235028; Dir Prof. Dr A. ZEHNDER.

Eidgenössische Forschungsanstalt für Wald, Schnee und Landschaft (WSL) (Federal Research Institute for Forest, Snow and Landscape): 8903 Birmensdorf; tel. 447392111; fax 447392215; Dir Dr M. F. BROGGI.

Eidgenössische Materialprüfungs- und Forschungsanstalt (EMPA) (Federal Laboratories for Materials Testing and Research): Überlandstr. 129, 8600 Dübendorf; tel. 448235511; fax 448216244; Dir Prof. Dr F. EGGIMANN.

Paul Scherrer Institut (PSI): Würenlingen und Villigen; tel. 563102111; fax 563102199; Dir Prof. Dr M. EBERLE.

Colleges

C. G. Jung Institute Zürich: Hornweg 28, 8700 Küsnacht; tel. 449141040; fax 449141050; e-mail info@jung.edu; internet www.jung.edu; f. 1948; private teaching and research institute for analytical psychology as conceived by the psychoanalyst, Carl Gustav Jung (1875–1961); clinical and professional training programme leading to a Diploma; courses and seminars in German and English for qualified auditors; special training in child-psychotherapy (for German-speaking students); several further education programmes; counselling centre; international picture archive and library; 100 teachers; 150 students; Pres. Dr phil. BRIGITTE SPILLMANN; Dir of Studies URSULA WEISS.

Franklin College Switzerland: Via Ponte Tresa 29, 6924 Sorengo (Lugano); tel. 919852260; fax 919944117; e-mail info@fc .edu; internet www.fc.edu; f. 1969; language of instruction: English; academic year September to May; mem. of Asscn of American International Colleges and Universities, Council of Independent Colleges; accredited by Middle States Asscn; undergraduate baccalaureate degree courses in business, communications, political science, languages, liberal arts and multidisciplinary programmes; special courses incl. academic travel; library: 32,000 vols, 30 subscription databases; 43 teachers; 300 students; Pres. ERIK O. NIELSEN; Dean of Academic Affairs ARMANDO L. ZANECCHIA.

Haute Ecole Pédagogique des Cantons de Berne, du Jura et de Neuchâtel—BEJEUNE: Rue du Banné 23, 2900 Porrentruy; tel. 328869912; fax 328869996; e-mail info@hep-bejune.ch; internet www .hep-bejune.ch; campuses at Bienne and La Chaux-de-Fonds; courses in teaching at preschool, primary, secondary and further education level; Rector MAURICE TARDIF; publs *Bulletin* (5 or 6 a year), *Revue Académique Electronique* (annually).

Institut de Hautes Etudes en Administration Publique (IDHEAP): Rte de la Maladière 21, 1022 Chavannes/ Lausanne; tel. 216940600; fax 216940609; e-mail idheap@idheap.unil.ch; internet www.idheap .ch; f. 1981; autonomous institution affiliated with Univ. of Lausanne and Federal Polytechnic; postgraduate courses in public administration, public management, public policy; library: 10,000 vols and 100 periodicals; 12 professors; 384 students; Pres. ARTHUR DUNKEL; Dir JEAN-LOUP CHAPPELET; publs *Bulletin* (quarterly), *Cahiers*.

Pädagogische Hochschule Aarau: Küttigerstr. 21, 5000 Aarau; tel. 628360460; fax 628360466; e-mail info.ph@fhnw.ch; internet www.fhnw.ch/ph; courses in pre-school, primary and secondary teaching, special psychology and pedagogy and research and development in applied pedagogy; Dir Prof. Dr RUDOLF KÜNZLI.

Pädagogische Hochschule Bern: Fabrikstr. 2, 3012 Bern; tel. 313092111; fax 313092199; e-mail info@phbern.ch; internet www.phbern.ch; f. 2005; institutes of pre-school and primary-level teaching, secondary-level teaching I and II, remedial pedagogy, further training and of educational media; 2,000 students; Rector Prof. Dr HANS PETER MÜLLER.

Pädagogische Hochschule St Gallen: Notkerstr. 27, 9000 St Gallen; tel. 712439420; e-mail phs_sekretariat@unisg .ch; internet www.phs.unisg.ch; f. 1983; campus at Gossau; courses in secondary-level teaching; Rector Prof. Dr MARK KÖNIG.

Schiller International University – Switzerland: (For general information, see entry for Schiller International University in Germany chapter)

Campuses:

Schiller International University – American College of Switzerland: 1854 Leysin; tel. 244930309; fax 244930300; e-mail siuacsadmissions@ bluewin.ch; internet www .american-college.com; f. 1963; degree courses in liberal arts and business administration; French and English Language Institute for EFL/ESL students (programme certificate); library of 48,000 vols; Pres. WALTER LEIBRECHT.

Schiller International University – Engelberg: Dorfstrasse 40, 6390 Engelberg; tel. 416397474; fax 416397475; e-mail info@schiller-university.ch; internet www .schiller-university.ch; f. 1978; Dir ROBERTA LO.

Staatsunabhängige Theologische Hochschule Basel (Basel Theological Seminary (State Independent)): Mühlestiegrain 50, 4125 Riehen BS; tel. 616468080; fax 616468090; e-mail info@sthbasel.ch; internet www.sthbasel.ch; f. 1970; masters and doctoral degree programmes in theology; distance-learning course in Hebrew and Greek; excavation project in Israel; Rector Dr JACOB THIESSEN.

Schools of Art and Music

ART

Ecole Cantonale d'Art de Lausanne: 4 ave de l'Elysée, 1006 Lausanne; tel. 213169933; fax 216163991; e-mail ecal@ecal .ch; internet www.ecal.ch; f. 1821; departments of fine arts, audiovisual studies, graphic design, multimedia and industrial design; 60 teachers; 200 students; Dir P. KELLER.

Ecole des Arts Décoratifs–Ecole Supérieure d'Arts Appliqués: Rue Jacques-Necker 2, 1201 Geneva; tel. 227320439; fax 227318734; internet www.geneve.ch/eaa; f. 1876; jewellery, ceramics, stylism, interior architecture, dressmaking, graphic art, art expression; 400 students; Dir ROGER FALLET.

Ecole Supérieure des Beaux-Arts: 9 blvd Helvétique, 1205 Geneva; tel. 223110510; fax 223101363; e-mail infoesba@etat.ge.ch; internet www.hesge.ch/esba; f. 1748; painting, drawing, sculpture, etching, mixed media, audio-visual depts; library: 12,000 vols; 59 teachers; 376 students; Dir J. MAGNIN (acting).

MUSIC

Conservatoire de Fribourg: 8 route Louis Braille, 1763 Granges-Paccot; tel. 264662222; fax 264666517; e-mail conservatoire@fr.ch; internet www.fr.ch/cof; f. 1904; music, singing, dance, theatre; 207 teachers; 5,000 students; Dir GIANCARLO GEROSA.

Conservatoire de Musique de Lausanne (Lausanne High School of Music): 2 rue de la Grotte, 1003 Lausanne; tel. 213213535; fax 213213536; e-mail reception@cdml.ch; internet www.regart.ch/cml; f. 1861 under the auspices of the State and of the City of Lausanne; 120 teachers; 1,400 students; Dir PIERRE WAVRE.

Conservatoire de Musique: Place Neuve, 1204 Geneva; tel. 223196060; fax 223196062; e-mail infosup@cmusge.ch; internet www .cmusge.ch; f. 1835; all branches of music, dramatic art and classical ballet; library: 80,000 music scores and 10,000 vols; 100 teachers; 500 full-time students; Dir PHILIPPE DINKEL; Librarian JACQUES TCHAMKERTEN; publ. *Bulletin* (monthly).

Conservatoire de Musique de Neuchâtel: Clos-Brochet 30–32, 2000 Neuchâtel; tel. 327252053; fax 327257024; e-mail conservatoire.ntel@ne.ch; internet www .conservatoire-ne.ch; f. 1918; Dir FRANÇOIS-XAVIER DELACOSTE; publ. *Duetto* (2 a year).

Konservatorium für Musik und Theater in Bern: Kramgasse 36, 3011 Bern; tel. 313116221; fax 313122053; f. 1858; 170 teachers; library: 50,000 vols; Pres. E. ZÖLCH; Dir Prof. J. STÄMPFLI.

Konservatorium und Musikhochschule Zürich: Florhofgasse 6, 8001 Zürich; tel. 442683040; fax 442518954; f. 1876; controlled by the public authorities; professional school, providing comprehensive musical courses for teachers, performers, composers, leading to State diplomas; department for children and amateurs (2,000 amateurs); library: *c.* 15,000 vols; 240 teachers; 500 students; Dir DANIEL FUETER; publ. *Der Bindebogen* (quarterly).

Musik-Akademie der Stadt Basel: Postfach, Leonhardsstr. 6, 4003 Basel; tel. 612645757; fax 612645713; e-mail info@ musakabas.ch; internet www.musakabas.ch/ ; f. 1867; comprises 3 institutes: music school providing non-professional musical education, conservatory providing professional musical education, Schola Cantorum Basiliensis providing specialized education in early music; library: 100,000 vols; 430 staff; 9,000 students; Dir EMANUEL ARBENZ.

Musikhochschule Winterthur: Tössertobelstr. 1, 8400 Winterthur; tel. 522681500; fax 522681501; e-mail zentrale.mw@hmt .edu; internet www.hmt.edu; f. 1873; 105 teachers; 224 students; Dir JOHANNES DEGEN.

SYRIA

The Higher Education System

Higher education institutions predate Syria's independence from France in 1946, with the oldest being University of Damascus, which was founded in 1903 (when Syria was part of the Ottoman Turkish Empire).

The Ministry of Higher Education is responsible for the universities, Intermediate Institutes (also attached to other Ministries) and higher institutes, and the Council of Higher Education is the co-ordinating body. Higher education policy is planned centrally but implementation is decentralized. There is a Supreme Council of Intermediate Institutes which supervises the Intermediate Institutes. In 2001 Legislative Decree No. 36 authorised the establishment of private institutions of higher education. There were 201,689 students enrolled in the four current universities in 2002/03.

Applicants are legally required to possess the General Secondary Certificate to be admitted to university. The specific grade requirements for admission to programmes are determined by the Council of Higher Education. The Bachelors (*Licence*—French, or *Ijâza fî*—Arabic) is often a four-year degree, although some disciplines require longer, such as engineering, pharmacy, architecture (five years) and medicine (six years). The first postgraduate degree is the Diploma of Higher Studies or Postgraduate Diploma, a full-time course lasting one or two years. Additionally, there is a Diploma of Qualification and Specialization, which is a professional qualification in commerce, medicine and teacher training. Following the award of the Diploma of Higher Studies, the Masters degree is a one- to three-year course consisting of both taught and research elements. Finally, the highest university degree is the Doctor of Philosophy (PhD), which comprises both taught and research elements and culminates with submission and defence of a thesis.

The Intermediate Institutes are the main institutions for the provision of post-secondary technical and vocational education. Courses last two years and are administered either by the Ministry of Higher Education or one of the relevant Ministries. Upon completion of the course, students are awarded the Certificate of Assistant Bachelor.

Learned Societies

GENERAL

Arabic Language Academy of Damascus: POB 327, Damascus; tel. (11) 3713103; fax (11) 3733363; f. 1919; Arabic Islamic legacy and linguistic studies and terminology; 20 mems; Pres. Dr SHAKER FAHAM; Sec.-Gen. Dr A. WASSEK CHAHID; publ. *Majallat Majmaa al-Lughah al-Arabiyyah bi-Dimashq* (review, quarterly).

LANGUAGE AND LITERATURE

British Council: Maysaloun St, Shalaan, POB 33105, Damascus; tel. (11) 3310631; fax (11) 3321467; e-mail general.enquiries@sy.britishcouncil.org; internet www.britishcouncil.org/syria; teaching centre; offers courses and exams in English language and British culture and promotes cultural exchange with the UK; attached office in Aleppo; library of 5,200 vols; additional electronic resources; Dir PAUL DOUBLEDAY; Teaching Centre Man. MARY STANSFELD.

Goethe-Institut: Adnan Malki St 8, POB 6100, Damascus; tel. (11) 3336673; fax (11) 3320849; e-mail goethedam@mail.sy; internet www.goethe.de/na/dam/deindex.htm; offers courses and exams in German language and culture and promotes cultural exchange with Germanygi; library of 5,200 vols; Dir MANFRED EWEL.

Instituto Cervantes: Muhayrin-Nazem, Pacha 400, Damascus; tel. (11) 3737061; fax (11) 3737062; e-mail damasco@cervantes.es; internet damasco.cervantes.es; offers courses and exams in Spanish language and culture and promotes cultural exchange with Spain and Spanish-speaking Latin and Central America; library: library of 10,000 vols; Dir CARLOS VARONA NARVIÓN.

Research Institutes

GENERAL

Institut Français d'Etudes Arabes: BP 344, Damascus; tel. (11) 3330214; fax (11) 3327887; e-mail ifead@net.sy; internet www.ifead.org; f. 1922; study of the classical Arab world, Islamic civilization, and history and studies of modern Syria; library of 100,000 vols, 1,500 periodicals; Dir FLORÉAL SANAGUSTIN; Joint Scientific Sec. NADINE MÉOUCHY; Joint Scientific Sec. SARAB ATTASSI; Librarian GENEVIÈVE JOLY; publ. *Bulletin d'Etudes Orientales* (annually).

AGRICULTURE, FISHERIES AND VETERINARY SCIENCE

Arab Center for the Study of Arid Zones and Dry Lands (ACSAD): POB 2440, Damascus; tel. (11) 5743087; fax (11) 5743063; e-mail acsad@net.sy; internet www.acsad.org; f. 1971 by the Arab League; studies problems of management conservation and development of agricultural resources, including water, soil, plant and animal resources; emphasis on resources survey and assessment, causes of degradation and desertification, processes of conservation and development, economic evaluation and social implications, proper management through appropriate technologies, technical training, processing and dissemination of pertinent scientific and technical knowledge and information; mems: 16 Arab states; library of 1,500 vols, 152 periodicals, 65,000 references; Dir-Gen. Dr HASSAN SEOUD; publs *Agriculture and Water in Arid Regions of the Arab World* (2 a year), *The Camel Newsletter* (2 a year).

EDUCATION

Arab Centre for Arabization, Translation, Authorship and Publication: Al-Afif St, 2 Senbul Jadet, POB 3752, Damascus; tel. (11) 3334876; fax (11) 3330998; e-mail acatap@net.sy; internet www.acatap.htmlplanet.com; f. 1990; attached to the Arab League Educational, Cultural and Scientific Organization (ALECSO); translates and prints recent educational, medical and scientific titles in Arabic; organizes seminars and workshops; library of 3,500 items; Dir Prof. Dr GHASSAN HALBOUNI; publ. *Arabization* (2 a year).

Libraries and Archives

Aleppo

Al Maktabah Al Wataniah: Bab El-Faradj, Aleppo; f. 1924; Librarian YOUNIS ROSHDI.

Damascus

Al Zahiriah (Public Library): Bab el Barid, Damascus; f. 1919; main subjects are miscellaneous sciences, literature and language, history, biography, religion; 100,000 vols, 50,000 periodicals; special collection: rare pre-1900 Arabic books; Librarian SAMA EL MAHASSINI; publ. brochure of new additions (quarterly).

Assad National Library: Malki St, POB 3639, Damascus; tel. (11) 3320803; internet www.alassad-library.gov.sy; f. 1984, in process of formation; national deposit library; publishes National Bibliography, trains librarians; 280 staff; 147,124 vols, 19,000 Arabic MSS; Gen. Dir GHASSAN LAHHAM; publs *National Bibliography* (annually), *Analytical Index of Syrian Periodicals*, *Index of Syrian University Theses*.

University of Damascus Library: POB 3003, Damascus; tel. and fax (11) 2119840; e-mail ucl-damasuniv@mail.sy; f. 1919; 150,000 vols, 2,700 periodicals; Librarian Dr NIZAR OYOUN EL-SOUD; publs *Conférences Générales* (annually), *Statistic Collection* (annually).

Homs

Dar al-Kutub al-Wataniah (Public Library): Homs.

Latakia

Public Library of Latakia: Latakia; f. 1944; 12,000 vols; Dir MOHAMAD ALI NTAYFI.

Museums and Art Galleries

Aleppo

Aleppo National Museum: Aleppo; tel. (21) 212400; f. 1931; archaeology and modern art; library of 4,000 vols; Head Curator Dr SHAWQI SHAATH.

Busra

Busra Museum: Busra; traditional arts and crafts; Dir of Archaeological Research Dr SULEIMAN MOGHDAD.

Damascus

Adnan Malki Museum: Damascus.

Agricultural Museum: Damascus.

Military Museum: Damascus.

Museum of Arabic Epigraphy: Damascus; f. 1974; Dir FAYEZ HOMSI.

National Museum: Syrian University St, Damascus 4; tel. (11) 2219148; fax (11) 2247983; e-mail antiquities@net.sy; f. 1919; Sections: Prehistory; Ancient Oriental; Greek, Roman and Byzantine; Arab and Islamic; Modern Art; of special interest is the reconstruction of the Palmyrene Hypogeum of Yarhai (2nd c. AD), of the Dura Synagogue (3rd c. AD), of the Umayyad Qasr El-Hair El-Gharbi (8th c. AD) and of the Damascus Hall (18th c. AD); houses the Directorate-General of Antiquities and Museums, established by decree in 1947 to conserve Syrian antiquities and to supervise the archaeological museums and the excavations; Dir-Gen. of Antiquities and Museums ALI AL-KAYYEM; publs *Les Annales Archéologiques Arabes Syriennes*, *Les Chroniques Archéologiques en Syrie*.

Popular Traditions Museum Qasrelazem: Bzourieh St, Damascus; tel. (11) 226160; f. 1954; traditions and crafts; library of 3,000 vols; Curator HASSAN KAMAL.

Deir ez-Zor

Deir ez-Zor Museum: Deir ez-Zor; f. 1974; archaeology; library of 1,000 vols; Dir ASSAD MAHMOUD; publ. *Les Annales Archéologiques de Syrie*.

Hama

Hama Museum: Hama; f. 1956; history and folklore.

Homs

Homs Museum: Homs dar Al-Thakafa; f. 1974; archaeology, folk and modern art; Curator MAJED EL-MOUSSLI.

Palmyra

Palmyra National Museum: Palmyra; f. 1961; archaeological finds from pre-history to 16th century; attached is the museum of Syrian desert folklore, traditional handcraft industry and agriculture; Dir KHALED AL-AS'AD.

Sweida

Sweida Museum: Sweida.

Tartos

Tartos Museum: Tartos; Islamic history.

Universities

AL-BAATH UNIVERSITY

POB 77, Homs
Telephone: (31) 431847
Fax: (31) 426716
E-mail: baath-univ@net.sy

Founded 1979
State control
Language of instruction: Arabic
Academic year: September to June
President: Prof. Dr YASSER HOURI
Vice-President (Administrative and Student Affairs): Prof. Dr HOUSAM BARAKAT
Vice-President (Scientific Affairs): Prof. Dr AUODI SALHA
Administrative Officer: KASSEM HAMMOUD
Director of International Relations: ABDUL ILAH AL-ABDOU
Librarian: LINA MAASRANI

Library of 63,000 vols
Number of teachers: 802
Number of students: 26,730

Publication: *University Magazine* (irregular)

DEANS

Faculty of Agriculture: Dr ABDULA AL-ISA
Faculty of Chemical and Petroleum Engineering: Dr SHARIF SADIQ
Faculty of Civil Engineering and Architecture: Dr MOHAMED HAKEMI (Architecture)
Faculty of Civil Engineering and Architecture: Dr BASSAM IBRAHIM (Civil Engineering)
Faculty of Dentistry: Dr MOUHAMED SABEH ARAB
Faculty of Education: Dr IBRAHIM KHADOUR
Faculty of Informatics: Dr MUHAMAD AL-RAJAB
Faculty of Literature: Dr AHMAD DAHMAN
Faculty of Mechanical and Electrical Engineering: Dr RADWAN AL-MASRI
Faculty of Medicine: Dr ISA TUMI
Faculty of Pharmacy: Dr IMAD HADAD
Faculty of Sciences: Dr MALEK ALI
Faculty of Veterinary Science (in Hama): Dr MOHAMED ALI AL-IMADI
Intermediate Institute of Computer Engineering: Dr MOHAMED AL-HAG YOUNES
Intermediate Institute of Engineering: Dr MOUFAK FAKHOURI
Intermediate Institute of Industry: Dr HASSAN FARAH
Intermediate Institute of Veterinary Medicine: Dr ASAD AL-ABID

UNIVERSITY OF ALEPPO

Aleppo
Telephone: (21) 236130
Fax: (21) 229184
Founded 1960
State control
Languages of instruction: Arabic, French, English
Academic year: September to June
Rector: Dr MOHAMMAD ALI HOURIEH
Vice-Rectors: Dr TAJEDDIN DIA (Academic Affairs), Dr MAHMOUD KARROUM (Administrative and Student Affairs)
Chief Administrator and Secretary: MOHAMMAD WATTAR
Registrar: MAHMUD ELWANI
Librarian: MUSTAFA JASSOUMEH

Number of teachers: 3,377
Number of students: 53,465

Publications: *Journal for the History of Arabic Science*, *Newsletter of the Institute for the History of Arabic Science*, *Research Journal of Aleppo University* (comprises the following series: Arts and Humanities; Medical Sciences; Agricultural Sciences; Basic Sciences; Engineering Sciences; *Adiyat Halab*)

DEANS

Faculty of Agriculture: Dr JEMMA IBRAHIM
Second Faculty of Agriculture: Dr MUHIEDD-EEN QARAWANI
Faculty of Architectural Engineering: Dr ABDUL GHANI AL-SHEHABI

Faculty of Arts and Humanities: Dr MOUSTAFA JATAL
Faculty of Civil Engineering: Dr SAMEH JAZMATI
Faculty of Dentistry: Dr MOHAMMAD IKBAL MUSHREF
Faculty of Economics: Dr AHMAD ASHKAR
Faculty of Electrical and Electronic Engineering: Dr MISHEL HALLAK
Faculty of Law: Dr KHALED AL-HAMOUD
Faculty of Mechanical Engineering: Dr SALMAN SAGHBINI
Faculty of Medicine: Dr MOUNZER BARAKAT
Faculty of Pharmacy: Dr SAMEER SA'AD
Faculty of Sciences: Dr NASSUH ALAYA

HEADS OF DEPARTMENTS

Faculty of Agriculture:

Animal Production: F. AL-YASIN
Basic Sciences: Dr WALID ASWAD
Economic and Agricultural Instruction: M. SAID FUTAYEH
Field Products: A. HAITHAM MUSHANTAT
Forestry: M. NABEEL SHALABI
Horticulture: Dr H. AL-WARA'
Nutritional Sciences: Dr A. ZIAD KEYALI
Plant Protection: Dr A. AMER HADJ KASEM
Rural Engineering: S. BARBARA
Soils: Dr ZUHAIR ABBASI

Second Faculty of Agriculture:

Animal Production: Dr ALI AL-ALI
Economy and Agricultural Instruction: Dr FAROUK BAKDASH
Field Products: Dr AHMED EL-FARHAN
Forestry and Ecology: Dr A. AL-JUM'A AL-DAKHIL
Nutritional Science: Dr ABOUD EL-SALEH
Pasture and Field Products: Dr ZIAD AL-HOUSSEIN
Plant Protection: Dr ISAM AL-MUGHIR
Rural Engineering: Dr ZIB IBRAHIM
Soil and Soil Reclamation: Dr A. AL-IBRAHIM

Faculty of Architectural Engineering:

Architectural Design: Dr GEORGE TUMA
Construction and Implementation: A. AL-DAKAR
Environment and Planning: Dr FATINA KURDI
History and Theories of Architecture: Dr JAMAL MUSELMANI

Faculty of Arts and Humanities:

Arabic Literature: Dr S. KAZZARA
Education and Psychology: Dr H. ABU HAMMUD
English Literature: Dr A. Y. KOTOB
French Literature: Dr N. ISMAEL

Faculty of Civil Engineering:

Communications and Transport: M. SATEH AL-HUSARI
Engineering Management and Construction: Dr M. HINDIEH
Environmental Engineering: Dr AMJAD MURAD AGHA
Geotechnical Engineering: Dr MARWAN HAMZEH
Hydraulic Engineering: M. NIZAR KAZAN
Principal Sciences: Dr N. NABGHALI
Structural Engineering: Dr A. KATKHUDA
Topographical Engineering: MICHAEL ASWAD

Faculty of Economics:

Accounting: Dr M. DABBAGHIYEH
Business Administration: Dr M. KHARSHUM
Economics and Planning: Dr J. BASH AGHA
Statistics: Dr A. RAFIK KASEM

Faculty of Electrical and Electronic Engineering:

Communication Engineering: W. HABBAL
Electrical Power Systems: M. SHAABAN
Electronic Engineering: M. G. TURMANINI
Information Engineering: Dr FADI FOWZ

Machinery and Electrical Conducting: ABDUL KARIM MANOUK
Mechanical Control and Electronics: Dr M. SAID AKIL
Principal Sciences: Dr DALAR BAYA'A

Faculty of Mechanical Engineering:

Agricultural Machines: I. DAMERJI
Applied Mechanics: Dr G. SALLUM
Mechanical Power: Dr YASER HAYANI
Principal Sciences: A. NADIM AKKAD
Production Engineering: Dr H. ABU SALEH

Faculty of Medicine:

Anaesthesiology and Resuscitation: M. TAHA AL-JASER
Anatomy: Dr A. ZAIDEH
Biochemistry: A. KARAZEH
Cerebral Diseases: S. AL-SAYED
Dermatology: Dr H. BALABAN
General Surgery: A. DAWLI
Gynaecology and Obstetrics: B. NASIF
Internal Medicine: R. ASFARI
Paediatrics: A. MATTAR
Pathology: Dr B. BAZERBASHI

Faculty of Sciences:

Animal Physiology: M. ADEL HAKIM
Chemistry: S. AL-KADRI
Geology: A. FUAD IBRAHIM BASHA
Mathematics: Dr M. KHER AHMAD
Physics: RIAD AL-RASHIH
Plant Physiology: Dr A. KASHLAN

ATTACHED INSTITUTES

Agricultural Research Centre: Meselmieh, Aleppo.

Institute for the History of Arabic Science: Dir Dr KHALED MAGOUT.

Intermediate Institute for Agriculture: Dir Dr MUSTAFA AL-JADDER.

Intermediate Institute for Commerce: Dir Dr A. RAHMAN AL-OBEID.

Intermediate Institute for Dentistry: Dir Dr ADEL AJAM.

Intermediate Institute for Engineering: Dir Dr N. SHEHADEH.

Intermediate Institute for Mechanical and Electrical Engineering: Dir Dr A. NAHHAS.

Intermediate Institute for Medicine: Dir Dr Y. KHANJI.

Intermediate Institute for Secretariat: Dir Dr H. IBRAHIM.

School of Nursing: Dir Dr B. NASSIF.

UNIVERSITY OF DAMASCUS

Damascus
Telephone: (11) 2232152
Fax: (11) 2236010
E-mail: damasuniv@net.sy
Internet: www.damasuniv.shern.net
Founded 1903

State control
Language of instruction: Arabic
Academic year: September to June
President: Dr ISAM AL-AWA
Vice-President (Academic): Prof. Dr MOHAMMAD BASHEER AL-MONAJED
Vice-President (Administrative): Prof. Dr NABEEL AL-BATAL
Secretary General: Dr RIYAD AL-AJLANI
Registrar: ESSAM JERJES
Librarian: KAIS SHAHEEN

Number of teachers: 2,688
Number of students: 85,512

Publications: *Aljami'a Journal, Historical Studies Journal* (4 a year), *Statistical Collections* (annually), *Damascus University Bulletin, Journal for the Arts, Humanities and Sciences* (4 a year), *Journal for the Economic and Legal Sciences* (4 a year), *Journal for Basic and Applied Sciences* (4 a year), *Journal for the Medical Sciences* (4 a year), *Dirasat Tarikhiyyah* (historical review, 4 a year)

DEANS

Faculty of Agriculture: Prof. Dr SULAIMAN SALHAB
Faculty of Architecture: Prof. Dr RIDWAN TAHLAWI
Faculty of Dentistry: Prof. Dr M. ISAM ALAWA
Faculty of Civil Engineering: ABDEL MUNEER NAJEM (Vice-Dean)
Faculty of Economics: Prof. Dr TAREK AL-KHAIR
Faculty of Fine Arts: Prof. Dr ABDEL RAZZAK MUAD
Faculty of Information Technology: Dr EMAD MUSTAFA
Faculty of Islamic Studies: Prof. M. FAROUQ AL-AKKAM
Faculty of Law: Prof. Dr ABBOUD AL-SARRAJ
Faculty of Letters: Prof. Dr M. HAMMADI
Faculty of Mechanical and Electrical Engineering: Prof. Dr FAISAL AL-ABBAS
Faculty of Medicine: Prof. Dr ADNAN SOUMAN
Faculty of Pharmacy: Prof. Dr ADEL NAWFAL
Faculty of Science: Prof. Dr M. SAED MAHASNEH
Nursing School: Dr KHITAN AL-KHATEEB

ATTACHED INSTITUTE

Higher Institute of Administrative Development: Dir Dr M. AL-HUSSEIN.

TISHREEN UNIVERSITY
(University of October)

Latakia
Telephone: (41) 437840
Fax: (41) 418504
E-mail: tuniv.lat@syriatel.net
Founded 1971 as University of Latakia
State control

Language of instruction: Arabic
Academic year: September to June
President: Prof. Dr NAJIB GHAZAWI
Vice-President for Academic Affairs: Dr MOHAMED YACINE-KASSAB
Vice-President for Students and Administrative Affairs: Dr AHMAD MANSOUR
Secretary: NAJAT OSMAN
Librarian: MOUHAMMAD NAJIB SAKER

Number of teachers: 845
Number of students: 25,621

Publications: *Journal of Agriculture, Journal of Arts and Humanities, Journal of Basic Science, Journal of Economics, Journal of Medical Science, Journal of Studies and Scientific Research*

DEANS

Faculty of Agriculture: Dr AHMAD JALLOUL
Faculty of Architecture: Dr NUHAD ABDALLA
Faculty of Arts: Dr MOHAMMAD JALAL OSMAN
Faculty of Civil Engineering: Dr ALI TURIKIEH
Faculty of Dentistry: Dr NAZIH ISSA
Faculty of Economics: Dr ALI HISMEH
Faculty of Education: Dr GHASSAN SALEH
Faculty of Electrical and Mechanical Engineering: Dr JARKAS TAJE DINE
Faculty of Medicine: Dr IBRAHIM SULAIMAN
Faculty of Nursing: NAJWA KERDOGHLI
Faculty of Pharmacology: Dr MAAROUF AL-KHAYER
Faculty of Physical Education: NOURI BARAKAT
Faculty of Science: Dr DAIFALLAH NASSOUR

Colleges

Arab Conservatory of Music: Sabil near Kalimeh Hospital, Aleppo; tel. (21) 2672600; fax (21) 2672600; f. 1963; depts of classical (Western) and Oriental (Middle Eastern) music; Children's Choir, Chamber Orchestra; 28 teachers; 600 students; Dir NABIL GHREWATI.

Higher Institute of Applied Sciences and Technology: POB 31983, Barzeh, Damascus; tel. (11) 5124639; fax (11) 2237710; e-mail hiast@mail.sy; f. 1983; awards BSc, MSc, PhD; depts of Informatics, Systems Engineering, Mathematics, Physics, Electronics, Management, Mechanics; language of instruction: Arabic; 120 teachers; 400 students; Dir Prof. Dr OMRAN KOUBA.

Higher Institute of Political Science: Al-Tall, Damascus; tel. (11) 5911704; fax (11) 5911526; f. 1976; depts of Administration and Public Relations, International Relations and Political Studies; library: 15,000 vols; 25 teachers; 434 students; Dean HUSEIN AL-SAYED HUSEIN.

TAJIKISTAN

The Higher Education System

Higher education institutions predate Tajikistan (formerly Tajik SSR)'s independence from the USSR in 1991, with the oldest being Tajik State Pedagogical University and Tajik Agricultural University, both of which were founded in 1931. In 2003 constitutional amendments abolished free higher education. In 2005/06 some 132,400 students were enrolled at 36 institutes of higher education.

The Diploma of Completed Secondary Education or the Diploma of Completed Vocational Education are the main requirements for admission to higher education. The Specialist Diploma is the Soviet-style undergraduate degree that lasts five or six years and grants students the right to enter directly into doctoral-level studies upon successful completion. Alternatively, the Bachelors (Bakalavr) degree is a four-year programme of study, after which a graduate may study for the Masters (Magister), the first postgraduate degree. The Masters is a two-year course culminating with submission of a thesis; students who have successfully completed the Masters may undertake doctoral-level studies. Both the Soviet-style Candidate of Science (Kandidat Nauk) and European-style Doctorate are available and are awarded after two to three years of independent research. The highest university degree is the Doctor of Sciences, which is purely an academic degree, aimed at students who wish to pursue a career in academia or research.

Technical and vocational education at the post-secondary level consists of two-year programmes of study leading to the title of Junior Specialist.

Learned Societies

GENERAL

Tajik Academy of Sciences: 734025 Dushanbe, Pr. Rudaki 33; tel. (372) 21-50-83; fax (372) 21-49-11; e-mail sarvay@ac.tajik.net; f. 1951; divs of Physical-Mathematical, Chemical and Geological Sciences (Chair. I. N. GHANIEV, Scientific Sec. R. I. KOSTOVA), Biological and Medical Sciences (Chair. H. A. ABDULLOEV, Scientific Sec. SH. H. QURBONOVA), Social Sciences (Chair. A. MUHAMMADKHOJAEV, Scientific Sec. F. B. BOBOEV); 32 mems; 49 corresp. mems; attached research institutes: see Research Institutes; library: see Libraries and Archives; Pres. Dr U. MIRSAYIDOV; Chief Academic Sec. G. H. SALIBAYEV; publs *Doklady* (Reports), *Problemy gastroenterologii*, *Izvestiya* (bulletins: Physical-Engineering and Geological Sciences, Biological Sciences, History and Philology, Philosophy, Econ. and Law).

LANGUAGE AND LITERATURE

British Council: see chapter on Uzbekistan.

Research Institutes

GENERAL

Khudzhand Scientific Centre: 735714 Khudzhand, Ul. Syrdarinskaya 26; tel. (379) 25-17-74; attached to Tajik Acad. of Sciences; Chair. M. R. DZHALILOV; Scientific Sec. M. SUBKHONOV.

Pamir Research Station: 736000 Khorog, Gorno-Badakhshan Autonomous Region; f. 1969; attached to Tajik Acad. of Sciences; Chair. U. KH. KHOLDOROV.

ARCHITECTURE AND TOWN PLANNING

Institute of Earthquake Engineering and Seismology: 734029 Dushanbe, Ul. Aini 121; tel. (372) 25-06-69; fax (372) 24-43-83; e-mail tisss@iscuk.td.silk.org; f. 1951; attached to Tajik Acad. of Sciences; library of 6,000 vols, 40 periodicals; Dir SOBIT KH. NEGMATULLAEV; Sec. PULAT A. YASUNOV; publs *Prognoz zemletryasenii* (in Russian, annual), *Zemletryaseniya Sredney Azii i Kazakhstana* (in Russian, annual).

BIBLIOGRAPHY, LIBRARY SCIENCE AND MUSEOLOGY

Institute of Manuscripts: 734025 Dushanbe, Kirov 35; tel. (372) 27-34-04; attached to Tajik Acad. of Sciences; Dir D. NAZRIYEV.

ECONOMICS, LAW AND POLITICS

Institute of Economics: 734000 Dushanbe, Ul. Aini 44; tel. (372) 21-67-50; fax (372) 21-57-65; f. 1951; attached to Tajik Acad. of Sciences; Dir R. K. RAKHIMOV.

Institute of Philosophy and Law: 734025 Dushanbe, Pr. Rudaki 33; tel. (372) 23-77-96; e-mail noibprez@ac.tajik.net; attached to Tajik Acad. of Sciences; f. 1991; Dir M. DINORSHOYEV.

HISTORY, GEOGRAPHY AND ARCHAEOLOGY

Donish Institute of History, Archaeology and Ethnography: 734025 Dushanbe, Pr. Rudaki 33; tel. (372) 22-37-42; f. 1932; attached to Tajik Acad. of Sciences; Dir R. M. MASOV.

LANGUAGE AND LITERATURE

Rudaki Institute of Language and Literature: 734025 Dushanbe, Pr. Rudaki 21; tel. (372) 21-60-11; f. 1932; attached to Tajik Acad. of Sciences; Dir A. M. MANIYAZOV.

MEDICINE

Institute of Gastroenterology: 734002 Dushanbe, Parvin 12; tel. (372) 21-77-82; fax (372) 23-49-17; e-mail mansurov@academy.td.silk.org; f. 1959; attached to Tajik Acad. of Sciences; library of 5,000 vols; Dir Prof. G. MIRODJEV; publ. *Problems of Gastroenterology* (4 a year).

NATURAL SCIENCES

Biological Sciences

Institute of Botany: 734017 Dushanbe, Ul. Karamova 27; tel. (372) 24-71-88; f. 1941; attached to Tajik Acad. of Sciences; Dir U. I. ISMOILOV.

Institute of Plant Physiology and Genetics: 734063 Dushanbe, Ul. Aini 299/2; tel. (372) 25-26-44; e-mail akotibbm@ac.tajik.net; f. 1964; attached to Tajik Acad. of Sciences; Dir Prof. KHURSHED KARIMOV.

Pavlovskii, E.N., Institute of Zoology and Parasitology: 734025 Dushanbe, Post Office 70; tel. (372) 25-58-71; f. 1941; attached to Tajik Acad. of Sciences; Dir A. K. GAFUROV.

Mathematical Sciences

Institute of Mathematics: 734063 Dushanbe, Ul. Aini 299; tel. (372) 25-77-76; e-mail usmanov@ac.tajik.net; f. 1973; attached to Tajik Acad. of Sciences; Dir Z. D. USMANOV.

Physical Sciences

Institute of Astrophysics: 734042 Dushanbe, Ul. Bukhoro 22; tel. (372) 27-46-14; e-mail astro@ac.tajik.net; f. 1958; attached to Tajik Acad. of Sciences; Dir KHURSAND I. IBADINOV; publ. *Bulletin* (2 a year).

Institute of Geology: 734063 Dushanbe, Ul. Aini 267; tel. (372) 25-32-67; f. 1941; attached to Tajik Acad. of Sciences; Dir M. R. DHALILOV.

Nikitin, V. I., Institute of Chemistry: 734063 Dushanbe, Ul. Aini 299/2; tel. (372) 25-26-04; e-mail sarvar@ac.tajik.net; f. 1946; attached to Tajik Acad. of Sciences; Dir U. M. MIRSAYIDOV.

RELIGION, SOCIOLOGY AND ANTHROPOLOGY

Institute of Oriental Studies and Written Heritage: 734025 Dushanbe, Kiroka 35; tel. (372) 27-23-36; e-mail ogonazar@ac.tajik.net; f. 1958; attached to Tajik Acad. of Sciences.

TECHNOLOGY

Umarov, S.U., Physical-Technical Institute: 734063 Dushanbe, Ul. Aini 299/1; tel. (37) 225-79-14; fax (37) 225-79-09; e-mail phti@tascampus.eastera.net; internet www.phti.tj; f. 1957; attached to Tajik Acad. of Sciences; theoretical and mathematical physics (classical and quantum statistics, field theory, non-linear science); materials science (crystal physics, polymer science); lasers and infrared spectroscopy; cryophysics; mathematical modelling of climate and climate change; application of nuclear physics methods; radiation safety and ecology; renewable energy sources; Dir Dr KHIKMAT KH. MUMINOV.

Libraries and Archives

Dushanbe

Central Scientific Library of the Tajik Academy of Sciences: 734025 Dushanbe, Pr. Rudaki 33; tel. (372) 22-42-24; f. 1933; 1,500,000 vols; Dir Dr A. A. ASLITDINOVA.

Firdavsi Tajik National Library: 734025 Dushanbe, Pr. Rudaki 36; tel. (372) 27-47-26; e-mail firdavsi@library.tajik.net; 3,037,310 vols; Dir S. MUKHIDDINOV.

Republican Scientific and Technical Library of Tajikistan: 734042 Dushanbe, Ul. Aini 14A; tel. (372) 27-58-77; fax (372) 21-71-54; f. 1965; 13,000,000 vols (incl. 11,000,000 patents); Dir K. I. ISMAILOV.

Tajik State University Library: 734016 Dushanbe, Pr. Rudaki 17; tel. (372) 23-39-81; f. 1948; 1,039,000 vols; Dir R. YARBABAYEV; publ. *Vestnik* (annually).

Museum

Dushanbe

Tajik State Historical Museum: 734012 Dushanbe, Ul. Aini 31; tel. (372) 23-15-44; history, culture, art; library of 14,000 vols; Dir M. MAKHMUDOV.

Universities

CENTRAL INSTITUTE OF ADVANCED QUALIFICATION OF TEACHERS

734013 Dushanbe, Chechova 13
Telephone: (372) 21-54-57
Fax: (372) 27-16-27
E-mail: ciftmail@tajnet.com
Founded 1935
State control
Rector: ABUNAZAR A. SOIROV
Vice-Rector: ABDUHALIM GAFFAROV
Number of students: 2,000
Faculties of Economics, Educational Administration, Foreign Languages Education, Pedagogy, Psychology, Science Education and Teacher Training.

HIGHER SCHOOL OF THE MINISTRY OF THE INTERIOR

734025 Dushanbe, Vose 123
Telephone: (372) 27-06-07
Fax: (372) 21-72-21
State Control
Faculties of History or Law.

KHOROG INSTITUTE OF SOCIAL SCIENCES

Khorog
Telephone: (352) 20-67-55
State Control
Rector: SH. YUSUFBEKOV
Faculties and History, Philology, Social Sciences.

KHOROG STATE UNIVERSITY

736000 Khorog
Telephone: (342) 20-22-18
Fax: (342) 20-43-99
Founded 1992
State Control
Rector: M. SHABOZOV
Faculties of Economics, History, Mathematics, Natural Sciences and Philology.

KHUJAND B. GAFUROV STATE UNIVERSITY

735700 Khujand, B. Mavlonbekova 1
Telephone: (342) 26-52-73
Fax: (342) 26-51-37
E-mail: hgu-rector@sugdien.com
Founded 1991
State control
Languages of instruction: Tajik, Russian, Uzbek, English
Rector: SALIMOV NOSIRJON
Library of 500,000 vols
Number of teachers: 754
Number of students: 10,599

DEANS

Art: G. JURAYEV
Cybernetics and World Economics: A. ABDULLOYEV
Drawing and Graphics: S. OLOV
Eastern Languages (Arabic and Persian): U. GAFFOROVA
Economics: A. ABDULLOYEV
Finance and Marketing: A. MAJIDOV
Foreign Languages: M. AZIMOVA
History: U. GAFFOROV
Law: IKROM KASIMOV
Mathematics: A. KASHIDOV
Natural Sciences: S. KARIMOV
Pedagogy: S. SHAROPOV
Physics and Technology: S. YAKUBOV
Russian and Literature: A. AZIZOV
Tajik Philology: N. F. FAIZULLAYEV
Uzbek Language: I. MAVLONBERDIYEV

KULYAB STATE UNIVERSITY

735360 Kulyab, Safarov 26
Telephone: (332) 22-35-06
State Control
Faculties of Economics, History, Mathematics, Pedagogy, Philology and Physics.

MODERN HUMANITARIAN UNIVERSITY

735700 Khujand, Microraion 17
Telephone: (342) 22-19-58
Fax: (342) 26-19-91
Founded 1998
State Control
Language of instruction: Russian
Rector: M. I. BAKIYEV
Number of teachers: 36
Number of students: 380

DEANS

Faculty of Computer Science: U. V. SIT
Faculty of Languages: SH. D. KHODJAYEV
Faculty of Law: N. T. RAKHIMOV
Faculty of Management: G. A. USUPOVA

REPUBLICAN INSTITUTE OF ADVANCED TEACHERS' STUDIES

734013 Dushanbe, Chehova 13
Telephone: (372) 21-64-67
State control.

TAJIK ABU-ALI IBN-CINA (AVICENNA) STATE MEDICAL UNIVERSITY

734003 Dushanbe, Pr. Rudaki 139
Telephone: (372) 24-12-53
Fax: (372) 24-36-87
E-mail: tgmu@tojikisyon.com
Founded 1993, fmrly Tajik Abu-Ali Ibn-Cina State Medical Institute
State control
Languages of instruction: Tajik, Russian
Number of teachers: 848

Number of students: 3,226
Rector: N. FAIZULLOYEV

DEANS

Medical Prevention: K. DABUROV
Medicine: K. KURBANOV
Pharmacology: S. KURBANOV
Stomatology: S. SUNHANOV

TAJIK INSTITUTE OF BUSINESS AND SERVICE

734025 Dushanbe, Borbad 45/5
Telephone: (372) 34-88-00
State control
Rector: H. U. UMAROV
Faculties of Business and Finance, Business and Services, Economics.

TAJIK INSTITUTE OF MANAGEMENT

Kairakkum
Telephone: (344) 32-24-85
State control
Rector: YU. MADJIDOV
Faculties of Management and Marketing.

TAJIK ISLAMIC UNIVERSITY

734001 Dushanbe, Shodmoni 58
Telephone: (372) 24-92-61
State control
Rector: ABDUJALOL ALIZODA
Faculties of General Studies, Islamic law and Religious Studies.

TAJIK OPEN UNIVERSITY

735500 Penjikent, Rudaki 108
Telephone: (347) 55-53-09
Fax: (347) 55-40-50
E-mail: tou@pnjk.tajik.net
Founded 1991
State control
Languages of instruction: Tajik, Russian
Principal: AHMADJON HOTAMOV
Number of teachers: 138 (full-time)
Number of students: 413
Divisions of Computing and Programming, Law and Management.

TAJIK–RUSSIAN SLAVONIC UNIVERSITY

734032 Dushanbe, M. Tursunzade 30
Telephone: (372) 22-35-50
Fax: (372) 21-05-79
State control
Principal: A. S. SATTAROV
Faculties of Economics, History, International Relations, Law and Philology.

TAJIK STATE INSTITUTE OF LANGUAGES

734064 Dushanbe, F. Muhammadiyeva 13
Telephone: (372) 32-95-29
Fax: (372) 32-95-15
E-mail: mabdullaeva@yandex.ru
Founded 1980
State control
Languages of instruction: Tajik, Russian
Rector: MAVLUDA ABDULLAYEVA
Vice-Rector: KHURSHED ZIYOYEV
Library of 113,000 vols
Number of teachers: 65
Number of students: 763

DEANS

Faculty of Foreign Languages: KHALIDA ASTANOVA
Faculty of Philology: KAHHOR AVAZOV

TAJIK STATE NATIONAL UNIVERSITY

734025 Dushanbe, Pr. Rudaki 17

Telephone: (372) 21-77-11
Fax: (372) 21-48-84
E-mail: tgnu@mail.ru
Internet: www.tsnu.tojikiston.com

Founded 1948 (present status 1997)
State control
Languages of instruction: Tajik, Russian
Academic year: September to July

Rector: Prof. KH. S. SAFIEV
Vice-Rector (Educational): Prof. D. KH. SAFAROV
Vice-Rector (International Relations): N. N. JUMAEV
Vice-Rector (Scientific): A. A. AMINJANOV
Librarian: R. I. YARBABAEV

Number of teachers: 1,228
Number of students: 13,060

Publications: *Guli murod* (Government and Law, 4 a year), *Science* (annually), *Vestnik* (4 a year)

DEANS

Faculty of Accounting: D. U. UROKOV
Faculty of Biology: Dr M. GIYOSOV
Faculty of Chemistry: L. KUDRATOVA
Faculty of Economics and Management: Prof. T. B. GANIEV
Faculty of Finance and Credit: SH. D. DUSTBOEV
Faculty of History: Prof. N. M. MIRZOEV
Faculty of Journalism and Translation Studies: Prof. A. SAIDULLOEV (acting)
Faculty of Law: M. A. MAKHMUDOV
Faculty of Mechanics and Mathematics: Dr R. M. MUSTAFOKULOV
Faculty of Mountain Geology: M. M. PHOZILOV
Faculty of Oriental Languages: S. SH. SHUKROEVA
Faculty of Philosophy: Prof. A. MUKHABATOV (acting)
Faculty of Physics: K. K. KOMILOV
Faculty of Tajik Philology: M. S. IMOMOV

TAJIK STATE PEDAGOGICAL UNIVERSITY

734001 Dushanbe, Rudaki 121

Telephone: (372) 24-13-83

Founded 1931
State control

Rector: KURBON RASULOV

Faculties of Economics and Management, Finance and Accountancy, History, Law, Mechanics and Mathematics, Pedagogics and Philology.

TAJIK STATE UNIVERSITY OF COMMERCE

734055 Dushanbe, Dehoti 1/2

Telephone: (372) 34-86-22
Fax: (372) 34-83-94
E-mail: kaa77@tajik.net

Founded 1991
State control
Languages of instruction: Russian, Tajik
Academic year: September to June

Rector: KHAMIDULLOKHON FAKIROV
Vice-Rector: N. SANGINOV

Number of teachers: 168
Number of students: 2,380

DEANS

Faculty of Customs: KHAMID MADJIDOV
Faculty of Distance Education: MUKHIDDIN KHOMIDOV
Faculty of Economics and Management: SAFIULLO HABIBOV
Faculty of World Economics and Financing: ZUYORATSHO AKOBIROV

TAJIK M. OSIMI TECHNICAL UNIVERSITY

734042 Dushanbe, Pr. Acad Rajabovs 10

Telephone: (372) 21-35-11
Fax: (372) 21-71-35
E-mail: techuni@tajnet.com

Founded 1956
State control
Languages of instruction: Tajik, Russian

Number of teachers: 530
Number of students: 6,000

Rector: SAIDMUHAMAD ODINAYEV

DEANS

Business Engineering: S. KAMOLIDDINOV
Chemical Technology and Metallurgy: A. SHARIFOV
Construction and Architecture: A. FAZILOV
Energy Engineering: R. JALILOV
Mechanical Technology: S. ZULFANOV
Transport and Road Engineering: A. TURSUNOV

TAJIK UNIVERSITY OF LAW, POLICY AND BUSINESS

Soghd Oblast, 735700 Khujand

Telephone: (342) 22-38-11
State control

Rector: H. R. PULATOV.

TECHNOLOGICAL UNIVERSITY OF TAJIKISTAN

734061 Dushanbe, N. Narabayev 63/3

Telephone: (372) 34-79-87
Fax: (372) 34-79-88
E-mail: rektorat@tat.tajik.net
Internet: www.tut.tajnet.com

Founded 1992
State control
Languages of instruction: Tajik, Russian, English
Academic year: September to June

Rector: AMIR H. KATAYEV
Vice-Rector: NURALI N. SHOYEV

Library of 70,000 vols
Number of teachers: 158

Number of students: 1,050

Publications: *Collection of Scientific Works* (biannually), *Herald of Ecology* (monthly)

DEANS

Faculty of Industrial Informatics: MIRZO YUSUPOV
Faculty of International Studies: NASRULLO HOJAYOROV
Faculty of Textile Technology and Mechanical Engineering: VALIJON M. MIRAKILOV

UNIVERSITY OF CENTRAL ASIA

c/o Aga Khan Development Network, POB 2049, 1211 Geneva 2, Switzerland
Internet: www.akdn.org/uca

Founded 2000; founding charter signed by the Aga Khan and the presidents of Tajikistan, Kyrgyzstan and Kazakhstan
Private control (independent Board of Trustees chaired by the Aga Khan)
Language of instruction: English

Joint Presidents: PRESIDENTS OF KYRGYZSTAN, KAZAKHSTAN AND TAJIKISTAN
Chancellor: HE The AGA KHAN
Rector: Dr S. FREDERICK STARR
Deans: Dr JOHN H. HERRING (School of Continuing Education), Dr BOHDAN KRAWCHENKO (School of Development)

Number of teachers: 153 full-time
Number of students: 2,700 resident and 3,000 non-resident

Campuses in Tekeli (Kazakhstan), Naryn (Kyrgyzstan) and Khorog (Tajikistan); Schools of Undergraduate Studies, Development, and Continuing Education.

Other Higher Educational Institutes

Tajik Agricultural University: 734017 Dushanbe, Pr. Rudaki 146; tel. (372) 24-72-07; fax (372) 24-49-43; e-mail rektorau@mail.ru; f. 1931; depts of agrochemistry and soil science, agronomy, fruit and vegetable growing, plant protection, veterinary science, animal husbandry, mechanization, electrification and automation, irrigation and land reclamation, economics and management, accounting, agrarian marketing, fruit and vegetables storage technology, cattle products processing, extra-mural and qualification improvement faculties; library: 400,000 vols; 482 teachers; 6,000 students; Rector SATTOROV IZATULLO TABAROVICH.

Tajik State Institute of Fine Arts: 734032 Dushanbe, Ul. Borbada 73A; tel. (372) 31-45-45; e-mail tgii@tajnet.com; internet www.art.tojikiston.com; f. 1967; faculties of cultural science, performing arts, library science and information, musical-pedagogical studies and theatre; 1,500 students; library: 70,000 vols; Rector Prof. TALABKHUJA SATTOROV.

TANZANIA

The Higher Education System

Higher education institutions predate the formation of the United Republic of Tanzania (by a merger of the independent states of Tanganyika and Zanzibar) in 1964, with the oldest being St Augustine University of Tanzania (formerly Nyegezi Social Training Centre), which was founded in 1961. In 2004 there were 16,347 students enrolled in 77 public and private institutions of higher education, which included universities, technical colleges, teacher training colleges and other higher education institutions. Higher education is administered by the Ministry of Science, Technology and Higher Education.

Students are required to gain three passes in the Advanced Certificate of Secondary Education and five passes at CSE level in order to gain admission to higher education. Examinations are administered by the National Examinations Council of Tanzania. Undergraduate Bachelors degrees usually last three years, although programmes of study in mainly professional fields of study last longer, such as engineering, nursing, pharmacy (four years) and medicine (five years). Following the award of the Bachelors, graduates may take the one-year Postgraduate Diploma or the Masters degree, which last one to three years. The highest university degree is the Doctor of Philosophy (PhD), a two-year period of research culminating with the submission of a thesis.

Post-secondary technical and vocational education is offered by technical colleges National Vocational Training Centres, Folk Development Colleges, Technical Secondary Schools, Private Vocational Schools and Training Schools. Qualifications include the Diploma and Advanced Diploma.

Learned Societies

GENERAL

Tanzania Society: Box 511, Dar es Salaam; f. 1936; a non-profit society catering for the geographical, ethnological, historical, and general scientific interests of Tanzania; 1,200 mems; publ. *Tanzania Notes and Records* (annually).

UNESCO Office Dar es Salaam: POB 31473, Dar es Salaam; Located at: Oyster bay, Uganda Ave, Plot No. 197A, Dar es Salaam; tel. (22) 2666623; fax (22) 2666927; e-mail dar-es-salaam@unesco.org; designated Cluster Office for Comoros, Madagascar, Mauritius, Seychelles and Tanzania; Dir CHEIKH TIDIANE SY.

AGRICULTURE, FISHERIES AND VETERINARY SCIENCE

Tanzania Veterinary Association: POB 3174, Chuo Kikuu Morogoro; tel. (23) 2604979; fax (23) 2604647; e-mail deanfvm@suanet.ac.tz; f. 1968; 350 mems; Chair. Prof. D. M. KAMBARAGE; publs *Annual Proceedings of the Tanzania Veterinary Association Scientific Conferences, Tanzania Veterinary Journal*.

BIBLIOGRAPHY, LIBRARY SCIENCE AND MUSEOLOGY

Tanzania Library Association: POB 33433, Dar es Salaam; tel. and fax (22) 2775411; e-mail tla_tanzania@yahoo.com; internet www.tlatz.org; f. 1965 as a br. of the East African Library Association, reorganized 1973 as an independent body; 200 mems; Chair. Dr ALLI MCHARAZO; Sec. P. MUNUBHI; publ. *Matukio* (Newsletter, irregular).

ECONOMICS, LAW AND POLITICS

East Africa Law Society: POB 6240, Arusha; 212 Ngorongoro Wing, AICC, Arusha; tel. and fax (27) 2508707; e-mail eals@habari.co.tz; f. 1996; 5,000 mems; CEO DONALD DEYA; publs *The East African Human Rights Report* (annually), *The East African Lawyer* (4 a year).

HISTORY, GEOGRAPHY AND ARCHAEOLOGY

Historical Association of Tanzania: c/o Department of History, University of Dar es Salaam, POB 35050, Dar es Salaam; tel. (22) 2410397; f. 1966; 2,000 mems; Chair. Prof. K. I. TAMBILA; Sec. Dr E. P. A. N. MIHANJO; publ. *Tanzania Zamani*.

LANGUAGE AND LITERATURE

Alliance Française: Ali Hassan Mwinyi Rd (behind Las Vegas Casino), Upanga, POB 2566, Dar es Salaam; tel. (22) 2111331; fax (22) 2666576; e-mail afdar@africaonline.co.tz; offers courses and exams in French language and culture and promotes cultural exchange with France; attached teaching centre in Arusha.

British Council: Samora Ave/Ohio St, POB 9100, Dar es Salaam; tel. (22) 2116574; fax (22) 2112699; e-mail info@britishcouncil.or.tz; internet www.britishcouncil.org/tanzania; teaching centre; offers courses and exams in English language and British culture and promotes cultural exchange with the UK; Dir TOM COWIN.

Research Institutes

GENERAL

Tanzania Commission for Science and Technology: POB 4302, Dar es Salaam; tel. (22) 2775313; fax (22) 2700745; e-mail costech@costech.or.tz; internet www.costech.or.tz; f. 1968; advises the government on science and technology policy and on all matters pertaining to the development of science and technology and their application to socio-economic development in the country; executive functions: co-ordinates all research in the country, promotes documentation and dissemination of information on science and technology and scientific research, collaborates with other research organizations; 60 mems; library of 8,000 vols; Dir.-Gen. Prof. Brig.-Gen. YADON M. KOHI; publ. *Tanzania Science and Technology Newsletter* (quarterly).

AGRICULTURE, FISHERIES AND VETERINARY SCIENCE

Agricultural Research Institute (Mlingano): Ministry of Agriculture, Livestock Development and Co-operatives, Private Bag, Ngomeni, Tanga; tel. (27) 42577; fax (27) 47647; e-mail mlingano@kaributanga.com; f. 1934; research on cultivation of sisal and other crops, soils, resourcing of efficient farming methods, horticulture; germplasm collection of tropical and subtropical fruits, spices and essential oils; Dir Dr A. NYAKI.

Forestry and Beekeeping Division: c/o Ministry of Natural Resources and Tourism, POB 426, Dar es Salaam; tel. (22) 2111062; e-mail fordev@africaonline.co.tz; forest surveying, mapping, industrial development, economics, management and education as part of the National Forest Policy and National Beekeeping Policy (both adopted 1998); library of 2,500 vols; Dir E. M. MNZAVA.

Livestock Production Research Institute: POB 202, Mpwapwa, Dodoma; tel. and fax (26) 2320853; f. 1905; research in dairy science, breeding and nutrition of livestock, Mpwapwa cattle and Malya goats, pastural agronomy and multidisciplinary research; National Livestock research Institute; research information documentation and dissemination; library of 4,000 vols, 40 periodicals; Dir Dr JULIUS BWIRE; publs *Annual Research Report, Progressive Stockman* (quarterly).

Mikocheni Agricultural Research Institute: POB 6226, Kinondoni District, Dar es Salaam; tel. (22) 2700552; fax (22) 2775549; e-mail mari@mari.or.tz; integrated pest management, with emphasis on biological control of coconut pests; Dir Dr ALOIS KULLAYA.

Tanzania Forestry Research Institute: Silviculture Research Centre, POB 95, Lushoto; f. 1951; library of 3,000 vols; Officer-in-Charge T. H. MSANGI; publs *TAFORI Newsletter, Tanzania Silviculture Research Notes* (4 a year), *Technical Notes*.

Tanzania Wildlife Research Institute: POB 661, Arusha; tel. (27) 2509871; fax (27) 2548240; e-mail info@tawiri.org; internet www.tawiri.org; research into wildlife, with the objective of providing scientific information and advice to the Govt of Tanzania and local wildlife management authorities on the sustainable conservation of wildlife; Chair Prof. PETER MSOLLA.

Tropical Pesticides Research Institute: POB 3024, Arusha; tel. (27) 2548813; fax (27) 2548217; e-mail tpri@habari.co.tz; internet www.habari.co.tz/tpri; f. 1962; research into all aspects of pesticide application and behaviour; library of 5,000 vols; Dir Dr GRATIAN BAMWENDA; publ. *Annual Report.*

HISTORY, GEOGRAPHY AND ARCHAEOLOGY

Tanzania Geological Survey: c/o Ministry of Energy and Minerals, POB 903, Dodoma; tel. (26) 2324943; e-mail mrd@twiga.com; internet tanzania.sgu.se; f. 1925; attached to Ministry of Energy and Minerals; regional mapping, mineral exploration and assessment; supporting laboratory facilities; reprints and maps; library of 4,000 books; Asst Commissioner for Mines S. J. MOHAMED; Chief Executive, Geological Survey of Tanzania B. A. MCHARO (acting); publs *Annual Reports, Bulletins, Records of the Geological Survey of Tanzania.*

LANGUAGE AND LITERATURE

Eastern African Centre for Research on Oral Traditions and African National Languages (EACROTANAL): POB 600, Zanzibar; f. 1979 as a regional and intergovernmental organization to encourage research and develop means of collection, analysis, conservation and diffusion of oral traditions and promotion of national languages; provides short-term training courses on these subjects; library of 3,000 vols (incl. 148 old Arabic MSS from Zanzibar); one of 3 African regional centres, set up by Burundi, Comoros, Ethiopia, Madagascar, Mauritius, Mozambique, Somalia, Sudan, Tanzania; Exec. Dir KHATIB MAKAME OMAR (acting); publs annotated bibliography of the Arabic MSS (every 2 years), *Paukwa Pakawa* (traditional tales, annually).

Institute of Kiswahili Research: POB 35110, Dar es Salaam; tel. (22) 2410757; e-mail tuki@ikr.udsm.ac.tz; internet www.udsm.ac.tz/ikr/; f. 1970; initiates and conducts fundamental research in all aspects of Kiswahili language; co-operates with local public authorities and int. organizations; promotes the standardization of orthography and the development of language generally; preparing new standard dictionary, technical dictionaries, grammars, monographs on oral literature; library of 3,000 vols; Dir Prof. M. M. MULOKOZI; publs *Kiswahili* (annually), *Mulika* (annually).

MEDICINE

National Institute for Medical Research (NIMR): Headquarters, Ocean Rd, POB 9653, Dar es Salaam; tel. (22) 2121400; fax (22) 2121360; e-mail headquarters@nimr.or .tz; internet www.nimr.or.tz; f. 1949 at Muheza as the Malaria Unit; investigation into human vector-borne diseases, especially malaria, bancroftian filariasis, and onchocerciasis; Dir Dr ANDREW KITUA; publ. *Annual Report.*

National Institute for Medical Research, Mwanza Centre: POB 1462, Mwanza; tel. (28) 250189; f. 1949; investigations into various tropical diseases with emphasis on bilharziasis, and other soil-transmitted helminths, bacterial diseases, sanitation and water, diarrhoeal diseases, sexually transmitted diseases, HIV/AIDS; library of 2,300 vols; Dir Dr R. M. GABONE; publs *Annual Report, NIMR Bulletin, Proceedings of the Annual NIMR Joint Scientific Conference.*

Libraries and Archives

Dar es Salaam

Tanzania National Archives: Vijibweni St, POB 2006, Dar es Salaam; tel. (22) 2151279; fax (22) 2150634; e-mail dram@intafrica.com; internet www.tanzania.go.tz/psrp/record1.html; f. 1963; German and British colonial archives, post-independence archives; Dir J. M. KARUGILA; publs *Annual Report, Guide to Archives.*

Tanzania Information Services Department: POB 9142, Dar es Salaam; tel. (22) 2122771; fax (22) 2113814; e-mail maelezo@pmo.go.tz; reference books on Tanzania, journalism, photography, social sciences, geography and history; newspapers and periodicals.

Tanzania Library Services Board: Bibi Titi Mohamed Rd, POB 9283, Dar es Salaam; tel. (22) 2150048; fax (22) 2151100; e-mail tlsb@africaonline.co.tz; f. 1964; 16 brs; Dir-Gen. ELIEZER A. MWINYIMVUA.

University of Dar es Salaam Library: POB 35092, Dar es Salaam; tel. and fax (22) 2410241; e-mail director@libis.udsm.ac.tz; internet www.udsm.ac.tz/library; f. 1961; legal deposit library; 600,000 vols; special collns: East Africana Colln, UN Colln, Law Colln; 8,000 periodicals; Dir Dr E. KIONDO.

Morogoro

Sokoine National Agricultural Library: POB 3022, Morogoro; tel. (23) 2604639; fax (23) 2604388; e-mail library@suanet.ac.tz; internet snalwww.suanet.ac.tz/index.html; 70,000 vols, 100 periodicals; Librarian F. W. DULLE.

Mwanza

Ladha Meghji Indian Public Library: POB 70, Mwanza; tel. (28) 2500482; fax (28) 2500222; e-mail desaitz@yahoo.com; f. 1935; 7,675 vols; runs English, French, oriental language and computer classes; Librarian RAMAN DESAI.

Zanzibar

Agricultural Department Library: POB 159, Zanzibar; 1,100 vols, 50 periodicals..

Museum Research Library: c/o Dept of Antiquities, Archives and Museum, Zanzibar National Archives, POB 116, Zanzibar; tel. (22) 30342; e-mail dama@zitec.org; f. 1930; reference library; 15,000 vols and 1,000 periodicals; Head of the Library SULEIMAN SEIF.

Zanzibar National Archives: POB 116, Zanzibar; tel. and fax (22) 35241; f. 1956; history and administration; 3,500 vols; Archivist HAMAD OMAR.

Museums and Art Galleries

Dar es Salaam

National Museums of Tanzania: POB 511, Dar es Salaam; tel. (22) 2122030; e-mail museumhq@omnisys.co.tz; internet www.museum.or.tz; f. 1937 as King George V Memorial Museum, name changed 1963; ethnography, palaeoanthropology, history and marine biology; houses the *Zinjanthropus* skull and other material from Olduvai Gorge and other Palaeolithic sites; also houses reference library; Dir-Gen. Dr N. A. KAYOMBO.

Branch museums:

Arusha Declaration Museum: POB 7423, Arusha; tel. (27) 2507800; e-mail adm-arusha@habari.co.tz; internet www

.arushamuseum.ac.tz; f. 1977; preservation and exhibition of political, social and economic history; Curators C. M. NYAMABONDO, JACKSON N.L. WASHA.

Arusha Natural History Museum: POB 2160, Arusha; tel. (27) 2507540; e-mail nnhm@habari.co.tz; internet www .museum.or.tz; Curator FELISTA MANGALU.

Village Museum: POB 511, Dar es Salaam; tel. (22) 2700437; e-mail villagemuseum@raha.com; f. 1967; traditional house styles and crafts; Curator JACKSON M. KIHIYO.

Zanzibar

Zanzibar Government Museum: POB 116, Zanzibar; tel. (24) 2230342; fax (24) 2235241; e-mail dama@zitec.org; internet www.museum.com/jb/museum?id=24191; f. 1925; operates Peace Memorial Museum at Mnazi Minoja (history, ethnography, natural history and archaeology of Zanzibar, f. 1925), Palace Museum at Mizingani (history of the Zanzibar sultans, f. 1994), Pemba Museum at Chake (history of Pemba Island, f. 2000), House of Wonders Museum at Forodhani (history and culture of Zanzibar and Swahili Coast civilization, f. 2001); Dir H. H. OMAR.

Universities

UNIVERSITY OF BUKOBA

POB 1725, Bukoba

Telephone: (28) 2220691
Fax: (28) 2222341
E-mail: uobtz@yahoo.comm
Internet: uobtz.tripod.com

Founded 1999
State Control
Language of instruction: English
Academic year: October to June

Chancellor: C. G. KAHAMA
Vice-Chancellor: Prof. M. HODD
Deputy Vice-Chancellor: Prof. ISRAEL KATOKE
Registrar: SAMUEL MUTASA

Library of 1,000 vols
Number of teachers: 20
Number of students: 50

DEANS

Faculty of Commerce and Management: JOSEPH MWABUKI
Faculty of Social and Natural Science: CHRISTOPHER RWIZA (acting)

UNIVERSITY OF DAR ES SALAAM

POB 35091, Dar es Salaam

Telephone: (22) 2410500
Fax: (22) 2410078
E-mail: vc@admin.udsm.ac.tz
Internet: www.udsm.ac.tz

Founded 1961; univ. status 1970
Language of instruction: English
Academic year: October to June (two semesters)

Chancellor: Ambassador P. BOMANI
Vice-Chancellor: Prof. M. L. LUHANGA
Chief Academic Officer: Prof. M. H. H. NKUNYA
Chief Administrative Officer: Prof. J. S. MSHANA
Director, Postgraduate Studies: Prof. P. A. K. MUSHI
Director, Research and Publications: Prof. M. C. Y. MBAGO

Library: see Libraries and Archives
Number of teachers: 540 full-time
Number of students: 10,850

Publications: *Annual Report, Research Bulletin* (2 a year)

DEANS

Faculty of Aquatic Sciences and Technology: Y. MGAYA
Faculty of Arts and Social Sciences: A. LIHAMBA
Faculty of Commerce and Management: Dr E. S. KAIJAGE
Faculty of Education: W. G. LUGOE
Faculty of Law: I. H. JUMA
Faculty of Mechanical and Chemical Engineering: (vacant)
Faculty of Science: Prof. R. T. KIVAISI
College of Engineering Technology: J. H. Y. KATIMA

DIRECTORS

Institute of Development Studies: H. M. MLAWA
Institute of Kiswahili Research: M. M. MULOKOZI
Institute of Marine Science: A. M. DUBI
Institute of Resource Assessment: R. B. B. MWALYOSI

PROFESSORS

CHACHAGI, C. S. L., Sociology and Anthropology
CHAMI, F. L., History
GALABAWA, J. C. J., Educational Planning and Administration
GONDWE, Z. S., Economic Law
HOWELL, K. M., Zoology and Marine Biology
KAMUZORA, C. L. A., Statistics
KIKULA, I. S., Resource Assessment
KIMAMBO, I. N., History
KIVAISI, R. T., Physics
LUGOE, W. L., Educational Psychology
MABOKO, M. A. II., Geology
MALEKELA, G. A., Educational Foundations
MASSAMBA, D. P. B., Kiswahili
MASUHA, J. R., Engineering, Design and Production
MATERU, P. N., Electrical Power Engineering
MBUNDA, F. L., Curriculum and Teaching
MBWETTE, T. S. A., Water Resource Engineering
MKILAHA, I. S. N., Energy Engineering
MKUDE, D. J., History
MLAMA, P. O. P., Fine and Performing Arts
MLAWA, H. M., Development Studies
MOSHA, H. J., Educational Planning and Administration
MPANGLA, G., Development Studies
MSAKI, P. K., Physics
MSAMBICHAKA, L. A., Economic Development
MSHANA, J. S., Materials Engineering
MSHIMBA, A. S. A., Mathematics
MUHONGO, S., Geology
MUKANDALA, R. S., Political Science and Public Administratiojn
MUNISHI, G. K. K., Political Science and Public Administratiojn
MUSHI, P. A. K., Adult Education and Extension
MUSHI, S. S., Political Science and Public Administratiojn
MWALYOSI, R. B. B., Resource Assessment
MWAMILA, B. L. M., Structural Engineering
MWANDOSYA, M. J., Computer and Systems Engineering
MWINYIWIWA, B. M. M., Electrical Power Engineering
NGWARE, S. S., Development Studies
NJAU, E. C., Physics
NKUNYA, M. H. H., Chemistry
OTHMAN, H. M., Development Studies
PETER, C. M., International Law
RUGUMAMU, S. M., Development Studies
RUGUMAMU, W., Geography
RUTASHOBYA, L. H. K., Marketing
SHIVJI, I. G., Constitutional and Administrative Law
TIBAIJUKA, A. K., Economic Development

ATTACHED INSTITUTES

College of Engineering and Technology: POB 35131, Dar es Salaam; Dir Prof. B. L. M. MWAMILA.
Institute of Development Studies: POB 35169, Dar es Salaam; Dir Prof. H. M. MLAWA.
Institute of Kiswahili Research: POB 35110, Dar es Salaam; Dir Prof. M. M. MULOKOZI.
Institute of Marine Sciences: POB 668, Zanzibar; f. 1950 as East African Marine Fisheries Research Organization; postgraduate studies and research; Dir Dr A. M. DUBI.
Institute of Resource Assessment: POB 35097, Dar es Salaam; Dir Dr R. B. B. MWALYOSI.
Muhimbili University College of Health Sciences: POB 65001, Dar es Salaam; tel. (22) 2151596; fax (22) 2150465; e-mail principal@muchs.ac.tz; f. 1991; Dir Prof. K. J. PALLANGYO

PROFESSORS

KILONZO, G. P., Psychiatry
LEMA, L. E. K., Surgery
MASELLE, A. Y., Clinical Pharmacology
MASELLE, S. Y., Microbiology and Immunology
MGAYA, H. N., Obstetrics and Gynaecology
MHALU, F. S., Microbiology and Immunology
MINJA, B. M., Otorhinolaryngology
MKONY, C. A., Surgery
MTABAJI, J. P., Physiology
PALLANGYO, K. J., Internal Medicine
SANGAWE, J. L., Ophthalmology
SWAI, A. B., Internal Medicine
University College of Lands and Architectural Studies: POB 35176, Dar es Salaam; e-mail uclas@uclas.ac.tz; f. 1996; Dir Prof. IDRIS S. KIKULA.

HUBERT KARIUKI MEMORIAL UNIVERSITY

POB 65300, 322 Regent Estate, Dar es Salaam
Telephone: (22) 2700021
Fax: (22) 2700024
E-mail: info@hkmu.ac.tz
Internet: www.hkmu.ac.tz

Founded 1997; university status 2000
Language of instruction: English
Academic year: September to August

Vice-Chancellor: Prof. ESTHER MWAIKAMBO
Deputy Vice-Chancellor for Finance, Planning and Administration: Dr PASCHALIS RUGARABAMU
Director of Postgraduate Studies and Research Institute: Dr SYLVESTER L. B. KAJUNA
Dean of Students: Prof. S. E. K. LUTAHOIRE
Senior Librarian: STANSLAUS NGADAYA

DEANS

Faculty of Medicine: Prof. FELICIAN RUTACHUNZIBWA
Faculty of Nursing: Prof. PAULINE P. MELLA

CHAIRS OF DEPARTMENTS

Department of Anatomy: (vacant)
Department of Behavioural Sciences and Ethics: (vacant)
Department of Biochemistry and Molecular Biology: Dr SYLVESTER L. B. KAJUNA
Department of Community Health Nursing: AMIRI MMAKA
Department of Community Medicine: Prof. JOAS LUGEMALILA
Department of Development Studies: (vacant)
Department of Fundamentals of Nursing and Basic Sciences: ELIZABETH MIKA

Department of Internal Medicine: Dr JULIUS KIBBASSA
Department of Maternal and Child Health Nursing: ELIZABETH KIJUGU
Department of Microbiology amd Parasitology: (vacant)
Department of Obstetrics and Gynaecology: Prof. MONICA CHIDUO
Department of Paediatrics and Child Health: Prof. FELICIAN RUTACHUNZIBWA
Department of Pathology: (vacant)
Department of Pharmacology and Therapeutics: (vacant)
Department of Physiology: IVAN ROLAND KARKADA
Department of Psychiatry: Dr ALPHAGE J. LIWA
Department of Surgery: Dr A. SHABHAY
Information Resource Unit: AMOS N. MADALA

PROFESSORS

KAAYA, E., Pathology
KILAMA, W. L., Medicine
LUTAHOIRE, S., Medicine
MELLA, P., Nursing
MWAIKAMBO, E., Medicine

INTERNATIONAL MEDICAL AND TECHNOLOGICAL UNIVERSITY

Mbeze Beach area, New Bagamoyo Rd, POB 77594, Dar es Salaam
Telephone: (22) 2647036
Fax: (22) 2647038
E-mail: iimtu@costech.or.tz
Internet: www.imtu.edu

Founded 1995 by Vignan Educational Foundation (India) and Tanzanian govt
Number of teachers: 23
Vice-Chancellor: Dr V. P. KIMATI
Deputy Vice-Chancellor for Academic Affairs: V. S. RAKESH
Director of Finance: P. B. KUMAR
Dean of Students: Dr RENJU THOMAS

HEADS OF DEPARTMENTS

Dermatology: MURALI MOHAN PASUMARTHY
General Surgery: H. D. BALLAL
Gynaecology: RICHARD SETH MASSANA LEMA
Medicine: S. H. VERMA
Ophthalmology: SOUMENDRA SAHOO
Otorhinolaryngology: (vacant)

MZUMBE UNIVERSITY

POB 1, Mzumbe
Telephone: (23) 2604381
Fax: (23) 2604382
E-mail: idm@raha.com
Internet: mzumbe.ac.tz/index.htm

Founded 1972 as Institute of Development Management; present name and status 2001
State control
Language of instruction: English
Academic year: October to June

Chancellor: IBRAHIM M. KADUMA
Vice-Chancellor: Prof. MOSES M. D. WARIOBA
Deputy Vice-Chancellor: Prof. JOSEPH A. KUZILWA
Registrar: Prof. HAMISI I. MAHIGI
Library of 40,000 books, 757 current periodicals
Number of teachers: 132
Number of students: 2,211
Publication: *Uongozi Journal* (quarterly)

DEANS

Faculty of Commerce: Dr DOMINICUS M. L. KASILO
Faculty of Law: ELEUTER G. MUSHI
Faculty of Public Administration and Management: ELEUTER G. MUSHI

Faculty of Science and Technology: Prof. DAMAS S. R. M. MUNA
Faculty of Social Science: Prof. JOSEPH T. NAGU

PROFESSOR

KUZILWA, J. A., Economics

ATTACHED INSTITUTES

Institute of Continuing Education: Dir ALTO A. D. SIMIME.

Institute of Development Studies: Dir Dr LEONARD J. SHIO.

Institute of Public Administration: Dir Dr MUJWAHUZI NJUNWA.

OPEN UNIVERSITY OF TANZANIA

Kawawa Rd, Kinondoni Municipality, POB 23409, Dar es Salaam
Telephone: (22) 2668992
Fax: (22) 2668759
E-mail: vc@out.ac.tz
Internet: www.openuniversity.ac.tz
Founded 1992
State control
Languages of instruction: English, Kiswahili
Academic year: January to December
Chancellor: Dr JOHN SAMWEL MALECELA
Vice-Chancellor: Prof. G. R. V. MMARI
Deputy Vice-Chancellor (Academic): Prof. DONATUS A. KOMBA
Registrar: Prof. USWEGE M. MINGA
Librarian: A. S. SAMZUGI
Library of 5,000 vols
Number of teachers: 33 full-time
Number of teachers: 80 part-time
Number of students: 3,811
Publication: *HURIA Journal*

HEADS OF UNIT

Faculty of Arts and Social Sciences: Prof. A. J. TEMU (Dean)
Faculty of Business Management: Prof. KWEKU O. AMAA (Dean)
Institute of Continuing Education: Dr C. K. MUGANDA (Dir)
Faculty of Education: Dr E. B. N. K. BABYEGEYA (Dean)
Institute of Educational Technology: Prof. SATOKE T. MAHENGE (Dir)
Faculty of Law: Dr M. C. MUKOYOGO (Dean)
Faculty of Science, Technology and Environmental Studies: Prof. C. A. KWANGA (Dean)

PROFESSORS

AMAA, K. O., Business Management
KIWANGA, C. A., Science, Technology and Environmental Studies
KOMBA, D. A., Education
MASENGE, R. W. P., Science, Technology and Environmental Studies
MUKOYOGO, M. C., Law
TEMU, A. J., Arts and Social Sciences

23 regional centres and 69 study centres.

ST AUGUSTINE UNIVERSITY OF TANZANIA

POB 307, Mwanza
Telephone: (28) 2552727
Fax: (28) 2550167
E-mail: saut@africaonline.co.tz
Founded 1960 as Nyegezi Social Training Centre; present status and name 1998
Private Control (Catholic Church)
Language of instruction: English
Academic year: October to June
Vice-Chancellor: Prof. CHARLES KITIMA
Library of 15,000 vols, 30 periodicals
Number of teachers: 44
Number of students: 404

DEANS

Faculty of Business Administration: ILDEFONS CHONYA (acting)
Faculty of Humanities and Mass Communication: JOSEPH MLACHA (acting)

SOKOINE UNIVERSITY OF AGRICULTURE

POB 3000, Chuo Kikuu, Morogoro
Telephone: (23) 2603511
Fax: (23) 2604651
E-mail: sua@suanet.ac.tz
Internet: www.suanet.ac.tz
Founded 1984, previously a faculty of University of Dar es Salaam
State control
Language of instruction: English
Academic year: August to June
Chancellor: AL NOOR KASSUM
Vice-Chancellor: Prof. A. B. LWOGA
Deputy Vice-Chancellor: Prof. P. M. MSOLLA
Director, Solomon Mahlangu Campus: Prof. R. D. MOSHA
Registrar: Assoc. Prof. H. O. DIHENGA
Librarian: F. W. DULLE
Library: see Libraries and Archives
Number of teachers: 244
Number of students: 2,399 (2,130 undergraduate, 269 postgraduate)
Publications: *Annual Report*, *Research Newsletter* (2 a year), *SUA Newsletter* (annually), *SUASA Newsletter* (annually)

DEANS

Faculty of Agriculture: Prof. N. S. Y. MDOE
Faculty of Forestry and Nature Conservation: Prof. G. C. MONELA
Faculty of Science: Dr Y. C. MUZANILA
Faculty of Veterinary Medicine: Prof. M. N. MGASA

HEADS OF DEPARTMENTS

Faculty of Agriculture (POB 3001, Chuo Kikuu, Morogoro; tel. and fax (23) 2604649; e-mail foa@suanet.ac.tz):

Agricultural Economics and Agribusiness: Assoc. Prof. E. M. SENKONDO
Agricultural Education and Extension: Assoc. Prof. Z. S. K. MVENA
Agricultural Engineering and Land Planning: Assoc. Prof. N. I. KIHUPI
Animal Science and Production: Prof. F. P. M. LEKULE
Crop Science and Production: Dr A. P. MAERERE
Food Science and Technology: Assoc. Prof. B. P. TIISEKWA
Soil Science: Dr J. J. T MSAKY

Faculty of Forestry and Nature Conservation (POB 3009, Chuo Kikuu, Morogoro; tel. and fax (23) 2604648; e-mail forestry@suanet.ac.tz):

Forest Biology: Assoc. Prof. P. K. T. MUNISHI
Forest Economics: Dr Y. M. NGAGA
Forest Engineering: Assoc. Prof. G. A. MIGUNGA
Forest Mensuration and Management: Prof. G. C. KAJEMBE
Wildlife Management: Assoc. Prof. S. L. S. MAGANGA
Wood Utilization: Dr P. R. GILLAH

Faculty of Science (POB 3038, Chuo Kikuu, Morogoro; tel. (23) 2601363; fax (23) 2603404; e-mail fos@suanet.ac.tz):

Biological Sciences: Dr P. L. MWANG'INGO
Biometry and Mathematics: G. K. KARUGILA
Physical Sciences: Dr J. K. MWALILINO
Social Sciences: Dr S. T. A. MAFU

Faculty of Veterinary Medicine (POB 3015, Chuo Kikuu, Morogoro; tel. and fax (23) 2604647; e-mail deanfvm@suanet.ac.tz):

Veterinary Anatomy: Prof. G. K. MBASSA
Veterinary Medicine and Public Health: Assoc. Prof. L. J. M. KUSILUKA
Veterinary Microbiology and Parasitology: Dr P. N. WAMBURA
Veterinary Pathology: Prof. G. L. MWAMENGELE
Veterinary Surgery and Theriogenology: Prof. E. K. BATAMUZI

PROFESSORS

ABELI, W. S., Forest Engineering
BITTEGEKO, S. B. P., Veterinary Surgery and Theriogenology
CHAMSHAMA, S. A. O., Forest Biology
GWAKISA, P. S., Veterinary Microbiology and Parasitology
KAMBARAGE, D. M., Veterinary Medicine and Public Health
KASSUKU, A. A., Veterinary Microbiology and Parasitology
KAZWALA, R. R., Veterinary Medicine and Public Health
KESSY, B. M., Veterinary Surgery and Theriogenology
KILONZO, B. S., Veterinary Microbiology and Parasitology
KIMAMBO, A. E., Animal Science and Production
KINABO, L. D. B., Veterinary Science
MALIMBWI, R. E., Forest Mensuration and Management
MASELLE, R. M., Veterinary Pathology
MATOVELO, J. A., Veterinary Pathology
MBASSA, G. K., Veterinary Anatomy
MGASA, M. N., Veterinary Surgery and Theriogenology
MGONGO, F. O. K., Veterinary Surgery and Theriogenology
MOSHA, R. D., Veterinary Science
MSOLLA, P. M., Veterinary Medicine and Public Health
MTAMBO, M. M. A., Veterinary Medicine and Public Health
MTENGA, L. A., Animal Science and Production
NGOMUO, A. J., Veterinary Science
O'KTING'ATI, A. E., Forest Economics
PEREKA, A. E., Veterinary Science
RUTATORA, D. F., Agricultural Education and Extension
SEMUGURUKA, W. D., Veterinary Pathology
SILAYO, R. S., Veterinary Microbiology and Parasitology

ATTACHED INSTITUTES

Computer Centre: POB 3218, Chuo Kikuu, Morogoro; e-mail ccentre@suanet.ac.tz; Dir Dr R. R. KAZWALA.

Development Studies Institute: POB 3024, Chuo Kikuu, Morogoro; e-mail dsi@suanet.ac.tz; Dir Dr E. A. MWAGENI.

Institute of Continuing Education: POB 3044, Morogoro; tel. (23) 2604549; fax (23) 2603718; e-mail ice@suanet.ac.tz; Dir Dr G. G. KIMBI.

Directorate of Research and Postgraduate Studies: POB 3151, Morogoro; tel. and fax (23) 2604388; e-mail drpgs@suanet.ac.tz; Dir Prof. J. A. MATOVELO.

SUA Centre for Sustainable Rural Development: POB 3035, Morogoro; tel. (23) 2604360; fax (23) 2604758; e-mail suajica@suanet.ac.tz; Dir Prof. D. F. RUTATORA.

SUA Pest Management Centre: POB 3110, Morogoro; tel. (23) 2604621; e-mail pestman@suanet.ac.tz; Dir Prof. R. S. MACHANG'U.

TUMAINI UNIVERSITY

POB 2200, Moshi
Telephone: (27) 2752291
Fax: (27) 2753612
Internet: www.elct.org/tumaini.html
Founded 1996; present status 2001
Private Control (Evangelical Lutheran Church in Tanzania)
Language of instruction: English
Vice-Chancellor: Prof. JOHN F. SHAO
Number of teachers: 145
Number of students: 789
Publication: *Tumaini Hill* (Newsletter, quarterly).

CONSTITUENT COLLEGES

IRINGA UNIVERSITY COLLEGE

POB 200, Iringa
Telephone: (26) 2720900
Fax: (26) 2720904
Founded 1993
Provost: NICOLAS BANGU

DEANS

Faculty of Arts and Social Sciences: SAMUEL MSHANA
Faculty of Business and Economics: GEORGE MPELUMBE
Faculty of Law: ANDREW MOLLEL
Faculty of Theology: FESTO BAHENDWA

KILAMANJARO CHRISTIAN MEDICAL COLLEGE

POB 2240, Moshi
Telephone: (27) 2754377
Fax: (27) 2754381
E-mail: kcmcadmin@kcmc.ac.tz
Internet: www.kcmc.ac.tz
Founded 1997
Provost: EGBERT M. KESSI

DEANS

Faculty of Medicine: AUGUSTINE L. MALLYA
Faculty of Nursing: MARCELINA H. MSUYA
Faculty of Rehabilitative Science: HAROLD G. SHANGALI

ATTACHED RESEARCH INSTITUTES

Institute of Allied Health Sciences: Dir HENNING GROSSMAN.

Institute of Postgraduate Medicine and Research: Dir WILHELMUS DOLMANS.

MAKUMIRA UNIVERSITY COLLEGE

POB 55, Usa River, Arusha
Telephone: (27) 2553634
Fax: (27) 2553493
E-mail: college@makumira.ac.tz
Internet: www.makumira.ac.tz
Founded 1954
Provost: Rev. Dr GWAKISA MWAKAGALI

DEANS

Faculty of Theology: Rev. ZAKAYO KIMARO

ZANZIBAR UNIVERSITY

POB 2440, Zanzibar
Telephone: (24) 2232242
Fax: (24) 2236388
E-mail: info@zanvarsity.ac.tz
Internet: www.zanvarsity.ac.tz
Founded 1998
State Control
Language of instruction: English
Vice-Chancellor: MUSTAFA A. A. ROSHASH (acting)
Library of 3,000 vols
Number of teachers: 24
Number of students: 393
Faculties of Arts and Social Science, Business Administration and Law and Shariah.

Colleges

College of African Wildlife Management, Mweka: POB 3031, Moshi; tel. (27) 2756451; fax (27) 2756414; e-mail mweka@mwekawildlife.org; internet www.mwekawildlife.org; f. 1963; professional and technical training, research and consultancy services in African wildlife management; qualifications awarded include certificate, diploma, advanced diploma and postgraduate diploma in wildlife management; library: 10,000 vols; 16 teachers; 150 students; Principal DEO-GRATIAS M. GAMASSA; publ. *Newsletter* (2 a year).

College of Business Education: POB 1968, Dar es Salaam; tel. (22) 2150177; e-mail principalcbe@yahoo.com; f. 1965; 55 teachers; 1,300 students; two- and three-year diploma courses in business administration and metrology; certificate course in business administration; postgraduate course in business administration; Principal S. M. HYERA.

Dar es Salaam Institute of Technology: Private Bag 2958, Dar es Salaam; tel. (22) 2150174; fax (22) 2152504; e-mail principaldit@intafrica.com; internet www.dit.ac.tz; f. 1957; civil, mechanical, electrical, electronics and telecommunications engineering courses; science and laboratory technology and computing studies courses; library: 27,000 vols; 180 teachers; 3,600 students (1,200 full-time, 2,400 part time); Principal Prof. J. W. A. KONDORO.

Eastern and Southern African Management Institute: POB 3030, Arusha; tel. (27) 2508384; fax (27) 2508285; e-mail esamihq@esamihq.ac.tz; internet www.esami-africa.org; f. 1974, reconstituted 1980; country offices in Kenya, Malawi, Mozambique, Namibia, Swaziland, Tanzania, Uganda, Zambia, Zimbabwe; conducts management development programmes; programmes in corporate entrepreneurship, energy and environment management, finance and banking, gender development and management, governance and public sector management, human resource management, information technology, transport and infrastructure development, health services management and administration; also Executive MBA and MBA in Transport Economics and Logistics Management; 44 teachers (24 full-time, 20 associate); library: 12,000 vols, 15,000 pamphlets; Dir-Gen. Dr BONARD MWAPE; publs *African Management Development Forum* (every 6 months), *ESAMI Newsletter* (quarterly).

Institute of Finance Management: Shaaban Robert St, POB 3918, Dar es Salaam; tel. (22) 2112931; fax (22) 2112935; e-mail principal@africaonline.co.tz; internet www.ifm.ac.tz; f. 1972; courses include certificates in insurance, social security administration, information technology and computer science; library: 32,000 vols, 100 periodicals; 80 teachers; 1,710 students; Chief Exec. Prof. JOSHUA DORIYE (acting); Dir of Studies Dr ISAYA JAIRO (acting); publ. *African Journal of Finance and Management* (2 a year).

Moshi University College of Co-operative and Business Studies: POB 474, Sokoine Rd, Moshi; tel. (27) 2751183; fax (27) 2750806; e-mail moshiuniversity@yahoo.com; internet www.muccobs.ac.tz; f. 1963; library: 37,000 vols; Gender Documentation Centre on co-operatives and development; Health Information Centre; 90 teachers; 900 students; Principal Prof. S. A. CHAMBO; publs *Journal of Co-operative and Business Studies* (2 a year), *Research Abstracts* (every 3 years), *Research Report Series*.

Kivukoni Academy of Social Sciences: POB 9193, Dar es Salaam; tel. (22) 2820041; fax (22) 2820816; e-mail kass@kasstz.org; internet www.kasstz.org; f. 1961; two-year diploma courses in social sciences, economic development and gender issues in development; one-year certificate in youth work; library: 27,000 vols; 30 teachers; 250 students; Principal Dr JOHN M. J. MAGOTTI.

National Social Welfare Training Institute: POB 3375, Dar es Salaam; tel. (22) 2700918; f. 1974; 20 teachers; 180 students; library: 7,172 vols; Principal T. F. NGALULA; publ. *Jamii Journal*.

University College of Lands and Architectural Studies: POB 35176, Dar es Salaam; tel. (22) 2775004; fax (22) 27755391; e-mail uclas@uclas.ac.tz; internet www.uclas.ac.tz; f. 1996; architecture, building economics, land management and valuation, land surveying, geomatics, environmental engineering, urban and rural planning; Institute of Human Settlements Studies (applied research and documentation services in housing, building, planning and environmental management), Centre for Information Communication Technology (geographic information systems, remote sensing and ICT Studies); library: 20,000 vols; special collections of UN publications, theses and masterplans; 111 teachers; 1,060 students; Principal Prof. IDRIS KIKULA; publ. *Journal of Building and Land Development* (3 a year).

The Higher Education System

The oldest institution of higher education is Chulalongkorn University, which was founded in 1917. Following the National Education Act (1999; amended 2002) and the Act for Streamlining of Ministries and Government Agencies (2003), the Ministry of Education, Ministry of University Affairs and Office of the National Education Commission were incorporated into a supra-Ministry of Education. Higher education is the responsibility of the Ministry of Education's Higher Education Commission. In 2004 there 1,891,693 students enrolled in 166 institutions under the authority of the Higher Education Commission.

The main requirements for admission to higher education are 12 years of secondary school education and the MAW 6 (M6) certificate. Applicants to state institutions must sit the Written Entrance Examination, and private institutions may also require applicants to fulfil additional criteria for admission. The principal undergraduate degree is the Bachelors, which is a four-year programme of study, although degrees in mainly professional fields of study may last longer, such as dentistry, architecture, pharmacy (five years) and medicine (six years). The first postgraduate degree is the Masters, which usually lasts two years and may be either a taught or a research degree. The highest university degree is the Doctor of Philosophy (PhD) which requires a minimum of three years and a maximum of eight years of classwork and research.

Post-secondary vocation and technical education is overseen by the Ministry of Education Vocational Education Commission. Qualifications offered include Diploma in Vocational Education, Higher Certificate (Technician Level) and Higher Diploma of Technical Education (all two years).

Learned Societies

GENERAL

Office of the National Culture Commission: Ratchadapisek Rd, Huay Khwang, Bangkok 10320; tel. 2470013; fax 248-5841; e-mail culturethai@hotmail.com; internet www.culture.go.th; f. 1979; advises the Ministerial Council on cultural policy, and promotes co-ordination and co-operation in cultural activities (e.g. ASEAN projects, UNESCO programmes, intra-regional music workshop, cultural exchanges, varied research); 300 mems; library of 30,000 vols; Sec.-Gen. ARTORN CHANDAVIMOL; publ. *Thai Culture Magazine* (weekly).

Royal Institute: The Royal Grand Palace Grounds, Thanon, Na Phra Lan Rd, Bangkok 10200; tel. 2214822; fax 2249910; e-mail royal_institute@mozart.inet.co.th; f. 1933 for the investigation and encouragement of all branches of knowledge, the exchange of knowledge and for advice to the Government; 151 mems; library of 25,000 vols; Pres. Prof. Dr PRAYOON KANCHANADUL; Sec.-Gen. CHAMNONG TONGPRASERT.

Siam Society under Royal Patronage: 131 Soi 21 (Asoke), Asokemontri Rd, Wattana, Bangkok 10110; tel. (2) 6616470; fax (2) 2583491; e-mail info@siam-society.org; internet www.siam-society.org; f. 1904; promotes the preservation of Thai heritage, culture, art, flora and fauna; 2,000 mems; library of 35,000 vols; Pres. M. R. CHAKRAROT CHITRABONGS; Hon. Sec. MONITA SINGHAKOWIN; publs *Journal, Natural History Bulletin* (2 a year).

BIBLIOGRAPHY, LIBRARY SCIENCE AND MUSEOLOGY

Thai Library Association: 273 Vibhavadee Rangsit Rd, Phyathai, Bangkok 10400; tel. 271-2084; f. 1954; 1,524 mems; Pres. M. CHAVALIT; Sec. K. SUCKCHAROEN; publs *TLA Bulletin, The World of Books*.

EDUCATION

Rectors' Conference of Thailand: Planning Division, Ministry of University Affairs, Si-Ayuthya Rd, Bangkok 10400; f. 1971; to exchange ideas and discuss problems of common concern to universities; 14 mems; Chair. Prof. Dr NATTH BHAMARAPRAVATI; Sec. Asst Prof. Dr UTHAI BOONPRASERT.

UNESCO Office Bangkok and Asia and Pacific Regional Bureau for Education: Prakanong Post Office, POB 10110, Bangkok; Located at: 920 Sukhumvit Rd, Bangkok 10110; tel. (2) 391-0577; fax (2) 391-0866; e-mail bangkok@unesco.org; internet www .unesco.org/bangkok; f. 1961; designated Cluster Office for Cambodia, Laos, Myanmar, Thailand and Viet Nam; Dir SHELDON SHAEFFER.

LANGUAGE AND LITERATURE

Alliance Française: 29 Thanon Sathorn Tai, Bangkok 10120; tel. (2) 2132122; fax (2) 2132064; e-mail bangkok@alliance-francaise .or.th; internet www.alliance-francaise.or.th; offers courses and exams in French language and culture and promotes cultural exchange with France; attached teaching centres in Chiang Mai, Chiang Rai and Phuket; Dir of Operations, Thailand ANDRÉ SCHMITT.

British Council: 254 Chulalongkorn Soi 64, Siam Sq., Phayathai Rd, Pathumwan, Bangkok 10330; tel. (2) 652-5480; fax (2) 253-5312; e-mail info@britishcouncil.or.th; internet www.britishcouncil.or.th; teaching centre; offers courses and exams in English language and British culture and promotes cultural exchange with the UK; attached teaching centres in Chiang Mai, Ladprao, Pinklao and Srinakarin; Dir PETER UPTON.

Goethe-Institut: 18/1 Soi Goethe, Sathorn 1 Rd, Bangkok 10120; tel. (2) 2870942; fax (2) 2871829; e-mail info@bangkok.goethe.org; internet www.goethe.de/bangkok; f. 1960; offers courses and exams in German language and culture and promotes cultural exchange with Germany; library of 8,000 vols; Dir WILFRIED ECKSTEIN.

MEDICINE

Medical Association of Thailand: 3 Silom St, Bangkok; f. 1921; 3,057 mems; Pres. Prof. Dr SONGKRANT NIYOMSEN; Hon. Sec. Prof. Dr SANONG UNAKOL; publ. *Journal*.

NATURAL SCIENCES

General

Science Society of Thailand: Faculty of Science, Chulalongkorn University, Phya Thai Rd, Bangkok 10330; tel. (2) 2527987; fax (2) 2527987; f. 1948; aims to promote education and research in all branches of natural science; 2,500 mems; Pres. Prof. Dr MONTRI CHULAVATNATOL; Sec.-Gen. Dr PIAMSOOK PONGSAWASDI; publs *Journal* (quarterly in English), *Science* (every 2 weeks).

Research Institutes

AGRICULTURE, FISHERIES AND VETERINARY SCIENCE

Fishery Technological Development Division: Dept of Fisheries, Ministry of Agriculture and Co-operatives, Charoen Krung Rd, Yannawa, Bangkok 10120; tel. (2) 2111261; f. 1954; fish handling, processing and utilization; analytical and sanitary certificate for export; Dir UDOM SUNDRARAVIPAT.

Forest Products Research and Development Division: Royal Forest Dept, Ministry of Agriculture and Co-operatives, 61 Paholyothin Rd, Jatujak, Bangkok 10900; f. 1935; wood and non-wood products research and utilization; library of 20,000 vols; Dir of Division WANIDA SUBANSENEE.

Rubber Research Centre: Hat Yai, Songkhla, Dept of Agriculture, Ministry of Agriculture, Bangkok.

NATURAL SCIENCES

Biological Sciences

Marine Biology Centre: Marine Fisheries Division, 89/1 Sapanpla, Yanawa, Bangkok 12; f. 1968; research and training of marine biologists; Dir DEB MENASWETA.

RELIGION, SOCIOLOGY AND ANTHROPOLOGY

Buddhist Research Centre: Wat Benchamabopitr, Bangkok; f. 1961; sponsored by Department of Religious Affairs, Ministry of Education; publs *Pali-Thai-English Dictionary, vol. 1*.

TECHNOLOGY

Department of Alternative Energy Development and Efficiency: Kasatsuk Bridge, Rama I Rd, Bangkok 10330; tel. (2)

2230021; fax (2) 2261416; e-mail dede@dede.go.th; internet www.dede.go.th; f. 1953; conducts research and inspection, surveys and gathers data on energy resources; lays down safety regulations, sets up standards for the sale of energy, promotes the use of energy to improve the economy; library of 13,000 vols; Dir-Gen. SIRIPORN SAILASUTA; publs *Thailand Energy Situation* (annually), *Oil and Thailand* (annually), *Electric Power in Thailand* (annually), *Thailand Alternative Energy Situation* (annually).

Department of Mineral Resources: Ministry of Industry, Rama VI Rd, Bangkok 10400; geological mapping, mineral prospecting, mining, mineral dressing and metallurgical research; Dir-Gen. Dr PRABHAS CHAKKAPHAK.

Department of Science Service: Rama VI Rd, Bangkok 10400; tel. 2461387-95; f. 1891; testing, calibration and analysis services; research in food technology, industrial fermentation, pulp and paper raw materials, chemical engineering processes, air and water pollution control; research in ceramics; scientific and technological information service; library: see Libraries; Dir-Gen. CHODCHOI EIUMPONG; publs *Annual Report*, *Journal* (3 a year).

Office of Atomic Energy for Peace: Vibhavadi Rangsit, Chatuchuk, Bangkok 10900; tel. 579-5230; fax 561-3013; f. 1961; 401 staff; library of 11,000 vols, 265 periodicals; Sec.-Gen. KRIENGSAK BHADRAKOM; publ. *OAEP Newsletter* (quarterly).

Thailand Institute of Scientific and Technological Research: 196 Phahonyothin Rd, Chatuchak, Bangkok 10900; tel. (2) 579-1121; fax (2) 561-1479; e-mail tistr@tistr.or.th; internet www.tistr.or.th; f. 1963; principal govt research agency; research depts: Pharmaceuticals and Natural Products, Food Industry, Chemical Industry, Biotechnology, Building Technology, Electronics Industry, Engineering Industry, Materials Technology, Agricultural Technology, Energy Technology, Environmental and Resources Management, Ecological Research, Thai Packaging Centre; 748 staff; Governor Dr NONGLUCK PANKURDDEE.

Libraries and Archives
Bangkok

Asian Institute of Technology Library: POB 4, Klong-Luang, Pathumthani 12120; tel. (2) 5245853; fax (2) 5245870; e-mail ref@ait.ac.th; internet www.library.ait.ac.th; f. 1959; provides services and training in library and information services; 250,000 vols, 900 periodicals; Head of Library BOONTHAREE PHOONCHAI.

Chulalongkorn University, Center of Academic Resources: Phya Thai Rd, Bangkok 10330; tel. 218-2905; fax 215-3617; e-mail webmaster@car.chula.ac.th; internet www.car.chula.ac.th; f. 1910; Central Library (995,264 vols), Thailand Information Center (73,400 vols), Audio-Visual Center (14,269 vols), International Information Center (20,147 vols), Academic Development and Service Center; Dir Dr KAMALES SANTIVEJKUL (acting).

Kasetsart University, Main Library: Bangkok 10903; tel. (2) 5611369; fax (2) 5611369; e-mail upvp@nontai.ku.ac.th; internet www.lib.ku.ac.th; f. 1943; 377,844 vols, 3,350 periodicals, 52,788 theses, 74,574 sheets of microfiche, 2,827 titles of audio-visual materials; Dir Mrs PIBOONSIN WATANAPONGSE; publ. *Buffalo Bulletin* (quarterly).

Library of the Scientific and Technological Information Division, Department of Science Service: Ministry of Science, Technology and Environment, Rama VI Rd, Ratchathewi District, Bangkok 10400; tel. (2) 245-5271; fax (2) 247-9468; e-mail info@dss.moste.go.th; internet www.dss.moeste.go.th; f. 1918; 450,000 vols; special library and technical information services including patents, standards and trade literature; Dir MAYUREE PONGPUDPUNTH.

National Archives of Thailand: Fine Arts Department, Samsen Rd, Bangkok 10300; tel. 2811599; f. 1952; historical and research resources services for official agencies, scholars and the public; four major classes of documentary material: textual (313,000 dossiers of public and personal records), 408,000 photos, 4,000 videos, 1,700 tapes, 51,000 posters, 5,600 microfilm reels, cartographic (24,000 maps and 1,753 aerial photographs), govt publs (3,660 titles), 1,026,000 film negatives and slides, 54,000 films and newsreels; Dir SAGARINDRA VISESHABANDHU.

National Library of Thailand: Samsen Rd, Bangkok 10300; tel. 2815212; fax 2810263; e-mail suwaksir@emisc.moe.go.th; internet www.span.com.au/nlt; f. 1905; 2,454,746 vols, 324,477 MSS, 2,567 periodicals, 700,318 audiovisual items; national research library; depository for UN publications and UNESCO documents and collns; controls International Standard Serial Number (ISSN–Thailand), ISSN Regional Centre for Southeast Asia (ISSN-SEA); Dir SUWAKHON SIRIWONGWORAWAT; publs *Thai National Bibliography*, *ISSN-SEA Bulletin*, *NLT Newsletter*.

Neilson Hays Library: 195 Suriwongse Rd, Bangkok; tel. (2) 2331731; fax (2) 2334999; e-mail neilson@loxinfo.co.th; internet www.neilsonhays.com; f. 1869; Librarian PRAPHEN CHITRAKDI.

Siriraj Medical Library, Mahidol University: Siriraj Hospital, Bangkok 10700; tel. 411-3112; fax 412-8418; f. 1897; 159,600 vols, 3,918 periodicals; Librarian K. CHOLLAMPE; publs *Siriraj Hospital Gazette*, *Journal of the Medical Association of Thailand*, *Newsletter* (monthly).

Srinakharinwirot University Library: Sukhumvit 23, Bangkok 10110; f. 1954; 196,011 vols (emphasis on education), 1,157 periodicals; audio-visual centre; Dir Asst Prof. Dr VIRA SUPAKIT; brs in Bangkhen, Bang Saen, Patoom Wan, Pitsanuloke, Songkla; publ. *New Books of the Month—A Bibliography*.

Thai National Documentation Centre: 196 Phahonyothin Rd, Chatuchak, Bangkok 10900; tel. (2) 579-1121; fax (2) 579-8594; e-mail tndc@tistr.or.th; internet www.tistr.or.th; f. 1961; documentation services to science and technology; 48,493 vols, monographs in Thai 14,782 vols, monographs in English 34,992 vols, periodicals (103 in English, 85 in Thai); Dir DARANEE PRABHASANOBOL.

Thammasat University Libraries: 2 Prachand Rd, Bangkok 10200; tel. (2) 6235171; fax (2) 6235173; e-mail tulib@tu.ac.th; internet www.library.tu.ac.th; f. 1934; 1,053,726 vols (social sciences and humanities, medical science, science and technology), 4,712 periodicals, 31 databases, 26,615 audio-visual items; 11 br. libraries; Librarian PRAPAIPHAN JARUTHAVEE; publs *Dom That* (2 a year), *Annual Report*.

United Nations Economic and Social Commission for Asia and the Pacific Library: United Nations Bldg, Rajdamnern Ave, Bangkok 10200; tel. (2) 288-1360; fax (2) 288-1000; e-mail escap_libref.unescap@un.org; internet www.unescap.org/unis/library/weblib.htm; economic and social development; 150,000 vols; Chief Librarian EVELYN DOMINGO-BARKER; publs *Asian and Pacific Bibliography* (annually), *ESCAP Documents and Publications* (annually).

Museum
Bangkok

National Museum Bangkok: Na Phra That Rd, PhraBorom Maha Ratchawang, Phra Nakhon, Bangkok 10200; tel. and fax 2241396; internet www.bangkok-museum.go.th; f. 1874; permanent exhibitions on Thai history, archaeology and art history of Thailand from the prehistoric period to the Bangkok period, decorative arts and ethnology; prehistoric artefacts, bronze and stone sculptures, costumes, textiles, ancient weapons, coins, wood-carvings, ceramics, royal regalia, theatrical masks and dresses, marionettes, shadow-play figures, funeral chariots, illustrated books, musical instruments, monuments, historic bldgs; lectures on Thai art and culture; library; Dir SOMCHAI NA NAKHONPANOM; publs *Guide to the National Museum, Official Guide to Ayutthaya and Bang Pa-in, Guide to Old Sukhothai, Thai Cultural Series*.

Universities and Technical Institutes

ASIAN INSTITUTE OF TECHNOLOGY

POB 4, Klong Luang, Pathumthani 12120
Telephone: (2) 5160110
Fax: (2) 5162126
E-mail: provost@ait.ac.th
Internet: www.ait.ac.th

Founded 1959

Independent graduate institute, open to graduates from all countries; 2 semesters per year leading to Diploma; 4 semesters (2 years) course leading to a Master's degree; further 3 years leading to Doctoral degree

Language of instruction: English
Academic year: January to December

President: Prof. MARIO T. TABUCANON (acting)
Provost: Prof. MARIO T. TABUCANON
Director of Promotion Activities: SANJEEV JAYASINGHE
Secretary: KARMA RANA

Library: see Libraries and Archives
Number of teachers: 110
Number of students: 2,000
Publication: *AIT Annual Report*

DEANS

School of Advanced Technologies: Prof. M. T. TABUCANON (acting)
School of Civil Engineering: Prof. CHONGRAK POLPRASERT (acting)
School of Environment, Resources and Development: Prof. CHONGRAK POLPRASERT
School of Management: Dr NAZRUL ISLAM (acting)

DIRECTORS

AIT Extension: Dr TERESITA DEL ROSARIO (acting)
Language Centre: MATTHEW LASZEWSKI
Library: BOONTHAREE PHOONCHAI

ASSUMPTION UNIVERSITY

Hua Mak Campus, 682 Ramkhamhaeng 24 Rd, Hua Mak, Bangkapi, Bangkok 10240
Bang Na Campus, 88 Moo 8, K. M. 26 Bang Na-Trad Rd, Samutprakarn 10540
Telephone: (2) 300-4543

Fax: (2) 300-4563
E-mail: abac@au.edu
Internet: www.au.edu

Founded 1969; became university in 1990; formerly Assumption Business Administration College
Private control (Catholic: Brothers of St Gabriel)
Language of instruction: English
Academic year: June to March

President: Rev. Bro. BANCHA SAENGHIRAN
Vice-President for Academic Affairs: Rev. Bro. VISITH SRIVICHAIRATANA
Vice-President for Administrative Affairs: Dr CHAVALIT MEENNUCH
Vice-President for Financial Affairs: Rev. Bro. ANUPATT P. YUTTACHAI
Vice-President for Information Technology: Prof. Dr SRISAKDI CHARMONMAN
Vice-President for Research Affairs: Asst Prof. Dr JIRAWAT WONGSWADIWAT
Vice-President for Student Affairs: Rev. Bro. LOECHAI LAVASUT
Registrar: KAMOL KITSAWAD
Director of Central Library: SUPRATA SINCH-AISUK

Library of 500,000 vols
Number of teachers: 1,233
Number of students: 20,000

Publications: *ABAC Journal, ABAC Today, AU Journal of Technology, Galaxy, Journal of Risk Management and Insurance, English Teacher, International Journal of Computer and Engineering Management (IJCEM), Prajna-Vihara (The Journal of Philosophy and Religion)*

DEANS

School of Architecture: PISIT VIRIYAVADHANA
School of Arts: Dr PIMPORN CHANDEE
School of Biotechnology: Dr CHURDCHAI CHEOWTIRAKUL
School of Business: Dr CHERDPONG SIBAN-RUANG
School of Communication Arts: CHALIT LIM-PANAVECH
School of Engineering: Dr SUDHIPORN PATUM-TAEWAPIBAL
School of Law: Assoc. Prof. PORNCHAI SOON-THORNPAN
School of Nursing Science: Dr NANTHAPHAN CHINLUMPRASERT
School of Risk Management and Industrial Services: BANCHA THEERASATIANKUL (acting)
School of Science and Technology: Asst Prof. SUPAVADEE NONTAKAO
Graduate School of Business: Rev. Bro. VINAI VIRIYADIDHAYAVONGS
Graduate School of Computer Engineering Management (MS Programme): Dr CHAM-NONG JUNGTHIRAPANICH
Graduate School of Computer Information Systems (MS Programme): Air Marshal Dr CHULIT MEESAJJEE
Graduate School of Computer Information Systems (PhD Programme): Asst Prof. Dr VICHIT AVATCHANAKORN
Graduate School of Counselling Psychology: Dr DOLORES DE LEON
Graduate School of Education: Assoc. Prof. Dr METHI PILANTHANANOND
Graduate School of Internet and E-Commerce Technology: Rear Admiral PRASART SRIBHADUNG
Graduate School of Philosophy and Religion: Asst Prof. Dr WARAYUTH SRIWARAKUEL

ATTACHED RESEARCH INSTITUTES

ABAC-KSC Internet Poll Research Centre: Dir NOPPADON KANNIKA.

Educational Research Centre: Dir Dr SAKESAN TONGKHAMBANJONG (acting).

Research Institute of Assumption University: Dir Dr JIRAWAT WONGSWADIWAT.

Social Sciences Research Centre: Dir Dr PREECHA METHAVASAPHAK.

BANGKOK UNIVERSITY

Rama 4 Rd, Klong-Toey, Bangkok 10110
Telephone: (2) 350-3500
Fax: (2) 249-6274
E-mail: buiao@bu.ac.th
Internet: www.bu.ac.th

Founded 1962 as Thai Polytechnic Institute; became Bangkok College 1965; university status 1984
Private control
Languages of instruction: Thai, English
Academic year: August to May

President: Dr THANU KULACHOL
Advisor to the President: Prof. Dr POTE SAPIANCHAI
Vice-Presidents: Dr MATHANA SANTIWAT (Academic Affairs), NARUMON OSATHANUGRAH (Administrative Affairs), RATCH OSATHANU-GRAH (Financial Affairs), Dr QUANCHAI AUNGTRAKUL (Planning and Development), Dr SUPONG LIMTHANAKOOL (Special Affairs), SUREE BURANATHANIT (Student Affairs)

Library of 400,000 vols
Number of teachers: 1,120
Number of students: 26,522 (25,742 undergraduate, 780 postgraduate)

Publications: *BU Academic Journal* (2 a year), *Executive Journal* (4 a year)

DEANS

School of Accounting: Dr SUTHA JIARANAIKUL-VANICH
School of Business Administration: Assoc. Prof. Dr SUTHINAN POMSUWAN
School of Communication: Dr SUDARAT DIS-AYAWATTANA
School of Economics: Asst Prof. THAMAKORN THARASRISUTHI
School of Engineering: Assoc. Prof. Dr TIPAR-ATANA WONGCHAROEN
School of Fine and Applied Arts: SUMITTRA SRIVIBOONE
School of Humanities: Dr NEENA SWASDISON
School of Law: Asst Prof. SURAVUDH KIJKUSOL
School of Science: KITTIPAT YINGPANYACHOK

BURAPHA UNIVERSITY

169 Saen Sook, Muang Chonburi 20131
Telephone: (38) 745900
Fax: (38) 390049
Internet: www.adm.buu.ac.th

Founded 1955
State control
Language of instruction: Thai
Academic year: June to March

President: Prof. Dr SUCHART UPATHAM
Vice-Presidents: Assoc. Prof. Dr RENA PON-RUENGPHANT (Academic Affairs), Assoc. Prof. BOONSERM POOHSANGUAN (Administration), Assoc. Prof. SUDA SUWANNAPIROM (Finance and Property Affairs), Asst Prof. PICHAN SAWANGWONG (International Relations), VIRAT KARAVAPITTAYAKULA (Planning and Development), Prof. Dr SOMSAK PHANTUWATTANA (Research Affairs), Asst Prof. BOOMKA THAIKRA (Student Affairs)
Librarian: Dr KWANCHADIL PHISALPHONG

Library of 231,635 vols
Number of teachers: 657
Number of students: 21,636 (8,000 undergraduate, 2,000 postgraduate)

Publication: *Journal of Science, Technology and Humanity*

DEANS

Faculty of Education: Assoc. Prof. Dr CHA-LONG TUBSEE
Faculty of Engineering: Asst Prof. Dr WIR-ONGA RUENGPHRATHUENGSUKA
Faculty of Fine and Applied Arts: Prof. THESAKAI THONANOPKONG
Faculty of Humanities and Social Sciences: Assoc. Prof. Dr CHARAN CHAKANDANG
Faculty of Marine Technology: Dr PINCHAI SONCHAENG
Faculty of Nursing: Asst Prof. Dr SUNTHAR-AWADEE THEMPICHET
Faculty of Public Health: Assoc. Prof. Dr SASTRI SAOWAKONTHA
Faculty of Science: Assoc. Prof. Dr KASHANE CHALERMWAT
Faculty of Science and Art: Asst Prof. RANOP PRAVATNGAM
Graduate School: Assoc. Prof. Dr PRATOOM MUONGMEE

CHIANG MAI UNIVERSITY

239 Huay Kaew Rd, Muang District, Chiang Mai 50200
Telephone: (53) 943661
Fax: (53) 219252
E-mail: opxxo004@chiangmai.ac.th
Internet: www.chiangmai.ac.th

Founded 1964
State control
Languages of instruction: Thai, English
Academic year: June to May

President: Prof. Dr PONGSAK ANGKASITH
Vice-Presidents: Asst Prof. Dr PONG-IN RAKARIYATHAM (Academic Affairs), Assoc. Prof. VAJARA RUJIWETPONGSTORN (Administrative Affairs), Asst Prof. Dr AKACHAI SANG-IN (Campus Management), Assoc. Prof. AMNAT YOUSUKH (Human Resources Development and Special Affairs), Assoc. Prof. Dr TANUN ANUMANRAJADHON (International Relations Affairs), Assoc. Prof. Dr PAIROTE WIRIYACHAREE (Planning and Development), Assoc. Prof. Dr DAOROONG KANGWANPONG (Research Affairs), Assoc. Prof. THEERA VISITPANICH (Student Development and Alumni Affairs)
Registrar: Asst Prof. AUNNOP KOONPHANDH
Librarian: Asst Prof. PRASIT MALUMPONG

Number of teachers: 2,171
Number of students: 26,000

Publications: *Bulletin of Chiang Mai Associated Medical Sciences* (quarterly), *Calendar of Arts and Culture* (monthly), *Chiang Mai Journal of Science* (3 a year), *Chiang Mai Medical Bulletin* (quarterly), *Chiang Mai University Journal* (3 a year), *Chiang Mai University Library Journal* (annual), *CM Dental Journal* (2 a year), *Engineering Journal* (3 a year), *Graduate School Bulletin* (every 2 years), *Humyon Journal* (2 a year), *Journal of Agriculture* (3 a year), *Journal of Asian Studies* (3 a year), *Journal of Economics* (3 a year), *Journal of Human Sciences* (2 a year), *Journal of Political Science* (2 a year), *Journal of Social Sciences* (3 a year), *Newsletter Rom Phayom* (quarterly), *Newletter of Women's Studies* (2 a year), *Nursing Newsletter* (quarterly), *PT & CT* (3 a year), *Regional Information Service Center for South East Asia on Appropriate Technology* (monthly), *Research Abstracts of the Institute for Science and Technology Research and Development* (annual), *Research Abstracts and On-going Research Projects* (annual), *Research and Development Technology Transfer (IST News)* (2 a year)

DEANS

Faculty of Agriculture: Assoc. Prof. Dr BOON-SERM CHEVA-ISARAKUL

Faculty of Agro-Industry: Asst Prof. Dr METHINEE H. CHAREN
Faculty of Architecture: Assoc. Prof. Dr SOMBAT THIRATRAKOOLCHAI
Faculty of Arts: Assoc. Prof. M. L. SURASAWADI SOOKASWADI
Faculty of Associated Medical Sciences: DECHA ROMCAI
Faculty of Business Administration: BOONSAWAT PRUCKSIGANON
Faculty of Dentistry: Assoc. Prof. VIRUSH PATANAPORN
Faculty of Economics: Dr SONGSAK SRIBOONCHITTA
Faculty of Education: Asst Prof. SERMKIAT JOMJENYONG
Faculty of Engineering: Assoc. Prof. Dr AKACHAI SANG-IN
Faculty of Humanities: Dr PRAPA SOOKGASEM
Faculty of Nursing: Assoc. Prof. Dr WIPADA KUNAVIKTIKUL
Faculty of Medicine: Prof. SUPOT WUDHIKARN
Faculty of Pharmacy: Assoc. Prof. AURAWAN TITWAN
Faculty of Science: Asst Prof. Dr MONGKON RAYANAKORN
Faculty of Social Sciences: Assoc. Prof. SEKSIN SRIVATANANUKULKIT
Faculty of Veterinary Medicine: Assoc. Prof. Dr SUVICHAI ROJANASATHIEN
Graduate School: Assoc. Prof. Dr SURASAK WATANESK

ATTACHED RESEARCH INSTITUTES

Institute for Science and Technology Research and Development: Dir Assoc. Prof. Dr CHESADA KASEMSET.

Research Institute for Health Sciences: Dir Prof. Dr THIRA SIRISANTHANA.

Social Research Institute: Dir Assoc. Prof. Dr MINGSARN KAOSA-ARD.

CHULALONGKORN UNIVERSITY

Phyathai Rd, Pathumwan, Bangkok 10330
Telephone: (662) 215-0871
Fax: (662) 215-4804
E-mail: info@chula.ac.th
Internet: www.chula.ac.th

Founded 1917
State control
Language of instruction: Thai
Academic year: June to March

Chair.: Prof. CHARAS SUWANWELA
President: Prof. SUCHADA KIRANADANA
Vice-Presidents: Prof. SOOTTIPORN CHITTMITTRAPAP, Assoc. Prof. BOONSOM LERDHIRUNWONG, Assoc. Prof. JOOMPOL RODCUMDEE, Assoc. Prof. WEERA SACHAKUL, Assoc. Prof. DUSADEE SANGUANCHART, Assoc. Prof. KAMALES SANTIVEJKUL, Assoc. Prof. SITHICHAI TADSRI, Assoc. Prof. WERASAK UDOMKICHDECHA, Prof. KUA WONGBOONSIN
Registrar: Assoc Prof. PRADISTHA INTARAKOSIT
Library: see Libraries and Archives
Number of teachers: 2,427
Number of students: 13,858 undergraduate, 5,135 postgraduate
Publications: *Annual Report, Chula Samphan* (every 2 weeks), *Data on Freshmen Entering Chulalongkorn University, Fact Book* (annually), *'Pra Keaw' Students' Handbook* (annually), *Research Journal* (annually), *University Newsletter* (quarterly)

DEANS

Faculty of Allied Health Sciences: Assoc. Prof. Dr WINAI DAHLAN
Faculty of Architecture: Assoc. Prof. Dr VIRA SACHAKUL
Faculty of Arts: Asst Prof. Dr M. R. KALAYA TINGSABADH

Faculty of Commerce and Accountancy: Asst Prof. Dr DANUJA KUNPANICHKIT
Faculty of Communication Arts: Prof. Dr SURAPOL WIRUNRAK
Faculty of Dentistry: Assoc. Prof. Dr SURASITH KIATPONGSAN
Faculty of Economics: Assoc. Prof. Dr SOTHITORN MALIKAMAST
Faculty of Education: Assoc. Prof. Dr PAITOON SINLARAT
Faculty of Engineering: Prof. Dr SOMSAK PANYAKEOW
Faculty of Fine and Applied Arts: Assoc. Prof. Dr CHANNARONG PORNRUNGROJ
Faculty of Law: Asst Prof. Dr TITHIPHAN CHUERBOONCHAI
Faculty of Medicine: Prof. Dr PIROM KAMOLRATANAKUL
Faculty of Nursing: Assoc. Prof. Dr JINTANA YUNIBHAND
Faculty of Pharmaceutical Science: Assoc. Prof. Dr BOONYONG TANTISIRA
Faculty of Political Science: Assoc. Prof. Dr AMARA PONGSAPICH
Faculty of Psychology: Assoc. Prof. Dr PUNTIP SIRIVUNNABOOD
Faculty of Science: Prof. Dr PIAMSAK MANASVATA
Faculty of Veterinary Science: Prof. Dr NARONGSAK CHAIYABUTR
Graduate School: Prof. Dr SUCHADA KIRANANDANA

HEADS OF DEPARTMENTS

Faculty of Allied Health Sciences:
Clinical Chemistry: Assoc. Prof. Dr RACHANA SANTIYANONT
Clinical Microscopy: Assoc. Prof. Dr PORNTHEP TIENSIWAKUL
Transfusion Medicine: Asst Prof. Dr WINAI DAHLAN

Faculty of Architecture:
Architecture: Assoc. Prof. VIRA BURANAKARN
Housing Development: Assoc. Prof. MANOP BONGSADADT
Industrial Design: Asst Prof. Dr AURAPIN PANTONG
Interior Architecture: Asst Prof. SURACHAI CHOLPRASERD
Landscape Architecture: Asst Prof. NILUBOL KLONGVESSA
Urban and Regional Planning: Asst Prof. Dr NIPAN VICHIENNOI

Faculty of Arts:
Dramatic Arts: NALINEE SITASUWAN
Eastern Languages: Asst Prof. Dr KANLAYANEE SITASUWAN
English: CHARURAT TANTRAPORN
Geography: Assoc. Prof. NAROTE PALAKAWONGSA NA AYUDHYA
History: Asst Prof. Dr PIYANART BUNNAG
Linguistics: Assoc. Prof. Dr THERAPHAN LUANGTHONGKUM
Library Science: Assoc. Prof. Dr PRAPAVADEE SUEBSONTHI
Philosophy: Assoc. Prof. Dr MARK TANTHAI
Thai: Assoc. Prof. Dr NAVAVAN BANDHUMEDHA
Western Languages: Asst Prof. PANITI HOONSWAENG

Faculty of Commerce and Accountancy:
Accountancy: ORAPIN CHARTABSORN
Banking and Finance: Asst Prof. VIRACH APHIMETEETAMRONG
Commerce: Dr ACHARA CHANDRACHAI
Marketing: Assoc. Prof. SURAPAT VACHARAPRATIP
Statistics: Assoc. Prof. PAKAVADI SIRIRANGSI

Faculty of Communication Arts:
Mass Communications: Assoc. Prof. Dr NUNTHAWAN SUCHATO

Motion Picture and Still Photography: Asst Prof. Dr YUTHAWAT PATHARAPANUPATH
Public Relations: Assoc. Prof. Dr THANAVADEE BOONLUE
Speech Communication and Performing Arts: Dr SAKDA PANNENGPETCH

Faculty of Dentistry:
Anatomy: Assoc. Prof. DOLLY METHATHRATHIP
Biochemistry: Asst Prof. LAMOONYONG POVATONG
Community Dentistry: Assoc. Prof. SOMPOL LEKFUANGFU
Microbiology: Asst Prof. RATANA SERINIRACH
Occlusion: Asst Prof. SUKNIPA VICHAICHALERMVONG
Operative Dentistry: Asst Prof. SAICHI MATHURASAI
Oral Medicine: Asst Prof. VILAIWAN ANEKSUK
Oral Pathology: VICHADE LEELAPRUTE
Oral Surgery: Assoc. Prof. SITHICHAI TUDSRI
Orthodontics: Asst Prof. KANOK SORATHESN
Paediatric Dentistry: Asst Prof. DHANIS HEMINDRA
Periodontology: Assoc. Prof. NOPHADOL SUPPIPAT
Pharmacology: WATANA KONTHIKAMEE
Physiology: Asst Prof. Dr CHOOKIAT SUCANTHAPREE
Prosthodontics: Asst Prof. SUPABOON BURNAVEJA
Radiology: PAIRAT DHIRAVARANGKURA

Faculty of Education:
Art Education: Asst Prof. SANYA WONGARAM
Audio-Visual Education: Asst Prof. SUGREE RODPOTHONG
Educational Administration: Asst Prof. Dr WEERAWAT UTAIRAT
Educational Research: Assoc. Prof. Dr VANNA PURANAJOTI
Elementary Education: Assoc. Prof. Dr DUANGDUEN ANNUAM
Foundations of Education: Assoc. Prof. Dr RERNGRATCHANEE NIMNUAL
Higher Education: Asst Prof. Dr THIDARAT BOONNUJ
Physical Education: Asst Prof. Dr LAWAN SUKKRI
Psychology: Assoc. Prof. Dr SOMPOCH IAMSUPASIT
Secondary Education: Asst Prof. Dr THERACHAI PURANAJOTI

Faculty of Engineering:
Chemical Engineering: Dr PIYASAN PRASERTHDAM
Civil Engineering: Prof. VATTANA THAMMONGKOL
Computer Engineering: Assoc. Prof. DUAN SINTUPUNPRATUM
Electrical Engineering: Prof. Dr SOMSAK PANYAKEOW
Environmental Engineering: Assoc. Prof. SUREE KHAODHIAN
Industrial Engineering: Prof. Dr SIRICHAN THONGPRASERT
Mechanical Engineering: Assoc. Prof. Dr WITHAYA YONGCHAREON
Metallurgical Engineering: Asst Prof. Dr CHATCHAI SOMSIRI
Mining Engineering and Mining Geology: Assoc. Prof. SARITHDEJ PATHANASETHPONG
Nuclear Technology: Asst Prof. NARES CHANKOW
Survey Engineering: SANYA SOWAPARB

Faculty of Fine and Applied Arts:
Creative Arts: SUCHINTANA SANGAUNMU
Dance: PUSADEE LIMSAKUL
Music: CHUMNONG SANICHIEN (acting)

Visual Arts: Asst Prof. PRAMUAN BURU-SPHAT

Faculty of Law:

Administrative Law: Assoc. Prof. Dr BOR-WORNSAK UWANNO
Civil and Commercial Law: Assoc. Prof. PHIJAISAKDI HORAYANGKURA
Criminal Law and Criminology: Assoc. Prof. VIRAPHONG BOONYOBHAS
International Law: Prof. VITIT MUNTARB-HORN
Procedural and Court Law: Assoc. Prof. PAITOON KONGSOMBOON

Faculty of Medicine:

Anaesthesiology: Assoc. Prof. POGCHIT PRA-MUAN
Anatomy: Asst Prof. ORASRI ROMYANAN
Biochemistry: Dr JERAPAN KRUNGKAI
Forensic Medicine: Assoc. Prof. VIRATT PANICHABHONGSE
Laboratory Medicine: Assoc. Prof. PAILIN UJJIN
Medicine: Prof. CHAIVEJ NUCHPRAYOON
Microbiology: Assoc. Prof. SOMJAI REIN-PRAYOON
Obstetrics and Gynaecology: Prof. PRA-MUAN VIRUTAMASEN
Ophthalmology: Prof. PRACHAK PRACHAK-VEJ
Orthopaedic Surgery: Assoc. Prof. CHAITHAVAT NGARMUKOS
Otolaryngology: Prof. AMNUAY CUTCHA-VAREE
Paediatrics: Prof. VIROJNA SUEBLINVONG
Parasitology: Assoc. Prof. MEDHI KULKUM-THORN
Pathology: Assoc. Prof. CHOOSAK VIRATCHAI
Pharmacology: Assoc. Prof. SOPIT THA-MAREE
Physiology: BUNGORN CHOMDEJ
Preventative and Social Medicine: Asst Prof. MUNEE SRESHTHABUTRA
Psychiatry: Prof. SUWATANA ARIBARG
Radiology: Prof. NITAYA SUWANWELA
Surgery: Assoc. Prof. YOD SUKOTHAMAN

Faculty of Pharmaceutical Science:

Biochemistry: Assoc. Prof. SUNATA PONGSA-MART
Food Chemistry: SUTHEE SUNTHORNTHUM
Manufacturing Pharmacy: Asst Prof. Dr POJ KULVANICH
Microbiology: Assoc. Prof. Dr VIMOLMAS LIPIPUN
Pharmaceutical Botany: Assoc. Prof. RAPEEPOL BAVOVADA
Pharmaceutical Chemistry: Assoc. Prof. SUTTATIP CHANTARASKUL
Pharmacognosy: Assoc. Prof. CHAIYO CHAI-CHANTIPYUTH
Pharmacology: Assoc. Prof. Dr PORNPEN PREMYOTHIN
Pharmacy: Assoc. Prof. PRAPAPUCK SILAPA-CHOTE
Physiology: Asst Prof. SUMLEE JAIDEE

Faculty of Political Science:

Government: Assoc. Prof. Dr PRAYAD HON-GTONGKUM
International Relations: Asst Prof. Dr CHAIWAT KHAMCHOO
Public Administration: Asst Prof. Dr THO-SAPORN SIRISUMPHAND
Sociology and Anthropology: Assoc. Prof. SUPATRA SOOPHARB

Faculty of Science:

Biochemistry: Asst Prof. TIPAPORN LIMPA-SENI
Biology: Assoc. Prof. Dr VITHAYA YODYIN-GYUAD
Botany: Assoc. Prof. Dr PREEDA BOON-LONG
Chemistry: Assoc. Prof. Dr SIRI VAROTHAI
Chemical Technology: Assoc. Prof. KUNCH-ANA BUNYAKIAT

Food Technology: Assoc. Prof. Dr CHAIYUTE THUNPITHAYAKUL
Geology: Assoc. Prof. SOMPOP VEDCHAKAN-CHANA
General Science: SA-ARD VIROCHRUT
Marine Science: Assoc. Prof. MANUWADEE HUNGSPREUGS
Material Science: Asst Prof. WERASAK UDOMKICHDECHA
Mathematics: Asst Prof. LA-OR CHONVIRIYA
Microbiology: Assoc. Prof. PRAKITSIN SIHA-NONTH
Photographic Science and Printing Technology: Assoc. Prof. PONTAWEE PUNGRAS-SAMEE
Physics: Asst Prof. SOMPHONG CHATRAP-HORN

Faculty of Veterinary Science:

Animal Husbandry: Assoc. Prof. SUCHIN JALAYANAGUPTA
Veterinary Anatomy: Assoc. Prof. PAYAT-TRA TANTILIPIKARA
Veterinary Medicine: Asst Prof. Dr JIROJ SASIPREEYAJAN
Veterinary Obstetrics, Gynaecology and Reproduction: Assoc. Prof. PRACHIN VIR-AKUL
Veterinary Pathology: Assoc. Prof. MANOP MUANGYAI
Veterinary Pharmacology: Assoc. Prof. Dr WARA PANICHKRIANGKRAI
Veterinary Physiology: Prof. Dr NARONG-SAK CHAIYABUTR
Veterinary Surgery: Asst Prof. Dr PHAI-WIPA KAMOLRAT

DIRECTORS

Academic Resource Centre: Assoc. Prof. Dr PRACHAK POOMVISES
American Studies Program: PRANEE TIP-PAYARATANA
Chula Unisearch: Assoc. Prof. Dr PRASIT PRAPINMONGKOLKARN
Computer Service Center: Assoc. Prof. KRAI-VIJIT TANTIMEDH
Cultural Center of Chulalongkorn University: CHUMNONG SANGVICHIEN
Energy Research and Training Center: Assoc. Prof. Dr KULTHORN SILAPABANLENG
General Education Project: Assoc. Prof. Dr PIRAWAN BHANTHUMNAVIN
Institute of Asian Studies: Assoc. Prof. Dr WITHAYA SITHAYA SUCHARITHANARUGSE
Institute of Biotechnology and Genetic Engineering: Assoc. Prof. Dr NALINE NILUBOL
Institute of Environmental Research: Assoc. Prof. Dr SUTHIRAK SUJARITTANONTA
Institute of Health Research: Assoc. Prof. VICHAI POSHYACHINDA
Institute of Middle East and Muslim World Studies: Asst Prof. Dr ARONG SUTHASASNA
Institute of Population Studies: Assoc. Prof. Dr KUO WONGBOONSIN
Institute of Security and International Studies: Assoc. Prof. SUKHUMBHAND PARIBATRA
Institute of Social Research: Prof. Dr KRAIYUDHT DHIRATAYAKINAN
Institute of Thai Studies: Assoc. Prof. Dr PRAKONG NIMMANHAEMINDA
Language Institute: Assoc. Prof. CHANIGA SILPA-ANAN
Merchant Marine Institute: Assoc. Prof. Dr ITTIPHOL PAN-NGUM
Metallurgy and Materials Science Research Institute: Asst Prof. Dr LEK UTTAMASIL
Petroleum and Petrochemical College: Assoc. Prof. Dr KAMCHAD MONGKOLKUL
Public Enterprise Institute: Asst Prof. Dr PIPAT THAIAREE
Sasin Graduate Institute of Business Administration: Prof. TOEMSAKDI KRISHNAMRA
Scientific and Technological Research Equipment Centre: Asst Prof. CHYAGRIT SIRI UPATHAM

Toban-N.E. Thai Project: Assoc. Prof. Dr PRAPANT SVETANANT

DHURAKIJPUNDIT UNIVERSITY

110/1-4 Prachacheun Rd, Laksi, Bangkok 10210

Telephone: (2) 9547300
Fax: (2) 9547904
E-mail: dpuic@dpu.ac.th
Internet: www.dpu.ac.th

Founded 1968
Private control
Languages of instruction: Thai, English
Academic year: June to October, November to February

President: Assoc. Prof. Dr VARAKORN SAMA-KOSES
Registrar: Aj. SUPACHAI UDOMRAT
Librarian: Aj. SUWAKHON SIRIWONGWORAWAT

Library of 165,719 vols
Number of teachers: 503
Number of students: 19,000

Publication: *Sudhiparidhasna* (University journal)

DEANS

Faculty of Accounting: Dr PORNSIRI POONA-KASEM
Faculty of Arts and Sciences: Lt. Gen. PRA-SONG PARNEHAROEN
Faculty of Business Administration: Assoc. Prof. Dr UPATHAM SAISANGJAN
Faculty of Communication Arts: Aj. PRADIT RATANAWIJARN
Faculty of Economics: Asst Prof. Dr OM HUVANANDANA
Faculty of Engineering: Asst Prof. CHALIE KOMOLSUT
Faculty of Information Technology: Assoc. Prof. Dr NUEHAREE PREMEHAISWADI
Faculty of Law: Prof. Dr KANIT NAVAKORN
Graduate School: Dr PHIRAPHAN PHAUSUK

HUACHIEW CHALERMPRAKIET UNIVERSITY

18/18 Bangna-Trad Rd, Bangplee District, Samutprakarn 10540

Telephone: (2) 312-6300
Fax: (2) 312-6237
E-mail: webmaster@hcu.ac.th
Internet: www.hcu.ac.th

Founded 1942 as Midwifery School; became a college 1981; present name and status 1992
Private control
Language of instruction: Thai
Academic year: June to May

President: Prof. KASEM WATANACHAI
Vice-Presidents: Dr URAIPAN JANVANICHYA-NONT (Academic Affairs), SANGUANSRI KENGKIJKOSOL (Administrative Affairs), Assoc. Prof. Dr CHIRADET OUSAWAT (Planning and Development), KANOGWAN CHANTHANAMONGKOL (Student Affairs)
Director of Library and Information Centre: SONGSAN UDOMSILP

Library of 90,000 books, 467 periodicals
Number of teachers: 299
Number of students: 6,195 (6,067 undergraduate, 128 postgraduate)

DEANS

Faculty of Business Administration: Prof. Lt-Gen. MONTHIEN PRACHUABDEE
Faculty of Liberal Arts: Assoc. Prof. Dr PAT NOISEANGSRI
Faculty of Medical Technology: Asst Prof. BUSABA MATRAKOOL
Faculty of Nursing: Assoc. Prof. Dr JARIYA-WAT KOMPAYAK
Faculty of Pharmaceutical Science: Assoc. Prof. Dr CHANTRA SHAIPANICH

Faculty of Physical Therapy: KITIMA CHUNTA-PANICH

Faculty of Public and Environmental Health: Assoc. Prof. Dr PRAMOTE THONGKRAJAI

Faculty of Science and Technology: Assoc. Prof. Dr SIRIPONGSE SRIBHIBHADH

Faculty of Social Work and Social Welfare: Assoc. Prof. Dr APORNPUN CHANSAWANG

Graduate School: Asst Prof. PANNARAI SANG-VICHIEN

KASETSART UNIVERSITY

50 Phahonyothin Rd, Chatuchak, Bangkok 10900

Telephone: (2) 942-8171
Fax: (2) 942-8170
E-mail: fro@ku.ac.th
Internet: www.ku.ac.th

Founded 1943
State control
Languages of instruction: Thai, English
Academic year: June to March (two semesters)

President: Assoc Prof. VIROCH IMPITHUKSA
Vice-Presidents: Prof. Dr SUPAMARD PANICH-SAKPATANA (Academic Affairs), Assoc Prof. Dr SARUN WATTANUTCHARIYA (Academic Service Affairs), Assoc Prof. Dr JESDA KAEWKULAYA (Academic Services), Assoc. Prof VUDTECHAI KAPILAKANCHANA (Administration), NAKORN LUANGPRASERT (Campus Development), Assoc Prof. Dr SOMCHAI CHANTSAVANG (Chalermprakiat Sakon Nakorn Campus), Assoc Prof. YUEN POO-VARAWAN (Informational Technology), Dr THANWA JITSANGUAN (International Affairs), Assoc. Prof. THONGCHAI MALA (Kamphaengsaen Campus), Dr SORNPRACH THANISAWANYANGKURA (Planning and Development), Assoc Prof. Dr JUTHATIP PATHRAWAT (Property Management), Assoc Prof. KAMOLPUN NAMWONGPROM (Quality Assurance), Assoc Prof. Dr SAMAKKEE BOO-NYAWAT (Research), Assoc. Prof. APIWAN KAMLANG-EK (Special Affairs), Assoc. Prof. Dr SANTI WIRIYAWIT (Sri Racha Campus), Assoc Prof. CHAICHAN MAHASAWASDE (Student Affairs)

Registrar: BAWPIT CHARUBHUN
Librarian: RANGSAN PITIPUNYA

Library: see Libraries and Archives
Number of teachers: 2,066
Number of students: 41,885 (31,657 undergraduate, 10,228 postgraduate)

Publications: *Kasetsart Journal* (natural sciences edition, 4 a year; social sciences edition, 2 a year), *Knowledge of the Land* (university's academic affairs, in English, annually), *Non See Newsletter* (university news, in English, monthly)

DEANS

Faculty of Agriculture: THARMMASAK SOMMAR-TYA

Faculty of Agriculture (Kamphaeng Saen): SOMBAT CHINAWONG

Faculty of Agro-Industry: SIREE CHAISERI

Faculty of Architecture: PASINEE SUNAKORN

Faculty of Business Administration: SAMPAN HANPAYON

Faculty of Economics: JEERASAK PONGPISANU-PICHIT

Faculty of Education: PANIT KHEMTONG

Faculty of Engineering: NONTAWAT JUNJAR-EON

Faculty of Engineering (Kamphaeng Saen): SOMYOT CHIRNAKSORN

Faculty of Engineering (Sri Racha): OUICHEAI CHIRACHON

Faculty of Fisheries: YONT MUSIG

Faculty of Forestry: UTIS KUTINTARA

Faculty of Humanities: NONGNUCH SRIUSSA-DAPORN

Faculty of Liberal Arts and Management Science: VICHITRA POONPERMSUB

Faculty of Liberal Arts and Science: KANAPOL JUTAMANEE

Faculty of Management Sciences: AMNART THEERAVANICH

Faculty of Natural Resources and Agro-Industry: CHANVIT VAJRABUKKA

Faculty of Resources and Environment: MINGKWAN MINGMUANG

Faculty of Science: VINIJ JIAMSAKUL

Faculty of Science and Engineering: PONGSAK SURIYAVANAGUL

Faculty of Social Science: PHUANGPHET SUR-ATANAKAWEEKUL

Faculty of Veterinary Medicine: DHANIRAT SANTIVATR

Graduate School: VINAI ARTKONGHARN

DIRECTORS

Agro-Ecological System Research and Development Institute: NARONGCHAI PIPATTANA-WONG

Inseechandrasatitya Institute for Crop Research and Development: ED SARABOL

Institute of Food Research and Product Development: WARUNEE VARANYANOND

Kasetsart Agro-Industrial Product Improvement Institute: VICHAI HARUTHAITHANASAN

Kasetsart University Research and Development Institute: RUNGSIT SUWANKETNIKOM

National Swine Research and Training Center: SRISUWAN CHOMCHAI

Rajanagarindra Institute of Linguistics and Cultural Studies: SUCHAO PLOYCHUM

Suwanvajokkasikit Animal Research and Development Institute: SEKSOM ATTAMANG-KUNE

PROFESSORS

ADIVADHANASIT, C., Sociology
CHANDRAPATYA, A., Entomology
KANCHANALAI, T., Civil Engineering
KETSA, S., Horticulture
LAUSUNTHORN, N., Literature
LIMPOKA, M., Veterinary Pharmacology
NA NAKORN, U., Aquaculture
PANICHSAKPATANA, S., Soil Science
PONGTONGKAM, P., Genetics
ROADRANGKA, V., Education
ROJANARIDPICHED, C., Agronomy
RUJOPAKARN, W., Transportation Engineering
SOMMARTYA, T., Plant Pathology
SRINIVES, P., Agronomy
SUWANKETNIKOM, R., Agronomy
TANGTHAM, N., Forest Conservation
TUDSRI, S., Agronomy
YINGJAJAVAL, S., Soil Physics
YONGSMITH, B., Microbiology

KHON KAEN UNIVERSITY

123 Mitraparb Rd, Amphur Muang, Khon Kaen 40002

Telephone: (4320) 222241
Fax: (4324) 1216
E-mail: info@kku.ac.th
Internet: www.kku.ac.th

Founded 1964
State control
Language of instruction: Thai
Academic year: June to March (two semesters)

President: Assoc. Prof. Dr SUMON SAKOLCHAI
Vice-President for Academic and International Affairs: Assoc. Prof. Dr KUTHILDA TUAMSUK

Vice-President for Administrative Affairs: Assoc. Prof. DUMRONG HORMDEE

Vice-President for Planning and Information Technology: Asst Prof. AROM TATAWASART

Vice-President for Research: Asst Prof. PUSAN SIRITHORN

Vice-President for Special Affairs: Asst Prof. WICHAI NEERATANAPHAN

Vice-President for Student Affairs: Asst Prof. Dr ANAN HIRANSALEE

Vice-President for Student Development: Assoc. Prof. LIKHIT AMARTTAYAKONG

Vice-President for University Facilities: SUR-ACHET MANGMEESRI

Library of 339,614 vols
Number of teachers: 1,810
Number of students: 18,457

Publications: *Academic Services Newsletter* (monthly), *Architecture Journal* (4 a year), *Bulletin of Medical Technology and Physical Therapy* (4 a year), *Humanities and Social Sciences Journal* (4 a year), *Information* (2 a year), *I-San Journal of International Medicine* (4 a year), *Journal of Library and Information Science* (4 a year), *Journal of Learning and Teaching Competency* (4 a year), *Journal of Learning and Teaching Innovation* (4 a year), *Journal of Medical Technology and Physical Therapy* (4 a year), *Journal of Mekong Societies* (4 a year), *Journal of Nursing* (4 a year), *Kaen Kaset* (4 a year), *Khon Kaen Agriculture Journal* (6 a year), *KKU Daily News*, *KKU Dental Journal* (2 a year), *KKU Engineering Journal* (4 a year), *KKU Engineering Quarterly*, *KKU Health Sciences Center Bulletin* (6 a year), *KKU Health Sciences Center Newsletter* (weekly), *KKU Journal of Education* (4 a year), *KKU Journal of Management Science* (annually), *KKU Newsletter* (every 2 weeks), *KKU Quality Assurance Journal* (2 a year), *KKU VET Journal* (2 a year), *Science Journal* (4 a year), *Srinagarind Medical Journal* (4 a year)

DEANS

Faculty of Agriculture: Asst Prof. ASSANEE PRACHINBURAVAN

Faculty of Architecture: Asst. Prof. TANOO POLWAT

Faculty of Associated Medical Sciences: Assoc. Prof. YUPA UAVIJTIAROON

Faculty of Dentistry: Asst Prof. Dr NIWUT JUNTAVEE

Faculty of Education: Assoc. Prof. Dr SAMPAN PANPURK

Faculty of Engineering: Assoc. Prof. Dr WINIT CHINSUWAN

Faculty of Fine and Applied Arts: Assoc. Prof. Dr CHALERMSAK PIKULSRI

Faculty of Humanities and Social Sciences: Assoc. Prof. SRIPANYA CHAIYAI

Faculty of Management Sciences: Assoc. Prof. SUMETH KAENMANEE

Faculty of Medicine: Asst Prof. SUCHART AREEMITR

Faculty of Nursing: Asst Prof. Dr WANAPA SRITANYARAT

Faculty of Pharmaceutical Sciences: Assoc. Prof. SUMON SAKOLCHAI

Faculty of Public Health: Assoc. Prof. AROON JIRAWATKUL

Faculty of Sciences: Asst Prof. Dr WANCHAI SOOMLEG

Faculty of Technology: Asst Prof. Dr KRIENG-SAK SRISUK

Faculty of Veterinary Medicine: Assoc. Prof. PRACKAK PUAPERMPOONSRI

Graduate School: Assoc. Prof. Dr SOMMAI PRIPREM

ATTACHED CENTERS

Center of Arts and Culture: Dir Asst Prof. CHOB DEESUANKOK.

Computer Center: Dir Assoc. Prof. CHARAT MONKOLSAWAS.

Educational Service Center: Dir Asst Prof. Dr VEERAPONG SEANJAN.

Instructional Resources Center: Dir APAI PRAKOBPOL.

Queen Sirikit Heart Center: Dir Assoc. Prof. Dr SUNCHAI THEERAPONGPAKDEE.

Research and Development Institute: Dir Assoc. Prof. SUCHINT SIMARAKS (acting).

KING MONGKUT'S INSTITUTE OF TECHNOLOGY LADKRABANG

Chalongkrung Rd, Ladkrabang District, Bangkok 10520

Telephone: (2) 3269157
Fax: (2) 3267333
E-mail: inter@kmitl.ac.th
Internet: www.kmitl.ac.th

Founded 1960
State control
Academic year: June to March

President: Assoc. Prof. PRAKIT TANGTISANON
Vice-Presidents: SUCHEEP SUKSUPATH (Academic Affairs), KITTI TIRASESTH (Administration), SURAPOL SETHABUTR (Chumporn Campus), AMNOUY PANITKULPONG (Development), WILAIWAN WONYODPUN (Finance and Property), DUSANEE THANABORIPAT (International Affairs), KULTHORN LUERNSHAVEE (Planning), PACHERNCHAI CHAIYASITH (Student Affairs)
Administrative Officer: RUAMPORN INTARAPRASONG
Director of Central Library: OUEN PIN-NGERN
Library of 67,000 vols
Number of teachers: 808
Number of students: 15,052

Publications: *IT Journal* (2 a year), *Journal* (2 a year), *Journal of Science – Ladkrabang* (2 a year), *Ladkrabang Engin* (4 a year), *Research Abstracts* (irregular)

DEANS

Faculty of Agricultural Technology: JUTARAT SETHAKUL
Faculty of Architecture: EKAPHONG CHULASANIE
Faculty of Engineering: TAWIL PAUNGMA
Faculty of Industrial Education: PREEYAPORN WONGANUTROHD
Faculty of Information Technology: SURASIT VANNAKRAIROJN
Faculty of Science: THEERAWAT MONGKOLAUSSAWARATNA
Graduate School: MANAS SANGWORASIL

HEADS OF DEPARTMENTS

Faculty of Agricultural Technology:

Agri-Business and Administration: SAOVAKON LERDKANCHANA
Agricultural Techniques: SUKHUMAPORN KHANSRI
Agro-Industry: RATIPORN HARUENKIT
Animal Production Technology: RONNCHAI SITTHIGRIPONG
Fisheries Science: PAVEENA TAVEEKIGAKARN
Horticulture: SOMCHAI GLAHAN
Pest Management Technology: WARADEJ CHANTRASORN
Plant Production Technology: VICHAI LIMKANCHANAPONG
Soil Science: ITTHISUNTHORN NUNTAGIJ

Faculty of Architecture:

Architecture: SUPANAT NILTAT
Communication Arts and Design: CHIRAPHONG BHUMICHITR
Fine Arts: KIETTISAK CHANONNART
Industrial Design: SURAPOL PLEEKRAM
Interior Architecture: PORNCHAI BOONCHAIWATTANA
Urban and Regional Planning: SOPAK PASUKNIRANT

Faculty of Engineering:

Agricultural Engineering: SONGVOOT SANGCHAN

Chemical Engineering: PAISAL NAKPIPAT
Civil Engineering: DANG REANSUWAN
Computer Engineering: SOMSAK MITATHA
Control Engineering: SUTHIAN KIATSUNTHON
Electrical Engineering: PRAPART PRISUWANNA
Electronics: KITIPHON CHITSAKUL
Food Engineering: SATHIP RATANAPASAKORN
Industrial Instrumentation: KASET SIRISANTISAMRIT
Industrial Technology: UTHAI SRITHEERAVIROJANA
Mechanical Engineering: AKKRADECH SINDHUPHAK
Telecommunications Engineering: THONGTHOOD VANISRI

Faculty of Industrial Education:

Agricultural Education: KUNYA TUNTIVISOOTTIKUL
Architectural Education: SMITH WANGCHAROEN
Engineering Education: THEERAPHON THEPHASADIN NA AYUTHYA
Industrial Education: RAVEWAN SHINATRAKOOL
Languages and Social Sciences: SUKHUMAN NILRAT

Faculty of Information Technology:

Information Science, Information Technology Management: CHANBOON SATHITWIRIYAWONG

Faculty of Science:

Applied Biology: PLANEE DHITAPHICHIT
Applied Physics: SURAPOL RUKVICHAI
Applied Statistics: VARARAT RUANGRATTANAMETEE
Mathematics and Computer Science: PRAIBOON PANTAVAKPONG

KING MONGKUT'S INSTITUTE OF TECHNOLOGY NORTH BANGKOK

1518 Pibulsongkram Rd, Bangsue, Bangkok 10800

Telephone: (2) 913-2500
Fax: (2) 587-4350
E-mail: iro@kmitnb.ac.th
Internet: www.kmitnb.ac.th

Founded 1959
State control
Languages of instruction: Thai, English
Academic year: June to March

President: Prof. Dr TERAVUTI BOONYASOPON
Vice-President (Academic Affairs): Assoc. Prof. Dr CHANASAK BAITIANG
Vice-President (Administration and International Affairs): Asst Prof. WATANA PINSEM
Vice-President (Finance): Asst Prof. ACHARA SUNGSUWAN
Vice-President (Prachinburi Campus): Asst Prof. WORAWIT CHATURAPANICH
Vice-President (Research and Quality Assurance): Assoc. Prof. CHARN THANADNGARN
Vice-President (Student Affairs): Asst Prof. WITTAYA WIPAWIWAT
Vice-President (University Development and Promotion): ARUN PUTHAYANGKURA
Registrar: SANGOB KONGKA
Director of Central Library: MONTREE KHEMRACH

Number of teachers: 626
Number of students: 16,445

Publications: *Journal of King Mongkut's Institute of Technology North Bangkok* (in Thai, 6 a year), *Technical Education Development* (in Thai, 4 a year)

DEANS

Faculty of Agro-Industry: Asst Prof. MALEE SIMSRISAKUL (acting)

Faculty of Applied Arts: Assoc. Prof. SURAPHI TONSIENGSOM (acting)
Faculty of Applied Science: Asst Prof. WICHAI SURACHERDKIATI
Faculty of Engineering: Asst Prof. Dr SIRISAK HARNCHOOWONG
Faculty of Information Technology: Assoc. Prof. Dr MONCHAI TIANTONG (acting)
Faculty of Technical Education: Asst Prof. Dr PISIT METHAPATARA
Faculty of Technology and Industrial Management: PEERASAK SAREKUL
College of Industrial Technology: Asst Prof. PREECHA ONG-AREE
Graduate College: Asst Prof. Dr VIBOON CHUNKAG

HEADS OF DEPARTMENTS

Faculty of Applied Arts (tel. (2) 587-2096; fax (2) 587-2096; internet arts.kmitnb.ac.th):

Humanities: Assoc. Prof. WIMOL MUANKID
Languages: NANTAWAN WIMANRAT
Social Sciences: PHONGSAK KALSAVAPACKKUL

Faculty of Applied Science (tel. (2) 587-8249; fax (2) 587-8250; e-mail wsc@kmitnb.ac.th; internet www.sci.kmitnb.ac.th):

Agro-Industrial Technology: WITHAYA HLEKLAI
Applied Statistics: Dr WINAI BODHISUWAN
Computer and Information Science: Dr YAOWADEE TEMTANAPAT
Industrial Chemistry: Asst Prof. Dr NARONG PUNGWIWAT
Industrial Physics and Medical Instrumentation: PRAJUAB YOONGSUNTIA
Mathematics: Asst Prof. PREEYA KHUMSUP

Faculty of Engineering (tel. (2) 587-4351; fax (2) 585-6149; e-mail shw@kmitnb.ac.th; internet www.eng.kmitnb.ac.th):

Chemical and Process Engineering: Asst Prof. Dr ANURUK PETIRUKSAKUL
Civil Engineering: CHANARONG KUNTHAWETHEP
Electrical Engineering: Asst Prof. Dr PRAYOOT AKKARAEKTHALIN
Industrial Electrical Technology: Assoc. Prof. JIRASAK CHANWITITUM
Industrial Engineering: Dr YONGYUT PRUKSACHAT
Material Handling Technology: Assoc. Prof. YANYONG SRISOM
Mechanical Engineering: Asst. Prof. Dr SUTHUM PATUMSAWAD
Production Engineering: PRAMUK JENKITTIYON
Production Technology: CHITTAKORN SRONGTOHERISAHUL

Faculty of Technical Education (tel. (2) 585-0634; fax (2) 586-9015; e-mail psn@kmitnb.ac.th; internet www.teched.kmitnb.ac.th):

Computer Education: Dr CHARUN SANRACH
Teacher Training in Civil Engineering: PLERNPHIT PANKAEW
Teacher Training in Electrical Engineering: KAJORN INWONG
Teacher Training in Mechanical Engineering: Asst Prof. Dr SURAT PROMCHUN
Technical Education Management: Assoc. Prof. Dr WORAPOJ SRIWONGKOL
Technological Education: Asst Prof. TUANGRAT SRIWONGKOL

Faculty of Technology and Industrial Management (129 Tambon Noenhom, Amphur Muang, Prachinburi 25230; tel. (37) 215-881; fax (37) 213-367; e-mail wcp@kmitnb.ac.th):

Agricultural Machinery Technology: CHOOCHEEP KEAWUBON
Construction Technology: PICHET SOOKSAKSUN
Industrial Management: RAPEEPUN SIRIWATPATARA
Information Technology: PRADIT PITAKSATHIENKUL

College of Industrial Technology (tel. (2) 585-0691; fax (2) 587-4356; e-mail poa@kmitnb.ac.th; internet cit.kmitnb.ac.th):

Electrical Technology: ANAN WETWATANA
Civil Construction and Woodworking Technology: SOMBOON KONGSOMSAKSIRI
Mechanical Technology: Assoc. Prof. WANCHAI CHANTAWONG
Social and Applied Science: Asst Prof. KHANTAROSE SANWONG

ATTACHED INSTITUTES

Institute of Computer and Information Technology: Dir Assoc Prof. UDOM JEENPRADUP.

Institute for Technical Education Development: Dir Asst Prof. SOMNOEK WISSUTTIPAT.

Institute of Technological Development for Industry: Dir Assoc. Prof. Dr KANIT CHALOEYJANYA.

Thai-French Innovation Centre: Dir PANARIT SETAKUL.

KING MONGKUT'S UNIVERSITY OF TECHNOLOGY THONBURI

91 Pracha-utit Rd, Bangmod, Thungkruh, Bangkok 10140

Telephone: (2) 470-8000
Fax: (2) 427-9860
E-mail: int.off@kmutt.ac.th
Internet: www.kmutt.ac.th

Founded 1960 as Thonburi Technical Institute; combined with two other Institutes to form King Mongkut's Institute of Technology 1971, but regained autonomy as King Mongkut's Institute of Technology Thonburi 1986; present name and status 1998
State control
Languages of instruction: Thai, English
Academic year: June to March

President: Dr KRISSANAPONG KIRTIKARA
Senior Vice-President (Academic Affairs): Assoc. Prof. Dr SOMCHAI CHANCHAONA
Senior Vice-President (Administrative Affairs, Property and Finance): Assoc. Prof. Dr KESRA VAMMASIRI
Vice-President (Human Resources): Asst Prof. Dr SUPANEE LERTTRILUCK
Vice-President (KMUTT Campuses): Asst Prof. Dr SOLOT SUWANNAYUEN
Vice-President (Planning and Development): Assoc Prof. Dr BOONCHAROEN SIRINAOVAKUL
Vice-President (Student Affairs): NITHI BURANAJANT
Registrar: APAKORN PADUNGSATAYAWONG
Director of Library and Information Centre: Asst Prof. NONGNUCH PATHARAKORN
Library of 120,000 books, 2,200 periodicals, 2,000 CD-ROMs, 14 online databases
Number of teachers: 576
Number of students: 12,453

Publication: *Research and Development Journal* (4 a year)

DEANS

Faculty of Engineering: Assoc. Prof. AKE CHAISAWASD
Faculty of Science: Assoc. Prof. DECH BUDCHAROENTHONG
School of Architecture: Assoc. Prof Dr KRAIWOOD KIATTIKOMOL
School of Bioresources and Technology: Assoc. Prof. BOOSYA BUNNAG
Joint Graduate School of Energy and Environment: Assoc. Prof. Dr BUNDIT FUNGTHAMMASAN
School of Energy and Materials: Assoc. Prof. Dr APICHIT THERDYOTHIN
School of Industrial Education: Assoc Prof. SAK KONGSUWAN
School of Information Technology: Asst Prof. Dr BORWORN PAPASARATORN

School of Liberal Arts: Asst Prof. SASITORN SUWANNATHEP
Graduate School of Management and Innovation: Assoc. Prof. Dr PASIT LORTEERAPONG

PROFESSORS

CHUCHEEPSAKUL, S., Civil Engineering
CHULLABODHI, C., Energy Management Technology
JIRARATANANON, R., Chemical Engineering
SOPONRONNARIT, S., Energy Technology
WONGWISES, S., Mechanical Engineering

ATTACHED INSTITUTE

Institute of Field Robotics: Dir Assoc. Prof. Dr DJITT LAOWATTANA.

KRIRK UNIVERSITY

43/1111 Ram-Indra Rd, Bangkhem, Bangkok 10220

Telephone: (2) 552-3500
Fax: (2) 552-3511
E-mail: phakaphan@krirk.ac.th
Internet: www.krirk.ac.th

Founded 1952
Private control
Academic year: June to May

President: DHATTONG VIRIYAVEJAKUL
Vice-Presidents: BENJA MANGALAPRUEK, Assoc. Prof. Dr MANOON PAHIRAH

Library of 68,000 books, 419 periodicals
Number of teachers: 130
Number of students: 3,445 (2,955 undergraduate, 490 postgraduate)

DEANS

Faculty of Business Administration: SANONG DEPRADIT
Faculty of Communication Arts and Liberal Arts: Prof. Maj.-Gen. SANITPONG KHEMTONG
Faculty of Economics: Asst Prof. Dr BUNSERM BUNCHAROENPOL
Faculty of Law: Pol. Maj.-Gen. Dr SAWADI SORALUM
Graduate School: Assoc. Prof. Dr MANOON PAHIRAH (acting)

MAE FAH LUANG UNIVERSITY

333 Moo 1, Muang District, Chiangrai 57100
Telephone: (53) 706-175
Fax: (53) 706-174
E-mail: postmaster@mua.go.th
Internet: www.mfu.ac.th

President: WANCHAI SIRICHANA (acting)

Schools of Agricultural Technology, Biotechnology, Information Technology, Liberal Arts, Management Science and Science.

MAEJO UNIVERSITY

Sansai, Chiang Mai 50290
Telephone: (53) 873-000
Fax: (53) 498-861
Internet: www.mju.ac.th

Founded 1934; present name 1992 (fmrly Maejo Institute of Agricultural Technology)
State control
Language of instruction: Thai
Academic year: June to March

President: Dr THEP PHONGPARNICH
Vice-President (Academic Affairs): Dr SONGVUT PHETPRADAP
Vice-President (Administration): Prof. ARKORN KANJANAPHACHOT
Vice-President (Education Quality Standards): Prof. PENRUT HONGWITAYAKO
Vice-President (Planning and International Affairs): Dr NUMCHAI THANUPON

Vice-President (Student Affairs): Prof. MANAS GUMPUKUL (acting)
Registrar: KRISSADA BHACKDEE
Librarian: WASSANA PHONGPAL

Library of 86,000 vols, 892 periodicals
Number of teachers: 1,190
Number of students: 8,809

Publications: *Journal of Agricultural Research and Extension* (every 2 months, in Thai, with English summaries), *Maejo Journal* (every 2 months, in Thai)

DEANS

Faculty of Agricultural Business: Prof. NAPAPORN MECKHAYAI
Faculty of Agricultural Production: Dr PISOOT NIUMSUP
Faculty of Engineering and Agro-Industry: Assoc. Prof. KITTIPONG VUTIJUMNONK
Faculty of Science: PRASAN WONGMANEERUNG

HEADS OF DEPARTMENTS

Faculty of Agricultural Business (tel. (53) 498-150; fax (53) 498-151):

Agricultural Economics and Co-operatives: Prof. VICHAI TANVATANAGUL
Agricultural Extension: Dr WEERAPON THONGMA
Business Administration and Agricultural Marketing: Prof. JONGKOL SAENG-ASAPHAWIRIYA
General Education: ADISORN KHUNTAROSE

Faculty of Agricultural Production (tel. (53) 878-088, fax (53) 498-157):

Agronomy: Prof. APICHAT SUNAKHAMGONG
Animal Technology: Dr SUKIT KHANTAPRAB
Fisheries Technology: Prof. APINAN SUWANNARAK
Horticulture: Dr YONGYUTH SRIGIEWFUN
Landscape and Environmental Conservation: SOPON MONGKOLWAT
Plant Protection: Prof. KAYAN SUWAN
Soil and Environmental Resources: Prof. BANPOTE TANT

Faculty of Engineering and Agro-Industry (tel. (53) 878-113; fax (53) 878-113):

Agriculture and Food Engineering: Prof. BUNDIT HIRANSATITPORN
Food Technology: Dr THANET KEOKAMNERD
Post-harvest Technology: Dr SURAT NUGLOR

Faculty of Science (tel. (53) 878-229; fax (53) 878-225):

Biology: Dr TAPANA CHUENBAL
Chemistry: SIRIRAT PAISANSUTHICOL
Computer Science: SNIT SITTHI
Mathematics and Statistics: Prof. PUENGPORN NIUMSUP
Physics: Prof. UTAIWAN TIWATHANON

MAHANAKORN UNIVERSITY OF TECHNOLOGY

51 Cheum Sampan Rd, Nong Chok, Bangkok 10530
E-mail: www@mut.ac.th
Internet: www.mut.ac.th

Founded 1990 as Mahanakorn College
Chancellor: Prof. Dr YONGYUT SATJAVANIT
Vice-Chancellor: YOUNGSAK KANATANAVANIT

Departments of Computer Engineering, Telecommunication Engineering, Control and Instrument Engineering, Electrical Engineering, Electrical Power Engineering, Mechanical Engineering, Chemical Engineering, Civil Engineering, Business Computer, Management, Finance and Banking, Marketing, Industrial Management, Business Communication Arts, Accountancy, Chemistry, Physics, Mathematics, Physiology, Anatomy, Microbiology, Pathology, Pharmacology and Parasitology.

MAHASARAKHAM UNIVERSITY

Tambon Kamriang, Kantarawichai District, Maha Sarakham 44150

Telephone: (43) 75-4241
Fax: (43) 75-4241
E-mail: webmaster@msu.ac.th
Internet: www.msu.ac.th

Founded 1994 from Mahasarakham College of Education and Mahasarakham campus of Srinakarinwirot University
State control
Academic year: June to March

President: Prof. Dr ADULYA VIRIYAVEJAKUL
Vice-Presidents: Dr CHINDA NGAMSUTDI (Educational Quality Enhancement), Asst Prof. SAKOL KONGBOON (Finance and President's Office), Asst Prof. Dr SANGKOM PUMIPUNTU (International Relations and Special Affairs), YUWADEE TAPANEEYAKORN (Planning and Budgeting), Dr SUPPHACHAI SAMAPPITO (Research and Academic Student Affairs), Asst Prof. Dr PISSAMAI SRI-AMPAI (Staff Development)
Director of Academic Resource Centre: Dr SUJIN BUTDISUWAN

Library of 155,000 books, 50,000 periodicals
Number of teachers: 792
Number of students: 24,878

DEANS

Faculty of Accounting and Management: MONGKHON MOUNGKIEO
Faculty of Architecture, Urban Design and Creative Arts: Assoc. Prof. MANEE PANICHKARN
Faculty of Education: Assoc. Prof. Dr PRASART ISARAPREEDA
Faculty of Engineering: Prof. Dr SOMCHART SOPONRONNARIT
Faculty of Fine and Applied Arts: NONTHIVATHN CHANDHANAPHALIN
Faculty of Graduate Studies: Assoc. Prof. PAITOOL SUKSRINGARM
Faculty of Humanities and Social Sciences: Asst Prof. Dr THAVEESILP SUBWATTANA
Faculty of Informatics: Asst Prof. Dr SANGKOM PUMIPUNTU
Faculty of Medicine: Prof. Dr SOMPORN POTINAM
Faculty of Nursing: Assoc. Prof. Dr DARUNEE RUJKORNKARN
Faculty of Pharmacy and Health Sciences: Dr BUDDHIPONG SATAYAVONGTHIP
Faculty of Public Health: Assoc. Prof. SOMJIT SUPANNATAS
Faculty of Science: Prof. Dr ROEN SAMANA
Faculty of Technology: Assoc. Prof. Dr SANHA PANICHAJAKUL
Faculty of Tourism and Hotel Management: TANES SRISATIT
College of Politics and Governance: Dr SOMCHAI PHATHARATHANANUNTH

ATTACHED RESEARCH INSTITUTES

Academic Resource Center: Dir KANNIGAR CHOLLAMPE.

Computer Center: Dir TAWEECHAI SITTISORN.

Palaeontological Research and Education Center: Dir Dr ERIC BUFFETAUT.

Research Institute of Northeastern Arts and Culture: Dir Dr SONGKOON CHANTAGHON.

Silk Innovation Center: Dir Asst Prof. Dr WANCHAI DE-EKNAMKUL.

Walai Rukhavej Botanical Research Institute: Dir Assoc. Prof. Dr PREECHA PRATHEPHA.

MAHIDOL UNIVERSITY

999 Phuttamonthon 4 Rd, Salaya, Phuttamonthon, Nakorn Pathom 73170

Telephone: (2) 849-6000
Fax: (2) 849-6222
E-mail: orbsw@mahidol.ac.th
Internet: www.mahidol.ac.th

Founded 1890 as Siriraj Medical School; present name 1969
State control

President: Prof. PORNCHAI MATANGKASOMBUT
Vice-President: Prof. AMARET BHUMIRATANA
Vice-President (Academic Infrastructures Development): Assoc. Prof. SUPACHAI TANGWONGSAN
Vice-President (Administration and Quality): Assoc. Prof. SUDHIN YOOSOOK
Vice-President (Campus): Asst Prof. NOPADUL CHAIKUM
Vice-President (Domestic and Overseas Networking Development): Prof. KHUNYING SURIYA RATANAKUL
Vice-President (Finance and Budgeting): Assoc. Prof. SOMPORN
Vice-President (Law and Regulation Development): Asst Prof. SINGHAPAN TONGSAWAS
Vice-President (Policy and Planning): Assoc. Prof. VIRAPONG PRACHAYASITTIKUL
Vice-President (Sports and Special Affairs): Assoc. Prof. PRASERT SARNVIVAT
Vice-President (Research): Prof. SRISIN KHUSMITH
Vice-President (Student Affairs Development): Assoc. Prof. SRIPRASIT BOONVISUT

Library of 1,000,000 vols and bound periodicals, 6,500 current periodicals, 800 audiovisual units, theses, reports, CD-ROMs and online databases; 13 br. libraries
Number of teachers: 2,819 (incl. 128 full professors, 788 assoc. professors, 818 asst professors)
Number of students: 18,135

Publications: *Bulletin of the Faculty of Medical Technology* (2 a year), *Journal of Ecosystem Perspectives* (3 a year), *Journal of Health Education* (2 a year), *Journal of Language and Culture* (3 a year), *Journal of Nursing* (3 a year), *Journal of Pharmaceutical Sciences* (4 a year), *Journal of Public Health* (3 a year), *Mahidol Journal* (2 a year), *Mahidol Dental Journal* (3 a year), *MU Annual Research Abstracts*, *Music Journal* (4 a year), *Ramathibodi Medical Journal* (4 a year), *Ramathibodi Nursing Journal* (3 a year), *Siriraj Hospital Gazette* (monthly)

DEANS

Faculty of Dentistry: Assoc. Prof. JURAI NAKAPARKSIN
Faculty of Engineering: Asst Prof. PIYA RATANASUWAN
Faculty of Environmental and Resource Studies: Assoc. Prof. ANUCHAT POUNGSOMLEE
Faculty of Graduate Studies: Assoc. Prof. RASSAMIDARAI HOONSAWAT
Faculty of Medical Technology: Assoc. Prof. CHATCHAI SORNCHAIL
Faculty of Medicine, Ramathibodi Hospital: Prof. PRAKIT VATHESATOGKIT
Faculty of Medicine, Siriraj Hospital: Clin. Prof. PIYASAKOL SAKOLSATHYATORN
Faculty of Nursing: Assoc. Prof. KOBKUL PHANCHAROENWORAKUL
Faculty of Pharmacy: Prof. PORNCHAI MATANGKASOMBUT (acting)
Faculty of Public Health: Assoc. Prof. CHALERMCHAI CHAOKITTIPORN
Faculty of Science: Prof. PRASERT SOBHON
Faculty of Social Sciences and Humanities: Asst Prof. SUREE KANJANAWONG
Faculty of Tropical Medicine: Prof. SORNCHAI LOAREESUWAN

Faculty of Veterinary Science: Asst Prof. PARNTEP RATANAKORN

DIRECTORS

Applied and Technological Service Center: Prof. AMARET BHUMIRATANA
ASEAN Institute for Health Development: Asst Prof. BOONYOUNG KIEWKANKA
College of Management: Asst Prof. LIANGCHAI LIMLOMWONGSE
College of Music: Assoc. Prof. SUGREE CHAREONSOOK
College of Religious Studies: Assoc. Prof. PINIT RATANAKUL
College of Sports Science and Technology: Asst Prof. PANYA KAIMUK
Institute for Innovation and Development of Learning Process: Prof. BINYO PANIJPAN
Institute for Population and Social Research: Assoc. Prof. BENCHA YODDUMNERN-ATTIG
Institute of Language and Culture for Rural Development: Assoc. Prof. SUWILAI PREMSRIRAT
Institute of Molecular Biology and Genetics: Prof. AMARET BHUMIRATANA
Institute of Nutrition: Assoc. Prof. EMORN WASANTWISUT
Institute of Science and Technology for Research and Development: Prof. KANOK PAVASUTHIPAISIT
National Doping Control Center: Assoc. Prof. TONGTAVUCH ANUKARAHANONTA
National Institute for Child and Family Development: Assoc. Prof. NITTAYA KOTCHABHAKDI
National Laboratory Animal Center: WANTANEE RATANASAK
Ratchasuda College: JITPRAPA SRI-ON
Salaya Center: Assoc. Prof. VIRAPONG PRACHAYASITTIKUL
University Computing Center: Assoc. Prof. JARERNSRI MITRPANONT
University International College: Prof. CHARIYA R. BROCKELMAN
University Library and Information Center: Assoc. Prof. SUPACHAI TANGWONGSAN

NARESUAN UNIVERSITY

Phitsanulok 65000

Telephone: (55) 261000
E-mail: international@nu.ac.th
Internet: www.nu.ac.th

Founded 1990
State control
Academic year: June to March

Library of 120,000 vols
Number of teachers: 867
Number of students: 21,435

Publications: *Naresuan University Journal*, *Naresuan University Newsletter* (monthly).

NATIONAL INSTITUTE OF DEVELOPMENT ADMINISTRATION

118 Seri Thai Rd, Klongchan, Bangkapi, Bangkok 10240

Telephone: (2) 377-7400
Fax: (2) 375-8798
E-mail: nisnida@nida.nida.ac.th
Internet: www.nida.ac.th

Founded 1966
State control
Languages of instruction: Thai, English
Academic year: June to May (3 semesters)

President: Assoc. Prof. Dr PREECHA JARUNGIDANAN
Vice-President for Academic Affairs: Assoc. Prof. Dr SAGOL JARIYAVIDYANONT
Vice-President for Administration: Assoc. Prof. CHAMAIPORN KUNAKEMAKORN
Vice-President for Planning: Prof. Dr CHARTCHAI NA CHIANGMAI

Library of 233,000 vols

Number of teachers: 155
Number of students: 10,391

Publications: *NIDA Annual Report, NIDA Bulletin* (6 a year), *Thai Journal of Development Administration* (4 a year)

DEANS

School of Applied Statistics: Assoc. Prof. Dr JIRAWAN JITHAVECH

School of Business Administration: Dr THAKOL NUNTHIRAPAKORN

School of Development Economics: Asst Prof. Dr WISARN PUPPHAVESA

School of Language and Communication: Assoc. Prof. Dr PATCHAREE POKASAMRIT

School of Public Administration: Prof. Dr SOMBAT THAMRONGTHANYAWONG

School of Social Development: Asst Prof. Dr TONG-ON MUNJAITON

DIRECTORS

Library and Information Center: SIRIPORN SUWANNA

Research Center: Assoc. Prof. Dr SAGOL JARIYAVIDYANONT (acting)

Training Center: Dr BOORAPA CHODCHOEY (acting)

Graduate Development Center: Assoc. Prof. Dr SAGOL JARIYAVIDYANONT (acting)

Graduate Programme in Human Resource Development: Asst Prof. Dr MANEEWAN CHAT-UTHAI (acting)

PROFESSORS

School of Applied Statistics (tel. (2) 375-8944; fax (2) 374-4061; e-mail jirawan@nida.nida.ac.th):

   SUWATTEE, P., Statistics

School of Business Administration (tel. (622) 375-8874; fax (662) 374-3282; e-mail thakol@nida.nida.ac.th):

   CHAMNONG, V., Organizational Behaviour

School of Public Administration (tel. (662) 375-1296; fax (662) 375-1297; e-mail sombat@nida.nida.ac.th):

   CHANGRIEN, P., Political Science
   PERMANJIT, G., City and Regional Planning
   THAMRONGTANYAWONG, S., Public Policy and Planning

School of Social Development (tel. (662) 375-9111; fax (662) 375-0941; e-mail tangon@nida.nida.ac.th):

   BHANTHUMNAVIN, D., Social Psychology
   NORANITPADUNGKARN, C., Social Sciences
   SMUCKARN, S., Social Psychology

PAYAP UNIVERSITY

Amphur Muang, Chiang Mai 50000

Telephone: (53) 851-478
Fax: (53) 241-983
E-mail: intexch@payap.ac.th
Internet: www.payap.ac.th

Founded 1974
Private control
Languages of instruction: Thai, English
Academic year: June to March (Thai Program);September to April (English Program)

President: Dr BOONTHONG POOCHAROEN
Vice-Presidents: Dr YUWALAK CHIVAKIDAKARN (Academic Affairs), Dr RUX PROHMPALIT (Finance), MARTHA G. BUTT (International Affairs), Dr TAWEESAK SUPASA (Planning and Development), Dr ESTHER WAKEMAN (Religious Affairs)
Librarian: SUNTREE RATAYA-ANANT

Library of 125,100 vols
Number of teachers: 390
Number of students: 9,000

Publication: *Payap Journal* (annually)

DEANS

Faculty of Accountancy, Finance and Banking: MANIT PABUT

Faculty of Business Administration: YUVALUCK CHIVAKIDAKARN

Faculty of Humanities: Dr NARONG PRACHAKHESUWAT

Faculty of Law: Dr KHETTAI LANGKARPINT

Faculty of Nursing: KAMOLWAN DISABUT

Faculty of Science: DUANGDUEN POOCHAROEN

Faculty of Social Science: MONTHATHIP RUNGRUANGSRI

Faculty of Theology: Rev. WILLIAM J. YODER

Graduate School: Dr RATANAPORN SETHAKUL

International College: Dr TAWAT BUNREUANG

ATTACHED INSTITUTES

Christian Communications Institute: Dir Rev. ROBERT S. COLLINS.

Institute for the Study of Religion and Culture: Dir JOHN W. BUTT.

Research and Development Institute: Dir Dr SUCHIRA PRAYULPITAK.

PRINCE OF SONGKLA UNIVERSITY

71/1 Moo. 5 Thanon Karnjanavanich Tambon Kor-Hong, POB Hat-Yai, Hat-Yai District, Songkla 90110

Fax: (74) 211030 (Hat-Yai Campus); (74) 212828
E-mail: hatyai-pr@psu.ac.th
Internet: www.psu.ac.th

Founded 1967
State control
Languages of instruction: Thai, English
Academic year: June to March (two semesters)

President: Assoc. Prof. Dr SUNTHORN SOTTHIBANDHU

Vice-President for Academic Affairs (Hat-Yai Campus): Dr PAIRAT SA-NGUANSAI

Vice-President for Academic Affairs (Pattani Campus): Asst Prof. Dr SUWIMON KIEWKAEW

Vice-President for Development: Asst Prof. Dr SUJITRA JARAJIT

Vice-President for Development Affairs (Pattani Campus): PRAMOTE KRAMUT

Vice-President, Hat-Yai Campus: Asst Prof. Dr METHI SUNBHANICH

Vice-President, Pattani Campus: Asst Prof. PRAPAN WISETRATTAKAM

Vice-President for Planning and Development: Assoc. Prof. UDOM CHOMCHAN

Vice-President for Research and International Relations: Assoc. Prof. Dr PRASERT CHITAPONG

Vice-President for Special Affairs (Pattani Campus): PANN YAUNLAIE

Assistant Presidents (Hat-Yai Campus): Asst Prof. Dr SUJITRA JORAJIT (Academic Affairs), PARIPON PATTANASATTAYAVONG (Physical Facilities), Asst Prof. SUPOTE KOVITAVA (Student Activities), JEDSADA MOKHAGUL (Student Development), Asst Prof. Dr WINIT JUNGCHAROENTHAM (System Development)

Assistant Presidents (Pattani Campus): Asst Prof. SUTHEP SANTIVARANON (Academic Affairs), SOMKIAT SUKNUNPONG (Administration), PHAYAM PHETKLA (International Relations), Asst Prof. WERA MANUSAVANICH (Student Affairs)

Number of teachers: 1,428
Number of students: 13,048

Publications: *PSU Arts and Culture, PSU Newsletter*

DEANS

Faculty of Agro-Industry (Hat-Yai Campus): Assoc Prof. PAIBOON THAMMARATWASIK

Faculty of Dentistry (Hat-Yai Campus): KRASSANAI WONGRANGSIMAKUL

Faculty of Education (Pattani Campus): Asst Prof. Dr WIRAT THUMMARPORN

Faculty of Engineering (Hat-Yai Campus): PICHIT RERNGSANGVATANA

Faculty of Environmental Management Establishment Project (Hat-Yai Campus): Asst Prof. Dr CHADCHAI RATANACHAI

Faculty Establishment Project of Hotel and Tourism Management: Assoc. Prof. MANAT CHAISAWAT (Dir)

Faculty of Humanities and Social Sciences (Pattani Campus): Asst Prof. PRAPAN WISETRATAKAN

Faculty of Management Science (Hat-Yai Campus): Asst Prof. Dr SOMPORN FUANGCHAN

Faculty of Medicine (Hat-Yai Campus): Assoc. Prof. PUNTIPYA SANGUANCHUA

Faculty of Natural Resources (Hat-Yai Campus): Assoc. Prof. Dr SOMKIAT SAITANOO

Faculty of Nursing (Hat-Yai Campus): Asst Prof. Dr SUNUTTRA TABOONPONG

Faculty of Pharmaceutical Science (Hat-Yai Campus): Asst Prof. Dr PITI TRISDIKOON

Faculty of Science (Hat-Yai Campus): Prof. PUANGPEN SIRIRUGSA

Faculty of Science and Technology (Pattani Campus): Asst Prof. PREECHA THANACHAI

College of Islamic Studies: Dr ISMA-AE ALEE (Dir)

Phuket Community College: Asst Prof. PUVADON BUTTRAT (Dir)

Surat Thani Community College: SORAT MAGBOON (Dir)

Trang Province Educational Extension Project: Assoc. Prof. SOMKAEW RUNGIERDKRIENGKRAI (Dir)

HEADS OF DEPARTMENTS

Hat-Yai Campus:

Faculty of Agro-Industry:

   Agro-industrial Technology: Assoc. Prof. PAIBOON THAMMARATWASIK (acting)
   Food Technology: Dr SUANYA CHANTHACHUM
   Industrial Biotechnology: Assoc. Prof. Dr POONSUK PRASERTSUB
   Material Product Technology: Dr CHAIRAT SIRIPATANA
   Graduate School: Asst Prof. Dr KHARN CHANPROMMA

Faculty of Dentistry:

   Conservative Dentistry: PRATINYA RATANACHONT
   Oral Biology and Occlusion: Asst Prof. SITTICHAI KUNTHONGKAWE
   Preventive Dentistry: SUPANEE SUNTHORNLOHANAKUL
   Prosthetic Dentistry: Asst Prof. POTJANARAT BENJAKUL
   Stomatology: Asst Prof. RAWE TEANPAISAN
   Surgery: Asst Prof. PRISANA PRIPATNANONT

Faculty of Engineering:

   Chemical Engineering: Asst Prof. CHAKRIT THONGURAI
   Civil Engineering: Asst Prof. Dr VACHARA THAONGCHAROEN
   Computer Engineering: WEERAPANT MUSIGASARN
   Electrical Engineering: Dr PRAKARN KURAHONGSA
   Industrial Engineering: SANE THANTHADALUGSANA
   Mechanical Engineering: PAIROJ KIRIRAT
   Mining and Metallurgical Engineering: Asst Prof. Dr DANUPON TANNAYOPAS

Faculty of Management Science:

   Business Administration: Asst Prof. PRALOM CHAIRATANAPONG
   Educational Foundation: SUNUNTRA CHUSCHART
   Public Administration: Asst Prof. TEERACHAI POOPAIBOOL

Faculty of Medicine:

Anaesthesiology: Asst Prof. LUKSAMEE CHARNVATE

Biomedical Sciences: SUVINA RATANA-CHAIYAVONG

Community Medicine: Asst Prof. Dr THA-WAN BENJAWONG

Internal Medicine: Asst Prof. UTHAI KHOW-EAN

Obstetrics and Gynaecology: Asst Prof. VERAPOL CHANDEYING

Ophthalmology: Asst Prof. SUCHITRA KANOK-KANTAPONG

Orthopaedic Surgery and Physical Therapy: Assoc. Prof. NIRAN KIATSIRIROJE

Otolaryngology: Asst Prof. SUMATE PERA-VUT

Paediatrics: Asst Prof. NARUMON PATARA-KITVANICH

Pathology: Asst Prof. SINEENART KALANU-WAKUL

Psychiatry: CHARNVIT NGENSRITRAKUL

Radiology: SOMCHAI WATTANAAARPORNCHAI

Surgery: Dr PRASERT VASINANUKORN

Faculty of Natural Resources:

Agricultural Development: Assoc. Prof. KRIANGSAK PATTAMARAKHA

Agricultural Economics and Agricultural Projects: Asst Prof. SOMBOON CHARERN-JIRATRAGUL

Animal Science: Asst Prof. PEERASAK SUT-TIYOTIN

Aquatic Science: Dr KIDCHAKAN SUPAMAT-TAYA

Earth Science: NIPA PANAPITUKKUL

Pest Management Unit: Asst Prof. Dr SURAKRAI PERMKAM

Plant Science: Asst Prof. Dr PRAVIT SOPA-NODON

Faculty of Nursing:

Administration in Nursing Education and Nursing Service: SAWITEE LYMCHAIAR-UNNRUNG

Fundamental Nursing: SIRIRATANA KOSAL-WATANA

Medical Nursing: JARUWAN MANASURAKAM

Obstetrical-Gynaecological Nursing and Midwifery: WATTANA SRIPOTEJANARD

Paediatric Nursing: Dr LADDA PRATEEP-CHAIKOOL

Public Health Nursing: Asst Prof. SUPANEE ONCHUNCHIT

Psychiatric Nursing: TIPPA CHETCHAOVALIT

Surgical Nursing: PINTIPAYA NARKDUM

Faculty of Pharmaceutical Science:

Clinical Pharmacy: Asst Prof. WANTANA LIANGMONGKOL

Pharmaceutical Chemistry: Dr VIMON TAN-TISHAIYAKUL

Pharmaceutical Technology: Asst Prof. ARUNSRI SUNTHORNPIT

Pharmacognosy and Pharmaceutical Botany: Asst Prof. ARUNPORN ITHARAT

Pharmacy Administration: AUTTAPORN SORNLERTLAMVANICH

Faculty of Science:

Anatomy: ARAYA ADUNTRAKOOL

Biochemistry: Assoc. Prof. PRAPAPORN UTARAPHUN

Biology: Assoc. Prof. JUTAMARD PHOLPUNTIN

Chemistry: Assoc. Prof. CHANITA PONGLI-MANONT

Foreign Languages: ADISA SAETEAU

General Science: Asst Prof. MANIDA PETCH-ARAT

Mathematics: Asst Prof. BUNCHERD PUD-TIKTI

Microbiology: VIVID SOMSARN

Pharmacology: PERARATCH THAINA

Physics: Dr WORAVUT LOHAVIJARN

Physiology: Assoc. Prof. PRADUP PRASART-KAEW

Pattani Campus:

Faculty of Education:

Demonstration School: Asst Prof. NONGNAT SATHAWARODOM (Dir)

Education: WITHADA SINPRAJUKPOL

Educational Administration: SOMKIAT PUANGROD

Educational Evaluation and Research: THAWEE THONGKUM

Educational Technology: Asst Prof. PORNTHEP MUANGMAN

Physical Education: CHARUS CHOOMUANG

Psychology and Guidance: PRASERT CHUS-ING

Faculty of Humanities and Social Sciences:

Eastern Languages: WORAWIT BARU

Geography: Asst Prof. PERM NILRAT

History and Art: SOMBOON THANASOOK

Library Science: Assoc. Prof. Dr DHIDA BODHIBUKKANA

Philosophy and Religion: Asst Prof. Dr PAITOON PATYAIYING

Social Sciences: Asst Prof. NIPA CHAISAVATE

Thai Language: Assoc. Prof. WANNAO YUDEN

Western Languages: CHAILERT KITPRASERT

Faculty of Science and Technology:

Home Economics: SUEBSAK GLINSORN

Mathematics and Computer Science: KANDA YANSAN

Rubber Technology and Polymer Science: ADISAI RUNGVICHANIWAT

Science: NOPPORN REINTHONG

Technology and Industry: SOMSAK LAO-CHAREONSUK

College of Islamic Studies:

Islamic Studies: ROHEEM NIYOMDECHA

RAMKHAMHAENG UNIVERSITY

Ramkhamhaeng Rd, Huamark, Bangkok 10240

Telephone: (2) 310-8118

Fax: (2) 310-8022

E-mail: admin@ram1.ru.ac.th

Internet: www.ru.ac.th

Founded 1971

State control

Languages of instruction: Thai, English

Academic year: June to March (two semesters)

Rector: Prof. RANGSAN SAENGSOOK

Vice-Rector for Academic Affairs and Research: Prof. Dr CHUTA THIANTHAI

Vice-Rector for Administration: Assoc. Prof. PRASAT SANGASILP

Vice-Rector for Amnartcharoen Province Regional Campus: Asst Prof. CHALERMCHAI PIWRUANGNONT

Vice-Rector for Campus Affairs: Assoc. Prof. KIM CHAISANSOOK

Vice-Rector for Cultural Affairs: Dr WICHAI SUNGPRAPAI

Vice-Rector for Development: Assoc. Prof. WIRAT SANGUANWONWAN

Vice-Rector for Educational Technology: Asst Prof. Dr PANYA SIRIROJ

Vice-Rector for Finance: Assoc. Prof. SOM-CHINTANA SIVALI

Vice-Rector for General Affairs: Assoc. Prof. ARUNTAVADEE PHATNIBUL

Vice-Rector for International Affairs: Assoc. Prof. RAMPAI SIRIMANAKUL

Vice-Rector for Khon Kaen Province Regional Campus: Assoc. Prof. VICHAI THARANONT

Vice-Rector for Legal Affairs and Property: Prof. SURACHAI SUWANPREECHA

Vice-Rector for Nakhornpanom Province Regional Campus: Asst Prof. VIBOON TOVA-NABOOT

Vice-Rector for Nakhornratsrima Province Regional Campus: Assoc. Prof. VISIT TAWEESET

Vice-Rector for Nakhornsrithammarat Province Regional Campus: Assoc. Prof. Dr AROM CHANUANCHIT

Vice-Rector for Policy and Planning: Assoc. Prof. MANOP PRAMANACHOTE

Vice-Rector for Prachinburi Province Regional Campus: Asst Prof. CHAMNAN TEM-MUANGPUK

Vice-Rector for Prae Province Regional Campus: Assoc. Prof. KULYANEE TARASUEB

Vice-Rector for Public Relations: Assoc. Prof. Dr WISANU SUWANA-PERM

Vice-Rector of the Rector's Office: Assoc. Prof. Dr KHOSIT INTAWONGSE

Vice-Rector for Sri Sa Ket Province Regional Campus: WICHIAN CHUENCHOB

Vice-Rector for Student Affairs: Assoc. Prof. SUMETH KAEWPRAG

Vice-Rector for Sukhothai Province Regional Campus: Asst Prof. SAMRAN SOMBOONPHOL

Vice-Rector for Trang Regional Campus: Assoc. Prof. PETJARAPORN JANTARASUT

Vice-Rector for University Affairs: Assoc. Prof SITTIPAN BUDDHAHUN

Vice-Rector for Uthaithani Province Regional Campus: Asst Prof. ROENGRAK JAMPANGOEN

Vice-Rector for Welfare: Assoc. Prof. NOPPA-KUN KUNACHEVA

Number of teachers: 852

Number of students: 340,231 (329,599 undergraduate, 10,632 graduate)

Publication: *Ramkhamhaeng University Newsletter* (weekly)

DEANS

Faculty of Business Administration: Prof. RANGSAN SAENGSOOK (acting)

Faculty of Economics: Assoc. Prof. VANCHAI RIMVITAGAYORN

Faculty of Education: Assoc. Prof. RAVIWAN SRIKRAMKRAN

Faculty of Engineering: Asst Prof. SUVAT SRIVITHAYARAKS

Faculty of Humanities: Assoc. Prof. Dr PIT SOMPONG

Faculty of Law: Assoc. Prof. JARAL LENGVIT-TAYA

Faculty of Political Science: Assoc. Prof. PRONCHAI DHEBPANYA

Faculty of Science: Assoc. Prof. SUPOTE CHAITIUMVONG

HEADS OF DEPARTMENTS

Business Administration (tel. (2) 310-8226; fax (2) 319-2160; internet www.bus.ru.ac.th):

Accounting: Asst Prof. Dr CHAINARIN WEER-ASTAVANICH

Advertising and Public Relations: Assoc. Prof. LADDAWAN YOMCHINDA

General Management: SOMPON THUNGWA

Marketing: Assoc. Prof. PANPIMOL KANKA-NOKE

Money and Banking: Assoc. Prof. ARUNEE NARINTRAKU NA AYUTHYA

Service Industries: Asst Prof. TIPPAVAN POOMMANEE

Economics (tel. (2) 310-8514; fax (2) 318-8905; internet www.eco.ru.ac.th):

Agricultural Economics: Assoc. Prof. KRI-SORN KUEPRAKONE

Development Economics: Assoc. Prof. Dr SOMBOON SUPASILPA

Economic History: Assoc. Prof. ASSUMPINA-PONG CHUTTRAKOM

Economic Theory: Assoc. Prof. SOMRUX RAKSASUB

Human Resource Economics: Assoc. Prof. SUNEE CHULTRAKOM

Industrial Economics: MALEEWAN PONGA-WASDI

International Economics: Assoc. Prof. VIR-ACH THANASUAN

Monetary Economics: Assoc. Prof. SUPAR-IRK SRINATE

Public Finance: NAKORN YIMSIRIVATTANA
Quantitative Economics: Asst Prof. PRAPAI TRAKARNVACHIRAHUT

Education (tel. (2) 310-8312; fax (2) 310-8312; internet www.edu.ru.ac.th):

Continuing Education: Dr SUMANA CHARANASOMBOON
Curriculum and Instruction: Assoc. Prof. NOPPORN YAMSANG
Educational Administration and Higher Education: Assoc. Prof. Dr PRACHAYA KLAPACHAN
Educational Foundation: Asst Prof. NOUNLAOR SAENGSOOK
Educational Technology: Assoc. Prof. Dr WEERA THAIPANICH
Evaluation and Research: Assoc. Prof. PENSEE SETTHAWONG
Geography: Asst. Prof. PAITOON PIYAPAKORN
Home Economics: Asst Prof. Dr WANDEE THAIPANICH
Physical Education: Dr CHARNCHAI CHOBTHAMASAKUL
Psychology: Assoc. Prof. Dr SIRIBOON SAIKOSOOM

Engineering (tel. (2) 310-8570; fax (2) 314-3783; e-mail krisada@ram1.ru.ac.th; internet www.ru.ac.th/eng1):

Civil Engineering: WARANON KONGSONG
Environmental Engineering: Assoc. Prof. MONTREE PIRIYAKUL
Industrial Engineering: Asst Prof. SUVAT SRIVITHAYARAKS

Humanities (tel. (2) 310-8260; fax (2) 310-8264; internet www.hum.ru.ac.th):

English and Linguistics: Assoc. Prof. Dr RAPIN TONGRA-AR
History: Assoc. Prof. PRAPASSORN BOONPRASERT
Library Science: Asst Prof. YUPA SAIMALA
Mass Communication: Asst Prof. SUPARASM THITIKULCHAROEN
Philosophy: Asst Prof. Dr NARUMON MARKMAN
Sociology and Anthropology: Asst Prof. Dr CHONGCIT SOPONKANAPORN
Thai and Oriental Languages: Asst Prof. ABHICHAN PANCHAROEN
Western Languages: Asst Prof. Dr ORAPIN KAMPANTHONG

Law (tel. (2) 310-8161; fax (2) 310-8165; internet www.law.ru.ac.th):

Civil Law: Assoc. Prof. JUTAMAS NISARAT
Commercial Law: Assoc. Prof. NAKORN SADEPURIVAT
Development Law: Assoc. Prof. SUKSAMAI SUTIBODI
General Law: Assoc. Prof. Dr SOMCHAI KASITIPRADIT
International Law: Dr SOMCHAI SIRISOMBOONWEJ
Procedural Law: Assoc. Prof. WINAI LAMLERT
Public Law: Asst Prof. Dr KWANCHAI SANTASAWANG

Political Science (tel. (2) 310-8483; fax (2) 310-8491; internet www.pol.sc.ac.th):

Government: Asst Prof. WUTISUK LAPCHAROENSAP
International Relations: Asst Prof. Dr KRISANA VAISAMRUAT
Public Administration: Asst Prof. KAWEE RUCKCHONE

Science (tel. (2) 310-8380; fax (2) 310-8381; internet www.sci.ru.ac.th):

Biology: Asst Prof. Dr WANNA MUSIG
Chemistry: Assoc. Prof. SUNANTA PHINYAWAT
Computer Science: Asst Prof. CHANIN VICHIENSON
Food Technology: Dr RANEE SURAKARNKUL

Materials Technology: PAKAMAS SADINDHAMASAK
Mathematics: Assoc. Prof. Dr SOMPORN SUTINANTOPAS
Physics: Assoc. Prof. DAMRONGSAK MANEEPONGSAWASDI
Statistics: Assoc. Prof. Dr ROSSUKON HUNGSPRUKE

RANGSIT UNIVERSITY

52/347, Muang Ake, Phaholyothin Rd, Tambon-Lakhok, 12000 Pathum Thani

Telephone: (2) 997-2200
Fax: (2) 533-9470
E-mail: info@rangsit.rsu.ac.th
Internet: www.rsu.ac.th

Founded 1985
Private control
Languages of instruction: Thai, English
Academic year: May to April

President: Dr ARTHIT OURAIRAT
Vice-Presidents: Asst Prof. Dr NARES PANTARATORN (Academic Affairs), DUMRONG INDHRAMEESUP (Administration), AKECHART SOMPONGSE (Student Affairs)
Library Director: UTHAI DHUTIYABHODHI
Library of 106,895 vols
Number of teachers: 703
Number of students: 13,713 (662 undergraduate, 13,051 postgraduate)
Publication: *Bulletin of Health, Science and Technology*

HEADS OF COLLEGES

Division of Art and Design:

College of Architecture: Asst Prof. Dr NARUPOL CHAIYOT
College of Fine and Applied Arts: AUMNOUVUT SARASALIN
Conservatory of Music: DENNY EUPRASERT

Division of Engineering and Technology:

College of Biotechnology: Asst Prof. Dr VARAPORN LAKSANALAMAI
College of Chemical and Environmental Engineering: Assoc. Prof. Dr DAMRONG KHUMMONGKOL
College of Civil Engineering: Asst Prof. Dr SEREE SUPHARATID
College of Electrical and Computer Engineering: Dr PISIT CHARNKEITKONG
College of Food Technology: Dr VARAPORN LAKSANALAMAI
College of Information Technology: Asst Prof. Dr CHONAWAT SRISAAN
College of Mechanical and Industrial Engineering: JESSADA TANDHASETTI

Division of Humanities and Social Sciences:

College of Accounting: Dr NAMUAN KHAEWRAT
College of Business Administration: Dr PHONGPHAT RAKAROM
College of Communication Arts: ANUSORN SRIKAEW
College of Economics: Assoc. Prof. Dr NATHABHOL KHANTHACHAI
College of Education: Dr MANITH BOONPRASERT (acting)
College of Law: Assoc. Prof. Dr TIVA NGERNYUANG
College of Liberal Arts: Asst Prof. Dr SUEBSANG PROMBOON
College of Social Innovation: WITAYAKORN CHIENGKUL
College of Tourism and the Hospitality Industry: SEREE WANGPAICHITR
Graduate College: Dr PHNOM KLEECHAYA
International College: Dr BRUCE WEEKS
Institute of Public Administration: Assoc. Prof. Dr PATOM MANIROJANA

Division of Medicine and Health Sciences:

College of Medical Technology: PISIT NAMJUNTRA

College of Medicine: Assoc. Prof. Dr KIJPRAMUK TANTAYAPORN
College of Nursing Science: Asst Prof. Dr AMPAPORN PUAVILAI
College of Oriental Medicine: Assoc. Prof. Dr SURAPOTE WONGYAI
College of Pharmacy: Assoc. Prof. Dr ORAPHAN MATANGKASOMBUT
College of Physical Therapy: SOMSAK NGERNSUTHIVORAKUL
College of Science: Assoc. Prof. Dr CHATCHAI TRAKULRUNGSI

SIAM UNIVERSITY

235 Petchkasem Rd, Phasi-Charoen, Bangkok 10160

Telephone: (2) 457-0068
Fax: (2) 457-3982
E-mail: siam@siam.edu
Internet: www.siam.edu

Founded 1973
Private control
Academic year: June to March

President: Dr PORNCHAI MONGKHONVANIT
Vice-Presidents: Prof. Dr NIPONE SOOKPREEDEE (Academic Affairs), Assoc. Prof. Dr WICHIAN PREMCHAISWADI (Information Technology), Dr PAYUNGSAK JANTRASURIN (Planning and Development), Assoc. Prof. Dr AMORNCHAI TANTIMEDH (Research), BUNCHA PORNPRAPA (Student Affairs)
Registrar: SURADEJ PRUGSAMATZ
Librarian: KANNIKA SIRIKHET
Library of 127,600 vols
Number of teachers: 547
Number of students: 14,522
Publications: *Cultural Approach* (2 a year), *Engineering Journal of Siam University* (2 a year), *Journal of Nursing, Siam University* (2 a year), *Siam Business Review* (3 a year), *Siam University Law Journal* (annual), *Siam University Review* (6 a year)

DEANS

School of Business Administration: Dr SUMRIT TIANDUM
School of Communication Arts: Assoc. Prof. Dr CHAMNONG VIBULSRI
School of Engineering: Assoc. Prof. SARAVUTH VORASUMANTA
School of Law: Dr SOMMAI CHANRUANG
School of Liberal Arts: Dr SUBORDAS WARMSINGH
School of Nursing Science: Assoc. Prof. PANAN BOON-LAUNG
School of Science: Dr JIRASAK KETSUWAN
Graduate School of Business: Dr ATTAPOL TREEMONKONG
Graduate School of Communication Arts: Assoc. Prof. Dr SMAN NGAMSNIT
Graduate School of Education: Assoc. Prof. Dr AMORNCHAI TANTIMEDH
Graduate School of Engineering: Dr TORSAK LERTSRISAKULRAT
Graduate School of Information Technology: Assoc. Prof. Dr WICHIAN PREMCHAISWADI
Graduate School of Public Administration: Assoc. Prof. Dr SANYA SANYAVIVAT

SILPAKORN UNIVERSITY

22 Boromrachachonnani Rd, Taling-Chan, Bangkok 10170

Telephone: (2) 880-7374
Fax: (2) 880-7372
E-mail: webmaster@su.ac.th
Internet: www.su.ac.th

Founded 1943
State control
Language of instruction: Thai
Academic year: June to March (2 semesters)

President: Assoc. Prof. Dr TRUNGJAI BURANA-SOMPHOB

Vice-Presidents: Prof. Dr THEERA NUHPIAM (Academic Affairs), Asst Prof. Dr NIKOM TANGKAPIPOP (Administrative Affairs), PANYA VIJINTHANASARN (Art and Culture), Asst Prof. Dr SOMPID KATTIYAPIKUL (International Affairs), Assoc. Prof. SINDHCHAI KCEOKITICHAI (Planning and Development), Asst Prof. PONGSAK ARAYANGKOON (Special Affairs), Assoc. Prof. KANIT KHEOVICHAI (Student Affairs)

Registrar: PRANEE TOADITHAP

Librarian: CHIRAYOO DARSRI

Number of teachers: 698

Number of students: 6,024

Publications: *Annual Report, Veridian* (newsletter).

CONSTITUENT CAMPUSES

Sanamchand Palace Campus: Rajmankhanakana Rd, Muang District, Nakhon Pathom 73000; tel. (34) 253840; fax (34) 255099; Vice-President Asst Prof. Dr NARONG CHIMPALEE; Librarian KANCHANA SUKONTHAMANEE

DEANS

Faculty of Arts: MANEEPIN PHROMSUTHIRAK

Faculty of Education: LIKHIT KARNCHANAPORN

Faculty of Industrial Technology: AMNARD SITTATTRAKUL

Faculty of Pharmacy: WANCHAI SUTANANTA

Faculty of Science: JARUNGSANG LAKSANABOONSONG

HEADS OF DEPARTMENTS

Faculty of Arts:

English: LAKANA GLINKONG
French: YAOWADEE PATANOTHAI
Geography: WORAPOT CHOBTHUM
German: WANPEN BANCHONGTAD
History: MANAS KIATTITHARAI
Library Science: RABIAB SUPAWIREE
Musical Art: CHOLLADA THONGTAWEE
Philosophy: TIRASAK OPASBUTR
Social Science: SUWIDA THAMMANEEWONG
Thai: KANYARAT VECHASAT

Faculty of Education:

Curriculum and Instruction: PRASERT MONGKOL
Educational Administration: PRAGOB KUNARAK
Educational Technology: THAPANEE THAMMETAR
Foundations of Education: MANEE SRIWIBOON
Non-formal Education: CHIDCHONG NANTANANATE
Psychology and Guidance: SOMSAP SOOKANAN

Faculty of Industrial Technology:

Biotechnology: PITTAYA LIEWSAREE
Food Technology: SUCHET SAMUHASANEETOO
Materials Technology: CHANPEN ANURATANANON

Faculty of Pharmacy:

Biopharmaceutical: ROCHAPORN WACHAROTAYANKUN
Community Pharmacy: RAPEEPUN CHALONGSUK
Pharmaceutical Chemistry: LAWAN SRIPONG
Pharmaceutical Technology: PRANEET OPANASOPIT
Pharmaceutics: INTIRA KANCHANAPHIBOOL
Pharmacognosy: CHAVALIT SITTISOMBUT
Pharmacology and Toxicology: PAJAREE CHOTNOPPARATPAT

Faculty of Science:

Biology: VILAIPORN BOONYAKITJINDA
Chemistry: PUANGNOI AKSORNTONG
Environmental Science: GUNTHAREE SRIPONGPAN
Mathematics: SUDA TRAGANTALENGSAK
Physics: SA-GUANSIRI ROONGKEADSAKOON

Thapra Palace Campus: 31 Na-Pra Lan Rd, Bangkok 10200; tel. (2) 623-6115; fax (2) 225-7258; Vice-President Asst Prof. SOMCHAI EKPANYAKUL

DEANS

Faculty of Archaeology: PIBUL SUPAKITVILEKAGARN

Faculty of Architecture: CHAICHARN THAVARAVET

Faculty of Decorative Arts: TEERA PALPRAME

Faculty of Painting, Sculpture and Graphic Arts: NONTHIVATH CHANDHANAPHALIN

HEADS OF DEPARTMENTS

Faculty of Archaeology:

Anthropology: MANEEWAN PEWNIM
Archaeology: PACHAREE SARIKABUTARA
Art History: CHITTIMA AMORNPICHETKUL
Oriental Languages: CHIRAPAT PRABANDVIDYA
Western Languages: POONSUK TEMIYANON

Faculty of Architecture:

Architectural Technology: CHARUNPAT PUVANANT
Architecture: SURIYA RANTANAPUTH
Related Arts and Architecture: SATHIT CHOOSANG
Urban Design and Planning: AMARA JUANGBHANICH

Faculty of Decorative Arts:

Applied Art Studies: PAIROJ JUMANI
Ceramics: SUPPHAKA PALPRAME
Interior Design: NIRANR KRAIRIKSH
Product Design: PRADIT KANCHANA-AKRADEJ
Visual Communication Design: NOPADON YUDHAMONTRI

Faculty of Painting, Sculpture and Graphic Arts:

Art Theory: MANOP ISARADEJ
Graphic Arts: YANAWIT KUNCHAETHONG
Painting: ROONG TRIRAPICHIT
Sculpture: VICHAI SITHIRATN
Thai Arts: THONGCHAI SRISUKPRASERT

SOUTH-EAST ASIA UNIVERSITY

19/1 Phetkasem Rd, Nona Khaem, Bangkok 10160

Telephone: (2) 807-4500

Fax: (2) 807-4528

E-mail: webmaster@sau.ac.th

Internet: www.sau.ac.th

President: Assoc. Prof. Dr NARONG SINSAWASDI

Founded 1973 as South-East Asia College; university status 1992

Library of 68,000 vols, 650 journals

Number of students: 5,191

Faculties of Engineering, Business Administration, Arts and Sciences and Law; Graduate School; Language Institute.

SRINAKHARINWIROT UNIVERSITY

114 Sukhumvit 23, Bangkok 10110

Telephone: (2) 664-1000

Fax: (2) 258-4006

E-mail: ird@swu.ac.th

Internet: www.swu.ac.th

Founded 1954; university status 1974

State control

Language of instruction: Thai

Academic year: June to May

President: Assoc. Prof. Dr SUMONTHA PROMBOON

Vice-Presidents: Assoc. Prof. Dr SAKCHAI NIRUNTHAWEE (Academic Affairs), Assoc. Prof. Dr PAISAL WANGPHANICH (Administrative Affairs), VINAI BHURAHONGSE (Arts and Culture), Assoc. Prof. Dr PINITI RATANANUKUL (Finance and Personnel), Dr SUTASSI SMUTHKOCHORN (International Relations), Asst Prof. Dr CHAVANEE TONGROACH (Planning and Development), Prof. Dr SERMSAK WISALAPORN (Research), Asst Prof. MANEE THONGGOOM (Student Affairs)

Registrar: ORAPIN KAEWLAI

Director of Central Library: Asst Prof. NONGNATH CHAIRAT

Library: see Libraries and Archives

Number of teachers: 1,523

Number of students: 16,877

Publication: Journals in humanities, nursing, pharmaceutical science, physical education and science, each 2 a year

DEANS

Faculty of Dentistry: Assoc. Prof. Dr TIPAPORN VONGSURASIT

Faculty of Education: Assoc. Prof. Dr KHOMPET CHATSUPAKUL

Faculty of Engineering: AREE HANSUEBSAI

Faculty of Fine Arts: Prof. Dr WIROON TUNGCHAROEN

Faculty of Health Science: Assoc Prof. Dr WITTAYA TONSUWONNONT

Faculty of Humanities: Asst Prof. SUPA PANCHAROEN

Faculty of Medicine: Assoc Prof. ARUNWONG THEPCHATRI

Faculty of Nursing: Assoc. Prof. Dr TASSANA BOONTHONG

Faculty of Pharmaceutical Sciences: Lt-Col Dr NOPDOL THONGNOPNUA

Faculty of Physical Education: Asst Prof. PHAN JIARANAI

Faculty of Science: Dr YUVADEE NAKAPADUNGRUT

Faculty of Social Sciences: Asst Prof. KAWEE WORRAKAWIN

Graduate School: Assoc. Prof. Dr NAPAPORN HAWANONDHA

DIRECTORS OF RESEARCH INSTITUTES

Arts and Culture Research Institute: Asst Prof. AMNARD YENSABYE

Behavioural Science Research Institute: Assoc. Prof. Dr DUSADEE YOELAO

Institute of Asia Pacific Studies: Asst Prof. PLUPLUNG KONGCHANA

Institute of Eco-Tourism: Assoc. Prof. Dr PHYOM THAMABUTHRA

Institute of Environment and Resources: Assoc. Prof. Dr VINAI VEERAVATNANOND

Institute for Research for the Gifted and Talented: Asst Prof. PRIT SUPASETSIRI

SRIPATUM UNIVERSITY

Bangkhen Campus, 61 Phaholyotin Rd, Jatujak, Bangkok 10900

Telephone: (2) 579-1111

Fax: (2) 561-1721

E-mail: webspu@spu.ac.th

Internet: www.spu.ac.th

Founded 1970

Languages of instruction: Thai, English

Academic year: August to April

President: RUTCHANEEPORN POOKAYAPORN PHUKKAMARN

Vice-Presidents: Asst Prof. Dr NIMNUAN SRICHAD (Academic Affairs), CHUA MAICHAROEN (Administration), SOPIT PANOMAI (Student Affairs), Assoc. Prof. Dr SUCHAI THANAWASTIEN (Technology)

Library Director: Asst Prof. Dr NAMTIP VIPAWIN

Library of 104,000 vols

Number of teachers: 493

Number of students: 16,442 (16,000 undergraduate, 442 postgraduate)

DEANS

Faculty of Accounting: KALAYAPORN BANMARUNG BURKE

Faculty of Architecture: Asst Prof. SUTHON VIRIYASOMBOON

Faculty of Business Administration: Dr KAMOL CHAIYAWAT

Faculty of Communication Arts: Assoc. Prof. ARUNEEPRAPA HOMSETHI

Faculty of Economics: SOMNUEK TANGEHAROEN

Faculty of Engineering: Assoc. Prof. NARONG U-THANOM

Faculty of Informatics: AMNUAY MUTHITAJAROEN

Faculty of Law: PARINYA PATHUMPONG

Faculty of Liberal Arts: Asst Prof. Dr GLORIA VIDHEECHAROEN

Graduate School: Dr NITINAI BUNNAG

SUKHOTHAI THAMMATHIRAT OPEN UNIVERSITY

Bangpood, Pakkred, Nonthaburi 11120

Telephone: (2) 503-2121

Fax: (2) 503-3607

E-mail: stou@samsorn.stou.ac.th

Internet: www.stou.ac.th

Founded 1978

State control

Language of instruction: Thai

Academic year: July to April (2 semesters)

President: Prof. Dr IAM CHAYA-NGAM

Vice-President for Academic Affairs: Assoc. Prof. Dr JUMPOL NIMPANICH

Vice-President for Administration: Assoc. Prof. NATEE KHLIBTONG

Vice-President for Development: Assoc. Prof. Dr CHOW ROJANASANG (acting)

Vice-President for Operations: Assoc. Prof. CHUTIMA SACCHANAND

Vice-President for Planning: Assoc. Prof. Dr CHOW ROJANASANG (acting)

Vice-President for Services: Assoc. Prof. NATEE KHLIBTONG (acting)

Vice-President for Special Affairs: Assoc. Prof. CHUTIMA SACCHANAND (acting)

Registrar: Assoc Prof. Dr SOMSAK MEESAPLAK

Library of 651,000 vols, 1,930 periodicals

Number of teachers: 393

Number of students: 221,269

DEANS

School of Agricultural Extension and Co-operatives: Asst Prof. Dr PONGPHAN THIENHIRUN

School of Communication Arts: Assoc. Prof. SUMON YUESIN

School of Economics: Asst Prof. Dr SOMCHIN SUNTAVARUK

School of Educational Studies: Assoc. Prof. Dr SOMPRASONG WITTAYAGIAT

School of Health Science: Asst Prof. Dr ADISAK SATTAM

School of Home Economics: Assoc. Prof. Dr JUMPOL NIMPANICH (acting)

School of Law: THIENCHAI NA NAKORN

School of Liberal Arts: Assoc. Prof. Dr PAITOON MIKUSOL

School of Management Science: Assoc. Prof. SUNA SITHILERTPRASIT

School of Political Science: Assoc. Prof. ROSALIN SIRIYAPHAN

School of Science and Technology (pending official approval): Assoc. Prof. Dr JUMPOL NIMPANICH

SURANAREE UNIVERSITY OF TECHNOLOGY

111 University Ave, Muang District, Nakhon Ratchasima 30000

Telephone: (44) 224-141

Fax: (44) 224-4140

E-mail: cenintaf@ccs.sut.ac.th

Internet: www.sut.ac.th

Founded 1990

State control

Languages of instruction: Thai, English

Academic year: May to April

Rector: Prof. Dr WICHIT SRISA-AN

Vice-Rectors: Assoc. Prof. Dr KASEM PRABRIPUTALOONG (Academic Affairs), Assoc. Prof. Dr THAI TIPSUWANNAKUL (Administrative Affairs), Assoc. Prof. Dr KANOK PHALARAKSH (Development), Dr WISITPORN WATANAWATIN (Planning), Asst Prof. Captain Dr KONTORN CHAMNIPRASART (Student Affairs)

Registrar: Asst Prof. Dr AIM-ORN TASSANASORN

Librarian: Assoc. Prof. Dr PRAPAVADEE SUEBSONTHI

Library of 55,000 books, 600 periodicals

Number of teachers: 205

Number of students: 4,623 (4,419 undergraduate, 204 postgraduate)

DEANS

Institute of Agricultural Technology: Assoc. Prof. Dr TERD CHAROENWATANA

Institute of Engineering: Asst Prof. Dr TAVEE LERTPANYAVIT

Institute of Medicine: Prof. VITOON OSATHANONDH

Institute of Science: Assoc. Prof. Dr TASSANEE SUKOSOL

Institute of Social Technology: Assoc. Prof. Dr KRICH SUEBSONTHI

THAKSIN UNIVERSITY

140 Kanjanawit Rd, Muang District, Song Khla 90000

Telephone: (74) 311-885

Fax: (74) 324-440

E-mail: tsuinter@tsu.ac.th

Internet: www.tsu.ac.th

Founded 1996

President: SOMBOON CHITPONG

Faculties of Education, Humanities and Social Sciences, Science; Institute of Southern Thai Studies.

THAMMASAT UNIVERSITY

2 Prachan Rd, Bangkok 10200

Telephone: (2) 221-6111

Fax: (2) 224-8099

E-mail: inter@tu.ac.th

Internet: www.tu.ac.th

Founded 1934

State control

Languages of instruction: Thai, English

Academic year: June to February (two semesters), Summer Session March to May

Rector: Assoc. Prof. NORANIT SETABUTR

Vice-Rector for Academic Affairs: Assoc. Prof. Dr ANEK LAOTHAMATAS

Vice-Rector for Academic Affairs at Rangsit Centre: Asst Prof. Dr BOONHONG CHONGKID

Vice-Rector for Administration at Rangsit Center: Assoc. Prof. Dr TWEKIAT MENAKANIST

Vice-Rector for Finance and Property Management: Asst Prof. JARUPORN VIYANANT

Vice-Rector for General Administration: Dr UDOM RATHAMARIT

Vice-Rector for International Affairs: Dr KAJIT JITTASEVI

Vice-Rector for Personnel Administration: Assoc. Prof. Dr CHINTANA DAMRONGLERD

Vice-Rector for Planning and Development: Assoc. Prof. GASINEE WITOONCHART

Vice-Rector for Student Affairs: Assoc. Prof. Dr KUNDHOL SRISERMBHOK

Registration Office Director: Asst Prof. SAKON VARANYUWATANA

Librarian: NUALCHAWEE SUTHAMWONG

Library: see Libraries

Number of teachers: 955

Number of students: 19,983

Publications: *Faculty Bulletin, Journal of Business Administration, Journal of Political Science, Social Work Journal, Thammasat Law Journal, Thammasat University Journal*, etc

DEANS

Faculty of Allied Health Science: Prof. Dr VITHOON VIYANANT

Faculty of Commerce: Assoc. Dr THANET NORABHOOMPIPAT

Faculty of Dentistry: Assoc. Prof. Dr PRATHIP PHANTUMVANIT

Faculty of Economics: Assoc. Prof. Dr SIRILAKSANA KHOMAN

Faculty of Engineering: JULSIRI JAROENPUNTARUK

Faculty of Journalism and Mass Communication: Assoc. Prof. PIYAGUL LAWANSIRI

Faculty of Law: Asst Prof. SUTEE SUPANIT

Faculty of Liberal Arts: Asst Prof. Dr SIRINEE CHENVIDYAKAM

Faculty of Medicine: Prof. SUCHATI INDRAPRASIT

Faculty of Nursing: Asst Prof. Dr SIRIPORN KHAMPLIKIT

Faculty of Political Science: Assoc. Prof. Dr CORRINE PHUANGKASEM

Faculty of Science and Technology: Assoc. Prof. VENUS PEACHAVANICH

Faculty of Social Administration: Dr DECHA SUNGKAWAN

Faculty of Sociology and Anthropology: PORNCHAI TRAKULWARANONT

Graduate School: Assoc. Prof. MANOON PAHIRAH

Sirindhon International Institute of Technology: Prof. Dr SAWASD TANTARATANA

ATTACHED INSTITUTES

Centre for Continuing Education and Social Service: Dir Assoc. Prof. SOMCHAI SRISUTTHIYAKORN.

College of Innovative Education: Dir Assoc. Prof. Dr NARIS CHAIYASOOT.

Human Resources Institute: Dir Assoc. Prof. Dr CHULACHEEB CHINWANNO.

Information Processing Institute for Education and Development: Dir M. R. PONGSVAS SVATIVAT.

Institute of East Asian Studies: Dir Assoc. Prof. YUPHA KLANGSUWAN.

Language Institute: Dir Asst Prof. Dr PRATIN PIMSARN.

Thai Khadi Research Institute: Dir Assoc. Prof. SUMITR PITIPHAT.

UBON RATCHATHANI UNIVERSITY

University Administrative Building Warinchamrap, Ubon Ratchathani 34190

Telephone: (45) 288-398

Fax: (45) 288-398

E-mail: ira@ubu.ac.th

Internet: www.ubu.ac.th

Founded 1974

State control

Academic year: May to March

President: Prof. Dr PHAITOON INGKASUWAN

Vice-Presidents: Asst Prof. Dr CHOTE CHITRANGSRI (Academic Affairs), Asst Prof. Dr MANAS LORSIRIKUL (Administrative Affairs), Asst Prof. WANWALAI ATHIVASPNG

(Development Affairs), Asst. Prof. APICHAI
SIVAPRAPAKORN (Finance and Procurement), Dr PRANEET NGAM-SANEH (Resources
and Environment), PRASERTSAK LOKAPAI-
BOONKUL (Student Affairs)

Librarian: SUOACHAI HATHONGKHAM

Library of 40,000 books, 600 periodicals

Number of teachers: 375

Number of students: 4,177 (undergraduate)

DEANS

Faculty of Agriculture: Asst Prof. DHERAPOL
BUNSIDDHI

Faculty of Engineering: Prof. Dr PRAKOB
WIROJANAKUD

Faculty of Liberal Arts: Assoc. Prof. ARUNEE
WIRIYAJITTRA (acting)

Faculty of Management Science: CHATRUDEE
LUMDUAN (acting Dir)

Faculty of Pharmaceutical Science: Assoc.
Prof. BUNG-ON SRIPANICHKULCHAI

Faculty of Science: Asst Prof. PICHIT TOSU-
KHOWONG

UNIVERSITY OF THE THAI CHAMBER OF COMMERCE

126/1 Vibhavadi Rangsit Rd, Bangkok 10320

Telephone: (2) 276-1040

Fax: (2) 276-2126

E-mail: nitima@morakot.nectec.or.th

Internet: www.utcc.ac.th

Founded 1940 as College of Commerce;
present name and status 1984

President: CHIRADET OUSAWAT

Library of 100,000 vols, 6,000 periodicals.

WALAILAK UNIVERSITY

222 Thaiburi, Thasala District, Nakhon Si
Thammarat 80160

Telephone: (75) 384-000

Fax: (75) 384-258

E-mail: wu@praduu.wu.ac.th

Internet: www.wu.ac.th

President: Dr SUPAT POOPAKA

Founded 1992

State control

Institutes of Agricultural Technology, Allied
Health Sciences and Public Health, Engineering and Resources Management,
Information Science, Liberal Arts, Management, Nursing and Science.

Colleges and Institutes
AGRICULTURE

Ayuthaya Agricultural College:
Ayuthaya.

Bang Phra Agricultural College: Bang
Phra, Cholburi; tel. (38) 777503 ext. 118; fax
(38) 341808; e-mail bp_library@hotmail.com;
internet www.bparg.rit.ac.th; f. 1957; teacher training, training in farming; library:
10,000 vols; 130 teachers; 1,600 students; Dir
Dr SURAPHOL SANGUANSRI.

**Rajamangola Institute of Technology,
Surin Campus:** Surin; tel. (44) 511022; fax
(44) 519034; e-mail webmaster@surin.rit.ac
.th; internet www.surin.rit.ac.th; f. 2001
(fmrly Surin Agricultural College); 143 teachers; 2,289 students; Dir Asst Prof. Dr
WIEHIEN OUNRUEN.

TECHNOLOGY

Mahanakorn University of Technology:
51 Chuem Sampan Rd, Krathumrai, Nong
Chok, Bangkok 10530; tel. 988-3655; fax 988-
3687; f. 1990; private institution; masters
degrees in engineering and business administration, bachelor degrees in science, engineering and veterinary medicine; Pres.
Assoc. Prof. Dr SITTHICHAI POOKAIYAUDOM;
publ. *Engineering Transactions* (3 a year).

Northern Technical Institute: Huay
Kaew Rd, Chiangmai; f. 1957; library:
50,777 vols; 2–3-year diploma courses; Dir
C. SUWATHEE.

**Rajamangala Institute of Technology,
Bangkok Technical Campus:** 2 Nang
Linchee Rd, Bangkok 10120; tel. 2863991; f.
1952; degree courses, 2- to 5-year certificate
and diploma courses; library: 61,048 vols; 431
teachers; 6,111 students; Dir SKUL VEJAKORN;
publs *Annual Report, Bulletin*

DEANS

Faculty of Agriculture: T. SARASOPHORN

Faculty of Business Administration: P. CHOT-
TIKHUN

Faculty of Education: M. KITTIPONG

Faculty of Engineering Technology: S. POVA-
TONG

Faculty of Fine Arts: B. PLAWONGSE

Faculty of Home Economics: A. CHAREONCHAI

Faculty of Liberal Arts: S. PICHYAPAIBOON

Faculty of Music and Drama: P. LAPKESORN

**Rajamangala Institute of Technology,
Khon Kaen Campus:** 150 Srichan Rd,
Khon Kaen; tel. (43) 236-451; f. 1963 (fmrly
Thai-German Technical Institute); specializes in industrial technology; 3-year vocational certificate course, 2-year higher
vocational diploma, 2-year BS; library:
11,186 vols (mainly industrial education);
Dir SUBHAN TUENGSOOK.

Southern Technical Institute: Songkla.

TIMOR-LESTE

The Higher Education System

Universidade Nasionál Timór Losora'e (formerly Universitas Timor Timur), which was founded in 1986, predates Timor-Leste (formerly East Timor)'s independence from Indonesia in 2002. It is Timor-Leste's principal institution of higher education. It was largely destroyed during civil unrest in 1999, but reopened in 2001. In that year there were an estimated 6,349 students enrolled in tertiary education. The Ministry of Education, Culture, Youth and Sport is responsible for the provision of higher education.

Research Institutes

LANGUAGE AND LITERATURE

Instituto Nacional de Linguística (National Institute of Linguistics): Liceu 'Dr Francisco Macado', Avda Cidade de Lisboa, Díli; tel. 3313-142; fax 3321-211; e-mail indldili@yahoo.com; internet www.shlrc.mq.edu.au/~leccles; f. 2001 to study, protect and foster the official languages of Timor-Leste, Tetum and Portuguese; official govt body with the charter of co-ordinating and overseeing all indigenous language research and development projects; attached to National University of East Timor; Dir-Gen. Prof. Dr BENJAMIM DE ARAÚJO E CORTE-REAL; Dir (Research and Publications) Prof. Dr GEOFFREY HULL; publ. *Research Bulletin* (electronic, 2 a year).

NATURAL SCIENCES

Centro Nacional de Investigação Científica (National Centre of Scientific Research): Liceu Dr Francisco Machado, Avda Cidade de Lisboa, Díli; tel. 3332-705; e-mail cnic_timor@yahoo.com; internet www.cnictimor.org; f. 2001 to develop the economic, social and political welfare of Timor-Leste by means of scientific research; areas of research: agriculture, business and economics, education, political and social sciences, technology; Dir Prof. HELDER DA COSTA.

Libraries and Archives

Díli

National University of Timor Lorosa'e Library: Avda Cidade de Lisboa, Díli; fmrly library of Universitas Timor Timur; large part of its collection removed or destroyed during civil unrest in 1999; University Librarian VENCESLAO DO REGO.

Xanana Gusmão Reading Room: Rua Belarmina Lobo Lecidere, POB 3, Díli; tel. 3322-831; e-mail xgrroom@mail.timortelecom.tp; internet www.xgrroom.org; f. 2000; Dir KIRSTY SWORD GUSMÃO.

University

UNIVERSIDADE NASIONÁL TIMÓR LOROSA'E
(National University of East Timor)

Avda Cidade de Lisboa, Díli
Telephone: 3321-210
Fax: 3322-535
E-mail: bcorte_real@hotmail.com

Founded 2000; succeeded Universitas Timor Timur, (f. 1986, under Indonesian control) which was largely destroyed during civil unrest in 1999
State control

Rector: Prof. Dr BENJAMIM DE ARAUJO E CORTE-REAL
University Librarian: VENCESLAU DO REGO
Number of students: 7,000.

ATTACHED INSTITUTE

Instituto Nacional de Linguística (National Institute of Linguistics): see Research Institutes.

The Higher Education System

The principal institution of higher education is the Université du Lomé (formerly University of Benin), which was founded in 1965 as the Institut Supérieur de Bénin (Advanced Institute of Benin) in conjunction with the neighbouring state of Benin. Higher education is the responsibility of the Ministry of Education and Ministry of Technical Education and Professional Training. The funding of higher education is administered by the General Higher Education Council (Grand Conseil des Universités), which determines institutional budgets following consultation with the institutions. Students' tuition fees account for approximately 5% of income.

The secondary school Baccalauréat is the main requirement for admission to higher education. Applicants without the Baccalauréat are required to sit an entrance examination. The university degree system is based on the French system of three cycles. The first cycle lasts two years and leads to the award of the undergraduate Diplôme d'Etudes Universitaires Générales. The second cycle consists of one year of study leading to the award of the Licence, followed by a further year leading to the award of the Maîtrise. Finally, the third cycle comprises firstly of a one- to two-year period of study leading to the award of the Diplôme d'Etudes Supérieures, Diplôme d'Études Supérieures Specialisées or Diplôme d'Études Approfondies, and secondly a two-year period of study culminating with the award of the Doctorat. Professional degrees lasting longer than four years are offered by faculties of the university and specialist schools, such as Diplôme d'Ingénieur Agronome (five years), Diplôme d'Ingénieur de Conception (five years) and Doctorat de Médecine (seven years).

Learned Societies

BIBLIOGRAPHY, LIBRARY SCIENCE AND MUSEOLOGY

Association Togolaise pour le Développement de la Documentation, des Bibliothèques, Archives et Musées: c/o Bibliothèque de l'Université de Bénin, BP 1515, Lomé; f. 1959; promotes research in the field of documentation and library science; participates in the education of adults and young people; holds conferences, etc.; 60 mems; Pres. KOFFI ATTIGNON; Sec.-Gen. EKOUE AMAH.

LANGUAGE AND LITERATURE

Goethe-Institut: 25, Rue Kokéti, angle Rue de l'Eglise, BP 914, Lomé; tel. 2210894; fax 2220777; e-mail info@lome.goethe.org; internet www.goethe.de/lome; offers courses and exams in German language and culture and promotes cultural exchange with Germany; Institut building and entire library holdings destroyed during civil unrest in April 2005; reconstructed and reopened to the public 2006; Dir Dr HERWIG KEMPF.

Research Institutes

GENERAL

Institut de Recherche pour le Développement (IRD): BP 375, Lomé; tel. 221-43-44; fax 221-03-43; e-mail ird_lome@netcom.tg; f. 1949; agronomy, geology, pedology, geography, sociology, hydrology, geophysics, library; Admin. Agent BERNADETTE NAKU; (see main entry under France).

AGRICULTURE, FISHERIES AND VETERINARY SCIENCE

Institut de Recherches Agronomiques Tropicales et des Cultures Vivrières (IRAT): BP 1163, Lomé; tel. 221-21-48; Dir M. SARAGONI; (see main entry under France).

Institut de Recherches du Café, du Cacao et Autres Plantes Stimulantes (IRCC): BP 90, Kpalimé; tel. 441-00-34; fax 441-00-60; f. 1967; research to improve quality and production of coffee, cocoa and other stimulants; experimental unit at Tové; Dir K. EDEM DJIEKPOR.

Institut Togolais de Recherche Agronomique/Centre Recherches Agro-Savanes Humides: BP 01, Kolokopé Anié; tel. 444-30-00; fax 444-30-02; e-mail crash@laposte.tg; f. 1948; Dir M. LAODJASSONDO; publs Rapports annuels, Coton et Fibres Tropicales; (see main entry under France).

NATURAL SCIENCES

General

Institut National de la Recherche Scientifique: BP 2240, Lomé; tel. 221-01-39; f. 1965; initiation of national scientific research; rural development research; 12 permanent staff; library of 5,000 vols; publ. Etudes Togolaises (2 a year).

TECHNOLOGY

Service des Mines du Togo: c/o Ministère des Mines, Ave de la Marina, Lomé; Dir-Gen. ANKOUM P. AREGBA.

Libraries and Archives

Lomé

Archives Nationales du Togo: POB 1002, Lomé; tel. 221-04-10; f. 1976; administered by the Nat. Ministry for Education and Scientific Research; 2,500 vols, specializing in colonial history, tropical agronomy, stock breeding, health; Curator SENGHOR MOUSSA.

Bibliothèque du Ministère de l'Intérieur: Rue Albert Sarraut, Lomé; Librarian KWAOVI GABRIEL JOHNSON.

Bibliothèque Nationale: BP 1002, Lomé; tel. 221-04-10; fax 222-19-67; e-mail dban@tg.refer.org; German and French archives; 18,050 vols, 400 periodicals (incl. 74 current); Dir WENMI-AGORE M. COULIBALEY.

Museum

Lomé

Direction du Musée National, des Sites et Monuments: BP 12156, Lomé; tel. 221-68-07; fax 221-43-80; f. 1974; Curator of the National Museum NAYONDJOUA DJANGUENANE.

Universities

UNIVERSITÉ DE KARA

BP 43, Kara
Telephone: 661-02-56
Fax: 660-12-74
Founded 2004
State Control
President: AÏSSAH AGBÉTRA

Number of teachers: 30
Number of students: 1,477

Faculties of Arts and Humanities, Economics and Management and Law and Politics.

UNIVERSITÉ DE LOMÉ

BP 1515, Lomé
Telephone: 221-35-00
Fax: 221-85-95
E-mail: ngayiber@tg.refer.org
Internet: www.ub.tg

Founded 1965 as a Higher Institute; university status 1970; includes all the institutions of higher education in the country
State control
Language of instruction: French
Academic year: October to June (three terms)

Pres.: Prof. NICOUÉ L. GAYIBOR
Vice-President: THIOU T. K. TCHAMIE
Secretary-General: ABALO KODJO TABO
Librarian: A. B. F. GBIKPI-BENISSAN

Library of 70,000 vols
Number of teachers: 650
Number of students: 14,168

Publications: Livret de l'Etudiant, Annales (Lettres, Sciences, Médecine, Droit-Economie), Actes des Journées Scientifiques, Annuaire statistique, Journal de la Recherche Scientifique, Campus Actualités

DEANS AND DIRECTORS

Faculty of Economics and Business Management: K. AYASSOU
Faculty of Law: Prof. PEDRO AKUETE SANTOS
Faculty of Letters and Humanities: Prof. KOMLA M. F. NUBUKPO
Faculty of Medicine: Prof. KOFFI N'DAKENA
Faculty of Sciences: Prof. M. GBEASSOR
CIC-CAFMICRO (Computer Centre): TSATSOU FIADJOE
Distance Learning Centre: MARYSE A. QUASHIE

Higher School of Agriculture: K. AGBEKO

Higher Secretarial School: A. MAGNAN

Medical Training School: Prof. BATOMA SOSSOU

National Higher School of Engineering: E. K.-S. BEDJA

National Institute of Education: A. KOMLAN

University Technical Institute of Food and Biological Sciences: Prof. COMLAN A. DE SOUZA

University Technical Institute of Management: N. BIGOU-LARE

Colleges

Centre de Formation Professionnelle Agricole de Tove: BP 401, Kpalimé; f. 1901; 21 teachers; 230 students; library: 3,500 vols; Dir S. N. KANKARTI; Sec.-Gen. I. KUEVI.

Ecole Africaine des Métiers d'Architecture et d'Urbanisme: BP 2067, Lomé; tel. 221-62-53; fax 222-06-52; f. 1975; specialist courses in architecture and town planning;

in-service courses for trained architects; library: 1,957 vols; 23 staff; 102 students; Dir AHMED ASKIA SIDI.

Ecole Nationale d'Administration: Ave de la Libération, Lomé; tel. 221-21-30; fax 221-35-29; f. 1958; provides training for Togolese civil servants; 100 teachers; 500 students; library: library of over 1,000 vols; Dir DAGO YABRE; Sec.-Gen. KOMIKUMA DOGBEVI.

TONGA

The Higher Education System

Institutions of higher education predate the independence of Tonga from the United Kingdom in 1970, with the oldest being the 'Atenisi Institute, which was founded in 1966. There were four technical and vocational colleges in 1999, with a total of 467 students, and one teacher-training college, with 288 students. In 1990 there were 230 Tongans studying overseas. Some degree courses are offered at the university division of the 'Atenisi Institute. The University of the South Pacific has a centre in Tonga. A new establishment offering higher education, the 'Unuaki 'o Tonga Royal University (UTRU), opened in 2004.

Among the qualifications required for admission to higher education are the Higher Leaving Certificate, New Zealand University Entrance Certificate and Pacific Secondary Certificate. There is also a one-year Preliminary or Foundation Programme for applicants to the University of the South Pacific. The Bachelors is the undergraduate degree and lasts three years, although the Bachelors in medicine at the Fiji School of Medicine is a four-year degree. Following completion of the Masters, graduates may study for the Masters, which is a one or two-year course of study. The highest university degree is the Doctorate, requiring a further two years of study following award of the Masters. The 'Atenisi Institute awards degrees, but these are not recognized by the Tongan Government.

The Government provides over half of all facilities and training for post-secondary vocational and technical education. Institutions providing such education include the Community Development Training Centre, Tonga Institute of Science and Technology, Civil Service Training Centre and Royal School of Science and Technology.

Learned Society

BIBLIOGRAPHY, LIBRARY SCIENCE AND MUSEOLOGY

Tonga Library Association: c/o USP Tonga Centre, POB 278, Nuku'alofa; tel. 29-055; fax 29-249; e-mail taufui_l@usp.ac.fj; f. 1981; training courses and library-related activities; 40 mems; Pres. LOSALINE TAUFU'I.

Libraries and Archives

Nuku'alofa

Ministry of Education Library: POB 123, Nuku'alofa; tel. 21-588; fax 24-105; f. 1976; provides supplementary reading and text books for students and public library service; 12,432 vols; special collection: Pacific (1,515 vols); Librarian TU'ILOKAMANA TUITA.

University of the South Pacific, Tonga Campus Library: POB 278, Nuku'alofa; tel. 29-240; fax 29-249; e-mail taufui_l@usp.ac.fj; 10,000 vols; Library Officer LOSALINE TAU-FU'I.

Museum

Nuku'alofa

Tupou College Museum: POB 25, Nuku'alofa; tel. 32-240; f. 1866; museum within Tupou College; artefacts from Tonga's history; Principal Rev. SIOSAIA PELE.

University

'UNUAKI-'O-TONGA ROYAL UNIVERSITY

Taufa'ahau Rd, Haveluloto Nuku'alofa, POB 2936, Tongatapu

Telephone: 25-663

Fax: 25-664

E-mail: admission@tongaroyaluniversity.com

Internet: www.tongaroyaluniversity.com

Founded 2004

Chair.: HRH Princess SALOTE MAFILE'O PILO-LEVU TUITA

Pres. and Vice-Chair.: Prof. 'ETUATE LAVU-LAVU

Vice-Pres. for Academic Affairs and Chief Exec. Dir: Prof. Dr MICHAEL FAIA

Exec. Vice-Pres.: SIONE TUALAU VIMAHI

Vice-Pres.: Prof. VINOD TRIVEDI

Dir for Admin. and Int. Relations: MELE LUPEHA'AMOA 'ILAIU

Dir of Technical and Vocational Training: PITA LIKILIKI PUA

Dir of Finance: MEHTA BHAVIK

Dir of Student Services: TELESIA LAVULAVU

Dir of Admissions: KALOLAINE KOLUSE

Dir of Research and Deputy Dir of Admissions: SIONA TALANOA FIFITA.

ATTACHED RESEARCH INSTITUTES

Asian Region Extension: 17, L/L, Harekrishna Complex opp. Kothawala Flats, Paldi Ahmedabad 380007, India; tel. 79-66613205; fax 79-26579891; e-mail ravishshah@tongaroyaluniversity.com; Exec. Dir Prof. VINOD TRIVEDI.

'Eua Community Education and Health Institute: Dir 'ANA FILI.

Ha'apai Community Education and Health Institute: Dir MO'ALE FINAU.

Tongatapu Community Health and Institute: Dir SIONE TUALAU VIMAHI.

Vava'u Community Education and Health Institute: Dir 'ETA HARRIS TAUMA-LOLO.

Colleges

'Atenisi Institute: POB 90, Nuku'alofa; tel. and fax 24-819; e-mail office@atenisi.edu.to; internet kalianet.to/atenisi; private control; f. 1966; language, literature, mathematics, philosophy, sociology; Founder/Dir Prof. FUTA HELU.

Hango Agricultural College: POB 16, Ohonua, Eua; tel. 50-044; fax 50-128; f. 1968; part of Free Wesleyan Church Education System; 1-year diploma course in para-veterinary studies, 1-year diploma course in horticulture/cropping, 2-year certificate course; library: 1,200 vols; 7 teachers; 55 students.

Tonga Institute of Science and Technology: POB 485, Nuku'alofa; tel. 22-667; fax 24-334; e-mail tist1uf@kalianet.to; f. 1985; offers training in maritime studies and technical trades; library: 300 vols; 20 teachers; 160 students; Principal Dr 'UHILA-MOE-LANGI FASI.

University of the South Pacific, Tonga Centre: POB 278, Nuku'alofa; tel. 29-240; fax 29-249; e-mail fukofuka_s@usp.ac.fj; extension centre with responsibilities for distance education, adult non-formal education; interests in village and community development and appropriate technology; library: see Libraries and Archives; Dir SALOTE FUKOFUKA.

TRINIDAD AND TOBAGO

The Higher Education System

The Trinidad campus of the University of the West Indies (UWI), at St Augustine, offers undergraduate and postgraduate programmes. The UWI Institute of Business offers postgraduate courses, and develops programmes for local companies. Other institutions of higher education are the Eric Williams Medical Sciences complex, the Polytechnic Institute and the East Caribbean Farm Institute. The country has one teacher training college and three government-controlled technical institutes and vocational centres, including the Trinidad and Tobago Hotel School. In the late 1990s the Government established the Trinidad and Tobago Institute of Technology, and the College of Science, Technology and Applied Arts of Trinidad and Tobago. In March 2004 a Steering Committee was appointed to conduct a strategic review of tertiary education, and distance and lifelong learning, in an attempt to improve consistency within the tertiary sector and in relation to the education system as a whole. In 2004 there were 16,752 students in three institutions of higher education.

Applicants are required to have a minimum of two GCE A-levels for admission to undergraduate courses, and either the Caribbean Examinations Council Secondary Education Certificate or GCE O-levels for admission to preliminary science, evening or part-time courses. Two-year Associate degrees are awarded by institutions such as the College of Nursing and the National Institute of Higher Education, and the undergraduate Bachelors degree is a three-year programme of study at the University of the West Indies. The postgraduate degrees are the two-year Masters and Doctorate programmes.

Post-secondary technical and vocational education is administered according to a framework of national vocational qualifications (TTNVQs). There are five levels: Pre-Craft, Craft, Technician, Professional, and Chartered or Advanced Professional. TTNVQs are offered by a range of professional institutes and centres.

Learned Societies

AGRICULTURE, FISHERIES AND VETERINARY SCIENCE

Agricultural Society of Trinidad and Tobago: POB 256, 112 St Vincent St, Port-of-Spain; tel. and fax 627-3087; e-mail agrisoc@tstt.net.tt; f. 1894; 528 mems; Pres. WENDY LEE YUEN; publ. *Journal* (annually).

Sugar Manufacture Association of Trinidad and Tobago: 80 Abercromby St, POB 230, Port-of-Spain; tel. 623-6106; f. 1967; to promote information of interest to the sugar industry; 272 mems; Pres. T. N. SKINNER; Sec. M. Y. KHAN; publ. *Proceedings*.

Tobago District Agricultural Society: Main St, Scarborough; Pres. Capt. R. H. HARROWER; Sec. S. A. DAVIES.

ARCHITECTURE AND TOWN PLANNING

Trinidad and Tobago Institute of Architects: POB 585, Port-of-Spain; tel. 624-8842; fax 624-5217; e-mail info@ttiarch.com; internet www.ttiarch.com; f. 1954 present name 1982; 90 mems (incl. overseas); Pres. MARK RAYMOND; Sec. STEVE JAMESON; publ. *Journal* (annually).

BIBLIOGRAPHY, LIBRARY SCIENCE AND MUSEOLOGY

Library Association of Trinidad and Tobago: POB 1275, Port-of-Spain; e-mail secretary@latt.org.tt; internet www.latt.org.tt; f. 1960; Pres. Dr LILLIBETH ACKBARALI; Exec. Sec. SALLY ANNE MONTSERIN; publ. *Bulletin*.

ECONOMICS, LAW AND POLITICS

Law Association of Trinidad and Tobago: POB 534, Port-of-Spain; tel. 625-9350; fax 625-9350; e-mail lawassoc@tstt.net.tt; internet www.lawassociationtt.com; f. 1986; 750 mems; Pres. S. RUSSELL MARTINEAU; Sec. PATRICIA DINDYAL; publ. *The Lawyer* (2 a year).

FINE AND PERFORMING ARTS

Trinidad Music Association: Bishop Anstey High School, Abercromby St, Port-of-Spain; f. 1941; 102 mems; Pres. Mrs ROBERT JOHNSTONE; Hon. Sec. Mrs VELMA JARDINE.

HISTORY, GEOGRAPHY AND ARCHAEOLOGY

Historical Society of Trinidad and Tobago: c/o POB 780, Port-of-Spain; f. 1932; 45 mems; Pres. MAX B. IFILL; Hon. Sec. and Treas. KENT VILLAFANA.

LANGUAGE AND LITERATURE

Alliance Française: 17 Alcazar St, Clair, POB 1288, Port-of-Spain; tel. 622-6728; fax 628-8226; e-mail aftnt@tstt.net.tt; internet www.geocities.com/alfrandett; offers courses and exams in French language and culture and promotes cultural exchange with France.

British Council: c/o British High Commission, 19 St Clair Ave, St Clair, POB 778, Port-of-Spain; tel. 628-0565; fax 622-2853; e-mail candice.fabien@britishcouncil.org.tt; internet www.britishcouncil.org/caribbean; offers courses and exams in English language and British culture and promotes cultural exchange with the UK; Man. HARRIET MASSINGBERD.

MEDICINE

Pharmacy Board of Trinidad and Tobago: Professional Centre Building, Wrightson Rd Extension, Port-of-Spain; tel. and fax 627-6731; e-mail pboftt@tstt.net.tt; f. 1899; 300 mems; Pres. (vacant); Hon. Sec. NORMA INNISS.

NATURAL SCIENCES

Physical Sciences

Geological Society of Trinidad and Tobago: POB 3524, La Romaine, Trinidad; tel. 679-6064; fax 679-6064; e-mail gstt@tstt.net.tt; internet www.gstt.org; f. 1976; 250 mems; library of 2,000 vols; Pres. Dr FAZAL HOSEIN; Pres. Elect CURTIS ARCHIE.

Research Institute

AGRICULTURE, FISHERIES AND VETERINARY SCIENCE

Caribbean Agricultural Research and Development Institute (CARDI): University Campus, St Augustine, Trinidad; tel. 645-1205; fax 645-1208; e-mail infocentre@cardi.org; internet www.cardi.org; f. 1975; sites in 13 Caribbean countries; Exec. Dir FRANK B. LAUCKNER.

Libraries and Archives

Port-of-Spain

Central Library of Trinidad and Tobago: POB 547, corner Duke and Pembroke Sts, Port-of-Spain; tel. 624-3120; fax 625-5369; e-mail nalis@trinidad.net; f. 1941; a division of the Office of the Prime Minister; 442,000 vols; public library; Heritage Library held jointly with Trinidad Public Library; 13 brs; Dir PAMELLA BENSON; publ. *Trinidad and Tobago National Bibliography*.

National Archives: The Government Archivist, POB 763, 105 St Vincent St, Port-of-Spain; tel. 625-2689; fax 625-2689; e-mail natt@tstt.net.tt; f. 1960; government and private archives; microfilm copies of Trinidad and Tobago records in other countries; Government Archivist HELENA LEONCE; publ. *Select Documents*.

Trinidad Public Library: corner Duke and Pembroke Sts, Port-of-Spain; tel. 624-3409; fax 624-1130; f. 1851; 70,000 vols; Heritage Library held jointly with Central Library of Trinidad and Tobago; 2 brs; Librarian LYNETTE COMISSIONG.

St Augustine

University of the West Indies, Main Library: St Augustine; tel. 662-2002 ext. 2132; fax 662-9238; e-mail mainlib@library.uwi.tt; internet www.mainlib.uwi.tt; f. 1926; 370,146 vols, 45,439 bound serials, 22,729 microfilms, 27,000 other non-book items, 1,253 maps, 3,107 multimedia items, 5,042 photographs, 10,590 vertical files, 273 video cassettes, 790 audio cassettes, 1,608 vinyl records; West Indiana, Oral and Pictorial Records Collections; Campus Librarian Dr MARGARET ROUSE-JONES; publs *CARINDEX: Science and Technology* (2 a year), *CARINDEX: Social Sciences and Humanities* (2 a year), *OPReP Newsletter*.

San Fernando

San Fernando Carnegie Free Library: Harris Promenade, San Fernando; tel. 652-2921; fax 653-9645; internet www.nalis.gov .tt; f. 1919; lending and reference service for children and adults; 36,109 vols; special collection: West Indies, Carnival; Librarian REYNOLD BASSANT.

Museum and Art Gallery

Port-of-Spain

National Museum and Art Gallery of Trinidad & Tobago: 117 Frederick St, Port-of-Spain; tel. 623-5941; fax 623-7116; e-mail museum@tstt.net.tt; f. 1892; art, archaeology, history, Carnival, petroleum technology, natural history; Curator VEL A. LEWIS.

University

UNIVERSITY OF THE WEST INDIES, ST AUGUSTINE CAMPUS

St Augustine, Trinidad

Telephone: 662-2002

Fax: 663-9684

Internet: www.uwi.tt

Founded 1948 by the Governments of the Caribbean Commonwealth Territories with the co-operation of the British Government. The University serves Jamaica, Trinidad and Tobago, Barbados and the Commonwealth Territories in the Caribbean

Autonomous

Language of instruction: English

Academic year: August to July

Chancellor: Sir GEORGE ALLEYNE

Vice-Chancellor: Prof. NIGEL HARRIS

Pro-Vice-Chancellor and Principal at St Augustine: Dr BHOENDRADATT TEWARIE

Pro-Vice-Chancellor (Research): Prof. WAYNE HUNTE

Deputy Principal: Prof. GURMOHAN KOCHHAR

Registrar of St Augustine: DAVID MOSES (acting)

Bursar of St Augustine: LYLLA BADA

Librarian at St Augustine: Dr MARGARET ROUSE-JONES

Library of 354,000 vols, 43,852 bound vols of periodicals, 736,611 unbound periodical issues, 15,280 current periodicals

Number of teachers: 520

Number of students: 12,604

Publications: *Caribbean Dialogue* (policy bulletin of Caribbean affairs), *Journal of Tropical Agriculture*, *St Augustine News*

DEANS

Faculty of Engineering: Prof. CLEMENT SANKAT

Faculty of Humanities and Education: Dr IAN ROBERTSON

Faculty of Medical Sciences: Prof. PHYLLIS PITT-MILLER

Faculty of Science and Agriculture: Prof. DYER NARINESINGH

Faculty of Social Sciences: Dr H. GHANY

PROFESSORS

ABIODUN, A., Public Health

ADDAE, J., Physiology

ADESIYUN, A., Public Health

AINA, A. O., Chemical Engineering

AKINGBALA, J. O., Food Science and Technology

BABAN, S. M. J., Surveying and Land Information

BARNES, J., Biochemistry

BHATT, B., Maths and Computer Science

BRERETON, B., History

BRKOVIC, B., Surveying and Land Information

BUTLER, D., Cocoa Research

COOPER, J., Veterinary Pathology

DAISLEY, H., Anatomical Pathology

DAWE, R. A., Petroleum Engineering

DEOSARAN, R., Sociology

EZEOKOLI, C., Veterinary Surgery

FARRELL, E. J., Mathematics

GAYLE, D. J., Strategic International Business

GHOSH, D. K., Finance

GIFT, S., Electrical and Computer Engineering

HALL, L., Chemistry

IMBERT, C., Mechanical Engineering

ISITOR, G., Veterinary Anatomy

LALLA, B., Linguistics

LEWIS, V., International Relations

McDAVID, C. R., Plant Science

McRAE, A., Human Anatomy (Pre-Clinical Sciences)

MELLOWES, W., Chemical Engineering

MELVILLE, G. N., Physiology

NARAYAN, C. V., Mechanical Engineering

NARAYNSINGH, V., Surgery

NARINESINGH, D., Chemistry

OMER, M., Child Health

PITT-MILLER, P., Anaesthetics

POSTHOFF, C., Computer Science

PRABHU, S. R., Oral Dentistry

PREMDAS, R., Public Policy

RAMKISSOON, H., Mathematics

RAMSARAN, R., International Relations

RAMSEWAK, S., Obstetrics and Gynaecology

REDDOCK, R. E., Gender and Development Studies

ROHLEHR, D. G., West Indian Literature

ROOPNARINESINGH, S., Obstetrics and Gynaecology

SAMAROO, B., History

SANKAT, C., Mechanical Engineering

SAUNDERS, R. M., Physics

SHARMA, A. K., Civil Engineering

SUITE, W., Civil Engineering

THEODORE, K., Economics

VENKOBACHAR, C., Environmental Engineering

ATTACHED INSTITUTES

Caribbean Centre for Monetary Studies: Dir Dr CLEMENT JACKSON.

Institute of Business: St Augustine; tel. 662-4681; fax 662-1411; e-mail corporate@uwi-iob.net; Dir Dr ROLPH BALGOBIN.

Institute of International Relations: St Augustine; tel. 662-5314; e-mail iirt@fss.uwi .tt; f. 1966; diplomatic training, postgraduate teaching and research in intl relations; Dir Prof. DENNIS GAYLE.

Sir Arthur Lewis Institute of Social and Economic Studies: St Augustine; fax 645-6329; e-mail salises@fss.uwi.tt; Dir Dr PATRICK WATSON.

TUNISIA

The Higher Education System

The University of Tunisia was founded in 1960, and divided in 1986 into three universities: Tunis, Center and Sfax-South. In 1987 the university at Tunis was divided into four subject-based institutions, which in turn were later reorganized into multi-disciplinary institutions. Several private universities have received accreditation since 2000. In 2004/05 a total of 311,569 students were enrolled at higher educational establishments in Tunisia. In 2005/06 there were 31,838 full-time students at 178 institutions of higher education. There is a Ministry of Higher Education and higher education is funded from the national budget.

The secondary school Baccalauréat is the main requirement for admission to higher education. University degrees are divided into three cycles: the first cycle ends with the awards of Diplôme Universitaire d'Etudes Scientifiques or Diplôme Universitaire d'Etudes Littéraires; the second cycle comprises the Licence or a Maîtrise; and the third cycle the doctoral-level degrees, specifically Diplôme d'Etudes Approfondies and Doctorat d'Etat. The professional title Diplôme d'Ingénieur is a second-cycle degree awarded after three years and the Docteur en Médecine is awarded after six years.

The leading qualification of post-secondary technical and vocational education is the Brevet de Technicien Supérieur, which requires the Baccalauréat or Brevet de Technicien Professionnel.

Learned Societies

GENERAL

Comité Culturel National: 105 ave de la Liberté, 1002 Tunis; tel. (71) 28-81-54; fax (71) 79-26-39; f. 1968; central body co-ordinating national and international cultural activities, sponsored by the Ministry of Culture and by foreign embassies; Regional and Local Cultural Committees throughout the country; 16 mems; Pres. MOHAMED TALBI; Sec.-Gen. SAMIR BELHAJ YAHIA.

BIBLIOGRAPHY, LIBRARY SCIENCE AND MUSEOLOGY

Association Tunisienne des Bibliothécaires, Documentalistes et Archivistes: BP 380, 1015 Tunis; f. 1965; information sciences; 250 mems; Pres. ABDELBAKI DALY; publ. *Rassid* (multilingual, 4 a year).

Comité National des Musées: Musée National du Bardo, Tunis; f. 1961; Pres. HABIB BEN YOUNES; publ. *Les musées de Tunisie*.

EDUCATION

Arab League Educational, Cultural and Scientific Organization (ALECSO) (Organisation Arabe pour l'Education, la Culture et la Science): BP 1120, Ave Mohamed V, Tunis; tel. (71) 78-44-66; fax (71) 78-49-65; e-mail alecso@email.ati.tn; internet www .alecso.org.tn; f. 1970 for the development of education, culture and sciences in Arab countries; mems: 21 Arab countries; library of 7,000 vols, 110 periodicals; Dir-Gen. MONGI BOUSNINA; publs *ALECSO Newsletter* (monthly), *Arab Journal of Culture* (2 a year), *Arab Journal of Education* (2 a year), *Arab Journal of Sciences and Information* (2 a year), *Fadha'at Newsletter* (2 a month), *Journal of Mass Education* (annually).

FINE AND PERFORMING ARTS

Union Nationale des Arts Plastiques: Musée du Belvédère, Tunis.

LANGUAGE AND LITERATURE

British Council: c/o British Embassy, 5 Place de la Victoire, BP 229, Tunis 1015 RP; tel. (71) 259053; fax (71) 353411; e-mail info@ tn.britishcouncil.org; internet www .britishcouncil.org.tn; offers courses and exams in English language and British culture and promotes cultural exchange with the UK; library of 8,000 vols; Dir WILL TODD (acting).

Teaching Centre:

Teaching Centre: 2nd/3rd Fl., 47 Ave Habib Bourguiba, Tunis 1001; tel. (71) 353568; fax (71) 353985; Teaching Centre Man. TANIA PUGLIESE (acting).

Goethe-Institut: 6 Place d'Afrique, rue du Sénégal, 1002 Tunis-Belvédère; tel. (71) 848266; fax (71) 841751; e-mail vogt@ tunis-goethe.org.tn; internet www.goethe.de/ wm/tun/deindex.htm; offers courses and exams in German language and culture and promotes cultural exchange with Germany; Dir ECKEHART VOGT.

Institut des Belles Lettres Arabes: 12 rue Jamâa al Haoua, 1008 Tunis Bab Menara; tel. (71) 560133; fax (71) 572683; e-mail ibla@ gnet.tn; internet www.iblatunis.org; f. 1930; cultural centre; language of instruction: Arabic, French; library of 32,000 vols on Tunisian studies and Arabic literature; Dir RAMÓN ECHEVERRÍA; publ. *IBLA* (2 a year).

Instituto Cervantes: 120 ave de la Liberté, 1002 Tunis Belvédère; tel. (71) 788847; fax (71) 793825; e-mail centun@cervantes.es; internet tunez.cervantes.es; offers courses and exams in Spanish language and culture and promotes cultural exchange with Spain and Spanish-speaking Latin and Central America; library of 16,000 vols; Dir FRANCISCO CORRAL SÁNCHEZ-CABEZUDO.

Union des Ecrivains Tunisiens: 20 ave de Paris, 1000 Tunis; f. 1970; 200 mems; Pres. MOHAMED LAROUSSI MÉTOUI; Sec. Gen. SOUF ABIOL; publ. *El Masson*.

Research Institutes

GENERAL

Centre d'Etudes Maghrébines à Tunis: 19 bis rue d'Angleterre, Impasse Menabrea, BP 404, 1049 Tunis-Hached; tel. (71) 32-62-19; fax (71) 32-83-78; e-mail cemat@planet .tn; internet www.la.utexas.edu/research/ mena/cemat; f. 1985; operated by American Institute for Maghreb Studies, Univ. of Arizona, Tucson; sponsors research by scholars of all nationalities and in all disciplines; gives research grants to Americans and Maghribis; facilitates liaison with North African scholars; holds annual research conference and frequent lectures; library of 2,000 vols, 1,000 dissertations; Dir LAURENCE MICHALAK.

Institut National de Recherche Scientifique et Technique (INRST): BP 95, Hammam Lif 2050; premises at: Route Touristique, Borj-Cedria, Soliman; tel. (72) 43-02-15; fax (72) 43-09-34; f. 1969; applied physics, biology, chemistry, biotechnology, earth sciences, development of the use of domestic and industrial waste; library of 1,500 vols, 100 in special collections; Dir MOHAMED ENNABLI; Sec.-Gen. MESSAOUD CHAHTOUR.

Institut de Recherche pour le Développement (IRD): see main entry under France: 5 impasse Chahrazed, BP 434, 1004 Tunis El Menzah; tel. (71) 75-00-09; fax (71) 75-02-54; f. 1958; pedology, hydrology, microbiology, medical entomology, agricultural economics, archaeology, desertification, remote detection; library; Dir J. CLAUDE.

AGRICULTURE, FISHERIES AND VETERINARY SCIENCE

Centre de Recherche du Génie Rural: BP 10, Ariana 2080; tel. (71) 71-80-55; f. 1959; agronomy, irrigation, etc.; Dir MOHAMED NEJIB REJEB; publ. *Cahier du CRGR*.

Institut National de la Recherche Agronomique de Tunisie (INRAT): Rue Hédi Karray 2049, Ariana; tel. (71) 23-00-24; fax (71) 75-28-97; e-mail netij.benmechlia@iresa .agrinet.tn; f. 1914; improvement of vegetable and livestock production through the use of appropriate agroecological and socio-economic methods; 7 research laboratories, 2 research units, 13 regional experimental stations; library of 8,000 vols, 1,500 periodicals; Dir Dr N. BEN MECHLIA; publ. *Annales* (annually).

Institut National de Recherches Forestières de Tunisie: BP 2-2080, Ariana; f. 1967 under present title; research in all aspects of forestry; library: Documentation Centre comprises 2,981 vols and 3,144 documents; Dir M. DAHMAN; publs *Bulletin d'Information* (2 or 3 a year), *Annales*, *Notes de Recherches*.

Institut National des Sciences et Technologies de la Mer: 28 rue 2 Mars 1934, 2025 Salammbô; tel. (71) 73-04-20; fax (71) 73-26-22; e-mail messaoudi.saida@instm.rnrt .tn; internet www.instm.rnrt.tn; f. 1924; fisheries research, aquaculture, fishing technology, marine environment, toxicology, algology; marine museum; library of 40,000 vols; Dir-Gen. Prof. RIDHA MRABET; publs *Bulletin* (annually), *Notes* (3 a year).

Institut de la Recherche Vétérinaire de Tunisie: Rue Djebel Lakhdhar La Rabta, 1006 Tunis; tel. (71) 56-26-02; fax (71) 56-96-92; f. 1897; veterinary research; library of 3,000 vols; Dir Dr MALEK ZRELLI.

BIBLIOGRAPHY, LIBRARY SCIENCE AND MUSEOLOGY

Institut National du Patrimoine: 4 place du Château, 1008 Tunis; tel. (71) 26-16-22; f. 1957; archaeology, museography, ethnography, research, protection and evaluation of the national heritage; library of 25,000 vols; Dir ABDELAZIZ DAOULATLI; publ. *Africa.*

EDUCATION

Institut National des Sciences de l'Education: 17 rue d'Irak, 1002 Tunis-Belvédère; tel. (71) 28-77-22; fax (71) 79-54-23; f. 1969; conducts research, undertakes assessment of curricula, books, students and teaching techniques, develops the use of audiovisual aids in education, organizes seminars and conferences; library of 30,000 vols; Dir NEJIB AYED; publs *Bulletin pédagogique, Cahiers de l'INSE, Revue Tunisienne des Sciences de l'Education.*

MEDICINE

Institut Pasteur: BP 74, 13 place Pasteur, 1002 Tunis Belvédère; tel. (71) 78-96-08; fax (71) 79-18-33; f. 1893; research in health sciences; library of 4,500 vols, 200 periodicals; Dir Prof. K. DELLAGI; publ. *Archives* (quarterly).

TECHNOLOGY

Centre National de l'Informatique: 17 rue Belhassen Ben Chaâbane, El-Omrane, 1005 Tunis; tel. (71) 78-30-55; fax (71) 78-18-62; e-mail mongi.miled@e-mail.ari.tn; f. 1976; assistance, training, development of computer applications and software, management of processing centres; library of 4,000 vols; Dir MONGI MILED.

Office National des Mines: BP 215, 1080 Tunis Cedex; premises at: 24 rue 8601, La Charguia, 2035 Tunis; tel. (71) 78-88-42; fax (71) 79-40-16; f. 1962; geological research and map-making; bibliographic database on geology of Tunisia; library of 15,000 vols, 450 periodicals; Pres. and Dir-Gen. MOHAMED FADHEL ZERELLI; publs *Annales des Mines et de la Géologie, Notes du service géologique.*

Libraries and Archives

Tunis

Archives Nationales: Le Premier Ministère, La Casbah, 1020 Tunis; tel. (71) 56-05-56; fax (71) 56-91-75; f. 1874; 5,000 vols, MSS in Arabic, Turkish, French, Italian and English; Dir MONCEF FAKHFAKH; publ. *Inventaires des documents d'archives conservés.*

Bibliothèque Nationale: BP 42, 20 Souk-el-Attarine, Tunis; tel. (71) 32-53-38; fax (71) 20-09-25; f. 1885; depository of books published in Tunisia (mostly in Arabic); documentation and information dept; 1,500,000 vols in 12 languages; 15,000 periodicals; 40,000 Arabic and Oriental MSS; Curator Dr HASSOUNA MZABI; publs *Catalogue général des manuscrits* (annually), *Le Livre Tunisien* (annually).

Bibliothèques Publiques: Head Office: 39 rue Asdrubal, Lafayette, 1002 Tunis; tel. (71) 78-25-52; fax (71) 79-77-52; f. 1965; 2,746,678 vols in 293 public libraries throughout the country, notably at Tunis, Béja, Bizerte, Gabès, Gafsa, Jendouba, Kairouan, Kasserine, El Kef, Medenine, Monastir, Nabeul, Sfax, Sousse, Siliana, Mahdia, Ariana, Ben Arous, Zagnouan, Sidi Bouzid, Tozeur, Kébili and Tetaouine; 233 children's libraries, 266 local and community libraries and 27 mobile libraries; Dir ALI FETTAHI; publs *Bulletin* (annually), *Répertoire, Statistics of public libraries.*

Centre de Documentation Nationale: 4 rue Ibn Nadim, 1002 Tunis-Belvédère; tel. (71) 89-42-66; fax (71) 79-22-41; f. 1966; 8,000 monographs, 2,400 periodicals, 10,000 press articles, 50,000 photographs; Dir-Gen. MOHAMED MAHFOUDH.

Museums and Art Galleries

Carthage

Musée National de Carthage: BP 3, 2016 Carthage; tel. (71) 73-00-36; fax (71) 73-00-99; f. 1964; library of 5,000 vols on archaeology (special collection: antiquity); Dir ABDELMAJID ENNABLI.

El Jem

Musée Archéologique d'El Jem: El Jem.

Kairouan

Musée d'Art Islamique: Kairouan.

Makthar

Musée Archéologique de Makthar: Makthar; Punic and Roman.

Monastir

Musée d'Art Islamique du Ribat: Monastir.

Sbeïtla

Musée de Sbeïtla: Sbeïtla; Roman antiquities.

Sfax

Musée Archéologique de Sfax: Sfax.

Sousse

Musée Archéologique de Sousse (Kasbah): Sousse.

Tunis

Maison des Arts: Parc du Belvédère, 1002 Tunis; tel. (71) 28-37-49; fax (71) 79-58-60; f. 1992; art exhibition, musical and cultural activities; library of 6,000 vols; Dir ALI LOUATI.

Musée National du Bardo: 2000 Le Bardo, Tunis; tel. (71) 51-36-50; fax (71) 51-40-50; f. 1888; contains prehistoric collections, relics of Punic, Greek and Roman art, and ancient and modern Islamic arts, largest collection in the world of Roman mosaics; library of 4,700 vols; Dir HABIB BEN YOUNES; publ. *Les Nécropoles Puniques de Tunisie.*

Universities

UNIVERSITÉ DU 7 NOVEMBRE À CARTHAGE

29 rue Asdrubal, 1002 Tunis

Telephone: (71) 78-75-02

Fax: (71) 78-87-68

E-mail: pu7nc@univ7nc.rnu.tn

Internet: www.univ7nc.rnu.tn/Fr/indexfr.htm

Founded 1988 as Université de Droit, d'Economie et de Gestion; present name 2000

President: Prof. TAÏEB HADHRI

Sec.-Gen.: MOHAMED AMEUR ISMAÏL

Number of teachers: 2,003

Number of students: 30,590

DEANS

Faculty of Economics and Management (Nabeul): EZZEDDINE ZOUARI

Faculty of Law, Political and Social Sciences (Tunis): (vacant)

Faculty of Sciences (Bizerte): CHAABANE CHEFI

DIRECTORS

Bizerte Preparatory Engineering Institute: CHAABANE CHEFI

Centre for Law and Justice Studies: SAIDA JAOUIDA GUIGA

Higher Institute of Applied Sciences and Technology (Mateur): HECHMI SAÏD

Higher Institute of Childcare Personnel Training: TAHAR ABID

Higher Institute of Environment, Urbanism and Building Technologies: MABROUK HTIRA

Higher Institute of Fine Arts (Nabeul): HAYET TLILI

Higher Institute of Fisheries and Aquaculture (Bizerte): EL HECHMI MISAOUI

Higher Institute of Languages (Tunis): MOHAMED MILED

Higher Institute of Statistics and Information Analysis: MEKKI KSOURI

Higher School of Agriculture (Kef): AHMED MAROUANI

Higher School of Agriculture (Mateur): HÉDI ABDOULI

Higher School of Agriculture (Mogren): ABDERRAZAK SOUISSI

Higher School of Communication: MOHAMED NACEUR AMMAR

Higher School of Food Industries: ABDELKADER CHÉRIF

Higher School of Rural Engineering: TIJANI EL MEHOUACHI

Higher School of Statistics and Information Analysis: MEKKI KSOURI

Higher School of Technology and Computer Science (Carthage): SAFIA M'DIMIGH BELGHITH

Institute of Advanced Business Studies (Carthage): KHALED MILED

Institute of Forestry: MOHAMED HABIB JEMLI

Nabeul Preparatory Engineering Institute: ABDELGHANI B. HADJ AMOR

National Agricultural Research Institute of Tunisia: NETIJ BEN MCHILA

National Institute of Agronomy (Tunis): MOHAMED MONCEF EL HARRABI

National Institute of Applied Sciences and Technology: MEKKI KSOURI

National Institute of Labour and Social Studies (Tunis): MUSTAPHA NASRAOUI

National Research Institute in Rural Engineering, Water and Forestry: MOHAMED NEJIB REJEB

National School of Architecture and Town Planning (Tunis): NACEUR AMMAR

Polytechnic School of Tunisia: JMAIEL BEN IBRAHIM

Preparatory Institute for Engineering Studies (Mateur): ABDELHAK BEN YOUNES

Preparatory Institute for Engineering Studies (Nabeul): ABDELGHANI BEN HADJ AMOR

Preparatory Institute for Scientific and Technical Studies (La Marsa): HASSAN MAAREF

UNIVERSITÉ DU CENTRE, SOUSSE

Rue Khalifa El Karoui Sahloul, BP 526, 4002 Sousse

Telephone: (73) 36-81-25

Fax: (73) 36-81-26

E-mail: universite.centre@uc.rnu.tn

Internet: www.uc.rnu.tn

Founded 1986 as Université de Monastir pour le Centre; present name 1991

State control

President: MOHAMED ALI HAMZA
Number of teachers: 2,585
Number of students: 51,490

DEANS

Faculty of Arts and Humanities, Khairouan: SAHBI ALLANI
Faculty of Arts and Humanities, Sousse: HÉDI JATLAOUI
Faculty of Dental Medicine, Monastir: KHALED BOURAOUI
Faculty of Economics and Management, Mahdia: ALI FRAJ
Faculty of Law, Economics and Political Science, Sousse: MONGI TARCHOUNA
Faculty of Medicine, Monastir: HABIB SABBAH
Faculty of Medicine, Sousse: BECHIR BEL HADJ ALI
Faculty of Pharmacy, Monastir: MOHAMED KALLEL
Faculty of Science, Monastir: MONGI BEN AMARA

ATTACHED RESEARCH INSTITUTES

Higher Institute of Applied Sciences and Technology, Sousse: Dir YOUNES BOUWEZRA.

Higher Institute of Applied Studies in Humanities, Mahdia: Dir HACHEMI BANNOUR.

Higher Institute of Biotechnology, Monastir: Dir AHMED NOURREDINE HELAL.

Higher Institute of Business Studies, Sousse: Dir LOFTI BELKASSEM.

Higher Institute of Crafts and Technical Training: Dir ABD-ESSATTAR EL-BARRAQ.

Higher Institute of Fashion, Monastir: Dir FATEN ELSHKIRI.

Higher Institute of Finance and Fiscal Studies: Dir NAJIB BELAID.

Higher Institute of Fine Arts, Sousse: Dir AZIZA MRABET.

Higher Institute of Information Technology and Communications Technology, Hammam Sousse: Dir RAFIK BRAHEM.

Higher Institute of Information Technology and Management, Kairouan: Dir ABD-ELSATTAR ELBARREK.

Higher Institute of Information Technology and Management, Monastir: Dir HABIB YOUSSEF.

Higher Institute of Management, Sousse: Dir FAÏÇAL MANSOURI.

Higher Institute of Modern Languages in Business and Tourism, Moknine: Dir MANSOUR MHENNI.

Higher Institute of Music, Sousse: Dir MOHAMED ZINELABIDINE.

Higher Institute of Transport and Planning, Sousse: Dir MUSTAPHA BELHARETH.

Higher School of Health Science and Technology, Monastir: Dir HABIB HASSINE.

Higher School of Health Science and Technology, Sousse: Dir RAFIAA NOURIA.

National School of Architecture, Chott Mariem: Dir MOHAMED HABIB BEN HAMOUDA.

National School of Engineering, Monastir: Dir SASSI BEN NASRALLAH.

Preparatory Institute for Engineering Studies, Monastir: Dir BECHIR BEN HASSINE.

UNIVERSITÉ EZZITOUNA

21 rue Sidi Jelizi, Place Maakel Ezzaïm, 1008 Tunis

Telephone: (71) 57-55-14
Fax: (71) 57-61-51
Internet: www.uz.rnu.tn

Founded 1988 from existing faculties
State control
President: SALEM BOUYAHIA
Faculties of Theology and Religious Studies
Publications: *Al-Miskat* (annually), *Ettanwir* (annually).

ATTACHED RESEARCH INSTITUTES

Centre for Islamic Studies: Dir HARRATH BOUALLAGUI.

Higher Institute of Islamic Civilization: Dir MEHREZ HAMDI.

Higher Institute of Theology: Dir MOHAMED BECHIR BOUZIDI.

UNIVERSITÉ DE LA MANOUBA

Campus Universitaire de la Manouba, la Manouba 2010

Telephone: (71) 60-14-99
Fax: (71) 60-22-11
E-mail: mail@uma.rnu.tn
Internet: www.uma.rnu.tn

Founded 2001
State control
President: SLAHEDDINE GHERISSI
Number of students: 32,565

DEAN

Faculty of Arts: MOHAMED ALI DRISSA

ATTACHED RESEARCH INSTITUTES

Higher Institute of Accounting and Business Administration: Dir SAMIR EL GHAZOUANI.

Higher Institute of Documentation: Dir KHALED MILED.

Higher Institute of the History of the National Movement: Dir MOHAMED LOFTI CHAIBI.

Higher Institute of Multimedia Arts: Dir HAMADI HASNI.

Higher Institute for the Promotion of the Handicapped: Dir LOFTI BELLALEHOM.

Higher Institute of Sport and Physical Education: Dir RIDHA LAOUNI.

Higher School of Commerce: Dir HASSAN MZALI.

Higher School of Sciences and Design Technology: Dir RAIF MALEK.

Institute of Press and Communications Science: Dir MOHAMED HAMDANE.

National School of Computer Sciences: Dir KHALID GHEDIRA.

School of Veterinary Medicine: Dir MOHAMED HABIB JEMLI.

UNIVERSITÉ DE SFAX POUR LE SUD

Route de l'Áeroport, 3029 Sfax

Telephone: (74) 24-44-23
Fax: (74) 24-09-13
E-mail: uss@uss.rnu.tn
Internet: www.mes.tn/uss/index.htm

Founded 1986 from existing faculties; campus at Gafsa
State Control
Languages of instruction: Arabic, French
President: MOHAMED HEDI KTARI
Secretary-General: MOHSEN BEN MANSOUR
Number of teachers: 2,495
Number of students: 48,514

DEANS

Faculty of Arts and Humanities: MOHSEN DHIEB
Faculty of Economics and Administration: ALI CHKIR
Faculty of Law: AHMED OMRANE
Faculty of Medicine: ADNANE HAMMAMI

Faculty of Science, Gafsa: (vacant)
Faculty of Science, Sfax: ABDELHAMID BEN SALAH

CONSTITUENT INSTITUTES

Higher Institute of Applied Humanities Studies, Gafsa: Dir IBRAHIM JADLA.

Higher Institute of Business Administration: Dir ABDELWAHEB REBAI.

Higher Institute of Business Administration, Gafsa: Dir MALEK OURIMI.

Higher Institute of Crafts and Technical Training: Dir NOURREDINE ELHENI.

Higher Institute of Electronics and Telecommunications Technology: Dir LOFTI KAMOUN.

Higher Institute of Industrial Management: Dir HABIB CHABCHOUB.

Higher Institute of Information Technology and Media Studies: Dir ABDELMAJID BEN HAMADOU.

Higher Institute of Management Training, Gafsa: Dir AMMAR AKRIMI.

Higher Institute of Music: Dir MOURAD SIALA.

Higher Institute of Sport and Physical Education: Dir JALEL MILADI.

Higher Institute of Technology, Gafsa: Dir JALEL KHDIRI.

Higher Institute of Technology, Sfax: Dir SLIMENE GABSI.

Institute of Advanced Business Studies: Dir FAIKA SCANDER CHARFI.

National School of Commerce: Dir ABDELKADER CHAABANE.

National School of Engineering: Dir BOUBAKER EL EUCH.

National School of Health Science and Technology: Dir MONGIA HACHICHA.

Olivier Institute: Dir TAÏ MILADI.

Preparatory Institute for Engineers: Dir FATHI LAADHAR.

RESEARCH CENTRE

Biotechnology Centre: Dir HAMADI AYADI.

UNIVERSITÉ DE SOUSSE

Ave Khelifa Karoui, Sahloul IV, Sousse

Telephone: 73368125
Fax: 73368126
E-mail: lmd@mes.rnu.tn
Internet: www.uc.rnu.tn

Founded 1986
State control
Language of instruction: French
Academic year: September to July
President: AHMED NOUREDDINE HELAL

Library of 200,000 vols
Number of teachers: 1,500
Number of students: 32,000
Faculties of Law, Economics and Politics, Medicine, Arts and Human Sciences.

ATTACHED RESEARCH INSTITUTES

Forestry Institute: Dir LAMJED TOUMI.

Higher Institute of Agriculture, Le Kef: Dir NASRAOUI BOUZID.

Higher Institute of Physical Education, Le Kef: Dir YOUSSEF BOUSSAIDI.

Higher School of Rural Engineering, Medjez El Bab: Dir TIJANI EL MEHOUACHI.

UNIVERSITÉ DE TUNIS

92 blvd du 9 Avril 1938, 1007 Tunis

Telephone: (71) 56-73-22
Fax: (71) 56-06-33

Founded 1988 as Université des Lettres, des Arts et des Sciences Humaines (Tunis I) from existing faculties; present name 2001

President: ABDERRAOUF MAHBOULI

Secretary-General: LAMJED MESSOUSSI

Library of 186,000 vols

Number of teachers: 1,280

Number of students: 32,000

Publications: *Les Annales de l'Université* (in Arabic), *Les Cahiers de Tunisie* (multilingual), *La Revue des Langues* (multilingual), *La Revue Tunisienne des Sciences de la Communication*, *Revue Géographique* (multilingual)

DEANS AND DIRECTORS

Faculty of Humanities and Social Sciences: HABIB DLALA

Faculty of Law, Economics and Management: CHOKRI MAMOGHLI

Faculty of Letters: (vacant)

Centre for Economic and Social Studies and Research: HACHMI LABAÏED

Higher Documentation Institute: HENDA HAJAMI BEN GHZALA

Higher Institute of Applied Studies in Humanities: JAMEL BEN TAHAR

Higher Institute of Cultural Studies and Heritage Professions of Tunis: HABIB BAKLOUTI

Higher Institute of Drama: MOHAMED MESSAOUD DRISS

Higher Institute of Education and Training: MALIKA TRABELSI

Higher Institute of Management: ABDELWAHED TRABELSI

Higher Institute of Music: MUSTAPHA ALOULOU

Higher Institute for Youth and Cultural Activity: MONCEF JAZZAR

Higher Teacher Training School: MABROUK EL MANNAÏ

National Institute of Heritage: BÉJI BEN MAMI

Preparatory Institute for Engineering Studies: MOHAMED ABEDELMANAF BEN ABDRABOU

Tunis College of Science and Technology: JILANI LAMLOUMI

Tunis Higher Institute of Fine Arts: MOHAMED BEN TAHER GUIGA

UNIVERSITÉ DE TUNIS EL MANAR

Campus Universitaire, Manar II, 2092 Tunis

Telephone: (71) 87-33-66

Fax: (71) 87-20-55

E-mail: unitumanar@tun2.rnu.tn

Founded 1988 as Université des Sciences, des Techniques et de Médecine de Tunis (Tunis

II) from existing faculties; present name 2001

President: Prof. YOUSSEF ALOUANE

Secretary-General: ISMAIL KHALIL

Number of teachers: 2,733

Number of students: 23,488

Publication: *Revue de l'Université* (every 2 months)

DEANS AND DIRECTORS

Faculties of Economics and Management: MOHAMED HADDAR

Faculty of Law and Political Science: CHAFIK SAÏED

Faculty of Mathematics, Physics and Natural Sciences: CHEDLI TOUBLI

Faculty of Medicine: RACHID MECHMECH

Bourguiba Institute of Modern Languages: ABED EL MAJID EL BEDOUI

El Khawarizmi Computer Centre: HENDA HADJAMI BEN GHEZELA

El Manar Preparatory School of Engineering: MOHAMED EL ABAAD

Higher Institute of Computer Science: SAMIR BEN AHMED

Higher Institute of Humanities: MOHAMED MAHJOUB

Higher Institute of Medical Technology: FATMA SLIM EL HILA

Higher Institute for Sport and Physical Education: ABDELAZIZ SFAR

Higher School of Food Technology: ABDELKADER CHERIF

Higher School of Health Sciences and Technology: MOHAMED HABIB JAAFOURA

Higher School of Posts and Telecommunications: NACEUR AMMAR

Higher School of Science and Technology: SLAHEDDINE EL-GHRISSI

Institute for the Advancement of Disabled People: RAOUF BEN AMMAR

Kef Higher School of Agriculture: BOUZID NASRAOUI

Kef Institute for Sport and Physical Education: YOUSSEF FEKIH

Mateur Higher School of Agriculture: HEDI ABDOULI

Mateur Preparatory School of Engineering: MOHAMED BEJAOUI

Medjez el Bab Higher School of Rural Engineering: ABDERRAZEK SUISSI

Mograne Higher School of Agriculture: TIJANI MAHOUACHI

Nabeul Preparatory Institute of Engineering: MONCEF HADDED

National Agricultural Research Institute: SALAH MEKNI

National Institute of Agronomy: MONCEF EL-HARRABI

National Research Institute of Rural Engineering for Water and Forests: NEJI RAJEB

National Research Institute of Sciences and Technology: MOHAMED NOBIL

National School of Computer Science: FAROUK KAMMOUN

National School of Engineering: KHALIFA MAÂLEL

National University Centre for Scientific and Technical Documentation: FATMA CHAMMAM BEN ABDALLAH

Pasteur Institute: KOUSSAI EDALAJI

Polytechnic Institute: TAIEB HADHRI

Preparatory Institute of Scientific Studies and Technology: FAOUZIA CHARFI

School of Civil Aviation and Meterorology: MOHAMED TOUIL

Sidi Thabet National School of Veterinary Medicine: ATEF MALEK

Tabarka Forestry School: HAMDA SAOUDI

Veterinary Research Institute: MALEK ZRELLI

Other Institutions of Higher Education

Centre Culturel International d'Hammamet: Ave des Nations Unies, 8050 Hammamet; tel. 72280410; fax 72280722; f. 1962; theatrical techniques, history and sociology of the theatre and video; Dir TAOUFIK BESBÈS.

Conservatoire National de Musique, de Danse et d'Arts Populaires: 20 ave de Paris, Tunis.

Ecole Nationale d'Administration: 24 ave du Docteur Calmette, Mutuelleville, Tunis; tel. 71288300; f. 1964; library: 53,000 vols; 1,050 students; Dir MAHER KAMOUN; publ. *Revue Tunisienne d'Administration Publique* (3 a year).

Ecole Nationale de la Statistique: BP 65, Tunis; f. 1969; 1- and 2-year diploma courses.

Institut d'Economie Quantitative: 27 rue de Liban, 1002 Tunis; tel. 71283633; fax 71787034; f. 1964; methodological research in planning and documentation in social and economic fields; library: 7,500 vols, 300 periodicals; Dir Gen. GHORBEL HÉDI.

Institut National du Travail et des Etudes Sociales: Z. I. Charguia II, BP 692, 1080 Tunis Cedex; tel. 71706207; fax 71703464; e-mail intes@intes.rnu.tn; internet www.intes.rnu.tn; language of instruction: Arabic; library: 5,000 vols; 110 teachers (34 full-time, 76 part-time); 2,200 students; Dir Prof. MUSTAPHA NASRAOUI; publ. *Travail et Développement* (2 a year).

TURKEY

The Higher Education System

Universities are administered by the YÖK (Council of Higher Education), which sets institutional budgets and defines criteria for the award of degrees. Institutions of higher education include universities, faculties, institutes, colleges, conservatories, vocational colleges and research centres. In 2003/04 some 1.8m. students attended 1,248 higher education institutes.

The main criteria for admission to higher education is the State University Entrance Examination (Ögrenci Secme Sinavi—ÖSS), administered by the Student Selection and Placement Centre (ÖSYM). Universities set their own entrance requirements based on scores in the ÖSS. Since 2002 the two-year Associate Degree (Ön Lisans Diplomasi) has been broadened to encompass technical and vocational education. The Bachelors (Lisans Diplomasi) is mostly a four-year programme of study, although some disciplines require longer periods of study, such as dentistry, architecture, veterinary medicine (five years) and medicine (six years). The first postgraduate degree is the Masters (Yüsek Lisans Diplomasi), which is a two-year programme and admission to which is on the basis of a competitive examination administered by the ÖSYM. The final university degree is the Doctor of Philosophy (Doktora); again, admission is on the basis of a competitive examination administered by the ÖSYM, and students are required to complete a four-year period of study and research for award of the final degree.

Technical and vocational education is legally defined as one of three categories: formal vocational education, apprenticeship training or vocational courses. Since 2002 students have been allowed to enter vocational higher education without taking an entrance examination. In terms of formal vocational training, the main institutions are specialist vocational schools attached to universities, in addition to two-year colleges of technology and commercial colleges. Students who successfully complete the course of study are awarded the ön lisans (followed by subject name) and title of tekniker (Technician). Apprenticeship training is offered largely at the secondary level, and vocational courses are aimed at adults who have left formal education.

Learned Societies

AGRICULTURE, FISHERIES AND VETERINARY SCIENCE

Türk Veteriner Hekimleri Birliği (Turkish Veterinary Medical Association): 73/8, Kocatepe, Ankara; tel. and fax (312) 435-54-15; e-mail merkezkonseyi@tvhb.org.tr; internet www.tvhb.org.tr; f. 1930.

BIBLIOGRAPHY, LIBRARY SCIENCE AND MUSEOLOGY

Türk Kütüphaneciler Derneği (Turkish Librarians' Association): Necatibey Cad. Elgün Sok. 8/8, 06440 Kızılay, Ankara; tel. (312) 230-13-25; fax (312) 232-04-53; e-mail tkd.dernek@gmail.com; internet www.kutuphaneci.org.tr; f. 1949; 2,000 mems; Pres. TUNCEL ACAR; Sec.-Gen. SUZAN AKYÜZ; publ. *Türk Kütüphaneciliği* (4 a year).

ECONOMICS, LAW AND POLITICS

Türk Hukuk Kurumu (Turkish Law Association): 2 Cad. 55/6 Bahçelievler, Ankara; f. 1934; publs *La Turquie* (Vie Juridique des Peuples, Paris), *Türk Hukuk Lûgati* (Turkish Law Dictionary).

EDUCATION

Türk Üniversite Rektörleri Komitesi (Committee of Turkish University Rectors): Yükseköğretim Kurulu, Bilkent, Ankara; tel. (312) 266-47-25; fax (312) 266-51-53; f. 1967; rectors of all Turkish universities, with five former rectors; advises the Higher Education Ccl and the Interuniversity Board on university affairs, promotes co-operation between universities; Pres. Prof. Dr KEMAL GÜRÜZ; Sec. Prof. Dr UĞUR BÜGET.

HISTORY, GEOGRAPHY AND ARCHAEOLOGY

Türk Tarih Kurumu (Turkish Historical Society): Kızılay Sok. 1, 06100 Sıhhiye Ankara; tel. (312) 310-23-68; fax (312) 310-16-98; e-mail ttkinfo@ttk.org.tr; internet www.ttk.org.tr; f. 1931; 40 mems; library of 228,577 vols; Pres. Prof. Dr YUSUF HALAÇO-ĞLU; publs *Belgeler* (annually), *Belleten* (3 a year).

LANGUAGE AND LITERATURE

British Council: Posta Kutusu 34, Çankaya, Ankara; tel. (312) 455-36-00; fax (312) 455-36-36; e-mail libinfo.ankara@britishcouncil.org.tr; internet www.britishcouncil.org/turkey; offers courses and exams in English language and British culture and promotes cultural exchange with the UK; attached offices in Istanbul (teaching centre) and Izmir; library of 7,500 vols, 72 periodicals; Dir of Operations, Turkey CHRIS BROWN.

Goethe-Institut: Atatürk Bulvarı 131, Bakanlıklar, 06640 Ankara; tel. (312) 419-52-83; fax (312) 418-08-47; e-mail il@ankara.goethe.org; internet www.goethe.de/om/ank; offers courses and exams in German language and culture and promotes cultural exchange with Germany; attached centres in Istanbul and Izmir; library of 15,000 vols; Dir SABINE HAGEMANN-ÜNLÜSOY.

Instituto Cervantes: Tarlabasi Bulvari, Zambak Sokak 33, 80080 Istanbul; tel. (212) 292-65-36; fax (212) 292-65-37; e-mail cenest@cervantes.es; internet estambul.cervantes.es; offers courses and exams in Spanish language and culture and promotes cultural exchange with Spain and Spanish-speaking Latin and Central America; library of 7,500 vols; Dir PABLO MARTÍN ASUERO.

PEN Yazarlar Derneği (Turkish PEN Centre): Istiklal Cad., 225, Beyoglu is Merkezi, B Blok, Kat. 2, 143, Beyoglu, Istanbul; e-mail pprtr@superonline.com; f. 1989; 200 mems; Pres. VECDI SAYAR; publ. *Turkish PEN Reader* (every 6 months, in English).

Türk Dil Kurumu (Turkish Language Institute): Atatürk Bulvarı 217, Kavaklıdere, 06680 Ankara; tel. (312) 428-61-00; fax (312) 428-52-88; e-mail bim@tdk.org.tr; internet www.tdk.org.tr; f. 1932; 40 mems; library of 35,000 vols on Turkish studies; Pres. Prof. Dr ŞÜKRÜ HALUK AKALIN; Sec.-Gen. CAFER ÇETIN; publs *Tercüme Yıllığı* (Yearbook of Translation), *Türk Dili Araştırmaları Yıllığı* (Yearbook of Turkic Studies), *Türk Dili Dergisi* (Journal of Turkish Language, monthly), *Türk Dünyası Dergisis* (Journal of Turkish World, 2 a year).

MEDICINE

Türk Cerrahi Derneği (Turkish Surgical Society): Koru Mah. Ihlamur Cad. 26, 06810 Çayyolu, Ankara; tel. (312) 241-99-90; fax (312) 241-99-91; e-mail turkcer@turkcer.org.tr; internet www.turkcer.org.tr; f. 1929.

Türk Mikrobiyoloji Cemiyeti (Turkish Microbiological Society): PK 57, Beyazit, Istanbul; tel. and fax (212) 531-70-89; e-mail tmc@tmc-online.org; internet www.tmc-online.org; f. 1931; 280 mems; Pres. Prof. Dr OZDEM ANĞ; Sec.-Gen. Prof. Dr ALI AĞAÇFIDAN; publs *Infeksiyon Dergisi* (Journal of Infection, quarterly), *Türk Mikrobiyoloji Cemiyeti Dergisi* (Journal, quarterly).

Türk Nöropsikiyatri Derneği (Turkish Neuropsychiatric Society): Op. Dr. Raif Bey Sok. 31/2, 34360 Sisli, Istanbul; tel. (212) 219-97-77; fax (212) 343-00-95; e-mail peykang@ixir.com; f. 1914; 1,200 mems; meetings to discuss aspects of psychiatry and neurology; Pres. Prof. PEYKAN GÖKOLP; publ. *Nöropsikiyatri Arşivi* (Archives of Neuropsychiatry, 4 a year).

Türk Ortopedi ve Travmatoloji Birliği Derneği (Turkish Association of Orthopaedics and Traumatology): Bayraktar Mahallesi Ikizdere Sok. 21/12, Kat:2 GOP, Ankara; tel. (312) 436-11-40; fax (312) 436-27-16; e-mail totbid@totbid.org.tr; internet www.totbid.org.tr; Pres. Prof. Dr N. ERTAN MERGEN.

Türk Oto-Rino-Larengoloji Cemiyeti (Turkish Oto-Rhino-Laryngological and Head and Neck Surgery Society): Buyudere Cad. Tankaya 18 Daire 1, Şişli, 80220 Istanbul; tel. (212) 233-11-26; fax (212) 233-11-27; e-mail orl@torl.org.tr; internet www.torl.org.tr; f. 1930; 2,500 mems; Pres. Prof. Dr ASIM KAYTAZ; Gen. Sec. Prof. Dr FERHAN ÖZ; publ. *Turkish Archives of Otolaryngology* (3 a year).

Türk Tabipleri Birliği (Turkish Medical Association): GMK Bul. Şehit Daniş Tunalıgil Sok. 2 Kat. 4, Maltepe, 06570 Ankara; tel. (312) 231-31-79; fax (312) 231-19-52; e-mail ttb@ttb.org.tr; internet www.ttb.org.tr; f. 1856; 312 mems; Pres. Dr FÜSUN SAYEK; Gen. Sec. Dr ORHAN ODABAŞI.

Türk Tibbi Elektro Radyografi Cemiyeti (Turkish Electro-Radiographical Society): Valikonagi Cad. 10, Harbiye, Istanbul; f. 1924.

Türk Tıp Tarihi Kurumu (Turkish Medical History Society): c/o Uludağ Üniversitesi, Tıp Fakültesi, Deontoloji ve Tıp Tarihi Anabilim Dalı, Bursa; tel. (532) 452-94-37; e-mail ademirer@yahoo.com; f. 1938; 120 mems; library of 70,000 vols; Pres. Prof. Dr AYŞEGÜL ERDEMIR DEMIRHAN.

Turk Tüberküloz ve Toraks Derneği (Turkish Association of Tuberculosis and Thorax): Ankara Üniversitesi, Tıp Fakültesi, Göğüs Hastalıkları Anabilim Dalı, 06100 Cebeci- Ankara; tel. (312) 319-00-27; fax (312) 319-00-46; e-mail akaya@medicine.ankara.edu.tr; internet www.tubtoraks.org; Dir Dr ÖZLEM ÖZDEMIR KUMBASAR; publ. *Journal* (4 a year).

Türk Üroloji Derneği (Turkish Urological Society): c/o Prof. Nurettin Öktem Sokak, Lale Palas Apt. 18/2, 34382 Şişli, Istanbul; tel. and fax (212) 232-46-89; e-mail uroturk@uroturk.org.tr; internet www.uroturk.org.tr; f. 1933; 1,093 mems; Pres. Prof. VURAL SOLOK; publ. *Türk Üroloji Dergisi* (Turkish Journal of Urology, quarterly).

NATURAL SCIENCES

Mathematical Sciences

Türkiye Matematik Derneği (Mathematical Society of Turkey): Sabancı Üniversitesi, Karaköy İletişim Merkezi, Bankalar Cad. 2, 80020 Karaköy, Istanbul; tel. (212) 292-49-39; e-mail emrah@su.sabanciuniv.edu; internet www.tmd.org.tr; f. 1948; development of mathematics among young people; 509 mems; Pres. Prof. Dr TOSUN TERZIOĞLU; Gen. Sec. Prof. Dr HÜLYA ŞENKON; publ. *Matematik Dünyası* (2 a year).

Physical Sciences

Türkiye Kimya Derneği (Chemical Society of Turkey): Halaskârgazi Cad. 53, D. 8 Uzay Apt, Harbiye, Istanbul; tel. (212) 240-73-31; e-mail tkd@turchemsoc.org; internet www.turchemsoc.org; f. 1919; 1,500 mems; Pres. Prof. Dr OSMAN YAVUZ ATAMAN'IN; publ. *Kimya ve Sanayi* (Chemistry and Industry).

PHILOSOPHY AND PSYCHOLOGY

Türkiye Felsefe Kurumu (Philosophical Society of Turkey): Ahmet Rasim Sok. 8/2, Çankaya, 06550 Ankara; tel. (312) 440-74-08; fax (312) 441-02-97; e-mail toc@tfk.org.tr; internet www.tfk.org.tr; f. 1974 to promote philosophy and philosophical education in Turkey, to encourage philosophical thinking in public life, and to secure international co-operation through seminars, symposia, courses etc.; 153 individual mems; Pres. IOANNA KUÇURADI; Sec.-Gen. CEMAL GÜZEL; publ. *Bülten* (3 a year).

Yeni Felsefe Cemiyeti (New Philosophical Society): Işık Lisesi, Nişantaşı, Istanbul; f. 1943.

TECHNOLOGY

TMMOB Jeoloji Mühendisleri Odası (Chamber of Geological Engineers of Turkey): PK 464, Yenişehir, 06444 Ankara; tel. (312) 434-36-01; fax (312) 434-23-88; e-mail jmo@jmo.org.tr; internet www.jmo.org.tr; f. 1974; 9,780 mems; library of 17,000 vols; Pres. AYDÝN CELEBI; Sec.-Gen. BAHATTIN

MURAT DEMIR; publs *Abstracts of the Geological Congress of Turkey* (annually), *Abstracts of Geological Research in Turkey* (annually), *Blue Planet* (2 a year), *Bulletin News* (4 a year), *Geological Bulletin of Turkey* (2 a year), *Journal of Geological Engineering* (2 a year).

Research Institutes

GENERAL

Research Centre for Islamic History, Art and Culture (IRCICA): POB 24, 34349 Beşiktaş, Istanbul; tel. (212) 259-17-42; fax (212) 258-43-65; e-mail ircica@superonline.com; internet www.ircica.org; f. 1979; a subsidiary of the Organization of the Islamic Conference; research and publication, organization of conferences, symposia, exhibitions, workshops, training courses and competitions; published books in various languages, newsletter appears quarterly in English, French and Arabic; library of 60,000 vols, 1,460 periodicals, 64,000 photographs; Dir-Gen. Dr HALIT EREN.

Türk Kültürünü Araştırma Enstitüsü (Turkish Cultural Research Institute): 17° Sok. 38, Bahçelievler, Ankara; tel. (312) 213-31-00; fax (312) 213-41-35; f. 1961; scholarly research into all aspects of Turkish culture; Dir Dr ŞÜKRÜ ELÇIN; publs *Cultura Turcica* (annually), *Türk Kültürü* (monthly), *Türk Kültürü Araştırmaları* (annually).

Türkiye Bilimsel ve Teknik Araştırma Kurumu (Scientific and Technical Research Council of Turkey): Tunus Cad. 80, 06100 Kavaklıdere, Ankara; tel. (312) 468-53-00; fax (312) 427-74-89; e-mail www-adm@tubitak.gov.tr; internet www.tubitak.gov.tr; f. 1963; library of 19,000 vols, 426 periodicals; government body which carries out, sponsors, promotes and co-ordinates research activities in pure and applied sciences; Pres. Prof. Dr NÜKET YETIS; Sec.-Gen. IBRAHIM BERBEROGLU (acting); publs *Bilim ve Teknik* (Science and Technology, monthly), *Turkish Journal of Agriculture and Forestry Sciences* (6 a year), *Turkish Journal of Biology* (6 a year), *Turkish Journal of Botany* (6 a year), *Turkish Journal of Chemistry* (6 a year), *Turkish Journal of Earth Sciences* (6 a year), *Turkish Journal of Electrical Engineering and Computer Sciences* (3 a year), *Turkish Journal of Engineering and Environmental Sciences* (6 a year), *Turkish Journal of Mathematics* (6 a year), *Turkish Journal of Medical Sciences* (6 a year), *Turkish Journal of Physics* (6 a year), *Turkish Journal of Veterinary and Animal Sciences* (6 a year), *Turkish Journal of Zoology* (6 a year).

Attached institutes:

Basic Science Research Institute.

Bilgi Teknolojileri ve Elektronik Araştırma Enstitüsü (Information Technologies and Electronics Research Institute): Middle East Technical University (ODTÜ) Campus, 06531 Ankara; tel. (312) 210-13-10; fax (312) 210-13-15; e-mail info@bilten.metu.edu.tr; internet www.bilten.metu.edu.tr; Dir Prof. Dr EROL KOCAOĞLAN.

Cukurova Advanced Agricultural Research and Development Institute.

Defence Research and Development Institute: PK 16 Mamak, 06261 Ankara; tel. (312) 399-03-38; fax (312) 212-37-49; Dir Prof. Dr ERES SÖYLEMEZ.

Gen Mühendisliği ve Biyoteknoloji Araştırma Enstitüsü (Research Institute for Genetic Engineering and Biotechnology): Anibal Cad. Barış Mah., PK 21, 41470 Gebze, Kocaeli; tel. (262) 641-23-00; fax

(262) 646-39-29; e-mail gmbae@rigeb.gov.tr; internet www.rigeb.gov.tr; f. 1983; Dir Doç. Dr KEMAL BAYSAL (acting).

Marmara Araştırma Merkezi (Marmara Research Centre): PK 21, 41470 Gebze, Kocaeli; tel. (262) 677-20-00; fax (262) 641-23-09; e-mail info@mam.gov.tr; internet www.mam.gov.tr; f. 1972; materials science, optoelectronics, earth sciences, food science, nutrition, information technology, chemistry, chemical technology, environmental technology and energy; library of 30,000 vols, 90,000 bound periodicals; Dir (vacant).

Ulusal Elektronik ve Kriptoloji Araştırma Enstitüsü (National Electronics and Cryptology Research Institute): PK 74, 41470 Gebze, Kocaeli; tel. (262) 648-10-00; fax (262) 648-11-00; e-mail uekae@uekae.tubitak.gov.tr; internet www.uekae.tubitak.gov.tr; library of 2,700 vols, 70 periodicals; Dir Prof. Dr AYHAN TÜRELI.

AGRICULTURE, FISHERIES AND VETERINARY SCIENCE

Kavak ve Hızlı Gelişen Tür Orman Ağaçları Araştırma Müdürlüğü (Poplar and Fast-Growing Forest Trees Research Institute): PK 1034, 41050 Izmit, Kocaeli; tel. (262) 311-69-64; fax (262) 311-69-72; e-mail kavak@kavak.gov.tr; internet www.kavak.gov.tr; f. 1962; attached to the Ministry of Forests; development of forest nursery and reafforestation techniques, introduction of new forest tree species, increase of wood production, research in poplar cultivation and management techniques; library of 3,700 vols; Dir Dr FARUK Ş. ÖZAY; publs *Annual Bulletin, Magazine, Technical Bulletin*.

Tarım ve Köyişleri Bakanlığı, Zirai Mücadele Araştırma Enstitüsü (Ministry of Agricultural and Rural Affairs, Plant Protection Research Institute): Bağdat Cad. 250, PK 49, Yenimahalle, Ankara; tel. (312) 344-74-30; fax (312) 315-15-31; f. 1934; depts dealing with research into combating plant diseases, pests and weeds; engaged in phytopathology, entomology, insect taxonomy and toxicology, nematology; analyses pesticides and crop pesticide residues; library of 5,000 vols; Dir Dr ZIYA ŞIMŞEK; publ. *Bitki Koruma Bülteni* (Plant Protection Bulletin, English, French or German summary, irregular).

HISTORY, GEOGRAPHY AND ARCHAEOLOGY

British Institute at Ankara: Tahran Cad. 24, 06700 Kavaklıdere, Ankara; tel. (312) 427-54-87; fax (312) 428-01-59; e-mail ggirdivan@biaatr.org; internet www.biaa.ac.uk *London Office*: c/o Gina Coulthard, British Institute of Archaeology at Ankara, British Academy, 10 Carlton House Terrace, London, SW1Y 5AH, UK; f. 1947 with the object of furthering archaeological research by British and Commonwealth students or scholars in Turkey; supports, promotes and publishes British research focused on Turkey and the Black Sea littoral, in all academic disciplines within the arts, humanities and social sciences; maintains a centre of excellence in Ankara, focused on the archaeology and related subjects of Turkey; library of 45,000 vols; Pres. Prof. OLIVER GURNEY; Dir Dr LUTGARDEN VANDEPUT; publs *Anatolian Archaeology* (annually), *Anatolian Studies* (annually).

Deutsches Archäologisches Institut İstanbul Şubesi (Deutsches Archäologisches Institut Istanbul Branch): Gümüşsuyu/Ayazpaşa Camii Sok 48, 34437 Istanbul; tel. (212) 244-07-14; fax (212) 252-

34-91; e-mail sekretariat@istanbul.dainst.org; internet www.dainst.de; f. 1929; research into archaeology and cultural history in Turkey from prehistory to the Ottoman period; library of 60,000 vols; Dir Prof. Dr-Ing. A. HOFFMANN; publs *Istanbuler Beihefte, Istanbuler Forschungen, Istanbuler Mitteilungen des DAI* (annually).

Hollanda Araştırma Enstitüsü (Netherlands Institute in Turkey): Istiklâl Cad., Nur-i Ziya Sokak 5, Beyoğlu, Istanbul; tel. (212) 293-92-83; fax (212) 251-38-46; e-mail nit@nit-istanbul.org; internet www.nit-istanbul.org; f. 1958; library of 16,000 vols; Dir Dr FOKKE GERRITSEN; Librarian GÜLTEN YILDIZ; publ. *Anatolica* (annual).

Institut Français d'Etudes Anatoliennes d'Istanbul (Fransız Anadolu Araştırmaları Enstitüsü/French Institute of Anatolian Studies, Istanbul): PK 54, Palais de France, Nuru Ziya Sok, 80072 Beyoğlu-Istanbul; tel. (212) 244-17-17; fax (212) 252-80-91; e-mail ifea@ifea-istanbul.net; internet www.ifea-istanbul.net; f. 1930; Anatolian studies from prehistory to contemporary period; 15 mems; library of 24,000 vols; Dir PIERRE CHUVIN; publs *Anatolia antiqua* (annually), *Anatolia moderna* (annually).

Orient-Institut der Deutschen Morgenländischen Gesellschaft, Istanbul (Alman Şarkiyat Cemiyeti'nin Orient Enstitüsü, İstanbul/Orient Institute of the German Oriental Society, Istanbul): Susam Sokak 16-18, D.8, 34433 Cihangir, Istanbul; tel. (212) 293-60-67; fax (212) 249-63-59; e-mail oiist@oidmg.org; internet www.oidmg.org; f. 1987; Turkish, Ottoman and Central Asian Studies; library of 25,000 vols, 1,000 periodicals; Dir Prof. Dr MANFRED KROPP; Dir in Istanbul Dr CLAUS SCHÖNIG.

MEDICINE

Çocuk Sağlığı Enstitüsü, Hacettepe Üniversitesi İhsan Doğramacı Çocuk Hastanesinde (Institute of Child Health at Hacettepe University Children's Hospital): İhsan Doğramacı Çocuk Hastanesi 2, Blok 3, 06100 Ankara; tel. (312) 324-42-91; fax (312) 324-32-84; e-mail tkutluk@hacettepe.edu.tr; internet www.cocuk.hacettepe.edu.tr; f. 1958; library incorporated in Medical Faculty Library; Dir Dr TEZER KUTLUK; publs *Çocuk Sağlığı ve Hastalıkları Dergisi* (abstracts in English, quarterly), *Turkish Journal of Paediatrics* (quarterly).

NATURAL SCIENCES

General

Istanbul Üniversitesi Deniz Bilimleri ve İşletmeciliği Enstitüsü (University of Istanbul Institute of Marine Sciences and Management): Müsküle Sok 1 Vefa, 34470 Istanbul; tel. (212) 528-25-39; fax (212) 526-84-33; e-mail cemga@istanbul.edu.tr; internet www.istanbul.edu.tr/enstituler/denizbilimleri/denizbilimleri.htm; f. 1993; library of 11,243 vols; Dir Prof. Dr ERTUĞRUL DOĞAN; publ. *Turkish Journal of Marine Science* (3 a year).

Türk Bilim Tarihi Kurumu (Turkish Society for History of Science): POB 234, 80692 Beşiktaş, Istanbul; tel. (212) 260-07-17; fax (212) 258-43-65; e-mail ircica@superonline.com; f. 1989; research and publication on history of science with emphasis on Ottoman history of science, organization of symposia; Pres. Prof. Dr EKMELEDDİN İHSANOĞLU; publ. *Newsletter* (2 a year).

Physical Sciences

Maden Tetkik ve Arama Genel Müdürlüğü (MTA) (General Directorate of Mineral Research and Exploration): İsmet İnönü

Bulvarı, Ankara; tel. (312) 287-34-30; fax (312) 287-91-88; e-mail mta@mta.gov.tr; internet www.mta.gov.tr; f. 1935; conducts the Geological Survey of Turkey and evaluates mineral resources; library: see Libraries and Archives; Dir-Gen. A. KEMAL ISIKER; publs *Bulletin of Mineral Research and Exploration* (2 a year, in English), annual reports and maps.

RELIGION, SOCIOLOGY AND ANTHROPOLOGY

Islâm Araştırmaları Merkezi (Centre for Islamic Studies): Altunizade, İcadiye Bağlarbaşı Cad. 40, Bağlarbaşı, 81200 Üsküdar, Istanbul; tel. (216) 474-08-50; fax (216) 474-08-74; e-mail isam@isam.org.tr; internet www.isam.org.tr; f. 1988; library of 160,000 vols, 2,400 periodicals; Chair. Prof. Dr M. AKIF AYDIN; publ. *Turkish Journal of Islamic Studies*.

TECHNOLOGY

Afet İşleri Genel Müdürlüğü Deprem Araştırma Dairesi (General Directorate of Disaster Affairs Earthquake Research Department): Yüksel Cad. 7/B, Yenişehir, Ankara; tel. (312) 287-36-45; e-mail zemin@deprem.gov.tr; internet www.deprem.gov.tr; f. 1969; 78 staff; attached to the Ministry of Public Works and Resettlement; establishment, operation and maintenance of nationwide strong ground motion recorder network; earthquake prediction; preparation of codes and regulations for earthquake-resistant design and construction; research on earthquake hazard minimization; education and information of the public; comprises Earthquake Engineering, Seismology and Laboratory Divisions; Dir MUSTAFA TAYMAZ; publ. *Bulletin* (quarterly).

Ankara Nükleer Araştırma ve Eğitim Merkezi (Ankara Nuclear Research and Training Centre): 06105 Saray, Ankara; tel. (312) 815-43-00; fax (312) 815-43-07; e-mail sinman@saray.anaem.gov.tr; internet www.anaem.gov.tr; f. 1967; attached to the Turkish Atomic Energy Authority; applied research in radiation chemistry and physics, electronics, nuclear agriculture, materials sciences and plasma physics; library of periodicals and technical reports; Dir O. GÜVEN; publ. *Turkish Journal of Nuclear Sciences* (2 a year).

Araştırma Dairesi Başkanlığı (Demiryollar, Limanlar ve Hava Meydanları İnşaatı Genel Müdürlüğünün) (Department of Research and Materials (General Directorate of Railways, Harbour and Airport Construction)): Macun mah. Serpme Sok 3, 06338 Yenimahalle, Ankara; tel. (312) 397-33-50; fax (312) 397-38-11; e-mail dlharastirma1@ttnet.net.tr; internet www.dlh.gov.tr/arastirma; f. 1948; road materials testing, pavement design, soil and rock mechanics and geotechnical investigations; 60 staff; library of 2,467 vols; Dir YUSUF ZIYA BOYACI; publ. *Research Bulletin*.

Devlet Su İşleri, Teknik Araştırma ve Kalite Kontrol Dairesi (State Hydraulic Works, Technical Research and Quality Control Department): Ismet Inonu Bul., 06100 Yücetepe, Ankara; tel. (312) 417-83-00; fax (312) 418-24-98; e-mail takk@dsi.gov.tr; internet www.dsi.gov.tr; f. 1958; research and laboratory work on hydraulic engineering, soil mechanics, construction materials and concrete, chemistry, isotopes for hydrology; *in situ* research on water works; library; Dir Prof. Dr VEYSEL EROĞLU; publ. *DSI Teknik Bülteni* (original papers, some in foreign languages).

Marmara Research Centre: POB 21, 41470 Gebze-Kocaeli; tel. (262) 641-23-00;

fax (262) 641-23-09; e-mail director@mam.gov.tr; f. 1972; research on basic and applied sciences, and industrial research; library of 90,000 vols, 746 periodicals; Dir Prof. ÖMER KAYMAKÇALAN; publ. publs research reports.

Libraries and Archives

Afyon

Gedik Ahmed Paşa Library: Dumlupınar Mah. Şeyh Mehmet, Cad. 1, Afyon; tel. and fax (272) 213-54-33; f. 1785; 30,000 vols.

Ankara

Ankara Üniversitesi, Kütüphane ve Dokümantasyon Daire Başkanlığı (Ankara University Libraries and Documentation Centre): Sevket Aziz Kansu Bldg, İncitaşı Sok, Beşevler, Ankara; tel. (312) 223-57-61; fax (312) 213-95-32; e-mail atilgan@ankara.edu.tr; internet www.ankara.edu.tr; f. 1946; 722,309 vols, 33,000 e-books, 621 printed periodicals, 11,000 e-journals, 4,308 audiovisual materials, 17,872 MSS, and 29,029 dissertations and theses; Library Dir Dr DOGAN ATILGAN.

Library of National Defence: Ankara; f. 1877; 8,678 vols in Turkish, 5,820 vols in other languages; State-governed.

Maden Tetkik ve Arama Genel Müdürlüğü Kütüphanesi (General Directorate of Mineral Research and Exploration Library): İsmet İnönü Bulvarı, Ankara; f. 1935; 180,000 vols in various languages, 2,118 periodicals; Librarian ÜMIT ERKMEN; publ. *Bulletin* (in Turkish and English).

Middle East Technical University Library: İsmet İnönü Bulvarı, 06531 Ankara; tel. (312) 210-27-80; fax (312) 210-11-19; e-mail lib-hot-line@metu.edu.tr; internet www.lib.metu.edu.tr; f. 1956; maintains custody of the university's recording, microfilm and projection equipment; 478,000 vols, 1,818 current periodicals, 6,941 electronic periodicals; Dir Prof. Dr BÜLENT KARASÖZEN.

Milli Kütüphane (National Library of Turkey): Bahçelievler, Ankara 06940; tel. (312) 222-38-12; fax (312) 223-04-51; e-mail info@mkutup.gov.tr; internet www.mkutup.gov.tr; f. 1946; 1,136,997 vols, 911,675 vols of periodicals, 35,024 MSS, 197,577 non-book items; Pres. TUNCEL ACAR; publs *Türkiye Bibliyografyası* (Turkish National Bibliography, monthly), *Türkiye Makaleler Bibliyografyası* (Bibliography of articles in Turkish periodicals, monthly).

Public Library: Ankara; f. 1922; 21,000 vols in Turkish, 10,200 vols in European languages, over 1,200 MSS in Arabic and Persian.

Türkiye Büyük Millet Meclisi Kütüphane ve Dokümantasyon Merkezi (Grand National Assembly Library and Documentation Centre): Ankara; tel. (312) 420-68-35; fax (312) 420-75-48; e-mail library@tbmm.gov.tr; internet www.tbmm.gov.tr; f. 1920; 271,298 vols in social sciences including 107,196 in Turkish, 24,788 in English, 10,847 in French, 1,000 in Arabic and Persian, 60 MSS, 59,134 vols of periodicals; Dir YSMET BAYDUR; publ. *Bilgi* (quarterly).

Antalya

Antalya Tekelioğlu İl Halk Kütüphanesi (Tekelioğlu Library): Ucgen Mah. 96. Sok. 54, Antalya; tel. (242) 344-51-37; f. 1924; 5,000 vols, nearly 2,000 MSS in Persian, Arabic and Turkish; Dir AYŞE D. SAVGUN.

Balıkeşir

Il Halk Kütüphanesi, Balıkeşir (Provincial Public Library, Balıkeşir): Bahçelievler Mah.Kıralı Sok., Balıkeşir; tel. (266) 241-32-33; fax (266) 243-04-12; f. 1901; 1,286 MSS in Turkish, Arabic and Persian, 49,000 vols in Turkish, Arabic and English, 766 in other languages, 5,088 periodicals; Dir A. ERCAN TIĞ.

Darende

Mehmet Paşa Library: Darende; f. 1776; 4,000 vols, 800 MSS.

Edirne

Selimiye Library: Edirne; f. 1575; 36,113 vols (including 3,172 MSS and 3,894 vols in Arabic); Librarian Mrs OZLEM AĞIRGAN.

Isparta

Halil Hamit Paşa Library: Isparta; f. 1783; 20,200 vols, over 850 MSS; Dir MAHMUT KAYICI.

Istanbul

Atatürk Kitaplığı (Ataturk Library): Mete Caddesi 45, Taksim, Istanbul; tel. (212) 249-56-83; fax (212) 251-79-72; f. 1929; public library; 184,000 vols.

Beyazıt Devlet Kütüphanesi (Beyazit State Library): Turan Emeksiz Sok 6, 344450 Beyazıt, Istanbul; tel. (212) 522-31-67; f. 1882; legal deposit library; 500,000 vols in various languages, 11,120 MSS, 32,992 photographs, 21,616 periodicals; Dir YUSUF TAVACI.

Boğaziçi University Library: Bebek, 80815 Istanbul; tel. and fax (212) 257-50-16; e-mail bulib@boun.edu.tr; internet www.library.boun.edu.tr; f. 1863; 375,000 vols in English and other languages, including a special colln of over 30,332 vols on the Near East, 10,000 rare books and MSS; 220 periodicals, 2,500 records and 200 CDs; Librarian HATICE ÜN.

Ecumenical Patriarchate Library: İstanbul Rum Patrikliği, Sadrazam Ali Paşa Caddesi 35, 34220 Fener, Istanbul; internet www.patriarchate.org; foundation dates from beginning of Patriarchate, reorganization 1890; 25,000 vols in main library, and 1,500 MSS; 45,000 vols in branch library at Orthodox Seminary of Heybeliada; Dir Rev. PANAĞHIOTIS THEODORIDIS (under the jurisdiction of the Holy Synod).

Institute of Turkology Library: Istanbul University, 34452 Beyazıt, Istanbul; f. 1924; 50,000 vols relating to Turkish language, literature, history and culture.

Istanbul Teknik Üniversitesi Kütüphane ve Dokümantasyon Daire (Istanbul Technical University Library and Documentation Division): Ayazağa Kampüsü, Maslak 34469, Istanbul; tel. (212) 285-35-96; fax (212) 285-33-02; e-mail kutuphane@itu.edu.tr; internet www.library.itu.edu.tr; f. 1795; six separate libraries on five university campuses; 372,000 vols; Dir of Libraries AYHAN KAYGUSUZ.

Istanbul University Library and Documentation Centre: University PTT 34452, Beyazıt, Istanbul; tel. (212) 455-57-83; fax (212) 455-57-84; e-mail uko@istanbul.edu.tr; internet www.kutuphane.istanbul.edu.tr; f. 1925; comprises the central university library and 17 faculty libraries; 500,000 vols, 18,606 MSS, 18,000 periodicals (3,100 current), 35,000 theses; Dir Doç. Dr ÜMIT KONYA.

Köprülü Yazma Eser Kütüphanesi (Köprülü Library): Divan Yolu Cad. 29, Cemberlitas-Eminonu, Istanbul; tel. (212) 516-83-13; f. 1677; 3,000 vols, 2,755 MSS, of which 193 are from early Ottoman presses,

and 42 handwritten works from before the 10th c.

Millet Kütüphanesi (Public Library): Macar Kardeşler Cad. 85, 34260 Fatih, Istanbul; tel. (212) 631-36-07; f. 1916; 33,980 vols, 8,844 MSS.

Nuruosmaniye Library: Camii Avlusu, Cagaloglu, Istanbul; tel. (212) 527-20-04; f. 1755; 6,000 vols, 5,000 MSS.

Süleymaniye Kütüphanesi (Süleymaniye Library): Aysekadin Hamami Sok. 35, Beyazit, Istanbul; tel. (212) 520-64-60; fax (212) 520-64-62; f. 1557; 113,068 vols and 66,117 MSS in Turkish, Uyghur, Arabic and Persian; 109 different collections including those from Ayasofya, Fatih and Husrev Pasha; MS restoration service; brs at Atif Efendi, Hacı Selim Ağa, Köprülü, Nuru-Osmaniye, Ragıppaşa; Dir Dr NEVZAT KAYA.

Women's Library and Information Center Foundation: Fener Mahallesi, Fener Vapur Iskelesi Karşısı, Fener Haliç, 34220 Istanbul; tel. (212) 534-95-50; fax (212) 523-74-08; e-mail kek@mail.archimac.org; 6,500 vols; Dir BEKIR KEMAL ATAMAN.

Izmir

National Library of Izmir: Milli Kütüphane Cad. 39, Konak- Izmir; f. 1912; 299,000 vols in Turkish, 40,000 vols in European languages, 19,000 vols in Oriental scripts, 4,000 MSS, 4,843 periodicals; Dir ALİ RIZA ATAY.

Konya

Public Library: Purcuklu Mah., Turbe Cad. 23, Karatoy, Konya; f. 1947; 20,000 vols, 6,000 MSS.

Nevşehir

Damat Ibrahim Paşa Library: Nevşehir; f. 1727; 5,500 vols, 600 MSS.

Museums and Art Galleries

Adana

Adana Bölge Müzesi (Adana Regional Museum): Adana; f. 1926; depts of archaeology and ethnography; conference hall, laboratories, library and administrative sections; more than 107,000 items from the Neolithic to Roman and Byzantine periods; unique statue of a god made from natural crystal dating from Hittite Empire.

Amasya

Amasya Müzesi: Atatürk Cad. 91 Amasya; tel. (358) 218-45-13; fax (358) 218-69-57; f. 1926, moved 1961 to the Gök Medrese Mosque; archaeological finds from the early Bronze Age to Ottoman period; includes mummies dating from the Imperial period.

Ankara

Anadolu Medeniyetleri Müzesi (Museum of Anatolian Civilizations): Samanpazarı, Ankara; tel. (312) 324-31-60; fax (312) 311-28-39; f. 1921; exhibits cover the Palaeolithic, Neolithic, Chalcolithic, Early Bronze Age, Hittite, Phrygian, Urartian and Classical periods; Hittite reliefs from Alaca, Carchemish, Sakcagözü and Aslantepe and Ankara regions; collections represent excavations at Karain, Çatal Hüyük, Hacılar, Can Hasan, Alacahöyük, Ahlatlıbel, Karaz, Alişar, Karaoğlan, Karayavşan, Oymaağaç, Merzifon, Beycesultan, Kültepe, Acemhöyük, İnandık, Boğazköy, Eskiyapar, Patnos, Adilcevaz, Uşak-İkiztepe, Pazarlı, Gordion, Altıntepe, with special sections for cuneiform tablets and coins; library of 6,567 vols; Dir İLHAN

TEMİZSOY; publs *The Anatolian Civilizations Museum Periodical*, *Museum Annual*, *Museum Conference Annual*, *Museum Lectures* (annually), *Museum News* (2 a year).

Anıtkabir Atatürk Müzesi (Atatürk's Mausoleum and Museum): Anıt Caddesi, Tandoğan, Ankara; tel. (312) 231-79-75; fax (312) 231-53-80; internet www.tsk.mil.tr./anitkabir/index.html; f. 1953; official and civil possessions of Mustafa Kemal Atatürk (1881–1938), founder of the Turkish Republic and its first President; colln incl. documents, medals, plaques and albums; panoramas and paintings of the most important battles in Turkish history; library of 3,123 vols from the private library of Atatürk.

Ethnographical Museum: Talatpasa Bulvari, Ankara; tel. (312) 311-95-56; f. 1930; specimens of Turkish and Islamic art, archives and Islamic seals; library of 6,245 vols; Dir Mrs SEMA KOÇ.

Kurtuluş Savaşl ve Cumhuriyet Müzeleri (Museums of the Turkish Independence War and Turkish Republic): Cumhuriyet Bulvari No. 14–22, Ulus, Ankara; f. 1961; located in former Grand National Assembly buildings; library of 60,000 vols and 20,000 documents; Dir MUSTAFA SÜEL.

Natural History Museum: MTA, Genel Müdürlüğü, Eskişehir Yolu Balgat, 06520 Ankara; tel. (312) 286-32-89; fax (312) 284-14-77; e-mail muze1@mta.gov.tr; internet www.mta.gov.tr; f. 1968; attached to General Directorate of Mineral Research and Exploration; Dir Dr ALAADIN VURAL.

Antakya

Hatay Museum: Gündüz Cad. 1, Antakya, Hatay; tel. (326) 214-61-68; fax (326) 213-33-86; f. 1934; collection of mosaics from Roman Antioch, also finds from Al-Mina, Atchana, Çatal Hüyük, Judeidah and Tainat excavations; Dir MEHMET ERDEM.

Antalya

Antalya Müzesi (Antalya Museum): Konyaaltı Caddesi, Antalya; tel. (242) 238-56-88; fax (242) 238-56-87; f. 1922; prehistory, archaeology, numismatics, ethnography, children's section and garden exhibition; library of 7,500 vols; Dir SELAHATTIN EYÜP AKSU.

Aydın

Aydın Müzesi: Hasan Efendi Mahallesi, Kapalı Spor Salonu yanı Aydın; tel. (256) 225-22-59; fax (256) 213-35-91; f. 1959; archaeology, ethnography, historical coins.

Bergama

Pergamon Museum: Cumhurıyet Cadd. 10, 35700 Bergama-Izmir; tel. (232) 631-28-83; fax (232) 631-07-77; f. 1936; houses the historical relics discovered as the result of excavations conducted at Pergamon; Dir ADNAN SARIOĞLU.

Bodrum

Bodrum Sualtı Arkeoloji Müzesi (Bodrum Museum of Underwater Archaeology): 48000 Bodrum; tel. (252) 316-25-16; fax (252) 313-76-46; e-mail bodrum-museum@yahoo.com; internet www.bodrum-museum.com; f. 1964 in the castle of Bodrum (built 15th c., by the Knights of St John from Rhodes); finds from land and underwater, incl. ceramics, metal, stone, gold and glass, from the Mycenaean, Attic, Hellenic, Roman, Byzantine and Ottoman eras; remains of late Bronze age ship; Dir (vacant).

Bursa

Bursa Arkeoloji Müzesi: Kültürpark, Bursa; tel. (224) 234-49-18; fax (224) 234-49-19; f. 1902; archaeological finds from

Bursa, Balıkesir and Bilecik; prehistoric, Roman and Byzantine finds, stone, ceramic, glass and metal objects, coins; library of 3,824 vols; Chief Officer SALIH KÜTÜK.

Bursa Türk ve Islâm Eserleri Müzesi (Bursa Turkish and Islamic Art Museum): Yeşil, Bursa; tel. (224) 327-75-39; f. 1975 in the Yeşil Medrese, built by the Ottoman Sultan Mehmet I Çelebi; items from 12th c. to late Ottoman period; illuminated MSS, samples of calligraphy, woodwork, metalwork, embroidery, costumes, ceramics; open-air museum of gravestones.

Çanakkale

Truva Müzesi (Troy Museum): Çanakkale; at the entrance to the ruins of Troy in Çanakkale is a small museum exhibiting pottery, figurines, statues, glass objects.

Eskişehir

Eskişehir Arkeoloji Müzesi: Akarbaşı Mahallesi, Hasan Polatkan Bul. 64, Eskişehir; tel. (222) 230-13-71; fax (222) 230-17-49; e-mail muze2603@kultur.gov.tr; f. 1935; plant and animal fossils; prehistory (ceramics, idols, stone and bone objects); the walls are decorated with late Roman mosaics found in excavations at Doryleum; Museum Head M. DURSUN ÇAĞLAR.

Istanbul

Âsiyan Museum: Aşiyan Yokuşu, 80810 Bebek, Istanbul; tel. (212) 263-69-86; home of Turkish poet and artist T. Fikret (1867-1915).

Askeri Müze ve Kültür Sitesi Komutanlığı (Military Museum and Cultural Centre): Harbiye, Istanbul; tel. (212) 233-27-20; fax (212) 296-86-18; e-mail askerimuze@hotmail.com; f. 1846; military uniforms, weapons, tents and trophies from ancient times; library of 18,395 vols; Dir Col H. İBRAHIM ÇIÇEKSIZ.

Ayasofya (Saint Sophia) Museum: Sultan Ahmet, 34400 Istanbul; tel. (212) 522-09-89; fax (212) 512-54-74; e-mail ayasofyamuzesi@hotmail.com; internet www.kultur.gov.tr; f. 1935; the Museum is housed in the Byzantine Basilica; built by Justinian and dedicated in AD 537, it was a church until 1453, after which it became a mosque; in 1935 it was made a state museum; contains Byzantine and Turkish antiquities; Dir MUSTAFA AKKAYA; publ. *The Annual of St Sophia*.

Istanbul Arkeoloji Müzeleri (Archaeological Museums of Istanbul): Gülhane, 34400 Istanbul; tel. (212) 520-77-40; fax (212) 527-43-00; f. 1891; includes Archaeological, Turkish Tiles and Ancient Orient museums, with Sumerian, Akkadian, Hittite, Assyrian, Egyptian, Urartu, Phrygian, Greek, Roman and Byzantine works of art; more than 1m. exhibits; library of 80,000 vols; Dir HALIL ÖZEKNLI.

Istanbul Deniz Müzesi (Istanbul Naval Museum): Deniz Müzesi K.hği, Beşiktaş, Istanbul; tel. (212) 261-00-40; fax (212) 236-68-93; f. 1897; cannons, important collection of historical caiques, models, torpedoes and mines, Turkish standards, medals, costumes, paintings; library of 20,000 vols, 22,436 archives files (Ottoman Empire period); Dir Cdr A. MUHLIS ERGIN.

Istanbul Resim ve Heykel Müzesi (Museum of Painting and Sculpture): Beşiktaş, Istanbul; tel. (212) 261-42-98; fax (212) 244-03-98; f. 1937; Turkish paintings and sculptures since 19th c.; international art exhibitions; Dir Prof. KEMAL İSKENDER.

Sabancı Üniversitesi Sakıp Sabancı Müzesi (Sabancı University Museum): İstinye Cad. 22, Emirgan 80850, Istanbul; tel. (212) 277-22-00; fax (212) 229-49-14; e-mail muze@sabanciuniv.edu; internet muze.sabanciuniv.edu; f. 2002 in the former private residence of the Sabancı family; calligraphic items since 15th c., paintings since 19th c.; Dir Dr NAZAN ÖLÇER.

Tanzimat Müzesi (Tanzimat Museum): Gülhane Parkı, 94400 Sirkeci, Istanbul; tel. (212) 512-63-04; e-mail tanzimatmuze@ibb-kutuphane.gov.tr; f. 1952 in Ihlamur Pavilion, current site since 1983; operated by Istanbul Metropolitan Municipality; documents, paintings and objects pertaining to the Tanzimat period of reform 1839–1876; Curator FADIME GELEŞ.

Topkapı Palace Museum: Sultanahmet 34400, Istanbul; tel. (212) 522-44-22; fax (212) 528-59-91; e-mail topkakisarayi@atlas.net.tr; internet www.kultur.gov.tr; palace built by Mehmed II; collections of Turkish armour, cloth, embroidery, glass and porcelain, copper- and silver-ware, treasure, paintings, miniatures, illuminated manuscripts, royal coaches, collections of Sèvres and Bohemian crystal and porcelain, clocks, important collection of Chinese and Japanese porcelain amassed by the Sultans, collection of manuscripts, Ottoman tent; Audience Hall, Council Hall of Viziers, Baghdad and Revan Köşks, Harem; library of 18,000 MSS and 200,000 archive documents; Dir FILIZ ÇAĞMAN.

Türk ve Islam Eserleri Müzesi (Museum of Turkish and Islamic Art): Ibrahim Paşa Sarayı, At Meydani 46, Sultanahmet, Istanbul 34400; tel. (212) 518-18-05; fax (212) 518-18-07; e-mail tiemist@superonline.com; internet www.tiem.org; f. 1914; Turkish and Islamic rugs, illuminated MSS, sculpture in stone and stucco, woodcarvings, metalwork and ceramics, traditional crafts and ethnographical material, all gathered from Turkish mosques and tombs; library: 4,142 MSS and 3,279 vols; Dir NAZAN ÖLCER.

Izmir

Izmir Arkeoloji Müzesi: Halit Rıfat Paşa Cad. 4, Konak, Izmir; tel. (232) 489-07-96; fax (232) 483-06-11; f. 1927; works from the Archaic, Classical and Hellenistic periods of the Ionian civilization.

Konya

Konya Museums: Il Kültür Müdürlüğü, Müze Müdürlüğü, Konya Valiliği; Dir of Museums Dr ERDOĞAN EROL.

Museums:

Atatürk Museum: collection of documents and objects connected with Atatürk, also Konya clothing and other ethnographic exhibits.

Classical Museum: collections of Neolithic, early Bronze Age, Hittite, Phrygian, Greek, Roman and Byzantine monuments.

Mevlâna Museum: f. in Mevlâna Turbe; Seljuk, Ottoman and Turkish collections, clothing, carpets, and Turkish collections, clothing, carpet, coins, library.

Seljuk Museum: f. in Ince Minare; contains stone and wooden works of the Seljuk period.

Sirçali Medresseh: Sarcophagus and inscription, collections of Seljuk and Ottoman period.

Turkish Ceramics Museum: f. in Karatay Medresseh; contains ceramics from 13th–18th c.

Polatlı

Gordion Museum: Polatlı, Ankara; tel. (312) 638-21-88; fax (312) 311-28-39; e-mail anmedmuz@marketweb.net.tr; f. 1965; built near the Great Tumulus believed to be that of the Phrygian king Midas; archaeological items found during excavations at Gordion (now Yassıhöyük); Dir ILHAN TEMIZSOY.

Selçuk

Efes Müzesi Müdürlügü (Ephesus Museum):Kusadasi Cad., 35920 Selçuk-Izmir; tel. (232) 892-60-10; fax (232) 892-70-02; f. 1929; of art (mostly statues and reliefs) excavated from Ephesus; library of 3,200 vols; Dir SELAHATTIN ERDEMGIL; publ. *Efes Müzesi Yıllıgı* (annually).

Selimiye

Side Müzesi: Manavgat-Antalya, Side (Selimiye); tel. (242) 753-10-06; fax (242) 753-27-49; f. 1962; museum is located in a Late Roman bath; statues and busts of Roman gods, goddesses and emperors; library of 985 vols; Dir ORHAN ATVUR.

Van

Van Müzesi:Şerefiye Mahallesi, Hacıosman Sokak 9 Van; tel. (432) 216-11-39; fax (432) 214-25-10; f. 1947; archaeological finds from the Urartu Civilization.

Universities

ABANT IZZET BAYSAL ÜNİVERSİTESİ

Yunus Emre Kampüsü, 14280 Gölköy- Bolu

Telephone: (374) 253-45-11
Fax: (374) 253-45-06
Internet: www.ibu.edu.tr
Founded 1992
State control

President: Prof. Dr YAŞAR AKBIYIK
Vice-Presidents: Prof. Dr M. TEKIN BABAÇ, Prof. Dr M. HAYRI ERKOL, Prof. Dr R. GÜL TÝRYAKÝ SÖNMEZ

Number of teachers: 393
Number of students: 7,500

DEANS

Faculty of Arts and Sciences: Prof. Dr NILHAT ÇELEBÝ
Faculty of Economics and Administrative Sciences: Prof. Dr NEVZAT YOSMAOĐLU
Faculty of Education: Prof. Dr ERSEGUL BALCIBUCAK
Faculty of Forestry: Prof. Dr NAFIZ URDU
Faculty of Medicine (Düzce): Prof. Dr AHMET ATAOĐLU
Faculty of Medicine (Yzzet): Prof. Dr CIHANGAR UYAN
Faculty of Technical Education: Prof. Dr YSMAIL ERCAN

ADNAN MENDERES ÜNİVERSİTESİ

Aytepe Mevkii, Merkez Kampus, 09010 Aydin

Telephone: (256) 212-76-79
Fax: (256) 225-32-40
Internet: www.adu.edu.tr
Founded 1992
State control
Academic year: September to June

Rector: Prof. Dr MUSTAFA GUREL
Vice-Rectors: Dr OSMAN KAYA, Prof. Dr ERGUN ONUR, Prof. Dr ISMAIL TURGUT
Sec. Gen.: ZIYAETTIN TEKMEN

Number of teachers: 960
Number of students: 10,000

Publications: *Bulletin* (quarterly), *Journal of Medical Faculty*

DEANS

Faculty of Agriculture: MUSTAFA ALI KAYNAK
Faculty of Economics and Administration: ERDOGAN GURSOY
Faculty of Medicine: TURGAY AKTUNE

Faculty of Science and Letters: ALI ERSIN KARAGOZLER
Faculty of Veterinary Science: HASAN ELEN

AFYON KOCATEPE ÜNİVERSİTESİ

Ahmet Necdet Sezer Kampüsü, Gazligol Yulu, 03200 Afyon

Telephone: (272) 444-03-03
Fax: (272) 228-14-08
E-mail: rektor@aku.edu.tr
Internet: www.aku.edu.tr

Founded 1974
State control

Rector: Prof. Dr HALIM SÖZBILIR
Vice-Rectors: Prof. Dr NALAN BAYSU SÖZBILIR, Prof. Dr YILMAZ DÜNDAR, Prof. Dr ADNAN ŞIŞMAN
General Secretary: RASIK ALTI
Librarian: Yrd. Doç. Dr NEVZAT BİLGİN

Number of teachers: 618
Number of students: 21,201 (12,883 undergraduate, 8,318 postgraduate)

DEANS

Faculty of Arts and Sciences: Prof. Dr MUHSIN KONUK
Faculty of Arts and Sciences (Uşak): Prof. Dr LÜTFI ÖZAV
Faculty of Economics and Administrative Sciences (Uşak): Prof. Dr H. HÜSEYIN BAYRAKLI
Faculty of Economics and Management Science: Prof. Dr KEMALETTIN CONKAR
Faculty of Education: Prof. Dr HAKKI YAZICI
Faculty of Education (Uşak): Prof. Dr ADNAN ŞIŞMAN
Faculty of Engineering: Prof. Dr ABDULLAH ÇAĞLAR
Faculty of Engineering (Uşak): Prof. Dr FIKRI ŞENOL
Faculty of Fine Arts: Prof. Dr NALAN BAYSU SÖZBİLIR
Faculty of Medicine: Prof. Dr AYŞE ÖNER
Faculty of Technical Education: Prof. Dr FATIH NURAY
Faculty of Veterinary Medicine: Prof. Dr RECEP ASLAN

AKDENİZ ÜNİVERSİTESİ

Dumlupınar Bulvarı Kampus, 07058 Antalya

Telephone: (242) 227-59-83
Fax: (242) 227-55-40
E-mail: international@akdeniz.edu.tr
Internet: www.akdeniz.edu.tr

Founded 1982; previously affiliated to Ankara University
State control
Language of instruction: Turkish
Academic year: October to June

Rector: Prof. Dr MUSTAFA AKAYDIN
Vice-Rectors: Prof. Dr MEHMET RIFKI AKTEKİN, Prof. Dr SADIK ÇAKMAKÇI, Prof. Dr MUSTAFA PEKMEZCI
General Secretary: NUSRET ÇELIK
Librarian: NEVZAT SABAN

Number of teachers: 1,646
Number of students: 19,090

Publications: *Journal of the Faculty of Agriculture, Journal of the Faculty of Medicine* (quarterly), *University Bulletin*

DEANS

Faculty of Agribusiness: Prof. Dr AHMET AKTAŞ
Faculty of Agriculture: Prof. Dr HALIL İBRAHIM UZUN
Faculty of Communications: Prof. Dr ÜMIT ATABEK
Faculty of Arts and Sciences: Prof. Dr MUSTAFA GÖKÇEOĞLU
Faculty of Economics and Administrative Sciences: Prof. Dr FULYA SARVAN

Faculty of Education: Prof. Dr MEHMET YALÇIN
Faculty of Engineering: Prof. Dr HIKMET RENDE
Faculty of Fine Arts: Prof. Dr ABDULLAH UZ
Faculty of Fisheries: Prof. Dr RAMAZAN İKIZ
Faculty of Law: Prof. Dr MERAL SAĞIR ÖZTOPRAK
Faculty of Medicine: Prof. Dr MUSTAFA MELİKOĞLU
Faculty of Veterinary Science: Prof. Dr BAYRAM ALI YUKARI

There are 4 Vocational Schools within Akdeniz University, 8 Vocational Schools in Antalya and 4 Graduate Schools.

ANADOLU ÜNİVERSİTESİ
(Anatolian University)

Yunus Emre Kampüsü, 26470 Eskişehir

Telephone: (222) 335-05-80
Fax: (222) 335-36-16
E-mail: webadmin@anadolu.edu.tr
Internet: www.anadolu.edu.tr

Founded 1958
State control
Languages of instruction: Turkish, English
Academic year: October to June

Rector: Prof. Dr ENGIN ATAÇ
Vice-Rectors: Prof. Dr ATİLA BARKANA, Prof. Dr NÜVIT GEREK, Prof. Dr FEVZI SÜRMELİ, Prof. Dr NEZİH VARCAN, Prof. Dr HALUK GÜRGEN
Registrar and Secretary-General: ALİ RIZA ÖNDER
Librarian: ADNAN YILMAZ

Number of teachers: 1,728
Number of students: 1,082,782 (including open-education students)

Publications: *Journal of Sciences and Technology* (2 a year), *Journal of Social Sciences* (2 a year), *Turkish Online Journal of Distance Education* (2 a year)

DEANS

Faculty of Business Administration: Prof. Dr B. FETHI ŞENIŞ
Faculty of Communication Sciences: Prof. Dr ALI ATIF BIR
Faculty of Economics: Prof. Dr AHMET ÖZMEN
Faculty of Economics and Administrative Sciences: Prof. Dr GÜNEŞ BERBEROĞLU
Faculty of Education: Prof. Dr GÜRHAN CAN
Faculty of Engineering and Architecture: Prof. Dr HASAN MANDAL
Faculty of Fine Arts: Prof. Dr ATILLA ATAR
Faculty of Law: Prof. Dr HASAN NÜVIT GEREK
Faculty of Letters: Prof. Dr CAHIT YALÇIN BILIM
Faculty of Open Education: Prof. Dr NAZMI ULUTAK
Faculty of Pharmacy: Prof. Dr ÜMIT UÇUCU
Faculty of Sciences: Prof. Dr AHMET ÖZATA

HEADS OF DEPARTMENTS

Faculty of Business Administration (tel. (222) 335-05-80 ext. 3260; fax (222) 335-59-47; internet www.anadolu.edu.tr/cindex.html):
Business Administration: Prof. Dr. B. FETHI ŞENIŞ
Faculty of Communication Sciences (tel. (222) 335-05-80 ext. 2612; fax (222) 320-45-20; e-mail iltfak@anadolu.edu.tr; internet www.ilt.anadolu.edu.tr):
Advertising and Public Relations: Prof. Dr ALI ATIF BIR
Cinema and Television: Prof. GÜLSEREN GÜÇHAN
Communication: Prof. Dr ALI ŞIMŞEK
Printing and Publishing: Prof. Dr XLADIR SUGUR

Faculty of Economics (tel. (222) 335-05-80 ext. 2743; fax (222) 320-13-04; e-mail ikfak@anadolu.edu.tr; internet www.anadolu.edu.tr/bindex.html):
Economics: Prof. Dr NÜVIT OKTAY
Labour Economics and Industrial Relations: (vacant)
Public Administration: Prof. Dr RAMAZAN GEYLAN
Public Finance: Prof. Dr NEZİH VARCAN

Faculty of Economics and Administrative Sciences (tel. (222) 335-05-80 ext. 3216; fax (222) 335-05-95; e-mail iibfak@anadolu.edu.tr; internet www.iibf.anadolu.edu.tr):
Business Administration: Prof. Dr FERRUH ÇÖMLEKÇI
Economics: Prof. Dr KEMAL YILDIRIM
Labour Economics and Industrial Relations: Prof. Dr Ö. ZÜHTÜ ALTAN
Public Finance: Prof. Dr FETHI HEPER

Faculty of Education (tel. (222) 335-05-80 ext. 3536; fax (222) 335-05-79; e-mail egtfak@anadolu.edu.tr; internet www.egt.anadolu.edu.tr):
Educational Sciences: Prof. Dr MUSTAFA SOĞLAM
Elementary School: Prof. Dr ŞEFİK YAŞAR
Special Education: Prof. Dr SÜLEYMAN ERİPEK
Teacher Training in Arts and Crafts: Prof. Dr ŞAHIN ÖZYÜKSEL
Teaching Computing and Technology: Prof. Dr FERHAN ODABAŞI
Teaching of Foreign Languages: Prof. Dr ZÜLAL BALPİNOR

Faculty of Engineering and Architecture (tel. (222) 335-05-80 ext. 6320; fax (222) 323-95-01; e-mail muhfak@anadolu.edu.tr; internet www.mmf.anadolu.edu.tr):
Architecture: Dr ALPER ÇABUK
Ceramics Engineering: Assoc. Prof. Dr HASAN MANDAL
Chemical Engineering: Prof. Dr MEHMET RIZA ALTIOKKA
Civil Engineering: Prof. Dr AHMET TUNCAN
Computer Engineering: Prof. Dr ALI GUNEŞ
Electrical and Electronic Engineering: Prof. Dr ALTUĞ İFTAR
Environmental Engineering: Prof. Dr SERAP KARA
Industrial Engineering: Prof. Dr MUSA ŞENEL

Faculty of Fine Arts (tel. (222) 335-05-80 ext. 4220; fax (222) 335-12-90; e-mail gzsfak@anadolu.edu.tr; internet www.gzs.anadolu.edu.tr):
Animation: Assoc. Prof. FETHİ KABA
Ceramics: Prof. ZEHRA ÇOBANLI
Graphics: Assoc. Prof. Dr FİKRET UÇAR
Interior Design: Asst Prof. MERAL NALÇAKAN
Painting: Prof. ABDULLAH DEMİR
Printing Arts: Prof. ATILLA ATAR
Sculpture: Prof. AYTAÇ KATI

Faculty of Law (tel. (222) 335-05-80 ext. 2205; fax (222) 320-09-53; e-mail hukfak@anadolu.edu.tr; internet www.hukuk.anadolu.edu.tr):
Public Finance and Economics: Asst Prof. Dr RANA EŞKINAT
Public Law: Asst Prof. AYSE TÜLIN YÖRÜK
Special Law: Prof. Dr AKAR ÖCAL

Faculty of Letters (tel. (222) 335-05-80 ext. 6036; fax (222) 320-61-01; e-mail edbfak@anadolu.edu.tr; internet www.edb.anadolu.edu.tr):
Art History: Dr EROL ALTINSAPAN
Classical Archaeology: Assoc. Prof. NEŸAT BILGES
History: Prof. Dr IHSAN GÜNEŞ
Sociology: Prof. Dr BILHAN KORTAL

Turkish Language and Literature: Dr
ABDULKEDIR GÜRER

Faculty of Open Education (tel. (222) 330-39-
80; fax (222) 335-06-33; e-mail aofak@
anadolu.edu.tr; internet www.aof.anadolu
.edu.tr):

Continuing Education: Prof. Dr FEVZI
SÜRMELI
Distance Education: Prof. Dr LEVEND KILIÇ
Economics and Business Administration:
Prof. Dr ALIEKREM ÖZKUL
Health Care: Prof. Dr NAZMI ULUTAK

Faculty of Pharmacy (tel. (222) 335-05-80
ext. 3625; fax (222) 315-01-27; e-mail eczfak@
anadolu.edu.tr; internet www.ecz.anadolu
.edu.tr):

Basic Pharmaceutical Sciences: Prof. Dr
MUZAFFER TUNÇEL
Pharmaceutical Technology: Prof. Dr YASE-
MIN YAZAN
Professional Pharmaceutical Sciences:
Prof. Dr ŞEREF DEMIRAYAK

Faculty of Sciences (tel. (222) 335-05-80 ext.
5155; fax (222) 320-49-10; e-mail fenfak@
anadolu.edu.tr; internet www.fen.anadolu
.edu.tr):

Biology: Prof. Dr MERIH KIVANÇ
Chemistry: Prof. Dr LALE ZOR
Mathematics: Doç. Dr MEHMET ÜREYEN
Physics: Prof. Dr ÖNDER ORHUN
Statistics: Prof. Dr ALI FUAT YÜZER

ATTACHED SCHOOLS

School of Civil Aviation: Dir Prof. Dr
MUSTAFA KARA.
School of Drama and Music: Dir NAZLI
GÜLMEZ.
School of Foreign Languages: Dir Assoc.
Prof. HANDAN YAVUZ.
School of Industrial Arts: Dir Prof. Dr
YAŞAR HOŞCAN.
**School of Physical Education and
Sports:** Dir Prof. Dr COŞKUN BAYRAK.
**School of Tourism and Hotel Manage-
ment:** Dir Prof. Dr DENIZ BÜLER.
College for the Handicapped: Dir Prof. Dr
AHMET KONROT.

ATTACHED RESEARCH CENTRES

Atatürk Research Centre for Music: Dir
Assoc. Prof. BÜLENT ALANER.
Centre for Health and Social Services:
Dir Dr TURGUT KUTLU.
**Research Centre for Archaeology and
Art History:** Dir Dr M. EROL ALTINSAPAN.
Research Centre for Civil Aviation: Dir
Asst Prof. HAKAN OKTAL.
Research Centre for Computer Studies:
Dir Prof. Dr ÖNDER ÖZKAZANÇ.
**Research Centre for Continuous Educa-
tion:** Dir Prof. Dr İLHAN ÜNLÜ.
**Research Centre for Culture and the
Environment:** Dir Prof. Dr İNAL C. AŞKUN.
**Research Centre for Economics and
Social Studies:** Dir Prof. Dr İLYAS ŞIKLAR.
**Research Centre for the Education of
Hearing-Impaired Children:** Dir Assoc.
Prof. Dr ÜMRAN TÜFEKÇIOĞLU.
**Research Centre for Environmental
Studies:** Dir Prof. Dr ÜLKER ÖGÜTVERN.
**Research Centre for the European
Union:** Dir Assoc. Prof. ELIF UÇKAN DAĞDE-
MIR.
Research Centre for Folklore: Dir Assoc.
Prof. Dr YAVUZ KILIÇ.
**Research Centre for Foreign Lan-
guages:** Dir Prof. Dr NAZMI ULUTAK.

**Research Centre for Medicinal and Aro-
matic Plants and Drugs:** Dir Prof. Dr
MUSTAFA ŞENYEL.
**Research Centre for Modern Turkish
History:** Dir Prof. Dr İHSAN GÜNEŞ.
**Research Centre for Televised Distance
Learning:** Dir Assoc. Prof. NAZMI ULUTAK.

GRADUATE SCHOOLS

Graduate School of Health Sciences: Dir
Prof. Dr YUSUF ÖZTÜRK.
Graduate School of Science: Dir Prof. Dr
ORHAN ÖZER.
Graduate School of Social Sciences: Dir
Prof. Dr ALTUĞ İFTAR.
Institute of Educational Sciences: Dir
Prof. Dr İLKNUR KEÇIK.
Handicapped Research Institute: Dir
Prof. Dr GÖNÜL SELVER KIRCAALÜ.
Institute of Communication Sciences:
Dir (vacant).
Institute of Fine Arts: Dir Prof. Dr ATILLA
ATAR.
**Institute of Satellite and Space
Sciences:** Dir Assoc. Prof. Dr CAN AYDAY.
Institute of Transport Economics: Dir
Prof. Dr NEZIH VARCAN.

ANKARA ÜNIVERSITESI

06100 Tandoğan, Ankara
Telephone: (312) 223-43-61
Fax: (312) 223-60-70
Internet: www.ankara.edu.tr
Founded 1946
State control
Language of instruction: Turkish
Academic year: October to June
Rector: Prof. Dr NUSRET ARAS
Vice-Rectors: Prof. Dr RAMAZAN ARSLAN, Prof.
Dr ÖMER L. GEBIZLIOĞLU, Prof. Dr ERKAN
İBIS
General Secretary: SERPIL GÜNER
Registrar: ZÜBEYDE AÇIK
Librarian: Doç. Dr DOĞAN ATILGAN

Number of teachers: 3,565
Number of students: 43,212

Publications: *Ankara Üniversitesi Yıllığı*
(Annals of the University), *Turkish Journal of Geographical Sciences*, and faculty
and research institute publications

DEANS

Faculty of Agriculture: Prof. Dr CEMAL TALUĞ
Faculty of Communications: Prof. Dr AHMET
TOLUNGÜÇ
Faculty of Dentistry: Prof. Dr NEJAT BORA
SAYAN
Faculty of Divinity: Prof. Dr MUALLA SEÇUK
Faculty of Education: Prof. Dr GÖNÜL AKÇA-
METE
Faculty of Education Health Sciences: Prof.
Dr NILGÜN SARP
Faculty of Engineering: Prof. Dr RIDVAN
BERBER
Çankırı Faculty of Forestry: Prof. Dr İLHAMI
KÖKSAL
Faculty of Law: Prof. Dr A. LALE SIRMEN
Faculty of Letters: Prof. Dr NECDET ADABAĞ
Faculty of Medicine: Prof. Dr TÜMER ÇOR-
APÇIOĞLU
Faculty of Pharmacy: Prof. Dr SEÇKIN ÖZDEN
Faculty of Political Science: Prof. Dr CELAL
GÖLE
Faculty of Science: Prof. Dr CEMAL AYDIN
Faculty of Veterinary Medicine: Prof. Dr
İBRAHIM BURGU

HEADS OF DEPARTMENTS

Faculty of Agriculture (e-mail agricul@agri
.ankara.edu.tr; internet www.agri.ankara
.edu.tr):

Agricultural Economics: Prof. Dr AYHAN
TUFAN
Agricultural Machinery: Prof. Dr RAHMI
KESKINIL
Agronomy: Prof. Dr CELAL ER
Animal Science: Prof. A. ÇETIN FIRATLI
Dairy Technology: Prof. Dr METIN ATAMER
Farm Structures and Irrigation: Prof. Dr
CENGIZ OKMAN
Fisheries: Prof Dr GÜLTEN KÖKSAL
Food Engineering: Prof. Dr RECAI ERCAN
Horticulture: Prof. Dr NILGÜN HALLORAN
Landscape Architecture: Prof. Dr HALIM
PERÇIN
Plant Protection: Prof. Dr FILIZ ERTUNÇ
Soil Science: Prof. Dr SÜLEYMAN TABAN

Faculty of Communication (e-mail ilef@
media.ankara.edu.tr; internet ilef.ankara
.edu.tr):

Journalism: Prof. Dr OYA TOKGÖZ
Public Relations: Prof. Dr METIN KAZANCI
Radio, Television and Cinema: Prof. Dr
BÜLENT CAPLI

Faculty of Dentistry (e-mail dekanlik@
dentistry.ankara; internet www.ankara.edu
.tr/faculties/dentistry):

Basic Dental Sciences: Prof. Dr ENDER
ERGUN
Clinical Dentistry: Prof. Dr NEJAT BORA
SAYAN

Faculty of Divinity (e-mail ilahiyat@divinity
.ankara.edu.tr; internet www.divinity
.ankara.edu.tr):

Basic Islamic Sciences: Prof. Dr AHMET
AKBULUT
Islamic History and Arts: Prof. Dr NUSRET
ÇAM
Philosophy and the Science of Religion:
Prof. Dr RECEP KILIÇINTAŞ

Faculty of Education (e-mail maytekin@
education.ankara.edu.tr; internet www
.ankara.edu.tr/faculties/educational):

Computing and Learning Technology:
Prof. Dr HAFIZE KEZER
Educational Sciences: Prof. Dr A. GÖNÜL
AKÇAMETE
Elementary Education: Prof. Dr MAHMUT
TEZCAN
Special Education: Prof. Dr BÜLBIN SUCUO-
ĞLU

Faculty of Engineering (e-mail dean@eng
.ankara.edu.tr; internet www.eng.ankara
.edu.tr):

Chemical Engineering: Prof. Dr AYLA
ÇALIMLI
Computer Engineering: Prof. Dr BAKI
KOYUNCU
Electronic Engineering: Prof. Dr MÜMTAZ
YILMAZ
Engineering Physics: Prof. Dr ÇELIK TAR-
IMCI
Food Engineering: Prof. Dr RECAI ERCAN
Geological Engineering: Prof. Dr NURETTIN
SONER
Geophysical Engineering: Prof. Dr NIZA-
METTIN KAZANCI

Faculty of Law (e-mail fac@law.ankara.edu
.tr; internet www.ankara.edu.tr/hukuk):

Private Law: Prof. Dr TUĞRUL ARAT
Public Finance and Economics: Prof. Dr
AHMET KUMRULU
Public Law: Prof. Dr ERDAL ONAR

Faculty of Letters (e-mail dtfc@humanity
.ankara.edu.tr; internet www.humanity
.ankara.edu.tr):

Anthropology: Prof. Dr ZAFER İLBARS
Archaeology: Prof. Dr HAYAT ERKANAL
Drama: Prof. Dr NURHAN KARADAĞ

Eastern Languages and Cultures: Prof. Dr MÜRSEL ÖZTÜRK
Folklore: Prof. Dr GÜRBÜZ ERGINER
Geography: Prof. Dr ALI ÖZÇAĞLAR
History: Prof. Dr MUSA CADIRCI
History of Art: Prof. Dr MEHMET TUNÇEL
Knowledge and Records Management: Prof. Dr SEKINE KARAKAŞ
Library Sciences: Prof. Dr SEKINE KARAKAŞ
Linguistics: Prof. Dr İCLAL ERGENÇ
Modern Turkish Dialects and Literature: Prof. Dr SEMA BARUTÇU ÖZÖNDER
Philosophy: Prof. Dr ŞAHIN YENIŞEHIRLIO-ĞLU
Physical Anthropology and Palaeoanthropology: Prof. Dr ERKSIN GÜLEÇ
Prehistoric Period Languages and Cultures: Prof. Dr İ. CEM KARASU
Psychology: Prof. Dr ALI DÖNMEZ
Sociology: Prof. Dr AYTUL KASAPOĞLU
Turkish Language and Literature: Prof. Dr HASAN ÖZDEMIR
Western Languages and Cultures: Prof. Dr TUNA ERTEM

Faculty of Medicine (e-mail btukel@medicine.ankara.edu.tr; internet www.ankara.edu.tr/faculties/medicine):
Basic Medicine: Prof. Dr CANAN AKBAY
Internal Medicine: Prof. Dr SÜKRÜ CIN
Surgery: Prof. Dr ORHAN GÖĞÜŞ

Faculty of Pharmacy (e-mail ankpharm@pharmacy.ankara.edu.tr; internet www.pharmacy.ankara.edu.tr):
Basic Pharmaceutical Sciences: Prof. Dr MEHMET AKIN
Pharmaceutical Technology: Prof. Dr TAMER BAYKARA
Professional Pharmaceutical Sciences: Prof. Dr ESIN ŞENER

Faculty of Political Science (internet www.ankara.edu.tr/faculties/political):
Business Administration: Prof. Dr GÜNEY DEVREZ
Economics: Prof. Dr ERCAN UYGUR
International Relations: Prof. Dr ERSIN ONULDURAN
Labour Economics and Industrial Relations: Prof. Dr ALPASLAN IŞIKLI
Public Administration: Prof. Dr YAVUZ SABUNCU
Public Finance: Prof. Dr YAVUZ SABUNCU

Faculty of Science (internet www.ankara.edu.tr/faculties/science):
Astronomy and Space Sciences: Prof. Dr CEMAL AYDIN
Biology: Prof. Dr CUMHUR ÇÖKMÜŞ
Chemical Engineering: Prof. Dr AYLA ÇALIMLI
Chemistry: Prof. Dr ATILLA ÖKTEMER
Electronic Engineering: Prof. Dr ÖNDER TÜZÜNALP
Engineering Physics: Prof. Dr ALI ULVI YILMAZER
Geological Engineering: Prof. Dr NURETTIN SONER
Geophysical Engineering: Prof. Dr AHMET TUĞRUL BAŞOKUR
Mathematics: Prof. Dr CEVAT KART
Physics: Prof. Dr SATILMIŞ ATAĞ
Statistics: Prof. Dr ÖMER L. GEBIZLIOĞLU

Faculty of Veterinary Medicine (e-mail vetmed@veterinary.ankara.edu.tr; internet www.ankara.edu.tr/faculties.veterinary):
Animal Husbandry and Animal Nutrition: Prof. Dr AHMET ERGIN
Basic Sciences of Veterinary Medicine: Prof. Dr REŞAR NURI AŞTI
Diseases and Clinical Sciences: Prof. Dr FARUK AKIN

DIRECTORS OF APPLIED RESEARCH CENTRES
Astronomy and Aerospace Sciences: Prof. Dr BERAHITDIN ALBAYRAK

Atatürk's Principles: Prof. Dr ÜNSAL YAVUZ
Autistic Children: Prof. Dr EFSER KERIMOĞLU
Biotechnology: Prof. Dr TUNCER ÖZDAMAR
Cardiology: Prof. Dr DERVIŞ ORAL
Children's Studies: Prof. Dr BEKIR ONUR
Communications: Prof. Dr ASKER KARTARI
Continuous Training: Prof. Dr NEJLA TURAL
Cyprus: Prof. Dr FÜSUN ARSAVA
Distance Learning: Doç. Dr NURETTIN ŞIMŞEK
Earthquake Science: Prof. Dr AHMET TUĞRUL BAŞOKUR
Education-Rehabilitation: Prof. Dr EFSER KERIMOĞLU
Environmental Problems: Prof. Dr NEVIN AKPINAR
European Communities: Prof. Dr M. NAIL ALKAN
Fishery Products: Prof. Dr GÜLTEN KÖKSAL
Foreign Language Teaching: Prof. Dr ERSIN ONULDURAN
Gastroenterology: Prof. Dr ALI ÖZDEN
Human Resource Management: Doç. Dr RECEP VARÇIN
Intellectual and Industrial Property: ARZU OĞUZ
International Agriculture: Prof. Dr NEŞET KILINÇER
Medical and Scented Plants: Prof. Dr SEMRA KURUNCU
Oncology: Prof. Dr FIKRI İÇLI
Ottoman History: Prof. Dr ESIN KAHYA
Pediatric Haemotology and Oncology: Prof. Dr ŞÜKRÜ CIN
Psychiatric Crisis: Prof. Dr IŞIK SAYIL
Public Finance and Politics: Prof. Dr AHMET KIRMAN
River, Lake and Sea Geology: Prof. Dr MUSTAFA ERGIN
Science and Technology: Prof. Dr TAMER BAYKARA
Strategic Research: Prof. Dr YAVUZ ERCAN
Turkish Geography: Doç. Dr ALI ÖZÇAĞLAR
Turkish Language Teaching Centre: Doç. Dr ENGIN UZUN
Women's Studies: SERPIL ÜŞÜR

ATTACHED INSTITUTES
Graduate Institute of Biotechnology: Dir Prof. Dr NEJAT AKAR.
Graduate Institute of Education: Dir Prof. Dr MERAL UYSAL.
Graduate Institute of Hepatology: Dir Prof. Dr S. CIHAN YURDAYDIN.
Graduate Institute of the History of the Turkish Revolution: Dir Prof. Dr YAVUZ ERCAN.
Graduate Institute of Medical Jurisprudence: Dir Prof. Dr HALIL GÜMÜŞ.
Graduate Institute of Medical Sciences: Dir Prof. Dr RIFAT VURAL.
Graduate Institute of Science: Dir Prof. Dr METIN OLGUN.
Graduate Institute of Social Sciences: Dir Prof. Dr CAN HAMAMCI.

ATTACHED SCHOOLS AND COLLEGES
Çankırı School of Health: Dir Prof. Dr MEHMET KIYAN.
School of Başkent: Dir Prof. Dr HANDE K. ERSOY.
School of Beypazarı: Dir Prof. Dr İLHAN KARAÇAL.
School of Çankırı: Dir Prof. Dr SABAHATTIN BALCI.
School of Cebeci Health Services: Dir Doç. Dr TÜLIN BEDÜK.
School of Dikimevi Health Services: Dir Prof. Dr AHMET DERYA AYSEV.
School of Foreign Languages: Dir Prof. Dr ERSIN ONULDURAN.
School of Home Economics (Faculty of Agriculture): Dir Prof. Dr EMINE GÖNEN.

School of Justice (Faculty of Law): Dir Doç. Dr HALUK KONURALP.
School of Kalecik: Dir Prof. Dr DOĞAN ERDOĞAN.
School of Kastamonu: Dir Prof. Dr BAHRI GÖKÇEBAY.
School of Physical Education and Sports: Dir Prof. Dr EMIN ERGEN.
State Conservatory: Dir Prof. Dr NURHAN KARADAĞ.

ATATÜRK ÜNIVERSITESI
Erzurum
Telephone: (442) 231-11-11
Fax: (442) 236-10-14
E-mail: ata@atauni.edu.tr
Internet: www.atauni.edu.tr

Founded 1957
State control
Language of instruction: Turkish
Academic year: October to June

Rector: Prof. Dr YAŞAR SÜTBEYAZ
Vice-Rectors: Prof. Dr NIHAT AKBULUT, Prof. Dr ÖMER KAYA
Chief Administrative Officer: Assoc. Prof. HÜSEYIN YURTTAŞ
Librarian: BÜNYAMIN OKUYUCU

Library of 285,000 vols and 200,000 journals
Number of teachers: 2,527 (incl. teaching assistants)
Number of students: 40,191

Publications: *Atatürk Dergisi* (2 a year), *Atatürk Üniversitesi Diş Hekimliği Fakültesi Dergisi* (quarterly), *Atatürk Üniversitesi Erzincan Hukuk Fakültesi Dergisi* (2 a year), *Atatürk Üniversitesi İlahiyat Fakültesi Dergisi* (2 a year), *Atatürk Üniversitesi Tıp Dergisi* (quarterly), *Erzincan Eğitim Fakültesi Dergisi* (2 a year), *Güzel Sanatlar Enstitüsü Dergisi* (2 a year), *Güzel Sanatlar Fakültesi Sanat Dergisi* (2 a year), *İktisadi ve İdari Bilimler Dergisi* (2 a year), *Kazım Karabekir Eğitim Fakültesi Dergisi* (2 a year), *Sosyal Bilimler Dergisi* (2 a year), *Sosyal Bilimler Enstitüsü Dergisi* (2 a year), *Türkiyat Araştırmaları Enstitüsü Dergisi* (2 a year), *Ziraat Fakültesi Dergisi* (quarterly)

DEANS
Faculty of Agriculture: Prof. Dr MÜKERREM KAYA
Faculty of Arts and Sciences: Prof. Dr ÜNIT DEMIR
Faculty of Arts and Sciences (Erzincan): Prof. Dr MUHARREM GÜLERYÜZ
Faculty of Communication and Journalism: Prof. Dr SEVIM AKTEN
Faculty of Dentistry: Prof. Dr RECEP ORBAK
Faculty of Economics and Administrative Sciences: Prof. Dr UĞUR GÜLLÜLÜ
Faculty of Education: Prof. Dr SEMIR BAYRAKÇEKEN
Faculty of Education (Ağrı): Prof. Dr BILGE SEYIDOĞLU
Faculty of Education (Bayburt): Prof. Dr AHMET GÜRSES
Faculty of Education (Erzincan): Prof. Dr ERDOĞAN BÜYÜKKASAP
Faculty of Engineering: Prof. Dr ŞAHIN GÜLABOĞLU
Faculty of Fine Arts: Prof. Dr SEVIM SAĞSÖZ
Faculty of Law School (Erzincan): Prof. Dr AHMET NEZIH KÖK
Faculty of Medicine: Prof. Dr CAHIT KARAKELLEOĞLU
Faculty of Pharmacy: Prof. Dr YUNUS KARA
Faculty of Theology: Prof. Dr BAHATTIN KÖK
Faculty of Veterinary Sciences: Prof. Dr LEYLA YILDIZ

HEADS OF DEPARTMENTS

Faculty of Agriculture (Atatürk Üniversitesi Ziraat Fakültesi, 25240 Erzurum; tel. (442) 231-22-04; fax (442) 236-09-58; e-mail ziraat@atauni.edu.tr):

Agricultural Economics: Prof. Dr ZIYA YURITAŞ

Agricultural Mechanization: Prof. Dr NIHAT TURGUT

Animal Feeding and Husbandry: Prof. Dr HAKKI EMSEN

Aquaculture: Prof. Dr SITKI ARAS

Engineering: Prof. Dr MUSTAFA OKUROĞLU

Entomology: Prof. Dr ŞABAN GÜÇLÜ

Field Crops: Prof. Dr ŞAHIN AKTEN

Food Science and Technology: Prof. Dr MÜKERREM KAYA

Horticulture: Prof. Dr İSMAIL GÜVENÇ

Landscape Architecture: Prof. Dr HASAN YILMAZ

Soil Science: Prof. Dr YILDIRIM SEZEN

Faculty of Arts and Sciences (Atatürk Üniversitesi Fen Edebiyat Fakültesi, 25240 Erzurum; tel. (442) 231-41-10; fax (442) 236-09-48; e-mail fenfak@atauni.edu.tr):

Archaeology and Fine Arts: Prof. Dr CEVAT BAŞARAN

Biology: Prof. Dr ÖMER FARUK ALGUR

Chemistry: Prof. Dr HASAN SEÇEN

English Language and Literature: Prof. Dr İBRAHIM YEREBAKAN

French Language and Literature: Prof. Dr AYTEN ER

Geography: Prof. Dr İHSAN BULUT

German Language and Literature: Prof. Dr YILMAZ ÖZBEK

History: Prof. Dr ENVER KONUKÇU

History of Art: Prof. HAMZA GÜNDOĞDU

Librarianship: Asst Prof. HALIS ALAR

Mathematics: Prof. Dr HÜSEYIN AYDIN

Modern Turk Languages and Literature: Assoc. Prof. METTIN AKKUŞ

Oriental Languages and Literature: Prof. Dr N. HAFIZ YANIK

Physics: Prof. Dr YUSUF ŞAHIN

Philosophy: Prof. Dr MUSTAFA YILDIRIM

Russian Language and Literature: Asst Prof. EROL KÜRKÇÜOĞLU

Sociology: Prof. Dr SEBAHATTIN GÜLLÜLÜ

Turkish Language and Literature: Prof. Dr BILGE SEYİDOĞLU

Faculty of Communication and Journalism (Atatürk Üniversitesi İletişim Fakültesi, 25240 Erzurum; tel. (442) 231-24-04; fax (442) 236-09-62; e-mail iletisim@atauni.edu.tr):

Journalism: Asst Prof. UĞUR YAVUZ

Public Relations: Asst Prof. FATMA GECIKLİ

Radio, Television and Cinema: Prof. ABDULKUDDÜS BİNGÖL

Faculty of Dentistry (Atatürk Üniversitesi Diş Hekimliği Fakültesi, 25240 Erzurum; tel. (442) 231-19-00; fax (442) 236-09-45; e-mail dishek@atauni.edu.tr):

Clinical Sciences: Prof. Dr RECEP ORBAK

Faculty of Economics and Administrative Sciences (Atatürk Üniversitesi İktisadi ve İdari Bilimler Fakültesi, 25240 Erzurum; tel. (442) 231-19-06; fax (442) 236-09-49; e-mail libf@atauni.edu.tr):

Business Management: Prof. Dr METIN TURKO

Economics: Prof. Dr MUAMMER YAYLALI

Faculty of Education (Atatürk Üniversitesi Eğtim Fakültesi, 25240 Erzurum; tel. (442) 231-40-01; fax (442) 236-09-55; e-mail kkegtfak@atauni.edu.tr):

Computer Education and Instructional Technology: Assoc. Prof. YAŞAR DEMIR

Counselling and Guidance: Asst Prof. MEHMET KÖK

Educational Sciences: Prof. Dr SIRM AKBABA

Fine Arts Training: Asst Prof. HALIL İBRAHIM YURTCAN

Foreign Languages Teaching: Prof. Dr FEHMI EFE

Physical Training and Sports: Prof. Dr İSMAIL BIRINCI

Primary School Education: Prof. Dr YAVUZ TAŞKESENLİGİL

Science and Mathematics for Secondary School Education: Prof. Dr AHMET GÜRSES

Social Sciences for Secondary School Education: Prof. Dr HAYATI DOĞDANAY

Turkish Teaching Education: Prof. Dr MUKIM SAĞIR

Faculty of Engineering (Atatürk Üniversitesi Mühendislik Fakültesi, 25240 Erzurum; tel. (442) 231-45-05; fax (442) 236-09-57; e-mail muhendis@atauni.edu.tr):

Chemistry: Prof. Dr AVNI ÇAKICI

Chemistry: Prof. Dr HANIFI SARAÇ

Civil Engineering: Prof. Dr TEMEL YETİMOĞLU

Computer Engineering: Prof. Dr SEDAT YÖRÜK

Electrical and Electronic Engineering: Prof. Dr HASAN EFEOĞLU

Industrial Engineering: Prof. Dr AVNI ÇAKICI

Machinery: Prof. Dr İHSAN EFEOĞLU

Metallurgical Engineering: Asst Prof. ZATER EKINCI

Faculty of Fine Arts (Atatürk Üniversitesi Güzel Sanatlar Fakültesi, 25240 Erzurum; tel. (442) 231-40-60; fax (442) 231-09-66; e-mail gsfsanat@atauni.edu.tr):

Basic Art Education: Asst Prof. ŞEYDA ALGAÇ

Music Sciences: Asst Prof. SERHAT YENER

Painting: Asst Prof. MEHMET KAVUKÇU

Performing Arts: Asst Prof. A. PINAR ÇIĞDEM

Photography: Asst Prof. NAFIA ÖZDEMIR HANYALOĞLU

Sculpture: Asst Prof. MUSTAFA BULAT

Traditional Turkish Handicrafts: Asst Prof. TASHIM PARLAK

Faculty of Law (Atatürk Üniversitesi Hukuk Fakültesi, Erzincan; tel. (446) 223-60-31; fax (446) 223-34-06; e-mail hukuk@atauni.edu.tr):

Common Law: Assoc. Prof. Dr ŞÜKRÜ YILDIZ

Economic and Financial Law: Asst Prof. MURAT NİŞANCI

Public Law and Administration: Assoc. Prof. Dr NIHAT BULUT

Faculty of Medicine (Atatürk Üniversitesi Tıp Fakültesi, 25240 Erzurum; tel. (442) 236-09-67; fax (442) 236-09-98; e-mail tipfak@atauni.edu.tr):

Basic Medicine: Prof. Dr AHMET AYYILDIZ

General Surgery: Prof. Dr MEHMET GÜNDOĞDU

Internal Medicine: Prof. Dr SELÇUK ATAMANALP

Faculty of Pharmacy (Atatürk Üniversitesi Eczacılık Fakültesi, 25240 Erzurum; tel. (442) 231-15-38; fax (442) 236-09-62; e-mail eczfak@atauni.edu.tr):

Basic Pharmaceutical Sciences: Prof. YÜCEL KADIOĞLU

Pharmaceutical Technology: Asst Prof. UFUK ÖZGEN

Pharmaceutical Vocational Education: Assoc. Prof. H. İNCI GÜL

Faculty of Theology (Atatürk Üniversitesi İlahiyat Fakültesi, 25240 Erzurum; tel. (442) 231-19-09; fax (442) 236-09-53; e-mail erilfak@atauni.edu.tr):

Basic Islamic Sciences: Prof. Dr NASRULLAH HACIMÜFTÜOĞ

Islamic Religion and Arts: Prof. Dr NACI OKÇU

Philosophy and Religious Sciences: Prof. Dr BHATTIN KÖK

Religious Sciences for Primary School Education: Assoc. Prof. Dr M. HANIFI PALABIYIK

Faculty of Veterinary Sciences (Atatürk Üniversitesi Veteriner Fakültesi, 25240 Erzurum; tel. (442) 231-39-75; fax (442) 631-41-88; e-mail vetfak@atauni.edu.tr):

Clinical Sciences: Prof. Dr ARMAĞAN ÇOLAK

Veterinary Basic Sciences and Diseases: Assoc. Prof. FIKRET ÇELEBİ

Zootechnology and Animal Nutrition: Asst Prof. MEHMET AKIF YÖRÜK

ATTACHED INSTITUTES

Fine Arts: Dir Prof. Dr HAMZA GÜNDOĞDU.

History of the Turkish Republic: Dir Prof. Dr SINEVER ESIN DAYI.

Medical Sciences: Dir Assoc. Prof. Dr ADNAN TEZEL.

Sciences: Dir Prof. Dr MEHMET ERTUĞRUL.

Social Sciences: Dir Prof. Dr VAHDETTIN BAŞCI.

Turkology: Dir Assoc. Prof. Dr TURGUT KARABEY.

ATILIM ÜNİVERSİTESİ

Kızılcaşar Köyü, 06836 İncek Gölbası, Ankara

Telephone: (312) 586-80-00

Fax: (312) 586-80-90

E-mail: iro@atilim.edu.tr

Internet: www.atilim.edu.tr

Private control

President: Prof. Dr ABDURRAHIM ÖZGENOĞLU

General Secretary: Prof. Dr ABDÜLAZIZ ŞEREN

Vice-Presidents: Prof. Dr İSMAIL BIRCAN, Prof. Dr İHSAN TARAKÇIOĞLU

DEANS

Faculty of Arts and Sciences: Prof. Dr OYA BATUM MENTEŞE

Faculty of Engineering: Prof. Dr KAMIL İBRAHIM AKMAN

Faculty of Law: Prof. Dr NAMI ÇAĞAN

Faculty of Management: Prof. Dr GÖKHAN ÇAPOĞLU

DIRECTORS

Graduate School of Natural and Applied Sciences: Prof. Dr SELÇUK SOYUPAK

Graduate School of Social Sciences: Prof. Dr ERTUĞRUL ÇETİNER

Preparatory School: AYTUNA KOCABIYIKOĞLU

BAHÇEŞEHİR ÜNİVERSİTESİ

34538 Bahçeşehir, Istanbul

Telephone: (212) 669-65-23

Fax: (212) 669-43-98

E-mail: info@bahcesehir.edu.tr

Internet: www.bahcesehir.edu.tr

Founded 1998

Rector: Prof. Dr SÜHEYL BATUM

Vice-Presidents: Prof. Dr NURBAY GÜLTEKIN, Prof. Dr ESER KARAKAŞ

Library of 43,095 vols, 22,000 e-books, 472 periodicals and 3,106 e-journals

Number of teachers: 150

Number of students: 1,207

DEANS

Faculty of Architecture: Prof. Dr ERHAN A. BALKAN

Faculty of Arts and Science: Prof. Dr ÖMER ASIM SAÇLI

Faculty of Engineering: Prof. Dr ŞENAY YALÇIN

Faculty of Law: Prof. Dr CUMHUR ÖZAKMAN

Faculty of Management: Prof. Dr İLKAY SUNAR

ATTACHED RESEARCH INSTITUTES

Entrepreneurship and Innovation Administration Centre: Dean RUHI KAYKAYOĞLU.

European Union Research Centre: Dean ESER KARAKAŞ.

Gap Collaboration Centre: Dean SÜHEYLA KIRCA.

Information and Cyber Technologies: Dean ESER KARAKAŞ.

Institute for Leadership and Public Affairs: Dir ADIL SAFTY.

Nobel Laureates Research Centre: Dir NAMIK ARAS.

Production Centre: Coordinator SINAN ÇETIN.

Social Sciences Research Centre: Dir ÜMIT EROL.

BALIKESİR ÜNİVERSİTESİ

Soma Cad., 10100 Balikesir
Telephone: (266) 245-96-50
Fax: (266) 245-96-63
E-mail: hacioglu@balikesir.edu.tr
Internet: www.balikesir.edu.tr
State control
Academic year: September to July
Rector: Prof. Dr NECDET HACIOĞLU
General Secretary: Prof. Dr FAIZ TÜRKAN
Library of 14,520 vols, 294 periodical subscriptions, 17 databases
Number of teachers: 607
Number of students: 22,141 full-time, 9,108 evening

DEANS

Faculty of Arts and Sciences: OKTAY ARSLAN
Faculty of Economics and Administration: ADEM ÇABUK
Faculty of Education: BEDRIYE TUNÇSIPER
Faculty of Engineering and Architecture: ŞERIF SAYLAN

DIRECTORS

Geothermal Research Institute: OSMAN ÇENET
Olive Trade and Agribusiness Institute: SAKIN VURAL VARLI

ATTACHED RESEARCH INSTITUTES

Applied Sciences Research Institute: Dir HAKAN KOÇKAR.

Atatürk's Principles and History of the Turkish Republic Research Institute: Dir NAHIDE ŞIMŞIR.

Balıkesir Local Culture Research Institute: Dir ALI DUYMAZ.

Boron Research Institute: Dir MEHMET DOĞAN.

Data Processing Research Institute: Dir MUSTAFA GÖKTEPE.

Environmental Studies Research Institute: Dir NURI NAKIPOĞLU.

European Union Research Institute: Dir CEVDET AVCIKURT.

Tourism Research Institute: Dir DÜRIYE BOZOK.

BAŞKENT ÜNİVERSİTESİ

Baglica Kampusu Eskisehir Yolu 20 km, Baglica 06530 Ankara
Telephone: (312) 212-80-16
Fax: (312) 223-57-91
E-mail: webmaster@baskent.edu.tr
Internet: www.baskent.edu.tr
Founded 1994

Private control
Rector: Prof. Dr MEHMET HABERAL
Library of 65,535 vols, 919 periodicals
Number of teachers: 947
Number of students: 4,052 undergraduate, 217 postgraduate, 324 associate

DEANS

Faculty of Commercial Sciences: Prof. Dr NEVIN CIĞERIM
Faculty of Communications: Dr M. SELÇUK USLU
Faculty of Dentistry: Dr NUR ALTINÖRS
Faculty of Economic and Administrative Sciences: Dr A. SELAMI SARGUT
Faculty of Education: Dr MUSTAFA KURU
Faculty of Engineering: Dr İMDAT KARA
Faculty of Fine Arts, Design and Architecture: (vacant)
Faculty of Health Sciences: Dr RIDVAN ÖZKER
Faculty of Law: Dr TURGUT AKINTÜRK
Faculty of Medicine: Prof. Dr FAIK SARIALIOĞLU
Faculty of Science and Letters: Dr İSMAIL ERDEM

BEYKENT ÜNİVERSİTESİ

34900 Beykent, Istanbul
Telephone: (212) 872-64-32
Fax: (212) 872-24-89
E-mail: info@beykent.edu.tr
Internet: www.beykent.edu.tr
Founded 1997
Language of instruction: English
Academic year: October to June
Rector: Prof. Dr MEHMET FIKRET GEZGIN
Vice-Rector: Prof. Dr MUSTAFA DELICAN, Prof. Dr ÜNSAL OSKAY
General Secretary: Prof. Dr NURETTIN ERDEM
Library and Learning Centre Manager: UĞUR BULGAN
Library of 27,500 vols, 165 periodicals, 2,000 CDs, 850 audio tapes
Number of teachers: 200
Number of students: 2,500

DEANS

Faculty of Arts and Science: ZAFER ASLAN
Faculty of Economics and Administrative Sciences: Prof. Dr MEHMET ZELKA
Faculty of Engineering and Architecture: Prof. Dr ERTAN ÖZKAN
Faculty of Fine Arts: Prof. Dr ÜNSAL OSKAY
Preparatory School: MUSTAFA MELEK (Dir)

BILKENT ÜNİVERSİTESİ

Bilkent, 06800 Ankara
Telephone: (312) 266-41-25
Fax: (312) 266-41-27
E-mail: bilinfo@bcc.bilkent.edu.tr
Internet: www.bilkent.edu.tr
Founded 1984
Private control (educational foundation)
Languages of instruction: Turkish, English
Academic year: September to June
President, Board of Trustees: Prof. İHSAN DOĞRAMACI
Rector: Prof. ALI DOĞRAMACI
Vice-Rector for Academic Affairs and Provost: Prof. ABDULLAH ATALAR
Vice-Rector for Administrative and Financial Affairs and General Secretary: Prof. KÜRŞAT AYDOĞAN
Vice-Rector for Student Affairs: Prof. EROL ARKUN
Vice-Rector and Librarian: Dr PHYLLIS L. ERDOĞAN
Number of teachers: 970
Number of students: 10,000

DEANS

Faculty of Art, Design and Architecture: Prof. BÜLENT ÖZGÜÇ
Faculty of Administration: Prof. DILEK ÖNKEL
Faculty of Economic, Administrative and Social Sciences: Prof. METIN HEPER
Faculty of Education: Prof. ZEKI KURUOĞLU
Faculty of Engineering: Prof. MEHMET BARAY
Faculty of Humanities and Letters: Prof. BÜLENT BOZKURT
Faculty of Law: Prof. TURGUT TÄN
Faculty of Music and Performing Arts: Assoc. Prof. IŞIN METIN
Faculty of Science: Prof. HASAN ERTEN
School of Applied Foreign Languages: JOHN O'DWYER
Vocational School of Computer Programming and Office Management: KAMER RODOPLU
Vocational School of Tourism and Hotel Services: KAMER RODOPLU

HEADS OF DEPARTMENTS

Faculty of Art, Design and Architecture (tel. (312) 266-44-71; fax (312) 266-41-36; e-mail ozguc@bilkent.edu.tr):

Communication and Design: Asst Prof. MAHMUT MUTMAN
Fine Arts: Asst. Prof. ZEKIYE SARIKARTAL
Graphic Design: Prof. BÜLENT ÖZGÜÇ
Interior Architecture and Environmental Design: Assoc. Prof. HALIME DEMIRKAN
Landscape Architecture and Urban Design: Asst Prof. ZUHAL ULUSOY

Faculty of Business Administration (tel. (312) 266-41-64; fax (312) 266-49-58; e-mail aydogan@bilkent.edu.tr):

Management: Prof. KÜRŞAT AYDOĞAN

Faculty of Economic, Administrative and Social Sciences (tel. (312) 266-41-37; fax (312) 266-49-60; e-mail mcelasun@bilkent.edu.tr):

Economics: Assoc. Prof. FATMA TAŞKIN
History: Asst Prof. MEHMET KALPAKLI
International Relations: Prof. ALI KARAOSMANOĞLU
Political Science and Public Administration: Prof. METIN HEPER

Faculty of Education (tel. (312) 266-43-38; fax (312) 266-41-52; e-mail kuruoglu@bilkent.edu.tr):

Teacher Education: Prof. MARGARET SANDS
Teaching English as a Foreign Language: Assoc. Prof. KIMBERLEY TRIMBLE

Faculty of Engineering (tel. (312) 266-41-33; fax (312) 266-41-26; e-mail baray@cs.bilkent.edu.tr):

Computer Engineering: Prof. H. ALTAY GÜVENIR
Electrical and Electronics Engineering: Prof. BÜLENT ÖZGÜLER
Industrial Engineering: Prof. BARBAROS TANSEL

Faculty of Humanities and Letters (tel. (312) 266-41-29; fax (312) 266-49-34; e-mail bbozkurt@bilkent.edu.tr):

American Culture and Literature: Asst Prof. CATHERINE MARIE SAMPBELL
Archaeology and History of Art: Assoc. Prof. MARIE-HENRIETTE GATES
English Language and Literature: Prof. BÜLENT BOZKURT
Philosophy: Prof. VAROL AKMAN
Turkish Literature: Prof. TALAT HALMAN

Faculty of Law (tel. (312) 290-3300; fax (312) 290-3282; e-mail ttan@bilkent.edu.tr):

Law: Prof. TERGUL TÄN

Faculty of Music and Performing Arts (tel. (312) 290-11-77; fax (312) 266-45-39; e-mail eerdinc@bilkent.edu.tr):

Music: Asst Prof. ISIN METIN
Performing Arts: Prof. CÜNEYT GÖKÇER

Faculty of Science (tel. (312) 290-43-80; fax (312) 266-45-79; e-mail ertcn@bilkent.edu.tr):

Chemistry: Prof. ŞEFIK SÜZER
Mathematics: Prof. MEFHARET KOCATEPE
Molecular Biology and Genetics: Prof. MEHMET ÖZTÜRK
Physics: Prof. BİLAL TANATAR

ATTACHED INSTITUTES

Economics and Social Sciences: Dir Prof. KÜRŞAT AYDOĞAN.

Engineering and Science: Dir Prof. Dr MEHMET BARAY.

Graduate School of Business Administration: Dir Prof. KÜRŞAT AYDOĞAN.

Fine Arts: Dir Prof. BÜLENT ÖZGÜÇ.

Music and Performing Arts: Dir Asst Prof. ISIN METIN.

World Systems, Economies and Strategic Research: Dir Prof. ORHAN GÜVENEN.

Centre for Studies in Society and Politics: Dir Prof. ERGUN ÖZBUDUN.

Bilkent Centre for Advanced Studies: Dir Prof. SALIM CIRACI.

Centre for Russian Studies: Dir Prof. NORMAN STONE.

Centre for Turkish Language and Speech Processing: Dir Prof. ENİS ÇET.

Communications and Spectrum Management Research Centre: Dir Prof. HAYRETTIN KÖYMEN.

Genetics and Biotechnology Research and Development Centre: Dir Prof. MEHMET ÖZTÜRK.

Graduate School of Education: Dir Prof. MARGARET SANDS.

Centre for Research in Transitional Societies: Dir Prof. GÜLIZ GER.

Centre for Turkish Literature: Dir Prof. TALAT HALMAN.

Centre for International Economics: Dir Prof. SUBIDEY TOGAN.

BOĞAZIÇI ÜNİVERSİTESİ
(Boğaziçi University)

34342 Bebek, Istanbul
Telephone: (212) 358-15-00
Fax: (212) 265-63-57
E-mail: halkilis@boun.edu.tr
Internet: www.boun.edu.tr
Founded 1863; formerly Robert College
State control
Languages of instruction: Turkish, English
Academic year: September to July
Rector: Dr AYSE SOYSAL
Vice-Rectors: Prof. Dr CEM BEHAR, Prof. Dr GULEN AKTAS GREENWOOD, Prof. Dr TURAN ÖZTURAN
Dean of Students: Prof. Dr ALI IZZET TEKCAN
Secretary-General: MINE KALENDEROĞLU
Registrar: ZELIHA BALKAN
Librarian: HATICE ÜN
Number of teachers: 984
Number of students: 9,973
Publications: *Boğaziçi University Journal* (annually), *Biomedical Engineering Bulletin* (4 a year), *Education Bulletin* (2 a year)

DEANS

Faculty of Arts and Sciences: Prof. Dr OMER OGUZ
Faculty of Economics and Administrative Sciences: Prof. Dr ESER BORAK
Faculty of Education: Prof. Dr CEM ALPTEKIN
Faculty of Engineering: Prof. Dr ALI RIZA KAYLAN

HEADS OF DEPARTMENTS

Faculty of Arts and Sciences (tel. (212) 265-71-31; fax (212) 265-80-02):

BAŞAK, O., Western Languages and Literature
ÇAĞLAYAN, H., Molecular Biology and Genetics
CANBEYLI, R., Psychology
DERINGIL, S., History
ESEN, N., Turkish Language and LIterature
IRZIK, G., Philosophy
KÜSEFOĞLU, S., Chemistry
OĞUZ, Ö., Physics
SIRMAN, N., Sociology
TANBAY, B., Mathematics

Faculty of Engineering (tel. (212) 265-05-33; fax (212) 265-84-88):

ÇAĞLAYAN, M. U., Computer Engineering
KIRDAR, B., Chemical Engineering
OR, İ., Industrial Engineering
ÖZÇALDIRAN, K., Electrical Engineering
ÖZTURAN, T., Civil Engineering
VARDAR, Ö., Mechanical Engineering

Faculty of Economics and Administrative Sciences (tel. (212) 263-73-79; fax (212) 263-73-79):

KAYTAZ, M., Economics
TAHA, P., Political Science and International Relations
UĞURLU, M., Management

Faculty of Education (tel. (212) 358-15-40 ext. 1358; fax (212) 257-50-36):

AKARSU, F., Teaching Secondary School Science and Mathematics
AKPINAR, Y., Educational Science
AKYEL, A., Foreign Languages
BEKMAN, S., Primary Education
FATMA, G., Educational Science

ATTACHED INSTITUTES

Institute of Biomedical Engineering: Dir Prof. Dr YORGO ISTEFANOPULOS.

Kandilli Observatory and Earthquake Research Institute: Dir Prof. Dr GÜLAY BARBAROSOĞLU.

Institute of Environmental Sciences: Dir Prof. Dr ORHAN YENIGÜN.

Institute for Graduate Studies in Engineering Sciences: Dir Prof. Dr METIN ARIK.

Institute for Graduate Studies in Social Sciences: Dir Prof. Dr CEVZA SEVGEN.

Atatürk Institute of Modern Turkish History: Dir Prof. Dr ZAFER TOPRAK.

ATTACHED SCHOOLS AND COLLEGES

School of Foreign Languages: Dir Prof. Dr ESER TAYLAN.

School of Vocational Education: Dir Prof. Dr MELTEM ÖZTURAN.

School of Applied Disciplines: Dir Prof. Dr MELTEM ÖZTURAN.

ÇAĞ ÜNİVERSİTESİ

Adana-Mersin, Karayolu, Üzeri, 33800 Yenice/Mersin
Telephone: (324) 651-48-00
Fax: (324) 651-48-11
E-mail: cag@cag.edu.tr
Internet: www.cag.edu.tr
Founded 1997
Private control
Languages of instruction: Turkish, English
Academic year: September to June
Rector: Prof. Dr YENER GULMEZ
Vice-Rectors: Prof. Dr YUCEL ERTEKIN, Prof. Dr M. TEVFIK ODMAN
Number of teachers: 90
Number of students: 1,400

Publication: *Journal of Social Sciences* (2 a year)
Faculties of Arts and Sciences, Economics and Administrative Sciences and Law; Higher Vocational School and Institute of Social Sciences.

ATTACHED RESEARCH INSTITUTE

Institute of Social Sciences: Dir Prof. Dr SULEYMEN TURKEL.

ÇANAKKALE ONSEKİZ MART ÜNİVERSİTESİ

Terziodlu Kampüsü, 17020 Çanakkale
Telephone: (286) 218-00-18
Fax: (286) 218-06-08
E-mail: comurek@comu.edu.tr
Internet: www.comu.edu.tr
Founded 1992
State control
Academic year: October to June
Rector: Prof. Dr RAMAZAN AYDIN
Assistant Rectors: Prof. Dr SUZAN ERBAŞ, Prof. Dr ALI ÖZPİNAR, Prof. Dr ALI OSMAN ÖZTÜRK
Number of teachers: 695
Number of students: 15,000

DEANS

Faculty of Agriculture: Prof. Dr KENAN KAYNAŠ
Faculty of Economics and Administrative Studies: Prof. Dr ALI AKDEMIR
Faculty of Education: Prof. Dr REMZI Y. KINCAL
Faculty of Engineering and Architecture: Prof. Dr SALIH ZEKI TUTKUN
Faculty of Fine Arts: Prof. Dr MUSTAFA APAYDIN
Faculty of Fisheries: Prof. Dr ŠÜKRAN CIRIK
Faculty of Sciences and Arts: Prof. Dr KAZIM KAYA
Faculty of Theology: Prof. Dr NASUHI ÜNAL KARAARSLAN

PROFESSORS

Faculty of Agriculture (Terziodlu Kampüsü, 17020 Çanakkale):

ALTAY, H.
BAYTEKIN, H.
GÖKKUŠ, A.
KAPTAN, H.
KAYNAŠ, K.
KUMUK, T.
ÖZPİNAR, A.
SENER, S.
SEREZ, M.

Faculty of Economics and Administrative Studies (Biga) (Biga, Çanakkale):

AKDEMIR, A.
ERDOĐAN, E.

Faculty of Education (Terziodlu Kampüsü, 17020 Çanakkale):

ERBAŠ, S.
METE TUNÇOKU, A.
OSMAN ÖZTÜRK, A.
Y KINCAL, R.
YILDIRIM, H.
YÜCE, K.

Faculty of Engineering and Architecture (Terziodlu Kampüsü, 17020 Çanakkale):

BILIŠLI, A.
GÜVEN, S.
YIĐITBAŠ, E.
ZEKI TUTKUN, S.

Faculty of Fine Arts (Terziodlu Kampüsü, 17020 Çanakkale):

APAYDIN, M.
UYANIK, M.

Faculty of Fisheries (Terziodlu Kampüsü, 17020 Çanakkale):

ALPASLAN, M.
CIRIK, S.
KARAFISTAN, A. İ.
TUNCER, S.

Faculty of Sciences and Arts (Terzioğlu Kampüsü, 17020 Çanakkale):

AYDIN, N.
AYDIN, R.
AYSEL, V.
BARAN, Y.
DEMIRCAN, O.
İBRAHIMOV, A.
KAYA, K.
ÖDEN, Z. G.
ÖZDEMIR, E.
ÖZEL, M. E.
TOK, V.
UĞUZMAN, T.
UYSAL, A. O.

Faculty of Theology (Terzioğlu Kampüsü, 17020 Çanakkale):

KARAARSLAN, N. Ü.

ATTACHED SCHOOLS AND INSTITUTES

School of Nursing: 17100 Çanakkale; Dir Prof. GÜNHAM ERDEM.

School of Tourism and Health Management: Terzioğlu Kampüsü, 17020 Çanakkale.

Natural and Applied Sciences Institute: Terzioğlu Kampüsü, 17020 Çanakkale; Dir Prof. Dr MEHMET EMIN ÖZEL.

Social Studies Institute: Terzioğlu Kampüsü, 17020 Çanakkale; Dir Assoc. Prof. R. CENGIZ AKÇAY.

ÇANKAYA ÜNİVERSİTESİ

Öğretmenler Cad. 14, Yüzüncü Yil, 06530 Balgat, Ankara

Telephone: (312) 284-45-00
Fax: (312) 285-96-31
E-mail: webadmin@cankaya.edu.tr
Internet: www.cankaya.edu.tr
Founded 1997
Private control
Languages of instruction: Turkish, English
Academic year: September to June
President: SITKI ALP
Vice-Presidents: İSMAIL AKINALTUĞ, YUSUF GUNGOR
Rector: Prof. Dr ZIYA AKTAŞ
Vice-Rector: Prof. Dr KENAN TAS
Secretary-General: LÜTFI ÖNSOY
Director of Library: FATIH KUMSEL

Library of 9,278 vols, 140 periodicals
Number of teachers: 207
Number of students: 3,182 (2,977 undergraduate, 205 postgraduate)

DEANS

Faculty of Arts and Sciences: Prof. Dr EMEL DOGRAMACI
Faculty of Economics and Administrative Sciences: Prof. Dr AHMED YALNIZ
Faculty of Engineering and Architecture: Prof. Dr ZIYA AKTAŞ
Faculty of Law: Prof. Dr TURGUT ÖNEN

DIRECTORS

Graduate School of Natural and Applied Sciences: Prof. Dr YURDAHAN GÜLER
Graduate School of Social Sciences: Prof. Dr ÖZHAN ULUATAM
Preparatory School: Prof. Dr CENGIZ TOSUN
Vocational School: Asst Prof. Dr NÜZHET AKIN

CELAL BAYER ÜNİVERSİTESİ

45000 Manisa
Telephone: (236) 237-28-86
Fax: (236) 237-24-42

E-mail: kutuphane@bayar.edu.tr
Internet: www.bayar.edu.tr
Founded 1992
State control
Rector: Prof. Dr CEMIL ÖZCAN
Vice-Rectors: Prof. Dr ÜLGEN OK, Prof. Dr CENGIZ YILMAZ
Number of teachers: 1,094
Number of students: 21,435
Publications: *Journal of Management and Economics* (2 a year), *Journal of Social Sciences* (2 a year)

DEANS

Faculty of Arts and Sciences: Prof. ŞULE AYCAN
Faculty of Economic and Administrative Sciences: Prof. SEMRA ÖNCÜ
Faculty of Education: Prof. NAZMI TOPÇU
Faculty of Engineering: Prof. ERGUN KÖSE
Faculty of Medicine: Prof. EROL ÖZMEN

ATTACHED RESEARCH INSTITUTES

Institute for Graduate Studies in Pure and Applied Sciences: e-mail fen@bayar.edu.tr.
Institute of Health Sciences: e-mail saglik@bayar.edu.tr.
Institute of Social Sciences: e-mail sosyal@bayar.edu.tr.

ÇUKUROVA ÜNİVERSİTESİ

Balcalı Kampüsü, 01330 Balcalı, Adana
Telephone: (322) 338-60-84
Fax: (322) 338-64-11
E-mail: international@cukurova.edu.tr
Internet: www.cukurova.edu.tr
Founded 1973
State control
Language of instruction: Turkish
Academic year: September to July
Rector: Prof. Dr ALPER AKINOĞLU
Vice-Rectors: Prof. Dr HASAN FENERCIOĞLU, Prof. Dr BANU İNANÇ, Prof. Dr İLHAMI YEĞINGIL
Secretary-General: MUSTAFA BERBEROĞLU
Librarian: TURHAN YILMAZ
Library of 110,000 vols
Number of teachers: 1,520
Number of students: 20,000
Publications: *University Bulletin* (2 a year), faculty journals (all 3 a year)

DEANS

Faculty of Agriculture: Prof. Dr AYZIN B. KÜDEN
Faculty of Arts and Sciences: Prof. Dr GÜLTEN GÜNEL
Faculty of Dentistry: Prof. Dr NAFIZ BOZDEMÝR
Faculty of Divinity: Prof. Dr M. SALIH KIRKGÖZ
Faculty of Economics and Administrative Sciences: Prof. Dr SERAP ÇABUK
Faculty of Education: Prof. Dr A. NECMI YAŞAR
Faculty of Engineering and Architecture: Prof. Dr TUNCAY YILMAZ
Faculty of Fisheries: Prof. Dr METIN KUMLU
Faculty of Medicine: Prof. Dr İSMET TAN

HEADS OF DEPARTMENTS

Faculty of Agriculture:

ABAK, K., Horticultural Science
BAŞÇETINÇELIK, A., Agricultural Mechanization
ÇEVIK, B., Farm Structures and Irrigation
FENERCIOĞLU, H., Food Science and Technology
GENÇ, I., Field Crops
ÖZBEK, H., Soil Science
ÖZKÜTÜK, K., Animal Science

UYGUN, N., Plant Protection
UZUN, G., Landscape Architecture
YURDAKUL, O., Agricultural Economics

Faculty of Arts and Sciences:

AKDENİZ, F., Mathematics
ÇOLAK, Ö., Biology
ERBATUR, G., Chemistry
KIYMAÇ, K., Physics
MENGI, M., Turkish Language and Literature

Faculty of Economics and Administrative Sciences:

CANBAŞ, S., Management
ÇABUK, A., Econometrics
ÖZSOYLU, A. F., Finance
TEKEOĞLU, M., Economics

Faculty of Education:

BALCI, T., Teaching of German Language
EKMEKÇI, Ö., Teaching of English Language
ERALDEMİR, B., Arts and Crafts
GÖMIEKSIZ, M., Primary School Teaching
İNANÇ, B., Educational Sciences
KAYRA, E., Teaching of French Language
ÖNGEL, Ü., Philosophy

Faculty of Engineering and Architecture:

ANIL, M., Mining Engineering
EROL, R., Industrial Engineering
ERTEN, E., Architecture
ERTUNÇ, A., Geological Engineering
GÜRÇINAR, Y., Interior Design
KIRKGÖZ, S., Civil Engineering
KOÇ, E., Textile Engineering
SERBEST, H., Electrical and Electronic Engineering
YILMAZ, T., Mechanical Engineering
YÜCEER, A., Environmental Engineering

Faculty of Medicine:

ACARTÜRK, S., Plastic Surgery
AKAN, E., Microbiology
AKBABA, M., Public Health
AKGALI, C., Otolaryngology
AKKIZ, H., Gastroenterology
ARIDOĞAN, N., Obstetrics and Gynaecology
BAYSAL, F., Pharmacology
BAYTOK, G., Orthopaedics-Traumatology
BIRAND, A., Cardiology
BOZDEMIR, N., Family Practice
DERE, F., Anatomy
DOĞAN, A., Physiology
ERKOÇAK, E. U., General Surgery
ERSOZ, T. R., Ophthalmology
IŞIK, G., Anaesthesiology
KARADAYI, A., Neurosurgery
KASAP, H., Medical Biology
KOCABAŞ, A., Thoracic Surgery
KOÇAK, R., Haematology
KÜMI, M., Paediatric Haematology
LEVENT, B. A., Psychiatry
MEMİSOĞLU, H., Dermatology
OĞUZ, M., Radiology
SAĞLIKER, Y., Nephrology
SARICA, Y., Neurology
TUNCER, I., Forensic Medicine and Pathology
TÜRKYILMAZ, R., Urology
YÜREĞIR, G., Biochemistry
ZORLUDEMIR, Ü., Paediatric Surgery

ATTACHED INSTITUTES

Institute of Health: Dir Prof. Dr G. YÜREĞIR.
Institute of Science: Dir Prof. Dr U. DINÇ.
Institute of Social Sciences: Dir Prof. Dr N. ERK.

CUMHURIYET ÜNİVERSİTESİ
(Republic University)

58140 Campus-Sivas
Telephone: (346) 219-11-58
Fax: (346) 219-11-03

E-mail: rektor@cumhuriyet.edu.tr
Internet: www.cumhuriyet.edu.tr
Founded 1974, reorganized 1982
State control
Language of instruction: Turkish
Academic year: October to June

Rector: Prof. Dr FERİT KOÇOĞLU
Vice-Rectors: Prof. Dr ZAFER KARS, Prof. Dr
HALDUN SÜMER, Prof. Dr ORHAN TATAR
Secretary-General: Dr EROL ŞANLI
Librarian: AYGÜL ÜNAL

Number of teachers: 1,322
Number of students: 20,000

DEANS

Faculty of Arts and Sciences: Prof. Dr RAIF
GÜLER
Faculty of Dentistry: Prof. Dr TIMUR ESENER
Faculty of Economic and Administrative
Sciences: Prof. Dr M. ALİ AKPINAR
Faculty of Education: Prof. Dr NEVZAT BAT-
TAL
Faculty of Engineering: Prof. Dr ALİ ÖZTÜRK
Faculty of Fine Arts: Prof. Dr KADİR KARKİN
Faculty of Medicine: Prof. Dr REYHAN EĞİL-
MEZ
Faculty of Theological Studies: Prof. Dr N.
YAŞAR AŞIKOĞLU YILMAZ

DIRECTORS OF INSTITUTES

Basic Sciences: Prof. Dr RAUF EMIROV
Medical Sciences: Prof. Dr ÖGE ÇETİNKAYA
Social Sciences: Prof. Dr BAYRAM KAGMAZO-
ĞLU

ATTACHED RESEARCH CENTRES

Atatürk's Principles Research Centre:
Dir Prof. Dr MEHMET AKÇAY.

**Environmental Problems Research Cen-
tre:** Dir Prof. Dr ALİ YILMAZ.

DICLE ÜNİVERSİTESİ
(Tigris University)

21280 Diyarbakır
Telephone: (412) 248-80-30
Fax: (412) 248-80-47
E-mail: fcan@dicle.edu.tr
Internet: www.dicle.edu.tr
Founded 1966 as branch of Ankara Univer-
sity, independent 1973
State control
Academic year: October to June

Rector: Prof. Dr FIKRI CANORUÇ
Vice-Rectors: Prof. Dr ERALP ARIKAN, Prof. Dr
ZÜLKÜF GÜLSÜN
General Secretary: MEHMET TEKDÖŞ
Librarian: SEVGİ EKMEKÇİLER
Academic year: October to May

Library of 72,000 books, 6,000 periodicals,
1,350 theses and 3 CD databases
Number of teachers: 700
Number of students: 9,000

Publications: *Medical Faculty Journal, University Annual*

DEANS

Faculty of Agriculture: Prof. Dr DOĞAN ŞAKAR
Faculty of Dentistry: Prof. Dr FATMA ATAKUL
Faculty of Education: Prof. Dr ÖMER SAYA
Faculty of Education (Siirt): Assoc. Prof.
YÜKSEL COŞKUN
Faculty of Engineering and Architecture:
Assoc. Prof. FIKRI KAHRAMAN
Faculty of Law: Assoc. Prof. Dr FAZIL HÜSNÜ
ERDEM
Faculty of Medicine: Assoc. Prof. Dr RECEP
IŞIK
Faculty of Science and Letters: Prof. Dr
HALİL HOŞGÖREN
Faculty of Technical Education (Batman):
Prof. Dr O. ZEKİ HEKİMOĞLU

Faculty of Theology: Assoc. Prof. ABDULKERİM
ÜNALAN
Faculty of Veterinary Medicine: Prof. Dr
SAVAŞ HATİPOĞLU

PROFESSORS

Faculty of Arts and Sciences:

BAŞARAN, D., Botany
BİLGİN, F. H., Zoology
GÜLSÜN, Z., Atomic and Molecular Physics
GÜMGÜM, B., Inorganic Chemistry
GÜNİGÜNİ, B., Inorganic Chemistry
TEZ, Z., Physical Chemistry
YILMAZ, A., General Physics

Faculty of Education:

ASLAN, E., Turkish Language and Literature
SÖNMEZ, A., Physics

Faculty of Medicine:

ARIKAN, E., Microbiology
AYDINOL, B., Biochemistry
BAHÇECİ, M., Internal Diseases
BAYHAN, N., Anaesthesiology
BUDAK, T., Medical Biology
CANORUÇ, F., Internal Diseases
ÇELİK, S., Biophysics
DEĞERTEKİN, H., Internal Diseases
DERİCİ, M., Dermatology
ERDOĞAN, F., Physical Rehabilitation
GÜL, T., Gynaecology and Obstetrics
GÜRGEN, F., Psychiatry
IŞIKOĞLU, B., Internal Diseases
İLÇİN, E., Public Health
KELLE, A., Medical Biology
METE, Ö., Microbiology
MÜFTÜOĞLU, E., Internal Diseases
NERGİS, Y., Histology
ÖZAYDIN, M., Pathology
ÖZGEN, G., Cardiovascular and Thoracic
Surgery
TAŞ, M. A., Public Health
TOPCU, İ., Otorhinolaryngology
TOPRAK, N., Internal Diseases
YILMAZ, N., Gynaecology and Obstetrics

ATTACHED INSTITUTES

College of Health: Dir ZEKİ YILDIRIM.

Institute of Medical Sciences: Dir Prof.
Dr ALİ KELLE.

Institute of Sciences: Dir Prof. Dr DAVUT
BAŞARAN.

Institute of Social Sciences: Dir Prof. Dr
ABDÜLBAKİ TURAN.

DOĞUS ÜNİVERSİTESİ

Acıbadem, Zeamet Sok 21, 81010 Kadıköy,
Istanbul
Telephone: (216) 327-11-04
Fax: (216) 327-96-31
E-mail: mozsari@dogus.edu.tr
Internet: www.dogus.edu.tr
Founded 1997
Private control
Languages of instruction: Turkish, English
Academic year: October to June

Rector: Prof. Dr A. TALHA DINIBÜTÜN
General Secretary: MEHMET ALİ ÖZSARI
Library and Information Resources Centre
Manager: SÖNMEZ ÇELIK

Library of 6,000 books, 35 periodicals
Number of teachers: 90
Number of students: 615 (580 undergradu-
ate, 35 postgraduate)

DEANS

Faculty of Arts and Sciences: Prof. Dr DILEK
DOLTAŞ
Faculty of Economic and Administrative
Sciences: Prof. Dr ALPTEKIN GÜNEL
Faculty of Engineering: Prof. Dr MITAT
UYSAL

Institute of Social Sciences: Prof. Dr CUDI
TUNCER GÜRSOY
Institute of Science and Technology: Prof. Dr
CEM GÖKNAR
Vocational School: GÜLSEN KAHRAMAN

DOKUZ EYLÜL ÜNİVERSİTESİ
(Ninth September University)

Cumhuriyet Bul. 144, 35210 Alsancak, Izmir
Telephone: (232) 464-8068
Fax: (232) 464-8135
E-mail: webadmin@deu.edu.tr
Internet: www.deu.edu.tr
Founded 1982 from existing faculties and
schools
State control
Academic year: October to July

President: Prof. Dr EMİN ALİCİ
Vice-Presidents: Prof. Dr ADIL ESEN, Prof. Dr
İREM ÖZKARAHAN, Prof. Dr ÖMÜR ÖZMEN
Secretary-General: Assoc. Prof. Dr SELMA
BAKTİR
Librarian: HALE BALTEPE

Library of 262,000 vols
Number of teachers: 2,938
Number of students: 41,000

Publications: *IIBF Dergisi* (Faculty of Economics and Administrative Sciences, 2 a
year), *İlahiyat Fakültesi Dergisi* (Faculty
of Theology Review), *Sosyal Bilimler Enstitüsü Dergisi* (Social Sciences Institute
Review, 2 a year), *Tip Fakültesi Dergisi*
(Faculty of Medicine Review)

DEANS

Faculty of Architecture: Prof. Dr ORCAN
GÜNDÜZ
Faculty of Arts and Sciences: Prof. Dr NİLGÜN
MORALI
Faculty of Business Administration: Prof. Dr
ORHAN İAÖZ
Faculty of Economics and Administrative
Sciences: Prof. Dr ŞENAY ÜÇDOĞRUK
Faculty of Education: Prof. Dr FERDA AYSAN
Faculty of Engineering: Prof. Dr CÜNEYT
GÜZELIŞ
Faculty of Fine Arts: Prof. Dr ÇETIN TÜRKAÜ
Faculty of Law: Prof. Dr ŞEREF ERTAŞ
Faculty of Medicine: Prof. Dr ŞEBNEM ÖZKAN
Faculty of Theology: Prof. Dr SELÄHATTIN
PARLADIR

DIRECTORS

School of Maritime Business and Manage-
ment: Prof. Dr GÜLDEM CERİT
School of Nursing: Prof. Dr GÜLSEREN KOCA-
MAN
School of Physical Therapy and Rehabilita-
tion: Prof. Dr SERAP ALPER
Graduate School of Atatürk Principles and
Turkish Revolution: Prof. Dr ERGÜN
AYBARS
Graduate School of Education: Prof. Dr
SEDEF GIDENER
Graduate School of Health Sciences: Prof. Dr
GÜL GÜNER
Graduate School of Science and Engineering:
Prof. Dr CAHİT HELVACI
Graduate School of Social Sciences: Prof. Dr
ALİ NAZIM SÖZER
Vocational School of Health Services: Prof.
Dr NEDİM GAKIR
Vocational School of Juridical Practice: Prof.
Dr HAKAN PEKCANITEZ
Vocational School of Religion: Prof. Dr DUR-
MUŞ TEZCAN
İzmir Vocational School: Prof. Dr RECEP
YAPAREL
Torbalı Vocational School: Prof. Dr BURHAN
ERDOĞAN
Institute of Marine Sciences and Technology:
Prof. Dr MUSTAFA ERGUN
Institute of Oncology: Prof. Dr NUR OLGUN

Conservatory: Prof. GÜLSER ERYÜMLÜ

HEADS OF DEPARTMENTS

Faculty of Architecture (Şehitler Cad. 12, Alsancak, Izmir; tel. (232) 464-8105; fax (232) 464-8063; e-mail mimarlik@deu.edu.tr; internet www.deu.edu.tr/mimarlik):

Architecture: Prof. Dr ÇETİN TÜRKÇÜ
Urban and Regional Planning: Prof. Dr TAYFUN TANER

Faculty of Arts and Sciences (DEÜ Kaynaklar Kampusu, Buca, Izmir; tel. (232) 453-5072; fax (232) 453-4181; e-mail fenedebiyat@deu.edu.tr; internet www.sci.deu.edu.tr):

American Studies: Prof. Dr AZİZE ÖZGÜVEN
Archaeology: Prof. Dr RECEP MERİÇ
Mathematics: Prof. Dr GONCA ONARGAN
Statistics: Prof. Dr NILGÜN MORALI

Faculty of Business (DEÜ Kaynaklar Kampusu, Buca, Izmir; tel. (232) 453-5072; fax (232) 453-5062; e-mail isletme@deu.edu.tr; internet tusec.deu.edu.tr):

Business Administration: Prof. Dr METE OKTAV
Economics: Prof. Dr ASIM YÜCEL
International Relations: Doç. Dr MUSTAFA TANYELI
Tourism Administration: Prof. Dr ORHAN İÇÖZ

Faculty of Economics and Administrative Sciences (24 Sokak 2, Dokuzçeşmeler, Buca, Izmir; tel. (232) 420-4180; fax (232) 420-1789; e-mail iibf@deu.edu.tr; internet teos.iibf.deu.edu.tr):

Business Administration: Prof. Dr MUAMMER DOĞAN
Econometrics: Prof. Dr LEVENT SENYEL
Economics: Prof. Dr MUZAFFER DEMIRÜ
Labour Economics and Industrial Relations: Prof. Dr FEVZI DEMIR
Public Administration: Prof. Dr EROL AKİ
Public Finance: Prof. Dr MEHMET TOSUNER

Faculty of Education (Menderes Cad., Istasyon Sokak 5, Buca, Izmir; tel. (232) 420-4882; fax (232) 420-4895; e-mail egitim@deu.edu.tr; internet www.deu.edu.tr/buca):

Educational Sciences: Prof. Dr REŞIDE KABADAYİ
Foreign Languages: Prof. Dr GÜLDEN ERTUĞRUL
Music: Prof. YÜKSEL USLAY
Painting and Crafts: Prof. İBRAHİM BOZKUŞ
Science: Prof. Dr TEOMAN KESERCIOĞLU, Prof. Dr ÖMER ERGIN
Social Sciences: Prof. Dr İBRAHİM ATALAY
Turkish Language and Literature: Prof. Dr İBRAHİM ATALAY

Faculty of Engineering (EÜ Kampusu, Bornova, Izmir; tel. (232) 388-0110; fax (232) 388-7864; e-mail muhendislik@deu.edu.tr; internet www.eng.deu.edu.tr):

Civil Engineering: Prof. Dr ÖMER ZAFER ALKU
Computer Engineering: Prof. Dr İREM ÖZKARAHAN
Electronics and Electrical Engineering: Prof. Dr CÜNEYT GÜZELIŞ
Environmental Engineering: Prof. Dr AYŞEN TÜRKMAN
Geological Engineering: Prof. Dr SACIT SÖZER
Geophysical Engineering: Prof. Dr ZAFER AKÇIĞ
Industrial Engineering: Prof. Dr HASAN ESKİ
Mechanical Engineering: Prof. Dr SAMI AKSOY
Mining Engineering: Prof. Dr MEVLÜT KEMAL

Faculty of Fine Arts (Gündoğdu Sokak 4, Narlidere, Izmir; tel. (232) 238-9075; fax (232) 239-0594; e-mail guzelsanatlar@deu.edu.tr):

Ceramics and Glass: Assoc. Prof. Dr SEVİM CIZER
Cinema and Television: Prof. Dr OĞUZ ADANIR
Drama and Theatre Arts: Prof. Dr MURAT TUNCAY
Musicology: Prof. Dr TURGUT ALDEMİR
Painting: Assoc. Prof. MÜMTAZ SAĞLAM
Photography: Assoc. Prof. Dr SİMBER ATAY
Sculpture: Assoc. Prof. CENGIZ ÇEKIL
Turkish Traditional Handicrafts: Assoc. Prof. Dr İSMAİL ÖZTÜRK

Faculty of Law (24 Sokak 2, Dokuzçeşmeler, Buca, Izmir; tel. (232) 420-4180; fax (232) 420-1827; e-mail hukuk@deu.edu.tr; internet www.deu.edu.tr/hukuk/index.htm):

Finance and Economics: Doç. Dr YUSUF KARAKOÇ
Private Law: Prof. Dr ÜNAL NARMANLIOĞLU
Public Law: Prof. Dr DURMUŞ TEZCAN

Faculty of Medicine (Mithatpasa Cad. 1606, 35340 Balçova, Izmir; tel. (232) 259-5959; fax (232) 259-0541; e-mail tip@deu.edu.tr; internet www.tip.deu.edu.tr):

Basic Medicine: Prof. Dr İ. NURAN YUHIĞ
Internal Medicine: Prof. ATILLA AKKOÇLU
Surgical Medicine: Prof. AYDANUR KARGI

Faculty of Theology (108/2 Sokak 18–20, Hatay, Izmir; tel. (232) 285-2932; fax (232) 224-1890; e-mail ilahiyat@deu.edu.tr; internet web.deu.edu.tr/ilahiyat):

Basic Islamic Sciences: Prof. Dr MUAMMER ÇELEBİ
History of Islam and Islamic Arts: Prof. Dr HAKKI ÖNKAL
Philosophy and Religion: Prof. Dr HANAFİ ÖZCAN

DUMLUPINAR ÜNİVERSİTESİ

M. Kampüs Rektörlük Binası Tavşanlı, Yolu 10 km 43100 Kütahya

Telephone: (274) 265-20-31
Fax: (274) 265-20-14
E-mail: ssevim@dumlupinar.edu.tr
Internet: www.dumlupinar.edu.tr

Founded 1992
State control
Academic year: November to July

Rector: Prof. Dr GÜNER ÖNCE
Vice-Rectors: Prof. Dr BAHRI ÖTEYAKA, Prof. Dr ALI SARIKOYUNCU
Secretary-General: YALÇIN KALAY
Registrar: MIKTAT BEKTAŞ
Head of Library: İSMAİL BAYRAM

Library of 28,000 books, 168 periodicals
Number of teachers: 515
Number of students: 19,000

DEANS

Faculty of Arts and Sciences: Prof. ALI SARIKOYUNCU
Faculty of Economic and Administrative Sciences (Bilecik): Prof. BAHRI ÖTEYAKA
Faculty of Education: Prof. Dr AHMET YAMIK
Faculty of Engineering: Prof. CEM ŞENSÖGÜT
Faculty of Fine Arts: Prof. Dr ADNAN TEPECİK
Faculty of Technical Education (Simav): Prof. GÜNER ÖNCE
Graduate School of Science and Engineering: Assoc. Prof. İSKENDER IŞIK
Graduate School of Social Sciences: Prof. AHMET KARAASLAN

EGE ÜNİVERSİTESİ
(Aegean University)

Bornova, Izmir
Telephone: (232) 388-01-10
Fax: (232) 339-90-90
E-mail: ulkubay@med.ege.edu.tr

Internet: www.ege.edu.tr

Founded 1955
State control

Languages of instruction: Turkish and, in some departments, English
Academic year: October to June

Rector: Prof. Dr ÜLKÜ BAYINDIR
Vice-Rectors: Prof. Dr HALUK BAYLAS, Prof. Dr FİKRET İKIZ, Prof. Dr MUSTAFA METIN
General Secretary: CIHANGIR SOYGÜL
Librarian: NURCAN ESLİK BAYKAL

Number of teachers and assistants: 992
Number of students: 30,887

Publications: Aegean Medical Journal, Fen Dergisi, Tıp Fakültesi Mecmuası, Ziraat Fakültesi Dergisi, and faculty publications

DEANS

Faculty of Agriculture: Prof. Dr SEMIH ERKAN
Faculty of Communications: Prof. Dr AHMET BÜLENT GÖKSEL
Faculty of Dentistry: Prof. Dr SELDA ERTÜRK
Faculty of Economics and Administrative Sciences: Prof. Dr REZAN TATLIDIL
Faculty of Education: Prof. Dr KADIR ASLAN
Faculty of Engineering: Prof. Dr MUSTAFA TÜRKSEVER
Faculty of Fisheries: Prof. Dr AHMET KOCATAŞ
Faculty of Medicine: Prof. Dr ATA ERDENER
Faculty of Pharmacy: Prof. Dr ERÇIN ERCIYAS
Faculty of Science: Prof. Dr BEKIR ÇETİNKAYA
Faculty of Science and Letters: Prof. Dr KASIM EĞIT

DIRECTORS

School of Nursing: Prof. Dr İNCI EREFE
School of Press and Publications: Prof. Dr ÖZCAN ÖZAL
School of Water Products: Prof. Dr ATILLA ALPBAZ
Professional School: Prof. Dr MEHMET DOKUZOĞUZ
Institute for Medical Sciences: Prof. Dr NECMETTİN ZEYBEK
Institute for Nuclear Sciences: Prof. Dr SELMAN KINACI
Institute for Science: Prof. Dr FERİDUN TOPALOĞLU
Institute for Solar Energy: Prof. Dr MEHMET AYDIN
Conservatory of Turkish Music: Prof. Dr REFET SAYGILI

RESEARCH CENTRES

Agricultural Research Center: Dir Prof. Dr TAYFUN ÖZKAYA.
Botanical Garden and Herbarium Research Center: Dir Prof. Dr ÖZCAN SEÇMEN.
Cancer Surveillance and Research Center: Dir Prof. Dr AYFER HAYDAROĞLU.
Centre for Strategic Studies.
Environmental Studies Research Center: Dir Prof. Dr ÜMIT ERDEM.
European Languages and Cultures Research Center (ADİKAM): Dir Prof. Dr GERTRUDE DURUSOY.
Family Planning and Infertility Research Center.
Genetic Disease Research Center: Dir Prof. Dr CIHANGIR ÖZKINAY.
Health Research Center (University Hospital).
Information and Communication Technologies Research Center: Dir Prof. Dr FAZIL APAYDIN.
Izmir Research Center: Dir Prof. Dr IŞIK TARAKÇIOĞLU.
Natural History Research Center (The Museum of Natural History): Dir Prof. Dr NIMET ÖKTEM.

Organ Transplantation Research Centre: Dir Prof. Dr ÖZDEMIR YARARBAŞ.

Principles of Atatürk and Recent Turkish History Research Center: Dir Prof. Dr FAZILET VARDAR-SUKAN.

Poison Research Center.

Science and Technology Research Center: Dir Prof. Dr S. ŞUHA SUKAN.

Seed Technology Research Center: Dir Prof. Dr BENIAN ESER.

Submarine Research Center.

Textile and Apparel Manufacturing Research Center: Dir Prof. Dr IŞIK TARAKÇIOGLU.

Women Studies Research Center.

ERCIYES ÜNIVERSITESI

38039 Kayseri
Telephone: (352) 437-49-22
Fax: (352) 437-49-31
E-mail: info@erciyes.edu.tr
Internet: www.erciyes.edu.tr
Founded 1978
State control
Language of instruction: Turkish
Academic year: November to June

Rector: Prof. Dr CENGIZ UTAŞ
Vice-Rectors: Prof. Dr ASUMAN GÖLGELI, Prof. Dr ŞENOL KARTAL, Prof. Dr IBRAHIM UZMAY
Registrar: Dr SEMA ASLAN
Librarian: GÜLNUR YAKAN

Number of teachers: 105
Number of students: 25,708

Publications: *Journal of the Faculty of Economics and Administrative Sciences, Journal of the Medical School, Journals of the Theology Faculty*

DEANS

Faculty of Architecture: Prof. Dr SEVGI LÖKÇE
Faculty of Arts and Science: Prof. Dr Ş. COŞKUN ÖNEM
Faculty of Arts and Science (Yozgat): Prof. Dr YUNUS AKÇAMUR
Faculty of Business Administration (Yozgat): Prof. Dr OSMAN UNUTULMAZ
Faculty of Business Administration and Management (Nevşehir): Prof. Dr MAHIR NAKIP
Faculty of Communication: Prof. Dr ŞÜKRÜ AKDOĞAN
Faculty of Dentistry: Prof. Dr BÜLENT KESIM
Faculty of Economics and Administrative Sciences: Prof. Dr CEMAL ÖZGÜVEN
Faculty of Education: Prof. Dr ERSOY TAŞDEMIRCI
Faculty of Engineering: Prof. Dr KERIM GÜNEY
Faculty of Engineering and Architecture (Yozgat): Prof. Dr RECEP KILIK
Faculty of Fine Arts: Prof. Dr SABRI YENER
Faculty of Law: Doç. Dr ISMAIL KAYAR
Faculty of Medicine: Prof. Dr RUHAN DÜŞÜNEL
Faculty of Pharmacy: Prof. Dr ERDOĞAN BERÇIN
Faculty of Theology: Prof. Dr CELAL KIRCA
Faculty of Veterinary Science: Prof. Dr ISMAIL HAKKI NUR

PROFESSORS

Faculty of Architecture (Erciyes University, 38039 Kayseri; tel. (352) 437-52-82; fax (352) 437-65-54; internet www.erciyes.edu.tr/mimart.htm):

LÖKÇE, S.
ÖZCAN, Z.
YURTSEVER, H.

Faculty of Arts and Science (Erciyes University, 38039 Kayseri; tel. (352) 437-52-62; fax (352) 437-49-33; internet www.matrix.erciyes.edu.tr):

AKÇAMUR, Y.
AKKURT, M.
AKTAN, A.
ALTINDIŞ, H.
ALTURAL, B.
ARGUNŞAH, H.
ARGUNŞAH, M.
AYYILDIZ, E.
AYYILDIZ, N.
BARAN, M.
BAYRAKTAR, B.
BOR, H.
ÇOBAN, A.
GÖRKEM, I.
GÜLENSOY, T.
GÜNDÜZ, M.
GÜZEL, Y.
HÜLAGÜ, M. M.
KARAÖRS, M. M.
KARTAL, Ş.
KESKIN, M.
KESKIN, M.
KÖK, T. R.
MANAŞLI, N.
MUCUK, O.
ÖNEM, Ş C.
ÖZDEMIR, M.
ÖZKAN, N.
ÖZSOY, S.
PATAT, Ş.
SARIPINAR, E.
SOYLAK, M.
TAŞDEMIRCI, E.
TOKATLI, U.
TUNÇBILEK, A. Ş.
TÜRKMEN, K.
ÜLGEN, A.
YILDIRIM, I.
YUVALI, A.

Faculty of Arts and Science (Yozgat) (Erciyes University, Yozgat; tel. (354) 263-82-70; fax (354) 263-82-71; internet www.yozgatfef.erciyes.edu.tr):

AKÇAMUR, Y.

Faculty of Communication (Erciyes University, 38039 Kayseri; tel. and fax (352) 437-52-61; internet iletsim.erciyes.edu.tr):

AKDOĞAN, Ş.
YERLIKAYA, I.

Faculty of Dentistry (Erciyes University, 38039 Kayseri; tel. and fax (352) 437-49-01; internet dent.erciyes.edu.tr):

KESIM, B.

Faculty of Economics and Administrative Sciences (Erciyes University, 38039 Kayseri; tel. (352) 437-49-13; fax (352) 437-52-39; e-mail iibf@erciyes.edu.tr; internet www.iibf.erciyes.edu.tr):

AKDOĞAN, M. Ş.
AKDOĞAN, A. A.
ANDAÇ, F.
ATALAY, M.
BILGINOĞLU, M. A.
ÇALIŞKAN, F.
DURA, C.
DURSUN, Y.
ERDEM, E.
NAKIP, M.
ÖZGÜVEN, C.
SAATÇI, M.
SÖNMEZ, I. H.
UNUTULMAZ, O.
YILDIZ, R.

Faculty of Economics and Administrative Sciences (Nevşehir) (Erciyes University, Nevşehir; tel. (384) 215-20-07; fax (384) 215-20-10; internet www.iibf.eunev.edu.tr):

YILDIZ, R.

Faculty of Economics and Administrative Sciences (Yozgat) (Erciyes University, Yozgat; tel. (354) 263-82-48; fax (354) 263-82-81; internet yiibf.erciyes.edu.tr):

UNUTULMAZ, O.

Faculty of Education (Erciyes University, 38039 Kayseri; tel. and fax (352) 437-32-06; internet egitim.erciyes.edu.tr):

TAŞDEMIRCI, E.

Faculty of Engineering (Erciyes University, 38039 Kayseri; tel. (352) 437-57-55; fax (352) 437-57-84; internet mf.erciyes.edu.tr):

ALÇI, M.
APALAK, M. K.
BILIŞIK, A.
DANIŞMAN, K.
GÜNEY, K.
HAKTANIR, T.
KARABOĞA, D.
KARAMIŞ, M. B.
KILIK, R.
TAŞPINAR, H.
UZMAY, I.
YAPICI, H.
YETIM, H.

Faculty of Engineering and Architecture (Yozgat) (Erciyes University, Yozgat; tel. (354) 263-82-72; fax (354) 263-82-76; internet ymmf.erciyes.edu.tr):

KILIK, R.

Faculty of Fine Arts (Erciyes University, 38039 Kayseri; tel. (352) 437-52-81; fax (352) 437-36-52; internet guzelsanat.erciyes.edu.tr):

YENER, S.

Faculty of Law (Erciyes University, 38039 Kayseri; tel. (352) 437-49-01; fax (352) 437-49-31; internet hukuk.erciyes.edu.tr):

KAYAR, I

Faculty of Medicine (Erciyes University, 38039 Kayseri; tel. (352) 437-49-10; fax (352) 437-52-85; internet tip.erciyes.edu.tr):

AKÇALI, Y. F.
AKDEMIR, H.
AKTAS, E.
ALTUNBAŞ, M.
ALTUNTAŞ, H.
ARGUN, M.
ARITAŞ, Y.
ARMAN, F.
AŞÇIOĞLU, M.
AŞÇIOĞLU, Ö.
AYCAN, K.
AYDOĞAN, S.
AYGEN, B.
AYGEN, E. M.
AYKUT, M.
BAKTIR, A.
BALKANLI, S.
BAŞBUĞ, M.
BAŞAR, E.
BAŞTÜRK, M.
BAYRAM, F.
BOYACI, A.
CANER, Y.
CEYHAN, O.
ÇETIN, N.
ÇETIN, S.
ÇETINKAYA, F.
ÇOKSEVIM, B.
DEMIR, R.
DEMIRTAŞ, H.
DOĞAN, H.
DOĞANAY, M.
DÜNDAR, M.
DÜNDAR, M.
DURAK, A. C.
DURSUN, N.
DÜŞÜNSEL, R.
EMIROĞULLARI, O. N.
ERENMEMIŞOĞLU, A.
ERGIN, A.

ERKAN, M.
ERKILIÇ, K.
ERSOY, A. Ö.
ESMAOĞLU, A.
GÖLGELİ, A.
GÜLEÇ, M.
GÜLMEZ, İ.
GÜLMEZ, İ.
GÜNAY, G. K.
GÜNAY, O.
GÜNDÜZ, Z.
GÜNEY, E.
GÜVEN, K.
KAHRAMAN, H. C.
KARACAGİL, M.
KARAKÜÇÜK, M. S.
KELEŞTİMUR, H. F.
KENDİRCİ, M.
KİLİÇ, H.
KİRNAP, M.
KOÇ, A. N.
KOÇ, R. K.
KONTAŞ, O.
KUMANDAŞ, S.
KURTOĞLU, S.
KÖSE, S. K.
KÜLAHLİ, İ.
KÜÇÜKAYDIN, M.
MADENOĞLU, H.
MİRZA, G. E.
MİRZA, M.
MÜDERRIS, İ. İ.
MUHTAROĞLU, S.
NARIN, N.
OKTEN, T.
OKUR, H.
OYMAK, O.
ÖZBAKİR, Ö.
ÖZBAL, Y.
ÖZCAN, N.
ÖZDAMAR, M. A.
ÖZDEMİR, M. A.
ÖZESMİ, Ç.
ÖZESMİ, M.
ÖZKUL, Y.
ÖZTÜRK, F.
ÖZTÜRK, M. A.
ÖZTÜRK, M. K.
ÖZTÜRK, Y.
PATIROĞLU, T.
PATIROĞLU, T. E.
SELÇUKLU, A.
SOFUOĞLU, S.
SOYUER, A.
SÖZÜER, E. M.
SÜER, C.
SÜMERKAN, A. B.
ŞAHİN, İ.
ŞAHİN, Y.
TALASLIOĞLU, A.
TATLIŞEN, A.
TAYYAR, M.
TEKOL, Y.
TERCAN, E.
TURAN, C.
TÜRK, C. Y.
TUTUŞ, A.
UKŞAL, Ü.
UTAŞ, C.
UTAŞ, S.
ÜNAL, A.
ÜNLÜ, Y.
ÜSTDAL, K. M.
ÜZÜM, K.
YAKAN, B.
YIĞITBAŞI, , O. G.
YILMAZ, Z.
YÜCESOY, M.

Faculty of Pharmacy (Erciyes University, 38039 Kayseri; tel. (352) 437-49-01; fax (352) 437-49-31; internet pharmacy.erciyes .edu.tr):

BERÇİN, E.

Faculty of Theology (Erciyes University, 38039 Kayseri; tel. (352) 437-60-64; fax

(352) 437-42-00; internet ilahiyat.erciyes .edu.tr):

APAYDIN, H. Y.
ATİK, M. K.
AYDIN, M. Ş.
BAĞÇECİ, M.
COŞKUN, A.
DEMİRCİ, A.
DUMAN, M. Z.
GÜNAY, Ü.
GÜNGÖR, H.
KIRCA, C.
KOÇ, T.
PAZARBAŞI, E.
POLAT, S.
SAMUR, S.
SEVERCAN, Ş.
ŞAHİN, H.
TAŞTAN, A.
TOKSARI, A.
TUNÇ, C.
UĞUR, A.

Faculty of Veterinary Science (Erciyes University, 38039 Kayseri; tel. (352) 339-94-84; fax (352) 337-27-40; internet www.erciyes .edu.tr/veterinert.htm):

ATASEVER, A.
AYDIN, F.
BEKYÜREK, T.
İNCİ, A.
İŞCAN, K. M.
LIMAN, B. C.
LIMAN, N.
NUR, İ. H.

ATTACHED INSTITUTES

Atatürk Higher School of Health: internet hbshmyo.erciyes.edu.tr; Dir Prof. Dr ÜMIT SEVİĞ.

Civil Aviation Higher School: internet havacilik.erciyes.edu.tr; Dir Prof. Dr HÜSEYIN YAPICI.

Gevher Nesibe Institute of the History of Medicine: Dir Prof. Dr EKREM AKTAŞ.

Halil Bayraktar Health Services Vocational School: internet hbshmyo.erciyes .edu.tr; Dir Prof. Dr ALİ ÖZDEMİR ERSOY.

High School of Foreign Languages: internet sfl.erciyes.edu.tr; Chair. Dr ADEM S. TURANLI.

High School of Physical Education and Sports: internet besyoerciyes.edu.tr; Dir Prof. Dr BEKIR ÇOKSEVIM.

Institute of Health Sciences: e-mail sagbilen@erciyes.edu.tr; internet sagen .erciyes.edu.tr; Dir Prof. Dr MERAL AŞÇIOĞLU.

Institute of Sciences: internet fbe.erciyes .edu.tr; Dir Prof. Dr NURSET AYYILDIZ.

Institute of Social Sciences: internet www .erciyes.edu.tr/enstitut.htm; Dir Prof. Dr MUSTAFA KESKIN.

Kayseri Vocational School: internet kmyo .erciyes.edu.tr; Dir Prof. Dr CEBRAIL ÇIF-TLIKLI.

Kocasinan Vocational School: internet kocmyo.erciyes.edu.tr; Dir ÖMER ŞENGÜL.

Nevşehir Higher School of Health: internet www.syo.eunev.edu.tr; Dir Prof. Dr NİMET KARATAŞ.

Nevşehir Higher School of Tourism and Hotel Management: internet www.eunev .edu.tr; Dir S. KUŞLUVAN.

Nevşehir Vocational School: internet www.myo.eunev.edu.tr; Dir Assoc. Asst Prof. KURTULUŞ KARAMUSTAFA.

Safiye Çikrikçioğlu Vocational School: internet scmyo.erciyes.edu.tr; Dir Assoc. Asst Prof. GÜNER BAYRAM.

Vocational School: internet myo.erciyes .edu.tr; Dir Assoc. Doç. Dr ALI KAYA.

Yozgat High School of Health: internet ysyo.erciyes.edu.tr; Dir MAHMUT KILIÇ.

Yozgat Vocational School: internet ymyo .erciyes.edu.tr; Dir Assoc. Asst Prof. ÖMER DEMİR.

FATİH ÜNİVERSİTESİ

34500 Büyükçekmece, Istanbul

Telephone: (212) 889-08-10
Fax: (212) 889-09-12
E-mail: registrar@fatih.edu.tr
Internet: www.fatih.edu.tr

Founded 1996
Private control
Language of instruction: English(in faculties)
Language of instruction: Turkish (in Vocational Schools)
Academic year: October to July

Rector: Prof. Dr TURGUT BALKAŞ (acting)
Vice-Rectors: Prof. Dr BAHATTIN ADAM, Prof. Dr KEMAL FIDANBOYLU (acting)
Registrar: MÜNEVVER GÜL UZUN
Library Manager: ERCÜMENT DEMIRBOZAN

Library of 25,000 books, 40 periodicals, 300 CD-ROMs
Number of teachers: 344
Number of students: 3,472

Publication: *Journal of Economic and Social Research* (2 a year)

DEANS

Faculty of Arts and Sciences: Prof. Dr ALPARSLAN AÇIKGENÇ
Faculty of Economics and Administrative Sciences: Prof. Dr FAHRETTIN GÜCIN
Faculty of Engineering: Prof. Dr MAZHAR ÜNSAL
Faculty of Medicine: Prof. Dr DAVUT AKTAŞ (acting)

FİRAT ÜNİVERSİTESİ
(Euphrates University)

23119 Elaziğ

Telephone: (424) 212-85-10
Fax: (424) 212-27-10
E-mail: okalem@firat.edu.tr
Internet: www.firat.edu.tr

Founded 1975
Language of instruction: Turkish
Academic year: October to June

Rector: Prof. Dr MEHMET HAMDI MUZ
Vice-Rectors: Prof. Dr A. Y. ERKIN OĞUR, Prof. Dr HARUN ÖZER
General Secretary: GAZI ÖZCAN
Librarian: Prof. Dr FAHRETTIN GÖKTAŞ

Number of teachers: 1,558
Number of students: 15,906

Publications: *Journal of Health Sciences* (2 a year), *Journal of Science and Engineering* (2 a year), *Journal of Social Sciences* (2 a year)

DEANS

Faculty of Agriculture (Bingöl): (vacant)
Faculty of Aquatic Sciences: Prof. Dr BÜLENT ŞEN
Faculty of Arts and Sciences: Prof. Dr İBRAHIM YILMAZÇELIK
Faculty of Communication: Prof. Dr ASAF VAROL
Faculty of Economic and Management Sciences (Tunceli): (vacant)
Faculty of Education: Prof. Dr MEHMET AYDOĞDU
Faculty of Education (Muş): (vacant)
Faculty of Engineering: Prof. Dr DURSUN PEHLİVAN
Faculty of Medicine: Prof. Dr ÖZGE ARDIÇO-ĞLU

Faculty of Technical Education: Prof. Dr ALI İNAN

Faculty of Theology: Doç. Dr MUSTAFA ÖZTÜRK

Faculty of Veterinary Medicine: Prof. Dr H. BASRI GÜLCÜ

HEADS OF DEPARTMENTS

Faculty of Aquatic Sciences (tel. (424) 212-2780; fax (424) 238-6287; e-mail bsen@firat.edu.tr):

Aquaculture: Prof. Dr MUSTAFA SARIEYYÜPOĞLU

Aquatic Basic Sciences: Prof. Dr BÜLENT ŞEN

Fisheries and Processing Technology: Doç. Dr ERDAL DUMAN

Faculty of Arts and Sciences (tel. (424) 218-7815; fax (424) 233-0062; e-mail mergut@firat.edu.tr):

Biology: Prof. Dr AHMET ŞAHİN
Chemistry: Prof. Dr MISIR AHMEDZADE
Geography: Prof. Dr SADETTİN TONBUL
History: Prof. Dr MUSTAFA ÖZTÜRK
Mathematics: Prof. Dr RIFAT ÇOLAK
Physics: Prof. Dr MEHMET CEYLAN
Sociology: Prof. Dr HALIL NARMAN
Turkish Language and Literature: Doç. Dr ESMA KILIÇ
Western Languages and Literature: Dr MEHMET AYGÜN

Faculty of Communication (tel. (424) 236-2660; fax (424) 238-8387; e-mail avarol@firat.edu.tr):

Journalism: (vacant)
Public Relations: (vacant)
Radio, Television and Cinema: Prof. Dr AŞAF VAROL

Faculty of Engineering (tel. (424) 421-5525; fax (424) 421-5526; e-mail dpehlivan@firat.edu.tr):

Chemical Engineering: Prof. Dr FIKRET TÜMEN

Civil Engineering: Prof. Dr ATAMAN HAKSEVER

Computer Engineering: Doç. Dr AHMET ARSLAN

Electrical and Electronic Engineering: Doç. Dr MUSTAFA POYRAZ

Environmental Engineering: Prof. Dr DURSUN PEHLİVAN

Geological Engineering: Prof. Dr ERKAN TANYOLU

Mechanical Engineering: Prof. Dr AYDİN TURGUT

Metallurgical and Materials Engineering: Dr MUSTAFA AKSOY

Faculty of Medicine (tel. (424) 212-29-60; fax (424) 237-91-38; e-mail sskilic@firat.edu.tr):

Fundamental Medical Sciences: Prof. Dr ENZER OZAN

Internal Medicine: Assoc. Prof. Dr BÜLENT MÜNGEN

Surgical Medicine: Prof. Dr REŞAT ÖZERCAN

Faculty of Technical Education (tel. (424) 218-4673; fax (424) 218-4674; e-mail mkaya@firat.edu.tr):

Automative Sciences Education: Prof. Dr NAZIF DİNÇER

Construction Sciences Education: Assoc. Prof. Dr MEHMET TUĞAL

Educational Sciences: Doç. Dr MEHMET GÜROL

Electrical Sciences Education: Asst Prof. Dr SEÇEK YILDIRIM

Electronics and Computer Education: Prof. Dr ASAF VAROL

Metallurgical Sciences Education: Prof. Dr MUSTAFA YILDIRIM

Faculty of Theology (tel. (424) 241-6032; fax (424) 241-6011; e-mail msoysaldi@firat.edu.tr):

Fundamental Islamic Sciences: Doç. Dr MEHMET SOYSALDI

Islamic History and Art: Assoc. Prof. Dr SİDDİK ÜNALAN

Philosophy and Religious Sciences: Assoc. Prof. Dr DAVUT KILIÇ

Faculty of Veterinary Medicine (tel. (242) 212-8525; fax (242) 238-8173; e-mail ndumanli@firat.edu.tr):

Animal Husbandry: Prof. Dr İ. HALIL ÇERÇI

Fundamental Veterinary Sciences: Prof. Dr SEMA OZAN

Internal Diseases and Surgical Sciences: Prof. Dr HÜSEYIN DEVECI

ATTACHED RESEARCH CENTRES

Advanced Technology Research Centre: Dir Doç. Dr SINAN SAYDAM.

Agriculture and Animal Research Centre: Dir Doç. Dr METIN BAYRAKTAR.

Biotechnology Research Centre: Dir Doç. Dr NIHAT DILSIZ.

Cardiology Research Centre: Dir Doç. Dr ERDOĞAN İLKAY.

Centre for Atatürk's Principles and the History of the Revolution: Dir Doç. Dr ERDAL AÇIKSES.

Computer Research Centre: Dir Asst Prof. Dr Y. TATAR.

Eastern Anatolia Research Centre: Dir Prof. Dr MUSTAFA ÖZTÜRK.

Environmental Pollution Research Centre: Dir (vacant).

Fırat Basin Research Centre: Dir Asst Prof. Dr Ö SOMUNKIRAN.

Fırat Medical Centre: Dir Doç. Dr İRFAN KAYGUSUZ.

Language Teaching and Training Research Centre: Dir Doç. Dr AHMET BURAN.

Leprosy Research Centre: Dir (vacant).

Natural Disasters Research Centre: Dir (vacant).

Research Centre for Environmental Pollution of the Keban Basin: Dir (vacant).

Research Centre for Hearing Difficulties: Dir (vacant).

Research Centre for University–Industry Relations: Dir TÜRKER GÜLER.

ATTACHED SCHOOLS AND COLLEGES

College of Health Sciences: Dir Prof. Dr EMINE ÜNSALDI.

College of Health Sciences (Elazig): Dir Prof. Dr ZÜLAL AŞCI TORAMAN.

College of Physical and Sports Education (Elazig): Dir Prof. Dr MEHMET ÜLKER.

College of Social Sciences (Elazig): Dir Doç. Dr ORHAN KILIÇ.

College of Technical Sciences (Elazig): Dir Doç. Dr NECATI KULOĞLU.

College of Vocational Education (Bingöl): Dir Prof. Dr MÜKREMIN APAYDIN.

College of Vocational Education (Maden): Dir Doç. Dr ALI İNAN.

College of Vocational Education (Malazgirt): Dir Prof. Dr KADIR SERVI.

College of Vocational Education (Muş): Dir Doç. Dr KADIR SERVI.

College of Vocational Education (Sivrice): Dir Prof. Dr HARUN ÖZER.

College of Vocational Education (Tunceli): Dir Prof. Dr SALIH ÖZÇELİK.

Fine Arts–Music: Dir Assoc. Prof. Dr GÜLDENIZ EKMEN AGIŞ.

Keban Sleyman Demırel College of Vocational Education: Dir Assoc. Prof. Dr HÜSAMETTIN KAYA.

Kemaliye Hacı Ali Akin College of Vocational Education: Dir Prof. Dr MEHMET CEBECI.

GALATASARAY ÜNİVERSİTESİ

Ciragan Cad. 36, 34357 Ortaköy, Istanbul
Telephone: (212) 227-44-80
E-mail: dyarsuvat@gsu.edu.tr
Internet: www.gsu.edu.tr
Founded 1992
Academic year: October to June
State control

Rector: Prof. Dr DUYGUN YARSUVAT
Vice-Rectors: Prof. Dr SEYFETTIN GÜRSEL, Prof. Dr PIERRE LE MIRE, Prof. Dr ETHEM TOLGA, Prof. Dr NECMI YÜZBAŞIOĞLU
General Secretary: Prof. Dr İSMAIL ÖZTÜRK

Library of 42,000 vols
Number of teachers: 140
Number of students: 1,674

DEANS

Faculty of Communications: Prof. Dr E. ÖZDEN CANKAYA

Faculty of Engineering and Technology: Prof. Dr ETHEM TOLGA

Faculty of Law: Prof. Dr HAMDI YASAMAN

Faculty of Science and Letters: Prof. Dr KENAN GÜRSOY

HEADS OF DEPARTMENTS

Department of Business Administration: Prof. Dr H. FUAT ÇELEBİOĞLU

Department of Computer Engineering: Prof. Dr ETHEM TOLGA

Department of Economics: Prof. Dr SEYFETTIN GÜRSEL

Department of Foreign Languages: Prof. Dr SIBEL YAMAK

Department of Industrial Engineering: Prof. Dr E. ERTUĞRUL KARSAK

Department of International Relations: Prof. Dr H. BERIL DEDEOĞLU

Department of Philosophy: Prof. Dr TÜLIN BUMIN

Department of Sociology: Prof. Dr ALI ERGUR

Institute of Sciences: Prof. Dr E. ERTUĞRUL KARSAK

Institute of Social Sciences: Prof. Dr İDIL KAYA

ATTACHED RESEARCH INSTITUTES

Centre of Research and Documentation of Europe: Dir Prof. Dr A. IŞIL KARAKAŞ.

Penalty Law and Criminology Research Centre: Dir Prof. Dr A. KÖKSAL BAYRAKTAR.

Strategic Research Center: Dir COŞKUN KIRCA.

GAZİ ÜNİVERSİTESİ

06500 Teknikokullar, Ankara
Telephone: (312) 212-68-40
Fax: (312) 221-32-02
E-mail: rektor@gazi.edu.tr
Internet: www.gazi.edu.tr
Founded 1982
State control
Language of instruction: Turkish
Academic year: September to June

Rector: Prof. Dr KADRI YAMAÇ
Vice-Rectors: Prof. Dr M.TUBA ONGUN, Prof. Dr TÜLIN OYGÜR, Prof. Dr SÜLEYMAN PAMPAL
Secretary General: Prof. Dr KIRALI MURTEZAOĞLU
Librarian: TÜNSEL CANATALI

Library of 86,000 vols
Number of teachers: 3,631

Number of students: 61,447 (56,114 undergraduate, 5,333 postgraduate)

Publication: *Gazi Üniversitesi Bülteni* (6 a year)

DEANS

Faculty of Architecture and Engineering: Prof. Dr Hüsnu Can

Faculty of Arts and Sciences: Prof. Dr Metin Aktaş

Faculty of Commerce and Tourism: Prof. Dr Mithat Üver

Faculty of Communication: Prof. Dr Nurettin Güz

Faculty of Dentistry: Prof. Dr İ. Levent Taner

Faculty of Economic and Administrative Sciences: Prof. Dr Burhan Aykaç

Faculty of Economics and Administrative Sciences (Çorum): Prof. Dr Hasan Kaval

Faculty of Education (Gazi): Prof. Dr Zekiye Suludere

Faculty of Education (Kastamonu): Prof. Dr Alemi Yetim

Faculty of Education (Kırşehir): Prof. Dr Selahattin Salman

Faculty of Engineering (Çorum): Prof. Dr Satilmiş Basan

Faculty of Forestry (Kastamonu): Prof. Dr Hasan Vurdu

Faculty of Industrial Arts Education: Prof. Dr İrfan Süer

Faculty of Law: Prof. Dr Kamil Turan

Faculty of Medicine: Prof. Dr Haluk Tokuloğlu

Faculty of Pharmacy: Prof. Dr Fethi Şahin

Faculty of Sciences (Kırşehir): Prof. Dr İrfan Akgün

Faculty of Technical Education: Prof. Dr Yalçin Örs

Faculty of Theology (Çorum): Prof. Dr Hasan Onat

Faculty of Vocational Education: Prof. Dr Rasih Demirci

GRADUATE SCHOOLS

Graduate School of Accident Research and Prevention: Dir Prof. Dr Ali Bumin.

Graduate School of Educational Sciences: Dir Prof. Dr Semih Yalçin.

Graduate School of Health Sciences: Dir Oktay Üner.

Graduate School of Natural Sciences: Maltepe, Ankara; Dir Prof. Dr Ahmet Biger.

Graduate School of Social Sciences: Kavaklıdere, Ankara; Dir Prof. Dr İhson Erdoğan.

GAZİOSMANPAŞA ÜNİVERSİTESİ

60110 Tokat

Telephone: (356) 252-14-52
Fax: (356) 252-14-52
E-mail: tokat@gop.edu.tr
Internet: www.gop.edu.tr
Founded 1992
State control
Academic year: October to June

Rector: Prof. Dr Zehra Seyfikli
Vice-Rectors: Prof. Dr Yaşar Akça, Prof. Dr Mehmet Durdu Karsli
Librarian: Mahmut İşeri

Library of 26,564 books, 117 periodicals
Number of teachers: 500
Number of students: 8,036 (7,932 undergraduate, 104 postgraduate)

DEANS

Faculty of Agriculture: Prof. Dr Cevdet Akdağ

Faculty of Arts and Sciences: Prof. Dr Zehra Seyfikli

Faculty of Economic and Administrative Sciences: Prof. Dr Osman Karakacier
Faculty of Education: Prof. Dr M. Durdu Karsli
Faculty of Medicine: Prof. Dr Murat Firat

GAZİANTEP ÜNİVERSİTESİ

POB 300, 27310 Gaziantep
Telephone: (342) 360-10-10
Fax: (342) 360-10-13
E-mail: gensek@gantep.edu.tr
Internet: www.gantep.edu.tr
Founded 1987
Academic year: October to June
Rector: Prof. Dr Erhan Ekinci

Number of teachers: 2,821
Number of students: 49,250

Publications: *Sosyal Bilimler Dergisi* (social sciences, annually), *Tıp Fakültesi Dergisi* (medicine, 2 a year)

DEANS

Faculty of Arts and Science: Ihsan Ünver
Faculty of Arts and Science (Kilis): Ömer Bakkaloglu
Faculty of Economics and Business Administration: Ismail H. Özsabuncuoğlu
Faculty of Education: Muhsin Macit
Faculty of Education (Adiyaman): Haci Duran
Faculty of Education (Kilis): Ali Riza Tekin
Faculty of Engineering: Mustafa Özakça
Faculty of Medicine: Abdurahman Kadayifçi

GEBZE YÜKSEK TEKNOLOJİ ENSTİTÜSÜ

PK 141, 41400, Gebze
Telephone: (262) 653-84-97
Fax: (262) 653-84-90
E-mail: okalem@gyte.edu.tr
Internet: www.gyte.edu.tr
State control

Rector: Prof. Dr Alinur Büyükaksoy
Vice-Rectors: Prof. Dr Vasfi Eldem, Prof. Dr Orhan Şahin

Library of 8,500 vols, 222 periodicals and 2,410 electronic journals
Number of students: 337 undergraduate; 1,478 graduate

Faculties of Architecture, Economics, Engineering and Science; Faculty of Technical Education in process of formation.

HACETTEPE ÜNİVERSİTESİ

Hacettepe, 06100 Ankara
Telephone: (312) 305-5000
Fax: (312) 310-5552
Internet: www.hacettepe.edu.tr
Founded 1206 in Kayseri; chartered 1967
State control
Languages of instruction: Turkish, English
Academic year: September to August

Rector: Prof. Dr Tunçalp Özgen
Vice-Rectors: Prof. Dr Hasan Bayhan, Prof. Dr Erol Belgin
Secretary-General: Attila Konaç
Registrar: Dr Nükhet Akin (Deputy Registrar)
Director of Libraries: Prof. Dr Ahmet Çelik (Deputy Director)

Library: Beytepe campus library of 150,000 vols, medical central library of 125,000 vols
Number of teachers: 3,645
Number of students: 22,513

Publications: *Hacettepe Tıp/Cerrahi Bülteni* (4 a year), and several faculty bulletins

DEANS
Beytepe Campus:

Faculty of Economics and Adminstrative Sciences: Prof. Dr Halil Can
Faculty of Education: Prof. Dr Haluk Soran
Faculty of Engineering: Prof. Dr Hüseyin Selçuk Geçim
Faculty of Fine Arts: Prof. Hasip Gençaydin
Faculty of Letters: Prof. Dr Tuğrul İnal
Faculty of Science: Prof. Dr Ali Kalaycioğlu

Hacettepe Campus:

Faculty of Dentistry: Prof. Dr Osman Taha Köseoğlu
Faculty of Medicine: Prof. Dr İskender Sayek
Faculty of Pharmacy: Prof. Dr A. Ahmet Başaran

DIRECTORS

School of Foreign Languages: Prof. Dr Güray Konig
School of Health Administration: Prof. Dr Hikmet Pekcan
School of Health Technology: Prof. Dr Türkan Merdol
School of Home Economics: Prof. Dr Müberra Babaoğlu
School of Nursing: Prof. Dr Gülümser Kubilay
School of Physical Therapy and Rehabilitation: Prof. Dr Hülya Kayihan
School of Social Work: Prof. Dr Ayşe Beril Tufan
Ankara State Conservatoire: Prof. Ali Doğan
Vocational School of Woodwork Technology: Prof. Dr Mehmet Doğan
Vocational School (Ankara): Prof. Dr İlhan Tomanbay
Vocational School of Health Services: Prof. Dr Erol Belgin
Kaman Vocational School: Doç. Dr M. Ali Hindistan
Polatlı Vocational School: Prof. Dr Ahmet Kart
Vocational School of Sports Sciences and Technology: Dr Caner Açikada
Polatlı Vocational School of Health Services: Prof. Dr Fatma Gül Şener

PROFESSORS

Faculty of Dentistry:

Alparslan, M. G., Oral and Dental Therapeutics
Altay, A., Paediatric Dentistry
Anil (Gazi), N., Prosthesis
Aslan, Y., Prosthesis
Avci, M., Prosthesis
Başeren, N. M., Oral and Dental Therapeutics
Berker, A. E., Periodontics
Bolay (Sarioğlu), Ş., Oral and Dental Therapeutics
Canay (Ölgun), R.Ş., Prosthesis
Çağlayan, F., Periodontics
Çağlayan, G., Periodontics
Çalt, T., Endodontics
Ciğer, S., Orthodontics
Dayangaç, B., Oral and Dental Therapeutics
Dayangaç, B., Prosthesis
Demirel (Uslu), F., Prosthesis
Durmaz, V., Oral and Dental Therapeutics
Eratalay, Y. K., Periodontics
Gökalp, S., Oral and Dental Therapeutics
Görücü, J., Oral and Dental Therapeutics
Görduysus, M., Endodontics
Gürgan, S., Oral and Dental Therapeutics
Hersek, N. E., Prosthesis
Kansu, A. Ö., Oral and Dental Therapeutics
Kansu, H., Oral and Dental Therapeutics
Keyf (Hamarat), F., Prosthesis
Kocadereli, İ., Orthodontics
Köprülü, H., Oral and Dental Therapeutics

Köseoğlu, O. T., Dental Surgery
Kuraner, T., Oral and Dental Therapeutics
Nazliel, H., Periodontics
Nohutçu, R. M., Periodontics
Öktemer, M., Prosthesis
Ölmez, M. S., Paediatric Dentistry
Önen, A., Oral and Dental Therapeutics
Özçelik, B., Oral and Dental Therapeutics
Özgünaltay, H. G., Oral and Dental Therapeutics
Saygili, G., Prosthesis
Serper, A., Endodontics
Şahin, E., Prosthesis
Şahin (Sökmen), S., Prosthesis
Şahmali, S., Prosthesis
Şengün, F. D., Periodontics
Taşar, F., Dental Surgery
Taşman, F., Endodontics
Tuncer, M., Periodontics
Uran, N., Oral Surgery
Yamalik, N., Periodontology
Yenigül, M., Prosthesis

Faculty of Economics and Administrative Sciences:

Akalin, G., Public Finance
Aktan, O. H., Economics
Bilici, N., Public Finance
Can, H., Economics
Çağlar, A., Public Administration
Erdoğan, M., Public Administration
İpçi, M. O., Accounting and Finance
Karan, M., Business Administration
Kazdağli, H., Economics
Morgil, O., Economics
Şahinöz, A., Economics
Şişik, Ü., Economics
Tanyeri, I, Economics
Telatar, M. E., Economics
Timur, H., Economics
Tokat, M., Economics
Uygun, H., Economics

Faculty of Education:

Abak, M., Physics
Acar, N., Counselling and Guidance
Akkoyunlu, B., Computer Education and Instructional Technologies
Akman, B., Pre-School Teaching
Aşkar, P., Computer Education and Instructional Technologies
Başar, H., Education
Başkan, A. G., Educational Administration, Supervision, Planning and Economics
Bülbül, A., Mathematics Teaching
Demirel, Ö., Education
Demirezen, M., Language Studies
Eratalay, N., French
Erçetin, Ş. Ş., Educational Administration, Supervision, Planning and Economics
Eren, A., Physics
Ersever, O. G., Counselling and Guidance
Ertem, C., Language and Literature
Genç, A., German Language Teaching
Haman, S., Physics Teaching
Kavak, Y., Education
Keskil, G., English Language Teaching
Kiran, A., Language Studies
Kiziroğlu, İ, Biology
Morgil, I., Analytical Chemistry
Önalp, B., Biology
Önsoy, R., Education
Öz, H., English Language Teaching
Patir, S., Chemistry
Sağlam, N., Biology
Salihoğlu, H., Language Studies
Senemoğlu, N., Education
Sipahiler, F., Biology
Soran, H., Biology
Sönmez, V., Education
Tuğrul, B., Pre-School Teaching

Faculty of Engineering:

Acar, J., Food

Aksu, Z., Process and Reactor Design
Alper, E., Chemistry
Apaydin, F., Physics
Arikan, A., Hydrogeology
Aydar, E., Mineralogy, Petrography
Aytaç, S., Food Sciences
Bayhan, H., Geology
Bayari, S. C., Hydrogeology
Beşkardeş, O., Chemistry
Birgül, Ö., Nuclear Physics
Bozdemir, M. T., Unit Operations and Thermodynamics
Cankurtaran, M., Physics
Çadirci, I., Electrical Engineering
Çağlar, A., Chemistry
Çelelbi, S. S., Chemistry
Çelik, H., Physics
Çelik, H., Physics
Çelik, S., Food Sciences
Çelik, T., Physics
Çiner, T. A., Geology
Çolak, Ü., Nuclear Physics
Demircioğlu, H., Electrical Engineering
Demirel, H., Mining Engineering
Duruboy, H. Z., Physics
Durusoy (Dörter), B. T., Mining Engineering
Eray, A., Solid State Physics
Ercan, B., Electrical Engineering
Erkan, Y., Geology
Firat, T., Physics
Geçim, S., Electrical Engineering
Girgin, İ, Mining Engineering
Gümüşderelioğlu, M., Chemistry
Gündüc, Y., Electrical Engineering
Hökelek, T., Physics
İde, S., General Physics
İnan, İ. D., Physics
Kaptan, Y., Physics
Karakaş, M. Ü., Computer Science Engineering
Karayiğit, A., Mineral Deposits, Geochemistry
Kasapoğlu, K. E., Geology
Kayhan, S., Telecommunications
Kendi, E., General Physics
Köksal, A., Electromagnetic Waves and Microwaves
Köksel, H., Food
Korkmaz, M., Physics
Kulaksiz, S., Mining and Mineral Processing
Kutsal, T., Chemistry
Mutlu, M., Food
Öktü, Ö., General Physics
Önder, M., Physics
Öner, M., Mining Engineering
Öner, M., Mining and Mineral Processing
Oral, B., Physics
Özbaş, Y., Food Technology
Özbay (Danaci), S., General Physics
Özbey, T., Physics
Özdural, A. R., Chemistry
Öztecin, E., Physics
Pişkin, E., Chemistry
Saatçi, A., Computer Science Engineering
Sağ, Y., Process and Reactor Design
Saldamli, İ., Food
Saraç, C., Mineral Deposits, Geochemistry
Saydam, A., Environmental Engineering
Sünnetçioğlu, M., Physics
Şafak, M., Electrical Engineering
Şenyur, M. G., Mining and Mineral Processing
Şimşek, S., Hydrogeology
Sungar, R., General Physics
Tabak, F., Physics
Tanyolaç, A., Chemistry
Temel, A., Mineral Deposits, Geochemistry
Temiz, A., Food
Tercan, A., Mining and Mineral Processing
Tolunay, H., Solid State Physics
Topaçli, C., Physics
Topaçli (Sungur), A., Atomic and Molecular Physics

Töreci, E., Computer Science Engineering
Tuncel, S. A., Process and Reactor Design
Tunoğlu, C., General Geology
Ulusay, R., Applied Geology
Us, F., Food
Ülkü, D., Physics
Ünver, B., Mining and Mineral Processing
Vural, H., Food Sciences
Yarimağan, Ü., Computer Science Engineering
Yazgan, E., Electrical Engineering

Faculty of Fine Arts:

Akyüz, U., Graphic Art
Aydinöz, A. A., Art
Dakak, H., Painting
Gencaydin, Z., Fine Arts
Kaya, İ., Graphic Art
Misman, H. A., Painting
Pekmezci, H., Painting
Pektaş, H., Graphic Art
Savaş, R., Sculpture

Faculty of Letters:

Akan, A. V., Sociology
Akkoyunlu, Z., Folklore Studies
Aksoy, B. M., English Translation and Interpretation
Aksoy, E., Western Language and Literature
Altay (Akansel), A., English Translation and Interpretation
Arikan (Gürer), G., Sociology
Aydin, O., Experimental Psychology
Bağci, S., History of Art
Baydur, K. G., Librarianship
Baykan, F., Philosophy
Bozbeyoğlu, S., French Language and Literature
Bozer, A. D., English Language and Literature
Çakin, İ., Librarianship
Çelik, A., Librarianship
Çelik-Şavk, Ü., Turkish Language and Literature
Dikeçligil, F. B., Sociometry
Doğan, Ş., German Language and Literature
Ercilasun, B., Literature
Ergan, N., Sociology
Erkenal, A., History of Art
Erlat, J., French Studies
Erol, B., English Language and Literature
Horata, O., Turkish Language and Literature
İçli, T., Sociology
İnal, T., French Studies
İzgi, O., General Turkish History
Karakaş, S., Experimental Psychology
Kiran, Z., French Studies
König, G., Linguistics
Kula, O., German Language and Literature
Kurbanoğlu, S. S., Librarianship
Ocak, A. Y., History
Ocak, F. T., History
Oppermann (Tunç), S., English Language and Literature
Ötüken, S. Y., Archaeology
Öz, M., History
Özbek, M., Social Anthropology
Özgen, E., Archaeology
Özmen, K., French Studies
Özönder, M. C., Sociology
Özyer, N., German Language and Literature
Sağlam, M. Y., German Language and Literature
Tepe, H., Philosophy
Tonta, Y., Librarianship
Umunç, H., English Language and Literature
Unan, F., History
Yimaz, E., Turkish Language and Literature
Yildirim, D., Literature
Yildiz, S., German Studies

Faculty of Medicine:

ABBASOĞLU, O., Internal Medicine
AÇAN, L., Biochemistry
ACAROĞLU, R.E., Orthopaedics
ADALAR, N., Internal Medicine
ADALIOĞLU, G., Paediatrics
AKALAN, N., Neurosurgery
AKALIN, N., Neurosurgery
AKAN, H. T., Dermatology
AKATA, D., Radiology
AKHAN, H. M. O., Radiology
AKIN, A., Community Health
AKINCİ, F.A., Physical Therapy and Rehabilitation
AKOVA, M., Internal Medicine
AKŞIT, D., Anatomy
AKSÖYEK, S., Cardiology
AKSU, A. T., Obstetrics and Gynaecology
AKYOL, F. H., Oncology
AKYOL, Ö., Biochemistry
AKYOL, U. M., Otorhinolaryngology
AKYÜZ (CELEPOĞLU), C., Oncology
ALAÇAM, R., Microbiology
ALEHAN, D., Paediatrics
ALPAR, C., Biostatistics
ALPARSLAN, M., Orthopaedics
ANLAR, B. F., Paediatrics
ARAN, Ö., Surgery
ARAS (SULHUN), T., Nuclear Medicine
ARIKAN, S., Microbiology
ARIOĞLU, S., Internal Medicine
ARİYÜREK, O.M., Radiology
ARSLAN, S., Internal Medicine
AŞAN, E., Morphology
ATAHAN, İ. L., Oncology
ATAKAN, Z. N., Dermatology
AYAS, K., Ear, Nose and Throat Surgery
AYDIN, E., Medical Ethics and History
AYDINGÖZ, Ü., Radiology
AYHAN, A., Obstetrics and Gynaecology
AYPAR, Ü., Anaesthesiology
AYSUN, S., Paediatrics
AYTAR, Ş., Medical Biology
BAKKALOĞLU, A., Paediatrics
BAKKALOĞLU, A. M., Urology
BALCI, S., Paediatrics
BALKANCI, F., Radiology
BARIŞTA, İ., Internal Medicine
BAŞAR, R., Anatomy
BAŞGÖZE, O., Physical Therapy and Rehabilitation
BATMAN, F., Internal Medicine
BAYRAKTAR, M., Internal Medicine
BAYRAKTAR, Y., Internal Medicine
BEKSAÇ, S., Obstetrics and Gynaecology
BELGİN, E., Ear, Nose and Throat Surgery
BENLİ, K., Neurosurgery
BEŞBAŞ, N., Paediatrics
BESİM, A., Radiology
BİLGİÇ, S., Ophthalmology
BİLİR, N., Community Health
BÖKE, E., Cardiovascular and Thoracic Surgery
BOZKURT, A., Pharmacology
BÜLBÜL, F. F., Plastic and Reconstructive Surgery
BÜYÜKPAMUKÇU, M., Oncology
BÜYÜKPAMUKÇU, N., Paediatric Surgery
ÇAĞLAR, M., Nuclear Medicine
ÇAĞLAR, M., Paediatrics
ÇAKAR, A. N., Morphology
ÇAKMAK, F., Urology
ÇALGÜNERİ, M., Internal Medicine
ÇANER, B. E., Nuclear Medicine
ÇEKIRGE, H., Radiology
ÇEKİRGE, I. S., Radiology
ÇELEBİOĞLU, B., Anaesthesiology
ÇELİK, H. H., Anatomy
ÇELİKER, A., Paediatrics
ÇELİKER, V., Anaesthesiology and Reanimation
ÇELİKER, A.R., Physical Therapy and Rehabilitation
ÇETIN, M., Paediatrics
ÇEYHAN, M., Paediatrics

ÇIFTÇI, A., Paediatrics
ÇIĞER, A., Institute of Neurological Sciences
CILA, A., Radiodiagnostics
ÇOKUĞRAŞ, N. A., Biochemistry
ÇÖPLÜ, L., Thoracic Diseases
ÇOSKUN, T., Paediatrics
ÇUHADAROĞLU, F., Psychiatry
ÇUMHUR, M., Morphology
DAĞDEVİREN, A., Histology and Embryology
DALKARA, N. E. T., Institute of Neurological Sciences
DEMIRCİN, M., Cardiovascular and Thoracic Surgery
DEMIRKAZİK, F., Radiology
DEMIRPENÇE (TANSEL), E., Biochemistry
DİNÇER, F., Physical Therapy and Rehabilitation
DİNÇER, P. R., Medical Biology
DOĞAN, P., Biochemistry
DOĞAN, R., Cardiovascular and Thoracic Surgery
DORAL, M. N., Orthopaedics
DUMAN, O., Physiology
DURUKAN, T., Obstetrics and Gynaecology
DÜNDAR, S., Internal Medicine
ELDEM, M. B., Ophthalmology
ELİBOL, B., Neurology
EMRE (DÖKMECI), S., Internal Medicine
ERBAŞ, A. T., Internal Medicine
ERBAŞ, B. H., Nuclear Medicine
ERDEM, Y., Internal Medicine
ERDENER, U., Ophthalmology
ERGEN, A., Urology
ERGÜVEN (DİKEL), S., Microbiology
ERK, Y., Plastic Surgery
ERKAN, İ., Urology
ERSOY, F. N., Paediatrics
ERSOY, Ü., Cardiovascular and Thoracic Surgery
ERTENLİ, A. İ., Internal Medicine
GEDİK, O., Internal Medicine
GEDIKOĞLU, G., Pathology
GÖKLER, B., Psychiatry
GÖKÖZ, A., Pathology
GÜÇ, D., Oncology
GÜÇ, M. O., Pharmacology
GÜLER, Ç., Community Health
GÜLER, E. N., Internal Medicine
GÜLLÜ, İ., Oncology
GÜMRÜK, F., Paediatrics
GÜNALP, G. S., Obstetrics and Gynaecology
GÜNGEN, Y. Y., Pathology
GÜR (AKMAN), D., Paediatrics
GÜRAKAN, H., Paediatrics
GÜRGAN, T., Obstetrics and Gynaecology
GÜRGERY, A., Paediatrics
GÜRKANYNAK, H. M., Oncology
GÜRLEK, Ö. A., Internal Medicine
GÜRSEL, B., Ear, Nose and Throat Surgery
HALILOĞLU, M., Radiology
HAMALOĞLU, E., General Surgery
HAŞÇELİK, A. G., Microbiology
HAŞÇELİK, H. Z., Physical Therapy and Rehabilitation
HAZNEDAROĞLU, C., Internal Medicine
HOŞAL, A., Otorhinology
İLGİ, N. S., Morphology
İLHAN, M., Pharmacology
İRKEÇ, M., Ophthalmology
KABAKÇİ, M.G., Cardiology
KALAYCİ, C., Paediatrics
KALE, G., Paediatrics
KALYONCU, A. F., Thoracic Diseases
KANBAK (SOYLU), M., Anaesthesiology and Reanimation
KANDEMIR, N., Paediatrics
KANSU, E., Oncology
KANSU, T., Institute of Neurological Sciences
KARAAĞAOĞLU, A. E., Medical Biology
KARABUDAK, R., Neurology
KARADUMAN, A., Dermatology
KARS, S. A., Internal Medicine
KART, A., Medical Biology
KAYA, S., Ear, Nose and Throat Surgery

KAYNAROLĞU, Z. V., Surgery
KEÇİK, A., Plastic Surgery
KENDİ, S., Urology
KES, S., Internal Medicine
KILINÇ, K., Biochemistry
KİPER, E. N., Childhood Health and Diseases
KIRATLI, H., Ophthalmology
KÖLEMEN, F., Dermatology
KÜÇÜKALİ, T., Pathology
KUŞ, M. S., Biochemistry
KUTLUK, M. T., Paediatrics
KUTSAL, F. Y., Physical Therapy and Rehabilitation
MAVİLİ, M. E., Plastic and Reconstructive Surgery
MOCAN, G., Pathology
MÜFTÜOĞLU, S., Histology and Embryology
MUŞDAL, Y., Orthopaedics and Traumatology
NAZLI, N., Internal Medicine, Cardiology
NURLU (ÖZGÜR), G., Neurology
ÖCAL, M. T., Anaesthesiology
ÖKTEM (BONCUK), F., Psychiatry
ONAT, D., Surgery
ÖNDEROĞLU, L. S., Obstetrics and Gynaecology
ÖNERCİ, T. M., Ear, Nose and Throat Surgery
ONUR, E. R., Pharmacology
ORAN, M. B., Radiology
ORER, H., Pharmacology
ORHAN, M., Ophthalmology
OTO, M. A., Internal Medicine
ÖĞRETMENOĞLU, O., Otorhinology
ÖĞÜŞ, İ. H., Biochemistry
ÖNDEROĞLU, S., Anatomy
ÖNER, Z. N., Surgery
ÖVÜNÇ, K., Cardiology
ÖZCAN, E. O., Neurosurgery
ÖZCEBE, L. H., Community Health
ÖZCEBE, O. İ., Internal Medicine
ÖZÇELİK, H., Paediatrics
ÖZDEMİR, A., Surgery
ÖZDEN, A. K., Medical Biology
ÖZEN, H., Paediatrics
ÖZEN, H. A., Urology
ÖZEN, S., Paediatrics
ÖZENÇ, A. M., Surgery
ÖZER, E. S., Paediatrics
ÖZER, N., Biochemistry
ÖZGEN, T., Institute of Neurological Sciences
ÖZGEN (ULUPİNAR), S., Anaesthesiology
ÖZGÜÇ, M., Medical Biology
ÖZGÜNEŞ, N., Biochemistry
ÖZIŞIK, Y. Y., Oncology
ÖZKAN, S., Ear, Nose and Throat Surgery
ÖZKARA (ŞAHİN), A., Biochemistry
ÖZKUTLU, H., Internal Medicine
ÖZKUTLU, S., Paediatrics
ÖZKUYUMCU, C., Microbiology
ÖZMEN, F., Internal Medicine
ÖZMEN, M. N., Radiology
ÖZMERT, E., Paediatrics
ÖZTEK, A. Z., Community Medicine
ÖZTÜRK, N., Biophysics
ÖZYAR, E., Radiation Oncology
ÖZYAZICI, A., Morphology
PALAOĞLU, Ö. S., Institute of Neurological Sciences
PEKCAN, H., Community Health
PURALİ, N., Biophysics
SANAÇ, A. Ş., Ophthalmology
SANAL, S. Ö., Paediatrics
SARGON, M. F., Anatomy
SAYEK, İ., Surgery
SAYGI (SÜTÇÜ), S., Neurology
SEÇMEER, G., Paediatrics
SELÇUK, Z., Chest Diseases
SELEKLER, K., Neurology
SENNAROĞLU, L., Ear Nose and Throat Surgery
ŞENOCAK, M. E., Paediatric Surgery
ŞİMŞEK, H., Internal Medicine
SİVRİ, B., Internal Medicine

SÖYLEMEZOĞLU, F., Pathology
SÖZEN, T., Internal Medicine
SÖZER, A. B., Ear, Nose and Throat Surgery
SUNGUR, A. A., Oncology
SURAT, A., Orthopaedics
ŞAFAK, T., Plastic and Reconstructive Surgery
ŞAHIN, A., Urology
ŞAHIN, A. A., Internal Medicine
ŞAHIN, S., Dermatology
ŞEFTALIOĞLU, A., Histology
ŞEKEREL, B., Paediatrics
ŞENER, B., Microbiology
ŞENER, E.C., Ophthalmology
TAN, M. E., Neurology
TANYEL, F. C., Paediatric Surgery
TASAR, C., Oncology
TATAR, G., Internal Medicine
TEKGÜL, S., Urology
TEKINALP, G., Paediatrics
TEKUZMAN, G., Oncology
TEZCAN, F., Biochemistry
TEZCAN, F. İ., Paediatrics
TEZCAN, S., Community Medicine
TOKATLI, A., Paediatrics
TOKGÖZOĞLU, M., Orthopaedics and Traumatology
TOKGÖZOĞLU, S. L., Internal Medicine
TOPALOĞLU, H., Paediatrics
TOPALOĞLU, R., Paediatrics
TOPÇU, M., Institute of Neurological Sciences
TUNCEL, H. M., Anatomy
TUNCER, A., Paediatrics
TUNCER, A. M., Paediatrics
TUNCER, M., Pharmacology
TUNCER, Z. S., Obstetrics and Gynaecology
TUNÇBILEK, E., Paediatrics
TUNÇKANAT, F. F., Microbiology
TURAN, E., Ear, Nose and Throat Surgery
TURGAN, Ç., Internal Medicine
UĞUR, Ö., Nuclear Medicine
ULUĞ, B., Psychiatry
ULUŞAHIN, N. A., Psychiatry
UNGAN, P., Biophysics
US (ERSÖZ), A. D., Microbiology
USMAN, A., Internal Medicine
USTAÇELEBI, S., Microbiology
UZUN (ÖZMEN), Ö., Internal Medicine
ÜNAL, M. F., Child Psychiatry
ÜNAL, S., Internal Medicine
ÜNSAL, M., Radiology
VARLI, K., Neurology
YALÇIN, Ş., Internal Medicine
YALÇINRIDVANAĞAOĞLU, A., Physiology
YARALI, H., Obstetrics and Gynaecology
YASAVUL, Ü., Internal Medicine
YAZICI, M., Orthopaedics
YAZICI, M. K., Psychiatry
YETKIN, S., Paediatrics
YIĞIT, Ş., Paediatrics
YILMAZ, E., Medical Biology
YORDAM, N., Paediatrics
YÖRÜKAN, S., Physiology
YURDAKÖK, K., Paediatrics
YURDAKÖK, M., Paediatrics
YÜCE, A., Childhood Health and Diseases
YÜCE, K., Obstetrics and Gynaecology
YURTER (ERDEM), H., Medical Biology
ZORLU, A. F., Radiation Oncology

Faculty of Pharmacy:
ALTINOZ SARISOY, S., Analytical Chemistry
BALKAN (TAYHAN), A., Pharmaceutical Chemistry
BAŞARAN, A. A., Pharmacognosy
BAŞARAN (GÜNDÜZ), N., Pharmaceutical Toxicology
BAŞÇI, N., Analytical Chemistry
BILGIN, A., Pharmaceutical Chemistry
ÇALIŞ, İ., Pharmacognosy
ÇALIŞ, Ü., Pharmaceutical Chemistry
ÇALIŞ, Y. S., Pharmaceutical Technology
ÇAPAN, Y., Pharmaceutical Technology
DALKARA, S., Pharmaceutical Chemistry

DEMIREZEN, L.Ö., Pharmacognosy
DEMIRDAMAR, S. R., Pharmacy
DEMIREZER, L. Ö., Pharmacognosy
ELDEM (ER), T., Pharmaceutical Biotechnology
ERDEMLI(ŞAHIN), İ., Pharmaceutical Toxicology
ERDOĞAN, H., Pharmaceutical Chemistry
ERSÖZ, T., Pharmacognosy
ERTAN, M., Pharmaceutical Chemistry
EZER, N., Pharmaceutical Botanics
HEKIMOĞLU (KONUR), S., Pharmarmaceutical Chemistry
HINCAL, A., Galenic Pharmacy
HINCAL, F., Pharmaceutical Toxicology
KIR (KOT), S., Analytical Chemistry
ÖNER, A. F., Pharmaceutical Chemistry
ÖNER, L., Pharmaceutical Chemistry
ÖZALTIN (LEBLEBIC), N., Analytical Chemistry
ÖZER, A. Y., Pharmaceutical Chemistry
ÖZER, İ., Biochemistry
ÖZGÜNES, H., Pharmaceutical Toxicology
PALASKA, E., Pharmaceutical Chemistry
PEKINER, C., Pharmacology
ŞAFAK, C., Pharmaceutical Toxicology
ŞAHIN, G., Pharmaceutical toxicology
SAKAR, M. K., Pharmaceutical Chemistry
SARAÇ, S., Pharmaceutical Chemistry
SARAÇOĞLU, İ., Pharmacognosy
ŞENEL, S., Pharmaceutical Technology
SÜMER (ILKIZ), N. A., Biochemistry
ŞUMLU, M., Pharmaceutical Technology
TEMIZER, A., Analytical Chemistry
UMA, S., Pharmaceutical Toxicology
ÜNLÜ (KARABABA), N., Pharmaceutical Technology
YEŞIADA, A., Pharmacy

Faculty of Science:
AKAY, M. T., Zoology
AKGÜN, A., Molecular Biology
AKSÖZ, E., Molecular Biology
AKSÖZ, N., General Biology
BALCIOĞLU, N., Organic Chemistry
BARLAS (EMIR), N., Zoology
BEKTAŞ, F. S., Analytical Chemistry
BOŞGELMEZ, A., Zoology
BOZCUK, A. N., Biology
BOZCUK, S., Biology
BROWN, L. M., Mathematics
ÇAĞATAY, N., Zoology
ÇAĞLAR, P., Analytical Chemistry
CANSUNAR, E., General Biology
CIHANGIR, N., Biotechnology
ÇIRAKOĞLU, Ç., Molecular Biology
ÇINGI, H., Statistics
DEMIREZEN, Ş., General Biology
DEMIRSOY, A., Zoology
DENIZLI, A., Biochemistry
DIRIL, N., Molecular Biology
DOĞAN, M., Analytical Chemistry
DURUSOY, M., Molecular Biology
DÜZ, S. F., Chemistry
EKMEKÇI, F. G., Hydrobiology
ERIK, S., Botany
ERK, A. F., Hydrobiology
EŞ, A. H., Mathematics
ESENSOY, Ö., Statistics
GÖKOĞLU, E., Analytical Chemistry
GÜNAY, S., Statistics
GÜNDÜZ, E., Hydrobiology
GÜNER, A., Polymer and Theoretical Chemistry
GÜVEN, O., Physical Chemistry
HARMANCI, A., Mathematics
İMAMOĞLU, Y., Analytical Chemistry
İNAL, Ç., Statistics
KALAYCIOĞLU, A., Molecular Biology
KARAN (ZÜMREOĞLU), B., Inorganic Chemistry
KAZANCI, N., Hydrobiology
KESKIN (ELDEM), N., Applied Biology
KILBARER, A. G., Physical Chemistry
KIŞ, M., Physical Chemistry
KOLANKAYA, D., Zoology

KOLANKAYA, N., General Biology
OKAY, G., Organic Chemistry
ORAL (HOCAOĞLU), G., Statistics
ÖNER, C., Molecular Biology
ÖNER (ÖZDÖNMEZ), R., Biotechnology
ÖZÇAĞ, E., Mathematics
PEKMEZ (ÖZÇIÇEK), N., Analytical Chemistry
PEKMEZ, K., Analytical Chemistry
RZAYEV, Z. M. O., Chemistry
SALIH, B., Physical Chemistry
SOLTANOV, K. N., Mathematics
SORKUN, K., Applied Biology
SÖZER, T., Statistics
ŞENEL (UYANIK), S., Physical Chemistry
TATLIDIL, H., Statistics
TERCAN, A., Algebra and Theory of Numbers
TERZIOĞLU, S., Botany
TIRAŞ, Y., Algebra and Theory of Numbers
TOKTAMIŞ, Ö., Statistics
TÜMER, M. A., General Biology
TÜNOĞLU, N., Organic Chemistry
ÜNALEROĞLU, C., Organic Chemistry
ÜNLÜ, H., General Biology
YALVAÇ, T., Mathematics, Geometry and Topology
YERLI, S. V., Hydrobiology
YILDIRIMLI, Ş., Botany
YILDIZ, A., Analytical Chemistry

ATTACHED INSTITUTES

Institute of Ataturk Principles and History of the Turkish Revolution: Dir Prof. Dr MUSTAFA YILMAZ.

Institute of Child Health: Dir Prof. Dr GÜLSEV KALE.

Institute of Fine Arts: Dir Prof. UĞURCAN AKYÜZ.

Institute of Health Sciences: Dir Prof. Dr HAKAN SEDAT ÖRER.

Institute of Medical Informatics: Dir Prof. Dr ERSIN TÖRECI.

Institute of Neurological Sciences and Psychology: Dir Prof. Dr TURGAY DALAKARA.

Institute of Nuclear Sciences: Dir Prof. Dr ENGIN KENDI.

Institute of Oncology: Dir Prof. Dr AYŞE KARS.

Institute of Population Studies: Dir Prof. Dr SABAHAT TEZCAN.

Institute of Public Health: Dir Prof. Dr NAZMI BILIR (Deputy Dir.

Institute of Science: Dir Prof. Dr AHMET RIFAT ÖZDURAL.

Institute of Social Sciences: Dir Assoc. Prof. Dr NURAN ÖZYER.

Institute of Turkish Research: Dir Prof. Dr CIHAT ÖZÖNDER.

HALIÇ ÜNIVERSITESI
(Haliç University)
Büyükdere Cad. 101, 34394 Mecidiyeköy, İstanbul
Telephone: (212) 275-20-20
Fax: (212) 274-81-22
E-mail: info@halic.edu.tr
Internet: www.halic.edu.tr

Founded 1998

President: Prof. Dr GÜNDÜZ GEDIKOĞLU

Library of 11,000 vols
Number of teachers: 200
Number of students: 1,200

Faculties of Arts and Science, Business Administration, Engineering and Medicine.

HARRAN ÜNİVERSİTESİ

Sanlıurfa

Telephone: (414) 312-84-56
Fax: (414) 312-81-44
E-mail: rektor@harran.edu.tr
Internet: www.harran.edu.tr

Founded 1992
State control

President: Prof. Dr Ugur Buyukburc
Vice-Presidents: Prof. Dr Ural Dınç, Prof. Dr I. Halil Mutlu, Prof. Dr Selcuk Yucesan
Number of teachers: 794
Number of students: 5,900

DEANS

Faculty of Agriculture: Prof. Dr Mehmet Aktas
Faculty of Arts and Sciences: Prof. Dr Göksenin Eseller
Faculty of Economics: Prof. Dr Mustafa Pirili
Faculty of Engineering: Prof. Dr Bilge Erdiller
Faculty of Medicine: Prof. Dr Selcuk Yucesan
Faculty of Theology: Prof. Dr Ibrahim Duzen
Faculty of Veterinary Sciences: Prof. Dr Nafiz Yurdaydin

DIRECTORS

Institute of Health Sciences: Prof. Dr A. Ziya Karakilcik
Institute of Natural Sciences: Prof. Dr İbrahim Bolat
Institute of Social Sciences: Prof. Dr Zuhal Karahan Kara

İNÖNÜ ÜNİVERSİTESİ

Elazığ Yolu 15. km, 44280 Malatya

Telephone: (422) 341-00-28
Fax: (422) 341-00-34
E-mail: rektor@inonu.edu.tr
Internet: www.inonu.edu.tr

Founded 1975
State control
Language of instruction: Turkish (but English in Faculty of Medicine)
Academic year: October to July

Rector: Prof. Dr Fatih Hilmioğlu
Vice-Rectors: Prof. Dr Sadik Keleş, Prof. Dr Mustafa Kiliç, Prof. Dr Hasan Küçükbay
Secretary-General: Reşat Özkan
Librarian: Neziha Üstüner
Number of teachers: 2,112
Number of students: 19,137

DEANS

Faculty of Economics and Administrative Sciences: Prof. Dr Mustafa Kiliç
Faculty of Education: Prof. Dr K. Bülent Birol
Faculty of Engineering: Prof. Dr Musa Sarikaya
Faculty of Fine Arts: (vacant)
Faculty of Medicine: Prof. Dr Özcan Ersoy
Faculty of Pharmacy: Prof. Dr Engin Şarer
Faculty of Religious Studies: Prof. Dr Aslan Aksoy
Faculty of Science and Literature: Prof. Dr Özfer Yeşilada
Adıyaman Faculty of Science and Literature: Prof. Dr Engin Şener

HEADS OF DEPARTMENTS

Faculty of Economics and Administrative Sciences (Central Campus, 44069 Malatya; tel. (422) 341-00-43; fax (422)341-00-43):

Business Studies: Prof. Dr Kazim Kirtiş
Econometrics: Asst Prof. Dr H. Hüseyin Doğan
Economics: Asst Prof. Dr Ali Yilmaz Gündüz

Public Administration: Prof. Dr Kemal Kartal

Faculty of Science and Literature (Central Campus, 44069 Malatya; tel. (422) 341-00-37; fax (422) 341-00-37):

Biology: Prof. Dr Eşref Yüksel
Chemistry: Prof. Dr Engin Şener
History: Prof. Dr Salim Çöhce
Mathematics: Prof. Dr Sadik Keleş
Physics: Prof. Dr Selçuk Atalay
Sociology: Asst Prof. Dr Abdullah Korkmaz
Turkish Language: Asst Prof. Dr Sadik Armutlu

Faculty of Education (Central Campus, 44069 Malatya; tel. (422) 341-00-31; fax (422) 341-00-42):

Art: Asst Prof. Dr Cemal Yurga
Computing and Teaching Technology: Asst Prof. Dr Mustafa Aktan
Educational Sciences: Prof. Dr Battal Aslan
High School Science Education: Prof. Dr Bayram Demirci
Language Teaching Programme (English): Asst Prof. Dr Zülküf Altan
Physical Training: Asst Prof. Dr Celal Taşkiran
Primary School Education: Prof. Dr Aslan Aksoy

DIRECTORS

Institute of Health Sciences: Asst Prof. Dr Tayfun Güldür
Institute of Science: Asst Prof. Dr Ali Şahin
Institute of Social Sciences: Prof. Dr Kemal Kartal

IŞIK ÜNİVERSİTESİ

Kumbaba Mevkii, 34980 Sile, Istanbul

Telephone: (216) 528-70-45
Fax: (216) 712-14-68
E-mail: isikun@isikun.edu.tr
Internet: www.isikun.edu.tr

Founded 1885; university status 1996
Private control
Academic year: October to June

President: Prof. Dr Ersin Kalaycioğlu

DEANS

Faculty of Arts and Sciences: Prof. Önder Pekcan
Faculty of Economics and Administrative Sciences: Prof. Dr Mehmet Kaytaz
Faculty of Engineering: Prof. Yorgo İstefanopulos
Institute of Science and Engineering: Prof. Dr Hüsnü A. Erbay
Institute of Social Sciences: Prof. Dr Toker Dereli

İSTANBUL ÜNİVERSİTESİ

Beyazıt, 34052 Istanbul

Telephone: (212) 440-00-00
Fax: (212) 440-00-10
E-mail: postmaster@istanbul.edu.tr
Internet: www.istanbul.edu.tr

Founded 1453, reorganized 1933
State control
Languages of instruction: Turkish, English
Academic year: October to February, March to July

Rector: Prof. Dr Mesut Parlak
Vice-Rectors: Prof. Dr Taylan Akkayan, Prof. Dr Osman Özdemir, Prof. Dr Nur Serter
Administrative Officer: Nurettin Erdem
Number of teachers and assistants: 5,000
Number of students: 49,000

DEANS

Faculty of Communication: Prof. Dr Suat Gezgin
Faculty of Dentistry: Prof. Dr Betül Tuncelli
Faculty of Economics: Prof. Dr Mithat Zeki Dinçer
Faculty of Engineering: Prof. Dr Cuma Bayat
Faculty of Fisheries and Aquatic Science: Prof. Dr Mehmet Salih Çelikkale
Faculty of Forestry: Prof. Dr Bülent Seçkin
Faculty of Law: Prof. Dr Tankut Centel
Faculty of Letters: Prof. Dr Taner Tarhan
Faculty of Management: Prof. Dr Hayri Ülgen
Faculty of Medicine: Prof. Dr Faruk Erzengin
Faculty of Medicine (Cerrahpaşa): Prof. Dr Fikret Sipahioğlu
Faculty of Pharmacy: Prof. Dr Aysel Gürsoy
Faculty of Political Science: Prof. Dr Feryal Orhon Basik
Faculty of Science: Prof. Dr Nurettin Meriç
Faculty of Theology: Prof. Dr Emrullah Yüksel
Faculty of Veterinary Science: Prof. Dr Ahmet Altinel

ATTACHED INSTITUTES

Institute of Application and Research in Experimental Medicine: Dir Prof. Dr Orhan Arioğlu.

Institute of Atatürk's Principles and Reforms: Dir Prof. Dr Yakut Iramak Özden.

Institute of Cardiology: Dir Prof. Dr İlhan Günay.

Institute of Child Health: Dir Prof. Dr Günay Saner.

Institute of Forensic Medicine: Dir Prof. Dr Sevil Atasoy.

Institute of Health Sciences: Dir Prof. Dr Emine Kökodlu.

Institute of Management: Dir Prof. Dr Cengiz Erdamar.

Institute of Marine Sciences and Geography: Dir Prof. Dr Mahmut Celal Barla.

Institute of Natural Sciences: Dir Prof. Dr Feyza Çiniciodlu.

Institute of Neurological Sciences: Dir Prof. Dr Cengiz Kuday.

Institute of Oncology: Dir Prof. Dr Erkan Topuz.

Institute of Social Sciences: Dir Prof. Dr Hülya Talu.

Institute of Thoracic Diseases and Tuberculosis: Dir Prof. Dr Müzeyyen Erk.

Institute of Turcology: Dir Prof. Dr Osman Fikri Sertkaya.

İSTANBUL BİLGİ ÜNİVERSİTESİ
(Istanbul Bilgi University)

İnönü Cad. 28, Kuştepe, 34387 Şişli, Istanbul

Telephone: (212) 311-50-00
Fax: (212) 216-24-00
E-mail: bilgi@bilgi.edu.tr
Internet: www.bilgi.edu.tr

Founded 1994 as Istanbul School of International Studies; present name and status 1996
Private control
Language of instruction: English
Academic year: October to July

Rector: Prof. Dr Aydin Uğur
Secretary-General: Prof. Dr Şule Kut
Registrar: M. Orhun Çavdar
Librarian: Michiel Paus

Library of 68,000 vols
Number of teachers: 574
Number of students: 8,640

Publications: *Bilgi Bellek, Foreign Policy* (every two months)

DEANS

Faculty of Communication: Prof. Dr NEZIH ERDOĞAN

Faculty of Economics and Administrative Sciences: Prof. Dr ŞULE KUT

Faculty of Law: Prof. Dr TURGUT TARHANLI

Faculty of Science and Letters: Prof. Dr İHSAN BILGIN

Social Science Institute (Graduate School): Prof. Dr BEYZA OBA

ATTACHED RESEARCH INSTITUTES

Center for Atatürk Studies: Dir Prof. Dr TANER BERKSOY.

English Language Programs: Dir OYA BAŞARAN.

European Documentation Center: Dir SAMI ÇUKADAR.

Human Rights Law Research Center: Dir Assoc. Prof. Dr TURGUT TARHANLI.

Research Center: Dir Prof. Dr GÜLTEN KAZGAN.

School of Advanced Vocational Studies: Dir Prof. Dr ULKA ARIBOĞAN.

İSTANBUL KÜLTÜR ÜNIVERSITESI

E5 Karayolu Üzeri, 22 Ataköy Metro Istasyonu Karşısı, Sirinevler, 34510 Istanbul

Telephone: (212) 639-30-24
Fax: (212) 551-11-89
E-mail: rektor@iku.edu.tr
Internet: www.iku.edu.tr

Founded 1997
Private control
Languages of instruction: Turkish, English
Academic year: October to May

Rector: Prof. Dr ÖNDER ÖZTUNALI
Vice-Rectors: Prof. Dr GETIN BOLCAL, Prof. Dr TAMER KOÇEL
Registrar: Asst Prof. Dr METIN BOLCAL

Library of 6,800 books
Number of teachers: 114
Number of students: 2,109 (2,064 undergraduate, 45 postgraduate)

Publication: *Journal* (4 a year)

DEANS

Faculty of Arts: Prof. Dr NÜKET GÜZ

Faculty of Business Administration: Prof. Dr TAMER KOÇEL

Faculty of Engineering and Architecture: Prof. Dr OKAY EROSKAY

Faculty of Law: Prof. Dr TAYFUN AKGÜNER

Faculty of Science and Letters: Prof. Dr LATIF TOPAKTAŞ

Vocational School: Prof. Dr TANER BULAT

İSTANBUL TEKNIK ÜNIVERSITESI

Ayazağa Kampüsü, 34469 Istanbul

Telephone: (212) 285-30-30
Fax: (212) 285-29-10
E-mail: karadogan@itu.edu.tr
Internet: www.itu.edu.tr

Founded 1773
State control
Languages of instruction: Turkish, English
Academic year: October to July (2 semesters)

Rector: Prof. FARUK KARUDOGAN
Vice-Rectors: Prof. A. FUAT ANDAY, Prof. HALUK KARADOĞAN, Prof. S. ERKIN NASUF
Provost: NEVZAT ÖZKÖK
Librarian: AYHAN KAYGUSUZ

Library: see Libraries and Archives
Number of teachers: 1,861
Number of students: 17,500

Publications: *ARI* (physical and engineering sciences, 4 a year), *Catalog* (biennially), *ITU'den Haberler* (4 a year)

DEANS

Faculty of Aeronautics and Astronautics: Prof. FEVZI ÜNAL

Faculty of Architecture: Prof. CENGIZ GIRITLIOĞLU

Faculty of Chemical and Metallurgical Engineering: Prof. HASAN CAN OKUTAN

Faculty of Civil Engineering: Prof. DERIN ORHON

Faculty of Electrical and Electronic Engineering: Prof. HAKAN KUNTMAN

Faculty of Management: Prof. AHMET FAHRI ÖZOK

Maritime Faculty: Prof. SAMI AYDIN ŞALCI

Faculty of Mechanical Engineering: Prof. TANER DERBENTLI

Faculty of Mines: Prof. MAHIR VARDAR

Faculty of Naval Architecture and Ocean Engineering: Prof. ÖMER GÖREN

Faculty of Science and Letters: Prof. FIGEN KADIRGAN (Deputy)

Faculty of Textile Technologies and Design: Prof. BÜLENT ÖZIPEK

Turkish Music Conservatory: Prof. CAN ETILI ÖKTEM

HEADS OF DEPARTMENTS

Faculty of Aeronautics and Astronautics (tel. (212) 285-33-41; fax (212) 285-31-39; e-mail dekanlik@uubf.itu.edu.tr; internet www .uubf.itu.edu.tr):

Aeronautics: M. FEVZI ÜNAL
Meteorological Engineering: YUNUS BORHAN
Space Science and Technology: ALSAN MERIÇ

Faculty of Civil Engineering (tel. (212) 285-38-55; fax (212) 285-65-87; internet www.ins .itu.edu.tr):

Civil Engineering: Prof. REHA ARTAN
Environmental Engineering: CUMALI KINACI
Geodesy and Photogrammetry: Prof. DOĞAN UÇAR

Faculty of Architecture (tel. (212) 245-27-53; fax (212) 251-48-95; e-mail dekanlik@atilla .mim.itu.edu.tr; internet www.mim.itu.edu .tr):

Architecture: MINE İNCEOĞLU
Industrial Design: NIGAN BAYAZIT
Interior Architecture: HASAN ŞENER
Landscape Architecture: CENGIZ YILDIZCI
Urban and Regional Planning: NURAN ZEREN GÜLERSOY

Faculty of Chemical and Metallurgical Engineering (tel. (212) 285-33-39; fax (212) 285-29-25; e-mail kimmet@itu.edu.tr; internet www.kmg.itu.edu.tr):

Chemical Engineering: NUSRET BULUTÇU
Food Engineering: DILEK BOYACIOĞLU
Metallurgical Engineering: MUSTAFA ÜRGEN

Faculty of Electrical and Electronics Engineering (tel. (212) 285-36-76; fax (212) 285-36-79; internet www.ee.itu.edu.tr):

Computer Engineering: Prof. EMRE HARMANCI
Electrical Engineering: Prof. SERHAT ŞEKER
Electronics and Communications Engineering: Prof. ERCAN TOPUZ

Faculty of Management (İ.T.Ü. Maçka, 80680 Istanbul; tel. (212) 246-20-46; fax (212) 240-72-60; internet www.isl.itu.edu.tr):

Industrial Engineering: F. NAHIT SERASLAN
Management Engineering: LERZAN ÖZKALE

Maritime Faculty (tel. (216) 395-10-43; fax (216) 395-45-00; e-mail oksag@itu.edu.tr; internet www.tdf.itu.edu.tr):

Deck Engineering: SÜREYYA ÖNEY
Marine Engines: NIL GÜLER

Faculty of Mechanical Engineering (tel. (212) 245-60-73; fax (212) 245-07-95; internet www .mkn.itu.edu.tr):

Mechanical Engineering: KADIR KIRKKÖPRÜ
Textile Engineering: BÜLENT ÖZIPEK

Faculty of Mining Engineering (tel. (212) 285-60-60; fax (212) 285-60-80; internet www .mines.itu.edu.tr):

Mining Engineering: NUH BILGIN
Geological Engineering: ERDOĞAN YÜZER
Geophysical Engineering: ILYAS CAGLAR
Petroleum and Natural Gas Engineering: Prof. MUSTAFA ONUR

Faculty of Naval Architecture and Ocean Engineering (tel. (212) 285-64-74; fax (212) 285-64-54; e-mail gemi@itu.edu.tr; internet www.gidb.itu.edu.tr):

Naval Construction: ALIM YILDIZ
Ocean Engineering: ABDI KÜKNER

Faculty of Sciences and Letters (tel. (212) 285-33-40; fax (212) 285-63-86; e-mail hunlu@itu.edu.tr; internet www.fe.itu.edu .tr):

Chemistry: OĞUZ OKAY
Engineering Sciences: FIKRET BALTA
Humanities and Social Sciences: GÖKHAN ÇETINSAYA
Mathematics: AYNUR UYSAL
Molecular Biology and Genetics: CANDAN TAMERLER
Physics: NIHAT BERKER

ATTACHED CONSERVATORY AND DEPARTMENTS

Department of Fine Arts: Dir AYLA ÖDEKAN.

Department of Languages and History: Dir ÖNER GÜNÇAVDI.

Turkish Music Conservatory: Dir CAN ETILI ÖKTEM.

Department of Physical Education and Sports: Dir EMIN TACER.

ATTACHED GRADUATE INSTITUTES

Institute of Energy: Dir HASAN SAYGIN.

Institute of Eurasia Earth Sciences: Dir OKAN TÜYSÜZ.

Institute of Informatics: Dir NÜZHET DALFES.

Institute of Science and Technology: Dir MEHMET KARACA.

Institute of Social Sciences: Dir NURAN ZEREN GÜLERSOY.

ATTACHED RESEARCH CENTRES

Bio-Engineering Research Centre: Dir ERTUĞRUL YAZGAN.

Building and Earthquake Project and Research Centre: Dir AHMET SAĞLAMER.

Building Research Centre: Dir METE TAPAN.

Electronics and Control Project Research Centre: Dir H. HAKAN KUTMAN.

Computer Centre: Dir MUTLU DAĞDELEN.

Energy Sciences and Technology Project Centre: Dir AHMET ARISOY.

Environment and Urban Planning Project and Research Centre: Dir NURAN ZEREN GÜLERSOY.

Geological and Underground Resources Project and Research Centre: Dir NUH BILGIN.

Istanbul Research Centre: Dir FERHAN YÜREKLI.

Machine Production Science and Technology Project and Research Centre: Dir İ. BARLAS ERYÜREK.

Materials Science and Production Technology Project and Research Centre: Dir OKAN ADDEMİR.

Oceanography and Aquatic Science Project and Research Centre: Dir SEDAT KAPDAŞLI.

Space Research Centre: Dir BİNGÜL YAZGAN.

Technological and Economic Development Research Centre: Dir YÜCEL CAN.

Transportation Vehicles Project and Research Centre: Dir EMİNE AĞAR.

İSTANBUL TİCARET ÜNİVERSİTESİ
(Istanbul Commerce University)

Ragıp Gümüşpala Cad. 84, 34378 Eminönü, Istanbul

Telephone: (212) 511-41-50
Fax: (212) 553-94-22
E-mail: rektorluk@iticu.edu.tr
Internet: www.iticu.edu.tr

President: Prof. Dr .A. HAYRI DURMUŞ
Library of 17,400 vols

DEANS

Faculty of Arts: Prof. Dr NECDET TEKİN
Faculty of Commercial Science: Prof. Dr MÜNEVVER TURANLI
Faculty of Communications: Prof. Dr JALE SARMAŞIK
Faculty of Engineering: Prof. Dr NECDET TEKİN
Faculty of Science: Prof. Dr AYSEL ÇELİKEL

İZMİR EKONOMİ ÜNİVERSİTESİ
(Izmir University of Economics)

Sakarya Cad. 156, 35330 Balcova, Izmir
Telephone: (232) 279-25-25
Fax: (232) 279-26-26
E-mail: rector@ieu.edu.tr
Internet: www.ieu.edu.tr

Founded 2001

Rector: Prof. Dr ATTILA SEZGİN
Vice-Rectors: Prof. Dr ERHAN ADA, Prof. Dr M. CEMALİ DİNÇER
Dean of Students: Yrd. Doç. Dr İSMAIL KIZILBAY
Librarian: ALI TUTAL
Number of teachers: 336
Number of students: 2,415

DEANS

Faculty of Administrative Sciences and Economics: Prof. Dr ERHAN ADA
Faculty of Communications: Prof. Dr ORHAN TEKELIOĞLU
Faculty of Computer Science: Prof. Dr İSMAIL BULMUŞ
Faculty of Fine Arts and Design: Prof. Dr TUNÇDAN BALCIOĞLU
Faculty of Science and Literature: Prof. Dr İSMIHAN BAYRAMOĞLU

DIRECTORS

School of Foreign Languages: B. BARUTLU
Graduate School of Social Sciences: Prof. Dr NEJAT TENKER
Vocational School: Prof. Dr TUNÇDAN BALCIOĞLU

İZMİR YÜKSEK TEKNOLOJİ ENSTİTÜSÜ
(İzmir Institute of Technology)

Gülbahçe Köyü, 35430 Urla, İzmir
Telephone: (232) 750-60-01
Fax: (232) 750-60-15
E-mail: semraulku@iyte.edu.tr

Internet: www.iyte.edu.tr
Founded 1992
State control
Languages of instruction: Turkish, English
Academic year: October to June

Rector: Prof. Dr SEMRA ÜLKÜ
Vice-Rectors: Prof. Dr CEMAL ARKON, Prof. Dr RECAI ERDEM
Librarian: GULIZAR USLU

Library of 21,492 books, 96 periodicals, 6,443 online scientific periodicals
Number of teachers: 423
Number of students: 1,733 (1,203 undergraduate, 530 postgraduate)

DEANS

Faculty of Architecture: Prof. Dr CEMAL ARKON
Faculty of Engineering: Prof. Dr MUHSIN ÇIFTIÇOGLU
Faculty of Science: Prof. Dr SEMRA ÜLKÜ
Graduate School of Engineering and Sciences: Assoc. Prof. SEMAHAT ÖZDEMIR

KADİR HAS ÜNİVERSİTESİ

Cibali Merkez Kampüsü, Hisarattı cad., 34230-01 Cibali-Fatih, Istanbul

Telephone: (212) 533-65-32
Fax: (212) 533-65-15
E-mail: info@khas.edu.tr
Internet: www.khas.edu.tr

Founded 1997
Private control (Foundation)
Languages of instruction: Turkish, English
Academic year: October to June

President: Prof. Dr YÜCEL YILMAZ
Vice-President: Prof. Dr NÜKHET TAN
General Secretary: Dr AHMET B. SÖĞÜTLÜOĞLU
Registrar: SELMA DÖNMEZ
Head Librarian: ERTUĞRUL ÇIMEN

Library of 13,857 vols
Number of teachers: 142
Number of students: 1,500

DEANS

Faculty of Arts and Sciences: Prof. Dr KEMAL YELEKÇ I
Faculty of Communications: Prof. Dr DENIZ BAYRAKDAR SEVGEN
Faculty of Economics and Business Administration: Prof. Dr EROL ÜÇDAL
Faculty of Engineering: Prof. Dr TUNCAY SAYDAM
Faculty of Fine Arts: Prof. Dr FATMA OYA BOYLA (acting)
Faculty of Law: Prof. Dr SELÇUK ÖZTEK

KAFKAS ÜNİVERSİTESİ

Rektörlüğü, Pasacayiri Mh., 36040 Kars
Telephone: (474) 242-68-00
Fax: (474) 242-68-47
E-mail: bidab@kafkas.edu.tr
Internet: www.kafkas.edu.tr

Founded 1992
State control

Rector: Prof. Dr NECATI KAYA
Number of teachers: 481
Number of students: 10,000

Publications: *University Bulletin* (annually), *University Gazette* (quarterly).

KAHRAMANMARAŞ SÜTÇÜ IMAM ÜNİVERSİTESİ

KSÜ Rektörlüğü, Avşar Kampüsü, 46100 Kahramanmaraş
Telephone: (344) 219-10-00
Fax: (344) 219-10-12
E-mail: baytorun@ksu.edu.tr
Internet: www.ksu.edu.tr

Founded 1992
State control
Academic year: October to June

Rector: Prof. Dr A. NAFI BAYTORUN
Vice-Rectors: Prof. Dr ORHAN DOĞAN, Prof. Dr CAFER MART, Prof. Dr CEMAL TUNCER
Secretary-General: RÜŞTÜ ERTUĞRUL
Librarian: ŞEREF AKBEN

Library of 25,000 books and periodicals
Number of teachers: 700
Number of students: 11,000

DEANS

Faculty of Agriculture: Prof. Dr ERFAN EFE
Faculty of Economics and Administrative Sciences: Prof. Dr AHMET HAMDI AYDIN
Faculty of Education: Prof. Dr ADNAN KÜÇÜKÖNDER
Faculty of Engineering and Architecture: Prof. Dr MEHMET NURI BODUR
Faculty of Forestry: Prof. Dr ORHAN ERDAŞ
Faculty of Medicine: Prof. Dr İLHAMI TANER KALE
Faculty of Sciences and Literature: Prof. Dr ALI DOĞAN
Faculty of Theology: Prof. Dr M. KAMAL ATİK

KARADENİZ TEKNİK ÜNİVERSİTESİ
(Karadeniz Technical University)

61080 Trabzon
Telephone: (462) 377-30-00
Fax: (462) 325-32-05
E-mail: head@ktu.edu.tr
Internet: www.ktu.edu.tr

Founded 1955
State control
Languages of instruction: Turkish, English
Academic year: October to August

Rector: Prof. Dr İBRAHIM ÖZEN
Vice-Rectors: Prof. Dr SELAHATTIN KÖSE, Prof. Dr NECATI TÜYSÜZ, Prof. Dr AHMET UĞUR TURHAN
General Secretary: Assoc. Prof. CÜNEYT ŞEN
Librarian: Prof. Dr MEHMET ARSLAN

Library of 100,214 vols
Number of teachers: 1,714
Number of students: 36,340

Publications: *KTÜ Bu Hafta* (university news bulletin, weekly), *KTÜ Bülteni* (bulletin, 2 a year), *KTÜ Education Activities* (annually)

DEANS

Faculty of Agriculture (Ordu): Prof. Dr Y. NURETTIN İSMAILÇELEBIOĞLU
Faculty of Architecture: Prof. Dr ŞINASI AYDEMIR
Faculty of Arts and Sciences: Prof. Dr KENAN İNAN
Faculty of Arts and Sciences (Giresun): Prof. Dr ZIYA YAPAR
Faculty of Arts and Sciences (Rize): Prof. Dr NAZMI TURAN OKUMUŞOĞLU
Faculty of Communication: Prof. Dr İBRAHIM ÖZEN
Faculty of Dentistry: Prof. Dr MEHMET TOSUN
Faculty of Economics and Administrative Sciences: Prof. Dr KAMIL YAZICI
Faculty of Economics and Administrative Sciences (Giresun): Prof. Dr METIN BERBER
Faculty of Education (Artvin): Prof. Dr OKTAY TORUL
Faculty of Education (Fatih): Prof. Dr ALIPAŞA AYAS
Faculty of Education (Giresun): Prof. Dr MEHMET TÜFEKÇI
Faculty of Education (Rize): Prof. Dr MEHMET AKBAŞ
Faculty of Engineering: Prof. Dr MUSTAFA AYTEKIN
Faculty of Engineering (Gümüşhane): Prof. Dr FIKRI BULUT

Faculty of Fine Arts: Prof. Dr MUSTAFA KANDİL

Faculty of Forestry: Prof. Dr ZAFER CEMAL ÖZKAN

Faculty of Marine Sciences: Prof. Dr İBRAHIM OKUMUŞ

Faculty of Marine Sciences (Sürmene): Prof. Dr ERTUĞ DÜZGÜNEŞ

Faculty of Medicine: Prof. Dr SÜLEYMAN BAYKALİL

Faculty of Pharmacy: Prof. Dr MEHMET TOSUN

Faculty of Technical Education: Prof. Dr KENAN GELİŞİ

Faculty of Theology: Prof. Dr S. KEMAL SANDIKÇI

PROFESSORS

Faculty of Agriculture (Ordu) (Ordu; tel. (452) 225-05-77; fax (452) 225-12-61; e-mail ziraat@ktu.edu.tr):

İSMAİLÇELEBİOĞLU, Y. N., Soil Science
ŞILBIR, Y., Field Crops

Faculty of Arts and Sciences (Kanuni Kampüsü, 61080 Trabzon; tel. (462) 325-31-41; fax (462) 325-31-95):

AKBAŞ, M., Mathematics
ALTUNBAŞ, M., Physics
ÇAVUŞ, A., Mathematics
ÇELEBİ, S., Physics
ÇİÇEK, K., History
DEMİRBAĞ, Z., Biology
GÖK, Y., Chemistry
GÜRSOY, O., Mathematics
KADIOĞLU, A., Biology
KAYGUSUZ, K., Chemistry
KOBYA, A. İ., Physics
ÖZDEMİR, M., Chemistry
ŞENTÜRK, H. B., Chemistry
YALÇINKAYA, M. A., History
YAPAR, C., Mathematics
YAYLI, N., Chemistry

Faculty of Arts and Sciences (Giresun) (Gazi Cad. Kışla Hamam Sok., Giresun; tel. (454) 216-25-20; fax (454) 216-45-18):

YANMAZ, E., Physics

Faculty of Arts and Sciences (Rize) (Engindere Mah., Köy Hizmetleri Yanı, 53100 Rize; tel. (464) 223-53-75; fax (464) 223-53-76):

OKUMUŞOĞLU, N. T., Physics

Faculty of Economics and Administrative Sciences (Kanuni Kampüsü, 61080 Trabzon; tel. (462) 325-32-12; fax (462) 325-72-81; e-mail iibf@ktu.edu.tr):

BOCUTOĞLU, E., Economics
ÇIFTÇİ, O., Labour Economics and Industrial Relations
ÇIKRIKÇI, M., Management
KESİM, A., Economics
ÖZYURT, H., Economics
TANDOĞAN, A., Economics
TÜREDİ, H., Management
YAZICI, K., Management

Faculty of Economics and Administrative Sciences (Giresun) (Giresun):

TÜFEKÇİ, M., Chemistry

Faculty of Education (Artvin) (Artvin):

TORUL, O., Chemistry

Faculty of Education (Fatih) (Söğütlü, Trabzon; tel. (462) 248-23-05; fax (462) 248-73-44):

AYAS, A. P., Science and Mathematical Education
BEKİROĞLU, N., Education
ÇAPA, M., History
KALE, R., Physical Training

Faculty of Education (Giresun) (Giresun; tel. (454) 215-53-72; fax (464) 215-53-75; e-mail gef@ktu.edu.tr):

TÜFEKÇİ, M., Chemistry

Faculty of Education (Rize) (Rize; tel. (464) 532-67-92; fax (464) 532-86-12; e-mail ktu .cayeli@superonline.com):

TORUL, O., Chemistry

Faculty of Engineering (Gümüşhane) (Gümüşhane; tel. (456) 233-74-27; fax (456) 233-74-27):

BULUT, F., Geology
DURMUŞ, A., Civil Engineering
UZMAN, Ü., Civil Engineering

Faculty of Engineering and Architecture (Kanuni Kampüsü, 61080 Trabzon; tel. (462) 325-31-72; fax (462) 325-74-05):

AKYOL, N., Geodesy and Photogrammetry
ARSLAN, F., Mechanical Engineering
AYDEMİR, S., Architecture
AYDEMİR, Ş., Architecture
AYTEKİN, M., Civil Engineering
BEKTAŞ, O., Geology
BERKÜN, M., Civil Engineering
BIYIK, C., Geodesy and Photogrammetry
BIYIKLIOĞLU, A., Mechanical Engineering
ÇAKIROĞLU, A. O., Civil Engineering
ÇEVİK, S., Architecture
DİLAVER, A., Geodesy and Photogrammetry
DİLEK, R., Geology
DURGUN, O., Mechanical Engineering
ERDÖL, R., Civil Engineering
GEDİK, İ, Geology
GENÇ, S., Geology
GÜR, Ş. O., Architecture
GÜRUNLÜ, C., Electronic and Electrical Engineering
KALENDER, A., Civil Engineering
KANDİL, M., Architecture
KARAALİ, C., Geodesy and Photogrammetry
KARADENİZ, S., Mechanical Engineering
KAYA, A., Geodesy and Photogrammetry
KORKMAZ, S., Geology
ONSOY, H., Civil Engineering
SADIKLAR, B., Geology
SAVAŞKAN, T., Mechanical Engineering
TÜDEŞ, T., Geodesy and Photogrammetry
TÜYSÜZ, N., Geology
UZUNER, B. A., Civil Engineering
ÜLKÜ, Z. A., Mechanical Engineering
YAVUZ, T., Mechanical Engineering
YOMRALIOĞLU, T., Geodesy and Photogrammetry

Faculty of Forestry (Kanuni Kampüsü, 61080 Trabzon; tel. (462) 325-31-83; fax (462) 325-74-99):

ACAR, H. H., Forest Engineering
ANŞİN, R., Forest Engineering
BAŞKENT, E. Z., Forest Engineering
BİLGİLİ, E., Forest Engineering
ÇOLAKOĞLU, G., Forest Industry Engineering
DEMİRCİ, A., Forest Engineering
EROĞLU, M., Forest Engineering
GERÇEK, Z., Forest Engineering
GÜMÜŞ, C., Forest Engineering
KALAY, H. Z., Forest Engineering
KIRCI, H., Forest Industry Engineering
KÖSE, S., Forest Engineering
MEREV, N., Forest Engineering
ÖZBİLEN, A., Landscape Design
ÖZKAN, Z., Landscape Design
TÜRKER, M. F., Forest Engineering
TÜRÜDÜ, O. A., Forest Engineering
ÜÇLER, A. Ö., Forest Engineering
USTA, M., Forestry Industry Engineering
YAHYAOĞLU, Z., Forest Engineering
YAVUZ, H., Forest Engineering

Faculty of Marine Sciences (Sürmene) (Sürmene, Trabzon; tel. (462) 752-24-19; fax (462) 752-21-58):

DÜZGÜNEŞ, E., Fisheries Technology Engineering
KARAÇAM, H., Fisheries Technology Engineering

Faculty of Medicine (Kanuni Kampüsü, 61080 Trabzon; tel. (462) 325-28-22; fax (462) 325-22-70):

AKYOL, N., Ophthalmology
ALHAN, E., Medical Surgery
ALPAY, K., Dermatology
ARSLAN, M. K., Internal Medicine
ARVASİ, H., Histology and Embryology
AYDIN, F., Internal Medicine
AYNACI, M., Child Surgery
BAHADIR, S., Dermatology
BAKİ, C., Orthopaedics
BAYKAL, S., Brain Surgery
BOZKAYA, H., Gynaecology
ÇAKIRBAY, H., Physical Rehabilitation
ÇALIK, A., Medical Surgery
CİNEL, A., General Surgery
DEĞER, O., Biochemistry
ERCİYES, H. N., Anaesthesiology
EREM, C., Internal Medicine
ERDURAN, E., Paediatrics
GEDİK, Y., Paediatrics
GÖR, A., Urology
GÜLER, M., Physical Rehabilitation
GÜMELE, H. R., Diagnostic Radiology
İMAMOĞLU, H. İ., Ophthalmology
İMAMOĞLU, M., Medical Surgery
KAPICIOĞLU, S., Internal Medicine
KARAGÜZEL, A., Medical Biology
KEHA, E., Biochemistry
KÖKSAL, İ., Internal Medicine
KUTLU, N., Surgical Medicine
KUZEYLİ, K., Brain Surgery
MUHTAR, H., Medical Surgery
OVALI, E., Internal Medicine
ÖKTEN, A., Paediatrics
ÖNCÜ, M., Internal Medicine
ÖNDER, Ç., Orthopaedics
ÖNDER, E., Biochemistry
ÖREM, A., Biochemistry
ÖZEN, İ., Anaesthesiology
ÖZGÜR, G. K., Urology
ÖZLÜ, T., Thoracic Diseases
ÖZORAN, Y., Pathology
ÖZYAVUZ, R., Urology
PİŞKİN, B., Medical Surgery
SARUHAN, H., Child Surgery
TELATAR, M., Internal Medicine
TESTERECİ, H., Biochemistry
TURGUTALP, H., Pathology
TURHAN, A. U., Orthopaedics
YANDI, M., General Surgery
YILDIZ, K., Pathology
YILDIZ, M., Orthopaedics

Faculty of Theology (Rize) (Atatürk Cad., Piri Çelebi Mah., Rize; tel. (464) 214-11-20; fax (464) 214-11-24; e-mail ilahiyat@ktu.edu.tr):

SANDIKÇI, S. K., Islamic Education

Faculty of Water Resource Sciences (Rize) (İyidere, Rize; tel. (464) 223-52-39; fax (464) 223-41-18):

KADIOĞLU, A., Biology

GRADUATE SCHOOLS

Graduate School of Health Sciences: Dir Assoc. Prof. ABDULKADİR REİS.

Graduate School of Natural and Applied Sciences: Dir Prof. Dr YUSUF AYVAZ.

Graduate School of Social Sciences: Dir Prof. Dr M. ALAADDİN YALÇINKAYA.

KIRIKKALE ÜNİVERSİTESİ

Ankara Karayolu 7 km, 71450 Kırıkkale

Telephone: (318) 357-36-94

Fax: (318) 357-36-94

E-mail: info@kku.edu.tr

Internet: www.kku.edu.tr

Founded 1992

State control

Academic year: October to July (two semesters)

Rector: Prof. Dr TAHSIN NURI DURLU

Vice-Rector: Prof. Dr ERSIN İSTANBULLUOĞLU

Library of 37,000 vols
Number of teachers: 700
Number of students: 12,000

DEANS

Faculty of Dentistry: Prof. Dr SEVIM ORKUN
Faculty of Economics and Administrative Sciences: Prof. Dr CEMALETTIN TAŞKIRAN
Faculty of Education: Prof. Dr İRFAN ALBAYRAK
Faculty of Engineering: Prof. Dr BILAL TOKLU
Faculty of Law: Prof. Dr ENVER BOZKURT
Faculty of Medicine: Prof. Dr ERTAN BATİSLAM
Faculty of Science and Literature: Prof. Dr MUSTAFA DIKICI
Faculty of Veterinary Medicine: Prof. Dr ERTUĞUL ELMA

KOÇ UNIVERSITY

Rumelifeneri Yolu, 34450 Sarıyer, Istanbul
Telephone: (212) 338-10-00
E-mail: information@ku.edu.tr
Internet: www.ku.edu.tr
Founded 1993
Private control
Languages of instruction: Turkish, English
Academic year: October to June
President: Prof. Dr ATTILA AŞKAR
Provost and Vice-President for Academic Affairs: Prof. Dr YAMAN ARKUN
Vice-President for Administration: Prof. Dr ÖMER YEDEKÇIOĞLU
General Secretary: MEHMET CELAYIR
Librarian: DIDAR BAYIR
Library of 82,000 vols
Number of teachers: 126
Number of students: 1,054

DEANS

College of Arts and Sciences: Prof. Dr ERSIN YURTSEVER
College of Administrative Sciences and Economics: Prof. Dr H. METE SONER
College of Engineering: Prof. Dr IRSADI AKSUN
School of Health Sciences: Prof. Dr ELIZABETH ANNE HERDMAN
School of Law: Prof. Dr TUĞRUL ANSAY
Graduate School of Business: Prof. BARIŞ TAN

KOCAELI ÜNİVERSİTESİ

Eski Istanbul Yolu 10 km., 413080 Limuteppe, Izmit/Kocaeli
Telephone: (262) 303-10-00
Fax: (262) 303-10-03
E-mail: intoffice@kou.edu.tr
Internet: www.kou.edu.tr
Founded 1992
State control
Academic year: October to June
Rector: Prof. Dr BAKI KOMSUOGLU
Vice-Rector (Academic Services): Prof. Dr YUNUS KISHALI
Vice-Rector (Administrative Services): Prof. Dr OZER KENAR
Vice-Rector (Financial Services): Prof. Dr YUSUF CAGLAR
Chief Librarian: MAHMUT SEMERCI
Library of 45,000 vols, 10,000 periodicals
Number of teachers: 1,752
Number of students: 10,521

Publications: *Journal of Social Sciences Institute* (2 a year), *Kocaeli University Communication Faculty Research Journal* (2 a year), *Kocaeli University Law Faculty Journal* (2 a year)

DEANS

Faculty of Arts: Prof. Dr NURI TEMIZSOYLU

Faculty of Communication: Prof. Dr HASRET COMAK
Faculty of Economics: Prof. Dr AHMET İSLAMOĞLU
Faculty of Education: Prof. Dr SERVETTIN BILIR
Faculty of Engineering: Prof. SAVAS AYBERK
Faculty of Law: Prof. Dr HAMDI YILMAZ
Faculty of Medicine: Prof. Dr ALI GÖKALP
Faculty of Science: Prof. Dr YÜKSEL GÜNEY
Faculty of Technical Education: Prof. Dr SATILMIŞ TEKINDAL

MALTEPE ÜNİVERSİTESİ

Marmara Eğitim Köyü, 34857 Maltepe, Istanbul
Telephone: (216) 626-10-50
Fax: (216) 626-10-70
E-mail: maltepe@maltepe.edu.tr
Internet: www.maltepe.edu.tr
Founded 1997
State control
Languages of instruction: Turkish, English
Academic year: October to June
Rector: Prof. Dr MESUT RAZBONYAH
Librarians: NAZAN KARAKAŞ, BURCU ESENER, ARZU ACAR
Library of 17,230 vols, 531 periodicals
Number of teachers: 240
Number of students: 2,220

Publications: *Fen-Edebiyat Fakültesi Dergisi* (Science and Letters Faculty Journal, 2 a year), *Hukuk Fakültesi Dergisi* (Law Faculty Journal, 2 a year), *İktisadi ve İdari Bilimler Fakültesi Dergisi* (Economics and Business Administration Faculty Journal, 2 a year), *İletişim Fakültesi Dergisi* (Communication Faculty Journal, 2 a year)

DEANS

Faculty of Architecture: Prof. Dr ERKUT ÖZEL
Faculty of Communication: Prof. Dr SABRI ÖZAYDIN
Faculty of Economics and Business Administration: Prof. Dr ERTAN OKTAY
Faculty of Education: Prof. Dr İSA EŞME
Faculty of Engineering: Prof. Dr MESUT RAZBONYALI
Faculty of Law: Prof. Dr AYDIN AYBAY
Faculty of Medicine: Prof. Dr ŞEFIK GÜNEY
Faculty of Science and Letters: Prof. Dr MÜCELLA ULUĞ

MARMARA ÜNİVERSİTESİ

Sultanahmet, 34413 Istanbul
Telephone: (212) 518-16-00
Fax: (212) 518-16-15
Internet: www.marun.edu.tr
Founded 1883, reorganized 1982
State control
Languages of instruction: Turkish, English
Languages of instruction: French, German
Academic year: September to July
Rector: Prof. Dr TUNÇ EREM
Vice-Rector: Prof. Dr AHMET HAYRI PURMUŞ
General Secretary: Dr ALTAN KİTAPÇI
Librarian: SEVINC KAZAZ
Number of teachers: 2,500
Number of students: 45,000
Publication: various faculty journals

DEANS

Faculty of Communication: Prof. Dr MELDA CINMAN ŞIMŞEK
Faculty of Dentistry: Prof. Dr SELÇUK BASA
Faculty of Economics and Business Administration: Prof. Dr AHMET HAYRI DURMUŞ
Atatürk Faculty of Education: Prof. Dr AYLA OKTAY

Faculty of Engineering: Prof. Dr A. ALP SAYAR
Faculty of Fine Arts: Prof. Dr HÜSAMETTIN KOÇAN
Faculty of Health Education: Prof. Dr NILGÜN SARP
Faculty of Law: Prof. Dr MERIH KEMAL OMAĞ
Faculty of Medicine: Prof. Dr TOLGA DAĞLI
Faculty of Pharmacy: Prof. Dr MÜRŞIT PEKIN
Faculty of Science and Letters: Prof. Dr EMINE GÜRSOY NASKALI
Faculty of Technical Education: Prof. Dr SEMRA ÜNAL
Faculty of Theology: Prof. Dr MUSTAFA FAYDA

ATTACHED INSTITUTES

Institute of Banking and Insurance: Dir Prof. Dr ILHAN ULUDAĞ.
Institute of Educational Studies: Dir Prof. Dr AYLA OKTAY.
Institute of European Union Studies: Dir Prof. Dr ASLAN GÜNDÜZ.
Institute of Fine Arts: Dir Prof. Dr ŞERMIN ALYANAK.
Institute of Gastroenterology: Dir Prof. Dr NURDAN TÖZÜN.
Institute of Health Sciences: Dir Prof. Dr SEVIM ROLLAS.
Institute of Middle Eastern and Islamic Country Studies: Dir Prof. Dr. AHMET TABAKOĞLU.
Institute of Neurology: Dir Prof. Dr NECMETTIN PAMIR.
Institute of Sciences: Dir Prof. Dr AHMET ALP SAYAR.
Institute of Social Sciences: Dir Prof. Dr ORHAN SEZGIN.
Institute of Turkic Studies: Dir Prof. Dr NADIR DEVLET.

MERSİN ÜNİVERSİTESİ

Çiftlik Köyü Kampüsü, 33343 Mersin
Telephone: (324) 361-00-22
Fax: (324) 361-00-15
E-mail: webadmin@mersin.edu.tr
Internet: www.mersin.edu.tr
Founded 1992
State control
Rector: Prof. Dr UĞUR ORAL
Librarian: HÜSEYIN GÖLALMIŞ
Number of teachers: 100
Number of students: 18,000

DEANS

Faculty of Architecture: Prof. Dr TAMER GÖK
Faculty of Communication: Prof. Dr SELIM AKSÖYEK
Faculty of Economics and Administrative Sciences: Prof. Dr TAYFUR ÖZŞEN
Faculty of Education: Prof. Dr ZAFER GÖKÇAKAN
Faculty of Engineering: Prof. Dr CEMIL CENGIZ ARCASOY
Faculty of Fine Arts: Prof. Dr E. BERIKA İPEKBAYRAK
Faculty of Fisheries: Prof. Dr GÜRKAN EKINGEN
Faculty of Medicine: Prof. Dr ESAT YILGÖR
Faculty of Pharmacy: Prof. Dr ATILLA YALÇIN
Faculty of Science and Letters: Prof. Dr AYHAN SEZER
Faculty of Technical Education (Tarsus): Prof. Dr ÖZDEN BAŞTÜRK

MİMAR SİNAN GÜZEL SANATLAR ÜNİVERSİTESİ
(Mimar Sinan Fine Arts University)

Fındıklı, 80040 Istanbul
Telephone: (212) 145-00-00
E-mail: ulik@msu.edu.tr

Internet: www.msu.cdu.tr
Founded 1883, university status 1982
State control
Language of instruction: Turkish
Rector: Prof. Dr ÝSMET VILDAN ALPTEKIN
Chief Administrative Officer: ERDAL KÜPELİ
Librarian: ASİYE ALAGÖZOĞLU

Library of 51,200 vols
Number of teachers: 420
Number of students: 3,509

DEANS

Faculty of Architecture: Prof. ÝLGI YÜCE AŞKÝN
Faculty of Fine Arts: Prof. RAHMI AKSUNGUR
Faculty of Sciences and Literature: Prof. Dr GÜLAY BAŞARÝR KÝROĞLU

HEADS OF DEPARTMENTS

Faculty of Architecture:

Architecture: Prof. N. ONAT
Industrial Design: Prof. Ö. KÜÇÜKERMAN
Urban and Regional Planning: Prof. Dr A. KARAMAN

Faculty of Fine Arts:

Applied Arts: Prof. B. SALDIRAY
Painting: Prof. A. AYAN
Sculpture: Prof. F. ÖZŞEN
Stage and Visual Arts: Prof. B. BUGAY
Traditional Turkish Arts: Doc. S. B. TURAN

Faculty of Sciences and Literature:

Archaeology: Prof. N. ATIK
History: R. SEŠEN
History of Art: Prof. Dr S. GERMANER
Mathematics: Doc. Dr BELGIN MAZLUMOĞLU
Sociology: Prof. Dr A. AKAY
Statistics: Prof. Dr K. YOĞURTÇUGIL
Turkish Language and Literature: Prof. Dr H. ERSOYLU

ATTACHED INSTITUTES

State Museum of Painting and Sculpture: Istanbul; Dir Prof. B. MUTLU.
State School of Music: Istanbul; Dir ERCI-VAN SAYDAM.

MUĞLA ÜNİVERSİTESİ

48000 Kötekli, Muğla
Telephone: (252) 211-10-00
Fax: (252) 211-15-00
E-mail: intoffice@mu.edu.tr
Internet: www.mu.edu.tr
Founded 1992; present status 2002
State control
Academic year: September to June
Rector: Prof. Dr ŞENER OKTIK
Vice-Rectors: Prof. Dr İBRAHIM YOKAŞ, Prof. Dr ATILA YÜCEL

Library of 76,000 vols, 750 periodicals, 60,000 electronic journals
Number of teachers: 660
Number of students: 17,140

DEANS

Faculty of Aquaculture and Fisheries Biology: Prof. Dr AHMET NURI TARKAN
Faculty of Arts and Sciences: Prof. Dr MURAT BARLAS
Faculty of Economics and Administrative Sciences: Prof. Dr CEMIL ERTUĞRUL
Faculty of Education: Prof. Dr ŞULE AYCAN
Faculty of Engineering: Prof. Dr ERDAL OZHAN
Faculty of Fine Arts: Prof. Dr ATILA YÜCEL (Deputy)
Faculty of Technical Education: Prof. Dr MUHAMMED ELTEZ

DIRECTORS

School of Foreign Languages: Prof. Dr MUS-TAFA KINSIZ

School of Health (Fethiye): Prof. Dr NESRIN AŞTI
School of Health (Muğla): Prof. Dr LALE AFRASYAP
School of Physical Education and Sports: Prof. Dr ERDAL ZORBA
School of Tourism and Hotel Management: Prof. Dr ASLAN EREN (Deputy)
Institute of Natural Sciences (Graduate School): Prof. Dr MUSTAFA DİLEK
Institute of Social Sciences (Graduate School): Prof. Dr ÖMER GÜRKAN

There are 8 Vocational Schools.

MUSTAFA KEMAL ÜNİVERSİTESİ

31000 Antakya, Hatay
Telephone: (326) 221-33-17
Fax: (326) 221-33-00
Internet: www.mku.edu.tr
Founded 1992
State control
Rector: Prof. Dr METIN GÜRKANLAR
Vice-Rectors: Prof. Dr KAMURAN GÜÇLÜ, Prof. Dr SERMIN ÖRNEKTEKIN, Prof. Dr CEMAL YÜKSELEN

Number of teachers: 650
Number of students: 13,000 undergraduate, 350 postgraduate

Faculties of Agriculture, Aquaculture, Economics and Business Administration, education, Engineering and Architecture, Fine Arts, Medicine, Public Administration, Science and Humanities and Veterinary Science.

NİĞDE ÜNİVERSİTESİ

Niğde Üniversitesi Rektörlüğü, 51100 Niğde
Telephone: (388) 232-10-10
Fax: (388) 232-10-11
E-mail: rektor@alp.nigde.edu.tr
Internet: www.nigde.edu.tr
Founded 1992
State control
Academic year: October to July
Rector: Prof. Dr HAMZA UYGUN
Vice-Rectors: Prof. Dr MEHMET ALI BILGINO-ĞLU, Prof. Dr ADNAN GÖRÜR
Secretary-General: MEVLÜT SEZGIN
Director of the Library and Documentation Department: MAZLUME VURAN

Library of 13,000 books, 100 periodicals
Number of teachers: 822
Number of students: 16,708 (15,433 under-graduate, 7,289 postgraduate)
Publications: *Natural Sciences, Social Sciences*

DEANS

Faculty of Arts and Science: ADIL KILIÇ
Faculty of Economics and Business Administration: KASIM KARAHAN
Faculty of Economics and Business Administration (Aksaray): H. FERHAT ESER
Faculty of Education: ADIL KILIÇ
Faculty of Engineering: REFIK KAYALI
Faculty of Engineering and Architecture: ADIL KILIÇ

DIRECTORS OF HIGHER SCHOOLS AND INSTITUTES

Higher School of Health: AHMET SAVRAN
Higher School of Physical Education and Sports: NEDIM ÇETIN
Higher School of Physical Education and Sports (Aksaray): AHMET ŞAHAN
Higher School of Vocational Education: (vacant)
Institute of Natural Sciences: AYDIN TOPÇU
Institute of Social Sciences: MUSA ŞAŞMAZ

OKAN ÜNİVERSİTESİ

Hasanpaşa Uzunçayır Cad. 6, Kadıköy, Istanbul
Telephone: (216) 325-48-18
Fax: (216) 339-61-36
E-mail: okan@okan.edu.tr
Internet: www.okan.edu.tr
Founded 2003
Rector: Prof. Dr SADIK KIRBAŞ
Vice-Rector: Prof. Dr CEVDET ÖĞÜT
Librarian: KENAN ÖZTOP
Number of students: 450

DEANS

Faculty of Arts and Sciences: Prof. Dr HASAN ÖZEKES
Faculty of Economics and Administrative Sciences: Prof. Dr SADIK KIRBAŞ
Faculty of Engineering: Asst Prof. Dr CEVDET ÖĞÜT

DIRECTORS

School of Computer Sciences and Tourism and Hotel Management: Prof. Dr ALI RIZA BÜYÜKUSLU
Social Institute: Asst Prof. Dr GONCA TELLI YAMAMOTO

ONDOKUZ MAYIS ÜNİVERSİTESİ

Kurupelit, 55139 Samsun
Telephone: (362) 457-60-00
Fax: (362) 457-60-91
E-mail: omuinter@omu.edu.tr
Internet: www.omu.edu.tr
Founded 1975
State control
Language of instruction: Turkish
Academic year: September to June
Rector: Prof. Dr FERİT BERNAY
Vice-Rectors: Prof. M. ERTUĞRUL BAKRAKTAR-KATALIR, Prof. Dr H. BARIŞ DİREN, Prof. Dr A. RIFAT ŞAHIN
Secretary-General: NAZIM ALKAN
Registrar: NURİYE GÜRKANLI
Librarian: ÖMER BOZKURT

Number of teachers: 1,809
Number of students: 25,579

Publications: *Faculty Journals* (monthly), *News Bulletin* (monthly)

DEANS

Faculty of Agriculture: Prof. Dr YUNUS PINAR
Faculty of Arts and Sciences: Prof. Dr ADEM GÜLEL
Faculty of Arts and Sciences (Ordu): Prof. Dr CEMIL YAPAR
Faculty of Arts and Sciences (Samsun): Prof. Dr İSMET ŞENEL
Faculty of Arts and Sciences (Sinop): Prof. Dr ŞEVKET BÜYÜKHATİPOĞLU
Faculty of Dentistry: Prof. Dr HÜLYA KÖPRÜLÜ
Faculty of Economics and Administrative Sciences (Boyabat): Prof. Dr HÜSEYİN ALPER GÜZEL
Faculty of Economics and Administrative Sciences (Samsun): Prof. Dr ERDAL YAVUZ
Faculty of Economics and Administrative Sciences (Ünye): Prof. Dr OSMAN ECEVİT
Faculty of Education (Amasya): Prof. Dr ZAFER EREN
Faculty of Education (Samsun): Prof. Dr BİLAL DİNDAR
Faculty of Education (Sinop): Prof. Dr ERDO-ĞAN BAŞAR
Faculty of Engineering: Prof. Dr OSMAN NURİ ERGÜN
Faculty of Fisheries (Sinop): Prof. Dr MUAM-MER ERDEM
Faculty of Marine Sciences (Fatsa): Prof. Dr HALUK KEFELİOĞLU
Faculty of Medicine: Prof. Dr ŞABAN SARIKAYA

Faculty of Theology: Prof. Dr OSMAN ZÜMRÜT
Faculty of Veterinary Medicine: Prof. Dr HAKAN MUĞLALI

PROFESSORS AND HEADS OF DEPARTMENTS
(H=Head of Dept)

Faculty of Agriculture (tel. (362) 457-60-86; fax (362) 457-60-34; e-mail iac-agric@omu.edu.tr; internet www.omu.edu.tr/akad/zf/zir-dekanlik/ziraat.htm):

ACAR, Z., Agronomy
APAN, M., Agricultural Structures and Irrigation (H)
BİLGENER, Ş., Horticulture
CİNEMRE, H. A., Agricultural Economics (H)
DEMİR, Y., Agricultural Structures and Irrigation
ECEVİT, O., Plant Protection (H)
GÜLÜMSER, A., Agronomy (H)
KEVSEROĞLU, K., Agronomy
KORKMAZ, A., Soil Science (H)
ODABAŞ, F., Horticulture (H)
ÖZCAN, M., Horticulture
ÖZDEMİR, N., Soil Science
ÖZTÜRK, T., Agricultural Structures and Irrigation
PINAR, Y., Agricultural Machinery (H)
SARICA, M., Animal Science
SARIÇİÇEK, B. Z., Animal Science (H)

Faculty of Arts and Sciences (Ordu) (Ordu Fen-Edebiyat Fakültesi, Perşembe, 52700 Ordu; tel. (452) 517-43-70; fax (452) 517-43-68; internet www.ome.edu.tr/akad/fklt/ordufen/index.html):

AKÇİN, Ö. E., Biology (H)
EKİNCİ, İ., History (H)
MAĞDEN, S., Mathematics
YAPAR, C., Mathematics

Faculty of Arts and Sciences (Samsun) (tel. (362) 457-60-80; fax (362) 457-60-81; internet www.omu.edu.tr/akad/fen/ana_sayfa.htm):

AFŞİN, B., Chemistry
ALPASLAN, F., Statistics
BATI, B., Chemistry
BİLGENER, M., Biology
BÜYÜKGÜNGÖR, O., Physics (H)
ÇALIŞKAN, M., Mathematics
ÇALIŞKAN, N., Physics
ÇELİK, F., Physics
DİNÇER, M., Physics
EDİNSEL, K., Psychology (H)
ERDÖNMEZ, A., Physics
EREN, Z., Biology
ERLER, M. Y., History (H)
GÖNÜLOL, A., Biology (H)
GÜLEL, A., Biology
GÜMRÜKÇÜOĞLU, İ. E., Chemistry (H)
GÜMÜŞ, H., Physics
GÜRKANLI, A. T., Mathematics (H)
IŞILDAK, İ., Chemistry
KARACAN, T., Turkish
KARTAL, V., Biology
KEFELİOĞLU, H., Biology
KILINÇ, M., Biology
KÖKSAL, F., Physics
KORKMAZ, H., Chemistry
KUTBAY, H. G., Biology
MENEK, N., Chemistry
NİŞANCI, A., Geography (H)
OKUMUŞOĞLU, N. T., Physics
ONAR, A. N., Chemistry
ÖLMEZ, H., Chemistry
ÖZBALCI, M., Turkish
ÖZKAPLAN, H., Physics
ÖZKANCA, R., Biology
ÖZKOÇ, İ., Biology
PANCAR, A., Mathematics
POLAT, N., Biology
ŞENEL, G., Biology
ŞENEL, İ., Physics (H)
TAPRAMAZ, R., Physics
TARAKÇI, C., Turkish
YAVUZ, M., Physics

YILMAZ, M., Mathematics
YILMAZ, V. T., Chemistry
ZEYBEKOĞLU, Ü., Biology

Faculty of Arts and Sciences (Sinop) (Sinop Fen-Edebiyat Fakültesi, Sinop; tel. (368) 271-55-20; fax (368) 271-55-24; e-mail sinopfenedebiyat@yahoo.com; internet www.omu.edu.tr/akad/sinopfen):

ÇANKAYA, E., Statistics (H)
DEMİRCİ, K., Mathematics (H)
SIVACI, R., Biology (H)

Faculty of Dentistry (tel. (362) 457-60-30; fax (362) 457-60-32; e-mail dentistry@omu.edu.tr; internet dentistry.omu.edu.tr):

AÇIKGÖZ, G., Periodontology (H)
ALKAN, A., Oral and Maxillofacial Surgery (H)
CEYLAN, G., Prosthodontics (H)
ÇELENK, P., Oral Diagnosis and Radiology (H)
KÖPRÜLÜ, H., Dental Diseases and Treatment (H)
KOYUTÜRK, A. E., Pedodontics (H)
TOLLER, M. Ö., Oral and Maxillofacial Surgery (H)
TÜRK, T., Orthodontics (H)

Faculty of Economics and Administrative Sciences (Ünye) (Ünye İktisadi ve İdari Bilimler Fakültesi, Ünye; tel. (452) 323-86-96; fax (452) 323-82-56; e-mail gurolo@omu.edu.tr):

ÖZCÜRE, G., Economics

Faculty of Education (Amasya) (Amasya Eğitim Fakültesi, Amasya; tel. (358) 252-62-30; fax (358) 252-62-22; e-mail amasyaeg@omu.edu.tr; internet www.omu.edu.tr/akad/fklt/aegt/amsegtgiris.htm):

KARAMUSTAFAOĞLU, O., Computers and Teaching Technology (H)
ORBAY, M., Primary Education (H)
ÜSTÜN, A., Education (H)
YİĞİT, M., Turkish (H)
ZİYAGİL, M. A., Physical Education and Sport (H)

Faculty of Education (Samsun) (tel. (362) 457-60-20; fax (362) 457-60-78; internet www.omuegitim.edu.tr/DesktopDefault.aspx):

AKBULUT, D. A., History (H)
BARUT, Y., Special Education (H)
BAŞAR, E., Primary Education
BAYRAKTARKATAL, E., Music (H)
BOLAT, H., Foreign Languages
ÇOLAK, M., Foreign Languages (H)
ÇORUH, U., Computer Education and Educational Technology
DİNDAR, B., Education (H)
ENGİN, A., Natural Sciences and Mathematics (H)
ERSANLI, K., Education
KIRCI, M., Turkish (H)
KOYUNCU, S., Fine Arts (H)

Faculty of Education (Sinop) (Sinop Eğitim Fakültesi, Sinop; tel. (368) 271-55-35; fax (368) 271-55-30; e-mail sinopegit@omu.edu.tr; internet www.ome.edu.tr/akad/sinop-egt):

AYDIN, H., Computers and Teaching Technology (H)
BAŞAR, E., Primary Education (H)
BOSTANCI, B. A., Foreign Languages (H)
MENTEŞE, S., Education (H)
ÖZDEMIR, O., Primary Education (H)

Faculty of Engineering (tel. (362) 457-60-94; fax (362) 457-60-35; e-mail onergun@omu.edu.tr; internet www.omu.edu.tr/akad/fklt/muh/muhendislik.htm):

BAYRAKLI, F., Environmental Engineering
BEKTAŞ, S., Geodesy and Photogrammetric Engineering (H)
BÜYÜKGÜNGÖR, H., Environmental Engineering (H)
EFENDİYEV, Ç., Telecommunications

ERGUN, O. N., Environmental Engineering
HURŞİT, A., Food Engineering (H)
KASIMZADE, A., Civil Engineering (H)
ÖNBİLGİN, G., Electrical and Electronic Engineering (H)
TOPALOĞLU, B., Machine Engineering (H)
ULUTAŞ, M., Computer Engineering (H)

Faculty of Fisheries (Sinop) (Su Ürünleri Fakültesi, Akliman Kampüsü, 57000 Sinop; tel. (368) 287-62-62; fax (368) 287-62-55; internet www.omu.edu.tr/akad/fklt/ssu/anamenu.html):

BAT, L., Basic Fisheries Sciences (H)
BİRCAN, R., Fish Breeding
BÜYÜKHATİPOĞLU, Ş., Fish Breeding
ERDEM, M., Fish Breeding
ERKOYUNCU, İ., Fishing and Fish Processing Technology (H)
KALMA, M., Fish Breeding
SAMSUN, O., Fishing and Fish Processing Technology

Faculty of Medicine (tel. (362) 457-60-70; fax (362) 457-60-41; internet www.omu.edu.tr/akad/fklt/tip/anamenu.htm):

ACAR, S., Paediatric Oncology
AĞAR, E., Physiology
AKAN, H., Radiodiagnostics
AKBAŞ, S., Child Psychiatry (H)
AKPOLAT, İ., Pathology
AKPOLAT, M. T., Nephrology
ALBAYRAK, D., Paediatric Haematology
ALPER, T., Obstetrics and Gynaecology
ALVUR, M., Biochemistry (H)
ANLAR, F. Y., Paediatrics
ARIK, A. C., Psychiatry
ARIK, N., Nephrology
ARITÜRK, E., Paediatric Surgery
AŞÇI, R., Urology
AYDIN, M., Paediatric Endocrinology
BAĞCI, H., Medical Biology (H)
BAKIR, T., Gastroenterology
BARIŞ, S., Pathology
BAŞOĞLU, A., Thoracic Surgery (H)
BAŞOĞLU, T., Nuclear Medicine (H)
BAYSAL, M. K., Paediatrics (H)
BEK, Y., Bio-statistics (H)
BERNAY, R. F., Paediatric Surgery (H)
BİLGİÇ, S., Anatomy
BÜYÜKALPELLİ, R., Urology (H)
CANTÜRK, F., Physical Medicine and Rehabilitation (H)
CANTÜRK, T., Dermatology
CENGİZ, K., Nephrology (H)
ÇELİK, F., Neurosurgery (H)
ÇELİK, S., Pharmacology (H)
ÇİFTÇİ, N., Histology and Embryology (H)
DABAK, N., Orthopaedics and Traumatology
DİKİCİ, M. F., Family Practice (H)
DİREN, H. B., Radio-diagnostics (H)
DURU, P., Paediatrics
DURUPINAR, B., Microbiology (H)
ELBİSTAN, M., Medical Biology
ERKAN, D., Ophthalmology (H)
ERKAN, L., Thoracic Diseases (H)
ERZURUMLU, K., General Surgery
GEPTİREMEN, A., Pharmacology
GÖKÇE, Ş. Ç., Radiation Oncology (H)
GÜLDOĞUŞ, F., Anaesthesiology
GÜLMAN, B., Orthopaedics and Traumatology (H)
GÜNAL, N., Paediatrics
GÜNAYDIN, M., Microbiology
GÜRMEN, N., Radiodiagnostics
GÜVEN, H., First Aid and Emergency Aid (H)
İÇTEN, N., Anatomy
İNCESU, L., Radiodiagnostics
İŞLEK, İ., Paediatrics
İYİGÜN, Ö., Neurosurgery
KAHRAMAN, H., Endocrinology
KALAYCI, A. G., Paediatrics
KANDEMİR, B., Pathology (H)
KAPLAN, S., Histology and Embryology

KARACALAR, A., Plastic and Reconstructive Surgery (H)
KARAGÖZ, F., Pathology
KARAİSMAİLOĞLU, N., Orthopaedics and Traumatology
KEÇELİGİL, H. T., Cardiovascular Surgery (H)
KESİM, M., General Surgery (H)
KESİM, Y., Pharmacology
KOCAKAVAK, C., Cardiology (H)
KÖKÇÜ, A., Obstetrics and Gynaecology (H)
KOLBAKIR, F., Cardiovascular Surgery (H)
KOPUZ, C., Anatomy (H)
KORKMAZ, A., Histology and Embryology
KOYUNCU, M., Otorhinolaryngology
KÜÇÜKÖDÜK, Ş., Paediatrics (H)
LEBLEBİCİOĞLU, H., Clinical Bacteriology and Infectious Diseases (H)
MALATYALIOĞLU, E., Obstetrics and Gynaecology
MALAZGİRT, Z., General Surgery
MARANGOZ, C., Physiology (H)
OĞUR, M. G., Paediatrics (H)
ONAR, M. K., Neurology (H)
ÖGE, İ., Ophthalmology
ÖKTEN, G., Medical Biology (H)
ÖZBENLİ, T., Neurology
ÖZEN, N., General Surgery
ÖZKAN, K., General Surgery
ÖZTÜRK, F., Paediatrics
PEKŞEN, Y., Public Health (H)
RAKUNT, C., Neurosurgery
RIZALAR, R., Paediatric Surgery
SANIÇ, A., Microbiology
SARIHASAN, B., Anaesthesiology
SARIKAYA, Ş., Urology
SELÇUK, M. B., Radiodiagnostics
ŞAHİN, A. R., Psychiatry (H)
ŞAHİN, M., Cardiology (H)
ŞAHİN, M., Nuclear Medicine (H)
ŞAHİNOĞLU, H., Anaesthesiology
ŞEŞEN, T., Otolaryngology
TANYERİ, F., Internal Medicine (Endocrinology) (H)
TANYERİ, Y., Otorhinolaryngology (H)
TAŞÇI, N., Physiology
TAŞDEMİR, H. A., Paediatrics
TEKAT, A., Otorhinolaryngology
TUNALI, G., Neurology
TURANLI, A. Y., Dermatology (H)
TURLA, A., Forensic Medicine (H)
TÜLEK, N., Clinical Bacteriology and Infectious Diseases
TÜR, A., Anaesthesiology (H)
TÜRE, U., Neurosurgery
ULUSOY, A. N., General Surgery
ÜNAL, R., Otorhinolaryngology
ÜSTÜN, C., Obstetrics and Gynaecology
ÜSTÜN, F. E., Anaesthesiology
YEŞİLDAĞ, O., Cardiology
YILMAZ, A. F., Urology
YÜCEL, İ., Internal Medicine (Oncology) (H)

Faculty of Theology (tel. (362) 457-60-83; fax (362) 457-60-83; e-mail ilhdek@omu.edu.tr; internet www.omu.edu.tr/akad/ilh):

DOĞAN, İ., Basic Islamic Sciences (H)
KAYA, M., Teaching Ethics and Religious Culture in Primary Education (H)
KOÇAK, M., Basic Islamic Sciences
PEKER, H., Philosophy and Religion (H)
TERZİ, M. Z., Islamic History and Art
TURAN, A., Basic Islamic Sciences (H)
YAZICI, İ., Basic Islamic Sciences
YETİK, E., Basic Islamic Sciences
ZÜMRÜT, O., Islamic History and Art (H)

Faculty of Veterinary Medicine (tel. (362) 457-60-00 ext. 2800; fax (362) 457-60-00 ext. 2801):

GÜVENÇ, T., Basic Veterinary Sciences (H)
MUĞLALI, H., Animal Science and Animal Nutrition (H)
UMUR, Ş., Diseases and Clinical Sciences (H)
YURDUSEV, N., Diseases and Clinical Sciences

DIRECTORS

Graduate School of Fine Arts: Asst Prof. AYDIN KAPTAN
Graduate School of Health Sciences: Prof. Dr SÜLEYMAN ÇELİK
Graduate School of Natural Sciences: Prof. Dr A. NUR ONAR
Graduate School of Social Sciences: Prof. Dr HASAN BOLAT

ORTA DOĞU TEKNİK ÜNİVERSİTESİ
(Middle East Technical University)

Ismet Inönü Bulvarı, Ankara 06531

Telephone: (312) 210-20-00
Fax: (312) 210-11-05
E-mail: rektorluk@metu.edu.tr
Internet: www.metu.edu.tr

Founded 1956
State control
Languages of instruction: Turkish, English
Academic year: October to June (two semesters)

President: Prof. Dr URAL AKBULUT
General Secretary: Prof. Dr HALUK DARENDELİLER
Registrar: NESRİN ÜNSAL
Librarian: Prof. Dr BÜLENT KARASÖZEN (acting)
Library: see Libraries and Archives
Number of teachers: 2,000
Number of students: 21,000

Publications: *METU Journal of Faculty of Architecture* (2 a year), *METU Journal of Human Sciences* (2 a year), *METU Studies in Development* (4 a year)

DEANS

Faculty of Architecture: Prof. Dr HALUK PAMIR
Faculty of Arts and Sciences: Prof. Dr O. YAVUZ ATAMAN
Faculty of Economic and Administrative Sciences: Prof. Dr ŞINASI AKOY
Faculty of Education: Prof. Dr MERAL AKSU
Faculty of Engineering: Prof. Dr MUSTAFA TOKYAY

DIRECTORS

Graduate School of Marine Sciences: Prof. Dr ŞÜKRÜ BEŞIKTEPE
Graduate School of Natural and Applied Sciences: Prof. Dr CANAN ÖZGEN
Graduate School of Social Sciences: Prof. Dr SENCER AYATA
School of Foreign Languages: Prof. Dr HÜSNÜ ENGINARLAR
Informatics Institute: Assoc. Prof. NAZIFE BAYKAL

PROFESSORS

Faculty of Architecture (tel. (312) 210-22-01; fax (312) 210-11-08; e-mail facultyweb@arc.metu.edu.tr; internet www.arch.metu.edu.tr):

AKTÜRE, S., City and Regional Planning
BAKIRER, Ö., Architecture
BALAMIR, M., City and Regional Planning
ERAYDIN, A., City and Regional Planning
ERSOY, M., City and Regional Planning
ERZEN, J. A., Architecture
EVYAPAN, G., Architecture
GEDİK, A., City and Regional Planning
GÜVEN, S., Architecture
İMAMOĞLU, V., Architecture
PAMIR, H., Architecture
SALTIK, E., Architecture
TUNA, N., City and Regional Planning
TÜREL, A., City and Regional Planning
YAVUZ, A., Architecture
YAVUZ, Y., Architecture

Faculty of Arts and Sciences (tel. (312) 210-31-01; fax (312) 210-12-79; e-mail wwwfef@metu.edu.tr; internet www.fef.metu.edu.tr):

ADALI, O., Biology
AKBULUT, U., Chemistry
AKGÜN, S., History
AKINOĞLU, G. B., Physics
AKKAYA, E. U., Chemistry
AKKAYA, M., Chemistry
AKŞİT, B., Sociology
AKYILDIZ, E., Mathematics
ALPAY, Ş., Mathematics
ALYÜRÜK, K., Chemistry
ARAS, L., Chemistry
ARINÇ, E., Biology
ATAMAN, O. Y., Chemistry
AYATA, S., Sociology
AYDIN, R., Physics
AYGÜN, R. S., Chemistry
AYHAN, H. Ö., Statistics
AYTUNA, A., Mathematics
BALCI, M., Chemistry
BAYIN, S. Ş., Physics
BAYKAL, A., Physics
BAYRAMLI, E., Chemistry
BİLHAN, M., Mathematics
BILIKMEN, K. S., Physics
CAN, C., Physics
ÇELEBİ, O., Mathematics
ÇEYLAN, Y., Philosophy
CIVELEK, F. R., Physics
DEMİR, A. S., Chemistry
DEMİRCİ, Ş., Chemistry
DOĞAN, M., Biology
ECEVİT, A., Physics
ECEVİT, M. C., Sociology
ECEVİT, Y., Sociology
ELLIALTIOĞLU, Ş., Physics
ERÇELEBİ, A. Ç., Physics
ERGUDEN, A., Philosophy
ERKOÇ, Ş., Physics
ERTÜRK, Y., Sociology
GÖKALP, A., Physics
GÖKMEN, A., Chemistry
GÖKMEN, İ. G., Chemistry
GÖKTÜRK, E. H., Chemistry
GÜLEN, D., Physics
GÜNAL, İ., Physics
GÜNDÜZ, U., Biology
GÜRAY, T., Biology
HACALOĞLU, J., Chemistry
HASIRCI, N., Chemistry
HASIRCI, V. N., Biology
İLTAN, E. O., Physics
İMAMOĞLU, O., Psychology
İNAM, A., Philosophy
İSCAN, M., Biology
İSÇİ, H., Chemistry
KARANCI, N. A., Psychology
KARASÖZEN, B., Mathematics
KARASU, A., Physics
KATIRCIOĞLU, B., Physics
KATIRCIOĞLU, Ş., Physics
KAYA, A., Mathematics
KAYA, Z., Biology
KAYRAN, H. C., Biology
KENCE, A., Biology
KILDIR, M., Chemistry
KIRBIYIK, H., Physics
KISAKÜREK, D., Chemistry
KIZILOĞLU, N., Physics
KIZILOĞLU, Ü., Physics
KOCABIYIK, S., Biology
KUZUCUOĞLU, M., Mathematics
KÜÇÜKYAVUZ, S., Chemistry
KÜÇÜKYAVUZ, Z., Chemistry
MUTLU, M. K., Sociology
MUTMAN, M., Sociology
NALBANTOĞLU, H. Ü., Sociology
NURLU, Z., Mathematics
ÖKTEM, H. A., Biology
ÖNAL, A. M., Chemistry
ÖNDER, T., Mathematics
ÖNSİPER, H., Mathematics
ÖZCENGİZ, G., Biology

ÖZDEMİR, S., Physics
ÖZKAN, H., Physics
ÖZKAN, İ., Chemistry
ÖZKAR, S., Chemistry
ÖZSAN, F. S., Physics
PAK, N. K., Physics
PEYNİRCİOĞLU, N. B., Chemistry
SAVCİ, M., Physics
SEVER, R., Physics
SEVERCAN, F., Biology
TALASLI, U., Psychology
TANYELİ, C., Chemistry
TARHAN, O., Chemistry
TAŞELİ, H., Mathematics
TATLI, A., Physics
TEZER, C., Mathematics
TEZER, M., Mathematics
TİNÇER, T., Chemistry
TOGAN, İ, Biology
TOGAN, İ, History
TOMAK, M., Physics
TOPPARE, L. K., Chemistry
TUNCEL, S., Chemistry
TURAN, G., Physics
TURAN, R., Physics
TÜRKER, L., Chemistry
ULA, A. T., Statistics
USANMAZ, A., Chemistry
UZUN, A., Statistics
VOLKAN, M., Chemistry
YİLMAZ, O., Physics
YURTSEVEN, H., Physics
YÜCEL, M., Biology
ZAFER, A., Mathematics
ZEYREK, T. M., Physics

Faculty of Economic and Administrative Sciences (tel. (312) 210-11-07; fax (312) 210-11-07; e-mail feas@feas.metu.edu.tr; internet www.feas.metu.edu.tr):

ACAR, A., Management
ACAR, A. F., Political Sciences and Public Administration
AKDER, H., Economics
AKSOY, Ş., Political Sciences and Public Administration
AYATA, A., Political Sciences and Public Administration
BAĞCI, H., International Relations
BÖLÜKBAŞIOĞLU, S., International Relations
ÇAKMAK, E. H., Economics
DAĞI, D. İ., International Relations
ERALP, Y. A., International Relations
ERLAT, G., Economics
ERLAT, H., Economics
EROL, C., Management
GITMEZ, A. S., Management
GÖKTAN, E., Management
KAYA, A. R., Political Sciences and Public Administration
MUĞAN, F. N. C., Management
ÖZUEREN, E., Economics
ŞENSES, F., Economics
TANSEL, A., Economics
TAYMAZ, E., Economics
TİLEYLİOĞLU, A., Management
TONAK, E., Economics

Faculty of Education (tel. (312) 210-40-01; fax (312) 210-11-12; e-mail top@metu.edu.tr; internet www.fedu.metu.edu.tr):

AKSU, M., Educational Sciences
ALPSAN, D., Science Education
AYDIN, A. G., Educational Sciences
BERBEROĞLU, G. H., Science Education
ÇİLELİ, M., Foreign Language Education
DEMIR, A. G., Educational Sciences
ENGİNARLAR, H., Foreign Language Education
ERTEPINAR, H., Science Education
GEBAN, Ö., Science Education
İÇÖZ, N., Foreign Language Education
KAŞ, A. D., Foreign Language Education
KÖNIG, W., Foreign Language Education
KORKUSUZ, F., Physical Education and Sports

ÖZDEN, Y., Computer Education and Instructional Technology
ŞIMŞEK, H., Educational Sciences
TEZER, E., Educational Sciences
YILDRIM, A., Educational Sciences
ZEYREK, D., Foreign Language Education

Faculty of Engineering (tel. (312) 210-25-01; fax (312) 210-11-10; e-mail engfac@eng.metu.edu.tr; internet www.eng.metu.edu.tr):

AKDENİZ, V., Metallurgical Engineering
AKGÖZ, Y. C., Engineering Sciences
AKGÜN, A. M., Aeronautical Engineering
AKIN, T., Electrical and Electronic Engineering
AKKÖK, M., Mechanical Engineering
AKMANDOR, İ. S., Aeronautical Engineering
AKSEL, H. M., Mechanical Engineering
AKYILMAZ, M. Ö., Civil Engineering
ALBAYRAK, K., Mechanical Engineering
ALEMDAROĞLU, N., Aeronautical Engineering
ALTINBİLEK, D. H., Civil Engineering
ALTINER, D., Geological Engineering
ANKARA, A., Metallurgical Engineering
ARIKAN, M. A. S., Mechanical Engineering
ARINÇ, F., Mechanical Engineering
AROL, A. İ., Mining Engineering
AŞKAR, M., Electrical and Electronic Engineering
ATALA, H., Metallurgical Engineering
ATALAY, Ü. M., Mining Engineering
ATIMTAY, A., Environmental Engineering
ATIMTAY, E., Civil Engineering
BAÇ, N., Chemical Engineering
BAĞCI, A. S., Petroleum and Natural Gas Engineering
BAKIR, U. B., Chemical Engineering
BALKAN, T., Mechanical Engineering
BAYINDIRLI, A., Food Engineering
BAYINDIRLI, L. A., Food Engineering
BAYKA, A. D., Mechanical Engineering
BAYKAL, A. D., Electrical and Electronic Engineering
BEŞIKÇI, C., Electrical and Electronic Engineering
BİLGEN, S., Electrical and Electronic Engineering
BIRAND, M. T., Electrical and Electronic Engineering
BİRLİK, G. A., Engineering Sciences
BOR, Ş., Metallurgical Engineering
BOZKURT, E., Geological Engineering
BOZOĞLU, F. T., Food Engineering
BOZŞAHIN, E. N. Ö., Industrial Engineering
BOZYIĞIT, M., Computer Engineering
BÖLÜKBAŞI, N., Mining Engineering
BÜYÜKDURA, O. M., Electrical and Electronic Engineering
CANATAN, F., Electrical and Electronic Engineering
ÇALIŞKAN, M., Mechanical Engineering
ÇELENLİGİL, M. C., Aeronautical Engineering
ÇİLİNGİR, F. C., Industrial Engineering
ÇOKÇA, E., Civil Engineering
ÇULFAZ, A., Chemical Engineering
DARENDELILER, H., Mechanical Engineering
DEMİRAL, B., Petroleum and Natural Gas Engineering
DEMİRBAŞ, K., Electrical and Electronic Engineering
DEMIREKLER, M., Electrical and Electronic Engineering
DİLEK, F. B., Environmental Engineering
DOĞAÇ, A., Computer Engineering
DOĞU, T., Chemical Engineering
DOYUM, A. B., Mechanical Engineering
DOYURAN, V., Geological Engineering
DURSUNKAYA, Z., Mechanical Engineering
ERALP, O. C., Mechanical Engineering
ERGİN, A., Civil Engineering
ERGÜL, R., Electrical and Electronic Engineering
ERGÜN, M. U., Civil Engineering

ERKİP, N., Industrial Engineering
ERKMEN, A., Electrical and Electronic Engineering
ERKMEN, İ., Electrical and Electronic Engineering
ERMİŞ, M., Electrical and Electronic Engineering
EROĞLU, İ., Chemical Engineering
EROL, A. O., Civil Engineering
ERSAK, A., Electrical and Electronic Engineering
ERTAN, B. H., Electrical and Electronic Engineering
ERTAŞ, A., Electrical and Electronic Engineering
ESİN, A., Food Engineering
EYÜBOĞLU, B. M., Electrical and Electronic Engineering
GEÇİT, M. R., Engineering Sciences
GENÇ, F. P., Computer Engineering
GENÇER, G. N., Electrical and Electronic Engineering
GEVECİ, A., Metallurgical Engineering
GÖĞÜŞ, M., Civil Engineering
GÖKÇAY, C. F., Environmental Engineering
GÖKLER, M. İ., Mechanical Engineering
GÖNCÜOĞLU, C., Geological Engineering
GÜLEÇ, N., Geological Engineering
GÜLKAN, P., Civil Engineering
GÜMRAH, F., Petroleum and Natural Gas Engineering
GÜNALP, T. N., Electrical and Electronic Engineering
GÜNDÜZ, G., Chemical Engineering
GÜRAN, H., Electrical and Electronic Engineering
GÜRBUZ, R., Metallurgical Engineering
GÜRKAN, T., Chemical Engineering
GÜRÜZ, G., Chemical Engineering
GÜVEN, A. N., Electrical and Electronic Engineering
GÜVEN, Ç., Industrial Engineering
GÜYAGÜLER, T., Mining Engineering
HALICI, U., Electrical and Electronic Engineering
HAMAMCI, H., Food Engineering
HIÇYILMAZ, C., Mining Engineering
HIZAL, A., Electrical and Electronic Engineering
HIZAL, M., Electrical and Electronic Engineering
HOŞTEN, Ç., Mining Engineering
İDER, S. K., Mechanical Engineering
İNAL, A., Civil Engineering
KAFTANOĞLU, B., Mechanical Engineering
KALKANLI, A., Metallurgical Engineering
KARAHANOĞLU, N., Geological Engineering
KARAKAYA, İ., Metallurgical Engineering
KARPUZ, C., Mining Engineering
KAYALIGIL, S., Industrial Engineering
KILIÇ, E. S., Mechanical Engineering
KINCAL, N. S., Chemical Engineering
KIPER, A., Computer Engineering
KIRCA, Ö., Industrial Engineering
KISAKÜREK, B., Chemical Engineering
KOCAOĞLAN, E., Electrical and Electronic Engineering
KOÇYİĞIT, A., Geological Engineering
KÖK, M. V., Petroleum and Natural Gas Engineering
KÖKSALAN, M., Industrial Engineering
KUZUOĞLU, M., Electrical and Electronic Engineering
LEBLEBİCİOĞLU, K., Electrical and Electronic Engineering
MEHMETOĞLU, T., Petroleum and Natural Gas Engineering
OKANDAN, E., Petroleum and Natural Gas Engineering
ORAL, S., Mechanical Engineering
ORÇAN, Y., Engineering Sciences
OSKAY, R., Mechanical Engineering
ÖGEL, B., Metallurgical Engineering
ÖGEL, Z. B. S., Food Engineering
ÖNAL, I., Chemical Engineering
ÖNDER, H., Civil Engineering

ÖZAY, N., Electrical and Electronic Engineering
ÖZBAYOĞLU, G., Mining Engineering
ÖZBELGE, Ö., Chemical Engineering
ÖZBELGE, T., Chemical Engineering
ÖZCEBE, G., Civil Engineering
ÖZENBAŞ, M., Metallurgical Engineering
ÖZGEN, C., Chemical Engineering
ÖZGÖREN, K., Mechanical Engineering
ÖZGÜVEN, N., Mechanical Engineering
ÖZHAN, E., Civil Engineering
ÖZKAN, M. Y., Civil Engineering
ÖZTÜRK, A., Metallurgical Engineering
ÖZTÜRK, T., Metallurgical Engineering
PARLAKTUNA, M., Petroleum and Natural Gas Engineering
PARNAS, L., Mechanical Engineering
PAYKOÇ, E., Mechanical Engineering
PLATİN, B. E., Mechanical Engineering
POLAT, F., Computer Engineering
SAATÇIOĞLU, Ö., Industrial Engineering
SAKA, M. P., Engineering Sciences
SARIOĞLU, F., Metallurgical Engineering
SAYAN, G. T., Electrical and Electronic Engineering
SELÇUK, E., Metallurgical Engineering
SELÇUK, N., Chemical Engineering
ŞENDİL, U., Civil Engineering
SEVERCAN, M., Electrical and Electronic Engineering
SEVAIOĞLU, O., Electrical and Electronic Engineering
SEVERCAN, M., Electrical and Electronic Engineering
SEVİNÇ, N., Metallurgical Engineering
SEVUK, A. S., Civil Engineering
ŞORMAN, A. Ü., Civil Engineering
SOYLU, R., Mechanical Engineering
SÖYLEMEZ, E., Mechanical Engineering
SOYLU, R., Mechanical Engineering
SUCUOĞLU, H., Civil Engineering
SÜRÜCÜ, G., Environmental Engineering
TANIK, Y., Electrical and Electronic Engineering
TANKUT, A. T., Civil Engineering
TEKİN, E., Metallurgical Engineering
TİMUÇİN, M., Metallurgical Engineering
TOKDEMİR, T., Engineering Sciences
TOKER, C., Electrical and Electronic Engineering
TOKYAY, M., Civil Engineering
TOPKAYA, Y., Metallurgical Engineering
TOSUN, İ., Chemical Engineering
TOPRAK, G. M. V., Geological Engineering
TULUNAY, E., Electrical and Electronic Engineering
TULUNAY, Y., Aeronautical Engineering
TUNCEL, G., Environmental Engineering
TÜMER, T. S., Mechanical Engineering
TUNCER, İ. H., Aeronautical Engineering
TURHAN, D., Engineering Science
TÜRKMENOĞLU, A. G., Geological Engineering
UNGAN, S., Food Engineering
UTKU, M., Civil Engineering
ÜÇTUĞ, Y., Electrical and Electronic Engineering
ÜNAL, E., Mining Engineering
ÜNER, D., Chemical Engineering
ÜNLÜ, K., Environmental Engineering
ÜNLÜSOY, Y. S., Mechanical Engineering
ÜNVER, Z., Electrical and Electronic Engineering
VURAL, F. T., Computer Engineering
VURAL, H., Mechanical Engineering
YALABIK, N., Computer Engineering
YAMAN, Y., Aeronautical Engineering
YANMAZ, M. A., Civil Engineering
YAZICI, A., Computer Engineering
YAZICIGİL, H., Geological Engineering
YEŞİN, A. O., Mechanical Engineering
YEŞİN, T., Mechanical Engineering
YETİŞ, U., Environmental Engineering
YILDIRIM, N., Electrical and Electronic Engineering
YILDIRIM, R. O., Mechanical Engineering

YILDIZ, F., Food Engineering
YILMAZ, Ç., Civil Engineering
YILMAZ, L., Chemical Engineering
YILMAZER, Ü., Chemical Engineering
YÜCEL, H., Chemical Engineering
YÜCEMEN, M. S., Civil Engineering
YÜKSEL, Y. Ö., Electrical and Electronic Engineering
YÜNCÜ, H., Mechancial Engineering

Graduate School of Marine Sciences (33731 Erdemli; tel. (324) 521-21-50; fax (324) 521-23-27; e-mail ilkay@imf.metu.edu.tr; internet www.ims.metu.edu.tr):

BİNGEL, F., Marine Sciences
KIDEYŞ, E. A., Marine Sciences
LATIF, M. A., Marine Sciences
OĞUZ, I. T., Marine Sciences
ÖZSOY, E., Marine Sciences
TUĞRUL, S., Marine Sciences
YILMAZ, A., Marine Sciences

ATTACHED RESEARCH CENTRES

Applied Ethics Research Centre: Dir CANAN ÖZGEN.

Audiovisual Research and Production Centre: Dir BİLGEHAN ÖGEL.

BİLTİR CAD/CAM/Robotics Application and Research Centre: Dir MUSTAFA GÖKLER.

Central Laboratory: Dir ÇIĞDEM ERÇELEBİ.

Centre for Black Sea and Central Asian Countries: Dir AYŞE AYATA.

Centre for Continuing Education: Dir HÜSEYIN VURA.

Centre for Research and Assessment of the Historic Environment: Dir NUMAN TUNA.

Centre for Welding Technology and Non-Destructive Testing: Dir ALPAY ANKARA.

Construction Industry Training and Research Centre: Dir UĞUR POLAT.

Disaster Management Implementation and Research Centre: Dir POLAT GÜLKAN.

METU–Southeast Anatolia Project Research Centre: Dir NURUNNİSA USUL.

Modelling and Simulation Centre: Dir MÜSLÜM BOZYIĞIT.

Petroleum Research Centre: Dir ENDER OKANDAN.

Research Centre for Science and Technology Policies: Dir ERKAN ERDIL.

OSMANGAZİ ÜNİVERSİTESİ

Meşelik Kampüsü, 26480 Eskişehir
Telephone: (222) 239-49-37
Fax: (222) 229-14-18
E-mail: ogubim@ogu.edu.tr
Internet: www.ogu.edu.tr
Founded 1970
State control
Languages of instruction: Turkish, English
Academic year: October to September
Chancellor (vacant)
Vice-Chancellor (vacant)
Rector: Prof. Dr NECAT A. AKGUN
Vice-Rectors: Prof. Dr MACIT YAMAN, Prof. Dr ATİLLA YILDIRIM
Registrar: ESAT ÇELİK
Library of 33,883 books, 7,521 periodicals
Number of teachers: 866
Number of students: 8,790 (7,930 undergraduate, 860 postgraduate)
Publications: *Journal of the Faculty of Engineering and Architecture* (2 a year), *Journal of the Faculty of Medicine* (2 a year)

DEANS

Faculty of Agriculture: Prof. Dr YAŞAR PANCAR

Faculty of Arts and Sciences: Prof. Dr YALÇIN ŞAHİN
Faculty of Economic and Administrative Sciences: Prof. Dr FAZIL TEKİN
Faculty of Education: Prof. Dr NACİ EKEM
Faculty of Engineering and Architecture: Prof. Dr ERCENGİZ YILDIRIM
Faculty of Medicine: Prof. Dr EROL GÖKTÜRK
Faculty of Theology: Prof. Dr MEHMET MAKSUDOĞLU

PAMUKKALE ÜNİVERSİTESİ

İncilipmar Campus, 20020 Denizli
Telephone: (258) 212-55-55
Fax: (258) 212-55-31
E-mail: pamukkale@pamukkale.edu.tr
Internet: www.pamukkale.edu.tr
State control

Rector: Prof. Dr HASAN KAZDAĞLI
Vice-Rectors: Prof. Dr HÜSEYIN BAĞCI, Prof. Dr YIĞIT GÜNDÜÇ, Prof. Dr İNAN ÖZER

DEANS

Faculty of Arts and Sciences: Prof. Dr LATIF ELÇİ
Faculty of Economic and Administrative Sciences: Prof. Dr İNAN ÖZER
Faculty of Education: Prof. Dr HÜSEYIN KIRAN
Faculty of Engineering: Prof. Dr SEBAHATTİN NAS
Faculty of Medicine: Prof. Dr HÜSEYIN BAĞCİ
Faculty of Technical Education: Prof. Dr YIĞIT GÜNDÜÇ

SABANCI ÜNİVERSİTESİ

Orhanli, 34956 Tuzla, Istanbul
Telephone: (216) 483-90-00
Fax: (216) 483-90-05
E-mail: db@sabanciuniv.edu
Internet: www.sabanciuniv.edu
Founded 1994
Private control
Languages of instruction: English, Turkish
Academic year: October to July
Rector: Prof. TOSUN TERZIOĞLU
General Secretary: HALUK BAL
Librarian: HILMI ÇELIK
Library of 60,000 vols, 56 databases
Number of teachers: 410
Number of students: 2,010

DEANS

Faculty of Arts and Social Sciences: Prof. AHMET ALKAN
Faculty of Engineering and Natural Sciences: Prof. KEMAL İNAN
Graduate School of Management: Prof. NAKIYE AVDAN BOYACIGILLER

ATTACHED CENTRES

Istanbul Policy Centre: Dir Prof. Dr USTUN ERGUDER.

Sabanci University Sakıp Sabancı Museum: Dir Dr NAZAN RAIBE OLCER.

SAKARYA ÜNİVERSİTESİ

Esentepe Kampüsü, 54187 Sakarya
Telephone: (264) 295-54-54
Fax: (264) 295-50-36
E-mail: basin@sakarya.edu.tr
Internet: www.sakarya.edu.tr
Founded 1992
State control
Languages of instruction: Turkish, English
Academic year: September to June
Rector: Prof. Dr MEHMET DURMAN
Vice-Rectors: Prof. Dr MEHMET ALPARGU, Prof. Dr MUZAFFER ELMAS, Prof. Dr H. RIZA GÜVEN

Rector: Dr Zafer Demir
Library of 50,000 vols
Number of teachers: 1,130
Number of students: 36,000
Publication: *Saü Bulletin*

DEANS

Faculty of Arts and Sciences: Prof. Dr Mehmet Alpargu
Faculty of Economic and Administrative Sciences: Prof. Dr Engin Yildirim
Faculty of Education: Prof. Vahdettin Sevinç
Faculty of Engineering: Prof. Dr Mehmet Ali Yalçin
Faculty of Fine Arts: Prof. Dr Ayşe Üstün
Faculty of Technical Education: Prof. Dr Hüseyin Ekiz
Faculty of Theology: Prof. Dr Ali Erbaşi

SELÇUK ÜNİVERSİTESİ

Vali Izzetbey Cad., Karatay Müzesi Karşisi, 42151 Konya
Telephone: (332) 350-70-05
Fax: (332) 352-09-98
E-mail: mesaj@selcuk.edu.tr
Internet: www.selcuk.edu.tr
Founded 1975
State control
Language of instruction: Turkish
Academic year: October to May
Rector: Prof. Dr Süleyman Okudan
Vice-Rectors: Prof. Dr Dinçer Bedük, Prof. Dr Şefik Bilir
Secretary-General: Assoc. Prof. Dr Kürşat Turgut
Librarian: Dr Ali Özgökmen
Number of teachers: 2,751
Number of students: 67,000
Publications: *Journal of Engineering and Architecture* (4 a year), *Journal of the Faculty of Medicine* (4 a year), *Journal of Veterinary Science* (6 a year)

DEANS

Faculty of Agriculture: Prof. Dr Mehmet Kara
Faculty of Arts and Sciences: Prof. Dr Mehmet Kara
Faculty of Communication: Prof. Dr Dursun Ali Dinç
Faculty of Dentistry: Prof. Dr Adnan Öztürk
Faculty of Economics and Administrative Sciences: Prof. Dr Coşkun Atayeter
Faculty of Economics and Administrative Sciences (Konya): Prof. Dr Orhan Gökçe
Faculty of Education: Prof. Dr Ömer Üre
Faculty of Engineering and Architecture: Prof. Dr Ali Sinan
Faculty of Fine Arts: Prof. Dr Behiç Coşkun
Faculty of Law: Prof. Dr Zehra Odyakmaz
Faculty of Medicine (Meram): Prof. Dr Uğur Erongun
Faculty of Medicine (Selcuklu): Prof. Dr Safa Kapicioğlu
Faculty of Science and Humanities: Prof. Dr Ramazan Özgan
Faculty of Technical Education: Prof. Dr Hüseyin Öğüt
Faculty of Theology: Prof. Dr Mehmet Aydin
Faculty of Veterinary Sciences: Prof. Dr Veysi Aslan
Faculty of Vocational Education: Prof. Dr Filiz Gündüz

ATTACHED INSTITUTES

Institute of Health Sciences: Dir Prof. Dr Saadettin Tipirdamaz.
Institute of Natural and Applied Sciences: Dir Prof. Dr Mustafa Yilmaz.
Institute of Social Sciences: Dir Assoc. Prof. Dr Remzi Duran.

Institute of Turkish Studies: Dir Assoc. Prof. Dr Yakup Karasoy.

SÜLEYMAN DEMİREL ÜNİVERSİTESİ

Merkez Kampüs, Çünür, 32260 Isparta
Telephone: (246) 211-10-00
Fax: (246) 237-04-31
E-mail: yaziisler@sdu.edu.tr
Internet: www.sdu.edu.tr
Founded 1992
State control
Academic year: September to July
Rector: Prof. Dr Metin Lutfi Baydar
Vice-Rectors: Prof. Dr İsmail Karaca, Prof. Dr Vecihi Kirdemir
General Secretary: Ahmet Tevfik Köse
Librarian: Uğur Bulgan
Library of 65,000 vols, 2,700 periodicals
Number of teachers: 1,850
Number of students: 44,000
Publications: *European Journal of Mineral Processing and Environmental Protection* (3 a year), *Journal of the Faculty of Administrative Sciences and Education* (in Turkish, 2 a year), *Journal of the Faculty of Forestry* (in Turkish, 2 a year), *Journal of Natural and Applied Sciences* (in Turkish, annually), *Medical Journal* (in Turkish, 4 a year)

DEANS

Faculty of Administrative Sciences and Economics: Prof. Dr Bilal Murat Özgüven
Faculty of Agriculture: Prof. Dr M. Atilla Aşkin
Faculty of Arts and Sciences: Prof. Dr Nurten Özçelik
Faculty of Dentistry: Prof. Dr M. Üstün Güldağ
Faculty of Education in Burdur: Prof. Dr Gökay Yildiz
Faculty of Engineering and Architecture: Prof. Dr Saim Saraç
Faculty of Fine Arts: Prof. Dr Kubilay Aktulum
Faculty of Fisheries in Eğirdir: Prof. Dr Öznur Diler
Faculty of Forestry: Prof. Dr Koray Sönmez
Faculty of Medicine: Prof. Dr Nevres Hürriyet Aydoğan
Faculty of Technical Education: Prof. Dr S. Nilay Keskin
Faculty of Theology: Prof. Dr Ekrem Sarikçioğlu
College of Health Sciences in Burdur: Prof. Dr Mehmet Zeki Yildirim
College of Health Sciences in Isparta: Prof. Dr Necat Imirzalioğlu
Institute of Basic Sciences: Prof. Dr Çiğdem Savaşkan
Institute of Health Sciences: Prof. Dr Halis Köylü
Institute of Social Sciences: Doç. Dr Mevlüt Albayrak

ATTACHED RESEARCH INSTITUTES

Agricultural Research and Implementation Centre.
Botanic Field and Herbarium Research and Implementation Centre.
CAD/CAM Implementation Centre.
Cancer Early Diagnosis Centre.
Centre for Strategic Research.
Ceramics Research and Implementation Centre.
Computer Sciences Research and Implementation Centre.
Continuous Education Research and Implementation Centre.
Earthquake and Geotechnics Research and Implementation Centre.

EU Documentation Research and Implementation Centre.
Experimental and Observatory Student Research and Implementation Centre.
Fashion Design and Ready-made Clothes Research and Implementation Centre.
Groundwater and Mineral Resources Research and Implementation Centre.
Music Culture Research and Implementation Centre.
Principles of Atatürk and History of the Turkish Revolution Research and Implementation Centre.
Pumice Research and Implementation Centre.
Radio and Television Research and Implementation Centre.
Remote Sensing Research and Implementation Centre.
Renewable Energy Resources Centre for Research and Application.
Research and Implementation Centre for Geothermal Energy.
Research and Implementation Hospital.
Rose and Rose Products Research and Implementation Centre.
Technological Materials Research & Development and Calibration Centre.
Turkish Language Research and Implementation Centre.
Women's Studies Research and Implementation Centre.

TRAKYA ÜNİVERSİTESİ

22050 Karaağaç, Edirne
Telephone: (284) 214-40-10
Fax: (284) 214-42-03
E-mail: rektorluk@trakya.edu.tr
Internet: www.trakya.edu.tr
Founded 1982 from existing faculties in Edirne
Academic year: October to June
Rector: Prof. Dr Enver Duran
Vice-Rectors: Prof. Dr Beyhan Karamanlioğlu, Prof. Dr Nizamettin Şenköylü, Prof. Dr Oğuz Taşkinalp
Librarian: Ender Bilar
Number of teachers: 1,428
Number of students: 23,809 full-time, 3,202 evening
Publications: *Journal of the Faculty of Agriculture* (2 a year), *Journal of the Faculty of Medicine* (4 a year), *Trakya University Journal of Scientific Research* (2 a year)

DEANS

Faculty of Agricultural Engineering (Tekirdağ): Prof. Birol Kayişoğlu
Faculty of Arts and Sciences: Prof. Nihat Aktaç
Faculty of Economics and Administrative Sciences: Prof. Sudi Apak
Faculty of Education: Prof. Nihat Aktaç
Faculty of Engineering (Çorlu): Prof. Ataman Haksever
Faculty of Engineering and Architecture: Prof. H. Erol Akata
Faculty of Medicine: Prof. Filiz Akata

ATTACHED INSTITUTES

Health Sciences Institute: Dir Prof. Dr Ismet Dökmeci.
Natural Sciences Institute: Dir Prof. Dr Ahmet Cihan.
Social Sciences Institute: Dir Prof. Dr Ilker Alp.

UFUK ÜNİVERSİTESİ

Mevlana Bulvarı (Konya Yolu) 86-88, 06520
  Balgat, Ankara

Telephone: (312) 284-77-77
Fax: (312) 287-23-90
E-mail: ufukuni@ufuk.edu.tr
Internet: www.ufuk.edu.tr

Founded 1972; present name and status 1999

Rector: Prof. Dr A. ERGÜN ERTUĞ
General Secretary: İSMET ATIK

Number of teachers: 23
Number of students: 66

Faculties of Arts and Science, Economics and
  Administration, Education, Law and Medicine.

ULUDAĞ ÜNİVERSİTESİ

Görükle Kampüsü, Rektörlük Uluslararası
  İlişkiler Ofisi, 16059 Bursa

Telephone: (224) 442-80-06
Fax: (224) 442-90-44
E-mail: intoffice@uludag.edu.tr
Internet: www.uludag.edu.tr

Founded 1975 as Bursa Üniversitesi; present
  name and structure 1982
State control
Language of instruction: Turkish
Academic year: September to June

Rector: Prof. Dr MUSTAFA YURTKURAN
Vice-Rectors: Prof. Dr ERDAL EMEL, Prof. Dr
  MEHMET GENÇ, Prof. Dr ALİ KARABULUT
Secretary-General: İSMET TOPUZ
Head of Libraries and Documentation Cen-
  tre: NEŞE ARAT

Library of 67,493 vols
Number of teachers: 2,102
Number of students: 41,057

Publications: *Agriculture* (annually), *Education* (annually), *Engineering* (annually),
  Medicine (annually), *Science and Literature* (annually), *Theology* (annually), *Veterinary Science* (annually)

DEANS

Faculty of Agriculture: Prof. Dr VAHAP
  KATKAT
Faculty of Economics and Administrative
  Sciences: Prof. Dr HALİS ERTÜRK
Faculty of Education: Prof. Dr MUSTAFA
  CEMİLOĞLU
Faculty of Engineering and Architecture:
  Prof. Dr SEDAT ÜLKÜ
Faculty of Medicine: Prof. Dr MÜFİT PARLAK
Faculty of Science and Letters: Prof. Dr
  MUSTAFA BAYRAKTAR
Faculty of Theology: Prof. Dr HÜSEYİN ALGÜL
Faculty of Veterinary Medicine: Prof. Dr
  HASAN BATMAZ

HEADS OF DEPARTMENTS

Faculty of Agriculture (tel. (224) 442-89-70;
fax (224) 442-80-77; e-mail ziraat@uludag
.edu.tr):

  Agricultural Construction and Irrigation:
    Prof. Dr İSMET ARICI
  Agricultural Economics: Prof. Dr ERKAN
    REHBER
  Agricultural Machines: Prof. Dr KAMİL
    ALİBAŞ
  Animal Husbandry: Prof. Dr ALİ KARABU-
    LUT
  Field Crops: Prof. Dr ESVET AÇIKGÖZ
  Food Science and Technology: Prof. Dr
    FIKRI BAŞOĞLU
  Horticulture: Prof. Dr VEDAT ŞENİZ
  Plant Protection: Prof. Dr NECATİ BAYKAL
  Soil Science: Prof. Dr AHMET ÖZGÜMÜŞ

Faculty of Economics and Administrative
Sciences (tel. (224) 442-89-40; fax (224) 442-
80-88; internet iktisat.uludag.edu.tr):

  Econometrics: Prof. Dr AHMET ÖZTÜRK

Economics: Prof. Dr ERCAN DÜLGEROĞLU
Finance: Prof. Dr MEHMET PALAMUT
International Relations: Prof. Dr MEHMET
  GENÇ
Labour Economics and Industrial Rela-
  tions: Prof. Dr YUSUF ALPER
Management: Prof. Dr ZEYYAT SABUNCUO-
  ĞLU
Public Administration: Prof. Dr HASAN
  ERTÜRK

Faculty of Education (tel. (224) 442-92-04;
fax (224) 442-92-14; internet egitim.uludag
.edu.tr):

  Computer Teaching Appliances: Yrd. Doç.
    Dr AYSAN ŞENTÜRK
  Education: Doç. Dr ERSİN ALTINTAŞ
  Fine Arts: Prof. Dr AYTEN SÜRÜR
  Foreign Language Education: Prof. Dr
    MUSTAFA DURAK
  Physical Training and Sport: Prof. Dr
    FÜSUN ÖZTÜRK KUTER
  Primary School Teacher Training: Yrd.
    Doç. Dr ASUDE BİLGİN
  Primary School Teaching of Turkish: Prof.
    Dr MUSTAFA CEMİLOĞLU

Faculty of Engineering and Architecture (tel.
(224) 442-81-74; fax (224) 442-80-21; internet
www.mm.uludag.edu.tr):

  Architecture: Doç. Dr NİLÜFER AKINCITÜRK
  Civil Engineering: Prof. Dr SEDAT ÜLKÜ
  Electronics Engineering: Prof. Dr ALİ
    OKTAY
  Environmental Engineering: H. SAVAŞ BAŞ-
    KAYA
  Industrial Engineering: Prof. Dr ERDAL
    EMEL
  Mechanical Engineering: Prof. Dr FERRUH
    ÖZTÜRK
  Textile Engineering: Prof. Dr RIFAT ALPAY

Faculty of Medicine (tel. (224) 442-82-00; fax
(224) 442-80-47; e-mail tipdek@uludag.edu
.tr; internet tip.uludag.edu.tr):

  Basic Medical Sciences: Prof. Dr İSMET KAN
  Internal Medical Sciences: Prof. Dr FARUK
    MEMİK
  Surgical Sciences: Prof. Dr BURÇIN KUTLAY

Faculty of Science and Letters (tel. (224) 442-
92-56; fax (224) 442-80-22; internet fened
.uludag.edu.tr):

  Archaeology and History of Art: Prof. Dr
    ZEREN TANINDI
  Biology: Prof. Dr GÖNÜL KAYNAK
  Chemistry: Prof. Dr NECATİ BEŞİRLİ
  History: Prof. Dr YUSUF OĞUZOĞLU
  Mathematics: Prof. Dr ERTUĞRUL ÖZDAMAR
  Philosophy: Prof. Dr SEVGİ İYİ
  Physics: Prof. Dr AYTAÇ YALÇINER
  Psychology: Prof. Dr NERMİN ÇELEN
  Sociology: Prof. Dr FÜGEN BERKAY
  Turkish Language and Literature: Prof. Dr
    COŞKUN AK

Faculty of Theology (tel. (224) 243-15-70; fax
(224) 243-15-73; internet ilahiyat.uludag.edu
.tr):

  Basic Islamic Sciences: Prof. Dr M. ALİ
    SÖNMEZ
  Islamic History and Arts: Prof. Dr HÜSEYİN
    ALGÜL
  Philosophy and Science of Religion: Prof.
    Dr HÜSEYİN AYDIN
  Primary School Religion and Teaching of
    Ethics: Prof. Dr MEHMET EMİN AY

Faculty of Veterinary Medicine (tel. (224)
442-92-00; fax (224) 442-80-25; internet
veteriner.uludag.edu.tr):

  Animal Husbandry and Feeding: Prof. Dr
    HASAN BAŞPINAR
  Basic Sciences of Veterinary Medicine:
    Prof. Dr ALİ BAHADIR
  Diseases and Clinics: Prof. Dr SELAHATTIN
    CEYLAN

YAŞAR ÜNİVERSİTESİ

Şehitler Cad. 1522, Sok 6, 35230 Alsancak,
  Izmir

Telephone: (232) 463-33-44
Fax: (232) 463-07-80
E-mail: info@yasar.edu.tr
Internet: www.ufuk.edu.tr

Founded 1998; present status 2001

Rector: Prof. Dr NECATİ SEN
General Secretary: DIDEM ÖKTEM

DEANS

Faculty of Business Economics and Admin-
  istration: Prof. Dr CENGIZ PINAR
Faculty of Communications: Prof. Dr CENGIZ
  PINAR (Deputy)
Faculty of Engineering and Architecture:
  Prof. Dr DEMIR ASLAN
Faculty of Law: Prof. Dr DEMIR ASLAN
  (Deputy)
Faculty of Science and Letters: Prof. Dr
  COŞKUN IŞCI

DIRECTORS

School of Foreign Languages: Asst Prof. Dr
  SENA TULPAR
Vocational School: Prof. Dr HASAN HÜSNÜ
  ÇATALCA

DIRECTORS OF GRADUATE SCHOOLS

Institute of Natural Sciences: Prof. Dr FEVZI
  ÜNLÜ
Institute of Social Sciences: Prof. Dr FEVZI
  ÜNLU (Deputy)

YEDİTEPE ÜNİVERSİTESİ

26 Agustos Yerlesimi, 81120 Kayisdagi,
  İstanbul

Telephone: (216) 578-00-00
Fax: (216) 578-02-44
E-mail: halklailiskiler@yeditepe.edu.tr
Internet: www.yeditepe.edu.tr

Founded 1997
Private control

Rector: Prof. Dr AHMET SERPİL
Vice-Rectors: Prof. Dr ATILLA DICLE (Pro-
  vost), Prof. Dr NILÜFER EĞRICAN, Prof. Dr
  SEDEFHAN OĞUZ
Secretary-General: MINE ÇAKALOZ
Number of students: 14,000

DEANS

Faculty of Architecture and Engineering:
  İBRAHIM FAHIR BORAK
Faculty of Arts and Sciences: Prof. Dr AHMET
  İNCE
Faculty of Commercial Sciences: Prof. Dr F.
  ÖMER GÖKAY
Faculty of Communication: Prof. Dr SUAT
  ANAR
Faculty of Dentistry: Prof. Dr TURKER SAN-
  DALLI
Faculty of Economics and Administrative
  Sciences: Prof. Dr HALUK ÜLMAN
Faculty of Education: Prof. Dr ÖMÜR AKYÜZ
Faculty of Fine Arts: Prof. Dr BIKE KOCAOĞLU
Faculty of Law: Prof. Dr HALUK KABAALIOĞLU
Faculty of Medicine: Prof. Dr ORAL PEKTAŞ
Faculty of Pharmacy: Prof. Dr DILEK EROL

YILDIZ TEKNİK ÜNİVERSİTESİ

80750 Beşiktaş, İstanbul

Telephone: (212) 259-70-70
Fax: (212) 261-42-84
E-mail: uerden@yildiz.edu.tr
Internet: www.yildiz.edu.tr

Founded 1911; reorganized 1982 (fmrly State
  Academy of Engineering and Architecture)
Academic year: October to July

Rector: Prof. Dr DURUL ÖREN

Vice-Rectors: Prof. Dr GÖRÜN ARUN (Research and Planning), Prof. Dr SALIH DURER (Administration), Prof. Dr ZEKERIYA POLAT (Education)
Secretary-General: ÜMIT ERDEN
Number of teachers: 1,111
Number of students: 17,000
Publication: *Periodical* (4 a year)

DEANS

Faculty of Architecture: Prof. Dr EMRE AYSU
Faculty of Art and Design: Prof. Dr TOMUR ATAGÖK
Faculty of Arts and Sciences: Prof. Dr DURUL OREN
Faculty of Chemical and Metallurgical Engineering: Prof. Dr SABRIYE PIŞKIN
Faculty of Civil Engineering: Prof. Dr YALÇIN YÜKSEL
Faculty of Economic and Administrative Sciences: Prof. Dr AYKUT POLATOĞLU
Faculty of Electrical and Electronic Engineering: Prof. Dr GALIP CANSEVER
Faculty of Mechanical Engineering: Prof. Dr HASAN HEPERKAN

ATTACHED INSTITUTES

Institute of Science and Technology: Dir Prof. Dr HÜSEYIN DEMIREL.

Institute of Social Sciences: Dir Prof. Dr MEHMET SÜMER.

ATTACHED COLLEGES

School of Foreign Languages: Dir Prof. Dr NÜKET ÖCAL.

School of Vocational Studies: Dir Assoc. Prof. Dr MUSTAFA SUNU.

YÜZÜNCÜ YIL ÜNİVERSİTESİ
(Centennial University)

65080 Van

Telephone: (432) 225-10-10
Fax: (432) 225-10-09
E-mail: yyu@yyu.edu.tr
Internet: www.yyu.edu.tr

Founded 1982
State control
Language of instruction: Turkish
Academic year: October to July

Rector: Prof. Dr YÜCEL AŞKIN
Vice-Rectors: Prof. Dr HASAN CEYLAN, Prof. Dr ALI FUAT DOĞU, Prof. Dr AYŞE YÜKSEL
General Secretary: Dr IŞIK TEPE
Librarian (vacant)

Library of 31,000 vols
Number of teachers: 300
Number of students: 6,100

Publications: *Artos* (Universities and Colleges in Literature, annually), *Eastern Journal of Physical Medicine and Rehabilitation* (monthly), *Journal of Agricultural Sciences* (annually), *Journal of the Faculty of Arts and Sciences (Sciences)* (irregular), *Journal of the Faculty of Education*

(Sciences) (monthly), *Journal of the Faculty of Education (Social Sciences)* (monthly), *Journal of the Faculty of Theology* (monthly), *Journal of the Faculty of Veterinary Science* (monthly), *Journal of the Graduate School of Sciences* (irregular), *Journal of Health Sciences* (monthly), *Journal of the Institute of Social Sciences* (irregular), *Rahva* (education, monthly), *University Bulletin* (monthly), *Van Medical Journal* (monthly), *Yeldegirmeni* (arts, monthly)

DEANS

Faculty of Agriculture: Prof. Dr FIRAT CENGIZ
Faculty of Arts and Sciences: Prof. Dr ERKSIN GÜLEÇ
Faculty of Economic and Administrative Sciences: Prof. Dr BÜLENT KARAKAŞ
Faculty of Education: Prof. Dr RAUF YILDIZ
Faculty of Education (Hakkari): Prof. Dr RECAI KARAHAN
Faculty of Engineering: Prof. Dr A. ÜMIT TOLLUOĞLU
Faculty of Fine Arts: Prof. Dr ZÜHRE ŞENTÜRK
Faculty of Medicine: Prof. Dr MANSUR KAMACI
Faculty of Theology: Prof. Dr SELAHATTIN KIYICI
Faculty of Veterinary Science: Prof. Dr NIHAT MERT

PROFESSORS

Faculty of Agriculture:

AKYUZ, N.
ASKIN, Y.
COKSOYLER, N.
ŞEN, S. M.
YASAR, B.

Faculty of Arts and Science:

AMIRALI, G.
CEYLAN, H.
KARAKAS, B.
ONLER, Z.
OZTURK, A.
RASIMGIL, R.
TILEKLIOĞLU, B.
ULUCAM, A.
YILMAZ, A.

Faculty of Education:

SAVAS, E.
TOZLU, N.

Faculty of Engineering:

ORCEN, S.
TOLLUOĞLU, A. U.

Faculty of Medicine:

AKSOY, H.
ATAY, G.
BURDURLU, Y.
CEYLAN, A.
DALKILIC, A. E.
DEMIRORS, A. P.
GOKSOY, T.
KAMACI, M.

ODABAS, D.
TURAN, F.
YAKUT, C.
YETKIN, Y.
YUKSEL, A.

Faculty of Veterinary Science:

AGAOĞLU, Z. T.
BOLAT, D.
BOYNUKARA, B.
KARADAG, H.
MERT, N.

ATTACHED INSTITUTES

Health Sciences.
Sciences.
Social Sciences.

ZONGULDAK KARAELMAS ÜNİVERSİTESİ

67100 Zonguldak

Telephone: (372) 257-41-30
Fax: (372) 257-21-40
Internet: www.karaelmas.edu.tr

Founded 1992
State control
Academic year: September to July

Rector: Prof. Dr BEKTAŞ AÇIKGÖZ
Vice-Rectors: Prof. Dr TURGAY ATALAY, Prof. Dr H. YILMAZ KAPTAN, Prof. Dr YADIGAR MÜFTÜOĞLU
Chief Librarian: FATMA CEYLAN

Library of 35,000 vols, 12,000 periodicals
Number of teachers: 1,194
Number of students: 10,194 full-time, 2,143 evening

Publications: *Journal of the Faculty of Engineering* (4 a year), *Journal of the Faculty of Forestry* (2 a year)

DEANS

Faculty of Arts and Science (Devrek): Prof. Dr TÜRKAN KOPAÇ
Faculty of Economics and Administration (Çaycuma): Prof. Dr GÜVEN MURAT
Faculty of Education (Ereğli): Prof. Dr BAKI HAZER
Faculty of Engineering: Prof. Dr H. YILMAZ KAPTAN
Faculty of Forestry (Bartın): Prof. Dr HÜDAVERDI EROĞLU
Faculty of Medicine: Prof. Dr GAMZE MOÇAN KUZEY
Faculty of Technical Education (Karabük): Prof. Dr ETEM SAIT ÖZ

DIRECTORS

Graduate School of Health Sciences: Prof. Dr Z. NUR BANOĞLU
Graduate School of Natural and Applied Sciences: Prof. Dr ETEM KIŞIOĞLU
Graduate School of Social Sciences: Prof. Dr TURHAN KORKMAZ

TURKMENISTAN

The Higher Education System

Institutions of higher education pre-date the independence of Turkmenistan (formerly Turkmen SSR) from the USSR in 1991, with the oldest being the Turkmen State Medical Institute, which was founded in 1932. Following independence, a policy of bilim (education) was initiated, aimed at distancing Turkmenistan from its Soviet (and hence, Russian) past; a key element in this policy was the reformation of the Turkmen language, primarily through the substitution of the Latin for the Cyrillic alphabet. Free education at Turkmenistan's universities was reported to have been abolished in 2003, while it was reported that the number of places for students in educational establishments had been sharply reduced since the mid-1990s. In 2004 a presidential decree invalidating all higher-education degrees received abroad came into effect; all teachers with such degrees were to be dismissed.

The main requirements for admission to higher education are the Secondary School Leaving Certificate and results in competitive entrance examinations. The main undergraduate qualifications are the Soviet-style Specialist Diploma, which lasts five years, and the Bachelors (Bakalavr), which lasts four years. Prior to university, students are expected to complete a period of work experience. There is no postgraduate education in Turkmenistan.

Post-secondary technical and vocational education consists of short-term courses of up to one-and-a-half years open to students who have completed nine years of secondary education. Qualifications studied for include Certificates and Diplomas.

Learned Societies

GENERAL

Academy of Sciences of Turkmenistan: 744000 Ashgabat, Neytralny Turkmenistan 15; tel. (12) 25-44-74; fax (12) 25-53-67; Pres. K. A. MAMEDOVICH; Dep. Pres. P. KOUWAN-DYK.

Research Institutes

GENERAL

Institute of Deserts, Flora and Fauna: 744000 Ashgabat, Neytralny Turkmenistan 15; tel. (12) 39-54-27; fax (12) 35-37-16; e-mail desert@online.tm; f. 1962; attached to Min. of Nature Protection; Dir Prof. A. G. BABAYEV; publ. *Problems of Desert Development* (6 a year).

AGRICULTURE, FISHERIES AND VETERINARY SCIENCE

Gara-Kala Experimental Station for Plant Genetic Resources: Balkan, Gara-Kala; tel. (48) 3-17-99; Dir A. SAPARMURADOV.

Scientific Research Institute of Farming: Ashgabat, ul. 2053 30; tel. (12) 34-74-35; fax (12) 35-74-12; Dir O. SOUNOV.

ECONOMICS, LAW AND POLITICS

Institute of Economics: 744032 Ashgabat, Bikrova sad keshi 28; tel. (12) 24-02-52; Dir G. M. MURADOV.

Institute of Philosophy and Law: 744000 Ashgabat, Neytralny Turkmenistan 15; tel. (12) 25-41-69; Dir O. MUSAYEV.

HISTORY, GEOGRAPHY AND ARCHAEOLOGY

Batyrov, S., Institute of History: 744000 Ashgabat, Neytralny Turkmenistan 15; tel. (12) 25-31-38; Dir N. V. ATAMEMEDOV.

Southern Turkmen Multidisciplinary Archaeological Expedition: Ashgabat, Neytralny Turkmenistan 15; tel. (12) 25-15-25; Man. K. KURBANSAKHATOV.

LANGUAGE AND LITERATURE

Bailyev Institute of Linguistics: 744000 Ashgabat, Neytralny Turkmenistan 15; tel. (12) 25-27-73; Dir M. SOYEGOV.

Magtymguly Institute of Literature: 744000 Ashgabat, Neytralny Turkmenistan 15; tel. (12) 25-35-09; Dir A. ORAZOV.

MEDICINE

Institute of Oncology: 744012 Ashgabat, Pervomaiskaya ul. 53; tel. (12) 24-66-45.

Scientific Clinical Center of Eye Diseases: Ashgabat, Ul. 1973 32; tel. and fax (12) 35-48-70; f. 1932; Dir A. SHAMURAT.

Turkmen Research Institute of Preventive and Clinical Medicine: 744006 Ashgabat, 2009 31; tel. (12) 29-01-88; fax (12) 24-11-93; f. 1989; Dir Dr NINA KERIMI.

NATURAL SCIENCES

Biological Sciences

Institute of Botany: 744000 Ashgabat, 2033 79; tel. (12) 25-37-58; Dir K. M. MURADOV.

Institute of Physiology: 744011 Ashgabat, 2053 30; tel. (12) 24-74-18; f. 1959; Dir K. AMMANEPESOV.

Institute of Zoology: 744000 Ashgabat, Ul. Engelsa 6; tel. (12) 25-37-91; Dir T. TOGKAYEV.

Physical Sciences

Institute of Chemistry: 744012 Ashgabat, Ul. Sovetskikh Pogranichnikov 92; tel. (12) 24-05-08; Dir A. KHODZHAMAMEDOV.

Institute of Geology: 744000 Ashgabat, Neytralny Turkmenistan 15; tel. (12) 29-14-85; Dir O. A. ODEKOV.

Research Institute of Seismology: 744000 Ashgabat, 1994 20A; tel. (12) 39-06-92; fax (12) 39-06-13; e-mail gaip@icctm.org; f. 1998; Dir Dr BATYR N. GAIPOV; publ. *Seismological Report* (2 a year).

TECHNOLOGY

Institute of Mathematics and Mechanics: 744000 Ashgabat, Neytralny Turkmenistan 15; tel. (12) 29-87-13; Dir M. B. ORAZOV.

Physical Engineering Institute: 744000 Ashgabat, Neytralny Turkmenistan 15; tel. (12) 25-42-85; Dir A. BERKELIYEV.

Libraries and Archives

Ashgabat

Central Scientific Library of the Academy of Sciences of Turkmenistan: 744007 Ashgabat, Ul. 2002 15A; tel. (12) 35-65-71; f. 1941; 2,130,000 vols; Dir A. B. YAZBERDIYEV.

Magtymguly Turkmen State University Library: 744005 Ashgabat, Sapamurat Turkmenbashi shayely 31; tel. (12) 5-39-22; 542,000 vols; Dir. A. T. VOROBEVA.

National Library of Turkmenistan: 744000 Ashgabat, Pl. 2001; tel. (12) 35-74-89; fax (12) 25-38-43; f. 1895; 5,500,000 vols; Dir MARAL JUMAEVA.

Museums and Art Galleries

Ashgabat

Central Botanical Garden: 744012 Ashgabat, Ul. Timiryazeva 17; tel. (12) 24-18-57; Dir D. KURBANOV.

National Museum of Turkmenistan: 744000 Ashgabat, Novofiruzinskoye 30; tel. (12) 51-90-20; fax (12) 51-90-22; e-mail vip@online.tm; f. 1998 by merger of National Museum of History and Ethnography of Turkmenistan, State Museum of History of Turkmenistan and Turkmen State Museum of Fine Art; history, ethnography, fine art; library of 8,830 vols; Dir OVEZMUHAMED MAMETNUROV.

Universities

MAGTYMGULY TURKMEN STATE UNIVERSITY

744014 Ashgabat, Saparmurat Turkembashi shayely 31

Telephone: (12) 39-89-97

Fax: (12) 35-11-59

E-mail: math3@online.tm

Founded 1950

State control

Rector: ASYRGELDI JUMAYEVICH GULGARAYEV

Pro-Rector: S. A. ATDAYEV

Number of teachers: 544

Number of students: 11,000

Faculties of Russian philology, Turkmen Philology, Foreign Languages, History, Law, Physics, Mathematics, Biology and Geography.

TURKMEN AGRICULTURAL UNIVERSITY

744012 Ashgabat, Ul. 2009 62

Telephone: (12) 34-26-52

Fax: (12) 34-68-80

State control

Library of 136,000 vols

Rector: ANNABERDY MAMEDOV

Depts of Agrochemistry, Fruit and Vegetable Growing, Viticulture, Veterinary Science, Animal Husbandry, Mechanization and Accounting.

Other Higher Educational Institutes

Turkmen Institute of National Economy: 744027 Ashgabat, Atamurad Nyyazov shayely 46; tel. (12) 41-90-36; fax (12) 46-98-05; faculties: economic planning, trade economics, accounting; Rector MUHAMED MAMEDOV.

Turkmen Polytechnic Institute: 744025 Ashgabat, Ul. 1916 62; tel. (12) 47-67-01; fax (12) 47-67-02; faculties: construction, oil, chemical technology, energy, economics, computer technology and sanitation technology; Rector KHYDYRMUHAMMED SAPARLYEV.

Turkmen State Medical Institute: 744001 Ashgabat, Ul. 2028 58; tel. (12) 25-40-96; fax (12) 35-19-53; f. 1932; library: 191,000 vols; Rector Dr KAKAGELDI KHODJANEPESOV.

Turkmen S. Seydi State Pedagogical Institute: 746100 Türkmenabat, Shabende 7; tel. (42) 26-21-30; fax (42) 26-20-31; teacher training, languages; Rector CHARY YAZLYEV.

TUVALU

The Higher Education System

There was no higher education in Tuvalu before 1979. In that year the University of the South Pacific (Fiji) established an extension centre at Funafuti. The Ministry of Education, Sports and Culture in Funafuti is responsible for higher education.

Libraries and Archives

Funafuti

National Library and Archives: POB 36, Funafuti; tel. 20711; fax 20832; depositary library for all govt documents; 19,500 vols, 150 periodicals; Librarian MILA TAFAO.

Parliamentary Library: Tuvalu Parliament, Vaiaku, Funafuti; tel. 20739; fax 20800; f. 1984; Librarian PAULSON PANAPA.

University

UNIVERSITY OF THE SOUTH PACIFIC, TUVALU CENTRE

POB 21, Funafuti
Telephone: 20811
Fax: 20704
E-mail: manuella_d@usp.ac.fj

Internet: www.usp.ac.fj/index.php?id =4502#tuvalu

Founded 1979
Dir: DAVID MANUELLA
Library of 3,000 vols.

UGANDA

The Higher Education System

Institutions of higher education predate Uganda's independence from the United Kingdom in 1962, the oldest being Makerere University in Kampala, which was founded in the 1920s as a technical college for students from British East Africa. After 1949 it was affiliated to University of London (United Kingdom) and in 1970 it was declared an independent university. There is also a university of science and technology at Mbarara, and a small Islamic university is Located at Mbale. Public institutions of higher education receive funding from the Ministry of Education and the Public Sector Commission. In 2004 there were 58,823 students enrolled at 18 universities.

Six passes in the Uganda Advanced Certificate of Education and two passes in the Uganda Certificate of Education are the main requirements for admission to undergraduate degrees. Sub-degree Certificate and Diploma courses lasting one or two years are offered in a range of subjects, often relating to professional fields of study. The principal undergraduate degree is the Bachelors, which is usually a three-year programme of study, although degrees in agriculture, engineering and veterinary science last four years, and degrees in medicine and pharmacy five years. The Bachelors is required for admission to a Masters degree programme. Masters degrees last between 18 months and three years, although gradually two years is becoming the norm. Following the Masters is the Doctorate, the highest university degree, which is awarded after a minimum of three-years' study.

Postsecondary technical and vocational education is offered by a range of institutions, among them technical colleges, colleges of commerce, vocational training institutes and co-operative colleges. There is no national framework of qualifications but awards are broadly classified as Craft, Technician or Higher Technician. The National Council for Higher Education is responsible for accreditation and quality assurance, and institutions seeking to award degrees or other programmes of higher education must fulfil a number of requirements. Once an institution has been awarded a provisional licence by the Council it then has three years to apply for chartered status.

Learned Societies

GENERAL

Uganda Society: POB 4980, Kampala; e-mail NCID@infocom.co.ug; internet www .africa.upenn.edu/ugandasoc/UgandaSociety .htm; f. 1923; present name 1933; premises in the Uganda Museum, Kira Rd, Kampala; membership open to persons of all nationalities and institutions, to promote interest in literary, historic, scientific and general cultural matters, discovering and recording facts about the country, arranging lectures and establishing contacts; library of 1,600 vols and periodicals; Pres. Prof. E. H. K. NSUBUGA; Sec. NANNY CARDER; publ. *The Uganda Journal* (2 a year).

BIBLIOGRAPHY, LIBRARY SCIENCE AND MUSEOLOGY

Uganda Library and Information Association: POB 40227, Kampala; tel. (77) 2495592; fax (41) 2540817; internet www.ou .edu/cas/slis/ULA/ula_index.htm; f. 1972; 356 mems; Chair. MAGARA ELISAM; Sec. C. BATAM-BUZE; publ. *Uganda Library and Information Science Journal* (2 a year).

EDUCATION

Association for Teacher Education in Africa: c/o Assoc. Prof. J. C. B. Bigala, Makerere University, POB 7062, Kampala; f. 1970; to develop and co-ordinate syllabuses and materials to be used in teacher education instns; 50 mem. instns in anglophone Africa; Pres. Prof. M. MOHAPELOA; Sec. Assoc. Prof. J. C. B. BIGALA; publs *Journal of West African Education*, *Education in Eastern Africa*.

Inter-University Council for East Africa: POB 7110, Kampala; tel. (41) 2256251; fax (41) 2342007; e-mail iuc@ infocom.co.ug; internet www.iucea.org; f. 1980 as a corporate body to succeed the Inter-University Committee for East Africa; aims to facilitate contact and co-operation between the universities of Kenya, Tanzania and Uganda, to provide a forum for discussion on academic matters, and to maintain comparable academic standards; also provides secretariat for the Asscn of Eastern and Southern African Universities (see under International); 36 mem. univs and colleges; Chair. Prof. F. I. B. KAYANJA (Vice-Chancellor, Mbarara University of Science and Technology); Exec. Sec. Prof. CHACHA NYAI-GOTTI-CHACHA; publs *Newsletter*, *Report* (annually).

LANGUAGE AND LITERATURE

Alliance Française: National Theatre, 1st Fl., POB 4314, Kampala; tel. (41) 2344490; fax (41) 2349812; e-mail afka@bushnet.net; offers courses and exams in French language and culture and promotes cultural exchange with France.

British Council: Rwenzori Courts, Plot 2 and 4a, Nakasero Rd, POB 7070, Kampala; tel. (41) 2234725; fax (41) 2254853; e-mail info@britishcouncil.or.ug; internet www .britishcouncil.org/uganda; offers courses and exams in English language and British culture and promotes cultural exchange with the UK; library of 5,000 vols, 40 periodicals; Dir KATE EWART-BIGGS.

MEDICINE

Uganda Medical Association: Plot 8, 41–43 Circular Rd, POB 2243, Kampala; tel. (41) 2321795; fax (41) 2345597; e-mail myers28@ hotmail.com; f. 1961; 1,500 mems; library of 700 vols; Pres. Dr MARGARET MUNGHERERA; Sec. Dr MYERS LUGEMWA; publ. *Uganda Medical Journal*.

Research Institutes

AGRICULTURE, FISHERIES AND VETERINARY SCIENCE

Animal Health Research Centre: POB 24, Entebbe; f. 1926; research and field work in animal diseases, husbandry and nutrition; herbarium; library of 13,950 vols; Dir Veterinary Research Services Prof. O. BWANGAMOI; Librarian H. R. KIBOOLE; publs *Research Index* (irregular), *Research Bulletin* (irregular), *Annual Report*.

Kawanda Agricultural Research Institute: POB 7065, Kampala; tel. and fax (41) 2567649; e-mail karidir@imul.com; f. 1937; research on bananas and coffee, horticulture, post-harvest soil and soil fertility management, integrated pest management, biometrics, plant breeding, plant pathology; 9 research staff; library of 2,600 vols; plant herbarium; insect museum; Dir of Research Dr MATTHIAS MAGUNDA.

Nakawa Forestry Research Centre: POB 8668, Kampala; tel. (41) 2256261; fax (41) 2241682; f. 1952; logging, milling and building research; preservation and seasoning tests; small specialized library.

Namulonge Agricultural and Animal Production Research Institute: POB 7084, Kampala; tel. (41) 2573016; fax (75) 2726554; e-mail fopio@naro-ug.org; internet www.naro.go.ug/Institute/Namulonge; f. 1949; aims to increase efficiency and yield of crop and livestock production; specific objectives are genetic improvement of crops and livestock, pest and disease control, management of mandate crops, feed resource development and management for livestock; 127 scientific staff; library of 1,700 vols, 155 periodicals; Dir of Research Dr FINA OPIO.

ECONOMICS, LAW AND POLITICS

Centre for Basic Research: 15 Baskerville Ave, Kololo, POB 9863, Kampala; tel. (41) 2342987; fax (41) 2235413; e-mail cbr@cbr-ug .org; internet www.cbr-ug.org; f. 1988; non-governmental organization active in social research; library of 14,000 vols; Exec. Dir Dr SIMON RUTABAJUUKA.

Makerere Institute of Social Research: POB 16022, Kampala; tel. (41) 2554582; fax (41) 2532821; e-mail misrlib@imul.com; internet www.uganda.co.ug/misr; f. 1948; conducts independent research into social, political and economic problems of East Africa; 6 Research Fellows, University staff in Departments of Economics, Political Science, Rural Economy and Extension, Environmental Studies, Women's Studies, Sociology, Social Work and Social Administration; library of 10,000 vols, 70 current periodicals; Dir Dr NAKANYIKE B. MUSISI;

Research Sec. PATRICK MULINDWA; publs working papers, USSC Conference papers (annually), *East African Studies* (irregular), *East Africa Linguistic Studies* (occasional), *Mawazo Journal* (2 a year), *Policy Abstracts and Research Newsletter*.

MEDICINE

Uganda Virus Research Institute: Entebbe; f. 1936 as Yellow Fever Research Institute; East African Virus Research institute 1950; present name 1977; attached to Uganda National Health Research Organization, under Ministry of Health control; carries out scientific research concerning communicable diseases, especially viral diseases threatening to public health, and advises the government on strategies for disease control and prevention.

NATURAL SCIENCES

Physical Sciences

Geological Survey and Mines Department: Plot 21, 29 Johnstone Rd, POB 9, Entebbe; tel. (41) 2320559; fax (41) 2320364; e-mail gsurvey@starcom.co.ug; f. 1919; library of 22,900 vols; Commissioner J. T. TUHUMWIRE.

Government Chemist Department: POB 2174, Kampala; tel. (41) 2250470; forensic chemical examination, bacteriological examination of foods and water, chemical analysis of water, food and drugs, pollution control, identification and assay of drugs, general chemical analysis of soils and ores, isolation and identification of active principles of medicinal plants; Dir GEOFFREY ONEN.

Libraries and Archives

Kampala

Cabinet Office Library: POB 7168, Kampala; tel. (41) 2254881; fax (41) 2235459; f. 1920; for government officials and for research workers; 10,000 vols; Librarian HERBERT R. KIBOOLE; publ. *Catalogue*.

Forestry Department Library: POB 7124, Kampala; tel. (41) 2347085; fax (41) 2347086; f. 1904; specialized library (open to students by special arrangement with the Commissioner for Forestry): literature on forestry and related sciences; 20,000 vols; Librarian W. M. BWIRUKA; publs *Forest Department Annual Report*, *The Woodsman Newsletter*.

Makerere University, Albert Cook Library: Makerere Medical School, POB 7072, Kampala; tel. (41) 2534149; fax (41) 2530024; e-mail cooklib@med.mak.ac.ug; f. 1946; 55,000 vols, 210 periodicals, covering all medical subjects, especially East African and tropical medicine; special collections: history of medicine, Mengo Notes, WHO publications, database of Ugandan health literature; Acting Deputy Librarian RACHEL NAKALEMBE (acting); publ. *Uganda Health Information Digest* (3 a year).

Makerere University Library Service: POB 16002, Kampala; tel. (41) 2531041; fax (41) 2540374; e-mail info@mulib.mak.ac.ug; internet www.makerere.ac.ug/mulib; f. 1940; consists of a Main Library, functioning as National Reference Library, with seven sub-libraries: five located on the main campus: East African School of Library and Information Science Library, Education Library, Institute of Adult and Continuing Education Library, Makerere Institute of Social Research Library and the Veterinary Library; and two off-campus: Albert Cook Library at the Medical School, Mulago; and Makerere University Agricultural Research Institute Library at the Agricultural Institute, Kabayoro; 384,000 vols, 330 current periodicals, special collections on East Africa, Uganda legal deposit, and private archives; book-bank system of basic textbooks kept in departmental libraries, comprising 182,000 vols; Librarian Dr MARIA G. N. MUSOKE; publ. publs incl. *East African Studies*, *Makerere Law Journal*, *Makerere Political Review*, *Mawazo*.

National Library of Uganda: Buganda Rd, POB 4262, Kampala; tel. (41) 233633; fax (41) 348625; e-mail library@infocom.co.ug; internet www.nlu.go.ug; f. 1964 as Public Libraries Board; present name 2003; organizes the collection and management of the nation's documented heritage, for current and future use; assists local govts in the management of public libraries; provides bibliographic control and aims to promote a reading culture among Ugandans, through reading tents and book donations to schools; provides an information referral service on Uganda; 157,000 vols, 200 serial titles; Dir GERTRUDE KAYAGA MULINDWA; publ. *National Bibliography of Uganda*.

Museums and Art Galleries

Entebbe

Entebbe Botanical Gardens: Lugard Rd, POB 295, Entebbe; tel. (41) 2320638; fax (41) 2321070; e-mail curator@infocom.co.ug; f. 1898; conservation and development of native and exotic plants, collection and planting of local medicinal plants; Curator JOHN MULUMBA-WASSWA; publ. *Index Seminum* (annually).

Game and Fisheries Museum, Aquarium and Library: Johnstone Rd, POB 4, Entebbe; collections of heads of game animals, reptiles, fish and butterflies, hunting and fishing implements and weapons; library of 1,100 vols; Commissioner for Fisheries CHRISTOPHER DHATEMWA; Commissioner for Wildlife MOSES OKUA.

Geological Survey Museum and Documentation Center: POB 9, Entebbe; tel. (41) 2320559; fax (41) 2320364; e-mail minerals@infocom.co.ug; f. 1919; attached to Geological Survey and Mines Department; about 37,500 specimens of rocks and minerals; library of over 9,850 vols and 3,850 periodicals.; Commissioner of the Geological Survey and Mines Department JOSHUA T. TUHUMWIRE.

Uganda Wildlife Education Centre: 56–57 Johnston St POB 369, Entebbe; tel. (41) 2322169; fax (41) 2320073; e-mail info@uweczoo.org; internet www.uweczoo.org; f. 1952; zoological colln of mammals, birds and reptiles; Exec. Dir and Chief Exec. Dr ANDREW G. SEGUYA.

Kampala

Uganda Museum: 5–7 Kira Rd, POB 365, Kampala; tel. (41) 2244060; fax (41) 2245580; f. 1908; natural history, geology, ethnology, archaeology, palaeontology; science and industry pavilion; special collection of African musical instruments; centre for archaeological research in Uganda; library of 4,000 vols; Curator Dr E. KAMUHANGIRE; publ. publs occasional papers, *Annual Report*.

Universities

GULU UNIVERSITY

POB 166, Gulu
Telephone: (47) 2132095
Founded 2002
State control
Language of instruction: English
Rector: JACK H. PEN-MOGI NYOKI
University Secretary: VINCENT M. OKOTH-OGOLA
Number of teachers: 79
Number of students: 640

Faculties of Business Administration, Development Studies and Education.

ISLAMIC UNIVERSITY IN UGANDA

POB 2555, Mbale
Telephone: (45) 2233512
Fax: (45) 2234452
E-mail: iuiumbalecampus@yahoo.com
Founded 1988
Private control
Languages of instruction: English, Arabic
Academic year: October to July
Rector: AHMAD K. SENGENDO
University Secretary: HARUNA KARENG CHE-MISTO
Academic Registrar: SULAIT D. KABALI
Librarian: M. T. ANSARI
Library of 16,500 books, 56 periodicals
Number of teachers: 263
Number of students: 2,705
Publication: *Islamic University Journal* (2 a year)

DEANS

Faculty of Arts and Social Sciences: JERMIL SERWANGA
Faculty of Education: HALIMA AKBAR WAKABI
Faculty of Islamic Studies and Arabic Language: ABDULQADIR BALONDE (acting)
Faculty of Law and Management Studies: HAROONAH NSUBUGA
Faculty of Science: SHAABAN OKRUT

ATTACHED RESEARCH INSTITUTE

Centre for Postgraduate Studies: Dir UMAR AHMAD KASULE.

KAMPALA UNIVERSITY

POB 25454, Kampala
Telephone: (41) 2258219
E-mail: kuniv@afsat.com
Private control
Vice-Chancellor: Prof. BADRU KATEREGA.

KYAMBOGO UNIVERSITY

POB 1, Kyambogo
Telephone: (41) 2285001
Fax: (41) 2220464
Internet: www.kyambogo.ac.ug
Founded 1954 as Uganda Polytechnic Kyambogo; university status 2001 following merger with Institute of Teacher Education Kyambogo and Uganda National Institute for Special Education
State control
Vice-Chancellor: ALBERT JAMES LUTALO-BOSA (acting)
Dean of Students: C. KABAGAMBE
Registrar: A. A. CULA (acting)
Librarian: J. KIYIMBA
Library of 80,000 vols, 10,100 periodicals
Number of students: 9,000

DEANS

Faculty of Arts and Social Sciences: FILDA L. OJOK
Faculty of Education: E. L. GUMISIRIZA
Faculty of Engineering: M. MUGISHA
Faculty of Science: A. WANYAMA
Faculty of Special Needs Education and Rehabilitation: (vacant)
Faculty of Vocational Studies: HABIB KATO

MAKERERE UNIVERSITY

POB 7062, Kampala
Telephone: (41) 2542803
Fax: (41) 2541068
E-mail: helpme@dicts.mak.ac.ug
Internet: www.makerere.ac.ug

Founded 1922 as technical school; became University College 1949, attained University status 1970
State control
Language of instruction: English
Academic year: October to June

Chancellor: H. E. THE PRESIDENT OF UGANDA
Vice-Chancellor: Prof. J. P. SEBUWUFU
Deputy Vice-Chancellor: Prof. J. EPELU-OPIO
Secretary: S. R. BYANAGWA
Academic Registrar: AMOS OLAL-ODUR
Librarian: J. MUGASHA

Number of teachers: 1,089
Number of students: 27,976

Publication: *Mawazo*

DEANS

Faculty of Agriculture: Assoc. Prof. E. N. SABIITI
Faculty of Arts: Dr O. NDOLERIIRE
Faculty of Commerce: WASWA-BALUNYWA
Faculty of Forestry and Nature Conservation: Dr J. KABOGGOZA
Faculty of Law: Assoc. Prof. J. OLOKA-ONYANGO
Faculty of Medicine: Assoc. Prof. N. SEWAN-KEMBO
Faculty of Science: Dr H. ORYEM-ORIGA
Faculty of Social Sciences: Dr JOY KWESIGA
Faculty of Technology: Dr B. M. KIGGUNDU
Faculty of Veterinary Medicine: Assoc. Prof. E. KATUNGA-RWAKISHAYA
School of Education: Dr C. MASEMBE-SSE-BUNGA
Margaret Trowell School of Industrial and Fine Arts: J. MUKASA

HEADS OF DEPARTMENTS

Faculty of Agriculture (tel. (41) 542277; fax (41) 531641; e-mail dean@foamak.ug.com):

Agricultural Economics: Dr B. BASHASHA (acting)
Agricultural Engineering: J. S. KIBALAMA
Agricultural Extension: Dr A. SEMANA (acting)
Animal Science: Prof. D. MUTETTIKA
Crop Science: Dr S. KYAMANYWA
Food Science and Technology: Dr J. K. KIKAFUNDA
Forestry: Dr J. R. S. KABOGGOZA
Soil Science: Dr J. R. F. ANIKU

Faculty of Arts (tel. (41) 542241; fax (41) 542265; e-mail faculty@arts.mak.ac.ug):

Geography: Dr J. B. NYAKAANA (acting)
History: Dr J. MULIRA
Literature: A. KWITONDA
Languages: Dr J. KALEMA
Mass Communications: M. CHIBITA
Music, Dance and Drama: Dr J. L. TAMU-SUZA
Philosophy: Dr J. KIGONGO
Religious Studies: Rev. Dr S. KABAZZI-KISIRINYA

Faculty of Commerce:

Accounting, Banking and Finance: J. KAKURU

Leisure and Hospitality: G. BAKUNDA
Marketing and Management: F. SEMUKONO

Faculty of Law (tel. (41) 542284; fax (41) 543110; e-mail lawdean@muklaw.ac.ug):

Commercial Law: Dr TUMWINE-MUKUBWA
Human Rights and Peace Centre: S. TIN-DIFA
Law and Jurisprudence: F. W. JJUUKO
Public and Comparative Law: Dr J. J. BARYA

Faculty of Medicine (POB 7072, Kampala; tel. (41) 530020; e-mail sewankam@infocom.co.ug):

Anaesthesia: Dr J. B. TINDIMWEBNA
Anatomy: Dr NZARUBARA
Biochemistry: J. P. KABAYO
Child Health and Development: Dr SSEMO-GERERE JITTA
Dentistry: Dr L. M. MUWAZI
Medical Illustration: W. SERUMAGA
Medical Microbiology: Dr C. F. NAJJUKA
Medicine: Dr R. D. MUGERWA
Nursing: S. MBABALI
Obstetrics and Gynaecology: Dr F. MIR-EMBE
Ophthalmology: Dr AMOS MWAKA
Orthopaedics: Dr NADDUMBA
Oto-rhino-laryngology: Dr TUMWEHEIRE
Radiology: M. G. KAWOOYA
Paediatrics: Dr J. S. MUKASA
Pathology: Dr H. R. WABINGA
Pharmacology and Therapeutics: Dr J. W. OGWAL-OKENG
Pharmacy: Dr E. OWINO (acting)
Physiology: J. N. NAKIBONEKA
Psychiatry: Dr G. NAKASI
Surgery: S. KIJAMBU
Institute of Public Health: Dr F. WABWIRE MANGENI

Faculty of Science (tel. (41) 532401; fax (41) 531061; e-mail dean@science.mak.ac.ug):

Biochemistry: Dr F. S. KIRONDE
Botany: Dr BUKENYA-ZIRABA
Chemistry: Prof. H. SEKAALO
Geology: A. MUWANGA
Physics: Dr J. V. M. NGABOYISONGA
Mathematics: Dr F. NABUGOOMU
Zoology: Dr J. B. KADDU

Faculty of Social Sciences (tel. (41) 545040; fax (41) 530815; e-mail deanfss@mak.ac.ug):

Economics: Dr J. ODUMBA-SENTAMU
Political Science: Dr C. N. BWANA
Social Work and Social Administration: N. ASINGWIRE (acting)
Sociology: E. K. KIRUMIRA
Women's Studies: GRACE BANTEBYA

Faculty of Technology (tel. (41) 545029; fax (41) 532780; e-mail dean@techmuk.ac.ug):

Architecture: Dr B. NAWANGWE
Civil Engineering: Dr J. A. MWAKALI
Electrical Engineering: Dr E. LUGUJJO
Mechanical Engineering: KARIKO-BUHWEZI
Surveying: N. A. BATUNGI

Faculty of Veterinary Medicine (tel. (41) 554685; fax (41) 554685; e-mail vetdean@imul.com):

Veterinary Anatomy: Dr B. BUKENYA
Veterinary Medicine: Dr E. K. KYEWALABYE
Veterinary Parasitology and Microbiology: Dr G. LUBEGA
Veterinary Pathology: Prof. OJOK-LONZY
Veterinary Physiological Sciences: Dr T. RUTAGWENDA
Veterinary Public Health and Preventive Medicine: Dr G. M. NASINYAMA
Veterinary Surgery and Reproduction: Dr J. OGAA

School of Education (tel. (41) 540733; e-mail deaneduc@mak.ac.ug):

Curriculum, Teaching and Media: P. MUGOMA (acting)

Educational Foundations and Management: Dr R. R. AKANKWASA
Language Education: MASAAZI MASAGAZI
Science and Technical Education: Dr J. O. OLUKA
Social Science and Arts Education: MAZINGA-KALYANKOLO

PROFESSORS

Faculty of Agriculture (tel. (41) 542277; fax (41) 531641; e-mail dean@foamak.ug.com; internet www.makerere.ac.ug):

ADIPALA-EKWAMU, Crop Science
BAREEBA, F. B., Animal Science
KITUNGULU-ZAKE, Y. J., Soil Science
KIWUWA, G. H., Animal Science
OSIRU, D. O., Crop Science
RUBAIHAYO, P. R.
RUYOOKA, D., Forestry

Faculty of Arts (tel. (41) 542241; fax (41) 542265; e-mail faculty@arts.mak.ac.ug):

BYARUHANGA-AKIIKI, A. B. T., Religious Studies and Philosophy
DALFOVO, A. T., Philosophy
MUKAMA, R.
TIBENDERANA, P. K., History

Faculty of Law (tel. (41) 542284; fax (41) 543110; e-mail lawdean@muklaw.ac.ug):

BAKIBINGA, D. J., Commercial Law
KAKOOZA, J. M. N., Law and Jurisprudence

Faculty of Medicine (tel. (41) 530020; fax (41) 531091; e-mail sewankam@infocom.co.ug):

ANOKBONGGO, W. W., Pharmacology and Therapeutics
BULWA, F. M., Obstetrics and Gynaecology
MMIRO, F. A., Obstetrics and Gynaecology
MUGERWA, J. W., Pathology
MUNUBE, J., Microbiology
NDUGWA, C. M., Paediatrics and Child Health
ODOI-ADOME, R., Pharmacy
OTIM, M. A., Medicine
OWOR, R., Pathology
SWEANKAMBO, N. K., Medicine

Faculty of Science (tel. (41) 541258; fax (41) 531061; e-mail deansci@mak.ac.ug):

BANAGE, W. B., Zoology
BANDA, E. K. J., Physics
ILUKOR, J. O., Physics
KAHWA, Y., Physics
KAKONGE, E., Biochemistry
LUBOOBI, L. S., Mathematics
MUGAMBE, P. E., Physics
MUGAMBI, P. E., Mathematics
OKWAKOL, M. N., Zoology
OLWA-ODYEK, Chemistry
POMEROY, D. E., Zoology
SEKAALO, H., Chemistry
TALIGOOLA, H. K., Botany
TUKAHIRWA, E., Environmental Science

Faculty of Social Sciences (tel. (41) 545040; fax (41) 530815; e-mail deanfss@mak.ac.ug):

AKIIKI-MUJAJU, A. B., Political Science
GINGYERA-PINYCWA, A. C. G., Political Science
MWAKA, V. M.

School of Education (tel. (41) 540733; e-mail deaneduc@mak.ac.ug):

MUSAAZI, J. S., Higher Education
OCITTI, J., Geography
ODAET, C. F., Educational Foundations and Management
OPOLOT, J. A., Psychology

Institute of Statistics and Applied Economics (tel. (41) 534224):

NTOZI, S. P. N.
TULYA-MUHIKA

ATTACHED INSTITUTES AND SCHOOLS

East African School of Librarianship: Kampala; f. 1963 to train librarians for all parts of East Africa; 3-year course leads to degree in Library and Information Science; Dir S. A. H. ABIDI.

Institute of Adult and Continuing Education: Kampala; f. 1953; three divisions: Adult Education and Communication Studies, Community Education and Extra-Mural Studies, Distance Education; one-year post-secondary school courses; shorter courses are also arranged both at the Centre and in surrounding rural areas; Dir Mr NUWA SENTONGO.

Institute of Statistics and Applied Economics: a joint enterprise of the Government of Uganda and the United Nations Development Programme; depts of Planning and Applied Statistics, Population Studies, and Statistical Methods; 3-year degree courses; Dir Dr X. R. MUGISHA.

Makerere Institute of Computer Science: Dir Dr V. BARYMUREEBA.

Makerere Institute of Social Research: see under Research Institutes.

MBARARA UNIVERSITY OF SCIENCE AND TECHNOLOGY

POB 1410, Mbarara
Telephone: (485) 221623
Fax: (485) 220782
E-mail: vcmust@infocom.co.ug
Internet: www.must.ac.ug
Founded 1989
Language of instruction: English
State control
Academic year: October to August
Chancellor: Prof. RAPHAEL OWOR
Vice-Chancellor: Prof. F. I. B. KAYANJA
Registrar: S. B. BAZIRAKE
Librarian: ANNE GAKIBAYO

Library of 22,100 vols
Number of teachers: 144
Number of students: 1,104

Publications: *Medical Journal* (annually), *Science Journal* (annually)

DEANS

Faculty of Development Studies: Prof. PAMELA MBABAZI
Faculty of Medicine: Prof. J. KABAKYENGA
Faculty of Science Education: Prof. J. BARANGA

PROFESSORS

BARANGA, J., Biology
BEGUMYA, Y. R., Physiology
JAEGER, B., Dermatology
KAYANJA, F. I. B., Histology
PEPPER, L., Medicine

ATTACHED INSTITUTE

Institute of Tropical Forest Conservation: POB 7487, Kampala; fax 245597; Dir Dr A. MCNEILAGE.

NAMASAGALI UNIVERSITY

POB 241, Kamuli
Telephone: (77) 2861961
Founded 1975; present status 1998
Private control
Vice-Chancellor: SAMWIRI KIGWANA

Library of 5,000 vols
Number of teachers: 58
Number of students: 531

DEANS

Faculty of Education: PETER MUBIRU
Faculty of Management and Development Studies: WILLIAM SAAZI

NDEJJE UNIVERSITY

POB 7088, Kampala
Telephone: (77) 2630319
Fax: (77) 2610132
Founded 1992
Private control
Academic year: October to June
Library of 40,000 vols
Number of teachers: 60
Number of students: 1,515
Vice-Chancellor: Bishop Dr MICHAEL SENYIMBA

Schools of Business Administration and Computer Science and Education.

UGANDA CHRISTIAN UNIVERSITY

POB 4, Mukono
Telephone: (41) 2290828
Fax: (41) 2290800
E-mail: ucu@ucu.ac.ug
Internet: www.ucu.ac.ug
Founded 1923 as Bishop Tucker Theological College; present name and status 1997
Private control; administered by Church of Uganda (Anglican)
Chancellor: Archbishop of Uganda Most Rev. LIVINGSTONE NKOYOYO
Vice-Chancellor: Rev. Dr STEPHEN F. NOLL
Academic Registrar: Dr ALEX KAGUME

Library of 50,000 vols, 70 periodicals
Number of teachers: 109
Number of students: 2,635

DEANS

Faculty of Business and Administration: JOSEPH OWOR

Faculty of Education, Mass Communication, Development Studies and Social Sciences: CHRISTOPHER BYARUHANGA
Faculty of Law: LILIAN TIBATEMWA-ERIKIKU-BINZA
Faculty of Technology: PATRICK MANGHENI
Faculty of Theology: ALFRED OLWA

UGANDA MARTYRS UNIVERSITY

POB 5498, Kampala
Telephone: (38) 2410611
Fax: (38) 2410100
E-mail: umu@umu.ac.ug
Internet: www.fiuc.org/umu
Founded 1993
Private control
Academic year: September to May
Chancellor: Rt Rev. Bishop PAUL KALANDA
Vice-Chancellor: Prof. Dr MICHEL LEJEUNE
Deputy Vice-Chancellor (Academic Affairs): Prof. Dr PETER KANYANDAGO
Registrar: INNOCENT BYUMA
Librarian: MASEREKA JOHN PIUS

Library of 23,000 vols
Number of teachers: 80
Number of students: 2,026 (459 full-time, 1,567 part-time and distance learning)

Publication: *Mtafiti Mwafrika* (African Researcher, 3 a year)

DEANS

Faculty of Agriculture: CHARLES SSEKYEWA
Faculty of Building Technology and Architecture: JACQUELINE WADULO
Faculty of Business Administration and Management: Dr ALEX IJO
Faculty of Education: Dr EMURWON OLUPOT
Faculty of Science: Asst Prof. Dr MARIE-ESTHER HAFLETT
School of Postgraduate Studies: Prof. Dr DEIRDRE CARABINE (Director)
Centre for Extra-Mural Studies: Dr MARTIN O'REILLY (Head)
Department of Health Sciences: Dr MANIPLE EVERD BIKAITWOHA
Department of Information and Communications Technology: GEORGE WILLIAM LULE (Head)
Department of Information Systems: Prof. Dr VICTOR VAN REIJSWOUD (Head)
Institute of Ethics and Development Studies: Dr JOSEPH KISEKKA (Director)

ATTACHED RESEARCH INSTITUTE

African Research and Documentation Centre: all aspects of African cultures; Dir Dr PETER KANYANDAGO.

UKRAINE

The Higher Education System

Institutions of higher education predate Ukraine (formerly Ukrainian SSR)'s independence from the USSR in 1991, the oldest being National University of Kyiv–Mohyla Academy which was founded in 1615. The next oldest institution is National University of Lviv 'Ivan Franko', which was founded in 1661. During the period of Soviet rule (1920–91) over 60 universities, academies and institutions of higher education were founded.

Since independence the Law on Education (1991) is the defining legislation for all levels of the education system, and a system of licensing, assessment and certification of educational establishments has been in place since 1992. Other than the Ministry of Education, institutions of higher education may also be attached to the relevant ministry. Ukraine participates in Bologna Process to establish a European Higher Education Area, the first phase of which is to adopt a credit-based system of comparable degrees with two main cycles (undergraduate and graduate). Higher education is classified into four levels, in ascending order: technical colleges (Level I), colleges (Level II), institutes (Level III) and universities, academies and institutes (Level IV). In 2003/04 there were 2,269,800 students enrolled in higher education.

The main requirements for admission to higher education are award of the general secondary education certificate (Atestat pro Povnu Zagal'nu Sersdniu Osvitu) and satisfactory performance in entrance examinations or interviews. Ukraine has introduced a two-tier Bachelors and Masters degree system in accordance with the principles of the Bologna Process; however, the old-style degrees are still available. The Bachelors (Dyplom Bakalavra) is an undergraduate degree of four years, and is offered parallel to the Specialist Diploma (Dyplom Spetsialista), an integrated five-year programme of study mostly offered by institutes. The first postgraduate degree under the new system is the Masters (Dyplom Magistra), and it lasts for one or two years after the award of the Bachelors or Specialist Diploma. Finally, doctoral-level studies consist of two awards, both lasting three years, Diploma of Candidate of Sciences (Dyplom pro Prysudzhenia Naukovogo Stupenia Kandydata Nauk) and Diploma of Doctor of Sciences (Dyplom pro Prysudzhenia Naukovogo Stupenia Doktora Nauk).

Learned Societies

GENERAL

National Academy of Sciences of Ukraine: 01601 Kyiv, Volodymirska 54; tel. (44) 225-22-39; fax (44) 224-32-43; e-mail prez@nas.gov.ua; internet www.nas.gov.ua; f. 1918; sections of Physical-Technical and Mathematical Sciences (Chair. A. K. SHIDLOVSKIY), Chemical and Biological Sciences (Chair. V. D. POKHODENKO), Social Sciences and Humanities (Chair. I. F. KURAS); depts of Mathematics (Academician-Sec. I. V. SKRYPNIK), Informatics (Academician-Sec. I. V. SERGIENKO), Mechanics (Academician-Sec. V. V. PYLYPENKO), Physics and Astronomy (Academician-Sec. A. G. NAUMOVETS), Earth Sciences (Academician-Sec. V. I. STAROSTENKO), Physical and Technical Problems of Materials Science (Academician-Sec. I. K. POKHODNYA), Physical and Technical Problems of Power Engineering (Academician-Sec. B. S. STOGNIY), Chemistry (V. V. GONCHARUK), Molecular Biology, Biochemistry and Experimental and Clinical Physiology (Academician-Sec. G. KH. MATSUKA), General Biology (Academician-Sec. D. M. GRODZINSKIY), Economics (Academician-Sec. V. M. GEYETS), History, Philosophy and Law (Academician-Sec. O. S. ONYSHCHENKO), Literature, Language and Art Criticism (Academician-Sec. I. M. DZYUBA); attached research institutes: see Research Institutes; 602 mems (180 ordinary, 298 corresp., 124 foreign); library: see Libraries and Archives; Pres. B.E. PATON; Chief Scientific Sec. A.P. SHPAK; publs in Ukrainian and English: *Dopovidi NAN Ukrainy*, *Ekonomika Ukrainy* (Economy of Ukraine, monthly), *Kosmichna Nauka i Tekhnologiya* (Space Science and Engineering, 6 a year), *Kyivska Starovyna* (Kiev Antiquities, 6 a year), *Visnyk NAN Ukrainy* (Journal of the National Academy of Sciences of Ukraine, in Ukrainian and English, monthly).

Shevchenko Scientific Society: 290013 Lviv, Vul. Gen. Chuprynka 21; tel. (322) 34-51-63; fax (322) 76-04-97; e-mail ntsh@ipm .lviv.ua; f. 1873; broad range of arts and sciences; library of 30,000 vols; Pres. Prof. O. M. ROMANIV; Sec. O. A. KUPCHYNSKY; publ. *Memoires* (2 a year).

AGRICULTURE, FISHERIES AND VETERINARY SCIENCE

Ukrainian Academy of Agricultural Sciences: 01010 Kyiv, vul. Suvorova 9; tel. (44) 290-10-85; fax (44) 290-94-73; e-mail uaan@ukrpack.net; internet www .aginukraine.com/uaas; f. 1990; 4,900 mems; attached research institutes: see Research Institutes; publ. *Visnyk Agrarnoi Nauky* (Bulletin of Agricultural Science, monthly).

ARCHITECTURE AND TOWN PLANNING

National Union of Architects of Ukraine: 01001 Kyiv, vul. Hrychenka 7; tel. (44) 279-98-09; fax (44) 228-13-11; Pres. IHOR SHPARA.

BIBLIOGRAPHY, LIBRARY SCIENCE AND MUSEOLOGY

Association of Libraries of Ukraine: 03039 Kyiv, pr. Richchya Zhovtnya 3; tel. (44) 265-81-04; fax (44) 264-33-98; e-mail nlu@csl.freenet.kiev.ua; internet www.nbuv .gov.ua; Pres. OLEKSIY S. ONYSCHENKO.

ECONOMICS, LAW AND POLITICS

Academy of Legal Sciences of Ukraine: 61024 Kharkiv, vul. Pushkinska 70; tel. (57) 704-19-01; fax (57) 704-19-10; e-mail aprnu@ online.kharkiv.com; internet www.aprnu .kharkiv.org; f. 1993; Pres. Acad. VASIL YA. TATSIY.

EDUCATION

Academy of Pedagogical Sciences of Ukraine: 04053 Kyiv, Artema vul. 52A; tel. (44) 211-94-01; fax (44) 226-31-80; e-mail info@apsu.org.ua; internet www.apsu.org.ua; f. 1992; 156 mems (51 ordinary, 84 corresponding, 21 foreign); Pres. Prof. VASYL H. KREMEN; publs *Biolohiya i Khimiya v Shkoli* (Biology and Chemistry at School, 4 a year), *Compyuter v Shkoli i Simyi* (Computer at School and at Home, 4 a year), *Defektolohiya* (Defectology, 4 a year), *Fizyka i Astronomiya v Shkoli* (Physics and Astronomy at School, 4 a year), *Heohrafiya i Osnovy Ekonomiky v Shkoli* (Geography and Fundamentals of Economics at School, 4 a year), *Istoriya v Shkolakh Ukrainy* (History in Ukrainian Schools, 4 a year), *Matemmatyka v Shkoli* (Mathematics at School, 4 a year), *Mystetstvo i Osvita* (Arts and Education, 4 a year), *Nauka i Osvita* (Science and Education, 2 a year), *Obdarovana Dytyna* (Gifted Child, 6 a year), *Pedahohichna Hazeta* (Pedagogical Newspaper, 12 a year), *Pedahohika i Psykholohiya* (Pedagogy and Psychology, 4 a year), *Praktychna Psykholohiya i Sotsialna Robota* (Applied Psychology and Social Work, monthly), *Profesiyno-Tekhnichna Osvita* (Vocational and Technical Education, 4 a year), *Shlyakh Osvity* (A Way of Education, 4 a year), *Ukrainska Literatura v Zahalnoosvitniy Shkoli* (Ukrainian Literature at Secondary School, 6 a year), *Ukrainska Mova i Literatura v Shkoli* (Ukrainian Language and Literature at School, 4 a year), *Vyshcha Osvita Ukrainy* (Higher Education in Ukraine, 4 a year), *Zarubizhna Literatura v Navchalnykh Zakladakh* (Foreign Literature at Educational Institutions, monthly).

FINE AND PERFORMING ARTS

National Artists' Union of Ukraine: 04053 Kyiv, vul. Sichovykh Striltsiv 1–5; tel. (44) 212-01-33; fax (44) 212-14-54; e-mail spilka@nbi.com.ua; internet www.nshu.org .ua; f. 1938; 33 regional constituent orgs; 4,330 mems; Head VOLODYMYR A. CHEPELNIK.

National Union of Cinematographers of Ukraine: 01033 Kyiv, vul. Saksahanskoho 6; tel. and fax (44) 287-75-57; e-mail ukrkino@ ln.ua; internet www.ukrkino.com.ua; f. 1958; 1,251 mems; Head BORIS I. SAVCHENKO.

National Writers' Union of Ukraine: 01024 Kyiv, vul. Bankova 2; tel. (44) 293-45-86; e-mail nspu@i.kiev.ua; internet www .nspu.kiev.ua; f. 1934 as part of the Writers'

Union of the former USSR; 1,600 mems; Head VOLODYMYR O. YAVORIVSKY.

HISTORY, GEOGRAPHY AND ARCHAEOLOGY

Ukrainian Geographical Society: 03022 Kyiv, vul. Vasilkivska 90; fax (44) 266-54-17; e-mail vpsh@icchq.univ.kiev.ua; Head PETRO H. SHISHCHENKO.

LANGUAGE AND LITERATURE

Alliance Française: 03150 Kyiv, c/o CCCL, 104 Vul. Gorki; tel. (44) 269-41-57; fax (44) 269-85-28; e-mail alliance.francaise@ifu.kiev.ua; offers courses and exams in French language and culture and promotes cultural exchange with France; attached offices in Dneprodzerzhinsk, Donetsk, Enerdogar, Feodossia, Gorlivka, Izmail, Kharkiv, Khmelnystkyi, Kramatorsk, Lougansk, Mykolaiv, Odessa, Oujgorod, Poltava, Rivne, Sebastopol, Simferopol, Slaviansk, Tchernivtsy, Ternopil, Vinnitsia and Zaporijjia.

British Council: 04070 Kyiv, 4/12 vul. Hryhoriya Skovorody; tel. (44) 490-56-00; fax (44) 490-56-05; e-mail enquiry@britishcouncil.org.ua; internet www.britishcouncil.org/ukraine; teaching centre; offers courses and exams in English language and British culture and promotes cultural exchange with the UK; attached offices in Donetsk, Kharkiv, Lviv and Odessa; training and professional development centre; Dir TERRY SANDELL; Teaching Centre Man. TONY HUBBARD.

Goethe-Institut: 04070 Kyiv, vul. Voloska, 12/4; tel. (44) 496-97-85; fax (44) 496-97-89; e-mail info@kiew.goethe.org; internet www.goethe.de/ins/ua/kie/; f. 1994; offers courses and exams in German language and culture and promotes cultural exchange with Germany; Dir MARION HAASE.

MEDICINE

Academy of Medical Sciences of Ukraine: 04050 Kyiv, vul. Gertsena 12; tel. (44) 213-34-11; fax (44) 219-39-81; e-mail beb@rcrm.kiev.ua; internet www.amnu.kiev.ua; f. 1993; 31 mems; 44 corresp. mems; 5 foreign mems; attached research institutes: see Research Institutes; Pres. Prof. OLEKSANDR F. VOZIANOV; Chief Scientific Sec. Prof. VOLODYMYR A. MIKHNOV; publ. *Journal* (4 a year).

Gerontology and Geriatrics Society: Institute of Gerontology, 252655 Kyiv 114, Vyshgorodska vul. 67; tel. (44) 430-40-68; fax (44) 432-99-56; e-mail admin@geront.kiev.ua; f. 1963; 250 mems; library of 72,000 vols; Chair. V. V. BEZRUKOV; Chief Learned Sec. O.K. KULTCHITSKY; publ. *Problems of Ageing and Longevity* (4 a year).

Ukrainian Association of Radiologists: 03022 Kyiv, vul. Lomonsova 33/43; tel. and fax (44) 258-97-86; e-mail aru-kiev@ukr.net; internet www.aruk.org; f. 1992; 6,000 mems; Chair. Prof. VLADIMIR E. MEDVEDEV; publ. *Radiodiagnostics and Radiotherapy* (4 a year).

Ukrainian Scientific Society of Cardiologists: c/o Institute of Cardiology 'M. D. Strazhevska', 03151 Kyiv, vul. Narodnogo Opolcheniya 5; tel. (44) 449-70-03; internet www.ukrcardio.org; Pres. VOLODYMYR KOVALENKO.

Ukrainian Scientific Society of Hygienists: 02660 Kyiv, vul. Popudrenka 50; tel. and fax (44) 559-90-90; e-mail regina@usch.kiev.ua; f. 1953; Head ANDRIY M. SERDYUK.

Ukrainian Society of Allergology and Clinical Immunology: c/o Dept of Immunology and Allergy, National Medical University 'O. Bohomolets', 04053 Kyiv, vul.

Kotsyubinskoho 9a; tel. (44) 216-54-03; fax (44) 216-24-02; Chair. Prof. H. DRANNIK.

Ukrainian Society of Ophthalmologists: c/o Institute of Eye Diseases and Tissue Therapy 'V. P. Filatov', 65061 Odesa, bul. Frantsuzsky 49/51; tel. (482) 22-20-35; fax (482) 68-48-51.

Ukrainian Physiological Society: 01024 Kyiv, vul. Bohomoltsya 4; tel. (44) 253-29-09; fax (44) 256-20-00; e-mail pkostyuk@biph.kiev.ua; internet uaphsoc.biph.kiev.ua; Head Acad. PLATON H. KOSTYUK; publ. *Fiziologichnyi Zhurnal* (Physiological Journal, 6 a year).

NATURAL SCIENCES

General

Scientific and Technical Societies—National Headquarters: 252053 Kyiv, Vul. Artema 21; tel. (44) 212-42-34.

Biological Sciences

Ukrainian Biochemical Society: c/o Palladin Institute of Biochemistry, 03680 Kyiv, vul. Leontovicha 9; tel. (44) 234-59-74; fax (44) 229-63-65; e-mail svk@biochem.kiev.ua; internet www.biochem.kiev.ua; f. 1925; Chair. Prof. SERGIY V. KOMISARENKO.

Physical Sciences

Ukrainian Physical Society: 03680 Kyiv, pr. Glushkova 2; tel. and fax (44) 266-40-36; e-mail nedilko@univ.kiev.ua; internet www.ups.kiev.ua; f. 1990; 6,000 mems; Pres. Prof. VOLODYMYR H. LITOVCHENKO.

Ukrainian Society of Geodesy, Aerospace Surveying and Cartography: c/o Ministry of Environment and Natural Resources of Ukraine, 02094 Kyiv, vul. Popudrenka 54; tel. (44) 268-21-09; fax (44) 559-73-89; e-mail ukrgeo@geomatica.kiev.ua; Pres. IHOR TREVOHO.

PHILOSOPHY AND PSYCHOLOGY

Ukranian Psychological Society: 01032 Kyiv, bul. T. Shevchenka 27A, Office 305; tel. and fax (44) 246-54-59; e-mail ucap@ukr.net; internet www.ucap.kiev.ua; Dir Dr VITALIY PANOK.

RELIGION, SOCIOLOGY AND ANTHROPOLOGY

Sociological Association of Ukraine: 01021 Kyiv, vul. Shovkovychna 12; tel. and fax (44) 291-52-46; e-mail sau@mail.kar.net; Dir Dr N. SHULGA.

TECHNOLOGY

Chornobyl Center for Nuclear Safety, Radioactive Waste and Radioecology: 07100 Kyiv, Slavutych, vul. Hvardeyskoi Divizii 77, 7/1; tel. (44) 792-30-16; fax (44) 792-81-44; e-mail center@chornobyl.net; internet www.chornobyl.net; f. 1996; Co-ordinating Dir Prof. YEVGEN V. GARIN.

Ukrainian Society of Mechanical Engineers: c/o Branch of Mechanics of the National Academy of Sciences of Ukraine, 49600 Dnipropetrovsk, vul. Leshko-Popelya 15; tel. (562) 45-12-38; fax (562) 47-34-13; e-mail itm@pvv.dp.ua; Pres. Acad. VIKTOR PYLYPENKO.

Ukrainian Society for Non-Destructive Testing: 03680 Kyiv, vul. Bozhenko 11; tel. (44) 227-26-66; fax (44) 220-94-82; e-mail usndt@ukr.net; internet www.usndt.com.ua; f. 1990; 170 mems; Pres. Prof. VOLODYMYR TROITSKIY.

Ukrainian Society for Soil Mechanics, Geotechnics and Foundation Engineering: 03680 Kyiv-37, vul. Ivana Klimenka 5/2; tel. (44) 249-72-34; fax (44) 248-89-09; e-mail

adm-inst@ndibk.kiev.ua; Pres. Prof. PETRO KRYVOSHEYEV.

Research Institutes

AGRICULTURE, FISHERIES AND VETERINARY SCIENCE

Dairy and Meat Technology Institute: 02660 Kyiv, M. Raskovoi 4A; tel. (44) 517-17-37; fax (44) 517-02-28; e-mail verb@timm.kiev.ua; internet www.timm.kiev.ua; f. 1959; attached to Ukrainian Acad. of Agricultural Sciences; library of 27,000 vols; Dir G. A. ERESKO; publ. *Meat and Milk* (6 a year).

Institute of Agricultural Economics: 03680 Kyiv, vul. Geroev Oborony 10; tel. (44) 261-43-21; fax (44) 266-05-65; e-mail info@iae.com.ua; f. 1956; attached to Ukrainian Acad. of Agricultural Sciences; Dir PETRO SABLUK; publ. *Economics of AIC* (monthly).

Institute of Agriculture: 08162 Kievska oblast, Kyevo-Svyatoshinsky raion, Chabani; tel. (44) 526-23-27; fax (44) 526-11-07; e-mail selectio@ukrpack.net; f. 1900; attached to Ukrainian Acad. of Agrarian Sciences; agriculture, crop-growing technologies, agricultural crops selection; library of 35,900 vols in scientific library; 100,000 in total; publs *Agriculture* (annually), *Proceedings of the International and All-Ukrainian Congresses*.

Institute of Beekeeping, P. I. Prokopovych: 03143 Kyiv, vul. Zabolotnogo 19; tel. (44) 266-67-98; fax (44) 266-31-89; e-mail prokopovych@ukr.net; f. 1989; attached to Ukrainian Acad. of Agrarian Sciences; library of 4,000 vols; Dir LEONID BODNARCHUK; publs *Apiary* (monthly), *Beekeeping* (annually), *Ukrainian Beekeeper*.

Institute of Cereals: 49600 Dnipropetrovsk, vul. Dzerzhinskogo 14; tel. (562) 44-45-49; fax (562) 36-26-18; f. 1930; attached to Ukrainian Acad. of Agrarian Sciences; maize, winter wheat, other cereals and leguminous plants; library of 110,000 vols; Dir Dr YEVGEN LEBID; publ. *Bulletin* (2 a year).

Institute for Fisheries: 03164 Kyiv, vul. Obukhivska 165; tel. (44) 423-74-61; fax (44) 423-74-58; e-mail vitbekh@online.com.ua; attached to Ukrainian Acad. of Agrarian Sciences; research and development into the exploitation of aquatic living resources in inland waters; fish genetics and selection; environmental safety; stock conservation and rehabilitation of rare and endangered species; and economic efficiency of Ukrainian fisheries; library of 50,000 vols; Dir OLEKSANDR TRETYAK; publ. *Rybne Gospodarstvo* (annually).

Institute for Mechanization of Animal Husbandry: 69017 Zaporizhzhya, Ostrov Khortitsa; tel. and fax (612) 286-53-23; f. 1930; attached to Ukrainian Acad. of Agrarian Sciences; Dir V. V. SHATSKY.

Institute of Plant Protection: 03022 Kyiv, 33 Vasilkovskaya; tel. (44) 257-11-24; fax (44) 257-21-85; e-mail plant_prot@ukr.net; internet ippuaan.by.ru; f. 1946; attached to Ukrainian Acad. of Agrarian Sciences; Dir Prof. VITALIY FEDORENKO; publ. *Zahayst i Karantyn Roslyn* (Plant Protection and Quarantine, 2 a year).

Institute of Veterinary Research of the Ukrainian Academy of Agricultural Sciences: 03151 Kyiv, vul. Donetska 30; tel. and fax (44) 245-78-05; e-mail vet@ivm.kiev.ua; internet www.ivm.kiev.ua; attached to Ukrainian Acad. of Agricultural Sciences; Dir ANATOLIY OBRAZHEV; publ. *Veterinary Biotechnology* (2 a year).

Land Use Research Institute: 03151 Kyiv, Narodnogo Opolcheniya 3; tel. (44) 275-73-88; e-mail kyiv@zempro.relc.com; f. 1961; attached to Ukrainian Acad. of Agrarian Sciences; Dir DMITRO S. DOBRYAK; publ. *Land-Use Systems* (4 a year).

Magarach Institute of the Vine and Wine: 334200 the Autonomous Republic of Crimea, Yalta, ul. Kirova 31; tel. (654) 32-55-91; fax (654) 23-06-08; e-mail magarach@yalita.yalta.iuf.net; f. 1828; Dir A. M. AVIDZBA; publs *Magarach–Vinogradarstvo i Vinodelie* (in Russian, also English summaries, 4 a year), *Proceedings of the Magarach Institute for Vine and Wine* (in Russian, 2 a year), *Proceedings of the Scientific Centre of Viticulture and Oenology* (in Russian, 2 a year).

Mironovka Institute of Wheat: 256816 Kievska oblast, P/o Mironovka; tel. (44) 747-41-35; fax (44) 747-41-60; f. 1911; attached to Ukrainian Acad. of Agricultural Sciences; library of 51,000 vols; Dir L. A. ZHIVOTKOV; publ. *Annual Collected Papers.*

Pig Breeding Institute 'O. V. Kvasnitsky': 36006 Poltava, Shvedska Mogila 1; tel. (532) 52-74-19; fax (532) 22-27-53; e-mail slsvin@e-mail.pl.ua; internet web.poltava.ua/firms/slsvin; f. 1930; library of 60,000 vols; Dir Prof. VALENTIN P. RYBALKO; publ. *Pig Breeding* (annually).

Plant Breeding and Genetics Institute: 65036 Odesa, Ovidiopolskaya doroga 3; tel. (0482) 39-54-01; fax (0482) 39-52-89; e-mail sgi_uaan@tekom.odessa.ua; f. 1912; attached to Ukrainian Acad. of Agricultural Sciences; development of breeding and seed production theory, as well as new varieties and hybrids of winter wheat, spring and winter barley, triticale, maize, sunflower, soybean, alfalfa, Sudan grass, sorghum; operates seven experimental farms for seed production; conferences and workshops on the problems of plant breeding; courses for agronomists and seed-growers; three-year post-doctoral courses; assistance to agricultural research stations and institutes; 103 research staff; library of 109,234 vols; Dir Dr VYACHESLAV SOKOLOV; publs *Collected Scientific Papers* (2 a year), *Scientific and Technical Bulletin* (3 or 4 a year).

Sugar Beet Research Institute: 03141 Kyiv, Klinichna vul. 25; tel. (44) 275-50-00; e-mail isb@isb.kiev.ua; internet www.sugarbeet.com.ua; f. 1922; attached to Ukrainian Acad. of Agrarian Sciences; library of 28,000 vols, 30,000 periodicals; Dir M. V. ROIK; publ. *Tsukrovi buryaky* (Sugar Beet, 6 a year).

Ukrainian Research Institute of Water Management and Ecological Problems: 252010 Kyiv, Inzhenerny prov. 4B; tel. and fax (44) 280-03-02; e-mail undiwep@ukrwecol.kiev.ua; internet www.nbuv.gov.ua/undiwep; f. 1974; library of 10,000 vols; Dir Prof. A. V. YATSYK.

Ukrainian Scientific Research Institute of Ecological Problems: 61166 Kharkiv, vul. Bakulina 6; tel. and fax (57) 702-15-92; e-mail director@niiep.kharkov.ua; internet www.niiep.kharkov.ua; f. 1971 as the All-Union Scientific Research Institute for Protection of Water; Dir Dr GRIGORY D. KOVALENKO (acting).

Zakarpatsky Institute of Agroindustrial Production: 90252 Zakarpatska oblast, Beregovo raion, Selo V. Bakhta; tel. and fax (3141) 2-34-04; e-mail insbakta@bereg.net.ua; f. 1989; 114 mems; library of 40,000 vols; Dir A. V. BAYLAN; publ. *Problems of Agroindustrial Complex of Karpaty* (every 2 years).

ARCHITECTURE AND TOWN PLANNING

Research Institute of Automated Systems in Construction: 03037 Kyiv, vul. M. Krivonosa 2A; tel. and fax (44) 249-72-30; e-mail office@ndiasb.kiev.ua; internet www.ndiasb.kiev.ua; Dir BORIS A. VOLOBOEV.

State Research Institute of Building Constructions: 03680 Kyiv, vul. I. Klymenko 5/2; tel. (44) 249-72-34; fax (44) 248-89-09; e-mail adm-inst@ndibk.kiev.ua; internet www.niisk.com; f. 1943; 500 mems; library of 30,000 vols, 72,000 patents; Dir VLADIMIR SENATOROV; publs *Building Construction* (2 a year), *World of Geotechnics* (2 a year).

Ukrainian Zonal Scientific and Research Design Institute of Civil Engineering: 01133 Kyiv, Bul. L. Ukrainki 26; tel. (44) 286-36-72; fax (44) 285-74-81; e-mail zniiep@adam.kiev.ua; internet www.zniiep.com.ua; f. 1963; library of 125,000 vols; Dir VLADIMIR B. SHEVELEV.

ECONOMICS, LAW AND POLITICS

Council for the Study of Productive Forces of Ukraine: 01032 Kyiv 32, Bul. T. Shevchenka 60; tel. (44) 216-90-70; fax (44) 244-66-70; e-mail rvps@folgat.net; attached to Nat. Acad. of Sciences of Ukraine; 6 attached scientific schools; Dir A. N. ALYMOV.

Institute of Economics: 01011 Kyiv, vul. Panasa Mirnogo 26; tel. (44) 290-84-44; fax (44) 290-86-63; e-mail instecon@ln.ua; f. 1936; attached to Nat. Acad. of Sciences of Ukraine; Dir I. I. LUKINOV.

Institute for Economic Research and Policy Consulting: 01034 Kyiv, Reytarska 8/5-A; tel. (44) 278-63-42; fax (44) 278-63-36; e-mail institute@ier.kiev.ua; internet www.ier.kiev.ua; Dir IGOR BURAKOVSKY.

Institute of Industrial Economics: 83048 Donetsk, Universitetska vul. 77; tel. (62) 55-78-44; fax (62) 345-06-71; e-mail admin@iep.donetsk.ua; f. 1969; attached to Nat. Acad. of Sciences of Ukraine; Dir A. I. AMOSHA; publ. *Ekonomika Promyslovosti* (Economics of Industry, in Ukrainian and Russian, 4 a year).

Institute of State and Law 'V. M. Koretsky': 01601 Kyiv, vul. Tryokhsviatitelskai 4; tel. (44) 278-51-55; fax (44) 278-54-74; e-mail jus@ukrpack.net; f. 1948; attached to Nat. Acad. of Sciences of Ukraine; research into the theory and practice of law and state-building; Dir YU. S. SHEMSHUCHENKO; publs *Lawful State* (annually), *Pravo Ukrainy* (Law of Ukraine, in Ukrainian and English, monthly).

Institute of World Economy and International Relations: 01030 Kyiv, vul. Leontovicha 5; tel. (44) 235-70-22; fax (44) 235-51-27; e-mail iweir_nas@iweir.org.ua; internet www.iweir.org.ua; f. 1992; attached to Nat. Acad. of Sciences of Ukraine; Dir Y. M. PAKHOMOV.

HISTORY, GEOGRAPHY AND ARCHAEOLOGY

Institute of Archaeology: 04210 Kyiv, Heroyiv Stalingrada 12; tel. (44) 418-27-75; fax (44) 418-33-06; e-mail sekretar@iananu.kiev.ua; internet www.iananu.kiev.ua; attached to Nat. Acad. of Sciences of Ukraine; Dir P. P. TOLOCHKO; publ. *Arkheologia* (Archaeology, in Ukrainian and English, 4 a year).

Krypiakevych, I., Institute of Ukrainian Studies: 79026 Lviv, Kozelnytska vul. 4; tel. (322) 70-70-22; fax (322) 70-70-21; e-mail inukr@inst-ukr.lviv.ua; internet www.inst-ukr.lviv.ua; f. 1951; attached to Nat. Acad. of Sciences of Ukraine; archaeology, history, philology, political science; library of 10,000 vols; Dir YAROSLAV D. ISAIEVYCH; publs *Istorychni ta kulturolohichni studii* (4 a year), *Shashkevychiana* (annually), *Ukrainska dialektna ta istorychna leksyka* (annually), *Ukraina: kulturna spadshchyna, natsionalna svidomist, derzhavnist* (2 a year).

Ukrainian Institute of History: 01001 Kyiv, vul. Hrushevskogo 4; tel. and fax (44) 229-63-62; e-mail institute@history.org.ua; internet www.history.org.ua; attached to Nat. Acad. of Sciences of Ukraine; Dir V. A. SMOLIY; publ. *Ukrainsky Istorychny Zhurnal* (Ukrainian Historical Journal, in Ukrainian and English, 6 a year).

LANGUAGE AND LITERATURE

Institute of Linguistics 'O. O. Potebni': 01001 Kyiv, vul. Hrushevskoho 4; tel. (44) 229-02-92; fax (44) 228-43-83; attached to Nat. Acad. of Sciences of Ukraine; Dir V. H. SKLIARENKO; publ. *Movoznavstvo* (Linguistics, in Ukrainian and English, 6 a year).

Institute of Literature 'Shevchenko, T. G.': 01001 Kyiv 1, Hrushevskoho 4; tel. (44) 229-10-84; fax (44) 228-52-81; e-mail ilnan@gilan.uar.net; f. 1926; attached to Nat. Acad. of Sciences of Ukraine; Dir M. G. ZHULYNSKY; publ. *Slovo i Chas* (Word and Time, in Ukrainian, monthly).

MEDICINE

Donetsk Scientific Research Institute of Traumatology and Orthopaedics: 83048 Donetsk, vul. Artema 106; tel. (62) 311-05-08; fax (62) 335-14-61; e-mail info@dniito.org.ua; internet www.dniito.org.ua; f. 1953; Dir Prof. Dr VOLODYMYR KLYMOVYTSKYY; publ. *Trauma* (4 a year).

Filatov Institute for Eye Diseases and Tissue Therapy: 65061 Odesa, vul. Frantsi 49–51; tel. (482) 22-20-35; fax (482) 68-48-51; e-mail filatov@farlep.net; internet www.ophthalmology.ru/~nauchnoiss291; f. 1936; library of 81,000 vols; Dir Prof. IVAN M. LOGAI; publ. *Ophthalmological Journal* (8 a year).

Institute of Cardiovascular Surgery, M. Amosov: 03110 Kiev, M. Amosova vul. 6; tel. and fax (44) 275-43-22; e-mail gvknyshov@ukr.net; f. 1983; 980 mems; Dir Prof. GENNADY V. KNYSHOV; Deputy Dir Prof. VITALY B. MAKSYMENKO; publ. *Annual of Cardiovascular Surgery* (annually).

Institute of Clinical Radiology: 04075 Kyiv, Pushcha-Voditsa, vul. Gamarnikova 42; attached to Ukrainian Acad. of Medical Sciences; Dir VOLODYMYR BEBESHKO.

Institute of Dermatology and Venereology: 61057 Kharkiv, Chernyshevska vul. 7/9; tel. (572) 43-17-83; fax (572) 47-65-82; e-mail uniidiv@vlink.kharkov.ua; f. 1924; attached to Acad. of Medical Sciences of Ukraine; library of 40,000 vols; Dir Prof. IVAN I. MAVROV; publ. *Journal of Dermatology and Venereology* (4 a year).

Institute of Epidemiology and Infectious Diseases 'L. V. Gromashevsky': 01601 Kyiv, vul. S. Razina 4; tel. (44) 277-37-11; Dir A. F. FROLOV.

Institute of Gerontology: 04114 Kyiv, Vyshgorodska vul. 67; tel. (44) 430-40-68; fax (44) 432-99-56; e-mail admin@geront.kiev.ua; f. 1958; attached to Ukrainian Acad. of Medical Sciences; Dir VLADISLAV V. BEZRUKOV; publ. *Problemy stareniya i dolgoletiya* (Problems of Ageing and Longevity, 4 a year).

Institute of Medical Radiology 'S. P. Hrihoryev': 61024 Kharkiv, vul. Pushkinska 82; tel. (57) 704-10-65; fax (57) 700-05-00; e-mail imr@ukr.net; internet www.imr.kharkov.ua; f. 1920; library of 70,000 vols;

Dir Prof. Dr MYKOLA I. PILIPENKO; publ. *Ukrainian Journal of Radiology* (quarterly).

Institute for Occupational Health: 01033 Kyiv, vul. Saksakanskogo 75; tel. (44) 220-80-30; fax (44) 220-66-77; e-mail yik@nanu.kiev.ua; f. 1928; library of 42,000 vols; Dir Prof. Y. I. KUNDIEV; publ. *Gigiyena Truda* (annually).

Institute of the Problems of Cryobiology and Cryomedicine of the National Academy of Sciences of Ukraine: 61015 Kharkiv, Pereyaslavskaya vul. 23; tel. (572) 373-41-43; fax (572) 373-30-84; e-mail cryo@online.kharkov.ua; internet www.cryo.org.ua; f. 1972; attached to Nat. Acad. of Sciences of Ukraine; library of 53,476 items; Dir Prof. Dr VALENTIN I. GRISCHENKO; publ. *Problemy Kriobiologii* (Problems of Cryobiology, in Ukrainian and English, quarterly).

Institute of Surgery and Transplantology: 03680 Kyiv, vul. Geroev Sevastopolya 30; tel. (44) 488-13-74; fax (44) 488-19-09; e-mail surgery@i.com.ua; internet www.surgery.org.ua; f. 1972; library of 25,000 vols; Dir Prof. VALERY SAYENKO; publ. *Clinical Surgery* (monthly).

Kavetsky, R. E., Institute of Experimental Pathology, Oncology and Radiobiology: 03022 Kyiv, Vasylkivska vul. 45; tel. (44) 259-01-83; fax (44) 258-16-56; e-mail inst@onconet.kiev.ua; internet www.onconet.kiev.ua; f. 1960; attached to Nat. Acad. of Sciences of Ukraine; library of 20,000 vols, 238 periodicals; Dir Prof. VASYL F. CHEKHUN; publs *Eksperimentalnaia onkologia* (Experimental Oncology, in Ukrainian and English, 4 a year), *Oncologia* (4 a year).

Kyiv 'N. D. Strazhesko' Research Institute of Cardiology: 03151 Kyiv, vul. Narodnogo Opolchenia 5; tel. (44) 277-66-22; fax (44) 228-72-72; f. 1936; 650 mems; library of 65,000 vols; Dir Prof. V. A. BOBROV.

Kyiv Research Institute of Oncology: Kyiv, vul. Lomonosova 33/43; tel. (44) 266 75-67; f. 1920; library of 27,000 vols; Dir V. L. GANUL.

Kyiv Research Institute of Otolaryngology: 03057 Kyiv, Zoologichna 3; tel. (44) 213-73-68; e-mail amtc@kndio.kiev.ua; f. 1960; library of 33,000 vols; publ. *Journal of Ear, Nose and Throat Diseases* (6 a year).

Lviv Scientific Research Institute of Hereditary Pathology: 79000 Lviv, vul. Lysenko 31A; tel. (322) 76-54-99; fax (322) 75-38-44; f. 1940; library of 28,000 vols; Dir O. Z. HNATEIKO; publ. *Medychna Genetyka* (every 2 years, in Ukrainian with Russian and English abstracts).

Medved, L. I., Institute of Ecohygiene and Toxicology (ECOHYNTOX): 03680 Kiev, vul. Heroiv Oborony 6; tel. (44) 250-72-00; fax (44) 251-96-43; e-mail office@medved.kiev.ua; internet www.medved.kiev.ua; f. 1964; library of 41,000 vols; Dir Prof. Dr MYKOLA PRODANCHUK; publs *Modern Problems of Toxicology* (6 a year), *Preventive Medicine* (4 a year), *Problems of Nutrition* (4 a year).

National Research Centre of Radiation Medicine: 254050 Kyiv, vul. Melnikova 53; tel. (44) 213-06-37; fax (44) 213-72-02; e-mail baz@rcrm.kiev.ua; f. 1986; attached to Ukrainian Acad. of Medical Sciences; library of 30,000 vols; Dir Prof. A. E. ROMANENKO; publs *International Journal of Radiation Medicine* (2 a year), *Problems of Radiation Medicine* (4 a year).

Phthisiology and Pulmonology Research Institute: vul. M. Amosova 10, 03680 Kyiv; tel. (44) 275-04-02; fax (44) 275-21-18; e-mail admin@ifp.kiev.ua; internet www.ifp.kiev.ua; f. 1922; Dir YURI I. FESCHENKO; publs *Asthma and Allergy* (4 a

year), *Ukrainian Chemotherapeutic Journal* (4 a year), *Ukrainian Journal of Pulmonology* (4 a year).

Research Centre for Radiation Medicine: 04050 Kyiv, vul. Melnikova 53; tel. (44) 213-06-37; fax (44) 213-72-02; e-mail baz@rcrm.kiev.ua; f. 1986; attached to Ukrainian Acad. of Medical Sciences; library of 30,000 vols; Dir Prof. V. G. BEBESHKO; publs *International Journal of Radiation Medicine* (6 a year), *Problems of Radiation Medicine* (4 a year).

Research Institute of Paediatrics, Obstetrics and Gynaecology: 04050 Kyiv, Manuilska vul. 8; tel. (44) 213-80-67.

Research Institute of Physical Methods of Treatment and Medical Climatology 'I. M. Sechenov': 98603 Yalta, Polikurovska vul. 25; tel. (654) 32-75-91; f. 1914; non-medical treatment and prophylaxis of lung diseases and diseases of the cardiovascular and nervous systems; Dir Prof. SERGEI SOLDATCHENKO.

Research Institute of Psychology 'G. S. Kostyuk': 03037 Kyiv, vul. Pankivska 2; tel. (44) 224-19-63; attached to Nat. Acad. of Pedagogical Sciences of Ukraine.

Romodanov, A., Institute of Neurosurgery: 04050 Kyiv, vul. Manuilskogo 32; tel. and fax (44) 213-95-73; e-mail brain@neuro.kiev.ua; internet www.neuro.kiev.ua; f. 1950; library of 70,000 vols; Dir Prof. Y. ZOZULIA; publ. *Ukrainian Neurosurgical Journal* (4 a year).

State Scientific Centre of Drugs: Kharkiv 310085, Astronomicheska vul. 33; tel. (57) 744-10-33; fax (57) 744-11-18; e-mail samatov@phukr.kharkov.ua; academic year farmacomua.narod.ru; f. 1920; production and development of finished drugs and technologies for preparation of phytochemicals; library of 28,000 vols; Dir Prof. V. P. GEORGIEVSKY; publ. *Pharmacom* (in Ukrainian and Russian, every 3 months).

Sytenko Institute of Spine and Joint Pathology: 61024 Kharkiv, Pushkinska vul. 80; tel. (57) 715-75-06; e-mail post@sytenko.org.ua; internet www.sytenko.org.ua; f. 1907; attached to Acad. of Medical Sciences of Ukraine; library of 40,500 vols; Dir Prof. MYKOLA O. KORZH; publ. *Orthopaedics, Traumatology and Prosthetics* (quarterly).

Ukrainian Institute of Public Health: 01601 Kyiv, vul. Dymytrova 5, korp. 10-A, 7th Fl.; tel. (44) 284-39-38; fax (44) 284-39-37; e-mail health@uiph.kiev.ua; internet www.uiph.kiev.ua; f. 1997; attached to Ukrainian Min. of Health; Dir Prof. V. M. PONOMARENKO; publ. *Bulletin of the Social Hygiene and Health Protection Organization of Ukraine* (4 a year).

Ukrainian Research Institute of Traumatology and Orthopaedics: 01601 Kyiv, vul. Vorovskogo 27; tel. (44) 216-42-49; fax (44) 216-44-62; e-mail travma@rql.net.ua; f. 1919; library of 57,000 vols; Dir G. V. GAIKO; publs *Statistical Data Report on Traumatological and Orthopaedic Aid to Ukrainians* (annually), *Vestnik Ortopedii, Travmatologii i Protezirovaniia* (Orthopaedics, Traumatology and Prosthesis, 4 a year).

Ukrainian Scientific Centre of Hygiene: 02094 Kyiv, vul. Popudrenko 50; tel. (44) 559-73-73; fax (44) 559-90-90; e-mail usch@usch.kiev.ua; f. 1931; incl. Institute of General and Communal Hygiene, and Institute of Medical Genetics; library of 102,213 vols; Dir Dr ANDRIY SERDIUK; publ. *Environment and Health* (4 a year).

NATURAL SCIENCES
Biological Sciences

Institute of Biology of Southern Seas: Pr. Nakhimov 2, 99011 Sevastopol; tel. (692) 54-41-10; fax (692) 55-78-13; e-mail ibss@ibss.iuf.net; internet www.ibss.iuf.net; f. 1871; attached to Nat. Acad. of Sciences of Ukraine; library of 150,000 vols; 350 mems; Dir Dr V. N. EREMEEV; publs *Ekologiya Morya* (Ecology of the Sea, 4 a year), *Morskoj Ekologicheskij Zhurnal* (Marine Ecological Journal, 3 a year).

Institute of Botany 'M. G. Kholodny': 01601 Kyiv, Tereshchenkivska vul. 2; tel. (44) 224-40-41; fax (44) 224-10-64; e-mail inst@botan.kiev.ua; f. 1921; attached to Nat. Acad. of Sciences of Ukraine; library of 106,000 vols; Dir K. M. SYTNIK; publs *Algologiya* (Algology, in Ukrainian and English, 4 a year), *Ukrainsky Botanichny Zhurnal* (Ukrainian Botanical Journal, in Ukrainian and English, 6 a year).

Institute of Cellular Biology and Genetic Engineering: 03143 Kyiv, Vul. Zabolotnogo 148; tel. (44) 526-71-09; fax (44) 526-71-04; e-mail cytogen@iicb.kiev.ua; internet www.cytgen.com; f. 1967; attached to Nat. Acad. of Sciences of Ukraine; Dir YA. B. BLUME; publ. *Tsitologia i Genetika* (Cytology and Genetics, in Ukrainian and English, 6 a year).

Institute of Hydrobiology: 04210 Kyiv-210, pr. Geroyiv Stalingrada 12; tel. (44) 419-39-81; fax (44) 418-22-32; e-mail hydrobiol@igb.ibc.com.ua; attached to Nat. Acad. of Sciences of Ukraine; Dir VIKTOR D. ROMANENKO; publ. *Gidrobiologichesky Zhurnal* (Hydrobiological Journal, in Ukrainian and English, 6 a year).

Institute of Molecular Biology and Genetics: 03143 Kyiv-143, vul. Zabolotnoho 150; tel. (44) 526-11-69; fax (44) 526-07-59; e-mail mishchuk@imbg.org.ua; internet www.imbig.org.ua; f. 1973; attached to Nat. Acad. of Sciences of Ukraine; library of 85,000 vols; Dir Prof. HANNA V. ELSKA; publ. *Biopolimery i Kletka* (Biopolymers and the Cell, in Ukrainian and English, 6 a year).

Institute of Plant Physiology and Genetics: 03022 Kyiv, Vasylkivska vul. 31/17; tel. (44) 257-01-14; fax (44) 257-51-50; e-mail editor@ifrg.freenet.kiev.ua; f. 1946; attached to Nat. Acad. of Sciences of Ukraine; Dir VLADIMIR V. MORGUN; publ. *Fiziologia i Biokhimia Kulturnykh Rastenii* (Physiology and Biochemistry of Cultivated Plants, in Ukrainian, Russian and English, 6 a year).

Institute for Sorption and Endoecology Problems: 03164 Kyiv, pr. Naumova 13; tel. (44) 452-93-28; fax (44) 452-93-27; e-mail ispe@ispe.kiev.ua; internet www.ispe.ldc.net; f. 1991; attached to Nat. Acad. of Sciences of Ukraine; Dir V. V. STRELKO.

Institute of Zoology 'I. I. Schmalhausen': 01601 Kyiv, vul. B. Khmelnytskoho 15; tel. (44) 225-10-70; e-mail iz@iz.freenet.kiev.ua; internet www.izan.kiev.ua; attached to Nat. Acad. of Sciences of Ukraine; Dir Prof. IGOR A. AKIMOV; publ. *Vestnik Zoologii* (Zoological Journal, in Ukrainian and English, 6 a year).

'O. O. Bohomolets' Institute of Physiology: 01601 Kyiv, vul. Bohomoltsa 4; tel. (44) 293-20-13; fax (44) 253-64-58; e-mail pkostyuk@serv.biph.kiev.ua; attached to Nat. Acad. of Sciences of Ukraine; Dir P. H. KOSTYUK; publs *Fiziologichny Zhurnal* (Physiological Journal, in Ukrainian and English, 6 a year), *Neirofiziologia* (Neurophysiology, in Ukrainian and English, 6 a year).

Palladin Institute of Biochemistry: 01601 Kyiv 30 vul. Leontovicha 9; tel. (44) 234-59-74; fax (44) 279-63-65; e-mail secretar@biochem.kiev.ua; internet www

.biochem.kiev.ua; f. 1925; attached to Nat. Acad. of Sciences of Ukraine; 360 ; Dir Prof. SERGIY KOMISARENKO; publ. *Ukrainsky Biokhimichny Zhurnal* (Ukrainian Biochemical Journal, in Ukrainian, Russian and English, 6 a year).

Zabolotny Institute of Microbiology and Virology: 03143 Kyiv, vul. Akademika Zabolotnogo 154; tel. (44) 266-11-79; fax (44) 266-23-79; e-mail smirnov@imv.kiev.ua; internet www.imv.kiev.ua; f. 1928; attached to Nat. Acad. of Sciences of Ukraine; library of 121,000 vols; Dir V. V. SMIRNOV; publ. *Mikrobiolohichny Zhurnal* (Microbiology Journal, in Ukrainian, Russian and English, 6 a year).

Mathematical Sciences

Institute of Mathematics: 01601 Kyiv, vul. Repina 3; tel. (44) 234-53-16; fax (44) 235-20-10; e-mail institute@imath.kiev.ua; internet www.imath.kiev.ua; attached to Nat. Acad. of Sciences of Ukraine; Dir A. M. SAMOILENKO; publ. *Ukrainsky Matematychny Zhurnal* (Ukrainian Mathematical Journal, in Ukrainian and English, monthly).

Physical Sciences

Bogatsky, A. V., Physico-Chemical Institute: 65080 Odesa, Lustdorfskaya doroga 86; tel. (482) 66-51-55; fax (482) 65-20-12; e-mail physchem@paco.odessa.ua; f. 1977; attached to Nat. Acad. of Sciences of Ukraine; 198 mems; Dir SERGEI ANDRONATI.

Boholyubov Institute for Theoretical Physics: vul. Metrologichna 14B, 03680 Kyiv-143; tel. (44) 492-14-23; fax (44) 526-59-98; e-mail itp@bitp.kiev.ua; internet www.bitp.kiev.ua; f. 1966; attached to Nat. Acad. of Sciences of Ukraine; Dir Prof. A. G. ZAGORODNY; publ. *Ukrainian Journal of Physics* (monthly).

Gas Institute: 03113 Kyiv, Degtiarivksa vul. 39; tel. (44) 456-44-71; fax (44) 456-88-30; e-mail eco@ukrpost.net; f. 1949; attached to Nat. Acad. of Sciences of Ukraine; library of 110,000 vols; Dir Prof. B. I. BONDARENKO; publ. *Ekotekhnologia i Resursosberezheniye* (Ecotechnology and Resource Saving, in Russian with summary in Ukrainian and English, 6 a year).

Institute of Bio-organic Chemistry and Petrochemistry: 02660 Kyiv, vul. Murmanska 1; tel. (44) 558-53-88; fax (44) 573-25-52; e-mail users@bpci.kiev.ua; f. 1987; attached to Nat. Acad. of Sciences of Ukraine; Dir Prof. V. P. KUKHAR; publ. *Katalys i Neftekhimiya* (Catalysis and Petrochemistry, 4 a year).

Institute of Colloid Chemistry and Water Chemistry 'A. V. Dumansky': 03680 Kyiv 142, Vernadsky pr. 42; tel. (44) 424-01-96; fax (44) 423-82-24; e-mail honch@iccwc.kiev.ua; f. 1968; attached to Nat. Acad. of Sciences of Ukraine; Dir V. V. GONCHARUK; publ. *Khimiya i Tekhnologiya Vody* (Water Chemistry and Engineering, in Russian and English, 6 a year).

Institute of General and Inorganic Chemistry 'V. I. Vernadsky': 03680 Kyiv, Pr. Akademika Palladina 32/34; tel. (44) 444-34-61; fax (44) 444-30-70; e-mail office@ionc.kar.net; internet www.ionc.kar.net; f. 1918; attached to Nat. Acad. of Sciences of Ukraine; Dir Prof. Dr SERGIY V. VOLKOV; publ. *Ukrainsky Khimichesky Zhurnal* (Ukrainian Journal of Chemistry, in Russian, Ukrainian and English, monthly).

Institute of Geochemistry, Mineralogy and Ore Formation: 03680 Kyiv-142, pr. Palladina 34; tel. (44) 424-01-05; fax (44) 424-12-70; e-mail pavlenko@igmr.relc.com; f. 1969; attached to Nat. Acad. of Sciences of Ukraine; library of 30,000 vols, 35 period-

icals; Dir MYKOLA P. SHCHERBAK; publ. *Mineralogichesky Zhurnal* (Mineralogical Journal, in Ukrainian and English, 6 a year).

Institute of Geological Sciences: 01054 Kyiv, vul. Honchar 55B; tel. (44) 216-94-46; fax (44) 216-98-34; e-mail info@igs.org.ua; f. 1926; attached to Nat. Acad. of Sciences of Ukraine; Dir Prof. PETRO F. HOZHYK; publ. *Geolohichny Zhurnal* (Geological Journal, in Ukrainian and English, 4 a year).

Institute of Geology and Geochemistry of Combustible Minerals: 79053 Lviv, Naukova vul. 3A; tel. (322) 63-15-03; fax (322) 63-22-09; e-mail igggk@ah.ipm.lviv.ua; f. 1951; attached to Nat. Acad. of Sciences of Ukraine and Naftogaz Ukrainy JSC; Dir V. E. ZABIGAILO; publ. *Geologia i Geokhimia Horiuchykh Kopalyn* (Geology and Geochemistry of Mineral Fuels, in Ukrainian and English, 4 a year).

Institute of Geophysics: 03680 Kyiv, pr. Akademika Palladina 32; tel. (44) 424-01-12; fax (44) 450-25-20; e-mail earth@igph.kiev.ua; internet www.igph.kiev.ua; f. 1960; attached to Nat. Acad. of Sciences of Ukraine; Dir V. I. STAROSTENKO; publ. *Geofizichesky Zhurnal* (Geophysical Journal, in Russian, Ukrainian and English, 6 a year).

Institute of the Ionosphere: 61002 Kharkiv, Chervonopraporna vul. 16; tel. and fax (572) 45-11-23; e-mail iion@kpi.kharkov.ua; f. 1991; attached to Nat. Acad. of Sciences of Ukraine and Kharkiv Polytechnical Institute (National Technical University); Dir Prof. VITALY TARAN.

Institute for Metal Physics 'G. V. Kurdyumov': 03142 Kyiv, vul. Vernadskoho 36; tel. (44) 444-10-05; fax (44) 444-25-61; e-mail metall@imp.kiev.ua; internet www.imp.kiev.ua; f. 1932; attached to Nat. Acad. of Sciences of Ukraine; Dir V. V. NEMOSHKALENKO; publs *Metallofizika i Noveishie Tekhnologii* (Metal Physics and Advanced Technology, in Ukrainian and English, monthly), *Uspehi Fiziki Metallov* (Developments in the Physics of Metals).

Institute of Nuclear Research: 03680 Kyiv, pr. Nauky 47; tel. (44) 265-23-49; fax (44) 265-44-63; e-mail interdep@kinr.kiev.ua; internet www.kinr.kiev.ua; attached to Nat. Acad. of Sciences of Ukraine; Dir IVAN M. VYSHNYEVSKIY; publ. *Scientific Papers* (irregular).

Institute of Organic Chemistry: 02660 Kyiv, Murmanska vul. 5; tel. (44) 552-71-50; fax (44) 573-26-43; e-mail iochkiev@ukrpack.net; f. 1939; Dir MYRON O. LOZYNSKIY.

Institute of Physical-Organic Chemistry and Coal Chemistry 'L. M. Litvinenko': 340114 Donetsk, vul. R. Lyuksemburga 70; tel. and fax (622) 55-85-24; e-mail postmaster@infou.donetsk.ua; f. 1975; attached to Nat. Acad. of Sciences of Ukraine; library of 34,000 vols, 44 periodicals; Dir ANATOLY F. POPOV.

Institute of Physics: 03028 Kyiv, pr. Nauky 46; tel. (44) 525-12-20; fax (44) 525-15-89; e-mail fizyka@iop.kiev.ua; internet www.iop.kiev.ua; f. 1929; attached to Nat. Acad. of Sciences of Ukraine; Dir M. S. BRODYN; publ. *Ukrainsky Fizychny Zhurnal* (Ukrainian Physics Journal, in Ukrainian and English, monthly).

Institute of Radio Astronomy: 61002 Kharkiv, Chervonopraporna vul. 4; tel. (57) 706-14-10; fax (57) 706-14-15; e-mail rai@ira.kharkov.ua; internet www.ira.kharkov.ua; f. 1985; attached to Nat. Acad. of Sciences of Ukraine; Dir LEONID M. LYTVYNENKO; publ. *Radiofizyka i Radioastronomiya* (Radiophysics and Radioastronomy, in Ukrainian, Russian and English, 4 a year).

Institute of Semiconductor Physics: 03028 Kyiv, pr. Nauky 45; tel. (44) 525-40-20; fax (44) 525-83-42; e-mail info@isp.kiev.ua; internet www.isp.kiev.ua; f. 1960; attached to Nat. Acad. of Sciences of Ukraine; Dir S. V. SVECHNIKOV; publs *Optoelektronika i Poluprovodnikovaya Tekhnika* (Optoelectronics and Semiconductor Technology, annually), *Semiconductor Physics, Quantum Electronics and Optoelectronics* (in English, 4 a year).

Institute of Single Crystals: 61001 Kharkiv, pr. Lenina 60; tel. (572) 332-23-31; fax (572) 332-02-73; e-mail info@isc.kharkov.com; internet www.isc.kharkov.com; f. 1961; attached to Nat. Acad. of Sciences of Ukraine; Dir Dr VYACHESLAV M. PUZIKOV; publ. *Functional Materials* (in English, 4 a year).

Institute of Surface Chemistry: 03164 Kyiv, vul. Naumovai 31; tel. (44) 444-96-04; fax (44) 424-35-67; e-mail user@surfchem.freenet.kiev.ua; f. 1986; attached to Nat. Acad. of Sciences of Ukraine; library of 20,000 vols; Dir Prof. V. M. OGENKO; publs *Chemistry, Physics and Surface Technology.*

Main Astronomical Observatory: 03680 Kyiv, vul. Akademika Zabolotnogo 27; tel. (44) 526-31-10; fax (44) 526-21-47; e-mail director@mao.kiev.ua; internet www.mao.kiev.ua; f. 1944; attached to Nat. Acad. of Sciences of Ukraine; Dir YA. S. YATSKIV; publs *Kinematika i Fizika Nebesnykh Tel* (Kinematics and Physics of Celestial Bodies, in Ukrainian and English, 6 a year), *Space Science and Technology* (4 a year).

Marine Hydrophysical Institute: 99011 Sevastopol, vul. Kapitanska 2; tel. (69) 254-04-52; fax (69) 255-43-53; e-mail vaivanov@alpha.mhi.iuf.net; internet www.mhi.iuf.net; attached to Nat. Acad. of Sciences of Ukraine; Dir Prof. VITALY A. IVANOV; publ. *Morskoy Gidrofizichesky Zhurnal* (Marine Hydrophysical Journal, in Ukrainian, Russian and English (*Physical Oceanography*), 6 a year).

Pisarzhevsky, L. V., Institute of Physical Chemistry: 03028 Kyiv, Pr. Nauki 31; tel. (44) 265-11-90; fax (44) 265-62-16; e-mail ipcukr@sovam.com; internet www.inphyschem_nas.kiev.ua; f. 1927; attached to Nat. Acad. of Sciences of Ukraine; Dir Prof. V. D. POKHODENKO; publ. *Teoreticheskaya i Eksperimentalnaya Khimiya* (Theoretical and Experimental Chemistry, in Russian and English, 6 a year).

Research and Design Institute of Basic Chemistry: 61002 Kharkiv, Mironositska vul. 25; tel. (57) 700-01-23; fax (57) 700-48-25; e-mail office@niochim.kharkov.ua; internet www.niochim.kharkov.ua/NIOCHIM1.htm; f. 1923; library of 185,000 vols; Dir V.I. MOLCHANOV.

Ukrainian State Geological Research Institute: 04114 Kyiv, vul. Avtozavodska 78; tel. (44) 430-70-24; fax (44) 430-41-76; e-mail ukrdgri@ukrdgri.gov.ua; internet www.ukrdgri.gov.ua; f. 1953; brs in Lviv, Chirnigiv, Poltava, Simferopol and Dnipropetrovsk; Dir MYKHAYLO D. KRASNOZHON.

PHILOSOPHY AND PSYCHOLOGY

Institute of Philosophy 'H. S. Skovoroda': 01001 Kyiv, vul. Tryokhsviatytelska 4; tel. (44) 278-06-05; fax (44) 278-63-66; e-mail ifukr@i.com.ua; internet www.filosof.com.ua; f. 1946; attached to Nat. Acad. of Sciences of Ukraine; Dir Prof MYROSLAV POPOVYCH; publs *Filosofska Dumka* (Philosophical Thought, in Ukrainian, every 2 months), *Filosofski Obrii* (Philosophical Horizons, in Ukrainian, 2 a year), *Praktychna Filosofia* (Practical Philosophy, quarterly), *Religiyna Panorama* (Religious Panorama, monthly).

RELIGION, SOCIOLOGY AND ANTHROPOLOGY

Institute of Art, Folklore Studies and Ethnography 'M. T. Rylsky': 01001 Kyiv, vul. Kirova 4; tel. (44) 266-20-08; e-mail etnolog@etnolog.kiev.ua; internet www.etnolog.kiev.ua; f. 1936; attached to Nat. Acad. of Sciences of Ukraine; Dir Prof. Dr H. A. SKRYPNYK; publ. *Folklore Studies*.

Institute of Sociology: 01021 Kyiv, Shovkovychna 12; tel. (44) 255-74-09; fax (44) 291-56-96; e-mail i-soc@i-soc.org.ua; internet www.i-soc.com.ua; f. 1990; attached to Nat. Acad. of Sciences of Ukraine; Dir Prof. VALERIY M. VORONA; publ. *Sotsiolohiya: Teoriya, Metody, Marketing* (Sociology: Theory, Methods, Marketing, in Ukrainian and English, 6 a year).

TECHNOLOGY

Frantsevich, I. N., Institute of Problems of Materials Science: 03142 Kyiv, vul. Krzhizhanovskoho 3; tel. (44) 424-01-02; fax (44) 424-21-31; e-mail dir@materials.kiev.ua; f. 1952; attached to Nat. Acad. of Sciences of Ukraine; Dir V. V. SKOROHOD; publ. *Poroshkovaya Metallurgia* (Powder Metallurgy, in Ukrainian and English, monthly).

Galkin, A., Donetsk Physical-Engineering Institute: 83114 Donetsk-114, vul. R. Lyuksemburg 72; tel. (62) 255-14-33; fax (62) 337-90-18; e-mail var@hpress.dipt.donetsk.ua; f. 1965; attached to Nat. Acad. of Sciences of Ukraine; library of 10,000 vols; Dir VIKTOR N. VARYUKHIN; publ. *Fizika i Tekhnika Vysokikh Davleniy* (High-pressure Physics and Technology, in Ukrainian and English, 4 a year).

G. S. Pisarenko Institute for Problems of Strength: 01014 Kyiv, Timiryazevska vul. 2; tel. (44) 285-16-87; fax (44) 286-16-84; e-mail postmaster@ipp.kiev.ua; internet www.ipp.kiev.ua; f. 1966; attached to Nat. Acad. of Sciences of Ukraine; Dir V. T. TROSHCHENKO; publ. *Problemy Prochnosti* (in Russian; publ. by Kluwer Academic/Plenum Publishers in English translation as Strength of Materials, 6 a year).

Institute for Superhard Materials: 04074 Kyiv, Avtozavodska vul. 2; tel. (44) 468-86-32; fax (44) 468-86-25; e-mail novikov@ism.ua; internet www.ism.ua; f. 1961; attached to Nat. Acad. of Sciences of Ukraine; Dir Prof. N. V. NOVIKOV; publs *Instumentalnyi Swit* (World of Tools, 6 a year), *Sverkhtviordye Materialy* (Superhard Materials, in Russian and English, 6 a year).

Institute of Applied Mathematics and Mechanics: 83114 Donetsk, vul. R. Lyuksemburg 74; tel. (622) 55-23-94; fax (622) 55-22-65; e-mail math@iamm.ac.donetsk.ua; internet www.iamm.ac.donetsk.ua; f. 1965; attached to Nat. Acad. of Sciences of Ukraine; library of 84,486 vols; Dir IGOR V. SKRYPNIK; publs *Mekhanika Tverdogo Tela* (irregular), *Nelineinye Granichnye Zadachi* (irregular), *Teoriya Sluchainykh Protsessov* (irregular), *Trudy Instituta Prikladnoi Matematiki i Mehaniki NAN Ukrainy* (irregular).

Institute of Cybernetics 'V. M. Hlushkov': 03680 Kyiv MSP, Glushkova 20; tel. (44) 266-20-08; fax (44) 266-74-18; e-mail aik@public.icyb.kiev.ua; internet www.icyb.kiev.ua; attached to Nat. Acad. of Sciences of Ukraine; Dir I. K. SERHIENKO; publs *Kibernetika i Sistemny Analiz* (Cybernetics and Systems Analysis, in Ukrainian and English, 6 a year), *Problemy Upravlenia i Informatiki* (Problems of Control and Informatics, in Ukrainian and English, 6 a year), *Uprav-*

lyauschie Sistemy i Mashiny (Control Systems and Computers, in Ukrainian and English, 6 a year).

Institute of Electrodynamics: 03680 Kyiv, Peremohy 56; tel. (44) 456-01-51; fax (44) 445-69-49; e-mail ied@ied.kiev.ua; internet www.ied.kiev.ua; attached to Nat. Acad. of Sciences of Ukraine; Dir. A. K. SHIDLOVSKIY; publ. *Tekhnichna Elektrodynamika* (Technical Electrodynamics, in Ukrainian and English, 6 a year).

Institute of Engineering Mechanics 'A. M. Pidhorny': 61046 Kharkiv, vul. Pozharskoho 2/10; tel. (572) 94-55-14; fax (572) 94-46-35; e-mail root@ipmach.kharkov.ua; internet www.ipmach.kharkov.ua; attached to Nat. Acad. of Sciences of Ukraine; Dir YURI M. MATSEVITIY; publ. *Problemy Mashinostroenia* (Problems of Mechanical Engineering, in Ukrainian and English, 4 a year).

Institute of Engineering Thermophysics: 03057 Kyiv, vul. Zhelyabova 2A, k. 102; tel. (44) 456-62-82; fax (44) 456-60-91; e-mail admin@ittf.kiev.ua; internet www.ittf.kiev.ua; attached to Nat. Acad. of Sciences of Ukraine; Dir ANATOLIY A. DOLINSKIY; publ. *Promyshlennaya Teplotekhnika* (Industrial Thermal Engineering, in Ukrainian and English, 6 a year).

Institute of Geotechnical Mechanics: 320095 Dnipropetrovsk, Simferopolska vul. 2A; tel. (562) 46-01-51; fax (562) 46-24-26; e-mail nanu@igtm.dp.ua; internet www.igtm.narod.ru; f. 1962; attached to Nat. Acad. of Sciences of Ukraine; library of 109,000 vols; Dir A.F. BULAT; publ. *Geotechnical Mechanics* (4 a year).

Institute of Hydromechanics: 03057 Kyiv, vul. Zhelyabova 8/4; tel. (44) 456-43-13; fax (44) 455-64-32; e-mail office@hydromech.com.ua; internet www.hydromech.kiev.ua; f. 1926; attached to Nat. Acad. of Sciences of Ukraine; library of 84,727 vols; Dir VIKTOR T. GRINCHENKO; publs *Acoustics Bulletin* (4 a year), *Applied Hydromechanics* (4 a year).

Institute for Information Recording: 03113 Kyiv, vul. Shpaka 2; tel. (44) 446-83-89; fax (44) 241-72-33; e-mail petrov@ipri.kiev.ua; internet www.ipri.kiev.ua; f. 1987; attached to Nat. Acad. of Sciences of Ukraine; optical storage, information-analytical systems, information security, digital transfer of Edison cylinders with audio-cultural heritage, expert decision-making support systems; 210 mems; Dir V. V. PETROV; publs *Reestracia Zberezenna i Obrobka Danih* (Data Recording, Storage and Processing, in Ukrainian, Russian and English, 4 a year), *Ukrainsky Referatyvny Zhurnal 'Dzherelo'* (Ukrainian Journal of Abstracts 'Dzherelo', in Ukrainian and English, 6 a year).

Institute of Low-Temperature Physics and Engineering 'B. I. Verkin': 61103 Kharkiv, pr. Lenina 47; tel. (57) 340-22-23; fax (57) 340-33-70; e-mail ilt@ilt.kharkov.ua; internet www.ilt.kharkov.ua; f. 1960; attached to Nat. Acad. of Sciences of Ukraine; library of 40,000 vols; Dir Prof. SERGEI LEONIDOVICH GNATCHENKO; publs *Fizika Nizkikh Temperatur* (Low-temperature Physics, in Ukrainian, Russian and English, monthly), *Matematicheskaya Fizika, Analiz, Geometria* (Mathematical Physics, Analysis, Geometry, in Ukrainian, Russian and English, 4 a year).

Institute of Mining and the Chemical Industry: 79026 Lviv, Striiska vul. 98; tel. (322) 97-13-77; fax (322) 34-40-61; e-mail ghp@ghp.lviv.ua; internet www.glrhimprom.narod.ru; f. 1956; Chair. I. I. ZOZULIA.

Institute of Modelling Problems in Energetics: 03164 Kyiv 164 vul. Generala

Naumova 15; tel. (44) 424-10-63; fax (44) 424-05-86; e-mail em@ipme.kiev.ua; internet www.ipme.kiev.ua; f. 1972; attached to Nat. Acad. of Sciences of Ukraine; 150 mems; Dir V. F. EVDOKIMOV; publ. *Elektronnoe Modelirovanie* (Electronic Modelling, in Russian and English, 6 a year).

Institute of Pulse Research and Engineering: 54018 Mykolayiv, Zhovtnevy pr. 43A; tel. (512) 22-41-13; fax (512) 22-61-40; e-mail iipt@iipt.com.ua; internet iipt.in.mk.ua; f. 1962; attached to Nat. Acad. of Sciences of Ukraine; library of 126,000 vols; Dir O. I. VOVCHENKO.

Institute of Radiophysics and Electronics 'O. Ya. Usikov': 61085 Kharkiv, Vul. Akademika Proskury 12; tel. (572) 44-83-19; fax (572) 44-11-05; e-mail ire@ire.kharkov.ua; internet www.ire.kharkov.ua; f. 1955; attached to Nat. Acad. of Sciences of Ukraine; Dir VLADIMIR M. YAKOVENKO.

Iron and Steel Institute 'Z. I. Nekrasov': 49050 Dnipropetrovsk, pl. Akademika Starodubova 1; tel. (56) 776-53-15; fax (56) 776-59-24; e-mail isi-nasu@a-teleport.com; internet www.isi.dnepr.net; f. 1939; attached to Nat. Acad. of Sciences of Ukraine; Dir Prof. Dr VADIM I. BOLSHAKOV; publ. *Fundamental and Applied Problems of the Steel Industry* (proceedings, annually).

Paton, Y. O., Institute of Electrical Welding: 03680 Kyiv, vul. Bozhenko 11; tel. (44) 287-31-83; fax (44) 528-04-86; e-mail office@paton.kiev.ua; internet www.paton.kiev.ua; f. 1934; attached to Nat. Acad. of Sciences of Ukraine; Dir B. E. PATON; publs *Automaticheskaya Svarka* (Automatic Welding, in Ukrainian and English, monthly), *Sovremennaya Elektrometallurgiya* (Electrometallurgy Today, in Russian, 4 a year), *Tekhnicheskaya Diagnostika i Nerazrushayushchiy Kontrol* (Technical Diagnostics and Non-destructive Testing, in Ukrainian and English, 4 a year).

Physical Mechanical Institute 'Karpenko': 79060 Lviv, vul. Naukova 5; tel. (322) 63-30-88; fax (322) 64-94-27; e-mail pminasu@ipm.lviv.ua; internet www.ipm.lviv.ua; f. 1951; attached to Nat. Acad. of Sciences of Ukraine; Dir V. V. PANASYUK; publs *Fizyko-Khimichna Mekhanika Materialiv* (Physical and Chemical Mechanics of Materials, in Ukrainian and English, 6 a year), *Vidbir i Obrobka Informatsii* (Information Extraction and Processing, in Ukrainian, 2 a year).

Pidstryhach Institute of Applied Problems of Mechanics and Mathematics: 79060 Lviv, Naukova str. 3B; tel. (322) 63-83-77; fax (322) 63-62-70; e-mail adm@iapmm.lviv.ua; internet www.iapmm.lviv.ua; f. 1973; attached to Nat. Acad. of Sciences of Ukraine; Dir Dr ROMAN M. KUSHNIR; publs *Applied Problems of Mechanics and Mathematics* (annually), *Mathematical Methods and Physicomechanical Fields* (4 a year).

Research and Development Institute of the Merchant Marine of Ukraine: 65026 Odesa, Lanzheronovska vul. 15A; tel. (48) 741-17-04; fax (48) 741-11-77; e-mail unii@paco.net; internet www.unii.odessa.ua; f. 1947; Dir ALEXANDER LESNIK.

Research Institute of the Sewn Goods Industry: 03680 Kyiv, vul. P. Lyubchenko 15; tel. (44) 528-55-41; fax (44) 528-64-57; e-mail legprom@i.kiev.ua; internet www.iptelecom.net.ua/~legprom; f. 1961; library of 22,500 vols; Dir V. P. KRYSKO.

State Research and Design Institute of Chemical Engineering 'Khimtekhnologiya': 93400 Luhansk oblast, Severodonetsk, vul. Vilesova 1; tel. (6452) 3-42-20; fax (6452) 2-50-42; e-mail office@ixt.lg.ua; internet www.ixt.lg.ua; f. 1950; library of 130,000 vols; Dir PETR P. BORISOV; publ. *Collected Research Papers* (monthly).

State Titanium Research and Design Institute: 69035 Zaporizhzhia, Lenina 180; tel. (612) 33-23-23; fax (612) 24-67-01; e-mail common@timag.org; internet www.timag .org; f. 1956; design and development of non-ferrous metallurgical processes, production of semiconductors and carbon-graphite materials; Dir Gen. Dr IGOR V. ZABELIN.

Timoshenko, S. P., Institute of Mechanics: 03057 Kyiv, vul. Nesterova 3; tel. (44) 456-93-51; fax (44) 456-03-19; e-mail ang@imech.freenet.kiev.ua; internet www .inmech.kiev.ua; library of 20,000 vols; f. 1918; mechanics of composite and inhomogenous materials; structural mechanics; mechanics of coupled fields in materials and structures; mechanics of fracture and fatigue; dynamics and stability of mechanical system motion; attached to Nat. Acad. of Sciences of Ukraine; Dir Prof. Dr ALEXANDER N. GUZ; publs *International Applied Mechanics* (in English, monthly), *Prikladnaya Mekhanika* (in Russian, monthly).

Ukrainian State Research and Design Institute of Mining Geology, Rock Mechanics and Mine Surveying (Ukr-NIMI): 83121 Donetsk, vul. Chelyuskintsev 291; tel. (622) 348-16-48; fax (622) 348-16-47; e-mail ukrnimi@ukrnimi.donetsk.ua; internet www.ukrnimi.donetsk.ua; f. 1929; attached to Nat. Acad of Science of Ukraine; Dir Dr A. V. ANTSIFEROV.

Vniichimprojekt Institute: 02002 Kyiv-2, vul. M. Raskovoi 11; tel. (44) 517-05-81; fax (44) 517-15-18; e-mail vniichim@nbi.com.ua; internet www.himpro.com.ua; f. 1970; develops synthetic detergents, personal care products and packaging materials; library of 38,800 vols; Pres. VALERY N. KRIVOSHEI; publs *Khimichna Promyslovist Ukrainy* (6 a year), *Upakovka* (6 a year).

Yuzhniigiprogaz Institute OJSC: 83121 Donetsk, Vul. Artema 169G; tel. (622) 55-10-68; fax (62) 305-71-76; e-mail ex@yuzh-gaz .donetsk.ua; internet www.ungg.org; f. 1933; library of 38,000 vols; Chair. B. A. SUMSKY.

Libraries and Archives
Chernivtsi

Chernivtsi National University 'Yuriy Fedkovych', Library: 58000 Chernivtsi, vul. Lesi Ukrainki 23; tel. (3722) 2-45-74; e-mail biblio@chnu.cv.ua; 2,600,000 vols; Dir OLEG I. SHLYUK.

Dnipropetrovsk

Dnipropetrovsk National University Library 'O. Gonchar': 49050 Dnipropetrovsk, vul. Kozakova 8; tel. (562) 46-61-95; internet www.dsu.dp.ua/lib.html; 1,417,000 vols; Dir S. V. KUBYSHKINA.

Donetsk

Scientific Library of Donetsk National University: 83055 Donetsk, Universitetska vul. 24; tel. (622) 99-23-78; fax (622) 92-71-12; e-mail bdongu@dongu.donetsk.ua; internet library.dongu.donetsk.ua; f. 1937; 1,052,763 vols; Dir N. A. KARYAGINA.

Kharkiv

Kharkiv V. N. Karazin National University Central Scientific Library: 61077 Kharkiv, pl. Svobody 4; tel. (57) 707-52-86; fax (57) 707-12-55; e-mail cnb@univ .kharkov.ua; internet www.univer.kharkov .ua/main/library; f. 1804; 3,400,000 vols, incl. 50,000 rare editions, 17 incunabula, more

than 1,000 manuscripts, books by classical writers and scholars published in their lifetimes; Dir IRINA G. LEVCHENKO (acting).

Kyiv

Archives of Ukraine.
Attached archives:

Central State Archive and Museum of Literature and Art of Ukraine: 01601 Kyiv, Volodymyrska vul. 22A; tel. (44) 228-44-81.

Central State Archive of Public Organizations of Ukraine: 01011 Kyiv, vul. Kutuzova 24; tel. (44) 295-55-32; e-mail cdago@online.com.ua.

Central State Archive of Supreme Bodies of Power and Government of Ukraine:tel. (44) 275-36-66; e-mail tsdavo@archives.gov.ua.

Central State CinePhotoFono Archive of Ukraine 'H.S.Pshenychniy':tel. (44) 275-37-37; e-mail sdkffa@archives.gov.ua.

Central State Historical Archive of Ukraine in Kyiv: 03110 Kiev, Solomyanska vul. 24; tel. (44) 275-30-02; fax (44) 275-30-02; e-mail cdiak@archives.gov .ua; internet www.archives.gov.ua; f. 1852; Dir OLGA MUZYCHUK.

State Archive of the City of Kyiv: 04060 Kyiv, vul. Oleny Telihy 23; tel. (44) 440-54-16; e-mail archiv@archiv.kyiv-city.gov.ua.

State Archive of Kyiv Oblast: 04119 Kyiv, vul. Melnykova 38; tel. (44) 213-75-72.

State Committee on Archives of Ukraine: 03110 MSP Kyiv-110, Solomyanska vul. 24; tel. (44) 275-27-77; fax (44) 275-36-55; e-mail mail@archives.gov .ua; internet www.archives.gov.ua; f. 1919; Dir-Gen. Prof. Dr HENNADIY BORYAK.

Kyiv National University 'Taras Shevchenko' Library: 01601 Kyiv, vul. Volodymyrska 58; tel. (44) 235-70-98; fax (44) 235-70-98; e-mail info@libcc.univ.kiev.ua; internet www.library.univ.kiev.ua; f. 1834; 3,559,000 vols; Dir VALENTINA G. NESTERENKO.

National Agricultural Library of the Ukrainian Academy of Agricultural Sciences: 03127 Kyiv, vul. Heroyiv Oborony 10; tel. (44) 266-05-09; e-mail dir@ucsal.nauu .kiev.ua; f. 1921; 964,000 vols; Dir Dr NADIA F. GRYTSENKO; publs *Agropromysloviy Complex Ukraiiny* (abstract journal, 4 a year), *Akademiky Ukrainskoi Akademii Agrarnykh Nauk* (bibliographic series, 6 a year), *Silskohospodarki Knyhy* (4 a year).

National Parliamentary Library of Ukraine: 01001 Kyiv, vul. M. Hrushevskoho 1; tel. (44) 228-85-12; fax (44) 228-85-12; e-mail npbu@nplu.kiev.ua; internet www .nplu.kiev.ua; f. 1866; 4,000,000 vols; Dir A. P. KORNIENKO; publ. *Kalendar znamennikh i pamyatnikh dat* (4 a year).

State History Library: 01015 Kyiv vul. Sichnevoho Povstannya 21; tel. (44) 290-46-17; e-mail shlu@shlu.freenet.kiev.ua; f. 1939; Dir OLENA VINOHRADOVA.

State Scientific Medical Library: 01033 Kyiv, vul. L. Tolstogo 7; tel. (44) 234-51-97; fax (44) 235-11-35; e-mail medlib@mail .library.gov; internet www.library.gov.ua; f. 1930; Dir RAISA I. PAVLENKO.

State Scientific and Technical Library of Ukraine: 03650 Kyiv, vul. Antonovicha 180; tel. (44) 528-21-85; fax (44) 529-34-91; e-mail gntb@uintei.kiev.ua; internet www .gntb.n-t.org; f. 1935; 20,000,000 vols, incl. books, documents and patents related to science and technology; Dir V. H. DRYGAYLO.

Ukrainian Institute of Scientific-Technical and Economic Information: 03680

Kyiv, vul. Horkogo 180; tel. (44) 268-25-79; fax (44) 268-25-41; Dir N. N. ERMOSHENKO.

Vernadsky National Library of Ukraine: 03039 Kyiv, pr. 40 Richja Zhovtnja 3; tel. (44) 265-81-04; fax (44) 264-33-98; e-mail nlu@csl .freenet.kiev.ua; internet www.nbuv.go.ua; f. 1919; over 14,000,000 vols; colln incl. books, newspapers, magazines, serials, maps, music scores, fine arts materials, manuscripts, old and rare books, incunabula, documents; colln of Slavic writings; archives of outstanding Ukrainian and foreign scientists; archives of the National Academy of Sciences of Ukraine; 40 departments and centres of preservation and restoration, culture and education, computer technologies, and publishing; Dir-Gen. O. S. ONYSHCHENKO; publs *Bibliotechnyi Visnyk* (Library Journal, in Ukrainian and English, 6 a year), *Naukovi Pratsi* (Scientific Works, 2 or 3 a year).

Lviv

Lviv Ivan Franko State University Library: 290602 Lviv, vul. Dragomanova 5; tel. (322) 73-04-94; 2,500,000 vols; Dir V. K. POTAICHUK.

Lviv Scientific Library of the National Academy of Sciences of Ukraine 'V. Stefanyk': 79000 Lviv, vul. Stefanyka 2; tel. (322) 74-43-72; fax (322) 76-51-58; e-mail library@lsl.lviv.ua; internet www.lsl.lviv.ua; f. 1940; 6,000,000 vols; Dir MIROSLAV. M. ROMANYUK.

Odesa

Scientific Library of Odesa National University 'I. I. Mechnikov': 65082 Odesa, vul. Preobrazhenska 24; tel. and fax (482) 26-04-01; e-mail libonu@ukr.net; f. 1817; 3,534,017 vols; Dir MARINA A. PODREZOVA.

Simferopol

Taurida National University 'V. I. Vernadsky', Library: 95007 Simferopol, pr. Vernaskogo 4; tel. (652) 51-69-98; fax (652) 51-71-35; e-mail library@crimea.edu; 776,000 vols; Librarian V. I. SPIROVA.

Uzhhorod

Uzhhorod National University Library: Uzhgorod, Kapytulna vul. 9; tel. (3122) 3-72-29; e-mail library@univ.uzhgorod.ua; internet www.univ.uzhgorod.ua/~library; 1,500,000 vols; Dir OLENA I. POCHEKUTOVA.

Museums and Art Galleries
Alupka

Alupka State Palace and Park Preserve: Alupka, Dvortsove shosse 10; tel. and fax (654) 72-29-51; f. 1921; Russian noble culture and way of life in 19th century; library of 10,000 vols; spec. colln of 17th c. maps of Europe and America; Dir K. K. KASPEROVICH.

Alushta

Alushta Literary Memorial Museum of S. M. Sergeev-Tsensky: Alushta, vul. Sergeeva-Tsenskogo 15; tel. (6560) 3-06-64; house where the author lived; Dir T. A. FEFYUZA.

Bakhchisarai

Bakhchisarai Historical and Cultural State Preserve: 98405 Crimea, Bakhchisarai, ul. Richna 133; tel. and fax (6554) 4-28-81; e-mail hansaray@crimeastar.net; internet www.hansaray.org.ua; f. 1917; works of art, architectural monuments, the Khan Palace of Bakhchisarai (built 1532), cave towns; library of 12,000 vols; Dir EVGENIY PETROV.

Chernihiv

Chernihiv Literary Museum 'Mikhailo Kotsyubinsky': 14000 Chernihiv, vul. Kotsyubinskogo 3; tel. (4622) 4-04-59; e-mail museummk@ic.com.ua; f. 1934; life and work of Kotsyubinsky; library of 11,000 books; Dir IGOR KOTSYUBINSKY; publ. *Collections* (every 5 years).

Chernivtsi

Chernivtsi Memorial Museum 'Yu. A. Fedkovych': Chernivtsi, vul. Pushkina 17; tel. (372) 2-56-78; f. 1945; life and work of the writer A. Fedkovich; Dir D. FYLYPCHUK.

Dniprodzerzhynsk

Dniprodzerzhynsk Museum of Town History: 51900 Dniprodzerzhynsk; tel. (5692) 3-02-24; f. 1931; library of 10,000 vols; Dir NINA TSIGANOK.

Dnipropetrovsk

Dnipropetrovsk Historical Museum 'D. I. Yavornystkiy': Dnipropetrovsk, vul. K. Marksa 16; tel. (562) 46-24-28; fax (562) 46-05-12; e-mail muzeum@a-teleport.com; internet www.museum.dp.ua; Dir NADEZHDA KAPUSTINA.

Dnipropetrovsk State Art Museum: 49044 Dnipropetrovsk, vul. Shevchenko 21; tel. (562) 47-32-65; e-mail info@globe.dp.ua; internet www.artmuseum.dp.ua; Dir LUDMILA TVERSKAYA.

Donetsk

Donetsk Botanical Gardens: 83059 Donetsk, pr. Ilicha 110; tel. (622) 94-12-80; fax (622) 94-61-57; e-mail horb@hcrb.dn.ua, f. 1964; attached to Nat. Acad. of Sciences of Ukraine; Dir A. Z. GLUKHOV.

Donetsk Art Museum: 83055 Donetsk, Pushkina 35; tel. (62) 304-83-03.

Kamyanets-Podilsky

Kamyanets-Podilsky State Historical Museum-Preserve: 32300 Khmelnitska oblast, Kamyanets-Podilsky, vul. Ioanno-Predtechenska 2; tel. (3849) 2-37-84; f. 1890; Dir L. P. STANISLAVSKA.

Kerch

Kerch State Archaeological Museum: 98300 Crimea, Kerch, Sverdlova 7; tel. and fax (65) 2-04-75; e-mail museum@kerch.com.ua; f. 1826; library of 20,000 vols; Dir P. I. IVANENKO; publ. *Arkheologiya i istoriya Bospora* (irregular).

Kharkiv

Kharkiv State Art Museum: 61002 Kharkiv, Sovnarkomivska vul. 11; tel. and fax (572) 43-02-10; f. 1934; Ukrainian, Russian and Western European artists; library of 18,000 vols; Dir V. V. MYZGINA.

Kharkiv State Historical Museum: 61003 Kharkiv, Universitetska vul. 10; tel. and fax (572) 23-20-94; Dir N. A. VOEVODIN.

Khomutovo

Ukrainian Steppe Nature Reserve: 87620 Donetsk oblast, Novoazov raion, Khomutove; tel. (62) 792-73-25; f. 1961; attached to Nat. Acad. of Sciences of Ukraine; Dir Dr ANATOLIY P. GENOV.

Kyiv

Bohdan and Varvara Khanenko Museum of Arts: 01004 Kyiv, Tereshchenkivska 15–17; tel. (44) 235-02-25; fax (44) 235-02-06; e-mail khanenkomuseum@ukr.net; f. 1919; holds more than 20,000 items of western European, Oriental and ancient art; Dir VIRA VYNOHRADOVA; publ. *Khanenko Readings* (annually).

Kyiv State Literary Museum 'Lessya Ukrainka': 01032 Kyiv, vul. Saksaganskogo 97; tel. (44) 220-57-52; f. 1962; life and work of the Ukrainian poets and artists of the 19th and early 20th centuries; library of 5,000 vols; Dir IRINA L. VEREMEYEVA.

Kyiv Museum of Russian Art: 01004 Kyiv, Tereshchenkivska vul. 9; tel. (44) 451-40-27; fax (44) 234-61-07; e-mail kmru@uninet.kiev.ua; f. 1922; library of 17,000 vols; Dir T.N. SOLDATOVA.

Museum of Theatrical, Musical and Cinematographic Art of Ukraine: 01015 Kyiv, vul. I. Mazepy 21/24; tel. and fax (44) 280-51-31; e-mail tmf-museum@ukr.net; internet www.tmf-museum.iatp.org.ua; f. 1923; library of 30,000 vols; Dir L. N. MATAT.

National Art Museum of Ukraine: 01001 Kyiv, vul. M. Hrushevskoho 6; tel. (44) 228-13-57; fax (44) 228-74-54; e-mail namu@i.com.ua; f. 1899; painting and wood-carving since the Middle Ages; Dir A. I. MELNIK.

National Botanical Gardens 'M. M. Gryshko': 01014 Kyiv, Timiryazevska vul. 1; tel. (44) 295-41-05; fax (44) 295-26-49; e-mail cherevchenko@botanical-garden.kiev.ua; f. 1935; attached to Nat. Acad. of Sciences of Ukraine; library of 39,041 vols; Dir Prof. Dr T. M. CHEREVCHENKO.

National Kyiv-Pechersk Lavra Museum: 01015 Kyiv, vul. Sichnevogo Povstannya 25; tel. (44) 254-22-57; e-mail lavra@lavra.kiev.ua; internet www.lavra.kiev.ua; ancient monastery, icons.

National Museum of the History of Ukraine: 01034 Kyiv, vul. Volodymyrska 2; tel. (44) 228-65-45; fax (44) 228-43-23, e-mail mhistory@i.com.ua; f. 1899; history, archaeology, religion, ethnography, 600,000 exhibits; Dir SERHIY CHAIKOVSKYI.

National Taras Shevchenko Museum: 12 Taras Shevchenko bulv., 01004 Kyiv; tel. (44) 234-25-23; e-mail m-shevchenka@ukr.net; life and work of the poet T. G. Shevchenko; f. 1940; Dir S. A. HALCHENKO.

St Sophia of Kiev National Conservation Area: 01034 Kyiv, Volodymyrska vul. 24; tel. (44) 278-26-20; fax (44) 278-67-06; e-mail stsophia@i.kiev.ua; internet www.sophia.org.ua; f. 1934; comprises 11th c. St Sofia cathedral (with early frescoes and mosaics) and other, 18th c. bldgs; attached museums incl. St Cyril Church Museum, St Andrew Church Museum, Golden Gates Museum (11th c. town gatehouse) and, in the Crimea, 6th–15th c. Sudak fortress; Dir.-Gen. NELYA M. KUKOVALSKA.

Ukrainian Museum of Folk and Decorative Art: 01015 Kyiv, vul. Sichnevoho Povstannya 21; tel. (44) 290-13-43; f. 1954; library of 3,180 vols; Dir V. G. NAGAI; publ. *Folk Creative Work and Ethnography*.

Kolomiya

Kolomiya State Museum of Folk Art: Ivano-Frankivska oblast, Kolomiya, Teatralna vul. 25; tel. (3433) 2-39-12; f. 1926; library of 6,000 vols; Dir Y. TKACHUK; publ. *People's House* (6 a year).

Lviv

Lviv Historical Museum: 79008 Lviv, pl. Rynok 4/6/24; tel. (322) 74-33-04; f. 1893; Dir BOGDAN CHAYKOVSKIY.

Lviv State Picture Gallery: 79000 Lviv, vul. Stefanika 3; tel. (322) 72-39-48; fax (322) 72-30-09; f. 1907; West European and Ukrainian contemporary art; library of 34,276 vols; Dir BORIS VOZNITSKY.

National Museum in Lviv 'Andrey Sheptytsky': 79008 Lviv–8, Svobody 20; tel. (322) 74-22-82; fax (322) 75-92-53; f. 1905; Dir IHOR KOZHAN.

State Museum of Ethnography, Arts and Crafts: Lviv, pr. Svoboda 15; tel. (322) 727012; f. 1873; attached to Nat. Acad. of Sciences of Ukraine.

State Natural History Museum: 79008 Lviv, Teatralna vul. 18; tel. and fax (322) 74-23-07; e-mail museum@museum.lviv.net; internet museum.lviv.net; f. 1870; attached to Nat. Acad. of Sciences of Ukraine; library of 69,000 vols; Dir Prof. YURIY M. CHORNOBAY; publ. *Proceedings* (annually).

Odesa

Odesa Archaeological Museum: 65026 Odesa, vul. Lanzheronovska 4; tel. 722-01-71; e-mail arhaeology@farlep.net; internet www.arhaeology.farlep.odessa.ua; f. 1825; history of the Northern Black Sea Coast area; library of 28,000 vols; Dir V. P. VANCHUGOV; Librarian H. P. UKRAINSKA.

Odesa Fine Arts Museum: 65082 Odesa, Sofievska vul. 5A; tel. (482) 23-82-72; fax (482) 23-83-93; e-mail ofam@farlep.net; f. 1899; Ukrainian and Russian art since 15th c.; library of 15,000 vols; Dir NATALYA S. POLISHCHUK.

Odesa Museum of Western and Eastern Art: 270026 Odesa, Pushkinsha vul. 9; tel. and fax (482) 22-48-15; e-mail oweamuseum@hotbox.ru; internet www.oweamuseum.odessa.ua; f. 1920; library of 14,000 vols; Dir VICTOR S. NIKIFOROV.

Poltava

Poltava Art Museum: 314020 Poltava, Spaska 11; tel. (5322) 7-27-11; f. 1919; library of 4,000 vols; Curator KIM SKALATSKY.

Poltava State Museum: Poltava, Lenina 2; life and work of the writers P. Mirnyi, J. Kotlyarevsky, V. G. Korolenko, N. V. Gogol; library of 80,000 vols; Dir GALINA P. BELOUS.

Sevastopol

National Preserve of Tauric Chersonesos: 99045 Crimea, Sevastopol, vul. Drevnyaya 1; tel. and fax (692) 55-02-78; e-mail info@chersonesos.org; internet www.chersonesos.org; f. 1892; archaeological park incorporating museum and ruins of Greek colony and Byzantine city of Tauric Chersonesos; library of 30,000 vols; Dir Dr LEONID V. MARCHENKO; publ. *Khersonesskyi Sbornik* (Chersonesos Collected Articles, annually).

Shevchenkovo

Shevchenko, T. G., State Memorial Museum: Cherkasska oblast, Zvenigorodsky raion, Shevchenkovo; f. 1939; life and work of T. G. Shevchenko; library of 3,000 vols; Dir T. V. GULAK.

Sumy

Sumy Art Museum 'Nukanor Onatsky': 40030 Sumy, Krasnaya pl. 1; tel. (542) 22-04-81; internet www.city.sumy.ua/artgalery; f. 1920; Dir GALINA V. AREFEVA.

Yalta

Nikita Botanical Gardens: 98648 Crimea, Yalta, Nikita; tel. (654) 33-55-30; fax (654) 33-53-86; e-mail nbg@yalta.crimea.ua; internet www.nbg.crimea.ua; f. 1812; attached to Ukrainian Acad. of Agrarian Sciences; library of 240,000 vols; Dir Prof. Dr V. N. EZHOV; publs *Bulletin* (3 a year), *Collected Scientific Works* (3 a year).

Universities

AGRARIAN UNIVERSITIES

BILA TSERKVA STATE AGRARIAN UNIVERSITY

09117 Kyivska obl., Bila Tserkva, bul. 50-Richchya Perermoti 96

Telephone: (04463) 3-11-01
E-mail: rector@btsau.kiev.ua
Internet: www.btsau.kiev.ua

Founded 1750; present name and status 1995

Rector: Dr Mykhailo M. Baranovskiy
First Pro-Rector: Prof. Dr Vitaliy P. Novak
Pro-Rector for Distance Studies: Prof. Dr Svetlana I. Tsekhmistrenko
Pro-Rector for Finance: Dr Tatyana V. Arbuzova
Pro-Rector for Research: Prof. Dr Ihor L. Yakimenko
Pro-Rector for Studies: Prof. Dr Lyliya V. Baranovskaya

Publication: Vestnik BSGAU (Bila Tserkva State Agrarian University Bulletin)

Faculties of Agronomy, Biotechnology, Culture and Art, Economics, External Studies, Languages, Law, Physical Education, Qualification Improvement and Veterinary Medicine..

ATTACHED RESEARCH INSTITUTES

Research Institute for Internal Animal Disease: Acad. Prof. Dr V. I. Levchenko.
Research Institute for Veterinary Medical Expertise and Products in Livestock Breeding: Dir Acad. Dr P. V. Mikityuk.

CRIMEAN STATE AGRARIAN UNIVERSITY

95492 Simferopol, Agrarnoye

Telephone: (652) 26-33-52
Fax: (652) 22-39-66
E-mail: rectorat@csau.crimea-ua.com
Internet: www.csau.crimea-ua.com

Founded 1922

Rector: Prof. M. M. Melnikov

Library of 542,425 vols
Number of teachers: 265
Number of students: 4,047

DEANS

Faculty of Accountancy and Finance: Prof. Anna N. Trubina
Faculty of Agricultural Mechanization: Prof. Anatoliy V. Baukov
Faculty of Agronomy: Prof. Nikolai I. Kopylov
Faculty of Economics and Management: Dr Valeriy A. Zagotov
Faculty of Humanities: Prof. Anatoliy P. Kazak
Faculty of Pomiculture and Viticulture: Dr Valeriy F. Vilchinskiy
Faculty of Technology: Dr Yuri B. Gerber
Faculty of Veterinary Medicine: Dr Galina V. Lukashik

DNIPROPETROVSK STATE AGRARIAN UNIVERSITY

49600 Dnipropetrovsk, vul. Voroshilova 25

Telephone: (56) 744-81-32
Internet: www.dsau.dp.ua

Founded 1922

Rector: Acad. Volodymyr I. Shemavnov
First Pro-Rector for Education: Prof. Dr Anatoliy S. Kobets
Pro-Rector for External and Postgraduate Studies: Dr Petro M. Makarenko

Pro-Rector for Research: Dr Petro M. Makarenko
Librarian: A. H. Bratchyk

Library of 372,000 vols
Number of teachers: 478
Number of students: 5,717 (3,793 full-time, 1,924 external)

Publications: Bulletin (2 a year), Transactions (2 a year)

DEANS

Faculty of Accounting and Finance: Doc. O. V. Nikitchenko
Faculty of Agricultural Mechanization: Dr V. I. Melnichenko
Faculty of Agronomy: Dr O. O. Mytsyk
Faculty of Biotechnology: Dr M. H. Povod
Faculty of Humanities: Dr I. I. Yaremenko
Faculty of Marketing and Management: T. M. Samilyk
Faculty of Veterinary Medicine: Dr I. A. Biben
Faculty of Water Management: Dr D. M. Onoprienko

KHARKIV STATE AGRARIAN UNIVERSITY 'V. V. DOKUCHAYEV'

62483 Kharkiv, P/O 'Komunist-1', vul. Mazepy 10

Telephone: (572) 93-71-46
Fax: (572) 93-60-67
Internet: www.hgau.narod.ru

Founded 1816

Rector: Prof. Mykola D. Yevtushenko

Library of 600,000 vols
Number of teachers: 258
Number of students: 5,195

Publications: Agrochemistry, Common Agriculture, Forestry, Plant Growing and Vegetable Production, Series on Crop Production, Series on Economics and Natural Sciences, Series on Soil Science

DEANS

Faculty of Agrochemistry and Soil Science: Vasyl Dekhtyaryov
Faculty of Agronomy: Yevgen Ogurtsov
Faculty of Continuing Education: Volodymyr Puzik
Faculty of Correspondence Studies: Volodymyr Biliusko
Faculty of Economics: Oleksandr Ulyanchenko
Faculty of Forestry: Anatoliy Polyvyaniy
Faculty of Land Management: Vasyl Balakyrsky
Faculty of Plant Protection: Volodymyr Turenko

LVIV STATE AGRARIAN UNIVERSITY

80381 Lviv oblast, Zhovkva raion, Dublyany

Telephone: (322) 79-33-45
E-mail: lday@mail.lviv.ua
Internet: www.lday.lviv.ua

Founded 1856

Library of 521,000 vols
Number of teachers: 390
Number of students: 9,000

Rector: Prof. Dr Volodymyr V. Snitynskyy

Publication: Transactions

Departments of Agronomy, Mechanization, Farm Building, Architecture, Economics, Agricultural Accounting.

NATIONAL AGRICULTURAL UNIVERSITY OF UKRAINE

03041 Kyiv, vul. Heroyiv Oborony 15

Telephone: (44) 267-81-19
Fax: (44) 261-42-34

E-mail: inter@nauu.kiev.ua
Internet: www.nauu.kiev.ua

Founded 1898

Rector: Dymtro O. Melnychuk

Library of 1,000,000 vols
Number of teachers: 2,827
Number of students: 22,034

Brs in Berezhany, Boyarka, Irpin, Nemishayiv, Nizhyn, Zalishchiky.

Publication: For Agricultural Specialists (6 a year)

DEANS

Faculty of Agricultural Biology: Anatoliy V. Bykin
Faculty of Agricultural Management: Kovtun O. Anatolivna
Faculty of Agricultural Mechanical Engineering: Yaroslav M. Mykhaylovych
Faculty of Animal Health: Vitaliy Y. Lubetskiy
Faculty of Animal Husbandry, Output Production and Processing Technology: Yuriy V. Zasukha
Faculty of Construction and Design: Konstyantyn H. Lopatko
Faculty of Ecology and Biotechnology: Natalya M. Ridey
Faculty of Economics: Serhiy M. Kvasha
Faculty of Electrification and Automation of Agriculture: Ivan P. Radko
Faculty of Forestry: Serhiy B. Kovalevsky
Faculty of Land Management: Bohdan I. Novak
Faculty of Law: Volodymyr I. Kurilo
Faculty of Landscape Engineering: Anatoliy I. Kushnir
Faculty of Quality and Safety of Agricultural Production: Olga M. Yakubchak
Faculty of Small Animal Health: Oleg F. Petrenko
Faculty of Social Pedagogy: Petro H. Luzan
Faculty of Water Resources and Aquaculture: Petro H. Shevchenko

NATIONAL FORESTRY ENGINEERING UNIVERSITY OF UKRAINE

79057 Lviv, vul. Gen. Chuprynka 103

Telephone: (32) 237-80-94
Fax: (32) 237-89-05
E-mail: ukrdltu@forest.lviv.ua
Internet: www.forest.lviv.ua

Rector: Yuriy Yu. Tunytsya
Vice-Rector: Hryhoriy T. Krynytskyy

Library of 450,000 vols
Number of teachers: 310
Number of students: 3,600

Publications: Naukovyy visnyk (Scientific bulletin), Ukrainski lis (Ukrainian Forest)

DEANS

Faculty of Engineering and Economy: Doc. P. K. Dinka
Faculty of Forestry: Doc. I. S. Vintoniv
Faculty of Forestry Mechanization: Doc. B. V. Bilyk
Faculty of Wood Treatment: Doc. V. M. Golubets
External Faculty: Doc. E. M. Matveev

STATE AGROECOLOGICAL UNIVERSITY

10008 Zhytomyr, Stary bul. 7

Telephone: (412) 37-49-31
Fax: (412) 22-14-02
Internet: www.academy.zt.ua

Founded 1922

Rector: V. P. Slavov

Library of 370,000 vols
Number of teachers: 276
Number of students: 2,859

Depts of Agricultural Ecology, Economics and Agribusiness, Animal Husbandry, Agricultural Engineering, Veterinary Medicine.

HUMANITIES AND SCIENCES UNIVERSITIES

CHERNIVTSI NATIONAL UNIVERSITY 'YURIY FEDKOVYCH'

58012 Chernivtsi, vul. Kotsyubinskoho 2
Telephone: (372) 22-62-35
Fax: (372) 55-29-14
E-mail: rector@chnu.cv.ua
Internet: www.chnu.cv.ua
Founded 1875
State control
Language of instruction: Ukrainian
Academic year: September to June
Rector: STEPAN V. MELNYCHUK
First Pro-Rector, Pro-Rector for Research: S. V. MELNYCHUK
Pro-Rector for Academic Affairs: ROMAN I. PETRYSHYN
Pro-Rector for Academic Development: TAMARA V. MARUSYK
Librarian: OLEG I. SHLYUK

Library: see Libraries and Archives
Number of teachers: 786
Number of students: 14,103 (7,421 full-time, 6,682 part-time)

Publications: *Scientific University Annual*, *Universitetsky Visnyk* (monthly)

DEANS

Faculty of Biology: M. M. MARCHENKO
Faculty of Chemistry: O. S. LYAVYNETS
Faculty of Computer Science: (vacant)
Faculty of Economics: L. S. BILYK
Faculty of Engineering and Technology: Prof. O. V. ANGELSKIY
Faculty of Foreign Languages: R. V. VATSEBA
Faculty of Geography: V. P. RUDENKO
Faculty of History, Politology and International Relations: O. V. DOBRZHANSKIY
Faculty of Law: P. S. PATSURKIVSKIY
Faculty of Applied Mathematics: R. I. PETRYSHYN
Faculty of Pedagogy: I. M. ZVARYCH
Faculty of Philology: B. I. BUNCHUK
Faculty of Philosophy and Theology: V. O. BALUKH
Faculty of Physics: I. V. GUTSUL

DNIPROPETROVSK NATIONAL UNIVERSITY

49050 Dnipropetrovsk, vul. Naukova 13
Telephone: (562) 46-00-95
Fax: (56) 776-58-33
E-mail: admin@dsu.dp.ua
Internet: www.dsu.dp.ua
Founded 1918
Languages of instruction: Ukrainian, Russian
Academic year: September to July
President: MYKOLA POLYAKOV
Vice-President (Academic): V. G. MUSIYAKA
Vice-President (Foreign Affairs): V. V. KOSTYRKO
Vice-President (President's Deputy): O. O. KOCHUBEY
Vice-President (Research): M. M. DRON
Librarian: L. S. KUBISHKINA
Library: see Libraries and Archives
Number of teachers: 1,233
Number of students: 13,260

Publication: *Dnipropetrovsk University Newspaper* (monthly)

DEANS

Faculty of Applied Mathematics: S. V. CHERNYSHENKO

Faculty of Biology and Ecology: O. Y. PAKHOMOV
Faculty of Chemistry: V. F. VARGALYUK
Faculty of Geology and Geography: V. V. BOGDANOVICH
Faculty of History: S. I. SVITLENKO
Faculty of International Economics: N. Y. BOYTSUN
Faculty of Law: P. I. GNATENKO
Faculty of Mass Media: V. D. DEMCHENKO
Faculty of Mechanics and Mathematics: V. O. SYASEV
Faculty of Medicine: J. S. SAPA
Faculty of Philology: O. V. RODNY
Faculty of Physics: R. S. TUTIK
Faculty of Psychology and Pedagogics: I. V. RASPOPOV
Faculty of Radio Physics: V. M. DOLGOV
Faculty of Ukrainian Philology and Art History: I. S. POPOVA
Institute of Economics: S. O. SMIRNOV
Institute of Physics and Technology: Y. A. DZUR

ATTACHED RESEARCH INSTITUTES

Scientific and Research Institute of Biology: Dir A. P. KULIK.
Scientific and Research Institute of Engineering: Dir V. G. BONDARENKO.
Scientific and Research Institute of Geology: Dir V. M. IVANOV.

DONETSK NATIONAL UNIVERSITY

83055 Donetsk, vul. Universytetska 24
Telephone: (62) 337-19-45
Fax: (62) 304-71-12
E-mail: postmaster@univ.donetsk.ua
Internet: www.donnu.edu.ua
Founded 1965; Donetsk State University until 2000
Languages of instruction: Ukrainian, Russian
Academic year: September to July
Rector: Prof. V. P. SHEVCHENKO
Vice-Rector: Prof. V. V. KHRYSTYANIVSKIY
Librarian: N. O. KORYAGINA
Library: see Libraries and Archives
Number of teachers: 900.
Number of students: 17,500

Publications: *Bulletin* (annually), *Donetsk Archaeological Bulletin* (annually), *Eastern Ukraine Linguistic Collected Articles* (2 a year), *Economical Cybernetics* (4 a year), *Finance, Accounting, Banks* (2 a year), *Historical and Political Studies* (4 a year), *Juridical Studies* (4 a year), *Management Models in Market Economy* (2 a year), *New Pages in the History of Donbass* (2 a year), *Philological Studies* (2 a year), *Theoretical and Applied Mechanics* (annually)

HEADS OF DEPARTMENTS

Faculty of Biology: S. V. BESPALOVA
Faculty of Chemistry: A. N. SHENDRIK
Faculty of Economics: G. A. CHERNICHENKO
Faculty of Finance: P. V. EGOROV
Faculty of Foreign Languages: B. D. KALIUSHCHENKO
Faculty of History: P. V. DOBROV
Faculty of Law: V. D. VOLKOV
Faculty of Mathematics: V. I. STOROZHEV
Faculty of Physics: A. G. MILOSLAVSKIY
Faculty of Russian and Ukrainian Philology: E. S. OTIN
Faculty of Interdisciplinary Professions: V. I. MASALSKIY
International Faculty: A. I. BILOBROVA

DONETSK STATE UNIVERSITY OF ECONOMICS AND TRADE 'M. TUHAN-BARANOVSKIY'

83050 Donetsk, vul. Shchorsa 31
Telephone: (62) 342-01-44
Fax: (512) 42-46-52
E-mail: info@donduet.edu.ua
Internet: www.donduet.edu.ua
Founded 1920
Rector: Dr ALEXANDR A. SHUBIN
Library of 600,000 vols
Number of teachers: 300
Number of students: 10,000

DEANS

Faculty of Accounting and Finance: V. A. ORLOVA
Faculty of Economics, Management and International Economic Relations: S. V. DROZHZHINA
Faculty of Marketing, Trade and Customs Affairs: Prof. I. KH. BASHIROV
Faculty of Public Catering: T. V. NUZHNAYA
Faculty of Processing and Catering Industry Equipment: Prof. V. A. SUKMANOV

EAST UKRAINIAN NATIONAL UNIVERSITY 'VOLODYMYR DAL'

91034 Luhansk, Kvartal Molodezhnyi 20A
Telephone: (642) 46-12-84
Fax: (642) 46-13-64
E-mail: uni@snu.edu.ua
Internet: www.snu.edu.ua
Founded 1921
Rector: Prof. Dr ALEXANDER L. GOLUBENKO
First Pro-Rector: Prof. Dr MIKHAIL F. SMIRNY
Pro-Rector for Education, Director of Postgraduate and Distance Education: Prof. Dr IRINA R. BUZKO
Library of 1,000,000 vols
Number of teachers: 1,200
Number of students: 20,000

Publications: *Alternative Technologies of Production and Materials Shaping in Mechanical Engineering* (monthly), *Bulletin* (6 a year)

Crimean Faculty (distance education); Faculty of European Studies in Essen, Germany

DEANS

Faculty of Computer Technologies and Automation: Prof. VITALIY A. ULSHIN
Faculty of Electrotechnical Engineering: Prof. VALERIY V. YAKOVENKO
Faculty of Engineering and Management (Krasnodon): Prof. LIDIYA I. LAZOR
Faculty of Finance and Economics: Prof. MYKHAIL D. APTEKAR
Faculty of History and Politology: Asst Prof. VOLODYMYR T. SAVCHENKO
Faculty of Law: Asst Prof. OLENA V. NOVAKOVA
Faculty of Linguistics, Journalism and Sociology: Prof. BORYS G. NAGORNIY
Faculty of Management: Prof. SULTAN K. RAMAZANOV
Faculty of Mathematics and Informatics: Asst Prof. MYKOLA M. KRAMAR
Faculty of Mechanical Engineering: Asst Prof. OLEG G. IGNATENKO
Faculty of Mining and Transport (Antratsit): Prof. VIKTORIYA K. SUCHANCEVA
Faculty of Natural Sciences: Asst Prof. ALLA A. GRYGORYEVA
Faculty of Philosophy: Prof. VIKTORIYA K. SUCHANCEVA

KHARKIV NATIONAL UNIVERSITY OF ECONOMICS

61001 Kharkiv, pr.Lenina
Telephone: (572) 30-23-04
Fax: (572) 30-23-01
E-mail: ksue@ksue.edu.ua
Internet: www.ksue.edu.ua
Founded 1930
Rector: Prof. Dr VLADIMIR S. PONOMARENKO
Pro-Rector for International Affairs: G. V. NAZAROVA
Library of 700,000 vols
Number of teachers: 612
Number of students: 12,000 (incl. 186 post-graduate and doctoral)

DEANS

Faculty of Accounting and Audit: Dr HRIHORIY F. AZARENKOV
Faculty of Economic Information Technologies: Dr VOLODYMYR I. GRACHOV
Faculty of Economics and Law: Dr TATYANA N. SERIKOVA
Faculty of Finance: Dr PAVLO V. PRONOZA
Faculty of International Economic Relations: Dr IVAN A. PODDUBNY
Faculty of Management and Marketing: Dr OLEKSANDR M. TIMONIN
Correspondence Faculty: Dr SERHIY V. LUKASHEV

KHARKIV NATIONAL UNIVERSITY 'V. N. KARAZIN'

61077 Kharkiv, Pl. Svobody 4
Telephone: (57) 705-12-47
Fax: (57) 705-12-48
E-mail: postmaster@univer.kharkov.ua
Internet: www.univer.kharkov.ua
Founded 1804
Languages of instruction: Russian, Ukrainian
Academic year: September to June
Library of 35,000,000 vols
Rector: Prof. V. S. BAKIROV
Vice-Rectors: Prof. V. V. ALEKSANDROV, Prof. YU. V. KHOLIN, Prof. O. I. NAVROTSKIY, Prof. I. I. ZALYUBOVSKIY
Librarian: I. G. LEVCHENKO
Number of teachers: 2,000
Number of students: 12,000
Publication: *Visnyk*

DEANS

School of Biology: Asst. Prof. L. I. VOROBYOVA
School of Chemistry: Prof. V. D. ORLOV
School of Computer Science: Asst Prof. O. F. TSELUYKO
School of Geology and Geography: Prof. K. A. NEMETS
School of Economics: Prof. L. I. BULAYENKO
School of Foreign Languages: Prof. V. G. PASYNOK
School of Fundamental Medicine: Prof. M. I. YABLUCHANSKIY
School of History: Prof. S. I. POSOKHOV
School of Mathematics and Mechanical Engineering: Prof. V. O. ZOLOTARYOV
School of Philology: Prof. YU. M. BEZKHUTRIY
School of Philosophy: Asst Prof. I. V. KARPENKO
School of Physics: Asst Prof. A. A. ZAVGORODNIY
School of Physics and Energy: (vacant)
School of Physics and Technology: Prof. I. O. GIRKA
School of Psychology: Prof. O. M. LAKTIONOV
School of Radiophysics: Prof. O. F. TYRNOV
School of Sociology: Prof. V. M. NIKOLAYEVSKIY
International Students Education Centre: Asst Prof. Z. F. NAZYROV

ATTACHED INSTITUTES

Research Institute of Astronomy: Dir Dr V. A. ZAKHOZHAY.
Research Institute of Biology: Dir Dr A. I. BOZHKOV.
Research Institute of Chemistry: Dir Prof. V. I. LARIN.
Research Institute of Regional Policy: Dir O. S. LOGVYNENKO.
Research Institute of High Technology: Dir Prof. M. O. AZARENKOV.

KHMELNYTSKY STATE UNIVERSITY

29016 Khmelnytsky, vul. Instytutska 11
Telephone: (382) 72-80-76
Fax: (3822) 2-32-65
E-mail: centr@mailhub.tub.km.ua
Internet: www.tup.km.ua
Founded 1962
Rector: MYKOLA SKYBA
Deputy Rectors: SERGIY KOSTOGRYZ (Academic Work), MYKHAYLO VOYNARENKO (Academic Work), ANATOLIY FOMOV (Administrative Work), VIKTOR NYZHNYK (Finance and Economic Activity), MYKOLA YOKHNA (International Relations), VITALIY KAPLUN (Scientific Work)
Number of teachers: 637teachers
Number of students: 12,976students
Publications: *Measuring and Computing Devices in Technological Processes* (2 a year), *Problems of Trybology International Scientific Journal* (2 a year), *University Herald* (6 a year)

DEANS

Faculty of Applied Mathematics and Computer Technologies: SERGIY KOVALCHUK
Faculty of Business: LIDIYA TORGOVA
Faculty of Correspondence Studies 1: VITALIY KARAZEY
Faculty of Correspondence Studies 2: VIRA BEGNYAK
Faculty of Distance Studies: MYKOLA MAZUR
Faculty of Economics: MYKOLA BONDARENKO
Faculty of Engineering Mechanics: GEORGIY DRAPAK
Faculty of Humanities and Pedagogics: LYUDMYLA STANISLAVOVA
Faculty of International Relations: VITALIY TRETKO
Faculty of Management: LYUDMYLA LYUBOKHYNETS
Faculty of Pre-University and Post-University Training: MYKOLA BABYCH
Faculty of Radio Electronics and Computer Engineering: VOLODYMYR KOSENKOV
Faculty of Technology and Design: DOMBROVSKIY

DIRECTORS

Institute of Correspondence and Distance Studies: YAROSLAV GLADKIY
Institute of Economy and Management: MYKOLA BONDARENKO
Institute of Humanities: VITALIY TRETKO
Institute of Mechanics and Computer Studies: GEORGIY DRAPAK
Institute of Technology, Design and Service: GEORGIY PARASKA
Institute of Telecommunication and Computer Systems: VOLODYMYR KOSENKOV

KYIV NATIONAL LINGUISTIC UNIVERSITY

03680 Kyiv GSP 150, vul. Chervonoarmiyska 73
Telephone: (44) 227-33-72
Fax: (44) 227-67-88
E-mail: knlu@uniling.kiev.ua
Internet: www.uniling.kiev.ua

Founded 1948
Rector: Dr HALIK I. ARTEMCHUK
Library of 1,000,000 vols
Number of teachers: 580
Number of students: 6,100
Publications: *Methods in Foreign Language Teaching, Philology of Foreign Languages* (both in Ukrainian and other languages, 4 a year)

DEANS

Faculty of English Language and Literature: ROMAN VASKO
Faculty of French Language and Literature: VALENTINA MELNIK
Faculty of German Language and Literature: MYKOLA HAMZYUK
Faculty of Slavic Languages: ALLA KENDYUSHENKO
Faculty of Spanish Language and Literature: ANATOLIY CHERNUHA
Faculty of Translation: NADYA HLADUSH

DIRECTORS OF INSTITUTES

Institute of Economics and Law: OLEKSANDR SHUTOV
Institute of Oriental Languages: SERHIY SOROKIN

KYIV NATIONAL UNIVERSITY OF ECONOMICS

03057 Kyiv, pr. Peremohi 54/1
Telephone: (44) 459-61-12
Fax: (44) 226-25-73
E-mail: rector@kneu.kiev.ua
Internet: www.kneu.kiev.ua
Founded 1906
Rector: Prof. Dr ANATOLIY F. PAVLENKO

DEANS

Faculty of Accounting: Prof. Dr VASYL I. YEFIMENKO
Faculty of Agroindustrial Economics: Prof. Dr MYKHAILO M. KOTSUPATRYY
Faculty of Credit and Economics: Prof. Dr MYKHAILO I. DYBA
Faculty of Economics and Management: Prof. Dr ANATOLIY P. NALIVAIKO
Faculty of Finance and Economics: Dr VOLODYMYR K. KHLIVNYY
Faculty of Information Systems and Technologies: Prof. Dr OLEKSANDR D. SHARAPOV
Faculty of International Economics and Management: Prof. Dr DMYTRO H. LUKYANENKO
Faculty of Law: Prof. Dr VITALIY F. OPRYSHKO
Faculty of Marketing: Prof. Dr VIKTOR YA. KARDASH

KYIV NATIONAL UNIVERSITY 'TARAS SHEVCHENKO'

01033 Kyiv, vul. Volodymyrska 64
Telephone: (44) 225-20-82
Fax: (44) 224-61-66
E-mail: svv@rector.univ.kiev.ua
Internet: www.univ.kiev.ua
Founded 1834
Rector: Prof. Dr VIKTOR V. SKOPENKO
First Pro-Rector: Prof. Dr OLEG V. TRETYAK
Pro-Rector: Prof. LEONID V. GUBERSKY
Pro-Rector for Academic Affairs: Prof. Dr MYKOLA E. DZERZHYNSKIY
Pro-Rector for Administrative and Economic Affairs: LARYSA O. KOMAROVA
Pro-Rector for Research: Prof. Dr OLEG K. ZAKUSYLO
Librarian: VALENTYNA G. NESTERENKO
Library: see Libraries and Archives
Number of teachers: 1,850
Number of students: 18,000

Publications: *Vestnik Kievskogo Universiteta*, etc

DEANS

Faculty of Biology: Prof. Dr LYUDMYLA I. OSTAPCHENKO
Faculty of Chemistry: Prof. MYKOLA S. SLOBODYANYK
Faculty of Cybernetics: Prof. ANATOLIY V. ANISIMOV
Faculty of Economics: Prof. VIKTOR D. BAZYLEVICH
Faculty of Geography: Prof. YAROSLAV B. OLIYNYK
Faculty of Geology: Prof. VOLODYMYR A. MIKHAILOV
Faculty of History: Prof. VIKTOR F. KOLESNIK
Faculty of Law: Prof. VOLODYMYR I. ANDREYTSEV
Faculty of Mechanics and Mathematics: Prof. IGOR O. PARASYUK
Faculty of Philosophy: Prof. ANATOLIY YE. KONVERSKIY
Faculty of Physics: Prof. LEONID A. BULAVIN
Faculty of Radiophysics: Prof. VALERIY I. HRIHORUK
Faculty of Sociology and Psychology: Prof. VOLODYMYR B. YEVTUKH
Preparatory Faculty: Prof. TETYANA V. TABENSKA

ATTACHED INSTITUTES

Astronomical Observatory: Dir B. I. HNATIK.

Centre for Ukrainian Studies: Dir Prof. VOLODYMYR I. SERHIYCHUK.

Information and Computing Centre: Dir Dr YURIY V. BOYKO.

Institute of International Relations: Dir Prof. LEONID V. HUBERSKIY.

Institute of Journalism: Dir Prof. VOLODYMYR V. RIZUN.

Institute of Management and Finance: Dir DMYTRO M. CHERVANOV.

Institute of Philology: Dir HRIHORIY F. SEMENYUK.

Institute of Postdiploma Studies: Dir Prof. VOLODYMYR V. RIZUN.

Military Institute: Dir Col VIKTOR V. BALABIN.

Scientific Research Institute: Pro-Rector Prof. Dr OLEG K. ZAKUSYLO.

Ukrainian Lyceum of Physics and Mathematics: Dir OLEKSIY A. LOBODA.

KYIV NATIONAL UNIVERSITY OF TRADE AND ECONOMICS

02156 Kyiv, vul. Kioto 19
Telephone: (44) 531-47-73
Fax: (44) 513-85-36
E-mail: rio@knteu.kiev.ua
Internet: www.knteu.kiev.ua

Rector: Prof. Dr ANATOLIY A. MAZARAKI
First Pro-Rector: Prof. Dr NINA M. USHAKOVA
Pro-Rector for Administrative and Economic Affairs: Prof. Dr VOLODYMYR I. FEDIRKO
Pro-Rector for Education: Prof. Dr OLEKSANDR P. KOROLCHUCK
Pro-Rector for International Relations: Prof. Dr VALERIY M. SAI
Pro-Rector for Organization and Development: Prof. Dr VIKTOR D. KUCHERENKO
Pro-Rector for Scientific Activity and Innovation: Prof. Dr VALENTYNA PASTUHOVA

Library of 800,000 vols
Number of students: 23,600

DEANS

Faculty of Banking: Dr IGOR V. SMOLIN
Faculty of Economics, Management and Law: Dr NATALIYA M. HULYAYEVA

Faculty of Finance: Prof. Dr ANATOLIY D. BUTKO
Faculty of the Restaurant, Hotel and Tourist Industry: Prof. Dr MYKHAILO I. PERESICHNYY
Faculty of Trade: Dr NADIYA K. KYSLYAK

NATIONAL UNIVERSITY OF KYIV-MOHYLA ACADEMY

04070 Kyiv, vul. Skovorody 2
Telephone: (44) 416-45-15
Fax: (44) 463-67-83
E-mail: rec@ukma.kiev.ua
Internet: www.ukma.kiev.ua
Founded 1615, closed 1817, re-established 1991, national university 1994
State control
Languages of instruction: Ukrainian, English
Academic year: September to June

President: VYACHESLAV BRYUKHOVETSKY
First Vice-President, Vice-President (Research and Development): MYKHAILO BRYK
Vice-President (Academic Affairs): VADYM ZUBKO
Vice-President (Development): NATALYA SHUMKOVA
Vice-President (Finance and Administration): LYUDMYLA DYACHENKO
Vice-President (Foreign Co-operation): VOLODYMYR PANCHENKO
Vice-President (Graduate and Post-Graduate Studies): LYUDMYLA DYACHENKO
Dean of Students: OLENA TRETYAKOVA
Registrar: NATALIA HRYBCHUK
Librarian: TETYANA YAROSHENKO

Library of 300,000 vols
Number of teachers: 157
Number of students: 2,300

Publications: *Magisterium* (4 a year), *Mandrivets* (Traveller, 6 a year), *Naukovi Zapysky* (Scientific Notes, 13 a year)

DEANS

Faculty of Computer Science: MYKOLA HLYBOVETS
Faculty of Economics: Prof. YURIY BAZHAL
Faculty of Humanities: Prof. VITALIY SCHERBAK
Faculty of Legal Sciences: Dr ANDRIY A. MELESHEVICH
Faculty of Natural Sciences: Dr IRYNA VYSHENSKA
Faculty of Social Sciences and Technology: Prof. SERHIY M. KVIT
Kyiv-Mohyla Business School: PAVLO M. SHEREMETA

NATIONAL UNIVERSITY OF LVIV 'IVAN FRANKO'

79000 Lviv, Universytetska vul. 1
Telephone: (322) 74-12-62
Fax: (322) 72-28-01
E-mail: dirlu@franko.lviv.ua
Internet: www.franko.lviv.ua
Founded 1661
Language of instruction: Ukrainian
Academic year: September to June

Rector: Prof. I. VAKARCHUK
Vice-Rector (Administrative Affairs): V. VLASEVYCH
Vice-Rector (Economic and Financial Affairs): I. KRUPKA
Vice-Rector (International Affairs): V. KYRYLYCH
Vice-Rector (Research): B. KOTUR
Vice-Rector (Student Affairs): P. STETCIUK
Vice-Rector (Teaching Affairs): V. VYSOCHANSKY
Vice-Rector (Teaching and Educational Affairs): M. ZUBRYTSKA

Librarian: B. YAKYMOVYCH
Library: see Libraries and Archives
Number of teachers: 1,161
Number of students: 22,000

Publications: *Filolohiya* (Philology), *Inozemna Filologiya* (Foreign Philology), *Matematychni Studii* (Mathematical Studies), *Mineralogichniy Zbirnyk* (Proceedings on Mineralogy), *Paleontologichniy Zbirnyk* (Proceedings on Palaeontology), *Teoretychna Elektrotekhnika* (Theoretical Electrical Engineering), *Ukrainske Literaturoznavstvo* (Ukrainian Literature Studies), *Ukraina Moderna* (Modern Ukraine), *Zhurnal Fizychnykh Doslidzhen* (Journal of Physical Research)

DEANS

Faculty of Applied Mathematics and Informatics: Prof. YAREMA G. SAVULA
Faculty of Biology: STEPAN HUDZ
Faculty of Chemistry: Prof. YAROSLAV M. KALYCHAK
Faculty of Economics: ZINOVIY VATAMANIUK
Faculty of Electronics: Prof. IGOR I. POLOVINKO
Faculty of Foreign Languages: Assoc. Prof. VOLODYMYR SULYM
Faculty of Geography: YURI FEDORYSHYN
Faculty of Geology: Prof. MYKOLA PAVLUN
Faculty of History: ROMAN SHUST
Faculty of International Relations: MARKYAN MALSKY
Faculty of Journalism: Assoc. Prof. MYKHAYLO PRYSYAZHNYI
Faculty of Law: Prof. VASYL NOR
Faculty of Mechanics and Mathematics: YAROSLAV PRTYIULA
Faculty of Philosophy: VOLODYMYR MELNYK
Faculty of Physics: YOSYP STAKIRA
Faculty of Pre-University Training: Assoc. Prof. ROMAN O. KROKHMALNY
Department of Pedagogy: Prof. DMYTRO HERTSYUK

ODESA NATIONAL UNIVERSITY 'I. I. MECHNIKOV'

65082 Odesa, Vul. Dvoryanska 2
Telephone: (48) 723-52-54
Fax: (048) 223-35-15
E-mail: oguint@paco.net
Internet: www.onu.edu.edu
Founded 1865
State control
Languages of instruction: Ukrainian, Russian
Academic year: September to July

Rector: Prof. VALENTIN SMYNTYNA
Pro-Rector (Academic): Prof. ALEXANDR ZAPOROZHCENKO
Pro-Rector (Academic and Methodological Work): Prof. EUGENIY STRELTSOV
Pro-Rector (Building and Maintenance): VYACHESLAV IGNATENKO
Pro-Rector (International Relations and External Economic Affairs): Assoc. Prof. SERGEY SKOROKHOD
Pro-Rector (Scientific Research): Prof. VLADIMIR IVANITSA
Librarian: MARINA PODREZOVA

Library: see Libraries and Archives
Number of teachers: 1,803
Number of students: 20,000

Publications: *Fisika aerodispersnikh sistem* (annually), *Fotoelektronika* (annually), *Odessa State University Herald* (annually), *Studies in Literature* (annually)

DEANS

Faculty of Biology: Prof. VLADLEN TOTZKIY
Faculty of Chemistry: Assoc. Prof. VASILIY MANCHUK

Faculty of Economics and Law: Prof. ANATO-
LIY VASILIEV
Faculty of Geology and Geography: Assoc.
Prof. Y. M. BILANCHIN
Faculty of History: Prof. VYACHESLAV KUSH-
NIR
Faculty of Philology: Prof. EVGENIY SHERNOI-
VANENKO
Faculty of Philosophy: Assoc. Prof. A. V.
CHAIKOVSKY
Faculty of Physics: Prof. G. G. CHEMERESYUK
Faculty of Romance and Germanic Philology:
Assoc. Prof. LIDIYA GOLUBENKO
Preparatory Faculty: Assoc. Prof. N. B.
PASCHENKO
College of Business and Social Work: Prof. O.
H. EREMENKO
Centre for Education and Science (Ilichevsk):
Prof. S. I. POKUTNUY (Dir)
Centre for Education and Science (Nikolaev):
N. SHYTYUK (Dir)
Centre for Education and Science (Pervo-
maysk): Assoc. Prof. N. NAVOEVA (Dir)
Institute of Innovation and Post-graduate
Education and Scientific Training Com-
plex: Prof. S. I. DMITRIEVA
Institute of Mathematics, Economics and
Mechanics: Prof. VIKTOR KRUGLOV
Institute of Social Studies: Prof. IGOR KOVAL
Preparatory Department for Foreign Citi-
zens: Assoc. Prof. SERGEY FEDORKO

ATTACHED INSTITUTES
Astronomical Observatory: Dir Prof. V. G.
KARETNIKOV.

**Institute of Combustion and Non-tradi-
tional Technologies:** Dir Prof. A. N.
ZOLOTKO.

Institute of Physics: Dir Prof. V. M.
BELOUS.

**Institute for the Protection of Nature
and Man from Physical and Chemical
Hazards:** Dir Prof. A. A. ENNAN.

V. I. Lipsky Botanical Garden: Dir A. S.
BONETSKY.

ODESA STATE ECONOMIC
UNIVERSITY

65026 Odesa, Preobrazhenska vul. 8
Telephone: (482) 23-61-58
Fax: (482) 32-04-46
E-mail: mail@oseu.odessa.ua
Internet: www.oseu.odessa.ua
Founded 1921
State control
Rector: M. I. ZVERYAKOV
Library of 359,000 vols
Number of teachers: 447
Number of students: 7,261.

POLTAVA UNIVERSITY OF
CONSUMERS' CO-OPERATIVES OF
UKRAINE

36014 Poltava, vul. Kovalya 3
Telephone: (532) 22-18-36
Fax: (532) 50-02-22
E-mail: uo@uccu.org.ua
Internet: www.uccu.org.ua
Founded 1974
Academic year: September to June
Rector: Prof. OLEKSIY O. NESTULYA
Vice-Rector: V. KOSARINA
Library of 400,000 vols
Number of teachers: 348
Number of students: 5,794

DEANS
Department of Economics and Management:
S. VACHTIN
Department of Finance and Accounting: O.
KOROSTASHOV

Department of Food Technology: V. SHKAR-
UPA
Department of Merchandise and Commerce:
N. TYAGUNOVA

ATTACHED INSTITUTE
**Institute of Continuing and Transition
Education:** courses in finance, accounting
and auditing, corporate economics, marketing, business and international management.

PRECARPATHIAN NATIONAL
UNIVERSITY 'VASYL STEFANYK'

Ivano-Frankivsk, vul. Shevchenka 57
E-mail: inst@pu.if.ua
Internet: www.pu.if.ua
Founded 1940
Rector: Prof. Dr BOHDAN. K. OSTAFIYCHUK
First Pro-Rector: Prof. Dr BOHDAN. V. VASYLY-
SHYN.

TAURIDA NATIONAL UNIVERSITY

95007 Simferopol, pr. Vernadskoho 4
Telephone: (652) 23-22-80
Fax: (652) 23-23-10
E-mail: rector@tnu.crimea.ua
Internet: www.tnu.crimea.ua
Founded 1918; present name 1999
State control
Language of instruction: Russian
Academic year: September to July
Rector: NIKOLAY V. BAGROV
Vice-Rectors: VLADIMIR N. BERZHANSKY, VIK-
TOR V. MILYUKOV, VIKTOR F. SHARAPA
Registrar: NIKOLAY V. PRAVDIN
Librarian: VIKTORIA I. SPIROVA
Library: see Libraries and Archives
Number of teachers: 800
Number of students: 15,000
Publications: *The Black Sea Peoples' Culture*
(annually), *Dynamic Systems* (annually),
*Ecological Aspects of Nature Protection in
the Crimea* (annually), *Ecological Study of
the Mountainous Crimea* (annually), *Eco-
systems of the Mountainous Crimea in
Studies of Nature Protection* (annually),
*Notes of Geologists, Pontida: Journal of
The Association for the Support of Biologi-
cal and Landscape Diversity* (annually),
Scientific Notes (annually)

DEANS
Faculty of Biology: SERGEY F. KOTOV
Faculty of Chemistry: VASSILY YA. CHIRVA
Faculty of Crimean Tatar and Oriental
Philology: AIDER M. MEMETOV
Faculty of Economics: ALEXANDER A. KANOV
Faculty of Foreign Languages: ALEXANDER D.
PETRENKO
Faculty of Geography: BORIS A. VAKHRUSHEV
Faculty of History: LEONID A. PASHKOVSKY
Faculty of Jurisprudence: ALEXANDER V.
TIMOSHCHYUK
Faculty of Management: VLADIMIR A. PODSO-
LONKO
Faculty of Mathematics: DONSKOY I. VLADI-
MIR
Faculty of Philosophy: ALEXEY D. SHORKIN
Faculty of Physical Training: VLADIMIR F.
KROVYAKOV
Faculty of Physics: TAMARA A. KOROSTELINA
Faculty of Psychology: VLADIMIR K. KALIN
Faculty of Slavic Philology and Journalism:
GALINA YU.. BOGDANOVICH
Faculty of Ukrainian Philology and Ukra-
nian Studies: VITALY M. VELIGODSKY

PROFESSORS
AKULOV, M. R., History of Ukraine
APATOVA, N. V., Information Systems in
Economics

ARIFOV, L. YA, Theoretical Physics
BERESTOVSKAYA, D. S., History of World
Culture
BERZHANSKY, V. N., Experimental Physics
BOKOV, V. A., Geography
BUROV, G. M., Ancient and Middle Ages
History
CHEKHOV, V. N., Theoretical and Applied
Mechanics
CHIRVA, V. YA, Organic and Analytical
Chemistry
DEMENTIEV, N. E., History of Russia
DONSKOY, V. I., Informatics
EMIROVA, A. M., Russian Language
FEDORENKO, A. M., Chemistry
FILIMONOV, S. B., History of Ukraine
GABRIELYAN, O. A., Political Science and
Sociology
GUBANOV, I. G., Geography
GUBAR, A. I., Ukrainian Language
KALIN, V. K., General Psychology, History of
Psychology
KALNOY, I. I., Social Philosophy
KASHENKO, S. G., History of Russian Law
KAZARIN, V. P., Russian and General Litera-
ture
KIRICHENKO, A. A., Law
KOPACHEVSKY, N. D., Mathematical Analysis
KORENYUK, I. I., Human and Animal Physiol-
ogy
KOZLOV, A. S., Greek Language
KRAMARENKO, V. I., Management
KRICHEK, P. M., Ukrainian Literature
KRYUCHKOV, I. V., Economics
KUDRYASHOV, A. P., Political Economy
KUZHEL, A. V., Theory of Functions and
Functional Analysis
LAZAREV, F. V., Philosophy
LYSENKO, N. I., General Land Science
MANAKOV, M. K., Physiology of Plants
MARTYNYUK, YU. N., Philosophy
MEMETOV, A. A., Philosophy
MISHNEV, V. G., Botany
NAGORSKAYA, M. N., Management
NIKOLKO, V. N., Philosophy
NOVIKOVA, M. A., Russian and General
Literature
OLIFEROV, A. N., Oceanology
OREKHOVA, L. A., Russian Literature
PERSIDSKY, S. K., Differential and Integral
Equations
PETRENKO, A. D., German Language
PODSOLONKO, V. A., Economics
POMERANETS, V. N., Economics
POPOV, V. K., Law
REGUSHEVSKY, E. S., Linguistics
RUDYAKOV, A. N., Linguistics
SHARAPA, V. F., History
SHEVLYAKOV, YU. M., Applied Mathematics
SHULGIN, V. F., Chemistry
SIDYAKIN, V. G., Human and Animal Physiol-
ogy
SOKOLOVSKAYA, ZH. P., Philology
STADNIK, I. P., Theoretical Physics
STASHKOV, A. M., Animal Biophysics
TEMURYANTS, N. A., Human and Animal
Physiology
TEREZ, E. K., Astronomy and Teaching
Methods of Physics
UNKOVSKAYA, T. E., Management
URSU, D. P., Modern and Contemporary
History
VOLYAR, A. V., Physics
YENA, V. G., Geography
YEFIMENKO, A. M., Theoretical Foundations
of Physical Culture
YURAKHNO, M. V., Zoology

TERNOPIL STATE ECONOMIC
UNIVERSITY

46000 Ternopil, vul. Lvivska 11
Telephone: (352) 43-61-33
Fax: (352) 43-61-33
E-mail: rektor@tane.edu.ua

Internet: www.tane.edu.ua
Founded 1971
Rector: Prof. SERHIY I. YURIY
Library of 300,000 vols
Number of teachers: 650
Number of students: 25,000

DEANS

Faculty of Accountancy and Auditing: Prof. YAROSLAV D. KRUPKA
Faculty of Agrarian Economics and Management: Prof. ROMAN HEVKO
Faculty of the Banking Industry: Dr BOGDAN LUTSIV
Faculty of Computing and Information Technologies: Prof. MYKOLA P. DIVAK
Faculty of Economics and Investment Management: Prof. BOGDAN LITVIN
Faculty of Economics and Management: Prof. EVGEN P. KACHAN
Faculty of Finance: Dr YOSIP M. BESKID
Faculty of International Business and Management: Prof. ANATOLIY M. TYBIN
Faculty of Law: Dr STEFANIYA S. OSADCHUK
Faculty of Postgraduate Education: Prof. MYHAILO V. SKYBNOVSKIY

ATTACHED CENTRES

Centre for European and International Studies: Dir Dr VITALINA KURILYAK.

Centre for Further Training: Dir LYUD-MYLA I. LEBEDYNSKA.

UZHHOROD NATIONAL UNIVERSITY

88000 Uzhhorod, vul. Pidhirna 46
Telephone: and fax (3122) 3-33-41
E-mail: admin@univ.uzhgorod.ua
Internet: www.univ.uzhgorod.ua
Founded 1945
State control
Language of instruction: Ukrainian
Academic year: September to July
Rector: Prof. Dr MYKOLA M. VEHESH
Pro-Rector for Academic Affairs: OLEXANDR H. SLYVKA
Pro-Rector for Administration and Economic Affairs: VOLODYMYR V. SHETELYA
Pro-Rector for Research: IHOR P. STUDENJAK
Pro-Rector for Social Development and Capital Construction: YAROSLAV S. HUK
Registrar: ROSTISLAV. V. ROMANYUK
Librarian: OLENA I. POCHEKUTOVA
Library: see Libraries and Archives
Number of teachers: 600
Number of students: 8,000
Publication: *Bulletin* (series: Biology, Medicine, Romance and Germanic Philology, Philology, Mathematics, Physics, Chemistry, 1 each a year)

DEANS

Faculty of Biology: Asst Prof. V. I. NIKOLAY-CHUK
Faculty of Chemistry: Asst Prof. VASYL LENDYEL
Faculty of Economics: Prof. VASIL MIKLOVDA
Faculty of Engineering: Asst Prof. IVAN TURYANYTSYA
Faculty of History: Asst Prof. VOLODYMYR FENYCH
Faculty of International Relations: Prof. M. A. LENDYEL
Faculty of Law: Prof. VASIL YAREMA
Faculty of Mathematics: Asst Prof. MYKHAYLO PAHYRYA
Faculty of Medicine: Asst Prof. BOLDIZHAR BOLDIZHAR
Faculty of Philology: Asst Prof. IVAN SABA-DOSH
Faculty of Physical Education and Sport: Asst Prof. STEPAN LASUR

Faculty of Physics: Prof. Dr VOLODYMYR LASUR
Faculty of Postgraduate Studies: Prof. IVAN MIKHAYLOVYCH
Faculty of Romance and Germanic Philology: Asst Prof. STEPAN BOBYNETS

ATTACHED INSTITUTES

Carpathian Institute: Dir Asst Prof. M. P. MAKARA.

Hungarian Philology Centre: Dir Prof. P. M. LIZANETS.

Institute of Herbal Medicine: Dir Prof. O. M. HANICH.

Institute for Solid State Physics and Chemistry: Dir Prof. YU. M. VYSOCHANSKI.

ZAPORIZHZHIA NATIONAL UNIVERSITY

69063 Zaporizhzhia, vul. Zhukovskoho 66
Telephone: (612) 64-45-46
Fax: (612) 62-71-61
E-mail: rektor@zsu.zp.ua
Internet: www.zsu.edu.ua
Founded 1985
State control
Languages of instruction: Russian, Ukrainian
Academic year: September to July
Rector: Prof. V. A. TOLOK
Pro-Rector (Administration): I. G. YAKUSHEV
Pro-Rector (Curriculum): V. V. HIRZHON
Pro-Rector (Research and International Cooperation): V. Z. HRYSTCHAK
Pro-Rector (Social Development): V. G. TKA-CHENKO
Registrar: S. A. EVSTAFENKO
Librarian: V. A. HERASYMOVA
Number of teachers: 541
Number of students: 8,200
Publications: *Antiquities of the Steppe, Black Sea Region and Crimea, Bulletin, Cultural Bulletin* (scientific-theoretical annual of the Lower Dnieper region), *New Paradigm, New Philology, Notes of the Scientific Research Laboratory of the Southern Ukraine, Problems of Bioindication, Renaissance Studies, Zaporizhzhya Legacy* (history of the Southern Ukraine in the 18th century)

DEANS

Faculty of Biology: Doc. V. I. DOMNICH
Faculty of Economics: Prof. V. V. KIRICHEVS-KIY
Faculty of Foreign Philology: Prof. V. I. SKIBINA
Faculty of History: Prof. F. G. TURCHENKO
Faculty of Law: Doc. T. A. DENISOVA
Faculty of Management: Doc. I. G. SHAVKUN
Faculty of Mathematics: Prof. N. G. TAMUROV
Faculty of Philology: Prof. O. D. TURGAN
Faculty of Physical Training: Doc. V. N. ZAYTSEVA
Faculty of Physics: Doc. A. Y. OSIPOV
Faculty of Postgraduate Education: Doc. Dr L. D. KRIVEGA
Faculty of Social Pedagogics: Prof. L. I. MISCHIK
Faculty of Sociology and Administration: Prof. V. P. BEKH

PROFESSORS

BAYKINA, N. G., Sports
BEKH, V. P., Politics and Theory of Administration
BESSONOVA, V. P., Biology
BOVT, V. D., Biology
BYLOUSENKO, P. I., Ukrainian Language
CHABANENKO, V. A., General Linguistics
FROLOV, A. K., Human Physiology
GRISTCHAK, V. Z., Applied Mathematics

IVANENKO, V. K., Methods of Teaching Philological Disciplines
KARAGODIN, A. I., History
KIRICHEVSKIY, V. V., Applied Mathematics
LYAKH, S. R., History of Ukraine
MISCHIK, L. I., Pedagogics and Psychology
MOROZOV, L. V., Finance and Credit
NAUMENKO, A. M., German Philology
NOVIKOV, Y. F., Theory and Practice of Management
PAKHOMOVA, T. A., Methods of Teaching Philological Disciplines
PROZOROVA, N. S., History and Theory of State and Law
PRYKHODKO, N. I., Problems of Administration and Social Pedagogics
PRYVARNIKOV, A. K., Algebra and Geometry
PSARYOV, V. I., Physics
SERGEYEV, A. V., Physics
TAMUROV, N. G., Applied Mathematics
TOLOK, V. A., Applied Mathematics
TURCHENKO, F. G., History of the Ukraine
TURGAN, O. D., Theory of Literature and Journalism
TYKHOMIROV, V. N., Foreign Literature
TYMCHENKO, S. M., History of the Ukraine
YESHENKO, V. A., Physiology and Civil Defence
ZATSNIY, Y. A., Theory and Practice of Translation

MEDICAL UNIVERSITIES

BUKOVINIAN STATE MEDICAL UNIVERSITY

58000 Chernivtsi, Teatralna pl. 2
Telephone: (372) 55-37-54
Fax: (372) 55-37-54
E-mail: bma@bsmu.edu.ua
Internet: www.bsmu.edu.ua
Founded 1944 as Chernivtsi State Medical Institute; as Bukovinian State Medical Academy 1997; present name and University status 2005
State control
Academic year: September to June
Rector: VASIL P. PISHAK
First Vice-Rector: MIHAILO Y. KOLOMOETS
Vice-Rector for International Relations: YURIY M. NECHYTAYLO
Library of 350,000 vols
Number of teachers: 435
Number of students: 3,100
Publications: *Bukovinian Medical Herald* (4 a year), *Clinical Anatomy and Operative Surgery* (4 a year), *Clinical and Experimental Pathology* (4 a year)

DEANS

VOLODYMYR HLUBOCHENKO
OLEKSANDR POLISCHUK
VIKTOR POLYOVIY
TAMILA SOROKMAN

CRIMEAN STATE MEDICAL UNIVERSITY 'S. I. GEORGIEVSKY'

95006 Simferopol, bul. Lenina 5/7
Telephone: (652) 27-44-62
Fax: (652) 27-20-92
E-mail: office@crsmu.com
Internet: www.crsmu.com
Founded 1931
Rector: Prof. A. A. BABANIN
Library of 634,371 vols
Number of teachers: 629
Number of students: 4,556
Publications: *Bulletin of Physiotherapy and Balneology* (4 a year), *Problems, Achievements and Perspectives of the Development of Biomedical Sciences and Practical Public Health of Ukraine* (colln of scientific works, 4 a year), *Tavrian Biomedical*

Bulletin (4 a year), *Tavrian Journal of Psychiatry* (4 a year)

DEANS

First Medical Faculty: Prof. A. I. KRADINOV
Second Medical Faculty: Prof. S. N. KRUTIKOV
Faculty of Stomatology: Prof. L. I. AVDONINA
International Faculty: Prof. M. N. GRISHIN
Postgraduate Faculty: Prof. N. P. BUGLAK

KHARKIV STATE MEDICAL UNIVERSITY

61022 Kharkiv, pr. Lenina 4
Telephone: (572) 40-26-96
Fax: (572) 47-52-38
E-mail: info@ksmu.kharkov.ua
Internet: www.ksmu.kharkov.ua

Founded 1805; present name and status 1994

Rector: Acad. ANATOLY YA. TSYGANENKO

Library of 938,451 vols
Number of teachers: 653
Number of students: 4,600

Publications: *Experimental Clinical Medicine* (4 a year), *Medical Practice* (6 a year), *Medicine Today and Tomorrow* (4 a year), *Ultrasonic Perinatal Diagnosis* (2 a year).

LUHANSK STATE MEDICAL UNIVERSITY

91045 Luhansk, Kvartal 50-richchya Oborony Luhanska 1
Telephone: (642) 54-84-03
Fax: (642) 53-20-36
E-mail: kanc@lsmu.edu.ua
Internet: www.lsmu.edu.ua

Founded 1956; present name and status 1994

Rector: Prof. VALERIY K. IVCHENKO

Library of 420,000 vols
Number of teachers: 394
Number of students: 2,815

Faculties of Dentistry, Healthcare, Nursing, Paediatrics and Pharmacy.

LVIV NATIONAL MEDICAL UNIVERSITY 'DANYLO HALYTSKIY'

79010 Lviv, Pekarska vul. 69
Telephone: (322) 72-26-60
Fax: (322) 76-79-73
E-mail: zimenkovsky@meduniv.lviv.ua
Internet: www.meduniv.lviv.ua

Founded 1784

Rector: Prof. Dr BORYS ZIMENKOVSKY

Library of 520,000 vols
Number of teachers: 1,123
Number of students: 5,176

DEANS

First Medical Faculty: IHOR YA. HRYTSKO
Second Medical Faculty: YURI YA. KRYVKO
Faculty of Nursing: VIRA I. PIROGOVA
Faculty of Pharmacy: TIMOFIY H. KALINYUK
Faculty of Stomatology: IVAN M. HOT
Faculty of Postgraduate Education: ROMAN I. ORACH
International Faculty: YELENA S. VARIVODA
External Faculty: ROMAN YE. DRAMOHRAI

NATIONAL MEDICAL UNIVERSITY 'O. BOHOMOLETS'

01601 Kyiv, bul. T. Shevchenka 13
Telephone: (44) 234-40-62
Fax: (44) 234-40-62
E-mail: nmu@nmu.edu.ua
Internet: www.nmu.edu.ua

Founded 1841

Rector: Prof. Dr VITALIY MOSCALENKO

Library of 750,000 vols

Number of teachers: 1,100
Number of students: 7,000

DEANS

First Medical Faculty: Prof. VOLODYMYR M. BLAHODAROV
Second Medical Faculty: Prof. VASYL Z. NETYAZHENKO
Third Medical Faculty: Prof. VIKTOR H. LIZOHUB
Fourth Medical Faculty: Prof. SERHIY T. OMELCHUK
Faculty of Medical Engineering: Prof. VALENTIN P. YATSENKO
Faculty of Pharmacy: Prof. IRINA V. NIZHENKOVSKA
Faculty of Stomatology: Prof. VALERIY P. NESPRYADKO
Foreign Students' Faculty: Prof. YURI O. KOPYOV
Preparatory Faculty for Doctors in the Ukrainian Armed Forces: Col OLEG M. VLASENKO

NATIONAL UNIVERSITY OF PHARMACY

61002 Kharkiv, vul. Pushkinskaya 53
Telephone: (57) 719-27-39
E-mail: congress@ukrfa.kharkov.ua
Internet: www.ukrfa.kharkov.ua

Founded 1805

Rector: Prof. VALENTIN P. CHERNYKH

Library of 500,000 vols

Publications: *Fisiologichno-Aktivni Rechovini* (Physiologically Active Substances, 2 a year), *Klinichna Farmatsiya* (Clinical Pharmacy, 4 a year), *Visnik Farmatsii* (Pharmacy Bulletin, 4 a year), *Zdorovya Cheloveky* (Health to Mankind, 4 a year)

Departments of Analytical Chemistry, Pharmacy Drug Technology, Biological Chemistry, Botany, Humanities, Industrial Drug Technology, Engineering and Informational Technologies, Foreign Languages, Clinical Pharmacy, Cosmetology and Aromology, Management and Marketing in Pharmacy, Microbiology, Physical, Colloidal and Inorganic Chemistry, Social Sciences, Organization and Economics of Pharmacy, Organic Chemistry, Pathological Physiology, Russian Language, Toxicological Chemistry, Ukrainian and Latin Studies, Quality Control in Pharmacy, Pharmacognosy, Pharmacology, Pharmacotherapy with Pharmacokinetics, Pharmaceutical Chemistry, Physics, Physiology, Physical and Health Training, Enterprise Economy, Economic Theory, Disaster Medicine and Military Medicine.

DEANS

First Faculty of Correspondence and Distance Learning: Dr VOLODYMYR I. STEPANENKO
Second Faculty of Correspondence and Distance Learning: Dr VOLODYMYR D. HORYACHIY
Faculty of Economics and Management: Dr VOLODYMYR V. MALY
Faculty of Industrial Pharmacy: Dr TATYANA KRUTSKIKH
Faculty of Medical Pharmacy: Dr OLGA I. NABOKA
First Faculty of Pharmacy: Prof. ANDREY A. TKACH
Second Faculty of Pharmacy: Dr LILIYA I. VYSHNEVSKAYA
Foreign Students' Faculty: Dr VOLODYMYR I. VELMA
Foreign Students' Preparatory Faculty: Dr TAMARA P. TSAPKO

NATIONAL UNIVERSITY OF PHYSICAL EDUCATION AND SPORTS OF UKRAINE

03680 Kyiv, vul. Fizkultury 1
Telephone: (44) 227-54-52
Fax: (44) 287-61-91
E-mail: rectorat@uni-sport.edu.ua
Internet: www.uni-sport.edu.ua

Founded 1930

Rector: Prof. Dr VOLODYMYR M. PLATONOV
First Pro-Rector for Education: Prof. Dr YURIY M. SHKREBTIY
Pro-Rector for Research: Dr TETYANA YU. KRUTSEVICH

Faculties of Olympic and Professional Sport, Physical Rehabilitation and Sports Medicine, Physical Education, Recreation and Health-Related Physical Culture; Faculty of External Studies.

TERNOPIL STATE MEDICAL UNIVERSITY 'I. HORBACHEVSKY'

46001 Ternopil, Maydan Voli 1
Telephone: (352) 52-44-92
Fax: (352) 52-41-83
E-mail: university@tdmu.edu.te.ua
Internet: www.tdma.edu.te.ua

Founded 1957

Rector: Prof. LEONID Y. KOVALCHUK

Library of 400,000 vols
Number of teachers: 548
Number of students: 2,819

Publications: *Achievements of Clinical and Experimental Medicine* (2 a year), *Hospital Surgery* (4 a year), *Infectious Diseases* (4 a year), *Medical Chemistry* (4 a year), *Medical Education* (4 a year), *Newsletter of Social Hygiene and Public Health Organization* (4 a year), *Scientific Research Newsletter* (4 a year)

DEANS

Faculty of Dentistry: Prof. STEPAN I. CHERKASHYN
Faculty of Medicine: Prof. ANATOLIY D. BEDENYUK
Faculty of Pharmacy: Prof. TARAS A. HROSHOVYI
Faculty of Postgraduate Education: Prof. YEVGEN M. STARODUB
Medical College: Prof. BORYS A. LOKAY

VINNYTSIA NATIONAL MEDICAL UNIVERSITY 'M. I. PYROHOV'

21018 Vinnytsya, pr. Lenina 9
Telephone: (432) 32-06-85
Fax: (432) 32-16-13
E-mail: admission@vsmu.vinnica.ua
Internet: www.vnmu.vn.ua

Founded 1921

Rector: Prof. Dr VASYL M. MOROZ

Library of 500,000 vols
Number of teachers: 554
Number of students: 3,600.

PEDAGOGICAL UNIVERSITIES

KHARKIV NATIONAL PEDAGOGICAL UNIVERSITY 'H. S. SKOVORODA'

61168 Kharkiv, vul. Blyukhera 2
Telephone: (57) 700-69-09
E-mail: rector@pu.ac.kharkov.ua
Internet: pu.ac.kharkov.ua

Founded 1811

Rector: Prof. Dr IVAN F. PROKOPENKO

Library of 714,689 vols

DEANS

Faculty of Art and Design: Prof. Dr NADIYA V. SHYLOVTSEVA

Faculty of Economics: Prof. Dr HANNA M. HUZENKO

Faculty of Elementary Education: Prof. Dr NATALIYA M. YAKUSHKO

Faculty of Foreign Languages: Dr NATALIYA V. TUCHYNA

Faculty of History: Prof. Dr ANATOLIY V. HUBA

Faculty of Law: Prof. Dr VIKTOR O. PROTSEVSKYY

Faculty of Music Education: Prof. Dr VALENTYN YE. POLYAKOV

Faculty of Natural Sciences: Prof. Dr LYUDMYLA P. KHARCHENKO

Faculty of Physical Education: Prof. Dr MYKOLA I. HORODYSKYY

Faculty of Physics and Mathematics: Prof. Dr OLEKSANDR I. HONCHAROV

Faculty of Pre-School Education: Prof. Dr TETYANA P. TANKO

Faculty of Psychology and Sociology: Prof. Dr OKSANA H. VOLKOVA

Faculty of Russian: Prof. Dr TAMARA P. STAKANKOVA

Faculty of Ukrainian Language and Literature: Prof. Dr STANISLAV B. STASEVSKYY

External Faculty: Prof. Dr OLENA A. OLEKSENKO

DIRECTORS

Institute of Post-Diploma Education: Prof. Dr MYKOLA V. HADETSKYY

Institute of World Languages: Prof. Dr TAMARA P. STAKANKOVA

NATIONAL PEDAGOGICAL UNIVERSITY 'M. DRAHOMANOV'

01030 Kyiv, vul. Pirohova 9

Telephone: (44) 234-11-08

Fax: (44) 234-22-51

E-mail: dirc@pntu.poltava.ua

Internet: www.npu.cdu.ua

Founded 1920; present name and status 1994

Rector: Acad. Prof. Dr VIKTOR P. ANDRUSHCHENKO

First Pro-Rector: Dr VOLODYMYR P. BEKH

Pro-Rector for Academic Affairs: Prof. Dr PETRO V. DMYTRENKO

Pro-Rector for Finance and Organisational Effectiveness: Dr OLEG S. PADALKA

Pro-Rector for Research and International Relations: Prof. Dr HRIHORIY I. VOLYNKA

Pro-Rector: Prof. Dr IVAN I. DROBOT.

TECHNICAL UNIVERSITIES

DNIPRODZERZHYNSK STATE TECHNICAL UNIVERSITY

51948 Dnipropetrovska oblast, Dniprodzerzhynsk, vul. Dniprobudivska

Telephone: (569) 55-13-89

Fax: (569) 55-13-07

E-mail: science@dstu.dp.ua

Internet: www.dstu.dp.ua

Founded 1920; present name and status 1994

Rector: Prof. IHOR O. PAVLYUCHENKOV

First Pro-Rector: Dr VITALIY M. HULYAYEV

DEANS

Faculty of Chemical Technology: Dr OLEH I. POLYANCHYKOV

Faculty of Economics and Management: Dr SERHIY H. DRONOV

Faculty of Electronics and Computer Technology: Prof. OLEKSANDR M. SYANOV

Faculty of Mechanical Engineering: Dr VOLODYMYR SOLOD

Faculty of Metallurgy: Dr OLEKSANDR V. HRESS

Faculty of Post-Diploma Education: Prof. I. V. HUBARYEV

Faculty of Power Engineering: Prof. ANATOLIY M. PAVLENKO

Faculty of Sociology and Philology: Prof. MYKOLA S. KONOKH

External Faculty: Prof. YEVHEN B. LEYKO

DNIPROPETROVSK NATIONAL TECHNICAL UNIVERSITY OF RAILWAY TRANSPORT 'V. LAZARYAN'

49700 Dnipropetrovsk-10, vul. Lazaryana 2

Telephone: (56) 776-59-47

Fax: (562) 47-18-66

E-mail: dnuzt@diit.edu.ua

Internet: www.diit.edu.ua

Founded 1930

Rector: Prof. Dr ALEXANDER N. PSHINKO

First Pro-Rector for Education: Prof. Dr BORIS E. BODNAR

Pro-Rector for Research: Dr SERHEY MYAMLYN

Library of 800,000 vols

Number of students: 4,200

Specialist faculties incl. Bridges and Tunnels, Mechanics, Management of Transport Processes in Railway Transport, Organization of Railway Construction and Track Maintenance, Industrial and Civil Engineering, Economics and Management in Transport, Technical Cybernetics and Military Training.

DONBASS STATE TECHNICAL UNIVERSITY

94204 Alchevsk, pr. Lenina 16

Telephone: (6442) 2-31-23

Fax: (6442) 2-68-87

E-mail: info@dmmi.edu.ua

Internet: www.dmmi.edu.ua

Rector: Prof. Dr ANATOLIY I. AKMAEV

First Pro-Rector for Academic Affairs: Dr VASILIY N. OKALELOV

Pro-Rector for Research: Dr NIKOLAY N. ZABLODSKIY

Library of 695,000 vols

Number of teachers: 470

Number of students: 12,000

Publication: *Impulse* (weekly)

Institutes of Automation and Electrotechnical Systems, Mechanics, Economics and Finance, Management, Contemporary Education, Retraining of Specialists; Faculties of Metallurgy, Mining, Civil Engineering, Linguistic and Educational Preparation for Foreign Students. Distance Faculties in Krasnodon, Lisichansk, Rovenki, Rubezhnoe and Sverdlovsk; Inter-University Satellite Tracking Centre; Industrial-Economic Institutes in Enakiev and Krasnoluch.

DONETSK NATIONAL TECHNICAL UNIVERSITY

83000 Donetsk, Artema 58

Telephone: (62) 337-17-33

Fax: (62) 304-12-78

E-mail: info@dgtu.donetsk.ua

Internet: www.donntu.edu.ua

Founded 1921

Rector: Prof. Dr ALEKSANDR A. MINAEV

First Pro-Rector: Prof. Dr ALEKSANDR A. TROYANSKIY

Pro-Rector for Academic Affairs: VLADIMIR I. KOSTENKO

Pro-Rector for Administration: HEORHIY A. ROMANKO

Pro-Rector for Internal Communications and Economic Affairs: ILYA P. NAVKA

Pro-Rector for Research: Prof. Dr EVGENIY A. BASHKOV

Librarian: TAMARA A. TIKHANKOVA

Library of 1,500,000 vols

Number of teachers: 1,500

Number of students: 23,000

Publications: *Development of Mining Minerals* (2 a year), *Problems of Ecology* (annually)

Brs in Gorlovka and Krasnoarmeysk.

DEANS

Faculty of Computing Technology and Information Science: Dr VLADIMIR V. LAPKO

Faculty of Ecology and Chemical Technology: Dr ALEKSANDR S. PARFENYUK

Faculty of Economics and Management: Prof. VYACHESLAV V. DEMENTYEV

Faculty of Electrotechnical Engineering: Dr ALEKSANDR V. LEVSHOV

Faculty of Geotechnology and Management in Manufacturing: Prof. YURI F. BULGAKOV

Faculty of Information Technologies and Automation: Dr ALEKSANDR V. KHORKHORDIN

Faculty of Mechanical Engineering: Dr SERGEY I. AVVAKUMOV

Faculty of Mining and Geology: Prof. OLEG I. KALINICHENKO

Faculty of Physics and Metallurgy: Dr NIKOLAY T. EGOROV

Faculty of Power Mechanics and Automation: Dr SERGEY A. SELIVRA

Faculty of Radiotechnology: Prof. PAVEL V. STEFANENKO

English-Language Technical Faculty: Prof. SERGEY A. KOVALEV

French-Language Faculty of Engineering: Dr GENNADIY S. KLYAGIN

German-Language Technical Faculty: Dr VIKTOR I. KALASHNIKOV

Polish-Language Technical Faculty: Dr ALEKSANDR YU. MAKEYEV

Foreign Students: Dr SERGEY I. AVVAKUMOV

DIRECTORS OF INSTITUTES

Institute of Mining: Dr SERGEY N. ALEKSANDROV

Institute of International Cooperation: Dr ILYA P. NAVKA

Automotive and Highways Institute: Prof. MIKHAIL N. CHALTSEV

Krasnoarmeysk Industrial Institute: Dr NIKOLAY N. SLED

Institute of Postgraduate Education: Dr VIKTOR YU. CHERNIKOV

IVANO-FRANKIVSK NATIONAL TECHNICAL UNIVERSITY OF OIL AND GAS

76019 Ivano-Frankivsk, vul. Karpatska 15

Telephone: (3422) 4-22-64

Fax: (3422) 4-21-39

E-mail: admin@nung.edu.ua

Internet: www.ifdtung.if.ua

Founded 1967

Rector: Y. I. KRYZHANIVSKY

Library of 790,000 vols

Number of teachers: 413

Number of students: 4,453

Faculties of Geological Prospecting, Gas and Oil Industry, Gas and Oil Pipelines, Automation and Electrification, Mechanical, Economics and Management, Mechanics and Technology, Engineering Ecology.

KHAI NATIONAL AEROSPACE UNIVERSITY 'M. YE. ZHUKOVSKYI'

61070 Kharkiv-70, Chkalova vul. 17

Telephone: (57) 744-98-56

Fax: (57) 744-11-31

E-mail: khai@khai.edu

Internet: www.khai.edu

Founded 1930

Rector: Prof. VLADIMIR S. KRIVTSOV

Library of 1,000,000 vols
Number of teachers: 2,950
Number of students: 9,500

DEANS

Faculty of Aircraft Control Systems: ANATO-
LIY S. KULIK
Faculty of Aircraft Design: VITALIY N. KOBRIN
Faculty of Aviation Engine-Building and
Power Systems: ANATOLIY I. DOLMATOV
Faculty of Aircraft Radio-Electronic Systems:
VIKTOR I. ILYUSHKO
Faculty of Economics and Management: IGOR
V. CHUMACHENKO
Faculty of Humanities: VOLODYMYR A. KOPI-
LOV
Faculty of Rocket Engineering: OLEKSIY G.
NIKOLAEV
Faculty of Distance Education: YAKOV V.
SAFRONOV
Faculty of Pre-University Training and Pro-
fessional Skills Improvement: VLADYSLAV
F. DEMENKO

KHARKIV NATIONAL AUTOMOBILE AND HIGHWAYS UNIVERSITY

61002 Kharkiv, vul. Petrovskoho 25

Telephone: (57) 700-38-65

Fax: (57) 700-38-66

E-mail: admin@khadi.kharkov.ua

Internet: www.khadi.kharkov.ua

Founded 1930

Rector: Prof. Dr ANATOLIY N. TURENKO
First Pro-Rector: Prof. Dr IVAN P. GLADKIY
Pro-Rector for Research: Prof. Dr VIKTOR A.
BOGOMOLOV

Library of 450,000 vols
Number of teachers: 458
Number of students: 10,956 full-time, 7,042
external

DEANS

Faculty of Automotive Technology: VOLODY-
MYR VOLKOV
Faculty of Business and Management: ILYA
DMITRIEV
Faculty of Distance Education: NIKOLAY
ALEKSA
Faculty of Road Construction: IGOR KIYASHKO
Faculty of Transport Systems: YURI BEKETOV
Faculty of Postgraduate Studies: NIKOLAY
KASLIN

KHARKIV NATIONAL UNIVERSITY OF RADIOELECTRONICS

61166 Kharkiv, pr. Lenina 14

Telephone: (57) 702-18-07

Fax: (57) 702-10-13

E-mail: info@kture.kharkov.ua

Internet: www.kture.kharkov.ua

Founded 1930

Rector: Prof. Dr MYKHAYLO F. BONDARENKO

Library of 750,000 vols
Number of students: 8,500

DEANS

Faculty of Applied Mathematics and Man-
agement: LEONID I. SHKLYAROV
Faculty of Computer Engineering and Man-
agement: GENNADIY F. KRIVULYA
Faculty of Computer Sciences: VLADIMIR P.
MASHTALIR
Faculty of Electronic Devices: VLADIMIR A.
STOROZHENKO
Faculty of Electronic Technology: YURI N.
ALEKSANDROV
Faculty of Radiotechnology: SERGEY N.
SAKALO

Faculty of Telecommunications and Electro-
nics: IGOR N. PRESNYAKOV
Foreign Students' Preparatory Faculty: VLA-
DIMIR P. NEMCHENKO
Postgraduate Faculty: ZOYA V. DUDAR

DIRECTORS OF INSTITUTES

Institute of Computing and Information
Technologies: VIKTOR M. LEVYKIN
Institute of Radioengineering and Electro-
nics: VLADIMIR M. SHOKALO
Institute of Telecommunications: VIKTOR M.
LEVYKIN

KHARKIV POLYTECHNICAL INSTITUTE (NATIONAL TECHNICAL UNIVERSITY)

61002 Kharkiv, vul. Frunze 21

Telephone: (572) 43-26-81

Fax: (572) 40-06-01

E-mail: omsroot@kpi.kharkov.ua

Internet: www.kpi.kharkov.ua

Founded 1885

Rector: LEONID L. TOVAZHNYANSKY
Pro-Rector for Education and International
Relations: VALERIY O. KRAVETS
Pro-Rector for Research: YEVGEN I. SOKOL

Number of teachers: 1,235
Number of students: 20,000

DEANS

Faculty of Automation and Instrument Mak-
ing: Prof. ANATOLIY I. HAPON
Faculty of Business Administration: Prof.
VIKTOR YA. ZARUBA
Faculty of Business and Finance: Prof.
OLEKSANDR M. HAVRIS
Faculty of Chemical Engineering: Dr OLEKSIY
M. PASSOKHA
Faculty of Computing and Information Tech-
nologies: Prof. MYKOLA I. ZAPOLOVSKIY
Faculty of Distance and Pre-University
Training: Dr MYKOLA M. SIRENKO
Faculty of Economics: Prof. PETRO H. PER-
ERVA
Faculty of Economics and Law: Prof. LEONID
M. IVIN
Faculty of Electrical Engineering: Prof.
VOLODYMYR V. VOINOV
Faculty of Engineering: Dr MIKHAILO S.
STEPANOV
Faculty of Engineering Physics: Dr DMITRO
V. BRESKLAVSKIY
Faculty of Information Science and Manage-
ment: Prof. VYACHESLAV H. BAZHENOV
Faculty of Inorganic Substances Technology:
Prof. MIKHAILO I. RISCHENKO
Faculty of Mechanics and Technology: Dr
MYKOLA POHRIBNIY
Faculty of Organic Substances Technology:
Prof. OLEKSANDR P. NEKRASOV
Faculty of Physics and Technology: Prof.
SERHIY M. KOSMACHOV
Faculty of Power Engineering: Prof. MYKOLA
O. TARASENKO
Faculty of Transport Engineering: Dr VITALIY
V. YEPIFANOV
German Technical Faculty: Dr VIRA M.
SHAMARDINA

KHARKIV STATE TECHNICAL UNIVERSITY OF CIVIL ENGINEERING AND ARCHITECTURE

61002 Kharkiv, Sumska ul. 40

Telephone: (572) 700-01-12

Fax: (572) 700-02-50

E-mail: office@kstuca.kharkov.ua

Internet: www.kstuca.kharkov.ua

Founded 1930

Rector: Prof. Dr MYKOLA S. BOLOTSKYKH

Library of 318,000 vols
Number of teachers: 470

Number of students: 5,000

Faculties of Construction, Sanitary Engineering, Architecture, Mechanical Engineering, Economics and Management,
Military Training, Part-Time Studies,
Postgraduate Study.

DEANS

Faculty of Architecture: Prof. OLEKSANDR B.
VASILENKO
Faculty of Construction: Dr YEVGEN A.
YAKOVLEV
Faculty of Economics and Management: Dr
DIMITRIY L. CHEREDNIK
Faculty of External Education: Dr OLEK-
SANDR F. PUGACHOV
Faculty of Mechanical-Technical Engineer-
ing: Dr MYKHAILO B. HUD
Faculty of Sanitary Engineering: Dr VIKTOR
V. SHYLIN
Faculty of Postgraduate Education: Dr GEN-
NADIY I. SUKHORUKOV
Faculty of Pre-University Preparation: Dr
OLEKSANDR A. SIROVATSKIY

KHERSON NATIONAL TECHNICAL UNIVERSITY

73008 Kherson, Beryslavske shose 24

Telephone: and fax (552) 55-40-11

E-mail: kstu@tlc.kherson.ua

Internet: www.kstu.edu.ua

Founded 1957

Rector: FRANTS B. ROHALSKIY

Library of 400,000 vols

Publication: *Proceedings* (2 a year)

DEANS

Faculty of Cybernetics: Prof. NADIYA A.
SOKOLOVA
Faculty of Distance Education: Prof. N. A.
PUSTOVAYA
Faculty of Economics: Prof. VOLODYMYR. E.
TURSH
Faculty of International Economics: Prof. V.
V. KRYUCHOVSKIY
Faculty of Machine Building: Prof. HRIHORIY
DYNEVICH
Faculty of Technology and Design: Prof. N. I.
VALKO
Preparatory Faculty: Prof. N. S. MYKOLAY-
CHUK

KIROVOHRAD NATIONAL TECHNICAL UNIVERSITY

25006 Kirovohrad, Universitetska 8

Telephone: (522) 55-93-59

Fax: (522) 55-92-53

E-mail: relintern@kdtu.kr.ua

Internet: www.kdtu.kr.ua

Founded 1929

Rector: Prof. Dr MYKHAILO I. CHERNOVOL
Pro-Rector for Education: Prof. MYKOLA M.
PETRENKO
Pro-Rector for Science and Research: Dr
VOLODYMYR M. KROPIVNIY

Library of 406,000 vols
Number of teachers: 400
Number of students: 7,000

DEANS

Faculty of Agricultural Mechanics: Prof.
VASYL M. SALO
Faculty of Automation, Power Engineering
and Programming: Prof. LARISA H. VIKH-
ROVA
Faculty of Economics: Prof. HRIHORIY M.
DAVIDOV
Faculty of Machine Design and Develop-
ment: Dr VOLODYMYR V. YATSUN
Faculty of Mechanics and Technology: Prof.
BORIS YE. NADVORNIY

Preparatory Faculty for Foreign Specialists: Prof. OLEKSANDR Y. MAZHEYKA

Preparatory and Specialists' Retraining Faculty: Prof. YEVGEN K. SOLOVYKH

KYIV NATIONAL UNIVERSITY OF CONSTRUCTION AND ARCHITECTURE

03037 Kyiv, Vozdukhoflotskii pr. 31

Telephone: (44) 248-49-05

Fax: (44) 248-49-01

E-mail: knuba@knuba.edu.ua

Internet: www.knuba.edu.ua

Founded 1930

Rector: A. M. TUGAY

Library of 1,213,000 vols

Number of teachers: 755

Number of students: 5,000

Faculties of Architecture, Automation of Construction, Construction, Constructional Technology, Urban Construction, Sanitary Engineering.

'KYIV POLYTECHNIC INSTITUTE' NATIONAL TECHNICAL UNIVERSITY OF UKRAINE

03056 Kyiv, pr. Peremohy 37

Telephone: (44) 236-69-13

Fax: (44) 236-69-13

E-mail: mzz@ntu-kpi.kiev.ua

Internet: www.ntu-kpi.kiev.ua

Founded 1898

Languages of instruction: Ukrainian, Russian, English

Academic year: September to June

Rector: Acad. MYKHAYLO Z. ZGUROVSKIY

Library of 3,000,000 vols

Number of students: 40,500students

Publications: *Kyivsky Politekhnik* (newspaper, weekly), *Vesti* (2 a year)

20 Educational depts, 9 educational-research institutes, 12 research institutes and 13 other scientific subdivisions (incl. design bureaux, eng. centres).

DEANS

Faculty of Applied Mathematics: Prof. OLEKSANDR A. MOLCHANOV

Faculty of Avionics and Space Systems: Prof. OLEKSANDR V. ZBRUTSKIY

Faculty of Biological Eng. and Biotechnology: Prof. OLEKSIY M. DUGAN

Faculty of Chemical Eng.: Prof. YEVGEN M. PANOV

Faculty of Chemical Technology: Prof. IHOR M. ASTRELIN

Faculty of Electric Power Technology and Automation: Prof. OLEKSANDR S. YANDULSKIY

Faculty of Electronics: Prof. VALERIY YA. ZHUYKOV

Faculty of Eng. Physics: Prof. PETRO I. LOBODA

Faculty of Information Science and Computing: Prof. OLEKSANDR A. PAVLOV

Faculty of Instrument Making: Prof. HRIHORIY S. TYMCHYK

Faculty of Law: Prof. ANATOLIY P. TUZOV

Faculty of Linguistics: Prof. NATALYA S. SAYENKO

Faculty of Management and Marketing: Prof. VASYL H. HERASIMCHUK

Faculty of Physical Education and Sport: Dr SERHIY O. SICHOV

Faculty of Physics and Mathematics: Acad. Prof. VIKTOR H. BARYAKHTER

Faculty of Radiotechnology: Prof. OLEKSANDR I. RYBIN

Faculty of Sociology: Prof. BORYS V. NOVIKOV

Faculty of Thermal Power Eng.: Prof. YEVGEN M. PISMENNIY

Faculty of Welding: SERHIY K. FOMICHOV

Inter-Univ. Medical Eng. Faculty: Prof. V. P. YATSENKO

DIRECTORS

Higher Institute of Telecommunications and Informatisation: ANATOLIY I. MINOCHKIN

Institute of Applied Systems Analysis: Acad. Prof. MYKHAILO Z. ZHUROVSKIY

Institute of Energy Conservation and Management: Prof. ARTUR V. PRAKHOVNIK

Institute of Mechanical and Machine Eng.: Prof. MYKOLA I. BOBYR

Institute of Physics and Technology: Prof. OLEKSIY M. NOVIKOV

Institute of Postgraduate Education: Prof. VOLODYMYR V. BOSSIY

Institute of Pre-Univ. Training and Professional Orientation: Prof. VASYL V. YASINSKIY

Institute of Printing and Publishing: PETRO O. KYRYCHOK

Institute of Telecommunications Systems: Prof. MYKHAILO YU. ILCHENKO

'LVIV POLYTECHNIC' NATIONAL UNIVERSITY

79013 Lviv, vul. St Bandery 12

Telephone: (322) 72-47-33

E-mail: rudavsky@polynet.lviv.ua

Internet: www.lp.edu.ua

Founded 1844

Rector: Prof. Dr YURIY K. RUDAVSKIY

First Pro-Rector: Prof. Dr PETRO P. KOSTROBIY

Pro-Rector for Education and Foreign Affairs: Prof. Dr YURIY M. RASHKEVYCH

Pro-Rector for Research: Prof. Dr YURIY YA. BODALO

Library of 3,000,000 vols

Number of teachers: 2,000

Number of students: 17,000

Publication: *Journal* (15 series annually)

DIRECTORS

Institute of Applied Mathematics and Fundamental Sciences: Prof. PETRO I. KALENYUK

Institute of Architecture: Prof. BOGDAN S. CHERKES

Institute of Chemistry and Chemical Technologies: Prof. YOSYP Y. YATCHYSHYN

Institute of Civil and Environmental Engineering: Prof. MYROSLAV A. SANYTSKY

Institute of Computer Sciences and Information Technologies: Prof. VOLODYMYR V. HRYTSYK

Institute of Computer Technologies, Automation and Metrology: Prof. BOHDAN I. STADNYK

Institute of Economics and Management: Prof. OLEH Y. KUZMIN

Institute of Engineering Mechanics and Transport: Prof. ZINOVIY A. STOTSKO

Institute of Geodesy: Prof. PETRO M. ZAZULYAK

Institute of Liberal Arts: Prof. LEONTIY E. DESCHYNSKIY

Institute of Power Engineering and Control Systems: Prof. PETRO M. ZAZULYAK

Institute of Telecommunications, Radioelectronics and Electronic Engineering: Prof. BOHDAN A. MANDZIY

Institute of Distance Education: Prof. BORYS M. ROMANYSHYN

NATIONAL AVIATION UNIVERSITY

03058 Kyiv, pr. Kosmonavta Komarova 1

Telephone: (44) 406-79-01

E-mail: post@nau.edu.ua

Internet: www.nau.edu.ua

Founded 1933

Rector: Prof. Dr VITALIY BABEK

Pro-Rector for Academic Affairs: Prof. Dr MYKOLA S. KULIK

Pro-Rector for Administrative and Financial Affairs: MYKOLA V. MYKHALKO

Pro-Rector for Corporate Affairs: Dr MAKSYM H. LUTSKYY

Pro-Rector for Economic Affairs: YURIY H. SYMONENKO

Pro-Rector for Research: Prof. Dr VOLODYMYR P. KHARCHENKO

Pro-Rector for Student Affairs: Dr YAROSLAV KOZACHOK

DIRECTORS

Institute of Aerospace Systems: Prof. Dr VALERYY M. SHMAROV

Institute of Aviation and Space Law: Prof. Dr TAMARA P. KUDLAI

Institute of Computer Technologies: Prof. Dr IGOR A. ZHUKOV

Institute of Continuing Education: Dr RINAT M. SALIMOV

Institute of Electronics and Control Systems: Prof. Dr VIKTOR M. SINYEGLAZOV

Institute of Extramural and Distance Education: Dr PAVLO S. BORSUK

Institute of Humanities: Prof. Dr ARTUR H. HUDMANYAN

Institute of Innovative Technologies: Prof. Dr VIKTOR V. KULISH

Institute of Information-Diagnostic Systems: Dr SERHIY F. FILONENKO (acting)

Institute of International Relations: Prof. Dr OLEKSANDR P. STEPANOV

Institute of Land Use and Information Technologies: Dr VIKTOR P. PARANICH

Institute of Management and Economics: Prof. Dr VOLODYMYR SHCHLNUKOV

Institute of Municipal Activity: Prof. Dr SERHIY V. IVANOV

Institute of Management Technologies: Dr VASYL D. SHPILOVYY

Institute of Management and Information Technologies: Prof. Dr DMYTRO F. BAISA

International Civil Aviation Organization (ICAO) Institute: Prof. Dr HALINA A. SUSLOVA

Preparatory Institute: Dr NATALIYA P. MURANOVA

NATIONAL MINING UNIVERSITY OF UKRAINE

49027 Dnipropetrovsk, pr. K. Marksa 19

Telephone: (562) 47-07-66

Fax: (562) 47-07-66

E-mail: dfr@nmuu.dp.ua

Internet: www.nmuu.dp.ua

Founded 1899

Rector: Prof. Dr GENNADIY PIVNYAK

Library of 1,300,000 vols

Number of teachers: 708

Number of students: 10,897

Faculties of Construction of Mines, Economics, Construction Electrical Engineering, Engineering, Geotechnology, Law, Mining and Prospecting

Publications: *University Monthly*, *University Newspaper* (weekly).

NATIONAL SHIPBUILDING UNIVERSITY 'ADMIRAL MAKAROV'

54025 Kyiv, Mikolaiv, pr. Heroiv Stalinhrada

Telephone: (512) 35-91-48

Fax: (512) 42-46-52

E-mail: vc@usmtu.edu.ua

Internet: www.usmtu.edu.ua

Founded 1929

Rector: Prof. Dr HEORHIY F. ROMANOVSKIY

First Pro-Rector: Prof. Dr OLEKSANDR M. DUBOVIY

Pro-Rector for Research: Prof. Dr VYACHE-SLAV F. KVASNITSKIY

DIRECTORS

Institute of Automation and Electrical Technology: Prof. VOLODYMYR S. BLINTSOV
Institute of External and Distance Education: Acad. Prof. OLEKSANDR O. MOCHALOV
Institute of Humanities: Prof. OLEKSANDR M. DUBOVIY
Institute of Machine Building: Prof. VIKTOR M. HORBOV
Institute of Shipbuilding: Prof. KOSTYANTIN KOSHKIN
Institute of Postgraduate Studies: Prof. MYKOLA V. FATEEV
1st of May Polytechnic Institute: Prof. TETYANA I. KOSTYUKOVA
Feodosia Polytechnic Institute: (vacant)

DEANS

Faculty of Engineering Economics: Prof. OLEKSANDR YU. YEGANOV
Preparatory Faculty: Prof. V. I. KONDRA-TENKO

NATIONAL TRANSPORT UNIVERSITY

01010 Kyiv, vul. Suvorova 1
Telephone: (44) 280-82-03
Fax: (44) 290-82-03
E-mail: general@ntu.edu.ua
Internet: www.ntu.edu.ua
Founded 1944
Rector: Prof. Dr MYKOLA F. DMYTRYCHENKO
First Pro-Rector: Prof. Dr MYKOLA O. BILYA-KOVYCH
Pro-Rector for Research: Prof. Dr MYKOLA M. DYMYTRIEV
Library of 440,000 vols
Number of teachers: 363
Number of students: 3,727

DEANS

Faculty of Motor Mechanics: YURIY HUTAR-EVICH
Faculty of Road Building: VYACHESLAV SAVENKO
Faculty of Transport Management: LYUDMILA KOZAK

DIRECTORS

Institute of Distance Education: SERHIY ANDRUSENKO
Preparatory Faculty and International Relations: MYKHAILO HONCHAR

NATIONAL UNIVERSITY OF FOOD TECHNOLOGIES

01033 Kyiv, Volodymyrska vul. 68
Telephone: (44) 220-64-00
E-mail: info@nuft.edu.ua
Internet: www.nuft.edu.ua
Founded 1930; present name and status 2002
Rector: Prof. I. S. GULYI
Library of 1,051,037 vols
Number of teachers: 805
Number of students: 13,106 full-time; 7,033 correspondence
Brs in Kamyanets-Podilsky, Lviv oblast, Poltava, Simferopol, Smila, Sumy.
Publications: *Latest Achievements in the Food Industry and Scientific Research, Scientific Works*

DEANS

Faculty of Automation and Computer Systems: IHOR ELPERIN
Faculty of Baking and Brewing Technology: PETRO SHIYAN
Faculty of Economics and Management: TATYANA MOSTENSKA

Faculty of Energy: MYKHAYLO MASLIKOV
Faculty of Mechanical Engineering: SERHIY BLAGHENKO
Faculty of Meat, Fat and Dairy Industry Technology: HEORHIY HONCHAROV
Faculty of Sugar Technology: HALYNA SIMAKHNYA

DIRECTOR

College of Restaurant Economy: YURIY SUKHENKO

NATIONAL UNIVERSITY OF WATER MANAGEMENT AND NATURAL RESOURCES

33028 Rivne, vul. Soborna 11
Telephone: (362) 22-10-86
Fax: (362) 22-21-97
Internet: rstu.rv.ua
Founded 1922
State control
Rector: VASYL A. HURYN
Pro-Rector for Academic Affairs: SERHIY V. KOVALYOV (acting)
Pro-Rector for Academic Affairs and Research: VIKTOR S. MOSHYNSKIY
Pro-Rector for Education, Administrative and Social Affairs: VOLODYMYR M. YAKYM-CHUK (acting)
Pro-Rector for Science and International Relations: LEONID F. KOZHUSHKO
Pro-Rector for Teaching Methods: VIKTOR S. MOSHYNSKY
Library of 829,000 vols
Number of teachers: 640
Number of students: 11,500
Publications: *Bulletin* (4 a year), *Hydroamelioration and Hydrotechnical Engineering* (annually), *Resource Saving Materials, Construction, Buildings and Structures* (4 a year)

DEANS

Faculty of Applied Mathematics and Computer-Integrated Systems (tel. (362) 23-14-60):
ANATOLIY P. VLASYUK
Faculty of Building and Architecture (tel. (362) 22-20-07):
HRYHORIY H. MASYUK
Faculty of Ecology and Natural Resource Application (tel. (362) 23-14-17):
MYKOLA O. KLYMENKO
Faculty of Economy and Business (tel. (362) 22-23-30):
SVITLANA O. LEVYTSKA
Faculty of Hydrotechnical Engineering and Hydroenergetics:
ANATOLIY M. MAKOVSKY
Faculty of Land Management and Geoinformation (tel. (362) 23-72-82):
PETRO H. CHERNYAGA
Faculty of Management (tel. (362) 23-00-95):
VITALIY P. OKORSKY
Faculty of Mechanical and Power Engineering (tel. (362) 22-35-11):
MYKOLA M. MARCHUK
Faculty of Water Management (tel. (362) 26-64-55):
ANATOLIY M. ROKOCHYNSKY

ATTACHED INSTITUTE

Institute of Pre-University Training and Post-Diploma Education: Dir ZINOVIY R. MALANCHUK.

ODESA NATIONAL POLYTECHNIC UNIVERSITY

65044 Odesa, pr. Shevchenko 1
Telephone: (482) 22-34-74
E-mail: ospu@ospu.odessa.ua
Internet: www.ospu.odessa.ua
Founded 1918
Rector: Prof. Dr VALERIY P. MALAKHOV
Pro-Rector for Studies and Education: Prof. Dr YURIY S. YAMOLSKY
Pro-Rector for Studies and Research: Prof. Dr VALERIY P. MALAKHOV
Library of 1,500,000 vols
Number of teachers: 4,000
Number of students: 20,000
Faculties of Mechanical Technology, Thermal Power, Nuclear Power, Radio Engineering, Automation and Electrification of Industry, Robot Systems, Automation and Computer Technology, Engineering Economics, Chemical Technology.

DIRECTORS

Institute of Basic Automation and Electrical Power Supply: Dr O. A. ANDRYUSCHENKO
Institute of Business, Economics and Informational Technologies: Dr HEORHIY N. VOSTROV
Institute of Computer Systems: Prof. SERHIY A. NESTERENKO
Institute of Industrial Technologies, Design and Management: Dr GENNADIY A. OBORS-KIY
Institute of Machine Engineering: Prof. ALEKSANDR F. DASCHENKO
Institute of Power Engineering: Prof. ANTON S. MAZURENKO
Institute of Radioelectronics and Telecommunications: Dr PORFIRIY YU. BARANOV
Institute of Pre-University Preparation: (vacant)

ODESA STATE ENVIRONMENTAL UNIVERSITY

65016 Odesa, vul. Lvivska 15
Telephone: (482) 63-62-09
Fax: (482) 42-77-67
E-mail: synop@ogmi.farlep.odessa.ua
Internet: www.odeku.edu.ua
Founded 1932
Academic year: September to June
Rector: Prof. SERHIY M. STEPANENKO
Vice-Rector: Dr MYKOLA H. SERBOV
Chief of International Department: V. M. SYTOV
Dean of Continuing Education and Training: L. M. POLETAEVA
Library of 273,000 vols
Number of teachers: 245
Number of students: 3,790
Publication: *Meteorology, Climatology and Hydrology* (4 a year)

DEANS

Faculty of Computer Science and Management: V. V. AUROV
Faculty of Environmental Studies: O. H. VOLODYMYROVA
Faculty of Hydrology, Hydrometeorological Institute: M. P. EKHNICH (Dir)
Faculty of Metrology: G. P. IVUS

PROFESSORS

Faculty of Computer Science:
KORBAN, V. KH.
KRUGLYAK, Y. M.
PREPELIZHA, G. P.

Faculty of Environmental Studies:
GERASIMOV, O. I.
LOEVA, I. D.
MINICHEVA, G. G.

SAFRANOV, T. A.
SOKOLOV, Y. M.
ZHYKALO, A. N.

Hydrometeorological Institute:
EFIMOV, V. A.
GOPCHENKO, E. D.
LOBODA, N. S.
MICHAYLOV, V. I.
MISCHENKO, Z. A.
POLEVOY, A. M.
SHKOLNY, E. P.
STEPANENKO, S. N.
TUCHKOVENKO, Y. S.

AFFILIATED COLLEGES

Kharkiv Hydrometeorological College:
Dir T. E. TKACHENKO.

Kherson Hydrometeorological College:
Dir S. V. AVGAYTIS.

POLTAVA NATIONAL TECHNICAL UNIVERSITY 'YU. KONDRATYUKA'

36601 Poltava-11, Pershotravnevyy pr-t 24

Telephone: (569) 55-13-89
Fax: (569) 55-13-07
E-mail: dirc@pntu.poltava.ua
Internet: www.pntu.edu.ua

Founded 1930; present name and status 1994

Rector: Prof. Dr VOLODYMYR O. ONYSHCHENKO
First Pro-Rector: Dr ANATOLIY V. HULYAYEV
Number of teachers: 450
Number of students: 8,500

DEANS

Faculty of Architecture: Dr V. V. RUSIN
Faculty of Construction: Dr O. A. KHARCH-ENKO
Faculty of Economics, Information Technology and Management: Dr V. F. PENTS
Faculty of Electro-Mechanical Engineering: (vacant)
Faculty of Finance and Economics: Dr RAYISA V. SHYNKARENKO
Faculty of Sanitary Engineering: Dr R. O. KOROBKO
External Faculty: Dr I. O. IVANYTSKA

SEVASTOPOL NATIONAL TECHNICAL UNIVERSITY

99053 Sevastopol, Streletsky Bay, Studgor-odok, ul. Mazepy 10

Telephone: (692) 23-50-08

Founded 1963

Rector: M. Z. LAVRINENKO

Library of 1,200,000 vols, special collns on machine-building and environmental monitoring
Number of teachers: 550
Number of students: 7,000.

UKRAINIAN STATE UNIVERSITY OF CHEMICAL ENGINEERING

49005 Dnipropetrovsk, pr. Gagarina 8

Telephone: (562) 47-08-13
Fax: (562) 47-08-13
E-mail: ugxtu@dicht.dp.ua
Internet: www.usuce.dp.ua

Founded 1930

Rector: Prof. Dr MIHAYLO V. BURMISTR
Library of 753,000 vols
Number of teachers: 520
Number of students: 6,032

Publications: *Chemist World*, *Chemistry and Chemical Technology Questions* (4 a year), *Scientific-Technological Digest* (4 a year)

DEANS

Faculty of Economics: BORIS A. KIOR

Faculty of High-Molecular Compounds Engineering: VIKTOR S. KOVALENKO
Faculty of Inorganic Chemistry: YURI D. GALIVETZ
Faculty of Mechanics: VLADIMIR I. SITAR
Faculty of Organic Resources Technology: VALERIY I. OVCHAROV
Faculty of Silicates Technology: VIKTOR I. HOLEUS

VINNYTSIA NATIONAL TECHNICAL UNIVERSITY

21036 Vinnytsia, Khmelnitske shose 95

Telephone: (432) 32-57-18
Fax: (432) 46-57-72
E-mail: vstu@vstu.vinnica.ua
Internet: www.vstu.edu.ua

Founded 1960

Rector: Prof. BORIS I. MOKIN
First Pro-Rector for Research, International Relations and Economic and Political Affairs: VOLODYMYR V. HRABKO
Library of 820,000 vols
Number of teachers: 542
Number of students: 7,492

Publications: *Proceedings* (6 a year), *University News* (monthly)

DIRECTORS

Institute of Civil Engineering and Gas Supply: HEORHIY S. RATUSHNYAK
Institute of Electronics and Computer Systems' Management: ANATOLIY S. VASYURA
Institute of Information Technologies and Computer Engineering: OLEKSIY D. AZAROV
Institute of Machine Building and Transport: YURIY A. BURYENNIKOV
Institute of Management: MYKOLA I. NEBAVA
Institute of Power Engineering, Ecology and Electrical Mechanics: MYKOLA P. SVRYDOV
Institute of Radioengineering, Telecommunications and Electronic Instrument Engineering: VASYL M. KYCHAK

ZAPORIZHZHIA NATIONAL TECHNICAL UNIVERSITY

69063 Zaporizhzhia, vul. Zhukovskoho 64

Telephone: (612) 64-25-06
Fax: (612) 64-21-41
E-mail: mail@zntu.edu.ua
Internet: www.zntu.edu.ua

Founded 1900

Rector: SERHIY B. BELIKOV
First Pro-Rector for Education: ANATOLIY D. KOVAL
Pro-Rector for Education: SERHIY T. YARYM-BASH
Librarian: LYUDMYLA I. KOZYRYATSKA
Library of 1,000,000 vols
Number of teachers: 600
Number of students: 9,200

Publications: *Bulletin of Propulsion Engineering*, *Computer Science and Control* (2 a year), *Electrotechnics and Electroenergetics*, *Journal* (monthly), *New Materials and Technology in Metallurgy and Machine Construction*, *Radio Electronics*

DIRECTORS

Institute of Continuous Training: Dr S. T. YARYMBASH
Institute of Economics and Humanities: Dr V. G. PRUSHIVSKIY
Institute of Information Science and Radioelectronics: Prof. D. M. LIZA
Institute of Machine Building: Acad. Prof. L. Y. IVSCHENKO
Institute of Physics and Technology: Acad. Prof. V. V. LUNOV

Academies

Dnipropetrovsk State Medical Academy: 49044 Dnipropetrovsk, Vul. Dzerzhinskoho 9; tel. (562) 45-15-65; fax (56) 370-96-38; e-mail dsma@dsma.dp.ua; internet www.dsma.dp.ua; f. 1916; main specialities: general practice, paediatrics, dentistry, clinical pharmacology, sanitary hygiene; library: 656,600 vols; 598 teachers; 4,045 students; Rector Dr GEORGY V. DZYAK; publs *Medical Perspectives* (4 a year), *Dermatology, Cosmetics and Sexual Pathology* (4 a year), *Urology* (4 a year).

Donbass State Academy of Civil Engineering and Architecture: 86123 Donetsk obl., Makeyevka vul. Derzhavina 2; tel. (622) 90-29-38; fax (622) 22-06-16; e-mail mailbox@dgasa.dn.ua; internet www.dgasa.dn.ua; f. 1972; faculties: basic and general engineering training, civil engineering, architecture, environmental engineering, mechanical engineering, economics, marketing and management; extra-mural preparatory dept for foreign students, humanities; library: 400,000 vols; 399 teachers; 5,769 students; Rector YEVHEN V. HOROKHOV; publs *Academy News* (monthly), *Bulletin* (6 a year), *Metal Construction* (4 a year).

Donbass State Engineering Academy: 84313 Kramatorsk, vul. Shkadinova 72; tel. (626) 41-67-94; fax (626) 41-63-15; e-mail postmaster@dgma.edu.donetsk.ua; faculties: engineering and economics, machine-building, automation, automation of metal-shaping processes, economics and humanities.

Ivano-Frankivsk State Medical Academy: 76000 Ivano-Frankivsk, Halytska 2; tel. and fax (3422) 2-42-95; e-mail ma@ifdma.if.ua; internet www.ifdma.if.ua; f. 1945; library: 319,000 vols; 389 teachers; 4,994 students; Rector Dr YE. NEIKO.

Kharkiv State Academy of Railway Transport: 61003 Kharkiv, pl. Feierbakha 7; tel. (57) 732 20-67; fax (572) 20-60-19; e-mail info@kart.kharkov.com; internet www.kart.edu.ua; f. 1930; faculties: traffic management, mechanics, automation, telemechanics and communication, construction, economics; library: 700,000 vols; brs in Donetsk, Kyiv; Rector NIKOLAY I. DANKO.

Kharkiv State Academy of Zooveterinary Science: 62341 Kharkiv obl., Dergachevskiy raion, P/O Malaya Danilovka; tel. (5763) 5-74-65; fax (5763) 5-70-76; e-mail zoovet@zoovet.kharkov.ua; f. 1851; library: 250,000 vols; 190 teachers; 2,500 students; Rector VALERY GOLOVKO.

Kharkiv State Municipal Academy: 61002 Kharkiv, vul. Revolyutsii 12; tel. (572) 43-21-62; fax (572) 47-65-00; e-mail root@ksma.kharkov.ua; f. 1930; faculties: management of public services and municipal finances, electric and underground transport, urban electric power supply and lighting, urban planning and development, engineering ecology, economics of civil engineering enterprises, economics of municipal economy enterprises, accounting and auditing, management in hotel business and tourism, architecture, landscape architecture, technical maintenance of buildings, retraining; electromechanical college, municipal economy college; library: 890,000 vols; 1,000 teachers; 12,000 students; Rector Prof. L. N. SHUTENKO.

Lviv Academy of Veterinary Medicine: 79301 Lviv, vul. Pekarska 50; tel. (322) 75-67-84; fax (322) 79-32-31; e-mail vetacademy@hotmail.com; internet www.vetacad.lviv.ua; f. 1784; faculties: veterinary medicine, biology and technology, food technology, economics and management and extra-mural studies; 292 teachers; 4,500 students; library: 333,000 vols; Rector Prof. Dr R. J. KRAVTSIV.

Lviv Commercial Academy: 79005 Lviv, vul. Tuhan-Baranovskoho 10; tel. (322) 75-65-50; e-mail academy@lac.lviv.ua; internet www.lac.lviv.ua; f. 1899; faculties: economics, management, international economic relations, law, commodity science and commerce; 300 teachers; 5,740 students; library: 600,000 vols; Rector YA. A. HONCHARUK.

National Metallurgical Academy of Ukraine: 49600 Dnipropetrovsk, pr. Gagarina 4; tel. (562) 45-31-56; fax (562) 47-44-61; e-mail dmeti@dmeti.dp.ua; internet dmeti.dp.ua; f. 1899; faculties: metallurgy, electrometallurgy, materials sciences and metal forming, mechanics and machine building, ecology and chemical technologies, economic cybernetics, computing systems and automation, energy and electromechanics, humanities, economics and management; library: 524,327 vols; 732 teachers; 12,199 students; Rector OLEKSANDR H. VELYCHKO; publ. *Theory and Practice of Metallurgy* (quarterly).

Odesa National Academy of Food Technologies: 65039 Odesa, vul. Kanatna 112; tel. (482) 29-11-40; fax (482) 25-32-84; e-mail fedosov@optima.com.ua; internet www.osaft.odessa.ua; f. 1902; State control; academic year September to June; faculties: economics, management and business; grain and grain products technology; technology of bread, confectionery and nutrition; food preserving technology and winemaking; meat and dairy products technology and ecology; mechanical engineering; automation of technological processes; 566 teachers (incl. 53 full professors); 10,400 students; library: 600,000 vols; Rector Prof. BOGDAN YEGOROV; publs *Collection of Scientific Works* (every 6 months), *Grain Products and Mixed Fodders* (quarterly).

Odesa National Maritime Academy: 65029 Odesa, Didrikhson 8; tel. (48) 777-57-74; fax (48) 234-52-67; e-mail info@ma.odessa.ua; internet www.ma.odessa.ua; f. 1944; faculties: navigation, marine engineering, electrical engineering, automation, radio electronics, maritime law; brs in Mariupol, Izmail, correspondence depts and the Maritime College of the Technical Fleet; library: 578,000 vols; 401 teachers; 7,134 (; Rector Prof. MYKHAYLO V. MIYUSOV; publs *Automization of Ship's Technical Devices* (2 a year), *Marine Transportation and Transport Complexes* (annually), *Navigation* (2 a year), *Sea Review* (4 a year), *Ship's Power Plants* (2 a year).

Odesa State Academy of Civil Engineering and Architecture: 65029 Odesa, Didrikhson 4; tel. (482) 20-41-82; fax (482) 23-35-10; e-mail rektorat@gs.org.ua; internet www.ogasa.odessa.ua; f. 1930; faculties: architecture, industrial and civil construction, technical engineering, construction engineering, power engineering, sanitary engineering; library: 600,000 vols; Rector Prof. VITALIY S. DOROFEEV.

Odesa State Academy of Refrigeration: 65026 Odesa, vul. Dvoryanska 1/3; tel. (482) 23-22-20; fax (482) 23-89-31; e-mail admin@osar.odessa.ua; internet www.osar.odessa.ua; f. 1922; faculties: refrigeration engineering, automation and robot engineering, systems of automatized projection, environmental protection and rational use of natural resources, heat technology, thermophysics, mechanical engineering, cryogenic engineering; library: 487,173 vols; 288 teachers; 3,500 students; Rector V. V. PRITULA; publ. *Refrigeration Engineering and Technology* (2 a year).

Poltava State Agrarian Academy: 314003 Poltava, vul. Skovorody 1/3; tel. (5322) 2-26-10; fax (5322) 2-29-57; e-mail antonov@agroak.poltava.ua; internet agroak.poltava.ua; f. 1920; depts: accounting and auditing, finance, economy of enterprises, management of organizations, farm mechanization, agronomy, zoological engineering, veterinary medicine; library: 315,000 vols; 247 teachers; 7,000 students; Rector Dr V. N. PISARENKO; publ. *Poltava Agrarian News* (4 a year).

Prydniprovska State Academy of Civil Engineering and Architecture: 49600 Dnipropetrovsk, Chernyshevskeho 24A; tel. and fax (562) 47-16-88; e-mail dik@pgasa.dp.ua; internet www.pgasa.dp.ua; f. 1930; faculties: civil engineering, building technology, economics, mechanics, architecture, construction, correspondence; library: 662,000 vols; 467 teachers; 6,392 students; Rector Prof. V. I. BOLSHAKOV.

State Academy of Food Technology and Management: 61051 Kharkiv, Klochkivska 333; tel. (572) 36-89-79; fax (572) 37-85-35; e-mail hdatoh@kharkov.com; internet www.hdatoh.kharkov.com; f. 1967; faculties: food technology, food science and food trade, economics, accountancy and auditing, industrial management, services management, food industry machines and equipment, marketing; 350 teachers; 5,000 students; library: 380,000 vols; Rector A. I. CHEREVKO; publ. *Zbirnyk naukovykh prats* (annually).

Ukrainian Engineering Pedagogics Academy: 61003 Kharkiv, Department of Foreign Relations, vul. Universytetska 16; tel. (572) 731-28-62; fax (572) 731-32-36; e-mail docents@vl.kharkov.ua; f. 1958; faculties: power engineering, mechanical and technological, machine-building, radioelectronics, electromechanics and computer systems, mining engineering, electrical and technological, social-economical; training centres for foreign citizens and engineering educators; library: 1,000,000 vols; 350 teachers; 11,000 students; Rector ELENA KOVALENKO.

Yaroslav Mudry National Law Academy of Ukraine: 61024 Kharkiv, Pushkinskaya ul. 77; tel. (57) 704-11-20; fax (57) 704-11-71; e-mail uracad@bestnet.kharkov.ua; internet www.uracad.kharkiv.edu; f. 1804; library: 1,000,000 vols, 1,000 dissertations, 29,000 rare books and manuscripts; 600 teachers; 15,000 students; Rector VASYL YA. TATSIY.

Zaporizhzhya State Engineering Academy: 69006 Zaporizhzhia, pr. Lenina 226; tel. (612) 15-90-34; fax (612) 12-38-87; e-mail admin@zgia.zp.ua; internet www.zgia.zp.ua; f. 1959; faculties: metallurgy, mechanics and technology, power engineering and energy-saving, building and water resources, electronics and electronic technologies, information technologies, management and finance, economics of enterprises, postgraduate studies; library: 501,777 vols; 350 teachers; 10,000 students; Rector Dr V. I. POZHUEV.

Institutes of Higher Education

Donetsk Musical-Pedagogical Institute: 340086 Donetsk, vul. Artema 44; tel. (622) 93-81-22; departments: piano, orchestral instruments, folk instruments, choral conducting, singing, composition, musicology.

Institute of National Economy: 03057 Kyiv, pr. Pobedy 54/1; tel. (44) 446-50-55; fax (44) 226-25-73; f. 1912; depts: economics and management, marketing, engineering economics, finance, agricultural management, accounting and audit, international relations; br. in Krivoi Rog; 600 teachers;

11,000 students; library: 800,000 vols; Rector ANATOLY PAVLENKO.

Kamyanets-Podilsk Institute of Agriculture: 32300 Khmelnytska r-n, Kamyanets-Podilsk, Ul. Shevchenko 13; tel. (3849) 2-52-18; fax (3849) 3-92-20; f. 1920; depts: agronomy, animal husbandry, veterinary medicine, economics, mechanization of agriculture; library: 600,000 vols; Rector M. I. SAMOKISH.

Kharkiv Institute of Agricultural Mechanization and Electrification: 61078 Kharkiv, vul. Artema 44; tel. (572) 22-37-86; f. 1929; library: 150,000 vols; Rector M. K. EVSEEV.

Kherson A. D. Tsuryupa Agricultural Institute: 325006 Kherson, vul. Rozy Lyuksemburga 23; tel. (55) 2-64-71; f. 1874; faculties of agronomy, animal husbandry, economics and agrobusiness jurisdiction, agricultural construction and hydromelioration; library: 300,000 vols; Rector V. A. USHKARENKO.

Kirovograd Higher Flying School of Civil Aviation: 316005 Kirovograd oblastnoi, vul. Dobrovolskogo 1; tel. (5222) 2-38-64; faculties: flying, air navigation, air traffic control.

Krivoi Rog Ore Mining Institute: 324027 Krivoi Rog, vul. XXII Partsezda 11; tel. (564) 23-22-30; fax (564) 74-84-12; f. 1922; faculties: geology and dressing, mine surveying and geodesy, underground mining, open-cast mining, electrical engineering, engineering, construction; geological museum; 4,500 students; library of 1.2m. vols; Rector V. F. BIZOV; publ. *Collection of Works* (2 a year).

Lugansk Agricultural Institute: 348008 Lugansk 8; tel. (642) 95-20-40; depts: agronomy, mechanization, economics, accounting.

Mariupol Metallurgical Institute: 87500 Mariupol, Republiki 7; tel. (629) 34-30-97; f. 1929; faculties: metallurgy, technology, welding, industrial energy, mechanical engineering; library: 580,000 vols; 444 teachers; 5,600 students; Rector I. V. ZHEZHELENKO.

Melitopol Institute of Agricultural Mechanization: 72300 Zaporizhzhya oblast, Melitopol, pr. B. Khmelnitskoho 18; tel. (612) 2-21-32; f. 1932; 315 teachers; 4,045 students; library: 330,000 vols; Rector N. L. KRIZHACHKOVSKII; publ. publs collections of scientific articles (quarterly).

Odesa Agricultural Institute: 270039 Odesa, Ul. Sverdlova 99; tel. (482) 22-37-23; fax (482) 24-01-84; f. 1918; depts: agronomy, fruit and vegetable growing, viticulture, animal husbandry, veterinary medicine, land management, mechanization, economics and management, accounting; 1,000 teachers; 5,200 students; library: 280,000 vols; br. in Nikolaev; Rector YU. S. TSUKANOV.

Odesa N. I. Pirohov Medical Institute: 270100 Odesa, per. Nariman Narimanova 2; tel. (482) 23-35-67; library: 433,000 vols.

Poltava Medical Stomatological Institute: 314024 Poltava, vul. Shevchenko 23; tel. (532) 2-88-25; Rector N. S. SKRIPNIKOV.

Ukrainian Institute of Printing: 290020 Lviv, vul. Podholosko 19; tel. (322) 59-94-01; faculties: mechanics, technology, economics, book illustration, editorial; library: 384,000 vols; Rector Dr STEPAN HUNKO; publ. *Journal of Printing and Publishing*.

Zaporizhzhia Medical Institute: 330074 Zaporizhzhia, vul. Mayakovskoho 26; tel. (612) 33-01-49; f. 1965; Rector I. I. TOKARENKO.

Schools of Art and Music

Kharkiv State Academy of Culture: 61003 Kharkiv, Bursatski Uzviz 4; tel. (57) 712-81-05; fax (57) 712-81-05; e-mail sheiko@ic.ac.kharkov.ua; internet www.ic.ac.kharkov.ua; f. 1929; departments: library and information science, cultural studies, documentation and information work, art, music, theatre, cinema and television; library: 400,000 vols; 257 teachers; 3,393 students; Rector Prof. VASYL M. SHEYKO; publs *Journal* (annually), *Kultura Ukrainy* (monthly).

Kyiv State Institute of Culture: 01133 Kyiv, vul. Shchorsa 36; tel. (44) 269-98-44; fax (44) 212-10-48; departments: library science, folk culture.

Kharkiv Institute of Industrial and Applied Arts: 61002 Kharkiv, vul. Krasnoznamennaya 8; tel. (572) 43-28-73; fax (572) 43-28-73; e-mail root@design.kharkov.ua; f. 1927 and renamed 1963; faculties: industrial design, interior design; library: 88,000 vols; 154 teachers; 577 students; Rector V. DANYLENKO.

Kharkiv State Institute of Arts: 310003 Kharkiv, pl. Sovetskoi Ukrainy 11/13; tel. (572) 22-56-28; piano, orchestral instruments, singing, choral conducting, composition, musicology, acting (puppets), directing (puppets), theatre studies; library: 100,000 vols.

Kyiv State Academy of Fine Arts and Architecture: 04053 Kyiv, vul. Smirnova-Lastochkina 20; tel. (44) 212-15-40; fax (44) 212-10-48; f. 1917; faculties: sculpture, painting, theatrical decorative art, graphic art, architecture, restoration, art history, arts management; 130 students; library: 130,000 vols; Rector Prof. ANDREI V. CHEBYKIN.

Lviv Academy of Arts: 79011 Lviv, vul. Kubiyovycha 38; tel. (322) 76-14-82; fax (322) 76-14-77; e-mail artacademy@mail.lviv.ua; internet www.artacademy.lviv.ua; f. 1946; faculties: design, decorative and applied arts, fine art and restoration, history and theory of art; library: 90,000 vols; 250 teachers; 1,000 students; Rector Prof. ANDRIY BOKOTEY; Vice-Rectors Prof. IGOR GOLOD, Prof. OREST HOLUBETZ; publ. *Scientific Messenger* (annually).

Odesa State Conservatoire 'A. V. Nezhdanova': 65021 Odesa, vul. Ostrovidova 63; tel. (482) 26-78-76; fax (482) 23-75-37; f. 1913; piano, orchestral and folk instruments, singing, choral conducting, composition, musicology; 140 teachers; 680 students; library: 100,000 vols; Rector OLEKSANDR V. SOKOL.

State Academy of Music 'Mykola Lysenko': 79005 Lviv, vul. Nyzhankivsky 5; tel. (322) 74-31-06; fax (322) 72-36-13; e-mail musinst@lviv.gu.net; internet musicacademy.lviv.ua; f. 1852; faculties: piano, orchestral instruments, folk instruments, operatic and symphonic conducting, choral conducting, musicology, composition, singing; library: 200,000 vols; 175 teachers; 550 students; Rector IHOR PYLATIUK.

Ukrainian National Academy of Music 'P. Tchaikovsky': 01001 Kyiv, Gorodetska vul. 1–3/11; tel. (44) 229-07-92; fax (44) 229-35-30; e-mail nmau@iptelecom.net.ua; f. 1913; faculties: piano, orchestral instruments, folk instruments, singing, choral conducting, opera and symphony orchestra conducting, composition, theory and history of music, music production, music education; 304 teachers; 1,156 students; library: 355,000 vols; Rector OLEG TIMOSHENKO; publ. *Ukrainian Musicology* (annually).

UNITED ARAB EMIRATES

The Higher Education System

The oldest current higher education institution is the United Arab Emirates University, founded in 1976. In September 1988 four higher colleges of technology (two for male and two for female students) opened, admitting a total of 425 students, all of whom were citizens of the United Arab Emirates; by 2002/03 71,194 students were enrolled in university and other higher education. In 2002/03 16,128 students were enrolled at the University at Al-Ain in Abu Dhabi. Many other students currently receive higher education abroad. There is a Ministry of Higher Education and Scientific Research. The Sorbonne University, based in Paris, France, signed an agreement in February 2006 with the Ministry of Higher Education and Scientific Research to open a branch in Abu Dhabi.

Admission to higher education is on the basis of an average score of at least 80% in the *Tawjihiyya* examinations. Students are awarded degrees on a credit basis. The undergraduate Bachelors degree is a four-year programme of study (medicine lasts seven years). The Masters degree is a one-year course following the Bachelors degree.

Post-secondary technical and vocational education is offered by higher colleges of technology and colleges. Higher colleges of technology are funded by the Ministry of Finance and provide training for professional and technology careers in the public and private sectors. Admission is on the basis of a score of at least 60% in the *Tawjihiyya* and the Common English Proficiency Examination. Among the qualifications offered by the higher colleges of technology are Certificates (two years), Diplomas (one to three years) and Higher Diplomas (three years).

Learned Societies

LANGUAGE AND LITERATURE

Alliance Française: POB 2646, Abu Dhabi; tel. (2) 6666232; fax (2) 6669044; e-mail allfr03@emirates.net.ae; internet www.chez.com/alliancead; offers courses and exams in French language and culture and promotes cultural exchange with France; attached teaching centre in Dubai.

British Council: Villa no. 7, Al Nasr St, Khalidya, Abu Dhabi, POB 46523; tel. (2) 6659300; fax (2) 6664340; e-mail information@ae.britishcouncil.org; internet www.britishcouncil.org/uae; teaching centre; offers courses and exams in English language and British culture and promotes cultural exchange with the UK; attached teaching centres in Dubai and Sharjah; Dir, United Arab Emirates JO MAHER; Deputy Dir PAUL MASON.

Research Institutes

GENERAL

Centre for Documentation and Research: POB 5884, Abu Dhabi; tel. (2) 4183333; fax (2) 4445811; e-mail dg@cdr.gov.ae; internet cdr.gov.ae; f. 1968; attached to Ministry of Presidential Court; documents, books, maps and articles relating to the Arabian Gulf and the Arabian Peninsula; publishes specialized research studies; convenes national, regional and international seminars and conferences; organizes exhibitions relating to the UAE; library of 32,000 vols in many languages, 6,481 microfiches, 7,000,000 documents; Dir Dr ABDULLAH MOHAMMED EL-REYES.

AGRICULTURE, FISHERIES AND VETERINARY SCIENCE

Agricultural Research Centre: POB 176, Ras Al Khaimah; f. 1975 as a UNDP-FAO assisted project, present name 1984; run by Ministry of Agriculture and Fisheries; conducts research into irrigation, plant protection, vegetable varieties, vegetables under plastic houses, soil fertility; *c.* 48 staff; library of 500 vols; Research Dir MOHAMMED HASSAN AL SHAMSI.

Libraries and Archives

Abu Dhabi

National Archives: POB 2380, Abu Dhabi; tel. (2) 4447797; fax (2) 4445639; internet www.cultural.org.ae; f. 1985; attached to the Cultural Foundation, an independent government body; cares for current and historical public records; Dir Dr NASSIR ALI AL-HIMIRI.

National Library: POB 2380, Abu Dhabi; tel. (2) 6336483; fax (2) 6217472; e-mail nlibrary@nsl.cultural.org.ae; internet www.cultural.org.ae; f. 1981; 900,000 vols, 1,500 periodical titles, 8,000 audiovisual items; UN Deposit Centre; Dir JUMAA ALQUBAISI; publs *National Bibliography* (in Arabic and English), *Union Catalogue of Periodicals in the UAE* (in Arabic and English).

Dubai

Dubai Municipality Public Libraries: POB 67, Dubai; tel. (4) 2262788; fax (4) 2266226; e-mail libraries@dm.gov.ae; internet www.dpl.gov.ae; f. 1963; 205,970 vols, 1,707 periodicals; special collection of Arab Islamic art books; Head MOHAMMAD JASSIM AL-ERIADI.

Museums and Art Galleries

Al Ain

Al-Ain Museum: POB 15715, Al Ain; tel. (3) 7641597; fax (3) 7658311; e-mail wyasin@emirates.net.ae; internet www.aam.gov.ae; f. 1971; archaeology and ethnography; library of 200 vols; archaeological sites at Al-Ain and Umm Al Nar island; Dirs SAIF BIN ALI AL DARMAKI, Dr WALID YASIN.

Sharjah

Sharjah Art Museum: POB 19989, Sharjah; tel. (6) 5688222; fax (6) 5686229; f. 1995; Dir SHIEKHA HOOR AL QASIMI.

Universities

AJMAN UNIVERSITY OF SCIENCE AND TECHNOLOGY (AUST)

POB 346, Ajman
Telephone: (6) 7466666
E-mail: webmaster@ajman.ac.ae
Internet: www.ajman.ac.ae
Founded 1988
President: Dr SAEED SALMAN

DEANS

Faculty of Business Administration: Dr YAHYA HADDAD
Faculty of Computer Science: Dr MAHMOUD ABO-NAAJ
Faculty of Dentistry: (vacant)
Faculty of Education and Basic Science: Dr SALEH AWADH OMAR ARAM
Faculty of Engineering: Prof. FAHAR HAYATI
Faculty of Foreign Languages: Dr THARWAT SAKRAN
Faculty of Information, Mass Communication and Public Relations: (vacant)
Faculty of Pharmacy and Health Sciences: Dr SAMIR ISSA BLOUKH

DUBAI UNIVERSITY COLLEGE

POB 14143, Dubai
Telephone: (4) 2242472
Fax: (4) 2225411
E-mail: info@duc.ac.ae
Internet: www.duc.ac.ae
Founded 1997
Under the control of the state-funded Dubai Chamber of Commerce and Industry
Languages of instruction: Arabic, English
President: M. OMAR HEFNI
Number of teachers: 48
Number of students: 630

DEANS

College of Business Administration: Assoc. Prof. ANANTH RAO
College of Design and Applied Arts: Dr MOHSEN ABOULNAGA (Chair)
College of Information Technology: Dr SAID SELIM

UNIVERSITY OF SHARJAH

POB 27272, Sharjah
Telephone: (6) 5585000
Fax: (6) 5585050
E-mail: info@sharjah.ac.ae
Internet: www.sharjah.ac.ae

Founded 1997
State-funded

Supreme President: Sheikh Dr SULTAN BIN MOHAMMED AL-QASSIMI
Chancellor: Dr ISAM H. ZABALAWI
Director of Admissions and Registration: MAHMOUD ABDALLA AL-ANSARI
Librarian: Dr BEHDJA MAKKI BOUMARAFI

DEANS

College of Arts and Sciences: Prof. SALIM SABRI
College of Business and Management: Dr JAMES C. MCBREARTY
College of Communication: Dr MUHAMMED AYISH
College of Engineering: Dr NABIL KALLAS (acting)
College of Fine Arts: Prof. PETER WHEELER
College of Health Sciences: Dr ANDREA BAUMANN
College of Law: (vacant)
College of Shari'a and Islamic Studies: Dr MOHAMED ZAUHAYLI (acting)

UNITED ARAB EMIRATES UNIVERSITY

POB 15551, Al Ain
Telephone: (3) 7544455
Fax: (3) 7548588
E-mail: uaeu@uacu.ac.ae
Internet: www.uaeu.ac.ae

Founded 1976
State control
Languages of instruction: Arabic, English
Academic year: September to June

Chancellor: H.H. Sheikh NAHAYAN MABARAK AL-NAHAYAN

Vice-Chancellor: Dr HADEF BIN JOUAN AL-DHAHERI
Deputy Vice-Chancellor (Academic Affairs): Dr ALI RASHID AL-NOAIMI
Deputy Vice-Chancellor (Community Services): Dr SAEED ABDULLAH HAREB
Deputy Vice-Chancellor (Planning): Dr AHMAD KHALIL AL-MUTAWA
Deputy Vice-Chancellor (Scientific Research): Dr MAYTHA SALEM AL-SHAMSI
Deputy Vice-Chancellor (Student Affairs): Dr MOHAMED IBRAHIM MANSOUR
Secretary-General: SHABIB M. AL-MARQOOZI
Librarian: Dr HOSAM SULTAN AL-ULIMA

Library of 450,000 vols
Number of teachers: 643
Number of students: 17,000

Publication: individual faculty journals published annually

DEANS

Faculty of Business and Economics: Dr DONALD L. BATES
Faculty of Education: Dr ABDULATIF HAIDAR
Faculty of Engineering: Dr JAMES RICHARD WILLIAMS
Faculty of Food Systems: Dr ABDULHALIM METWALLI
Faculty of Humanities and Social Sciences: Prof. ADEL AL SAFTY
Faculty of Information Technology: Dr RAFIC Z. MAKKI
Faculty of Medicine and Health Sciences: Dr GEORGE CARRUTHERS
Faculty of Science: Prof. JOSEPH HILL
Faculty of Sharia and Law: Dr MOHAMMED AL-MURSI ZAHRA

RESEARCH CENTRE

Central Laboratories Unit.

ZAYED UNIVERSITY

POB 19282, Dubai
Telephone: (4) 2648899
Fax: (4) 2648689
Internet: www.zu.ac.ae.

Colleges

Dubai University College: POB 14143, Dubai; tel. (4) 2242472; fax (4) 2242151; e-mail info@duc.ac.ae; internet www.duc.ac.ae; f. 1997; languages of instruction: Arabic, English; Dir Prof. M. OMAR HERFNI.

Emirates Institute for Banking and Financial Studies: POB 4166, Sharjah; tel. and fax (6) 5728880; e-mail customerservice@eibfs.com; internet www.eibfs.com; f. 1983; Diploma and short courses; br. in Abu Dhabi; Gen. Man. HUMAID AL-QUTAMI.

Etisalat College of Engineering: POB 980, Sharjah; tel. (6) 5611333; internet www.ece.ac.ae; f. 1989; awards B.Eng. degree in Communications; library: 7,000 vols; 23 teachers; 130 students; College Man. SALIM MOHAMMAD AL-OWAIS.

Higher Colleges of Technology: POB 32092, Abu Dhabi; tel. (2) 6815654; fax (2) 6812637; e-mail enquiries@hct.ac.ae; internet www.hct.ac.ae; f. 1988; library: 120,000 vols; 950 teachers; 15,000 students; Chancellor H. E. SHEIKH NAHAYAN MABARAK AL-NAHAYAN; Vice-Chancellor JIM HORTON; Librarian FREIDE WIEBE

DIRECTORS

Abu Dhabi Men's College: Dr TAYEB KAMALI
Abu Dhabi Women's College: Dr NICHOLAS GARA
Al Ain Men's College: Dr NEAL MANGHAM
Al Ain Women's College: Dr NEAL MANGHAM
Dubai Men's College: NORMAN J. GRAY
Dubai Women's College: Dr HOWARD E. REED
Fujairah Women's College: Dr WILLIAM LEX
Ras Al Khaimah Men's College: Dr BERRY CALDER
Ras Al Khaimah Women's College: Dr BERRY CALDER
Sharjah Men's College: Dr FARID OHAN
Sharjah Women's College: Dr FARID OHAN

UNITED KINGDOM

The Higher Education System

Institutions of higher education date from the 13th century, with the oldest being the University of Oxford, the oldest college of which was founded in 1249; the next oldest university is the University of Cambridge, the oldest college of which was founded in 1284. The oldest Scottish universities are the University of St Andrews and the University of Aberdeen, which were both founded in the 15th century. The 19th century saw a great expansion of the higher education system, with the foundation of over 90 universities, colleges and institutes in the United Kingdom. In 2003/04 there were 89 universities (including the Open University) and 60 other higher education institutions, together with the privately funded University of Buckingham, offering courses of higher education. Notable legislation pertaining to higher education includes the Further and Higher Education Act 1992, which brought to an end the binary system by which universities and polytechnics were treated separately and enabled former polytechnics to achieve university status, and the Higher Education Act 2004, which brought in changes to the funding of higher education by introducing a scheme whereby students contributed towards their tuition. Institutions of higher education include universities, university colleges, colleges of higher education and some further education colleges. Institutions of higher education are established by a Royal Charter and most receive some funding from the government. However, they are autonomous bodies in which admissions, staffing and teaching are administered independently of the government.

Up until 2007 the Secretary of State for Education and Skills was responsible, in principle, for all sectors of education in England. In that year some of these responsibilities, as well as some of those from the Department of Trade and Industry, were transferred to a newly-created Department for Innovation, Universities and Skills. In practice the individual Local Education Authorities (LEAs) have substantial autonomy over the education system in their area. The Secretary of State for Wales is responsible for all non-university education in Wales and, since April 1993, for the University of Wales College, Newport. Government finance for publicly funded higher education institutions is distributed by the Higher Education Funding Council (HEFC) in England, the Scottish Funding Council in Scotland, the Department for Education, Culture and Welsh Language in Wales, and the Department for Employment and Learning in Northern Ireland. Student loans are the main form of support for assistance with living costs for higher education students. The amount of loan depends on where a student lives or studies, the length of the academic year, the course of study, the year of the course and the student's and their family's income. Since 2006/07 universities have been entitled to set variable fees. Since the academic year 2000/01, eligible full-time Scottish-domiciled or EU students who are studying in Scotland no longer pay tuition fees. Other additional forms of student support include dependant's allowances, young and mature student bursaries, hardship funds, disabled students' allowance and care leavers' grant, and the Higher Education (HE) Grant, introduced in September 2004.

Students in England, Wales and Northern Ireland enter university upon completion of 13 years of education. Universities set their own standards for admission, which are usually based on a student's performance in their A-Level examinations. However, other awards at level 3 on the National Qualifications Framework (NQF) may also be accepted, for example the BTEC National Diploma. All undergraduate admissions in the UK (including Scotland) are dealt with by the University and College Admissions Service (UCAS). This organization does not set admission standards, which are established by each individual institution, but it oversees the process of university admission and provides information to students on entry requirements for specific courses. The principal undergraduate degrees are the Bachelor of Arts (BA Hons) and Bachelor of Science (BSc Hons). These are usually full-time, three-year courses but can also be taken as longer part-time courses and may be available through distance learning. In Scotland, where students usually start a year earlier, a full-time first degree generally takes four years for Honours and three years for the broad-based Ordinary degree. The Foundation degree is a new higher education qualification (since 2001) of one year, with a vocational focus. It aims to increase the number of people qualified at higher technician and associate professional level (e.g. legal executives, engineering technicians, personnel officers, laboratory technicians, teaching assistants). Both full- and part-time courses are offered in a variety of work-related subjects and offer progression to a full Honours degree. The Higher National Diploma (HND) or Diploma of Higher Education (Dip HE) are two-year, full-time programmes, and there is the option of turning them into an Honours degree by studying for a further year. Some students go on to do postgraduate studies, usually leading to a masters degree, such as a Master of Arts (MA), or Master of Science (MSc), or to a Doctorate (PhD). A Masters degree usually lasts one year full-time or two years part-time. A PhD usually lasts three years full-time or six years part-time. Since 2003 a four-year PhD has been introduced.

The Learning and Skills Act 2000 integrated all planning and funding for post-compulsory learning below higher education, including that provided in schools, into one overarching sector under the auspices of the Learning and Skills Council (LSC), which consists of a network of 10 regional directors and local branches. From 1986 onwards the National Council for Vocational Qualifications (NCVQ) established a framework on National Vocational Qualifications (NVQs) in England, Wales and Northern Ireland. In 1997 the Council's work was taken over by the Qualifications and Curriculum Authority. The framework is based on five defined levels of achievement, ranging from Level 1, broadly equating to foundation skills in semi-skilled occupations, to Level 5, equating to professional/senior management occupations. The competence-based system has also been extended in Scotland through a system of Scottish Vocational Qualifications (SVQs) along similar lines to the NVQs. General National Vocational Qualifications (GNVQs), along with General Scottish Vocational Qualifications (GSVQs) have also been introduced. The work of the Qualifications, Curriculum and Assessment Authority for Wales has been taken over by the Welsh Assembly Government.

The principal vocational qualifications now awarded in England, Wales and Northern Ireland are Vocational A-levels, introduced in September 2000, and the new A-Levels in applied subjects. These were designed to replace the Advanced GNVQ, with the aim of improving the standing of vocational qualifications and increasing flexibility within the system. Since September 2002, the Vocational GCSE has also replaced the Foundation, Intermediate and Part One GNVQs. The LSC is responsible for funding the further education sector in England. It is also responsible for funding provision for non-prescribed higher education in further education sector colleges and further education provided by LEA maintained and other institutions, referred to as 'external institutions'. In Wales, the Department for Education, Culture and Welsh Language funds further education provision made by further education institutions via a third party or sponsored arrangements. The Scottish Funding Council funds further education colleges in Scotland, while the Department for Employment and Learning funds further education colleges in Northern Ireland. Further and higher education may be pursued through vocational or academic courses, on a full-time, part-time or 'sandwich' basis.

Regulatory and Representative Bodies

GOVERNMENT

England, Scotland and Wales

Department for Children, Schools and Families: Sanctuary Bldgs, Great Smith St, London, SW1P 3BT; tel. 0870-000-2288; fax (1928) 794248; e-mail info@dfes.gsi.gov.uk; internet www.dcsf.gov.uk; Secretary of State EDWARD (ED) BALLS; Minister of State for Schools JIM KNIGHT.

Department for Culture, Media and Sport: 2–4 Cockspur St, London, SW1Y 5DH; tel. (20) 7211-6200; fax (20) 7211-6032; e-mail enquiries@culture.gov.uk; internet www.culture.gov.uk; Secretary of State JAMES PURNELL.

Department for Education, Culture and Welsh Language: Welsh Assembly Govt, Cathays Park, Cardiff, CF10 3NQ; tel. (845) 010-3300; e-mail education.training@wales.gsi.gov.uk; internet new.wales.gov.uk/about/departments/dells/?lang=en; Minister CARWYN JONES.

Department for Innovation, Universities and Skills: London; tel. (20) 7215-5555; internet www.dius.gov.uk; f. 2007 to carry out functions of the fmr Depts of Education and Skills and of Trade and Industry, incl. responsibilities for science, innovation, further and higher education and skills; Secretary of State JOHN DENHAM; Ministers of State for Higher Education and Lifelong Learning BILL RAMMELL, IAN PEARSON.

Northern Ireland

Department of Culture, Arts and Leisure: Interpoint, 20–24 York St, Belfast, BT15 1AQ; tel. (28) 9025-8825; fax (28) 9025-8906; e-mail dcal@dcalni.gov.uk; internet www.dcalni.gov.uk; Minister EDWIN POOTS.

Department of Education: Rathgael House, Balloo Rd, Bangor, Co Down, BT19 7PR; tel. (28) 9127-9279; fax (28) 9127-9100; e-mail mail@deni.gov.uk; internet www.deni.gov.uk; Minister CAITRÍONA RUANE.

Department for Employment and Learning: Adelaide House, 39–49 Adelaide St, Belfast, BT2 8FD; tel. (28) 9025-7777; fax (28) 9025-7778; e-mail del@nics.gov.uk; internet www.delni.gov.uk; Minister Sir REG EMPEY.

ACCREDITATION

ENIC/NARIC United Kingdom: Nat. Recognition Information Centre, UK NARIC, Oriel House, Oriel Road, Cheltenham, Glos., GL50 1XP; tel. (870) 990-4088; fax (870) 990-1560; e-mail info@naric.org.uk; internet www.naric.org.uk; Head Dr BAI-YUN CLOUD.

Open and Distance Learning Quality Council: 16 Park Crescent, London, W1B 1AH; tel. (20) 7612-7090; fax (20) 7612-7092; e-mail info@odlqc.org.uk; internet www.odlqc.org.uk; f. 1968; official accrediting body for providers of open and distance learning; Chief Exec. Dr DAVID MORLEY.

Qualifications and Curriculum Authority (QCA): 83 Piccadilly, London, W1J 8QA; tel. (20) 7509-5555; fax (20) 7509-6666; e-mail info@qca.org.uk; internet www.qca.org.uk; f. 1986 by merger of the Nat. Council for Vocational Qualifications and the School Curriculum and Assessment Authority; a public body, sponsored by the Dept for Children, Schools and Families; maintains and develops the nat. curriculum and associated assessments, tests and examinations; accredits and monitors qualifications in schools, colleges and the workplace; offices in London and Northern Ireland; Chair. Sir ANTHONY GREENER; Chief Exec. Dr KEN BOSTON.

Scottish Qualifications Authority (SQA): The Optima Bldg, 58 Robertson St, Glasgow, G2 8DQ; tel. (845) 279-1000; fax (141) 242-2244; e-mail customer@sqa.org.uk; internet www.sqa.org.uk; sponsored by the Scottish Exec. Education Dept; SQA is the nat. body in Scotland responsible for the devt, accreditation, assessment and certification of qualifications other than degrees; SQA qualifications incl. Higher Nat. Certificates and Diplomas, and Scottish Vocational Qualifications; has offices in Glasgow and Dalkeith; Chair. JOHN MCCORMICK; Chief Exec. Dr JANET BROWN.

FUNDING

Higher Education Funding Council for England: Northavon House, Coldharbour Lane, Bristol, BS16 1QD; tel. (117) 931-7317; fax (117) 931-7203; e-mail hefce@hefce.ac.uk; internet www.hefce.ac.uk; f. 1992; promotes and funds teaching and research; aims to meet the needs of students, the economy and society; Chair. DAVID YOUNG; Chief Exec. Prof. DAVID EASTWOOD.

Higher Education Funding Council for Wales: Linden Court, Ilex Close, Llanishen, Cardiff, CF14 5DZ; tel. (29) 2076-1861; fax (29) 2076-3163; e-mail info@hefcw.ac.uk; internet www.hefcw.ac.uk; f. 1992; promotes internationally excellent higher education in Wales, for the benefit of individuals, society and the economy; Chair. Prof. Sir ROGER WILLIAMS; Chief Exec. Prof. PHILIP GUMMETT.

Learning and Skills Council (LSC): Cheylesmore House, Quinton Rd, Coventry, CV1 2WT; tel. (870) 900-6800; fax (24) 7682-3675; e-mail info@lsc.gov.uk; internet www.lsc.gov.uk; f. 2001; works to improve the skills of England's young people and adults to ensure a workforce of world-class standard; is responsible for planning and funding high-quality education and training for everyone in England other than those in univs; offices in Coventry and London; Chair. CHRISTOPHER N. BANKS; Chief Exec. MARK HAYSOM.

Scottish Funding Council: Donaldson House, 97 Haymarket Terrace, Edinburgh, EH12 5IID; tel. (131) 313-6500; fax (131) 313-6501; e-mail info@sfc.ac.uk; internet www.sfc.ac.uk; f. 2005 to replace the Scottish Further Education Funding Council and the Scottish Higher Education Funding Council; a Non-Departmental Public Body of the Scottish Exec.; allocates resources for teaching and learning, research and other activities in Scotland's colleges and univs; Chair. JOHN MCCLELLAND; Chief Exec. ROGER MCCLURE.

Sector Skills Development Agency: 3 Callflex Business Park, Golden Smithies Lane, Wath-upon-Dearne, S Yorkshire, S63 7ER; tel. (1709) 765444; e-mail info@ssda.org.uk; internet www.ssda.org.uk; responsible for funding, supporting and monitoring the network of 25 Sector Skills Councils (SSCs); ensures consistent, high-quality standards across the Skills for Business network; Chair. MARGARET SALMON; Chief Exec. MARK FISHER.

NATIONAL BODIES

British Educational Communications and Technology Agency (Becta): Milburn Hill Rd, Science Park, Coventry, CV4 7JJ; tel. (24) 7641-6994; fax (24) 7641-1418; e-mail becta@becta.org.uk; internet www.becta.org.uk; f. 1998; govt agency for Information and Communications Technology (ICT) in education; supports and develops the use of technology to raise educational standards; Chair DAVID HARGREAVES.

City & Guilds: 1 Giltspur St, London, EC1A 9DD; tel. (20) 7294-2800; fax (20) 7294-2400; e-mail enquiry@city-and-guilds.co.uk; internet www.city-and-guilds.co.uk; f. 1878; awards vocational qualifications at all levels in 500 subjects at 8,500 training centres globally; Dir-Gen. Dr CHRIS HUMPHRIES; publs Broadsheet (2 a year), Report and Accounts (annually).

College of Teachers: Institute of Education, University of London, 57 Gordon Square, London, WC1H 0NU; tel. and fax (20) 7947-9536; e-mail enquiries@cot.ac.uk; internet www.collegeofteachers.ac.uk; f. 1846, incorporated by Royal Charter 1849; offers membership to educationists, awards qualifications by examination to experienced teachers of Associate, Licentiate (equivalent to university first degree), Diploma in the Advanced Study of Education, and Fellow; 1,630 mems; Pres. Prof. JOHN D. TURNER; publ. Education Today (4 a year).

Council for the Curriculum, Examinations and Assessment: 29 Clarendon Rd, Clarendon Dock, Belfast, BT1 3BG; tel. (28) 9026-1200; fax (28) 9026-1234; e-mail info@ccea.org.uk; internet www.ccea.org.uk; f. 1994; reports to the Dept of Education of the Northern Ireland Exec.; advises Govt on what should be taught in Northern Ireland's schools and colleges, ensures that the qualifications and examinations offered by awarding bodies in Northern Ireland are of an appropriate quality and standard, and awards qualifications incl. GCSEs and GCE A and AS levels; Chief Exec. NEIL ANDERSON (acting).

Education and Training Inspectorate: Inspection Services Br., Dept of Education, Rathgael House, 43 Balloo Rd, Bangor, Co Down, BT19 7PR; tel. (28) 9127-9726; fax (28) 9127-9721; e-mail inspectionservices@deni.gov.uk; internet www.etini.gov.uk; provides inspection services for, and information about the quality of education in N Ireland to, the Dept of Education, Dept of Culture, Arts and Leisure, and Dept for Employment and Learning; promotes the highest possible standards of learning, teaching and achievement throughout the education, training and youth sectors; Chief Inspector MARION MATCHETT.

Educational Institute of Scotland: 46 Moray Place, Edinburgh, EH3 6BH; tel. (131) 225-6244; fax (131) 220-3151; e-mail enquiries@eis.org.uk; internet www.eis.org.uk; f. 1847; to promote sound learning and advance the interests of teachers and lecturers in Scotland; 54,782 mems; Pres. JACK BARNETT; Gen. Sec. RONALD A. SMITH; publ. Scottish Educational Journal (around 8 per session).

Estyn: Anchor Court, Keen Rd, Cardiff, CF24 5JW; tel. (29) 2044-6446; fax (29) 2044-6448; e-mail enquiries@estyn.gsi.gov.uk; internet www.estyn.gov.uk; the office of Her Majesty's Inspectorate for Education and Training in Wales; has offices in Cardiff and Mold; Chief Inspector S. LEWIS.

General Teaching Council for England: Victoria Sq. House, Victoria Sq., Birmingham, B2 4AJ; tel. (870) 001-0308; fax (121) 345-0100; e-mail info@gtce.org.uk; internet www.gtce.org.uk; f. 2000; ind. body that aims to help improve standards of teaching and the quality of learning; maintains a register of more than 500,000 qualified teachers in England and regulates the teaching profession in the public interest; the GTC is the awarding body for qualified teacher status (QTS) in England; has offices in Birmingham and London; Chief Exec. KEITH BARTLEY; publ. *Teaching* (3 a year).

GuildHE: Woburn House, 20 Tavistock Sq., London, WC1H 9HB; tel. (20) 7387-7711; fax (20) 7387-7712; e-mail info@guildhe.ac.uk; internet www.guildhe.ac.uk; f. 1978 as SCOP (the Standing Conference of Principals Ltd); new name 2006; acts as the rep. org. for higher education colleges, specialist instns and some univs; promotes institutional diversity and distinctiveness within the UK higher education sector; Chair. PAMELA TAYLOR; Exec. Sec. PATRICIA AMBROSE.

Her Majesty's Inspectorate of Education: Scottish Exec. Education Dept, Victoria Quay, Edinburgh, EH6 6QQ; tel. (1506) 600200; e-mail enquiries@hmie.gov.uk; internet www.hmie.gov.uk; ind. agency accountable to the Scottish Ministers; promotes and contributes to sustainable improvements in standards, quality and achievements for all learners in a Scottish education system which is inclusive; Sr Chief Inspector GRAHAM DONALDSON.

Higher Education Wales: PO Box 413, Cardiff, CF10 3UF; tel. (29) 2078-6216; fax (29) 2078-6222; e-mail hew@wales.ac.uk; internet www.hew.ac.uk; f. 1996; provides an expert resource on all aspects of higher education in Wales; 13 mem. univs and other instns; Chair. Prof. MERFYN JONES; Dir AMANDA WILKINSON.

Independent Schools Inspectorate: CAP House, 9–12 Long Lane, London, EC1A 9HA; tel. (20) 7600-0100; fax (20) 7776-8849; e-mail info@isinspect.org.uk; internet www.isinspect.org.uk; responsible under Statute for inspecting the 1,200 ind. schools in England that are members of the Ind. Schools Council; promotes and safeguards the welfare and education of the children in these schools through inspections which are rigorous, careful and objective; Chair. JUNE TAYLOR.

National Conference of University Professors: c/o Chemistry Dept, University of Wales, Singleton Park, Swansea, SA2 8PP; tel. and fax (1792) 295261; e-mail ncup@swansea.ac.uk; internet www.swan.ac.uk/ncup; f. 1989 to support university professors in carrying out their responsibilities for the maintenance of academic standards; to provide a forum for discussion and a corporate voice on matters of concern to the nation's university system; to improve public understanding of the work of universities, and to act as a means of collecting and disseminating information relevant to universities; mems: 640 univ. profs; Pres. Prof. GAVIN C. REID; Sec. MARGARET GOODE.

National Institute of Adult Continuing Education (England and Wales): 21 DeMontfort St, Leicester, LE1 7GE; tel. (116) 204-4200; fax (116) 285-4514; e-mail enquiries@niace.org.uk; internet www.niace.org.uk; f. 1921 by incorporation of the British Institute of Adult Education and the Nat. Foundation for Adult Education to promote understanding and co-operation between bodies and individuals engaged in adult education, to encourage research and training and serve as a centre of information; conferences and meetings; library; develops co-operative relations with foreign and int. orgs; both corporate and individual membership; 220 individual mems, 520 corporate mems; 37 hon. life mems; library of 20,000 vols; Dir ALAN TUCKETT; publs *Adults Learning* (monthly), *Studies in the Education of Adults* (2 a year), *Convergence* (quarterly), *CONCEPT—Journal of Contemporary Community Education Practice Theory* (3 a year), *Journal of Adult and Continuing Education*

(2 a year), *Journal of Access Policy and Practice* (2 a year).

National Society for Education in Art and Design: The Gatehouse, Corsham Court, Corsham, Wilts., SN13 0BZ; tel. (1249) 714825; fax (1249) 716138; e-mail anneingall@nsead.org; internet www.nsead.org; f. 1888; the recognized professional body and trade union for principals, lecturers and teachers employed in colleges and schools of art and all specialist teachers of art, craft and design; 2,500 mems; Gen. Sec. JOHN STEERS; publ. *Journal of Art and Design Education* (3 a year).

Nord Anglia Education PLC: Nord House, Third Avenue, Centrum 100, Burton-upon-Trent, Staffs., DE14 2WD; tel. (845) 225-3030; fax (845) 225-3031; e-mail enquiries@nordanglia.com; internet www.nordanglia.com; provider of education, training and childcare within the UK and overseas; aims to deliver quality learning experiences to people at every stage of their lives; comprises Int. Schools Div., Learning Services Div. and Leapfrog Day Nurseries; has offices in Burton-upon-Trent, Cheadle and London; CEO ANDREW FITZMAURICE.

Office for Fair Access: Northavon House Coldharbour Lane, Bristol, BS16 1QD; tel. (117) 931-7171; fax (117) 931-7479; e-mail enquiries@offa.org.uk; internet www.offa.org.uk; f. 2004; promotes fair access to higher education, in particular for low income and other under-represented groups; Dir Sir MARTIN HARRIS.

Office for Standards in Education, Children's Services and Skills (Ofsted): Royal Exchange Bldgs, St Ann's Sq., Manchester, M2 7LA; tel. (8456) 404045; e-mail enquiries@ofsted.gov.uk; internet www.ofsted.gov.uk; f. 2007 by merger of the Office for Standards in Education (Ofsted) and the Adult Learning Inspectorate; inspects and regulates care for children and young people, and inspects education and training for learners of all ages; it is required to promote service improvement, ensure that services focus on the interests of their users, and see that services are efficient, effective and promote value for money; reports directly to Parliament (and to the Lord Chancellor about children and family courts administration); has offices in Manchester, London, Nottingham and Bristol; Chair. ZENNA ATKINS; publ. *Ofsted News* (online magazine).

Quality Assurance Agency for Higher Education: Southgate House, Southgate St, Gloucester, GL1 1UB; tel. (1452) 557000; fax (1452) 557070; e-mail comms@qaa.ac.uk; internet www.qaa.ac.uk; f. 1997; ind. body funded by subscriptions from univs and colleges of higher education, and through contracts with the main higher education funding bodies; safeguards the public interest in sound standards of higher education qualifications, and encourages continuous improvement in the management of the quality of higher education; has offices in Gloucester and Glasgow; Chief Exec. PETER WILLIAMS; publ. *higher quality* (news bulletin, irreg.).

Quality Improvement Agency: Friars House, Manor House Dr., Coventry, CV1 2TE; tel. (870) 162-0632; fax (870) 162-0633; internet www.qia.org.uk; responsibilities are to accelerate improvement in the performance of the learning and skills sector, build the sector's capacity for self-improvement, help the sector respond to strategic reforms, and lead the sector quality improvement strategy; Chair. Sir GEOFFREY HOLLAND; Chief Exec. ANDREW THOMSON.

Scottish Further Education Unit: Argyll Court, Castle Business Park, Stirling, FK9

4TY; tel. (1786) 892000; fax (1786) 892001; e-mail sfeu@sfeu.ac.uk; internet www.sfeu.ac.uk; f. 1985 as Curriculum Advice and Support Team, present name 1991; delivers a range of high quality services which promote and support changes in Scotland's colleges leading to excellence in learning effectiveness and in college devt; Chair. CHRISTINA POTTER; Chief Exec. BRIAN LISTER.

Standing Conference of Arts and Social Sciences: SOCSI, Cardiff University, Glamorgan Building, King Edward VII Ave, Cardiff, CF10 3WT; tel. (29) 2087-4035; fax (29) 2087-4175; e-mail renton@cardiff.ac.uk; internet www.scass.org.uk; f. 1984 to interpret, explain and safeguard the role of university teaching and research in the Arts and Social Sciences; organizes conferences, lobbies government and agencies on behalf of arts and social sciences orgs; Convenor Dr S. DELAMONT.

Training and Development Agency for Schools: 151 Buckingham Palace Rd, London, SW1W 9SZ; tel. (20) 7023-8001; internet www.tda.gov.uk; aims to secure an effective school workforce that improves children's life chances; Chief Exec. GRAHAM HOLLEY; publ. *tdaNews* (monthly).

UK Council for Graduate Education: Lichfield Centre, The Friary, Lichfield, WS13 6QG; tel. (1503) 308602; fax (1503) 308604; e-mail ukcge@ukcge.ac.uk; internet www.ukcge.ac.uk; f. 1994; promotes a distinct identity for graduate education and research in higher education; 125 full institutional mems, 8 assoc. institutional mems, 9 individual mems; Chair Prof. MALCOLM McCRAE; Hon. Gen. Sec. Prof. STUART POWELL.

Universities and Colleges Admissions Service (UCAS): Rosehill, New Barn Lane, Cheltenham, Glos., GL52 3LZ; tel. (1242) 222444; e-mail enquiries@ucas.ac.uk; internet www.ucas.com; the central org. that processes applications for full-time undergraduate courses at UK univs and colleges; Chief Exec. ANTHONY McCLARAN.

Universities Scotland: 53 Hanover St, Edinburgh, EH2 2PJ; tel. (131) 226-1111; fax (131) 226-1100; e-mail info@universities-scotland.ac.uk; internet www.universities-scotland.ac.uk; represents, promotes and campaigns for the Scottish higher education sector; 21 mem. univs and other instns; Dir DAVID CALDWELL.

Universities UK: Woburn House, 20 Tavistock Sq., London, WC1H 9HQ; tel. (20) 7419-4111; fax (20) 7388-8649; e-mail info@universitiesuk.ac.uk; internet www.universitiesuk.ac.uk; aims to promote, encourage and develop British univs, and to promote understanding of the role, achievements and objectives of univs; mems: 128 exec. heads of British univs; Pres. Prof. DRUMMOND BONE; Chief Exec. DIANA WARWICK.

University and College Union: 27 Britannia St, London, WC1X 9JP; tel. (20) 7837-3636; fax (20) 7837-4403; e-mail hq@ucu.org.uk; internet www.ucu.org.uk; f. 2006 by merger of Asscn of Univ. Teachers (f. 1919) and Nat. Asscn for Teachers in Further and Higher Education (f. 1976); UCU is the largest trade union and professional asscn for academics, lecturers, trainers, researchers and academic-related staff working in further and higher education throughout the UK; Pres. LINDA NEWMAN; Gen. Sec. SALLY HUNT.

Learned Societies

GENERAL

Academy of Learned Societies for the Social Sciences: Berkshire House, 252–256 Kings Rd, Reading, RG1 4HP; tel. (118) 953-3770; e-mail caroline.bucklow@acss.org.uk; internet www.acss.org.uk; f. 1999; co-operates with govt and other bodies, on behalf of the social science community; organizes meetings and seminars about social science for practitioners; sponsors schemes which promote social science; 400 academicians, 30 mem. socs; Exec. Sec. CAROLINE BUCKLOW; Sec. DENISE DANT; publs *21st Century Society* (3 a year), *Newsletter* (3 a year).

British Academy: 10 Carlton House Terrace, London, SW1Y 5AH; tel. (20) 7969-5200; fax (20) 7969-5300; e-mail secretary@britac.ac.uk; internet www.britac.ac.uk; f. 1950; sections of Classical Antiquity, of African and Oriental Studies, of Theology and Religious Studies, of Linguistics and Philology, of Early Modern Languages and Literature, of Modern Languages, Literature and Other Media, of Archaeology, of Medieval Studies: History and Literature, of Early Modern History to 1800, of Modern History from 1800, of History of Art and Music, of Philosophy, of Law, of Economics and Economic History, of Social Anthropology and Geography, of Sociology, Demography and Social Statistics, of Political Studies: Political Theory, Government and International Relations, of Psychology; 700 mems; Pres. Viscount RUNCIMAN; Sec. P. W. H. BROWN; Foreign Sec. Prof. C. N. J. MANN; publs *Proceedings*, *Annual Report*.

British Council: 10 Spring Gardens, London, SW1A 2BN; tel. (20) 7930-8466, fax (20) 7389-6347; e-mail general.enquiries@britishcouncil.org; internet www.britishcouncil.org; f. 1934; promotes a wider knowledge of the United Kingdom and the English language abroad and develops closer cultural relations with other countries; operates in 109 countries; maintains English Teaching Centres in 53 countries, and 209 overseas libraries and information centres; arranges for the invigilation overseas of British examinations and, in collaboration with the University of Cambridge Local Examinations Syndicate, offers service to test English-language proficiency of foreign students seeking admission to British instns; grants scholarships and other awards to overseas scholars and research workers to enable them to pursue their studies in the United Kingdom, and is responsible for administering in the United Kingdom a number of Fellowships schemes on behalf of other bodies including the UN and the Foreign and Commonwealth Office; promotes liaison between scientists in the United Kingdom and abroad and provides information on British science, medicine and technology; promotes British writers, actors and other artists abroad; organizes overseas exhibitions of British books and periodicals; Chair. NEIL KINNOCK; Chief Exec. MARTIN DAVIDSON.

Commonwealth Institute: Kensington High St, London, W8 6NQ; tel. (20) 7603-4535; fax (20) 7602-7374; e-mail information@commonwealth.org.uk; internet www.commonwealth.org.uk; aims to advance primary and secondary education across the Commonwealth; Company Sec. JUDY CURRY.

Attached centre:

Centre for Commonwealth Education: jt venture between the Commonwealth Institute and the Faculty of Education at the University of Cambridge; Dir Prof. CHRISTOPHER COLCLOUGH.

English-Speaking Union (of the Commonwealth): Dartmouth House, 37 Charles St, Berkeley Sq., London, W1J 5ED; tel. (20) 7529-1550; fax (20) 7495-6108; e-mail esu@esu.org; internet www.esu.org; f. 1918; int. voluntary org. which through its educational programmes is devoted to the promotion of understanding and friendship; 35,000 mems world-wide; library of 13,000 vols; Pres. HRH PRINCE PHILIP, DUKE OF EDINBURGH; Chair. Lord HUNT OF WIRRAL; Dir-Gen. VALERIE MITCHELL; publ. *Newsletter* (6 a year).

Royal Society: 6–9 Carlton House Terrace, London, SW1Y 5AG; tel. (20) 7451-2500; fax (20) 7930-2170; e-mail info@royalsoc.ac.uk; internet www.royalsoc.ac.uk; f. 1660; science, technology and engineering; 1,410 mems (1,280 fellows, 130 foreign mems); library: see Libraries and Archives; Pres. Prof. MARTIN REES, LORD REES OF LUDLOW; Biological Sec. Prof. DAVID READ; Foreign Sec. Prof. Dame JULIA HIGGINS; Physical Sec. Prof. MARTIN TAYLOR; Exec. Sec. STEPHEN COX; publs *Biology Letters* (quarterly), *Journal of the Royal Society Interface* (quarterly), *Notes and Records*, *Philosophical Transactions*, *Proceedings*.

Royal Society for the Encouragement of Arts, Manufactures and Commerce (RSA): 8 John Adam St, London, WC2N 6EZ; tel. (20) 7930-5115; e-mail general@rsa.org.uk; internet www.theRSA.org; f. 1754 for the promotion of arts, manufactures and commerce; 21,000 Fellows; library of 8,000 vols, 11,000 MSS; Pres. HRH Prince PHILIP DUKE OF EDINBURGH; Chair. Sir PAUL JUDGE; Dir PENNY EGAN; publ. *Journal* (6 a year).

Royal Society of Edinburgh: 22–26 George St, Edinburgh, EH2 2PQ; tel. (131) 240-5000; fax (131) 240-5024; e-mail rse@royalsoced.org.uk; internet www.royalsoced.org.uk; f. 1783; arts and sciences; 1,466 fellows (1,356 ordinary, 67 hon., 43 corresp.); Pres. Sir MICHAEL ATIYAH; Gen. Sec. Prof. ANDREW MILLER; publs *Proceedings A* (mathematics, 6 a year), *Transactions* (earth sciences, quarterly).

Saltire Society: 9 Fountain Close, 22 High St, Edinburgh, EH1 1TF; tel. (131) 556-1836; fax (131) 557-1675; e-mail saltire@saltiresociety.org.uk; internet www.saltiresociety.org.uk; f. 1936 to conserve and foster the Scottish way of life through education, literature, arts and crafts, and architecture; brs throughout Scotland; 1,270 mems; Pres. Lord CULLEN OF WHITEKIRK; Administrator KATHLEEN MUNRO.

AGRICULTURE, FISHERIES AND VETERINARY SCIENCE

Agricultural Economics Society: AES Secretariat, Tangley Mount, Tangley, Andover, SP11 0SH; tel. (1264) 730872; fax (1264) 730869; e-mail aesoc@btopenworld.com; internet www.aes.ac.uk; f. 1926 to promote the study and teaching of all disciplines relevant to agricultural economics as they apply to the agricultural, food and related industries; 500 mems; Pres. ALLAN BUCKWELL; publs *Journal of Agricultural Economics* (3 a year), *EuroChoices* (3 a year).

British Agricultural History Society: Dept of History, University of Exeter, Amory Building, Rennes Drive, Exeter, EX4 4RJ; tel. (1392) 263284; fax (1392) 263305; e-mail bahs@exeter.ac.uk; internet www.bahs.org.uk; f. 1952; 800 mems; Treasurer Prof. M. OVERTON; publ. *Agricultural History Review* (2 a year).

British Society of Animal Science: POB 3, Penicuik, Midlothian, EH26 0RZ; tel. (131) 445-4508; fax (131) 535-3120; e-mail bsas@sac.ac.uk; internet www.bsas.org.uk; f. 1944; United Kingdom mem. org. of the European Assen for Animal Production; 1,000 mems; Pres. Prof. GEOFF SIMM; Chief Exec. MIKE STEELE; publ. *ANIMAL* (animal bioscience, monthly).

British Society of Soil Science: c/o Dr J. H. Gauld, Macaulay Land Use Research Institute, Craigiebuckler, Aberdeen, AB15 8QH; tel. (1224) 318611; fax (1224) 208065; e-mail j.gauld@mluri.sari.ac.uk; internet www.soils.org.uk; f. 1947 to advance the study of the soil itself and its management in agriculture, forestry, environmental matters and other fields; 950 mems; Pres. Prof. D. POWLSON; publs *European Journal of Soil Science* (4 a year), *Soil Use and Management* (4 a year).

British Veterinary Association: 7 Mansfield St, London, W1G 9NQ; tel. (20) 7636-6541; fax (20) 7436-2970; e-mail bvahq@bva.co.uk; internet www.bva.co.uk; f. 1881 to advance the veterinary art by means of publications and conferences, and to promote and protect the interests of mems of the veterinary profession; more than 10,000 mems; Pres. Dr DAVID CATLOW; publs *In Practice* (10 a year), *Off The Record* (10 a year), *The Veterinary Record* (weekly).

Institute of Chartered Foresters: 7A St Colme St, Edinburgh, EH3 6AA; tel. (131) 225-2705; fax (131) 220-6128; e-mail icf@charteredforesters.org; internet www.charteredforesters.org; f. 1925, Royal Charter 1982; to maintain and improve the standards of practice and understanding of forestry, and to be the rep. body of the forestry profession; 1,150 mems; Exec. Dir SHIREEN CHAMBERS; publs *Forestry* (5 a year), *The Chartered Forester* (members' magazine; quarterly).

Institution of Agricultural Engineers: West End Rd, Silsoe, Bedford, MK45 4DU; tel. (1525) 861096; fax (1525) 861660; e-mail secretary@iagre.org; internet www.iagre.org; f. 1938; professional body for all involved in land-based sectors incl. agriculture, horticulture, forestry, amenities and the environment; 2,100 mems; Sec. CHRISTOPHER R. WHETNALL; publ. *Landwards* (4 a year).

Royal Agricultural Society of England: National Agricultural Centre, Stoneleigh Park, Warwicks., CV8 2LZ; tel. (24) 7669-6969; fax (24) 7669-6900; e-mail info@rase.org.uk; internet www.rase.org.uk; f. 1838 (Royal Charter 1840); 11,000 mems; established National Agricultural Centre at Stoneleigh in 1963 to promote advancements in British Agriculture and disseminate information; organizes the Royal Show; arranges regular courses, conferences etc.; agricultural history library; Chief Exec. CHARLES RUNGE; publ. *RASE Journal* (annually).

Royal College of Veterinary Surgeons: Belgravia House, 62–64 Horseferry Rd, London, SW1P 2AF; tel. (20) 7222-2001; fax (20) 7222-2004; e-mail admin@rcvs.org.uk; internet www.rcvs.org.uk; f. 1844; governing body of the veterinary profession in the United Kingdom; maintains the Statutory Registers and the discipline of the profession and has supervisory functions in relation to veterinary education in British univs; possesses the foremost veterinary library in the United Kingdom, open to veterinary surgeons and *bona fide* scientific workers; 22,000 mems; Pres. SHEILA CRISPIN; Registrar JANE C. HERN; publ. *Directory of Veterinary Practices* (annual).

Royal Forestry Society: 102 High St, Tring, Herts, HP23 4AF; tel. (1442) 822028; fax (1442) 890395; e-mail rfshq@rfs.org.uk; internet www.rfs.org.uk; f. 1882 as the English Arboricultural Soc. to advance the knowledge and practice of forestry and arboriculture, and to disseminate knowledge of the sciences on which they are based; 4,000 mems; library of 1,500 vols; Chief Exec. Dr J. E. JACKSON; publs *E-news* (electronic, fortnightly), *Quarterly Journal of Forestry*.

Royal Highland and Agricultural Society of Scotland: Royal Highland Centre, Ingliston, Edinburgh, EH28 8NF; tel. (131) 335-6200; fax (131) 333-5236; e-mail info@rhass.org.uk; internet www.rhass.org.uk; f. 1784, inc. by Royal Charter 1787, for the promotion of agriculture and related industries and education; 14,000 mems; library of 6,000 vols; Chief Exec. R. J. JONES; Sec. G. M. BARWICK.

Royal Horticultural Society: Exhibition Halls, Library and Offices, 80 Vincent Square, London, SW1P 2PE; tel. (20) 7834-4333; e-mail info@rhs.org.uk; internet www.rhs.org.uk; Gardens and School, Wisley, Woking, Surrey; Gardens at Rosemoor, Great Torrington, Devon, Hyde Hall, Chelmsford, Essex and Harlow Carr, Harrogate, North Yorkshire; f. 1804; 230,000 mems; library of 50,000 vols (Lindley Library); Pres. Sir RICHARD CARE POLE; Dir-Gen. Dr ANDREW COLQUHOUN; Sec. ANDREW SMITH; publs *The Garden* (monthly), *The New Plantsman*, *Proceedings*, *Wisley Handbooks*, etc.

Royal Scottish Forestry Society: Hagg on Esk, Canonbie, Dumfriesshire, DG14 0XE; tel. (13873) 71518; fax (13873) 71418; e-mail rsfs@ednet.co.uk; internet www.rsfs.org; f. 1854; 1,400 mems; Pres. JAMES J. BROWN; Dir ANDREW G. LITTLE; publ. *Scottish Forestry* (quarterly).

Royal Welsh Agricultural Society: Llanelwedd, Builth-Wells, Powys, LD2 3SY; tel. (1982) 553683; fax (1982) 553563; e-mail requests@rwas.co.uk; internet www.rwas.co.uk; f. 1904; organizes Royal Welsh Show, Royal Welsh Agricultural Winter Fair and Royal Welsh Smallholder and Garden Festival; promotes agriculture, horticulture, forestry and conservation, particularly in Wales; 14,000 mems; Chief Exec. D. WALTERS; publ. *Royal Welsh Journal* (annually).

Society of Dairy Technology: POB 12, Appleby in Westmorland, Cumbria, CA16 6YJ; tel. (1768) 354034; fax (1768) 352546; e-mail execdirector@sdt.org; internet www.sdt.org; f. 1943 for the advancement of dairy technology and for the encouragement of technical education and scientific enquiry in the dairy industry; 600 mems; Pres. MICHAEL HICKEY; publ. *International Journal of Dairy Technology* (quarterly).

ARCHITECTURE AND TOWN PLANNING

Architectural Association (Inc.): 34–36 Bedford Sq., London, WC1B 3ES; tel. (20) 7887-4000; fax (20) 7414-0782; internet www.aaschool.ac.uk; f. 1847; 3,200 mems worldwide; library of 35,000 vols, 49,000 classified periodical articles, 150,000 slides; runs the AA School of Architecture, offering facilities for architectural studies to undergraduates and graduates; professional courses; research programmes; Pres. ERIC PARRY; Company Sec. KATHLEEN FORMOSA; publs *AA Files* (3 a year), *Projects Review* (annual).

Association of Building Engineers: Lutyens House, Billing Brook Rd, Northampton, NN3 8NW; tel. (1604) 404121; fax (1604) 784220; e-mail building.engineers@abe.org.uk; internet www.abe.org.uk; f. 1925; training, examining and qualifying professional body for those specializing in the technology of building; 7,000 mems; Chief Exec. DAVID GIBSON; Hon. Sec. PATRICK REDDIN; publ. *Building Engineer* (monthly).

Campaign to Protect Rural England (CPRE): 128 Southwark St, London, SE1 0SW; tel. (20) 7981-2800; fax (20) 7981-2899; e-mail info@cpre.org.uk; internet www.cpre.org.uk; f. 1926; nat. charity which helps people to protect and enhance their local countryside; 60,000 mems; Pres. Sir MAX HASTINGS; Dir KATE PARMINTER; publs *Annual Review*, *Countryside Voice* (3 a year).

Civic Trust: 17 Carlton House Terrace, London, SW1Y 5AW; tel. (20) 7930-0914; fax (20) 7321-0180; e-mail pride@civictrust.org.uk; internet www.civictrust.org.uk; f. 1957 to improve and regenerate the environment where people live and work; registered charity; supports over 1,000 local amenity societies; Chief Exec. MARTIN BACON; publ. *Civic Focus* (4 a year).

Council for the Care of Churches: Church House, Great Smith St, London, SW1P 3AZ; tel. (20) 7898-1866; fax (20) 7898-1881; e-mail enquiries@ccb.c-of-e.org.uk; f. 1921 to maintain the highest standards in the preservation, restoration and alteration of Anglican churches and their contents by making available sound artistic and technical advice; library of 12,000 vols; Chair. Very Rev. GRAEME KNOWLES; Sec. PAULA GRIFFITHS.

Landscape Institute: 33 Great Portland St, London, W1W 8QG; tel. (20) 7299-4500; fax (20) 7299-4501; e-mail mail@landscapeinstitute.org; internet www.landscapeinstitute.org; f. 1929; objects: advancement of the art of landscape architecture, theory and practice of landscape design, promotion of research and education therein, maintenance of a high standard of professional qualification, promotion of the highest standard of professional service; the Institute is the chartered institute in the UK for landscape architects, incorporating designers, scientists and managers; 5,194 mems (comprising students, assocs, mems and fellows); library of 15,313 vols, journal articles and landscape drawings; visits to library and archive by non-members by appointment; Dir-Gen. MARION BOWMAN; publs *Landscape* (11 a year), *Vista* (11 a year), *E-Vista* (online).

London Society: Mortimer Wheeler House, 46 Eagle Wharf Rd, London, N1 7ED; tel. (20) 7253-9400; e-mail info@londonsociety.org.uk; internet www.londonsociety.org.uk; f. 1912 to encourage a wider concern for the beauty of the capital city, the preservation of its charms and the careful consideration of its development; library: collection of books and manuscripts including journals since 1912, now housed at Mortimer Wheeler House; 746 mems; Pres. HRH THE DUKE OF GLOUCESTER; Chair. Exec. Cttee FRANK KELSALL; Hon. Sec. J. D. HILL; publ. *Journal* (2 a year).

National Trust for Places of Historic Interest or Natural Beauty: 36 Queen Anne's Gate, London, SW1H 9AS; tel. (20) 7222-9251; fax (20) 7222-5097; e-mail enquiries@thenationaltrust.org.uk; internet www.nationaltrust.org.uk; f. 1895 for the purpose of promoting the permanent preservation of, and public access to, land of natural beauty and buildings of historic interest; 2,300,000 mems; Chair. Sir WILLIAM PROBY; Dir-Gen. FIONA REYNOLDS; publs *Annual Report*, *Members' and Visitors' Handbook*, *Newsletter*.

National Trust for Scotland: Wemyss House, 28 Charlotte Square, Edinburgh, EH2 4ET; tel. (131) 243-9300; fax (131) 243-9301; e-mail information@nts.org.uk; internet www.nts.org.ul; f. 1931; promotes the preservation of places of historical or architectural interest or natural beauty in Scotland; 250,000 mems.

Open Spaces Society: 25A Bell St, Henley-on-Thames, RG9 2BA; tel. (1491) 573535; fax (1491) 573051; e-mail hq@oss.org.uk; internet www.oss.org.uk; f. 1865; campaigns to protect common land, village greens, open spaces and public paths, and people's right to enjoy them; 2,440 mems; Chair. RODNEY LEGG; Gen. Sec. KATE ASHBROOK; publ. *Open Space* (3 a year).

Oxford Preservation Trust: 10 Turn Again Lane, St Ebbes, Oxford, OX1 1QL; tel. (1865) 242918; fax (1865) 251022; e-mail info@oxfordpreservation.org.uk; internet www.oxfordpreservation.org.uk; f. 1927 to preserve and enhance for the benefit of the public the amenities of the City of Oxford and its surroundings; takes an active role in local planning; awards grants and runs an annual Environmental Award Scheme to acknowledge projects which contribute to the conservation or enhancement of the built or natural environment; 1,000 mems; Chair. Sir DAVID YARDLEY; Dir DEBORAH DANCE.

ROOM—the National Council for Housing and Planning: 41 Botolph Lane, London, EC3R 8DL; tel. (20) 7929-9494; fax (20) 7929-9490; e-mail room@rtpi.org.uk; internet www.room.org.uk; f. 1900 as the National Housing Reform Council to secure the abolition of unhealthy and socially undesirable houses; a campaigning organization with mems in both public and private sectors, seeking to promote the best standards of housing and planning; and to disseminate information on housing, planning and regeneration; 600 mems; Chair. CATHERINE CHATER; publ. *Axis* (6 a year).

Royal Incorporation of Architects in Scotland: 15 Rutland Sq., Edinburgh, EH1 2BE; tel. (131) 229-7545; fax (131) 228-2188; e-mail info@rias.org.uk; internet www.rias.org.uk; f. 1916 as a professional org.; 4,000 mems; Pres. ARNIE DUNN; Chief Exec. MARY WRENN; publs *Practice Information* (quarterly), *Newsletter* (quarterly).

Royal Institute of British Architects: 66 Portland Place, London, W1B 1AD; tel. (20) 7580-5533; fax (20) 7255-1541; e-mail info@inst.riba.org; internet www.architecture.com; f. 1834; 28,000 corporate mems; library: library: see entry for British Architectural Library; Pres. JACK PRINGLE; CEO RICHARD HASTILOW; publs *RIBA Journal* (monthly), *Directory of Practices* (annually).

Royal Institution of Chartered Surveyors: 12 Great George St, Parliament Square, London, SW1P 3AD; tel. (20) 7222-7000; fax (20) 7222-9430; e-mail info@rics.org; internet www.rics.org; f. 1868; 110,000 mems; library of 35,000 vols; Chief Exec. LOUIS ARMSTRONG; Chief Operating Officer TIM SULIVAN; publs *RICS Business* (monthly), *Library Information Service Weekly Briefing*, *Abstracts and Reviews* (monthly).

Royal Town Planning Institute: 41 Botolph Lane, London, EC3R 8DL; tel. (20) 7929-9494; fax (20) 7929-9490; e-mail online@rtpi.org.uk; internet www.rtpi.org.uk; f. 1914 to further the science and art of town planning for the benefit of the public; 20,000 mems; library of 10,000 vols; Pres. JIM CLAYDON; Sec.-Gen. ROBERT UPTON; publs *RTPI News* (weekly), *Planning Theory and Practice* (quarterly).

Society for the Protection of Ancient Buildings: 37 Spital Square, London, E1 6DY; tel. (20) 7377-1644; fax (20) 7247-5296; e-mail info@spab.org.uk; internet www.spab.org.uk; f. 1877 by William Morris to prevent the destruction of old buildings and to advise on their conservative repair through courses, campaigns, etc.; c. 8,500 mems; Pres. THE DUKE OF GRAFTON; Sec. PHILIP VENNING; publ. *Annual Report*.

Town and Country Planning Association: 17 Carlton House Terrace, London, SW1Y 5AS; tel. (20) 7930-8903; fax (20) 7930-

3280; e-mail tcpa@tcpa.org.uk; internet www .tcpa.org.uk; f. 1899 to campaign for garden cities; now concerns itself with all aspects of planning and the environment; campaigns for improvement to the environment by effective planning, community participation and sustainable development; holds conferences and study tours; 1,000 mems; Chair. Dr DAVID LOCK; Dir GIDEON AMOS; publ. *Town and Country Planning* (11 a year).

Victorian Society: 1 Priory Gardens, Bedford Park, London, W4 1TT; tel. (20) 8994-1019; fax (20) 8747-5899; e-mail admin@ victoriansociety.org.uk; internet www .victoriansociety.org.uk; f. 1958; aims to preserve the finest Victorian and Edwardian architecture, and to study the art and built environment of the period; makes suggestions to the Dept of the Environment for bldgs to be added to the statutory list; judges applications for listed bldgs to be demolished or altered; represented at public inquiries on preservation of bldgs; 3,500 mems; Chair. Dr GEOFF BRANDWOOD; Dir Dr IAN DUNGAVELL; publ *The Victorian Magazine* (3 a year), *Journal* (irregular).

BIBLIOGRAPHY, LIBRARY SCIENCE AND MUSEOLOGY

Arlis UK and Ireland/Art Libraries Society of United Kingdom and Ireland: 18 College Rd, Bromsgrove, Worcs., B60 2NE; tel. (1527) 579298; fax (1527) 579298; e-mail sfrench@arlis.demon.co.uk; internet www.arlis.org.uk; f. 1969; aims to promote art librarianship particularly by acting as a forum for the interchange of information and materials; 710 mems (360 UK and Ireland, 350 overseas); Chair. MARGARET YOUNG; Admin. SONIA FRENCH; publ *Art Libraries Journal* (quarterly), *News-sheet* (every 2 months), *Directory* (annually).

Aslib (The Association for Information Management): Holywell Centre, 1 Phipp St, London, EC2A 4PS; tel. (20) 7613-3031; fax (20) 7613-5080; e-mail aslib@aslib.com; internet www.aslib.com; f. 1924; asscn of industrial and commercial firms, govt depts, research assens and instns, univs and learned socs in the UK and 80 other countries; provides enquiry service covering areas incl. knowledge management, online information retrieval methods, library automation and modern library and information resources management; consultancy; short courses on all aspects of information work; organizes nat. and int. conferences and meetings; 2,100 mem. orgs; library: see Libraries and Archives; Man. Dir R. N. BOWES; publs *The Journal of Documentation* (5 a year), *Aslib Proceedings* (10 a year), *Managing Information* (10 a year), *Aslib Book Guide* (monthly), *Program* (quarterly), *Forthcoming International Scientific and Technical Conferences* (quarterly), *Records Management Journal* (3 a year), *Current Awareness Abstracts* (10 a year), *Online & CD Notes* (10 a year), *Performance, Measurement and Metrics* (3 a year).

Association of Independent Libraries: c/o Catherine Levy, The Leeds Library, 18 Commercial St, Leeds, LS1 6AL; tel. (113) 245-3071; e-mail enquiries@leedslibrary.co .uk; internet www.independentlibraries.co .uk; f. 1989; 27 mems; Pres. (vacant); publs *Newsletter* (2 a year), *Directory*.

Bibliographical Society: c/o Inst. of English Studies, Univ. of London, Senate House, Malet St, London, WC1E 7HU; tel. (20) 7862-8679; fax (20) 7862-8720; e-mail secretary@ bibsoc.org.uk; internet www.bibsoc.org; f. 1892; 1,000 mems; promotes study and research in the fields of historical, analytical, descriptive and textual bibliography and the

history of printing, publishing, bookselling, bookbinding and collecting; holds meetings, at which papers are read and discussed; prints and publishes a journal and books concerned with bibliography; maintains bibliographical library; awards medals for services to bibliography, and grants and bursaries to support bibliographical research; Pres. Dr ELISABETH LEEDHAM-GREEN; Hon. Sec. M. L. FORD; publ. *The Library* (quarterly).

Booktrust: Book House, 45 East Hill, London, SW18 2QZ; tel. (20) 8516-2977; e-mail info@booktrust.co.uk; internet www .booktrust.org.uk; ind. educational charity; f. 1925 as The Nat. Book Council to extend the use and enjoyment of books of all kinds; provides book lists and a book information service; administers literary prizes, the Children's Laureate, Children's Book Week and Bookstart (books for babies); over 1,000 mems; Pres. DORIS LESSING; Chief Exec. CHRIS MEADE.

Cambridge Bibliographical Society: Univ. Library, Cambridge, CB3 9DR; tel. (1223) 333123; fax (1223) 333160; e-mail cbs@ula.cam.ac.uk; f. 1949; historical bibliography and history of the book trade; lectures and visits; 500 mems; Hon. Sec. NICHOLAS SMITH; publs *Monographs* (irreg.), *Transactions* (annual).

Chartered Institute of Library and Information Professionals: 7 Ridgmount St, London, WC1E 7AE; tel. (20) 7255-0500; fax (20) 7255-0501; e-mail info@cilip.org.uk; internet www.cilip.org.uk; f. 2002 following merger of Library Association and Institute of Information Scientists; advice and publs on librarianship and information management in all sectors; 25,000 mems; Pres. IAN SNOWLEY.

Chartered Institute of Library and Information Professionals Scotland (CILIPS)/frmrly Scottish Library Association: 1st Floor, Block C, Brandon gate, Leechlee Rd, Hamilton, ML3 6AU; tel. (1698) 458888; fax (1698) 283170; e-mail cilips@ slainte.org.uk; internet www.slainte.org.uk; f. 1908; attached to CILIP; 2,200 mems; Pres. MOIRA METHVEN; Dir ELAINE FULTON; publs *Information Scotland* (6 a year), *Scottish Library and Information Resources* (annually).

Chartered Institute of Library and Information Professionals Wales (CILIP Wales): c/o The Executive Officer, Dept of Information Studies, Llanbadarn Fawr, Aberystwyth, Ceredigion, SY23 3AS; tel. (1970) 622174; fax (1970) 622190; e-mail cilip-wales@aber.ac.uk; internet www.cilip .org.uk/wales; f. 1931; a branch of the Chartered Institute of Library and Information Professionals; a professional body of librarians and information professionals in Wales concerned with all aspects of librarianship and related matters; 850 mems; Exec. Officer SUE MACE; publs *Y Ddolen* (3 a year), *Wales Current Awareness* (email bulletin every 2 weeks).

Edinburgh Bibliographical Society: c/o National Library of Scotland, George IV Bridge, Edinburgh, EH1 1EW; tel. (131) 623-3893; fax (131) 623-3888; e-mail j .marshall@nls.uk; internet www.edbibsoc.lib .ed.ac.uk; f. 1890 for discussion and elucidation of questions connected with books, printed or manuscript, especially Scottish, the promotion and encouragement of bibliographical studies, and the printing of bibliographical works; 150 mems; Pres. Dr DAVID FINKELSTEIN; Hon. Sec. Dr WARREN McDOUGALL; publ. *Journal* (annual).

Friends of the National Libraries: c/o Dept of Manuscripts, The British Library, 96

Euston Rd, London, NW1 2DB; tel. (20) 7412-7559; e-mail secretary@fnlmail.org.uk; internet www.friendsofnationallibraries.org .uk; f. 1931 to promote the acquisition of printed books, MSS and archives of historical, literary or artistic significance for libraries and record offices; 900 mems; Chair. Lord EGREMONT; Hon. Sec. MICHAEL BORRIE; publ. *Annual Report*.

Museums Association: 24 Calvin St, London, E1 6NW; tel. (20) 7426-6970; fax (20) 7426-6961; e-mail info@museumsassociation .org; internet www.museumsassociation.org; f. 1889 to promote and improve museums and galleries and the training of museum staff; 5,196 mems; Pres. JANE GLAISTER; publs *Museum Journal* (monthly), *Museums and Galleries Yearbook*, *Museums Practice* (3 a year).

Resource: The Council for Museums, Archives and Libraries: 16 Queen Anne's Gate, London, SW1H 9AA; tel. (20) 7273-1444; fax (20) 7273-1404; e-mail info@ resource.gov.uk; internet www.resource.gov .uk; f. 2000; advises the Govt on museum, library and archive affairs; executive functions: allocates grants to Regional Agencies and co-ordinates funding and monitoring of other sectoral agencies; 15 mems; Chair. Lord EVANS OF TEMPLE GUITING; Chief Exec. CHRIS BATT (acting); publ. *Annual Report*.

Society of College, National and University Libraries (SCONUL): 102 Euston St, London, NW1 2HA; tel. (20) 7387-0317; fax (20) 7383-3197; e-mail info@sconul.ac.uk; internet www.sconul.ac.uk; f. 1950 to promote the work of the national and university libraries of the UK and Ireland; 156 mem. institutions; Chair. A. GREEN; Sec. A. J. C. BAINTON; publ. *Annual Library Statistics*.

ECONOMICS, LAW AND POLITICS

Association of Chartered Certified Accountants: 29 Lincoln's Inn Fields, London, WC2A 3EE; tel. (20) 7059-7000; fax (20) 7059-7070; e-mail info@accaglobal.com; internet www.accaglobal.com; f. 1904; inc. by Royal Charter; 105,000 mems; Pres. CHRISTOPHER FORSTER; Chief Exec. ALLEN BLEWITT; publs *Accounting & Business* (monthly), *Accountants' Guide*, *Student Accountant* (monthly), *Teach Accounting* (quarterly).

British Academy of Forensic Sciences: Haematology, ICMS, Barts and the London, 4 Newark St, London, E1 2AT; tel. (20) 7882-2276; fax (20) 7882-2182; e-mail y.d .syndercombe-court@qmul.ac.uk; internet www.bafs.org.uk; f. 1959 to advance forensic science in all its aspects to the benefit of justice and the law; scientific and medico-legal meetings; publication of articles of interest to lawyers, doctors, scientists and law-enforcement officers; over 400 mems; Sec.-Gen. Dr DENISE SYNDERCOMBE-COURT; publ. *Medicine, Science and the Law* (quarterly).

British Institute of International and Comparative Law: Charles Clore House, 17 Russell Sq., London, WC1B 5JP; tel. (20) 7862-5151; fax (20) 7862-5152; e-mail info@ biicl.org; internet www.biicl.org; f. 1958 by the amalgamation of the Grotius Society and the Society of Comparative Legislation and Int. Law; organizes the Commonwealth Legal Advisory Service and research in comparative law, int. law, and law of the European Communities; holds conferences, meetings and lectures in int. and comparative law; Chair. Lord BINGHAM OF CORNHILL; Dir Prof. GILLIAN TRIGGS; publs *International and Comparative Law Quarterly*, *Bulletin of International Legal Developments* (every 2 weeks), and other occasional pubs on int. and comparative law.

Chartered Institute of Bankers in Scotland: Drumsheugh House, 38B Drumsheugh Gardens, Edinburgh, EH3 7SW; tel. (131) 473-7777; fax (131) 473-7788; e-mail info@ciobs.org.uk; internet www.ciobs.org.uk; f. 1875 to improve the qualifications of those engaged in banking, and to raise their status and influence; 13,000 mems; Chief Exec. Prof. C. W. MUNN; publ. *The Scottish Banker* (6 a year).

Chartered Institute of Management Accountants (CIMA): 26 Chapter St, London, SW1P 4NP; tel. (20) 7663-5441; fax (20) 7663-5442; e-mail student.services@cimaglobal.com; internet www.cimaglobal.com; f. 1919, Royal Charter granted 1975; professional examining and membership body for chartered management accountants throughout the world; membership is gained through examination and practical experience; 62,000 mems in 155 countries; Pres. C. O. IGHODARO; Sec. C. TILLEY; publs *Financial Management* (monthly), *CIMA Insider* (monthly).

Chartered Institute of Public Finance and Accountancy: 3 Robert St, London, WC2N 6RL; tel. (20) 7543-5600; fax (20) 7543-5700; e-mail webCo-ordinator@cipfa.org; internet www.cipfa.org.uk; f. 1885; professional accountancy body for public services; provides education and training in accountancy and financial management, and monitors professional standards; 13,500 mems; 3,000 students; CEO STEVE FREER; publs *Public Finance* (weekly), *PMPA* (4 a year).

Chartered Insurance Institute: The Hall, 20 Aldermanbury, London, EC2V 7HY; tel. (20) 8989-8464; fax (20) 7726-0131; e-mail info@cii.co.uk; internet www.cii.co.uk; f. 1897; inc. by Royal Charter 1912 with the object of providing and maintaining a central organization for the promotion of professionalism and progress among insurance and financial services employees; primarily an educational and examining body; 70,000 mems; library of 15,000 vols; Dir-Gen. D. E. BLAND; Librarian R. L. CUNNEW; publ. *Journal* (every 2 months).

Confederation of British Industry (CBI): Centre Point, 103 New Oxford St, London, WC1A 1DU; tel. (20) 7379-7400; fax (20) 7240-1578; internet www.cbi.org.uk; represents the interests of private enterprise and industry and seeks to influence govt policy-making; Pres. MARTIN BROUGHTON; Dir-Gen. RICHARD LAMBERT; publs *Business Voice* (monthly), *CBI Distributive Trades Survey* (monthly), *Economic Situation Report* (monthly), *Industrial Trends Survey* (quarterly/monthly).

David Davies Memorial Institute of International Studies: c/o Dept of International Politics, University of Wales, Aberystwyth, SY23 3DA; e-mail ddmstaff@aber.ac.uk; f. 1951 to commemorate and continue the work of Lord Davies (1880–1944), on the means of establishing a viable world order; aims: to advance and promote the development of international relations in the political, economic, legal, social, educational, ecological and other fields, and to carry out and instigate research; works through *ad hoc* groups, seminars, conferences, bringing together experts in the relevant fields and publishing its findings; 1,000 mems; Dir Prof. NICHOLAS J. WHEELER.

Economics and Business Education Association: The Forum, 277 London Rd, Burgess Hill, W. Sussex, RH15 9QU; tel. (1444) 240150; fax (1444) 240101; e-mail office@ebea.org.uk; internet www.ebea.org

.uk; f. 1948 to promote and extend the study of econ., business studies and related subjects in schools and colleges; to act as a rep. body for econ. and business studies teachers in educational matters; and to promote knowledge of and interest in econ. and related subjects among the general public; annual conference; 1,600 mems; Pres. Prof. DAVID MYDDLETON; Chair. IAN MARCOUSÉ; publ. *Teaching Business and Economics* (3 a year).

Electoral Reform Society: 6 Chancel St, Blackfriars, London, SE1 0UU; tel. (20) 7928-1622; fax (20) 7401-7789; e-mail ers@reform.demon.co.uk; internet www.electoral-reform.org.uk; f. 1884 as Proportional Representation Society, to secure an effective vote for every parliamentary and local government elector, by the adoption of the single transferable vote form of proportional representation, at all elections of representative bodies, and similarly for elections in all voluntary organizations; comprehensive reference library and archive; Electoral Reform (Ballot Services) Ltd (tel. (20) 8365-8909, fax (20) 8365-8587) provides advice and electoral administration service for UK organizations; Electoral Reform (International Services) (tel. (20) 7620-3794, fax (20) 7928-4366) provides advice for overseas organizations; the McDougall Trust is a charitable organization whose principal objective is to advance the knowledge of elections, voting systems and representative democracy; 2,000 mems; Pres. EARL RUSSELL; Chair. KEITH BEST; Chief Exec. KEN RITCHIE; publ. *Electoral Bulletin* (monthly).

European Movement: 7 Holyrood St, London, SE1 2EL; tel. (20) 7940-5252; fax (20) 7940-5253; e-mail info@euromove.org.uk; internet www.euromove.org.uk; f. 1948 to promote European integration and unity at nat. and intl level; Pres. (vacant).

Fabian Society: 11 Dartmouth St, London, SW1H 9BN; tel. (20) 7227-4900; fax (20) 7976-7153; e-mail info@fabian-society.org.uk; internet www.fabian-society.org.uk; f. 1884; public policy think-tank and socialist soc.; conducts research, organizes conferences and seminars; 6,000 mems; Gen. Sec. SUNDER KATWALA; publs *Fabian Pamphlets* (6 a year), *Fabian Review* (quarterly).

Faculty of Actuaries: MacLaurin House, 18 Dublin St, Edinburgh, EH1 3PP; tel. (131) 240-1300; fax (131) 240-1313; e-mail faculty@actuaries.org.uk; internet www.actuaries.org.uk; f. 1856; 1,220 (1174 fellows, 11 hon. fellows, 35 affiliates); library of 9,000 vols; 784 students; Sec. RICHARD MACONACHIE; publ. *British Actuarial Journal* (4 or 5 a year).

Faculty of Advocates: Advocates Library, Parliament House, Edinburgh, EH1 1RF; tel. (131) 226-5071; fax (131) 225-3642; internet www.advocates.org.uk; f. 1532; the sole professional body for Advocates (Barristers) in Scotland; it maintains professional standards, examines Intrants and represents its members; 739 mems; library: copyright library in respect of legal works of 100,000 law books associated with National Library of Scotland; Dean ROY MARTIN; Clerk ANDREW F. STEWART; Keeper of the Library STEPHEN E. WOOLMAN.

Federal Trust for Education and Research: 7 Graphite Square, Vauxhall Walk, London, SE11 5EE; tel. (20) 7735-4000; fax (20) 7735-8000; e-mail info@fedtrust.co.uk; internet www.fedtrust.co.uk; f. 1945 to promote and carry out research and education into federal solutions to national, European and global problems, in particular the European Union; 500 mems; Dir BRENDAN DONNELLY.

General Council of the Bar: 289–293 High Holborn, London, WC1V 7HZ; tel. (20) 7242-0082; fax (20) 7831-9217; internet www.barcouncil.org.uk; f. 1894, present constitution 1987; governing body for the barristers' profession in England and Wales; Chief Exec. DAVID HOBART; publs *Code of Conduct, Counsel* (incorporating *Bar News*) (monthly).

Hansard Society: 9 Kingsway, London, WC2B 6XF; tel. (20) 7395-4000; fax (20) 7395-4008; internet www.hansardsociety.org.uk; f. 1944; promotes parliamentary democracy, political education, political research and informed discussion of all aspects of modern parliamentary government; 400 mems; Pres. SPEAKER OF THE HOUSE OF COMMONS; Dir CLARE ETTINGHAUSEN; publ. *Parliamentary Affairs* (quarterly).

Institute for Fiscal Studies: 7 Ridgmount St, London, WC1E 7AE; tel. (20) 7291-4800; fax (20) 7323-4780; e-mail mailbox@ifs.org.uk; internet www.ifs.org.uk; f. 1969 to provide high-quality economic analysis of public policy; produces briefing notes and working papers and organizes conferences, seminars and briefings; *c.* 750 individual mems; 250 corporate and institutional mems; Dir ROBERT CHOTE; Research Dir RICHARD BLUNDELL; publ. *Fiscal Studies* (quarterly).

Institute of Actuaries: Staple Inn Hall, High Holborn, London, WC1V 7QJ; tel. (20) 7632-2100; fax (20) 7632-2111; Located at: Education Service and Library, Napier House, 4 Worcester St, Oxford, OX1 2AW; tel. (1865) 268200; fax (1865) 268211; e-mail institute@actuaries.org.uk; internet www.actuaries.org.uk; f. 1848, Royal Charter 1884, to develop the role and standing of the actuarial profession and to enhance its reputation in serving the public interest; sets examinations, courses in continuing professional devt; professional codes and disciplinary standards; 14,428 mems, 6,833 Fellows; library of 15,000 vols (Oxford), colln of rare books (London); Pres. NICHOLAS J. DUMBRECK; Chief Exec., Actuarial Profession CAROLINE M. INSTANCE; Head of Education and CPD Dr TREVOR WATKINS; publs *Annals of Actuarial Science* (with Faculty of Actuaries, 2 a year), *British Actuarial Journal* (with Faculty of Actuaries, 5 a year).

Institute of Chartered Accountants in England and Wales: Chartered Accountants' Hall, Moorgate Place, London, EC2P 2BJ; tel. (20) 7920-8100; fax (20) 7920-0547; internet www.icaew.co.uk; f. 1880 by Royal Charter; special collection of early European books on book-keeping; internationally important research library on the British accounting and tax systems; 128,000 mems; library of 40,000 vols, 40,000 journal records; Pres. DAVID ILLINGWORTH; Deputy Pres. RICHARD DYSON; publ. *Accountancy* (monthly).

Institute of Chartered Accountants of Scotland: CA House, 21 Haymarket Yards, Edinburgh, EH12 5BH; tel. (131) 347-0100; fax (131) 347-0105; e-mail enquiries@icas.org.uk; internet www.icas.org.uk; f. 1854 to deal with professional matters concerning its members; runs research centre in conjunction with the Scottish Accountancy Research Trust; library of 3,000 books, 140 periodicals, online and CD-ROM databases; 16,000 mems; Pres. NORMAN MURRAY; Chief Exec. and Sec. DESMOND HUDSON; publ. *CA Magazine* (monthly).

Institute of Chartered Secretaries and Administrators: 16 Park Crescent, London, W1B 1AH; tel. (20) 7580-4741; fax (20) 7323-1132; e-mail info@icsa.co.uk; internet www.icsa.org.uk; f. 1891 as a professional organization for secretaries of incorporated bodies;

44,000 mems; Information Manager SHEILA DOYLE; publs *Best Practice Guides* (irregular), *Chartered Secretary* (monthly), *Company Secretarial Practice* (quarterly), *The Company Secretary* (monthly).

Institute of Economic Affairs: 2 Lord North St, Westminster, London, SW1P 3LB; tel. (20) 7799-3745; fax (20) 7799-2137; e-mail iea@iea.org.uk; internet www.iea.org.uk; f. 1955; to improve understanding of economics and its application to business and public policy; Dir-Gen. JOHN BLUNDELL; publs *Hobart Papers, Research Monographs, IEA Readings, Occasional Papers, Current Controversies, Choice in Welfare, Economic Affairs, Journal* (quarterly).

Institute of Financial Services: IFS House, 4–9 Burgate Lane, Canterbury, Kent, CT1 2XJ; tel. (1227) 818609; fax (1227) 763788; e-mail institute@ifslearning.com; internet www.ifslearning.com; f. 1879; provides the educational foundation and qualifications for a career in banking, building societies or other financial services; publishes textbooks for the financial sector; 41,000 mems; library of 30,000 vols; Pres. IAN HARLEY; Chief Exec. GAVIN SHREEVE; publs *Eclectic* (4 a year), *IFS News* (monthly), *Financial World* (monthly).

Law Society: 113 Chancery Lane, London, WC2A 1PL; tel. (20) 7242-1222; fax (20) 7831-0344; e-mail info.services@lawsociety.org.uk; internet www.lawsociety.org.uk; f. 1825; regulator and representative body for solicitors in England and Wales; 93,000 mems; library: see Libraries and Archives; Chief Exec. JULIA PARASKEVA; publ. *Gazette* (weekly).

Political Studies Association of the United Kingdom: Dept of Politics, Univ. of Newcastle, Newcastle upon Tyne, NE1 7RU; tel. (191) 222-8021; fax (191) 222-3499; e-mail psa@ncl.ac.uk; internet www.psa.ac.uk; f. 1950 to promote the devt of political studies; 1,600 mems; Chair. Prof. JON TONGE; Hon. Sec. Prof. PAUL CARMICHAEL; publs *British Journal of Politics and International Relations* (quarterly), *Political Studies* (quarterly), *Politics* (3 a year).

Royal Economic Society: Dept of Economics, London Business School, Regents Park, London, NW1 4SA; tel. (20) 7000-8420; fax (20) 7724-1598; e-mail eburke@london.edu; internet www.res.org.uk; f. 1890; 3,500 mems; Pres. Prof. Sir JOHN VICKERS; Sec.-Gen. Prof. RICHARD PORTES; publs *The Economic Journal* (8 a year), *The Econometrics Journal* (on-line), *Newsletter* (quarterly).

Royal Faculty of Procurators in Glasgow: 12 Nelson Mandela Place, Glasgow, G2 1BT; internet www.rfpg.org; f. inc. long prior to 1668, and by Royal Charter 1796; a legal society; 500 mems; library of 20,000 vols; Dean RAYMOND WILLIAMSON; Gen. Mgr IAIN C. PEARSON; Librarian JOHN M. McKENZIE.

Royal Institute of International Affairs: Chatham House, 10 St James's Sq., London, SW1Y 4LE; tel. (20) 7957-5700; fax (20) 7957-5710; e-mail contact@chathamhouse.org.uk; internet www.chathamhouse.org.uk; f. 1920 to facilitate the scientific study of int. affairs; c. 3,500 mems (all categories); studies of economic, political and security trends in int. relations; research into Middle East, Asia-Pacific, Africa, Europe, Russia and Central Asia, and into energy and the environment, int. economics, law and security; library: see Libraries and Archives; Pres Lord HURD OF WESTWELL, Lord ROBERTSON OF PORT ELLEN, Lord ASHDOWN OF NORTON-SUB-HAMDON; Dir Dr ROBIN NIBLETT; Dir of Research ROSEMARY HOLLIS; publs *International Affairs* (6 a year), *The World Today* (monthly).

Royal Statistical Society: 12 Errol St, London, EC1Y 8LX; tel. (20) 7638-8998; fax (20) 7256-7598; e-mail rss@rss.org.uk; internet www.rss.org.uk; f. 1834; 6,000 mems; Pres. Prof. TIM HOLT; Dir-Gen. IVOR GODDARD; publs *Applied Statistics* (journal, 4 a year), *Statistical Methodology* (journal, 4 a year), *Statistics in Society* (journal, 3 a year), *The Statistician* (journal, 4 a year).

Selden Society: c/o School of Law, Queen Mary–University of London, Mile End Rd, London, E1 4NS; tel. (20) 7882-5136; fax (20) 8981-8733; e-mail selden-society@qmw.ac.uk; internet www.selden-society.qmw.ac.uk; f. 1887; 1,700 mems; Pres. Sir JAMES HOLT; Hon. Treas. CHRISTOPHER WRIGHT; Literary Dir Prof. Sir JOHN BAKER; Sec. VICTOR TUNKEL; publ. publs more than 130 vols on sources and other aspects of English legal history; publs *Selden Society Main Series* (annual), *Selden Society Supplementary Series* (irregular).

Stair Society: c/o Thomas H Drysdale, 14 Murrayfield Drive, Edinburgh, EH12 6EB; e-mail stairsecretary@aol.com; internet www.stairsociety.org; f. 1934 to encourage the study and advance the knowledge of the history of Scots Law; 490 mems; Pres. Lord HOPE OF CRAIGHEAD; Chair. of Council Dr JOHN CAIRNS; Sec. THOMAS H. DRYSDALE.

EDUCATION

Advisory Centre for Education (ACE) Ltd: 1 C Aberdeen Studios, 22–24 Highbury Grove, London, N5 2DQ; tel. (20) 7354-8318; fax (20) 7354-9069; e-mail enquiries@ace.dialnet.com; internet www.ace-ed.org.uk; f. 1960; aims to provide information on education for parents and others, to encourage close home–school relationships, and to arouse discussion on education issues; publs *ACE Bulletin* (every 2 months), *Stop Press* (monthly).

British Educational Management and Administration Society: c/o Sheffield Hallam University, Collegiate Crescent, Sheffield, S10 2BP; tel. (114) 225-2328; fax (114) 225-5649; e-mail info@belmas.org.uk; internet www.belmas.org.uk; f. 1971; to advance the practice of and research into educational administration; to maintain close contact with national and intl organizations and to encourage the foundation of local groups; 1,400 mems; Chair. BARBARA VANN; Hon. Sec. Dr NIGEL BENNETT; publs *Educational Management and Administration, Management in Education* (both quarterly), *Networks*.

Council for Education in World Citizenship: Hampton Community College, Hanworth Rd, Hampton, Middx, TW12 3HB; tel. (20) 8941-9854; e-mail info@cewc.org.uk; internet www.cewc.org.uk; f. 1939; an independent, non-political organization to assist schools and colleges in the teaching of international affairs and promote a more global perspective in curricula; 1,000 mem. schools; library: library of resources and reference material; Dir LES STRATTON; publs *Broadsheet, Broadsheet Digest, Activities Sheet, Newsletter* (all 5 a year).

University Association for Contemporary European Studies: King's College London, Strand, London, WC2R 2LS; tel. (20) 7240-0206; fax (20) 7836-2350; e-mail admin@uaces.org; internet www.uaces.org; f. 1968; to bring together academics with a common interest in European studies (and specifically in European integration) with practitioners active in European affairs; circulates information to mems about developments in European studies; holds conferences and seminars; provides documentation on European Studies; 820 individual, 110 corporate mems; Exec. Dir. SUSAN DAVIS; publs *Directory of Expertise on Europe:* *European Studies Research Interests of UACES Members* (every 3 years), *Courses in European Studies in Universities & Colleges* (online), *Journal of Common Market Studies* (5 a year), *European Union Annual Review, Contemporary European Studies Book Series, Journal of Contemporary European Research* (online).

Workers' Educational Association (WEA): 70 Clifton St, London, EC2A 4HB; tel. (20) 7426-3450; fax (20) 7426-3451; e-mail national@wea.org.uk; internet www.wea.org.uk; f. 1903; voluntary provider of adult education; co-operates with univs and other voluntary asscns through all English regions and in Scotland for the provision of classes; these classes, although provided independently, are grant-aided by the Learning and Skills Council in England, the Scottish Office Education Dept, local education authorities and other funding bodies; 19,000 mems; 96,000 students; Gen. Sec. RICHARD BOLSIN.

FINE AND PERFORMING ARTS

Arts Council of England: 14 Great Peter St, London, SW1P 3NQ; tel. (20) 7333-0100; fax (20) 7973-6590; e-mail enquiries@artscouncil.org.uk; internet www.artscouncil.org.uk; f. 1940 as the Council for the Encouragement of Music and the Arts (CEMA), in 1945 became the Arts Council of Great Britain, present name 1994; nat. ind. and non-political body working to develop, sustain and promote the arts; distributes public money from govt and the National Lottery to artists and arts orgs, both directly and through the regional arts boards; Chair. Sir CHRISTOPHER FRAYLING; Chief Exec. PETER HEWITT; publs *Annual Report, Development Funds.*

Arts Council of Wales: 9 Museum Pl., Cardiff, CF10 3NX; tel. (29) 2037-6500; fax (29) 2022-1447; e-mail info@artswales.org.uk; internet www.artswales.org.uk; funded by the Welsh Assembly Government and distributor of National Lottery funding; 18 mems; Chair. Prof. DAI SMITH; Chief Exec. PETER TYNDALL.

British Academy of Composers and Songwriters: British Music House, 26 Berners St, London, W1T 3LR; tel. (20) 7636-2929; fax (20) 7636-2212; e-mail info@britishacademy.com; internet www.britishacademy.com; f. 1999, following merger of Association of Professional Composers, British Academy of Songwriters, Composers and Authors, and Composers' Guild of Great Britain; represents the interests of composers and songwriters, providing initial career support and services and benefits for members, protects copyright, and promotes British songwriting and composition; 3,000 mems; Chief Exec. CHRIS GREEN.

British and International Federation of Festivals: Festivals House, 198 Park Lane, Macclesfield, Cheshire, SK11 6UD; tel. (8707) 744290; fax (8707) 744292; e-mail info@festivals.demon.co.uk; internet www.festivals.demon.co.uk; f. 1921; headquarters of the Amateur Festival Movement; 800 mems; Patron HM THE QUEEN; Chief Exec. E. WHITEHEAD; publ. *Year Book.*

British Film Institute: 21 Stephen St, London, W1T 1LN; tel. (20) 7255-1444; fax (20) 7436-7950; internet www.bfi.org.uk; f. 1933; nat. agency with responsibility for encouraging the arts of film and television and conserving them in the nat. interest; among its divisions and activities are the National Film and Television Archive (*q.v.*), the National Film Theatre, the London Film Festival, the London Lesbian and Gay Film Festival, education and library services,

DVD and book publishing; 24,000 mems; in receipt of annual government grant; Dir AMANDA NEVILL; publs *Annual Review*, *Sight and Sound* (monthly, illustrated).

British Institute of Professional Photography: Fox Talbot House, Amwell End, Ware, Herts., SG12 9HN; tel. (1920) 464011; fax (1920) 487056; e-mail info@bipp.com; internet www.bipp.com; f. 1901; professional qualifying body; awards the designatory letters FBIPP, ABIPP and LBIPP; represents professional photographers and photographic technicians; aims to improve the quality of photography, to establish recognized examinations and standards of conduct and to safeguard the interests of the public and the profession; 3,500 mems; publ. *The Photographer* (12 a year).

British Society of Painters: c/o Margaret Simpson, 2 The Brambles, Ilkley, West Yorks., LS29 9DH; tel. (1943) 609075; e-mail info@britpaint.co.uk; internet www.britpaint.co.uk; f. 1986; 62 mems (12 fellows, 50 mems); holds two exhibitions annually; awards prizes; Pres. DAVID SHEPHERD; Dir LESLIE SIMPSON.

Attached societies:

British Watercolour Society: c/o Margaret Simpson, 2 The Brambles, Ilkley, West Yorks., LS29 9DH; tel. (1943) 609075; f. 1911; holds two exhibitions annually; awards prizes; 150 mems; Pres. KENNETH ELMSLEY; Dir MARGARET SIMPSON.

Society of Miniaturists: c/o Margaret Simpson, 2 The Brambles, Ilkley, West Yorks., LS29 9DH; tel. (1943) 609075; fax (1943) 603753; e-mail info@britpaint.co.uk; internet www.britpaint.co.uk; f. 1895; 35 mems; holds two exhibitions annually; awards prizes.

Commission for Architecture and the Built Environment (CABE): The Tower Building, 11 York Rd, London, SE1 7NX; tel. (20) 7960-2400; fax (20) 7960-2444; e-mail enquiries@cabe.org.uk; internet www.cabe.org.uk; f. 1999; 11 mems; Chair. Sir STUART LIPTON; CEO JON ROUSE.

Contemporary Art Society: Bloomsbury House, 74–77 Great Russell St, London, WC1B 3DA; tel. (20) 7612-0730; fax (20) 7631-4230; e-mail cas@contempart.org.uk; internet www.contempart.org.uk; f. 1910 to promote the development of contemporary art and to acquire works by living artists for loan or gift to public galleries; 1,500 mems; Chair. OLIVER PRENN; Exec. Dir GILL HEDLEY.

English Folk Dance and Song Society: Cecil Sharp House, 2 Regent's Park Rd, London, NW1 7AY; tel. (20) 7485-2206; fax (20) 7284-0534; e-mail info@efdss.org; internet www.efdss.org; f. 1932 (Folk Song Society 1898, English Folk Dance Society 1911); to collect, study and preserve English folk dances and songs and other folk music, and to encourage their performance; 5,000 mems; library: see Vaughan Williams Memorial Library; Chief Officer HAZEL MILLER; publs *Folk Music Journal* (annually), *English Dance and Song* (quarterly).

Federation of British Artists: 17 Carlton House Terrace, London, SW1Y 5BD; tel. (20) 7930-6844; fax (20) 7839-7830; e-mail info@mallgalleries.com; internet www.mallgalleries.org.uk; f. 1961; administers The Mall Galleries, The Mall, London, SW1, and holds annual exhibitions, open to all artists, for mem. socs.

Member societies:

Hesketh Hubbard Art Society: 17 Carlton House Terrace, London, SW1Y 5BD; tel. (20) 7930-6844; fax (20) 7839-7830; e-mail info@mallgalleries.com; internet www.mallgalleries.org.uk; f. 1930 by the Royal Soc. of British Artists; weekly drawing sessions in Mall Galleries from life models; 165 mems; Pres. SIMON WHITTLE.

New English Art Club: 17 Carlton House Terrace, London, SW1Y 5BD; tel. (20) 7930-6844; fax (20) 7839-7830; e-mail info@mallgalleries.com; internet www.mallgalleries.org.uk; f. 1886; exhibition held in autumn, open to all artists to submit work for selection; 55 mems (51 ordinary, 4 hon.); Pres. TOM COATES.

Pastel Society: 17 Carlton House Terrace, London, SW1Y 5BD; tel. (20) 7930-6844; fax (20) 7839-7830; e-mail info@mallgalleries.com; internet www.mallgalleries.org.uk; f. 1898; 60 mems; annual open exhibition; Pres. MOIRA HUNTLY.

Royal Institute of Oil Painters: 17 Carlton House Terrace, London, SW1Y 5BD; tel. (20) 7930-6844; fax (20) 7839-7830; e-mail info@mallgalleries.com; internet www.mallgalleries.org.uk; f. 1882; 65 mems; annual exhibition; Pres. DENNIS SYRETT.

Royal Institute of Painters in Water Colours: 17 Carlton House Terrace, London, SW1Y 5BD; tel. (20) 7930-6844; fax (20) 7839-7830; e-mail info@mallgalleries.com; internet www.mallgalleries.org.uk; f. 1831; annual exhibition (March) open to all artists to submit work for selection; 61 mems, incl. 2 hon. retd mems; Pres. RONALD MADDOX.

Royal Society of British Artists: 17 Carlton House Terrace, London, SW1Y 5BD; tel. (20) 7930-6844; fax (20) 7839-7830; e-mail info@mallgalleries.com; internet www.mallgalleries.org.uk; f. 1823; annual open exhibition (May); 119 mems (97 ordinary, 16 assoc., 6 hon.); Pres. ROMEO DI GIROLAMO.

Royal Society of Marine Artists: 17 Carlton House Terrace, London, SW1Y 5BD; tel. (20) 7930-6844; fax (20) 7839-7830; e-mail info@mallgalleries.com; internet www.mallgalleries.org.uk; f. 1939; annual open exhibition (October); 40 mems; Pres. GEOFF HUNT.

Royal Society of Portrait Painters: 17 Carlton House Terrace, London, SW1Y 5BD; tel. (20) 7930-6844; fax (20) 7839-7830; e-mail info@mallgalleries.com; internet www.mallgalleries.org.uk; f. 1891; 41 mems; mems limited to 50; annual exhibition (May); Pres. ANDREW FESTING.

Society of Wildlife Artists: 17 Carlton House Terrace, London, SW1Y 5BD; tel. (20) 7930-6844; fax (20) 7839-7830; e-mail info@mallgalleries.com; internet www.mallgalleries.org.uk; f. 1963; annual open exhibition (September); 66 mems; Pres. ANDREW STOCK.

Guild of Church Musicians: c/o John Ewington, 'Hillbrow', Godstone Rd, Blechingley, Surrey, RH1 4PJ; tel. (1883) 743168; e-mail johnmusicsure@orbix.co.uk; internet www.churchmusicians.org; f. 1888; runs courses and seminars, conducts examinations for the Archbishops' Certificate in Church Music and the Archbishops' Certificate in Public Worship, and runs a Fellowship Programme (FGCM) at postgraduate diploma level; 700 mems; Pres. Dr MARY ARCHER; Warden Very Rev. Dr RICHARD FENWICK; Gen. Sec. JOHN EWINGTON; publs *Laudate* (2 or 3 a year), *Year Book*.

Incorporated Association of Organists: 17 Woodland Rd, Northfield, Birmingham, B31 2HU; tel. (121) 475-4408; fax (121) 475-4408; e-mail w.j.stormont@btinternet.com; internet iao.org.uk; f. 1913; 100 affiliated associations with 6,500 mems worldwide; aims to improve and advance the knowledge of organs, organ music and teaching methods by organizing an Annual Congress, residential and day courses, master-classes, recitals and lectures; administers a Benevolent Fund for organists; Pres. Dr SIMON LINDLEY; Hon. Sec. JOHN STORMONT; publ. *Organists' Review* (4 a year).

Incorporated Society of Musicians: 10 Stratford Place, London, W1C 1AA; tel. (20) 7629-4413; fax (20) 7408-1538; e-mail membership@ism.org; internet www.ism.org; f. 1882; professional association for all musicians (performers, teachers and composers); 5,000 mems; Pres. ROBERT LLOYD; Chief Exec. NEIL HOYLE; publs *Yearbook and Register of Members*, *Register of Professional Private Music Teachers* (annually), *Music Journal* (monthly), *Register of Performers and Composers* (annually), *Register of Musicians in Education* (annually).

Institute of Contemporary Arts: Nash House, The Mall, London, SW1Y 5AH; tel. (20) 7930-0493; fax (20) 7873-0051; internet www.ica.org.uk; f. 1947; contemporary cultural centre; organizes exhibitions, lecture series, films, performances and musical events, etc.; c. 6,000 mems; Dir EKOW ESHUN; Chair. ALAN YENTOB; publs *Monthly Bulletin of Events*, *ICA Documents*.

Oriental Ceramic Society: POB 517, Cambridge, CB21 5BE; tel. (1223) 881328; e-mail ocslondon@btinternet.com; internet www.ocs-london.com; f. 1921 to increase knowledge and appreciation of Eastern Ceramics and other arts; 800 mems; Pres. ROSEMARY SCOTT; Sec. MARY PAINTER; publ. *Transactions* (annual).

Plainsong and Mediaeval Music Society: c/o RSCM, Cleveland Lodge, Westhumble, Dorking, Surrey, RH5 6BW; tel. (1306) 872800; fax (1306) 887260; e-mail pmms@rscm.com; f. 1888 for the promotion of the study and appreciation of plainsong and medieval music, especially by publication and performance; 150 mems; Chair. Prof. JOHN HARPER; Sec. Dr DAVID MATEER; publ. *Plainsong & Medieval Music* (2 a year).

Royal Academy of Arts in London: Burlington House, Piccadilly, London, W1V 0DS; tel. (20) 7300-8000; fax (20) 7300-8001; internet www.royalacademy.org.uk; f. 1768; fine arts; runs art school; 80 Acads; Pres. Sir NICHOLAS GRIMSHAW; Sec. MARY ANNE STEVENS; Keeper MAURICE COCKRILL; publs *RA Magazine* (quarterly), *RA Illustrated* (summer exhibition souvenir, annual).

Royal British Society of Sculptors: 108 Old Brompton Rd, London, SW7 3RA; tel. (20) 7373-8615; fax (20) 7370-3721; e-mail info@rbs.org.uk; internet www.rbs.org.uk; f. 1904 for the promotion and advancement of the art of sculpture; Pres. Prof. BRIAN FALCONBRIDGE; Administrator FLORENCIA GUILLEN; publ. *Sculpture97*.

Royal Cambrian Academy of Art: Crown Lane, Conwy, LL32 8AN; tel. (1492) 593413; fax (1492) 593413; e-mail rca@rcaconwy.org; internet www.rcaconwy.org; f. 1882 for the promotion of the arts of painting, engraving, sculpture, and other forms of art in Wales; 100 mems; Pres. KYFFIN WILLIAMS; Hon. Sec. ANN LEWIS; Curator GWYNETH JONES.

Royal Fine Art Commission for Scotland: Bakehouse Close, 146 Canongate, Edinburgh, EH8 8DD; tel. (131) 556-6699; fax (131) 556-6633; e-mail plan@royfinartcomforsco.gov.uk; internet www.royfinartcomforsco.gov.uk; f. 1927; independent body advising ministers and local authorities on the visual impact and quality of design of construction projects; during the Edinburgh International Festival an annual exhibition is held on a topic related to the

Commission's work; 12 mems; Sec. CHARLES PROSSER.

Royal Musical Association:; tel. (161) 861-7542; fax (161) 861-7543; e-mail jeffrey .dean@stingrayoffice.com; internet www.rma .ac.uk; f. 1874, inc. 1904, for the investigation and discussion of subjects connected with the art, science and history of music; annual conference, research students' conference, 4–6 annual regional study days; 925 mems; Pres. Prof. JOHN DEATHRIDGE; Sec. Dr JEFFREY DEAN; Hon. Treasurer LAWRENCE WRAGG; publs *Journal of the Royal Musical Association* (2 a year), *Royal Musical Association Monographs* (annual), *Royal Musical Association Research Chronicle* (annual).

Royal Photographic Society of Great Britain: Fenton House, 122 Wells Rd, Bath, BA2 3AH; tel. (1225) 325733; fax (1225) 448688; e-mail rps@rps.org; internet www.rps.org; f. 1853 for the advancement of the science and art of photography; 9,500 mems; library of 20,000 vols and periodicals; permanent colln of 200,000 photographs and 8,000 items of photographic equipment; Pres. Prof. RAYMOND CLARK; Sec.-Gen. BARRY LANE; publs *RPS Journal* (10 a year), *The Imaging Science Journal* (quarterly), *Imaging Abstracts* (6 a year).

Royal Scottish Academy: The Mound, Edinburgh, EH2 2EL; tel. (131) 225-6671; fax (131) 220-6016; e-mail info@ royalscottishacademy.org; internet www .royalscottishacademy.org; f. 1826; Scottish art (paintings, drawings, sculpture, architectural drawings); books and catalogues on Scottish art; archives relating to the instn and Scottish art; 129 mems (98 Acads, 31 hon. Acads) Programme Dir COLIN R. GREENSLADE; Collns Curator Dr JOANNA SODEN; Acad. Co-ordinator PAULINE COSTIGANE; publ. *Report* (irreg.).

Royal Watercolour Society: Bankside Gallery, 48 Hopton St, Blackfriars, London, SE1 9JH; tel. (20) 7928-7521; fax (20) 7928-2820; e-mail info@banksidegallery.com; internet www.banksidegallery.com; f. 1804; small archive and diploma collection; 83 mems; Pres. FRANCIS BOWYER; Sec. JUDY DIXEY; publ. *Bankside Bulletin* (quarterly).

Royal West of England Academy: Queen's Rd, Clifton, Bristol, BS8 1PX; tel. (117) 973-5129; fax (117) 923-7874; e-mail info@rwa .org.uk; internet www.rwa.org.uk; f. 1844 to encourage, advance and promote the appreciation of the fine arts by exhibitions and occasional lectures and meetings; 160 academicians; library: small library, mainly exhibition catalogues; Pres. and Chair. of Council DEREK BALMER.

Scottish Arts Council: 12 Manor Place, Edinburgh, EH3 7DD; tel. (131) 226-6051; fax (131) 225-9833; e-mail administrator@ scottisharts.org.uk; internet www.sac.org.uk; f. 1967; provides funding, development support and information on the arts in Scotland; Dir GRAHAM BERRY; publ. *Information Bulletin* (6 a year).

Society for Theatre Research: c/o Theatre Museum, 1E Tavistock St, London, WC2E 7PA; e-mail e.cottis@btinternet.com; internet www.str.org.uk; f. 1948; encourages research into the history and technique of the British theatre; holds monthly lectures in the winter season; distributes research grants annually and offers an annual theatre book prize; 750 individual and corporate mems; Pres. TIMOTHY WEST; publ. *Theatre Notebook* (3 a year).

Society of Architectural Illustration: Bankfield House, 13 Wallbridge, Stroud, Glos., GL5 3JA; tel. (1453) 766958; fax (1453) 763913; e-mail info@sai.org.uk; internet www.sai.org.uk; f. 1975; has established a professional body and a recognized qualification for mems of the design professions who specialize in architectural illustration; confers SAI (Member), FSAI (Fellow), Hon.FSAI (Hon. Fellow); 359 mems; Pres. PHILIP CROWE; Admin. ERIC MONK; publs *Newsletter*, *Yearbook*, journals.

Society of Scribes and Illuminators: c/o 6 Queen Square, London, WC1N 3AT; tel. and fax (1524) 251534; fax (1524) 251534; e-mail scribe@calligraphyonline.org; internet www .calligraphyonline.org; f. 1921; aims to re-establish and perpetuate the tradition of craftsmanship, calligraphy and fine lettering; advanced training scheme; reference library; 500 mems (63 fellows, 440 lay mems); Hon. Sec. GILLIAN HAZELDINE; publs *Newsletter* (3 a year), *The Scribe* (2 a year).

SPNM–Promoting New Music: St Margaret's House, 4th Floor, 18–20 Southwark St, London, SE1 1TJ; tel. (20) 7407-1640; fax (20) 7403-7652; e-mail spnm@spnm.org.uk; internet www.spnm.org.uk; f. 1943; 1,700 mems; concerts and workshop performances of new music; educational projects and collaborations with venues and ensembles in United Kingdom; professional development and training for emerging composers; Pres. Sir PETER MAXWELL DAVIES; Exec. Dir ABIGAIL POGSON; publ. *New Notes* (monthly).

HISTORY, GEOGRAPHY AND ARCHAEOLOGY

Ancient Monuments Society: St Ann's Vestry Hall, 2 Church Entry, London, EC4V 5HB; tel. (20) 7236-3934; fax (20) 7329-3677; e-mail office@ancientmonumentssociety.org .uk; internet www .ancientmonumentssociety.org.uk; f. 1924 for the study and conservation of ancient monuments, historic buildings and fine old craftsmanship, in partnership with the Friends of Friendless Churches; 2,000 mems; Pres. Prof. R. W. BRUNSKILL; Chair. GILES QUARME; Sec. M. J. SAUNDERS; publs *Newsletter* (in 3 series), *Transactions* (annually).

Baptist Historical Society: Baptist House, POB 44, 129 Broadway, Didcot, OX11 8RT; internet www.baptisthistory.org.uk; f. 1908 to promote the study of and record the history of the Baptists; assists researchers, and gives advice to Churches on care and preservation of records; library administered jointly with Angus Library, Regent's Park College, Oxford; 550 mems; Pres. Rev. Dr P. SHEPHERD; Sec. Rev. S. L. COPSON; publ. *The Baptist Quarterly*.

British Archaeological Association: c/o John McNeill, 18 Stanley Rd. Oxford, OX4 1QZ; internet www.britarch.ac.uk/baa/; f. 1843; 700 mems; Hon. Pres. Dr NICOLA COLDSTREAM; Hon. Sec. JOHN McNEILL; publs *Journal* (annually), *Conference Transactions* (annually).

British Cartographic Society: c/o Royal Geographic Society, 1 Kensington Gore, London, SW7 2AR; tel. (1823) 665775; fax (1823) 665775; e-mail admin@cartography .org.uk; internet www.cartography.org.uk; f. 1963; 700 mems; promotes the art and science of map-making through cartography, history of cartography, map library curatorship, GIS, technical developments and automation in cartography, design and technology and education and careers in cartography; Pres. MARY SPENCE; Administrator KEN ATHERTON; Hon. Sec. Dr TIM RIDEOUT; publs *Cartographic Journal* (3 a year), *Cartographiti* (newsletter of the map curators' group, 3 a year), *Maplines* (newsletter, 3 a year).

British Numismatic Society: c/o Warburg Institute, Woburn Sq., London, WC1H 0AB; tel. (1223) 332915; e-mail secretary@ britnumsoc.org; internet www.britnumsoc .org; f. 1903; 636 mems; Pres. Dr M. A. S. BLACKBURN; Sec. Dr E. M. SCREEN; publ. *British Numismatic Journal* (annual).

British Records Association: c/o Finsbury Library, 245 St John St, London, EC1V 4NB; tel. (20) 7833-0428; fax (20) 7833-0416; e-mail britrecassoc@hotmail.com; internet www.britishrecordsassociation.org.uk; f. 1932 for the preservation and use of records (archives), and for the co-ordination of the work of institutions and individuals interested in the subject; 1,000 mems; annual conference; Pres. RT HON. THE MASTER OF THE ROLLS; Hon. Sec. ELIZABETH HUGHES; publ. *Archives* (2 a year).

Cambrian Archaeological Association: c/o Rev. M. Coombe, 28 Gipsy Lane, Exmouth, EX8 3HN; tel. (1395) 272923; internet www.cambrians.org.uk; f. 1846; 832 mems; Pres. Dr J. L. DAVIES; Gen. Sec. Rev. M. COOMBE; publ. *Archaeologia Cambrensis* (annually).

Canterbury and York Society: c/o Borthwick Institute, Univ. of York, York, YO10 5DD; internet www.york.ac.uk/inst/bihr/cys; f. 1904; 249 mems; Pres. Prof. D. M. SMITH; Sec. Dr C. FONGE; publ. *Medieval Bishops' Registers and other Ecclesiastical Records*.

Catholic Record Society: c/o Hon. Sec., 12 Melbourne Place, Wolsingham, Wolsingham, DL13 3EH; tel. (1388) 527747; e-mail LeoGooch@wolsinghamdl133eh.frceserve.co .uk; internet www.catholic-history.org.uk/ crs/; f. 1904; publishes documentary material on Catholic history in England and Wales since the Reformation; intl membership; Hon. Sec. Dr LEO GOOCH; publ. *Monographs* (irregular).

Council for British Archaeology: St Mary's House, 66 Bootham, York, YO30 7BZ; tel. (1904) 671417; fax (1904) 671384; e-mail info@britarch.ac.uk; internet www .britarch.ac.uk; f. 1944; works to promote the study and safeguarding of Britain's historic environment, to provide a forum for archaeological opinion, and to improve public knowledge of Britain's past; 600 institutional mems, 5,600 individual mems; Pres. N. MERRIMAN; Dir M. HEYWORTH; publ. *British Archaeology* (6 a year).

Council of British Geography: c/o Royal Geographical Society (with the Institute of British Geographers), 1 Kensington Gore, London, SW7 2AR; tel. (20) 7591-3000; fax (20) 7591-3021; f. 1988 to provide a formal organization linking all British geographical societies for the advancement of British geography; co-ordinates policies of mem. societies, and takes initiatives in educational, academic, research or policy matters; Chair. Prof. A. KENT; Hon. Sec. Dr R. HALL.

Ecclesiastical History Society: c/o Dr S. Martin, 7 Churchcroft, Harborne, Birmingham, B17 0SL; e-mail martin.s@ocr.org.uk; internet www.ehsoc.org.uk; f. 1961; aims to further the study of ecclesiastical history and to maintain relations between British ecclesiastical historians and scholars abroad; 900 mems; Pres. D. H. McLEOD; Sec. S. M. HAMILTON; publs *Studies in Church History* (annually), *Subsidia* (irregular).

Economic History Society: Dept of Economic and Social History, Univ. of Glasgow, Lilybank House, Bute Gardens, Glasgow, G12 8RT; tel. (141) 330-4662; fax (141) 330-4889; e-mail ehsocsec@arts.gla.ac.uk; internet www.ehs.org.uk; f. 1927; provides Fellowships; training course for postgraduate students; annual conference; 1,250 mems; Pres. Prof. R. M. SMITH; Hon. Sec. Prof. P. S. FEARON; publ. *Economic History Review* (quarterly).

Egypt Exploration Society: 3 Doughty Mews, London, WC1N 2PG; tel. (20) 7242-1880; fax (20) 7404-6118; e-mail contact@ees.ac.uk; internet www.ees.ac.uk; f. 1882; excavation in Egypt and publication of work, lectures and study days; 3,000 mems; library: see Libraries and Archives; Sec. Gen. PATRICIA SPENCER; Librarian and Membership and Outreach Sec. KAREN EXELL; publs *Archaeological Survey* (irreg.), *Egyptian Archaeology* (2 a year), *Excavation Memoirs* (irreg.), *Graeco-Roman Memoirs* (annual), *Journal of Egyptian Archaeology* (annual).

English Place-Name Society: School of English Studies, University of Nottingham, Nottingham, NG7 2RD; tel. (115) 951-5919; fax (115) 951-5924; e-mail janet.rudkin@nottingham.ac.uk; internet www.nottingham.ac.uk/english/ins; f. 1923 for the publication of a yearly volume on the place-names of a county, or part of a county; 650 mems; Hon. Dir RICHARD COATES; publ. *Journal* (annually).

Friends Historical Society: c/o Friends House, Euston Rd, London, NW1 2BJ; f. 1903; 400 mems; Clerk of Exec. DUDLEY BARLOW; publ. *Journal* (annual).

Geographical Association: 160 Solly St, Sheffield, S1 4BF; tel. (114) 296-0088; fax (114) 296-7176; e-mail info@geography.org.uk; internet www.geography.org.uk; f. 1893 to further the interests of teachers of geography and the study and teaching of geography generally; 7,000 mems; CEO Dr DAVID LAMBERT; publs *Geography* (3 a year), *Teaching Geography* (3 a year), *Primary Geographer* (3 a year).

Hakluyt Society: c/o Map Library, British Library, 96 Euston Rd, London, NW1 2DB; tel. (1428) 641850; e-mail office@hakluyt.com; internet www.hakluyt.com; f. 1846; publishes primary source material of early exploratory voyages, travel and other geographical records; 2,350 mems; Pres. Prof. R. C. BRIDGES; Hon. Sec. and Series Editor Prof. W. F. RYAN.

Harleian Society: c/o College of Arms, Queen Victoria St, London, EC4V 4BT; tel. (20) 7236-7728; fax (20) 7248-6448; e-mail info@harleian.co.uk; internet harleian.co.uk; f. 1869, inc. 1902, for the transcribing, printing and publishing of the Heraldic Visitations of Counties, Parish Registers or any MSS relating to genealogy, family history and heraldry; 300 subscribers; Chair. T. WOODCOCK; Hon. Sec. and Treas. T. H. S. DUKE (Chester Herald of Arms).

Heraldry Society: POB 772, Guildford, Surrey, GU3 3ZX; tel. (1483) 237373; fax (1483) 237373; e-mail secretary@theheraldrysociety.com; internet www.theheraldrysociety.com; f. 1947 to further the study of heraldry, armory, chivalry, genealogy and kindred subjects; 1,000 mems; Patron THE DUKE OF NORFOLK; publs *The Coat of Arms* (4 a year), *The Heraldry Gazette* (4 a year).

Historic Buildings and Monuments Commission for England (English Heritage): POB 569, Swindon, SN2 2YP; tel. (870) 333-1181; fax (1793) 414-926; e-mail customers@english-heritage.org.uk; internet www.english-heritage.org.uk; f. 1983; executive non-departmental public body sponsored by the Department for Culture, Media and Sport; responsible for all aspects of protecting and promoting historic buildings and landscapes throughout England; funded by the UK Government and from revenue earned from its historic properties; Chair. Sir NEIL COSSONS; publs *Buildings at Risk Register* (annually), *Conservation Bulletin* (quarterly), *Register of Parks and Gardens*.

Attached Organizations:

Centre for Archaeology: Fort Cumberland, Fort Cumberland Rd, Eastney, Portsmouth, Hampshire, PO4 9LD; tel. (23) 9285-6700; e-mail cfa@english-heritage.org.uk.

National Monuments Record Centre: Kemble Drive, Swindon, SN2 2GZ; tel. (1793) 414600; e-mail nmrinfo@english-heritage.org.uk.

Historical Association: 59A Kennington Park Rd, London, SE11 4JH; tel. (20) 7735-3901; fax (20) 7582-4989; e-mail mstiles@history.org.uk; internet www.history.org.uk; f. 1906; aims to advance the study and teaching of history at all levels, to increase public interest in all aspects of the subject and to develop it as an essential element in the education of all; 60 brs nationally; 8,500 mems; history textbook collection; Pres. HARRY DICKINSON; Chief Exec. MADELINE STILES; publs *The Historian* (quarterly), *History* (quarterly), *Primary History* (3 a year), *Teaching History* (quarterly).

Honourable Society of Cymmrodorion: 30 Eastcastle St, London, W1W 8DJ; tel. (20) 7631-0502; e-mail aelodau1751we@yahoo.co.uk; internet www.cymmrodorion1751.org.uk; f. 1751; promotes the practice and development of literature, the arts and sciences insofar as they are of special interest to Wales, the Welsh people and those interested in Wales; Royal Charter 1951; 900 mems; Patron HRH THE PRINCE OF WALES; Pres. Prof. PRYS MORGAN; Hon. Sec. JOHN SAMUEL; publs *Dictionary of Welsh Biography*, *Transactions* (annually).

Huguenot Society of Great Britain and Ireland: The Huguenot Library, University College London, Gower St, London, WC1E 6BT; tel. (20) 7679-5199; e-mail library@huguenotsociety.org.uk; internet www.huguenotsociety.org.uk; f. 1885; 1,385 mems (9 hon. fellows, 1,376 ordinary fellows); Pres. ROBERT WALLACE-TURNER; Hon. Sec. BARBARA JULIEN; publs *Huguenot Families* (genealogy, 2 a year), *Proceedings* (annual), *Quarto Series* (irreg.), *New Series* (irreg.).

Institute of Heraldic and Genealogical Studies: 79–82 Northgate, Canterbury, Kent, CT1 1BA; tel. (1227) 768664; fax (1227) 765617; e-mail admin@ihgs.ac.uk; internet www.ihgs.ac.uk; f. 1961; provides courses in family history and related subjects using traditional classroom methods and a correspondence course available online or by post, leading to accredited qualifications; spec. collns; 250 mems; library of 35,000 vols, 20,000 case studies; Pres. Rt Hon. the Earl of LYTTON; Principal C. R. HUMPHERY-SMITH; Reg. CELIA HERITAGE; publs *Atlas and Index of Parishes*, *Family History* (quarterly), *Syllabus of Study*, *Teacher's Aids*.

Jewish Historical Society of England: 33 Seymour Place, London, W1H 5AP; tel. (20) 7723-5852; fax (20) 7723-5852; e-mail info@jhse.org; internet www.jhse.org; f. 1893; Jewish Studies Library, University College, London; 800 mems; Administrator DAVID FREEMAN; Hon. Sec. Dr GERRY BLACK; publ. *Transactions* (annually).

London and Middlesex Archaeological Society: c/o Museum of London, London Wall, London, EC2Y 5HN; tel. (20) 7814-5734; e-mail postmaster@london-arch-soc.demon.co.uk; internet www.lamas.org.uk; f. 1855; promotes and publishes archaeological and historical research in London area; 656 mems; Pres. Dr SIMON THURLEY; Hon. Sec. JACKIE KEILY; publ. *Transactions* (annual).

London Record Society: c/o Institute of Historical Research, Senate House, Malet St, London, WC1E 7HU; tel. (20) 7862-8798; fax (20) 7862-8793; e-mail heather.creaton@sas.ac.uk; internet www.history.ac.uk/cmh; f. 1964 to publish original sources for the history of London and generally to encourage public interest in archives relating to London; 380 mems; Hon. Sec. HEATHER CREATON.

London Topographical Society: 36 Old Deer Park Gardens, Richmond, Surrey, TW9 2TL; tel. (20) 8940-5419; e-mail frazer@topsoc.org; internet www.topsoc.org; f. 1880; 1,050 mems; publishes material to assist in the study and appreciation of London's history, growth and topography, incl. reproductions of historic maps and views of London; Patron HRH THE DUKE OF EDINBURGH; Hon. Sec. PATRICK FRAZER; publs *London Topographical Record* (every 5 years), *Newsletter* (2 a year), maps, views and books.

Manchester Geographical Society: Friends' Meeting House, 6 Mount St, Manchester, M2 5NS; tel. (161) 834-2965; e-mail mangeogsoc@fsnet.co.uk; internet www.mangeogsoc.org.uk; f. 1884 to promote the study of all branches of geographical science; 160 mems; library of 4,500 vols (now on permanent loan to the University of Manchester); Pres. JOHN MITCHELL; Hon. Sec. Dr PAUL HINDLE; publ. *North West Geography* (e-journal, 2 a year).

Monumental Brass Society: c/o H. M. Stuchfield, Lowe Hill House, Stratford St Mary, Suffolk, CO7 6JX; e-mail martin.stuchfield@intercitygroup.co.uk; internet www.mbs-brasses.co.uk; f. 1887 to promote the study of and interest in, better preservation of monumental brasses, and to compile and publish a full and accurate list of all extant and lost brasses, English and foreign; Pres. Rev. Canon D. G. MEARA; Hon. Sec. H. M. STUCHFIELD; publs *Transactions* (annually), *Portfolio* (irregular), *Bulletin* (3 a year).

Palestine Exploration Fund: 2 Hinde Mews, Marylebone Lane, London, W1V 2AA; tel. (20) 7935-5379; fax (20) 7486-7438; e-mail execsec@pef.org.uk; internet www.pef.org.uk; f. 1865; 900 subscribers; promotes research into the archaeology and history, manners, customs and culture, topography, geology and natural sciences of biblical Palestine and the Levant (modern-day Syria, Lebanon, Jordan and Israel); library of 5,000 vols; Exec. Curator FELICITY COBBING; Hon. Librarian RUPERT CHAPMAN; publ. *Palestine Exploration Quarterly* (3 a year).

Prehistoric Society: c/o Institute of Archaeology, University College London, 31–34 Gordon Square, London, WC1H 0PY; internet www.ucl.ac.uk/prehistoric; f. 1908; furthers prehistoric archaeology; 2,000 mems; Pres. Prof. GRAEME BARKER; Hon. Sec. Dr ALEX GIBSON; publs *Proceedings* (annually), *Past* (3 a year).

Regional Studies Association: POB 2058, Seaford, East Sussex, BN25 4QU; tel. (1323) 899698; fax (1323) 899798; e-mail rsa@mailbox.ulcc.ac.uk; internet www.regional-studies-assoc.ac.uk; f. 1965; an interdisciplinary group exclusively concerned with regional issues; provides a forum for the exchange of ideas and information on regional problems, publishes the results of regional research, and stimulates studies and research in regional planning and related fields; holds meetings, conferences and seminars; organizes study groups; 14 branches; 600 individual, 200 corporate mems, including government depts, ministries, local authorities, educational institutions, etc; Chair. MIKE DANSON; Dir SALLY HARDY; Hon. Sec. ANNE GREEN; publs *Regional Studies* (9 a year), *Newsletter* (6 a year).

Royal Archaeological Institute: c/o Society of Antiquaries, Burlington House, Piccadilly, London, W1J 0BE; tel. (116) 2433839; fax (116) 2433839; e-mail admin@royalarchaeolinst.org; internet www.royalarchaeolinst.org; f. 1843; has a lecture programme, holds meetings for mems, awards grants for archaeological research and excavations; 1,500 mems; Pres. JONATHAN COAD; Hon. Sec. Dr GILL HEY; publ. *Archaeological Journal* (annual).

Royal Geographical Society (with the Institute of British Geographers): 1 Kensington Gore, London, SW7 2AR; tel. (20) 7591-3000; fax (20) 7591-3001; e-mail info@rgs.org; internet www.rgs.org; f. 1830; furtherance of geographical research, teaching and expeditions; Expedition Advisory Centre for scientific expeditions overseas; 14,000 mems; library of 130,000 books, 800,000 maps and charts, 4,500 atlases, 100,000 mid-19th-century to contemporary pictures and photographs; Pres. Sir NEIL COSSONS; Dir and Sec. Dr RITA GARDNER; publs *Geographical Journal* (4 a year), *Geographical* (monthly), *Transactions* (4 a year), *Area* (4 a year).

Royal Historical Society: Univ. College London, Gower St, London, WC1E 6BT; tel. (20) 7387-7532; fax (20) 7387-7532; e-mail royalhistsoc@ucl.ac.uk; internet www.rhs.ac.uk; f. 1868; 3,000 mems; library of 3,000 vols; Pres. Prof. MARTIN J. DAUNTON; Exec. Sec. SUE CARR; publs *Transactions* (annual), *Camden* (5th series, 2 vols a year).

Royal Numismatic Society: c/o Dept of Coins and Medals, British Museum, London, WC1B 3DG; tel. (20) 7323-8272; fax (20) 7323-8171; e-mail numismatics@numismatics.org.uk; internet www.numismatics.org.uk; f. 1836; 1,000 mems; Pres. J. CRIBB; Secs V. S. CURTIS, S. MOORHEAD; publ. *Numismatic Chronicle* (annual).

Royal Philatelic Society London: 41 Devonshire Pl., London, W1G 6JY; tel. (20) 7486-1044; fax (20) 7486-0803; e-mail secretary@rpsl.org.uk; internet www.rpsl.org.uk; f. 1869; 1,600 mems; Pres. S. JOHN SACHER; Sec. BRIAN J. TROTTER; publ. *The London Philatelist* (10 a year).

Royal Scottish Geographical Society: Graham Hills Bldg, 40 George St, Glasgow, G1 1QE; tel. (141) 552-3330; fax (141) 552-3331; e-mail rsgs@strath.ac.uk; internet www.rsgs.org; f. 1884 to further the science of geography in all its branches; symposia, illustrated talks and schools conferences; provides research grants and support to scientific expeditions; library of 20,000 vols, 30,000 maps, 200 current periodicals, special collection of early maps of Scotland; 2,200 mems; Pres. The EARL OF LINDSAY; Dir DAVID M. MUNRO; publs *Geogscot* (newsletter, 3 a year), *The Scottish Geographical Journal* (4 a year).

Scottish History Society: Dept of Scottish History, Univ. of St Andrews, St Katharine's Lodge, The Scores, St Andrews, KY16 9AL; e-mail katie.stevenson@st-andrews.ac.uk; internet www.scottishhistorysociety.org; f. 1886 for the printing of unpublished documents illustrating the history of Scotland; 800 mems; Pres. Dr IAIN HUTCHISON; Hon. Sec. Dr KATIE STEVENSON.

Society for Army Historical Research: c/o National Army Museum, Royal Hospital Rd, London, SW3 4HT; internet www.sahr.co.uk; f. 1921; army and regimental history; military antiquities and pictures, uniforms, badges and medals, arms and equipment, customs and traditions and the history of land warfare in general; 1,000 mems; Pres. Field Marshal Sir JOHN CHAPPLE; Hon. Sec. GEORGE EVELYN; publ. *Journal* (quarterly).

Society for Medieval Archaeology: c/o Institute of Archaeology, University College London, 31–34 Gordon Square, London, WC1H 0PY; tel. (20) 7679-1522; fax (20) 7383-2572; e-mail a.reynolds@ucl.ac.uk; internet www.socmedarch.org; f. 1957 for the study of archaeology of the post-Roman period; 1,500 mems; Pres. Prof. ROBERTA GILCHRIST; Hon. Sec. Dr ANDREW REYNOLDS; publs *Medieval Archaeology* (annually), *Monograph Series* (irregular).

Society for Nautical Research: c/o 6 Ashmeadow Rd, Arnside, via Carnforth, Lancs., LA5 0AE; tel. (1524) 761616; e-mail honsecretary.snr@btopenworld.com; internet www.snr.org; f. 1910; 1,500 mems; Pres. HRH the DUKE OF YORK; Chair. Prof. R. HARDING; Sec. P. D. WINTERBOTTOM; publs *The Mariners' Mirror* (quarterly), *Newsletter* (quarterly).

Society for Post-Medieval Archaeology Ltd: c/o David Cranstone, 267 Kells Lane, Low Fell, Gateshead NE9 5HU; tel. (191) 482-1037; fax (191) 482-2343; e-mail cranconsult@btinternet.com; internet www.spma.org.uk; f. 1967; 400 mems; Pres. Dr DAVID GAIMSTER; Sec. DAVID CRANSTONE; publs *Post-Medieval Archaeology* (2 a year), *Newsletter* (2 a year).

Society for Renaissance Studies: c/o Michelle O'Malley, Centre for Research in the History of Art, University of Sussex, Falmer, Brighton, BN1 9RQ; e-mail m.o-malley@sussex.ac.uk; internet www.sas.ac.uk/srs/Default.htm; f. 1967 to advance scholarship in the Renaissance, including literature, philosophy, science, art and music; 550 mems; Hon. Chair. Dr DAVID CHAMBERS; Hon. Sec. Dr MICHELLE O'MALLEY; publs *Renaissance Studies* (quarterly), *Bulletin* (2 a year).

Society of Antiquaries of London: Burlington House, Piccadilly, London, W1J 0BE; tel. (20) 7734-0193; fax (20) 7287-6967; e-mail admin@sal.org.uk; internet www.sal.org.uk; f. 1707; 2,200 fellows; library: see Libraries and Archives; Pres. Prof. R. J. CRAMP; Sec. D. MORGAN EVANS; publs *Archaeologia* (irregular), *The Antiquaries Journal* (annually).

Society of Antiquaries of Scotland: Royal Museum, Chambers St, Edinburgh, EH1 1JF; tel. (131) 247-4133; fax (131) 247-4163; e-mail socants@nms.ac.uk; internet www.socantscot.org; f. 1780; study of Scottish antiquities and history, particularly by archaeological research; grants and awards available for research relating to Scotland; 3,500 mems; Pres. Dr J. N. G. RITCHIE; Dir F. M. ASHMORE; publ. *Proceedings* (annually).

Society of Archivists: Prioryfield House, 20 Canon St, Taunton, Somerset, TA1 1SW; tel. (1823) 327030; fax (1823) 271719; e-mail societyofarchivists@archives.org.uk; internet www.archives.org.uk; f. 1947; 2,000 mems; Pres. VICTOR GRAY; Exec. Sec. PATRICK S. CLEARY; publs *Journal* (2 a year), *ARC Magazine* (monthly).

Society of Genealogists: 14 Charterhouse Bldgs, Goswell Rd, London, EC1M 7BA; tel. (20) 7251-8799; fax (20) 7250-1800; e-mail library@sog.org.uk; internet www.sog.org.uk; f. 1911; 11,500 mems; promotes the study, science and knowledge of genealogy and family history, through education and library programmes; library of 120,000 vols and other items, incl. video cassettes, microfiches and CDs; Pres. PATRIC DICKENSON; Dir JUNE PERRIN (acting); publ. *Genealogists' Magazine* (quarterly).

United Reformed Church History Society: Westminster College, Madingley Rd, Cambridge, CB3 0AA; tel. (1223) 741300; e-mail mt212@cam.ac.uk; f. 1972 to incorporate the Congregational Historical Soc. (f. 1899), the Presbyterian Historical Soc. of England (f. 1913) and the Churches of Christ Historical Soc. (f. 1981); 300 mems; library of 5,000 vols; Hon. Sec. Rev. ELIZABETH J. BROWN; publ. *Journal* (2 a year).

Wesley Historical Society: c/o Dr John A. Hargreaves, 7 Haugh Shaw Rd, Halifax, HX1 3AH; tel. (1422) 250780; e-mail johnahargreaves@blueyonder.co.uk; internet www.wesleyhistoricalsociety.org.uk; f. 1893 to promote the study of the history and literature of all branches of Methodism; annual lecture, residential conference every three years; 600 mems; library at Westminster Institute of Education, Oxford Brookes Univ., Harcourt Hill Campus, Oxford, OX2 9AT; Pres. Rev. Dr JOHN A. NEWTON; Gen. Sec. Dr E. D. GRAHAM; publ. *Proceedings* (3 a year).

LANGUAGE AND LITERATURE

Academi Gymreig, Yr/Welsh Academy, The: Mount Stuart House, 3rd Floor, Mount Stuart Sq., Cardiff, CF10 5FQ; tel. (29) 2047-2266; fax (29) 2049-2930; e-mail post@academi.org; internet www.academi.org; f. 1959; promotes the writers and literatures of Wales; 600 mems (220 in Welsh-language section, 380 in English-language section); Pres. (English language) DANNIE ABSE; Pres. (Welsh language) T. LLEW JONES; Co-Chairs Dr HARRI PRITCHARD-JONES, Dr JOHN PIKOULIS; Chief Exec. PETER FINCH; publs *Taliesin* (3 a year), *A470* (5 a year).

Alliance Française: 1 Dorset Sq., London, NW1 6PU; tel. (20) 7723-6439,; fax (20) 7224-1865; e-mail info@alliancefrancaise.org.uk; internet www.alliancefrancaise.org.uk; offers courses and exams in French language and culture and promotes cultural exchange with France; attached offices in Bath, Belfast, Bristol, Cambridge, Exeter, Glasgow, Jersey, Loughborough, Manchester, Milton Keynes, Oxford, Totnes, York; Dir CHRYSTEL HUG.

Alliance of Literary Societies: 22 Belmont Grove, Havant, Hants., PO9 3PU; tel. (2392) 475855; fax (870) 0560330; e-mail rosemary@sndc.demon.co.uk; internet www.sndc.demon.co.uk; f. 1973; aims to provide a single voice for literary and authors' societies in defence of sites and legacies of literary importance; annual general meeting; 110 mem. socs; Pres. AERONWY THOMAS; Sec. ROSEMARY CULLEY; publs *Handbook*, *Newsletter* (2 a year).

Association for Language Learning: 150 Railway Terrace, Rugby, CV21 3HN; tel. (1788) 546443; fax (1788) 544149; e-mail langlearn@all-languages.org.uk; internet www.all-languages.org.uk; f. 1990; offers help, in-service training and support to language teachers; promotes the learning and use of foreign languages; 3,500 mems; Dir LINDA PARKER; publs *Language Learning Journal*, *Rusistika* (annually), *Tuttitalia*, *Vida Hispánica*, *Deutsch: Lehren und Lernen*, *Francophonie* (all 2 a year), *Language World* (quarterly).

Association of British Science Writers: Wellcome Wolfson Bldg, 165 Queen's Gate, London, SW7 5HE; tel. (870) 770-3361; e-mail absw@absw.org.uk; internet www.absw.org.uk; f. 1947 to assist those who write about science and technology, and to improve the standard of science journalism in the UK; 600 mems; Chair. Dr TED NIELD; Administrator BARBARA DRILLSMA; publ. *Science Reporter* (quarterly).

British Association for Applied Linguistics: c/o Dovetail Management Consultancy, POB 6688, London, SE15 3WB; tel. (20) 7639-0090; fax (20) 7635-6014; e-mail admin@baal.org.uk; internet www.baal.org.uk; f. 1967 to promote the study of language in use, to foster interdisciplinary collaboration and to provide a common forum for those engaged in the theoretical study of language and those interested in its practical use; 750 individual mems, 30 mem. publishers and university depts; Chair. SUSAN HUNSTON; Sec. GRAHAM TURNER; publs *Applied Linguistics* (3 a year, in asscn with American Asscn for Applied Linguistics), *British Studies in Applied Linguistics* (Edited Proceedings of Annual Meetings), *Newsletter* (3 a year).

British Association of Academic Phoneticians: Phonetics Laboratory, Dept of English Language, University of Glasgow, G12 8QQ; tel. (141) 330-4596; fax (141) 330-3531; e-mail m.macmahon@englang.arts.gla.ac.uk; internet www.phon.ucl.ac.uk/home/baap; f. 1984; 150 mems; Sec. and Archivist Prof. M. K. C. MACMAHON.

Brontë Society: The Brontë Parsonage Museum, Haworth, Keighley, West Yorks., BD22 8DR; tel. (1535) 642323; fax (1535) 647131; e-mail bronte@bronte.org.uk; internet www.bronte.org.uk; f. 1893, inc. 1902, to collect and act as guardian of Brontë letters, MSS, and personal belongings which are housed in the Brontë Parsonage Museum, former home of the Brontës and now in the care of the Society; 3,000 mems; Pres. (vacant); Chair. RICHARD WILCOCKS; publ. *Brontë Studies* (3 a year).

Charles Lamb Society: BM Elia, London, WC1N 3XX; f. 1935; to promote the study of the lives and works of Charles Lamb and his circle and to form a collection of Eliana; 300 mems; library: library housed in the Guildhall Library, Corporation of London; Pres. Prof. J. R. WATSON; Chair. NICHOLAS POWELL; publ. *The Charles Lamb Bulletin* (4 a year).

Chartered Institute of Linguists: Saxon House, 48 Southwark St, London, SE1 1UN; tel. (20) 7940-3100; fax (20) 7940-3101; e-mail info@iol.org.uk; internet www.iol.org.uk; f. 1910; promotes proficiency in modern languages worldwide amongst professional linguists, including translators, interpreters and educationalists, as well as those in the public and private sectors for whom languages are an important skill; helps to ensure equal access for all to the public services (law, health, local govt) by providing interpreting qualifications in most of the languages spoken in the United Kingdom and running the Nat. Register of Public Service Interpreters (NRPSI Ltd); a wholly owned subsidiary IoL Language Services Ltd offers translation, production and recruitment services, validation of language qualifications and assessments as well as training courses; IoL Educational Trust, an associated charity, is an accredited awarding body offering high level examinations; 6,500 mems; library of 6,000 vols; Chief Exec. JOHN HAMMOND; publ. *The Linguist* (every 2 months).

Classical Association: c/o Clare Roberts, Senate House, Malet St, London, WC1E 7HU; tel. (20) 7862-8706; fax (20) 7255-2297; e-mail office@classicalassociation.org; internet www.classicalassociation.org; f. 1903; 3,500 mems; Joint Secs Prof. DOUGLAS CAIRNS, BARBARA FINNEY; publs *CA News* (2 a year), *Classical Quarterly* (2 a year), *Classical Review* (2 a year), *Greece and Rome* (2 a year).

Dickens Fellowship: Dickens House, 48 Doughty St, London, WC1N 2LF; tel. (20) 7405-2127; fax (20) 7831-5175; internet www.dickens.fellowship.btinternet.co.uk; f. 1902 to knit together in a common bond of friendship lovers of Charles Dickens, and to assist in the preservation and purchase of buildings and objects associated with Dickens or mentioned in his works; 7,000 mems; Pres. HENRY DICKENS HAWKSLEY; Hon. Gen. Secs THELMA

GROVE, Dr TONY WILLIAMS; publs *The Dickensian* (3 a year), *Mr Dick's Kite* (3 a year).

Early English Text Society: Lady Margaret Hall, Oxford, OX2 6QA; internet www.eets.org.uk; f. 1864; texts published annually; 900 mems; Hon. Dir Prof. ANNE HUDSON; Exec. Sec. Prof. VINCENT A. GILLESPIE.

English Association: Univ. of Leicester, University Rd, Leicester, LE1 7RH; tel. (116) 252-3982; fax (116) 252-2301; e-mail engassoc@le.ac.uk; internet www.le.ac.uk/engassoc; f. 1906 to promote knowledge and appreciation of the English language and its literature, through conferences, lectures and publs; 2,500 mems; Pres. Prof. ELAINE TREHARNE; Chair. Prof. PETER KITSON; Chief Exec. HELEN LUCAS; publs *English 4–11* (3 a year), *English* (3 a year), *English Association Newsletter* (3 a year), *Essays and Studies*, *The Use of English* (3 a year), *The Year's Work in Critical and Cultural Theory*, *The Year's Work in English Studies*.

English Centre of International PEN: 6–8 Amwell St, London, EC1R 1UQ; tel. (20) 7713-0023; fax (20) 7837-7838; e-mail enquiries@englishpen.org; internet www.englishpen.org; f. 1921; 990 mems; Pres. Dr ALISTAIR NIVEN; Dir SUSANNA NICKLIN.

English Speaking Board: 26A Princes St, Southport, Merseyside, PR8 1EQ; e-mail admin@esbuk.org; internet www.esbuk.org; tel. (1704) 501730; fax (1704) 539637; f. 1953; promotes and encourages all aspects of oral communication in English; brings together people from educational, professional and industrial spheres who are concerned with oral education as a means of communication; individual and corporate mems in 34 countries; arranges courses and examinations in spoken English at all levels, from primary to higher education; certificates and diplomas awarded to teachers, professional speakers; assessments for individuals studying English as an acquired language; 450 mems; Hon. Pres. JOCELYN BELL; Chair. PETER BLUNT; publ. *Speaking English* (2 a year).

Francis Bacon Society Inc.: c/o G. N. Salway, Flat 1, Lee House, 75A Effra Rd, London, SW19 8PS; tel. (20) 8542-4689; e-mail info@baconsocietyinc.org; internet www.baconsocietyinc.org; f. 1886; registered charity; for the study of the works and life of Francis Bacon, and investigation into evidence suggesting Bacon's authorship of plays attributed to Shakespeare; library; Pres. PETER A. WELSFORD; Sec. GERALD N. SALWAY; publ. *Baconiana*.

Goethe-Institut: 50 Princes Gate, Exhibition Rd, London, SW7 2PH; tel. (20) 7596-4000; fax (20) 7594-0240; e-mail mail@london.goethe.org; internet www.goethe.de/london; offers courses and exams in German language and culture and promotes cultural exchange with Germany; attached centres in Glasgow and Manchester; library of 17,000 vols; Dir Dr ROLAND GOLL.

Institute of Translation and Interpreting: Fortuna House, South Fifth St, Milton Keynes, MK9 2EU; tel. (1908) 325250; fax (1908) 325259; e-mail info@iti.org.uk; internet www.iti.org.uk; f. 1986; promotes high standards in translation and interpreting; provides information on these services to govt, industry, the media and the general public; offers guidance to those entering the profession and advice to those who offer language services and their customers; 2,850 mems; Gen. Sec. ALAN WHEATLEY; publ. *ITI Bulletin* (6 a year).

Instituto Cervantes: 102 Eaton Sq., London, SW1W 9AN; tel. (20) 7235-0353; fax (20) 7235-0329; e-mail cenlon@cervantes.es; internet londres.cervantes.es; f. 1991; offers

courses and exams in Spanish language and culture and promotes cultural exchange with Spain and Spanish-speaking Latin and Central America; attached centre in Manchester; library: library of 20,000 vols; Dir JUAN PEDRO APARICIO.

Joseph Conrad Society: P. O. S. K., 238-246 King St, London, W6 ORF; e-mail theconradian@aol.com; internet www.josephconradsociety.org; f. 1973 to provide a forum and resource for scholars of Conrad's work; 200 mems; library of 800 vols; Sec. HUGH EPSTEIN; publ. *The Conradian* (2 a year).

Kipling Society: 6 Clifton Rd, London, W9 1SS; tel. (20) 7286-0194; fax (20) 7286-0194; e-mail jane@keskar.fsworld.co.uk; internet www.kipling.org.uk; f. 1927 to honour and extend the influence of Rudyard Kipling; 800 mems; Pres. Sir GEORGE ENGLE; Hon. Sec. JANE KESKAR; publ. *The Kipling Journal* (quarterly).

Linguistics Association of Great Britain: Dr Andrew Hippisley, School of Electronics and Physical Sciences, University of Surrey, Guildford, Surrey, GU2 7XH; e-mail a.hippisley@surrey.ac.uk; internet www.lagb.org; f. 1959 to promote the study of linguistics and provide a forum for discussion and co-operation in the field; annual general meeting; 600 mems; Pres. Prof. APRIL MCMAHON; Hon. Sec. Dr AD NEELEMAN; publ. *Journal of Linguistics* (2 a year).

Malone Society:; tel. (020) 7862-8679; e-mail wim.van-mierlo@sas.ac.uk; internet www2.sas.ac.uk/ies/malone/; f. 1906 for the study, editing and publishing of English drama up to 1642; 670 mems; Chair. LEAH SCRAGG; Exec. Sec. Prof. JOHN CREASER.

Philological Society: School of Oriental and African Studies, Univ. of London, Thornhaugh St, Russell Sq., London, WC1H 0XG; fax (20) 7898-4399; e-mail secretary@philsoc.org.uk; internet www.philsoc.org.uk; f. 1842, inc. 1879, to investigate and promote the study and knowledge of the structure, affinities, and history of languages; 691 mems; Pres. Prof. NICHOLAS SIMS-WILLIAMS; Secs Prof. ANDREW LINN, Dr LUTZ MARTEN, Dr PAUL ROWLETT; publ. *Transactions* (3 a year).

Poetry Society: 22 Betterton St, London, WC2H 9BX; tel. (20) 7240-9880; fax (20) 7240-4818; e-mail info@poetrysociety.org.uk; internet www.poetrysociety.org.uk; f. 1909 to promote the study, appreciation and enjoyment of poetry; poetry reading, educational activities, organizers of National Poetry Day; 3,000 mems; Dir JULES MANN; publs *Poetry Review* (quarterly), *Poetry News* (quarterly).

Royal Society of Literature of the United Kingdom: Somerset House, Strand, London, WC2R 1LA; tel. (20) 7845-4676; fax (20) 7845-4679; e-mail info@rslit.org; internet www.rslit.org; f. 1820; lectures and literary discussions; awards 3 prizes annually; 850 fellows and mems; Pres. Sir MICHAEL HOLROYD; Chair Dr MAGGIE GEE; Sec. MAGGIE FERGUSSON; publ. *News* (annual).

Society for the Promotion of Hellenic Studies: Senate House, Malet St, London, WC1E 7HU; tel. (20) 7862-8730; fax (20) 7862-8731; e-mail hellenic@sas.ac.uk; f. 1879; 3,500 mems; library: see entry for Societies for the Promotion of Hellenic and Roman Studies Joint Library; Pres. Prof. R. G. OSBORNE; Hon. Sec. Prof. B. A. SPARKES; Exec. Sec. R. W. SHONE; publs *Journal of Hellenic Studies* (annually), *Journal of Roman Studies* (annually), *Britannia* (annually).

Society for the Promotion of Roman Studies: Senate House, Malet St, London,

WC1E 7HU; tel. (20) 7862-8727; fax (20) 7862-8728; e-mail office@romansociety.org; internet www.romansociety.org; f. 1910; 3,700 mems; library: see entry for Socs for the Promotion of Hellenic and Roman Studies Joint Library; Pres. Prof. M. G. FULFORD; publs *Britannia* (annual), *Journal of Roman Studies* (annual).

Society for the Study of Medieval Languages and Literature: c/o Dr Corinne Saunders, Department of English Studies, University of Durham, Hallgarth House, 77 Hallgarth St, Durham, DH1 3AY; internet www.mod-langs.ox.ac.uk/ssmll/; f. 1932; Editors Dr E. KENNEDY, Prof. N. PALMER, Dr C. SAUNDERS; publ. *Medium Ævum* (2 a year).

Society of Authors: 84 Drayton Gardens, London, SW10 9SB; tel. (20) 7373-6642; fax (20) 7373-5768; e-mail authorsoc@writers.org .uk; internet www.writers.org.uk/society; f. 1884 to promote and protect the rights of authors in all the media; 6,800 mems; Gen. Sec. MARK LE FANU; publ. *The Author* (quarterly).

Wells, H. G., Society: c/o Dr S. McLean, 56 Riseholme Rd, Gainsborough, Lincolnshire DN21 1YT; internet hgwellsusa.50megs.com; f. 1960 to promote an interest in and an appreciation of the life, work and thought of H. G. Wells; 200 mems; library of 300 vols (H. G. Wells Collection, Library, London Metropolitan University—North London campus); Sec. Dr STEVE MCLEAN; publs *Newsletter* (3 a year), *The Wellsian* (annually).

MEDICINE

Academy of Medical Sciences: 10 Carlton House Terrace, London, SW1Y 5AH; tel. (20) 7969-5288; fax (20) 7969-5298; e-mail apollo@acmedsci.ac.uk; internet www .acmedsci.ac.uk; f. 1998; 763 mems; Pres. Sir KEITH PETERS; Exec. Dir MARY MANNING.

Anatomical Society of Great Britain and Ireland: Anatomy Dept, Windle Bldg, University College, Cork City, Ireland; tel. (21) 902115; e-mail j.fraher@ucc.ie; internet www .anatsoc.org.uk; f. 1887; 700 mems; Pres. Prof. B. MOXHAM; Hon. Sec. Prof. J. FRAHER; publs *Journal of Anatomy* (monthly), *Aging Cell*.

Apothecaries of London, Worshipful Society of: Apothecaries' Hall, Black Friars Lane, London, EC4V 6EJ; tel. (20) 7236-1180; fax (20) 7329-3177; e-mail examoffice@ apothecaries.org; internet www.apothecaries .org; f. 1617 by King James I; grants a registrable medical qualification (LMSSA Lond.), also the post-graduate diplomas in Medical Jurisprudence (DMJ), in Genitourinary Medicine (DipGUM), HIV Medicine (DipHIV), the History of Medicine (DHMSA), Philosophy of Medicine (DPMSA), Musculo Skeletal Medicine (DMSM), Medical Care of Catastrophes (DMCC), Clinical Pharmacology (DCPSA), Forensic Medical Sciences (DFMS); Forensic Human Identification (DFIIID); Mastership in Medical Jurisprudence (MMJ); 1,600 mems; Master Sir WILLIAM SHAND; Clerk ANDREW WALLINGTON-SMITH; Registrar KIM EDMUNDS.

Association for the Study of Medical Education: 12 Queen St, Edinburgh, EH2 1JE; tel. (131) 225-9111; fax (131) 225-9444; e-mail info@asme.org.uk; internet www .asme.org.uk; f. 1957 to exchange information and promote research into medical education; 1,200 individual mems, 85 corporate mems; Pres. Prof. Sir KENNETH CALMAN; Chair Prof. GRAHAM BUCKLEY; Chief Exec. Prof. FRANK SMITH; publs *Bulletin* (6 a year), *Medical Education* (monthly), *The Clinical Teacher* (2 a year), *Annual Report*.

Association of Anaesthetists of Great Britain and Ireland: 21 Portland Place, London, W1B 1PY; tel. (20) 7631-8801; e-mail info@aagbi.org; internet www.aagbi.org; f. 1932 to promote the development and study of anaesthetics and their administration and to maintain the high standard of this branch of medicine; 7,000 mems; Pres. Prof. LEO STRUNIN; Hon. Sec. Dr ROBERT BUCKLAND; publs *Anaesthesia* (monthly), *Anaesthesia News* (monthly).

Association of British Neurologists:; tel. (20) 7405-4060; fax (20) 7405-4070; e-mail info@theabn.org; internet www.theabn.org; f. 1933 to support neurologists and neurological trainees in their clinical practice and research, and advance the understanding of the nervous system and its disorders; 1,139 mems; Pres. Prof. DAVID CHADWICK; Hon. Sec. Dr DAVID BATEMAN.

Association of Surgeons of Great Britain and Ireland: c/o The Royal College of Surgeons, 35–43 Lincoln's Inn Fields, London, WC2A 3PN; tel. (20) 7973-0300; fax (20) 7430-9235; e-mail admin@asgbi.org.uk; internet www.asgbi.org.uk; f. 1920 for the advancement of the science and art of surgery; Pres. DENIS C. WILKINS; Hon. Sec. JONATHAN K. PYE.

British Association of Plastic Surgeons: c/o The Royal College of Surgeons, 35–43 Lincoln's Inn Fields, London WC2A 3PE; tel. (20) 7831-5161; fax (20) 7831-4041; e-mail secretariat@baps.co.uk; internet www.baps .co.uk; f. 1946 to protect and preserve public health by the promotion and development of plastic surgery; Pres. M. A. P. MILLING; Hon. Sec. C. M. CADDY; publ. *British Journal of Plastic Surgery* (8 a year).

British Association for Sexual Health and HIV: c/o Simon Croker, RSM, 1 Wimpole St, London, W1G 0AE; tel. (20) 7290-2968; fax (20) 7290-2989; f. 1922 as Medical Society for the Study of Venereal Diseases, to study sexually transmitted and allied diseases, incl., more recently,HIV/AIDS; 900 mems; Pres. Dr SIMON BARTON; Hon. Sec. Dr KEITH RADCLIFFE; publ. *Sexually Transmitted Infections* (6 a year).

British Dental Association: 64 Wimpole St, London, W1G 8YS; tel. (20) 7935-0875; fax (20) 7487-5232; e-mail enquiries@bda .org; internet www.bda.org; f. 1880 as a professional asscn and subsequently became the trade union for the dental profession; 20,000 mems, 3,500 student numbers; library of 10,000 vols; Chief Exec. Dr P. WARD; publ. *British Dental Journal* (every 2 weeks).

British Dietetic Association: 5th Fl., Charles House, 148–9 Great Charles St Queensway, Birmingham, B3 3HT; tel. (121) 200-8080; e-mail info@bda.uk.com; internet www.bda.uk.com; f. 1936; 5,000 mems; Chair. SUSAN JONES; Sec. LORETTA COX; publ. *Journal of Human Nutrition and Dietetics* (every 2 months).

British Geriatrics Society: 31 St John's Square, London EC1M 4DN; tel. (20) 7608-1369; fax (20) 7608-1041; e-mail info@bgs.org .uk; internet www.bgs.org.uk; f. 1947 to improve standards of medical care for elderly patients and to encourage research in the problems of old age; 2,000 mems; Chief Exec. ALEX MAIR; publ. *Age and Ageing*.

British Institute of Radiology: 36 Portland Place, London, W1B 1AT; tel. (20) 7307-1400; fax (20) 7307-1414; e-mail admin@bir .org.uk; internet www.bir.org.uk; f. 1897; a centre for consultation on the medical, physical and biological applications of radiology; current and historic radiological library; 1,700 mems; Pres. PETER SHARPE; Gen. Sec. TONY HUDSON; publs *The British Journal of Radiology* (monthly), *Imaging* (4 a year).

British Medical Association: BMA House, Tavistock Square, London, WC1H 9JP; tel. (20) 7387-4499; fax (20) 7383-6400; e-mail info.web@bma.org.uk; internet www.bma.org .uk; f. 1832; voluntary professional association for doctors; scientific and educational body, publisher of the British Medical Journal and provides services for members; 137,000 mems; library: see Libraries and Archives; Pres. Prof. ANTHONY KUMAR; Chair. JAMES JOHNSON; publs *BMA News* (weekly), *British Medical Journal* (weekly), and numerous journals on specialized medical subjects.

British Nutrition Foundation: High Holborn House, 52–54 High Holborn, London, WC1V 6RQ; tel. (20) 7404-6504; fax (20) 7404-6747; e-mail postbox@nutrition.org.uk; internet www.nutrition.org.uk; f. 1967; Hon. Pres. Prof. Dame BARBARA CLAYTON; Dir-Gen. Prof. R. S. PICKARD; Sec. P. D. LEIGH; publ. *Bulletin* (4 a year).

British Orthodontic Society: c/o David Barnett, BOS Office, Eastman Dental Hospital, Grays Inn Rd, London, WC1X 8LD; tel. and fax (20) 7837-2193; internet www.bos.org .uk; f. 1994; Chair. W. G. WEBB; Sec. D. C. TIDY; publ. *British Journal of Orthodontics* (quarterly).

British Orthopaedic Association: c/o The Royal College of Surgeons, 35-43 Lincoln's Inn Fields, London, WC2A 3PN; tel. (20) 7405-6507; fax (20) 7831-2676; e-mail secretary@boa.ac.uk; internet www.boa.ac .uk; f. 1918; the advancement of the science and art of orthopaedic surgery; 3,486 mems; Pres. C. S. B. GALASKO, Hon. Sec. N. J. FIDDIAN; Chief Exec. D. C. ADAMS; publ. *Journal of Bone and Joint Surgery*.

British Pharmacological Society: 16 Angel Gate, City Rd, London, EC1V 2SG; tel. (20) 7417-0113; fax (20) 7417-0114; e-mail sjs@bps.ac.uk; internet www.bps.ac .uk; f. 1931; 2,500 mems; Exec. Officer S.-J. STAGG; publs *British Journal of Pharmacology* (2 a month), *British Journal of Clinical Pharmacology* (monthly).

British Psycho-Analytical Society: 114 Shirland Rd, London, W9 2EQ; tel. (20) 7563-5000; fax (20) 7563-5001; e-mail bpasadmin@ compuserve.com; internet www .psychoanalysis.org.uk; f. 1919 for the advancement of psychoanalysis as a science; 400 mems; library of 50,000 vols; Pres. D. CAMPBELL; Hon. Sec. C. POLMEAR; publ. *The International Journal of Psycho-Analysis* (every 2 months).

British Society for Research on Ageing: c/o Dr Sian Henson, University College London, 46 Cleveland St, London, W1T 4JF; e-mail web@brsa.org; internet www.bsra.org .uk; f. 1945 to encourage gerontological research in Great Britain by acting as a forum for the report and discussion of new advances in ageing research; open to all who are engaged in experimental gerontology; Chair. Prof. JANET LORD; Sec. Dr SIAN HENSON; publs *Mechanisms of Ageing and Development*, *Lifespan* (2 a year).

British Society for Rheumatology: Bride House, 18–20 Bride Lane, London, EC4Y 8EE; tel. (20) 7842-0900; fax (20) 7842-0901; e-mail bsr@rheumatology.org.uk; internet www.rheumatology.org.uk; f. 1984 to promote the devt of rheumatology and scientific knowledge of musculo-skeletal diseases; 1,400 mems; Pres. Dr ANDREW BAMJI; Exec. Sec. S. PETERS; publ. *Rheumatology*.

British Society of Gastroenterology: 3 St Andrews Pl., Regent's Park, London, NW1 4LB; tel. (20) 7935-3150; fax (20) 7487-3734;

e-mail bsg@mailbox.ulcc.ac.uk; internet www.bsg.org.uk; f. 1937; 3,000 mems; Pres. Prof. MIKE FARTHING; Sec. Dr A. HARRIS; publ. *Gut* (monthly).

Central Council of Physical Recreation: Francis House, Francis St, London, SW1P 1DE; tel. (20) 7854-8500; fax (20) 7854-8501; e-mail info@ccpr.org.uk; internet www.ccpr.org.uk; f. 1935 to formulate and promote measures to improve and develop sport and physical recreation; Pres. HRH THE PRINCE PHILIP, DUKE OF EDINBURGH; Chair. of Exec. Cttee HOWARD WELLS; publ. *Annual Report.*

Chartered Society of Physiotherapy: 14 Bedford Row, London, WC1R 4ED; tel. (20) 7306-6666; fax (20) 7306-6611; e-mail enquiries@csp.org.uk; internet www.csp.org.uk; f. 1894, inc. by Royal Charter 1920; professional, educational and trade union body for chartered physiotherapists and physiotherapy students in the UK; 47,000 mems; Pres. Baroness ILORA FINLAY OF LLANDAFF; Chief Exec. PHIL GRAY; publs *Physiotherapy Frontline* (2 a month), *Physiotherapy Journal* (monthly).

College of Optometrists: 42 Craven St, London, WC2N 5NG; tel. (20) 7839-6000; fax (20) 7839-6800; e-mail optometry@college-optometrists.org; internet www.college-optometrists.org; f. 1980 (by The British Optical Association, The Scottish Association of Opticians and The Worshipful Company of Spectacle Makers) for the improvement and conservation of human vision; also includes a library and museum; 10,968 mems; library of 7,000 vols; Pres. KEVIN LEWIS; Sec. BRYONY PAWINSKA; publ. *Ophthalmic and Physiological Optics* (on-line, 6 a year).

Diabetes UK: 10 Parkway, London, NW1 7AA; tel. (20) 7424-1000; fax (20) 7424-1001; e-mail info@diabetes.org.uk; internet www.diabetes.org.uk; f. 1934 to help all people with diabetes and those interested in diabetes, to promote greater public understanding of the condition and to support research into diabetes; 190,000 mems; Chair. of Board of Trustees Sir MICHAEL HIRST; Chief Exec. PAUL STREETS; publs *Balance Magazine* (6 a year), *Diabetes Update* (4 a year), *Diabetic Medicine* (10 a year), *Balance for Beginners* (updated annually).

Harveian Society of London: 11 Chandos St, London, W19 9EB; tel. (20) 7580-1043; f. 1831 to promote the advance of medical science; 448 mems; Pres. Prof. ROBERT DOUGLAS; Hon. Sec. Prof. JOHN WALKER-SMITH; Exec. Sec. Col R. D. KINSELLA-BEVAN.

Institute of Biomedical Science: 12 Coldbath Square, London, EC1R 5HL; tel. (20) 7713-0214; fax (20) 7436-4946; e-mail mail@ibms.org; internet www.ibms.org; f. 1912; promotes and develops biomedical science and its practitioners, and establishes and maintains professional standards; 16,000 mems; Chief Exec. ALAN R. POTTER; publs *British Journal of Biomedical Science* (quarterly), *The Biomedical Scientist* (monthly).

Medical Society of London: Lettsom Ho., 11 Chandos St, London, W1M 0EB; tel. (20) 7580-1043; f. 1773; 558 mems; library of 4,500 vols; Pres. MICHAEL PUGH; Senior Sec. Maj.-Gen. LOUIS LILLYWHITE; publ. *Transactions* (annually).

MIND: Granta House, 15–19 Broadway, London, E15 4BQ; tel. (20) 8519-2122; fax (20) 8522-1725; e-mail contact@mind.org.uk; internet www.mind.org.uk; f. 1946; charity which works for a better life for people with experience of mental distress; 1,600 mems, 210 local asscns, 7 regional offices; Chair. DAVID PERYER; Chief Exec. RICHARD BROOK; publ. *OPENMind* (6 a year).

Nutrition Society: 10 Cambridge Court, 210 Shepherds Bush Rd, London, W6 7NJ; tel. (20) 7602-0228; fax (20) 7602-1756; e-mail office@nutsoc.org.uk; internet www.nutritionsociety.org.uk; f. 1941 to advance the scientific study of nutrition and its application to the maintenance of human and animal health; over 2,200 mems; Pres. Prof. J. C. MATHERS; publs *Proceedings* (6 a year), *British Journal of Nutrition* (monthly), *Public Health Nutrition* (8 a year), *Nutrition Research Reviews* (2 a year).

Pathological Society of Great Britain and Ireland: 2 Carlton House Terrace, London, SW1Y 5AF; tel. (20) 7976-1260; fax (20) 7976-1267; e-mail administrator@pathsoc.org.uk; internet www.pathsoc.org.uk; f. 1906; 1,500 mems; Chair. Prof. F. WALKER; Meetings Secs Prof. M. WELLS, Dr C. G. GEMMELL; publs *Journal of Pathology*, *Journal of Medical Microbiology*, *Reviews in Medical Microbiology*.

Royal Association for Disability and Rehabilitation: 12 City Forum, 250 City Rd, London, EC1V 8AF; tel. (20) 7250-3222; fax (20) 7250-0212; e-mail radar@radar.org.uk; internet www.radar.org.uk; f. 1977; covers the whole field of disability; a co-ordinating organization concerned with the needs and rights of disabled people; Dir KATE NASH.

Royal College of Anaesthetists: Churchill House, 35 Red Lion Sq., London, WC1R 4SG; tel. (20) 7092-1500; fax (20) 7092-1730; e-mail info@rcoa.ac.uk; internet www.rcoa.ac.uk; f. 1948; responsible for the science of anaesthesia throughout the United Kingdom and for ensuring the quality of patient care through the maintenance of standards in anaesthesia, critical care and pain management; 13,500 fellows, mems and trainees; Pres. Dr JUDITH HULF; publs *British Journal of Anaesthesia* (monthly), *Bulletin* (6 a year).

Royal College of General Practitioners: 14 Princes Gate, London, SW7 1PU; tel. (20) 7581-3232; fax (20) 7225-3047; e-mail info@rcpg.org.uk; internet www.rcgp.org.uk; f. 1952 to ensure the highest possible standards in general medical practice; 21,000 mems; Chair. Dr MAYUR LAKHANI; Hon. Sec. Dr MAUREEN BAKER; publ. *British Journal of General Practice* (monthly).

Royal College of Nursing of the United Kingdom: 20 Cavendish Square, London, W1M 0AB; tel. (20) 7409-3333; fax (20) 7355-1379; internet www.rcn.org.uk; f. 1916 to represent the interests of nurses and advance the provision of healthcare generally; library of 60,000 vols; Pres. SYLVIA DENTON; publ. *Nursing Standard* (weekly).

Royal College of Obstetricians and Gynaecologists: 27 Sussex Place, Regent's Park, London, NW1 4RG; tel. (20) 7772-6200; fax (20) 7723-0575; e-mail coll.sec@rcog.org.uk; internet www.rcog.org.uk; f. 1929; 10,705 mems; library of 11,000 vols; Pres. Prof. ALLAN TEMPLETON; College Administrator P. A. BARNETT; publs *British Journal of Obstetrics and Gynaecology* (monthly), *The Obstetrician and Gynaecologist* (4 a year).

Royal College of Ophthalmologists: 17 Cornwall Terrace, London, NW1 4QW; tel. (20) 7935-0702; fax (20) 7935-9838; internet www.rcophth.ac.uk; f. 1988 for the cultivation and promotion of ophthalmology; 3,200 mems; Pres. ALLAN TEMPLETON; Hon. Sec. BRENDA BILLINGTON; publ. *Eye* (6 a year).

Royal College of Paediatrics and Child Health: 50 Hallam St, London, W1W 6DE; tel. (20) 7307-5600; fax (20) 7307-5601; e-mail enquiries@rcpch.ac.uk; internet www.rcpch.ac.uk; f. 1928 to advance for the benefit of the public, education in paediatrics and to relieve sickness by promoting the

improvement of paediatric practice; 7,800 mems; Pres. Prof. ALAN CRAFT; Registrar Dr SHEILA SHRIBMAN; publ. *Archives of Disease in Childhood* (monthly, with British Medical Association).

Royal College of Pathologists: 2 Carlton House Terrace, London, SW1Y 5AF; tel. (20) 7451-6700; fax (20) 7451-6701; e-mail info@rcpath.org; internet www.rcpath.org; f. 1962; 7,500 fellows and mems; library of 2,100 vols (spec. colln); Pres. Prof. ADRIAN NEWLAND; Chief Exec. DANIEL ROSS; publ. *Bulletin* (quarterly).

Royal College of Physicians: 11 St Andrews Pl., London, NW1 4LE; tel. (20) 7224-1539; fax (20) 7487-5218; e-mail infocentre@rcplondon.ac.uk; internet www.rcplondon.ac.uk; f. 1518; aims to promote the values of the medical profession, improve standards of clinical practice, support physicians in their practice of medicine through education and training, communicate with govt, the public and the profession and provide leadership on health and healthcare issues; 22,000 mems (13,000 fellows, 9,000 collegiate members); library: see Libraries and Archives; Pres. Prof. I. GILMORE; Registrar Prof. R. BURNHAM; Sec. M. ELSE; publ. *Clinical Medicine* (6 a year).

Royal College of Physicians and Surgeons of Glasgow: 232–242 St Vincent St, Glasgow, G2 5RJ; tel. (141) 221-6072; fax (141) 221-1804; e-mail registrar@rcpsglasg.ac.uk; internet www.rcpsglasg.ac.uk; f. 1599; a medical licensing corporation; 7,298 Fellows and Members in medicine, surgery and dentistry; library: see Libraries and Archives; Pres. Prof. G. TEASDALE; Hon. Sec. Dr K. PATERSON.

Royal College of Physicians of Edinburgh: 9 Queen St, Edinburgh, EH2 1JQ; tel. (131) 225-7324; fax (131) 220-3939; internet www.rcpe.ac.uk; f. 1681; 7,000 mems; library: see Libraries and Archives; Pres. Prof. N. J. DOUGLAS; Sec. Dr J. COLLINS; publ. *Journal* (quarterly).

Royal College of Psychiatrists: 17 Belgrave Square, London, SW1X 8PG; tel. (20) 7235-2351; fax (20) 7245-1231; e-mail rcpsych@rcpsych.ac.uk; internet www.rcpsych.ac.uk; f. 1971 by Charter, previously Royal Medico-Psychological Association; 8,000 Fellows and mems; Pres. Dr M. SHOOTER; Registrar Dr A. FAIRBAIRN; Chief Exec. Mrs V. CAMERON; publs *British Journal of Psychiatry* (monthly), *Psychiatric Bulletin* (monthly), *Advances in Psychiatric Treatment* (6 a year).

Royal College of Radiologists: 38 Portland Place, London, W1B 1JQ; tel. (20) 7636-4432; fax (20) 7323-3100; e-mail enquiries@rcr.ac.uk; internet www.rcr.ac.uk; f. 1939; practice of radiology and oncology; 6,600 mems; Chief Exec. ANDREW HALL; publs *Clinical Radiology* (monthly), *Clinical Oncology* (8 a year).

Royal College of Surgeons of Edinburgh: Nicolson St, Edinburgh, EH8 9DW; tel. (131) 527-1600; fax (131) 557-6406; e-mail information@rcsed.ac.uk; internet www.rcsed.ac.uk; f. 1505; postgraduate education and assessment in surgery; 15,000 Fellows; Pres. J. A. R. SMITH; Chief Exec. J. R. C. FOSTER; publs *The Surgeon* (6 a year), *Surgeon News* (4 a year).

Royal College of Surgeons of England: 35–43 Lincoln's Inn Fields, London, WC2A 3PE; tel. (20) 7405-3474; fax (20) 7831-9438; internet www.rcseng.ac.uk; f. 1800; supervises training of surgeons in approved posts; provides educational and practical workshops for surgeons and other medical professionals; promotes surgical research; 14,300 fellows and mems; library: c. 100,000 vols;

Pres. BERNARD RIBEIRO; publs *Annals* (8 a year), *Bulletin* (monthly, except August and December).

Royal Institute of Public Health: 28 Portland Place, London, W1B 1DE; tel. (20) 7580-2731; fax (20) 7580-6157; e-mail info@riphh.org.uk; internet www.riphh.org.uk; f. 1898; 3,000 mems; Chief Exec. NICHOLA WILKINS; publs *Health and Hygiene* (quarterly), *Public Health* (6 a year).

Royal Medical Society: Students' Centre, Bristo Sq., Edinburgh, EH8 9AL; tel. (131) 650-2672; e-mail enquiries@royalmedicalsociety.co.uk; internet www.royalmedicalsociety.co.uk; f. 1737; 2,000 mems; library of 2,000 vols; Pres. HANNAH BECKWITH; Sec. ANDREW MOOREHEAD; publ. *Res Medica* (2 a year).

Royal Pharmaceutical Society of Great Britain: 1 Lambeth High St, London, SE1 7JN; tel. (20) 7735-9141; fax (20) 7735-7629; e-mail enquiries@rpsgb.org; internet www.rpsgb.org; f. 1841; 45,439 mems (1,284 fellows, 40,676 mems); library of 80,000 vols, pamphlets and MSS, 300 journals; Pres. HEMANT PATEL; Sec. and Registrar A. M. LEWIS; publs *Annual Register of Pharmaceutical Chemists*, *British National Formulary* (published jointly with the British Medical Association), *The Hospital Pharmacist* (6 a year), *The International Journal of Pharmacy Practice* (quarterly), *Journal of Pharmacy and Pharmacology* (monthly), *Martindale: The Extra Pharmacopoeia*, *Medicines and Ethics*, *Pharmaceutical Codex*, *The Pharmaceutical Journal* (weekly), *Pharmaceutical Sciences* (monthly).

Royal Society for the Promotion of Health: 38A St George's Drive, London, SW1V 4BH; tel. (20) 7630-0121; fax (20) 7976-6847; e-mail rsph@rsph.org; internet www.rsph.org; f. 1876 for the protection and preservation of health and the advancement of health-related sciences; an examining body for food hygiene and other health-related examinations; holds conferences, lectures; 5,000 mems; Patron HM THE QUEEN; Chief Exec. ANDREW BARFIELD (acting); publ. *Journal of the Royal Society for the Promotion of Health* (6 a year).

Royal Society of Medicine: 1 Wimpole St, London, W1G 0AE; tel. (20) 7290-2900; fax (20) 7290-2992; e-mail membership@rsm.ac.uk; internet www.rsm.ac.uk; f. 1805, first Royal Charter 1834; 55 Sections covering the field of medicine and surgery; publishes own material, journals for other orgs and proceedings of sponsored meetings; postgraduate medical library; 20,000 mems world-wide; library: see Libraries and Archives; Pres. Prof. Baroness ILORA FINLAY OF LLANDAFF; publs *Journal of Integrated Care Pathways* (3 a year), *Journal of Health Services Research and Policy* (online, quarterly), *Journal of Medical Biography* (quarterly), *Journal of Telemedicine and Telecare* (online, 6 a year), *Laboratory Animals* (online, quarterly), *Health Information on the Internet* (online, 6 a year), *Handbook of Practice Management* (online, quarterly), *Clinical Risk* (online, 6 a year), *Annals of Clinical Biochemistry* (online, 6 a year), *Clinical Governance Bulletin* (6 a year, also online), *Journal of the Royal Society of Medicine* (monthly, also online), *Tropical Doctor* (quarterly), *International Journal of STD and AIDS* (monthly, also online), *Journal of Laryngology and Otology* (monthly, also online), *Aids and Hepatitis Digest* (6 a year), *Effective Health Care* (6 a year, also online), *Journal of Medical Screening* (quarterly, also online), *Phlebology* (quarterly, also online), *Health Services Management Research* (quarterly,

also online), *Journal of the British Menopause Society* (quarterly, also online).

Royal Society of Tropical Medicine and Hygiene: 50 Bedford Sq., London, WC1B 3DP; tel. (20) 7580-2127; fax (20) 7436-1389; e-mail mail@rstmh.org; internet www.rstmh.org; f. 1907 to promote and advance the study, control and prevention of disease in humankind and other mammals in warm climates, and to facilitate the discussion and exchange of information among those interested in tropical diseases; 2,000 mems; Pres. Prof. D. H. MOLYNEUX; Hon. Secs Prof. G. PASVOL, Dr J. R. STOTHARD; publs *Transactions* (monthly), *Year Book* (every 2 years).

St John's Hospital Dermatological Society: St John's Institute of Dermatology, St Thomas' Hospital, Lambeth Palace Rd, London, SE1 7EH; tel. (20) 7188-6404; meeting at St John's Hospital for Diseases of the Skin; f. 1911 to promote the knowledge and study of dermatology by presentation and discussion of rare and interesting cases; 250 Fellows; Pres. Dr CHARLES DARLEY; Hon. Sec. Dr NEIL WALKER; publ. *Clinical and Experimental Dermatology* (every 2 months).

Society for Endocrinology: 17/18 The Courtyard, Woodlands, Bradley Stoke, Bristol, BS32 4NQ; tel. (1454) 642200; fax (1454) 642222; e-mail info@endocrinology.org; internet www.endrocrinology.org; f. 1939 to promote the advancement of public education in endocrinology; 1,900 mems; Chair. S. FRANKS; publs *Journal of Endocrinology* (monthly), *Journal of Molecular Endocrinology* (every 2 months), *The Endocrinologist* (4 a year), *Endocrine-Related Cancer* (4 a year).

Society of British Neurological Surgeons: c/o Suzanne Murray, 35–43 Lincoln's Inn Fields, London, WC2A 3PE; tel. (20) 7869-6892; fax (20) 7869-6890; e-mail admin@sbns.freeserve.co.uk; internet www.sbns.org.uk; f. 1926; promotes high standards of professional practice through the Soc's involvement in the education and the examination of neurosurgeons and through its meetings and associated activities in the continual professional devt of neurosurgeons; 384 mems; Pres. Prof. JOHN PICKARD; Hon. Sec. PHILIP VAN HILLE; publ. *Proceedings* (in *British Journal of Neurosurgery*).

Society of Occupational Medicine: 6 St Andrew's Place, London, NW1 4LB; tel. (20) 7486-2641; fax (20) 7486-0028; e-mail admin@som.org.uk; internet www.som.org.uk; f. 1935; concerned with the protection of the health of people at work and the prevention of occupational diseases and injuries; stimulates research and education in occupational medicine; 2,000 mems; Pres. Dr G. PARKER; Hon. Sec. Dr E. S. WILKINSON; publ. *Occupational Medicine* (8 a year).

Stroke Association: 240 City Rd, London, EC1V 2PR; tel. (845) 303-3100; e-mail info@stroke.org.uk; internet www.stroke.org.uk; f. 1899, fmrly The Chest, Heart and Stroke Association; aims to provide practical support to people who have had strokes and to their families, through community services and welfare grants, and to prevent strokes through health education; Chair. of Council Prof. AVERIL MANSFIELD; Chief Exec. JON MERRICK; publ. *Stroke News* (quarterly).

Tavistock Institute of Medical Psychology: The Tavistock Centre, 120 Belsize Lane, London, NW3 5BA; tel. (20) 7435-7111; fax (20) 7435-1080; e-mail timp@tccr.org.uk; internet www.tccr.org.uk; f. 1929; promotes the study and practice of psychotherapy and provides grants for related small research projects; administers the Tavistock Centre for Couple Relationships, which offers a professional service to couples experiencing difficulty in relationships and trains counsel-

lors; and Relationship Counselling for London, which provides a counselling consultation service and trains counsellors; Chair. Dr A. OBHOLZER; Company Sec. D. OBADINA; publ. *In Brief* (annually).

NATURAL SCIENCES

General

Association for Science Education: College Lane, Hatfield, Herts., AL10 9AA; tel. (1707) 283000; fax (1707) 266532; e-mail membership@ase.org.uk; internet www.ase.org.uk; f. 1901; organizes meetings and workshops locally and nationally; aims to improve science teaching and to provide a medium of expression for science teachers; 21,000 mems; Chief Exec. Dr D. S. MOORE; publs *School Science Review* (quarterly), *Education in Science* (5 a year), *Primary Science Review* (5 a year), *Science Teacher Education* (3 a year).

British Association for the Advancement of Science: Wellcome Wolfson Bldg, 165 Queen's Gate, London, SW7 5HD; tel. (870) 770-7101; fax (870) 770-7102; e-mail info@the-ba.net; internet www.the-ba.net; f. 1831; promotes and advances public understanding and awareness of science and technology and their effect on society; 2,000 mems; Chief Exec. Dr ROLAND JACKSON; publ. *Science and Public Affairs* (quarterly).

British Society for the History of Science: 5 Woodcote Green, Fleet, Hants., GU51 4EY; tel. (1252) 641135; fax (1252) 641135; e-mail execsec@bshs.org.uk; internet www.bshs.org.uk; f. 1947; promotes and furthers the study of the history and philosophy of science, technology and medicine, organizes meetings and conferences; 750 mems; Exec. Sec. P. E. CRANE; publs *British Journal for the History of Science* (4 a year), *Viewpoint* (newsletter, 3 a year).

Cambridge Philosophical Society: Central Science Library, Arts School, Bene't St, Cambridge, CB2 3PY; tel. (1223) 334743; e-mail philosoc@hermes.cam.ac.uk; internet www.cam.ac.uk/societies/cps; f. 1819 to promote scientific enquiry and to facilitate the communication of facts connected with the advancement of science; 1,900 mems; Exec. Sec. B. LARNER; publs *Mathematical Proceedings* (6 a year), *Biological Reviews* (4 a year).

Council for Environmental Education: 94 London St, Reading, RG1 4SJ; tel. (118) 950-2550; fax (118) 959-1955; e-mail enquiries@cee.org.uk; internet www.cee.org.uk; f. 1968 to increase the effectiveness of the environmental education movement by developing and influencing policy and supporting and encouraging good practice; umbrella org. for national and associated orgs working in environmental and sustainable development education; library: reference library and resource centre; 84 mems; Dir LIBBY GRUNDY; publs *Earthlines* (3 a year), *CEEview* (4 a year), *CEEmail* (3 a year).

Environment Council: 212 High Holborn, London, WC1V 7BF; tel. (20) 7836-2626; fax (20) 7242-1180; e-mail info@envcouncil.org.uk; internet www.the-environment-council.org.uk; f. 1969, fmrly Ccl for Environmental Conservation; works with business, industry, government, non-governmental organizations and the community to find sustainable solutions to environmental problems; 2,000 mems; Chief Exec. STEVE ROBINSON; publ. *elements* (6 a year).

Field Studies Council: Preston Montford, Montford Bridge, Shrewsbury, SY4 1HW; tel. (1743) 852100; fax (1743) 852101; e-mail fsc.headoffice@field-studies-council.org; internet www.field-studies-council.org; f. 1943;

independent educational charity; operates 17 residential and day centres throughout the UK, offering a range of courses for schools and colleges; leisure learning and professional development courses are offered in the UK and overseas; provides outreach education, training and consultancy; publishes a number of titles to support is work, incl. identification guides; 4,000 mems; Pres. Prof. I. D. MERCER; Chair. Prof. T. P. BURT; Dir A. D. THOMAS; publ. *Annual Report*.

Foundation for Science and Technology: 10 Carlton House Terrace, London, SW1Y 5AH; tel. (20) 7321-2220; fax (20) 7321-2221; e-mail office@foundation.org.uk; internet www.foundation.org.uk; f. 1977; debates science, engineering, technology and medical science policy; Chief Exec. Dr DOUGAL GOODMAN; publ. *FST Journal* (quarterly).

Institution of Environmental Sciences: 1, 38 Ebury St, London, SW1W 0LU; tel. (20) 7730-5516; fax (20) 7730-5519; e-mail ies-uk@breathemail.net; internet www.ies-uk.org.uk; f. 1971 for consultation in matters of an environmental nature; aims to promote interdisciplinary studies of the environment, to diffuse information relating to environmental sciences at nat. and int. levels, and to bring together into a corporate professional body all persons throughout the world possessing responsibilities for environmental affairs; 820 individual mems, 7 collective mems; Chair. CAROLYN ROBERTS; Hon. Sec. J. R. BLUMHOF; publ. *The Environmental Scientist* (6 a year).

London Natural History Society: c/o Dr J. Edgington, 19 Mecklenburgh Sq., London, WC1N 2AD; tel. (20) 7837-7800; e-mail ugap136@aol.com; internet www.lnhs.org.uk; f. 1858 for the study of natural history, archaeology and related subjects, especially within a radius of 20 miles from St Paul's Cathedral; 1,250 mems; library of 3,000 vols; Asst Treasurer ROBIN BLADES; publs *The London Naturalist* (annually), *London Bird Report* (annually).

Royal Institution of Great Britain: 21 Albemarle St, London, W1S 4BS; tel. (20) 7409-2992; fax (20) 7629-3569; e-mail ri@ri.ac.uk; internet www.rigb.org; f. 1799; promotes science to the public through lectures and discussions; Davy Faraday Research Laboratory conducts research into the chemistry and physics of materials; active heritage dept; 3,200 mems; library: library: see Libraries and Archives; museum: see Museums and Art Galleries; Pres. HRH THE DUKE OF KENT; Sec. Prof. ALAN MARIES; Dir Prof. Baroness GREENFIELD; Dir of the Davy Faraday Research Laboratory Prof. C. R. A. CATLOW.

Scottish Field Studies Association: Kindrogan Field Centre, Enochdhu, Blairgowrie, Perthshire, PH10 7PG; tel. (1250) 881286; fax (1250) 881433; e-mail kindrogan@btinternet.com; internet www.kindrogan.com; f. 1945; provides residential courses and a venue for fieldwork in biology and geography; 400 mems; Chair. ROBIN NOBLE; publ. *Newsletter* (2 a year).

United Kingdom Science Park Association: Chesterford Research Park, Little Chesterford, Cambridge, CB10 1XL; tel. (1799) 532050; fax (1799) 532049; e-mail admin@ukspa.prestel.co.uk; internet www.ukspa.org.uk; f. 1984 to act as a forum for those concerned with the planning and management of science parks, and to promote awareness of science parks and provide information on their objectives and achievements; mems: 65 science parks; Chair. N. HALFORD; Sec. D. KIRBY; publs *Directory*, *The Development and Operation of Science Parks*.

Wildlife Trusts: The Kiln, Waterside, Mather Rd, Newark, NG24 1WT; tel. (1636) 677711; fax (1636) 670001; internet www.wildlife.org.uk; f. 1912 as Royal Society for Nature Conservation; inc. by Royal Charter 1916 and 1976, to promote the conservation of nature for study and research and to educate the public in the understanding and appreciation of nature, the awareness of its value and the need for its conservation; acts as the national office for the 46 Wildlife Trusts, Urban Wildlife Groups and Wildlife Watch (junior branch); 320,000 mems; Pres. Prof. DAVID BELLAMY; publs annual report, *Natural World* (3 a year).

Biological Sciences

Association for the Study of Animal Behaviour: c/o Prof. F. Huntingford, Graham Kerr Building, University of Glasgow, Glasgow, G12 8QQ; tel. (141) 330-6643; fax (141) 330-5971; e-mail gbza10@udcf.gla.ac.uk; internet www.societies.ncl.ac.uk/asab; f. 1936; 2,000 mems; Pres. Prof. F. HUNTINGFORD; Sec. Dr C. MAGNHAGEN; publ. *Animal Behaviour* (monthly).

Association of Applied Biologists: c/o Horticulture Research International, Wellesbourne, Warwick, CV35 9EF; tel. (1789) 470382 ext. 186; fax (1789) 470234; e-mail carol.aab@hri.ac.uk; internet www.aab.org.uk; f. 1904 to promote the study and advancement of all branches of biology, with special reference to their applied aspects; 1,000 mems; Pres. Prof. C. DUFFAS; Hon. Sec. M. MAY; publ. *Annals of Applied Biology* (every 2 months).

Biochemical Society: 3rd Fl., Eagle House, 16 Procter St, London, WC1V 6NX; tel. (20) 7280-4100; fax (20) 7280-4170; e-mail genadmin@biochemistry.org; internet www.biochemistry.org; f. 1911 for the advancement of the science of biochemistry; 8,000 mems; Chair. Prof. C. J. LEAVER; Chief Exec. Dr C. J. KIRK; publs *Biochemical Journal* (every 2 weeks), *Biochemical Society Transactions* (6 a year), *Clinical Science* (monthly), *Essays in Biochemistry* (2 a year), *Symposia* (annually), *The Biochemist* (6 a year), *Biology of the Cell* (on behalf of the Société de Biologie Cellulaire de France and the Société Française des Microscopies, 12 a year), *Biotechnology and Applied Biochemistry* (on behalf of the International Union of Biochemistry and Molecular Biology, 6 a year).

Biosciences Federation: 76 Portland Place, London, W1B 1NT; tel. (20) 7269 5711; e-mail info@bsf.ac.uk; internet www.bsf.ac.uk; An umbrella organisation for UK bioscientists, representing 27 independently-functioning societies and institutions; President Prof. C. P. DOWNES; Chief Executive Officer MIKE WITHNALL.

Botanical Society of Scotland: c/o Royal Botanic Garden Edinburgh, 20A Inverleith Row, Edinburgh, EH3 5LR; tel. (131) 552-7171; internet www.botsocscot.org.uk; f. 1836 (fmrly Botanical Soc. of Edinburgh); incorporates the Cryptogamic Soc. of Scotland; 300 mems and fellows; Pres. Prof. R. J. ABBOTT; Hon. Gen. Sec. Dr M. P. COCHRANE; publ. *Botanical Journal of Scotland* (2 a year).

Botanical Society of the British Isles: c/o Dept. of Botany, Natural History Museum, Cromwell Rd, London, SW7 5BD; tel. (20) 7942-5002; internet www.bsbi.org.uk; f. 1836 for study of British native flowering plants and ferns; exhibitions, conferences, field meetings; c. 2,800 mems; Hon. Gen. Sec. D. A. PEARMAN; publs *BSBI News* (3 a year), *Watsonia* (2 a year).

British Biophysical Society: c/o Dr R. Cooke, GlaxoSmithKline, New Frontiers Science Park, Third Avenue, Harlow, Essex, CM19 5AW; tel. (1279) 627981; fax (1279) 622790; e-mail Rob_M_Cooke@gsk.com; internet www.cryst.bbk.ac.uk/BBS/bbs.html; f. 1960; 800 mems; Sec. Dr R. COOKE.

British Ecological Society: 26 Blades Court, Deodar Rd, Putney, London, SW15 2NU; tel. (20) 8871-9797; fax (20) 8871-9779; e-mail general@ecology.demon.co.uk; internet www.britishecologicalsociety.org; f. 1913; 5,000 mems; Exec. Sec. Dr HAZEL J. NORMAN; publs *Symposium* (annually), *Journal of Ecology* (6 a year), *Journal of Animal Ecology* (6 a year), *Journal of Applied Ecology* (6 a year), *Functional Ecology* (6 a year).

British Lichen Society: C/o Dept of Botany, Natural History Museum, Cromwell Rd, London, SW7 5BD; tel. (20) 7942-5617; fax (20) 7942-5529; e-mail bls@nhm.ac.uk; internet www.thebls.org.uk; f. 1958; 600 mems; library of 500 vols, 5,000 reprints; Sec. P. A. WOLSELEY; publs *The Lichenologist* (6 a year), *Bulletin* (2 a year).

British Mycological Society: Joseph Banks Building, Royal Botanic Gardens, Kew, Richmond, Surrey, TW9 3AB; tel. (23) 9284-2024; fax (23) 9252-5902; e-mail info@britmycolsoc.org.uk; internet www.britmycolsoc.org.uk; f. 1896; promotion of mycology through scientific meetings, publications and education; 1,206 mems and 644 assocs; Pres. Prof. GEOFF GADD; Gen. Sec. Dr GEOFFREY D. ROBSON; publs *Field Mycology* (4 a year), *Mycological Research* (monthly), *Mycologist* (4 a year).

British Ornithologists' Union: Department of Zoology, University of Oxford, South Parks Rd, Oxford, OX1 3PS; tel. and fax (1865) 8281842; e-mail bou@bou.org.uk; internet www.bou.org.uk; f. 1858 for the advancement of the science of ornithology; 1,800 ordinary mems, plus hon. mems and corresp. mems; Pres. Prof. C. M. PERRINS; Hon. Sec. N. J. BUCKNELL; publ. *Ibis* (quarterly).

British Society for Plant Pathology: Marlborough House, Basingstoke Rd, Spencers Wood, Reading, Berks., RG7 1AG; e-mail secretary@bspp.org.uk; internet www.bspp.org.uk; f. 1981; 650 mems; Pres. Prof. PETER MILLS; Sec. BILL RENNIE; publs *Molecular Plant Pathology* (every 2 months), *New Disease Reports* (quarterly), *Plant Pathology* (every 2 months), *BSPP News* (quarterly).

British Trust for Ornithology: The Nunnery, Thetford, Norfolk, IP24 2PU; tel. (1842) 750050; fax (1842) 750030; e-mail bto.staff@bto.org; internet www.bto.org; f. 1933; promotes and encourages the wider understanding, appreciation and conservation of birds through scientific studies using the combined skills and enthusiasm of its members, other bird watchers and staff; projects include Nat. Bird Ringing Scheme, Nest Records Scheme, Wetland Bird Survey, Breeding Bird Survey, Garden Bird Watch; offers advisory services to ecologists, land use planners, conservationists, developers; 13,000 mems; library: library; Pres. Baroness YOUNG OF OLD SCONE; Dir Dr F. A. CLEMENTS; publs *BTO News* (6 a year), *Bird Study* (3 a year), *Ringing and Migration* (2 a year), *Bird Table* (quarterly).

Fauna and Flora International: Great Eastern House, Tenison Rd, Cambridge, CB1 2DT; tel. (1223) 571000; fax (1223) 461481; e-mail info@fauna-flora.org; internet www.fauna-flora.org; f. 1903; world's oldest international wildlife conservation society working to save endangered species from extinction; especially concerned with the prevention of illegal trade; publishes information and news about wildlife conservation throughout the world; c. 5,000 mems;

Chair. RONALD HAYCOCK; publ. *Oryx* (quarterly).

Freshwater Biological Association: The Ferry House, Ambleside, Cumbria, LA22 0LP; tel. (15394) 42468; fax (15394) 46914; e-mail info@fba.org.uk; internet www.fba.org.uk; f. 1929 to promote the investigation of the biology of animals and plants found in fresh (including brackish) water; River Laboratory, East Stoke, Wareham, Dorset sited on River Frome; Ferry House Laboratory on shores of Windermere, Cumbria; 1,650 mems; library of 150,000 books and reprints, 10,000 vols. of scientific periodicals; Pres. Sir MARTIN HOLDGATE; Chair. of Council Prof. A. G. HILDREW; Sec. and Dir Dr R. A. SWEETING; publs *FBA News* (4 a year), *Freshwater Forum* (2 a year).

Genetics Society: c/o Jayne Richards, Roslin Institute, Roslin, Midlothian, EH25 9PS; tel. (131) 200-6391; fax (131) 200-6401; e-mail mail@genetics.org.uk; internet www.genetics.org.uk; f. 1919; all aspects of genetics, pure and applied; 2,000 mems; Pres. Prof. JONATHAN HODGKIN; Hon. Sec. Dr JOHN ARMOUR; publs *Genes and Development* (every 2 weeks), *Genetics Society News* (monthly), *Heredity* (monthly).

Institute of Biology: 20–22 Queensberry Place, London, SW7 2DZ; tel. (20) 7581-8333; fax (20) 7823-9409; e-mail info@iob.org; internet www.iob.org; f. 1950 to advance the science and practice of biology; 18 regional brs; 70 affiliated socs; 15,000 mems; Pres. Dr. NANCY LANE; Chief Exec. Prof. A. D. B. MALCOLM; publs *Biologist*, *Journal of Biological Education*.

Linnean Society of London: Burlington House, Piccadilly, London, W1J 0BF; tel. (20) 7434-4479; fax (20) 7287-9364; e-mail adrian@linnean.org; internet www.linnean.org; f. 1788; possesses the unique colln of Linnaeus's plants and animals and other collns; 2,100 Fellows, incl. 50 Foreign Members and 20 Hon. Fellows, 20 Associates (under the age of 30) and 6 Student Associates (under the age of 25); library: see Libraries; Exec. Sec. ADRIAN THOMAS; Hon. Pres. Prof. G. MCGREGOR REID; Hon. Sec. (Botany) Dr J. R. EDMONDSON; Hon. Sec. (Zoology) Dr V. R. SOUTHGATE; Hon. Sec. (Editorial) Dr D. F. CUTLER; publs *Annual Report* (annually), *Botanical Journal* (monthly), *Biological Journal* (monthly), *Zoological Journal* (monthly), *The Linnean Newsletter and Proceedings* (4 a year), *Synopses of the British Fauna* (irregular), *Symposium* (volumes).

Malacological Society of London: c/o Dr V. Flari, Cental Science Laboratory, Sand Hutton, York, YO4 1LZ; tel. (1904) 462349; e-mail vasiliki@flari.fsnet.co.uk; internet www.malacsoc.org.uk; f. 1893 to promote all aspects of the study of Mollusca; library: Radley Library deposited at University College London; 300 mems; Hon. Sec. Dr VASILIKI FLARI; publs *Journal of Molluscan Studies* (quarterly), *The Malacologist* (bulletin of the Society, 3 a year).

Marine Biological Association of the United Kingdom: The Laboratory, Citadel Hill, Plymouth, Devon, PL1 2PB; tel. (1752) 633207; fax (1752) 633102; e-mail sec@mba.ac.uk; internet www.mba.ac.uk; f. 1884 to promote scientific research into all aspects of life in the sea and to make public the results; the Asscn receives grants from univs, research charities and other public bodies and an annual grant-in-aid from the Natural Environment Research Council; 1,250 mems; library: National Marine Biological Library; 60,000 vols; Pres. Sir NEIL CHALMERS; Sec. and Dir Prof. STEPHEN J. HAWKINS; publs

Journal (6 a year), *MBA News* (2 a year), *JMBA Global* (2 a year).

Physiological Society: POB 11319, London, WC1E 7JF; tel. (20) 7631-1458; fax (20) 7631-1462; e-mail admin@physoc.org; internet www.physoc.org; f. 1876 to promote the advancement of physiology and facilitate communication between physiologists at home and abroad; 1,795 mems; Chief Exec. ESTHER WILLIAMS; publs *The Journal of Physiology* (monthly), *Experimental Physiology* (6 a year), *The Physiological Society Magazine* (4 a year).

Ray Society: c/o Natural History Museum, Cromwell Rd, London, SW7 5BD; tel. (20) 7942-5653; e-mail a.polaszek@nhm.ac.uk; f. 1844 to publish works primarily concerned with the natural history of the British Isles and north-west Europe; 325 mems; Pres. Prof. G. A. BOXSHALL; Hon. Sec. Dr A. POLASZEK; publ. *Annual Report of the Council.*

Royal Entomological Society of London: 41 Queens Gate, London, SW7 5HR; tel. (20) 7584-8361; fax (20) 7581-8505; e-mail reg@royensoc.co.uk; internet www.royensoc.co.uk; f. 1833; 2,025 Fellows; library of 11,000 vols, 750 periodicals, 30,000 reprints; Pres. Dr HUGH LOXDALE; Registrar W. H. F. BLAKEMORE; publs *Ecological Entomology*, *Physiological Entomology*, *Systematic Entomology*, *Medical and Veterinary Entomology*, *Insect Molecular Biology*, *Agricultural and Forest Entomology*, *Antenna* (all quarterly).

Royal Society for the Protection of Birds: The Lodge, Sandy, Bedfordshire, SG19 2DL; tel. (1767) 680551; fax (1767) 692365; internet www.rspb.org.uk; f. 1889 (inc. 1904) to protect wild birds and their natural habitat; 1m. mems; library of 9,000 vols; Chair. IAN NEWTON; Chief Exec. GRAHAM WYNNE; publs *Birds* (quarterly), *Bird Life* (every 2 months), and occasional titles.

Royal Zoological Society of Scotland: Scottish National Zoological Park, Edinburgh, EH12 6TS; tel. (131) 334-9171; fax (131) 316-4050; e-mail info@rzss.org.uk; internet www.edinburghzoo.org.uk; f. 1909, inc. by Royal Charter 1913, to promote, through the presentation of the Soc.'s living collns, the conservation of animal species and wild places by captive breeding, environmental education and scientific research; 13,000 mems; Chief Exec. DAVID WINDMILL (acting); publ. *Arkfile* (quarterly).

Scottish Association for Marine Science: Dunstaffnage Marine Laboratory, Dunbeg, Oban, Argyll, PA34 4AD; tel. (1631) 559000; fax (1631) 559001; e-mail mail@dml.ac.uk; internet www.sams.ac.uk; f. 1897 for research and education in marine science; 470 mems; Pres. Prof. Sir JOHN ARBUTHNOTT; Dir Prof. GRAHAM SHIMMIELD; publs *Annual Report*, *Newsletter* (2 a year).

Selborne Society: c/o R. J. Hall, 89 Daryngton Dr., Greenford, Middx, UB6 8BH; tel. (20) 8578-3181; internet www.biochem.ucl.ac.uk/~dab/selborne.html; f. 1885 to perpetuate the memory of Gilbert White of Selborne and to promote the study of natural history, esp. among schoolchildren; 800 mems; Hon. Sec. R. J. HALL; publ. *Newsletter* (3 a year).

Society for General Microbiology: Marlborough House, Basingstoke Rd, Spencers Wood, Reading, RG7 1AG; tel. (118) 988-1800; fax (118) 988-5656; e-mail admin@sgm.ac.uk; internet www.sgm.ac.uk; f. 1945 to promote the advancement of microbiology, providing a common meeting ground for those working in specialized fields including medical, veterinary, agricultural and economic microbiology; 5,300 individual mems, 350 schools; Pres. Prof. T. H. PENNINGTON; Exec. Sec. Dr R. S. S. FRASER; publs *Micro-*

biology (monthly), *Journal of General Virology* (monthly), *Microbiology Today* (4 a year), *International Journal of Systematic and Evolutionary Microbiology* (6 a year), *Journal of Medical Microbiology* (monthly).

Systematics Association: c/o Dr Z. Lawrence, CABI Bioscience, Bakeham Lane, Egham, Surrey, TW20 9TY; tel. (1491) 829000; fax (1491) 829100; e-mail z.lawrence@cabi.org; internet www.systass.org; f. 1937 to study systematics in relation to biology and evolution; 500 mems; Pres. Dr B. S. C. LEADBEATER; Secs Dr W. BAKER (Programmes), Dr J. HAWKINS (Grants and Awards), Dr Z. LAWRENCE; publ. *Newsletter* (3 a year).

Zoological Society of London: Regent's Park, London, NW1 4RY; tel. (20) 7722-3333; fax (20) 7449-6411; internet www.zsl.org; f. 1826; consists of: ZSL London Zoo and ZSL Whipsnade Zoo; conservation programmes, library and fellowship services; 20,000 mems; library: c. 180,000 vols, 1,300 periodicals; Pres. Sir PATRICK BATESON; Dir-Gen. RALPH ARMOND; publs *Animal Conservation* (6 a year), *Conservation Science and Practice Book Series* (2 a year), *International Zoo Yearbook* (annual), *Journal of Zoology* (monthly), *Nomenclator Zoologicus* (9 vols).

Mathematical Sciences

British Society for the History of Mathematics: 20 Dunvegan Close, Exeter, Devon, EX4 4AF; internet www.bshm.org; f. 1971; provides a forum for all interested in the history and development of mathematics and related disciplines; organizes conferences, workshops, visits; 500 mems; Hon. Sec. TONY MANN; publ. *Bulletin* (3 a year).

Institute of Mathematics and its Applications: Catherine Richards House, 16 Nelson St, Southend-on-Sea, Essex, SS1 1EF; tel. (1702) 354020; fax (1702) 354111; e-mail post@ima.org.uk; internet www.ima.org.uk; f. 1964 to extend and diffuse knowledge of mathematics and of the applications of mathematics in science, engineering, economics, etc; to promote education in mathematics; 5,400 mems; Pres. Prof. PETER GRINDROD; publs *IMA Journal of Applied Mathematics* (6 a year), *IMA Journal of Management Mathematics* (4 a year), *IMA Journal of Mathematical Control and Information* (4 a year), *IMA Journal of Numerical Analysis* (4 a year), *IMA Journal of Teaching Mathematics and its Applications* (4 a year), *Mathematical Medicine and Biology: A Journal of the IMA* (4 a year).

London Mathematical Society: De Morgan House, 57–58 Russell Square, London, WC1B 4HS; tel. (20) 7637-3686; fax (20) 7323-3655; e-mail lms@lms.ac.uk; internet www.lms.ac.uk; f. 1865 for the promotion and extension of mathematical knowledge; 2,450 mems; Pres. Prof. J. F. TOLAND; Hon. Sec. Prof. N. L. BIGGS; Exec. Sec. P. R. COOPER; publs *Bulletin* (6 a year), *Journal* (6 a year), *Nonlinearity* (6 a year), *Proceedings* (6 a year).

Physical Sciences

Association of Public Analysts: Burlington House, Piccadilly, London W1V 0BN; tel. (1224) 491648; fax (1224) 276873; e-mail nmichie@aberdeencity.gov.uk; internet www.the-apa.co.uk; f. 1953 as a body to support analysts engaged in the public protection enforcement service, where chemical analysis and related testing are undertaken, especially in relation to the composition of foodstuffs, fertilizers, animal feed and other areas of consumer protection; 120 mems and Associate mems; Pres. NORMAN MICHIE; Hon. Sec. RON ENNION; publ. *Journal of the Association of Public Analysts* (on-line).

British Astronomical Association: Burlington House, Piccadilly, London, W1J 0DU; internet www.britastro.org; f. 1890; asscn of amateur astronomical observers; 3,250 mems; publs *Handbook* (annual), *Journal* (6 a year).

British Cryoengineering Society: POB 41, Leatherhead, KT22 9YY; tel. (1372) 376544; fax (1372) 376544; e-mail admin@bcryo.org.uk; internet www.bcryo.org.uk; f. 1967 to foster and encourage the development and application of cryogenics in Britain by means of contacts, education and research; 10 mem. instns; Chair. N. P. HEGARTY; Hon. Sec. J. S. HARRIS; publ. *British Cryogenics Council Newsletter* (4 a year).

British Horological Institute: Upton Hall, Upton, Newark, Notts., NG23 5TE; tel. (1636) 813795; fax (1636) 812258; e-mail clocks@bhi.co.uk; internet www.bhi.co.uk; f. 1858 to promote the science and practice of horology; 4,500 mems; library; Pres. The MASTER OF THE WORSHIPFUL COMPANY OF CLOCKMAKERS; Sec. M. TAYLOR; publ. *The Horological Journal* (monthly).

British Interplanetary Society: 27/29 South Lambeth Rd, London, SW8 1SZ; tel. (20) 7735-3160; fax (20) 7820-1504; e-mail mail@bis-spaceflight.com; internet www.bis-spaceflight.com; f. 1933 to promote the science, eng. and technology of astronautics, to support and engage in research studies and to disseminate the results thereof; 3,300 mems (1,800 fellows, 1,500 mems); Pres. JOHN HARLOW; Exec. Sec. SUSZANN PARRY; publs *Spaceflight* (monthly), *Journal* (monthly), *Space Chronicle* (2 a year).

British Nuclear Energy Society: 1–7 Great George St, London, SW1P 3AA; tel. (20) 7665-2241; fax (20) 7799-1325; e-mail andrew.tillbrook@ice.org.uk; internet www.bnes.com; f. 1962 in succession to British Nuclear Energy Conference to provide a forum for discussion, and directed to the broader aspects of nuclear energy, covering engineering and scientific disciplines; 12 constituent institutions; 1,200 mems; Sec. ANDREW TILLBROOK; publs *Nuclear Energy* (every 2 months), *Conference Proceedings* (irregular).

Challenger Society for Marine Science: c/o Southampton Oceanography Centre, Waterfront Campus, Southampton, SO14 3ZH; tel. (23) 8059-6097; fax (23) 8059-6149; e-mail jxj@soc.soton.ac.uk; internet www.challenger-society.org.uk; f. 1903 for the promotion of the study of oceanography; 500 mems; Pres. Prof. CHRIS GERMAN; Hon. Sec. JANE READ; publ. *Ocean Challenge* (3 a year).

Geological Society of London: Burlington House, Piccadilly, London, W1J 0BG; tel. (20) 7434-9944; fax (20) 7439-8975; e-mail enquiries@geolsoc.org.uk; internet www.geolsoc.org.uk; f. 1807 to investigate the mineral structure of the Earth; 9,000 mems; library: see Libraries and Archives; Pres. Prof. PETER STYLES; Exec. Sec. E. NICKLESS; publs *Geochemistry, Exploration, Environment, Analysis* (4 a year), *Journal* (6 a year), *Petroleum Geoscience* (4 a year), *Quarterly Journal of Engineering Geology and Hydrogeology* (4 a year).

Geologists' Association: Burlington House, Piccadilly, London, W1J 0DU; tel. (20) 7434-9298; fax (20) 7287-0280; e-mail geol.assoc@btinternet.com; internet www.geologist.demon.co.uk; f. 1858 to foster the progress and diffusion of the science of geology and to encourage research and the development of new methods; 2,000 mems; Pres. Dr ROBIN COCKS; Exec. Sec. SARAH STAFFORD; publs *Proceedings* (quarterly), *GA Magazine* (quarterly).

Institute of Acoustics: 77A St Peter's St, St Albans, Herts., AL1 3BN; tel. (1727) 848195; fax (1727) 850553; e-mail education@ioa.org.uk; internet www.ioa.org.uk; f. 1974; 2,700 mems; Pres. COLIN ENGLISH; Chief Exec. KEVIN NACAN-LIND; publ. *Acoustics Bulletin* (6 a year).

Institute of Physics: 76 Portland Place, London, W1B 1NT; tel. (20) 7470-4800; fax (20) 7470-4848; e-mail physics@iop.org; internet www.iop.org; f. 1918, chartered 1970; professional body for physicists in the UK and Ireland; 34,500 mems; Pres. Sir JOHN ENDERBY; Hon. Sec. Prof. JOHN BEEBY; Chief Exec. Dr ROBERT KIRBY-HARRIS; publs *Journal of Physics* (series A—50 a year, B—24 a year, CM—50 a year, D—24 a year and G—12 a year), *Chinese Physics* (12 a year), *Chinese Physics Letters* (12 a year), *Combustion Theory and Modelling* (4 a year), *European Journal of Physics* (6 a year), *Inverse Problems* (6 a year), *Journal of Cosmology and Astroparticle Physics* (online only), *Journal of High Energy Physics* (online only), *Journal of Micromechanics and Microengineering* (12 a year), *Journal of Radiological Protection* (4 a year), *Journal of Turbulence* (online only), *Measurement Science and Technology* (12 a year), *Metrologia* (6 a year), *Modelling and Simulation in Materials Science and Engineering* (8 a year), *Nanotechnology* (12 a year), *New Journal of Physics* (online only, at www.njp.org), *Nonlinearity* (6 a year), *Nuclear Fusion* (12 a year), *Physics Education* (6 a year), *Physics in Medicine and Biology* (24 a year), *Physiological Measurement* (6 a year), *Plasma Physics and Controlled Fusion* (12 a year), *Plasma Sources Science and Technology* (4 a year), *Reports on Progress in Physics* (12 a year), *Semiconductor Science and Technology* (12 a year), *Smart Materials and Structures* (6 a year), *Superconductor Science and Technology* (12 a year).

Mineralogical Society of Great Britain and Ireland: 12 Baylis Mews, Amyand Park Rd, Twickenham, Middx, TW1 3HQ; tel. (20) 8891-6600; fax (20) 8891-6599; e-mail info@minersoc.org; internet www.minersoc.org; f. 1876 by Joseph Henry Collins; scientific publishing and promotion of the mineral sciences through scientific meetings and special interest groups; 1,000 mems; Pres. Prof. BEN HARTE; Gen. Sec. Dr MARK HODSON; Exec. Sec. Dr ADRIAN LLOYD-LAWRENCE; publs *Clay Minerals* (quarterly), *MINABS Online*, *Mineralogical Magazine* (6 a year).

Palaeontographical Society: c/o Dept of Palaeontology, Natural History Museum, Cromwell Rd, London, SW7 5BD; tel. (20) 7942-5195; fax (20) 7942-5546; e-mail s.long@nhm.ac.uk; internet www.nhm.ac.uk/hostedsites/palsoc; f. 1847 for the illustration and description of British fossils; 181 individual mems, 174 mem. orgs; Pres. Prof. R. A. FORTEY; Sec. Dr S. L. LONG; publ. *Monograph of the Palaeontographical Society* (annual).

Quekett Microscopical Club: c/o Natural History Museum, Cromwell Rd, London, SW7 5BD; tel. (20) 7942-5213; e-mail secretary@quekett.org; internet www.quekett.org; f. 1865 to encourage the study of every branch of microscopical science; 500 mems; library of 1,000 vols; publ. *Quekett Journal of Microscopy* (2 a year).

Royal Astronomical Society: Burlington House, Piccadilly, London, W1J 0BQ; tel. (20) 7734-4582; fax (20) 7494-0166; e-mail info@ras.org.uk; internet www.ras.org.uk; f. 1820, granted Royal Charter in 1831; 3,200 mems; library: see Libraries; Pres. Prof. K. WHALER; Exec. Sec. D. ELLIOTT; publs *Geophysical Journal International* (monthly), *Astronomy and Geophysics* (6 a year), *Monthly Notices of the Royal Astronomical Society* (every 10 days).

Royal Meteorological Society: 104 Oxford Rd, Reading, Berks, RG1 7LS; tel. (1734) 568500; fax (1734) 568571; e-mail execdir@rmets.org; internet www.rmets.org; f. 1850; 3,000 mems; Pres. Prof. C. G. COLLIER; Gen. Sec. Dr P. RYDER; publs *Quarterly Journal*, *International Journal of Climatology* (15 times a year), *Weather* (monthly), *Meteorological Applications* (quarterly), *Atmospheric Science Letters* (online), *Weather Front* (monthly).

Royal Microscopical Society: 37–38 St Clements, Oxford, OX4 1AJ; tel. (1865) 248768; fax (1865) 791237; e-mail info@rms.org.uk; internet www.rms.org.uk; f. 1839, granted Royal Charter in 1866; for the promotion of microscopical science and its applications in the academic and industrial fields; 1,400 mems; Pres. Prof. CHRIS HAWKS; Exec. Dir ROBERT FLAVIN; publs *Journal of Microscopy* (monthly), *Proceedings* (quarterly).

Royal Society of Chemistry: Thomas Graham House, Science Park, Milton Rd, Cambridge, CB4 0WF; tel. (1223) 420066; fax (1223) 426017; e-mail sales@rsc.org; internet www.rsc.org; f. 1980 from unification of the Chemical Soc. (f. 1841) and the Royal Inst. of Chemistry (f. 1877); 46,000 fellows and mems (designated Chartered Chemists), assoc. mems and affiliates, incl. 4,000 students; library: see Libraries and Archives; Pres. Prof. JIM FEAST; Chief Exec. Dr RICHARD PIKE; publs *The Analyst* (monthly), *Analytical Abstracts* (monthly), *Catalysts and Catalysed Reactions* (monthly), *Chemical Communications* (weekly), *Chemical Society Reviews* (monthly), *Chemical Technology* (monthly), *Chemistry World* (monthly), *Chromatography Abstracts* (published in collaboration with the Chromatographic Soc., monthly), *CrystEngComm* (electronic only, monthly), *Dalton Transactions* (weekly), *Education in Chemistry* (6 a year), *Faraday Discussions* (3 a year), *Green Chemistry* (monthly), *Journal of Analytical Atomic Spectroscopy* (monthly), *Journal of Environmental Monitoring* (monthly), *Journal of Materials Chemistry* (weekly), *Lab on a Chip* (monthly), *Laboratory Hazards Bulletin* (monthly), *Mass Spectrometry Bulletin* (monthly), *Methods in Organic Synthesis* (monthly), *Molecular BioSystems* (monthly), *Natural Product Reports* (6 a year), *Natural Product Updates* (monthly), *New Journal of Chemistry* (published on behalf of the CNRS, monthly), *Organic and Biomolecular Chemistry* (every 2 weeks), *PCCP–Physical Chemistry Chemical Physics* (jtly owned by Royal Soc. of Chemistry, Deutsche Bunsen-Gesellschaft für Physikalische Chemie and the chemical societies of Denmark, Finland, Ireland, Israel, Italy, the Netherlands, Norway, Spain, Sweden, Switzerland and Turkey, weekly), *Photochemical and Photobiological Sciences* (published on behalf of European Soc. for Photobiology (ESP), European Photochemistry Asscn (EPA), the Asia and Oceania Soc. for Photobiology (AOSP) and the Korean Soc. of Photoscience (KSP), monthly), *Soft Matter* (monthly), *Chemical Biology* (monthly), *Chemical Science* (monthly).

SCI (Society of Chemical Industry): International Headquarters, 14/15 Belgrave Square, London, SW1X 8PS; tel. (20) 7598-1500; fax (20) 7598-1545; e-mail secretariat@soci.org; internet www.soci.org; f. 1881; interdisciplinary network connecting industry, research and consumer affairs at all levels throughout the world; provides opportunities for people working in the areas of process and materials technologies, energy, water, agriculture, food, pharmaceuticals, construction and environmental protection to exchange ideas and gain new perspectives on markets, technologies and strategies; 6,000 mems; Pres. THOMAS M. SWAN; Gen. Sec. RICHARD DENYER; publs *Chemistry & Industry* (2 a month), *Journal of Chemical Technology and Biotechnology* (monthly), *Journal of the Science of Food and Agriculture* (15 a year), *Pest Management Science* (monthly), *Polymer International* (monthly), *SCI Bulletin* (monthly).

Yorkshire Geological Society: c/o Dr T. J. Morse, 19 Thorngate, Barnard Castle, Co. Durham, DL12 8QB; tel. (1833) 638893; e-mail tjm4@tutor.open.ac.uk; internet www .yorksgeolsoc.org.uk; f. 1837; 800 mems; library of 5,000 vols; Pres. Dr J. POWELL; Gen. Sec. Dr T. J. MORSE; publ. *Proceedings* (2 a year).

PHILOSOPHY AND PSYCHOLOGY

Aristotelian Society: Room 281, Stewart House, Russell Sq., London, WC1B 5DN; tel. (20) 7862-8685; e-mail mail@ aristoteliansociety.org.uk; internet www .aristoteliansociety.org.uk; f. 1880 for the systematic study of philosophy, its historic devt and its methods and problems; 700 individual mems, 1,357 mem. libraries; Exec. Sec. R. E. CARTER; publs *Proceedings* (annual; online journal, 3 a year), *Supplementary Volume* (annual).

British Psychological Society: St Andrews House, 48 Princess Rd East, Leicester, LE1 7DR; tel. (116) 254-9568; fax (116) 247 0787; e-mail mail@bps.org.uk; internet www.bps.org.uk; f. 1901; 40,000 mems; Pres. Dr GRAHAM POWELL; Hon. Gen. Sec. Prof. ANN COLLEY; publs *The Psychologist* (monthly), *Psychology and Psychotherapy: Theory, Research and Practice* (4 a year), *British Journal of Educational Psychology* (4 a year), *British Journal of Mathematical & Statistical Psychology* (4 a year), *British Journal of Social Psychology* (4 a year), *British Journal of Clinical Psychology* (4 a year), *Journal of Occupational & Organisational Psychology* (4 a year), *British Journal of Developmental Psychology* (4 a year), *British Journal of Psychology* (4 a year), *Selection & Development Review* (4 a year), *Legal and Criminological Psychology* (4 a year), *British Journal of Health Psychology* (4 a year).

British Society of Aesthetics: c/o Prof. Graham McFee, The Chelsea School, Univ. of Brighton, 1 Denton Rd, Eastbourne, BN20 7SP; e-mail kathleen@british-aesthetics.org; internet www.british-aesthetics.org; f. 1960 to promote study, research and discussion in aesthetics and the growth of artistic taste among the public, and to facilitate communications between scholars at an international and European level; Pres. RICHARD WOLLHEIM; Sec. KATHLEEN STOCK; publs *Newsletter* (every 6 months), *British Journal of Aesthetics* (quarterly).

Experimental Psychology Society: Dept of Experimental Psychology, Univ. of Bristol, 12A Priory Rd, Bristol BS8 1TU; internet www.eps.ac.uk; f. 1946; to further scientific enquiry in the field of psychology; 693 mems; Pres. Prof. U. FRITH; Hon. Sec. Dr C. JARROLD; publ. *Quarterly Journal of Experimental Psychology*.

Leeds Philosophical and Literary Society Ltd: c/o The Town Hall, Leeds, LS1 3AD; internet www.leedsphilandlit.org .uk; f. 1820 to promote the advancement of science, literature and the arts in the city of Leeds and elsewhere; organizes public lectures and visits; provides assistance for scholarly research and publication; 135 mems; Sec. Dr J. LYDON.

Manchester Literary and Philosophical Society: MMU Business School, Aytoun St, Manchester, M1 3GH; tel. (161) 247-6774; fax (161) 247-6773; e-mail admin@manlitphil .co.uk; internet www.manlitphil.co.uk; f. 1781 to promote the advancement of education and the widening of public interest in, and appreciation of, any form of literature, science, the arts and public affairs; varied lectures throughout the academic year; 500 mems; library of 4,000 vols; Administrators ALLAN JEFFERIS, SARAH IRVING; Sec. Prof. PATRICIA VERDIN; publ. *Manchester Memoirs* (annual).

Mind Association: c/o Prof. B. W. Hooker, Philosophy Dept, Univ. of Reading, Reading, RG6 6AA; tel. (118) 378-6631; fax (118) 378-8295; e-mail b.w.hooker@reading.ac.uk; internet www.mind.oupjournals.org; f. 1900 to publish the journal *Mind*, and help organize annual conferences jointly with the Aristotelian Soc.; 685 mems; Hon. Sec. Prof. B. W. HOOKER; publ. *MIND* (4 a year).

Philosophical Society of England: 6 Craghall Dean Ave, Newcastle upon Tyne, NE3 1QR; tel. (191) 222-6796; fax (191) 284-1223; e-mail m.c.bavidge@ncl.ac.uk; internet atschool.eduweb.co.uk/cite/staff/philosopher/ philsocindex.htm; f. 1913 to spread a knowledge of philosophy among the general public; 150 mems; Pres. Prof. BRENDA ALMOND; Chair. MICHAEL BAVIDGE; publ. *The Philosopher* (2 a year).

Royal Institute of Philosophy: 14 Gordon Square, London, WC1H 0AR; tel. (20) 7387-4130; fax (20) 7387-4061; e-mail j.garvey@ royalinstitutephilosophy.org; internet www .royalinstitutephilosophy.org; f. 1925; 700 mems; Pres. Lord QUINTON; Chair. Lord SUTHERLAND OF HOUNDWOOD; Dir Prof. A. O'HEAR; Sec. Dr JAMES GARVEY; publs *Philosophy* (4 a year), *Conference Proceedings* (annually), *Think* (4 a year).

Royal Philosophical Society of Glasgow: POB NAT 8268, Glasgow, G46 7BR; tel. (141) 433-4484; fax (141) 330-4112; e-mail info@ royalphil.org; internet myweb.tiscali.co.uk/ royalphil/rps; f. 1802; organizes lectures and promotes philosophical debate; 200 mems; Pres. Prof. NEIL SPURWAY; Sec. Dr CHRIS LINDSAY; publ. *Society Journal*.

Victoria Institute, or Philosophical Society of Great Britain (operates as Faith and Thought): 41 Marne Ave, Welling, Kent, DA16 2EY; tel. and fax (20) 8303-0465; internet www.faithandthought.org.uk; f. 1865; Pres. Sir JOHN HOUGHTON; publs *Faith and Thought* (2 a year), *Science and Christian Belief* (jointly with Christians in Science, 2 a year).

William Morris Society: Kelmscott House, 26 Upper Mall, London, W6 9TA; tel. (20) 8741-3735; fax (20) 8748-5207; e-mail william .morris@care4free.net; internet www .morrissociety.org; f. 1955 to encourage wider appreciation and understanding of the life, work and influence of William Morris and his circle; 1,400 mems; library of 2,000 vols; Hon. Sec. PETER FAULKNER; publs *Journal* (2 a year), *Newsletter* (4 a year).

RELIGION, SOCIOLOGY AND ANTHROPOLOGY

African Studies Association of the United Kingdom: c/o SOAS, Thornhaugh St, London, WC1H 0XG; tel. (20) 7898-4390; fax (20) 7898-4389; e-mail asa@soas.ac.uk; f. 1963 to advance academic studies relating to Africa by providing facilities for the interchange of information and ideas; holds inter-disciplinary conferences, symposia; 600 mems; Hon. Pres. Prof. GRAHAM FURNISS; Hon. Sec. Dr INSA NOLTE.

British Association for the Study of Religions: c/o Dr James Cox, University of Edinburgh, New College, Mound Place, Edinburgh, EH1 2LX; tel. (131) 650-8942; fax (131) 650-7952; e-mail J.Cox@ed.ac.uk; internet basr.open.ac.uk; f. 1954; affiliated to Intl Association for the History of Religions; organizes an annual conference; 250 mems; Pres. and Chair Dr JAMES COX; Hon. Sec. Dr GRAHAM HARVEY; publ. *Bulletin* (3 a year).

British Society for Middle Eastern Studies: Institute for Middle Eastern and Islamic Studies, University of Durham, Al-Qasimi Bldg, Elvet Hill Rd, Durham, DH1 3TU; tel. (191) 334-4517; fax (191) 334-5661; e-mail a.l.haysey@durham.ac.uk; internet www.dur.ac.uk/brismes; f. 1973; to promote the study of the Middle Eastern region from the end of classical antiquity and the rise of Islam, encouraging discussion and debate and fostering co-operation among teachers, researchers and students of the Middle East, both within the UK and internationally; co-operation with similar societies is being consolidated and expanded; 550 mems; Pres. Dr NOEL BREHONY; Sec. Dr CIGDEM BALIM; publs *British Journal of Middle Eastern Studies* (2 a year), *Newsletter* (3 a year).

British Sociological Association: Bailey Suite, Palatine House, Belmont Business Park, Belmont, Durham, DH1 1TW; tel. (191) 383-0839; fax (191) 383-0782; e-mail enquiries@britsoc.org.uk; internet www .britsoc.co.uk; f. 1951 to promote interest in sociology, to advance its study and application in the United Kingdom, and to encourage contacts between workers in all relevant fields of enquiry; holds conferences, seminars and workshops; 2,500 mems; Pres. Prof. SUE SCOTT; Exec. Committee Chair Prof. GAYLE LETHERBY; Exec. Officer JUDITH MUDD; publs *Sociology* (6 a year), *Work Employment and Society* (4 a year), *Network* (3 a year), *Cultural Sociology* (3 a year).

Ecclesiological Society: 143 Leathwaite Rd, London, SW11 6RW; tel. (20) 8851-1521; e-mail cooper@ecclsoc.org; internet www.ecclsoc.org; f. 1839 as The Cambridge Camden Society; collections of books, pamphlets and photographs; 900 mems; Pres. D. R. BUTTRESS (Surveyor Emeritus of Westminster Abbey); Chair. TREVOR COOPER; publ. *Journal* (3 a year).

Folklore Society: c/o Warburg Inst., Woburn Sq., London, WC1H 0AB; tel. (20) 7862-8564; e-mail folklore.society@talk21 .com; internet www.folklore-society.com; f. 1878; c. 1,000 mems and subscribers; library of 11,000 vols; Pres. Prof. W. F. RYAN; Hon. Sec. Dr J. WOOD; publ. *Folklore* (3 a year).

Galton Institute: 19 Northfields Prospect, Northfields, London, SW18 1PE; tel. (20) 8874-7257; e-mail betty.nixon@talk21.com; f. 1907 to promote the study of eugenics, genetics and population problems; 400 mems; Pres. STEVE JONES; Gen. Sec. B. NIXON; publ. *Galton Institute Newsletter* (quarterly).

Henry Bradshaw Society: 5A Green Place, Oxford, OX1 4RF; e-mail hbs@rolvenden .freeserve.co.uk; internet www .henrybradshawsociety.org; f. 1890; publishes facsimiles and editions of rare texts relating to the liturgy of the medieval Christian church; 190 institutional mems, 110 individual mems; Chair. Prof. MICHAEL LAPIDGE; Sec. PETER JACKSON.

Institute of Community Studies: 18 Victoria Park Square, London, E2 9PF; tel. (20) 8980-6263; fax (20) 8981-6719; e-mail info@

icstudies.ac.uk; internet icstudies.ac.uk; f. 1954; social research on poverty, deprivation and comparative social policy; housing, urban planning and community; education; Dir Dr GEOFF MULGAN.

Institute of Race Relations: 2–6 Leeke St, King's Cross Rd, London, WC1X 9HS; tel. (20) 7837-0041; fax (20) 7278-0623; e-mail info@irr.org.uk; internet www.irr.org.uk; f. 1958 to promote scientific study and publication on race and racism, and to make information and proposals available on race relations; Dir A. SIVANANDAN; publ. *Race & Class* (4 a year).

Maghreb Studies Association: c/o The Maghreb Bookshop, 45 Burton St, London, WC1H 9AL; tel. and fax (20) 7388-1840; e-mail maghreb@maghrebreview.com; internet www.maghrebreview.com; f. 1981 to promote the study of the history, politics and environment of North Africa and the broader Middle East and Islamic world; Chair. Prof. HÉDI BOURAOUI; Exec. Sec. M. BEN-MADANI; publ. *Maghreb Review* (quarterly).

Modern Churchpeople's Union: c/o Rev. Jonathan Clatworthy, 9 Westward View, Liverpool, L17 7EE; tel. (845) 345-1909; e-mail office@modchurchunion.org; internet www.modchurchunion.org; f. 1898 for the advancement of liberal religious thought; 700 mems; Pres. Rt Rev. JOHN SAXBEE; Chair. Rev. JOHN PLANT; Gen. Sec. Rev. JONATHAN CLATWORTHY; publ. *Modern Believing* (quarterly).

National Society (Church of England) for Promoting Religious Education: Church House, Great Smith St, Westminster, SW1P 3AZ; tel. (20) 7898-1518; fax (20) 7898-1493; e-mail info@natsoc.c-of-e.org.uk; internet www.natsoc.org.uk; f. 1811; promotes religious education in accordance with the principles of the Church of England; Chair The BISHOP OF PORTSMOUTH; Gen. Sec. Rev. JANINA AINSWORTH.

Royal African Society: SOAS, Thornhaugh St, Russell Square, London, WC1H 0XG; tel. (20) 7898-4390; fax (20) 7898-4389; e-mail ras@soas.ac.uk; internet www.royalafricansociety.org; f. 1901; hosts regular programme of lectures in London, Bristol and Edinburgh; 1,000 mems; Chair. Lord HOLME OF CHELTENHAM; Sec. LINDSAY ALLAN; publ. *African Affairs* (quarterly).

Royal Anthropological Institute of Great Britain and Ireland: 50 Fitzroy St, London, W1T 5BT; tel. (20) 7387-0455; fax (20) 7388-8817; e-mail admin@therai.org.uk; internet www.therai.org.uk; f. 1843; conferences and film festivals; manages various trust and scholarship funds; awards medals and prizes; raises funds for research; 1,500 mems; library with borrowing rights to 120,000 vols; film-hire library; photographic archive; Pres. Prof. ALAN BILSBOROUGH; Dir HILARY CALLAN; Hon. Sec. Dr ERIC HIRSCH; publs *Anthropology Today* (6 a year), *Journal of the Royal Anthropological Institute* (incorporating *Man*, 5 a year).

Royal Asiatic Society of Great Britain and Ireland: 60 Queen's Gardens, London, W2 3AF; tel. (20) 7724-4742; fax (20) 7706-4008; e-mail info@royalasiaticsociety.org; internet www.royalasiaticsociety.co.uk; f. 1823 for the study of the history, religions, institutions, customs, languages, literature and art of Asia; 600 subscribing libraries; brs in various Asian cities; 800 mems; library: see Libraries; Sec. ADRIAN THOMAS; publ. *Journal* (quarterly).

Royal Commonwealth Society: 18 Northumberland Ave, London, WC2N 5BJ; tel. (20) 7930-6733; fax (20) 7930-9705; e-mail info@rcsint.org; internet www.rcsint.org; f. 1868;

10,000 mems worldwide; publ. *Newsletter* (3 a year).

Royal Society for Asian Affairs: 2 Belgrave Square, London, SW1X 8PJ; tel. (20) 7235-5122; fax (20) 7259-6771; e-mail info@rsaa.org.uk; internet www.rsaa.org.uk; f. 1901; 1,200 mems with knowledge of, and interest in, Asia; library of 7,500 vols; Pres. Lord DENMAN; Chair. Sir HAROLD WALKER; Sec. NORMAN J. M. CAMERON; publ. *Asian Affairs* (3 a year).

Society for South Asian Studies: c/o Royal Asiatic Society, 14 Stephenson Way (Second Floor), London, NW1 2HD; e-mail ssas@btconnect.com; internet www.societyforsouthasianstudies.org; tel. (20) 7388-5490; f. 1972; supports research and training in the arts, humanities and social sciences of South Asia; 300 mems; Chair. Prof. PETER ROBB; Sec. Dr JAVED MAJEED; publ. *South Asian Studies* (annual).

Swedenborg Society: 20–21 Bloomsbury Way, London, WC1A 2TH; tel. (20) 7405-7986; e-mail swed.soc@netmatters.co.uk; internet www.swedenborg.org.uk; f. 1810 for the translation and publication of the writings of Emanuel Swedenborg, Swedish scientist, philosopher and theologian; approx. 1,000 mems; Pres. DAVID LORIMER; Sec. MADELINE G. WATERS; publ. *Journal* (annually).

TECHNOLOGY

British Computer Society: 1 Sanford St, Swindon, Wilts., SN1 1HJ; tel. (1793) 417417; fax (1793) 480270; e-mail bcshq@bcs.org.uk; internet www.bcs.org.uk; f. 1957; industry body for Information Technology professionals; sets standards for education and training through the BCS Professional Examination and through the inspection and accreditation of university courses and company training schemes; awards the Chartered IT Professional (CITP) qualification; licensed by the Engineering Council and the Science Council to appoint chartered and incorporated engineers and chartered scientists; 45,000 mems; joint library with Instn of Electrical Engineers; Pres. DAVID MORRISS; Registrar MANDY BRYAR; publs *The Computer Journal* (6 a year), *IT Now* (6 a year), *IEE Proceedings – Software* (6 a year, in conjunction with IEE), *Interacting with Computers Journal* (4 a year), *Formal Aspects of Computing Journal* (6 a year).

British Masonry Society: Shermanbury, 6 Church Rd, Whyteleafe, Surrey, CR3 0AR; tel. (20) 8660-3633; fax (20) 8668-6983; e-mail kenneth@fisher5053.fsnet.co.uk; internet www.masonry.org.uk; f. 1986; 400 mems; Sec. Dr K. FISHER; publ. *Masonry International* (3 a year).

British Society of Rheology: c/o Dr G. J. Brownsey, Institute of Food Research, Norwich Research Park, Colney, Norfolk, NR4 7UA; tel. (1603) 255201; fax (1603) 507723; e-mail tnp@aber.ac.uk; internet www.ncl.ac.uk/rheology/bsr/; f. 1940 to promote rheology, the science of the deformation and flow of matter; 600 mems; Pres. Prof. G. C. MAITLAND; Sec. Dr TIMOTHY N. PHILLIPS; library at University of Wales, Aberystwyth; publs *Rheology Abstracts*, *Bulletin* (quarterly).

BSI Group (British Standards Institution): 389 Chiswick High Rd, London, W4 4AL; tel. (20) 8996-9000; fax (20) 8996-7400; e-mail cservices@bsi-global.com; f. 1901 as an Engineering Standards Committee; inc. 1918 as British Engineering Standards Association, f. 1929 under Royal Charter and Supplemental Charter in 1931, when scope

was extended; independent certification of management systems and products; product-testing services; operates BSI British Standards, the national standards body of the UK, which develops standards for industry and the population in general; 15,000 subscribing mems; CEO STEVAN BREEZE; Dir of Legal Affairs and Company Sec. RICHARD CATT; publs *Annual Report*, *British Standards*, *BSI Catalogue* (annually), *Business Standards* (quarterly), *Standards Update* (monthly).

Chartered Institute of Building: Englemere, Kings Ride, Ascot, Berks, SL5 7TB; tel. (1344) 630700; fax (1344) 630777; e-mail reception@ciob.org.uk; internet www.ciob.org.uk; f. 1834, inc. by Royal Charter 1980; professional body for managers in the construction industry; 39,000 mems; Pres. STUART HENDERSON; Chief Exec. CHRIS BLYTHE; publs *Construction Information Quarterly* (4 a year), *New Constructor* (3 a year), *Construction Manager / Construction Computing* (10 a year).

Chartered Institute of Logistics and Transport: 11–12 Buckingham Gate, London, SW1E 6LB; tel. (20) 7592-3116; fax (20) 7592-3111; e-mail cyril.bleasdale@ciltinternational.org; internet www.cilt-international.com; f. 1919, inc. by Royal Charter 1926 to promote, encourage, and co-ordinate the study and advancement of the science and art of transport in all its branches, and to provide a source of authoritative views on transport; brs in Argentina, Australia, Bangladesh, Canada, Cyprus, Ghana, Greece, Hong Kong, India, Ireland, Kenya, Malawi, Malaysia, Malta, Mauritius, Nepal, New Zealand, Nigeria, Pakistan, Singapore, South Africa, Spain, Sri Lanka, Thailand, Uganda, United Arab Emirates, USA, West Indies, Zambia, Zimbabwe and elsewhere; 32,000 mems; Pres. RICHARD HUNT; Dir-Gen. CYRIL BLEASDALE; publ. *CILT World* (newsletter, 3 a year).

Chartered Institute of Patent Attorneys: 95 Chancery Lane, London, WC2A 1DT; tel. (20) 7405-9450; fax (20) 7430-0471; e-mail mail@cipa.org.uk; internet www.cipa.org.uk; f. 1882, chartered 1891, present name 2006; professional and examining body; 3,250 mems; Sec. MICHAEL RALPH; publs *CIPA* (monthly), *Register of Patent Agents* (annual).

Chartered Institution of Building Services Engineers: 222 Balham High Rd, London, SW12 9BS; tel. (20) 8675-5211; fax (20) 8675-5449; e-mail enquiries@cibse.org; internet www.cibse.org; promotes the science and practice of such engineering services as are associated with the built environment and industrial processes and the advancement of education and research in building services engineering; 15,000 mems; Chief Exec. and Sec. JULIAN AMEY; publs *Building Services Journal* (monthly), *Lighting Research and Technology* (quarterly), *Building Services Engineering Research and Technology* (quarterly).

Chartered Institution of Water and Environmental Management: 15 John St, London WC1N 2EB; tel. (20) 7831-3110; fax (20) 7405-4967; e-mail admin@ciwem.org.uk; internet www.ciwem.org.uk; f. 1895; to advance the science and practice of water and environmental management for the public benefit and to promote education, training, study and research in those areas; 12,000 mems; Pres. PETER TREADGOLD; Exec. Dir NICK REEVES; publs *Journal* (quarterly), *Water and Environment Magazine* (monthly).

Chartered Management Institute: 2 Savoy Court, Strand, London, WC2R 0EZ;

and Management House, Cottingham Rd, Corby, Northants., NN17 1TT; tel. (1536) 204222; fax (1536) 201651; e-mail member@ managers.org.uk; internet www.managers .org.uk; f. 1947 as British Institute of Management, name changed 1992; granted Royal Charter 2002; encourages and supports the lifelong development of managers; influences policy-makers and opinion-formers on management isues; 84,000 individual mems, 600 company mems; library: 80,000 items, 200 periodicals; Dir-Gen. MARY M. CHAPMAN; Sec. VALERIE HAMILL; publ. *Professional Manager* (6 a year).

Chartered Society of Designers: 5 Bermondsey Exchange, 179–181 Bermondsey St, London, N1 3UW; tel. (20) 7357-8088; fax (20) 7407-9878; e-mail csd@csd.org.uk; internet www.csd.org.uk; f. 1930, incorporated by Royal Charter 1976; professional body for designers practising in product design, fashion and textiles design, interiors and graphics, design management, education and professional development; 4,000 mems; Pres. ADRIANNE LeMAN; publ. *CSD Magazine* (4 a year).

Crafts Council: 44A Pentonville Rd, London, N1 9BY; tel. (20) 7278-7700; fax (20) 7837-6891; e-mail reference@craftscouncil .org.uk; internet www.craftscouncil.org.uk; f. 1971 as the Crafts Advisory Cttee, present name 1979; directly funded by Arts Council England; nat. org. for contemporary crafts in Great Britain, offering exhibition and education programmes; maintains an Index of Selected Makers, electronic picture library, a Nat. Register of Makers, Reference Library, Loan Colln, Reference Desk; offers maintenance and/or equipment grants; library of 6,580 vols, 142 periodicals; Chair. JOANNA FOSTER; Dir ROSY GREENLEES; publ. *Crafts* (6 a year).

Design Council: 34 Bow St, London, WC2E 1DL; tel. (20) 7420-5200; fax (20) 7420-5300; e-mail info@design-council.org.uk; internet www.design-council.org.uk; f. 1944 to inspire, in the world context, the best use of design by the UK to improve prosperity and well-being; Chair. of Council Prof. CHRISTOPHER FRAYLING; Chief Exec. ANDREW SUMMERS.

Energy Institute: 61 New Cavendish St, London, W1G 7AR; tel. (20) 7467-7100; fax (20) 7255-1472; e-mail info@energyinst.org .uk; internet www.energyinst.org.uk; f. 2003 following the merger of the Institute of Petroleum (f. 1913) and the Institute of Energy (f. 1927), to promote the safe, environmentally responsible and efficient supply and use of energy; research into oil, gas and other primary fuels and renewable sources of energy; power generation, transmission and distribution, sustainable development, demand-side management and energy efficiency; publishes codes of safe practice, measurement manuals, test methods, journals; organizes conferences, courses and offers an extensive library and information service; 12,000 individual mems and 400 group mems; library of 15,000 vols, 200 periodicals; Pres. Sir JOHN COLLINS; Chief Exec. LOUISE KINGHAM; Hon. Sec. JOANNE WADE; publs *Energy World* (11 a year), *Petroleum Review* (monthly).

Engineering Council UK: 10 Maltravers St, London, WC2R 3ER; tel. (20) 7240-7891; fax (20) 7379-5586; e-mail info@engc.org.uk; internet www.engc.org.uk; f. 1981 by Royal Charter; aims to advance the education and training of engineers and technologists, to improve the supply of qualified engineers and technologists and to set up and maintain relevant professional, educational and train-

ing standards; Senate Chair Sir COLIN TERRY; Exec. Dir ANDREW RAMSAY.

Ergonomics Society: The Elms, Elmsgrove, Loughborough, Leics., LE11 1RG; tel. (1509) 234904; fax (1509) 235666; e-mail ergsoc@ergonomics.org.uk; internet www .ergonomics.org.uk; f. 1949 to promote ergonomics and the work of ergonomists in solving problems that arise between man, his working environment and things that he uses; 1,400 mems; Pres. M. E. GALLEY; Hon. Gen. Sec. D. H. O'NEILL; publs *Ergonomics*, *Applied Ergonomics*, *Work and Stress*, *Behaviour and Information Technology*.

Faculty of Royal Designers for Industry: RSA, 8 John Adam St, London, WC2N 6EZ; tel. (20) 7930-5115; fax (20) 7839-5805; e-mail rdi@rsa.org.uk; internet www.rsa.org .uk; f. 1936 to further the development of design and in particular its application to industrial purposes; number of holders of RDI limited to 100 (90 at present plus 40 Hon.); Pres. Sir STUART HAMPSON; Master MARTIN HUNT; Sec. PENNY EGAN.

Gemmological Association and Gem Testing Laboratory of Great Britain: 27 Greville St, London, EC1N 8TN; tel. (20) 7404-3334; fax (20) 7404-8843; e-mail gagtl@ btinternet.com; internet www.gem-a.info; f. 1931 for promotion of the study of gemmology and the scientific and industrial study of all materials and articles used or dealt in by persons interested in the science of gems; 4,000 mems; publs *Journal of Gemmology* (quarterly), *Gem and Jewellery News* (quarterly).

Institute of Corrosion: Corrosion House, Vimy Court, Vimy Rd, Leighton Buzzard, Beds, LU7 1FG; tel. (1525) 851771; fax (1525) 376690; e-mail admin@icorr.demon.co.uk; internet www.icorr.org; f. 1975; 1,600 mems; Pres. DAVID DEACON; Hon. Sec. JIM BURNELL-GRAY; publs *Corrosion Management* (6 a year), *Corrosion Science* (monthly).

Institute of Food Science and Technology: 5 Cambridge Court, 210 Shepherd's Bush Rd, London, W6 7NJ; tel. (20) 7603-6316; fax (20) 7602-9936; e-mail info@ifst .org; internet www.ifst.org; f. 1964 to promote the knowledge, devt and application of science and technology of food, and the provision of a professional body for food scientists and technologists; 2,800 mems; Pres. Dr R. BURT; Hon. Sec. S. TOMLINSON; Chief Exec. H. G. WILD; publs *International Journal of Food Science and Technology* (10 a year), *Food Science and Technology* (quarterly).

Institute of Management Services: Brooke House, 24 Dam St, Lichfield, Staffs., WS13 6AA; tel. (1543) 266909; fax (1543) 257848; e-mail admin@ims-stowe.fsnet.co .uk; internet www.ims-productivity.com; f. 1941; promotion, practice and devt of methodologies and techniques for the improvement of productivity and quality; 1,700 mems; Chair. J. LUCEY; publ. *Management Services Journal* (quarterly).

Institute of Marine Engineering, Science and Technology (IMarEST): 80 Coleman St, London, EC2R 5BJ; tel. (20) 7382-2600; fax (20) 7382-2670; e-mail info@ imarest.org; internet www.imarest.org; f. 1889 as Institute of Marine Engineers, present name 2002; professional society representing those involved in marine engineering, science and technology; 15,000 mems; library: library and Marine Information Centre; Sec. K. F. READ; publs *Marine Engineers' Review* (10 a year), *Journal of Offshore Technology* (6 a year), *The Marine Scientist* (4 a year), *Proceedings* (Parts A and B), *Maritime Electronics* (6 a year).

Institute of Materials, Minerals and Mining: 1 Carlton House Terrace, London, SW1Y 5DB; tel. (20) 7451-7300; fax (20) 7839-1702; e-mail admin@iom3.org; internet www.iom3.org; f. 2002 following merger of Institute of Materials and Institution of Mining and Metallurgy; advances the science and practice of engineering; facilitates the acquisition and preservation of knowledge pertaining to the associated professions; establishes, upholds and advances the industry standards of education, training and competence; organizes meetings and conferences worldwide; administers scholarships and fellowships; 22,000 mems; library of 65,000 vols, 1,000 periodicals; Pres. Dr R. DOLBY; Chief Exec. Dr B. A. RICKINSON; publs *Steel World* (2 a year), *Materials World* (monthly), *Surface Engineering* (4 a year), *Materials Science and Technology* (monthly), *International Materials Reviews* (6 a year), *Ironmaking and Steelmaking* (6 a year), *British Corrosion Engineering, Science and Technology* (4 a year), *Powder Metallurgy* (4 a year), *Plastics, Rubber and Composites* (10 a year), *Interdisciplinary Science Reviews* (4 a year), *Science and Technology of Welding and Joining* (6 a year), *British Ceramic Transactions* (6 a year), *Historical Metallurgy* (2 a year), *Transactions* of the former Institute of Mining and Metallurgy (9 a year), *Abstracts* of the former Institute of Mining and Metallurgy (4 a year).

Institute of Measurement and Control: 87 Gower St, London, WC1E 6AF; tel. (20) 7387-4949; fax (20) 7388-8431; e-mail education@instmc.org.uk; internet www .instmc.org.uk; f. 1944, inc. by Royal Charter 1975; to promote the advancement and application of the science and practice of measurement and control; to co-ordinate and disseminate information and to conduct examinations; 4,100 mems; Sec. MICHAEL YATES; publs *Measurement and Control* (10 a year, incl. *Inst MC Interface*, of which 2 a year), *Transactions* (5 a year), *Instrument Engineer's Yearbook*.

Institute of Physics and Engineering in Medicine: Fairmount House, 230 Tadcaster Rd, York, YO24 1ES; tel. (1904) 610821; fax (1904) 612279; e-mail office@ipem.org.uk; internet www.ipem.org.uk; f. 1995; objective is to promote, for the public benefit, the advancement of physics and engineering applied to medicine and biology and to advance public education in the field; 3,100 mems; Pres. Prof. PETER C. WILLIAMS; Gen. Sec. ROBERT W. NEILSON; publs *Medical Engineering and Physics* (8 a year), *Physiological Measurement* (quarterly), *Physics in Medicine and Biology* (every 2 weeks).

Institute of Quarrying: 7 Regent St, Nottingham, NG1 5BS; tel. (115) 941-1315; fax (115) 948-4035; e-mail mail@quarrying .org; internet www.quarrying.org; f. 1917; professional body to provide a professional qualification, to improve science and practice of quarrying and to provide a forum for technical discussion; over 5,000 home and overseas mems; Exec. Dir J. W. BERRIDGE; Sec. L. BRYDEN; publ. *Quarry Management* (monthly).

Institute of Refrigeration: Kelvin House, 76 Mill Lane, Carshalton, Surrey, SM5 2JR; tel. (20) 8647-7033; fax (20) 8773-0165; e-mail ior@ior.org.uk; internet www.ior.org .uk; f. 1899 (as the Cold Storage and Ice Association) for the general advancement of refrigeration in all its applications; 2,600 mems; Pres. J. ELLIS; Sec. M. J. HORLICK; publ. *Proceedings*.

Institute of Science Technology: Stowe House, Netherstowe, Lichfield, Staffs., WS13 6TJ; tel. (1543) 266823; fax (1543) 266833;

e-mail office@istonline.org.uk; internet www .istonline.org.uk; f. 1954 from the Science Technologists' Association (f. 1948); professional and qualifying body for laboratory technicians; provides training for vocational qualifications and continuing professional development; gives awards, prizes and travelling scholarships; 1,000 mems; Pres. B. HARDWICK; Chair. J. D. ROBINSON; Hon Sec. A. TAYLOR; publ. *Science Technology* (2 a year).

Institute of Scientific and Technical Communicators: POB 522, Peterborough, Cambs., PE2 5WX; tel. (1733) 390141; fax (1733) 390126; e-mail istc@istc.org.uk; internet www.istc.org.uk; f. 1972; aims to establish and maintain professional codes of practice for people engaged in all branches of scientific and technical communication; 1,500 mems; Pres. GAVIN IRELAND; Sec. CAROL HEWITT; publs *Communicator* (quarterly), *Newsletter* (monthly).

Institution of Chemical Engineers: 165–189 Railway Terrace, Rugby, CV21 3HQ; tel. (1788) 578214; fax (1788) 560833; e-mail tjevans@icheme.org.uk; internet www .icheme.org; f. 1922, incorporated by Royal Charter to promote the science and practice of chemical engineering, to improve the standards and methods of education therein, and to act as a qualifying body for chemical engineers, etc.; 25,000 mems; Chief Exec. Dr T. J. EVANS; publs *Chemical Engineering Research and Design* (12 a year), *Process Safety and Environmental Protection* (6 a year), *Food and Bioproducts Processing* (4 a year), *The Chemical Engineer* (monthly).

Institution of Civil Engineers: 1 Great George St, Westminster, London, SW1P 3AA; tel. (20) 7222-7722; fax (20) 7222-7500; e-mail secretariat@ice.org.uk; internet www .ice.org.uk; f. 1818; inc. by Royal Charter in 1828 for the general advancement of mechanical science and more particularly for promoting the acquisition of knowledge which constitutes the profession of a Civil Engineer, namely the art of directing natural sources of power for the use and convenience of man; two principal roles: i) qualifying body for all three levels of registration: Chartered Engineers, Incorporated Engineers and Engineering Technicians; ii) learned society; as a qualifying body the Institution is concerned with academic and professional achievements and with continuing education, and as a learned society it is concerned with the acquisition and dissemination of knowledge; 80,000 corporate and non-corporate mems; library of 95,000 vols; Pres. Prof. COLIN J. CLINTON; Dir-Gen. and Sec. TOM FOULKES; publs *Proceedings* (in 6 parts: *Civil Engineering, Geotechnical Engineering, Structures & Building, Municipal Engineer, Transport, Water, Maritime & Energy*, all 4 a year), *Geotechnique* (4 a year), *Nuclear Energy, Advances in Cement Research, Magazine of Concrete Research, Ground Improvement*.

Institution of Electronics: 34 Colmore Ave, Spital, Wirral, L63 9NL; internet www .i-e.org.uk; f. 1930, inc. 1935, for the furtherance of the science of electronics and other scientific subjects; over 2,500 mems; Gen. Sec. W. BIRTWISTLE; publ. *Proceedings* (quarterly).

Institution of Engineering and Technology: Savoy Place, London, WC2R 0BL; tel. (20) 7240-1871; fax (20) 7240-7735; e-mail postmaster@theiet.org; internet www.theiet .org; f. 1871 (and inc. by Royal Charter in 1921, inc. the Institution of Radio and Electronic Engineers 1988 and Institution of Manufacturing Engineers 1991 and the Institution of Incorporated Engineers 2006);

to promote the general advancement of science, engineering and technology, and to facilitate the exchange of information and ideas on those subjects; fmrly Institution of Electrical Engineers; 150,000 mems; library: see Libraries and Archives; Pres. Sir ROBIN SAXBY; CEO Dr A. ROBERTS; publs *Communications Engineer* (6 a year), *Computing and Control Engineering* (6 a year), *Electronics Education* (3 a year), *Electronics Letters* (every 2 weeks), *Electronics Systems and Software* (6 a year), *Engineering Management* (6 a year), *Engineering & Technology* (monthly), *Flipside* (6 a year), *Information Professional* (6 a year), *Manufacturing Engineer* (6 a year), *Power Engineer* (6 a year), *Proceedings* (6 a year), *Systems Biology* (4 a year).

Institution of Engineering Designers: Courtleigh, Westbury Leigh, Westbury, Wilts., BA13 3TA; tel. (1373) 822801; fax (1373) 858085; e-mail staff@ied.org.uk; internet www.ied.org.uk; f. 1945 to advance education in engineering, particularly in engineering and product design and to constitute a body of members qualified to a recognized high standard; a nominated body of the Engineering Council; 5,300 mems; Sec. ELIZABETH BRODHURST; publ. *Engineering Designer* (6 a year).

Institution of Engineers and Shipbuilders in Scotland: 1 Atlantic Quay, Broomielaw, Glasgow, G2 8JE; tel. (141) 248-3721; f. 1857 to facilitate the exchange of information and ideas amongst its mems, and to promote the advancement of the science and practice of engineering and shipbuilding; 800 mems; Pres. I. C. BROADLEY; Exec. Sec. E. W. BELL; publs *Transactions* (annually), *Year Book and List of Members* (every 2 years).

Institution of Fire Engineers: London Rd, Moreton-in-Marsh, GL56 0RH; tel. (1608) 812580; fax (1608) 812581; e-mail info@ife .org.uk; internet www.ife.org.uk; f. 1918, and inc. 1924, to promote, encourage, and improve the science of fire engineering and technology; 11,000 home and overseas mems; CEO ELLEN JESSETT; publ. *Fire Prevention and Fire Engineers Journal* (monthly, online).

Institution of Gas Engineers and Managers: Charnwood Wing, Holywell Park, Ashby Rd, Loughborough, LE11 3GH; tel. (1509) 282728; fax (1509) 283110; e-mail general@igem.org.uk; internet www.igem .org.uk; f. 1863; Royal Charter 1929, to promote by research, discussion and education the sciences necessary for the better production, distribution or utilization of gas and of the by-products of its production; 5,000 mems; library of 10,000 vols; Chief Exec. JOHN WILLIAMS; publ. *Journal*.

Institution of Highways and Transportation: 6 Endsleigh St, London, WC1H 0DZ; tel. (20) 7387-2525; fax (20) 7387-2808; e-mail info@iht.org; internet www.iht.org; f. 1930 as the Institution of Highway Engineers; present name 1987; concerned with the design, construction, maintenance and operation of sustainable transport systems and infrastructure; serves as a representative body for the profession, to implement best practice and technical excellence, to bring fellow professionals and ideas together and to provide training and professional competence; 11,000 UK-based mems, several hundred overseas mems; 18 UK-based brs, several overseas brs incl. Republic of Ireland, Hong Kong and Malaysia; Chief Exec. MARY LEWIS; publ. *Transportation Professional* (10 a year).

Institution of Incorporated Engineers (IIE): Savoy Hill House, Savoy Hill, London,

WC2R 0BS; tel. (20) 7836-3357; fax (20) 7497-9006; e-mail info@iie.org.uk; internet www .iie.org.uk; f. 1998; 40,000 mems; Sec. and Chief Exec. PETER F. WASON; publ. *Engineering Technology* (monthly).

Institution of Lighting Engineers: Regent House, Regent Place, Rugby, Warwicks., CV21 2PN; tel. (1788) 576492; fax (1788) 540145; e-mail info@ile.org.uk; internet www.ile.org.uk; f. 1924 to promote, encourage and improve the science and art of efficient lighting in all fields, and to facilitate the exchange of information and ideas on this subject; 1,900 mems; Pres. DEREK ROGERS; Chief Exec. RICHARD FROST; publ. *Lighting Journal* (6 a year).

Institution of Mechanical Engineers: 1 Birdcage Walk, London, SW1H 9JJ; tel. (20) 7222-7899; fax (20) 7222-4557; internet www .imeche.org.uk; f. 1847, inc. by Royal Charter 1930; principal organization for professional mechanical engineers in the UK, and qualifying body for chartered and incorporated mechanical engineers; 75,000 mems worldwide; library of 60,000 books and various other documents; Pres. WILLIAM EDGAR; Chief Exec. ANDREW IVES; publs *Automotive Engineer* (10 a year), *Environmental Engineering* (quarterly), *Institution of Diesel and Gas Turbine Engineers* (6 a year), *Journal of Strain Analysis, Professional Engineering* (22 a year).

Institution of Nuclear Engineers: Allan House, 1 Penerley Rd, London, SE6 2LQ; tel. (20) 8698-1500; fax (20) 8695-6409; e-mail inucewh@aol.com; internet www.inuce.org .uk; f. 1959 for the advancement of nuclear engineering technology and its related fields; 1,700 mems; Pres. Dr P. A. BEELEY; publ. *The Nuclear Engineer* (every 2 months).

Institution of Structural Engineers: 11 Upper Belgrave St, London, SW1X 8BH; tel. (20) 7235-4535; fax (20) 7235-4294; e-mail mail@istructe.org; internet www.istructe .org; f. 1908 as the Concrete Inst., present name 1922; inc. by Royal Charter 1934, to promote the general advancement of the science and art of structural eng.; library of 15,000 vols; 21,000 mems; Pres. DAVID HARVEY; Chief Exec. Dr KEITH J. EATON; publ. *The Structural Engineer* (2 a month).

National Society for Clean Air and Environmental Protection: 44 Grand Parade, Brighton, East Sussex, BN2 9QA; tel. (1273) 878770; fax (1273) 606626; e-mail admin@nsca.org.uk; internet www.nsca.org .uk; f. 1899 as Coal Smoke Abatement Soc. and merged with the Smoke Abatement League of Great Britain in 1929; air pollution, contaminated land and noise control, environmental protection; 1,500 mems, incl. learned socs, local authorities, industrial concerns, etc.; Pres. Lord JULIAN HUNT; Chief Exec. PHILIP MULLIGAN (acting); publs *NSCA Briefing* (monthly), *NSCA Pollution Handbook* (overview of pollution control legislation, annual).

Newcomen Society for the Study of the History of Engineering and Technology: Science Museum, Exhibition Rd, South Kensington, London, SW7 2DD; tel. and fax (20) 7371-4445; e-mail office@newcomen.com; internet www.newcomen.com; f. 1920 to encourage the study of the history of eng. and technology world-wide; 1,000 mems; Exec. Sec. DICK SWANN; publs *Transactions* (2 a year), *Bulletin* (quarterly).

Oil and Colour Chemists' Association: Priory House, 967 Harrow Rd, Wembley, Middlesex, HA0 2SF; tel. (20) 8908-1086; fax (20) 8908-1219; e-mail enquiries@occa .org.uk; internet www.occa.org.uk; f. 1918 to promote by discussion and scientific investigation the technology of the paint, oil, printing ink, and allied industries; 2,400 mems; Pres. D. FOULGER; Gen. Sec. C. PACEY-DAY; publs *Surface Coatings International Part A* (10 a year), *Surface Coatings International Part B* (4 a year), *Surface Coating Reviews, Surface Coating Monographs*.

Radio Society of Great Britain: Lambda House, Cranborne Rd, Potters Bar, EN6 3JE; tel. (1707) 659015; fax (1707) 45105; e-mail sales@rsgb.org.uk; internet www.rsgb.org; f. 1913 to promote interest in the science of radio-communication by amateurs, and to safeguard the interests of those of its members who operate or aspire to operate amateur transmitting stations; 30,000 mems; Gen. Man. PETER A. KIRBY; publ. *Radio Communication* (monthly).

Remote Sensing and Photogrammetry Society: c/o School of Geography, Univ. of Nottingham, Nottingham, NG7 2RD; tel. (115) 951-5435; fax (115) 951-5249; e-mail rspsoc@nottingham.ac.uk; internet www .rspsoc.org; f. 2001; theory, techniques, instrumentation, applications in surveying, engineering, mapping, geographic information; 1,000 mems; library of 2,000 vols; Hon. Gen. Sec. Dr PHILIPPA MASON; publs *The Photogrammetric Record* (quarterly), *International Journal of Remote Sensing* (24 a year).

Royal Academy of Engineering: 29 Great Peter St, London, SW1P 3LW; tel. (20) 7227-0500; fax (20) 7233-0054; internet www .raeng.org.uk; f. 1976; conducts engineering and educational studies, sponsors links between industry and higher education, co-sponsors with industry academic posts at higher education instns; 1,353 mems (1,239 fellows, 91 foreign mems, 23 hon. fellows); Pres. Sir ALEC BROERS; Chief Exec. P. GREENISH; publs *Annual Report, Ingenia* (4 a year).

Royal Aeronautical Society: 4 Hamilton Place, London, W1J 7BQ; tel. (20) 7499-3515; fax (20) 7499-6230; internet www.aerosociety .com; f. 1866; 18,500 mems; library of 27,000 books, 1,300 periodicals (of which 300 current), 20,000 technical reports, 100,000 photographs; Dir KEITH MANS; publs *Aerospace Professional* (monthly), *The Aeronautical Journal* (monthly), *Aerospace International* (monthly).

Royal Institution of Naval Architects: 10 Upper Belgrave St, London, SW1X 8BQ; tel. (20) 7235-4622; fax (20) 7245-6959; e-mail hq@rina.org.uk; internet www.rina.org.uk; f. 1860, to advance naval architecture and marine technology; 7,100 mems; Pres. GERAINT PRICE; Chief Exec. TREVOR BLAKELEY; publs *Transactions Part A: International Journal of Maritime Engineering* (4 a year), *Transactions Part B: International Journal of Small Craft Technology* (2 a year), *The Naval Architect* (10 a year), *Ship and Boat International* (10 a year), *Ship Repair and Conversion Technology* (4 a year), *Significant Ships* (annually), *Significant Small Craft* (annually), *Warship Technology* (5 a year).

Royal Television Society: Holborn Hall, 100 Gray's Inn Rd, London, WC1X 8AL; tel. (20) 7430-1000; fax (20) 7430-0924; e-mail info@rts.org.uk; internet www.rts.org.uk; f. 1927 for the advance of the art of television, and as a forum for discussion and debate on all aspects of the profession; annual awards; 14 regional centres; over 3,000 mems; Pres. Sir ROBERT PHILLIS; Chief Exec. SIMON ALBURY; publ. *Television* (10 a year).

Society for Underwater Technology: 80 Coleman St, London, EC2R 5BJ; tel. (20) 7382-2601; fax (20) 7382-2684; e-mail info@ sut.org; internet www.sut.org.uk; f. 1966; to promote the further understanding of the underwater environment, and to advance the development of the techniques and tools needed to explore, study and exploit the oceans; provides sponsorship for undergraduate and 1-year postgraduate students studying in an appropriate subject area; 1,000 individual and 110 corporate mems; Exec. Sec. I. N. L. GALLETT; publ. *Underwater Technology* (4 a year).

Society of Consulting Marine Engineers and Ship Surveyors: 202 Lambeth Rd, London, SE1 7JW; tel. (20) 7261-0869; fax (20) 7261-0871; e-mail sec@scmshq.org; internet www.scmshq.org; f. 1920 to provide a central org. for consulting marine engineers, naval architects and ship surveyors, and generally to elevate the status and procure the advancement of the interests of the profession; Sec. P. R. OWEN.

Society of Designer Craftsmen: 24 Rivington St, London, EC2A 3DU; tel. (20) 7739-3663; fax (20) 7739-3663; e-mail info@ societyofdesignercraftsmen.org.uk; internet www.societyofdesignercraftsmen.org.uk; f. 1888; 750 mems; Pres. Prof. CHRISTOPHER FRAYLING; Chair. STEPHEN MAER; Hon. Secs ALICIA MERRETT, JOANNA HAYES; publ. *The Designer Craftsman* (annually).

Society of Dyers and Colourists: Perkin House, POB 244, 82 Grattan Rd, Bradford, W. Yorks., BD1 2JB; tel. (1274) 725138; fax (1274) 392888; e-mail secretariat@sdc.org .uk; internet www.sdc.org.uk; f. 1884 to promote the advancement of the science and technology of colour and coloration; examining and awarding body for chartered qualifications; colour experience; 2,500 mems, 800 subscribers; Pres. ADRIAN ABEL; Chief Exec. and Gen. Sec. KENNETH M. MCGHEE; publs *Colour Index, Coloration Technology* (6 a year).

Society of Engineers: Guinea Wiggs, Nayland, Colchester, Essex, CO6 4NF; tel. (1206) 263332; fax (1206) 262624; e-mail chiefexcecutive@society-of-engineers.org.uk; internet www.society-of-engineers.org.uk; f. 1854; library of 2,000 vols; Pres. I. A. C. WRIGHT; Chief Exec. L. C. A. WRIGHT; publ. *Engineering World* (2 a year).

Society of Glass Technology: Unit 9, Twelve O'Clock Court, 21 Attercliffe Rd, Sheffield, S4 7WW; tel. (114) 263-4455; fax (114) 263-4411; e-mail info@sgt.org; internet www.sgt.org; f. 1916 to promote the association of persons interested in glass technology; publishes books, journals and conference proceedings; hosts and organizes int. and local conferences on glass; provides information and holds a library and archive on glass; supports students with travel bursaries and final year project prizes; British representative on int. bodies such as the Int. Commission on Glass and European Soc. of Glass Science and Technology; 900 mems; library of 10,000 vols; Located at Univ. of Sheffield Applied Science Library; Hon. Sec. JOHN HENDERSON; publs *Glass Technology: European Journal of Glass Science and Technology Part A* (6 a year), *Physics and Chemistry of Glasses: European Journal of Glass Science and Technology Part B* (6 a year).

Society of Operations Engineers: 22 Greencoat Place, London, SW1P 1PR; tel. (20) 7630-1111; fax (20) 7630-6677; e-mail soe@soe.org.uk; internet www.soe.org.uk; f. 2000 by merger of Institute of Road Transport Engineers (IRTE) and Institution of Plant Engineers (IPlantE), to represent members of the road transport, plant engineering and engineer surveying industries; professional body; 21,800 mems; Pres. MIKE EDWARDS; Chief Exec. TRACEY FISHER; publs *Operations Engineer, Plant Engineer* (6 a year), *Transport Engineer* (12 a year).

South Wales Institute of Engineers: Empire House, Mount Stuart Square, Cardiff, CF10 5FN; tel. (29) 20481726; fax (29) 20451953; e-mail info@swie.org.uk; internet www.swie.org.uk; f. 1857 for the encouragement and advancement of engineering science and practice; 272 mems; Pres. G. EVANS; Hon. Sec. D. M. MORGAN; publ. *Proceedings* (every 2 years).

SCI (Steel Construction Institute): Silwood Park, Ascot, Berks, SL5 7QN; tel. (1344) 636525; fax (1344) 636570; e-mail reception@ steel-sci.com; internet www.steel-sci.org; f. 1986; develops and promotes the proper and effective use of steel as a construction material; 850 mems; library of 11,000 vols; Dir Dr G. W. OWENS; publ. *New Steel Construction* (every 2 months).

Textile Institute: see under International Organizations (Engineering and Technology).

TWI: Granta Park, Great Abington, Cambridge, CB21 6AL; tel. (1223) 899000; fax (1223) 892588; e-mail twi@twi.co.uk; internet www.twi.co.uk; f. 1946 to undertake general and contract research, to advance welding technology in all aspects, to provide consultancy and laboratory services, to provide education and training and to improve the professional status and qualification of members; specialized information services on materials-joining technology; training courses in welding engineering, welding inspection, practical welding, non-destructive testing, structural integrity, microjoining; 10,500 mems (3,500 research, 7,000 professional); library of 10,000 vols; Chief Exec. R. JOHN; publs *Connect* (6 a year), *Contact* (news video, annual).

Research Institutes

AGRICULTURE, FISHERIES AND VETERINARY SCIENCE

Animal Health Trust: Lanwades Park, Kentford, Newmarket, Suffolk, CB8 7UU; tel. (8700) 502424; fax (8700) 502425; e-mail info@aht.org.uk; internet www.aht.org.uk; f. 1942; aims to advance veterinary science and provide specialist clinical services for all companion animals; Pres. HRH The PRINCESS ROYAL; CEO Dr PETER WEBBON.

Biotechnology and Biological Sciences Research Council (BBSRC): Polaris House, North Star Ave, Swindon, Wilts., SN2 1UH; tel. (1793) 413200; fax (1793) 413201; internet www.bbsrc.ac.uk; f. 1994; responsible to the Office of Science and Technology; supports fundamental and strategic multidisciplinary research, with emphasis on the biological sciences, biotechnology and engineering, in its institutes and univs; Chair. Dr PETER RINGROSE; Chief Exec. Prof. JULIA GOODFELLOW.

Institutes and units:

Babraham Institute: Babraham Hall, Babraham, Cambridge, CB2 4AT; tel. (1223) 496000; fax (1223) 496021; internet www.babraham.ac.uk; f. 1948; research to advance understanding of function in animal cells and systems, with emphasis on cell signalling, recognition mechanisms and mammalism devt; Dir Dr R. J. BICKNELL (acting).

Institute for Animal Health: Compton, Nr Newbury, Berks., RG20 7NN; tel. (1635) 578411; fax (1635) 577237; internet www.iah.ac.uk; undertakes basic, strategic and applied research required for the understanding of the aetiology, pathogenesis, epidemiology and diagnosis of diseases of farm animals, including those exotic diseases that could spread to the United Kingdom, the study of newly recognized diseases and the influence of disease control measures on food safety and quality; Dir of Research Prof. M. W. SHIRLEY (acting).

Sites:

Institute for Animal Health—Compton Laboratory: Compton, Nr Newbury, Berks., RG20 7NN; tel. (1635) 578411; fax (1635) 577237.

Institute for Animal Health—Pirbright Laboratory: Ash Rd, Pirbright, Woking, Surrey, GU24 0NF; tel. (1483) 232441; fax (1483) 232448; Head Dr A. I. DONALDSON.

Neuropathogenesis Unit: Ogston Bldg, West Mains Rd, Edinburgh, EH9 3JF; tel. (131) 667-5204; fax (131) 668-3872.

Institute of Food Research: Norwich Research Park, Colney Lane, Norwich, NR4 7UA; tel. (1603) 255000; fax (1603) 507723; internet www.ifr.ac.uk; investigates the relationship between diet and health and seeks to improve the safety, quality and nutritional value of foods for consumers; contributes to the improvement of dietary guidelines and advice and generates and evaluates new options for safe and efficient food manufacture; Dir Prof. DAVID WHITE.

Institute of Grassland and Environmental Research: Plas Gogerddan, Aberystwyth, SY23 3EB; tel. (1970) 828255; fax (1970) 828357; internet www.iger.bbsrc.ac.uk/igerweb; basic and strategic research into grassland and environmental research related to non-arable agriculture; seeks to increase understanding of genetic and competitive processes in pastures and natural plant populations in response to grazing and climatic variables, to elucidate processes controlling intake, growth, body composition and lactation in ruminants, to investigate consequences of climatic and management changes on grassland agriculture and the opportunities for alternative animals and crops, and to study the fluxes of nutrients and utilization efficiencies of inputs with reference to losses and environmental pollution; Research Dir Prof. C. J. POLLOCK.

Sites:

Institute of Grassland and Environmental Research—Aberystwyth Research Centre: Plas Gogerddan, Aberystwyth, Dyfed, SY23 3EB; tel. (1970) 828255; fax (1970) 828357; Dir (vacant).

Institute of Grassland and Environmental Research—Bronydd Mawr Research Centre: Trecastle, Brecon, Powys, LD3 8RD; tel. (1874) 636480; fax (1874) 636542; Officer in charge J. M. M. MUNRO.

Institute of Grassland and Environmental Research—North Wyke Research Station: Okehampton, Devon, EX20 2SB; tel. (1837) 883500; Head of Site (vacant).

John Innes Centre: Colney Lane, Norwich, NR4 7UH; tel. (1603) 450000; fax (1603) 450045; internet www.jic.ac.uk; aims to assist the agricultural and biotechnological industries by carrying out fundamental research on plants and bacteria; to understand and describe the basis of the control of plant and bacterial form, behaviour and metabolism so that genetically modified plants and bacteria may be improved or changed to offer new industrial potentialities; Dir Prof. CHRIS LAMB.

Roslin Institute (Edinburgh): Roslin, Midlothian, EH25 9PS; tel. (131) 527-4200; fax (131) 440-0434; internet www.ri.bbsrc.ac.uk; basic and strategic research on farm animals; Dir HARRY GRIFFIN.

Rothamsted Research: Rothamsted, Harpenden, Herts., AL5 2JQ; tel. (1582) 763133; fax (1582) 760981; internet www.rothamsted.ac.uk; f. 1843; basic, strategic and applied research on soils and crop plants; Dir Prof. IAN R. CRUTE.

Attached site:

Broom's Barn Research Station: Higham, Bury St Edmunds, Suffolk, IP28 6NP; tel. (1284) 812200; fax (1284) 811191; e-mail brooms.barn@bbsrc.ac.uk; internet www.broomsbarn.ac.uk; research into sugar beet; Dir BILL CLARK.

Central Science Laboratory: Sand Hutton, York, N. Yorks., YO41 1LZ; tel. (1904) 462000; fax (1904) 462111; e-mail science@csl.gov.uk; internet www.csl.gov.uk; f. 1992; exec. agency of the Dept for Environment, Food and Rural Affairs; research and advice in the fields of: plant health; the authenticity, chemical and microbiological safety and nutritional value of the food supply; pesticide safety (including the monitoring of residues in food); veterinary drug residues; proficiency testing schemes; the control of pests and diseases of growing and stored crops; the impact of food production on the environment and the consumer; alternative crops and biotechnology; animal health and welfare; and conservation and wildlife management; Chief Exec. Prof. T. M. ROBERTS.

Centre for the Environment, Fisheries and Aquaculture Science (CEFAS): Pakefield Rd, Lowestoft, Suffolk, NR33 0HT; tel. (1502) 562244; fax (1502) 513865; e-mail lowlibrary@cefas.co.uk; internet www.cefas.co.uk; an exec. agency of the Dept for the Environment, Food and Rural Affairs; provides contract research, consultancy and training services in environmental impact assessment, environmental research and monitoring, aquaculture health and hygiene, and fisheries science and management; extensive research library; brs at Weymouth and Burnham-on-Crouch; Chief Exec. R. JUDGE.

Forest Research: Alice Holt Lodge, Wrecclesham, Farnham, Surrey, GU10 4LH; tel. (1420) 22255; fax (1420) 23653; internet www.forestresearch.gov.uk; f. 1919 to advance research and technology related to forestry; comprises two research stations with biological sections for silviculture and seeds, tree improvement, woodland ecology, entomology, pathology, environmental research, development of forest machinery and working methods, woodland surveys, and service sections for statistics and computing, mensuration, photography; research resources and technical support; library of 20,000 vols; Chief Exec. JIM LYNCH; publ. *Annual Report*.

Research stations:

Alice Holt Research Station: Alice Holt Lodge, Wrecclesham, Farnham, Surrey, GU10 4LH; tel. (1420) 22255; fax (1420) 23653; e-mail j.parker@forestry.gov.uk; Chief Research Officer P. H. FREER-SMITH.

Northern Research Station: Roslin, Midlothian, EH25 9SY; tel. (131) 445-2176; fax (131) 445-5124; e-mail nrs@forestry.gsi.gov.uk; Chief Exec. J. DEWAR.

Henry Doubleday Research Association: Ryton Organic Gardens, Coventry, CV8 3LG; tel. (24) 7630-3517; fax (24) 7663-9229; e-mail enquiry@hdra.org.uk; internet www.hdra.org.uk; f. 1954; conducts research in organic agriculture, with focus on commercial organic horticulture in temperate regions and subsistence agriculture in developing countries; maintains vegetable seed colln; sets standards for organic amenity horticulture; services to the public incl. membership of the Asscn and access to organic display gardens; Dir of Research Dr MARGI LENNARTSSON.

NIAB: Huntingdon Rd, Cambridge, CB3 0LE; tel. (1223) 276381; fax (1223) 277602; e-mail info@niab.com; internet www.niab.com; f. 1919 to promote the improvement of existing varieties of seeds, plants and crops in the United Kingdom; includes the Official Seed Testing Station for England and Wales, and other depts which are particularly concerned with crop variety testing and description, seed certification and seed production techniques; library of 10,000 vols; Dir Prof. BRIAN J. LEGG; Sec. J. W. HALL; publs *Annual Report*, *Plant Genetic Resources Characterization and Utilization* (print and online), *Varieties of Cereals, Oilseeds, Pulses* (2 a year), *Grass and Herbage Legumes Variety Book* (annually), *Potato Variety Handbook*.

Oxford Forestry Institute: University of Oxford, Department of Plant Sciences, South Parks Rd, Oxford, OX1 3RB; tel. (1865) 275000; fax (1865) 275074; e-mail ofi@plants.ox.ac.uk; internet www.plants.ox.ac.uk/ofi/; f. 1924 (as Imperial, later Commonwealth Forestry Inst.), for research and higher studies in forestry; library of 200,000 vols, in conjunction with CAB International; Dir Prof. J. BURLEY.

Scottish Agricultural Science Agency: 1 Roddinglaw Rd, Edinburgh, EH12 9FJ; tel. (131) 244-8890; fax (131) 244-8940; e-mail info@sasa.gsi.gov.uk; internet www.sasa.gov.uk; f. 1992; govt agency carrying out scientific executive work, associated research and consultation on: seed testing, testing of candidate cultivars of crop plants for Nat. Listing and Plant Breeders' Rights, certification of seed and planting stock, production of disease-tested clonal stocks of potatoes, statutory aspects of pest and disease control, pesticide usage assessment, pesticide residues, ecology of mammals and birds of actual or potential pest status; Chief Exec. Dr GORDON C. MACHRAY.

Scottish Executive Environment and Rural Affairs Department: Pentland House, 47 Robb's Loan, Edinburgh, EH14 1TY; tel. (131) 556-8400; e-mail ceu@scotland.gsi.gov.uk; internet www.scotland.gov.uk.

Research institutes:

Hannah Research Institute: Ayr, KA6 5HL; tel. (1292) 674000; fax (1292) 674003; internet www.hri.sari.ac.uk; f. 1928; research into human health and nutrition; programme areas: metabolism; life and death of the cell; CHARIS (food science and technology research); Dir Prof. C. KNIGHT (acting).

Macaulay Institute: Craigiebuckler, Aberdeen, AB15 8QH; tel. (1224) 498200; fax (1224) 311556; e-mail enquries@macaulay.ac.uk; internet www.macaulay.ac.uk; f. 1930; interdisciplinary research across the environmental and social sciences; aims to support the protection of natural resources, creation of integrated land-use systems and the devt of sustainable rural communities; Chief Exec. Prof. BILL RITCHIE.

Moredun Research Institute: Pentlands Science Park, Bush Loan, Penicuik, Midlothian, EH26 0PZ; tel. (131) 445-5111; fax (131) 445-6235; internet www.mri.sari.ac .uk; f. 1920; research on livestock diseases that undermine biological efficiency, impair welfare or threaten public health; Dir Prof. JULIE FITZPATRICK.

Rowett Research Institute: Greenbank Rd, Bucksburn, Aberdeen, AB21 9SB; tel. (1224) 712751; fax (1224) 715349; internet www.rowett.ac.uk; f. 1913; research into how nutrition can prevent disease, into improving health and into enhancing the quality of food production in agriculture; Dir Prof. PETER MORGAN.

Scottish Crop Research Institute: Invergowrie, Dundee, DD2 5DA; tel. (1382) 562731; fax (1382) 562426; internet www.scri.sari.ac.uk; f. 1981; research into potatoes, barley and soft fruit crops; Dir Prof. PETER GREGORY.

Veterinary Laboratories Agency: Woodham Lane, Addlestone, Surrey, KT15 3NB; tel. (1932) 341111; fax (1932) 347046; internet www.defra.gov.uk/corporate/vla; exec. agency of the Dept for Environment, Food and Rural Affairs; f. 1917; Dir S. EDWARDS.

Woburn Experimental Station (Lawes Agricultural Trust): Husborne Crawley, Bedford; f. 1876 for the investigation of manurial and other problems of British crops; run as outstation of Rothamsted Experimental Station; Dir L. FOWDEN; publ. *Annual Report*.

ARCHITECTURE AND TOWN PLANNING

The Prince's Foundation: 19–22 Charlotte Rd, London, EC2A 3SG; tel. (20) 7613-8500; fax (20) 7613-8599; e-mail enquiry@ princes-foundation.org; internet www .princes-foundation.org; f. 1992; research into all areas of architecture, planning, regeneration, building, methods of construction and the crafts; public lectures, seminars and exhibitions; educational courses and consultancy; library of 5,000 vols; Administrator RIRIKO SUZUKI.

ECONOMICS, LAW AND POLITICS

Economic Research Council: 7 St James's Square, London, SW1Y 4JU; tel. (20) 7439-0271; e-mail info@ercouncil.org; internet www.ercouncil.org; f. 1943 as a non-profit-making research and educational organization in the field of economics and monetary practice; Pres. Lord BIFFEN; Chair. DAMON DE LASZLO; Hon. Sec JIM BOURLET; publ. *Britain and Overseas* (quarterly).

International Institute for Strategic Studies: Arundel House, 13–15 Arundel Street, London, WC2R 3DX; tel. (20) 7379-7676; fax (20) 7836-3108; e-mail iiss@iiss.org; internet www.iiss.org; f. 1958; aims to promote discussion and research on the problems of international security arising from all causes; international membership, Council, and staff; 2,141 mems (1,623 ordinary, 391 assoc., 127 student), 165 corporate mems; Chair. of the Council FRANÇOIS HEISBOURG; Dir Dr JOHN CHIPMAN; publs *Strategic Comments* (electronic publ., 10 a year), *Survival* (4 a year), *The Military Balance* (annually), *Strategic Survey* (annually), *Adelphi Papers* (8–10 a year).

National Institute of Economic and Social Research: 2 Dean Trench St, Smith Square, London, SW1P 3HE; tel. (20) 7222-7665; fax (20) 7654-1900; e-mail enquiries@ niesr.ac.uk; internet www.niesr.ac.uk; f. 1938; library of 10,000 vols, 300 periodicals; Pres. Lord BURNS; Dir M. WEALE; publ. *National Institute Economic Review* (4 a year).

Overseas Development Institute: 111 Westminster Bridge Rd, London, SE1 7JD; tel. (20) 7922 0300; fax (20) 7922 0399; e-mail odi@odi.org.uk; internet www.odi.org.uk; f. 1960 to act as an independent think-tank on international development and humanitarian issues; works to inspire and inform policy and practice which lead to the reduction of poverty, the alleviation of suffering and the achievement of sustainable livelihoods in developing countries; has 14 research and policy groups and programmes; works with partners in the public and private sectors, in both developing and developed countries; library of 20,000 vols; Chair. Baroness MARGARET JAY OF PADDINGTON; Dir SIMON MAXWELL; publs *Development Policy Review* (quarterly), *Disasters: The Journal of Disaster Studies and Management* (quarterly), research work in the form of books, opinions, briefing papers and working papers.

Royal United Services Institute for Defence and Security Studies: Whitehall, London, SW1A 2ET; tel. (20) 7930-5854; fax (20) 7321-0943; e-mail information@rusi.org; internet www.rusi.org; f. 1831; professional forum in the UK for those concerned with national and international defence and security; research programmes, lectures, conferences and seminars; individual, corporate and diplomatic mems; library: see Libraries and Archives; Dir Rear Admiral RICHARD COBBOLD; publs *Chinese Military Update* (monthly), *Documents of British Foreign and Security Policy* (irregular, jointly with the Stationery Office), *Homeland Security and Resilience Monitor* (10 a year), *Journal* (6 a year), *Newsbrief* (12 a year), *World Defence Systems* (3 a year).

EDUCATION

Institute for Cultural Research: POB 2227, London, NW2 3BW; tel. (20) 8452-0960; fax (20) 8438-0311; e-mail adm@i-c-r .org.uk; internet i-c-r.org.uk; f. 1966; to promote and conduct research and advance public education in man's heritage of knowledge; 200 mems; Chair. of Council DAVID WADE; Hon. Sec. HENRI BORTOFT.

National Foundation for Educational Research in England and Wales: The Mere, Upton Park, Slough, Berks., SL1 2DQ; tel. (1753) 574123; fax (1753) 691632; e-mail enquiries@nfer.ac.uk; internet www .nfer.ac.uk; f. 1946; to study problems arising within the nat. educational system, to disseminate information on its findings and to collaborate on a nat. and int. basis with other educational and research bodies; Pres. Sir BRIAN FENDER; Chair. RICHARD BUNKER; Dir SUE ROSSITER; publs *Educational Research* (3 a year), *Educational Research News*, research reports (various).

SCRE Centre: St Andrew's Bldg, 11 Eldon St, Glasgow G3 6NH; tel. (141) 330-3490; fax (141) 330-3491; e-mail scre.info@scre.ac.uk; internet www.scre.ac.uk; f. 1928 as Scottish Council for Research in Education; conducts educational research of the highest quality and supports the use of research outcomes through the dissemination of findings; Dir Prof. PAUL BRNA.

Society for Research into Higher Education Ltd: 76 Portland Place, London, W1B 1NT; tel. (20) 7637-2766; fax (20) 7637-2781; e-mail srheoffice@srhe.ac.uk; internet www .srhe.ac.uk; f. 1964 to encourage research and development in higher education and collect and disseminate the results; 237 corporate mems; Pres. (vacant); Dir HELEN PERKINS; publs *Research into Higher Education Abstracts* (3 a year), *Studies in Higher Education* (4 a year), *Higher Education Quarterly, Newsletter* (3 a year), *International Newsletter* (3 a year).

HISTORY, GEOGRAPHY AND ARCHAEOLOGY

German Historical Institute: 17 Bloomsbury Sq., London, WC1A 2NJ; tel. (20) 7309-2050; e-mail ghil@ghil.ac.uk; internet www .ghil.ac.uk; f. 1976; research in modern and comparative British and German history; study of int., esp. Anglo-German, relations; European history; 9 research fellows; library of 70,000 vols, 180 periodicals; Dir Prof. Dr ANDREAS GESTRICH; Admin. Officer WOLFGANG HAACK; publ. *Bulletin* (2 a year).

Institute of Contemporary British History: Institute of Historical Research, Senate House, Malet St, London, WC1E 7HU; tel. (20) 7862-8810; fax (20) 7862-8812; e-mail icbh@icbh.ac.uk; internet www.icbh.ac.uk/ icbh; f. 1986; Dir Dr HARRIET JONES (acting); publs *Contemporary British History* (4 a year), *Modern History Review* (4 a year).

Royal Archaeological Institute: c/o Society of Antiquaries, Burlington House, Piccadilly, London, W1J 0BE; tel. (116) 2433839; fax (116) 2433839; e-mail admin@ royalarchaeolinst.org; internet www .royalarchaeolinst.org; f. 1843; has a lecture programme, holds meetings for mems, awards grants for archaeological research and excavations; 1,500 mems; Pres. JONATHAN COAD; Hon. Sec. Dr GILL HEY; publ. *Archaeological Journal* (annual).

Scott Polar Research Institute: Lensfield Rd, Cambridge, CB2 1ER; tel. (1223) 336540; fax (1223) 336549; e-mail enquiries@spri.cam .ac.uk; internet www.spri.cam.ac.uk; f. 1920; research and information centre on the Polar regions (glaciology, geophysics, oceanography, remote sensing, history, anthropology, socio-economics); exhibits; library of 100,000 vols, 700 periodicals; archives; photographic library; Dir Prof. J. A. DOWDESWELL; publs *Polar and Glaciological Abstracts, Polar Record*.

LANGUAGE AND LITERATURE

Arts and Humanities Research Board: Whitefriars, Lewins Mead, Bristol, BS1 2AE; tel. (117) 987-6500; internet www.ahrb.ac .uk; f. 1998 by the higher education funding councils for England, Scotland and Wales, for Employment and Learning in Northern Ireland, and the British Academy, as the first stage in the establishment of the Arts and Humanities Research Council, to provide financial and practical support for research and postgraduate training in the arts and humanities, as well as funding for museums and art galleries; Chief Exec. (vacant); Chair. Prof. Sir BRIAN FOLLETT; publ. *Arcady Newsletter* (irregular).

CILT, the National Centre for Languages: 20 Bedfordbury, London, WC2N 4LB; tel. (20) 7379-5101; fax (20) 7379-5082; e-mail info@cilt.org.uk; internet www.cilt.org .uk; f. 1966; independent, registered charity, supported by govt grants; nat. centre for information on learning and teaching languages and on languages for employment; has an enquiry service, specialized library and multimedia colln, training and conference programme; library of 14,000 titles; Chief Exec. ISABELLA MOORE.

Modern Humanities Research Association: 1 Carlton House Terrace London, SW1Y 5DB; e-mail mail@mhra.org.uk; internet www.mhra.org.uk; f. at Cambridge Univ. in 1918 to encourage advanced studies in modern and medieval languages and literatures; publishes journals and monographs; provides funding assistance for academic publishing, research and conferences; 400 mems; Hon. Sec. Prof. DAVID GILLESPIE; publs *Annual Bibliography of English Language and Literature*, *Austrian Studies*, *Modern Language Review* (quarterly), *Oxford German Studies*, *Portuguese Studies* (2 a year), *The Slavonic and East European Review* (quarterly), *Yearbook of English Studies* (2 a year), *The Year's Work in Modern Language Studies*.

MEDICINE

Arthritis Research Campaign: POB 177, Chesterfield, Derbyshire, S41 7TQ; tel. (1246) 558033; fax (1246) 558007; e-mail info@arc.org.uk; internet www.arc.org.uk; f. 1936 to raise funds for medical research into the causes, treatment and cure of arthritis and related musculoskeletal conditions; educates medical students, doctors and allied healthcare professionals about arthritis; provides information to people affected by arthritis and to the general public; Chief Exec. F. LOGAN; publ. *Arthritis Today* (4 a year).

Burden Neurological Institute: Frenchay Park Rd, Bristol, BS16 1JB; tel. (117) 918-6720; e-mail burdeninstitute@hotmail.com; internet www.bristol.ac.uk/neuroscience/clinical/bni; f. 1939 to conduct research in neurology, neurophysiology, neuropsychology and psychiatry; stem cell research into multiple sclerosis; library of 4,000 vols; Dir Prof. NEIL J. SCOLDING; Sec. RODNEY C. NORTH.

Cancer Research UK: 61 Lincoln's Inn Fields, London, WC2A 3PX; tel. (20) 7242-0200; fax (20) 7269-3101; internet www.cancerresearchuk.org; f. 2002, by merger of Imperial Cancer Research Fund (f. 1902) and Cancer Research Campaign (f. 1923); library of 4,000 vols, 300 periodicals; Chair. DAVID NEWBIGGING; Chief. Exec. Prof. ALEX MARKHAM; publs *Annual Report*, *Scientific Report* (annually).

Cancer Research UK Beatson Laboratories: Garscube Estate, Switchback Rd, Bearsden, Glasgow, G61 1BD; tel. (141) 330-3953; fax (141) 942-6521; e-mail beatson@gla.ac.uk; internet www.beatson.gla.ac.uk; f. 1990; incorporates Beatson Institute for Cancer Research and the University of Glasgow depts of Medical Oncology and Radiation Oncology; research in molecular and cell biology of cancer and related diseases; library of 1,000 textbooks, 83 journals; Dir of the Beatson Institute for Cancer Research Prof. J. A. WYKE; publ. *Scientific Report* (annually).

Centre for Applied Microbiology and Research: Porton Down, Salisbury, Wilts, SP4 0JG; tel. (1980) 612100; fax (1980) 611096; e-mail research@camr.org.uk; internet www.camr.org.uk; f. 1979; Special Health Authority administered by the Microbiological Research Authority; WHO Reference Laboratory for pathogenic viruses; undertakes research and development in health care and environmental fields; also production and consultancy contracts in all its principal activities, and maintains strong links with government, academia and industry, in the UK and overseas; HIV/AIDS research; biotechnology; pharmaceutical manufacturing; role of microorganisms in chronic diseases; vaccine research and development (and production at clinical trial level); molecular genetics of bacteria and yeast; microbiological safety; European Collection of Cell Cultures; protein isolation and characterization; manufactures a number of biologically derived drug compounds from both wild-type and recombinant microorganisms; has specialist facilities for work with pathogenic microorganisms and their products; library of 5,000 vols, 200 periodicals; research Dir Dr CHARLES R. PENN.

Institute for Ageing and Health: c/o Lynn Patterson, Wolfson Research Centre, Newcastle General Hospital, Newcastle upon Tyne, NE4 6BE; tel. (191) 256-3014; fax (191) 256-3011; e-mail l.patterson@ncl.ac.uk; internet www.ncl.ac.uk/iah/; f. 1994 to undertake clinical research into gerontology and the health-related issues of the ageing process; 200 mems; small specialist library; Dir Prof. TOM KIRKWOOD.

Institute of Cancer Research: see under University of London.

Liverpool School of Tropical Medicine: Pembroke Place, Liverpool, L3 5QA; tel. (151) 708-9393; fax (151) 705-3370; e-mail robbinsv@liverpool.ac.uk; internet www.liv.ac.uk/lstm; f. 1898 and received its Charter of Incorporation 1905; affiliated to the University of Liverpool; its objects are to train medical and paramedical personnel in all aspects of individual or community medicine in the tropics, to conduct original research into tropical diseases and their control, and to organize and conduct clinical and prophylactic measures against tropical diseases; also undertakes research and technical assistance work in other health sector areas; library of 50,000 vols and periodicals, incl. Ronald Ross collection; Dir Prof. JANET HEMINGWAY; publs *Annals of Tropical Medicine and Parasitology*, *Annals of Tropical Paediatrics*.

Medical Research Council (MRC): 20 Park Crescent, London, W1B 4AL; tel. (20) 7636-5422; fax (20) 7436-6179; e-mail corporate@headoffice.mrc.ac.uk; internet www.mrc.ac.uk; f. 1913.; principal objectives are to promote the balanced devt of medical and related biological research and to advance knowledge that will lead to the maintaining and improvement of human health; the Council employs its own research staff in about 40 research establishments; it also provides grants to scientists who are not members of its own staff, to undertake research programmes and projects, thus complementing the research resources of the univs and hospitals; research training is supported by means of fellowships and studentships; Chair. Sir ANTHONY CLEAVER; Chief Exec. Prof. COLIN BLAKEMORE; publ. *Research Strategy* (annual).

Attached research establishments:

Centre for Mechanisms of Human Toxicity: Hodgkin Bldg, Univ. of Leicester, POB 138, Lancaster Rd, Leicester, LE1 9HN; tel. (116) 252-5525; fax (116) 252-5616; internet www.le.ac.uk/cmht; f. 1993; Dir Prof. G. C. K. ROBERTS.

MRC Anatomical Neuropharmacology Unit: Mansfield Rd, Oxford, OX1 3TH; tel. (1865) 271865; fax (1865) 271647; internet mrcanu.pharm.ox.ac.uk; f. 1984; Dir Prof. P. SOMOGYI.

MRC Biomedical Nuclear Magnetic Resonance Centre: Nat. Institute for Medical Research, The Ridgeway, Mill Hill, London, NW7 1AA; tel. (20) 8816-2026; fax (20) 8906-4477; internet www.nmrcentre.mrc.ac.uk; Dir Dr T. FRENKIEL.

MRC Biostatistics Unit: Institute of Public Health, Univ. Forvie Site, Robinson Way, Cambridge, CB2 2SR; tel. (1223) 330300; fax (1223) 330388; internet www.mrc-bsu.cam.ac.uk; f. 1970; Hon. Dir Prof. S. THOMPSON.

MRC Cambridge Centre for Brain Repair: Dept of Clinical Neurosciences, Univ. of Cambridge, E. D. Adrian Bldg, Forvie Site, Robinson Way, Cambridge, CB2 2PY; tel. (1223) 331160; fax (1223) 331174; internet www.brc.cam.ac.uk; Chair. Prof. J. W. FAWCETT.

MRC Centre, Cambridge: Hills Rd, Cambridge, CB2 0QH; tel. (1223) 248011; fax (1223) 213556; internet www2.mrc-lmb.cam.ac.uk; Head Dr M. B. DAVIES.

MRC Centre, London: University College London, 3rd Floor, Stephenson House, 158–160 North Gower St, London, NW1 2ND; tel. (20) 7383-5894; fax (20) 7383-5902; internet www.centre-london.mrc.ac.uk; Head of Centre Dr IAN VINEY.

MRC Centre, Oxford: Manor House, John Radcliffe Hospital, Headington, Oxford, OX3 9DU; tel. (1865) 222580; fax (1865) 222549; Head Dr ANNE-MARIE CORIAT.

MRC Centre for Protein Engineering: Hills Rd, Cambridge, CB2 2QH; tel. (1223) 402100; fax (1223) 402140; internet www.mrc-cpe.cam.ac.uk; f. 1989; Dir Prof. A. FERSHT.

MRC Centre for Synaptic Plasticity: Dept of Anatomy, School of Medical Sciences, University Walk, Bristol, BS8 1TD; tel. (117) 928-7420; fax (117) 929-1687; internet www.bris.ac.uk/synaptic; Dir Prof. G. L. COLLINGRIDGE.

MRC Clinical Sciences Centre: Faculty of Medicine, Imperial College London, Hammersmith Hospital Campus, Du Cane Rd, London, W12 0NN; tel. (20) 8383-8249; fax (20) 8383-8337; internet www.csc.mrc.ac.uk; f. 1993; Dir Prof. C. HIGGINS.

MRC Clinical Trials Units: 222 Euston Rd, London, NW1 2DA; tel. (20) 7670-4700; fax (20) 7670-4818; e-mail contact@ctu.mrc.ac.uk; internet www.ctu.mrc.ac.uk; f. 1998; Dir Prof. J. DARBYSHIRE.

MRC Cognition and Brain Sciences Unit: 15 Chaucer Rd, Cambridge, CB2 7EF; tel. (1223) 355294; fax (1223) 359062; e-mail info@mrc-cbu.cam.ac.uk; internet www.mrc-cbu.cam.ac.uk; f. 1944; investigates fundamental human mental processes such as attention, emotion, memory and knowledge, speech and language; conducts behavioural experiments to probe the functional properties of psychological systems and build computer models of their operation; carries out neuropsychological and neuroimaging (PET, fMRI, MEG, EEG) studies of the underlying neural mechanisms in the brain and explores the clinical implications of our research for patient therapy and rehabilitation; Dir Prof. WILLIAM D. MARSLEN-WILSON.

MRC Dunn Human Nutrition Unit: Wellcome Trust/MRC Bldg, Addenbrooke's Site, Hills Rd, Cambridge, CB2 2XY; tel. (1223) 252700; fax (1223) 252715; internet www.mrc-dunn.cam.ac.uk; Dir Sir JOHN E. WALKER.

MRC Epidemiology Resource Centre: Southampton General Hospital, Southampton, SO16 6YD; tel. (23) 8077-7624; fax (23) 8070-4021; e-mail postmaster@mrc.soton.ac.uk; internet www.mrc.soton.ac.uk; Dir Dr C. COOPER.

MRC Functional Genetics Unit: Univ. of Oxford, Dept of Physiology, Anatomy and Genetics, South Parks Rd, Oxford, OX1 3QX; tel. (1865) 285867; fax (1865) 285862; internet www.mrcfgu.ox.ac.uk; Hon. Dir Prof. KAY DAVIES.

MRC Harwell (Mammalian Genetics Unit): Harwell, Oxon., OX11 0RD; tel. (1235) 841000; fax (1235) 841200; internet www.mgu.har.mrc.ac.uk; Dir Prof. S. BROWN.

MRC Harwell (Mouse Genome Centre): Harwell, Didcot, Oxon., OX11 0RD; tel. (1235) 834393; fax (1235) 834776; internet www.mgc.har.mrc.ac.uk; f. 1996; Dir Prof. S. BROWN.

MRC Harwell (Radiation and Genome Stability Unit): Harwell, Didcot, Oxon., OX11 0RD; tel. (1235) 834393; fax (1235) 834776; internet www.ragsu.har.mrc.ac.uk; Dir Prof. D. T. GOODHEAD.

MRC Health Services Research Collaboration: Univ. of Bristol, Canynge Hall, Whiteladies Rd, Bristol, BS8 2PR; tel. (117) 928-7343; fax (117) 928-7236; internet www.epi.bristol.ac.uk/hsrc; f. 1998; Dir Prof. P. DIEPPE.

MRC Human Genetics Unit: Western General Hospital, Crewe Rd, Edinburgh, EH4 2XU; tel. (131) 332-2471; fax (131) 343-2620; internet www.hgu.mrc.ac.uk; f. 1967; Dir Prof. N. D. HASTIE.

UK Human Genome Mapping Project Resource Centre: Hinxton Hall, Cambridge, CB10 1SB; tel. (1223) 494500; fax (1223) 494512; internet www.hgmp.mrc.ac.uk; Dir Dr D. CAMPBELL.

MRC Human Immunology Unit: Weatherall Institute of Molecular Medicine, John Radcliffe Hospital, Headington, Oxford, OX3 9DS; tel. (1865) 222336; fax (1865) 222600; internet www.imm.ox.ac.uk/groups/mrc-hiu; Dir Prof. ANDREW McMICHAEL.

MRC Human Reproductive Sciences Unit: Centre for Reproductive Biology, 37 Chalmers St, Edinburgh, EH3 9EW; tel. (131) 229-2575; fax (131) 228-5571; internet www.hrsu.mrc.ac.uk; Dir Prof. R. P. MILLAR.

MRC Immunochemistry Unit: Univ. Dept of Biochemistry, South Parks Rd, Oxford, OX1 3QU; tel. (1865) 275354; fax (1865) 275729; internet www.bioch.ox.ac.uk/immunoch; Dir Prof. K. B. M. REID.

Institute for Environment and Health: Cranfield Univ., Silsoe, Beds., MK45 4DT; tel. (1525) 863192; fax (1525) 863420; e-mail ieh@cranfield.ac.uk; internet www.silsoe.cranfield.ac.uk/ieh; f. 1993; aims to promote a healthier environment through identifying and evaluating environment and health issues and conducting and managing research programmes on the adverse effects of chemicals; areas of specialization incl. air pollution, chemical toxicology and regulatory affairs, endocrine disruption, food and diet, human exposure and risk assessment, health impact assessment, occupational and environmental toxicology; Dir Dr PAUL HARRISON.

MRC Institute of Hearing Research: Univ. of Nottingham, Nottingham, NG7 2RD; tel. (115) 922-3431; fax (115) 951-8503; e-mail postmaster@ihr.mrc.ac.uk; internet www.ihr.mrc.ac.uk; Dir Prof. M. P. HAGGARD.

MRC Interdisciplinary Research Centre for Cognitive Neuroscience: Univ. Laboratory of Physiology, Parks Rd, Oxford, OX1 3PT; tel. (1865) 272497; fax (1865) 272488; e-mail admin@cogneuro.ox.ac.uk; internet www.cogneuro.ox.ac.uk; Dir (vacant).

MRC Interdisciplinary Research Centre in Cell Biology: MRC Laboratory for Molecular Cell Biology, University College London, Gower St, London, WC1E 6BT; tel. (20) 7679-7806; fax (20) 7679-7805; internet www.ucl.ac.uk/lmcb; Dir Prof. C. R. HOPKINS.

MRC Laboratories, The Gambia: POB 273, Banjul, Gambia; tel. 4495442; fax 4495919; e-mail psnell@mrc.gm; internet www.mrc.gm; f. 1957; research into improvement of health care for developing countries; areas of speciality include virology, malaria, bacterial diseases and genetics; Dir Prof. T. CORRAH.

MRC Laboratory of Molecular Biology: Hills Rd, Cambridge, CB2 0QH; tel. (1223) 248011; fax (1223) 213556; internet www2.mrc-lmb.cam.ac.uk; f. 1962; Dir Dr HUGH PELHAM.

MRC Molecular Haematology Unit: Institute of Molecular Medicine, John Radcliffe Hospital, Headington, Oxford, OX3 9DU; tel. (1865) 222359; fax (1865) 222500; internet www.imm.ox.ac.uk/groups/mrc_molhaem; Hon. Dir Prof. Sir DAVID WEATHERALL.

MRC Muscle and Cell Motility Unit: New Hunts House, GKT School of Biomedical Sciences, London Bridge, London, SE1 1UL; tel. (20) 7848-6434; fax (20) 7848-6435; internet www.kcl.ac.uk/depsta/biomedical/randall/mrcmcmu.html; Hon. Dir Prof. R. M. SIMMONS.

MRC Prion Unit: Institute of Neurology, Queen Sq., London, WC1N 3BG; tel. (20) 7837-4888; fax (20) 7837-8047; e-mail pacollinge@prion.ucl.ac.uk; internet www.prion.ucl.ac.uk; f. 1999; Dir Prof. JOHN COLLINGE.

MRC Protein Phosphorylation Unit: Sir James Black Centre, College of Life Sciences, Univ. of Dundee, Dundee, DD1 5EH; tel. (1382) 384241; fax (1382) 223778; internet www.dundee.ac.uk/lifesciences/mrcppu; f. 1990; Hon. Dir Prof. Sir PHILIP COHEN.

MRC Resource Centre for Human Nutrition Research: Elsie Widdowson Laboratory, Fulbourn Rd, Cambridge, CB1 9NL; tel. (1223) 426356; fax (1223) 437515; internet www.mrc-hnr.cam.ac.uk; Dir Dr ANN PRENTICE.

MRC Social and Public Health Sciences Unit: 4 Lilybank Gardens, Glasgow, G12 8RZ; tel. (141) 357-3949; fax (141) 357-2389; internet www.msoc-mrc.gla.ac.uk; f. 1998; Dir Prof. SALLY MACINTYRE.

MRC Social, Genetic and Developmental Psychiatry Centre: Institute of Psychiatry, De Crespigny Park, Denmark Hill, London, SE5 8AF; tel. (20) 7740-5121; fax (20) 7740-5123; Dir Prof. P. McGUFFIN.

MRC Technology: 20 Park Crescent, London, W1B 1AL; tel. (20) 7636-5422; fax (20) 7436-6179; e-mail info@tech.mrc.ac.uk; internet www.mrctechnology.org; CEO Dr ROBERTO SOLARI.

MRC Toxicology Unit: Hodgkin Bldg, Univ. of Leicester, POB 138, Lancaster Rd, Leicester, LE1 9HN; tel. (116) 252-5537; fax (116) 252-5616; internet www.le.ac.uk/cmht/tox_unit.htm; f. 1947; Dir Prof. G. COHEN (acting).

MRC Virology Unit: Institute of Virology, Church St, Glasgow, G11 5JR; tel. (141) 330-4017; fax (141) 337-2236; internet www.mrcvu.gla.ac.uk; Dir Prof. D. J. McGEOCH.

National Institute for Medical Research: The Ridgeway, Mill Hill, London, NW7 1AA (a relocation to the University College London campus (*q.v.*) was announced in early 2005); tel. (20) 8959-3666; fax (20) 8906-4477; internet www.nimr.mrc.ac.uk; f. 1920; Dir Prof. Sir JOHN SKEHEL.

Oxford Centre for Molecular Sciences: New Chemistry Laboratory, Univ. of Oxford, South Parks Rd, Oxford, OX1 3QT; tel. (1865) 275627; fax (1865) 275905; internet www.ocms.ox.ac.uk; Dir Prof. C. M. DOBSON.

National Asthma Campaign: Providence House, Providence Place, London, N1 0NT; tel. (20) 7226-2260; fax (20) 7704-0740; internet www.asthma.org.uk; f. 1990; ind. UK charity; funds research into asthma and provides advice and information; 40,000 mems; Chair. Prof. DUNCAN GEDDES; Chief Exec. DONNA COVEY; publs *Asthma News* (4 a year), *Airways Extra*.

Paterson Institute for Cancer Research: Christie Hospital (NHS) Trust, Wilmslow Rd, Withington, Manchester, M20 9BX; tel. (161) 446-3000; fax (161) 446-3109; e-mail inquiries@picr.man.ac.uk; internet www.paterson.man.ac.uk; f. 1932; conducts basic and clinical cancer research; Dir NIC JONES.

Public Health Laboratory Service: 61 Colindale Ave, London, NW9 5HT; tel. (20) 8200-4400; fax (20) 8200-7874; internet www.phls.co.uk; f. 1946; library of 35,000 vols; Dir (vacant); publs *PHLS Library Bulletin* (weekly), *PHLS HIV Bulletin*, *PHLS Food and Environment Bulletin* (monthly), *Communicable Disease and Public Health* (4 a year), *Communicable Disease Report* (weekly).

Strangeways Research Laboratory: Worts' Causeway, Cambridge, CB1 8RN; tel. (1223) 740145; fax (1223) 740147; internet www.srl.cam.ac.uk; f. 1912; research into cell biology, developmental biology, cancer; primary research into cancer genetics, epidemiology, cardiovascular disease and diabetes; Dirs Prof. J. DANESH, Prof. B. PONDER.

NATURAL SCIENCES

General

Engineering and Physical Sciences Research Council: Polaris House, North Star Ave, Swindon, SN2 1ET; tel. (1793) 444100; fax (1793) 444005; e-mail infoline@epsrc.ac.uk; internet www.epsrc.ac.uk; f. 1994; supports basic, strategic and applied research and related postgraduate training in engineering and the physical sciences; Chair. JOHN ARMITT; Chief Exec. Dr RANDAL RICHARDS; publs *Connect*, *Newsline*, *Spotlight*.

Natural Environment Research Council (NERC): Polaris House, North Star Ave, Swindon, SN2 1EU; tel. (1793) 411500; fax (1793) 411501; e-mail requests@nerc.ac.uk; internet www.nerc.ac.uk; f. 1965; funds and conducts research to help find sustainable solutions to problems concerning biodiversity, environmental risks and hazards, global change, natural resource management, and pollution and waste; trains independent environmental scientists; Chair. ROB MARGETTS; Chief Exec. Prof. JOHN LAWTON.

Component institutes of the Council:

British Antarctic Survey: High Cross, Madingley Rd, Cambridge, CB3 0ET; tel. (1223) 221400; fax (1223) 362616; e-mail information@bas.ac.uk; internet www.antarctica.ac.uk; f. 1945 as Falkland

Islands Dependencies Survey; present name 1962; operates 5 research stations, 2 Royal Research Ships and 5 aircraft in and around Antarctica; undertakes a programme of science in the Antarctic and related regions and aims to address key global and regional issues; undertakes joint research projects and over 120 nat. and int. collaborations; library of 8,500 vols, 350 periodicals; Dir Prof. C. RAPLEY.

British Geological Survey: Kingsley Dunham Centre, Nicker Hill, Keyworth, Nottingham, NG12 5GG; tel. (115) 936-3100; fax (115) 936-3200; internet www.bgs.ac.uk; Dir Dr D. FALVEY.

Centre for Ecology and Hydrology: Maclean Bldg, Benson Lane, Crowmarsh Gifford, Wallingford, Oxon, OX10 8BB; tel. (1491) 838800; fax (1491) 692424; e-mail director@ceh.ac.uk; internet www.ceh.ac.uk; Dir Prof. PATRICIA NUTTALL.

Constituent institutes:

CEH Banchory: Hill of Brathens, Glassel, Banchory, Aberdeenshire, AB31 4BW; tel. (1330) 826300; fax (1330) 823303; internet banchory.ceh.ac.uk; Dir Prof. STEVE ALBON.

CEH Bangor: University of Wales, Deinol Rd, Bangor, Gwynedd, LL57 2UP; tel. (1248) 370045; fax (1248) 355365; internet bangor.ceh.ac.uk; Dir Dr BRIDGET EMMETT.

CEH Dorset: Winfrith Technology Centre, Dorchester, Dorset, DT2 8ZD; tel. (1305) 213500; fax (1305) 213600; internet dorset.ceh.ac.uk; Dir Prof. ALAN GRAY.

CEH Edinburgh: Bush Estate, Penicuik, Midlothian, EH26 0QB; tel. (131) 445-4343; fax (131) 445-3943; internet www.ceh.ac.uk; Dir Prof. J. NEIL CAPE.

CEH Lancaster: Lancaster Environment Centre, Library Ave, Bailrigg, Lancaster, LA1 4AP; tel. (1524) 595800; e-mail lancaster@ceh.ac.uk; internet www.ceh.ac.uk/sites/lancaster.html; Head of Site Dr BRENDA HOWARD.

CEH Oxford: Mansfield Rd, Oxford, OX1 3SR; tel. (1865) 281630; fax (1865) 281696; e-mail enquiries@ceh.ac.uk; internet www.nerc-oxford.ac.uk/cehoxford; Dir Prof. P. NUTTALL.

CEH Wallingford: Maclean Bldg, Crowmarsh Gifford, Wallingford, Oxon., OX10 8BB; tel. (1491) 838800; fax (1491) 629424; e-mail jsw@ceh.ac.uk; internet www.nwl.ac.uk; Dir Prof. JIM WALLACE.

CEH Windermere: The Ferry House, Far Sawry, Ambleside, Cumbria, LA22 0LP; tel. (15394) 42468; fax (15394) 46914; Dir Dr PETER MATTHIESSEN.

Proudman Oceanographic Laboratory: 6 Brownlow St, Liverpool, L3 5DA; tel. (151) 795-4800; fax (151) 795-4801; e-mail polenquiries@pol.ac.uk; internet www.pol.ac.uk; Dir Dr ED HILL.

Centre for Atmospheric Science: Dept of Chemistry, Univ. of Cambridge, Lensfield Rd, Cambridge, CB2 1EP; tel. (1223) 336473; fax (1223) 336473; internet www.atm.ch.cam.ac.uk/acmsu/; Dir Dr J. A. PYLE.

Centre for Population Biology: Imperial College London, Silwood Park Campus, Ascot, Berks., SL5 7PY; tel. (20) 7594-2475; fax (1344) 873173; internet www.imperial.ac.uk/cpb; Dir Prof. GEORGIA MACE.

Environmental Systems Science Centre: Univ. of Reading, Harry Pitt Bldg, 3 Earley Gate, Reading, RG6 6AL; tel. (118) 931-8741; fax (118) 931-6413; e-mail admin@mail.nerc-essc.ac.uk; internet www.nerc-essc.ac.uk; Head Prof. R. J. GURNEY.

National Centre for Atmospheric Science (NCAS): Dept of Meteorology, Univ. of Reading, POB 243, Earley Gate, Reading, RG6 6BB; tel. (118) 378-8315; fax (118) 378-8316; e-mail n.d.bray@reading.ac.uk; internet www.cgam.nerc.ac.uk; Dir for Climate Prof. JULIA SLINGO.

National Oceanography Centre: Univ. of Southampton Waterfront Campus, European Way, Southampton, SO14 3ZH; tel. (23) 8059-6666; fax (23) 8059-6032; internet www.noc.soton.ac.uk; Dir Prof. ED HILL.

Plymouth Marine Laboratory: Prospect Pl., Plymouth, PL1 3DH; tel. (1752) 633100; fax (1752) 633101; internet www.pml.ac.uk; Dir Prof. NICK OWENS.

Scottish Association for Marine Science: Dunstaffnage Marine Laboratory, POB 3, Oban, Argyll, PA34 4AD; tel. (1631) 562244; fax (1631) 565518; internet www.sams.ac.uk/dml; Dir Prof. G. B. SHIMMIELD.

Sea Mammal Research Unit: Gatty Marine Laboratory, Univ. of St Andrews, St Andrews, Fife, KY16 8LB; tel. (1334) 462630; fax (1334) 462632; e-mail smru.office@smru.st-and.ac.uk; internet smub.st-and.ac.uk; Dir Prof. P. HAMMOND.

Tyndall Centre for Climate Change Research: School of Environmental Sciences, Univ. of East Anglia, Norwich, Norfolk, NR4 7TJ; tel. (1603) 592267; fax (1603) 593901; internet www.tyndall.ac.uk; Dir Prof. ANDREW WATKINSON.

Biological Sciences

Bristol University Botanic Garden: Bracken Hill, North Rd, Leigh Woods, Bristol, BS8 3PF; tel. (117) 973-3682; fax (117) 974-1929; internet www.bris.ac.uk/Depts/BotanicGardens/; f. 1882 to advance public education in and promote research into botany and its related subjects; Curator NICHOLAS WRAY; publs *Annual Report, Annual Seed List.*

Cambridge University Botanic Garden: Cory Lodge, Bateman St, Cambridge, CB2 1JF; tel. (1223) 336265; fax (1223) 336278; e-mail enquiries@botanic.cam.ac.uk; internet www.botanic.cam.ac.uk; f. 1762 (1846 on present site); teaching and research in botany and horticulture; library of 11,000 (incl. early vols of *Gardeners Chronicle* annotated by Charles Darwin); Dir Prof. J. S. PARKER; publ. *Seed List* (annually).

Chelsea Physic Garden: 66 Royal Hospital Rd, London, SW3 4HS; tel. (20) 7352-5646; fax (20) 7376-3910; internet www.chelseaphysicgarden.co.uk; f. 1673; botanic garden and centre for research and education on plants, conservation of rare plants, and a public amenity; specializes in medicinal plants; library: restricted-access library of 300 vols, incl. Society of Apothecaries Dale bequest; Curator R. ATKINS; publ. *Index Seminum* (annually).

Institute of Zoology: Zoological Society of London, Regent's Park, London, NW1 4RY; tel. (20) 7449-6601; fax (20) 7586-2870; e-mail enquiries@ioz.ac.uk; internet www.zsl.org; f. 1977; studies aimed at the scientific advancement of conservation, breeding and management of animals in the wild and in captivity; research groups in reproductive biology (gamete biology, endocrinology, physiological ecology), genetics (population genetics, molecular genetics), veterinary science (incl. wildlife disease and comparative medicine), ecology (behavioural ecology and population dynamics); incorporates Nuffield Laboratories of Comparative Medicine and Wellcome Laboratories of Comparative Physiology; library and publs: see Zoological Society of London; Dir Dr W. V. HOLT

(acting); publ. *Science for Conservation* (annually).

National Institute for Biological Standards and Control: Blanche Lane, South Mimms, Potters Bar, Herts, EN6 3QG; tel. (1707) 654753; fax (1707) 646730; e-mail enquiries@nibsc.ac.uk; internet www.nibsc.ac.uk; f. 1976; the National Biological Standards Board is responsible for control and standardization of biological substances used in human medicine, and its functions are executed through the Institute; biological substances include all vaccines such as poliomyelitis, measles, rubella and whooping cough, also blood products, certain hormones and a number of antibiotics; research and development work is an important part of the Institute's activities; designated a WHO Int. Laboratory for Biological Standards; library of 4,000 vols, 200 periodicals; Dir Dr G. C. SCHILD; publs *Annual Report, Biological Reference Materials.*

Royal Botanic Garden, Edinburgh: 20A Inverleith Row, Edinburgh, EH3 5LR; tel. (131) 552-7171; fax (131) 248-2901; e-mail D&M@rbge.org.uk; internet www.rbge.org.uk; f. 1670; int. centre for the study of plant biodiversity and conservation; courses leading to HND in horticulture with plantsmanship; MSC course in plant taxonomy; Inverleith House Gallery with art exhibitions inspired by nature; regional gardens—Benmore Botanic Garden, near Dunoon, Argyll; Logan Botanic Garden, Stranraer, Wigtownshire; Dawyck Botanic Garden, Stobo, Peeblesshire; Herbarium of c. 2,000,000 specimens; library: see Libraries and Archives; Regius Keeper Prof. STEPHEN BLACKMORE; publ. *Edinburgh Journal of Botany* (3 a year).

Royal Botanic Gardens, Kew: Richmond upon Thames, Surrey, TW9 3AB; tel. (20) 8332-5000; fax (20) 8332-5197; e-mail info@rbgkew.org.uk; internet www.rbgkew.org.uk; f. 1759, became a public institution in 1841; taxonomic botany, horticulture, conservation, economic aspects, biochemistry, genetics, propagation and seed storage; also gardens and facilities at Wakehurst Place, West Sussex; library: see Libraries and Archives; Dir Prof. Sir PETER CRANE; publs *Kew Record of Taxonomic Literature* (4 a year), *Kew Bulletin* (4 a year), *Curtis's Botanical Magazine* (4 a year).

Attached institute:

Millennium Seed Bank Project: Wakehurst Place, Ardingly, Haywards Heath, W. Sussex, RH17 6TN; tel. (1444) 894100; fax (1444) 894110; e-mail msbscl@kew.org; internet www.rbgkew.org/msbp; aims to save 10% (24,000) of the world's plant species from extinction by 2010 through collection and conservation of seeds, incl. all UK native seed-bearing flora; undertakes UK and international programmes of seed collection; Convention to Combat Desertification established to protect drylands flora species; Head of Seed Conservation ROGER SMITH.

University of Oxford Botanic Garden: Rose Lane, Oxford, OX1 4AX; tel. (1865) 286690; fax (1865) 286693; e-mail postmaster@obg.ox.ac.uk; internet www.botanic-garden.ox.ac.uk; f. 1621 for teaching purposes; 6,000 different plant species in glasshouses, walled garden, water garden, rock garden and seasonal borders; educational lectures and tours; Harcourt Arboretum south of Oxford; library of 1,000 vols on horticulture; Dir TIMOTHY WALKER; publ. *Guide.*

Wildfowl & Wetlands Trust: Slimbridge, Glos., GL2 7BT; tel. (1453) 891900; fax (1453) 890827; e-mail enquiries@wwt.org.uk;

internet www.wwt.org.uk; f. 1946; concerned with all aspects of biology/ecology of wetlands and wildfowl, particularly those related to conservation, research, education and recreation; the world's largest comparative collection of living wildfowl is maintained at Slimbridge; other centres open to the public all year round at Arundel, Sussex; Castle Espie, Co. Down; Martin Mere, Lancs.; Washington, Tyne and Wear; Welney, Norfolk; Llanelli, Dyfed; Caerlaverock, Dumfriesshire; Barnes, London; education staff and facilities at all centres; 100,000 mems; library: research library at Slimbridge; Man. Dir MARTIN SPRAY; publs *Wildfowl* (annually), *Wildfowl and Wetlands* (quarterly).

Mathematical Sciences

National Computing Centre: Oxford Rd, Manchester, M1 7ED; tel. (161) 242-2121; fax (161) 242-2499; e-mail info@ncc.co.uk; internet www.ncc.co.uk; f. 1966; a membership organization run on a commercial basis to promote the effective use of information technology; acts as a focus for its mems and represents their views at nat. and intl level; provides consultancy and training services, software packages and other products; co-operates with other bodies to foster standards and best practices; Exec. Chair. MICHAEL GOUGH; Man. Dir STEFAN FOSTER.

Physical Sciences

Cambridge University Institute of Astronomy: Madingley Rd, Cambridge, CB3 0HA; tel. (1223) 337548; fax (1223) 337523; e-mail ioa@ast.cam.ac.uk; internet www.ast.cam.ac.uk; incorporating former Observatory (f. 1824), Solar Physics Observatory (f. 1913) and Institute of Theoretical Astronomy (f. 1967); work on observational and theoretical astrophysics; library of 17,500 vols; Dir Prof. D. O. GOUGH.

Council for the Central Laboratory of the Research Councils: Chilton, Didcot, Oxon., OX11 0QX; tel. (1235) 821900; fax (1235) 445808; e-mail enquiries@cclrc.ac.uk; internet www.cclrc.ac.uk; f. 1995; provides advanced and large-scale laboratory facilities, and expertise, to support univ. and industrial research; Chief Exec. of governing ccl Prof. JOHN WOOD; publ. *Science and Technology* (3 a year).

Laboratories:

Daresbury Laboratory: Keckwick Lane, Daresbury Science and Innovation Campus, Warrington, Cheshire, WA4 4AD; tel. (1925) 603000; fax (1925) 603100; e-mail enquiries@stfc.ac.uk; internet www.scitech.ac.uk; f. 1958; operates synchrotron X-ray source; provides advanced surface science and other materials facilities, and computational support in a broad range of disciplines; Chief Exec. Prof. KEITH MASON.

Rutherford Appleton Laboratory: Harwell Science and Innovation Campus, Didcot, Oxon., OX11 0QX; tel. (1235) 445000; fax (1235) 445808; e-mail enquiries@stfc.ac.uk; internet www.scitech.ac.uk; f. 1957; operates pulsed source of neutrons and muons (ISIS), high-power lasers, microelectronic design and micro-engineering facilities, and space engineering and data centres; provides supercomputing, detector technology and particle physics support; Chief Exec. Prof. KEITH MASON.

Jodrell Bank Observatory/University of Manchester: Macclesfield, Cheshire; tel. (1477) 571321; fax (1477) 571618; internet www.jb.man.ac.uk; f. 1945; the observatory uses seven large steerable radio telescopes, including the Lovell (fmrly Mark 1A) 250-ft diameter radio telescope; these can be connected into MERLIN array which extends to Cambridge (baseline: 230 km) to study radio objects in any part of the sky; research on galactic and extra-galactic astrophysical continuum and spectral line radio emissions and cosmic micro-wave background; observations of radio emission from quasars, pulsars and stars; multi-telescope interferometry and very long base-line interferometry; Dir Prof. A. G. LYNE.

Met Office: Fitzroy Rd, Exeter, EX1 3PB; tel. (0870) 900 0100 (within UK); tel. (1392) 885680 (from overseas); fax (1392) 885681; e-mail enquiries@metoffice.gov.uk; internet www.metoffice.gov.uk; f. 1854; provides a national meteorological service and is responsible for implementing the objectives of the World Meteorological Organisation (see International Organizations); provides comprehensive forecasting and consultative services; involved with major research into all aspects of meteorology, climatology and atmospheric science, partly in co-operation with universities and other national and international agencies; work on the physics and dynamics of the atmosphere ranges in scale from global numerical analyses and forecasts to the microphysics of clouds; library: see Libraries and Archives; Chief Exec. D. ROGERS; publs *Annual Report*, *Scientific and Technical Review*.

Attached Research Centre:

Hadley Centre for Climate Prediction and Research: Fitzroy Rd, Exeter, EX1 3PB; tel. (870) 900-0100 (within UK); fax (870) 900-5050 (within UK); e-mail hadley@metoffice.gov.uk; internet www.metoffice.com/research/hadleycentre/index.html; to monitor, understand and predict global and regional climate variability and change; Dir Dr DAVID GRIGGS; publ. *COP Climate Change* (annually).

Mullard Radio Astronomy Observatory: Astrophysics Group, Cavendish Laboratory, Madingley Rd, Cambridge, CB3 0HE; tel. (1223) 337295; fax (1223) 354599; internet www.mrao.cam.ac.uk; f. 1945; Dir Prof. R. E. HILLS; publ. numerous scientific papers.

Science and Technology Facilities Council: Polaris House, North Star Ave, Swindon, SN2 1SZ; tel. (1793) 442000; fax (1793) 442002; internet www.scitech.ac.uk; operates large-scale research facilities; manages int. research projects in support of a broad cross-section of the UK community; Chair. PETER WARRY; Chief Exec. Prof. KEITH MASON.

Attached centre:

Astronomy Technology Centre: Blackford Hill, Edinburgh, EH9 3HJ; tel. (131) 668-8313; fax (131) 668-8314; internet www.roe.ac.uk; manages the 3.8-m infrared telescope and the James Clerk Maxwell mm-wave telescope in Hawaii, USA; responsible for the optical telescope at La Palma Observatory, Canary Islands, Spain; houses the Dept of Astronomy of Edinburgh Univ.; has a Starlink data processing centre and a Super-COSMOS high-speed plate scanning machine; Dir Dr ADRIAN RUSSELL.

United Kingdom Atomic Energy Authority: Harwell, Didcot, Oxon., OX11 0RA; tel. (1235) 436900; fax (1235) 436899; internet www.ukaea.org.uk; f. 1954; has responsibility for the safe management and decommissioning of the nuclear reactors and other research and development facilities used to develop the UK's nuclear power programme, together with the safe disposal of the radioactive waste; implements the UK's contribution to the European fusion programme; sites at Dounreay (Caithness), Windscale (Cumbria), Risley (Cheshire), Culham (Oxfordshire), Harwell (Oxfordshire), Winfrith (Dorset); Chair. Sir KENNETH EATON; Chief Exec. Dr JOHN MCKEOWN.

University of London Observatory: 553 Watford Way, Mill Hill Park, London, NW7 2QS; tel. (20) 8959-0421; fax (20) 8238-8872; e-mail vmp@star.ucl.ac.uk; internet www.ulo.ucl.ac.uk; f. 1929; part of Dept of Physics and Astronomy, University College, London; teaching and research in astronomy; specialized astronomical library; Dir Dr M. DWORETSKY; publ. *Communications* (irregular, online only).

PHILOSOPHY AND PSYCHOLOGY

Anna Freud Centre: 21 Maresfield Gardens, London, NW3 5SD; tel. (20) 7794-2313; fax (20) 7794-6506; e-mail info@annafreud.org; internet www.annafreudcentre.org; f. 1940 by Anna Freud, daughter of Sigmund; psychoanalytical treatment of troubled children and young people; offers clinical and academic training in child psychotherapy and conducts research into psychotherapeutic techniques and the emotional development of children; Dirs PETER FONAGY, LINDA MAYES, MARY TARGET.

RELIGION, SOCIOLOGY AND ANTHROPOLOGY

Economic and Social Research Council: Polaris House, North Star Ave, Swindon, SN2 1UJ; tel. (1793) 413000; fax (1793) 413001; internet www.esrcsocietytoday.ac.uk; f. 1965; ind. org. funded mainly by Govt; research and training agency; aims to provide research on issues of importance to business, public sector and govt; Chair. FRANCES CAIRNCROSS; Chief Exec. Prof. IAN DIAMOND; publs *Annual Report*, *The Edge* (3 a year), *Social Sciences* (3 a year).

Institute of Ismaili Studies: 42–44 Grosvenor Gardens, London, SW1W 0EB; tel. (20) 7881-6000; fax (20) 7881-6040; e-mail info@iis.ac.uk; internet www.iis.ac.uk; f. 1977 by the Aga Khan; research into Islam, with emphasis on Shi'ism and Ismaili tariqah; library of 25,000 vols, MSS and audiovisual items; Dir Prof. AZIM NANJI.

ISTD: Centre for Crime and Justice Studies: King's College London, 75–79 York Rd, London, SE1 7AW; tel. (20) 7401-2425; fax (20) 7401-2436; e-mail istd.enq@kcl.ac.uk; internet www.kcl.ac.uk/orgs/istd; f. 1931; is an independent objective forum for all criminal justice professionals and those with a lay interest in crime; arranges conferences, courses and visits; Pres. The Baroness HILTON OF EGGARDON; Chair. of Council Sir GRAHAM SMITH; Dir UNA PADEL; publs *British Journal of Criminology* (quarterly), *Annual Report*, *Criminal Justice Matters* (quarterly).

London Middle East Institute: Rm 479, SOAS, Russell Square, London, WC1H 0XG; tel. (20) 7898-4330; fax (20) 7898-4329; e-mail lmei@soas.ac.uk; internet www.lmei.soas.ac.uk; attached to the School of Oriental and African Studies (SOAS), University of London; Dir Prof. ROBERT SPRINGBORG; publ. *The Middle East in London* (monthly).

Muslim Institute: 109 Fulham Palace Rd, London, W6 8JA; tel. (20) 8563-1995; fax (20) 8563-1993; e-mail info@musliminstitute.com; internet www.musliminstitute.com; f. 1972; research in early history of Islam, Islamic economics, philosophy of science, international relations, global Islamic movement; teaching (short courses) in political thought, philosophy of science, Arabic language, journalism; monthly meetings of academics, writers and activists dealing with issues such as reform within Islam, Islamic identity and citizenship and the future of Islam in Europe; library of 600 vols; Dir Dr FARIDA OWAISI.

Tavistock Institute: 30 Tabernacle St, London, EC2A 4UE; tel. (20) 7417-0407; fax (20) 7417-0566; e-mail central.admin@ tavinstitute.org; internet www .tavistockinstitute.org; f. 1947; study of human relations in conditions of well-being, conflict or breakdown in the family, the work group, the community and the larger organization; disciplines range from social science to organizational development; Sec. DEBBIE SORKIN; publs *Human Relations* (monthly), *Evaluation* (4 a year).

TECHNOLOGY

BHR Group Ltd: Fluid Eng. Centre, Cranfield, Beds., MK43 0AJ; tel. (1234) 750422; fax (1234) 750074; e-mail solutions@ bhrgroup.com; internet www.bhrgroup.com; f. 1947; provides research, devt and consultancy on all aspects of fluid eng. and process technology, for a wide range of industries; specializes in abrasive water-jet cutting, fluid power, hydraulics, mixing, pumping, process intensification, chemical reaction eng., micromaterials and nanomaterials technology, multiphase flow, pipe networks, sealing and containment, slurry transport; biodiesel; field studies; conferences and specialist training courses; technical information services; Chief Exec. J. A. R. MUIR.

BMT Group Ltd: Goodrich House, 1 Waldegrave Rd, Teddington, TW11 8LZ; tel. (20) 8943-5544; fax (20) 8943-5347; internet www .bmt.org; f. 1985; provides industry with high-level research and technical assistance; solutions to the problems of designers and operators of structures and vehicles on land, coastal terrain and at sea; 22 subsidiary and assoc. operating companies; Chair. Dr NEIL CROSS; Chief. Exec. PETER FRENCH; publs *BMT Abstracts* (monthly), *Focus*.

British Textile Technology Group (BTTG): Wira House, West Park Ring Rd, Leeds, LS16 6QL; tel. (113) 259-1999; fax (113) 278-0306; e-mail info@bttg.co.uk; internet www.bttg.co.uk; f. 1918; engaged in research, development, testing and evaluation for textile and related industries; undertakes product development and testing, international consulting work, etc; Man. Dir A. J. KING.

Building Research Establishment Ltd: Bucknalls Lane, Garston, Watford, Herts., WD25 9XX; tel. (1923) 664000; fax (1923) 664010; e-mail enquiries@bre.co.uk; internet www.bre.co.uk; f. 1921; research and consultancy covering building, construction and the prevention and control of fire; certification of building products; Chief Exec. Dr MARTIN WYATT; publs *BRE: Constructing the Future* (4 a year), *BRE Digest series* (4 a year), *BRE Report Series*.

CERAM Research Ltd: Queens Rd, Penkhull, Stoke-on-Trent, Staffs., ST4 7LQ; tel. (1782) 764444; fax (1782) 412331; e-mail enquiries@ceram.com; internet www.ceram .com; f. 1948; research into ceramics and materials processing, manufacture of ceramic components and the use of ceramic products for clients involved in metals, composites, construction and the environment; services incl. contract research and development, manufacturing consultancy, testing and analysis; library of 13,000 vols and 60,000 pamphlets; Chair. DAVID DRY; Chief Exec. Dr NEIL SANDERSON; publ. *World Ceramics Abstracts* (online).

CIRIA: Classic House, 174–180 Old St, London, EC1V 9BP; tel. (20) 7549-3300; fax (20) 7253-0523; e-mail enquiries@ciria.org; internet www.ciria.org; f. 1960 to improve the quality, efficiency, cost-effectiveness and safety of both the provision and operation of the modern built environment; Chief Exec. Dr T. W. BROYD; publs *Annual Review*, *CIRIA News* (4 a year).

Defence Science and Technology Laboratory (DSTL): Porton Down, Salisbury, Wilts, SP4 0JQ; tel. (1980) 613121; fax (1980) 613085; e-mail central-enquiries@dstl .gov.uk; internet www.dstl.gov.uk; f. 2001 following re-organisation of the former Defence Evaluation and Research Agency (DERA); part of the Ministry of Defence; locations: Alverstoke, Bedford, Bincleaves, Farnborough, Fort Halstead, Malvern, Pershore, Porton Down, Portsdown West, Winfrith; library: MOD Scientific Reports Collection of 750,000 items from WWII to the present; publs *Defence Reports Abstracts* (monthly; available only to the MOD, its agencies and contractors), *Defence Technology Alerts* (monthly, information about technological developments in the defence community; available only to the MOD, its agencies and contractors).

Infoterra Ltd: Delta House, Southwood Crescent, Southwood, Farnborough, Hants., GU14 0NL; tel. (1252) 362000; fax (1252) 375016; e-mail info@infoterra-global.com; internet www.infoterra-global.com; f. 1989 to commercialize the National Remote Sensing Centre and Earth Observation Centre; supplier of products and services based on information extracted from data acquired by Earth observation satellites and aerial photography; consultancy services; Marketing Dir ANTHONY DENNISS.

National Physical Laboratory: Hampton Rd, Teddington, Middx, TW11 0LW; tel. (20) 8977-3222; fax (20) 8943-6458; e-mail enquiry@npl.co.uk; internet www.npl.co.uk; f. 1900; national standards laboratory; establishes measurement standards, and undertakes research into improved techniques, engineering materials and information technology; Dir Dr BOB McGUINESS; publ. *Metromnia* (newsletter, quarterly).

Natural Resources Institute: University of Greenwich, Central Ave, Chatham Maritime, Kent, ME4 4TB; tel. (1634) 880088; fax (1634) 880066; e-mail nri@greenwich.ac.uk; internet www.nri.org; f. 1987; became an institute of the Univ. of Greenwich 1996; supplier of research, consultancy and training services in the environment and natural resources sector to support development assistance programmes, sustainable management of natural resources, environmental sciences, cost-effective and environmentally safe pest management, development and transfer of technologies to improve food security, social, economic and institutional analysis to enhance the impact of development projects and policies; training (some courses accredited for postgraduate qualifications); library of 300,000 vols and information service; Dir Dr GUY POULTER (acting); publ. *NRI Bulletin*.

NEL: East Kilbride, Glasgow, G75 0QU; tel. (1355) 220222; fax (1355) 272999; e-mail info@nel.uk; internet www.nel.uk; f. 1947; applied engineering research, development; calibration, consultancy and prototype manufacture for private and public sectors; Gen. Man. Dr F. KINGHORN; publs *Conference Proceedings*, technical papers, reports.

Pera International: Melton Mowbray, Leics., LE13 0PB; tel. (1664) 501501; fax (1664) 501264; f. 1946; a multi-disciplinary technology centre specializing in all aspects of manufacture, incl. materials, quality training, methods, computer applications, human resources and manufacturing integration.

QinetiQ: Cody Technology Park, Ively Rd, Farnborough, Hants, GU14 0LX; tel. (08700) 100942; e-mail customercontact@qinetiq .com; internet www.qinetiq.com; f. 2001 as government-owned UK plc following re-organisation of the former Defence Evaluation and Research Agency (DERA); researches and develops services and technologies in a variety of fields: defence, maritime, aviation, security, energy and power, automative, finance, health, highways and traffic, public sector, rail, space, telecoms, media and electronics; locations: Aberporth, Bedford, Bincleaves, Bishopton, Boscombe Down, Bridgwater, Bristol, Buckingham Gate (London), Burntisland, BUTEC (Rosshire), Chertsey, Cobbett Hill, Defford, Eskmeals, Farnborough, Fort Halstead, Foulness, Fraser (Portsmouth), Funtington (Chichester), Haslar, Hebrides, Kirkcudbright, Larkhill, Llanbedr, Loch Goil, Malvern, Pendine, Pershore, Plymouth, Portland Bill, Portsdown West, Portsdown, Rona, Rosneath, Rosyth, Shoeburyness, Skipness, Sundridge, West Freugh, Weston-Super-Mare, Winfrith; CEO Sir JOHN CHISHOLM.

Scottish Universities Environmental Research Centre: East Kilbride, Glasgow, G75 0QF; tel. (1355) 223332; fax (1355) 229898; e-mail Director@suerc.gla.ac.uk; internet www.gla.ac.uk/suerc; f. 1963; provides research and teaching facilities in radioactive and stable isotopes in the environment, ultratrace analysis, radiation mapping, nuclear waste disposal, thermoluminescence dating and dosimetry, food irradiation, radiochemistry, environmental studies, geochronology, isotope geology, stable isotope geochemistry, carbon dating and cosmogenic isotope analysis, including accelerator mass spectrometry; Dir Prof. ANTHONY E. FALLICK.

Smith Institute: POB 183, Guildford, Surrey, GU2 7GG; tel. (1483) 579108; fax (1483) 568710; e-mail office@smithinst.ac.uk; internet www.smithinst.ac.uk; f. 1993; non-profit organization; mathematics and computing depts of univs throughout the UK; joint industry/academic institute for research in industrial mathematics and system engineering; Dir Dr ROBERT LEESE.

TRL Ltd: Crowthorne House, Nine Mile Ride, Wokingham, Berks., RG40 3GA; tel. (1344) 773131; fax (1344) 770356; e-mail info@trl.co.uk; internet www.trl.co.uk; f. 1933; independent research-and-development and consultancy org. specializing in road materials and construction, structures, road safety and traffic, vehicle safety, environment; library of 200,000 books and pamphlets, 250 current journals, int. roads and transport database; Chief Exec. Dr SUSAN SHARLAND; publ. *TRL Journal of Research* (3 or 4 a year).

Tun Abdul Razak Research Centre: Brickendonbury, Hertford, SG13 8NL; tel. (1992) 584966; fax (1992) 554837; f. 1938; research and development on natural rubber; library of 3,000 books and 200 periodicals, information retrieval system containing 100,000 items; Dir of Research Dr C. S. L. BAKER; publs *Annual Report*, *Rubber Developments*.

WRc PLC: Frankland Rd, Blagrove, Swindon, Wilts., SN5 8YF; tel. (1793) 865000; fax (1793) 865001; e-mail solutions@wrcplc.co .uk; internet www.wrcplc.co.uk; independent research and development and consultancy organization specializing in water and environmental management; Chief Exec. RON CHAPMAN.

Libraries and Archives

Aberdeen

Aberdeen City Council Library and Information Services: Central Library, Rosemount Viaduct, Aberdeen, AB25 1GW; tel. (1224) 652500; fax (1224) 641985; e-mail centrallibrary@aberdeencity.gov.uk; internet www.aberdeencity.gov.uk/libraries; f. 1884; 500,000 vols; spec. collns incl.: Scottish genealogy, local photographs, North Sea oil, British patent abstracts, 10,000 standard specifications, trade marks, business information; 17 brs; Central Library – Adult Lending Library, Children's Library, Media Centre, Internet access, Aberdeen College Learning Centre, Community Reference and Local Studies; Community Contacts Directory; Careers Information Point; Scottish Parliament Partner Library; Nat. Library of Scotland Partner; Europe Direct Centre Enquiry and Research service, Enquire online nat. reference service; Library and Information Services Manager FIONA CLARK.

Robert Gordon University Library: Garthdee Rd, Aberdeen, AB10 7QE; tel. (1224) 263450; fax (1224) 263460; e-mail library@rgu.ac.uk; internet www.rgu.ac.uk/library; f. 1992; 205,470 vols; Dir of Knowledge and Information Services CAROLE MUNRO.

University of Aberdeen: Library and Historic Collections: Queen Mother Library, Meston Walk, Aberdeen, AB24 3UE; tel. (1224) 272579; fax (1224) 273596; e-mail library@abdn.ac.uk; internet www.abdn.ac.uk/library; f. 1495; 1,200,000 vols; McBean Jacobite collection, O'Dell railway collection, Biesenthal Hebrew collection, Taylor psalmody collection, G. W. Wilson photographic collection, Gregory, Melvin and other special collections; consists of Queen Mother Library, Taylor Library and European Documentation Centre, Medical Library; Special Libraries and Archives on King's College Campus; Acting Librarian and Man. of Library Services WENDY PIRIE.

Aberystwyth

Ceredigion County Library: Public Library, Corporation St, Aberystwyth, SY23 2BU; tel. (1970) 633703; fax (1970) 625059; e-mail llyfrgell.library@ceredigion.gov.uk; f. 1996; 290,000 vols, 5,000 vols; 7 brs; County Libraries Officer WILLIAM H. HOWELLS.

National Library of Wales: Aberystwyth, Ceredigion, SY23 3BU; tel. (1970) 632800; fax (1970) 615709; internet www.llgc.org.uk; f. 1907; one of the six copyright libraries of the British Isles; 5,000,000 printed books, 30,000 MSS, over 3,500,000 deeds and documents and 200,000 maps, prints and drawings, including the finest existing Welsh collection; diaries and correspondence of David Lloyd George; Librarian ANDREW M. W. GREEN; publ. *The National Library of Wales Journal* (2 a year).

University of Wales Aberystwyth, Hugh Owen Library: Penglais, Aberystwyth, Ceredigion, SY23 3DZ; tel. (1970) 622391; fax (1970) 622404; e-mail libinfo@aber.ac.uk; internet www.aber.ac.uk; f. 1872; 756,000 vols, 3,647 periodicals; spec. collns in Hugh Owen Library incl. Celtic Colln (13,000 vols), Gregynog Press books and private press books since beginning of 20th century, George Powell Colln (19th-century English and French literature, fine art and music), James Camden Hotten Collection, Rudler Collection of geological pamphlets, Duff Colln of pamphlets (Classics), League of Nations and UN Documents, microforms incl. Early American Imprints 1639–1800, David De Lloyd Papers (Welsh folksongs), Lily Newton Papers (water pollution), Thomas Webster letters (19th-century geologist), British Soc. of Rheology Library; spec. collns in Thomas Parry Library (incl. Welsh Institute of Rural Studies Library) incl. Horton Colln (early children's books), Appleton Colln (Victorian colour printing and binding); Dir of Information Services Dr M. HOPKINS.

Aldershot

Prince Consort's Library: Knollys Rd, Aldershot, Hants., GU11 1PS; tel. (1252) 349381; fax (1252) 349382; e-mail pcl@dstl.gov.uk; f. 1860; public access by written appointment only; military history library; 60,000 vols; Head of Library Services TIM WARD.

Ashton under Lyne

Tameside Metropolitan Borough Council Education and Leisure Services Department: Council Offices, Wellington Rd, Ashton under Lyne, OL6 6DL; tel. (161) 342-8355; fax (161) 342-3744; e-mail barry.delve@nxcorp1.tameside.gov.uk; internet www.tameside.gov.uk/libraries/index.html; f. 1974; 288,078 vols, 150 periodicals; special collections: local studies and archives, sound recordings, video cassettes, computer software; Head of Library Services CATHERINE SIMENSKY.

Aylesbury

Buckinghamshire County Library: County Offices, Walton St, Aylesbury, Bucks., HP20 1UU; tel. (1296) 383206; fax (1296) 382259; e-mail library@buckscc.gov.uk; internet www.buckscc.gov.uk/libraries; f. 1918; 927,000 vols; 34 brs; Library Systems Manager HAZEL EDWARDS.

Bangor

University of Wales, Bangor, Information Services: Bangor, LL57 2DG; tel. (1248) 382961; fax (1248) 382979; e-mail library@bangor.ac.uk; internet www.bangor.ac.uk/is/library; f. 1884; 500,000 vols; Bangor Cathedral Library; local Estate archives; 6 brs; Dir EINION WYN THOMAS; publ. *Annual Report*.

Barry

Vale of Glamorgan Library and Information Service: Civic Offices, Holton Rd, Barry, CF63 4RU; tel. (1446) 709381; fax (1446) 709448; internet www.valeofglamorgan.gov.uk/libraries; 10 brs; Vale Librarian SIAN E. JONES.

Bath

University of Bath Library: Bath, BA2 7AY; tel. (1225) 388388; fax (1225) 386229; e-mail library@bath.ac.uk; internet www.bath.ac.uk/library; 440,000 vols; contains Sir Isaac Pitman's Library; Univ. Librarian H. D. NICHOLSON.

Bedford

Bedfordshire Libraries: County Hall, Bedford, MK42 9AP; tel. (1234) 363222; fax (1234) 228993; e-mail bedfordshirelibraries@bedfordshire.gov.uk; internet www.bedfordshire.gov.uk; f. 1925; 17 brs; 4 mobile libraries; 950,000 vols; spec. collns: Mott-Harrison colln of Bunyan life and works; aeronautics, agriculture, slides, audio-visual including videos, DVDs, CDs and computer software; special services for hospitals, housebound readers, prisons, local govt, schools and young people; Head of Libraries B. S. GEORGE.

Birmingham

Aston University Library and Information Services: Aston Triangle, Birmingham, B4 7ET; tel. (121) 204-4525; fax (121) 204-4530; e-mail library@aston.ac.uk; internet www.aston.ac.uk/lis; f. 1895; 276,000 vols, 470 print journal titles, 3,850 e-journal titles, 18,495 unique journal titles, incl. full-text journal databases; Dir Dr N. R. SMITH.

Birmingham Library Services: Central Library, Chamberlain Sq., Birmingham, B3 3HQ; tel. (121) 303-4511; fax (121) 233-9702; e-mail libraries@birmingham.gov.uk; internet www.birmingham.gov.uk/libraries; f. 1861; 1,362,708 vols including 134 incunabula; 41 community libraries; reference library (f. 1866); depts: archives (incl. Diocesan Record Office and Boulton and Watt colln); arts, business information, language and literature (including John Ash Oberammergau Passion Play colln, King's Norton Parish Library, Sheldon Rector's Library, Parker colln of early children's books and games, Samuel Johnson, Milton, Cervantes, Baskerville and war poetry collns, early printed books, fine bindings and private press books, and Shakespeare Library—f. 1864, 45,000 vols in 90 languages), local studies and history (incl. Priestley colln, Sir Benjamin Stone colln of photographs, Marston Rudland colln of engraved portraits, Francis Frith negative archive, Bedford Photographic colln, and Warwickshire Photographic Survey), Music Library, Science and Technology (incl. patents), Social Sciences (incl. railways colln and UN depository), Learning Centre; Head of Library and Archives Services BRIAN GAMBLES.

Orchard Learning Resources Centre (University of Birmingham): Hamilton Drive, Weoley Park Rd, Selly Oak, Birmingham, B29 6QW; tel. (121) 415-8454; fax (121) 415-8476; e-mail olrc@bham.ac.uk; internet www.olrc.bham.ac.uk; f. 1997; anthropology and world area studies, communications, development economics, Islamics, Christian theology and missiology, social studies, world religions, education, child and youth studies; 225,000 vols; Greek papyri; spec. collns incl. Harold W. Turner Colln on New Religious Movements; Mingana Collection of Arabic and Syriac MSS, archives relating to Christian mission and Christian education; Resource Centre Man. DOROTHY VUONG.

University of Birmingham Library: Edgbaston, Birmingham, B15 2TT; tel. (121) 414-5816; fax (121) 471-4691; internet www.is.bham.ac.uk; f. 1880 (as Mason Science College Library); 2,655,251 vols, 7,500 current periodicals, 3,000,000 MSS; special collections include: archives of Joseph, Austen and Neville Chamberlain, Anthony Eden, W. H. Dawson, Francis Brett Young, Harriet Martineau, Bishop E. W. Barnes, Sir Oliver Lodge, Church Missionary Society Archives (pre-1950), YMCA archives; St Mary's, Warwick and Bengeworth parish libraries, Wigan Library from Bewdley, Worcs, Baskerville collection; Birmingham and Midland Institute pamphlet collection; Librarian M. I. SHOEBRIDGE.

Blackburn

Blackburn with Darwen Library and Information Service: Central Library, Town Hall St, Blackburn, BB2 1AG; tel. (1254) 661221; fax (1254) 678898; e-mail library@blackburn.gov.uk; internet www.blackburn.gov.uk/libraries; Head of Cultural Services SUSAN LAW.

Blackpool

Blackpool Library Service: Leisure, Culture and Community Learning, Progress House, Clifton Road, Blackpool, FY4 4US; tel. (1253) 478105; fax (1253) 476059; e-mail library.info@blackpool.gov.uk; 149,547 vols, 70 periodicals; Head of Cultural Services ANNE ELLIS.

Bournemouth

Bournemouth Libraries: 22 The Triangle, Bournemouth, BH2 5RQ; tel. (1202) 454848; fax (1202) 454840; e-mail bournemouth@ bournemouthlibraries.org.uk; 277,404 vols, 41,237 audiovisual items, 13,276 sheet music, 16,720 microforms, 2,339 maps, 532 newspapers and periodicals; Area Services and Arts Manager CAROLYN DATE.

Bracknell

Bracknell Forest Borough Library and Information Service: Bracknell Library, Town Square, Bracknell, RG12 1BH; tel. (1344) 423149; fax (1344) 411392; e-mail bracknell.library@bracknell-forest.gov.uk; internet www.bracknell-forest.gov.uk/ libraries; f. 1998; 9 brs; Head of Libraries, Arts and Information RUTH BURGESS.

Bradford

Bradford Libraries: Prince's Way, Bradford, BD1 1NN; tel. (1274) 753600; fax (1274) 395108; e-mail public.libraries@bradford.gov .uk; internet www.bradford.gov.uk; f. 1887; 1,000,000 vols; 32 libraries and 3 mobile libraries, provide general collections; Central Library specializes in: local history, business information, Asian languages, and audio and video services; Head of Service JOHN TRIFFITT.

University of Bradford Library: Bradford, Yorks., BD7 1DP; tel. (1274) 233400; fax (1274) 233398; e-mail library@bradford.ac .uk; internet www.bradford.ac.uk/library; f. 1966; 580,000 vols; J. B. Priestley Library; Academic Librarian JOHN J. HORTON; publs *Annual Report*, occasional bibliographies and guides.

Bridgend

Bridgend County Borough Library and Information Service: Coed Parc, Park St, Bridgend, Mid Glam., CF31 4BA; tel. (1656) 754800; fax (1656) 645719; e-mail blis@ bridgend.gov.uk; 13 brs; Co Borough Librarian JOHN WOODS.

Bridgwater

Somerset County Library: Mount St, Bridgwater, Somerset, TA6 3ES; tel. (1278) 451201; fax (1278) 452787; e-mail lbhq.gen@ somerset.gov.uk; f. 1919; 1,135,429 vols and sound recordings; 34 brs, 8 mobile libraries; Head of Cultural Services ROB FROUD.

Brighton

Brighton and Hove Libraries: c/o Brighton Central Library, Vantage Point, New England St, Brighton, BN1 2GW; tel. (1273) 290800; fax (1273) 296951; e-mail libraries@brighton-hove.gov.uk; internet www.citylibraries.info; Head of ICT and Libraries SALLY MCMAHON.

Constituent Library:

Jubilee Library: Jubilee St, Brighton, BN1 1GE; tel. (1273) 290800; e-mail brightonlibrary@brighton-hove.gov.uk; internet www.citylibraries.info/jubilee/ default.asp; f. 2005; holdings include 45,000 rare and historical books.

University of Sussex Library: Falmer, Brighton, BN1 9QL; tel. (1273) 606755; fax (1273) 678441; e-mail library@sussex.ac.uk; internet www.sussex.ac.uk/library; f. 1961; 750,000 vols; Librarian DEBORAH SHORLEY.

Bristol

Bristol City Council–Culture and Leisure: Central Library, College Green, Bristol, BS1 5TL; tel. (117) 903-7200; fax (117) 922-1081; 27 brs, 1 mobile library; reference library; business learning centre; 876,332 vols; Dir S. WRAY.

University of Bristol Library: Tyndall Ave, Bristol, BS8 1TJ; tel. (117) 928-9000; fax (117) 925-5334; internet www.bris.ac.uk/ is; f. 1909; 1,500,000 vols and pamphlets; special collections include the English novel to 1850, the Sir Allen Lane Penguin collection, business histories, early geology, medicine, mathematics, chemistry and physics, Pinney Papers (17th–19th c.), Brunel workbooks and papers, British philosophers, landscape gardening, courtesy books, General Election addresses (part of the National Liberal Club Library), Wiglesworth Ornithological Library, EDC, Addington Symonds Papers, Papers of the Somerset Miners' Association; Dir of Library Services PETER KING.

Caernarfon

Gwynedd Library and Information Service: Development Directorate, Gwynedd Council, Council Offices, Caernarfon, LL55 1SH; tel. (1286) 679504; fax (1286) 677347; e-mail library@gwynedd.gov.uk; internet www.gwynedd.gov.uk; f. 1996; 361,506 vols; 17 brs; Dir IWAN TREFOR JONES.

Cambridge

British and Foreign Bible Society's Library: Cambridge Univ. Library, West Rd, Cambridge, CB3 9DR; tel. (1223) 333000 ext. 33075; fax (1223) 333160; e-mail bslib@lib.cam.ac.uk; internet www.lib .cam.ac.uk; f. 1804; large colln of printed Bibles, over 35,000 vols of Scripture in more than 2,500 languages; archives of the Bible Society from 1804; Librarian P. M. MEADOWS.

Cambridge University Library: West Rd, Cambridge, CB3 9DR; tel. (1223) 333000; fax (1223) 333160; e-mail library@lib.cam.ac.uk; internet www.lib.cam.ac.uk; f. 1400; a legal deposit library; 7,115,065 printed books and serial vols, numerous spec. collns, 157,186 MSS, large collns of papers and correspondence, 1,151,087 maps, 1,800,324 microforms; the collns have been accumulating since the beginning of the 15th century; Librarian P. K. FOX.

College libraries:

Christ's College Library: Cambridge, CB2 3BU; tel. (1223) 334950; fax (1223) 334973; e-mail library@christs.cam.ac.uk; internet www.christs.cam.ac.uk; f. 1448; refounded 1505; 100,000 vols, incunabula, periodicals; spec. collns: works of John Milton, including items published before 1700, Charles Lesingham Smith collection of early mathematical and scientific books, William Robertson Smith Oriental Library, Sir Stephen Gaselee colln of Coptic studies, A. H. Wratislaw colln of Slavonic language and literature, W. H. D. Rouse colln of Indian studies and 16th-century English books; Librarian Dr GAVIN ALEXANDER.

Churchill College Library: Cambridge, CB3 0DS; tel. (1223) 336138; fax (1223) 336160; e-mail librarian@chu.cam.ac.uk; internet www.chu.cam.ac.uk; f. 1960; 50,000 vols; spec. collns incl. political, military and scientific archives mainly since late 19th century, Powys colln, Winston Churchill's books on Napoleon; Librarian MARY KENDALL.

Clare College Library: Memorial Court, Clare College, Cambridge, CB3 9AJ; tel. (1223) 333202; fax (1223) 765560; e-mail library@clare.cam.ac.uk; internet www .clare.cam.ac.uk/academic/libraries/index .html; f. 1326; 33,000 vols; comprises Fellows' Library (8,000 vols) and Forbes Mellon Library (25,000 vols); spec. collns: Cecil Sharp MSS; Fellows' Librarian Dr H.

JAHN; Forbes Mellon Librarian ANNE C. HUGHES.

Corpus Christi College: Parker Library: Trumpington St, Cambridge, CB2 1RH; tel. (1223) 338025; fax (1223) 338041; e-mail parker-library@corpus.cam .ac.uk; internet www.corpus.cam.ac.uk; f. 1352; 20,000 books, 600 MSS; spec. collns: Parker bequest of MSS and early printed books, Lewis colln of coins, gems and other antiquities (at present on loan to the Fitzwilliam Museum); Stokes colln on Jewish history; readers by appointment; Librarian Dr C. DE HAMEL.

Downing College: The Maitland Robinson Library: Regent St, Cambridge, CB2 1DQ; tel. (1223) 334829; fax (1223) 363852; internet www.dow.cam.ac .uk; f. 1800; Maitland Robinson Library opened 1993; 46,000 vols; spec. collns of Bowtell MSS relating to the city and univ. of Cambridge; library of 500 vols of naval history and navigation and large colln of law, Civil War and Interregnum newspapers; College Librarian KAREN LUBARR.

Emmanuel College Library: St Andrew's St, Cambridge, CB2 3AP; tel. (1223) 334233; e-mail library@emma.cam .ac.uk; internet www.emma.cam.ac.uk/ teaching/library; f. 1584; 72,000 vols rare book collns, incl. the Graham Watson Colln and library of William Sancroft, Archbishop of Canterbury; 400 MSS (readers by appointment only); Librarian Dr H. C. CARRON.

Fitzwilliam College Library: Cambridge, CB3 0DG; tel. (1223) 332042; fax (1223) 477976; e-mail library@fitz.cam.ac .uk; internet www.fitz.cam.ac.uk/library; f. 1963; 800 mems; 38,000 vols; Librarian MARION A. MACLEOD.

Girton College Library: Cambridge, CB3 0JG; tel. (1223) 338970; fax (1223) 339890; e-mail library@girton.cam.ac.uk; internet www-lib.girton.cam.ac.uk; f. 1869; 95,000 vols, 120 periodicals; special collns: Blackburn Colln of women's rights materials, Newall Colln of Scandinavian material, Frere Colln of Hebrew MSS, Crews Colln of Judeo-Spanish material, Somerville Colln of science and mathematics, Bibas Colln of 18th-century French works; College Archive covers the history of higher education for women via the College's institutional records and numerous collns of personal papers; Librarian FRANCES GANDY.

Gonville and Caius College Library: Cambridge, CB2 1TA; tel. (1223) 332419; e-mail library@cai.cam.ac.uk; internet www.cai.cam.ac.uk; f. 1348; 80,000 vols, 900 incunabula, 1,000 MSS related to medieval law and science; Fellow Librarian Prof. D. S. H. ABULAFIA.

Jesus College Old Library: Jesus College, Cambridge, CB5 8BL; tel. (1223) 339405; fax (1223) 324910; f. 1500; 8,600 vols, 39 incunabula, 80 medieval MSS from north-country monasteries, 17 Oriental MSS; spec. collns: Civil War tracts, military science, library of the Malthus family, large theological colln; Keeper of the Old Library Prof. S. C. HEATH.

King's College Library: Cambridge, CB2 1ST; tel. (1223) 331232; fax (1223) 331891; e-mail library@kings.cam.ac.uk; internet www.kings.cam.ac.uk/library; f. 1441; 125,000 vols; spec. collns: MSS of Sir Isaac Newton (available on microfilm in the Univ. Library), 20th-century MSS, notably major collns of Rupert Brooke, E. M. Forster, T. S. Eliot, J. M. Keynes, Joan Robinson; includes the Rowe Music

Library; f. 1928; 25,000 vols; Librarian P. M. JONES.

Magdalene College Old Library: Cambridge, CB3 0AG; tel. (1223) 332100; fax (1223) 332187; e-mail library@magd.cam.ac.uk; MSS of works by Thomas Hardy, Rudyard Kipling, T. S. Eliot, I. A. Richards and 38 medieval MSS, including a 13th-century Apocalypse; papers of Ferrar family of Little Gidding; incunabula, foreign-printed books of 16th, 17th and 18th centuries, early theological works; Diaries of A. C. Benson and W. R. Inge; 17,000 vols; Keeper Dr RICHARD LUCKETT.

Newnham College Library: Cambridge, CB3 9DF; tel. (1223) 335740; e-mail librarian@newn.cam.ac.uk; internet www.newn.cam.ac.uk/nclcl; f. 1871; 90,000 vols; 9 medieval MSS, incunabula, early editions of poets, dramatists and chroniclers of 16th and 17th centuries; Skilliter Centre for Ottoman Studies holds 4,500 vols relating to Ottoman history; Librarian DEBORAH HODDER.

Pembroke College Library: Cambridge, CB2 1RF; tel. (1223) 338121; fax (1223) 338163; e-mail lib@pem.cam.ac.uk; f. 1347; 45,000 vols, 317 medieval MSS; spec. collns: papers of Gray, C. Smart, William Mason, R. Storrs; Librarian PATRICIA ASKE.

Pepys Library (Magdalene College): Cambridge, CB3 0AG; tel. (1223) 332115; fax (1223) 332187; e-mail pepyslibrary@magd.cam.ac.uk; f. 1724 in its present location; 3,000 vols in original bookcases; Pepys's own colln (MSS, books, music, maps, prints and drawings), not added to since 1703; Pepys's own catalogue; spec. collns: Pepys MSS (incl. Diary), medieval MSS, naval and historical MSS (mostly English, 16th- and 17th-century), colln of calligraphy, prints of London and Westminster, incunabula, broadside ballads, plays; Librarian Dr RICHARD LUCKETT.

Peterhouse (Perne) Library: Cambridge, CB2 1RD; tel. (1223) 338251; fax (1223) 337578; e-mail lib@pet.cam.ac.uk; internet www.pet.cam.ac.uk; f. 1594; 5,000 vols, 80 incunabula, 280 medieval MSS, 16th- and 17th-century musical MSS (on permanent deposit in Univ. Library); spec. collns incl. first editions of classics in science, 16th-century theological books; Librarian S. H. MANDELBROTE.

Queens' College Old Library: Cambridge, CB3 9ET; tel. (1223) 335549; fax (1223) 335522; e-mail librarian@queens.cam.ac.uk; internet www.queens.cam.ac.uk; f. 1448; 22 medieval MSS, 31 incunabula, library of over 28,000 vols; catalogue by Thomas Hartwell Horne (1827); Milner colln of works on history of Reformation and 18th-century science and mathematics; Thomas Smith colln of Renaissance humanist writings; Keeper of the Old Library Dr I. PATTERSON.

St Catharine's College Library: Cambridge, CB2 1RL; tel. (1223) 338343; fax (1223) 338340; e-mail librarian@caths.cam.ac.uk; internet www.caths.cam.ac.uk/library; f. 1473; 69,000 vols (44,000 vols in undergraduate library; 25,000 vols in spec. collns: 17th-century political and religious tracts, 184 vols of 18th-century medical works (Addenbrooke collection), medieval Romance literature, Spanish books and MSS of 16th and 17th centuries; MSS, 30 incunabula); Fellow Librarian Dr R. S. K. BARNES.

St John's College Library: Cambridge, CB2 1TP; tel. (1223) 338662; fax (1223) 337035; e-mail library@joh.cam.ac.uk; internet www.joh.cam.ac.uk/library; f. 1511; MSS; spec. collns: 15th-century

books, Matthew Prior bequest, Sir Soulden Lawrence law colln, Thomas Baker's colln of printed books and MSS, Samuel Butler colln, Smith colln of Rabelais literature, Wordsworthiana, papers of Sir Cecil Beaton, mathematical works of historical interest from libraries of Adams, Todhunter and Pendlebury, Udny Yule colln of Thomas à Kempis edns, Hugh Gatty colln, Sparrow bequest of Samuel Parr books, papers of Sir Fred Hoyle; Librarian Dr MARK NICHOLLS.

Selwyn College Library: Grange Rd, Cambridge, CB3 9DQ; tel. (1223) 335880; e-mail lib@sel.cam.ac.uk; internet www.sel.cam.ac.uk/library; f. 1896; 40,000 vols, MSS, incunabula; spec. collns incl. diaries and papers of George Augustus Selwyn (1809–78) Primate of New Zealand and later Bishop of Lichfield, large colln of theological works including 19th-century sermons, 19th-century missionary colln with particular emphasis on Melanesia and New Zealand, and 3,000 19th-century English ecclesiastical pamphlets; Librarian SARAH STAMFORD.

Sidney Sussex College Library: Cambridge, CB2 3HU; tel. (1223) 338852; fax (1223) 338884; e-mail librarian@sid.cam.ac.uk; internet www.sid.cam.ac.uk/indepth/lib/library.html; f. 16th-century; 35,000 vols, 70 periodicals; Muniment Room: 7,300 vols, 106 MSS, incunabula; spec. collns incl. 18th- and 19th-century mathematical books; Taylor Mathematical Library (separately administered); Librarian HEATHER E. LANE.

Trinity College Library: Cambridge, CB2 1TQ; tel (1223) 338488; fax (1223) 338532; e-mail trin-lib@lists.cam.ac.uk; internet www.trin.cam.ac.uk; f. 1546; 300,000 vols; spec. collns incl. medieval western and oriental MSS; literary MSS of Milton, Tennyson, Housman, Capell colln of Shakespeareana; Rothschild library of 18th-century English literature; Isaac Newton's library; papers of economists, philosophers, politicians since 19th century; Librarian Prof. D. McKITTERICK.

Trinity Hall Library: Cambridge, CB2 1TJ; tel. (1223) 332546; fax (1223) 332537; e-mail library@trinhall.cam.ac.uk; f. 1350; 24,000 vols, 31 MSS; spec. collns incl. early canon law, Larman Bequest of books and MSS relating to Reformation and Tudor periods, particularly heraldry, ecclesiastical history and theology; Dir of Library Services DOMINIQUE RUHLMANN.

Special libraries:

Balfour and Newton Libraries: Univ. of Cambridge, Dept of Zoology, Downing St, Cambridge, CB2 3EJ; tel. (1223) 336648; fax (1223) 336676; e-mail library@zoo.cam.ac.uk; internet www.zoo.cam.ac.uk/library; Balfour Library f. 1883, Newton Library f. 1907; 155,000 vols, 25,000 periodicals, over 110,000 reprints; Librarian C. M. CASTLE.

Churchill Archives Centre: Churchill College, Cambridge, CB3 0DS; tel. (1223) 336087; fax (1223) 336135; e-mail archives@chu.cam.ac.uk; internet www.chu.cam.ac.uk/archives; f. 1973; houses papers of Sir Winston Churchill, Lady Thatcher and many other senior political figures; Dir of the Archives ALLEN PACKWOOD.

Marshall Library of Economics: Sidgwick Ave, Cambridge, CB3 9DB; tel. (1223) 335217; f. 1925; 97,000 vols; Librarian ROWLAND THOMAS.

Squire Law Library: 10 West Rd, Cambridge, CB3 9DZ; tel. (1223) 330077; fax

(1223) 330048; f. 1904; 130,000 vols; spec. collns incl. Roman law, legal history, comparative law, conflict of laws, int. law, environmental law, intellectual property, political biographies; research library; Librarian D. F. WILLS.

Cambridgeshire Libraries and Information Service: 7 Lion Yard, Cambridge, Cambs., CB2 3QD; tel. (845) 045-5225; fax (1223) 717079; e-mail your.library@cambridgeshire.gov.uk; internet www.cambridgeshire.gov.uk/leisure/libraries; f. 1974; 1,155,000 vols; 32 brs, 8 mobile libraries; Head of Libraries and Information LESLEY NOBLETT; Cambridge Central Library closed for refurbishment, due to reopen in spring 2008.

Needham Research Institute: East Asian History of Science Library, 8 Sylvester Rd, Cambridge, CB3 9AF; tel. (1223) 311545; fax (1223) 362703; e-mail admin@nri.org.uk; internet www.nri.org.uk; f. 1976 from collns assembled since 1942 by Dr Joseph Needham and Dr Lu Gwei-Djen, from sources in China and the West, primarily intended for the research on which is based the series 'Science and Civilization in China' (23 vols of which have so far been published); governed by the Needham Research Institute Trust (fmrly East Asian History of Science Trust, f. 1968), an educational charity; a unique collection specialized in works in the history of science, technology and medicine in East Asia and consisting of books, periodicals, off-prints, MSS in Asian and European languages, also archival and iconographic material (notes, photographs, maps, microfilms, etc.); open to research scholars by appointment; Dir Dr CHRISTOPHER CULLEN; Librarian JOHN P. C. MOFFETT.

Tyndale House Library: 36 Selwyn Gardens, Cambridge, CB3 9BA; tel. (1223) 566602; fax (1223) 566608; e-mail librarian@tyndale.cam.ac.uk; internet www.tyndale.cam.ac.uk; f. 1944; a residential centre for biblical research; intended for postgraduate study in biblically-related fields, with a view to promoting evangelical scholarship; 40,000 vols; Librarian Dr ELIZABETH MAGBA; publ. *Tyndale Bulletin* (2 a year).

Canterbury

Canterbury Cathedral Archives and Library: The Precincts, Canterbury, Kent, CT1 2EH; tel. (1227) 865330 (Archives); tel. (1227) 865287 (Library); fax (1227) 865222; e-mail archives@canterbury-cathedral.org; internet www.canterbury-cathedral.org; f. c.597; books and archives have been used and maintained here throughout the cathedral's existence; documents since 8th century; MSS of Christ Church Cathedral Priory and the Dean and Chapter of Canterbury; archives of the Diocese of Canterbury; archives of Canterbury City and District Parish; records for parishes in the Archdeaconry of Canterbury (eastern Kent); 52,000 printed books: early printed books, Bibles, prayer books, Catholic and anti-Catholic writings, natural science, travel, theology, history, 17th–19th century pamphlets, material on the slave trade, music; 2 parish libraries (Elham and Preston-next-Wingham); Librarian KEITH O'SULLIVAN; Archivist CRESSIDA ANNESLEY.

University of Kent, The Templeman Library: Canterbury, CT2 7NU; tel. (1227) 764000; fax (1227) 823984; e-mail library-enquiry@kent.ac.uk; internet www.kent.ac.uk; f. 1964; 800,000 vols; special collections include Cartoon Centre (80,000 original political cartoons), Victorian and Edwardian Popular Theatre (Pettingell, Melville and Reading-Rayner MSS and printed plays, mainly 19th century), Maddison collection (history of science), C. P. Davies Wind and Watermill collection, the papers of Lord Weatherill; Dir of Information Services and Librarian MARGARET M. COUTTS.

Cardiff

Cardiff County Libraries: Central Library, St David's Link, Frederick St, Cardiff, CF10 2DU; tel. (29) 2038-2116; fax (29) 2087-1599; e-mail p.sawyer@cardiff.gov.uk; 750,000 vols; 19 br libraries, 2 mobile libraries; Community Learning Officer PAUL SAWYER.

Central library:

Cardiff Central Library and County Library Headquarters: St David's Link, Frederick St, Cardiff, CF1 4DT; f. 1862; main library includes lending and reference books; music and sound recordings library; video and DVD colln; children's library; local studies library includes maps, prints and MSS, large collection of Welsh history; facilities for disabled.

Cardiff University Library Service: Information Services Directorate, 40–41 Park Pl., Cardiff, CF10 3BB; tel. (29) 2087-4876; fax (29) 2087-4285; e-mail library@cardiff.ac.uk; internet www.cardiff.ac.uk/1495; f. 1883; consists of 18 libraries: Aberconway (Business, Economics and Transport), Archie Cochrane (Medicine), Architecture, Arts and Social Studies, Biomedical Sciences, Brian Cooke Dental, Bute, Cancer Research Wales, Law, Legal Practice, Music, Nursing and Healthcare Studies, School of Nursing and Midwifery Studies, Science, Senghennydd (Mathematics and Lifelong Learning), Sir Herbert Duthie (Medicine), Trevithick (Engineering and Science), Whitchurch Postgraduate Medical Centre; research collections: Ann Griffiths collection, Architecture Rare Books collection, Arts and Social Studies Special collection, Cochrane archive, Cudlipp collection, David Bainton archive, European Documentation Centre, First Edition archive, Historical Book collection (Healthcare), Osman archive (Photojournalism), Salisbury collection (Welsh History), UCAC (Undeb Cenedlaethol Athrawon Cymru) archive; University Librarian JANET PETERS.

Amgueddfa Cymru – National Museum-Wales Library: Cathays Park, Cardiff, CF10 3NP; tel. (29) 2057-3202; fax (29) 2057-3216; internet www.museumwales.ac.uk; f. 1907; 200,000 vols, books and periodicals relevant to the museum collns; spec. collns: Tomlin (conchology), Willoughby Gardner (early natural history), Vaynor (James) Colln (early works on astronomy); also houses libraries of Cardiff Naturalists' Soc. and Cambrian Archaeological Asscn; Librarian J. R. KENYON.

Carlisle

Cumbria County Library: County Heritage Services, Arroyo Block, The Castle, Carlisle, CA3 8UR; tel. (1228) 607300; fax (1228) 607299; e-mail herithq@dial.pipex.com.

Carmarthen

Carmarthenshire County Library: Public Library, St Peter's St, Carmarthen, SA31 1LN; tel. (1267) 224824; fax (1267) 221839; 762,000 vols; 33 brs, 5 mobile libraries; special collections: coal mine plans, Theodore Nichol Collection, the library of the Carmarthenshire Antiquarian Society; Prin. Officer, Libraries and Community Learning DEWI THOMAS.

Chelmsford

Anglia Polytechnic University Library: Rivermead Campus, Bishop Hall Lane, Chelmsford, CM1 1SQ; tel. (1245) 493131; fax (1245) 490835; 250,000 vols; Librarian NICOLA KERSHAW.

Essex County Council Libraries: County Hall, Market Rd, Chelmsford, Essex, CM1 1LH; tel. (845) 603-7628; e-mail answers.direct@essexcc.gov.uk; internet www.essexcc.gov.uk/libraries; 73 brs, 15 mobile libraries; Libraries Man. MARTIN PALMER (acting).

Chester

Cheshire Libraries: Cheshire County Council, Libraries and Culture, Room 286, County Hall, Chester, CH1 1SF; tel. (1244) 606034; fax (1244) 602767; e-mail webmaster@cheshire.gov.uk; internet www.cheshire.gov.uk/library/home.htm; f. 1922; 1,500,000 vols; 35 full-time, 6 part-time, 3 dual use brs, 6 mobile libraries and 1 research library; HQ special collections; Education Library Service; County Libraries Officer I. DUNN.

Chichester

West Sussex County Council Library Service: Greyfriars, 61 North St, Chichester, West Sussex, PO19 1NB; tel. (1243) 756700; fax (1243) 756714; e-mail county.libraries@westsussex.gov.uk; internet www.westsussex.gov.uk; f. 1925; 1,117,000 vols; 35 brs, 3 mobile libraries; County Librarian S. HOUGHTON.

Colchester

University of Essex, The Albert Sloman Library: Wivenhoe Park, Colchester, CO4 3SQ; tel. (1206) 873333; fax (1206) 872289; internet www.essex.ac.uk; f. 1964; 982,000 vols and microforms, 7,619 current periodicals; spec. collns: Latin America, fmr USSR, Social Democratic Party (SDP) archives, SDP papers of Lord Rodgers of Quarrybank, Tawney Soc. archives, Nat. Viewers' and Listeners' Asscn archives, Boundary Comm. for England archives (1992–93 public enquiries), papers and publs of the Cttee on Standards in Public Life (Nolan Cttee), Sigmund Freud and related collns (papers and publs), papers of Lord Alport, Sir Vincent Evans colln, Paul Sieghart memorial archive, SCOPE-ENUWAR archive, papers of Lord Brimelow, Gaudier-Brzeska colln, Royal Statistical Soc. (historical) colln, Essex Soc. for Archaeology and History Library, John Hassall colln, Lord Hill of Wivenhoe papers, T. E. Lawrence letters, Samuel Harsnett Library (Archbishop of York, 1629–31), Ellis East European Elections colln, Windscale Inquiry (1977) papers, archives of the Talking Newspaper Asscn of the UK, Margery Allingham/Philip Youngman Carter colln, Bernie Hamilton (Human Rights) archive; Librarian R. BUTLER.

Conwy

Conwy County Borough Council Library, Information and Culture Service: Bodlondeb, Conwy, LL32 8DU; tel. (1492) 576140; fax (1492) 592061; e-mail llyfr.lib.pencadlys.hq@conwy.gov.uk; f. 1996; 200,000 vols; 13 brs, 1 mobile library; special collections: local history, Welsh language and literature; Head of Service: Library, Information and Culture RONA ALDRICH.

Coventry

Coventry Libraries and Information Services: Central Library, Smithford Way, Coventry, CV1 1FY; tel. (24) 7683-2314; fax (24) 7683-2440; e-mail central.library@coventry.gov.uk; f. 1868; 480,000 vols; spec.

collns on the motor industry, cycle industry, local history, George Eliot, trade unions and industrial relations; Head of Libraries and Information Services ANDREW GREEN.

University of Warwick Library: Gibbet Hill Rd, Coventry, CV4 7AL; tel. (24) 7652-3523; fax (24) 7652-4211; e-mail library@warwick.ac.uk; internet library.warwick.ac.uk; f. 1963; 1,000,000 vols; special collections: British and foreign statistical serials (trade, finance, production), current and retrospective, pre-1948 collections of Howard League for Penal Reform, Modern Records Centre (labour history, employers' records, industrial relations), Modern German Literature; Librarian ANNE BELL.

Cwmbran

Monmouthshire Libraries and Information Service: Chepstow Library, Manor Way, Chepstow, NP16 5HZ; tel. (1291) 635731; fax (1291) 635736; e-mail infocentre@monmouthshire.gov.uk; internet libraries.monmouthshire.gov.uk; f. 1996; 177,000 vols; 6 brs, 1 mobile library; Principal Librarian ANN JONES.

Darlington

Darlington Libraries: Central Library, Crown St, Darlington, DL1 1ND; tel. (1325) 462034; fax (1325) 381556; e-mail crown.street.library@darlington.gov.uk; internet www.darlington.gov.uk/library; Libraries Man. LYNNE LITCHFIELD.

Derby

Derby City Libraries: Roman House, Heritage Gate, Friary St, Derby, DE1 1XB; tel. (1332) 716607; fax (1332) 715549; e-mail libraries@derby.gov.uk; internet www.derby.gov.uk/libraries; f. 1879; re-f. 1997; Head of Library Services DAVID POTTON.

Dorchester

Dorset County Library: Colliton Park, Dorchester, Dorset, DT1 1XJ; tel. (1305) 225000; fax (1305) 224344; e-mail dorsetlibraries@dorsetcc.gov.uk; internet www.dorsetcc.gov.uk; f. 1920, reorganized 1997; 625,000 items; 34 brs; 5 mobile libraries; special collections: Dorset Collection, Thomas Hardy Collection, Powys Collection; Head of Cultural Services P. LEIVERS; publ. *Subject Index* (annually).

Dundee

Dundee City Council Central Library: The Wellgate, Dundee, DD1 1DB; tel. (1382) 434318; fax (1382) 434036; e-mail library@dundeecity.gov.uk; f. 1869; 13 brs, mobile library; special collections: local history and genealogy, commerce, music, Wighton Collection of National Music (620 vols), British Standards, Audio Library, video library; Chief Neighbourhood Resource Officer FRASER PATRICK.

University of Dundee Library: Dundee, DD1 4HN; tel. (1382) 344087; fax (1382) 229190; e-mail library@dundee.ac.uk; internet www.dundee.ac.uk/library; f. 1881; 750,000 vols; Librarian J. M. BAGNALL.

Durham

Durham Arts, Libraries and Museums Department: POB, County Hall, Durham, DH1 5TY; tel. (191) 383-3595; fax (191) 384-1336; e-mail alm@durham.gov.uk; f. 1923; 876,000 vols; 38 full-time brs, 2 trailers, 4 mobile and 3 travelling libraries, 1 bookbus for the elderly; Dir PATRICK CONWAY.

University of Durham Library: Main University Library, Stockton Rd, Durham, DH1 3LY; tel. (191) 334-2968; fax (191) 334-2971; e-mail main.library@durham.ac.uk; internet www.dur.ac.uk/library; f. 1833;

1,000,000 printed items on four sites, incl. European Documentation Centre, Middle East Documentation Unit; dept of Archives and Special Collections houses extensive special collections of early printed books, MSS, maps, prints, photographs; printed book special collections include those formed by Bishop Cosin, M. J. Routh, Bishop Maltby, Dr Winterbottom, and the Sharp Library from Bamburgh Castle; 200 incunabula, 2,200 STC, 10,000 Wing; collections of MSS and archives include medieval MSS, modern literary MSS (C. C. Abbott, Basil Bunting, William Plomer Collections), Earl Grey Papers, Malcolm MacDonald Papers, Durham Cathedral Archives, Durham diocesan and probate records, Howard of Naworth Papers and other collections of local family and estate records, Sudan Archive; Librarian Dr J. T. D. HALL; publ. *Durham University Library Publications* (occasional).

Ebbw Vale

Blaenau Gwent Libraries: Facilities Section, Municipal Offices, Civic Centre, Ebbw Vale, NP23 6XB; tel. (1495) 355311; fax (1495) 355468; e-mail libraries@ blaenau-gwent.gov.uk; 120,000 vols; 7 brs, 2 mobile libraries; County Borough Librarian MARY JONES.

Edinburgh

Edinburgh City Libraries and Information Services: Central Library, George IV Bridge, Edinburgh, EH1 1EG; tel. (131) 242-8000; fax (131) 242-8009; e-mail eclis@ edinburgh.gov.uk; internet www.edinburgh .gov.uk/libraries; f. 1890; 1,365,000 items; 25 community libraries, 4 mobile libraries; Central Reference (incl. business information, British Standards, electronic information; 346,229 items); special collections: Edinburgh Room (contains information on life in Edinburgh and on Scott, Stevenson, Ballantyne; press cuttings; illustrations; playbills; 120,000 items), Scottish (especially genealogy, history and Scottish Parliament information; 97,000 items), Music and Audio (CDs, scores, Scottish music; 148,000 items), Fine Art (includes costume, fashion and photography; slides, Japanese prints, videos, artists' books, press cuttings on Scottish art, architecture, design and photography; 90,000 items); City Librarian BILL WALLACE.

Edinburgh University Library, Museums and Galleries: George Square, Edinburgh, EH8 9LJ; tel. (131) 650-3384; fax (131) 650-3380; e-mail library@ed.ac.uk; internet www.lib.ed.ac.uk; f. 1580; 3,462,947 printed items, 279,814 microforms, 111,832 maps in sheets, 7,700 metres of MSS and archives, 33,808 theses, 6,826 audiovisual items, 4,417 electronic and 4,430 print current periodicals; Drummond (of Hawthornden) Collection; Laing Charters and MSS; Halliwell-Phillipps Collection; MSS on Scottish history and the Scottish literary renaissance; Arthur Koestler MSS and part library; Corson Sir Walter Scott Collection; New Zealand Studies Collection; MSS and printed books on early 20th c. English literature; Scottish Enlightenment; history of science and medicine; African, East Asian, Islamic and Middle Eastern studies; includes the Main Library, Law and Europa Library, Moray House Library (Education), New College Library (Divinity), Science Libraries and Royal (Dick) School of Veterinary Studies Libraries, Royal Infirmary Library, Reid Concert Hall Museum of Instruments (John Donaldson Collection), St Cecilia's Hall Museum of instruments (Raymond Russell Collection of Early Keyboard Instruments) and the Talbot Rice Gallery; Dir of Library Services SHEILA E. CANNELL; publ. *Annual report* (online only).

Heriot-Watt University Library: Riccarton, Edinburgh, EH14 4AS; tel. (131) 451-3570; fax (131) 451-3164; e-mail library@hw .ac.uk; internet www.hw.ac.uk; f. 1821; 145,000 vols, 1,500 periodicals; Librarian M. L. BREAKS.

National Archives of Scotland: HM General Register House, Edinburgh, EH1 3YY; tel. (131) 535-1314; fax (131) 535-1360; e-mail enquiries@nas.gov.uk; internet www .nas.gov.uk; f. 1993 as an Executive Agency; national archives of Scotland; local and church records, and records of Scottish government and law since 12th c.; also contains many private and business collns; Keeper of the Records of Scotland GEORGE P. MACKENZIE.

National Library of Scotland: George IV Bridge, Edinburgh, EH1 1EW; tel. (131) 623-3700; fax (131) 623-3701; e-mail enquiries@ nls.uk; internet www.nls.uk; f. 1680 as the Advocates' Library; under Copyright legislation may claim any book, etc., published in the United Kingdom and Ireland; contains 13,000,000 vols and pamphlets and a large collection of MSS; Library's Inter-Library Services (33 Salisbury Pl., Edinburgh, EH9 1SL) maintain a stock (120,000 vols) of scarce books to supplement the reserves of Scottish public libraries, act as the headquarters for Scottish inter-library co-operation, and house Scottish Union Catalogue; Chair. of the Trustees Prof. MICHAEL ANDERSON; National Librarian MARTYN WADE; publ. *Discover NLS* (quarterly).

Attached library:

National Library of Scotland Map Library: 33 Salisbury Pl., Edinburgh, EH9 1SL; tel. (131) 466-3813; fax (131) 466-3812; e-mail maps@nls.uk; internet www.nls.uk; f. 1958; modern topographic and thematic map coverage of most parts of the world; particular interest in early/ modern maps with Scottish association; Head D. WEBSTER.

National Museums of Scotland Library: Chambers St, Edinburgh, EH1 1JF; tel. (131) 247-4153; fax (131) 247-4311; e-mail library@ nms.ac.uk; internet www.nms.ac.uk; f. 1854; 300,000 vols, esp. European decorative arts, northern European archaeology and Scottish history; MS collns incl. Society of Antiquaries of Scotland, Harvie Brown (natural sciences), William Spiers Bruce (Antarctic exploration), Sir William Jardine (natural sciences); Head of Library ELIZE ROWAN.

Royal Botanic Garden Library: Edinburgh, EH3 5LR; Located at: 20A Inverleith Row, Edinburgh, EH3 5LR; tel. (131) 522-7171; fax (131) 248-2901; e-mail library@rbge .org.uk; internet www.rbge.org.uk; f. 1670; incorporates the botanical libraries of the Plinian (1841), Wernerian (1858) and Botanical (1872) societies of Edinburgh, Dr John Hope (1899), Cleghorn Memorial Library (1941) and Mr Robert Scarlett (1975); compiles indexes to Monographs, Floras, Gardens, botanists, botanical expeditions, etc.; 100,000 vols, including pre-Linnean literature on botany, horticulture, agriculture and medicine; 100,000 pamphlets and separates; 4,000 (1,500 current) periodicals; extensive collection of botanical drawings and prints, photographs, cuttings, etc., correspondence, diaries, maps, plans, MSS, etc., relating to the early Regius Keepers and Curators and botanists and horticulturists in the United Kingdom and abroad; Librarian H. J. HUTCHEON; publs *British Fungus Flora* (irreg.), *Catalogue of Plants* (irreg.), *Edinburgh Journal of Botany* (3 a year), *Sibbaldia: an* occasional series of horticultural notes (irreg.).

Royal College of Physicians of Edinburgh Library: 9 Queen St, Edinburgh, EH2 1JQ; tel. (131) 225-7324; fax (131) 220-3939; e-mail library@rcpe.ac.uk; internet www.rcpe.ac.uk; f. 1681; 50,000 books, 1,000 vols of MSS; open to all *bona fide* enquirers; particularly rich in the early sources of medical knowledge; colln of periodicals; Librarian I. A. MILNE.

Royal College of Surgeons of Edinburgh Library and Archive: Nicolson St, Edinburgh, EH8 9DW; tel. (131) 527-1630; fax (131) 557-6406; e-mail library@rcsed.ac.uk; internet www.rcsed.ac.uk; f. 1505; 40,000 vols, 170 periodicals; historical and contemporary medical and surgical stock; images library; college archive since 1505; private library for Fellows and members (access to researchers by appointment); CEO J. R. C. FOSTER; publs *The Surgeon, Surgeons' News*.

Signet Library: Parliament Square, Edinburgh, EH1 1RF; tel. (131) 225-4923; fax (131) 220-4016; e-mail library@wssociety.co .uk; internet www.signetlibrary.co.uk; f. date of foundation 1594, but there were Writers to Her Majesty's Signet as early as 1460; 90,000 vols; the Library of the Society of Writers to Her Majesty's Signet is devoted chiefly to Scots law and Scottish history and genealogy, and is the library of a private society; Librarian AUDREY R. WALKER.

Eton

Eton College Library: Eton College, Windsor, Berks SL4 6DB; tel. (1753) 671221; fax (1753) 801507; e-mail collections@etoncollege .org.uk; f. 1440; 85,000 items, incl. 200 medieval MSS, 200 incunabula; important collns of edns of classical writers and related material (16th–18th centuries), early science, Elizabethan, Jacobean and Restoration drama, large colln of Civil War and early 18th-century English pamphlets, 16th-century Italian books; bindings, English and Continental, since 12th century; Topham colln of drawings and engravings after the antique (c. 2,500 items); Etoniana colln (c. 5,000 printed books, drawings, prints, scrapbooks, MSS); School Books colln; Parikian colln of Armenian printed books 1500–1900; Kessler colln of books on China and Russia; English literature since 19th century, incl. Elizabeth Barrett Browning, Anne Thackeray Ritchie, Thomas Hardy, Edward Gordon Craig, Moelwyn Merchant collections; mezzotint colln (1,000 items); Librarian M. C. MEREDITH; Archivist P. C. HATFIELD.

Exeter

Devon Library and Information Services: Great Moor House, Bittern Rd, Sowton, Exeter, EX2 7NL; tel. (1392) 384315; fax (1392) 384316; e-mail devlibs@devon.gov.uk; internet www.devon.gov.uk/libraries; f. 1924; 1,188,826 vols; 55 brs, 11 mobile libraries; Head of Library and Information Services L. OSBORNE.

Exeter Cathedral Library: Diocesan House, Palace Gate, Exeter, EX1 1HX; tel. (1392) 272894; fax (1392) 285986; e-mail library@exeter-cathedral.org.uk; internet www.exeter-cathedral.org.uk/admin/library .html; f. 11th century when Bishop Leofric gave 66 MS vols to the Cathedral Church; 20,000 items; MS vols incl. Exeter Book of Old English Poetry and Exon Domesday Book; spec. collns incl. Cathedral MSS and archives, early printed books in medicine and science, Cook Colln (16th–19th century works, early linguistics), printed tracts (mainly English Civil War period), Harington Collection (16th–19th century theology, ecclesiastical history, history); archive of

50,000 items; Cathedral Librarian PETER W. THOMAS; Cathedral Archivist ANGELA DOUGHTY.

National Meteorological Library and Archive: Met Office, Fitzroy Rd, Exeter, EX1 3PB; tel. (1392) 884841; fax (1392) 885681; e-mail metlib@metoffice.gov.uk; internet www.metoffice.gov.uk; f. 1870; 300,000 vols and 5,000 images; the nat. library and archive for meteorology, climatology; incl. comprehensive records of data published by British and foreign institutions; early weather diaries; official weather records and charts; ships' weather log books; open to the public; Library and Archive Man. SARA OSMAN.

University of Exeter Library: Stocker Rd, Exeter, EX4 4PT; tel. (1392) 263869; fax (1392) 263871; e-mail library@exeter.ac.uk; internet www.library.ex.ac.uk; f. 1937; 1,200,000 vols; administers Library of Devon and Exeter Institution (36,000 vols); Dir of Academic Services MICHELE SHOEBRIDGE.

Falkirk

Falkirk Council Library Services: Public and Schools Library Service, Victoria Bldgs, Queen St, Falkirk, FK2 7AF; tel. (1324) 506800; fax (1324) 506801; e-mail library .support@falkirk.gov.uk; internet www .falkirk.gov.uk; local history colln; Falkirk Council Libraries Man. IRENE MCINTYRE; publ. *Current Awareness Bulletin* (weekly).

Glasgow

Department for International Development Library: Abercrombie House, Eaglesham Rd, East Kilbride, Glasgow, G75 8EA; tel. (1355) 843880; internet www.dfid.gov.uk.

Glasgow Caledonian University Library: City Campus, Cowcaddens Rd, Glasgow, G4 0BA; tel. (141) 331-3867; fax (141) 331-3968; e-mail library@gcal.ac.uk; internet www.lib.gcal.ac.uk; f. 1993; 220,000 vols; Chief Librarian FLORA SMITH (acting).

Glasgow City Libraries and Archives: Glasgow, G3 7DN; tel. (141) 287-2999; fax (141) 287-2815; 32 district libraries; 2,145,000 vols; special collections of foreign literature and local history; Dir (vacant).

Attached library:

Mitchell Library: North St, Glasgow, G3 7DN; f. 1874; 1,235,000 vols; special collections: on Glasgow (20,000 vols), music (43,000 vols), Robert Burns (5,000 vols), Scottish poetry (12,000 vols) and Patent Depositary Library; business users' service; receives a copy of every publication issued by HMSO, and is also a Depository Library for the unrestricted publications of the United Nations, Unesco and FAO; Librarian F. MACPHERSON.

Royal College of Physicians and Surgeons of Glasgow Library: 234 St Vincent St, Glasgow, G2 5RJ; tel. (141) 227-3204; fax (141) 221-1804; e-mail library@rcpsg.ac.uk; internet www.rcpsg.ac.uk; f. 1599; 150,000 vols; Librarian JAMES BEATON.

University of Glasgow Library: Hillhead St, Glasgow, G12 8QE; tel. (141) 330-6704; fax (141) 330-4952; e-mail library@lib.gla.ac .uk; internet www.lib.gla.ac.uk; f. 15th century; 2,038,650 vols; incorporates Trinity College Glasgow Library (Church of Scotland); Hunterian Books and MSS, Euing Collections of the Bible and music, Farmer Music Collection, Laver, MacColl and Wright Papers on fine art, Hamilton Collection of philosophy, Ferguson Collection of the history of chemistry, Stirling Maxwell Collection of Emblem books, J. M. Whistler archive, David Murray regional history collection, Scottish Theatre Archive, Edwin Morgan Papers, Trotsky Collection; Dir of Library Services HELEN DURNDELL (acting).

University of Strathclyde Library: 101 St James' Rd, Glasgow, G4 0NS; tel. (141) 548-3701; fax (141) 552-3304; e-mail library@ strath.ac.uk; internet www.lib.strath.ac.uk; f. 1796; 1,000,000 vols, 6,290 periodicals; spec. collns include Anderson colln (founder's library), Young colln (alchemy and early chemistry), Laing colln (mathematics vols from the 18th and 19th centuries), Robertson colln (Scottish history and topography); Librarian DEREK G. LAW.

Gloucester

Gloucestershire County Library, Arts and Museums Service: Shire Hall, Quayside House, Gloucester, GL1 2HY; tel. (1452) 425020; fax (1452) 425042; e-mail clams@ gloscc.gov.uk; internet www.gloscc.gov.uk; spec. collns incl. Gloucestershire Colln; Head of Library Services COLIN CAMPBELL.

Grays

Thurrock Libraries: Grays Library, Orsett Rd, Grays, RM17 5DX; tel. (1375) 383611; fax (1375) 370806; e-mail grays.library@ thurrock.gov.uk; internet www.thurrock.gov .uk/libraries; 10 brs, 1 mobile library; Head of Libraries ANN HALLIDAY.

Guildford

University of Surrey Library: Guildford, Surrey, GU2 7XH; tel. (1483) 683325; fax (1483) 689500; e-mail library-enquiries@ surrey.ac.uk; internet www.surrey.ac.uk/ library; f. 1894; 500,000 vols, 3,800 periodicals; spec. collns incl. National Resource Centre for Dance, E. H. Shephard archive; Dir of Information Services T. J. A. CRAWSHAW.

Hatfield

Hertfordshire Library Service: New Barnfield, Travellers Lane, Hatfield, Herts., AL10 8XG; tel. (1438) 737333; fax (1438) 737334; e-mail hertsdirect@hertscc.gov.uk; internet www.hertsdirect.org; f. 1925; 1,408,462 vols, other media 119,852 items; 48 brs, 13 mobile libraries, 6 hospital libraries, 1 prison library; special collns: performing arts, local history, business information, official publns; Head of Libraries GLENDA WOOD.

Haverfordwest

Pembrokeshire County Library: Dew St, Haverfordwest, Pembs., SA61 1SU; tel. (1437) 775244; fax (1437) 769218; e-mail sandra.matthews@pembrokeshire.gov.uk; internet www.pembrokeshire.gov.uk; reference library, incl. the Pembrokeshire Colln; local studies colln; 14 br. lending libraries; Information and Cultural Services Man. NEIL BENNETT.

Hawarden

St Deiniol's Residential Library: Hawarden, Deeside, Flintshire, CH5 3DF; tel. (1244) 532350; fax (1244) 520643; e-mail deiniol.visitors@connect.com; internet www .st-deiniols.org; f. 1896 by William Ewart Gladstone (1809–1898); 200,000 vols, 50,000 pamphlets, and MSS material; theology, philosophy, history (esp. 19th c.), classics, English literature, Gladstonian Studies; accommodation for 37 residents; Warden Rev. PETER FRANCIS; Librarian PATRICIA WILLIAMS.

Hereford

Herefordshire Council Libraries: Shire Hall, Hereford HR1 2HX; tel. (1432) 261644; 11 brs; Policy and Communications Man. ALAN BLUNDELL; Principal Libraries Officer JAMES ANTHONY.

Huddersfield

Kirklees Cultural Services: Headquarters, Red Doles Lane, Huddersfield, West Yorks., HD2 1YF; tel. (1484) 226300; fax (1484) 446842; f. 1974; 1,250,000 vols; Head of Cultural Services JONATHAN DRAKE.

University of Huddersfield Learning Centre: Queensgate, Huddersfield, HD1 3DH; tel. (1484) 473888; fax (1484) 517987; internet www.hud.ac.uk; f. 1841; 450,000 vols; Dir of Library Services PHIL SYKES.

Ipswich

Suffolk County Council—Libraries, Archives and Information: Endeavour House, Russell Rd, Ipswich, IP1 2BX; tel. (1473) 264285; fax (1473) 216847; e-mail help@suffolklibraries.co.uk; internet www .suffolklibraries.co.uk; f. 1974 by amalgamation of fmr Suffolk library authorities; Head of Service Devt, Libraries, Archives and Information ROGER MCMASTER.

Keele

University of Keele Library: Keele, Staffs., ST5 5BG; tel. (1782) 583535; fax (1782) 584502; e-mail help@lib.keele.ac .uk; internet www.keele.ac.uk/depts/li; f. 1949; 620,000 vols; Librarian P. R. REYNOLDS.

Keyworth

British Geological Survey Library: British Geological Survey, Keyworth, Nottingham, NG12 5GG; tel. (115) 936-3205; fax (115) 936-3200; e-mail libuser@bgs.ac.uk; internet www.bgs.ac.uk; f. 1837; 500,000 vols, 3,000 current periodicals, 200,000 maps, 20,000 archives, nat. collns of 100,000 photographs largely illustrating British scenery and geology; regional office library at Edinburgh; Chief Librarian KEN HOLLYWOOD.

Kingston upon Hull

Kingston upon Hull Libraries: Central Library, Albion St, Hull, HU1 3TF; tel. (1482) 210000; fax (1482) 616827; internet www.hullcc.gov.uk; Head of Libraries JO EDGE.

University of Hull, Academic Services Libraries: Cottingham Rd, Hull, North Humberside, HU6 7RX; tel. (1482) 466581; fax (1482) 466205; e-mail libhelp@hull.ac.uk; internet www.hull.ac.uk/lib; f. 1929; 1,000,000 vols; special collections: South East Asia, India, British Labour history; Dir of Academic Services and Librarian R. G. HESELTINE.

Kirkcaldy

Fife Council Libraries, Central Area: East Fergus Place, Kirkcaldy, Fife, KY1 1XT; tel. (1592) 412930; fax (1592) 412941; 400,000 vols; Librarian DOROTHY MILLER.

Lampeter

University of Wales, Lampeter Library: Lampeter, Ceredigion, SA48 7ED; tel. (1570) 422351; fax (1570) 423875; e-mail library@ lamp.ac.uk; internet www.lamp.ac.uk; f. 200,000 vols, incl. Tract colln of 11,000 items; Librarian A. PRESCOTT (acting); publ. *Trivium*.

Lancaster

University of Lancaster Library: Bailrigg, Lancaster, LA1 4YH; tel. (1524) 592515; fax (1524) 63806; f. 1963; 936,000 vols, pamphlets and other items, 3,000 current serials; special collections: business history, Quaker, Redlich (music), Socialist, European Documentation Centre; Librarian JACQUE-

LINE WHITESIDE; publ. *Report of the Librarian.*

Branch library:

Ruskin Library: University of Lancaster, Bailrigg, Lancaster, LA1 4YH; tel. (1524) 593587; fax (1524) 593580; e-mail Ruskin.Library@lancaster.ac.uk; internet www.lancs.ac.uk/users/ruskinlib; Whitehouse colln of documents related to the writer and thinker, John Ruskin (1819–1900), (incl. 1,700 works of art by Ruskin and his circle, Ruskin's exhaustive diaries, 8,000 of his letters, 200 MSS, 3,500 books and 1,000 original photographs); Curator STEPHEN WILDMAN.

Leeds

Leeds Library and Information Services: Central Library, Municipal Bldgs, Calverley St, Leeds, LS1 3AB; tel. (113) 2478282; fax (113) 3951833; e-mail businessandresearch@leedslearning.net; internet www.leeds.gov.uk/libraries; 2m. vols; 54 brs, 5 mobile libraries; numerous spec. collns incl. early botanical books, fine arts, Jewish and Hebrew books, military history, music books, scores and audiovisual items, patents, business information, family and local historical documents, maps and photographic prints; Chief Librarian CATHERINE BLANSHARD.

Leeds University Library: Leeds, LS2 9JT; tel. (113) 233-6388; fax (113) 233-5561; f. 1874; 2,500,000 vols, pamphlets and microforms including the Brotherton Collection which contains over 50,000 vols and pamphlets and a large number of MSS, deeds and letters; includes fmr Ripon Cathedral Library containing early MSS, Service Books, Books of Hours, MSS since 13th c., important printed books from 15th–18th c.; Liddle Collection of First World War archive materials; Librarian M. COUTTS; publs *Al-Masaq, Journal of Educational Administration and History, Leeds Studies in English, Leeds Texts and Monographs, Northern History, Proceedings of the Leeds Philosophical and Literary Society: literary and historical section, Proceedings of the Leeds Philosophical and Literary Society: scientific section, Proceedings of the Yorkshire Geological Society, Publications of the Thoresby Society, University of Leeds Review.*

Leicester

De Montfort University Library: Kimberlin Library, The Gateway, Leicester, LE1 9BH; tel. (116) 255-1551; fax (116) 255-0307; Head of Library Services KATHRYN ARNOLD.

Leicester City Libraries: New Walk Centre, Welford Place, Leicester, LE1 6ZG; tel. (116) 252-6762; fax (116) 255-9257; e-mail libraries@leicester.gov.uk; internet www.leicester.gov.uk/departments/page.asp?pgid=2089; Head of Library and Information Services PATRICIA FLYNN.

Leicestershire Library Services: County Hall, Glenfield, Leicester, LE3 8SS; tel. (116) 265-7376; fax (116) 265-7370; e-mail libraries@leics.gov.uk; internet www.leics.gov.uk/libraries; f. 1974.

University of Leicester Library: POB 248, University Rd, Leicester, LE1 9QD; tel. (116) 252-2042; fax (116) 252-2066; e-mail library@le.ac.uk; internet www.le.ac.uk/library; f. 1921; 1,000,000 items; special collections of local history of England and Wales, papers of Joe Orton; Librarian C. FYFE.

Lewes

East Sussex Library and Information Service: C15G, County Hall, 44 St Anne's Crescent, Lewes, East Sussex, BN7 1SW; tel. (1273) 481870; fax (1273) 481716; 1,409,700 vols; 30 full-time and part-time brs; Asst Dir: Libraries, Culture and Community Learning Dr IRENE CAMPBELL.

Lichfield

Dean Savage Reference Library: 19B The Close, Lichfield, Staffs., WS13 7LD; tel. (1543) 306240; f. 1924; 6,000 vols, mostly theology and ecclesiastical history; for use, apply to above address.

Lincoln

Lincolnshire County Council Communities Directorate–Libraries: County Offices, Newland, Lincoln, LN1 1YL; tel. (1522) 553207; fax (1522) 552811; e-mail library.support@lincolnshire.gov.uk; internet www.lincolnshire.gov.uk; f. 1974 from 7 former Lincolnshire library authorities; 1,528,773 vols; 46 brs, 11 mobile libraries; spec. collns: Music, Drama, Lincolnshire material, Alfred Lord Tennyson, Elvin and Longmire Collns; Head of Libraries, Sport and Support Services JOHN PATEMAN.

Liverpool

Liverpool Libraries and Information Services: Central Library, William Brown St, Liverpool, L3 8EW; tel. (151) 233-5835; fax (151) 233-5886; e-mail refbt.central.library@liverpool.gov.uk; f. 1852; 1,500,000 vols, pamphlets, MSS etc; reference services (includes Hornby Library: rare books, fine bindings, MSS, prints etc. and patents library), services to business, record office, family history service; EU depository library; Head of service JOYCE LITTLE.

University of Liverpool Library: POB 123, Liverpool, L69 3DA; tel. (151) 794-2674; fax (151) 794-2681; e-mail library@liverpool.ac.uk; f. 1881; over 1,400,000 vols, 4,900 current periodicals; special collections include 254 incunabula, the T. G. Rylands collection (early cartography, Lancashire and Cheshire history), the William Blake collection, the Scott Macfie collection (gypsy studies), the William Noble collection (Kelmscott and other private presses), the Knowsley collection (17th- to 19th-century English pamphlets), the Peers collection (Spanish Civil War), and the Fraser collection (c. 900 books and pamphlets on tobacco; also much material on positivism and secularism) Robert Graves Collection, Merseyside poets; modern MS holdings include the Rathbone, Blanco White, Brunner and Glasier papers, Science Fiction Foundation Collection, Olaf Stapledon collection; the Education Library contains an important collection of children's books; Librarian F. M. THOMSON; publs *Guide to Special Collections, Annual Report.*

Llandrindod Wells

Powys Library and Archive Service: Cefnllys Lane, Llandrindod Wells, Powys, LD1 5LD; tel. (1597) 826860; fax (1597) 826872; f. 1974; 300,000 vols; 18 brs; special local history collections; County Librarian T. L. ADAMS.

Llangefni

Isle of Anglesey County Library: Llangefni Library, Lon-y-Felin, Llangefni, Anglesey, LL77 7RT; tel. (1248) 752092; fax (1248) 750197; e-mail jrtlh@ynysmon.gov.uk; internet www.ynysmon.gov.uk; Head of Services JOHN REES THOMAS.

London

Aslib-IMI Information and Library Service: Temple Chambers, 3–7 Temple Ave, London, EC4Y 0HP; tel. (20) 7583-8900; fax (20) 7583-8401; e-mail aslib@aslib.co.uk; internet www.aslib.com/info; *c.* 16,000 vols on information management, incl. documentation, information science, special libraries and related subjects, 370 current periodicals of the world and about 25,000 references to articles, reports, etc., on library and information science; publs *Aslib Guide to Copyright* (3 a year), *Aslib Book Guide* (monthly), *Aslib Proceedings* (10 a year), *Current Awareness Abstracts* (10 a year), *Forthcoming International Scientific and Technical Conferences* (4 a year), *Journal of Documentation* (5 a year), *Managing Information* (10 a year), *Online and CD Notes* (10 a year), *Program: Electronic Library and Information Systems* (4 a year), *Records Management Journal* (3 a year).

Barking and Dagenham Public Libraries: Central Library, Vicarage Field Shopping Centre, Barking, Essex, IG11 8DQ; tel. (20) 8724-1312; fax (20) 8724-1316; e-mail libraries@ibbd.gov.uk; internet www.lbbd.gov.uk/4-libraries/libraries-menu.html; f. 1888; 600,000 vols; Head of Library Service TREVOR BROWN.

Barnet Education–Libraries: Bldg 4, North London Business Park, Oakleigh Rd South, London, N11 1NP; internet www.barnet.gov.uk; f. 1965; 66,000 vols; special collection of Sociology; Head of Libraries, Museums and Local Studies P. A. LITTLE.

Bexley Library Service: Ground Floor, Footscray Offices, Maidstone Rd, Sidcup, Kent, DA14 5HS; tel. (20) 8309-4100; fax (20) 8309-4142; e-mail libraries@bexley.gov.uk; internet www.bexley.gov.uk; 600,000 vols; 12 brs; 3 mobile libraries, reference library; Local Studies and Archive Centre; Library Services Manager J. MITLIN (acting).

Brent Library Service: Brent Council, Town Hall, Forty Lane, Wembley, Middx, HA9 9HD; tel. (20) 8937-3144; fax (20) 8937-3023; e-mail libraryservice@brent.gov.uk; internet www.brent.gov.uk/library.nsf; f. 1965; 580,000 vols; 12 brs, mobile library, housebound service, Grange Museum of Local History; Head of Library Service KAREN TYERMAN.

British Architectural Library: RIBA, 66 Portland Pl., London, W1B 1AD; tel. (20) 7580-5533; fax (20) 7631-1802; e-mail info@inst.riba.org; internet www.architecture.com; f. 1834; 150,000 vols, 700 current serials, 1,400 dead runs, 1.5m. photographs, 300,000 negatives, 700 m of MSS, and a colln of 600,000 drawings (housed at the Henry Cole Wing, Victoria and Albert Museum, London); one of the most comprehensive architectural libraries in the world; Dir Dr IRENA MURRAY; publs *Architectural Periodicals Index and Books catalogued by the British Architectural Library* (quarterly), *RIBA List of Recommended Books* (annual), *APId: Architectural Publications Index* (on disc, quarterly).

British Film Institute (BFI), National Film and Television Archive and National Library: 21 Stephen St, London, W1T 1LN; tel. (20) 7255-1444; fax (20) 7580-7503; e-mail information.unit@bfi.org.uk; internet www.bfi.org.uk/filmtvinfo/library; f. 1935 as a division of the British Film Institute; 275,000 feature films and short films since 1894, 210,000 television programmes; preserves for posterity, and makes available for study, cinematograph films and television programmes, stills, posters and set designs of artistic and historical value; incl. J. Paul Getty Jr Conservation Centre (in Berkhamsted), National Film and Television Archive and Independent Television Commission Library; Head of Collections and Information DARREN LONG.

British Geological Survey London Information Office: Natural History Museum (Earth Galleries), Exhibition Rd, London, SW7 2DE; tel. (20) 7589-4090; fax (20) 7584-8270; e-mail bgslondon@bgs.ac.uk; internet www.bgs.ac.uk; f. 1986; information and advisory service; public reference colln of British Geological Survey; publs incl. geological maps, memoirs, reports, research reports and information illustrating the geology of the British Isles; online access to British Geological Survey databases; some overseas maps and textbooks; Man. CLARE M. TOMBLESON.

British Library: 96 Euston Rd, London, NW1 2DB; tel. (870) 444-1500; e-mail press-and-pr@bl.uk; internet www.bl.uk; f. 1973; legal deposit library; 150m. items in most known languages, incorporating books, newspapers, periodicals, manuscripts, maps, prints and drawings, music scores, patents and the National Sound Archive; document supply service at Boston Spa, Wetherby, West Yorks., LS23 7BQ; Chair. Lord EATWELL; Chief Exec. LYNNE BRINDLEY; publ. *British Library Journal* (online only).

British Library of Political and Economic Science: London School of Economics, 10 Portugal St, London, WC2A 2HD; tel. (20) 7955-7218; fax (20) 7955-7454; e-mail j.sykes@lse.ac.uk; internet www.lse.ac.uk/library; f. 1896; 4m. bibliographic items comprising journals, govt publs from all over the world, other serial publs and 1.2m. monographs; colln mainly covers economics, political science, law (esp. int), sociology, history and geography; Librarian and Dir of Information Technology Services JEAN SYKES; publ. *The International Bibliography of the Social Sciences* (annual, also on-line).

British Medical Association Library: BMA House, Tavistock Sq., London, WC1H 9JP; tel. (20) 7383-6625; fax (20) 7388-2544; e-mail bma-library@bma.org.uk; internet www.bma.org.uk; f. 1887; 50,000 vols, 3,000 periodicals, 3,500 films and videos; Librarian JACKY BERRY; publ. *BMA Library Bulletin* (online only).

Bromley Public Libraries: Central Library, High St, Bromley, BR1 1EX; tel. (20) 8460-9955; fax (20) 8313-9975; e-mail reference.library@bromley.gov.uk; internet www.bromley.gov.uk; f. 1894; 631,508 vols, 44,581 audiovisual items, 1,399 multimedia items, 98,878 microtext items; special collections: Crystal Palace, Walter de la Mare, H. G. Wells; Asst Dir LINDA SIMPSON.

Camden Leisure and Community Services (Libraries, Arts and Tourism): The Crowndale Centre, 218–220 Eversholt St, London, NW1 1BD; tel. (20) 7974-1647; fax (20) 7974-1615; 759,537 vols; Head of Libraries DAVID JONES.

Canning House Library: The Hispanic and Luso-Brazilian Council, Canning House, 2 Belgrave Square, London, SW1X 8PJ; tel. (20) 7235-2303; fax (20) 7235-3587; e-mail enquiries@canninghouse.com; internet www.canninghouse.com; f. 1943; attached to Hispanic and Luso Brazilian Council; a non-political, not-for-profit organisation, founded to stimulate understanding between Britain, Spain, Portugal and Latin America; 60,000 vols on Latin America, Caribbean, Spain and Portugal; Library and Information Services Man. ALAN BIGGINS; publ. *British Bulletin of Publications on Latin America, the Caribbean, Portugal and Spain* (2 a year).

City of Westminster Libraries and Archives: Dept of Environment and Leisure, Westminster City Hall, Victoria St, London, SW1E 6QP; tel. (20) 7641-6571; fax (20) 7641-6594; 11 community libraries, total stock: 1,196,903 books and other materials; Asst Dir, Lifelong Learning DAVID RUSE.

Constituent libraries include:

City of Westminster Archives Centre: 10 St Ann's St, London, SW1P 2DE; tel. (20) 7641-5180; e-mail archives@westminster.gov.uk; internet www.westminster.gov.uk/archives; 200,000 archive items.

Westminster Music Library: 160 Buckingham Palace Rd, London, SW1W 9UD; tel. (20) 7641-4292; 62,400 items on music (not recordings).

Westminster Reference Library: 35 St Martin's St, London, WC2H 7HP; tel. (20) 7641-5286; 432,000 vols covering the humanities, pure sciences, business and technology; 700 current periodicals; British and foreign directories; access to CD-ROM online databases; Art and Design Library; 3,300 maps.

College of Arms: Queen Victoria St, London, EC4V 4BT; tel. (20) 7248-2762; fax (20) 7248-6448; e-mail enquiries@college-of-arms.gov.uk; internet www.college-of-arms.gov.uk; f. 1484; 30,000 vols; genealogical and heraldic collns; Archivist R. C. YORKE.

Croydon Public Libraries: Katharine St, Croydon, CR9 1ET; tel. (20) 8726-6900; fax (20) 8253-1004; internet www.croydon.gov.uk; f. 1888; 695,017 vols, 23,592 audio items; Libraries Officer A. BATT.

Department for Education and Skills Library: LG01 Sanctuary Bldgs, Great Smith St, London, SW1P 3BT; tel. (20) 7925-5040; fax (20) 7925-5085; e-mail enquiries.library@dfes.gsi.gov.uk; internet www.dfes.gov.uk; f. 1854; 210,000 vols; Chief Librarian GILL BAKER.

Department of Health Library: Skipton House, 80 London Rd, London, SE1 6LH; tel. (20) 7972-6541; fax (20) 7972-5976; e-mail library.skh@dh.gsi.gov.uk; internet www.dh.gov.uk; f. 1834; 200,000 vols and pamphlets, 650 print periodicals and various databases and e-journals on public health, health services policy and management, medicine, hospitals, and social care; Head of Library and Information Services PEK LAN BOWER; Senior Librarian JAMES DENMEAD; publs *DH-Data Thesaurus* (print), *DH-Data* (online), *HMIC* (online and CD-ROM).

Associated Library:

Department of Health Library (Leeds): Room 5W58A, Quarry House, Quarry Hill, Leeds, LS2 7UE; tel. (113) 2545080; fax (113) 2545084; e-mail libqh@dh.gsi.gov.uk; Senior Librarian KERRY HANSON.

Dr Williams's Library: 14 Gordon Square, London, WC1H 0AR; tel. (20) 7387-3727; e-mail enquiries@DWLib.co.uk; f. 1729; a lending and reference library of theological, philosophical and historical works, relating in particular to religious nonconformity and especially to congregational, English Presbyterian and Unitarian traditions; 150,000 vols; Dir Dr DAVID L. WYKES; publs *Bulletin* (annually), *Lectures of Friends of Dr Williams's Library* (annually).

Attached library:

Congregational Library: 15 Gordon Square, London, WC1H 0AG; f. 1831; c. 40,000 vols, mainly relating to Church history, the history and activities of the Nonconformists, theology, religious liberty and hymnology.

Ealing Library and Information Service: Perceval House, 14/16 Uxbridge Rd, London, W5 2HL; tel. (20) 8579-2424; f. 1965; 650,000 vols; Borough Librarian ANDREW SCOTT.

Enfield Libraries: Central Library, Cecil Rd, Enfield, Middx, EN2 6TW; tel. (20) 8379-8366; fax (20) 8379-8401; e-mail central.library@enfield.gov.uk; internet www.enfield.gov.uk; f. 1965; 620,000 vols; 14 brs, 3 reference libraries, mobile library; spec. collns: linguistics, local history; Head of Library Services JULIE GIBSON.

Foreign and Commonwealth Office Library: King Charles St, London, SW1A 2AH; tel. (20) 7008-3925; e-mail library.enquiries@fco.gov.uk; internet www.fco.gov.uk; the library, which is for the use of internal staff, specializes in publs on int. relations and diplomacy, the history, economy, politics and law of foreign countries; diplomatic memoirs, maps and treaty collns; the Foreign Office and Colonial Office historical collns of books have transferred to King's College London, and the photograph collns to the Nat. Archives; Chief Librarian CARRYL ALLARDICE.

Geological Society of London Library: Burlington House, Piccadilly, London, W1J 0BG; tel. (20) 7432-0999; fax (20) 7439-3470; e-mail library@geolsoc.org.uk; internet www.geolsoc.org.uk; f. 1807; 300,000 vols, 40,000 maps; lending restricted to the United Kingdom, via British Library Document Supply Centre; reference access by appointment; Chief Librarian SHEILA MEREDITH.

Gray's Inn Library: South Square, Gray's Inn, London, WC1R 5EU; f. *c.*1522; 40,000 vols; Legal Reference Library, for members of Gray's Inn, others admitted on application; special collections: 12th–14th century MSS, Baconiana; Librarian Mrs T. L. THOM.

Greenwich Libraries: Library Support Services, Plumstead Library, 232 Plumstead High St, London, SE18 1JL; tel. (20) 8317-4466; internet www.greenwich.gov.uk/council/publicservices/libraries.htm; f. 1905; 750,833 vols, 85,213 sound recordings; Borough Librarian and Head of Community Services JULIA NEWTON.

Guildhall Library, City of London: Aldermanbury, London, EC2V 7HH; tel. (20) 7332-1868; fax (20) 7600-3384; e-mail printedbooks.guildhall@cityoflondon.gov.uk; internet www.cityoflondon.gov.uk/guildhalllibrary; f. *c.*1425; public reference library, particularly rich in books on all aspects of London history; 229,000 vols; 250,000 series of MSS, consisting mainly of City parochial records, records of the City Livery Cos, London diocesan records, and records of major London commercial instns; major collns on business history, marine history, clocks and watchmaking, wine and food; 30,000 prints, 30,000 maps; Dir of Libraries and Guildhall Art Gallery DAVID BRADBURY.

Branch library:

City Business Library, Corporation of London: 1 Brewers' Hall Garden, London, EC2V 5BX; tel. (20) 7332-1812; fax (20) 7332-1847; e-mail cbl@cityoflondon.gov.uk; internet www.cityoflondon.gov.uk/citybusinesslibrary; f. 1970; finance, investment and banking; contains co financial data, country information (including global markets) and market research information; Business Librarian G. CONSIDINE.

Hackney Library Services: Hackney Central Library, 1 Reading Lane, London, E8 1GQ; e-mail reference.library@hackney.gov.uk; internet www.hackney.gov.uk/cl-libraries; f. 1965; c. 900,000 vols; 7 brs, ref. library; special collections: mechanic trades, woodwork and furniture, local history, John Dawson Collection; Head of Library Services, Archives and Information Services NICOLA BAKER.

Hammersmith and Fulham Public Libraries: Hammersmith Library, Shepherds Bush Rd, London, W6 7AT; tel. (20) 8753-3813; fax (20) 8753-3815; internet www .lbhf.gov.uk; f. 1888; 550,000 vols, 48,000 audio items; special collections: law, politics, Christianity, HMSO publs since 1970, video and audio cassettes, DVDs, CDs; Head of Libraries DAVID HERBERT.

Haringey Libraries: Central Library, High Rd, Wood Green, London, N22 6XD; tel. (20) 8888-1292; Head of Libraries JEAN EARLEY.

Harrow Public Library Service: POB 4, Civic Centre, Station Rd, Harrow, HA1 2UU; tel. (20) 8424-1055; fax (20) 8424-1971; e-mail libraries@harrow.gov.uk; internet www.harrow.gov.uk; f. 1965; 412,000 vols; 38,000 audiovisual items; spec. collns: architecture and building; 11 brs; Group Man., Library Services R. J. R. MILLS.

Havering Library Service: Central Library, St Edward's Way, Romford, Essex, RM1 3AR; tel. (1708) 432389; fax (1708) 432391; f. 1964; c. 500,000 vols; 9 brs; Chief Librarian (vacant).

Hillingdon Libraries, Planning and Community Service: Central Library, 14 High St, Uxbridge, Middx., UB8 1HD; tel. (1895) 250600; fax (1895) 239794; e-mail clibrary@hillingdongrid.org; internet www .hillingdon.gov.uk/libraries; f. 1965; 843,105 vols; Dir (vacant).

Home Office Library and Information Team: Seacole Bldg, 2 Marsham St, London, SW1P 4DF; tel. (20) 7035-4041; fax (20) 7035-4022; e-mail library@homeoffice.gsi.gov.uk; internet www.homeoffice.gov.uk; 42,000 vols, 100,000 microforms, 2,000 periodicals; social sciences, especially official publications, criminal law and administration of justice, criminology, police, immigration, nationality, probation and community relations; regular access for Home Office staff only; access for staff from other govt depts by appointment; Head of Information Services Unit P. GRIFFITHS.

Hounslow Library Network: CIP, CentreSpace, Treaty Centre, High St, Hounslow, Middx, TW3 1ES; tel. (845) 456-2800; fax (845) 456-2880; e-mail hounslowlibraries@cip .org.uk; internet www.hounslow.info; Dir of Culture and Heritage (vacant).

House of Commons Library: London, SW1A 0AA; tel. (20) 7219-4272; e-mail hcinfo@parliament.uk; f. 1818; over 150,000 vols, plus Parliamentary Papers; reference library files contain more than 1,500 periodicals and newspapers; research div. issues internal reference sheets and background papers on subjects of current interest to Mems; library private to MPs; Information Office handles enquiries on Parliament from the general public; Librarian JOHN PULLINGER; publs *Weekly Information Bulletin, Sessional Digest, Research Papers.*

House of Lords Library: London, SW1A 0PW; tel. (20) 7219-5242; fax (20) 7219-6396; e-mail hllibrary@parliament.uk; f. 1826; 120,000 vols, legal and Parliamentary history, general literature and reference; Dir of Information Services and Librarian Dr ELIZABETH HALLAM SMITH.

Imperial College of London Libraries: South Kensington, London, SW7 2AZ; tel. (20) 7594-8820; fax (20) 7594-8876; e-mail library@imperial.ac.uk; internet www .imperial.ac.uk/library; central library and 5 departmental libraries on South Kensington campus; 5 Faculty of Medicine libraries at Charing Cross, Chelsea and Westminster, Royal Brompton, St Mary's and Wellcome Library, Hammersmith campuses; also Michael Way Library at Silwood Park and

The Kempe Centre at Wye campus; 580,000 vols, 17,000 e-journal titles, 1,000 print titles; Dir of Library Services CLARE JENKINS.

InfoSource (Department of Trade and Industry Information Services): 1 Victoria St, London, SW1H 0ET; tel. (20) 7215-5006; fax (20) 7215-5713; f. 1950; virtual library service for the Dept of Trade and Industry; paper archive colln of material from the current dept and predecessor Dept of Energy, Board of Trade and Ministry of Technology; public access by appointment only; Man. ALISON COTTERILL.

Inner Temple Library: Inner Temple, London, EC4Y 7DA; tel. (20) 7797-8217; fax (20) 7583-6030; e-mail library@innertemple .org.uk; internet www.innertemplelibrary .org.uk; f. 1500; 80,000 vols, mostly legal and historical; contains, in addition to British law and legal history, an extensive colln of law relating to the Commonwealth. Spec. colln of 10,000 MSS, including Petyt MSS, available to the public (by written application, access granted at Librarian's discretion) for historical research; Librarian MARGARET CLAY.

Institute of Advanced Legal Studies Library: Univ. of London, 17 Russell Sq., London, WC1B 5DR; tel. (20) 7862-5790; fax (20) 7862-5850; e-mail ials@sas.ac.uk; internet www.ials.sas.ac.uk; f. 1947; serves academic researchers nationally and internationally; a premium information service is available for clients outside the higher education sector; 290,000 vols, 2,870 current serials; comprehensive colln of legal literature (except for Oriental laws and literature of East European law in East European languages), with spec. emphasis on the legal systems of the UK, the Commonwealth, the USA, Western Europe and Latin America; comparative law; int. law; incl. the Foreign and Commonwealth Office Commonwealth Law Library; the Records of Legal Education Archives; Dir of Institute Prof. AVROM SHERR; Librarian and Assoc. Dir of Institute JULES WINTERTON.

Institute of Contemporary History—Wiener Library: 4 Devonshire St, London, W1W 5BH; tel. (20) 7636-7247; fax (20) 7436-6428; e-mail info@wienerlibrary.co.uk; internet www.wienerlibrary.co.uk; f. in Amsterdam in 1933 by Dr Alfred Wiener, moved to London 1939; 60,000 vols incl. books and pamphlets; 3,000 periodicals; 900 catalogued documents on the Holocaust, anti-Semitism, the Third Reich, Fascism, Neo-Fascism, contemporary German-Jewish history and exile studies; Dir BEN BARKOW; Senior Librarian KATHARINA HÜBSCHMANN; publs *Journal of Contemporary History, Wiener Library News.*

Institute of Historical Research Library: Univ. of London, Senate House, London, WC1E 7HU; tel. (20) 7862-8760; e-mail ihr.library@sas.ac.uk; internet www .history.ac.uk; f. 1921; 169,000 vols; Librarian ROBERT LYONS.

Institution of Engineering and Technology Library and Archives: Savoy Place, London, WC2R 0BL; tel. (20) 7344-5461; fax (20) 7497-3557; e-mail libdesk@theiet.org; internet www.theiet.org/library; f. 1871; 75,000 books, 200,000 bound vols of periodicals, 850 current periodicals, 20,000 reports and pamphlets; spec. collns of historical electrical works; Sir Francis Ronalds Colln (6,000 vols and pamphlets), Sylvanus P. Thompson Library (4,500 vols and 8,000 pamphlets), Faraday MSS, and library, notebooks and MSS of Oliver Heaviside; holds library of British Computer Society; produces INSPEC database and provides specialized information services; Man. of Library and Archives Services JOHN W. COUPLAND; publs

Electronics Letters (2 a month), *Engineering and Technology* (monthly), *IET Proceedings* (6 a year).

Islington Libraries: Central Library, 2 Fieldway Crescent, London, N5 1PF; tel. (20) 7527-6900; fax (20) 7527-6939; e-mail library.informationunit@islington.gov.uk; internet www.islington.gov.uk/libraries; f. 1905; 544,357 vols; Head of Library and Cultural Service ROSEMARY DOYLE.

Kensington and Chelsea Library Service: Central Library, Phillimore Walk, London, W8 7RX; tel. (20) 7361-3010; e-mail libraries@rbkc.gov.uk; internet www.rbkc .gov.uk/libraries; f. 1888; 620,000 vols; system incl.: Central Library, Phillimore Walk; Chelsea Library, Chelsea Old Town Hall, Kings Rd, London, SW3 5EZ; 4 brs; spec. collns: genealogy and heraldry, biography, languages, folklore, costume and local history; Head of Libraries JANE BATTYE.

King's College London Library: Strand, London, WC2R 2LS; tel. (20) 7848-2139; fax (20) 7848-1777; e-mail libraryenquiry@kcl.ac .uk; internet www.kcl.ac.uk/library; f. 1829; sites incl. Chancery Lane (humanities, law, science), Denmark Hill Campus (medicine, dentistry), Guy's Campus (medicine, dentistry, biomedical sciences), St Thomas's Campus (medicine) and Waterloo Campus (life sciences, nursing and midwifery, education, management); 1,200,000 vols; Dir of Library Services (vacant).

Kingston-upon-Thames Public Libraries: Fairfield Rd, Kingston-uponThames, Surrey, KT1 2PS; tel. (20) 8547-6413; fax (20) 8547-6426; internet www .kingston.gov.uk/browse/leisure/libraries .htm; f. 1882; 230,000 vols; Head of Library Services BARBARA LEE.

Lambeth Library Service: International House, Canterbury Crescent, Brixton, London, SW9 7QE; tel. (20) 7926-0750; fax (20) 7926-0751; e-mail infoservice@lambeth.gov .uk; internet www.lambeth.gov.uk; f. 1888; 9 brs; mobile library and home visit library service; archives and local history service; over 600,000 vols; Head of Service LESLEY RAY.

Lambeth Palace Library: Lambeth Palace Rd, London, SE1 7JU; tel. (20) 7898-1400; fax (20) 7928-7932; e-mail lpl.staff@c-of-e.org.uk; internet www.lambethpalacelibrary.org; f. 1610; 200,000 printed items (esp. Church history) and 4,500 vols of MSS since 9th century; Sion College Library MSS and early printed books; archives; Librarian and Archivist Dr RICHARD PALMER.

Law Society Library: 113 Chancery Lane, London, WC2A 1PL; tel. (870) 606-2511; fax (20) 7831-1687; e-mail library@lawsociety .org.uk; internet www.lawsociety.org.uk; f. 1828; private library for solicitors who are mems of the Law Society of England and Wales; 45,000 vols; Librarian CHRIS HOLLAND.

Lewisham Library Service: Education and Culture, Lewisham Council, 3rd Floor, Laurence House, 1 Catford Rd, London, SE6 4RU; tel. (20) 8314-8527; fax (20) 8314-3151; e-mail frankie.sulke@lewisham.gov.uk; f. 1890; 700,000 vols; 12 brs, Central Reference Library, Local Studies Centre, Open Learning Centre; Head of Libraries JULIA NEWTON (acting); publs *Looking Back at Lewisham,* local history publs.

Library of Anti-Slavery International: Thomas Clarkson House, The Stableyard, Broomgrove Rd, London, SW9 9TL; tel. (20) 7501-8939; fax (20) 7738-4110; e-mail library@antislavery.org; internet www .antislavery.org; f. 1839; literature, photographs and videos on historical and contemporary slavery and human rights issues (modern issues incl. bonded labour, child labour, descent-based slavery, forced labour, indigenous peoples and trafficking; historical issues incl. the Transatlantic Slave Trade and colonialism); Librarian JEFF HOWARTH.

Library of the Religious Society of Friends in Britain: Friends House, Euston Rd, London, NW1 2BJ; tel. (20) 7663-1135; fax (20) 7663-1001; e-mail library@quaker .org.uk; internet www.quaker.org.uk/library; f. 1673; 20,000 vols, 60,000 pamphlets, and 4,000 vols of MSS, as well as prints and photographs; central archives; visitors must complete a registration form; Librarian HEATHER ROWLAND.

Library of the Theosophical Society in England: 50 Gloucester Place, London, W1U 8EA; tel. (20) 7563-9816; fax (20) 7935-9543; e-mail info@theosoc.org.uk; internet www .theosophical-society.org.uk; f. 1875; 14,000 vols; Librarian BARRY THOMPSON; publ. *Insight*.

Lincoln's Inn Library: Holborn, London, WC2A 3TN; tel. (20) 7242-4371; fax (20) 7404-1864; e-mail library@lincolnsinn.org .uk; internet www.lincolnsinn.org.uk; f. by 1475; 170,000 vols on law and 2,000 vols of MSS, including the Hale Colln; Librarian G. F. HOLBORN.

Linnean Society Library: Burlington House, Piccadilly, London, W1J 0BF; tel. (20) 7434-4479; fax (20) 7287-9364; e-mail library@linnean.org; internet www.linnean .org; f. 1788; 90,000 vols on natural history, including Linnaeus's own library and a collection of MSS, engravings and portraits; Librarian LYNDA BROOKS; publs *The Linnean Newsletter and Proceedings, Synopses of the British Fauna (New Series)*.

London Borough of Redbridge Libraries Service: Central Library, Clements Rd, Ilford, Essex, IG1 1EA; tel. (20) 8708-2415; fax (20) 8708-2431; e-mail ros.willis-fear@ redbridge.gov.uk; internet www.redbridge .gov.uk; f. 1965; adult, children's, reference and reserve: 633,104 vols; Central Library Man. ROS WILLIS-FEAR.

London Library: 14 St James's Sq., London, SW1Y 4LG; tel. (20) 7930-7705; fax (20) 7766-4766; e-mail membership@ londonlibrary.co.uk; internet www .londonlibrary.co.uk; f. 1841; open to subscribing members; an educational charity; 1,000,000 vols mainly in the humanities and social sciences; Librarian INEZ T. P. A. LYNN.

London Oratory Library: The Oratory, Brompton Rd, South Kensington, London, SW7 2RP; tel. (20) 7808-0900; fax (20) 7584-1095; e-mail webmaster.brompton-oratory@ ntlworld.com; internet www .bromptonoratory.com; f. 1854; contains 40,000 vols and 3,000 pamphlets on Theology and Church History; separate library (4,000 vols) of David Lewis, Tractarian convert; Librarian and Archivist Rev. Dr U. M. LANG.

London School of Hygiene and Tropical Medicine Library: Keppel St, London, WC1E 7HT; tel. (20) 7927-2283; fax (20) 7927-2273; e-mail library@lshtm.ac.uk; internet www.lshtm.ac.uk/library; f. 1924; tropical and preventive medicine in all aspects; many series of medical reports; archives incl. the papers of Sir Ronald Ross and many other eminent public health and tropical medicine professionals; Head of Library and Archives Service CAROLINE LLOYD.

Marx Memorial Library: Marx House, 37A Clerkenwell Green, London, EC1R 0DU; tel. (20) 7253-1485; fax (20) 7251-6039; internet www.marxlibrary.net; f. 1933; 150,000 vols; pamphlets, files of Labour, Socialist and Communist periodicals; spec. collns: Peace Movement, Spanish Civil War, USA, and the Hunger Marches; James Klugmann colln of Chartist and early British working-class history; research, reading and lending; lectures and discussion conferences; Librarian Dr JOHN CALLOW; publ. *Bulletin* (2 a year).

Merton Libraries and Heritage Service: Merton Civic Centre, London Rd, Morden, Surrey, SM4 5DX; tel. (20) 8545-3783; fax (20) 8545-3237; e-mail library.enquiries@ merton.gov.uk; internet www.merton.gov.uk; f. 1887; 500,000 vols; spec. collns: William Morris, Nelson; Head of Library and Heritage Services INGRID LACKAJIS.

Middle Temple Library (The Hon. Society of the): Middle Temple Lane, London, EC4Y 9BT; tel. (20) 7427-4830; fax (20) 7427-4831; e-mail library@middletemple .org.uk; internet www.middletemplelibrary .org.uk; f. 1641; private library for members of The Honourable Soc. of the Middle Temple; non-members admitted at the discretion of the Keeper of the Library; contains 125,000 vols of works on British, American, Public Int. and European Communities law; spec. collns: 80 incunabula, misc. tracts, mainly 17th century, 83 vols from John Donne's library; Librarian and Keeper of the Records V. HAYWARD.

Ministry of Defence, Information Services: Ministry of Defence Main Bldg, Whitehall, London, SW1A 2HB; tel. (20) 7218-4445; fax (20) 7218-5413; e-mail info-svcslibrary-office@mod.uk; covers defence policy, defence forces, military, naval and aviation strategy and technology, int. relations, politics, management and computer science; 50,000 vols, 300 periodicals; Chief Librarian PATRICK RYAN.

National Archives: Ruskin Ave, Kew, Richmond upon Thames, Surrey, TW9 4DU; tel. (20) 8876-3444; fax (20) 8878-8905; e-mail enquiry@nationalarchives.gov.uk; internet www.nationalarchives.gov.uk; f. 2003 following merger of the Public Record Office (f. 1838) and the Historical Manuscripts Commission (f. 1869); national archives for England and Wales and for the United Kingdom; holds the records of central government and the central courts of law since 11th century; central UK advisory body on archives and manuscripts relating to British history; Keeper of Public Records and Historical Manuscripts Commissioner SARAH TYACKE; publ. *National Register of Archives* (previously publ. by the Historical Manuscripts Commission and containing 43,000 indexed unpublished lists of manuscripts).

National Art Library: Victoria and Albert Museum, Cromwell Rd, London, SW7 2RL; tel. (20) 7942-2400; fax (20) 7942-2401; e-mail nal.enquiries@vam.ac.uk; internet www.vam.ac.uk; f. 1837; attached to Victoria and Albert (V&A) Museums; reference library for the int. documentation of art and design; 1,000,000 vols on art and allied subjects; spec. collns: Dyce (1869) and Forster (1876) literary libraries, Clements Colln of armorial book-bindings, Piot Colln of festival literature, and many others; Keeper of the Word and Image Dept SUSAN LAMBERT.

Attached archive:

Archive of Art and Design: 23 Blythe Rd, Olympia, London W14 0QX; tel. (20) 7603-1514; fax (20) 7602-0980; e-mail archive@vam.ac.uk; internet www.vam.ac .uk/resources/archives/aad/index.html; f. 1978; colln of principally 20th-century archives of designers, design asscns and cos involved in the design process; Keeper of the Word and Image Dept JULIUS BRYANT.

Natural History Museum, Library and Information Services: Cromwell Rd, London, SW7 5BD; tel. (20) 7942-5460; fax (20) 7942-5559; e-mail internet www.nhm.ac.uk; f. 1881; 1,000,000 vols covering botany, entomology, museum techniques, palaeontology, mineralogy, parasitology, physical anthropology, zoology, ornithology; spec. collns: Carl Linnaeus, Sir Joseph Banks, Alfred Russel Wallace; 1,800 MS colln, 400,000 original works of art; Head, Library and Information Services GRAHAM HIGLEY; publs *Journal of Systematic Palaeontology* (quarterly), *Systematics and Biodiversity* (quarterly).

Newham Public Libraries: East Ham Library, High St South, London, E6 4EL; tel. (20) 8472-1430; f. 1965; 500,530 vols, 57,243 reference stock, 14,031 audio items; Chief Librarian (vacant).

Newsroom, Guardian and Observer Archive and Visitor Centre: 60 Farringdon Rd, London, EC1R 3GA; tel. (20) 7886-9898; fax (20) 7490-8359; internet www .guardian.co.uk/newsroom; f. 2002; archives of organizations and people associated with the Guardian and Observer newspapers; photographic libraries; microfilm, bound hard-copy and digital back-issues; permanent display details history of the two newspapers; Dir LUKE DODD.

Partnership House Mission Studies Library: 157 Waterloo Rd, London, SE1 8XA; tel. (20) 7803-3215; fax (20) 7928-3627; e-mail library.phmslib@cms-uk.org; internet phmsl.soutron.com; f. 1988 from post-1945 collections of fmr Church Missionary Society and United Society for the Propagation of the Gospel libraries; 29,000 vols on missiology, growth of the Church worldwide and its social concerns, comparative religion, ecumenical movement; houses the CMS Max Warren collection of pre-1945 books; Librarian ELIZABETH WILLIAMS; publ. *Library Bulletin* (6 a year).

Queen Mary, University of London, Library: Mile End Rd, London, E1 4NS; tel. (20) 7882-3300; fax (20) 8981-0028; e-mail library-enquiries@qmul.ac.uk; internet www.library.qmul.ac.uk; f. 1887; 600,000 vols on the arts, sciences, engineering, medicine, social studies and law; European Documentation Centre; Librarian B. MURPHY.

Medical libraries:

St Bartholomew's and the Royal London, Queen Mary's School of Medicine and Dentistry, Libraries: Turner St, London, E1 2AD; tel. (20) 7882-7112; fax (20) 7882-7113; internet www.library.qmul .ac.uk; incl. Whitechapel, West Smithfield, London Chest Hospital, Wolfson Institute of Preventive Medicine.

Richmond upon Thames Public Libraries: Central Lending Library, Little Green, Richmond upon Thames, Surrey, TW9 1QL; Central Reference Library: Old Town Hall, Whittaker Ave, Richmond upon Thames, Surrey, TW9 1TP; tel. (20) 8940-0981 (CLL); tel. (20) 8940-5529 (CRL); fax (20) 8940-7516 (CLL); fax (20) 8940-6899 (CRL); f. 1880; includes Borough Local Studies Collection; Head of Libraries and Culture AILEEN CAHILL.

Royal Academy of Arts Library: Burlington House, London, W1J 0BD; tel. (20) 7300-5737; fax (20) 7300-5765; e-mail library@ royalacademy.org.uk; internet www .royalacademy.org.uk; f. 1768; 35,000 vols on the fine arts and standard reference books; also original drawings, MSS and engravings; Head of Library Services ADAM WATERTON.

Royal Academy of Music Library: Marylebone Rd, London, NW1 5HT; tel. (20) 7873-7323; fax (20) 7873-7322; e-mail library@ram.ac.uk; internet www.ram.ac.uk; f. 1822; 150,000 vols, 5,500 sets of orchestral parts, sound recordings; special collections include MSS and early editions, Sir Henry Wood Library, Angelina Goetz Library, David Munrow Library, Sullivan Archive, Robert Spencer Collection, Foyle Menuhin Archive; Librarian KATHRYN ADAMSON.

Royal Asiatic Society Library: 14 Stephenson Way, London, NW1 2HD; tel. (20) 7388-4539; fax (20) 7391-9429; e-mail library@royalasiaticsociety.org; internet www.royalasiaticsociety.org; f. 1823; 50,000 vols dealing with Asia, and 1,500 Oriental MSS; Librarian KATHY LAZENBATT; publ. *Journal* (quarterly).

Royal Astronomical Society Library: Burlington House, Piccadilly, London, W1V 0NL; tel. (20) 7734-4582; fax (20) 7494-0166; e-mail info@ras.org.uk; internet www.ras.org.uk; f. 1820; 31,000 vols, plus archives, dealing with astronomy, history of astronomy and geophysics; Librarian P. D. HINGLEY.

Royal Botanic Gardens, Kew, Library & Archives: Kew, Richmond upon Thames, Surrey, TW9 3AE; tel. (20) 8332-5414; fax (20) 8332-5430; e-mail library@rbgkew.org.uk; internet www.rbgkew.org.uk; f. 1852; 150,000 vols, 4,000 periodicals, 140,000 pamphlets, 200,000 plant illustrations; approved place of deposit for own records; botany (esp. taxonomic, floristic and economic aspects), horticulture, conservation, also biochemistry, anatomy, genetics, molecular systematics, propagation and seed storage; registered files and 250,000 letters and MSS; Head of Library and Archives CHRISTOPHER MILLS.

Royal College of Art Library: Kensington Gore, London, SW7 2EU; tel. (20) 7590-4224; fax (20) 7590-4217; e-mail library@rca.ac.uk; internet www.rca.ac.uk; f. 1953; 70,000 vols on the visual arts, history and philosophy of design, history and criticism of the arts; Colour Reference Library: comprehensive colln of books and articles on all aspects of colour; admittance by appointment only; Head of Information and Learning Services PETER HASSELL; Library Man. DARLENE MAXWELL.

Royal College of Music Library: Prince Consort Rd, South Kensington, London, SW7 2BS; tel. (20) 7591-4325; fax (20) 7589-7740; e-mail library@rcm.ac.uk; internet www.rcm.ac.uk; f. 1883; c. 400,000 vols, incl. MSS and early printed music; admission for reference only; Chief Librarian PAMELA THOMPSON.

Royal College of Physicians' Library (Heritage Centre and Information Centre): 11 St Andrews Pl., Regent's Park, London, NW1 4LE; tel. (20) 7224-1539; fax (20) 7486-3729; e-mail infocentre@rcplondon.ac.uk; internet www.rcplondon.ac.uk; f. 1518; 60,000 vols (mostly related to history of medicine, but some on current medical issues), 100 incunabula, 200 linear m of MSS, 30,000 portrait photographs and other pictorial items; Information Centre Man. JULIE BECKWITH; publs *Evan Bedford Library of Cardiology: catalogue*, *Munk's Roll* (Lives of Fellows of the College, 11 Vols 1878–2004).

Royal College of Surgeons of England Library and Lumley Study Centre: 35-43 Lincoln's Inn Fields, London, WC2A 3PE; tel. (20) 7869-6555; fax (20) 7405-4438; e-mail library@rcseng.ac.uk; internet www.rcseng.ac.uk; f. 1800; 150,000 vols on surgery and dentistry, 400 current periodicals; Librarian THALIA KNIGHT; publ. *Annals*.

Royal College of Veterinary Surgeons Trust Library: Belgravia House, 62–64 Horseferry Rd, London, SW1P 2AF; tel. (20) 7222-2021; fax (20) 7222-0751; e-mail library@rcvstrust.org.uk; internet www.rcvslibrary.org.uk; f. 1842; open to qualified veterinary surgeons and veterinary nurses; open to members of the public by appointment; 30,000 vols; Librarian (vacant).

Royal Geographical Society (with the Institute of British Geographers) Library: Kensington Gore, London, SW7 2AR; tel. (20) 7591-3044; fax (20) 7591-3001; e-mail enquiries@rgs.org; internet www.rgs.org; f. 1830; 250,000 books and bound periodicals; 500 current periodicals; map room contains 1m. maps and charts, 3,000 atlases, large selection of gazetteers and expedition reports; picture library of 500,000 images; archives; Prin. Librarian E. M. RAE; Map Curator F. HERBERT; publs *Area*, *Geographical Journal*, *Transactions*.

Royal Institute of International Affairs Library: 10 St James's Sq., London, SW1Y 4LE; tel. (20) 7957-5723; fax (20) 7957-5710; e-mail libenquire@chathamhouse.org.uk; internet www.chathamhouse.org.uk; f. 1920; 130,000 vols, 300 current periodicals and newspapers; 5m. classified cuttings from the int. press from 1924 to 1939 (on microfilm) and 1972 to July 1997: (further 5m. cuttings for 1940–71 at British Library Newspaper Library); Senior Librarian MARY BONE.

Royal Institution of Great Britain Library: 21 Albemarle St, London, W1S 4BS; tel. (20) 7409-2992; fax (20) 7629-3569; e-mail ril@ri.ac.uk; internet www.rigb.org; f. 1799; 50,000 vols on all branches of science; 150 periodicals currently received; special collections: solid state chemistry, catalysis, scientific biography, social relations of science, popular science, history of science, early scientific books and journals especially of 18th–19th c.; archives and MSS of many scientists who have worked at the Institution, including Davy, Faraday, Tyndall, Dewar, the Braggs and Porter; Head of Collections and Heritage Prof. FRANK JAMES.

Royal National Institute for Deaf People (RNID) Library: 330–332 Gray's Inn Rd, London, WC1X 8EE; tel. (20) 7915-1553; f. 1911; 18,000 books and 200 current journals on all aspects of deafness and other communication disorders; Librarian MARY PLACKETT.

Royal Society Library: 6–9 Carlton House Terrace, London, SW1Y 5AG; tel. (20) 7451-2606; fax (20) 7930-2170; e-mail library@royalsoc.ac.uk; internet www.royalsoc.ac.uk; f. 1660; history of science and scientists, science policy, science education, science and the public; 150,000 vols; Library Man. RUPERT BAKER.

Royal Society of Chemistry Library and Information Centre: Burlington House, Piccadilly, London, W1J 0BA; tel. (20) 7440-3373; fax (20) 7287-9798; e-mail library@rsc.org; internet www.rsc.org; f. 1841; 100,000 vols; Librarian NIGEL LEES.

Royal Society of Medicine Library: 1 Wimpole St, London, W1G 0AE; tel. (20) 7290-2940; fax (20) 7290-2939; e-mail library@rsm.ac.uk; internet www.rsm.ac.uk; f. 1805; 500,000 vols, 1,200 current periodicals, 10,000 back titles; lending restricted to members; back-up library to British Library; worldwide mail order photocopy service; historical colln from 1474; medical portrait colln; Dir of Library Services WAYNE SIME.

Royal United Services Institute for Defence and Security Studies Library: Whitehall, London, SW1A 2ET; tel. (20) 7930-5854; fax (20) 7747-2636; e-mail library@rusi.org; internet www.rusi.org; f. 1831; 15,000 vols on all issues relating to nat. and int. defence and security; Librarian JOHN MONTGOMERY; publs *Whitehall Papers and Reports* (irreg.), *Homeland Security and Resilience Monitor* (10 a year), *Newsbrief (International Security Studies Department)* (monthly), *RUSI Defence Systems* (3 a year), *RUSI Journal* (6 a year).

St Bride Library: Bride Lane, Fleet St, London, EC4Y 8EE; tel. (20) 7353-4660; fax (20) 7583-7073; e-mail nigelroche@stbridefoundation.org; internet www.stbride.org; f. 1891; printing, papermaking, bookbinding, illustration, graphic design; 50,000 books and pamphlets, 3,500 periodical titles; early technical literature, drawings, MSS, prospectuses, patents, materials for printing and type founding; programme of exhibitions and lectures; 3 annual conferences; educational outreach programme for schools; library tours and talks; Librarian NIGEL ROCHE; publ. *Ultrabold*.

St Paul's Cathedral Library: London, EC4M 8AE; tel. (20) 7246-8345; fax (20) 7248-3104; e-mail library@stpaulscathedral.org.uk; internet www.stpauls.co.uk; f. 1707; 13,500 vols and 11,500 pamphlets; early printed books of theology and Greek and Latin classics, 20 medieval MSS; Librarian JO WISDOM.

School of Oriental and African Studies Library: University of London, Thornhaugh St, Russell Square, London, WC1H 0XG; tel. (20) 7898-4160; fax (20) 7898-4159; internet www.soas.ac.uk; f. 1916; 859,000 vols and pamphlets, 4,500 periodicals, 2,700 MSS and archive collections dealing with Asian and African languages, literature, philosophy, religions, history, law, cultural anthropology, art and archaeology, social sciences; back-up library to the British Library for loans; Librarian ANNE POULSON.

Science Museum Library: Imperial College Rd, South Kensington, London, SW7 5NH; tel. (20) 7942-4242; fax (20) 7942-4243; e-mail smlinfo@nmsi.ac.uk; internet www.sciencemuseum.org.uk/library; f. 1883; 600,000 vols including 21,000 periodicals, of which 500 titles are current; historical, biographical and archival collns; Head of Library IAN CARTER (acting).

Sir John Soane's House and Museum Library: 13 Lincoln's Inn Fields, London, WC2A 3BP; tel. (20) 7440-4251; fax (20) 7831-3957; e-mail library@soane.org.uk; internet www.soane.org; f. 1837; contains Sir John Soane's colln of 8,000 vols on art, antiquities, architecture, classical and general literature, architectural drawings, personal and business archive; Librarian STEPHANIE COANE.

Societies for the Promotion of Hellenic and Roman Studies Joint Library: Senate House, Malet St, London, WC1E 7HU; tel. (20) 7862-8709; fax (20) 7862-8735; e-mail colin.annis@sas.ac.uk; internet www.sas.ac.uk/icls; f. 1879; since 1953 run in association with Univ. of London's Institute of Classical Studies Library; classical archaeology, art, history, religion, philosophy, language and literature; 120,000 books, 18,000 periodicals, 630 current periodicals; classified colln of 6,800 coloured slides, 125 CD-ROMs; Librarian COLIN ANNIS.

Society of Antiquaries Library: Burlington House, Piccadilly, London, W1J 0BE; tel. (20) 7479-7084; fax (20) 7287-6967; e-mail library@sal.org.uk; internet www.sal.org.uk; f. 1707; 100,000 vols, 650 current periodicals on British and foreign archaeology and history, heraldry, genealogy, etc.; MSS, prints, drawings, early printed books, brass rubbings, seal casts; Librarian E. B. NURSE; publ. *Antiquaries Journal* (annual).

Southwark Libraries: Headquarters, 15 Spa Rd, London, SE16 3QW; tel. (20) 7525-1993; fax (20) 7525-1505; 600,000 vols; special collection: computer science; 50,000 tapes, CDs, videos; 12 brs; Art Gallery; 2 museums; Arts, Libraries and Museums Man. ADRIAN OLSEN.

Supreme Court Library: Royal Courts of Justice, Dept for Constitutional Affairs, Strand, London, WC2A 2LL; tel. (20) 7947-6587; fax (20) 7947-6661; internet www .justice.gov.uk; f. 1970; 300,000 vols; spec. collns: Court of Appeal (Civil Div.) Transcripts 1950–; old edns of legal textbooks (in Supreme Court Library—Bar—f. 1883); Librarian J. ROBERTSON.

Surrey Libraries: Enquiries Direct, Guildford Library, 77 North St, Guildford, GU1 4AL; tel. (1483) 543599; fax (1483) 543597; e-mail libraries@surreycc.gov.uk; internet www.surreycc.gov.uk; offers a public library service to Surrey; 52 brs and an enquiries dept; 1,913,000 vols, 78,400 audiovisual items; Head of Libraries and Culture YVONNE REES.

Sutton Library Service: Central Library, St Nicholas Way, Sutton, Surrey, SM1 1EA; tel. (20) 8770-4700; fax (20) 8770-4777; f. 1936; 9 libraries; 316,100 vols; 26,759 audio items, 9,067 visual items; spec. colln: genealogy and heraldry; Heads of Libraries and Heritage C. MCDONOUGH, A. FLETCHER.

Thames Valley University Learning Resource Centre: St Mary's Rd, London, W5 5RF; tel. (20) 8231-2246; fax (20) 8231-2631; e-mail lrs@tvu.ac.uk; internet www.tvu .ac.uk; f. 1992; 259,000 vols; Head of Learning Resources J. I. WOLSTENHOLME.

Tower Hamlets Public Libraries: c/o Head of Libraries, Bancroft Library, Bancroft Rd, London, E1 4DQ; tel. (20) 8980-4366; f. 1965; 627,564 vols; special collections: General, American, French, German, Portuguese literature and texts; Local History library; collection of books in Urdu, Bengali, Punjabi, Hindi, Gujarati, Chinese and Vietnamese; gramophone records and tape cassettes; video cassettes, compact discs; Head of Libraries ANNE CUNNINGHAM.

Treasury and Cabinet Office Library: Parliament St, London, SW1P 3AG; tel. (20) 7270-5290; fax (20) 7270-5681; 120,000 vols; 1,500 periodicals; covers economics, finance and public administration; Librarian JEAN CLAYTON.

UCL Library Services: Gower St, London, WC1E 6BT; tel. (20) 7679-7700; fax (20) 7679-7373; e-mail library@ucl.ac.uk; internet www.ucl.ac.uk/library; f. 1828; comprises Main (Arts and Humanities) and Science sites at Gower St; Cruciform and Royal Free medical libraries; libraries of Bartlett (Faculty of the Built Environment), Human Communication Science, Institute of Archaeology, Institute of Laryngology and Otology (incorporating RNID), Institute of Orthopaedics, UCL School of Slavonic and East European Studies; libraries of Eastman Dental Institute; Institute of Child Health, Institute of Neurology, Institute of Ophthalmology, Spec. Collns; 2,000,000 vols; Dir of UCL Library Services PAUL AYRIS.

University of Greenwich Information and Library Services: Old Royal Naval College, Greenwich, London, SE10 9LS; tel. (20) 8331-8196; fax (20) 8331-9084; internet www.gre.ac.uk/lib; Head of Learning Services ANN MURPHY.

University of London Library: Senate House, Malet St, London, WC1E 7HU; tel. (20) 7862-8500; fax (20) 7862-8480; e-mail ull@ull.ac.uk; internet www.ull.ac.uk; f. 1838; 2,000,000 titles; research library principally in the arts, humanities and social sciences, for reference and loan, including special collections, e.g., Goldsmiths' Library of Economic Literature, Harry Price Collection, Sterling Library, Durning-Lawrence Library, Eliot-Phelips Collection, Bromhead Library, Carlton Shorthand Collection, Porteus Library, Malcolm Morley Theatre Collection and the Libraries of the Canadian and Australian High Commissions; Librarian EMMA ROBINSON.

Upper Norwood Joint Library: Westow Hill, London, SE19 1TJ; tel. (20) 8670-2551; fax (20) 8670-5468; e-mail unjl@unisonfree .net; f. 1900; 60,000 vols; collections on the Crystal Palace and its historical background, the Gerald Massey collection, the J. B. Wilson collection; Librarian BRADLEY MILLINGTON.

Vaughan Williams Memorial Library: English Folk Dance and Song Soc., Cecil Sharp House, 2 Regents Park Rd, London, NW1 7AY; tel. (20) 7485-2206; fax (20) 7284-0523; e-mail library@efdss.org; internet library.efdss.org; f. 1930; maintained by the English Folk Dance and Song Soc. (*q.v.*); England's main source of information on traditional song, dance, customs and folk culture; 20,000 vols,, MS collns, microfilms, press cuttings, broadsides, 10,000 audiovisual items, 15,000 photographic images; open to the public for reference; Librarian MALCOLM TAYLOR; publs *Folk Music Journal* (annual), *English Dance and Song (EDS)* (quarterly).

Victoria and Albert Museum, Library of the: see National Art Library.

Waltham Forest Public Libraries: Central Library, High St, Walthamstow, London, E17 7JN; tel. (20) 8520-3031; fax (20) 8509-9539; internet www.lbwf.gov.uk; f. 1893; 448,427 vols; special collections: Cookery, Domestic Economy, Fiction Authors U, V; Librarian COLIN RICHARDSON.

Wandsworth Public Libraries: Town Hall, Wandsworth High St, London, SW18 2PU; tel. (20) 8871-6364; fax (20) 8871-7630; e-mail libraries@wandsworth.gov.uk; internet www.wandsworth.gov.uk/home/ leisureandtourism/libraries; f. 1883; 721,101 vols; 12 brs; reference library, 2 music libraries, local history library, home delivery library service; special collections: architecture, town planning, European history, geography and travel, occult sciences, local history, early children's books, G. A. Henty; Head of Libraries, Museums and Arts JANE ALLEN.

Warburg Institute Library: Woburn Sq., London, WC1H 0AB; tel. (20) 7862-8949; fax (20) 7862-8939; e-mail warburg@sas.ac.uk; internet www.sas.ac.uk/warburg; f. 1922; cultural and intellectual history of Europe from Classical Antiquity to modern times, including history of art, literature, science, religion, humanism; houses libraries of the Royal and British Numismatic Societies; 330,000 vols, 1,300 current serials; Librarian Prof. JILL KRAYE; publ. *Journal of the Warburg and Courtauld Institutes* (annual).

Wellcome Library: 183 Euston Rd, London, NW1 2BE; tel. (20) 7611-8722; fax (20) 7611-8369; e-mail library@wellcome.ac.uk; internet library.wellcome.ac.uk; f. 1890, opened to the public in 1949; records medicine and its role in society, past and present; includes popular science, biomedical ethics and the public understanding of science; more than 700 incunabula; 700,000 books; ephemera; 55,000 pamphlets, 2,700 periodical titles; 9,000 Western MSS; 12,000 Oriental MSS in 43 languages; 200,000 prints, drawings, photographs, paintings; 700 collns of medical archives; 2,500 films; Librarian FRANCES NORTON.

Westminster Abbey Library and Muniment Room: London, SW1P 3PA; tel. (20) 7654-4830; fax (20) 7654-4827; e-mail library@westminster-abbey.org; internet www.westminster-abbey.org; f. 1623; 20,000 vols since the 16th century, predominantly theological but also general literature and music; Abbey records and other documents since the 11th century; Librarian Dr TONY TROWLES; Keeper of Muniments Dr R. MORTIMER.

Women's Library: Old Castle St, London, E1 7NT; tel. (20) 7320-2222; fax (20) 7320-2333; e-mail moreinfo@thewomenslibrary.ac .uk; internet www.thewomenslibrary.ac.uk; f. 1926; documents changing role of women in society; attached to London Metropolitan Univ.; 43,000 books, 2,500 periodicals, 17,000 pamphlets; Head of Library Services BEVERLEY KEMP.

Zoological Society of London Library: Regent's Park, London, NW1 4RY; tel. (20) 7449-6293; fax (20) 7586-5743; e-mail library@zsl.org; internet www.zsl.org; f. 1826; contains 180,000 vols, 1,300 current periodicals connected with zoology and animal conservation; photograph library; archives of Zoological Soc. of London; Librarian ANN SYLPH; publs *Animal Conservation, International Zoo Yearbook, Journal of Zoology.*

Loughborough

Loughborough University: Pilkington Library: Loughborough, Leics, LE11 3TU; tel. (1509) 222360; fax (1509) 223993; internet www.lboro.ac.uk; f. 1911; 550,000 vols, 4,000 periodicals; includes the University Archives; University Librarian M. D. MORLEY.

Luton

Luton Libraries: Luton Libraries, St George's Sq., Luton, LU1 2NG; tel. (1582) 547420; fax (1582) 547461; e-mail referencelibrary@luton.gov.uk; internet www.luton.gov.uk/libraries; Libraries Man. JEAN GEORGE.

Maidenhead

Royal Borough of Windsor and Maidenhead Libraries: Maidenhead Library, St Ives Rd, Maidenhead, SL6 1QU; tel. (1628) 796967; fax (1628) 796971; Head of Library Services MARK TAYLOR.

Maidstone

Kent Libraries and Archives: Springfield, Maidstone, Kent, ME14 2LH; tel. (1622) 696511; fax (1622) 696494; e-mail libraries .informationservices@kent.gov.uk; internet www.kent.gov.uk/libraries; f. 1921; 3,300,000 vols; Head of Libraries and Archives CATH ANLEY.

Manchester

Chetham's Library: Long Millgate, Manchester, M3 1SB; tel. (161) 834-7961; fax (161) 839-5797; e-mail librarian@chethams .org.uk; internet www.chethams.org.uk; f. 1653 as a free public reference library; 100,000 vols, incl. many works from the 17th and 18th centuries; local history records; Librarian Dr MICHAEL POWELL.

John Rylands University Library, University of Manchester: Oxford Rd, Manchester, M13 9PP; tel. (161) 275-3751; fax (161) 273-7488; e-mail libtalk@fs1.li.man.ac .uk; internet www.library.manchester.ac.uk; f. 2004 by merger of the John Rylands University Library of Manchester (f. 1972 by merger of John Rylands Library—f. 1900 with Manchester University Library—f.

1851) and the Library of UMIST (f. 1824); 4,500,000 printed books, 1,000,000 MSS or archival items, 800,000 titles on microform, 9,000 serials currently received; numerous special collections, several of international renown such as Althorp Library of 2nd Earl Spencer and manuscript portion of Bibliotheca Lindesiana, containing, *inter alia*, 220,000 books printed before 1801, among them 4,500 incunabula and 1,500 Aldines; Librarian and Dir WILLIAM G. SIMPSON; publ. *Bulletin* (3 a year).

Manchester Libraries and Theatres: Central Library, St Peter's Square, Manchester, M2 5PD; tel. (161) 234-1900; fax (161) 234-1963; internet www.manchester.gov.uk/libraries; f. 1852; 2,430,000 vols, 141,000 audio-visual items; includes social sciences, commercial, arts, music, Chinese, languages and literature, technical, local studies and archives, European information and general libraries, and a unit for visually impaired people: two library theatres with resident company; 23 brs, offering Afro-Caribbean, Asian, Vietnamese and community resource services, with 3 mobile libraries and a housebound readers' service; libraries in old people's homes, hospitals and prisons; special collections incl. the Newman Flower, Henry Watson, and Gaskell; Library Theatre Company; Dir LIS PHELAN.

Manchester Metropolitan University Library: Sir Kenneth Green Library, All Saints, Manchester Metropolitan University, Manchester, M15 6BH; tel. (161) 247-6104; fax (161) 247-6349; internet www.mmu.ac.uk/library; f. 1970; 1,000,000 vols; Librarian Prof. COLIN HARRIS.

Matlock

Derbyshire County Council Libraries and Heritage: County Hall, Matlock, Derbyshire, DE4 3AG; tel. (1629) 580000; fax (1629) 585363; f. 1923; 1,100,000 vols; 46 brs; Dir of Libraries and Heritage MARTIN MOLLOY.

Merthyr Tydfil

Merthyr Tydfil County Borough Library: Central Library, High St, Merthyr Tydfil, CF47 8AF; tel. (1685) 723057; fax (1685) 370690; e-mail library.services@merthyr.gov.uk; internet www.libraries.merthyr.gov.uk; f. 1935; Public Library Service with active colln and promotion of local history; 163,210 vols; 2 brs; Head of Libraries GERAINT H. JAMES.

Middlesbrough

Middlesbrough Libraries and Information: Central Library, Victoria Square, Middlesbrough, TS1 2AY; tel. (1642) 729001; fax (1642) 729953; 400,000 vols; central library, 12 brs; Libraries and Information Man. CHRYS MELLOR.

University of Teesside Library: Library and Information Services, Borough Rd, Middlesbrough, TS1 3BA; tel. (1642) 342103; fax (1642) 342190; 290,000 vols; Dir IAN C. BUTCHART.

Milton Keynes

Milton Keynes Council Library Service: Milton Keynes Central Library, 555 Silbury Blvd, Central Milton Keynes, MK9 3HL; tel. (1908) 254050; fax (1908) 254089; e-mail central.library@milton-keynes.gov.uk; internet www.mkweb.co.uk/library-services; f. 1981; Reference and Information Librarian HELEN BOWLT.

Open University Library: Walton Hall, Milton Keynes, MK7 6AA; tel. (1908) 653138; fax (1908) 653571; e-mail library-marketing@open.ac.uk; internet www.open.ac.uk/library; f. 1969; 220,000 books, 12,000 print period-

icals, 16,5000 online journals; Dir of Library Services NICKY WHITSED.

Mold

Flintshire Library and Information Service: County Hall, Mold, CH7 6NW; tel. (1352) 704400; fax (1352) 753662; e-mail flintslib@dial.pipex.com; 20 libraries, 2 mobile libraries, 1 library for the housebound; special collections: Arthurian literature, local studies; Wales Euro Information Centre; Head of Libraries and Archives LAWRENCE RAWSTHORNE.

Morpeth

Northumberland County Library: Beachfield, Gas House Lane, Morpeth, Northumberland, NE61 1TA; tel. (1670) 534514; fax (1670) 534513; e-mail referencelibrary@northumberland.gov.uk; internet www.northumberland.gov.uk; f. 1924; 635,000 vols; 35 brs, 5 mobile libraries; special collections: local history, vocal scores, cinema, drama, Northern Poetry Library; Divisional Dir (Libraries, Arts and Heritage) D. E. BONSOR.

Newbury

West Berkshire Libraries: West Berkshire District Council, Market St, Newbury, Berks., RG14 5LD; tel. (1635) 519900; fax (1635) 519906; e-mail newburylibrary@westberks.gov.uk; internet www.westberks.gov.uk; Library and Information Strategic Development Man. CHRISTINE OWEN.

Newcastle upon Tyne

Newcastle Libraries and Information Service: POB 88, Newcastle upon Tyne, NE99 1DX; tel. (845) 002-0336; fax (191) 277-4137; e-mail information@newcastle.gov.uk; internet www.newcastle.gov.uk/libraries; f. 1880; 600,000 vols, 50,000 audio-visual items; extensive local and family history resources; Thomas Bewick Colln (first edns, engravings, original woodblocks, Bewick's worktable and toolbox), Thomlinson Library (4,351 vols from the 16th, 17th and 18th centuries, mainly theological); City Library and 17 brs; Head of Culture, Libraries and Lifelong Learning TONY DURCAN.

University of Newcastle upon Tyne, The Robinson Library: Newcastle upon Tyne, NE2 4HQ; tel. (191) 222-7662; fax (191) 222-6235; e-mail library@ncl.ac.uk; internet www.ncl.ac.uk/library; f. 1871 as Library of Durham College of Physical Science; 1,000,000 vols, 4,500 periodicals; special collections include: Pybus (medical history), Robert White, Gertrude Bell, Runciman Papers, Trevelyan Papers, Catherine Cookson, Library of Japanese Science and Technology, Wallis; Librarian Dr T. W. GRAHAM.

Newport (Gwent)

Newport Community Learning and Libraries: Central Library, John Frost Square, Newport, NP20 1PA; tel. (1633) 265539; fax (1633) 222615; e-mail central.library@newport.gov.uk; internet www.newport.gov.uk/libraries; 11 brs; Community Learning and Libraries Man. GILL JOHN.

Newport (Isle of Wight)

Isle of Wight Council Library Services: Library Headquarters, Parkhurst Rd, Newport, Isle of Wight, PO30 5TX; tel. (1983) 825717; fax (1983) 528047; e-mail tblackmore@iwight.gov.uk; internet www.iwight.com/thelibrary; f. 1904; 11 brs; Head of Libraries and Information Services TIM BLACKMORE.

Northallerton

North Yorkshire County Library: County Library Headquarters, Grammar School Lane, Northallerton, North Yorks., DL6 1DF; tel. (1609) 767800; fax (1609) 780793; e-mail julie.blaisdale@northyorks.gov.uk; 1,059,000 vols; 45 brs; Head of Libraries, Archives and Arts JULIE BLAISDALE.

Northampton

Northamptonshire Libraries and Information Service: POB 216, John Dryden House, 8–10 The Lakes, Northampton, NN4 7DD; tel. (1604) 236236; fax (1604) 237937; f. 1927; 1,224,000 vols; 107,000 sound recordings and videotapes; 35 brs, 6 mobile libraries; County Libraries and Information Officer ERIC WRIGHT.

Norwich

Norfolk Library and Information Service: County Hall, Norwich, NR1 2UA; tel. (1603) 222049; fax (1603) 222422; e-mail libraries@norfolk.gov.uk; internet www.library.norfolk.gov.uk; f. 1925, reorganised 1974; 1,307,000 vols; 4 core libraries; 44 brs; 2 shop libraries; 13 mobile libraries; Dir of Cultural Services T. TURNER.

Norwich Cathedral Library: 12 The Close, Norwich, Norfolk, NR1 4DH; tel. (1603) 218443; fax (1603) 766032; a medieval monastic (Benedictine) foundation; 20,000 vols modern theology loan colln; 8,000 vols historic colln, some incunabula and MSS; houses 450 vols of the Swaffham Parochial Church Library and other parish books; Canon Librarian Archdeacon C. OFFER; Librarian G. WARREN.

University of East Anglia Library: Norwich, NR4 7TJ; tel. (1603) 592425; fax (1603) 259490; e-mail library@uea.ac.uk; internet www.lib.uea.ac.uk; f. 1962; 725,000 vols; Dir of Library and Learning Resources JEAN STEWARD.

Nottingham

Nottingham City Libraries and Information Service: Central Library, Angel Row, Nottingham, NG1 6HP; tel. (115) 915-2828; fax (115) 915-2840; e-mail enquiryline@nottinghamcity.gov.uk; internet www.nottinghamcity.gov.uk/libraries; f. 1868; 480,000 vols, 33,000 sound recordings; spec. collns include local history, D. H. Lawrence, Byron and Robin Hood; Asst Dir of Leisure Services (Libraries, Information and Museums) BRIAN ASHLEY.

University of Nottingham Information Services: University Park, Nottingham, NG7 2RD; tel. (115) 951-4555; fax (115) 951-4558; internet www.nottingham.ac.uk/is; f. (University College) 1881; 1,000,000 vols and pamphlets, 5,450 current periodicals, 7,600 electronic journals; MSS and archives (Portland, Newcastle, Middleton, Manvers, etc.) 3,000,000 items; special collections include D. H. Lawrence, early children's books, French Revolution, meteorology, ornithology; includes Hallward Library (arts, social sciences and law), George Green Library of Science and Engineering, James Cameron Gifford Library of Agricultural and Food Sciences (Sutton Bonington), Greenfield Medical Library and Djanogly Learning Resources Centre (education, business and computer science); Dir of Information Services K. A. STANTON.

Oakham

Rutland Library Service: Oakham Library, Catmos St, Oakham, Rutland, LE15 6HW; tel. (1572) 722918; fax (1572) 724906; e-mail libraries@rutland.gov.uk; internet www.rutland.gov.uk/libraries; f. 1997; County Librarian ROBERT CLAYTON.

Oxford

Bodleian Library: Oxford, OX1 3BG; tel. (1865) 277000; fax (1865) 277182; e-mail enquiries@bodley.ox.ac.uk; internet www .bodley.ox.ac.uk; f. 1602; the principal library of Oxford University; includes the Old Library, the Radcliffe Camera, New Library and the following dependent libraries: Radcliffe Science Library, Hooke Library, Bodleian Law Library, Indian Institute Library, Bodleian Library for Commonwealth and African Studies (at Rhodes House), Vere Harmsworth Library (for the history of the United States), Bodleian Japanese Library, Philosophy Library, Oriental Institute Library and Institute for Chinese Studies Library; a legal deposit library, entitled to a free copy of every book published in the UK; 7,800,000 printed vols, 248,000 MSS; Librarian SARAH E. THOMAS; publ. *The Bodleian Library Record* (2 a year).

Oxfordshire County Libraries Headquarters: Cultural and Adult Learning Services, Central Library, Westgate, Oxford, OX1 1DJ; tel. (1865) 810191; fax (1865) 810187; e-mail cultural.services@oxfordshire .gov.uk; internet www.oxfordshire.gov.uk/ libraries; 1,081,000 vols, 11,000 maps, 3,600 prints, 272,000 photographs and slides, 40,000 scores, 48,000 sound recordings, 39,000 videos and DVDs; 43 static libraries, 5 mobile libraries; County Librarian CAROLINE TAYLOR.

Sackler Library: St John St, Oxford, OX1 2LG; tel. (1865) 288190; fax (1865) 278098; e-mail enquiries@saclib.ox.ac.uk; internet www.saclib.ox.ac.uk; f. 2001, fmrly Ashmolean Library (since 1683); 270,000 vols; archaeology, ancient history and ancient Near Eastern studies, and Byzantine studies, numismatics, classical languages and literature, Western art and architecture. Special collections include Grenfell and Hunt Papyrological Library, Griffith Egyptological Library, Haverfield and Richmond Archives and original documentation of principal archaeological expeditions and explorations and classification of artefacts; Librarian-in-Charge Dr G. PIDDOCK.

Taylor Institution Library: Oxford Univ. Library Services, St Giles', Oxford, OX1 3NA. tel. (1865) 278158; fax (1865) 278165; e-mail enquiries@taylib.ox.ac.uk; internet www .taylib.ox.ac.uk; f. 1847; 600,000 vols; medieval and modern continental European (and related) languages and literature (esp. French, German, Italian, Spanish, Portuguese incl. the languages and literature of Latin America, the literature of Canada, and North and sub-Saharan Africa); Dutch, Yiddish, Celtic, Afrikaans, Romanian; linguistics and philology; spec. collns incl.: Voltaire and the French Enlightenment; Dante and Futurist holdings; the G. B. Guarini colln; Golden Age literature; literature of the former German Democratic Republic; Luther *Flugschriften* and the Fiedler colln; letters and papers of Modern European writers; and the Strachan colln of *livres d'artistes*; Slavonic, East European and Modern Greek languages and literature housed separately at 47 Wellington Sq., Oxford, OX1 2JF; the Taylor Instn houses the Taylor Instn Modern Languages Faculty Library, as well as the Main Library; Librarian in Charge A. J. PETERS.

University of Oxford Libraries.

Constituent Libraries:

Balliol College Library: Oxford, OX1 3BJ; tel. (1865) 277709; fax (1865) 277803; e-mail library@balliol.ox.ac.uk; internet www.balliol.ox.ac.uk; f. 1263; 110,000 vols; Librarian Dr P. A. BULLOCH.

Brasenose College Library: Oxford, OX1 4AJ; tel. (1865) 277827; e-mail library@bnc.ox.ac.uk; internet www.bnc.ox .ac.uk; f. 1509; 60,000 vols; Fellow Librarian Dr E. H. BISPHAM; College Librarian LIZ KAY.

Christ Church Library: Oxford, OX1 1DP; tel. (1865) 276169; e-mail library@ chch.ox.ac.uk; internet www.chch.ox.ac .uk; f. 1546; 130,000 vols.

Codrington Library (All Souls College): Oxford, OX1 4AL; tel. (1865) 279318; fax (1865) 279299; e-mail codrington.library@all-souls.ox.ac.uk; internet www.all-souls.ox.ac.uk; f. 1710; 178,000 vols; spec. collns: medieval and modern history, military history, strategic studies and law; Librarian Prof. I. MACLEAN.

Corpus Christi College Library: Oxford, OX1 4JF; tel. (1865) 276744; fax (1865) 276767; e-mail library.staff@ corpus-christi.ox.ac.uk; internet www.ccc .ox.ac.uk/library/library.htm; f. 1517; 80,000 vols, MSS; spec. collns: incunabula, early English printed books, 17th- and 18th-century Italian books, English, French and German books on 19th-century philosophy; Fellow Librarian J. HOWARD-JOHNSTON; Librarian J. SNELLING.

Exeter College Library: Oxford, OX1 3DP; tel. (1865) 279600; fax (1865) 279630; e-mail library@exeter.ox.ac.uk; f. 1314; Librarian Dr J. R. MADDICOTT.

Green College Library: Oxford, OX2 6HG; tel. (1865) 274770; fax (1865) 274796; e-mail gill.edwards@green.ox.ac .uk; internet library.green.ox.ac.uk; f. 1979; 7,000 vols; Medicine and Social Science Librarian GILL EDWARDS.

Hertford College Library: Oxford, OX1 3BW; tel. (1865) 279409; e-mail susan .griffin@hertford.ox.ac.uk; internet www .hertford.ox.ac.uk; 50,000 vols; 17th-century colln from Magdalen Hall (forerunner of Hertford College); Fellow Librarian Dr T. C. BARNARD; Librarian S. M. GRIFFIN.

Jesus College Library: Oxford, OX1 3DW; tel. (1865) 279704; e-mail librarian@jesus.ox.ac.uk; internet www .jesus.ox.ac.uk; 70,000 vols, incl. periodicals; Celtic colln; Fellows' Library (f. 1571): 12,000 early printed books, 150 MSS; spec. collns: library of Lord Herbert of Chirbury, material relating to T. E. Lawrence (of Arabia); Meyricke Library (f. 1865): undergraduate library; Fellow Librarian Dr T. HORDER; College Librarian S. A. COBBOLD; Archivist R. DUNHILL.

Keble College Library: Oxford, OX1 3PG; tel. (1865) 272797; e-mail library@ keb.ox.ac.uk; f. 1876; 40,000 vols in working library; spec. collns: medieval MSS, incunabula and early printed books, Brooke colln, Millard colln, Hatchett-Jackson colln, Port-Royal, John Keble's own library, part of Henry Liddon's library, 19th-century archive material; Librarian M. M. SZURKO.

Lincoln College Library: Oxford, OX1 3DR; tel. (1865) 279831; e-mail library@ lincoln.ox.ac.uk; f. 1427; 40,000 vols; Librarian F. M. PIDDOCK.

Magdalen College Library: Oxford, OX1 4AU; tel. (1865) 276045; fax (1865) 276057; e-mail library@magd.ox.ac.uk; internet www.magd.ox.ac.uk/college_life/libraries_ and_archives.shtml; f. 1458; 120,000 vols; spec. collns: 16th- to 18th-century books, late medieval English history, late medieval MS books, early printed botanical books, early printed medical books; Fellow Librarian Dr C. Y. FERDINAND.

Merton College Library: Oxford, OX1 4JD; tel. (1865) 276380; fax (1865) 276361; e-mail library@admin.merton.oxford.ac .uk; internet www.merton.ox.ac.uk; f. 1264; 70,000 vols; Librarian Dr JULIA WALWORTH.

New College Library: Holywell St, Oxford, OX1 3BN; tel. (1865) 279580; fax (1865) 279590; e-mail naomi.vanloo@new .ox.ac.uk; internet www.new.ox.ac.uk/ the_library; f. 1379; 100,000 vols; spec. collns: medieval MSS, incunabula, early archives, modern papers of Milner Colln (deposited in Bodleian Library); Librarian NAOMI VAN LOO.

Nuffield College Library: Oxford, OX1 1NF; tel. (1865) 278550; fax (1865) 278621; e-mail librarian@nuffield.ox.ac.uk; internet www.nuffield.ox.ac.uk/library; f. 1937; 200,000 vols; postgraduate research library in the social sciences covering politics, int. relations, sociology and economics; spec. collns: modern political MSS, labour history, trade unions, political parties, William Cobbett, Daniel Defoe, William Morris, Lord Nuffield; Librarian ELIZABETH MARTIN.

Oriel College Library: Oxford, OX1 4EW; tel. (1865) 276558; e-mail library@ oriel.ox.ac.uk; f. 1326; 100,000 vols; spec. colln of personages who attended Oriel College; Librarian MARJORY SZURKO.

Pembroke College, McGowin Library: Oxford, OX1 1DW; tel. (1865) 276409; fax (1865) 276418; e-mail library@pmb.ox.ac .uk; internet www.pmb.ox.ac.uk; f. 1624; 40,000 vols; Chandler colln of Aristotelia; Fellow Librarian Dr C. MELCHERT.

Queen's College Library: High St, Oxford, OX1 4AW; tel. (1865) 279130; fax (1865) 790819; e-mail library@queens.ox .ac.uk; internet www.queens.ox.ac.uk/ library; f. 1340; 150,000 vols; Librarian A. J. SAVILLE.

St Edmund Hall Library: Queen's Lane, Oxford, OX1 4AR; tel. (1865) 279000; internet www.seh.ox.ac.uk/index .cfm?do=library; f. 17th century; 54,000 vols; spec. collns: Emden (naval and military history), Aularian (Hall members' publs), John Oldham, Thomas Hearne; Librarian DEBORAH EATON.

St John's College Library: Oxford, OX1 3JP; tel. (1865) 277300; fax (1865) 277435; e-mail library@fyfield.sjc.ox.ac.uk; internet www.sjc.ox.ac.uk; f. c.1555; 80,000 vols; Librarian Dr P. HACKER.

Trinity College Library: Oxford, OX1 3BH; tel. (1865) 279863; fax (1865) 279902; e-mail alison.felstead@trinity.ox.ac.uk; internet www.trinity.ox.ac.uk/college/ library; Librarian ALISON FELSTEAD.

University College Library: Oxford, OX1 4BH; tel. (1865) 276621; fax (1865) 276987; e-mail library@university-college .ox.ac.uk; internet www.lib.ox.ac.uk/ libraries/guides/uni.html; f. 1249; 50,000 vols; spec. collns, incl. the Attlee Papers, are deposited in the Bodleian Library (see above); Librarian C. M. RITCHIE.

Wadham College Library: Oxford, OX1 3PN; tel. (1865) 277900; e-mail library@ wadh.ox.ac.uk; f. 1613; 55,000 vols; spec. collns: 16th-century theology, 17th-century science; Persian history and literature; Fellow Librarian Prof. R. W. FIDDIAN.

Worcester College Library: Oxford, OX1 2HB; tel. (1865) 278354; fax (1865) 278387; internet www.lib.ox.ac.uk/ libraries/guides/wor/html; f. 1714; 75,000 vols; spec. collns: Clarke Papers (Civil War and Commonwealth documents), architectural books and drawings (Inigo Jones,

Hawksmoor), English poetry and drama from 1550–1750, Pottinger colln of 19th-century pamphlets, 17th- and 18th-century print colln; Librarian JOANNA PARKER.

Paisley

Renfrewshire Libraries: Abbey House, Paisley, Renfrewshire, PA1 1AJ; tel. (141) 840-3003; fax (141) 840-3004; e-mail libraries .els@renfrewshire.gov.uk; internet www .renfrewshire.gov.uk/libraries; 418,000 vols; 17 libraries, incl. Paisley Central Reference Library; toy library; 329,500 vols, 20,500 CDs, 1,000 DVDs; Libraries Man. VIVIAN KERR.

University of Paisley Library: High St, Paisley, PA1 2BE; tel. (141) 848-3758; fax (141) 848-3761; e-mail library@paisley.ac.uk; internet library.paisley.ac.uk; 365,000 vols, 12,000 online journals; Chief Librarian TERESA GILBERT (acting).

Peterborough

Peterborough Cathedral Library: c/o Chapter Office, Minster Precincts, Peterborough, PE1 1XS; tel. (1733) 562125; fax (1733) 552465; e-mail fiona.west@ peterborough-cathedral.org.uk; f. c. 1670 by Dean Duport; 8,000 vols, some important medieval MSS and some early printed books (books and MSS printed before 1800 are now deposited in the Cambridge University Library, save those of local concern); Librarian Canon J. HIGHAM.

Peterborough City Libraries: Peterborough Central Library, Broadway, Peterborough, PE1 1RX; tel. (1733) 742700; fax (1733) 555277; e-mail libraries@peterborough.gov .uk; internet www.peterborough.gov.uk/ council/libraries; 8 brs, 2 mobile libraries; Library Service Man. ELAINE JEWELL.

Plymouth

City of Plymouth Libraries and Information Services: Central Library, Drake Circus, Plymouth, Devon, PL4 8AL; tel. (1752) 305923; fax (1752) 305929; e-mail library@plymouth.gov.uk; internet www .plymouth.gov.uk/libraries; 16 brs; City Librarian ALASDAIR MACNAUGHTAN.

Pontllanfraith

Caerphilly Libraries: Unit 7, Woodfieldside Business Park, Penman Rd, Pontllanfraith, Blackwood, NP12 2DG; tel. (1495) 235587; fax (1495) 235567; e-mail caer.libs@ dial.pipex.com; 20 brs; Principal Officer Libraries MARY PALMER.

Pontypool

Torfaen Libraries: Torfaen County Borough Council, Civic Centre, Pontypool, NP4 6YB; tel. (1633) 628941; fax (1633) 628935; e-mail sue.johnson@torfaen.gov.uk; 116,000 vols; 4 brs; Cultural Services Manager SUE JOHNSON.

Poole

Borough of Poole Libraries: Poole Central Library, Dolphin Centre, Poole, Dorset, BH15 1QE; tel. (1202) 262437; fax (1202) 262442; e-mail poolelibrary@poole.gov.uk; internet www.poole.gov.uk; Head of Cultural Services CLAIRE CHIDLEY.

Port Talbot

Neath Port Talbot Library and Information Service: Reginald St, Velindre, Port Talbot, SA13 1YY; tel. (1639) 899829; fax (1639) 899152; e-mail npt.libhq@ neath-porttalbot.gov.uk; internet www .neath-porttalbot.gov.uk; f. 1996; 391,000 vols; 18 brs, 2 mobile libraries; Co-ordinator (Cultural Services) J. L. ELLIS.

Porth

Rhondda Cynon Taff County Borough Library Services: Ty Trevithick, Abercynon, Mountain Ash, CF45 4UQ; tel. (1443) 744029; fax (1443) 744023; 550,000 vols; 29 brs, 4 mobile libraries; Head of Libraries and Museums Education Department GILL EVANS.

Portsmouth

Portsmouth City Libraries: Central Library, Guildhall Square, Portsmouth, PO1 2DX; tel. (23) 9281-9311; fax (23) 9283-9855; e-mail library.admin@portsmouthcc .gov.uk; internet www.portsmouth.gov.uk/ leisure/libraries; f. 1976; Library Services Man. COLIN BROWN (acting).

University of Portsmouth Library: Frewen Library, University of Portsmouth, Cambridge Rd, Portsmouth, PO1 2ST; tel. (23) 9284-3222; fax (23) 9284-3233; e-mail library@port.ac.uk; internet www.libr.port .ac.uk; 600,000 vols; Librarian IAN BONAR.

Preston

Lancashire County Library: Bowran St, Preston, PR1 2UX; tel. (1772) 534003; fax (1772) 534200; f. 1924; 3,018,000 vols; 84 brs, 12 mobile libraries, 2 trailer libraries; Admin. Officer LINDA WHITFIELD.

Reading

Reading Borough Libraries: Central Library, Abbey Sq., Reading, RG1 3BQ; tel. (118) 901-5950; fax (118) 901-5954; e-mail info@readinglibraries.org.uk; internet www .readinglibraries.org.uk; f. 1883; 280,000 vols; 7 brs, 2 mobile libraries; Local Studies Library; Head of Cultural Services AMAR DAVE.

Reading University Library: Main Library, Whiteknights, POB 223, Reading, RG6 6AE; tel. (118) 378-8770; fax (118) 378-6636; e-mail library@reading.ac.uk; internet www.library.rdg.ac.uk; f. 1892; 1,181,800 vols, 3,300 current periodicals; special collns incl. Overstone Library, Stenton Library on English history, Cole Library on early zoology, Beckett colln of material by or about Samuel Beckett, Finzi collns of music and English poetry, Turner colln of French Revolution pamphlets, Stendhal colln, agricultural history, children's books, archives of British publishers, papers of Lord and Lady Astor; European Documentation Centre; Librarian JULIA MUNRO.

Rochester

Medway Council Directorate of Leisure, Arts and Libraries: Civic Centre, Strood, Rochester, Kent, ME2 4AU; tel. (1634) 306000; fax (1634) 332869; e-mail rose .gardner@medway.gov.uk; internet www .medway.gov.uk; f. 1998; 16 brs, 1 mobile library, Medway Archives and Local Studies Centre; Asst Dir for Arts, Libraries and Heritage JANICE MASKORT.

Runcorn

Halton Borough Libraries: Halton Lea Library, Halton Lea, Runcorn, WA7 2PF; tel. (1928) 715351; fax (1928) 790221; e-mail haltonlea.lib@halton-borough.gov.uk; internet www.halton.gov.uk; f. 1998; 4 brs; Head of Libraries PAULA RILEY-COOPER.

Ruthin

Denbighshire Library Service: Yr Hen Garchar, 46 Clwyd St, Ruthin, Denbighshire, LL15 1HP; tel. (1824) 708204; fax (1824) 708202; e-mail library.services@ denbighshire.gov.uk; internet www .denbighshire.gov.uk; 8 libraries, 1 mobile library, 1 home library service; special collections: Welsh music, local history;

219,260 vols; Head of Libraries R. ARWYN JONES.

St Andrews

University of St Andrews Library and Information Services: North St, St Andrews, Fife, KY16 9TR; tel. (1334) 462281; fax (1334) 462282; e-mail lis .library@st-and.ac.uk; internet library .st-andrews.ac.uk; f. 1412; 780,000 vols, MSS, maps and numerous special collections, including Donaldson (Classics and Education), J. D. Forbes (Science), and Von Hügel (Theology and Philosophy); Dir of Library Services J. PURCELL.

Salford

HM Customs and Excise Library: Ralli Quays, 3 Stanley St, Salford, M60 9LA; tel. (161) 827-0465; fax (161) 827-0491; f. 1991; also at Revenue and Customs Library, 1 Parliament St, London, SW1A 2BQ; tel. (20) 7147-0469; fax (20) 7147-0232; f. 1671; c. 35,000 vols; Chief Librarian LORNA BANKES.

University of Salford Information Services Division: Clifford Whitworth Bldg, Peel Park Campus, The Crescent, Salford, M5 4WT; tel. (161) 295-2444; fax (161) 295-5888; e-mail isd-servicedesk@salford.ac.uk; internet www.isd.salford.ac.uk; f. 1896; 675,000 items, 5,000 periodicals; Dir of Information Services TONY LEWIS.

Salisbury

Salisbury Cathedral Library: The Cathedral, Salisbury, Wilts., SP1 2EN; f. 11th century; contains printed books and medieval MSS; open only to bona fide research students by appointment; an exhibition of books and documents incl. an original Magna Carta is on show in the Chapter House from March to December; Librarian SUZANNE EWARD.

Sheffield

Sheffield Hallam University Learning Centre: Adsetts Centre, City Campus, Sheffield, S1 1WB; tel. (114) 225-2109; fax (114) 225-3859; e-mail learning.centre@shu.ac.uk; 498,000 vols, 2,600 journal titles; Dir GRAHAM BULPITT.

Sheffield Libraries and Information Services: Central Library, Surrey St, Sheffield, S1 1XZ; tel. (114) 273-4712; fax (114) 273-5009; e-mail libraries@sheffield.gov.uk; internet www.sheffield.gov.uk; f. 1856; 915,000 vols (excluding MSS); 27 br. libraries, 5 mobile libraries; 4 hospital libraries, central library (incl. private press books, books printed in England 1765–79); business, science and technology standards, local studies, circulation services (incl. Whitworth Colln of organ books, Sports Library and Information Service), Sheffield Archives (incl. Strafford papers, Edmund Burke papers, Edward Carpenter papers, Fairbank map colln); City Librarian JANICE MASKORT.

University of Sheffield Library: Western Bank, Sheffield, S. Yorks, S10 2TN; tel. (114) 222-7200; fax (114) 222-7290; e-mail library@ sheffield.ac.uk; internet www.shef.ac.uk/ library; f. 1905; 1,400,000 vols; special collections: Sir Charles Firth's collection of 17th c. tracts and 19th c. broadside ballads, the Samuel Hartlib Papers, the papers of Sir Hans Krebs (FRS and Nobel Laureate), National Fairground Archive, Sir Thomas Beecham Music Library; Dir of Library Services and University Librarian M. J. LEWIS.

Shrewsbury

Shropshire County Library Service: Shirehall, Abbey Foregate, Shrewsbury, Shropshire, SY2 6ND; tel. (1743) 255000;

fax (1743) 255050; e-mail libraries@shropshire-cc.gov.uk; internet www.shropshire.gov.uk/library.nsf; f. 1925; 510,000 vols, audiovisual collns; 22 brs, 8 mobile libraries; Head of Libraries and Information JIM ROADS.

Slough

Slough Borough Council Libraries and Information Service: Slough Library, High St, Slough, SL1 1EA; tel. (1753) 535166; fax (1753) 825050; e-mail library@slough.gov.uk; internet www.sloughlibrary.org.uk; 3 brs, 1 mobile library; Head of Libraries and Information YVONNE COPE.

Southampton

Southampton City Libraries: Central Library, Civic Centre, Southampton, SO14 7LW; tel. (23) 8083-2459; fax (23) 8033-6305; e-mail e.whale@southampton.gov.uk; internet www.southampton.gov.uk/education/libraries/main.htm; City Librarian H. A. RICHARDS.

University of Southampton Library: Southampton, SO17 1BJ; tel. (23) 8059-2180; fax (23) 8059-3007; e-mail libenqs@soton.ac.uk; internet www.library.soton.ac.uk; f. 1862 as Hartley Institution; main and branch libraries; 1,300,000 vols, 8,000 current periodicals, Wessex Medical Library, Ford Collection of Parliamentary Papers (since 1801), Wellington Papers, Broadlands Archives (Palmerston, Shaftesbury, Mountbatten), Cope collection of Hampshire material, Perkins Agricultural Library, Parkes Library (relationship between Jewish and non-Jewish worlds), archive collections relating to Anglo-Jewry, Hampshire Field Club Library; Librarian Dr MARK BROWN.

Southend on Sea

Southend on Sea Borough Council Education and Libraries Department: Central Library, Victoria Ave, Southend on Sea, Essex, SS2 6EX; tel. (1702) 534100; 7 brs; Head of Service SIMON MAY.

Stafford

Staffordshire Library and Information Services: 16 Martin St, Stafford, ST16 2LG; tel. (1785) 278311; fax (1785) 278319; internet www.staffordshire.gov.uk; f. 1916; 1,265,000 vols, 13,000 CDs, 5,000 DVDs and videos; 43 static libraries, 11 mobile libraries; County Librarian OLIVIA SPENCER.

Stirling

Stirling Council Library Services: Borrowmeadow Rd, Stirling, FK7 7TN; tel. (1786) 432383; fax (1786) 432395; e-mail libraryheadquarters@stirling.gov.uk; internet www.stirling.gov.uk; 330,000 vols; Libraries and Archives Man. R. RUTHVEN.

University of Stirling Library: Stirling, FK9 4LA; tel. (1786) 467235; fax (1786) 466866; e-mail library@stir.ac.uk; internet www.is.stir.ac.uk; f. 1966; 500,000 vols, 6,000 periodicals, colln of works by Sir Walter Scott and contemporaries, John Grierson archive, Lindsay Anderson archive, Howietoun Fish Farm archive, labour history collection; facilities for online information retrieval; Dir of Information Services and Univ. Librarian Dr PETER KEMP.

Stockport

National Library for the Blind: Far Cromwell Rd, Bredbury, Stockport, SK6 2SG; tel. (161) 355-2000; fax (161) 355-2098; e-mail enquiries@nlbuk.org; internet www.nlb-online.org; f. 1882; contains 400,000 vols, including music, in Braille and Moon types; Grant Print Library; Chief Exec.

HELEN BRAZIER; publs *NLB Focus* (3 a year), *Read On* (4 a year), *Annual Review*.

Stoke on Trent

Staffordshire University Library: POB 664, College Rd, Stoke on Trent, ST4 2XS; tel. (1782) 294443; fax (1782) 295799; 300,000 vols; Librarian LIZ HART.

Stoke on Trent City Council Libraries, Information and Archives: City Central Library, Bethesda St, Hanley, Stoke on Trent, ST1 3RS; tel. (1782) 238455; fax (1782) 238499; e-mail central.library@swift.stoke.gov.uk; internet www.stoke.gov.uk/libraries; 460,000 vols; Solon ceramics colln; Library and Archives Services Manager IAN VAN ARKADIE.

Stratford upon Avon

Shakespeare Centre Library: Henley St, Stratford upon Avon, Warwicks., CV37 6QW; tel. (1789) 201813; fax (1789) 296083; e-mail library@shakespeare.org.uk; internet www.shakespeare.org.uk; f. 1964; 55,000 vols, comprising the combined collns of the Shakespeare Birthplace Trust and the Royal Shakespeare Company, incl. its administrative and production archives; leaflets, photographs, programmes, press clippings, playbills and ephemera; Head of Library and Information Resources SYLVIA MORRIS.

Swansea

City and County of Swansea Library and Information Service: Library HQ, County Hall, Oystermouth Rd, Swansea, SA1 3SN; tel. (1792) 636430; fax (1792) 636235; e-mail swansea.libraries@swansea.gov.uk; internet www.swansea.gov.uk/culture; 986,546 vols; special collections: Dylan Thomas, Deffett Francis, Welsh and Local History; Head of Libraries PETER GAW.

Swansea University Library: Singleton Park, Swansea, SA2 8PP; tel. (1792) 295697; fax (1792) 295851; e-mail library@swansea.ac.uk; internet www.swan.ac.uk/lis/index.asp; f. 1920; 800,000 items; Dir of Library and Information Services CHRISTOPHER WEST.

Swindon

Swindon Borough Libraries: Swindon Reference Library, Regent Circus, Swindon, SN1 1QG; tel. (1793) 463240; fax (1793) 541319; e-mail reference.library@swindon.gov.uk; internet www.swindon.gov.uk; f. 1943; Libraries and Heritage Manager DAVID ALLEN.

Telford

Telford and Wrekin Libraries: Telford Town Centre Library, St Quentin Gate, Telford, TF3 4JG; tel. (1952) 292151; fax (1952) 292078; e-mail telfordlibrary@hotmail.com; internet twlibraries.enta.net; 9 brs, 1 mobile library; Libraries and Heritage Services Man. PAT DAVIS.

Torquay

Torbay Library Service: Torquay Library, Lymington Rd, Torquay, TQ1 3DT; tel. (1803) 208310; fax (1803) 208311; e-mail tqadminlib@torbay.gov.uk; internet www.torbay.gov.uk; f. 1998; 3 brs, 1 mobile library; local studies colln; Head of Library Services PETER J. BOTTRILL.

Trowbridge

Wiltshire Libraries and Heritage: Bythesea Rd, Trowbridge, Wilts, BA14 8BS; tel. (1225) 713700; fax (1225) 713993; internet www.wiltshire.gov.uk; f. 1919; 869,000 vols, cassettes, compact discs, videos, etc.; 31 brs, 4 mobile libraries; special collections: Wiltshire, agriculture, life of Christ, anthropol-

ogy and sociology of the family; public and private archives for Wiltshire and the Diocese of Salisbury; Assistant Dir, Libraries and Heritage PAULINE PALMER; publ. *Annual Report*.

Truro

Cornwall Library Service: Unit 17, Threemilestone, Truro, Cornwall, TR4 9LD; tel. (1872) 324676; fax (1872) 223509; e-mail library@cornwall.gov.uk; internet www.cornwall.gov.uk/library; f. 1925; 835,000 vols; 29 brs; Asst Dir, Education, Arts and Libraries CHRIS RAMSEY.

Warrington

Warrington Borough Libraries: Warrington Library, Museum St, Warrington, WA1 1JB; tel. (1925) 442890; fax (1925) 411395; e-mail library@warrington.gov.uk; internet www.warrington.gov.uk; f. 1848; 13 brs, 1 mobile library; Head of Libraries, Museum and Archives MARTIN GAW.

Warwick

Warwickshire Library and Information Service: Barrack St, Warwick, CV34 4TH; tel. (1926) 412657; fax (1926) 412471; e-mail librarieslearningandculture@warwickshire.gov.uk; internet www.warwickshire.gov.uk/libraries; f. 1920; 1,105,000 vols; 32 libraries; 5 mobile libraries; community service vehicle; special collns: Warwickshire Colln, George Eliot Colln; Head of Libraries, Learning and Culture EDWINA CORDWELL.

West Bretton

National Arts Education Archive, Lawrence Batley Centre for: University of Leeds, Special Collections, Bretton Hall Campus, West Bretton, West Yorks., WF4 4LG; tel. (1924) 832020; fax (1924) 832077; e-mail s.kielty@leeds.ac.uk; internet naea.leeds.ac.uk; f. 1985; to establish an illustrated 'trace' of work in art and design education 1880 to date, to make this available to scholars and the general public, and to promote academic research and more informed teaching through its use; colln of works of art illustrating the development of the Child Art and Basic Design movements in art education; includes many thousands of original papers, letters, slides, films, videos, tapes and books; Senior Library Asst SONJA KIELTY.

Winchester

Hampshire Library and Information Service: 81 North Walls, Winchester, Hampshire, SO23 8BY; tel. (1962) 826600; fax (1962) 856615; e-mail library@hants.gov.uk; internet www3.hants.gov.uk/library/library-finder.htm; f. 1974; 2,840,000 vols; 54 brs; 17 mobile libraries; County Librarian R. WARD.

Worcester

Worcestershire Library and Information Service: Cultural Services, Worcestershire County Council, County Hall, Spetchley Rd, Worcester, WR5 2NP; tel. (1905) 766231; fax (1905) 766930; e-mail librarieshq@worcestershire.gov.uk; internet www.worcestershire.gov.uk/libraries; f. 1998; 23 brs, 5 public mobile libraries; Library Services Man. CATHY EVANS.

Wrexham

Wrexham County Borough Council, Library and Information Service: Education and Leisure Services Directorate, Roxburgh House, Hill St, Wrexham, LL11 1SN; tel. (1978) 297430; fax (1978) 297422; 214,746 vols; 12 libraries, 2 mobile libraries, 1 library for the housebound; special collections: open learning, Japanese life and culture; business information centre; Chief Officer ALAN WATKIN.

York

City of York Libraries: York Central Library, Museum St, York, YO1 7DS; tel. (1904) 655631; fax (1904) 552835; internet www.york.gov.uk/libraries; f. 1893; Head of Library Service FIONA WILLIAMS.

University of York Library: Heslington, York, YO10 5DD; tel. (1904) 433865; fax (1904) 433866; e-mail lib-enquiry@york.ac .uk; internet www.york.ac.uk/services/ library; f. 1963; 1,000,000 vols; Univ. Librarian ELIZABETH M. HEAPS.

York Minster Library: Dean's Park, York, YO1 7JQ; tel. (1904) 625308; fax (1904) 611119; f. 7th–8th century; 125,000 vols, 115 incunabula, 101 medieval MSS, 200 music MSS; spec. collns include Civil War Tracts and Yorkshire local history (120,000 vols); Librarian JOHN POWELL; Archivist PETER YOUNG.

Museums and Art Galleries

Aberdeen

Aberdeen Art Gallery and Museums: Schoolhill, Aberdeen, AB10 1FQ; tel. (1224) 523700; fax (1224) 632133; e-mail info@aagm .co.uk; internet www.aberdeencity.gov.uk; Officer in Charge CHRISTINE REW (acting).

Selected museums and galleries:

Aberdeen Art Gallery: Schoolhill, Aberdeen, AB10 1FQ; tel. (1224) 523700; fax (1224) 632133; e-mail info@aagm.co.uk; internet www.aberdeencity.gov.uk; f. 1884; fine and decorative arts; major collections of British art since 18th c.

Aberdeen Maritime Museum: Shiprow, Aberdeen, AB11 5BY; tel. (1224) 337700; fax (1224) 213066; e-mail info@aagm.co.uk; internet www.aberdeencity.gov.uk; f. 1984; displays covering all aspects of Aberdeen and the North East of Scotland's maritime heritage.

Alloway

Burns Cottage and Museum: Murdoch's Lone, Alloway, Ayr, Ayrshire, KA7 4PQ; tel. (1292) 443700; fax (1292) 441750; e-mail info@burnsheritagepark.com; internet www .burnsheritagepark.com; f. 1881; birthplace of the poet Robert Burns; MSS and correspondence; Visitor Services Supervisor JOHN MANSON.

Anstruther

Scottish Fisheries Museum: St Ayles, Harbourhead, Anstruther, Fife, KY10 3AB; tel. (1333) 310628; e-mail enquiries@ scotfishmuseum.org; internet www .scotfishmuseum.org; f. 1969; visual historical record of every aspect of the Scottish fishing industry from prehistoric times to the present; touring boat; library: reference library and archive of 1,000 vols (open by appointment); photographic archive; Dir TOM SUNTER; publ. *Newsletter* (annually).

Bangor

Gwynedd Museum and Art Gallery, Bangor: Ffordd Gwynedd, Bangor, Gwynedd, LL57 1DT; tel. (1248) 353368; fax (1248) 370149; e-mail gwyneddmuseum@ gwynedd.gov.uk; internet www.gwynedd.gov .uk/museums; f. 1884; artefacts relating to North Wales, incl. archaeology, furniture, costume and Welsh textiles; Curator ESTHER ROBERTS.

Barnard Castle

Bowes Museum: Barnard Castle, Co. Durham, DL12 8NP; tel. (1833) 690606; fax (1833) 637163; e-mail info@ thebowesmuseum.org.uk; internet www .thebowesmuseum.org.uk; f. 1869; collections formed 1862–75 by John and Josephine Bowes mainly of all forms of European Fine and Decorative Arts; f. at Barnard Castle 1869, since when there have been additions of British Decorative Arts, including series of English rooms from 16th–19th c., music, costumes, local history and archaeology galleries; reference library; administered by Durham County Council; Dir ADRIAN JENKINS.

Bath

American Museum in Britain: Claverton Manor, Bath, BA2 7BD; tel. (1225) 460503; fax (1225) 469160; e-mail info@ americanmuseum.org; internet www .americanmuseum.org; f. 1959; illustrates the devt of American decorative arts from the 17th to the 19th century; textile colln; printed maps from the 15th and 16th centuries; Native American colln; library: reference library of 10,500 vols; Dir SANDRA BARGHINI.

Holburne Museum of Art: Great Pulteney St, Bath, BA2 4DB; tel. (1225) 466669; e-mail holburne@bath.ac.uk; internet www.bath.ac .uk/holburne; f. 1893; paintings, silver, sculpture, porcelain and furniture in an 18th c. building; Dir ALEXANDER STURGIS.

Beamish

Beamish, The North of England Open Air Museum: Beamish, Co. Durham, DH9 0RG; tel. (191) 370-4000; fax (191) 370-4001; e-mail museum@beamish.org.uk; internet www.beamish.org.uk; f. 1970 to study, collect, preserve and exhibit buildings, machinery, objects and information illustrating the development of industry, social history, agriculture and way of life in the North of England; the museum covers more than 300 acres and includes a colliery village, railway station, a working farm and The Town of around 1913; Pockerley Manor and horse yard illustrate yeoman farming lifestyle in early 19th c.; working replica of George Stephenson's *Locomotion No. 1* railway engine, and *Steam Elephant* of 1815; library of 20,000 vols, 10,000 trade catalogues; photographic archive containing 250,000 photographs; oral history colln with 800 tape recordings; Dir MIRIAM HARTE.

Beaulieu

National Motor Museum: John Montagu Building, Beaulieu, Brockenhurst, Hants., SO42 7ZN; tel. (1590) 614650; fax (1590) 612655; e-mail nmmt@beaulieu.co.uk; internet www.beaulieu.co.uk; f. 1968; houses the Shell Art Collection (commercial art); library: reference library, film library, photograph library; Dir MARION BUDGETT.

Birmingham

Birmingham Museums and Art Gallery: Chamberlain Sq., Birmingham, B3 3DH; tel. (121) 303-2834; fax (121) 303-1394; e-mail bmag_enquiries@birmingham.gov.uk; internet www.bmag.org.uk; f. 1867; Departments of Fine and Applied Art (foreign schools from Renaissance, English from 17th c., early English watercolours and Pre-Raphaelite paintings and drawings, modern art, sculpture, silver, metalwork, costume, glass, stained glass, ceramics and textile collections); Archaeology, Ethnography and Local History (collections from Ancient Egypt, Ur, Nineveh, Jericho, Nimrud, Vinca, Jerusalem, Petra and Vounos—Cyprus)—Mexico and Peru, Prehistoric, Roman and British Medieval antiquities, British 20th century); Pacific ethnography collection; British coin collection; restricted access to comprehensive collections of minerals, gemstones and molluscs, British birds, lepidoptera and coleoptera; Midlands flora; prints (access by appointment only); br. museums incl. Aston Hall, Blakesley Hall, Weoley Castle, Sarehole Mill, Soho House, Museum of the Jewellery Quarter; picture library; Head RITA McLEAN (acting).

Thinktank, Birmingham Museum: Millennium Point, Curzon St, Birmingham, B4 7XG; tel. (121) 202-2222; e-mail findout@ thinktank.ac; internet www.thinktank.ac; consists of 10 galleries of interactive exhibits on science, technology, medicine, natural and local history; also planetarium;; Chief Exec. NICK WINTERBOTHAM.

Bishop's Stortford

Bishop's Stortford Museum: South Rd, Bishop's Stortford, Herts., CM23 3JG; tel. (1279) 651746; fax (1279) 467171; e-mail museum@rhodesbishopsstortford.org.uk; internet www.rhodesbishopsstortford.org; f. 1938 as the Rhodes Memorial Museum; present name 2005; exhibits relating to the life and times of colonialist Cecil Rhodes (1853–1902); African art and culture; also incorporates local history museum; Curator SARAH TURNER.

Blackburn

Blackburn Museum and Art Gallery: Museum St, Blackburn, Lancs., BB1 7AJ; tel. (1254) 667130; fax (1254) 685541; f. 1874; local history, Indian and Pakistani textiles and jewellery, military history, icons, coins, books, MSS, early printed books, fine and decorative arts, Japanese prints.

Bradford

National Media Museum: Bradford, West Yorks., BD1 1NQ; tel. (870) 701-0200; fax (1274) 723155; e-mail talk@ nationalmediamuseum.org.uk; internet www .nationalmediamuseum.org.uk; f. 1983 as part of the National Museum of Science and Industry; explores the history, art and science of photography, film and television, with interactive exhibits; photographic colln incorporates the Kodak Museum colln and colln of the Royal Photographic Society; cinematography colln focuses on film-making; also exhibits of books, posters, designs and ephemera; the Museum houses an IMAX projection system, with cinema screen and a Cinerama cinema; library: access to the Kraszna-Krausz personal library and to other relevant books, MSS and periodicals; Head COLIN PHILPOTT.

Brighton

Booth Museum of Natural History: 194 Dyke Rd, Brighton, BN1 5AA; tel. (1273) 292777; fax (1273) 292778; e-mail boothmus@ pavilion.co.uk; internet www.booth .virtualmuseum.info; f. 1874; displays of British birds in re-created natural settings, and galleries of butterflies from all over the world and geology and vertebrate evolution; reference collections of eggs, insects, minerals, palaeontology, osteology, skins and herbaria; Keeper of Biology Dr GERALD LEGG; Asst Keeper Natural Sciences JEREMY M. ADAMS.

Brighton Museum and Art Gallery: Royal Pavilion Gardens, Brighton, East Sussex, BN1 1EE; tel. (1273) 290900; fax (1273) 292871; e-mail museums@brighton-hove.gov .uk; internet www.brighton.virtualmuseum .info; f. 1873; collection of paintings since 15th c., drawings and prints; English pottery and porcelain, including the Willett Collection; decorative art and furniture of Art Nouveau and Art Deco periods; fashion gallery; ethnography; local history; Assistant Dir of Heritage PAULINE SCOTT-GARRETT.

Royal Pavilion: Brighton, East Sussex, BN1 1EE; tel. (1273) 290900; fax (1273) 292871; e-mail visitor.services@ brighton-hove.gov.uk; internet www .royalpavilion.org.uk; f. 1851; Regency seaside palace of King George IV with Mughal-style exterior and Chinese-style interiors; Asst Dir of Heritage PAULINE SCOTT-GARRETT.

Bristol

Bristol City Museums and Art Gallery: Queen's Rd, Bristol, BS8 1RL; tel. (117) 922-3571; fax (117) 922-2047; e-mail general_museum@bristol-city.gov.uk; internet www.bristol-city.gov.uk/museums; galleries incl. Old Masters, French School, British collection, Modern Art and Bristol School; decorative arts collection incl. Eastern Art, ceramics, silverware and glassware; minerals, fossils and natural history collections; archaeological collection; also 16th c. Red Lodge (Park Row), Georgian House (Gt George St), Blaise Castle House Museum (Henbury), Bristol Industrial Museum (Princes Wharf); Kingsweston Roman Villa; Dir KATE BRINDLEY; publ. *Events* (3 a year).

British Empire and Commonwealth Museum: Clocktower Yard, Temple Meads, Bristol, BS1 6QH; tel. (117) 925-4980; fax (117) 925-4983; e-mail admin@ empiremuseum.co.uk; internet www .empiremuseum.co.uk; f. 2002; charts the history of the British empire and examines its legacy in contemporary Britain; holds 553,000 individual items covering documents. photographs, film, paintings, prints, costumes, textiles, domestic and personal artefacts, books, music and an extensive oral history archive; Dir Dr GARETH GRIFFITHS.

Burnley

Towneley Hall Art Gallery and Museums: Towneley Hall, Towneley Park, Burnley, Lancs, BB11 3RQ; tel. (1282) 424213; fax (1282) 436138; e-mail towneleyhall@burnley.gov.uk; internet www .towneleyhall.org.uk; f. 1902; collections incl. natural history, Egyptology, local history, textiles, decorative art and furniture; art collection focuses on 19th c. British artists; Curator J. SUSAN BOURNE.

Caernarfon

Segontium Roman Fort Museum: Beddgelert Rd, Caernarfon, Gwynedd, LL55 2LN; tel. (1286) 676767; fax (1286) 676767; e-mail info@segontium.org.uk; internet www .segontium.org.uk; f. 1924; exhibits relating to the Roman occupation of Wales, relics from Segontium Roman fort.

Cambridge

Fitzwilliam Museum: Trumpington St, Cambridge, CB2 1RB; tel. (1223) 332900; fax (1223) 332923; e-mail fitzmuseum-enquiries@lists.cam.ac.uk; internet www.fitzmuseum.cam.ac.uk; f. 1816; art collns of the Univ. of Cambridge; paintings, drawings, prints, sculpture; coins and medals; ceramics, glass, textiles, arms and armour, and other applied arts; Greek, Roman, Cypriot, western Asiatic and Egyptian antiquities; library of 250,000 vols and medieval, literary and music MSS, autograph letters, early printed books, printed music, books on history of art; Dir DUNCAN ROBINSON; publ. *Biennial Review.*

University Museum of Archaeology and Anthropology: Downing St, Cambridge, CB2 3DZ; tel. (1223) 333516; fax (1233) 333517; e-mail cumaa@hermes.cam.ac.uk; internet museum.archanth.cam.ac.uk; f. 1884; anthropology and prehistoric archaeology of all parts of the world; also local archaeology of all periods; Dir and Curator Prof. D. W. PHILLIPSON.

University Museum of Zoology: Downing St, Cambridge, CB2 3EJ; tel. (1223) 336650; fax (1223) 336679; e-mail umzc@zoo.cam.ac .uk; internet www.zoo.cam.ac.uk/museum; f. 1815; collns of recent and fossil zoological species; Collns Man. RAY SYMONDS.

Cardiff

Amgueddfa Cymru – National Museum Wales: Cathays Park, Cardiff, CF10 3NP; tel. (29) 2057-3951; fax (29) 2057-3321; internet www.museumwales.ac.uk; f. 1907; Pres. PAUL LOVELUCK; Dir MICHAEL HOULIHAN.

Associated museums:

Big Pit: National Coal Museum: Blaenafon, Torfaen, NP4 9XP; tel. (1495) 790311; internet www.museumwales.ac .uk/en/bigpit; f. 1980; working coal mine and exhibits relating to Welsh mining history; Man. PETER WALKER.

National Museum Cardiff: Cathays Park, Cardiff, CF10 3NP; tel. (29) 2039-7951; internet www.museumwales.ac.uk/ en/cardiff; f. 1907; houses the Welsh nat. clln of fine and applied art; also archaeological, numismatic, natural history and geological cllns; library of 2,000,000 ; also print and drawings study room open by appointment; Dir MICHAEL TOOBY.

National Roman Legion Museum: High St, Caerleon, Gwent, NP18 1AE; tel. (1633) 423134; internet www.museumwales.ac .uk/en/caerleon; f. 1930; former Roman fortress, comprising ruins and relevant exhibits; library: library open by appointment; Man. BETHAN LEWIS.

National Slate Museum: Llanberis, Gwynedd, LL55 4TY; tel. (1286) 870630; fax (1286) 871906; internet www .museumwales.ac.uk/en/slate; f. 1972; machinery, relics and bldgs relating to north Wales slate industry; library: open by appointment; Keeper DAFYDD ROBERTS.

National Waterfront Museum: Oystermouth Rd, Maritime Quarter, Swansea, SA1 3RD; tel. (1792) 638950; internet www .museumwales.ac.uk/en/swansea; 15 themed display areas on the effect of the Industrial Revolution on Welsh life.

National Wool Museum: Dre-fach Felindre, near Newcastle Emlyn, Llandysul, Carmarthenshire, SA44 5UP; tel. (1559) 370929; fax (1559) 371592; internet www.museumwales.ac.uk/en/wool; f. 1976; displays of bldgs and artefacts relating to the Welsh woollen industry; library: library open by appointment; Man. SALLY MOSS.

St Fagans National History Museum: St Fagans, Cardiff, CF5 6XB; tel. (29) 2057-3500; internet www.museumwales .ac.uk/en/stfagans; f. 1948; museum of Welsh social history, with over 40 original bldgs re-erected on site; library: library open by appointment; Dir JOHN WILLIAMS-DAVIES.

Turner House Gallery: Plymouth Rd, Penarth, CF64 3DM; tel. (29) 2070-8870; e-mail post@nmgw.ac.uk; internet www .nmgw.ac.uk; f. 1921; art gallery; Dir MICHAEL TOOBY.

Carmarthen

Carmarthenshire County Museum: Abergwili, Carmarthen, SA31 2JG; tel. (1267) 228696; fax (1267) 223830; e-mail museums@carmarthenshire.gov.uk; internet www.carmarthenshire.gov.uk; f. 1978; local authority museum; geology, archaeology, social history, folk life, furniture, ceramics, art, costume; Heritage Manager C. J. DELANEY.

Chawton

Jane Austen's House: Chawton, Alton, Hampshire; tel. (1420) 83262; e-mail enquiries@jane-austens-house-museum.org .uk; internet www .jane-austens-house-museum.org.uk; f. 1949; portraits, documents, furniture and objects relating to Jane Austen and her family; Dir T. F. CARPENTER.

Cirencester

Corinium Museum: Park St, Cirencester, Glos.; tel. (1285) 655611; e-mail judy.mills@ cotswold.gov.uk; internet www.cotswold.gov .uk; important collection of Roman material; mosaic pavements, sculpture, military and civil tombstones, household domestic utensils, personal ornaments, and Samian and coarse pottery, all giving ample evidence of the importance and wealth of Corinium, which was the second largest town in Roman Britain; regional museum for the Cotswolds; Museums Service Man. Dr JOHN PADDOCK.

Colchester

Colchester Museums: Museum Resource Centre, 14 Ryegate Rd, Colchester, Essex, CO1 1YG; tel. (1206) 282931; fax (1206) 282925; internet www.colchestermuseums .org.uk; f. 1860 from the collections of Essex Archaeological Society; local human and natural history; large collections in the Norman Castle, with extensive Roman section; three branch museums (covering Natural History, social history, Colchester Clocks); Head of Museums PETER BERRIDGE.

Devizes

Wiltshire Heritage Museum, Gallery and Library: The Museum, 41 Long St, Devizes, Wilts., SN10 1NS; tel. (1380) 727369; fax (1380) 722150; e-mail wanhs@ wiltshireheritage.org.uk; internet wiltshireheritage.org.uk; f. 1853; archaeological and historical collns from Wiltshire, incl. Stonehenge, with emphasis on Bronze Age period; Wiltshire art colln; archives relating to Wiltshire; library of 8,000 vols; Chair. W. A. PERRY; Curator Dr P. H. ROBINSON; Librarian Dr L. HAYCOCK; publ. *Wiltshire Archaeological and Natural History Magazine* (annually).

Doncaster

Doncaster Museum and Art Gallery: Chequer Rd, Doncaster, South Yorks., DN1 2AE; tel. (1302) 734293; fax (1302) 735409; e-mail museum@doncaster.gov.uk; internet www.doncaster.gov.uk/museums; f. 1909; regional natural history, geology, archaeology and local history collections; permanent art collection, paintings, ceramics and glass; Regimental collection of the King's Own Yorkshire Light Infantry; Man. G. PREECE.

Dorchester

Dorset County Museum and Dorset Natural History and Archaeological Society: High West St, Dorchester, Dorset, DT1 1XA; tel. (1305) 262735; fax (1305) 257180; e-mail dorsetcountymuseum@ dor-mus.demon.co.uk; internet www .dorsetcountymuseum.org; f. 1846 (Museum), merged with Society (f. 1875) in 1928; natural history, palaeontology, archaeology, fine arts, geology, literature (incl. Thomas Hardy), and the local history of Dorset; lectures, conferences and seminars are held in the Museum during the first half of the calendar year; Pres. CAROLINE MONTAGU, COUNTESS OF SANDWICH; Dir of the Museum and Sec. to the Society JUDY LINDSAY; publ. *The Proceedings of the Dorset Natural History and Archaeological Society* (annually).

Dumfries

Dumfries Museums: The Observatory, Rotchell Rd, Dumfries, DG2 7SW; tel. (1387) 253374; fax (1387) 265081; e-mail dumfriesmuseum@dumgal.gov.uk; internet www.dumgal.gov.uk/museums; f. 1835 as an observatory; building erected as a windmill *c.* 1790; exhibits Roman relics, Stone and Bronze Age artefacts, natural and local history from Dumfries and Galloway; incorporates Dumfries Museum, Thornhill Museum, Langholm Museum and Myrseth Museum collections; MSS concerning Carlyle and Barrie; camera obscura; period rooms at Old Bridge House (1660) nearby; Robert Burns Centre in Dumfries Town Mill (1781): exhibitions on Burns and his life in South West Scotland; Burns House: period house occupied by Burns 1793–96 and where he died: exhibits incl. MSS, first editions, personal belongings; Sanquhar Museum in Adam-designed Town House (1735) covers local history and geology; Curator ELAINE KENNEDY.

Dundee

Dundee City Council: Leisure and Communities: McManus Art Galleries and Museum, Albert Sq., Dundee, DD1 1DA; tel. (1382) 432350; fax (1382) 432369; e-mail mcmanus.galleries@dundeecity.gov.uk; internet www.dundeecity.gov.uk; f. 1873; McManus Galleries (Victorian Scottish paintings, contemporary art and photography, decorative arts, local history displays from time of earliest settlers to modern era, costume gallery, natural history), Broughty Castle Museum (history of Broughty Ferry, Dundee's whaling industry, natural history of the seashore), Mills Observatory; Arts and Heritage Man. JOHN STEWART-YOUNG.

Durham

Killhope, the North of England Lead Mining Museum: nr Cowshill, Upper Weardale, Co. Durham, DL13 1AR; tel. (1388) 537505; e-mail killhope@durham.gov.uk; internet www.durham.gov.uk/killhope; f. 1984 as Killhope Lead Mining Centre; present name 2000; fully restored 19th c. lead mine; Man. IAN FORBES.

University of Durham, Oriental Museum: Elvet Hill, off South Rd, Durham, DH1 3TH; tel. (191) 334-5694; fax (191) 334-5694; e-mail oriental.museum@durham.ac.uk; internet www.dur.ac.uk/oriental.museum; f. 1960; Duke of Northumberland's colln of Egyptian antiquities; MacDonald colln of Chinese ceramics; Charles Hardinge colln of Chinese jades; Henry de Laszlo colln of Chinese art and other examples of oriental art and archaeology covering Ancient Egypt and the Near East, the Indian sub-continent, Japan and S. E. Asia; Curator CRAIG P. BARCLAY.

Edinburgh

Edinburgh City Museums and Art Galleries: City Art Centre, 2 Market St, Edinburgh, EH1 1DE; tel. (131) 529-3993; fax (131) 529-3977; e-mail cac.admin@edinburgh.gov.uk; internet www.cac.org.uk; comprise Museum of Edinburgh, 142 Canongate (local history), People's Story, Canongate Tolbooth, 163 Canongate (life and work of Edinburgh's people), Museum of Childhood, 42 High St, Writers' Museum, Lawnmarket (collection of Scott, Burns and Stevenson), City Art Centre (museum headquarters), Market St (temporary exhibitions and artists since 19th c.), Lauriston Castle, Cramond Rd South (furniture collection in Edwardian interior), Queensferry Museum, South Queensferry (local history); Newhaven (local history); Brass Rubbing Centre, Chalmers Close, Royal Mile; Head of Museums and Arts LYNNE HALFPENNY.

National Galleries of Scotland: The Mound, Edinburgh, EH2 2EL; tel. (131) 624-6200; fax (131) 623-7126; e-mail enquiries@nationalgalleries.org; internet www.nationalgalleries.org; f. 1859; Dir-Gen. JOHN LEIGHTON; publ. *Bulletin* (describing new acquisitions and exhibitions of the 4 Nat. Galleries, every 2 months).

Constituent galleries:

Dean Gallery: 73 Belford Rd, Edinburgh, EH4 3DS; tel. (131) 624-6200; fax (131) 623-7126; e-mail deaninfo@nationalgalleries.org; internet www.nationalgalleries.org; f. 1999; Paolozzi gift of sculpture and graphic art, works from the Penrose colln; Gabrielle Keiller colln; library and archive; Dir RICHARD CALVO-CORESSI.

National Gallery of Scotland: The Mound, Edinburgh, EH2 2EL; tel. (131) 624-6200; fax (131) 220-0917; e-mail nginfo@nationalgalleries.org; internet www.nationalgalleries.org; f. 1859; European and Scottish paintings etc. up to 1900; also drawings, prints and sculpture; Dir MICHAEL CLARKE.

Royal Scottish Academy: The Mound, Edinburgh, EH2 2EL; tel. (131) 225-6671; fax (131) 220-6016; internet www.royalscottishacademy.org; f. 1826; collns of painting, sculpture and architecture from academicians since 1831; collns of contemporary art; William Gillies colln; library: library of material on fine arts and architecture open by appointment; Pres. IAN MCKENZIE-SMITH.

Scottish National Gallery of Modern Art: 75 Belford Rd, Edinburgh, EH4 3DR; tel. (131) 624-6200; fax (131) 343-2802; e-mail gmainfo@nationalgalleries.org; internet www.nationalgalleries.org; f. 1960; Scottish and European paintings, drawings, prints and sculptures since beginning of 20th century; library of 50,000 vols; Dir RICHARD CALVOCORESSI.

Scottish National Portrait Gallery: 1 Queen St, Edinburgh, EH2 1JD; tel. (131) 624-6200; fax (131) 558-3691; e-mail pginfo@nationalgalleries.org; internet www.nationalgalleries.org; f. 1882; portraits of Scottish historical interest; an extensive reference section of engravings and photographs of portraits; the nat. photography colln; Dir JAMES HOLLOWAY.

National Museums of Scotland: Chambers St, Edinburgh, EH1 1JF; tel. (131) 247-4422; fax (131) 220-4819; e-mail info@nms.ac.uk; internet www.nms.ac.uk; f. 1985; Dir Dr GORDON RINTOUL.

Constituent museums:

Museum of Flight: East Fortune Airfield, East Lothian, EH39 5LF; tel. (1620) 880308; fax (1620) 880355; e-mail info@nms.ac.uk; internet www.nms.ac.uk/flight; collection of aircraft, rockets and aeroengines displayed in the hangars of a former RAF wartime station; houses a decommissioned Concorde aircraft; Curator ALISTAIR DODDS.

Museum of Scotland: Chambers St, Edinburgh, EH1 1JF; tel. (131) 247-4422; fax (131) 220-4819; e-mail info@nms.ac.uk; internet www.nms.ac.uk/scotland; f. 1998; history and geology of Scotland; Dir Dr GORDON RINTOUL.

Museum of Scottish Country Life: Philipshill Rd, Wester Kittochside, East Kilbride, G76 9HR; tel. (131) 247-4377; fax (1355) 571290; e-mail info@nms.ac.uk; internet www.nms.ac.uk/countrylife; f. 2001; includes Georgian farmhouse and a 1950s working farm; Gen. Man. DUNCAN DORNAN.

National War Museum of Scotland: Edinburgh Castle, Edinburgh, EH1 2NG; tel. (131) 247-4413; fax (131) 225-3848; e-mail info@nms.ac.uk; internet www.nms.ac.uk/war; f. 1930; collections covering the Scottish experience of war and military service since 1700; Curator ALLAN CARSWELL.

Royal Museum: Chambers St, Edinburgh, EH1 1JF; tel. (131) 247-4422; fax (131) 220-4819; e-mail info@nms.ac.uk; internet www.nms.ac.uk/royal; f. 1854; international collections covering decorative arts, archaeology, ethnography, natural history, geology, science and technology; Dir Dr GORDON RINTOUL.

Shambellie House Museum of Costume: New Abbey, Dumfriesshire, DG2 8HQ; tel. (1387) 850375; fax (1387) 850461; e-mail info@nms.ac.uk; internet www.nms.ac.uk/costume; f. 1977; 19th c. country house; changing exhibitions of costume from the 1850s–1950s; Man. MARGARET ROBERTS.

Gateshead

BALTIC The Centre for Contemporary Art: South Shore Rd, Gateshead, NE8 3BA; tel. and fax (191) 440-4944; e-mail info@balticmill.com; internet www.balticmill.com; f. 2002; Dir PETER DOROSHENKO (acting).

Glasgow

Glasgow Museums: Cultural and Leisure Services, 20 Trongate, Glasgow, G1 5ES; tel. (141) 271-8310; fax (141) 271-8354; e-mail museums@cls.glasgow.gov.uk; internet www.glasgowmuseums.com; colln displayed in 13 museums across the city of Glasgow; Martyrs' School open by appointment only; Museum Man. HARRY DUNLOP; publ. *Preview Magazine* (quarterly).

Constituent museums:

Burrell Collection: Pollok Country Park, 2060 Pollokshaws Rd, Glasgow G43 1AT; tel. (141) 287-2550; fax (141) 287-2597; e-mail museums@cls.glasgow.gov.uk; internet www.glasgowmuseums.com; f. 1983; colln bequeathed to City of Glasgow by Sir William Burrell 1944; antiquities from Iraq, Egypt, Greece and Italy; Oriental art, incl. Chinese ceramics, bronzes and jades, Japanese prints, Near Eastern carpets, rugs, ceramics and metal work; European decorative arts of 14th–18th centuries including tapestries, stained glass, sculpture, furniture, glass, silver and ceramics; fine art, especially French 19th-century works by Degas, Boudin, Monet and Daumier; Museum Man. MURIEL KING.

Gallery of Modern Art (GOMA): Royal Exchange Sq., Glasgow G1 3AH; tel. (141) 229-1996; fax (141) 204-5316; e-mail museums@cls.glasgow.gov.uk; internet www.glasgowmuseums.com; f. 1996; exhibits work by local, nat. and int. artists; aims to address contemporary social issues through major biannual projects; museum bldg combines old and new architecture and incorporates a number of artists' commissions; Man. VICTORIA HOLLOWS.

Glasgow Museums Resource Centre (GMRC): 200 Woodhead Rd, Nitshill,

Glasgow, G53 7NN; tel. (141) 276-9300; fax (141) 276-9305; e-mail museums@cls .glasgow.gov.uk; internet www .glasgowmuseums.com; f. 2003; publicly accessible store of 200,000 items held by Glasgow's museum service; home of the Open Museum; daily public tours and formal and informal learning programmes; research facilities; Man. CHRISTINE MCLELLAN.

Kelvingrove Art Gallery and Museum: Argyle St, Glasgow, G3 8AG; tel. (141) 287-2699; fax (141) 287-2690; e-mail museums@cls.glasgow.gov.uk; internet www.glasgowmuseums.com; f. 1901; collns incl. Dutch and French Impressionist paintings, Scottish colourists, arms and armour, Charles Rennie Mackintosh and the Glasgow Style, natural history, technology, costume; discovery and study centres; Man. CAROLINE BARR.

McLellan Galleries: 270 Sauchiehall St, Glasgow, G2 3EH; tel. (141) 565-4137; fax (141) 565-4111; e-mail museums@cls .glasgow.gov.uk; internet www .glasgowmuseums.com; f. 1854 to house the colln of Glasgow industrialist and coachmaker Archibald McLellan; closed June 2006; Man. CAROLINE BARR.

Museum of Transport: Kelvin Hall, 1 Bunhouse Rd, Glasgow, G3 8DP; tel. (141) 287-2720; fax (141) 287-2692; e-mail museums@cls.glasgow.gov.uk; internet www.glasgowmuseums.com; f. 1964; history of transport and technology; displays incl. Glasgow trams and buses, Scottish-built cars, commercial vehicles, cycles and motor cycles, railway locomotives, fire engines, horse-drawn vehicles, ship models; toy cars, prams, the oldest surviving pedal cycle in the world and a reproduction of a typical Glasgow street of 1938; Manager LAWRENCE FITZGERALD.

People's Palace and Winter Gardens: Glasgow Green, Glasgow G40 1AT; tel. (141) 271-2962; fax (141) 271-2960; e-mail museums@cls.glasgow.gov.uk; internet www.glasgowmuseums.com; f. 1898; local and social history museum; story of the city of Glasgow and its inhabitants since 1750; the Winter Gardens houses exotic palms and plants; Curator FIONA HAYES.

Pollok House: Pollok Country Park, 2060 Pollokshaws Rd, Glasgow, G43 1AT; tel. (141) 616-6410; fax (141) 616-6521; internet www.nts.org.uk; 18th-century Palladian house with Edwardian additions, furnished c. 1750–1820 and with Stirling Maxwell collection of Spanish and European paintings; managed by the National Trust of Scotland on behalf of Glasgow Museums; Man. ROBERT FERGUSON.

Provand's Lordship: 3 Castle St, Glasgow, G4 0RB; tel. (141) 553-2557; fax (141) 552-4744; e-mail museums@cls.glasgow .gov.uk; internet www.glasgowmuseums .com; built 1471, the oldest house in Glasgow, with period room displays; home to the St Nicholas Garden, a herb garden containing 15th-century medicinal plants, the Tontine Faces (colln of carved stone faces originally carved for the new Town Hall 1740); Man. HARRY DUNLOP.

St Mungo Museum of Religious Life and Art: 2 Castle St, Glasgow, G4 0RH; tel. (141) 553-2557; fax (141) 552-4744; e-mail museums@cls.glasgow.gov.uk; internet www.glasgowmuseums.com; f. 1993; art objects associated with religious faiths; displays on religion in art, world faiths, religion in Scottish history; permanent Zen garden; Man. HARRY DUNLOP.

Scotland Street School Museum: 225 Scotland St, Glasgow, G5 8QB; tel. (141) 287-0500; fax (141) 287-0515; e-mail museums@cls.glasgow.gov.uk; internet www.glasgowmuseums.com; f. 1906; designed by Charles Rennie Mackintosh between 1903 and 1906; history of Scotland Street Public School, and developments in education in Scotland; reconstructed classrooms from the Victorian period, World War II, the 1950s and 1960s; colln of old school photographs; Man. CAROLINE BARR.

Hunterian Museum and Art Gallery: University of Glasgow Main/Gilbert-Scott Bldg, University Ave, Glasgow, G12 8QQ; tel. (141) 330-4221; fax (141) 330-3617; e-mail hunter@museum.gla.ac.uk; internet www.hunterian.gla.ac.uk; f. 1807; based around the collns of the surgeon extraordinary to Queen Charlotte, William Hunter (1718–1783); geological, prehistoric, Roman, ethnographical and coin collns, scientific instruments; zoological, anatomical and pathological collns in university depts of Zoology, Anatomy and Pathology; books and MSS in university library; main hall closed for refurbishment until 2007; Dir EWEN SMITH.

Attached gallery:

Hunterian Art Gallery: University of Glasgow, 82 Hillhead St, Glasgow, G12 8QQ; tel. (141) 330-5431; fax (141) 330-3618; e-mail hunter@museum.gla.ac.uk; internet www.gla.ac.uk/museum/; f. 1980; collections of C. R. Mackintosh and J. M. Whistler; works by Chardin, Stubbs and Reynolds; Scottish painting since 18th c.; Old Master and modern prints; Dir EWEN SMITH.

Gloucester

City Museum and Art Gallery: Brunswick Rd, Gloucester, GL1 1HP; tel. (1452) 396131; fax (1452) 410898; e-mail city.museum@ gloucester.gov.uk; internet www.gloucester .gov.uk; f. 1859; natural history, archaeology (before 1500AD), fine and applied art; temporary art, science, archaeology, natural sciences and textile exhibitions; collns online at livinggloucester.co.uk.

Gloucester Folk Museum: 99–103 Westgate St, Gloucester, GL1 2PG; tel. (1452) 396868; fax (1452) 330495; e-mail folk .museum@gloucester.gov.uk; internet www .gloucester.gov.uk/folkmuseum; f. 1935; local history, crafts, trades and industries of City and County of Gloucester since 1500; housed in Tudor and Jacobean timber-framed buildings with new extensions; regular special exhibitions, activities and events; social history reference colln (access by appointment); Man. CHRIS MORRIS.

Grasmere

Dove Cottage and the Wordsworth Museum, The Wordsworth Trust (Centre for British Romanticism): Dove Cottage, Grasmere, Ambleside, Cumbria, LA22 9SH; tel. (15394) 35544; fax (15394) 35748; internet www.wordsworth.org.uk; f. 1890; fmr home of William and Dorothy Wordsworth and, later, of Thomas de Quincey; contains original furniture and personal effects, and a museum containing MSS, books, paintings, objects relating to the poet, and to Grasmere life of the period; library: major research library for the Romantic period; access by appointment; Dir and Chief Exec. DAVID WILSON; publ. *Friends of the Wordsworth Trust—Newsletter* (quarterly).

Grays

Thurrock Museum: Thameside Complex, Orsett Rd, Grays, Essex, RM17 5DX; tel.

(1375) 385484; fax (1375) 392666; e-mail thurrock.museum@thurrock.gov.uk; internet www.thurrock.gov.uk/museum; f. 1956; archaeology and history of Thurrock with accent on the growth of technology in a Thameside landscape; Deputy Curator T. CARNEY.

Haverfordwest

Pembrokeshire Museum Service: The County Library, Dew St, Haverfordwest, Pembs., SA61 1SU; tel. (1437) 779500; fax (1437) 779500; internet www.pembrokeshire .gov.uk; f. 1967; Museums Officer NICK SUFFOLK.

Attached museums:

Penrhos Cottage: Pembrokeshire Museum Service, The County Library, Dew St, Haverfordwest, Pembs., SA61 1SU; Located at: Llanycefn, Clunderwen; tel. (1437) 779500; fax (1437) 779500; f. 1971; traditional thatched Welsh cottage with original furniture; open by appointment only; Museums Officer NICK SUFFOLK.

Scolton Manor Museum: Spittal, Haverfordwest; tel. (1437) 731328; fax (1437) 779500; f. 1972; regional history of Pembrokeshire; includes period rooms in early Victorian manor, World War II exhibition, railway exhibits, geology, river fishing, coal mining, servant life, costume; history of the domestic iron; Museums Officer NICK SUFFOLK.

High Wycombe

Disraeli Museum: Hughenden Manor, High Wycombe, Bucks., HP14 4LA; tel. (1494) 755573; fax (1494) 474284; e-mail hughenden@nationaltrust.org.uk; internet www.nationaltrust.org.uk; f. 1947; contains Disraeli's books, furniture, paintings and personal effects; property of the National Trust (q.v); library of 4,000 vols; Property Man. NICK PHILLIPS; Regional Curator CHARLES PUGH.

Huddersfield

Tolson Memorial Museum: Ravensknowle Park, Wakefield Rd, Huddersfield, HD5 8DJ, West Yorks; tel. (1484) 223830; fax (1484) 223843; e-mail tolson.museum@kirklees.gov .uk; f. 1922; illustrates natural and human history of the district; prehistory, folk-life, development of woollen industry, collection of vehicles.

Ironbridge

Ironbridge Gorge Museums: Coach Rd, Coalbrookdale, Shropshire, TF8 7DQ; tel. (1952) 884391; fax (1952) 435999; e-mail information@ironbridge.org.uk; internet www.ironbridge.org.uk; f. 1968; explains and interpret the industrial and social history of the East Shropshire Coalfield, regarded as the 'Birthplace of the Industrial Revolution'; 6-mile site on the River Severn comprising: Coalbrookdale Museum of Iron and Darby Furnace, Ironbridge with the Museum of the Gorge, the world's first Iron Bridge (built 1779), Blists Hill Victorian Town, Coalport China Museum, Jackfield Tile Museum, Ironbridge Institute at Coalbrookdale, Rosehill and Dale House (restored home of the Darby family), Tar Tunnel (200-year-old source of natural bitumen), Broseley Pipeworks, 'Enginuity' (engineering and technological exhibits); designated a World Heritage Site by UNESCO; library of 50,000 vols; Chief Exec. (vacant).

Kendal

Abbot Hall Art Gallery and Museum of Lakeland Life: Kendal, Cumbria, LA9 5AL; tel. (1539) 722464; fax (1539) 722494; e-mail info@abbothall.org.uk; internet www .abbothall.org.uk; f. 1962 (gallery), 1971 (museum); gallery provides changing exhibitions of local and international interest; houses permanent collections of 18th c. furniture, paintings and *objets d'art*, modern paintings, sculpture and drawings; museum features the working and social life of the area; Arthur Ransome Room; Captain Flint's Locker; Dir EDWARD KING.

Attached museum:

Blackwell–The Arts and Crafts House: Bowness-on-Windermere, Cumbria, LA23 3JR; tel. (1539) 446139; fax (1539) 488486; e-mail info@blackwell.org.uk; internet www.blackwell.org.uk; f. 2001; bldg designed by Baillie Scott and built 1898-1900; period house with Arts and Crafts interiors and exhibitions of historic and contemporary crafts; Dir EDWARD KING.

Kendal Museum of Natural History and Archaeology: Station Rd, Kendal, LA9 6BT; tel. (1539) 721374; fax (1539) 737976; internet www.visitcumbria.com/sl/kennhm .htm; f. 1796; Westmorland Gallery of local history and archaeology, World Wildlife gallery, Natural History gallery of geology, flora and fauna of the district; Dir (vacant).

Kirkcaldy

Kirkcaldy Museum and Art Gallery: War Memorial Gardens, Kirkcaldy, Fife, KY1 1YG; tel. (1592) 583213; e-mail kirkcaldy .museum@fife.gov.uk; internet www .fifedirect.org.uk/museums; f. 1925; local history, archaeology, earth and natural sciences, industrial history, decorative arts, costume, ceramics; Scottish paintings since 19th century; Museums Co ordinator DALLAS MECHAN.

Leeds

Leeds Museums and Galleries: 7th Fl., Merrion House, Leeds, LS2 8DT; tel. (113) 247-7241; fax (113) 247-7747; e-mail tim .corum@leeds.gov.uk; internet www.leeds .gov.uk; f. 1820; Dir TIM CORUM; publ. *Museums and Galleries Review* (annually).

Selected museums and galleries:

Abbey House Museum: Abbey Walk, Kirkstall, Leeds, LS5 3EH; tel. (113) 230-5492; fax (113) 230-5499; e-mail abbey .house@leeds.gov.uk; internet www.leeds .gov.uk/abbeyhouse; f. 1927; gatehouse of Kirkstall Abbey (www.leeds.gov.uk/kirk-stallabbey), recreation of Victorian Leeds; Curator SAMANTHA FLAVIN.

Armley Mills (Leeds Industrial Museum): Canal Rd, Armley, Leeds, LS12 2QF; tel. (113) 263-7861; fax (113) 263-7861; e-mail armley.mills@leeds.gov .uk; internet www.leeds.gov.uk/ armleymills; f. 1969; textiles, printing, cinematography, history of engine and locomotive manufacturing in Leeds; manager's and mill-workers' houses; Senior Curator (vacant).

Leeds City Art Gallery: The Headrow, Leeds, LS1 3AA; tel. (113) 247-8248; e-mail city.art.gallery@leeds.gov.uk; internet www.leeds.gov.uk/artgallery; f. 1888; 19th-century English and European paintings; early English watercolours, including Kitson and Lupton collns; modern paintings and sculpture; library: Print Room and Art Library; linked with Henry Moore Institute Archive and Library supporting the study of sculpture; Curator (vacant).

Lotherton Hall: Lotherton Lane, Aberford, Leeds, LS25 3EB; tel. (113) 281-3259; fax (113) 281-2100; internet www.leeds.gov .uk/lothertonhall; f. 1969; country house dating from the 19th and 20th centuries; Gascoigne Colln of furniture, silver, cera-

mics, costume and paintings from the 17th to 19th centuries; modern crafts; oriental gallery; Curator ADAM WHITE.

Temple Newsam House: Temple Newsam Rd, off Selby Rd, Leeds, LS15 0AE; tel. (113) 264-5535; fax (113) 260-2285; e-mail temple.newsam@leeds.gov.uk; internet www.leeds.gov.uk/temple .newsam; f. 1923; Tudor-Stuart house, birthplace of Lord Darnley; contains extensive collns of old master and Ingram family paintings and the decorative arts; Curators ANTHONY WELLS-COLE, JAMES LOMAX.

Royal Armouries Museum: Armouries Drive, Leeds, LS10 1LT; tel. (113) 220-1999; fax (113) 220-1955; e-mail enquiries@ armouries.org.uk; internet www .royalarmouries.org; f. 1996; nat. colln of arms and armour; Chief Executive PAUL EVANS; publ. *Arms and Armour: Journal of the Royal Armouries*.

Leicester

Leicestershire Museums: Community Services Dept, Leicester County Council, Leicester Rd, Glenfield, Leicester, LE3 8TB; tel. (116) 265-6783; fax (116) 265-6844; e-mail museums@leics.gov.uk; internet www.leics .gov.uk/museums; f. 1849; local museums include Charnwood Museum, Donington-le-Heath Manor House, Harborough Museum, Melton Carnegie Museum, Snibston Discovery Park and the Record Office at Wigston Magna; Leicester 'Open Museum' comprises exhibits for hire within the county; museums concentrate on archaeology, natural life, cultural life, working life, Leicestershire history and education; Head H. E. BROUGHTON.

National Space Centre: Exploration Dr., Leicester, LE4 5NS; fax (116) 261-0261; e-mail info@spacecentre.co.uk; internet www.spacecentre.co.uk; f. 2001; displays about space and space exploration; incl. space science research unit; Chief Exec. CHAS BISHOP.

Lincoln

Lincolnshire Heritage Services: Cultural Services Branch, Lincolnshire County Council Offices, Newland, Lincoln, LN1 1YQ; tel. (1522) 552222; e-mail education@lincolnshire .gov.uk; internet www.lincolnshire.gov.uk; f. 1974; operates 6 museums (see below) and several other sites, incl. Lincoln Castle, Judges Lodgings, Battle of Britain Memorial Flight Visitor Centre, Lincolnshire Archives, and windmills in Alford, Burgh le Marsh, Heckington and Lincoln; Head of Heritage and Regeneration HEATHER CUMMINS.

Attached museums:

Church Farm Museum: Church Rd South, Skegness, Lincs., PE25 2HF; tel. (1754) 766658; fax (1754) 898243; e-mail churchfarmmuseum@lincolnshire.gov.uk; f. 1976; a complex of 18th- and 19th-century farmhouse and agricultural bldgs with displays of agricultural equipment typical of the area; farmhouse furnished to period c. 1900; Principal Keeper MATT STEPHENS.

The Collection: Art and Archaeology in Lincolnshire: Danes Terrace, Lincoln, LN2 1LP; tel. (1522) 550990; fax (1522) 550991; e-mail thecollection@lincolnshire .gov.uk; comprises exhibits from the former City and County Museum (artefacts since medieval era, incl. collns of coins, medals, arms and natural science) and the Usher Gallery (fine, decorative and contemporary arts); Senior Keeper ANDREA MARTIN.

Gainsborough Old Hall: Parnell St, Gainsborough, Lincs., DN21 2NB; tel.

(1427) 612669; fax (1427) 612779; e-mail gainsborougholdhall@lincolnshire.gov.uk; f. 1974; 15th-century manor house with great hall, medieval kitchen; Principal Keeper SUSAN SCOTT.

Grantham Museum: St Peter's Hill, Grantham, Lincs., NG31 6PY; tel. (1476) 568782; fax (1476) 592457; e-mail grantham.museum@lincolnshire.gov.uk; f. 1923; local prehistoric artefacts, Roman and Saxon archaeology, Grantham local history, trades and industries, display of Victorian dolls, and a colln devoted to notable figures born locally, incl. Sir Isaac Newton and Margaret Thatcher; Principal Keeper RON FRAYNE.

Museum of Lincolnshire Life: Burton Rd, Lincoln, LN1 3LY; tel. (1522) 528448; fax (1522) 521264; e-mail lincolnshire_museum@lincolnshire.gov.uk; f. 1969; displays illustrating the social, agricultural and industrial history of Lincolnshire over the 17th–20th centuries; also contains Lincolnshire Regiment Museum; manages the Ellis Windmill; Principal Keeper JANET EDMOND.

Stamford Museum: Broad St, Stamford, Lincs., PE9 1PJ; tel. (1780) 766317; fax (1780) 480363; e-mail stamford_museum@ lincolnshire.gov.uk; f. 1980; local archaeology and history incl. Stamford Ware pottery, the visit of Daniel Lambert and the Stamford Tapestry; Principal Keeper TRACEY CRAWLEY.

Usher Gallery: Lindum Rd, Lincoln, LN2 1NN; tel. (1522) 527980; fax (1522) 550991; e-mail usher.gallery@lincolnshire.gov.uk; internet www.thecollection.lincoln .museum; houses the Usher colln of watches, miniatures and decorative art, and a colln of fine art, sculpture and coins, incl. works by De Wint, Lowry, Turner and contemporary artists Grayson Perry and Terry Frost; attached to The Collection (county archaeological collns; see above); Area Service Man. JEREMY WEBSTER.

Liverpool

National Museums Liverpool: internet www.liverpoolmuseums.org.uk; f. 1986 as National Museums and Galleries on Merseyside; present name 2003; groups the 7 museums of Liverpool; Chair. of Board of Trustees LOYD GROSSMAN; Dir DAVID FLEMING.

Constituent Museums and Galleries:

Conservation Centre: Whitechapel, Liverpool, L1 6HZ; tel. (151) 478-4999; internet www.liverpoolmuseums.org.uk/ conservation; f. 1996; illustrates the arts and science of the conservation of museum exhibits; depts of ceramics, conservation science, frames, metals, organics, paintings, paper, sculpture, shipkeeping, taxidermy and textiles; Head of Conservation SALLY ANN YATES.

HM Customs and Excise National Museum: Albert Dock, Liverpool, L3 4AQ; tel. (151) 478-4499; internet www .liverpoolmuseums.org.uk/customs; f. 1994; exhibits relating to smuggling and revenue collection since 1700; holds national colln of Dept of Customs and Excise; displays of equipment, prints, paintings and photographs.

Lady Lever Art Gallery: Port Sunlight Village, Wirral, CH62 5EQ; tel. (151) 478-4136; fax (151) 478-4140; internet www .liverpoolmuseums.org.uk/ladylever; f. 1922; colln of English 18th and 19th c. paintings and furniture, Chinese porcelain, Wedgwood pottery and Victorian paintings.

Merseyside Maritime Museum: Albert Dock, Liverpool, L3 4AQ; tel. (151) 478-4499; fax (151) 478-4590; internet www .liverpoolmuseums.org.uk/maritime; f. 1980; set in Liverpool's docklands; displays and exhibits on the region's maritime past; gallery of maritime paintings; library: reference library of maritime material, incl. archives and records.

Sudley House: Mossley Hill Rd, Liverpool; tel. (151) 724-3245; internet www .sudleyhouse.org.uk; f. 1986; fmr home of 19th c. shipowner; 18th and 19th c. art including works by Gainsborough, Landseer and artists of the Pre-Raphaelite movement; closed to the public until 2007; Keeper of Art Galleries JULIAN TREUHERZ.

Walker Art Gallery: William Brown St, Liverpool, L3 8EL; tel. (151) 478-4199; fax (151) 478-4190; internet www .liverpoolmuseums.org.uk/walker; collns of European art since 1300; sculpture gallery; Keeper JULIAN TREUHERZ.

World Museum Liverpool: William Brown St, Liverpool, L3 8EN; tel. (151) 478-4399; fax (151) 478-4390; internet www.liverpoolmuseums.org.uk/wml; f. 1851, rebuilt 1964–69; present name 2005; special collns include the Mayer-Fejérvàry Gothic ivories, the Bryan Fausset group of Anglo-Saxon antiquities, the Lord Derby and Tristram ornithological collections; Vivarium, Aquarium, Historic Transport, Archaeology, Ethnology, Time and Space Gallery, Planetarium, National History Centre; Keeper JOHN MILLARD.

London

Bank of England Museum: Threadneedle St, London, EC2R 8AH; tel. (20) 7601-5545; fax (20) 7601-5808; e-mail museum@ bankofengland.co.uk; internet www .bankofengland.co.uk/education/museum; f. 1988; illustrates the history of the Bank and its current work; collns incl. banknotes and coins, furniture, pictures and photographs, silver; Curator JOHN KEYWORTH.

British Museum: Great Russell St, London, WC1B 3DG; tel. (20) 7323-8000; e-mail information@thebritishmuseum.ac.uk; internet www.thebritishmuseum.ac.uk; f. 1753 in pursuance of the will of Sir Hans Sloane, and with the addition of the Cottonian and Harleian Libraries; opened 1759, present bldgs begun 1823, completed 1852; collns and exhibitions of prehistoric, Egyptian, Assyrian, medieval, oriental and other archaeological collns, ethnography, prints, drawings, ceramics, coins, medals and banknotes; many catalogues and reproductions are published; Chair. of Board of Trustees NIALL FITZGERALD; Dir NEIL MACGREGOR; Keepers of Depts JONATHAN KING (Africa, Oceania and the Americas), VIVIAN DAVIES (Ancient Egypt and Sudan), Dr JOHN CURTIS (Ancient Near East), JAN STUART (Asia), JOE CRIBB (Coins and Medals), DAVID SAUNDERS (Conservation, Documentation and Scientific Research), Dr DYFRI WILLIAMS (Greek and Roman Antiquities), JONATHAN WILLIAMS (Prehistory and Europe), ANTHONY GRIFFITHS (Prints and Drawings).

British Postal Museum and Archive: Freeling House, Phoenix Place, London, WC1X 0DL; tel. (20) 7239-2570; fax (20) 7239-2576; e-mail info@postalheritage.org .uk; internet www.postalheritage.org.uk; f. 1966; collection of stamps, essays, drawings and official documents dating back to Rowland Hill's proposals for Uniform Penny Postage in 1837–39; also the Post Office collection of stamps of the world and of British stamps since early 20th c., and the

philatelic archives (1855–1965) of Thomas De La Rue and Co., security printers, on microfilm; postboxes and other postal exhibits; Chief Executive Officer TONY CONDER.

Carlyle's House: 24 Cheyne Row, Chelsea, London, SW3 5HL; tel. (20) 7352-7087; e-mail carlyleshouse@nationaltrust.org.uk; built 1708; occupied by the Victorian writer, Thomas Carlyle (1834–81) and his wife; National Trust property; contains books, paintings, furniture, and personal relics.

Courtauld Institute Gallery: Courtauld Institute of Art, Somerset House, Strand, London, WC2R 0RN; tel. (20) 7848-2526; fax (20) 7848-2589; e-mail galleryinfo@courtauld .ac.uk; internet www.courtauld.ac.uk/ gallery; f. 1932; Old Master, Impressionist and Post-Impressionist paintings, prints and drawings, (incl. works by Botticelli, Cézanne, Goya, Manet, Michelangelo, Rembrandt, Renoir, Rubens, Tiepolo, Turner and Van Gogh); sculpture and applied arts; Senior Curator Dr ERNST VEGELIN.

Cuming Museum (Borough of Southwark): 151 Walworth Rd, London, SE17 1RS; tel. (20) 7525-2332; fax (20) 7525-2345; e-mail cuming.museum@southwark.gov.uk; internet www.southwark.gov.uk; f. 1906; worldwide collections of the Cuming family joined with the local history of Southwark, from Roman times to the present; Cllns Man. CATHERINE HAMILTON.

Design Museum: Butler's Wharf, 28 Shad Thames, London, SE1 2YD; tel. (20) 7403-6933; fax (20) 7378-6540; internet www .designmuseum.org; f. 1981; ind. museum set up by the Conran Foundation, to promote awareness of the importance of design in education, industry, commerce and culture; colln of mass-produced design; Chair. LUQMAN ARNOLD; Dir (vacant).

Dulwich Picture Gallery: Gallery Rd, London, SE21 7AD; tel. (20) 8693-5254; fax (20) 8299-8700; e-mail info@ dulwichpicturegallery.org.uk; internet www .dulwichpicturegallery.org.uk; f. 1811; built 1814 by Sir John Soane to house collection of Old Masters including Rembrandt, Rubens, Cuyp, Van Dyck, Teniers, Poussin, Claude, Watteau, Raphael, Tiepolo, Gainsborough, Murillo, etc.; schedule of temporary exhibitions and educational activities; Dir IAN DEJARDIN.

Estorick Collection of Modern Italian Art: 39A Canonbury Sq., London, N1 2AN; tel. (20) 7704-9522; fax (20) 7704-9531; e-mail curator@estorickcollection.com; internet www.estorickcollection.com; f. 1998; 20th-century Italian art, especially Futurist; also sculpture; library of 2,000 vols, periodicals and catalogues: library open by appointment; Dir ROBERTA CREMONCINI.

Fashion and Textile Museum: 83 Bermondsey St, London, SE1 3XF; tel. (20) 7407-8664; fax (20) 7403-0555; e-mail info@ ftmlondon.org; internet www.ftmlondon.org; f. 2003; British and world fashion and textile design.

Foundling Museum: 40 Brunswick Square, London, WC1N 1AZ; tel. (20) 7841-3600; fax (20) 7841-3601; e-mail enquiries@ foundlingmuseum.org.uk; internet www .foundlingmuseum.org.uk; f. 2004; documents the history of the Foundling Hospital (f. 1739), London's first home for abandoned children, and of its founder, Thomas Coram (1697–1764); permanent exhibition of art and social history; Gerald Coke Handel Collection; Dir RHIAN HARRIS.

Freud Museum: 20 Maresfield Gardens, London, NW3 5SX; tel. (20) 7435-2002; fax (20) 7431-5452; e-mail info@freud.org.uk;

internet www.freud.org.uk; f. 1986; fmr London home of Sigmund Freud and his daughter Anna; incl. Sigmund Freud's colln of antiquities, including 1,500 Egyptian, Greek, Roman and Oriental antiquities; his psychoanalytical couch, library and furniture; also a psychoanalysis research center; library of 1,600 vols from Sigmund Freud's colln; reference library relating to the history of psychoanalysis; archive containing Freud family documents and photographs; Dir MICHAEL MOLNAR; Librarian KEITH DAVIES.

Geffrye Museum: 136 Kingsland Rd, London, E2 8EA; tel. (20) 7739-9893; fax (20) 7729-5647; e-mail info@geffrye-museum.org .uk; internet www.geffrye-museum.org.uk; f. 1914; English furniture, textiles, domestic objects and paintings arranged in a series of period rooms from 1600; herb and period gardens; library: reference library of books and periodicals on the arts and social history; Dir DAVID DEWING.

Hampton Court Palace: Surrey, KT8 9AU; tel. (870) 751-5175; internet www.hrp.org.uk; contains a collection of paintings and tapestries, including Andrea Mantegna's nine great tempera paintings of 'The Triumphs of Julius Caesar'; Palace Dir RODNEY GIDDINS; Superintendent of the Royal Collection C. STEVENS.

Hayward Gallery: South Bank Centre, Belvedere Rd, London, SE1 8XZ; tel. (20) 7921-08138; fax (20) 7401-2664; e-mail hginfo@hayward.org.uk; internet www .hayward.org.uk; f. 1968; contemporary perspectives on art past and present, focusing on individual artists, historical themes and artistic movements, other cultures, and contemporary art; administers national touring exhibitions and the Arts Council Collection (7,500 items); Dir CAROLINE FELTON (acting).

Horniman Museum and Gardens: 100 London Rd, Forest Hill, London, SE23 3PQ; tel. (20) 8699-1872; fax (20) 8291-5506; e-mail enquiry@horniman.ac.uk; internet www.horniman.ac.uk; f. 1901; three major collns: ethnography, natural history and musical instruments (incl. archive documents); Aquarium; 16 acres of gardens; library of 35,000 vols, mainly on African history, entomology, botany, ethnography, natural history and musical instruments; Dir JANET VITMAYER.

Hunterian Museum at the Royal College of Surgeons: 35–43 Lincoln's Inn Fields, London, WC2A 3PE; tel. (20) 7869-6560; fax (20) 7869-6564; e-mail museums@rcseng.ac .uk; internet www.rcseng.ac.uk/museums; f. 1800, built around the colln of anatomist and surgeon John Hunter (1728–1793); collns of comparative anatomy and pathology specimens, skeletons, skulls and teeth, teaching models, historical surgical and dental instruments, paintings, drawings and sculpture; temporary exhibitions, lectures, family events and educational workshops; Keeper of the College Collections STELLA MASON; Senior Curator SIMON CHAPLIN; Head of Conservation Unit MARTYN COOKE.

Imperial War Museum: Lambeth Rd, London, SE1 6HZ; tel. (20) 7416-5321; fax (20) 7416-5374; e-mail mail@iwm.org.uk; internet www.iwm.org.uk; f. in 1917, to illustrate and record the operations in which the Armed Forces of the British Commonwealth have been engaged since 1914; nat. museum and picture gallery; contains many exhibits on all aspects of war, incl. 19,000 works of art, 6m. photographs, 120m. ft of film and 46,000 hours of sound and video recordings; library of 270,000 items, incl. pamphlets, periodicals, maps and drawings; Chair. of the Board of Trustees Sir PETER SQUIRE; Dir-Gen. ROBERT

CRAWFORD; publ. *Imperial War Museum Review* (annual).
Branches:

Cabinet War Rooms: Clive Steps, King Charles St, London, SW1A 2AQ; tel. (20) 7930-6961; fax (20) 7839-5897; e-mail cwr@iwm.org.uk; internet cwr.iwm.org.uk; Churchill's underground headquarters; incorporates the Churchill Museum (churchillmuseum.iwm.org.uk), exploring the life of Winston Churchill (1874–1965); Dir P. REED.

HMS Belfast: Morgans Lane, Tooley St, London, SE1 2JH; tel. (20) 7940-6300; fax (20) 7403-0719; internet hmsbelfast.iwm.org.uk; Second World War cruiser moored in the Pool of London; Dir E. J. WENZEL.

Imperial War Museum Duxford: Duxford, Cambridge, CB2 4QR; tel. (1223) 835000; e-mail duxford@iwm.org.uk; internet duxford.iwm.org.uk; f. 1977; airfield which featured in the Battle of Britain (1940), housing historic colln of aircraft, military vehicles, tanks and artillery; incl. American Air Museum (aam.iwm.org.uk); Dir RICHARD ASHTON.

Imperial War Museum North: The Quays, Trafford Wharf, Trafford Park, Manchester, M17 1TZ; tel. (161) 836-4000; fax (161) 836-4012; e-mail iwmnorth@iwm.org.uk; internet north.iwm.org.uk; f. 2002; war and its impact on the 20th and 21st centuries, through exhibits, audiovisual shows and interactive exhibits; Dir JIM FORRESTER.

Iveagh Bequest: Kenwood, Hampstead Lane, London, NW3 7JR; tel. (20) 8348-1286; left to the nation by Edward Cecil Guinness, first Earl of Iveagh, in 1927; includes paintings of British, Dutch, Flemish and French Schools, housed in an 18th c. mansion (Kenwood House) designed by Robert Adam, containing an ornate library; exhibitions on aspects of 18th c. art; Admin. Trustee English Heritage (HBMC); Dir of E.H. London Region REBECCA KANE; publs catalogues.

Livesey Museum for Children: 682 Old Kent Rd, London, SE15 1JF; tel. (20) 7635-5829; fax (20) 7277-5384; e-mail livesey.museum@southwark.gov.uk; internet www.liveseymuseum.org.uk; f. 1974; annual interactive exhibition for children under 12 on a variety of themes; Exhibitions and Museum Man. THERESA DHALIWAL.

London Transport Museum: 39 Wellington St, Covent Garden, London, WC2E 7BB; tel. (20) 7379-6344; fax (20) 7565-7254; e-mail enquiry@ltmuseum.co.uk; internet www.ltmuseum.co.uk; f. 1978, opened on present site 1980; governing body: Transport for London; conserves and explains London's transport heritage; exhibits of vehicles, posters, equipment, uniforms, film and video recordings, maps, signs and models; film and photo library; museum closed until autumn 2007; library of 12,000 vols on London's transport and associated art, architecture and design; Dir SAM MULLINS; publ. *Annual Report*.

Museum of London: London Wall, London, EC2Y 5HN; tel. (870) 444-3850; fax (870) 444-3853; e-mail info@museumoflondon.org.uk; internet www.museum-london.org.uk; formed from amalgamation of London Museum and Guildhall Museum; social history of London from prehistory to 20th century; exhibits include the Lord Mayor's coach, 18th-century prison cell, Victorian shop fronts; Chair. of Board of Govs MICHAEL CASSIDY; Dir Prof. JACK LOHMAN.

National Army Museum: Royal Hospital Rd, Chelsea, London, SW3 4HT; tel. (20) 7730-0717; fax (20) 7823-6573; e-mail info@national-museum.ac.uk; internet www.national-army-museum.ac.uk; f. 1960; displays depicting the history of the British Army since 1485, the Indian Army until Independence in 1947, and colonial land forces; reference collections of 43,000 books, 30,000 pamphlets, 1,000 ft of archives, 40,000 prints and drawings, 1,000,000 photographs; uniforms including decorations and badges; weapons; painting, silver, china, models; personal relics; Dir Dr ALAN J. GUY.

National Gallery: Trafalgar Square, London, WC2N 5DN; tel. (20) 7747-2885; fax (20) 7747-2423; e-mail information@ng-london.org.uk; internet www.nationalgallery.org.uk; f. 1824; contains examples of all the principal schools of Western European painting from 1250 to 1900; a selection of British painters from Hogarth to Turner; guided tours and public lectures; picture library; Chair. PETER SCOTT; Senior Curator DAVID JAFFÉ; Dir of Collections SUSAN FOISTER; Dir of Conservation MARTIN WYLD; Dir of Scientific Research Dr ASHOK ROY.

National Maritime Museum: Park Row, Greenwich, London, SE10 9NF; tel. (20) 8858-6516; fax (20) 8312-6599; internet www.nmm.ac.uk; f. 1934; established 1934, opened 1937; illustrates British maritime history; the collection includes portraits and sea pieces, models, ship's plans, instruments, maps and charts, weapons, medals, a library of books and MSS; photo library of 330,000 images and negatives; Queen's House: 17th c. royal apartments of Queen Henrietta Maria; also the Royal Observatory Greenwich, where the displays illustrate themes concerned with astronomy, time and navigation, the meridian line, and a planetarium; library: library of 20,000 vols on maritime history; Dir ROY CLARE; publ. *Journal for Maritime Research*.

National Portrait Gallery: St Martin's Pl., London, WC2H 0HE; tel. (20) 7306-0055; fax (20) 7306 0056; internet www.npg.org.uk; f. 1856; portraits of the most eminent people in British history; library of 40,000 vols; Dir SANDY NAIRNE; Chair. of Trustees Prof. DAVID CANNADINE.

Natural History Museum: Cromwell Rd, South Kensington, London, SW7 5BD; tel. (20) 7942-5000; internet www.nhm.ac.uk; originates from the Natural History Depts of the British Museum, and a br. comprising the Natural History Museum at Tring, Herts; separate instn 1963; incorporates the Geological Museum; library: see Libraries and Archives; Chair. of the Board of Trustees OLIVER STOCKEN; Dir Dr MICHAEL DIXON; Science Dir RICHARD PAUL LANE; Keeper of Botany Dr JOHANNES VOGEL; Keeper of Entomology Dr MALCOLM SCOBLE; Keeper of Mineralogy Dr ANDREW FLEET; Keeper of Palaeontology Prof. NORMAN MACLEOD; Keeper of Zoology Prof. PHIL RAINBOW.

Polish Institute and Sikorski Museum: 20 Princes Gate, London, SW7 1PT; tel. (20) 7589-9249; f. 1945; archives, museum, research centre and publishing house; includes the Sikorski Collection (personal belongings, memorabilia, wartime diary, etc. of Gen. Wladyslaw Sikorski, 1881–1943), militaria (over 10,000 items), maps, paintings and engravings, sculptures, porcelain, miniatures, coins and medals.

Royal Academy of Arts: Burlington House, Piccadilly, London, W1J 0BD; tel. (20) 7300-8000; internet www.royalacademy.org.uk; f. 1768 by Joshua Reynolds, first President of the Academy; permanent colln includes works by Turner, Gainsborough, Reynolds and Hockney; temporary exhibitions of works borrowed from major instns worldwide; Pres. Sir NICHOLAS GRIMSHAW.

Royal Air Force Museum: Grahame Park Way, London, NW9 5LL; tel. (20) 8205-2266; fax (20) 8200-1751; e-mail london@rafmuseum.org; internet www.rafmuseum.org.uk; f. 1963, opened 1972; grant-aided through the Ministry of Defence; exhibits 100 full-size British and foreign aircraft from 1909 to the present day, together with supporting material recording the history of the Royal Air Force and the development of aviation generally; activities cover many aspects of aviation, including military, civil, artistic, scientific, industrial and political; br. at Cosford (West Midlands); library of 100,000 vols, and archives and photographic collection; Dir Dr MICHAEL FOPP.

Royal Armouries: HM Tower of London, London, EC3N 4AB; tel. (20) 7480-6358; fax (20) 7481-2922; e-mail enquiries@armouries.org.uk; internet www.royalarmouries.org and Royal Armouries Museum, Armouries Drive, Leeds, W. Yorks., LS10 1LT; tel. (113) 220-1999; fax (113) 220-1995 and Artillery Collection, Fort Nelson, Down End Rd, Portsdown Hill, Fareham, PO17 6AN; tel. (1329) 233734; fax (1329) 822092; the nat. museum of arms and armour and museum of the Tower of London, originating from the working arsenal at the Tower and the collection of royal armours begun by Henry VIII; first open to the public c. 1660; the national and royal collections cover the development of arms and armour since c. 1000; Leeds-based picture library of 167,000 prints, transparencies and slides; archives relating to the history of the museum and the Royal Small Arms Factory; library: Leeds-based reference library of 40,000 vols; also libraries at the Tower of London and Fort Nelson; Chief Exec. PAUL EVANS; Chair. ANN GREEN; Museum Dir PETER ARMSTRONG; publ. *Arms and Armour* (2 a year).

Royal College of Music Museum of Instruments: Prince Consort Rd, South Kensington, London, SW7 2BS; tel. (20) 7591-4842; fax (20) 7589-7740; e-mail museum@rcm.ac.uk; internet www.cph.rcm.ac.uk; f. 1970; colln of instruments and accessories since 1480, incl. Donaldson, Tagore, Hipkins, Ridley, Hartley, Fleming, Walton and Steele-Perkins collns; Curator JENNY NEX.

Royal Institution of Great Britain Faraday Museum: 21 Albemarle St, London, W1S 4BS; tel. (20) 7409-2992; fax (20) 7629-3569; e-mail ril@ri.ac.uk; internet www.rigb.org; f. 1799; Michael Faraday's Magnetic Laboratory, where many of his most important discoveries were made, was restored in 1972 to the form it was known to have in 1845; the adjacent museum has a unique collection of original apparatus, diaries, note-books and personal effects; Head of Collections and Heritage Prof FRANK JAMES.

Saatchi Gallery: Duke of York's Headquarters, King's Rd, Sloane Sq., Chelsea, London; internet www.saatchi-gallery.co.uk; f. 1985; colln of mostly modern art from contemporary British artists (incl. Damien Hirst, Tracey Emin, Sarah Lucas, Jenny Saville, Chapman brothers); also exhibits work of lesser-known int. artists.

Science Museum: South Kensington, London, SW7 2DD; tel. (870) 870-4771; fax (20) 7942-4302; internet www.sciencemuseum.org.uk; f. 1857; official title the National Museum of Science and Industry; Dir (vacant); Science Library: see Libraries and Archives.

Sir John Soane's House and Museum: 13 Lincoln's Inn Fields, London, WC2A 3BP; tel. (20) 7440-4251; fax (20) 7831-3957; e-mail library@soane.org.uk; internet www.soane .org; f. 1837 (built by Sir John Soane 1812, est. by Act of Parliament for the promotion of the study of architecture and allied arts 1833); collection includes paintings by Hogarth, the Egyptian Sarcophagus of Seti I, Italian bronzes, paintings, antique sculpture, 18th-century English sculpture, models, 30,000 architectural drawings; library: library: see Libraries and Archives; Dir TIM KNOX.

South London Gallery: 65 Peckham Rd, London, SE5 8UH; tel. (20) 7703-6120; fax (20) 7252-4730; e-mail mail@ southlondongallery.org; internet www .southlondongallery.org; f. 1891; regular exhibitions of innovative contemporary art supported by a full programme of education events and workshops; Dir MARGOT HELLER; Curator KIT HAMMONDS.

Tate: Millbank, London, SW1P 4RG; tel. (20) 7887-8888; fax (20) 7887-8007; e-mail information@tate.org.uk; internet www.tate .org.uk; f. 1897; Dir Sir NICHOLAS SEROTA.

Constituent museums:

Tate Britain: Millbank, London, SW1P 4RG; tel. (20) 7887-8008; fax (20) 7887-8007; e-mail information@tate.org.uk; internet www.tate.org.uk; f. 1897 by Sir Henry Tate; nat. gallery of British art since 1500, incl. works by Hogarth, Blake, Constable and the Pre-Raphaelites, with the Turner Collection housed in the Clore Gallery; Dir STEPHEN DEUCHAR.

Research centre:

Hyman Kreitman Research Centre: Tate Britain, Millbank, London, SW1P 4RG; tel. (20) 7887-8838; fax (20) 7887-8901; e-mail research.centre@tate.org .uk; internet www.tate.org.uk/research/ researchservices; f. 2002; library: art library and archive; 150,000 exhibition catalogues, 4,000 artists' bookworks; artists' and institutional archives documenting British art since 1900; Head of Library and Archive KATE SLOSS.

Tate Liverpool: Albert Dock, Liverpool, L3 4BB; tel. (151) 702-7400; e-mail visiting .liverpool@tate.org.uk; internet www.tate .org.uk/liverpool; f. 1988; home of the Nat. Colln of Modern Art in the North; 4 floors displaying work selected from the Tate Colln and spec. exhibitions of artwork loaned from around the world; modern and contemporary art since 1900, incl. painting and sculpture, photography, video installations; tours and lectures; Dir CHRISTOPH GRUNENBERG.

Tate Modern: Bankside, London, SE1 9TG; tel. (20) 7887-8008; fax (20) 7887-8007; e-mail information@tate.org.uk; internet www.tate.org.uk; f. 2000; int. modern art since 1900; Dir VICENTE TODOLÍ.

Tate St Ives: Porthmeor Beach, St Ives, Cornwall TR26 1TG; tel. (1736) 796226; e-mail tatestives@tate.org.uk; internet www.tate.org.uk; f. 1993; modern painting, sculpture and ceramics by artists associated with St Ives, as well as int. figures; incl. Barbara Hepworth Museum and Sculpture Garden; Dir SUSAN DANIEL-MCELROY.

Victoria and Albert (V&A) Museums.
CONSTITUENT MUSEUMS:

Museum of Childhood: Cambridge Heath Rd, London, E2 9PA; tel. (20) 7983-5200; fax (20) 8983-5225; e-mail bgmc@vam.ac.uk; internet www .museumofchildhood.org.uk; f. 1872; children's toys, games, costume, nursery furniture; Dir DIANE LEES.

Theatre Museum—National Museum for the Performing Arts: Reading Room, Blythe House, 23 Blythe Rd, London, W14 0QX; tel. (20) 7943-4727; fax (20) 7943-4777; e-mail tmenquiries@vam.ac.ul; internet www.vam.ac.uk/tco; f. 1974, opened to the public 1987; nat. record of stage performance; history, craft and practice of the performing arts in Britain; library of 100,000 vols (incorporating British Theatre Asscn colln and library of the Soc. for Theatre Research); spec. archive collns incl. D'Oyly Carte Co, English Stage Co, Engish Shakespeare Co, Arts Council of Great Britain, Diaghilev's Ballets Russes and Edward Gordon Craig; spec. photographic archives incl. Houston Rogers, Gordon Anthony and Anthony Crickmay; Nat. Video Archive of Performance; future exhibitions will be held at the V&A; new permanent gallery will be open by 2009; Dir GEOFFREY MARSH.

Victoria and Albert Museum (V&A): South Kensington, London, SW7 2RL; tel. (20) 7942-2000; e-mail vanda@vam.ac.uk; internet www.vam.ac.uk; f. 1852; all forms of art and design, with collns of ceramics, furniture, fashion, glass, jewellery, metalwork, sculpture, textiles and paintings; library: library: see entry for Nat. Art Library; Dir MARK JONES; Keepers BETH MCKILLOP (Asian Dept), C. WILK (Furniture, Textiles and Fashion Dept), JULIUS BRYANT (Prints, Drawings and Painting/ Nat. Art Library Dept), Dr P. WILLIAMSON (Sculpture, Metalwork, Ceramics and Glass Dept).

Wallace Collection: Hertford House, Manchester Square, London, W1U 3BN; tel. (20) 7935-9500; fax (20) 7224-2155; e-mail enquiries@wallacecollection.org; internet www.wallacecollection.org; f. 1900; collns of 18th c. French pictures, furniture, Sèvres porcelain and sculpture, 17th c. paintings, armoury and *objets d'art*, bequeathed to the nation in 1897 by Lady Wallace; Dir ROSALIND SAVILL.

White Cube: 48 Hoxton Sq., London, N1 6PB; tel. (20) 7930-5373; fax (20) 7749-7480; e-mail enquiries@whitecube.com; internet www.whitecube.com; f. 2000; modern British art; Man. Dir JAY JOPLING.

Whitechapel Art Gallery: Whitechapel High St, London, E1 7QX; tel. (20) 7522-7888; fax (20) 7377-1685; e-mail info@ whitechapel.org; internet www.whitechapel .org; f. 1901; temporary exhibitions, principally of modern or contemporary art; no permanent collection; charitable trust supported by the Arts Council, local authorities, charitable bodies and the business community; Chair. of Trustees KEIR MCGUINNESS; Dir IWONA BLAZWICK.

Manchester

Manchester City Galleries: Mosley St, Manchester, M2 3JL; tel. (161) 235-8888; fax (161) 235-8899; internet www .manchestergalleries.org; f. 1823; dept of Manchester City Council, operates 4 galleries in and around Manchester.

Constituent galleries:

Gallery of Costume: Platt Hall, Rusholme, Manchester, M14 5LL; tel. (161) 224-5217; fax (161) 256-3278; e-mail mageducation@manchester.gov.uk; internet www.manchestergalleries.org; 18th-century fmr textile merchant's house; 20,000 items of clothing and fashion accessories from 17th century to the present; library of 18,000 vols.

Heaton Hall: Heaton Park, Prestwich, Manchester, M25 5SW; tel. (161) 773-2581; fax (161) 235-8805; e-mail

galleryeducation@notes.manchester.gov .uk; internet www.manchestergalleries .org; Grade 1 listed, 18th-century neoclassical country house; interiors restored to illustrate life as it was in the late 18th and 19th centuries.

Manchester Art Gallery: Mosley St, Manchester, M2 3JL; tel. (161) 235-8888; fax (161) 235-8899; e-mail galleryeducation@notes.manchester.gov .uk; internet www.manchestergalleries .org; f. 2002 following re-organization of the fmr Manchester City Art Gallery; 25,000 items; fine art colln includes 2,000 oil paintings, 3,000 watercolours and drawings, 250 sculptures, 90 miniatures, 1,000 prints, notable works by the Pre-Raphaelites: Rossetti, Millais, Hunt, Burne-Jones; colln of decorative arts ranges from ancient Greek pottery to contemporary furniture; contemporary local art and design, incl. works by Lowry; gallery of craft and design.

Wythenshawe Hall: Wythenshawe Park, Northenden, Manchester, M23 0AB; tel. (161) 990-5083; fax (161) 235-8805; e-mail galleryeducation@notes.manchester.gov .uk; internet www.manchestergalleries .org; f. 1926; Tudor house.

Manchester Museum: Univ. of Manchester, Oxford Rd, Manchester, M13 9PL; tel. (161) 275-2634; fax (161) 275-2676; internet www.museum.manchester.ac.uk; f. 1821; archaeology, Egyptology, ethnology, geology, botany, zoology, entomology, archery, numismatics; education and exhibition services; Dir Dr NICHOLAS MERRIMAN.

Museum of Science and Industry in Manchester: Liverpool Rd, Castlefield, Manchester, M3 4FP; tel. (161) 832-2244; e-mail collections@msim.org.uk; internet www.msim.org.uk; f. 1983; housed in the world's oldest passenger railway station; explores the history, science and industry of Manchester, with displays focusing on textiles, communications, utilities, steam power and the railways, cameras, aircraft; Xperiment! (interactive science centre); Dir IAN GRIFFIN (acting).

Urbis: Cathedral Gardens, Manchester, M4 3BG; tel. (161) 605-8200; e-mail info@urbis .org.uk; internet www.urbis.org.uk; f. 2002; exhibits on social, historical and cultural aspects of city life, with interactive galleries; Learning Administrator ALEXIA ANTHONY.

Newcastle upon Tyne

Museum of Antiquities of the University and the Society of Antiquaries of Newcastle upon Tyne: University of Newcastle upon Tyne, Newcastle upon Tyne, NE1 7RU; tel. (191) 222-7849; fax (191) 222-8561; e-mail m.o.antiquities@ncl.ac.uk; internet museums.ncl.ac.uk; f. 1813; prehistoric, Roman and medieval collections, scale models of Hadrian's Wall, reproductions of Roman arms and armour, and reconstruction of a Temple of Mithras; library: departmental library of 18,000 items relating to Hadrian's Wall, British, Continental and Mediterranean archaeology; Museums Officer L. ALLASON-JONES.

Tyne and Wear Museums: Discovery Museum, Blandford Square, Newcastle upon Tyne, NE1 4JA; tel. (191) 232-6789; fax (191) 230-2614; e-mail info@twmuseums .org.uk; internet www.twmuseums.org.uk; f. 1974; Dir ALEC COLES.

Selected museums and galleries:

Arbeia Roman Fort: Baring St, South Shields, NE33 2BB; tel. (191) 456-1369; fax (191) 427-6862; e-mail info@twmuseums .org.uk; internet www.twmuseums.org.uk/ arbeia; f. 1953; Roman coins, military equipment, pottery, jewellery; excavations and reconstructions; Curator ALEX CROOM.

Discovery Museum: Blandford Square, Newcastle upon Tyne, NE1 4JA; tel. (191) 232-6789; fax (191) 230-2614; e-mail discovery@twmuseums.org.uk; internet www.twmuseums.org.uk/discovery; f. 1934; displays of fashion, military history, social history and maritime history, and ship *Turbinia*; Curator GRAHAM BRADSHAW.

Hancock Museum: Barras Bridge, Newcastle upon Tyne, NE2 4PT; tel. (191) 222-6765; fax (191) 261-7537; e-mail hancock .museum@ncl.ac.uk; internet www .twmuseums.org.uk/hancock; f. 1829; general zoology, ornithology, geology, botany and enthnography; Egyptology; closed until 2009, when it will reopen as The Great North Museum; Curator STEVE McLEAN.

Laing Art Gallery: New Bridge St, Newcastle upon Tyne, NE1 8AG; tel. (191) 232-7734; e-mail laing@twmuseums.org.uk; internet www.twmuseums.org.uk/laing; f. 1904; British oil paintings and watercolours since 1700 (incl. works by Reynolds, Gainsborough, Turner, Landseer, Burne-Jones, Holman Hunt, Spencer, etc.); silver, ceramics and glass (incl. display of enamelled glass by William Beilby); Curator JULIE MILNE.

Monkwearmouth Station Museum: North Bridge St, Sunderland, SR5 1AP; tel. (191) 567-7075; fax (191) 510-9415; e-mail info@twmuseums.org.uk; internet www.twmuseums.org.uk/monkwearmouth; f. 1973; collns relating to transport, incl. rolling stock, printed material, photographs and models; closed until 2007; Curator JULIET HORSLEY.

Segedunum Roman Fort, Baths and Museum: Buddle St, Wallsend, NE28 6HR; tel. (191) 236-9347; fax (191) 295-5858; e-mail info@twmuseums.org.uk; internet www.twmuseums.org.uk/ segedunum; f. 2000; Roman collection incl. defensive missiles from the fort; Industry Gallery has artefacts associated with coal-mining and shipbuilding, incl. model of the ship *Carpathia*; Curator GEOFF WOODWARD.

Shipley Art Gallery: Prince Consort Rd, Gateshead, NE8 4JB; tel. (191) 477-1495; e-mail shipley@twmuseums.org.uk; internet www.twmuseums.org.uk/shipley; f. 1917; contemporary craft; British paintings and old masters; local industrial history; Curator AMY BARKER.

South Shields Museum and Art Gallery: Ocean Rd, South Shields, NE33 2JA; tel. (191) 456-8740; fax (191) 456-7850; e-mail info@twmuseums.org.uk; internet www.twmuseums.org.uk/southshields; local history in relation to South Tyneside; Catherine Cookson gallery; local art and crafts; Curator ALISDAIR WILSON.

Stephenson Railway Museum: Middle Engine Lane, North Shields, NE29 8DX; tel. and fax (191) 200-7146; e-mail info@ twmuseums.org.uk; internet www .twmuseums.org.uk/stephenson; colln of steam, diesel and electric locomotives, incl. the early locomotive *Billy*; social history relating to railways; Curator JOHN CLAYSON.

Sunderland Museum and Winter Gardens: Burdon Rd, Sunderland SR1 1PP; tel. (191) 553-2323; fax (191) 553-7828; e-mail sunderland.museum@twmuseums .org.uk; internet www.twmuseums.org.uk/ sunderland; f. 1846; archaeology, local history, geology, glass, pottery, paintings

(incl. by Lowry), natural history; ethnography; Curator JULIET HORSLEY.

Newport (Gwent)

Newport Museum and Art Gallery: John Frost Square, Newport, South Wales, NP20 1PA; tel. (1633) 840064; e-mail museum@ newport.gov.uk; internet www.newport.gov .uk; f. 1888; collns of Roman material from Caerleon and Caerwent; oils, early English watercolours and prints, and other paintings (incl. by Lowry); teapot displays; ceramics; natural and local history collections; Museums Officer (Collections) BRUCE CAMPBELL; Museums and Heritage Officer MIKE LEWIS.

Norwich

Norfolk Museums and Archaeology Service: The Shirehall, Market Ave, Norwich, Norfolk, NR1 3JQ; tel. (1603) 493625; fax (1603) 493623; e-mail museums@norfolk.gov .uk; internet www.museums.norfolk.gov.uk; Head of Museums VANESSA TREVELYAN.

Selected museums:

Ancient House Museum: White Hart St, Thetford; tel. (1842) 752599; e-mail ancient .house.museum@norfolk.gov.uk; 15th c. timber-framed building; local history; Curator OLIVER BONE.

Bridewell Museum: Bridewell Alley, Norwich, NR2 1AQ; tel. (1603) 629127; fax (1603) 614018; e-mail hannah.madox@ norfolk.gov.uk; local industries and crafts in medieval house; Curator HANNAH MADDOX.

Cromer Museum: Cromer; tel. (1263) 513543; e-mail cromer.museum@norfolk .gov.uk; local history, archaeology, geology, natural history; Curator ALISTAIR MURPHY.

Elizabethan House Museum: Great Yarmouth; tel. (1493) 745526; fax (1493) 745459; domestic life, toys, porcelain, glassware.

Gressenhall Farm and Workhouse: Gressenhall; tel. (1362) 860563; e-mail gressenhall.museum@norfolk.gov.uk; historic workhouse; social and rural history displays and collections; farm with rare breeds of animal.

Lynn Museum: Market St, King's Lynn, PE30 1NL; tel. (1553) 75001; e-mail lynn .museum@norfolk.gov.uk; social history, natural history, archaeology and geology of West Norfolk.

Norwich Castle Museum and Art Gallery: Castle Meadow, Norwich, NR1 3JN; tel. (1603) 493625; fax (1603) 493623; e-mail museums@norfolk.gov.uk; f. 1894; Norman Keep; fine art, ceramics, social history, natural history, archaeology.

Royal Norfolk Regimental Museum: Market Ave, Norwich, NR1 3JQ; tel. (1603) 493650; e-mail museums@norfolk .gov.uk; social history of the county regiment since 1685.

Time and Tide: Great Yarmouth; tel. (1493) 743930; various aspects of East Anglian maritime history.

Tolhouse Museum: Great Yarmouth; tel. (1493) 745526; fax (1493) 745459; history of crime and punishment in Great Yarmouth.

Town House: 46 Queen St, King's Lynn, PE30 5DQ; tel. (1553) 773450; social history of King's Lynn.

Sainsbury Centre for Visual Arts: University of East Anglia, Norwich, Norfolk, NR4 7TJ; tel. (1603) 593199; e-mail scva@ uea.ac.uk; internet www.scva.org.uk; f. 1978; modern European art and art, sculpture and design of other cultures and periods; library

of 13,000 vols (mainly non-Western art and anthropology); Dir NICHOLA JOHNSON.

Nottingham

Nottingham Castle Museum: Friar Lane, off Maid Marian Way, Nottingham, NG1 6EL; tel. (115) 915-3700; fax (115) 915-3653; e-mail castle@ncmg.org.uk; internet www .nottinghamcity.gov.uk; f. 1878; archaeology and ethnography, fine and applied arts, military, social and local history; Dir MICHAEL WILLIAMS.

Nottingham Natural History Museum: Wollaton Hall, Nottingham, NG8 2AE; tel. (115) 915-3900; fax (115) 915-3940; internet www.nottinghamcity.gov.uk; f. 1867; collections of botanical, zoological, and geological material; extensive British and foreign herbaria, Crowfoot collection of exotic butterflies, Pearson collection of European butterflies, Fowler collection of British Coleoptera, Hollier collection of Wenlock Limestone fossils, Carrington series of Mountain Limestone fossils; library of 3,500 vols; Nottinghamshire environmental database; controlled by Nottingham City Council; Senior Keeper G. WALLEY.

Overton

National Coal Mining Museum for England: Caphouse Colliery, New Rd, Overton, Wakefield, West Yorks., WF4 4RH; tel. (1924) 848806; fax (1924) 840694; e-mail info@ncm.org.uk; internet www.ncm.org.uk; f. 1988; mine workings and mine exhibits; library: library of material on all aspects of coal-mining; Dir Dr MARGARET FAULL.

Oxford

Ashmolean Museum, University of Oxford: Beaumont St, Oxford, OX1 2PH; tel. (1865) 278000; fax (1865) 278018; internet www.ashmol.ox.ac.uk; f. 1683; contains the art and archaeological collections of the University of Oxford; British, European, Mediterranean, Egyptian and Near Eastern archaeology; Italian, Dutch, Flemish, French and English oil paintings; Old Master and modern drawings, water-colours and prints; miniatures; European ceramics; sculpture and bronzes; English silver; objects of applied art; Hope collection of engraved portraits; coins and medals of all countries and periods; Chinese and Japanese porcelain, paintings and lacquer; Chinese bronzes, Tibetan art; Indian sculpture and painting; Islamic pottery and metalwork; Dir Dr CHRISTOPHER BROWN; publ. *Annual Report*.

Modern Art Oxford: 30 Pembroke St, Oxford, OX1 1BP; tel. (1865) 722733; fax (1865) 722573; internet www .modernartoxford.org.uk; f. 1965; exhibitions of contemporary and 20th-century painting, sculpture, design, photography, architecture, film and video; Dir ANDREW NAIRNE.

Pitt Rivers Museum, University of Oxford: South Parks Rd, Oxford, OX1 3PP; tel. (1865) 270927; fax (1865) 270943; e-mail prm@prm.ox.ac.uk; internet www.prm.ox.ac .uk; f. 1884; attached to Univ.'s School of Anthropology and Museum Ethnography; contains the ethnographic, archaeological and related photographic and manuscript collns of the Univ.; library of 30,000 vols, 250 periodicals; spec. collns of historic photographs and MSS; Dir Dr MICHAEL O'HANLON.

Plymouth

Plymouth City Museum and Art Gallery: Drake Circus, Plymouth, Devon PL4 8AJ; tel. (1752) 304774; fax (1752) 304775; e-mail plymouthmuseum@plymouth.gov.uk; internet www.plymouth.gov.uk; f. 1897 to illustrate the arts and sciences of the West Country; comprises the Cottonian Colln of early printed and illuminated books, Old Master engravings and drawings, and portraits by Sir Joshua Reynolds; general collns of Fine Art (since 16th c.) and of Decorative Arts including Plymouth silver and William Cookworthy's Plymouth and Bristol porcelain; natural history, ethnography, archaeology and local history; the Merchant's House (f. 1977), 33 St Andrew's St (16–17th c.); the Elizabethan House (f. 1929), 32 New St (16th c.) and Smeaton's Tower lighthouse, The Hoe; Curator NICOLA MOYLE.

Portsmouth

Portsmouth City Museum and Records Office: Museum Rd, Portsmouth, Hants., PO1 2LJ; tel. (23) 9282-7261; fax (23) 9287-5276; e-mail mvs@portsmouthcc.gov.uk; internet www.portsmouthmuseums.co.uk; f. 1972; local history, fine and decorative art; Records Office contains the official records of the City of Portsmouth since 14th century; Museums and Records Services Man. PAUL RAYMOND.

Branch museums:

Charles Dickens Birthplace: 393 Old Commercial Rd, Portsmouth, Hants., PO1 4QL; tel. (23) 9282-7261; fax (23) 9287-5276; e-mail mvs@portsmouthcc.gov.uk; internet www.portsmouthmuseums.co.uk; f. 1904; built 1805; birthplace of Charles Dickens in 1812; a small terraced house restored, decorated and furnished in the Regency style; Dickens memorabilia and exhibition; Museums and Records Services Man. Dr JANE MEE.

D-Day Museum and Overlord Embroidery: Clarence Esplanade, Southsea, Hants., PO5 3NT; tel. (23) 9282-7261; fax (23) 9287-5276; e-mail mvs@portsmouthcc .gov.uk; internet www.ddaymuseum.co.uk; f. 1984; houses the 'Overlord Embroidery', commemorating the D-Day Landings; displays of original archive material, vehicles, uniforms and artefacts; Museums and Records Services Man. Dr JANE MEE.

Southsea Castle: Clarence Esplanade, Southsea, Hants., PO5 3PA; tel. (23) 9282-7261; fax (23) 9287-5276; e-mail mvs@portsmouthcc.gov.uk; internet www .portsmouthmuseums.co.uk; f. 1967; built 1544 by Henry VIII to protect Portsmouth harbour; 'Life in the Castle' experience; Tudor, Civil War and Victorian history; artillery and underground passages; Museums and Records Services Man. Dr JANE MEE.

Preston

Harris Museum and Art Gallery: Market Sq., Preston, Lancs., PR1 2PP; tel. (1772) 258248; fax (1772) 886764; e-mail harris .museum@preston.gov.uk; internet www .harrismuseum.org.uk; f. 1893; fine art, decorative art, costumes and textiles, archaeology, local history, photography; Head of Arts and Heritage Services ALEXANDRA WALKER.

Reading

Museum of English Rural Life: Univ. of Reading, Redlands Rd, Reading, Berks., RG1 5EX; tel. (118) 378-8660; fax (118) 378-5632; e-mail merl@reading.ac.uk; internet www .merl.org.uk; f. 1951; nat. colln of objects, photographs, archives, records and publs relating to English rural and agricultural history; c 1m. photographic prints and negatives; library of 70,000 vols incl. large sections on agricultural sciences and technology and pre-1950 agricultural devt overseas; Head of Univ. Museums and Collns Services K. ARNOLD-FOSTER.

Museum of Reading: Blagrave St, Reading, Berks, RG1 1QH; tel. (118) 939-9800; fax

(118) 939-9881; e-mail curator@ readingmuseum.org.uk; internet www .readingmuseum.org.uk; f. 1883; local history and industry; works of art from the Reading Foundation for Art; collection of Romano-British remains at Silchester; Blake's Lock Riverside Museum treats Reading's industry, commerce and waterways; Senior Curator MATTHEW WILLIAMS.

Salisbury

Salisbury and South Wiltshire Museum: The King's House, 65 The Close, Salisbury, Wilts., SP1 2EN; tel. (1722) 332151; fax (1722) 325611; e-mail museum@ salisburymuseum.org.uk; internet www .salisburymuseum.org.uk; f. 1860; archaeology, local history, ceramics, costume, Pitt Rivers colln, topographical pictures, numismatics; temporary exhibitions; Dir P. R. SAUNDERS.

Selborne

Gilbert White's House and Garden and the Oates Museum: The Wakes, High St, Selborne, Alton, Hants; tel. (1420) 511275; f. 1954; private collections funded by the Oates Memorial Trust; furnished period rooms, original MSS about the natural history of Selborne; 18th c. plants grown in the garden; exploration in Africa by Frank Oates and in Antarctica by Capt. Lawrence Oates; Oates Memorial Library.

Sheffield

Kelham Island Museum: Alma St, Sheffield, S3 8RY; tel. (114) 272-2106; fax (114) 275-7847; e-mail postmaster@simt.co.uk; internet www.simt.co.uk/kelham; f. 1982; objects, pictures and archives relating to Sheffield's industrial heritage; Exec. Dir JOHN HAMSHERE.

Weston Park Museum: Western Bank, Sheffield, S10 2TP; tel. (114) 278-2600; e-mail info@sheffieldgalleries.co.uk; internet www.sheffieldgalleries.org.uk; f. 1875 as Sheffield City Museum and Mappin Art Gallery; collns of Sheffield cutlery, Old Sheffield Plate, British and European cutlery, coins and medals, ceramics, local archaeology, natural sciences, local geology, etc.; Victorian paintings, Old Masters; Dir NICK DODD.

Singleton

Weald and Downland Open Air Museum: Singleton, Chichester, W. Sussex, PO18 0EU; tel. (1243) 811363; fax (1243) 811475; e-mail courses@wealddown.co.uk; internet www .wealddown.co.uk; f. 1967 to save interesting examples of vernacular architecture from South-east England which have been threatened with demolition; more than 45 buildings ranging from early medieval times to 19th c. have been re-erected on the site; working exhibits include a watermill and treadwheel; working farm with animals; continuing education courses for adults in building conservation, traditional building methods and traditional rural trades and crafts; diverse curriculum of subjects offered to schools, Master's degree course in Timber Building Conservation; library: research library and archive; Dir RICHARD HARRIS; Head of Learning DIANA ROWSELL.

Southampton

Southampton City Art Gallery: Civic Centre, Commercial Rd, Southampton, Hants., SO14 7LP; tel. (23) 8083-2277; fax (23) 8083-2153; e-mail art.gallery@ southampton.gov.uk; internet www .southampton.gov.uk/leisure/arts; f. 1916 by a bequest fund for purchase and display of works of art; opened 1939; collections include

Old Masters, French 19th- and 20th c. Schools, British painting since 18th c., with emphasis on the Camden Town School; large collection of British contemporary painting and sculpture; library of 1,500 vols; Curator TIM CRAVEN.

Southport

Atkinson Art Gallery: Lord St, Southport, Merseyside, PR8 1DH; tel. (1704) 533133 ext. 2110; fax (151) 934-2109; f. 1878 for the exhibition of the town's permanent colln; British oils and watercolours since the 18th century; contemporary sculpture, paintings and prints; Arts and Cultural Services Man. (Museums and Galleries) JOANNA JONES.

Stoke on Trent

Chatterley Whitfield Mining Museum: Tunstall, Stoke on Trent, North Staffs, ST6 8UN; tel. (1782) 813337; f. 1979 at a former colliery; aims to demonstrate the realities of mining development; recreation of surface and underground conditions; reference library; mining artefacts, photographs, films, documents, maps and plans, and oral history recordings; Dir JAMES HUTCHINSON; publs *Chatterley Whitfield News*, *Primary Teachers' Pack*, *Schools Roadshow Pack*.

Stoke on Trent Museums: Bethesda St, Hanley, Stoke on Trent, ST1 3DW; tel. (1782) 232323; fax (1782) 232500; e-mail museums@ stoke.gov.uk; internet www.stoke.gov.uk/ museums; Head of Museums IAN LAWLEY.

Constituent Museums:

Etruria Industrial Museum: Lower Bedford St, Etruria, Stoke on Trent, ST4 7AF; tel. (1782) 233144; fax (1782) 233141; e-mail museums@stoke.gov.uk; steam-powered potter's mill.

Ford Green Hall: Ford Green Rd, Smallthorne, Stoke on Trent, ST6 1NG; tel. (1782) 233195; fax (1782) 233194; e-mail ford.green.hall@stoke.gov.uk; 17th -century timber-framed bldg and period garden.

Gladstone Pottery Museum: Uttoxeter Rd, Longton, Stoke on Trent, ST3 1PQ; tel. (1782) 237777; fax (1782) 237076; e-mail gladstone@stoke.gov.uk; fmr Victorian pottery factory.

Potteries Museum and Art Gallery: Bethesda St, City Centre, Stoke on Trent, ST1 3DW; tel. (1782) 232323; fax (1782) 232500; e-mail museums@stoke.gov.uk; Staffordshire pottery and porcelain, art, natural history, archaeology, local history.

Swansea

National Waterfront Museum: Oystermouth Rd, Maritime Quarter, Swansea, SA1 3RD; tel. (1792) 638956; fax (1792) 459641; e-mail waterfrontmuseum@nmgw .ac.uk; internet www.waterfrontmuseum.co .uk; f. 2005; exhibits on the history of the industrialization of Welsh society since the 18th c.; major collection of printed books and copy photographs covering the industrial history of Wales; Dir STEPHANOS MASTORIS.

Wakefield

Wakefield Metropolitan District Council Access and Culture–Libraries and Museums: Wakefield Art Gallery, Wentworth Terrace, Wakefield, W. Yorks., WF1 3QW; tel. (1924) 305796; fax (1924) 305770; e-mail cmacdonald@wakefield.gov.uk; internet www.wakefield.gov.uk/culture; f. 1934; museums and sites incl. Wakefield Art Gallery, Wakefield Museum, Pontefract Museum, Castleford Museum Room, Pontefract Castle, Sandal Castle, Clarke Hall Educational Museum; Head of Libraries and Museums COLIN MACDONALD.

Weybridge

Brooklands Museum: Brooklands Rd, Weybridge, Surrey, KT13 0QN; tel. (1932) 857381; fax (1932) 855465; e-mail info@brooklandsmuseum.com; internet www.brooklandsmuseum.com; f. 1991; cars, motorcycles, aircraft, historic Brooklands racetrack, interactive science gallery; Dir ALLAN WINN.

Widnes

Catalyst—Science Discovery Centre: Mersey Rd, Widnes, Cheshire, WA8 0DF; tel. (151) 420-1121; fax (151) 495-2030; e-mail info@catalyst.org.uk; internet www.catalyst.org.uk; f. 1987; to inform the public about the role of chemistry in society past and present, incl. its relationship to the environment; to enthuse school pupils about science through workshops, science demonstrations and interactive galleries; colln of relevant artefacts; library: reference library on history of the chemical industry; archive of historical photographs; Dir JULIE BURGESS-WILSON.

Wolverhampton

Wolverhampton Art Gallery and Museums: Lichfield St, Wolverhampton, W. Midlands, WV1 1DU; tel. (1902) 552055; fax (1902) 552053; f. 1884; collections of fine art since 18th c.; Branch museums: Bantock House (English enamels, porcelain, japanned ware); Bilston Craft Gallery (contemporary craft and temporary exhibitions); Arts and Museums Officer CORINNE MILLER.

York

Jorvik–The Viking City: Coppergate, York, YO1 9WT; tel. (1904) 543403; fax (1904) 627097; e-mail enquiries@vikingjorvik.com; internet www.vikingjorvik.com; f. 1984; reconstruction of part of the Viking city of Jorvik, based on archaeological evidence; many artefacts from the York Archaeological Trust's excavation are on display in the Gallery; Head of Attractions SARAH MALTBY.

National Railway Museum: Leeman Rd, York, YO26 4XJ; tel. (1904) 621261; fax (1904) 611112; e-mail nrm@nmsi.ac.uk; internet www.nrm.org.uk; f. 1975; part of the Science Museum (*q.v.*); houses a large part of the National Railway Collection reflecting over 150 years of British railway heritage; full-size rolling stock of diesel, electric and steam locomotives, carriages and wagons, models, signalling equipment, railway relics, posters, prints, films, technical drawings, photographs and paintings; Institute of Railway Studies, based at the Museum, provides university-level teaching on history and heritage of rail and urban transport; library of 15,000 vols; closed until October 2007; Head ANDREW SCOTT.

York Castle Museum: Eye of York, York, YO1 9RY; tel. (1904) 687687; e-mail castle.museum@ymt.org.uk; internet www.yorkcastlemuseum.org.uk; f. 1938; England's first major folk museum; Kirk collection illustrates English life since 17th c., including reconstructed shops and streets; also costumes, arms and armour, craft workshops; Museums Man. IAN CARLISLE.

York City Art Gallery: Exhibition Square, York, YO1 7EW; tel. (1904) 687687; fax (1904) 697966; e-mail art.gallery@ymt.org.uk; internet www.yorkartgallery.org.uk; f. 1879; paintings of the Italian, Dutch, Flemish, German, French, Spanish and British Schools; William Etty colln; large colln of 20th c. studio ceramics; library of 7,000 vols; Museums Man. JOSEPHINE MARTIN; Curator CAROLINE WORTHINGTON.

Yorkshire Museum: Museum Gardens, York, YO1 7FR; tel. (1904) 687687; e-mail yorkshire.museum@ymt.org.uk; internet www.yorkshiremuseum.org.uk; f. 1822; archaeology (Roman, Anglo-Saxon, Viking and medieval life), natural history, geology, numismatics and ceramics; Museums Man. HELEN YOUNG.

Universities

UNIVERSITY OF ABERDEEN

Aberdeen, AB24 3FX

Telephone: (1224) 272000

Fax: (1224) 276054

E-mail: pubrel@abdn.ac.uk

Internet: www.abdn.ac.uk

Founded 1495

Chancellor: ROBIN HARPER
Principal and Vice-Chancellor: Prof. C. DUNCAN RICE
Provost: NEVA HAITES
Sr Vice-Principal: Prof. STEPHEN LOGAN
Vice-Principals: Prof. CHRIS GANE (Learning and Information Services), Prof. B. MACASLAN (Learning and Teaching), Prof. D. H. HOULIHAN (Research and Commercialisation)
Sec.: STEVE CANNON
Librarian: WENDY PIRIE
Library: see Libraries
Number of teachers: 842
Number of students: 12,000

Publications: *Aberdeen University Review*, *Gaudeamus* (annual)

VICE-PRINCIPALS AND DEANS

Faculty of Arts and Social Sciences: Prof. BRYAN MACGREGOR
Faculty of Life Sciences and Medicine: NEVA HAITES
Faculty of Physical Sciences: Prof. A. RODGER

PROFESSORS

Faculty of Arts and Social Sciences (Univ. of Aberdeen, King's College, Aberdeen, AB24 3FX; tel. (1224) 272084; fax (1224) 272082; e-mail adf076@abdn.ac.uk):

ADAMS, C. D., Land Economy
ARTER, D., Politics and Int. Relations
BEAUMONT, P. R., Law
BEBBINGTON, K. J., Accountancy
BLAIKIE, J. A. D., Sociology and Anthropology
BRIDGES, R. C., History and Economic History
BRITTON, C. M., French
BRUCE, C., Sociology
BRYDEN, J. M., Geography
BUCKLAND, R., Accountancy
BURGESS, G. J., German
CAMERON, J. R., Philosophy
CAREY-MILLER, D. L., Law
CHAPMAN, K., Geography
CLARK, B., Geography
DAWSON, P. M., Management Studies
DEVINE, T. M., Research Institute of Irish and Scottish Studies
DUFF, P. R., Law
DUKES, P., History and Economic History
DUNKLEY, J., French
EDWARDS, K. J., Geography
ELLIOTT, R. F., Econ.
EVANS-JONES, R., Law
FERGUSSON, D. A. S., Divinity with Religious Studies
FORTE, A. D. M., Law
FRASER, P., Accountancy
GANE, C. H. W., Law
GRAHAM, L. G., Philosophy
HARRIS, D. R., Hispanic Studies
HARRISON, R. T., Management Studies

HEALD, D. A., Accountancy
HENDERSHOTT, P. H., Land Economy
HENDRY, L. B., Centre for Educational Research
HEWITT, D. S., English
HOESLI, M. E. R., Accountancy
HOTSON, H., Early Modern History
INGOLD, T., Sociology and Anthropology
JOHNSTONE, W., Divinity with Religious Studies
JORDAN, A. G., Politics and Int. Relations
KEATING, M. J., Politics and Int. Relations
KEMP, A. G., Econ.
KIDD, M., Econ.
LEBOUTTE, R. F. M. P., History
LEE, C. H., Econ.
LYALL, F., Law
MACDONALD, I. R., Hispanic Studies
MACGREGOR, B. D., Land Economy
MACINNES, A. I., History
MCKEE, L., Management Studies
MANNINGS, D., History of Art
MATHER, A. S., Geography
MATTHEWS, E. H., Philosophy
MEEK, D. E., Celtic
MILLER, D., Law
MURRAY, I., English
O'BOYLE, C. J. M., Celtic
OHLMEYER, J., History
PAYNE, P. L., History and Economic History
PORTER, J. W., English (Elphinstone Institute)
ROBERTS, C., Accountancy
ROBERTSON, R., Sociology
ROWAN-ROBINSON, J. R., Law
SALMON, T. C., Politics and Int. Relations
SAUNDERS, A. M., French
SEWEL, J. B., Politics and Int. Relations
SHEEHAN, M. J., Politics and Int. Relations
SHUCKSMITH, D. M., Land Economy
SOULSBY, C., Geography
SWANSON, P., Hispanic Studies
THEODOSSIOU, I., Econ.
THOMANECK, J. K. A., German
TORRANCE, I. R., Divinity with Religious Studies
URWIN, D. W., Politics and Int. Relations
VAN DER MERWE, C. G., Law
WALKER, N. C., Law
WALKER, S., Geography
WATSON, F. B., Divinity with Religious Studies
WATSON, G. J. B., English

Faculty of Life Sciences and Medicine (Univ. of Aberdeen, Polworth Bldg, Foresterhill, Aberdeen, AB25 2ZD; tel. (1224) 552504; fax (1224) 840708; internet w3.abdn.ac.uk/medicine):

ALEXANDER, D. A., Mental Health
ASHFORD, M. L. J., Biomedical Sciences
BOOTH, I. R., Microbiology
BROWN, A. J. P., Molecular and Cell Biology
CASSIDY, J., Medicine and Therapeutics (Oncology)
CATTO, G. R. D., Medicine and Therapeutics
DOCHERTY, K., Molecular and Cell Biology (Biochemistry)
EL-OMAR, E. M., Medicine and Therapeutics
FORRESTER, J. V., Ophthalmology
FOTHERGILL, J. E., Molecular and Cell Biology (Biochemistry)
GILBERT, F. J., Radiology
GODDEN, D. J., Highlands and Islands Health Research Institute
GOLDEN, M. H. N., Medicine and Therapeutics
GOODAY, G. W., Molecular and Cell Biology
GOW, N. A. R., Molecular and Cell Biology
GRANT, A. M., Public Health
GREAVES, M., Medicine and Therapeutics (Haematology)

HAITES, N. E., Medicine and Therapeutics, and Molecular and Cell Biology
HAMILTON, W. A., Medical Microbiology
HANNAFORD, P., Primary Care
HARRIS, W. J., Molecular and Cell Biology (Genetics)
HAWKSWORTH, G. M., Biomedical Sciences, and Medicine and Therapeutics
HELMS, P. J. B., Child Health
HUHTANIEMI, I. T., Obstetrics and Gynaecology
HUKINS, D. W. L., Biomedical Physics and Bioengineering
HUTCHISON, J. D., Surgery (Orthopaedics)
KIDD, C., Biomedical Sciences (Physiology)
LITTLE, J., Medicine and Therapeutics (Epidemiology)
LOGAN, S. D., Biomedical Sciences (Neuroscience)
MCCAIG, C. D., Biomedical Sciences
MACLEOD, A. M., Medicine and Therapeutics
MAUGHAN, R. J., Environmental and Occupational Medicine
NEEDHAM, G., Medical Faculty
NORMAN, J. N., General Practice and Primary Care
ODDS, F. C., Molecular and Cell Biology
PENNINGTON, T. H., Medical Microbiology
PERTWEE, R. G., Biomedical Sciences
POPE, M. H., Medicine and Therapeutics
PRICE, D. B., General Practice and Primary Care
PROSSER, J. I., Molecular and Cell Biology
RALSTON, S. H., Medicine and Therapeutics
REES, A. J., Medicine and Therapeutics
REID, D. M., Medicine and Therapeutics
RITCHIE, L. D., General Practice and Primary Care
RUSSELL, E. M., Public Health
SEATON, A., Environmental and Occupational Medicine
SEYMOUR, D. G., Medicine and Therapeutics, and General Practice and Primary Care
SHARP, P. F., Biomedical Physics and Bioengineering
SHAW, D. J., Molecular and Cell Biology
SMITH, W. C. S., Public Health
TEMPLETON, A. A., Obstetrics and Gynaecology
VAN DER MOLEN, T., General Practice and Primary Care
WALKER, F., Pathology
WEBSTER, N. R., Medicine and Therapeutics (Anaesthesia and Intensive Care)
WHALLEY, L. J., Mental Health
WISCHIK, C. M., Mental Health

Faculty of Physical Sciences (Univ. of Aberdeen, King's College, Aberdeen, AB24 3FX; tel. (1224) 272081; fax (1224) 272082; e-mail adf073@abdn.ac.uk):

ALEXANDER, I. J., Plant and Soil Sciences
ARCHBOLD, R. J., Mathematical Sciences
BAKER, M. J., Eng.
BOYLE, P. R., Zoology
CHANDLER, H. W., Eng.
CRAWFORD, J. E., Psychology
DELLA SALA, S. F., Psychology
DEREGOWSKI, J. B., Psychology
DUFFY, J. A., Chemistry
ENGLISH, P. R., Agriculture
FLIN, R., Psychology
FORRESTER, A. R., Chemistry
FREESTON, M. W., Computing Science
GLASSER, F. P., Chemistry
GORMAN, D. G., Eng.
GRAY, P. M. D., Computing Science
HALL, G. S., Mathematical Sciences
HOULIHAN, D. F. J., Zoology
HOWE, R. F., Chemistry
HUBBUCK, J. R., Mathematical Sciences
HUNTER, J., Computing Science
HURST, A., Geology and Petroleum Geology
INGRAM, M. D., Chemistry

JOLLIFFE, I. T., Mathematical Sciences
KILLHAM, K. S., Plant and Soil Sciences
LOGIE, R. H., Psychology
LOMAX, M. A., Agriculture
MACDONALD, D. I. M., Geology and Petroleum Geology
MEHARG, A. A., Plant and Soil Sciences
MILLER, H. G., Agriculture and Forestry
MITCHELL, C. P., Agriculture and Forestry
MORDUE, W., Zoology
NAYLOR, R. E. L., Agriculture
PENMAN, J., Eng.
PLAYER, M. A., Eng.
PRIEDE, I. G., Zoology
RACEY, P. A., Zoology
ROBINSON, D., Plant and Soil Sciences
RODGER, A. A., Eng.
SECOMBES, C. J., Zoology
SLEEMAN, D. H., Computing Science
SPEAKMAN, J. R., Zoology
SPRACKLEN, C. T., Eng.
SPEAKMAN, J. R., Zoology
THOMSON, K. J., Agriculture
VAS, P., Eng.
WIERCIGROCH, M., Eng.
WILLETTS, B. B., Eng.

ATTACHED RESEARCH INSTITUTES

Aberdeen Centre for Energy Regulation and Obesity: Chair Prof. J. SPEAKMAN.

Aberdeen University Centre for Organic Agriculture: Dir Dr C. LEIFERT.

Arkleton Centre for Rural Development Research: Dirs Prof. J. BYRDEN, Prof. M. SHUCKSMITH.

Centre for Advanced Studies in Nursing: Dir Dr A. KIGER.

Centre for Austrian Studies: based in Univs of Aberdeen and Edinburgh; Dirs Dr JANET STEWART (Aberdeen) Prof. ANDREW BARKER (Edinburgh).

Centre for Early Modern Studies: Dir Prof. H. HOTSON.

Centre for Educational Research: Dir J. SHUCKSMITH.

Centre for Entrepreneurship: Dir Prof. R. HARRISON.

Centre for European Labour Market Research: Dir Prof. I. THEODOSSIOU.

Centre for Nordic Policy Studies: Dir Prof. D. ARTER.

Centre for Philosophy, Technology and Society: Dir Prof. G. GRAHAM.

Centre for Property Research: Dir Prof. B. D. MACGREGOR.

Centre for Research on the 18th Century: Dir Dr J. DUNKLEY.

Centre for Russian, East and Central European Studies: Dir Prof. P. DUKES.

Centre for Scottish Studies: Dir Dr J. S. SMITH.

Centre for Space Policy: Dir A. MCLEAN.

Centre for Study of the Hispanic Avant Garde: Dir Prof. D. HARRIS.

Centre for the Study of Religions: Dir J. A. THROWER.

Centre for Trauma Research: Dir Prof. D. A. ALEXANDER.

Computer Based Learning in Land Use and Environmental Science: Dir Dr S. HEATH.

Dugald Baird Centre on Women's Health: Dir Dr W. GRAHAM.

Elphinstone Institute: Dir Dr I. RUSSELL.

Highlands and Islands Health Research Institute: Dir Prof. D. GODDEN.

Language Centre: Dir C. BURGESS (acting).

Oil and Gas Centre: Dir L. BOWIE.

Research Institute of Irish and Scottish Studies: Dir Prof. T. DEVINE.

School of Physics: Head of School Prof. D. W. L. HUKINS.

Scottish Centre for International Security: Dir Prof. M. SHEEHAN.

ASSOCIATED INSTITUTES

Institute of Terrestrial Ecology (NERC): see under Natural Environment Research Council.

Macaulay Land Use Research Institute: see under Research Institutes.

Marine Laboratory of the Department of Agriculture and Fisheries for Scotland: Dir Prof. A. D. HAWKINS.

Rowett Research Institute: see under Research Institutes.

UNIVERSITY OF ABERTAY DUNDEE

Bell St, Dundee, DD1 1HG
Telephone: (1382) 308000
Fax: (1382) 308877
E-mail: sro@abertay.ac.uk
Internet: www.abertay.ac.uk
Founded 1888 as Dundee Technical Institute, present name and status 1994
Academic year: October to June

Chancellor: Rt Hon. EARL OF AIRLIE
Vice-Chancellor and Principal: Prof. BERNARD KING
Vice-Principal: Prof. MICHAEL T. SWANSTON
Head of Information Services: IVOR G. LLOYD
Library of 110,000 items
Number of teachers: 380 (230 full-time, 150 part-time)
Number of students: 5,144 (4,228 full-time, 916 part-time)

HEADS OF SCHOOL

Dundee Business School: Prof. MARY MALCOLM
School of Computing and Advanced Technologies: Prof. LACHLAN MACKINNON
School of Contemporary Sciences: Prof. JOHN W. PALFREYMAN
School of Social and Health Sciences: Prof. STEVE OLIVIER

ATTACHED RESEARCH INSTITUTES

International Centre for Computer Games and Virtual Entertainment (ICCAVE): Head of School Prof. LACHLAN MACKINNON.

Manufacturing and Intelligent Systems Technology (MIST): Dir Prof. DAVID A. BRADLEY.

Scottish Informatics, Mathematics, Biology and Statistics (SIMBIOS): Dir Prof. JOHN W. PALFREYMAN.

Scottish Institute for Wood Technology: Senior Research Dir Prof. JOHN W. PALFREYMAN.

Tayside Economic Research Centre (TERC): Dir NEIL C. MCGREGOR.

Urban Water Technology Centre: Head Dr CHRIS JEFFERIES.

ANGLIA RUSKIN UNIVERSITY

Chelmsford Campus: Bishop Hall Lane, Chelmsford, CM1 1SQ
Cambridge Campus: East Rd, Cambridge, CB1 1PT
Telephone: (1245) 493131 (Chelmsford); (1223) 363271 (Cambridge)
Fax: (1245) 490835
E-mail: answers@apu.ac.uk
Internet: www.anglia.ac.uk

Founded as a university (Anglia Polytechnic University) by merger of existing institutions 1992; present name 2005

Academic year: September to July

Chancellor: Lord ASHCROFT
Vice-Chancellor: Prof. MIKE THORNE
Deputy Vice-Chancellor: Prof. ANTHONY POWELL
Pro Vice-Chancellors: PETER CREAMER, Prof. STEVE MARSHALL, Prof. ROBIN SMITH
Librarian: NICOLA KERSHAW
Number of teachers: 709
Number of students: 14,000

DEANS

Arts and Social Science: MONIKA THOMAS
Design and Communication Systems: RICHARD WOOLLEY
Education: Dr JOAN ADAMS
Law: Prof. JOHN WHITE
Science and Technology: Prof. ADRIAN MOORE
Ashcroft International Business School: PHILIP KNOWLES (acting)
Graduate School: Prof. JOHN DAVIES
Institute of Health and Social Care: MIKE COOK

UNIVERSITY OF THE ARTS LONDON

65 Davies St, London, W1K 5DA
Telephone: (20) 7514-6000
Fax: (20) 7514-6131
E-mail: info@arts.ac.uk
Internet: www.arts.ac.uk
Founded 2004
Rector: Sir MICHAEL BICHARD.

COLLEGES OF THE UNIVERSITY

Camberwell College of Arts

Peckham Rd, London, SE5 8UF
Telephone: (20) 7514-6302
Fax: (20) 7514-6310
E-mail: enquiries@camberwell.arts.ac.uk
Internet: www.camberwell.arts.ac.uk
Founded 1898

Main subject areas: ceramics, design products, conservation, drawing, graphic design, illustration, painting, photography, sculpture.

Head: JUDE FREEMAN.

Central Saint Martins College of Art and Design

Southampton Row, London, WC1B 4AP
Telephone: (20) 7514-7022
Fax: (20) 7514-7254
E-mail: enquiries@csm.arts.ac.uk
Internet: www.csm.arts.ac.uk
Founded 1896

Main subject areas: fashion and textiles; film, video and photography; fine art; graphics and communication design; interdisciplinary art and design; theatre and performance; three-dimensional design.

Library of 80,000 vols.

Chelsea College of Art and Design

Millbank London, SW1P 4RJ
Telephone: (20) 7541-7751
E-mail: enquiries@chelsea.arts.ac.uk
Internet: www.chelsea.arts.ac.uk
Founded 1895

Main subject areas: fine art, communication design, interior and spatial design, textile design, history and theory of visual and multimedia cultures.

Head: Prof. ROGER WILSON.

London College of Communication

Elephant and Castle, London, SE1 6SB
Telephone: (20) 7514-6569
Fax: (20) 7514-6535
E-mail: info@lcc.arts.ac.uk
Internet: www.lcc.arts.ac.uk
Founded 1894

Schools of: graphic design, marketing, media, and printing and publishing.

London College of Fashion

20 John Princes St, London, W1G 0BJ
Telephone: (20) 7514-7407
Fax: (20) 7514-7484
E-mail: enquiries@fashion.arts.ac.uk
Internet: www.fashion.arts.ac.uk
Founded 1957

Rector: SANDRA HOLTBY
Dean (Quality Assurance): ELIZABETH ROUSE
Library Manager: DIANE MANSBRIDGE
Library of 57,000 books, 390 periodicals
Number of teachers: 140
Number of students: 3,150

DEANS

School of Fashion Design and Technology: ROY PEACH
School of Fashion Promotion and Management: ANN PRIEST

ASTON UNIVERSITY

Aston Triangle, Birmingham, B4 7ET
Telephone: (121) 359-3611
Fax: (121) 333-6350
E-mail: prospectus@aston.ac.uk
Internet: www.aston.ac.uk
Founded as Birmingham Municipal Technical School 1895, Central Technical College 1927, College of Advanced Technology 1956, University Charter 1966
Academic year: October to June

Chancellor: Sir MICHAEL BETT
Vice-Chancellor: Prof. M. T. WRIGHT
Senior Pro-Vice-Chancellor: Prof. B. J. TIGHE
Pro-Vice-Chancellors: Prof. N. B. R. REEVES, Dr F. HEWITT
University Secretary and Registrar: R. D. A. PACKHAM
Director of Library and Information Services: Dr N. R. SMITH
Library: see Libraries and Archives
Number of teachers: 343
Number of students: 6,623 (5,700 full-time, 923 part-time)
Publication: *Annual Report and Accounts*

HEADS OF SCHOOLS

Aston Business School: Prof. J. A. SAUNDERS
School of Engineering and Applied Science: Prof. A. K. KOCHHAR
School of Languages and European Studies: Prof. A. F. STEVENS
School of Life and Health Sciences: Prof. D. C. BILLINGTON

PROFESSORS

BENNETT, D., Aston Business School
BENNION, I., Electronic Engineering and Computer Science
BLOW, K., Engineering and Applied Science
BOOTH, R. T., Civil and Mechanical Engineering
BRETT, P., Mechanical Engineering
BRIDGWATER, T., Chemical Engineering and Applied Chemistry
BRODBECK, F., Aston Business School
CARDWELL, M. J., Electronic Engineering and Computer Science
CHILTON, P. A., Languages and European Studies
DAVIS, E. W., Aston Business School

DORAN, N. J., Electronic Engineering and Computer Science
FOSTER, D. H., Vision Sciences
GAFFNEY, J., Languages and European Studies
GILMARTIN, B., Life and Health Sciences
GÖRNER, R., Languages and European Studies
GREENLEY, G. E., Aston Business School
HARDING, G. F. A., Psychology and Human Biology
HARRIS, M., Aston Business School
HAYNS, M. R., Civil and Mechanical Engineering
HOMER, J., Chemical Engineering and Applied Chemistry
HOOLEY, G. J., Aston Business School
IRWIN, W. J., Pharmaceutical Sciences
JONES, B., Engineering
KETTLE, R., Civil and Mechanical Engineering
KHAYAT, M., Engineering and Applied Science
KOCHHAR, A., Engineering and Applied Science
LATHAM, R. V., Computer Science and Applied Mathematics
LEWIS, C. D., Aston Business School
LI WAN PO, A., Pharmaceutical Sciences
LOVE, J., Aston Business School
LOWE, D., Electronic Engineering and Computer Science
MARTIN, I., Pharmaceutical Sciences
NORRIS, T., Civil and Mechanical Engineering
OSBORNE, S., Aston Business School
PAGE, C., Civil Engineering and Applied Chemistry
PARKER, D., Aston Business School
REEVES, N. B. R., Languages and European Studies
SAAD, D., Information Engineering
SAUNDERS, J., Aston Business School
STEVENS, A., Languages and European Studies
SULLIVAN, J., Engineering and Applied Science
THANASSOULIS, E., Aston Business School
TIGHE, B. J., Chemical Engineering and Applied Chemistry
TISDALE, M. J., Pharmaceutical Sciences
WEST, M., Aston Business School

AFFILIATED INSTITUTE

Aston Science Park/Birmingham Technology Ltd: Chief Exec. D. W. HARRIS.

UNIVERSITY OF BATH

Claverton Down, Bath, BA2 7AY
Telephone: (1225) 386386
Fax: (1225) 386559
E-mail: registry@bath.ac.uk
Internet: www.bath.ac.uk
Founded 1856, designated College of Advanced Technology 1960, independent institution with direct-grant status 1962, University Charter 1966
Academic year: September to June

Chancellor: Lord TUGENDHAT
Vice-Chancellor: Prof. GLYNIS BREAKWELL
Pro Vice-Chancellors: Prof. KEVIN EDGE, Prof. IAN JAMIESON, Prof. G. G. LUNT
Registrar: J. A. BURSEY
Librarian: H. NICHOLSON
Library: see Libraries and Archives
Number of teachers: 500
Number of students: 12,000

DEANS

Faculty of Engineering and Design: Prof. A. K. DAY
Faculty of Humanities and Social Sciences: Prof. GEOF WOOD

Faculty of Science: Prof. CHRISTOPHER JENNISON

School for Health: Prof. P. H. REDFERN (acting)

School for Management: Prof. A. PETTIGREW

PROFESSORS

ACHARYA, K. R., Biology and Biochemistry
AGGARWAL, R. K., Electronic and Electrical Engineering
ALMOND, D. P., Materials Science
BENDING, S. J., Physics
BIRD, D. M., Physics
BLAKE, D. R., Medical Sciences
BRAMLEY, A. N., Engineering and Applied Sciences
BRITTON, N., Mathematical Sciences
BROOKS, S. W., European Studies and Modern Languages
BROWN, A. D., Management
BUDD, C. J., Applied Mathematics
BULL, A., European Studies and Modern Languages
BURSTALL, F. E., Mathematical Sciences
CARUSO, A., Architecture and Civil Engineering
CHARNLEY, A. K., Biology and Biochemistry
CHAUDHURI, J. B., Chemical Engineering
COLEMAN, P. G., Physics
CRITTENDEN, B. D., Chemical Engineering
CRONIN, N. J., Physics
DANIELS, H. R., Education
DANSON, M. J., Biochemistry
DAVENPORT, J. H., Information Technology
DAVIDSON, M. G., Chemistry
DAVIES, J. J., Physics
EATWELL, R., European Studies and Modern Languages
EGGLESTONE, C., Psychology
EDGE, K., Mechanical Engineering
EISENTHAL, R., Biology and Biochemistry
FFRENCH-CONSTANT, R., Biology and Biochemistry
FINEMAN, S., Management
FITCH, J. P., Software Engineering
FORD, I. D., Management
FRAENKEL, L. E., Mathematical Sciences
GALAKTIONOV, V. A., Mathematical Sciences
GARLAND, C. J., Pharmacy and Pharmacology
GILLESPIE, D., Russian
GOODING, D. C., Psychology
GOUGH, I. R., Social Sciences
GOULD, N., Social and Policy Sciences
GRAHAM, I. G., Mathematical Sciences
GREEN, R. H., Management
GURSUL, I., Mechanical Engineering
GUY, R., Pharmacy and Pharmacology
HAMMOND, G. P., Environmental Engineering
HARLAND, C. M., Management
HASTE, H. E., Psychology
HAWLEY, J. G., Mechanical Engineering
HOLMAN, G. D., Biochemistry
HOPE, V., Management
HORROCKS, M., School for Health
HUDSON, J. R., Economics and International Development
HUNT, G. W., Mechanical Engineering
HURST, L. D., Biology
IBELL, T. J., Architecture and Civil Engineering
IOANNIDIS, C., Management
JENNISON, C., Statistics
JOHNSON, P., Computer Science
JONES, P. R., Economics and International Development
KERWIN, D. G., Sport and Exercise Science
KNIGHT, J. C., Physics
KOLACZKOWSKI, S. T., Chemical Engineering
LAUDER, H., Education
LEWIS, A., Psychology
LEWIS, M. A., Management
LOGEMANN, H., Mathematical Sciences
MCKAY, A., Economics and International Development
MARKANDYA, A., Economics and International Development

MARSH, R. J., Modern Languages
MARSHALL, J., Management
MARTIN, B., Marketing
MAYER, M., Strategic Management
MEDLAND, A. J., Design Engineering
MILEHAM, A. R., Mechanical Engineering
MILES, A. W., Mechanical Engineering
MILLAR, J., Social Policy
MITCHELL, N., Electronic and Electrical Engineering
MOLLOY, K., Chemistry
MONRO, D. M., Electronics
MORTON, K. W., Mathematical Sciences
NANDEIBAM, S., Economics and International Development
NAUDE, P., Management
ORTON, P., School for Health
PACE, N. G., Physics
PARKER, S. C., Chemistry
PENROSE, M., Mathematical Sciences
PETER, L. M., Physical Chemistry
POTTER, B. V. L., Pharmacy
POWELL, P., Management
PURCELL, J., Management
PYM, D., Computer Science
RAITHBY, P. R., Chemistry
REASON, P., Management
REDFERN, P., School for Health
REYNOLDS, S. E., Biology
RICKELLS, P., Architecture
RODGER, D., Electronic and Electrical Engineering
ROOM, G. J., Social Sciences
RUSSELL, P. ST. J., Physics
RYAN, E. P., Mathematical Sciences
SCOTT, R. J., Biology and Biochemistry
SCOTT, W. A. H., Education
SKEVINGTON, S. M., Psychology
SLACK, J. M. W., Cell and Molecular Biology
SMITH, A. W., Pharmacy
SMYSHLYAEV, V., Mathematical Sciences
SPENCE, A., Numerical Analysis
STABLES, A. W., Education
STEVENS, R., Engineering and Applied Science
TATE, G. D., European Studies and Modern Languages
TAVERNOR, R. W., Architecture
TAYLOR, J. T., Electronic and Electrical Engineering
TOLAND, J. F., Mathematics
TURNBULL, D., Architecture and Civil Engineering
TYRELL, R. M., Pharmacy and Pharmacology
VASSILIEV, D. G., Mathematical Sciences
VIDGEN, R, Management
VINCENT, J. F. V., Mechanical Engineering
WALLACE, A. M., Education
WANG, W. N., Physics
WARD, S., Pharmacy and Pharmacology
WELHAM, M., Pharmacy and Pharmacology
WHITMAN, R., Politics
WILKINSON, B., Management
WILLIAMS, I., Chemistry
WILLIAMS, J. M. J., Chemistry
WILLIS, P. J., Mathematical Sciences
WONNACOTT, S. J., Biology and Biochemistry
WOOD, G. D., Economics and International Development

BATH SPA UNIVERSITY

Newton Park Campus: Newton St Loe, Bath, BA2 9BN

Telephone: (1225) 875875 (Newton Park)
Fax: (1225) 875444 (Newton Park)

Sion Hill Campus: Lansdown, Bath, BA1 5SF

Telephone: (1225) 875875 (Sion Hill)
Fax: (1225) 875666 (Sion Hill)
E-mail: enquiries@bathspa.ac.uk
Internet: www.bathspa.ac.uk

Founded 1898; renamed Bath College of Higher Education 1975; granted taught degree-awarding powers 1992; present name and status 2005

Director: FRANK MORGAN
Registrar: CHRISTOPHER ELLICOTT
Head, Library Services: JULIE PARRY
Number of teachers: 570
Number of students: 5,200

Schools of Art and Design, Education, English and Creative Studies, Graduates, Historical and Cultural Studies, International Students, Music and Performing Arts and Science and the Environment and Social Sciences.

UNIVERSITY OF BIRMINGHAM

Edgbaston, Birmingham, B15 2TT

Telephone: (121) 414-3344
Fax: (121) 414-3971
Internet: www.bham.ac.uk

Founded 1900
Academic year: September to June

Chancellor: Sir DOMINIC CADBURY
Vice-Chancellor and Principal: Prof. MICHAEL STERLING
Vice-Principal: Prof. MICHAEL CLARKE
Pro-Vice-Chancellors: Prof. A. M. CRUISE, Prof. G. E. PETTS, Prof. C. R. RICKWOOD
Registrar and Secretary: JONATHAN NICHOLLS
Librarian: M. SHOEBRIDGE (acting)
Library: see Libraries
Number of teachers: 1,241
Number of students: 17,993 (full-time)

Publications: *Court Reporter* (annual), *The Birmingham Magazine* (annually), *Bulletin* (every 2 weeks, in term-time), *Medlines* (2 a year)

DEANS

Arts and Social Sciences: Prof. A. J. RANDALL
Life and Health Sciences: Prof. S. J. W. BUSBY
Physical Sciences and Engineering: Prof. L. A. CLARK

PROFESSORS

ABELL, S., Functional Materials
ADAMS, D. H., Hepatology
AHMED, A., Reproductive Physiology
AL-RUBEAI, M., Biotechnology
ALCOCK, P., Social Policy and Administration
ALEXANDER, D., Accounting
ALLEMANN, R., Chemical Biology
AMANN, R., Soviet Politics
ARNULL, A. M., European Law
BACKHOUSE, R. E., History and Philosophy of Economics
BACON, P. A., Rheumatology
BALDWIN, J., Judicial Administration
BALE, J. S., Environmental Biology
BANFIELD, S. D., Music
BARBER, K., African Popular Culture
BARKER, A., Classics
BARNDEN, J., Artificial Intelligence
BARNETT, A. H., Diabetic Medicine
BATLEY, P. R. A., Development Administration
BEEVERS, D. G., Medicine
BELL, T., Metallurgy
BESRA, G., Biosciences
BIDDLESTONE, A. J., Chemical Engineering
BIRKETT, J., French Studies
BLACKBURN, S., Solids Processing
BLAKE, J. R., Applied Mathematics
BOOTH, D. A., Psychology
BOOTH, I. W., Paediatric Gastroenterology and Nutrition
BOWEN, P., Mechanical Metallurgy
BOWERY, N. G., Pharmacology
BRADBURY, A., Vascular Surgery
BREUILLY, J. J., Modern History
BROOKS, N. P., Medieval History
BROWN, N. L., Molecular Genetics and Microbiology
BROWNE, K., Forensic and Family Psychology
BRYAN, S., Health Economics
BUCKLEY, C., Rheumatology

BURKE, F., Primary Dental Care
BUSBY, S. J. W., Biochemistry
BUTLER, M. G., Modern German Literature
BUTLER, P. J., Comparative Physiology
CAESAR, M. P., Italian
CALLOW, J. A., Botany
CAMPBELL, J., Casting Technology
CARROLL, D., Applied Psychology
CHAPPLE, I., Periodontology
CHENG, K. K., Public Health and Epidemiology
CHILD, J., Commerce (International Management and Organization)
CHIPMAN, J., Cell Toxicology
CLARK, L. A., Structural Engineering
CLARKE, M., Public Policy
CLIFFORD, C. M., Nursing
COCHRANE, R., Psychology
COLE, J. A., Microbial Physiology and Biochemistry
COOPER, J. M., Russian Economic Studies
COOTE, J. H., Physiology
COULTHARD, R. M., English Language and Linguistics
COX, A. W., Business Strategy and Procurement
CROFT, S. J., International Relations
CROSSLEY, E. C. D., 19th-Century French Studies
CRUIKSHANK, G. S., Neurosurgery
CRUISE, A. M., Astrophysics and Space Research
CURTIS, R., Combinatorial Algebra
DADSON, T. J., Hispanic Studies
DANIELS, H. R. J., Special Education and Educational Psychology
DANIELS, P. W., Geography
DAVIES, G., Engineering
DAVIES, L., English
DAVIES, M. L., International Education
DAVIS, A., Social Work
DAWE, D. J., Structural Mechanics
DE CHERNATONY, L., Brand Marketing
DEAN, T. A., Manufacturing Engineering
DEB, S., Neuropsychiatry and Intellectual Disability
DELECLUSE, H.-J., Molecular Pathology
DENT, N. J. H., Philosophy
DICKENSON, D., Global Ethics
DOE, W., Medicine
DOLING, J. F., Housing Studies
DOWDEN, K., Classics
DUDA, J., Sports Psychology
DUTTA, J., Economics
EDWARDS, A., Education
EDWARDS, P. P., Inorganic Chemistry
ELLIS, E. D., Public Law
ELLIS, S., English Literature
ENONCHONG, N., Law
EVANS, H., Metallurgy and Materials
FADDY, M., Statistics
FELDMAN, D. J., Jurisprudence
FENDER, J., Macroeconomics
FORGAN, E. M., Condensed Matter Physics
FRAME, J. W., Oral Surgery
FRANKLIN, F., Plant Molecular Biology
FRANKLYN, J. A., Medicine
FREEMANTLE, N., Clinical Epidemiology and Biostatistics
FRYER, P. J., Chemical Engineering
GALLIMORE, P. H., Cancer Studies
GARVEY, J., Particle Physics
GORDON, J., Cellular Immunology
GRAY, R., Medical Statistics
GREAVES, C., Solid State Chemistry
GUNN, J. M. F., Theoretical Physics
HALDON, J. F., Byzantine Studies
HALL, P. S., Communications Engineering
HAM, C. J., Health Policy and Management
HARBER, C., International Education
HARRIS, I. R., Materials Science
HARRIS, J., Law
HARRIS, K. D. M., Structural Chemistry
HARRISON, R. M., Environmental Health
HAWKEY, P., Immunology
HAY, C., Political Analysis

HEATH, J. K., Biochemistry
HENDERSON, W., Continuing Education
HICKS, C., Health Care Psychology
HOBBS, F. D. R., Primary Care and General Practice
HUGHES, A., 20th-century French Literature
HUMPHREYS, G. W., Cognitive Psychology
HUNTER, J. R., Ancient History and Archaeology
HUTTON, P., Anaesthetics and Intensive Care
JACKSON, J. B., Bioenergetics
JEFFERIS, R., Molecular Immunology
JEFFERY, C., German Politics
JEFFERYS, J. G. R., Basic Neuroscience
JENKINSON, E. J., Experimental Immunology
JENNINGS, J., Political Theory
JOHNSON, P., Oncology and Translational Research
JONES, D. A., Sport and Exercise Sciences
JONES, E. L., Pathology
JONES, I. P., Physical Metallurgy
JONES, P. M., French History
JONES, R. H., Public Sector Accounting
JUNG, A., Computer Science
KAPLAN, J., Drama and Theatre Arts
KEARSEY, M., Biometrical Genetics
KEIGHLEY, M. R. B., Surgery
KELSEY, D., Economic Theory
KENDALL, K., Chemical Engineering
KENDALL, M., Clinical Pharmacology
KERALI, R., Highway Engineering and Management
KILDY, M., Maternal and Fetal Medicine
KINSON, J. B., High Energy Physics
KLAPPER, J., Foreign Language Pedagogy
KNIGHT, D., Water Engineering
KNOTT, J. F., Metallurgy and Materials
KNOWLES, P. J., Theoretical Chemistry
KWIATKOWSKA, M., Computer Science
LAIRD, W. R. E., Prosthetic Dentistry
LANCASTER, M., Communications Engineering
LAWRANCE, A. J., Statistics
LE SUEUR, A., Jurisprudence
LEATHER, P., Urban and Regional Studies
LERNER, I., Theoretical Physics
LEWIS, A., Special Education and Educational Psychology
LILFORD, R., Public Health and Epidemiology
LLOYD-BOSTOCK, S., Law and Psychology
LOGAN, A., Molecular Neuroscience
LOTE, C., Experimental Nephrology
LUCAS, W., American Studies
LUESLEY, D. M., Gynaecology
LYDDIATT, A., Process Biotechnology
MACARTHUR, C., Maternal and Child Epidemiology
MACASKIE, L., Applied Microbiology
McCASKIE, T., Asante History
MACKAY, R., Hydrogeology
MacLENNAN, I. C. M., Immunology
McLEOD, D. H., Church History
MADELIN, K. B., Civil Engineering
MAHER, E., Medical Genetics
MALLIN, C., Business Finance
MARQUIS, P. M., Biomaterials
MARSH, D., Political Science and International Studies
MARSHALL, J. M., Cardiovascular Science
MARTIN, G. R., Avian Sensory Science
MENON, A., European Studies
MICHELL, R. H., Biochemistry
MILLER, C. J., English Law
MINNIKIN, D., Microbial Chemistry
MOAYYEDI, P., Primary Care and General Practice
MORRISON, K., Neurology
MORTON, D. B., Biomedical Science and Biomedical Ethics
MOSS, P. A. H., Haematology
MULLINEUX, A. W., Global Finance
MURIE, A., Urban and Regional Studies
MURINDE, V., Developmental Finance
MURRAY, P. I., Ophthalmology
NASH, G., Cardiovascular Rheology

NEAL-STURGESS, C. E., Automotive Engineering
NELSON, J. M., Nuclear Physics
NIELSEN, J., Theology
NIENOW, A. W., Biochemical Engineering
NOONAN, H., Philosophy
NORTON, J. P., Control Engineering
OLIVER, C., Clinical Psychology
ORFORD, J. F., Clinical and Community Psychology
PALIWODA, S., Marketing
PALLEN, M., Infection
PALMER, R. E., Experimental Physics
PARKER, D., Textual Criticism and Palaeography
PARLE, J., Primary Care
PARRATT, J., Third-World Theologies
PATERSON, W. E., German Studies
PECK, E., Health Services Management
PENN, C., Molecular Microbiology
PERRIE, M., Russian History
PERRY, J. G., Civil Engineering
PETTS, G., Physical Geography
PETTS, J., Environmental Risk Management
PIDDOCK, L., Microbiology
PILKINGTON, H., Sociology and Russian Area Studies
PONMAN, T., Astrophysics
PRESTON, P., Political Sociology
PREWETT, P., Microsystems Manufacture
RAFTERY, J. P., Health Economics
RAINE, J., Management in Criminal Justice
RAKODI, C., Public Policy
RANDALL, A. J., English Social History
RANSON, P. R. S., Education
REDDY, U., Computer Science
REDMOND, J., European Studies
RICHARDS, S., Public Management
RICKINSON, A. B., Cancer Studies
RIDDOCH, M., Cognitive Neuropsychology
ROBINSON, G., Pure Mathematics
ROGERS, C., Geotechnical Engineering
RUSSELL, M., Electronic and Electrical Engineering
SALMON, M., Experimental Rheumatology
SAMUELS, J. M., Business Finance
SAVAGE, C., Nephrology
SCASE, W., Medieval English Literature
SCHOFIELD, A., Theoretical Physics
SCOTT, I. R., Law
SEN, S., Development Economics
SEVILLE, J. P. K., Chemical Engineering
SHARPLES, M., Educational Technology
SHEPPARD, M. C., Medicine
SHUTE, S., Criminal Law and Criminal Justice
SIEBERT, W. S., Labour Economics
SIMNETT, G. M., High-Energy Astrophysics
SINCLAIR, P. J. N., Economics
SKELCHER, C., Local Government Studies
SLOMAN, A., Artificial Intelligence and Cognitive Science
SMALL, I. C., English Literature
SMITH, A., Oral Biology
SMITH, M., Experimental Neurology
SORAHAN, T., Occupational Epidemiology
SOUTHWOOD, T., Paediatric Rheumatology
SPEIRS, R. C., German
SPENCER, K. M., Local Policy
SPURGEON, P. C., Health Services Management
STEVENS, A., Public Health
STEWART, P. M., Medicine
STRAIN, A., Biochemistry
SUGDEN, R., Commerce
SUGIRTHARAJAH, R., Biblical Hermeneutics
SWANSON, R., Medieval Ecclesiastical History
TANN, J., Commerce
TAYLOR, A., Economics
TAYLOR, A. M. R., Cancer Genetics
TAYLOR, E. W., Animal Physiology
TAYLOR, M., World Faiths Development Dialogue
TELLAM, J., Hydrogeology
TEMPLE, J. G., Surgery
TEUBERT, W., English

THEOBALD, M. F., Accounting
THOMAS, C. M., Molecular Genetics
THOMAS, C. R., Biochemical Engineering
THOMAS, H. R., Economics of Education
TIMMS, C. R., Music
TOOLAN, M., Applied English Linguistics
TRAYER, I. P., Biochemistry
TURNBULL, P., Marketing
TURNER, B. M., Experimental Genetics
TZIOVAS, D. P., Modern Greek Studies
USTORF, W., Mission
VERDI, R., Fine Art and Art History
VINZENT, M., Theology
WAKELAM, M. J. O., Molecular Pharmacology
WALMSLEY, A., Dentistry
WALSH, M., English Literature
WALTON, D., Mechanical Engineering
WEBBER, J., Theology
WEST, S., Art History
WESTBROOK, G. K., Geophysics
WESTBURY, D. R., Physiology
WHARTON, C., Biochemistry
WHEATLEY, K., Medical Statistics
WHENHAM, E., Music History
WHITEHAND, J. W. R., Urban Geography
WHITTLE, M. J., Fetal Medicine
WICKHAM, C. J., Early Medieval History
WILSON, J. S., Pure Mathematics
WILSON, R., Group Theory
WING, A. M., Human Movement
WINTERBOTTOM, J., Chemical Reaction Engineering
WOOD, D. M., French Literature
WOODMAN, G., Comparative Law
WRIGHTSON, P., Physiotherapy
YAO, X., Computer Science
YOUNG, F. M., Theology
YOUNG, L. S., Cancer Biology

ATTACHED RESEARCH INSTITUTES

Accident Research Centre: Dir Prof. C. E. NEAL-STURGESS.

Assessment Research Unit: Dir Dr R. J. RIDING.

Biosciences Graduate Research School: Dir Prof. C. M. THOMAS.

Centre for Advanced Research in English: Dir Dr M. KNOWLES.

Centre for English Language Studies: Dir C. J. KENNEDY.

Centre for International Education and Research: Dir Dr H. R. J. DANIELS.

Centre for Russian and East European Studies: Dir Prof. HILARY A. PILKINGTON.

Centre for Studies in Security and Diplomacy: Dir Sir DAVID LOGAN.

Centre for the History of Medicine: Dir R. G. ARNOTT.

Centre for the Study of Leopardi and the Age of Romanticism: Dir Dr F. D'INTINO.

Dictionary Research Centre: Dir Dr R. MOON.

European Research Institute: Dir Prof. A. MENON.

Institute for Advanced Research in Arts and Social Sciences: Hon. Dir Prof. E. W. IVES.

Institute of Applied Social Studies: Dir DAVE MARSH.

Institute of Child Health: Dir Prof. I. W. BOOTH.

Institute of European Law: Dir Prof. A. M. ARNULL.

Institute of Judicial Administration: Dir Prof. J. BALDWIN.

Interdisciplinary Research Centre in Materials Processing: Head Dr S. BLACKBURN.

Ironbridge Institute: Ironbridge Gorge Museum, Coalbrookdale, Telford, Shropshire, TF8 7DX; tel. (1952) 432751; e-mail ironbridge@bham.ac.uk; Academic Dir Dr R. H. WHITE.

Postgraduate Centre of the Study of Drama: Dir Prof. J. KAPLAN.

Shakespeare Institute: Mason Croft, Stratford upon Avon, Warwicks., CV37 6HP; tel. (1789) 293138; e-mail shakespeare@bham.ac.uk; Dir Prof. KATE MCLUSKIE.

Wave Solutions: Dir Prof. P. S. HALL.

UNIVERSITY OF BOLTON

Deane Rd, Bolton, BL3 5AB
Telephone: (1204) 900600
Fax: (1204) 399074
E-mail: enquiries@bolton.ac.uk
Internet: www.bolton.ac.uk

Founded 1989; granted university status 2005

State control

Academic year: September to July

Vice-Chancellor and Chief Executive: Dr GEORGE HOLMES

Pro-Vice-Chancellor (Strategic Planning and Communications): KARYN BRINKLEY

Dean of Students: SARAH RICHES

Library Manager: KAREN SENIOR

Library of 171,000 books, 2,587 periodicals

Number of teachers: 250

Number of students: 7,833 (6,401 undergraduate, 1,432 postgraduate)

Publication: *The Bolt* (quarterly)

Departments of Art and Design, Built Environment, Business Logistics and Information, Business Studies, Computing and Electronic Technology, Cultural and Creative Studies, Education, Engineering and Safety, Health and Social Studies, Management, Product Design and Development, Psychology and Life Science and Sport, Leisure and Tourism Management.

BOURNEMOUTH UNIVERSITY

Fern Barrow, Poole, Dorset, BH12 5BB
Telephone: (1202) 524111
Fax: (1202) 702736
E-mail: marketing@bournemouth.ac.uk
Internet: www.bournemouth.ac.uk

Founded 1976 as Dorset Institute of Higher Education; became Bournemouth Polytechnic 1990; present name and status 1992

Academic year: September to July

Chancellor: Lord TAYLOR OF WARWICK

Vice-Chancellor: Prof. GILLIAN SLATER

Pro-Vice-Chancellor (Academic): Prof. PAUL LUKER

Pro-Vice-Chancellor (Corporate Development and Finance): DAVID WILLEY

Registrar: NOEL RICHARDSON

Librarian: DAVID BALL

Library of 150,000 vols

Number of teachers: 391

Number of students: 13,617 (9,680 full-time, postgraduate and sandwich, 3,937 part-time)

HEADS OF SCHOOLS

School of Conservation Sciences: Prof. MARK BRISBANE

School of Design, Engineering and Computing: Prof. RICHARD WYNNE

School of Finance and Law: Prof. NICK GRIEF

School of Service Industries: Prof. NIGEL HEMMINGTON

Business School: Prof. DAVID JONES

Bournemouth Media School: ROGER LAUGHTON

Institute of Health and Community Studies: ANGELA SCHOFIELD

UNIVERSITY OF BRADFORD

Bradford, West Yorks., BD7 1DP
Telephone: (1274) 233081
Fax: (1274) 236260
E-mail: enquiries@bradford.ac.uk
Internet: www.bradford.ac.uk

Founded 1957 as Bradford Institute of Technology; University Charter 1966

Academic year: September to June (two semesters)

Chancellor: IMRAN KHAN

Vice-Chancellor and Principal: Prof. CHRISTOPHER TAYLOR

Pro-Vice-Chancellors: Prof. G. ALDERSON, Prof. A. M. POLLARD, Prof. J. LUCAS

Registrar and Secretary: N. J. ANDREW

Director of Learning Resources Unit: Dr S. J. HOUGHTON

Librarian: J. J. HORTON (Academic), P. M. KETLEY (Resources Management)

Library: see Libraries

Number of teachers: 600

Number of students: 9,901

Publication: *Vice-Chancellor's Research Report* (annually)

DEANS

Archaeological and Environmental Sciences: Dr CARL HERON

Engineering, Design and Technology: Prof. ANDREW DAY

Health Studies: G. BRADSHAW

Informatics: Prof. R. A. EARNSHAW

Life Sciences: Prof. B. WINN

Lifelong Education and Development: Prof. G. LAYER

Management: Prof. A. FRANCIS

Social and International Studies: Prof. JOHN CUSWORTH

PROFESSORS

ALDERSON, G., Medical Microbiology
ANDERSON, D., Biomedical Sciences
ASHLEY, R. M., Urban Water
ASHMORE, M. R., Environmental Science
BAILES, P. J., Process Engineering
BALMER, J. M. T., Corporate Identity
BARRY, B. W., Pharmaceutical Technology
BENKREIRA, H., Coating and Polymer Processing
BIBBY, M. C., Cancer Research
CHALMERS, M. G., International Politics
CHOUDHRY, T., Finance
CHRYSTYN, H., Clinical Pharmacy
CLARK, B. J., Pharmaceutical Technology
COATES, P. D., Polymer Engineering
COSTALL, B., Neuropharmacology
COWLING, P. I., Computing
CUSWORTH, J. W., International Development Management
DANDO, M. R., International Security
DAY, A. J., Quality Engineering
DOUBLE, J. A., Experimental Cancer Chemotherapy
DOWNS, M. G., Dementia Studies
DUNCAN, S. S., Comparative Social Policy
EARNSHAW, R. A., Electronic Imaging
EDWARDS, H. G. M., Molecular Spectroscopy
EXCELL, P. S., Applied Electromagnetics
FELL, A. F., Pharmaceutical Chemistry
FILOTOTCHEV, I. R., Strategic Management
FRANCIS, F. A. S., Management
GALLAGHER, T. G. P., Ethnic Conflict and Peace
GARDINER, J. G., Electronic Engineering
GARDNER, M. L. G., Physiological Biochemistry
GRAVES-MORRIS, P. R., Numerical Analysis
GREEN, J. N., Romance Linguistics
HOGARTH-SCOTT, S., Marketing and Entrepreneurship
HOPE, C. A., Service Quality
HUSBAND, C. H., Social Analysis
JAMES, A. L., Social Sciences

JAMES, P. W., Environmental Sciences
JENKINS, T. C., Drugs Design
JIANG, J., Electronic Imaging and Media Communications
JOBBER, D., Marketing
KOUVATSOS, D. D., Computer Systems Modelling
LAYER, G. M., Lifelong Learning
LUCAS, J., Learning and Teaching
McCOLM, I. J., Ceramic Materials
MELLORS, C., Political Science
MIRZA, H. R., International Business
MUHLEMANN, A. P., Operations Management
NAYLOR, R. J, Pharmacology
NEWELL, R. J., Nursing Research
O'HEAR, A., Philosophy
OSTELL, A. E., Organizational Health and Behaviour
PEARCE, J. V., Latin American Politics
PIKE, R. H., Finance and Accounting
POLLARD, A. M., Archaeological Sciences
PRICE, D. H. R., Operational Research
RADAELLI, C. M., Public Policy
RAMSBOTHAM, O. P., Peace Studies
RANDALL, V. A., Biomedical Sciences
ROGERS, P. F., Peace Studies
SCHALLREUTER, K. U., Clinical and Experimental Dermatology
SEAWARD, M. R. D., Environmental Biology
SHEPHERD, S. J., Cryptography and Computer Communications Security
SHERIFF, R. E., Mobile Communications
SMALL, N. A., Community and Primary Care
TAYLOR, W. A., Business Information Systems
TOROPOV, V. V., Computational Mechanics
VOURDAS, A., Computing
WALLS, J. R., Chemical Engineering
WEISS, J. A., Development Economics
WHALLEY, R., Mechanical Engineering
WHITAKER, D. J., Optometry
WILLIAMS, A. C., Contemporary German Studies
WINN, B., Optometry
WOOD, J. M., Medical Biochemistry
WOODHOUSE, T., Conflict Resolution
WOODWARD, M. E., Telecommunications
YORK, P., Physical Pharmaceutics
ZAIRI, M., Best Practice Management

ATTACHED INSTITUTES

Institute of Cancer Therapeutics: Dir Prof. LAURENCE PATTERSON (acting).

Institute for Pharmaceutical Innovation: Dir PAUL THORNING (acting).

UNIVERSITY OF BRIGHTON

Lewes Rd, Brighton, BN2 4AT
Telephone: (1273) 600900
Fax: (1273) 642607
E-mail: intrel@brighton.ac.uk
Internet: www.brighton.ac.uk
Founded 1970 as Brighton Polytechnic, present name and status 1992
Academic year: September to June
Vice-Chancellor
Deputy Vice-Chancellor: DAVID HOUSE (acting)
Pro-Vice-Chancellor (Academic Affairs): Prof. STUART LAING
Pro-Vice-Chancellor (Business and Marketing): COLIN MONK
Registrar and Secretary: CHRISTINE MOON
Director of Information Services: MARK TOOLE
Library of 550,000 vols
Number of teachers: 843 (full-time)
Number of students: 10,261 (full-time)

DEANS

Faculty of Arts and Communications: Prof. BRUCE BROWN

Faculty of Education and Sport: PAUL GRIFFITHS
Faculty of Health: Prof. MICHAEL WHITING
Faculty of Management and Information Sciences: Prof. DAVID ARNOLD
Faculty of Science and Engineering: Prof. FRED MAILLARDET
Brighton and Sussex Medical School: Prof. JON COHEN

HEADS OF SCHOOLS

Faculty of Arts and Communications:
  School of Architecture and Design: ANNE BODDINGTON
  School of Arts and Communication: BILL BEECH
  School of Historical and Critical Studies: Dr PADDY MAGUIRE
Faculty of Education and Sport:
  School of Education: MAGGIE CARROLL
  School of Languages: Prof. BRIAN HILL
  Chelsea School: PAUL McNAUGHT-DAVIS
Faculty of Health:
  School of Applied Social Science: DAVID TAYLOR
  School of Healthcare Professions: MARION TREW
  Postgraduate Medical School: Prof. RICHARD VINCENT
Faculty of Management and Information Sciences:
  School of Computing, Mathematical and Information Sciences: Dr JOHN TAYLOR
  School of Service Management: Dr PAUL FROST
  Brighton Business School: Prof. AIDAN BERRY
  Centre for Research in Innovation Management (CENTRIM): Prof. HOWARD RUSH
Faculty of Science and Engineering:
  School of Engineering: Dr MARK JONES
  School of the Environment: Prof. CALLUM FIRTH
  Information Technology Research Institute: Prof. DONIA SCOTT

UNIVERSITY OF BRISTOL

Bristol, BS8 1TH
Telephone: (117) 928-9000
Fax: (117) 925-1424
Internet: www.bristol.ac.uk
Founded 1909, previously established as University College, Bristol, 1876
Academic year: October to July
Chancellor: Rt Hon. Baroness HALE
Pro-Chancellors: Sir DEREK HIGGS, STELLA CLARKE, PETER DURIE
Vice-Chancellor: Prof. ERIC THOMAS
Pro-Vice-Chancellors: Prof. PATRICIA BROADFOOT, Prof. D. N. CLARKE, Prof. S. A. R. KNOX
Registrar: D. W. M. PRETTY
University Secretary (vacant)
Deputy Registrar and Director of Information Services: A. ALLDEN
Library: see Libraries and Archives
Number of teachers: 1,617
Number of students: 15,000 (full-time and part-time)

DEANS

Faculty of Arts: Dr ROBERT FOWLER
Faculty of Engineering: Prof. DAVID MUIR WOOD
Faculty of Medical and Veterinary Sciences: Prof. GARETH WILLIAMS
Faculty of Medicine and Dentistry: Prof. GARETH WILLIAMS
Faculty of Science: Dr WILLIAM BOYD

Faculty of Social Sciences and Law: Prof. HARRIET BRADLEY

PROFESSORS
(some professors serve in more than one faculty)

Faculty of Arts (Senate House, Tyndall Ave, Bristol, BS8 1TH; tel. (117) 928-8897; internet www.bris.ac.uk/Depts/ArtsPGC/facart.htm):

BANFIELD, S. D., Music
BANN, S., History of Art
BENNETT, A. J., English
BIRD, A. J., Philosophy
BROOKSHAW, D. R., Luso-Brazilian Studies
BRYCE, J. H., Italian
BUXTON, R. G. A., Greek Language and Literature
CLARK, E. G., Ancient History
CORNWELL, N. J., Russian and Comparative Literature
DOYLE, W., History
FOWLER, R. L. H., Greek
FREEMAN, M. J., French Language and Literature
HARRISON, R. J., European Prehistory
HOOK, D., Hispanic Studies
HOPKINS, D. W., English Literature
HUTTON, R. E., History
KENNEDY, D. F., Latin Literature and Theory of Criticism
KERSHAW, B. R., Drama
KOSENINA, A., German
LOWE, R., Contemporary History
MARTINDALE, C. A., Latin
OFFORD, D. C., Russian Intellectual History
PARKIN, J., French Literary Studies
PARRY, M. M., Italian Linguistics
POOLE, G. R., Composition
PUNTER, D. G., English
SAMPSON, R. B. K., Romance Philology
STREET, S. C. J., Film
UNWIN, T. A., French
VINCENT, J. R., History
WEBB, E. T., English
WHITE, M. E., Theatre
WILLIAMS, P. M., Indian and Tibetan Philosophy

Faculty of Engineering (Queen's Building, University Walk, Bristol, BS8 1TR; tel. (117) 928-9760; internet www.fen.bris.ac.uk):

ADAMS, R. D., Applied Mechanics
BEACH, M. A., Radio Systems Engineering
BLOCKLEY, D. I., Civil Engineering
BOWES, S. R., Electrical and Electronic Engineering
BULL, D. R., Digital Systems Processing
CANAGARAJAH, C. N., Multimedia Signal Processing
CHALMERS, A. G., Computer Graphics
CHAMPNEYS, A. R., Applied Non-linear Mathematics
CLUCKIE, I. D., Worldwide Water Management
DAGLESS, E. L., Microelectronics
FLACH, P. A., Artificial Intelligence
FRISWELL, M. I., Aerospace Engineering
HOGAN, S. J., Mathematics
JOSZA, R. O., Computer Science
KRAUSKOPF, B., Applied Non-linear Mathematics
LIEVEN, N. A. J., Aerospace Dynamics
McGEEHAN, J. P., Communications Engineering
MAY, M. D., Computer Science
MELLOR, P. H., Electrical Engineering
MUIR WOOD, D., Civil Engineering
NIX, A. R., Wireless Communication Systems
PRADHAN, D. K., Computer Science
QUARINI, G. L., Process Engineering
RAILTON, C. J., Electrical and Electronic Engineering

RARITY, J. G., Optical Communications Systems
SMART, N. P., Cryptology
SMITH, D. J., Mechanical Engineering
STOTEN, D. P., Dynamics and Control
TAYLOR, C. A., Earthquake Engineering
WISNOM, M. R., Aerospace Structures

Faculty of Medical and Veterinary Sciences (University Walk, Bristol BS8 1TD; tel. (117) 331-7484; internet www.bristol.ac.uk/fmvs/):

BANTING, G. S., Molecular Cell Biology
BASHIR, Z. I., Cellular Neuroscience
BENNETT, P. M., Bacterial Genetics
BRADY, R. L., Biochemistry
BROWN, M. W., Anatomy and Cognitive Neuroscience
CLARKE, A. R., Biochemistry
COLLINGRIDGE, G., Neuroscience in Anatomy
CULLEN, P. J., Biochemistry
DAY, M. J., Veterinary Pathology
DENTON, R. M., Biochemistry
DUFFUS, W. P. H., Veterinary Medicine
GRUFFYDD-JONES, T. J., Feline Medicine
HALESTRAP, A. P., Biochemistry
HALFORD, S. E., Biochemistry
HALL, L., Molecular Genetics
HALL, E. J., Companion Animal Studies
HASSAN, A. B., Adult Oncology
HEADLEY, P. M., Physiology
HENDERSON, G., Pharmacology
HENLEY, J. M., Molecular Neuroscience
HEYDERMAN, R. S., Infectious Diseases and International Health
HOLT, P. E., Veterinary Surgery
HUMPHREY, T. J., Veterinary Zoonotic Bacteriology
KUWABARA, P. E., Genomics
LAWSON, S. N., Physiology
LISNEY, S. J. W., Physiology
MACGOWAN, A. P., Clinical Microbiology and Antimicrobial Therapeutics
MARRION, N. V., Neuroscience
MARTIN, P. B., Cell Biology
MOLNAR, E., Anatomy
MULLER, R. L., Neuroscience
NICOL, C. J., Animal Welfare
ORCHARD, C. H., Physiology
PARASKEVA, M. M., Experimental Oncology
PATON, J. F. R., Physiology
PIGNATELLI, M., Histopathology
RIVETT, A. J., Biochemistry
ROBERTS, P. J., Neurochemical Pharmacology
RUTTER, G. A., Biochemistry and Cell Biology
SIDDELL, S. G., Virology
STOKES, C. R., Mucosal Immunology
TAVARE, J. M., Biochemistry
VAZQUEZ-BOLAND, J. A., Veterinary Molecular Biology
VIRJI, M., Molecular Microbiology
WATERMAN-PATERSON, A. E., Veterinary Anaesthesia
WILLIAMS, N. A., Immunology
WOOD, J. D., Food Animal Science
WRAITH, D. C., Pathological Sciences

Faculty of Medicine and Dentistry (Senate House, Tyndall Ave, Bristol BS8 1TH; tel. (117) 928-9951; internet www.medici.bris.ac.uk/medf):

ADDY, M., Periodontology
ALDERSON, D., Gastrointestinal Surgery
ANGELINI, G., Cardiac Surgery
ARMITAGE, W. J., Opthalmology
BINGLEY, P. J., Diabetes
CAMPBELL, A. V., Ethics in Medicine
COLLINGRIDGE, G., Neuroscience in Anatomy
COWPE, J. G., Oral Surgery
DAVEY SMITH, G., Clinical Epidemiology
DICK, A. D., Ophthalmology
DONOVAN, J. L., Social Medicine
EBRAHIM, S. B. J., Epidemiology of Ageing
EMOND, A. M., Community Child Health

EVESON, J. W., Head and Neck Pathology
FINN, A. H. R., Paediatrics
FLEMING, P. J., Infant Health and Developmental Psychology
FRANKEL, S. J., Epidemiology and Public Health Medicine
GALE, E. A. M., Diabetic Medicine
GOLDING, M. J., Paediatric and Perinatal Epidemiology
GUNNELL, D. J., Epidemiology
HANKS, G. W. C., Palliative Medicine
HARRISON, G. L., Mental Health
HOLLANDER, A. P., Rheumatology and Tissue Engineering
HOLLY, J. M. P., Clinical Sciences
JAGGER, D. C., Restorative Dentistry
JENKINSON, H. F., Oral Microbiology
KARSCH, K. R., Cardiology
KIRWAN, J. R., Rheumatic Diseases
LEARMONTH, I. D., Orthopaedic Surgery
LEWIS, G. H., Psychiatric Epidemiology
LIGHTMAN, S. L., Medicine
LOPEZ BERNAL, A., Human Reproductive Biology
LOVE, S., Neuropathology
MATHIESON, P. W., Renal Medicine
MURPHY, D., Experimental Medicine
NEWBY, A. C., Vascular Cell Biology
NUTT, D. J., Psychopharmacology
PETERS, T. J., Primary Health Care Services Research
PIGNATELLI, M. M., Histopathology
PRIME, S. S., Experimental Pathology
REES, M. R., Clinical Radiology
SALISBURY, C. J., Primary Health Care
SANDY, J. R., Orthodontics
SCOLDING, N. J., Clinical Neurosciences
SHARP, D. J., Primary Health Care
SOOTHILL, P. W., Maternal and Foetal Medicine
STEVENS, M. C. G., Paediatric Oncology
THORESEN, M., Neo-natal Neuroscience
UNEY, J. B., Molecular Neuroscience
WHITELAW, A. G. L., Neonatal Medicine
WILCOCK, G. K., Care of the Elderly
WILLIAMS, G., Medicine and Dentistry
WOLF, A. R., Anaesthesia
WYNICK, D., Molecular Medicine

Faculty of Science (Senate House, Tyndall Ave, Bristol, BS8 1TH; tel. (117) 928-9957; internet www.bris.ac.uk/depts/science/sciweb.htm):

AGGARWAL, V. K., Synthetic Organic Chemistry
ALAM, M. A., Physics
ALLAN, N. L., Physical Chemistry
ALLEN, G. C., Materials Science
ANDERSON, M. G., Geography
ANNETT, J. F., Physics
ASHFOLD, M. N. R., Physical Chemistry
BALINT-KURTI, G. G., Theoretical Chemistry
BAMBER, J. L., Geography
BATES, P. D., Hydrology
BENTON, M. J., Vertebrate Palaeontology
Sir BERRY, MICHAEL, Physics
BIRKINSHAW, M., Cosmology and Astrophysics
BLUNDY, J. D., Petrology
BRERETON, R. G., Chemometrics
CHERNS, D., Physics
CLOKE, P. J., Geography
CONNELLY, N. G., Inorganic Chemistry
CONREY, J. B., Number Theory
COSGROVE, T., Physical Chemistry
CUTHILL, I. C., Behavioural Ecology
DAVIS, A. P., Supramolecular Chemistry
EASTOE, J. G., Chemistry
EDWARDS, K. J., Cereal Functional Genomics
EGGERS, J. G., Applied Mathematics
EVANS, D. V., Applied Mathematics
EVANS, R., Physics
EVERSHED, R. P., Chemistry
FOSTER, B., Physics

FRANKS, N. R., Animal Behaviour and Ecology
FREEMAN, N. H., Cognitive Development
GALLAGHER, T. C., Organic Chemistry
GIBSON, W. C., Protozoology
GOLDSTEIN, H., Statistics
GREEN, B. J., Pure Mathematics
GREEN, P. J., Statistics
HANNAY, J. H., Theoretical Physics
HARRIS, S., Environmental Sciences
HAWKESWORTH, C. J., Earth Sciences
HAYDEN, S. M., Physics
HAYES, P. K., Biology
HEATH, G. P., Physics
HELFRICH, G. R., Seismology
HENSHAW, D. L., Physics
HOOD, B. M., Development Psychology
HOUSTON, A. I., Theoretical Biology
JONES, G., Biological Sciences
JONES, K., Human Quantitative Geography
KEATING, J. P., Mathematical Physics
KEMPSON, H. E., Personal Finance and Social Policy Research
KENDALL, J.-M., Earth Sciences
LARNER, W. J., Human Geography and Sociology
LINDEN, N., Theoretical Physics
LISKEVICH, V., Mathematics
LLOYD-JONES, G. C., Chemistry
McNAMARA, J. M., Mathematics and Biology
MANN, S., Chemistry
MANNERS, I., Inorganic Materials and Chemistry
MILES, M. J., Physics
NASON, G. P., Statistics
OBERAUER, K., Psychology
ORPEN, A. G., Structural Chemistry
ORR-EWING, A. J., Chemistry
PEREGRINE, D. H., Applied Mathematics
POPESCU, S., Physics
PRENTICE, I. C., Earth System Science
PRINGLE, P. G., Inorganic Chemistry
RAGNARSDOTTIR, K. V., Environmental Geochemistry
RICHARDSON, R. M., Physics
RICKARD, J. C., Mathematics
ROBERT, D., Bionanoscience
ROBERTS, A., Zoology
ROGERS, P. J., Biological Psychology
SCHOFIELD, A. H., Pure Mathematics
SHERMAN, D. M., Geochemistry
SIEGERT, M. J., Physical Geography
SIMPSON, T. J., Organic Chemistry
SMART, P. L., Geography
SPARKS, R. S. J., Geology
STEEDS, J. W., Physics
STOBART, A. K., Plant Biochemistry
TICKELL, A. T., Human Geography
TINSLEY, R. C., Zoology
TRANTER, M., Geography
TROSCIANKO, T. S., Psychology
VALDES, P. J., Physical Geography
VAN DEN BERG, M., Pure Mathematics
VINCENT, B., Physical Chemistry
VINEY, M. E., Biological Sciences
WALL, R. L., Zoology
WALSBY, A. E., Botany
WELCH, P. D., Mathematics
WIGGINS, S. R., Applied Mathematics
WILLIS, C. L., Organic Chemistry
WOOD, B. J., Earth Sciences
WORRALL, D. M., Physics

Faculty of Social Sciences and Law (Senate House, Tyndall Ave, Bristol, BS8 1TH; tel. (117) 928-7797; internet www.bris.ac.uk/depts/socsci):

ASHTON, D. J., Accountancy and Finance
ATTFIELD, C. L. F., Econometrics
BAILEY-HARRIS, R. J., Law
BRADLEY, H. K., Sociology
BREWER, A. A., History of Economics
BURGESS, S. M., Economics
CARVER, T. F., Political Theory
COWAN, D. S., Law and Policy

CROSSLEY, M. W., Comparative and International Education
DEEM, R., Education
DOYAL, L., Health and Social Care
DUGDALE, D., Management Accounting
FARMER, E. R. G., Child and Family Studies
FENTON, C. S., Sociology
FORREST, R. S., Urban Studies
FORSTER, A. W., Politics and International Relations
FOX, K. R., Exercise and Health Sciences
FRIEDMAN, A. L., Management and Economics
GORDON, D., Social Justice
GREGG, P. A., Economics
GROUT, P. A., Political Economy
HESTER, M., Gender, Violence and International Policy
HILL, J. D., Law
HUGHES, R. M., Education
JOHNSON, M. L., Health and Social Policy
KERRIDGE, J. R., Law
KYLE, J. G., Deaf Studies
LEVITAS, R., Sociology
LITTLE, R., International Politics
MCFARLANE, A. E., Education
MCLENNAN, G., Sociology
MCMEEL, G. P., Law
MODOOD, T., Sociology, Politics and Public Policy
MOK, K. J., East Asian Studies
OSBORN, M. J., Education
PARK, I.-U., Industrial Organisation
PARTINGTON, T. M., Law
PRIDHAM, G. F. M., European Politics
PROPPER, C., Economics
PROSSER, J. A. W., Public Law
QUINTON, D. L., Psychosocial Development
REA-DICKINS, P. M., Applied Linguistics in Education
ROBERTSON, S. L., Education (Sociology)
ROSE, F. D., Commercial Law
STANTON, K. M., Law
SKULTANS SHELLEY, V., Social Anthropology
SUFRIN, B. E., Law
SUTHERLAND, R. J., Education
TEMPLE, J. R. W., Economics
WARD, L. M., Disability and Social Policy
WEBSTER, A., Educational Psychology

ASSOCIATED INSTITUTIONS

Baptist College: The Promenade, Clifton, Bristol, BS8 3NF; f. 1679; Principal Rev. C. ELLIS.

Long Ashton Research Station: see under Research Institutes.

Trinity College: Stoke Hill, Bristol, BS9 1JP; f. 1971; Anglican; Principal Rev. F. W. BRIDGER.

Wesley College: Henbury Hill, Bristol, BS10 7QD; f. 1842; Methodist; Principal Dr N. G. RICHARDSON.

BRUNEL UNIVERSITY

Uxbridge, Middx, UB8 3PH
Telephone: (1895) 274000
Fax: (1895) 232806
E-mail: admissions@brunel.ac.uk
Internet: www.brunel.ac.uk

Founded 1957 as Brunel College of Technology; College of Advanced Technology 1962; University Charter 1966; incorporated West London Institute into the University in 1995
Academic year: September to June
Chancellor: Lord WAKEHAM
Pro-Chancellor: D. KINGSMILL
Vice-Chancellor and Principal: Prof. CHRIS JENKS
Vice-Principal: Prof. M. SARHADI
Pro-Vice-Chancellors: Prof. S. HODKINSON (Development and External Relations),

Prof. Y.-H. SONG (Graduate Studies), Prof. L. THOMAS (Quality), Prof. C. JENKS (Research)
Academic Registrar: E. J. WEALE
Managing Director (Resources and Operations): P. BOWLER

Number of teachers: 665 (598 full-time, 67 part-time)
Number of students: 12,910

HEADS OF SCHOOLS

School of Arts: Prof. S. DIXON
Brunel Business School: Prof. D. LLOYD
School of Engineering and Design: Prof. S. TASSOU
School of Health Sciences and Social Care: Prof. L. DE SOUZA
School of Information Systems, Computing and Mathematics: Prof. R. MACREDIE
School of Social Sciences and Law: Prof. A. OLOWOFOYEKU
School of Sport and Education: Prof. L. THOMAS

PROFESSORS

ALLOTEY, P., Race and Diversity
ANDREWS, B., Health and Social Care
ANGELIDES, M., Information Systems and Computing
BALACHANDRAN, W., Systems Engineering
BENNETT, J., Economics and Finance
BERESFORD, P., Health and Social Care
BUTLER, C., Design and Systems Engineering
BUXTON, M., Economics and Finance
CAPEL, S., Sport Sciences
CAPORALE, G., Economics and Finance
CHIGARA, B., Law
CHOO, A., Law
CLARK, C., Systems Engineering
COSMAS, J. P., Electronic and Computer Engineering
CORTAZZI, M., Education
DARBY-DOWMAN, K. H., Mathematical Sciences
DAVIS, E. P., Economics
DE SOUZA, L. H., Health Studies
DICKSON, K. E., School of Business and Management
DIXON, S., Arts
DODSON, J., Institute for the Environment
ESAT, I. I., Mechanical Engineering
EVANS, R. E., Education
FAN, Z., Centre for Advanced Solidification Technology
FITZGERALD, G., Information Systems and Computing
FOX-RUSHBY, J., Health Studies
FYODOROV, Y. V., Mathematical Sciences
GLEES, A., School of International Studies
GOBET, F., Human Sciences
GOODWIN, R., Human Sciences
GRIMES, S. M., Graduate School
HARRISON, D. J., Design
HARWIN, J., Health and Social Care
HEALD, S. S., Human Sciences
HENDRY, J., School of Business and Management
HEVER, N., Mathematics
HEY, V., Education
HIERONS, R., Informations Systems and Computing
HOLLAND, A., Electrical and Computer Engineering
HORNSBY, P. R., Wolfson Centre
IOANNIDIS, C., Economics and Finance
IOSSA, E., Economics
IRANI, Z., Information Systems and Computing
IRVING, M. R., Electronic and Computer Engineering
JAFFEY, P., Law
KLEINBERG, S. J., Faculty Office of Arts and Social Sciences
KOSHY, V., Informations Systems and Computing

KUPER, A. J., Human Sciences
LAM, A. C. L., Business Management
LEA, R. M., Electronic and Computer Engineering
LEROY, S., Geography and Earth Sciences
LIU, X., Information Systems and Computing
LLOYD, D. J., Business School
MCCONNELL, A., Sport Sciences
MACREDIE, R. D., Information Systems and Computing
MARTIN, C., Economics and Finance
MITRA, G., Mathematical Sciences
MORAN, M. F., English
MORGAN, K. J., School of International Studies
NEWBOLD, R. F., Biological Sciences
OLOWOFOYEKU, A., Law
PEACOCK, J., Health Sciences
PETLEY, J., Performing Arts
POLDEN, P., Law
REIDPATH, D., Health Studies
ROBINSON, I., Human Sciences
RODGERS, G., Mathematical Sciences
SEALE, C., Human Sciences
SONG, J. H., Mechanical Engineering
SONG, Y. H., Electronic and Computer Engineering
STANTON, N. A., Design
STEWARD, F., School of Business and Management
STOLARSKI, T. A., Mechanical Engineering
STONHAM, T. J., Electronic and Computer Engineering
SUMPTER, J. P., Biology Sciences
SUTHERLAND, I. A., Brunel Institute of Bioengineering
TASSOU, S., Mechanical Engineering
THOMAS, L. M., Education
TOREN, C., Human Sciences
TULLOCH, J., Mathematical Sciences
TWIZELL, E. H., Mathematical Sciences
VASEGHI, S., Electronic and Computer Engineering
WATTS, S. T., Electronic and Computer Engineering
WHITEMAN, J. R., Mathematical Sciences
WIEGOLD, P., Performing Arts
WOODS, A., School of Business and Management
WRIGHT, D., Design and Systems Engineering
WRIGHT, M. J., Human Sciences
WROBEL, L. C., Mechanical Engineering
WYDELL, T., Human Sciences
YOUNG, T., Information Systems and Computing
ZHAO, H., Mechanical Engineering

ATTACHED INSTITUTES

Analysis, Testing, Slicing Search and Transformation Group: Dir Prof. R. HIERONS.

BFSS National Religious Centre: Dir L. BROADBENT.

Bioengineering Research Group: Dir Prof. C. CLARKE.

Body Space and Technology Research Group: Dir Dr S. BROADHURST.

Brunel Able Child Education Centre: Dir Dr V. KOSHY.

Brunel Centre for Advanced Solidification Technology (BCAST): Dir Prof. Z. FAN.

Brunel Centre of Contemporary Literature (BCCL).

Brunel Centre for Democratic Evaluation: Dir Dr J. FISHER.

Brunel Centre for Intelligence and Security Studies (BCISS): Dir Prof. A. GLEES.

Brunel Centre for Manufacturing Metrology: Dir Prof. B. JONES.

Brunel Centre for Packaging Technology (BCPT): Dir Dr L. GABRIELSON.

Brunel Enterprise Centre: Dir K. ROBSON.

Brunel Information and Technology Laboratory (BITLAB): Dir Prof. S. J. WATTS.

Brunel Institute of Cancer Genetics and Pharmacogenomics: Dir Prof. R. NEWBOLD.

Brunel Institute for Power Systems and Control: Dir Prof. M. R. IRVING.

Brunel Organisation and Systems Design Centre: Dir Dr N. PATEL.

Brunel Research into Enterprise, Sustainability and Ethics (BRESE).

CARISMA: Dir Prof. G. MITRA.

Centre for Applied Simulation Modelling: Dir Prof. R. PAUL.

Centre for Black Professional Practice.

Centre for Cell Chromosome Biology Group: Dirs Dr D. GRIFFIN, Dr I. KILL.

Centre for Child-Focused Anthropological Research: Dir Dr C. TOREN.

Centre for Child-Focused Research: Dir Prof. J. HARWIN.

Centre for Consumer and Commercial Law Research: Dir Prof. G. WOODROFFE.

Centre for Criminal Justice Research: Dir Dr C. CORBETT.

Centre for Health Informatics and Computing: Dir Prof. T. YOUNG.

Centre for Citizen Participation: Dir Prof. P. BERESFORD.

Centre for Cognition and Neuroimaging: Dir Prof. M. WRIGHT.

Centre for Epidemiological Research: Dir L. DE SOUZA.

Centre for Knowledge and Business Process Management: Dir Dr V. HLUPIC.

Centre for International and Public Law: Dir Prof. B. CHIGARA.

Centre for Living Information Systems Thinking: Dir Prof. R. PAUL.

Centre for Media Communications Research (CMCR): Dir Dr L. HENDERSON.

Centre for Research into Emotion Work (CREW): Dir Dr N. CORNELIUS.

Centre for Research in Rehabilitation: Dir L. DE SOUZA.

Centre for the Study of Law and the Family: Dirs F. KAGANAS, Prof. M. KING.

Centre for the Study of Health, Sickness and Disablement: Dir I. ROBINSON.

Centre for Youth Work Studies: Dir Dr S. BRADFORD.

Convergence of IP-based Services for Mobile Users and Networks in DVB-T and UMTS Systems (CISMUNDUS): Dir Prof. J. COSMAS.

Combustion Engines Research Group: Dir Prof. H. ZHAO.

Communications and Signal Processing Group: Dir Prof. S. VASEGHI.

Creative Practice Music Research Group: Dir F. GRIFFITH.

Culture, Race and Diversity in Health and Social Care (CRD): Dir Prof. P. ALLOTEY.

Design, Organisation and Systems Design Centre (OSDC): Dir Dr N. PATEL.

e2v Centre for Electronic Imaging: Dir Prof. A. HOLLAND.

Engineering Management Systems Group (EMSG): Dir Dr M. OZBAYRAK.

Experimental Techniques Centre: Dir Dr R. BULPETT.

Health Economics Research Group: Dir Prof. M. J. BUXTON.

Health Services and Epidemiology Research Group: Dir Prof. J. PEACOCK.

Imaging for Space and Terrestrial Applications: Dir Prof. A. HOLLAND.

Information Systems Evaluation and Integration Group (ISEing): Dir Prof. Z. IRANI.

INSTINCT for Convergence: Dir Dr T. J. OWENS.

Institute for Bioengineering: Dir Prof. I. SUTHERLAND.

Institute of Computational Mathematics: Dir Prof. J. R. WHITEMAN.

Institute for the Environment: Dir Prof. J. DODSON.

Intelligent Data Analysis Research Group (IDA): Dir Prof. X. LIU.

Microarray Facility: Dir Prof. X. LIU.

Molecular Immunology: Dir Dr S.-L. LI.

Multi-Agent and Distributed Intelligence Research Alliance: Dir Prof. G. RZEVSKI.

Multidisciplinary Assessment of Technology Centre for Healthcare (MATCH): Dir D. LAWES.

Public Health: Dir A. SCRIVEN.

Screen Media: Dir Dr M. AARON.

Statistics and Operational Research: Dir Prof. K. DARBY-DOWMAN (acting).

The Vivid Centre – Vivid Visualization Developments: Dir Dr C. CHEN.

Wolfson Centre for Materials Processing: Dir Prof. P. R. HORNSBY.

3D Murale: Dir Prof. J. COSMAS.

UNIVERSITY OF BUCKINGHAM

Hunter St, Buckingham, MK18 1EG

Telephone: (1280) 814080

Fax: (1280) 822245

E-mail: admissions@buck.ac.uk

Internet: www.buckingham.ac.uk

Founded 1973 (first student intake 1976); Royal Charter 1983

Private control

Academic year: January to December (4 10-week terms)

Chancellor: Sir MARTIN JACOMB
Chairman of Council: ROBERT TOMKINSON
Vice-Chancellor: Dr TERENCE KEALEY
Secretary and Registrar: Prof. JOHN CLARKE
Librarian and Director of Information Services: JOAN HOLAH

Number of teachers: 83 (59 full-time, 24 part-time)

Number of students: 750

Publication: *Denning Law Journal* (annually)

DEANS OF ACADEMIC DEPARTMENTS

Accounting and Finance: LAWRIE DRURY
Business School: Prof. PHIL DOVER
Education: ANTHONY O'HEAR
English Studies: GERRY LOFTUS
Humanities: Prof. MARTIN RICKETTS
Information Systems: Dr JUDITH JEFFCOATE
Law: CHARLOTTE WALSH
Management: Dr JIM RAFFERTY
Medical School: KAREL SIKORA (Dean-Elect)
Metabolic Research: Prof. MICHAEL CAWTHORNE
Modern Foreign Languages: Dr JILL HILL
Psychology: Dr PHILIP FINE

PROFESSORS

ADAMS, C. J., Information Systems
ALCOCK, A., Corporate Law
ARCH, J., Metabolic Research

BARRY, N. P., Social and Political Theory
CAWTHORNE, M. A., Metabolic Research
CLARKE, J. C., History
DURAND, A., European Law
EDWARDS, S., Law
O'KEEFE, D., Education
SMITHERS, A., Education
WOODHEAD, C., Education

ATTACHED RESEARCH INSTITUTES

Centre for Education and Employment Research: Dir Prof. ALAN SMITHERS.

Clore Laboratory: Dir Prof. MICHAEL CAWTHORNE.

UNIVERSITY OF CAMBRIDGE

Cambridge CB2 1TN

Telephone: (1223) 337733 (Central Switchboard); (1223) 332200 (Central Administration)

E-mail: webmaster@admin.cam.ac.uk

Internet: www.cam.ac.uk

Founded 13th century

Academic year: October to June

Chancellor: HRH THE PRINCE PHILIP, DUKE OF EDINBURGH

Vice-Chancellor: Prof. ALISON RICHARD
Pro Vice-Chancellors: Prof. A. CLIFF, Prof. I. LESLIE, Prof. M. MCKENDRICK, Prof. T. MINSON, Dr K. PRETTY
High Steward: Dame BRIDGET OGILVIE
Registrar: Dr T. J. MEAD
Librarian: P. K. FOX

Fitzwilliam Museum: see Museums

Number of teachers: 1,500

Number of students: 15,821 (11,160 undergraduate, 4,661 postgraduate)

PROFESSORS

Faculty of Archaeology and Anthropology (Downing St, Cambridge, CB2 3DZ; tel. (1223) 333500; fax (1223) 333503; e-mail archanth-enquires@lists.cam.ac.uk; internet www.archanth.cam.ac.uk):

HUMPHREY, C., Asian Anthropology (King's College)
JONES, M. K., Archaeological Science (Peterhouse)
MACFARLANE, A. D. J., Anthropological Science (King's College)
MASCIE-TAYLOR, C. G. N., Biological Anthropology (Churchill College)
MELLARS, P. A., Prehistory and Human Evolution (Corpus Christi College)
Lord RENFREW, Archaeology (Jesus College)
Dame STRATHERN, MARILYN, Social Anthropology (Girton College)

Faculty of Architecture and History of Art (1–5 Scroope Terrace, Trumpington St, Cambridge, CB2 1PX; tel. (1223) 332950; fax (1223) 332960; internet www.arct.cam.ac.uk):

ECHENIQUE, M. H., Land Use and Transport Studies (Churchill College)
HOWARD, D. J., History of Art
SAINT, A. J., Architecture
SPENCE, R., Architectural Engineering

Faculty of Biology (Old Press Site, Silver St, Cambridge, CB3 9EW; tel. (1223) 766894; fax (1223) 332355; e-mail facbiol@mole.bio.cam.ac.uk):

AKAM, M. E., Zoology (King's College)
ASHBURNER, M., Genetics (Churchill College)
BATE, C. M., Developmental Neurobiology (King's College)
BATESON, P. P. G. B., Ethology (King's College)
Sir BLUNDELL, TOM, Biochemistry (Sidney Sussex College)
BURROWS, M., Zoology (Wolfson College)

CLUTTON-BROCK, T. H., Animal Ecology (Magdalen College)

COLLINS, V. P., Histopathology

COOKE, A., Pathology (King's College)

CRAWFORD, A. C., Neurophysiology (Trinity College)

DAVIES, N. B., Behavioural Ecology (Pembroke College)

DICKINSON, A., Experimental Psychology (Hughes Hall)

ELLAR, D. J., Biochemistry (Gonville and Caius College)

ELLINGTON, C. P., Zoology (Downing College)

EVERITT, B. J., Behavioural Neuroscience (Downing College)

GILLIGAN, C. A., Plant Sciences (King's College)

GLOVER, D. M., Genetics (Fitzwilliam College)

GRAY, J. C., Plant Molecular Biology (Robinson College)

GRIFFITHS, H., Plant Sciences

HARRIS, W. A., Anatomy (Clare College)

HERBERT, J., Anatomy (Gonville and Caius College)

HUGHES, C., Pathology (Trinity College)

IRVINE, R. F., Molecular Pharmacology (Corpus Christi College)

JACKSON, R. J., Biochemistry (Pembroke College)

JACKSON, S. P., Zoology (St John's College)

JOHNSON, M. H., Anatomy (Christ's College)

KEVERNE, E. B., Behavioural Neuroscience (King's College)

KOUZARIDES, T., Pathology

LAMB, T. D., Neuroscience (Darwin College)

LASKEY, R. A., Animal Embryology (Darwin College)

LAUE, E. D., Biochemistry (St John's College)

LAUGHLIN, S. B., Zoology (Churchill College)

LEADLAY, P. F., Biochemistry (Clare College)

LEIGH, R. A., Botany (Girton College)

McNAUGHTON, P. A., Pharmacology (Christ's College)

METCALFE, J. C., Mammalian Cell Biochemistry (Darwin College)

MINSON, A. C., Virology (Wolfson College)

MOLLON, J. D., Visual Neuroscience (Gonville and Caius College)

MOORE, B. C. J., Experimental Psychology (Wolfson College)

PARKER, J. S., Plant Cytogenetics (St Catharine's College)

PERHAM, R. N., Structural Biochemistry (St John's College)

ROBBINS, T. W., Experimental Psychology (Downing College)

SALMOND, G. P. C., Biochemistry (Wolfson College)

SMITH, J. C., Zoology (Christ's College)

STANLEY, M. A., Pathology (Christ's College)

SURANI, M. A. H., Physiology of Reproduction (King's College)

TAYLOR, C. W., Pharmacology (Downing College)

THOMAS, J. O., Macromolecular Biochemistry (St Catherine's College)

THOMAS, R. C., Physiology (Downing College)

TROWSDALE, J., Pathology

TRUMP, D., Molecular Genetics

TYLER, L. K., Experimental Psychology (Clare College)

WARING, M. J., Pharmacology (Jesus College)

WYLLIE, A. H., Pathology (St John's College)

Faculty of Classics (Sidgwick Site, Sidgwick Ave, Cambridge, CB3 9DA; tel. (1223) 335151; fax (1223) 335960; internet www.classics.cam.ac.uk):

AUSTIN, C. F. L., Greek (Trinity Hall)

CARTLEDGE, P. A., Greek History (Clare College)

DIGGLE, J., Greek and Latin (Queens' College)

GAMSEY, P., History of Classical Antiquity (Jesus College)

GOLDHILL, S., Greek Literature and Culture (King's College)

HENDERSON, J., Classics (King's College)

HORROCKS, G. C., Comparative Philology (St John's College)

MILLETT, M. J., Classical Archaeology (Fitzwilliam College)

OSBORNE, R., Ancient History (King's College)

REEVE, M. D., Latin (Pembroke College)

SCHOFIELD, M., Ancient Philosophy (St John's College)

SEDLEY, D. N., Ancient Philosophy (Christ's College)

School of Clinical Medicine (Addenbrooke's Hospital, Hills Rd, Cambridge, CB2 2SP; tel. (1223) 336700; fax (1223) 336709; e-mail school-enquiries@medschl.cam.ac.uk; internet www.medschl.cam.ac.uk):

ALLAIN, J.-P., Transfusion Medicine (Corpus Christi College)

BARON, J. C., Medicine

BARON-COHEN, S., Psychiatry (Trinity College)

BENNETT, M. R., Medicine

BLACKWELL, J. M., Molecular Parasitology (Newnham College)

BOBROW, M., Medical Genetics (Wolfson College)

BRADLEY, J. A., Surgery

BRAYNE, C. E. G., Public Health (Darwin College)

BROWN, M. J., Clinical Pharmacology (Gonville and Caius College)

BULLMORE, E. T., Psychiatry

CARRELL, R. W., Haematology (Trinity College)

CHATTERJEE, V. K. K., Medicine (Churchill College)

CHILVERS, E. R., Respiratory Medicine (St Edmund's College)

COMPSTON, D. A. S., Neurology (Jesus College)

COX, T. M., Medicine (Sidney Sussex College)

DANESH, J., Public Health and Primary Care

DAY, N. E., Public Health and Primary Care (Hughes Hall)

DIXON, A. K., Radiology (Peterhouse)

DUNGER, D. B., Paediatrics

EDWARDS, A. W. F., Public Health and Primary Care (Gonville and Caius College)

FAWCETT, J. W., Medicine (King's College)

FEARON, D. T., Medicine (Trinity College)

FFRENCH-CONSTANT, C. K., Neurological Genetics (Pembroke College)

GASTON, J. S. H., Rheumatology (St Edmund's College)

GOODYER, I. M., Child and Adolescent Psychiatry (Wolfson College)

GREEN, A. R., Haematology

HODGES, J. R., Medicine (King's College)

HOLLAND, A. J., Psychiatry

HUGHES, I. A., Paediatrics (Clare Hall)

JONES, P. B., Psychiatry

KHAW, K.-T., Clinical Gerontology (Gonville and Caius College)

KINMONTH, A.-L., General Practice (St John's College)

LEVER, A. M. L., Medicine (Peterhouse)

LOMAS, D. J., Respiratory Biology (Trinity College)

LUZIO, J. P., Clinical Biochemistry (St Edmund's College)

MENON, D. K., Medicine (Queens' College)

MURPHY, G., Oncology

NEAL, D. E., Surgery

O'RAHILLY, S., Metabolic Medicine (Churchill College)

PETERS, A. M., Nuclear Medicine (New Hall)

Sir PETERS, KEITH, Physic (Christ's College)

PICKARD, J. D., Neurosurgery (St Catharine's College)

PONDER, B. A. J., Clinical Oncology (Jesus College)

READ, R. J., Haematology

ROSENGARD, B. R., Surgery

SIDDLE, K., Clinical Biochemistry (Churchill College)

SISSONS, J. G. P., Medicine (Darwin College)

SMITH, G. C. S., Obstetrics and Gynaecology

SUTTON, S. R., Public Health and Primary Care

TODD, J. A., Medical Genetics (Gonville and Caius College)

VENKITARAMAN, A. R., Cancer Research (New Hall)

WEISSBERG, P. L., Cardiovascular Medicine (Wolfson College)

Department of Clinical Veterinary Medicine (Madingley Rd, Cambridge, CB3 0ES; tel. (1223) 337701; fax (1223) 337610; e-mail enquiries@vet.cam.ac.uk; internet www.vet.cam.ac.uk):

ALLEN, W. R., Equine Reproduction (Robinson College)

BLAKEMORE, W. F., Neuropathology (Wolfson College)

BROOM, D. M., Animal Welfare (St Catharine's College)

JEFFCOTT, L. B., Veterinary Clinical Studies (Pembroke College)

McCONNELL, I., Veterinary Science (Clare Hall)

MASKELL, D. J., Farm Animal Health, Food Science and Food Safety (Wolfson College)

Faculty of Divinity (West Rd, Cambridge, CB3 9BS; tel. (1223) 763002; fax (1223) 763002; e-mail divinity-office@lists.cam.ac.uk; internet www.divinity.cam.ac.uk):

DAVIES, G. I., Old Testament Studies (Fitzwilliam College)

DE LANGE, N. R. M., Hebrew and Jewish Studies (Wolfson College)

DUFFY, E., History of Christianity (Magdalene College)

FORD, D. F., Divinity (Selwyn College)

GORDON, R., Hebrew (St Catharine's College)

HORBURY, W., Jewish and Early Christian Studies (Corpus Christi College)

LIPNER, J., Hiduism and Comparative Study of Religion (Clare Hall)

RILEY-SMITH, J., Ecclesiastical History (Emmanuel College)

STANTON, G. N., Divinity – Lady Margaret's (Fitzwilliam College)

TURNER, D. A., Divinity – Norris-Hulse (Peterhouse College)

Department of Earth Sciences and Geography (Downing St, Cambridge, CB2 3EQ; tel. (1223) 333400 (Earth Sciences), (1223) 333399 (Geography); fax (1223) 333450 (Earth Sciences), (1223) 333392 (Geography); internet www.esc.cam.ac.uk):

BENNETT, R. J., Geography (St Catharine's College)

BICKLE, M. J., Tectonics, Basin and Crustal Development and Sedimentology (Queens' College)

CARPENTER, M. A., Mineralogy and Mineral Physics (Magdalene College)

CLIFF, A. D., Theoretical Geography (Christ's College)

CONWAY MORRIS, S., Evolutionary Palaeoecology (St John's College)

DOVE, M., Mineralogy and Mineral Physics

DOWDESWELL, J. A., Physical Geography (Jesus College)

ELDERFIELD, H., Environmental Change and Marine Geochemistry (St Catharine's College)

HAINING, R. P., Geography (Fitzwilliam College)

HUPPERT, H., Geophysics (King's College)

JACKSON, J., Geophysics

MARTIN, R. L., Geography (St Catharine's College)

McCAVE, I. N., Environmental Change and Marine Geochemistry (St John's College)

McKENZIE, D. P., Geophysics (King's College)

RICHARDS, K. S., Geography (Emmanuel College)

RICKARDS, R. B., Palaeobiology and Palaeoecology (Emmanuel College)

SALJE, E. K. H., Mineralogy and Petrology (Darwin College)

SCOTT, J. F., Mineralogy and Mineral Physics

VAN ANDEL, R. P., Environmental Change and Marine Geochemistry

WHITE, R. S., Geophysics (St Edmund's College)

WOODS, A. W., Earth Sciences (St John's College)

Faculty of Economics and Politics (Austin Robinson Building, Sidgwick Ave, Cambridge, CB3 9DD; tel. (1223) 335200; fax (1223) 335475; e-mail faculty@econ.cam.ac.uk; internet www.econ.cam.ac.uk):

BROWN, W. A., Industrial Relations (Wolfson College)

DASGUPTA, P. S., Economics (St John's College)

Lord EATWELL, Economics (Queens' College)

HARRIS, C. J., Economics (King's College)

HARVEY, A. C., Econometrics (Corpus Christi College)

HONKAPOHJA, S., Macroeconomics

Sir MIRRLEES, JAMES, Political Economy (Trinity College)

NEWBERY, D. M. G., Applied Economics (Churchill College)

PESARAN, M. H., Economics (Trinity College)

ROWTHORN, R. E., Economics (King's College)

SINGH, A., Economics (Queens' College)

Faculty of Education (17 Trumpington St, Cambridge, CB2 1QA; tel. (1223) 332888; fax (1223) 332894; internet www.educ.cam.ac.uk):

GRAY, J. M., Education (Homerton College)

MACBEATH, J. E. C., Education (Hughes Hall)

McINTYRE, D. I., Education (Hughes Hall)

RUDDUCK, J., Education (Homerton College)

Faculty of Engineering (Trumpington St, Cambridge, CB2 1PZ; tel. (1223) 332600; fax (1223) 332662; e-mail reception@eng.cam.ac.uk; internet www.eng.cam.ac.uk):

AINGER, C., Engineering

AMARATUNGA, G. A. J., Engineering (Churchill College)

BOLTON, M. D., Engineering (Churchill College)

BRITTER, R. E., Engineering (Pembroke College)

CALLADINE, C., Engineering

CAMPBELL, A. M., Engineering (Christ's College)

CARDWELL, D., Engineering

CIPOLLA, R., Engineering (Jesus College)

COLES, H. J., Engineering

COLLINGS, N., Engineering (Robinson College)

COLOURIS, G., Engineering

CONTI, R., Engineering

DAWES, W. N., Aeronautical Engineering (Churchill College)

DENTON, J. D., Turbomachinery, Aerodynamics (Trinity Hall)

DOWLING, A. P., Mechanical Engineering (Sidney Sussex College)

EARL, C. F., Engineering

FFOWCS WILLIAMS, J. E., Engineering (Emmanuel College)

FITZGERALD, W., Engineering

FLECK, N. A., Mechanics of Materials (Pembroke College)

GLOVER, K., Engineering (Sidney Sussex College)

GREGORY, M. J., Manufacturing Engineering (Churchill College)

GUTHRIE, P., Engineering

HARVEY, J., Engineering

HOCHGREB, S., Engineering

HODSON, H. P., Engineering (Girton College)

HOPPER, A., Communications (Corpus Christi College)

HUTCHINGS, I. M., Manufacturing Engineering (St John's College)

IWAI, Y., Engineering

KELLY, M. J., Engineering (Trinity Hall)

KITTELSON, D., Engineering

LANGLEY, R. S., Mechanical Engineering (Fitzwilliam College)

LIDDELL, W. I., Engineering

MAIR, R. J., Engineering (St John's College)

MIGLIORATO, P., Engineering (Trinity College)

MILNE, W. I., Electrical Engineering (Churchill College)

NEWLAND, D. E., Engineering (Selwyn College)

PALMER, A. E., Engineering

PELLEGRINO, S., Engineering (Corpus Christi College)

RAYNER, P. J. W., Signal Processing (Christ's College)

ROBERTSON, J., Engineering (Churchill College)

WALLACE, K. M., Engineering (Selwyn College)

WELLAND, M. E., Engineering (St John's College)

WHITE, I. H., Electrical Engineering (Jesus College)

WOODHOUSE, J., Engineering (Clare College)

YOUNG, J. B., Engineering (King's College)

YOUNG, S. J., Information Engineering (Emmanuel College)

Faculty of English (27 Trumpington St, Cambridge, CB3 1QA; tel. (1223) 765786; fax (1223) 765776; e-mail english-faculty@lists.cam.ac.uk; internet www.english.cam.ac.uk):

BARTON, A., English (Trinity College)

Dame BEER, GILLIAN (Clare Hall)BEER, J. (Peterhouse College)

BROWN, G., English as an International Language (Clare College)

COLLINI, S. A., English (Clare Hall)

DONALDSON, I., English (King's College)

DUMVILLE, D. N., Anglo-Saxon, Norse and Celtic (Girton College)

ERSKINE-HILL, H. H., Literary History (Pembroke College)

JACOBUS, M. L., English (Churchill College)

KERRIGAN, J. F., English (St John's College)

SIMPSON, W. J., English (Girton College)

WINDEATT, B. A., English (Emmanuel College)

Faculty of History (West Rd, Cambridge, CB3 9EF; tel. (1223) 335340; fax (1223) 335968; e-mail gen.enq@hist.cam.ac.uk; internet www.hist.cam.ac.uk):

ABULAFIA, D. S. H., History of the Mediterranean Countries in Middle Ages (Gonville and Caius College)

ANDREW, C. M., Modern and Contemporary History (Corpus Christi College)

BADGER, A. J., American History since 1930 (Clare College)

BAYLY, C. A., South Asian Studies Centre (St Catharine's College)

BLANNING, T. C. W., Modern European History (Sidney Sussex College)

BRADING, D. A., Latin American History (Clare Hall)

BURKE, U. P., Cultural History (Emmanuel College)

CLARKE, P. F., Modern British Political History (Trinity College)

DAUNTON, M. J., Economic History (Churchill College)

DUFFY, E., Religious History (Magdalene College)

EVANS, G., Medieval Intellectual History

EVANS, R. J., Modern European History (Gonville and Caius College)

GARNSEY, P. D. A., Ancient History (Jesus College)

HATCHER, M. J., Economic and Social History (Corpus Christi College)

ILIFFE, J., African History (St John's College)

McKITTERICK, R. D., Medieval History (Newnham College)

MAYALL, J. B. L., International Relations (Sidney Sussex College)

MORRILL, J. S., British and Irish History (Selwyn College)

RILEY-SMITH, J. S. C., Crusading History (Emmanuel College)

SKINNER, Q. R. D., Modern History (Christ's College)

STEDMAN JONES, G., Political Economy (King's College)

Faculty of Law (10 West Rd, Cambridge, CB3 9DZ; tel. (1223) 330033; fax (1223) 330055; e-mail admin@law.cam.ac.uk; internet www.law.cam.ac.uk):

ALLAN, T., Public Law and Jurisprudence (Pembroke College)

ALLOTT, P. J., International Public Law (Trinity College)

BAKER, J. H., English Legal History (St Catharine's College)

Sir BEATSON, J., Laws of England (St John's College)

BELL, J. S., Law (Pembroke College)

Sir BOTTOMS, ANTHONY, Criminology (Fitzwilliam College)

CHEFFINS, B. R., Corporate Law (Trinity Hall)

CLARKE, M. A., Commercial Contract Law (St John's College)

CORNISH, W. R., Intellectual Property Law (Magdalene College)

CRAWFORD, J. R., International Law (Jesus College)

DASHWOOD, A. A., European Law (Sidney Sussex College)

FARRINGTON, D. P., Psychological Criminology (Darwin College)

GRAY, K. J., Law (Trinity College)

IBBETSON, D. J., Civil Law (Corpus Christi College)

SMITH, A. T. H., Criminal and Public Laws (Gonville and Caius College)

SPENCER, J. R., Law (Selwyn College)

TILEY, J., Law of Taxation (Queens' College)

TONRY, M., Institute of Criminology

WIKSTROM, P. O. H., Criminology (Girton College)

Faculty of Mathematics (Centre for Mathematical Sciences, Wilberforce Rd, Cambridge, CB3 0WA; tel. (1223) 337900

(Applied Mathematics and Theoretical Physics), (1223) 337999 (Pure Mathematics and Mathematical Statistics); fax (1223) 337918 (Applied Mathematics and Theoretical Physics), (1223) 337920 (Pure Mathematics and Mathematical Statistics); internet www .maths.cam.ac.uk):

BAKER, A., Pure Mathematics (Trinity College)

BARROW, J. D., Applied Mathematics (Clare Hall)

COATES, J. H., Pure Mathematics (Emmanuel College)

DRUMMOND, I. T., Applied Mathematics and Theoretical Physics (Robinson College)

EKERT, A. K., Applied Mathematics

FOKAS, A. S., Applied Mathematics

GIBBONS, G. W., Theoretical Physics (Clare College)

GOWERS, W. T., Mathematical Studies (Trinity College)

GREEN, M. B., Theoretical Physics (Clare Hall)

GRIMMETT, G. R., Mathematical Statistics (Churchill College)

HAWKING, S. W., Mathematics (Gonville and Caius College)

HINCH, E. J., Fluid Mechanics (Trinity College)

HUPPERT, H. E., Theoretical Geophysics (King's College)

ISERLES, A., Applied Mathematics and Theoretical Physics (King's College)

KELLY, F. P., Mathematics of Systems (Christ's College)

LANDSHOFF, P. V., Mathematical Physics (Christ's College)

LICKORISH, W. B. R., Geometric Topology (Pembroke College)

MCINTYRE, M. E., Atmospheric Dynamics (St John's College)

MAHADEVAN, L., Complex Physical Systems

MANTON, N. S., Mathematical Physics (St John's College)

PEDLEY, T. J., Fluid Mechanics (Gonville and Caius College)

PROCTOR, M. R. E., Applied Mathematics and Theoretical Physics (Trinity College)

ROGERS, L. C. G., Pure Mathematics (St John's College)

SCHOLL, A. J., Pure Mathematics

SHEPHERD-BARRON, N. I., Pure Mathematics and Mathematical Statistics (Trinity College)

STONE, J. M., Applied Mathematics

THOMAS, C. B., Pure Mathematics (Robinson College)

TOTARO, B. J., Pure Mathematics and Mathematical Statistics

TOWNSEND, P. K., Theoretical Physics (Queen's College)

TUROK, N., Mathematical Physics (Clare Hall)

WEBER, R. R., Mathematics for Operational Research (Queens' College)

WEISS, N. O., Mathematical Astrophysics (Clare College)

WILLIS, J. R., Theoretical Solid Mechanics (Fitzwilliam College)

WILSON, P. M. H., Pure Mathematics (Trinity College)

Faculty of Modern and Medieval Languages (Sidgwick Ave, Cambridge, CB3 9DA; tel. (1223) 335000; fax (1223) 335062; e-mail mml-faculty-office@lists.cam.ac.uk; internet www.mml.cam.ac.uk):

BARANSKI, Z. G., Italian (New Hall)

BAYLEY, P. J., French (Gonville and Caius College)

BOYDE, P., Italian (St John's College)

BOYLE, N., German (Magdalene College)

CROSS, A. G., Slavonic Studies (Fitzwilliam College)

FRANKLIN, S., Slavonic Studies (Clare College)

HAWKINS, S., Linguistics (Clare Hall)

KAY, H. S., French (Girton College)

MCKENDRICK, M. C., Spanish and Portuguese (Girton College)

NISBET, H. B., German (Sidney Sussex College)

PAULIN, R. C., German (Trinity College)

ROBERTS, I. G., Linguistics (Downing College)

SMITH, P. J., Spanish and Portuguese (Trinity Hall)

Faculty of Music (11 West Rd, Cambridge, CB3 9DP; tel. (1223) 335184; fax (1223) 335067; e-mail admin@mus.cam.ac.uk; internet www.mus.cam.ac.uk):

HOLLOWAY, R. G., Music (Gonville and Caius)

PARKER, R., Music (St John's College)

Faculty of Oriental Studies (Sidgwick Ave, Cambridge, CB3 9DA; tel. (1223) 335106; fax (1223) 335110; e-mail webmaster@oriental .cam.ac.uk; internet www.oriental.cam.ac .uk):

BOWRING, R. J., Modern Japanese Studies (Downing College)

GORDON, R. P., Hebrew (St Catharine's College)

KORNICKI, P. F., Japanese History and Bibliography (Robinson College)

MCMULLEN, D. L., Chinese (St John's College)

POSTGATE, J. N., Assyriology (Trinity College)

REIF, S. C., Medieval Hebrew Studies (St John's College)

Faculty of Philosophy (Sidgwick Ave, Cambridge, CB3 9DA; tel. (1223) 335090; fax (1223) 335091; e-mail phil-admin@lists.cam .ac.uk; internet www.phil.cam.ac.uk):

BLACKBURN, S. W., Philosophy (Trinity College)

CRAIG, E. J., Philosophy (Churchill College)

HEAL, B. J., Philosophy (St John's College)

Faculty of Physics and Chemistry (Institute of Astronomy, Madingley Rd, Cambridge, CB3 0HA; tel. (1223) 337089; fax (1223) 337523):

AHMED, H., Microelectronics (Corpus Christi College)

BHADESHIA, H. K. D. H., Materials Science and Metallurgy (Darwin College)

BLAND, J. A. C., Physics (Selwyn College)

BONFIELD, W., Materials Science and Metallurgy

CARTER, J. R., Physics (Newnham)

CLYNE, T. W., Materials Science and Metallurgy (Downing College)

DOBSON, C. M., Chemistry

DONALD, A. M., Experimental Physics (Robinson College)

EFSTATHIOU, G. P., Astrophysics (King's College)

ELLIOTT, S. R., Chemistry (Trinity College)

EVETTS, J. E., Device Materials (Pembroke College)

Sir FERSHT, A. R., Organic Chemistry (Gonville and Caius College)

FIELD, J. E., Applied Physics (Magdalene College)

FRAY, D. J., Materials Chemistry (Fitzwilliam College)

FRIEND, R. H., Physics (St John's College)

GILMORE, G. F., Institute of Astronomy (King's College)

GLEN, R. C., Chemistry (Clare College)

GOUGH, D. O., Theoretical Astrophysics (Churchill College)

HANDY, N. C., Quantum Chemistry (St Catharine's College)

HANSEN, J.-P., Chemistry (Corpus Christi College)

HILLS, R. E., Physics (St Edmund's College)

HOLMES, A. B., Organic and Polymer Chemistry (Clare College)

HUMPHREYS, C. J., Materials Science (Selwyn College)

JOHNSON, B. F. G., Chemistry (Fitzwilliam College)

JOSEPHSON, B. D., Physics (Trinity College)

KING, D. A., Physical Chemistry (Downing College)

KLINOWSKI, J., Chemistry (Peterhouse)

LAMBERT, R. M., Chemistry (King's College)

LASENBY, A. N., Physics (Queens' College)

LEY, S. V., Organic Chemistry (Trinity College)

LIANG, W. Y., Superconductivity (Gonville and Caius College)

LITTLEWOOD, P. B., Physics (Trinity College)

LONGAIR, M. S., Natural Philosophy (Clare Hall)

LONZARICH, G. G., Condensed-Matter Physics (Trinity College)

OSTRIKER, J., Astronomy (Clare College)

PATERSON, I., Chemistry (Jesus College)

PAYNE, M. C., Physics (Pembroke College)

PEPPER, M., Physics (Trinity College)

PRINGLE, J. E., Astronomy (Emmanuel College)

PYLE, J. A., Chemistry (St Catharine's College)

Sir REES, MARTIN, Astronomy (King's College)

SANDERS, J. K. M., Inorganic Chemistry (Selwyn College)

WARNER, M., Physics (Corpus Christi College)

WEBBER, B. R., Physics (Emmanuel College)

WILLIAMS, D. H., Biological Chemistry (Churchill College)

WINDLE, A. H., Materials Science (Trinity College)

Faculty of Social and Political Sciences (New Museums Site, Cambridge, CB2 3RF; tel. (1223) 334520; fax (1223) 334550; e-mail sps-enquiries@lists.cam.ac.uk; internet www .sps.cam.ac.uk):

DUNN, J. M., Political Theory (King's College)

HAWTHORN, G. P., International Politics (Clare Hall)

MITCHELL, J. C. W., Social and Political Sciences (Jesus College)

RICHARDS, M. P. M., Family Research (Trinity College)

THOMPSON, J. B., Sociology (Jesus College)

TURNER, B. S., Sociology

Institute of Biotechnology (Tennis Court Rd, Cambridge, CB2 1QT; tel. (1223) 334160; fax (1223) 334162; e-mail admin@biotech.cam.ac .uk; internet www.biot.cam.ac.uk):

LOWE, C. R., Biotechnology (Trinity College)

Department of Chemical Engineering (New Museums Site, Pembroke St, Cambridge, CB2 3RA; tel. (1223) 334799; fax (1223) 334796; e-mail research@cheng.cam.ac.uk; internet www.cheng.cam.ac.uk):

BRIDGWATER, J., Chemical Engineering (St Catharine's College)

GLADDEN, L. F., Chemical Engineering (Trinity College)

HAYHURST, A. N., Chemical Engineering (Queens' College)

MACKLEY, M. R., Chemical Engineering (Robinson College)

SLATER, N. K. H., Chemical Engineering (Sidney Sussex College)

Computer Laboratory (William Gates Building, J. J. Thomson Ave, Cambridge, CB3 0FD; tel. (1223) 763500; fax (1223) 334678; e-mail departmental-secretary@cl.cam.ac.uk; internet www.cl.cam.ac.uk):

CROWCROFT, J. A., Communications Systems (Trinity College)

GORDON, M. J. C., Computer Assisted Reasoning (King's College)

LESLIE, I. M., Computer Science (Christ's College)

PITTS, A. M., Computer Science (Darwin College)

WINSKEL, G., Computer Science (Emmanuel College)

Department of History and Philosophy of Science (Free School Lane, Cambridge, CB2 3RH; tel. (1223) 334500; fax (1223) 334554; e-mail hps-admin@lists.cam.ac.uk; internet www.hps.cam.ac.uk):

FORRESTER, J. P., History and Philosophy of Psychoanalysis and Human Science (King's College)

JARDINE, N., History and Philosophy of the Sciences (Darwin College)

KUSCH, M., Philosophy of Language and Mind

LIPTON, P., History and Philosophy of Science (King's College)

SCHAFFER, S., History of Physical Science

SECORD, J., Social History of Science

Department of Land Economy (19 Silver St, Cambridge, CB3 9EP; tel. (1223) 337147; fax (1223) 337130; internet www.landecon.cam .ac.uk):

GLASCOCK, J., Real Estate Finance

Judge Institute of Management Studies (Trumpington St, Cambridge, CB2 1AG; tel. (1223) 339700; fax (1223) 339701; e-mail enquiries@jims.cam.ac.uk; internet www .jims.cam.ac.uk):

DAWSON, S. J. N., Management Studies (Sidney Sussex College)

DEAKIN, S. F., Corporate Governance (Peterhouse)

DEMPSTER, M. A. H., Management Studies

Lord EATWELL, Financial Policy (Queens' College)

HUGHES, A., Enterprise Studies (Sidney Sussex College)

MEEKS, G., Financial Accounting

NOLAN, P. H., Chinese Management (Jesus College)

OLIVER, N., Management Studies (Wolfson College)

PHILLIPS, N. W., Management Studies

SCHOLTES, S., Management Science

WALSHAM, G., Management Studies

WILLMOTT, H., Management Studies

WOMEN'S COLLEGES

Lucy Cavendish College: Lady Margaret Rd, Cambridge, CB3 0BU; tel. (1223) 332190; fax (1223) 332178; internet www.lcc.cam.ac .uk; f. 1965; Pres. Dame VERONICA SUTHERLAND.

New Hall: Huntingdon Rd, Cambridge, CB3 0DF; tel. (1223) 762100; fax (1223) 352941; internet www.newhall.cam.ac.uk; f. 1954; Pres. A. M. LONSDALE.

Newnham College: Sidgwick Ave, Cambridge, CB3 9DF; tel. (1223) 335700; fax (1223) 359155; internet www.newn.cam.ac .uk; f. 1871; Principal Baroness ONORA O'NEILL.

MIXED COLLEGES

Christ's College: St Andrew's St, Cambridge, CB2 3BU; tel. (1223) 334900; fax (1223) 334967; internet www.christs.cam.ac .uk; f. 1505 for men; women admitted 1978; Master Prof. FRANK KELLY.

Churchill College: Storey's Way, Cambridge, CB3 0DS; tel. (1223) 336000; fax (1223) 336480; internet www.chu.cam.ac.uk; f. 1960 for men; women admitted 1972; Master Sir DAVID WALLACE.

Clare College: Trinity Lane, Cambridge, CB2 1TL; tel. (1223) 333200; fax (1223) 333219; internet www.clare.cam.ac.uk; f. 1326 for men; women admitted 1972; Master Prof. A. J. BADGER.

Corpus Christi College: Trumpington St, Cambridge, CB2 1RH; tel. (1223) 338000; fax (1223) 338061; internet www.corpus.cam.ac .uk; f. 1352 for men; women admitted 1983; Master Prof. H. AHMED.

Downing College: Regent St, Cambridge, CB2 1DQ; tel. (1223) 334800; fax (1223) 467934; internet www.dow.cam.ac.uk; f. 1800 for men; women admitted 1978; Master Prof. B. EVERITT.

Emmanuel College: St Andrew's St, Cambridge, CB2 3AP; tel. (1223) 334200; fax (1223) 334426; internet www.emma.cam.ac .uk; f. 1584 for men; women admitted 1978; Master Lord RICHARD WILSON.

Fitzwilliam College: Huntingdon Rd, Cambridge, CB3 0DG; tel. (1223) 332000; fax (1223) 464162; internet www.fitz.ac.uk; f. 1966 for men; women admitted 1978; Master Prof. B. F. G. JOHNSON.

Girton College: Huntington Rd, Cambridge, CB3 0JG; tel. (1223) 338999; fax (1223) 338896; internet www.girton.cam.ac .uk; f. 1869 for women; men admitted 1977; Mistress Prof. Dame MARILYN STRATHERN.

Gonville and Caius College: Trinity St, Cambridge, CB2 1TA; tel. (1223) 332400; fax (1223) 332456; internet www.cai.cam.ac.uk; f. 1348 for men; women admitted 1978; Master N. MCKENDRICK.

Homerton College: Hills Rd, Cambridge, CB2 2PH; tel. (1223) 507111; fax (1223) 507120; internet www.homerton.cam.ac.uk; f. 1824 as a Training College (Approved Society 1976); men re-admitted 1978; Principal Dr K. B. PRETTY.

Hughes Hall: Mortimer Rd, Cambridge, CB1 2EW; tel. (1223) 334898; fax (1223) 311179; internet www.hughes.cam.ac.uk; f. 1885 as the Cambridge Training College for Women (Approved Foundation 1968); Pres. Prof. PETER RICHARDS.

Jesus College: Jesus Lane, Cambridge, CB5 8BL; tel. (1223) 339339; fax (1223) 324910; internet www.jesus.cam.ac.uk; f. 1497 for men; women admitted 1978; Master Prof. ROBERT J. MAIR.

King's College: King's Parade, Cambridge, CB2 1ST; tel. (1223) 331100; fax (1223) 331315; internet www.kings.cam.ac.uk; f. 1441 for men; women admitted 1972; Provost Dame JUDITH MAYHEW JONAS.

Magdalene College: Magdalene St, Cambridge, CB3 0AG; tel. (1223) 332100; fax (1223) 363637; internet www.magd.cam.ac .uk; f. 1428 for men; women admitted 1987; Master D. D. ROBINSON.

Pembroke College: Trumpington St, Cambridge, CB2 1RF; tel. (1223) 338100; fax (1223) 338163; e-mail enquiries@pem.cam .ac.uk; internet www.pem.cam.ac.uk; f. 1347 for men; women admitted 1983; Master Sir ROGER TOMKYS.

Peterhouse: Trumpington St, Cambridge, CB2 1RD; tel. (1223) 338200; fax (1223) 337578; internet www.pet.cam.ac.uk; f. 1284 for men; women admitted 1984; Master Lord WILSON OF TILLYORN.

Queens' College: Silver St, Cambridge, CB3 9ET; tel. (1223) 335511; fax (1223) 335522; e-mail enquiries@quns.cam.ac.uk; internet www.quns.cam.ac.uk; f. 1448 for men; women admitted 1979; Pres. Lord EATWELL.

Robinson College: Grange Rd, Cambridge, CB3 9AN; tel. (1223) 339100; fax (1223) 351794; internet www.robinson.cam.ac.uk; f. 1979; Warden DAVID YATES.

St Catharine's College: Trumpington St, Cambridge, CB2 1RL; tel. (1223) 338300; fax (1223) 338340; internet www.caths.cam.ac .uk; f. 1473 for men; women admitted 1978; Master Prof. Dame JEAN THOMAS.

St Edmund's College: Mount Pleasant, Cambridge, CB3 0BN; tel. (1223) 336250; fax (1223) 336111; e-mail college.office@ st-edmunds.cam.ac.uk; internet www .st-edmunds.cam.ac.uk; f. 1896 for men; (Approved Foundation 1975); women admitted 1978; Master Sir BRIAN HEAP.

St John's College: St John's St, Cambridge, CB2 1TP; tel. (1223) 338600; fax (1223) 337720; e-mail enquiries@joh.cam.ac.uk; internet www.joh.cam.ac.uk; f. 1511 for men; women admitted 1981; Master Prof. P. GODDARD.

Selwyn College: Grange Rd, Cambridge, CB3 9DQ; tel. (1223) 335846; fax (1223) 335837; internet www.sel.cam.ac.uk; f. 1882 for men; women admitted 1976; Master Prof. R. BOWRING.

Sidney Sussex College: Sidney St, Cambridge, CB2 3HU; tel. (1223) 338800; fax (1223) 338884; e-mail enquiries@sid.cam.ac .uk; internet www.sid.cam.ac.uk; f. 1596 for men; women admitted 1976; Master Prof. S. J. N. DAWSON.

Trinity College: Trinity St, Cambridge, CB2 1TQ; tel. (1223) 338400; fax (1223) 338564; e-mail college.office@trin.cam.ac.uk; internet www.trin.cam.ac.uk; f. 1546 for men; women admitted 1977; Master Prof. A. K. SEN.

Trinity Hall: Trinity Lane, Cambridge, CB2 1TJ; tel. (1223) 332500; fax (1223) 332537; internet www.trinhall.cam.ac.uk; f. 1350 for men; women admitted 1977; Master Prof. P. F. CLARKE.

MIXED COLLEGES FOR GRADUATE STUDENTS

Clare Hall: Herschel Rd, Cambridge, CB3 9AL; tel. (1223) 332360; fax (1223) 333219; e-mail receptionist@clarehall.cam.ac.uk; internet www.clarehall.cam.ac.uk; f. 1965 (Approved Foundation); Pres. Prof. E. SALJE.

Darwin College: Silver St, Cambridge, CB3 9EU; tel. (1223) 335660; fax (1223) 335667; e-mail deanery@dar.cam.ac.uk; internet www.dar.cam.ac.uk; f. 1964; Master Prof. W. A. BROWN.

Wolfson College: Barton Rd, Cambridge, CB3 9BB; tel. (1223) 335900; fax (1223) 335908; e-mail college-secretary@wolfson .cam.ac.uk; internet www.wolfson.cam.ac.uk; f. 1965; Pres. Dr G. JOHNSON.

ATTACHED INSTITUTES

Cambridge Programme for Industry: Assistant Sec. V. A. COURTICE (New Hall).

Centre of African Studies: Free School Lane, Cambridge CB2 3RQ; tel. (1223) 334396; fax (1223) 334396; e-mail african-studies@lists.cam.ac.uk; internet www.african.cam.ac.uk; Dir Dr L. A. QUAYSON (Pembroke College).

Centre for Applied Research in Educational Technologies: Dir JOHN NORMAN.

Centre of International Studies: 1st Fl., 17 Mill Lane, Cambridge, CB2 1RX; tel. (1223) 767235; fax (1223) 767236; e-mail intstudies@lists.cam.ac.uk; internet www .intstudies.cam.ac.uk; Dir J. B. L. MAYALL (Sidney Sussex College).

Centre of Latin American Studies: Second Floor, 17 Mill Lane, Cambridge, CB2 1RX; tel. (1223) 335390; fax (1223) 335397; e-mail clas-enquiries@lists.cam.ac.uk; internet www.latin-american.cam.ac.uk; Dir Dr C. A. JONES (Wolfson College).

Centre of Middle Eastern and Islamic Studies: Sidgwick Ave, Cambridge, CB3 9DA; tel. (1223) 335103; fax (1223) 335103; internet www.cmeis.cam.ac.uk; Dir Dr A. BENNISON.

Centre for Research in the Arts, Social Sciences and Humanities: DAMTP, Silver St, Cambridge, CB3 9EW; tel. (1223) 766886; fax (1223) 765276; e-mail crassh-admin@lists .cam.ac.uk; internet www.crassh.cam.ac.uk; Dir Prof. C. I. E. DONALDSON (King's College).

Centre of South Asian Studies: Laundress Lane, Cambridge, CB2 1SD; tel. (1223) 338094; fax (1223) 316913; Dir R. S. CHANDAVARKAR (Trinity College).

Department of Medical Genetics: Cambridge; tel. (1223) 331154; fax (1223) 331206; Chair. Prof. M. BOBROW.

ESRC Centre for Business Research: Judge Institute of Management Studies, Trumpington St, Cambridge, CB2 1AG; tel. (1223) 765320; fax (1223) 765338; e-mail enquiries@cbr.cam.ac.uk; internet www.cbr .cam.ac.uk; Dir A. HUGHES (Sidney Sussex College).

Institute of Continuing Education: Madingley Hall, Madingley, Cambridge, CB3 8AO; tel. (1954) 280280; fax (1954) 280200; Dir M. E. RICHARDSON (Wolfson College).

Institute for Stem Cell Biology: Dir Prof. AUSTIN SMITH.

Interdisciplinary Environmental Centre: Chair. Prof. E. SALJE.

Isaac Newton Institute for Mathematical Sciences: 20 Clarkson Rd, Cambridge, CB3 0EH; tel. (1223) 335999; fax (1223) 330508; e-mail info@newton.cam.ac.uk; internet www.newton.cam.ac.uk; Dir Sir DAVID WALLACE (Churchill College).

Language Centre: Old Music School, Downing Place, Cambridge, CB2 3EL; tel. (1223) 335058; fax (1223) 335040; e-mail enquiries@langcen.cam.ac.uk; internet www .langcen.cam.ac.uk; Dir A. N. KING (Churchill College).

Research Centre for English and Applied Linguistics: Keynes House, Trumpington St, Cambridge, CB2 1QA; tel. (1223) 332340; fax (1223) 330253; internet www .rceal.cam.ac.uk; Dir Prof. J. HAWKINS.

School of Arts and Humanities: 22 Trumpington St, Cambridge, CB2 1QA; tel. (1223) 766222; fax (1223) 766221; internet www .csah.cam.ac.uk; Sec. M. P. CHALK (New Hall).

School of the Biological Sciences: Old Press Site, Silver St, Cambridge, CB3 9EW; tel. (1223) 766894; fax (1223) 332355; e-mail facbiol@mole.bio.cam.ac.uk; internet www .bio.cam.ac.uk; Sec. K. S. DOUGLAS.

School of the Humanities and Social Sciences: 22 Trumpington St, Cambridge, CB2 1QA; fax (1223) 766221; internet www .chass.cam.ac.uk; Sec. C. C. HEWETSON (Hughes Hall).

School of the Physical Sciences: 17 Mill Lane, Cambridge, CB2 1RX; tel. (1223) 334197; fax (1223) 330257; internet www .cam.ac.uk/cambuniv/schools/physsci; Sec. A. T. WINTER (Christ's College).

School of Technology: Old Press Site, Silver St, Cambridge, CB3 9EW; tel. (1223) 332795; fax (1223) 332994; internet www .cam.ac.uk/cambuniv/schools/technology; Sec. S. T. LAM (Trinity College).

Wellcome Trust/Cancer Research UK Institute of Cancer and Developmental Biology: Tennis Court Rd, Cambridge, CB2 1QR; tel. (1223) 334088; fax (1223) 334089; e-mail info@welc.cam.ac.uk; internet www .welc.cam.ac.uk; Chair. Prof. J. C. SMITH (Christ's College).

CANTERBURY CHRIST CHURCH UNIVERSITY

North Holmes Rd, Canterbury, CT1 1QU
Telephone: (1227) 767700
Fax: (1227) 470442
E-mail: admissions@canterbury.ac.uk
Internet: www.canterbury.ac.uk

Founded 1962 as a Church of England Teacher Training College; University College 1995; present name and status 2005

Vice-Chancellor: Prof. MICHAEL WRIGHT
Pro-Vice-Chancellor: Dr PAUL DALTON
Pro-Chancellor: Bishop STEPHEN VENNER

Number of teachers: 1,000
Number of students: 13,500

Campuses in Canterbury, Medway, Thanet and Tunbridge Wells; Faculties of Arts and Humanities, Business and Sciences, Education and Health.

CARDIFF UNIVERSITY

Cardiff, CF10 3XQ
Telephone: (29) 2087-4000; (29) 2037-4457
E-mail: prospectus@cardiff.ac.uk
Internet: www.cardiff.ac.uk

Founded 2004 by merger of Cardiff University (f. 1883) and University of Wales College of Medicine (f. 1931)
Academic year: September to June

President: Lord KINNOCK
Vice-Chancellor: Dr DAVID GRANT
Provost and Deputy Vice-Chancellor: Prof. STEPHEN TOMLINSON
Provost: Prof. HADYN ELLIS
Pro Vice-Chancellors: Prof. KEN WOODHOUSE (External Affairs), Prof. NIGEL PALASTANGA (Learning and Teaching), Prof. RICHARD WHIPP (Research), Prof. TERESA REES (Student and Staff Issues)

Library: see entry for Cardiff University Libraries
Number of teachers: 2,628 (2,176 full-time, 452 part-time)
Number of students: 21,258 (16,451 undergraduate, 5,077 postgraduate)

Publication: *Annual Report*

HEADS OF SCHOOLS

College of Humanities and Sciences:
  Architecture: Prof. PHIL JONES
  Business School: Prof. ROGER MANSFIELD
  Chemistry: Prof. GRAHAM HUTCHINGS
  City and Regional Planning: Prof. TERRY MARSDEN
  Computer Science: Prof. NICK FIDDIAN
  Earth, Ocean and Planetary Sciences: Prof. DIANNE EDWARDS
  Engineering: Prof. HYWEL THOMAS
  English, Communication and Philosophy: Prof. MARTIN A. KAYMAN
  European Studies: Prof. PAUL FURLONG
  History and Archaeology: Prof. J. OSMOND
  Journalism, Media and Cultural Studies: Prof. TERRY THREADGOLD
  Law School: Prof. DAVID MIERS
  Lifelong Learning: Dr R. EVANS (Dean)
  Mathematics: Prof. J. D. GRIFFITHS
  Music: Prof. ROBIN STOWELL
  Physics and Astronomy: Prof. MIKE EDMUNDS
  Religious and Theological Studies: Prof. STEPHEN PATTISON
  Social Sciences: Prof. HUW BEYNON
  Welsh: Prof. SIONED DAVIES

Wales College of Medicine, Biology, Life and Health Sciences:
  Biosciences: Prof. J. L. HARWOOD
  Dentistry: Prof. M. L. JONES

  Healthcare Studies: MARTIN BOOY
  Medicine: Prof. KEN WOODHOUSE
  Nursing and Midwifery Studies: Prof. ANN TUCKER
  Optometry and Vision Sciences: Prof. MICHAEL BOULTON
  Pharmacy: Prof. S. P. DENYER
  Postgraduate Medical and Dental Education: Prof. SIMON A. SMAIL
  Psychology: Prof. DYLAN JONES

PROFESSORS

College of Humanities and Sciences
  Architecture:

WESTON, R.

  Business School:

BLYTON, P. R.
BOYNE, G. A.
CHANDLER, R. A.
CLARKE, R.
COLLIE, D. R.
COPELAND, L.
DAVIES, A. J.
DELBRIDGE, R. I.
EDWARDS, J. R.
EZZAMEL, M. A.
FOREMAN-PECK, J.
FOSH, P.
FOXALL, G. R.
HARRIS, L. C.
HEERY, E. J.
HINES, P. A.
HUGHES HALLET, A.
JONES, D. T.
JONES, M. J.
KNOTT, J. H.
McNABB, R.
MAKEPEACE, G. H.
MARTIN, S. J.
MATTHEWS, K. G. P.
MELLETT, H. J.
MINFORD, A. P. L.
MORRIS, J. L.
NAIRN, M. M.
OGBONNA, E.
PEATTIE, K. J.
PEEL, M. J.
PENDLEBURY, M. W.
POOLE, M. J. F.
REED, M. I.
RHYS, D. G.
SILVER, M. S.
TOWILL, D. R.
TURNBULL, P. J.
WALKER, S. P.
WHITFIELD, K. L.
XU, X.

  Chemistry:

ATTARD, G. A.
BOWKER, M.
CAVELL, K. J.
EDWARDS, P. G.
HARRIS, K. D. M.
HEWLINS, M. J. E.
JONES, C.
KNIGHT, D. W.
KNOWLES, P. J.
McKEOWN, N. B.
ROBERTS, M. W.
WELLS, P. B.
WILLIAMS, D. R.
WIRTH, T.

  City and Regional Planning:

ALDEN, J. D.
CLAPHAM, D. F.
COOKE, P. N.
GUY, C. M.
HOOPER, A. J.
LOVERING, J.
MORGAN, K. J.
MURDOCH, J. L.
PUNTER, J. V.
WEBSTER, C. J.
WILLIAMS, H. C. W. L.

Computer Science:

AVIS, N. J.
BATCHELOR, B. G.
BROWN, B. M.
GRAY, W. A.
JONES, A. J.
JONES, C. B.
MARTIN, R. R.
WALKER, D. W.

Earth, Ocean and Planetary Sciences:

BOWEN, D. Q.
CARTWRIGHT, J. A.
EDWARDS, D.
HARRIS, C.
LISLE, R. J.
O'HARA, M. J.
PARKES, R. J.
PEARCE, J. A.
PEARSON, P. N.
RICKARD, D. T.
SCHULTZ, A.
WRIGHT, V. P.
ZAHN, R.

Engineering:

BARR, B. I. G.
BARROW, D. A.
BORODICH, F. M.
CHAMBERS, J. A.
EVANS, H. P.
DIMOV, S. S.
FALCONER, R. A.
HUGHES, T. G.
KARIHALOO, B. L.
LEVER, K. V.
MILES, J. C.
MORGAN, D. V.
MOSES, A. J.
PHAM, D. T.
POOLEY, F. D.
ROWE, D. M.
SNIDLE, R. W.
SYRED, N.
TASKER, P. J.
WATTON, J.
WILLIAMS, F. W.

English, Communication and Philosophy:

ATTFIELD, R.
BELSEY, C.
COUPLAND, N. J. R.
KAYMAN, M. A.
KNIGHT, S. T.
NORRIS, C. C.
SARANGI, S. K.
SKILTON, D. J.
VAN LEEUWEN, T.
WEEDON, C. M.

European Studies:

BERENDSE, G.-J.
BOUCHER, D.
BRYDEN, K. M.
COLE, A. M.
DYSON, K. H. F.
HADDOCK, B. A.
HANLEY, D. L.
JACKSON, D. A.
LOUGHLIN, J. P.

History and Archaeology:

BENTON, G.
COSS, P. R.
EDBURY, P. W.
FREESTONE, I. C.
FISHER, N. R. E.
HINES, J.
HUDSON, P.
PRINGLE, R. D.
WHITTLE, A. W. R.

Journalism, Media and Cultural Studies:

HARGREAVES, I. R.
KITZINGER, J.
LEWIS, J. W.
MILLER, B. T. A.
TAIT, R.

Law School:

CAMPBELL, I. D.
CHURCHILL, R. R.
DOE, C. N.
DOUGLAS, G. F.
FENNELL, P. W. H.
HARPWOOD, V.
HOLM, S.
LEE, R. G.
LEWIS, R. K.
LOWE, N. V.
MIERS, D. R.
MORGAN, D. M.
MURCH, M.
NELKEN, D.
SMITH, K. J. M.
THOMAS, P. A.
WELLS, C. K.
WYLIE, J. C. W.

Mathematics:

BOURENKOV, K.
EVANS, D. E.
EVANS, W. D.
HOOLEY, C.
HUXLEY, M. N.
PHILLIPS, T. N.
WICKRAMASINGHE, N. C.
ZHIGLJAVSKY, A. A.

Music:

THOMAS, A. T.
TYRELL, J.
WALSH, S.

Physics and Astronomy:

ADE, P. A. R.
BLOOD, P.
DISNEY, M. J.
GEAR, W. K.
GRIFFIN, M. J.
GRISHCHUK, L.
INGLESFIELD, J. E.
IVANOV, A. L.
SATHYAPRAKASH, B. S.
WHITWORTH, A. P.

Religious and Theological Studies:

SAMUEL, G. B.
TREVETT, C.

Social Sciences:

ADAM, B. E.
ATKINSON, P.
BROWN, P.
COLLINS, H. M.
CROZIER, W. R.
DAVIES, W. B.
DRAKEFORD, M.
EPSTEIN, D. A.
FAIRBROTHER, P.
FEVRE, R. W.
FITZ, J.
GLASNER, P. E.
LAWN, M.
LEVI, M.
MAGUIRE, E. M. W.
MOORE, L. A. R.
NICHOLS, W. A. T.
POWER, S. A. R.
PRIOR, L. F.
REES, G. M.
REES, T. L.
WALKERDINE, V.
WALTERS, D.
WILLIAMS, G. H.

Welsh:

JONES, R. O.
THOMAS, P. W.
WILLIAMS, C. H.

Wales College of Medicine, Biology, Life and Health Sciences

Biosciences:

ARCHER, C. W.
BENJAMIN, M.
BODDY, L.
BOWEN, I. D.

BRUFORD, M. W.
BUCHMAN, V.
CATERSON, B.
CLARKE, A. R.
COAKLEY, W. T.
CRUNELLI, V.
DALE, T. C.
DAVIES, A. M.
DUANCE, V. C.
DUNNETT, S. B.
ECCLES, R.
EHRMANN, M.
FOX, K. D.
FRY, J. C.
HARWOOD, A. J.
HARWOOD, J. L.
JACOB, T. J. C.
JOHN, R. A.
KAY, J.
MOXHAM, B. J.
ORMEROD, S. J.

Dentistry:

DUMMER, P. M. H., Adult Dental Health
GLANTZ, P.-O. J., Adult Dental Health
JONES, M. L., Dental Health and Development
LEWIS, M. A. O., Oral Medicine
MACKENZIE, I. C., Adult Dental Health
RICHMOND, S., Dental Health and Development
SHEPHERD, J. R., Oral Surgery and Pathology
TREASURE, E. T., Dental Public Health
WHITTAKER, D. K., Basic Dental Science
WILTON, J. M. A., Adult Dental Health

Healthcare Studies:

PALASTANGA, N.

Medicine:

BURNETT, A. K., Haematology
CAMPBELL, A. K., Medical Biochemistry
CLARKE, A. J., Medical Genetics
COOPER, D. N., Human Molecular Genetics
DAVIES, D. P., Child Health
DUERDEN, B. I., Medical Microbiology
EVANS, W. H., Medical Biochemistry
FELCE, D., Mental Handicap Research
FIANDER, A., Obstetrics and Gynaecology
FINLAY, A. Y., Dermatology
FINLAY, I. G., Palliative Care
FRENNEAUX, N. P., Cardiology
GRIFFITH, T. M., Medical Imaging
HARDING, K. G., Rehabilitation Medicine
HARMER, M., Anaesthetics and Intensive Care Medicine
HARPER, P. S., Medical Genetics
HOUSTON, H. L. A., General Practice
KRAWCZAK, M., Mathematical Genetics
LAI, F. A., Cell Signalling
LEWIS, M. J., Cardiovascular Pharmacology
MANSEL, R. E., Surgery
MASON, M., Clinical Oncology
MORGAN, B. P., Medical Biochemistry
O'DONOVAN, M. C., Psychological Medicine
OWEN, M. J., Neuropsychiatric Genetics
OWENS, D. R., Diabetes
PALMER, S. R., Epidemiology, Statistics and Public Health
PILL, R., General Practice
ROUTLEDGE, P., Clinical Pharmacology
ROWE, M., Cell Biology
SAMPSON, J. R., Medical Genetics
SCANLON, M. F., Endocrinology
SHALE, D. J., Respiratory and Communicable Diseases
SIBERT, J. R., Community Child Health
SMITH, P. J., Cancer Biology
STEPHENS, S. D. G., Audiology
THAPAR, A., Child and Adolescent Psychiatry
WHEELER, M. H., Surgery
WILES, C. M., Neurology
WILKINSON, C., General Practice
WILLIAMS, B. D., Rheumatology

WILLIAMS, G. T., Pathology
WILLIAMS, J. D., Nephrology
WOODCOCK, J. P., Bioengineering
WOODHOUSE, K. W., Geriatric Medicine
WORWOOD, M., Haematology
WYNFORD-THOMAS, D., Pathology

Nursing and Midwifery Studies:

BURNARD, P., Nursing and Midwifery Education
LYNE, P. A., Nursing Research
TUCKER, A., Nursing and Midwifery

Optometry and Vision Sciences:

MEEK, K. M. A.
ROVAMO, J. M.
WESS, T. J.
WILD, J.

Welsh School of Pharmacy:

AKHTAR, S.
BROADLEY, K. J.
DUNCAN, R.
LUSCOMBE, D. K.
MCGUIGAN, C.
MRSNY, R. J.
NICHOLSON, R. I.
RUSSELL, A. D.
WALKER, R. D.

Psychology:

AGGLETON, J. P.
ELLIS, H. D.
HALLIGAN, P.
HAY, D. F.
HONEY, R. C.
MANSTEAD, A. S. R.
OAKSFORD, M. R.
PAYNE, S. J.
PEARCE, J. M.
PIDGEON, N.
SMITH, A. P.
SNOWDEN, R. J.
SPEARS, R.
WRIGHT, P.

RESEARCH CENTRES

Advanced Chinese Engineering Centre.
Biobank.
Biostatistics and Bioinformatics Unit.
Cancer Studies.
Cardiff Centre for Ethics, Law and Society.
Cardiff Centre for the History of the Crusades.
Cardiff Centre for Medicines Research.
Cardiff Centre for Mobile Communications.
Cardiff Centre for Modern German History.
Cardiff Centre for Molecular Modelling.
Cardiff Centre for Multidisciplinary Microtechnology.
Cardiff Family Studies Research Centre.
Cardiff Genetics and Society Research Centre.
Cardiff Geotechnical Centrifuge Centre.
Cardiff Institute for Society, Health and Ethics.
Cardiff Institute of Tissue Engineering and Repair.
Cardiff University Brain and Repair Imaging Centre.
Cardiovascular Sciences.
Central European Music Research Centre.
Centre for Advanced Software and Intelligent Systems.
Centre for Advanced Studies in the Social Sciences.
Centre for Applied Ethics.

Centre for Applied Spin Resonance.
Centre for Astrobiology.
Centre for Automotive Industry Research.
Centre for Critical and Cultural Theory.
Centre for Editorial and Intertextual Research.
Centre for Education in the Built Environment.
Centre for Energy Research and Services.
Centre for Health Sciences Research.
Centre for Housing Management and Development.
Centre for International Family Law Studies.
Centre for Journalism Studies.
Centre of Knowledge, Expertise and Science.
Centre for Language and Communication Research.
Centre for Law and Religion.
Centre for Local and Regional Government Research.
Centre for Medico-Legal Studies.
Centre for Neuroscience.
Centre for Pest Management and Ecotoxicology.
Centre for Rural Environment and Society.
Centre for Social Work Studies.
Centre for the Study of Medieval Society and Culture.
Centre for the Study of Religion in Late Antiquity.
Centre for Sustainable Energy and Process Management.
CETIC Centre for Research in the Built Environment.
Collaborative Research Centre.
Collingwood and British Idealism Centre.
Common Cold and Nasal Research Centre.
Crime, Law and Justice.
eCommerce Innovation Centre.
ESRC Research Centre for Business Relationships, Accountability, Sustainability and Society.
Genomic Approaches to Health and Disease.
Geoenvironmental Research Centre.
Health Communication Research Centre.
Hydroenvironmental Research Centre.
IBM Cynefin Centre for Organisational Complexity.
Immunology, Infection and Inflammation.
Institute for Medical Engineering and Medical Physics.
Interdisciplinary Protein Research Centre.
International Centre for Planning Research.
Japanese Studies Centre.
Land Regeneration Institute.
Lean Enterprise Research Centre.
Logistics Systems Dynamics Group.
Llysdinam Field Centre.
Mitutoyo Metrology Centre.
Regeneration Institute.
Repair, Replacement and Regeneration.

Seafarers International Research Centre for Safety and Occupational Health.
Skin Research Centre.
National Centre for ENDOR Spectroscopy.
Regional Training Centre for High Performance Computing.
Tenovus Centre for Cancer Research.
Tom Hopkinson Centre for Media Research.
UnumProvident Centre for Psychosocial and Disability Research.
Wales Cancer Bank.
Wales Heart Research Institute.
Wales Waste and Resources Research Centre.
Welsh Centre for Learning Disabilities.
Welsh Governance Centre.
Welsh Institute for Research in Economics and Development.
Welsh School of Pharmacy Centre for Socioeconomic Research.
Wolfson Centre for Magnetics Technology: Dir DAVID JILES.
Wound Healing Research Unit.

UNIVERSITY OF CENTRAL ENGLAND IN BIRMINGHAM

Perry Barr, Birmingham, B42 2SU

Telephone: (121) 331-5000
Fax: (121) 331-6740
E-mail: ucechoices@uce.ac.uk
Internet: www.uce.ac.uk

Founded 1971 as City of Birmingham Polytechnic, later became Birmingham Polytechnic, present name and status 1992

Academic year: October to July

Chancellor: The Lord Mayor of Birmingham, Cllr MICHAEL NANGLE
Vice-Chancellor: Prof. DAVID TIDMARSH
Secretary and Registrar: M. PENLINGTON

Library of 900,000 vols
Number of teachers: 700
Number of students: 20,650 (10,750 full-time, 9,900 part-time)

DEANS

Birmingham Institute of Art and Design: Prof. M. DURMAN
Faculty of Computing, Information and English: Prof. JOHN ROUSE
Faculty of Education: Prof. R. WOODS
Faculty of Health and Community Care: Prof. S. BUCHANAN
Faculty of Law and Social Services: Prof. JOHN ROUSE
UCE Business School: Prof. U. PARDESI
Technology Innovation Centre: GRAHAM ROGERS
Birmingham Conservatoire: Prof. G. CAIRD (Principal)

HEADS OF DEPARTMENTS AND SCHOOLS

Accountancy: T. ELLIOT
Architecture and Landscape: Prof. J. LOW
Art: Prof. R. PILLING
Arts and Education: T. DAVIES
Banking: D. WINSTONE
Birmingham Conservatoire Junior School: TIM ENGLISH
Brass: D. PURSER
Business: T. ELLIOT
Composition: A. DOWNES
Creative Studies: Prof. A. DOWNES
Defence School of Healthcare Studies: C. WILLIAMS
Early Years Education: G. BAPTISTE
Economics: M. RICHARDSON
Electronic Communications and Software: M. WILKES

Fashion, Textiles and Three-Dimensional Design: R. SNELL (acting)
Finance: T. ELLIOT
Foundation and Community Studies (Art and Design): Prof. T. JONES
Health and Policy Studies: Prof. M. FILBY
Information and English: Dr D. ROBERTS
Jazz: J. PRICE
Jewellery: Prof. N. CHERRY
Keyboard Studies: Prof. M. WILSON
Law: M. SPENCER
Management: K. TREHAN
Marketing: M. RICHARDSON
Mathematics, Science and Technology (Teacher Training): C. BENSON
Mechanical and Manufacturing Engineering: Prof. RAY McCAFFERTY
Media and Communication: Prof. R. PILLING
Music Technology: L. COCCIOLI
Nursing Studies: L. WILLIAMS
Operating Department Practice: C. REAY
Organ and Harpsichord: D. SAINT
Piano: M. WILSON
Planning and Housing: V. COATHAM
Post-compulsory Education: Prof. J. HOSKYNS
Postgraduate Studies: L. GARNETT
Primary Education: M. HARRIS
Primary Health Care: E. PAJAK
Property and Construction: J. BADMAN
Radiography: Prof. R. KLEM
Research: P. JOHNSON
Secondary Education: H. COLL
Social Sciences: Prof. C. PAINTER
Social Work and RNIB Rehabilitation Studies: R. DOLTON
Speech and Language Therapy: J. NETTLETON
Strings: J. TODD
Theoretical and Historical Studies: Prof. K. QUICKENDEN
Visual Communication: Prof. D. KNIGHT
Voice and Opera: J. PIKE
Women's Health Studies: S. JONES
Woodwind: M. HARRIS

UNIVERSITY OF CENTRAL LANCASHIRE

Preston, PR1 2HE
Telephone: (1772) 201201
Fax: (1772) 892911
E-mail: cenquiries@uclan.ac.uk
Internet: www.uclan.ac.uk

Founded 1956 as Harris College, 1973 as Preston Polytechnic, 1984 as Lancashire Polytechnic; present name and status 1992
Academic year: September to July

Chancellor: Sir RICHARD EVANS
Vice-Chancellor: Dr MALCOLM McVICAR
Deputy Vice-Chancellor: ALAN ROFF
Librarian: KEVIN ELLARD

Number of teachers: 1,006
Number of students: 26,900 (15,500 full-time, 11,400 part-time)

Publication: *Annual Report*

DEANS

Faculty of Cultural, Legal and Social Studies: (vacant)
Faculty of Design and Technology: PETER ROBERTSON
Faculty of Health: EILEEN MARTIN
Faculty of Science: DAVID PHOENIX
Lancashire Business School: DAVID HAMBLIN

HEADS OF DEPARTMENTS

Faculty of Cultural, Legal and Social Studies (tel. (1772) 893017; fax (1772) 892908):

Combined Honours Unit: MIKE ABRAMSON
Education and Social Sciences: KEN PHILLIPS
Humanities: JOHN JOUGHIN
Lancashire Law School: Prof. RICHARD TAYLOR

Languages and International Studies: JOHN SHAW
Faculty of Design and Technology (tel. (1772) 893165; fax (1772) 892901):

Art and Fashion: GLENDA BRINDLE
Built Environment: ANDREW PLATTEN
Computing: MARTIN BROWN
Technology: DJAMAL AIT-BOUDAOUD
Visual Communication and Three Dimensional Design: MARK LAMEY
Faculty of Health (tel. (1772) 893840; fax (1772) 892995):

Lancashire School of Health and Postgraduate Medicine: PETER AGGETT
Midwifery Studies: MAGGIE MORGAN
Nursing: BERNARD GIBBON
Social Work: BRIAN CORBY
Faculty of Science (tel. (1772) 893485; fax (1772) 892903):

Biological Sciences: PETER ROBINSON
Environmental Management: Dr NIGEL SIMONS
Forensic and Investigative Science: Dr LEE CHATFIELD
Mathematics, Physics and Astronomy: Prof. MIKE HOLMES
Psychology: PAUL POLLARD
Lancashire Business School (tel. (1772) 894606; fax (1772) 892904):

Information and Finance: PHIL BAUGH
Journalism: MIKE WARD
Strategy and Innovation: GRAHAM BALDWIN
Tourism and Leisure Management: (vacant)

UNIVERSITY OF CHESTER

Parkgate Rd, Chester, CH1 4BJ
Telephone: (1244) 511000
Fax: (1244) 512471
E-mail: enquiries@chester.ac.uk
Internet: www.chester.ac.uk

Founded 1839; present status 2005
Principal: Prof. TIMOTHY WHEELER
Number of teachers: 413
Number of students: 10,105

Campuses in Chester and Warrington; Schools of Applied and Health Sciences, Arts and Media, Business Management and Law, Creative and Media Arts, Education, Health and Social Care, Humanities and Social Sciences; Graduate School; Research Centres in Exercise and Nutrition Science, Public Health Research, Research in the Arts, Religion and Biosciences, Science Communication, Stress Research, Sport and Society, Victorian studies and Work-related Studies; Institute for Social and Health Research.

CITY UNIVERSITY

Northampton Square, London, EC1V 0HB
Telephone: (20) 7477-8000
Fax: (20) 7477-8560
E-mail: registry@city.ac.uk
Internet: www.city.ac.uk

Founded 1894 as Northampton Institute, Northampton College of Advanced Technology 1957, University Charter 1966
Academic year: September to July

Chancellor: THE LORD MAYOR OF LONDON
Vice-Chancellor and Principal: Prof. DAVID RHIND
Pro-Vice Chancellors: M. DOCKRAY, C. TH. GRAMMENOS, S. MILLER, J. WEINBERG
Academic Registrar (vacant)
Librarian: B. M. CASEY

Library of 350,000 vols
Number of teachers: 438
Number of students: 8,966

Publication: *Annual Report*

HEADS OF SCHOOLS

School of Engineering and Mathematical Sciences: Prof. C. ARCOUMANIS
School of Informatics: D. J. BOLTON
School of Social Sciences: Prof. TONY WOODIWISS
St Bartholomew School of Nursing and Midwifery: Prof. SALLY GLEN
Sir John Cass City of London Business School: Lord CURRIE OF MARYLEBONE

HEADS OF DEPARTMENTS NOT UNDER A SCHOOL

Arts Policy and Management: Prof. E. MOODY
Continuing Education: Dr YVONNE HILLIER
Journalism: ROD ALLEN
Law: Prof. C. L. RYAN
Music: Prof. DENIS SMALLEY

PROFESSORS

ATKINSON, J. H., Soil Mechanics
BADEN-FULLER, C., Business Strategy
BARBUR, J. L., Optics and Visual Science
BARONE-ADESI, G., Financial Engineering
BATCHELOR, R., Banking and Finance
BOOTH, P., Real Estate Finance
BOSWELL, L. F., Civil Engineering
BOWERS, L., Psychiatric Nursing
BOYLAN, P. J., Arts Policy and Management
BRADLEY, K., Management
BRYER, R.
BUCKLEY, R. J., Ocular Medicine
BURN, E. H., Law
BURRIDGE, P., Economics
BYNG, S., Communication Disability
CAPIE, F. H., Economic History
CARSON, E. R., Systems Science
COHEN, B., Computing
COLLINS, M. A., Marketing Research
CONNELL, T. J., Languages for the Professions
COYLE, A., Sociology
CRESSY, R., Accounting and Finance
CROMPTON, R., Sociology
CUBBIN, J., Economics
D'ANDREA, V., Educational Development
DANIELS, P. G., Applied Mathematics
DICKINSON, G. M., International Insurance
DINENIS, E., Investment and Risk Management
DOCKRAY, M. S., Law
DONE, G. T. S., Aeronautics
DOUGLAS, R. H., Visual Science
FAHLE, M., Optometry
FINKELSTEIN, L., Measurement and Instrumentation
GARDINER, J. M., Psychology
GEMMILL, G. T., Finance
GLEN, S., Nursing
GLYCOPANTIS, D., Economics
GOLOMBOK, J. M., Psychology
GRAMMENOS, C. TH., Shipping, Trade and Finance
GRANT, R. M., Management
GRATTAN, K. T. V., Measurement and Instrumentation
GREENSLADE, R., Journalism
HABERMAN, S., Actuarial Science
HAINES, C. R., Mathematics Education
HAMPTON, J., Psychology
HEFFERNAN, S. A., Banking and Finance
HENDRY, C., Organizational Behaviour
HEYMAN, B., Nursing
HINES, M., Psychology
HOLTHAM, C. W., Information Management
KARCANIAS, N., Control Theory and Design
LASSFER, M., Finance
LEVIS, M., Finance
LITTLEWOOD, B., Software Engineering
LOVELAND, I., Law
McGUIRE, A. J., Economics
MARKS, D., Psychology
MARTIN, P. P., Mathematical Physics
MATHON, J., Mathematical Physics
MENOU, M., Information Policy
MEYER, J., Adult Nursing

MINTZ, B., Engineering Materials
MOODY, E., Arts Policy and Management
NEWBY, J., Statistical Science
PALMER, A. W., Electrical Engineering
PARKIN, D., Health Economics
PEAKE, D. J., Aero and Fluid Dynamics
PHYLAKTIS, E., International Finance
PRICE, S., Economics
PURDUE, H. M., Law
RAHMAN, A., Photonic Devices
RAPER, J. F., Information Science
RATTANSI, A., Sociology
RYAN, C. L., Law
SALMON, M., Financial Markets
SAMUEL, R., Music
SANDALL, J., Midwifery
SELIM, G., Internal Auditing
SMALLEY, D., Music
SMITH, I. K., Applied Thermodynamics
STEPHENSON, H., Journalism
STOSIC, N., Positive Displacement Compressor Technology
STRIGINI, L., Systems Engineering
TAYLOR, R. N., Geotechnical Engineering
THOMAS, P.
THORLEY, A. R. D., Fluid Engineering
TUMBER, H., Sociology
TUNSTALL, C. J., Sociology
VERRALL, R., Actuarial Science and Statistics
VIRDI, K. S., Structural Engineering
WATTS, M., Psychology
WEINBERG, J.
WILLETTS, P., Global Politics
WILLIAMS, A. P. O., Organizational and Occupational Psychology
WOLL, B., Sign Language and Deaf Studies
WOOD, G., Economics
WOODIWISS, A., Sociology
WOODWARD, E. G., Optometry and Visual Science
WOOTTON, L. R., Engineering

AFFILIATED INSTITUTION

Inns of Court School of Law: 4 Gray's Inn Place, Gray's Inn, London, WC1R 5DX; tel. (20) 7404-5787; fax (20) 7831-4188; e-mail lpc@icsl.ac.uk; internet www.icsl.ac.uk.

COVENTRY UNIVERSITY

Priory St, Coventry, CV1 5FB
Telephone: (24) 7688-7688
Fax: (24) 7688-8638
E-mail: info.rao@coventry.ac.uk
Internet: www.coventry.ac.uk

Founded 1970 as Lanchester Polytechnic, later became Coventry Polytechnic; present name and status 1992
Academic year: September to June
Vice-Chancellor: Prof. MADELAINE ATKINS
Pro-Vice-Chancellors: JOHN LATHAM (Business Development), Prof. ASHRAF JAWAID (International Affairs), Prof. D. PENNINGTON (Learning and Student Experience), DAVID SOUTTER (Resources)
Academic Registrar: KATE QUANTRELL
Librarian: P. NOON

Library of 400,000 vols
Number of teachers: 600
Number of students: 18,000

Publications: *Biological Agriculture and Horticulture* (4 a year), *Coventry University Law Journal* (2 a year), *The Holocene*, *International Journal of Media and Cultural Politics*, *Quaternary Newsletter*, *Ultrasonics – Sonochemistry*

HEADS OF SCHOOL

Art and Design: Prof. M. TOVEY
Business: Prof. D. GILLINGHAM
Engineering: Prof. A. JAWAID
Health and Social Sciences: Dr L. MERRIMAN
Mathematical and Information Sciences: Prof. I. M. MARSHALL

Science and the Environment: Prof. B. ILBERY, RAY HULSE (acting)

CRANFIELD UNIVERSITY

Cranfield campus: Cranfield, Beds., MK43 0AL
Telephone: (1234) 750111
Fax: (1234) 750875

Silsoe campus: Silsoe, Beds., MK45 4DT
Telephone: (1525) 863000
Fax: (1525) 863001

Shrivenham campus: Shrivenham, Swindon, Wilts., SN6 8LA
Telephone: (1793) 782551
Fax: (1793) 783878
E-mail: info@cranfield.ac.uk
Internet: www.cranfield.ac.uk

Founded 1946 as College of Aeronautics; became Cranfield Institute of Technology 1969; incorporated National College of Agricultural Engineering (Silsoe) 1975; took responsibility for academic work at Royal Military College of Science, Shrivenham, 1984; present name 1993
Academic year: October to September

Chancellor: Lord VINCENT OF COLESHILL
Vice-Chancellor: Prof. JOHN O'REILLY
Academic Registrar and Secretary: D. J. BUCK

Library of 490,706 vols, 7,299 journals (electronic and print)
Number of students: 3,075 degree-course (mostly postgraduate), 8,721 short-course

Schools at Cranfield: Industrial and Manufacturing Science, Engineering, Management. School at Shrivenham: Defence Technology. Units at Silsoe: Institute of Bioscience and Technology, Institute of Water and Environment, National Soil Resources Institute

PROFESSORS

ALAMDARI, F. N., Air Transport and Management
ALLEN, D. M., Microengineering
ALLEN, P. M., Evolutionary Complex Systems
ASHWELL, G. J., Nano-Materials
BELLAMY, C. D., Military Science and Doctrine
BESSANT, J., Innovation Management
BOWMAN, C. C., Business Strategy
BRAITHWAITE, M., Chemical Physics
BROOKER, P., Air Traffic Management and Environmental Policy
CARTER, R. C., International Water Development
CHRISTOPHER, M. G., Marketing and Logistics
COLLINS, B. S.
CROWLEY, A. B., Ballistics
DEASLEY, P. J., Mechatronics
DRIKAKIS, D., Fluid Mechanics and Computational Science
EDWARDS, C., Management Information Systems
EVANS, S., Life Cycle Engineering
FIELDING, J. P., Aircraft Design
GARRY, K., Experimental Aerodynamics
GODWIN, R. J., Agricultural Engineering
GREENHALGH, D. A., Non-Intrusive Measurement of Combustion and Flow
GRIFFIN, K. R. H., Innovation and New Product Development
HARRIS, J. A., Environmental Technology
HARRISON, A. S., Operations and Logistics
HETHERINGTON, J. G., Engineering Design
HIGSON, S. P. J., Bio- and Electro-analysis
HOLMES, E. R., Military and Security Studies
HUTCHINSON, P., Statistical Fluid Mechanics
IRVING, P. E., Damage Tolerance
IVEY, P. C., Turbomachinery
JAMES, K., Executive Learning
JOHN, P., Systems Engineering for Defence

JUDD, S., Membrane Technology
KAKABADSE, A., Management Development
KAY, J. M., Manufacturing Systems Engineering
KIBBLEWHITE, M. G., National Soils Resources Institute (Dir)
KIRK, G. J. D., Soil Systems
KNOX, S., Brand Marketing
LEEDS-HARRISON, P. B., Soil and Water Management
MAGAN, N., Applied Mycology
MATTHEWS, R. G., Defence Economics
MAYS, G. C., Civil Engineering
MORRIS, J., Resource Economics and Management
MOSS, J. B., Thermofluids and Combustion
MUIR, H. C., Aerospace Psychology
MYDDELTON, D. R., Finance and Accounting
NEELY, A. D., Operations Strategy and Performance
NELLIS, J. G., International Management Economics
NICHOLLS, J. R., Coatings Technology
ORMONDROYD, R. F., Communications and Wireless Network
OSBALDESTON, M., Cranfield School of Management (Dir)
PARKER, D., Business Economics and Strategy
PARTRIDGE, I. K., Polymer Composition
PATEL, M., School of Engineering (Head)
PAYNE, A. F. T., Services and Relationship Marketing
PICKETT, A. K., Automotive Materials
PILETSKY, S. A., Bio-organic Polymer Chemistry
PILIDIS, P., Gas Turbine Performance Engineering
POLL, D. I. A., Aerospace Engineering
POLLARD, S., Waste Technology
RAMSDEN, J., Nanotechnology
RITZ, K., Soil Biology
SACKETT, P. J., Integrated Systems
SAINI, S., Analytical Science
SAMMES, A. J., Computer Science
SANDERSON, M. L., Fluid Instrumentation
SAVILL, M., Computational Aerodynamics Design
SHORE, P., Ultraprecision Engineering
SINGH, R., Gas Turbine Engineering
STEPHENS, W., Water and Environment
STEPHENSON, D. J., Materials Processing
STEPHENSON, T., Water Sciences
STRUTT, J. E., Reliability Engineering and Risk Management
SUDARSANAM, P., Finance and Corporate Control
SWEENEY, M. T., Operations Management
TAFFLER, R. J., Accounting and Finance
TATAM, R. P., Engineering Photonics
TAYLOR, J. C., Land Resources Monitoring and Remote Sensing
TAYLOR, T., Defence Analysis and Security Management (Head)
THOMPSON, C. P., Applied Computation
TRANFIELD, D., Management
TURNER, A. P. F., Biosensor Technology
TYSON, S. J. J., Human Resource Management
VAUGHAN, N. D., Automative Engineering
VIGNJEVIC, R., Structural Mechanics
VINNICOMBE, S., Organizational Behaviour and Diversity Management
WALLACE, I., Environmental and Ordnance Systems
WANG, R., Biomedical Optics
WARD, J. M., Strategic Information Systems
WARNER, P. J., Industrial Molecular Biology
WHATMORE, R. W., Engineering Nanotechnology
WHITE, B. A., Control and Guidance
WHITE, S. M., Integrated Catchment Management
WOODMAN, A. C., Translational Medicine

DE MONTFORT UNIVERSITY

The Gateway, Leicester, LE1 9BH
Telephone: (116) 255-1551
Fax: (116) 250-6204
E-mail: enquiry@dmu.ac.uk
Internet: www.dmu.ac.uk

Founded 1969 as City of Leicester Polytechnic, later became Leicester Polytechnic; present name and status 1992

Chancellor: Baroness USHA PRASHAR
Chief Executive and Vice-Chancellor: PHILIP TASKER
Pro Vice-Chancellors: Prof. D. ASCH, Prof. S. BASKERVILLE, Prof. J. SIMMONS
Academic Registrar: E. CRITCHLOW
University Librarian: K. ARNOLD
Number of teachers: 1,500
Number of students: 27,500 (21,500 full-time, 6,000 part-time)

DEANS OF FACULTY

Faculty of Art and Design: Dr G. MORAN
Faculty of Business and Law: Prof. D. WILSON
Faculty of Computing and Engineering: Prof. M. MIHSEIN
Faculty of Health and Life Sciences: Prof. G. GRANT
Faculty of Humanities: Prof. P. MARTIN
Bedford Faculty: Prof. K. JACQUES

UNIVERSITY OF DERBY

Kedleston Rd, Derby, DE22 1GB
Telephone: (1332) 590500
Fax: (1332) 294861
E-mail: enquiries-admissions@derby.ac.uk
Internet: www.derby.ac.uk

Founded 1851 with college status, later Derbyshire College of Higher Education; present name and status 1993; merged with High Peak College 1998
Academic year: September to June
Chancellor: Prof. LESLIE WAGNER
Vice-Chancellor: Prof. JOHN COYNE
Deputy Vice-Chancellors: JENNIFER FRY, Prof. FREDA TALLANTYRE
Pro Vice-Chancellor: HARI PUNCHIHEWA
Librarian: GORDON BREWER
Library of 275,000 vols
Number of teachers: 700
Number of students: 22,000 (15,000 higher education, 7,000 further education)

DIRECTORS

School of Arts, Design and Technology: Prof. DAVID MANLEY
Derbyshire Business School: Prof. MARY CARSWELL
School of Education, Health Care and Sciences: Prof. DAWN FORMAN
University of Derby College, Buxton: Prof. DAVID DAVIES

UNIVERSITY OF DUNDEE

Dundee, DD1 4HN
Telephone: (1382) 344000
Fax: (1382) 201604
E-mail: secretary@dundee.ac.uk
Internet: www.dundee.ac.uk

Founded 1881 as University College, Dundee, Royal Charter 1967
Academic year: October to June
Chancellor: Sir JAMES BLACK
Rector: CRAIG MURRAY
Principal and Vice-Chancellor: Sir ALAN LANGLANDS
Vice-Principals: Prof. D. H. BOXER, Prof. J. CALDERHEAD
Secretary: D. DUNCAN
Librarian: J. M. BAGNALL

Library: see Libraries and Archives
Number of teachers: 693 full-time
Number of students: 9,495 full-time

DEANS

Faculty of Arts and Social Sciences: Prof. C. A. WHATLEY
Faculty of Education and Social Work: Prof. R. ELDER
Faculty of Engineering and Physical Sciences: Prof. M. R. C. DAVIES
Faculty of Law and Accountancy: Prof. C. T. REID
Faculty of Life Sciences: Prof. C. P. DOWNES
Faculty of Medicine, Dentistry and Nursing: Prof. B. BURCHELL
Faculty of Duncan of Jordanstone College: Prof. G. L. P. FOLLETT

PROFESSORS

Faculty of Arts and Social Sciences (Tower Extension, Dundee, DD1 4HN; tel. (1382) 344180; ; tel. (1382) 345527; e-mail j.y .forbes@dundee.ac.uk; internet www.dundee .ac.uk/facartsoc):

CHALKLEY, M. J., Economics
CHATTERJI, M., Applied Economics
DEWHURST, J. H. L., Regional Economics
DOBSON, A. P., Politics
FINDLAY, A. M., Geography
HARLEY, T. A., Cognitive Psychology
HARRIS, R., British History
KENNEDY, R. A., Psychology
KITSON, P. J., English Literature
LLOYD, M. G., Town and Regional Planning
MACDONALD, M. J., History of Scottish Art
MCKEAN, C. A., Scottish Architectural History
MOLANA, H. H., Economics
NEWTON, K. M., Literary Theory
WADE, N. J., Visual Psychology
WERRITTY, A., Physical Geography
WHATLEY, C. A., Modern History

Faculty of Education and Social Work (Gardyne Rd, Dundee, DD5 1NY; tel. (1382) 464000; fax (1382) 464900; e-mail edusocwk@dundee.ac.uk; internet www .dundee.ac.uk/facedusoc):

BALDWIN, N., Child Care and Protection
DANIEL, D. M., Child Care and Protection
HARTLEY, J. D., Educational Theory and Policy
TOPPING, K. J., Educational and Social Research

Faculty of Engineering and Physical Sciences (Carnegie Bldg, Dundee, DD1 4HN; tel. (1382) 344190; fax (1382) 344389; e-mail engineering@dundee.ac.uk; internet www .dundee.ac.uk/facengphys):

ABEL, E. W., Biomedical Engineering
ARNOTT, J. L., Communications Systems
CHAPLAIN, M. A., Mathematical Biology
DAVIES, M. C. R., Civil Engineering
DAVIES, P. A., Fluid Dynamics
DHIR, R. K., Concrete Technology
FITZGERALD, A. G., Physics
FLETCHER, R., Mathematics
GOODMAN, T. N. T., Applied Analysis
HORNER, R. M. W., Engineering Management
NEWELL, A. F., Electronics and Microcomputer Systems
PANFILOV, A., Mathematical Biology
RICKETTS, I. W., Assistive Systems and Healthcare Computing
VARDY, A. E., Civil Engineering
WATSON, G. A., Numerical Analysis

Faculty of Law and Accountancy (Scrymgeour Bldg, Dundee, DD1 4HN; tel. (1382) 344185; fax (1382) 345094; e-mail lawandaccy@dundee.ac.uk; internet www .dundee.ac.uk/faclawacc):

BELCHER, C. A., Law
BISSETT-JOHNSON, A., Private Law

CAMERON, P. D., International Energy Law and Policy
FERGUSON, P. R., Scots Law
GRINYER, J. R., Accountancy
HELLIER, C. V., Accountancy and Business Finance
NIXON, W. A. J., Accountancy
PAGE, A. C., Public Law
PALMER, K. F., Mineral Policy
POUNDER, D. J., Forensic Medicine
POWER, D. M., Business Finance
REID, C. T., Environmental Law
STEVENS, P., Petroleum Policy and Economics
WALDE, T. W., International Economic, Energy and Natural Resources Law

Faculty of Life Sciences (Wellcome Biocentre, Dundee, DD1 4HN; tel. (1382) 344182; fax (1382) 345519; e-mail science@dundee.ac.uk; internet www.dundee.ac.uk/lifesciences):

BARTON, G. J., Bioinformatics
BLOW, J. J., Chromosome Maintenance
BOXER, D. H., Microbial Biochemistry
CANTRELL, D. A., Immunology
Sir COHEN, PHILIP, Enzymology
CROCKER, P. R., Glycoimmunology
EDDY, F. B., Zoology
GADD, G. M., Microbiology
HARDIE, D. G., Cellular Signalling
HERBERT, R. A., Microbial Ecology
HUNTER, W. N., Structural Biology
PROUD, C. G., Biochemical Physiology
STARK, M. J. R., Yeast Molecular Biology
TICKLE, C. A., Developmental Biology
WATTS, C., Immunobiology
WEIJER, C. J., Developmental Physiology
WILLIAMS, J. A., Developmental Biology

Faculty of Medicine, Dentistry and Nursing (Ninewells Hospital and Medical School, Dundee, DD1 9SY; tel. (1382) 632763; fax (1382) 644267; internet www.dundee.ac.uk/ facmedden):

ANDERSON, A. S., Food Choice
ASHFORD, M. L. J., Neuroscience
BALFOUR, D. J. K., Behavioural Pharmacology
BARBOUR, R., Health and Social Care
BELCH, J. J. F., Vascular Medicine
BURCHELL, A., Molecular Medicine
BURCHELL, B., Medical Biochemistry
CADDEN, S. W., Oral Biology
CHISHOLM, D. M., Dental Surgery
CROMBIE, I. K., Public Health
CUMMINGS, J. H., Experimental Gastroenterology
DAVEY, P. G., Pharmacoeconomics
FAHEY, T. P., General Practice
FLEMING, S., Cellular and Molecular Pathology
HAYES, J. D., Molecular Carcinogenesis
HUME, R., Developmental Medicine
HUNT, S. C., Nursing and Midwifery
LAMBERT, J. J., Neuropharmacology
Sir LANE, DAVID, Molecular Oncology
LANG, C. C., Cardiology
LEVISON, D. A., Pathology
LIPWORTH, B. J., Allergy and Respiratory Medicine
MACDONALD, T. M., Clinical Pharmacology and Pharmacoepidemiology
MACFARLAINE, G. T., Bacteriology
MCLEAN, W. H. I., Human Genetics
MCMURDO, M. E. T., Ageing and Health
MATTHEWS, K., Psychiatry
MORRIS, A. D., Diabetic Medicine
MOSSEY, P. A., Craniofacial Development and Dentofacial Orthopaedics
MUNRO, A. J., Radiation Oncology
MURPHY, D. J., Obstetrics and Gynaecology
OGDEN, G. R., Oral and Maxillofacial Surgery
PIPPARD, M. J., Haematology
PITTS, N. B., Dental Health
RANKIN, E. M., Cancer Medicine

ROWLEY, D. I., Orthopaedic and Trauma Surgery
SAUNDERS, W. P., Endontology
SCHOR, S. L., Oral Cell Biology
STEELE, R. J., Surgery
STIRRUPS, D. R., Orthodontics
STRUTHERS, A. D., Cardiovascular Medicine and Therapeutics
SULLIVAN, F. M., General Practice and Primary Care
THOMPSON, A. M., Surgical Oncology
WILDSMITH, J. A. W., Anaesthesia
WOLF, C. R., Molecular Pharmacology
WRIGHT, E. G., Experimental Haematology
WYATT, J., Health Informatics

Faculty of Duncan of Jordanstone College (Perth Rd, Dundee, DD1 4HT; tel. (1382) 345213; fax (1382) 227304; internet www .dundee.ac.uk/facdjcad):

COLVIN, C., Fine Art Photography
FISHER, G. R., Sculpture
FOLLETT, G. L. P., Design
INNS, T. G., Design
PARTRIDGE, S., Media Art
ROBB, A., Fine Art
UNWIN, S. D. A., Architecture

UNIVERSITY OF DURHAM

University Office, Old Elvet, Durham, DH1 3HP(191) 334-2000
Fax: (191) 334-6250
E-mail. pro.directory@durham.ac.uk
Internet: www.dur.ac.uk

Founded 1832

Academic year: October to June (three terms)

Chancellor: BILL BRYSON
Vice-Chancellor: Prof. CHRISTOPHER HIGGINS
Deputy Vice-Chancellor: Prof. P. JONES (Sub-Warden)
Pro-Vice-Chancellor: Prof. A. BILSBOROUGH
Registrar and Secretary: LEE SANDERS

Library: see Libraries and Archives
Number of teachers: 677
Number of students: 17,320

DEANS

Faculty of Arts and Humanities: Prof. SETH KUNIN
Faculty of Science: Dr K. J. ORFORD
Faculty of Social Sciences and Health: Prof. R. J. ALLISON
Colleges and Student Support Services: Prof. T. BURT

PROFESSORS

Faculty of Arts and Humanities:

ARCHER, R. L. A., Spanish
BAGULEY, D., French
BARCLAY, J. M. G., Divinity
BARNES, G. L., Japanese
BROOKS, C. W., History
BROWN, D. W., Divinity
CLARK, T. J. A., English Studies
COOPER, D. E., Philosophy
COWLING, D. J., French
DAVIES, D. J., Study of Religion
DIBBLE, J. C., Music
HALL, E. M., Greek Cultural History
HARRIS, E., Classics and Ancient History
HARRIS, H. J., History
HAYWARD, C. T. R., Hebrew
LOUTH, A., Patristic and Byzantine Studies
LOWE, E. J., Philosophy
MANNING, P. D., Music
MICHIE, R. C., History
O'MEARA, P., Russian
O'NEILL, M. S. C., English Studies
PADDISON, M. H., Music
PRESTWICH, M. C., History
REGAN, S., English Studies
RHODES, P. J., Ancient History
ROLLASON, D. W., History
ROWE, C. J., Greek

SANDERS, A. L., English Studies
SAUL, N. D. B., German
STUCKENBRUCK, L. T., Biblical Studies
TAYLOR, J. H. M., French
WAUGH, P., English Studies
WILLIAMSON, P. A., History

Faculty of Science:

ABRAM, R. A., Physics
ABRASHKIN, V. A., Mathematics
ADAMS, C. S., Physics
APPLETON, E., Engineering
BADYAL, J. P., Chemistry
BENNETT, K. H., Engineering
BOWER, R. G., Physics
BROERSMA, H. J., Computer Science
BRYCE, M. R., Chemistry
CAMPBELL, A. C., Psychology
CHAMBERLAIN, J. M., Applied Physics
CROUCH, R., Engineering
DAVIDSON, J. P., Earth Sciences
DOREY, P. E., Mathematics
EDWARDS, R., Biological and Biomedical Sciences
FARBER, M. S., Pure Mathematics
FINDLAY, J. M., Psychology
FLOWER, D. R., Physics
FOULGER, G. R., Earth Sciences
FRENK, C. S., Fundamental Physics
GATHERCOLE, S. E., Psychology
GLOVER, E. W. N., Physics
GOLDSTEIN, M., Statistics
GOULTY, N. R., Earth Sciences
HATTON, P. D., Physics
HE, L., Engineering
HEYWOOD, C. A., Psychology
HOLDSWORTH, R. E., Earth Sciences
HOWARD, J. A. K., Chemistry
HUNTLEY, B., Biological and Biomedical Sciences
HUSSEY, P. J., Plant Molecular Cell Biology
HUTCHISON, C. J., Animal Cell Biology
HUTSON, J. M., Chemistry
LINDSAY, S. W., Biological and Biomedical Sciences
LINDSEY, K., Plant Molecular Biology
MANSFIELD, P., Mathematics
MARDER, T. B., Chemistry
MAROPOULOS, P., Engineering
MENSHIKOV, M. V., Statistics
MILNER, A. D., Cognitive Neuroscience
MONKMAN, A. P., Physics
MUNRO, M., Computer Science
NIU, Y., Earth Sciences
PARKER, D., Chemistry
PENNINGTON, M. R., Mathematical Sciences and Physics
PETTY, M. C., Engineering
PURVIS, A., Engineering
QUINLAN, R. A., Biomedical Sciences
SALOUS, S., Engineering
SEARLE, R. C., Geophysics
SHANKS, T., Physics
SHARPLES, R. M., Physics
SLABAS, A. R., Plant Sciences
STEWART, I. A., Computer Science
STIRLING, W. J., Mathematical Sciences and Physics
STRAUGHAN, B., Numerical Analysis
TANNER, B. K., Physics
TAVNER, P., Engineering
THOMPSON, R. N., Geology
TUCKER, M. E., Geological Sciences
UNSWORTH, A., Engineering
WALMSLEY, A. R., Infectious Diseases
WARD, M. J., Physics
WARD, R. S., Mathematics
ZAKRZEWSKI, W. J., Mathematics

Faculty of Social Sciences and Health:

ABHYANKAR, A., Finance
ALLEN, T., Law
ALLISON, R. J., Geography
AMIN, A., Geography
ANTONIOU, A., Business School
BAILEY, D., Applied Social Sciences
BAILIFF, I. K., Archaeology

BARR, D. G., Business School
BASU, P., Economics
BILSBOROUGH, A., Anthropology
BLACKMAN, T. J., Applied Social Sciences
BOHLANDER, M., Law
BOYNE, R. D., Sociology and Social Policy
BURT, T. P., Geography
BYRAM, M. S., Education
BYRNE, D. S., Applied Social Sciences
CAMPBELL, D., Cultural and Political Geography
CAMPBELL, I. D., Law
CARRITHERS, M. B., Anthropology
CLARK, T., Organizational Behaviour
COCKERILL, T. A. J., Business Management and Economics
COOPER, B., Education
DARNELL, A. C., Business School
DEGELING, P., Clinical Management Development
DIXON, R., Managerial Accounting
EHTESHAMI, A., Middle Eastern and Islamic Studies
ELLIOTT, J., Education
EVANS, H. M., Humanities in Medicine
FENWICK, H. M., Law
FERGUSON, R. I., Physical Geography
GLOVER, G. R., Public Mental Health
GOTT, R., Education
GRAHAM, S., Geography
GREAVES, R.-M., European Law
HAMILTON, J. D., Academic Director of Phase 1 Medicine
HOBBS, R. F., Law
HOLMES, P. R., Business School
HUDSON, R., Geography
HUNGIN, A. P. S., Health
HUNTER, D. J., Health Policy and Management
JOHNSON, P. S., Business School
KOUKRAKOS, P., Law
LAFFIN, M., Public Policy and Management
LANE, S., Geography
LAYTON, R. H., Anthropology
LEIGH, I. D., Law
LINSTEAD, S., Organizational Analysis
LONG, A. J., Geography
MASON, J., Health
McGLYNN, C. M. S., Law
McKENDRICK, D. G., Strategy
MEYER, J. H. F., Education
MOORE, G., Business School
NEWTON, L. D., Education
PAINTER, J. M., Geography
PALMER-COOPER, J. A., Education
PARKER, S. C., Entrepreneurship
PAUDYAL, K., Business School
POLOS, L., Business School
PRICE, A. J., Archaeology
READ, D., Business School
REDMAN, T., Business School
RIDGWAY, J. E., Education
RIGG, J. D., Geography
ROBERTS, C. A., Archaeology
SCOTT, S. J., Applied Social Sciences
SHENNAN, I., Geography
SHONE, R., Business School
SILLITOE, P., Anthropology
SMITH, R. D., Education
SMITH, S. J., Human Geography
SULLIVAN, G. R., Law
TOWNSEND, A. R., Regional Regeneration and Development Studies
TYMMS, P. B., Education
VAN WITTELOOSTUIJN, A., Strategy
WARBRICK, C. J., Law
WATSON, R., Financial Management
WILLIAMS, R. J., Politics
WILSON, R. J. A., Middle Eastern and Islamic Studies
WRIGHT, G., Management

COLLEGES

College of St Hild and St Bede: Durham; f. 1975; Principal Dr J. A. PEARSON.

Collingwood College: Durham; f. 1972; Principal Prof. J. H. M. TAYLOR.

George Stephenson College: Stockton; f. 2001; Principal Prof. A. C. DARNELL.

Grey College: Durham; f. 1959; Master Prof. J. M. CHAMBERLAIN.

Hatfield College: Durham; f. 1846; Master ANGEL B. SCOTT (acting).

John Snow College: Stockton; f. 2001; Principal Prof. H. M. EVANS.

Josephine Butler College: Durham; f. 2001; Principal ADRIAN SIMPSON.

St Aidan's College: Durham; f. 1895, known as St Aidan's Society until 1961; Principal J. S. ASHWORTH.

St Chad's College: Durham; f. 1904; Principal Rev. Canon Dr J. P. M. CASSIDY.

St Cuthbert's Society: Durham; f. 1888, known as non-Collegiate until 1947; Principal Prof. R. D. BOYNE.

St John's College with Cranmer Hall: Durham; f. 1909; Principal Rev. Dr DAVID WILKINSON.

St Mary's College: Durham; f. 1899; Principal J. HOBBS.

Trevelyan College: Durham; f. 1966; Principal Dr N. MARTIN.

University College: Durham; f. 1832; Master Prof. M. E. TUCKER.

Queen's Campus, Stockton: f. 1992 as University College Stockton, to award joint qualifications of Universities of Durham and Teesside; now part of the University of Durham.

Ushaw College: Durham; f. 1808; Rector Rev. T. P. DRAINEY.

Ustinov College (Graduate Society): Durham; f. 1965; Principal Dr PENELOPE WILSON (acting).

Van Mildert College: Durham; f. 1963; Principal Prof. P. O'MEARA.

UNIVERSITY OF EAST ANGLIA

Norwich, Norfolk NR4 7TJ
Telephone: (1603) 456161
Fax: (1603) 458553
Internet: www.uea.ac.uk
Founded 1963
Academic year: September to June

Chancellor: Sir BRANDON GOUGH
Vice-Chancellor: Dr BILL MACMILLAN
Pro-Vice-Chancellors: Prof. ALAN DAWSON, Prof. G. BENTHAM, Prof. N. NORRIS
Registrar and Secretary: B. SUMMERS
Librarian: JEAN C. STEWARD

Library of 800,000 items (700,000 books, CDs and DVDs, 100,000 print periodicals)
Number of teachers: 646
Number of students: 14,047

Publications: *Pretext* (literary, 2 a year), *Reactions* (literary, annually), *Scandinavica* (modern Norvic studies, 2 a year), *Tiempo* (climate research)

DEANS

School of American Studies: Prof. RICHARD CROCKATT
School of Biological Sciences: Prof. J. TURNER
School of Chemical Sciences and Pharmacy: Prof. MIKE COOK
School of Computing Sciences: Prof. ANDREW BANGHAM
School of Developmental Studies: Prof. M. STOCKING
School of Economics: Dr ALISTAIR MUNRO
School of Education and Lifelong Learning: Prof. CHRIS HUSBANDS
School of Environmental Sciences: Prof. CHRIS VINCENT

School of Film and Television Studies: Prof. ANDREW HIGSON
School of History: Prof. J. CHARMLEY
School of Language, Linguistics and Translation Studies: Dr MARIE-MADELEINE KENNING
School of Law: Prof. ALISTAIR MULLIS
School of Literature and Creative Writing: Prof. CLIVE SCOTT
School of Management: Prof. NIKOLAOS TZOKAS
School of Mathematics: Prof. TOM WARD
School of Medicine: Prof. S. LEINSTER
School of Music: JONATHAN IMPETT
School of Nursing and Midwifery: K. GUYON
School of Philosophy: Dr CATHERINE OSBORNE
School of Political, Social and International Studies: Prof. JOHN GREENAWAY
School of Social Work and Psychological Sciences: Prof. DAVID HOWE
School of World Arts Studies and Museology: T. S. HESLOP

PROFESSORS

School of American Studies (tel. (1603) 592220; fax (1603) 507728; e-mail wwweas@uea.ac.uk; internet www.uea.ac.uk/eas):

BIGSBY, C. W. E.
CROCKATT, R.
HOMBERGER, E.

School of Biological Sciences (tel. (1603) 593503; fax (1603) 592250; e-mail diana.cook@uea.ac.uk; internet www.uea.ac.uk/bio):

DAWSON, A., Biology
DUNCAN, G., Biology
EDWARDS, D. R., Cancer Studies
HEWITT, G. M., Biology
JOHNSTON, A. W. B., Biology
REYNOLDS, J., Biology
RICHARDSON, D. J.
SUTHERLAND, W. J., Biology
WATKINSON, A. R., Ecology

School of Chemical Sciences and Pharmacy (tel. (1603) 593145; fax (1603) 592003; e-mail k.e.bezants@uea.ac.uk; internet www.uea.ac.uk/cap):

ANDREWS, D. L., Chemistry
BELTON, P., Chemistry
BOCHMANN, M., Chemistry
COOK, M. J., Chemistry
CRAIG, D., Pharmacy
FIELD, R., Chemistry
MOORE, G. R., Chemistry
ROBINSON, B. H., Chemistry
RUSSELL, D., Chemistry
THOMSON, A. J., Chemistry

School of Computing Sciences (tel. (1603) 592847; fax (1603) 593345; e-mail www-admin@uea.ac.uk; internet www.cmp.vea.uea.ac.uk):

BANGHAM, J. A., Electronic Systems Engineering
GLAUERT, J., Computing Science
FINLAYSON, G., Information Systems
FORREST, A. R., Computing Science
RAYWARD-SMITH, V. J., Computing Science
SLEEP, M. R., Computing Science

School of Developmental Studies (tel. (1603) 592807; fax (1603) 451999; e-mail dev.general@uea.ac.uk; internet www.uea.ac.uk/dev):

ELLIS, F. T., Development Studies
JENKINS, R., Development Studies
SEDDON, D., Development Studies
STOCKING, M. A., Development Studies

School of Economics (tel. (1603) 592070; fax (1603) 250434; e-mail m.watling@uea.ac.uk; internet www.uea.ac.uk/eco):

CUBITT, R., Economics
DAVIES, S. W., Economics
HARGREAVES HEAP, S. P., Economics
LAWSON, S., International Relations

LOOMES, G., Economics
LYONS, B. R., Economics
SUGDEN, R., Economics

School of Education and Lifelong Learning (tel. (1603) 591451; fax (1603) 593446; e-mail edv.reception@uea.ac.uk; internet www.uea.ac.uk/edu):

BRIDGES, D., Education
ELLIOTT, J., Education
NORRIS, N. F. J., Education
SCHOSTAK, J. F., Education
TICKLE, L., Education
WALKER, R., Education

School of Environmental Sciences (tel. (1603) 592542; fax (1603) 592327; e-mail env@uea.ac.uk; internet www.uea.ac.uk/env):

BATEMEN, I., Environmental Sciences
BENTHAM, C. G., Environmental Sciences
BRIMBLECOMBE, P., Environmental Sciences
HEY, R. D., Environmental Sciences
HULME, M., Environmental Sciences
JICKELLS, T. D., Environmental Sciences
LEEDER, M. R., Environmental Sciences
LISS, P. S., Environmental Sciences
O'RIORDAN, T., Environmental Sciences
PENKETT, S. A., Environmental Sciences
PIDGEON, N. F., Environmental Sciences
PLANE, J. M. C., Environmental Sciences
SCHELLNHUBER, J., Environmental Sciences
TURNER, R. K., Environmental Studies
VINCENT, C. E., Environmental Sciences
WATKINSON, A. R., Ecology
WIGLEY, T. M. C., Environmental Sciences

School of Film and Television Studies (tel. (1603) 593820; fax (1603) 507728; e-mail k.durnford@uea.ac.uk; internet www.uea.ac.uk/eas):

BARR, C. J. A., Film Studies
HIGSON, A., Film Studies
JANCOVICH, M., Film Studies
TASKER, Y., Contemporary Popular Culture

School of History (tel. (1603) 593521; fax (1603) 593519; e-mail h.ashdown@uea.ac.uk; internet www.uea.ac.uk/his):

CHARMLEY, J. D., Modern British History
DAVIS, J. C., English History
HARPER-BILL, C., English History
HOWE, A. C., Modern History
RAWCLIFFE, C., English History
SANDERSON, M., Modern Social History
VINCENT, N., English and European History

School of Language, Linguistics and Translation Studies (tel. (1603) 592750; fax (1603) 250599; e-mail pg.llt@uea.ac.uk; internet www.uea.ac.uk/llt):

CHILTON, P., Linguistics

School of Law (tel. (1603) 593042; fax (1603) 250245; e-mail pglaw@uea.ac.uk; internet www.uea.ac.uk/law):

HVIID, M., Competition and Contract Law
MULLIS, A., International Commercial Law
PATTENDEN, R. D., Law
PRIME, T., Law
SMITH, I. T., Employment Law
WINSHIP, P., Law

School of Literature and Creative Writing (tel. (1603) 593820; fax (1603) 507728; e-mail k.durnford@uea.ac.uk; internet www.uea.ac.uk/eas):

DUNCKER, P., Creative Writing
HOLMES, R., Literature
ROBERTS, M., Creative Writing
ROBINSON, M., Scandinavian Studies
SAGE, V., Literature
SALES, R., English Literature
SCOTT, C., European Literature (French)
YARROW, R., Drama

School of Management (tel. (1603) 593029; fax (1603) 593343; e-mail pg.mgt@uea.ac.uk; internet www.mgt.uea.ac.uk):

DREW, S., Management
FLETCHER, K. P., Management
TZOKAS, N., Customer Relationship Management
WADDAMS, C., Management

School of Mathematics (tel. (1603) 592597; fax (1603) 593868; e-mail ann.barnes@uea.ac.uk; internet www.mth.uea.ac.uk):

EVEREST, G. R., Mathematics
JOHNSON, J. A., Mathematics
VANDER-BROECK, J. M., Applied Mathematics
WARD, T., Pure Mathematics
ZALESSKII, A., Pure Mathematics

School of Medicine, Health Policy and Practice (tel. (1603) 593061; fax (1603) 593752; e-mail e.newport@uea.ac.uk; internet www.med.uea.ac.uk):

BACHMANN, M., Healthcare Interfaces
BARRETT, A., Clinical Oncology
HARVEY, I., Epidemiology and Public Health
HOWE, A. C., Clinical Professor
HUNTER, P. R., Clinical Professor
MACGREGOR, A., Public Health
MUGFORD, M., Health Economics
REYNOLDS, S., Medicine

School of Music (tel. (1603) 592452; fax (1603) 250454; e-mail n.swan@uea.ac.uk; internet www.uea.ac.uk/mus):

CHADD, D., Music

School of Nursing and Midwifery (tel. (1603) 421422; fax (1603) 421505; e-mail nam.admissions@uea.ac.uk; internet www.uea.ac.uk/nam):

SALTER, B., Health Services Research

School of Philosophy (tel. (1603) 593717; fax (1603) 250434; e-mail m.watling@uea.ac.uk; internet www.uea.ac.uk/phi):

O'HAGAN, T., Philosophy

School of Political, Social and International Studies (tel. (1603) 593717; fax (1603) 250434; e-mail m.watling@uea.ac.uk; internet www.uea.ac.uk/psi):

GOODWIN, B., Politics
LAWSON, S., International Relations
STREET, J. R., Politics

School of Social Work and Psychosocial Sciences (tel. (1603) 592068; fax (1603) 593552; e-mail pgswk@uea.ac.uk; internet www.uea.ac.uk/swk):

HOWE, D. K., Social Work
THOBURN, J., Social Work

Schools of World Art Studies and Museology (tel. (1603) 592817; fax (1603) 593642; e-mail pgwam1@uea.ac.uk; internet www.uea.ac.uk/art):

HODGES, R. A., Visual Arts
JORDANOVA, L., Visual Arts
ONIANS, J. B., Visual Arts

ASSOCIATED RESEARCH INSTITUTES

British Trust for Ornithology: see separate entry under Learned Societies.

Centre for Environmental Fisheries and Aquaculture Science (CEFAS): Pakefield Rd, Lowestoft, NR33 0HT; tel. (1502) 562244.

Department of Family Medicine: Norfolk and Norwich University Hospital, Colney Lane, Norwich, NR4 7UY; tel. (1603) 286286.

Department of Medical Physics and Bioengineering: Norfolk and Norwich University Hospital, Colney Lane, Norwich, NR4 7UY; tel. (1603) 286286.

IACR–Broom's Barn: Higham, Bury St Edmunds, Suffolk, IP28 6NP; tel. (1284) 812200.

Institute of Food Research Norwich Laboratory: Norwich Research Park, Colney, Norwich NR4 7UA; tel. (1603) 255000.

John Innes Centre: see under Research Institutes.

Morley Research Centre: Morley, Wymondham, NR18 9DB; tel. (1953) 713200.

National Institute of Agricultural Botany: Huntington Rd, Cambridge, CB3 0LE; tel. (1223) 276381.

Norfolk and Norwich Institute for Medical Education: Norfolk and Norwich University Hospital, Colney Lane, Norwich, NR4 7UY; tel. (1603) 286286.

Sainsbury Institute for the Study of Japanese Arts and Culture: 8A The Close, Norwich, NR1 4DH; tel. (1603) 624349.

Sainsbury Laboratory: John Innes Centre, Norwich Research Park, Colney, Norwich, NR4 7UH; tel. (1603) 450000.

Tyndall Centre for Climate Change Research: School of Environmental Sciences, Norwich, NR4 7TJ; tel. (1603) 593900; fax (1603) 593901; e-mail tyndall@uea.ac.uk; internet www.tyndall.ac.uk; Dir Prof. MIKE HULME.

UNIVERSITY OF EAST LONDON

Longbridge Rd, Dagenham, Essex, RM8 2AS

Telephone: (20) 8223-3000
Fax: (20) 8223-4072
E-mail: admiss@uel.ac.uk
Internet: www.uel.ac.uk

Founded 1970 as North East London Polytechnic, later became Polytechnic of East London; present name and status 1992

Organized in three campuses: Stratford Campus, Romford Rd, Stratford, London, E15 4LZ (health, bioscience, law, psychology); Barking Campus, Longbridge Rd, Dagenham, Essex, RM8 2AS (education, business, computing and technology); Docklands Campus, 4–6 University Way, London, E16 2RD (art and design, media and cultural studies, architecture, social sciences)

Academic year: September to July

Chancellor: Lord RIX
Vice-Chancellor (vacant)
Pro-Vice-Chancellors: Dr SUSAN PRICE, Prof. ALAN SIBBALD
Registrar: ALAN INGLE
Librarian: ANDREW McDONALD
Library of 248,000 vols, 1,400 current periodicals
Number of teachers: 530 (485 full-time, 45 part-time)
Number of students: 16,000

HEADS OF SCHOOL

School of Architecture and the Visual Arts: CLIFFORD NICHOLLS
Business School: TIM McINTYRE-BHATTY (acting)
School of Computing and Technology: Dr PAUL SMITH
School of Education: ANN SLATER
School of Health and Bioscience: Dr DAVID HUMBER
School of Law: FIONA FAIRWEATHER
School of Psychology: Prof. DAVID ROSE
School of Social Sciences, Media and Cultural Studies: Dr GAVIN POYNTER

UNIVERSITY OF EDINBURGH

Old College, South Bridge, Edinburgh, EH8 9YL

Telephone: (131) 650-1000
Fax: (131) 650-2147
E-mail: communications.office@ed.ac.uk
Internet: www.ed.ac.uk

Founded 1583
Academic year: September to June
Chancellor: HRH THE PRINCE PHILIP, DUKE OF EDINBURGH
Vice-Chancellor and Principal: Prof. T. O'SHEA
Rector: MARK BALLARD
Sec.: M. CORNISH
Academic Registrar and Deputy Sec. for Academic Affairs: Dr D. B. NELSON
Dir of Student Recruitment and Admissions: E. LISTER
Dir of Finance: J. GORRINGE
Dir of Int. Office: A. MACKAY
Dir of Research Services: D. WADDELL
Librarian (vacant)
Library: see Libraries and Archives
Number of teachers: 2,730
Number of students: 24,620 (21,423 full-time, 3,197 part-time)
Publications: *EDIT Magazine* (2 a year), *Scottish Affairs* (quarterly), *Scottish Studies* (annual), *The University of Edinburgh Journal* (2 a year)

HEADS OF COLLEGES

College of Humanities and Social Science: Prof. V. BRUCE
College of Medicine and Veterinary Medicine: Prof. J. SAVILL
College of Science and Eng.: Prof. G. BULFIELD

PROFESSORS

College of Humanities and Social Science (Administration Office, 55–56 George Sq., Edinburgh, EH8 9JU; tel. (131) 650-4646; fax (131) 650-6512; internet www.hss.ed.ac.uk):

ADLER, M. E., Socio-Legal Studies
ABHYONKAR, A., Financial Markets
ALTHAUS-REID, M., Contextual Theology
ANDERSON, R. D., Modern History
ANGOLD, M. J., Byzantine History
ANSELL, J. I., Risk Management
ARCHIBALD, T. W., Business Modelling
BAILEY, P., Modern Chinese History
BANKOWSKI, Z., Legal Theory
BANNER, M. C., Ethics and Public Policy in Life Sciences
BARKER, A. W., Austrian Studies
BARNARD, A. J., Anthropology of Southern Africa
BARRINGER, J. M., Greek Art and Archaeology
BARSTAD, H. M., Hebrew and Old Testament Studies
BLOOR, D., Sociology of Science
BLOXHAM, D., Modern History
BOYLE, A. E., Public International Law
BRAY, F., Social Anthropology
BRODIE, D., Employment Law
BROWN, S. J., Ecclesiastical History
BRUCE, V., Psychology
CAIRNS, D. L., Classics
CAIRNS, J. W., Legal History
CAMPBELL, I., Scottish and Victorian Literature
CARR, C. H., Corporate Strategy
CARR, D., Philosophy of Education
CARSTEN, J. F., Social and Cultural Anthropology
CASTLES, F. G., Social and Public Policy
CLARK, A., Logic and Metaphysics
CLARK, C., Social Work Ethics
CLASON, J., Comparative Social Policy
COGLIANO, F. D., American History
COLEBROOK, C. M., Literary Theory
COLVIN, S., German
COWLING, E. G., 20th-Century European Art
Cox, J. L., Religious Studies
COYNE, A. R., Architectural Computing
CREE, V. E., Social Work Studies
CROOK, J. N., Business Econ.

CURRIE, C., Child and Adolescent Health
DAVIDSON, R., Social History
DAWSON, J., Reformation History
DAYAN, P., French
DEARY, I. J., Differential Psychology
DELLA SALA, S., Human Cognitive Neuroscience
DEVINE, T. M., Scottish History and Palaeography
DUFFY, J. H., French
ERSKINE, A., Ancient History
FABRE, C., Political Theory
FERGUSSON, D., Divinity
FERREIRA, F., Language and Cognition
FRANSMAN, M., Econ.
FROTH, S., Music
GENTZ, N., Chinese
GIEGERICH, H. J., English Linguistics
GILLIES, W., Celtic Languages, Literature, History and Antiquities
GILMORE, W. C., Int. Criminal Law
GOODE, A., Social Anthropology in Practice
GREASLEY, D. G., Economic History
GREEN, J., Medieval History
GRETTON, G. L., Law
GRIFFITHS, A., Anthropology of Law
GRIFFITHS, M., Classroom Learning
HARDING, D. W., Archaeology
HARDMAN MOORE, J. H., Political Economy
HAYWARD, T., Environmental Political Theory
HAYWOOD, J., Education and Technology
HENDERSON, J., Visual Cognition and Cognitive Neuroscience
HENLEY, J. S., Int. Management
HEYCOCK, C., Syntax
HIGGINS, P., Outdoor and Environmental Education
HILLENBRAND, C., Islamic History
HILLENBRAND, R., Islamic Art
HIMSWORTH, C. M. G., Admin. Law
HOPKINS, E. H. K., Econ.
HOUNSELL, D., Higher Education
HURFORD, J. R., General Linguistics
HURTADO, L. W., New Testament Language, Literature and Theology
JACKSON, A., History
JAMIESON, L. H. A., Sociology of Families and Relationships
JEFFERY, C., Politics
JEFFERY, P. M., Sociology
JEFFERY, R., Sociology of South Asia
JEFFREYS-JONES, R., American History
JOSEPH, J. E., Applied Linguistics
KREBER, C., Teaching and Learning in Higher Education
LADD, D. R., Linguistics
LAPSLEY, I. McL., Accountancy
LAURIE, G. T., Medical Jurisprudence
LIM, T. M., Hebrew Bible and Second Temple Judaism
LINGARD, R., Education
LOGIE, R. H., Human Cognitive Neuroscience
MACCORMICK, D. N., Public Law and the Law of Nature and Nations
MACDONALD, A. J., Architectural Studies
MACINNES, J., Sociology
MACKENZIE, D. A., Sociology
MACQUEEN, H. L., Private Law
MAHER, G., Criminal Law
MAIN, B. G. M., Business Econ.
MANNING, S., English Literature
MARDER, R., Midwifery
MARSHALL, D. W., Marketing and Consumer Behaviour
MCCRONE, D., Sociology
MCDOUGALL, B. S., Chinese
MCMAHON, A., English Language
MCMILLAN, J. F., History
MEEK, D. E., Scottish and Gaelic Studies
MELIA, K. M., Nursing Studies
MEYERHOFF, M., Sociolinguistics
MITCHELL, F., Management Accounting
MOLINA, A. H., Technology Strategy
MUNN, P., Curriculum Research

MUNRO, C. R., Constitutional Law
MYERS, A., Organology
NELSON, P., Music and Technology
NICHOLSON, C. E., 18th-century and Modern Literature
NORTHCOTT, M. S., Ethics
NUGENT, P., Comparative African History
NUTLEY, S., Public Management
O'DONOVAN, O., Christian Ethics and Practical Theology
OLIVER, N., Management
OSBORNE, N., Music
OSBORNE, S., Int. Public Management
OZGA, J., Educational Research
PATERSON, L., Educational Policy
PEDRESCHI, R., Architectural Technology
PELTENBURG, E. J., Archaeology
PETERSON, J., Int. Politics
PICKERING, M., Psychology of Language and Communication
POLLOCK, A., Health Policy
POWER, M. J., Clinical Psychology
PRITCHARD, D., Philosophy
PULLUM, G., General Linguistics
RAAB, C. D., Govt
RAFFE, D., Sociology of Education
RALSTON, I., Prehistoric European Archaeology
REID, K. G. C., Property Law
RIDDELL, S., Inclusion and Diversity
RIDGE, M. R., Moral Philosophy
ROBBINS, J. M. W., Hispanic Studies
RODGER, R., Economic and Social History
ROSA, P., Entrepreneurship and Family Business
SAKOVICS, J., Economic Theory
SANDERS, R., Sport Science
SCALTSAS, T., Ancient Philosophy
SCHOFIELD, J., Healthcare Management
SCOTT, A. G., European Union Studies
SHAW, J., European Institutions
SNELL, A. J., Econ. and Econometrics
SORACE, A., Developmental Linguistics
SPARKS, R., Criminology
SPENCER, J., Anthropology of South Asia
STANLEY, E., Sociology
STEPHENSON, A. J. R., Modern German History
STEVENSON, R., 20th-Century Literature
TAFFER, R., Finance and Investment
TETT, L., Community Education and Lifelong Learning
THOMAS, J. P., Econ.
THOMSON, R., Fine Art
USHER, J., Italian
WASOFF, F., Family Policies
WATERHOUSE, L. A. M., Social Work
WEBB, J., Sociology of Organizations
WHYTE, I. B., Architectural History
WHYTE, W. J., Social Work
WILLIAMS, R., Social Research on Technology
WISHART, J. G., Developmental Disabilities in Childhood
YEARLEY, S., Sociology of Scientific Knowledge

College of Medicine and Veterinary Medicine (The Queen's Medical Research Institute, 47 Little France Crescent, Edinburgh, EH16 4TJ; tel. (131) 242-9300; fax (131) 242-9301; e-mail mvm@ed.ac.uk; internet www.mvm.ed.ac.uk):

AMOS, A., Health Promotion
AMYES, S. G. B., Microbial Chemotherapy
ANDERSON, R., Clinical Reproductive Science
ARGYLE, D., Veterinary Clinical Studies
BACKETH-MILLBURN, K. C., Sociology of Families and Health
BALL, K., Biochemistry and Cell Signalling
BARD, J., Bio-informatics and Devt
BATEMAN, D. N., Clinical Toxicology
BELL, J. E., Neuropathology
BEST, J. J. K., Medical Radiology
BHOPAL, R., Public Health

BLACKWOOD, D., Psychiatric Genetics
BOYD, K. M., Medical Ethics
BROPHY, P. J., Veterinary Anatomy and Cell Biology
CALDER, A. A., Obstetrics and Gynaecology
CAMPBELL, H., Genetic Epidemiology and Public Health
CLUTTON, E., Veterinary Anaesthesiology
CORCORAN, B. M., Veterinary Cardiopulmonary Medicine
CRAWFORD, D. H., Bacteriology
CRITCHLEY, H., Reproductive Medicine
CUMMING, A. D., Medical Education
CUNNINGHAM-BURLEY, S. J., Medical and Family Sociology
DAVIES, J., Experimental Anatomy
DENNIS, M. S., Stroke Medicine
DEWHURST, D., Student Learning (e-Learning)
DIXON, P. M., Equine Surgery
DONALDSON, K., Respiratory Toxicology
DOUGLAS, N. J., Respiratory and Sleep Medicine
DROUSFIELD, I., Leukocyte and Lung Cell Biology
DUNLOP, M. G., Coloproctology
EBMEIER, K. P., Psychiatry
ELSE, R. W., Diagnostic Veterinary Pathology
FALLON, M. T., Palliative Medicine
FAZAKERLEY, J., Virology
FEARON, K. C. H., Surgical Oncology
FFRENCH-CONSTANT, C., Multiple Sclerosis
FLEETWOOD-WALKER, S. M., Sensory Neuroscience
FORBES, S. J., Transplantation and Regenerative Medicine
FOWKES, F. G. R., Epidemiology
FOX, K. A. A., Cardiology
GALLY, D. L., Microbial Genetics
GARDEN, O. J., Clinical Surgery
GHAZAL, P., Molecular Genetics and Biomedicine
GOVAN, J. R. W., Microbial Pathogenecity
GRANT, S. G. N., Molecular Neuroscience
GREENING, A. P., Pulmonary Disease
GREGORY, C. D., Inflammatory Cell Biology
GUNN-MOORE, D., Feline Medicine
HARKISS, G. D., Veterinary Immunopathology
HARMAR, A. J., Molecular Pharmacology
HARRISON, D. J., Pathology
HASLETT, C., Respiratory Medicine
HAYES, P. C., Hepatology
HECK, M., Cell Biology and Genetics
VAN HEYNINGEN, S., Learning and Teaching
HILLIER, S. G., Reproductive Endocrinology
HOOPER, M. L., Molecular Pathology
HOPKINS, J., Veterinary Immunology
HOWIE, S. E. M., Immunopathology
HUPP, E., Cancer Research
IBBETSON, R. J., Dental Primary Care
IREDALE, J., Medicine
IRONSIDE, J. W., Clinical Neuropathology
JARMAN, A. P., Developmental Cell Biology
JODRELL, D., Cancer Therapeutics
JOHNSTONE, E. C., Psychiatry
KAUFMAN, M. H., Anatomy
LAMB, J. R., Veterinary Clinical Immunology
LAWRIE, S. M., Psychiatric Imaging
LENG, G., Experimental Physiology
LINCOLN, Q. A., Biological Tuning
LUDWIG, M., Neurophysiology
MACNEE, W., Respiratory and Environmental Medicine
MACPHERSON, S. G., Postgraduate Medical Education
MARSHALL, I., Magnetic Resonance Physics
MASON, J. I., Clinical Biochemistry
MCCULLOCH, J., Neuropharmacology
MCDICKEN, W. N., Medical Physics and Medical Eng.
MCGORUM, B. C., Equine Medicine
MCINTOSH, N., Child Life and Health
MCKEEVER, D., Veterinary Clinical Science

McQUEEN, D. S., Sensory Pharmacology
MELTON, D. W., Somatic Cell Genetics
MIMS, R. A., Paediatric Neurology
MORRIS, R. G. M., Neuroscience
MURRAY, G. D., Medical Statistics
MURRAY, S. A., Primary Palliative Care
NASH, A. A., Veterinary Pathology
NEWBY, D., Cardiology
OWENS, D. G. C., Clinical Psychiatry
PETTIGREW, G. W., Bioenergetics
PORTEOUS, D. J., Human Molecular Genetics and Medicine
POWER, I., Anaesthetics, Critical Care and Pain
POXTON, I. R., Microbial Infection and Immunity
PRESCOTT, R. J., Health Technology Assessment
PRICE, D. J., Developmental Neurobiology
RALSTON, S. H., Rheumatology
REES, J. L., Dermatology
RHIND, S. M., Veterinary Medical Education
ROCHESTER, R. R., Cellular Neuroscience
ROSS, J. A., Liver Cell Biology
ROSSI, A., Respiratory and Inflammation Pharmacology
RUSSELL, J. A., Neuroendocrinology
SALLER, D. M., Osteoarticular Pathology
SANDERCOCK, P., Medical Neurology
SATSANGI, J., Gastroenterology
SAVILL, J. S., Experimental Medicine
SECKL, J. R., Molecular Medicine
SETHI, T. J., Respiratory and Lung Cancer Biology
SHARPE, M., Psychological Medicine and Symptoms Research
SHEIKH, A., Primary Care Research and Devt
SHIPSTON, M. J., Physiology
SIMMONDS, P., Virology
SIMPSON, A. H. R. W., Orthopaedic Surgery
SIMPSON, J. W., Canine Medecine
SMYTH, J. F., Medical Oncology
TAYLOR, D. W., Tropical Animal Health
THODAY, K. L., Veterinary Dermatology
TURNER, A. N., Nephrology
TURNER, M., Cellular Therapy
WALKER, B. R., Endocrinology
WARDLAW, J. M., Applied Neuroimaging
WARLOW, C. P., Medical Neurology
WATSON, E. D., Veterinary Reproduction
WEBB, D. J., Clinical Pharmacology
WELBURN, S., Medical and Veterinary Molecular Epidemiology
WELLER, D., General Practice
WHITTLE, I. R., Surgical Neurology
WILL, R. G., Clinical Neurology
WILMUT, I., Reproductive Science
WOOLHOUSE, M. E. J., Veterinary Public Health and Quantitative Epidemiology

College of Science and Engineering (Weir Bldg, King's Bldgs, West Mains Rd, Edinburgh, EH9 3JY; tel. (131) 650-5759; fax (131) 650-5738; e-mail sciengmail@ed.ac.uk; internet www.scieng.ed.ac.uk):

ACKLAND, G. J., Computer Simulation
AITKEN, A., Protein Biochemistry
AITKEN, C. G. G., Forensic Statistics
ALLEN, J. E., Immunology
ALLSHIRE, R., Chromosome Biology
ANDERTON, X., Therapeutic Immunology
ARSLAN, T., Integrated Electronic Systems
ATKINSON, M. P., e-Science
ATTFIELD, J. P., Materials Science at Extreme Conditions
BALL, R. D., Mathematical Physics
BARLOW, P. N., Structural Biology
BARTHOLEMIE, R. J., Renewable Energy
BARTON, N. H., Evolutionary Genetics
BAXTER, R. L., Chemical Biology
BEGGS, J. D., Molecular Biology
BIALEK, J. W., Electrical Eng.
BIRD, A. P., Genetics
BISHOP, C. M., Computer Science

BLAXTER, M. L., Evolutionary Genomics
BONDI, E., Social Geography
BOULTON, G. S., Geology
BOWNES, M., Developmental Biology
BRADEN, H. W., Integrable Systems
BRADLEY, M., Chemical Biology
BRAND, P. W. J. L., Astrophysics
BRANDONI, S., Chemical Eng.
BRANFORD, D., Photonuclear Physics
BRUCE, A. D., Statistical Physics
BRYDON, I. G., Renewable Energy
BULFIELD, G., Animal Genetics
BUNDY, A. R., Automated Reasoning
BUNEMAN, P., Database Systems
CAMPBELL, D. M., Musical Acoustics
CARBERY, A., Mathematics
CATES, M., Natural Philosophy
CHAPMAN, S. K., Biological Inorganic Chemistry
CHEUNG, R., Nanoelectronics
CLARKE, P., e-Science
COOPER, J. M., Micro- and Nanosystems
CRAIN, J., Applied Physics
CROWLEY, T., Earth Systems Science
DAVIE, A. M., Mathematical Analysis
DAVIES, M., Signal Processing
DAVIS, I., Cell Biology
DONOVAN, R. J., Chemistry
DUGMORE, A. J., Geosciences
DUNLOP, J. S., Extragalactic Astronomy
EASSON, W. J., Fluid Mechanics
FAN, W., Web Data Management
FARMER, J. G., Environmental Geochemistry
FIGUEROA-O'FARRILL, J., Geometric Physics
FINNEGAN, D. J., Molecular Genetics
FISHER, R. B., Computer Vision
FITTON, J. G., Igneous Petrology
FORDE, M. C., Civil Eng. Construction
FOURMAN, M. P., Computer Systems
FRY, S. C., Plant Biochemistry
GILLESPIE, T. A., Mathematical Analysis
GONDZIS, J., Optimization
GORDON, I., Mathematics
GORYANIN, I., Systems Biology
GRACE, J., Environmental Biology
GRAHAM, C. M., Experimental Geochemistry
GRANT, P. M., Electronic Signal Processing
GRAY, D., Immunology
GYÖNGY, I. J., Probability
HALL, C., Materials
HALLIDAY, I., Physics
HARLEY, S. L., Lower Crustal Processes
HARRISON, A., Solid-State Chemistry
HARTE, B., Metaphorism
HASZELDINE, S., Sedimentary Geology
HEAVENS, A. F., Theoretical Astrophysics
HEGGIE, D. C., Mathematical Astronomy
HILLSTON, J., Quantitative Modelling
HUDSON, A. D., Developmental Genetics
HUZLEY, A., Physics, Quantum Ordering at Extreme Positions
ILLIUS, A. W., Animal Ecology
JACK, M. A., Electronic Systems
JACOBS, J. M., Cultural Geography
JERRUM, M. R., Algorithms and Complexity
KEIGHTLEY, P. D., Evolutionary Genetics
KENNEDY, A. D., Computational Science
KENWAY, R. D., Mathematical Physics
KLEIN, E., Cognitive Systems
KROON, D., Geology
LAWRENCE, A., Astronomy
LEACH, D. R. F., Molecular Genetics
LEIGH, D. A., Organic Chemistry
LEIGH BROWN, A. J., Evolutionary Genetics
LEIM-KUHLER, B., Applied Mathematics
LENAGAN, T. H., Non-commutative Algebra
LIBKIN, L., Foundations of Data Management
LOAKE, G. J., Molecular Plant Sciences
LU, Y., Structural Mechanics
MADDON, P., Physical Chemistry
MAIN, I. G., Seismology and Rock Physics
MAIZELS, R. M., Zoology
MATTHEWS, K., Parasite Biology

McKINNON, K. I. M., Operational Research
McLAUGHLIN, S., Electronic Communications Systems
McMAHON, M., High Pressure Physics
McNABB, H., Heterocyclic Chemistry
MEDVINSKY, A., Haematopoietic Stem Cell Biology
METCALFE, S. E., Environmental Change
MILLER, A. J., Systems Biology
MONCRIEFF, J., Micrometeorology
MOORE, J. D., Artificial Intelligence
MULGREW, B., Signals and Systems
MULHEIM, F., Particle Physics
MURRAY, A. F., Neural Electronics
NEE, S., Social Evolution
NELMES, R. J., Physical Crystallography
O'BOYLE, M., Computer Science
OBERLANDER, J., Epistemics
OOI, J., Particulate Solid Mechanics
OPARKA, K. J., Plant Science
PARKER, D. F., Applied Mathematics
PARSONS, S., Crystallography
PEACOCK, J. A., Cosmology
PEMBERTON, J. M., Molecular Ecology
PLAYFER, S. M., Experimental Particle Physics
PLOTKIN, G. D., Computation Theory
PONTON, J. W., Chemical and Process Systems Eng.
POON, W. C. K., Condensed Matter Physics
PUSEY, P. N., Physics
RANICKI, A. A., Algebraic Surgery
RANKIN, D. W. H., Structural Chemistry
READ, A. F., Natural History
REID, G. A., Molecular Microbiology
RENALS, S., Speech Technology
RESBOL, N. D., Fungal Cell Biology
ROBERTSON, A. H. F., Geology
ROTTER, J. M., Civil Eng.
ROUNSEVELL, M., Rural Economy and Environmental Sustainability
SANNELLA, D. T., Computer Science
SAWYER, L., Biomolecular Structure
SCHÄFER, A., Environmental Eng.
SEATON, N. A., Interfacial Eng.
SHEIKHDESLAMI, R., Chemical Process Eng.
SHOTTER, A. C., Experimental Physics
SIEGERT, M. J., Geoscience
SINGER, M., Geometry
SMOKTURNOWICZ, A., Algebra
STAEHELI, L., Geography
STEEDMAN, M., Cognitive Science
STENNING, K., Human Communications
STIRLING, C., Computation Theory
SUGDEN, D. E., Geography
SUMMERFIELD, M. A., Geomorphology
TASKER, P. A., Industrial Chemistry
TATE, A., Knowledge-based Systems
TELEMAN, C., Mathematics
TETT, S. F. B., Earth Systems Dynamics
THOMPSON, R., Environmental Geophysics
TOPHAM, N. P., Computer Systems
TORERO, J. L., Fire Safety Eng.
TREW, A. S., Computational Science
TUDHOPE, A. W., Climate Science
TYER, S. M. D., Systems Biology
UNDERHILL, J. R., Seismic Stratigraphy
UNDERWOOD, I., Electronic Displays
USAMI, A. S., Structural Eng. and Computational Mechanics
VOLBERG, A., Mathematical Sciences
WALKINSHAW, M. D., Structural Biochemistry
WALDER, P., Theoretical Computer Science
WALLACE, A. R., Renewable Energy Systems
WALTON, A. J., Microelectronic Manufacturing
WEBBER, B., Intelligent Systems
WEST, S. A., Evolutionary Ecology
WHALER, K. A., Geophysics
WHITTEMORE, C. T., Agriculture and Rural Economy
WILLIAMS, C. K. I., Machine Learning
WILLIAMS, W., Mineral Physics

WILLSHAW, D., Computational Neurobiology
WITHERS, C. W. J., Geography
WOODS, P. J., Nuclear Physics
WRIGHT, J., Mathematical Analysis
YELLOWLEES, L. J., Inorganic Electrochemistry
ZIOLKOWSKI, A. M., Petroleum Geoscience

CONSTITUENT COLLEGE

New College: Mound Pl., Edinburgh, EH1 2LX; f. 1846; Principal Rev. Prof. A. G. AULD.

ATTACHED INSTITUTES

Institute for Advanced Studies in the Humanities: Hope Park Sq., Edinburgh, EH8 9NW; Dir S. MANNING.

Institute for Applied Language Studies: 21 Hill Pl., Edinburgh, EH8 9BP; Dir E. H. GLENDINNING.

Scottish Agricultural College Edinburgh: see under Colleges.

UNIVERSITY OF ESSEX

Wivenhoe Park, Colchester, CO4 3SQ
Telephone: (1206) 873333
Fax: (1206) 873598
Internet: www.essex.ac.uk
Founded 1961
Academic year: October to July
Chancellor: Lord PHILLIPS OF SUDBURY
Vice-Chancellor: Prof. Sir I. M. CREWE
Pro-Vice-Chancellor (Academic Development): Prof. M. J. SHERER
Pro-Vice Chancellor (Academic Standards): Dr SAM STEEL
Pro-Vice-Chancellor (Research and Business Development): Prof. R. E. MASSARA
Pro-Vice-Chancellor (Resources): Prof. J. RICHMOND
Registrar and Secretary: Dr TONY RICH
Librarian: ROBERT BUTLER

Library: see Libraries and Archives
Number of teachers: 453
Number of students: 6,686

DEANS

School of Humanities and Comparative Studies: Dr FIONA VENN
School of Law: Prof. JANE E. A. WRIGHT
School of Science and Engineering: Prof. DAVID NEDWELL
School of Social Sciences: Prof. JOHN SCOTT
Graduate School: Prof. JOAN BUSFIELD
Collaborative Education: BOB MACK

PROFESSORS

ADAMS, M. J., Electronic Systems Engineering
ADES, J. D., Art History and Theory
ANDERMAN, S. D., Law
ARNOLD, A. J., Accounting, Finance and Management
ATKINSON, R. M., Language and Linguistics
BAKER, N. R., Biological Sciences
BENEKE, R., Biological Sciences
BENTON, E., Sociology
BERTHOUD, R., Institute for Social and Economic Research
BHASKAR, V., Economics
BLACKBURN, R. O., Sociology
BOOTH, A. L., Institute for Social and Economic Research
BORSLEY, R., Language and Linguistics
BOYLE, C. K., Law
BUDGE, I., Government
BURDETT, K., Economics
BUSFIELD, N. J., Sociology
CHAMBERS, M. J., Economics
CLAHSEN, H., Language and Linguistics
COAKLEY, J., Accounting, Finance and Management
COLBECK, I., Biological Sciences

COLES, M. G., Economics
COOPER, C. E., Biological Sciences
COXON, A. P. M., Sociology
CRITCHLEY, S. J., Philosophy
CROSSICK, G. J., History
DEWS, P. K., Philosophy
DINE, J. M., Law
DOWDEN, J. M., Mathematics
DOWNTON, A. C., Electronic Systems Engineering
ELSON, D., Sociology
ERMISCH, J. F., Institute for Social and Economic Research
FERNANDEZ, N., Biological Sciences
FOWERAKER, J. W., Government
FOX, E. M., Psychology
FRASER, V., Art History and Theory
GEIDER, J., Biological Sciences
GERSHUNY, J. I., Institute for Social and Economic Research
GHANBARI, M., Electronic Systems Engineering
GILBERT, G. S., Law
GILLIES, J., Literature
GLUCKSMANN, M. A., Sociology
GOBERT, J. J., Law
GRAY, R. J., Literature
HADFIELD, B., Law
HAMILTON, C. P., Law
HAMMERSLEY, R., Health and Social Services Institute
HAMPSON, F. J., Law
HANLEY, J. R., Psychology
HATTON, T. J., Economics
HAWKSFORD, M. J., Electronic Systems Engineering
HENNING, I., Electronic Systems Engineering
HIGGINS, P. M., Mathematics
HOLT, A. R., Mathematics
HULME, P. D., Literature
HUNT, P. H. M., Law
IVERSEN, M. D., Art History and Theory
JENKINS, S. P., Institute for Social and Economic Research
KIRCHNER, E. J., Government
LAHIRI, S., Economics
LEADER, S. L., Law
LIND, L. F., Electronic Systems Engineering
LINSTEAD, S., Accounting, Finance and Management
LUBBOCK, J. A., Art History and Theory
LYNN, P., Institute for Social and Economic Research
McKAY, D. H., Government
McSWEENEY, L. B., Accounting, Finance and Management
MASON, C. F., Biological Sciences
MASSARA, R. E., Electronic Systems Engineering
MEDDIS, R., Psychology
MIRSHEKAR, D., Electronic Systems Engineering
MORRIS, L. D., Sociology
MUTHOO, A., Economics
NEARY, I. J., Government
NEDWELL, D. B., Biological Sciences
NORTON, J., Biological Sciences
OLIVER, J., Computer Science
O'MAHONY, M. J., Electronic Systems Engineering
ORBELL, S., Psychology
PATRICK, P., Language and Linguistics
PLACK, C. J., Psychology
PLUMMER, K. J., Sociology
POLI, R., Computer Science
PRETTY, J., Biological Sciences
PUTTFARKEN, T., Art History and Theory
RADFORD, A., Language and Linguistics
RANDALL, M. V., Government
REYNOLDS, C. A., Biological Sciences
RICHMOND, J., Economics
ROCA, I. M., Language and Linguistics
RODLEY, N. S., Law
ROSE, D. I., Institute for Social and Economic Research
SACKS, M. D., Philosophy

SANDERS, D. J., Government
SCHÜRER, K., Data Archive
SCOTT, J. P., Sociology
SEAL, W. B., Accounting, Finance and Management
SHERER, M. J., Accounting, Finance and Management
SIKKA, P. N., Accounting and Financial Management
SMITH, S. A., History
SORELL, T. E., Philosophy
SOUTH, N., Sociology
SPENCER, A. J., Language and Linguistics
STANWAY, G., Biological Sciences
STONE, P. A., Law
SUNKIN, M. S., Law
TATHAM, M. A. A., Language and Linguistics
TEMPLE, C. M., Psychology
THORNALLEY, P. J., Biological Sciences
TIMMIS, K., Biological Sciences
TSANG, E. P. K., Computer Science
TURNER, R., Computer Science
VERGO, P. J., Art History and Theory
WALTER, J. D., History
WEALE, A. P., Government
WHITELEY, P. F., Government
WILKINS, A. J., Psychology
WILSON, M. T., Biological and Chemical Sciences

ATTACHED INSTITUTES

Data Archive: computerized social science data archive; Dir Prof. K. SCHÜRER.

Health and Social Services Institute: applied teaching, training and research in health and social services; Dir Prof. N. SOUTH.

Institute for Social and Economic Research: annual panel survey of 5,000 British households, examines income distribution etc., labour market behaviour, household formation and dissolution; Dir Prof. J. I. GERSHUNY.

UNIVERSITY OF EXETER

Exeter, EX4 4QJ
Telephone: (1392) 661000
Fax: (1392) 263108
E-mail: intoff@exeter.ac.uk
Internet: www.exeter.ac.uk
Founded 1922 as University College, University 1955
Academic year: October to July
Chancellor: Lord ALEXANDER OF WEEDON
Vice-Chancellor: Prof. STEVE SMITH
Deputy Vice-Chancellors: Prof. MALCOLM COOK, Prof. R. J. P. KAIN, Prof. PAUL WEBLEY
Registrar and Secretary: DAVID ALLEN
Librarian: ALASDAIR PATERSON

Library: see Libraries and Archives
Number of teachers: 879 (753 full-time, 126 part-time)
Number of students: 12,284 (9,622 full-time, 2,662 part-time)
Publications: *Bracton Law Journal* (annually), *Cornish Studies* (annually), *FACT: focus on alternative and complementary therapies* (4 a year), *New Arabian Studies* (annually), *Studies in Theatre Production* (2 a year)

PROFESSORS

School of Biological and Chemical Sciences (Biological Sciences, Hatherly Laboratories, Prince of Wales Rd, Exeter, EX4 4PS; tel. (1392) 264674; fax (1392) 263700; e-mail m.j .finn@ex.ac.uk; internet www.ex.ac.uk/ biologyChemical Sciences, Stocker Rd, Exeter, EX4 4QD; tel. (1392) 263488; fax (1392) 263434; e-mail chemistry@exeter.ac.uk; internet www.exeter.ac.uk/chemweb):

ANDERSON, J. M., Ecology

BROWN, J. A., Fish Physiology
BRUCE, D. W., Inorganic Chemistry
BRYANT, J. A., Biological Sciences
FOWLER, P. W., Theoretical Chemistry
LAPPIN-SCOTT, H. M., Environmental Microbiology
LEGON, A. C., Physical Chemistry
LITTLECHILD, J. A., Biological Chemistry
MACNAIR, M. R., Evolutionary Genetics
MOODY, C. J., Organic Chemistry
TALBOT, N. J., Molecular Genetics
TYLER, C. R., Biological Sciences

School of Business and Economics (Streatham Court, Rennes Drive, Exeter, EX4 4PU; tel. (1392) 263218; fax (1392) 263242; e-mail sobe@ex.ac.uk; internet www.exeter.ac.uk/sobe):

ARNOLD, A. J., Accounting
BULKLEY, I. G., Economics
CHIA, R., Strategy and Organization
COOKE, T. E., Accounting
CORRADI, V., Econometrics
DE MEZA, D. E., Economics
DRAPER, P. R., Finance
ELLIOTT, R. H., Marketing and Consumer Research
GREGORY, A., Corporate Finance
HARRIS, R. D. F., Finance
MARIOTTI, M., Economics
MURRAY, G. C., Management
MYLES, G. D., Economics
NEWTON, T., Organization and Society
TIPPETT, M., Accounting
WREN-LEWIS, S., Business Economics

School of Classics, Ancient History and Theology (The Queen's Building, The Queen's Drive, Exeter, EX4 4QW; tel. (1392) 264200; fax (1392) 264377; internet www.ex.ac.uk/classics):

BRAUND, D. C., Mediterranean and Black Sea History
GILL, C. J., Ancient Thought
GORRINGE, T., Theological Studies
MITCHELL, S., Hellenistic Culture
SEAFORD, R. A. S., Greek Literature
WILKINS, J. M., Greek Literature
WISEMAN, T. P., Classics and Ancient History

School of Education and Lifelong Learning (St Luke's Campus, Heavitree Rd, Exeter, EX1 2LU; tel. (1392) 264892; fax (1392) 264922; internet www.cx.ac.uk/education):

BIESTA, G. J. J., Education
BURDEN, R. A., Applied Educational Psychology
BURGHES, D. N., Education
COPLEY, T. D., Religious Education
DILLON, P. J., ICT and Telematics in Education
ERNEST, P., Philosophy of Mathematics Education
NORWICH, B., Educational Psychology and Special Educational Needs
PREECE, P. F. W., Education
REYNOLDS, D., Leadership and School Effectiveness
RICHARDSON, W., Education

School of Engineering, Computer Science and Mathematics (Department of Engineering, Harrison Building, North Park Rd, Exeter, EX4 4QF; tel. (1392) 217965Department of Computer Science, The Old Library, Prince of Wales Rd, Exeter, EX4 4PT; tel. (1392) 263628; fax (1392) 264067; internet www.secs.ex.ac.uk):

DAVIES, T. W., Thermofluids Engineering
DEITMAR, A., Pure Mathematics
EVANS, K. E., Materials Engineering
JONES, C. A., Applied Mathematics
KRZANOWSKI, W. J., Statistics
NARAYANAN, A., Artificial Intelligence
PARTRIDGE, D., Computer Science
SAVIC, D. A., Hydroinformatics
SOWARD, A. M., Applied Mathematics

THURBURN, J., Geophysical Fluid Dynamics
TOWNLEY, S., Applied Mathematics
VAMOS, P., Pure Mathematics
WALTERS, G. A., Water Engineering
WRAGG, A. A., Electrochemical Engineering
WRIGHT, C., Electronics and Computer Engineering
ZHANG, D., Mechanical Engineering
ZHANG, K., Fluid Dynamics

School of English (The Queen's Building, The Queen's Drive, Exeter, EX4 4QH; tel. (1392) 264268; e-mail english@ex.ac.uk; internet www.ex.ac.uk/english):

DENTITH, S., English
GAGNIER, R., English Literature
MACCABE, C., English
RYLANCE, R., English
TAYLOR, H. R., English

School of Geography, Archaeology and Earth Resources (Amory Building, Rennes Drive, Exeter, EX4 4QE; tel. (1392) 263341 (Geography); ; tel. (1392) 264350 (Archaeology); e-mail geography@ex.ac.uk; e-mail archaeology@ex.ac.uk; internet www.ex.ac.uk/schools/geogarch):

BROWN, A. G., Physical Geography and Palaeoenvironmental Analysis
CASELDINE, C., Environmental Change
COLES, B. J., Prehistoric Archaeology
KAIN, R. J. P., Geography
MAXFIELD, V. A., Roman Archaeology
SHAW, G., Human Geography
WALLING, D. E., Geography
WEBB, B. W., Physical Geography
WILLIAMS, A. M., Human Geography and European Studies
WINTER, M., Rural Policy

School of Historical, Political and Sociological Studies (Amory Building, Rennes Drive, Exeter, EX4 4RJ, tel. (1392) 264631; fax (1392) 263305; e-mail j.e.ashby@ex.ac.uk; internet www.ex.ac.uk/shipss):

ARMSTRONG, J. D., International Relations
BARNES, S. B., Sociology
BLACK, J. M., History
BURT, R., Mining History
DENORA, T., Sociology
DOERN, G. B., Public Policy
DUPRÉ, J., Philosophy of Science
HAMPSHER-MONK, I. W., Political Theory
ORME, N. I., History
OVERTON, M., Economic and Social History
RODGER, N., Naval History
RUSH, M. D., Politics
SZAJKOWSKI, B., Pan-European Politics
THORPE, A. J., Modern British History
WILKS, S. R. M., Politics
WITKIN, R. W., Sociology

School of Law (Amory Building, Rennes Drive, Exeter, EX4 4RJ; tel. (1392) 263380; fax (1392) 263196; e-mail S.O.Hammond@ exeter.ac.uk; internet www.cx.ac.uk/law):

ECONOMIDES, K. M., Legal Ethics
MCEWAN, J., Criminal Law
STEBBINGS, C., Modern Legal History
TETTENBORN, A. M., Law
USHER, J., European Law

Peninsula Medical School (Tamar Science Park, Davy Rd, Plymouth, PL6 8BX; tel. (1752) 764261; fax (1752) 764226; internet www.pms.ac.uk):

BLIGH, J., Medical Education
ERNST, E., Complementary Medicine
HATTERSLEY, A. J., Molecular Medicine
SHELDON, B., Evidence-based Social Services
SNEYD, R., Anaesthesia
SHORE, A., Vascular Physiology
TOOKE, J. E., Vascular Medicine

Camborne School of Mines (Redruth, Cornwall, TR15 3SE; tel. (1209) 714866; fax (1209) 716977; e-mail admissions@csm.exeter.ac.uk; internet www.exeter.ac.uk/csm):

ATKINSON, K., Mining Geology
GLASS, H. J., Mining and Minerals Engineering
PINE, R. J., Geotechnical Engineering
SCOTT, P. W., Industrial Geology

School of Modern Languages (The Queen's Building, The Queen's Drive, Exeter, EX4 4QH; tel. (1392) 264391; fax (1392) 264391; internet www.ex.ac.uk/schools/sml):

COOK, M. C., French 18th-Century Studies
DIFFLEY, P. B., Italian
HAYWARD, S., French
HITCHCOCK, R., Hispano-Arabic Studies
LAUSTER, M., German
ORR, M. M., Modern French Studies
ROBERTSHAW, A. T., German Medieval Studies
SORRELL, M. R. M., French Poetry and Literary Translation
WALTERS, G., Spanish

School of Performance Arts (Thornlea, New North Rd, Exeter, EX4 4LA; tel. (1392) 264580; fax (1392) 264594; e-mail drama@ exeter.ac.uk; internet www.ex.ac.uk/coverpage/dramus):

MCCULLOUGH, C., Drama
ZARRILLI, P., Drama

School of Physics (Stocker Hill, Exeter, EX4 4QL; tel. (1392) 264151; fax (1392) 264111; e-mail physics@exeter.ac.uk; internet newton.ex.ac.uk):

BARNES, W. L., Photonics
INKSON, J. C., Theoretical Physics
JONES, R., Computational Physics
NAYLOR, T., Astrophysics
SAMBLES, J. R., Experimental Physics
SAVCHENKO, A. K., Condensed Matter Physics
SRIVASTAVA, G. P., Theoretical Condensed Matter Physics
WINLOVE, C. P., Biophysics

School of Psychology (Washington Singer Laboratories, Perry Rd, Exeter, EX4 4QE; tel. (1392) 264626; fax (1392) 264623; e-mail psyadmin@ex.ac.uk; internet www.ex.ac.uk/psychology):

HASLAM, S. A., Social Psychology
KAY, J. M., Psychology
LEA, S. E. G., Psychology
MITCHELL, O. C., Experimental Psycholinguistics
MONSELL, S., Cognitive Psychology
WEBLEY, P., Economic Psychology

School of Sport and Health Sciences (St Lukes, Exeter, EX1 2LU; tel. (1392) 264726; fax (1392) 403007; internet www.ex.ac.uk/exsport):

ARMSTRONG, N., Paediatric Physiology
FORSYTHE, W. J., History of Social Policy
JORDAN, W. J. O., Social Policy
SPARKES, A. C., Social Theory
TAYLOR, A. H., Exercise and Health Psychology

Institute of Arab and Islamic Studies (IAIS Building, Stocker Rd, Exeter, EX4 4ND; tel. (1392) 264036; fax (1392) 264035; e-mail iais-info@ex.ac.uk; internet www.ex.ac.uk/iais):

EL-ENANY, R., Modern Arabic Literature
GULLY, A., Arabic Studies
MORRIS, J. W., Islamic Studies
NIBLOCK, T., Arab Gulf Studies

ATTACHED INSTITUTES

Bill Douglas Centre for the History of Cinema and Popular Culture: f. 1996; Dir Dr D. PETRIE.

Centre for Children's Health and Exercise Research: f. 1987; Dir Prof. N. ARMSTRONG.

Centre for Educational Development and Cooperation: f. 1985; Dir (vacant).

Centre for Energy and the Environment: Exeter; f. 1975; Dir Dr TREVOR W. PRIEST.

Centre for European Legal Studies: Dir (vacant).

Centre for European Studies: Exeter; f. 1979; Dir Prof. B. SZAJKOWSKI.

Centre for Evidence-Based Social Services: f. 1997; Dir Prof. B. SHELDON.

Centre for Finance and Investment: Dir IAN TONKS.

Centre for Innovation in Mathematics Teaching: Dir Prof. D. N. BURGHES.

Centre for Leadership Studies: f. 1997; Dir JONATHAN GOSLING.

Centre for Legal Practice: f. 1992; Dir Prof. V. J. SHRUBSALL.

Centre for Maritime Historical Studies: Dir Dr M. DUFFY.

Centre for Medical History and Related Social Studies: f. 1997; Dir MARK A. JACKSON.

Centre for Mediterranean Studies: Dir Dr MOHAMED-SALAN OMRI.

Centre for Research for the Learning Society: Dir Prof. W. RICHARDSON.

Centre for Research on Teaching and Learning: f. 1987; Dir Prof. N. BENNETT.

Centre for South-West Historical Studies: f. 1985; Dir Prof. R. BURT.

Centre for Systems and Control Engineering: f. 1991; Dir (vacant).

Centre of Telematics for Education: f. 1997; Dir Prof. P. DILLON.

Centre for Theology and Public Issues: Dir Prof. T. GORRINGE.

Centre for Wetland Research: f. 1997; Dir Prof. B. COLES.

Economic and Social Research Council Centre for Genomics in Society (Egenis Centre): f. 2003; Dir Prof. JOHN DUPRÉ.

English Language Centre: f. 1991; Dir (vacant) Dr KEVIN DUNSEATH.

Foreign Language Centre: Dir D. LEWIS.

Institute of Arab and Islamic Studies: Exeter; f. 1999; Dir Prof. T. NIBLOCK.

Institute of Cornish Studies: Truro; f. 1970; Dir Prof. P. J. PAYTON.

UNIVERSITY OF GLAMORGAN

Pontypridd, Mid Glamorgan, CF37 1DL(1443) 480480
Fax: (1443) 480558
E-mail: enquiries@glam.ac.uk
Internet: www.glam.ac.uk

Founded 1913 as South Wales and Monmouth School of Mines; in 1956 became Glamorgan College of Technology; became Glamorgan Polytechnic in 1970, later Polytechnic of Wales; present name and status 1992

Academic year: September to July

Chancellor: Lord MORRIS OF ABERAVON
Vice-Chancellor: Prof. DAVID HALTON
Deputy Vice-Chancellor: Prof. L. HOBSON
Pro-Vice-Chancellor (Academic): Prof. JOY CARTER
Pro-Vice-Chancellor (Operations): Dr ALDWYN COOPER
Academic Registrar: J. O'SHEA
University Secretary: LEIGH BRACEGIRDLE
Librarian: J. ATKINSON

Library of 245,000 vols, 1,745 current periodicals
Number of teachers: 616
Number of students: 18,000

DEANS

Faculty of Advanced Technology: PETER HODSON
Faculty of Health, Sport and Science: DONNA MEAD
Faculty of Humanities and Social Sciences: ROD DUBROW-MARSHALL
Cardiff School of Creative and Cultural Industries: PETER ROBERTSON
Further Education and Collaborative Activities: JOHN O'SHEA
Glamorgan Business School: ALAN LOVELL

UNIVERSITY OF GLASGOW

Glasgow, G12 8QQ
Telephone: (141) 330-2000
Fax: (141) 330-4808
E-mail: publicityservices@gla.ac.uk
Internet: www.gla.ac.uk

Founded 1451, reconstituted 1577
Academic year: October to June

Chancellor: Sir KENNETH CALMAN
Vice-Chancellor and Principal: Sir MUIR RUSSELL
Vice-Principals: Prof. MALCOLM D. MCLEOD (Advancement), Prof. CHRISTOPHER D. MORRIS (Arts, Social Sciences and Marketing), Prof. PETER H. HOLMES (Biomedicine), Prof. ROBIN E. LEAKE (Physical Sciences and Engineering), Prof. STEVE P. BEAUMONT (Research and Enterprise)
Clerk of Senate: Prof. ANDREW S. NASH
Rector: MORDECHAI VANUNU
Secretary of Court: DAVID NEWALL
Librarian: CHRISTINE A. BAILEY
Library: see Libraries and Archives
Number of teachers: 1,727
Number of students: 19,972
Publications: *Avenue* (2 a year), *News Review* (2 a year)

DEANS

Arts: Prof. JOHN M. CAUGHIE
Biomedical and Life Sciences: Prof. JOHN R. COGGINS
Education: Dr HIREK S. KWIATKOWSKI
Engineering: Prof. JOHN W. HANCOCK
Information and Mathematical Sciences: Prof. DAVID R. FEARN
Law and Financial Studies: Prof. NOREEN BURROWS
Medicine: Prof. DAVID H. BARLOW (Executive Dean)
Physical Sciences: Prof. DAVID H. SAXON
Social Sciences: Prof. NOREEN BURROWS (acting)
Veterinary Medicine: Prof. STUART W. J. REID

PROFESSORS

Faculty of Arts (6 University Gardens, Glasgow, G12 8QQ; tel. (141) 330-6319; fax (141) 330-4537; e-mail dean@arts.gla.ac.uk; internet www.arts.gla.ac.uk):

ABRAMS, L. C., Gender History
ADAMS, A. R., Emblem Studies
BISHOP, P. C., German
BLACK, C. F., Italian History
BROADIE, A., Logic and Rhetoric
BUTT, J. A., Music (Gardiner Chair)
CAIE, G. D., English Language
CARTER, A. B., Moral Philosophy
CASTILLO, S., American Literature (John Nichol Chair)
CAUGHIE, J. M., Film and Television Studies
CLANCY, T. O., Celtic
COHN, S. K., Medieval History
COWAN, E. J., Scottish History
CRONIN, R., English Literature
GERAGHTY, C., Film and TV Studies
GEYER-KORDESCH, J. M., European Natural History and Medicine
GIFFORD, D. G., Scottish Literature

GONZALEZ, M. A., Latin American Studies
GRANT, R. A., Cultural and Political Thought
GREEN, R. P., Humanity
HAIR, G. B., Music
HANSON, W. S., Roman Archaeology
HAZLETT, W. I., Ecclesiastical History
HOPKINS, D., Art History
JASPER, D., Literature and Theology
KAY, C. J., English Language
KIDD, C., Modern History (Chair)
KIRK, J., Scottish History
KNAPP, A. B., Mediterranean Archaeology
KNOWLES, D. R., Political Philosophy
LEASK, N., English Language and Literature (Regius)
LEONARD, T. A., Creative Writing
MACKENZIE, A. L., Spanish (Ivy McClelland Research Chair)
MACMAHON, M. K. C., Phonetics
MCDONALD, J. B., Drama (James Arnott Chair)
MCLEOD, M. D., African Studies
MALEY, W. T., Renaissance Studies
MARSHALL, W. J., Modern French Studies
MAWDSLEY, E., International History
MOIGNARD, E. A., Classical Art and Archaeology
MORRIS, C. D., Archaeology
MOSS, M. S., Archival Studies
NEWLANDS, G. M., Divinity
NEWMAN, S. P., American Studies (Sir Denis Brogan Chair)
O MAOLALAIGH, R., Celtic
O'DOCHARTAIGH, C. N. O., Celtic
PEACOCK, N. A., French (Marshall Chair)
READER, K. A., Modern French Studies
RIACH, A. S., Scottish Literature
ROBERTSON, P. B., Mackintosh Studies
ROSS, S., Humanities Informatics and Digital Curation
RYCROFT, M. E., Music
SCHMIDT-LEUKEL, P. H., World Religions for Peace
SMITH, J. J., English Philology
STALLEY, R. F., Ancient Philosophy
STEPHENSON, R. H., German Language and Literature; Modern Languages (William Jacks Chair)
TAYLOR, R. C., Social Policy and Social Work
THORP, N. R., History of Art
TODD, J., English Literature (Francis Hutcheson Chair)
WARD, M. G., German Language and Literature
YARRINGTON, A. W., Fine Art (Richmond Chair)

Faculty of Biomedical and Life Sciences (Room 237, West Medical Building, Glasgow, G12 8QQ; tel. (141) 339-8855; fax (141) 330-4758; e-mail ilbs-acstaff@bio.gla.ac.uk; internet www.gla.ac.uk/ibls/faculty/html):

BIRKBECK, T. H., Marine Microbiology
BLATT, M. R., Botany (Regius Chair)
CAMPBELL, A. M., Biochemical Immunology
CLEMENTS, J. B., Virology
COGDELL, R. J., Botany (Hooker Chair)
COGGINS, J. R., Molecular Enzymology
COOMBS, G. H., Biochemical Parasitology
CROZIER, A., Plant Biochemistry and Human Nutrition
CUSHLEY, W., Molecular Immunology
DAVIES, R. W., Biotechnology (Robertson Chair)
DOW, J. A. T., Molecular and Integrative Physiology
ELLIOTT, R. M., Molecular Virology
EVANS, D. J., Virology
FERRELL, W. R., Clinical Physiology
FURNESS, R. W., Seabird and Fishing Interactions
GILLESPIE, D. A. F., Molecular and Cell Biology
GOULD, G. W., Membrane Biology

HAGAN, P., Parasitology
HOUSLAY, M. D., Biochemistry (Gardiner Chair)
HOUSTON, D. C., Zoology
HUNTINGFORD, F. A., Functional Ecology
JENKINS, G. I., Plant Cell and Molecular Biology
KENNEDY, M. W., Infection Biology
KOLCH, W., Molecular and Cellular Biology
LA THANGUE, N. B., Biochemistry (Cathcart Chair)
LINDSAY, J. G., Medical Biochemistry
MACLEAN, M. R., Pulmonary Pharmacology
MCGRATH, J. C., Physiology (Regius Chair)
MARTIN, W., Cardiovascular Pharmacology
MAXWELL, D. J., Neuroanatomy
METCALFE, N. B., Behavioural Ecology
MILLIGAN, G., Molecular Pharmacology
MILNER-WHITE, E.J., Structural Bioinformatics
MITCHELL, T. J., Microbiology
MONCKTON, D. G., Human Genetics
MONAGHAN, P., Animal Ecology
MORRIS, B. J., Molecular Neurobiology
MUTRIE, N., Physical Activity and Health Science
NIMMO, H. G., Plant Biochemistry
PAGE, R. D., Taxonomy
PAYNE, A. P., Anatomy
PHILLIPS, R. S., Parasitology
PRICE, N. C., Protein Science
RUXTON, G. D., Theoretical Ecology
SMITH, G. L., Cardiovascular Physiology
STARK, W. M., Molecular Genetics
STONE, T. W., Pharmacology
TAYLOR, A. C., Physiological Ecology
TODD, A. J., Neuroscience
TURNER, C. M. R., Parasitology
WHITE, R. J., Gene Transcription

Faculty of Education (St Andrew's Building, Glasgow, G12 8QQ; tel. (141) 330-3700; fax (141) 330-3005; e-mail faculty@educ.gla.ac.uk; internet www.gla.ac.uk/faculties/education):

BARON, S., Urban Education
BARR, J. L., Adult and Continuing Education
CONROY, J. C., Religious and Philosophical Education
MCGETTRICK, B. J., Educational Studies
MCGONIGAL, J., English in Education
MENTER, I. J., Teacher Education
PETERS, M. A., Education
PREECE, J., Adult and Lifelong Education
WHITEHEAD, R. R., Theoretical Physics
WILKINSON, J. E., Education

Faculty of Engineering (James Watt South Building, Glasgow, G12 8QQ; tel. (141) 330-3733; fax (141) 330-4722; internet www.eng.gla.ac.uk):

ACHA, E., Electrical Power Systems
AITCHISON, J. S., Photonics
ARNOLD, J. M., Applied Electromagnetics
ASENOV, A. M., Device Modelling
BARKER, J. R., Electronics
BARLTROP, N. D. P., Naval Architecture and Ocean Engineering (John Elder Chair)
BICANIC, N. J. D., Civil Engineering (Regius Chair)
CARTMELL, M. P., Mechanical Engineering
COOPER, J. M., Bioelectronics and Bioengineering
COTON, F. N., Low Speed Aerodynamics
COWLING, M. J., Marine Technology
CUMMING, D., Microelectronics
DAS, P. K., Marine Structures
DAVIES, J. H., Physical Electronics
DE LA RUE, R. M., Optoelectronics
ERVINE, D. A., Water Engineering
GALBRAITH, R. A. M., Engineering (Shoda Chair)
HANCOCK, J. W., Mechanical Engineering
HUNT, K. J., Mechanical Engineering (Wylie Chair)

HUTCHINGS, D., Optical and Quantum Electronics
IRONSIDE, C. N., Quantum Electronics
MCINNES, C. R., Space Systems Engineering
MARSH, J. H., Optoelectronic Systems
MILLER, T. J. E., Electrical Engineering
MURRAY-SMITH, D. J., Engineering Systems and Control
O'REILLY, J., Control Engineering
SEWELL, J. I., Electronic Systems
STANLEY, C. R., Semiconductor Materials
THAYNE, I., Ultrafast Systems
VASSALOS, D., Naval Architecture
WEAVER, J. M. R., Applied Nanofabrication
WHEELER, S. J., Civil Engineering (Cormack Chair)
WILKINSON, C. D. W., Electrical Engineering (James Watt Chair)

Faculty of Information and Mathematical Science (Room 311, Boyd Orr Building, Glasgow, G12 8QQ; tel. (141) 330-4269; fax (141) 330-2359; e-mail gs@fims.gla.ac.uk; internet www.gla.ac.uk/faculties/ims):

ANDERSON, A. H., Psychology
ATKINSON, M. P., Computing Science
BOWMAN, A. W., Statistics
BREWSTER, S. A., Human Computer Interaction
BROWN, K. A., Mathematics
BURTON, A. M., Psychology
CALDER, M., Formal Methods
COHEN, S. D., Number Theory
FEARN, D. R., Applied Mathematics
FORD, I., Biostatistics
GARROD, S. C., Cognitive Psychology
GILBERT, D. R., Biomedical Informatics
HILL, N. A., Mathematics (Simson Chair)
JOHNSON, C. W., Computing Science
JONES, B. T., Psychology
KROPHOLLER, P. H., Mathematics
O'DONNELL, P.
OGDEN, R. W., Mathematics (George Sinclair Chair)
PRIDE, S. J., Mathematics
SANFORD, A. J., Psychology
SCHWEINBERGER, S. R., Psychology
SCHYNS, P. G., Visual Cognition
SCOTT, E. M., Environmental Statistics
SENN, K.S. J., Statistics
SMITH, P. F., Mathematics
SVENTEK, J., Communications Systems
TITTERINGTON, D. M., Statistics
VAN RIJSBERGEN, K.J., Computing Science
WATT, D. A., Computing Science
WEBB, J. R. L., Mathematics
WELLAND, R. C., Software Engineering

Faculty of Law and Financial Studies (5–9 Stair Building, The Square, Univ. of Glasgow, Glasgow, G12 8QQ; tel. (141) 330-6075; fax (141) 330-4900; e-mail faculty@law.gla.ac.uk; internet www.gla.ac.uk/faculties/law):

BEATTIE, V. A., Accounting
BURROWS, N., European Law
CRERAR, L. D., Banking Law
DANBOLT, J., Finance
DAVIDSON, F. P., (Law, Commercial Law (Alexander Stone Chair)
EMMANUEL, C. R., Accountancy
FARMER, L. A., Law
GRAY, R. H., Accounting
HOLLAND, J. B., Accountancy
KINNON, D. H., Accounting (Johnstone Smith Chair)
MCLEAN, S. A., Law and Ethics in Medicine (International Bar Assoc Chair)
MCPHAIL, K., Social and Ethical Accounting
MULLEN, T. J., Law
MURDOCH, J. L., Public Law
OPONG, K. K., Finance and Accounting
ORUCU, E., Comparative Law
REES, W., Accountancy
RENNIE, R., Conveyancing
SHACKLETON, J. K., Accounting History

THOMSON, J. M., Law (Regius Chair)
TOMKINS, A., Public Law (John Millar Chair)
WOOLFSON, C. A., Labour Studies

Faculty of Medicine (Wolfson Medical Building, University Ave, University of Glasgow, Glasgow, G12 8QQ; tel. (141) 330-5921; fax (141) 330-3360; e-mail postmaster@student.gla.ac.uk; internet www.gla.ac.uk/faculties/medicine):

AYOUB, A. F., Oral Surgery
BAGG, J., Clinical Microbiology
BAKER, A. H., Molecular Medicine
BARLOW, D. H., Reproductive Medicine
BROWN, R., Cancer Therapeutics
CASSIDY, J., Oncology
COBBE, S. M., Medical Cardiology (Walton Chair)
CONNELL, J. M. C., Endocrinology
CONNOR, J. M., Medical Genetics (Burton Chair)
COOKE, T. G., Surgery (St Mungo Chair)
COOPER, S. A., Learning Disabilities
DOMINICZAK, A. F., Cardiovascular Medicine
ELLIOTT, A. T., Clinical Physics
ESPIE, C. A., Clinical Psychology
EVANS, T. J., Molecular Microbiology
EVANS, J. J., Applied Neuropsychology
FRANKLIN, I. M., Transfusion Medicine
GARSIDE, P., Immunobiology
GEMMELL, C. G., Bacterial Infection and Epidemiology
GEORGE, W. D., Surgery (Regius Chair)
GRAHAM, G. J., Molecular and Structural Immunology
GREER, I. A., Obstetrics and Gynaecology (Muirhead Chair)
GUSTERSON, B. A., Pathology
HANLON, P. W., Public Health
HARNETT, M. M., Immune Signalling
HILLAN, E. M., Midwifery
HILLIS, W. S., Cardiovascular and Exercise Medicine
HOLE, D. J., Epidemiology and Biostatistics
HOLYOAKE, T., Experimental Haematology
JUDGE, K. F., Health Promotion Policy (HEBS Chair)
KEITH, W. N., Molecular Oncology
KENNEDY, P. G. E., Neurology (Burton Chair)
KENNY, G. N. C., Anaesthesia
LANGHORNE, P., Stroke Care
LEAN, M. E. J., Human Nutrition (Rank Chair)
LEES, K. R., Cerebrovascular Medicine
LIEW, F. Y., Immunology (Gardiner Chair)
LOWE, G. D. O., Vascular Medicine
LUMSDEN, M. A., Medical Education and Gynaecology
LYALL, F., Maternal and Fetal Health
MACDONALD, D. G., Oral Pathology
MACFARLANE, P. W., Electrocardiology
MACRAE, I. M., Neuroscience
MCCOLL, K. E. L., Gastroenterology
MCINNES, I. B., Experimental Medicine
MCINNES, G. T., Clinical Pharmacology
MCKILLOP, J. H., Medicine (Muirhead Chair)
MCMILLAN, T., Clinical Neuropsychology
MCMURRAY, J. I. V., Medical Cardiology
MILLAR, K., Behavioural Science
MORRISON, J. M., General Practice
MOWAT, A. M., Mucosal Immunology
MURRAY, T. S., General Practice
O'DWYER, P. J., Gastrointestinal Surgery
OLIVER, J. S., Forensic Toxicology
RAMPLING, R. P., Neuro-Oncology
REID, J. L., Materia Medica, Medicine and Therapeutics (Regius Chair)
REID, M., Professor of Women's Health
SATTAR, N. A., Metabolic Medicine
SHEPHERD, J., Pathological Biochemistry
SMITH, L. N., Nursing Studies
STONE, D. H., Paediatric Epidemiology

STOTT, D. J., Geriatric Medicine (David Cargill Chair)
STURROCK, R. D., Rheumatology (McLeod/Arthritis and Rheumatism Council Chair)
THOMSON, N. C., Respiratory Medicine
WATT, G. C. M., General Practice (Norrie-Miller Chair)
WEAVER, L. T., Child Health (Samson Gemmell Chair)
WELBURY, R. R., Paediatric Dentistry
WELSH, J., Palliative Medicine (Dr Olav Kerr Chair)
WHEATLEY, D. J., Cardiac Surgery
WILLISON, H. J., Neurology
WRAY, D., Oral Medicine

Faculty of Physical Sciences (Room 234, Kelvin Building, University of Glasgow, Glasgow, G12 8QQ; tel. (141) 330-4374; fax (141) 330-4371; e-mail physci@gla.ac.uk; internet www.facps.gla.ac.uk):

BARRON, L. D., Physical Chemistry (Gardiner Chair)
BISHOP, P. M., Geography
BRIGGS, J. A., Geography
BROWN, J. C., Astrophysics, Astronomy (Regius Chair)
BROWN, R. W., Earth Sciences
CHAPMAN, J. N., Physics
COOPER, A., Biophysical Chemistry
CRAVEN, A. J., Physics
DAVIES, C. T., Physics
DOYLE, A. T., Physics
FALLICK, A. E., Isotope Geosciences
FROGGATT, C. D., Physics
GILMORE, C. J., Crystallography
HOEY, T., Numerical Geoscience
HOUGH, J., Physics
ISAACS, N. W., Protein Crystallography (Joseph Black Chair)
JACKSON, S. D., Catalysis Science
KOCOVSKY, P., Chemistry (Ramsay Chair)
LEAKE, R. E., Endocrine Oncology
LONG, A. R., Physics
PADDISON, R., Geography
PADGETT, M. J., Physics
PHILO, C., Geography
ROBERTSON, N. A., Experimental Physics
ROBINS, D. J., Bio-organic Chemistry
ROSNER, G., Natural Philosophy (Cargill Chair)
RUSSELL, M. J., Applied Geology (Dixon Chair)
SAXON, D. H., Physics (Kelvin Chair)
STRAIN, K. A., Physics
WILSON, C., Chemistry (Regius Chair)
WINFIELD, J. M., Inorganic Chemistry

Faculty of Social Sciences (Adam Smith Building, 40 Bute Gardens, Glasgow, G12 8RT; tel. (141) 330-0347; fax 9141) 330-3547; e-mail enquiries@socsci.gla.ac.uk; internet www.gla.ac.uk/faculties/socialsciences):

ADAMS, C. D., Ian Mactaggart Chair of Property and Urban Studies
BEAUMONT, P. B., Employee Relations
BERRY, C. J., Political Theory
BURMAN, M., Criminology
CORRIN, C. A., Feminist Politics
CROWTHER, M. A., Social History
FERGUSON, H., Sociology
FRENCH, M. J., Economic History
FRISBY, D. P., Sociology
FURLONG, A., Sociology
GIRVIN, B., Comparative Politics
GOODLAD, R., Housing and Urban Studies
GORDON, E. J., Gender and Social History
HARRIS, R., Cairncross Professor of Applied Economics
HILL, M., Study of the Child (St Kentigern Chair)
KEARNS, A. J., Urban Studies
LAING, A. W., Business and Management
MACBETH, D. K., Supply Chain Management

MACDONALD, R., Bonar-Macfie Chair of Economics
MACLENNAN, D., Urban Studies, Economics and Finance (Mactaggart Chair of Urban Studies)
MCGREGOR, A. M., Housing and Urban Studies
MCKEGANEY, N. P., Drug Misuse Research
MALLEY, J., Economics
MILLER, W. L., Politics (Edward Caird Chair)
MOUTINHO, L. A., Marketing
MUSCATELLI, A., Economics (Daniel Jack Chair)
NOORBAKHSH, F., Development Economics
ORME, J. E., Social Work
PARR, J. B., Regional and Urban Economics
PATON, R. A., Management
PETCH, A. J., Nuffield Trust Professor of Community Care
PETERSON, J. C., European Politics (Jean Monnet Chair)
PHILO, G., Communications and Social Change
SCHENK, C., International Economic History
STOKES, R. G., International Industrial History
TUROK, I. N., Urban Economic Development
VIRDEE, S., Sociology
WATSON, N., Disability Studies
WEAVER, R., Entrepreneurship
WHITE, S. L., Government
WHITE, J. D., Russian and East European History
WILSON, F. M., Organisational Behaviour

Faculty of Veterinary Medicine (464 Bearsden Rd, Glasgow, G61 1QH; tel. (141) 330-5700; fax (141) 942-7215; internet www.gla.ac.uk/faculties/vet):

BARRY, J. D., Molecular Parasitology
BENNETT, D., Small Animal Clinical Studies
CAMERON, E. R., Molecular and Cellular Oncology
CAMPO, M. S., Viral Oncology
CARMICHAEL, S., Veterinary Clinical Studies
DEVANEY, E., Parasite Immunobiology
ECKERSALL, P. D., Veterinary Biochemistry
FITZPATRICK, J. L., Farm Animal Medicine
GRIFFITHS, I., Comparative Neurology
HOLMES, P. H., Veterinary Physiology
JARRETT, R. F., Molecular Pathology
LOVE, S., Equine Clinical Studies
MOTTRAM, J. C., Molecular and Cellular Parasitology
NASH, A. S., Small Animal Medicine
NEIL, J. C., Virology and Molecular Oncology
NOLAN, A., Veterinary Pharmacology
O'SHAUGHNESSY, P. J., Reproductive Biology
ONIONS, D. E., Veterinary Pathology
PALMARINI, M., Molecular Pathogenesis
PARKINS, J. J., Animal Health
REID, J., Veterinary Anaesthesia
REID, S. W. J., Veterinary Informatics and Epidemiology
ROBERTS, M., Molecular Bacteriology
STEAR, M. J., Veterinary Medicine
SULLIVAN, M., Veterinary Surgery and Diagnostic Imaging
TAIT, A., Veterinary Parasitology
TAYLOR, D. J., Veterinary Bacteriology and Public Health

Hunterian Museum and Art Gallery (see Museums and Art Galleries)

SILBER, E. A.

ASSOCIATED INSTITUTIONS
Free Church College, Edinburgh.

Glasgow School of Art: see separate entry in UK Colleges section.
Scottish Agricultural College, Edinburgh: see separate entry in UK Colleges section

ATTACHED INSTITUTIONS
Cancer Research UK Beatson Laboratory: see separate entry in UK Research Institutes.
Centre for History of Medicine: 5 University Gardens, Glasgow, G12 8QQ.
Medical Research Council Social and Public Health Sciences Unit: see separate entry for MRC in Research Institutes.
Medical Research Council Virology Unit: see separate entry for MRC in Research Institutes.
Scottish Universities Environmental Research Centre: see separate entry in Research Institutes.
Wellcome Surgical Institute: Garscube Estate, Bearsden Rd, Glasgow, G61 1QH.

GLASGOW CALEDONIAN UNIVERSITY

Cowcaddens Rd, Glasgow, G4 0BA
Telephone: (141) 331-3000
Fax: (141) 331-3005
E-mail: helpline@gcal.ac.uk
Internet: www.caledonian.ac.uk
Founded 1971 as Glasgow Polytechnic; merged with The Queen's College; present name and status 1993
State control
Academic year: September to June

Chancellor (vacant)
Pro-Vice-Chancellor for Academic Affairs: MIKE SMITH
Pro-Vice-Chancellor for Operations: CAROLINE MACDONALD
Principal: PAMELA GILLIES
Vice-Principal: Prof. MIKE SMITH
Head of Academic Admin.: E. B. FERGUSON
Librarian: JOHN CRAWFORD
Number of students: 14,500
Publication: *Research Report* (annual)

DEANS
School of Built and Natural Environment: Prof. C. HARDCASTLE
School of Computing and Mathematical Sciences: Prof. M. MANNION
School of Eng., Science and Design: Prof. G. GALBRAITH
School of Health and Social Care: Prof. B. DURWARD
School of Law and Social Sciences: Prof. ELAINE MCFARLAND (acting)
School of Life Sciences: Prof. D. PARKER
School of Nursing, Midwifery and Community Health: Prof. B. PARFITT
Caledonian Business School: Prof. IAN ROBSON

HEADS OF DIVISIONS
School of the Built and Natural Environment (tel. (141) 331-3300; fax (141) 331-3370; e-mail schoolbne@gcal.ac.uk; internet www.sbne.gcal.ac.uk):
    Construction Management and Econ.: Dr I. CAMERON
    Environment, Design and Construction: T. KILPATRICK
School of Computing and Mathematical Sciences (tel. (141) 331-3277; fax (141) 331-8445; e-mail pgit@gcal.ac.uk; internet www.gcal.ac.uk/cms):
    Computing: Dr C. PARKER
    Mathematics: Dr B. GARDINER

School of Engineering, Science and Design (tel. (141) 331-3529; fax (141) 331-3690; e-mail j.n.dixon@gcal.ac.uk; internet www .sesd.gcal.ac.uk):

Analytical Science Measurement and Control: Prof. J. PUGH
Creative Technologies: Prof. D. HARRISON
Electronic and Electrical Eng.: T. WEST-WOOD
Mechanical Eng.: Dr M. MACDONALD

School of Health and Social Care (tel. (141) 331-8151; fax (141) 331-8112; e-mail f .brannan@gcal.ac.uk; internet www.gcal.ac .uk/shsc):

Occupational Therapy: V. MCKAY
Physiotherapy: M. CURR
Podiatry: S. BAIRD
Radiography: B. ELLIS (acting)
Social Work: I. BRODIE

School of Law and Social Sciences (tel. (141) 331-3256; fax (141) 331-3439; e-mail lss@gcal .ac.uk; internet www.lss.gcal.ac.uk):

Law: A. O'DONNELL
Social Sciences: Dr BILL HUGHES

School of Life Sciences (tel. (141) 331-3600; fax (141) 331-3500; e-mail lifesciences@gcal .ac.uk; internet www.caledonian.ac.uk/sls):

Biological and Biomedical Sciences: Prof. M. FINBOW
Psychology: Dr A. DRUNDELL
Vision Sciences: Prof. A. TOMLINSON

School of Nursing, Midwifery and Community Health (tel. (141) 331-3467; fax (141) 331-8312; e-mail nursing@gcal.ac.uk; internet www.gcal.ac.uk/nch):

Community Health: Dr D. FERGUSSON
Midwifery: Prof. V. FLEMMING
Post-reg. Nursing and Health: K. CURRIE
Pre-reg. Nursing: Dr K. STRACHAN

Caledonian Business School (tel. (141) 331-3117; fax (141) 331-3172; e-mail cbs@gcal.ac .uk; internet www.cbs.gcal.ac.uk):

Accounting and Finance: A. RUSSELL
Business Information Management: Dr D. EDGAR
Econ. and Enterprise: J. WILSON (acting)
Human Resource Management and Devt: Dr R. BEATTIE
Media, Culture and Leisure Management: Prof. M. FOLEY
Marketing: Dr G. BIRTWHSITLE
Management: Prof. R. LEVY
Risk: Dr L. T. DRENNAN

UNIVERSITY OF GLOUCESTERSHIRE

POB 220, The Park, Cheltenham, Glos., GL50 2QF

Telephone: (1242) 532700
Fax: (1242) 532810
E-mail: intoffice@glos.ac.uk
Internet: www.glos.ac.uk

Founded 1990 as Cheltenham and Gloucester College of Further Education through merger of existing colleges; present name and status 2001
State control

Chancellor: Lord CAREY OF CLIFTON
Vice-Chancellor: Prof. PATRICIA BROADFOOT
Deputy Vice-Chancellor: Dr PETER EASY
University Registrar and Secretary: PAUL VAN ROSSUM
Head of Learning Centres: ANN MATHIE

Number of teachers: 293
Number of students: 9,092 (5,525 full-time and sandwich, 3,567 part-time)

Publications: *Business School Research Journal* (4 a year), *Contexts* (2 a year), *Journal of Learning and Teaching* (2 a year), *Landscape Issues* (2 a year)

HEADS OF SCHOOLS
School of Art, Media and Design: DAVE KESKEYS
School of Education: PETER MANSFIELD
School of Environment: CAROLYN ROBERTS
School of Health and Social Sciences: GUY DALY
School of Humanities: LINDEN PEACH
School of Sport and Leisure: MIKE COGGER
Gloucestershire Business School: JIM SIMPSON

ATTACHED RESEARCH UNIT

Countryside and Community Research Unit: Dir Prof. BILL SLEE.

UNIVERSITY OF GREENWICH

30 Park Row, Greenwich, London, SE10 9LS

Telephone: (20) 8331-8000
Fax: (20) 8331-8145
E-mail: courseinfo@greenwich.ac.uk
Internet: www.greenwich.ac.uk

Founded 1890, later became Thames Polytechnic; present name and status 1992
Academic year: September to July

Chancellor: Rt Hon. Lord HOLME OF CHELTENHAM
Vice-Chancellor: Baroness TESSA BLACKSTONE
Pro-Vice-Chancellors: Prof. J HUMPHREYS (Academic Planning), Prof. M. CROSS (Research, Consultancy and Outreach), Prof. D. WILLS (Resources)
Director of Student Affairs: C. H. ROSE
University Secretary: LINDA CORDING
Librarian: D. HEATHCOTE

Library of 610,000 vols
Number of teachers: 709
Number of students: 20,197

Publications: *Applied Mathematical Modelling* (monthly), *Computational Fluid Dynamics News* (4 a year)

HEADS OF SCHOOLS
Avery Hill Faculty (Mansion Site, Bexley Rd, London, SE9 2PQ):

Architecture and Construction: Prof. R. HAYWARD
Education and Training: R. M. YOUNG (acting)
Health and Social Care: Prof. L. MEERABEAU
Social Sciences and Law: Prof. D. CHAMBERS

University of Greenwich at Medway (Central Ave, Chatham Maritime, Kent, ME4 4AW):

Medway School of Engineering: Prof. NDY EKERE
Pharmacy: Prof. C. A. MACKIE
Science: Prof J. W. NICHOLSON
Natural Resources Institute: GUY POULTER (Dir)

Maritime Greenwich Faculty (Old Royal Naval College, Park Row, Greenwich, London, SE10 9LS):

Business: Prof LES JOHNSON
Computing and Mathematical Sciences: Prof. MARTIN EVERETT
Education and Training: Dr R. M. YOUNG (acting)
Humanities: Dr JANE LONGMORE

HERIOT-WATT UNIVERSITY

Edinburgh Campus, Edinburgh, EH14 4AS
Scottish Borders Campus, Netherdale, Galashiels, TD1 3HF

Telephone: (131) 449-5111 (Edinburgh); (1896) 753351 (Scottish Borders)
Fax: (131) 449-5153 (Edinburgh); (1896) 758965 (Scottish Borders)
E-mail: enquiries@hw.ac.uk

Internet: www.hw.ac.uk

Founded 1821 as Edinburgh School of Arts; became Heriot-Watt College 1885; present name and status 1966
Academic year: October to September

Chancellor: Baroness SUSAN GREENFIELD
Principal and Vice-Chancellor: Prof. JOHN S. ARCHER
Vice-Principal: Prof. J. E. L. SIMMONS
Deputy Principal (Academic,Business Development and International): Prof. B. G. D. SMART
Deputy Principal (Research): Prof. D. R. HALL
Deputy Principal (Resources): Prof. A. C. WALKER
Director of Finance and Information Technology: P. MCNAULL
Secretary: P. L. WILSON
Librarian: M. L. BREAKS

Number of teachers: 410
Number of students: 16,500

HEADS OF SCHOOLS
School of the Built Environment: Prof. J. A. SWAFFIELD
School of Engineering and Physical Sciences: Prof. J. D. C. JONES
School of Life Sciences: Prof. F. G. PRIEST
School of Management and Languages: Prof. J. FERNIE
School of Mathematical and Computer Sciences: Prof. K. J. CORNWELL
Institute of Petroleum Engineering: Prof. P. CORBETT
School of Textiles and Design: Prof. R. H. WARDMAN (acting)
Edinburgh Business School: Prof. K. G. LUMSDEN (Dir: Prof. C. M. BROWN (Exec Dir)

PROFESSORS

School of the Built Environment (tel. (131) 451-4644; fax (131) 451-4617; e-mail a.j .ormston@hw.ac.uk):

ASPINALL, P. A., Environmental Science
BANFILL, P. F. G., Construction Materials
BRAMLEY, G. R., Planning and Housing
CARLEY, M., Planning and Housing
CRAIK, R. J. M., Acoustics
GRANT, I., Fluid Loading and Instrumentation
HAGUE, C., Planning and Housing
JONES, C. A., Estate Management
JOWITT, P. W., Dir, Scottish Institute of Sustainable Technology
KAKA, A. P., Construction Management
MCCARTER, W. J., Concrete Technology and Soil Mechanics
MAY, I. M., Civil Engineering
MUNRO, M., Planning and Housing
PENDER, G., Civil Engineering
PRIOR, A. A., Planning and Housing
SWAFFIELD, J. A., Building Services Engineering
WOLFRAM, J., Offshore Research and Development

School of Engineering and Physical Sciences (tel. (131) 451-3082; fax (131) 451-3136; e-mail l.bruce@hw.ac.uk):

GALBRAITH, I., Physics
GREENAWAY, A. H., Physics
HALL, D. R., Optoelectronics
HAND, D. P., Physics
HARRISON, R. G., Physics
JOHN, P., Chemistry
JONES, J. D. C., Physics
LANE, D. M., Ocean Systems
MCKENDRICK, K. G., Physical Chemistry
NEWBOROUGH, M., Energy
NI, X., Process and Reaction Engineering
OCONE, R., Chemical Engineering
REUBEN, R. L., Materials Engineering

SANGSTER, A. J., Electrical and Electronic Engineering
SIMMONS, J. E. L., Mechanical Engineering
TOPPING, B. H. V., Structural Engineering
WALKER, A. C., Physics
WALLACE, A. M., Electrical and Electronic Engineering
WELCH, A. J., Inorganic Chemistry
WHERRETT, B. S., Theoretical Physics
WILLIAMS, B. W., Electrical Engineering
WILSON, J. I. B., Physics

School of Life Sciences (tel. (131) 451-3456; fax (131) 451-3009; e-mail j.e.j.lodder@hw.ac.uk):

AUSTIN, B., Microbiology
BROTHERTON, C. J., Psychology
PALMER, G. H. O., Brewing
PAUL, M., Engineering and Environmental Geology
PRIEST, F. G., Microbial Physiology
SCHWEIZER, H. M., Biological Sciences
STEWART, G. G., Brewing and Distilling

School of Management and Languages (tel. (131) 451-8143; fax (131) 451-3498; e-mail enquiries@sml.hw.ac.uk):

CRAIG, V., Employment Law
FERNIE, J., Retail Marketing
HARE, P. G., Economics
HATIM, B. A., Arabic Studies
KEENAN, T., Business Organization
LANG, M. F., Languages
MCKINNON, A. C., Logistics
MARSTON, C. L., Accounting
MASON, I., Interpreting and Translating
SCHAFFER, M. E., Economics
SHARWOOD SMITH, M. A., Languages

School of Mathematical and Computer Sciences (tel. (131) 451-3420; fax (131) 451-3327; e-mail enquiries@macs.hw.ac.uk):

AYLETT, R., Computer Science
BEEVERS, C. E., Mathematics
BROWN, K. J., Mathematics
CAIRNS, A. J. G., Actuarial Mathematics and Statistics
CARR, J., Mathematics
CORNWELL, K. J., Engineering Heat Transfer
EILBECK, J. C., Applied Numerical Analysis
FOSS, S., Actuarial Mathematics and Statistics
GIBSON, G. J., Statistics
HOWIE, J., Mathematics
JOHNSTON, D. A., Mathematics
KAMAREDDINE, F. D., Computer Science
KHANIN, K., Mathematics
KUKSIN, S., Mathematics
LACEY, A. A., Mathematics
MACDONALD, A. S., Actuarial Mathematics and Statistics
POOLEY, R. J., Computer Science
SHERRATT, J. A., Mathematics
SZABO, R., Mathematics
WATERS, H. R., Actuarial Mathematics and Statistics
WILKIE, A. D., Actuarial Mathematics and Statistics
WILLIAMS, M. H., Computing

Institute of Petroleum Engineering (tel. (131) 451-3567; fax (131) 451-3127; e-mail jane.wells@pet.hw.ac.uk):

CHRISTIE, M. A., Reservoir Engineering
CORBETT, P. W. M., Geoengineering
DANESH, S. A., Reservoir Engineering
FORD, J. T., Petroleum Engineering
MACBETH, C., Reservoir Geophysics; Time-lapse and Multi Components
SIDE, J., Civil Engineering
SMART, B. G. D., Coal and Uranium Mining; Geotechnical Engineering
SORBIE, K. S., Petroleum Engineering
TODD, A. C., Petroleum Engineering

School of Textiles and Design (tel. (1896) 753351; fax (1896) 758965; e-mail l.a.lindsay@hw.ac.uk):

STYLIOS, G. K., Textiles

Edinburgh Business School (tel. (131) 451-3090; fax (131) 451-3002; e-mail enquiries@ebs.hw.ac.uk):

BROWN, C. M., Executive Director
LOTHIAN, N., Accounting
LUMSDEN, K. G., Director
O'FARRELL, P. N., Consultant

ATTACHED RESEARCH INSTITUTES

Centre for Biomedical Textiles Research: Dir Dr A. FOTHERINGHAM.

Centre for Economic Reform and Transformation: Dir Prof. M. E. SCHAFFER.

Centre for Genetics and Insurance Research: Dir Prof. A. S. MACDONALD.

Centre for Logistics Research: Dir Prof. A. C. MACKINNON.

Centre for Marine Biodiversity and Biotechnology: Dir Dr P. F. KINGSTON.

Centre for Photonics: Dir Prof. J. D. C. JONES.

Centre for Theoretical Modelling in Medicine: Dir Prof. J. A. SHERRATT.

Centre for Translation and Interpreting Studies in Scotland: Dir Prof. I. MASON.

International Centre for Brewing and Distilling: Dir Prof. G. G. STEWART.

International Centre for Island Technology: Old Academy Building, Back Rd, Stromness, Orkney, KW16 2AW; Dir Prof. J. SIDE.

International Centre for Mathematical Sciences: 14 India St, Edinburgh; Dir T. DART.

Microsystems Engineering Centre: Dir Dr M. DESMULLIEZ.

Ocean Systems Laboratory: Dir Prof. D. M. LANE.

Research Institute for Flexible Materials: Dir Prof. G. STYLIOS.

Scottish Institute of Sustainable Technology: Dir Prof. P. JOWITT.

Scottish Manufacturing Institute: Dir Prof. J. E. L. SIMMONS.

Social Enterprise Institute: Dir D. JONES.

Technology and Research Services: Dir G. E. MCFADZEAN.

UNIVERSITY OF HERTFORDSHIRE

College Lane, Hatfield, Herts., AL10 9AB
Telephone: (1707) 284800
Fax: (1707) 284870
E-mail: admissions@herts.ac.uk
Internet: www.herts.ac.uk

Founded 1952 as Hatfield College of Technology, became Hatfield Polytechnic in 1969; present name and status 1992

Main campus in Hatfield and Law campus in St Albans

Academic year: October to June

Chancellor: Lord MACLAURIN OF KNEBWORTH
Vice-Chancellor: Prof. TIM WILSON
Pro-Vice-Chancellors: Prof. H. R. HANAHOE (Strategic Planning), T. M. NEVILLE (Finance), Prof. R. M. PITTILO (Academic Quality Assurance and Enhancement)
Secretary and Registrar: P. E. WATERS
Librarian: D. MARTIN

Library of 350,000 vols
Number of teachers: 699
Number of students: 17,000

DEANS

Faculty of Art and Design: C. MCINTYRE

Faculty of Engineering and Information Sciences: Prof. J. SENIOR
Faculty of Health and Human Sciences: V. FISHER
Faculty of Humanities and Education: Prof. G. HOLDERNESS
Faculty of Interdisciplinary Studies: A. C. WEIR
Faculty of Law (St Albans Campus): Prof. D. TRIBE
Faculty of Natural Sciences: Prof. J. HOUGH
Business School: M. TIMBRELL

UNIVERSITY OF HUDDERSFIELD

Queensgate, Huddersfield, W. Yorkshire, HD1 3DH
Telephone: (1484) 422288
Fax: (1484) 516151
E-mail: admissions@hud.ac.uk
Internet: www.hud.ac.uk

Founded 1841, formerly Huddersfield College of Technology, became Polytechnic of Huddersfield in 1970; present name and status 1992

Academic year: September to June

Chancellor: PATRICK STEWART
Vice-Chancellor and Principal: Prof. J. TARRANT
Pro-Vice-Chancellor: Prof. B. J. EVANS
Deputy Vice-Chancellor: Prof. F. ARTHUR
University Secretary: A. MEARS
Academic Registrar: Dr V. P. JEFFS

Library of 416,000 vols
Number of teachers: 1,194 (649 full-time, 545 part-time)
Number of students: 17,347 (10,432 full-time, 6,915 part-time)

DEANS OF SCHOOLS

Applied Sciences: Prof. M. I. PAGE
Business: D. SMITH
Computing and Engineering: Dr D. HALL (acting)
Design Technology: G. CALDERBANK
Education: F. BRIDGE
Human and Health Sciences: Prof. SUE FROST
Music and Humanities: Dr DAVID TAYLOR

UNIVERSITY OF HULL

Cottingham Rd, Hull, HU6 7RX
Telephone: (1482) 346311
Fax: (1482) 465936
Internet: www.hull.ac.uk

Founded 1927 as University College of Hull, University Charter 1954

Academic year: September to June

Chancellor: Baroness BOTTOMLEY
Vice-Chancellor: Prof. D. DREWRY
Deputy Vice-Chancellor (Pro-Vice Chancellor for Academic Affairs): Prof. J. W. BRUCE
Pro Vice-Chancellors: Prof. B. WINN V. MALIN
Quality Director, University Registrar and Secretary: FRANCES OWEN
Librarian and Academic Services Director: Dr R. G. HESELTINE
Library: see Libraries and Archives
Number of teachers: 570 (517 full-time, 53 part-time)
Number of students: 17,412 (11,345 full-time, 6,067 part-time)

DEANS

Faculty of Arts and Social Sciences: Dr ALAN BEST
Faculty of Science: Dr D. F. SEWELL
Business School: Prof. M. JACKSON
Hull York Medical School: Prof. W. GILLESPIE
Postgraduate Medical School: Prof. N. STAFFORD
School of Nursing, Social Work and Applied Health Studies: R. HOGSTON
Institute for Learning: Prof. G. CHESTERS

PROFESSORS

ALEKSEEVSKY, D., Mathematics
ATTENBOROUGH, K., Engineering
BENNETT, J., Hull York Medical School
BINKS, B., Chemistry
BIRKINSHAW, P. J., Law
BOSCH, P., Mathematics
BOTTERY, M., Educational Studies
BROOKES, G. R., Computer Science
BURGESS, M., Politics
BURGESS, P., History
CAMPION, P. D., Public Health and Primary Care Medicine
CARVALHO, G., Biological Science
CHESTERS, G., IfL Office
CLELAND, J., Cardiology
COLQUHOUN, D., Educational Studies
CRAIG, G., Comparative and Applied Social Sciences
CROUCH, D., History
CUMMINGS, A., Engineering Design and Manufacture
CUTLAND, N. J., Pure Mathematics
DAVIES, K., International Leadership Centre
DYER, P. E., Physics
ELTIS, D., Economic Studies
FLETCHER, P. D., Chemistry
FROSTICK, L. E., Geography and Earth Resources
GIBBS, D. C., Geography and Earth Resources
GILBERT, P., Philosophy
GILLESPIE, W., Hull York Medical School
GOODBY, J. W., Chemistry
GRABBE, L. L., Theology
GREEN, R., Economics
GRIFFIN, G., Gender Studies
HARDISTY, J. H., Geography and Earth Resources
HARRIS, R. J., Politics
HASWELL, S., Chemistry
HAUGHTON, G., Geography
HAYWOOD, S., Engineering
HOPPEN, T., History
JACKSON, M., Business School
JESSHOPE, C., Computer Science
JOHNSTON, R., Psychology
KILLICK, S. R., Obstetrics and Gynaecology
KING, V. T., Politics
KITCHEN, P., Business School
LA TORRE, M., Law
LEIGHTON, A., English
LIND, M. J., Oncology
LLOYD, H. A., History
LOVEJOY, P., History
McCOLLUM, P. T., Surgery
McNAUGHTON, L., Sport Science
MAUNDERS, K. T., Accounting, Business and Finance
MONSON, J. R. T., Surgery
MORICE, A. H., Respiratory Medicine
MORTIMER, A., Psychiatry
Lord NORTON OF LOUTH, Politics
OKELY, J. M., Comparative and Applied Social Sciences
O'SULLIVAN, N. K., Politics
PATTON, R. J., Electronic Engineering
PHILLIPS, R., Computer Science
RATLEDGE, C., Biological Science
RICHARDSON, P. D., Economic Studies
RIGBY, B., English
SANDERS, V., English Literature
SCHLUDERMANN, B., Dutch Studies
SHNIRELMAN, A., Mathematics
SMITH, P. M., French
STAFFORD, N., Otolaryngology and Head and Neck Surgery
SWIFT, K. G., Engineering Design and Manufacture
TOWNSHEND, A., Chemistry
TURNBULL, L. W., Magnetic Resonance Investigation
TURNER, G., Biological Science
TURNER, M. E., Economic Studies
VLADIMIROV, V., Mathematics

WALKER, L., Rehabilitation
WATSON, R., Care of the Older Person
WILLIAMS, D., French

ATTACHED INSTITUTES AND CENTRES

Applied Statistics Centre: Dir (vacant).

Centre for City and Regional Studies: Dirs Prof. D. GIBBS, Prof. G. HAUGHTON.

Centre for Community Nursing: Dir (vacant).

Centre for Educational Studies: Head Prof. M. BOTTERY.

Centre for Internet Computing: Head Dr C. GASKELL.

Centre for Learning Development: Head Prof. G. CHAMBERS (acting).

Centre for Lifelong Learning: Head D. VULLIAMY.

Centre for Magnetic Resonance Investigations: Dir Prof. L. W. TURNBULL.

Centre for Metabolic Bone Disease: Dir (vacant).

Centre for Waste and Pollution Research: Dir Prof. L. E. FROSTICK.

Design Enterprise Centre: Centre Man. M. POOLE.

Family Assessment and Support Unit: Dir T. ALLCOTT.

Graduate School: Dir Prof. V. T. KING.

Hull Institute for Mathematical Science and Applications (HIMSA): Dir Prof. V. VLADIMIROV.

Hull Medical Engineering Centre (Hul-MEC): Dir Prof. R. PHILLIPS.

Institute for Chemistry in Industry: Dir Prof. A. TOWNSHEND.

Institute of Estuarine and Coastal Studies: Dir Dr M. ELLIOTT.

Institute of European Public Law: Dir Prof. P. BIRKINSHAW.

Institute for Learning: Dir Prof. G. CHESTERS.

Institute of Rehabilitation: Dir Prof. L. G. WALKER.

International Leadership Centre: Dir Prof. B. DAVIES.

Research Institute for Environmental Science and Management: Dir Prof. L. FROSTICK.

Scarborough Centre for Business and Leisure Management: Head (vacant).

Scarborough Centre for Coastal Studies: Head (vacant).

University of Hull International Fisheries Institute (HIFI): Dir Dr I. COWX.

Wetland Archaeology and Environments Research Centre: Manager Dr M. LILLIE.

UNIVERSITY OF KEELE

Keele, Staffordshire, ST5 5BG
Telephone: (1782) 621111
E-mail: undergraduate@keele.ac.uk
Internet: www.keele.ac.uk

Founded as University College of North Staffordshire 1949, present name 1962
Academic year: September to August
Chancellor: Prof. Sir DAVID WEATHERALL
Vice-Chancellor: Prof. JANET FINCH
University Secretary and Registrar: SIMON MORRIS
Director of Academic Affairs: CHRIS BURDON
Director of Finance: PAT CRAWFORD
Librarian: ALLAN FOSTER
Library: see Libraries and Archives
Number of teachers: 360

Number of students: 7,100 (5,200 undergraduate, 1,900 postgraduate)
Publications: *British Journal for the History of Philosophy, Sociological Review*

DEANS

Faculty of Health: Prof. SUSAN DILLY
Faculty of Humanities: Prof. SUE SCOTT
Faculty of Natural Sciences: Prof. JOHANNA LAYBOURN-PARRY
Faculty of Social Sciences: Prof. RICHARD SPARKS

PROFESSORS

ALLAN, G., Social Relations
ANDREW, J., Russian Literature
ARME, C., Life Sciences
BAILEY, C. J., American Politics
BAINBRIDGE, S. J. J., English Literature
BALE, J. R., Education
BELL, I. F. A., American Studies
BERNARD, M., Social Gerontology
BIGGS, S. J., Social Gerontology
BLADEN-HOVELL, R. C., Economics
BLENKINSOPP, A., Practice of Pharmacy
BOTTING, D. C. F., English Literature
BOWEN, J. M., English Literature
BRENTON, O. P., Computer Science
BUDGEN, D., Computer Science
BUTLER, I. G., Social Work
CHAPMAN, S. R., Prescribing Studies
CLAYTON, R. N., Medicine
COCKS, R. C. J., Law
COOPER, D., Law
COX, J. L., Psychiatry
CRAWFORD, M. S., American Studies
CROFT, P., Epidemiology
CROME, I., Psychiatry
CROME, P., Geriatric Medicine
CROOK, M., French History
CULLEN, C., Psychology
DANCHEV, A., International Relations
DAVID, M. E., Education
DAVIES, S. J., Medicine
DEEN, S. M., Computer Science
DILLY, S. A., Medicine
DOBSON, J. P., Biomedical Engineering
DUGDALE, A. M., Law
DUMBRELL, J. W., American Studies
EGGLESTON, P., Molecular Entomology
EKINS, P. W., Sustainable Development
EL HAJ, A., Cell Engineering
EVANS, A., Astrophysics
FINCH, J. V., Social Relations
FISCHMAN, R. A., Music
FRASCINA, F. A., Visual Arts
FU, Y., Applied Mathematics
GREENHOUGH, T. J., Life Sciences
HALEY, M. A., Property Law
HARTLEY, R., Economics
HAWKINS, C., Medicine
HAY, E., Medicine
HAYS, R., Medical Education
HERMAN, D. K., Law
HEYWOOD, B. R., Inorganic Chemistry
HOPE, T. J., Criminology
HOWELL, J. A. S., Organometallic Chemistry
HUGHES, A. L., Early Modern History
HURD, H., Life Sciences
JACKSON, P. A., History
JEFFERSON, T., Criminology
JONES, K. W., Education
JONES, P. W., Statistics
KARSTEDT, S., Criminology
KITCHENHAM, B., Quantitative Software Engineering
KNIGHTS, D., Organizational Analysis
LANOT, G., Economics
LEE, K., Health Planning and Management
LOADER, I. S., Criminology
LUCY, W. N. R., Law
McCALL, I., Medicine
MacKENZIE, G., Medical Statistics
MAFFULI, N., Medicine
MUNRO, R., Organization Theory

O'BRIEN, P. M. S., Medicine
O'KANE, R., Comparative Political Theory
O'SHAUGHNESSY, N. J., Management
ONG, B. N., Health Services Research
ORMEROD, R. M., Inorganic Materials Chemistry
PATON, C. R., Health Policy
PHILLIPSON, C. R., Applied Social Studies
POGUNTKE, T., International Relations
PROOPS, J. L. R., Ecological Economics
QUINNEY, D. A., Mathematics
RAMSDEN, C. A., Chemistry
ROBINSON, E. J., Psychology
ROTENBERG, K. J., Psychology
SCRIVENS, E. E. J., Health Policy
SEIFERT, R. V., Industrial Relations
SHELDON, S., Law
SHRIRA, V., Mathematics
SIM, J. W., Physiotherapy Studies
SLOBODA, J. A., Psychology
SOUTHALL, D. P., Paediatrics
SPARKS, J. R., Criminology
SPITERI, M., Medicine
STENNING, P., Criminology
STRANGE, P., Theoretical Physics
STRANGE, R., Medicine
STYLES, P., Geophysics
SUGANAMI, H., Philosophy of International Relations
THORNBERRY, P., International Relations
TOWNSHEND, C. J. N., History
VAUGHAN, M. P., Music
VOGLER, J. F., International Relations
WALKER, R. B. J., International Relations
WARD, R. D., Biological Sciences
WASIK, M., Criminal Justice
WERBNER, P., Sociology
WILLIAMS., G. D., Earth Sciences
WILLIAMS, G. T., Biochemistry
WILLIS, P., Management
WILLMOTT, A. J., Mathematics
WINCHESTER, J. A., Earth Sciences
WORRALL., A. J., Criminology
WORRALL., T. S., Economics

UNIVERSITY OF KENT AT CANTERBURY

The Registry, Canterbury, Kent, CT2 7NZ
Telephone: (1227) 764000
Fax: (1227) 452196
Internet: www.ukc.ac.uk

Founded 1965
State control
Academic year: September to June

Chancellor: Sir CRISPIN TICKELL
Vice-Chancellor: Prof. DAVID MELVILLE
Deputy Vice-Chancellor: DAVID R. NIGHTIN-
GALE
Secretary and Registrar: NICK MCHARD
Librarian: MARGARET COUTTS

Number of teachers: 850
Number of students: 10,602

Publication: *Annual Report*

DEANS

Faculty of Humanities: Dr FRANCIS LOUGH
Faculty of Science, Technology and Medical
Studies: URSULA FULLER
Faculty of Social Sciences: Prof. CHRISTOPHER
HALE

PROFESSORS

Faculty of Humanities (Cornwallis West,
University of Kent at Canterbury, Canterbury, CT2 7NF; tel. (1227) 823490; fax (1227)
827134):

ANDERSON, G., Classics
ANDREWS, M. Y., Victorian and Visual
Studies
BAUGH, C., Drama
BOLT, C. A., American History
CARDINAL, R. T., Literary and Visual
Studies

CLARKE, G. N. G., Photography and Visual
Studies
CUNNINGHAM, H. S. C., Social History
DOCHERTY, T., English
DURRANI, O., German
ELLIS, D., English
FLOWER, J., French
GILL, R., Theology
INNES, C. L., Post-Colonial Literatures
IRWIN, M., English Literature
NORMAN, R. J., Moral Philosophy
ROBINSON, P., French
SMITH, C. W., History of Science
SMITH, M., Film Studies
TURLEY, D., Cultural and Social History
WELCH, D. A., Modern European History

Faculty of Science, Technology and Medical
Studies (Institute of Mathematics and Statistics, University of Kent at Canterbury,
Canterbury, CT2 7NF; tel. (1227) 823913; fax
(1227) 827154):

BROWN, P. J., Medical Statistics
BULL, A., Microbial Technology
BURNS, R. G., Environmental Microbiology
CHADWICK, A. V., Physical Chemistry
CLARKSON, P., Mathematics
COLCHESTER, A. C. F., Clinical Neu-
roscience and Medical Image Computing
COOK, C. C. H., Psychiatry of Alcohol
Misuse
DAVIES, P. A., Optical Communications
DORE, J., Condensed-Matter Physics
FAIRHURST, M. C., Computer Vision
FLEISCHMAN, P., Mathematics
FREEDMAN, R. B., Biochemistry
GEEVES, M. A., Physical Biochemistry
GULLICK, W., Biosciences
HALE, A. S., Psychiatry of Mental Illness
HATTON, L., Software Reliability
JACKSON, D. A., Applied Optics
JAMES, R., Oncology
JEFFRIES, P., Mycology
JONES, R., Polymer Science
LANGLEY, R. J., Antenna Systems
LININGTON, P. F., Computer Communica-
tion
LITTLE, L. T., Millimetre Wave Astronomy
MANDER, K., Computer Science
MORGAN, B. J. T., Applied Statistics
NEWPORT, R., Materials Physics
PANNELL, C. N., Optical Physics
SHACKELL, J. R., Mathematics and Compu-
tation
SOBHY, M. I., Electronic Engineering
STACEY, K., Molecular Biology
STEEL, M., Statistics
STRANGE, J. H., Experimental Physics
THOMPSON, S., Computer Science
TUITE, M., Molecular Biology
WELCH, P. H., Parallel Computing
WHITE, G., Space Sciences

Faculty of Social Sciences (Keynes College,
University of Kent at Canterbury, Canterbury, CT2 7NP; tel. (1227) 823655; fax (1227)
823959):

ABRAMS, W. D. J., Social Psychology
ALASZEWSKI, A., Sociology of Health Stu-
dies
BALDOCK, J., Social Policy
BARRY, C., Cognitive Psychology
BROWN, R. J., Social Psychology
CALNAN, M., Sociology of Health Studies
CARRUTH, A., Economics
CHURCH, C., European Studies
CONAGHAN, J., Law
ELLEN, R. F., Anthropology and Human
Ecology
EVANS, M. S., Women's Studies
FROST, M., International Relations
FUREDI, F., Sociology
GREEN, F., Economics
GROOM, A. J. R., Government
HALE, C., Criminology
HARROP, S., Wildlife Management Law
HOWARTH, W., Environmental Law

HUGHES, J. J., Industrial Relations
JENKINS, W. I., Public Policy Management
LEADER-WILLIAMS, N., Biodiversity Man-
agement
LUI, S. W., Management Science and
Computational Mathematics
MANSELL, J., Applied Psychology of Learn-
ing Disability
MUCHLINSKI, P., International Business
Law
MURPHY, G., Applied Psychology of Learn-
ing Disability
PAHL, J., Social Policy
PICKVANCE, C. G., Urban Studies
RAY, L., Sociology
RUBIN, G., Law
RUTHERFORD, B. A., Accounting
RUTTER, D., Health Psychology
SAKWA, R., Russian and European Politics
SAMUEL, G., Law
SAYERS, J., Psychoanalytic Psychology
SCASE, R., Sociology and Organizational
Behaviour
SEYMOUR-URE, C. K., Government
SHARP, J. A., Management
STEPHENSON, G., Social Psychology
TAYLOR-GOOBY, P., Social Policy
THIRLWALL, A. P., Applied Economics
TWIGG, J., Social Policy and Sociology
UGLOW, S., Criminal Justice
VICKERMAN, R. W., Regional and Transport
Economics
WILLIAMS, A., International Relations

ATTACHED INSTITUTES

Centre for American Studies: Dirs Dr D.
TURLEY, Dr GUY REYNOLDS.

Centre for Applied Ethics: Dir Prof. R.
GILL.

**Centre for Colonial and Postcolonial
Research:** Dir R. EDMOND.

**Centre for Comparative Literary Stu-
dies:** Dir Dr ELIZABETH SCHÄCHTER.

Centre for Criminal Justice Studies: Dir
Dr S. UGLOW.

**Centre for European, Regional and
Transport Economics:** Dir Prof. R. VICKER-
MAN.

Centre for Geography: Dir Prof. C. G.
PICKVANCE.

Centre for Health Service Studies: Dir
Prof. A. ALASZEWSKI.

**Centre for History and Cultural Studies
of Science:** Dir Prof. CROSBIE SMITH.

Centre for Materials Research: Dir Prof.
BOB NEWPORT.

Centre for Medieval and Tudor Studies:
Dir (vacant).

**Centre for Research in Health Beha-
viour:** Dir Prof. D. RUTTER.

**Centre for Social Anthropology and
Computing:** Dir Dr M. FISHCHER.

**Centre for the Study of Group Pro-
cesses:** Dir Prof. D. ABRAMS.

Centre for the Study of Propaganda: Dir
Prof. D. WELCH.

**Centre for the Study of Social and
Political Movements:** Dir C. ROOTES.

Centre for Women's Studies: Dir Prof. M.
EVANS.

European Institute of Social Services:
Dir ANDREW SWITHINBANK.

Institute for Social Research: Dir D.
MORGAN.

**Kent Energy Economics Research
Group:** Dir Dr J. PIERSON.

**Kent Institute of Medicine and Health
Sciences:** Dir Dr MARK RAKE.

**London Centre for International Rela-
tions:** Dir Dr V. JABRI.

Personal Social Services Research Unit: Dir Dr ANN NETTEN.

Tizard Centre: Dir P. MCGILL.

Unit for Astrophysics and Planetary Science: Dir Prof. GLENN WHITE.

Urban and Regional Studies Unit: Dir Prof. C. PICKVANCE.

KINGSTON UNIVERSITY

River House, 53–57 High St, Kingston upon Thames, Surrey, KT1 1LQ

Telephone: (20) 8547-2000
Fax: (20) 8547-7980
E-mail: admissions-info@kingston.ac.uk
Internet: www.kingston.ac.uk

Founded 1970 as Kingston Polytechnic, present name and status 1992
Academic year: October to July

Chancellor: Sir PETER HALL
Vice-Chancellor: Prof. PETER SCOTT
Deputy Vice-Chancellor: Prof. MARY STUART
University Secretary: RAFICQ ABDULLA
Head of Library Services: GRAHAM BULPITT

Library of 400,000 vols
Number of teachers: 661
Number of students: 17,000

DEANS

Faculty of Art, Design and Music: Prof. PENELOPE SPARKE
Faculty of Arts and Social Sciences: Dr GAIL CUNNINGHAM
Faculty of Business: Prof. GWYNETH PITT
Faculty of Health and Social Care Sciences: Prof. FIONA ROSS
Faculty of Science: Prof. REG DAVIS
Faculty of Technology: Prof. JOHN ROBERTS

HEADS OF SCHOOL/DEPARTMENT

Accounting and Finance: Dr JOHN ARCHBOLD
Architecture: Prof. PETER JACOB
Art and Design History: FRAN LLOYD
Chemical and Pharmaceutical Sciences: Dr WILLIAM BLAND
Computer Science and Electronic Systems: (vacant)
Earth Sciences and Geography: Prof. ANDY RANKIN
Economics: VINCENT DALY
Education: Dr MARY BOUSTED
Engineering: Prof. ANDREW SELF
Fashion: JOHN MCKITTERICK
Fine Art: Prof. BRUCE RUSSELL
Foundation Studies: PAUL STAFFORD
Graphic Design: PENNY HUDD
Humanities: JOHN IBBETT
Human Resource Management: Prof. CHRISTINE EDWARDS
Languages: TERESA LAWLOR
Law: ROGER HOLMES
Life Sciences: Dr DAVID MACKINTOSH
Marketing: WENDY LOMAX
Mathematics: Prof. JOHN MORRIS
Music: Prof. EDWARD HO
Operations Management and Quantitive Methods: Prof. RICHARD ENNALS
Postgraduate and In-Service Teacher Training: PETER STAMMERS
Social Science: Prof. JOE BAILEY
Social Work: PAUL DONNELLY
Surveying: SARAH SAYCE
Three-Dimensional Design: NIGEL ORDISH

UNIVERSITY OF LANCASTER

Lancaster, LA1 4YW

Telephone: (1524) 65201
Fax: (1524) 843087
E-mail: ugadmissions@lancaster.ac.uk
Internet: www.lancs.ac.uk

Founded 1964
Academic year: October to July

Chancellor: Sir CHRISTIAN BONINGTON
Pro-Chancellor: B. GRAY
Vice-Chancellor: Prof. P. WELLINGS
Deputy Vice-Chancellor: BOB MCKINLAY
Pro-Vice-Chancellors: Prof. C. L. COOPER, Prof. R. D. MCKINLAY, Prof. R. MACDONALD, A. WHITAKER
Secretary: F. AIKEN
Librarian: J. M. WHITESIDE

Library: see Libraries
Number of teachers: 800
Number of students: 10,380 full-time (7,916 undergraduates, 2,464 postgraduates)

DEANS

Faculty of Applied Sciences: Prof. MARY SMYTH
Faculty of Arts and Humanities: Prof. D. W. WHITTON
Faculty of Environmental and Natural Sciences: Prof. TREVOR MCMILLAN
Faculty of Social Sciences: Prof. BOB MCKINLAY
Graduate School: Prof. CHRIS PARK
Management School: Prof. SUE COX

PROFESSORS

ACKROYD, S. C., Organizational Behaviour
ALDERSON, J. C., Linguistics and English Language Education
ALLSOP, D., Neuroscience
ARAUJO, L., Industrial Marketing
ARCHARD, D., Philosophy
ASTON, E., Theatre Studies
BARDGETT, R. D., Ecology
BARTON, D., Language and Literacy
BELLANY, I., Politics
BEVEN, K. J., Environmental Science
BINLEY, A., Hydrogeophysics
BLACKLER, F. H. M., Behaviour in Organizations
BLAIR, G. S., Distributed Systems
BLINKHORN, R. M., History
BLOOMFIELD, B., Organizational Behaviour
BRADLEY, S., Economics
BRAY, R. W., Music
BREMNER, J. G., Developmental Psychology
BURGOYNE, J. G., Management Learning
BYGATE, M., Linguistics
CARTER, R. G., Electronic Engineering
CHADWICK, R., Philosophy
CHAPMAN, G. P., Geography
CHETWYND, A. G., Mathematics and Statistics
CLARK, D., Medical Sociology
CLARKE, I., Marketing
COLLINSON, D., Management Learning
COULSON, G., Distributed Systems
COX, S. J., Safety and Risk Management
CROUCHLEY, R., Applied Statistics
DAVIES, N.A. J., Computing
DAVIES, W. J., Environmental Physiology
DAVISON, W., Environmental Chemistry
DENVER, D. T., Politics
DIGGLE, P. J., Mathematics and Statistics
DILLON, G. M., Politics
DIX, A., Computing
DUFFIELD, M., Politics
EASTERBY-SMITH, M. P. V., Management Learning
EASTON, G., Marketing
EMERSON, E., Clinical Psychology
EVANS, E. J., Social History
FAIRCLOUGH, N. L., Linguistics
FALKO, V., Condensed Matter Theory
FIDDLER, A., German and Austrian Studies
FILDES, R. A., Management Science
FINDLAY, A., Renaissance Drama
FORDE, B., Plant Biotechnology
FOX, S., Social and Management Learning
FRANCIS, B. J., Social Statistics
FRANKLIN, S., Sociology
GELLERSEN, H.-W., Computing
GATRELL, A. C., Health
GRAHAM, H., Social Policy

HAMILTON, M. E., Adult Learning and Literacy
HANLEY, K. A., English Literature
HARMAN, P. M., History of Science
HATTON, C. R., Psychology, Health and Social Care
HEELAS, P. L. F., Religion and Modernity
HENDERSON, R., Biostatistics
HETHERINGTON, A. M., Plant Cell Physiology
HEWITT, C. N., Atmospheric Chemistry
HONARY, B., Communications Engineering
HONARY, F., Space Plasma and Radio Science
HOPKINS, J. B., Psychology
HUGHES, J. A., Sociological Analysis
HUTCHISON, D., Computing
INTRONA, L., Organisation, Technology and Ethics
IVANIC, R., Linguistics and Education
JESSOP, R. D., Sociology
JOHNES, G., Economics
JOHNSON, K., Linguistics and Language Education
JONES, K. C., Environmental Chemistry and Ecotoxicology
KATAMBA, F. X., Linguistics
KIRBY, M. W., Economic History
KRIER, A., Semiconductor Physics
KUHN, A. F., Film Studies
LAMBERT, C. J., Theoretical Condensed Matter Physics
LAMBRECHT, B. M., Accounting and Finance
LAW, J., Sociology
LEA, P. J., Biological Sciences
LEWIS, C. N., Family and Developmental Psychology
LYTH, D., Astro-Particle Physics
MCCLINTOCK, P. V. E., Physics
MACDONALD, R., Environmental Science
MCENERY, A. M., English Language and Linguistics
MCMILLAN, T. J., Cancer Biology
MCNEILL, M., Women's Studies and Cultural Studies
MAHER, B., Geography
MAY-CHAHAL, C., Applied Social Science
MORRIS, P. E., Psychology
MULLETT, M. A. A., Cultural and Religious History
NIEDUSZYNSKI, I. A., Connective Tissue Biochemistry
O'HANLAN, J. F., Finance
O'NEILL, J. F., Philosophy
ORMEROD, T., Cognitive Psychology
OTLEY, D. T., Accounting and Finance
PAYNE, J. P., German Studies
PEARCE, L., Literary Theory and Women's Writing
PEASNELL, K. V., Accounting and Finance
PENN, R. D., Economic Sociology and Statistics
PERCY, K. A., Adult Continuing Education
PICCIOTTO, S., Law
PICKETT, G. R., Low Temperature Physics
PIDD, M., Management Science
PINKERTON, H., Physical Volcanology
POOLEY, C. G., Geography
POPAY, J., Social and Public Health
POPE, P. F., Accounting and Finance
POWER, D. J., Mathematics
RATOFF, P. N., Experimental Particle Physics
READER, I. J., Religious Studies
REYNOLDS, P. M., Management Learning
RICHARDS, J. M., Cultural History
RICHARDSON, A. M. D., Miccrosystems Engineering
ROBERTS, G., Mathematics
RODWELL, J. S., Plant Ecology
ROGERS, C. G., Educational Research
ROSE, M., Entrepreneurship
ROTHSCHILD, R., Economics
ROWE, P., Law
SAUNDERS, M. S., Evaluation in Education and Work
SAYER, R. A., Sociology
SEGAL, R., Theories of Religion
SEWARD, D. W., Engineering Design

SHAPIRO, D. Z., Sociology
SHORT, M. H., Linguistics
SIEWIERSKA, A. M., Linguistics
SMITH, D. B., Criminology
SMITH, L., Educational Research
SMYTH, M. M., Experimental Psychology
SOMMERVILLE, I. F., Computing
SOOTHILL, K. L., Social Research
STACEY, J., Women's Studies and Cultural Studies
STRINGER, K. J., Medieval British History
SUCHMAN, L., Sociology
SUGARMAN, D., Law
TAWN, J. A., Statistics
TAYLOR, J., Economics
TAYLOR, S. J., Finance
THORPE, D. H., Applied Social Science
TIHANOV, G., Comparative Literature
TROWLER, P., Higher Education
TUCKER, R. W., Mathematical Physics
TURVEY, G. J., Engineering Mechanics
URRY, J. R., Sociology
WEBER, C. L., Politics
WHITELEY, N. S., Visual Arts
WHITTAKER, J. B., Biological Sciences
WHITTON, D. W., French Theatre
WHYTE, I. D., Historical Geography
WIGMORE, J. K., Condensed Matter Physics
WILSON, L., Environmental Science
WILSON, R. F., Renaissance Studies
WISE, S., Social Justice
WYNNE, B. E., Science Studies
XYDEAS, C. S., Communications Engineering
YADAV, P. K., Accounting and Finance

ATTACHED INSTITUTE

Institute for Advanced Studies: Dir BOB JESSOP.

UNIVERSITY OF LEEDS

Leeds, LS2 9JT
Telephone: (113) 243-1751
Fax: (113) 244-3923
E-mail: enquiry@leeds.ac.uk
Internet: www.leeds.ac.uk

Founded 1874 as Yorkshire College of Science, University Charter 1904
Academic year: September to June

Chancellor: The Right Hon. Lord BRAGG
Pro-Chancellor: D. ANSBRO
Vice-Chancellor: Prof. MICHAEL ARTHUR
Secretary: J. R. GAIR
Academic Registrar and Deputy Secretary: A. J. PARKINSON
Librarian and Keeper of the Brotherton Collection: MARGARET M. COUTTS
Library: see Libraries and Archives
Number of students: 32,241; 32,062 enrolled on short courses

DEANS

Faculty of Arts: Prof. MARGARET ATACK
Faculty of Biological Sciences: Prof. ANTHONY J. TURNER
Faculty of Earth and Environment: Prof. PETER J. MACKIE
Faculty of Education, Social Sciences and Law: Prof. JOHN LEACH (acting)
Faculty of Engineering: Prof. ROGER D. POLLARD
Faculty of Mathematics and Physical Sciences: Prof. MICHAEL WILSON
Faculty of Medicine and Health: Prof. EDWARD HILLHOUSE
Faculty of Performance, Visual Arts and Communications: Prof. DAVID COOPER
Leeds University Business School: Prof. ANDREW R. LOCK

PROFESSORS AND HEADS OF DEPARTMENTS

Faculty of Arts:

AGIUS, D. A., Arabic and Islamic Material Culture

ATACK, M. K., French
BLACK, R. D., Renaissance History
BROCK, R. W., Renaissance History
BUTLER, M. H., Renaissance Drama
CANTOR, G. N., History of Science
CHARTRES, J. A., Social and Economic History
CHILDS, J. C. R., Military History
DIXON, S. M., Modern History
ELLIOTT, J. K., New Testament Textual Criticism
FAIRER, D., 18th c. English Literature
FINLAY, F. J., German
FRENCH, S. R. D., Philosophy of Science
GARNER, P., Spanish
GIDLEY, CM., American Literature
GOOCH, J., International History
HAMMOND, P., 17th-century English Literature
HARTLEY, T., Translation Studies
HEATH, M. F., Greek Language and Literature
HILL, J., Visiting Professor
HOLMES, D., French
HUGGAN, G., Commonwealth and Post-Colonial Literatures
JOHNSON, S., Linguistics
JONES, V., 18th c. Gender and Culture
KILLICK, R., Quebec Studies and 19th-century French Studies
KING, V. T., South-East Asian Studies
KNIGHT, R. A., Language Centre
KNOTT, K., Religious Studies
LARRISSY, E., English Literature
LEVENE, D. S., Latin Language and Literature
KOCIENSKI, P., Chemistry
LINDLEY, D., Renaissance Literature
LOOSELY, D. L., Contemporary French Culture
LOUD, G. A., Medieval Italian History
McFADYEN, A. I., Theology and Religious Studies (H)
MALTBY, R., Latin Philology
MORRIS, R. H., Medieval Studies
NAGIB, L., Centenary Professor of World History
NELSON, M. T., Philosophy
NETTON, I. R., Arabic Studies
PLATTEN, D. P., French
POIDEVIN, R. Le, Metaphysics
RICHARDSON, B. F., Italian
SILVERMAN, M., Modern French Studies
SIMONS, P. M., Philosophy
SPIERS, E. M., Strategic Studies
SUTTON, J. F., Russian
TABERNER, S. J., German
TOLLIDAY, S. W., Economic History
WAWN, A., Anglo-Icelandic Studies
WILLIAMS, M. B., East Asian Studies (H)
WILSON, K. M., International Politics
WOOD, I. N., Early Medieval History

Faculty of Biological Sciences:

ALEXANDER, R. M., Biology
ALTRINGHAM, J. D., Biomechanics
ATKINSON, H. J., Nematology
BALDWIN, S. A., Biochemistry
BAUMBERG, S., Bacterial Genetics
BEECH, D. J., Cellular and Molecular Physiology
BENTON, T. G., Population Ecology
BOOTH, A. G., On-Line Learning
BROWN, S. B., Biochemistry
BUCKLEY, N. J., Neuroscience
CARDING, S., Molecular Immunology
CHOPRA, I., Microbiology
FINDLAY, J. B. C., Biochemistry
FORBES, J. M., Agricultural Sciences
GILMARTIN, P. M., Plant Molecular Genetics
HANDYSIDE, A., Developmental Biology
HENDERSON, P. J. F., Biochemistry and Molecular Biology
HOLDEN, A. V., Computational Biology
HOLLAND, K. T., Microbiology

HOMANS, S. W., Structural Biology
HOOPER, N. M., Biochemistry
HUGHES, I. E., Pharmacology Education
INGHAM, E., Medical Immunology
ISAAC, R. E., Comparative Biochemistry
KILLINGTON, R. A., Visiology Education
KRAUSE, J., Behavioural Ecology
McPHERSON, M. J., Biochemistry and Molecular Biology
MEYER, P., Plant Genetics
ORCHARD, C. H., Physiology
PHILLIPS, S. E. V., Biophysics
RADFORD, S. E., Structural Molecular Biology
RAYNER, J. M. V., Zoology
ROBERTSON, B., Neurobiology
ROWLANDS, D. J., Molecular Virology
SHORROCKS, B., Population Biology
SMITH, J. E., Parasitology
STOCKLEY, P. G., Biological Chemistry
TRINICK, J. A., Animal Cell Biology
TURNER, A. J., Biochemistry
WARD, S. A., Sport and Exercises
WILCOX, M. H., Medical Microbiology
WITHINGTON, D. J., Auditory Neuroscience
WOOD, E. J., Biochemistry
WRAY, D. A., Pharmacology
YATES, M. S., Biomedical Sciences (H)

Faculty of Earth and Environment:

ALEXANDER, R. M., Biology
BAILEY, A. J., Population Geography (H)
BELL, M., Traffic and Environmental Pollution
BEST, J. L., Process Sedimentology
BONSALL, P. W., Transport Planning
CARSTEN, O., Transport Safety
CLARKE, G. P., Business Geography
CLARKE, M. C., Geographic Modelling
FAIRHEAD, J. D., Applied Geophysics
FORBES, R. D., Business Geography
FRANCIS, J. E., Paleoclimatology
GUBBINS, D., Geophysics
HAISEMAN, G. A., Geophysics
KNEALE, P. E., Applied Hydrology
KNIPE, R. J., Structural Geology
KROM, M. D., Marine and Environmental Geochemistry
LLOYD, J. J., Centenary Professor of Earth Science Systems
McDONALD, A. T., Environmental Management
MACKIE, P. J., Transport Studies
MAY, A. D., Transport Engineering
MOBBS, S. D., Atmospheric Dynamics
NASH, C. A., Transport Economics
RAISWELL, R. W., Sedimentary Geochemistry
REES, P. H., Population Geography
SMITH, M. H., Atmospheric Physics
SMITH, N. J., Project and Transport Infrastructure Management (joint post with Faculty of Engineering)
STILLWELL, J. C. H., Migration and Regional Development
TZEDAKIS, P. C., Quarternary Earth System History
VALENTINE, G., Human Geography
WATLING, D., Centenary Professor of Transport Analysis
WILSON, B. M., Igneous Petrogenesis
YARDLEY, B. W. D., Metamorphic Geochemistry

Faculty of Education, Social Sciences and Law:

ACKERS, H. L., European Law
BAGGULEY, P., Sociology and Social Policy (H)
BARNES, C., Disability Studies
BATES, I., Education and Work
BAYNHAM, M. J., TESOL
BELL, D. S., French Government and Politics
BLUTH, C., International Studies
CAMERON, L. J., Applied Linguistics
CHASE, M. S., Continuing Education (H)

CRAWFORD, T. A., Criminology and Criminal Justice
DEACON, A. J., Social Policy
DONNELLY, J. F., Science Education
HALSON, D. R., Law
HODKINSON, P. M., Lifelong Learning
KEAY, A., Corporate and Commercial Law
KERR, A., Sociology
LEACH, J., Science Education
LODGE, J., European Studies
McCARGO, D., Politics and International Studies
McMULLEN, J., Labour Law
ORMEROD, D., Law
OSLER, A. H., Education
PEARSON, R., Development Studies
RADICE, H. K., International Political Economy
ROSENEIL, S., Sociology and Gender Studies
SCOTT, P., Science Education
SHORROCKS-TAYLOR, D., Assessment and Evaluation in Education
SUBEDI, S. P., International Law
SUGDEN, D. A., Special Needs in Education
THEAKSTON, K., British Government
VINCENT-JONES, P., Law
WALKER, C. P., Criminal Justice
WALL, D. S., Legal History
WILLIAMS, F., Social Policy
ZUKAS, M., Adult Education

Faculty of Engineering:

ANDREWS, G. E., Combustion Engineering
BARTON, D. C., Solid Mechanics
BELL, A. J., Electronic Materials
BERZINS, M., Scientific Computation
BIGGS, S. R., Particle Science and Technology
BONSALL, P. W., Transport Planning
BOYLE, R. D., Computing
BRADLEY, D., Mechanical Engineering
BRODLIE, K. W., Visualization
CHILDS, T. H. C., Manufacturing Engineering
COHN, A. G., Automated Reasoning
DAVIES, A. G., Electronic and Photonic Engineering
DEW, P. M., Computer Science
DOWSON, D., Mechanical Engineering
DYER, M. E., Theoretical Computer Science
EDMONDS, D. V., Metallurgy
FAIRWEATHER, RM., Thermofluids and Combustion
FISHER, J., Mechanical Engineering
GASKELL, P. H., Fluid Mechanics
GHADIRI, M., Chemical Engineering
HARRISON, P. H., Quantum Electronics
HOGG, D. C., Artificial Intelligence
HOWES, M. J., Electronic Engineering
HOYLE, B. S., Vision and Image Systems
HUNTER, I. C., Microwave Signal Processing
JHA, A., Applied Materials Science
JIMACK, P., Scientific Computing
JIN, Z. M., Computational Biomechanics/Bioengineering
LINFIELD, E., Terahertz Electronics
McINTOSH, A. C., Thermodynamics and Combustion Theory
MARA, D. D., Civil Engineering
MARKARIAN, G., Communication Systems
MILES, R. E., Semiconductor Electronics
NEVILLE, A., Engineering Tribology
PAGE, C. L., Civil Engineering Materials
DE PENNINGTON, A., Computer-Aided Engineering
POLLARD, R. D., High-Frequency Measurements
POURKASHANIAN, M., High Temperature Combustion Processes
PRIEST, M., Engineering Tribology
RAND, B., Ceramics
RHODES, J. D., Electronic and Electrical Engineering
ROBERTS, K. J., Chemical Engineering

ROBERTSON, I. D., Centenary Professor of Microwave and Millimetre Wave Circuits
SHEPPARD, C. G. W., Applied Thermodynamics and Combustion Science
SMITH, N. J., Project and Transport Infrastructure Management (joint position with Transport Studies)
VIRK, G. S., Robotics and Control
WILLIAMS, P. T., Environmental Engineering
WILLIAMS, R. A., Mineral and Process Engineering
XU, J., Computing

Faculty of Mathematics and Physical Sciences:

BATCHELDER, D. N., Physics
BEDDARD, G., Chemical Physics
BLOOR, M. I. G., Applied Mathematics
BODEN, N., Physical Chemistry
BRINDLEY, J., Applied Mathematics
COOPER, S. B., Pure Mathematics
CRAWLEY-BOEVEY, W. W., Pure Mathematics
CYWINSKI, R., Experimental Physics
DALES, H. G., Pure Mathematics
DICKINSON, E., Food Colloids
DYSON, J. E., Astronomy
EVANS, S. D., Molecular and Nanoscale Physics
FALLE, S. A. E. G., Astrophysical Fluid Dynamics
FORDY, A. P., Nonlinear Mathematics
GREIG, D., Physics
GRIFFITHS, J. F., Functional Dye Chemistry
GRIGG, R. E., Organic Chemistry
GUTHRIE, J. T., Polymer and Surface Coatings, Science and Technology
HAMLEY, I. W., Polymer Materials
HARTQUIST, T. W., Astrophysics
HEARD, D. E., Atmospheric Chemistry
HICKEY, B., Physics
HILLAS, A. M., Physics
HUGHES, D. W., Applied Mathematics
INGHAM, D. B., Applied Mathematics
JOHNSON, A. P., Computational Chemistry
KENNEDY, J. D., Inorganic Chemistry
KENT, J. T., Statistics
KOCIEŃSKI, P. J., Organic Chemistry
LANCE, E. C., Pure Mathematics
LAWRIE, I. D., Theoretical Physics
LEWIS, D. M., Colour Chemistry
LUO, M. R., Colour and Imaging Science
McLEISH, T. C. B., Polymer Physics
MACPHERSON, H. D., Pure Mathematics
MARDIA, K. V., Applied Statistics
MERKIN, J. H., Applied Mathematics
MIKHAILOV, A. V., Mathematical Physics
MORGAN, A. J., Theoretical Physics
MORGAN, M. R., Food Biochemistry
NIJHOFF, F. W., Mathematical Physics
PARTINGTON, J. R., Pure Mathematics
PILLING, M. J., Physical Chemistry
POVEY, M. J. W., Food Physics
RATHJEN, M., Pure Mathematics
READ, C. J., Pure Mathematics
ROBINSON, D. S., Food Science
ROBSON, J. C., Pure Mathematics
SAVAGE, M. D., Thin Liquid Films and Coatings
SCOTT, S. K., Mathematical Chemistry
SLEEMAN, B. D., Applied Mathematics
TAYLOR, C. C., Statistics
TRUSS, J. K., Pure Mathematics
VEDRAL, V., Centenary Professor of Quantum Information Science
VERETENNIKOV, A. Y., Statistics
WAINER, S. S., Pure Mathematics
WARD, I. M., Physics
WATSON, A. A., Physics
WEDZICHA, B. L., Food Science
WHITAKER, B. J., Chemical Physics
WILSON, M. J., Applied Mathematics
WOOD, J. C., Pure Mathematics

Faculty of Medicine and Health:

ADAMS, C., Adult Psychiatry and Mental Health Services Research
ALIMO-METCALFE, B. M., Leadership Studies
BALL, S. G., Cardiology
BARKHAM, M., Clinical and Counselling Psychology
BIRD, H. A., Pharmacological Rheumatology
BISHOP, T., Genetic Epidemiology
BLUNDELL, J. E., Psychobiology
BONIFER, C., Experimental Haematology
BONTHRON, D. T., Molecular Medicine
BOYLSTON, A. W., Pathology
BRUNTON, P. A., Restorative Dentistry
CADE, J., Nutritional Epidemiology and Public Health
CHEATER, F., Public Health Nursing
CLEREHUGH, M. A., Periodontology
CLOSS, J., Nursing Research
COTTRELL, D. J., Child and Adolescent Psychiatry
CUCKLE, H. S., Reproductive Epidemiology
DICKSON, R. A., Orthopaedic Surgery
DRIFE, J. O., Obstetrics and Gynaecology
DUGGAL, M. S., Child Dental Health
EMERY, P., Rheumatology
FORMAN, D., Cancer Epidemiology
GIANNOUDIS, P. P., Orthopaedic Surgery
GRANT, P. J., Molecular Vascular Medicine
GREEN, A., International Health Planning
GUILLOU, P. J., Surgery
HALE, C., Clinical Nursing
HALL, A. S., Clinical Cardiology
HANBY, A. M., Breast Pathology
HAWARD, R., Cancer Studies
HAY, A., Environmental Toxicology
HEWISON, J., Healthcare Psychology
HEYWOOD, P. L., Primary Care
HILLHOUSE, E., Dean of the School of Medicine and Health
HOPKINS, P. M., Anaesthesia
HOUSE, A. O., Liaison Psychiatry
HOWDLE, P. D., Clinical Education
HULL, M. A., molecular Gastroenterology
HUME, W. J., Oral Pathology
INGLEHEARN, C., Molecular Ophthalmology
KAPLAN, R. S., Clinical Cancer Studies
KEEN, J., Health Politics and Information Management
KELLETT, M., Restorative Dentistry (H)
KIRKHAM, J., Oral Biology
KNOWLES, M., Experimental Cancer Research
LEVENE, M. I., Paediatrics and Child Health
LONG, A., Health Systems Research
McDERMOTT, M., Experimental Rheumatology
McGONAGLE, D., Investigative Rheumatology
McMAHON, M. J., Surgery
McWILLIAM, P. N., Cardiovascular Physiology
MACLENNAN, K., Tumour Pathology
MARKHAM, A. F., Medicine
MARSH, P. D., Oral Microbiology
MORLEY, S. J., Clinical Psychology
MURDOCH-EATON, D., Medical Education
PEERS, C. S., Cellular Physiology
QUIRKE, P., Pathology
RAYNOR, D. K., Pharmacy Practice, Medicine and their Users
ROBERTS, T. E., Medical Education
ROBINSON, C., Oral Biology
RODGERS, R. J., Behavioural Pharmacology
SANDLE, G. I., Clinical Science
SELBY, P. J., Cancer Medicine
SEYMOUR, M., Gastro-intestinal Medicine
TENNANT, A., Rehabilitation Studies
TWELVES, C. J., Clinical Pharmacology and Oncology
WALKER, J. J., Obstetrics and Gynaecology
WILD, C., Molecular Epidemiology

WILLIAMS, S. A., Oral Health Services Research
WISTOW, G., Health and Social Care
WOOD, D. J, Dental Materials
WOOD, E. J., Biochemistry

Faculty of Performance, Visual Arts and Communications:

BARBER, G. D., Performance Studies (Music)
BOON, R., Performance Studies
BROWN, C., Applied Musicology
BROWN, R. C. M., International Communications
BURKINSHAW, S. M., Textile Chemistry
CASSIDY, T., Design
COOPER, D. G., Music
DANIELS, S. M., Performance and Cultural Industries
GREEN, V., Fine Art, Film and Media
HANN, M. A., Design Theory
HAY, K. G., Contemporary Art Practice
HILL, D., Fine Art
LAWRENCE, C. A., Textile Engineering
MCQUILLAN, M., Fine Art, History of Art and Cultural Studies
MORRISON, D. E., Communications Research
ORTON, L. F., Art History and Theory
PALMER, R., Fine Art
POLLOCK, G. F. S., Social and Critical Histories of Art
RASTALL, G. R., Historical Musicology
TAYLOR, P. M., International Communications
WALLIS, M., Performance and Culture
WESTLAND, S., Colour Science and Technology

Leeds University Business School:

BUCKLEY, P. J., International Business
CLEGG, L. J., European Integration and International Business Management
COLLINS, M., Financial History
GERRARD, W. J., Sport Management and Finance
HAYES, J., Management Studies
HILLIER, D., Financial Markets
HODGKINSON, G. P., Organizational Behaviour and Strategic Management
KATSIKEAS, C. S., Marketing and International Management
KEASEY, K., Financial Services
LOCK, A. R., Marketing and Business Administration
MACKIE, P. J., Transport Studies
MCNULTY, T. H., Management and Governance
MAULE, A. J., Human Decisions
MICHELL, P. C. N., Marketing and Communications
MOIZER, P., Accounting
NASH, C. A., Transport Economics
NOLAN, P. J., Industrial Relations
OAKLAND, J. S., Business Excellence and Quality Management
PEARMAN, A. D., Management Decision Analysis
PÉROTIN, V., Economics
SAWYER, M. C., Economics
SCHENK-HOPPÉ, K. R., Renaissance History
SHIN, Y., Applied Econometrics
STUART, M., Human Resources Management and Employment Relations
THORPE, R., Management Development
WILSON, N., Credit Management

ACCREDITED COLLEGES

Trinity and All Saints College: Brownberrie Lane, Horsforth, Leeds, LS18 5HD; tel. (113) 283-7100; f. 1966; 2,200 students; Principal Dr M. J. COUGHLAN.

York St John College: Lord Mayor's Walk, York, YO31 7EX; tel. (1904) 624624; f. 1841; 7,837 students; Principal Prof. D. WILLCOCKS.

LEEDS METROPOLITAN UNIVERSITY

City Campus, Leeds, LS1 3HE
Telephone: (113) 283-2600
E-mail: vc@leedsmet.ac.uk
Internet: www.leedsmet.ac.uk
Founded 1970 as Leeds Polytechnic; present name and status 1992

Vice-Chancellor: Prof. SIMON LEE
Deputy Vice-Chancellors: F. GRIFFITHS, Dr D. G. HITCHINS, Prof. G. TAYLOR
Secretary and Registrar: STEVE DENTON
Director of Learning and Information Services: JOHN HEAP
Library of 405,000 vols, 5,500 periodicals
Number of teachers: 1,425
Number of students: 41,100 (15,581 full-time, 1,309 sandwich, 24,210 part-time)

DEANS

Faculty of Cultural and Education Studies: MARY HEYCOCK
Faculty of Health and the Environment: Dr MICHAEL HOLMES
Faculty of Information and Engineering Systems: ALAN MILLS
Leeds Business School: Prof. STEPHEN PARKINSON
Harrogate College: JOHN DISHMAN

UNIVERSITY OF LEICESTER

University Rd, Leicester, LE1 7RH
Telephone: (116) 252-2522
Fax: (116) 252-2200
Internet: www.le.ac.uk
Founded 1918 as University College; Charter 1950; University Charter 1957
Academic year: September to June

Chancellor: Sir PETER WILLIAMS
Vice-Chancellor: Prof. R. G. BURGESS
Pro Vice-Chancellor: Prof. MARK THOMPSON
Registrar: K. J. JULIAN
Librarian: C. FYFE

Library: see Libraries and Archives
Number of teachers: 652 full-time
Number of students: 9,060 full-time

DEANS

Faculty of Arts: Prof. A. W. YARRINGTON
Faculty of Education and Continuing Studies: Prof. K. R. FOGELMAN
Faculty of Law: Prof. R. C. A. WHITE
Faculty of Medicine and Biological Sciences: Prof. W. J. BRAMMAR
Faculty of Science: Prof. J. C. FOTHERGILL
Faculty of the Social Sciences: Prof. M. JACKSON

PROFESSORS

Faculty of Arts (tel. (116) 252-2679; fax (116) 252-5213; e-mail arts@le.ac.uk; internet www.le.ac.uk/arts):

BARKER, G. W., Archaeology
BONNEY, R. J., Modern History
CAMPBELL, G. R., Renaissance Literature
CULL, N. J., American Studies
EKSRDJIAN, D., History of Art and Film
FOXHALL, L., Ancient History
HOOPER-GREENHILL, E. R., Museum Studies
HOUSLEY, N. J., History
LITTLEJOHNS, R., Modern Languages
MATTINGLY, D. J., Roman Archaeology
NEWEY, V., English
PALMER, M., Industrial Archaeology
PEARCE, S. M., Museum Studies
RUGGLES, C. L. N., Archaeoastronomy
SHATTOCK, E. J., Victorian Literature
SHIPLEY, D. G. J., Ancient History
STANNARD, M. J., Modern English Literature
TREHAME, E. M., English

WALKER, G. M., Early Modern Literature and Culture
WOOD, S., Modern Languages
YARRINGTON, A., Art History

Faculty of Education and Continuing Studies (tel. (116) 252-3688; fax (116) 252-3653; e-mail soed@le.ac.uk; internet www.le.ac.uk/education):

BELL, L. A., Educational Management
COOPER, P. W., Education
DIMMOCK, C. A. J., Educational Management
FOGELMAN, K. R., Education

Faculty of Law (tel. (116) 252-2363; fax (116) 252-5023; e-mail law@le.ac.uk; internet www.le.ac.uk/law):

BRADNEY, A. G. D., Law
CLARKSON, C. M. V., Law
GRAHAM, C., Law
MCHALE, J. V., Law
SHAW, M. N., International Law
SZYSZCZAK, E. M., Competition and Labour Law
THOMPSON, M. P., Law
WHITE, R. C. A., Law

Faculty of Medicine and Biological Sciences (tel. (116) 252-2969; fax (116) 252-3013; e-mail med-admis@le.ac.uk; internet www.le.ac.uk/medicine):

ABRAMS, K. R., Epidemiology and Public Health
ANDREW, P. W., Microbial Pathogenesis
BAGSHAW, C. R., Biochemistry
BAKER, R. H., Quality in Health Care
BARER, M. R., Clinical Microbiology
BARNETT, D. B., Clinical Pharmacology
BELL, P. R. F., Surgery
BELL, S. C., Reproductive Sciences
BRAMMAR, W. J., Biochemistry
BRUGHA, T. S., Psychiatry
BURTON, P. R., Genetic Epidemiology
CAMP, R. D. R., Dermatology
CHERRYMAN, G. R., Radiology
COLLEY, A. M., Psychology
COLMAN, A. M., Psychology
CRITCHLEY, D. R., Biochemistry
CUNDLIFFE, E., Biochemistry
DAVIES, G. M., Psychology
DAVIES, M., Diabetes Medicine
DUGGAN, C. F., Forensic Mental Health
DYER, M. J. S., Pathology
EPERON, I. C., Biochemistry
EVANS, D. H., Medical Physics
FIELD, D. J., Neonatal Medicine
FORSYTHE, I. D., Neuroscience
FRASER, R. C., General Practice
FURNESS, P. N., Renal Pathology
GALINANES, M., Cardiac Surgery
GOTTLOB, I., Ophthalmology
GRANT, W. D., Environmental Microbiology
HALLIGAN, A. W. F., Foetal-Maternal Medicine
HARPER, W. M., Orthopaedic Surgery
HESLOP-HARRISON, J. S., Plant Cell Biology, Molecular Cytogenetics
HOLLIN, C. R., Criminological Psychology
JAGGER, C., Epidemiology
Sir JEFFREYS, A., Genetics
JONES, D. R., Medical Statistics
JOSEPH, M. H., Behavioural Neuroscience
KETLEY, J. M., Genetics
KYRIACOU, C. P., Behavioural Genetics
LAUDER, I., Pathology
LINDESAY, J. E. B., Psychiatry for the Elderly
LONDON, N. J. M., Surgery
LOUIS, E. J., Genetics
LUNEC, J., Chemical Pathology
MELLON, J. K., Urology
NAHORSKI, S. R., Pharmacology and Therapeutics
NG, L. L., Medicine and Therapeutics
NICHOLSON, K. G., Infectious Diseases
NICHOLSON, M. L., Transplant Surgery

O'CALLAGHAN, C. L. P., Paediatrics
PANERAI, R. B., Physiological Measurement
PARKER, G., Community Care
PASI, K. J., Haematology
PETERSEN, S. A., Medical Education
POTTER, J. F., Medicine for the Elderly
REVELEY, M. A., Psychiatry
ROBERTS, G. C. K., Biochemistry
ROWBOTHAM, D. J., Anaesthesia and Pain Management
RUTTY, G. N., Forensic Pathology
SAMANI, N. J., Cardiovascular Medicine
SCHWAEBLE, W. J., Microbiology and Immunology
SCRUTTON, N. S., Biochemistry
SILVERMAN, M., Child Health
SMITH, G., Anaesthesia
SMITH, R. H., Biology
STACE, C. A., Plant Taxonomy
STAMMERS, R. B., Occupational Psychology
STANDEN, N. B., Physiology
STEWARD, W. P., Oncology
TAYLOR, D. J., Obstetrics and Gynaecology
THOMPSON, J. R., Ophthalmology
THURSTON, H., Medicine
TREMBATH, R. C. P., Medical Genetics
TWELL, D., Plant Biology
VOSTANIS, P., Child and Adolescent Psychiatry
WALKER, R. A., Pathology
WARDLAW, A. J., Respiratory Medicine
WHITELAM, G. C., Plant Molecular Physics
WILLIAMS, B., Medicine
WILLIAMS, P. H., Microbiology
WOODS, K. L., Therapeutics
ZIEGLER-HEITBROCK, H.-W. L., Immunology

Faculty of Science (tel. (116) 252-5012; fax (116) 252-2770; e-mail science@le.ac.uk; internet www.le.ac.uk/science):

ALDRIDGE, R. J., Palaeontology
BENDELL, A., Quality and Reliability Management
BINNS, C., Physics and Astronomy
BOWLER, I. R., Human Geography
BRADSHAW, M. J., Human Geography
COCKS, A. C. F., Mechanical Engineering
COWLEY, S. W. H., Solar-Planetary Physics
CULLIS, P. M., Organic Chemistry
DISSADO, L. A., Engineering
FISHER, P. F., Geographical Information
FOTHERGILL, J. C., Engineering
FRASER, G. W., Detector Physics
GOSTELOW, J. P., Engineering
HARVEY, P. K. H., Geomathematics
HILLMAN, A. R., Physical Chemistry
HOLLOWAY, J. H., Inorganic Chemistry
HOPE, E. G., Inorganic Chemistry
KING, A. R., Astrophysics
KOENIG, S. C., Pure Mathematics
LEIMKUHLER, B. J., Applied Mathematics
LESTER, M., Physics and Astronomy
LEWIS, G. T., Human Geography
LIGHT, W. A., Mathematics
LOVELL, M. A., Petrophysics
MAGUIRE, P. K. H., Geophysics
MILLINGTON, A. C., Physical Geography
NORRIS, C., Surface Physics
PAN, J., Mechanics and Materials
PARRISH, R. R., Isotope Geology
PARSONS, A. J., Physical Geography
PERCY, J. M., Chemistry
POLLOCK, C., Electrical Engineering
PONTER, A. R. S., Engineering
POSTLETHWAITE, I., Engineering
RAMAN, R., Computer Science
ROBINSON, T. R., Space Plasma Physics
SAUNDERS, A. D., Geochemistry
SIVETER, D. J., Palaeontology
SPURGEON, S. K., Engineering
STEWART, A., Computer Science
THOMAS, R. M., Mathematics and Computer Science
WARD, M. J., X-Ray Astronomy
WARWICK, R. S., X-Ray Astronomy

Faculty of the Social Sciences (tel. (116) 252-2842; fax (116) 252-5073; e-mail socsci@le.ac.uk; internet www.le.ac.uk/socsci):

BARBALET, J. M., Sociology
BENDELL, A., Quality and Reliability Management
BENYON, J. T., Political Studies
BRESNEN, M., Organisational Behaviour
BURRELL, G., Organization Theory
CHAREMZA, W., Economics
COTTRELL, P. L., Economic and Social History
DEMETRIADES, P. O., Financial Economics
DYER, C. C., Regional and Local History
FEARON, P. S., Modern Economic and Social History
FIELDING, D. J., Economics
FRASER, C. D., Economics
GILL, M., Criminology
HANLON, G., Organisations and Society
HOFFMAN, J. A., Political Theory
HYDE-PRICE, A. G. V., Politics and International Relations
JACKSON, P. M., Economics; Public Sector Economics
KOOP, G., Economics
LAYDER, D. R., Social Theory
LEE, K. C., Economics
MUELLER, F., Management
OSWICK, C., Organisation Theory and Development
PARKER, M., Organisation Management
PUDNEY, S. E., Economics
RODGER, R. G., Urban History
SCHOTT, D. M. S., History of Urban Planning
SNELL, K. D. M., English Local History
SREBERNY, A., Mass Communications
THOMPSON, R. S., Economics
UNWIN, L. W., Vocational Education
WILLIAMS, C., Management

ATTACHED INSTITUTE

Leicester Institute for Lifelong Learning: Dir Prof. J. T. BENYON.

UNIVERSITY OF LINCOLN

Brayford Pool, Lincoln, LN6 7TS

Telephone: (1522) 882000
Fax: (1522) 882088
E-mail: enquiries@lincoln.ac.uk
Internet: www.lincoln.ac.uk

Founded 1861 as School of Art and Design; as Humberside College of Higher Education 1978; Humberside Polytechnic 1990; University of Humberside 1992; University of Lincolnshire and Humberside 1996; incorporated Lincoln School of Art and Lincolnshire School of Agriculture 2001; present name and status 2001

Vice-Chancellor: Prof. DAVID CHIDDICK
Pro-Vice-Chancellors: Prof. FRANCES MANNSÅKER, Prof. MIKE SAKS, Dr JIM WHITTINGHAM, Prof. BRIAN WINSTON
Registrar: EDMUND FITZPATRICK
Director of Learning Support: MICHELLE ANDERSON

Library of 240,000 vols, 1,000 periodicals
Number of teachers: 513
Number of students: 9,963

Publication: *Institute of Communication Ethics* (quarterly)

DEANS

Faculty of Applied Computing Sciences: Prof. GRAEME WILKINSON
Faculty of Art, Architecture and Design: Prof. VINCENT SHACKLOCK
Faculty of Business and Law: Dr DON WHITE
Faculty of Health, Life and Social Sciences: Prof. BRIAN McGAW
Faculty of Media and Humanities: Prof. ALLEN McLAURIN

ATTACHED RESEARCH INSTITUTES

Centre for Health Improvement and Leadership in Lincoln (CHILL): Dir Prof. DAVID CHIDDICK.

International Institute for Education Leadership: Dir FERGUS O'SULLIVAN.

Lincolnshire School of Agriculture, Holbeach: Dir CLIVE BOUND.

School of Professional and Continuing Information: Dir CLIVE BOUND.

School of Theology and Ministry Studies: Dir Canon Dr MIKE WEST.

UNIVERSITY OF LIVERPOOL

Liverpool, L69 3BX

Telephone: (151) 794-2000
Fax: (151) 708-6502
Internet: www.liv.ac.uk

Founded 1881 as University College, Royal Charter 1903

Chancellor: Rt Hon. Lord OWEN
Pro-Chancellor: LAWRENCE HOLDEN
Vice-Chancellor: Prof. J. DRUMMOND BONE
Pro-Vice-Chancellors: Prof. J. W. BRUCE, Prof. J. M. CRAMPTON, G. DOCKRAY, Prof. K. D. EVEREST
Registrar: M. D. CARR
Librarian: F. M. THOMSON

Library: see Libraries and Archives
Number of teachers: 1,075
Number of students: 13,960

Publications: *Bulletin of Hispanic Studies* (quarterly), *Third World Planning Review* (quarterly), *Town Planning Review* (quarterly)

DEANS

Faculty of Arts: Prof. JOHN BELCHEM
Faculty of Engineering: Prof. IFHAN OWEN
Faculty of Medicine: Prof. JOHN CALDWELL
Faculty of Science: Prof. JONATHAN SAUNDERS
Faculty of Social and Environmental Studies: Prof. PETER BATEY
Faculty of Veterinary Science: Prof. ALEXANDER TREES
Dental Studies: Prof. GRAHAM EMBERY

PROFESSORS

Faculty of Arts:

BATE, A. J., English Literature
BELCHEM, J. C., History
CLARK, S. R. L., Philosophy
DAVIES, J. K., Ancient History and Classical Archaeology
ELLIOTT, M., Irish Studies
EVEREST, K. D., Modern English
FISHER, J. R., Latin-American History
FORSDICK, C., French
GASKIN, R. M., Philosophy
GOWLETT, J. A. J., Archaeology, Classics and Oriental Studies
HIGGINS, J., Latin American Literature
HOEY, M. P., English Language
LEE, W. R., Economic and Social History
MEE, C., Archaeology, Classics and Oriental Studies
MILLARD, A. R., Hebrew and Ancient Semitic Languages
MILLS, A. D., English Language and Literature
SAUL, N. D. B., German
SEED, D., English
SEVERIN, D. S., Spanish
SHAW, J., Archaeology, Classics and Oriental Studies
SLATER, E. A., Archaeology
STAFFORD, P. A., History
TALBOT, M. O., Music
WRIGHT, R. H. P., Hispanic Studies

Faculty of Engineering:

BACON, D. J., Materials Science and Engineering
BUNGEY, J. H., Civil Engineering
BURROWS, R., Environmental Hydraulics
CANTWELL, W. J., Engineering
CHALKER, P. R., Engineering
ECCLESTON, W., Electronic Engineering
ESCUDIER, M. P., Mechanical Engineering
FANG, M. T. C., Applied Electromagnetism
GOODHEW, P. J., Materials Engineering
HALL, S., Electrical Engineering and Electronics
HON, K. K. B., Manufacturing Systems
JONES, G. R., Electrical Engineering and Electronics
JONES, N., Mechanical Engineering
LUCAS, J., Electrical Engineering and Electronics
MOTTERSHEAD, J. E., Applied Mechanics
NANDI, A. K., Electrical Engineering and Electronics
OWEN, I., Mechanical Engineering
PADFIELD, G. D., Engineering
POND, R. C., Materials Science and Engineering
TATLOCK, G. J., Engineering
WATKINS, K. G., Engineering
WU, Q. H., Electrical Engineering

Faculty of Medicine:

ASHFORD, R. W., Parasite and Vector Biology
BACK, D. J., Pharmacology and Therapeutics
BURGOYNE, R. D., Physiology
CALVERLEY, P. M. A., Rehabilitation Medicine
CAPEWELL, S. J., Public Health
CARTY, H. M. L., Paediatric Radiology
CAWLEY, J. C., Haematology
CHADWICK, D. W., Neurology
COOKE, R. W. I., Paediatric Medicine
DIMALINE, R., Physiology
DOCKRAY, G. J., Physiology
DOWRICK, C. F., Primary Care
EMBERY, G., Clinical Dental Sciences
FIELD, J. K., Molecular Oncology
FOSTER, C. S., Pathology
FRASER, W. D., Clinical Chemistry
FROSTICK, S. P., Orthopaedics
GALLAGHER, J. A., Human Anatomy and Cell Biology
GARNER, P. A., Tropical Medicine
GOSDEN, C. M., Medical Genetics
GOWERS, S. G., Adolescent Psychiatry
GRIERSON, I., Experimental Ophthalmology
GRIFFITHS, R. D., Medicine
HART, C. A., Medical Microbiology
HART, G., Medicine
HILL, J., Child and Development Psychiatry
HOMMEL, M., Tropical Medicine
HUNTER, J. M., Anaesthesia
JACKSON, M. J., Cellular Pathophysiology
JOHNSON, P. M., Immunology
KROEGER, A., International Community Health
LEUWER, M., Anaesthesia
LLOYD, D. A., Paediatric Surgery
MOLYNEUX, M. E., Tropical Medicine
MORRISS, R. K., Psychiatry
NEILSON, J. P., Obstetrics and Gynaecology
NEOPTOLEMOS, J. P., Surgery
NURMIKKO, T. J., Neurology
PARK, B. K., Pharmacology and Therapeutics
PETERSEN, O. H., Physiology
PINE, C. M., Clinical Dental Sciences
PIRMOHAMED, M., Pharmacology and Therapeutics
QUINN, J. P., Human Anatomy and Cell Biology
RHODES, J. M., Medicine
ROBERTS, J. N., Magnetic Resonance
SALMON, P., Clinical Psychology

SCOTT, J., Oral Diseases
SHENKIN, A., Clinical Chemistry
SMYTH, R. L., Child Health
STEWART, J. P., Medical Microbiology
TEPIKIN, A. V., Physiology
THEAKSTON, R. D. G., Tropical Medicine
TOWNSON, H., Medical Entomology
TRAYHURN, P., Medicine
TREES, A. J., Tropical Medicine
VARRO, A., Physiology
WALLEY, T. J., Clinical Pharmacology
WARD, S., Tropical Medicine
WARENIUS, H. M., Research Oncology
WARNKE, P. C., Neurology
WATSON, A. J. M., Medicine
WATTS, A., Restorative Dentistry
WEINDLING, A. M., Child Health
WHITEHEAD, M. M., Public Health
WILKINSON, D. G., Liaison Psychiatry
WILLIAMS, D. F., Clinical Engineering
WILLIAMS, G., Medicine
WILSON, K. C. M., Psychiatry of Old Age
WINSTANLEY, P. A., Pharmacology and Therapeutics
WRAY, S. C., Physiology

Faculty of Science:

ALLPORT, P., Physics
APPLEBY, P. G., Mathematical Sciences
BEGON, M. E., Biological Sciences
BHANSALI, R. J., Mathematical Sciences
BOWCOCK, T. J. V., Physics
BRUCE, J. W., Pure Mathematics
CANTER, D. V., Psychology
COOPER, S. J., Psychology
COSSINS, A. R., Biological Sciences
CRAMPTON, J. M., Molecular Biology
DAINTON, J. B., Physics
DEROUANE, E. G. J., Chemistry, Innovative Catalysis
DONALD, I., Psychology
DUNBAR, R. I. M., Psychology
EDWARDS, C., Biological Sciences
EDWARDS, S. W., Biological Sciences
ELLIOTT, T. J., Geology
FISHER, M. D., Computer Science
FLINT, S. S., Earth Sciences
GIBLIN, P., Mathematical Sciences
GORYUNOV, W., Mathematical Sciences
HEATON, B. T., Inorganic Chemistry
HETHERINGTON, M. M., Psychology
HOLLOWAY, S., Chemical Physics
IRVING, A. C., Mathematical Sciences
JONES, A. C., Chemistry
KEMP, S. J., Biological Sciences
KUSZNIR, N. J., Geophysics
MCCARTHY, A. J., Biological Sciences
MCLENNAN, A. G., Biological Sciences
MARRS, R. H., Applied Plant Biology
MAYES, A. R., Psychology
MICHAEL, C., Theoretical Physics
MORTON, H. R., Mathematical Sciences
MOSS, B., Botany
MOVCHAN, A., Mathematical Sciences
MUELLER, M. M., Psychology
NIKULIN, W., Mathematical Sciences
NORTON, T. A., Marine Biology
PARKER, G. A., Zoology
RAVAL, R., Chemistry
REES, H. H., Biological Sciences
REES, S. M., Mathematical Sciences
RITCHIE, D. A., Genetics
ROBERTS, S. M., Organic Chemistry
ROSSEINSKY, M. J., Chemistry
RUDLAND, P. S., Biochemistry
SAUNDERS, J. R., Genetics and Microbiology
SCHIFFRIN, D. J., Physical Chemistry
SHAW, J., Earth Sciences
STIRLING, W. G., Experimental Physics
TOMSETT, A. B., Biological Sciences
VAN DEN BERG, C. M. G., Earth Sciences
VAN DER HOEK, W., Computer Science
VEDRINE, J., Chemistry
WEIGHTMAN, P., Physics
WOOLDRIDGE, M. J., Computer Science

Faculty of Social and Environmental Studies:

ARORA, A., Law
BARON, J. S., Management
BATEY, P. W. J., Town and Regional Planning
CORNER, J., Politics and Communication Studies
DEARING, J. A., Geography
DELANTY, G., Sociology
DRUMMOND, H., Decision Sciences
DUNSTER, D., Architecture
ELLIOTT, D., Management
GIBBS, B. M., Acoustics
GILLESPIE, R., Politics
GOULD, W. T. S., Geography
HADRI, K., Economics and Accounting
HARVEY, A. M., Geography
HILL, J. J., Management
HOJMAN, D. E., Economics and Accounting
JONES, C., Social Policy and Social Work
JONES, M. A., Law
KAVANAGH, D. A., Politics and Communication Studies
KEHOE, D. F., Management
LYON, C. M., Common Law
MCCABE, B. P. M., Economics
MCGOLDRICK, D., Law
MACLEOD, J. K., Law
MUNCK, R. P., Sociology
NEUWAHL, N. A. E. M., European Law
OLDHAM, D. J., Building Engineering
PEPPER, S. M., Architecture and Building Engineering
ROBERTS, K., Sociology
RUSSELL, T., Centre for Research into Primary Science and Technology
SADLER, D., Geography
SAPSFORD, D. R., Economics and Accounting
SMITH, D., Management
SMITHERS, A. G., Education
TAYLOR, P. J., Economics and Accounting
WARBURTON, J., Law
WONG, Y. L. C., Civic Design
WOODS, R. I., Geography

Faculty of Veterinary Science:

BENNETT, M., Veterinary Pathology
BEYNON, R. J., Veterinary Pre-Clinical Science
CARTER, S. D., Veterinary Science
DOBSON, H., Veterinary Reproduction
EDWARDS, G. B., Equine Studies
GASKELL, C. J., Small Animal Studies
GASKELL, R. M., Veterinary Pathology
HURST, J. L., Animal Science
INNES, J. F., Veterinary Clinical Science and Animal Husbandry
MORGAN, K. L., Epidemiology
SHIRAZI-BEECHEY, S. P., Veterinary Pre-Clinical Science

AFFILIATED INSTITUTION

Liverpool School of Tropical Medicine: see Research Institutes.

LIVERPOOL HOPE UNIVERSITY

Hope Park, Liverpool, L16 9JD

Telephone: (151) 291-3000
Fax: (151) 291-3100
E-mail: admission@hope.ac.uk
Internet: www.hope.ac.uk

Founded 1844; present name and status 2005
Academic year: September to July

Rector and Chief Exec.: Prof. GERALD PILLAY
Number of students: 7,000

Deaneries: Arts and Humanities; Education; Business and Computer Sciences, Sciences and Social Sciences.

LIVERPOOL JOHN MOORES UNIVERSITY

Rodney House, 70 Mount Pleasant, Liverpool L3 5UX

Telephone: (151) 231-5090
Fax: (151) 231-3194
Internet: www.livjm.ac.uk

Founded 1970 as Liverpool Polytechnic, present name and status 1992
Academic year: September to May

Chancellor: CHERIE BOOTH
Vice-Chancellor: Prof. MICHAEL BROWN
Pro Vice-Chancellor (Administration) and University Secretary: ALISON WILD
Pro Vice-Chancellor (Delivery): Prof. GERRY KELLEHER
Pro Vice-Chancellor (Development): STEPHEN KENNY
Pro Vice-Chancellor (Infrastructure): ALLAN BICKERSTAFFE
Director of Learning and Information Services: MAXINE MELLING
Number of teachers: 2,800
Number of students: 20,000

DEANS

Faculty of Business and Law: Prof. JAMES KIRKBRIDE
Faculty of Education, Community and Leisure: Dr DIANE BURTON
Faculty of Health and Applied Social Sciences: Prof. GODFREY MAZHINDU
Faculty of Media, Arts and Social Science: Prof. ROGER WEBSTER
Faculty of Science: Prof. PETER WHEELER
Faculty of Technology: Prof. DIANE MEEHAN

DIRECTORS OF ACADEMIC DEPARTMENTS

Faculty of Business and Law:
 Accounting, Finance and Economics: DAVE GARDNER
 Business Information: DOUG HAYNES
 Law: Prof. ROGER EVANS
 Languages: Prof. LINDA ARCHIBALD
 Management: JOHN VAUGHAN

Faculty of Education, Community and Leisure:
 Education: Dr TRICIA MEERS
 Outdoors, Leisure and Food: ELAINE PRISK
 Physical Education, Sports and Dance: Prof. PAT SHENTON

Faculty of Health and Applied Social Sciences:
 Applied Social Sciences: PHIL LEE
 Midwifery and Child Health: ANGELA HAWTIN
 Nursing and Healthcare Studies: PAT FIRBY
 Centre for Public Health: (vacant)

Faculty of Media, Arts and Social Science:
 International Centre for Digital Content: Prof. PETER FOWLER
 Liverpool School of Art and Design: Prof. CECILIA CRIGHTON
 Media, Critical and Creative Arts: Dr TAMSIN SPARGO
 Social Science: Dr MARGARET EDWARDS

Faculty of Science:
 Astrophysics Research Institute: Prof. MIKE BODE
 Biological and Earth Sciences: Dr SIMON DOWELL
 Biomolecular Sciences: Prof. HILARY EVANS
 Pharmacy and Chemistry: Dr TERRY NOLAN
 Psychology: Prof. ANDY TATTERSALL
 Sports and Exercise Science: Prof. TIM CABLE

Faculty of Technology and Environment:
 Built Environment: Prof. PETER MORGAN

Computing and Mathematical Sciences: Prof. MADJID MERABTI
Engineering: Dr IAN JENKINSON
European Institute for Urban Affairs: Prof. MICHAEL PARKINSON

UNIVERSITY OF LONDON

Senate House, Malet St, London, WC1E 7HU

Telephone: (20) 7862-8000
Fax: (20) 7862-8358
E-mail: enquiries@lon.ac.uk
Internet: www.lon.ac.uk

Founded 1836 as an examining body; became also a teaching body in 1898

Chancellor: HRH THE PRINCESS ROYAL
Vice-Chancellor: Prof. Sir GRAEME DAVIES
Deputy Vice-Chancellor: Prof ADRIAN SMITH
Dir of Admin.: CATHERINE SWARBRICK
Academic Registrar: GILLIAN ROBERTS
Library: see Libraries and Archives
Number of teachers: 7,881
Number of students: 155,000 (125,000 based in the 19 constituent colleges; 30,000 external).

COLLEGES OF THE UNIVERSITY

Birkbeck, University of London

Malet St, London, WC1E 7HX

Telephone: (20) 7631-6000
Fax: (20) 7631-6270
Internet: www.bbk.ac.uk

Founded 1823; Charter of Incorporation 1926
State control
Academic year: September to July

Master: Prof. DAVID S. LATCHMAN
Vice-Master: Prof. PHILIP DEWE
Dean of College: Prof. PAUL BARNES
Sec.: KEITH HARRISON
Registrar: B. A. HARWOOD
Librarian: PHILIP PAYNE
Library of 364,102
Number of teachers: 927 (incl. 575 part-time)
Number of students: 7,266

Depts of Applied linguistics, Computational biology, Computer science, Cultural history, Economics, German, History, International business, Law, Mathematical finance, Modern British history, Nineteenth-century literature, Philosophy, Political aesthetics, Psychology, Shakespeare studies, Structural biology

DEANS

Faculty of Arts: Prof. MATTHEW INNES
Faculty of Continuing Education: Prof. JOHN ANNETTE
Faculty of Science: Dr STEVE WALKER
Faculty of Social Science: Dr ROGER JOHNSON

PROFESSORS

ANNETTE, J., Citizenship and Lifelong Learning
ARCHIBUGI, D., Innovation, Governance and Public Policy
BARNES, J., Psychology
BARNES, P., Applied Crystallography
BELSKY, J., Psychology
BOURKE, J., History
BRAH, A., Sociology
BRAKE, L., Literature and Print Culture
BRINER, R., Organizational Psychology
BRUMMELHUIS, R., Mathematical Finance
CHRISTIE, I., Film and Media History
CLARK, S., Renaissance Literature
CONNOR, S., Modern Literature and Theory
COOLE, D., Political and Social Theory
COOMBES, A., Material and Visual Culture
DAVIES, D., Chemistry
DENCH, E., Ancient History
DEWE, P., Organizational Behaviour

DICKENSON, D., Medical Ethics and Humanities
DOUZINAS, C., Law
DOWNES, H., Geochemistry
DRIFFILL, J., Econ.
EDWARDS, C., Ancient History and Culture
EIMER, M., Psychology
FIGES, O., History
FITZPATRICK, P., Law
FRASER, H., Nineteenth-Century Studies
FROSH, S., Psychology
GOLDSWORTHY, G. J., Biology
GRAYLING, A., Applied Philosophy
HEALY, T., Renaissance Studies
HILEY, B., Physics
HORNSBY, J., Philosophy
HOUNSELL, E., Biological Chemistry
HOWELLS, R., French
HUNTER, M., History
JAMES, S., Philosophy
JENKINS, R., Political Science
JOHNSON, M. H., Psychology
JONES, R. C., Creative Writing
KELLY, J., Industrial Relations
LEVENE, M., Computer Science
LOVENDUSKI, J., Politics
MCAUSLAN, P., Law
MACMILLAN, F., Law
MAYBANK, S., Computer Science
MELHUISH, E., Psychology
MIRKIN, B., Computer Science
MORAN, L., Law
MOSS, D., Biomolecular Structure
MULCAHY, L., Law and Society
MÜLLER, H., Cognitive Psychology
MULVEY, L., Film Studies
NEAD, L., History of Art
OUGHTON, C., Management
POLLARD, P., French
POULOVASSILIS, A., Computer Science
PRICE, G. D., Mineral Physics
PSARADAKIS, Z., Econometrics
ROWE, W., Poetics
SAIBIL, H., Structural Biology
SEGAL, L., Psychology and Gender Studies
SHEPHERD, J., Geography
SIBERT, A., Econ.
SINGH, R., Politics
SMITH, R., Applied Econ.
SNOWER, D. J., Econ.
SOLA, M., Econ.
THOMPSON, W., Political Economy
USHER, M., Psychology
WAKSMAN, G., Structural Molecular Biology
WALLACE, B., Crystallography
WELLS, D. A., German

Courtauld Institute of Art

Somerset House, Strand, London, WC2R 0RN

Telephone: (20) 7848-2777
Fax: (20) 7848-2410
E-mail: ugadmissions@courtauld.ac.uk
Internet: www.courtauld.ac.uk

Founded 1932; became an independent college of the Univ. of London 2002
Academic year: September to July

Undergraduate and postgraduate courses in the history of Western art; diploma courses in conservation of easel paintings and in the history of art; MA degree courses in the history of art and the conservation of wall paintings; PhD in history of art

Dir: Prof. JAMES CUNO
Sec. and Registrar: MICHAEL ARTHUR
Academic Registrar: Dr R. J. WALKER
Head of Academic Information Services: Dr S. PRICE
Number of teachers: 29
Number of students: 381 (329 full-time, 52 part-time)
Publication: *Journal of the Warburg and Courtauld Institutes* (annual)

PROFESSORS

CORMACK, R., History of Art
CROSSLEY, P., History of Art
CUNO, J., History of Art
GREEN, C., History of Art
HOUSE, J., History of Art
LOWDEN, J., History of Art
RIBEIRO, A., History of Dress
RUBIN, P., History of Art
SOLKIN, D., History of Art

Goldsmiths College

New Cross, London, SE14 6NW
Telephone: (20) 7919-7171
Fax: (20) 7919-7903
E-mail: ext-comms@gold.ac.uk
Internet: www.goldsmiths.ac.uk
Founded 1891

Undergraduate and postgraduate internal degrees; professional and postgraduate diploma and certificate courses in visual and performing arts, design, social, computing and behavioural sciences, humanities, English, languages, media and communication studies, cultural studies, educational studies (incl. teacher training), counselling and psychodynamic studies, and professional and community education

Academic year: September to June

Warden: Prof. GEOFFREY CROSSICK (acting)
Pro-Warden for Academic Affairs: Dr HELEN CARR
Pro-Warden for Research: Prof. SIMON McVEIGH
Pro-Warden of Students: Dr PHILLIP BROADHEAD
College Sec.: SHARON PAGE
Dir of Information Services: JOAN PATEMAN

Library of 221,000 vols
Number of teachers: 331 and 560 visiting tutors
Number of students: 8,677 (5,259 full-time, 3,418 part-time)

Publications: *African Affairs* (historical and cultural studies), *African Identities*, *Death and Dying* (sociological), *Economy and Society* (quarterly), *Goldsmiths Journal of Education* (2 a year), *History Workshop Journal* (quarterly), *Journal of Buddhist Ethics* (historical and cultural studies), *Scriblerian* (English language and literature, 2 a year), *Sikh Formations*, *Social Identities*, *Third Text* (historical and cultural studies)

PROFESSORS

AHLUWALIA, P., Politics
ALEXANDER, S., History
BACK, L., Sociology
BAILEY, J., Music
BALDICK, C., English and Comparative Literature
BERRY, C., Media and Communications
BLAMIRES, A., English and Comparative Literature
BURGIN, V., Visual Arts
CARR, H., English
CAYGILL, H., History
CHITTY, C., Educational Studies
CURRAN, J. P. P., Media and Communications
DAVIDOFF, J., Psychology
DE VILLE, N., Visual Arts
DOWNIE, A., English and Comparative Literature
DRYDEN, W., Professional and Community Education
DUTTMAN, A., Visual Cultures
FALCONBRIDGE, B., Visual Arts
FRENCH, C., Psychology
GREGORY, E., Educational Studies
HARRIS, O., Anthropology
HEIDENSOHN, F. M., Politics
HEMSWORTH, G., Visual Arts
IVASHKIN, A., Music

JEFFERIES, J., Visual Arts
KEITH, M., Sociology and Centre for Urban and Community Research
KEOWN, D., History
KIMBELL, R. A., Design
LASH, S., Cultural Studies
LURY, C., Sociology
McROBBIE, A., Media and Communications
McVEIGH, S., Music
MAYO, M., Professional and Community Education
MICHAEL, M., Sociology
MOORE-GILBERT, B., English and Comparative Literature
MORLEY, D., Media and Communications
MORRISON, B., English and Comparative Literature
NEGUS, K., Music
PEARSON, G., Professional and Community Education
POWELL, J., Psychology
PRING, L., Psychology
RAO, N., Politics
ROBINS, K., Media and Communications
ROGOFF, I., Visual Cultures
SEIDLER, V., Sociology
SHEVTSOVA, M., Drama
SILVESTER, J., Psychology
SKEGGS, B., Sociology
SMITH, P. K., Psychology
SOKOL, B. J., English and Comparative Literature
THOMAS, N., Anthropology
VALENTINE, T., Psychology
VELMANS, M., Psychology
WALLER, D., Professional and Community Education
WIGGINS, G., Computing
ZIMMER, R., Computing

Heythrop College

Univ. of London, Kensington Sq., London, W8 5HQ
Telephone: (20) 7795-6600
Fax: (20) 7795-4200
E-mail: enquiries@heythrop.ac.uk
Internet: www.heythrop.ac.uk
Founded 1614; became part of Univ. of London 1970
Academic year: September to June

Principal: Rev. Dr JOHN McDADE
Sec. and Registrar: ANNABEL CLARKSON
Assistant Registrar: ROSALIE BOLLAND

Library of 250,000 vols
Number of teachers: 30
Number of students: 580

Publications: *Heythrop Journal* (quarterly), *Heythrop Studies in Contemporary Philosophy, Religion and Theology* (2 a year)

Specialist courses in theology and philosophy. The college does not receive an HEFCE grant.

Imperial College London

South Kensington Campus, London, SW7 2AZ
Telephone: (20) 7589-5111
Fax: (20) 7584-7596
E-mail: info@imperial.ac.uk
Internet: www.imperial.ac.uk
Founded 1907 by fed. of Royal College of Science, Royal School of Mines, and City and Guilds College, (1988) St Mary's Hospital Medical School, (1995) National Heart and Lung Institute, (1997) Charing Cross and Westminster Medical School and Royal Postgraduate Medical School, and (2000) Wye College
Academic year: October to June

Rector: Sir RICHARD SYKES
Deputy Rector: Prof. Sir L. BORYSIEWICZ
Pro-Rector for Educational Quality: Prof. R. D. RAWLINGS

Pro-Rector for Int. Relations: Prof. D. J. EWINS
Pro-Rector for Postgraduate Affairs: Prof. M. A. RITTER
Pro-Rector for Public and Corporate Affairs: Prof. T. MAINI
Pro-Rector for Research: Prof. CHRISTOPHER L. HANKIN
College Sec.: K. A. MITCHESON
Dir of Library Services: CLARE JENKINS
Number of teachers: 1,180
Number of students: 12,056 (11,152 full-time, 904 part-time)

PRINCIPALS

Faculty of Eng.: (vacant)
Faculty of Life Sciences: Prof. MICHAEL P. HASSELL
Faculty of Medicine: Prof. STEPHEN SMITH
Faculty of Physical Sciences: Prof. FRANK G. LEPPINGTON
Business School: Prof. DAVID BEGG (Dir)
Humanities: Dr CHARMIAN BRINSON (Dir)

PROFESSORS

ADCOCK, I. M., Respiratory Cell and Molecular Biology
ALBANESE, C., Mathematical Finance
ALBERTI, J. G. M. M., Metabolic Medicine
ALIABADI, F. M. H., Aerostructures
ALLDAY, M. J., Virology
ALLEN-MERSH, T. G., Gastrointestinal Surgery
ALTON, E. W. F. W., Gene Therapy
AMIS, A. A., Orthopaedic Biomechanics
ANAND, P., Clinical Neurology
ANDERSON, D., Energy and Environmental Studies
ANDERSON, R. M., Infectious Disease Epidemology
APSIMON, H. M., Air Pollution Studies
ARMSTRONG, A., Organic Chemistry
ARST, H. N., Microbial Genetics
ATKINSON, A., Materials Chemistry
ATKINSON, C., Applied Mathematics
BALDING, D. J., Statistical Genetics
BALOGH, A., Space Physics
BANGHAM, C., Immunology
BARBER, J., Biochemistry
BARLOW, J. G., Technology and Innovation Management
BARNES, P. J., Thoracic Medicine
BARNES, T. R. E., Clinical Psychiatry
BARNHAM, K. W. J., Physics
BARRETT, A. G. M., Organic Chemistry
BARRETT, J. W., Numerical Analysis
BEDDINGTON, J. R., Applied Population Biology
BEGG, D. K. H., Econ.
BELL, A. R., Plasma Physics
BELL, J. N. B., Environmental Pollution
BELL, M. G. H., Transport Operations
BELVISI, M., Respiratory Pharmacology
BENNETT, P. R., Obstetrics and Gynaecology
BLACKMOND, D. G., Catalysis
BLANE, D., Medical Sociology
BLOMLEY, M. J., Radiology
BLOOM, S. R., Metabolic Medicine
BLUNT, M. J., Petroleum Eng.
BOOBIS, A. R., Biochemical Pharmacology
BOSANQUET, N. F. G., Health Policy
BOTTO, M., Rheumatology
BRADLEY, D. D. C., Experimental Solid State Physics
BRANDON, N. P., Sustainable Development in Energy
BRENNAN, F. M., Immunopathology
BRIDSON, M. R., Pure Mathematics
BRIGGS, D. J., Public Health
BRINSON, C. E. J., German Studies
BRISCOE, B. J., Interface Eng.
BRONSTEIN, A. M., Clinical Neurology
BROOKS, D. J., Neurology
BROSENS, J. J., Reproductive Sciences
BUCHANAN, D. L., Mining Geology

BUCK, K. W., Plant and Fungal Virology
BUCK, M., Molecular Microbiology
BUCKINGHAM, J. C., Pharmacology
BUENFELD, N. R., Concrete Structures
BULPITT, C. J., Geriatric Medicine
BUSH, A., Paediatric Respirology
BUTLER, D., Water Eng.
CALLAN, M. F. C., Immunology and Rheumatology
CARGILL, P. J., Physics
CASH, J. R., Numerical Analysis
CASS, A. E. G., Chemical Biology
CAWLEY, P., Mechanical Eng.
CHADWICK, D., Applied Catalysis
CHATURVEDI, N., General Practice
CHEN, Y., Mathematical Physics
CHEUNG, P., Digital Systems
CHRISTOFIDES, N., Operational Research
CHUNG, K. F., Respiratory Medicine
CLARK, K. L., Computational Logic
COLLINS, P., Clinical Cardiology
CONNERADE, J.-P., Atomic and Molecular Physics
CONSTANTINIDES, A. G., Signal Processing
CONWAY, G. R., Int. Devt
COOK, H. T., Renal Pathology
COOKSON, W. O. C., Respiratory Genetics
COOMBES, R. C. D. S., Medical Oncology
COUCHMAN, J. R., Cell Biology
COUTELLE, C. C., Gene Therapy
COWBURN, R. P., Nanotechnology
COWIE, M. R., Cardiology
COWLEY, S. R., Plasma Physics
CRAIG, D. D. C., Organic Synthesis
CRASTER, R. V., Applied Mathematics
CRAWLEY, M. J., Community Ecology
CRISANTI, A., Molecular Parasitology
CROWDER, M. J., Stochastic Modelling
CUMPSTY, N. A., Mechanical Eng.
CUTHBERTSON, K., Finance
DAINTY, J. C., Applied Optics
DALLMAN, M. J., Immunology
DAMZEN, M. J., Experimental Laser Physics
DARLINGTON, J., Programming Methodology
DARZI, A., Minimal Access Surgery
DAVIS, M. H. A., Mathematics
DE BELLEROCHE, J. S., Neurochemistry
DE MELLO, A. J., Chemical Nanosciences
DELL, A., Carbohydrate Biochemistry
DERWENT, R. G., Atmospheric Chemistry
DJAMGOZ, M. B. A., Neurobiology
DOKAL, I. S., Haematology
DONALDSON, S. K., Pure Mathematics
DONNELLY, C., Statistical Epidemiology
DORNAN, P. J., Experimental Particle Physics
DOUGHERTY, M. K., Space Physics
DREW, J. E., Astrophysics
DRIVER, C., Econ.
DUGWELL, D. R., Chemical Eng.
DURHAM, S. R., Allergy and Clinical Immunology
DURUCAN, S., Mining and Environmental Eng.
EDALAT, A., Computer Science and Mathematics
EDGERTON, D. E. H., History of Science, Technology and Medicine
EDWARDS, A. D., Neonatology
ELGIN, J. N., Applied Mathematics
ELLAWAY, P. H., Physiology
ELLIOTT, P., Epidemiology and Public Health Medicine
EVANS, A. W., Risk Management
EVANS, J., Tropical Forestry
EWINS, D. J., Vibration Eng.
FARRELL, P. J., Tumour Virology
FELDMAN, M., Cellular Immunology
FENNER, R. T., Eng. Computation
FENWICK, A., Tropical Parasitology
FERENCZI, M. J., Physiological Sciences
FERGUSON, N. M., Mathematical Biology
FIRMIN, D., Biomedical Imaging
FIRTH, J. A., Anatomy
FISK, D. J., Eng. for Sustainable Devt
FISK, N. M., Obstetrics and Gynaecology
FOSTER, R. G., Molecular Neurology

FOULKES, W. M. C., Physics
FOXWELL, B. M., Immune Cell Signalling
FRANKEL, G., Molecular Pathenogenesis
FRANKS, N. P., Biophysics
FRANKS, S., Reproductive Endocrinology
FRASER, R. W., Agricultural Econ.
FREEMONT, P. S., Structural Biology
FRENCH, P. M. W., Physics
FRIEDLAND, J. S., Infectious Diseases and Microbiology
FROGUEL, P., Genomic Medicine
GABRA, H., Medical Oncology
GABRIEL, J., Organizational Theory
GANN, D. M., Technology and Innovation Management, Built Environment
GARNETT, G., Microparasite Epidemiology
GARRALDA HUALDE, M. E., Child and Adolescent Psychiatry
GAUNTLETT, J. P., Theoretical Physics
GELENBE, S. E., Computer and Communication Networks
GEORGE, A., Molecular Immunology
GHATEI, M., Peptide Endocrinology
GHOSH, S., Gastroenterology
GIBBON, J. D., Applied Mathematics
GIBSON, S. E., Chemistry
GIBSON, V. C., Organic Chemistry
GILKS, C. F., Int. Health
GILLON, R., Medical Ethics
GLAISTER, S., Transport and Infrastructure
GLOVER, V. A., Perinatal Psychobiology
GODFRAY, H. C. J., Evolutionary Biology
GOGOLIN, A. O., Mathematical Physics
GORDON, M. Y. A., Experimental Haematology
GOSMAN, A. D., Computational Fluid Dynamics
GOTCH, F. M., Immunology
GRAEBER, M. R., Neuroscience
GRAHAM, J. M. R., Unsteady Aerodynamics
GRAHAM, N. J. D., Environmental Eng.
GRASBY, P. M., Psychiatry
GREENHALGH, R. M., Surgery
GRIFFITHS, D. S., Human Resource Management
GRIGORYAN, A., Pure Mathematics
GRIMES, R. W., Materials Science
GRIMM, S. W., Toxicology
GRINGARTEN, A., Petroleum Eng.
GRUZELIER, J. G., Psychology
GUO, Y., Computing Science
HABIB, N. A., Hepto-biliary Surgery
HAIGH, J. D., Atmospheric Physics
HAJNAL, J. V., Imaging Science
HALL, G., Physics
HALL, P., Applied Mathematics
HALL, S. G. F., Econ.
HALLIWELL, J. J., Theoretical Physics
HAND, D. J., Statistics
HANKINS, M. W., Visual Neuroscience
HARDIE, R. J., Insect Physiology
HARDING, S., Cardiac Pharmacology
HARRIES, J. E., Earth Observation
HARRISON, N., Chemistry
HARRISON, P. G., Computing Science
HASKARD, D. O., Cardiovascular Medicine
HASSELL, M. P., Insect Ecology
HENCH, L. L., Ceramic Materials
HENRY, J. A., Accident and Emergency Medicine
HIGGINS, C. F., Clinical Sciences
HIGGINS, J. S., Polymer Science
HILL, B., Policy Analysis
HILLIER, R., Compressible Flow
HINDS, E. A., Quantum Optics
HODKINSON, I., Logic and Computation
HODSON, M. E., Respiratory Medicine
HOLDEN, D. W., Molecular Microbiology
HOLM, D. D., Applied Mathematics
HOLMES, A. B., Organic and Polymer Chemistry
HOPKINS, C. R., Biochemistry
HUDSON, J. A., Rock Mechanics
HUGHES, A. D., Clinical Pharmacology
HUGHES, S. F. R., Orthopaedic Surgery
HUHTANIEMI, I. T., Reproductive Biology

HULL, C., Theoretical Physics
IMREGUN, M., Computational Eng. Dynamics
ISHAM, C. J., Theoretical Physics
IVANOV, A. A., Pure Mathematics
IWATA, C. J., Biochemistry
JACKSON, G., Chemical Physics
JAMES, G. D., Pure Mathematics
JARDINE, R. J., Geomechanics
JARVELIN, M., Lifecourse Epidemiology
JEGER, M., Agroecology
JENSEN, H. J., Mathematics
JOHNSON, H. D., Petroleum Geology
JOHNSTON, D. G., Clinical Endocrinology
JOHNSTON, S. L., Respiratory Medicine
JONES, T. S., Physical Chemistry
JONES, W. G., High Energy Physics
JONES, W. P., Combustion
KANDIYOTI, R., Chemical Eng.
KELSALL, G. H., Electrochemical Eng.
KENNARD, C., Clinical Neurology
KILNER, J. A., Materials Science
KING, P. R., Petroleum Eng.
KINLOCH, A. J., Adhesion
KITNEY, R. I., Biomedical Systems Eng.
KLUG, D., Chemical Biophysics
KLUMPES, P. J. M., Accounting
KNIGHT, P. L., Quantum Optics
KORNYSHEV, A. A., Chemical Physics
KRAMER, J., Distributed Computing
KRUSHELNICK, K. M., Plasma Physics
KYDD, J., Agricultural Econ. and Business Management
LALANI, E. M. A., Molecular and Cell Pathology
LANE, D. A., Molecular Haematology
LAWRENCE, C., Fluid Mechanics
LAYCOCK, J. F., Endocrine Physiology
LEATHERBARROW, R., Chemical Biology
LESCHZINER, R., Computational Aerodynamics
LESTER, J. N., Water Technology
LEUNG, K. K., Internet Technology
LEVER, M. J., Physiological Mechanics
LEVIN, M., Paediatrics
LIEBECK, M. W., Pure Mathematics
LIMEBEER, D. J. N., Control Eng.
LINDSTEDT, R. P., Thermofluids
LIVINGSTON, A. G., Chemical Eng.
LLOYD SMITH, D., Structural Mechanics
LOMAX, M. A., Animal Sciences
LONG, K. R., Experimental Particle Physics
LUCKHAM, P. F., Particle Technology
LUK, W. W.-C., Computer Eng.
MACCHIETTO, S., Process Systems Eng.
MACCULLOCH, R. J., Econ.
MACDERMOT, J., Clinical Pharmacology
MACKINNON, A., Theoretical Solid State Physics
MADEN, A., Psychiatry
MAGEE, A. I., Membrane Biology
MAGEE, J. N., Computing Science
Sir MAINI, R. N., Rheumatology
MAJEED, F. A., Primary Healthcare and General Practice
MAMDANI, E. H., Telecommunications Strategy and Services
MANSFIELD, J., Biology
MARANGOS, J. J., Laser Physics
MAROS, I., Computational Methods of Operations Research
MARSTON, S. B., Cardiovascular Biochemistry
MATHIAS, C. J., Neurovascular Medicine
MATTHEWS, S. J., Chemical and Structural Biology
MAXWELL, P. H., Nephrology
MAZE, M., Anaesthetics
MEADE, N., Quantitative Finance
MCCLURE, M. O., Retrovirology
MEIKLE, W. P. S., Astrophysics
MILLER, A., Organic Chemistry and Structural Biology
MITCHELL, J., Pharmacology in Critical Care
MOORE, G. E., Molecular Genetics
MUGGLETON, S. H., Bioinformatics
MUMFORD, J., Natural Resource Management
MUNTONI, F., Paediatric Neurology

NAGASE, H., Rheumatology
NETHERCOT, D. A., Civil Eng.
NEW, G. H. C., Non-Linear Optics
NICHOLSON, J. K., Biological Chemistry
NORTHOVER, J. M. A., Intestinal Surgery
OPENSHAW, P. J. M., Experimental Medicine
OWENS, I., Evolutionary Ecology
PANTELIDES, C. C., Chemical Eng.
PARKER, K. H., Physiological Fluid
PARKER, M. G., Obstetrics and Gynaecology
PARRY, A. O., Statistical Physics
PARRY, G., Applied Physics
PARRY, S., Radiochemistry
PARTRIDGE, M. R., Respiratory Medicine
PASVOL, G., Infection and Tropical Medicine
PAVLOVIC, M., Structural Eng. and Mechanics
PENDRY, J. B., Theoretical Solid-State Physics
PENNELL, D. J., Cardiology
PEPPER, J., Caradiothoracic Surgery
PERRAUDIN, W. R. M., Finance
PETERS, N. S., Cardiac Electrophysiology
PHILLIPS, C. C., Experimental Solid-State Physics
PHILLIPS, D., Physical Chemistry
PISTIKOPOULOS, E. N., Chemical Eng.
PLANT, J. A., Applied Geochemistry
PLAYFORD, R., Gastroenterology
PLENIO, M. B., Quantum Physics
POLAK, J. M., Endocrine Pathology
POOLE-WILSON, P. A., Cardiology
POTTS, D. M., Analytical Soil Mechanics
POULTER, N. R., Preventative Cardiovascular Medicine
PRABHU, J. C., Marketing
PUSEY, C. D., Renal Medicine
QUIRKE, N., Physical Chemistry
RAWLINGS, R. D., Materials Science
REED, M. J., Steroid Biochemistry
REGAN, L., Obstetrics and Gynaecology
REYNOLDS, R., Cellular Neurobiology
RICHARDS, B., Computing Science
RICHARDSON, S., Public Health
RICHARDSON, S. M., Chemical Eng.
RITTER, M. A., Immunology
RIVERS, R. J., Theoretical Physics
ROBB, M. A., Chemistry
ROBERTS, I., Paediatrics Haematology
ROSE, M. L., Transport Immunology
ROWAN-ROBINSON, G. M., Astrophysics
RUDD, C. E., Haematology
RUSSELL, N. J., Biology
RUSTEM, B., Computational Methods in Operations
RZEPA, H. S., Computational Fluid Dynamics
SAKLATVALA, J., Experimental Pathology
SANDERSON, D. J., Geology
SCHROTER, R. C., Biological Mechanics
SCHWARTZ, S. J., Space Physics
SCOTT, J., Medicine
SCREATON, G. R., Medicine
SEABRA, M. C., Molecular Genetics
SECKL, M., Molecular Cancer Medicine
SEDDON, J. M., Physical Chemistry
SEFTON, J. A., Econ.
SELKIRK, M. E., Biochemical Parasitology
SENSKY, J., Applied Mathematics
SERGOT, M. J., Computational Logic
SEVER, P. S., Clinical Pharmacology and Therapeutics
SEVERS, N. J., Cell Biology
SHAH, N., Process Systems Eng.
SHAUNAK, S., Infectious Diseases
SHAW, R. J., Thoracic Medicine
SHERIDAN, D. J., Clinical Cardiology
SINDEN, R. E., Parasite Cell Biology
SKOROBOGATOV, A. N., Pure Mathematics
SLOMAN, M. S., Distributed Systems Management
SMITH, G. L., Experimental Pathology
SMITH, R. A., Mechanical Eng.
SMITH, R. W., Physics
SOBEY, R. J., Fluid Mechanics
SOUTHWOOD, D. J., Physics
SPIKES, H. A., Lubrication
SPRATT, B. G., Molecular Microbiology

SQUIRE, J. M., Structural Biophysics
STAMP, G. W. M., Histopathology
STARK, J., Applied Mathematics
STEER, P. J., Obstetrics and Gynaecology
STELLE, K. S., Physics
STERNBERG, M. J. E., Structural Bioinformatics
STUCKEY, D. C., Biochemical Eng.
SUGDEN, P. H., Cellular Biochemistry
SUMMERFIELD, J. A., Experimental Medicine
SUMNER, T. J., Experimental Astrophysics
SUTTON, A. P., Nanotechnology
SWAN, C., Hydrodynamics
SYMS, R. R., Microsystems
SZYMANSKI, S. A., Econ.
TAYLOR, A., Neurophysiology
TAYLOR, A. M. K. P., Thermofluids
TAYLOR, J. R., Ultrafast Physics and Technology
TAYLOR, K. M., Cardiac Surgery
TEMPLER, R., Biophysical Chemistry
THIRTLE, C. G., Agricultural Econ.
THOMAS, H. C., Medicine
THOMPSON, R. C., Experimental Physics
TOUMAZOU, C., Analogue Circuit Design
TRUSLER, J. P. M., Thermophysics
TSEYTLIN, A., Theoretical Physics
TYRER, P. J., Community Psychiatry
UNDERWOOD, S. R., Cardiac Imaging
VAN HEEL, M., Structural Biology
VASSILICOS, C., Fluid Mechanics
VAZ DE MELO, J., Molecular Haematology
VENABLES, P. J., Viral Immunorheumatology
VINEIS, P., Environmental Epidemiology
VINTER, R. B., Control Theory
VIRDEE, T. S., Physics
VVEDENSKY, D., Theoretical Solid-State Physics
WAAGE, J. K., Applied Ecology
WALDEN, A. T., Statistics
WANG, Y., Reservoir Geophysics
WARK, D. L., High Energy Physics
WARNER, M. R., Geophysics
WARWICK, A. C., History of Science
WAXMAN, J., Medical Oncology
WEBER, J. N., Genito-Urinary Medicine and Communicable Diseases
WEBSDALE, D. M., Physics
WEBSTER, J. P. G., Agricultural Business Management
WHEATER, H. S., Hydrology
WILKINS, M. R., Clinical Pharmacology
WILLIAMS, A. J., Membrane Biophysics
WILLIAMS, T. J., Applied Pharmacology
WINSTON, R. M., Fertility Studies
WISE, C. M., Civil Eng. Design
WISE, R. J. S., Neurology
WOOD, D. A., Clinical Epidemiology
WOODS, J. D., Oceanography
WRIGHT, D. J., Pest Management
YANG, G. Z., Medical Image Computing
YOUNG, D. B., Medical Microbiology
ZEGARLINSKI, B., Pure Mathematics

Institute of Education

20 Bedford Way, London, WC1H 0AL

Telephone: (20) 7612-6000
Fax: (20) 7612-6126
E-mail: info@ioe.ac.uk
Internet: www.ioe.ac.uk

Founded as London Day Training College in 1902, transferred to control of Univ. of London in 1932, became a School of the Univ. in 1987

Postgraduate initial teacher training and BEd for serving teachers; advanced diplomas, certificates, Masters degrees and research degrees in education and related aspects of the social sciences, health and professional practice; NPQH and other courses for heads and school leaders; short courses, incl. INSET, for teachers at all levels and in related occupations

Academic year: September to June

Dir: Prof. Sir DAVID WATSON
Sec.: DAVID WARREN
Academic Registrar: Dr LORETO LOUGHRAN
Librarian: ANNE PETERS

Library of 270,000 vols, 1,160 periodicals
Number of teachers: 176
Number of students: 4,424 (1,372 full-time, 3,052 part-time)

Publication: *London Review of Education* (3 a year)

PROFESSORS

AGGLETON, P., Education
ALDERSON, P., Childhood Studies
ALDRICH, R., History of Education
BALL, S., Sociology of Education
BARNETT, R., Higher Education
BARTON, L., Inclusive Education
BLATCHFORD, P., Education and Psychology
BRANNEN, J., Sociology of the Family
BRIGHOUSE, H., Philosophy of Education
BUCKINGHAM, D., Education
BYNNER, J., Education
CAMERON, D., Languages
DAVID, N., Educational Technology
DOCKRELL, J., Psychology and Special Needs
DOLTON, P., Education
ELBOURNE, D., Evidence-Informed Policy and Practice
EVANS, K., Education (Lifelong Learning)
GILLBORN, D., Education
GOLDSTEIN, H., Statistical Methods
GORDON, P., History of Education
GREEN, A., Education
GUNDARA, J., Education
HALPIN, D., Education
HIRST, P., Education
HOYLES, C. M., Mathematics Education
JOSHI, H., Education
KENT, A., Geography Education
KRESS, G., English
LAWTON, D., Education
LEONARD, D., Sociology of Education and Gender
LEVACIC, R., Econ. and Finance of Education
LITTLE, A., Education with spec. reference to Developing Countries
LUNT, I., Educational Psychology
MACGILCHRIST, B., Education
MAYALL, B., Childhood Studies
MOSS, P., Early Childhood Provision
NOSS, R., Mathematics Education
OAKLEY, A. R., Sociology and Social Policy
POWER, S., Education
REISS, M., Science Education
ST JAMES ROBERTS, I., Child Dev.t
SAMMONS, P., Education
SHATTOCK, M., Higher Education Management
SIRAJ-BLATCHFORD, I., Early Childhood Education
WELCH, G., Music Education
WHITE, J, Philosophy of Education
WHITTY, G. J., Sociology of Education
WOLF, A., Education

ATTACHED RESEARCH INSTITUTES

Bedford Group for Lifecourse and Statistical Studies: 20 Bedford Way, London, WC1H 0AL; f. 2002; combines Centre for Longitudinal Studies, Centre for Multilevel Modelling, DfES Centre for the Econ. of Education, DfES Centre for Research on the Wider Benefits of Learning, DfES Nat. Centre for Research and Devt in Adult Literacy and Numeracy and Int. Centre for Research on Assessment; Dir Prof. JOHN BYNNER.

Social Science Research Unit: 18 Woburn Sq., London, WC1H 0NR; f. 1990 with a remit to develop a programme of policy-relevant work in the broad areas of education and health; Dir Prof. ANN OAKLEY.

Thomas Coram Research Unit: 27–28 Woburn Sq., London, WC1H 0AA; f. 1973 with support from the Dept of Health and Social Security, Thomas Coram Fndn, and other bodies; now a multidisciplinary designated research unit of the Dept of Health; research in health, education and devt of children; Dir Prof. PETER AGGLETON.

King's College London

James Clerk Maxwell Bldg, 57 Waterloo Rd, London, SE1 8WA

Strand, London WC2R 2LS

Guy's campus: London Bridge, London, SE1 1UL

St Thomas' campus: Lambeth Palace Rd, London, SE1 7EH

King's Denmark Hill campus: Bessemer Rd, London, SE5 9PJ

Telephone: (20) 7836-5454 (Strand), (20) 7955-5000 (Guy's), (20) 7928-9292 (St Thomas')

E-mail: ceu@kcl.ac.uk

Internet: www.kcl.ac.uk

Founded 1829; merged with Queen Elizabeth College and Chelsea College 1985, with the Institute of Psychiatry 1997, and with United Medical and Dental Schools of Guy's and St Thomas' Hospitals 1998

Academic year: September to June

Principal: Prof. RICK TRAINOR (acting)

Vice-Principals: Prof. Sir LAWRENCE FREEDMAN, Prof. Sir GRAEME CATTO

Sec. and Registrar: HARRY T. MUSSELWHITE

Academic Registrar: BRIAN E. SALTER

Library: see Libraries and Archives

Number of teachers: 1,535

Number of students: 19,100 (incl. School of Medicine and Dentistry)

Publications: *Dispatches* (3 a year), *King's College Law Journal* (2 a year)

HEADS OF SCHOOLS

Guy's, King's and St Thomas' School of Biomedical Sciences: Prof. ROBERT HIDER

Guy's, King's and St Thomas' School of Dentistry: Prof. NAIRN WILSON

School of Education: Prof. DERYN WATSON

School of Health and Life Sciences: Prof. PHILIP WHITFIELD

School of Humanities: Dr DAVID RICKS

School of Law: Prof. JOHN PHILLIPS

Guy's, King's and St Thomas' School of Medicine: Prof. GWYN WILLIAMS

Florence Nightingale School of Nursing and Midwifery: Dr ANNE MARIE RAFFERTY

School of Physical Sciences and Eng.: Prof. COLIN BUSHNELL

School of Social Science and Public Policy: Prof. MICHAEL CLARKE

Institute of Psychiatry: Prof. GEORGE SZMUKLER

PROFESSORS

Guy's, King's and St Thomas' School of Biomedical Sciences (1st Floor, Henrietta Raphael House, London SE1 1UL; tel. (20) 7848-6400; fax (20) 7848-6399; e-mail biomed.admin@kcl.ac.uk):

BERRY, M., Anatomy
BRAIN, S. D., Pharmacology
BUCKLAND-WRIGHT, J. C., Radiological Anatomy
CICLITIRA, P. J., Gastroenterology
FILE, S. E., Psychopharmacology
FRASER, L. R., Reproductive Biology
GOULD, H. G., Biophysics
HALLIWELL, B., Biochemistry
HEARSE, D. J., Cardiovascular Biochemistry
HOLDER, N. H., Anatomy
HOWELL, S. L., Physiology
JENNER, P. G., Pharmacology
JONES, G. E., Cell Biology

LITTLETON, J. M., Pharmacology
LUMSDEN, A. G. S., Developmental Neurobiology
MCMAHON, S. B., Physiology
MCNAUGHTON, P. A., Physiology
MADEN, M., Developmental Biology
MANN, G. E., Vascular Physiology
MARSHALL, J., Ophthalmology
NAFTALIN, R. J., Physiology
NEAL, M. J., Pharmacology
PAGE, C. P., Pharmacology
PATIENT, R. K., Molecular Genetics
PEARSON, J. D., Physiology
PRICE, R. G., Biochemistry
QUINN, P. J., Biochemistry
RICE-EVANS, C., Biochemistry
RITTER, J. M., Clinical Pharmacology
RUTTER, M., Psychopathology
SIMMONS, R., Biophysics
STANDRING, S. M., Applied Neurobiology
THURSTON, C. F., Microbiology
TIMBRELL, J. A., Biochemical Toxicology
WEBSTER, K., Anatomy
WILLIAMS, W. P., Environmental Science

Guy's, King's and St Thomas' School of Dentistry (Guy's Tower, Guy's Hospital, London SE1 9RT; tel. (20) 7188-7188; fax (20) 7188-1159):

BEIGHTON, D., Oral Microbiology
CHALLACOMBE, S. J., Oral Medicine
ELEY, B. M., Periodontology
GELBIER, S., Dental Public Health
GIBBONS, D. E., Oral Health Services Research
JOHNSON, N., Dental Sciences
KIDD, E. A., Cariology
LANGDON, J., Oral and Maxillofacial Surgery
LINDEN, R., Craniofacial Biology
MCGURK, M., Oral and Maxillofacial Surgery
MEIKLE, M. C., Orthodontics
MEREDITH SMITH, M., Evolutionary Dento-Skeletal Biology
PALMER, R. M., Implant Dentistry and Periodontology
PITT-FORD, T. R., Endodontology
SHARPE, P. T., Craniofacial Biology
SMITH, B. G. N., Conservative Dental Surgery
SMITH, N. J. D., Dentistry
WADE, W. G., Oral Microbiology
WATSON, R., Prosthetic Dentistry

School of Education (Franklin-Wilkins Bldg (WBW), Waterloo Rd, London SE1 9NN; tel. (20) 7848-3183; fax (20) 7848-3182):

BROWN, M. L., Education
COX, M. J., Information Technology in Education
DUSCHL, R., Science Education
JOHNSON, D. C., Education
STREET, B. U., Language in Education
WILLIAM, D. A. P. R., Educational Assessment

School of Health and Life Sciences (Franklin-Williams Bldg, 150 Stamford St, London SE1 9NN; e-mail health-life@kcl.ac.uk):

ASKHAM, J. M., Gerontology
CAMMACK, R., Health and Life Siences
COWAN, D. A., Pharmaceutical Toxicology
COWLEY, S. A., Community Practice Development
EBRINGER, A. M. A., Immunology
FRANK, L. S., Children's Nursing Research
GEISSLER, C. A., Nutrition
HALL, D. O., Health and Life Sciences
HIDER, R. C., Pharmacy
MARRIOTT, C., Pharmacy
REDFERN, S. J., Nursing Studies
ROSS MURPHY, S. B., Life Sciences
SANDERS, T. A., Nutrition
STAINES, N. A., Immunology
TINKER, A. M., Gerontology
WHILE, A. E., Nursing Studies

WILSON-BARNETT, J., Nursing Studies

School of Humanities (Strand, London WC2R 2LS; tel. (20) 7848-2374; fax (20) 7848-2415; e-mail humanities@kcl.ac.uk):

ADLER, J. D., German
BANNER, M. C., Moral and Social Theology
BEATON, R. M., Modern Greek
BIRTWISTLE, H., Musical Composition
BOND, B. J., War Studies
BRIDGE, C., Australian Studies
BUSH, C., American Literature
BUTT, J. W., Modern Hispanic Studies
CHABAL, P. E., Lusophone-African Studies
CLARKE, M., Defence Studies
CLARKE, P. B., History and Sociology of Religion
DANDEKER, C., Military Sociology
DEATHRIDGE, J. W., King Edward Chair of Music
DOCKRILL, M. L., Diplomatic History
DREYFUS, L., Music
FREEDMAN, L. D., War Studies
GANZ, D., Palaeography
GARNETT, J., Defence Studies
GAUNT, S. B., French Language and Literature
GILLIES, D. A., Philosophy of Science and Mathematics
GRIFFITHS, R. M., French Studies
HAMNETT, C., Human Geography
HEATH, M. J., French Literature
HELM, P., Theology and Religious Studies
HERRIN, J. E., Late Antique and Byzantine Studies
HOGGART, K., Geography
HOOK, D., Spanish Medieval Studies
IFE, B. W., Spanish and Spanish-American Studies
JORDANOVA, L., Modern History
KARSH, E., Mediterranean Studies
KNIBB, M. A., Old Testament Studies
LAPPIN, S., Linguistics
LIEU, J., New Testament Studies
MCCABE, M. M. A., Ancient Philosophy
MACEDO, H. M., Portuguese and Brazilian Studies
MACHOVER, M., Philosophy
MAYER, R. G. M., Classics
NELSON, J. L., Medieval History
NEWITT, M. D. D., History
NEWSON, L. A., Geography
NOKES, D. L., English Literature
ORMOND, L., Victorian Studies
OVERY, R. J., Modern History
PAPINEAU, D. C., Philosophy
PORTER, A. N., History
PROUDFOOT, G. R., English
ROBERTS, J. A., English Language and Medieval Literature
ROSEVEARE, H. G., History
RUSSELL, C. S. R., History
SABIN, P. A. G., Strategic Studies
SAINSBURY, R. M., Philosophy
SAVILE, A. B., Philosophy
SCHIESARO, A., Latin Language and Literature
SILK, M. S., Latin Language and Literature
SORABJI, R. R. K., Philosophy
STOKES, J., English Literature
THORNES, J. B., Geography
WAYWELL, G. B., Classics
WHITE, J. J., German

School of Law (Strand, London WC2R 2LS; tel. (20) 7836-5454; e-mail gen.genlaw@kcl.ac.uk):

BLACKBURN, R., Law
EECKHOUT, P. O. V., Law
EWING, K. D., Law
GEARTY, C. A., Human Rights Law
GLOVER, J. C. B., Ethics (Dir)
GUEST, A. G., Law
HAYTON, D. J., Law
LOMNICKA, E. Z., Law
MARTIN, J. E., Law
MORSE, C. G., Law

MULLERSON, R., Int. Law
NORRIE, A. W., Criminal Law and Criminal Justice
PHILLIPS, J. C., Law
WHISH, R., Law

Guy's, King's and St Thomas' School of Medicine (1st Fl., Hodgkin Bldg, London SE1 9RT; tel. (20) 7848-6971; fax (20) 7848-6969):

ADAM, A., Interventional Radiology
ADAMS, A. P., Anaesthetics
AMIEL, S., Diabetic Medicine
BANATVALA, J. E., Clinical Virology
BATES, G. P., Nuerogenetics
BENJAMIN, I., Surgery
BOURAS, N., Psychiatry of Learning Difficulties
BRAUDE, P. R., Obstetrics and Gynaecology
BURNAND, K. G., Vascular Surgery
BURNEY, P. G. J., Public Health Medicine
COLLINS, W. P., Obstetrics and Gynaecology
CRAIG, T. K., Community Psychiatry
DAVID, A., Cognitive Neuropsychiatry
DAVIS, H. M., Child Health Psychology
DOHERTY, P., Cell Biology
EADY, R. A., Experimental Dermatopathology
EASTERBROOK, P. J., Medicine
EYKYN, S. J., Clinical Microbiology
FABRE, J., Clinical Sciences
FARZANEH, F., Molecular Medicine
FENTIMAN, I. S., Surgical Oncology
FOGELMAN, I., Nuclear Medicine
FORSLING, M. L., Neuroendocrinology
FRENCH, G. L., Medical Microbiology
GARETY, P. A., Clinical Psychology
GIANNELLI, F. B., Molecular Genetics
GLEESON, M. J., Otolaryngology
GREAVES, M. W., Dermatology
GREENOUGH, A., Clinical Respiratory Physiology
HART, I. R., Cancer Research
HAWK, J. L. M., Dermatological Photobiology
HAWKES, D. J., Computational Imaging
HAY, R. J., Cutaneous Medicine
HAYCOCK, G. B., Paediatrics
HAYDAY, A. C., Immunobiology
HEATLEY, F. W., Orthopaedic Surgery
HENDRY, B., Renal Medicine
HIGGINSON, I., Palliative Care
HIGGS, R., General Practice
HUGHES, R. A. C., Neurology
JACKSON, S., Clinical Gerontology
JONES, R. H., General Practice
KALRA, L., Stroke Medicine
KEMENY, D. M., Immunology
KOPELMAN, M. D., Neuropsychiatry
LEE, T. H., Allergy and Respiratory Medicine
LEHNER, T., Basic and Applied Immunology
LOWY, C., Endocrinology
LUCAS, S. B., Clinical Histopathology
MACDONALD, A. J. D., Old-Age Psychiatry
McGREGOR, A., Medicine
MAISEY, M. N., Radiological Sciences
MARTEAU, T. M., Health Psychology
MATHEW, C. G. P., Molecular Genetics
MILLS, K. R., Clinical Neurophysiology
MILNER, A. D., Neonatology
MUFTI, G., Haematological Oncology
NICOLAIDES, K., Obstetrics and Gynaecology
PANAYI, G. S., Rheumatology
PEARSON, T. C., Haematology
PETERS, T. J., Clinical Biochemistry
POLKEY, C., Neurosurgery of Epilepsy
POSTON, L., Foetal Health
RAMIREZ, A. J., Liaison Psychiatry
RICHARDS, M. A., Palliative Medicine
ROBERTS, V. C., Clinical Prof.
ROBINSON, R. O., Paediatric Neurology
ROSS, E., Community Paediatrics
RUBENS, R. D., Clinical Oncology

SACKS, S. H., Nephrology
SAVIDGE, G. F., Coagulation Medicine
SCOTT, D. L., Clinical Rheumatology
SELLER, M. J., Developmental Genetics
SHEPHERD, G. W., Mental Health Rehabilitation
SIMONOFF, E. A., Child and Adolescent Psychiatry
SOLOMON, E., Human Genetics
SONKSEN, P. H., Endocrinology
SWAMINATHAN, R., Clinical Biochemistry
SWIFT, C., Health Care of the Elderly
TYNAN, M. J., Paediatric Cardiology
VIBERTI, G., Diabetes and Metabolic Medicine
WATSON, J. P., Psychiatry
WEINMAN, J. A., Psychology Applied to Medicine
WESSELEY, S., Liaison Psychiatry
WILLIAMS, D. G., Medicine

Florence Nightingale School of Nursing and Midwifery (James Clerk Maxwell Bldg, 57 Waterloo Rd, London, SE1 8WA; tel. (20) 7848-4698; e-mail nightingale@kcl.ac.uk; internet www.kcl.ac.uk/nursing):

COWLEY, S.
FRANCK, L.
HUMPHREY, C.
NORMAN, I.
RICHARDSON, A.
SANDALL, J.
WHILE, A.

School of Physical and Engineering Sciences (Strand, London WC2R 2LS; tel. (20) 7848-2267; fax (20) 7848-2766; e-mail pse .schooloffice@kcl.ac.uk):

AGHVAMI, A. H., Telecommunications Eng.
BUSHNELL, C. J., Mathematics
CLARKSON, T. G., Electrical Eng.
COLLINS, A. T., Physics
DAVIES, A. C., Electrical Eng.
DAVIES, E. B., Mathematics
DAVIES, G., Physics
GABBAY, D. M., Logic
GAUNT, D. S., Physics
GIBSON, S. E., Chemistry
GOSPEL, H. F., Management
HALL, T. J., Optoelectronics
HEATH, C. C., Work and Orgs
HIBBERT, F., Chemistry
HOLWILL, M. E. J., Biological Physics
HOWE, P. S., Applied Mathematics
HUGHES, M. N., Chemistry
LAUGHLIN, R., Physical and Eng. Sciences
PIKE, E. R., Physical and Eng. Sciences
PRESSLEY, A. N., Mathematics
ROBB, M. A., Chemistry
ROBINSON, D. C., Mathematics
ROGERS, A. J., Electrical Eng.
SAFAROV, Y., Mathematics
SANDLER, M. B., Signal Processing
SARKAR, S., Theoretical Physics
SAUNDERS, P. T., Mathematics
STREATER, R. F., Mathematics
SWANSON, J. G., Electrical Eng.
TURNER, C. W., Electrical Eng.
UFF, J., Eng. Law
WEST, P. C., Mathematics
WINDER, R., Computer Science
YIANNESKIS, M., Fluid Mechanics

Institute of Psychiatry (De Crespigny Park, London, SE5 8AF; tel. (20) 7836-5454; e-mail spjgams@iop.kcl.ac.uk; internet www.iop.kcl .ac.uk):

ANDERTON, B. H., Neuroscience
BANERJEE, S. S., Mental Health and Ageing
BARKER, G. J., Magnetic Resonance Physics
BOLTON, D., Philosophy and Psychopathology
CHALDER, T., Psychological Medicine
CRAIG, T. K. J., Psychological Medicine
GOODMAN, R., Child and Adolescent Psychiatry
HEMSLEY, D. R., Psychology

HOTOPF, M., General Hospital Psychiatry
HUXLEY, P. J., Social Work
JONES, E., History of Medicine and Psychiatry
KNAPP, M. R. J., Health Economics
MACDONALD, A. J. D., Psychological Medicine
McGUFFIN, P., Social, Genetic and Developmental Psychiatry
MORRIS, R. G., Neuropsychology
SALKOVSKIS, P. M., Psychology
STOLERMAN, I., Behavioural Pharmacology
STRANG, J., Addiction Research
WESSELY, S., Epidemiological and Liaison Psychiatry

ATTACHED CENTRE

Centre for Defence Studies: King's College London, Strand, London, WC2R 2LS; tel. (20) 7848-2338; fax (20) 7848-2748; e-mail cds@kcl.ac.uk; internet www.kcl.ac .uk/depsta/rel/cds; f. 1990; Dir Prof. MICHAEL CLARKE; publ. *Conflict, Security and Development* (3 a year).

London Business School

Regent's Park, London, NW1 4SA

Telephone: (20) 7262-5050

Fax: (20) 7724-7875

Internet: www.london.edu

Founded 1965

Academic year: October to July

Dean: LAURA D'ANDREA TYSON

Number of teachers: 100

Number of students: 1,150 (postgraduate)

PROFESSORS

BARWISE, P., Management and Marketing
BUNN, D. W., Decision Science
CONGER, J., Organizational Behaviour
COOPER, I. A., Finance
DEGRAVE, Z., Decision Sciences
DENHAAN, W. J., Econ.
DIMSON, E., Finance
DOW, J., Finance
DUTTA, S., Marketing
EARL, M. J., Information Management
EARLEY, P. C., Organizational Behaviour
ESTRIN, S., Econ.
FRANKS, J. R., Finance
GEROSKI, P. A., Econ.
GHOSHAL, S., Strategic Leadership
GOFFEE, R. E., Organizational Behaviour
MARKIDES, C., Strategic and Int. Management
MARSH, P. R., Finance
NICHOLSON, A., Operations Management
NICHOLSON, N., Organizational Behaviour
PORTES, R., Econ.
PUTSIS, W., Marketing
SCHAEFER, S. M., Finance
SERVAES, H., Finance
TALMOR, E., Accounting
TYSON, L., Econ.
UPPAL, R., Finance
VILCASSIM, N., Marketing
VOSS, C., Total Quality Management
WAVERMAN, L., Econ.
YIP, G., Strategic and Int. Management

London School of Economics and Political Science

Houghton St, London, WC2A 2AE

Telephone: (20) 7405-7686

Fax: (20) 7955-6001

E-mail: stu.rec@lse.ac.uk

Internet: www.lse.ac.uk

Founded 1895

Academic year: October to July

Dir: Sir HOWARD DAVIES

Deputy Dirs: Prof. JUDITH REES, Dr RAY RICHARDSON, Prof. HENRIETTA MOORE

Sec. (vacant)

Library: see Libraries and Archives

Number of teachers: 430 (full-time)

Number of students: 8,467 (7,611 full-time, 856 part-time)

Publications: *Economica* (quarterly journal of econ., economic history and statistics), *The British Journal of Sociology* (quarterly), *British Journal of Industrial Relations* (quarterly), *Journal of Transport Economics and Policy* (3 a year), *The International Bibliography of the Social Sciences* (4 volumes published once a year), *Government and Opposition* (quarterly), *Population Studies* (3 a year), *Journal of Political Studies* (quarterly)

PROFESSORS

ALPERN, S. R., Mathematics
ANDERSON, R. W., Accounting and Finance
ANGELL, I. O., Information Systems
BALDWIN, R., Law
BALFOUR, S., Govt
BARKER, E. V., Sociology
BARKER, R. S., Govt
BARR, N. A., European Institute
BEAN, C. R., Econ./CEP
BESLEY, T. J., Econ.
BHATTACHARYA, S., Accounting and Finance
BIGGS, N. L., Mathematics
BLOCH, M. E. F., Anthropology
BRIGHTWELL, G. R., Mathematics
BROMWICH, M., Accounting and Finance
BROWN, C. J., Int. Relations
BUZAN, B. G., Int. Relations
CARTWRIGHT, N. L. D., Philosophy
CHANT, S. H., Geography and Environment
CHARVET, J. C. R., Govt
CHESHIRE, P. C., Geography and Environment
CHINKIN, C. M., Law
CIBORRA, C., Information Systems
COHEN, S., Sociology
COLEMAN, J., Govt
COLLEY, L. J., European Institute
COLLINS, H. G., Law
CONNOR, G., Accounting and Finance
CORBRIDGE, S. E., Geography and Environment
COWELL, F. A., Econ.
COX, M., Int. Relations
CRAFTS, N. F. R., Economic History/CEP
DAVIES, P. L., Law
DESAI, LORD, Econ.
DOWDING, K. M., Govt
DOWNES, D. M., Social Policy
DUNLEAVY, P., Govt
DYSON, T. P., Population Studies
EPSTEIN, S. R., Economic History
FEATHERSTONE, K., European Institute
FELLI, L., Econ.
FREEMAN, R. B., CEP
FULLER, C. J., Anthropology
GALLIERS, R., Information Systems
GASKELL, G. D., Social Psychology
GEARTY, C. A., Sociology
GORDON, I. R., Geography and Environment
GRAY, J. N., Govt
GREENWOOD, C. J., Law
HALLIDAY, F., Int. Relations
HARDMAN MOORE, J., Econ.
HARRISS, J. C., Devt Studies Institute
HARTLEY, T. C., Law
HELD, D., Govt
HEMMER, T., Accounting and Finance
HIDALGO, F. J., Econ.
HILL, C. J., Int. Relations
HILLS, J. R., STICERD
HOBCRAFT, J. N., Population Studies, Social Policy
HOWSON, C., Philosophy
HUMPHREY, N. K., Centre for Philosophy of Natural and Social Science
HUMPHREY, P. C., Social Psychology
HUTTER, B. M., Centre for Analysis of Risk and Regulation

HYMAN, R., Industrial Relations
JACKMAN, R. A., Econ.
JOHNSON, P. A., Economic History
JONES, D. K. C., Geography and Environment
JONES, G. W., Govt
KALDOR, M. H., Centre for the Study of Global Governance
KELLY, J. E., Industrial Relations
KIERNAN, K. E., Social Policy
KIYOTAKI, N., Econ.
KNAPP, M. R. J., Social Policy
KNOX, M. B., Int. History
LACEY, N. M., Law
LAYARD, P. R. G., Econ./CEP
LE GRAND, J., Social Policy
LIEVEN, D. C. B., Govt
LIGHT, M. M., Int. Relations
LINTON, O., Econ.
LIVINGSTONE, S. M., Social Psychology
LOUGHLIN, M., Law
McGUIRE, A. J., Social Policy
MACVE, R. H., Accounting and Finance
MANNING, A. P., Econ.
MANSELL, R. E., Sociology
MARSDEN, D. W., Industrial Relations
METCALF, D. H., Industrial Relations/CEP
MILLER, P. B., Accounting and Finance
MOORE, H. L., Anthropology
MORGAN, M. S., Economic History
MOUZELIS, N. P., Sociology
MURPHY, M. J., Population Studies
MURPHY, T., Law
NEWBURN, W. H. T., Social Policy
NICKELL, S. J., Econ.
NORBERG, R., Statistics
O'LEARY, B., Govt
PAGE, E. C., Govt
PARRY, J. P., Anthropology
PHILIP, G. D. E., Govt
PHILLIPS, A. M., Gender Institute
PIACHAUD, D. F. J., Social Policy
PICCIONE, M., Econ.
PISCHKE, J. S., Econ.
PISSARIDES, C. A., Econ.
POWER, A. E., Social Policy
POWER, M. K., Accounting and Finance
PRESTON, P., Int. History
QUAH, D., Econ.
RAWLINGS, R., Law
REES, J. A., Geography and Environment
REINER, R., Law
REYNIERS, D. J., Interdisciplinary Institute of Management
ROBERTS, S. A., Law
ROBINSON, P. M., Econ.
ROCK, P. E., Sociology
RODRIGUEZ-SALGADO, M., Int. History
ROSE, N. S., Sociology
ROSENHEAD, J. V., Operational Research
RYDIN, Y. J., Geography and Environment
SAITH, A., Devt Studies Institute
SASSEN, S., Geography and Environment
SENNETT, R., Sociology
SHIN, H. S., Accounting and Finance
SMITH, A. D. S., Govt
STERN, N. H., Econ.
STEVENSON, D., Int. History
SUTTON, J., Econ.
TAYLOR, P. G., Int. Relations
TEUBNER, G., Law
TIMMERMANN, A. G., Accounting and Finance
TONG, H., Statistics
VENABLES, A. J., Econ.
WADE, R., Devt Studies Institute
WALLACE, W., Int. Relations
WEBB, D. C., Accounting and Finance
WHITEHEAD, C. M. E., Econ.
WILLIAMS, H. P., Operational Research
WORRALL, J., Philosophy
YAHUDA, M. B., Int. Relations
YAO, Q., Statistics

ATTACHED INSTITUTES

Asia Research Centre: f. 1997; conducts social science research on Asia; Dir Dr C. HUGHES.

BIOS: f. 2003; Dir Prof. NIKOLAS ROSE.

Business History Unit: f. 1978 jointly with Imperial College London to promote research into business history, including technological aspects; Dir Dr T. GOURVISH.

Centre for Analysis of Risk and Regulations: f. 2000; Dirs Prof. B. HUTTER, Prof. M. POWER.

Centre for Analysis of Social Exclusion: f. 1997; Dir Prof. J. HILLS.

Centre for Civil Society: f. 1999 to conduct research on problems and issues in the management of voluntary agencies and NGOs; Dir Prof. J. HOWELL.

Centre for Discrete and Applicable Mathematics: f. 1995 to raise the profile of mathematics in the social sciences; Dir Prof. N. BIGGS.

Centre for Economic Performance: f. 1990 to conduct interdisciplinary research on economic performance, focusing particularly on the performance of firms; Dirs Prof. J. VAN REENEN, Prof. RICHARD FREEMAN.

Centre for Educational Research: f. 1990 to carry out research into current educational topics including choice of schools, schools' admissions, the Nat. Curriculum, the funding of education, and European and int. issues; Dir Dr A. WEST.

Centre for International Studies: f. 1967 to promote research in all aspects of international studies; Chair. of Steering Committee Dr JOHN KENT.

Centre for Philosophy of Natural and Social Science: f. 1990 to promote the study of philosophical and methodological issues; Dir Dr CARL HOEFER.

Centre for Research into Economics and Finance in Southern Africa: f. 1990; undertakes research into the management of int. finance, foreign-exchange policy and domestic financial policy in South Africa, and macroeconomic and financial issues in the southern African region; Dir Dr J. LEAPE.

Centre for the Analysis of Time Series: f. 2000, Dir Dr LEONARD SMITH.

Centre for the Economics of Education: f. 2000; Dir Prof. S. MACHIN.

Centre for the Study of Global Governance: f. 1992 to investigate the origin and nature of urgent problems amenable to a multinational co-operative solution and to promote debate and propose solutions; Dir Prof. Lord DESAI.

Centre for the Study of Human Rights: f. 1998; Dir Prof. C. GEARTY.

Cities Programme: f. 1996; undertakes design-based teaching and research on the social, technical and economic aspects of cities and urban systems; Dir R. BURDETT.

Computer Security Research Centre: f. 1991 to study computer security issues from organizational, management, social and technical perspectives; Dir Dr J. BACKHOUSE.

Development Studies Institute: f. 1990; a multi-disciplinary centre for teaching economic research and devt studies, covering problems from around the globe, of the third world and Eastern Europe; Head Prof. JOHN HARRISS.

European Institute: f. 1991 to co-ordinate and develop research and research training on European issues; Dir Prof. PAUL TAYLOR.

Financial Markets Group: f. 1987 to undertake first rate basic research into the nature and operation of financial markets; Dir Prof. D. WEBB.

Greater London Group: f. 1958 to undertake research and publication on the govt and economy of Greater London and the South-East Region; consists of academic teachers of the School with a small professional research staff; Chair. Prof. G. W. JONES; Dir TONY TRAVERS.

Interdisciplinary Institute of Management: f. 1990; concerned with promoting interdisciplinary research into management; research is closely linked with the Centre for Economic Performance; Dir Prof. DIANE REYNIERS.

LSE Gender Institute: f. 1993; a multidisciplinary centre established to address the major intellectual challenges posed by contemporary changes in gender relations; Dir Prof. ANNE PHILLIPS.

LSE Health and Social Care: f. 2000; undertakes research, consultancy and training in int. comparative health policy; co-ordinates the European Health Policy Research Network; Dirs Dr E. MOSSIALOS, Prof. MARTIN KNAPP.

LSE Housing: f. 1989; a centre for research, devt and consultancy work in the areas of housing policy and management; residents' consultation and involvement, tenant involvement, inner-city problems, difficult estates; European housing issues; Co-ordinator Dr ANNE POWER.

LSE London: f. 1998 to study the economic and social issues of the London region, as well as the problems and potential of other urban and metropolitan regions; Dir Prof. I. GORDON.

Mannheim Centre of Criminology and Criminal Justice: f. 1990 to co-ordinate research in the field of criminology and criminal justice; Dir Prof. DAVID DOWNES.

Media@lse: f. 2000; Dir Prof. R. SILVERSTONE.

Methodology Institute: established at LSE in 1991 jtly with external research bodies, to research methodological aspects of social surveys; Dir Prof. G. GASKELL.

Population Investigation Committee: f. 1936 to promote and undertake research into population questions and to promote the study of demography in both its quantitative and qualitative aspects; Chair. Prof. J. HOBCRAFT.

Public Policy Group: f. 1998; Chair Prof. PATRICK DUNLEAVY.

Simulating Social Policy in an Ageing Society (SAGE): f. 1999; Co-Dir Prof. P. JOHNSON.

Suntory and Toyota International Centres for Economics and Related Disciplines: f. 1978 to promote research into applied economics and related fields; incl. Centre for the Analysis of Social Exclusion; Dir Prof. TIMOTHY BESLEY.

London School of Hygiene and Tropical Medicine

Keppel St, London, WC1E 7HT

Telephone: (20) 7636-8636
Fax: (20) 7436-5389
E-mail: registry@lshtm.ac.uk
Internet: www.lshtm.ac.uk

Founded 1899
Academic year: September to September

Dir: Prof. Sir ANDREW HAINES
Sec. and Registrar: WENDY SURRIDGE

Library: see Libraries
Number of teachers: 432 (incl. research staff)
Number of students: 1,800

Publications: *Health Policy and Planning, Journal of Tropical Medicine and Hygiene*

Depts of Epidemiology and population health, Infectious and tropical diseases, Public health and policy

PROFESSORS
ACKERS, J., Postgraduate Education in Public Health
BERRIDGE, V., History
BLACK, N. A., Health Services Research
CAIRNCROSS, A. M., Environmental Health
CAIRNS, J., Health Econ.
CLELAND, J., Medical Demography
COLEMAN, M. P., Epidemiology and Vital Statistics
COUSENS, S. N., Epidemiology and Medical Statistics
CROFT, S. L., Parasitology
CURTIS, C., Medical Entomology
DOCKRELL, H., Immunology
DOWIE, J., Health Impact Analysis
ELBOURNE, D., Health Care Evaluation
FINE, P. E. M., Communicable Disease Epidemiology
FLETCHER, A., Epidemiology and Ageing
FOSTER, A., Int. Eye Health
GREENWOOD, B. M., Communicable Diseases
GRUNDY, E., Demographic Gerontology
HALL, A. J., Infectious Disease Epidemiology
HAYES, R. J., Epidemiology and Int. Health
HILL, A. A., Community Nutrition
KAYE, P. M., Cellular Immunology
KELLY, J. M., Molecular Biology
KENWARD, M. G., Biostatistics
KIRKWOOD, B. R., Epidemiology and Int. Health
LEON, D., Epidemiology
MABEY, D., Communicable Diseases
MCADAM, K. P. W., Clinical Tropical Medicine
MCKEE, C. M., European Public Health
MILES, M. A., Medical Protozoology
MILLS, A. J., Health Econ. and Policy
MULHOLLAND, K., Infectious Disease Epidemiology
NOAH, N. D., Public Health
PETO, J., Cancer Epidemiology
POCOCK, S. J., Medical Statistics
PRENTICE, A., Int. Nutrition
RILEY, E. M., Infectious Disease Immunology
ROBERTS, I., Epidemiology and Public Health
RODRIGUES, L., Infectious Disease Epidemiology
ROY, P., Virology
SMITH, P. G., Tropical Epidemiology
TAYLOR, M. G., Medical Helminthology
WALT, G., Int. Health Policy
WELLINGS, K., Sexual and Reproductive Health
WHITWORTH, J. A., Int. Public Health
WREN, B. W., Microbial Pathogenesis
UAUY, R., Public Health Nutrition

Queen Mary, University of London

Mile End Rd, London, E1 4NS

Telephone: (20) 7882-5555
Fax: (20) 7882-5500
E-mail: international-office@qmul.ac.uk
Internet: www.qmul.ac.uk

Founded 1989 as Queen Mary and Westfield College, following merger of Queen Mary College (f. 1934) and Westfield College (f. 1882); present name 2000
Academic year: September to June

Principal: Prof. ADRIAN SMITH
Vice-Principal for Academic Planning and Devt: A. D. OLVER
Vice-Principal for Humanities and Law: P. OGDEN
Vice-Principal for Science and Eng.: M. A. H. MACCALLUM

Library: see Libraries and Archives
Number of teachers: 1,000
Number of students: 9,000

DEANS
Faculty of Arts: Dr C. COOK

Faculty of Eng. and Mathematical Sciences: Prof. I. WILLIAMS
Faculty of Law and Social Sciences: Dr M. GRAY
Faculty of Natural Sciences: Prof. J. DUCKETT
Barts and the London School of Medicine and Dentistry: Prof. NICHOLAS WRIGHT (Warden)

PROFESSORS
Faculty of Arts:
BARRETT, M., English
CHESHIRE, J. L., Linguistics
COOLE, D., Political Studies
DEYERMOND, A. D., Spanish
DUNKERLEY, J. C., Political Studies
EVANS, P. W., Hispanic Studies
HAMILTON, P. W. A., English
HENNESSY, P. J., Contemporary History
HOBSON JEANNERET, M. E., French Language and Literature
JACKSON, J., History
JANOWITZ, A., English
JARDINE, L. A., English and Drama
KAY, S., Medieval Studies
MILLER, J. L., History
MORIARTY, M. M., French Literature and Thought
OLSCHNER, L. M., German
PARSONS, D. W., Public Policy
PENNY, R. J., Romance Philology
RAMSDEN, J. A., Modern History
RANAWAKE, S. A., German
RAYFIELD, D., Russian
REES, G. C., English
ROSE, J., English
RUBIN, M., History
SASSOON, D., History
SHIACH, M., Cultural History
TERRY, A. H., Catalan
VAREY, J. E., Hispanic Studies and Italian
WHITFORD, M. L., Modern French Thought
WOOTTON, D., History
YOUNG, K., Political Studies

Faculty of Engineering and Mathematical Sciences:
ALIABADI, M. H., Eng.
ANDREWS, E. H., Materials
ARROWSMITH, D. K., Mathematics
ASHBY, D., Mathematics
BADER, D. L., Eng.
BAILEY, R. A., Statistics
BULLET, S. R., Mathematics
CAMERON, P. J., Mathematics
CARR, B. J., Mathematics and Astronomy
CLARRICOATS, P., Electrical Eng.
CROOKES, R., Combustion Eng.
CUTHBERT, L. G., Electronic Eng.
DAVIES, K. L., Materials
DONKIN, S., Pure Mathematics
DRIKAKIS, D., Eng.
EDIRISINGHE, M., Materials
EVANS, J., Materials
GASTER, M., Experimental Aerodynamics
GOLDSHEID, I., Probability Theory
GUO, Z. X., Materials
HODGES, W. A., Mathematics
HOGG, P., Materials
LAUGHTON, M. A., Electrical and Electronic Eng.
LAWN, C. J., Thermo-Fluids Eng.
LEEDHAM-GREEN, C. R., Pure Mathematics
LESCHZINER, M. A., Eng.
LINDSAY, P., Electrical Eng.
MACCALLUM, M. A. H., Applied Mathematics
MURRAY, C. D., Mathematics and Astronomy
O'HEARN, P., Computer Science
OLVER, A. D., Electrical and Electronic Eng.
PAKER, Y., Parallel Computing
PAPALOIZOU, J. C. B., Mathematics and Astronomy
PARINI, C., Antenna Eng.

ROBINSON, E., Computer Science
ROSE, J. W., Mechanical Eng.
ROXBURGH, I. W., Mathematics and Astronomy
SCHWARTZ, S. J., Space Plasma Physics
STARK, J. P. W., Aeronautical Eng.
TANNER, K., Materials
WEHRFRITZ, B. A. F., Pure Mathematics
WILLIAMS, I. P., Mathematics and Astronomy

Faculty of Law and Social Sciences:

ADAMS, J., Property Law
ATKINSON, B. W., Geography
BAILLIE, R. T., Econ.
BLAKENEY, M., Intellectual Property Law
COTTERRELL, R. B. M., Legal Theory
CURTIS, S., Geography
FITZPATRICK, P., Law
FLETCHER, I. F., Commercial Law
GHIGLINO, C., Econ.
HASKEL, J., Econ.
LAHORE, J. C., Intellectual Property Law
LEE, R., Geography
McCONVILLE, S. D. M., Criminal Justice
NORTON, J. J., Banking Law
O'DONOVAN, K., Law
OGDEN, P. E., Geography
REED, C., Electronic Commerce Law
RICHARDSON, G. M., Public Law
SMITH, D. M., Geography
SORGER, G., Econ.
SPENCE, N. A., Human Geography
THOMAS, G., Equity and Property Law
TZAVALIS, E., Econ.
VAN BUEREN, G., Int. Human Rights Law
YELLAND, J. L., Law

Faculty of Natural Sciences:

ADE, P. A. R., Experimental Astrophysics
AYLETT, B. J., Chemistry
BONNETT, R., Research Chemistry
BRADLEY, D. C., Chemistry
BUGG, D. V., Nuclear Physics
CARTER, A. A., Particle Physics
CHARAP, J. M., Theoretical Physics
CLEGG, P. E., Astrophysics
COVNEY, P. V., Physical Chemistry
DUCKETT, J. G., Botany
DUNSTAN, D. J., Experimental Physics
EDGINGTON, J. A., Physics
EMERSON, J., Physics
GRIFFITHS, D. V., Organic Chemistry
HILDREW, A. G., Ecology
KALMUS, P., Physics
LICHTENSTEIN, C. P., Molecular Biology
MARTIN, D., Physics
PERCIVAL, I. C., Physics
PYE, J. D., Biological Sciences
RANDALL, E. W., Research Chemistry
SEWELL, G., Physics
SULLIVAN, A., Inorganic Chemistry
THOMPSON, G., Physics
THORPE, A., Biology
UTLEY, J. H. P., Organic Chemistry
VLCEK, A., Inorganic Chemistry
WARREN, M. J., Biological Sciences
WHITE, G. J., Physics and Astronomy
WILSON, E. G., Physics

Barts and the London School of Medicine and Dentistry (Turner St, London, E1 2AD; tel. (20) 7377-7611; fax (20) 7377-7612; e-mail medicaladmissions@qmul.ac.uk; internet www.mds.qmul.ac.uk):

ANSEAU, M. R., Institute of Dentistry
ARMSTRONG, P., Haematology, Oncology and Imaging
ARMSTRONG-JAMES, M. A., Biomedical Sciences
ASHBY, D., Wolfson Institute of Preventive Medicine
BENJAMIN, N., Pharmacology
BERRY, C. L., Molecular Pathology, Infection and Immunity
BESSER, G. M., Metabolism
BRADLEY, P. F., Institute of Dentistry

BRITTON, K. E., Haematology, Oncology and Imaging
BROCKLEHURST, K., Biomedical Sciences
BURRIN, J., Metabolism
CARTER, Y. H., Community Sciences
CHARD, T., Haematology, Oncology and Imaging
CLARK, A. J. L., Metabolism
COHEN, R. D., Metabolism
COID, J. W., Community Sciences
COSTELOE, K., Metabolism
CURTIS, M., Oral Microbiology
DAVIES, R. J., Molecular Pathology, Infection and Immunity
DOYAL, L., Metabolism
ELLIOTT, J. C., Institute of Dentistry
FELDMAN, R. A., Surgery, Clinical Neuroscience and Intensive Care
FLOWER, R. J., Pharmacology
GALTON, D., Metabolism
GOODE, A. W., Surgery, Clinical Neuroscience and Intensive Care
GOWLAND, G., Pharmacology
GROSSMAN, A., Metabolism
GRUDZINSKAS, J. G., Community Sciences
HAJEK, P., Clinical Psychology
HARDIE, J. M., Institute of Dentistry
HAJ, M., Metabolism
HEATH, M., Institute of Dentistry
HILLIER, S. M., Community Sciences
HITMAN, G. A., Metabolism
HUGHES, F., Periodontology
ILES, R. A., Metabolism
JACOBS, I., Gynaecological Oncology
JEFFRIES, R. A., Molecular Pathology, Infection and Immunity
KOPELMAN, P. G., Metabolism
KUMAR, P., Clinical Medical Education
LEIGH, I. M., Haematology, Oncology and Imaging
LESLIE, R. D. G., Metabolism
LILLEYMAN, J. S., Metabolism
LISTER, T. A., Haematology, Oncology and Imaging
LOWE, D. G., Molecular Pathology, Infection and Immunity
LUMLEY, J. S., Surgery, Clinical Neurosurgery and Intensive Care
MACDONALD, T. T., Metabolism
MARTIN, J. E., Molecular Pathology, Infection and Immunity
MILLER, G., Epidemiology
MILLER, N. E., Metabolism
MONSON, J., Clinical Endocrinology
NEWLAND, A. C., Haematology, Oncology and Imaging
OLIVER, R. T. D., Haematology, Oncology and Imaging
OXFORD, J., Molecular Pathology, Infection and Immunity
PERRETT, D., Metabolism
PHILLIPS, I. R., Biomedical Sciences
PINCHING, A. J., Molecular Pathology, Infection and Immunity
PRICE, C. P., Metabolism
PRIEBE, S., Community Sciences
PRIESTLEY, J. V., Biomedical Sciences
REES, L. H., Metabolism
REZNEK, R., Haematology, Oncology and Imaging
SANDERSON, I. R., Metabolism
SAVAGE, M., Metabolism
STRUNIN, L., Surgery, Clinical Neuroscience and Intensive Care
SUGDEN, M. C., Biomedical Sciences
SWAIN, C., Gastrointestinal Endoscopy
SWASH, M., Surgery, Clinical Neuroscience and Intensive Care
TABAQCHALI, S., Molecular Pathology, Infection and Immunity
THIEMERMANN, C., Pharmacology
TOMLINSON, D. R., Biomedical Sciences
TROTT, K. R., Haematology, Oncology and Imaging
VINSON, G. P., Biomedical Sciences

WALD, N. J., Wolfson Institute of Preventive Medicine
WHITTLE, B. J., Pharmacology
WILLIAMS, D. M., Institute of Dentistry
WILLIAMS, N. S., Surgery, Clinical Neuroscience and Intensive Care
WILLOUGHBY, D. A., Pharmacology
WINGATE, D. L., Metabolism

ATTACHED CENTRES

Astronomy Unit: nat. centre conducting research in most areas of astronomy; the UK Cluster Science Centre is located in the Unit.

Bone and Joint Research Unit: f. 1975.

Centre for Commercial Law Studies: f. 1980; serves as focus for advanced teaching and research in commercial and business law.

Centre for Medieval and Renaissance Studies: interdisciplinary modular taught courses in Medieval and Renaissance Studies, leading to MA.

Centre for Modern European Studies: administers MA in European Languages, Literatures and Thought and holds regular colloquia and research seminars.

Centre for Oral Bio-metrics: f. 2000; oral health and disease.

Centre for the Study of Migration: f. 1994 as focal point for those engaged in the study of migration locally, nationally and internationally.

Computer Related Crime Research Centre: f. 1996.

Environmental Science Unit: an interdisciplinary teaching and research unit that co-ordinates and administers Environmental Science teaching (BSc) within the College.

Genome Centre: f. 2001; facilitates projects within the college that require high throughput DNA sequencing, linkage and association analysis, mutation and polymorphism screening and DNA expression analysis along with crucial bioinformatic support.

Health and Health Care Research Centre: f. 1985; links researchers in several disciplines working on health service research, incl. assessment of local need for health care, health and service utilization of particular population groups, and health policy evaluation procedures.

Institute of Community Health Sciences: f. 2001; complementary research in social geography, econ. and health policy.

Interdisciplinary Research Centre in Biomedical Materials: f. 1991; funded by EPSRC as nat. centre; innovation of analogue biomaterials for tissue and joint replacement; second generation implants and prostheses for medical and dental applications; offers PhD, MD and MS degrees.

Mathematics Research Centre: f. 1997.

Public Policy Research Unit: f. 1988 as vehicle for research grants and contracts and policy discussion within the Dept of Political Studies; oversees the MSc degree in Policy Studies.

William Harvey Research Institute: f. 1989.

Wolfson Institute of Preventive Medicine: f. 1991.

Royal Academy of Music

Marylebone Rd, London, NW1 5HT

Telephone: (20) 7873-7373
Fax: (20) 7873-7374
E-mail: go@ram.ac.uk
Internet: www.ram.ac.uk

Founded 1822; inc. by Royal Charter 1830
State control

Pres.: HRH The Duchess of GLOUCESTER
Principal: CURTIS PRICE
Academic Registrar: PHILIP WHITE

Library of 125,000 vols, incl. colln of early
sheet music and MSS
Number of teachers: 155
Number of students: 600

Publication: *RAM Magazine* (2 a year).

Royal Holloway, University of London

Egham, Surrey, TW20 0EX

Telephone: (1784) 434455
Fax: (1784) 437520
E-mail: liaison-office@rhbnc.ac.uk
Internet: www.rhul.ac.uk

Founded 1985 by merger of Bedford College
(f. 1849) and Royal Holloway College (f.
1886)

Principal: Prof. STEPHEN HILL
Head of Registry: PHIL McGEEVOR
Librarian: SARAH E. GERRARD

Library of 520,000 vols
Number of teachers: 339
Number of students: 5,361

DEANS

Faculty of Arts: MÀIRE DAVIES
Faculty of History and Social Sciences: Prof.
JOANNE WRIGHT
Faculty of Science: Prof. MICHAEL GREEN
Graduate School: Dr KLAUS DODDS

PROFESSORS

Faculty of Arts:
ALSTON, R., Classics
ARMSTRONG, T. D., English Literature
BOEHMER, E. D., English
BOWIE, A., German
BRADBY, D. H., Drama and Theatre Studies
BRATTON, J. S., Theatre and Cultural
History
BRUZZI, S., Film Studies
CARROLL, J. F. M., Philosophy and German
CAVE, R. A., Drama and Theatre Studies
CHARLTON, D. P., Music
COOK, N. J., Music
DZELAINIS, M. M., Early Modern Literature
and Thought
ELLIS, J. C. P., Media Arts
EVERSON, J. E., Italian Literature
GARNETT, A., Media Arts
GIBSON, A. W., Modern Literature and
Theory
GOULD, W. L., English Literature
GUNDLE, S., Italian
HAMPSON, R. G., Modern Literature
HILL, W. J., Media Arts
HUGHES, E. J., Modern French Literature
HUGHES, J., German and Comparative
Literature
KAHANE, A., Classics
LEE SIX, A. E., Hispanic Studies
LONGERICH, P., German History
MERCK, A. J., Media Arts
MOTION, A., Creative Writing
O'BRIEN, J. P., French Renaissance Litera-
ture
PIKE, L., Music
POWELL, J. G. F., Classics
RINK, J., Music
ROBERTSON, E., French
RYAN, K. J. P., English Language and
Literature
SAMSON, J., Music
SCHAFER, E. J., Drama
TOSI, A., Italian Studies
VILAIN, R. L., German and Comparative
Literature
VILASECA, D., Spanish
WATHEY, A., Music History
WHITE, I. A., German

WILES, D., Theatre
WILLIAMS, J., French Literature and Film

Faculty of History and Social Sciences:
ANSARI, K. H., Islam and Culture
BARN, R., Health and Social Care
BARRON, C. M., History of London
BROADBENT, P. J., Management
CESARANI, D., History
CHAMPION, J. A. I., Early Modern Ideas
CLAEYS, G. R., History of Political Thought
CORFIELD, P. J., History
CROFT, J. P., Early Modern History
DENNEY, D., Applied Social Studies
DREWRY, G., Public Admin.
EDWARDS, J. R., Social Policy
FAULKNER, D. O., Management
FERLIE, E. B., Management
FRANK, J. L., Econ.
GRAHAM, H. E., History
HACKLEY, C. E., Marketing
HEYES, A., Econ.
LEE, R. M., Social Research Methods
MANDLER, M., Econ.
MATTEN, D., Management
McSWEENEY, L. B., Management
NEWELL, S. M., Management
NORMAN, H., Econ.
PILBEAM, P., Modern European History
ROBINSON, F. C. R., History of Southeast
Asia
ROSENBERG, D., Information and Commu-
nication Management
SAUL, N. E., Medieval History
SELZER, A., Econ.
SMITH, C. D., Organization Studies
SPAGAT, M., Economics
STONE, D., Modern History

Faculty of Science:
ANDREWS, B. D., Abnormal Psychology
BLACKBURN, S., Mathematics
BLAIR, G. A., Physics
BOLWELL, G. P., Plant Biochemistry
BOWYER, J. R., Plant Biochemistry
BRADLEY, C., Health Psychology
BRAMLEY, P. M., Biochemistry
BRYSBAERT, M. M. C., Psychology
CASTIELLO, U., Psychology
CATCHPOLE, C. K., Animal Behaviour
CHERVONENKIS, A. Y., Computer Science
COHEN, D. A., Computer Science
COLLINSON, M. E., Plant Palaeobiology
COWAN, B. P., Physics
CRANG, P. A., Geography
DAVIES, E. R., Machine Vision
DICKSON, J. G., Molecular Cell Biology
DRIVER, F. F., Human Geography
DUDEN, R., Biological Sciences
EBINGER, C. J., Tectonics
EYSENCK, M. W., Psychology
FOWLER, C. M. R., Geography
FUNNELL, E., Neuropsychology
GAMBLE, C. S., Geography
GAMMERMAN, A., Computer Science
GREEN, M. G., Particle Physics
GUTIN, Z., Computer Science
HALL, R., Geology
HARMAN, G., Mathematics
HARRIS, M., Psychology
IMRIE, R. F., Human Geography
JANSEN, V., Mathematical Biology
KEMP, R. A., Physical Geography
LEA, M. J., Physics
LOEWENTHAL, C., Psychology
LOWE, J. J., Geography
LUO, Z., Computer Science
MACLEOD, A. K., Psychology
McCLAY, K. R., Structural Geology
MENZIES, M. A., Geochemistry
MITCHELL, C. J., Information Security
MOORE, A. M., Crystallography
MURPHY, S. P., Mathematics
MURTAGH, F., Computer Science
NISBET, E. G., Geology
O'MAHONY, P. F., Applied Mathematics
PATERSON, K. G., Mathematics

PETRASHOV, V. T., Physics
ROSE, J., Geography
SAUNDERS, J., Low Temperature Physics
SCHACK, R., Mathematics
SCOTT, A. C., Applied Palaeobotany
SIMON, D., Devt Geography
SMITH, A. T., Psychology
SOLOVYEV, W., Computer Science
STRONG, J. A., Experimental Physics
THIRLWALL, M. F., Isotope Geochemistry
UNWIN, P. T., Geography
VAPNIK, V., Computer Science
VOVK, V. G., Computer Science
WILD, P. R., Mathematics
ZANKER, J. M., Neuroscience

Royal Veterinary College

Royal College St, London, NW1 0TU

Telephone: (20) 7468-5000
Fax: (20) 7388-2342
E-mail: registry@rvc.ac.uk
Internet: www.rvc.ac.uk

Founded 1791
Academic year: September to July

Principal: Prof. QUINTIN McKELLAR
Sec. and Registrar: A. N. SMITH
Librarian: SIMON JACKSON

Number of teachers: 109
Number of students: 1,058

PROFESSORS

BROWNLIE, J., Veterinary Pathology
CHANTLER, P. D., Veterinary Molecular and
Cellular Biology
CHURCH, D. B., Small Animal Studies
ELLIOTT, J., Pharmacology
GOODSHIP, A. E., Orthopaedic Sciences
GREGORY, N. G., Animal Welfare Physiology
HOWARD, C. R., Veterinary Microbiology and
Parasitology
JACOBS, D. E., Veterinary Parasitology
JOHNSTON, A. M., Veterinary Public Health
LANYON, L., Veterinary Anatomy
LEES, P., Veterinary Pharmacology
LLOYD, D. H., Veterinary Dermatology
McGOWAN, M., Farm-Animal Medicine and
Surgery
MAY, S. A., Equine Medicine and Surgery
PFEIFFER, D. U., Veterinary Epidemiology
SCARAMUZZI, R. J., Veterinary Physiology
SKERRY, T. M., Developmental Biology
SMITH, R., Equine Orthopaedics
STICKLAND, N. C., Veterinary Anatomy
STOKER, N. G., Molecular Bacteriology
WATHES, D. C., Veterinary Reproduction
WATSON, P. F., Reproductive Biology
WILLIAMS, A. E., Veterinary Pathology

St George's Hospital Medical School

Cranmer Terrace, London, SW17 0RE

Telephone: (20) 8672-9944
Fax: (20) 8725-3426
E-mail: webmaster@stgeorges.nhs.uk
Internet: www.sghms.ac.uk

Founded 1751
Academic year: September to August

Principal: Prof. MICHAEL FARTHING
School Sec.: C. SWARBRICK
Academic Sec.: G. JONES
Academic Registrar: P. BROWN

Library of 150,000 vols
Number of teachers: 400
Number of students: 6,068

PROFESSORS

ANDERSON, H. R., Epidemiology and Public
Health
AUSTEN, B. M., Protein Science
BELL, B. A., Neurosurgery
BENNETT, D. C., Anatomy
BENNETT, E. D., Anaesthesia
BLAND, J. M., Medical Statistics
BOLTON, T. B., Pharmacology

Brown, N., Anatomy and Developmental Biology
Burns, T. P., Community Psychiatry
Camm, A. J., Clinical Cardiology
Campbell, S., Obstetrics and Gynaecology
Cappuccio, F., General Practice and Primary Care
Carter, N. D., Developmental Biochemistry
Chalmers, R. A., Paediatric Metabolism
Chambers, T. J., Tissue Pathology
Clemens, M. J., Biochemistry
Coates, A. R. M., Medical Microbiology
Collier, J. G., Clinical Pharmacology
Cook, D., Epidemiology
Dalgleish, A. G., Oncology
Duff, M. J. B., Physiological Medicine
Eastman, N. L. G., Psychiatry
Fisher, L. M., Biochemistry
Ghodse, A. H., Psychiatry of Addictive Behaviour
Gillberg, C., Psychiatry
Gordon-Smith, E. C., Haematology
Griffin, G. E., Infectious Diseases and Medicine
Griffiths, J. R., Medical Biochemistry
Hall, G. M., Anaesthesia
Hay, F. C., Immunology
Hermon-Taylor, J., Surgery
Hilton, S. R., General Practice and Primary Care
Hollins, S. C., Psychiatry of Learning Disability
Horton, R., Clinical Pharmacology
Howlin, P. A., Clinical Psychology
Johnstone, A. P., Molecular Immunology
Jones, I., Sociology of Health and Illness
Jones, P. W., Medicine
Kaski, J. C., Cardiological Sciences
Krishna, S., Infectious Diseases
Lacey, J. H., Psychiatry
Large, W. A., Pharmacology
Levick, J. R., Physiology
MacGregor, G. A., Cardiovascular Medicine
McKenna, W. J., Cardiac Medicine
Malik, M., Cardiology
Markus, H., Clinical Neuroscience
McLaren, S., Nursing
Mortimer, P. S., Physiological Medicine
Oliveira, D. B. G., Renal Medicine
Patton, M., Medical Genetics
Ross, F., Nursing Primary Care
Seymour, C. A., Clinical Biochemistry and Metabolism
Strachan, D. P., Public Health
Victor, C. R., Public Health Sciences
Waller, G., Psychiatry
Walters, D. V., Child Health
West, R. J., Psychology
Whincup, P. H., Public Health Sciences
Whipp, B. J., Physiology
Xu, Q., Cardiological Sciences

School of Oriental and African Studies

Thornhaugh St, Russell Sq., London, WC1H 0XG

Telephone: (20) 7898-4034
Fax: (20) 7898-4039
E-mail: study@soas.ac.uk
Internet: www.soas.ac.uk
Founded 1916
Academic year: September to June
Dir and Principal: Prof. Paul Webley
Pro-Dir: Prof. Peter Robb
Vice-Principal for External Relations: Prof. Elisabeth Croll
Registrar: Sharon Page
Academic Registrar: T. Harvey
Library: see Libraries and Archives
Number of teachers: 200
Number of students: 3,700
Publications: *The Bulletin, The China Quarterly, Journal of African Law*

DEANS

Faculty of Arts and Humanities: Prof. Tom Tomlinson
Faculty of Languages and Cultures: Prof. Graham Furniss
Faculty of Law and Social Sciences: Prof. Stephen Chan

PROFESSORS

Abdel-Haleem, M. A. S., Islamic Studies
Abu-Deeb, K. M., Arabic
Arnold, D., History of South Asia
Ash, R. F., Taiwan Studies
Barrett, T. H., East Asian History
Behrens-Abouseif, D., Islamic Art and Archaeology
Bernstein, H., Devt Studies
Bocking, B., Study of Religions
Booth, A. E., Econ. (Asia)
Braginsky, V. I., South East Asian Languages and Literatures
Brown, I., Economic History (South East Asia)
Clarence-Smith, W. G., Economic History (Asia and Africa)
Croll, E., Chinese Anthropology
Cruise O'Brien, D. B., Politics of Africa
Dikotter, F., Modern Chinese History
Fardon, R., Anthropology (West Africa)
Fine, B., Econ.
Furniss, G., African Languages, Literature and Popular Culture
George, A., Babylonian
Gerstle, C. A., Japanese Studies
Hafez, S., Modern Arabic
Hale, W., Turkish Politics
Harding, A., Law
Harris, L., Econ.
Hawkins, J. D., Ancient Anatolian Languages
Hawting, G., History (Near and Middle East)
Hewitt, B. G., Caucasian Languages
Howe, C., Chinese Business and Management
Ingham, B., Arabic Linguistic Studies
Kratz, U., Indonesian and Malay
Palmer, M., Law
Peel, J. D. Y., Anthropology and Sociology (Africa)
Picton, J., African Art
Pottier, J., Anthropology (Africa)
Rathbone, R. J. A. R., Modern African History
Robb, P. G., History of India
Ruben, D.-H., Philosophy
Sender, J., Econ. (Africa)
Shackle, C., Modern Languages of South Asia
Sims-Williams, N., Iranian and Central Asian Studies
Tapper, R. L., Anthropology (Middle East
Weeks, J., Devt Econ.
Wright, O., Musicology of the Middle East

School of Pharmacy

29–39 Brunswick Sq., London, WC1N 1AX

Telephone: (20) 7753-5800
Fax: (20) 7278-0622
E-mail: registry@pharmacy.ac.uk
Internet: www.pharmacy.ac.uk
Founded 1842
Academic year: October to June
Dean: Prof. A. Smith
Clerk to the Council and Sec.: Dr J. C. Axe
Number of teachers: 53
Number of students: 1,200

PROFESSORS

Alpar, H. O., Drug Delivery Research
Barber, N. D., Practice and Policy
Bates, I., Pharmacy Education
Brocchini, S., Chemical Pharmaceuticals
Buckton, G., Pharmaceutics
Florence, A. T., Pharmacy

Hadgraft, J., Biophysical Pharmaceutics
Heinrich, H., Pharmacognosy and Phytotherapy
Kellaway, I., Pharmaceutics
Moffat, A. C., Pharmaceutical Analysis
Neidle, S., Chemical Biology
Patterson, L. H., Medicinal Chemistry
Smith, F., Pharmacy Practice
Stephenson, F. A., Molecular Neuroscience
Taylor, D., Pharmaceutical and Public Health Policy
Taylor, K., Clinical Pharmaceutics
Taylor, P., Microbiology
Thomson, A. M., Pharmacology
Thurston, D., Pharmaceutical and Biological Chemistry

University College London

Gower St, London, WC1E 6BT

Telephone: (20) 7679-2000
Fax: (20) 7387-8057
E-mail: international@ucl.ac.uk
Internet: www.ucl.ac.uk
Founded 1826; merged with Royal Free Hospital School of Medicine 1998
Provost and Pres.: Prof. Malcolm Grant
Vice-Provosts: Marilyn J. Gallyer, Prof. Dave Delpy, Prof. Richard Frackowiak, Prof. Michael J. Worton, Prof. K. Michael Spyer
Registrar: Martin H. Butcher
Library: see Libraries and Archives
Number of teachers: 3,800
Number of students: 20,700
Publications: *UCL Universe, The World of UCL*

DEANS

Faculty of Arts and Humanities: Prof. Gerard J. P. O'Daly
Faculty of the Built Environment: Prof. Christine E. Hawley
Faculty of Eng. Sciences: Prof. Christopher W. Pitt
Faculty of Laws: Prof. Michael Bridge
Faculty of Life Sciences: Prof. A. Bob Lieberman
Faculty of Mathematical and Physical Sciences: Prof. Fred L. Pearce
Faculty of Biomedical Sciences: Prof. K. Michael Spyer (Interim)
Faculty of Social and Historical Sciences: Prof. Hugh D. Clout
Royal Free and University College Medical School: Prof. K. Michael Spyer (Principal)

PROFESSORS

Adler, M. W., Sexually Transmitted Diseases
Aeppli, G., Physics
Aghion, P., Econ. of Public Policy
Aiello, L. C., Biological Anthropology
Aiken, J., Fine Art
Akbar, A. N., Immunology
Allsop, R. E., Transport Studies
Anderson, J. E., Organic Chemistry
Anderson, J. M., Mathematics
Anderson, P. N., Experimental Neuroscience
Anderson, R. H., Paediatric Cardiac Morphology
Andrews, D. J., Eng. Design
Arridge, S. R., Image Processing
Ashmore, J. F., Biophysics
Ashton, R. D., English Language and Literature
Atkinson, J., Psychology
Attanasio, O. P., Econ.
Attwell, D. I., Physiology
Ayazi Shamlou, P., Biochemical Eng.
Aynsley-Green, A., Child Health
Babiker, A. G., Medical Statistics and Epidemiology
Ball, K. M., Mathematics
Banister, D. J., Transport Planning

BARENDT, E. M., Law of Media of Communication and Expression
BARKER, J. A., Hydrogeology
BARLOW, M. J., Astrophysics
BARNES, M. P., Scandinavian Studies
BARTLETT, R. P., Russian History
BARTLEY, M., Medical Sociology
BATE, S. P., Health Services Management
BATTARBEE, R. W., Environmental Change
BATTY, J. M., Spatial Analysis and Planning
BAYVEL, P., Optical Communications and Networks
BEBBINGTON, P. E., Social and Community Psychiatry
BEGENT, R. H. J., Oncology
BERGER, M. A., Mathematics
BETTERIDGE, D. J., Endocrinology and Metabolism
BEVAN, S. J., Pharmacology
BEVERLEY, P. C. L., Tumour Immunology
BHATTACHARYA, S. S., Experimental Ophthalmology
BINDMAN, D., History of Art
BIRD, A. C., Clinical Ophthalmology
BISHOP, S. R., Non-linear Dynamics
BLUNDELL, R., Econ.
BLUNN, G. W., Biomedical Eng.
BOGLE, I. D. L., Chemical Eng.
BOLSOVER, S. R., Cell Physiology
BORDEN, I. M., Architecture and Urban Culture
BORGERS, T., Econ.
BOSHOFF, C. H., Cancer Medicine
BOSTOCK, H., Neurophysiology
BOULOS, P. B., Surgery
BOWLING, A., Health Services Research
BOWMAKER, J., Visual Research
BOWN, S. G., Laser Medicine and Surgery
BOYD, I. W., Electronic Materials
BRAMWELL, S. T., Physical Chemistry
BREWIN, C. R., Clinical Psychology
BRIDGE, M. G., Commercial Law
BROCKES, J. P., Cell Biology
BRODY, M. B., Linguistics
BROWN, D. A., Pharmacology
BROWN, M. M., Stroke Medicine
BROWN, R. A., Tissue Eng.
BROWN, S. N., Mathematics
BROWNE, E. J., History of Medicine
BRUCKDORFER, K. R., Biochemistry
BRYSON, W. N., History and Theory of Art
BURGESS, J. A., Geography
BURK, K. M., Modern and Contemporary History
BURNHAM, P. C., Social Anthropology
BURNSTOCK, G., Anatomy
BURROUGHS, A. K., Hepatology
BUTLER, W. E., Comparative Law
BUTTERWORTH, B. L., Cognitive Neuropsychology
BUXTON, B. F., Information Processing
BYNUM, W. F., History of Medicine
CALLARD, R., Immunology
CAMPBELL, J. A., Computer Science
CAMPBELL, R., Communication Disorders
CARLIN, W. J., Econ.
CATLOW, C. R. A., Chemistry
CHAIN, B. M., Immunology
CHARLES, I. G., Molecular Biology
CHESHER, A. D., Econ.
CLARK, J. B., Neurochemistry
CLARK, R. J. H., Chemistry
CLARKE, P. E. L., Physics
CLAYTON, P. T., Paediatric Metabolic Disease and Hepatology
CLOUT, H. D., Geography
COCKCROFT, S., Cell Physiology
COLHOUN, H. M., Clinical Epidemiology
COLLINGE, J., Neurodegenerative Disease
COLLINS, M. K. L., Immunology
COLQUHOUN, D., Pharmacology
CONWAY, S. R., History
COOK, P. F. C., Architecture
COOTER, R. J.
COPP, A. J., Developmental Neurobiology
COVENEY, P. V., Physical Chemistry

CRAGGS, M. D., Applied Neurophysiology
CRAIG, G., Paediatric Genetics
CRANE, T. M., Philosophy
CRAWFORD, M. H., Ancient History
CROLL, J. G. A., Civil and Environmental Eng.
CROSS, P. A., Geomatic Eng.
CULHANE, J. L., Physics
CULL-CANDY, S. G., Pharmacology
CURRAN, H. V., Psychopharmacology
CUZNER, M. L., Neurochemistry
DACRE, J. E., Medical Education
DANPURE, C. J., Molecular Cell Biology
DARBYSHIRE, J. H., Epidemiology
DAVIDSON, B. R., Surgery
DAVIES, S. W., Experimental Neuropathology
DAVIES, W. E., History
D'AVRAY, D. L., History
DAWID, A. P., Statistics
DAYAN, P., Computational Neuroscience
DEAN, M. C., Anatomy
DEEMING, A. J., Chemistry
DELETANT, D. J., Romanian Studies
DELHANTY, J. D. A., Human Genetics
DELPY, D. T., Medical Photonics
DENNIS, I. H., English Law
DEZATEUX, C. A., Paediatric Epidemiology
DHILLON, A. P., Histopathology
DICKENSON, A. H., Neuropharmacology
DIMITRIOU, H., Planning Studies
DOLAN, R., Neuropsychiatry
DOLPHIN, A., Pharmacology
DOWD, P. M., Dermatology
DOWMAN, I. J., Photogrammetry and Remote Sensing
DRIVER, J. S., Psychology
DUCHEN, M. R., Physiology
DUNCAN, J. S., Clinical Neurology
DUNNILL, P., Biochemical Eng.
DUSHEIKO, G. M., Medicine
DWORKIN, R. M., Jurisprudence
EDWARDS, J. C. W., Connective-Tissue Medicine
EDWARDS, Y. H., Human Genetics
EKINS, R. P., Biophysics
ELL, P. J., Nuclear Medicine
ELTON, L., Higher Education
EMERY, V. C., Virology
EVANS, A. W., Transport Safety
EVANS, M. C. W., Plant Chemistry
FEARN, T., Applied Statistics
FERGUSSON-PELL, M., Neuromuscular Restoration and Rehabilitation
FINE, L. G., Medicine
FINKELSTEIN, A. C. W., Software Systems Eng.
FINNEY, J. L., Physics
FISH, D. R., Clinical Neurophysiology and Epilepsy
FISHER, A. J., Physics
FISHER, E. M. C., Neurogenetics
FITZGERALD, M., Developmental Neurobiology
FITZKE, F. W., Visual Optics
FLETCHER, I. F., Int. Commercial Law
FONAGY, P., Psychoanalysis
FOOT, M. M., Library and Archive Studies
FOREMAN, J. C., Immunopharmacology
FORGACS, D. A., Italian
FORGE, A., Auditory Cell Biology
FORTY, J. A., History of Architecture
FOURNIER, C. L., Architecture and Urban Planning
FOWLER, C. J., Uro-neurology
FRACKOWIAK, R. S. J., Cognitive Neurology
FRANCK, L. S., Children's Nursing Research Studies
FREEMAN, M. D. A., English Law
FRENCH, D. W., History
FRISTON, K. J., Imaging Neuroscience
FRITH, C. D., Neuropsychology
FRITH, U., Cognitive Devt
FRY, C. H., Cellular Physiology
FULBROOK, M. J. A., German History
FULLER, J. H., Clinical Epidemiology
FURNHAM, A. F., Psychology
GABELLA, G., Histology and Cytology

GAGE, S. A., Innovative Technology in Architecture
GALLIVAN, S., Mathematics
GARB, T., History of Art
GARDINER, R. M., Paediatrics
GARDNER-MEDWIN, A. R., Physiology
GARTHWAITE, J., Experimental Neuroscience
GELLER, M. J., Jewish Studies
GENN, H. G., Socio-Legal Studies
GILBERT, A. G., Geography
GILLAN, M. J., Physics
GILLESPIE, S. H., Medical Microbiology
GOADSBY, P. J., Clinical Neurology
GODOVAC-ZIMMERMANN, J., Protein Biochemistry
GOLDSPINK, G., Anatomy
GOLDSTEIN, D. B., Evolutionary and Population Genetics
GOLDSTONE, A. H., Haematology
GOODSHIP, A. E., Orthopaedic Sciences
GOODWIN, P. B., Transport Policy
GOSWAMI, U., Cognitive Developmental Psychology
GRAFFY, J. J., Russian Literature and Cinema
GRANTHAM-MCGREGOR, S. M., Child Health and Nutrition
GRASS, A. J., Fluid Mechanics
GREEN, C. J., Surgery
GREENHALGH, P. M., Primary Care Devt
GREENWOOD, J., Biomedical Research
GREGORY, J., Water Chemistry
GRIFFITHS, H. D., Electronics
GRIFFITHS, P. D., Virology
GUERRINI, R., Paediatric Neurology
GUEST, J. E., Planetary Science
GUEST, S. F. D., Legal Philosophy
GURLING, H. M., Molecular Psychiatry
HALE, K. J., Chemistry
HALL, A., Molecular Biology
HALL, C., Modern British Social and Cultural History
HALL, C. M., Paediatric Radiology
HALL, P. G., Planning Studies
HAMILTON-MILLER, J. M. T., Medical Microbiology
HAMMOND, P., Dental and Medical Informatics
HANN, I., Paediatric Haematology and Oncology
HANSON, J. M., House Form and Culture
HARRIS, J. M., Linguistics
HARRIS, R., Geography
HARRISON, C. M., Geography
HARRISON, M. J. G., Clinical Neurology
HART, S. M., Hispanic Studies
HARTLEY, J. A., Cancer Studies
HARVEY, N. J. W., Judgement and Decision Research
HASSAN, F. A., Archaeology
HATCH, D. J., Paediatric Anaesthesia
HAUSSER, M. A., Neuroscience
HAWKINS, P. N., Medicine
HAWLEY, C., Architectural Studies
HAWORTH, S. G., Developmental Cardiology
HAZELL, R. J. D., Govt and the Constitution
HEBDEN, J. C., Biomedical Optics
HERMANS, T. J., Dutch and Comparative Literature
HERTZMAN, C., Paediatric Radiology
HEYDECKER, B. G., Transport Studies
HEYES, C. M., Psychology
HILLIARD, J., Fine Art Media
HILLIER, W. R. G., Architectural and Urban Morphology
HILLSON, S. W., Bioarchaeology
HITCHINGS, R. A., Glaucoma and Allied Studies
HOARE, M., Biochemical Eng.
HOBKIRK, J. A., Dental Prosthetics
HOBSON, R. P., Developmental Psychopathology
HOCKEY, S. M., Library and Information Studies
HODGSON, H., Medicine
HOMEWOOD, K. M., Human Ecology

HOPPIT, J., British History
HORNBLOWER, N. S. R., Classics and Ancient History
HORNE, F. P., English Language and Literature
HORTON, M. A., Bone Biology and Mineral Metabolism
HOSKING, G. A., Russian History
HOWARTH, I. D., Astronomy
HOWELL, P., Experimental Psychology
HUDSON, R. A., Linguistics
HUGHES, L. A. J., Russian History
HUMBERSTON, J. W., Physics
HUMPHRIES, S. E., Cardiovascular Genetics
HUNT, D. M., Molecular Genetics
HUNT, J. C. R., Climate Modelling
HUNT, N. P., Orthodontics
HUNT, S. P., Molecular Neurobiology
HYAMS, J. S., Cell Biology
ICHIMURA, H., Econ.
INGRAM, D., Health Informatics
ISENBERG, D. A., Rheumatology
ISHAM, V. S., Probability and Statistics
JANOSSY, G., Immunology
JARVIS, M. J., Health Psychology
JAUNIAUX, E. R. M., Obstetrics and Fetal Medicine
JAYNE, J. E., Mathematics
JEHIEL, P., Econ.
JESSEN, K. R., Developmental Neurobiology
JOHNSON, A. M., Primary Care and Population Sciences
JOHNSON, E. R., Mathematics
JOHNSON, F. E. A., Mathematics
JOHNSTON, A., Psychology
JONES, A. G., Chemical Eng.
JONES, D. T., Bioinformatics
JONES, J. S., Human Genetics
JONES, T. W., Physics
JORDAN, D., Physiology
JOWELL, J. L., Public Law
KAPLAN, B. J., Dutch History
KARLIN, D. R., English
KATONA, C. L. E., Psychiatry of the Elderly
KATZ, D. R., Immunopathology
KEMP, D. T., Auditory Biophysics
KHAW, P. T., Glaucoma Studies and Wound Healing
KING, M., Primary Care Psychiatry
KINNON, C., Molecular Immunology
KIRBY, D. G., Modern History
KIRSTEIN, P. T., Computer Systems
KLIER, J. D., Modern Jewish History
KOERNER, J. L., History of Art
KOLANKIEWICZ, J. M., Sociology
KUHRT, A. T. L., Ancient Near Eastern History
KULLMANN, D. M., Neurology
LARMAN, D. G., Mathematics
LAST, D. M., Anthropology
LATCHMAN, D. S., Human Genetics
LAURENT, G. J., Pulmonary Biochemistry
LAWRENCE, C. J., History of Medicine
LAYCOCK, G. K., Crime Science
LEES, A. J., Clinical Neurology
LEES, W. R., Medical Imaging
LEMON, R. N., Neurophysiology
LEONARD, J. V., Paediatric Metabolic Disease
LEWIS, A. D. E., Comparative Legal History
LIEBERMAN, A. R., Anatomy
LIGHTMAN, S. L., Clinical Ophthalmology
LIM, L., Neurochemistry
LINCH, D. C., Clinical Haematology
LINDON, J. M. A., Italian Studies
LITTLEWOOD, R., Anthropological Psychiatry
LLOYD, M. H., General Practice
LONDEI, M., Autoimmunity
LONGLEY, P. A., Geographic Information
LUMLEY, R., Italian Cultural History
LUND, V. J., Rhinology
LUTHERT, P. J., Pathology
LUXON, L. M., Audiological Medicine
LYDYARD, P. M., Immunology
MCARTHUR, J. M., Geochemistry
MCCARTHY, M., Public Health
MCDOWELL, L. M., Economic Geography

MCEWEN, K. A., Physics
MCGUIRE, W. J., Geological Hazards
MACHIN, S. J., Econ.
MACHIN, S. J., Haematology
MACKETT, R. L., Transport Studies
MACLEAN, A. B., Obstetrics and Gynaecology
MCLEAN, P., Fine Art
MCMANUS, I. C., Psychology and Medical Education
MCMILLAN, P. F., Solid State Chemistry
MCMILLIN, A. B., Russian Literature
MCMULLEN, P., Mathematics
MACRORY, R. B., Environmental Law
MAJEED, F. A., Primary Care and Public Health
MALLET, J., Biological Diversity
MALONE-LEE, J. G., Geriatric Medicine
MARGETTS, H. Z., Political Science
MARKESINIS, B., Common Law and Civil Law
MARMOT, M. G., Epidemiology and Public Health
MARTIN, B. R. C., Physics
MARTIN, J. F., Cardiovascular Medicine
MARTIN, M. G. F., Philosophy
MARTIN, P., Tissue Repair
MASON, K. O., Astronomy
MASTERS, J. R. W., Experimental Pathology
MATHEWS, T. P., French
MATHIAS, C. J., Neurovascular Medicine
MEGHIR, C. H. D., Econ.
MEREDITH, P. G., Rock Physics
MIDWINTER, J. E., Electrical Eng.
MILLA, P. J., Paediatric Gastroenterology
MILLER, A. I., History and Philosophy of Science
MILLER, D. H., Clinical Neurology
MILLER, D. J., Physics
MILLER, D. M. S., Anthropology
MIRSKY, R., Developmental Neurobiology
MOBBS, P. G., Physiology
MONCADA, S., Experimental Biology and Therapeutics
MUNK, M., Molecular Embryology
MOORE, A. T., Ophthalmology
MORRIS, P. W. G., Construction and Project Management
MOSS, S. E., Biomedical Research
MOSS, S. J., Molecular Pharmacology and Cell Biology
MOTHERWELL, W. B., Chemistry
MULLER, J.-P. A. L., Image Understanding and Remote Sensing
MUNDY, A. R., Urology
MUNTON, R. J. C., Geography
MYTHEN, M. G., Paediatric Anaesthesia
NAZARETH, I. D., Primary Care and Population Science
NEILD, G. H., Nephrology
NEVILLE, B., Paediatric Neurology
NEWELL, M. L., Paediatric Epidemiology
NEWELL, W. R., Physics
NEWMAN, A. F., Econ.
NEWMAN, S. P., Health Psychology
NORTH, J. A., History
NUGENT, J. H. A., Plant Biochemistry
NUTT, B. B., Facility and Environment Management
NUTTON, V., History of Medicine
O'DALY, G. J. P., Latin
O'HARE, M. J., Cell Biology
O'HIGGINS, P., Anatomy
O'KEEFE, J., Cognitive Neuroscience
O'KEEFFE, D., European Law
O'NEILL, M. E., Mathematics
O'REILLY, J. J., Telecommunications
ODA, H., Japanese Law
OLIVER, A. D. H., Constitutional Law
OLSEN, I., Cell Biology and Tissue Eng.
ONO, S. J., Ocular Immunology
ORDIDGE, R. J., Medical Physics
ORENGO, C. A., Bioinformatics
ORESZCZYN, T., Energy and Environment
ORTON, C. R., Quantitative Archaeology
OWEN, J. S., Molecular Medicine
PALMER, N. E., Law of Art and Cultural Property

PARKIN, I. P., Chemistry
PARMAR, M. K. B., Medical Statistics and Epidemiology
PARNAVELAS, J. G., Neuroanatomy
PARTRIDGE, L., Biometry
PATTISON, J. R., Medical Microbiology
PEARCE, D. W., Econ.
PEARCE, F. L., Biological Chemistry
PECKHAM, C., Paediatric Epidemiology
PEPYS, M., Medicine
PERKINS, R. M., Norse Studies
PERKINS, S. J., Structural Biochemistry
PETTET, B. G., Company and Capital Markets Law
PHILLIPS, A., Epidemiology and Biostatistics
PICKERING, K. T., Sedimentology and Stratigraphy
PIERRO, A., Paediatric Surgery
PIPER, P. W., Molecular Microbiology
PITT, C. W., Electrical Eng.
PLATT, J. P., Geology
PLOTKIN, H. C., Psychobiology
POLLOCK, A. M., Health Services Policy
POMIANKOWSKI, A., Genetics
PORTER, J. B., Haematology
PORTER, S. R., Oral Medicine
POULTER, L. W., Immunology
POUNDER, R. E., Medicine
POVEY, M. S., Human Somatic Cell Genetics
POWER, C., Epidemiology and Public Health
POWIS, S. H., Renal Medicine
PRASHER, D. K., Audiology
PREECE, M., Child Health and Growth
PREISS, D., Pure Mathematics
PRICE, C. A., Archaeological Conservation
PRICE, G. D., Mineral Physics
PRICE, S. D., Chemical Physics
PRICE, S. L., Chemistry
PROWSE, P., Theatre Design
PYNSENT, R. B., Czech and Slovak Literature
QUINN, N. P., Clinical Neurology
RADEMACHER, T. W., Molecular Medicine
RAWSON, P. F., Geology
REHREN, T. H. H., Archaeological Materials and Technologies
REVELL, P. A., Histopathology
RICH, P. R., Bioenergetics
RICHARDS, C. D., Experimental Physiology
RICHARDS, P., Anthropology
RICHARDSON, W. D., Biology
ROBERTS, B. P., Chemistry
ROBERTS, G. J., Children's Dentistry
ROBERTSON, M. M., Neuropsychiatry
RODECK, C. H., Obstetrics and Gynaecology
ROEMER, C. E., Papyrology
RON, M. A., Neuropsychiatry
ROOK, G. A. W., Medical Microbiology
ROSEN, F. R., History of Political Thought
ROSEN, S., Speech and Hearing Sciences
ROTHWELL, J. C., Human Neurophysiology
ROWLAND, S. C. W., Higher Education
ROWLANDS, M. J. J., Material Culture
RUBIN, G. S., Visual Function and Rehabilitation
RUSSELL, M. A., Addiction
RYAN, J. M., Post-Conflict Recovery
SAGGERSON, E. D., Biochemistry
SALT, J., Geography
SALT, T. E., Visual Science
SALVERDA, R., Dutch Language and Literature
SAMMONDS, P. R., Geophysics
SANDER, J. W. A., Epilepsy
SANDS, P. J., Law
SAUNDERS, M. I., Oncology
SCAMBLER, G. N., Medical Sociology
SCAMBLER, P. J., Molecular Medicine
SCARAVILLI, F., Neuropathology
SCHAPIRA, A. H. V., Neurology
SCHOFIELD, T. P., History of Legal and Political Thought
SCULLY, C. M., Special Needs Dentistry
SEEDS, A. J., Opto-Electronics
SEGAL, A. W., Medicine
SENN, S. J., Pharmaceutical and Health Statistics

SEYMOUR, R. M., Mathematics
SHALLICE, T., Psychology
SHANKS, D. R., Experimental Psychology
SHARPLES, R. W., Classics
SHEIHAM, A., Dental Public Health
SHENNAN, S. J., Theoretical Archaeology
SHEPHARD, E. A., Molecular Biology
SHEPHERD, P. R., Cellular Signalling
SHERR, L., Clinical and Health Psychology
SHORVON, S. D., Clinical Neurology
SILLITO, A. M., Visual Science
SIMONS, S. J. R., Chemical Eng.
SINDET-PEDERSEN, S., Oral Implantology
SINGER, A., Gynaecological Research
SINGER, M., Intensive Care Medicine
SLATER, M., Virtual Environments
SMART, T. G., Pharmacology
SMITH, A., Detector Physics
SMITH, A. H., Political Economy
SMITH, F. T., Mathematics
SMITH, N. V., Linguistics
SMITH, S. R., Econ.
SNOWDON, P. F.
SOMMER, V., Evolutionary Anthropology
SOUTHGATE, L. J., Primary Care and Education
SPEIGHT, P. M., Oral Pathology
SPELLER, R. D., Medical Physics
SPIRO, S. G., Respiratory Medicine
SPOOR, C. F., Evolutionary Anatomy
SPYER, K. M., Physiology
STANFORD, J. L., Medical Microbiology
STEADMAN, J. P., Urban and Built Form Studies
STEPHENS, J. A., Physiology
STEPTOE, A. P. A., Psychology
STOCKMAN, A., Investigative Eye Research
STOCKS, J., Respiratory Medicine
STONEHAM, A. M., Physics
STOREY, P. J., Physics
STROBEL, S., Paediatrics and Clinical Immunology
SURTEES, R. A. H., Paediatric Neurology
SUTHERLAND, J. A., Modern English Literature
SUTTON, S. R., Social and Health Psychology
SWALES, M. W., German
SWALLOW, D. M., Biology
SWANN, P. F., Molecular Oncology
SWANSON, T. M., Law and Econ.
TAIT, W. J., Egyptology
TAYLOR, B., Community Child Health
TAYLOR, I., Surgery
TEDDER, R. S., Medical Virology
TENNYSON, J., Physics
THIMBLEBY, H. W., Human Interaction with Systems
THOMAS, D. G. T., Neurological Surgery
THOMAS, K. D., Human Palaeoecology
THOMPSON, A. J., Clinical Neurology and Neurorehabilitation
THOMPSON, E. J., Neurochemistry
THORNTON, J. M., Biomolecular Structure
THRASHER, A. J., Paediatric Immunology
TILLEY, C. Y., Anthropology and Archaeology
TITCHENER-HOOKER, N. J., Biochemical Engineering
TOBIAS, J. S., Cancer Medicine
TODD, C. J., Network Science
TODD-POKROPEK, A. E., Medical Physics
TOFTS, P. S., Medical Physics
TOMKINS, A. M., Int. Child Health
TONETTI, M., Periodontology
TOOK, J. F., Dante Studies
TRELEAVEN, P. C., Computer Science
TRIMBLE, M. R., Behavioural Neurology
TURNER, M. W., Molecular Immunology
TURNER, R., Anthropology
TWINING, W. L., Jurisprudence
TYLER, N. A., Communities and Transport
UCKO, P. J., Comparative Archaeology
UNWIN, R., Nephrology and Physiology
VALLANCE, P., Clinical Pharmacology
VAN DER LELY, H. K. J., Developmental Language Disorders and Cognitive Neuroscience

VAN GRIETHUYSEN, W. J., Naval Architecture
VAN REENEN, J. M., Econ.
VARGHA-KHADEM, F., Developmental Cognitive Neuroscience
VERGANI, D., Immunopathology
WAKELY, P. I., Urban Devt
WALTON, S. J., Norwegian
WARDLE, F. J., Clinical Psychology
WARNER, A. E., Developmental Biology
WASHBROOK, J., Computer Science
WATERFIELD, M. D., Biochemistry
WEIS, R. J., English
WEISS, R. A., Viral Oncology
WELLER, I. V. D., Sexually Transmitted Diseases
WELLS, J. C., Phonetics
WESTON, H. D., History of Art
WHITEHOUSE, R. D., Archaeology
WIGZELL, F. C. M., Russian Literature and Culture
WILBUR, S. R., Distributed Systems
WILKIN, C., Physics
WILLIAMS, G. H., Histopathology
WILLIAMS, R. S., Hepatology
WILLIS, A. J., Astronomy
WILSON, D. S. M., Linguistics
WILSON, E. J., Latin American Literature
WILSON, M., Microbiology
WILSON, S. W., Developmental Genetics
WINCHESTER, B. G., Biochemistry
WINGHAM, D. J., Climate Physics
WINSLET, M. C., Surgery
WINTER, R. M., Clinical Genetics
WOLEDGE, R. C., Experimental Physiology
WOLFF, J., Philosophy
WOLPERT, D. M., Motor Neuroscience
WOLPERT, L., Biology as applied to Medicine
WOO, P. M. M., Paediatric Rheumatology
WOOD, N. W., Clinical Neurogenetics
WOOD, P. A., Geography
WOOLF, A. S., Nephrology
WORTON, M. J., French Language and Literature
WOTTON, R. S., Biology
WOUDHUYSEN, H. R., English Language and Literature
WRIGHT, A., Otorhinolaryngology
WU, G., Computational Fluid Dynamics
WYATT, J. S., Neonatal Paediatrics
YANG, Z., Statistical Genetics
YATES, J. G., Chemical Eng.
YELLON, D. M., Cellular Cardiology
YIP, M. J., Linguistics
YOUSRY, T. A., Neuroradiology
YUDKIN, J. S., Medicine
ZEKI, S., Neurobiology
ZUMLA, A., Infectious Diseases and International Health

SCHOOL OF THE COLLEGE

UCL School of Slavonic and East European Studies: Univ. of London, London, WC1E 7HU; tel. (20) 7636-8000; f. 1915, merged with University College London 1999; 60 teachers; 500 students (460 full-time, 40 part-time); Dir: Prof. M. A. BRANCH; Academic Registrar CAROL PEARCE; publ. *The Slavonic and East European Review* (quarterly)..

INSTITUTES OF THE COLLEGE

Centre for Allergy Research and Environmental Health: Dir Prof. JONATHAN BROSTOFF.

Institute of Child Health: 30 Guilford St, London, WC1N 1EH; tel. (20) 7242-9789; is the Medical School of the Hospitals for Sick Children, Great Ormond St, and the Queen Elizabeth Hospital for Children, Hackney Rd; Dean Prof. R. J. LEVINSKY; Sec. I. R. MIDDLETON.

Institute of Neurology: The National Hospital, Queen Sq., London, WC1N 3BG; tel. (20) 7837-3611; library of 16,000 vols; Dean Prof. D. N. LANDON; Sec. R. P. WALKER.

Institute of Ophthalmology: Bath St, London, EC1V 9EL; tel. (20) 7608-6800; (associated with Moorfields Eye Hospital)f. 1947; postgraduate teaching and research in eye disease and prevention of blindness; library of 13,000 vols; Dir of Research and Teaching Prof. A. M. SILLITO; Sec. CHRISTINE GRIFFITHS.

Jill Dando Institute for Crime Science: Third Floor, 1 Old St, London, EC1V 9HL; tel. (20) 7324-3000; fax (20) 7324-3003; e-mail jdi@ucl.ac.uk; internet www.jdi.ucl.ac.uk; f. 2001; Dir Prof. GLORIA LAYCOCK..

ASSOCIATED INSTITUTE

Eastman Dental Institute: Eastman Dental Hospital, Gray's Inn Rd, London, WC1X 8LD; tel. (20) 7915-1000; fax (20) 7915-1012; Dean Prof. C. B. A. SCULLY; Sec. R. N. TAYLOR..

UNIVERSITY INSTITUTES

University of London Institute in Paris

11 rue de Constantine, 75340 Paris Cedex 07, France

Telephone: (1) 44-11-73-73
Fax: (1) 45-50-31-55
E-mail: l.mitchell@ulip.lon.ac.uk
Internet: www.ulip.lon.ac.uk

Founded 1894 as 'Guilde Franco-Anglaise', attached to Univ. of Paris 1927, now an institute of advanced study of Univ. of London; partner of Queen Mary and Royal Holloway, Univ. of London

Academic year: September to July

Dir: Dr DAVID SHEPHEARD
Admin. Officer: SIMON STONE

Number of teachers: 41
Number of students: 2,660

Publication: *Franco-British Studies* (2 a year)

PROFESSORS

WARD, D., English
WILLIAMSON, E., French

University Marine Biological Station Millport

Millport, Isle of Cumbrae, Scotland, KA28 0EG

Telephone: (1475) 530581
Fax: (1475) 530601
E-mail: tracy.price@millport.gla.ac.uk
Internet: www.gla.ac.uk/acad/marine

Founded 1970 in asscn with Univ. of Glasgow for teaching and research in marine biology

Library of 5,000 vols

Dir: Prof. P. G. MOORE (acting)
Sec.: DAVID MURDEN

PROFESSORS

ATKINSON, R. J. A., Marine Biology
MOORE, P. G., Marine Biology.

CONSTITUENT INSTITUTES OF THE SCHOOL OF ADVANCED STUDY

Dean of the School of Advanced Study: Prof. C. N. J. MANN

Institute of Advanced Legal Studies

17 Russell Sq., London, WC1B 5DR

Telephone: (20) 7862-5800
Fax: (20) 7862-5850
E-mail: ials@sas.ac.uk
Internet: www.ials.sas.ac.uk
Academic year: October to December

Founded 1947

Provides a centre for postgraduate legal studies, professional legal education and legal research; MA in advanced legislative studies, a research methodology course and a wide range of public lectures and seminars

Dir: Prof. AVROM SHERR
Administrator: Prof. PETER NIVEN
Library: see Libraries and Archives
Publication: *Amicus Curiae*

PROFESSORS

DAINTITH, T. C., Constitutional and Admin. Law, Economic Law
RIDER, B. A. K., Company Law, Commercial Criminal Law
SHERR, A. S., Legal Education, the Legal Profession

Institute of Classical Studies

Senate House, London, WC1E 7HU
Telephone: (20) 7862-8705
Fax: (20) 7862-8722
E-mail: icls.publications@sas.ac.uk
Internet: www.icls.sas.ac.uk/institute/publicat.htm
Founded 1953

Dir: Prof. MIKE EDWARDS (acting)
Sec.: Dr OLGA KRZYSZKOWSKA

Library of basic research books complemented by the library of the Hellenic and Roman Societies (jt library of 100,000 vols); research courses and seminars held for postgraduate students
Publications: *Bulletin* (annual), *Bulletin Supplements*.

Institute of Commonwealth Studies

28 Russell Sq., London, WC1B 5DS
Telephone: (20) 7262-8844
Fax: (20) 7262-8820
E-mail: ics@sas.ac.uk
Internet: www.sas.ac.uk/commonwealthstudies

Founded 1949 for postgraduate study in social sciences and recent history relating to the Commonwealth; relocating to Senate House, Malet St in 2008 (see above)
Academic year: September to June

Dir: Prof. RICHARD CROOK
Admin. Man.: DENISE ELLIOTT
Information Resources Manager: DAVID CLOVER

Library of 170,000 vols
Number of teachers: 5 (full-time)
Number of students: 80
Publication: *Journal of Imperial and Commonwealth History* (quarterly)

PROFESSORS

CROOK, R., Commonwealth Studies and Local Governance
HOLLAND, R., Imperial and Commonwealth History

ATTACHED INSTITUTE

Commonwealth Policy Studies Unit (CPSU): internet www.cpsu.org.uk; Head R. BOURNE.

Institute of English Studies

School of Advanced Study, Senate House, Malet St, London, WC1E 7HU
Telephone: (20) 7862-8675
Fax: (20) 7862-8720
E-mail: ies@sas.ac.uk
Internet: www.sas.ac.uk/ies
Founded 1991 as Centre for English Studies; present name 1999
State control
Academic year: September to June

Dir: Prof. WARWICK GOULD
Administrators: JOANNE GRUBB (Admin. Sec.), Dr WIM VAN MIERLO (Finance Officer,

Postgraduate, Alumni Scheme and Bibliographical Society), GINA VITELLO (Centre for Manuscript and Print Studies, Nat. Research Training Scheme)
Number of teachers: 20
Number of students: 32.

Institute of Germanic and Romance Studies

Senate House, Malet St, London, WC1E 7HU
Telephone: (20) 7862-8677
Fax: (20) 7862-8672
E-mail: igrs@sas.ac.uk
Germanic Studies Library: 29 Russell Sq., London, WC1B 5DP
Telephone: (20) 7862-8965
Fax: (20) 7862-8970
E-mail: igslib@sas.ac.uk
Internet: igrs.sas.ac.uk
Founded 2004 by merger of Institute of Germanic Studies (f. 1950) and Institute of Romance Studies (f. 1989)
Academic year: October to June

Dir: Prof. NAOMI SEGAL
Admin. Secretary: ROSEMARY LAMBETH
Librarian: WILLIAM ABBEY; 1,320 mems
Library of 100,000 vols
Number of teachers: 6
Number of students: 25
Publications: *London German Studies* (irreg.), *Journal of Romance Studies* (3 a year).

Institute of Historical Research

Senate House, Malet St., London, WC1E 7HU
Telephone: (20) 7862-8740
Fax: (20) 7862-8745
E-mail: ihr@sas.ac.uk
Internet: www.history.ac.uk
Founded 1921 as the Univ.'s centre for postgraduate study in history, it is also a nat. and int. meeting place for scholars of history and related disciplines
Academic year: October to June

Dir: Prof. DAVID BATES
Institute Administrator: ELAINE WALTERS
Library: Library: see Libraries and Archives
Number of teachers: 8
Number of students: 13
Publications: *Historical Research* (quarterly), *Teachers of History* (annual), *Theses in Progress and Theses Completed* (annual)

PROFESSORS

BATES, D., Medieval History
CANNADINE, D., Contemporary British History
KEENE, D., Comparative Metropolitan History
THANE, P., Contemporary British History

Institute of Musical Research

Senate House, Malet St, London, WC1E 7HU
Telephone: (20) 7664-4865
Fax: (20) 7862-8657
E-mail: music@sas.ac.uk
Internet: music.sas.ac.uk
Founded 2005, began operating 2006
Funded by HEFCE; fosters collaborative research; hosts visiting scholars; organizes conferences and other events; runs publication programmes; provides research training support for postgraduate students
Dir: Prof. KATHARINE ELLIS
Administrator: VALERIE JAMES.

Institute of Philosophy

Senate House, Malet St, London, WC1E 7HU
Telephone: (20) 7862-8683

Fax: (20) 7862-8639
E-mail: philosophy@sas.ac.uk
Internet: www.philosophy.sas.ac.uk
Founded 2005
Aims to make philosophy of the highest quality available to the widest possible audience, both inside and outside the UK's academic community.
Dir: Prof. TIM CRANE
Administrator: Dr SHAHRAR ALI.

Institute for the Study of the Americas

31 Tavistock Sq., London, WC1H 9HA
Telephone: (20) 7862-8870
Fax: (20) 7862-8886
E-mail: americas@sas.ac.uk
Internet: www.americas.sas.ac.uk
Founded 2004 by merger of Institute of Latin American Studies (f. 1964) and Institute of United States Studies (f. 1965) to promote, co-ordinate and provide a focus for research and postgraduate teaching of Latin American studies, United States studies and comparative American studies
Academic year: October to July

Dir: Prof. JAMES DUNKERLEY
Librarian: SHEREEN COLVIN
Number of teachers: 22
Number of students: 80
Publication: *Journal of Latin American Studies* (quarterly)

PROFESSORS

DUNKERLEY, J., Politics
MOLYNEUX, M., Sociology
MORGAN, I., United States Studies

Warburg Institute

Woburn Sq., London, WC1H 0AB
Telephone: (20) 7862-8949
Fax: (20) 7862-8955
E-mail: warburg@sas.ac.uk
Internet: www.warburg.sas.ac.uk
Founded 1921 for the study of cultural and intellectual history and the history of the classical tradition
Academic year: October to September

Dir: Prof. C. HOPE
Sec. and Registrar: ANITA C. POLLARD
Librarian: Prof. JILL KRAYE
Library: see Libraries and Archives
Number of teachers: 5
Number of students: 20
Publications: *Journal of the Warburg and Courtauld Institutes* (annual), *Warburg Institute Colloquia* (annual), *Warburg Studies and Texts* (irreg.)

PROFESSORS

BURNETT, C. S. F., History of Islamic Influences in Europe
HOPE, C., History of the Classical Tradition
KRAYE, J. A., History of Renaissance Philosophy
MCGRATH, E., History of Art.

ASSOCIATE INSTITUTION

The following institution has recognized teachers of the University of London on its staff and offers courses leading to degrees of the University.
Institute of Cancer Research: 123 Old Brompton Rd, London, SW7 3RP; tel. (20) 7352-8133; fax (20) 7370-5261; internet www.icr.ac.uk; f. 1909; library of 25,000 vols; Chief Exec. Prof. PETER RIGBY; Sec. J. M. KIPLING.

LONDON METROPOLITAN UNIVERSITY

London City campus: 133 Whitechapel High St, London, E1 7QA
North London campus: 166–220 Holloway Rd, London, N7 8DB
E-mail: admissions@londonmet.ac.uk
Internet: www.londonmet.ac.uk

Founded 2002 following merger of University of North London and London Guildhall University
President: Sir RODERICK CASTLE FLOUD
Vice-Chancellor and Chief Executive: BRIAN ROPER
Deputy Vice-Chancellor (Academic): BOB AYLETT
Deputy Vice-Chancellor (Planning and Resources): MAX WEAVER
Deputy Vice-Chancellor (Research and Development): CHRIS TOPLEY
Academic Registrar: JILL GRINSTEAD
Number of students: 33,000

HEADS OF DEPARTMENTS

Accounting, Banking and Information Systems Management Services: FRED SMITH
Applied Social Studies: SUE PIKE
Architecture and Spatial Design: ROBERT MULL
Art, Media and Design: BOB MORGAN
Computing: JEFF NAYLOR
Cultural and Language Studies: PAULINE DODGSON-KATIYO
Economics, Finance and International Business: GEORGE HADJIMATHEOU
Education: JON DAVISON
Health and Human Sciences: BRIAN BOINTON
Law, Governanace and International Relations: CONNIE OSTMANN
Management and Professional Development: ANDY INGLIS
Polymers Unit: MIKE O'BRIEN
Psychology: STUART MILLAR

LONDON SOUTH BANK UNIVERSITY

103 Borough Rd, London, SE1 0AA
Telephone: (20) 7928-8989
Fax: (20) 7815-8155
E-mail: enquiry@lsbu.ac.uk
Internet: www.lsbu.ac.uk

Founded 1970 as South Bank Polytechnic; present name and status 1992
State control
Academic year: September to July
Chancellor: Sir TREVOR McDONALD
Vice-Chancellor: Prof. DEIAN HOPKIN
Deputy Vice-Chancellor: Prof. TREVOR WATKINS (Academic)
Registrar: R. PHILLIPS
Librarian: J. AKEROYD

Library of 280,000 vols
Number of teachers: 652
Number of students: 20,281

Publication: *Prospectuses* (annually)

DEANS

Faculty of the Built Environment: Prof. LAWRENCE WOOD
Faculty of Engineering, Science and Technology: Prof. CHRIS CLARE
Faculty of Health: Prof. DAVID SINES
Faculty of Humanities and Social Sciences: Prof. JEFFREY WEEKS
Business School: Prof. NICHOLAS ROWE

HEADS OF SCHOOL/AREA

Faculty of the Built Environment:
  Construction: Prof. R. HOWES
  Urban Design and Policy: Prof. B. REDDING
Faculty of Engineering and Science:
  Computing, Information Systems and Mathematics: Prof. A. HASHIM
  Electrical, Electronic and Information Engineering: Prof. B. BRIDGE
  Engineering Systems and Design: Prof. R. MATTHEWS
  Applied Science: T. G. EVANS
Faculty of Humanities and Social Sciences:
  Education, Politics and Social Sciences: Prof. J. WEEKES
  Redwood College: Prof. K. AGBOLEGBE
Business School:
  Undergraduate Office: N. RICHARDS
  Postgraduate Office: D. GREEN

LOUGHBOROUGH UNIVERSITY

Loughborough, Leics., LE11 3TU
Telephone: (1509) 263171
Fax: (1509) 223901
Internet: www.lboro.ac.uk

Founded 1966 as univ.; formerly Loughborough College of Advanced Technology
Academic year: September to June

Chancellor: Sir JOHN JENNINGS
Vice-Chancellor: Sir DAVID WALLACE
Deputy Vice-Chancellor: Prof. PHIL ROBERTS
Pro-Vice-Chancellors: Prof. MORAG BELL, Prof. NEIL A. HALLIWELL
Senior Pro-Chancellor: Sir BRYAN CARSBERG
Pro-Chancellors: ROGER BOISSIER, RICHARD PARRY-JONES
Registrar: JOHN TOWN
Librarian: MARY MORLEY

Library of 600,000 vols
Number of teachers: 554
Number of students: 14,515

Publication: *Annual Report*

DEANS

Faculty of Engineering: Prof. C. BACKHOUSE
Faculty of Science: Prof. K. C. PARSONS
Faculty of Social Sciences and Humanities: Prof. T. KAVANAGH

PROFESSORS

ALEXANDROV, A. S., Theoretical Physics
ALLEN, D., European and International Politics
ALTY, J. L., Computer Science
ANDERSON, J., Physical Geography
ANDREWS, J., Risk and Reliability Analysis
ANUMBA, C., Construction Engineering and Informatics
ARNOLD, J., Organizational Behaviour
AUSTIN, S., Structural Engineering
BABITSKY, V. I., Dynamics
BACKHOUSE, C., Product Innovation
BAGILHOLE, B., Social Policy and Equal Opportunities
BEAVERSTOCK, J., Economic Geography
BECKER, S., Social Policy and Social Care
BELL, M., Cultural Geography
BIDDLE, S., Exercise and Sport Psychology
BILLIG, M. G., Social Sciences
BINNER, J., Ceramic Materials
BOUCHLAGHEM, D., Architectural Engineering
BOWMAN, R., Organic Chemistry
BRYMAN, A E., Social Research
BUCK, T., International Business
BURNS, N. D., Manufacturing Systems
CAMERON, N., Human Biology
CASE, K., Computer Aided Engineering
CHIVERS, G. E., Risk and Professional Development
CHUNG, P., Computer Science
DAMODARAN, L., Participative Design and Change Management
DANIELS, K., Organizational Psychology
DAVIDSON, I., Accounting and Finance
DICKENS, P., Manufacturing Technology
DOBSON, P., Competitive Economics
EDWARDS, D. E., Psychology
EVANS, J., Sociology of Education and Physical Education

FARRELL, G., Criminology
FAULKNER, R. G., Physical Metallurgy
FEATHER, J. P., Library and Information Studies
FITZGERALD, L., Management Accounting
FLETCHER, S., Physical Chemistry
FORBES, W., Accounting and Finance
GANE, M., Sociology
GARNER, C., Applied Thermodynamics
GIBB, A., Construction Engineering Management
GILBERT, C., Polymer Technology
GLEESON, M., Exercise Biochemistry
GOLDING, P., Sociology
GOODALL, R. M., Control Systems Engineering
GORDON, T., Automative Systems Engineering
GREEN, C. J., Banking and Finance
GRIFFITHS, J. B., Applied Mathematics
GRIMSHAW, R. H. J., Mathematical Sciences
HALL, M., Banking and Financial Regulation
HALLIWELL, N. A., Optical Engineering
HANKINSON, G., Chemical Engineering
HANSON, C., English
HANTRAIS, L., European Social Policy
HASLAM, R., Health and Safety Ergonomics
HENRY, I., Leisure Policy and Management
HILL, M. R., Russian and East European Industrial Studies
HOBBY, E., 17th century Studies
HORNE, J. A., Psychophysiology
HOULIHAN, B., Sport Policy
HOURSTON, D. J., Polymer Technology
HOWCROFT, B., Retail Banking
HUNTLEY, J., Applied Mechanics
INFIELD, D., Renewable Energy Systems
JONES, R., Sports Technology
JONES, R. C. F., Organic and Biological Chemistry
KALAWSKY, R. S., Human Computer Integration
KAVANAGH, T., Design
KING, M., Management Sciences
KIRK, D., Physical Education and Sport
KONG, M., Bioelectrics Engineering
KRYLOV, V., Acoustics and Vibration
KURYLEV, S., Mathematics
KUSMARTSEV, F., Condensed Matter Theory
LANSDALE, M., Experimental Psychology
LISTER, M. R. A., Social Policy
LLEWELLYN, D. T., Money and Banking
LOUGHLAN, J., Aerospace Structures
LOVEDAY, D., Building Physics
MAGUIRE, J., Sociology of Sport
MASON, G., Chemical Engineering
MAUGHAN, R., Sport and Exercise Nutrition
McCAFFER, R., Construction Management
McGUIGAN, J., Cultural Analysis
McGUIRK, J. J., Aerodynamics
McIVER, P., Applied Mathematics
McKEE, V., Inorganic Chemistry
McKNIGHT, C., Information Studies
MILLER, J. N., Analytical Chemistry
MILLS, T. C., Applied Statistics and Econometrics
MORGAN, K., Gerontology
NASSEHI, V., Chemical Engineering
ODDEY, A., Drama and Theatre Studies
OPPENHEIM, C., Information Science
OVERTON, W., Literature
PAGE, P., Organic Chemistry
PARISH, D., Communication Networks
PARKIN, R. M., Mechatronics
PARSONS, K. C., Environmental Ergonomics
PENTECOST, E., Economics
PEPPARD, J., Information Systems
PORTER, J. M., Design Ergonomics
POTTER, J. A., Discourse Analysis
PRICE, A., Construction Project Management
PUGH, C., Mathematics
RADLEY, A., Social Psychology
RAHNEJAT, H., Dynamics
RAMAN, K., Marketing
RAOOF, M., Structural Engineering
REID, I., Physical Geography

RENDELL, H., Physical Geography
RHODES, C., Art History and Theory
RIELLY, C., Chemical Engineering
ROBERTS, P. H., Design and Technology
ROTHBERG, S., Vibration Engineering
SAKER, J., Ford Faculty
SCHAD, J., Victorian Studies
SHIONO, K., Environmental Hydrodynamics
SILBERSCHMIDT, V., Mechanics of Materials
SLATER, D., Human Geography
SMITH, D., Sociology
SMITH, I. R., Electrical Power Engineering
SMITH, M., European Politics
SMITH, P., Photonics Engineering
SMITH, R., Applied Mathematics
SMITH, R., Mathematical Engineering
SMITH, R. M., Analytical Chemistry
STAROV, V., Chemical Engineering
STURGES, P., Library Studies
SUMMERS, R., Information Science
TAYLOR, P. J., Geography
THOMSON, R., Materials Engineering
THORPE, A., Construction Information Technology
THRING, R., Fuel Cell Engineering
TIPPETT, M., Accounting and Finance
TIWARI, A., Renewable Energy Systems
VARDAXOGLOU, Y., Wireless Communications
VESELOV, A. P., Mathematics
WAKEMAN, R. J., Chemical Engineering
WARD, H., Child and Family Research
WARWICK, P., Environmental Radiochemistry
WELLS, P., Animation
WESTON, R. H., Flexible Automation
WEYMAN-JONES, T. G., Industrial Economics
WHEATLEY, A. D., Water Technology
WILKINSON, A., Human Resource Management
WILKINSON, S., Feminism and Health Studies
WILLIAMS, C., Sports Science
WILLIAMS, D., Healthcare Engineering
WILSON, J., Operational Research
WOOD, N., Literature
WOODHEAD, M., Systems Engineering
WOODWARD, B., Underwater Acoustics
YEADON, F., Computer Simulation in Sport
ZIEBECK, K. R. A., Physics

ATTACHED INSTITUTES

Banking Centre: Dir J. B. HOWCROFT.

Centre for Hazard & Risk Management (CHaRM): tel. (1509) 228275; fax (1509) 222723; internet www.lboro.ac.uk/departments/bs; Dir CHARLES HANCOCK.

Centre for Innovative Construction Engineering (CICE): Dir Prof. C. ANUMBA.

Centre for Renewable Energy Systems Technology: Dir Prof. D. G. INFIELD.

Centre for Research in Social Policy: Dirs B. STAFFORD, S. MIDDLETON.

Communications Research Centre: Dirs Prof. M. BILLIG, Prof. P. GOLDING.

Ergonomics and Safety Research Institute (ESRI): Dir J. RICHARDSON (acting).

European Construction Institute: Chair. IMRIE CSOTI.

Institute of Development Engineering: Dir I. SMOUT.

Institute of Polymer Technology and Materials Engineering (IPTME): Dir J. HARPER.

Interactive Multimedia in Process Control and Communication Research Centre (IMPACT): Dir Prof. J. L. ALTY.

Library and Information Statistics Unit: Dir Dr E. DAVIES.

Loughborough Materials Characterisation Centre: Dir D. HOURSTON.

Management Development Centre: Dir J. WHITTAKER.

Mathematics Education Centre: Dir T. CROFT.

Midlands Centre for Criminology and Criminal Justice: Dir G. FARRELL.
Parallel Algorithm and Architectures Research Centre (PAARC): Dir HELMUT BEZ.
Systems Engineering Innovation Centre (SEIC): Dir Prof. M. WOODHEAD.

UNIVERSITY OF LUTON

Park Square, Luton, Bedfordshire, LU1 3JU
Telephone: (800) 389-6633
Fax: (1582) 486260
E-mail: info@luton.ac.uk
Internet: www.luton.ac.uk
Founded 1993; fmrly Luton College of Higher Education
Academic year: October to June
Chancellor: Sir ROBIN BIGGAM
Vice-Chancellor: Prof. LES EBDON
Deputy Vice-Chancellors: Prof. KATE ROBINSON, Dr STEPHEN PETTITT
Registrar: Dr JIM FRANKLIN
Librarian: TIM STONE
Library of 200,000 vols
Number of teachers: 700
Number of students: 12,300

DEANS

Faculty of Creative Arts and Technology: JAMES CRABBE
Faculty of Health and Social Science: Prof. SANDRA JOWETT
Luton Business School: Prof. PAUL BURNS

UNIVERSITY OF MANCHESTER

Oxford Rd, Manchester, M13 9PL
Telephone: (161) 306 6000
E-mail: ipro@manchester.ac.uk
Internet: www.manchester.ac.uk
Founded 2004 following merger of University of Manchester (f. 1851) and UMIST (f. 1824)
Academic year: September to June
Chancellors: ANNA FORD, Sir TERRY LEAHY
President and Vice-Chancellor: Prof. ALAN GILBERT
Pro-Chancellors: NORMAN ASKEW (Chair of the Governing Body), Admiral Sir JOHN KERR
Registrar, Secretary and Head of Administration: DUGALD MACKIE
Administrative Directors: JANE RATCHFORD (Business, Careers and Community), ALAN FERNS (Communications and Marketing Services), DIANA HAMPSON (Estates), GEOFF HOPE-TERRY (Finance), Prof. MARK CLARK (Information Systems), TIM WESTLAKE (International Development), ALBERT MCMENEMY (Planning and Academic Services), IAN HAWORTH (Public and Government Relations), ANDREW YATES (Sport, Trading and Residential Services), DELYTH CHAMBERS (Student Recruitment)
Librarian: BILL SIMPSON
Library: See John Rylands University Library of Manchester
Number of teachers: 2,000
Number of students: 18,000

VICE PRESIDENTS AND DEANS

Vice-President for Communications and External Relations: Prof. PAUL LAYZELL
Vice-President and Dean of the Faculty of Engineering and Physical Sciences: Prof. JOHN PERKINS
Vice-President and Dean of the Faculty of Humanities: Prof. ALISTAIR ULPH
Vice-President and Dean of the Faculty of Life Sciences: Prof. ALAN NORTH

Vice-President and Dean of the Faculty of Medical and Human Sciences: Prof. DAVID GORDON
Vice-President for Innovation and Economic Development: Prof. ROD COOMBS
Vice-President for Research: Dame Prof. NANCY ROTHWELL
Vice-President for Teaching and Learning: Prof. BOB MUNN

HEADS OF SCHOOLS

Faculty of Engineering and Physical Sciences (internet www.eps.manchester.ac.uk):
    School of Chemical Engineering and Analytical Science: Prof. RICHARD SNOOK
    School of Chemistry: Prof. PAUL O'BRIEN
    School of Computer Science: Prof. CHRIS TAYLOR
    School of Earth, Atmospheric and Environmental Sciences: Prof. RICHARD PATTRICK
    School of Electrical and Electronic Engineering: Prof. STEVE WILLIAMSON
    School of Materials: Prof. BOB YOUNG
    School of Mathematics: Prof. PAUL GLENDINNING
    School of Mechanical, Aerospace and Civil Engineering: Prof. GRAHAM THOMPSON
    School of Physics and Astronomy: Prof. JOHN DURELL

Faculty of Humanities (internet www.art.man.ac.uk):
    School of Arts, Histories and Cultures: Prof. PENNY SUMMERFIELD
    School of Education: Prof. MEL WEST
    School of Environment and Development: Prof. CLIVE AGNEW
    School of Informatics: Prof. BOB WOOD
    School of Languages, Linguistics and Culture: Prof. STEVE PARKER
    School of Law: Prof. ANDREW SANDERS
    Manchester Business School: Prof. JOHN ARNOLD
    School of Social Sciences: Prof. PETER HALFPENNY

Faculty of Life Sciences (internet www.fs.man.ac.uk):
    School of Life Sciences: Prof. ALAN NORTH

Faculty of Medical and Human Sciences (internet www.mhs.manchester.ac.uk):
    School of Dentistry: Prof. KEVIN O'BRIEN
    School of Medicine: Prof. ANDREW GARNER
    School of Nursing, Midwifery and Social Work: Prof. KAREN A. LUKER
    School of Pharmacy and Pharmaceutical Sciences: Dr LARRY GIFFORD
    School of Psychological Sciences: Prof. GEOFF BEATTIE

PROFESSORS

Faculty of Engineering and Physical Sciences
    School of Chemical Engineering and Analytical Sciences:
        ALDER, J. F.
        CILLIERS, J.
        DAVEY, R.
        DEWHURST, R.
        DYAKOWSKI, T.
        FIELDEN, P.
        GODDARD, N.
        GRIFFITHS, R.
        HEGGS, P.
        MANN, R.
        MAVITUNA, F.
        MCCARTHY, J.
        PERSAUD, K.
        ROBERTS, S.
        SHARRATT, P.
        SMITH, R.
        SNOOK, R.
        TIDDY, G.
        VICKERMAN, J.
        WEBB, C.

School of Chemistry:

ANDERSON, N. W.
BAILEY, P. D.
CLARKE, J. H. R.
CLAYDEN, J. P.
CONNOR, J. N. L.
GASKELL, S. J.
HELLIWELL, J. R.
HILLIER, I. H.
KELL, D. B.
LIVENS, F. R.
MORRIS, G. A.
MUNN, R. W.
O'BRIEN, P.
STOODLEY, R. J.
SUTHERLAND, J.
TAIT, P. J. T.
THOMAS, E. J.
TURNER, M.
VICKERMAN, J. C.
WAUGH, K. C.
WINPENNY, R.
WOODPENNY, L. V.

School of Computer Science:

ACZEL, P.
BARRINGER, H.
BARTON, S.
BREE, D.
FURBER, S.
GOBLE, C.
GURD, J.
HORROCKS, I.
HUBBOLD, R.
KAHN, H.
MIDDLETON, B.
PATON, N.
RECTOR, A.
TAYLOR, C.
VORONKOV, A.
WARBOYS, B.
WATSON, I.

School of Earth, Atmospheric and
Environmental Sciences:

CHOULARTON, T. W., Atmospheric Physics
CURTIS, C., Geochemistry
GAWTHORPE, R., Sedimentation and Tectonics
HENDERSON, M., Petrology
JONAS, P. R., Atmospheric Physics
PATTRICK, R., Earth Sciences
RUTTER, E., Earth Sciences
SELDEN, P., Earth Sciences
TURNER, G., Earth Sciences
VAUGHAN, D., Mineralogy
VAUGHAN, G., Atmospheric Sciences
ZUSSMAN, Z., Earth Sciences

School of Electrical and Electronic
Engineering:

ALLINSON, N. M.
BROWN, A. K.
DAVIS, L. E.
GOTT, G. F.
HICKS, P. J.
JENKINS, N.
KIRSCHEN, D.
MCCANN, H.
MISSOUS, M.
MUNRO, N.
PEAKER, A. R.
REZAZADEH, A.
STRBAC, G.
WANG, H.
WILLIAMSON, S.
YORK, T. A.

School of Materials:

DERBY, B., Materials Science
FREER, R., Materials Science
HUMPHREYS, F. J., Materials Science
LORIMER, G., Materials Science
LOVELL, P., Polymer Science
O'BRIEN, P., Inorganic Materials, Chemistry
ROBERTS, J., Textiles and Paper

SALE, F., Chemical Metallurgy and Materials Science
SHERRY, A., Corrosion and Protection
STANFORD, J., Polymer Materials Science
STOTT, H., Corrosion and Protection
THOMPSON, G., Corrosion and Protection
WITHERS, P., Materials Science
YOUNG, R., Polymer Science and Technology

School of Mathematics:

ABRAHAMS, I. D., Applied Mathematics
ACZEL, P. H., Mathematical Logic and Computing Science
BOROVIK, A., Pure Mathematics
BROOMHEAD, D., Applied Mathematics
BRYANT, R., Pure Mathematics
DODSON, K., Geometry
DOLD, J., Applied Mathematics
DONEY, R. A., Probability Theory
DUCK, P. W., Applied Mathematics
GLENDINNING, P., Applied Mathematics
HIGHAM, N. J., Applied Mathematics
PARIS, J. B., Pure Mathematics
PLYMEN, R. J., Pure Mathematics
PREMET, A. A., Algebra
PREST, M., Pure Mathematics
RAY, N., Pure Mathematics
ROWLEY, P., Mathematics
RUBAN, A., Computational Fluid Dynamics
SILVESTER, D., Applied Mathematics
SUBBA RAO, T., Statistics
TAYLOR, M. J., Pure Mathematics
WOOD, R. M. W., Algebra

School of Mechanical, Aerospace and Civil
Engineering:

AL-HASSANI, S. T. S., Mechanical Engineering
BAILEY, C., Structural Engineering
BALL, A. D., Maintenance Engineering
COOPER, J. E., Engineering
DAVIES, M., Structural Engineering
HAYHURST, D. R., Design, Manufacture and Materials
HINDUJA, S., Mechanical Engineering
JACKSON, J. D., Mechanical and Nuclear Engineering
LAUNDER, B. E., Mechanical Engineering
LAURENCE, D., Computational Fluid Dynamics
LEUNG, A., Engineering
LEVERMORE, G., Built Environment
LI, L., Laser Engineering
MARSDEN, B., Nuclear Graphite Technology
REID, S. R., Mechanical Engineering
SANDOZ, D. J., Control Engineering
SMITH, I., Geotechnics
STANSBY, P., Hydrodynamics
THOMPSON, G., Mechanical Engineering
TURAN, A., Mechanical Engineering
VARLOW, B. R., Industrial Liaison
WINCH, G., Construction Project Management
WOOD, N., Aerospace Engineering
WRIGHT, J. R., Mechanical Engineering

School of Physics and Astronomy:

BARLOW, S. J., Particle Physics
BISHOP, R. F., Theoretical Physics
BRAY, A. J., Theoretical Physics
DIAMOND, P. D., Astronomy and Astrophysics
DURELL, J. L., Nuclear Physics
FLAVELL, W. R., Photon Physics
FORSHAW, J. R., Particle Physics
GEIM, A. K., Condensed Matter Physics
GLEESON, H. F., Nonlinear and Liquid Crystal Physics
KING, G. C., Photon Physics
KING, T. A., Photon Physics
LAFFERTY, G. D., Particle Physics
LU, J., Biological Physics
LYNE, A. G., Astronomy and Astrophysics
MARSHALL, R., Particle Physics
MILLAR, T. J., Astronomy and Astrophysics

MOORE, M. A., Theoretical Physics
MULLIN, T., Nonlinear and Liquid Crystal Physics
WALET, N. R., Theoretical Physics
WILKINSON, P. N., Astronomy and Astrophysics
WYATT, T. R., Particle Physics
ZIJLSTRA, A. A., Astronomy and Astrophysics

Faculty of Humanities

School of Arts, Histories and Culture:

ADAMSON, S., Linguistics and Literary History
ALEXANDER, P., Post-Biblical Jewish Studies
BERGIN, J., Modern History
BROOKE, G. J., Biblical Studies
CASKEN, J., Music
CAUSEY, A., Modern Art History
COOPER, B., Music
CORNELL, T., Ancient History
CROWLEY, T., Modern English Literature
DENISON, D., English Linguistics
EAGLETON, T., Cultural Theory
FALLOWS, D., Music
FANNING, D., Music
FOURACRE, P., History
GARDNER, V., Theatre Studies
GATRELL, P., Modern History
GRAHAM, E. L., Social and Pastoral Theology
GRANGE, P., Music
HAMMOND, G., English Literature
HOGG, R. M., English Language and Medieval English Literature
JACKSON, B. S., Modern Jewish Studies
JANTZEN, G. M., Philosophy of Religion
JONES, A., History of Art
JOYCE, P., Modern History
LANGSLOW, D., Classics
LING, R., Archaeology
MILLWARD, R., Economic History
PARKIN, T., Ancient History
PEARSON, J., English Literature
PITTOCK, M., Scottish and Romantic Literature
SCRAGG, D., Anglo-Saxon Studies
SHARROCK, A., Classics
SUMMERFIELD, P., Modern History
THOMAS, J., Archaeology
WARD, B., American Studies
WARD, G., Contextual Theology
WOOLFORD, J., 19th Century Literature and Culture

School of Education:

AINSCOW, M., Education
BAMFORD, J., Audiology and Deaf Education
CONTI-RAMSDEN, G., Specific Language Impairment
DAVIES, A., Education
DYSON, A., Education
FARRELL, P., Educational Psychology
THOMPSON, L., Language and Literacy Studies
WEST, M., Educational Leadership
WILLIAMS, J. S., Mathematics Education

School of Environment and Development:

AGNEW, C., Geography
ALLOTT, T., Geography
BEBBINGTON, A., Management in International Development
BRADFORD, M., Geography
CASTREE, N., Geography
COOK, P., Economics and Development Policy
DOUGLAS, I., Geography
HANDLEY, J., Land Restoration and Management
HEBBERT, M., Town Planning
HENDERSON, J., International Economic Sociology
HULME, D., Development Studies
KIRKPATRICK, C., Development Economics

MacDougall, G., Architecture and Advanced Technology
Robson, B., Geography
Stonehouse, R., Architecture
Thomas, R., Geography
Williams, G., Urban Planning and Development
Wood, C., Environmental Planning

School of Informatics:

Blenkhorn, P., Interactive Systems Design
Keane, J., Data and Decision Engineering
Loucopoulos, P., Information Systems
Macaulay, L., System Design
Ramsay, A., Data and Decision Engineering
Sutcliffe, A., Interactive Systems Design
Wastell, D., Information Systems
Wood, J., Information Systems
Wood-Harper, A., Information Systems

School of Languages, Linguistics and Cultures:

Alexander, P. S., Middle Eastern Studies
Berger, S., Modern German and Comparative European History
Durrell, M., German
Günsberg, M., Italian
Lawrance, J., Spanish
Parker, S., German
Perriam, C., Hispanic Studies
Smith, G. R., Middle Eastern Studies
Tolz, V., Russian

School of Law:

Brazier, M., Law
Brazier, R., Law
Dobash, R., Law
Dobash, R., Law
Duxbury, N., Law
Gibbons, T., Law
Harris, J., Law
Harris, N., Law
Hayry, M., Law
Jaconelli, J., Law
McCormack, G., Law
McGee, A., Law
Millman, D., Law
Ogus, A., Law
Qureshi, A., Law
Sanders, A., Law
Shaw, J., Law
Tsujii, J., Text Mining

Manchester Business School:

Barrar, P., Operations Management
Bowe, M., International Finance
Bruce, M., Design Management and Retailing
Chittenden, F., Small Business Finance
Conyon, M., Corporate Governance
Coombs, R., Technology Management
Davidson, M., Managerial Psychology
Davies, G., Corporate Reputation
Easingwood, C., Marketing
Edwards, P., Accountancy
French, S., Information and Decision Sciences
Garrett, I., Accounting and Finance
Georghiou, L., Technology and Entrepreneurship Management and Policy
Ghauri, P., International Business
Green, K., Technology and Entrepreneurship Management and Policy
Hassard, J., Organizational Analysis
Higgins, J., Health Policy
Howells, J., Innovation and Competition
Humphrey, C., Accounting
Jackson, P., Corporate Communications
Kang, J., Marketing
Lewis, B., Marketing
Littler, D., Strategic Management
Marchington, M., Human Resource Management
McGoldrick, P., Retailing
Miles, I., Technology and Entrepreneurship Management and Policy

Naudé, P., Marketing
Newman, M., Management Accounting and Information Systems
Oakey, R., Business Development
Ogden, S., Accounting and Finance
O'Leary, T., Accounting
Paxson, D., Finance
Poon, S.-H., Finance
Rickards, T., Creativity and Organizational Change
Robson, K., Accounting
Rubery, J., Comparative Employment Systems
Sanghavi, N., Retail Marketing and Strategy
Scapens, R., Management Accounting and Information Systems
Sparrow, P., International Human Resource Management
Stapleton, R., Finance
Stark, A., Accounting
Stephen, F., Regulation
Strong, N., Finance
Turley, S., Accounting
Waddington, J., Human Resource Management
Walker, M., Finance and Accounting
Walsh, V., Innovation Management
Walshe, K., Health Policy and Management
Williams, K., Accounting and Political Economy
Yang, J.-B., Decision Sciences and Operations Management

School of Social Sciences:

Agénor, P.-R., Economics
Blackburn, K., Economics
Callahan, W., International Politics
Colman, D., Economics
Evstigneev, I., Economics
Gledhill, J., Social Anthropology
Harvey, P., Social Anthropology
Henley, P., Social Anthropology
Madden, P., Economics
Mason, J., Sociology
Metcalfe, S., Economics
Nixson, F., Economics
Osborn, D., Economics
Smart, C., Sociology
Wade, P., Social Anthropology
Werbner, R., Social Anthropology
Young, T., Economics

Faculty of Life Sciences:

Abadi, R.
Attwood, T.
Balment, R.
Barnes, G.
Brass, A.
Brown, T. A.
Bulleid, N.
Case, M.
Charman, W.
Cronly-Dillon, J.
Crossman, A.
David, R.
Dixon, M.
Dunne, M.
Eddy, A.
Efron, N.
Ferguson, M.
Foster, D.
Garrod, D.
Grant, M.
Grencis, R.
Hardingham, T.
High, S.
Humphries, M.
Hutchinson, I.
Hyde, J. E.
Itzhaki, R.
Kadler, K.
Kauppinen, R.
Kielty, C.
Kulikowski, J.
Lian, L. Y.

Loudon, A.
Moore, A.
McCarthy, J. E. G.
North, R. A.
Oliver, S.
Pickstone, J.
Poller, L.
Roberts, I.
Rothwell, N.
Sharrocks, A.
Sibley, C.
Stern, P.
Stirling, C.
Streuli, C.
Terenghi, G.
Tomlinson, D.
Trinci, A.
Turner, S.
Verkhratsky, A.
Weston, A.
Whetton, A. D.
White, A.
Worboys, M.

Faculty of Medical and Human Sciences

School of Dentistry:

Blinkhorn, A. S., Oral Health
Dixon, M. J., Dental Genetics
Ferguson, M. W. J., Basic Dental Sciences
O'Brien, K. D., Orthodontics
Shaw, W. C., Orthodontics and Dentofacial Development
Sloan, P., Experimental Oral Pathology
Thornhill, M. H., Medicine in Dentistry (H)
Wilson, N. H. F., Restorative Dentistry

School of Medicine:

Adams, J. E., Diagnostic Radiology (H)
Agius, R., Occupational and Environmental Medicine
Birch, J. M., Cancer Research Campaign, Paediatric and Familial Cancer Research Group
Boulton, A. J. M., Medicine
Burnie, J. P., Medical Microbiology (H)
Case, R. M., Physiology
Cherry, N. M., Occupational and Environmental Medicine
Crossman, A. R., Anatomy
David, T. J., Child Health and Paediatrics (H)
Davis, J. R. E., Medicine
Dunn, G., Biomedical Statistics
Durrington, P. N., Medicine
Eden, O. B., Paediatric Oncology
Eisner, D., Cardiac Physiology
Freemont, A. J., Tissue Pathology
Galasko, C. S. B., Orthopaedic Surgery (H)
Gallagher, S. T., Oncology
Garrod, D. R., Developmental Biology
Gordon, D., Medicine
Grant, M. E., Medical Biochemistry
Green, R., Physiology
Grencis, R. K., Immunology
Griffiths, C. E. M., Dermatology
Hawkins, R. E., Medical Oncology
Heagerty, A., Medicine (H)
Heller, R., Public Health
Herholz, K., Clinical Neurosciences
Hickman, J., Molecular Pharmacology
Horan, M. A., Geriatric Medicine (South) (H)
Howell, A., Medical Oncology
Hutchinson, I. V., Immunology
Irving, M. H., Surgery
Jackson, A., Neuroradiology
Kiernan, C. C., Behavioural Studies in Mental Handicap
Kirkwood, T. B. L., Biological Gerontology
Kitchener, H. C., Gynaecological Oncology (H)
Lowenstein, P. R., Molecular Medicine and Gene Therapy
McAllister, I., Medicine
McClure, J., Pathology

McCOLLUM, C. N., Surgery (H)

McCORD, J. F., Restorative Care of the Elderly

McLEOD, D., Ophthalmology (H)

MALLICK, N. P., Renal Medicine

MAWER, E. B., Bone and Mineral Metabolism

MAYES, A., Cognitive Neuroscience

MÜLLER, R., Pharmaceutics, Biopharmaceutics and Biotechnology

O'BRIEN, K. D., Orthodontics

OLLIER, W. E. R., Immunogenetics

POLLARD, B. J., Anaesthesia

PRICE, P., Radiation Oncology

READ, A. P., Human Genetics

RECTOR, A. L., Medical Informatics

ROLAND, M. O., General Practice

SCARFFE, J. H., Oncology

SEYMOUR, L., Gene Therapy

SIBBALD, B. S., Health Services Research

SIBLEY, C. P., Child Health and Physiology

SILMAN, A. J., Rheumatic Diseases Epidemiology

STANLEY, J. K., Hand Surgery

TALLIS, R. C., Geriatric Medicine (Salford) (H)

TAYLOR, C. J., Medical Biophysics (H)

THATCHER, N., Oncology

THOMPSON, D. G., Gastroenterology

VADGAMA, P., Clinical Biochemistry (H)

WHITE, A., Endocrine Sciences

WHITEHOUSE, C. R., Teaching Medicine in the Community

WILKIN, D., Health Services Research (H)

WOODMAN, C. B. J., Cancer Epidemiology and Public Health

YATES, D. W., Accident and Emergency Surgery

School of Nursing, Midwifery and Social Work:

CARLISLE, E., Education in Nursing and Midwifery

LUKER, K., Nursing and Midwifery

THOMSON, A., Midwifery

TODD, C., Primary Care and Community Health

WATERMAN, H., Nursing and Midwifery

School of Pharmacy and Pharmaceutical Sciences:

ATTWOOD, D.

CANTRILL, J.

CLARKE, D.

COLLETT, J.

DIVE, C.

DOUGLAS, K.

GIFFORD, L.

GILBERT, P.

HOUSTON, J. B.

NOYCE, P.

ROWLAND, M.

STRATFORD, I.

School of Psychological Sciences:

BAMFORD, J.

BARROWCLOUGH, C.

BEATTIE, G.

BENTALL, R.

CONTI-RAMSEN, G.

DAVIS, A.

LAMBON-RALPH, M.

LIEVEN, E.

MEUDELL, P.

PARKER, D.

TARRIER, N.

WEARDEN, J. H.

MANCHESTER METROPOLITAN UNIVERSITY

All Saints, Manchester, M15 6BH

Telephone: (161) 247-2000

Fax: (161) 236-6390

E-mail: enquiries@mmu.ac.uk

Internet: www.mmu.ac.uk

Founded 1970 as Manchester Polytechnic; present name and status 1992

Academic year: September to July

Chancellor: Rt Hon. Dame JANET SMITH

Pro-Chancellor: ALAN BENZIE

Vice-Chancellor: Prof. JOHN BROOKS

Deputy Vice-Chancellor and Academic Director: Prof. B. S. PLUMB

Academic Registrar: J. D. M. KARCZEWSKI-SLOWIKOWSKI

Librarian: Prof. C. HARRIS

Library: Library: see Libraries and Archives

Number of teachers: 1,300

Number of students: 32,085 (18,690 full-time, 3,309 on sandwich courses, 10,086 part-time)

PRO-VICE-CHANCELLORS AND DEANS OF FACULTY

Faculty of Art and Design: Prof. M. WAYMAN

Faculty of Food, Clothing and Hospitality Management: Prof. R. MURRAY

Faculty of Health, Social Care and Education: Prof. V. K. RAMPROGUS

Faculty of Humanities, Law and Social Science: Prof. J. BEER

Faculty of Science and Engineering: Prof. M. NEAL

Business School: HUW MORRIS

MMU Cheshire: D. DUNN

HEADS OF ACADEMIC DEPARTMENTS

Faculty of Art and Design (Ormond Bldg, Lower Ormond St, Manchester, M15 6BX; tel. (161) 247-1705; fax (161) 247-6393; e-mail artdes.fac@mmu.ac.uk; internet www .mmu.ac.uk/artanddesign):

Manchester School of Architecture: J. JESSOP

School of Art: (vacant)

School of Design: Prof. D. CROW

Manchester Institute for Research and Innovation in Art and Design: Prof. J. HYATT

Department of the History of Art and Design: Prof. L. A. HUNT

Resource Planning: M. STARLING

Faculty of Food, Clothing and Hospitality Management (Old Hall Lane, Manchester, M14 6HR; tel. (161) 247-2603; fax (161) 247-6872; e-mail hollings-fac@mmu.ac.uk; internet www.mmu.ac.uk/hollings):

Clothing Design and Technology: C. FAIRHURST

School of Food, Consumer, Tourism and Hospitality Management: Prof. R. C. MOODY

Faculty of Health, Social Care and Education (799 Wilmslow Rd, Didsbury, Manchester, M20 2RR; tel. (161) 247-2020; fax (161) 247-6392; e-mail commstud.fac@mmu.ac.uk; internet www.did.stu.mmu.ac.uk):

School of Health, Psychology and Social Care: PENNY RENWICK

Education and Social Research Institute: Prof. HARRY TORRANCE (acting)

Institute of Education: Prof. M. TOTTERDELL

Research Institute for Health and Social Care: Prof. CAROLYN KAGAN

Faculty of Humanities, Law and Social Science (Geoffrey Manton Building, Rosamond St West, Manchester, M15 6LL; tel. (161) 247-1751; fax (161) 247-6308; e-mail humanities-fac@mmu.ac.uk/hiss):

Economics: Prof. J. VINT

English: Prof. SUE ZLOSNIK

History and Economic History: Prof. D. NICHOLLS

Information and Communications: Prof. R. J. HARTLEY

Languages: Dr S. HANDLEY

Politics and Philosophy: Prof. P. CAMMACK

Sociology: B. LEACH

Faculty of Science and Engineering (John Dalton Bldg, Chester St, Manchester, M1 5GD; tel. (161) 247-2975; fax (161) 247-6831; e-mail se.courses@mmu.ac.uk; internet www .sci-eng.mmu.ac.uk):

Biological Sciences: Prof. T. LOOKER

Chemistry and Materials: Prof. J. B. LEACH

Combined Honours and Foundation Studies: Dr K. MOORE

Computing and Mathematics: Prof. D. CAUSON

Engineering and Technology: Prof. K. S. HURST (acting)

Environmental and Geographical Studies: (vacant)

Business School (Aytoun Bldg, Aytoun St, Manchester, M1 3GH; tel. (161) 247-3711; fax (161) 236-5319; e-mail business@mmu.ac .uk; internet www.business.mmu.ac.uk):

Business Information Technology: S. LYON (acting) (Exec. Head)

Corporate Reporting and Compliance: Prof. R. SWEETING (Exec. Head)

Human Resources Management and Organisational Behaviour: S. SHAW (Exec. Head)

Retail and Marketing: D. MUSKETT (Exec. Head)

Strategy and Entrepreneurship: S. LYON (Exec. Head)

MMU Cheshire (Crewe Green Rd, Crewe, CW1 5DU; tel. (161) 247-2991; fax (161) 247-6376; e-mail crewe.fac@mmu.ac.uk; internet www.mmu.ac.uk/cheshire):

Business and Management Studies: Prof. D. LEESE (acting)

Contemporary Arts: S. LACEY (acting)

Exercise and Sports Science: Prof. L. BURWITZ

Institute of Education: Prof. M. TOTTERDELL

Interdisciplinary Studies: Dr J. PIPER

Centre for Social Inclusion: Prof. G. HEATHCOTE

MIDDLESEX UNIVERSITY

North London Business Park, Oakleigh Rd South, London, N11 1QS

Telephone: (20) 8411-5898

Fax: (20) 8411-5649

E-mail: admissions@mdx.ac.uk

Internet: www.mdx.ac.uk

Founded 1973 as Middlesex Polytechnic, present name and status 1992; comprises the former Enfield and Hendon Colleges of Technology, Hornsey College of Art, New College of Speech and Drama, Trent Park College of Education, the College of All Saints and North London College of Health Studies

Academic year: September to July

Chancellor: Lord SHEPPARD OF DIDGEMERE

Vice-Chancellor: Prof. MICHAEL DRISCOLL

Deputy Vice-Chancellor and Director of Middlesex International: Dr TERRY BUTLAND

Deputy Vice-Chancellor and Director of Middlesex UK: Prof. MARGARET HOUSE

Deputy Vice-Chancellor and Director of Finance and Director, Middlesex Business Services: MELVYN KEEN

Assistant Vice-Chancellor and Director of Middlesex Research: Prof. WAQAR AHMAD

Pro-Vice-Chancellors: Prof. GABRIELLE PARKER (School of Arts), Prof. NORMAN REVELL (School of Computing Science), Prof. MARGARET HOUSE (School of Health and Social Sciences), Prof. RICHARD TUFNELL (School of Lifelong Learning and Education), Prof. DENNIS PARKER (Middlesex University Business School), ROBERT CRICK (Dean of Students), PAULA VICKERS (Computing and Communications Service), WILLIAM MARSTERSON (Information and Learning

Resources), BARRY JACKSON (Learning Development), Prof. DENNIS HARDY (Projects), Prof. EDMUND PENNING-ROWSELL (Research)

Library of 540,000 vols, 130,000 vols of periodicals

Number of teachers: 853

Number of students: 25,563 (19,303 full-time and sandwich courses, 6,260 part-time)

DEANS

School of Arts: Prof. GABRIELLE PARKER

School of Computing Science: Prof. NORMAN REVELL

School of Health and Social Sciences: Prof. MARGARET HOUSE

School of Lifelong Learning and Education: Prof. RICHARD TUFFNELL

Middlesex University Business School: Prof. DENNIS PARKER

NAPIER UNIVERSITY

Craiglockhart Campus, 219 Colinton Rd, Edinburgh, EH14 1DJ

Telephone: (131) 455-2801

Fax: (131) 455-6363

E-mail: info@napier.ac.uk

Internet: www.napier.ac.uk

Founded 1964 as Napier College of Science and Technology, later became Napier Polytechnic, present name and status 1992

Academic year: September to July

Chancellor: Viscount YOUNGER OF LECKIE

Principal: Prof. JOAN STRINGER

Vice-Principals: Dr PETER EASY, Dr JENNY REES

Sec. and Academic Registrar: Dr GERRY WEBBER

Librarian: C. PINDER

Number of teachers: 560 full-time

Number of students: 12,500

DEANS

Faculty of Eng., Computing and Creative Industries: Prof. RAO BHAMIDMARRI

Faculty of Health, Life and Social Sciences: Prof. MORAG PROWSE

Business School: GEORGE STONEHOUSE

DEPARTMENTS AND SCHOOLS

Faculty of Engineering, Computing and Creative Industries (Craighouse Campus, Craighouse Rd, Edinburgh, EH10 5LG; fax (131) 455-6370; depts of Creative industries, Eng. and built environment, Computing):

Faculty of Health, Life and Social Sciences (10 Colinton Rd, Merchiston Campus, Edinburgh, EH10 5DT; tel. (131) 455-2801; fax (131) 455-2400; Schools of Health and social sciences, Life sciences, and Nursing, midwifery and social care):

Business School (Craiglockhart Campus, Edinburgh, EH14 1DJ; tel. (131) 455-2801; fax (131) 536-5621; Schools of Accounting, econ. and financial services, Management and law, and Marketing, tourism and languages):

UNIVERSITY OF NEWCASTLE UPON TYNE

Registrar's Office, 6 Kensington Terrace, Newcastle upon Tyne, NE1 7RU

Telephone: (191) 222-6000

Fax: (191) 261-1182

E-mail: postmaster@ncl.ac.uk

Internet: www.ncl.ac.uk

Founded 1851, incorporated as separate University in 1963

Academic year: September to June

Chancellor: Rt. Hon. CHRISTOPHER PATTEN

Vice-Chancellor: Prof. C. R. W. EDWARDS

Deputy Vice-Chancellor: JOHN GODDARD

Pro-Vice-Chancellor for External Relations and Research Liaison: Prof. T. F. PAGE

Pro-Vice-Chancellor for Humanities and Social Sciences: Prof. A. STEVENSON

Pro-Vice-Chancellor for Medical Sciences: Prof. O. F. W. JAMES

Pro-Vice-Chancellor for Science, Agriculture and Engineering: Prof. M. YOUNG

Pro-Vice-Chancellor for Teaching and Learning: Dr E. RITCHIE

Registrar: J. V. HOGAN

Librarian: Dr T. W. GRAHAM

Number of teachers: 2,060

Number of students: 17,281

Publication: *Annual Report*

PROVOSTS AND DEANS

Faculty of Humanities and Social Sciences: Prof. SIMON C. GUY (Dean of Research: Prof. G. DOCHERTY (Dean of Business Development)

Faculty of Medical Sciences: Prof. OLIVER JAMES (Dean of Research: JAMES, O. F. W. (Provost)

Faculty of Science, Agriculture and Engineering: Prof. MALCOLM P. YOUNG (Provost: Prof. E. MARTIN (Dean of Research: Prof. B. CLARKE (Dean of Business Development)

PROFESSORS

Faculty of Humanities and Social Sciences:

ALDER, J. E., Law

ANDERSON, L. R., Modern English and American Literature

APPLEYARD, A. R., Accounting and Finance

BABINGTON, B. F., Film Studies

BALLANTYNE, A. N., Architectural Science

BATCHELOR, J. B., English Literature

BONNETT, A., Social Geography

BURTON-ROBERTS, N. C., English Language and Linguistics

CAIN, T. G. S., Early Modern Literature

CARRINGTON, L. B., Education

CHARLES, D. R., Business Innovation

CHEDGZOY, K., Renaissance Literature

COLLIER, R. S., Law and Social Theory

COOK, V. J., Applied Linguistics

COOMBES, M. G., Geographic Information

DAVIS, P. S., Museology

DOLKON, P. J., Economics

FIRTH, J. E., Law

GILLESPIE, A. E., Communications Geography

GRAHAM, D. F., Poetry

GUY, S. C., Law

HAIMES, E. V., Sociology

HANSEN, R., Politics

HILLIER, J. S., Town and Country Planning

HOLMBERG, J. A., Theoretical Linguistics

HOWARD, D., Research Development

JONES, P. N., Political Philosophy

KARANASOS, M., Financial Economics

LAMONT, C., English Romantic Literature

LEOPOLD, J. W., Human Resources Management

LI, W., Applied Linguistics

MAC AN GHAILL, M., Education

MADANI POUR, A., Urban Design

MARSHALL, J. N., Economic Geography

MIDDLETON, R., Music

MINCA, C., Human Geography

MOLES, J. L., Latin

MOULAERT, F., European Planning and Development

MYLES, F., French Linguistics

NEWSON, M. D., Physical Geography

PERRIAM, C. G., Hispanic Studies

PINCOMBE, M. J., Tudor and Elizabethan Literature

POWRIE, P. P., French Cultural Studies

REYNOLDS, K. K., Children's Literature

RICHARDSON, L. D., Sociology and Social Policy

RIORDAN, C. B., German

RODGERS, C. P., Law

SAUNDERS, D. B., History of the Russian Empire

SHUCKSMITH, D. M., Town Planning

SPAWFORTH, A. J. S., Ancient History

STANLEY, L., Sociology

STIMPSON, B. E., French Studies

TOMANEY, J., Regional Governance

TOOLEY, J. N., Policy Studies in Education

VAN DER ELJK, P. J., Greek

WALKER, J. A., Family Policy

WARD, I., Law

WHALEY, D. C., Law

WHEELOCK, J., Socio-economics

WILLIS, K. G., Economics of the Environment

WRIGHT, T. R., English Literature

WYNARCZYK, P., Small Enterprise Research

Faculty of Medical Sciences:

AGIUS, L., Metabolic Biochemistry

ARGENT, B. E., Cellular Physiology

BARER, D. H., Clinical Geriatric Medicine

BARTON, J. R., Clinical Medicine

BASSENDINE, M. F., Hepatology

BATES, D., Clinical Neurology

BILOUS, R. W., Clinical Medicine

BLAIN, P. G., Environmental Medicine

BLAMIRE, A. M., Magnetic Resonance Physics

BOND, J., Social Gerontology and Health Services Research

BOND, S., Nursing Research

BURN, J., Clinical Genetics

BURT, A. D., Pathology

BUSHBY, K. M. D., Neuromuscular Genetics

CALVERT, A. H., Medical Oncology

CARDING, P., Voice Pathology

CAWSTON, T. E., Rheumatology

CHINNERY, P. F., Neurogenetics

CONNOLLY, B. A., Biochemistry

CORRIS, P. A., Thoracic Medicine

CRAFT, A. W., Child Health

DALY, A. K., Pharmacogenetics

DARK, J. H., Cardiothoracic Surgery

DARRINGTON, A. M., Psychology, Brain and Behaviour

DAY, C. P., Liver Medicine

DICKINSON, A. M., Marrow Transplant Biology

DONALDSON, C., Health Economics

DUNLOP, W., Obstetrics and Gynaecology

ECCLES, M. P., Primary Care Research

EDWARDSON, J. A. E., Neuroendocrinology

ELLISON, D. W., Neuropathology

EYRE, J. A., Paediatric Neuroscience

FERRIER, I. N., Psychiatry

FLECKNELL, P. A., Comparative Biology

FORD, G. A., Pharmacology of Old Age

FREESTON, M., Clinical Psychology

GATEHOUSE, A. M. R., Invertebrate Molecular Biology

GIBSON, G. J., Respiratory Medicine

GILBERT, H. J., Agricultural Biochemistry and Nutrition

GILLESPIE, J. I., Human Physiology

GOODSHIP, J. A., Medical Genetics

GOODSHIP, T. H. J., Renal Medicine

GOSLING, L. M., Animal Behaviour

GRAY, C. S., Clinical Geriatric Medicine

GRIFFITHS, T. D., Cognitive Neurology

GRUBIN, D., Forensic Psychiatry

HALL, A. G., Experimental Haematology

HARRIS, J. B., Experimental Neurology

HARWOOD, C. R., Molecular Microbiology

HAWKINS, A. R., Molecular Genetics

HEASMAN, P. A., Periodontology

HENDRICK, D. J., Occupational Respiratory Medicine

HESKETH, J. E., Mammalian Molecular Biology

HILL, P. M., Postgraduate Medical Education

HIRST, B. H., Cellular Physiology
HOME, P. D., Diabetes Medicine
HUGHES, M. A., Plant Molecular Genetics
INGRAM, C. D., Psychobiology
ISAACS, J., Clinical Rheumatology
JAMES, O. F. W., Geriatric Medicine
JONES, D. E. J., Liver Immunology
KEHOE, M. A., Microbiology
KENNY, R. A., Cardiovascular Research
KIRBY, J. A., Immunobiology
KIRKWOOD, T. B. L., Medicine
LAKEY, J. H., Structural Biochemistry
LE COUTEUR, A. S., Child and Adolescent Psychiatry
LENNARD, T. W. J., Breast and Endocrine Surgery
LEUNG, H. Y., Urological Oncology
LIGHTOWLERS, R. N., Molecular Neuroscience
LYDALL, D. A., Biology of Ageing
MCCABE, J. F., Dental Materials Science
MCCASKIE, A. W., Orthopaedic Surgery
MCGUCKIN, C., Regenerative Medicine
MCKEITH, I. G., Old Age Psychiatry
MCNEIL, C. J., Biological Sensor Systems
MARSHALL, S. M., Diabetes
MATHERS, J. C., Human Nutrition
MAY, C., Medical Sociology
MENDELOW, A. D., Neurosurgery
MORGAN, B. A., Yeast Molecular Biology
NEWELL, D. R., Cancer Therapeutics
O'BRIEN, J. T., Old Age Psychiatry
PARKER, L., Paediatric Epidemiology
PEARSON, A. D. J., Paediatric Oncology
PERRY, E. K., Neurochemical Pathology
PERRY, R. H., Neuropathology
PETRIE, M., Behavioural Ecology
PROCTOR, S. J., Haematological Oncology
PURVES, I. N., Health Informatics
RAWLINS, M., Clinical Pharmacology
REYNOLDS, N. J., Dermatology
ROBINSON, J. H., Immunology
ROBINSON, N. J., Molecular Genetics
ROBSON, S. C., Fetal Medicine
RUSSELL, R. R. B., Oral Biology
SELF, C. H., Clinical Biochemistry
SEYMOUR, R. A., Restorative Dentistry
SIMMONS, N. L., Epithelial Physiology
SLATER, C. R., Neuroscience
SOAMES, J. V., Oral Pathology
SPENCER, J. A., Medical Education in Primary Health Care
STANSBY, G., Vascular Surgery
STEELE, J. G., Dental Sciences
STRACHAN, T., Human Molecular Genetics
STRAUB, V. W., Medicine
TAYLOR, R., Medicine and Metabolism
THOMASON, J. M., Prosthodontics and Oral Rehabilitation
THIELE, A., Visual Neuroscience
THOMSON, P. J., Oral and Maxillofacial Surgery
THOMSON, R. G., Epidemiology and Public Health
TURNBULL, D. M., Neurology
VAN ZWANENBERG, T. D., Postgraduate General Practice
VON ZGLINICKI, T., Cellular Gerontology
WALKER, M., Molecular Diabetic Medicine
WALLS, A. W. G., Restorative Dentistry
WESTLEY, B. R., Molecular Pathology
WHITAKER, M. J., Physiology
WILLIAMS, F. M., Toxicology
WILSON, J. A., Otolaryngology and Head and Neck Surgery
YOUNG, A. H., General Psychiatry

Faculty of Science, Agriculture and Engineering:

AKAY, G., Chemical Engineering
ANDERSON, G. K., Environmental Engineering
ANDERSON, T., Computing Science
APLIN, A. C., Petroleum Geosciences
ATLAR, M., Ship Hydrodynamics
BARENGHI, C. F., Fluid Dynamics

BIRMINGHAM, R. W., Small Craft Design
BLYTHE, P. T., Transport
BRAIDEN, P. M., Manufacturing Engineering
BRUCE, G. J., Shiprepair and Conversion
BULL, S. J., Surface Engineering
BURDESS, J. S., Engineering Dynamics
CALDER, I. R., Land Use and Water Resources Management
CARRASCO, R. A., Mobile Communications
CLARE, A. S., Marine Science
CLARKE, B. G., Geotechnical Engineering
CLEGG, W., Structural Crystallography
CRAM, W. J., Plant Biology
CROWE, A., Physics
CULLINANE, K., Marine Transport and Management
DICKINSON, A. S., Theoretical Atomic Physics
DONNELLY, T., Integrated Pollution Control
EDWARDS, S. A., Agriculture
EMBLEY, T. M., Evolutionary Molecular Therapy
FINCH, J. W., Electrical Control Engineering
FRID, C. L., Marine Systems Geology
GIBSON, A. G., Composite Materials Engineering
GOLDING, B. T., Organic Chemistry
GOODFELLOW, M., Microbial Systematics
GRIFFIN, R. J., Medicinal Chemistry
HALL, J. W., Animal Behaviour
HARRIMAN, A. M., Physical Chemistry
GOSLING, L. M., Animal Behaviour
HALL, J. W., Earth System Engineering
HARRISON, M. D., Informatics
HARVEY, D. R., Agricultural Economics
HENDERSON, O. R., Statistics
HENDERSON, R. A., Inorganic Chemistry
HINTON, O. R., Signal Processing
HOFMANN, D. A., Gear Systems Design and Development
INCECIK, A., Offshore Engineering
JACK, A. G., Electrical Engineering
JAROS, M., Philosophical Studies
JOHNSON, G. R., Rehabilitation Engineering
JONES, C. B., Computing Science
JONES-LEE, M. W., Economics
KAPOOR, A., Mechanical Engineering Innovation
KOUTNY, M., Computing Science
LARTER, S. R., Geology
LEE, P. A., Computing Science
LEIFERT, C., Ecological Agriculture
LI, F., E-Business Development
LOWE, P. D., Rural Economy
MCLOUGHLIN, I. P., Management
MANNING, D. C., Soil Science
MARTIN, E. B., Industrial Statistics
MATTHEWS, J. N. S., Medical Statistics
MECROW, B. C., Electrical Power Engineering
METCALFE, I. S., Chemical Engineering
MITRANI, I., Computing Science
MONTAGUE, G. A., Bioprocess Control
MOORE, P., Geomatics
MORRIS, A. J., Process Control
MOSS, I. G., Theoretical Cosmology
NELSON, J. D., Public Transport Systems
NORTH, M., Organic Chemistry
O'CONNELL, P. E., Water Resources Engineering
O'DONNELL, A. G., Soil Microbiology and Molecular Ecology
OLIVE, P. J. W., Reproductive Biology
O'NEILL, A. G., Microelectronics
PAGE, T. F., Engineering Materials
PARKER, D., Geomatics
PROCTER, S., Management
REEKS, M. W., Multiphase Flow
RITSON, C., Agricultural Marketing
ROBERTSON, A. G., Pure Mathematics
ROSKILLY, A. P., Marine Engineering
RYAN, P. Y. A., Computing Science
SCOTT, K., Electrochemical Engineering

SEN, P., Marine Design and Construction
SERGEEV, Y. A., Engineering Mathematics
SHARIF, B. S., Digital Communications
SHRIVASTAVA, S. K., Computing Science
SHUKUROV, A., Astrophysics and Fluid Dynamics
SNOWDON, K. J., Research Development
THOMAS, K. M., Carbon Science
THOMPSON, D. P., Engineering Ceramics
UPSTILL-GODDARD, R. C., Marine Biogeochemistry
WAGNER, T., Earth Systems Science
WATSON, P., Computer Science
WHITE, J. R., Polymer Science and Engineering
WRIGHT, A. R., Chemical Engineering
WRIGHT, N. G., Electronic Materials
YAKOVLEV, A. V., Computing Systems Design
YOUNG, N. J., Pure Mathematics
YOUNGER, P. L., Hydrogeochemical Engineering

UNIVERSITY OF NORTHAMPTON

Park Campus, Boughton Green Rd, Northampton, NN2 7AL

Telephone: (1604) 735500
Fax: (1604) 710703
E-mail: study@northampton.ac.uk
Internet: www.northampton.ac.uk

Founded as University College Northampton; present status 2005

Rector: ANN TATE
Pro-Rectors: Prof. PETER BUSH (Academic), Dr FRANK BURDETT (Research and Business Development), DIANE HAYES (Resources)

Library of 175,000 vols, 1,000 periodicals
Number of teachers: 465
Number of students: 10,000

Schools of Applied Sciences, Arts, Business, Education, Health and Social Sciences.

NORTHUMBRIA UNIVERSITY

22 Ellison Place, Newcastle upon Tyne, NE1 8ST

Telephone: (191) 232-6002
Fax: (191) 227-4017
E-mail: er.pressoffice@northumbria.ac.uk
Internet: www.northumbria.ac.uk

Founded 1969 as Newcastle upon Tyne Polytechnic, present name and status 1992
Academic year: September to July

Chancellor: The Lord STEVENS OF KIRKWHELPINGTON
Vice-Chancellor and Chief Executive: Prof. KEL FIDLER
Deputy Vice-Chancellor (Resources): DAVID CHESSER
Pro-Vice-Chancellor (Learning and Teaching): Prof. BOB CRYAN
Pro-Vice-Chancellor (Student and Staff Affairs): Dr PETER SLEE
Director of Corporate Planning: VAL WILSON
Registrar: PAUL KELLY
Director of Learning Resources: Prof. JANE CORE

Library of 500,000 vols
Number of teachers: 924 (full-time)
Number of students: 29,500 (21,250 full-time and sandwich, 8,250 part-time)

DEANS

School of Applied Sciences: Prof. JULIE MENNELL
School of Arts and Social Sciences: Prof. LINDEN PEACH
School of Built Environment: STEPHEN HODGSON (acting)
School of Computing, Engineering and Information Science: Prof. ALISTAIR SAMBELL
School of Health, Community and Education Studies: Prof. ROYSTON STEPHENS

School of Law: Prof. PHILLIP KENNY
School of Psychology and Sports Sciences: Prof. PAM BRIGGS
Newcastle Business School: Prof. PAUL CRONEY

UNIVERSITY OF NOTTINGHAM

University Park, Nottingham, NG7 2RD
Telephone: (115) 951-5151
Fax: (115) 951-3666
Internet: www.nottingham.ac.uk
Founded as Univ. College 1881, Univ. Charter 1948

Chancellor: Prof. FUJIA YANG
Vice-Chancellor: Sir COLIN CAMPBELL
Pro-Vice-Chancellors: Prof. D. BIRCH, Prof. D. GREENAWAY, Prof. D. GRIERSON, Prof. D. RILEY, Prof. H. F. SEWELL, Prof. D. G. TALLACK
Registrar: K. H. JONES
Dir of Information Services: K. A. STANTON
Library: see Libraries and Archives
Number of teachers: 2,000
Number of students: 26,500

DEANS

Arts: Prof. D. G. TALLACK
Education: Prof. D. HOPKINS
Eng.: Prof. A. H. DODSON
Law and Social Sciences: Prof. C. R. THORNE
Medicine and Health Sciences: Prof. P. C. RUBIN
Science: Prof. P. J. BUTTERY
Veterinary Medicine and Science: Prof. G. ENGLAND
Graduate School: Prof. S. J. B. TENDLER

PROFESSORS

AITKENHEAD, A., Anaesthesia and Intensive Care
ALDRICH, R. J., Politics
ARCHER, D. B., Microbiology
ARMOUR, E. A. G., Mathematical Physics
ARROWSMITH, S. L., Law
ASHER, G. M., Electrical and Electronic Eng.
ASHWORTH, J., American and Canadian Studies
AZZOPARDI, B. J., Chemical, Environmental and Mining Eng.
BACKHOUSE, R. C., Computer Science and Information Technology
BAILEY, S. H., Law
BALL, F. G., Statistics
BARNARD, C. J., Animal Behaviour and Ecology
BATES, C., Physics and Astronomy
BATH, P., Stroke Medicine
BECKER, A. A., Mechanical Eng.
BECKETT, J. V., History
BEHNKE, J. M., Infections and Immunity
BELAVKIN, V., Mathematical Physics
BENFORD, S. D., Computer Science and Information Technology
BENNETT, M. J., Plant Science
BENNETT, T., Biomedical Sciences
BENSON, T. M., Electrical and Electronic Eng.
BERRY, R. H., Accounting and Finance
BETON, P. H., Physics and Astronomy
BINKS, M. R., Institute for Enterprise and Innovation
BIRCH, D. J., Law
BLACK, C. R., Plant Science
BLEANEY, M. F., Econ.
BOWLEY, R. M., Physics and Astronomy
BOWTELL, R. W., Physics and Astronomy
BRADLEY, J. E., Infections and Immunity
BRADSHAW, C. M., Psychiatry
BRAILSFORD, D. F., Computer Science and Information Technology
BRIGGS, D., Pharmaceutical Sciences
BRINCAT, M. P., Nurture Unit
BRITTON, J., Respiratory Medicine
BROOK, J. D., Genetics

BROUGHTON-PIPKIN, F., Obstetrics and Gynaecology
BROWN, A. D., Business School
BROWN, S. F., Civil Eng.
BRUCE, A. C., Econ. and Insurance
BURKE, E. K., Computer Science and Information Technology
BURKHARDT, H., Education
BUTTERY, P. J., Nutritional Biochemistry
BYCROFT, B. W., Pharmaceutical Sciences
CALLEN, A. E., Art History
CAMPBELL, K. H., Animal Physiology
CARDWELL, R. A., Hispanic and Latin American Studies
CARTER, R. A., English Studies
CASEY, P. M., Theology
CHALLIS, R. E., Electrical and Electronic Eng.
CHESTERS, M. A., Physical Chemistry
CHOI, K.-S., Fluid Mechanics
CHOONARA, I., Human Devt
CHRISTOPOULOS, C., Electrical and Electronic Eng.
CLARK, J. S., Organic Chemistry
CLARKE, B., Genetics
CLARKE, D. D., Psychology
COLES, P., Physics and Astronomy
COLLIS, J., Atmospheric Environment
CONNERTON, I., Food Sciences
COOKE, M., Music
COX, K., Nursing
COX, T. R., Institute of Work, Health and Orgs
CREMONA, J. E., Mathematical Sciences
CURRIE, G., Business School
CURRIE, G., Philosophy
DANCHEV, A., Int. Relations
DANIELS, S., Geography
DAVIES, M. C., Pharmaceutical Sciences
DAVIS, S. S., Pharmaceutical Sciences
DAVIS, T., Orthopaedic and Accident Surgery
DAY, C., Education
DENBY, B., Chemical, Environmental and Mining Eng.
DERRINGTON, A. M., Psychology
DEVLIN, J., Marketing
DIACON, S. R., Business School
DINGWALL, R. W. J., Institute for the Study of Genetics, Biorisks and Society
DISNEY, R. F., Econ.
DODSON, A. H., Civil Eng.
DONNELLY, R., Vascular Medicine
DOWD, K., Centre for Risk Insurance Studies
DRYDEN, I. L., Statistics
DUNCAN, A. S., Econ.
EAVES, L., Physics and Astronomy
ELLIMAN, D. G., Computer Science and Information Technology
ENNEW, C. T., Business School
EVETTS, J. A., Sociology and Social Policy
FALVEY, R. E., Econ.
FAWCETT, A. P., Architecture
FAWCETT, J. J., Law
FENN, P. T., Business School
FESENKO, I., Pure Mathematics
FINCH, R., Microbiology and Infectious Diseases
FLINT, A. P. F., Animal Physiology
FORBES, I., Politics
FORD, G. A., Theology
FORD, G. C., Computer Science and Information Technology
FOXON, C. T. B., Physics and Astronomy
FRANCIS, R. A., French
FRASER, D., Midwifery
GARDINER, S. M., Biomedical Sciences
GARNER, C. D., Inorganic Chemistry
GARVEY, S. D., Mechanical Eng.
GEARY, R. J., History
GILL, P. M. W., Physical Chemistry
GILLIES, P. A., Public Health Sciences
GINDY, N. N. Z., Manufacturing Eng. and Operations Management
GLASS, R. E., Genetics
GOW, I. T., Business School
GRAVELLS, N. P., Law
GREENAWAY, D., Econ.

GREENHAFF, P. L., Biomedical Sciences
GRIERSON, D., Plant Science
GRIFFITHS, A., Institute of Work, Health and Orgs
HALL, I., Therapeutics
HAMMOND, B. S., English Studies
HARDING, S. E., Food Sciences
HARGREAVES, A., Education
HARRIS, D. J., Law
HARRISON, C., Education
HASLAM, C., Institute of Work, Health and Orgs
HEFFERNAN, M. J., Geography
HENDERSON, J., Archaeology
HEPTINSTALL, S., Cardiovascular Medicine
HERVEY, T. K., Law
HEWITT, N., French
HEYWOOD, P. M., Politics
HILL, S. J., Biomedical Sciences
HOLLIS, C., Psychiatry
HOPKINSON, B., Vascular Surgery
HOWDLE, S. M., Inorganic Chemistry
HYDE, T. H., Mechanical Eng.
IRVING, W., Microbiology and Infectious Diseases
JACKSON, S., Psychology
JAKEMAN, E., Theoretical Mechanics
JAKEMAN, E., Electrical and Electronic Eng.
JAMES, R., Microbiology and Infectious Diseases
JAMES, V. C., Nursing
JENSEN, O. E., Theoretical Mechanics
JESCH, J., English Studies
JOHNSON, C. M., French
JOHNSON, I. R., Human Devt
JONES, R. G., Physical Chemistry
JORDAN, T. R., Psychology
KENDALL, D. A., Biomedical Sciences
KENNER, J., European Law
KING, J. R., Theoretical Mechanics
KING, R. H., American and Canadian Studies
KNIGHT, D. M., French
LANGLEY-EVANS, S., Human Nutrition
LARKINS, E., Electrical and Electronic Eng.
LAYBOURN-PARRY, J., Life and Environmental Sciences
LEDGEWAY, T., Vision Research
LEICESTER, M., Continuing Education
LEYBOURNE, S. J., Econ.
LEYSHON, A., Geography
LINCOLN, N. B., Psychology
LLOYD, R. G., Genetics
MCCARTNEY, D. G., Materials Engineering and Materials Design
MCCORQUODALE, R. G., Law
MCCOUSTRA, M., Chemical Physics
MACDONALD, I. A., Biomedical Sciences
MCGUIRK, B. J., Hispanic and Latin American Studies
MCRAE, J., English Studies
MADELEY, R., Community Health Sciences
MAHAJAN, R., Anaesthesia and Intensive Care
MANNING, N. P., Sociology and Social Policy
MARLOW, N., Human Devt
MARSDEN, C. A., Biomedical Sciences
MATHER, P. M., Geography
MAYER, R. J., Biomedical Sciences
MAYHEW, T. M., Biomedical Sciences
MELLER, H. E., History
MEPHAM, B., Biosciences
MERRIFIELD, M. R., Physics and Astronomy
MESSENT, P. B., American and Canadian Studies
MILES, N. J., Chemical, Environmental and Mining Eng.
MILLINGTON, M. I., Hispanic and Latin American Studies
MILNE, L. M., Russian and Slavonic Studies
MILNER, C. R., Econ.
MITCHELL, J. R., Food Sciences
MITCHELL, P., Psychology
MITHEN, R. F., Agricultural Sciences
MONTEITH, S., American Studies
MOON, J., Int. Centre for Corporate Social Responsibility

MOORE, T., Eng. Surveying and Space Geodesy
MORGAN, W. J., Continuing Education
MORRIS, P. G., Physics and Astronomy
MORSE, G. K., Law
MURPHY, R. J. L., Education
MURPHY, S., Biomedical Sciences
NEWBOLD, P., Econ.
NEWMAN, J. A., American and Canadian Studies
O'BRIEN, C., Manufacturing Eng. and Operations Management
O'CONNELL-DAVIDSON, J., Sociology and Social Policy
O'SHEA, P. S., Biomedical Sciences
OC, T., Built Environment
PARKER, S., Continuing Education
PASHBY, I. R., Manufacturing Eng. and Operations Management
PATIENT, R. K., Genetics
PATTENDEN, G., Chemistry
PEBERDY, J. F., Institute for Enterprise and Innovation
PERKINS, A., Human Devt
PIERSON, C., Politics
POLIAKOFF, M., Inorganic Chemistry
POWER, H., Mechanical Eng.
PRINGLE, M., General Practice
PRITCHARD, D. I., Pharmaceutical Sciences
RAY, D., Biomedical Sciences
REES, W., Int. Security
REEVE, D. E., Civil Eng.
RIFFAT, S. B., Built Environment
RILEY, D. S., Theoretical Mechanics
ROBERTS, J. A., Plant Science
RODDEN, T. A., Computer Science and Information Technology
ROSSLYN, W., Russian and Slavonic Studies
ROWLANDS, B. J., Gastrointestinal Surgery
RUDD, C. D., Mechanical Eng.
RUSSELL, N., Haematology
SABLITZKY, F., Genetics
SARRE, P. J., Physical Chemistry
SCHOLEFIELD, J., Surgery
SCHRODER, M., Inorganic Chemistry
SEABROOK, M. F., Agricultural Sciences
SEDDON, A. B., Materials Engineering and Materials Design
SHAKESHEFF, K., Pharmaceutical Sciences
SHARP, P. M., Genetics
SHAW, P. E., Biomedical Sciences
SHAW, R., Obstetrics and Gynaecology
SHAYLER, P. J., Mechanical Eng.
SIMESTER, A. P., Law
SIMPKINS, N. S., Organic Chemistry
SINCLAIR, M. T., Business School
SNAPE, C. E., Chemical, Environmental and Mining Eng.
SOCKET, E., Bacterial Genetics
SOMEKH, M. G., Electrical and Electronic Eng.
SOMMERSTEIN, A. H., Classics
SPIESS, M. K., Pure Mathematics
STARKEY, K. P., Business School
STARMER, C. V., Econ.
STEPHENSON, T., Child Health
STEVENS, M. F. G., Pharmaceutical Sciences
STILL, J. M., French
TALLACK, D. G., American and Canadian Studies
TATTERSFIELD, A., Respiratory Medicine
TAYLOR, A. J., Food Sciences
TENDLER, S. J. B., Pharmaceutical Sciences
THORNE, C. R., Geography
THORNTON, J., Obstetrics and Gynaecology
TOMS, J. S., Business School
TUCK, B., Electrical and Electronic Eng.
TUCKER, G. A., Nutritional Biochemistry
TURVILLE-PETRE, T. F. S., English Studies
TYNAN, A. C., Business School
UNDERWOOD, G., Psychology
VAN ZYL SMIT, D., Law
WAITES, W. M., Food Sciences
WALKER, R. L., Sociology and Social Policy
WALLACE, W. A., Orthopaedic and Accident Surgery

WARD, C., Rehabilitation and Ageing
WEBB, R., Agricultural Sciences
WESTHEAD, P., Business School
WHITE, N. D., Law
WHYNES, D. K., Econ.
WILCOX, R. G., Cardiovascular Medicine
WILKINSON, R., Epidemiology and Public Health Sciences
WILLIAMS, H., Medical and Surgical Sciences
WILLIAMS, P., Pharmaceutical Sciences
WILLIAMS, P., Institute of Infections and Immunity
WILSON, J., Business School
WILSON, J. R., Manufacturing Eng. and Operations Management
WILSON, R. J. A., Archaeology
WINGFIELD, J., Pharmaceutical Sciences
WOOD, A. T., Statistics
WOOD, D. J., Psychology
WOOD, J. V., Materials Eng. and Materials Design
WOODS, R. A. M., German
WORTHEN, J., English Studies
WRIGHT, D. M., Business School
WRIGHT, N., Environmental Fluid Mechanics
WRIGLEY, C. J., History
YOUNG, J. W., History
YOUNG, L., Molecular Embryology
YU, H., Civil Eng.

ATTACHED CAMPUSES

China Campus: 199 Taikang East Rd, Ningbo 315100, Zhejiang Province, China; tel. (574) 88180000; fax (574) 88222276; e-mail recruitment-china@nottingham.ac.uk; internet www.nottingham.edu.cn; language of instruction: Englishf. 2005; 2,000 students; Provost Prof. PETER BUTTERY; Vice-Pres. and CEO Designate Prof. ROGER WOODS.

Malaysia Campus: Wisma MISC, Jalan Conlay, 50450 Kuala Lumpur, Malaysia; tel. (3) 21485288; fax (3) 21458837; e-mail enquiries@nottingham.edu.my; internet www.unim.nottingham.ac.uk; 1,200 students; Chair. of Campus Dato' SERI AHMAD RITHAUDDEEN BIN TENGKU ISMAIL.

NOTTINGHAM TRENT UNIVERSITY

Burton St, Nottingham, NG1 4BU
Telephone: (115) 941-8418
Fax: (115) 848-4852
E-mail: cor.web@ntu.ac.uk
Internet: www.ntu.ac.uk
Founded 1970; university status 1992
Academic year: September to July
Vice-Chancellor: Prof. NEIL GORMAN
Pro-Vice-Chancellors: Prof A. T. P. JONES, Prof. T. PALMER
Director of Corporate Affairs: JENNIFER SPENCER
Director of Finance and Operations: STEPHEN JACKSON
Director of Human Resources: FRANCESCA FOWLER
Registrar: D. W. SAMSON
Librarian: SUE McKNIGHT
Library of 467,299 vols, 2,550 periodicals, 7,150 electronic journals, 261 databases
Number of teachers: 927 (767 full-time, 160 part-time)
Number of students: 26,101
Publications: *Nottingham Law Journal* (2 a year), *Gearing and Transmissions Journal* (2 a year), *Journal of Construction Procurement* (2 a year), *Loess Letter* (2 a year), *Mercian Geologist* (annually), *Journal for Critical Realism* (3 a year), *Journal7 of Strategic Change* (8 a year), *Collapsing Soil Communique* (2 a year), *John Clare Society Journal* (annually), *Interventions Journal* (3 a year), *Comparative American Studies* (quarterly), *Studies in Travel Writing* (2 a year)

HEADS OF COLLEGES

College of Art and Design and the Built Environment: Prof. SIMON LEWIS
College of Business, Law and Social Sciences: Prof. DAVID WEBB
College of Education, Communication and Culture: Prof. NIGEL HASTINGS
College of Science and Technology: Prof. YVONNE BARNETT

DEANS

School of Animal, Rural and Environmental Sciences: DAVID BUTCHER
School of Arts, Communication and Culture: Prof. M. S. HOWARTH
School of Art and Design: JEAN WILLIAMSON
School of Biomedical and Natural Sciences: Prof. BOB REES
School of the Built Environment: Prof. G. KENNEDY
School of Computing and Informatics: Prof. ADRIAN HOPGOOD
School of Education: Dr GILL SCOTT
School of Social Sciences: Prof. DAVID MASON
Nottingham Business School: Prof. M. REYNOLDS
Nottingham Law School: Prof. M. J. GUNN

HEADS OF DEPARTMENTS

Accounting: Dr A. T. A. LOVELL
Animal, Rural and Environmental Sciences: Prof. DAVID BUTCHER
Biomedical and Natural Sciences: Prof. BOB REES
Built Environment: Prof. G. KENNEDY
Computing and Mathematics: Prof. A. HOPGOOD
Design: Prof. G. KENNEDY
Economics and Politics: P. D. PERITON
School of Engineering: Prof. J. B. HULL
English and Media Studies: K. P. G. CURTIS (acting)
Fashion and Textiles: J. WILLIAMSON (acting)
Finance and Business Information Systems: Prof. M. REYNOLDS
Health and Human Services: Prof. P. E. HIGHAM
Human Resource Management: Prof. J. W. LEOPOLD
Informatics, Computing and Intelligent Systems: Prof. ADRIAN HOPGOOD
International Studies: Dr L. PETTIFORD (acting)
Land-based Studies: Prof. D. BUTCHER
Literature, Language, Communication and Culture: Prof. MARIANNE HOWARTH
Modern Languages: Prof. M. HOWARTH
Nottingham Law School: Prof. M. J. GUNN
Primary Education: Prof. N. HASTINGS
Professional Legal Studies: Prof. A. T. P. JONES
School of Science: Dr N. A. A. MACFARLANE
Secondary and Tertiary Education: Prof. S. LAW
Social Sciences: DAVID MASON
Strategic Management and Marketing: Prof. P. C. JOYCE
School of Propety and Construction: Prof. P. GALLIMORE
Visual and Performing Arts: Prof. S. E. LEWIS

OPEN UNIVERSITY

Walton Hall, Milton Keynes, Bucks., MK7 6AA
Telephone: (1908) 274066
Fax: (1908) 653744
E-mail: general-enquiries@open.ac.uk
Internet: www.open.ac.uk
Founded 1969
Academic year: February to October (for undergraduate studies); teaching takes

place over nine months, with examinations in October

Distance learning courses supported by personal tuition and, where appropriate, fully integrated with broadcasts on BBC television and radio, audio and video cassette material, computing, and residential summer schools. Students are over the age of 18, resident in the UK, the European Union, or certain other countries where the Open University has agreed to register students, mainly in full-time employment and studying in their spare time. Courses can be taken as single entities or accumulated towards a BA or BSc degree. Short courses in professional and vocational areas are also available, leading to advanced and professional diplomas and certificates. There is also a higher degrees programme for the BPhil, MPhil and PhD by research, and 11 taught masters degrees (incl. MBA). Apart from the headquarters, there are 13 regions administering 290 study centres throughout the UK and in parts of Europe

Chancellor: Baroness BOOTHROYD

Pro-Chancellor: CHRISTOPHER HASKINS

Vice-Chancellor: Prof. BRENDA GOURLEY

Pro-Vice-Chancellors: Dr LINDA JONES (Curriculum and Awards), Dr PAUL CLARK (Learning Technologies and Teaching), Prof. BRIGID HEYWOOD (Research and Staff), Prof. DAVID VINCENT (Strategy, Planning and Partnership), Prof. ALAN COCHRANE (Students, Quality and Standards)

Secretary: FRASER WOODBURN

Director of Library Services: NICK WHITSED

Number of teachers: 8,527 (1,124 full-time, 7,403 part-time)

Number of students and clients: 195 full-time, 189,613 part-time

Publications: *Courses, Diplomas and BA/ BSc Degrees, Open Business School Brochure, PGCE Brochure, Research Degree Prospectus, Studying with the Open University, Taught Master's Degree Prospectuses*

DEANS

Faculty of Arts: Dr RICHARD F. ALLEN

School of Education and Languages: ALAN TAIT

School of Health and Social Welfare: LESLEY-ANNE CULL

School of Management: Prof. JAMES FLECK

Faculty of Mathematics and Computing: Prof. D. BRANNAN

Faculty of Science: Dr PHILIP POTTS

Faculty of Social Sciences: PEGOTTY GRAHAM

Faculty of Technology: Dr ANDREW LANE

DIRECTORS OF UNITS

Institute of Educational Technology: Prof. PETER WRIGHT

Student Services: Prof. D. SEWART

REGIONAL DIRECTORS

London Region: ROSEMARY HAYES

South Region: PAT ATKINS

South East Region: LIZ GRAY

South West Region: LINDA BRIGHTMAN

West Midlands Region: Dr MICHAEL ROOKES

East Midlands Region: G. LAMMIE

East of England Region: ANGELA SCHOFIELD

Yorkshire Region: NICK BARRY

North West Region: CAROLE BAUME

North Region: J. SHIPLEY

Wales: HEATHER GRAHAM

Scotland: P. G. SYME

Ireland: Dr R. HAMILTON

PROFESSORS

ALDGATE, P. J., Social Care

ALLEN, J. R., Social Science
APPLEBY, C., Business Development
ATKINSON, D., Learning Disability
BASSINDALE, A., Organometallic Chemistry
BENNETT, T., Sociology
BENTON, T. J., Art History
BERRY, F., Inorganic Chemistry
BISSELL, C. C., Telematics
BLOWERS, A. T., Social Sciences
BORNAT, J., Oral History
BRAITHWAITE, N., Engineering Physics
BRANNAN, D. A., Pure Mathematics
BROWN, S., Philosophy
BURROWS, D. J., Music
BURTON, K. W., Isotope Geochemistry
BUSH, P.
CANDLIN, C. N., Applied Linguistics
CHAMBERS, E.
CHATAWAY, J. C., development Manager
CLARKE, J., Social Policy
COCHRANE, A., Public Policy
COCKELL, C. S., Geomicrobiology
COLEMAN, J. A., Languages
COLLINS, R. E., Media Studies
COOK, G., Education
CRITCHLEY, F., Statistics
CROSS, N. G., Design Studies (Technology)
DANIEL, E. M., Information Management
DAVIES, C., Health Care
DE ROECK, A. N., Computing
DOBSON, A. N. H., Politics
DU GAY, P. L. J., Sociology
EARL, C., Engineering Product Design
EDWARDS, L., Structural Integrity
EISENSTADT, M., Artificial Intelligence
ELLIOTT, D., Technology Policy
EMSLEY, C., Arts
ENGLANDER, R., History
FORRESTER-PATON, R., Social Enterprise
GARTHWAITE, P. H., Statistics
GELLATLY, A. R. H., Cognitive Psychology
GLATTER, R. G., Education
GOODMAN, D. C., History of Science and Technology
GOWER, J. C., Statistics
GRANNELL, M. J., Pure Mathematics
GRANT, J., Education in Medicine
GRAY, J. J., History of Mathematics
GRIGGS, T. S., Pure Mathematics
HALL, P. A. V., Computing
HALLIDAY, T. R., Evolutionary Biology
HAMMERSLEY, M., Educational and Social Research
HARDWICK, L. P., Classical Studies
HARRIS, N. B. W., Tectonics
HARRISON, C. T., Art History
HERBERT, T., Music
HIMMELWEIT, S. F., Economics
HOLLWAY, W., Psychology
INCE, D. C., Computing
ISON, R. L., Systems
JOHNSON, J., Complexity, Science and Design
JONES, B. W., Astronomy
JONES, M. C., Statistics
KAYE, G. R., Information Management
KING, C., Art History
LAING, A. W., Marketing
LAURENCE, E. A., History
LENTIN, A., History
LEWIS, V., Education
McCORMICK, R., Learning Schools Programme
McDONNELL, J. A., Planetary Space Science
MACKINTOSH, M., Economics
MALE, D., Immunology
MASON, J. H., Mathematics Education
MASON, N., Physics
MASON, R., Educational Technology
MASSEY, D. B., Geography
MERCER, N., Education
MONK, J. S., Digital Systems
MOON, R. E., Education
MUNCIE, J. P., Criminology
NAUGHTON, J., Public Understanding of Technology
NEWMAN, J. E., Social Policy

NUSEIBEH, B., Computing
O'DAY, R., History
OWENS, W. R., Art
PETERS, G., Systems Strategy
PHOENIX, A. A., Psychology
PILLINGER, C. T., Planetary Sciences
PLUMBRIDGE, W. J., Materials
POND-JANZEN, C. M., Biological Sciences
QUINTAS, P. R., Knowledge Management
RICHARDS, D., Applied Mathematics
RICHARDSON, J. T. E., Student Learning and Assessment
ROSE, S. P. R., Biology
ROY, R., Design and Environment
RUTTERFORD, J., Financial Management
SALAMAN, G., Organization Studies
SAWARD, M., Politics
SCANLON, E., Educational Technology
SEGAL-HORN, S., International Strategy
SELF, S., Volcanology
SHUKER, D. E. G., Organic Chemistry
SILVERTOWN, J. W., Ecology
SLAPPER, G., Law
SLATER, J. B.
SPICER, R. A., Earth Sciences
STEWART, D.
STEWART, M. G., Neuroscience
STOREY, J., Human Resource Management
SWITHENBY, S. J., Physics
THOMPSON, G. F., Political Economy
THORPE, M. S., Educational Technology
WALDER, D. J., Literature
WATSON, S., Sociology
WETHERELL, M., Business
WHATMORE, S. J., Geography
WIELD, D. V., Innovation and Development
WILKINSON, M., Applied Mathematics
WILSON, R. C. L., Earth Sciences
WOLFFE, J. R., Religious History
ZARNECKI, J., Space Sciences

UNIVERSITY OF OXFORD

Univ. Offices, Wellington Sq., Oxford, OX1 2JD

Telephone: (1865) 270000

Fax: (1865) 270708

Internet: www.ox.ac.uk

Founded 12th century

Academic year: October to June

Chancellor: Rt Hon. CHRISTOPHER PATTEN

High Steward: Rt Hon. the Lord BINGHAM OF CORNHILL

Vice-Chancellor: Dr JOHN HOOD

Pro-Vice-Chancellors: Dr JON DELLANDREA (Devt and External Relations), Prof. ELIZABETH FALLAIZE (Education), Dame FIONA CALDICOTT (Personnel and Equal Opportunities), Prof. ANTHONY MONACO (Planning and Resources), Prof. EWAN McKENDRICK (Research, Academic Services and Univ. Collns)

Registrar: Dr JULIE MAXTON

Sec. of Faculties and Academic Registrar: MICHAEL SILBY

Dir, Library Services: RONALD MILNE (acting)

Library: see Bodleian Library

Ashmolean Museum: see Museums

Number of teachers: 1,400

Number of students: 17,664

PROFESSORS

Note: Faculties, Schools, Depts, etc. are grouped by Div. (each div. has a full-time head and an elected board who are responsible for day-to-day operations incl. finance and planning) as follows: *Humanities Div.* (Faculty of Classics, Faculty of English Language and Literature, Faculty of Medieval and Modern European Languages and Literatures, Faculty of Modern History, Faculty of Music, Faculty of Oriental Studies, Faculty of Philosophy, Ruskin School of Drawing and Fine Art, Faculty of Theology);

Life and Environmental Sciences Div. (School of Anthropology, School of Archaeology, Dept of Biochemistry, School of Geography and the Environment, Dept of Plant Sciences, Dept of Zoology); *Mathematical and Physical Sciences Div.* (Dept of Chemistry, Computing Laboratory, Dept of Earth Sciences, Dept of Eng. Science, Dept of Materials, Mathematical Institute, Dept of Physics, Dept of Statistics); *Medical Sciences Div.* (Clinical Depts: Nuffield Dept of Anaesthetics, Dept of Cardiovascular Medicine, Nuffield Dept of Clinical Laboratory Sciences, Nuffield Dept of Clinical Medicine, Dept of Clinical Neurology, Dept of Clinical Pharmacology, Medical Oncology, Weatherall Institute of Molecular Medicine, Nuffield Dept of Obstetrics and Gynaecology, Nuffield Laboratory of Ophthalmology, Nuffield Dept of Orthopaedic Surgery, Dept of Paediatrics, Dept of Psychiatry, Div. of Public Health and Primary Health Care, Nuffield Dept of Surgery; Non-Clinical Depts: Dept of Experimental Psychology, Dept of Human Anatomy and Genetics, Sir William Dunn School of Pathology, Dept of Pharmacology, Dept of Physiology); *Social Sciences Div.* (Area and Devt Studies, Dept of Econ., Dept of Educational Studies, Oxford Internet Institute, Faculty of Law, Faculty of Management (Saïd Business School), Dept of Politics and Int. Relations, Queen Elizabeth House (Devt Studies), Dept of Social Policy and Social Work, Dept of Sociology). *Dept of Continuing Education* is not part of a Div.

Nuffield Department of Anaesthetics (Radcliffe Infirmary, Oxford, OX2 6HE; tel. (1865) 727342; fax (1865) 794191; internet www.nda.ox.ac.uk):

HAHN, C. W. W., Anaesthetic Science (Green College)
McQUAY, H. J., Pain Relief (Balliol College)
SEAR, J. W., Anaesthetics (Green College)

School of Anthropology and Museum Ethnography (51 Banbury Rd, Oxford, OX2 6PE; tel. (1865) 274624; fax (1865) 274630; internet www.anthropology.ox.ac.uk):

BANKS, M. J., Visual Anthropology (Wolfson College)
BARNES, R. H., Social Anthropology (St Antony's College)
JAMES, W. R., Social Anthropology (St Cross College)
PARKIN, D. J., Social Anthropology (All Souls College)
ULIJASZEK, S., Human Ecology (St Cross College)
VERTOVEC, S., Transnational Anthropology (Linacre College)

School of Archaeology (34–36 Beaumont St, Oxford, OX1 2PG; tel. (1865) 278240; fax (1865) 278254; internet www.arch.ox.ac.uk):

BARTON, R. N. E., Archaeology (Hertford College)
CUNLIFFE, B. W., European Archaeology (Keble College)
GOSDEN, C. H., Archaeology (St Cross College)
HEDGES, R. E. M., Archaeology (St Cross College)
MAYHEW, N. J., Numismatics and Monetary History (St Cross College)
POLLARD, A. M., Archaeological Science (Linacre College)
ROBINSON, M. A., Environmental Archaeology
SHERRATT, A. G., Archaeology (Linacre College)
VICKERS, M. J., Archaeology (Jesus College)
WILSON, A., Archaeology of the Roman Empire (All Souls College)

Department of Biochemistry (South Parks Rd, Oxford, OX1 3QU; tel. (1865) 275263; fax (1865) 275259; e-mail admin@bioch.ox.ac.uk; internet www.bioch.ox.ac.uk):

ARMITAGE, J. P., Biochemistry (Merton College)
CAMPBELL, I. D., Structural Biology (St John's College)
DRICKAMER, K., Biochemistry
DWEK, R. A., Glycobiology (Exeter College)
ENDICOTT, T. J., Structural Biology (Magdalen College)
FERGUSON, S. J., Biochemistry (St Edmund Hall)
HANDFORD, P. A., Biochemistry (St Catherine's College)
HODGKIN, J. A., Genetics (Keble College)
Dame JOHNSON, L., Molecular Biophysics (Corpus Christi College)
MAHADEVAN, L. C., Biochemistry (Trinity College)
NASMYTH, K., Biochemistry (Trinity College)
NOBLE, M. E. M., Structural Biology
REID, K. B. M., Immunochemistry (Green College)
SANSOM, M. S. P., Molecular Biophysics (Christ Church)
SHERRATT, D. J., Microbiology (Linacre College)
SOUTHERN, E. M., Biochemistry (Trinity College)
STUART, D. I., Structural Biology (Hertford College)
WATTS, A., Biochemistry (St Hugh's College)
WENTWORTH, P., Medicinal Chemistry
YUDKIN, M. D., Biochemistry (Kellogg College)

Department of Cardiovascular Medicine (Level 5, John Radcliffe Hospital, Headington, Oxford, OX3 9DU; tel. (1865) 220257; fax (1865) 768844; e-mail postmaster@cardiov.ox.ac.uk; internet www.cardiov.ox.ac.uk):

BHATTACHARYA, S., Cardiovascular Medicine
CHANNON, K. M., Cardiovascular Medicine (Lady Margaret Hall)
FARRALL, M., Cardiovascular Genetics (Keble College)
NEUBAUER, S., Cardiovascular Medicine (Christ Church)
WATKINS, H. C., Cardiovascular Medicine (Exeter College)

Department of Chemistry (Central Chemistry, South Parks Rd, Oxford, OX1 3QH; tel. (1865) 275990; fax (1865) 275905; internet www.chem.ox.ac.uk):

ANDERSON, H. L., Chemistry (Keble College)
ATKINS, P. W., Chemistry (Lincoln College)
ARMSTRONG, F. A., Chemistry (St John's College)
Sir BALDWIN, J., Chemistry (Magdalen College)
BATTLE, P. D., Chemistry (St Catherine's College)
BAYLEY, H., Chemical Biology (Hertford College)
BEER, P. D., Chemistry (Wadham College)
BROWN, J. M., Chemistry (Exeter College)
CLARY, D. C., Chemistry (Magdalen College)
COMPTON, R. G., Chemistry (St John's College)
DAVIES, S. G., Chemistry (New College)
DENNING, R. G., Chemistry (Magdalen College)
DILWORTH, J. R., Chemistry (St Anne's College)
DONOHOE, T. J., Chemistry (Magdalen College)
EDWARDS, P. P., Inorganic Chemistry (St Catherine's College)
EGDELL, R. G., Inorganic Chemistry (Trinity College)

ELAND, J. H. D., Physical Chemistry (Worcester College)
FLEET, G. W., Chemistry (St John's College)
FOORD, J. S., Chemistry (St Catherine's College)
GREEN, J. C., Chemistry (St Hugh's College)
HANCOCK, G., Chemistry (Trinity College)
HORE, P. J., Physical Chemistry (Corpus Christi College)
HOWARD, B. J., Chemistry (Pembroke College)
KLEIN, J., Chemistry (Exeter College)
LOGAN, D. E., Chemistry (Balliol College)
MADDEN, P. A., Chemistry (The Queen's College)
MINGOS, D. M. P., Chemistry (St Edmund Hall)
O'HARE, D. M., Chemistry (Balliol College)
RICHARDS, W. G., Chemistry (Brasenose College)
SCHOFIELD, C. J., Chemistry (Hertford College)
SOFTLEY, T. P., Chemical Physics (Merton College)
WAYNE, R. P., Chemistry (Christ Church)

Faculty of Classics (Classics Centre, The Old Boys' School, George St, Oxford, OX1 2RL; tel. (1865) 288391; fax (1865) 288386; internet www.classics.ox.ac.uk):

BOWIE, E. L., Classical Languages and Literature (Corpus Christi College)
BOWMAN, A. K., Ancient History (Brasenose College)
CAMERON, A. M., Late Antique and Byzantine History (Keble College)
HARDIE, P. R., Latin Language and Literature (Corpus Christi College)
HARRISON, S. J., Classical Languages and Literature (Corpus Christi College)
HUTCHINSON, G. O., Greek and Latin Languages and Literature (Exeter College)
JENKYNS, R. H. A., The Classical Tradition (Lady Margaret Hall)
KURTZ, D. C., Classical Art (Wolfson College)
PARKER, R. C. T., Ancient History (New College)
PELLING, C. B. R., Greek (Regius) (Christ Church)
SMITH, R. R. R., Classical Archaeology and Art (Lincoln College)
TAPLIN, O. P., Classical Languages and Literature (Magdalen College)
WILLI, A., Comparative Philology (Worcester College)

Nuffield Department of Clinical Laboratory Sciences (Level 4, Academic Block, John Radcliffe Hospital, Headington, Oxford, OX3 9DU; tel. (1865) 220556; fax (1865) 220078; internet www.ndcls.ox.ac.uk):

BELL, J. I., Medicine (Regius) (Magdalen College)
FERGUSON, D. J. P., Ultrastructural Morphology
GATTER, K. C., Pathology (St John's College)
HIGGS, D. R., Haematology
LA THANGUE, N. B., Clinical Laboratory Science (Linacre College)
MASON, D. Y., Cellular Pathology (Pembroke College)
MURPHY, M. F., Blood Transfusion Medicine
ROBERTS, D. J., Haematology
WAINSCOAT, J. S., Haematology
WILKIE, A. O. M., Pathology

Nuffield Department of Clinical Medicine (John Radcliffe Hospital, Headington, Oxford, OX3 9DU; tel. (1865) 221325; fax (1865) 222901; internet www.jr2.ox.ac.uk/ndm):

ALTMAN, D. G., Statistics in Medicine

BUCHAN, A. M., Clinical Geratology (Green College)

CERUNDOLO, V., Immunology (Merton College)

CLARKE, M. J., Clinical Epidemiology

COOKSON, W. O. C. M., Genetics (Green College)

DARBY, S. C., Medical Statistics

FRAYN, K. N., Human Metabolism (Green College)

GIBBONS, G. F., Human Metabolism

HILL, A. V. S., Human Genetics (Exeter College)

HOLMAN, R. R., Diabetic Medicine (Green College)

JEWELL, D. P., Gastroenterology (Green College)

JONES, E. Y., Protein Crystallography

KEY, T., Epidemiology

MCCARTHY, M., Diabetic Medicine (Green College)

MCKENNA, W. G., Radiation Oncology and Biology (Wolfson College)

MARSH, K., Tropical Medicine

MATTHEWS, D. R., Diabetic Medicine (Harris Manchester College)

MONACO, A. P., Human Genetics

NEWBOLD, C. I., Tropical Medicine (Green College)

Sir PETO, RICHARD, Medical Statistics and Epidemiology (Green College)

PETO, T. E. A., Medicine

PHILLIPS, R. E., Clinical Medicine (Wolfson College)

PUGH, C. W., Renal Medicine (Green College)

RATCLIFFE, P. J., Medicine (Jesus College)

RORSMAN, P., Diabetic Medicine (Harris Manchester College)

ROWLAND-JONES, S. L., Immunology (Christ Church)

STAMMERS, D. K., Structural Biology

STRADLING, J. R., Respiratory Medicine

STUART, D. I., Biochemistry (Hertford College)

TAGGART, D. P., Cardiovascular Surgery

THAKKER, R. V., Medicine (Somerville College)

TOWNSEND, A. R. M., Molecular Immunology (Linacre College)

WARRELL, D. A., Tropical Medicine and Infectious Diseases (St Cross College)

WASS, J. A. H., Endocrinology (Green College)

WHITE, N. J., Tropical Medicine

WOJNAROWSKA, F. T., Dermatology

WORDSWORTH, B. P., Rheumatology (Green College)

Department of Clinical Neurology (Radcliffe Infirmary, Oxford, OX2 6HE; tel. (1865) 224805; fax (1865) 790493; internet www.clneuro.ox.ac.uk):

BEESON, D. M. W., Neurosciences

EBERS, G. C., Clinical Neurology (St Edmund Hall)

ESIRI, M. M., Neuropathology (St Hugh's College)

JEZZARD, P., Neuroimaging

MARSHALL, J. C., Neuropsychology

MATTHEWS, P. M., Neurology (St Edmund Hall)

ROTHWELL, P. M., Clinical Neurology

VINCENT, A. C., Neuroimmunology (Somerville College)

WADE, D. T., Neurological Disability

WILLCOX, H. N. A., Neurosciences

Department of Clinical Pharmacology (Radcliffe Infirmary, Oxford, OX2 6HE; tel. (1865) 224524; fax (1865) 791712; internet www.clinpharm.ox.ac.uk):

KERR, D. J., Therapeutic Sciences and Clinical Pharmacology (Corpus Christi College)

Computing Laboratory (Wolfson Bldg, Parks Rd, Oxford, OX1 3QD; tel. (1865) 273838; fax (1865) 273839; e-mail enquiries@comlab.ox.ac.uk; internet web.comlab.ox.ac.uk/oucl):

ABRAMSKY, S., Computing (Wolfson College)

BIRD, R. S., Computing Science (Lincoln College)

BRENT, R. P., Computing Science (St Hugh's College)

DE MOOR, O., Computing Science (Magdalen College)

GAVAGHAN, D. J., Computational Biology (New College)

GILES, M., Computational Fluid Mechanics (St Hugh's College)

GOTTLOB, G., Computing Science (St Anne's College)

JEAVONS, P., Computing Science (St Anne's College)

MCCOLL, W. F., Computing Science (Wadham College)

MELHAM, T. F., Computing Science (Balliol College)

ONG, C. H. L., Computing Science (Merton College)

ROSCOE, A. W., Computing Science (University College)

SÜLI, E. E., Numerical Analysis (Linacre College)

TREFETHEN, L. N., Numerical Analysis (Balliol College)

Continuing Education (1 Wellington Sq., Oxford, OX1 2JA; tel. (1865) 270360; fax (1865) 270309; e-mail enquiries@conted.ox.ac.uk; internet www.conted.ox.ac.uk):

AIRS, M. R., Conservation and the Historic Environment (Kellogg College)

DAWKINS, C. R., Public Understanding of Science (New College)

Queen Elizabeth House (Development Studies) (21 St Giles, Oxford, OX1 3LA; tel. (1865) 273600; fax (1865) 273607; internet www.qeh.ox.ac.uk):

CASTLES, S., Migration and Refugee Studies (Green College)

DERCON, S., Devt Econ. (Wolfson College)

HARRISS-WHITE, B., Devt Studies (Wolfson College)

LALL, S., Devt Econ. (Green College)

STEWART, F. J., Devt Econ. (Somerville College)

WOOD, A., Int. Devt (Wolfson College)

Department of Earth Sciences (Parks Rd, Oxford, OX1 3PR; tel. (1865) 272000; fax (1865) 272072; e-mail enquiries@earth.ox.ac.uk; internet www.earth.ox.ac.uk):

BRASIER, M. D., Palaeobiology (St Edmund Hall)

ENGLAND, P. C., Geology (University College)

FRASER, D. G., Earth Sciences (Worcester College)

HALLIDAY, A. N., Geochemistry (St Hugh's College)

KNOWLES, C. J., Eng. Science (Linacre College)

Sir O'NIONS, KEITH, Physics and Chemistry of Materials (St Hugh's College)

PARSONS, B. E., Geodesy and Geophysics (St Cross College)

WATTS, A. B., Marine Geology and Geophysics (Wolfson College)

WOODHOUSE, J. H., Geophysics (Worcester College)

Department of Economics (Manor Road Building, Manor Rd, Oxford, OX1 3UQ; tel. (1865) 271089; fax (1865) 271094; e-mail reception@economics.ox.ac.uk; internet www.economics.ox.ac.uk):

ALLEN, R. C., Economic History (Nuffield College)

ANAND, S., Econ. (St Catherine's College)

BLISS, C. J., Int. Econ. (Nuffield College)

COLLIER, P., Econ. (St Antony's College)

HENDRY, D. F., Econ. (Nuffield College)

KLEMPERER, P. D., Econ. (Nuffield College)

KNIGHT, J. B., Econ. (St Edmund Hall)

MALCOMSON, J. M., Econ. (All Souls College)

MUELLBAUER, J. N. J., Econ. (Nuffield College)

OFFER, A., Economic History (All Souls College)

ROBERTS, K. S. W., Econ. (Nuffield College)

SHEPHARD, N., Econ. (Nuffield College)

VICKERS, J. S., Political Economy (All Souls College)

VINES, D. A., Econ. (Balliol College)

Department of Educational Studies (15 Norham Gardens, Oxford, OX2 6PY; tel. (1865) 274023; fax (1865) 274027; internet www.edstud.ox.ac.uk):

FURLONG, J., Educational Studies (Green College)

PHILLIPS, D., Comparative Education (St Edmund Hall)

SYLVA, K. D., Educational Psychology (Jesus College)

WALFORD, G., Education Policy (Green College)

Department of Engineering Science (Parks Rd, Oxford, OX1 3PJ; tel. (1865) 273000; fax (1865) 273010; internet www.eng.ox.ac.uk):

BORTHWICK, A. G. L., Eng. Science (St Edmund Hall)

Sir BRADY, MIKE, Information Eng. (Keble College)

CLARKE, D. W., Control Eng. (New College)

COCKS, A. C. F., Eng. Science (St Anne's College)

CUI, Z., Chemical Eng. (Hertford College)

DANIEL, R. W., Eng. Science (Brasenose College)

DARTON, R. C., Eng. Science (Keble College)

DEXTER, A. L., Eng. Science (Worcester College)

EATOCK TAYLOR, W. R., Mechanical Eng. (St Hugh's College)

EDWARDS, D. J., Eng. Science (Wadham College)

HILLS, D. A., Eng. Science (Lincoln College)

HOULSBY, G. T., Civil Eng. (Brasenose College)

IRELAND, P. T., Eng. Science (St Anne's College)

JONES, T. V., Turbomachinery (St Catherine's College)

KOUVARITAKIS, B., Eng. Science (St Edmund Hall)

MURRAY, D. W., Eng. Science (St Anne's College)

NOBLE, J. A., Eng. Science (Oriel College)

NOWELL, D., Eng. Science (Christ Church)

OLDFIELD, M. L. G., Eng. Science (Keble College)

RAYNES, E. P., Optoelectronic Eng. (St Cross College)

ROBERTS, S. J., Information Eng. (Somerville College)

SILLS, G. C., Eng. Science (St Catherine's College)

TARASSENKO, L., Electrical and Electronic Eng. (St John's College)

WILSON, T., Eng. Science (Hertford College)

ZISSERMAN, A. P., Eng. Science

Faculty of English Language and Literature (St Cross Bldg, Manor Rd, Oxford, OX1 3UQ; tel. (1865) 271055; fax (1865) 271054; internet www.english.ox.ac.uk):

BUSH, R. L., American Literature (St John's College)

BUTLER, I. C., English Language and Literature (Christ Church)

CAMERON, D. J., Language and Communication (Worcester College)

COOPER, E. H., English Language and Literature (University College)

CUNNINGHAM, V. D., English Language and Literature (Corpus Christi College)

GILL, S. C., English Language and Literature (Lincoln College)

GILLESPIE, V. A., English Language and Literature (St Anne's College)

GILLESPIE, V. A., Medieval English Language and Literature (Lady Margaret Hall)

GODDEN, M. R., Anglo-Saxon (Pembroke College)

HANNA, R., Palaeography (Keble College)

KELLY, J. S., English Language and Literature (St John's College)

LEE, H., English Literature (New College)

MACLEAN, I. W. F., Renaissance Studies (All Souls College)

McCABE, R. A., English Language and Literature (Merton College)

NEWLYN, L. A., English Language and Literature (St Edmund Hall)

NORBROOK, D. G. E., English Literature (Merton College)

RICKS, C., Poetry (Balliol College)

ROMAINE, S., English Language (Merton College)

STROHM, P., English Language and Literature (St Anne's College)

SUTHERLAND, K., Bibliography and Textual Criticism (St Anne's College)

WOMERSLEY, D. J., English Literature (St Catherine's College)

WU, S., English Language and Literature (St Catherine's College)

YOUNG, R. J. C., English and Critical Theory (Wadham College)

Department of Experimental Psychology (South Parks Rd, Oxford, OX1 3UD; tel. (1865) 271444; fax (1865) 310447; e-mail general@psy.ox.ac.uk; internet www.psych.ox.ac.uk):

BISHOP, D. V. M., Developmental Neuropsychology (St Hugh's College)

BRADDICK, O. J., Psychology (Magdalen College)

HEWSTONE, M. R. C., Social Psychology (New College)

MARTIN, R. M. A., Abnormal Psychology (St Edmund Hall)

PASSINGHAM, R. E., Cognitive Neuroscience (Wadham College)

PLUNKETT, K. R., Cognitive Neuroscience (St Hugh's College)

RAWLINS, J. N. P., Behavioural Neuroscience (University College)

ROGERS, B. J., Experimental Psychology (Lady Margaret Hall)

ROLLS, E. T., Experimental Psychology (Corpus Christi College)

School of Geography and the Environment (Mansfield Rd, Oxford, OX1 3TB; tel. (1865) 271919; fax (1865) 271929; internet www.geog.ox.ac.uk):

CLARK, G. L., Geography (St Peter's College)

LIVERMAN, D. M., Environmental Science (Linacre College)

McDOWELL, L. M., Human Geography (St John's College)

PEACH, G. C. K., Social Geography (St Catherine's College)

SWYNGEDOUW, E., Geography (St Peter's College)

THOMAS, D. S. G., Geography (Hertford College)

WHATMORE, S. J., Environment and Public Policy (Linacre College)

WHITTAKER, R. J., Biogeography (St Edmund Hall)

Department of Human Anatomy and Genetics (South Parks Rd, Oxford, OX1 3QX; tel. (1865) 272169; fax (1865) 272420; e-mail enquiries@anat.ox.ac.uk; internet www.anat.ox.ac.uk):

DAVIES, K. E., Anatomy (Hertford College)

MORRIS, J. F., Human Anatomy (St Hugh's College)

MORRISS-KAY, G. M., Developmental Anatomy (Balliol College)

POMTING, C. P., Bioinformatics

SATTELLE, D. B., Molecular Neurobiology

School of Interdisciplinary Studies (12 Bevington Rd, Oxford, OX2 6LH; tel. (1865) 284991; internet www.areastudies.ox.ac.uk):

BEINART, W., Race Relations (St Antony's College)

BROWN, A. H., Politics (St Antony's College)

CRAMPTON, R. J., East European History (St Edmund Hall)

GOODMAN, R. J., Japanese Studies (St Antony's College)

SHUE, V., Contemporary China (St Antony's College)

Oxford Internet Institute (1 St Giles, Oxford, OX1 3JS; tel. (1865) 287210; fax (1865) 287211; e-mail enquiries@oii.ox.ac.uk; internet www.oii.ox.ac.uk):

DUTTON, W. H., Internet Studies (Balliol College)

MARGETTS, H., Society and the Internet (Mansfield College)

ZITTRAIN, J., Internet Governance and Regulation (Keble College)

Faculty of Law (St Cross Bldg, St Cross Rd, Oxford, OX1 3UL; tel. (1865) 271490; fax (1865) 271493; e-mail lawfac@law.ox.ac.uk; internet www.law.ox.ac.uk):

ASHWORTH, A. J., English Law (All Souls College)

BRIGGS, A., Private Int. Law (St Edmund Hall)

BURROWS, A. S., Commercial and Financial Law (St Hugh's College)

CRAIG, P. P., English Law (St John's College)

FINNIS, J. M., Law and Legal Philosophy (University College)

FREDMAN, S. D., Law (Exeter College)

FREEDLAND, M. R., Employment Law (St John's College)

FREEDMAN, J. A., Taxation Law (Worcester College)

GALLIGAN, D. J., Socio-Legal Studies (Wolfson College)

GARDNER, J. B., Jurisprudence (University College)

HAWKINS, K. O., Law and Society (Oriel College)

LOADER, I., Criminology (All Souls College)

LOWE, A. V., Public Int. Law (All Souls College)

McBARNET, D. J., Socio-Legal Studies (Wolfson College)

McCRUDDEN, J. C., Human Rights Law (Lincoln College)

McKENDRICK, E. G., English Private Law (Lady Margaret Hall)

PRENTICE, D. D., Corporate Law (Pembroke College)

RAZ, J., Philosophy of Law (Balliol College)

VAVER, D., Intellectual Property and Information Technology Law (St Peter's College)

VOGENAUER, S., Comparative Law (Brasenose College)

WEATHERILL, S. R., European Community Law (Somerville College)

WYATT, D. A., Law (St Edmund Hall)

Faculty of Management (Saïd Business School, Park End St, Oxford, OX1 1HP; tel. (1865) 288800; fax (1865) 288805; e-mail enquiries@sbs.ox.ac.uk; internet www.sbs.ox.ac.uk):

EARL, M. J., Information Management (Templeton College)

HOLT, D. B., Marketing (Worcester College)

HOPWOOD, A. G., Operational Management (Christ Church)

MAYER, C. P., Management Studies (Wadham College)

MORRIS, T. J., Management Studies (Templeton College)

RAYNER, S., Science and Civilisation (Keble College)

SAKO, M., Management Studies (Templeton College)

WESTBROOK, R., Operational Management (St Hugh's College)

WHITTINGTON, R. C., Strategic Management (New College)

WILLMAN, P. W., Management Studies (Balliol College)

WOOLGAR, S. W., Marketing (Green College)

Department of Materials (Parks Rd, Oxford, OX1 3PH; tel. (1865) 273700; fax (1865) 273789; e-mail enquiries@materials.ox.ac.uk; internet www.materials.ox.ac.uk):

BRIGGS, G. A. D., Nanomaterials (St Anne's College)

BROOK, R. J., Materials Science (St Cross College)

CEREZO, A., Materials (Wolfson College)

COCKAYNE, D. J. H., Physical Examination of Materials (Linacre College)

COCKS, A., Materials Eng. (St Anne's College)

GRANT, P. S., Materials Science (St Catherine's College)

GROVENOR, C. R. M., Materials (St Anne's College)

PETFORD-LONG, A. K., Materials (Corpus Christi College)

PETTIFOR, D. G., Metallurgy (St Edmund Hall)

SMITH, G. D. W., Materials (Trinity College)

SUTTON, A. P., Materials Science (Linacre College)

Mathematical Institute (24–29 St Giles, Oxford, OX1 3LB; tel. (1865) 273525; fax (1865) 273583; internet www.maths.ox.ac.uk):

BALL, J. M., Natural Philosophy (The Queen's College)

BATTY, C. J. K., Analysis (St John's College)

CANDELAS, P., Mathematics (Wadham College)

CHAPMAN, S. J., Mathematics and its Applications (Mansfield College)

DE SAUTOY, M. P. F., Mathematics (All Souls College)

ETHERIDGE, A. M., Probability (Magdalen College)

HAYDON, R. G., Mathematics (Brasenose College)

HEATH-BROWN, D. R., Pure Mathematics (Worcester College)

HITCHIN, N. J., Geometry (New College)

JOYCE, D. D., Mathematics (Lincoln College)

KIRWAN, F. C., Mathematics (Balliol College)

LYONS, T. J., Mathematics (St Anne's College)

MAINI, P. K., Mathematical Biology (Brasenose College)

QUILLEN, D. G., Pure Mathematics (Magdalen College)

SEGAL, D., Mathematics (All Souls College)

TILLMANN, U., Mathematics (Merton College)

TOD, K. P., Mathematical Physics (St John's College)

VAUGHAN-LEE, M. R., Mathematics (Christ Church)

WELSH, J. A. D., Mathematics (Merton College)

WILKIE, A. J., Mathematical Logic (Wolfson College)

WOOD, J. S., Mathematics

ZILBER, B., Mathematical Logic (Merton College)

Medical Oncology Unit (Churchill Hospital, Oxford, OX3 7LJ; tel. (1865) 226184; fax (1865) 226179):

HARRIS, A. L., Clinical Oncology (St Hugh's College)

HICKSON, I. D., Molecular Oncology

Faculty of Medieval and Modern European Languages and Literatures (41 and 47 Wellington Sq., Oxford, OX1 2JF; tel. (1865) 270570; fax (1865) 270757; e-mail enquiries@mod-langs.ox.ac.uk; internet www .mod-langs.ox.ac.uk):

BROWN, H. M., German (St Hilda's College)

CHARLES-EDWARDS, T. M. O., Celtic (Jesus College)

COOPER, R. A., French (Brasenose College)

EARLE, T. F., Portuguese Studies (St Peter's College)

ENGEL, M., New German Literature (Queen's College)

FALLAIZE, E. A., French (St John's College)

FIDDIAN, R. W., Spanish (Wadham College)

HOWELLS, C. M., French (Wadham College)

JEFFERYS, E. M., Byzantine and Modern Greek Language and Literature (Exeter College)

KELLY, C. H. M., Russian (New College)

MCLAUGHLIN, M. L., Italian Studies (Magdalen College)

MAIDEN, M. D., Romance Languages (Trinity College)

PALMER, N. F., German Medieval and Linguistic Studies (St Edmund Hall)

PARISH, R. J., French (St Catherine's College)

PEARSON, R. A. G., French (Queen's College)

PULMAN, S. G., General Linguistics (Somerville College)

ROBERTSON, R. N. N., German (St John's College)

SHEPPARD, R. W., German (Magdalen College)

SHERINGHAM, M. H. T., French Literature (All Souls College)

VIALA, A., French Literature (Lady Margaret Hall)

WATANABE-O'KELLY, H., German Literature (Exeter College)

WICKHAM, C. J., Medieval History (All Souls College)

WILLIAMSON, E. H., Spanish Studies (Exeter College)

ZANCANI, D., Italian (Balliol College)

ZORIN, A. L., Russian (New College)

Faculty of Modern History (Broad St, Oxford, OX1 3BD; tel. (1865) 277256; fax (1865) 250704; internet www.history.ox.ac.uk):

BROCKLISS, L. W. B., Early Modern French History (Magdalen College)

BROWN, J. M., History of the British Commonwealth (Balliol College)

CARWARDINE, R. J., American History (St Catherine's College)

CORSI, P., History of Science (Linacre College)

EVANS, R. J. W., Modern History (Regius) (Oriel College)

FOSTER, R. F., Irish History (Hertford College)

FOX, R., History of Science (Linacre College)

GILDEA, R. N., Modern French History (Merton College)

HARRIS, J. F., Modern History (St Catherine's College)

HUMPHRIES, K. J., Economic History (All Souls College)

KEMP, M. J., History of Art (Trinity College)

KNIGHT, A. S., History of Latin America (St Antony's College)

MACLEAN, I. W. F., Renaissance Studies (All Souls College)

OFFER, A., Economic History (All Souls College)

POGGE VON STRANDMANN, H. J. O., Modern History (University College)

ROPER, L. A., Early Modern History (Balliol College)

SERVICE, R. J., Russian History (St Antony's College)

SHARPE, R., Diplomatic (Wadham College)

SLACK, P. A., Early Social Modern History (Linacre College)

STRACHAN, H. F. A., History of War (All Souls College)

Weatherall Institute of Molecular Medicine (John Radcliffe Hospital, Headington, Oxford, OX3 9DS; tel. (1865) 222443; fax (1865) 222737; internet www.imm.ox.ac.uk):

BICKNELL, R., Cancer Cell Biology

DAVIS, S. J., Molecular Immunology

ELLIOTT, T. J., Immunology

ENVER, T., Molecular Haematology

FUGGER, L., Clinical Immunology

JACKSON, D. G., Human Immunology

MCMICHAEL, A. J., Molecular Medicine (Corpus Christi College)

WOOD, W. G., Haematology

Faculty of Music (St Aldate's, Oxford, OX1 1DB; tel. (1865) 276125; fax (1865) 276128; internet www.music.ox.ac.uk):

CALDWELL, J. A., Music (Jesus College)

FRANKLIN, P. R., Music (St Catherine's College)

STROHM, R., Music (Wadham College)

Nuffield Department of Obstetrics and Gynaecology (John Radcliffe Hospital, Oxford, OX3 9DU; tel. (1865) 221004; fax (1865) 769141; internet www.medicine.ox.ac .uk/ndog):

BARLOW, D. H., Obstetrics and Gynaecology (Oriel College)

KEHOE, S. T. (St Peter's College)

MARDON, H. J., Reproductive Science (St Catherine's College)

POULTON, J., Mitochondrial Genetics

REDMAN, C. W. G., Obstetric Medicine (Lady Margaret Hall)

SARGENT, I. L., Reproductive Science (Mansfield College)

Nuffield Laboratory of Ophthalmology (Walton St, Oxford, OX2 6AW; tel. (1865) 248996; fax (1865) 794508; e-mail enquiries@eye.ox .ac.uk; internet www.eye.ox.ac.uk):

HARDING, J. J., Ocular Biochemistry

OSBORNE, N. N., Ocular Neurobiology (Green College)

Faculty of Oriental Studies (Oriental Institute, Pusey Lane, Oxford, OX1 2LE; tel. (1865) 278200; fax (1865) 278190; internet www.orinst.ox.ac.uk):

ALLAN, J. W., Eastern Art (St Cross College)

BAINES, J. R., Egyptology (The Queen's College)

DUDBRIDGE, G., Chinese (University College)

GOODMAN, M. D., Jewish Studies (Wolfson College)

HOLES, C. D., Contemporary Arab World (Magdalen College)

MINKOWSKI, C. Z., Sanskrit (Balliol College)

Dame RAWSON, JESSICA, Chinese Art and Archaeology (Merton College)

SANDERSON, A. G. J. S., Eastern Religions and Ethics (All Souls College)

SHEIKHOLESLAMI, A. R., Persian Studies (Wadham College)

SMITH, M. J., Egyptology (University College)

SUBRAHMANYAM, S., Indian History and Culture (St Cross)

VAN GELDER, G. J. H., Arabic (St John's College)

VAN LINT, T. M., Armenian Studies (Pembroke)

WILLIAMSON, H. G. M., Hebrew (Regius) (Christ Church)

Nuffield Department of Orthopaedic Surgery (Nuffield Orthopaedic Centre, Windmill Rd, Headington, Oxford, OX3 7LD; tel. (1865) 227374; fax (1865) 737640; internet www .ndos.ox.ac.uk):

ATHANASOU, N. A., Osteoarticular Pathology (Wadham College)

BROWN, M., Musculoskeletal Sciences (St Peter's College)

BULSTRODE, C. J. K., Orthopaedic Surgery (Green College)

CARR, A. J., Orthopaedic Surgery (Worcester College)

MURRAY, D., Orthopaedic Surgery

RUSSELL, R. G. G., Musculoskeletal Sciences (St Peter's College)

TRIFFITT, J. T., Bone Metabolism

WILLETT, K. M., Orthopaedic Trauma Surgery (Wolfson College)

Department of Paediatrics (John Radcliffe Hospital, Headington, Oxford, OX3 9DU; tel. (1865) 221077; fax (1865) 220479; internet www.medicine.ox.ac.uk/paediatrics):

HARRIS, A., Paediatric Molecular Genetics (St Cross College)

KWIATKOWSKI, D. P., Tropical Paediatrics (St John's College)

MOXON, E. R., Paediatrics (Jesus College)

WILKINSON, P. R., Paediatrics (All Souls College)

Sir William Dunn School of Pathology (South Parks Rd, Oxford, OX1 3RE; tel. (1865) 275500; fax (1865) 275501; internet www .path.ox.ac.uk):

BARCLAY, A. N., Molecular Immunology (Oriel College)

BROWNLEE, G. G., Chemical Pathology (Lincoln College)

COOK, P. R., Cell Biology (Lincoln College)

ERRINGTON, J., Microbiology (Magdalen College)

GORDON, S., Cellular Pathology (Exeter College)

GRIFFITHS, G. M., Experimental Psychology

GULL, K., Molecular Microbiology (Lincoln College)

HALE, G., Therapeutic Immunology

POWRIE, F., Immunology

PROUDFOOT, N. J., Molecular Biology (Lincoln College)

VAN DER MERWE, P. A., Molecular Immunology

WALDMANN, H., Pathology (Lincoln College)

Department of Pharmacology (Mansfield Rd, Oxford, OX1 3QT; tel. (1865) 271850; fax (1865) 271853; e-mail info@pharm.ox.ac.uk; internet www.pharm.ox.ac.uk):

BOLAM, J. P., Anatomical Neuropharmacology

BRADING, A. F., Pharmacology (Lady Margaret Hall)

GALIONE, A. G., Pharmacology (New College)

Baroness GREENFIELD, SUSAN, Pharmacology (Lincoln College)

SIM, E., Pharmacology (St Peter's College)

SMITH, A. D., Pharmacology (Lady Margaret Hall)

Faculty of Philosophy (10 Merton St, Oxford, OX1 4JJ; tel. (1865) 276926; fax (1865) 276932; e-mail enquiries@philosophy.ox.ac .uk; internet www.philosophy.ox.ac.uk):

BROOME, J. R., Moral Philosophy (Corpus Christi College)

KINSEY DAVIES, M., Mental Philosophy

EDGINGTON, D., Metaphysical Philosophy (Magdalen College)

FREDE, M., History of Philosophy (Keble College)

HAWTHORNE, J., Philosophy (Magdalen College)

MOORE, A. W., Philosophy (St Hugh's College)

SAVULESCU, J., Applied Ethics (St Cross College)

WILLIAMSON, T., Logic (New College)

Department of Physics (Clarendon Laboratory, Parks Rd, Oxford, OX1 3PU; tel. (1865) 272200; fax (1865) 272400; internet www.physics.ac.uk):

ABRAHAM, D. B., Statistical Mechanics (Wolfson College)

ALLISON, W. W. M., Physics (Keble College)

ANDREWS, D. G., Physics (Lady Margaret Hall)

BINNEY, J. J., Physics (Merton College)

BLUNDELL, S. J., Physics (Mansfield College)

BURNETT, K., Physics (St John's College)

CHALKER, J. T., Physics (St Hugh's College)

COOPER, S., Experimental Physics (St Catherine's College)

COWLEY, R. A., Experimental Philosophy (Wadham College)

DAVIES, R. L., Astrophysics (Christ Church)

DEVENISH, R. C. E., Physics (Hertford College)

EWART, P., Physics (Worcester College)

FOOT, C. J., Physics (St Peter's College)

FOSTER, B., Experimental Physics (Balliol College)

GLAZER, A. M., Physics (Jesus College)

HARNEW, N., Physics (St Anne's College)

JELLEY, N. A., Physics (Lincoln College)

JOHNSON, N. F., Physics (Lincoln College)

JORDAN, C., Physics (Somerville College)

NICHOLAS, R. J., Physics (University College)

RAWLINGS, S. G., Physics (St Peter's College)

READ, P. L., Physics (Trinity College)

RENTON, P. B., Physics

ROSS, G. G., Theoretical Physics (Wadham College)

RYAN, J. F., Physics (Christ Church)

SHERRINGTON, D., Physics (New College)

SILK, J. I., Astronomy (New College)

SILVER, J. D., Physics (New College)

STEANE, A., Physics (Exeter College)

STONE, N. J., Physics (St Edmund Hall)

TAYLOR, F. W., Atmospheric Physics (Jesus College)

TURBERFIELD, A. J., Physics (Magdalen College)

WALMSLEY, I. R., Experimental Physics (St Hugh's College)

WARK, J. S., Physics (Trinity College)

YEOMANS, J. M., Physics (St Hilda's College)

Department of Physiology (Parks Rd, Oxford, OX1 3PT; tel. (1865) 272500; fax (1865) 272469; e-mail enquiries@physiol.ox.ac.uk; internet www.physiol.ox.ac.uk):

ASHCROFT, F. M., Physiology (Trinity College)

ASHLEY, C. C., Physiology (Corpus Christi College)

BLAKEMORE, C. B., Physiology (Magdalen College)

CLARKE, K., Physiological Biochemistry

ELLORY, J. C., Physiology (Corpus Christi College)

KING, A. J., Neurophysiology (Merton College)

MIALL, R. C., Neuroscience

PAREKH, A. K., Physiology

PARKER, A. J., Physiology (St John's College)

PATERSON, D. J., Cardiovascular Physiology (Merton College)

POWELL, T., Physiology (New College)

ROBBINS, P. A., Physiology (The Queen's College)

STEIN, J. F., Physiology (Magdalen College)

VAUGHAN-JONES, R. D., Cellular Physiology (Exeter College)

Department of Plant Sciences (South Parks Rd, Oxford, OX1 3RB; tel. (1865) 275000; fax (1865) 275074; e-mail reception@plants.ox.ac.uk; internet www.plants.ox.ac.uk):

DICKINSON, H. G., Botany (Magdalen College)

GURR, S. J., Molecular Plant Pathology (Somerville College)

LEAVER, C. J., Plant Science (St John's College)

RATCLIFFE, R. G., Plant Sciences (New College)

SMITH, J. A. C., Plant Sciences (Magdalen College)

Department of Politics and International Relations (Manor Rd, Oxford, OX1 3UQ; tel. (1865) 278707; fax (1865) 278725; internet www.politics.ox.ac.uk):

BOGDANOR, V. B., Politics and Govt (Brasenose College)

BROWN, A. H., Politics (St Antony's College)

CEADEL, M. E., Politics (New College)

COHEN, G. A., Social and Political Theory (All Souls College)

CRAMPTON, R. J., East European History (St Edmund Hall)

FOOT, R. J., Int. Relations (St Antony's College)

FREEDEN, M. S., Politics (Mansfield College)

HOOD, C. C., Govt (All Souls College)

KING, D. S., American Govt (Nuffield College)

MACFARLANE, S. N., Int. Relations (St Anne's College)

MILLER, D. L., Political Theory (Nuffield College)

ROBERTS, E. A., Int. Relations (Balliol College)

ROBERTSON, D. B., Politics (St Hugh's College)

RYAN, A. J., Politics (New College)

SHLAIM, A., Int. Relations (St Anthony's College)

WARE, A. J., Politics (Worcester College)

Department of Psychiatry (Warneford Hospital, Oxford, OX3 7JX; tel. (1865) 226451; fax (1865) 793101; internet www.psychiatry.ox.ac.uk):

BAILEY, A. J., Psychiatry (St John's College)

BURNS, T. P. (Kellogg College)

COWEN, P. J., Psychopharmacology

CROW, T. J., Psychiatry

FAIRBURN, C. J. A. G., Psychiatry

GEDDES, J., Epidemiological Psychiatry

GOODWIN, G. M., Psychiatry (Merton College)

HARRISON, P. J., Psychiatry (Wolfson College)

HAWTON, K. E., Psychiatry (Green College)

JACOBY, R. J., Old Age Psychiatry (Linacre College)

MAYOU, R. A., Psychiatry (Nuffield College)

STEIN, A. J., Child and Adult Psychiatry (Linacre College)

STORES, G., Developmental Neuropsychiatry (Linacre College)

WILLIAMS, J. M. G., Clinical Psychology

Division of Public Health and Primary Health Care (Old Rd, Headington, Oxford, OX3 7LF; tel. (1865) 226666; fax (1865) 227036; internet www.dphpc.ox.ac.uk):

BERAL, V., Epidemiology (Green College)

COLLINS, R. E., Medicine and Epidemiology

FITZPATRICK, R. M., Public Health and Primary Health Care (Nuffield College)

GLASZIOU, P., Evidence-based Medicine (Kellogg College)

GOLDACRE, M. J., Public Health (Magdalen College)

GRAY, A. M., Health Econ.

HOPE, R. A., Medical Ethics (St Cross College)

JAFFE, H. W., Public Health (St Cross College)

JENKINSON, C. P., Health Services Research (Green College)

MANT, D. C., General Practice (Kellogg College)

NEIL, H. A. W., Clinical Epidemiology (Wolfson College)

PARKER, M. J., Bioethics (St Cross College)

SNOW, R. W., Tropical Public Health

Ruskin School of Drawing and Fine Art (74 High St, Oxford, OX1 4BG; tel. (1865) 276940; fax (1865) 276949; internet www.ruskin-sch.ox.ac.uk):

CATLING, B. D., Fine Art (Linacre College)

CHEVSKA, M., Fine Art (Brasenose College)

WENTWORTH, R., Fine Art (St Edmund Hall)

Department of Social Policy and Social Work (Barnett House, 32 Wellington Sq., Oxford, OX1 2ER; tel. (1865) 270325; fax (1865) 270324; internet www.apsoc.ox.ac.uk):

COLEMAN, D. A., Demography

NOBLE, M. W. J., Social Policy (Green College)

RINGEN, S., Sociology and Social Policy (Green College)

Department of Sociology (Manor Rd, Oxford, OX1 3UQ; tel. (1865) 286170; fax (1865) 286171; e-mail enquiries@sociology.oxford.ac.uk; internet www.sociology.ox.ac.uk):

EVANS, G., Sociology of Politics (Nuffield College)

GALLIE, D. I. D., Sociology (Nuffield College)

GAMBETTA, D., Sociology (All Souls College)

GERSHUNY, J., Sociology (St Hugh's College)

HEATH, A. F., Sociology (Nuffield College)

Department of Statistics (1 South Parks Rd, Oxford, OX1 3TG; tel. (1865) 272860; fax (1865) 272595; internet www.stats.ox.ac.uk):

DONNELLY, P. G., Statistical Science (St Anne's College)

ETHERIDGE, A. M., Probability (Magdalen College)

GITTINS, J. C., Statistics (Keble College)

HEIN, J. J., Bioinformatics (University College)

LAURITZEN, S. L., Statistics (Jesus College)

MCDIARMID, C. J. H., Operations Research (Corpus Christi College)

REINERT, G., Statistics (Keble College)

RIPLEY, B. D., Applied Statistics (St Peter's College)

SILVERMAN, B. W., Statistics (St Peter's College)

Nuffield Department of Surgery (John Radcliffe Hospital, Headington, Oxford, OX3 9DU; tel. (1865) 220532; fax (1865) 768876; internet www.surgery.ox.ac.uk):

AUSTYN, J. M., Immunobiology (Wolfson College)

AZIZ, T. Z., Neurosurgery

FRIEND, P. J., Transplantation (Green College)

GRAY, D. W. R., Experimental Surgery (Oriel College)

MEAKINS, J. L., Surgery (Balliol College)

MORTENSON, N. J., Colorectal Surgery

WOOD, K. J., Immunology

Faculty of Theology (Theology Faculty Centre, 41 St Giles, Oxford, OX1 3LW; tel. (1865)

270790; fax (1865) 270795; internet www .theology.ox.ac.uk):

ADAMS, M. M., Divinity (Regius) (Christ Church)

Rev. BARTON, J., Interpretation of Holy Scripture (Oriel College)

BROOKE, J. H., Science and Religion (Harris Manchester College)

DAY, J., Old Testament Theology (Lady Margaret Hall)

FIDDES, P. S., Systematic Theology (Regent's Park College)

LEFTOW, B., Philosophy of the Christian Religion (Oriel College)

MACCULLOCH, D. N. J., History of the Church (St Cross College)

Rev. MCGRATH, A. E., Historical Theology (Wycliffe Hall)

Rev. O'DONOVAN, O. M. T., Moral and Pastoral Theology (Regius) (Christ Church)

PATTISON, G. L., Divinity (Christ Church)

ROWLAND, C. C., Exegesis of Holy Scripture (The Queen's College)

TUCKETT, C. M., New Testament Studies (Wolfson College)

Department of Zoology (South Parks Rd, Oxford, OX1 3PS; tel. (1865) 271234; fax (1865) 310447; internet www.zoo.ox.ac.uk):

CAVALIER-SMITH, T., Evolutionary Biology

DAWKINS, C. R., Public Understanding of Science (New College)

DAWKINS, M. E. S., Animal Behaviour (Somerville College)

GARDNER, R. L., Zoology (Royal Society's Henry Dale Research) (Christ Church)

GRAFEN, A., Theoretical Biology (St John's College)

GRAHAM, C. F., Animal Devt (St Catherine's College)

HARVEY, P., Zoology (Jesus College)

HOLLAND, P. W. H., Zoology (Merton College)

KACELNIK, A., Behavioural Ecology (Pembroke College)

KENNEDY, W. J., Natural History (Kellogg College)

Sir KREBS, J., Zoology (Jesus College)

MACDONALD, D. W., Wildlife Conservation (Lady Margaret Hall)

MAIDEN, M. C. J., Molecular Epidemiology

MCLEAN, A. R., Mathematical Biology (St Catherine's College)

RANDOLPH, S. E., Parasite Ecology (Oriel College)

ROGERS, D. J., Ecology (Green College)

SHELDON, B. C., Field Ornithology (Wolfson College)

SIMPSON, S. J., Hope Entomological Collections (Jesus College)

DIRECTORS AND HEADS OF UNIVERSITY INSTITUTIONS AND DEPARTMENTS

Institute for the Advancement of University Learning (Littlegate House, 16/17 St Ebbe's St, Oxford, OX1 1PT; tel. (1865) 286808; fax (1865) 286801; e-mail services@learning.ox .ac.uk; internet www.learning.ox.ac.uk):

G. GIBBS, Teaching and Learning in Higher Education

Institute of Archaeology (34–36 Beaumont St, Oxford, OX1 2PG; tel. (1865) 278240; fax (1865) 278254; internet www.archinst.ox.ac .uk):

G. LOCK (Kellogg College)

Research Laboratory for Archaeology and the History of Art (6 Keble Rd, Oxford, OX1 3QJ; tel. (1865) 283033; fax (1865) 273932; internet www.rlaha.ox.ac.uk):

A. M. POLLARD, Archaeological Science (Linacre College)

University Archives (Bodleian Library, Broad St, Oxford, OX1 3BG; tel. (1865)

277145; fax (1865) 277187; e-mail enquiries@oua.ox.ac.uk; internet www.oua .ox.ac.uk):

Keeper S. BAILEY (Linacre College)

Ashmolean Museum of Art and Archaeology (Beaumont St, Oxford, OX1 2PH; tel. (1865) 278000; fax (1865) 278018; internet www .ashmol.ox.ac.uk):

C. P. H. BROWN (Worcester College)

Bodleian Library (Broad St, Oxford, OX1 3BG; tel. (1865) 277000; fax (1865) 277182; e-mail enquiries@bodley.ox.ac.uk; internet www.bodley.ox.ac.uk):

Dir of Univ. Library Services and Bodley's Library R. P. CARR (Balliol College)

Botanic Garden (High St, Oxford, OX1 4AZ; tel. (1865) 286690; fax (1865) 286693; e-mail postmaster@botanic-garden.ox.ac.uk; internet www.botanic-garden.ox.ac.uk):

Keeper T. WALKER

Brazilian Studies Centre (92 Woodstock Rd, Oxford, OX2 7ND; tel. (1865) 284460; fax (1865) 284461; e-mail enquiries@brazil.ox.ac .uk; internet www.brazil.ox.ac.uk):

Dir L. BETHELL (St Antony's College)

Chemical Crystallography (Chemistry Research Laboratory, 12 Mansfield Rd, Oxford, OX1 3TA; tel. (1865) 285000; fax (1865) 285102; internet www.cryst.chem.ox .ac.uk):

Dir D. J. WATKIN

Institute for Chinese Studies (Clarendon Institute Bldg, Walton St, Oxford, OX1 2HG; tel. (1865) 280387; fax (1865) 280435; e-mail enquiries@chinese.ox.ac.uk; internet www.orinst.ox.ac.uk/ea/chinese):

F. PIEKE (St Cross College)

Centre for Criminology (Manor Rd, Oxford, OX1 3UQ; tel. (1865) 274444; fax (1865) 281924; e-mail ccr@crim.ox.ac.uk; internet www.crim.ox.ac.uk):

I. LOADER (All Souls College)

Environmental Change Institute (1A Mansfield Rd, Oxford, OX1 3SZ; tel. (1865) 281180; fax (1865) 281202; e-mail enquiries@eci.ox.ac .uk; internet www.eci.ox.ac.uk):

Dir D. LIVERMAN, Environmental Science (Linacre College)

Institute of European and Comparative Law (St Cross Bldg, St Cross Rd, Oxford, OX1 3UL; tel. (1865) 281610; fax (1865) 281611; e-mail enquiries@eurocomplaw.ox.ac.uk; internet www.iecl.ox.ac.uk):

S. VOGENAUER, Comparative Law (Brasenose College)

European Humanities Research Centre (c/o Prof. C. Kelly, New College, Oxford, OX1 3BN; e-mail enquiries@ehrc.ox.ac.uk; internet www.ehrc.ox.ac.uk):

C. H. M. KELLY, Russian (New College)

Glycobiology Institute (Dept of Biochemistry, South Parks Rd, Oxford, OX1 3QU; tel. (1865) 275342; fax (1865) 275216; internet www.bioch.ox.ac.uk/glycob):

Dir R. A. DWEK, Glycobiology (Exeter College)

Department of the History of Art and Centre for Visual Studies (Littlegate House, St Ebbes, Oxford, OX1 2PT; tel. (1865) 286830; fax (1865) 286831; internet www.hoa.ox.ac .uk):

Head M. J. KEMP, History of Art (Trinity College)

Wellcome Unit for the History of Medicine (45–47 Banbury Rd, Oxford, OX2 6PE; tel. (1865) 274600; fax (1865) 274605; internet www.wuhmo.ox.ac.uk):

Dir M. HARRISON (Green College)

Museum of the History of Science (Old Ashmolean Bldg, Broad St, Oxford, OX1 3AZ; tel. (1865) 277280; fax (1865) 277288; internet www.mhs.ox.ac.uk):

Keeper J. A. BENNETT (Linacre College)

Inorganic Chemistry Laboratory (South Parks Rd, Oxford, OX1 3QR; tel. (1865) 272600; fax (1865) 272690; internet www .chem.ox.ac.uk/icl):

Head P. P. EDWARDS, Inorganic Chemistry (St Catherine's College)

Nissan Institute of Japanese Studies (27 Winchester Rd, Oxford, OX2 6NA; tel. (1865) 274570; fax (1865) 274574; e-mail secretary@nissan.ox.ac.uk; internet www .nissan.ox.ac.uk):

Dir B. A. WASWO (St Antony's College)

Language Centre (12 Woodstock Rd, Oxford, OX2 6HT; tel. (1865) 283360; fax (1865) 283366; e-mail admin@lang.ox.ac.uk; internet www.lang.ox.ac.uk):

Dir R. N. VANDERPLANK (Kellogg College)

Latin American Centre (St Antony's College, Oxford, OX2 6JF; tel. (1865) 274486; fax (1865) 274489; e-mail enquiries@lac.ox.ac .uk; internet www.lac.ox.ac.uk):

R. THORP (St Antony's College)

Centre for Linguistics and Philology (Walton St, Oxford, OX1 2HG; tel. (1865) 280400; fax (1865) 280412; e-mail enquiries@ling-phil.ox .ac.uk; internet www.ling-phil.ox.ac.uk):

Curator S. G. PULMAN, General Linguistics (Somerville College)

Oxford Centre for Molecular Science (Central Chemistry Laboratory, South Parks Rd, Oxford, OX1 3QH; tel. (1865) 275345; fax (1865) 275253; internet www.ocms.ox.ac.uk):

Dir I. D. CAMPBELL, Structural Biology (St John's College)

Microbiology Unit (Dept of Biochemistry, South Parks Rd, Oxford, OX1 3QU; tel. (1865) 285360; fax (1865) 275297; internet www.bioch.ox.ac.uk):

Head D. J. SHERRATT, Microbiology (Linacre College)

University Museum of Natural History (Parks Rd, Oxford, OX1 3PW; tel. (1865) 272950; fax (1865) 272970; e-mail info@oum .ox.ac.uk; internet www.oum.ox.ac.uk):

Dir W. J. KENNEDY, Natural History (Kellogg College)

National Perinatal Epidemiology Unit (Institute of Health Sciences, Old Rd Campus, Headington, Oxford, OX3 7LF; tel. (1865) 227000; fax (1865) 227002; internet www .npeu.ox.ac.uk):

Dir P. BROCKLEHURST

Organic Chemistry Laboratory (Chemistry Research Laboratory, 12 Mansfield Rd, Oxford, OX1 3TA; tel. (1865) 285000; fax (1865) 275632; internet www.chem.ox.ac.uk/ oc):

Head Sir JACK BALDWIN, Organic Chemistry (Magdalen College)

Oriental Institute (Pusey Lane, Oxford, OX1 2LE; tel. (1865) 278200; fax (1865) 278190; e-mail orient@orinst.ox.ac.uk; internet www .orinst.ox.ac.uk):

Chair. of Curators G. J. H. VAN GELDER, Arabic (St John's College)

Philosophy Centre (10 Merton St, Oxford, OX1 4JJ; tel. (1865) 276926; fax (1865) 276932; e-mail enquiries@philosophy.ox.ac .uk; internet www.philosophy.ox.ac.uk):

Curator W. J. MANDER (Harris Manchester College)

Phonetics Laboratory (41 Wellington Sq., Oxford, OX1 2JF; tel. (1865) 270444; fax

(1865) 270445; e-mail enquiries@phon.ox.ac.uk; internet www.phon.ox.ac.uk):

Dir J. S. COLEMAN (Wolfson College)

Physical and Theoretical Chemistry Laboratory (South Parks Rd, Oxford, OX1 3QZ; tel. (1865) 275400; fax (1865) 275410; e-mail ptcl.information@chem.ox.ac.uk; internet ptcl.chem.ox.ac.uk):

Head J. KLEIN, Chemistry (Exeter College)

Pitt Rivers Museum (South Parks Rd, Oxford, OX1 3PP; tel. (1865) 270927; fax (1865) 270943; e-mail prm@prm.ox.ac.uk; internet www.prm.ox.ac.uk):

Dir M. O'HANLON (Linacre College)

Ruskin School of Drawing and Fine Art (74 High St, Oxford, OX1 4BG; tel. (1865) 276940; fax (1865) 276949; internet www.ruskin-sch.ox.ac.uk):

Master R. WENTWORTH, Fine Art (St Edmund Hall)

Saïd Business School (Park End St, Oxford, OX1 1HP; tel. (1865) 288800; fax (1865) 288805; e-mail enquiries@sbs.ox.ac.uk; internet www.sbs.ox.ac.uk):

Dir A. HOPWOOD, Operations Management (Christ Church)

Institute of Social and Cultural Anthropology (51 Banbury Rd, Oxford, OX2 6PF; tel. (1865) 274670; fax (1865) 274630; internet www.isca.ox.ac.uk):

Head D. J. PARKIN, Social Anthropology (All Souls College)

Centre for Socio-Legal Studies (Manor Rd, Oxford, OX1 3UQ; tel. (1865) 284220; fax (1865) 284221; internet www.csls.ox.ac.uk):

Dir D. J. GALLIGAN, Socio-Legal Studies (Wolfson College)

Transport Studies Unit (11 Bevington Rd, Oxford, OX2 6NB; tel. (1865) 274715; fax (1865) 515194; internet www.tsu.ox.ac.uk):

Dir J. M. PRESTON (St Anne's College)

COLLEGES

All Souls College: Oxford, OX1 4AL; tel. (1865) 279379; f. 1438; for Fellows only; Warden Dr JOHN DAVIES.

Balliol College: Oxford, OX1 3BJ; tel. (1865) 277777; internet www.balliol.ox.ac.uk; f. 1263; Master ANDREW GRAHAM.

Brasenose College: Oxford, OX1 4AJ; tel. (1865) 277830; internet www.bnc.ox.ac.uk; f. 1509; Principal Prof. ROGER CASHMORE.

Christ Church: Oxford, OX1 1DP; tel. (1865) 276150; internet www.chch.ox.ac.uk; f. 1546; Dean The Very Rev. CHRISTOPHER LEWIS.

Corpus Christi College: Oxford, OX1 4JF; tel. (1865) 276700; internet www.ccc.ox.ac.uk; f. 1517; Pres. Sir TIM LANKESTER.

Exeter College: Oxford, OX1 3DP; tel. (1865) 279600; internet www.exeter.ox.ac.uk; f. 1314; Rector FRANCES CAIRNCROSS.

Green College: Oxford, OX2 6HG; tel. (1865) 274770; internet www.green.ox.ac.uk; f. 1979, for graduates; Warden Prof. COLIN BUNDY.

Harris Manchester College: Oxford, OX1 3TD; tel. (1865) 271006; internet www.hmc.ox.ac.uk; f. 1786, for mature students; Principal The Rev. Dr RALPH WALLER.

Hertford College: Oxford, OX1 3BW; tel. (1865) 279400; internet www.hertford.ox.ac.uk; f. 1740; Principal Dr JOHN LANDERS.

Jesus College: Oxford, OX1 3DW; tel. (1865) 279700; internet www.jesus.ox.ac.uk; f. 1571; Principal Lord KREBS.

Keble College: Oxford, OX1 3PG; tel. (1865) 272727; internet www.keble.ox.ac.uk; f. 1870; Warden Prof. Dame AVERIL CAMERON.

Kellogg College: Oxford, OX2 6PN; tel. (1865) 612000; internet www.kellogg.ox.ac.uk; f. 1990, for continuing education and graduate students; Pres. Dr GEOFFREY THOMAS.

Lady Margaret Hall: Oxford, OX2 6QA; tel. (1865) 274300; internet www.lmh.ox.ac.uk; f. 1878; Principal Dr FRANCES LANNON.

Linacre College: Oxford, OX1 3JA; tel. (1865) 271650; internet www.linacre.ox.ac.uk; f. 1962, as Linacre House, for graduates; Principal Prof. PAUL SLACK.

Lincoln College: Oxford, OX1 3DR; tel. (1865) 279800; internet www.linc.ox.ac.uk; f. 1427; Rector Prof. PAUL LANGFORD.

Magdalen College: Oxford, OX1 4AU; tel. (1865) 276000; internet www.magd.ox.ac.uk; f. 1458; Pres. Prof. DAVID CLARY.

Mansfield College: Oxford, OX1 3TF; tel. (1865) 270999; internet www.mansfield.ox.ac.uk; f. 1886; Principal Dr DIANA WALFORD.

Merton College: Oxford, OX1 4JD; tel. (1865) 276310; internet www.merton.ox.ac.uk; f. 1264; Warden Prof. Dame JESSICA RAWSON.

New College: Oxford, OX1 3BN; tel. (1865) 279555; internet www.new.ox.ac.uk; f. 1379; Warden Prof. ALAN RYAN.

Nuffield College: Oxford, OX1 1NF; tel. (1865) 278500; internet www.nuff.ox.ac.uk; f. 1958, for graduates; Warden Prof. STEPHEN NICKELL.

Oriel College: Oxford, OX1 4EW; tel. (1865) 276555; internet www.oriel.ox.ac.uk; f. 1326; Provost Sir DEREK MORRIS.

Pembroke College: Oxford, OX1 1DW; tel. (1865) 276444; internet www.pmb.ox.ac.uk; f. 1624; Master GILES HENDERSON.

Queen's College, The: Oxford, OX1 4AW; tel. (1865) 279120; internet www.queens.ox.ac.uk; f. 1340; Provost Sir ALAN BUDD.

St Anne's College: Oxford, OX2 6HS; tel. (1865) 274800; internet www.st-annes.ox.ac.uk; f. 1879 (as Society of Oxford Home Students); Principal TIM GARDAM.

St Antony's College: Oxford, OX2 6JF; tel. (1865) 284700; internet www.sant.ox.ac.uk; f. 1953, for graduates; Warden Prof. MARGARET MACMILLAN.

St Catherine's College: Oxford, OX1 3UJ; tel. (1865) 271700; internet www.stcatz.ox.ac.uk; f. 1868, reconstituted as a full College 1962; Master Prof. ROGER AINSWORTH.

St Cross College: Oxford, OX1 3LZ; tel. (1865) 278490; internet www.stx.ox.ac.uk; f. 1965, for graduates; Master Prof. ANDREW GOUDIE.

St Edmund Hall: Oxford, OX1 4AR; tel. (1865) 279000; internet www.seh.ox.ac.uk; c.1278; Principal Prof. MIKE MINGOS.

St Hilda's College: Oxford, OX4 1DY; tel. (1865) 276884; internet www.st-hildas.ox.ac.uk; f. 1893; Principal SHEILA FORBES.

St Hugh's College: Oxford, OX2 6LE; tel. (1865) 274900; internet www.st-hughs.ox.ac.uk; f. 1886; Principal ANDREW DILNOT.

St John's College: Oxford, OX1 3JP; tel. (1865) 277300; internet www.sjc.ox.ac.uk; f. 1555; Pres. Sir MICHAEL SCHOLAR.

St Peter's College: Oxford, OX1 2DL; tel. (1865) 278900; internet www.spc.ox.ac.uk; f. 1929 as St Peter's Hall; Master Prof. BERNARD SILVERMAN.

Somerville College: Oxford, OX2 6HD; tel. (1865) 270600; academic year www.some.ox.ac.uk; f. 1879; Principal Dame FIONA CALDICOTT.

Templeton College: Oxford, OX1 5NY; tel. (1865) 422500; fax (1865) 425501; internet www.templeton.ox.ac.uk; f. 1995; Dean Prof. MICHAEL EARL.

Trinity College: Oxford, OX1 3BH; tel. (1865) 279900; internet www.trinity.ox.ac.uk; f. 1555; Pres. Sir IVOR ROBERTS.

University College: Oxford, OX1 4BH; tel. (1865) 276602; internet www.univ.ox.ac.uk; f. 1249; Master Lord BUTLER OF BROCKWELL.

Wadham College: Oxford, OX1 3PN; tel. (1865) 277900; internet www.wadham.ox.ac.uk; f. 1612; Warden Sir NEIL CHALMERS.

Wolfson College: Oxford, OX2 6UD; tel. (1865) 274100; internet www.wolfson.ox.ac.uk; f. 1965, for graduates; Pres. Prof. JON STALLWORTHY (acting).

Worcester College: Oxford, OX1 2HB; tel. (1865) 278300; internet www.worc.ox.ac.uk; f. 1714; Provost RICHARD SMETHURST.

PERMANENT PRIVATE HALLS

Blackfriars: Oxford, OX1 3LY; tel. (1865) 278400; internet www.bfriars.ox.ac.uk; f. 1921; Regent Dr RICHARD FINN.

Campion Hall: Oxford, OX1 1QS; tel. (1865) 286100; internet www.campion.ox.ac.uk; f. 1896; Master Rev. Dr PETER L'ESTRANGE.

Greyfriars: Oxford, OX4 1SB; tel. (1865) 243694; internet www.greyfriars.ox.ac.uk; f. 1910; Warden Dr NICHOLAS RICHARDSON.

Regent's Park College: Oxford, OX1 2LB; tel. (1865) 288120; internet www.rpc.ox.ac.uk; f. 1810; Principal Rev. Dr ROBERT ELLIS.

St Benet's Hall: Oxford, OX1 3LN; tel. (1865) 280556; internet www.st-benets.ox.ac.uk; f. 1897; Master Rev. LEO CHAMBERLAIN.

St Stephen's House: Oxford, OX4 1JX; tel. (1865) 247874; internet www.ssho.ox.ac.uk; f. 1876; Principal Rev. Canon Dr ROBIN WARD.

Wycliffe Hall: Oxford, OX2 6PW; tel. (1865) 274200; internet www.wycliffe.ox.ac.uk; Principal Rev. Dr RICHARD TURNBULL.

ASSOCIATED INSTITUTIONS

Maison Française d'Oxford: Norham Rd, Oxford, OX2 6SE; tel. (1865) 274220; fax (1865) 274225; e-mail maison@herald.ox.ac.uk; internet www.mfo.ac.uk; f. 1946; Dir Prof. J.-C. SERGEANT.

NERC Centre for Ecology and Hydrology: see under Research Institutes.

Oxford Centre for Hebrew and Jewish Studies: Yarnton Manor, Yarnton, Oxford, OX5 1PY; tel. (1865) 377946; fax (1865) 375079; internet users.ox.ac.uk/~ochjs; f. 1972; Master of Studies (MSt) degree; library: Leopold Muller Memorial Library: Kressel colln of 30,000 vols and pamphlets and 400,000 newspaper cuttings, Elkoshi colln of 17,000 vols, Yizkor colln of 450 Holocaust memorial books; Pres. P. OPPENHEIMER (Christ Church).

Oxford Centre for Islamic Studies: George St, Oxford, OX1 2AR; tel. (1865) 278730; fax (1865) 248942; e-mail islamic.studies@oxcis.ac.uk; internet www.oxcis.ac.uk; f. 1985; Dir FARHAN AHMAD NIZAMI (Magdalen College).

Oxford Institute for Energy Studies: 57 Woodstock Rd, Oxford, OX2 6FA; tel. (1865) 311377; fax (1865) 310527; e-mail information@oxfordenergy.org; internet www.oxfordenergy.org; f. 1982; Dir R. G. SKINNER.

Oxford International Centre for Palliative Care: Churchill Hospital, Oxford OX3 7LJ; Dir R. G. TWYCROSS (St Peter's College).

OXFORD BROOKES UNIVERSITY

Gipsy Lane, Headington, Oxford, OX3 0BP

Telephone: (1865) 741111
Fax: (1865) 483073
Internet: www.brookes.ac.uk

Founded 1865 as Oxford School of Art; became Oxford Polytechnic 1970; university status 1992
State control
Academic year: September to July

Chancellor: JON SNOW
Vice-Chancellor: Prof. GRAHAM UPTON
Deputy Vice-Chancellor: Dr PETRA WEND
Deputy Vice-Chancellor and Registrar: REX KNIGHT
Director of Academic and Student Affairs: MIKE RATCLIFFE
Director of Learning Resources: Dr HELEN WORKMAN
Academic Registrar: STEPHEN MARSHALL

Library of 500,000 vols
Number of teachers: 750
Number of students: 17,500

DEANS

Arts and Humanities: Prof. LINDA FITZSIM-MONS
Biological and Molecular Sciences: Prof. LINDA KING
Built Environment: Prof. JOHN RAYTERY
Business: SIMON WILLIAMS
Education: Dr DAVID LANGFORD
Health and Social Care: JUNE GIRVIN
Social Sciences and Law: Prof. DEREK ELSOM
Technology: Dr DENISE MORREY
Undergraduate Modular Programme: D. SCURRY

UNIVERSITY OF PAISLEY

Paisley, Renfrewshire, PA1 2BE

Telephone: (141) 848-3000
Fax: (141) 887-0812
E-mail: uni-direct@paisley.ac.uk
Internet: www.paisley.ac.uk

Founded 1897 as Paisley College of Technology, present name and status 1992
Academic year: October to June

Chancellor: Sir ROBERT SMITH
Principal and Vice-Chancellor: Prof. SEAMUS McDAID (acting)
Vice-Principal: Prof. JUDITH VINCENT (acting)
Assistant Principals: Prof. ROBERT CHAPMAN (acting), Prof. ALAN GODFREY
Registrar and Secretary: DAVID RIGG
Librarian: STUART JAMES

Number of teachers: 455 full-time
Number of students: 10,313 (6,195 full-time, 3,118 part-time)

Publication: *Annual Report*

DEANS

School of Education: IAN SMITH
School of Engineering and Science: Prof. ROGER McLEAN
School of Health, Nursing and Midwifery: Prof. JACK RAE
School of Information Communication Technologies: Dr CHRIS HALSALL
School of Media: ALEX GILKISON
School of Social Sciences: Dr TONY CLARKE
Paisley Business School: ALAN GODFREY

HEADS OF DEPARTMENTS

Accounting and Finance: A. I. M. FLEMING
Adult Nursing: N. FINLAY
Biological Sciences: Dr G. BICKERSTAFF
Chemistry and Chemical Engineering: Dr H. VAUGHAN
Civil, Structural and Environmental Engineering: J. YOUNGER
Computing and Information Systems: Prof. T. CONNOLLY

Economics and Entrepreneurship: Prof J. J. STRUTHERS
School of Education: I. SMITH
Electronic Engineering and Physics: Dr J. ANDERSON
Information Operations and Quality Management: A. BURNS
Land Economics and Law: R. McMASTER
Languages: S. STUART
Marketing: Prof. D. BATHIE
Mathematics and Statistics: Dr N. PITCHER
Mechanical and Manufacturing Engineering and the Quality Centre: J. WOOD
School of Media: A. GILKINSON
Mental Health Nursing: J. ROBERTSON
Midwifery: L. STORRIE
Politics: B. SLOCOCK
Professional and Community Education: S. CARR
Psychology: S. HOBBS
Social Policy and Social Work: Dr J. RODGER
Social Studies: Prof. J. O. FOSTER
Sociology: Dr G. NAIR
Strategic and Human Resource Management: Prof. R. RIMMER

ATTACHED INSTITUTES

Advanced Concrete and Masonry Centre: Dir Prof. P. BARTOS.

Centre for Alcohol and Drug Studies: Dir K. BARRIE.

Centre for Environmental and Waste Management: Dir Dr J. McQUAID-COOK.

Centre for Gerontology and Health Studies: Dir Prof. M. GILHOOLY.

Centre for Particle Characterization and Analysis: Man. Dr A. HURSTHOUSE.

Electromagnetic Compatibility Centre: Dir F. GALBRAITH.

Enterprise Research Centre: Dir Prof. D. DEAKINS.

Environmental Technologies: Dir Prof. P. TUCKER.

Land Value Information Unit: Dir D. MARTIN.

Microelectronics in Business Unit: Man. F. GALBRAITH.

Network and Information Management Services: Dir A. SHAW.

Technology and Business Centre: Manager B. G. CROSS.

Thin Film Centre: Dir Prof. F. PLACIDO.

UNIVERSITY OF PLYMOUTH

Drake Circus, Plymouth, PL4 8AA

Telephone: (1752) 600600
Fax: (1752) 232293
E-mail: publicrelations@plymouth.ac.uk
Internet: www.plymouth.ac.uk

Founded 1970 as Plymouth Polytechnic; name changed to Polytechnic South West in 1989; present name and status 1992
Academic year: September to June

Vice-Chancellor: Prof. ROLAND LEVINSKY
Deputy Vice-Chancellors: PETER JOHN, GRAHAM RAIKES
Deputy Vice-Chancellors (Academic Affairs): Prof. MICHAEL BEVERIDGE, Dr MARK CLEARY
Pro-Vice-Chancellor (Health): Prof. MARY WATKINS
Pro-Vice-Chancellor (Research): Prof. STEVE NEWSTEAD
Pro-Vice-Chancellor (Teaching and Learning Development): IVAN SIDGREAVES
Dean of Students: Dr ANITA JELLINGS
University Secretary and Academic Registrar: JANE HOPKINSON
Director of Information and Learning Facilities: MARTIN BERKIEN (acting)

Library of 500,000 vols, 2,850 periodicals
Number of teachers: 977

Number of students: 24,000 (16,000 full-time and sandwich, 8,000 part-time)

Publications: *Annual Review, Research Report*

DEANS

Faculty of Arts: Prof. STEVEN PARISSIEN
Faculty of Education: Prof. PETER JOHN
Faculty of Health and Social Work: Prof. JOHN CLIBBENS (acting)
Faculty of Science: RODDY WILLIAMSON
Faculty of Social Science and Business: Prof. JOAN CHANDLER
Faculty of Technology: Prof. NEIL JAMES
University of Plymouth Colleges: Dr IAN TUNBRIDGE
Peninsula Medical School: Prof. JOHN TOOKE

HEADS OF DEPARTMENTS

Faculty of Arts (Earl Richards Rd North, Exeter, EX2 6AS; tel. (1392) 475009; fax (1392) 475012; e-mail fae-admissions@plymouth.ac.uk; internet www.fae.plymouth.ac.uk):

Art and Design: M. HOPE
Arts and Humanities: Prof. L. FITZSIMMONS
Graduate Studies in Arts and Education: Dr G. TAYLOR

Faculty of Education:
Rolle School of Education: G. PAYNE

Faculty of Health and Social Work (tel. (1752) 233200; fax (1752) 233194; e-mail humansciences@plymouth.ac.uk; internet www.hs.plymouth.ac.uk):

Sociology: Prof. D. MASON
Graduate School: Dr J. CHANDLER
Institute of Health Studies: Prof. M. WATKINS

Faculty of Science (tel. (1752) 233093; fax (1752) 233095; e-mail sciences@plymouth.ac.uk; internet www.science.plymouth.ac.uk):

Biological Sciences: Prof. M. JONES
Environmental Sciences: Prof. S. HILL
Geographical Sciences: Prof. D. PINDER
Geological Sciences: Dr J. GRIFFITHS
Institute of Marine Studies: Prof. D. HUNTLEY

Faculty of Social Science and Business:
Accounting and Law: Dr P. ATRILL
Business and Management: N. WISEMAN
International Business: Prof. D. HEAD
Politics: Prof. M. THRASHER
Psychology: Prof. J. EVANS
Social Work and Social Policy: J. LEWIS
Graduate School: L. LINDLEY

Faculty of Technology (tel. (1752) 233322; fax (1752) 233310; e-mail technology@plymouth.ac.uk; internet www.tech.plymouth.ac.uk):

Agriculture and Food Studies: Dr M. FULLER
Architecture: Prof. M. WIGGINTON
Civil and Structural Engineering: Dr C. WILLIAMS
Computing: Prof. P. PEARCE
Electronic, Communication and Electrical Engineering: Prof. W. CLEGG
Land Use and Rural Management: M. F. WARREN
Mathematics and Statistics: Prof. P. DYKE
Mechanical and Marine Engineering: Dr J. CHUDLEY

UNIVERSITY OF PORTSMOUTH

University House, Winston Churchill Ave, Portsmouth, PO1 2UP

Telephone: (23) 9284-8484
Fax: (23) 9284-3082
E-mail: info.centre@port.ac.uk
Internet: www.port.ac.uk

Founded 1869 as Portsmouth School of Science and Art, became Portsmouth Polytechnic in 1969; present name and status 1992

Academic year: September to June

Chancellor: Lord PALUMBO

Vice-Chancellor: Prof. J. CRAVEN

Pro-Vice-Chancellors: Dr D. ARRELL, Dr M. BATEMAN

Academic Registrar: A. REES

Librarian: I. BONAR

Library of 600,000 vols

Number of teachers: 1,000

Number of students: 18,000

DEANS

Faculty of the Environment: B. WEBSTER

Faculty of Humanities and Social Sciences: Prof. I. KENDALL

Faculty of Science: Prof. D. ROGERS

Faculty of Technology: Dr S. CLARIDGE

Portsmouth Business School: A. RIDLEY

HEADS OF DEPARTMENTS

Faculty of the Environment (Portland Building, Portland St, Portsmouth, PO1 3AH; tel. (23) 9284-2956; fax (23) 9284-2516; e-mail env.admissions@port.ac.uk):

Architecture: TOD WAKEFIELD

Art, Design and Media: B. MILLIGAN

Civil Engineering: Prof. B. LEE

Environmental Design and Management: T. GOODHEAD

Geography: I. WHITE

Maritime and Heritage Studies: L. SHURMER-SMITH

Faculty of Humanities and Social Sciences (Park Building, King Henry I St, Portsmouth, PO1 2OZ; tel. (23) 9284-8299; fax (23) 9284-6254; e-mail humanities.admissions@port.ac.uk):

Criminal Justice Studies: Prof. S. SAVAGE

Education and Continuing Studies: M. COESHOTT

Languages and Area Studies: B. BRIERLEY

Social, Historical and Literary Studies: F. CARR

Faculty of Science (St Michael's Building, White Swan Rd, Portsmouth, PO1 2DT; tel. (23) 9284-3005; fax (23) 9284-3335; e-mail sci.admissions@port.ac.uk):

Biological Sciences: Dr R. GREENWOOD

Earth and Environmental Sciences: D. HUGHES

Institute of Marine Sciences: R. EATON

Pharmacy: Dr J. WONG

Psychology: Prof. C. SINHA

Radiography: DEREK ADRIAN-HARRIS

Sport and Exercise Science: A. REES

Portsmouth Institute of Medicine, Health and Social Care: Prof. L. REYNOLDS

Faculty of Technology (Liongate Building, Lion Terrace, Portsmouth, PO1 3HT; tel. (23) 9284-2555; fax (23) 9284-2584; e-mail technology-admissions@port.ac.uk):

Computer Science and Software Engineering: J. CHANDLER

Cosmology and Gravitation: Prof. R. MAARTENS

Creative Technologies: Dr S. HAND

Electronic and Computer Engineering: Dr M. FILIP

Information Systems and Computer Applications: Dr R. BERESFORD

Mathematics: Dr A. OSBALDESTIN

Mechanical and Design Engineering: J. FOSTER

Technology Extended Campus: Dr J. BRITT

Portsmouth Business School (Richmond Bldg, Portland St, Portsmouth, PO1 3DE; tel. (23) 9284-8200; fax (23) 9284-4059; e-mail bus.admissions@port.ac.uk):

Accounting and Management Science: C. CALLAGHAN

Business and Management: D. ADAM-SMITH

Economics: D. BIBBY

UNIVERSITY OF READING

Reading, Berks., RG6 6AH

Telephone: (118) 987-5123

Fax: (118) 931-4404

E-mail: information@reading.ac.uk

Internet: www.reading.ac.uk

Founded 1892 as University Extension College; university status 1926

Academic year: October to July

Chancellor: The Rt Hon. Lord CARRINGTON

Vice-Chancellor: Prof. GORDON MARSHALL

Pro-Vice-Chancellors: Prof. TONY DOWNES, Prof. MICHAEL FULFORD, Prof. PETER GREGORY

Registrar: DAVID FRAMPTON

Librarian: J. H. MUNRO

Library: see Libraries and Archives

Number of teachers: 2,005

Number of students: 12,320

Publications: *Annual Report, R & D Research Digest* (3 a year)

DEANS

Faculty of Arts and Humanities: Prof. CEDRIC BROWN

Faculty of Economic and Social Sciences: Prof. DIANNE BERRY

Faculty of Life Sciences: Prof. ROB ROBSON

Faculty of Science: Prof. DAVID RICE

PROFESSORS

(Some professors serve in more than one faculty)

Faculty of Arts and Humanities (Whiteknights, POB 218, Reading, RG6 6AA; tel. (118) 931-8063; fax (118) 931-0748):

ARNOLD, B. C. B., History

BARANSKI, Z., Italian Studies

BARBER, M. C., History

BIDDISS, M. D., History

BROWN, C. C., English and American Literary Studies

BUCKLEY, S., Arts and Communication Design

BULL, J., Arts and Communication Design

BULLEN, J. B., English and American Literary Studies

COOK, G.W. D., Linguistics and Applied Language Studies

COOPER, P. J., Psychology

COTTINGHAM, J. G., Humanities

CURRY, A. E., History

DANCY, J. P., Humanities

DUNSBY, J. M., Arts and Communication Design

ELIOT, S. J., English and American Literary Studies; Arts and Communication Design

EVANS, A. W., Environmental Economics

GARMAN, M. A. G., Linguistics and Applied Language Studies

GILCHRIST, R., Archaeology

HOOKER, B., Humanities

HOULBROOKE, R.A., History

HOWELLS, C. A., English and American Literary Studies

JAMES, E. F., History

LUNA, P., Arts and Communication Design

NOBLE, P. S., Modern Languages

PARRINDER, J. P., English and American Literary Studies

PILLING, J., English and American Literary Studies

POTTS, A., Humanities

ROACH, P. J., Lingustic and Applied Language Studies

ROBEY, D. J. B., Modern Languages

RUTHERFORD, I. C., Humanities

SANDFORD, J. E., Modern Languages

SEGAL, N., Modern Languages

STRAWSON, G. J., Humanities

TUCKER, G. H., Modern Languages

WALLACE-HADRILL, A. F., Humanities

WARBURTON, I. P., Linguistic Science

WILKINS, D. A., Linguistics and Applied Language Studies

WOODWARD, P. R., Politics

Faculty of Economic and Social Sciences (Whiteknights, POB 218, Reading, RG6 6AA; tel. (118) 931-8183; fax (118) 931-6658; e-mail fasug@reading.ac.uk):

BELLAMY, R., Politics and Sociology

BREHENY, M. J., Business

BUCKLEY, R. A., Law

BUSH, A. W., Education

CANTWELL, J. A., Business

CASSON, M. C., Business

CROLL, P., Education

CROSBY, F. N., Business

DAVIES, J. C. H., Politics and Sociology

DOWNES, T. A., Law

EDWARDS, V. K., Education

EVANS, A. W., Business

FIDLER, F. B., Education

FRANZONI, R., Politics and Sociology

GHANDI, P. R., Law

GILBERT, J. K., Education

GRAY, C. S., Politics and Sociology

JONES, G. G., Business

KEENE, J., Health and Social Care

LIZIERI, C. M., Business

MALVERN, D. D., Education

MURDOCH, J. R., Law

NOBES, C. W., Business

PATTERSON, K. D., Business

PEMBERTON, J., Business

POPE, M. L., Education

RICHARDS, B. J., Education

SCOTT-QUINN, B., Business

SOUTHWORTH, G. W., Education

STYCHIN, C., Law

UTTON, M. A., Business

WADDINGTON, P. A. J., Politics and Sociology

WARD, C. W., Business

WOODWARD, P. R., Politics and Sociology

Faculty of Life Sciences (Whiteknights, POB 200, Reading, RG6 6AF; tel. (118) 931-8342; fax (118) 931-5509; e-mail sciug@reading.ac.uk):

BARNETT, J. R., Plant Sciences

BEEVER, D. E., Agriculture, Policy and Development

BISBY, F. A., Plant Sciences

BROWN, V. K., Agriculture, Policy and Development

CALIGARI, P. D. S., Plant Sciences

COLLINS, M. D., Food Biosciences

CRABBE, M. J. C., Animal and Microbial Sciences

DUNWELL, J. M., Plant Sciences

ELLIS, R. H., Agriculture, Policy and Development

FRANCE, J., Agriculture, Policy and Development

GARFORTH, C. J., Agriculture, Policy and Development

GIBSON, G. R., Food Biosciences

HADLEY, P., Plant Sciences

HOLLAND, P. W. H., Animal and Microbial Sciences

JOHN, P., Plant Sciences

JONES, I. M., Animal and Microbial Sciences

KNIGHT, P. G., Animal and Microbial Sciencesy

LEDWARD, D. A., Food Biosciences

LOWRY, P. J., Animal and Microbial Sciences

MOTTRAM, D. V., Food Biosciences

OWEN, E., Agriculture, Policy and Development

PAGEL, M., Animal and Microbial Sciences

PAYNE, C. C., Plant Sciences

PYLE, D. L., Food Biosciences
ROBSON, R. L., Animal and Microbial Sciences
SCHOFIELD, J. D., Food Biosciences
SIBLY, R. M., Animal and Microbial Sciences
STRANGE, P., Animal and Microbial Sciences
SWINBANK, A., Agriculture, Policy and Development
TRAILL, B., Agriculture, Policy and Development
WHITEHEAD, J. R., Applied Statistics
WILLIAMS, C. M., Food Biosciences

Faculty of Science (Whiteknights, POB 200, Reading, RG6 6AF; tel. (118) 931-8342; fax (118) 975-5509; e-mail sciug@reading.ac.uk):

ALLOWAY, B. J., Human and Environmental Sciences
ANDREWS, B., Computer Science, Cybernetics and Electronic Engineering
ASTILL, G. G., Human and Environmental Sciences
ATKINS, A. G., Construction Management and Engineering
BAKER, K. D., Computer Science, Cybernetics and Electronic Engineering
BASSETT, D. C., Mathematics, Meteorology and Physics
BERRY, D. C., Psychology
BON, R., Construction Management and Engineering
BOWKER, M., Chemistry
BRADLEY, R. J., Human and Environmental Sciences
BROWNING, K. A., Mathematics, Meteorology and Physics
CARDIN, D. J., Chemistry
CHAPLIN, C. R., Construction Management and Engineering
CHAPMAN, R. W., Human and Environmental Sciences
CLEMENTS-CROOME, T. D. J., Construction Management and Engineering
CODLING, K., Mathematics, Meteorology and Physics
COLEMAN, M. L., Human and Environmental Sciences
COLQUHOUN, H. M., Chemistry
COOPER, P. J., Psychology
DREW, M. G. B., Chemistry
FISHER, G. N., Construction Management and Engineering
FLANAGAN, R., Construction Management and Engineering
FULFORD, M. G., Human and Environmental Sciences
GILBERT, A., Chemistry
GILCHRIST, R., Human and Environmental Sciences
GREGORY, P. J., Human and Environmental Sciences
GURNEY, R., Mathematics, Meteorology and Physics
HAINES, K., Mathematics, Meteorology and Physics
HARRISON, R., Computer Science, Cybernetics and Electronic Engineering
HARWOOD, L. M., Chemistry
HILTON, A. J. W., Mathematics, Meteorology and Physics
HOSKINS, B. J., Mathematics, Meteorology and Physics
JERONIMIDIS, G., Construction Management and Engineering
MCKENNA, F. P., Psychology
MEGSON, G. M., Computer Science, Cybernetics and Electronic Engineering
MITCHELL, G. R., Mathematics, Meteorology and Physics
MITHEN, S. J., Human and Environmental Sciences
MURRAY, L., Psychology
NEEDHAM, D. J., Mathematics, Meteorology and Physics

NICHOLS, N. K., Mathematics, Meteorology and Physics
O'NEILL, A., Mathematics, Meteorology and Physics
PORTER, D., Mathematics, Meteorology and Physics
RICE, D. A., Chemistry
SELLWOOD, B. W., Human Sciences
SHARKEY, P. M., Computer Science, Cybernetics and Electronic Engineering
SHINE, K. P., Mathematics, Meteorology and Physics
SLINGO, G. M., Mathematics, Meteorology and Physics
SMITH, P. T., Psychology
THORPE, A. J., Mathematics, Meteorology and Physics
VALDES, P. J., Mathematics, Meteorology and Physics
WADGE, G. M., Mathematics, Meteorology and Physics
WALSH, R., Chemistry
WANN, J. P., Psychology
WARBURTON, D. M., Psychology
WARWICK, K., Computer Science, Cybernetics and Electronic Engineering
WHITEHEAD, P. G., Human and Environmental Sciences
WRIGHT, A. C., Mathematics, Meteorology and Physics
WRIGHT, J. D. M., Mathematics, Meteorology and Physics

Rural History Centre (Whiteknights, POB 229, Reading, RG6 6AG; tel. (118) 931-8342; fax (118) 931-5509; e-mail rhc@reading.ac.uk):

HOYLE, R. W.

AFFILIATED INSTITUTION

College of Estate Management: see under Colleges.

ROBERT GORDON UNIVERSITY

Schoolhill, Aberdeen, AB10 1FR
Telephone: (1224) 262000
Fax: (1224) 263000
Internet: www.rgu.ac.uk
Founded 1750, present name and status 1992
Academic year: September to July
Chancellor: Sir IAN WOOD
Principal and Vice-Chancellor: Prof. MICHAEL PITTILO
Secretary: Dr ADRIAN GRAVES
Academic Registrar: HILARY DOUGLAS
Chief Librarian: ELAINE DUNPHY
Library of 250,946 vols, 1,901 periodicals, 4,939 online journals
Number of teachers: 702 (full-time)
Number of students: 13,309 (7,780 full-time, 5,529 part-time)
Publication: *Annual Review*

ASSISTANT PRINCIPALS

Faculty of Design and Technology: Prof. IAN PIRIE
Faculty of Health and Social Care: Prof. VAL MAEHLE
Aberdeen Business School: Prof. RITA MARCELLA

HEADS OF SCHOOLS

Faculty of Design and Technology (Scott Sutherland School, Garthdee Rd, Aberdeen, AB10 7QB; tel. (1224) 263750; fax (1224) 263757; e-mail c.black@rgu.ac.uk):

School of Computing: Prof. SUSAN CRAW
School of Engineering: Prof. JOHN WATSON
Gray's School of Art: Prof. MIKE PRESS
Scott Sutherland School: Prof. ROBERT W. POLLOCK

Faculty of Health and Social Care (Garthdee Rd, Aberdeen, AB10 7QG; tel. (1224) 263050;

fax (1224) 263053; e-mail s.barnett@rgu.ac.uk):

Applied Social Studies: Prof. JOYCE LISHMAN
Health Sciences: ELIZABETH HANCOCK
Life Sciences: Prof. MAUREEN MELVIN
Nursing and Midwifery: JENNIE PARRY
Pharmacy: Prof. TERENCE M. HEALEY

Aberdeen Business School (Garthdee Rd, Aberdeen, AB10 7QE; tel. (1224) 263550; fax (1224) 263838; e-mail j.dey@rgu.ac.uk):

Accounting and Finance: ELIZABETH GAMMIE
Business and Management: MORAG HAMILTON
Information and Media: IAN M. JOHNSON
Public Administration and Law: VERONICA STRACHAN

ROEHAMPTON UNIVERSITY

Erasmus House, Roehampton Lane, London, SW15 5PU
Telephone: (20) 8392-3000
E-mail: enquiry.desk@roehampton.ac.uk
Internet: www.roehampton.ac.uk
Founded 1841; granted university status 2004
Vice-Chancellor: Prof. PAUL O'PREY
Deputy Vice-Chancellor: Dr PETER WESTON
Pro Vice-Chancellor (External Partnerships), and Principal, Southlands College: Dr PETER BRIGGS
Pro Vice-Chancellor (Services), and Principal, Whitelands College: Dr TRISH ROBERTS
Principal, Digby Stuart College: FRANCES SPACKMAN
Principal, Froebel College: Prof. MIKE WATTS

HEADS OF SCHOOLS

School of Arts: PETER REYNOLDS
School of Business, Social Sciences and Computing: Prof. YVONNE GUERRIER
School of Education Studies: (vacant)
School of English and Modern Languages: LINDA THOMAS
School of Humanities and Cultural Studies: LYNDIE BRIMSTONE
School of Initial Teacher Education: JEANNE KEAY
School of Life and Sport Sciences: Dr CLIVE BULLOCK
School of Psychology and Therapeutic Studies: MICHAEL BARHAM

PROFESSORS

School of Arts:

FISHER, A., Art History
JORDAN, S., Dance
READ, A., Drama and Theatre Studies

School of Business, Social Sciences and Computing:

BALES, K., Sociology
EADE, J., Sociology and Anthropology
FENNELL, G., Sociology and Social Policy
GLOVER, J., Employment Studies
GUERRIER, Y., Organizational Studies

School of Education Studies:

BREHONY, K. J., Early Childhood Studies
HARGREAVES, D., Child Development
MAHONY, P., Education
MASON, R., Art Education
WATTS, M., Education

School of English and Modern Languages:

COATES, J., English Languages and Linguistics
DOBSON, M., English Literature
HARTLEY, J., English Literature
HEADLAM-WELLS, R., English Literature
LEADER, Z., English Literature
PRIESTMAN, M., English Literature

School of Humanities and Cultural Studies:
DEAN, T., Medieval History
EDWARDS, P., History
GIBSON, A., Philosophy
TOSH, J., History

School of Initial Teacher Education:
BEST, R., Education

School of Life and Sport Sciences:
MACLARNON, A., Evolutionary Anthropology

School of Psychology and Therapeutic Studies:
BEAUMONT, G., Neuropsychology
ESSAU, C., Developmental Psychopathology
REID, M., Nutritional Psychology
VOGELE, C., Clinical and Health Psychology

ATTACHED RESEARCH INSTITUTES

AHRB Research Centre for Cross-Cultural Music and Dance Performance: tel. (20) 7898-4687; e-mail kh@soas.ac.uk; Directors Dr KEITH HOWARD, Dr ANDRÉE GRAU.

Centre for Art Education and International Research: e-mail r.mason@roehampton.ac.uk; Dir Prof. RACHEL MASON.

Centre for Dance Research: e-mail s.jordan@roehampton.ac.uk; Dir Prof. STEPHANIE JORDAN.

Centre for International Research in Music Education: e-mail CIRME@roehampton.ac.uk; Dir Prof. DAVID HARGREAVES.

Centre for Research in Animals in Society and Culture: tel. (20) 8392-3170; e-mail g.marvin@roehampton.ac.uk; Dir Dr GARRY MARVIN.

Centre for Research in Ecology and the Environment: tel. (20) 8392-3457; Dir Dr PETER SHAW.

Centre for Research in English and Local History: e-mail p.edwards@roehampton.ac.uk; Dir Prof. PETER EDWARDS.

Centre for Research in Evolutionary Anthropology: tel. (20) 8392-3645; e-mail a.maclarnon@roehampton.ac.uk; Dir Prof. ANN MACLARNON.

Centre for Research in Film and Audio-visual Cultures: tel. (20) 8392-3513; e-mail p.mcDonald@roehampton.ac.uk; Dir Dr PAUL MCDONALD.

Centre for Research in Francophone Studies: Dir Dr PATRICK CORCORAN.

Centre for Research in Human Rights: tel. (20) 8392-3661; fax (20) 8392-3231; e-mail l.gearon@roehampton.ac.uk; Dir Dr LIAM GEARON.

Centre for Research in Learning and Teaching in Higher Education.

Centre for Research in Religious Education and Development: tel. (20) 8392-3338; e-mail d.rose@roehampton.ac.uk; Dir Dr DAVID ROSE.

Centre for Research in Renaissance Studies: e-mail r.headlam_wells@roehampton.ac.uk; Dir Prof. ROBIN HEADLAM-WELLS.

Centre for Research in Testing, Evaluation and Curriculum in ELT: tel. (20) 8392-3348; e-mail c.weir@roehampton.ac.uk; Dir (vacant).

Centre for Scientific and Cultural Research in Sport.

Clinical and Health Psychology Research Centre.

Early Childhood Research Centre: tel. (20) 8392-3689; e-mail ecc@roehampton.ac.uk; Dir Prof. KEVIN J. BREHONY.

Hispanic Research Centre: tel. (20) 8392-3572; e-mail i.santaolalla@roehampton.ac.uk; Dir Dr ISABEL SANTAOLALLA.

National Centre for Research in Children's Literature: tel. (20) 8392-3346; e-mail k.reynolds@roehampton.ac.uk; internet www.ncrcl.ac.uk; Dir Prof. KIM REYNOLDS.

Professional Education Research Centre: tel. (20) 8392-3224; e-mail h.johnson@roehampton.ac.uk; Dir Dr HELEN JOHNSON.

Research Centre for Cognition, Emotion and Interaction.

Research Centre for Therapeutic Education.

UNIVERSITY OF ST ANDREWS

St Andrews, Fife, KY16 9AJ
Telephone: (1334) 476161
Internet: www.st-and.ac.uk

Founded 1411

Chancellor: Sir MENZIES CAMPBELL
Principal and Vice-Chancellor: Dr BRIAN LANG
Deputy Principal: D. J. CORNER
Master: Prof. K. BROWN
Secretary to the University Court: A. E. W. WORK
Vice-Principal (External Relations): S. MAGEE
Vice-Principal (Research): Prof. A. MILLER
Vice-Principal (Teaching): Prof. R. PIPER
Quaestor and Factor: D. WATSON
Library: see Libraries and Archives
Number of teachers: 417
Number of students: 5,868

DEANS

Faculty of Arts: Prof. C. J. SMITH
Faculty of Divinity: Dr M. I. AGUILAR
Faculty of Medicine: Prof. R. H. MACDOUGALL
Faculty of Science: Prof. P. G. WILLMER

PROFESSORS

Faculty of Arts:
BARTLETT, R. J., Medieval History
BEATH, J. A., Economics and Finance
BEBBINGTON, J., Management
BENTLEY, M. J., Modern History
BROADIE, S., Moral Philosophy
BROWN, K. M., Scottish History
CARRADICE, I. A., Art History
CHAMBERS, H. E., German
CHIA, R., Management Centre for Business Education
CRAWFORD, R., English
DAVIES, H. T. O., Management
DE GROOT, G. J., Modern History
DENNIS, N., Spanish
DUNN, D. E., English
FERGUSON, R., French
FITZROY, F. R., Economics and Finance
GIFFORD, P., French
GIVEN-WILSON, C. J., Medieval History
GOW, P., Philosophical and Anthropological Studies
GRATWICK, A., Classical Philology
GRAY, R. H., Management
HALDANE, J. J., Moral Philosophy
HALLIWELL, F. S., Greek
HARRIES, J. D., Ancient History
HINE, H. M., Latin, Classics
HINNEBUSCH, R., International Relations
HOUSTON, R. A., Modern History
HUDSON, J., History
HUGHES-HALLETT, A., Economics and Finance
HUMFREY, P., Art History
JENSEN-BUTLER, C. N., Economics and Finance
KENNEDY, H. N., Medieval History

LITTLER, C., Management Centre for Business Education
LODDER, C. A., Art History
LODGE, R. A., French
MCKIERNAN, P., Management
MCKINLAY, A., Management
MAGDALINO, P., Medieval History
NOLAN, C., Economics and Finance
NUTLEY, S., Management
PETTEGREE, A. D. M., Modern History
POLLMANN, K., Classics
PRESS, J. I., Russian
PRIEST, G., Philosophy
RAPPORT, N. J., Social Anthropology
READ, P., French
REID, G. C., Economics and Finance
RENGGER, N. J., International Relations
RHODES, N., English
ROE, N. H., English
SCOTT, H. M., Modern History
SCOTT, M., French
SELLERS, S. C., English
SKORUPSKI, J., Moral Philosophy
SMITH, C. J., Classics
SMITH, G., Art History
SUTHERLAND, A. J., Economics and Finance
WALKER, W. B., International Relations
WILKINSON, P., International Relations
WOOLF, G. D., Classics
WRIGHT, C. J. G., Logic and Metaphysics

Faculty of Divinity:
BAUCKHAM, R. J., Divinity
ESLER, P. F., Divinity
HART, T. A., Divinity
PIPER, R. A., Divinity
SEITZ, C. R., Divinity
TORRANCE, A. J., Divinity

Faculty of Medicine:
HERRINGTON, S., Medicine
HUMPHRIS, G., Medicine
MACDOUGALL, R. A., Medicine
RICHES, A., Medicine

Faculty of Science:
BALLANTYNE, C. K., Geography and Geosciences
BIRD, M., Geography and Geosciences
BOYD, I., Biology
BOYLE, P. J., Geography and Geosciences
BROWN, V., Psychology
BRUCE, P. G., Chemistry
BUCKLAND, S. T., Mathematics and Statistics
BYRNE, R. W., Psychology
CAIRNS, R. A., Applied Mathematics
CAMERON, A. C., Physics and Astronomy
COLE-HAMILTON, D. J., Chemistry
COTTRELL, G., Biology
DEARLE, A., Computer Science
DHOLAKIA, K., Physics and Astronomy
DRITSCHEL, D. G., Mathematics
DUNN, M. H., Photonics
FALCONER, K. J., Mathematics and Statistics
FEDAK, M. A., Biology
FLOWERDEW, R., Geography and Geosciences
HARWOOD, J., Biology
HAY, R. T., Biochemistry
HOOD, A. W., Mathematics
HORNE, K. D., Physics and Astronomy
IRVINE, J. T. S., Chemistry
JOHNSTON, I. A., Comparative Physiology
KRAUSS, T. F., Physics and Astronomy
LEE, S., Physics and Astronomy
LEONHARDT, U., Physics and Astronomy
MACKENZIE, A., Physics and Astronomy
MACLEOD, M., Psychology
MAGURRAN, A. E., Biology
MEAGHER, T. R., Biology
MILLER, A., Physics
MORRIS, R., Chemistry
MORRISON, R., Software Engineering
NAISMITH, J. H., Chemistry
O'HAGAN, D., Chemistry

PATERSON, D. M., Biology
PERRETT, D. I., Psychology
PRIEST, E. R., Theoretical Solar Physics
RANDALL, R. E., Biology
REICHER, S., Psychology
RICHARDSON, N. V., Chemistry
RITCHIE, M. G., Biology
ROBERTS, B., Mathematics
ROBERTSON, E. F., Mathematics
SAMUEL, I., Physics and Astronomy
SIBBETT, W., Natural Philosophy
SILLAR, K. T., Biology
SLATER, P. J. B., Natural History
TAYLOR, G. L., Biology
TODD, C. D., Biology
TUCKER, J. B., Cell Biology
WALTON, J. C., Chemistry
WHITEN, D. A., Psychology
WILLMER, P. G., Biology
WINN, P., Psychology
WOOLLINS, J. D., Chemistry

UNIVERSITY OF SALFORD

Salford, Greater Manchester, M5 4WT

Telephone: (161) 295-5000
Fax: (161) 295-5999
E-mail: office-exrel@salford.ac.uk
Internet: www.salford.ac.uk

Founded 1896 as the Royal Technical Institute, later Royal College of Advanced Technology, University Charter granted 1967

Academic year: October to July

Chancellor: Sir WALTER BODMER
Vice-Chancellor: Prof. M. HARLOE
Pro-Vice-Chancellors: Prof. P. BARRETT, Prof. P. BOWKER, H. JANE HANSTOCK, Prof. J. POWELL
Registrar and Secretary: ADRIAN GRAVES
Director of Academic Information Services and Librarian: TONY LEWIS
Number of teachers: 800
Number of students: 18,000

DEANS

Arts, Media and Social Sciences: Prof. C. BRYANT
Business and Informatics: CAROLE ROBERTS
Health and Social Care: M. GARRITY
Science, Engineering and the Environment: Prof. S. DONELLY

PROFESSORS

ALEXANDER, K., Construction and Property Management
ALSHAWI, M., Surveying
AOUAD, G., Surveying
ARMOUR, D. G., Physics
ARNELL, R. D., Aeronautical, Mechanical and Manufacturing Engineering
AVIS, N., Information Technology Institute
AYLETT, R., Information System Institute
BAKER, R. D., Accounting, Economics and Management Service
BARIC, L. F., Information Technology Institute
BARRETT, P. S., Surveying
BETTS, M. P., Surveying
BLAKEMORE, D. L., Modern Languages
BOARDMAN, A. D., Physics
BOOTH, J. G., Physics
BOTHAM, D., Management
BOWKER, P., Rehabilitation
BRANDON, P. S., Surveying
BROWN, G. R., Surveying
BRYANT, C. G. A., Sociology
BULL, M. J., Politics and Contemporary History
CALDWELL, D., Electronic and Electrical Engineering
CARTER, G., Physics
CHADWICK, D. W., Information System Institute

CHRISTER, A. H., Computer and Mathematics Science
COLLIER, C. G., Civil and Environmental Engineering
COLLIGON, J. S., Electronic and Electrical Engineering
COLLINS, D. N., Geography
COLQUHOUN, H. M., Chemistry and Applied Chemistry
COOK, R., Media and Performance
COOPER, G., Information Technology
COOPER, I., Centre for Regional Development and Sustainability
COOPER, R., Art and Design Technology
CRAIG, P. S., Biological Sciences
CROSSLEY, T. R., Aeronautical, Mechanical and Manufacturing Engineering
DANGERFIELD, B. C., Accounting, Economics and Management Science
DANSON, F. M., Environment and Life Sciences
DAVIES-COOPER, R., Art and Design Technology
DONNELLY, S. E., Physics
EASSON, A. W., English
EDGELL, S. R., Sociology
EDWARDS, J., Rehabilitation
EKERE, N. N., Aeronautical, Mechanical and Manufacturing Engineering
FERNANDO, T. P., Information Systems Institute
FLYNN, R., Sociology
GARSIDE, P. L., European Studies Research Institute
GERBER, R., Physics
GLEAVE, M. B., Geography
GOLDSMITH, M. J. F., Politics and Contemporary History
GRAY, J. O., Electronic and Electrical Engineering
GRUNDY, P. J., Physics
HARDING, A., Regional Development and Urban Politics
HARRIS, G. T., Modern Languages
HICKEY, L. D., Modern Languages
HILL, R., Computer and Mathematical Sciences
HORNER, A., English
HUGHES, R., Chemistry and Applied Chemistry
KAY, S., Health and Social Care
KEIGER, J. F. V., Modern Languages
KOBBACY, K. A. H., Accounting, Economics and Management Science
LAM, Y. W., Acoustics and Electronic Engineering
LARMOUTH, J., Information Technology Institute
LAWSON, R., Biological Sciences
LEONARD, J., Sciences
LINGE, N., Electronic and Electrical Engineering
LONG, A. F., Healthcare Practice
LONGHURST, B. J., English, Sociology, Politics and Contemporary History
LORD, D., Physics
MARVIN, S., Centre for Regional Development and Sustainability
MASON, R. S., Business Studies
MAY, T., Sociology
MELBOURNE, C., Civil and Environmental Engineering
MORGAN, C. G., Biological Sciences
NAGY, F. L. N., Information Technology
NEAL, F., European Studies
PEMBLE, M. E., Chemistry and Applied Chemistry
POPAY, J., Public Health Research and Resource Centre
POWELL, J. A., Information Technology
PROCTER, G., Chemistry and Applied Chemistry
RAYNES, N., Health and Social Care
REZGUI, Y., Information Systems Institute
RICHARDS, J., Science
ROSS, D. K., Physics

SAMPSON, A. A., Economics
SANGER, D. J., Aeronautical, Mechanical and Manufacturing Engineering
SARSHAR, M., Construction and Property Management
SCOTT, D. B., Music
SHARDLOW, S. M., Social Work
SIMMONS, C., Accounting, Economics and Management Science
STEELE, A., Environment and Life Sciences
STOREY, D. M., Biological Sciences
TAYLOR, I. R., Sociology
TOLZ, V., English, Sociology, Politics and Contemporary History
TOMLINSON, P., Languages
TONGE, J., English, Sociology, Politics and Contemporary History
TOWELL, R. J., Modern Languages
VADERA, S., Sciences
WALKDEN, F., Computer and Mathematics Science
WEBSTER, P. J., Civil and Environmental Engineering
WHITEHEAD, C., Physics
WHITELEY, S., Media, Music and Performance
WHITELOCK, J., Management
WOOD, J. R. G., Information and Educational and Materials Development, Computer and Mathematical Sciences
WOOD, L., Business and Informatics
WOOD-HARPER, A. T., Computer and Mathematics Science
WRIGHT, F., Surveying
WYN JONES, E., Chemistry and Applied Chemistry

DIRECTORS OF INSTITUTES OF THE RESEARCH AND GRADUATE COLLEGE

Biosciences Research Institute: Dr ROGER BISBY
European Studies Research Institute: Prof. JOHN KEIGER
Institute for Health and Social Care Research: Prof. N. RAYNES
Institute for Materials Research: Prof. K. ROSS
Institute for Public Health Research and Policy: Dr P. BELLABY
Institute for Social Research: Prof. ROB FLYNN
Research Institute for Advanced Engineering: Prof. NIGEL LINGE
Research Institute for Business and Informatics: Prof. J. R. G WOOD
Telford Institute for Environmental Science Research: Prof. M. DANSON

UNIVERSITY OF SHEFFIELD

Sheffield, S10 2TN

Telephone: (114) 222-2000
Fax: (114) 279-8603
E-mail: pr@shef.ac.uk
Internet: www.shef.ac.uk

Founded 1897 as University College, Royal Charter 1905

Academic year: September to June

Chancellor: Sir PETER MIDDLETON
Pro-Chancellors: K. E. RIDDLE, P. W. LEE G. H. N. PEEL
Vice-Chancellor: Prof. R. F. BOUCHER
Pro-Vice-Chancellors: Prof. M. BEAULIEU, Prof. A. D. H. CROOK, Prof. P. J. FLEMING, Prof. G. R. TOMLINSON, Prof. P. E. WHITE
Registrar and Secretary: Dr D. E. FLETCHER
Librarian: M. J. LEWIS

Library: see Libraries and Archives
Number of teachers: 1,296
Number of students: 23,194 (19,383 full-time, 3,811 part-time)

DEANS

Faculty of Architectural Studies: Prof. B. R. LAWSON
Faculty of Arts: Prof. D. H. WALKER

Faculty of Engineering: Prof. D. H. OWENS
Faculty of Law: Prof. M. S. M. LLEWELYN
Faculty of Medicine: Prof. A. H. BROOK
Faculty of Pure Science: Prof. J. A. LEE
Faculty of Social Sciences: Prof. W. CARR

PROFESSORS
(Some staff serve in more than one faculty)
Faculty of Architectural Studies:

BLUNDELL JONES, P. M., Architecture
CAMPBELL, H., Town and Regional Planning
CROOK, A. D. H., Town and Regional Planning
HENNEBERRY, J., Town and Regional Planning
KANG, J., Architecture
LAWSON, B. R., Architecture
PLANK, R. J., Architecture
SWANWICK, C. A., Landscape
TILL, J., Architecture
TREGENZA, P. R., Architecture

Faculty of Arts:

AINSWORTH, P. F., French
Canon ALEXANDER, L. C. A., Biblical Studies
BARRETT, J. C., Archaeology
BELL, D. A., Philosophy
BENNET, J., Archaeology
BRADDICK, M. J., History
BRANIGAN, K., Archaeology
BROOKSBANK JONES, A., Hispanic Studies
CLARKE, E. F., Music
CLINES, D. J. A., Biblical Studies
COLLIS, J. R., Archaeology and Prehistory
COOK, R. J., History
CROSS, M. F., French
DENNELL, R. W., Archaeology
DIVERS, J., Philosophy
DUFFIELD, N. G., English Language and Linguistics
ENGLAND, J. P., Hispanic Studies
EXUM, J. C., Biblical Studies
GREENGRASS, M., History
HAFFENDEN, J., English Literature
HATTAWAY, M., English Literature
HILL, P. H. A. W., Music
HOOKWAY, C. J., Philosophy
HOPKINS, R., Philosophy
JONES, G. E. M., Archaeology
Sir KERSHAW, I., Modern History
KING, E. J., History
LEATHERBARROW, W. J., Russian and Slavonic Studies
LINN, A. R., English Language and Linguistics
MCMAHON, A. M. S., English Language and Linguistics
OWENS, D. J., Philosophy
PERRAUDIN, M. F., Germanic Studies
PHIMISTER, I. P., International History
ROBERTS, N. J., English Literature
RUSSELL, R., Russian and Slavonic Studies
SAUL, J. M., Philosophy
SHELLARD, D. M., English Literature
SHEPHERD, D. G., Russian and Slavonic Studies
SHOEMAKER, R. B., History
SHUTTLEWORTH, S. A., English Literature
SIMEONE, N. A., Music
STAUB, M. H., History
STERN, R. A., Philosophy
STOCK, J. P. J., Music
SWANSON, P., Hispanic Studies
WALKER, D. H., French
WHITELAM, K. W., Biblical Studies
ZVELEBIL, M., Archaeology

Faculty of Engineering:

ALLEN, R. W. K., Chemical and Process Engineering
ALLERTON, D. J., Automatic Control and Systems Engineering
ALLINSON, N. M., Electronic and Electrical Engineering

ANDERSON, W. F., Civil and Structural Engineering
ASHLEY, R. M., Civil and Structural Engineering
ASKES, H., Civil and Structural Engineering
BANKS, S. P., Automatic Control and Systems Engineering
BANWART, S. A., Civil and Structural Engineering
BEYNON, J. H., Metallurgy
BOLLER, C., Mechanical Engineering
BILLINGS, S. A., Control Engineering
BROWN, M. W., Mechanical Engineering
BURGESS, I. W., Civil and Structural Engineering
CHAMBERS, B., Electronic and Electrical Engineering
CULLIS, A. G., Electronic and Electrical Engineering
DALEY, S., Automatic Control and Systems Engineering
DAVID, J. P. R., Electronic and Electrical Engineering
DAVIES, H. A., Engineering Materials
FLEMING, P. J., Automatic Control and Systems Engineering
GIBBS, M. R. J., Engineering Materials
HARDING, J., Engineering Materials
HOUNSLOW, M. J., Chemical and Process Engineering
HOUSTON, P. A., Electronic and Electrical Engineering
HOWARD, I. C., Mechanical Engineering
HOWE, D., Electrical Engineering
JAMES, P. F., Engineering Materials
JOHNSON, C. M., Electronic and Electrical Engineering
JONES, F. R., Engineering Materials
JONES, H., Engineering Materials
LEE, W. E., Engineering Materials
LERNER, D. N., Civil Engineering
MAC NEIL, S., Tissue Engineering
MATTHEWS, A., Engineering Materials
OWENS, D. H., Automatic Control and Systems Engineering
PAVIC, A., Civil and Structural Engineering
PILAKOUTAS, K., Civil and Structural Engineering
QIN, N., Mechanical Engineering
RAINFORTH, W. M., Engineering Materials
REES, G. J., Electronic and Electrical Engineering
RIDGWAY, K., Mechanical Engineering
SAUL, A. J., Civil and Structural Engineering
SHARIFI, V. N., Chemical and Process Engineering
SHORT, R. D., Engineering Materials
SOUTIS, C., Aerospace Engineering
SWITHENBANK, J., Chemical and Process Engineering
TOMLINSON, G. R., Engineering Dynamics
UNGAR, G., Engineering Materials
WALDRON, P., Civil and Structural Engineering
WEST, A. R., Engineering Materials
WILSON, C. W., Mechanical Engineering
WORDEN, K., Mechanical Engineering
WRIGHT, P. C., Chemical and Process Engineering
WRIGHT, P. V., Engineering Materials
YATES, J. R., Mechanical Engineering
ZHU, Z. Q., Electronic and Electrical Engineering

Faculty of Law (fax (114) 222-6832):

ADAMS, J. N., Intellectual Property
BEYLEVELD, D., Law
BIRDS, J. R., Commercial Law
BRADGATE, J. R., Commercial Law
BRADNEY, T. A., Law
DIGNAN, J., Criminology and Restorative Justice
DITTON, J., Criminology
HARDEN, I., Law

HOLDAWAY, S. D., Sociology
KINDERLERER, J., Biotechnical Law
LEWIS, N. D., Constitutional Law, Sociology of Law
LUXTON, P., Property Law
MERRILLS, J. E. G., International Law
SHAPLAND, J. M., Criminal Justice

Faculty of Medicine (Beech Hill Rd, Sheffield, S10 2RX; fax (114) 271-3960):

AHMEDZAI, S., Palliative Medicine
AKEHURST, R. L., Health Economics
BARBER, D. C., Medical Imaging and Medical Physics
BAX, N. D. S., Medical Education
BISHOP, N. J., Paediatric Bone Disease
BOISSONADE, F. M., Oral and Maxillofacial Surgery
BRAZIER, J. E., Health Economics
BROOK, A. H., Oral Health and Development
BROOK, I. M., Oral and Maxillofacial Surgery
BROOKER, C. G. D., Mental Health
BROWN, B. H., Medical Physics
BROWN, B. L., Cell Signalling and Endocrinology
BROWN, N. J., Surgical Sciences
CAMPBELL, M. J., Medical Statistics
CANNINGS, C., Mathematics and Informatics
COLEMAN, R., Medical Oncology
CROSSMAN, D. C., Cardiology
CROUCHER, P. I., Bone Biology
DOLAN, P. H. R., Health Economics
DOWER, S. K., Molecular Immunology
DUFF, G. W., Molecular Medicine
EASTELL, R., Bone Metabolism
EL-NAHAS, A. M., Nephrology
ENDERBY, P. M., Community Rehabilitation
FORREST, A. R. W., Clinical Chemistry
GERRISH, K., Nursing Practice Development
GRANT, G. W. B., Cognitive Disability
GRIFFITHS, P. D., Academic Radiology
Sir HALL, D. M. B., Community Paediatrics
HAMDY, F., Urology
HANCOCK, B. W., Clinical Oncology
HATTON, P. V., Adult Dental Care
HELLEWELL, P. G., Vascular Biology
HENDERSON, I. W., Functional Genomics
HUTCHINSON, A., Public Health Medicine
INCE, P., Neuropathology
KERSHAW, B., Nursing and Midwifery
KIRKHAM, M. J., Midwifery
LEDGER, W. L., Obstetrics and Gynaecology
LENNON, M. A., Oral Health and Development
LEWIS, C. E., Molecular and Cellular Pathology
MAC NEIL, S., Tissue Engineering
MATHERS, N., General Practice
MEUTH, M., Cellular Genetics
MILROY, C. M., Forensic Pathology
MOORE, H. D. M., Reproductive Biology
NICHOLL, J. P., Medical Care Research Centre
NICOLSON, P., Health Psychology
NOLAN, M. R., Gerontological Nursing
PALEY, M. N. J., Magnetic Resonance Physics
PARKER, S. G., Health Care for Elderly People
PARRY, G. D., Applied Psychological Therapies
PAYNE, S., Palliative Care Nursing
PEAKE, I. R., Molecular Medicine
PERKINS, M. R., Human Communications Science
PHILP, I., Health Care for Elderly People
POCKLEY, A. G., Immunobiology
POWERS, H. J., Nutritional Biochemistry
QWARNSTRÖM, E. E., Cell Biology
READ, R. C., Infectious Diseases

READ, S. M., Acute and Critical Care Nursing
REED, M. W. R., Surgical Oncology
REILLY, C. S., Anaesthesia
RENNIE, I. G., Ophthalmology
ROBINSON, P. G., Oral Health and Development
ROBINSON, P. P., Oral and Maxillofacial Surgery
ROLF, C. G., Sports Medicine
ROSS, R. J. M., Endocrinology
SAYERS, J. R., Functional Genomics
SHAW, P. J., Neurology
SPEIGHT, P. M., Oral Pathology
STACKHOUSE, R. J., Human Communication Science
TANNER, M. S., Paediatrics
TANTAM, D. J. H., Psychotherapy
TAYLOR, C. J., Paediatric Gastroenterology
THOMPSON, D. R., Acute and Critical Care
TUCKER, G. T., Molecular Pharmacology and Pharmacogenetics
UNDERWOOD, J. C. E., Pathology
VAN NOORT, R., Adult Dental Care
WALSH, T. F., Adult Dental Care
WARNES, A. M., Social Gerontology
WEETMAN, A. P., Medicine
WELLS, M., Gynaecological Pathology
WELLS, W. B., Human Communication Science
WHYTE, M. K. B., Respiratory Medicine
WOLL, P. J., Medical Oncology
WOODRUFF, P. W. R., Academic Clinical Psychiatry

Faculty of Pure Science:

ANDERSON, C. W., Mathematics and Statistics
ANDREWS, P. W., Biomedical Science
ARMS, S. P., Chemistry
ARMSTRONG, H. W., Geography
ARTYMIUK, P. J., Molecular Biology and Biotechnology
ATKIN, R. J., Applied Mathematics
BAILEY, G. J., Applied Mathematics
BEERLING, D. J., Palaeoclimatology
BIGG, G. R., Geography
BIGGINS, J. D., Probability and Statistics
BINGHAM, N. H., Probability and Statistics
BIRKHEAD, T. R., Zoology
BLACKSTOCK, W., Molecular Biology and Biotechnology
BULLOUGH, P. A., Molecular Biology and Biotechnology
BURKE, T. A., Molecular Ecology
BUTLIN, R. K., Evolutionary Biology
CALLAGHAN, T. V., Arctic Ecology
CALOW, P., Zoology
CARSWELL, D. A., Geology
CHATWIN, P. C., Applied and Computational Mathematics
CIRAVEGNA, F., Computer Science
COOKE, M. P., Computer Science
DEAN, P., Psychology
DERRICK, J., Computer Science
DORLING, D. F. L., Geography
EBDON, J. R., Chemistry
EISER, C., Psychology
EISER, J. R., Psychology
FÁY-SIEBENBÜRGEN, R. VON, Applied Mathematics
FLEMING, A. J., Plant Sciences
FOSTER, S. J., Molecular Biology and Biotechnology
FRISBY, J. P., Psychology
GAIZAUSKAS, R., Computer Science
GASTON, K. J., Biodiversity and Conservation
GEHRING, G. A., Solid State Physics
GREEN, J., Molecular Biology and Biotechnology
GREEN, P. D., Computer Science
GREENLEES, J. P. C., Probability and Statistics
GREGSON, N., Geography
GRUNDY, D., Biomedical Science

HARDY, G., Clinical Psychology
HEATHWAITE, A. L., Geography
HIGGINS, J. A., Molecular Biology and Biotechnology
HOCKEY, G. R. J., Psychology
HOLCOMBE, W. M. L., Computer Science
HOLLEY, M. J., Biomedical Science
HORTON, P., Molecular Biology and Biotechnology
HUGHES, D. W., Physics and Astronomy
HUNTER, C. A., Chemistry
HUNTER, C. N., Molecular Biology and Biotechnology
INGHAM, P. W., Biomedical Science
JACKSON, P. A., Human Geography
JACKSON, R. F. W., Synthetic Chemistry
JONES, R. A. L., Physics
JORDAN, D. A., Pure Mathematics
KELLY, D. J., Molecular Biology and Biotechnology
LEE, J. A., Environmental Biology
LEEGOOD, R. C., Plant Biochemistry
LEGGETT, G. J., Nanoscale Analytical Science
McLEOD, C. W. M., Chemistry
MALTBY, L., Environmental Biology
MANN, B. E., Chemistry
MAYHEW, J. E. W., Psychology
MOERDIJK, I., Pure Mathematics
MOORE, H. D. M., Reproductive Biology
MOORE, R., Computer Science
NICOLSON, R. I., Psychology
NIRANJAN, M., Computer Science
O'HAGAN, A., Probability and Statistics
OUTHWAITE, C. W., Mathematics and Statistics
PARSONS, L. M., Psychology
PATTIE, C. J., Geography
PICKUP, B. T., Chemistry
PIPER, P., Molecular Biology and Biotechnology
PLACZEK, M., Biomedical Science
POOLE, R. K., Molecular Biology and Biotechnology
PRESS, M. C., Physiological Ecology
QUEGAN, S., Applied and Computational Mathematics
QUICK, W. P., Plant Physiology
RATNIEKS, F. L. W., Apiculture
READ, D. J., Plant Sciences
REDGRAVE, P., Psychology
REES, M., Plant Ecology
RICE, D. W., Molecular Biology and Biotechnology
ROSZKOWSKI, L., Physics and Astronomy
RUDERMAN, M. S., Applied Mathematics
RYAN, A. J., Chemistry
SCHOLES, J. D., Plant and Microbial Science
SHARKEY, N. E., Computer Science
SHARP, R. Y., Pure Mathematics
SHEERAN, P., Psychology
SIEGAL, M., Psychology
SKOLNICK, M. S., Experimental Condensed Matter
SLADE, P., Clinical Psychology
SMALLWOOD, R., Computer Science
SMYTHE, C., Biomedical Science
SMYTHE, E., Biomedical Science
SNAITH, V. P., Pure Mathematics
SPENCER, C. P., Psychology
SPOONER, N. J. C., Physics
STRICKLAND, N. P., Pure Mathematics
SURPRENANT, A., Biomedical Science
TADHUNTER, C. N., Physics and Astronomy
THOMPSON, M.J., Applied Mathematics
TURNER, G., Genetics
TURPIN, G., Clinical Psychology
VALENTINE, G., Geography
WALL, T. D., Psychology
WALKER, M., Computer Science
WALTHO, J. P., Molecular Biology and Biotechnology
WARD, M. D., Chemistry
WHITE, P. E., Geography
WILKS, Y., Computer Science

WILLIAMSON, M. P., Molecular Biology and Biotechnology
WOODWARD, F. I., Plant Ecology
WYATT, L. R., Applied Mathematics
ZINOBER, A. S. I., Applied Mathematics

Faculty of Social Sciences:

ADCOCK, C. J., Financial Econometrics
ARMSTRONG, D., Education
BEAULIEU, M., Management
BOOTH, T. A., Social Policy
BROOKES, R. G., Education
CARR, W., Education
CASSELL, C. M., Management
CHAPPELL, D., Mathematical Economics
CLEGG, C. W., Work Psychology
COLE, P., Journalism
CORRALL, S., Librarianship and Information Management
FORD, N. J., Information Studies
FRANKLIN, R., Media Communications
GAMBLE, A. M., Politics
GEDDES, A. P., Politics
GRAYSON, J. H., East Asian Studies
GRUGEL, J. B., Politics
GUNTER, B., Journalism
HANNON, P. W., Education
HEALD, D. E. A, Management
HOCKEY, J. L., Sociological Studies
HOOK, G. D., Japanese Studies
HOOPER, B. J., East Asian Studies
JAMES, A., Sociological Studies
JENKINS, R., Sociology
KENNEDY-PIPE, C., International Relations, Politics
MACDONALD, S., Management
MALTBY, J. A., Management
MARSH, P., Child and Family Welfare
McCONNELL, D., Education
MOSLEY, P., Economics
NIXON, J. D., Education
NORRIS, C. A., Sociology
PARRY, G., Education
PAYNE, A. J., Politics
REDMAN, T. A., Management
SMITH, M. J., Politics
STANDISH, P., Education
TAYLOR, A J., Politics
TAYLOR, P. D., Leisure Management
TYLECOTE, A. B., Economics and Management of Technological Change
USHERWOOD, R. C., Information Studies
VINCENT, A. W., Politics
WALKER, A. C., Social Policy
WEBB, S. C., Institute of Lifelong Learning
WELLINGTON, J. J., Education
WHITTAKER, S. J., Information Studies
WILLETT, P., Information Studies
WOOD, S. J., Work Psychology
WRIGHT, T., East Asian Studies

ATTACHED SCHOOLS

School of Health and Related Research: Dean Prof. R. L. AKEHURST.

School of Management: Dir Prof. M. BEAULIEU.

SHEFFIELD HALLAM UNIVERSITY

City Campus, Howard St, Sheffield, S1 1WB

Telephone: (114) 225-5555
Fax: (114) 225-3398
E-mail: admissions@shu.ac.uk
Internet: www.shu.ac.uk

Founded 1969 as Sheffield Polytechnic, later Sheffield City Polytechnic; present name and status 1992
Academic year: September to June

Chancellor: Lord WINSTON
Vice-Chancellor: Prof. DIANA GREEN
Pro-Vice-Chancellors: Prof. R. ANDERSON, Prof. P. GARRAHAN, Prof. C. HAWKES
Director of Human Resources: ROSALIND EDWARDS
University Secretary: LIZ WINDERS

Academic Registrar: GWYN ARNOLD
Library of 540,000 vols
Number of teachers: 955
Number of students: 28,249 (20,993 under-
graduate, 7,286 postgraduate)

DEANS

Faculty of Arts, Computing Engineering and
Sciences: GRAHAM BUTTON
Faculty of Development and Society: Prof.
KEVIN BONNETT
Faculty of Health and Wellbeing: Prof.
RHIANNON BILLINGLSEY
Faculty of Organisation and Management:
CHRISTINE BOOTH

UNIVERSITY OF SOUTHAMPTON

Highfield, Southampton, SO17 1BJ
Telephone: (23) 8059-5000
Fax: (23) 8059-3939
Internet: www.soton.ac.uk
Founded 1952; opened as the Hartley Insti-
tution 1862; incorporated as the Hartley
University College 1902
Academic year: October to July

Chancellor: LORD SELBORNE
Vice-Chancellor: Prof. BILL WAKEHAM
Deputy Vice-Chancellors: Prof. P. J. GREG-
SON, Prof. K. E. McLUSKIE, Prof. A. A.
WHEELER
Secretary and Registrar: J. F. D. LAUWERYS
Director of Student Services (vacant)
Librarian: Dr M. BROWN

Library: see Libraries
Number of teachers: 950
Number of students: 19,896 (15,446 full-time,
4,450 part-time)

DEANS

Faculty of Engineering, Science and Mathe-
matics: Prof. J. K. HAMMOND
Faculty of Law, Arts and Social Sciences:
Prof. NICK FOSKETT
Faculty of Medicine, Health and Life
Sciences: Prof. D. WILLIAMS

PROFESSORS

Faculty of Engineering, Science and Mathematics (tel. (23) 8059-4184):

ALLEN, R., Institute of Sound and Vibration
Research
ARNELL, N. W., Geography
ASHBURN, P., Electronics and Computer
Science
ATTARD, G. S., Chemistry
BAILEY, A. G., Electronics and Computer
Science
BARBER, K. E., Geography
BARNES, K. J., Physics and Astronomy
BARTLETT, P. N., Chemistry
BAUMBERG, J. J., Physics and Astronomy
BEDUZ, C., Cryogenics
BOWDITCH, B. H., Mathematics
BRADLEY, M., Chemistry
BROWN, A. D., Electronics and Computer
Science
BROWN, T., Chemistry
BRYDEN, H., Oceanography
BUTLER, M. J., Electronics and Computer
Science
CARLING, P. A., Geography
CASTRO, I. P., Aeronautics and Astronau-
tics
CHAPLIN, J. R., Civil and Environmental
Education
CHARLES, P. A., Physics and Astronomy
CHENG, R. C. H., Mathematics
CLARK, M. J., Geography
CLAYTON, C. R. I., Civil and Environmental
Education
COLES, H. J., Physics and Astronomy
COLLINS, M. B., Oceanography
CURRAN, P. J., Geography

DAVIES, A. E., Electrical Engineering
DEAN, A. J., Physics and Astronomy
DE GROOT, P. A. J., Physics and Astronomy
DE ROURE, D. C., Electronics and Compu-
ter Science
D'INVERNO, R. A, Mathematics
DUNMUR, D. A., Chemistry
DYKE, J. M., Chemistry
EASON, A. B., Opto-electronics Research
Centre
EASON, R. W., Physics and Astronomy
ELLIOTT, S. J., Institute of Sound and
Vibration Research
EVANS, A. G. R, Electronics and Computer
Science
EVANS, J., Chemistry
FASHAM, M. J. R., Oceanography
FITT, A. D., Mathematics
FOODY, G. M., Geography
FRAMPTON, C. S., Chemistry
GREGSON, P. J., Engineering Materials
GRIFFIN, M. J., Institute of Sound and
Vibration Research
GRIFFITHS, G., Oceanography
GRUDININ, A. B., Opto-electronics Research
Centre
HALL, W., Electronics and Computer
Science
HAMMOND, J. K., Institute of Sound and
Vibration Research
HANNA, D. C., Physics and Astronomy
HANZO, L., Electronics and Computer
Science
HARNAD, S. R., Electronics and Computer
Science
HARRIS, C. J., Electronics and Computer
Science
HAYDEN, B. E., Chemistry
HEARN, G. E., Ship Science
HENDERSON, P., Electronics and Computer
Science
HEY, A. J. G., Electronics and Computer
Science
HOLLIGAN, P. M., Oceanography
HUGHES, J. F., Electrical Engineering
HURSTHOUSE, M. B., Chemistry
JENKINS, W. J., Chemical Oceanography
JENNINGS, N. R., Electronics and Computer
Science
JONES, G. A., Mathematics
KEANE, A. J., Mechanical Engineering
KEMP, A. E. S., Oceanography
KILBURN, J. D., Chemistry
KILLWORTH, P. D., Oceanography
KING, R. C., Mathematics
KING, S. F., Physics and Astronomy
LEE, M. M. K., Civic and Environmental
Engineering
LEIGHTON, T. G., Institute of Sound and
Vibration Research
LEVASON, W., Chemistry
LEVITT, M. H., Chemistry
LEWIS, S., Mathematics
LOCKWOOD, M., Physics and Astronomy
LUCKHURST, G. R., Chemistry
LUTMAN, M. E., Institute of Sound and
Vibration Research
McBRIDE, J. W., Mechanical Engineering
McDONALD, M., Civil and Environmental
Engineering
McHARDY, I. M., Physics and Astronomy
MAROTZKE, J., Oceanography
MARTIN, D. J., Geography
MASON, C., Geography
MELLOR, J., Chemistry
MORFEY, C. L., Institute of Sound and
Vibration Research
MURRAY, J. W., Geology
NELSON, P. A., Institute of Sound and
Vibration Research
NESBITT, R. W., Oceanography
PALMER, M. R., Oceanography
PARKER, G. I., Electronics and Computer
Science
PAYNE, D. N., Opto-electronics Research
Centre

PLEASE, C. P., Mathematics
PLETCHER, D., Chemistry
POTTS, C. N., Mathematics
POWRIE, W., Civil and Environmental
Engineering
PRESCOTT, P., Mathematics
PRICE, W. G., Ship Science
RAINFORD, B. D., Physics and Astronomy
REDMAN-WHITE, W., Electronics and Com-
puter Science
RICHARDSON, D. J., Opto-electronics
Research Centre
ROBINSON, I. S., Oceanography
ROE, H. S., Oceanography
ROGERS, E. T. A., Electronics and Compu-
ter Science
ROSS, D. A., Physics and Astronomy
RUTT, H. N., Electronics and Computer
Science
SACHRAJDA, C. T. C., Physics and Astron-
omy
SANDHAM, N. D., Aeronautics and Astro-
nautics
SASSONE, V., Electronics and Computer
Science
SHADBOLT, N. R., Electronics and Compu-
ter Science
SHENOI, R. A., Ship Science
SHEPHERD, J., Oceanography
SINGERMAN, D., Mathematics
SINHA, M. C., Oceanography
SLUCKIN, T. J., Mathematics
SNAITH, V., Mathematics
STOW, D. A., Oceanography
SYKULSKI, J. K., Electrical Engineering
TANTON, T. W., Civil and Environmental
Engineering
TEMAREL, P., Ship Science
THOMSON, J., Oceanography
TROPPER, A. C., Physics and Astronomy
TYLER, P. A., Oceanography
VICKERS, J. A., Mathematics
WEAVER, P. P. E., Oceanography
WELLER, M. T., Chemistry
WELSH, A. H., Mathematics
WHEELER, A. A., Mathematics
WHITBY, R. J., Chemistry
WILKINSON, J. S., Opto-electronics
Research Centre
WILSON, P. A., Ship Science
WILLOUGHBY, A. F. W., Engineering Mate-
rials
WRIGLEY, N., Geography
ZERVAS, M. N., Opto-electronics Research
Centre
ZHANG, X., Aeronautics and Astronautics
ZHELUDEV, N. I., Physics and Astronomy

Faculty of Law, Arts and Social Sciences (tel.
(23) 8059-2206; fax (23) 8059-3987; e-mail
artsrec@soton.ac.uk; internet www.soton.ac
.uk/~arts):

ANDERLINI, L., Economics
ARNOLD, D. R., Archaeology
BANCE, A. F., German
BOURNE, G. M., Education
BRADLEY, B., Psychology
BRUMFIT, C. J., Education
CALVERT, P. A. R., Politics
CANOVA, F., Economics
CESARANI, D., History
CHAMBERS, R. L., Social Statistics
CHAMPION, T. C., Archaeology
CHAPMAN, C. B., Management
CHEYETTE, B. H., English
CLIFF, D., Electronics and Computer
Science
COLEMAN, P. G., Social Work Studies
COLLIER, A. S., Philosophy
COOK, N. J., Music
COOK, P., Film and Media Studies
CREMER, J., Economics
CROUAN, K. M., Winchester School of Art
DALE, R. S., Management
DOMINELLI, L. R., Social Work Studies
DEBATTISTA, C., Law

EVERIST, M. E., Music
FINNISSY, M., Music
FOSKETT, N., Education
GAMBLE, C. S., Archaeology
GASKELL, N. J., Law
GIBBONS, J., Winchester School of Art
GODDARD, A. R., Management
GRIME, R. P., Law
HAMLIN, A., Economics
HILLIER, G. H., Economics
HANNIGAN, B. M., Law
HINTON, D. A., Archaeology
JOHNSON, J. E. V., Management
KAPLAN, C., English
KARP, L., Economics
KEAY, S. J., Archaeology
KELLY, M. H., French
KUSHNER, A. R., History
LABANYI, J., Spanish
LUSTGARTEN, L., Law
McCORMICK, B., Economics
McGREW, A., Politics
McKENZIE, G. W., Management
McLUSKIE, K. E., English
MAR-MOLINERO, C., Spanish
MARTIN, R., Management
MASON, A., Politics
MEINHOFF, U., German
MERKIN, R., Law
MITCHELL, R., Management
MIZON, G. E., Economics
MOGG, K., Psychology
MONK, R., Philosophy
MONTGOMERY, J. R., Law
NAPIER, C. J., Management
NEWTON, K., Politics
NICHOLLS, D., Music
PEACOCK, D. P. S., Archaeology
PILGRIM, P. J., Winchester School of Art
Lord PLANT OF HIGHFIELD, Politics
PRINGLE, R., Sociology
RAPAPORT, H., English
REMINGTON, R. E., Psychology
REUTER, T. A., History
ROSEMAN, M., History
RUTHERFORD, A. F., Law
SEDIKEDES, C., Psychology
SHARPE, K. M., History
SIMONS, H., Education
SIMPSON, J., Politics
SKINNER, C. J., Social Statistics
SONUGA-BURKE, E., Psychology
STEVENSON, J. E., Psychology
SUTCLIFFE, C. M. S., Management
TAYLOR, B., Winchester School of Art
TAYLOR, M., History
THOMAS, C. A., Politics
THOMAS, L., Management
THOMAS, S. H., Management
TRIDIMAS, T., European Community Law
ULPH, A. M., Economics
UNGERSON, C. E., Sociology and Social Policy
VALIMAKI, J., Economics
WIKELEY, N. J., Law
ZILLIBOTI, F., Economics

Faculty of Medicine, Health and Life Sciences
(Some professors also serve in the Faculty of Engineering, Science and Mathematics)

ANTHONY, C., Biochemistry
ARTHUR, M. J. P., Medicine
ASHBURN, A. M., Rehabilitation
BARKER, D. J. P., Clinical Epidemiology
BARNITT, R., Occupational Therapy
BRIGGS, R. S. J., Geriatric Medicine
BYRNE, C. D. T., Endocrinology
CAMERON, I. T., Obstetrics
CHURCH, M. K., Experimental Immunopharmacology
CLARKE, I. N., Virology
COGGON, D., Environmental Epidemiology
COLEMAN, P. G., Social Gerontology

COOPER, C., Rheumatology
CROSS, N. C., Human Genetics
DAY, I. N. M., Genetics
ELIA, M., Human Nutrition
ELLIOTT, T. J., Oncology
FLEMING, T. P., Biological Sciences
FOX, K. R., Biological Sciences
FREW, A. J., Molecular Biology
FRIEDMAN, P., Dermatology
GABBAY, J., Public Health Medicine
GETLIFFE, K., Nursing
GLASPER, E. A., Nursing Studies
GLENNIE, M., Immunochemistry
GRIMBLE, R. F., Nutrition
HALL, J. L., Biological Sciences
HAMBLIN, T. J., Immunohaematology
HANSON, M. A., Foetal Origins of Adult Disease
HAWKINS, S. J., Biology
HECKELS, J. E., Molecular Microbiology
HOLGATE, S. T., Immunopharmacology
JACKSON, A. A., Human Nutrition
JACOBS, P. A., Genetics
JOHNSON, P., Medical Oncology
KENDRICK, T., Primary Medical Care
KINGDON, D., Mental Health Care Delivery
LATHLEAN, J., Nursing
LEE, A. G., Biochemistry
MacDONALD, T. T., Tissue Repair
MACLEAN, N., Biological Sciences
McLELLAN, D. L., Rehabilitation
Dame MACLEOD CLARK, J., Nursing
NICOLL, J. A., Clinical Neurosciences
O'CONNOR, D., Biological Sciences
PERRY, V. H., Biological Sciences
PEVELER, M., Psychiatry
PRIMROSE, J. N., Surgery
RENWICK, A., Clinical Pharmacology
ROCHE, W. R., Pathology
SEDGWICK, E. M., Neurophysiology
SHEARMAN, C. P., Human Nutrition
SHOOLINGIN-JORDAN, P. M., Biochemistry
STEVENSON, F. K., Cancer Sciences
THOMPSON, C., Psychiatry
THORNTON, R., Neurosurgery
WALKER, R. J., Physiology and Pharmacology
WARD, M. E., Medical Microbiology
WARNER, J. O., Child Health
WELLER, R. O., Neuropathology
WHEAL, H. V., Physiology and Pharmacology
WILSON, D. I., Human Genetics
WOOD, S. P., Biological Sciences

SOUTHAMPTON SOLENT UNIVERSITY

East Park Terrace, Southampton, SO14 0YN
Telephone: (23) 8031-9000
Fax: (23) 8033-4161
E-mail: enquiries@solent.ac.uk
Internet: www.solent.ac.uk

Founded 1855 as a school of art; became an independent higher education corporation 1989, present name and status 2005

Vice-Chancellor: Prof. ROGER BROWN
Number of students: 16,000

Faculties of Media, Arts and Society and Technology; Southampton Business School.

STAFFORDSHIRE UNIVERSITY

College Rd, Stoke on Trent, ST4 2DE
Telephone: (1782) 292720
Fax: (1782) 292796
E-mail: international@staffs.ac.uk
Internet: www.staffs.ac.uk

Founded 1970 as North Staffordshire Polytechnic, became Staffordshire Polytechnic 1988; present name and status 1992
Academic year: September to July

Chancellor: Sir BILL MORRIS

Vice-Chancellor: Prof. CHRISTINE KING
Deputy Vice-Chancellor (External Developments): P. RICHARDS
University Secretary: KEN SPROSTON
Academic Registrar: FRANCESCA FRANCIS
Librarian: LIZ HART
Library of 300,000 vols, 2,000 periodicals
Number of teachers: 589
Number of students: 16,575 (10,991 full-time undergraduate, 1,972 postgraduate, 3,612 part-time)
Publications: *Annual Review*, *Horizon* (journal for former students; 3 a year), *Research Report* (annually), *University News* (2 a month)

PRO-VICE-CHANCELLORS

Faculty of Arts, Media and Design: ANN PARRY
Faculty of Business and Law: Prof. RICHARD PAINTER
Faculty of Computing, Engineering and Technology: Prof. TOM RUXTON
Faculty of Health and Sciences: Dr TEERANLALL RAMGOPAL

UNIVERSITY OF STIRLING

Stirling, FK9 4LA
Telephone: (1786) 473171
Fax: (1786) 463000
Internet: www.external.stir.ac.uk
Founded 1967
Academic year: September to May (two semesters)
Chancellor: Dame DIANA RIGG
Principal and Vice-Chancellor: Prof. C. HALLETT
Deputy Principals: Prof. J. FIELD, Prof. N. KEEBLE, Prof. S. MARSHALL
Secretary: K. CLARKE
Deputy Secretary: Dr D. FARRINGTON
Clerk to the Court: J. WHITLEY
Director of Information Services and University Librarian: Dr P. KEMP
Library: see Libraries and Archives
Number of teachers: 420
Number of students: 8,400
Publication: *Annual Report*

DEANS

Faculty of Arts: Prof. S. MARSHALL
Faculty of Human Sciences: Prof. D. TIMMS
Faculty of Management: Prof. R. BALL
Faculty of Natural Sciences: Prof. C. SOMMERVILLE

PROFESSORS AND HEADS OF DEPARTMENT
(H=Head of Department)
Faculty of Arts (tel. (1786) 467491; fax (1786) 451335; e-mail arts1@stir.ac.uk):
BEBBINGTON, D. W., History
BERMUDEZ, J., Philosophy (H)
DOYLE, G. M., Film and Media Studies
DRAKAKIS, J., English Studies
DUFF, R. A., Philosophy
FLOOD, G., Religious Studies (H)
FRITH, S., Film and Media Studies
INGLE, S. J., Politics
IZOD, J., Film and Media Studies
KEEBLE, N. H., English Studies
KIDD, W., Modern Languages (H)
LAW, R. C., History
McKEAN, R. B., History (H)
MACK, D. S., English Studies
MARSHALL, S., Philosophy
MILES, R., English Studies
MILLAR, A., Philosophy
MURDOCH, B. O., Modern Languages
PEDEN, G., History
REYNOLDS, S., Modern Languages
SCHLESINGER, P., Film and Media Studies
SMITH, A., English Studies

STACHURA, P. D., History
TIMMINS, G., Politics (H)
WATSON, R., English Studies (H)

Faculty of Human Sciences (tel. (1786) 467595; fax (1786) 466292; e-mail hums1@stir.ac.uk):

ALLAN, J., Education
BOREHAM, N., Education
BOWES, A., Applied Social Science (H)
BROWN, S., Education
CLASEN, J., Applied Social Science
COPE, P., Education (H)
EDWARDS, R., Education
HALLETT, C., Applied Social Science
JOHNSTONE, M., Education
KEARNEY, N., Nursing and Midwifery
McIVOR, G., Applied Social Science
MARKOVA, I., Psychology
MARSHALL, M., Applied Social Sciences
MURPHY-BLACK, T., Nursing and Midwifery
NIVEN, K., Nursing and Midwifery
O'CARROLL, R., Psychology
OSBORNE, J., Education
PHILLIPS, W., Psychology
POWER, K., Psychology
PROUT, A., Applied Social Science
ROWLINGS, C., Applied Social Science
STARRS, T., Nursing and Midwifery
TIMMS, D, Applied Social Science
WATT, R., Psychology (H)
WATTERSON, A., Nursing and Midwifery
WILSON, J., Psychology
WOERGOETTER, F., Psychology

Faculty of Management (tel. (1786) 467277; fax (1786) 467279; e-mail mgts1@stir.ac.uk):

BALDRY, C., Management and Organization (H)
BALL, R., Management and Organization
BEATTIE, V., Accounting, Finance and Law
BELL, D., Economics
BROWNLIE, D., Marketing
BURT, S., Marketing (H)
COALTER, F., Sports Studies
DOW, S., Economics (H)
FREATHY, J., Marketing
HART, R., Economics
HUGHES, M., Management and Organization
JARVIE, G., Sports Studies (H)
KING, D., Economics
LIMMACK, R., Accounting, Finance and Law
LOASBY, B., Economics
McINNES, W., Accounting, Finance and Law
MAGILL, E., Computing Science and Mathematics
PAGE, S., Marketing
RIORDAN, J., Sports Studies
ROWLINSON, P., Computing Science and Mathematics
SHARP, C., Sports Studies
SMITH, L., Computing Science and Mathematics
SPARKS, L., Marketing
STOPFORTH, D., Accounting, Finance and Law
TURNER, K., Computing Science and Mathematics
VAMPLEN, W., Sports Studies
WRIGHT, R., Economics
YOUNG, J., Marketing

Faculty of Natural Sciences (tel. (1786) 467550; fax (1786) 466896; e-mail nats1@stir.ac.uk):

BRYANT, D., Biological and Environmental Sciences
DAVIDSON, D., Environmental Science
FERGUSON, H., Aquaculture
GEORGE, S., Aquaculture
HOPKINS, D., Biological and Environmental Sciences
McANDREW, B., Aquaculture
MUIR, J., Aquaculture

PROCTOR, J., Biological and Environmental Sciences
REID, J., Biological Sciences
RICHARDS, R., Aquaculture (H)
ROSS, L., Aquaculture
SIMPSON, I., Biological and Environmental Sciences
SMITH, K., Biological and Environmental Sciences
SOMMERVILLE, C., Aquaculture
TEALE, A., Aquaculture
THOMAS, M., Biological and Environmental Sciences
USHER, M., Biological and Environmental Sciences
WILSON, H., Biological and Environmental Sciences

NON-PROFESSORIAL HEADS OF DEPARTMENT

Faculty of Arts (tel. (1786) 467490; fax (1786) 451335; e-mail arts1@stir.ac.uk):

DOYLE, G. M., Film and Media Studies
KIDD, W., Modern Languages
McKEAN, R., History
TIMMINS, G., Politics

Faculty of Human Sciences (tel. (1786) 467595; fax (1786) 466292; e-mail hums1@stir.ac.uk):

STARRS, T., Nursing and Midwifery

Faculty of Management (tel. (1786) 467277; fax (1786) 467279; e-mail mgts1@stir.ac.uk):

CLARK, R., Computing Science and Mathematics
LITTLE, G., Accounting, Finance and Law
McAULEY, A, Marketing

ATTACHED INSTITUTES

Academic Innovation and Continuing Education: Dir Prof. J. FIELD.

Anxiety and Stress Research Centre: Dir Prof. K. POWER.

Augmentative and Alternative Communication Research Unit: Dir (vacant).

Centre for English Language Teaching: Dir S. TYTLER.

Centre for Environmental History: Dir Dr F. WATSON.

Centre for Publishing Studies: Dir A. WHEATCROFT.

Centre for Research in Polish History: Dir Dr P. STACHURA.

Centre for Scottish Studies: Dir Prof. R. WATSON.

Centre for Social Research in Dementia: Dir (vacant).

Centre of Commonwealth Studies: Dir Prof. A. SMITH.

Dementia Services Development Centre: Dir Prof. M. MARSHALL.

Housing Policy and Practice Unit: Dir Dr D. ROBERTSON.

Institute for Retail Studies: Dir Prof. S. BURT.

Management Development Unit: Dir C. TAYLOR.

Nursing Research Initiative for Scotland: Dir (vacant).

Scottish Centre for Information on Language Teaching and Research: Dir Prof. R. JOHNSTONE.

Scottish Economic Policy Network: Dir Prof. D. BELL.

Scottish Network for Chronic Pain Research: Dir Dr E. BRODIE.

Scottish School of Primary Care: Dir (vacant).

Social Work Research Centre: Dir Prof. G. McIVOR.

Stirling Media Research Institute: Dir Prof. P. SCHLESINGER.

UNIVERSITY OF STRATHCLYDE

16 Richmond St, Glasgow, G1 1XQ

Telephone: (141) 552-4400
Fax: (141) 552-0775
E-mail: scls@mis.strath.ac.uk
Internet: www.strath.ac.uk

Founded 1796 under the title of Anderson's Institution; affiliated to the University of Glasgow between 1913 and 1964; University Charter 1964; merged with Jordanhill College of Education 1993

Academic year: September to June

Chancellor: The Rt Hon. Lord HOPE
Principal and Vice-Chancellor: Prof. ANDREW HAMNETT
Vice-Principal: Prof. SUSAN A. SHAW
Secretary: PETER W. A. WEST
Librarian: Prof. DEREK LAW

Number of teachers: 942 (full-time)
Number of students: 14,500 (full-time)

Publications: *Annual Report, Continuing Education Programme, Postgraduate Prospectus, Undergraduate Prospectus, University Calendar*

DEANS

Faculty of Arts and Social Sciences: BARRIE WALTERS
Faculty of Education: IAIN SMITH
Faculty of Engineering: Prof. NEAL JUSTER
Faculty of Science: Dr BRIAN FURMAN
Strathclyde Business School: Prof. CHARLES HARVEY

PROFESSORS

ACKERMANN, F., Management Science
AINSWORTH, M., Mathematics
ALEXANDER, J., Immunology
ANDERSON, J., Bioscience
ANDONOVIC, I., Electronic and Electrical Engineering
ASHCROFT, B. K., Economics
BACHTLER, J., European Policy
BALENDRA, R., Design, Manufacture and Engineering Management
BANKS, W. M., Advanced Materials
BARNETT, S., Quantum Optics
BARON, S., Education
BATES, T., Law
BATH, M., English
BAUM, T. G., Hospitality Management
BEDFORD, T., Management Science
BELTON, V., Management Science
BINGHAM, R., Physics
BIRCH, D. J. S., Photophysics
BITITCI, U., Design, Manufacture and Engineering Management
BLACKIE, J. W. G., Scots Law
BOYD, B., Language Education
BOYLE, J. T., Mechanics of Materials
BRIDGES, A., Architecture
BROWN, C., History
BRYCE, T. G. K, Education
CARTER, S., Marketing
CHAKRABARTI, M., Social Work
CLARK, N., Environmental Studies
CLARKE, J. A., Energy Systems
COMMON, M., Environmental Studies
CONNOLLY, P., Bioengineering
CONNOR, R., Computer and Information Sciences
COOPER, C., Accounting and Finance
CORCORAN, M., Architecture
COURTNEY, J. M., Bioengineering
CRESTANI, F., Computer and Information Sciences
CROSS, R. B., Economics
CULSHAW, B., Optoelectronics
CURTICE, J., Government
DAVIES, J. B., Psychology

DONALDSON, G. B., Applied Physics
DUNLOP, J., Communications Engineering
DURRANI, T., Signal Processing
DUXBURY, G., Chemical Physics
EDEN, C., Graduate School of Business
ELPHINSTONE, M., Writing
FABB, N., English
FAIRLEY, J., Environmental Planning
FARRELL, J., Modern Languages
FERGUSON, A. I., Photonics
FINN, G., Educational Studies
FIRTH, W. J., Experimental Physics
FISCHER, C., History
FOOT, H. C., Psychology
FRASER, W. H., History
GENNARD, J., Human Resource Management
GETTINBY, G. C., Statistics
GIBB, F., Computer and Information Sciences
GORDON, G., Academic Practice
GORMAN, D., Mechanical Engineering
GRANT, C. D., Chemical Engineering
GRANT, M., Bioengineering
GRAY, T. G. F., Fracture Mechanics
GRIMBLE, M. J., Industrial Systems
GURNEY, A., Pharmacology
GURNEY, W. S. C., Mathematical Ecology
HALL, P., Chemical Engineering
HALLIDAY, J., Educational Studies
HALLING, P. J., Biocatalyst Science
HARNETT, W., Immunology
HART, S., Marketing
HARVEY, A. L., Pharmacology
HASTINGS, G., Marketing
HAYWARD, G., Signal Processing
HENDRY, A., Metallurgy and Engineering Materials
HIGHAM, D., Mathematics
HILLIER, D., Accounting and Finance
HOGWOOD, B. W., Politics
HOOD, N., Business Policy
HOWE, C., Psychology
HUDSON, S., Pharmaceutical Care
HUMES, W., Educational Studies
HUNTER, I., Molecular Microbiology
HUTTON, N., Law
HUXHAM, C., Management Science
JACKSON, M., Environmental Health
JACOBS, N., Training and Education in Prosthetics
JAROSZYNSKI, D., Physics
JOHNSON, G., Strategic Management
JOHNSON, M., Electronic and Electrical Engineering
JUDGE, D., Politics
JUSTER, N., Design and Manufacture
KANE, K., Physiology and Pharmacology
KARTVEDT, P., Architecture
KAY, N. M., Business Economics
KENDRICK, A., Childcare Initiative
KERR, W., Pure and Applied Chemistry
LANGFORD, D. A., Construction
LAW, D., Computer and Information Sciences
LEDINGHAM, K., Physics
LEITHEAD, W., Electronic and Electrical Engineering
LITTLEJOHN, D., Analytical Chemistry
LLOYD, I. J., Law
LO, K. L., Power Engineering
LOVE, J., Economics
MCBRIDE, A., Mathematics
MCCALL, J., Education
MACDONALD, J., Power Engineering
MACDONALD, R., International Finance
MACFARLANE, C. J., Subsea Engineering
MCGETTRICK, A. D., Computer and Information Sciences
MCGOWN, A., Civil Engineering
MCGREGOR, P., Economics
MACGREGOR, S., Electronic and Electrical Engineering
MACKAY, G., Educational Support and Guidance
MCKEE, S., Mathematics
MCNAB, A., Electronic and Electrical Engineering
MCNICOLL, I. H., Applied Economics

MANGAN, J. A., Cultural Studies in Education
MAO, X., Statistics
MARSHALL, A., Accounting and Finance
MASON, C., Entrepreneurship
MAVER, T. W., Computer-Aided Design
MEARNS, D., Counselling Unit
MILBURN, R., Community Education
MILLAN, C. G., French Studies
MILLER, K., Employment Law
MILLS, A., Pure and Applied Chemistry
MITCHELL, J., Government
MULVEY, R. E., Inorganic Chemistry
MURDOCH, A., Mathematics
MURPHY, J., Preparative Chemistry
NICOL, A., Bioengineering
NICOLSON, D., Law
NIMMO, M., Exercise Physiology
NIXON, P., Computer and Information Sciences
NORRIE, K., Law
O'DONNELL, K., Physics
OPPO, G.-L., Physics
OSIPOV, M., Mathematics
PACIONE, M., Geography
PADGETT, S., Government
PATERSON, A. A., Law
PETHRICK, R. A., Physical Chemistry
PHELPS, A., Plasma Physics
PLEVIN, R., Physiology and Pharmacology
PYNE, N., Physiology and Pharmacology
REID, S., Veterinary Informatics
RENSHAW, E., Statistics and Modelling Science
RHODES, J., Mechanics of Materials
ROBERTSON, B., Physiology and Pharmacology
ROBERTSON, C., Statistics
ROBSON, P., Law
RODGER, B., Law
SAREN, M., Marketing
SAWDAY, J., English
SCULLION, H., Human Resource Management
SHAW, S. A., Marketing
SHERRINGTON, D. C., Polymer Chemistry
SLOAN, D. McP., Numerical Analysis
SMITH, W. E., Inorganic Chemistry
SPIER, S., Architecture
STACK, M., Mechanical Engineering
STEPHEN, F. H., Economics
STEVENS, H., Pharmaceutical Sciences
STIMSON, W. H., Immunology
SUCKLING, C. J., Chemistry
SUMMERS, H. P., Theoretical Atomic Physics
SUPPLE, J., French
SWALES, J., Economics
THOMPSON, P., Human Resource Management
THOMSON, J., Psychology
UCHEGBU, I., Pharmaceutical Sciences
UTTAMCHANDANI, D., Electronic and Electrical Engineering
VASSALOS, D., Naval Architecture and Marine Engineering
WADSWORTH, R., Physiology and Pharmacology
WAIGH, R. D., Pharmacy
WALLS, L., Management Science
WATSON, J., Biochemistry
WEETMAN, P., Accounting and Finance
WEIR, A. D., Education
WHITTY, N., Law
WILLIAMS, H., Management Science
WILLIAMS, T., Management Science
WILSON, C. G., Pharmacy
WISLON, S., Mathematics
WOOD, R. C., Hospitality Management
WRIGHT, G., Business Administration
WRIGHT, R., Business
WRIGHT, H. D., Structural Engineering
YADAV, P. K., Accounting and Finance
YEO, E., History
YOUNG, S., Marketing
YUILL, D., European Policies

UNIVERSITY INSTITUTES

Centre for Electrical Power Engineering: Royal College Bldg, 204 George St, Glasgow, G1 1XW; Dir Prof. O. FARISH.

Centre for Professional Legal Studies: Stenhouse Bldg, 173 Cathedral St, Glasgow, G4 0RQ; Dir Prof. R. HARPER.

Centre for Scottish Cultural Studies: Level 6, Livingstone Tower, 26 Richmond St, Glasgow, G1 1XA; Dir Dr K. G. SIMPSON.

Centre for Social Marketing: Stenhouse Bldg, 173 Cathedral St, Glasgow, G4 0RQ; Dir Dr G. HASTINGS.

Centre for the Study of Public Policy: McCance Bldg, 16 Richmond St, Glasgow, G1 1XQ; Dir Prof. R. ROSE.

David Livingstone Institute of Overseas Development Studies: McCance Bldg, 16 Richmond St, Glasgow, G1 1XQ; Dir Prof. J. PICKETT.

European Policies Research Centre: EAC Bldg, 141 St James' Rd, Glasgow, G4 0LT; Dirs Prof. D. M. YUILL, Prof. K. J. ALLEN.

Fraser of Allander Institute for Research on the Scottish Economy (Dept of Economics): Curran Bldg, 131 St James' Rd, Glasgow, G4 0LS; Dir B. K. ASHCROFT.

Graduate School of Environmental Studies: Level 7, Graham Hills Bldg, 50 Richmond St, Glasgow, G1; Dir Ms J. FORBES.

Industrial Control Centre: Marland House, 40 George St, Glasgow, G1 1BA; Dir Prof. M. GRIMBLE.

Institute of Photonics Wolfson Centre: Chief Exec. Dr KAREN NESS.

John Logie Baird Centre for Research in Television and Film: Livingstone Tower, 26 Richmond St, Glasgow G1 1XH; Dir Prof. S. W. FRITH.

National Centre for Training and Education in Prosthetics and Orthotics: Curran Bldg, 131 St James' Rd, Glasgow G4 0LS; Dir Prof. J. HUGHES.

Scottish Local Authorities Management Centre: Curran Bldg, 131 St James's Rd, Glasgow, G4 0LS; Dir Prof. A. ALEXANDER.

Scottish Transputer Centre & DTI Centre for Parallel Signal Processing: Royal College Bldg, 204 George St, Glasgow, G1 1XW; Dir Prof. T. DURRANI.

Senior Studies Institute: McCance Bldg, 16 Richmond St, Glasgow, G1 1XQ; Dir L. A. HART.

Smart Structures Research Institute: Royal College Bldg, 204 George St, Glasgow, G1 1XW; Dir P. GARDINER.

Strathclyde Fermentation Centre: Royal College Bldg, Glasgow, G1 1XW; Dir Prof. B. KRISTIANSEN.

Strathclyde Formulation Research Unit: Royal College Bldg, 204 George St, Glasgow, G1 1XW; Dir Dr A. J. BAILLIE.

Strathclyde Institute for Drug Research: Royal College Bldg, 204 George St, Glasgow G1 1XW; Dir Prof. A. L. HARVEY.

UNIVERSITY OF SUNDERLAND

Langham Tower, Ryhope Rd, Sunderland, SR2 7EE

Telephone: (191) 515-2000
Fax: (191) 515-2960
E-mail: student-helpline@sunderland.ac.uk
Internet: www.sunderland.ac.uk

Founded 1969 as Sunderland Polytechnic; present name and status 1992
Academic year: September to June

Chancellor: Lord PUTTNAM OF QUEENSGATE

Vice-Chancellor and Chief Executive: Prof. PETER FIDLER
Deputy Vice-Chancellors: Prof. JEFF BROWN, JIM BRADSHAW
Secretary and Clerk to the Board: J. D. PACEY
Director of Information Services: Prof. ANDREW MACDONALD

Library of 280,000 vols
Number of teachers: 494
Number of students: 8,439 full-time

DEANS

School of Arts, Design, Media and Culture: Prof. F. SWANN
Sunderland Business School: VICKY HOUSTON
School of Computing and Technology: Prof. P. SMITH
School of Education and Lifelong Learning: Prof. G. SHIELD
School of Health, Natural and Social Sciences: M. D. BURKE

PROFESSORS

ALABASTER, T., Environmental Informatics
ARTHUR, W. W., Population Biology
BAINBRIDGE, E., Fine Art
BRAYNE, H., Law
CHILTON, P., Politics and Peace Studies
COCKTON, G., Computer Software Engineering
COX, C. S., Control Engineering
CRISELL, A. P., Broadcasting Studies
CROZIER, G., Education
DARBY, J., Humanities
EDWARDS, H. M., Computer Software Engineering
ELLIOTT, J., Education
ELLIS, P., Performance Arts
FLETCHER, E. J., Applied Computing
GROUNDWATER, P. W., Organic Chemistry
HANMER, J., Humanities
HARVEY, B. P., Humanities
HEPBURN, A., Modern Irish History
HESTER, M., Social Studies
HARRISON, R., Renewable Energy
ITZIN, C., Health and Community Studies
LEES, G., Neurophysiology and Neuropharmacology
LILLEY, T. H., Physical Chemistry
MACINTYRE, J., Computer Software Engineering
MALIN, N. A., Health Services Research
MOSCARDINI, A. O., Mathematical Modelling
O'BRIEN, M., Librarian, Communication and Media Studies
OVER, D. E., Philosophical Logic
PALOVA, Z., Design and Creative Arts
PETROVA, S., Glass
PODCZECK, G. F., Pharmaceutics
PRENTICE, R. C., Tourism
PRINGLE, K., Comparative Social Policy
REED, M. A., Criminal and Private International Law
RICHARDS, D. S., International Business and Cross-Cultural Management
SIM, S. D., Critical Theory
SINGH, G., Pharmacy
STOREY, J. C., Librarian, Communication and Media Studies
TAIT, J. I., Computer Software Engineering
THOMPSON, B., Design and Creative Arts
THORNHAM, S., Librarian, Communication and Media Studies
TINDLE, J., Computer Software Engineering
VAN LEEUWEN, C. C., Psychology
VAN ZON, H., Social Studies
WALDRON, P., Modern European History
WERMTER, S., Information Systems
WILSON, P. H., Early Modern History

UNIVERSITY OF SURREY

Guildford, Surrey, GU2 5XH

Telephone: (1483) 300800
Fax: (1483) 300803

Internet: www.surrey.ac.uk
Founded as Battersea Polytechnic Institute 1891; designated a College of Advanced Technology 1956; University Charter 1966
Academic year: September to May
Chancellor: HRH The Duke of KENT
Vice-Chancellor and Chief Executive: Prof. CHRISTOPHER M. SNOWDEN
Deputy Vice-Chancellor: Prof. JOHN A. TURNER
Pro-Vice-Chancellors: Prof. BARRY G. EVANS (Research and Enterprise), Prof. BERNARD L. WEISS (Staff Development), Prof. DAVID W. AIREY (Teaching and Learning), Prof. ANDY ROBERTSON
University Secretary and Clerk to the Council: J. W. A. STRAWSON
Registrar: P. W. BEARDSLEY
Director of Information Services and University Librarian: T. J. A. CRAWSHAW
Number of teachers: 970 (incl. 350 part-time associate lecturers)
Number of students: 10,730

Publications: *Prospectus, Prospectus of Research and Postgraduate Studies, Report of the Vice-Chancellor* (annually), *Surrey Matters*

HEADS OF SCHOOLS

School of Arts: Prof. COLIN GRANT
School of Biomedical and Life Sciences: Prof. JOHN HAY
School of Electronics and Physical Sciences: Prof. M. KEARNEY
School of Engineering: Prof. P. A. SMITH
European Institute of Health and Medical Sciences: Prof. R. POPE
School of Human Sciences: Prof. N. EMLER
School of Management: Prof. R. M. O'KEEFE
Postgraduate Medical School: Prof. STEVEN MYINT

PROFESSORS

School of Arts:

ANDERMAN, G. M., Translation Studies
BARTA, P., Russian and Cultural Studies
CORBETT, G. G., Linguistics and Russian Language
EADE, J.
FLOCKTON, C. H., European Economic Studies
FLOOD, C. G., European Studies
FORBES, S.
GRANT, C. B., Communication Studies
HOLFORD, J. A. K.
HUTCHINGS, S. C., Russian
JARVIS, P., Continuing Education
JUDGE, A., French
LANSDALE, J. H., Dance Studies
LUTZEIER, P. R., German
MCNAIR, S., Education
MIDDLEHURST, R. M., Higher Education
MOORE, A., Music
UPEX, R. V., Law

School of Biomedical and Life Sciences:

ADAMS, M. R., Food Microbiology
BUSHELL, M. E., Microbial Physiology
CLIFFORD, M. N., Food Safety
DALE, J. W., Molecular Microbiology
DANIL DE NAMOR, A., Chemistry
FERNS, G. A. A., Metabolic and Molecular Medicine
GIBSON, G. G., Molecular Toxicology
GOLDFARB, P. S. G., Molecular Biology
HAY, J. N., Materials Chemistry
HEYES, D. M., Chemistry
HINDMARCH, I., Human Psychopharmacology
HOURANI, S. M. O., Pharmacology
HOWELL, N. K., Food Science
KITCHEN, I., Neuropharmacology
LYNCH, J. M., Life Sciences
MCFADDEN, J., Molecular Genetics
MILLWARD, D. J., Nutrition

ROBERTSON, W. R.
SERMON, P., Physical Chemistry
SKENE, D. J., Neuroendocrinology
SLADE, R. C. T., Inorganic Chemistry
SMITH, C., Functional Genomics

School of Electronics and Physical Sciences:

ADAMS, A. R.
AHMAD, KH., Artificial Intelligence
ALLAM, J., Ultra-Fast Optoelectronics
BRIDGES, T. J., Mathematics
CLOUGH, A. S.
COWERN, N. E. B., Nanoscale Materials Processing
EVANS, B. G., Information Systems
GELLETLY, W.
HESS, O., Computational Quantum Electronics
HOMEWOOD, K. P., Semiconductor Optoelectronics
ILLINGWORTH, J., Machine Vision
KEARNEY, M. J., Electronic Device Engineering
KITTLER, J. V., Machine Intelligence
KONDOZ, A. M., Multimedia Communication Systems
KRAUSE, P. J., Software Engineering
MCDONALD, P. J.
MELBOURNE, I., Mathematics
PAVLOU, G., Communication and Information Systems
PETROU, M., Image Analysis
REED, G. T., Optoelectronics
ROBERTS, R. M., Mathematics
ROGERS, A. J.
SANDSTEDE, B., Mathematical Sciences
SCHNEIDER, S. A., Computing
SEALY, B. J., Solid State Devices and Ion Beam Technology
SILVA, S. R. P., Solid State Electronics
SPYROU, N. M.
Sir SWEETING, MARTIN, Satellite Engineering
TAFAZOLLI, R., Mobile Communications
THOMPSON, I. J.
TOSTEVIN, J. A.
WALKER, P. M.
WEBB, R. P., Ion Beam Physics
WEISS, B. L., Microelectronics

School of Engineering:

AZAPAGIC, A., Sustainable Engineering
CHEW, J. W., Mechanical Engineering
CHRYSSANTHOPOULOS, M. K., Structural Systems
CLIFT, R., Environmental Technology
CROCOMBE, A. D., Structural Mechanics
GILLAN, M. A., Aerospace Engineering
GORINGE, M. J., Materials
HOLLAWAY, L. C., Composite Structures
JACKSON, T., Sustainable Development
JEFFERIS, S., Civil Engineering
KOKOSSIS, A. C., Process Systems Engineering Optimization
LAWSON, M., Construction Systems
LLOYD, B. J., Environmental Health Engineering
NOOSHIN, H., Space Structures
PARKE, C. A. R., Structural Engineering
PARKER, G. A., Mechanical Engineering
ROBINS, A. G., Environmental Fluid Mechanics
SMITH, P. A., Composite Materials
THORPE, R., Multiphase Engineering
TOY, N., Fluid Mechanics
TSAKIROPOULOS, P., Metallurgy
TÜZÜN, U., Process Engineering
WATTS, J. F., Materials Science

School of Human Sciences:

ARBER, S. L., Sociology
BAG, P., Economics
BARRETT, M. D., Psychology
BIRD, G. R., Economics
BROWN, J. M., Forensic Psychology
BULMER, M. I. A., Sociology
CRAWFORD, I., Economics

DAVIES, I. R. L., Psychology
EMLER, N., Social Psychology
FIELDING, N. G., Sociology
GILBERT, G. N., Sociology
GROEGER, J. A., Cognitive Psychology
HAMPSON, S. E., Psychology and Health
HUNT, L. C., Economics
LEVINE, P., Economics
OGDEN, J., Health Psychology
RICKMAN, N. J., Economics
SHEPHERD, R., Psychology
STERR, A., Cognitive Neuroscience and Neuropsychology
TARLING, R., Sociology
UZZELL, D. L., Environmental Psychology
ZIJLSTRA, F., Occupational and Organizational Psychology

School of Management:

AIREY, D. W., Tourism Management
ARCHER, G. S. H., Financial Management
BUTLER, R. W., Tourism
DESOMBRE, T., Healthcare Management
GILBERT, D., Marketing
HALES, C., Organizational Behaviour
JONES, P. L. M., Productions and Operations Management
KIRBY, D., Entrepreneurship
LIU, X., International Business
LOCKWOOD, A. J., Hospitality Management
LOWE, M., Retail Management
O'KEEFE, R. M., Information Management
PHILLIPS, P. A., Hotel Management
RILEY, M. J., Organizational Behaviour
SADLER-SMITH, E., Management Development and Organizational Behaviour

Postgraduate Medical School:

FARMER, R. D. T., Epidemiology
THOMAS, H., Oncology

European Institute of Health and Medical Sciences:

BRYAN, K., Clinical Practice
BUCKLE, P., Health Ergonomics
HUNT, G.
POPE, R., Nurse Education
ROBBINS, I., Mental Health Practice
SMITH, P. A., Nurse Education
STUBBS, D. A., Ergonomics

ATTACHED INSTITUTES

Advanced Technology Institute: Dir Prof. S. R. P. SILVA.

Centre for Communication Systems Research: Dir Prof. B. G. EVANS.

Centre for Environmental Strategy: Dir Prof. R. CLIFT.

Centre for Policy and Change: Dir Prof. S. MCNAIR.

Centre for Research on Nationalism, Multiculturalism and Ethnicity: Dir Prof. J. EADE.

Centre for Vision, Speech and Signal Processing: Dir Prof. J. V. KITTLER.

Digital World Research Centre: Dir Prof. D. FROHLICH.

Engineering Fluids and Systems Research Centre: Dir Prof. J. W. CHEW.

Engineering Structures and Materials Research Centre: Dir Prof. J. F. WATTS.

European Institute of Health and Medical Sciences: Dir Prof. R. POPE.

Food, Consumer and Health Research Centre: Co-Dirs Prof. R. SHEPHERD, Dr M. RAATS.

Language Centre: Dir M. J. THACKER.

Surrey Centre for Ion Beam Applications: Dir Prof. B. J. SEALY.

Surrey Satellite Technology Ltd: CEO Prof. Sir MARTIN SWEETING.

Surrey Space Centre: Dir Prof. Sir MARTIN SWEETING.

UNIVERSITY OF SUSSEX

Falmer, Brighton, Sussex, BN1 9RH
Telephone: (1273) 606755
Fax: (1273) 678335
E-mail: information@sussex.ac.uk
Internet: www.sussex.ac.uk

Founded 1961
Academic year: October to June

Chancellor: Lord ATTENBOROUGH OF RICHMOND UPON THAMES
Vice-Chancellor: Prof. ALASDAIR SMITH
Deputy-Chancellor: Prof. A. L. MOORE
Pro-Vice-Chancellors: Prof. J. N. DEARLOVE, Prof. N. G. LLEWELLYN, Dr M. STUART
Registrar and Secretary: PHILIP HARVEY
Librarian: D. C. SHORLEY

Library: see Libraries and Archives
Number of teachers: 515
Number of students: 11,725

DEANS

School of African and Asian Studies: Dr M. H. JOHNSON
School of Biological Sciences: Prof. T. J. FLOWERS
School of Chemistry, Physics and Environmental Science: Dr R. C. SMITH
School of Cognitive Sciences: Prof. R. COATES
School of Cultural and Community Studies: C. KEDWARD
School of Engineering and Information Technology: Prof. P. LISTER
School of English and American Studies: Dr A. CROZIER
School of European Studies: Dr J. A. LANE
School of Humanities: Dr S. F. BURMAN
School of Legal Studies: Prof. H. H. RAJAK
School of Life Sciences: Prof. J. P. BACON
School of Mathematical Sciences: Prof. C. GOLDIE
School of Science and Technology: Prof. J. B. H. DU BOULAY
School of Social Science: Dr R. A. BOND
School of Social Sciences and Cultural Studies: Prof. J. M. HOLMWOOD
Sussex Institute: Prof. F. G. GRAY

PROFESSORS

ABBS, P. F., Creative Writing
ABRAHAM, J. W., Sociology
ABRAHAM, S. C. S., Psychology
ARMES, S. P., Chemistry
BACON, J. P., Neuroscience
BAILIN, D., Theoretical Physics
BEEBEE, J. J. C., Molecular Ecology
BENJAMIN, P. R., Neuroscience
BILLINGHAM, N. C., Chemistry
BLISS, J. F., Education
BODEN, M. A., Philosophy and Psychology
BUXTON, H., Visual Intelligence
CAWSON, A., Digital Media
CHATWIN, C. R., Manufacturing Systems
CHERRY, D., History of Art
CLARK, A. J., Philosophy
CLARK, T. D., Physical Electronics
CLOKE, F. G. N., Chemistry
CLUNAS, A. C., History of Art
COATES, R. A., Linguistics
COLCLOUGH, C. L., Development Studies
COLLETT, T. S., Neurobiology
COPELAND, E. J., Theoretical Physics
DARWIN, C. J., Experimental Psychology
DAVEY, G. C. L., Psychology
DEARLOVE, J. N., Politics
DOMBEY, N. D., Theoretical Physics
DU BOULAY, J. B. H., Artificial Intelligence
DUNFORD, M. F., Economic Geography
DYHOUSE, C. A., History
ERAUT, M. R., Education
FAIRHEAD, J., Social Anthropology
FALLOWFIELD, L. J., Psycho-Oncology
FENDER, S. A., American Studies
FIELDING, A. J., Human Geography
FLOWERS, T. J., Plant Physiology

GANN, D. M., Science and Technology Policy Research
GARDINER, J. M., Psychology
GARNHAM, A., Experimental Psychology
GAZDAR, G. J. M., Computational Linguistics
GOLDIE, C. M., Statistics
GOUGH, M. P., Space Science
GRAY, F. G., Continuing Education
GRIFFITH-JONES, S., Development Studies
GRILLO, R. D., Social Anthropology
GRIMSDALE, R. L., Electronic Engineering
HANSON, J. R., Chemistry
HART, V. M., American Studies
HENNESSY, M., Computer Science
HINDS, E. A., Experimental Physics
HIRSCHFELD, J. W. P., Mathematics
HOBDAY, M. G., Science and Technology Policy Research
HOLMWOOD, J. M., Sociology
HOWKINS, A. J., Social History
HUMPHREY, C. J., Development Studies
HUTCHINGS, M. J., Ecology
JAYAWANT, B. V., Electrical and Systems Engineering
KAPLINSKY, R. M., Development Studies
KEDWARD, H. R., History
KING, R. L., Geography
Sir KROTO, H. W., Chemistry
LAND, M. F., Neurobiology
LEACH, M. A., Development Studies
LEHMANN, A. R., Molecular Genetics
LEWIN, K. M., Education
LIDDLE, A. R., Astrophysics
LISTER, P. F., Electronics
LLEWELLYN, N. G., History of Art
McCAFFERY, A. J., Chemistry
MANOR, J. G., Development Studies
MARTIN, B. R., Science and Technology Policy Research
MATHER, G. W., Experimental Psychology
MELLOR, D. A., History of Art
MILNER-GULLAND, R. R., Russian
MITTER, P., History of Art
MOORE, A. L., Biochemistry
MOORE, M. P., Development Studies
MURPHY, R. J., German, Comparative Literature and Film
NICHOLLS, P. A., English and American Literature
NIXON, J. F., Chemistry
O'SHEA, M. R., Neuroscience
OAKHILL, J. V., Experimental Psychology
OSMOND-SMITH, D., Music
OUTHWAITE, R. W., Sociology
PAIN, V. M., Biochemistry
PARSONS, P. J., Organic Chemistry
PAVITT, K. L. R., Science and Technology Policy Studies
PENDLEBURY, J. M., Experimental Physics
PERRY-ROBINSON, J. P., Science and Technology Policy Research
PLATT, J. A., Sociology
POWNER, E. T., Electronic Engineering
PRASSIDES, K., Chemistry
RAJAK, H. H., Law
RICHARDS, R. L., Chemistry
RÖHL, J. C. G., History
ROLLO, J. M. C., European Economic Integration
ROPER, T. J., Biology
ROSS, M. G., European Law
ROYLE, N. W. O., English
RUSSELL, I. J., Neurobiology
RYAN, C. J., Italian
SAMPSON, G. R., Natural Language Computing
SCHMITZ, H., Development Studies
SHAW, M., International Relations and Politics
SHORT, B. M., Geography
SINFIELD, A. J., English
SKELDON, R., Geography
SMITH, L. J., English
SMITH, P. H., Media Studies
SMITH, P. B., Social Psychology
SOBOLEV, A. V., Mathematics

STACE, A. J., Chemistry
STEINMUELLER, W. E., Science and Technology Policy Research
STEPHENS, D. N., Experimental Psychology
STOBART, R. K., Automotive Engineering
SUMNER, M. T., Economics
TAPPER, E. R., Politics
TAYLOR, I. J., Social Care and Social Work
TEMKIN, J., Law
TIDD, J., Science and Technology Policy Research
TIMMS, E. F., German Studies
TORRANCE, H., Education
TOWNSEND, P. D., Experimental Physics
TROSCIANKO, T., Psychology
TURNER, A. B., Mechanical Engineering
VAN DER PIJL, K., International Relations
VAN GELDEREN, M. A. J., Intellectual History
VANCE, R. N. C., English
VINCENT, R., Medical Science
VON TUNZELMANN, G., Economics of Science and Technology
WAGSTAFF, R. A. S., Economics
WALLIS, M., Biochemistry
WARK, D. L., Physics
WATTS, C. T., English
WEBB, P. D., Politics
WILKINSON, R. G., Trafford Centre for Graduate Medical Education and Research
WINTERS, L. A., Economics
WORDEN, A. B., Early Modern History
YOUNG, D. W., Chemistry
ZHANG, K., Pure Mathematics

ATTACHED INSTITUTES

Genome Damage and Stability Centre: see under Research Institutes.

Institute of Development Studies: University of Sussex, Falmer, Brighton, Sussex, BN1 9RE; tel. (1273) 606261; f. 1966; national centre concerned with Third World development and the relationships between rich and poor countries; offers teaching and supervision for university graduate degrees; library of 200,000 vols; an official depository for United Nations publications; Dir KEITH BEZANSON; publ. *IDS Bulletin* (quarterly).

Institute of Employment Studies: University of Sussex, Falmer, Brighton, Sussex, BN1 9RH; Dir R. PEARSON.

SPRU–Science and Technology Policy Research: Dir Prof. B. MARTIN.

Trafford Centre for Medical Research: University of Sussex, Falmer, Brighton, Sussex, BN1 9RH; Dir Prof. A. L. MOORE (acting).

UNIVERSITY OF TEESSIDE

Borough Rd, Middlesbrough, TS1 3BA
Telephone: (1642) 218121
Fax: (1642) 342067
E-mail: registry@tees.ac.uk
Internet: www.tees.ac.uk
Founded 1929 as Constantine College of Technology, became Teesside Polytechnic 1970, present name and status 1992
Chancellor: TOM SAWYER
Vice-Chancellor: Prof. GRAHAM HENDERSON
Deputy Vice-Chancellors: Prof. GRAHAM HENDERSON, Prof. KATHERINE LENI OGLESBY, HELEN PICKERING, Prof. MIKE SMITH
University Secretary: J. MORGAN MCCLINTOCK
Head of Academic Registry (vacant)
Director, Library and Information Services: IAN BUTCHART

Library of 369,641 vols
Number of teachers: 511 (467 full-time, 44 part-time)
Number of students: 18,500

DIRECTORS OF SCHOOLS

Arts and Media: GERDA ROPER

Computing and Mathematics: Prof. DEREK SIMPSON
Health and Social Care: PAUL KEANE
Science and Technology: Prof. BRIAN HOBBS
Social Sciences and Law: Prof. LIZ BARNES
Teesside Business School: Dr J. WILSON

THAMES VALLEY UNIVERSITY

St Mary's Rd, Ealing, London, W5 5RF
Telephone: (20) 8579-5000
Fax: (20) 8566-1353
E-mail: learning.advice@tvu.ac.uk
Internet: www.tvu.ac.uk

Wellington St, Slough, Berks, SL1 1YG
Telephone: (1753) 534585

Founded as Ealing College of Higher Education, Thames Valley College of Higher Education, Queen Charlotte's College of Health Care Studies and the London College of Music; merged to become Polytechnic of West London in 1991; present name and status 1992
Academic year: September to July
Campuses in Ealing and Slough
Chancellor: KARAN BILIMORIA
Vice-Chancellor: Prof. KENNETH BARKER
Deputy Vice-Chancellor: GEOFF CRISPIN
Head of Registry Services (vacant)
Library of 244,000 vols, 2,930 periodicals
Number of teachers: 638 (388 full-time, 250 part-time)
Number of students: 25,741 (9,004 full-time and sandwich, 16,737 part-time and distance learning)

DEANS

Faculty of Health and Human Sciences: LOIS CROOKE
Faculty of Professional Studies: Prof. DAVID GREEN
London College of Music and Media: Prof. COLIN LAWSON

UNIVERSITY OF WALES

University Registry, King Edward VII Ave, Cathays Park, Cardiff, CF10 3NS
Telephone: (29) 2038-2656
Fax: (29) 2039-6040
E-mail: uniwales@wales.ac.uk
Internet: www.wales.ac.uk
Founded 1893
Chancellor: HRH Prince CHARLES, PRINCE OF WALES
Pro-Chancellor: The Most Revd Dr BARRY MORGAN, ARCHBISHOP OF WALES
Senior Vice-Chancellor: Prof. ANTONY CHAPMAN
Secretary-General: Dr LYNN E. WILLIAMS.

MEMBER INSTITUTIONS

University of Wales, Aberystwyth

Old College, King St, Aberystwyth, Ceredigion, SY23 2AX
Telephone: (1970) 623111
Fax: (1970) 611446
E-mail: lnh@aber.ac.uk
Internet: www.aber.ac.uk
Founded 1872
Languages of instruction: English, Welsh
Academic year: October to June
President: Lord ELYSTAN MORGAN
Vice-Presidents: HUW WYNNE-GRIFFITH, WINSTON RODDICK
Vice-Chancellor: Prof. NOEL LLOYD
Pro-Vice Chancellors: Prof. J. BARRETT, Prof. LYN PYKETT
Registrar and Secretary: Dr CATRIN HUGHES
Library: Library: see entry for University of Wales Aberystwyth, Hugh Owen Library

Number of teachers: 588 (326 full-time, 262 part-time)
Number of students: 9,708 (incl. 1,558 postgraduate)
Publication: *Prom* (annually)

DEANS

Faculty of Arts: Prof. ALED JONES
Faculty of Science: Dr JOHN HARRIES
Faculty of Social Sciences: Prof. LEN SCOTT

PROFESSORS

ADAMS, W. A., Biological Sciences
AKEHURST, G. P., School of Management and Business
ALEXANDER, M. S., International Politics
ALEXANDER, N. S., School of Management and Business
AP GWILYM, O. M., School of Management and Business
BARKER, M. J., Theatre, Film and Television Studies
BARRETT, J., Biological Sciences
BARRY, P., English
BIRKINSHAW, K., Mathematical and Physical Sciences
BOOTH, K., International Politics
CLARK, I., International Politics
CRESSWELL, T. J., Institute of Geography and Earth Sciences
DAUGHERTY, R. A., Education
DAVIES, A. R., Mathematical and Physical Sciences
DOUST, J. H., Sports Science
DRAPER, J., Biological Sciences
EDKINS, J. A., International Politics
ELLIS, D., Dept of Information Studies
FOLEY, M., International Politics
GOUGH, R., Theatre, Film and Television Studies
GREAVES, G. N., Physics
GWILLIAM, D. R., School of Management and Business
HAMBREY, M. J., Institute of Geography and Earth Sciences
HARDING, C., Law
HARESIGN, W., Rural Sciences
HARVARD, R. G., European Languages
HARVEY, J., Art
HOLLAND, K. M., School of Management and Business
JONES, A. G., History and Welsh History
JONES, M. R., Institute of Geography and Earth Sciences
KAY, D., Institute of Geography and Earth Sciences
KING, R. D., Computer Science
LEE, M. H., Computer Science
LINKLATER, A., International Politics
MCINNES, C. J., International Politics
MACKLIN, M. G., Institute of Geography and Earth Sciences
MAVRON, V., Mathematical and Physical Sciences
MIDMORE, P. R., Rural Sciences
NEIL, P. S., Education and Lifelong Learning
NEWBOLD, C. J., Rural Sciences
O'MALLEY, T. P., Theatre, Film and Television Studies
PEARSON, M. J., Theatre, Film and Television Studies
PIOTROWICZ, R. W., Law
POMEROY, J. W., Institute of Geography and Earth Studies
POSTER, J. P., English
PRICE, C. J., Computer Science
PRICE, R. D., History and Welsh History
PYKETT, L., English
RABEY, D. I., Theatre, Film and Television Studies
ROWLAND, D., Law
RUBENSTEIN, W. D., History and Welsh History
SCHOFIELD, P. R., History and Welsh History
SCOTT, L. V., International Politics

SHEN, Q., Computer Science
SIMS-WILLIAMS, P., Welsh Language
STEPHENS, E. C., Theatre, Film and Television Studies
SUGANAMI, H., International Politics
TROTTER, D., European Languages
WATHERN, P., Biological Sciences
WATT, P. D., English
WHEELER, N. J., International Politics
WILLIAMS, G. A., Welsh Language and Literature
WILLIAMS, H. L., International Politics
WILLIAMS, I., Theatre, Film and Television Studies
WILLIAMS, M. C., International Politics
WILLIAMS, J. R., Law
WOODS, T. S., English
YOUNG, M., Biological Sciences

University of Wales, Bangor

Bangor, Gwynedd, LL57 2DG
Telephone: (1248) 351151
Fax: (1248) 370451
Internet: www.bangor.ac.uk
Founded 1884
Academic year: September to June
Chancellor: HRH THE PRINCE OF WALES
President: Lord ELIS-THOMAS OF NANT CONWY
Vice-Chancellor: Prof. R. M. JONES
Pro-Vice-Chancellors: Prof. M. S. BAIRD, Prof. T. N. CORNS, Prof. C. F. LOWE, Prof. H. G. FF. ROBERTS
Secretary and Registrar: Dr D. M. ROBERTS
Library: see entry for University of Wales, Bangor, Information Services
Number of teachers: 755
Number of students: 8,637
Publication: *Annual Review*

DEANS

Faculty of Arts and Social Sciences: R. M. MORRIS
Faculty of Education: J. A. ELLIOTT
Faculty of Health Studies: P. J. PYE
Faculty of Science and Engineering: Prof. M. A. LOCK

PROFESSORS

Faculty of Arts and Social Sciences:
  BUSHELL, A., Modern Languages
  CORNS, T. N., English
  DAVIS, H., Social Sciences
  FRANCIS, L., Theology and Religious Studies
  GARDENER, E. P. M., Banking
  JARVIS, B., Welsh
  McLEAY, S. J., Treasury
  MOLYNEUX, P., Banking and Finance
  MORGAN, D. D., Theology and Religious Studies
  PASCALL, R. J., Music
  TANNER, D. M., History and Welsh History
  THOMAS, J. A., Linguistics
  WATKIN, T. G., Law

Faculty of Education:
  BAKER, C. R., Education
  ROBERTS, H. G. FF., Education

Faculty of Science and Engineering:
  BAIRD, M. S., Chemistry
  COX, W. M., Psychology of Addictive Behaviours
  DANDO, A. G., Ocean Sciences
  DAVIES, S. L., Informatics
  EDWARDS-JONES, G., Agricultural and Forest Sciences
  ELLIOTT, A. J., Ocean Sciences
  FARRAR, J. F., Biological Sciences
  GODBOLD, D. L., Agricultural and Forest Sciences
  HARDY, L., Sport, Health and Exercise Studies
  HOPE, S., Computer Science
  HUGHES, R. N., Biological Sciences

IRVINE, S. J. C., Chemistry
JOHN, N. W., Computing
LANE, P. M., Communications Systems
LAST, J. D., Informatics
LOWE, C. F., Psychology
OWENS, G., Forensic Clinical Psychology
PAYNE, J. W., Biological Sciences
PETHIG, R., Informatics
PORTER, T., Pure Mathematics
PRICE, C., Agricultural and Forest Sciences
RAFAL, R. D., Clinical Neuroscience and Neuropsychology
RAYMOND, J., Experimental Consumer Psychology
RUSSELL, I., Public Health
SHAPIRO, K., Psychology
SEED, R., Marine Geology
SHORE, K. A., Electronic Engineering
SIMPSON, J. H., Physical Oceanography
STUART, N. S. A., Biological Sciences
TAYLOR, D. M., Electronic Engineering
THORPE, R. S., Biological Sciences
TIPPER, S. P., Cognitive Science
TOMOS, A. D., Biological Sciences
VIHMAN, M. M., Developmental Psychology
WILLIAMS, P. A., Biological Sciences
WOODS, R. T., Clinical Psychology

ATTACHED INSTITUTES

Biocomposites Centre: f. 1991; conducts contract research on the processing of wood and plant materials; Dir Dr P. FOWLER.

Centre for Advanced Welsh Music Study: Dir Dr SALLY HARPER.

Centre for Applicable Mathematics: f. 1988; Dir Dr G. W. ROBERTS.

Centre for Applied Marine Sciences: f. 1977; Dir Prof. A. J. ELLIOTT.

Centre for Arid Zone Studies: f. 1984; specializes in natural resource management and rural development in drought-prone areas; Dir Dr W. I. ROBINSON.

Centre for Attention Perception and Motor Control: studies the interaction between vision and movement and the role of selective attention and memory in the control of goal-directed behaviour; Dir Prof. S. TIPPER.

Centre for Comparative Criminology and Criminal Justice: f. 1992; Dir Dr J. WARDHAUGH.

Centre for Computational Chemistry: develops industrial applications of modelling in materials science for natural and advanced materials; Dir Dr J. N. MACDONALD.

Centre for Enterprise and Regional Devlopment: Dir S. JONES.

Centre for Experimental Consumer Psychology: Dir Prof. J. RAYMOND.

Centre for Social Policy Research and Development: f. 1986; scientific research primarily in areas of human development, health studies and social care provision; Dir V. BURHOLT.

Centre for the Advanced Study of Religion in Wales: Dir Dr G. TUDUR.

Centre for the Standardisation of Terminology: develops standardized dictionaries and glossaries of contemporary technical terms in Welsh; Dir D. PRYS.

Department of Lifelong Learning: organizes a range of degree and modular courses throughout the region; Dir M. HUWS.

Dyslexia Unit: Dir A. COOKE.

Humanities Research Centre: incorporates the R. S. Thomas Study Centre; Dir Prof. D. TANNER.

Industrial Development Bangor (UWB) Ltd: f. 1968; an engineering company owned by the College which carries out design, development and manufacture of a range of

electrical and electronic equipment; Man. Dir E. D. JONES.

Institute of Bioelectronic and Molecular Microsystems: f. 1983; Dir Prof. D. M. TAYLOR.

Institute of Economic Research: Bangor; f. 1969; research in regional economics, economics of developing countries, tourism and economics of ports, policy-making and planning; data analysis; Dir Prof. R. R. MACKAY.

Institute of Environmental Science: Dir Prof. J. FARRAR.

Institute of European Finance: Bangor; f. 1973; Dir Prof. E. P. M. GARDENER.

Institute of Medical and Social Care Research: f. 1998; Dir Prof. I. T. RUSSELL.

Menai Technology Enterprise Centre (MENTEC): f. 1986; Dir (vacant).

Research Centre Wales: f. 1985; Dir Prof. C. R. BAKER.

Research Institute for Enhancing Learning: Dir Dr J. A. FAZEY.

Welsh Institute for Social and Cultural Affairs: Dir Prof. D. TANNER.

Welsh National Centre for Religious Education: f. 1980; promotes the development of religious education in schools, colleges and churches of all types throughout Wales; Dir Prof. L. FRANCIS.

University of Wales, Lampeter

Lampeter, Ceredigion, SA48 7ED
Telephone: (1570) 422351
Fax: (1570) 423423
Internet: www.lamp.ac.uk
Founded 1822; opened as College on St David's Day 1827; first Royal Charter granted 1827, with later Charters 1852, 1865, 1896, 1963 and 1990; affiliated to Oxford Univ. 1880 and Cambridge Univ. 1883; inc. as constituent college of the University of Wales 1971 and as constituent institution 1987
Academic year: October to June
Visitor: The Bishop of ST DAVIDS
Vice-Chancellor: Prof. R. PEARCE
Pro-Vice-Chancellor: Dr B. C. BURNHAM
Registrar and Secretary: Dr T. D. RODERICK
Library: Library: see entry for University of Wales, Lampeter Library
Number of teachers: 100
Number of students: 2,000
Publications: *Annual Report, Trivium*

PROFESSORS

AUSTIN, D., Archaeology
BADHAM, P., Theology and Religious Studies
BEAUMONT, P., Geography
BORSAY, P., History
COCKBURN, D., Philosophy
COHN-SHERBOK, D., Jewish Studies
ELDRIDGE, C. C., History
MANNING, J., English
ROFFE, I. M., Centre for Enterprise, Entrepreneurial and European Studies
THORNE, D. A., Welsh
YAO, X., Theology and Religious Studies
YATES, N., Ecclesiastical History

University of Wales, Swansea

Singleton Park, Swansea, SA2 8PP
Telephone: (1792) 205678
Internet: www.swan.ac.uk
Founded 1920
Academic year: September to June
Vice-Chancellor: Prof. RICHARD B. DAVIES
Pro-Vice-Chancellors: Prof. JOHN BAYLIS, Prof. PATRICK O'FARRELL, Prof. NIGEL WEATHERILL, Prof. RHYS WILLIAMS

Dean of Student Admissions: Prof. R. W. WILLIAMS

Registrar and Pro-Vice-Chancellor: Prof. P. TOWNSEND

Library: see entry for University of Wales Swansea Library

Number of teachers: 800

Number of students: 10,400

DEANS

Faculty of Arts and Social Studies: Prof. J. FRANCE

Faculty of Business, Economics and Law: Prof. L. MAINWARING

Faculty of Educational and Health Studies: Dr M. J. ISAAC

Faculty of Engineering: Dr S. HARDY

Faculty of Science: Dr P. W. GRANT

PROFESSORS

Faculty of Arts and Social Studies:

BAYLIS, J., Politics and International Relations

BEDANI, G. L. C., Italian

BELL, I., English Language and Literature

BOYCE, D. G., Political Theory and Government

BYRON, R., Social Sciences and International Development

CHARLES, N., Social Sciences and International Development

CLARK, D. S., History

COLTON, M. J., Social Sciences and International Development

FULTON, H., English

GAGEN, D. H., Hispanic Studies

HARDING, G. N., Political Theory and Government

HOWELL, D. W., History

JOHNSTON, D. R., Welsh Language and Literature

LLOYD, A. B., Classics and Ancient History

MEARA, P. M., Applied Language Studies

PHILLIPS, D. Z., Philosophy

RAYNOR, P., Social Sciences and International Development

REW, A. W., Social Sciences and International Development

ROTHWELL, A. J., French

SULLIVAN, M. J., Social Sciences and International Development

TAYLOR, R., Political Theory and Government

THOMAS, A. R., Social Sciences and International Development

THOMAS, M. W., English Language and Literature

THOMPSON, N. W., History

WALTERS, V., Social Sciences and International Development

WILLIAMS, K. M., Media and Communication Studies

WILLIAMS, R. W., German

Faculty of Business, Economics and Law:

ADAMS, M. B., European Business Management

BISCHOFF, E. E., European Business Management

BLACKABY, D., Economics

DAVIES, I. R., Law

HAWKES, A. G., Statistics

JACOBS, G. C., European Business Management

JONES, T. H., Law

LEVIN, J., Law

MAINWARING, L., Economics

MURPHY, P. D., Economics

SIMINTIRAS, A., Business Management

SLOANE, P. J., Economics

THOMAS, D. R., Law

Faculty of Education and Health Studies:

CLARK, J., Community Nursing

GOLDBERG, C. B., Health Science

GREEN, B. F., Nursing, Midwifery and Health Care

HUGHES, D. J., Health Science

LOWE, R. A., Education

WHITEHEAD, M., Education

WILLIAMS, A. M., Nursing

Faculty of Engineering:

BOARD, K., Electrical Engineering

BONET, J., Engineering

BOWEN, W. R., Chemical Engineering

CLEMENT, R. M., Engineering

ELMIRGHANI, J. M., Engineering

EVANS, R. W., Materials Engineering

EVANS, W. J., Materials Engineering

GETHIN, D. T., Engineering

LEES, A. W., Engineering

LEWIS, R. W., Mechanical Engineering

MAWBY, P. A., Engineering

MORGAN, K., Civil Engineering

OWEN, D. R. J., Civil Engineering

PANDE, G. N., Civil Engineering

PARKER, J. D., Materials Engineering

PERIC, D., Engineering

PREECE, P. E., Chemical Engineering

RANDLE, V., Engineering

WEATHERILL, N. P., Civil Engineering

WILLIAMS, P. R., Engineering

WILSHIRE, B., Materials Engineering

Faculty of Science:

BARNSEY, M. J., Physical Geography

BENTON, D., Psychology

BRAIN, P. F., Zoology

BRENTON, A. G., Mass Spectrometry

CHARLTON, M., Physics

CHEN, M., Computer Science

CLARK, D. R., Psychology

DAVIES, A. J., Physics

DOEL, M. A., Geography

ELWYN, G., Swansea Clinical School

FOLKARD, S., Psychology

GALLON, J., Biochemistry

GAMES, D. E., Mass Spectrometry

HERBERT, D. T., Geography

LYONS, R. A., Swansea Clinical School

MATTHEWS, J. A., Physical Geography

MOLLER, F. G., Computer Science

MORGAN, G., Swansea Clinical School

MORLEY, J. O., Computational Chemistry

NEWTON, R. P., Biological Sciences

PARRY, J. M., Genetics

PASTUR, L., Mathematics

RATCLIFFE, N. A., Zoology

ROWLEY, A. F., Immunology

SHORE, G. M., Physics

SKIBINSKI, D. O. F., Biological Sciences

SMITH, K., Chemistry

STREET-PERROTT, F. A., Physical Geography

TELLE, H. H., Physics

TRUMAN, A., Mathematics

TUCKER, J. V., Computer Science

WALSH, R. P., Geography

WATERS, R., Genetics

WATKINS, J., Sports Science

WEBSTER, M. F., Computer Science

WILLIAMS, D., Mathematics

WILLIAMS, J. G., Swansea Clinical School

WOOD, R. L., Psychology

University of Wales College, Newport

Caerleon Campus, POB 179, Newport, NP18 3YG

Telephone: (1633) 432432

Fax: (1633) 432850

E-mail: uic@newport.ac.uk

Internet: www.newport.ac.uk

Vice-Chancellor: Prof. JAMES R. LUSTY

Deputy Vice-Chancellor: Dr PETER NOYES

Pro Vice-Chancellors: ANNE CARLISLE, GEOFF EDGE

DEANS

School of Art, Media and Design: Prof. PAUL SEAWRIGHT (acting)

School of Business and Management: MIKE TRAVIS

School of Computing and Engineering: ALAN HAYES

School of Education: Dr CARL PETERS

School of Humanities and Science: Dr HILARY MATHESON

School of Social Studies: AMELIA LYONS

Centre for Community and Lifelong Learning: VIV DAVIES

University of Wales Institute, Cardiff

Llandaff Campus, Western Ave, Cardiff, CF5 2SG

Telephone: (29) 2041-6070

Fax: (29) 2041-6286

E-mail: uwicinfo@uwic.ac.uk

Internet: www.uwic.ac.uk

Founded 1976

Academic year: October to July

Principal and Chief Executive: Prof. ANTHONY J. CHAPMAN

Number of students: 8,000

HEADS OF SCHOOLS

Cardiff School of Art and Design: C. O'NEIL

Cardiff School of Education: PAUL THOMAS

School of Applied Sciences: Dr S. M. BOWEN

Cardiff School of Health Sciences: MAUREEN BOWEN

School of Lifelong Learning: P. TREADWELL

School of Product and Engineering Design: Dr G. GORST

Cardiff School of Sports: DAVE COBNER

UWIC Business School: M. NEWTH

Welsh School of Hospitality, Tourism and Leisure: Dr E. JONES

UNIVERSITY OF WARWICK

Coventry, CV4 7AL

Telephone: (24) 7652-3523

Fax: (24) 7646-1606

Internet: www.warwick.ac.uk

Founded 1965

Academic year: September to June

Chancellor: Sir NICHOLAS SCHEELE

Pro-Chancellor: J. LEIGHFIELD

Vice-Chancellor: Prof. NIGEL THRIFT

Deputy Vice-Chancellor: S. PALMER

Pro-Vice-Chancellors: R. G. DYSON, J. JONES, S. PALMER, M. WHITBY

Registrar: J. BALDWIN

Librarian: ANNE BELL

Number of teachers: 839

Number of students: 15,833 (incl. part-time)

PROFESSORS

Faculty of Arts (internet www2.warwick.ac.uk/fac/arts):

BASSNETT, S. E., Centre for Translation and Comparative Cultural Studies

BATE, J., English and Comparative Literary Studies

BEACHAM, R. C., Theatre Studies

BELL, M., English

BENNETT, O., Theatre Studies

BERG, M. L., History

BRUNSDON, C. M., Film and Television Studies

BURNS, R. A., German Studies

CAESAR, A., Italian

CAPP, B. S., History

CLARK, C. F., History

DABYDEEN, D., Caribbean Studies

DAVIS, C. J., French Studies

DAVIS, J., Theatre Studies

DOCHERTY, T., English and Comparative Literary Studies

DYER, R. W., Film and Television Studies

GARDNER, J., History of Art

HEUMAN, G. J., Caribbean Studies, History

HINDLE, S., History

HILL, L. J., French Studies
HINTON, J. S., History
HUGHES, D. W., English
JONES, C. D. H., History
KING, J. P., History
LAZARUS, N., English
MACK, P. W. D., English
MCFARLANE, A. J., History
MULRYNE, J. R., English
NYE, D., History
O'BRIEN, K., English and Comparative Literary Studies
PATERSON, L. M., French Studies
READ, C. J., History
ROSENTHAL, M. J., History of Art
RUTTER, C. C., English and Comparative Literary Studies
SHARPE, K., English
STEEDMAN, C. K., Social History
SWAIN, S. C. R., Classics
TREGLOWN, J. D., English
VINCENDEAU, G. O. R., Film and Television Studies
WHITBY, L. M., Classics

Faculty of Medicine (internet www2.warwick .ac.uk/fac/med):

Warwick Medical School (Leicester–Warwick Medical Schools)

CARTER, Y., Dean, Warwick Medical School
DALE, J., Division of Health in the Community
FULFORD, K. W. N., Philosophy and Mental Health
GRIFFIN, D., Orthopaedics and Trauma
HUNDT, G. A., School of Health and Social Studies
KUMAR, S., Medicine, Diabetes and Metabolism
LAMB, S., Physiotherapy and Rehabilitation
LEHNERT, H., Medicine
PEILE, E., Medical Education
SINGER, D., Clinical Pharmacology
SPANSWICK, D., Molecular Neurosciences
STANFIELD, P. R., Dept of Biological Sciences
STEWART-BROWN, S., Public Health
THORNTON, S., Biological Sciences
THOROGOOD, M., Epidemiology
WEICH, S., Psychiatry

Faculty of Science (internet www2.warwick .ac.uk/fac/sci):

some members also serve in the Faculty of Medicine

ANDERSON, D., Civil and Mechanical Engineering
BALL, R. C., Theoretical Physics
BARKLEY, D., Mathematics
BHATTACHARYYA, S. K., Manufacturing Systems
BRIGHT, S.
BROWN, G. D. A., Psychology
BRYANSTON-CROSS, P. J., Civil and Mechanical Engineering
BUGG, T. D. H., Biological Chemistry
BURNS, I.
CAMPBELL-KELLY, M., Computer Science
CARPENTER, P. W., Mechanical Engineering
CHAPMAN, S. C., Physics
CHATER, N., Psychology
CHETWYND, D. G., Civil and Mechanical Engineering
COOPER, M. J., Physics
COPAS, J. B., Statistics
CRITOPH, R. E., Civil and Mechanical Engineering
DALE, N., Biological Sciences
DALTON, H., Biological Sciences
DAVEY, J., Biological Sciences
DERRICK, P. J., Chemistry
DIMMOCK, N. J., Biological Sciences

DOWSETT, M. G., Physics
DOWSON, C. G., Biological Sciences
DUPREE, R., Physics
EASTON, A. J., Biological Sciences
ELWORTHY, K. D., Mathematics
FIRTH, D., Statistics
FLOWER, J. O., Engineering
FREEDMAN, R. B., Biological Sciences
FRIESECKE, G., Mathematics
FULFORD, K. W. M., Philosophy and Mental Health
FULOP, V., Biological Sciences
GARDNER, J. W., Electronic Engineering
GODFREY, K. R., Electrical and Electronic Engineering
GREEN, R. J., Electronic Communication Systems
HADDLETON, D. M., Chemistry
HARRISON, P. F., Physics
HOLT, D. F., Mathematics
HUANG, T., Civil and Mechanical Engineering
HUTCHINS, D. A., Electrical and Electronic Engineering
HUTTON, J. L., Statistics
JONES, G. V., Psychology
JONES, J. D. S., Mathematics
KEMP, T. J., Chemistry
KENDALL, W. S., Statistics
KERR, R., Mathematics
KERR, R. M., Civil and Mechanical Engineering
LAMBERTS, K., Psychology
LAWRENCE, A. J., Statistics
LEWIS, M. H., Physics
LORD, J. M., Biological Sciences
MCCONVILLE, C. F., Physics
MCCRAE, M. A., Biological Sciences
MACKAY, R., Mathematics
MANN, N. H., Biological Sciences
MARSH, T., Physics
MAYOR, E. A., Psychology
MEDLEY, G. F. H., Biological Sciences
MILLAR, A. J., Biological Sciences
MILLS, P.
MOND, D. M. Q., Mathematics
MOORE, P., Chemistry
MURRELL, J. C., Biological Sciences
NUDD, G. R., Computer Science
PARKER, E. H. C., Semiconductor Physics
PATERSON, M. S., Computer Science
PAUL, D. McK., Physics
PELED, D., Computer Science
POLLICOTT, M., Mathematics
RAND, D. A., Mathematics
RAWNSLEY, J. H., Mathematics
REID, M. A., Mathematics
ROBERTS, L. M., Biological Sciences
ROBINSON, C., Biological Sciences
RODGER, P. M.
ROURKE, C. P., Mathematics
SCOTT, R., Chemistry
SERIES, C. M., Mathematics
SHIPMAN, M., Chemistry
SMITH, J. Q., Statistics
SMITH, M. E., Physics
STANFIELD, P. R., Biological Sciences
STAUNTON, J. B., Physics
STEEL, M. F., Statistics
STEWART, I. N., Mathematics
STRIEN, S. VAN, Mathematics
STUART, A., Mathematics
TAYLOR, P. R., Chemistry
THOMAS, B.
THORNTON, S., Obstetrics and Gynaecology
UNWIN, P. R., Chemistry
WALTERS, P., Mathematics
WELLINGTON, E. M. H., Biological Sciences
WHALL, T. E., Physics
WHIPPS, J.
WILLS, M., Chemistry
WILSON, A. J., Medical Physics
WILSON, R. G., Computer Science
WILSON, T. M. A., Biological Sciences
WOODLAND, H. R., Biological Sciences
WOODRUFF, D. P., Physics

Faculty of Social Studies (internet www2 .warwick.ac.uk/fac/soc):

some members also serve in the Faculty of Medicine

ALI, S. S., Law
ANSELL-PEARSON, K., Philosophy
ANWAR, M., Ethnic Relations
ARCHER, M. S, Sociology
ARULAMPALAM, S. W., Economics
AUBREY, C., Institute of Education
BAXI, U., Law
BEALE, H. G., Law
BECKFORD, J. A., Sociology
BENINGTON, J., Business Studies
BLACKORBY, A. B., Economics
BRESLIN, S., Politics and International Studies
BREWER, B., Philosophy
BRIDGES, L. T., Law
BROADBERRY, S. N., Economics
BRYER, R. A., Accounting and Finance
BURNELL, P. J., Politics and International Studies
BURNHAM, P., Politics and International Studies
BURRIDGE, R. H. M., Law
CAMPBELL, R. J., Institute of Education
CARNALL, C., Business Studies
CAVE, M., Centre for Management under Regulation
CHARLES, N., Sociology
CLARKE, S. R. C., Sociology
CLUBB, C., Accounting and Finance
COWLING, K. G., Industrial Economics
COHEN, R., Sociology
CROUCH, C., Governance and Public Management
CURRIE, W., Information Systems
DALE, J., Primary Care
DAVIES, R., Business Studies
DEVEREUX, M. P., Economics and Business Studies
DICKENS, L. J., Business Studies
DUTTA, B., Economics
DYSON, R. G., Business Studies
EDWARDS, P. K., Business Studies
EILAN, N. H., Philosophy
ELIAS, D. P. B., Employment Research
ELLIOTT, R., Business Studies
FAUNDEZ, J., Law
FINE, R. D., Sociology
FULFORD, K. W. M., Philosophy and Mental Health
FULLER, S., Sociology
GEMMILL, G., Accounting and Finance
GHOSAL, S., Economics
GLEESON, D., Institute of Education
GRANT, W. P., Politics and International Studies
HARRIS, A., Institute of Education
HARRIS, J., Health and Social Studies
HARRISON, R. M., Economics
HARTLEY, J., Local Government Centre
HIGGOTT, R. A., Politics and International Studies
HODGES, S. D., Financial Management
HOSKIN, K. W., Business Studies
HOULGATE, S., Philosophy
HUDDLESTON, P. J., Institute of Education
HURLEY, S., Politics and International Studies
IRELAND, N. J., Economics
JACKSON, R. M. D., Institute of Education
JOHNSTON, R., Business Studies
JOLY, D., Centre for Research in Ethnic Relations
LAYTON-HENRY, Z. A., Politics and International Studies
LEGGE, K., Business Studies
LEWANDO-HUNDT, G., Social Sciences and Health
LINDLEY, R. M., Employment Research
LINDSAY, G. A., Special Educational Needs
LOCKWOOD, B., Economics

LOVELL, T. A., Women and Gender
LUNTLEY, M., Philosophy
McCONVILLE, M. J., Law
McELDOWNEY, J. F., Law
McGEE, J., Marketing and Strategic Management
MARGINSON, P., Industrial Relations
MASSON, J. M., Law
MAWSON, J., Local Government Centre
MILLER, M. H., Economics
MITCHELL, C., Centre for Management under Regulation
MORGAN, G., Industrial Relations
MULLENDER, A., Social Work
NAYLOR, R. A., Economics
NEAL, A., Law
NEUBERGER, A., Accounting and Finance
OSWALD, A. J., Economics
PALIWALA, A., Law
PERRONI, C., Economics
PIERCY, N., Marketing and Strategic Management
POGANY, S. I., Law
PHIZACKLEA, A. M., Sociology
RAI, S. M., Politics and International Studies
RANKIN, N., Economics
RATCLIFFE, P. B., Sociology
REEVE, A. W., Politics and International Studies
SALMON, M., Accounting and Finance
SARNO, L., Business Studies
SCARBOROUGH, H., Business Studies
SCHOLTE, J. A., Politics and International Studies
SKIDELSKY, R., Political Economy
SLACK, N. D. C., Manufacturing and Strategy Policy
SLADE, M., Economics
SMITH, H., Politics and International Studies
SMITH, R. J., Economics
SPENCER, N. J., Community Paediatrics
STEWART, M. B., Economics
STONEMAN, P., Business Studies
STOREY, D. J., Business Studies
STURDY, A., Industrial Relations and Organizational Behaviour
SWAN, J. A., Organizational Behaviour
SZCZEPURA, A., Business Studies
TALL, D. O., Institute of Education
TAYLOR, M. P., Economics
TERRY, M. A., Business Studies
THOMAS, H., Business Studies
TRIGG, R. H., Philosophy
TSOUKOS, H., Industrial Relations and Organizational Behaviour
WAGNER, P., Sociology
WALKER, I., Economics
WARHURST, A., Corporate Citizenship Unit
WATERSON, M. J., Economics
WENSLEY, J. R. C., Marketing and Strategic Management
WHALLEY, J., Development Economics
WHITE, B., Politics and International Studies
WHITESIDE, N., Sociology
WILLCOCKS, L., Information Management and e-Business
WILSON, D. C., Strategic Management
WOODERS, M., Economics
WRAY, D., Institute of Education

ATTACHED RESEARCH CENTRES

AHRB Centre for the Study of Renaissance Elites and Court Cultures: Dir Prof. S. HINDLE.

Centre for Advanced Materials: f. 1984; Dir Prof. M. H. LEWIS.

Centre for Caribbean Studies: f. 1984; Dir Dr C. JONES.

Centre for Comparative Labour Studies: f. 1994; Dir Dr T. ELGER.

Centre for Cultural Policy Studies: Dir O. BENNETT.

Centre for Education and Industry: f. 1986; Dir P. HUDDLESTON.

Centre for Educational Development, Appraisal and Research: f. 1986; Dir Prof. G. LINDSAY.

Centre for English Language Teacher Education: f. 1983; Dir J. KHAN.

Centre for Health Service Studies: f. 1994; Dir Prof. A. K. SZCZEPURA.

Centre for the History of Medicine: f. 1999; Dir H. MARLAND.

Centre for Management under Regulation: f. 1998; Dir Prof. M. CAVE.

Centre for New Technologies Research in Education: Dir Dr D. C. PRATT.

Centre for Nuclear Magnetic Resonance: f. 1985; Dir Prof. R. DUPREE.

Centre for Research in East Roman Studies: f. 1993; Dir Prof. S. SWAIN.

Centre for Research in Ethnic Relations: f. 1985 (fmrly ESRC Research Unit on Ethnic Relations, University of Aston); Dir Prof. D. JOLY.

Centre for Research in Philosophy and Literature: f. 1985; Dir Dr C. BATTERSBY.

Centre for Scientific Computing: Dir (vacant).

Centre for Small and Medium Sized Enterprises: f. 1985 as the Small Business Centre; Dir Prof. D. J. STOREY.

Centre for the Study of Democratisation: f. 1994; Dir Dr C. I. P. FERDINAND.

Centre for the Study of Globalisation and Regionalisation: f. 1997; Dir Prof. R. HIGGOTT.

Centre for the Study of the Renaissance: f. 1993; Dir Prof. J. GARDNER.

Centre for the Study of Safety and Well-Being (SWELL): Dir Dr C. HUMPHREYS.

Centre for the Study of Sport in Society: f. 1994; Dir Dr A. PARKER.

Centre for the Study of Women and Gender: f. 1993; Co-Dirs Dr C. HUGHES, Dr D. STEINBURG.

Centre for Translation and Comparative Cultural Studies: f. 1992; Dir Dr P. KUHIWCZAK.

Corporate Citizenship Unit: Dir Prof. A. WARHURST.

Division of Clinical Sciences: Head of Division Prof. D. SINGER.

Division of Health in the Community: Dir Prof. J. DALE.

Division of Medical Education: Chair. Prof. E. PEILE.

ESRC Centre on Skills, Knowledge and Organizational Performance: in conjunction with the University of Oxford; Dir K. MAYHEW (Oxford).

Financial Options Research Centre: Dir Dr N. WEBBER.

Fluid Dynamics Research Centre: f. 1996; Dir Prof. P. W. CARPENTER.

Forum for Research in Health, Medicine and Society: Co-Dirs Dr A. DOLAN, Dr H. BRADBY.

Humanities Research Centre: f. 1985; Dir Prof. R. W. DYER.

Industrial Relations Research Unit: f. 1970; Dir Prof. P. MARGINSON.

Innovation, Knowledge and Organizational Networks (IKON) Research Centre: Dir Prof. J. SWAN.

Institute for Employment Research: f. 1981; Dir Prof. R. M. LINDLEY.

Institute of Governance and Public Management: Dir Prof. J. BENINGTON.

Institute of Health: Co-Dirs H. BRADBY, G. LEWANDO-HUNDT.

Institute of Mass Spectrometry: f. 1988; Dir Prof. P. J. DERRICK.

International Automotive Research Centre: Dir Prof. Lord BHATTACHARYYA.

International Centre for Education in Development: f. 1990; Dir Dr R. PRESTON.

International Manufacturing Centre: Dir Prof. Lord BHATTACHARYYA.

Legal Research Institute: f. 1978; Dir Prof. S. I. POGANY.

Local Government Centre: f. 1989; Dir Prof. J. MAWSON.

Mathematical Interdisciplinary Research at Warwick: Dir Prof. R. S. MACKAY.

Mathematics Research Centre: f. 1965; Dir Prof. M. REID.

NatWest/Royal Bank of Scotland Financial Capability Centre: National Co-ordinator K. CURRY.

Risk Initiative and Statistical Consultancy Unit: f. 1996; Dir J. FENLON.

Social Theory Centre: Dirs Dr C. TURNER, Dr R. ROGOWSKI.

UK Centre for Legal Education: Dir R. H. M. BURRIDGE.

UNIVERSITY OF THE WEST OF ENGLAND

Frenchay Campus, Coldharbour Lane, Bristol, BS16 1QY

Telephone: (117) 965-6261
Fax: (117) 328-2810
E-mail: admissions@uwe.ac.uk
Internet: www.uwe.ac.uk

Founded 1969 as Bristol Polytechnic; present name and status 1992

Academic year: September to June

Vice-Chancellor: Sir HOWARD NEWBY
Deputy Vice-Chancellor: JOHN RUSHFORTH
Pro-Vice-Chancellor: Prof. COLIN FUDGE
Academic Registrar: TESSA HARRISON
Academic Secretary: C. WEBB
Librarian: C. REX

Library of 593,000 vols, 8,400 periodicals
Number of teachers: 957
Number of students: 18,998 full-time and sandwich; 7,432 part-time

DEANS

Faculty of Applied Sciences: Prof. W. PURCELL
Faculty of Art, Media and Design: Prof. P.L GOUGH
Bristol Business School: (vacant): WARWICK JONES
Faculty of the Built Environment: Prof. C. FUDGE
Faculty of Computing, Engineering and Mathematical Sciences: Prof. S. E. J. HODDELL
Faculty of Education: Prof. R. RITCHIE
Faculty of Health and Social Care: Prof. S. WEST
Faculty of Humanities, Languages and Social Sciences: Prof. G. CHANNON
Faculty of Law: Prof. A. R. BENSTED

UNIVERSITY OF WESTMINSTER

309 Regent St, London, W1B 2UW

Telephone: (20) 7911-5000
Fax: (20) 7911-5858
E-mail: admissions@wmin.ac.uk
Internet: www.wmin.ac.uk

Founded 1838 as Polytechnic Institution; became Royal Polytechnic Institution

1839 and Polytechnic of Central London 1970; present name and status 1992

Academic year: September to August

Vice-Chancellor and Rector: Dr GEOFFREY COPLAND

Deputy Vice-Chancellor: Dr MAUD TYLER

Academic Registrar: EVELYNE RUGG

Provosts: Prof. MAUD TYLER (Cavendish Campus): Prof. KEITH PHILLIPS (Harrow Campus): Prof. MARTIN EVERETT (Marylebone Campus): Prof. MYSZKA GUZKOWSKA (Regent Campus)

Library of 410,000 vols
Number of teachers: 1,204
Number of students: 23,000

DEANS OF SCHOOL

School of Architecture and the Built Environment: Prof. ALAN JAGO

School of Biosciences: Prof. SIMON JARVIS

Harrow School of Computer Science: VASSILIS KONSTANTINON

School of Informatics: Prof. STEPHEN WINTER

School of Integrated Health: Dr PETER DAVIES

School of Law: Prof. ANDY BOON

School of Media, Arts and Design: SALLY FELDMAN

School of Social Sciences, Humanities and Languages: Prof. RICKY MORGAN-TAMOSUMAS

Harrow Business School: Dr MARK PATTON

Westminster Business School: Prof. LEN SHACKLETON

Westminster International University in Tashkent: ABDUJABBOR ABDUVAHIDOV

ATTACHED INSTITUTES

Diplomatic Academy of London: University of Westminster, 309 Regent St, London, W1B 2UW; postgraduate diploma in Diplomatic Studies, MA, MPhil, PhD; Dir NABIL AYAD.

Policy Studies Institute (PSI): 100 Park Village East, London, NW1 3SR; tel. (20) 7468-0468; fax (20) 7388-0914; internet www .psi.org.uk; f. 1978; wholly-owned subsidiary company of Univ. of Westminster; conducts research promoting economic well-being and quality of life; Dir MALCOLM RIGG; publ. *Cultural Trends* (4 a year), *Policy Studies* (4 a year).

UNIVERSITY OF WINCHESTER

Sparkford Rd, Winchester, SO22 4NR

Telephone: (1962) 841515
Fax: (1962) 842280
E-mail: helpdesk@winchester.ac.uk
Internet: www.winchester.ac.uk

Founded 1840; present name and status 2005

Chancellor: MARY FAGAN
Vice-Chancellor: Prof. JOY CARTER

Number of teachers: 550
Number of students: 5,500 (3,000 full-time, 2,500 part-time)

Undergraduate and postgraduate degree programmes in arts, business, health and applied social studies, humanities, performing arts, social sciences and teacher education.

UNIVERSITY OF WOLVERHAMPTON

Molineux St, Wolverhampton, WV1 1SB

Telephone: (1902) 321000
Fax: (1902) 322680
E-mail: enquiries@wlv.ac.uk
Internet: www.wlv.ac.uk

Founded 1969 as Wolverhampton Polytechnic; present name and status 1992

Constituent Colleges: City of Wolverhampton College, Dudley College, Rodbaston College, Sandwell College, South Birmingham College, Telford College of Arts and Technology, Walsall College of Arts and Technology

Chancellor: Rt Hon. Lord PAUL OF MARYLEBONE

Vice-Chancellor (vacant)

Pro-Vice-Chancellors: Prof. GEOFF HURD (Academic Development and Quality), Prof. G. F. BENNETT (Marketing and Development), GARRY SPROSTON (Services), Prof. R. W. NEWTON (Strategic Planning and Resources)

Registrar: JANE NELSON

Director of Learning Resources: MARY HEANEY

Library of 363,471 vols
Number of teachers: 848
Number of students: 23,908

DEANS OF SCHOOLS

Applied Sciences: PATRICK ROBOTHAM
Art and Design: BRYONY CONWAY
Computing and Information Technology: Prof. ROBERT MORETON
Education: Sir GEOFFREY HAMPTON
Engineering and the Built Environment: Prof. PAUL OLOMALAIYE
Health Sciences: Prof. MEL CHEVANNES
Humanities and Social Sciences: BARBARA GWINETT
Legal Studies: BRIAN MITCHELL
Sport, Leisure and Performing Arts: Prof. CRAIG MAHONEY
Wolverhampton Business School: (vacant)

UNIVERSITY OF WORCESTER

Henwick Grove, Worcester, WR2 6AJ

Telephone: (1905) 855000
E-mail: admissions@worc.ac.uk
Internet: www.worc.ac.uk

Founded as University College Worcester; present name and status 2005

Academic year: September to May

Vice-Chancellor and Chief Executive: Prof. DAVID GREEN

Pro-Vice-Chancellor and Deputy Chief Executive: Prof. JUDITH ELKIN

Pro-Vice-Chancellor (Resources): Dr MARTIN DOUGHTY

Registrar and University Secretary: JOHN RYAN

Library of 130,000 vols, 800 periodicals
Number of students: 7,193

HEADS OF DEPARTMENTS

Applied Sciences, Geography and Archaeology: Dr JOHN FAGG
Arts, Humanities and Social Sciences: Dr RICHARD PEARSON
Institute of Education: CHRIS ROBERTSON
Institute of Health, Social Care and Psychology: LOUISE JONES
School of Sport and Exercise Science: MALCOLM ARMSTRONG
Worcester Business School: MARK RICHARDSON

UNIVERSITY OF YORK

Heslington, York, YO10 5DD

Telephone: (1904) 430000
Fax: (1904) 433433
E-mail: admissions@york.ac.uk
Internet: www.york.ac.uk

Founded 1963

Academic year: October to June (three terms)

Chancellor: Dame JANET BAKER
Pro-Chancellors: Sir MICHAEL CARLISLE, K. H. M. DIXON, GORDON HORSFIELD
Vice-Chancellor: Prof. B. CANTOR
Registrar and Secretary: SALLY NEOCOSMOS
Librarian: A. E. M. HEAPS

Library: see Libraries
Number of teachers: 430
Number of students: 7,800
Publication: *Annual Review*

PROFESSORS

ABADIR, K., Mathematics, Economics
AFSHAR, H., Politics
ANDREWS, R., Educational Studies
ARTHURS, A. M., Mathematics
ATTRIDGE, D., English
BABIKER, M., Physics
BALDWIN, T. R., Philosophy
BARRELL, J. C., English
BEHRINGER, W., History
BERTHOUD, J. A., English
BESSEL, R., History
BILLER, P., History
BOWLBY, R., English
BOWLES, D. J., Biology
BRADSHAW, J. R., Social Policy
BRAUNSTEIN, S., Quantum Computing
BURNS, A., Computer Science
BURR, A., Electronics
CALLINICOS, A., Politics
CAMPBELL, C., Sociology
CARR-HILL, R., Health Economics
CARVER, M. O., Archaeology
CLARK, J. H., Chemistry
CORRIGAN, E., Mathematics
CRESSER, M., Environment
CULYER, A. J., Economics
DE FRAJA, G., Economics
DITCH, J. S., Social Policy and Social Work
DIVALL, C., Railway Studies
DIXON, H. D., Economics
DODSON, E., Chemistry
DODSON, G. G., Chemistry
DODSON, M., Mathematics
DOLLIMORE, J., English
DRUMMOND, M. F., Health Economics
EL-GOMATI, M. M., Electronics
ELLIS, A. W., Psychology
FITTER, A.H., Biology
FORD, J. R., Housing Policy
FORREST, A. I., History
FOUNTAIN, J., Mathematics
GILBERT, B. C., Chemistry
GODBY, R., Physics
GODFREY, C., Health Services, Centre for Health Economics
GODFREY, L. G., Social and Economic Statistics
GRAHAM, I., Biology
GRAVELLE, H. S. E., Economics
GUEST, H., English
HALL, G., Psychology
HARRISON, M. D., Computer Science
HARTLEY, K., Economics
HEY, J. D., Social and Economic Statistics
HITCH, G., Psychology
HOLMAN, J., Chemistry
HOWARD, D., Electronics
HOWELL, D., Politics
HUBBARD, R., Chemistry
HULME, C., Psychology
HUTTON, J. P., Economics and Econometrics
INESON, P., Biology
JACKSON, S. F., Women's Studies
JONES, A., Economics
KEMP, P., Social Policy Research Unit
KITZINGER, C., Sociology
KLEIJNEN, J. E., Centre for Reviews and Dissemination
LAMARQUE, P., Philosophy
LAMBERT, P., Economics
LEESE, H. J., Biology
LeFANU, N., Music
LEWIN, R. J., Health Studies
LINDSAY SMITH, J., Chemistry
LOCAL, J. K., Linguistics
McDERMID, J. A., Computer Science
McDOUGALL, C., Criminal Justice
MacPHAIL, E., Psychology
McQUEEN-MASON, S., Biology

MAITLAND, N. J., Biology
MARKS, R., History of Art
MARSH, R., Music
MARVIN, A. C., Electronics
MATTHEW, J. A. D., Physics
MAYNARD, A. K., Health Studies
MAYNARD, M. A., Social Policy and Social Work
MAYSTON, D. J., Public Sector Economics
MENDUS, S., Politics
MILLAR, R., Educational Studies
MILNER, A. J., Biology
MINNIS, A. J., Medieval Literature
MONK, A., Psychology
MULKAY, M., Sociology
MULLER-DETHLEFS, K., Chemistry
O'CONNOR, T., Archaeology
O'GRADY, K., Physics
ORMROD, M., History
PARRY, G., English
PERRINGS, C., Environment
PERT, G. J., Computational Physics
PERUTZ, R. N., Chemistry
PHILLIPS, P., Economics
POSNETT, J., York Health Economics Consortium
PRUTTON, M., Physics
QURESHI, H., Social Policy and Social Work
RAFFAELLI, D., Environment
RAINEY, L. S., English
RIDDY, F J., English
ROBARDS, A. W., Biology
ROBINSON, J., Electronics
ROYLE, E., History
RUNCIMAN, C., Computer Science
RUSSELL, I. T., Health Sciences
SANDERS, D., Biology
SHARPE, J. A., History
SHAW, I., Social Work
SHELDON, T., Health Sciences
SIMMONS, P. J., Economics
SINCLAIR, I. A. C., Social Work
SLOPER, P., Social Policy Research Unit
SMITH, D. M., Borthwick Institute
SMITH, P. C., Economics
SNOWLING, M. S., Psychology
SOUTHGATE, J., Biology
SPARROW, J., Biology
STEIN, M., Social Work
SUDBERY, A., Mathematics
TAYLOR, R. J. K., Chemistry
THOMPSON, D. R., Health Studies
TYRRELL, A. M., Electronics
VULLIAMY, G., Educational Studies
WALTON, P., Chemistry
WALVIN, J., History
WAND, I. C., Computer Science
WARD, N. A.-M. F., English
WARNER, A. R., Language
WATT, I. S., Health Studies
WEBSTER, A., Sociology
WELLINGS, A. J., Computer Science
WICKENS, M. R., Economics
WILKINSON, A. J., Chemistry
WILLIAMS, A. H., Economics
WILSON, K., Chemistry
WILSON, R. A., Biology
WOOLHOUSE, R., Philosophy
YEARLEY, S., Sociology
YOUNG, A. W., Psychology
YOUNG, J. P. W., Biology

ATTACHED INSTITUTES

Borthwick Institute of Historical Research: St Anthony's Hall, Peaseholme Green, York, YO1 2PW; Dir Prof. D. M. SMITH.

Cancer Research Unit: Dir Prof. N. J. MAITLAND.

Centre for Cell and Tissue Research: Man. Dr A. J. WILSON.

Centre for Defence Economics: Dir Prof. K. HARTLEY.

Centre for Eighteenth Century Studies: King's Manor, York, YO1 2EP; Co-Dirs Dr H. GUEST, Dr G. CUBITT.

Centre for Experimental Economics: Dir Prof. J. D. HEY.

Centre for Health Economics: Dir Prof. M. DRUMMOND.

Centre for Housing Policy: Dir Prof. J. FORD.

Centre for Medieval Studies: King's Manor, York, YO1 2EP; Dir Prof. W. H. ORMROD.

Centre for Women's Studies: Dir Prof. S. JACKSON.

Environmental Archaeology Unit: Dir H. K. KENWARD.

Institute of Railway Studies: Dir Prof. C. DIVALL.

Institute for Research in the Social Sciences: Dir Prof. J. R. BRADSHAW.

Jack Birch Unit for Environmental Carcinogenesis: Dir Prof. J. SOUTHGATE.

Microbiology Research Unit: Dir Dr W. B. BETTS.

NHS Centre for Reviews and Dissemination: Dir Prof. J. E. KLEIJNEN.

Social Policy Research Unit: Dir Prof. P. KEMP.

Stockholm Environment Institute at York: Dir Dr J. KUYLENSTIERNA.

Tropical Marine Research Unit: Dir (vacant).

York Cancer Research Group P53: Dir Prof. J. MILNER.

York Electronics Centre: Man. P. G. LONG.

York Health Economics Consortium: Dir Dr P. WEST.

University Colleges

University colleges have taught degree-awarding powers only and do not carry out research.

Buckinghamshire Chilterns University College: Queen Alexandra Rd, High Wycombe, HP11 2JZ; tel. (1494) 522141; fax (1494) 524392; internet www.bcuc.ac.uk; f. 1893; present name and status 1999; Dir RUTH FALWELL; Faculties of Applied Social Sciences and Humanities, Design, Health Studies, Leisure and Tourism and Technology; Buckinghamshire Business School.

University College Chichester: College Lane, Chichester, PO19 6PE; tel. (1243) 816000; e-mail admissions@ucc.ac.uk; internet www.ucc.ac.uk; f. 1839; present name and status 1999; campuses in Chichester and Bognor Regis; Departments of Animal Sciences, Business and Management, Dance, English, Exercise and Health Sciences, Fine Art, History, International Studies, Information Technology, Media Studies and Media Production, Music, Physical Education, Performing Arts, Social Studies, Sport, Teacher Education, Theology and Tourism; Dir Prof. PHILIP ROBINSON.

Harper Adams University College: Newport, Shropshire; tel. (1952) 820280; fax (1952) 814783; e-mail admissions@harper-adams.ac.uk; internet www.harper-adams.ac.uk; f. 1901; undergraduate and postgraduate taught courses and research degrees in agriculture, animal health, agri-business marketing and management, agricultural engineering, rural enterprise and land management, rural environmental management; food and consumer studies, countryside and environment management, food technology, animal care, equestrian management, inter-nation agri-business, business management and marketing; also HND, HNC and university access course; 83 teachers; 1,600 students; Principal Prof. E. W. JONES.

University College for the Creative Arts at Canterbury, Epsom, Farnham, Maidstone and Rochester: internet www.ucreative.co.uk; f. 2005 following merger of the institutions listed below; Rector ELAINE THOMAS (acting); Deputy Rector Prof. DAVID BUSS (acting); Chief Exec. VALERIE STEAD (acting).

Constituent Institutions:

Kent Institute of Art & Design: Oakwood Park, Maidstone, Kent, ME16 8AG; tel. (1622) 757286; fax (1622) 621100; e-mail info@kiad.ac.uk; internet www.kiad.ac.uk; f. 1987 by merger of existing colleges; 269 teachers (60 full-time, 58 part-time, 151 sessional); library of 86,000 vols, 100,000 slides, 414 periodicals and 12 electronic titles total holdings across all three constituent colleges; Chief Admin. Officer RAY MOON.

Constituent colleges:

Kent Institute of Art & Design at Canterbury: New Dover Rd, Canterbury, Kent, CT1 3AN; tel. (1227) 769371; fax (1227) 817500; 83 teachers (18 full-time, 15 part-time, 50 sessional); 852 students; Admin. Man. WAYNE CAMPBELL.

Kent Institute of Art & Design at Maidstone: Oakwood Park, Maidstone, Kent, ME16 8AG; tel. (1622) 757286; fax (1622) 621100; 91 teachers (16 full-time, 19 part-time, 56 sessional); 889 students; Admin. Man. WAYNE CAMPBELL.

Kent Institute of Art & Design at Rochester-upon-Medway: Fort Pitt, Rochester, Kent, ME1 1DZ; tel. (1634) 830022; fax (1634) 820300; 95 teachers (26 full-time, 24 part-time, 45 sessional); 1,251 students; Admin. Man. WAYNE CAMPBELL.

Surrey Institute of Art & Design, University College: Falkner Rd, Farnham, Surrey, GU9 7DS; tel. (1252) 722441; fax (1252) 892616; e-mail registry@surrart.ac.uk; internet www.surrart.ac.uk; f. 1969 as West Surrey College of Art and Design; University College status 1999; honours degree courses in Fine Art, Printed and Woven Textiles, Photography, Film and Video, Animation, Fashion, Fashion Promotion and Illustration, Three-Dimensional Design, Design Management, Graphic Design, Packaging Design, Interior Design, Graphic Design (Visual Communication), Journalism, Time-Based New Media, Fashion Journalism, Graphic Design (New Media), Arts and Media and Product Design Sustainable Futures; National Diploma in Fine Art; foundation course, Masters degree in Art and Design; library of 60,000 vols; 3,000 students; Dir Prof. ELAINE THOMAS.

Queen Margaret University College: Clerwood Terrace, Edinburgh, EH12 8TS; tel. (131) 317-3000; fax (131) 317-3256; e-mail admissions@qmuc.ac.uk; internet www.qmuc.ac.uk; f. 1875; Faculties of Business and Arts and Health and Social Sciences; library: 100,000 vols and 1,400 periodicals; 174 teachers; 3,500 students; Principal and Vice-Patron Prof. ANTHONY P. COHEN; Academic Registrar IRENE R. HYND; Librarian PENNY AITKEN.

Colleges

Due to limitations of space, we are restricted to giving a selection of the larger and more established colleges in the UK.

AGRICULTURE

Myerscough College: Myerscough Hall, Bilsborrow, Preston, PR3 0RY; tel. (1995) 642211; fax (1995) 642333; e-mail enquiries@myerscough.ac.uk; internet www .myerscough.ac.uk; f. 1894; agriculture, horticulture, arboriculture, veterinary nursing, animal welfare, equine science, ecology and conservation, sport and leisure, creative design, landscape, mechanization, motor sport; 200 teachers; 6,000 students; library: 25,000 vols, 110 current journals, 8,000 bound journals; Chief Exec. and Principal (vacant).

Royal Agricultural College: Cirencester, Glos. GL7 6JS; tel. (1285) 652531; fax (1285) 650219; e-mail admissions@rac.ac.uk; internet www.rac.ac.uk; f. 1845; courses at certificate, diploma, degree and postgraduate levels in agriculture, agribusiness, land management, equine and related subjects; library: 26,500 vols; 45 teachers; 650 full-time students; Principal Prof. J. D. LEAVER.

Scottish Agricultural College: Ayr Campus, Auchincruive Estate, Ayr, KA6 5HW; tel. (1292) 525343; fax (1292) 525349; e-mail recruitment@au.sac.ac.uk; internet www.sac .ac.uk/education; f. 1900; campuses at Ayr (associated with Univ. of Glasgow), Aberdeen (associated with Univ. of Aberdeen) and Edinburgh (associated with Univ. of Edinburgh); courses in horticulture, garden design and landscape, applied bioscience, business and rural resource management, environmental studies, leisure and tourism, food technology, agriculture; animal science; courses at all levels from HNC/D to honours degree and taught and research postgraduate; 250 teachers; 1,200 students; Principal Prof. WILLIAM McKELVEY.

Welsh Institute of Rural Studies: University of Wales, Llanbadarn Fawr, Aberystwyth, Ceredigion, SY23 3AL; tel. (1970) 624471; fax (1970) 611264; e-mail irs-enquiries@aber.ac.uk; internet www.irs .aber.ac.uk; f. 1971; BSc (Hons), MSc, HND and University Postgraduate Diploma courses in fields relating to animal science, agriculture, countryside conservation and management, tourism and equine studies; library: 53,000 vols; 32 teachers; 600 students; Dir Prof. WILLIAM HARESIGN.

Writtle College: Lordship Rd, Chelmsford, CM1 3RR; tel. (1245) 424200; fax (1245) 420456; e-mail info@writtle.ac.uk; internet www.writtle.ac.uk; f. 1893; courses at Master and Bachelor levels, foundation degrees in agriculture, horticulture, sport, design, leisure management, rural resource management, business management, animal science, landscape design and construction, equine studies and adventure tourism; 1,800 full-time students; Registrar BRENDA JORDT.

ART AND DESIGN

The colleges listed below (unless otherwise stated) are those which offer courses leading to the Diploma in Art and Design.

City and Guilds of London Art School: 124 Kennington Park Rd, London, SE11 4DJ; tel. (20) 7735-2306; fax (20) 7582-5361; e-mail info@cityandguildsartschool.ac.uk; internet www.cityandguildsartschool.ac.uk; f. 1879; 1-year foundation course; 3-year BA (Hons) degrees in Fine Arts, in Painting and Sculpture; 3-year graduate diploma course in

Applied Arts: Decorative Arts, Architectural Glass; 3-year BA (Hons) degrees in Conservation Studies; 3-year graduate diploma courses in Wood-carving and Gilding, Stone Carving; 60 part-time teachers; 200 students; Principal TONY CARTER.

Courtauld Institute of Art: part of University of London (see entry).

Edinburgh College of Art: Lauriston Place, Edinburgh, EH3 9DF; tel. (131) 221-6000; fax (131) 221-6001; e-mail marketing@eca.ac.uk; internet www.eca.ac.uk; f. 1907; Schools of Architecture and Landscape Architecture; Schools of Drawing and Painting, Design and Applied Arts, Visual Communication and Sculpture; 1,800 students; Principal Prof. IAN HOWARD; Sec. MICHAEL W. WOOD.

Falmouth College of Arts: Woodlane, Falmouth, Cornwall TR11 4RA; tel. (1326) 211077; fax (1326) 211205; internet www .falmouth.ac.uk; f. 1902; ABC Diploma in Foundation Art and Design; BA (Hons) programmes in Broadcasting Studies, Textile Design, Film Studies, Spatial Design, History of Modern Art and Design, English with Media Studies, Fine Art, Graphic Design, Illustration, Journalism Studies, Photographic Communication, Studio Ceramics, 3D Design; Postgraduate Diplomas in Broadcast Journalism, Creative Advertising, Professional Writing, Photography, Creative Enterprise, Broadcast Television; PG Dip/MA in History of Modern Art and Design; MA in Contemporary Visual Arts, Illustration, Interactive Design; MPhil in Research; 80 teachers; 1,700 students; library: 25,000 vols, 200 periodicals; Principal Prof. ALAN LIVINGSTON.

Glasgow School of Art: 167 Renfrew St, Glasgow, G3 6RQ; tel. (141) 353-4500; fax (141) 353-4746; e-mail info@gsa.ac.uk; internet www.gsa.ac.uk; f. 1845; BA, MA and MPhil courses in Architecture, Fine Art and Design; all degree courses validated by University of Glasgow; 1,400 full-time students; library: 50,000 vols, 59,000 slides; Dir Prof. S. REID.

Hamilton Kerr Institute: Whittlesford, Cambridge, CB2 4NE; tel. (1223) 832040; fax (1223) 837595; e-mail hki-admin@lists .cam.ac.uk; f. 1976; dept of Fitzwilliam Museum, Univ. of Cambridge; postgraduate course in conservation and restoration of easel paintings; 5 teachers; 10 students (4 full-time, 6 intern); Dir I. McCLURE.

Norwich School of Art and Design: Francis House, 3–7 Redwell St, Norwich, Norfolk, NR2 4SN; tel. (1603) 610561; fax (1603) 615728; e-mail info@nsad.ac.uk; internet www.nsad.ac.uk; f. 1846; Bachelor degree courses in Fine Art, Creative Writing Studies, Graphic Design, Contemporary Textile Practices, Visual Studies; Master's degree courses in Animation and Sound Design, Art, Design and Education, Digital Practices, Fine Art, Photographic Studies, Textile Culture, Writing the Visual; doctorates; 1,000 students; Principal SUSAN TUCKETT.

Ravensbourne College of Design and Communication: Walden Rd, Chislehurst, Kent, BR7 5SN; tel. (20) 8289-4900; fax (20) 8325-8320; e-mail info@rave.ac.uk; internet www.rave.ac.uk; f. 1962; degree courses in graphic design, product design, furniture design, interior design, fashion design, interaction design, moving image design, professional broadcasting, broadcast engineering and communication and technology; BTEC HNDs in broadcast operations, engineering and production; BTEC HNCs in broadcast post production, and digital technology for the creative industries; BTEC NC in broad-

cast engineering; foundation course in art design and media; MA in Interactive Digital Media; 94 teachers (34 full-time, 60 part-time); 900 students; Dir Prof. ROBIN BAKER; Head of Academic Affairs SARAH GERSHON.

Royal Academy Schools: Burlington Gardens, Piccadilly, London, W1J 0BD; tel. (20) 7300-5920; fax (20) 7300-5856; internet www .royalacademy.org.uk; f. 1768; Schools of Painting and Sculpture; Keeper MAURICE COCKRILL; Sec. LAURA SCOTT.

Royal College of Art: Kensington Gore, London, SW7 2EU; tel. (20) 7590-4444; fax (20) 7590-4500; e-mail admissions@rca.ac.uk; internet www.rca.ac.uk; f. 1837, awarded Charter 1967 empowering it to grant its own degrees; postgraduate institution receiving direct grant from HEFCE; library: 70,000 vols, 200 periodicals; 800 students; Visitor HRH The DUKE OF EDINBURGH; Provost Sir TERENCE CONRAN; Rector and Vice-Provost Prof. Sir CHRISTOPHER FRAYLING; Registrar ALAN SELBY

COURSE DIRECTORS

Animation: Prof. JOAN ASHWORTH
Architecture and Design: Prof. NIGEL COATES
Ceramics and Glass: Prof. MARTIN SMITH
Communication Art and Design: Prof. DAN FERN
Conservation: WILLIAM LINDSAY
Critical and Historical Studies: JOE KERR
Curating Contemporary Art: TERESA GLEADOWE
Design Products: Prof. RON ARAD
Fashion: Prof. WENDY DAGWORTHY
Goldsmithing, Silversmithing, Metalwork and Jewellery: Prof. DAVID WATKINS
History of Design: Prof. JEREMY AYNSLEY
Industrial Design Engineering: Prof. TOM BARKER
Interaction Design: Prof. HILARY FRENCH
Painting: Prof. GRAHAM CROWLEY
Photography: OLIVIER RICHON
Printed Textiles and Constructed Textiles: Prof. CLARE JOHNSTON
Printmaking: Prof. CHRIS ORR
Sculpture: Prof. GLYNN WILLIAMS
Vehicle Design: DALE HARROW

Ruskin School of Drawing and Fine Art: 74 High St, Oxford, OX1 4BG; f. 1871; dept of the University of Oxford; 3-year degree course in Fine Art; 60 students; Principal STEPHEN FARTHING.

School of Architecture, Architectural Association: 34–36 Bedford Square, London, WC1B 3ES; tel. (20) 7887-4000; fax (20) 7414-0782; e-mail info@aaschool.ac.uk; internet www.aaschool.ac.uk; f. 1847; private; academic year August to July; 1-year foundation course; 5-year course leading to AA Dipl.; postgraduate courses and research in Architecture, Building Conservation, Conservation (Landscape and Gardens), Emergent Technologies and Design, Environment and Energy, Histories and Theories of Architecture, Housing and Urbanism, Landscape Urbanism; 3,200 mems; library: 35,000 vols, 150,000 slides; 120 teachers; 580 students; Chair. MOHSEN MOSTAFAVI; publs AA Files (2 a year), Projects Review (annually).

Slade School of Fine Art: University College London, Gower St, London, WC1E 6BT; tel. (20) 7679-2313; fax (20) 7679-7801; e-mail slade.enquiries@ucl.ac.uk; internet www.ucl.ac.uk/slade; f. 1871; BA (Hons) degree course in Fine Art (painting, sculpture or fine art media); MA in Fine Art; MFA in Fine Art; MPhil/PhD in Fine Art; 38 teachers; 260 students; Slade Professor JOHN AIKEN; Admissions Officer CAROLINE NICHOLAS.

Wimbledon School of Art: Merton Hall Rd, Wimbledon, London, SW19 3QA; tel. (20)

8408-5000; fax (20) 8408-5050; e-mail info@ wimbledon.ac.uk; internet www.wimbledon .ac.uk; f. 1890; MA in Theatre: Visual Language of Performance, Drawing, Painting, Sculpture and Graphic Media; BA (Hons) in Painting, Sculpture, Theatre Design for Performance, Costume Design, Costume Interpretation, Technical Arts and Special Effects, Set Design for Stage and Screen and Graphic Media; Edexcel Foundation Diploma; library: 28,000 vols; 47 teachers (full-time); 900 students; Principal Prof. R. BUGG.

BUSINESS AND COMMERCE

Aberdeen College: Gallowgate Centre, Gallowgate, Aberdeen, AB25 1BN; tel. (1224) 612000; fax (1224) 612001; f. 1959; courses include English as a foreign language, EX training (electrical work in hazardous environments), interpreter/translator, business studies, journalism, communication, hospitality, social studies, offshore industries, mechanical engineering, electrical and electronic engineering, art and design, systems analysis and design, sports coaching and development, agriculture; 266 full-time teachers; 6,000 full-time, 18,000 part-time students; library: 25,000 vols; Principal RAE ANGUS; Librarian DAVID MORLEY.

Ashridge: Berkhamsted, Herts., HP4 1NS; tel. (1442) 841000; fax (1442) 841036; e-mail info@ashridge.org.uk; internet www .ashridge.com; f. 1959; MBA, MSc, Diploma and executive development programmes; 83 full-time teachers; 6,000 students; Chief Exec. KAI PETERS.

Central College of Commerce: 300 Cathedral St, Glasgow, G1 2TA; tel. (141) 552 3941; f. 1962; courses in accounting, computing, office studies, business studies, distribution, marketing, advertising, librarianship, art and design, sports therapy, hairdressing and beauty therapy; 120 full-time, 50 part-time teachers; 1,980 full-time, 3,750 part-time students; library: 30,000 vols; Principal P. W. DUNCAN.

College of Estate Management: Whiteknights, Reading, Berks., RG6 6AW; tel. (118) 986-1101; fax (118) 975-0188; e-mail prospectuses@cem.ac.uk; internet www.cem .ac.uk; f. 1919; undergraduate and professional distance learning courses include the BSc degrees in Estate Management, Quantity Surveying, Construction Management, and Building Surveying of the University of Reading; courses meet fully the academic requirements of the Royal Instn of Chartered Surveyors or the Chartered Inst. of Building; access course – Diploma in Surveying Practice (leading to Tech RICS); MBA in Construction and Real Estate (University of Reading), MSc degrees (University of Reading) in Real Estate, Surveying, Conservation of the Historic Environment and Facilities Management; postgraduate diplomas in Project Management, Facilities Management, Property Investment, Conservation of the Historic Environment, Arbitration and Surveying; 270 teachers (245 external, 25 internal); 2,700 students; Principal PETER E. GOODACRE; Dir of Student Services PAUL J. S. BATHO.

Dundee College: Old Glamis Rd, Dundee, DD3 8LE; tel. (1382) 834834; fax (1382) 858117; e-mail enquiry@dundeecoll.ac.uk; internet www.dundeecollege.ac.uk; f. 1956; professional courses in management and financial accountancy, postgraduate courses in management and personnel management, HND and HNC and NC courses; library: 65,000 vols; 380 teachers (300 full-time and 80 part-time); 9,500 students; Principal I. S. OVENS.

European Business School London: Regent's College, Inner Circle, Regent's Park, London, NW1 4NS; tel. (20) 7487-7507; fax (20) 7487-7425; e-mail ebs@ regents.ac.uk; f. 1979 in UK, centres also in Germany, France, Italy, Japan, Russia, Spain and USA; BA (Hons) degree in European Business Administration, and other degrees with business and language mix; summer courses; 750 full-time students in London; library: 25,500 vols; Academic Dir Prof. ERIC DE LA CROIX.

Henley Management College: Greenlands, Henley-on-Thames, Oxfordshire, RG9 3AU; tel. (1491) 418803; fax (1491) 418899; e-mail mba@henleymc.ac.uk; internet www .henleymc.ac.uk.mba; f. 1945 as the Administrative Staff College; residential courses for managers and administrators already holding important positions to prepare them for still greater responsibilities; special courses; research projects; higher degrees and postgraduate courses; 113 teachers (53 full-time, 60 associate); 121 residential course mems, 6,500 students globally; library: 18,000 vols; Principal Prof. STEPHEN WATSON; Librarian JANE GOLDSMITH; publ. *Journal of General Management*.

Regents Business School London: Inner Circle, Regent's Park, London, NW1 4NS; tel. (20) 7477-2990; fax (20) 7477-2991; e-mail info@rbslondon.ac.uk; internet www .rbslondon.ac.uk; f. 1997; BA (Hons) degrees (validated by Open University) awarded in International Business, in International Finance and Accounting, in International Business with Design Management, and in International Marketing; also courses leading to Certificate of Higher Education and Diploma of Higher Education; LLB degree (validated by Bournemouth University); MA degrees (validated by Bournemouth University) awarded in International Management, in International Marketing Management, and in International Business Administration; 60 teachers; 430 students; Academic Dir Dr RICHARD GREGSON; Commercial Dir MOHAMED MALADWALA.

Roffey Park Institute: Forest Rd, Horsham, West Sussex, RH12 4TD; tel. (1293) 851644; fax (1293) 851565; e-mail info@ roffeypark.com; internet www.roffeypark .com; f. 1946; issues MBA degree (validated by Univ. of Sussex) and MSc in People and Organisational Development (validated by Univ. of Salford); 17 teachers; 70 students on two-year courses and 50 per week on executive short courses; Chief Exec. VALERIE HAMMOND.

LAW

BPP Law School: 67–69 Lincoln's Inn Fields, London, WC2A 3JB; tel. (20) 7430-2304; fax (20) 7404-1389; e-mail law@bpp.co .uk; internet www.bpp.co.uk; f. 1992; private instn offering Bar Vocational Course, Postgraduate Diploma in Law, Legal Practice Course and several other courses; library: 6,200 vols; 64 teachers; 600 full-time postgraduate students; Chief Exec. JACQUELINE SIERS.

College of Law: Braboeuf Manor, St Catherines, Guildford, Surrey, GU3 1HA; tel. (1483) 460200; fax (1483) 460305; postgraduate courses; brs in Guildford, London, Chester and York; Chief Exec. of Board of Management Prof. NIGEL SAVAGE.

MUSIC AND DRAMATIC ART

Bristol Old Vic Theatre School: 1 and 2 Downside Rd, Clifton, Bristol, BS8 2XF; tel. (117) 925-4495; fax (117) 923-9371; e-mail enquiries@oldvic.drama.ac.uk; f. 1946;

courses in acting, theatre design, wardrobe, stage management and technical aspects of the theatre; Principal CHRISTOPHER DENYS.

Central School of Speech and Drama: Embassy Theatre, 64 Eton Ave, London, NW3 3HY; tel. (20) 7722-8183; fax (20) 7722-4132; e-mail enquiries@csdd.ac.uk; internet www.cssd.ac.uk; f. 1906; 90 staff; 750 students; courses in art, design and the performing arts, in education and in therapy; Principal Prof. GARY CROSSLEY; Academic Registrar PHILIPPA JOWETT.

Guildhall School of Music and Drama: Silk St, Barbican, London, EC2Y 8DT; tel. (20) 7628-2571; fax (20) 7256-9438; e-mail info@gsmd.ac.uk; internet www.gsmd.ac.uk; f. by the Corporation of London in 1880 and administered by the Board of Governors; 300 professorial staff; 700 students; Principal BARRY IFE; Dir of Music DAMIAN CRANMER; Dir of Drama WYN JONES; Dir of Technical Theatre Studies SUE THORNTON.

Liverpool Institute for the Performing Arts: Mount St, Liverpool, L1 9HF; tel. (151) 330-3000; fax (151) 330-3131; e-mail reception@lipa.ac.uk; internet www.lipa.ac .uk; f. 1996; 80 teachers; 650 students; degrees administered by Liverpool John Moores University; Chief Executive and Principal MARK FEATHERSTONE-WITTY.

London Academy of Music and Dramatic Art: Tower House, 226 Cromwell Rd, London, SW5 0SR; tel. (20) 7373-9883; f. 1861; professional theatrical training, acting and stage management; Principal PETER JAMES.

National Film and Television School: Beaconsfield Studios, Station Rd, Beaconsfield, Bucks., HP9 1LG; tel. (1494) 671234; fax (1494) 674042; e-mail info@nftsfilm-tv.ac .uk; internet www.nftsfilm-tv.ac.uk; f. 1970; postgraduate and professional training for film and television production; two-year MA courses in animation direction, cinematography, composing for film and television, editing, fiction directing, producing, production design, post-production sound and screenwriting; diploma courses in digital post-production, fiction directing, producing for television entertainment, sound recording for film and television and visual and special effects producing; 30 teachers; other visiting lecturers and tutors; 150 students; library: research and information library; Chair. MICHAEL KUHN; Dir NIK POWELL; Dir (Full-time Programme) ROGER CRITTENDEN.

Royal Academy of Dramatic Art (RADA): 62–64 Gower St, London, WC1E 6ED; tel. (20) 7636-7076; fax (20) 7323-3865; e-mail enquiries@rada.ac.uk; internet www.rada .org; f. 1904; courses: Acting (9 terms), Theatre Technical Arts Diploma (6 terms), Scenic Arts, Scenic Construction, Stage Electrics, Property Making, Wardrobe (each 4 terms); library: 17,500 vols; Principal NICHOLAS BARTER.

Royal Academy of Music: see University of London.

Royal College of Music: Prince Consort Rd, South Kensington, London, SW7 2BS; tel. (20) 7589-3643; fax (20) 7589-7740; e-mail info@rcm.ac.uk; internet www.rcm.ac .uk; f. 1883; 4–year B Mus in performance, I-year M Mus, 1–2 year PGDip, DMus; 610 students; library: see Libraries and Archives; Pres. HRH THE PRINCE OF WALES; Dir Prof. COLIN LAWSON; Sec. and Registrar KEVIN PORTER.

Royal College of Organists: 7 St Andrew St, Holborn, London, EC4A 3LQ; tel. (20) 7936-3606; fax (20) 7353-8244; e-mail admin@rco.org.uk; internet www.rco.org.uk;

f. 1864, inc. by Royal Charter 1893; Senior Exec. ALAN DEAR.

Royal Military School of Music: Kneller Hall, Twickenham, Middx, TW2 7DU; f. 1857; 21 teachers; 42 students; 120 pupils; Commandant Col R. G. ROWE; Principal Dir of Music (Army) Lt-Col G. A. KINGSTON.

Royal Northern College of Music: 124 Oxford Rd, Manchester, M13 9RD; tel. (161) 907-5200; fax (161) 273-7611; e-mail info@rncm.ac.uk; internet www.rncm.ac.uk; f. 1973; library: library contains extensive collection of MSS, reference works, gramophone records, tape cassettes, CDs, videos, periodicals, and important archive material including an historical instrument collection; 150 teachers; 600 students; Pres. THE DUCHESS OF KENT; Principal Prof. EDWARD GREGSON.

Royal School of Church Music: Cleveland Lodge, Westhumble St, Dorking, Surrey, RH5 6BW; tel. (1306) 872800; fax (1306) 887260; e-mail enquiries@rscm.com; internet www.rscm.com; f. 1927, inc. 1930; centre for training church musicians; publication of church music; world-wide membership of individuals and affiliated churches; Chair. of Council Sir DAVID HARRISON; Dir Prof. JOHN HARPER; publs *Church Music Quarterly*, *Sunday by Sunday* (liturgy planner, 4 a year).

Royal Scottish Academy of Music and Drama: 100 Renfrew St, Glasgow, G2 3DB; tel. (141) 332-4101; fax (141) 332-8901; e-mail registry@rsamd.ac.uk; internet www.rsamd.ac.uk; f. 1847 as The Glasgow Athenaeum, became The Scottish National Academy of Music 1928, The Royal Scottish Academy of Music 1944 and the Royal Scottish Academy of Music and Drama 1968; international performing arts academy; venue for performing arts productions; 300 teachers; 700 students; library: 80,120 music vols, 13,750 books, 7,570 sound recordings; Principal JOHN WALLACE; Dir of the School of Music RITA McALLISTER; Dean of the School of Drama RUSSELL BOYCE.

Royal Welsh College of Music and Drama: Castle Grounds, Cathays Park, Cardiff, CF1 3ER; tel. (29) 2039-2854; fax (29) 2039-1301; internet www.rwcmd.ac.uk; full- and part-time courses for performers, and degree and diploma courses validated by the Univ. of Wales; Principal EDMOND FIVET.

Trinity College of Music: King Charles Court, Old Royal Naval College, Greenwich, London, SE10 9JF; tel. (20) 8305-4444; fax (20) 8305-9444; e-mail info@tcm.ac.uk; internet www.tcm.ac.uk; f. 1872; full-time 4-year BMus. (Hons) course; MMus, Postgraduate, Diploma, Advanced Diploma; foundation course; individualized programme of study; 150 teachers; 570 students (500 full-time, 70 part-time); Patron HRH THE DUKE OF KENT; Pres. Sir CHARLES MACKERRAS; Principal GAVIN HENDERSON; publ. *The Trinity Magazine* (3 a year).

SCIENCE AND TECHNOLOGY

Camborne School of Mines, University of Exeter: Pool, Redruth, Cornwall, TR15 3SE; tel. (1209) 714866; fax (1209) 716977; e-mail admissions@csm.ex.ac.uk; internet www.ex.ac.uk/CSM; f. 1859; library: 30,000 vols; 25 teachers; 300 students; Dir Prof. R. J. PINE; publ. *Annual Journal*.

Glasgow Metropolitan College: 60 North Hanover St, Glasgow, G1 2BP; tel. (141) 566 6222; fax (141) 566 6626; e-mail adminofficer@glasgowmet.ac.uk; internet www.glasgowmet.ac.uk; f. 2005 by merger of Glasgow College of Building and Printing (f. 1972) and Glasgow College of Food Technology (f. 1972); library: 32,000 vols; 270 teachers; 17,369 students (3,987 full-time, 13,382 part-time); Principal Prof. THOMAS B. WILSON.

Hull York Medical School: University of York, Heslington, YO10 5DD; tel. (1904) 321695; fax (1904) 321696; internet www.hyms.ac.uk/statichome.htm University of Hull, Hull HU6 7RX; f. 2003; Dean Prof. W. J. GILLESPIE.

Wessex Institute of Technology: Ashurst Lodge, Ashurst, Southampton, Hants., SO40 7AA; tel. (23) 8029-3223; fax (23) 8029-2853; f. 1986; 19 teachers; 30 students; library: 10,000 vols; Dir Prof. C. A. BREBBIA; Registrar Dr W. BLAIN; Librarian P. HODGSON

HEADS OF DEPARTMENTS

Damage Mechanics: (vacant)
Environmental Fluid Mechanism: Dr V. POPOV
Industrial Research: Dr R. A. ADEY
Information and Communications Technology: Dr A. PERATTA

NORTHERN IRELAND

Learned Societies

FINE AND PERFORMING ARTS

Arts Council of Northern Ireland: MacNeice House, 77 Malone Rd, Belfast, BT9 6AQ; tel. (28) 9038-5200; fax (28) 9066-1715; e-mail info@artscouncil-ni.org; internet www.artscouncil-ni.org; f. 1943; the mission of the council is to develop the arts in Northern Ireland; Chair. ROSEMARY KELLY; Chief Exec. ROISÍN McDONOUGH; publ. *Article* (2 a year).

HISTORY, GEOGRAPHY AND ARCHAEOLOGY

Ulster Archaeological Society: c/o Dept of Archaeology and Ethnography, Ulster Museum, Botanic Gardens, Belfast, BT9 5AB; e-mail arcethno.um@nics.gov.uk; internet www.varcsoc.org; f. 1853; 300 mems; Pres. Dr C. LYNN; Hon. Sec. KEN PULLIN; publs *Ulster Journal of Archaeology* (annual), *Newsletter* (quarterly).

Research Institutes

AGRICULTURE, FISHERIES AND VETERINARY SCIENCE

Agricultural Research Institute of Northern Ireland: Large Park, Hillsborough, Co. Down, BT26 6DR; tel. (28) 9268-2484; fax (28) 9268-9594; e-mail arini@dardni.gov.uk; internet www.arini.ac.uk; f. 1927; Dir Dr C. S. MAYNE; Sec. M. J. McGUINNESS.

Veterinary Sciences Division: Stormont, Belfast, BT4 3SD; tel. (28) 9052-5690; fax (28) 9052-5755; e-mail bill.ellis@dardni.gov.uk; part of Department of Agriculture and Rural Development, and of School of Agriculture and Food Science, Queen's University Belfast; library of 11,000 vols; Dir Prof. W. A. ELLIS.

ECONOMICS, LAW AND POLITICS

Northern Ireland Economic Research Centre: 46-48 University Rd, Belfast, BT7 1NJ; tel. (28) 9026-1800; fax (28) 9033-0054; internet www.qub.ac.uk/nierc; f. 1985; independent, funded by Queen's University Belfast, NI Govt and private industry; research and detailed studies into all aspects of the Northern Ireland economy and related issues in regional economics with a view to improving Northern Ireland's growth and employment prospects; library with special emphasis on NI economy; Dir Dr M. ANYADIKE-DANES; publs *Working Papers* (print and online, irregular), *NIERC Reports* (print and online, irregular), *Northern Ireland Studies* (print and online, irregular).

NATURAL SCIENCES

Physical Sciences

Armagh Observatory: College Hill, Armagh, BT61 9DG; tel. (28) 3752-2928; fax (28) 3752-7174; e-mail meb@arm.ac.uk; internet www.arm.ac.uk; f. 1790 by Primate Robinson; library of 15,000 vols; Dir Prof. MARK E. BAILEY; Administrator LAWRENCE YOUNG.

Libraries and Archives

Armagh

Armagh Public Library: 43 Abbey St, Armagh, BT61 7DY; tel. (28) 3752-3142; fax (28) 3752-4177; e-mail armroblib@aol.com; internet www.armaghrobinsonlibrary.org; f. 1771 by Primate Richard Robinson; library includes Ref. Dept with 35,000 vols; Dean Swanzy's special collection of genealogical works and Army Lists; history, theology, philosophy; largely antiquarian; MSS include copies of Primatial Registers since 1362; Keeper Very Rev. PATRICK ROOKE.

Southern Education and Library Board Library Service: Library Headquarters, 1 Markethill Rd, Armagh, BT60 1NR; tel. (28) 3752-5353; fax (28) 3752-6879; e-mail info.selb@ni-libraries.net; internet www.ni-libraries.net; f. 1973; 23 brs, 11 mobile libraries; 1,450,000 vols; Chief Librarian K. RYAN.

Ballymena

North-Eastern Education and Library Board, Library Service: Demesne Ave, Ballymena, Co. Antrim; tel. (28) 2566-4100; fax (28) 2563-2038; e-mail info.neelb@ni-libraries.net; internet www.neelb.org.uk; f. 1922; 2,000,000 vols; 28 brs, 8 mobile libraries; Head of Libraries and Corporate Services ANNE CONNOLLY.

Ballynahinch

South-Eastern Education and Library Board: Library Headquarters, Windmill Hill, Ballynahinch, Co Down BT24 8DH; tel. (28) 9756-6400; fax (28) 9756-5072; e-mail info.seelb@ni-libraries.net; internet www.ni-libraries.net; f. 1973; 24 brs, 5 mobile libraries; 652,000 vols, 6,000 maps, 18,000 microforms, 22,000 CDs, 3,000 video recordings, 2,000 DVDs; Chief Librarian BETH PORTER.

Belfast

Belfast Education and Library Board: Belfast Central Library, Belfast, BT1 1EA; tel. (28) 9050-9150; e-mail info.belb@ni-libraries.net; internet www.belb.org.uk; f. 1888; Central Library, 20 community libraries and 2 mobile libraries; Central Lending Library 57,000 vols; Central Reserve Colln 100,000 vols; Humanities and General Reference Library 120,000 vols; Irish Library 40,000 books, pamphlets and MSS on all aspects of Ireland, Ulster and Belfast; Fine Arts and Literature 74,000 vols; Music Library 12,000 vols, 24,000 scores, 24,000 records and cassettes; Business, Science and Technology Library 68,000 vols; other spec. collns: Bibliographies, Govt and Agency Publs, Patents, Rare Books, microfilms; Chief Librarian KATHERINE MCCLOSKEY.

Linen Hall Library (Belfast Library and Society for Promoting Knowledge): 17 Donegall Sq. N., Belfast, BT1 5GB; tel. (28) 9032-1707; fax (28) 9043-8586; e-mail info@linenhall.com; internet www.linenhall.com; f. 1788; 200,000 vols; noted for its Irish collection of 70,000 vols, including early Ulster printing and major collection of political ephemera relating to civil conflict since 1968; 5,000 17th c. pamphlets, 18th and 19th c. travel, biography; Librarian JOHN C. GRAY.

Public Record Office of Northern Ireland: 66 Balmoral Ave, Belfast, BT9 6NY; tel. (28) 9025-5905; fax (28) 9025-5999; e-mail proni@dcalni.gov.uk; internet www.proni.gov.uk; f. 1923; an exec. agency within the Dept of Culture, Arts and Leisure for Northern Ireland; retains official and private records relating mainly to the history of Northern Ireland; Chair. and Chief Exec. Dr GERRY SLATER.

Queen's University Library: Belfast, BT7 1LS; tel. (28) 9097-5023; fax (28) 9032-3340; e-mail library@qub.ac.uk; internet www.qub.ac.uk/lib; f. 1849; 1,200,000 books, periodical vols, pamphlets, MSS, theses and microforms; spec. collns: Hibernica Colln (incl. R. M. Henry Colln, O'Rahilly Colln), Antrim Presbytery Library, MacDouall Colln (Philology), Hamilton Harty Music Colln, Thomas Percy Library; Asst Dir (Information Services) E. TRAYNOR; publs *Irish Naturalists Journal* (quarterly), *Northern Ireland Legal Quarterly*, *Wiles Lectures* (annual), *Inaugural Lectures*, *Statistical and Social Inquiry Society of Ireland Journal* (annual).

Newtownabbey

University of Ulster Library: Shore Rd, Newtownabbey, Co Antrim, BT37 0QB; tel. (28) 9036-6399; fax (28) 9036-6849; e-mail library@ulster.ac.uk; internet www.ulster.ac.uk/library; f. 1985; 729,000 vols (all campuses); Dir of Information Services NIGEL MACARTNEY (acting); Asst Dir (Library) ELAINE URQUHART.

Campus libraries:

Belfast Campus Library: York St, Belfast, Co Antrim, BT15 1ED; tel. (28) 9026-7270; 68,226 vols, mostly arts-related: painting, history of art and architecture, sculpture, design, fashion, film and photography, museum studies, Irish language.

Coleraine Campus Library: Cromore Rd, Coleraine, Co Londonderry, BT52 1SA; tel. (28) 7032-3128; 297,689 vols; European Documentation Centre; spec. collns: First and Second World Wars, Nenry Davis Gift of incunabula, Hentry Morris Colln of Irish material, Stelfox natural history colln.

Jordanstown Campus Library:; 273,004 vols; American and women's studies; UK, US and Irish radical newspapers and periodicals on microfilm.

Magee Campus Library: Northland Rd, Londonderry, BT48 7JL; tel. (28) 7137-5240; 78,361 vols; informatics, law and social work; Irish Colln of 5,400 books and 800 pamphlets, Rare Books Colln.

Omagh

Western Education and Library Board: 1 Spillars Place, Omagh, Co. Tyrone, BT78 1HL; tel. (28) 8224-4821; fax (28) 8224-6716; e-mail info@ni-libraries.net; internet www.welbni.org; provides library services in the council areas of Omagh, Fermanagh, Londonderry, Strabane and Limavady; Chief Librarian HELEN OSBORN.

Museums and Art Galleries

Belfast

National Museums Northern Ireland: Botanic Gardens, Belfast, BT9 5AB; tel. (28) 9038-3000; fax (28) 9038-3006; internet www.magni.org.uk; Chief Exec. TIM COOKE.

Constituent Museums:

Armagh County Museum: The Mall East, Armagh, BT61 9BE; tel. (28) 3752-3070; internet www.armaghcountymuseum.org.uk; f. 1935; local history, antiquities, natural history; photographic and map collns; library: extensive reference library; Curator CATHERINE McCULLOUGH.

Ulster American Folk Museum: Castletown, Omagh, Co Tyrone, BT78 5QY; tel. (28) 8224-3292; internet www.folkpark.com; f. 1976; open-air museum illustrating history of emigration from Ulster to the USA during 18th–19th centuries; reconstructions of bldgs and activities; full-size reconstruction of 19th-century sailing ship; Curator Dr PHILIP MOUNT.

Ulster Folk and Transport Museum: Cultra, Holywood, Co Down, BT18 0EU; tel. (28) 9042-8428; internet www.uftm.org.uk; f. 1964; nat. museum comprising open-air museum with authentic bldgs illustrating Ulster folk life, both rural and urban; separate transport museum; library of 18,000 vols; Chair. of Board of Trustees M. ELLIOTT; Divisional Head JONATHAN BELL; publ. *Ulster Folklife* (annual).

Ulster Museum: Botanic Gardens, Belfast, BT9 5AB; tel. (28) 9038-3000; internet www.ulstermuseum.org.uk; f. 1833; fine and applied arts, archaeology, ethnography, history, botany, geology, zoology; Head (vacant); closed for redevelopment until spring 2009.

Universities

QUEEN'S UNIVERSITY BELFAST

University Rd, Belfast, BT7 1NN

Telephone: (28) 9024-5133

Fax: (28) 9024-7895

Internet: www.qub.ac.uk

Founded 1845 as Queen's College, original University Charter 1908, present Charter 1982

State control

Language of instruction: English

Academic year: September to September

Chancellor: Senator GEORGE MITCHELL
Pro-Chancellors: B. MCLAUGHLIN, C. GIBSON
President and Vice-Chancellor: Prof. PETER GREGSON
Pro-Vice-Chancellors: Prof. K. L. BELL, Prof. K. D. BROWN, Prof. JOHN MANN, Prof. F. G. MCCORMAC
Registrar: J. P. J. O'KANE
Librarian (vacant)

Library: see Libraries and Archives
Number of teachers: 1,600 full-time
Number of students: 17,500 (full-time and part-time); 10,000 part-time students enrolled at the Institute of Lifelong Learning

DEANS

Faculty of Arts, Humanities and Social Sciences: Prof ELLEN DOUGLAS-COWIE
Faculty of Engineering and Physical Sciences: Prof. K. L. BELL (acting)
Faculty of Medicine, Health and Life Sciences: Prof. J. MCELNAY

PROFESSORS

Faculty of Arts, Humanities and Social Sciences (73 University Rd, Belfast, BT7 1NN; tel. (28) 9033-5347; fax (28) 9024-9864; e-mail humanities-faculty@qub.ac.uk; internet www.qub.ac.uk/fhum):

ALCORN, M., Music and Sonic Arts
ANDREW, M., English
BALES, R., Languages, Literatures and (Performing) Arts
BELL, D., Languages, Literatures and (Performing) Arts
BEW, P., Politics, International Studies and Philosophy
BOWLER, P., History and Anthropology
BURNETT, M., English
CAMPBELL, J., History and Anthropology
CARAHER, B., English
CAREY, M., Management and Economics
CARSON, C., English
CLOUGH, P., Education
CONNOLLY, P., Education
CONNOLLY, S., History and Anthropology
CULLEN, B., Politics, International Studies and Philosophy
DALY, M., Sociology, Social Policy and Social Work
DAVIES, S., Languages, Literatures and (Performing) Arts
DAWSON, N., Law
DEMIRAG, S., Management and Economics
DICKSON, B., Law
DONNAN, H., History and Anthropology
DOUGLAS-COWIE, E., Arts, Humanities and Social Sciences
ELWOOD, J., Education

ENGLISH, R., Politics, International Studies and Philosophy
EVANS, J., Politics, International Studies and Philosophy
FORKER, J., Management and Economics
GALLAGHER, A., Education
GARDNER, J., Arts, Humanities and Social Sciences
GEOGHEGAN, V., Politics, International Studies and Philosophy
GORMAN, J., Politics, International Studies and Philosophy
GRAY, P., History and Anthropology
GREEN, I., History and Anthropology
GUELKE, A., Politics, International Studies and Philosophy
HARVEY, C., Law
HAYTON, D., History and Anthropology
HELLAWELL, P., Music and Sonic Arts
HILLYARD, P., Sociology, Social Policy and Social Work
HYNDMAN, N., Management and Economics
JACKSON, J., Law
JEFFCUTT, P., Management and Economics
JEFFERY, K., History and Anthropology
JOHNSTON, D., Languages, Literatures and (Performing) Arts
KENNEDY, L., History and Anthropology
LEITH, P., Law
MACDONALD, C., Politics, International Studies and Philosophy
MAGENNIS, H., English
MANN, M., Sociology, Social Policy and Social Work
McEVOY, J., Politics, International Studies and Philosophy
McEVOY, K., Law
McKILLOP, D., Management and Economics
McLAUGHLIN, E., Sociology, Social Policy and Social Work
MILTON, K., History and Anthropology
MOORE, M., Management and Economics
MORISON, J., Law
MULLETT, M., History and Anthropology
O, R., Languages, Literatures and (Performing) Arts
O'DOWD, L., Sociology, Social Policy and Social Work
O'DOWD, M., History and Anthropology
O'HEARN, D., Sociology, Social Policy and Social Work
O'NEILL, S., Politics, International Studies and Philosophy
PHILIP, G., Management and Economics
PINKERTON, J., Sociology, Social Policy and Social Work
PRIOR, L., Sociology, Social Policy and Social Work
SCRATON, P., Law
SHEEHAN, E., English
SIMPSON, P., English
SMACZNY, J., Music and Sonic Arts
TEAGUE, P., Management and Economics
THOMPSON, J., English
TURNER, J., Management and Economics
TURNER, S., Law
WALKER, B., Politics, International Studies and Philosophy
WALKER, G., Politics, International Studies and Philosophy
WHEELER, S., Law
WHITEHEAD, D., History and Anthropology
WHITEHOUSE, H., History and Anthropology
WIENER, A., Politics, International Studies and Philosophy
WILFORD, R., Politics, International Studies and Philosophy
WILLIAMS, F., Arts, Humanities and Social Sciences
WOODFIELD, I., Music and Sonic Arts

Faculty of Engineering and Physical Sciences (NI Technology Centre, Cloreen Park, Belfast, BT9 5HN; tel. (28) 9033-5443; fax (28) 9066-3715; e-mail g.holmes@qub.ac.uk; internet www.qub.ac.uk/feng):

ALLEN, S. J., Chemical Engineering
ARMITAGE, D. H., Pure Mathematics
ARMSTRONG, C. G., Mechanical and Manufacturing Engineering
ARMSTRONG, G. A., Electrical and Electronic Engineering
ATKINSON, R., Physics and Astronomy
BASHEER, P. A. M., Civil Engineering
BELL, D. A., Computer Science
BELL, K. L., Applied Mathematics and Theoretical Physics
BLAIR, G. P., Mechanical and Aerospace Engineering
BOYD, D. R., Chemistry
BURCH, R., Chemistry
CAMPBELL, B., Geography
CLELAND, D. J., Civil Engineering
CLINT, M., Computer Science
COWAN, C. F. N., Electrical and Electronic Engineering
COWIE, R., Psychology
CRAWFORD, R., Mechanical and Aerospace Engineering
CROOKES, D., Computer Engineering
CROTHERS, D. S. F., Applied Mathematics and Theoretical Physics
CROSSLEY, P., Electrical and Electronic Engineering
DOUGLAS, R., Mechanical and Manufacturing Engineering
DUFTON, P. L., Physics and Astronomy
FEE, A. J., Mechanical and Manufacturing Engineering
FINNIS, M. W., Physics and Astronomy
FLECK, R., Mechanical and Manufacturing Engineering
FUSCO, V. F., Electrical and Electronic Engineering
GAMBLE, H. S., Electrical and Electronic Engineering
GRAHAM, W. G., Physics and Astronomy
HALL, V., Archaeology and Palaeoecology
HARDACRE, C., Chemistry
HARKIN-JONES, E. M. A., Mechanical and Manufacturing Engineering
HEPPER, P., Psychology
HIBBERT, A., Applied Mathematics and Theoretical Physics
HOWE, J., Environmental Planning
HU, P., Chemistry
IRWIN, G. W., Electrical and Electronic Engineering
KALIN, R. M., Civil Engineering
KEENAN, F. P., Applied Mathematics and Theoretical Physics
LATIMER, C. J., Physics and Astronomy
LEWIS, C. L. S., Physics and Astronomy
LIVINGSTONE, D. N., Mechanical and Aerospace Engineering
McCANNY, J. V., Electrical and Electronic Engineering
McCORMAC, G., Archaeology and Palaeoecology
McELDOWNEY, J. M., Environmental Planning
McGARVEY, J. J., Chemistry
McGUINNESS, C., Psychology
MAGEE, T. R. A., Chemical Engineering
MALLORY, J., Archaeology and Palaeoecology
MANN, J., Chemistry
MARSHALL, A. J., Electrical and Electronic Engineering
ORFORD, J. D., Geography
ORR, J. P., Mechanical and Manufacturing Engineering
PERROTT, R. H., Computer Science
RAGHUNATHAN, S. R., Aeronautical Engineering
SCOTT, N. S., Computer Science
SEDDON, K. R., Chemistry
SHEEHY, N., Psychology
DE SILVA, A. P., Chemistry

SMITH, B., Geography
SMYTH, A., Environmental Planning
TAYLOR, K. T. A., Applied Mathematics and Theoretical Physics
WALMSLEY, D. G., Physics and Astronomy
WALTERS, H. R. J., Applied Mathematics and Theoretical Physics
WHALLEY, W. B., Geography
WHITAKER, M. A. B., Physics and Astronomy
WICKSTEAD, A. W., Pure Mathematics
WILLIAMS, I., Physics and Astronomy
WOODS, R., Electrical and Electronic Engineering
WOOLLEY, T. A., Architecture

Faculty of Medicine, Health and Life Sciences (Whitla Medical Bldg, 97 Lisburn Rd, Belfast, BT9 7BL; tel. (28) 9027-2010; fax (28) 9033-0571; e-mail s.mcmillan@qub.ac.uk; internet www.qub.ac.uk/fmhs):

AMES, J., Biological and Food Sciences
CAMPBELL, F., Biomedical Sciences
CHAKRAVARTHY, U., Biomedical Sciences
COSBY, S., Biomedical Sciences
DAVIES, R., Biological and Food Sciences
DRING, M., Biological and Food Sciences
ELBORN, J., Medicine and Dentistry
ELWOOD, R., Biological and Food Sciences
ENNIS, M., Medicine and Dentistry
EVANS, A., Medicine and Dentistry
FEE, J., Medicine and Dentistry
FREEMAN, R., Medicine and Dentistry
GORMAN, S., Pharmacy
HALL, P., Medicine and Dentistry
HAMILTON, P., Biomedical Sciences
HARKIN, D., Biomedical Sciences
HAY, R., Medicine and Dentistry
HIRST, D., Pharmacy
HUGHES, A., Medicine and Dentistry
HUGHES, C., Pharmacy
HUTCHINSON, G., Biological and Food Sciences
JOHNSTON, G., Medicine and Dentistry
JOHNSTON, J., Biomedical Sciences
JOHNSTON, P., Biomedical Sciences
JONES, D., Pharmacy
KEE, F., Medicine and Dentistry
LAMEY, P., Medicine and Dentistry
LAPPIN, T., Biomedical Sciences
LARKIN, M., Biological and Food Sciences
LEWIS, S., Medicine and Dentistry
LINDEN, G., Medicine and Dentistry
LYNCH, E., Medicine and Dentistry
MAGGS, C., Biological and Food Sciences
MAULE, A., Biological and Food Sciences
MAXWELL, A., Medicine and Dentistry
McCLURE, N., Medicine and Dentistry
McDERMOTT, B., Medicine and Dentistry
McELNAY, J., Medicine, Health and Life Sciences
McVEIGH, G., Biomedical Sciences
MIRAKHUR, R., Medicine and Dentistry
MONTGOMERY, W., Biological and Food Sciences
ORR, J., Nursing and Midwifery
PORTER, S., Nursing and Midwifery
REILLY, P., Medicine and Dentistry
REYNOLDS, G., Medicine and Dentistry
RIMA, B., Biomedical Sciences
SAVAGE, J., Medicine and Dentistry
SHAW, C., Pharmacy
SHIELDS, M., Medicine and Dentistry
STITT, A., Biomedical Sciences
STOUT, R., Medicine and Dentistry
TRIMBLE, E., Medicine and Dentistry
VANDENBROECK, K., Pharmacy
WALKER, B., Pharmacy
WOOLFSON, D., Pharmacy
YOUNG, I., Medicine and Dentistry

UNIVERSITY INSTITUTES AND CENTRES

Centre for Computer-Based Learning: Dir Dr L. GREENWOOD.

Centre for Human Rights: Dir Prof. S. LIVINGSTONE.

Centre for Marine Resources and Mariculture: Man. Dr N. McDONOUGH.

Centre for Social Research: Dir M. TOMLINSON.

Centre for Women's Studies: Dir Dr M. HILL.

Centre of Canadian Studies: Co-Dirs S. HODGETT, Dr S. ROYLE.

Gibson Institute for Land, Food and Environment: Dir Dr J. M. STEPHENS (acting).

Institute for Childcare Research: Dir Prof. D. IWANIEC.

Institute of Byzantine Studies: Dir Prof. M. E. MULLETT.

Institute of Criminology and Criminal Justice: Dir Prof. J. JACKSON.

Institute of European Studies: Dir Prof. M. L. SMITH.

Institute of Governance, Public Policy and Social Research: Dir Prof. E. MEEHAN.

Institute of Irish Studies: Dir B. M. WALKER.

Institute of Lifelong Learning: Dir P. NOLAN.

Institute of Professional Legal Studies: Dir A. FENTON.

Institute of Theology: Dir Dr J. LEWIS.

Northern Ireland Centre for Postgraduate Pharmaceutical Education and Training: Dir Dr C. ADAIR.

Northern Ireland Semi-Conductor Research Centre: Dir H. S. GAMBLE.

Northern Ireland Technology Centre: Dir T. EDGAR.

Polymer Processing Research Centre: Dir R. MURPHY.

Queen's University Environmental, Science and Technology Research Centre (QUESTOR): Dir Dr W. McGAREL.

RECOGNIZED COLLEGES

Belfast Bible College: Glenburn House, Glenburn Rd South, Dunmorry, BT17 9JP; tel. (28) 9030-1551; Principal Rev. G. J. CHEESEMAN.

Edgehill Theological College: Lennoxvale, Belfast, BT9 5BY; tel. (28) 9066-5870; Methodist; Principal Rev. W. D. D. COOKE.

Greenmount College of Agriculture and Horticulture: 21 Greenmount Rd, Antrim, BT41 4PU; tel. (28) 9442-6666; Principal R. J. McCLENAGHAN.

Irish Baptist College: 67 Sandown Rd, Belfast, BT5 6GU; tel. (28) 9047-1908; Principal Rev. H. MOORE.

Loughry College of Agriculture and Food Technology: Cookstown, Co. Tyrone, BT80 9AA; tel. (28) 8676-2491; Principal J. G. S. SPEERS.

St Mary's College: 191 Falls Rd, Belfast, BT12 6FE; tel. (28) 9032-7678; Principal Rev. M. O'CALLAGHAN.

Seamus Heaney Centre for Poetry: Dir CIARAN CARSON.

Stranmillis College: Stranmillis Rd, Belfast, BT9 5DY; tel. (28) 9038-1271; courses in education; Principal J. R. McMINN.

Union Theological College: Botanic Ave, Belfast, BT7 1JT; tel. (28) 9032-5374; Presbyterian; Principal Rev. Prof. T. S. REID.

UNIVERSITY OF ULSTER

Cromore Rd, Coleraine, Co. Londonderry, BT52 1SA

Telephone: (28) 7034-4141
Fax: (28) 7032-4927
E-mail: online@ulster.ac.uk

Internet: www.ulster.ac.uk

Founded 1984 by merger of the New University of Ulster and the Ulster Polytechnic

State control

Academic year: October to June

Chancellor: Sir RICHARD NICHOLS

Pro-Chancellor: Prof. ROY SPENCE

Vice-Chancellor: Prof. RICHARD BARNETT (acting)

Pro-Vice-Chancellors: Prof. NORMAN BLACK (Academic Development and Student Services), Prof. JIM ALLEN (Communication and Institutional Development), Prof. DENISE McALISTER (Quality Assurance and Enhancement, and Provost at Jordanstown), Prof. BERNIE HANNIGAN (Research and Development)

Number of teachers: 850

Number of students: 24,244 (16,497 full-time, 7,747 part-time)

DEANS

Faculty of Arts: Prof. ROBERT WELCH

Faculty of Business and Management: Prof. ROBERT HUTCHINSON

Faculty of Engineering and Built Environment: Dr RICHARD MILLAR (acting)

Faculty of Life and Health Sciences: Prof. HUGH McKENNA

Faculty of Social Sciences: Prof. ANNE MORAN

PROFESSORS

Faculty of Arts:

ARTHUR, P. J., History, Philosophy and Politics

BRADFORD, R. W., Literary History and Theory

CROTTY, P. J., Irish and Scottish Literary History

FRASER, T. G., History

GARGETT, G., French Culture and Ideas

GRAHAM, B. J., Irish Cultural Heritage

HILL, B. J., Textiles Technology

HILL, W. J., Media Studies

JEFFERY, K. J., Modern History

JONES, G. J., Social and Intellectual History

KELLY, W., Irish Visual Culture

LARRES, K., History and International Affairs

LINDLEY, K. J., Early Modern British History

McBRIDE, R., Modern Languages

McCARTHY, G. F., Theatre Studies

McCLELLAND, B., Design

MacLENNAN, A. M., Fine Art

MacMATHÚNA, S., Irish Studies

McMINN, J. M., Anglo-Irish Literature

MORGAN, V., History, Philosophy and Politics

NIC CRAITH, M., Irish Culture and Language

O CORRAIN, A. P., Modern Irish Studies

O'KEEFFE, T. M.

ROBINSON, H., Politics of Art

SHARP, A. J., International Studies

STURDY, D. J., Early Modern History

WELCH, R. A., English

WILLEMEN, P., Media Studies

YORK, R. A., European Literature

Faculty of Business and Management:

ALEXANDER, N. S., Services Management

BELL, J. D., International Business Entrepreneurship

BROWN, S., Marketing Research

CAREY, M., Management Science

CARSON, D., Marketing

CLARKE, W. M., European Marketing

CROMIE, S., Management Education

EWART, R. W.

FOX, A. F., Financial Management

GILMORE, A. J., Services Marketing

GLASS, J. C., Applied Financial Economics

HUTCHINSON, R. W., Business Finance

KIRK, R. J., Accounting and Finance

McHUGH, M. L., Organizational Behaviour

McNAMEE, P. B., International Business

O'NEILL, K. E., Enterprise and Small Business Development

O'REILLY, M. D., International Business Strategy

WARD, J. D., Taxation

Faculty of Engineering and Built Environment:

ADAIR, A. S., Real Estate Development

ANDERSON, J. Mc C., Electronics

ANDERSON, T. J., Interactive Computing

BLACK, N. D., Medical Informatics

BROWN, N. M. D., Chemistry (Surface Science)

BUSTARD, D. W., Computing Science

DUBITZKY, W., Bioinformatics

EAMES, P. C., Solar Energy Applications

FARAHMAND, K., Mathematics

HINE, J. P., Transport

HOUSTON, S. K., Mathematical Studies

HULL, M. E. C., Computing Science

McCLEAN, S. I., Mathematics

McGINNITY, T. M., Intelligent Systems Engineering

McGREAL, W. S., Property Research

McILHAGGER, R., Engineering Components

McKEAG, D., Product Development

McKEVITT, P., Digital Multimedia

McLAUGHLIN, J. A., Advanced Functional Materials

McMULLAN, J. T.

McTEAR, M., Knowledge Engineering

MITCHELL, R. H., Electronics

MOLKOV, V., Fire Safety Science

PARR, G. P., Telecommunications

SHIELDS, T. J., Built Environment

WOODSIDE, A. R., Highways Engineering

Faculty of Life and Health Sciences:

ALLEN, J. M., Physiology

ANDERSON, R. S., Vision Science

BALMER, A. E., Sports Studies

BARNETT, C. R., Science and Technology Innovation

BARNETT, Y. A., Biomedical Sciences

BAXTER, G. D., Rehabilitation Sciences

BOORE, J. R. P., Nursing

BOREHAM, C. A. G., Sport and Exercise Science

BROWN, J., Primary Health Care – General Practice

CAIRNS, S. E., Psychology

CHAMBERS, M. G., Mental Health Nursing

DOLK, H. M., Epidemiology and Health Services Research

DOWNES, C. S., Cancer Biology

DUBITZKY, W., Bioinformatics

EAKIN, P. A., Occupational Therapy

EASTWOOD, D. A., Environmental Studies

FLATT, P. R., Biological and Biomedical Sciences

HANNIGAN, B. M., Biomedical Sciences

HIRST, D. G., Radiation Science

HOWARD, V., Bioimaging

KERNOHAN, W. G., Health Research

LESLIE, J., Psychology

LIVINGSTONE, M. B. E., Nutrition

McCABE, A. M., Quaternary Science

McCLOSKEY, J., Geophysics

McCONKEY, R. A., Developmental Disabilities

McCORMACK, B., Nursing Research

McDOWELL, D. A., Food Studies

McHALE, A. P., Medical Biotechnology

McKENNA, H. P., Nursing

McKEOWN, S. R., Cancer Biology

McNULTY, H. M., Nutritional Science

PARAHOO, K. A., Nursing and Health Research

POULTON, B. C., Community Health Nursing

MARCHANT, R., Microbial Biotechnology

RAE, G., Psychology

ROWLAND, I. R., Human Nutrition (Diet and Health)
SHAW, C., Biotechnology
SMYTH, W. F., Bio-analytical Chemistry
STRAIN, J. J., Human Nutrition
STRINGER, M., Psychology
THURNHAM, D. I., Human Nutrition
WALSH, D. M., Rehabilitation Research
WEINREICH, P., Psychology
WHITTINGTON, D., Health Psychology
WILCOCK, D. N., Environmental Studies

Faculty of Social Sciences:

BAMFORD, D. R., Social Work
BELL, C. M., Public International Law
BIRRELL, W. D., Social Administration and Policy
BOROOAH, V. K., Applied Economics
CAMPBELL, C., Law
DICKSON, S. B., Law
ERRIDGE, A. F., Public Policy and Management
GOODLUCK, H., Linguistic Science
HARGIE, O. D. W., Communication
HENRY, A. M., Linguistics

HILLYARD, P., Social Policy and Administration
KNOX, C. G., Comparative Public Policy
MCALEAVY, G. J., Further and Higher Education
MCALISTER, D. A., Health Policy
MCWILLIAMS, M. M., Women's Studies
MORAN, A., Education
NI AOLAIN, F., Law
O'CONNOR, J. S., Social Policy
OFFER, J. W., Social Theory and Policy
OSBORNE, R. D., Applied Policy Studies
OSMANI, S. R., Applied Economics
PARIS, C. T., Housing Studies
PATTERSON, H. H., Politics
PRITCHARD, R., Education
ROLSTON, W. J., Sociology
SMITH, A.
THAIN, C., Politics
WILSON, J., Communication

International Centre of Excellence for the Study of Peace and Conlict (International Conflict Research–INCORE):

ROBINSON, G., Initiative and Conflict Resolution and Ethnicity (Dir)

College

BELFAST INSTITUTE OF FURTHER AND HIGHER EDUCATION

College Square East, Belfast, BT1 6DJ
Telephone: (28) 9026-5000
Fax: (28) 9026-5451
E-mail: information_services@belfastinstitute.ac.uk
Internet: www.belfastinstitute.ac.uk
Founded 1991 from College of Technology (f. 1901), College of Business Studies and Rupert Stanley College

Director: Prof. PATRICK MURPHY
Number of students: 9,800 full-time.

Academic departments: business and management, community education and training, computing and administrative studies, continuing education, creative and health studies, general education, hospitality, leisure and tourism, technology.

BERMUDA

Learned Societies
GENERAL

Bermuda National Trust: POB HM 61, Hamilton IIM AX; Located at: Waterville, 29 The Lane, Paget PG 05; tel. 236-6483; fax 236-0617; e-mail palmetto@bnt.bm; internet www.bnt.bm; f. 1970; promotes the preservation and appreciation of lands, buildings and artefacts of natural or historic interest; 4,000 mems; Pres. WAYNE JACKSON; Exec. Dir STEVE CONWAY; publ. *Architectural Heritage–Bermuda* (irregular).

FINE AND PERFORMING ARTS

Bermuda Society of Arts: POB HM 1202, Hamilton HM FX; Located at: The City Hall Arts Centre, 17 Church St, Hamilton; tel. 292-3824; fax 296-0699; e-mail bsoa@ibl.bm; internet www.bsoa.bm; f. 1956; 700 mems; Pres. ELDON TRIMINGHAM III; Gallery Dir PETER R. LAPSLEY.

HISTORY, GEOGRAPHY AND ARCHAEOLOGY

Bermuda Historical Society: 13 Queen St, Hamilton HM 11; tel. 295-2487; f. 1895; 130 mems; Pres. ANDREW BERMINGHAM.

St George's Historical Society: Cnr Duke of Kent St and Featherbed Alley, POB 279, St George's GE BX; tel. 297-0423; e-mail albatross@ibl.bm; f. 1922; operates the Mitchell House, early 18th c. period museum, contains antique furniture, paintings, porcelain and textiles; 150 mems; Pres. JEANNIE OLANDER; Sec. and Treas. TONY SAUNDERS.

MEDICINE

Bermuda Medical Society: King Edward VII Memorial Hospital, 7 Point Finger Rd, Paget DV 04; tel. 236-2345; fax 239-6324; e-mail brenda.gorman@bermudahospitals

.bm; f. 1970; 70 mems; Pres. Dr JONATHAN MURRAY; Sec. Dr GERHARD BOONSTRA.

NATURAL SCIENCES
Biological Sciences

Bermuda Audubon Society: POB HM 1328, Hamilton HM FX; tel. 297-2623; e-mail info@audubon.bm; internet www.audubon.bm; f. 1954; 300 mems; environmental protection and education; Pres. ANDREW DOBSON; publ. *Newsletter*.

Physical Sciences

Astronomical Society of Bermuda: POB HM 1046, Hamilton HM EX; tel. 236-3780; fax 232-1402; e-mail eddimac@ibl.bm; f. 1962; 10 mems; Pres. EDWARD MCGONAGLE; Sec. C. MCGONAGLE.

Research Institutes
AGRICULTURE, FISHERIES AND VETERINARY SCIENCE

Bermuda Department of Environmental Protection: POB HM 834, Hamilton HM CX; tel. 236-4201; fax 236-7582; e-mail tsleeter@gov.bm; f. 1898; management and development of horticulture, environmental protection and Bermudan natural history; Dir THOMAS D. SLEETER; publs *Annual Report*, *Envirotalk* (monthly).

NATURAL SCIENCES
Biological Sciences

Bermuda Biological Station for Research, Inc.: Ferry Reach, St George's GE 01; tel. 297-1880; fax 297-8143; internet www.bbsr.edu; f. 1903; research in most aspects of marine sciences and oceanography and environmental sciences; courses organized during long vacation in marine invertebrates, ecology, pollution, etc., and high school and college facilities for instruction in marine sciences; library of 20,000 vols; Chair. ROBERT E. CAWTHORN; Dir Dr ANTHONY H. KNAP; publ. *Currents* (2 a year and online).

Libraries and Archives
Hamilton

Bermuda Archives: Government Administration Bldg, 30 Parliament St, Hamilton HM 12; tel. 295-5151; fax 295-8751; internet www.gov.bm; f. 1949; repository for official and non-governmental records; Archivist KARLA HAYWARD.

Bermuda National Library: 13 Queen St, Par-la-Ville, Hamilton HM 11; tel. 295-2905; fax 292-8443; e-mail bdanatlib@gov.bm; internet www.bermudanationallibrary.bm; f. 1839; national and public library services; 113,792 vols; special collection of Bermudiana; extensive talking book and large print collns; Head Librarian C. JOANNE BRANGMAN; publ. *Bermuda National Bibliography* (4 a year; also online).

Museums and Art Galleries
Flatts

Bermuda Aquarium, Museum and Zoo: POB FL 145, Flatts FL BX; 40 North Shore Rd, Flatts FL 04; tel. 293-2727; fax 293 3176; e-mail idwalker@gov.bm; internet www.bamz.org; f. 1928; live zoological collection, aquarium with large reef tank, local natural history and other exhibits; library of 3,000 vols; Principal Curator Dr IAN WALKER (acting); publ. *Critter Talk* (quarterly).

Mangrove Bay

Bermuda Maritime Museum: POB MA 133, Mangrove Bay, MA BX; tel. 234-1333; fax 234-1735; e-mail marmuse@ibl.bm; internet www.bmm.bm; f. 1975; area includes fortress of Bermuda Dockyard and exhibits representing Bermuda maritime history; Dir Dr EDWARD C. HARRIS; Curator CHARLOTTE ANDREWS; publs *Bermuda Journal of Archaeology and Maritime History* (annually), *Maritimes* (members' magazine).

St George's

National Trust Museum: POB HM 61, Hamilton HM AX; Located at: 32 Duke of York St, St George's; tel. 297-1423; fax 236-0617; e-mail palmetto@bnt.bm; internet

www.bnt.bm; f. 1970; displays depicting Bermuda's role in the American Civil War; collection of antique furniture; Dir AMANDA OUTERBRIDGE.

Tucker House Museum: POB HM-61, Hamilton HM AX; Located at: 5 Water St, St George's; tel. 297-0545; fax 236-0617; e-mail palmetto@bnt.bm; internet www.bnt .bm; f. 1970; administered by the Bermuda National Trust: 18th-century house with period furniture; Dir AMANDA OUTERBRIDGE.

Smith's Parish

Verdmont House Museum: POB HM-61, Hamilton HM AX; Located at: 6 Verdmont Lane, off Collector's Hill, Smith's Parish; tel. 236-7639; fax 236-0617; e-mail palmetto@bnt

.bm; internet www.bnt.bm; administered by Bermuda National Trust; 18th c. house with period furniture; Dir AMANDA OUTERBRIDGE.

College

Bermuda College: POB PG 297, Paget PG BX; Located at: Stonington Ave, South Rd, Paget PG 04; tel. 236-9000; fax 239-4008; e-mail info@bercol.bm; internet www.bercol .bm; f. 1974; 65 teachers; 1,350 students; library: 30,000 vols; divisions of applied science and technology, business, liberal arts, hospitality; Pres. Dr CHARLES GREEN.

GIBRALTAR

Learned Societies

NATURAL SCIENCES

Biological Sciences

Gibraltar Ornithological and Natural History Society: Gibraltar Natural History Field Centre, Jews' Gate, Upper Rock Nature Reserve; tel. 72639; fax 74022; e-mail info@ gonhs.org; internet www.gonhs.org; f. 1978; research, conservation, education; 450 mems; Gen. Sec. Dr JOHN CORTES; publs *Alectoris* (annual), *Gibraltar Nature News* (2 a year), *Report of the Strait of Gibraltar Bird Observatory* (annual).

Libraries and Archives

Gibraltar

Gibraltar Garrison Library: POB 374; Located at: 2 Library Gardens; tel. 77418; fax 79927; e-mail gibgarlib@gibnynex.gi; f. 1793; Gibraltar and Western Mediterranean; 45,000 vols; Trust Sec. BRENDA BOAST.

Gibraltar Government Archives: 6 Convent Place; tel. 79461; fax 79461; e-mail gibarchives@gibnynex.gi; f. 1969; repository for official Government records; Archivist T. J. FINLAYSON.

John Mackintosh Hall Library: Gibraltar; tel. 78000; fax 40843; e-mail gfjmh@gibraltar .gi; f. 1964; attached European Documentation Centre; 33,000 vols; Librarian Dr G. FINLAYSON.

Museums and Art Galleries

Gibraltar

Gibraltar Museum: 18–20 Bomb House Lane; tel. 74289; fax 79158; e-mail jcfinlay@ gibnet.gi; internet www.gib.gi/museum; f. 1930; collection of local natural history, archaeology and palaeontology (especially Palaeolithic, Neolithic and Phoenician) and military history; Dir Dr J. C. FINLAYSON.

GUERNSEY

Learned Societies

GENERAL

Alderney Society: The Alderney Society Museum, High St, GY9 3TG, Alderney; tel. (1481) 823222; e-mail alderneymuseum@ alderney.net; internet www .alderneymuseum.org; f. 1966; 600 mems; publ. *Bulletin* (annually).

Société Guernesiaise: Candie Gardens, St Peter Port, GY1 1UG; tel. (1481) 725093; fax (1481) 726248; e-mail societe@cwgsy.net; internet www.societe.org.gg; f. 1882; sections: Archaeology, Astronomy, Botany,

Entomology, Family History, Geology, Historic Buildings, History, Marine Biology, Nature Conservation, Ornithology; also manages island's nature reserves; Pres. RICHARD HOCART; Sec. LAWNEY MARTIN; publs *Newsletter* (3 a year), *Transactions* (annual).

HISTORY, GEOGRAPHY AND ARCHAEOLOGY

Alderney Maritime Trust: St Anne's House, Queen Elizabeth II St, St Annes, GY9 3AA, Alderney; tel. (1481) 822249; f. 1994 by the States of Alderney for the

preservation, protection and management of historic shipwrecks off the coast of Alderney.

Libraries and Archives

St Peter Port

Guille-Allès Library: Market St, St Peter Port, GY1 1HB; tel. (1481) 720392; fax (1481) 712425; e-mail ga@library.gg; internet www .library.gg; f. 1882; administered by the Guille-Allès Trust to provide free library services for the community; Chief Librarian MAGGIE FALLA.

UNITED STATES OF AMERICA

The Higher Education System

Institutions of higher education pre-date the USA's independence from the United Kingdom in 1776, the oldest being Harvard University, which was founded in 1636. Over 500 universities and colleges were founded during the 19th century, particularly following the Morrill Land-Grants Acts of 1862 and 1890, which gave over Federal lands to the States for the purpose of establishing and funding educational institutions; the so-called 'A&M' (agricultural and mechanical) universities are among the most prominent of these institutions. There is no Federal system of higher education, which is primarily provided by State governments and private institutions. However, the Federal Department of Education is responsible for promoting education at all levels, dispensing Federal aid and enforcing civil rights statutes. The Bill of Rights of the US Constitution guarantees academic freedom at all levels. Higher education is offered by universities and two-year, four-year and community colleges. In 2001 there were 4,197 two-year and four-year universities and colleges, with a total enrolment of an estimated 16.6m. students in 2005.

Admission to higher education is often on the basis of the High School Graduation Diploma and results in Scholastic Aptitude Tests (SATS), with institutions also applying their own criteria. Two-year Associate degrees are offered by both four-year institutions and two-year junior, technical and community colleges (junior colleges are usually privately run institutions and community colleges are funded by State and local governments). Students who have been awarded Associate degrees may transfer into four-year universities and colleges to complete full degrees. The Bachelors is the main under-graduate degree and lasts four years, consisting of two years of general education and then two years of study in a 'major' subject. Bachelors degrees in specialist or technical fields last five years. Most degrees are awarded on a 'credit-semester' basis, under which the student is required to accumulate a specified number of credits each semester in order to graduate. The minimum number of credits required for the award of the Bachelors degree is 120.

Postgraduate education in US institutions is referred to as 'graduate school' because degrees at this level are administered by university graduate schools. Admission to graduate school requires the Bachelors and an application supported by transcripts, statements of purpose and letters of recommendation. Applicants will also be required to achieve good scores in at least one of several standardized tests, depending on the subject area. Among these tests are Graduate Record Examinations, Miller Analogies Test, Graduate Management Admissions Test, Law School Admissions Test and the Medical College Admission Test. Masters degrees last between one and three years and are available on a taught or research basis, the difference being that taught degrees prepare students for professional entry and research degrees prepare students for further postgraduate studies. The PhD is the most common doctoral-level degree, and lasts between five to 10 years following the award of the Masters. The PhD consists of a period of intensive study leading to examinations before the student undertakes research for a doctoral dissertation, which is presented and defended before a panel.

There is no established Federal framework of post-secondary technical and vocational qualifications. Occupational training takes place in the workplace and educational certificates, diplomas and degrees consist of both classroom-based learning and practical experience.

Accreditation of universities and colleges is administered by the six main regional accrediting bodies, which are recognized by the Department of Education and are members of the Council on higher Education Accreditation. They are: Middle States Association of Schools and Colleges (MSA), The Northwest Association of Schools and Colleges (NASC), North Central Association of Schools and Colleges (NCA), New England Association of Schools and Colleges, Inc. / Commission on Institutions of Higher Education (NEASC–CIHE), Southern Association of Colleges and Schools / Commission on Colleges (SACS–CC) and Western Association of Schools and Colleges / Accrediting Commission for Senior Colleges and Universities (WASC–Sr). There are also professional bodies and single-subject agencies which accredit specialist schools and individual programmes.

Regulatory and Representative Bodies

GOVERNMENT

Department of Education: 400 Maryland Ave, SW, Washington, DC 20202; tel. (202) 401-2000; fax (202) 401-0596; internet www.ed.gov; Secretary of Education MARGARET SPELLINGS.

ACCREDITATION

Council for Higher Education Accreditation: Suite 510, 1 Dupont Circle, NW, Washington, DC 20036; tel. (202) 955-6126; fax (202) 955-6129; e-mail chea@chea.org; internet www.chea.org; nat. advocate and institutional voice for self-regulation of academic quality through accreditation; recognizes 60 institutional and programmatic accrediting orgs; 3,000 mems (degree-granting colleges and univs); Chair. JOHN D. WILEY; Pres. JUDITH S. EATON.

ENIC/NARIC United States of America: United States Network for Education Information (USNEI)/US ENIC, Int. Affairs Office/OS, U.S. Dept of Education, 400 Maryland Ave, SW, Washington, DC 20202-8401; tel. (202) 401-3710; fax (202) 401-2508; e-mail stephen.hunt@ed.gov; internet www.ed.gov/nle/usnei; Dir, Planning and Policy Dr E. STEPHEN HUNT.

Middle States Association of Colleges and Schools: Middle States Commission on Higher Education: 3624 Market St, Philadelphia, PA 19104; tel. (267) 284-5000; e-mail info@msche.org; internet www.msche.org; f. Asscn 1887 as the College Asscn of Pennsylvania, present name 1975; the Comm. is a voluntary, non-governmental, membership assen that defines, maintains, and promotes educational excellence across instns with diverse missions, student populations and resources; it accredits degree-granting colleges and univs in the Middle States region, which includes DE, DC, MD, NJ, NY, PA, Puerto Rico, the US Virgin Islands and several locations internationally; Chair. of Comm.'s Exec. Cttee Dr JESSICA S. KOZLOFF; Pres. of Comm. JEAN AVNET MORSE; publ. *MSCHE Letter* (electronic newsletter, 3 a year).

New England Association of Schools and Colleges, Inc.: Commission on Institutions of Higher Education: New England Assen of Schools and Colleges, 209 Burlington Rd, Suite 201, Bedford, MA 01730-1433; tel. (781) 271-0022; fax (781) 271-0950; e-mail cihe@neasc.org; internet www.neasc.org/cihe/cihe.htm; f. Assen 1885; the Comm. is the regional accreditation agency for over 225 colleges and univs in the 6 New England states: CT, ME, MA, NH, RI and VT; 2 instns in Greece, 1 in Bulgaria and 3 in Switzerland are also affiliated with CIHE; Chair. of Comm. JUDITH R. GORDON; Dir of Comm. Dr BARBARA E. BRITTINGHAM.

North Central Association of Colleges and Schools: Higher Learning Commission: Suite 2400, 30 North LaSalle St, Chicago, IL 60602-2504; tel. (312) 263-0456; fax (312) 263-7462; internet www.ncahigherlearningcommission.org; ind. corpn that accredits degree-granting educational instns in the N Central region: AR, AZ, CO, IA, IL, IN, KS, MI, MN, MO, ND, NE, OH, OK, NM, SD, WI, WV and WY; Pres. of Comm. STEVEN D. CROW; Dir of Operations BERNADETTE A. IVERS.

Northwest Commission on Colleges and Universities: Suite 100, 8060 165th Ave, NE, Redmond, WA 98052; tel. (425) 558-4224; fax (425) 376-0596; internet www.nwccu.org; f. 1917; ind., non-profit membership org. recognized as the regional authority on educational quality and institutional effectiveness of higher education institutions in the seven-state Northwest region of AK, ID, MT, NV, OR, UT and WA; it fulfils its mission by establishing accreditation criteria and evaluation procedures by which the region's 160 instns are reviewed; Pres. Dr SANDRA E. ELMAN.

Southern Association of Colleges and Schools: Commission on Colleges: 1866 Southern Lane, Decatur, GA 30033; tel. (404) 679-4500; fax (404) 679-4558; internet www.sacscoc.org; recognized regional accrediting body in the 11 US Southern states (AL, FL, GA, KY, LA, MS, NC, SC, TN, TX and VA) and in Latin America for those instns of higher education that award associate, baccalaureate, masters or doctoral degrees; Chair. of Comm. PHILIP C. STONE; Pres. of Comm. Dr BELLE S. WHEELAN.

Western Association of Schools and Colleges: Accrediting Commission for Senior Colleges and Universities: 985 Atlantic Ave, Suite 100, Alameda, CA 94501; tel. (510) 748-9001; fax (510) 748-9797; e-mail wascsr@wascsenior.org; internet www.wascsenior.org; f. Asscn 1962 to promote the welfare, interests and devt of education in the Western Region; the Comm. accredits 151 instns in CA, HI and the Pacific Basin; Chair. of Comm. JOHN D. WELTY.

FUNDING

Alfred P. Sloan Foundation: Suite 2550, 630 Fifth Ave, New York, NY 10111; tel. (212) 649-1649; fax (212) 757-5117; internet www.sloan.org; f. 1934; makes grants for projects in science and technology, standard of living and economic performance, and education and careers in science and technology; Pres. RALPH E. GOMORY; publ. *Report* (annual).

American Association for Higher Education: 1 Dupont Circle, NW, Suite 360, Washington, DC 20036-1143; tel. (202) 293-6440; fax (202) 293-0073; e-mail info@aahe.org; internet www.aahe.org; f. 1969; sponsors projects and programmes in fields of teaching and learning that will improve the quality of American higher education; 9,500 mems; Pres. CLARA M. LOVETT; publs *AAHE Bulletin* (monthly Sept to June), *Change* (6 a year).

Foundation Center: 79 Fifth Ave, New York City, NY 10003; tel. (212) 620-4230; fax (212) 691-1828; internet fdncenter.org; offices in Washington, DC, San Francisco, Cleveland and Atlanta; f. 1956; makes available information about philanthropic foundations; maintains a full collection of foundation reports; library of 2,500 vols, 3,250 pamphlets and articles, 500 foundation reports, computer files of foundation grants, aperture card system containing foundation IRS returns; Pres. SARA ENGELHARDT; publs *Foundation Grants Index* (quarterly, and annual cumulation), *Foundation Directory* (annual), *Foundation 1000* (annual), *Guide to US Foundations, Their Officers, Trustees and Donors* (annual), *Foundation Grants to Individuals* (every 2 years), *Foundation Fundamentals, Grant Guides in 30 Subjects* (annual).

Kellogg, W. K., Foundation: 1 Michigan Avenue, E, Battle Creek, MI 49017-4012; tel. (269) 968-1611; fax (269) 968-0413; internet www.wkkf.org; f. 1930; philanthropic nonpartisan org. administering funds for activ-

ities in the fields of youth and education, health, food systems and rural devt, and philanthropy and volunteerism, in the USA, Latin America, the Caribbean and southern Africa; Pres./CEO STERLING K. SPEIRN.

Rockefeller Foundation: 420 Fifth Ave, New York, NY 10018; tel. (212) 869-8500; internet www.rockfound.org; f. 1913 to promote the well-being of mankind; makes grants in the fields of: agriculture, health, population sciences, the global environment, African initiatives, organized under the Int. Program to Support Science-Based Devt; arts and humanities; equal opportunity; school reform; Chair. of Board JAMES ORR, III.

Woodrow Wilson International Center for Scholars: 1 Woodrow Wilson Plaza, 1300 Pennsylvania Ave, NW, Washington, DC 20004-3027; tel. (202) 691-4000; fax (202) 691-4001; internet www.wilsoncenter.org; f. 1968; nonpartisan instn supported by public and private funds; provides a link between the world of ideas and the world of policy; fosters research, study, discussion and collaboration among a full spectrum of individuals concerned with policy and scholarship in nat. and world affairs; library of 20,000 vols, 250 periodicals; Pres. and Dir LEE H. HAMILTON (acting); Chair of Board of Trustees JOSEPH GILDENHORN.

NATIONAL BODIES

American Association of Collegiate Registrars and Admissions Officers: Suite 520, 1 Dupont Circle, NW, Washington, DC 20036; tel. (202) 293-9161; fax (202) 872-8857; e-mail sullivanj@aacrao.org; internet www.aacrao.org; provides professional devt, guidelines and voluntary standards to be used by higher education officials regarding the best practices in records management, admissions, enrolment management, admin. information technology and student services; more than 10,000 mems in 30 countries; Pres. PAUL AUCOIN; Exec. Dir JEROME SULLIVAN; publ. *College & University* (quarterly).

American Association of Community Colleges: Suite 410, 1 Dupont Circle, NW, Washington, DC 20036; tel. (202) 728-0200; fax (202) 833-2467; internet www.aacc.nche.edu; f. 1920 as American Asscn of Junior Colleges, present name 1992; aims to build a nation of learners by advancing America's community colleges; more than 1,100 mem. instns; Pres. and CEO GEORGE R. BOGGS.

American Association of State Colleges and Universities: 1307 New York Ave NW, 5th Floor, Washington, DC 20005-4701; tel. (202) 293-7070; fax (202) 296-5819; internet www.aascu.org; f. 1961 to improve higher education within its member institutions through co-operative planning, through studies and research on common educational problems, and through the development of a more unified programme of action; 425 mems; Pres. Dr CONSTANTINE W. CURRIS; publ. *Memo* (monthly).

American Association of University Professors: Suite 500, 1012 14th St NW, Washington, DC 20005-3465; tel. (202) 737-5900; fax (202) 737-5526; e-mail aaup@aaup.org; internet www.aaup.org; f. 1915; 44,000 mems; Pres. JANE L. BUCK; Gen. Sec. ROGER W. BOWEN; publ. *Academe: Bulletin of the AAUP* (6 a year).

American Council on Education: 1 Dupont Circle, Washington, DC 20036; tel. (202) 939-9300; fax (202) 833-4760; internet www.acenet.edu; f. 1918; 1,800 mem. instns and asscns; Pres. LAWRENCE BACOW; publs *ACE/Oryx Series on Higher Education, Educational Record* (quarterly), *Higher Education and National Affairs* (fortnightly).

American Federation of Teachers: 555 New Jersey Ave, NW, Washington, DC 20001; tel. (202) 879-4400; internet www.aft.org; f. 1916 to represent the economic, social and professional interests of classroom teachers; 1.4m. mems; Pres. EDWARD J. McELROY; publs *American Teacher* (8 a year), *American Educator* (quarterly), *PSRP Reporter* (newsletter for paraprofessionals and school-related personnel, quarterly), *Healthwire* (newspaper of the healthcare div. 6 a year), *AFT On Campus, Public Employee Advocate* (6 a year), *American Academic* (higher education policy, irreg.), *AFT e-Activist Network* (electronic), *AFT-Africa AIDS Campaign* (electronic), *AFT Healthcare General News* (electronic, 1 or 2 a week), *AFT Healthcare School Nurse List* (electronic, c. 5 a week), *AFT Higher Education News from the National* (electronic), *AFT Human Rights News* (electronic, quarterly), *AFT PLUS F.Y.I. Blast* (electronic, 2 a month), *AFT PSRP e-news* (electronic, 2 a week), *AFT Retiree e-news* (electronic, 20 a year).

American Vocational Association, Inc.: 1410 King St, Alexandria, VA 22314; tel. (703) 683-3111; fax (703) 683-7424; f. 1925; 40,000 mems; Exec. Dir BRET LOVEJOY; publs *Techniques* (magazine), *Vocational Education Weekly, School To Work Reporter*.

Association of American Colleges and Universities: 1818 R St, NW, Washington, DC 20009; tel. (202) 387-3760; fax (202) 265-9532; e-mail pub_desk@aacu.org; internet www.aacu.org; f. 1915 to improve undergraduate curriculum through research, projects, publications and meetings; to extend the opportunity of a liberal education to all potential students, regardless of academic specialization or intended career; 900 mems; Pres. CAROL SCHNEIDER; publs *Liberal Education* (quarterly), *Peer Review* (quarterly), *Diversity Digest* (3 a year).

Association of American Universities: Suite 550, 1200 New York Ave, NW, Washington, DC 20005; tel. (202) 408-7500; internet www.aau.edu; f. 1900; 62 mems; Pres. NILS HASSELMO.

Association of Community College Trustees: Suite 301, 1233 20th St, NW, Washington, DC 20036; tel. (202) 775-4667; fax (202) 223-1297; internet www.acct.org; promotes effective board governance through advocacy and education; Chair. KITTY BOYLE; Pres. and CEO J. NOAH BROWN.

Association of Governing Boards of Universities and Colleges: Suite 400, 1 Dupont Circle, Washington, DC 20036; tel. (202) 296-8400; fax (202) 223-7053; e-mail info@agb.org; internet www.agb.org; strengthens and protects the country's unique form of institutional governance through its research, services and advocacy; Pres. RICHARD D. LEGON.

Center for Quality Assurance in International Education: Suite 520, 1001 North Fairfax St, Alexandria, VA 22314; tel. (703) 519-0922; fax (703) 519-0997; e-mail cqaie@cqaie.org; internet www.cqaie.org; facilitates the comparative study of nat. quality and competency assurance mechanisms to improve efforts within countries and promote mobility among nat. systems; assists countries in the devt or enhancement of quality assurance systems for higher education; promotes the globalization of the professions; monitors issues of quality in the transnational movement of higher education; Chair. CAROL BOBBY; Exec. Dir Dr MARJORIE PEACE LENN.

College Board, The: 45 Columbus Ave, New York, NY 10023; tel. (212) 713-8000; internet www.collegeboard.com; f. 1900; not-for-profit membership asscn; mission is to connect students to college success and opportunity; offices in New York, Albany, NY, Bala Cynwyd, PA, Rosemont, IL, Waltham, MA, Duluth, GA, Tallahassee, FL, Austin, TX, San Jose, CA, and Sacramento, CA; more than 5,200 mem. schools, colleges, univs, and other educational orgs; Pres. GASTON CAPERTON.

Council on International Educational Exchange: 7 Custom House St, 3rd Floor, Portland, ME 04101; tel. (207) 553-7600; fax (207) 553-7699; e-mail studyinfo@ciee.org; internet ciee.org; f. 1947 as Council on Student Travel, present name 1967; creates and administers programmes that allow high school and univ. students and educators to study and teach abroad; offices in Portland and Boston, MA; Chair. MICHAEL STOHL; Pres. and CEO STEVAN TROOBOFF.

Education Commission of the States: Suite 1200, 700 Broadway, Denver, CO 80203-3460; tel. (303) 299-3600; fax (303) 296-8332; e-mail ecs@ecs.org; internet www.ecs.org; f. 1967; helps states develop effective policy and practice for public education by providing data, research, analysis and leadership; Chair. KATHLEEN SEBELIUS; Pres. RODERICK G. W. CHU; publs *The Progress of Education Reform* (research summaries, irreg.), *ECS e-Clips* (electronic newsletter on education news, daily), *ECS e-Connection* (electronic newsletter with links to key education information, weekly), *Citizenship Matters* (electronic newsletter on improving citizenship education in schools, 6 a year), *ECS Governance Notes* (electronic newsletter with links to key information on education governance, 6 a year), *ECS Leadership Links* (electronic newsletter with links to key information on education leadership, 6 a year), *ECS TQ Update* (electronic newsletter on improving the quality of teaching, 6 a year).

Institute of International Education: 809 United Nations Plaza, 2nd Floor, New York, NY 10017-3580; tel. (212) 883-8200; fax (212) 984-5452; internet www.iie.org; f. 1919; ind. non-profit org. working to promote closer educational relations between the people of the USA and those of other countries, strengthen and link instns of higher learning globally, rescue threatened scholars and advance academic freedom, build leadership skills and enhance the capacity of individuals and orgs to address local and global challenges; offices in Washington, DC, Chicago, Denver, Houston, San Francisco, China, Egypt, Hungary, India, Indonesia, Mexico, Qatar, Russia, Thailand, Ukraine and Vietnam; 900 mem. instns; Chair. THOMAS S. JOHNSON; Pres. and CEO Dr ALLAN E. GOODMAN; publ. *Opening Minds*.

NAFSA: Association of International Educators: 1307 New York Ave, NW, 8th Floor, Washington, DC 20005-4701; tel. (202) 737-3699; fax (202) 737-3657; e-mail inbox@nafsa.org; internet www.nafsa.org; f. 1948 as Nat. Asscn of Foreign Student Advisers, present name 1990; promotes int. education and provides professional devt opportunities; sets and upholds standards of good practice, and provides training opportunities; 9,000 mems; Pres RONALD MOFFATT; Exec. Dir and CEO MARLENE M. JOHNSON; publs *International Educator* (6 a year), *NAFSA.news* (electronic newsletter, weekly), *Policy Brief* (electronic, irreg.).

National Academy of Education: Suite 1049, 500 Fifth St, NW, Washington, DC 20001; e-mail nae.info@nyu.edu; internet www.nae.nyu.edu; f. 1965; up to 150 mems, 25 foreign assocs; Pres. NEL NODDINGS; Exec Dir AMY SWAUGER.

National Association of State Boards of Education: Suite 100, 277 South Washington St, Alexandria, VA 22314; tel. (703) 684-4000; fax (703) 836-2313; e-mail brendaw@nasbe.org; internet www.nasbe.org; f. 1958; works to strengthen state leadership in educational policy-making, promote excellence in the education of all students, advocate equality of access to educational opportunity, and assure continued citizen support for public education; Pres. W. BRADLEY BRYANT; Exec. Dir BRENDA L. WELBURN.

National Association of State Directors of Career Technical Education Consortium: The Hall of States, 444 North Capitol St, NW, Suite 830, Washington, DC 20001; tel. (202) 737-0303; fax (202) 737-1106; e-mail kgreen@careertech.org; internet www.careertech.org; f. 1920; provides leadership for career technical education's role in education, workforce preparation and economic devt; 200 mems; Pres. RICH KATT; Exec. Dir KIMBERLY A. GREEN.

National Association of State Directors of Teacher Education and Certification: 1225 Providence Rd, PMB 116, Whitinsville, MA 01588; tel. (508) 380-1202; fax (508) 278-5342; e-mail rje@nasdtec.com; internet www.nasdtec.org; represents professional standards boards and comms and state depts of education in all 50 states, DC, the Dept of Defense Education Activity, the US Territories, AB, BC, and ON that are responsible for the preparation, licensure, and discipline of educational personnel; promotes high standards for educators, teacher mobility across state lines, comprehensive personnel screening and a database on teacher discipline; Pres. PETER DONOVAN; Exec. Dir ROY EINREINHOFER; publ. *The Communicator* (irreg.).

National Association of State Universities and Land-Grant Colleges: Suite 400, 1307 New York Ave, NW, Washington, DC 20005-4722; tel. (202) 478-6040; fax (202) 478-6046; internet www.nasulgc.org; f. 1887; a voluntary, non-profit asscn supporting high-quality public higher education and its mem. instns as they perform their teaching, research, and public service roles; provides a forum for the discussion and devt of policies affecting higher education and the public interest; 215 mem. instns; Chair. Dr NANCY L. ZIMPHER; Pres. PETER MCPHERSON.

National Education Association of the United States: 1201 16th St, NW, Washington, DC 20036-3290; tel. (202) 833-4000; fax (202) 822-7974; internet www.nea.org; f. 1857; 2,700,000 mems; 100,000 life mems; Pres. REG WEAVER; Dir in each State; publs *NEA Today* (9 a year), *This Active Life*, *Thought and Action* (2 a year), *Tomorrow's Teachers* (annual).

National Society for the Study of Education: Univ. of Illinois College of Education, 1040 West Harrison St, M/C 147, Chicago, IL 60607; tel. (312) 996-4529; fax (312) 996-8134; e-mail nsse@uic.edu; internet www.uic.edu/educ/nsse; f. 1901; 2,000 mems; Sec. DEBRA MIRETZKY.

State Higher Education Executive Officers: Suite 100, 3035 Center Green Dr., Boulder, CO 80301-2251; tel. (303) 541-1600; fax (303) 541-1639; e-mail sheeo@sheeo.org; internet www.sheeo.org; f. 1954; works to develop and sustain excellent systems of higher education; emphasizes the importance of state planning and co-ordination for higher education by promoting effective strategic planning and statewide co-ordination and governance; speaks as a nat. org. in public and private forums, promoting the interests of the states in effectively planning and

financing higher education; Chair. ROBERT T. PERRY; Pres. PAUL LINGENFELTER.

United States Network for Education Information: Nat. Library of Education, 400 Maryland Ave, SW, Washington, DC 20202-5523; tel. (800) 424-1616; fax (202) 205-6688; e-mail usnei@ed.gov; internet www.ed.gov/about/offices/list/ous/international/usnei/edlite-index.html; f. 1996; provides a focused description and guide to American education and to foreign systems of education to facilitate int. educational mobility; Man. Dr E. STEPHEN HUNT.

Learned Societies
GENERAL

American Academy of Arts and Letters: 633 West 155th St, New York, NY 10032-7599; tel. (212) 368-5900; fax (212) 491-4615; f. 1898; 250 mems; Pres. LOUIS AUCHINCLOSS; Exec. Dir VIRGINIA DAJANI; publ. *Proceedings* (annually).

American Academy of Arts and Sciences: Norton's Woods, 136 Irving St, Cambridge, MA 02138; tel. (617) 576-5000; fax (617) 576-5050; e-mail aaas@amacad.org; internet www.amacad.org; f. 1780; 4,600 mems (4,000 American fellows, 600 foreign hon. mems); Pres. PATRICIA MEYER SPACKS; Sec. EMILIO BIZZI; Senior Exec. Officer LESLIE C. BERLOWITZ; publs *Daedalus* (4 a year), *Bulletin* (4 a year), *Records* (annually).

American Council of Learned Societies: 633 Third Ave, New York, NY 10017-6795; tel. (212) 697-1505; fax (212) 949-8058; e-mail grants@acls.org; internet www.acls.org; f. 1919; supports humanities research through fellowships and grants awarded to individuals, groups and institutions; represents humanities scholars and promotes the scholarly humanities in the USA and international public and policy arenas; provides a forum for learned societies to discuss and suggest improvements in scholarship, education and communication among humanities scholars; 68 mem. socs concerned with the advancement of humanistic studies in the humanities and social sciences; Pres. PAULINE YU; publs *Annual Report*, *Occasional Paper series*.

American Philosophical Society: 104 South Fifth St, Philadelphia, PA 19106-3387; tel. (215) 440-3400; fax (215) 440-3436; internet www.amphilsoc.org; f. 1743 by Benjamin Franklin, the oldest learned society in the USA; mems are elected by the Society on the basis of distinction in any field of learning; there are five classes of membership: mathematical and physical sciences, biological sciences, social sciences, humanities, and the professions, arts and affairs; the Society meets twice a year (April, November) for symposia, lectures and presenting awards; it makes grants for research, operates a distinguished library rich in historical MSS, chiefly relating to the history of science in America (see Special Libraries), and awards prizes including the Magellanic Premium, the oldest American scientific award; publishes several books each year and engages in community service; it owns four buildings: Philosophical Hall (1789, a National Historical Landmark), Library Hall (105 S. Fifth St), Benjamin Franklin Hall (427 Chestnut St) and Richardson Hall (431 Chestnut St); the first two buildings contain numerous valuable portraits (paintings and statuary) of distinguished former members; museum and exhibition programme; 912 mems (766 US citizens, 146 foreign); Pres.

BARUCH S. BLOMBERG; publs *Transactions, Proceedings, Memoirs, Year Book*.

Asia Foundation: POB 3223, San Francisco, CA 94119 (Main Office); tel. (415) 982-4640; fax (415) 392-8863; e-mail info@asiafound-dc.org; internet www.asiafoundation.org; offices in Washington, DC, and 13 Asian and Pacific island countries; f. 1954; library of 3,370 vols on current Asian and world affairs; assists Asian economic and social development through private American support to Asian institutions, organizations and individuals working towards constructive social change, stable political development and equitable economic growth within their societies; provides small grants, primarily in fields of law and public administration, rural and community development, communications and libraries, Asian regional co-operation; Books for Asia Program distributes books and journals to libraries and institutions in Asia; Pres. DOUG BEREUTER; Exec. Vice-Pres. BARNETT F. BARON; publ. *Annual Report*.

Connecticut Academy of Arts and Sciences: POB 208211, Yale University, New Haven, CT 06520-8211; tel. (203) 432-3113; fax (203) 432-5712; e-mail caas@yale.edu; internet www.yale.edu/caas; f. 1799; 400 mems; library merged with Yale University Library; Pres. FRANKLIN ROBINSON; Sec. MARGOT KOHORN; publs *A Manual of the Writings in Middle English* (all irregular), *Memoirs, Transactions*.

English-Speaking Union of the United States: 144 East 39th St, New York, NY 10016; tel. (212) 818-1200; fax (212) 867-4177; internet www.esuus.org; f. 1920; to increase communication and understanding among people of all nationalities through the medium of the English language; initiates and implements innovative educational programmes; non profit; 10,000 mems; 76 brs in USA; library of 6,000 vols; Chair. WILLIAM R. MILLER; Pres. and Exec. Dir ALICE BOYNE; publ. *E-SU Today*.

Hispanic Society of America: 613 West 155th St, New York, NY 10032; tel. (212) 926-2234; fax (212) 690-0743; e-mail info@hispanicsociety.org; internet www.hispanicsociety.org; f. 1904; 400 mems; professional research staff; reference library and museum; Dir MITCHELL A. CODDING.

National Academies of Sciences and Engineering, Institute of Medicine and National Research Council: 2101 Constitution Ave NW, Washington, DC 20418; tel. (202) 334-2000; internet national-academies .org; f. 1863; established by Congressional charter; linked group of instns, co-ordinating their advice to fed. govt; publ. *Proceedings of the National Academy of Sciences* (weekly).

Individual institutions:

Institute of Medicine: 500 Fifth St, NW, Washington, DC 20001; tel. (202) 334-2352; fax (202) 334-1412; e-mail iomwww@nas.edu; internet www.iom.edu; f. 1970; 1,060 mems; Pres. HARVEY V. FINEBERG; Exec. Officer SUSANNE A. STOIBER; publ. *IOM News* (quarterly).

National Academy of Engineering: 500 Fifth St, NW, Washington, DC 20001; tel. (202) 334-3200; fax (202) 334-2290; internet www.nae.edu; f. 1964; 1,622 mems; Pres. WILLIAM A. WULF; Home Sec. W. DALE COMPTON; Foreign Sec. GEORGE BUGLIARELLO; Exec. Officer LANCE DAVIS.

National Academy of Sciences: 2101 Constitution Ave NW, Washington, DC 20418; internet www.nas.edu; f. 1863; sections: Mathematics; Astronomy; Physics; Chemistry; Geology; Geophysics; Biochemistry; Cellular and Developmental Biology; Physiology and Pharmacology; Cellular and Molecular Neuroscience; Plant Biology; Genetics; Evolutionary Biology; Systems Neuroscience; Biophysics and Computational Biology; Engineering Sciences; Applied Mathematical Sciences; Applied Physical Sciences; Computer and Information Sciences; Medical Genetics, Haematology and Oncology; Medical Physiology and Metabolism; Immunology; Microbial Biology; Anthropology; Psychology; Social and Political Sciences; Economic Sciences; Animal, Nutritional and Applied Microbial Sciences; Plant, Soil and Microbial Sciences; Environmental Sciences and Ecology, Human Environmental Sciences; 2,350 mems (2,000 ordinary, 350 foreign assoc.); President BRUCE ALBERTS; Home Sec. JOHN I. BRAUMAN; Foreign Sec. MICHAEL T. CLEGG.

National Research Council: 2101 Constitution Ave NW, Washington DC 20418; internet www.national-academies.org/nrc; f. 1916 by the National Academy of Sciences as the operating arm of the National Academy of Sciences and the National Academy of Engineering.; Chair, National Research Council BRUCE M. ALBERTS; Vice-Chair WILLIAM A. WULF.

National Foundation on the Arts and the Humanities: Washington, DC 20506; f. 1965 as an independent agency in the Executive Branch of Government to develop and promote a broadly conceived national policy of support for the humanities and the arts in the United States.

Constituent institutions:

National Council on the Arts: Washington, DC 20506; tel. (202) 682-5433; fax (202) 682-5538; f. 1964; advises the Chairman of the National Endowment for the Arts on policies, programmes and procedures and reviews applications for financial assistance; Chair. of Council is Chair. of the Arts Endowment; 20 mems (14 private citizens appointed by the President for a 6-year term, 6 ex-officio from Congress).

National Council on the Humanities: Washington, DC 20506; f. 1965; advises the Chairman of the National Endowment for the Humanities on policies, programmes and procedures and reviews applications for financial assistance; 26 private citizen mems appointed by the President for six-year terms (approx. one-third of the appointments expire every two years); Chair. of Council is Chair. of the Humanities Endowment.

National Endowment for the Arts: 1100 Pennsylvania Ave, NW Washington, DC 20506; tel. (202) 682-5400; e-mail webmgr@arts.endow.gov; internet arts .endow.gov; f. 1965 to establish and carry out a programme of grants-in-aid to non-profit groups, individuals of exceptional talent and state art agencies, which will promote progress in the arts; Chair. DANA GIOIA (acting).

National Endowment for the Humanities: 1100 Pennsylvania Ave, NW Washington, DC 20506; e-mail info@neh .gov; internet www.neh.gov; f. 1965 to establish and carry out a programme supporting projects of research, education and public activity in the humanities; Chair. Prof. BRUCE COLE.

Federal Council on the Arts and the Humanities: Washington, DC 20506; f. 1965 to co-ordinate the activities of the two Endowments with related federal agencies and to carry out the federal indemnity programme; mems include the Chairmen of the two Endowments; the Secs of the Depts of Education, Interior, State, Commerce, Transportation, Housing and Urban Development, and Labor; the Commissioners of the Fine Arts Commission, Administration on Aging, and Public Buildings Service; the Administrators of the Veterans Administration and the General Services Administration; the Dirs of the National Science Foundation, and Institute of Museum and Library Services; the Librarian of Congress; the Archivist of the United States; and the Chairman of the National Museum Services Board; mems who do not vote on indemnity include the Dir, National Gallery of Art; Sec. of the Senate; Sec., Smithsonian Institution; Member, House of Representatives.

New York Academy of Sciences: 2 East 63rd St, New York, NY 10021; tel. (212) 838-0230; fax (212) 888-2894; e-mail nyas@nyas .org; internet www.nyas.org; f. 1817; sections of Anthropology, Atmospheric Sciences and Geology, Biochemical Pharmacology, Chemical Biology, Chemical Biology, Computational Biology and Bioinformatics, Emerging Infectious Diseases, Environmental Sciences, Genome Integrity, Genomic Medicine, History and Philosophy of Science, Imaging, Microbiology, Nanobiotechnology, Neurogenerative Diseases, Neuroimmunology, Psychology, RNAi, Science Education, Systems Biology, Vision Research, Women Investigators Network, Women in Science; 22,000 mems; Pres. ELLIS RUBINSTEIN; publ. *The Annals*.

North American Spanish Language Academy/Academia Norteamericana de la Lengua Española: GPO Box 349, New York, NY 10116; tel. (718) 761-0556; fax (718) 761-0556; e-mail acadnorteamerica@aol.com; f. 1973; mem. of Asociación de Academias de la Lengua Española; corresp. of Real Academia, Spain; 36 mems; Dir ODÓN BETANZOS-PALACIOS; Joint Sec. GUMERSINDO YÉPEZ; Joint Sec. GERARDO PIÑA-ROSALES; publs *Boletín* (every 2 years), *Glosas* (4 a year).

Smithsonian Institution: Washington, DC 20560; tel. (202) 357-2700; e-mail info@si .edu; internet www.si.edu; f. 1846 for the 'increase and diffusion of knowledge' by bequest of English scientist James Smithson; a museum, education and research complex; 17 mems of the Board of Regents, incl. the Chief Justice of the USA and the Vice-Pres. of the USA, three mems of the Senate and of the House of Representatives, and nine citizen mems; Chancellor THE CHIEF JUSTICE OF THE UNITED STATES; Secretary (Presiding Officer) CRISTIÁN SAMPER (acting); Deputy Secretary SHEILA BURKE; Under Secretaries DAVID L. EVANS (Science), NED RIFKIN (Art); publs *Smithsonian Contributions to Anthropology, Smithsonian Contributions to Astrophysics, Smithsonian Studies in Air and Space, Smithsonian Contributions to Botany, Smithsonian Contributions to the Earth Sciences, Smithsonian Contributions to the Marine Sciences, Smithsonian Contributions to Paleobiology, Smithsonian Contributions to Zoology, Smithsonian Studies in History and Technology, American Art Journal, Archives of American Art Journal*.

Constituent libraries and archives; (unless indicated otherwise, each institution listed below has a separate entry in the USA chapter):

Air and Space Museum Archives: see entry for National Air and Space Museum.

Ralph Rinzler Folklife Archives and Collections: see entry for Center for Folklife and Cultural Heritage.

Smithsonian Institution Libraries: 22–branch library system: for details of individual libraries, see under entries for

Smithsonian instns. For general details of the system, see main Smithsonian libraries entry.

Smithsonian Institution Archives.

Archives of American Art.

Archives of American Gardens: see entry for Smithsonian Horticulture Services Division.

Eliot Elisofon Photographic Archives: see entry for African Art Museum.

Juley Photographic Archive: see entry for Smithsonian American Art Museum and its Renwick Gallery.

American History Museum Archives Center: see entry for National Museum for American History.

National Anthropological Archives and Human Studies Film Archives: see entry for National Museum of Natural History.

Constituent museums and art galleries; (unless indicated otherwise, each institution listed below has a separate entry in the USA chapter):

Anacostia Museum and Center for African American History and Culture.

Arts and Industries Building.

Cooper-Hewitt, National Design Museums.

Freer Gallery of Art and Arthur M. Sackler Gallery.

Hirshhorn Museum and Sculpture Garden.

National Air and Space Museums.

National Museum of African Art.

National Museum of American History, Behring Center.

National Museum of the American Indian.

National Museum of Natural History.

National Portrait Gallery.

National Postal Museum.

National Zoological Park.

Smithsonian American Art Museum and the Renwick Gallery.

Smithsonian Institution Building–the Castle: see main Smithsonian entry for address and contact details.

Constituent science centres; (unless indicated otherwise, each institution listed below has a separate entry in the USA chapter):

Astrophysical Observatory (SAO): see entry for Harvard-Smithsonian Center for Astrophysics.

Carrie-Bow Marine Field Station – Caribbean Coral Reef Ecosystems (CCRE): see entry in Belize chapter.

Center for Earth and Planetary Studies.

Conservation and Research Center: see entry for Smithsonian National Zoological Park.

Environmental Research Center (SERC).

Marine Science: network of Smithsonian instns — see entries for Environmental Research Center (SERC), Marine Station at Fort Pierce, CCRE, Tropical Research Institute, National Museum of Natural History, and National Zoological Park.

Migratory Bird Center: see entry for Smithsonian National Zoological Park.

Natural History Museum Research and Collections: see entry for National Museum of Natural History.

Tropical Research Institute (STRI): see entry in Panama chapter.

Conservation research units; (unless indicated otherwise, each institution listed below has a separate entry in the USA chapter):

African Art Museum Conservation Research Department: see entry for National Museum of African Art.

Center for Materials Research and Education.

Freer and Sackler Galleries Department of Conservation and Scientific Research: see entries for Freer Gallery of Art and Arthur M. Sackler Gallery.

Cultural and scholarly programmes; (unless indicated otherwise, each institution listed below has a separate entry in the USA chapter):

Asian Pacific American Program:; f. 1997 to provide leadership and support for all Asian Pacific America (APA) activities at the Smithsonian; Dir FRANKLIN ODO.

Center for Education and Museum Studies.

Center for Folklife and Cultural Heritage.

Jerome and Dorothy Lemelson Center for the Study of Invention and Innovation.

Latino Initiatives: see entry for Smithsonian Center for Latino Initiatives.

National Science Resources Center.

AGRICULTURE, FISHERIES AND VETERINARY SCIENCE

Agricultural History Society: Business Office: Economic Research Service, Room 2103, 1800 M St NW, Washington, DC 20036-5831; tel. (202) 694-5348; f. 1919 to encourage interest in, promote the study of, and facilitate research and publication on the history of agriculture; incorporated 1924 as a non-profit organization; 1,400 mems; Pres. LORENA S. WALSH; Sec. LOWELL K. DYSON; publ. *Agricultural History* (quarterly).

American Dairy Science Association: 1111 N. Dunlap Ave, Savoy, IL 61874; tel. (217) 356-5146; fax (217) 398-4119; e-mail adsa@assochq.org; internet www.adsa.org; f. 1906; 4,654 mems; Pres. MICHAEL F. HUTJENS; Exec. Dir BRENDA CARLSON; publ. *Journal of Dairy Science* (monthly).

American Forests: POB 2000, Washington, DC 20013; tel. (202) 737-1944; internet www.americanforests.org; f. 1875; 35,000 mems; Chair. KEVIN DAUGHERTY.

American Society for Horticultural Science: 113 South West St, Ste 200, Alexandria, VA 22314-2851; tel. (703) 836-4606; fax (703) 836-2024; internet www.ashs.org; f. 1903; 5,000 mems; field of activities: to promote and encourage scientific research and education in all branches of horticulture; Chair CARY MITCHELL; Pres. FREDERICK S. DAVIES; publs *Hort Science* (every 2 months), *Journal* (every 2 months), *HortTechnology* (quarterly).

American Society of Agricultural Engineers: 2950 Niles Rd, St Joseph, MI 49085; tel. (269) 429-0300; fax (269) 429-3852; e-mail hq@asae.org; internet www.asae.org; f. 1907; 9,000 mems; Exec. Vice-Pres. MELISSA MOORE; publs *Applied Engineering in Agriculture* (6 a year), *Agricultural Safety and Health* (4 a year), *Resource Magazine* (monthly), *Transactions* (6 a year), *Standards* (annually).

American Society of Agronomy: 677 South Segoe Rd, Madison, WI 53711; tel. (608) 273-8080; fax (608) 273-2021; e-mail headquarters@agronomy.org; internet www

.agronomy.org; f. 1907; 12,600 mems; Exec. Vice-Pres. ELLEN BERGFELD; publs *Agronomy Journal* (every 2 months), *Crop Science* (6 a year), *Journal of Environmental Quality* (6 a year), *Journal of Natural Resources and Life Sciences Education* (annually), *Soil Science Society of America* (6 a year), *Soil Survey Horizons* (quarterly), *Vadose Zone* (4 a year).

American Society of Animal Science: c/o Dr Ellen Bergfeld, 1111 N. Dunlap St, Savoy, IL 61874-9604; tel. (217) 356-9050; fax (217) 398-4119; e-mail asa@assochq.org; internet www.asas.org; f. 1908; promotes development of sciences beneficial to animal production; 6,500 mems; Pres. Dr JAMES R. MALES; Exec. Dir Dr JEROME F. BAKER; publ. *Journal of Animal Science* (monthly).

American Veterinary Medical Association: 1931 N. Meacham Rd, Schaumburg, IL 60173-4360; tel. (847) 925-8070; fax (847) 925-1329; e-mail avmainfo@avma.org; internet www.avma.org; f. 1863; 58,000 mems; Exec. Vice-Pres. Dr BRUCE LITTLE; library of 5,000 vols, 400 periodicals; publs *Journal of the AVMA* (every 2 weeks), and, *American Journal of Veterinary Research* (monthly).

Association for International Agricultural and Extension Education: POB 110540, Gainesville, FL 32611-0540; tel. (353) 392-0502; fax (353) 392-9585; internet www.aiaee.org; f. 1984 to provide a professional association and network of agricultural educators with the aim of improving and strengthening agricultural education programmes and institutions, especially in developing countries; c. 200 mems; Pres. JIM PHELAN; Sec. MIKE MCGIRR; publs *The Informer* (4 a year), *Journal* (4 a year).

Council for Agricultural Science and Technology: 4420 West Lincoln Way, Ames, IA 50014-3447; tel. (515) 292-2125; fax (515) 292-4512; e-mail cast@cast-science.org; internet www.cast-science.org; f. 1972; non-profit consortium of scientific societies, organizations, companies, scientists and citizens interested in public policy and the science of food and agriculture; compiles scientific information for Congress, the public, journalists and educators; 4,000 mems; Pres. STANLEY M. FLETCHER; Exec. Vice-Pres. Dr TERESA A. GRUBER; publ. *NewsCAST*.

Poultry Science Association Inc.: 1111 N. Dunlap St, Savoy, IL 61874; tel. (217) 356-3182; fax (217) 398-4119; internet www.poultryscience.org; f. 1908; 1,800 mems; Pres. PATRICIA Y. HESTER; publs *Applied Poultry Research* (monthly), *Poultry Science* (monthly).

Society of American Foresters: 5400 Grosvenor Lane, Bethesda, MD 20814-2198; tel. (301) 897-8720; fax (301) 897-3690; e-mail safweb@safnet.org; internet www.safnet.org; f. 1900; 18,000 mems; Pres. HARRY V. WIANT Jr; Exec. Vice-Pres. WILLIAM H. BANZHAF; publs *Journal of Forestry* (monthly), *Forestry Source* (monthly), *Forest Science* (quarterly), *Southern Journal of Applied Forestry* (quarterly), *Northern Journal of Applied Forestry* (quarterly), *Western Journal of Applied Forestry* (quarterly).

Soil Science Society of America: c/o Ellen Bergfeld, 677 South Segoe Rd, Madison, WI 53711; tel. (608) 273-8080; fax (608) 273-2021; e-mail headquarters@soils.org; internet www.soils.org; f. 1936; 5,363 mems; Exec. Vice-Pres. ELLEN BERGFELD; publs *Soil Science Society of America Journal* (6 a year), *Journal of Environmental Quality* (6 a year).

ARCHITECTURE AND TOWN PLANNING

American Institute of Architects: 1735 New York Ave, NW, Washington, DC 20006;

tel. (202) 626-7300; fax (202) 626-7547; e-mail infocentral@aia.org; internet www .aia.org; f. 1857; 74,000 mems; library of 30,400 vols; Pres. DOUGLAS L. STEIDL; publ. *AIArchitect*.

American Planning Association: 122 S. Michigan Ave, Suite 1600, Chicago, IL 60603-6107; tel. (312) 431-9100; fax (312) 431-9985; internet www.planning.org; f. 1909; non-profit research, educational and professional organization for city planners and others involved in land use and community development; 30,000 mems; includes American Institute of Certified Planners (AICP); Pres. APA DAVID M. SIEGEL; Pres. AICP SUE SCHWARTZ; publs *APA Journal* (quarterly), *Planning* (monthly), *Planning and Environmental Law* (monthly), *PAS Memo*, *Zoning Practice* (monthly), *Practicing Planner* (quarterly, online), *The Commissioner* (quarterly).

National Trust for Historic Preservation in the United States: 1785 Massachusetts Ave, NW, Washington, DC 20036-2117; tel. (202) 588-6000; fax (202) 588-6038; internet www.nationaltrust.org; f. 1949 to encourage preservation of buildings, sites and objects significant in American history and culture; 200,000 mems; library: library (at Architecture School, Univ. of Maryland, College Park) of 14,000 vols, 400 periodicals; Pres. RICHARD MOE; Exec. Vice-Pres. DAVID J. BROWN; publs *Historic Preservation* (every 2 months), *Historic Preservation Forum*, *Historic Preservation News* (monthly), *Preservation Law Reporter*.

Society of Architectural Historians: 1365 N. Astor St, Chicago, IL 60610-2144; tel. (312) 573-1365; fax (312) 573-1141; e-mail info@sah.org; internet www.sah.org; f. 1940; 3,500 mems; Pres. THERESE O'MALLEY; First Vice-Pres. BARRY BERGDOLL; Sec. ROBERT CRAIG; publs *Journal* (quarterly), *Newsletter* (every 2 months).

BIBLIOGRAPHY, LIBRARY SCIENCE AND MUSEOLOGY

American Association of Law Libraries: 53 West Jackson Blvd, Chicago, IL 60604; tel. (312) 939-4764; fax (312) 431-1097; internet www.aallnet.org; f. 1906; 5,000 mems; Pres. CLAIRE M. GERMAIN; publs *Law Library Journal* (quarterly), *Index to Foreign Legal Periodicals* (quarterly), *Directory of Law Libraries* (annually), *AALL Spectrum* (10 times a year).

American Association of Museums: Suite 400, 1575 Eye St, NW, Washington, DC 20005; tel. (202) 289-1818; fax (202) 289-6578; internet www.aam-us.org; f. 1906; promotes museums as cultural resources and represents interests of museum profession; 15,000 mems; programmes incl. Accreditation, Museum Assessment, Technical Information Service, Continuing Education, Govt Affairs, int. programmes and AAM/ICOM; the Asscn is governed by a board of dirs, who are museum professionals; Chair. ED ABLE; publs *Aviso* (monthly), *Museum News* (every 2 months), *The Official Museum Directory* (annual).

American Library Association: 50 East Huron St, Chicago, IL 60611; tel. (312) 944-6780; fax (312) 440-9374; e-mail library@ala .org; internet www.ala.org; f. 1876; promotes effective library and information services and public access to information; offers professional services and publications to mems and non-mems; 64,000 mems; library of 24,000 vols; Pres. MICHAEL GORMAN; Exec. Dir KEITH MICHAEL FIELS; publs *American Libraries* (monthly), *Booklist* (every 2 weeks), *Children and Libraries: The Journal of the Association for Library Service to Children (ALSC)* (3 a year), *Choice* (monthly), *College and Research Libraries* (every 2 months), *Information Technology and Libraries* (quarterly), *Documents to the People (DttP)* (quarterly), *EMIE Bulletin* (quarterly), *Federal Librarian* (quarterly), *Information Technology and Libraries (ITAL)* (quarterly), *Interface* (quarterly), *Knowledge Quest* (5 a year), *Library Administration & Management* (quarterly), *Library Resources and Technical Services* (quarterly), *Library Technology Reports* (every 2 months), *Newsletter on Intellectual Freedom* (every 2 months), *Public Libraries* (6 a year), *RBM: A Journal of Rare Books, Manuscripts, and Cultural Heritage* (2 a year), *RUSQ* (quarterly), *School Library Media Research*, *Young Adult Library Services* (quarterly).

American Society for Information Science and Technology (ASIST)/formerly American Society for Information Science (ASIS): Suite 510, 1320 Fenwick Lane, Silver Spring, MD 20910; tel. (301) 495-0900; fax (301) 495-0810; e-mail asis@ asis.org; internet www.asis.org; f. 1937 as American Documentation Institute, renamed American Society for Information Science 1968, current name 2000; concerned with the development of advanced methodologies and techniques that contribute to the more efficient use of information; acts as a bridge between research and development and the requirements of diverse types of information systems; comprises managers, designers and users of information systems and technology; 4,000 mems; Pres. NICHOLAS J. BELKIN; Exec. Dir RICHARD HILL; publs *Journal*, *Bulletin* (every 2 months), *Annual Review of Information Science and Technology*, *Annual Proceedings*.

American Theological Library Association: 250 S Wacker Drive, Suite 1600, Chicago, IL 60606-5889; tel. (312) 454-5100; fax (312) 454-5505; e-mail atla@atla.com; internet www.atla.com; f. 1946; 1,000 mems; library of 30,000 monologue titles preserved on microfiche and microfilm, 2,000 microfilm serial titles; Exec. Dir DENNIS A. NORLIN; publs *Newsletter* (4 a year), *Summary of Proceedings* (annually), *Theology Cataloging Bulletin* (4 a year), *Annual Report*.

Art Libraries Society of North America (ARLIS/NA): Suite 232, 329 March Rd, Box 11, Kanata, ON K2K 2E1, Canada; tel. (800) 817-0621; fax (919) 599-7027; e-mail arlisna@ igs.net; internet www.arlisna.org; f. 1972; sponsors conferences and workshops, distributes publications, grants awards for art book publishing and student essays on visual librarianship; affiliated with ARLIS (UK), ARLIS (Australia-New Zealand), ARLIS (Norge), ARLIS (Norden), American Library Asscn, Visual Resources Asscn and College Art Asscn; 20 US and Canadian chapters, 1,365 mems worldwide; Pres. JEANNE M. BROWN; Exec. Dir ELIZABETH CLARKE; publs *Art Documentation* (2 a year), *ARLIS/NA Update* (6 a year), *Occasional Papers* (irregular), *Topical Papers* (irregular), *Handbook and List of Members* (annually).

Association for Library and Information Science Education: 1055 Commerce Park Drive, Suite 110, POB 4219, Oak Ridge, TN 37830; tel. (865) 425-0155; fax (865) 481-0390; e-mail contact@alise.org; internet www .alise.org; f. 1915; 83 institutional mems; 650 personal mems; Pres. JOHN BUDD; Exec. Dir DEBORAH YORK; publs *Journal of Education for Library and Information Science* (quarterly), *Library and Information Science Education Statistical Report* (annually).

Association of Academic Health Sciences Library Directors: c/o Houston Academy of Medicine—Texas Medical Center Library, 1133 M. D. Anderson Blvd, Houston, TX 77030; tel. (713) 790-7060; fax (713) 790-7052; f. 1978; 125 mems; Pres. JUDITH MESSERLE; Sec. SANDRA WILSON; publs *AAHSLD News*, *Annual Report*, *Annual Statistics of Medical School Libraries in the United States and Canada*, *Membership Directory*.

Association of Art Museum Directors: 41 East 65th St, New York, NY 10021; tel. (212) 249-4423; fax (212) 535-5039; e-mail canagnos@aamd.org; internet www.aamd .org; f. 1916 to promote the development of a scholarly and creative role for art museums and their directors in the cultural life of the nation; to apply its members' knowledge and experience in the field of art to the promotion of the public good; to encourage communication among art museums and their directors; 168 mems; Pres. MATTHEW TEITELBAUM; Sec. ANNE HAWLEY.

Association of Research Libraries: 21 Dupont Circle, Suite 800, Washington, DC 20036; tel. (202) 296-2296; fax (202) 872-0884; e-mail arlhq@arl.org; internet www.arl .org; f. 1932; 123 institutional mems; Pres. ANN WOLPERT; publs *ARL: A Bimonthly Report on Research Library Issues and Actions from ARL, CNI, and SPARC* (6 a year), *ARL Annual Salary Survey* (statistical compilation; annually), *ARL Statistics* (statistical compilation), *ARL Proceedings* (online).

Association of Vision Science Librarians: c/o Bette Anton, Optometry Library, University of California, Berkeley, 490 Minor Hall, Berkeley, CA 94720-2020; tel. (510) 642-1020; internet spectacle.berkeley.edu/ ~library/AVSL.HTM; f. 1968 to foster collective and individual acquisition and dissemination of visual science information, to improve services to those seeking such information and to develop libraries' standards; 100 individual mems, and 75 institutes; Chair. ELAINE WELLS; publs *Vision Union List of Serials* (every 3 years), *PhD Theses in Physiological Optics*.

Bibliographical Society of America: POB 1537, Lenox Hill Station, New York, NY 10021; tel. and fax (212) 452-2710; e-mail bsa@bibsocamer.org; internet www .bibsocamer.org; f. 1904, inc. 1927; 1,000 mems; Pres. JOHN BIDWELL; Exec. Sec. MICHELE RANDALL; publ. *Papers* (quarterly).

Bibliographical Society of the University of Virginia: POB 400152, Alderman Library, Charlottesville, VA 22904; tel. (434) 924-7013; e-mail ar3g@virginia.edu; internet etext.lib.virginia.edu/bsuva; f. 1947; an int. soc. promoting the study of books, MSS, printing and the graphic arts, bibliography and textual criticism; 650 mems; Pres. G. THOMAS TANSELLE; Sec. and Treasurer ANNE RIBBLE; publ. *Studies in Bibliography* (annual).

California Library Association: 717 20th St, Suite 200, Sacramento, CA 95814; tel. (916) 447-8541; fax (916) 447-8394; e-mail info@cla-net.org; internet www.cla-net.org; f. 1896; 2,400 mems; Exec. Dir SUSAN E. NEGREEN; Pres. DANIS KREIMEIER; publ. *California Libraries* (monthly).

California School Library Association: 717 K St, Suite 515, Sacramento, CA 95814-3477; tel. (916) 447-2684; fax (916) 447-2695; e-mail csla@pacbell.net; internet www .schoolibrary.org; f. 1977; Pres. ANNE H. WICK; Exec. Dir PENNY KASTANIS; publ. *CSLA Journal* (2 a year).

Catholic Library Association: c/o Jean R. Bostley SSJ, 100 North St, Suite 224, Pittsfield, MA 01201-5109; tel. (413) 443-2252; fax (413) 442-2252; e-mail cla@cathla.org;

internet www.cathla.org; f. 1921; 1,000 mems; Exec. Dir. JEAN R. BOSTLEY; publs *Catholic Library World* (quarterly), *Catholic Periodical and Literature Index* (quarterly).

Council on Library and Information Resources: 1755 Massachusetts Ave NW, Suite 500, Washington, DC 20036; tel. (202) 939-4750; fax (202) 939-4765; e-mail info@clir.org; internet www.clir.org; f. 1956; to develop resources and services of libraries and information services; Pres. NANCY DAVENPORT; publs reports, 8–10 a year, *CLIR Issues* (6 a year).

Medical Library Association: 65 East Wacker Place, Suite 1900, Chicago, IL 60601-7246; tel. (312) 419-9094; fax (312) 419-8950; internet www.mlanet.org; f. 1898; 4,500 mems; non-profit educational org.; provides information for the delivery of health care, the education of health professionals, the conduct of research, and the public's understanding of health; Exec. Dir CARLA J. FUNK; publ. *Journal* (quarterly).

Music Library Association: 8551 Research Way, Suite 180, Middleton, WI 53562; tel. (608) 836-5825; fax (608) 831-8200; e-mail mla@areditions.com; internet www.musiclibraryassoc.org; f. 1931; 2,900 mems; Pres. BONNA BOETTCHER; Exec. Sec. NANCY B. NUZZO; publs *Notes* (quarterly), *Music Cataloging Bulletin* (monthly), *MLA Newsletter* (quarterly), *Index and Bibliography Series* (irregular), *Technical Reports—Information for Music Media Specialists* (irregular).

Society of American Archivists: 527 South Wells St, 5th Floor, Chicago, IL 60607; tel. (312) 922-0140; fax (312) 347-1452; e-mail info@archivists.org; internet www.archivists.org; f. 1936; a professional association for archivists and institutions interested in the preservation and use of archives, manuscripts and current records; 3,400 individual and institutional mems; Exec. Dir NANCY PERKIN BEAUMONT; publs *The American Archivist* (journal), *Archival Outlook* (newsletter).

Special Libraries Association: 331 South Patrick St, Alexandria, VA 22314-3501; tel. (703) 647-4900; fax (703) 647-4901; e-mail sla@sla.org; internet www.sla.org; f. 1909; activities: professional development, résumé referral service, employment clearing-house and career advisory service (at annual conference only), chapters and division services, book publishing, government relations, public relations; Information Resources Center provides telephone reference service; research; 14,000 mems; library: specialized library of 3,000 vols; Pres. ETHEL SALONEN; Exec. Dir JANICE R. LACHANCE; publ. publs include *Information Outlook* (monthly).

Theatre Library Association: c/o New York Public Library for the Performing Arts, 40 Lincoln Center Plaza, New York, NY 10023; tel. (212) 944-3895; fax (212) 944-4139; internet tla.library.unt.edu; f. 1937; 300 mems; Pres. MARTHA S. LOMONACO; Treas. PAUL NEWMAN; publs *Broadside* (4 a year), *Performing Arts Resources* (annually).

ECONOMICS, LAW AND POLITICS

Academy of Political Science: 475 Riverside Drive, Suite 1274, New York, NY 10115-1274; tel. (212) 870-2500; fax (212) 870-2202; e-mail aps@psqonline.org; internet www.psqonline.org; f. 1880; 8,000 mems; Pres and Exec. Dir DEMETRIOS CARALEY; Chair. GEORGE B. MUNROE; publ. *Political Science Quarterly*.

American Academy of Political and Social Science: 3814 Walnut St, Philadelphia, PA 19104-6197; tel. (215) 746-6500; fax (215) 898-1202; internet www.aapss.org; f.

1889; 5,000 mems; Pres. LAWRENCE W. SHERMAN; Exec. Dir ROBERT W. PEARSON; publ. *The Annals* (every 2 months).

American Accounting Association: 5717 Bessie Drive, Sarasota, FL 34233-2399; tel. (941) 921-7747; fax (941) 923-4093; e-mail office@aaahq.org; internet aaahq.org; f. 1916; professional society for educators, practitioners and students of accounting; 13,000 mems; Pres. JANE F. MUTCHLER; Exec. Dir TRACEY SUTHERLAND; publs *The Accounting Review*, *Accounting Horizons*, *Issues in Accounting Education, monographs, surveys.*

American Arbitration Association: 335 Madison Ave, Floor 10, New York, NY 10017-4605; tel. (212) 716-5800; fax (212) 716-5905; e-mail websitemail@adr.org; internet www.adr.org; f. 1926; a public-service, not-for-profit org. offering a broad range of dispute resolution services to business executives, attorneys, individual employees, trade asscns, unions, management, consumers, families, communities and all levels of govt; also conducts seminars, conferences, etc.; 5,400 mems, over 50,000 arbitrators on national panel; library of 23,500 vols, 244 periodical titles; Pres. WILLIAM K. SLATE II; publs *Arbitration Journal, Arbitration Times, The Claims Forum, Forum New York, Lawyers' Arbitration Letter* (quarterly), *Summary of Labor Arbitration Awards, Arbitration in the Schools, Labor Arbitration in Government, New York No-Fault Arbitration Reports* (monthly), *Annual Report.*

American Bar Association: 321 North Clark St, Chicago, IL 60610; tel. (312) 988-5000; internet www.abanet.org; f. 1878; 400,000 mems; library of 50,000 vols; Pres. ROBERT J. GREY; publs *Bar Leader* (every 2 months), *Journal* (monthly), *Reports* (annually).

American Economic Association: 2014 Broadway, Suite 305, Nashville, TN 37203-2418; tel. (615) 322-2595; fax (615) 343-7590; internet www.aeaweb.org; f. 1885 to encourage economic discussion, research and the issue of publications on economic subjects; 19,000 mems; Pres. DANIEL MCFADDEN; publs *American Economic Review, Papers and Proceedings, Journal of Economic Literature, Journal of Economic Perspectives.*

American Finance Association: University of California Berkeley, Haas School of Business, 545 Student Services Bldg., Berkeley, CA 94720-1900; tel. and fax (510) 642-2397; e-mail pyle@haas.berkeley.edu; internet www.afajof.org; f. 1940 to make available knowledge on current developments in the field of finance; 7,000 mems; Exec. Sec. and Treas. Prof. DAVID PYLE; publ. *Journal of Finance* (6 a year).

American Judicature Society: 180 N. Michigan Ave, Suite 600, Chicago, IL 60601; tel. (312) 558-6900; internet www.ajs.org; f. 1913 to promote the effective administration of justice; 6,000 mems; Exec. Dir ALLAN SOBEL; publ. *Judicature* (every two months).

American Law Institute: 4025 Chestnut St, Philadelphia, PA 19104; tel. (215) 243-1600; fax (215) 243-1664; f. 1923; promotes the clarification and simplification of the law; research work; publishes Restatements of the Law, and model and uniform codifications; 3,685 mems; library of 5,000 vols; Pres. MICHAEL TRAYNOR; Dir LANCE LIEBMAN; publs *Proceedings of ALI Annual Meetings* (annually), *ALI Reporter* (newsletter, 4 a year).

American Law Institute-American Bar Association Committee on Continuing Professional Education: 4025 Chestnut St, Philadelphia, PA 19104; tel. (215) 243-1600; fax (215) 243-1664; internet www

.ali-aba.org; f. 1947 to organize, develop and carry out a national programme of continuing education of the bar; library of 5,000 vols; Exec. Dir JULENE FRANKI; publs *ALI-ABA Business Law Course Materials Journal* (6 a year), *ALI-ABA CLE Review* (monthly), *ALI-ABA Estate Planning Course Materials Journal* (6 a year), *The Practical Lawyer* (6 a year), *The Practical Litigator* (6 a year), *The Practical Real Estate Lawyer* (6 a year), *The Practical Tax Lawyer* (4 a year).

American Peace Society: 1319 Eighteenth St, NW, Washington, DC 20036-1802; f. 1828; Pres. Dr EVRON M. KIRKPATRICK; Sec. L. EUGENE HEDBERG; publ. *World Affairs* (quarterly).

American Political Science Association: 1527 New Hampshire Ave, NW, Washington, DC 20036-2106; tel. (202) 483-2512; fax (202) 483-2657; e-mail apsa@apsanet.org; internet www.apsanet.org; f. 1903; 15,000 mems; Exec. Dir MICHAEL BRINTNALL; publs *American Political Science Review* (quarterly), *Perspectives on Politics* (quarterly), *PS: Political Science and Politics* (quarterly).

American Society for Political and Legal Philosophy: c/o The Sec./Treas., Prof. Jacob T. Levy, University of Chicago, 5828 S. University Ave., Chicago, IL 60637; tel. (773) 702-8052; fax (773) 702-1689; internet www.political-theory.org/asplp .html; f. 1955; 500 mems; Pres. WILL KYMLICKA; publ. *NOMOS* (Yearbook).

American Society for Public Administration: 1120 G St NW, Suite 700, Washington, DC 20005; tel. (202) 393-7878; fax (202) 638-4952; e-mail info@aspanet.org; internet www.aspanet.org; f. 1939; 11,000 mems; national and regional conferences, management institutes; chapters in local centres; Exec. Dir MARY HAMILTON; publs *PA Times* (monthly), *Public Administration Review* (every 2 months).

American Society of International Law: 2223 Massachusetts Ave NW, Washington, DC 20008; tel. (202) 939-6000; fax (202) 797-7133; e-mail library@asil.org; internet www.asil.org; f. 1906, inc. 1950; 4,300 mems; library of 22,000 vols; Pres. JAMES H. CARTER; Exec. Dir CHARLOTTE KU; publs *The American Journal of International Law* (4 a year), *International Legal Materials* (6 a year), *Newsletter* (6 a year), *Proceedings* (annually).

American Statistical Association: 1429 Duke St, Alexandria, VA 22314-3415; tel. (703) 684-1221; fax (703) 684-2037; e-mail asainfo@amstat.org; internet www.amstat .org; f. 1839; 16,000 mems; Pres. FRITZ J. SCHEUREN; publs *Journal of the American Statistical Association* (4 a year), *The American Statistician* (4 a year), *Technometrics* (4 a year), *Journal of Educational and Behavioral Statistics* (4 a year), *Journal of Business and Economic Statistics* (4 a year), *Journal of Computational and Graphical Statistics* (4 a year), *Journal of Agricultural, Biological and Environmental Statistics* (4 a year), *Chance Magazine* (4 a year).

Association of American Law Schools: 1201 Connecticut Ave NW, Suite 800, Washington, DC 20036; tel. (202) 296-8851; fax (202) 296-8869; e-mail aals@aals.org; internet www.aals.org; f. 1900 for the improvement of the legal profession through legal education; 165 institutional mems; Exec. Dir CARL C. MONK; publs *Proceedings* (annually), *Directory of Law Teachers* (annually), *Journal of Legal Education* (quarterly), *Newsletter* (quarterly), *Placement Bulletin* (irregular).

Atlantic Council of the United States: 1101 15th St NW, 11th Fl., Washington, DC 20005; tel. (202) 463-7226; fax (202) 463-7241; e-mail info@acus.org; internet www

.acus.org; f. 1961; nat., non-partisan, non-profit public policy centre that addresses the advancement of US global interests within the Atlantic and Pacific communities; the council engages the US executive and legislative branches, the nat. and int. business community, media and academia, and diplomats and other foreign leaders in an integrated programme of policy studies and round-table discussions, briefings, dialogues and conferences, designed to encourage its selected membership and other constituencies to reflect and plan for the future; funded by corporations, foundations, private individuals, and govt grants and contracts; 130 board mems, 200 councillors, 400 acad. assocs; Pres. (Finance and Admin.) DREW A. JUBERT; publs *Bulletin* (irreg.), *Policy Papers* (irreg.), *Occasional Papers* (irreg.).

Carnegie Endowment for International Peace: 1779 Massachusetts Ave NW, Washington, DC 20036; tel. (202) 483-7600; fax (202) 483-1840; e-mail info@CarnegieEndowment.org; internet www.CarnegieEndowment.org; f. 1910; private, non-profit and non-partisan organization dedicated to advancing co-operation between nations and promoting active international engagement by the USA; 130 mems (incl. Carnegie Moscow Center); library of 8,000 vols; Pres. JESSICA T. MATHEWS; publs *Pro et Contra* (annually), *Foreign Policy* (6 a year).

Century Foundation: 41 East 70th St, New York, NY 10021; tel. (212) 535-4441; fax (212) 535-7534; e-mail info@tcf.org; internet www.tcf.org; f. 1919 by the late Edward A. Filene as an endowed foundation for public policy research on major economic, political and social institutions and issues; Chair. of the Board of Trustees ALAN BRINKLEY; Vice-Chair. of the Board and Chair. of Exec. Cttee JAMES A. LEACH; Pres. RICHARD C. LEONE; publ. *Annual Report*.

Council for European Studies: 1203A, International Affairs Bldg, Columbia University, 420 W. 118th St., New York, NY 10027; tel. (212) 854-4172; fax (212) 854-8808; e-mail ces@columbia.edu; internet europanet.org; f. 1970; a consortium of European studies programs at over 80 universities in the USA; affiliated with Columbia Univ.; aims to encourage greater scholarly interest in Europe, to emphasize the commonality of problems that face the nations of Europe and North America; sponsors research, information services, graduate student training; holds conferences, etc.; 1,200 individual mems, 115 mem. institutions; Chair KATHLEEN THELEN; publs *European Studies Newsletter* (3 a year), *Guides to libraries and archives of Germany, France and Italy*.

Council of State Governments: 2760 Research Park Drive, POB 11910, Lexington, KY 40511; tel. (859) 244-8000; fax (859) 244-8001; e-mail sales@csg.org; internet www.csg.org; f. 1933; offices in Washington, DC, New York, Atlanta, Chicago and San Francisco; a non-partisan organization established by the States for service to the States; Pres. RUTH ANN MILLER; Exec. Dir DANIEL M. SPRAGUE; publs *State Government News* (monthly), *Suggested State Legislation* (annually), *Spectrum* (4 a year), *CSG State Directories* (annually), *Book of the States* (2 a year).

Council on Foreign Relations, Inc.: 58 East 68th St, New York, NY 10021; tel. (212) 434-9400; fax (212) 434-9800; internet www.cfr.org; f. 1921; 2,905 mems; library: Foreign Relations library of 18,000 vols, 300 periodicals, clippings files; Chair. PETER G. PETERSON; Pres. RICHARD N. HAASS; publs *Foreign Affairs* (6 a year), *Critical Issues*.

Economic History Association: c/o Dept of Economics, 500 El Camino Real, Santa Clara University, Santa Clara, CA 95053-0385; tel. (408) 554-4348; fax (408) 554-2331; e-mail eha@falcon.cc.ukans.edu; internet www.eh.net/eha; f. 1940 to encourage and promote teaching, research and publication in all fields of economic history; 1,200 individual mems; 2,210 library mems; Exec. Dir THOMAS WEISS; publ. *Journal of Economic History* (quarterly).

Federal Bar Association: 2215 M St NW, Washington, DC 20037; tel. (202) 785-1614; fax (202) 785-1568; e-mail fba@fedbar.org; internet www.fedbar.org; f. 1920; 16,000 mems; 99 Chapters; more than 100 committees in fields of federal law; Pres. THOMAS R. SCHUCK; publ. *The Federal Lawyer*.

Foreign Policy Association, Inc.: 470 Park Ave South, New York, NY 10016; tel. (212) 481-8100; fax (212) 481-9275; internet www.fpa.org; f. 1918; object: to promote citizen education in world affairs, to assist organizations, communities and educational institutions, to develop programmes for citizen understanding and constructive participation in world affairs, and to advance public understanding of foreign policy problems through national programmes and publications of a non-partisan character based upon the principles of freedom, justice and democracy; Chair. GONZALO DE LAS HERAS; Pres. and CEO NOEL V. LATEEF; publs *Great Decisions* (yearly), *Headline Series* (quarterly).

History of Economics Society: c/o Prof. J. Patrick Raines, Dept of Economics, University of Richmond, Richmond, VA 23173; f. 1973 to promote interest and inquiry into the history of economics and related parts of intellectual history; 750 mems in the USA and other countries; Sec.-Treas. Prof. J. PATRICK RAINES; publ. *Bulletin* (2 a year).

Institute for Mediterranean Affairs: 50 Sutton Place South 3H, New York, NY 10022; tel. (212) 759-6576; fax (212) 921-0248; established under charter of the University of the State of New York to evolve a better understanding of the historical background and contemporary political and socio-economic problems of the nations and regions that border on the Mediterranean Sea; to analyse the various tensions in the Eastern Mediterranean and to investigate the basic problems of the area; special attention is given to the Israeli–Arab conflict; 250 Academic Advisory mems; Pres. Prof. SEYMOUR M. FINGER; Dir SAMUEL A. MERLIN; publ. *The Mediterranean Survey* (bulletin, irregular).

Institute for Operations Research and the Management Sciences: 7240 Parkway Drive, Suite 310, Hanover, MD 21076; tel. (443) 757-3500; fax (443) 757-3515; e-mail informs@mail.informs.org; internet www.informs.org; f. 1953; 11,000 mems; Pres. MARK S. DASKIN; Exec. Dir MARK G. DOHERTY; publs *Decision Analysis* (quarterly), *Information Systems Research* (quarterly), *INFORMS Journal on Computing* (quarterly), *Interfaces* (6 a year), *Management Science* (monthly), *Manufacturing & Service Operations Management* (quarterly), *Marketing Science* (6 a year), *Mathematics of Operations Research* (quarterly), *Operations Research* (6 a year), *Organization Science* (6 a year), *Transportation Science* (quarterly).

Society of Actuaries: 475 N Martingale Rd, Suite 600, Schaumburg, IL 60173-2226; tel. (847) 706-3500; fax (847) 706-3599; e-mail webmaster@soa.org; internet www.soa.org; f. 1949; educational, research and professional membership society for actuaries in life and health insurance and pension planning; 16,595 mems; library of 3,900 vols; special collections, reports and transactions from US, Canadian and international actuarial organizations; Pres. STEPHEN G. KELLISON; publs *The Actuary* (newsletter, monthly), *The Future Actuary* (newsletter, 3 a year), *The North American Actuarial Journal* (4 a year).

World Peace Foundation: 79 John F. Kennedy St, Cambridge, MA 02138-4952; tel. (617) 496-9812; fax (617) 491-8588; e-mail world_peace@harvard.edu; internet www.worldpeacefoundation.org; f. 1910; an operating foundation which does not give outside grants; policy-oriented studies in world affairs; Pres. ROBERT I. ROTBERG; publ. sponsors publ. *International Organization* (4 a year).

EDUCATION

Carnegie Corporation of New York: 437 Madison Ave, New York, NY 10022; tel. (212) 371-3200; fax (212) 754-4073; internet www.carnegie.org; f. 1911 by Andrew Carnegie for the advancement and diffusion of knowledge and understanding among peoples of the USA and, with subsequent amendment of the charter, of some of the current or former British overseas Commonwealth; primary interests: education, international affairs, democracy; 17 trustees; Pres. VARTAN GREGORIAN; Chair HELENE L. KAPLAN; publs *Annual Report, Carnegie Newsline, Carnegie Quarterly, Challenge Papers, Reporter, Results of Carnegie Journalism Reports*.

Institute of International Education: 809 United Nations Plaza, New York, NY 10017; tel. (212) 883-8200; fax (212) 984-5452; internet www.iie.org; f. 1919; private non-profit agency which develops, administers and programs educational and cultural exchange between the USA and more than 150 other countries; conducts special studies and seminars to analyse and evaluate development in the field of educational exchange; information centre; six regional offices, overseas offices in Bangkok, Budapest, Jakarta, Hong Kong, Mexico City and Moscow; library of 5,000 vols; Pres. ALLAN GOODMAN; publs *Annual Report, Open Doors, Vacation Study Abroad, Academic Year Abroad* (all annually), *Funding for US Study, Financial Resources for International Study, English Language and Orientation Programs*.

International Montessori Society: 9525 Georgia Ave, Suite 200, Silver Spring, MD 20910; tel. (301) 589-1127; fax (301) 589-0733; e-mail havis@imsmontessori.org; internet www.imsmontessori.org; f. 1979 to support the effective application of Montessori educational principles throughout the world; provides teacher education through correspondence; occasional workshops; mail-order book sales; audio CD and study guide of distinctive IMS technology for Montessori teaching; 600 mems; small library; Exec. Dir LEE HAVIS; publs *Montessori News* (2 a year), *Montessori Observer* (quarterly).

Philosophy of Education Society: c/o Alexander Sidorkin, PES Exec. Dir, University of Northern Colorado, McKee 208, Greeley, CO 80639; tel. (970) 351-2701; internet philosophyofeducation.org; f. 1941; 550 mems; exists to promote discussion and analysis of philosophy and education and to improve the teaching and research in philosophy and education; Pres. SUSAN LAIRD; publs *Educational Theory* (quarterly), *Philosophy of Education Newsletter* (3 a year), *Yearbook*.

FINE AND PERFORMING ARTS

American Council for the Arts: 1 East 53rd St, New York, NY 10022-4201; tel. (212) 223-2787; fax (212) 223-4415; f. 1960 to promote the interests of the arts; 1,500 mems; library of 5,000 items; Pres. and CEO LUIS R. CANCEL; Chair. DONALD R. GREENE; publ. *ACA UpDate* (monthly).

American Federation of Arts: 41 East 65th St, New York, NY 10021-6594; tel. (212) 988-7700; fax (212) 861-2487; e-mail pubinfo@afaweb.org; internet www.afaweb .org; f. 1909 by act of Congress; works to strengthen the ability of museums to enrich the public's experience and understanding of art; organizes national and international travelling art exhibitions and develops educational programmes in co-operation with the museum community; Chair. BARBARA WEEDEN; Pres. GILBERT H. KINNEY; Dir JULIA BROWN; publ. *Memo to Members* (4 a year).

American Musicological Society: 6010 College Station, Brunswick, ME 04011-8451; tel. (207) 798-4243; fax (207) 789-4254; e-mail ams@ams-net.org; internet www.ams-net.org; f. 1934; 3,500 mems; Pres. CHARLES ATKINSON; Exec. Dir ROBERT JUDD; publs *Journal* (3 a year), *Newsletter* (2 a year), *Abstracts of Papers read at the Annual Meeting* (annually).

American Society for Aesthetics: Marquette University, 707 N. 11th, Room 322, Milwaukee, WI 53201-1881; tel. (414) 288-7831; fax (414) 288-5415; e-mail asastcar@ marquette.edu; internet www .aesthetics-online.org; f. 1942; aesthetics and the arts; 800 mems; Pres. CAROLYN KORSMEYER; Sec. CURTIS L. CARTER; publs *Journal of Aesthetics and Art Criticism* (4 a year), *Newsletter* (3 a year).

American Society for Theatre Research: c/o Erickson and Associates, 6000 Ridgewood Circle, Downers Grove, IL 60516; tel. (630) 964-7241; fax (630) 964-7141; e-mail NEricksn@aol.com; internet www.astr.umd .edu; f. 1956; serves needs of theatre and performance studies historians and fosters knowledge of the theatre in the USA and overseas; 706 mems; Pres. Prof. BRUCE McCONACHIE; Sec. Prof. GAY GIBSON CIMA; publ. *Theatre Survey* (2 a year).

American Society of Composers, Authors and Publishers (ASCAP): 1 Lincoln Plaza, New York, NY 10023; tel. (212) 621-6000; fax (212) 595-3342; e-mail info@ ascap.com; internet www.ascap.com; f. 1914; a non-profit-making society that issues licences for public performance of members' copyright works; 180,000 mem. songwriters, composers and music publishers; Pres. MARILYN BERGMAN; publs *ASCAP Playback* (quarterly), *ASCAP Biographical Dictionary*.

Center for Creative Photography: University of Arizona, 1030 N. Olive Rd, Tucson, AZ 85721-0103; tel. (520) 621-7968; fax (520) 621-9444; e-mail oncenter@ccp.arizona.edu; internet www.creativephotography.org; f. 1975; a unique resource for the study and history of photography; extensive collection of prints and other materials related to the life and works of photographers since the beginning of the 20th c.; comprises a computer-catalogued archive; houses the life-time archives of Ansel Adams, Wynn Bullock, Harry Callahan, Dean Brown, Louise Dahl-Wolfe, Andreas Feininger, Sonya Noskowiak, Aaron Siskind, Frederick Sommer, W. Eugene Smith, Edward Weston, etc.; 500 mems; library of 11,000 vols, 100 periodicals; Dean of the Libraries and the Center for Creative Photography CARLA STUFFLE; publ. *The Archive* (every 2 years).

College Art Association: 275 Seventh Ave, New York, NY 10001; tel. (212) 691-1051; fax (212) 627-2381; e-mail nyoffice@collegeart .org; internet www.collegeart.org; f. 1911 to further scholarship and excellence in the teaching and practice of art and art history; 13,000 individual, 2,000 institutional mems;

Exec. Dir SUSAN BALL; publs *Art Bulletin* (quarterly), *Art Journal* (quarterly), *CAA News*.

Graphic Arts Technical Foundation: 200 Deer Run Rd, Sewickley, PA 15143-2600; tel. (412) 741-6860; fax (412) 741-2311; e-mail info@gatf.org; internet www.gatf.org; f. 1924; 14,000 mems in 60 countries; library: library of over 6,000 vols and periodicals; non-profit scientific research and technical education organization serving the international graphic communications community; conducts technical workshops, in-plant assessments, seminars worldwide on various aspects of graphic communications; Pres. GEORGE H. RYAN; publs *GATFWORLD* (every 2 months), *SecondSight* (technical reports), *Learning Modules*.

National Academy of Design: 1083 Fifth Ave, New York, NY 10128; tel. (212) 369-4880; fax (212) 360-6795; e-mail nmalloy@ nationalacademy.org; internet www .nationalacademy.org; f. 1825; membership composed exclusively of artists; sections: painting, sculpture, water colour, graphic arts, architecture; art museum, art library and art school attached; 450 mems; Pres. GREGORY AMENOFF; Corresp. Sec. STANLEY BLEIFELD; Dir Dr ANNETTE BLAUGRUND; publ. *Bulletin* (2 a year).

National Sculpture Society: 237 Park Ave, New York, NY 10017; tel. (212) 764-5645; fax (212) 764-5651; e-mail info@ nationalsculpture.org; internet www .nationalsculpture.org; f. 1893, inc. 1896; to disseminate knowledge of American sculpture; 3,000 mems (incl. 320 professional mems); Pres. DAN OSTERMILLER; Exec. Dir GWEN PIER; publ. *Sculpture Review* (4 a year).

Society for Ethnomusicology, Inc.: Morrison Hall 005, 1165 E. 3rd St, Bloomington, IN 47405-3700; tel. (812) 855-6672; fax (812) 855-6673; e-mail sem@indiana.edu; internet www.ethnomusicology.org; f. 1955; 2,400 mems; Pres. DEBORAH WONG; Sec. JANET STURMAN; publs *Ethnomusicology* (3 a year), *Newsletter* (4 a year).

HISTORY, GEOGRAPHY AND ARCHAEOLOGY

American Antiquarian Society: 185 Salisbury St, Worcester, MA 01609-1634; tel. (508) 755-5221; fax (508) 753-3311; e-mail library@mwa.org; internet www .americanantiquarian.org; f. 1812; a learned society and research library concerned with American history before 1877; library of 680,000 vols, 2,000 linear ft MSS collections, 3m. newspaper issues, 200,300 items of graphic art; 656 mems; Pres. ELLEN S. DUNLAP; publs *Almanac* (society newsletter), *The Book: Newsletter of the Program in the History of the Book in American Culture* (3 a year), *Proceedings* (2 a year).

American Association for State and Local History: 1717 Church St, Nashville, TN 37203-2991; tel. (615) 320-3203; fax (615) 327-9013; e-mail history@aaslh.org; internet www.aaslh.org; f. 1940; 6,000 mems; successor to Conference of Historical Societies; objects: exchange of information on local and regional history and historical societies, and dissemination in scholarly and popular publications of professional material and interpretative articles; Pres. and CEO TERRY L. DAVIS; publs *History News* (4 a year, professional news), *History News Dispatch* (monthly).

American Catholic Historical Association: The Catholic University of America, Mullen Library 320, Washington, DC 20064; tel. (202) 319-5079; fax (202) 319-5079; e-mail acha@cua.edu; internet research.cua

.edu/acha; f. 1919 to promote interest in the history of the Catholic Church broadly considered; research work; 890 mems; Sec. and Treasurer Prof. TIMOTHY MEAGHER; publ. *Catholic Historical Review* (4 a year).

American Historical Association: 400 A St SE, Washington, DC 20003; tel. (202) 544-2422; fax (202) 544-8307; e-mail aha@ historians.org; internet www.historians.org; f. 1884; 16,000 mems; Pres. Prof. LINDA K. KERBER; Exec. Dir ARNITA A. JONES; Controller RANDY NORELL; publs *American Historical Review* (5 a year), *Annual Report*, *Perspectives* (9 a year), *Program of the Annual Meeting*.

American Irish Historical Society: 991 Fifth Ave, New York, NY 10028; tel. (212) 288-2263; fax (212) 628-7927; e-mail info@ aihs.org; internet aihs.org; f. 1897; research in the history of the Irish in America; 800 mems; library of 10,000 vols; Dir WILLIAM COBERT; Chair. DONALD R. KEOUGH; Librarian Rev. JOSEPH A. O'HARE; publ. *The Recorder* (2 a year).

American Jewish Historical Society: 15 West 16th St, New York, NY 10011; tel. (212) 294-6160; fax (212) 294-6161; e-mail ajhs@ ajhs.org; internet www.ajhs.org; f. 1892 to collect and publish material bearing upon the history of Jews in America and to promote the study of American-Jewish history; 3,200 mems; library of 50,000 vols, 30,000,000 MSS, contains many rare and valuable MSS since the 16th century, American-Jewish periodicals since the 18th century; Chair. Prof. DEBORAH DASH MOORE; Exec. Dir DAVID SOLOMON; publs *American Jewish History*, *Heritage* (occasional newsletter).

American Numismatic Society: Broadway at 155th St, New York, NY 10032; tel. (212) 234-3130; fax (212) 234-3381; e-mail info@ amnumsoc.org; internet www.amnumsoc .org; f. 1858; 2,077 mems; collection encompasses all periods and fields of interest; library of 100,000 vols; Pres. DONALD PARTRICK; Exec. Dir UTE WARTENBERG; publs regular journals, *American Journal of Numismatics* (annually), *Numismatic Literature* (2 a year); publs irregular journals, *Numismatic Notes and Monographs*, *Numismatic Studies*, *Sylloge Nummorum Graecorum*, *The Collection of the American Numismatic Society*, *Ancient Coins in the North American Collections*, *Proceedings of the Coinage of the Americas Conference*, *Magazine* (3 a year).

American Society for Eighteenth-Century Studies: Wake Forest University, Winston-Salem, NC 27109; tel. (336) 727-4694; fax (336) 727-4697; e-mail asecs@wfu .edu; internet asecs.press.jhu.edu; f. 1969, inc. 1970; independent society; works through publications and meetings to foster interest and encourage investigation in the achievements of the 18th c. in America and Europe; mems: 50 institutions, 1,077 libraries, 2,500 individuals; Pres. Prof. MARGARET ANNE DOODY; Exec. Dir BYRON R. WELLS; publs *ASECS News Circular* (quarterly), *Eighteenth-Century Studies* (quarterly), *Studies in Eighteenth-Century Culture* (annually).

American Society of Church History: 409 Prospect St, New Haven, CT 06511; e-mail asch@yale.edu; internet www .churchhistory.org; f. 1888, reorganized 1906; 1,500 mems; Sec. HENRY W. BOWDEN; publ. *Church History* (quarterly).

Archaeological Institute of America: 656 Beacon St, Boston, MA 02215; tel. (617) 353-9361; fax (617) 353-6550; e-mail aia@bu.edu; internet www.archaeological.org; f. 1879; 8,000 mems; Pres. JANE C. WALDBAUM; Exec. Dir BONNIE R. CLENDENNING; publs

American Journal of Archaeology (4 a year), *Archaeology* (illustrated, 6 a year), *Dig Magazine* (6 a year).

Arizona Archaeological and Historical Society: Arizona State Museum, Univ. of Arizona, Tucson, AZ 85721; internet www .statemuseum.arizona.edu/aahs/aahs.shtml; f. 1916; 1,150 mems; Pres. Dr JAMES E. AYRES; publs *Glyphs* (monthly), *Kiva* (quarterly).

Association of American Geographers: 1710 16th St, NW, Washington, DC 20009-3198; tel. (202) 234-1450; fax (202) 234-2744; e-mail gaia@aag.org; internet www.aag.org; f. 1904; 9,000 mems; Pres. VICTORIA A. LAWSON; Exec. Dir DOUGLAS RICHARDSON; publs *Annals* (quarterly), *The Professional Geographer* (quarterly), *AAG Newsletter* (monthly).

Brooklyn Historical Society: 128 Pierrepont St, Brooklyn, NY 11201; tel. (718) 222-4111; fax (718) 222-3794; internet www .brooklynhistory.org; f. 1863; 1,250 mems; museum colln of objects relating to Brooklyn; library of 155,000 bound vols, 100,000 graphic images, 2,000ft of MSS, 2,000 maps and atlases; Pres. JESSIE M. KELLY.

California Historical Society: 678 Mission St, San Francisco, CA 94105; tel. (415) 357-1848; fax (415) 357-1850; e-mail info@ calhist.org; internet www .californiahistoricalsociety.org; f. 1871; non-profit-making institution; 6,000 mems; library of 55,000 vols, rare MSS, pamphlets and maps, 500,000 historic photographs; Exec. Dir STEPHEN BEEKER; Pres. Board of Trustees JOHN K. VAN DE KAMP; publ. *California History* (magazine, 4 a year).

Dallas Historical Society: POB 150038, Dallas, TX 75315; Located at: The Hall of State at Fair Park, 3939 Grand Ave., Dallas, TX 75210; tel. (214) 421-4500; fax (214) 421-7500; internet www.dallashistory.org; f. 1922; encourages historical enquiry; collects, preserves and exhibits historical materials; the Society has the custody of the Hall of State (see under Museums and Galleries), which it operates as a museum and archives of Texas and Dallas history; 2,000 mems; library of 10,000 vols, 3,000,000 archival items, 10,000 museum artefacts and 30,000 photographs; Exec. Dir MICHAEL DUTY; Chief Operations Officer FRANK WILSON; publs *Legacies* (published jtly with other organizations, 2 a year), *The Register* (newsletter).

Historical Society of Pennsylvania: 1300 Locust St, Philadelphia, PA 19107; tel. (215) 732-6200; fax (215) 732-2680; e-mail hsppr@ hsp.org; internet www.hsp.org; f. 1824; historical and genealogical collns; 2,300 mems; library of 600,000 vols and pamphlets, more than 19 m. MSS, 300,000 graphics; Pres. DAVID MOLTKE-HANSEN; Chair. COLIN F. MCNEIL; publs *Pennsylvania Legacies Newsmagazine* (2 a year), *The Pennsylvania Magazine of History and Biography* (quarterly).

Maryland Historical Society: 201 West Monument St, Baltimore, MD 21201-4647; tel. (410) 685-3750; fax (410) 385-2105; internet www.mdhs.org; f. 1844; 5,000 mems; museum and library: see under Museums; Pres. STANARD T. KLINEFELTER; Dir DENNIS A. FIORI; publs *Maryland Historical Magazine* (quarterly), *Maryland Magazine of Genealogy* (2 a year), *News and Notes*.

Massachusetts Historical Society: 1154 Boylston St, Boston, MA 02215-3695; tel. (617) 536-1608; fax (617) 859-0074; internet www.masshist.org; f. 1791; oldest historical society in US; library: see Libraries; Dir WILLIAM M. FOWLER; Librarian PETER DRUMMEY; publs *Proceedings*, etc.

Medieval Academy of America: 104 Mt Auburn St, 5th Floor, Cambridge, MA 02138; tel. (617) 491-1622; fax (617) 492-3303; e-mail speculum@medievalacademy.org; internet www.medievalacademy.org; f. 1925; promotes research, publication and instruction in medieval records, literature, languages, art, archaeology, history, philosophy, science, life, and all other aspects of medieval civilization; 4,300 mems; Pres. BARBARA HANAWALT; Exec. Dir RICHARD K. EMMERSON; publ. *Speculum: A Journal of Medieval Studies* (quarterly).

Minnesota Historical Society: 345 Kellogg Blvd W, St Paul, MN 55102-1906; tel. (612) 296-6126; fax (612) 297-3343; internet www.mnhs.org; f. 1849; history museum; state historic preservation office; state archives; collection of artefacts; archaeology; 8,000 mems; library: library of over 500,000 vols; newspaper and audiovisual library, 78,000 cu. ft of MSS; 23 historic sites; Pres. DAVID A. KOCH; Dir NINA ARCHABAL; publs *Member News* (6 a year), *Minnesota History* (quarterly).

National Geographic Society: 1145 17th St NW, Washington, DC 20036; tel. (202) 857-7000; fax (202) 775-6141; internet www .nationalgeographic.com; f. 1888 for the increase and diffusion of geographic knowledge; 8,000,000 mems; library: see Libraries and Archives; Pres. and CEO JOHN M. FAHEY, Jr; publs *National Geographic* (monthly), *National Geographic Kids* (monthly), *National Geographic Traveler* (8 a year), *National Geographic Adventure* (10 a year), *National Geographic Explorer* (classroom magazine available only in USA, 6 a year).

New York Historical Society: 170 Central Park West, New York, NY 10024-5194; tel. (212) 873-3400; fax (212) 874-8706; internet www.nyhistory.org; f. 1804; 3,300 mems; museum of 17th–19th c. American art, antiques and history including portraits, landscapes and genre paintings; library of 630,000 vols, 2,000,000 MSS, 10,000 maps and atlases, large collection of pre-1820 newspapers, sheet music, 20,000 broadsides, 1 m. prints and photographs; Pres. and CEO Dr LOUISE MIRRER; Dir Dr LINDA S. FERBER.

Omohundro Institute of Early American History and Culture: POB 8781, Williamsburg, VA 23187-8781; tel. (757) 221-1110; fax (757) 221-1047; e-mail ieahc1@wm.edu; internet oieahc.wm.edu; f. 1943 by the College of William and Mary and the Colonial Williamsburg Foundation; awards post-doctoral fellowships, sponsors conferences, publishes three to four book titles annually; 1,000 associate mems; library of 7,000 vols, 880 periodicals, 2,000 microfilms; Dir Prof. RONALD HOFFMAN; publs *Uncommon Sense* (newsletter, 2 a year), *William and Mary Quarterly*.

Oregon Historical Society: 1200 SW Park Ave, Portland, OR 97205-2483; tel. (503) 222-1741; fax (503) 221-2035; e-mail orhist@ohs .org; internet www.ohs.org; f. 1873; 6,500 mems; library of 35,000 books, 2,000,000 photographs, 25,000 maps, MSS, thousands of pamphlets, serials and newspapers; museum artefacts from neolithic period to discovery, settlement of Oregon Country, Pacific Northwest; Dir JOHN HERMAN; publ. *Oregon Historical Quarterly* (4 a year).

Organization of American Historians: 112 North Bryan Ave, Bloomington, IN 47408; tel. (812) 855-7311; fax (812) 855-0696; e-mail oah@oah.org; internet www.oah .org; f. 1907 to promote historical study in American history; attached to Indiana University; 9,300 indiv. mems, 2,400 institutional mems; Pres. JAMES O. HORTON; Exec.

Dir LEE W. FORMWALT; publ. *Journal of American History* (4 a year).

Pilgrim Society: 75 Court St, Plymouth, MA 02360; tel. (508) 746-1620; fax (508) 747-4228; internet www.pilgrimhall.org; f. 1820; 850 mems; library of 12,000 vols and Rare Manuscript Collections dealing with the Plymouth Colony; the Society maintains Pilgrim Hall Museum, the oldest public museum in North America; collections of Pilgrim decorative arts, furnishings, prehistoric Native American collections; maintains the National Monument to the Forefathers; Dir PEGGY MACLACHLAN BAKER.

Presbyterian Historical Society: 425 Lombard St, Philadelphia, PA 19147-1516; tel. (215) 627-1852; fax (215) 627-0509; e-mail refdesk@history.pcusa.org; internet www.history.pcusa.org; f. 1852; 700 mems; library of 200,000 vols and 17,000 cu. ft archive material; Exec. Dir FREDERICK J. HEUSER JR; publ. *The Journal of Presbyterian History* (4 a year).

Renaissance Society of America: The City University of New York, 365 Fifth Ave, Room 5400, New York, NY 10011; tel. (212) 817-2130; fax (212) 817-1544; e-mail rsa@rsa .org; internet www.rsa.org; f. 1954; 2,400 individual mems, 1,100 library mems; Pres. JESSIE ANN OWENS; Exec. Dir JOHN MONFASANI; publs *Renaissance Quarterly*, *Renaissance News & Notes*.

Rhode Island Historical Society: 110 Benevolent St, Providence, RI 02906; tel. (401) 331-8575; fax (401) 351-0127; internet www.rihs.org; f. 1822; administers: John Brown House, 52 Power St: 18th c. museum house; decorative arts, furniture, paintings, silver and pewter; library: library, 121 Hope St, 200,000 vols; historical and genealogical; large graphics and MSS collection; Museum of Work and Culture: 42 South Main St, Woonsocket, RI; 1,700 mems; Pres. ROGER N. BEGIN; Exec. Dir BERNARD P. FISHMAN; publ. *Rhode Island History* (quarterly).

Society of American Historians: Butler Library, Box 2, Columbia University, New York, NY 10027; tel. (212) 854-5943; internet www.historians.org/affiliates/soc_am_hisn .htm; f. 1939; 350 fellows; Pres. ROBERT DALLEK; Exec. Sec. MARK C. CARNES.

State Historical Society of Wisconsin: 816 State St, Madison, WI 53706-1488; tel. (608) 264-6400; fax (608) 264-6404; f. 1846; 7,200 mems; library of 1,085,000 vols including pamphlets and government documents; 1,888,000 microforms, 39,000 cu. ft MSS, 49,000 cu. ft public records, 25,000 maps and atlases, 1,000,000 pictures and negatives, 14,000 cinema and television films from major Hollywood Studios, 2,000,000 motion picture and theatre promotional graphics; Dir GEORGE VOGT; publs *Wisconsin Magazine of History* (quarterly), *Columns*, *Wisconsin Public Documents* (both every 2 months).

Vermont Historical Society: 60 Washington St, Barre, VT 05641-4209; tel. (802) 479-8500; fax (802) 479-8510; e-mail vhs@vhs .state.vt.us; internet www.vermonthistory .org; f. 1838; objects: educational work in Vermont and American history; collection of books, documents, and MSS relating to Vermont; publication of historical magazines and books; maintenance of State Museum (located at: 109 State St, Montpelier, VT 05609-0901); 2,500 mems; library of 40,000 vols, early Vermont imprints; Pres. PETER MALLARY; Dir J. KEVIN GRAFFAGNINO; publs *Vermont History* (2 a year), *In Context* (4 a year).

Western Reserve Historical Society: 10825 East Blvd, Cleveland, OH 44106; tel. (216) 721-5722; fax (216) 721-0645; f. 1867; maintains a historical museum, family and regional history library, auto-aviation museum, five historical sites; 6,400 mems; library of 235,000 vols, 25,000 vols of newspapers, 30,500 rolls of microfilm, 1,000,000 prints and photos, 6,000,000 MSS; Pres. JAMES A. SCHOFF; Exec. Dir PATRICK H. REYMANN; publ. *News* (6 a year).

LANGUAGE AND LITERATURE

Alliance Française: c/o French Embassy, 4101 Reservoir Rd NW, Washington, DC; tel. (202) 944-63-53; fax (202) 944-63-47; e-mail dgi@afusa.org; internet www.alliance-us.org; offers courses and exams in French language and culture and promotes cultural exchange with France; attached teaching offices in Albuquerque (NM), Atlanta (GA), Austin (TX), Berkeley (CA), Beverly Hills (CA), Bloomfield Hills (MI), Bonita Springs (FL), Boston (MA), Buffalo (NY), Chicago (IL), Cincinnati (OH), Denver (CO), Doylestown (PA), Earlysville (VA), Evanston (IL), Fort Lauderdale (FL), Fresno, (CA), Greenwich (CT), Hartford (CT), Hawaii (HI), Houston (TX), Jackson (MS), Jacksonville (FL), Kansas City (MO), Louisville (KY), Lynchburg (VA), Madison (WI), Miami (FL), Milwaukee (WI), Minneapolis-St.Paul (MI), Missoula (MT), Napa (CA), Naperville (TN), New Haven (CT), New York (NY), Newport Beach (CA), Norfolk (VA), New Orleans (LA), Orlando (FL), Pasadena (CA), Philadelphia (PA), Phoenix (AZ), Pittsburg (PA), Portland (OR), Providence (RI), Sacramento (CA), Saint-Louis (MO), Salt Lake City (UT), San Antonio (TX), San Diego (CA), San Francsico (CA), San Rafael (CA), Santa Clara Valley (CA), Santa Cruz County (CA), Sarasota (FL), Saratoga (CA), Seattle (WA), Toledo (OH), Tulsa (OK), Washington, DC, White Plains (NY), Wilmington (DE), Woodbury (CT); Dir of Operations, USA PIERRE HUDE-LOT.

American Center of PEN: 588 Broadway, Suite 303, New York, NY 10012; tel. (212) 334-1660; fax (212) 334-2181; e-mail pen@pen.org; internet www.pen.org; f. 1922 to promote friendship and intellectual co-operation among writers, the exchange of ideas and freedom of expression; conferences, workshops, emergency fund for writers, translation prize; administers PEN/Nabokov Award and other literary awards; programme for inmate-writers in American prisons; 2,700 mems; library of 1,000 vols; Pres. Sir SALMAN RUSHDIE; Exec. Sec. MICHAEL ROBERTS; publs *Grants and Awards Available to American Writers* (every 2 years), *PEN America* (2 a year), *PEN News* (4 a year).

American Classical League: Miami University, Oxford, OH 45056; tel. (513) 529-7741; fax (513) 529-7742; e-mail info@aclclassics.org; internet www.aclclassics.org; f. 1919; 3,400 mems; Pres. KEN KITCHELL; Sec. TAMARA BAUER; publ. *The Classical Outlook* (quarterly).

American Comparative Literature Association: University of Texas at Austin Program in Comparative Literature, 1 University Station, B5003, Austin, TX 78712-0196; tel. (512) 471-8020; e-mail info@acla.org; internet www.acla.org; f. 1960 to further the growth of comparative literature in the USA, 1,000 mems; Pres. MARGARET HIGONNET; Sec. and Treas. ELIZABETH RICHMOND-GARZA; publ. *Comparative Literature Journal* (4 a year).

American Dialect Society: c/o Allan Metcalf, Dept of English, MacMurray College, Jacksonville, IL 62650; tel. (217) 479-7117; fax (217) 245-0405; e-mail aallan@aol.com; internet www.americandialect.org; f. 1889; 550 mems; study of the English language in North America, together with other languages or dialects of other languages influencing it or being influenced by it; sponsor of *Dictionary of American Regional English*; Pres. MICHAEL B. MONTGOMERY; Exec. Sec. ALLAN METCALF; publs *Newsletter* (3 a year), *American Speech* (4 a year, with annual supplement).

American Philological Association: 292 Logan Hall, University of Pennsylvania, 249 South 36th St, Philadelphia, PA 19104-6304; tel. (215) 898-4975; fax (215) 573-7874; e-mail apaclassics@sas.upenn.edu; internet www.apaclassics.org; f. 1869; study of classical languages, literatures and history; 3,200 mems; Exec. Dir ADAM D. BLISTEIN; publs *Newsletter* (6 a year), *Transactions* (annually).

British Council: British Embassy, 3100 Massachusetts Ave NW, Washington, DC 20008-3600; tel. (202) 588-6500; fax (202) 588-7918; e-mail info@us.britishcouncil.org; internet www.britishcouncil.org/usa; offers courses and exams in English language and British culture and promotes cultural exchange with the UK; Educational Advisor ANDY MCKAY.

Goethe-Institut: 1014 5th Ave, New York, NY 10028; tel. (212) 439-8700; fax (212) 439-8705; e-mail soetje@newyork.goethe.org; internet www.goethe.de/uk/ney/enindex.htm; offers courses and exams in German language and culture and promotes cultural exchange with Germany; attached centres in Boston, Chicago, Los Angeles, San Francisco and Washington, DC; library of 12,000 vols, 150 periodicals; Dir and Regional Dir for USA, Canada and Mexico PETER SOETJE.

Instituto Cervantes: Amster Yard, 211–215 E 49th St, New York, NY 10017; tel. (212) 308-7720; fax (212) 308-7721; e-mail cenny@cervantes.es; internet nyork.cervantes.es; offers courses and exams in Spanish language and culture and promotes cultural exchange with Spain and Spanish-speaking Latin and Central America; attached centres in Albuquerque (NM) and Chicago (IL); library of 40,000 vols; Exec. Dir ANTONIO MUÑOZ MOLINA.

Linguistic Society of America: 1325 18th St NW, Suite 211, Washington, DC 20035-6501; tel. (202) 835-1714; fax (202) 835-1717; e-mail lsa@lsadc.org; internet www.lsadc.org; f. 1924; linguistic institute; 2,100 libraries, foreign and domestic; 7,000 mems; Pres. MARK ARONOFF; Sec.-Treas. GREGORY WARD; Exec. Dir MARGARET W. REYNOLDS; publ *Language* (quarterly), *LSA Bulletin* (quarterly).

Modern Language Association of America: 26 Broadway, New York, NY 10004-1789; tel. (646) 576-5000; fax (646) 458-0030; e-mail info@mla.org; internet www.mla.org; f. 1883; 30,000 mems; Exec. Dir Prof. ROSEMARY G. FEAL; publs *PMLA* (6 a year), *MLA International Bibliography of Books and Articles on the Modern Languages and Literatures* (annually).

National Communication Association: 1765 N St NW, Washington, DC 20036; tel. (202) 464-4622; fax (202) 464-4600; internet www.natcom.org; f. 1914; 7,000 mems; Exec. Dir JAMES L. GAUDINO; publs *Quarterly Journal of Speech*, *Communication Monographs* (quarterly), *Communication Education* (quarterly), *Critical Studies in Mass Communication* (quarterly), *Directory* (annually), *International and Intercultural Communication Annual*, *Text and Performance Quarterly*, *The Communication Teacher* (quarterly), *Journal of Applied Communication Research* (quarterly).

Poetry Society of America: 15 Gramercy Park, New York, NY 10003; tel. (212) 254-9628; fax (212) 673-2352; e-mail poetrysoc@aol.com; internet www.poetrysociety.org; f. 1910; 2,000 mems; service organization for poets and readers of poetry; sponsor readings, lectures, workshops and annual prize-giving; library of 8,000 vols of American poetry; Pres. WILLIAM LOUIS-DREYFUS; Exec. Dir ALICE QUINN; publ. *Journal* (2 a year).

Society of Biblical Literature: 825 Houston Mill Rd, Atlanta, GA 30329; tel. (404) 727-3100; fax (404) 727-3101; e-mail sbl.exec@sbl-site.org; internet www.sbl-site.org; f. 1880; study of biblical and related literature, language, history, religions; 7,000 mems; Exec. Dir KENT RICHARDS; publ. *Journal of Biblical Literature* (quarterly).

MEDICINE

Aerospace Medical Association: 320 S. Henry St, Alexandria, VA 22314-3579; tel. (703) 739-2240; fax (703) 739-9652; internet www.asma.org; f. 1929; advancement of aerospace medicine, life sciences, bio-astronautics and environmental medicine; annual awards; 3,500 mems; Pres. Dr RICHARD JENNINGS; Exec. Dir Dr RUSSELL B. RAYMAN; publ. *Aviation, Space and Environmental Medicine* (monthly).

American Academy of Allergy, Asthma and Immunology: 555 East Wells St, Suite 1100, Milwaukee, WI 53202-3823; tel. (414) 272-6071; e-mail info@aaaai.org; internet www.aaaai.org; f. 1943; 5,200 mems; Pres. Dr F. ESTELLE R. SIMONS; publ. *The Journal of Allergy and Clinical Immunology*.

American Academy of Family Physicians: 11400 Tomahawk Creek, Leawood, KS 66211; tel. (800) 274-2237; fax (913) 906-6080; internet www.aafp.org; f. 1947; promotes and maintains high standards in the general/family practice of medicine; 94,000 mems; Pres. Dr MARY E. FRANK; Exec. Vice-Pres. Dr DOUGLAS E. ENLEY; publs *American Family Physician* (24 a year), *Family Practice Management* (10 a year), *Annals of Family Medicine* (6 a year), *Caring for Hispanic Patients* (annually).

American Academy of Ophthalmology: 655 Beach St, POB 7424, San Francisco, CA 94120-7424; tel. (415) 561-8500; fax (415) 561-8533; internet www.aao.org; f. 1896; 20,777 mems; Pres. SUSAN H. DAY; Exec. Vice-Pres. H. DUNBAR HOSKINS Jr; publs *Ophthalmology*, *Argus* (monthly).

American Academy of Otolaryngology–Head and Neck Surgery: One Prince St, Alexandria, VA 22314-3357; tel. (703) 836-4444; fax (703) 688-5100; e-mail info@entnet.org; internet www.entnet.org; f. 1896; offers more than 500 continuing medical educational courses at annual meetings and through correspondence courses throughout the USA and abroad; 12,000 US and non-US fellows, scientific and associate mems; Exec. Vice-Pres. and CEO Dr DAVID R. NIELSEN; publs *The Bulletin* (news magazine, monthly), *Otolaryngology–Head and Neck Surgery* (peer-reviewed scientific journal, monthly).

American Academy of Pediatrics: 141 Northwest Point Blvd, Elk Grove Village, IL 60007-1098; tel. (847) 434-4000; fax (847) 434-8000; e-mail kidsdocs@aap.org; internet www.aap.org; f. 1930; 60,000 mems; Pres. Dr CAROL D. BERKOWITZ; Exec. Dir Dr JERROL R. ALDEN; publs *AAP Grand Rounds* (monthly and online), *Neoreviews* (online, monthly), *Pediatrics* (monthly and online), *Pediatrics in Review* (monthly and online).

American Academy of Periodontology: 737 N. Michigan Ave, Chicago, IL 60611-2690; tel. (312) 787-5518; fax (312) 787-3670; internet www.perio.org; f. 1914; 7,200 mems;

Exec. Dir GERALD M. BOWERS; publ. *Journal of Periodontology* (monthly).

American Association of Anatomists: 9650 Rockville Pike, Bethesda, MA 20814-3998; tel. (301) 634-7910; fax (301) 634-7965; e-mail exec@anatomy.org; internet www.anatomy.org; f. 1888; 2,753 mems; Pres. Dr ROBERT S. MCCUSKEY; Exec. Dir ANDREA PENDLETON; publs *Anatomical Record*, *Developmental Dynamics*, *New Anatomist*.

American Association of Immunologists: 9650 Rockville Pike, Bethesda, MD 20814; tel. (301) 634-7178; fax (301) 634-7887; e-mail infoaai@aai.org; internet www.aai.org; f. 1913; independent body for the exchange of information and advancement of knowledge in immunology and related fields; 6,000 mems; Chair. Dr LINDA SHERMAN; Exec. Dir Dr M. MICHELE HOGAN; publ. *Journal of Immunology*.

American Cancer Society Inc.: 19 W. 56th St, New York, NY 10019; internet www.cancer.org; f. 1913; voluntary health agency; library of more than 16,000 vols (located at 4 West 35th St, New York, NY 10001); Pres. STEPHEN F. SENER; publs *Ca-A* (cancer journal for clinicians, 6 a year), *Cancer* (2 a month), *Cancer News* (2 a year), *World Smoking & Health* (3 a year).

American College of Obstetricians and Gynecologists: 409 12th St, SW, POB 96920, Washington, DC 20090-6920; tel. (202) 638-5577; internet www.acog.org; f. 1951; 38,000 mems; Exec. Dir Dr RALPH HALE; publ. *Obstetrics and Gynecology* (monthly).

American College of Physicians: Independence Mall West, Sixth St at Race, Philadelphia, PA 19106; internet www.acponline.org; f. 1915; 116,000 mems; Pres. CHARLES K. FRANCIS; publ. *Annals of Internal Medicine* (every 2 weeks).

American College of Rheumatism: 1800 Century Place, Suite 250, Atlanta, GA 30345-4300; tel. (404) 633-3777; fax (404) 633-1870; internet www.rheumatology.org; 4,000 mems; Exec. Sec. ELIZABETH TINDALL.

American College of Surgeons: 633 N St Clair St, Chicago, IL 60611-3211; tel. (312) 202-5000; fax (312) 202-5001; e-mail postmaster@facs.org; internet www.facs.org; f. 1913; 63,421 fellows; Dir THOMAS R. RUSSELL; Sec. Dr KATHRYN D. ANDERSON; publs *Bulletin* (monthly), *Journal of the American College of Surgeons* (monthly).

American Dental Association: 211 East Chicago Ave, Chicago, IL 60611; tel. (312) 440-2547; fax (312) 440-3526; e-mail adaf@ada.org; internet www.ada.org; f. 1859; 146,000 mems; library of 50,000 vols; Exec. Dir Dr JAMES BRAMSON; publs *Journal* (monthly), *ADA News* (every 2 weeks), *American Dental Directory* (annually).

American Dietetic Association: 120 South Riverside Plaza, Chicago, IL 60606-6995; tel. (312) 899-0040; fax (312) 899-0008; e-mail membrshp@eatright.org; internet www.eatright.org; f. 1917 to improve the nutrition of human beings; to advance the science of dietetics; to promote education in these and allied fields; 70,000 mems; library of 1,000 vols; publ. *Journal* (monthly).

American Geriatrics Society, Inc.: Suite 801, Empire State Building, 350 Fifth Ave, New York, NY 10118; tel. (212) 308-1414; fax (212) 832-8646; e-mail info@americangeriatrics.org; internet www.americangeriatrics.org; f. 1942; 6,500 mems; holds Annual Meeting, runs postgraduate courses; Pres. Dr MEGHAN GERETY; Exec. Vice-Pres. LINDA HIDDEMEN BARONDESS; publs *Annals of Long-term Care*, *Clinical Geriatrics*, *Geriatrics Review Syllabus*, *Journal of the American Geriatrics Society* (monthly), *Newsletter* (every 2 months).

American Gynecological and Obstetrical Society: University of Virginia Health System, POB 800566, Charlottesville, VA 22908; f. 1993; 200 Fellows, 92 Life Fellows, 43 Hon. Fellows; Sec. Dr PAUL B. UNDERWOOD.

American Heart Association: 7272 Greenville Ave, Dallas, TX 75231; tel. (214) 373-6300; fax (214) 706-1341; internet www.americanheart.org; f. 1924; 3,629,000 mems; dedicated to the reduction of disability and death from cardiovascular diseases and stroke; supports cardiovascular research and brings its benefits to the public through professional education and community service programmes, to co-ordinate efforts of all medical and lay groups in combating cardiovascular diseases, and to inform the public of progress in the cardiovascular field; CEO M. CASS WHEELER; publs *Arteriosclerosis, Circulation, Circulation Research, Currents in Emergency Cardiac Care* (4 a year), *Hypertension, Stroke, Thrombosis and Vascular Biology*.

American Hospital Association: One N. Franklin, Chicago, IL 60606; tel. (312) 422-3000; internet www.aha.org; f. 1898 to advance the health of individuals and communities; leads, represents and serves hospitals, health systems and other related organizations that are accountable to the community and committed to health improvement; 37,000 personal mems, 5,000 institutional mems; library of 63,000 vols; Pres. and Chief Operating Officer RICHARD UMBDENSTOCK; Executive Vice-Presidents NEIL J. JESUELE, RICHARD J. POLLACK; Senior Vice-Pres. and Sec. MICHAEL P. GUERIN; publs *AHA News* (weekly), *Hospitals and Health Networks* (monthly), *Trustee* (monthly).

American Institute of the History of Pharmacy: Pharmacy Bldg, 777 Highland Ave, Madison, WI 53705-2222; tel. (608) 262-5378; e-mail aihp@aihp.org; internet www.pharmacy.wisc.edu/aihp; f. 1941; documentation and preservation of pharmaceutical heritage; 1,000 mems; Exec. Dir Dr GREGORY J. HIGBY; publ. *Pharmacy in History* (4 a year).

American Laryngological, Rhinological and Otological Society, Inc. (Triological Society): 555 N 30th St, Omaha, NE 68131; tel. (402) 346-5500; fax (402) 346-5300; e-mail info@triological.org; internet www.triological.org; f. 1895; 1,200 mems; Pres. Dr PATRICK E. BROOKHOUSER; Exec. Sec. Dr GERALD B. HEALY; publ. *The Laryngoscope*.

American Lung Association: 61 Broadway, New York, NY 10006; tel. (212) 315-8700; fax (212) 265-5642; internet www.lungusa.org; f. 1904; 115 affiliated associations nationally; the Medical Section of the ALA, the American Thoracic Society, has a membership of over 11,000, including some 2,000 pulmonary physicians in foreign countries; Pres. and Chief Exec. JOHN L. KIRKWOOD; Sec. JAMES M. ANDERSON; publs *American Journal of Respiratory Cell and Molecular Biology* (monthly), *American Journal of Respiratory and Critical Care Medicine*.

American Medical Association: 515 North State St, Chicago, IL 60610-4377; tel. (312) 464-5000; internet www.ama-assn.org; f. 1847; 296,000 mems; Exec. Vice-Pres. Dr MICHAEL MAVES; publs *American Medical Directory* (irregular), *American Medical News* (weekly), *Jama* (weekly).

American Medical Technologists: 710 Higgins Rd, Park Ridge, IL 60068; tel. (847) 823-5169; fax (847) 823-0458; e-mail amtmail@aol.com; internet www.amt1.com; f. 1939; 29,000 mems; Pres. DAVE MCCULLOUGH; publs *AMT Events* (4 a year), *Journal of Continuing Education Topics* (3 a year).

American Neurological Association: Administrative Office, 5841 Cedar Lake Rd, Suite 204, Minneapolis, MN 55416; tel. (952) 545-6284; fax (952) 545-6073; e-mail ana@llmsi.com; internet www.aneuroa.org; f. 1875; 1,000 mems; Pres. JOHN W. GRIFFIN; Sec. ROBERT L. MACDONALD; publ. *Annals of Neurology*.

American Occupational Therapy Association, Inc.: 4720 Montgomery Lane, Bethesda, MD 20814; tel. (301) 652-6611; fax (301) 652-7711; e-mail ajotsis@aota.org; internet www.aota.org; f. 1917; 35,000 mems; library of 4,000 vols; Pres. CAROLYN BAUM; Exec. Dir FREDERICK P. SOMERS; publs *American Journal of Occupational Therapy* (6 a year), *OT Practice* (every 2 weeks), *OT Week*.

American Optometric Association, Inc.: 243 N. Lindbergh Blvd, St. Louis, MO 63141; tel. (314) 991-4100; fax (314) 991-4101; internet www.aoanet.org; f. 1898 to promote the art and science of optometry, to improve vision care and health of the public; 31,000 mems; Pres. Dr WESLEY E. PITTMAN; publs *AOA News* (every 2 weeks), *Optometry* (monthly).

American Pediatric Society: 3400 Research Forest Drive, Suite B7, The Woodlands, TX 77381; tel. (281) 296-0052; fax (281) 296-0082; e-mail info@aps-spr.org; internet www.aps-spr.org; f. 1888; 855 active mems; Pres. ELIZABETH R. MCANARNEY; Exec.-Dir DEBBIE ANAGNOSTELIS; publ. *Paediatric Research* (monthly).

American Physical Therapy Association: 1111 N. Fairfax St, Alexandria, VA 22314; tel. (703) 684-2782; fax (703) 684-7343; internet www.apta.org; f. 1921, inc. 1930; to develop the art and science of physical therapy, and to represent and promote the profession; 65,000 mems; CEO FRANCIS J. MALLON; publs *Physical Therapy* (journal, monthly), *PT – The Magazine of Physical Therapy* (monthly).

American Physiological Society: 9650 Rockville Pike, Bethesda, MD 20814-3991; tel. (301) 634-7164; fax (301) 634-7241; e-mail info@aps.faseb.org; internet www.the-aps.org; f. 1887; 10,600 mems; Pres. D. NEIL GRANGER; Exec. Dir MARTIN FRANK; publs *Advances in Physiology Education* (4 a year and online), *American Journal of Physiology (Consolidated)* (2 a year), *Cell Physiology* (online), *Endocrinology and Metabolism* (online), *Gastrointestinal and Liver Physiology* (online), *Heart and Circulatory Physiology* (online), *Journal of Applied Physiology* (monthly and online), *Journal of Neurophysiology* (monthly and online), *Lung Cellular and Molecular Physiology* (online), *Physiological Genomics* (online), *Physiological Reviews* (4 a year), *The Physiologist* (6 a year and online), *Physiology* (6 a year and online), *Regulatory, Integrative and Comparative Physiology* (online), *Renal Physiology* (online).

American Psychiatric Association: 1000 Wilson Boulevard, Suite 1825, Arlington, VA 22209-3901; tel. (703) 907-7300; e-mail apa@psych.org; internet www.psych.org; f. 1844; 35,000 mems; library of 10,000 vols; Med. Dir MELVIN SABSHIN; publs *American Journal of Psychiatry* (monthly), *Psychiatric News* (every 2 weeks), *Psychiatric Services* (monthly).

American Public Health Association: 800 I St NW, Washington, DC 20001-3710; tel. (202) 777-2742; fax (202) 777-2534; e-mail comments@apha.org; internet www.apha.org; f. 1872; interests include environment, personal health services, social factors, manpower and training in public health, global and international health; 32,000 mems; Exec. Dir Dr GEORGES BENJAMIN; publs *American Journal of Public Health* (monthly), *The Nation's Health* (monthly).

American Roentgen Ray Society: 44211 Slatestone Court, Leesburg, VA 20176; tel. (703) 729-3353; fax (703) 729-4839; e-mail info@arrs.org; internet www.arrs.org; f. 1900; international organization of physicians and scientists working in radiology and related fields; 13,000 mems; Exec. Dir SUSAN BROWN CAPPITELLI; publ. *American Journal of Roentgenology* (monthly).

American Society for Clinical Laboratory Science: 6701 Democracy Blvd, Suite 300, Bethesda, MD 20817; tel. (301) 657-2768; fax (301) 657-2909; e-mail ascls@ascls .org; internet www.ascls.org; f. 1933; 13,000 mems; local, state and regional societies; activities include education, education and research funding, professional affairs and membership services; formerly ASMT; Pres. BARBARA BROWN; Sec. SCOTT AIKEY; publs *Clinical Laboratory Science* (4 a year), *ASCLS Today* (monthly).

American Society for Clinical Pathology: 2100 West Harrison St, Chicago, IL 60612-3798, tel. (312) 738-1336, e-mail info@ ascp.org; internet www.ascp.org; f. 1922; a non-profit medical society for the promotion of pathology and laboratory medicine; 140,000 mems; library of 25,500 vols; Pres. Dr DAVID KEREN; Sec. Dr FRED RODRIGUEZ, JR; publs *American Journal of Clinical Pathology* (monthly), *Laboratory Medicine* (monthly), *Pathology Patterns Reviews* (2 a year).

American Society for Investigative Pathology, Inc.: 9650 Rockville Pike, Bethesda, MD 20814-0990, tel. (301) 634-7130; fax (301) 634-7990; e-mail asip@asip .org; internet www.asip.org; f. 1976; 2,500 mems; Pres. Dr PETER HOWLEY; Sec.-Treas. Dr STANLEY COHEN; Executive Officer Dr MARK E. SOBEL; Director of Finance and Operations JAMES S. DOUGLAS; publs *American Journal of Pathology* (monthly), *The Journal of Molecular Diagnostics* (5 a year).

American Society for Microbiology: 1752 N St NW, Washington, DC 20036; tel. (202) 737-3600; fax (202) 942-9368; internet www .asm.org; f. 1899; present name 1961; 48,000 mems; Exec. Dir MICHAEL I. GOLDBERG; publs *Antimicrobial Agents and Chemotherapy* (monthly), *Abstracts of the Annual Meeting* (annually), *Applied and Environmental Microbiology* (monthly), *ASM News* (monthly), *Clinical and Diagnostic Laboratory Immunology* (monthly), *Clinical Microbiology Reviews* (4 a year), *Eukaryotic Cell* (monthly), *Infection and Immunity* (monthly), *Journal of Bacteriology* (24 a year), *Journal of Clinical Microbiology* (monthly), *Journal of Virology* (24 a year), *Microbiology and Molecular Biology Reviews* (quarterly), *Molecular and Cellular Biology* (monthly).

American Society for Nutritional Sciences: 9650 Rockville Pike, Bethesda, MD 20814; tel. (301) 634-7050; fax (301) 571-1892; f. 1928 to develop and extend knowledge of nutrition and to facilitate personal contact between investigators in nutrition and related fields of interest; 3,100 mems; Pres. STEVEN H. ZEISEL; Sec. SHARON M. DONOVAN; publs *The Journal of Nutrition* (monthly), *Nutrition Notes* (4 a year).

American Society for Pharmacology and Experimental Therapeutics, Inc.: 9650 Rockville Pike, Bethesda, MD 20814-3995; tel. (301) 634-7060; fax (301) 634-7061; e-mail info@aspet.org; internet www.aspet .org; f. 1908; 4,900 mems; holds an annual

meeting on experimental biology; Pres. ELAINE SANDERS-BUSH; Exec. Officer CHRISTINE K. CARRICO; publs *Drug Metabolism and Disposition* (monthly), *Journal of Pharmacology and Experimental Therapeutics* (monthly), *Molecular Interventions* (6 a year), *Molecular Pharmacology* (monthly), *Pharmacological Reviews* (4 a year), *The Pharmacologist* (4 a year).

American Society of Clinical Hypnosis: 140 N. Bloomingdale Rd, Bloomingdale, IL 60108-1017; tel. (630) 980-4740; fax (630) 351-8490; e-mail info@asch.net; internet www.asch.net; f. 1957; an independent organization of professional people in medicine, dentistry, and psychology who share scientific and clinical interests in hypnosis; aims to provide educational programmes to further understanding and acceptance of hypnosis as an important tool of ethical clinical medicine and scientific research; 2,400 mems; Pres. JORDAN I. ZARREN; Sec. THOMAS J. BARR; publ. *The American Journal of Clinical Hypnosis* (quarterly).

American Society of Tropical Medicine and Hygiene: 60 Revere Drive, Suite 500, Northbrook, IL 60062; tel. (847) 480-9592; fax (847) 480-9282; e-mail astmh@astmh.org; internet www.astmh.org; f. 1951; 3,000 mems; Exec. Dir BRIAN MADDOX; publs *American Journal of Tropical Medicine and Hygiene* (monthly), *Tropical Medicine and Hygiene News* (6 a year).

American Speech-Language-Hearing Association: 10801 Rockville Pike, Rockville, MD 20852; tel. (301) 897-5700; fax (301) 571-0457; e-mail actioncenter@asha.org; internet www.asha.org; f. 1925; 118,000 mems; Exec. Dir FREDERICK T. SPAHR; publs *American Journal of Audiology* (3 a year), *American Journal of Speech-Language Pathology* (quarterly), *Asha* (quarterly), *Journal of Speech, Language, and Hearing Research* (every 2 months), *Language Speech and Hearing Services in Schools* (quarterly).

American Surgical Association: 900 Cummings Center, Suite 221-U, Beverly, MA 01915; tel. (978) 927-8330; fax (978) 524-8890; e-mail asa@prri.com; internet www.americansurgical.info; f. 1880; 1,000 mems; Pres. Dr HIRAM C. POLK, JR; Sec. Dr MICHAEL W. MULHOLLAND; publs *Transactions* (annually), *Annals of Surgery* (12 a year).

American Urological Association, Inc.: 1000 Corporate Boulevard, Linthicum, MD 21090; tel. (410) 689-3700; fax (410) 689-3800; e-mail aua@auanet.org; internet www .auanet.org; f. 1902; 14,500 mems; Pres. Dr BRENDAN M. FOX; Sec. Dr CARL A. OLSSON; publs *The Journal of Urology* (monthly), *AUA News* (6 a year).

Armed Forces Institute of Pathology: 6825 16th St, NW, Washington, DC 20306-6000; est. 1862 as Army Medical Museum, present name 1949; it is the central laboratory of pathology for the Department of Defense serving both the military and civilian sectors in education, consultation and research in the medical, dental and veterinary sciences; research into leprosy, malaria, HIV/AIDS, sickle cell disease, radiation injury, trauma, drug toxicity and aerospace pathology; organized into: Center for Advanced Pathology, Center for Clinical Laboratory Medicine, Center for Administrative Services, Center for Education, Repository and Research Services, Office of the Armed Forces Medical Examiner, and National Museum of Health and Medicine; Dir Col MICHAEL J. DICKERSON (USAF).

Association of American Medical Colleges: 2450 N St, NW, Washington, DC 20037-1126; tel. (202) 828-0400; fax (202)

828-1125; internet www.aamc.org; f. 1876; 126 US and 16 Canadian medical schools, more than 400 teaching hospitals and 87 academic and professional societies; Chair. Dr DEBORAH E. POWELL; publs *Academic Medicine* (monthly), *AAMC Curriculum Directory* (annually), *AAMC Directory of Medical Education* (annually), *AAMC Reporter* (monthly), *Medical School Admission Requirements* (annually).

Association of American Physicians: Harvard University, Department of Medicine, Microbiology and Molecular Genetics, Channing Lab., 181 Longwood Ave. Boston, MA 02155; tel. (617) 277-0551; fax (617) 731-1541; e-mail lmialot@aap-online.org; internet www.aap-online.org; f. 1886; 1,200 mems; Pres. RALPH SNYDERMAN; publ. *Transactions* (annually).

Center for the Study of Aging and Human Development: Box 3003, Duke University Medical Center, Durham, NC 27710; tel. (919) 660-7500; fax (919) 684-8569; internet www.geri.duke.edu; f. 1955; supports and trains researchers and clinicians with emphasis on post-doctoral training in all aspects of normal aging (gerontology) as well as diseases and disorders of human aging (geriatrics); lectures, seminars and publications; Geriatric Evaluation and Treatment Clinic for direct service and in-service professional training; geriatric training for health professionals; co-sponsors Osher Lifelong Learning Institute; Dir HARVEY JAY COHEN.

College of Physicians of Philadelphia: 19 South 22nd St, Philadelphia, PA 19103; tel. (215) 563-3737; e-mail histref@ collphyphil.org; internet www.collphyphil .org; f. 1787; to increase understanding between health professions and the general public; includes the College Library, the Mutter Museum (pathology and anatomy) and the Francis C. Wood Institute for the History of Medicine; 1,500 Fellows; library of 340,000 vols; CEO MARK HOCHBERG; College Librarian and Dir, Wood Institute EDWARD T. MORMAN.

Commonwealth Fund: 1 East 75th St, New York, NY 10021; tel. (212) 606-3800; fax (212) 606-3500; e-mail cmwf@cmwf.org; internet www.cmwf.org; f. 1918; to enhance the common good through its efforts to help Americans live healthy and productive lives and to assist specific groups with serious and neglected problems; current fund initiatives include helping young people realize their potential through mentoring and educational enhancement programmes, improving health care services, promoting healthier life styles and bettering the health care of minorities; awards Harkness Fellowships which enable future leaders of the UK, Australia and New Zealand to study social issues in the USA; Chair. of Board SAMUEL O. THIER; Pres. KAREN DAVIS; publ. *Annual Report*.

Gerontological Society of America: 1030 15th St NW, Suite 250, Washington, DC 20005; tel. (202) 842-1275; fax (202) 842-2088; e-mail geron@geron.org; internet www .geron.org; f. 1945; multidisciplinary sciences org., incl. an educational unit, AGHE (Association for Gerontology in Higher Education) and a policy institute, NAAS (National Academy on an Aging Society); 5,000 mems; Exec. Dir CAROL A. SCHUTZ; Pres. TERRY T. FULMER; publs *AGHExchange* (4 a year), *Journals of Gerontology*, (Series A: Biological Sciences and Medical Sciences; Series B: Psychological Sciences and Social Sciences), *Public Policy and Aging Report* (4 a year), *The Gerontologist*.

Industrial Health Foundation, Inc.: 34 Penn Circle West, Pittsburgh, PA 15206; f.

1935; a non-profit organization for the advancement of healthy working conditions in industry; 120 member companies and associations; library of 2,000 vols; publs *Industrial Hygiene Digest* (monthly), special technical bulletins.

John A. Hartford Foundation, Inc.: 55 East 59th St, New York, NY 10022; tel. (212) 832-7788; fax (212) 593-4913; e-mail mail@jhartfound.org; internet www.jhartfound.org; f. 1929 by John A. Hartford and George L. Hartford; ageing and health programme; Chair. of the Board NORMAN H. VOLK; Exec. Dir CORINNE H. RIEDER; publ. *Annual Report*.

Medical Society of the State of New York: POB 5404, Lake Success, New York, NY 11042; tel. (516) 488-6100; fax (516) 488-1267; e-mail mssny@mssny.org; internet www.mssny.org; f. 1807; 30,000 mems; library of 45,000 vols; Pres. Dr WILLIAM B. ROSENBLATT; Exec. Vice-Pres. WILLIAM R. ABRAMS; publs *News of New York* (every 2 weeks), *Medical Directory of New York State* (every 2 years).

National Association for Biomedical Research: 818 Connecticut Ave, Suite 900, Washington, DC 2006; tel. (202) 857-0540; fax (202) 659-1902; e-mail info@nabr.org; internet www.nabr.org; f. 1979; 350 institutional mems; Pres. FRANKIE L. TRULL; Exec. Vice-Pres. BARBARA RICH; publs *NABR Alert*, *NABR Update* (both every 2 weeks), *State Laws*, *NABR Annual Report*.

National Mental Health Association: 12th Fl., 2000 N Beauregard St, Alexandria, VA 22311; tel. (703) 684-7722; fax (703) 684-5968; internet www.nmha.org; f. 1909; 340 affiliates nationally; Chair. of the Board DAN AKENS; Pres./CEO MICHAEL M. FAENZA; publs *FOCUS*, *Legislative Alert*.

New York Academy of Medicine: 1216 Fifth Ave, New York, NY 10029; tel. (212) 822-7200; fax (212) 876-6620; internet www.nyam.org; f. 1847; 3,000 mems; library: see Libraries and Archives; Pres. Dr JEREMIAH A. BARONDESS.

Radiological Society of North America, Inc.: 820 Jorie Blvd, Oak Brook, IL 60523-2251; tel. (630) 571-2670; fax (630) 571-7837; internet www.rsna.org; f. 1915; continuing medical education in radiology; 30,000 mems; Chair. Dr R. GILBERT JOST; Pres. Dr DAVID H. HUSSEY; publs *Radiology* (monthly), *Radio-Graphics* (6 a year), *Index to Imaging Literature* (online index of 38 journals), *News* (monthly).

Society of Medical Jurisprudence: POB 20678, New York, NY 10021-0073; f. 1883; investigation, study and advancement of the science of medical jurisprudence, and the attainment of a higher standard of medical testimony; members must be physicians, lawyers, chemists, forensic odontologists or health professionals of good standing in their respective professions, or teachers in approved Law or Medical Schools; 250 mems; publ. *Proceedings* (monthly, October–June).

NATURAL SCIENCES

General

Academy of Natural Sciences of Philadelphia: 1900 Benjamin Franklin Parkway, Philadelphia, PA 19103-1195; tel. (215) 299-1000; fax (215) 299-1028; internet www.acnatsci.org; f. 1812; natural history museum; research in systematics and evolutionary biology, ecology, limnology and geology, and environmental monitoring; 24m. specimen collections of plants, animals and fossils of world-wide scope; teaching at all levels; 200,000 mems; library: see Libraries and Archives; Pres. IAN DAVISON (acting);

publs *Annual*, *Notulae Naturae*, *Occasional*, *Proceedings*.

American Association for the Advancement of Science: 1200 New York Ave, NW, Washington, DC 20005; tel. (202) 326-6400; fax (202) 789-0455; e-mail media@aaas.org; internet www.aaas.org; f. 1848; 128,000 mems; 262 affiliates serving 10m. mems; aims to advance science and serve society through initiatives in science policy; international programmes; science education; Chair. Dr GILBERT S. OMENN; Pres. Dr JOHN HOLDREN; Chief Exec. Dr ALAN I. LESHNER; publ. *Science* (weekly).

American Society of Limnology and Oceanography: 5400 Bosque Boulevard, Suite 680, Waco, TX 76710-4446; tel. (254) 399-9635; fax (254) 776-3767; internet aslo.org; f. 1936; 3,800 mems; Pres. JONATHAN COLE; publs *Limnology and Oceanography* (every 2 months), *Limnology and Oceanography Bulletin* (4 a year).

Buffalo Society of Natural Sciences: 1020 Humboldt Parkway, Buffalo, NY 14211; tel. (716) 896-5200; fax (716) 897-6723; internet www.sciencebuff.org; f. 1861; administers the Buffalo Museum of Science and Tifft Nature Preserve; samples of natural life in the USA; cultures from other eras to the present; Whem Ankh: The Cycle of Life in Ancient Egypt; Dinosaurs and Company; research in anthropology, botany, entomology, geology, mycology, ornithology, palaeontology, vertebrate zoology, with collections in these fields; 11,000 mems; library of 40,000 vols; publ. *Bulletin* (irregular).

California Academy of Sciences: 875 Howard St, San Francisco, CA 94103-3009; tel. (415) 321-8000; e-mail info@calacademy.org; internet www.calacademy.org; f. 1853 for the advancement of natural sciences through public education and research; incorporated under the laws of the State of California 1871; 20,000 mems incl. 300 Fellows; maintains a public museum of natural history; the Steinhart Aquarium (Dir ROBERT JENKINS); the Morrison Planetarium (Chair. STEVEN B. CRAIG), a scientific library of 100,000 vols (Librarian THOMAS MORITZ), and research departments with large scientific collections; Departments: Anthropology (Curator NINA JABLONSKI), Aquatic Biology (Curator JOHN E. McCOSKER), Botany (Curator TOM DANIEL), Entomology (Curator CHARLES GRISWOLD), Exhibits (Chair. LINDA KULIK), Herpetology (Curator ROBERT DREWES), Invertebrate Zoology and Geology (Curator GARY WILLIAMS), Ornithology and Mammalogy (Curator LUIS BAPTISTA), Ichthyology (Curator WILLIAM ESCHMEYER); Pres. Dr WILLIAM CLEMENS; Exec. Dir Dr EVELYN E. HANDLER; publs *Annual Report*, *California Wild*, *Memoirs*, *Newsletter* (monthly), *Occasional Papers*, *Pacific Discovery* (quarterly), *Proceedings*.

Chicago Academy of Sciences: 2430 N. Cannon Drive, Chicago, IL 60614; tel. (773) 755-5100; e-mail cas@chias.org; internet www.chias.org; f. 1857; 2,200 mems; research colln of plants, animals, fossils and minerals; also maintains Peggy Notebaert Nature Museum, with interactive displays treating the relationship between people and nature; library: a technical scientific library of 3,000 vols, 2,000 periodicals; Chair. PATRICK F. DALY; publs *Bulletin*, *Natural History Miscellanea*.

Cranbrook Institute of Science: 1221 N. Woodward Ave, POB 801, Bloomfield Hills, MI 48303-0801; tel. (810) 645-3259; fax (810) 645-3050; f. 1930; a non-profit-making organization with exhibits and educational programmes in astronomy, mineralogy, geology, botany, zoology, ecology, anthropology,

mathematics and physics; 4,000 mems; library of 18,000 vols; Dir DANIEL E. APPLEMAN.

Franklin Institute: 222 North 20th St, Philadelphia, PA 19103; tel. (215) 448-1200; internet sln.fi.edu; f. 1824; a non-profit science centre dedicated to public science education and to advancing knowledge in the physical sciences; its committee on Science and the Arts awards several medals, including the Franklin Medal, for contributions to science and technology; also administers the Bower Awards for science and business; the Institute incorporates the Franklin Institute Science Museum (*q.v.*), the Fels Planetarium, The Tuttleman Omniverse Theater and the Musser Choices Forum, and houses the Benjamin Franklin National Memorial; there is an observatory open to the public; Pres. and CEO Dr DENNIS M. WINT; publ. *Journal*.

History of Science Society: c/o University of Florida, POB 117360, 3310 Turlington Hall, Gainesville, FL 32611; tel. (352) 392-1677; fax (352) 392-2795; e-mail info@hssonline.org; internet www.hssonline.org; f. 1924; 5,000 mems; Exec. Dir ROBERT J. MALONE; Pres. MICHAEL SOKAL; publs *Isis* (4 a year), *Osiris* (annually).

Maryland Academy of Sciences: 601 Light St, Baltimore, MD 21230; tel. (410) 685-2370; fax (410) 545-5974; internet www.mdsci.org; f. 1797, as an educational and scientific institution, and for the diffusion and explanation of scientific information to the public; controls Maryland Science Center; (10,000 mems); Chair. THOMAS S. BOZZUTO; Pres. (vacant); Exec. Dir GREGORY P. ANDORFER; publ. *Maryland Science Center News* (quarterly).

Mellon Institute: see Carnegie-Mellon University under Universities.

National Science Teachers Association: 1840 Wilson Blvd, Arlington, VA 22201-3000; tel. (703) 243-7100; internet www.nsta.org; f. 1895, reorganized 1944; advances science teaching and science education at elementary, secondary and college levels; 53,000 mems; Pres. ANNE TWEED; Exec. Dir GERALD WHEELER; publs *Journal of College Science Teaching*, *Science and Children*, *Science Scope*, *The Science Teacher*.

Ohio Academy of Science: 1500 West Third Ave, Suite 223, Columbus, OH 43212-2817; tel. (614) 488-2228; fax (614) 488-7629; e-mail oas@iwaynet.net; internet www.ohiosci.org; f. 1891; 2,000 mems; CEO LYNN E. ELFNER; publs *The Ohio Academy of Science News* (irregular), *The Ohio Journal of Science* (5 a year).

Sigma Xi, the Scientific Research Society: 3106 East NC Highway 54, POB 13975, Research Triangle Park, NC 27709; tel. (919) 549-4691; fax (919) 549-0090; e-mail memberinfo@sigmaxi.org; internet www.sigmaxi.org; f. 1886 for the encouragement of scientific research; 70,000 mems; Pres. FRANCISCO J. AYALA; Exec. Dir PATRICK D. SCULLY; publ. *American Scientist* (6 a year).

Southern California Academy of Sciences: c/o Natural History Museum of Los Angeles County, 900 Exposition Blvd, Los Angeles, CA 90007; tel. (909) 607-2836; fax (909) 621-8588; internet scas.jsd.claremont.edu; f. 1891; 400 mems; Pres. Dr JOHN DORSEY (acting); publs *Bulletin* (3 a year), *Memoirs* (irregular).

World Future Society: 7910 Woodmont Ave, Suite 450, Bethesda, MD 20814; tel. (301) 656-8274; fax (301) 951-0394; e-mail wfsinfo@wfs.org; internet www.wfs.org; f. 1966; Pres. TIMOTHY C. MACK; private, non-profit organization promoting free discussion and study of alternative futures especially on technological and social themes; 30,000 mems; publs *The Futurist* (10 a year), *Futures Research Quarterly*, *Future Survey* (monthly).

Biological Sciences

American Genetic Association: POB 257, Buckeyestown, MD 21717; tel. (301) 695-9292; fax (301) 695-9292; e-mail agajoh@mail .ncifcrf.gov; internet www.theaga.org; f. 1903; Pres. Dr SHOZO YOKOYAMA; Sec. Dr LINDA STRAUSBAUGH; publ. *Journal of Heredity* (6 a year).

American Institute of Biological Sciences: 1444 I St NW, Suite 200, Washington, DC 20005; tel. (202) 628-1500; fax (202) 628-1509; internet www.aibs.org; f. 1947; mems: 34 professional societies and 6 industrial firms; 240,000 mems; Pres. MAR-VALEE WAKE; Exec. Dir Dr RICHARD O'GRADY; publs *BioScience* (monthly), *Forum* (every 2 months), *Membership Directory and Handbook* (every 2 years).

American Malacological Society: Dept of Zoology, University of Rhode Island, Kingston, RI 02881; internet erato.acnatsci.org/ ams; f. 1931; study of phylum Mollusca–systematics, ecology, functional morphology, evolution; medical, neotological and palaeontological aspects; 750 mems; Pres. DIANNA K. PADILLA; Sec. PAUL CALLOMON; publs *American Malacological Bulletin* (2 a year), *AMS News* (irregular).

American Ornithologists' Union: 1313 Dolly Madison Blvd, Suite 402, McLean, VA 22101; tel. (703) 790-1745; fax (703) 790-2672; e-mail aou@burkinc.com; internet www.aou.org; f. 1883; scientific study of birds; 5,000 mems; Pres. FRED COOKE; Sec. M. ROSS LEIN; publs *The Auk* (4 a year), *Check-List of North American Birds* (irregular), *Ornithological Newsletter* (6 a year).

American Phytopathological Society: 3340 Pilot Knob Rd, St Paul, MN 55121; tel. (651) 454-7250; fax (651) 454-0766; e-mail aps@scisoc.org; internet www.apsnet.org; f. 1908; detection and control of plant diseases; plant health management; plant management network; 5,000 mems; Pres. (vacant); Exec. Vice-Pres. STEVEN C. NELSON; publs *Phytopathology* (monthly), *Plant Disease* (monthly), *Molecular Plant-Microbe Interactions* (monthly).

American Society for Photobiology: POB 1897, Lawrence, KS 66044; tel. (785) 843-1235; fax (785) 843-1287; e-mail phot@ allenpress.com; internet www.pol-us.net/ ASP_Home; f. 1972; 1,600 mems; Pres. FRANCES NOONAN; publs *Newsletter* (every 2 months), *Photochemistry and Photobiology* (monthly).

American Society of Human Genetics: 9650 Rockville Pike, Bethesda, MD 20814; tel. (301) 634-7300; e-mail society@ashg.org; internet genetics.faseb.org/genetics/ashg/ ashgmenu.htm; f. 1948; 7,500 mems; Exec. Dir ELAINE STRASS; publ. *American Journal of Human Genetics* (monthly).

American Society of Ichthyologists and Herpetologists: c/o Maureen A. Donnelly, Florida International University, Department of Biological Sciences, University Park, Miami, FL 33199; tel. (305) 348-1235; fax (305) 348-1986; e-mail asih@fiu.edu; internet www.asih.org; f. 1913; 3,500 mems (2,500 individual, 1,000 subscriber); Pres. LYNNE R. PARENTI; Sec. MAUREEN A. DONNELLY; publ. *Copeia* (quarterly).

American Society of Mammalogists: 810 E. 10th St, Lawrence, KS 66044; tel. (785) 843-1235; fax (785) 843-1274; e-mail asm@ aibs.org; internet www.mammalsociety.org; f. 1919, inc. 1920; 4,500 mems; object of the

Society is the promotion of interest in mammalogy by holding meetings, issuing serial or other publications, and aiding research; five classes of mems, all elective: Annual, Life, Patron, Honorary and Emeritus; the Society is affiliated with the American Institute of Biological Sciences, the American Association for the Advancement of Science and the International Union for the Conservation of Nature; Pres. GUY CAMERON; Sec. and Treas. RONALD A. VAN DEN BUSSCHE; publs *Journal of Mammalogy* (quarterly), *Mammalian Species* (irregular).

American Society of Naturalists: 4328 Storer Hall, University of California, Davis, CA 95616-8755; tel. (530) 752-1114; e-mail rkgrosberg@ucdavis.edu; internet www .amnat.org; f. 1883; 1,835 mems; Pres. Dr RICHARD GROSBERG; Sec. Dr JUDITH L. BRONSTEIN; publ. *The American Naturalist* (monthly).

American Society of Parasitologists: c/o John Janovy, Jr, School of Biological Sciences, University of Nebraska Lincoln, Lincoln, NE 68588-0118; tel. (402) 472-2754; fax (402) 472-2083; e-mail jjanovy1@unl.edu; internet asp.unl.edu; f. 1924; 1,500 mems; Sec. and Treas. JOHN JANOVY, JR; publ. *The Journal of Parasitology* (6 a year).

Biophysical Society: 9650 Rockville Pike, Room L-0512, Bethesda, MD 20814; tel. (301) 634-7114; fax (301) 634-7133; e-mail society@ biophysics.org; internet www.biophysics.org; f. 1957; 7,000 mems; Pres. YALE GOLDMAN; Sec. JILL TREWHELLA; Exec. Dir ROSALBA KAMPMAN; publ. *Biophysical Journal* (monthly).

Botanical Society of America, Inc.: POB 299, St Louis, MO 63166-0299; tel. (314) 577-9566; fax (314) 577-9515; e-mail bsa-manager@botany.org; internet www .botany.org; f. 1893; 3,000 mems; Pres. CHRISTOPHER HAUFLER, Sec. STEVE WELLER, Exec. Dir BILL DAHL; publs *American Journal of Botany* (monthly), *Directory* (every 2 years), *Guide to Graduate Study in the US and Canada* (irregular), *Plant Science Bulletin* (quarterly).

Ecological Society of America: 1707 H St NW, Suite 400, Washington, DC 20006; tel. (202) 833-8773; fax (202) 833-8775; e-mail esahq@esa.org; internet www.esa.org; f. 1915; 8,300 mems; Exec. Dir KATHERINE S. MCCARTER; publs *Bulletin* (4 a year), *Ecology* (monthly), *Ecological Monographs* (4 a year), *Ecological Applications* (6 a year), *Frontiers in Ecology and the Environment* (10 a year).

Entomological Society of America: 10001 Derekwood Lane, Suite 100, Lanham, MD 20706; tel. (301) 731-4535; fax (301) 731-4538; e-mail esa@entsoc.org; internet www .entsoc.org; f. 1953 by the union of the American Association of Economic Entomologists (f. 1889) and the former Entomological Society of America (f. 1906); 6,000 mems; Exec. Dir PAULA G. LETTICE; publs *American Entomologist* (4 a year), *Annals* (6 a year), *Anthropod Management Tests* (annually), *Environmental Entomology* (6 a year), *Journal of Economic Entomology* (6 a year), *Journal of Medical Entomology* (6 a year).

Environmental Mutagen Society: 1821 Michael Faraday Drive, Suite 300, Reston, VA 20190; tel. (703) 438-8220; fax (703) 438-3113; e-mail emshq@ems-us.org; internet www.ems-us.org; f. 1969; 800 mems; promotion of basic and applied studies of mutagenesis; makes an annual award; Exec. Dir TONIA MASSON; publ. *Environmental and Molecular Mutagenesis* (8 a year).

Federation of American Societies for Experimental Biology: 9650 Rockville Pike, Bethesda, MD 20814; tel. (301) 634-7000; fax (301) 634-7001; internet www.faseb

.org; f. 1912; Full Member Societies: American Physiological Society, American Society for Biochemistry and Molecular Biology, American Society for Pharmacology and Experimental Therapeutics, American Society for Investigative Pathology, American Society for Nutritional Sciences, American Association of Immunologists, Biophysical Society, American Association of Anatomists, The Protein Society, American Society for Bone and Mineral Research, American Society for Clinical Investigation, The Endocrine Society, The American Society of Human Genetics, Society for Developmental Biology; Associate Member Societies: Association of Biomolecular Resource Facilities, American Peptide Society, Society for the Study of Reproduction, Teratology Society, Radiation Research Society, Society for Gynecologic Investigation, Environmental Mutagen Society; library of 2,500 vols; Pres. Dr PAUL W. KINCADE; Sec. and Exec. Dir Dr FREDERICK R. RICKLES; publ. *The FASEB Journal* (monthly).

Genetics Society of America: 9650 Rockville Pike, Bethesda, MD 20814-3998; tel. (301) 634-7300; fax (301) 634-7079; internet www.genetics-gsa.org; f. 1932; 4,000 mems; Pres. Dr TERRY ORR-WEAVER; Sec. Dr ANITA K. HOPPER; Exec. Dir ELAINE STRASS; publ. *Genetics* (monthly).

Mycological Society of America: c/o Dr Faye Murrin, Dept of Biology, Memorial University, St John's, NL A1B 3X9, Canada; tel. (709) 737-8018; fax (709) 737-3018; e-mail fmurrin@morgan.ucs.mun.ca; internet msafungi.org; f. 1931; 1,300 mems; Sec. Dr FAYE MURRIN; publs *Mycologia* (every 2 months), *Inoculum* (newsletter, every 2 months), *Mycologia Memoirs* (irregular).

National Audubon Society: 700 Broadway, New York, NY 10003-9562; tel. (212) 979-3000; fax (212) 979-3188; internet www .audubon.org; f. 1905; membership: 550,000, 518 local chapters; Dir GEOFFREY COBB RYAN; publs *Audubon* (every 2 months), *Audubon Field Notes* (quarterly).

National Wildlife Federation: 11100 Wildlife Center Drive, Reston, VA 20190-5362; tel. (703) 790-4000; fax (703) 790-4075; internet www.nwf.org; f. 1936; 4 m. mems; Pres. and CEO LARRY J. SCHWEIGER; publs *Conservation Directory*, *International Wildlife Magazine*, *National Wildlife Magazine*, *Ranger Rick*, *Your Big Backyard*.

Nature Conservancy: Suite 100, 4245 North Fairfax Drive, Arlington, VA 22203-1606; tel. (800) 628-6860; e-mail comment@ tnc.org; internet nature.org; f. 1951; international non-profit organization committed to preserving biological diversity by protecting lands and waters; 1,000,000 mems; Pres. STEVEN J. MCCORMICK; publ. *Nature Conservancy* (6 a year).

Society for Developmental Biology: 9650 Rockville Pike, Bethesda, MD 20814-3998; tel. (301) 634-7815; fax (301) 634-7825; e-mail sdb@faseb.org; internet www .sdbonline.org; f. 1939; the purpose of the society is to further the study of development in all organisms and at all levels, to represent and promote communication among students of development, and to promote the field of developmental biology; 2,100 mems; Pres. JUDITH KIMBLE; publ. *Developmental Biology* (every 2 weeks).

Society for Economic Botany: Dept of Anthropology, Univ. of Missouri, Columbia, MO 65211; tel. (314) 882-3038; internet www .econbot.org; f. 1959; 1,000 mems; Pres. BRAD BENNETT; Sec. WILL MCCLATCHEY; publ. *Economic Botany* (quarterly).

Society for Experimental Biology and Medicine: 197 W Spring Valley Ave, Maywood, NJ 07607-1727; tel. (201) 291-9080; fax (201) 291-2988; e-mail sebm@inch.com; internet www.sebm.org; f. 1903; 1,500 mems, 1,300 subscribers; Exec. Dir FELICE O'GRADY; publ. *Experimental Biology and Medicine* (11 a year).

Society of Vertebrate Paleontology: Suite 500, 60 Revere Drive, Northbrook, IL 60062; tel. (847) 480-9095; fax (847) 480-9282; e-mail svp@vertpaleo.org; internet www.vertpaleo.org; f. 1941; 2,000 mems; Pres. ANNALISA BERTA; Sec. CATHERINE BADGLEY; publs *Bibliography of Fossil Vertebrates, Journal of Vertebrate Paleontology* (4 a year), *Palaeontologia Electronica, SVP News Bulletin* (3 a year).

Wildlife Conservation Society: Bronx Zoo, 2300 Southern Blvd, Bronx, NY 10460; tel. (718) 220-5100; fax (718) 220-2685; e-mail lcorcoran@wcs.org; internet www.wcs.org; f. 1895; operates the Bronx Zoo, New York Aquarium, Central Park Zoo, Queens Zoo, Prospect Park Zoo; 100,000 mems; library of 6,000 vols; Chair. DAVID SCHIFF; Pres. and CEO Dr STEVEN E. SANDERSON; publ. *Wildlife Conservation* (6 a year).

Wildlife Management Institute: 1101 Fourteenth St, NW, Suite 801, Washington, DC 20036; tel. (202) 371-1808; fax (202) 408-5059; e-mail wmihq@aol.com; internet www.wildlifemanagementinstitute.org; inc. 1946; Pres. STEVEN A. WILLIAMS; Exec. Vice-Pres. RICHARD E. MCCABE; publs *North American Wildlife and Natural Resources Conference Transactions* (annually), *Outdoor News Bulletin* (monthly).

Wildlife Society, Inc.: 5410 Grosvenor Lane, Suite 200, Bethesda, MD 20814-2144; tel. (301) 897-9770; fax (301) 530-2471; e-mail tws@wildlife.org; internet www.wildlife.org; f. 1937 to develop and promote sound stewardship of wildlife resources and of the ecosystems upon which wildlife and humans depend, to undertake an active role in preventing human-induced environmental degradation, to increase awareness and appreciation of wildlife values, and to seek the highest standards in all activities of the wildlife profession; 9,100 mems; Exec. Dir HARRY E. HODGDON; publs *Journal of Wildlife Management* (4 a year), *Wildlife Society Bulletin* (4 a year).

Mathematical Sciences

American Mathematical Society: 201 Charles St, Providence, RI 02904; tel. (401) 455-4000; fax (401) 331-3842; e-mail ams@ams.org; internet www.ams.org; f. 1888; sponsors meetings, symposia, seminars and institutes, and provides employment services in the mathematical sciences; 27,000 mems; Exec. Dir JOHN EWING; publs *Bulletin* (4 a year), *Journal* (4 a year), *Proceedings* (monthly), *Transactions* (monthly), *Mathematical Reviews* (monthly), *Mathematics of Computation* (4 a year), *Electronic Research Announcements* (electronic only), *Notices* (11 a year), *Conformal Geometry and Dynamics* (electronic only), *Representation Theory* (electronic only), *Abstracts of Papers Presented to the American Mathematical Society* (4 a year), *Current Mathematical Publications* (every 3 weeks), *Employment Information in the Mathematical Sciences* (5 a year), *Memoirs* (6 a year), *St Petersburg Mathematical Journal* (6 a year), *Sugaku Expositions* (2 a year), *Theory of Probability and Mathematical Statistics* (2 a year), *Transactions of the Moscow Mathematical Society* (annually).

Dozenal Society of America: Mathematics Dept, Nassau Community College, Garden City, NY 11530; tel. (631) 669-0273; e-mail contact@dozens.org; internet www.dozenal.org; f. 1944 as the Duodecimal Society of America; 144 mems; library of 120 vols; Chair. Prof. GENE ZIRKEL; Pres. Prof. JAY SCHIFFMAN; publ. *Duodecimal Bulletin* (2 a year).

Mathematical Association of America, Inc.: 1529 18th St, NW, Washington, DC 20036; tel. (202) 387-5200; fax (800) 741-9415; internet www.maa.org; f. 1915; 30,000 mems; Pres. CARL C. COWEN; Sec. MARTHA J. SIEGEL; Exec. Dir TINA H. STRALEY; publs *American Mathematical Monthly* (10 a year), *College Mathematics Journal* (5 a year), *Focus* (newsletter, 6 a year), *Journal of Online Mathematics and its Applications, Mathematics Magazine* (5 a year), *Math Horizons* (quarterly).

Society for Industrial and Applied Mathematics Society: 3600 University City Science Center, Philadelphia, PA 19104; tel. (215) 382-9800; fax (215) 386-7999; e-mail siam@siam.org; internet www.siam.org; f. 1951 to promote a better understanding of how mathematics may be used in the solution of complex problems in industry; 10,000 individual mems, 500 institutional mems; Pres. MARTIN GOLUBITSKY; Sec. L. PAMELA COOK; publs *SIAM review* (quarterly), 12 specialist journals, mainly quarterly.

Physical Sciences

Acoustical Society of America: 2 Huntington Quadrangle, Melville, NY 11747-4502; tel. (516) 576-2360; fax (516) 576-2377; e-mail asa@aip.org; internet asa.aip.org; f. 1929; 6,900 mems; Pres. WILLIAM A. YOST; Exec. Dir CHARLES E. SCHMID; publs *Journal* (monthly), *Acoustics Research Letters Online* (quarterly).

American Association of Petroleum Geologists: Box 979, Tulsa, OK 74101-0979; tel. (918) 584-2555; fax (918) 584-0469; e-mail bulletin@aapg.org; internet www.aapg.org; f. 1917; world's largest professional geoscience organization; 31,995 mems; Exec. Dir RICK FRITZ; publs *AAPG Bulletin* (monthly), *AAPG Explorer* (monthly), *Environmental Geosciences* (quarterly).

American Astronomical Society: Dept of Terrestrial Magnetism, 5241 Broad Branch Rd NW, Washington, DC 200151; tel. (202) 478-8867; fax (202) 478-8821; e-mail aassec@aas.org; internet www.aas.org; f. 1899, inc. 1928; 6,500 mems; Exec. Officer Dr JOHN A. GRAHAM; publs *The Astronomical Journal* (monthly), *Bulletin* (4 a year), *The Astrophysical Journal* (3 a month).

American Chemical Society: 1155 16th St NW, Washington, DC 20036; tel. (202) 872-4600; fax (202) 872-4615; e-mail help@acs.org; internet www.chemistry.org; f. 1876; 155,000 mems; Pres. WILLIAM F. CARROLL, JR; Exec. Dir Dr MADELEINE JACOBS; publs *Analytical Chemistry, Biochemistry, Bioconjugate Chemistry, Biomacromolecules, Chemical and Engineering News, Chemical Research in Toxicology, Chemical Reviews, Chemistry of Materials, Crystal Growth & Design, Energy & Fuels, Environmental Science & Technology, Journal of Chemical Information and Modeling, Journal of Chemical Theory and Computation, Journal of Combinatorial Chemistry, Industrial & Engineering Chemistry Research, Inorganic Chemistry, Journal of Agricultural and Food Chemistry, Journal of the ACS, Journal of Chemical & Engineering Data, Journal of Medicinal Chemistry, Journal of Organic Chemistry, Journal of Physical Chemistry A, Journal of Physical Chemistry B, Journal of Proteome Research, Langmuir, Macromolecules, Molecular Pharmaceutics, Nano Letters, Organic Letters, Organic Process Research & Development, Organometallics*.

American Crystallographic Association: c/o POB 96, Ellicott Station, Buffalo, NY 14205-0096; tel. (716) 898-8690; fax (716) 898-8695; e-mail aca@hwi.buffalo.edu; internet www.hwi.buffalo.edu/aca/; f. 1949; 2,200 mems; crystallography and the application of diffraction methods to the study of the arrangement of atoms in matter; Pres. LOUIS DELBAERE; publs *Newsletter* (quarterly), *Program and Abstracts* (annually), *Transactions* (annually).

American Geological Institute: 4220 King St, Alexandria, VA 22302-1502; tel. (703) 379-2480; fax (703) 379-7563; e-mail agi@agiweb.org; internet www.agiweb.org; f. 1948; comprises 35 Earth science societies; Exec. Dir MARCUS E. MILLING; publs *Geotimes* (monthly), *Bibliography and Index of Geology* (monthly).

American Geophysical Union: 2000 Florida Ave NW, Washington, DC 20009-1277; tel. (202) 462-6900; fax (202) 328-0566; e-mail service@agu.org; internet www.agu.org; f. 1919; publishes journals and books; sponsors scientific meetings; sections: Geodesy; Seismology; Atmospheric Sciences; Geomagnetism and Paleomagnetism; Ocean Sciences; Volcanology, Geochemistry and Petrology; Tectonophysics; Planetary Sciences; Space Physics and Aeronomy; Hydrology; 40,000 mems; Pres. JOHN A. ORCUTT; Exec. Dir A. F. SPILHAUS, Jr; publs *Earth Interactions* (electronic journal), *Eos* (weekly), *Geochemistry, Geophysics, Geosystems* (online), *Geophysical Research Letters* (every 2 weeks), *Global Biogeochemical Cycles* (4 a year), *International Journal of Geomagnetism and Aeronomy* (4 a year), *Journal of Geophysical Research* (7 sections, monthly), *Nonlinear Processes in Geophysics* (4 a year), *Paleoceanography* (6 a year), *Radio Science* (6 a year), *Reviews of Geophysics* (4 a year), *Space Weather* (4 a year), *Tectonics* (6 a year), *Water Resources Research* (monthly), *Virtual Choice* (online).

American Institute of Chemists: 315 Chestnut St, Philadelphia, PA 19106-2702; tel. (215) 873-8224; fax (215) 925-1954; e-mail info@theaic.org; internet www.theaic.org; f. 1923; professional aspects of chemical practice, including national certification programme, involvement in governmental activities, awards, and sponsorship, through the AIC Foundation, of unique programme annually to honour top college chemistry seniors; 6,000 mems; Pres. RICHARD BRADLEY; Exec. Dir SHARON DOBSON; publs *AIC Professional Directory* (annually), *The Chemist* (9 a year).

American Institute of Physics: 1 Physics Ellipse, College Park, MD 20740-3843; tel. (301) 209-3100; fax (301) 209-0843; e-mail aipinfo@aip.org; internet www.aip.org; f. 1931; composed of ten mem. societies with total membership of 95,000; 18 affiliated socs, 94 Corporate Assocs, 550 student chapters; Niels Bohr Library; Chair. MILDRED DRESSELHAUS; Exec. Dir and CEO. MARC BRODSKY; 46 publs, including *Physics Today*, journals, bulletins, translated Russian and Chinese journals and secondary information services.

American Meteorological Society: c/o Dr Richard E. Hallgren, 45 Beacon St, Boston, MA 02108; tel. (617) 227-2425; fax (617) 742-8718; e-mail amsinfo@ametsoc.org; internet www.ametsoc.org; f. 1919, inc. 1920; 11,850 mems; Pres. SUSAN AVERY; Exec. Dir RONALD D. MCPHERSON; Deputy Exec. Dir KEITH L. SEITTER; publs *Bulletin of the American Meteorological Society, Meteorological Mono-*

graphs, *Meteorological and Geoastrophysical Abstracts*, *Journal of Physical Oceanography*, *Journal of the Atmospheric Sciences*, *Journal of Climate*, *Journal of Applied Meteorology*, *Monthly Weather Review*, *Journal of Atmospheric and Oceanic Technology*, *Weather and Forecasting*, *Historical Monographs*, *Journal of Hyrdrometeorology*.

American Microscopical Society: Dept of Biology, Washington College, Chestertown, Maryland 21620; tel. (410) 778-2800; internet www.amicros.org; f. 1878; 695 mems and 645 subscribers; Pres. Dr VICKI PEARSE; Treas. Dr D. BRUCE CONN; publ. *Invertebrate Biology* (quarterly).

American Nuclear Society: 555 North Kensington Ave, La Grange Park, IL 60526; tel. (708) 352-6611; fax (708) 352-0499; e-mail nucleus@ans.org; internet www.ans .org; f. 1954; 17 professional divisions: Fusion Energy, Education and Training, Environmental Sciences, Isotopes and Radiation, Materials Science and Technology, Mathematics and Computation, Nuclear Criticality Safety, Fuel Cycle and Waste Management, Human Factors, Nuclear Reactor Safety, Radiation Protection and Shielding, Power and Operations, Reactor Physics, Robotics and Remote Systems Technology, Thermal Hydraulics, Biology and Medicine, Decommissioning, Decontamination and Reutilization, Accelerator Applications; 52 local sections, 8 overseas local sections (Japan, South Korea, Latin America, Austria, Switzerland, Italy, France, Taiwan); 51 student branches; 80 organization mems; Pres. E. JAMES REINSCH; Exec. Dir HARRY A. BRADLEY; publs *Nuclear Science and Engineering* (9 a year), *Nuclear News* (monthly), *ANS News* (6 a year), *Nuclear Technology* (monthly), *Fusion Technology* (6 a year plus supplements), *Transactions* (2 a year), *Buyers' Guide* (annually), nuclear standards.

American Pharmacists Association: 2215 Constitution Ave NW, Washington, DC 20037; tel. (202) 628-4410; fax (202) 783 2351; e-mail webmaster@aphanet.org; internet www.aphanet.org; f. 1852; 50,000 mems; library of 6,000 vols; Exec. Vice-Pres. and CEO Dr JOHN A. GANS; publs *Journal of the American Pharmacists Association* (6 a year), *Journal of Pharmaceutical Sciences* (monthly), *Pharmacy Today* (monthly), *APhA Drug Infoline* (monthly), *Pharmacy Student* (6 a year).

American Physical Society: One Physics Ellipse, College Park, MD 20740; tel. (301) 209-3200; fax (301) 209-0865; e-mail exoffice@aps.org; internet www.aps.org; f. 1899; 40,000 mems; Pres. MARVIN L. COHEN; Exec. Officer Dr JUDY R. FRANZ; publs *Bulletin*, *Physical Review* (in 5 series), *Physical Review Letters*, *Physical Review Special Topics – Accelerators and Beams* (monthly), *Reviews of Modern Physics*.

American Society for Biochemistry and Molecular Biology: 9650 Rockville Pike, Bethesda, MD 20814; tel. (301) 634-7145; fax (301) 634-7126; e-mail asbmb@asbmb.org; internet www.asbmb.org; f. 1906; 12,000 mems; Pres. HEIDI HAMM; Exec. Officer BARBARA A. GORDON; publs *Journal of Biological Chemistry* (weekly), *Journal of Lipid Research* (monthly), *Molecular and Cellular Proteomics* (monthly).

Electrochemical Society: 65 South Main St, Pennington, NJ 08534; tel. (609) 737-1902; fax (609) 737-2743; e-mail ecs@ electrochem.org; internet www.electrochem .org; f. 1902; approx. 8,000 individual mems, 100 corporate mems; conducts two international technical meetings annually on various topics in electrochemistry, solid-state science and related fields; Exec. Dir ROQUE J.

CALVO; publs *Electrochemical and Solid-State Letters* (print ed. published monthly, articles published online), *Interface* (quarterly, print and online), *Journal* (print ed. published monthly, articles published online).

Geochemical Society: Department of Earth and Planetary Sciences, Washington University, 1 Brookings Drive, St Louis, MO 63130-4899; tel. (314) 935-4131; fax (314) 935-4121; e-mail gsoffice@gs.wustl.edu; internet gs.wustl.edu; f. 1955; 1,800 mems; Pres. SUSAN BRANTLEY; Sec. JEREMY B. FEIN; publs *Geochimica et Cosmochimica Acta*, *Geochemistry Geophysics Geosystems* (online).

Geological Society of America, Inc.: POB 9140, 3300 Penrose Place, Boulder, CO 80301-9140; tel. (303) 447-2020; fax (303) 357-1070; e-mail comm@geosociety.org; internet www.geosociety.org; f. 1888; 16,000 mems; Exec. Dir JOHN W. HESS; publs *Abstracts with programs* (annually), *Environmental and Engineering Geoscience* (quarterly), *Geology* (monthly), *GSA Bulletin* (monthly), *GSA Today* (monthly).

Microscopy Society of America: Bostrom Corp., Suite 400, 230 East Ohio, Chicago, IL 60611; tel. (312) 644-1527; fax (312) 644-8557; e-mail businessoffice@microscopy.org; internet www.microscopy.org; f. 1942; annual meeting, presenting technical papers and exhibits; aims to increase and diffuse knowledge of microscopy and related instruments and results obtained through their use; 5,000 mems; Pres. JAY JEROME; Sec. JANET H. WOODWARD; publs *Journal* (6 a year), *Proceedings* (annually).

Mineralogical Society of America: 1015 Eighteenth St NW, Suite 601, Washington, DC 20036-5212; tel. (202) 775-4344; fax (202) 775-0018; e-mail business@minsocam.org; internet www.minsocam.org; f. 1919; mineralogy, petrology, crystallography, geochemistry; 2,200 mems; Exec. Dir J. ALEX SPEER; publs *The American Mineralogist* (8 a year), *Reviews in Mineralogy and Geochemistry* (3 to 6 a year).

Oak Ridge Associated Universities, Inc.: POB 117, 130 Badger Ave, Oak Ridge, TN 37831-0117; tel. (865) 576-3000; fax (865) 576-3643; e-mail smitha@orau.gov; internet www.orau.org; f. 1946; consortium of 87 universities; promotes collaborative partnerships with universities, federal laboratories and industry; manages the Oak Ridge Institute for Science and Education for the US Department of Energy; carries out research and development, training and education, technical assistance activities for DOE and other federal and private organizations; concentrates on the following major areas: science/engineering education, worldwide emergency response and training, workforce health and safety research and training, technical training systems and environmental monitoring; manages educational programmes for undergraduate, graduate and postdoctoral students and academic staff; develops training processes that encompass the design, delivery and evaluation of training networks; performs radiological site investigations and verification surveys; manages University Radioactive Ion Beam (UNI-RIB) user facility; maintains medical, training and energy/environment library; Pres. Dr RONALD D. TOWNSEND; publ. *Annual Report*.

Optical Society of America: 2010 Massachusetts Ave, NW, Washington, DC 20036; tel. (202) 223-8130; fax (202) 223-1096; e-mail info@osa.org; internet www.osa.org; f. 1916; a national organization devoted to the advancement of optics and the service of

all who are interested in any phase of that science; 15,452 mems; Pres. G. MICHAEL MORRIS; Exec. Dir ELIZABETH ROGAN; publs *Journal of the Optical Society of America A* (optics, image science and vision; monthly), *Journal of the Optical Society of America B* (optical physics; monthly), *Optics and Photonics News* (monthly), *Optics Letters* (2 a month), *Applied Optics* (3 a month), *Journal of Lightwave Technology* (monthly), *Optics and Spectroscopy* (monthly), *Journal of Optical Technology* (monthly), *Chinese Journal of Lasers B* (6 a year), *Journal of Optical Networking* (monthly, online only), *Optics Express* (monthly, online only).

Palaeontological Society: c/o Roger D. K. Thomas, Department of Earth and Environment, Franklin and Marshall College, Lancaster, PA 17604-3003; tel. (717) 291-4135; fax (717) 291-4186; internet www.paleosoc .org; f. 1908 to publish and disseminate palaeontological research; 1,710 mems; 1,000 institutional subscribers; associated with the Geological Society of America; Pres. DAVID J. BOTTJER; Sec. ROGER D. K. THOMAS; publs *Newsletter* (2 a year), *Journal of Paleontology* (every 2 months), *Paleobiology* (quarterly), *The Paleontological Society Memoirs* (irregular), *Short Course Notes* (annually).

Seismological Society of America: 201 El Cerrito Plaza Professional Bldg, El Cerrito, CA 94530; tel. (510) 525-5475; fax (510) 525-7204; e-mail info@seismosoc.org; internet www.seismosoc.org; f. 1906; 1,900 mems; seismology, earthquake engineering, earthquake geology, etc.; Pres. STEVEN D. MALONE; Sec. JOE J. LITEHISER, JR; Exec. Dir SUSAN B. NEWMAN; publs *Bulletin* (6 a year), *Seismological Research Letters* (6 a year).

Society for Sedimentary Geology (SEPM): 6128 East 38th St, Suite 308, Tulsa, OK 74135-5814; tel. (918) 610-3361; fax (918) 621-1685; internet www.sepm.org; f. 1926; 5,000 mems; Pres. J. FREDERICK SARG; Exec. Dir HOWARD HARPER; publs *Journal of Sedimentary Research* (6 a year), *PALAIOS* (6 a year).

Society of Economic Geologists: 7811 Shaffer Parkway, Littleton, CO 80127-3732; tel. (720) 981-7882; fax (720) 981-7874; e-mail seg@segweb.org; internet www .segweb.org; f. 1920; 3,500 mems; Pres. MURRAY HITZMAN; publ. *Economic Geology* (8 a year).

PHILOSOPHY AND PSYCHOLOGY

American Philosophical Association: 31 Amstel Ave, University of Delaware, Newark, DE 19716; tel. (302) 831-1112; fax (302) 831-8690; e-mail apaonline@udel.edu; internet www.apa.udel.edu/apa; f. 1900; to promote the exchange of ideas among philosophers, to encourage creative and scholarly activity in philosophy and to facilitate the professional work of teachers of philosophy; 10,800 mems; Chair. JUDITH THOMSON; Exec. Dir MICHAEL KELLY.

American Psychological Association: 750 First St, NE, Washington, DC 20002-4242; tel. (202) 336-5500; internet www.apa .org; f. 1892; 155,000 mems; Pres. GERALD P. KOOCHER; Exec. Vice-Pres. and CEO NORMAN B. ANDERSON; library of 2,500 vols; publs *American Psychologist*, *APA Monitor*, *Psychological Abstracts* (monthly), and 47 others.

Metaphysical Society of America: c/o Brian Martine, Dept of Philosophy, University of Alabama in Huntsville, AL 35899; tel. (205) 895-6555; fax (205) 895-6954; e-mail martineb@email.uah.edu; internet www.acls .org/metaphys.htm; f. 1950 to study metaphysical problems without regard to sectarian divisions; 700 mems; Sec. and Treas. BRIAN MARTINE; Pres. FREDERICK FERRE.

Philosophy of Science Association: c/o George Gale, Dept of Philosophy, University of Missouri, Kansas City, MO 64110-2499; internet philosophy.wisc.edu/psa; f. 1934 to further studies and free discussion in the field of philosophy of science; 1,000 mems; Pres. ELLIOTT SOBER; Exec. Sec. GEORGE GALE; publs *Newsletter* (quarterly), *Philosophy of Science* (quarterly), *Proceedings of Biennial Meetings*.

Psychometric Society: c/o Terry Ackerman, 207 Curry Bldg, POB 26171, University of North Carolina at Greensboro, Greensboro, NC 27402-6171; tel. (336) 334-3474; e-mail taackerm@uncg.edu; internet www .psychometrika.org; f. 1935; 750 mems; Pres. BOB CUDECK; Sec. TERRY ACKERMAN; publ. *Psychometrika* (quarterly).

RELIGION, SOCIOLOGY AND ANTHROPOLOGY

African Studies Association: Rutgers University, Douglass Campus, 132 George St, New Brunswick, NJ 08901-1400; tel. (732) 932-8173; fax (732) 932-3394; e-mail members@rci.rutgers.edu; internet www .africanstudies.org; f. 1957; encourages research and collects and disseminates information on Africa; 2,500 mems; Pres. Dr SANDRA BARNES; Exec. Dir Dr CAROL C. MARTIN; publs *African Studies Review* (3 a year), *ASA News* (3 a year), *Issue* (2 a year), *History in Africa* (annually).

American Academy of Religion: Suite 300, 825 Houston Mill Rd, Atlanta, GA 30329-4246; tel. (404) 727-3049; fax (404) 727-7959; e-mail adminasst@aarweb.org; internet www.aarweb.org; f. 1909; int. learned soc. and professional asscn of teachers and research scholars in the field of religion and religious studies; 8,500 mems; publs *Journal of the American Academy of Religion (JAAR)* (quarterly), *Religious Studies News* (quarterly).

American Anthropological Association: Suite 600, 2200 Wilson Blvd, Arlington, VA 22201-3357; tel. (703) 528-1902; fax (703) 528-3546; e-mail members@aaanet.org; internet www.aaanet.org; f. 1902; 11,000 mems; Exec. Dir WILLIAM E. DAVIS III; publs *Culture and Agriculture* (2 a year), *Anthropology of Work Review* (3 a year), *Visual Anthropology Review* (2 a year), *Transforming Anthropology* (2 a year), *Political and Legal Anthropology Review* (2 a year), *Museum Anthropology* (2 a year), *Journal of the Society for the Anthropology of Europe* (2 a year), *Anthropology of Consciousness* (2 a year), *Journal of Latin American Anthropology* (2 a year), *City and Society* (2 a year), *American Anthropologist* (4 a year), *American Ethnologist* (4 a year), *Ethos* (4 a year), *Cultural Anthropology* (4 a year), *Medical Anthropology Quarterly* (4 a year), *Anthropology and Education Quarterly* (4 a year), *Anthropology News* (9 a year), *Guide to Departments of Anthropology* (annually), *Anthropology and Humanism* (2 a year), *Journal of Linguistic Anthropology* (2 a year), *Archaeological Publications* (annually), *National Association for the Practice of Anthropology Bulletin* (annually), *Central States Anthropology Society (CSAS)* (2 a year), *General Anthropology Bulletin* (2 a year), *North American Dialogue* (2 a year), *Society of Lesbian and Gay Anthropologists (SOLGAN) Newsletter* (2 a year), *Teaching Anthropology/Society for Anthropology in Community Colleges* (2 a year), *Voices* (annually).

American Counseling Association: 5999 Stevenson Ave, Alexandria, VA 22304; tel.

(703) 823-9800; fax (703) 823-6862; internet www.counseling.org; f. 1952; counselling, guidance and student personnel services; 43,000 mems; divisions: American College Counseling Asscn, Asscn for Counselor Education and Supervision, National Career Development Asscn, Counseling Asscn for Humanistic Education and Development, American School Counselor Asscn, American Rehabilitation Counseling Asscn, Asscn for Assessment in Counseling, National Employment Counseling Asscn, Asscn for Multicultural Counseling and Development, Asscn for Spiritual, Ethical and Religious Values in Counseling, Internat. Asscn of Addictions and Offender Counselors, American Mental Health Counselors Asscn, Asscn for Counselors and Educators in Government, Asscn for Adult Development and Aging, Asscn for Gay, Lesbian and Bisexual Issues in Counseling, Internat. Asscn of Marriage and Family Counselors; Asscn for Creativity in Counseling; Asscn for Specialists in Group Work; Counselors for Social Justice; Pres. Dr PATRICIA ARREDONDO; Exec. Dir RICHARD YEP (acting); publs 16 periodicals on aspects of counselling, guidance and human development.

American Folklore Society: c/o Timothy Lloyd, Mershon Center, Ohio State University, 1501 Neil Ave, Columbus, OH 43201-2602; tel. (614) 292-3375; fax (614) 292-2407; internet afsnet.org; f. 1888; 2,200 mems; Pres. BILL IVEY; Exec. Dir TIMOTHY LLOYD; publs *Journal of American Folklore* (4 a year), *Newsletter*.

American Oriental Society: Hatcher Graduate Library, University of Michigan, Ann Arbor, MI 48109-1205; e-mail jrodgers@ umich.edu; internet www.umich.edu/~aos; f. 1842; 1,350 mems; library of 22,000 vols; Pres. PAUL W. KROLL; Sec. and Treas. J. RODGERS; publ. *Journal* (quarterly).

American Society for Ethnohistory: Dept of Anthropology, McGraw Hall, Cornell University, Ithaca, NY 14853; tel. (607) 277-0109; internet ethnohistory.org; f. 1954; 1,200 mems; scholarly organization devoted to the study of the histories of cultures and societies in all areas of the world; Pres. K. TSIANINA LOMAWAIMA; Sec. and Treas. CAROLYN PODRUCHNY; publ. *Ethnohistory* (quarterly).

American Sociological Association: 1307 New York Ave NW, Suite 700, Washington, DC 20005; tel. (202) 383-9005; fax (202) 638-0882; internet www.asanet.org; f. 1905; 14,000 mems; Pres. TROY DUSTER; Exec. Officer SALLY T. HILLSMAN; publs *The American Sociological Review* (6 a year), *City & Community* (4 a year), *Contemporary Sociology* (6 a year), *Contexts* (4 a year), *Employment Bulletin* (monthly), *Footnotes* (9 a year), *Journal of Health and Social Behavior* (4 a year), *Social Psychology Quarterly* (4 a year), *Sociological Methodology* (annually), *Sociological Theory* (2 a year), *Sociology of Education* (4 a year), *Teaching Sociology* (4 a year).

Association for Asian Studies, Inc.: 1021 East Huron St, Ann Arbor, MI 48104; tel. (734) 665-2490; fax (734) 665-3801; e-mail postmaster@aasianst.org; internet www .aasianst.org; f. 1941; 8,000 mems; Pres. MARY ELIZABETH BERRY; Exec. Dir MICHAEL PASCHAL; publs *Asian Studies Newsletter* (5 a year), *Bibliography of Asian Studies Online* (electronic database, updated 4 times a year), *Education about Asia* (3 a year), *Journal of Asian Studies* (quarterly).

Association for the Study of Afro-American Life and History, Inc.: c/o Dr Edward Beasley, 4826 Sorter Drive, Kansas City, KS 66104; tel. (913) 287-8465; internet www

.dpw-archives.org/asalh.html; f. 1915; 2,200 mems; publs *The Journal of Negro History* (quarterly), *The Negro History Bulletin* (quarterly).

National Institute of Social Sciences: 150 Amsterdam Ave, New York, NY 10023; f. 1899; 850 mems; Pres. J. SINCLAIR ARMSTRONG; Sec. BRUCE E. BALDING.

Pacific Sociological Association: Dept of Sociology, California State University, Sacramento, CA 95819-6005; tel. (916) 278-5254; fax (916) 278-6281; e-mail psa@csus.edu; internet www.csus.edu/psa; f. 1930; 900 mems; Exec. Dir DEAN S. DORN; publs *Sociological Perspectives* (quarterly), *The Pacific Sociologist*.

Population Association of America, Inc.: 8630 Fenton St, Suite 722, Silver Spring, MD 20910-3812; tel. (301) 565-6710; fax (301) 565-7850; e-mail info@popassoc.org; internet www.popassoc.org; f. 1931; 3,000 mems; Pres. CHARLES HIRSCHMAN; Exec. Dir STEPHANIE D. DUDLEY; publ. *Demography* (4 a year).

Population Council: 1 Dag Hammarskjold Plaza, New York, NY 10017; tel. (212) 339-0500; fax (212) 755-6052; e-mail pubinfo@ popcouncil.org; internet www.popcouncil.org; f. 1952; int. non-profit non-governmental org. seeking to improve the well-being and reproductive health of current and future generations around the world and to help achieve a humane, equitable and sustainable balance between people and resources; activities incl. fundamental biomedical research in reproduction, developing contraceptives and other products for improvement of reproductive health, conducting studies to improve the quality and outreach of services related to family planning, HIV/AIDS and reproductive health, conducting research on reproductive health and behaviour, family structure and function, and causes and consequences of population growth, and strengthening professional resources in developing countries through collaborative research, awards, fellowships and training; Pres. Dr PETER J. DONALDSON; Vice-Pres. International Programs Division Dr ANRUDH JAIN; Vice-Pres. Distinguished Scholar Dr JOHN BONGAARTS; Chief Financial Officer KENNETH L. PAYNE; publs *Momentum* (2 a year), *Population Briefs* (3 a year), *Population and Development Review* (4 a year), *Studies in Family Planning* (4 a year).

Religious Research Association: 618 SW 2nd Ave, Galva, IL 61434-1912; tel. (309) 932-2727; fax (309) 932-2282; e-mail bill4329@hotmail.com; internet rra.hartsem .edu; f. 1951; aims to increase understanding of the function of religion in persons and society through application of social scientific and other scholarly methods; to promote religious research; to co-operate with other societies and individuals interested in the study of religion; 600 mems; Pres. DANIEL V. A. OLSON; Exec. Sec. W. H. SWATOS, Jr; publ. *Review of Religious Research* (quarterly).

Russell Sage Foundation: 112 East 64th St, New York, NY 10021; tel. (212) 750-6000; fax (212) 371-4761; e-mail info@rsage.org; internet www.russellsage.org; f. 1907; promotes improvement of social and living conditions in the United States; supports projects on the future of work, immigration and the social psychology of cultural contact; Chair. ROBERT E. DENHAM; Pres. ERIC WANNER; publ. *Biennial Report*.

Society for Applied Anthropology: POB 2436, Oklahoma City, OK 73101-2436; tel. (405) 843-5113; fax (405) 843-8553; e-mail info@sfaa.net; internet www.sfaa.net; f. 1941; application of the social and behavioural sciences to contemporary problems; 3,000 mems; Exec. Dir Dr JUDE THOMAS MAY;

publs *Human Organization* (4 a year), *Practicing Anthropology* (4 a year), *SfAA Newsletter* (4 a year).

Society for the Scientific Study of Religion Inc.: Arthur L. Greil, Alfred University Division of Social Sciences Saxon Drive, Alfred, NY 14802; tel. (607) 871-2215; fax (607) 871-2085; e-mail sssr@alfred.edu; internet las.alfred.edu/~soc/SSSR; f. 1949; dedicated to research and scholarly publs relating to religious phenomena; examining the consequences of religious beliefs on individual and social behaviour, the impact of religious organizations on other institutions, and problems of continuity and change within religious groups; *c.* 1,500 mems; Pres. NANCY AMMERMAN; Exec. Officer LARRY GREIL; publs *Journal* (quarterly), *Newsletter*.

Society for the Study of Evolution: c/o Allen Marketing and Management, POB 1897, Lawrence, KS 66044; tel. (785) 843-1235; fax (785) 843-1274; e-mail sse@allenpress.com; internet lsvl.la.asu.edu/evolution; f. 1946 to promote the study of organic evolution and the integration of the various fields of science concerned with evolution; 3,000 mems; Pres. DOLPH SCHLUTER; Exec. Vice-Pres. JESSICA GUREVITCH; publ. *Evolution* (6 a year).

TECHNOLOGY

American Ceramic Society: POB 6136, Westerville, OH 43086-6136; tel. (614) 890-4700; fax (614) 899-6109; e-mail info@ccramics.org; internet www.ceramics.org; f. 1899; 10,400 mems; library of 11,000 vols; Pres. WARREN W. WOLF; Sec. and Exec. Dir GLENN F. HARVEY; runs Ceramic Correspondence Inst.; publs *Applied Ceramic Technology* (6 a year), *Ceramic Engineering and Science Proceedings* (5 a year), *Ceramics Monthly*, *Ceramic Society Bulletin* (monthly), *Ceramic Source* (annually), *Journal of the American Ceramic Society* (monthly), *Pottery Making Illustrated* (5 a year).

American Council of Engineering Companies: 1015 15th St, NW, Washington, DC 20005-2605; tel. (202) 347-7474; fax (202) 898-0068; e-mail acec@ncec.org; internet www.accc.org; f. 1956; 5,800 mems; Pres. DAVID A. RAYMOND; publs *American Consulting Engineer*, *Directory*, *Engineering Inc.*

American Institute of Aeronautics and Astronautics: 1801 Alexander Bell Drive, Suite 500, Reston, VA 20191; f. 1930; 35,000 mems; Exec. Dir CORT DUROCHER; publs *Aerospace America* (includes *AIAA Bulletin*), *Journal of Spacecraft and Rockets*, *Journal of Aircraft*, *AIAA Journal*, *AIAA Student Journal*, *Journal of Guidance, Control and Dynamics*, *Journal of Propulsion and Power*, *Journal of Thermophysics and Heat Transfer*, *Journal of Aerospace Computing, Information and Communication* (monthly, online only).

American Institute of Chemical Engineers: 3 Park Ave, New York, NY 10016-5991; tel. (212) 591-8100; fax (212) 591-8888; e-mail xpress@aiche.org; internet www.aiche.org; f. 1908; 40,000 mems; Pres. JEFFREY J. SIIROLA; Exec. Dir JOHN SOFRANKO; publs *AIChE Journal* (monthly), *Biotechnology Progress* (6 a year), *Chemical Engineering Progress* (monthly), *Chemical Engineering Faculty Directory* (annually), *Environmental Progress* (4 a year), *Process Safety Progress* (4 a year).

American Institute of Mining, Metallurgical and Petroleum Engineers, Inc.: POB 270728, Littleton, CO 80127-0013; tel. (303) 948-4255; fax (303) 948-4260; e-mail aime@aimehq.org; internet www.aimehq.org; f. 1871; 90,523 mems via member societies; Exec. Dir J. RICK ROLATER.

Member societies:

Association for Iron and Steel Technology: 186 Thorn Hill Rd, Warrendale, PA 15086-7528; tel. (724) 776-6040; fax (724) 776-1880; e-mail info@aistech.org; internet www.aistech.org; 11,268 mems; Exec. Dir RONALD E. ASHBURN; publ. *Iron and Steel maker* (monthly).

Minerals, Metals and Materials Society: 184 Thorn Hill Rd, Warrendale, PA 15086-7528; tel. (724) 776-9000; fax (724) 776-3770; e-mail tmsgeneral@tms.org; internet www.tms.org; Exec. Dir ALEXANDER R. SCOTT; publs *Journal of Metals* (monthly), *Metallurgical Transactions A* (monthly), *B* (4 a year).

Society for Mining, Metallurgy and Exploration, Inc.: 8307 Shaffer Parkway, Littleton, CO 80127-7002; tel. (303) 973-9550; fax (303) 973-3845; e-mail sme@smenet.org; internet www.smenet.org; 9,836 mems; Exec. Dir DAVID L. KANAGY; publs *Mining Engineering* (monthly), *Transactions* (annually), *Minerals & Metallurgical Processing* (quarterly).

Society of Petroleum Engineers: POB 833836, Richardson, TX 75083-3836; tel. (972) 952-9393; fax (972) 952-9435; e-mail postmaster@spe.org; internet www.spe.org; 60,559 mems; Exec. Dir MARK A. RUBIN; publs *Journal of Petroleum Technology* (monthly), *Transactions*.

American Iron and Steel Institute: 1140 Connecticut Ave, NW, Suite 705, Washington, DC 20036; tel. (202) 452-7100; internet www.steel.org; f. 1908; 31 corporate mems; Pres. and CEO ANDREW G. SHARKEY.

American National Standards Institute: 25 West 43rd St, New York, NY 10036; tel. (212) 642-4900; fax (212) 398-0023; internet www.ansi.org; f. 1918; co-ordinates the development of voluntary national standards, approves American National Standards, and represents US interests in the ISO and the IEC; mems: 1,000 companies, organizations, academic and government bodies, Chair. Dr ROBERT W. NOTH; Pres. and CEO S. JOE BHATIA; publ. *ANSI Reporter* (monthly).

American Society for Engineering Education: 1818 N St, NW, Suite 600, Washington, DC 20036-2479; tel. (202) 331-3500; fax (202) 245-8504; internet www.asee.org; f. 1893; for the improvement of higher and continuing education for engineers and engineering technologists including teaching, counselling, research, ethics, etc.; 12,000 individual mems, 500 institutional mems; Pres. SHERRA E. KERNS; Exec. Dir FRANK L. HUBAND; publs *ASEE Prism*, *Chemical Engineering Education*, *Civil Engineering Education*, *Computers in Education Journal*, *Directory of Engineering and Engineering Technology*, *Engineering Design Graphics Journal*, *The Engineering Economist*, *Journal of Engineering Education*, *Journal of Industrial Engineering Design*, *Mechanical Engineering News*.

American Society for Photogrammetry and Remote Sensing: 5410 Grosvenor Lane, Suite 210, Bethesda, MD 20814-2160; tel. (301) 493-0290; fax (301) 493-0208; e-mail asprs@asprs.org; internet www.asprs.org; f. 1934; aerial photography, photogrammetry, photo-interpretation, remote sensing, geographic information systems (GIS), surveying, mapping, cartography; 7,000 mems; Pres. KAREN L. SCHUCKMAN; Treas. DONALD T. LAUER; publ. *Photogrammetric Engineering and Remote Sensing* (monthly).

American Society of Civil Engineers: 1801 Alexander Bell Drive, Reston, VA 20191-4400; tel. (703) 295-6300; fax (703)

295-6222; internet www.asce.org; f. 1852; 105,000 mems; Pres. WILLIAM P. HENRY; Exec. Dir PATRICK J. NATALE; publs *ASCE* (monthly), *ASCE News*, *Journal of Aerospace Engineering* (quarterly), *Journal of Architectural Engineering* (quarterly), *Journal of Energy Engineering* (3 a year), *International Journal of Geomechanics* (quarterly), and 25 online journals, *Publications Information* (every 2 months).

American Society of Heating, Refrigerating and Air-Conditioning Engineers, Inc.: 1791 Tullie Circle NE, Atlanta, GA 30329; tel. (404) 636-8400; fax (404) 321-5478; e-mail ashrae@ashrae.org; internet www.ashrae.org; f. 1959 by merger of the American Society of Heating and Ventilating Engineers and the American Society of Refrigerating Engineers; 55,000 mems; Sec. and Exec. Vice-Pres. JEFF H. LITTLETON; publs *ASHRAE Journal* (monthly), *ASHRAE Handbook* (annually), *ASHRAE Transactions* (2 a year), *HVAC&R Research* (4 a year), *IAQ Applications* (4 a year).

American Society of Mechanical Engineers: 3 Park Ave, New York, NY 10016-5990; tel. (212) 591-7722; fax (212) 591-7674; e-mail infocentral@asme.org; internet www.asmc.org; f. 1880; 120,000 mems; Pres. HARRY ARMEN; Exec. Dir VIRGIL R. CARTER; publs *Applied Mechanics Reviews* (monthly), *Mechanical Engineering* (monthly), *Transactions* (divided into 17 periodicals, each published quarterly): *Journal of Applied Mechanics*, *Biomechanical Engineering*, *Dynamic Systems, Measurement and Control*, *Energy Resources Technology*, *Engineering for Industry*, *Engineering for Gas Turbines and Power*, *Engineering Materials and Technology*, *Fluids Engineering*, *Heat Transfer*, *Mechanisms*, *Transmissions and Automation in Design*, *Pressure Vessel Technology*, *Solar Energy Engineering*, *Tribology*, *Vibration and Acoustics*, *Electronic Packaging*, *Turbomachinery*, *Manufacturing Review* (4 a year).

American Society of Naval Engineers, Inc.: 1452 Duke St, Alexandria, VA 22314-3458; tel. (703) 836-6727; fax (703) 836-7491; e-mail asnehq@navalengineers.org; internet www.navalengineers.org; f. 1888; 6,000 mems; Pres. Rear Adm. (Retd) DAVID P. SARGENT, Jr; Exec. Dir Capt. (Retd) DENNIS KRUSE; publ. *Naval Engineers Journal* (4 a year).

American Welding Society: 550 NW Le Jeune Rd, Miami, FL 33126; tel. (305) 443-9353; fax (305) 443-7559; e-mail education@aws.org; internet www.aws.org; f. 1919; welding education seminars and conferences, qualification and certification, annual int. exposition; 46,000 mems; Exec. Dir R. W. SHOCK; publs *Welding Journal* (monthly), *Inspection Trends* (4 a year), *Welding Handbook* (every 3 years), 200 welding standards, references, training guides.

ASM International: 9639 Kinsman Rd, Materials Park, OH 44073-0002; tel. (440) 338-5151; fax (440) 338-4634; e-mail cust-srv@asminternational.org; internet www.asm-intl.org; f. 1913; 43,000 mems; technical society concerned with advanced materials technology; Pres. Dr BHAKTA B. RATH; Man. Dir and Sec. STANLEY C. THEOBALD; publs *Advanced Materials and Processes* (monthly, containing *ASM News*), *Alloy Digest* (monthly), *Electronic Device Failure Analysis*, *International Materials Reviews* (6 a year, with Institute of Materials), *Journal of Failure Analysis and Prevention*, *Journal of Phase Equilibria and Diffusion* (6 a year), *Journal of Materials Engineering and Performance* (6 a year), *Journal of Thermal Spray Technology* (4 a year), *Metallurgical Transactions A & B (6 a year) (with TMS–AIME)* (monthly).

Association of Consulting Chemists and Chemical Engineers, Inc.: POB 297, Sparta, NJ 07871; tel. (973) 729-6671; fax (973) 729-7088; e-mail info@chemconsult.org; internet www.chemconsult.org; f. 1928; 160 mems; Pres. Dr JOSPEH V. PORCELLI; publ. *Consulting Services Directory*.

ASTM International: 100 Barr Harbor Drive, POB C700, West Conshohocken, PA 19428-2959; tel. (610) 832-9585; fax (610) 832-9555; e-mail service@astm.org; internet www.astm.org; f. 1898; non-profit organization providing a global forum for the development and publication of voluntary consensus standards for materials, products, systems and services; 30,000 mems from 100 countries; Pres. JAMES THOMAS; publs *Journal of ASTM International (JAI), Cement, Concrete & Aggregates, Geotechnical Testing Journal, Journal of Composites, Technology and Research, Journal of Forensic Sciences, Journal of Testing and Evaluation*.

Edison Electric Institute: 701 Pennsylvania Ave, NW, Washington, DC 20004-2696; tel. (202) 508-5000; fax (202) 508-5360; internet www.eei.org; f. 1933; mems US shareholder-owned electric power companies, int. affiliates and associates (200 US mems, 50 int. mems, 140 assoc. mems); Pres. THOMAS R. KUHN; publ. *Electric Perspectives* (6 a year).

Illuminating Engineering Society of North America: 120 Wall St, New York, NY 10005; f. 1906; 10,000 mems; Exec. Vice-Pres. W. HANLEY; publs *Lighting Design and Application* (monthly), *LEUKOS* (online—quarterly, printed compilation—annually), *IES Lighting Handbooks*.

Industrial Designers Society of America: 45195 Business Court, Suite 250, Dulles, VA 20166-6717; tel. (703) 707-6000; fax (703) 787-8501; e-mail idsa@idsa.org; internet www.idsa.org; f. 1965; 3,300 mems; Exec. Dir KRISTINA GOODRICH.

Institute of Electrical and Electronics Engineers, Inc.: 3 Park Ave, 17th Fl., New York, NY 10016-5997; tel. (212) 419-7900; fax (212) 752-4929; internet www.ieee.org; f. 1884; 365,000 mems; Exec. Dir JOHN H. POWERS; publs *IEEE Potentials* (monthly), *IEEE Spectrum/The Institute, Proceedings* (monthly), *Society and Council Transactions*, etc.

Institute of Food Technologists: 525 W. Van Buren, Suite 1000, Chicago, IL 60607; tel. (312) 782-8424; fax (312) 782-8348; e-mail info@ift.org; internet www.ift.org; f. 1939; 26,000 mems; Exec. Vice-Pres. BARBARA BYRD KEENAN; publs *Food Technology* (monthly), *Journal of Food Science* (every 2 months).

Institute of Industrial Engineers: 3577 Parkway Lane, Suite 200, Norcross, GA 30092; tel. (770) 449-0460; fax (770) 441-3295; internet www.iienet.org; f. 1948; 30,000 mems; Pres. ALLEN L. SOYSTER; Exec. Dir DON GREENE; publs *The Engineering Economist* (quarterly), *IIE Transactions* (monthly), *Industrial Engineer* (monthly), *Industrial Management* (every 2 months).

Instrument Society of America: POB 12277, 67 Alexander Drive, Research Triangle Park, NC 27709; tel. (919) 549-8411; fax (919) 549-8288; internet www.isa.org; f. 1945; 33,000 mems; Exec. Dir ROB RENNER; Pres. DON ZEE; conferences and exhibitions, symposia, special interest divisions, training, certification, consensus standards; publs *Industrial Computing* (monthly), *InTech* (monthly), *ISA Directory of Instrumentation* (annually), *Motion Control* (8 a year).

International Communication Association: c/o Michael L. Haley, Executive Director, 1730 Rhode Island NW, Suite 300, Washington, DC 20036; tel. (202) 530-9855; fax (202) 530-9851; e-mail ica@icahdq.org; internet www.icahdq.org; f. 1950 to bring together academics and professionals concerned with research and application of human communication theory; 3,200 mems; Pres. ROBERT T. CRAIG; Exec. Dir MICHAEL L. HALEY; publs *Human Communication Research* (4 a year), *Communication Theory* (4 a year), *Journal of Communication* (4 a year), *ICA Newsletter* (10 a year), *The Communication Yearbook* (annually).

Markle Foundation: 10 Rockefeller Plaza, 16th Floor, New York, NY 10020-1903; tel. (212) 713-7600; fax (212) 765-9690; e-mail info@markle.org; internet www.markle.org; f. 1927 through an endowment given by John Markle; seeks to improve mass media and realize the potential of communications technology; Pres. ZOË BAIRD.

National Society of Professional Engineers: 1420 King St, Alexandria, VA 22314-2794; tel. (703) 684-2800; fax (703) 836-4875; internet www.nspe.org; f. 1934; professional aspects of engineering; administers licensure and licensure preparation; operates a Board of Ethical Review; 60,000 mems; Pres. BOBBY E. PRICE; Exec. Dir ALBERT C. GRAY; publ. *Engineering Times* (monthly).

Society for the History of Technology: Dept. of History, 603 Ross Hall, Iowa State University, Ames, IA 50011; tel. (515) 294-8469; fax (515) 294-6390; e-mail shot@iastate.edu; internet www.shot.jhu.edu; f. 1958; concerned with history of technological devices and processes, relations of technology with science, politics, social change, the arts and humanities, and economics; affiliated to the American Assocation for the Advancement of Science, the American Council of Learned Societies; 2,600 mems; Pres. ROSALIND WILLIAMS; Sec. AMY SUE BIX; publs *SHOT Newsletter* (both quarterly), *Technology and Culture*.

Society of Automotive Engineers, Inc.: 400 Commonwealth Drive, Warrendale, PA 15096-0001; tel. (724) 776-4841; fax (724) 772-1851; e-mail magazines@sae.org; internet www.sae.org; f. 1905; 84,000 mems; Pres. J. E. ROBERTSON; publs *Aerospace Engineering* (monthly), *Automotive Engineering International* (monthly), *Off-Highway Engineering* (6 a year), *SAE Handbook* (annually), *SAE Transactions* (annually), *SAE Update* (monthly).

Society of Manufacturing Engineers: POB 930, Dearborn, MI 48121-0930; tel. (313) 271-1500; fax (313) 425-3401; internet www.sme.org; f. 1932 to advance scientific knowledge in the field of manufacturing and to apply its resources to research, writing, publishing and disseminating information; 62,000 mems; library of 7,000 vols; Pres. GENE NELSON; Exec. Dir and Gen. Man. NANCY BERG; publs *Composites in Manufacturing* (4 a year), *Electronics Manufacturing Engineering* (4 a year), *Finishing Line* (4 a year), *Forming and Fabricating* (monthly), *Integrated Design and Manufacturing* (monthly), *Machining Technology* (4 a year), *Journal of Manufacturing Processes* (4 a year), *Journal of Manufacturing Systems* (6 a year), *Manufacturing Engineering* (monthly), *Molding Systems* (monthly), *Rapid Prototyping* (4 a year), *Robotics Today* (4 a year), *Vision* (4 a year).

Society of Naval Architects and Marine Engineers: 601 Pavonia Ave, Suite 400, Jersey City, NJ 07306; tel. (201) 798-4800; fax (201) 798-4975; internet www.sname.org; f. 1893; 10,000 mems; Exec. Dir PHILIP B.

KIMBALL; publs *Journal of Ship Production* (quarterly), *Journal of Ship Research* (quarterly), *Marine Technology* (quarterly), *Transactions* (annually).

Society of Rheology: c/o Janis Bennett, American Institute of Physics, Suite 1NO1, 2 Huntington Quadrangle, Melville, NY 11747-4502; tel. (516) 576-2403; fax (516) 576-2223; e-mail rheology@aip.org; internet www.rheology.org; f. 1929; 1,700 ; Pres. ANDREW J. KRAYNIK; Sec. A. JEFFREY GIACOMIN; publs *Journal of Rheology* (every 2 months), *Rheology Bulletin* (2 a year).

Research Institutes

GENERAL

Getty Research Institute: Suite 1100, 1200 Getty Center Dr., Los Angeles, CA 90049-1688; tel. (310) 440-7335; fax (310) 440-7778; e-mail griweb@getty.edu; internet www.getty.edu/research; f. 1983; an operating programme of the J. Paul Getty Trust; promotes innovative scholarship in the arts and humanities, bridging traditional academic boundaries; library of 900,000 vols, incl. reference rare materials serials and auction catalogues; Dir Dr THOMAS CROW; Chief Librarian Dr SUSAN M. ALLEN.

National Humanities Center: 7 Alexander Dr., POB 12256, Research Triangle Park, NC 27709; tel. (919) 549-0661; f. 1977; an institute for advanced study created to encourage scholarship in the humanities and to enhance the usefulness and influence of the humanities in the USA; awards Fellowships (40 a year) to pursue advanced post-doctoral research and writing at the Center, organizes seminars, lectures, conferences; library has reference works, bibliographical aids, microfilm catalogue; Chair. FRANCIS OAKLEY; Pres. and Dir GEOFFREY GALT HARPHAN; Sec. JOHN ADAMS.

RAND Corporation: 1776 Main St, POB 2138 Santa Monica, CA 90407-2138; tel. (310) 393-0411; fax (310) 393-4818; internet www.rand.org; f. 1948; brs in Arlington, VA, Pittsburgh, PA, New York City, NY, Cambridge (UK), Berlin (Germany), Delft (Netherlands) and Doha (Qatar); research on matters affecting the public interest; education, civil and criminal justice, health sciences, int. affairs, labour and population, science and technology, national security, information processing systems; non-profit instn receiving funds from federal, state and local government, foundations and the private sector; 718 research professionals; Pres. Dr JAMES A. THOMSON; Chair. ANN MCLAUGHLIN KOROLOGOS; publs *Rand Research Review* (3 a year), *RAND Journal of Economics* (online), *research reports*.

AGRICULTURE, FISHERIES AND VETERINARY SCIENCE

Agricultural Research Institute: 236 Massachusetts Ave NE, Suite 401, Washington, DC 20002; tel. (202) 544-5534; fax (202) 544-5749; f. 1951; 100 mems; forum for agricultural research administrators to discuss agricultural research programmes and needs; Exec. Dir RICHARD A. HERRETT; publs *Newsletter* (every 2 months), *Proceedings* (annually).

Forest Products Society: 2801 Marshall Court, Madison, WI 53705-2295; tel. (608) 231-1361; fax (608) 231-2152; internet www.forestprod.org; f. 1947; Technology transfer concerning all areas of the forest products industry; 2,000 mems in more than 30 countries; Pres. BOB LITTLE; Exec. Vice-Pres. CAROL LEWIS; publs *Forest Products*

Journal (10 a year), *Journal of Forest Products Business Research* (online), *Wood Design Focus* (quarterly).

BIBLIOGRAPHY, LIBRARY SCIENCE AND MUSEOLOGY

Getty Conservation Institute: 1200 Getty Center Dr., Suite 700, Los Angeles, CA 90049-1684; tel. (310) 440-7325; fax (310) 440-7702; e-mail gciweb@getty.edu; internet www.getty.edu/conservation; f. 1983; a programme of the J. Paul Getty Trust; works for the preservation of the world's cultural heritage; library of 55,000 vols; Dir TIMOTHY P. WHALEN; publs *Art and Archaeology Technical Abstracts* (online at aata.getty.edu/nps), *Conservation: the GCI Newsletter* (3 a year).

Institute for Scientific Information: 3501 Market St, Philadelphia, PA 19104; internet www.isinet.com; f. 1960; periodicals library of 8,000 titles; Pres. and CEO MICHAEL TANSEY; publs *Science Citation Index, Social Sciences Citation Index, Arts and Humanities Citation Index, CompuMath Citation Index, Index to Scientific and Technical Proceedings, Index to Scientific Reviews, Index to Social Sciences and Humanities Proceedings, Index Chemicus, Current Chemical Reactions, Index to Scientific Book Contents;* Current Contents in the following editions: *Agriculture, Biology and Environmental Sciences; Social and Behavioural Sciences; Arts and Humanities; Engineering, Technology and Applied Sciences; Life Sciences; Clinical Medicine; Physical, Chemical and Earth Sciences; Biotechnology Citation Index, Neuroscience Citation Index, Mathematical Science Citation Index, Chemistry Citation Index, Materials Science Citation Index, Biochemistry and Biophysics Citation Index;* online databases include: *Scisearch, Social Scisearch, Arts & Humanities Search, Computer & Mathematics Search, Current Contents Search, ISTP Search, ISTP & B Search, Research Alert Direct* (Products available in print and in electronic form.).

National Federation of Abstracting and Information Services: 1518 Walnut St, Suite 1004, Philadelphia, PA 19102; tel. (215) 893-1561; fax (215) 893-1564; e-mail nfais@nfais.org; internet www.nfais.org; f. 1958; aims to serve the world's information community through education, research, and publication; Pres. LINDA SACKS; Exec. Dir BONNIE LAWLOR; publ. *NFAIS Newsletter* (monthly).

Smithsonian Center for Education and Museum Studies: Rm 2235, Arts and Industries Bldg, 900 Jefferson Drive, SW, Washington, DC; tel. (202) 633-1000; e-mail educate@si.edu; internet museumstudies.si.edu; interprets the collective knowledge of the Smithsonian Institution and serves as a gateway to the Institution's education resources; library: merged library of collections from the Museum Reference Center and Central Reference and Loan Services branch libraries; part of the Smithsonian Institution Libraries system; publ. *Center for Museum Studies Bulletin*.

Smithsonian Institution Museum Conservation Institute: Museum Support Centre, 4210 Silver Hill Rd, Suitland, MD 20746; tel. (301) 238-1240; fax (301) 238-3709; e-mail mciweb@si.edu; internet www.si.edu/mci; f. 1963; research in the fields of conservation and the scientific study of collection materials; Dir ROBERT J. KOESTLER.

ECONOMICS, LAW AND POLITICS

Brookings Institution: 1775 Massachusetts Ave NW, Washington, DC 20036; tel. (202) 797-6000; fax (202) 797-6004; internet www.brook.edu; f. 1916; research, education, and publishing in the fields of economics, government, and foreign policy; 61 professional mems; library of 75,000 vols, 700 periodical titles, files of pamphlets and govt documents, selected UN documents; Pres. STROBE TALBOTT; Chair. JOHN L. THORNTON; publs *Brookings Papers on Economic Activity* (3 a year), *Brookings Papers on Education Policy, The Brookings Review* (4 a year), *Brookings Trade Forum* (annually), *Brookings–Wharton Papers on Financial Services, Brookings–Wharton Papers on Urban Affairs*.

Center for Strategic and International Studies (CSIS): 1800 K St NW, Washington, DC 20006; tel. (202) 887-0200; fax (202) 775-3199; e-mail mschoeff@csis.org; internet www.csis.org; research into new challenges to national and international peace and security; helps to develop new methods of governance for the global age through programmes in technology and public policy, energy, and international trade and finance; Pres. and CEO JOHN H. HAMRE; publ. *Washington Quarterly*.

Center for the Study of Democratic Institutions: 10951 West Pico Blvd, Suite 300, Los Angeles, CA 90064; tel. (310) 474-0011; fax (310) 474-8061; e-mail npq@pacificnet.net; internet www.digitalnpq.org; f. 1959, fmrly Robert Maynard Hutchins Center for the Study of Democratic Institutions; Exec. Dir NATHAN GARDELS; publ. *New Perspectives Quarterly*.

Counterpart International, Inc.: 1200 18th St NW (Suite 1100), Washington, DC 20036; tel. (202) 296-9676; fax (202) 296-9679; e-mail communications@counterpart.org; internet www.counterpart.org; f. 1965 as Foundation for the Peoples of the South Pacific to develop civil society, promote economic self-sufficiency and public health and encourage sustainable environmental management; present name 1992; attached offices in New York and Los Angeles; operates programmes in Armenia, Azerbaijan, Belarus, Bosnia and Herzegovina, Bulgaria, Fiji, Georgia, Guatemala, India, Iraq, Kazakhstan, Kiribati, Kyrgyzstan, Moldova, Papua New Guinea, Russia, Samoa, Senegal, Solomon Islands, Tajikistan, Tonga, Turkmenistan, Tuvalu, Ukraine, Uzbekistan, Vanuatu and Vietnam; Pres. and CEO LELEI LELAULU; publ. *Annual Report*.

East-West Center: 1601 East-West Rd, Honolulu, HI 96848-1601; tel. (808) 944 7111; fax (808) 944 7376; e-mail ewcinfo@eastwestcenter.org; internet www.eastwestcenter.org; f. 1960; a public, non-profit educational institution with an international board of governors; research fellows, graduate students, and professionals in government, academia and business each year work with the Center's international staff in co-operative study, training, and research; they examine major issues related to international relations, population, resources, economic development, and the environment in Asia, the Pacific and the United States; Pres. Dr CHARLES E. MORRISON; publs *Asia Pacific Issues Paper* (irregular), *Observer* (4 a year), *Annual Report*.

International Center for Economic Growth: University of the Pacific, 3601 Pacifica Ave, Stockton, CA 94104; tel. (209) 946-3265; fax (209) 496-2650; e-mail rhodam@iceg.org; internet www.iceg.com; f. 1985 to promote economic growth and human development in developing and post-socialist countries, by strengthening the capacity of local research institutes to provide project leadership; operates in conjunction with 370 mem. institutes globally; sponsors conferences and seminars; CEO ROBERT HODAM; publ. *Newsletter*.

International Marketing Institute: 314 Hammond St, Suite 52, Chestnut Hill, MA 02167-1206; tel. (617) 552-8690; fax (617) 552-2590; f. 1960; affiliated to Boston College Graduate School of Management; international executive development and management training programmes in management education, with marketing as the primary focus; Exec. Dir JOSEPH B. GANNON.

Marketing Science Institute: 1000 Massachusetts Ave, Cambridge, MA 02138-5396; tel. (617) 491-2060; fax (617) 491-2065; e-mail msi@msi.org; internet www.msi.org; f. 1961; non-profit marketing consortium that stimulates, supports, and reports research in order to advance marketing knowledge and practice; sponsors and publishes academic research on all areas of marketing; 65 mem. companies; Chair. GORDON A. WYNER; Exec. Dir LEIGH MCALISTER; publ. *MSI Reports* (quarterly).

National Bureau of Economic Research: 1050 Massachusetts Ave, Cambridge, MA 02138; tel. (617) 868-3900; fax (617) 868-2742; internet www.nber.org; f. 1920; fundamental qualitative analysis of the US economy; 50 Dirs; Pres. and CEO MARTIN FELDSTEIN; publs *Digest* (12 a year), *NBER Reporter* (quarterly).

Scripps Foundation for Research in Population Problems and Gerontology Center: Scripps Gerontology Center, 396 Upham Hall, Oxford, OH 45056; tel. (513) 529-2914; fax (513) 529-1476; e-mail scripps@muohio.edu; internet www.scripps.muohio.edu; f. 1922; 20 mems; library of 4,000 vols; Dir SUZANNE R. KUNKEL.

EDUCATION

American Educational Research Association: 1230 17th St, NW, Washington, DC 20036-3078; tel. (202) 223-9485; fax (202) 775-1824; internet www.aera.net; f. 1916; 22,000 mems; Pres. WILLIAM TATE; publs *American Educational Research Journal, Educational Evaluation and Policy Analysis, Educational Researcher, Journal of Educational and Behavioral Statistics, Review of Educational Research, Review of Research in Education*.

National Science Resources Center: 901 D Street, SW, Suite 704B, Washington, DC 20024-0952; tel. (202) 633-2978; fax (202) 287-2070; e-mail nsrcsite@si.edu; internet www.nsrconline.org; f. 1985; operated by the Smithsonian Institution, National Academy of Sciences, National Academy of Engineering and Institute of Medicine to improve the teaching of science in schools; Exec. Dir SALLY GOETZ SHULER.

Office of Educational Research and Improvement (OERI): 555 New Jersey Ave NW, Washington, DC 20208; f. 1980 by Congress; main government agency supporting educational research; aims to improve the quality of educational practice; consists of five principal components: Fund for the Improvement and Reform of Schools and Teaching, Library Programs, Program for the Improvement of Practice, Office of Research, and National Center for Education Statistics; publs statistical and research reports.

HISTORY, GEOGRAPHY AND ARCHAEOLOGY

Center for Reformation Research: 801 Seminary Pl., St Louis, MO 63105; tel. (314) 505-7199; f. 1957; microfilm library of original MSS and printed materials of the 15th and 16th centuries; reference library; Exec. Dir ROBERT ROSIN.

Leo Baeck Institute, Inc.: Center for Jewish History, 15 West 16th St, New York, NY 10011; tel. (212) 744-6400; fax (212) 988-1305; e-mail lbaeck@lbi.cjh.org; internet www.lbi.org; f. 1955; research and documentation on German Jewish history; exhibitions and lectures; library of 70,000 vols in German, English and Hebrew, archives of family papers, community histories, business and public records, 1300 personal memoirs, 20,000 photographs (access to archive and library materials is available only through reading room of the Center for Jewish History); art collection; 1,100 mems; Exec. Dir CAROL KAHN STRAUSS; Head Librarian RENATE EVERS; publs *Bulletin des Leo Baeck Instituts, Jüdischer Almanach des LBI, LBI Yearbook, News, Overview.*

Mississippi Office of Geology: POB 20307, Jackson, MS 39289; tel. (601) 961-5500; fax (601) 961-5521; internet www.deq.state.ms.us/mdeq.nsf/page/geology_home; f. 1850; research into the geology and mineral resources of the State; library of 60,000 vols; Dir MICHAEL B. E. BOGRAD; publs *Mississippi Geology,* bulletins, maps.

Paleontological Research Institution: 1259 Trumansburg Rd, Ithaca, NY 14850; tel. (607) 273-6623; fax (607) 273-6620; internet www.priweb.org; f. 1932; 1,000 mems; library of 50,000 vols; collection of 2 m. specimens; Dir Dr WARREN D. ALLMON; publs *American Paleontologist* (quarterly), *Bulletins of American Paleontology* (2 a year), *Palaeontographica Americana* (irregular).

School for Advanced Research on the Human Experience: POB 2188, Santa Fe, NM 87504-2188; tel. (505) 954-7200; fax (505) 989-9809; internet www.sarweb.org; f. 1907; centre for advanced studies in anthropology and the humanities; grants to 6 resident scholars, incl. 1 native American annually; native artist fellows; advanced seminars in anthropology; anthropological publs; extensive collns in south-west Indian art; 2,000 mems; library of 6,000 vols; Pres. JAMES F. BROOKS; Chair. JEREMY SABLOFF.

MEDICINE

American Association for Cancer Research, Inc.: c/o Dr Margaret Foti, 615 Chestnut St, 17th Floor, Philadelphia, PA 19106-4404; tel. (215) 440-9300; fax (215) 440-9313; e-mail meetings@aacr.org; internet www.aacr.org; f. 1907; to facilitate communication and dissemination of knowledge among scientists and others dedicated to cancer research; 20,000 mems; Pres. Dr KAREN S. H. ANTMAN; CEO Dr MARGARET FOTI; publs *Cancer Research* (2 a month), *Molecular Cancer Research* (monthly), *Cancer Epidemiology, Biomarkers & Prevention* (monthly), *Clinical Cancer Research* (monthly), *Molecular Cancer Therapeutics* (monthly).

American Federation for Medical Research: 900 Cummings Center, Suite 221-U, Beverly, MA 01915; tel. (978) 927-8330; fax (978) 524-8890; e-mail afmr@prri.com; internet www.afmr.org; f. 1940; 5,300 mems; Pres. Dr MARK R. BURGE; Secretary and Treasurer DAVID A. D'ALESSIO; publ. *Journal of Investigative Medicine* (6 a year).

Association for Research in Nervous and Mental Disease, Inc.: Weill Medical College of Cornell University, Department of Psychiatry, 1300 York Ave, Box 171, Room F-1231, New York, NY 10021; tel. (570) 839-0296; fax (570) 839-0297; e-mail amgooder@med.cornell.edu; internet www.arnmd.org; f. 1920; annual meeting for continuing medical education credits on research topics of interest to neurologists and psychiatrists; 850 mems; Chair. JACK D. BARCHAS; publ. *Clinical Neuroscience Research* (6 a year).

Association for Research in Vision and Ophthalmology, Inc.: 12300 Twinbrook Parkway, Suite 250, Bethesda, MD 20852-1606; tel. (240) 221-2900; fax (240) 221-0370; e-mail mem@arvo.org; internet www.arvo.org; f. 1928; 10,800 mems; Exec. Vice-Pres. Dr PAUL KAUFMAN; publs *Investigative Ophthalmology and Visual Science, Journal of Vision* (irregular).

California Pacific Medical Center Research Institute: 2340 Clay St (5th Fl.), San Francisco, CA 94115; tel. (415) 561-1601; fax (415) 561-1753; internet www.cpmc.org/professionals/research/; f. 1959; non-profit research division of medical centre conducting patient-oriented research in arthritis, HIV/AIDS, cancer, including leukemia and monoclonal antibodies, heart disease, immunology and infectious diseases, artificial heart research, organ transplantation and preservation, neurology, maternal foetal medicine, child health and human development; Dir WARREN S. BROWNER.

Fox Chase Cancer Center: 333 Cottman Ave, Philadelphia, PA 19111-2497; tel. (215) 728-6900; fax (215) 728-3655; internet www.fccc.edu; f. 1926; library of 22,000 vols including 5,000 monographs and 440 scientific journals; Pres. Dr ROBERT C. YOUNG.

Huntington Medical Research Institutes: 734 Fairmount Ave, Pasadena, CA 91105; tel. (818) 397-5436; fax (818) 397-3330; internet www.hmri.org; f. 1952; oncology, cell biology, differentiated cell culture, cancer genetics, prostatic cancer, immunotherapy, biomedical magnetic resonance spectroscopy, cardiology, development of neural prosthetic devices; Exec. Dir WILLIAM OPEL; publ. *Newsletter.*

Jackson Laboratory: 600 Main St, Bar Harbor, Maine 04609-1500; tel. (207) 288-6000; fax (207) 288-6079; e-mail pubinfo@jax.org; internet www.jax.org; f. 1929; research in molecular genetics, cell biology, biochemistry, immunology and physiological genetics; library of 3,000 vols, 20,000 bound journals, 370 current journals, 46,000 article reprints; Dir Dr RICHARD WOYCHIK; publs *Annual Report, Inside the Jackson Laboratory* (quarterly), *Scientific Report* (annually), *Training for Research* (annually).

Lovelace Respiratory Research Institute: 2425 Ridgecrest Drive, SE, Albuquerque, NM 87108-5127; tel. (505) 348-9400; fax (505) 348-8541; f. 1947 to conduct biomedical research and technology development; 300 mems; library of 10,000 books and 116 current journals; Pres. and CEO ROBERT RUBIN; publs *Advances, Annual Report.*

Mayo Foundation: Rochester, MN 55905; tel. (507) 284-2658; f. 1919; clinical medicine, medical research, graduate and undergraduate education; library of 275,000 vols and 3,500 periodicals; Chair. Board of Trustees E. W. SPENCER; Pres. R. R. WALLER; Admin. J. H. HERRELL; publ. *Mayo Clinic Proceedings* (monthly).

Memorial Sloan-Kettering Cancer Center: 1275 York Ave, New York, NY 10021; tel. (212) 639-2000; internet www.mskcc.org; f. 1948; research in physical and biological sciences relating to cancer; postdoctoral research training in laboratory investigation with scientific staff; graduate instruction with Cornell University; Pres. Dr HAROLD VARMUS; publ. *Annual Report.*

Menninger: 2801 Gessner Drive, POB 809045, Houston, TX 77280-9045; tel. (713) 275-5000; fax (713) 275-5117; e-mail webmaster@menninger.edu; f. 1925 as a non-profit mental health centre for inpatient and outpatient treatment of mental illness through preventive psychiatry, clinical treatment, research and professional education; library: medical library of 50,000 vols; Pres. and CEO IAN AITKEN; publs *Menninger Perspective* (quarterly), *Bulletin of the Menninger Clinic* (quarterly).

National Institutes of Health: US Department of Health and Human Services, Public Health Service, Bethesda, MD 20892; tel. (301) 496-4000; fax (301) 496-0019; internet www.nih.gov; f. 1887; principal agency of DHHS for biomedical research, research training, and biomedical communications; National Library of Medicine: see Libraries and Archives; Dir Dr ELIAS A. ZERHOUNI.

Constituent institutes:

National Cancer Institute: Bldg 31, Room 11A4, 31 Center Dr., Bethesda, MD 20892; tel. (301) 496-5615; fax (301) 402-0338; internet www.nci.nih.gov; f. 1937; principal Federal govt agency for cancer research; supports research into the causes, prevention, early detection and treatment of cancer, and into supportive care; co-operates with State and local health agencies and voluntary bodies; Dir Dr ANDREW C. VON ESCHENBACH.

National Eye Institute: c/o National Institutes of Health, 31 Center Dr., MSC 2510, Bethesda, MD 20892-2510; tel. (301) 496-2234; fax (301) 496-9970; internet www.nei.nih.gov; f. 1968; conducts and supports research relating to disorders of the eye and visual system, and to rehabilitation and other related fields; research performed in Institute's own laboratories and through contracts; supports training, and directs Nat. Eye Health Education Program; Dir Dr PAUL A. SIEVING.

National Heart, Lung and Blood Institute: c/o US Department of Health and Human Services, Public Health Service, Bethesda, MD 20892; tel. (301) 496-5166; fax (301) 402-0818; internet www.nhlbi.nih.gov; f. 1948 as National Heart Institute, redesignated 1969 and 1976; performs and supports research in diseases of the heart, blood vessels, lungs (exclusive of pulmonary malignancies) and blood; Dir Dr ELIZABETH NABEL.

National Human Genome Research Institute (NHGRI): Bldg 31, Room 4B09, 31 Center Dr., MSC 2152, 9000 Rockville Pike Bethesda, MD 20892-2152; tel. (301) 402-0911; fax (301) 402-2218; internet www.genome.gov; f. 1989; directs and supports work on the sequencing of the human genome; funds research on the genome's structure, function, and role in health and disease; and supports studies on the ethical, legal and social implications (ELSI) of genome research; Dir Dr FRANCIS S. COLLINS.

National Institute on Aging: Bldg 31, Room 5C27, 31 Center Dr., MSC 2292, Bethesda, MD 20892; tel. (301) 496-1752; fax (301) 496-1072; e-mail webmaster@nia.nih.gov; internet www.nia.nih.gov; f. 1974; conducts and supports biomedical, social and behavioural research and training related to the ageing process and diseases and other special problems and needs of the aged; Dir Dr RICHARD J. HODES.

National Institute on Alcohol Abuse and Alcoholism (NIAAA): 5635 Fishers Lane, MSC 9304, Bethesda, MD 20892-9304; internet www.niaaa.nih.gov; f. 1970; conducts and supports research in a wide range of scientific areas incl. genetics, neuroscience, epidemiology, health risks and benefits of alcohol consumption, prevention and treatment; Dir Dr TING-KAI LI.

National Institute of Allergy and Infectious Diseases: 6610 Rockledge Dr., MSC 6612, Bethesda, MD 20892-6612; tel. (301) 496-5717; fax (301) 402-3573; e-mail ocpostoffice@niaid.nih.gov; internet www.niaid.nih.gov; f. 1948; supports basic and applied research to prevent, diagnose and treat infectious diseases such as HIV/AIDS and other sexually transmitted infections, influenza, tuberculosis, malaria and illness from potential agents of bioterrorism; supports research on transplantation and immune-related illnesses, including autoimmune disorders, asthma and allergies; Dir Dr ANTHONY S. FAUCI.

National Institute of Arthritis and Musculoskeletal and Skin Diseases: 1 AMS Circle Bethesda, MD 20892-3675; tel. (301) 495-4484; fax (301) 718-6366; e-mail niamsinfo@mail.nih.gov; internet www .niams.nih.gov; f. 1986; research into the causes, treatment and prevention of arthritis and musculoskeletal and skin diseases; training of basic and clinical scientists to carry out this research; dissemination of information on progress in research; Dir Dr STEPHEN I. KATZ.

National Institute for Biomedical Imaging and Bioengineering (NIBIB): 6707 Democracy Blvd, Suite 202, Bethesda, MD 20892-5477; tel. (301) 451-6768; internet www.nibib.nih.gov; f. 2000; Dir Dr RODERIC PETTIGREW.

National Institute of Child Health and Human Development: c/o US Dept of Health and Human Service, Public Health Service, Bethesda, MD 20892; tel. (301) 496-5133; fax (301) 496-7101; internet www.nichd.nih.gov; f. 1963; supports, fosters and co-ordinates research and training in areas of maternal health, child health and human development, focusing on the continuing process of growth and development, biological and behavioural; also supports research in the population sciences, incl. contraceptive development and evaluation, reproductive health, behavioural and demographic research, and medical rehabilitation; Dir Dr DUANE ALEXANDER.

National Institute on Deafness and Other Communication Disorders: Bldg 31, Room 3C02, 31 Center Dr., MSC 2320, Bethesda, MD 20892-2320; tel. (301) 496-7243; fax (301) 402-0018; internet www.nidcd.nih.gov; f. 1988; supports and conducts research on the normal processes and diseases of human communication, incl. hearing, balance, smell, taste, voice, speech and language; fosters training and disseminates science-based health information; Dir Dr JAMES F. BATTEY.

National Institute of Dental and Craniofacial Research: National Institutes of Health, 31 Center Dr., MSC 2290, Bethesda, MD 20892-2290; tel. (301) 496-9469; fax (301) 402-2185; internet www .nidcr.nih.gov; f. 1948; conducts and supports research and training with the aim of preventing, diagnosing and treating dental, oral and craniofacial diseases and conditions; Dir Dr LAWRENCE TABAK.

National Institute of Diabetes and Digestive and Kidney Diseases: c/o US Dept of Health and Human Services, Public Health Service, Bethesda, MD 20892; tel. (301) 496-3583; fax (301) 496-7422; e-mail NIDDK_Inquiries@nih.gov; internet www.niddk.nih.gov; f. 1950, renamed 1986; conducts and supports research into diabetes, endocrinology,

metabolic diseases, digestive diseases, nutrition, kidney and urologic diseases and haematology; information and education activities; Dir Dr ALLEN M. SPIEGEL.

National Institute on Drug Abuse (NIDA): 6001 Executive Blvd, Room 5213, Bethesda, MD 20892-9561; tel. (301) 443-1124; e-mail Information@lists .nida.nih.gov; internet www.nida.nih.gov; f. 1974; Dir Dr NORA VOLKOW.

National Institute of Environmental Health Sciences: c/o US Dept of Health and Human Services, Public Health Service, Research Triangle Park, NC 27709; tel. (919) 541-1919; fax (919) 541-2260; internet www.niehs.nih.gov; f. 1969; conducts, fosters and co-ordinates research on the biological effects of chemical, physical, and biological substances present in or introduced into the environment; Dir Dr DAVID SCHWARTZ; publ. *Environmental Health Perspectives* (monthly).

National Institute of General Medical Sciences: c/o US Dept of Health and Human Services, Public Health Service, Bethesda, MD 20892; tel. (301) 594-2172; fax (301) 402-0156; e-mail cassmanm@nih .gov; internet www.nigms.nih.gov; f. 1962; supports a programme of research and training in the basic medical sciences; Dir Dr JEREMY M. BERG.

National Institute of Mental Health (NIMH): 6001 Executive Blvd, Room 8184, MSC 9663, Bethesda, MD 20892-9663; tel. (301) 443-4513; fax (301) 443-4279; e-mail nimhinfo@nih.gov; internet www.nimh.nih .gov; f. 1946; aims to improve mental health through biomedical research on the mind, brain and behaviour; Dir Dr THOMAS R. INSEL.

National Institute of Neurological Disorders and Stroke: Brain Resources and Information Network (BRAIN), POB 5801, Bethesda, MD 20824; tel. (301) 496-5751; e-mail braininfo@ninds.nih.gov; internet www.ninds.nih.gov; f. 1950; conducts, supports, fosters, and co-ordinates research on the causes, prevention, diagnosis and treatment of disorders of the brain and nervous system; Dir Dr STORY C. LANDIS.

National Institute of Nursing Research: c/o US Dept of Health and Human Services, Public Health Service, Bethesda, MD 20892; internet www.nih .gov/ninr; f. 1993; supports and conducts scientific research and research training to strengthen nursing practice and health care for prevention and amelioration of disease and disability; Dir Dr PATRICIA GRADY.

Naval Aerospace Medicine Institute: Pensacola, FL 32508-1047; f. 1939; training in aviation and aerospace medicine; library of 20,000 vols; Commanding Officer Capt. R. E. HAIN.

Radiation Research Society: 810 E. 10th St, Lawrence, KS 66044; tel. (630) 571-2881; fax (785) 843-1274; e-mail info@radres.org; internet www.radres.org; f. 1952; 1,990 mems; Pres. GEORGE ILIAKIS; Sec. and Treas. KATHY MASON; publs *Newsletter* (quarterly), *Radiation Research* (monthly).

Schepens Eye Research Institute: 20 Staniford St, Boston, MA 02114; tel. (617) 912-0100; fax (617) 912-0101; e-mail geninfo@vision.eri.harvard.edu; internet www.theschepens.org; f. 1950; basic and clinical research on causes, prevention and treatment of eye diseases, development of diagnostic and therapeutic devices, instruments and techniques for ophthalmology, study of the processes of vision; library of

200 vols, 100 journals; Chair. KENNETT F. BURNES; publ. *Sundial*.

Society for Pediatric Research: 3400 Research Forest Drive, Suite B7, The Woodlands, TX 77381; tel. (281) 419-0052; fax (281) 419-0082; e-mail info@aps-spr.org; internet www.aps-spr.org; f. 1929; Exec. Dir. DEBBIE ANAGNOSTELIS; Exec. Sec. BRENDA PAPKE; publ. *Pediatric Research Journal*.

Southwest Foundation for Biomedical Research: POB 760549, San Antonio, TX 78425-0549; tel. (210) 258-9400; internet www.sfbr.org; f. 1941; basic research in biomedical sciences; designated in 1999 one of the regional primate research centres (Southwest Regional Primate Research Center); library of 50,000 journal vols; 6,700 books; Chair. JOHN C. KERR; Scientific Dir Dr ROBERT E. SHADE; publs *Progress in Biomedical Research* (irregular), *Annual Report*.

Wistar Institute of Anatomy and Biology: 36th and Spruce Sts, Philadelphia, PA 19104; tel. (215) 898-3700; fax (215) 573-2097; internet www.wistar.org; f. 1892; cellular and subcellular research in human diseases; library of 10,000 vols; Dir Dr RUSSEL E. KAUFMAN.

NATURAL SCIENCES
General

Battelle Memorial Institute: 505 King Ave, Columbus, OH 43201-2693; tel. (614) 424-3304; fax (614) 424-5263; e-mail solutions@battelle.org; internet www.battelle .org; f. 1929; serves industry and Govt in the generation, application and commercialization of technology; supports research and devt activities of clients in 30 countries; major areas of activity are health and environment, products and processes, technology management consulting, nat. security, energy; research operations in the USA and Europe; offices worldwide; library: library of more than 150,000 vols; Pres. and Chief Exec. CARL F. KOHRT.

Carnegie Institution of Washington: 1530 P St, NW, Washington, DC 20005; tel. (202) 387-6400; fax (202) 387-8092; internet www.carnegieinstitution.org; f. 1902'to encourage, in the broadest and most liberal manner, investigation, research, and discovery, and the application of knowledge to the improvement of mankind'; research and education in the biological, physical, earth and planetary sciences; 80 faculty mems; Chair. Board of Trustees MICHAEL GELLERT; Pres. RICHARD MESERUE; publ. *Spectra* (quarterly).

Attached departments:

Department of Embryology: 115 West University Parkway, Baltimore, MD 21210; tel. (410) 554-1200; f. 1914; Dir ALLAN C. SPRADLING.

Department of Global Ecology: 260 Panama St, Stanford, CA 94305; tel. (650) 325-1521; f. 2002; Dir CHRISTOPHER FIELD.

Department of Plant Biology: 290 Panama St, Stanford, CA 94305; tel. (650) 325-1521; f. 1903 as Desert Laboratory; Dir CHRISTOPHER SOMERVILLE.

Department of Terrestrial Magnetism: 5241 Broad Branch Rd, NW, Washington, DC 20015; tel. (202) 478-8820; f. 1904; Dir SEAN C. SOLOMON.

Geophysical Laboratory: 5251 Broad Branch Rd, NW, Washington, DC 20015; tel. (202) 478-8900; f. 1906; Dir WESLEY HUNTRESS.

Observatories of the Carnegie Institution: 813 Santa Barbara St, Pasadena, CA 91101; tel. (626) 577-1122; internet www

.ociw.edu; f. 1904 as Mount Wilson Observatory; Dir WENDY FREEDMAN.

Midwest Research Institute: 425 Volker Blvd, Kansas City, MO 64110; tel. (816) 753-7600; fax (816) 753-8420; e-mail info@mriresearch.org; internet www.mriresearch.org; f. 1944; 1,300 mems; specialization in chemistry, biological sciences, toxicology, health sciences, environmental sciences, engineering, energy, economics, management sciences, human services, safety, agriculture and food safety; Pres. Dr JAMES SPIGARELLI; Chair. LOUIS W. SMITH; publ. *Annual Report.*

Smithsonian Environmental Research Center (SERC): POB 28, 647 Contees Wharf Rd, Edgewater, MD 21037; tel. (443) 482-2200; fax (443) 482-2380; internet www.serc.si.edu; f. 1965; administered by the Smithsonian Institution; multi-disciplinary instn dedicated to increasing knowledge of the biological and physical processes that sustain life on earth; scientific programmes: animal–plant interactions, bio-geochemistry, chemical ecology, ecological modelling, estuarine zoology, forest ecology, invasion studies, micro zooplankton, plant ecophysiology, plant ecology, plant physiology, phytoplankton, solar radiation, terrestrial animal ecology; part of the Smithsonian Marine Science Network; library: branch library of the Smithsonian Institution Libraries system: 12,500 books and bound journals, 120 current journals, collection of *Chesapeakiana*; Dir ANSON HINES; Librarian ANGELA HAGGINS.

Southern Research Institute: POB 55305, Birmingham, AL 35255-5305; tel. (205) 581-2000; fax (205) 581-2726; internet www2.southernresearch.org; f. 1941; contract scientific research in the areas of pharmaceutical discovery and development, engineering, environmental and energy-related sciences; library of 40,000 vols; Pres. and CEO ROBERT C. LONERGAN; Chair. CAROL GARRISON; publ. *Annual Report.*

World Resources Institute: 10 G St NE, Suite 800, Washington, DC 20002; tel. (202) 729-7600; fax (202) 729-7610; e-mail front@wri.org; internet www.wri.org; f. 1982; provides information about global resources and environmental conditions, analysis of emerging issues, and development of creative yet workable policy responses; seeks to deepen public understanding by publishing a variety of reports and papers, undertaking briefings, seminars and conferences, and offering material for use in the press and on the air; Pres. JONATHAN LASH; Sec. and Treas. MARJORIE BEANE.

Biological Sciences

Boyce Thompson Institute for Plant Research, Inc.: Cornell University, Tower Rd, Ithaca, NY 14853; tel. (607) 254-1234; fax (607) 254-1242; internet bti.cornell.edu; f. 1924; non-profit affiliate of Cornell University; research on plants and human health, including molecular biology, biochemistry, plant physiology, plant pathology, entomology, air and water pollution; library of 4,700 vols; President and CEO DAVID B. STERN; Vice-President for Research GARY BLISSARD; Vice-President for Finance and Administration JOHN M. DENTES; publ. *Annual Report.*

Cold Spring Harbor Laboratory: POB 100, Cold Spring Harbor, NY 11724; tel. (516) 367-8397; fax (516) 367-8496; internet www.cshl.org; f. 1890, chartered under present title 1962; research on cancer biology, molecular neuroscience, structural biology, plant genetics, professional education, DNA literacy; library of 30,000 vols; special collections on history of science and genetics; Pres.

and CEO Dr BRUCE W. STILLMAN; publs *Symposia on Quantitative Biology* (annually), *CSH Monographs* (irregular), *Abstracts of Papers, Annual Report, CSH Current Communications in Cell and Molecular Biology, Banbury Reports* (irregular), *Cancer Surveys, Genes and Development* (every 2 months), *Genome Research* (monthly), *Learning and Memory* (every 2 months).

Marine Biological Laboratory: 7 MBL St, Woods Hole, MA 02543; tel. (508) 548-3705; fax (508) 540-6902; e-mail comm@mbl.edu; internet www.mbl.edu; f. 1888; research and teaching instn; offers courses and seminars on ecology, behaviour, developmental biology, microbiology, neurobiology, parasitology, cell and molecular biology and biological techniques, global infectious diseases; library of 150,000 vols, 3,000 periodicals; Dir WILLIAM T. SPECK; Chair. of Board ALFRED ZEIEN; publs *Guide to Research and Education* (annually), *Annual Report, Lab Notes* (3 a year), *Biological Bulletin* (6 a year).

Missouri Botanical Garden: POB 299, St Louis, MO 63166-0299; tel. (314) 577-5100; fax (314) 577-9595; internet www.mobot.org; f. 1859; botanical research, exploration, education and display, with emphases on monographic and floristic studies in North America, tropical Latin America and Africa; library of 123,000 vols, special collections: Pre-Linnaean, Linnaean, Rare Books; archives and non-book materials, herbarium collection (4.3 million vascular plants and 300,000 bryophytes); Dir PETER H. RAVEN; publs *Annals* (quarterly), *Bulletin* (7 a year), *Flora of China Newsletter, Flora of North America Newsletter* (every 2 months), *Herbarium News* (monthly), *Monographs in Systematic Botany* (irregular), *Novon* (quarterly).

Moss Landing Marine Laboratories: POB 450, Moss Landing, CA 95039; tel. (831) 771-4400; fax (831) 632-4403; internet www.mlml.calstate.edu; f. 1966; research, undergraduate and postgraduate education in the marine sciences; library of 10,000 vols; Dir Dr KENNETH COALE.

Mote Marine Laboratory, Inc.: 1600 Ken Thompson Parkway, Sarasota, FL 34236-1096; tel. (941) 388-4441; fax (941) 388-4312; e-mail info@mote.org; internet www.mote.org; f. 1955; independent, non-profit marine research organization; research includes environmental assessment, estuarine and coastal ecology, marine chemistry, toxicology, biology and behaviour of fishes, marine mammals, sea turtles and biomedical research; aquarium and environmental education programmes; library of 20,000 vols, 10,000 books and documents, 400 journal titles, 3,000 reprints; Chair. MICHAEL MCKEE; Pres. KUMAR MAHADEVAN; publs *Collected Papers* (every 3 years), *Mote Magazine* (3 a year), *Mote Technical Reports* (irregular).

New England Aquarium: Central Wharf, Boston, MA 02110; tel. (617) 973-5200; internet www.neaq.org; f. 1969; 11,000 mems; public aquarium, research programmes; library of 3,000 vols; Pres. and CEO EDMUND C. TOOMEY; publ. *Aqualog* (quarterly).

New York Botanical Garden: 200th St and Kzimiroff Blvd, Bronx, NY 10458-5126; tel. (718) 817-8632; fax (718) 220-6405; e-mail malvarez@nybg.org; internet www.nybg.org; f. 1891; 10,800 mems; 250 acres of gardens, plant collections and wild areas, including a National Landmark conservatory; museum building includes herbarium housing some 7m. specimens; library of over

1 million items, inc. 196,000 vols; Pres. GREGORY LONG; publs *Economic Botany* (quarterly), *Botanical Review* (quarterly), *North American Flora* (irregular), *Memoirs* (irregular), *Brittonia* (quarterly), *Contributions* (irregular), *Advances in Economic Botany* (irregular), *Flora Neotropica* (irregular), *Intermountain Flora* (irregular).

Salk Institute for Biological Studies: POB 85800, San Diego, CA 92186-5800; tel. (858) 453-4100; fax (858) 552-8285; e-mail communications@salk.edu; internet www.salk.edu; f. 1960; 550 mems; advanced biological research into HIV/AIDS, cancer, neuroendocrinology, developmental neurobiology, peptide biology, molecular biology, plant biology, prebiotic chemistry, language studies, neuropsychology, immunology, molecular neurobiology and neurophysiology; library of 15,000 vols; Pres. Dr RICHARD A. MURPHY.

Smithsonian Horticulture Services Division: Arts and Industries Bldg, 900 Jefferson Drive, SW, Rm 2282, Washington, DC 20560-0420; tel. (202) 357-1926, (202) 633-7570 (Archives); fax (202) 786-2026; internet gardens.si.edu; f. 1972; research and educational programmes; manages grounds of the Smithsonian Institution museums and creates horticultural exhibitions; library: Archives of American Gardens: 80,000 photographic images, records of historic and contemporary American gardens; special collns: Garden Club of America (40,000 images), J. Horace McFarland (glass lantern slides and photographs), Thomas Warren Sears (glass negatives).

Smithsonian Marine Station at Fort Pierce: 701 Seaway Drive, Fort Pierce, FL 34949; tel. (772) 465-6630; fax (772) 461-8154; e-mail webmaster@sms.si.edu; internet www.sms.si.edu; f. 1969; attached to the National Museum of Natural History of the Smithsonian Institution; research into marine biodiversity and ecosystems of Florida; Head Scientist Dr VALERIE PAUL.

Smithsonian National Zoological Park: 3001 Connecticut Ave, NW, Washington, DC 20008; tel. (202) 673-4717; e-mail nationalzoo@nzp.si.edu; internet natzoo.si.edu; f. 1889; administered by the Smithsonian Institution; animal collection of 2,800 specimens from 435 species; part of the Smithsonian Marine Science Network; Dir DAVID L. EVANS; publs *ZooGoer* (publ. by Friends of the National Zoo, 6 a year), *CRC World* (publ. by the Conservation and Research Center Foundation, 4 a year).

Attached research institutes:

Conservation and Research Center: *Rock Creek Research Laboratories*: National Zoo, Rock Creek Park, Washington, DC; *Front Royal Campus*: Front Royal, VA; conservation biology research: Fort Royal Campus – Geographic information Systems (GIS), endocrine and gamete laboratories, veterinary clinic, 14 field stations; Rock Creek Research Laboratories – department of conservation biology, nutrition laboratory, department of reproductive sciences; Amazonia Science Gallery.

Smithsonian Migratory Bird Center: National Zoological Park, Washington, DC 20008; research into bird migration; Dir RUSSELL GREENBERG.

Physical Sciences

Argonne National Laboratory: 9700 South Cass Ave, Argonne, IL 60439; tel. (630) 252-2000; internet www.anl.gov; f. 1946; multipurpose research laboratory with primary focuses on basic research in the physical, life and environmental sciences, and on technology-directed research in fission, fossil and fusion energy as well as conservation and renewable energy; library of 65,000 vols and 1,000,000 technical reports; Dir Dr ROBERT ROSNER; publs *Explorer* (2 a year), *Frontiers* (annually), *LOGOS* (4 a year).

Association of Universities for Research in Astronomy, Inc. (AURA): Suite 350, 1200 New York Avenue NW, Washington, DC 20005; tel. (202) 483-2101; fax (202) 483-2106; internet www.aura-astronomy.org; f. 1957; operates the Space Telescope Science Institute, Baltimore, MD, and the National Optical Astronomy Observatories, Tucson, AZ, which consist of the Kitt Peak National Observatory, AZ, the National Solar Observatory, AZ and NM; and Cerro Tololo Inter-American Observatory, Chile; manages the International Gemini Project, Tucson, AZ; library of 30,000 vols; Pres. Dr GOETZ K. OERTEL; Vice-Pres. HARRY W. FEINSTEIN.

Byrd Polar Research Center: 1090 Carmack Rd, Ohio State University, Columbus, OH 43210-1002; tel. (614) 292-6531; fax (614) 292-4697; e-mail lay.l@osu.edu; internet www-bprc.mps.ohio-state.edu; f. 1960; geology, glaciology, atmospheric sciences, pedology, history, palaeontology, geophysics and remote sensing, palaeoclimatology and environmental policy in polar regions; library of 12,000 vols; papers and memorabilia of Richard E. Byrd, Sir Hubert Wilkins and other polar explorers; Dir C. J. VAN DER VEEN; publs *Report* (irregular), *Technical Report* (irregular).

Center for Earth and Planetary Studies (CEPS): Smithsonian Institution, POB 37012, National Air and Space Museum, MRC 315, Washington, DC 20013-7012; tel. (202) 357-1424; internet www.nasm.si.edu/ceps; attached to the Collections and Research Department of the Smithsonian Institution's National Air and Space Museum (Washington, DC); research into planetary and terrestrial geology and geophysics, application of remote sensing data from Earth-orbiting satellites and space missions; designated Regional Planetary Image Facility (RPIF); colln of Space Shuttle photographs; responsible for museum galleries 'Exploring the Planets' and 'Looking at Earth'; Dept Chair. JAMES R. ZIMBELMAN; Program Manager PRISCILLA STRAIN.

Fermi National Accelerator Laboratory: POB 500, Batavia, IL 60510-0500; tel. (708) 840-3000; fax (708) 840-4343; e-mail fermilab@fnal.gov; internet www.fnal.gov; f. 1967; research in high energy physics; run by Universities Research Asscn, Inc for US Dept of Energy; library of 15,000 vols, 250 periodicals; Dir MICHAEL S. WITHERELL; publs *Fermilab Report*, *Symmetry* (12 a year).

Goddard Institute for Space Studies: 2880 Broadway, New York, NY 10025; tel. (212) 678-5500; fax (212) 678-5552; internet www.giss.nasa.gov; f. 1961; global climate, biogeochemical cycles, cloud studies, planetary atmospheres, global habitability; library of 15,000 vols; Dir Dr JAMES HANSEN.

Harvard–Smithsonian Center for Astrophysics (CfA): 60 Garden St, Cambridge, MA 02138; tel. (617) 495-7461; fax (617) 495-7468; internet sao-www.harvard.edu; f. 1973 as a formal collaboration between the Harvard College Observatory (f. 1839) and the Smithsonian Astrophysical Observatory (f. 1890); scientific divisions: atomic and molecular physics, high energy astrophysics, optical and infrared astronomy, radio and geoastronomy, solar, stellar and planetary sciences, theoretical astrophysics, science education; library: John G. Wolbach Library and Information Resource Center (combines

libraries of the SAO and HCO) of 75,000 vols, 40,000 astronomic photographic plates; Dir IRWIN SHAPIRO.

Lamont-Doherty Earth Observatory of Columbia University: POB 1000, Palisades, NY 10964-8000; tel. (845) 359-2900; fax (845) 365-8162; e-mail director@ldeo.columbia.edu; internet www.ldeo.columbia.edu; f. 1948; research in earth and ocean sciences; library of 25,000 vols; Dir G. MICHAEL PURDY (acting); publs *Earth Matters* (newsletter), *Year Book*, *List of Scientific Publications*.

Lick Observatory: Mount Hamilton, CA 95140; internet mthamilton.ucolick.org; attached to the University of California, Santa Cruz Campus; f. 1888; optical astronomy and astrophysics; Dir J. S. MILLER.

Lowell Observatory: 1400 W. Mars Hill Rd, Flagstaff, AZ 86001; tel. (928) 774-3358; fax (928) 774-6296; internet www.lowell.edu; f. 1894; library: astronomical research library of 12,000 vols; Dir R. L. MILLIS; publ. *The Lowell Observer*.

Lunar and Planetary Institute: 3600 Bay Area Blvd, Houston, TX 77058; tel. (281) 486-2139; fax (281) 486-2127; e-mail info@lpi.usra.edu; internet www.lpi.usra.edu; f. 1968 to promote and support research in lunar and planetary studies; library of 55,000 vols, 210 periodicals, also photographic and cartographic data from planetary spacecraft missions; library is a NASA Regional Planetary Image Facility; Dir STEPHEN MACKWELL; publ. *Lunar and Planetary Information Bulletin* (quarterly).

Maria Mitchell Observatory: The Nantucket Maria Mitchell Asscn, 4 Vestal St, Nantucket, MA 02554; tel. (508) 228-9198; fax (508) 228-1031; e-mail vladimir@mmo.org; internet www.mmo.org; f. 1902; astronomical research, research training, public lectures and viewings; library of 4,000 vols; Dir Dr VLADIMIR STRELNITSKI; publ. *Annual Report*.

Mount Graham International Observatory (MGIO): 1480 West Swift Trail, Safford, AZ 85546; tel. (928) 428-2739; fax (928) 428-2854; internet mgpc3.as.arizona.edu; Dir BUDDY E. POWELL.

Constituent centres:

Vatican Observatory Research Group (VORG): Univ. of Arizona, Tucson, AZ 85721; tel. (520) 621-3225; fax (520) 621-1532; e-mail ccorbally@as.arizona.edu; internet clavius.as.arizona.edu/vo/rr1024/vo.html; f. 1993; attached to Vatican Observatory, Vatican City; operates the 1.8-m Alice P. Lennon Telescope with its Thomas J. Bannan Astrophysics Facility, known together as the Vatican Advanced Technology Telescope; Vice-Dir of the Vatican Observatory for VORG Dr CHRISTOPHER J. CORBALLY.

Arizona Radio Observatory (ARO): Univ. of Arizona, 933 North Cherry Ave, Tucson, AZ 85721; tel. (520) 621-5290; fax (520) 621-5554; e-mail opersmt@as.arizona.edu; internet aro.as.arizona.edu; operates the Heinrich Hertz Submillimeter Telescope (HHSMT); Dir Dr LUCY ZIURYS.

Large Binocular Telescope Observatory (LBTO): Univ. of Arizona, 933 North Cherry Ave, Tucson, AZ 85721; tel. (520) 626-7088; fax (520) 626-9333; e-mail rgreen@as.arizona.edu; internet medusa.as.arizona.edu/lbto; f. 1988, operational 2007; the world's most powerful optical telescope; consists of 2 8.4-m mirrors on a common mount; a collaboration between the Italian astronomical community (represented by the Istituto Nazionale di Astrofisica (q.v.)), the Univ. of Arizona,

Arizona State Univ., Northern Arizona Univ., the LBT Beteiligungsgesellschaft in Germany, the Ohio State Univ., Research Corpn in Tucson, and the Univ. of Notre Dame; Dir RICHARD F. GREEN.

National Astronomy and Ionosphere Center: Space Sciences Building, Cornell University, Ithaca, NY 14853-6801; tel. (607) 255-3735; fax (607) 255-8803; e-mail jtm14@cornell.edu; internet www.naic.edu; f. 1963; national research facility funded by the US National Science Foundation and operated by Cornell Univ.; research in areas of radio and radar astronomy and in space atmospheric sciences; Arecibo Observatory: see chapter on Puerto Rico; Dir Dr ROBERT L. BROWN; Admin. Dir DIANNA MARSH; publs *Astronomical Journal* (irregular), *Astrophysical Journal* (irregular), *Journal of Geophysical Research* (irregular), *Astronomy and Astrophysics* (irregular), *Publication of the Astronomical Society of the Pacific* (irregular), *Journal of Atmospheric and Solar-Terrestrial Physics* (irregular).

National Center for Atmospheric Research (NCAR): POB 3000, Boulder, CO 80307-3000; tel. (303) 497-1000; fax (303) 497-1194; internet www.ncar.ucar.edu; f. 1960; sponsored by National Science Foundation; operated by the University Corpn for Atmospheric Research (UCAR); research in weather prediction, causes of climatic trends, solar processes and influences of the sun on weather and climate, convective storms, and global air quality; library: 100,000 items, 900 current journals; Dir TIM KILLEEN; publs *UCAR* (quarterly), *Biannual Report*, *Annual Scientific Report*.

National Radio Astronomy Observatory: 520 Edgemont Rd, Charlottesville, VA 22903-2475; and POB 2, Green Bank, WV 24944-0002; and 949 N. Cherry Ave, Tucson, AZ 85721-0655; and POB O, Socorro, NM 87801-0387; tel. (434) 296-0221; fax (434) 296-0278; e-mail brodrigu@nrao.edu; internet www.nrao.edu; f. 1956; a facility of the National Science Foundation, operated under co-operative agreement by Associated Universities Inc.; research in radio astronomy, radio astronomy electronics, design of radio telescopes; observing radio telescopes include a 27-element array of 82-ft radio telescopes in New Mexico, a 10-element array of 82-ft radio telescopes located in 7 states and the US Virgin Islands, dedicated to very long baseline interferometry and a 100-metre fully steerable telescope in West Virginia; library of 27,000 vols; Dir FRED K. Y. LO.

National Solar Observatory: NSO Tucson, 950 N. Cherry Ave, Tucson, AZ 85719-4933; tel. (520) 318-8000 NSO Sacramento Peak, POB 62, Sunspot, NM 88349-0062; tel. (505) 434-7000; internet www.nso.edu; f. 1952; operated by AURA, Inc. (q.v.); national centre for solar research; offers telescope use to astronomical community; 50 staff, including 11 astrophysicists; library of 8,000 vols; Dir STEPHEN L. KEIL; publs research papers.

Rare-earth Information Center (RIC): Institute for Physical Research and Technology, Iowa State University, Ames, IA 50011-3020; tel. (515) 294-2272; fax (515) 294-3709; e-mail ric@ameslab.gov; f. 1966; emphasis on metallurgy and solid state physics of rare earth metals, alloys and compounds; Dir R. W. McCALLUM; publs *Rare-earth Information Center News* (quarterly), *RIC Insight* (monthly).

Scripps Institution of Oceanography: Mail Code 0233, La Jolla, CA 92093-0233; tel. (619) 534-3624; fax (619) 534-5306; internet www.sio.ucsd.edu; f. 1903; graduate school and research division of Univ. of

California, San Diego; main depts: Geosciences Research, Marine Biology Research, Physical Oceanography, Marine Physical Laboratory, Center for Marine Biotechnology and Biomedicine, Marine Life Research Group, Center for Coastal Studies, Climate Research, Marine Research, Center for Atmospheric Sciences, Scripps Graduate Department; associated Univ. of California institutes: Institute of Geophysics and Planetary Physics, California Space Institute; special facilities include hydraulics laboratory; operates four research vessels and one platform; public aquarium and museum; library of 225,000 vols, 3,800 periodicals; Dir CHARLES F. KENNEL; publs *Bulletin* (irregular), *Contributions* (annually), *Explorations* (quarterly).

Sproul Observatory: Swarthmore, PA 19081; tel. (610) 328-8272; f. 1911; attached to Swarthmore College; 61-cm Long Focus Refractor, 61-cm reflector and echelle spectrometer; astrometry and stellar spectroscopy; library of 9,000 vols.

United States Naval Observatory: 3450 Massachusetts Ave, NW, Washington, DC 20392-5420; tel. (202) 762-1437; fax (202) 762-1461; f. 1830; positional astronomy, astrometry, proper motions, stellar parallaxes, photometry, double stars, earth rotation, master clock, precise time measurement, celestial mechanics; library of 75,000 vols; substation at Flagstaff, Ariz.; Superintendent Capt. K. W. FOSTER; Scientific Dir Dr KENNETH JOHNSTON; publs *Astronomical Almanac*, *Nautical Almanac*, *Air Almanac*, *Multi-year Interactive Computer Almanac*, *Astronomical Phenomena*, *NavObs Circulars*, *Astronomical Papers*, *Time Service Bulletins*, star catalogs.

Vanderbilt Dyer Observatory: 1000 Oman Drive, Brentwood, TN 37027; tel. (615) 373-4897; fax (615) 371-3904; e-mail nancy.dwyer@vanderbilt.edu; internet www.dyer.vanderbilt.edu; f. 1953; specializes in research on local structure of the Milky Way, photo-electric photometry of eclipsing binaries and variable stars, pre-planetary discs around young stars; equipped with combination 60-cm reflecting and Baker-Schmidt telescope, 40-cm computer controlled automatic telescope, 30-cm and 40-cm Cassegrain reflecting telescopes and 15-cm refracting telescope; library: Observatory library of 12,000 vols; Dir RICK CHAPPELL; publ. *IAPPP Communications* (quarterly).

Warner and Swasey Observatory: Case Western Reserve University, Cleveland, OH 44106; tel. (216) 368-3728; fax (216) 368-5203; f. 1920; astronomical research and education (observational facility of the department of astronomy at Case Western Reserve University); staff: 3 academic, 7–10 others; library of 15,000 vols; Dir R. EARLE LUCK; publs *Publications*, *Reprints*.

Woods Hole Oceanographic Institution: Woods Hole, MA 02543; tel. (508) 548-1400; fax (508) 457-2034; e-mail information@whoi.edu; internet www.whoi.edu; f. 1930; research in physical, chemical and biological oceanography, marine geology and marine geophysics, ocean acoustics, ocean engineering and marine policy; conducts joint PhD programme with Massachusetts Inst. of Technology, postdoctoral fellowship programme and summer student fellowship programme; joint library with Marine Biological Laboratory of 150,000 vols and 5,000 periodical titles; Pres. and Dir ROBERT B. GAGOSIAN; publs *Abstracts of Papers* (annually), *Oceanus* (3 a year).

Yale Observatory: Yale University, Dept of Astronomy, 260 Whitney Ave, POB 208101, New Haven, CT 06520-8101; tel. (203) 432-3000; fax (203) 432-5048; internet www.astro.yale.edu; publs *Bright Star Catalogue* (and supplement), *General Catalogue of Trigonometric Stellar Parallaxes*, *Transactions*.

Yerkes Observatory: 373 W. Geneva St, Williams Bay, WI 53191; tel. (262) 245-5555; fax (262) 245-9805; internet astro.uchicago.edu/yerkes; f. 1897; research branch of the Dept of Astronomy and Astrophysics of the Univ. of Chicago; library of 25,000 books and journals; Dir Dr K. M. CUDWORTH.

PHILOSOPHY AND PSYCHOLOGY

American Society for Psychical Research, Inc.: 5 West 73rd St, New York, NY 10023; tel. (212) 799-5050; fax (212) 496-2497; e-mail aspr@aspr.com; internet www.aspr.com; f. 1885; study of paranormal phenomena such as telepathy, clairvoyance, precognition, psychokinesis etc.; 2,000 mems; library of 9,000 vols; Chester Carlson Research Fellow Emeritus Dr KARLIS OSIS; Exec. Dir PATRICE KEANE; publs *Journal*, *Newsletter* (quarterly), *Proceedings* (occasional).

RELIGION, SOCIOLOGY AND ANTHROPOLOGY

American Institutes for Research: 1000 Thomas Jefferson St, Washington, DC 20007; tel. (202) 403-5000; fax (202) 403-5001; e-mail inquiry@air.org; internet www.air.org; f. 1946; independent, non-profit organization conducting research, development, analysis and evaluation studies in the behavioural and social sciences for clients in government and the private sector; Pres. and Chief Exec. Officer SOL H. PELAVIN; publ. *Newsletter* (annually).

American Research Center in Egypt (ARCE): US office, Mailstop 1256/001/1AC, Emory University Briarcliff Campus, Atlanta, GA 30322; tel. (404) 712-9854; fax (404) 712-9849; e-mail arce@emory.edu; internet www.arce.org Cairo office: 2 Midan Simón Bolívar, Garden City, Cairo, 11461; tel. (2) 796-4681; fax (2) 794-8622; e-mail arce@internetegypt.com; f. 1948; independent, non-profit-making; promotes research on Egypt and the Middle East in the fields of archaeology, art, architecture, history, culture, social sciences; library: library (in Cairo) of 25,000 vols; *c*. 1,200 mems; Pres. CAROL REDMOUNT; Assoc. Dir. for US Operations SUSANNE THOMAS; Cairo Dir GERRY DEE SCOTT, III; publs *Newsletter* (3 a year), *Journal* (annually).

American Schools of Oriental Research: 656 Beacon St, 5th Floor, Boston, MA 02215-2010; tel. (617) 353-6570; fax (617) 353-6575; e-mail asor@bu.edu; internet www.asor.org; f. 1900; promote research into the cultures of the Near East and support activities of independent archaeological institutions abroad: Albright Institute of Archaeological Research (Jerusalem, Israel), American Center of Oriental Research (Amman, Jordan), and Cyprus American Archaeological Research Institute (Nicosia, Cyprus); 1,500 mems; Pres. LAWRENCE T. GERATY; publs *Near Eastern Archaeology* (4 a year), *Bulletin* (4 a year), *Journal of Cuneiform Studies* (annually), *The Annual*, *Newsletter* (4 a year).

Arctic Studies Center: Dept of Anthropology, National Museum of Natural History, Smithsonian Institution, Washington, DC 20560-0112; *Alaska Office*: 121 West 7th Ave, Anchorage, AK 99501; tel. (202) 357-2682 (Washington), (907) 343-6162 (Anchorage); fax (202) 357-2684 (Washington), (907) 343-6130 (Anchorage); e-mail arctics@nmnh.si.edu; internet www.mnh.si.edu/arctic; f. 1988; attached to Dept of Anthropology of the Smithsonian Institution's National Museum of Natural History; research into peoples, history, archaeology and social change in the circumpolar regions; Dir WILLIAM W. FITZHUGH; publ. *Newsletter* (annually).

Center for Advanced Study in the Behavioral Sciences: 75 Alta Rd, Stanford, CA 94305-8090; tel. (650) 321-2052; fax (650) 321-1192; e-mail info@casbs.org; internet www.casbs.org; f. 1954; Dir Dr CLAUDE M. STEELE; publ. *Annual Report*.

Harry Ransom Humanities Research Center, The University of Texas at Austin: POB 7219, Austin, TX 78713-7219; tel. (512) 471-8944; fax (512) 471-9646; internet www.hrc.utexas.edu; f. 1957; specializes in American, British and French literature and art since 19th c.; library of 1,000,000 vols, 40,000,000 MSS, 5,000,000 photographs; Dir THOMAS F. STALEY.

Middle American Research Institute: Tulane University, New Orleans, LA 70118-5698; tel. (504) 865-5110; fax (504) 862-8778; e-mail mari@tulane.edu; internet www.tulane.edu/~mari; f. 1924; for research, education, and publs related to Mexico and Central America; supports publication, archaeological excavation and research in humanities and social sciences; small museum gallery; anthropological collections; Dir E. WYLLYS ANDREWS V.

Middle East Institute: 1761 N St, NW, Washington, DC 20036-2882; tel. (202) 785-1141; fax (202) 331-8861; e-mail mideasti@mideasti.org; internet www.mideasti.org; f. 1946; a non-profit, non-advocating resource centre; promotes American understanding of the Middle East, North Africa, the Caucasus and Central Asia; co-ordinates cultural presentations; library of 25,000 vols; 1,300 mems; Pres. EDWARD S. WALKER, Jr; publ. *Middle East Journal* (quarterly).

Smithsonian Center for Folklife and Cultural Heritage: POB 37012, Victor Bldg, Suite 4100, MRC 953, Washington, DC 20013-7012; Located at: 750 9th St, NW, Suite 4100, Smithsonian Institution, Washington, DC 20560-0953; tel. (202) 275-1150; fax (202) 275-1119; e-mail folklife-info@si.edu; internet www.folklife.si.edu; promotes the understanding and continuity of contemporary grassroots cultures in the USA and abroad; runs Smithsonian Folklife Festival, Smithsonian Folkways Recordings, exhibitions, documentary films, symposia; library: Ralph Rinzler Folklife Archives and Collections: 17,300 commercial discs, 4,000 acetate discs, 45,000 audiotapes, 2,000 CDs, 1,000,000 stills, 2,500 videotapes, 500,000 ft of motion picture film; Moses and Frances Asch collection, consisting of recordings and material relating to Folkways Records; records and archives of the center; Dir RICHARD KURIN.

Smithsonian Center for Latino Initiatives: 900 Jefferson Drive, SW, Rm 1465, MRC 448, Washington, DC 20560-0448; tel. (202) 633-1240; fax (202) 786-2477; internet latino.si.edu; f. 1998; co-ordinates all Smithsonian-related Latino exhibitions, initiatives, research and educational programmes; library: archive of papers of Latino and Latin American artists; Dir LUBEN MONTOYA (acting).

Social Science Research Council: 810 Seventh Ave, New York, NY 10019; tel. (212) 377-2700; fax (212) 377-2727; e-mail info@ssrc.org; internet www.ssrc.org; f. 1923; to advance research in the social sciences by: appointment of committees of scholars to set priorities and make plans for critical areas of social research; improvement of research training through training institutes and fellowship programmes; support of individual research through postdoctoral grants; sponsorship of research conferences, often interdisciplinary and international; sponsorship of books and other research publications that may result from these activities; Pres. CRAIG CALHOUN; publ. *Items* (quarterly).

Wenner-Gren Foundation for Anthropological Research, Inc.: 470 Park Ave South, 8th Fl., New York, NY 10016; tel. (212) 683-5000; fax (212) 683-9151; e-mail inquiries@wennergren.org; internet www.wennergren.org; f. 1941 as the Viking Fund; supports research in all branches of anthropology and closely related disciplines concerned with human origins, development and variation; grants to aid individual research, including dissertation research, fellowships and post-PhD research grants; Conference Grants Program; Historical Archives Program; Professional Development International Fellowships and International Collaborative Research Grants; Pres. Dr LESLIE AIELLO; publ. *Current Anthropology* (5 a year).

TECHNOLOGY

Brookhaven National Laboratory: POB 5000, Upton, Long Island, NY 11973-5000; tel. (631) 344-8000; internet www.bnl.gov; f. 1947; operated by Brookhaven Science Assocs. under contract with the US Dept of Energy; basic and applied research by staff and visiting scientists in the fields of energy, particle accelerators, physics, medicine, biology, chemistry, applied sciences, mathematics, and the environment, including the design, development, acquisition and operation of large-scale facilities too costly or complex for an individual university; training of scientists and engineers; dissemination of scientific and technical knowledge; library of 82,000 vols; staff: 644 research, 621 professional, 759 technicians, 1,129 general; Dir Dr PRAVEEN CHAUDHARI; publs *Brookhaven Bulletin, Brookhaven Highlights*.

Building Research Board: 2101 Constitution Ave, NW, Washington, DC 20418; tel. (202) 334-3376; f. 1949 as a unit of the Nat. Academy of Sciences—Nat. Research Council; undertakes activities concerned with the development and application of technology to serve society's needs for the built environment: infrastructure, housing, building and related community and environmental design and development; Chair. HAROLD J. PARMELEE; Dir ANDREW C. LEMER.

Combustion Institute: 5001 Baum Blvd, Pittsburgh, PA 15213-1851; tel. (412) 687-1366; fax (412) 687-0340; e-mail office@combustioninstitute.org; internet www.combustioninstitute.org; f. 1954; 3,600 mems; non-profit educational scientific society which promotes and disseminates research in combustion science; offices in 26 countries; Pres. Prof. BRIAN S. HAYNES; Exec. Sec. SUE S. TERPACK; publs *Combustion and Flame* (monthly), *Proceedings of Symposium (International) on Combustion* (every 2 years).

Herty Foundation: POB 7798, Savannah, GA 31418-7798; tel. (912) 963-2600; fax (912) 963-2614; internet www.herty.com; f. 1938; non-profit contractual research and development of wood, non-wood and synthetic fibres; Dir Dr KARL M. COUNTS.

Industrial Research Institute, Inc.: 2200 Clarendon Blvd, Suite 1102, Arlington, VA 22201-3331; tel. (703) 647-2580; fax (703) 647-2581; e-mail iriinc_info@mailback.com; internet www.iriinc.org; f. 1938; 208 mem. companies; Pres. Dr F. M. ROSS ARMBRECHT, Jr; publ. *Research-Technology Management* (every 2 months).

Institute of Textile Technology: 2401 Research Drive, Box 8301, Raleigh, NC 27695-8301; tel. (919) 513-7704; fax (919) 882-9410; internet www.itt.edu; f. 1944; research, graduate education and information programmes for the textile industry; library of 50,000 vols; Pres. Dr GILBERT O'NEAL; Dir, Research Dr HENRY BOYTER; publs *Textile Technology Digest* (monthly), *Textile Technology Digest on CD-ROM* (4 a year), *Vital Textile Literature* (every 2 weeks).

Jerome and Dorothy Lemelson Center for the Study of Invention and Innovation: National Museum of American History, Rm 1016, Smithsonian Institution, POB 37012 Washington, DC 20013-7012; tel. (202) 633-3450; fax (202) 357-4517; internet invention.smithsonian.org; f. 1995 to document, interpret and disseminate information about invention and innovation, and to encourage inventive creativity in young people; part of the Smithsonian Institution National Museum of American History; Dir ARTHUR MOLELLA.

National Aeronautics and Space Administration (NASA): 300 E St SW, Washington, DC 20546; e-mail public-inquiries@hq.nasa.gov; internet www.nasa.gov; Administrator MICHAEL D. GRIFFIN.

Main research centres:

Ames Research Center: NASA, Moffet Field, CA 94035; tel. (650) 604-5000; internet www1.nasa.gov/centers/ame; f. 1939; Dir Dr G. SCOTT HUBBARD.

Dryden Flight Research Center: PO Box 273, Edwards, CA 93523-0273; tel. (661) 276-3311; internet www.nasa.gov/centers/dryden; research in aeronautics and space technology; Dir KEVIN L. PETERSEN.

George C. Marshall Space Flight Center: National Aeronautics and Space Administration, AL 35812; f. 1960; Dir D. A. KING.

Glenn Research Center: NASA, 21000 Brookpark Rd, Cleveland, OH 44135; tel. (216) 433-4000; internet www.nasa.gov/centers/glenn; f. 1942; Dir JULIAN EARLS.

Goddard Space Flight Center: NASA, Greenbelt, MD 20771; tel. (301) 286-8955; fax (301) 286-1707; internet www1.nasa.gov/centers/goddard; f. 1959; space research; 3,500 mems; library of 57,000 vols, 35,000 periodicals; Dir Dr EDWARD J. WEILER.

Jet Propulsion Laboratory: 4800 Oak Grove Drive, Pasadena, CA 91109; tel. (818) 354-4321; internet www.nasa.gov/centers/jpl; centre for robotic exploration of the solar system; operated by California Institute of Technology; Dir Dr CHARLES ELACHI.

John F. Kennedy Space Center: NASA, FL 32899; internet www1.nasa.gov/centers/kennedy; f. 1962; previously Launch Operations Center; space vehicle launch facility; library of 32,000 vols, 106,000 documents and reports, 589 periodicals; 160,000 specifications and standards; Dir JAMES W. KENNEDY.

Langley Research Center: NASA, Hampton, VA 23665; internet www1.nasa.gov/centers/langley; f. 1917; Dir ROY BRIDGES.

Lyndon B. Johnson Space Center: NASA, Houston, TX 77058; tel. (281) 483-0123; internet www.nasa.gov/centers/johnson; f. 1961; the Johnson Space Center is responsible for the design, development and testing of manned spacecraft and associated systems, for the selection and training of astronauts and for the operation of manned space flights; operates White Sands Test Facility at Las Cruces, NM; library: Johnson Space Center Technical library of 49,000 vols, 550,000 technical reports, 600 periodicals; Dir JEFFERSON D. HOWELL, Jr.

Stennis Space Center: tel. (228) 688-3341; e-mail pao@ssc.nasa.gov; internet www.nasa.gov/centers/stennis; Dir THOMAS Q. DONALDSON.

National Institute of Standards and Technology: Gaithersburg, MD 20899-1000; and at Boulder, CO 80303-3328; tel. (301) 975-3057; fax (301) 926-1630; e-mail inquiries@nist.gov; internet www.nist.gov; f. 1901; a non-regulatory agency of the Commerce Department's Technology Administration; works with industry to develop and apply technology, measurements and standards; laboratory research focused on infrastructural technologies; Dir WILLIAM JEFFREY.

National Renewable Energy Laboratory: 1617 Cole Blvd, Golden, CO 80401-3393; tel. (303) 275-3000; fax (303) 275-4091; internet www.nrel.gov; f. 1977; a national centre for federally sponsored long-range high-risk renewable energy research and development; library of 105,000 books and reports, 350 journals; Dir Dr DAN ARVIZU; publs *AFDC Update*, *Biofuels Update*.

Southwest Research Institute: 6220 Culebra Rd, Post Office Drawer 28510, San Antonio, TX 78228-0510; tel. (210) 684-5111; fax (210) 522-3547; internet www.swri.edu; f. 1947; independent non-profit organization conducting research and development in the engineering and physical sciences for government, business and industry around the world; library of 50,000 vols; Pres. J. DAN BATES; publ. *Technology Today* (3 a year).

SRI International: 333 Ravenswood Ave, Menlo Park, CA 94025-3493; tel. (415) 326-6200; internet www.sri.com; f. 1946 (fmrly Stanford Research Institute); non-profit-making; centres for diversified research for industry and government in pure and applied science and engineering; br in Washington, DC; overseas offices in Tokyo, Japan, Seoul, Republic of Korea, Zurich, Switzerland, Cambridge, UK and London, UK; Pres. and CEO CURTIS R. CARLSON.

TRI Princeton: POB 625, Princeton, NJ 08542; tel. (609) 924-3150; fax (609) 683-7836; e-mail info@triprinceton.org; internet www.triprinceton.com; f. 1930; fundamental and applied research and continuing education in the physical and engineering sciences relating to fibrous materials, films, polymers, human hair, and porous and nanoporous materials; 169 individual mems; library of 5,000 vols; Pres. Dr GAIL R. EATON; Sec. of the Board of Trustees ELEANOR LEHMAN; publ. *Textile Research Journal* (monthly).

Libraries and Archives

Alabama

Birmingham Public Library: 2100 Park Pl., Birmingham, AL 35203; tel. (205) 226-3610; internet www.bplonline.org; f. 1909; 1,094,390 vols; spec. collns: Agee Cartographical Colln (incl. Joseph H. Woodward Colln), Catherine Collins Colln of Dance, Scruggs Philately Colln, Tutwiler Colln of Southern History and Literature, govt documents, archives, MSS, musical recordings, film and video; DIALOG Online Computer Reference Service, Books by Mail Service; 19 brs; Dir BARBARA SIRMANS.

University of Alabama Library: POB 870266, Tuscaloosa, AL 35487-0266; tel.

(205) 348-6047; internet www.lib.ua.edu; f. 1831; regional depository for federal documents; deptl libraries for business, education, engineering, sciences; special collns on Alabama and Southern history and literature; 1,814,178 vols; Dean of Libraries LOUIS A. PITSCHMANN.

Alaska

Alaska State Library: POB 110571, Juneau, AK 99811-0571; tel. (907) 465-2910; fax (907) 465-2665; e-mail asl@eed.state.ak.us; internet www.library.state.ak.us; f. 1900; govt services 61,597 vols, historical collns of 59,494 vols, 484 photographic collns, and 814 MSS; 2,842 vols in Anchorage office; genealogy resources; Dir KATHRYN SHELTON.

Arizona

Arizona State Library, Archives and Public Records: Suite 200, 1700 West Washington, Phoenix, AZ 85007; tel. (602) 542-4035; fax (602) 542-4972; e-mail services@lib.az.us; internet www.lib.az.us; f. 1864; law, govt, Arizona and Southwest history, genealogy, federal and state documents; library extension, archives, library for the blind and physically handicapped, museums, public records; 1,127,196 vols; Dir GLADYSANN WELLS.

City of Phoenix Public Library: 1221 North Central, Phoenix, AZ 85004; tel. (602) 262-4636; fax (602) 495-5841; internet www.phoenixpubliclibrary.org; f. 1901; 1,754,000 vols, 4,315 periodical titles; 15 brs; audiovisual material; Arizona and South-west materials; Dir TONI GARVEY.

University of Arizona Library: Main Library A349, POB 210055, Tucson, AZ 85721-0055; Located at: 1510 East University Blvd, Tucson, AZ 85721-0055; tel. (520) 621-2101; fax (520) 621-9733; internet www.library.arizona.edu; f. 1891; 4,844,241 vols; spec. collns: history of science, Southwestern Americana and borderlands history, fine and theatre arts, British and American literature; Dir Libraries CARLA STOFFLE.

Arkansas

Arkansas History Commission Library: 1 Capitol Mall, Little Rock, AR 72201; tel. (501) 682-6900; e-mail state.archives@arkansas.gov; internet www.ark-ives.com; f. 1905; official state archives; MSS, books, microfilm, newspapers, maps, photographs; Dir Dr WENDY RICHTER.

Arkansas State Library: 1 Capitol Mall, Little Rock, AR 72201; tel. (501) 682-2053; fax (501) 682-1529; e-mail shawkes@asl.lib.ar.us; internet www.asl.lib.ar.us; f. 1979; Librarian CAROLYN ASHCRAFT.

University of Arkansas Libraries: 365 North McIlroy Ave, Fayetteville, AR 72701-4002; tel. (479) 575-4104; fax (479) 575-6656; internet dante.uark.edu; spec. collns: local politics, Civil War, women's records, 100,000 pictures and photographs, maps; Dir CAROLYN HENDERSON.

California

California State Library: POB 942837, Sacramento, CA 94237-0001; tel. (916) 654-0174; fax (916) 654-00641; e-mail csl-adm@library.ca.gov; internet www.library.ca.gov; f. 1850; 696,000 vols, 3,011,835 govt publs; library service to State Govt; preservation of CA materials; govt document depository; law library; books for the blind, and physically handicapped service; administrator of the state and federal aid to public libraries; State Librarian SUSAN HILDRETH; publs *California Library Directory* (annual), *California Library Laws* (annual), *California Library Statistics* (annual), *California State Publications* (monthly).

Hoover Institution on War, Revolution and Peace: Stanford, CA 94305; tel. (650) 723-1754; fax (650) 723-1687; internet www-hoover.stanford.edu; f. 1919; centre of documentation and research on int. and domestic political, social and economic change since beginning of the 20th century; 60m. documents, 100,000 political posters; 4,772 archival units on the causes and consequences of war and revolutionary movements, and on efforts to achieve peace; with emphasis on int. rivalries and global co-operation; research programme on political, economic and social problems in the USA; independent, within the framework of Stanford Univ.; Dir Dr JOHN RAISIAN; publs *China Leadership Monitor* (quarterly), *Education Next* (quarterly), *Hoover's Digest* (quarterly), *Policy Review* (6 a year).

Huntington Library, Art Collections and Botanical Gardens: 1151 Oxford Rd, San Marino, CA 91108; tel. (626) 405-2100; fax (626) 449-5720; e-mail publicinformation@huntington.org; internet www.huntington.org; f. 1919 by the late Henry E. Huntington as a free research library, art gallery, museum, and botanical garden; 7,000,000 vols; collns incl. 500,000 rare books, 6,000,000 MSS, working reference library of 500,000 vols and 600,000 photographs; available to scholars and others engaged in research work on application to the Registrar; collns concentrate on British and American history, literature and art; particular strengths incl. English medieval and Renaissance, British drama, American colonial, American Civil War, American frontier, MSS since 19th century, early science; separate reference libraries located in the Botanical Dept and Art Gallery, the latter incl. 300,000 photographs, paintings and 6,000 British drawings; public programmes, lectures, exhibitions; Pres. ROBERT A. SKOTHEIM; Dir Library DAVID S. ZEIDBERG; See also Museums and Art Galleries; publ. *Huntington Frontiers* (2 a year).

Los Angeles County Law Library: 301 West First St, Los Angeles, CA 90012-3100; tel. (213) 629-3531; fax (213) 613-1329; e-mail lacll@lalaw.lib.ca.us; internet www.lalaw.lib.ca.us; f. 1891; 700,000 vols; brs in Compton, Long Beach, Norwalk, Pasadena, Pomona, Santa Monica, Torrance and Van Nuys; spec. colln 7,500 vols on Roman, canon, civil, English law; Dir MARCIA J. KOSLOV.

Los Angeles Public Library: 630 West Fifth St, Los Angeles, CA 90071; tel. (213) 228-7000; fax (213) 228-7069; e-mail cenadmin@lapl.org; internet www.lapl.org; f. 1872; 6,222,418 vols; 70 brs; Californiana, children's literature, cookery, genealogy, North American Indians, modern languages, orchestral scores, US patents, standards and specifications, English language, theatre, congressional documents and hearings, business and finance, corporate annual reports, videos, DVDs, CDs, audiobooks, telephone and trade directories; Dir Central Library ANNE CONNOR; Dir Branch Libraries CECILIA RIDDLE.

Sacramento Public Library: 828 I St, Sacramento, CA 95814; tel. (916) 264-2770; fax (916) 264-2755; e-mail contact@saclibrary.org; internet www.saclibrary.org; central library, 27 brs, 2 mobile units; 2,000,000 vols; spec. collns: Sacramento current and historical information, California colln, business colln, printing history, Sacramento area authors, art and music colln; Dir ANNE MARIE GOLD.

San Diego County Public Law Library: 1105 Front St, San Diego, CA 92101-3904; tel. (619) 531-3900; fax (619) 238-7716; e-mail refdesk@sdcpll.org; internet www.sdcpll.org; f. 1891; 346,151 vols; Dir ROBERT RIGER.

San Diego Public Library: 820 East St, San Diego, CA 92101-6478; tel. (619) 236-5800; fax (619) 236-5878; e-mail weblibrary@sandiego.gov; internet www.sandiego.gov/public-library; f. 1882; 2,335,811 vols; Dir ANNA TATÁR.

San Francisco Law Library: Rm 400, 401 Van Ness Ave, San Francisco, CA 94102; tel. (415) 554-6821; fax (415) 554-6820; internet www.sfgov.org/sfll; 246,000 vols, main library; 30,367 vols, br. libraries; 3 brs; open to public; Dir MARCIA BELL.

San Francisco Public Library: 100 Larkin St, San Francisco, CA 94102-4733; tel. (415) 557-4400; fax (415) 557-4239; e-mail info@sfpl.org; internet sfpl.org; 2,309,166 vols; City Librarian LUIS HERRERA.

Stanford University Libraries and Academic Information Resources (SULAIR): Stanford, CA 94305; tel. (650) 723-9108; e-mail ic@sulmail.stanford.edu; internet www-sul.stanford.edu; f. 1885; 7.7m. vols, incl. the Green Library (2,837,863 vols), Hoover Institution on War, Revolution and Peace (1,257,466 vols) and 45 departmental and school libraries, of which the major ones are: Lane Medical Library (371,725 vols), Robert Crown Law Library (437,896 vols), Cubberley Education Library (175,849 vols), Branner Earth Sciences Library (132,446 vols), J. Hugh Jackson Business Library (548,639 vols), Linear Accelerator Center Library (8,840 vols), Falconer Biology Library (105,106 vols), Hopkins Marine Station Library (38,478 vols), Mathematical and Computer Sciences Library (127,396 vols), Swain Chemistry Library (55,529 vols), Art and Architecture (180,933 vols), Music (108,443 vols), Archive of Recorded Sound (6,382 items), Physics (59,401 vols), Eng. (114,039 vols); spec. collns: Transportation, Music, British and American Literature, History of Science, Book Arts and History of the Book, Children's Literature, Judaica and Hebraica; Univ. Librarian and Dir of Academic Information Resources MICHAEL A. KELLER.

University of Southern California Library: Los Angeles, CA 90089-0182; tel. (213) 740-2543; fax (213) 749-1221; e-mail library@usc.edu; internet www.usc.edu/isd/libraries; f. 1880; 4,000,000 vols, 6m. microform items, 3,000,000 photographs, 30,000 periodicals; spec. collns: Cervantes, Lewis Carroll, Max Reinhardt; American literature; cinema and television, European philosophy; German exile literature; gerontology; int. relations; Korean studies, Latin American studies, natural history, Southern California history, Univ. Archives; Dean of Libraries CATHERINE QUINLAN.

Colorado

Boulder Laboratories Library: 325 Broadway/MC5, Boulder, CO 80305; tel. (303) 497-3271; fax (303) 497-3890; e-mail boulderlabs.mMain.library@noaa.gov; internet library.bldrdoc.gov; f. 1951; attached to US Dept of Commerce; 45,000 vols, 580 current journals, 29,000 bound journal vols, 700 e-journals; Dir JOHN WELSH.

Denver Public Library: 10 West 14th Ave, Pkwy, Denver, CO 80204-2731; tel. (720) 865-1111; fax (303) 640-6374; internet denverlibrary.org; f. 1889; 2,455,965 items; 22 brs; specializes in Western US history, conservation of natural resources, energy and the environment, genealogy, fine printing, folk music, US 10th Mountain Div. soldiers; City Librarian SHIRLEY AMORE.

University of Colorado at Boulder Libraries: 184 UCB, Boulder, CO 80309-

0184; tel. (303) 492-8705; fax (303) 492-1881; e-mail reflib@colorado.edu; internet ucblibraries.colorado.edu; f. 1876; spec. collns: mountaineering, photobooks, peace and justice, western Americana; 2,920,335 vols; Dean of Libraries JAMES F. WILLIAMS.

Connecticut

Connecticut State Library: 231 Capitol Ave, Hartford, CT 06106; tel. (860) 757-6500; fax (860) 757-6503; e-mail isref@cslib.org; internet www.cslib.org; f. 1854; Connecticut newspapers, genealogy, history, law, legislative reference, public policy, Connecticut and US govt publs; 1,139,624 vols, 1,724,681 govt docs, 28,000 cu ft of archival records and state archives; State Librarian KENDALL F. WIGGIN.

University of Connecticut Library: 369 Fairfield Way, Storrs, CT 06269-2005; tel. (860) 486-2518; fax (860) 486-0584; e-mail elibrary@uconn.edu; internet www.lib.uconn .edu; f. 1881; largest public research colln in the state; 2,600,000 vols, 6,000 current print periodicals, 41,000 electronic journals, 2.8m. microforms, 35,000 reference sources, 200,000 maps and a large repository of electronic information resources; Vice-Provost for Libraries BRINLEY FRANKLIN; publ. *University of Connecticut Libraries* (6 a year).

Yale University Library: POB 208240, 130 Wall St, New Haven, CT 06520-8240; tel. (203) 432-1818; fax (203) 432-1294; e-mail smlref@yale.edu; internet www.library.yale .edu; f. 1701; 10,500,544 vols; each of the 12 Undergraduate Colleges has its own library; Univ. Librarian ALICE PROCHASKA.

Delaware

Delaware Division of Libraries, Department of State: 43 South DuPont Highway, Dover, DE 19901; tel. (302) 739-4748; fax (302) 739-6787; internet www.state.lib.de.us; f. 1901; spec. collns: US govt documents, talking books; State Librarian and Dir ANNE E. C. NORMAN.

District of Columbia

Archives of American Art: Reference Services/ILL, AAA, Smithsonian Institution, POB 37012, Victor Bldg, Rm 2200, MRC, 937, Washington, DC 20013-7012; *Washington, DC Center*: Suite 2200, 750 Ninth St, NW, Washington, DC 20560-0937; tel. (202) 275-2156; fax (202) 275-1955; *New York City Research Center*: 1285 Ave of the Americas, Lobby Level, New York, NY 10019; tel. (212) 399-5015; fax (212) 307-4501; e-mail yeckleyk@aaany.si.edu; internet www.aaa.si .edu; f. 1954, bureau of the Smithsonian Instn since 1970; 900 mems; 14,000,000 items; Dir JOHN W. SMITH; publ. *Journal* (quarterly).

Department of Commerce Library: 14th and Constitution Ave, NW, Washington, DC 20230; f. 1913; 50,000 vols, 2,000 vols microform; Dir ANTHONY J. STEINHAUSER.

Independent libraries within the Dept of Commerce include:

Bureau of the Census Library: Federal Office Bldg No. 3, Room 2455, Washington, DC 20233; tel. (301) 763-1484; fax (301) 585-7976; f. 1952; 250,000 vols; Project Man. CATHERINE EARLES.

National Oceanic and Atmospheric Administration, Environmental Data and Information Service, Environmental Science Information Center, Library and Information Services Division: 1315 East-West Highway, 2nd Floor, SSMC3, Silver Spring, MD 20910; tel. (301) 713-2600; fax (301) 713-4598; e-mail library.reference@noaa.gov; internet www.lib.noaa.gov; 1,000,000 vols; 35 libraries and information centres holding spec. collns; Dir JANICE BEATTIE.

Department of Justice Library: 950 Pennsylvania Ave, NW, Washington, DC 20530-0001; tel. (202) 514-3775; fax (202) 514-3546; internet www.usdoj.gov; f. 1831; 300,000 vols, principally Anglo-American legal and related materials, 1m. items of microfiche and microfilm; 11 br. libraries (total 300,000 vols); specialized areas of American law; Library Dir BLANE K. DESSY.

Department of the Interior Libraries: Washington, DC 20240.

Constituent libraries:

US Geological Survey Library: 950 National Center, 12201 Sunrise Valley Dr., Reston, VA 20192; tel. (703) 648-4302; fax (703) 648-6373; e-mail library@ usgs.gov; internet library.usgs.gov; f. 1879; 1,000,000 vols, 450,000 maps, 270,000 pamphlets; 8,500 serial and periodical titles received; comprehensive working and research library; interlibrary loan service; open to the public; Chief Information Officer ROBERT BIER.

Library of the US Department of the Interior: Room 1151, 1849 C St, NW, Washington, DC 20240; tel. (202) 208-5815; internet library.doi.gov; f. 1949 by amalgamation of 8 existing Interior Libraries at Washington; 850,000 vols; 15,000 serials and 2,500 periodicals received; subjects incl. the conservation and devt of natural resources; automated information services; interlibrary loans service; copy facilities; open to the public; Dir VICTORIA NOZERO; publ. *Bibliographies* (available from US Nat. Technical Information Service).

Department of the Treasury Library: Main Treasury Bldg, 1500 Pennsylvania Ave, NW, Washington, DC 20220; tel. (202) 622-0990; fax (202) 622-2611; e-mail treasury .libraryref@treas.sprint.com; f. *c.*1817; 74,000 vols, 495,000 microfiches and 7,800 reels of microfilm; spec. collns: taxation, public finance, int. economic affairs, Treasury history.

Department of Veterans Affairs, Headquarters Library: 193A, 810 Vermont Ave, NW, Washington, DC 20420; tel. (202) 273-8523; fax (202) 273-9125; internet www.va .gov; planning, policy, devt, training, centralized support services for the VA Library Network (VALNET); this comprises 176 library services at 172 VA facilities; combined library holdings 1,398,000 vols, 145,000 audiovisual items, 75,655 journal subscriptions; Chief GINNY DUPONT.

District of Columbia Public Library: 901 G St, NW, Washington, DC 20001; tel. (202) 727-0321; fax (202) 727-1129; internet www .dclibrary.org; f. 1896; Martin Luther King, Jr Memorial Library (central library), 26 brs, Library for the Blind and the Physically Handicapped; spec. collns: Washingtoniana, Washington Star Colln, Black Studies, Musical Scores; 2,672,488 vols; Chief Librarian GINNIE COOPER.

Dumbarton Oaks Research Library and Collection: 1703 32nd St, Washington, DC 20007; tel. (202) 339-6401; fax (202) 339-6419; e-mail DumbartonOaks@doaks.org; internet www.doaks.org; f. 1940; research library of 200,000 vols; collns of early Christian and Byzantine art, and of Pre-Columbian art of Mexico, Central and South America; research programmes in Byzantine and Pre-Columbian studies, and studies in landscape architecture; Dir EDWARD J. KEENAN; publs *Colloquium Papers* (Landscape Architecture, irreg.), *Conference Proceedings* (Pre-Columbian, irreg.), *Dumbarton Oaks Papers* (Byzantine, annual), *Dumbarton Oaks Studies* (Byzantine, irreg.), *Studies in Pre-Columbian Art and Archaeology* (irreg.).

Folger Shakespeare Library: 201 East Capitol St, SE, Washington, DC 20003; tel. (202) 544-4600; fax (202) 544-4623; e-mail reference@folger.edu; internet www.folger .edu; f. 1932; administered by Trustees of Amherst College; collns incl.: original editions and reprints of Shakespeare; English Renaissance books 1475–1640; 16th and 17th centuries Continental European books; 17th and 18th centuries strozzi MSS; Dryden colln; English plays 1641–1700; 250,000 play bills; 55,000 MSS since 16th century relating to the life and times of Shakespeare and the history of drama and Shakespearean scholarship; 50,000 literary and theatrical prints and engravings; Fellowships; Folger Institute; public and educational programmes; theatre; lectures; poetry readings; concerts; exhibitions; Dir Dr GAIL KERN PASTER; publs *Folger News* (3 a year), *Shakespeare Quarterly* (quarterly).

House of Representatives Library: Cannon House Office Bldg B-18, Washington, DC 20515; internet www.house.gov; f. 1792; 250,000 vols, and spec. bound collns of all House of Representatives publs since c. 1800; Librarian E. RAYMOND LEWIS.

Library of Congress: 101 Independence Ave, SE, Washington, DC 20540; tel. (202) 707-5000; internet www.loc.gov; f. 1800; Library's priority is service to the Congress of the United States, but it now performs, in its role as the nat. library, services to other libraries, which incl.: (i) the devt of scientific schemes of classification (Library of Congress and Dewey Decimal), subject headings, and cataloguing embracing the whole field of printed matter, (ii) a centralized acquisition and cataloguing programme in which publs are acquired worldwide and cataloguing data distributed to other libraries, (iii) a 755-vol. *National Union Catalog: Pre-1956 Imprints*, (iv) an inter-library loan system (only within USA); registers creative work for copyright; 29m. books and pamphlets (incl. Orientalia colln, with 139,000 vols in Hebraic, 175,000 vols in other Near Eastern languages and 2,000,000 vols in Chinese, Japanese, Korean and languages of southern Asia, colln of 1m. vols on Hispanic and Portuguese culture, and colln of Russian literature), newspapers and periodicals, 750,000 rare books and incunabula, 45,301,000 MSS relating to American history and civilization, 4,346,000 maps, 10,316,000 microforms, colln of books and recordings for the blind and physically handicapped (copies available through co-operating regional and sub-regional libraries), Folklife colln (incl. 45,000 hours of recordings dating back to 1890, and 625,000 selections of folk song, folk music, folk tales and oral history), Law colln (American and foreign material), Music colln (8m. items), colln of Motion Pictures, Broadcasts and Sound Recordings (incl. film dating back to 1894, 720,000 moving image items, 3m. sound recordings, copyright deposits of recordings since 1972, jazz and popular music on 78 rpm discs, NBC radio colln of 75,000 broadcasts, House of Representatives debates), colln of Prints and Photographs (15,676,000 items, incl. early daguerreotypes); Librarian of Congress JAMES H. BILLINGTON.

Moorland-Spingarn Research Center: Howard Univ., Washington, DC 20059; tel. (202) 806-7240; fax (202) 806-6405; internet www.founders.howard.edu/moorland-spingarn; f. 1914; one of the world's largest and most comprehensive repositories for collns documenting the history and culture of people of African descent in the Americas, Africa and Europe; 175,000 vols, 500 MSS and archival collns, many thousands of microforms, sheet music, tapes, transcripts, photographs, records and artefacts; Dir Dr THOMAS C. BATTLE.

National Archives and Records Administration: National Archives Bldg, 700 Pennsylvania Ave, NW, Washington, DC 20408-0001; tel. (202) 501-5400 National Archives at College Park, 8601 Adelphi Rd, College Park, MD 20740-6001; tel. (301) 837-2000; fax (301) 837-0483; internet www .archives.gov; f. 1934; ensures, for citizens and Federal officials, ready access to essential evidence that documents the rights of American citizens, the actions of Federal officials, and the nat. experience; establishes policies and procedures for managing US Govt records and assists Federal agencies in documenting their activities, administering record management programmes, scheduling records, and retiring non-current records; obtains, arranges, describes, preserves, and provides access to the essential documentation of the 3 branches of Govt, manages the Presidential Libraries system, and publishes the laws, regulations, and Presidential and other public documents; assists the Information Security Oversight Office, which manages Federal classification and declassification policies, and the Nat. Historical Pubs and Records Commission, which makes grants nationwide to help non-profit orgs identify, preserve, and provide access to materials that document American history; consists of 33 facilities nationwide, incl. 18 Regional Records Services Facilities and 10 Presidential Libraries; on permanent display in the Exhibition Hall are the Declaration of Independence, the Constitution of the United States, and the Bill of Rights; Archivist of the United States ALLEN WEINSTEIN; publ. *Prologue: Quarterly Journal of the National Archives and Records Administration.*

National Geographic Society Library: 1145 17th St, NW, Washington, DC 20036-4688; tel. (202) 857-7783; fax (202) 429-5731; e-mail library@ngs.org; internet www .nationalgeographic.com/library; f. 1920; reference reading room open to the public for research by appointment; spec. colln(s): polar, natural history, exploration and discovery, soc. publs; 45,000 vols, 150 periodicals; Vice-Pres., Libraries and Information Services SUSAN FIFER CANBY.

National Library of Education: 400 Maryland Ave, SW, Washington, DC 20202; tel. (800) 424-1616; fax (202) 401-0547; e-mail library@ed.gov; internet ies.ed.gov/ncee/projects/nat_ed_library.asp; f. 1870 as Bureau of Education library, present name 1994; fed. govt's primary resource centre for education information; 60,000 vols, c. 800 periodicals, the complete ERIC (Education Resources Information Center) microfiche colln, archives of official print and electronic documents published by the Dept of Education, and histories and documentation of education legislation passed by the Congress; depositary library; Dir CHRISTINA DUNN.

Navy Department Library: Washington Navy Yard, 805 Kidder Breese St, SE, Washington, DC 20374-5060; tel. (202) 433-4132; fax (202) 433-9553; e-mail navylibrary@navy.mil; internet www.history .navy.mil/library; f. 1800; 170,000 vols; Dir JEAN HORT.

Pentagon Library: 6605 Army Pentagon, Washington, DC 20310–6605; Located at: Taylor Bldg (NC3), Rm 12W66, 2531 Jefferson Davis Highway, Cystal Dr., Arlington, VA 22202-3905; tel. (703) 695-1997; fax (703) 695-3983; internet www.hqda.army.mil/library; f. 1944; 100,000 vols, 1,800 periodicals and 1m. documents; combines the resources of 28 former War Dept libraries into one central colln in the Pentagon; spec. collns on military arts and sciences, unit histories, military law; and Army admin., training and technical pubs.

Ralph J. Bunche Library of the Department of State: 2201 C St, NW, Washington, DC 20520-2442; tel. (202) 647-1099; fax (202) 647-2971; e-mail library@state.gov; f. 1789; 550,000 vols; materials relate primarily to the economic, political and social conditions in foreign areas, treaties and agreements, int. relations and diplomatic history; Chief Librarian ELAINE CLINE.

Senate Library: Russell Senate Office Bldg, Washington, DC 20510; tel. (202) 224-7106; fax (202) 224-0879; e-mail gregory_harness@ sec.senate.gov; f. 1871; 250,000 vols, incl. spec. colln of legislative proceedings and documents from 1774; the work of the Senate Library is essentially that of research and reference for the use of the Senate and its committees; principal services rendered incl. legislative and general reference, automated information retrieval, Micrographics Center and photoduplication facilities; Head of Information Services KIMBERLEY FERGUSON.

Smithsonian Institution Archives: POB 37012, MRC 507, Washington, DC 20013-7012; Located at: Capital Gallery Bldg, Suite 3000, 600 Maryland Ave, Washington, DC 20024-2520; tel. (202) 357-1420; fax (202) 357-2395; e-mail osiaref@osia.si.edu; internet www.si.edu/archives; repository for the official records of the Instn since its foundation in 1846, and official repository for numerous other orgs; personal papers of noted Smithsonian staff, artists, researchers and museum founders; 14,000 cu ft of materials; Dir ANNE VAN CAMP.

Smithsonian Institution Libraries: National Museum of Natural History Bldg, POB 37012, Room 22, MRC 154, Washington, DC 20013-7012; located at National Museum of Natural History Bldg, 10th and Constitution Ave, NW, Washington, DC 20013-7012; tel. (202) 633-2240; fax (202) 786-2866; e-mail libmail@sil.si.edu; internet www.sil.si .edu; f. 1968; 1,500,000 vols in 21 brs, incl. 50,000 rare books, over 50,000 pieces of trade literature, World's Fair collection, history of science and technology; attached to the Smithsonian Instn; exhibition gallery and annual colln-based curated exhibition; displays in SI Castle, Nat. Air and Space Museum and Nat. Museum of Natural History; active exhibition loan programme; Dir Dr NANCY E. GWINN; publ. *Information* (newsletter, quarterly).

Wirtz Labor Library, Department of Labor: Rm N2445, 200 Constitution Ave, NW, Washington, DC 20210; tel. (202) 693-6600; fax (202) 693-6642; e-mail library@dol .gov; internet www.dol.gov/oasam/library; f. 1917; 550,000 vols, 300 current periodical titles; Library Director JEAN BOWERS.

Florida

Broward County Division of Libraries: 100 South Andrews Ave, Fort Lauderdale, FL 33301; tel. (954) 357-7555; internet www .broward.org/library/welcome.htm; f. 1974; 919,048 vols; consists of a flagship Main Library, the African-American Research Library and Cultural Center, the Alvin-Sherman Library, Research, and Information Technology Center at Nova Southeastern Univ., 5 regional libraries, 30 br. libraries and 2 reading centres; spec. collns: Black Heritage, Spanish Language, Floridiana; Main Library is a depository for govt documents; Dir DOROTHY KLEIN ROBERT E. CANNON.

Florida State University Library: 105 Dogwood Way, Tallahassee, FL 32306-2047; tel. (850) 644-2706; fax (850) 644-5016; internet www.lib.fsu.edu; f. 1853; 2,947,702 vols and bound serials; Dir F. WILLIAMS SUMMERS.

Miami-Dade Public Library System: 101 West Flagler St, Miami, FL 33130-1523; tel. (305) 375-2665; fax (305) 375-3048; internet www.mdpls.org; f. 1971; 4,142,711 vols; spec. collns incl. Florida history, Spanish books, urban affairs, genealogy; main library, 43 brs with further 13 scheduled to open; 2 mobile libraries; Dir RAYMOND SANTIAGO.

University of Florida Libraries: POB 117001, Gainesville, FL 32611-7001; tel. (352) 392-0342; fax (352) 392-7251; internet www.uflib.ufl.edu; f. 1853; 4,000,000 vols; spec. collns: children's literature in English before 1900, contemporary American and British poetry, contemporary American creative writing, Floridiana, history of printing and book arts, Judaica, Latin Americana, New England literature before 1900, performing arts, United States Borderlands (Florida), Irish literature; Dean of Univ. Libraries JUDITH RUSSELL.

Georgia

Atlanta-Fulton Public Library: 1 Margaret Mitchell Sq., NW, Atlanta, GA 30303; tel. (404) 730-1700; internet www.af.public .lib.ga.us; f. 1867; 2,177,267 vols, 70,000 recordings and cassettes; 34 brs; Dir JOHN F. SZABO.

Hawaii

Hawaii State Public Library System: 478 South King St, Room B-1, Honolulu, HI 96813; tel. (808) 586-3500; e-mail esss@ librarieshawaii.org; internet www .librarieshawaii.org; 3,328,602 vols; 51 brs; State Librarian JO ANN SCHINDLER; publ. *Holo I Mua* (newsletter, monthly).

Illinois

Abraham Lincoln Presidential Library and Museum: *Library*: 112 North 6th St, Springfield, IL; *Museum*: 212 North 6th St, Springfield, IL; tel. (217) 558-8844; fax (217) 558-8878; internet www.alplm.org; f. 2002; fmr Illinois State Historical Library (f. 1889) of 12,000,000 items; spec. colln: Henry Horner Lincoln Colln of 46,000 items incl. 1,500 signed MSS, 10,000 books and pamphlets, 1,000 posters, 1,000 prints and photographs, Gettysburg Address, Second Inaugural Address, Anti-Slavery Statement; Exec. Dir RICK BEARD.

American Medical Association. James S. Todd Memorial Library: 515 North State St, Chicago, IL 60610; tel. (312) 464-4855; fax (312) 464-5226; e-mail amalibrary@ama-assn .org; internet www.ama-assn.org; f. 1911; 18,000 vols, 1,100 journal titles; spec. collns: history of US medicine, AMA publs; Dir SANDRA R. SCHEFRIS.

Chicago Public Library: 400 South State St, Chicago, IL 60605-1203; tel. (312) 747-4300; internet www.chipublib.org; f. 1872; 4,764,000 vols; Pres. JAYNE CARR THOMPSON.

Cook County Law Library: 2900 Richard J. Daley Center, 50 West Washington St, 29th Floor, Chicago, IL 60602; tel. (312) 603-5131; fax (312) 603-4716; internet www.co .cook.il.us/agencydetail.php?pagencyid=10; f. 1966; 234,000 vols; 7 brs; Dir JEAN WENGER; publs *CCLL Newsletter*, *CCLL Selected New Acquisitions*.

Illinois State Library: 300 South Second St, Springfield, IL 62701-1796; tel. (217) 782-2994; fax (217) 785-4326; internet www

.cyberdriveillinois.com/departments/library/home.html; f. 1839; 5,000,000 items and documents; State Librarian JESSE WHITE; Dir ANNE CRAIG; publs *Insight* (6 a year), *Illinois Literacy* (quarterly), *Illinois Libraries* (irreg.).

John Crerar Library of the University of Chicago: 5730 South Ellis Ave, Chicago, IL 60637; tel. (773) 702-7715; fax (773) 702-3317; e-mail crerar-reference@lib.uchicago.edu; internet www.lib.uchicago.edu/e/crerar; f. 1892, merged with Univ. of Chicago 1984; 1,350,000 vols on the biomedical and physical sciences, incl. history of science and medicine; rare books and MSS from the Crerar collns are in the Univ. Joseph Regenstein Library; Dirs BARBARA KERN, ANDREA TWISS-BROOKS.

Library of International Relations: 565 West Adams, Chicago, IL 60661; tel. (312) 906-5615; fax (312) 906-5685; internet library.kentlaw.edu; f. 1932; 1992 became part of Illinois Institute of Technology; supported by voluntary contributions; f. to encourage interest and research in int. affairs; specialized library of 175,000 vols, serials and periodicals; official depository of the UN and EU; open to the public; Dir KEITH ANN STIVERSON.

Newberry Library: 60 West Walton St, Chicago, IL 60610; tel. (312) 255-3676; internet www.newberry.org; f. 1887; ind. research institution of more than 1,500,000 vols in the humanities, with spec. collns on the American Indians, the history of printing, music, American and English history and literature, exploration and early cartography, Portugal, the Renaissance in England and Europe, European history from the Renaissance to 1815, the Philippine Islands; Latin American history and literature of the colonial period; maintains research and educational programmes in its Center for the History of Cartography, Center for History of the American Indian, Center for Renaissance Studies and Family and Community History Center; Pres. and Librarian DAVID SPADAFORA.

Northwestern University Libraries: 1970 Campus Dr., Evanston, IL 60208-2300; tel. (847) 491-7658; fax (847) 491-8306; e-mail library@northwestern.edu; internet www.library.northwestern.edu; f. 1856; 3,893,000 vols; Northwestern Univ. Library (humanities and social sciences, with spec. collns on Africa: comprehensive historically on sub-Sahara, Francophone West Africa and South Africa; extensive holdings in Art Nouveau, Dada, Surrealism, Futurism and Expressionism, Samuel Johnson, Siege and Commune of Paris 1870–71, Women's Liberation movement; libraries for music and transportation); br. libraries for science-eng., geology and mathematics; professional libraries (dentistry, law, medicine) and the Schaffner Library in Chicago; Univ. Librarian SARAH M. PRITCHARD.

University of Chicago Library: 1100 East 57th St, Chicago, IL 60637-1502; tel. (773) 702-8740; fax (773) 702-6623; e-mail ill-lending@lib.uchicago.edu; internet www.lib.uchicago.edu; f. 1892; 7,363,549 vols; comprises Regenstein (humanities and social sciences), Crerar (science, medicine, technology), Harper (college), D'Angelo (law), and 4 other dept libraries; research collns incl. the Spec. Collns Research Center for research in most areas in humanities, law, business, and the social, biological and physical sciences; Dir JUDITH NADLER.

University of Illinois (Urbana-Champaign) Library: 1408 West Gregory Dr., Urbana, IL 61801; tel. (217) 333-2290; internet www.library.uiuc.edu; f. 1867;

8,840,000 vols, 7,457,000 MSS, maps, microtexts and other items; 40 departmental libraries; spec. collns in classical literature and history, English literature incl. Milton and Shakespeare, Western US history, Lincolniana, Italian history, music, architecture, science and technology; Univ. Librarian PAULA T. KAUFMAN.

Indiana

Allen County Public Library: 900 Webster St, POB 2270, Fort Wayne, IN 46801; tel. (260) 421-1200; fax (260) 421-1386; e-mail ask@acpl.info; internet www.acpl.lib.in.us; f. 1894; 2,000,000 vols; Fred J. Reynolds Historical Genealogy Collection; 13 brs; Dir JEFFREY R. KRULL.

Indiana State Library: 140 North Senate Ave, Indianapolis, IN 46204-2296; tel. (317) 232-3675; fax (317) 232-3728; internet www.statelib.lib.in.us; f. 1825; to provide library service to state government, advice and counsel to the libraries and librarians of the state, reference service and materials for local school, public, special, and academic libraries; genealogy and special research collections; Indiana history collection; service to the blind and physically handicapped; library for Indiana Academy of Science; 1,703,621 items; Dir BARBARA R. MAXWELL; publs *Indiana Libraries* (quarterly), *Focus on Indiana Libraries* (monthly).

Indiana University Libraries: 1320 East Tenth St, Bloomington, IN 47405; tel. (812) 855-8028; fax (812) 855-2576; e-mail libref@indiana.edu; internet www.libraries.iub.edu; f. 1829; 6,770,498 vols, 4,966,561 microforms, 7,400,000 MSS, 226,758 music scores, 329,041 slides, 665,883 maps and charts, 253,835 audio recordings, 18,116 serials, 379,540 graphic materials, 1,102,108 government publications; Dean of Libraries SUZANNE THORIN.

Indianapolis-Marion County Public Library: 40 East St Clair St, POB 211, Indianapolis, IN 46206; tel. (317) 269-1700; fax (317) 269-1768; internet www.imcpl.org; f. 1873; 1,815,942 vols; 22 brs, 3 bookmobiles; CEO LINDA MIELKE; publ. *Reading in Indianapolis* (monthly).

Purdue University Libraries: 504 West State St, West Lafayette, IN 47907; tel. (765) 494-2831; fax (765) 494-0156; internet www.lib.purdue.edu; f. 1869; 2,200,000 vols; 14 brs; Dean JAMES MULLINS.

University of Notre Dame Libraries: Notre Dame, IN 46556; tel. (574) 631-6258; fax (574) 631-6772; internet www.library.nd.edu; f. 1873; 2,500,000 vols; special collections: Ambrosiana, American Catholic Studies, O'Neill Irish Music, Joyce Sports Research, medieval education, Descartes, Jacques Maritain, Dante, orchids, historical botany, Irish Maps and Sea Charts, Irish Rebellion of 1798, Irish postage stamps; Dir JENNIFER A. YOUNGER.

Iowa

Herbert Hoover Presidential Library and Museum: 210 Parkside Dr., POB 488, West Branch, IA 52358; tel. (319) 643-5301; fax (319) 643-6045; e-mail hoover.library@nara.gov; internet hoover.archives.gov; f. 1962; administered by the Nat. Archives and Records Admin.; official and personal papers of 31st Pres. of USA; also 150 MS collns; 18,000 vols, 8,247,000 MSS, 43,000 photos, 522 hours sound recordings and 156,000 ft of film, 2,770 rolls of microfilm, 11,864 pages of oral history, 5,300 museum objects covering history since beginning of the 20th century, econ. and political science; Dir TIMOTHY WALCH; publ. *Historical Materi-*

als in the Herbert Hoover Presidential Library.

Iowa State University Library: cnr of Osborn Dr. and Morrill Rd, Ames, IA 50011-2140; tel. (515) 294-3642; fax (515) 294-5525; internet www.lib.iastate.edu; f. 1870; 2,473,075 vols, 3,491,798 microforms, 46,798 electronic journals, 108,440 photographs and maps; spec. collns: Archives of American Agriculture, Archives of American Veterinary Medicine, American Archives of the Factual Film, Women in Science and Eng. Archives, Univ. Archives; fed. depository; books on science and technology, incl. agriculture, entomology, botany, ornithology and veterinary medicine; Dean OLIVIA M. A. MADISON.

University of Iowa Libraries: Iowa City, IA 52242-1420; tel. (319) 335-5299; fax (319) 335-5900; e-mail lib-ref@uiowa.edu; internet www.lib.uiowa.edu; f. 1847; 3,823,000 vols, 11 departmental libraries; spec. colln: Iowa Women's Archives; Univ. Librarian NANCY L. BAKER; publs *Bindings* (newsletter, 2 a year), *Libraries News* (2 a year).

Kansas

Dwight D. Eisenhower Library: 200 Southeast Fourth St, Abilene, KS 67410; tel. (785) 263-6700; fax (785) 263-6718; e-mail eisenhower.library@nara.gov; internet www.eisenhower.archives.gov; f. 1962; MSS, presidential and personal papers related to former Pres. Eisenhower, and MSS of important persons in Eisenhower"s admin. and military career; 22,000,000 MSS items, 31,500 pages oral history transcripts, 24,000 vols, 211,000 still photographs, audio tapes and films; Dir DAN HOLT; publ. *Overview* (quarterly).

Kansas State Historical Society: 6425 Southwest Sixth St, Topeka, KS 66615-1099; tel. (913) 272-8681; fax (913) 272-8682; internet www.kshs.org; f. 1875; 300,000 vols; state archives, newspapers and census, archaeology; manuscript, photograph and maps dept, museum, folk arts dept, education dept; 3,000 mems; Exec. Dir JENNIE CHIN; publs *Kansas History: A Journal of the Central Plains* (quarterly), *Kansas Heritage* (quarterly), *Kansas Kaleidoscope* (6 a year).

Kansas State University Libraries: Manhattan, KS 66506; tel. (785) 532-7400; e-mail library@ksu.edu; internet www.lib.ksu.edu; f. 1863; 1,209,000 vols, 31,867 serials, 4,000,000 microforms, 1,840,000 govt docs, 100,000 maps, 8,400 scores, 32,000 pieces of audio visual material, 5 brs (Veterinary Medical, Eng., Maths and Physics, Architecture and Technology and Aviation); spec. collns in cookbooks, Linnaeana, Robert Graves, and Diderot's *Encyclopédie*; Dean of Libraries LORI GOETSCH; publs *KSU Library Cassette Series on Library Technology* (irreg.), *Library Bibliography Series* (irreg.).

University of Kansas Libraries: Suite 502, 1425 Jayhawk Blvd, Lawrence, KS 66045-7544; tel. (785) 864-8983; fax (785) 864-5311; e-mail sroyer@ku.edu; internet www.lib.ku.edu; f. 1866; 3,800,000 vols, 322,000 maps, 3,370,000 microforms, 3,000,000 graphics (mostly photographs), 30,000 sound recordings, 691,000 govt docs, 15,000 linear ft MSS; Dean of Libraries LORRAINE HARICOMBE.

Kentucky

Kentucky Department for Libraries and Archives: 300 Coffee Tree Rd, Frankfort, KY 40601; tel. (502) 564-8300; internet www.kdla.ky.gov; 116,000 vols; 3,400 films, 5,000 videos; 646 periodicals; 44,000 fed. documents; State Librarian WAYNE ONKST.

Louisville Free Public Library: 301 York St, Louisville, KY 40203-2257; tel. (502) 574-1611; fax (502) 561-8657; internet www.lfpl .org; f. 1902; 976,500 vols; 36,000 phonodiscs, 70,000 programmes on electronic tape, operates 2 FM radio stations for music and educational programmes; 17 brs, 1 bookmobile; spec. Kentucky History Colln; houses a 'Louisville Art Gallery'; Talking Book Library for the blind and physically handicapped; Dir CRAIG BUTHOD; publs *Alivebrary*, *Book Paths*.

University of Kentucky Libraries: Lexington, KY 40506-0456; tel. (859) 257-0500; fax (859) 257-8379; internet www.uky.edu/ libraries; f. 1909; 3,286,731 vols, 6,347,361 microforms, 30,250 current serials, 257,418 maps, 1,125,174 govt documents, more than 300 licensed networked electronic resources, 25,000 electronic journals; 15 br. and collegiate libraries; regional depository for govt publs and a depository for EU and Canadian publs, British Parliamentary Papers, Kentucky govt publs, and technical reports from US fed. agencies; King Library Press; Univ. and audiovisual archives; large colln of Kentuckiana, spec. collns of 19th-century British literature, French and Spanish drama from 1600–1900, modern political manuscript collns, broadsides, ballads and chapbooks, Cortot colln of music theory, typography, history of books, Appalachian Regional Commission archives, oral history colln; Center for Digital Programs creates digital content for the Kentuckiana Digital Library, incl. electronic texts, digitized photographs, images and archival finding aids; Dean of Libraries CAROL PITTS DIEDRICHS.

Louisiana

Louisiana State University Libraries: Baton Rouge, LA 70803; tel. (225) 578-5652; fax (225) 578-6825; internet www.lib.lsu.edu; f. 1860; UN, fed. and state depositories; spec. collns incl. E. A. McIlhenny Natural History Colln, Louisiana Colln, sugar technology, Southern history, agriculture, plant pathology, petroleum, bibliography colln, aquaculture, incl. crawfish, wetlands research and marine biology; archives on Lower Mississippi Valley; 3,175,014 vols, 5,375,405 microforms; Dean JENNIFER CARGILL; publ. *Library Lectures*.

New Orleans Public Library: 219 Loyola Ave, New Orleans, LA 70112; tel. (504) 596-2550; fax (504) 596-2609; internet nutrias .org; f. 1843; 1,043,471 vols; 12 brs; spec. collns: city archives colln, civil and criminal courts colln, carnivals, maps, photographs, rare books, early sheet music, early jazz recordings and MSS; incls African American Resource Center and Business and Science Div.; Chair. IRVIN MAYFIELD; Head of Main Public Services LINDA MARSHALL HILL.

Tulane University Libraries: 7001 Freret St, New Orleans, LA 70118; tel. (504) 865-5605; fax (504) 865-6773; internet library .tulane.edu; f. 1834; 2,331,250 vols (incl. law, medicine and 6 other collns); spec. collns on New Orleans, Louisiana and Southern US history; Latin America, architecture and jazz; Dean of the Library LANCE QUERY.

Maryland

Enoch Pratt Free Library: 400 Cathedral St, Baltimore, MD 21201-4484; tel. (410) 396-5430; fax (410) 837-5837; internet www.pratt .lib.md.us; f. 1886; spec. collns: H. L. Mencken colln, Maryland history colln; 2,290,042 vols, 91,000 maps, 5,000 films, 19,094 video cassettes, 38,450 slides, 486 filmstrips, 34,802 recordings; Dir CARLA D. HAYDEN; publs *Menckeniana* (quarterly),

Pratt Matters (quarterly), *Staff Reporter* (monthly).

Johns Hopkins University Libraries: Baltimore, MD 21218; tel. (410) 516-8335; internet webapps.jhu.edu/jhuniverse/ libraries; f. 1876; network of libraries incl. the Milton S. Eisenhower Library, 1 of the Sheridan libraries and the principal research library of the univ.; spec. collns in medicine, int. affairs, music and earth and space science; 2,961,160 vols; Dean of Univ. Libraries WINSTON TABB.

National Agricultural Library: Abraham Lincoln Bldg, 10301 Baltimore Ave, Beltsville, MD 20705-2351; tel. (301) 504-5755; fax (301) 504-5472; internet www.nal.usda.gov; f. 1862; 3,300,000 vols; agriculture and the related sciences; spec. collns: Layne R. Beaty Papers (farm radio and television broadcasting); foreign and domestic nursery seed trade catalogues; flock, herd and stud books; audiovisual colln on food and nutrition; apiculture; Forest Service and USDA Photo Colln on optical laser discs; M. Truman Fossum Colln (floriculture); James M. Gwin Colln (poultry); Charles E. North Colln (milk sanitation); Pomology Colln (original pomological art); Charles Valentine Riley Colln (entomology); plant exploration photo colln; food and nutrition micro-computer software; MAPP colln of family life education materials; computer database (AGRICOLA) of 3m. records for books and journal articles in agriculture; information centres on agricultural trade and marketing, alternative farming systems, animal welfare, aquaculture, biotechnology, food and nutrition, plant genome, rural information, technology transfer, water quality and youth devt; Dir PETER YOUNG; publs *Agriculture Libraries Information Notes* (monthly), *Quick Bibliography* (irreg.).

National Institute of Standards and Technology Research Library: West End Admin. Bldg, Rm 101 E Wing, Route 70 S and Quince Rd, Gaithersburg, MD 20899; e-mail inquiries@nist.gov; internet www.nist .gov; f. 1912; 200,000 vols, 1000 journals; spec. collns: science, eng. and technology; Dir WILLIAM A. JEFFREY; Deputy Dir JAMES TURNER; Librarian PAUL VASSALLO.

National Institutes of Health Library: Bldg 10, Room 1L25, 10 Center Dr., Bethesda, MD 20892-1150; tel. (301) 496-2447; fax (301) 402-0254; internet nihlibrary .nih.gov; f. 1903; serves the specialized research programs of the NIH; 70,000 books, 160,000 periodicals, 26,500 microforms; biology, medicine, health sciences, chemistry, physiology, physics; Chief Librarian SUZANNE GREFSHEIM.

National Library of Medicine: 8600 Rockville Pike, Bethesda, MD 20894; tel. (301) 496-6308; fax (301) 496-4450; e-mail custserv@nlm.nih.gov; internet www.nlm .nih.gov; f. 1836; 7,000,000 items; books, journals, technical reports, MSS, microfilms, photographs and images; world's largest medical library; houses old and rare medical works; materials, information and research services in all areas of biomedicine and healthcare; Dir DONALD A. B. LINDBERG; publ. *Index Medicus* (monthly).

University of Maryland Libraries: College Park, MD 20742-7011; tel. (301) 405-0800; internet www.lib.umd.edu; f. 1856; consists of 8 campus libraries: McKeldin Library, Hornbake Library, Art Library, Architecture Library, Eng. and Physical Sciences Library, Michelle Smith Performing Arts Library, Shady Grove Library and Medi Center, White Memorial (Chemistry) Library, and a number of spec. collns; 2,288,796 vols; Dean CHARLES LOWRY.

Massachusetts

Boston Athenaeum: 10½ Beacon St, Boston, MA 02108-3777; tel. (617) 227-0270; fax (617) 227-5266; internet www .bostonathenaeum.org; f. 1807; ind. research library; 750,000 vols; history, biography, English and American literature, fine and decorative arts; spec. collns incl. Confederate States imprints, books from libraries of George Washington, Gen. Henry Knox and the Adams Family, the King's Chapel Colln (1698), Gypsy literature, private press pbls, 19th-century tracts, early US Govt documents, maps, charts and atlases, and the Charles E. Mason print colln; Bartlett Hayes poster colln; 19th-century photographs; Head of Reference STEPHEN NONACK.

Boston Public Library: 700 Boylston St, Boston, MA 02116; tel. (617) 536-5400; fax (617) 236-4306; e-mail info@bpl.org; internet www.bpl.org; f. 1848; the oldest free municipal library supported by public taxation in the world; 28 brs; 15,000,000 vols; Pres. BERNARD A. MARGOLIS.

Boston University Libraries: 771 Commonwealth Ave, Boston, MA 02215; tel. (617) 353-3704; e-mail ask@bu.edu; internet www .bu.edu/library; f. 1839; 1,920,000 vols, 28,000 periodicals; 5 major libraries, Mugar Memorial Library (7 brs humanities and social sciences), Howard Gotlieb Archival Research Center (rare books and MSS), Pappas Law Library, Medical Library, School of Theology Library; Dir ROBERT HUDSON.

Francis A. Countway Library of Medicine: 10 Shattuck St, Boston, MA 02115; tel. (617) 432-2142; fax (617) 432-0693; internet www.countway.harvard.edu; f. 1965; serves the Harvard Medical School, Harvard School of Public Health, Harvard School of Dental Medicine, Boston Medical Library and the Massachusetts Medical Soc.; 630,000 vols, 3,500 journals, 10,000 non-current biomedical journals; Dir Dr ISAAC KOHANE; Dir of Center for the History of Medicine SCOTT PODOLSKY.

Harvard University Library: Cambridge, MA 02138; tel. (617) 495-3650; fax (617) 495-0370; e-mail administration@hulmail .harvard.edu; internet hul.harvard.edu; f. 1638; 13,143,330 vols divided among c. 80 libraries; the oldest library in the USA; the central collns are housed in the Widener, Houghton, Pusey, Lamont, Hilles, Cabot Science, Harvard-Yenching, Littauer, Loeb Music, Tozzer, Fine Arts and Geological Sciences Libraries; important collns in nearly every field of learning, and 4,000 vols printed before 1501; Dir ROBERT DARNTON; Harvard College Librarian NANCY CLINE; publ. *Harvard Library Bulletin*.

Massachusetts Historical Society Library: 1154 Boylston St, Boston, MA 02215; tel. (617) 536-1608; fax (617) 859-0074; e-mail library@masshist.org; internet www.masshist.org/library; f. 1791; 250,000 vols; 3500 MSS collns; personal papers of individuals and families who lived in Massachusetts; Librarians PETER DRUMMEY, STEPHEN T. RILEY; publs *Miscellany* (quarterly), *Proceedings* (annual).

Massachusetts Institute of Technology Libraries: 14S 216, 77 Massachusetts Ave, Cambridge, MA 02139-4307; tel. (617) 253-5651; fax (617) 253-8894; internet libraries .mit.edu; f. 1861; 2,667,215 vols and pamphlets, 17,000 current journals, 30,000 electronic journals, 478 online databases; 5 major subject libraries, for Architecture and planning, Eng., Humanities, Science, Management and social science, as well as 5 specialized libraries and the Institute archives; Dir of Libraries ANN J. WOLPERT.

Springfield Library: 220 State St, Springfield, MA 01103; tel. (413) 263-6828; fax (413) 263-6817; e-mail askalibrarian@springfieldlibrary.org; internet www.springfieldlibrary.org; f. 1857; 668,856 vols, 32,490 audio recordings, 20,804 video cassettes, 3,933 CD-ROMs, 296 periodicals; 6 brs; Dir EMILY BADER.

State Library of Massachusetts: 341 State House, Boston, MA 02133; tel. (617) 727-2590; fax (617) 727-5819; e-mail library .director@state.ma.us; internet www.mass .gov/lib; f. 1826; 822,083 vols; a govt and public affairs library serving the information and research needs of the exec. and legislative branches of Massachusetts State govt; depository for printed documents of the same and for selected fed. documents; collns espec. strong in public law, public affairs, state and local history; State Librarian LESLIE A. KIRWAN; publ. *Commonwealth of Massachusetts Publications Received by the State Library* (quarterly).

Worcester Public Library: 3 Salem Squ., Worcester, MA 01608; tel. (508) 799-1690; internet www.worcpublib.org; f. 1859; 586,000 vols; 3 sites: main library at Salem Sq., Frances Perkins Library at Greendale and Great Brook Valley Branch Library; largest selective depository of fed. documents in central Massachusetts; Librarian PENELOPE B. JOHNSON.

Michigan

Detroit Public Library: 5201 Woodward Ave, Detroit, MI 48202; tel. (313) 833-4036; internet www.detroitpubliclibrary.org; f. 1865; 2,655,156 vols, 163,158 maps, 754,397 microforms, 788,464 pictures, 20,000 videos; special collections on Automotive history, Burton Historical Collection (Michigan, Great Lakes and Old North-west Territory), Labor History Collection, Azalia Hackley Memorial Collection of Negro Music, Dance and Drama; 24 brs; Dir NANCY SKOWRONSKI.

Library of Michigan: 702 W. Kalamazoo, POB 30007, Lansing, MI 48909-7507; tel. (517) 373-1300; fax (517) 373-5853; e-mail librarian@michigan.gov; internet www .michigan.gov/libraryofmichigan, f. 1828; 5,500,000 vols; operates a main library, Law Library, Service for the Blind and Physically Handicapped; specializes in Michigan history and current information, public policy issues, genealogy; State Librarian NANCY R. ROBERTSON; publs *Directory of Michigan Libraries* (online), *LM4X* (online newsletter, quarterly), *District Library Law, Michigan Genealogist* (online newsletter, quarterly), *Michigan Library Statistics*.

Michigan State University Libraries: East Lansing, MI 48824; tel. (517) 353-8700; internet www.lib.msu.edu; f. 1855; 4.5 m. vols and 14 departmental libraries and special collections; Dir CLIFFORD H. HAKA.

University of Michigan Libraries: Ann Arbor, MI 48109-1205; tel. (734) 764-9356; fax (734) 763-5080; internet www.lib.umich .edu; f. 1817; 7,000,000 vols, including special collections in ancient papyri, early economics, early military science, Elsevier imprints, English and American drama, Frost and Faulkner collections, fine printing, French historical pamphlets (16th–17th c.), imaginary voyages, music and musicology (17th–19th c.); William L. Clements Library of American History; Michigan Historical Collections; Dir JAMES HILTON.

Wayne State University Libraries: 5150 Anthony Wayne Dr., Detroit, MI 48202; tel. (313) 577-0243; fax (313) 577-6777; e-mail am4886@wayne.edu; internet www.lib .wayne.edu; 3,342,000 vols in 5 library units: the David Adamany Undergraduate Library

(general), the Neef Law Library, the Purdy/Kresge Library (arts), the Science and Engineering Library and the Shiffman Medical Library; Dean of Library Services SANDRA YEE.

Minnesota

James Jerome Hill Reference Library: 80 West 4th St, Saint Paul, MN 55102; tel. (651) 265-5500; e-mail info@jjhill.org; internet www.jjhill.org; f. 1916; 140,000 vols; applied business and commerce; business papers of James Jerome Hill and Louis W. Hill, Sr; Exec. Dir (vacant).

Minneapolis Public Library: 250 South Marquette, Minneapolis, MN 55401; tel. (612) 630-6000; fax (612) 630-6210; internet www.mplib.org; f. 1885; 3,271,000 vols; 14 brs; spec. colns incl. Heffelfinger Aesop's and Others' Fables, 19th-century American studies, Kittleson World War II, Minneapolis history, Mark Twain, Huttner Abolition and Anti-Slavery, Environmental Conservation Library, Foundations, US Patents, Early American Exploration and Travel, North American Indians, Spencer Natural History; Dir KATHERINE G. HADLEY.

Minnesota Historical Society Library: 345 Kellogg Blvd, Saint Paul, MN 55102-1906; tel. (651) 296-6980; fax (651) 296-9961; e-mail reference@mnhs.org; internet www .mnhs.org; f. 1849; 300,000 vols; North American history particularly relating to Minnesota and the Upper Midwest (especially travel accounts, fur trade, Scandinavian and other immigration, labour, political and church history, railroad records, local history and genealogy); several million pamphlets, documents, newspapers, films, maps, photographs, tapes, artefacts and MSS; Asst Dir for Library and Archives MICHAEL FOX.

Office of Library Development and Services, Minnesota Department of Children, Families and Learning: 1500 Highway 36 West, Roseville, MN 55113; tel. (651) 582-8722; fax (651) 582-8897; e-mail cfl .library@state.mn.us; internet cfl.state.mn .us; f. 1899; 10,000 vols, 200 periodicals, films, cassettes; inter-agency resource and information centre with 4,500 computer search services, periodicals, reports, on education, planning, vocational rehabilitation and related fields; Dir JOYCE C. SWONGER; publ. *Minnesota Libraries*.

Saint Paul Public Library: 90 West 4th St, Saint Paul, MN 55102; tel. (651) 266-7000; fax (651) 266-7060; internet www.sppl.org; f. 1882; 1,131,578 vols; Dir KATHLEEN FLYNN.

University of Minnesota Libraries: 309–19 Ave S, Minneapolis, MN 55455; tel. (612) 624-4520; fax (612) 626-9353; e-mail lib-web@tc.umn.edu; internet www.lib.umn .edu; f. 1851; 6,200,669 vols, 36,900 current journals; general and 15 departmental libraries; special collections: law, immigration history, social welfare history, data processing, medicine, children's literature, horticulture, literary MSS; Librarian WENDY PRADT LOUGEE.

Missouri

Harry S. Truman Library: Independence, MO 64050; tel. (816) 268-8200; fax (816) 268-8295; e-mail truman.library@nara.gov; internet www.trumanlibrary.org; f. 1957; manuscripts, printed materials, photographs, sound recordings, oral history interviews and 30,000 museum objects relating to the career and administration of President Harry S. Truman (1945–1953); 15,000,000 MSS, 110,000 photographs, 38,102 vols, 80,000 other printed items; administered by

the National Archives and Records Administration; Dir MICHAEL DEVINE.

Kansas City Public Library: 14 West 10th St, Kansas City, MO 64105; tel. (816) 701-3400; fax (816) 701-3401; internet www .kclibrary.org; f. 1873; 2,007,420 vols; 10 brs; special historical collections include the Missouri Valley Collection (local history), Ramos Collection (African American history) and Western expansion materials; Dir DOROTHY ELLIOTT.

Linda Hall Library: 5109 Cherry St, Kansas City, MO 64110-2498; tel. (816) 363-4600; fax (816) 926-8790; e-mail requests@lindahall.org; internet www.lindahall.org; f. 1946; independent, non-profit, public access science, engineering and technology library, specializing in periodicals and scientific and technical research materials; document supplier; fee-based literature search services; collections: 1,000,000 vols, 13,500 current periodicals, 48,000 total serial titles, 273,800 monographs, 1,550,000 govt-contracted technical reports, incl. 70,000 maps, 160,000 standards and specifications, History of Science Colln (6,000 vols), US patent and trademark colln; Pres. C. LEE JONES.

Missouri State Library & Wolfner Library for the Blind and Physically Handicapped: 600 W. Main St, POB 387, Jefferson City, MO 65101; tel. (573) 751-0970; fax (573) 751-3612; e-mail wolfner@sos .mo.gov; internet www.sos.mo.gov/library; f. 1945; 87,000 vols, 495 periodicals; special collection: Missouri state documents; Wolfner Library holds; 360,000 vols and 70 periodicals; State Librarian SARA PARKER; publs *Census Update* (4 a year), *Missouri Library World* (quarterly), *Newsline* (monthly).

St Louis County Library: 1640 S Lindbergh Blvd, St Louis, MO 63131-3598; tel. (314) 994-3300; internet www.slcl.lib.mo.us; f. 1946; 2,028,498 vols; 20 brs and 19 bookmobiles; Dir DAN WILSON.

St Louis Public Library: 1301 Olive St, St Louis, MO 63103-2389; tel. (314) 241-2288; fax (314) 539-0393; internet www.slpl.lib.mo .us; f. 1865; 4,895,532 vols, 115,000 maps; 14 brs; special collections include the Julia Davis Collection (African American history and culture); genealogical sources dating from 1902; Steedman Collection (architecture); Federal Documents Depository since 1866; Exec. Dir WALLER McGUIRE; publ. *Missouri Union List of Serial Publications*.

St Louis University Library: 3650 Lindell Blvd, St Louis, MO 63108; tel. (314) 977-3100; fax (314) 977-3108; e-mail piusref@slu .edu; internet www.slu.edu/html/libraries .html; f. 1818; 2,225,000 vols; Vatican Microfilm Collection; Dir Dr FRANCES BENHAM; publ. *Manuscripta* (3 a year).

University of Missouri Libraries: Columbia, MO 65201-5149; tel. (573) 882-4701; fax (573) 882-8044; internet mulibraries .missouri.edu; f. 1839; 3,205,927 vols, 14,548 journals; 7 brs; special collections of Western Historical MSS and Missouriana; Dir of Libraries JAMES COGSWELL.

Nebraska

University of Nebraska Libraries: Lincoln, NE 68588-4100; tel. (402) 472-2526; fax (402) 472-5131; internet iris.unl.edu; f. 1869; 2,900,000 vols in combined libraries plus UN and federal and map depositories; 44,000 serials; microfacsimile and archive depts; collections supporting 9 colleges, 5 schools and 48 PhD programmes; Dean JOAN R. GIESECKE.

New Hampshire

New Hampshire State Library: 20 Park St, Concord, NH 03301-6314; tel. (603) 271-2144; fax (603) 271-2205; internet www.state .nh.us; special collections: historical children's books, New Hampshire government, town records and history; 600,000 vols; State Librarian MICHAEL C. YORK; publ. *Granite State Libraries* (4 a year).

New Jersey

New Jersey State Library: 185 West State St, POB 520, Trenton, NJ 08625-0520; tel. (609) 292-6220; fax (609) 292-2746; e-mail nblake@njstatelib.org; internet www .njstatelib.org; f. 1796; 2,000,000 vols and documents, 1,500 current periodicals, 750,000 items on microfiche and microfilm; State Librarian NORMA E. BLAKE (acting).

Newark Public Library: 5 Washington St, POB 630, Newark, NJ 07101-0630; tel. (973) 733-7784; e-mail reference@npl.org; internet www.npl.org; f. 1888; 1,180,492 catalogued vols, 924,814 catalogued non-book items, 1,696,441 uncatalogued items, 411,531 periodicals, 1,015,095 prints, pictures, and art slides; collns: art, music, science, technology, business, depository for US patents, US govt documents, New Jersey documents, New Jersey history, fine printing, black studies, Newark Evening News Morgue; 10 brs; Dir WILMA J. GREY (acting).

Princeton University Libraries: 1 Washington Rd, Princeton, NJ 08544; tel. (609) 258-1470; fax (609) 258-0441; e-mail libhr@princeton.edu; internet libweb .princeton.edu; f. 1746; 5,000,000 vols; spec. collns incl. 450 medieval and Renaissance codices, 10,000 Islamic MSS, cuneiform tablets, stone seals and papyri, pre-Columbian indigenous materials (especially Mayan), George Cruikshank and Aubrey Beardsley, American Theatre (incl. papers of Max Gordon and Otto Kahn), archives of American publishers, especially Charles Scribner's Sons, the Morris L. Parrish Colln of Victorian Novelists, early American family papers, especially Edward Livingston and Blair-Lee, public policy papers since early 20th century, especially John Foster Dulles, Adlai Stevenson and the American Civil Liberties Union, 'Boom' period Latin American writers (incl. Mario Vargas Llosa); Univ. Librarian KAREN A. TRAINER; publ. *Princeton University Library Chronicle*.

Rutgers University Libraries: 169 College Ave, CAC, New Brunswick, NJ 08901-1163; tel. (732) 932-7505; fax (732) 932-7637; internet www.libraries.rutgers.edu; f. 1766; 3,000,000 vols; 26 libraries on Rutgers campuses in Camden, Newark and New Brunswick, with spec. collns in medicine, physics, chemistry, mathematics, microbiology, art, alcohol studies, labour/management relations, urban research, law and music; Univ. Librarian MARIANNE GAUNT.

New Mexico

New Mexico State Library: 1209 Camino Carlos Rey, Santa Fe, NM 87505; tel. (505) 476-9700; fax (505) 476-9701; internet www .stlib.state.nm.us; f. 1929; provides state agencies with library resources and services, and serves as a primary reference source for libraries in the state; 2,000,000 vols; special collections: *Southwest Resources* (books, journals and newspapers on the history of the southwestern area of the USA), *New Mexico Documents* (publs of the various depts, agencies, commissions comprising the state govt); State Librarian RICHARD AKEROYD (acting); publs *Directory of New Mexico Libraries*, *Hitchhiker* (weekly).

New York

American Museum of Natural History Library: Central Park West at 79th St, New York, NY 10024; tel. (212) 769-5400; fax (212) 769-5009; internet library.amnh.org; f. 1869; 450,000 vols, 19,000 periodicals, 1,000,000 photographs, 3,000 films, 13,000 rare vols; subject areas include anthropology, astronomy, geology, paleontology, zoology, exploration and travel, history of science, and museology; Dir TOM MORITZ; publs *Anthropological Papers* (all irregular), *Bulletin*, *Novitates*.

Association of the Bar of the City of New York Library: 42 West 44th St, New York, NY 10036; tel. (212) 382-6666; fax (212) 302-8219; internet www.abcny.org/Library; f. 1870; 600,000 vols; law; Dir NATHAN A. ROSEN.

Brooklyn Public Library: Grand Army Plaza, Brooklyn, NY 11238; tel. (718) 230-2100; internet www.brooklynpubliclibrary .org; f. 1897; 7,189,998 items; spec. collns incl. Brooklyn history; 58 brs, Business Library, Central Library, bookmobile; Exec. Dir GINNIE COOPER.

Buffalo and Erie County Public Library: 1 Lafayette Square, Buffalo, NY 14203; tel. (716) 858-8900; fax (716) 858-6211; internet www.buffalolib.org; f. 1954 following merger; 5,295,000 vols; 51 brs, of which 15 are City Branch libraries; Dir MICHAEL C. MAHANEY.

Center for Jewish History: 15 West 16th St, New York, NY 10011; tel. (212) 294-8301; fax (212) 294-8302; e-mail inquiries@cjh.org; internet www.cjh.org; f. 2000 through collaboration between American Jewish Historical Society, American Sephardi Federation, Leo Baeck Institute, Yeshiva University Museum, YIVO Institute for Jewish Research; repository for the cultural and historical legacy of the Jewish people; combined library and archive holdings of 500,000 books, 10,000,000 documents; photographs, paintings, textiles; Chair. BRUCE SLOVIN; Exec. Dir PETER A. GEFFEN.

Central Library of Rochester and Monroe County: 115 South Ave, Rochester, NY 14604-1896; tel. (585) 428-7300; internet www.libraryweb.org/central; f. 1912; 1,344,621 vols; audiovisual dept; pictures and photographs on 2,000 subjects; local history archive collection of MSS, directories, histories, newspapers, city and county publs; 20 brs; Dir P. SMITH; publ. *Rochester History* (quarterly).

Columbia University Libraries: 535 West 114th St, New York, NY 10027; tel. (212) 854-7309; fax (212) 854-5082; e-mail lio@ columbia.edu; internet www.columbia.edu/ cu/lweb; f. 1754; 9,400,000 vols; 23 deptl and professional school libraries with important collns in architecture, business, humanities, history, law, medicine, engineering, the sciences and social sciences; Vice-Pres. for Information Services and Univ. Librarian JAMES G. NEAL.

Cornell University Library: Ithaca, NY 14853; tel. (607) 255-4144; fax (607) 255-9091; internet www.library.cornell.edu; f. 1865; 7,298,409 vols, 7,992,461 microforms; special collections: French Revolution, East Asia, South and South-east Asia, Iceland, history of science, Dante, Petrarch, slavery, Wordsworth, witchcraft; Librarian SARAH E. THOMAS.

Department of Records and Information Services: 31 Chambers St, New York, NY 10007; tel. (212) 788-8602; fax (212) 788-8614; internet www.nyc.gov/html/records/ home.html; f. 1977; comprises Municipal Archives of the City of New York, City Hall Library, and Municipal Records Management Division; Commissioner BRIAN G. ANDERSSON.

Franklin D. Roosevelt Presidential Library: 4079 Albany Post Rd, Hyde Park, New York 12538; tel. (845) 486-7760; fax (845) 486-1147; e-mail roosevelt.library@ nara.gov; internet www.fdrlibrary.marist .edu; f. 1939; manuscripts, photographs, printed and museum materials concerning life and times of Franklin and Eleanor Roosevelt, incl. 4,700 lin. ft of his papers, many papers of his contemporaries and associates; 17 m. MSS pages, 130,000 photographs, 47,000 books, 78,000 other printed items, 25,000 museum items; administered by the National Archives and Records Administration; Dir Dr CYNTHIA M. KOCH.

Hispanic Society of America Library: Broadway, between 155th and 156th Sts, New York, NY 10032; tel. (212) 926-2234; fax (212) 690-0743; e-mail library@ hispanicsociety.org; internet www .hispanicsociety.org; f. 1904; art, history and literature of Spain, Portugal and Hispanic America; 200,000 manuscripts; 18,000 books printed before 1701, including 300 incunabula; 250,000 later books; Curator of Modern Books GERALD J. MACDONALD; Curator of Manuscripts and Rare Books JOHN O'NEILL.

Jewish Theological Seminary of America Library: 3080 Broadway, New York, NY 10027; tel. (212) 678-8080; fax (212) 678-8998; e-mail library@jtsa.edu; internet www .jtsa.edu/library; f. 1903; 375,000 vols, 11,000 MSS, 30,000 leaves of Cairo Genizah, Archives, Louis Ginzberg Microfilm library (foreign collections of Hebrew MSS); incunabula; Bible, Rabbinics, Jewish history, liturgy, theology, Early Yiddish, Hebrew literature, history of science and medicine; Haggadahs; Megillot (Esther scrolls); Ketuboth (marriage contracts); prints and photographs; musical scores; microfilms; videos; sound recordings; Librarian DAVID KRAEMER.

Medical Research Library of Brooklyn: 450 Clarkson Ave, Box 14, Brooklyn, NY 11203; tel. (718) 270-7400; fax (718) 270-7413; internet library.downstate.edu/; f. 1962 as the joint library of the Academy of Medicine of Brooklyn, Inc. (f. 1845) and the State University of New York Downstate Medical Center (f. 1860); 255,000 vols; Dir of Libraries RICHARD E. WINANT.

Morgan Library: 29 East 36th St, New York, NY 10016; tel. (212) 685-0610; fax (212) 481-3484; e-mail media@morganlibrary.org; internet www.morganlibrary.org; f. 1924; public museum and research library; collns formed by Pierpont Morgan, with additions made by his son and subsequent directors; among its treasures are: Medieval and Renaissance MSS from 5th–16th c.; a colln of 10,000 drawings by artists since 15th c.; colln of Rembrandt prints; Pierre Matisse Gallery Archives; major monuments in the history of printing and typography, from Gutenberg and Caxton to modern times; comprehensive group of fine bindings; literary and historical MSS, incl. Dickens, Ruskin, the Brontës, Austen, Thoreau and Steinbeck; Carter Burden Colln of American Literature; colln of autograph scores, incl. works by Beethoven, Mahler, Mozart and Stravinsky; extensive Gilbert and Sullivan archive; regular public lectures and exhibitions; Dir CHARLES ELIOT PIERCE, Jr.

New York Academy of Medicine Library: 1216 Fifth Ave, New York, NY 10029; tel. (212) 876-8200; fax (212) 423-0275; e-mail library@nyam.org; internet www.nyam.org; f. 1847; 696,951 vols, 182,910 catalogued pamphlets, 275,788 catalogued illustrations and portraits, 2,700 serials; special collns: Medical Americana, history of medicine, medical biography, rare medical books and incunabula, food and cookery; Pres. JO IVEY BOUFFORD; publ. *Bulletin of the New York Academy of Medicine.*

New York Law Institute Library: 120 Broadway, New York, NY 10271-0043; tel. (212) 732-8720; fax (212) 406-1204; internet www.nyli.org; f. 1828; 300,000 vols; 1,450 reels of microfilm; 16,300 microfiches; law library for practising attorneys; special collns and editions incl. George Washington's copy of the Code de Louis XIII: the Plantation Laws of Virginia, autographed by Richard Henry Lee; Librarian NANCY G. JOSEPH; publ. *New Acquisitions Bulletin.*

New York Public Library: Fifth Ave and 42nd St, New York, NY 10018; tel. (212) 930-0800; fax (212) 930-9299; e-mail webmaster@ nypl.org; internet www.nypl.org; f. 1895 by the consolidation of Astor, Tilden and Lenox Libraries; 11,300,000 vols, 40,000 periodicals and newspapers, 26,000,000 manuscripts, maps, microfilms, films, video and audio cassettes, phonorecords, prints and sheet music; spec. collns incl. Berg collection of English and American literature, Arents collection of books on tobacco and books in parts, and the Spencer collection of illustrated books; 85 local brs and 4 research centres (Humanities and Social Sciences Library, Library for the Performing Arts, Science, Industry and Business Library, Schomburg Center for Research in Black Culture) with 4,400,000 vols and 5,900,000 non-book items; research libraries: 10,000,000 vols, 8,000,000 manuscripts; Pres. PAUL LECLERC.

New York State Library: Albany, NY 12230; tel. (518) 474-5355; fax (518) 474-5279; internet www.nysl.nysed.gov; American and New York State History, law, medicine, education, technology and genealogy; MSS and special collections; US govt depository; Talking Book and Braille Library; 19 m. items; State Librarian JANET WELCH; publ. *Checklist of Official Publications of the State of New York* (monthly).

New York University Libraries: 70 Washington Square South, New York, NY 10012; tel. (212) 998-2505; fax (212) 995-4070; e-mail libweb@nyu.edu; internet www .nyu.edu/library; f. 1835; 4,057,000 vols; 9 brs: Bobst Library has 3 specialized research centres (digital projects, arts, labour history), Courant Institute of Mathematical Sciences focuses on research-level material in mathematics, computer science, and related fields, Stephen Chan Library of Fine Arts houses collections in art history and archaeology, Jack Brause Real Estate Library, Frederick L. Ehrman Medical Library, the Dental Center's Waldman Memorial Library and the Law Library; Dean CAROL A. MANDEL.

Queens Borough Public Library: 89-11 Merrick Blvd, Jamaica, NY 11432; tel. (718) 990-0700; fax (718) 291-8936; e-mail webmaster@queenslibrary.org; internet queenslibrary.org; f. 1896; 9,700,000 vols; spec. collns incl. Long Island history and genealogy; 500,000 pictures; 62 brs; Dir THOMAS W. GALANTE.

Syracuse University Library: 222 Waverly Ave, Syracuse, NY 13244-2010; tel. (315) 443-2573; fax (315) 443-2060; internet libwww.syr.edu; f. 1870; 2,650,000 vols; 8 campus sites (audio lab, science and technology, mathematics, physics, geology, law, architecture and African American history); special collections: Leopold von Ranke, Kipling, Crane, letters and publishing history since early 20th c., cartoon art; Univ. Librarian SUZANNE THORIN (acting); publ. *Associates Courier* (annually).

Union Theological Seminary (The Burke Library): 3041 Broadway at 121st St, New York, NY 10027; tel. (212) 851-5607; fax (212) 851-5613; e-mail refdesk@uts .columbia.edu; internet www.columbia.edu/ cu/lweb/indiv/burke/index.html; f. 1836; 700,000 vols, 163,000 pieces in microform, 1,500 periodical subscriptions, 1,800 audio and visual tapes; incorporates Missionary Research Library; includes Archives of Women in Theological Scholarship; Library Dir SARA J. MYERS.

United Nations Library—Dag Hammarskjöld Library: United Nations Plaza, New York, NY 10017; tel. (212) 963-7443; fax (212) 963-2388; internet www.un.org/depts/ dhl; f. 1949, dedicated 1961; comprehensive collections of documents on the UN, Specialized Agencies and the League of Nations; collections of books, periodicals and government documents on topics of concern to the UN; activities and history of the UN; international affairs since 1918; official gazettes of all countries and newspapers of most member states in their official languages; 600,000 vols, 10,000 serials, 5,000,000 documents, 80,000 maps; Head Librarian PHYLLIS DICKSTEIN.

United States Military Academy Library: West Point, NY 10996-1799; tel. (914) 938-2230; f. 1802; 500,000 bound vols; military-historical, academic, government documents, MSS, rare books and special collections; Library Dir KENNETH W. HEDMAN.

University of Rochester Libraries: Rochester, NY 14627-0055; tel. (585) 275-4461; fax (585) 273-5309; internet www.lib .rochester.edu; f. 1850; 3,120,000 vols; libraries comprise the River Campus Libraries (7 deptl libraries), the Sibley Music Library at the Eastman School of Music, the Edward G. Miner Library (medicine and dentistry) and the Charlotte Whitney Allen Library at the Memorial Art Gallery; Dean RONALD DOW.

North Carolina

Duke University Library: Perkins Library, POB 90193, Durham, NC 27708-0193; tel. (919) 660-5800; fax (919) 660-5923; internet library.duke.edu; f. 1838; 5,560,966 vols, 51,827 linear ft of MSS and archives; British history and literature of 17th–19th centuries; general European history since 1870; French Revolution; Church history of Reformation; E Asia; advertising history; American and Latin American history; S Americana; women's history; history of economic thought; labour history; French, English, Italian, German Baroque and American literature; int. law; 6 br. libraries and 4 professional school libraries: Law (Ford Library), Medicine, Business and Divinity; Univ. Librarian and Vice-Provost for Library Affairs DEBORAH JAKUBS; publ. *Duke University Libraries* (3 a year).

Public Library of Charlotte and Mecklenburg County: 310 North Tryon St, Charlotte, NC 28202; tel. (704) 336-2725; fax (704) 336-2002; internet www.plcmc.org; f. 1903; 1.5m. vols; colln of foreign language publs, local history and genealogy; 23 br. libraries; Dir of Libraries CHARLES M. BROWN.

University of North Carolina Library: Chapel Hill, NC 27514-8890; tel. (919) 962-1301; fax (919) 843-8936; e-mail reference@ unc.edu; internet www.lib.unc.edu; f. 1795; 4,263,684 vols, 3,897,013 microforms; spec. colls on NC, S Americana, on the history of the book, incunabula, 16th-century books, incl. large colln of Estienne imprints, *crónicas* of the discovery and conquest of the New

World, also Johnson, Boswell, Dickens, Shaw and selected contemporary authors, Napoleon and the French Revolution, World War I and World War II materials, early Americana, Confederate imprints, Spanish, Catalan and Portuguese drama, John Murray and Smith, Elder & Co imprints, Afro-American materials, Fed. and State documents, Latin America, Mazarinades, Music, Social Science, Marine Sciences, Ageing, Marine Science, Journalism and S historical MSS; 10 departmental libraries in scientific and other fields; Institute of Govt Library; separate libraries in Law, Health Sciences, Planning; Data Library; Univ. Librarian SARAH C. MICHALAK.

Ohio

Akron-Summit County Public Library: 55 South Main St, Akron, OH 44326; tel. (330) 643-9000; internet ascpl.lib.oh.us; f. 1874; 1,118,000 vols; special collections in genealogy and local history; 17 brs, 1 bookmobile; Dir DAVID JENNINGS; publs *Annual Report, Shelf Life.*

Case Western Reserve University Library: 11055 Euclid Ave, Cleveland, OH 44106-7151; tel. (216) 368-3506; fax (216) 368-6950; internet www.cwru.edu/UL/ homepage.html; f. 1826; 1,500,000 vols, more than 1,290,000 monographs, 7,363 serial titles, US Govt publications, company annual reports, newspapers, CDs, technical reports, 9,000 DVDs; spec. collns incl. Early American Children's Books, German Literature and Philology, History of Medicine, History of Printing, History of Science and Technology, Environmental Sciences, Natural History, Public Housing and Urban Development; Dir JOANNE EUSTIS.

Cleveland Public Library: 325 Superior Ave, Cleveland, OH 44114-1271; tel. (216) 623 2800; fax (216) 623 7015; e-mail info@cpl .org; internet www.cpl.org; f. 1869; 9,745,655 vols; 28 neighbourhood brs; home-bound services; the John G. White endowed collection of Folklore, Orientalia and Chess; large circulating collection of video cassettes and sound recordings; services to hospitals, the homebound, the physically handicapped and the blind; telephone reference service; fee-based research service; Dir ANDREW A. VENABLE, Jr; publ. *Cleveland News Index* (monthly).

Columbus Metropolitan Library: 96 S. Grant Ave, Columbus, OH 43215; tel. (614) 645-2800; fax (614) 645-2050; internet www .columbuslibrary.org; 2,815,300 vols; 20 brs; Dir PATRICK A. LOSINSKI.

Dayton Metro Library: 215 East Third St, Dayton, OH 45402; tel. (937) 227-9500; tel. (937) 227-9539; internet www .daytonmetrolibrary.org; f. 1805; 1,509,623 vols, 23 brs; bookmobile service; service to homebound, elderly and blind; circulating collection of 16 mm. films, records and cassettes; Dir JOHN S. WALLACH; publs *Annual Report, Business Industry Technology Service, Spotlight on your Library.*

Ohio State University Libraries: 1858 Neil Ave. Mall, Columbus, OH 43210-1286; tel. (614) 292-6154; fax (614) 292-7859; e-mail library@osu.edu; internet www.lib .ohio-state.edu; f. 1873; Main (Thompson) Library and 26 departmental and affiliated libraries; 5,700,000 vols, 5,749,143 microforms, 43,000 serials; spec. collns incl. American fiction, theatre, cartoons and cartooning, medieval Slavic MSS on microfilm; Dir of Libraries JOSEPH J. BRANIN.

Public Library of Cincinnati and Hamilton County: 800 Vine St, Library Square, Cincinnati, OH 45202-2009; tel. (513) 369-6900; fax (513) 369-6993; internet www

.cincinnatilibrary.org; f. 1853; 4,887,372 books, 150,000 maps; US Documents Depository; spec. collns incl. local history, genealogy, theology, art, music, theatre, US patents and trademarks, Inland Rivers Library, Bibles, English language dictionaries, Cincinnatiana, first editions of English and American authors; 41 brs; Regional Library for the Blind and Physically Handicapped; Exec. Dir KIMBER L. FENDER.

State Library of Ohio: 274 East First Ave, Columbus, OH 43201; tel. (614) 644-7061; fax (614) 466-3584; internet winslo.state.oh.us; f. 1817; 1.4 m. vols; a special library for state government, incl. periodicals, documents, pamphlets, services and microforms; special collection of management, genealogy, local history, education and health; State Librarian JO BUDLER.

Toledo-Lucas County Public Library: 325 Michigan St, Toledo, OH 43624; tel. (419) 259-5200; fax (419) 255-5207; internet www.toledolibrary.org; f. 1970; 1,900,000 vols; 18 brs; 1 outreach service; Dir CLYDE S. SCOLES.

University of Cincinnati Libraries: Cincinnati, OH 45221-0033; tel. (513) 556-1515; fax (513) 556-0325; internet www.libraries.uc .edu; f. 1819; 3,123,318 vols; comprises a general library, medical, law, departmental and branch libraries; includes special collections on classics, modern Greek, medicine, fine arts, modern poetry, 18th-century literature; Dean and University Librarian Dr VICTORIA MONTAVON; publ. *Source* (newsletter).

Oklahoma

University of Oklahoma Libraries: Norman, OK 73019; tel. (405) 325-2611; f. 1892; 4,000,000 vols; special collections in western history, business and economic history, history of science, English, European and American literatures; Librarian SUL H. LEE.

Oregon

Multnomah County Library: 801 Southwest 10th Ave, Portland, OR 97205; tel. (503) 988-5402; fax (503) 998-5441; internet www .multcolib.org; f. 1864; 1,587,291 vols; 14 brs; Dir MOLLY RAPHAEL.

Oregon State Library: 250 Winter St, NE, Salem, OR 97301-3950; tel. (503) 378-4243; fax (503) 588-7119; e-mail reference@library .state.or.us; internet www.oregon.gov/osl; f. 1905; 1,140,680 vols; provides service to state agencies and print-disabled persons; develops local library services; special collns: Oregon and Oregon authors; State Librarian JIM SCHEPPKE.

University of Oregon Library: 1501 Kincaid St, Eugene, OR 97403-1299; tel. (541) 346-3053; fax (541) 346-3485; internet libweb .uoregon.edu; f. 1876; 2,548,402 vols, 481,414 govt documents; 730,983 maps; 2,887,172 microfilm units; 1,217 computer files; Dean of Libraries DEBORAH A. CARVER.

Pennsylvania

American Philosophical Society Library: 105 South 5th St, Philadelphia, PA 19106-3386; tel. (215) 440-3400; fax (215) 440-3423; internet www.amphilsoc.org; f. 1743; 300,000 vols, 8,000,000 MSS, microfilms; special collections on Benjamin Franklin, Thomas Paine, history of science, genetics, quantum physics, Darwinism, American Indian linguistics; Librarian MARTIN L. LEVITT; publ. *Mendel Newsletter* (annually).

Carnegie Library of Pittsburgh: 4400 Forbes Ave, Pittsburgh, PA 15213-4080; tel. (412) 622-3114; fax (412) 622-6278; e-mail info@carnegielibrary.org; internet www

.carnegielibrary.org; f. 1895; adjacent to Carnegie Institute; 3,304,674 vols, 3,306,849 other materials; main library, library for the blind and physically-handicapped; 18 local brs; Dir BARBARA MISTICK.

Ewell Sale Stewart Library of the Academy of Natural Sciences: 1900 Benjamin Franklin Parkway, Philadelphia, PA 19103-1195; tel. (215) 299-1040; fax (215) 299-1144; e-mail library@ansp.org; internet www.ansp .org/library; f. 1812; 200,000 vols, 2,500 current periodicals, 250,000 MSS; collns in the field of natural history since the 18th century; expedition literature, including the works of scientists such as Lewis and Clark, and the published journals of amateur naturalists; illustrated works in natural sciences, from the pre-Linnaean classics of Gesner, Aldrovandi and Catesby (published before 1750) through the great bird books of Gould, Audubon, Elliot, and Wilson and the flora of Redouté, Sowerby, and the Bauers, to the modern masters of wildlife art, F. L. Jaques, L. A. Fuertes, and Terence Shortt; Librarian LORENA BOYLAN.

Free Library of Philadelphia: 1901 Vine St, Philadelphia, PA 19103-1189; tel. (215) 686-5322; internet www.library.phila.gov; 55 brs throughout the city; f. 1891; 7,881,335 vols; special collections include: Fleisher orchestral music; Carson history of the common law; Widener incunabula; Drinker Choral Library; Lewis Illuminated MSS, European and Oriental; History of the Automobile; Elkins Americana, Dickens, Goldsmith, Gimbel Poe; Lewis cuneiform tablets; Rosenbach children's books of the 18th–19th c.; children's illustrators, Beatrix Potter, Kate Greenaway, Arthur Rackham; theatre collection; map collection (over 130,000 single-sheet maps, also atlases, etc.); Pres. and Dir E. L. SHELKROT.

Pennsylvania State University Libraries: 515 Paterno Library, University Park, PA 16802; tel. (814) 865-0401; fax (814) 865-3665; e-mail s2w@psulias.psu.edu; internet www.libraries.psu.edu; f. 1859; 4,779,165 vols; 5,135,467 microforms, 461,603 maps, 1,500,000 government documents, 57,235 serials; comprises a central library (Pattee Library and Paterno Library) which houses 9 subject libraries, 6 departmental brs, 12 Commonwealth College Libraries, Penn State Erie, The Behrend College, Penn State Great Valley, Penn State Abington, Abington College, Penn State Altoona, Altoona College, Berks-Lehigh Valley College, Capital College, Penn State Mont Alto, Dickinson School of Law; Special Collections Library includes: American Literature; Australian Art and Literature; Gift Books, Emblem Books; German Literature in translation (Allison-Shelley); Joseph Priestley; Renaissance; Williamscote Library (18th c. English, History, Theology and Classics); Utopian Literature; Labour History; Australiana; Vance Packard; John O'Hara; Conrad Richter, Theodore Roethke, Kenneth Burke, Arnold Bennett, C. R. Carpenter; Nunzio J. Palladino Nuclear Regulatory Commission Papers; University Archives; US Steel Workers of America Archives; United Mineworkers of America; Stapleton Collection of Pennsylvania Imprints; Dean of Libraries NANCY L. EATON.

State Library of Pennsylvania: 333 Market St, Harrisburg, PA 17126-1745; tel. (717) 787-2646; fax (717) 783-2070; e-mail ra-reference@state.pa.us; internet www .statelibrary.state.pa.us; f. 1745; 992,500 vols; American history, education, political science, sociology, library science, law, genealogy; Pennsylvania history, newspapers, maps, original Pennsylvania Assembly Collection; Dir CARYN CARR.

University of Pennsylvania Library: 3420 Walnut St, Philadelphia, PA 19104-6206; tel. (215) 898-7555; fax (215) 898-0559; e-mail library@pobox.upenn.edu; internet www.library.upenn.edu; f. 1750; 5,027,301 vols; central library and 14 departmental and affiliated libraries; Archaeology, Anthropology, Leibniz, Descartes, History of Philosophy and Science, Lithuanian History and Literature, History of Chemistry, Criminology, French Revolution, Judaica, Modern Jewish History, Modern Hebrew Literature, Aristotelianism, Occam, Medieval History, Medieval Church History, Inquisition, Middle East and Islamic Studies, Italian Renaissance Literature, Spanish Literature of the Golden Age, Shakespeareana (Furness Library), Restoration Drama, 18th- and early 19th-century English fiction, Jonathan Swift, Thomas Paine, American drama, fiction, and poetry: Walt Whitman, Washington Irving, Robert Montgomery Bird, Theodore Dreiser, James Farrell; Middle-High German, Old French, Indic MSS., South Asia, History of Economics, History of Education, Programmschriften, Elzevir Imprints, Franklin Imprints, early Americana, the American West; Dir of Libraries JOHN KEANE.

University of Pittsburgh Libraries: Pittsburgh, PA 15260; tel. (412) 648-7747; fax (412) 648-7887; internet www.pitt.edu/ libraries.html; f. 1873; 22 separate libraries on or near Main Campus and 4 regional campus libraries in Bradford, Greensburg, Johnstown and Titusville; 3,700,000 vols, 3,700,000 micro-units; Dir RUSH MILLER.

Rhode Island

Brown University Library: Providence, RI 02912; tel. (401) 863-2167; fax (401) 863-1272; e-mail rock@brown.edu; internet www .brown.edu/Facilities/University_Library; f. 1764; 3,509,710 vols; University Librarian HARRIETTE HEMMASI.

John Carter Brown Library: POB 1894, Providence, RI 02912; tel. (401) 863-2725; fax (401) 863-3477; e-mail jcbl_information@ brown.edu; internet www.jcbl.org; f. 1846; independently funded and administered centre for advanced research in history and the humanities at Brown University; contains primary historical sources pertaining to the colonial period of the Americas 1492–1825; 45,000 rare books, 16,000 reference books; Dir Dr NORMAN FIERING.

Providence Public Library: 225 Washington St, Providence, RI 02903; tel. (401) 455-8005; fax (401) 455-8080; e-mail pplref@ provlib.org; internet www.provlib.org; f. 1876; 1,000,000 vols; Dir M. DALE THOMPSON.

Tennessee

Jean and Alexander Heard Library, Vanderbilt University: 419 21st Ave S, Nashville, TN 37240-0007; tel. (615) 322-7110; fax (615) 343-8279; internet www .library.vanderbilt.edu/; f. 1873; 2,500,000 vols housed in Central, Science-Engineering, Biomedical, Divinity, Education, Law, Management and Music Libraries; Librarian PAUL GHERMAN.

Memphis Public Library and Information Center: 3030 Poplar Ave, Memphis, TN 38111-3527; tel. (901) 725-8855; fax (901) 725-8883; internet www.memphislibrary.org; f. 1893; 4.5 m. vols; CATV and colour videotaping studio; information and referral service (LINC-Library Information Center); Dir J. A. DRESCHER; publs *Kaleidoscope* (monthly), *Staff Newsline* (monthly).

University of Tennessee, Knoxville Libraries: 1015 Volunteer Boulevard, Knoxville, TN 37996-1000; tel. (865) 974-4465; fax (865) 974-4259; e-mail bdewey@utk.edu;

internet www.lib.utk.edu; f. 1794; 2,376,414 vols; spec. collns incl. Tennesseana, North American Indians; Dean BARBARA I. DEWEY.

Texas

Austin Public Library: 800 Guadalupe St, Box 2287, Austin, TX 78768-2287; tel. (512) 974-7444; fax (512) 974-7403; internet www.ci.austin.tx.us/library; f. 1926; 1,550,145 vols; 20 facilities; system maintains a comprehensive collection of books, magazines, newspapers, recordings, audio cassettes and videocassettes; Austin History Center contains materials on history of Austin and Travis County; Dir BRENDA BRANCH.

Dallas Public Library: 1515 Young St, Dallas, TX 75201-5499; tel. (214) 670-1400; e-mail dpldir@dallaslibrary.org; internet www.dallaslibrary.org; f. 1901; 6,143,644 items; Dir RAMIRO SALAZAR.

Fort Worth Public Library: 500 W. 3rd St, Fort Worth, TX 76102-7305; tel. (817) 871-7701; fax (817) 871-7734; internet www.fortworthlibrary.org; f. 1901; 2,066,000 vols; 15 brs; special collections: genealogy, local history, sheet music, postcards, bookplates; US and Texas govt depository; Dir Dr GLENIECE ROBINSON.

George Bush Presidential Library and Museum: 1000 George Bush Drive West, College Station, TX 77845; tel. (979) 691-4000; fax (979) 691-4050; e-mail library.bush@nara.gov; internet bushlibrary.tamu.edu; 38,000,000 pages of official and personal papers, 1,000,000 photographs, 2,500 hrs of videotape; museum of 70,000 items relating to the life and career of President George Bush (1989–1993); Dir Dr DOUGLAS MENARCHIK.

Houston Public Library: 500 McKinney St, Houston, TX 77002; tel. (832) 393-1313; fax (832) 393-1266; e-mail website@hpl.lib.tx.us; internet www.houstonlibrary.org; f. 1901; 4,561,000 vols; 35 brs; special collections: Bibles, Civil War, Salvation Army posters, early Houston photographs, early printing and illuminated MSS, juvenile literature, petroleum, sheet music, Texana, US and Texas depository; specializes in genealogy, art, architecture, business, management; jazz, Afro-American and Hispanic archives; Dir TONI LAMBERT.

University of Texas System Libraries: Austin, TX 78713-8916; internet www.lib.utexas.edu; f. 1883; 6,835,983 vols; also Arlington; 893,155 vols; El Paso; 746,308 vols; Permian Basin; 215,945 vols; San Antonio; 367,583 vols; Health Science Center, Houston; 54,000 vols; Health Science Center, Dallas; 224,732 vols; Health Science Center, San Antonio; 173,143 vols; Medical Branch, Galveston 291,326.

Utah

Family History Library of the Church of Jesus Christ of Latter-day Saints: 35 North West Temple St, Salt Lake City, UT 84150-3400; tel. (801) 240-2584; fax (801) 240-3718; e-mail fhl@ldschurch.org; internet www.familysearch.org; f. 1894; 300,000 bound vols, 2,200,000 reels of microfilm, 734,000 microfiches; Dir DAVID E. RENCHER.

University of Utah Library: 295 S. 1500 E., Salt Lake City, UT 84112-0860; tel. (801) 581-8558; fax (801) 581-3464; internet www.lib.utah.edu; f. 1850; 2,000,000 vols, 13,000 serial titles; special collections: archives, Middle East, MSS, rare books, Western Americana, oral history; US State and UN documents depository; Dir (vacant).

Virginia

Fairfax County Public Library: 12000 Government Center Parkway, Suite 324, Fairfax, VA 22035; tel. (703) 324-3100; internet www.co.fairfax.va.us/library; f. 1939; 3,000,000 vols; 21 brs; also CD-ROMs, microfilm, audio and video cassettes, periodicals, recorded and talking books, CATV hookup; Dir EDWIN S. CLAY III.

Library of Virginia: 800 East Broad St, Richmond, VA 23219-1905; tel. (804) 692-3500; internet www.lva.lib.va.us; f. 1823; 700,000 vols, 834 current periodicals; Virginiana, Southern US History, Civil War, genealogy; archive collection of 55,000 cu. ft; Librarian NOLAN T. YELICH; publ. *Virginia Cavalcade* (quarterly).

Mariners' Museum Research Library and Archives: 100 Museum Drive, Newport News, VA 23606-3759; tel. (757) 591-7782; fax (757) 591-7310; e-mail library@mariner.org; internet www.mariner.org/library; f. 1933 by Archer M. and Anna H. Huntington; library of materials related to human interaction with the world's waterways; more than 75,000 vols, 350,000 photographs, 1,000,000 archival items such as ships' logs, charts, manuscripts, blueprints and memorabilia; special collections: Edwin Levick Collection of photographs of passenger ships, yachts, and America's Cup Races; A. Aubrey Bodine Collection of images of life on the Chesapeake Bay; Chris-Craft Collection documenting the construction of boats by one of America's most important pleasure boat builders; Dir SUSAN BERG.

Patent and Trademark Office Scientific and Technical Information Center: Madison West Building, Room 1C35, 600 Dulany St, Alexandria, VI; tel. (571) 272-3547; internet www.uspto.gov/web/patents/sticlibinfo.htm; f. 1836; 200,000 vols; foreign patent documents since 1617; Program Man. HENRY ROSICKY.

Richmond Public Library: 101 East Franklin St, Richmond, VA 23219; tel. (804) 646-4256; fax (804) 646-7685; internet www.richmondpubliclibrary.org; f. 1924; 810,066 vols; Dir HARRIET HENDERSON.

University of Virginia Library: POB 400114, Charlottesville, VA 22904-4111; tel. (804) 924-3026; fax (804) 924-1431; internet www.lib.virginia.edu; f. 1819; 5,053,162 vols, 53,015 journals, 150,362 maps, 447,020 slides and photographs, 87,642 video and audio recordings, 16,700,000 MSS; spec. collns incl. American history and literature, including McGregor Library of American History and the Barrett Library of American Literature, Massey-Faulkner collection, Streeter collection on Southeastern Railways, Optics, Evolution, Thomas Jefferson, Scott Sporting Collection, Victorian fiction, Greek and Latin literature, Music, International Law, History of Printing, Gothic novels, Matthew Arnold, Jorge Luis Borges collection, Gordon collection of French books, Tibetan collection, Paul Mellon collection of Americana and Virginiana; Librarian KARIN WITTENBORG.

Washington

Seattle Public Library: 1000 4th Ave, Seattle, WA 98104; tel. (206) 386-4100; f. 1891; 1,668,000 vols; special collections: Aeronautics, Pacific Northwest Americana; 23 br. libraries; Librarian DEBORAH JACOBS.

University of Washington Libraries: Box 352900, Seattle, WA 98195-2900; tel. (206) 543-1763; fax (206) 685-8727; e-mail libquest@u.washington.edu; internet www.lib.washington.edu; f. 1862; 6,546,072 vols; 55,932 current serials, 7,588,453 microforms; includes Law Library (separately administered; Librarian PENNY HAZELTON), Health Sciences Library, Odegaard Undergraduate Library, East Asia Library, Special Collns Division and 14 br. libraries; Dir and Dean, University of Washington Libraries LIZABETH WILSON.

Washington State Library: POB, 40220, Olympia, WA 98504-0220; tel. (360) 902-4151; fax (360) 586-7575; internet www.secstate.wa.gov/library; f. 1853; 488,916 books and periodicals, 1,545,899 federal and state documents; 483,118 microfiche, 42,734 microfilm, 8,914 films, 8,744 audio and video tapes; special collections: Washington Authors, Pacific Northwest, Washington State Documents, Washington State Newspapers, Transportation, Labor and Industries, Utilities; State Librarian JAN WALSH.

West Virginia

West Virginia University Libraries: POB 6069, Morgantown, WV 26506-6069; 1549 University Ave, Morgantown, WV 26506-6069; tel. (304) 293-4040; fax (304) 293-6638; e-mail ask_a_librarian@mail.wvu.edu; internet www.libraries.wvu.edu; f. 1867; 1,497,710 vols; spec.collns incl. W. Virginia historical art, Appalachian, Myers, rare book; 1.9m. microforms; 4m. archives; Dean FRANCES O'BRIEN.

Wisconsin

American Geographical Society Collection of the University of Wisconsin–Milwaukee Library: POB 604, Milwaukee, WI 53201; 2311 East Hartford Ave, Milwaukee, WI 53211; tel. (414) 229-4785; fax (414) 229-3624; e-mail agsc@uwm.edu; internet www.uwm.edu/lLibraries; f. 1851; 210,000 vols, 500,000 maps, 9,000 atlases, 84 globes, 33,676 pamphlets, 207,320 Landsat images, 159,063 photographs and slides, 1,387 CD-ROMs; Dir EWA BARCZYK; publ. *Current Geographical Publications / Online Geographical Bibliography (GEOBIB)* (online).

Milwaukee Public Library: 814 West Wisconsin Ave, Milwaukee, WI 53233; tel. (414) 286-3000; fax (414) 286-2794; internet www.mpl.org; f. 1878; 3,170,711 vols; spec. collns incl. Great Lakes marine colln, Milwaukee Road archives, Omar Khayyam colln, Arkham House colln, Philosopher Press colln, cookbooks, H. G. Wells, definitive edns of collected works of British and American authors, Charles King colln, Harry Franck colln, genealogy; depository for US Fed. Documents, US Geologic Survey, US Defense Mapping Agency maps and US Patent Office; 12 br. libraries, Wisconsin Regional Library for the Blind and Physically Handicapped headquarters, 1 mobile library, 2 library vans; City Librarian PAULA KIELY.

University of Wisconsin Library: 728 State St, Madison, WI 53706; tel. (608) 262-3193; fax (608) 265-2754; internet www.library.wisc.edu; f. 1848; 7,300,000 vols; 55,000 serial titles, 6.2m. microforms, 160 linear ft of MSS, 7m. govt documents, maps, musical scores; spec. collns on pharmacy, Scandinavian literature, Gaelic literature and history, modern Polish literature, history of science, history of Calvinism, socialist and labour movements; English, American, French, German, Icelandic, Irish, Spanish literature and history; Dir-Gen. of Library System KENNETH FRAZIER.

Museums and Art Galleries

Alabama

Alabama Museum of Natural History, University of Alabama: POB 870340, Tuscaloosa, AL 35487-0340; tel. (205) 348-7550; e-mail programs@bama.ua.edu; internet amnh.ua.edu; exhibits and collns incl. the Hodges meteorite, the only meteorite known to have struck a human being, fossils, minerals and palaeontology; Dir Dr IAN W. BROWN.

Alaska

Alaska State Museum: 395 Whittier St, Juneau, AK 99801–1718; tel. (907) 465-2901; fax (907) 465-2976; internet www.museums .state.ak.us; f. 1900, opened to the public 1920; Alaskan history, Alaska's native people, Russian America, art, natural history and ethnographic materials; state-wide assistance to museums in Alaska; Alaska State Chief Curator BRUCE KATO.

Attached museum:

Sheldon Jackson Museum: 104 College Dr., Sitka, AK 99835-7657; tel. (907) 747-8981; fax (907) 747-3004; internet www .museums.state.ak.us; f. 1888; Alaska Native artefacts; Chief Curator BRUCE KATO.

Arizona

Arizona State Museum: POB 210026, Univ. of Arizona, Tucson, AZ 85721-0026; Located at: 1013 East University Blvd, Tucson, AZ 85721-0026; tel. (520) 621-6302; fax (520) 621-2976; internet www .statemuseum.arizona.edu; f. 1893; archaeology, anthropology and ethnology of Arizona and surrounding regions; research colln incl. Hohokam, Mogollon and other archaeological material, osteological remains, vertebrate zoo-archaeological and herbarial specimens, 1,500 linear ft of archive material and 250,000 photographs; collns Southwest Indian pottery, Navajo textiles; library of 50,000 vols, 1,500 periodicals; Dir HARTMAN H. LOMAWAIMA.

Arkansas

Arkansas Arts Center: POB 2137, Little Rock, AR 72203; Located at: 501 East Ninth St, Little Rock, AR 72202; tel. (501) 372-4000; fax (501) 375-8053; internet www.arkarts .com; incl. Children's Theatre and Museum School; spec. colln American and European art from Renaissance to present, paintings by Diego Rivera, Odilon Redon, Francesco Bassano; sculpture by Henry Moore, Louise Nevelson, Roy Lichtenstein; prints by Rembrandt, Whistler, Dürer; contemporary crafts; library of 5,000 vols; Dir Dr ELLEN PLUMMER.

Arkansas Museum of Science and History: Suite 150, 500 President Clinton Ave, Little Rock, AR 72201; tel. (501) 396-7050; fax (501) 396-7054; e-mail erandolph@amod .org; internet www.amod.org; Egyptian sarcophagus from 6th century BC, multicultural masks, 51 species of animals; Exec. Dir NAN SELZ.

Historic Arkansas Museum: 200 East Third St, Little Rock, AR 72201; tel. (501) 324-9351; fax (501) 324-9345; e-mail info@ historicarkansas.org; internet www .arkansashistory.com; f. 1939; 5 pre-Civil War houses; collns of decorative, mechanical and fine arts; Dir BILL WORTHEN.

California

Asian Art Museum of San Francisco, The Avery Brundage Collection: 200 Larkin St, San Francisco, CA 94102; tel. (415) 581-3500; fax (415) 581-4700; e-mail pr@asianart .org; internet www.asianart.org; f. 1969; museum and centre of research on outstanding collns of Chinese, Japanese, Korean, Indian, Southeast Asian, Himalayan and Islamic art; library of 30,000 vols; Chair. DIXON R. DOLL.

California Palace of the Legion of Honor: Lincoln Park, 34th Ave and Clement St, San Francisco, CA 94121; tel. (415) 750-3600; fax (415) 750-7686; e-mail mediarelations@famsf.org; internet www .legionofhonor.org; f. 1924; attached to Fine Arts Museums of San Francisco; European decorative arts and paintings; ancient art; sculpture by Auguste Rodin; Achenbach Foundation for Graphic Arts has largest colln of prints and drawings in the Western USA (see also de Young Museum); Dir JOHN E. BUCHANAN, Jr; publ. *Fine Arts Magazine* (3 or 4 a year).

de Young Museum: 50 Hagiwara Tea Garden Dr., Golden Gate Park, San Francisco, CA 94118; tel. (415) 863-3330; fax (415) 750-7692; internet www.deyoungmuseum .org; f. 1895; reopened 2005; attached to Fine Arts Museums of San Francisco; collns of American art from the 17th to the 21st century; art of the native Americas, Africa, and the Pacific (see also California Palace of the Legion of Honor); Dir JOHN E. BUCHANAN, Jr; publ. *Fine Arts Magazine* (3 or 4 a year).

Getty, J. Paul, Museum: Suite 1000, 1200 Getty Center Dr., Los Angeles, CA 90049-1687; tel. (310) 440-7330; fax (310) 440-7751; e-mail gettymuseum@getty.edu; internet www.getty.edu; f. 1954; Greek, Roman and Etruscan antiquities, European paintings; drawings, manuscripts, decorative arts; European and American photographs, modern and contemporary European and American outdoor sculpture; conservation work and symposia; Dir MICHAEL BRAND.

Getty Villa: 17985 Pacific Coast Highway, Malibu, CA 90265-5799; e-mail gettymuseum@getty.edu; internet www .getty.edu/museum/home.html; f. 1953, reopened in 2006 after major renovations; incl. re-creation of a Roman seaside villa, the Villa dei Papiri, which was destroyed by the eruption of Vesuvius in AD 79; houses permanent colln of 44,000 Greek, Roman and Etruscan antiquities, 1,200 of which are on public display; a library and other facilities for scholars supports research programmes and the comparative study of ancient art and cultures, both western and non-western; Dir MICHAEL BRAND.

Griffith Observatory and Planetarium: 2800 East Observatory Rd, Los Angeles, CA 90027; tel. (213) 473-0800; fax (213) 473-0816; internet www.griffithobs.org; f. 1935; 3 main divs: the Observatory, with Zeiss twin 12-inch and 9-inch refracting telescopes and 3 solar telescopes; more than 100 exhibits; the Samuel Oschin Planetarium, with its Zeiss star projector and space travel projectors; Dir Dr E. C. KRUPP; publ. *The Griffith Observer* (illustrated, monthly).

Huntington Library, Art Collections and Botanical Gardens: 1151 Oxford Rd, San Marino, CA 91108; tel. (626) 405-2100; fax (626) 449-5720; e-mail publicinformation@huntington.org; internet www.huntington.org; f. 1919; British and French paintings from 18th–19th centuries (incl. full-length portraits by Reynolds, Gainsborough and Lawrence); 18th-century French sculpture, furniture and porcelain; European decorative arts from 16th–18th centuries; American painting, furniture and decorative arts from 1730–1930; botanical gardens of 120 acres with 15,000 plant species; library of 500,000 rare books, 500,000 ref. books, 6,000,000 MSS, prints, 600,000 photographs and maps; Pres. STEVEN S. KOBLIK; Dir Art Collns JOHN MURDOCH; See also Libraries and Archives; publ. *Huntington Frontiers* (2 a year).

Natural History Museum of Los Angeles County: 900 Exposition Blvd, Los Angeles, CA 90007; e-mail info@nhm.org; internet www.nhm.org; f. 1910; Western USA and American History, New World ethnology and archaeology, palaeontology, geology, mineralogy, botany, ichthyology, mammalogy, entomology, herpetology, invertebrate zoology, ornithology; active research centre in areas of living and fossil invertebrates, vertebrates, mineralogy, anthropology (Native American, Pre-Columbian and Pacific) and history (CA and Southwestern); incl. Page Museum at La Brea Tar Pits and William S. Hart Museum; 15,000 mems; library of 100,000 vols; Pres. Board of Governors ED. N. HARRISON; Chair. Museum Foundation STEPHEN R. ONDERDONK; Dir JAMES L. POWELL; publs *Contributions in Science* (irreg.), *Science Series* (irreg.), *Terra* (every 2 months).

San Diego Museum of Art: Balboa Park, POB 122107, San Diego, CA 92112-2107; 1450 El Prado, Balboa Park, San Diego, CA; tel. (619) 232-7931; fax (619) 232-9367; e-mail information@sdmart.org; internet www.sdmart.org; f. 1925; Renaissance and Baroque paintings of Spanish, Italian, Dutch, Flemish and French schools; major works by El Greco, Zurbarán, Goya, Crivelli, Tiepolo, Guardi, Rubens, Rembrandt, Ruysdael, Hals, Matisse, Braque; early and contemporary American artists; Asiatic arts and sculpture, graphics and decorative arts from many countries; Latin American art; lectures, concerts and classes; library of 27,000 vols, 12,000 periodicals; Dir DERRICK R. CARTWRIGHT.

San Diego Natural History Museum: POB 121390, San Diego, CA 92112-1390; tel. (619) 232-3821; fax (619) 232-0248; e-mail library@sdnhm.org; internet www .sdnhm.org; f. 1874 to further the knowledge of natural history and the conservation of natural resources; depts of botany, herpetology, birds and mammals, entomology, palaeontology and marine invertebrates; library of 92,000 vols, 900 journals and series; archives; Laurence Klauber Herpetology Colln; Pres. and CEO Dr MICHAEL W. HAGER; Library Dir MARGARET DYKENS; publ. *Proceedings*.

San Francisco Museum of Modern Art: 151 Third St, San Francisco, CA 94103; tel. (415) 357-4000; fax (415) 357-4037; internet www.sfmoma.org; f. 1935 by the San Francisco Art Asscn; contemporary art; permanent colln: early Modernism, Analytical Cubism, Abstract Expressionism and other major schools since the beginning of the 20th century; also German Expressionism, Modernist Mexican painting, figurative art of the San Francisco Bay area; important photography dept with colln of images since the 1840s; dept of architecture and design focusing on works by architects and designers of the Pacific region; dept of media arts incl. multimedia, videotape, film and other works created in moving-image or image-reproduction media; library of 80,000 vols, 1,860 periodicals, 56,000 monographs, catalogues raisonnés and exhibition catalogues; Dir NEAL BENEZRA.

University of California, Berkeley, Art Museum & Pacific Film Archive: 2625 Durant Ave, Berkeley, CA 94720-2250; tel. (510) 642-0808; fax (510) 642-4889; e-mail bampfa@berkeley.edu; internet www.bampfa .berkeley.edu; f. 1970; 10 exhibition galleries, sculpture garden; permanent colln of Asian and western art; Hans Hofmann colln; 10,000 film colln and programme; serves the univ. and San Francisco Bay Area community with exhibitions, study collns, etc.; organizes and receives travelling exhibitions from major museums internationally; screens 550–600 films annually; Dir KEVIN E. CONSEY.

Colorado

Denver Art Museum: 100 West 14th Ave Parkway, Denver, CO 80204-2788; tel. (720) 865-5000; fax (720) 913-0001; e-mail info@ denverartmuseum.org; internet www .denverartmuseum.org; f. 1893 as Artists' Club of Denver; art education programmes for children and adults; permanent collns incl. Architecture, Design and Graphics; Asian; Modern and Contemporary; Native Art (incl. American Indian, African and Oceanic artworks); New World (incl. Pre-Columbian and Spanish Colonial); Painting and Sculpture (incl. American and European); Western American art; Textile Art; 28,000 mems for academic research; visiting scholars by appointment; Dir Dr LEWIS I. SHARP; publs *On and Off the Wall* (newsletter, 6 a year), *Western Passages* (annual).

Denver Museum of Nature and Science: 2001 Colorado Blvd, Denver, CO 80205-5798; tel. (303) 322-7009; fax (303) 331-6492; e-mail feedback@dmns.org; internet www .dmns.org/main/en; f. and inc. 1900; depts of Anthropology and Archaeology, Archives, Photographic Archives, Earth Sciences, Zoology, Conservation, Exhibitions, Youth Programmes, Adult Programmes; Gates Planetarium, Hall of Life, IMAX® Theater, auditorium; library of 40,000 vols, 800 periodicals; Chief Curator Dr KIRK JOHNSON; Pres. and CEO GEORGE W. SPARKS; publs *Museum Monthly* (newsletter), *Museum Quarterly*.

Connecticut

Connecticut State Museum of Natural History and Archaeology Center: 2019 Hillside Rd, Storrs, CT 06269-1023; tel. (860) 486-4460; fax (860) 486-0827; internet www .cac.uconn.edu; attached to Univ. of Connecticut; Archaeological Center f. 2004; 500,000 archaeological and ethnographic items primarily of Native North and South American origin, including 19th-century Plains Indian shirts and Paleolithic stone tools dating from over 250,000 years ago; State Archaeologist Dr NICHOLAS BELLANTONI; Dir LEANNE KENNEDY HARTY.

Discovery Museum and Planetarium: 4450 Park Ave, Bridgeport, CT 06604; tel. (203) 372-3521; fax (203) 374-1929; internet www.discoverymuseum.org; independent; f. 1958; incl. CineMuse Theater, Henry B. duPont Planetarium, Challenger Learning Center, interactive science galleries and educational programmes; Exec. Dir LINDA MALKIN; Admin. Dir LYNN HAMILTON.

Peabody Museum of Natural History: POB 208118, New Haven, CT 06520-8118; tel. (203) 432-5050; fax (203) 432-9816; internet www.peabody.yale.edu; f. 1866 by a gift of George Peabody, banker and philanthropist; affiliated with Yale Univ.; extensive collns in the fields of anthropology, meteorites, botany, palaeobotany, invertebrate palaeontology, mineralogy, vertebrate palaeontology, invertebrate zoology and vertebrate zoology, historic scientific instruments, each with its own Curator; also Yale Peabody Museum Field Station; Dir MICHAEL J. DONOGHUE; publs *Bulletin*, *Discovery*, *Postilla*.

Wadsworth Atheneum Museum of Art: 600 Main St, Hartford, CT 06103; tel. (860) 278-2670; fax (860) 527-0803; e-mail info@ wadsworthatheneum.org; internet www .wadsworthatheneum.org; f. 1842; early American furniture, Hudson River School landscapes, Renaissance and Baroque paintings, African-American art; Meissen and Sèvres porcelains; costume and textiles; 19th-century French and Impressionist paintings; modernist and surrealist masterpieces; MATRIX Gallery for Contemporary Art; library: Auerbach library of 40,000 vols; Dir WILLARD HOLMES.

Delaware

Winterthur, An American Country Estate (Museum, Gardens and Library): Winterthur, DE 19735; tel. (302) 888-4600; fax (302) 888-4820; e-mail webmaster@ winterthur.org; internet www.winterthur .org; f. 1951; American antiquities from 1640–1860, 60-acre naturalistic garden; MA program in Early American Culture and MS program in Art Conservation, both in conjunction with Univ. of Delaware; colln of over 85,000 articles and antiques; 23,000 mems; library of 500,000 vols, MSS, microfilm, periodicals, photographs; Dir and CEO LESLIE GREENE BOWMAN; publ. *Winterthur Portfolio* (quarterly).

District of Columbia

Anacostia Museum and Center for African American History and Culture: 1901 Fort Pl., SE, Washington, DC 20020; tel. (202) 633-4020; fax (202) 287-3183; e-mail aminfo@si.edu; internet www.anacostia.si .edu; attached to the Smithsonian Instn; Dir JAMES C. EARLY (acting).

Arthur M. Sackler Gallery: Smithsonian Institution, 1050 Independence Ave, SW, Washington, DC 20560; tel. (202) 653-4880; fax (202) 357-4911; internet www.asia.si.edu; f. 1982, opened 1987; initial colln gift of Arthur M. Sackler; part of the Smithsonian Instn, and interlinked with the Freer Gallery of Art; int. loan exhibitions and displays of permanent colln, incl. ancient Egyptian art, arts of the Islamic world, Chinese art, Japanese art, Korean art and Southeast Asian art; public programmes and publs aim to promote artistic and cultural traditions of Asia; joint Sackler and Freer scientific and research dept; library of 80,000 vols; Dir JULIAN RABY.

Arts and Industries Building: 900 Jefferson Dr., SW, Washington, DC; tel. (202) 633-1000; e-mail info@si.edu; internet www.si .edu/ai; f. 1881 for the inaugural ball of Pres. James A. Garfield, to host exhibits from the Centennial Exposition in Philadelphia; attached to the Smithsonian Instn; exhibitions from the Smithsonian Instn and other museums and collns; closed for renovation.

Corcoran Gallery of Art: 700 17th St, NW, Washington, DC 20006-4840; tel. (202) 639-1700; internet www.corcoran.org; f. 1869 from colln of banker William Corcoran; 14,000 items from 19th and 20th centuries American and European painting, sculpture and photography, incl. works by Cuyp, Degas, Delacroix, Hopper, Elsworth Kelly, Monet, Picasso, Man Ray, Renoir, Rodin, Sargent, Warhol, Whistler; also houses the Corcoran Gallery of Art and Design; Dir and Pres. PAUL GREENHALGH.

Freer Gallery of Art: Jefferson Dr. at 12th St, SW, Washington, DC 20560; tel. (202) 633-4880; fax (202) 357-4911; e-mail asiainfo@asia.si.edu; internet www.asia.si .edu; f. 1923 (est. 1906), based on gift of the late Charles L. Freer, of Detroit (1854–1919); part of the Smithsonian Instn, and interlinked with the Arthur M. Sackler Gallery; devoted to research and exhibition of the outstanding collns of Chinese, Japanese, Korean, Indian, Near Eastern and late 19th–20th century American art; works of James McNeill Whistler; joint Sackler and Freer scientific and research dept; library of 80,000 vols, (approx. half in Chinese and Japanese); Dir JULIAN RABY; publs *Ars Orientalis*, *Oriental Studies*.

Hirshhorn Museum and Sculpture Garden: POB 37012 HMSG/MRC 350, Washington, DC 20013-7012; Located at: Independence Ave at 7th St, SW, Washington, DC 20560; tel. (202) 633-4674; fax (202) 786-2682; e-mail hmsginquiries@si.edu; internet hirshhorn.si.edu; f. 1966; administered by the Smithsonian Instn; modern and contemporary int. art; sculpture since 19th century; library: research library of 57,000 vols, 50 serials, 13,000 slides from 900 contemporary artists; Chair. J. TOMILSON HILL.

International Spy Museum: 800 F St, NW, Washington, DC 20004; tel. (202) 393-7798; fax (202) 393-7797; e-mail jsaxon@ spymuseum.org; internet www.spymuseum .org; f. 2002; history and contemporary role of espionage from a global perspective; Exec. Dir PETER EARNEST; Chief Operating Officer PAUL BOSCH.

National Air and Space Museum: 6th and Independence Ave, SW, Washington, DC 20013-7012; tel. (202) 633-1000; fax (202) 633-81742426; e-mail info@si.edu; internet www.nasm.si.edu; f. 1946 to record the nat. devt of aeronautics and astronautics; administered by the Smithsonian Instn; collects, preserves, and displays aeronautical and astronautical equipment of historical interest and significance; provides educational material for the historical study of aeronautics and astronautics; colln contains original full-size aircraft, spacecraft, recovered space exploration vehicles, engines, instruments, flight clothing, accessories of technical, historical, and biographical interest, photographs, scale models, and extensive reference data; Paul E. Garber Preservation, Restoration and Storage Facility and Steven F. Udvar-Hazy Center; library of 40,000 vols and journals; archives: 11,000 cu ft of materials, 1.7m. photographs, 700,000 ft of film, 2m. technical drawings; Dir JOHN R. DAILEY.

Attached research institute:

Center for Earth and Planetary Studies: see separate entry.

National Gallery of Art: 2000B South Club Dr., Landover, MD 20785; located between Third and Ninth St, NW, on Constitution Ave, Washington, DC 20565; tel. (202) 737-4215; fax (202) 789-2681; internet www.nga .gov; f. 1937; ind. establishment of the US govt; European and American paintings, sculpture and graphic arts since 12th century; photographic archives; slide colln; library of 350,000 vols, 2,321 periodicals; Pres. VICTORIA P. SANT; Dir EARL A. POWELL, III; Administrator DARRELL R. WILLSON; publ. *Studies in the History of Art*.

National Museum of African Art, Smithsonian Institution: 950 Independence Ave, SW, Washington, DC 20560-0708; tel. (202) 633-4649; fax (202) 357-4879; e-mail nmafaweb@nmafa.si.edu; internet africa.si .edu; f. 1964, merged with Smithsonian Instn 1979; 8,000 items from throughout Africa, incl. traditional and contemporary art; library: research facilities include the Warren M. Robbins library of 25,000 vols and the Eliot Elisofon Photographic Archives (300,000 photographic prints and transparencies, 120,000 ft of motion picture film and videotape); Dir Dr SHARON F. PATTON.

National Museum of American History: 14th St and Constitution Ave, NW, Washington, DC 20560; tel. (202) 357-2700; fax (202) 357-1853; internet americanhistory.si.edu; administered by the Smithsonian Instn; f. 1964; devoted to the colln, care, study and exhibition of objects which reflect the experience of the American people, incl. c. 3m. artefacts; programme of lectures and concerts; library: Archives Center of 700 collns; Dir BRENT D. GLASS; Curator, Archives Center JOHN A. FLECKNER.

Attached research institute:

Jerome and Dorothy Lemelson Center for the Study of Invention and Innovation: see separate entry.

National Museum of Natural History: POB 37012, Smithsonian Institution, NW, Washington, DC 20013-7012; tel. (202) 357-2661; fax (202) 357-4779; internet www.mnh.si.edu; f. 1846; administered by the Smithsonian Instn; depository of the nat. collns, containing more than 120m. catalogued items; it is especially rich in the natural science and anthropology of the Americas, including zoology, entomology, botany, geology, palaeontology, archaeology, ethnology, and physical anthropology; also houses exhibits relating to the natural sciences and anthropology; research: 100 scientists working in 4 depts: Anthropology, Mineral Sciences, Paleobiology, Systematic Biology; part of the Smithsonian Marine Science Network; library: Nat. Anthropological Archives: 400,000 ethnological and archaeological photographs, 20,000 works of native art, 1,200 aluminum discs recorded by J. P. Harrington; Human Studies Film Archives: 8m. ft of film and video; Acting Dir Dr PAUL RISSER; publ. *Smithsonian Contributions* (separate series for Anthropology, Botany, Earth Sciences, Paleobiology, Zoology and Marine Sciences).

Attached research institutes:

Arctic Research Centre: see separate entry.

Carrie-Bow Marine Field Station – Caribbean Coral Reef Ecosystems (CCRE): see separate entry in Belize chapter.

Marine Station at Fort Pierce: see separate entry.

National Portrait Gallery: POB 37012, Victor Bldg, Suite 8300, MRC 973, Washington, DC 20013-7012; tel. (202) 275-1738; fax (202) 275-1895; e-mail npgnews@si.edu; internet www.npg.si.edu; administered by the Smithsonian Instn; f. 1962; portraits of persons who have made significant contributions to the history, devt or culture of the people of the USA; library of 90,000 vols; Dir MARC PACHTER; publ. *PROFILE* (quarterly).

National Postal Museum: 2 Massachussetts Ave, NE, Washington, DC 20002; tel. (202) 633-5555; fax (202) 633-9393; internet www.postalmuseum.si.edu; f. 1993 in the bldg of the former Washington, DC post office (1914–1986); Nat. Philatelic Colln (f. 1886); controlled by the Smithsonian Instn with the support of the United States Postal Service; Nat. Philatelic Colln of 6m. items; delivery vehicles, mailboxes and mailbags, uniforms and equipment and other items of postal history; library of 40,000 vols, journals, catalogues, archival documents (part of the Smithsonian Instn Libraries system); Dir ALLEN KANE; Librarian PAUL McCUTCHEON.

Smithsonian American Art Museum and its Renwick Gallery: 750 Ninth St, NW, Rm 3100, Washington, DC 20013-7012; tel. (202) 275-1500; fax (202) 275-1424; e-mail info@saam.si.edu; internet americanart.si.edu; administered by the Smithsonian Instn; f. 1829; largest colln of American art in the world; 41,000 artworks since 18th century.; recently renovated museum bldg houses Lunder Conservation Center (permanent displays of the museum's preservation work) and provides information on conservation science and techniques; other centres incl. Luce Foundation Center for American Art (art storage and study centre): 3,300

objects on display, incl. a discussion of each artwork, artist biographies, audio interviews, video-clips and still images; specialized art research databases of 500,000 records, incl. Inventory of American Paintings and Sculpture; pre-1877 Art Exhibition Catalogue Index and findings from the Save Outdoor Sculpture programme; Photographic Archives of 250,000 photographs, negatives and slides; Peter A. Juley and Son colln (127,000 images documenting the work of 11,000 American artists from the 1890s to 1975); and the Water Rosenblum colln (7,500 black-and-white photographs documenting the New York art scene from 1945–1970); Graphic Arts Study Center (28,000 works on paper, including prints, drawings, watercolours and photographs) and the Joseph Cornell Study Center; Renwick Gallery of craft work; now part of the Donald W. Reynolds Center; library: library of 180,000 vols specializing in American art, history and biography; shared by the Smithsonian American Art Museum and the Nat. Portrait Gallery; Dir ELIZABETH BROUN; Chief of Art Information Resources CHRISTINE HENNESSEY; publ. *American Art* (3 a year).

Florida

John and Mable Ringling Museum of Art/State Art Museum of Florida: 5401 Bay Shore Rd, Sarasota, FL 34243; tel. (941) 359-5700; fax (941) 359-7704; e-mail info@ringling.org; internet www.ringling.org; f. 1927, bequested to the State of Florida 1936; attached to Florida State Univ.; comprises Museum of Art (European, American and Non-Western art), 2 Circus Museums including the Tibbals Learning Center, home of the world's largest miniature circus, Cà d'Zan Mansion (former Ringling winter residence), Historic Asolo Theater (18th-century Venetian theatre from Asolo, Italy), 66-acre waterfront estate; library of 60,000 vols and exhibition catalogues, 100 periodicals; Exec. Dir Dr JOHN WETENHALL; Curators Dr STEPHEN BORYS, DEBORAH WALK (Circus Museum) JOANNA WEBER (Museum of Art).

Marineland Foundation Inc. (Marineland of Florida): 9600 Oceanshore Blvd, St Augustine, FL 32080; tel. (904) 471-1111; fax (904) 460-1330; e-mail reservations@marineland.net; internet www.marineland.net; f. 1937; incl. 2 Oceanariums, 11 marine and fresh water exhibits; houses C. V. Whitney Laboratory; ref. library on aquatic sciences (not open to the public); Gen. Man. ROBIN B. FRIDAY, Sr.

Georgia

Roosevelt's Little White House: 401 Little White House Rd, Warm Springs, GA 31830; tel. (706) 655-5870; fax (706) 655-5872; internet www.fdr-littlewhitehouse.org; f. 1946; under direction of Georgia Dept of Natural Resources; remains as it was when Pres. Franklin Delano Roosevelt died here in 1945; exhibits and film of Roosevelt in Georgia; Franklin Delano Roosevelt Memorial Museum opened in April 2004 with expanded and updated exhibits and films; Superintendent (vacant); Volunteer Coordinator LYNN BARFIELD.

Hawaii

Bernice P. Bishop Museum: 1525 Bernice St, Honolulu, HI 96704; tel. (808) 847-3511; fax (808) 841-8968; e-mail library@bishopmuseum.org; internet www.bishopmuseum.org; f. 1889; devoted to the study of natural and cultural history in the Pacific; depts of Hawaiian and Pacific Studies (ethnology and archaeology), Natural Sciences (botany, entomology, zoology, ichthyology, malacology, vertebrate and

invertebrate zoology), Education, Library and Archives; lectures, films, education programmes, permanent and temporary exhibits; Richard T. Mamiya Science Adventure Center; library of 115,000 vols, 1m. historic photographs; Pres. MICHAEL T. CHINAKA; publ. *Ka'Elele* (monthly).

Attached institutes:

Hawaii Maritime Center: Pier 7, Honolulu Harbor, Honolulu, HI 96813; tel. (808) 563-6373; maritime history; two ships, Hōkūle'a (Polynesian double-hulled canoe) and The Falls of Clyde (18th-century, 4-masted, fully rigged).

Amy B.H. Greenwell Ethnobotanical Garden: POB 1053, Captain Cook, HI 96704; tel. (808) 323-3318; fax (808) 323-2394; e-mail agg@bishopmuseum.org; 200 species of endemic, indigenous and Polynesian introduced plants; insect house; archaeological site.

Museum of the Honolulu Academy of Arts: 900 South Beretania St, Honolulu, HI 96814-1495; tel. (808) 532-8700; fax (808) 532-8787; e-mail info@honoluluacademy.org; internet www.honoluluacademy.org; f. 1927; museum and art school; Western and Asian art collns; educational programmes for adults and young people; Doris Duke Theatre with frequent films, lectures, concerts and performances; outdoor gardens; arts festivals; guided tours/gallery talks; art classes and educational programmes for children and adults; spec. exhibitions; Robert Allerton Art Research Library; 8,865 mems; library of 45,000 vols; spec. colln 8,000 woodblock prints; Dir STEPHEN LITTLE; publ. *Calendar News* (bulletin for members, 6 a year).

Shangri La: 4055 Papu Circle, Honolulu, HI 96816; tel. (808) 734-1941; fax (808) 732-4361; internet www.shangrilahawaii.org; f. 2002 as a bequest of the collector Doris Duke; 3,500 items of Islamic art and craft: architectural features, furniture, ceramics, textiles and paintings; attached to the Doris Duke Foundation for Islamic Art; library of 600 vols; Exec. Dir DEBORAH POPE; Curator Dr AMY LANDAU.

Idaho

Boise Art Museum: 670 Julia Davis Dr., Boise, ID 83702; tel. (208) 345-8330; internet www.boiseartmuseum.org; private, non-profit; f. 1931 as the Boise Art Asscn; regional and nat. artwork; permanent colln of 2,300 works of 20th-century American art with emphasis on artists of the Pacific Northwest, American Realism and ceramics; education programme; Exec. Dir MELANIE FALES.

Nez Perce National Historical Park: 39063 US Highway 95, Spalding, ID 83540; tel. (208) 843-7001; fax (208) 843-7003; e-mail nepe_visitor_information@nps.gov; internet www.nps.gov/nepe; govt, Nat. Park Service; Nez Perce (Nimiipuu) history and culture; 38 sites marking important event related to war of 1877; incl. White Bird Battlefield, Big Hole National Battlefield and Bear Paw Battlefield.

Illinois

Adler Planetarium: 1300 South Lake Shore Dr., Chicago, IL 60605-2403; tel. (312) 922-7827; fax (312) 322-2257; internet www.adlerplanetarium.org; f. 1930 by Max Adler; the circular planetarium chamber seats 280 persons, with a hemispherical dome 68 ft wide and Zeiss VI projector; the exhibition area houses one of the world's finest collns of astronomical artifacts, incl. the world's oldest known window sundial (dated 1529) and a telescope made by William Herschel; some of the oldest artefacts in the colln date back to 12th-century Persia; exhibits in astronomy and related sciences; 190-seat theatre featuring real-time interactive virtual environments; library: library of c. 5,000 vols; classrooms; photographic laboratories; solar telescope; several telescopes incl. 20-inch diam. Cassegrain reflector equipped with a charge-coupled device (in the Doane Observatory, east of the planetarium); programme incl. sky shows, classes in astronomy, navigation and telescope making; grade school programme; public observation sessions, demonstrations, lectures and films; Pres. Dr PAUL H. KNAPPENBERGER, Jr.

Art Institute of Chicago: 111 South Michigan Ave, Chicago, IL 60603-6404; tel. (312) 443-3600; e-mail webmaster@artic.edu; internet www.artic.edu; f. 1879; American painting and sculpture; European painting since 13th century, medieval and Renaissance art; prints and drawings; sculpture; Asian arts (of 5,000 years); African and Amerindian art; textiles; decorative arts; photography; architecture; School of Art; Ryerson Library, f. 1901; Burnham Library of Architecture, f. 1912; library: total of 180,000 vols and 340,000 slides on art and architecture; also Kraft Education Center; Dir JAMES CUNO; publs *News and Events* (6 a year), *Museum Studies* (2 a year).

Field Museum: 1400 South Lake Shore Dr., Chicago, IL 60605; tel. (312) 922-9410; fax (312) 427-7269; internet www.fieldmuseum .org; f. by Marshall Field in 1893; depts of Anthropology, Botany, Geology, Zoology (birds, fishes, insects, invertebrates, mammals, reptiles and amphibians); library of 215,000 vols; large colln of books on China, incl. several thousand in Chinese; Ornithological Section incl. many rare and beautifully illustrated vols; Pres. JOHN W. McCARTER, Jr; publs *Fieldiana* (technical publications in anthropology, botany, geology, and zoology), *The Field Museum Bulletin*, *General Guide*.

Illinois State Museum: Spring and Edwards Sts, Springfield, IL 62706; tel. (217) 782-7386; fax (217) 782-1254; internet www.museum.state.il.us; f. 1877; natural history and anthropology (recreations of American Indian villages and natural habitats); 'At Home in the Heartland' exhibition of decorative arts in Illinois since 1750; historic and contemporary works by Illinois artists are exhibited in the fine and applied arts galleries, and *A Place for Discovery* is a 'hands on' learning centre; library: library of over 10,000 vols mainly relative to collns; Dir BONNIE W. STYLES; publs *Events and Activities* (quarterly), *Impressions* (quarterly), *The Living Museum* (quarterly).

Attached museums and galleries:

ISM Chicago Gallery: James R. Thompson Center, Chicago, IL 60601-3219; tel. (312) 814-5322; fax (312) 814-3471; internet ; exhibitions of art created by past and contemporary Illinois artists and artisans.

Dickson Mounds Museum: 10956 North Dickson Mounds Rd, Lewistown, IL 61542; tel. (309) 547-3721; fax (309) 547-3189; internet www.museum.state.il.us/ismsites/ dickson/geninfo.html; on-site archaeological museum covering 12,000 years of Illinois history; Dir Dr MICHAEL WIANT (acting).

Illinois State Museum at Springfield: Spring and Edwards Sts, Springfield, IL 62706-5000; tel. (217) 782-7386; fax (217) 782-1254; e-mail info@museum.state.il.us; internet www.museum.state.il.us/ismsites/ main/geninfo.html; natural and cultural heritage of Illinois; Dir BONNIE W. STYLES.

Lockport Gallery: 201 West 10th St, Lockport, IL 60441; tel. (815) 838-7400; fax (815) 838-7448; e-mail lockport-Info@ museum.state.il.us; internet www .museum.state.il.us/ismsites/lockport/gen-info.html; f. 1987; exhibitions of art created by past and contemporary Illinois artists and artisans; Dir JIM ZIMMER.

John G. Shedd Aquarium: 1200 South Lake Shore Dr., Chicago, IL 60605; tel. (312) 939-2435; fax (312) 939-8069; e-mail contactus@sheddaquarium.org; internet www.sheddaquarium.org; f. 1930; exhibits both fresh-water and salt-water species; oceanarium re-creates a Pacific Northwest Coast environment and a Falkland Islands habitat; 90,000-gallon Coral Reef exhibit; Wild Reef re-creates a coral reef in the Philippines and offers a diverse shark habitat; Pres. and CEO TED A. BEATTIE.

Lincoln Park Zoological Gardens: 2001 North Clark St, Chicago, IL 60614-3895; tel. (312) 742-2000; fax (312) 742-2137; e-mail info@lpzoo.org; internet www.lpzoo.org; f. 1868; specimens of mammals, birds, reptiles, and amphibians; farm; specialities: great apes, primates, perching birds, snakes, big cats; spec. programmes: Farm in the Zoo, Travelling Zoo and Endangered Species educational programmes; scientific studies incl. nutrition, behaviour, reproductive biology, physiology, African, Asian and South American field work; library of 2,000 vols; Dir KEVIN J. BELL; publs *Animal Inventory* (annual), *Lincoln Park Zoo Magazine* (quarterly).

Research centres:

Lester E. Fisher Center for the Study and Conservation of Apes:; f. 2004; multidisciplinary ape research and conservation programme; initiatives in animal health, epidemiology, nutrition, behaviour, population biology and conservation of wild populations and study of ape cognition, endocrinology and citizen science; Dir Dr ELIZABETH V. LONSDORF.

Alexander Center for Applied Population Biology:; f. 2005; research in small population biology; Population Management Centre conducts population biology-based analyses for captive populations at North American zoos; Dir Dr JOANNE EARNHARDT.

Davee Center for Epidemiology and Endocrinology:; f. 2001; studies on health in captive and wild animal populations; Dir DOMINIC A. TRAVIS.

Museum of Science and Industry: 57th St and Lake Shore Dr., Chicago, IL 60637; tel. (773) 684-1414; fax (773) 684-7141; e-mail msi@msichicago.org; internet www .msichicago.org; f. 1933; metals, power, physics, chemistry, electronics, transportation, petroleum, food, space eng., communications and medical sciences; over 2,000 exhibit units incl. re-creation of a coal mine, German submarine, walk-through model of human heart, Colleen Moore's Fairy Castle, 'Yesterday's Main Street', actual Apollo 8 spacecraft, Henry Crown Space Center, 'Omnimax' theater, and exhibits on space exploration and energy research; Pres. and CEO DAVID MESENA.

Oriental Institute Museum: 1155 East 58th St, Chicago, IL 60637; tel. (773) 702-9514; fax (773) 702-9853; e-mail oi-museum@ uchicago.edu; internet oi.uchicago.edu; f. 1919; holds 180,000 registered objects from Egypt, Iran, Iraq, Israel, Jordan, Palestinian Territories, Syria, Sudan and Turkey; research arm supports archaeological excavations in Iran, Turkey, Syria, Sudan and Egypt; Institute has dictionary projects in Demotic Egyptian, Sumerian, Akkadian and Hittite; library of 60,000 vols; Museum Dir GEOFF EMBERLING; Head Registrar HELEN McDONALD; publ. *Journal of Near Eastern Studies*.

Indiana

Indiana State Museum: 650 West Washington St, Indianapolis, IN 46204; tel. (317) 232-1637; e-mail museumcommunication@dnr.in.gov; internet www.in.gov/ism; f. 1888; cultural and natural history ranging from prehistoric fossils to current popular culture items; Dir of Collns REX GARNIEWICZ.

Indianapolis Museum of Art: 4000 Michigan Rd, Indianapolis, IN 46208-3326; tel. (317) 923-1331; e-mail ima@ima.museum; internet www.ima-art.org; f. 1883; library of 10,000 vols; files on 28,000 artists, incl. 3,800 Indiana artists; spec. collns incl. Samuel Josefowitz Colln of Gauguin and the School of Pont-Aven, Holliday Colln of Neo-Impressionism, featuring the work of Georges Seurat and his followers, the largest colln of works by J. M. W. Turner outside the UK, a comprehensive Chinese colln, Japanese Edo-period paintings, more than 2,000 objects in the African art colln; also fashion arts, textiles and West Asian rugs; incl. Virginia B. Fairbanks Art and Nature Park and Oldfields–Lilly House and Gardens.

Iowa

Iowa Museum Association: POB 65314, West Des Moines, IA 50265; tel. (515) 274-1355; e-mail imabailey@mchsi.com; internet www.iowamuseums.org; 184 mems; Pres. SANDI YODER; Exec. Dir JENNIE BAILEY.

Museum of Art: 150 North Riverside Dr., Iowa City, IA 52242-1789; tel. (319) 335-1727; fax (319) 335-3677; e-mail uima@uiowa .edu; internet www.uiowa.edu/uima; attached to Univ. of Iowa; f. 1969; European and American Art since 1900, prints and drawings before 1900, Arts of Africa, Art of the Ancient Americas, Native North American Art and Ceramic Arts; Provost MICHAEL J. HOGAN.

Museum of Natural History and Old Capitol Museum: 10 Macbride Hall, Iowa City, IA 52242; tel. (319) 335-0480; fax (319) 335-0653; internet www.uiowa.edu/~nathist; attached to Univ. of Iowa; spec. collns incl. geology, ecology and native cultures; giant Ice Age sloth; North American birds; Mammal Hall incl. a skeleton of an Atlantic Right Whale; Dir PAMELA TRIMPE.

Kansas

Natural History Museum, University of Kansas: Dyche Hall, 1345 Jayhawk Blvd, Lawrence, KS 66045-7561; tel. (785) 864-4540; fax (785) 864-5335; e-mail kunhm@ku .edu; internet www.nhm.ku.edu; f. 1870; attached to Univ. of Kansas; 8m. specimens of plants and animals, from prehistoric to living species and from every continent and ocean; collns: entomology, herbarium, herpetology, ichthyology, ichthyology tissue, invertebrate palaeontology, invertebrate zoology, mammalogy, ornithology, palaeobotany, vertebrate palaeontology; Dir LEONARD KRISHTALKA.

Spencer Museum of Art, University of Kansas: 1301 Mississippi St, Lawrence, KS 66045-7500; tel. (785) 864-4710; fax (785) 864-3112; e-mail spencerart@ku.edu; internet www.spencerart.ku.edu; f. 1928; specializes in medieval art, European painting and sculpture, American painting and graphics, photography, Japanese Edo prints and painting and modern Chinese painting; also houses Kress Foundation Dept of Art History and the Murphy Library of Art and Architecture; library of 105,000 vols in

Murphy Library of Art and Architecture; Dir SARALYN REECE HARDY; publs *The Franklin D. Murphy Lecture* (annual), *Register* (annual).

Kentucky

Behringer-Crawford Museum: 1600 Montague Rd, Devou Park, Covington, KY 41011; tel. (859) 491-4003; e-mail info@bcmuseum.org; internet www.bcmuseum.org; f. 1888; regional cultural history, minerals, fossils, and American Indian artifacts.

Kentucky Historical Society: 100 West Broadway, Frankfort, KY 40601; tel. (502) 564-1792; e-mail khstours@ky.gov; internet history.ky.gov; incl. Thomas D. Clark Center for Kentucky History, Old State Capitol, and Kentucky Military History Museum; incl. a 'Historymobile' and 'Museums to go'.

Museums:

Thomas D. Clark Center for Kentucky History: prehistoric times to the present: First Kentuckians (10,000 BC to AD 1750), The Kentucky Frontier (1750–1800), The Antebellum Age (1800–1860), War and Aftermath (1860–1875), Continuity and Change (1875–1900), The New Century (1900–1930), Depression and War (1930–1950), and Many Sides of Kentucky (1950 to present); Pure Kentucky highlights the lives and contributions of famous Kentuckians through artifacts.

Old State Capitol:; f. 1830; nat. historical landmark introduced Greek-Revival architecture to the USA west of the Appalachian Mountains; bldg served as capitol of the Commonwealth of Kentucky from 1830 to 1910; site of the assassination of William Goebel, the only governor in US history to die in office as a result of assassination; recreation of State Law Library.

Kentucky Military History Museum: the Old State Arsenal, a 2-storey brick Gothic-Revival 'castle' standing on a cliff overlooking the Kentucky River and the downtown area, built in 1850, houses the weapons and equipment of the Kentucky Militia, State Guard, and other volunteer military orgs; collns of firearms, edged weapons, artillery, uniforms, flags, photographs, personal items.

Louisiana

New Orleans Museum of Art: POB 19123, New Orleans, LA 70179; 1 Collins Diboll Circle, City Park, New Orleans, LA 70124; tel. (504) 488-2631; fax (504) 484-6662; e-mail webmaster@noma.org; internet www.noma.org; f. 1911; paintings, sculpture, prints, drawings, photographs and decorative arts; spec. colln(s) incl. history of glass; 150-year colln of photographs; Japanese paintings of the Edo Period; Chinese pottery and stone sculpture; 17th- to 20th-century French paintings; Italian and Spanish paintings from Renaissance and Baroque periods; 16th- to 18th-century Low Countries paintings; tribal arts of sub-Saharan Africa; 18th- and 19th-century French porcelain; 20th-century American art and pottery; Spanish colonial Latin American paintings and sculpture; English and Continental portrait miniatures; P. C. Fabergé jewelled objects; 18th- to 20th-century American and English silver; arts of pre-Columbian Mexico, and of Central and South America; North American Indian arts; Sculpture Garden containing 50 works by Henry Moore, Fernando Botero, Elisabeth Frink, Barbara Hepworth and others; library of 30,000 vols; Dir E. JOHN BULLARD; publ. *Arts Quarterly*.

Maine

Maine Archives and Museums: POB 5024, Augusta, ME 04333; tel. (207) 441-1410; e-mail mam@gwi.net; internet www.mainemuseums.org; directory of 201 museums in Maine; Pres. EDWARD S. ALLEN.

Maryland

Baltimore Museum of Art: 10 Art Museum Dr., Baltimore, MD 21218-3898; tel. (443) 573-1700; fax (443) 573-1582; internet www.artbma.org; f. 1914; total colln of 90,000 items; Cone Colln of post-impressionist and modern art (incl. 500 works by Matisse, and examples by Picasso, Cézanne and Van Gogh); West Wing for Contemporary Art housing 16 galleries of art since 1960s; Old Master and 19th-century European paintings and sculpture; prints, drawings and photographs since 15th century; American paintings, sculpture, and decorative arts from 17th–19th centuries; Maryland period rooms; African, Asian, Native American, and Oceanic art; 3-acre sculpture garden; library of 55,000 vols; Chair. SUZANNE F. COHEN; Dir DOREEN BOLGER; publ. *BMA Today* (members' magazine, quarterly).

Maryland Historical Society, Museum and Library of Maryland History: 201 W Monument St, Baltimore, MD 21201; tel. (410) 685-3750; fax (410) 385-2105; internet www.mdhs.org; f. 1844; exhibits Francis Scott Key's original MS of The Star-Spangled Banner and the war of 1812; 3,000 paintings and miniatures; 700 pieces of furniture; sculpture, drawings, silver; ceramics; jewellery, textiles; library: library of over 90,000 vols, etc.; MS room incls Calvert Papers, papers of Benjamin Henry Latrobe, over 1,300 letters and documents of the Lords Baltimore and their families, genealogical colln and many hundreds of prints and drawings; maritime colln emphasizing crafts of Chesapeake Bay; Dir ROB ROGERS; publs *Maryland Historical Magazine* (quarterly), *News and Notes* (quarterly).

Attached museums:

Baltimore Civil War Museum: President Street Station, 601 President St, Baltimore, MD 21202; tel. (410) 385-5188.

Fells Point Maritime Museum: 1724 Thames St, Baltimore, MD 21231; tel. (410) 732-0278.

Walters Art Museum:; e-mail croberts@thewalters.org 600 North Charles St, Baltimore, MD 21201; tel. (410) 547-9000; fax (410) 783-7969; internet www.thewalters.org; f. 1931; collns range from pre-dynastic Egypt to 20th-century Europe; Chinese, Japanese and Indian art, Ancient Egyptian, Greek and Roman art, Byzantine art, Romanesque, early Gothic art, later Gothic art, Renaissance sculpture and decorative arts, manuscript illumination, incunabula, arms and armour, old master paintings, 19th-century paintings, decorative arts; library of 120,000 vols; Dir GARY VIKAN; publs *Journal* (annual), *The Walters Magazine* (quarterly).

Massachusetts

Adams National Historical Park: 135 Adams St, Quincy, MA 02169-1749; tel. (617) 773-1177; fax (617) 472-7562; e-mail ADAM_Visitor_Center@nps.gov; internet www.nps.gov/adam; donated to the USA in December 1946 by the Adams Memorial Soc.; designated a nat. historic site under the admin. of the Nat. Park Service of the Dept of the Interior; built in 1731 by Major Leonard Vassall of Boston; bought by John Adams in 1787; at the end of his term he lived in the house until his death in 1826; the house then passed to his son, John Quincy Adams, in the middle of his term as sixth Pres.; the Adams family continued to live there until 1927; the house, contents, and garden are as the Adams family left them; the separate stone library, standing in the garden, was built in 1870 by Charles Francis Adams, and contains c. 14,000 vols, comprising most of the libraries of John Quincy Adams and Charles Francis Adams and some of the libraries of John Adams, Charles Francis Adams II, Henry and Brooks Adams.

Concord Museum: 200 Lexington Rd, Concord, MA 01742; tel. (978) 369-9763; fax (978) 369-9660; e-mail cm1@concordmuseum.org; internet www.concordmuseum.org; f. 1886; history and decorative arts museum with 16 period rooms and galleries, with artefacts from Concord area; museum rooms chronicle life in Concord from Native American habitation to present; spec. collns incl. relics from the battle at North Bridge, the largest colln of Thoreau artifacts from his stay at Walden Pond, and the contents of Emerson's study; Dir DESIRÉE CALDWELL; publ. *Newsletter* (quarterly).

Harvard University Art Museums: 32 Quincy St, Cambridge, MA 02138; tel. (617) 495-9400; internet www.artmuseums.harvard.edu; f. 1891; incorporates the Fogg Art Museum (Western art from the Middle Ages to the present), Busch-Reisinger Museum (art of German-speaking countries), Arthur M. Sackler Museum (ancient, Asian, Islamic and later Indian art); library of 300,000 vols; 1.6m. slides; study and historic photographs; Dir THOMAS W. LENTZ.

Museum of Fine Arts, Boston: 465 Huntington Ave, Boston, MA 02115-5523; tel. (617) 267-9300; fax (617) 267-0280; e-mail webmaster@mfa.org; internet www.mfa.org; f. 1870; colln incl. 450,000 objects; rare and important works incl. masters of American painting, Impressionist art, Asian scrolls and Egyptian mummies; library of 200,000 vols and catalogues; Dir MALCOLM ROGERS.

Museum of Science: Science Park, Boston, MA 02114; tel. (617) 723-2500; fax (617) 589-0454; e-mail information@mos.org; internet www.mos.org; f. 1830; exhibits on astronomy, natural history, physical science, technology, medicine, etc.; educational programmes with more than 550 interactive exhibits; houses the Charles Hayden Planetarium, the Mugar Omni Theater and the Lyman Library; library of 40,000 vols and journals; Pres. and Dir IOANNIS N. MIAOULIS; publ. *Magazine* (2 a year).

Peabody Essex Museum: East India Sq., Salem, MA 01970-3738; tel. (978) 745-9500; fax (978) 744-6776; internet www.pem.org; f. 1799; maritime art and history, Asian, Oceanic, African and Native American art; American art and architecture; incl. Phillips Library; library of 400,000 vols; Dir DAN L. MONROE; publs *American Neptune* (quarterly), *Quarterly Review of Archaeology*.

Peabody Museum of Archaeology and Ethnology: Harvard Univ., 11 Divinity Ave, Cambridge, MA 02138; tel. (617) 496-1027; fax (617) 495-7535; e-mail peabody@fas.harvard.edu; internet www.peabody.harvard.edu; f. 1866 by George Peabody; works in close co-operation with the Dept of Anthropology of Harvard, and much of the research is jtly determined; since its founding more than 800 expeditions have been sent to every continent, resulting, with the addition of important gifts and purchases, in the building up of one of the most comprehensive collns of ethnology, archaeology and physical anthropology in the USA; the first scientific studies of Maya archaeology were made under its direction, and its collns from this area, and from Middle America generally, are extremely important; there are also collns of Old World archaeology; in ethnology, the material from the Pacific Islands is important, and the Museum is also rich in material representing the native tribes of Africa, of South America, and of the Plains and North-west Coast Indians of North America, where some of the objects date from the Lewis and Clark expedition of 1806; the archaeology of the south-western USA, incl. the Pueblo Indian area, is also strongly represented; the Tozzer Library with its 250,000 vols and pamphlets, covers the entire field of anthropology; Dir WILLIAM L. FASH; publs *Papers, Memoirs, Bulletin.*

Smith College Museum of Art: Northampton, MA 01063; tel. (413) 585-2770; fax (413) 585-2782; e-mail artmuseum@smith .edu; internet www.smith.edu/artmuseum; f. 1879; collns incl. examples from most periods and cultures with special emphasis on European and American paintings, sculpture, drawings, prints and photographs since 17th century; Dir and Chief Curator JESSICA NICOLL.

Worcester Art Museum: 55 Salisbury St, Worcester, MA 01609; tel. (508) 799-4406; fax (508) 799-4767; e-mail information@ worcesterart.org; internet www.worcesterart .org; f. 1898; 40,000-piece colln of paintings, sculptures, decorative arts, photographs, prints, drawings and new media illustrating the evolution of art from early Egyptian civilization to modern times; espec. notable are ancient Egyptian, Greek, Roman, Asian and medieval sculpture; mosaics from Antioch; a French Romanesque Chapter House; Italian and other European schools of painting from 13th century to present; American collns from 17th century to the present; pre-Columbian art; Japanese and Western prints; offers a year-round studio art and art appreciation programme; library of 45,000 vols; Dir JAMES A. WELU.

Michigan

Detroit Institute of Arts: 5200 Woodward Ave, Detroit, MI 48202; tel. (313) 833-7900; fax (313) 833-2357; internet www.dia.org; f. 1885; comprehensive fine arts collection from prehistoric to contemporary times; collection of American, Dutch, Flemish, French, Italian and German Expressionist painting; Ancient, African, Oceanic and New World Cultures; Asian, Native American, Islamic and art since the beginning of the 20th c.; graphic arts; American and European decorative arts since the beginning of the 20th c.; theatre arts collection; library of 160,000 vols; Dir GRAHAM W. J. BEAL; publs *Bulletin of the DIA* (2 a year), *Your DIA* (monthly).

Henry Ford Museum and Greenfield Village: 20900 Oakwood Blvd, POB 1970, Dearborn, MI 48121; tel. (313) 982-6001; internet www.hfmgv.org; f. 1929; indoor and outdoor museum of US history from European settlement to the present; domestic life, agriculture and industry, leisure and entertainment, transportation and communication; historic structures; archival and library holdings include 37,600 books, 146,000 periodicals, 18,500 trade catalogues, 9,000 linear feet of archival material including records of the Ford Motor Co, 1,000,000 photographic images and 50,000 graphic items; Chair. of Board WILLIAM CLAY FORD, Jr; Pres. STEVEN K. HAMP.

Minnesota

Minneapolis Institute of Arts: 2400 Third Ave South, Minneapolis, MN 55404; tel. (612) 870-3046; fax (612) 870-3004; internet www .artsmia.org; f. 1883; library of 20,000 vols; collection of 100,000 objects representing nearly every school and period of art, including European and American paintings, sculpture, decorative arts, period rooms, prints and drawings, photography, Oriental, African, Oceanic, North and South American Arts since 1500 BC; Minnich collection of botanical, zoological and fashion prints, paintings by Poussin, Rembrandt, El Greco, Goya, Manet, Monet, Renoir, Van Gogh, Matisse; Alfred F. Pillsbury collection of ancient Chinese jades and bronzes, etc.; Dir EVAN M. MAURER.

Science Museum of Minnesota: 120 W Kellogg Blvd, St. Paul, MN 55102; tel. (651) 221-9444; fax (651) 221-4777; e-mail info@ smm.org; internet www.smm.org; f. 1907; research in anthropology, biology, palaeontology, ethnology, zoology, archaeology, geology and geography; collections in the field of biology, anthropology, palaeontology, geology; outdoor research centre; a 300-seat omnitheatre; nature centre; Pres. ERIC JOLLY.

Walker Art Center: 1750 Hennepin, Minneapolis, MN 55403; tel. (612) 375-7600; fax (612) 375-7618; e-mail info@walkerart.org; internet www.walkerart.org; f. 1927; modern paintings, drawings, prints, sculpture, photography; extensive music, dance, film and video, theatre and education programmes; includes Minneapolis Sculpture Garden; library of 35,000 vols; audio and film and video archive; Dir KATHY HALBREICH; publ. *Monthly Calendar of Events.*

Mississippi

Mississippi Museum of Art: 380 South Lamar St, Jackson, MS 39201; tel. (601) 960-1515; fax (601) 960-1505; internet www .msmuseumart.org; f. 1903 by Bessie Cary Lemly as the Art Study Club; 1911 became Mississippi Art Association; 1978 current name; permanent colln of 3,800 pieces with an emphasis on mid-19th and 20th-century American art; incl. paintings, sculptures, prints, drawings, and photographs by Albert Bierstadt, Arthur B. Davies, Robert Henri, George Inness, Georgia O'Keeffe, Thomas Sully, J. A. M. Whistler; photographs and works on paper incl. works by Thomas Hart Benton, Alexander Calder, William Eggleston, Walker Evans, Andy Warhol, Eudora Welty; Annie Laurie Swaim Hearin Memorial Exhibition Series hosts world-class exhibitions every 2 years; educational programmes for adults and children; Dir BETSY BRADLEY.

Mississippi Museum of Natural Science: 2148 Riverside Dr., Jackson, MS 39202-1353; tel. (601) 354-7303; fax (601) 354-7227; internet www.msnaturalscience.org; an aquarium system with over 200 living species of native fish, reptiles, amphibians, and aquatic invertebrates; 1,700 sq. ft greenhouse called 'The Swamp' with another 20,000 gallon aquarium, provides a home for alligators, turtles, fish, and a lush native plant garden; 200 seat auditorium, library, biological archives; Exec. Dir Dr SAM POLLES.

Walter Anderson Museum of Art: 510 Washington Ave, Ocean Springs, MS 39564-4632; tel. (228) 872-3164; fax (228) 875-4494; e-mail wama@walterandersonmuseum.org; internet www.walterandersonmuseum.org; f. 1991; watercolors, drawings, oils, block prints, ceramics, and carvings by the 3 Anderson brothers; Exec. Dir GAYLE PETTY-JOHNSON.

Missouri

Kansas City Museum: 30 West Pershing Rd, Kansas City, MO 64108-2422; tel. (816) 460-2020; fax (816) 460-2260; internet www .unionstation.org/kcmuseum.cfm; f. 1939; administered by Kansas City Museum Association; science and technology exhibitions, American Indian artefacts, costume and textile collection, natural history exhibits, planetarium, archives and reference library; Pres. Dr DAVID A. UCKO.

Nelson-Atkins Museum of Art: 4525 Oak St, Kansas City, MO 64111; tel. (816) 751-1178; fax (816) 561-4011; internet www .nelson-atkins.org; f. 1933; departments: Asian art, prints, photography, modern and contemporary art, American art, American Indian art, European art, decorative arts, ancient art, African art, education, Kansas City Sculpture Park (incl. monumental bronzes by Henry Moore); works by Thomas Hart Benton; library of 135,000 vols, 500 serials; Dir MARC F. WILSON; publ. *Calendar of Events.*

St Louis Art Museum: Forest Park, St Louis, MO 63110; f. 1907; publicly owned collection of about 30,000 art objects; important collections of American, European and Asian painting, sculpture and decorative arts, pre-Columbian and Oceanic art; library of 35,000 vols; Dir JAMES D. BURKE; publs *Bulletin, Annual Report.*

Montana

Montana Historical Society Museum: POB 201201, 225 North Roberts, Helena, MT 59620-1201; tel. (406) 444-2694; e-mail mhslibrary@mt.gov; internet mhs.mt.gov/ museum; f. 1865; collects, preserves, and interprets fine art, historical, archaeological, and ethnological artifacts that pertain to Montana and its adjoining geographic region; incl. Original Governor's Mansion and Moss Mansion Historic House; research centre; State Historic Preservation Officer Dr MARK BAUMLER; publ. *Montana The Magazine of Western History* (quarterly).

Museum of the Rockies: 600 West Kagy Blvd, Bozeman, MT 59717; tel. (406) 444-2694; e-mail wwwmor@montana.edu; internet museumoftherockies.org; f. 1957, gifted by Dr Caroline McGill; attached to Montana State Univ.; independent, non-profit; cultural and natural history; paleontology colln; on-site 19th-century farm; incl. Planetarium, dinosaur complex and Tyrannosaurus rex; Dean and Dir SHELDON McKAMEY.

Yellowstone Art Museum: 401 North 27th St, Billings, MT 59101; tel. (406) 256-6804; e-mail artinfo@artmuseum.org; internet yellowstone.artmuseum.org; f. 1964 as Yellowstone Arts Center; contemporary and historic art; Montana Colln of 3,000 regional artefacts; Virginia Snook Colln incl. illustrations from Will James, paintings and drawings from Joseph Henry Sharp, Charles M. Russell; Exec. Dir ROBYN G. PETERSON.

Nebraska

Nebraska State Historical Society: POB 82554, 1500 R St, Lincoln, NE 68501; internet www.nebraskahistory.org; state; state-wide network of historical sites and museums; incl. Chimney Rock Nat. Historic Site, Fort Robinson Museum, Gerald R. Ford Conservation Center, John G. Neihardt State Historic Site, K St Govt Records Facility, Lincoln Childrens Museum, Museum of Nebraska History, Neligh Mill State Historic Site, Senator George W. Norris State Historic Site, Thomas P. Kennard House Nebraska Statehood Memorial, Willa Cather State Historic Site; Pres. PETER BLEED.

University of Nebraska State Museum: 307 Morrill Hall, Lincoln, NE 68588-0338; tel. (402) 472-2642; internet www.museum .unl.edu; incl. Planetarium; collns and research in following: Anthropology, Botany, Entomology, Invertebrate Paleontology,

Parasitology, Vertebrate Paleontology, Zoology; Dir PRISCILLA C. GREW.

Affiliated Museums:

Ashfall Fossil Beds State Historical Park: 6930 517th Ave, Royal, NE 68773; tel. (402) 893-2000; e-mail ashfall2@unl.edu; internet ashfall.unl.edu; fossil site of int. significance left intact for public viewing; Superintendent RICK OTTO.

Trailside Museum of Natural History: Fort Robinson State Park, Crawford, NE 69339; tel. (308) 665-2929; internet trailside.unl.edu; geological and natural history.

Lester F. Larsen Tractor Test and Power Museum: POB 830833, Lincoln, NE 68583-0833; tel. (402) 472-8389; fax (402) 472-8367; e-mail tractormuseum2@unl.edu; internet tractormuseum.unl.edu; to collect, preserve, research and interpret the traditions and technologies of agriculture; Dir BILL SPLINTER.

Nevada

Fleischmann Planetarium and Science Center: POB 272, 1650 North Virginia St, Reno, NV 89557; tel. (775) 784-4812; fax (775) 784-4822; internet planetarium.unr.nevada.edu; attached to Univ. of Nevada, Reno; f. 1964; public star shows and large-format films; Spitz SciDome digital projector; Dir Dr DEE HENDERSON.

Nevada Museum of Art: 160 West Liberty St, Reno, NV 89501; tel. (702) 486-5205; fax (702) 486-5172; internet www.nevadaart.org; f. 1931; Altered Landscape incl. 600 pieces of contemporary landscape photographs; Contemporary Colln focuses on West Coast and Nevada-based artists; Sierra Nevada/Great Basin Colln surveys artists' impressions of the landscape over 150 years; Historical Colln incl. paintings and sculptures; work-ethic themed E. L. Wiegand Colln; Curator ANN WOLF.

Nevada State Museum and Historical Society: 700 Twin Lakes Dr., Las Vegas, NV 89107; tel. (702) 486-5205; fax (702) 486-5172; internet www.springspreserve.org/html/nsm.html; Biological Sciences, Earth Sciences, Regional History; Dir DAVID MILLMAN.

New Hampshire

Currier Museum of Art: 201 Myrtle Way, Manchester, NH 03104-4393; tel. (603) 669-6144; fax (603) 669-7194; internet www.currier.org; f. 1929; art museum featuring European and American paintings, decorative arts, photographs and sculptures; permanent collection includes words by Picasso, Matisse, Monet, O'Keeffe, Calder and Wyeth; owns Frank Lloyd Wright's 1950 Zimmerman House; year-round exhibitions, tours and classical music performances; Dir SUSAN STRICKLER.

New Jersey

Montclair Art Museum: 3 South Mountain Ave, Montclair, NJ 07042-1747; tel. (973) 746-5555; fax (973) 746-9118; e-mail mail@montclair-art.com; internet www.montclair-art.com; opened 1914; American art since mid-18th century, incl. paintings, sculpture, works on paper, costumes and bookplates; Native American art and artefacts; library: LeBrun library of 50,000 vols; 20,000 colour slides; Pres. WILLIAM H. TURNER, III; Dir ELLEN S. HARRIS; publ. *Members Bulletin* (6 a year).

New Mexico

Museum of New Mexico: POB 2087, Santa Fé, NM 87504-2087; internet www.museumofnewmexico.org; f. 1909; a state agency, under Board of Regents appointed by Governor, divisions in anthropology, history, fine arts, international folk art, Indian arts and culture, state monuments located in separate buildings; library: custody of combined libraries approx. 26,000 vols; Dir THOMAS A. LIVESAY; publ. *El Palacio* (quarterly).

Constituent museums:

Museum of Fine Arts: 107 West Palace Ave, Santa Fe, NM 87501; tel. (505) 476-5072; fax (505) 476-5076; internet www.mfasantafe.org; f. 1917; 23,000 objects, focusing on the areas of photography and works on paper; paintings, sculpture and furniture since the beginning of the 20th c.; Curator TIM RODGERS.

Museum of Indian Arts and Culture: 708-710 Camino Lejo, Santa Fe, NM 87505; tel. (505) 476-1250; fax (505) 476-1330; internet www.miaclab.org; Native art and material culture; includes Laboratory of Anthropology; Curator JULIA CLIFTON.

Museum of International Folk Art: 706 Camino Lejo, Santa Fe, NM 87505; tel. (505) 476-1200; fax (505) 476-1300; internet www.moifa.org; 130,000 artefacts.

Palace of the Governors: 105 West Palace Ave, Santa Fe, NM 87501; tel. (505) 476-5100; fax (505) 476-5104; internet www.palaceofthegovernors.org; constructed in the early 17th c. as Spain's seat of government in what is today the American South-West; chronicles the history of Santa Fe, as well as New Mexico and the wider region; Dir FRANCES LEVINE.

Wheelwright Museum of the American Indian: 704 Camino Lejo, POB 5153, Santa Fe, NM 87502; tel. (505) 982-4636; fax (505) 989-7386; e-mail info@wheelwright.org; internet www.wheelwright.org; f. 1937; access by appointment; houses collections of artefacts, archives, sound recordings and photographs, documenting Native American (especially Navajo) culture, both historic and contemporary; contemporary and traditional American Indian art; Dir JONATHAN BATKIN.

New York

Albright-Knox Art Gallery: 1285 Elmwood Ave, Buffalo, NY 14222; tel. (716) 882-8700; fax (716) 882-1958; e-mail corlick@albrightknox.org; internet www.albrightknox.org; f. 1862; colln of paintings since the 18th century, with emphasis on American and European contemporary artists; sculpture; prints and drawings; photographs; Dir of Art Gallery LOUIS GRACHOS; Sr Curator Dr DOUGLAS DREISHPOON.

American Museum of Natural History: Central Park West at 79th St, New York, NY 10024-5192; tel. (212) 769-5100; internet www.amnh.org; f. 1869; depts of anthropology, earth and planetary sciences, entomology, herpetology, ichthyology, invertebrates, mammalogy, mineral sciences, ornithology, vertebrate palaeontology; library: see Libraries and Archives; Chair. Board of Trustees LEWIS W. BERNARD; Pres. ELLEN V. FUTTER; publs *American Museum Novitates, AMNH Bulletin, Anthropological Papers, Curator, Natural History, Rotunda.*

Attached institution:

Hayden Planetarium: Rose Center for Earth and Space, 81st St and Central Park West, New York, NY 10024; f. 1935; Zeiss Star Projector and more than 250 special effects projectors are used on a 75-ft diameter dome; c. 9,000 stars are projected in the Planetarium heavens; new sky-show several times a year; lectures, educational courses; Chair. Dr WILLIAM A. GUTSCH, Jr.

Brooklyn Botanic Garden: 1000 Washington Ave, Brooklyn, NY 11225; tel. (718) 623-7200; fax (718) 622-7839; e-mail publicaffairsoffice@bbg.org; internet www.bbg.org; f. 1910; living colln of 12,000 species and varieties; herbarium with 200,000 specimens; education programmes, children's garden, art and horticulture classes, cultural programmes, guided tours, plant information service; library of 55,000 vols; Chair. of the Board EARL D. WEINER; Pres. SCOTT MEDBURY; publ. *Plants & Gardens News* (3 a year).

Brooklyn Children's Museum: 145 Brooklyn Ave, Brooklyn, NY 11213; tel. (718) 735-4400; fax (718) 604-7442; internet www.brooklynkids.org; f. 1899; world's first children's museum; teaching colln of more than 27,000 ethnographic objects and natural science specimens, interactive technological exhibits on science and culture; Children's Resource Library; Portable Colln Loan Program for schools; special cultural performances, participatory activities for gen. public, school classes, groups, workshops; Pres. CAROL ENSEKI.

Brooklyn Museum of Art: 200 Eastern Parkway, Brooklyn, NY 11238-6052; tel. (718) 638-5000; fax (718) 638-3731; e-mail information@brooklynmuseum.org; internet www.brooklynmuseum.org; f. 1890; native American art; Peruvian textiles; pre-Columbian gold; Costa Rican sculpture; collns from Africa, Melanesia and Polynesia; collns from China, Korea, Southeast Asia, Japan, India and Persia; Colonial South American art; American period rooms; sculpture garden; American and European paintings; Prints and Drawings; Ancient Art of the Near East, Egypt, Greece and Rome; American and European costumes; American glass, pewter and silver; contemporary paintings and sculpture; art reference library and Egyptological library (170,000 vols and periodicals); Dir Dr ARNOLD L. LEHMAN.

Buffalo Museum of Science: 1020 Humboldt Parkway, Buffalo, NY 14211; tel. (716) 896-5200; fax (716) 897-6723; internet www.sciencebuff.org; f. 1861; administered by Buffalo Society of Natural Sciences; exhibit halls feature insects, dinosaurs and other fossils, birds, wild flowers and fungi, vertebrates, minerals, flora and fauna of the Niagara Frontier, life in ancient Egypt, solar system and space exploration, geology; solar and lunar observatory; loan collns, lectures, day and evening classes, etc.; library of 45,000 vols, 400 journals; Pres. and CEO CARROLL SIMON.

Cooper-Hewitt, National Design Museum, Smithsonian Institution: 2 East 91st St, New York, NY 10128; tel. (212) 849-8400; fax (212) 860-6909; internet ndm.si.edu; f. 1895 as the Cooper Union Museum; administered by the Smithsonian Instn; 250,000 items, incl. collns of original drawings and designs for architecture and the decorative arts; prints since 15th century; textiles, lace, woodwork and furniture, ceramics, glass, etc.; drawings and paintings by F. E. Church, W. Homer and other 19th-century American artists; exhibitions change regularly, each one focusing on aspects of contemporary or historical design; incl. Design Resource Center, a modern study facility, housing the depts of Product Design and Decorative Arts, Textiles, and Wall-coverings; the Center is linked to the Andrew Carnegie Mansion by the Agnes Bourne Bridge Gallery; the Library, the Drue Heinz Study Center for Drawings and Prints, and the Henry Luce Study Room for American Art are located in the Carnegie Mansion; library of 70,000 vols, incl. 6,500 rare books; Dir PAUL WARWICK THOMPSON.

Dia: Beacon Riggio Galleries: 3 Beekman St, Beacon, NY 12508; tel. (845) 440-0100; fax (845) 440-0092; e-mail info@diaart.org; internet www.diacenter.org; f. 2003; administered by Dia Art Foundation; works by artists who have come to prominence since the early 1960s; additional site in New York, Dia: Chelsea; Chair. LEONARD RIGGIO.

Frick Collection: 1 East 70th St, New York, NY 10021; tel. (212) 288-0700; fax (212) 628-4417; e-mail info@frick.org; internet www .frick.org; f. 1920; European paintings from 13th–19th centuries; Italian Renaissance bronzes and furniture; Limoges enamels of the Renaissance; French 18th-century sculpture, furniture and porcelains; Oriental porcelains; the works of art, most of them assembled by the industrialist Henry Clay Frick; attached reference library; Dir ANNE L. POULET.

Guggenheim, Solomon R., Museum: 1071 Fifth Ave at 89th St, New York, NY 10128-0173; tel. (212) 423-3500; fax (212) 423-3650; internet www.guggenheim.org; f. 1937; bldg designed by Frank Lloyd Wright; permanent colln of 6,000 works since the Post-Impressionist era, augmented by the Justin K. Thannhauser Colln of Impressionist and Post-Impressionist masterpieces, incl. large collns of Brancusi sculptures, Kandinsky paintings and graphics, and works by Klee, Braque, Chagall, Delaunay, Dubuffet, Léger, Marc, Mondrian and Picasso, and the Panza Colln of American Minimalist paintings and sculptures and Conceptual pieces; a continuous programme of loan exhibitions is presented, drawn from its own colln and from leading public and private collns throughout the world; library: research library of c. 20,000 vols; Dir THOMAS KRENS; Sr Curator GERMANO CELANT; Chief Operating Officer MARC STEGLITZ.

Attached museum:

    Guggenheim Museum SoHo: 575 Broadway, New York, NY 10012-4233; tel. (212) 423-3500.

Hispanic Society of America Museum: Broadway, between 155th and 156th Sts, New York, NY 10032; tel. (212) 926-2234; fax (212) 690-0743; e-mail info@hispanicsociety .org; internet www.hispanicsociety.org; f. 1904; free museum concentrated on the culture of the Iberian Peninsula and Latin America: paintings, prints and drawings (14th century to present), sculpture (13th century to present), archaeology, decorative arts (ceramics, textiles, metalwork, furniture); reference library and photograph files; Dir Dr MITCHELL A. CODDING; Curator of Paintings and Drawings MARCUS BURKE; Curator of Iconography PATRICK LENAGHAN.

Jewish Museum: 1109 Fifth Ave at 92nd St, New York, NY 10128; tel. (212) 423-3200; fax (212) 423-3232; e-mail info@thejm.org; internet www.thejewishmuseum.org; f. 1904; most comprehensive colln of Judaica in the USA; changing contemporary art and other exhibits of Jewish interest; spec. events, films, lectures, etc.; Dir HELEN GOLDSMITH MENSCHEL.

Metropolitan Museum of Art: 1000 Fifth Ave at 82nd St, New York, NY 10028-0198; tel. (212) 535-7710; internet www .metmuseum.org; f. 1870; depts of Art of Africa, Oceania and the Americas, American Paintings and Sculpture, American Decorative Arts, Ancient Near Eastern Art, Asian Art, Costume Institute, Drawings and Prints, European Paintings, European Sculpture and Decorative Arts, Greek and Roman Art, Islamic Art, Robert Lehman Colln, Medieval Art, Musical Instruments, Photographs, Twentieth-century Art; 2m. works of art and 6,500 objects; library of 240,000 vols,

1,400 periodicals; photograph and slide library; Pres. (vacant) EMILY K. RAFFERTY; Sr Vice-Pres. and Chief Financial Officer OLENA PASLAWSKY; Dir PHILIPPE DE MONTEBELLO; publ. *The Bulletin.*

Museum of Modern Art: 11 West 53rd St, New York, NY 10019-5497; tel. (212) 708-9400; fax (212) 708-9889; e-mail info@moma .org; internet www.moma.org; f. 1929; int. permanent colln and temporary exhibitions of paintings, drawings, prints, sculptures, industrial and graphic design, photographs, architecture and design since 1880s; large colln of American, British, French, German and Russian films, 1,200 of which are available to educational organizations; daily film showings; organizes exhibitions worldwide in all the visual arts; library: modern art library of 140,000 vols; Dir GLENN D. LOWRY.

Museum of Sex: 233 Fifth Ave at 27th St, New York, NY 10016; tel. (212) 689-6337; e-mail info@museumofsex.com; internet www.museumofsex.com; f. 2002; seeks to preserve and present the history, evolution and cultural significance of human sexuality; collns on pornography and burlesque theatre; Pres. RUTH ABRAM (founder); Curator REBECCA AMES.

The Paley Center for Media: 25 West 52nd St, New York, NY 10019; tel. (212) 621-6800; fax (212) 621-6700 *Museum in Los Angeles*, 465 North Beverly Dr., Beverly Hills, CA 90210; tel. (310) 786-1025; internet www.mtr.org; f. 1975; fmrly Museum of Television and Radio; prior to that Museum of Broadcasting; colln of 100,000 programmes and exhibition reflecting radio and television history; seminars and education programmes for groups and students; Pres. and Chief Exec. PAT MITCHELL.

Museum of the City of New York: Fifth Ave at 103rd St, New York, NY 10029; tel (212) 534-1672; fax (212) 423-0758; e-mail mcny@mcny.org; internet www.mcny.org; f. 1923; colln of 1.4m. paintings, sculptures, prints, photographs, costumes, toys reflecting historical and modern New York city; Dir SUSAN HENSHAW JONES.

The National Cartoon Museum: POB 17M, New York, NY 10118-0069; tel. (561) 391-2200; fax (561) 391-2721; e-mail inquiry@cartoon.org; internet www.cartoon .org; f. 1974; 160,000 original drawings from the following genres: animation, comic books, comic strips, gag cartoons, illustration, editorial, cartoons, greeting cards, caricature, graphic novels, sports cartoons, and computer-generated art; the colln also includes over 10,000 books on cartoons and 1,000 hours of film and tape of animated cartoons, interviews, and cartoon documentaries; as of May 2007 looking to relocate; Dir JEANNE GREEVER; publ. *Inklings* (quarterly).

National Museum of the American Indian, Smithsonian Institution: *George Gustav Heye Center*, 1 Bowling Green, New York, NY 10004; tel. (212) 514-3700; fax (212) 514-3800 *Cultural Resources Center*, 4220 Silver Hill Rd, Suitland, MD 20746; tel. (301) 238-1435 *NMAI on the National Mall*, Fourth St and Independence Ave, Washington, DC 20560; tel. (202) 633-1000; e-mail nin@ic.si .edu; internet www.nmai.si.edu; f. 1989 by Act of Congress; part of the Smithsonian Instn; dedicated to the preservation, study, exhibition and collection of the material culture of the Native peoples of the Western Hemisphere; 800,000 items, mostly from the colln of George Gustav Heye (1874–1957); library of 40,000 vols, 90,000 photographs and negatives; Dir W. RICHARD WEST.

Neue Galerie New York: 1048 Fifth Ave, New York, NY 10028; tel. (212) 628-6200; fax

(212) 628-8824; e-mail museum@neuegalerie .org; internet www.neuegalerie.org; f. 2001; early 20th-century German and Austrian art and design; Dir RENÉE PRICE.

Rochester Museum and Science Center: 657 East Ave at Goodman St, Rochester, NY 14607; tel. (585) 271-4320; internet www .rmsc.org; f. 1912; natural science, anthropology, regional history, and technology; library of 25,000 vols; Strasenburgh Planetarium: computerized, Zeiss projector, exhibits, daily astronomy and space-science shows in Star Theater; 800-acre Cumming Nature Center in the nearby Bristol Hills; environmental education facility; Gannett School of Science and Man; Pres. KATE BENNETT.

Whitney Museum of American Art: 945 Madison Ave at 75th St, New York, NY 10021; tel. (212) 570-3676; fax (212) 570-1807; e-mail feedback@whitney.org; internet www.whitney.org; f. 1930; established for the encouragement and advancement of contemporary American art; spec. exhibitions incl. Whitney biennial and historical surveys; highlights from the permanent colln of over 8,500 paintings, sculptures and works on paper; Pres. ROBERT J. HURST; Dir ADAM D. WEINBERG.

North Carolina

Morehead Planetarium and Science Center: Univ. of North Carolina at Chapel Hill, Chapel Hill, NC 27599; tel. (919) 962-1236; fax (919) 962-1238; e-mail mhplanet@ unc.edu; internet www .moreheadplanetarium.org; f. 1947; educational programmes for adults and children; daily planetarium shows; digital video theatre; Star Theatre; exhibitions; Dir TODD BOYETTE; publ. *Sundial.*

North Dakota

North Dakota Museum of Art: 261 Centennial Dr., Grand Forks, ND 58202; tel. (701) 777-4195; fax (701) 777-4425; e-mail ndmoa@ndmoa.com; internet www.ndmoa .com; private, non-profit; f. 1985; contemporary, int. art in all media starting with the early 1970s; colln contemporary Native American art; Pres. LAUREL REUTER.

State Historical Society of North Dakota Museum: 612 East Boulevard Ave, Bismarck, ND 58505-0830; tel. (701) 328-2666; fax (701) 328-3710; internet www.nd.gov/ hist; history, natural history, archeology, and ethnology; 1,050,000 items ranging from a 10,000-year-old mastodon, to a 1915 homesteader's claim shack, to 1990s youth soccer equipment; Pres. MARVYN L. KAISER; publ. *North Dakota History: Journal of the Northern Plains* (quarterly).

Attached Museums:

    Pembina State Museum: PO Box 456, Exit 215, Off Interstate 29, 805 Highway 59 Pembina, ND 58271; tel. (701) 825-6840; e-mail shspembina@nd.gov; 2 exhibition galleries; observation tower offering a grand view of the Red River Valley; preglacial fossils; bone and stone tools; frontier military forts.

Ohio

Cincinnati Art Museum: 953 Eden Park Drive, Cincinnati, OH 45202; tel. (513) 639-2995; fax (513) 721-0129; e-mail cincyart@ fuse.net; internet www.cincinnatiartmuseum .org; f. 1881; permanent collns grouped in 88 galleries: Art of the Ancient World, Near Eastern Art, Far Eastern Art, Medieval Art, Arts of Africa and the Americas, Musical Instruments, Continental and English Decorative Arts, American Decorative Arts, European Painting and Sculpture, American

Painting and Sculpture, Prints, Drawings and Photographs, Costumes and Textiles; Nabataean antiquities from Khirbet Tannur; large collection of Old Master prints and modern Japanese and East European prints; contemporary art; temporary exhibitions; library of 52,000 vols, 250,000 pamphlets and clippings; Pres. JOHN W. BEATTY; Dir ANITA J. ELLIS (acting); publs *Annual Report*, *CANVAS* (every 2 months).

Cleveland Museum of Art: 11150 East Blvd, Cleveland, OH 44106; tel. (216) 421-7340; fax (216) 421-0411; e-mail info@levelandart.org; internet www.clemusart.com; inc. 1913, opened 1916; collections include paintings, sculpture, prints and drawings, textiles and decorative arts from the ancient world, Asia, Europe, the Americas, Africa and Oceania; library of 315,000 books and periodicals; 6m. images; Pres. MICHAEL J. HORVITZ; Dir KATHARINE LEE REID; publs *Cleveland Studies in the History of Art* (annual), *Members' Magazine* (10 a year).

Cleveland Museum of Natural History: 1 Wade Oval Drive, University Circle, Cleveland, OH 44106-1767; tel. (216) 231-4600; fax (216) 231-5919; e-mail info@cmnh.org; internet www.cmnh.org; f. 1920; comprises Natural History Museum, Shafran Planetarium, Observatory, and 26 separate natural areas in northern Ohio; collns in all fields with particular emphasis on the northern half of Ohio, including Upper Devonian Fossil Fishes; also vertebrates, insects, shells, minerals, precious and semi-precious stones, and botanical and ethnological materials; dept of physical anthropology responsible for the discovery and naming of new species of early man, *A. afarensis*; the Museum has sponsored or participated in several expeditions to Africa, islands of the South Atlantic, Antarctica, the Azuero Peninsula of Panama, and various parts of North America; many study collections, including herbarium, the Hamann-Todd Skeletal collection; mounted Jurassic cetiosaurid, Haplocanthosaurus; library of 60,000 vols; Exec. Dir Dr BRUCE M. LATIMER; publs *The Cleveland Bird Calendar*, *The Explorer* (quarterly), *Kirtlandia* (scientific papers), *Tracks* (every 2 months, members' newsletter).

Health Museum: 8911 Euclid Ave, Cleveland, OH 44106; tel. (216) 231-5010; fax (216) 231-5129; f. 1940; permanent exhibitions and interactive displays to educate the public in decision-making for healthy lifestyle choices; formalized youth education in 13 laboratory classrooms and 'Health on Wheels' travelling programme; adult education programme of seminars, lectures and health promotion activities; permanent installations include: Juno, the Museum's symbol, a transparent woman who talks to visitors about body systems and functions; 'Wonder of New Life' depicted by Dickinson Birth Models; the 'Giant Tooth' complex; and the participatory Family Discovery centre; Pres. Dr BERNADINE HEALY; Dir MICHAEL J. MARKS; publs *Classes and Services Booklet* (annually), *Healthwise* (quarterly).

National Museum of the United States Air Force: Wright-Patterson Air Force Base, 1100 Spaatz St, OH 45433; tel. (937) 255-3286; internet www.wpafb.af.mil/museum; f. 1923; displays of historical events, individuals and materials incl. aircraft and missiles; preservation of milestones in aerospace technology; study of aviation and aerospace history; Research Center with 400,000 photographs, and 4,500,000 video tapes, technical orders, books, drawings, logbooks, diaries, periodicals and other documents; Dir Maj.-

Gen. (Retd) CHARLES D. METCALF; publ. *Friends' Journal*.

Oklahoma

Oklahoma Historical Society History Center and Museum: 2401 North Laird Ave, Oklahoma, OK 73105; tel. (405) 522-5248; fax (405) 522-5402; e-mail okhc@okhistory.org; internet www.okhistorycenter.org; 50 topics and 2,000 artifacts reflecting Oklahoma's past; Dir Dr DEE HENDERSON.

Attached Museums:

Spiro Mounds Archaeological Park: POB 339AA, Spiro, OK 74959; tel. (918) 962-2062; internet www.spiro.lib.ok.us/mounds.htm; 140-acre site encompassing 12 southern mounds containing evidence of an Indian culture that occupied the site from AD 850 to 1450; Dir DENNIS PETERSON; other museums incl. Pioneer Woman, Cherokee Strip, Chisholm Trail, State Capital Publishing House, Route 66.

Oregon

Jordan Schnitzer Museum of Art: 1223 University of Oregon, Eugene, OR 97403-1233; 1430 Johnson Lane, Eugene, OR 97403; tel. (541) 346-3027; fax (541) 346-0976; e-mail mnh@uoregon.edu; internet uoma.uoregon.edu; attached to Univ. of Oregon; galleries featuring American, European, Korean, Chinese and Japanese art; Gordon Gilkey Research Center; Pres. CONNIE HULING.

Museum of Natural and Cultural History: 1680 East 15th Ave, Eugene, OR 97403; tel. (541) 346-3024; fax (541) 346-5334; e-mail mnh@uoregon.edu; internet natural-history.uoregon.edu; attached to Univ. of Oregon; Native American cultural and archaeological artifacts, spanning 15,000 years; incl. cache of 10,000-year-old sagebrush bark sandals, extensive fossil collections, several hundred western Indian baskets made before 1900; Dir JOHN ERLANDSON.

Oregon Historical Society Museum: 1200 Southwest Park Ave, Portland, OR 97205; tel. (503) 222-1741; e-mail orhist@ohs.org; internet www.ohs.org; 85,000 artifacts of local history; library of 32,000 vols, 25,000 maps, 12,500 linear ft of MSS, 4,000 serials titles, 6,000 vertical files, 18,000 reels of newspaper microfilm, 8.5m. ft of film and videotape, 10,000 oral history tapes, c. 2.5m. photographs; Exec. Dir GEORGE VOGT.

Pennsylvania

American Swedish Historical Museum: 1900 Pattison Ave, Philadelphia, PA 19145; tel. (215) 389-1776; fax (215) 389-7701; e-mail info@americanswedish.org; internet www.americanswedish.org; f. 1926; contributions by Swedes and Swedish-Americans since the mid-17th century; 14 galleries dedicated to all major historical and cultural aspects of Swedish accomplishments; exhibition on New Sweden Colony (1638–1655); library of 11,000 vols, primary source genealogical documents and sources; colln of letters, documents and designs by John Ericsson; Chair. SANDRA S. PFAFF; Dir TRACEY BECK; publ. *Newsletter*.

Barnes Foundation Gallery, Collections and Arboretum: 300 North Latch's Lane, Merion, PA 19066-1729; tel. (610) 667-0290; fax (610) 664-4026; e-mail info@barnesfoundation.org; internet www.barnesfoundation.org; f. 1922 by Dr Albert C. Barnes; offers courses in visual literacy and the philosophy and appreciation of art; colln of 1,000 paintings, including works by El Greco, Titian, Goya, Rubens, Cézanne, Renoir, Modigliani, Soutine, Picasso, Matisse

and Van Gogh; also sculpture, antique furniture and wrought iron; Arboretum, school with courses in botany, horticulture and landscape design; Teacher Institute with courses in visual arts and environmental and horticultural studies; school programmes for children from kindergarten level to grade 12; Chair. Dr BERNARD C. WATSON.

Carnegie Science Center: One Allegheny Ave, Pittsburgh, PA 15212-5850; tel. (412) 237-3400; fax (412) 237-3375; internet www.carnegiesciencecenter.org; f. 1991 to develop scientific literacy and promote participation in science and technology among the residents of Pennsylvania and neighbouring states; c. 400 interactive exhibits; 3 live demonstration theatres; 4-storey IMAX dome theatre; interactive planetarium; 36,000 sq. ft science-of sport exhibition; Cold War submarine moored on Pittsburgh's Ohio River; model-railroad display; working foundry; Tesla coil and Van de Graaff generator; interactive exhibits featuring robotics, cryogenics and lasers; Dir JOANNA HAAS.

Franklin Institute Science Museum: Benjamin Franklin Parkway at 20th St, Philadelphia, PA 19103; tel. (215) 448-1200; fax (215) 448-1235; internet sln.fi.edu; f. 1824; planetarium, Omnimax Theater, interactive theatre; exhibits and demonstrations in physical sciences and technology; workshops and teacher training; Pres. and CEO Dr DENNIS M. WINT; publ. *Journal*.

Pennsylvania Academy of the Fine Arts: 118 North Broad St., Philadelphia, PA 19102; tel. (215) 972-7600; fax (215) 569-0153; internet www.pafa.org; f. 1805; colln of American paintings since 18th century, sculpture, graphics; spec. exhibitions annually; archive; library of 12,000 vols; Pres. DEREK A. GILLMAN; Chair. DONALD R. CALDWELL; Dir EDNA S. TUTTLEMAN; publ. *Newsletter* (quarterly).

Philadelphia Museum of Art: POB 7646, Philadelphia, PA 19101-7646; tel. (215) 763-8100; fax (215) 236-4465; e-mail pr@philamuseum.org; internet www.philamuseum.org; f. 1876; 250,000 works of art, incl. paintings, prints, sculpture and silver from medieval to contemporary times representing European, American, and Far Eastern Art; Dir and CEO ANNE D'HARNONCOURT.

Attached museums:

Rodin Museum: Benjamin Franklin Parkway at 22nd St., Philadelphia, PA 19101-7646; tel. (215) 763-8100; internet www.rodinmuseum.org; f. 1929; houses 124 sculptures; Chair (vacant).

University of Pennsylvania Museum of Archaeology and Anthropology: 3260 South St, Philadelphia, PA 19104; tel. (215) 898-4000; fax (215) 898-0657; e-mail websiters@museum.upenn.edu; internet www.museum.upenn.edu; f. 1887; items from ancient Egypt, Mesopotamia, Africa, Asia, Polynesia, the ancient Mediterranean world and the Americas; library of 100,000 vols, archives with 300,000 photographic items and more than 600 m of textual records; Dir Dr JEREMY A. SABLOFF; publ. *Expedition* (3 a year).

Rhode Island

Haffenreffer Museum of Anthropology: 300 Tower St, Bristol, RI 02809; tel. (401) 253-8388; fax (401) 253-1198; internet www.brown.edu/facilities/haffenreffer; attached to Brown Univ.; library of 10,000 vols; 110,000 items of ethnographic and archaeological interest mainly from North America but also from Latin America, Africa, Middle East and Asia; Herbert Spinden Photographic Archive of 20,000 images and documents related to Central American archaeology and ethnography from the early 20th century, incl. many images of important archaeological sites that have since been altered or destroyed; Kensinger Colln with 5,000 photographs and related field notes and texts from Anthropologist Ken Kensinger's research with the Cashinahua of Peru in 1960s; Conti Colln has c. 3000 photographs dating from the late 1950s to early 1970s taken by Rhode Island photographer Gino Conti, primarily on the Hopi, Apache and Navaho reservations, and also in Mexico; Dir Shepard Krech, III.

National Museum of American Illustration: Vernon Court, 492 Bellevue Ave, Newport, RI 02840; tel. (401) 851-8949; fax (401) 851-8974; e-mail art@americanillustration.org; internet www.americanillustration.org; private, non-profit; f. 1998 by Judy and Laurence Cutler; housed in Vernon Court, an adaptation of a 17th-century French chateau built in 1898; American Imagist Colln of originals by Maxfield Parrish, Norman Rockwell, J.C. Leyendecker, Howard Pyle, N.C. Wyeth, Charles Dana Gibson, Henry Hutt, James Montgomery Flagg, Howard Chandler Christy, John Falter; comprises original art works, prints (open and limited edns), as well as significant memorabilia, vintage materials, artifacts (such as Rockwell's first paint box and Parrish's stippling paint brushes) and photographic materials.

South Carolina

Gibbes Museum of Art: 135 Meeting St, Charleston, SC 29401; tel. (843) 722-2706; fax (843) 720-1682; internet www.gibbesmuseum.org; f. 1903; local visual arts; 18th, 19th and early 20th-century paintings, works on paper (prints, drawings, watercolours, photographs), miniature portraits, and sculpture; Dir Todd Smith.

South Carolina State Museum: POB 100107, Columbia, SC 29202-3107; 301 Gervais St, Columbia, SC 29202; tel. (803) 898-4921; e-mail publicrelations@museum.state.sc.us; internet www.museum.state.sc.us; art, cultural history, natural history, science and technology; Stringer Discovery Center; travelling exhibits.

South Dakota

Museum of the South Dakota State Historical Society: 900 Governors Dr., Pierre, SD 57501-2217; tel. (605) 773-3458; fax (605) 773-6041; internet www.sdhistory.org/mus/museum.htm; 5 galleries of local history; travelling exhibits; Curators Ronette Rumpca, Daniel Brosz, Kathryn Higdon.

South Dakota Art Museum: Medary Ave at Harvey Dunn St, Brookings, SD 57007; tel. (605) 688-5423; internet www.southdakotaartmuseum.com; f. 1970; collns incl. Harvey Dunn, Native American Art, Marghab Linens, Paul Goble; Dir Lynn Vershoor.

Tennessee

American Museum of Science and Energy: 300 South Tulane Ave, Oak Ridge, TN 37830; tel. (865) 576-3200; e-mail information@amse.org; internet www.amse.org; f. 1949; operated for the US Dept of Energy by Enterprise Advisory Services, Inc.; one of the world's largest energy exhibitions, with live demonstrations, computers and films on all energy forms and uses; Dir David Sincerbox.

Texas

Dallas Museum of Art: 1717 North Harwood, Dallas, TX 75201; tel. (214) 922-1200; fax (214) 954-0174; internet www.dallasmuseumofart.org; f. 1903; arts of Africa, Asia and Pacific; Indonesian textiles; architectural and shrine objects from S Asia; Egyptian antiquities; contemporary art since 1945; American art from pre-Columbian times to the mid-20th century; 19th century and early modern European paintings and sculpture; N American and European decorative arts; Wendy and Emery Reves Colln, Faith and Charles Bybee Colln of American Furniture; prints, drawings, photographs; library: reference library of 25,000 vols, special collns: ethnography, artists' files; Dir Dr John R. Lane.

Hall of State: c/o Dallas Historical Society, POB 150038, Dallas, TX 75315-0038; 3939 Grand Ave, Dallas, TX 75210; tel. (214) 421-4500; fax (214) 421-7500; internet www.dallashistory.org; f. 1936; museum and archives of Texas and Dallas history; operated by Dallas Historical Society (see Learned Societies); library of 14,000 vols, 15,000 museum artefacts and 2m. archival items; Chief Operating Officer Franklin K. Wilson; Collns Dir Alan Colson.

Museum of Fine Arts: 1001 Bissonnet St, Houston, TX 77005; tel. (713) 639-7300; fax (713) 639-7399; internet www.mfah.org; inc. 1900; c. 55,000 artworks; art of the ancient world; European painting and sculpture; Far Eastern art; art of Africa, Oceania and the Americas; decorative arts; prints and drawings; film and video; modern art; photography; textiles and costume; 2 major museum bldgs, the Caroline Wiess Law Bldg and the Audrey Jones Beck Bldg; 2 facilities for the Glassell School of Art, the Studio School for Adults and the Glassell Jr School; 2 house museums that exhibit decorative arts, Bayou Bend Colln and Gardens and Rienzi, the Lillie and Hugh Roy Cullen Sculpture Garden; 18 acres of public gardens; library: reference library of 80,000 vols, 83,000 slides, Dir Peter C. Marzio; publ. *MFA Today* (6 a year).

San Jacinto Museum of History: 1 Monument Circle, La Porte (Houston), TX 77571-9585; tel. (281) 479-2421; fax (281) 479-2428; e-mail sjm@sanjacinto-museum.org; internet www.sanjacinto-museum.org; f. 1939; exhibits revisualize the history of Texas region from 1519 to 1900; library of 25,000 vols; MSS and documents since the 15th century; Pres. Paul G. Bell, Jr; Dir J. C. Martin.

Texas Memorial Museum: 2400 Trinity St, Campus of the Univ. of Texas, Austin, TX 78705; tel. (512) 471-1604; fax (512) 471-4794; internet www.utexas.edu/tmm; f. 1936; natural history of Texas, the Southwest and Latin America, minerals, fossils, palaeontology, vertebrate and invertebrate zoology, geology, entomology; Dir Edward C. Theriot; publ. *Pearce-Sellards Series*.

Utah

Earth Science Museum: 1683 North Canyon Rd, Provo, UT 84602-3300; tel. (801) 422-3680; fax (801) 422-7919; internet cpms.byu.edu/esm; f. 1976; attached to Brigham Young Univ.; fossil vertebrate colln of over 17,000 specimens ranging from Devonian fish (380m. years ago) to Pleistocene mammoths and cave fossils (15,000 years ago), with primary focus on dinosaurs from the Intermountain West; Curator and Manager Dr Rodney D. Scheetz.

Utah Museum of Fine Arts: 410 Campus Center Dr, Salt Lake City, UT 84112-0350; tel. (801) 581-7332; internet www.umfa.utah.edu; attached to Univ. of Utah; collns of

African Art, American Art, American Indian Art, Ancient Greek and Roman Art, Art of the Pacific Islands, Austrian Art, Cambodian Art, Chinese Art, Decorative Arts, Dutch Art, Egyptian Art, English Art, Flemish Art, French Art, German Art, Italian Art, Japanese Art, Nazi-Era Provenance Research Project, Pre-Columbian Art, Scottish Art, Spanish Art, Thai Art.

Virginia

Colonial Williamsburg Foundation: POB 1776, Williamsburg, VA 23187-1776; tel. (757) 229-1000; fax (757) 565-8797; internet www.colonialwilliamsburg.org; f. 1926; 301-acre outdoor living history museum with nearly 500 preserved, restored and reconstructed bldgs; 90 acres of period gardens and greens; demonstration of 18 historic trades; incl. DeWitt Wallace Decorative Arts Museum, Bassett Hall, Kimball Theatre and Abby Aldrich Rockefeller Folk Art Museum; library: John D. Rockefeller, Jr Library of 75,000 vols, 45,000 MSS, 55,000 architectural plans; Pres. and Chair. Colin G. Campbell; publ. *Colonial Williamsburg* (quarterly).

Mariners' Museum: 100 Museum Dr., Newport News, VA 23606; tel. (757) 596-2222; fax (757) 591-7310; e-mail info@mariner.org; internet www.mariner.org; f. 1930; int. maritime colln of c. 35,000 artefacts; incl. Peter W. Ifland Colln of Navigation Instruments (169 navigation pieces covering 5 centuries), Edwin Levick Colln of c. 30,000 photographs (yachting events and America's Cup races), artifacts and archives of the Civil War ironclad USS Monitor; library: see Libraries and Archives; Pres. and Chief Exec. John B. Hightower.

Virginia Museum of Fine Arts: 200 North Blvd, Richmond, VA 23220-4007; tel. (804) 340-1400; fax (804) 340-1548; e-mail contact@vmfa.museum; internet www.vmfa.museum; f. 1936; state-wide network of local and regional arts orgs and loan programme offering exhibition material to affiliated groups; film programmes; permanent collns incl. Russian Imperial jewelled objects by Fabergé, ancient Greek, Roman and Byzantine objects and sculptures; Indian, Chinese, Japanese, medieval, renaissance, and baroque paintings and sculptures; Himalayan colln; Art Nouveau and Art Deco colln; European and American decorative arts, prints, sculpture and paintings; contemporary art; library of 134,500 vols; Assoc. Dir Sandra C. Rusak; publ. *Calendar* (6 a year).

Washington

Seattle Art Museum: 1300 First Ave, Seattle, WA 98101-2003; tel. (206) 625-8900; fax (206) 654-3135; e-mail boxoffice@seattleartmuseum.org; internet www.seattleartmuseum.org; permanent collns of Aboriginal and Oceanic Art, African Art, American Art, Ancient Mediterranean and Islamic Art, Decorative Arts, European Arts, Japanes and Korean Art, Modern and Contemporary Art, Native and Mesoamerican Art, Textiles.

Attached Museums:

Seattle Asian Art Museum: 1400 East Prospect St, Volunteer Park, Seattle, WA 98112-3303; tel. (206) 654-3100; fax (206) 654-3191; Chinese, South Asian and Southeast Asian Art.

Olympic Sculpture Park: 2901 Western Ave, Seattle, WA 98121; tel. (206) 332-1377; fax (206) 332-1371; f. 1999; waterfront site for exhibition of sculptures.

Washington State History Museum: 1911 Pacific Ave, Tacoma, WA 98402; tel. (253) 272-3500; fax (253) 272-9518; internet www

Universities and Colleges
(Arranged alphabetically by State)

.washingtonhistory.org/wshm; Washington State Historical Society; Great Hall of Washington History, History Lab Learning Center; Dir PATRICIA TOBIASON; publ. *Columbia* (annual).

West Virginia

Huntington Museum of Art: 2033 McCoy Rd, Huntington, WV 25701; tel. (304) 529-2701; fax (304) 529-7447; internet www.hmoa.org; collns incl. Folk Art, Prints, Silver, Touma, Glass; Herman P. Dean Firearms; Daywood Colln; library of 20,000 vols in James D. Francis Art Library; incl. C. Fred Edwards Conservatory of subtropical plants; Exec. Dir MARGARET MARY LANE.

West Virginia State Museum and Cultural Center: Capitol Complex, 1900 Kanawha Blvd, E, Charleston, WV 25305-0300; tel. (304) 558-0220; fax (304) 558-2779; internet www.wvculture.org/agency/cultcenter.html; local art and history; also houses State Archives; Dir ADAM HODGES; publ. *Artworks* (quarterly).

Wisconsin

Milwaukee Art Museum: 700 North Art Museum Dr., Milwaukee, WI 53202; tel. (414) 224-3200; fax (414) 271-7588; e-mail mam@mam.org; internet www.mam.org; f. 1957 as Milwaukee Art Center; private, non-profit; collns in Ancient Art, Early European Art, 19th Century Art, American Art to 1900, Modern Art, Contemporary Art, Photography, Asian Art, Haitian Colln, African Art, Folk, Self-Taught and Outsider Art; Brooks Stevens Archive of Industrial Design; Rogovin Colln of photographs of working-class families; Dir and CEO DAVID GORDON.

Wisconsin Historical Museum: 816 State St, Madison, WI 53706-1417; 30 North Carroll St, Madison, WI 53703; tel. (608) 264-6555; e-mail museumstore@wisconsinhistory.org; internet www.wisconsinhistory.org/museum; Wisconsin Historical Society; spec. collns incl. Anthropolgy, Business and Technology, Costumes and Textiles, Domestic Life, Political Life; Pres. MARK L. GAJEWSKI.

Wyoming

National Museum of Wildlife Art: 2820 Rungius Rd, Jackson Hole, WY 83002; tel. (307) 733-5771; e-mail info@wildlifeart.org; internet www.wildlifeart.org; 2,000 pieces of art portraying wildlife, dating from 2000BC to the present, focusing primarily on European and American painting and sculpture; colln of American art from the 19th and 20th centuries recording European exploration of the American West; spec. collns incl. Carl Rugius Colln; Art Library and Archives; incl. National Elk Refuge; Pres. and CEO JAMES McNUTT.

Wyoming Dinosaur Center and Dig Sites: 110 Carter Ranch Rd, Thermopolis, WY 82443; tel. (307) 864-2997; fax (307) 864-5762; e-mail wdinoc@wyodino.org; internet www.wyodino.org; museum with interpretive displays, dioramas, life-size dinosaur mounts, exhibits covering all facets of early life; Fossil Preparation Laboratory; 60 dig sites in Warm Springs Ranch; Research Center; Casting Laboratory; Dir of Science SCOTT HARTMAN.

Wyoming State Museum: Barrett Bldg, 2301 Central Ave., Cheyenne, WY 82002; tel. (307) 777-7022; fax (307) 777-5375; e-mail wsm@state.wy.us; internet wyomuseum.state.wy.us; themed galleries: Barber Gallery, Drawn to this Land, Hands-on History Room, Living in Wyoming, RIP – Rex in Pieces, Swamped with Coal, The Wild Bunch, Wyoming's Story; travelling exhibits; Dir MANNY VIGIL.

ALABAMA

ALABAMA AGRICULTURAL AND MECHANICAL UNIVERSITY

4900 Meridian St, Huntsville, AL 35811
POB 1357, Normal, AL 35762
Telephone: (205) 851-5230
Fax: (205) 851-5244
Internet: www.aamu.edu
Founded 1875
Academic year: August to May
Pres.: Dr VIRGINIA CAPLES
Vice-Pres. for Academic Affairs: Dr VIRGINIA CAPLES
Vice-Pres. for Business and Finance: ARTHUR J. HENDERSON
Vice-Pres. for Research and Devt: Dr ROSE M. YATES
Vice-Pres. for Student Affairs: Dr JEROME ROBERTS
Registrar: Dr SHIRLEY HOUZER
Library of 339,272 vols
Number of teachers: 340
Number of students: 5,700

DEANS

Agricultural and Environmental Studies: JAMES W. SHUFORD
Arts and Sciences: JERRY R. SHIPMAN
School of Business: Dr BARBARA A. P. JONES
School of Education: Dr JOHN VICKERS, Jr
School of Eng. and Technology: Dr ARTHUR J. BOND
School of Graduate Studies: Dr CHANDRA REDDY
Univ. College: Dr THOMAS McALPINE (acting)
J. F. Drake Memorial Learning Resources Center: Dr CLARENCE TOOMER

ALABAMA STATE UNIVERSITY

915 South Jackson St, POB 271, Montgomery, AL 36101-0271
Telephone: (205) 293-4100
Fax: (205) 834-6861
Internet: www.alasu.edu
Founded 1867 as college, attained univ. status 1969
Pres.: Dr JOE A. LEE
Vice-Pres. (Academic Affairs): Dr EVELYN WHITE
Vice-Pres. (Fiscal Affairs): FREDDIE GALLOT
Vice-Pres. (Student Affairs): RICKY DRAKE
Vice-Pres. (Admin. Services): Dr LEON FRAZIER
Vice-Pres. (Institutional Advancement): Dr WILLIAM BROCK
Dir (Univ. Relations): JULIE DeBARDELABEN
Library of 218,850 vols
Number of teachers: 415
Number of students: 5,608
Publications: *Alabama State University Bulletin* (annual), *ASU Today*

DEANS

College of Education: Dr PETE MACCHIA (acting)
College of Business Admin: Dr PERCY VAUGHN
College of Arts and Sciences: Dr THELMA IVERY
Univ. College: Dr T. CLIFFORD BIBB
School of Graduate Studies: Dr ALLEN STEWART (acting)
Division of Aerospace Studies: Col KEITH SINGLETON
School of Music: Dr HORACE B. LAMAR, Jr

ATHENS STATE UNIVERSITY

300 North Beaty St, Athens, AL 35611-1999
Telephone: (205) 233-8100
Internet: www.athens.edu
Founded 1822
Pres.: Dr JERRY F. BARTLETT
Dir of Admissions: NECEDAH HENDERSON
Library Dir: ROBERT BURKHARDT
Library of 100,000 vols
Number of teachers: 69
Number of students: 3,200

DEANS

School of Arts and Sciences: (vacant)
School of Business: Dr LINDA SHONESY
School of Education: DEBRA BAIRD

AUBURN UNIVERSITY

Auburn Univ., AL 36849
Telephone: (334) 844-4000
Fax: (334) 844-6179
Internet: www.auburn.edu
Founded 1856 as The East Alabama Male College; became Alabama Agricultural and Mechanical College 1872, Alabama Polytechnic Institute 1899, Auburn Univ. 1960
Land grant State Univ.
Academic year: August to July
Pres.: Dr EDWARD R. RICHARDSON
Exec. Vice-Pres. and Chief Financial Officer: Dr DONALD L. LARGE, Jr
Vice-Pres: Dr C. MICHAEL MORIARTY (Research), Dr WES WILLIAMS (Student Affairs), Dr DAVID WILSON (Univ. Outreach), DEBORAH SHAW (Alumni Affairs), ROBERT McGINNIS (acting) (Alumni Devt)
Provost: Dr JOHN G. HEILMAN (acting)
Dean of Libraries: SHERI DOWNER (acting)
Library of 2,724,011 bound vols, 2,592,641 microforms, 35,015 current periodicals, 134,000 maps, govt documents
Number of teachers: 1,177
Number of students: 22,928
Publications: *The Auburn Plainsman*, *AU Report* (weekly), *Auburn Magazine*, *AES Highlights* (monthly), *Southern Humanities Review*, *Public Sector*, *Circle*, *The Auburn Pharmacist*, *The Auburn Veterinarian* (all quarterly), *Glomerata*, *Engineering Research Activities*, *Auburn University Research*, *The Auburn Bulletin*, *The Auburn Graduate Bulletin*, *The Tiger Cub* (all annual), *Facts & Figures* (every 2 years)

DEANS

Agriculture: Dr JOHN W. JENSEN
Architecture, Design and Construction: DANIEL BENNETT
Business: Dr PAUL M. BOBROWSKI
Education: Dr BONNIE WHITE
Eng.: Dr LARRY BENEFIELD
Forestry and Wildlife Sciences: Dr RICHARD W. BRINKER
Human Sciences: Dr JUNE M. HENTON
Liberal Arts: Dr JOSEPH ANSELL
Nursing: BARBARA S. WITT
Pharmacy: Dr R. LEE EVANS
Sciences and Mathematics: Dr STEWART W. SCHNELLER
Veterinary Medicine: Dr TIMOTHY R. BOOSINGER
Graduate School: Dr STEPHEN McFARLAND (acting)

BIRMINGHAM-SOUTHERN COLLEGE

900 Arkadelphia Rd, Birmingham, AL 35254
Telephone: (205) 226-4600
Fax: (205) 226-4627
Internet: www.bsc.edu

Founded 1856 (Southern Univ.) and 1898 (Birmingham College); instns merged to form Birmingham-Southern College 1918
Pres.: Dr DAVID POLLICK
Provost: Dr WAYNE SHEW
Vice-Pres. for Admission: SHERI SALMON
Vice-Pres. for Business and Finance: WAYNE ECHOLS
Vice-Pres. for Communications: BILL WAGNON
Vice-Pres. for Devt: GEORGE L. JENKINS
Vice-Pres. for Student Affairs: DUDLEY LONG
Librarian: BILLY PENNINGTON
Library of 250,000 vols, 57,000 govt documents, 1,030 current periodicals, 47,000 microfiches, 13,500 microfilms, audiovisual items, recordings, slides
Number of teachers: 106
Number of students: 1,425

DEANS

Div. of Behavioural and Social Sciences: BOB SLAGTER
Business and Graduate Programmes: Dr TARA SUDDERTH
Div. of Education: CLINT E. BRUESS
Div. of Fine and Performing Arts: LESTER SEIGEL
Div. of Humanities: JOHN TATTER
Div. of Science and Mathematics: CLYDE STANTON

FAULKNER UNIVERSITY

5345 Atlanta Highway, Montgomery, AL 36109

Telephone: (334) 272-5820
Internet: www.faulkner.edu

Founded 1942 as Montgomery Bible College; changed name to Alabama Christian College 1953; present name 1985
Campuses at Huntsville, Birmingham, Montgomery and Mobile
Private control
Academic year: August to July
Pres.: Dr BILLY D. HILYER
Dir of Admissions: KEITH MOCK
Dir of Libraries: BRENDA G. TURNER
Library: Nichols Main Library of 100,000 vols; also George H. Jones Jr Law Library

DEANS

Arts and Sciences: Prof. DAVE RAMPERSAD
College of Biblical Studies: Prof. CECIL MAY
College of Business: Prof. DAVE A. KHADANGA
Jones School of Law Administration: CHARLES NELSON

HERITAGE CHRISTIAN UNIVERSITY

POB HCU, Florence, AL 35630
E-mail: hcu@hcu.edu
Internet: www.hcu.edu

Founded 1971 as International Bible College; present name 2000
Private control
Academic year: August to July
Pres.: DENNIS JONES
Academic Dean: Dr BILL BAGENTS
Dean of Students: Dr NATHAN SEGARS
Dean of Men: TRAVIS HARMON
Dean of Women: HOLLY YOUNG
Registrar: SARA GOLDMAN
Librarian: JAMIE COX
Library of 61,000 vols.

HUNTINGDON COLLEGE

1500 East Fairview Ave, Montgomery, AL 36106

Telephone: (334) 833-4222
E-mail: info@huntingdon.edn
Internet: www.huntingdon.edu

Founded 1854
Pres.: J. CAMERON WEST
Dean of Students: RICHARD JONES
Dir of the Library: ERIC A. KIDWELL
Library of 110,000 vols
Number of teachers: 68
Number of students: 673

CHAIRS OF DEPTS

Biology and Chemistry: Dr ERASTUS C. DUDLEY
Business, Global Leadership and Political Science: Dr SAMIR R. MOUSSALLI
Education, Human Performance and Psychology: SHELBY SEARCY
English and Communication Studies: Dr JACKIE TRIMBLE
History, Modern Languages and Religious Studies: Dr FRANK W. BRUCKNER
Mathematics and Computer Science: Dr ANTHONY JACK CARLISLE
Music, Theatre and Fine Art: Dr JAMES W. GLASS

JACKSONVILLE STATE UNIVERSITY

700 Pelham Rd North, Jacksonville, AL 36265-1602

Telephone: (256) 782-5881
E-mail: info@jsucc.jsu.edu
Internet: www.jsu.edu

Founded 1883
Pres.: BILL MEEHAN
Vice Pres. for Academic and Student Affairs: Dr REBECCA O. TURNER
Vice-Pres. for Admin. and Business Affairs: WILLIAM FIELDING (acting)
Librarian: WILLIAM HUBBARD
Library of 583,365 vols
Number of teachers: 384 (265 full-time, 119 part-time)
Number of students: 8,478

DEANS

College of Arts and Sciences: J. E. WADE
College of Commerce and Business Admin.: WILLIAM FIELDING
College of Education and Professional Studies: Dr CYNTHIA HARPER
College of Nursing and Health Sciences: MARTHA LAVENDER
College of Graduate Studies and Continuing Education: WILLIAM D. CARR

MILES COLLEGE

POB 3800, Birmingham, AL 35208
Located at: 5500 Myron Massey Blvd Fairfield, AL 35064

Telephone: (205) 929-1000
Fax: (205) 929-1453
E-mail: info@mail.miles.edu
Internet: www.miles.edu

Founded 1905
Private control
Number of students: 1,700
Pres.: ALBERT J. H. SLOAN II
Dean of Academic Affairs: HATTIE G. LAMAR
Dean of Students: CAROLYN D. RAY.

UNIVERSITY OF MOBILE

5735 College Highway, Mobile, AL 36663-0220

Telephone: (251) 675-5990
Fax: (251) 675-6293
Internet: www.umobile.edu

Founded 1961
Private control
Pres.: Dr MARK R. FOLEY
Chancellor: Dr WILLIAM K. WEAVER, Jr
Vice-Pres. for Academic Affairs: Dr AUDREY C. EUBANKS

Vice-Pres. for Business Affairs: J. STEPHEN LEE
Vice-Pres. for Institutional Advancement: MICHAEL R. BLAYLOCK
Vice-Pres. for Student Development: KIMBERLY B. LEOUSIS
Dean of Academic Services and Registrar: Dr DONALD BERRY
Dir of Library Services: JEFFREY D. CALAMETTI
Library of 64,504 vols, 143,605 microfiches, 950 periodical titles
Number of teachers: 111 full-time
Number of students: 1,987

DEANS

School of Business: Dr ANNE LOWERY
School of Christian Studies: Dr CECIL TAYLOR
School of Education: Dr LARRY V. TURNER
School of Nursing: Dr ELIZABETH M. FLANAGAN
College of Arts and Sciences: Dr CHARLES M. CLARK

OAKWOOD COLLEGE

7000 Adventist Blvd NW, Huntsville, AL 35896

Telephone: (256) 726-7000
Fax: (256) 726-7596
E-mail: info@oakwood.edu
Internet: www.oakwood.edu

Founded 1896
private control, affiliated to Seventh-day Adventist Church
Academic year: July to June
Pres.: Dr DELBERT W. BAKER
Provost and Sr Vice-Pres.: Dr MERVYN A. WARREN
Vice-Pres. for Academic Affairs: Dr JOHN E ANDERSON
Dir of Admissions: JASON McCRACKEN
Dir of Library Services: PAULETTE MacLEAN JOHNSON
Library of 119,760 vols
Number of teachers: 162 (103 full-time, 59 part-time)
Number of students: 1,787.

SAMFORD UNIVERSITY

800 Lakeshore Dr., Birmingham, AL 35229

Telephone: (205) 726-2011
Fax: (205) 726-2654
E-mail: web@samford.edu
Internet: www.samford.edu

Founded 1841
Academic year: June to May
Pres. (vacant): THOMAS E. CORTS
Provost: J. BRADLEY CREED
Vice-Pres. for Business Affairs and Gen. Counsel: JOSEPH W. MATHEWS, Jr
Vice-Pres. and Dean of Students: RICHARD H. FRANKLIN
Vice-Pres. for Facilities: DON M. MOTT
Vice-Pres. for Univ. Relations: MICHAEL MORGAN
Librarian: JEAN THOMASON
Number of teachers: 252
Number of students: 4,377
Publication: *Bulletin*

DEANS

School of Business: MARLENE REED (acting)
Beeson School of Divinity: Dr TIMOTHY F. GEORGE
School of Education: Dr JEAN ANN BOX (acting)
Cumberland School of Law: Dr JOHN L. CARROLL
Ida V. Moffett School of Nursing: NENA SANDERS

McWhort School of Pharmacy: Dr JOSEPH O. DEAN, Jr
Howard College of Arts and Sciences: DAVID CHAPMAN
Metro College: Dr CINDY KIRK
Div. of Music: Dr MILBURN PRICE
Theatre Dept: Dr DON SANDLEY (Chair.)

SOUTHEASTERN BIBLE COLLEGE

2545 Valleydale Rd, Birmingham, AL 35244-2083

Telephone: (205) 970-9200
Fax: (205) 970-9207
E-mail: info@sebc.edu
Internet: www.sebc.edu

Founded 1935 as Birmingham School of the Bible; name changed to Southeastern Bible School 1943; present name 1950
Private control
Academic year: August to May
Pres.: Dr DONALD W. HAWKINS
Vice-Pres. (Academics): Dr ED GLASSCOCK
Vice-Pres. (Business Affairs): PETE WALKER
Dean of Students: RANDY HOFHEINS
Dir of Institutional Effectiveness and Research: Dr PETER REOCH
Registrar: LUCRETIA MOBBS
Dir of Library Services: REBECCA KNIGHT
Library of 35,000 vols.

SOUTHERN CHRISTIAN UNIVERSITY

POB 240240, Montgomery, AL 36124-0240
Located at: 1200 Taylor Rd, Montgomery, AL 361170-3553
Telephone: (334) 387-3877
Fax: (334) 387-3878
E-mail: admissions@southernchristian.edu
Internet: www.southernchristian.edu

Founded 1967 as Alabama Christian School of Religion; present name 1991
Private control
Academic year: August to August
President: Dr REX A. TURNER
Vice-President (Academic Affairs): Dr STANLEY PATTERSON
Registrar: ELAINE TARENCE
Librarian: TERRY SHERIDAN

DEANS

School of Leadership and Human Services: Dr TERRY GUNNELLS
Turner School of Theology: Dr WINSTON TEMPLE (acting)
College of General Studies: JAMES CRABTREE (acting)

SPRING HILL COLLEGE

4000 Dauphin St, Mobile, AL 36608
Telephone: (251) 380-4000
Internet: www.shc.edu

Founded 1830
Academic year: August to May
Pres.: Rev. GREGORY F. LUCEY
Exec. Vice-Pres.: CHARMANE P. MAY
Provost and Vice-Pres. for Academic Affairs: Dr NOREEN M. CARROCCI
Vice-Pres. for Business and Finance: RHONDA M. SHIRAZI
Vice-Pres. for Devt: KEN HOKENSON
Vice-Pres. for Student Affairs and Dean of Students: JOE DEIGHTON
Dir of Library Services: BRUCE WHITMAN
Library of 170,000 vols
Number of teachers: 138 (72 full-time, 66 part-time)
Number of students: 1,497 (1,299 undergraduates, 198 graduates)

DEANS

Faculty of Business: Dr ANDREW SHARP

Faculty of Communication Arts: THOMAS LOEHR
Faculty of English: Dr MARGARET DAVIS, Dr JOHN HAFNER, Dr MICHAEL KAFFER, Dr DAVID SAUER
Faculty of Fine Arts: RUTH BELASCO
Faculty of History: Dr NEIL HAMILTON, Dr PATRICIA HARRISON
Faculty of Foreign Languages: Dr CHARLES KARGLEDER
Faculty of Mathematics: Dr CHARLES CHENEY, Dr DANIEL CYPHERT
Faculty of Nursing: Dr CAROL HARRISON
Faculty of Philosophy: Dr MELVIN BRANDON, Dr KARL KOBELJA
Faculty of Physics: Dr JOHN KANE
Faculty of Political Science: Dr NADER ENTESSAR
Faculty of Psychology: Dr ROBERT MACALEESE
Faculty of Sociology: Dr LARRY HALL
Faculty of Teacher Education: Dr LOIS SILVERNAIL
Faculty of Theology: Dr TIMOTHY CARMODY, Dr GEORGE GILMORE, Rev. FREDERICK GUNTI, Rev. CHRIS VISCARDI

STILLMAN COLLEGE

POB 1430, Tuscaloosa, AL 35403
E-mail: admissions@stillman.edu
Internet: www.stillman.edu

Founded 1876 as Tuscaloosa Institute; renamed Stillman Institute 1898; present name 1948
Private control
Academic year: August to July
Pres.: Dr ERNEST MCNEALEY
Vice-Pres. (Academic Affairs): Dr CHRISTOPHER JEFFRIES
Dean (Enrollment Management): GEORGE LEE
Vice-Pres. (Fiscal Affairs): SAMA MONDEH
Vice-Pres. (Student Affairs): Dr SHARON WHITTAKER
Dean of the Library: ROBERT J. HEATH
Library of 117,500 vols, 410 periodicals

DEANS

Arts and Sciences: Dr CHARLOTTE CARTER

TALLADEGA COLLEGE

627 West Battle St, Talladega, AL 35160
Telephone: (256) 761-6212
Fax: (256) 362-2268
E-mail: olprater@talladega.edu
Internet: www.talladega.edu

Founded 1867 as Swayne School; present name 1869
Private control
Academic year: August to May
Pres.: OSCAR L. PRATER
Provost and Vice-Pres. (Academic Affairs): Dr ARTHUR BACON
Vice-Pres. (Admin. and Finance) (vacant)
Vice-Pres. (Institutional Advancement): SANDRA D. COOLEY (acting)
Dean of Student Affairs: DAMEON MADISON
Registrar: FLORETTA DORTCH
Librarian: JULIETTE SMITH
Library of 130,000 vols

DEANS

Division of Business and Admin.: MICHAEL TAKU (acting)
Division of Humanities and Fine Arts: Dr TRELLIE JEFFERS (acting)
Division of Natural Sciences and Mathematics: Dr LEONARD COLE (acting)
Division of Social Sciences and Education: Dr EDWARD HALL

TROY STATE UNIVERSITY

Troy, AL 36082
Telephone: (334) 670-3000
Fax: (334) 670-3735
E-mail: intlprog@troyst.edu
Internet: www.troy.edu

Founded 1887
Academic year: August to May
Chancellor: Dr JACK HAWKINS, Jr
Sr Vice-Chancellor for Admin.: Dr DOUGLAS C. PATTERSON
Vice Chancellor for Academic and Student Affairs: Dr ED ROACH
Asst to Provost: VICKIE MILES
Librarian: Dr HENRY R. STEWART

Library of 334,000 vols
Number of teachers: 265
Number of students: 5,100.

CONSTITUENT UNIVS

Troy State Univ., Dothan

500 Univ. Dr., Dothan, AL 36303
Telephone: (334) 9836556
Fax: (334) 9836322
Internet: dothan.troy.edu

Founded 1887 as Troy State Normal School; name changed to Troy State Teachers College 1929, Troy State College 1957, present name 1996
Academic year: August to August
Pres.: Dr BARBARA ALFORD
Exec. Sec.: KAREN MCGAHEE
Dir, Academic Records and Registrar: LYNDA SALISBURY
Dir, Continuing Education Center: MICHAEL H. TEW
Dir, Information Services: RONNIE CREEL
Dir of Student and Community Services: BOB WILLIS
Dir, Fort Rucker Location: GAYE PEACOCK
Dir of Library Services: JULIA SMITH
Number of students: 1,855 (part-time and full-time undergraduates and graduates)

DEANS

College of Arts and Sciences: Dr ALAN BELSCHES
College of Business Admin.: Dr ADAIR GILBERT
College of Education: Dr SANDRA LEE JONES

Troy State Univ., Montgomery

231 Montgomery St, P.O. Drawer 4419, Montgomery, AL 36103-4419
E-mail: m01admissions@troy.edu
Internet: montgomery.troy.edu
Academic year: August to May
Pres.: Dr CAMERON MARTINDALE
Vice-Pres. (Academic Affairs): Dr TERRY DIXON
Vice-Pres. (Admin. and Financial Affairs): RAY WHITE
Exec. Asst to Pres.: SANDRA GOUGE
Dean of Distance Learning: Dr MAC ADKINS
Dean of Student Affairs: Dr CHARLES WESTERN
Registrar: LYNN LEWIS
Library Dir: KAY FOWLER

DEANS

College of Arts and Sciences: Dr WILLIAM S. RICHARDSON
College of Education: Dr LEN KITCHENS
Division of Business: Dr JAMES SIMPSON

Troy State Univ., Phenix City

1 Univ. Pl., Phenix City, AL 36869
Telephone: (334) 448-5106
Internet: phenix.troy.edu
Academic year: August to August
Vice-Chancellor: Dr CURTIS PITTS

Dir, Admin.: KENNY MARCUM
Dir, Institutional Advancement: KATHY NINAS
Academic Dean: Dr JOHN IRWIN
Dir, Student Services and Registrar: DARLENE SCHMURR-STEWART

DEANS

College of Business Admin.: Dr CHERIE FRETWELL
College of Counselling and Psychology: Dr KATHRYN NESS
College of Education: Dr LARRY THACKER

TUSKEGEE UNIVERSITY

Tuskegee, AL 36088
Telephone: (334) 727-8011
Fax: (334) 727-5276
E-mail: admi@tuskegee.edu
Internet: www.tuskegee.edu

Founded 1881
Academic year: August to May

Pres.: Dr BENJAMIN F. PAYTON
Provost and Vice-Pres. for Academic Affairs: Dr LUTHER S. WILLIAMS
Vice-Pres. for Admissions and Enrollment Management: ROBERT L. LANEY
Dean of Students: PETER J. SPEARS
Vice-Pres. for Business and Fiscal Affairs: LESLIE V. PORTER
Registrar: EDRICE LEFTWICH
Dir of Library Services: JUANITA ROBERTS
Library of 250,000 vols, 1,000 periodicals
Number of teachers: 266
Number of students: 3,000

DEANS

College of Agriculture and Environmental and Natural Sciences: Dr WALTER H. HILL
College of Business and Information Science: Dr ALICIA JACKSON
College of Engineering, Architecture and Physical Science: Dr LEGAND L. BURGE
College of Liberal Arts and Education: Dr BENJAMIN BENFORD
College of Veterinary Medicine, Nursing and Allied Health: (vacant)

UNITED STATES SPORTS ACADEMY

One Academy Drive, Daphne, AL 36526
Telephone: (251) 626-3303
Fax: (251) 625-1035
E-mail: academy@ussa.edu
Internet: www.ussa.edu

Founded 1972
Private control
Academic year: September to August

President and Chief Executive Officer: Dr THOMAS P. ROSANDICH
Vice-President: Dr T. J. ROSANDICH
Executive Secretary: RENEE KIRSCHENBAUM
Dean of Academic Affairs and Director of Doctoral Affairs: Dr. ALBERT G. APPLIN
Director of Continuing Education: BETSY SMITH
Director of Doctoral Studies: Dr. CYNTHIA RYDER
Director of Student Services: BOBBI SPURGEON-HARRIS
Registrar: BOBBI SPURGEON-HARRIS
Library Director: NANCY GRAY
Library of 1,000,000 vols
Publications: *The Academy* (quarterly), *The Sport Journal* (quarterly), *The Sport Supplement* (quarterly)

CHAIRMEN OF DEPARTMENTS

Fitness Management: Dr DAVID MORRIS
Sports Coaching: SALLY FORD
Sports Management: Dr CLIFF McPEAK
Sports Medicine: Dr ENRICO ESPOSITO
Sports Studies: (vacant)

UNIVERSITY OF ALABAMA

POB 870100, Tuscaloosa, AL 35487
Telephone: (205) 348-6010
Fax: (205) 348-9046
E-mail: admissions@ua.edu
Internet: www.ua.edu

Founded 1831
Academic year: August to May

Pres.: Dr ROBERT E. WITT
Provost and Vice-Pres. for Academic Affairs: Dr JUDY L. BONNER
Vice-Pres. for Financial Affairs and Treas.: LYNDA GILBERT
Vice-Pres. for Student Affairs: Dr MARGARET KING
Vice-Pres. for Univ. Advancement: ROBERT E. WITT
Dean of Libraries: LOUIS A. PITSCHMANN
Library: see Libraries and Archives
Number of teachers: 1,051
Number of students: 20,929

Publications: *Alabama Business* (monthly), *Alabama Law Review* (monthly), *Alabama Heritage* (quarterly), *Alabama Review* (quarterly), *Alabama Alumni Magazine* (6 a year), *Law and Psychology Review* (annual), *Alabama Research Magazine* (annual)

DEANS

College of Arts and Sciences: Dr ROBERT F. OLIN
College of Commerce and Business Admin.: Dr BARRY MASON
College of Communication and Information Sciences: E. CULPEPPER CLARK
College of Community Health Sciences: Dr EUGENE MARSH
College of Continuing Studies: Dr CAROLYN DAHL
College of Education: Dr JAMES McLEAN
College of Engineering: Dr KEITH McDOWELL
College of Human Environmental Sciences: Dr MILLA BOSCHUNG
Capstone College of Nursing: SARA E. BARGER
Graduate School: Dr RONALD ROGERS
Honors College: Dr ROBERT HALLI
School of Law: Dr KENNETH RANDALL
School of Social Work: Dr JAMES P. (IKE) ADAMS, Jr

UNIVERSITY OF ALABAMA AT BIRMINGHAM

1530 Third Ave S., Birmingham, AL 35294
Telephone: (205) 934-4011
Internet: main.uab.edu

Founded 1969

Pres.: Dr CAROL Z. GARRISON
Provost: Dr ELI CAPILOUTO
Vice-Pres. and Dean of the School of Medicine: Dr ROBERT RICH
Vice-Pres. for Financial Affairs and Admin.: RICHARD L. MARGISON
Library of 1,409,945 vols (Mervyn H. Sterne Library), 358,858 vols (Lister Hill Library of the Health Sciences); 2,125 current periodicals (Sterne), 1,809 current periodicals (Lister Hill)
Number of teachers: 1,988 (1,839 full time)
Number of students: 16,516

Publications: *UAB Magazine* (quarterly), *UAB Reporter* (weekly)

DEANS

School of Arts and Humanities: BERT BROUWER
School of Business: Dr ROBERT HOLMES (acting)
School of Dentistry: MARY LYNNE CAPILOUTO (acting)
School of Education: Dr MICHAEL FRONING
School of Engineering: LINDA C. LUCAS

School of Health Related Professions: CHARLES L. JOINER
School of Medicine: Dr ROBERT RICH
School of Natural Sciences and Mathematics: LOWELL E. WENGER
School of Nursing: Dr RACHEL Z. BOOTH
School of Optometry: AROL AUGSBURGER
School of Public Health: Dr MAX MICHAEL, III
School of Social and Behavioural Sciences: Dr TENNANT S. McWILLIAMS
Graduate School: JAMES B. McCLINTOCK (acting)

UNIVERSITY OF ALABAMA IN HUNTSVILLE

301 Sparkman Drive, Huntsville, AL 35899
Telephone: (256) 824-1000
Fax: (256) 890-6538
Internet: www.uah.edu

Founded 1950

President: Dr FRANK A. FRANZ
Provost and Vice-President for Academic Affairs: Dr LEWIS J. RADONOVICH
Vice-President for Finance and Administration: RAY M. PINNER
Vice-President for Research: Dr RON GREENWOOD
Vice-President for Student Affairs: DELOIS SMITH
Vice-President for University Advancement: Dr J. DERALD MORGAN
Dean of Library: Dr WILSON LUQUIRE
Library of 326,399 vols, 1,169 current periodicals, microforms, MSS, sound recordings, govt documents (M. Louis Salmon Library)
Number of teachers: 459
Number of students: 7,036

DEANS

College of Administrative Science: Dr C. DAVID BILLINGS
College of Engineering: Dr JORGE I. AUÑÓN
College of Liberal Arts: Dr SUE W. KIRKPATRICK
College of Nursing: Dr C. FAY RAINES
College of Science: Dr JACK D. FIX (acting)
School of Graduate Studies: Dr DEBRA MORIARITY

UNIVERSITY OF MONTEVALLO

Montevallo, AL 35115
Telephone: (205) 665-6000
Fax: (205) 665-6003
Internet: www.montevallo.edu

Founded 1896

Pres.: PHILIP C. WILLIAMS
Provost and Vice-Pres. for Academic Affairs: Dr WAYNE C. SEELBACH
Vice-Pres. for Student Affairs: Dr GLENDA E. ISENHOUR
Vice-Pres. for Business Affairs: CYNTHIA S. JARRETT
Dir of Admissions: IRA L. GURGANUS
Dir of Libraries: ROSEMARY H. ARNESON
Library of 248,132 vols, 751,618 microform items, 2,523 audio-visual items, 868 current periodicals
Number of teachers: 199
Number of students: 2,935

DEANS

College of Arts and Sciences: Dr MICHAEL L. ROWLAND
College of Business: Dr NANCY BELL
College of Education: Dr BETH COUNCE
College of Fine Arts: KENNETH J. PROCTER
Graduate Studies: Dr TERRY G. ROBERSON

UNIVERSITY OF NORTH ALABAMA

Florence, AL 35632-0001
Telephone: (205) 765-4100

Fax: (205) 765-4329
Internet: www.una.edu
Founded 1830 as a private instn; became a state instn 1872
Pres.: WILLIAM G. CALE, JR
Vice-Pres. for Academic Affairs, and Provost: Dr ROOSEVELT NEWSON
Vice-Pres. for Fiscal Affairs: Dr STEVE SMITH
Vice-Pres. for Student Affairs, and Univ. Counsel: Dr DAVID P. SHIELDS, JR
Vice-Pres. for Univ. Advancement and Admin.: Dr G. DANIEL HOWARD
Dean of Information Technologies: Dr G. GARRY WARREN
Library of 328,456 vols, 900,000 microform items, 7,800 audio-visual items, 2,145 current periodicals
Number of teachers: 285 (201 full-time, 84 part-time)
Number of students: 5,601

DEANS

College of Arts and Sciences: Dr VAGN HANSEN
College of Business: Dr KERRY GATLIN
College of Education: Dr MARK EDWARDS
College of Nursing and Allied Health: Dr BIRDIE I. BAILEY

UNIVERSITY OF SOUTH ALABAMA

307 University Blvd, Mobile, AL 36688-0002
Telephone: (251) 460-6101
Internet: www.southalabama.edu
Founded 1963
Pres.: GORDON MOULTON
Sr Vice-Pres.: Dr PAT C. COVEY
Dean and Vice-Pres. for Medical Affairs: Dr ROBERT A. KREISBERG
Vice-Pres. for Student Affairs: Dr DALE T. ADAMS
Vice-Pres. for Finance: M. WAYNE DAVIS
Registrar: MELISSA WOLD
Dean of Libraries: Dr RICHARD J. WOOD
Library of 548,800 vols
Number of teachers: 981
Number of students: 13,538

DEANS

College of Allied Health Professions: Dr RICHARD TALBOTT
College of Arts and Sciences: Dr G. DAVID JOHNSON
Mitchell College of Business: Dr CARL C. MOORE
College of Education: Dr RICHARD HAYES MITCHELL
College of Engineering: Dr JOHN STEADMAN
College of Medicine: Dr ROBERT KREISBERG
College of Nursing: Dr DEBRA C. DAVIS
School of Computer and Information Sciences: Dr DAVID L. FEINSTEIN
School of Continuing Education and Special Programs: Dr THOMAS L. WELLS
Graduate School: Dr JUDY STOUT

UNIVERSITY OF WEST ALABAMA

Livingston, AL 35470
Telephone: (205) 652-3400
Internet: www.uwa.edu
Founded 1835
Pres.: RICHARD HOLLAND
Provost: DAVID M. TAYLOR
Vice-Pres. for Financial Affairs: T. RAIFORD NOLAND
Vice-Pres. for Institutional Advancement: CLEMIT W. SPRUIELL
Vice-Pres. for Student Affairs: DANNY BUCK-ALEW
Dir of the Library: MONROE C. SNIDER
Library of 250,000 vols
Number of teachers: 92

Number of students: 2,153

DEANS

College of Business: Dr HABIB BAYZARI
College of Education: Dr TOM DeVANEY
College of Liberal Arts: Dr MICHAEL A. COOKE
College of Natural Sciences and Mathematics: Dr JUDY MASSEY
Div. of Nursing: SYLVIA HOMAN (Chairperson)
School of Graduate Studies: JOE B. WILKINS, Jr

ALASKA

ALASKA BIBLE COLLEGE

POB 289, Glennallen, AK 99588
Telephone: (907) 822-3201
Fax: (907) 822-5027
E-mail: info@akbible.edu
Internet: www.akbible.edu
Founded 1966
Private control
Academic year: August to May
Pres.: Dr GARY J. RIDLEY
Number of teachers: 10
Number of students: 45.

ALASKA PACIFIC UNIVERSITY

4101 University Dr., Anchorage, AK 99508
Telephone: (907) 564-8248
Fax: (907) 562-4276
E-mail: infodesk@alaskapacific.edu
Internet: www.alaskapacific.edu
Founded 1957
Academic year: September to August
Pres.: Dr DOUGLAS McKAY NORTH
Academic Dean: MARILYN R. BARRY
Registrar: JEANETTE BROOKS
Library of 400,000 vols, shared with Univ. of Alaska, Anchorage
Number of teachers: 80
Number of students: 689.

SHELDON JACKSON COLLEGE

801 Lincoln St, Sitka, AK 99835
Telephone: (907) 747-5220
Internet: www.sheldonjackson.edu
Founded 1878 as Sitka Training School; name changed to Sheldon Jackson School 1911; present name 1966
Private control
Academic year: August to May
Pres.: Rev. Dr DAVID DOBLER
Dir of Admissions: ANDY LEE
Chief Financial Officer: JIM SHARPE
Dir of Communications: HOLLY KEEN
Dean of Academic Affairs: Dr MARY LOUISE VAN WINKLE
Dean of Student and Community Affairs: CHRIS BRYNER
Grants Administrator: CARNIELLE CALL
Library of 80,000
Number of students: 250 (full-time and part-time).

UNIVERSITY OF ALASKA STATEWIDE SYSTEM

POB 755000, Fairbanks, AK 99775
Telephone: (907) 450-8000
Fax: (907) 450-8002
E-mail: sypres@alaska.edu
Internet: www.alaska.edu
Founded 1917 as Alaska Agricultural College and School of Mines; univ. status 1935; consists of 3 multi-campus 4-year univs, community college
Pres.: MARK R. HAMILTON
Vice-Pres. for Finance: JOSEPH M. BEEDLE

Vice-Pres. for Research: Dr CRAIG DORMAN
Vice-Pres. for Univ. Relations: WENDY REDMAN
Number of teachers: 2,332 (statewide)
Number of students: 32,711 (statewide)
Publs program catalogues from various units of the univ.

CONSTITUENT UNIVERSITIES

University of Alaska Anchorage: 3211 Providence Dr., Anchorage, AK 99508; tel. (907) 786-1800; Chancellor Dr ELAINE P. MAIMON.

University of Alaska Fairbanks: POB 757520, Fairbanks, AK 99775; tel. (907) 474-7581; Chancellor Dr STEPHEN JONES.

University of Alaska Southeast: 11120 Glacier Highway, Juneau, AK 99801; tel. (907) 465-6457; Chancellor JOHN PUGH.

ARIZONA

AMERICAN INDIAN COLLEGE

10020 North 15th Ave, Phoenix, AZ 85021-2199
Telephone: (602) 944-3335
Fax: (602) 943-8299
E-mail: aicadm@aicag.edu
Internet: www.aicag.edu
Founded 1957
Private control
Pres.: Rev. JAMES V. COMER (acting)
Vice-Pres. and Academic Dean: Dr DAVID L. DeGARMO (acting)
Dean of Institutional Assessment: Dr JOSEPH J. SAGGIO (acting)
Dean of Institutional Research: JIM DEMPSEY (acting)
Dean of Students: VINCE ROUBIDEAUX (acting)
Registrar: SANDRA M. GONZALES (acting)
Library Dir: JOHN S. ROSE (acting)
Library of 20,000 vols
Number of teachers: 21 (7 full-time, 14 part-time)
Number of students: 59.

ARIZONA STATE UNIVERSITY

Tempe, AZ 85287
Telephone: (602) 965-9011
E-mail: askasu@asu.edu
Internet: www.asu.edu
Founded 1885
Pres.: Dr MICHAEL M. CROW
Exec. Vice-Pres. and Provost: ELIZABETH D. CAPALDI
Exec. Vice-Pres. and Chief Financial Officer: CAROL CAMPBELL
Vice-Pres. and Provost, Phoenix Campus: MERNOY HARRISON
Vice-Pres. and Provost, Polytechnic Campus: ALBERT McHENRY
Vice-Pres. and Provost, West Campus: MARJORIE ZATZ
Vice-Pres. for Academic Personnel: MARK SEARLE
Vice-Pres. for Academic Affairs: DAVID YOUNG
Vice-Pres. for Research and Economic Affairs: JONATHAN FINK
Vice-Pres. for Admin. and Legal Affairs: PAUL WARD
Vice-Pres. for Univ. Student Initiatives: JAMES RUND
Vice-Pres. for Univ. Athletics: LISA LOVE
Vice-Pres. for Global Engagement: ANTHONY ROCK
Vice-Pres. and Univ. Technology Officer: ADRIAN SANNIER
Vice-Pres. for Public Affairs: VIRGIL RENZULI
Librarian: SHERRIE SCHMIDT

Library of 2,500,000 vols
Number of teachers: 1,800 full-time
Number of teachers: 800 part-time
Number of students: 60,000

DEANS

College of Design: WELLINGTON REITER
Carey School of Business: ROBERT MITTEL-STAEDT
East College: DAVID SCHWALM
College of Education: SARAH HUDELSON
College of Engineering: DEIRDRE MELDRUM
College of Fine Arts: KWANG-WU KIM
School of Global Management and Leadership: GARY WAISSI
Graduate Studies: MARIA T. ALLISON
Barrett Honors College: MARK JACOBS
College of Human Services: JOHN HEPBURN
New College of Interdisciplinary Arts and Sciences: BARRY RITCHIE
School of Journalism and Mass Communication: CHRISTOPHER CALLAHAN
College of Law: PATRICIA D. WHITE
College of Liberal Arts and Sciences: QUENTIN WHEELER
School of Management and Agribusiness: PAUL PATTERSON
College of Nursing and Healthcare Innovation: BERNADETTE MELNYK
College of Public Programs: DEBRA FRIEDMAN
College of Science and Technology: TIMOTHY LINDQUIST
College of Teacher Education and Leadership: MARI KOERNER, University College: GAIL HACKETT

GRAND CANYON UNIVERSITY

POB 11097, Phoenix, AZ 85061-1097
Located at: 3300 West Camelback Rd, Phoenix, AZ 85017-3030
Telephone: (602) 249-3300
Internet: www.grand-canyon.edu
Founded 1949 as Grand Canyon College; present name 1989
Private control
Academic year: August to August
Pres.: DON ANFORFER
CEO: BRENT RICHARDSON
Vice-Pres. for Academic Affairs and Provost: Dr LEANNA HALL
Vice-President for Finance: PHIL DANIELS
Vice-Pres. for Student Affairs: Dr JEAN-NOEL THOMPSON
Chancellor: Dr BILL R. WILLIAMS
Library of 117,000 books, government documents and audiovisual materials
Number of students: 11,000

DEANS

College of Liberal Arts and Science: JAMES BEGGS
College of Nursing and Health Sciences: FRAN ROBERTS
College of Education: JODY SUMMERFORD
College of Business: KATHY PLAYER

NORTHERN ARIZONA UNIVERSITY

Flagstaff, AZ 86011
Telephone: (928) 523-9011
Internet: www.nau.edu
Founded 1899
Academic year: August to May
Pres.: Dr JOHN D. HAEGER
Provost: Dr LIZ GROBSMITH
Vice-Provost for Undergraduate Studies: Dr KAREN PUGLIESI
Vice-Pres. for Admin. and Finance: KATHE SHINHAM
Vice-Pres. for Univ. Advancement: JAMES S. HILL
Vice-Pres. for Enrollment Management and Student Affairs: DAVID BOUSQUET

Dean of Students: RICK BRANDEL
Dir. of Libraries: CYNTHIA CHILDERY
Library of 1,400,000 vols, incl. 560,000 books, 240,000 govt documents, 35,000 maps, 373,000 microforms, 18,000 sound recordings, 10,000 videos, 136,000 periodicals
Number of teachers: 706
Number of students: 18,000

DEANS

College of Arts and Letters: Dr MICHAEL VINCENT
College of Business Admin.: Dr MASON S. GERETY
College of Social and Behavioral Sciences: Dr KATHRYN CRUZ-URIBE
College of Engineering and Natural Sciences: Dr LAURA HUENNEKE
College of Education: Dr DANIEL L. KAIN
School of Forestry: Dr ROBERT CLARK
School of Health Professions: Dr JOHN SCIACCA
School of Nursing: Dr ILENE DECKER
School of Hotel and Restaurant Management: Dr GALEN R. COLLINS

PRESCOTT COLLEGE

220 Grove Ave, Prescott, AZ 86301
Telephone: (877) 350-2100
E-mail: admissions@prescott.edu
Internet: www.prescott.edu
Founded 1966
Private control
Academic year: September to August
Pres.: Dr DAN GARVEY
Chief Operating Officer: STEVEN M. COREY
Dean of Adult Degree Program: Dr PAUL BURKHARDT
Dean of Master of Arts Program: Dr PAUL BURKHARDT
Dean of Resident Degree Program: Dr GRET ANTILLA
Library Dir: EILEEN CHALFOUN
Registrar: LAURIE GILBRETH
Library of 23,900 vols
Number of teachers: 60 (full-time)
Number of students: 1,000

Publications: *Alligator Juniper*, *Wolfberry Sun*

Resident Degree, Adult Degree, MA and PhD programs in: Human Development, Ecopsychology, Abstract Art, Environmental Education and Interpretation, Teacher Education, Human Ecology, Agroecology, Creative Writing, Outdoor Adventure Education, Management, Counselling, and Wilderness Leadership.

BRANCH CAMPUS

Prescott College Tucson Center: 2233 East Speedway Blvd, Tucson, AZ 85719; tel. (520) 319-9868; fax (520) 319-1032; Exec. Dir. BILL WALTON.

SOUTHWESTERN COLLEGE

2625 East Cactus Rd, Phoenix, AZ 85032
Telephone: (602) 992-6101
E-mail: swc@swcaz.edu
Internet: www.southwesterncollege.edu
Founded 1960
Private control
Academic year: August to August
Pres.: Dr BRENT GARRISON
Exec. Vice-Pres.: DAVID M. BARNES
Vice-Pres. for Academics and Student Devt: SHERRY HAEHL
Vice-Pres. for Devt. PAUL HENDRICKS
Dir of Enrollment Management: BRIAN HAEHL
Registrar: LAMBERT CRUZ
Librarian: ALICE EICKMEYER

Undergraduate courses in Christian ministries, biblical studies, elementary and secondary education, business admin., counselling, music.

THUNDERBIRD SCHOOL OF GLOBAL MANAGEMENT

15249 North 59th Ave, Glendale, AZ 85306-6000
Telephone: (602) 9787000
E-mail: admissions@thunderbird.edu
Internet: www.thunderbird.edu
Founded 1946 as The American Institute for Foreign Trade; present name 1997
Private control
Academic year: September to August
Pres.: Dr ÁNGEL CABRERA
Chief Operating Officer and Treasurer: TIM PROPP
Senior Vice-Pres. for Academic Programs: Dr ROBERT E. WIDING
Vice-Pres. for Institutional Advancement: JOAN NEICE
Dean of Faculty: Dr F. JOHN MATHIS
Dir of Corporate Learning: BETH STOOPS
Depts of: Accounting, Culture and Languages, Economics, Entrepreneurship, Finance, Int. Studies, Management, Marketing, Operations and Supply Chain Management

Publication: *Thunderbird International Business Review* (6 a year)

DEANS

Accounting: DALE L. DAVISON
Economics: JOHN F. MATHIS
Executive Education: DAVID BOWEN

PROFESSORS

Management: DAVID BOWEN
Supply Chain Management: JOSEPH CAVINATO
Applied Accounting: DALE DAVISON
Global Entrepreneurship: ROBERT HISRICH
Management: ANDREW INKPEN
Management: MANSOUR JAVIDAN
Int. Finance: JOHN F. MATHIS
Risk Management: JOHN O'CONNELL
Management: CHRISTINE PEARSON
Applied Family Business: ERNESTO POZA
Management: KANNAN RAMASWAMY
Int. Studies: MARTIN SOURS
Applied Entrepreneurship: STEVEN STRALSER
Global Management: MARY TEAGARDEN
Marketing: ROBERT WIDING

UNIVERSITY OF ADVANCING TECHNOLOGY

2625 West Baseline Rd, Tempe, AZ 85283-1056
Telephone: (602) 383-8228
Fax: (602) 383-8228
E-mail: admissions@uat.edu
Internet: www.uat.edu
Founded 1983 as CAD Institute; name changed to Univ. of Advancing Computer Technology 1997; present name 2002
Private control
Academic year: September to August
Pres.: DOMINIC P. PISTILLO
Vice-Pres. of Finance: ROBERT WRIGHT
Provost: DAVID B. BOLMAN
Dean of Admissions and Student Support: CHRYS PISTILLO
Dean of Academic Affairs: REBECCA R. WHITEHEAD
Dean of Institutional Accreditation: BILL PEACE
Dean of Student and Employer Affairs: MEREDITH BARHAM
Registrar: JUDITH DRAYER
Academic Librarian: SUSAN WHITE

Library of 10,000 books, CD-ROMs and videotapes
Number of students: 1,201 (267 online, 51 graduates)
Number of teachers: 64

15 Technology disciplines incl. Game Design, Game Programming, Artificial Life Programming, Network Security and Computer Forensics

Publication: *Journal of Advancing Technology* (2 a year).

UNIVERSITY OF ARIZONA

Tucson, AZ 85721
Telephone: (520) 621-2211
Fax: (602) 621-9118
Internet: www.arizona.edu

Founded 1885
Academic year: August to May (two terms)
Pres.: ROBERT N. SHELTON
Vice-Pres.: EDITH AUSLANDER
Senior Vice-Pres. for Business Affairs: JOEL VALDEZ
Exec. Vice-Pres. and Provost: GEORGE H. DAVIS
Vice-Pres. for External Relations: STEPHEN J. MacCARTHY
Vice-Pres. for Learning and Information Technologies (vacant)
Vice-Pres. for Legal Affairs and General Counsel: JUDITH LEONARD
Vice-Pres. for Enrollment Management: PATTI OTA
Vice-Pres. for Research, Graduate Studies and Economic Development: LESLIE TOLBERT
Vice-Pres. for Outreach: EUGENE SANDER
Dean of Students: MELISSO VITO
Dean of Univ. Libraries: CARLA STOFFLE

Library: see Libraries and Archives
Number of teachers: 1,723
Number of students: 34,000

Publications: *Arizona Law Review*, *Arizona Quarterly* (literature), *Arizona and the West* (quarterly, history), *Books of the Southwest*, *Bulletin*, *Business and Economic Review* (monthly), *Hispanic American Historical Review* (quarterly), *Record*

DEANS

College of Agriculture and Life Sciences: EUGENE SANDER
College of Architecture and Landscape Architecture: CHARLES ALBANESE
College of Management: PAUL R. PORTNEY
College of Education: RONALD W. MARX
College of Engineering: TOM PETERSON
College of Fine Arts: Dr MAURICE SEVIGNY
College of Humanities: CHARLES TATUM
College of Law: Prof. TONI MASSARO
College of Optical Sciences: Prof. JAMES C. WYANT
College of Science: Dr JOAQUIN RUIZ
College of Social and Behavioural Sciences: EDWARD DONNERSTEIN

PROFESSORS

College of Agriculture and Life Sciences:
ALLEN, R. E., Animal Science; Nutritional Sciences
AX, R. L., Animal Science; Obstetrics and Gynaecology
BEATTIE, B. R., Agricultural and Resource Economics
BOURQUE, D. P., Biochemistry; Molecular and Cellular Biology
BOWERS, W. S., Entomology
BRUSSEAU, M. L., Soil, Water and Environmental Sciences; Hydrology and Water Resources
BURAS, N., Hydrology and Water Resources
BYRNE, D. N., Entomology

CALDWELL, R. L., Soil, Water and Environmental Sciences; Communication
CATE, R. M., Family and Consumer Sciences
CHANDLER, V. L., Plant Science; Molecular and Cellular Biology
CHRISTENSON, J. A., Agricultural and Resource Economics
COATES, W. E., Arid Lands
COLBY, B. G., Agricultural and Resource Economics; Hydrology and Water Resources
COLLIER, R. J., Animal Science
COLLINS, J. K., Veterinary Science and Microbiology
CORY, D. C., Agricultural and Resource Economics
COX, D. E., Agriculture Education
DANIEL, T. C., Renewable Natural Resources; Psychology
DENISE, R. K., Animal Science
DENNEHY, T. J., Entomology
DESTEIGUER, J. E., Renewable Natural Resources
FFOLLIOTT, P. F., Watershed Management; Arid Lands
FOSTER, K. E., Arid Lands
GALBRAITH, D. W., Plant Science
GAY, L. W., Watershed Management
GERBA, C. P., Soil, Water and Environmental Sciences; Microbiology and Immunology
GIACOMELLI, G. A., Agricultural and Biosystems Engineering
GIMBLETT, H. R., Renewable Natural Resources; Landscape Architecture
GLENN, E. P., III, Soil, Water and Environmental Sciences; Wildlife and Fisheries Science
GOLL, D. E., Nutritional Sciences; Biochemistry
GUNATILAKA, L., Arid Lands
HAGEDORN, H. H., Entomology
HARTSHORNE, D. J., Nutritional Sciences; Biochemistry
HATCH, K. L., Agricultural and Biosystems Engineering
HAWES, M. C., Plant Pathology
HAWKINS, R. H., Watershed Management; Hydrology and Water Resources
HUETE, A. R., Soil, Water and Environmental Sciences
INNES, R. D., Agricultural and Resource Economics; Economics
JENSEN, M. H., Plant Science
JOENS, L. A., Veterinary Science and Microbiology
KALTENBACH, C., Animal Science
KENNEDY, C. K., Plant Pathology; Molecular and Cellular Biology
KNIGHT, J. A., Jr, Agriculture Education
LARKINS, B. A., Plant Science; Molecular and Cellular Biology
LEONARD, R. T., Plant Science
LIGHTNER, D. V., Veterinary Science and Microbiology
MAIER, R. M., Soil, Water and Environmental Sciences
MANNAN, R. W., Wildlife and Fisheries Science
MARCHELLO, J. A., Animal Science; Nutritional Sciences
MARSH, S. E., Arid Lands; Geography and Regional Development; Renewable Natural Resources
McCLARAN, M. P., Range Management
McCLURE, M. A., Plant Pathology
McDANIEL, R. G., Plant Science
McLAUGHLIN, S. P., Arid Lands
McPHERSON, G. R., Renewable Natural Resources
MILLER, G. M., Agriculture Education
MONKE, E. A., Agricultural and Resource Economics
MORAN, N. A., Ecology and Evolutionary Biology; Entomology

PEPPER, I. L., Soil, Water and Environmental Sciences
POE, S. E., Agricultural and Biosystems Engineering
RAY, D. T., Plant Science
REID, C. P., Renewable Natural Resources
RIDLEY, C. A., Family and Consumer Sciences; Psychology
ROHRBAUGH, M. J., Family and Consumer Sciences; Psychology
ROTH, R. L., Agricultural and Biosystems Engineering
ROWE, D. C., Family and Consumer Sciences; Psychology
RUYLE, G. B., Range Management
SANDER, E. G., Biochemistry; Nutritional Sciences
SCHOWENGERDT, R., Arid Lands; Electrical and Computer Engineering; Optical Sciences
SCHURG, W. A., Veterinary Science and Microbiology; Animal Science
SHAW, W. W., Wildlife and Fisheries Science
SHIM, S., Family and Consumer Sciences
SILVERTOOTH, J. C., Soil, Water and Environment Sciences; Plant Science
SLACK, D. C., Agricultural and Biosystems Engineering
SONGER, J. G., Veterinary Science and Microbiology
STERLING, C. R., Veterinary Science and Microbiology
TABASHNIK, B., Entomology
THOMPSON, G. D., Agricultural and Resource Economics
VANETTEN, H. D., Plant Pathology
VIERLING, E., Biochemistry; Molecular and Cellular Biology
WARRICK, A. W., Soil, Water and Environmental Sciences; Hydrology and Water Resources
WHEELER, D. E., Entomology
WIERENGA, P. J., Soil, Water and Environmental Sciences
WILSON, P. N., Agricultural and Resource Economics
WOLFE, F. H., Nutritional Sciences
ZWOLINSKI, M. J., Watershed Management

College of Architecture, Planning and Landscape Architecture:
ALBANESE, C. A., Architecture
CHALFOUN, N. V., Architecture
ERIBES, R. A., Planning; Architecture
MALO, A., Architecture
MATTER, F. S., Planning; Architecture
ROSENBLOOM, S., Planning; Architecture
SAN MARTIN, I. J., Architecture
STAMM, W. P., Architecture

Eller College of Business and Public Administration:
BLOCK, M. K., Economics
BRUCKS, M. L., Marketing
BURGOON, J. K., Communication
CHEN, H., Management Information Systems
CONNOLLY, T., Management and Policy
COX, J. C., Economics
DROR, M., Management Information Systems
DYL, E. A., Finance
FELIX, W. L., Accounting
FISHBACK, P. V., Economics
GILLILAND, S. W., Management and Policy
HECKLER, S. E., Marketing
IACOBUCCI, D. M., Marketing
ISAAC, M. R., Economics
KANTOR, S. E., Economics
LIBECAP, G. D., Economics
McCABE, K. A., Economics
MILWARD, H. B., Public Administration and Policy; Management and Policy
NUNAMAKER, J. F., Jr, Management Information Systems
OAXACA, R. L., Economics

RAM, S., Management Information Systems
RAPORPORT, A., Management and Policy
SHENG, O. R. L., Management Information Systems
SILVERS, A. L., Public Administration and Policy
SMITH, K. R., Economics
TAYLOR, L. D., Economics
WALKER, M. A., Economics
WALLENDORF, M., Marketing
WALLER, W. S., Accounting
ZUPAN, M. A., Economics

College of Education:

ALEAMONI, L. M., Special Education, Rehabilitation and School Psychology
AMES, W. S., Teaching and Teacher Education
ANDERS, P. L., Language, Reading and Culture
ANTIA, S. D., Special Education, Rehabilitation and School Psychology
CARTER, K. J., Teaching and Teacher Education
DOYLE, W., Teaching and Teacher Education
GOOD, T. L., Educational Psychology
GOODMAN, Y. M., Language, Reading and Culture
GRIFFEY, D. C., Physical Education
LESLIE, L., Higher Education
LEVIN, J. R., Educational Psychology
LEVIN, J. S., Higher Education
MAKER, C. J., Special Education, Rehabilitation and School Psychology
MCCARTY, T. L., Language, Reading and Culture
MISHRA, S. P., Special Education, Rehabilitation and School Psychology
MOLL, L. C., Language, Reading and Culture
MORRIS, R. J., Special Education, Rehabilitation and School Psychology
OBRZUT, J. E., Special Education, Rehabilitation and School Psychology
RHOADES, G. D., Higher Education (H)
RUIZ, R., Language, Reading and Culture
SABERS, D. L., Educational Psychology
SALES, A. P., Special Education, Rehabilitation and School Psychology
SHORT, K. G., Language, Reading and Culture
SLAUGHTER, S. A., Higher Education
STREITMATTER, J. L., Educational Psychology
TAYLOR, J. L., Educational Administration
UMBREIT, J., Special Education, Rehabilitation and School Psychology
VALMONT, W. J., Language, Reading and Culture
WOODARD, D. B., Higher Education

College of Engineering and Mines:

ARNOLD, R. G., Chemical Engineering
ASKIN, R. G., Systems and Industrial Engineering
BAHILL, A. T., Systems and Industrial Engineering
BALES, R. C., Hydrology and Water Resources
BALSA, T. F., Aerospace and Mechanical Engineering
BASSETT, R. L., Hydrology and Water Resources
BIRNIE, D. P. III, Materials Science and Engineering; Electrical and Computer Engineering
BREWS, J. R., Electrical and Computing Engineering
BUDHU, M., Civil Engineering and Engineering Mechanics
BURAS, N., Hydrology and Water Resources
CALVERT, P. D., Materials Science and Engineering
CELLIER, F. E., Electrical and Computer Engineering

CETAS, T. C., Aerospace and Mechanical Engineering; Electrical and Computer Engineering
CHAMPAGNE, F. H., Aerospace and Mechanical Engineering
CHEN, C. F., Aerospace and Mechanical Engineering
COLBY, B. G., Hydrology and Water Resources
CONTRACTOR, D., Civil Engineering and Engineering Mechanics
DAVENPORT, W. G., Materials Science and Engineering
DAVIS, D. R., Hydrology and Water Resources
DESAI, C., Civil Engineering and Engineering Mechanics
DEYMIER, P. A., Materials Science and Engineering
EHSANI, M. R., Civil Engineering and Engineering Mechanics
FASEL, H. F., Aerospace and Mechanical Engineering
FRANTZISKONIS, G. N., Civil Engineering and Engineering Mechanics
GANAPOL, B. D., Hydrology and Water Resources
HALDAR, A., Civil Engineering and Engineering Mechanics
HAWKINS, R. H., Hydrology and Water Resources
HEINRICH, J. C., Aerospace and Mechanical Engineering
HIGLE, J. L., Systems and Industrial Engineering
HISKEY, J. B., Materials Science and Engineering
JACKSON, K. A., Materials Science and Engineering; Optical Sciences
KECECIOGLU, D. B., Aerospace and Mechanical Engineering
KERSCHEN, E. J., Aerospace and Mechanical Engineering
KOSTUK, R. K., Electrical and Computer Engineering; Optical Sciences
KULATILAKE, P., Mining and Geological Engineering
KUNDU, T., Civil Engineering and Engineering Mechanics
LOURI, A., Electrical and Computer Engineering
LYNCH, D. C., Materials Science and Engineering
MADDOCK, T., III, Hydrology and Water Resources
MADENCI, E., Aerospace and Mechanical Engineering
MARCELLIN, M. W., Electrical and Computer Engineering
MIRCHANDANI, P. B., Systems and Industrial Engineering; Electrical and Computer Engineering
NEUMAN, S. P., Hydrology and Water Resources
NIKRAVESH, P. E., Aerospace and Mechanical Engineering
OHANLON, J. F., Electrical and Computer Engineering
PALUSINSKI, O. A., Electrical and Computer Engineering
PETERSON, T. W., Chemical and Environmental Engineering (H)
POIRIER, D. R., Materials Science and Engineering
PRINCE, J. L., III, Electrical and Computer Engineering
RAGHAVAN, S., Materials Science and Engineering
RAMBERG, J. S., Systems and Industrial Engineering
RAMOHALLI, K. N., Aerospace and Mechanical Engineering
REAGAN, J. A., Electrical and Computer Engineering; Optical Sciences
ROZENBLIT, J. W., Electrical and Computer Engineering

SAADATMANESH, H., Civil Engineering and Engineering Mechanics
SCHOOLEY, L. C., Electrical and Computer Engineering
SCHOWENGERDT, R., Electrical and Computer Engineering; Optical Sciences
SEN, S., Systems and Industrial Engineering
SHADMAN, F., Chemical Engineering
SHUTTLEWORTH, W. J., Hydrology and Water Resources
SIMMONS, J. H., Materials Science and Engineering; Optical Sciences
SIMON, B. R., Aerospace and Mechanical Engineering
SOROOSHIAN, S., Hydrology and Water Resources; Systems and Industrial Engineering
STERNBERG, B. K., Mining and Geological Engineering
STRICKLAND, R. N., Electrical and Computer Engineering; Optical Sciences
SUNDARESHAN, M. K., Electrical and Computer Engineering
SZIDAROVSZKY, F., Systems and Industrial Engineering; Hydrology and Water Resources
SZILAGYI, M. N., Electrical and Computer Engineering
UHLMANN, D. R., Materials Science and Engineering; Optical Sciences
VALDES, J. B., Civil Engineering and Engineering Mechanics; Hydrology and Water Resources
VARADY, R. G., Hydrology and Water Resources
VRUDHULA, S. B. K., Electrical and Computer Engineering
WANG, F., Systems and Industrial Engineering
WEINBERG, M. C., Materials Science and Engineering
WENDT, J. O. L., Chemical and Environmental Engineering
WILLIAMS, J. G., Nuclear and Energy Engineering
WILLIAMS, S. K., Materials Science and Engineering
WYGNANSKI, I. J., Aerospace and Mechanical Engineering
YEH, T.-C. J., Hydrology and Water Resources
ZEIGLER, B. P., Electrical and Computer Engineering
ZIOLKOWSKI, R. W., Electrical and Computer Engineering

College of Fine Arts:

ASIA, D. I., Music
BOELTS, J. G., Art
CALDWELL, C. B., Media Arts
CHABOT, A. M., Art
CHAMBERLAIN, B. B., Music
COOK, G. D., Music
CROFT, M. F., Art
CUTIETTA, R. A., Music
DEMING, C. J., Media Arts
DIETZ, W. D., Music
DIXON, H. W., Theatre Arts
ERVIN, T. R., Music
FAN, P., Music
FERNANDEZ, N., Music
GEOFFRION, M. M., Art
GREER, W. D., Art
HAMMAN, D. L., Music
HAMMOND, H., Art
HANCOCK, J. L., Dance
HANSON, G. I., Music
HASKELL, J. R., Music
HEDDEN, S. K., Music
HITNER, C. V., Art
JONES, H. H., Art
KASHY, J. L., Music
KIRKBRIDE, J. E., Music
KOLOSICK, J. T., Music
LOWE, M., Dance

McLAUGHLIN, C. M., Music
MURPHY, E. W., Music
O'BRIEN, J. P., Music
PARRY, E. C., III, Art
PATTERSON, R. T., Music
POLK, A. W., Art
POWELL, G. C., Music
QUIROZ, A. J., Music
ROE, C. R., Music
ROGERS, B. J., Art
SEVIGNY, M. J., Art
TUCCI, A. D., Theatre Arts
TUNKARA, M. S., Art
WIMMER, G. E., Art
WINSLOW, D. J., Theatre Arts
ZUMBRO, N. L., Music

College of Humanities:

AIKEN, S. H., English
ARIEW, R. A., French and Italian
BABCOCK, B. A., English
BECK, J., French and Italian
BOWEN, R., English
CANFIELD, J. D., English
CHANDOLA, A. C., East Asian Studies
CHISHOLM, D. H., German Studies
CLASSEN, A., German Studies
COMPITELLO, M. A., Spanish and Portuguese
DAHOOD, R., English
DAYAN, J., English
DRYDEN, E. A., English
ENOS, T., English
EPSTEIN, W. H., English
EVANS, E. J., English
EVERS, L. J., English
FIELDER, G. E., Russian and Slavic Languages
FIORE, R. L., Spanish and Portuguese
GARRARD, J. G., Russian and Slavic Languages
GILABERT, J. J., Spanish and Portuguese
GONZALEZ, R. D., English
GUTSCHE, G. J., Russian and Slavic Languages
GYURKO, L. A., Spanish and Portuguese
HOGLE, J. E., English
HOUSTON, R. W., English
KIEFER, F. P., Jr, English
KINKADE, R. P., Spanish and Portuguese
KOLODNY, A., English
KUNNIE, J. E., African-American Studies
LEONARD, A., Jr, Classics; Near Eastern Studies
MARTINSON, S. D., German Studies
McKNIGHT, B. E., East Asian Studies
MEDINE, P. E., English
MILLER, J. R., English
MILLER, T. P., English
MOMADAY, N. S., English
MONSMAN, G. C., English
NANTELL, J. A., Spanish and Portuguese
ORLEN, S. L., English
PENNER, J. D., English
PIALORSI, F. P., English
POVERMAN, C. E., English
PROMIS, J. M. O., Spanish and Portuguese
RAVAL, S. S., English
RIVERO, E. S., Spanish and Portuguese
SALDATE, M. IV, Education Foundations and Administration
SAVILLE-TROIKE, M., English
SCHULZ, R. A., German Studies
SCRUGGS, C. W., English
SHELTON, R. W., English
SKINNER, M. B., Classics
SOLOMON, J., Classics
SOREN, H. D., Classics
TAO, C-L. P., East Asian Studies
TAO, J-S., East Asian Studies
TAPAHONSO, L., American Indian Studies
TATUM, C. M., Spanish and Portuguese
TERPENING, R. H., French and Italian
TROIKE, R. C., English
ULREICH, J. C., Jr, English
VANCE, T. J., East Asian Studies

VOYATZIS, M. E., Classics
WAUGH, L. R., French and Italian
WILD, P. T., English
WITTIG, M. M., French and Italian; Women's Studies

James E. Rogers College of Law:

ANAYA, S. J.
ANDREWS, A. W.
ATWOOD, B. A.
AUSTIN, G. W.
BRAUCHER, J.
CHIORAZZI, M. G.
DOBBS, D. B.
GANTZ, D. A.
GLENNON, R. J., Jr, Law and Public Policy
HEGLAND, K. F.
HENDERSON, R. C.
KORN, J. B.
KOZOLCHYK, B.
MASSARO, T. M.
MAUET, T. A.
OBIORA, L. A.
RATNER, J. R.
SCHNEYER, T. J.
SCHUESSLER, T. L.
SILVERMAN, A.
SPECE, R. G., Jr
WEISS, E. J.
WILLIAMS, R. A., Jr
WOODS, W. D., Jr

College of Medicine:

AHMANN, F. R., Medicine; Surgery
AKPORIAYE, E., Microbiology and Immunology
ALBERTS, D. S., Medicine; Pharmacology; Public Health
ALECK, K. A., Clinical Paediatrics
ALPERT, J. S., Medicine
AMPEL, N. M., Medicine
ATWATER, A. E., Physiology
BALDWIN, A. L., Physiology
BARANKO, P. V., Clinical Professor
BARKER, S. J., Anaesthesiology
BARNES, G. R., Jr, Clinical Professor
BARRETT, H. H., Optical Sciences; Radiology
BARTON, L. L., Paediatrics
BERG, R. A., Paediatrics
BERNSTEIN, H., Microbiology and Immunology
BOWDEN, G. T., Radiation Oncology; Pharmacology and Toxicology
BOYWER, T. D., Medicine
BRANDENBURG, R. O., Medicine
BRAUN, E. J., Physiology
BUCHSBAUM, H. W., Clinical Neurology
BURT, J. M., Physiology; Surgery
BUXER, J. B., Clinical Professor
CANFIELD, L. M., Public Health
CARMONA, R. H., Clinical Surgery
CARTER, D. E., Pharmacology and Toxicology
CETAS, T. C., Radiation Oncology
CHAMBLISS, L., Clinical Obstetrics and Gynaecology
CLEWELL, W. H., Clinical Professor
COULL, B. M., Neurology; Medicine
COULTHARD, S. W., Clinical Surgery
CRAIG, A. D., Jr, Cell Biology and Anatomy
CROSS, H. E., Clinical Ophthalmology
CUNNIFF, C. M., Paediatrics; Clinical Obstetrics and Gynaecology
CUNNINGHAM, J. T., Clinical Medicine
DALLAS, W. J., Optical Sciences; Radiology
DALTON, W. S., Medicine
DANTZLER, W. H., Physiology
DASPIT, C. P., Clinical Surgery
DAVIS, T. P., Pharmacology
DELLON, A. L., Clinical Professor
DEMEURE, M. J., Surgery
DORR, R. T., Pharmacology
DRESNER, M. L., Clinical Surgery
DRYDEN, R. M., Clinical Opthalmology
DUCKWORTH, W. C., Clinical Medicine
DUNCAN, B. R., Paediatrics; Public Health

ELLIOT, J., Clinical Obstetrics and Gynaecology
ERENBERG, A., Clinical Paediatrics
ESCOBAR, P. L., Clinical Medicine
EWY, G. A., Medicine
FAGAN, T. C., Medicine
FELICETTA, J. V., Clinical Medicine
FISHBURNE, J. I., Jr, Clinical Obstetrics and Gynaecology
FLINK, I. L., Medicine
FREGOSI, R. F., Physiology
FRENCH, E. D., Pharmacology
FREUNDLICH, I. M., Clinical Professor
FRIEDMAN, R. L., Microbiology and Immunology
GALGIANI, J. N., Medicine
GANDOLFI, A. J., Anaesthesiology; Pharmacology and Toxicology
GAREWAL, H. S., Medicine
GATENBY, R. A., Radiology
GELENBERG, A. J., Psychiatry
GERNER, E. W., Radiation Oncology
GHISHAN, F. K., Paediatrics; Physiology
GILLIES, R. J., Radiology
GLATTKE, T. J., Surgery
GLEASON, D. M., Clinical Surgery
GLICKMAN, S. I., Clinical Surgery
GMITRO, A. F., Radiology; Optical Sciences
GOLDMAN, S., Surgery; Medicine
GORE, R. W., Physiology; Cell Biology and Anatomy
GRAHAM, A. R., Pathology
GRANA, W. A., Orthopaedic Surgery
GREEN, S. A., Public Health
GROGAN, T. M., Pathology
GROSS, R. A., Clinical Medicine
GROSSMAN, M., Clinical Medicine
GRUENER, R. P., Physiology
HABIB, M. P., Clinical Medicine
HADJIPAVLOU, A. G., Clinical Surgery
HALE, F. A., Clinical Family and Community Medicine
HALONEN, M. J., Pharmacology; Microbiology; Medicine
HAMEROFF, S. R., Anaesthesiology
HAMILTON, A. J., Surgery; Clinical Radiation Oncology; Psychology
HANSEN, R. C., Medicine; Paediatrics
HARRIS, D. T., Microbiology and Immunology
HATCH, K. D., Obstetrics and Gynaecology
HAUSSLER, M. R., Biochemistry
HAYNES, R. J., Clinical Surgery
HEINE, M. W., Obstetrics and Gynaecology
HENDIN, B. A., Clinical Neurology
HERMAN, R. M., Pharmacology
HERSH, E. M., Medicine; Microbiology and Immunology
HOYER, P. B., Physiology
HUNT, K. R., Clinical Radiology
HUNTER, T. B., Radiology
HUTTER, J. J., Paediatrics
ISERSON, K. V., Emergency Medicine
JOHNSON, D. G., Medicine; Pharmacology
KALIVAS, J., Clinical Medicine
KAPLAN, A. M., Clinical Paediatrics
KATZ, M. A., Medicine; Physiology
KAY, M., Microbiology and Immunology; Medicine
KERN, K. B., Medicine
KLOTZ, S. A., Medicine
LANCE, M. P., Medicine
LANE, R. D., Psychiatry
LEIBOWITZ, A. I., Clinical Medicine
LESLIE, J. B., Clinical Anaesthesiology
LEVINE, B. E., Clinical Medicine
LEVINE, N., Medicine
LEVINE, R. B., Neurobiology; Physiology
LEVY, P., Clinical Medicine
LIEN, Y-H. H., Medicine; Physiology
LISSE, J. R., Medicine
LOHMAN, T. G., Physiology
LUKAS, R. J., Pharmacology
MALAN, T. P., Anaethesiology
MALONE, J. M., Clinical Surgery

MARCHALONIS, J. J., Microbiology and Immunology; Pathology; Medicine
MARSHALL, J. R., Public Health; Medicine
MARSHALL, W. N., Jr, Clinical Paediatrics
MARTINEZ, F., Paediatrics
MATTOX, J. H., Public Health; Clinical Obstetrics and Gynaecology
McCARTY, R. J., Clinical Medicine
McCLURE, C. L., Clinical Family and Community Medicine
McCUSKEY, R. S., Cell Biology and Anatomy; Physiology
McDONAGH, P. F., Surgery; Physiology
McLOONE, J. B., Clinical Psychiatry
McMULLEN, N. T., Cell Biology and Anatomy; Neurology
MEISLIN, H. W., Emergency Medicine
MICHAEL, U. F., Clinical Medicine
MILLER, J. M., Ophthalmology; Optical Sciences
MILLER, T. P., Medicine
MILLS, J. L., Surgery
MOHER, L. M., Clinical Family and Community Medicine
MORGAN, W. J., Paediatrics; Physiology
MORKIN, E., Medicine; Physiology; Pharmacology
MORRISON, D. A., Medicine; Radiology
NAGLE, R. B., Pathology; Cell Biology and Anatomy; Surgery
NOLTE, J., Cell Biology and Anatomy
OBER, R. R., Clinical Ophthalmology
OLESON, J. R., Radiation Oncology
ORTIZ, A., Public Health
OTTO, C. W., Anaesthesiology
OUTWATER, E. K., Radiology
OVITT, T. W., Radiology
PALMER, C. M., Clinical Anaesthesiology
PAYNE, C. M., Microbiology and Immunology
PEIRCE, J. C., Clinical Medicine
PELLETIER, K. R., Clinical Professor
PENG, Y-M., Medicine
PETERSEN, E. A., Medicine; Family and Community Health; Public Health
PETERSEN, S. R., Clinical Professor
PHIBBS, B. P., Clinical Medicine
PINNAS, J. L., Clinical Professor
PORRECA, F., Pharmacology; Anaethesiology
PORTER, J. M., Clinical Surgery
POTTER, R. L., Psychiatry
POWIS, G., Pathology; Pharmacology
PURDON, T. F., Clinical Obstetrics and Gynaecology
PUST, R. E., Family and Community Medicine; Public Health
PUTNAM, C. W., Surgery; Pharmacology
QUAN, S. F., Medicine; Anaesthesiology
RACY, J. C., Psychiatry
RAMSAY, E. G., Surgery
RANCE, N. E., Pathology; Neurology; Cell Biology and Anatomy
RAY, C. G., Clinical Pathology
REED, K. L., Obstetrics and Gynaecology
REICHLIN, S., Medicine
REIMAN, E. M., Psychiatry
REKATE, H. L., Clinical Surgery
REYNA, V. F., Surgery; Medicine
RIMSZA, M. E., Clinical Paediatrics
RIZKALLAH, T. H., Clinical Obstetrics and Gynaecology
ROBBINS, R. A., Medicine
ROEHRIG, H., Radiology
ROESKE, W. R., Medicine; Pharmacology
ROSENFELD, P. A., Clinical Obstetrics and Gynaecology
RUNYAN, R. B., Cell Biology and Anatomy
RYAN, K. J., Pathology; Microbiology and Immunology
SABBAGH, A. H., Clinical Professor
SAMPLINER, R. E., Medicine
SANDERS, A. B., Emergency Medicine
SANOWSKI, R. A., Clinical Medicine
SATTENSPIEL, E., Clinical Obstetrics and Gynaecology

SCHIFF, M., Clinical Surgery
SCHILLER, W. R., Clinical Surgery
SCHMITZ, G. L., Clinical Surgery
SCHORR, W. F., Clinical Medicine
SCHUMACHER, M. J., Paediatrics; Medicine
SECOMB, T. W., Physiology
SEEGER, J. F., Radiology
SETHI, G. K., Surgery
SHAH, J. H., Medicine; Radiology
SHAPIRO, W. R., Clinical Neurology
SHEHAB, Z. M., Clinical Paediatrics; Clinical Pathology
SHISSLAK, C. M., Public Health; Family and Community Medicine, Psychology
SIBLEY, W. A., Neurology
SILVERMAN, H. D., Clinical Family and Community Medicine
SIPES, I. G., Pharmacology and Toxicology; Anaesthesiology
SKINNER, P. H., Family and Community Medicine
SLOVITER, R. S., Pharmacology; Neurology
SNYDER, R. W., Ophthalmology
SOBONYA, R. E., Pathology
SONNTAG, V. K. H., Clinical Surgery
SPAITE, D. W., Emergency Medicine
SPETZLER, R. F., Surgery
STERN, L. Z., Medicine
STERN, R. G., Clinical Radiology
STONE, H. H., Clinical Surgery
STUART, D. G., Physiology
SURWIT, E. A., Clinical Obstetrics and Gynaecology
SZIVEK, J. A., Orthopaedic Surgery
TAETLE, R., Medicine
TISCHLER, M. E., Biochemistry; Medicine; Physiology
TOLBERT, L. P., Neurobiology; Cell Biology and Anatomy
ULMER, D. D., Clinical Medicine
UNGER, E. C., Radiology
VALENZUELA, T. D., Emergency Medicine
VAN WYCK, D., Medicine
VILLAR, H. V., Surgery; Radiation Oncology
WEIL, A. T., Clinical Public Health
WEINSTEIN, R. S., Pathology
WEISS, B. D., Clinical Family and Community Medicine
WEISS, J. C., Clinical Paediatrics
WHITNEY, P. J., Clinical Surgery
WILLIAMS, C. L., Surgery
WILLIAMS, R. L., Clinical Paediatrics
WILLIAMS, S. K., Surgery; Physiology
WITTE, C. L., Surgery
WITTE, M. H., Surgery
WITTEN, M. L., Paediatrics
WOOLFENDEN, J. M., Radiology
WOOSLEY, R. L., Pharmacology; Medicine
WRIGHT, S. H., Physiology
YAMAMURA, H. I., Pharmacology; Biochemistry; Psychiatry
YATES, A., Clinical Family and Community Medicine
YUDELL, A., Clinical Neurology

College of Nursing:

BADGER, T. A.
GLITTENBERG, J. E.
ISENBERG, M. A.
MOORE, I. M.
PARSONS, L. C.
PHILLIPS, L. R.
REED, P. G.
VERRAN, J. A.
WOODTLI, M. A.

College of Pharmacy:

BOOTMAN, J. L., Pharmacy Practice and Science; Pharmaceutical Sciences; Public Health
CARTER, D. E., Pharmacology and Toxicology
COLE, J. R., Medicinal Chemistry; Pharmaceutical Sciences
CONSROE, P. F., Pharmacology and Toxicology

COONS, S. J., Pharmacy Practice and Science; Public Health
DRAUGALIS, J., Pharmacy Practice and Science; Pharmaceutical Sciences
GANDOLFI, A. J., Pharmacology; Pharmacology and Toxicology
HURLEY, L., Medicinal Chemistry–Pharmacology and Toxicology; Medicinal Chemistry–Pharmaceutical Sciences
JACOBSON, E. L., Pharmacology and Toxicology
JACOBSON, M. K., Medicinal Chemistry–Pharmacology and Toxicology
LIEBLER, D. C., Pharmacology and Toxicology
MAYERSOHN, M., Pharmaceutical Sciences
McQUEEN, C. A., Pharmacology and Toxicology
MURPHY, J. E., Pharmacy Practice and Science; Pharmaceutical Sciences
NOLAN, P. E., Pharmacy Practice and Science; Pharmaceutical Sciences
REGAN, J. W., Pharmacology and Toxicology
SCHRAM, K. H., Pharmaceutical Sciences
SIPES, I. G., Pharmacology and Toxicology
SLOVITER, R. S., Pharmacology
TIMMERMANN, B., Pharmacology and Toxicology; Pharmaceutical Sciences
TONG, T. G., Pharmacy Practice and Science; Pharmacology and Toxicology
YALKOWSKY, S. H., Pharmaceutical Sciences

College of Science:

ADAMOWICZ, L., Chemistry
ANDREWS, G. R., Computer Science
ANGEL, J. R. P., Astronomy; Optical Sciences
APOSHIAN, H. V., Molecular and Cellular Biology; Pharmacology
ARMSTRONG, N. R., Chemistry; Optical Sciences
ARNETT, W. D., Astronomy
ATKINSON, G. H., Chemistry; Optical Sciences
BALDWIN, T. O., Biochemistry
BARRETT, B. R., Physics
BARTON, M. D., Geosciences
BAYLES, K. A., Speech and Hearing Science
BECK, S. L., Geosciences
BETTERTON, E. A., Atmospheric Sciences
BICKEL, W. S., Physics
BIRKY, C. W., Jr, Ecology and Environmental Biology
BOURQUE, D. P., Biochemistry; Molecular and Cellular Biology
BOWDEN, G. T., Radiation Oncology; Pharmacology and Toxicology; Molecular and Cellular Biology
BOYNTON, W. V., Lunar and Planetary Laboratory; Planetary Sciences
BREDAS, J-L. E., Chemistry
BRILLIANT, M. H., Paediatrics; Molecular and Cellular Biology
BROWER, D. L., Molecular and Cellular Biology; Biochemistry
BROWN, M. F., Chemistry; Biochemistry
BROWN, R. H., Planetary Sciences; Lunar and Planetary Laboratory; Astronomy
BURD, G. D., Molecular and Cellular Biology; Cell Biology and Anatomy; International Studies
BURROWS, A. S., Physics; Astronomy
BUTLER, R. F., Geosciences; Arizona Research Laboratories
CALDER, W. A., III, Ecology and Evolutionary Biology
CRANFIELD, L. M., Biochemistry; Public Health
CHANDLER, V. L., Plant Science; Molecular and Cellular Biology
CHASE, C. G., Geosciences
COHEN, A. S., Geosciences; Ecology and Environmental Biology

CRESS, A. E., Radiation Oncology; Molecular and Cellular Biology
CUSANOVICH, M. A., Biochemistry; Chemistry
CUSHING, J. M., Mathematics
DAVIES, R., Atmospheric Sciences
DAVIS, O. K., Geosciences
DEAN, J. S., Dendrochronology; Anthropology
DEBRAY, S. K., Computer Science
DECELLES, P. G., Geosciences
DENTON, M. B., Chemistry; Geosciences
DIECKMANN, C. L., Biochemistry; Molecular and Cellular Biology
DOWNEY, P. J., Computer Science
DRAKE, M. J., Planetary Sciences; Lunar and Planetary Laboratory; Arizona Research Laboratories; Geosciences
ENEMARK, J. H., Chemistry
ERCOLANI, N. M., Mathematics
ERICKSON, R. P., Paediatrics; Molecular and Cellular Biology
FANG, L-Z., Physics
FARIS, W. G., Mathematics
FINK, U., Lunar and Planetary Laboratory; Planetary Sciences
FLASCHKA, H., Mathematics
FLESSA, K. W., Geosciences
FORSTER, K. I., Psychology
FRIEDLANDER, L., Mathematics
GANGULY, T., Geosciences
GARCIA, J. D., Physics
GAY, D. A., Mathematics
GEHRELS, A. M. J. T., Lunar and Planetary Laboratory; Planetary Sciences
GEHRELS, G. E., Geosciences
GLASS, R. S., Chemistry
GLATTKE, T. J., Speech and Hearing Science; Surgery
GREENBERG, R. J., Planetary Sciences; Teaching and Teacher Education
GREENLEE, W. M., Mathematics
GRIMES, W. J., Biochemistry; Molecular and Cellular Biology
GROVE, L. C., Mathematics
GUPTA, R., Computer Science
HALLICK, R. B., Biochemistry
HAUSSLER, M. R., Biochemistry
HAYNES, C. V., Geosciences
HERMAN, B. M., Atmospheric Sciences
HILDEBRAND, J. G., Neurobiology; Biochemistry
HOLLAND, A. L., Speech and Hearing Science
HRUBY, V. J., Chemistry; Arizona Research Laboratories; Biochemistry
HSIEH, K C., Physics
HUBBARD, W. B., Lunar and Planetary Laboratory; Planetary Sciences
HUGHES HALLETT, D. J., Mathematics
HUGHES, M. K., Dendrochronology; Watershed Management
IMPEY, C. D., Astronomy
JOHNS, K. A., Physics
JOHNSON, R. A., Geosciences
JOKIPII, J. R., Planetary Sciences; Lunar and Planetary Laboratory; Astronomy
KELLER, P. C., Chemistry
KENNEDY, C. K., Plant Pathology; Molecular and Cellular Biology
KENNEDY, T. G., Mathematics; Physics
KENNICUTT, R. C., Astronomy
KRIEG, P. A., Cell Biology and Anatomy; Molecular and Cellular Biology
KUKOLICH, S. G., Chemistry
LARSON, H. P., Lunar and Planetary Laboratory; Planetary Sciences
LEAVITT, S. W., Dendrochronology
LEVERMORE, C. D., Mathematics
LEWIS, J. S., Lunar and Planetary Laboratory; Planetary Sciences
LICHTENBERGER, D. L., Chemistry
LIEBERT, J. W., Astronomy
LITTLE, J. W., Biochemistry; Molecular and Cellular Biology
LOMEN, D. O., Mathematics

LOVELOCK, D., Mathematics
LUNINE, J. I., Planetary Sciences; Lunar and Planetary Laboratory; Arizona Research Laboratories; Physics
MAIER, R., Mathematics; Physics
MARDER, S. R., Chemistry; Optical Sciences
MARKOW, T. A., Ecology and Environmental Biology
MASH, E. A., Jr, Chemistry
MAZUMDAR, S., Physics; Optical Sciences
MCCALLUM, W. G., Mathematics
MCCULLEN, J. D., Physics
MCINTYRE, L., Jr, Physics
MELIA, F., Physics; Astronomy
MELOSH, H. J., Lunar and Planetary Laboratory; Planetary Sciences; Geosciences
MENDELSON, N. H., Molecular and Cellular Biology
MICHOD, R. E., Ecology and Evolutionary Biology
MIESFELD, R. L., Biochemistry; Molecular and Cellular Biology
MITTAL, Y. D., Mathematics
MOLONEY, J. V., Mathematics; Optical Sciences
MORAN, N. A., Ecology and Environmental Biology; Entomology
MOUNT, D. W., Molecular and Cellular Biology; Ecology and Environmental Biology; Biochemistry
MULLEN, S. L., Atmospheric Sciences; Hydrology and Water Resources
MYERS, E. W., Jr, Computer Science; Molecular and Cellular Biology
NEWELL, A. C., Mathematics; Arizona Research Laboratories
O'BRIEN, D. F., Chemistry; Biochemistry
OCHMAN, H., Biochemistry; Ecology and Environmental Biology; Molecular and Cellular Biology
OVERPECK, J. T., Geosciences
PALMER, J. N., Mathematics
PARKER, R. R., Molecular and Cellular Biology; Biochemistry
PARRISH-JONES, J. T., Geosciences
PATCHETT, P. J., Geosciences; Arizona Research Laboratories
PATRASCIOIU, A. N., Physics
PEMBERTON, J. E., Chemistry
POLT, R. L., Chemistry
POMEAU, Y., Mathematics
RAFELSKI, J., Physics; Arizona Research Laboratories
RIEKE, G. H., Astronomy; Planetary Sciences; Lunar and Planetary Laboratory
RIEKE, M. J., Astronomy
ROSENZWEIG, M. L., Ecology and Evolutionary Biology
RUIZ, J., Geosciences
RUTHERFOORD, J. P., Physics
RYCHLIK, M. R., Mathematics
SALZMAN, W. R., Chemistry
SARCEVIC, I., Physics
SCADRON, M. D., Physics
SCHAFFER, W. M., Ecology and Evolutionary Biology
SCHLICHTING, R. D., Computer Science
SCHMIDT, G. D., Astronomy
SHAKED, M., Mathematics
SHUPE, M. A., Physics
SMITH, M. A., Chemistry
SNODGRASS, R. T., Computer Science
STEIN, D. L., Physics
STEVENSON, F. W., Mathematics
STRITTMATTER, P. A., Astronomy
SWETNAM, T. W., Dendrochronology
SWINDLE, T. D., Lunar and Planetary Laboratory; Planetary Sciences; Geosciences
TABOR, M., Mathematics; Applied Mathematics; Physics
THAKUR, D. S., Mathematics
THOMPSON, R. I., Astronomy
TIFFT, W. G., Astronomy

TISCHLER, M. E., Biochemistry; Medicine; Physiology
TITLEY, S. R., Geosciences
TOMASKO, M. G., Lunar and Planetary Laboratory
TOUBASSI, E., Mathematics
TOUSSAINT, W. D., Physics
VANETTEN, H. D., Plant Pathology; Molecular and Cellular Biology
VELEZ, W. Y., Mathematics
VENABLE, D. L., Ecology and Evolutionary Biology
VIERLING, E., Biochemistry; Molecular and Cellular Biology
VON HOFF, D. D., Medicine; Pathology; Molecular and Cellular Biology
WALKER, F. A., Chemistry; Biochemistry
WALLACE, T. C., Jr, Geosciences
WARD, S., Molecular and Cellular Biology; Ecology and Environmental Biology
WELLS, M. A., Biochemistry
WILLOUGHBY, S. S., Mathematics
WINFREE, A. T., Ecology and Environmental Biology
WING, W. H., Physics; Optical Sciences; Arizona Research Laboratories; International Studies
WOJTKOWSKI, M. P., Mathematics
WOOLF, N. J., Astronomy
WYSOCKI, V. H., Chemistry; Biochemistry
YELLE, R. V., Planetary Sciences; Lunar and Planetary Laboratory
ZAKHAROV, V. E., Mathematics
ZANDT, G., Geosciences
ZIURYS, L. M., Chemistry; Astronomy

College of Social and Behavioral Sciences:
ADAMS, E. C., Anthropology
ANDERSON, K. S., History
ANNAS, J. E., Philosophy
BARNES, C. A., Psychology
BASSO, E. B., Anthropology
BECHTEL, R. B., Psychology; Renewable Natural Resources
BECKER, D. V., Psychology; Psychiatry
BEEZLEY, W. H., History
BERGENSEN, A. J., Sociology
BERNSTEIN, A. E., History
BERNSTEIN, G. L., History
BEVER, T. G., Psychology; Linguistics; Cognitive Science
BONINE, M. E., Near Eastern Studies; Geography and Regional Development
BOOTZIN, R. R., Psychology; Psychiatry
BUCHANAN, A. E., Philosophy
CHALMERS, D. J., Philosophy
CHAVES, M. A., Sociology
CLARKE, J. W., Political Science
COSGROVE, R. A., History
DANIEL, T. C., Psychology; Renewable Natural Resources
DE LA TORRE, A. I., Mexican American Studies – Public Health
DEAN, J. S., Dendrochronology; Anthropology
DEMERS, R. A., Linguistics
DEUTSCH, S. J., History
DEVER, W. G., Near Eastern Studies
DINNERSTEIN, L., History
DINNERSTEIN, M., Women's Studies
DOBSON, M. V., Ophthalmology
EATON, R. M., History
ESTRADA, A. L., Mexican American Studies
FERNANDEZ, C., Sociology
FINAN, T. J., Anthropology
FISH, P. R., Anthropology
FORSTER, K. I., Psychology
FUCHS, E., Near Eastern Studies; Judaic Studies
GALASKIEWICZ, J. J., Sociology
GAMAL, A. S., Near Eastern Studies
GARCIA, J. A., Political Science
GARCIA, J. R., History
GARRETT, M. F., Psychology; Linguistics; Speech and Hearing Studies
GIBSON, L. J., Geography

GLISKY, E. L., Psychology
GLITTENBERG, J. E., Nursing; Psychiatry; Anthropology
GOLDMAN, A. I., Philosophy
GREENBERG, J. B., Anthropology
GUMERMAN, G. J., Anthropology
HAMMOND, M., Linguistics
HARNISH, R. M., Philosophy; Linguistics
HEALEY, R. A., Philosophy
HILL, J. H., Anthropology
HURT, C. D., Information Resources and Library Science; Communication
JACOB, C. S., Communication
JOHNSON, J. W., Journalism
KARANT-NUNN, S. C., History
KASZNIAK, A. W., Psychology; Psychiatry; Neurology
KENNEDY, E. J., Women's Studies; Anthropology
KING, J. E., Psychology; Anthropology
KRAMER, C., Anthropology
LANGENDOEN, D. T., Linguistics
LANSING, J. S., Anthropology
LONGACRE, W. A., Anthropology
MALONEY, J. C., Philosophy
MARSH, S. E., Arid Lands; Geography and Regional Development
MARSTON, S., Geography and Regional Development
MARTINEZ, O., History
MCNAUGHTON, B. L., Psychology; Physiology
MCPHERSON, J. M., Sociology
MISHLER, W. T., II, Political Science
MOLM, L. D., Sociology
MORBECK, M. E., Anthropology
MORILL, C. K., Sociology; Psychology; Communication
MULLIGAN, G. F., Geography and Regional Development
NADEL, L., Psychology
NADER, H., History
NICHOLS, R. L., History
NICHTER, M., Anthropology; Public Health
NORRANDER, B., Political Science
OLSEN, J. W., Anthropology
PAREZO, N. J., American Indian Studies; Anthropology
PETERSON, M. A., Psychology
PHILIPS, S. U., Anthropology
PIATTELLI-PALMARINI, M., Cognitive Science
PLANE, D., Geography and Regional Development
POLLOCK, J. L., Philosophy
RAGIN, C. C., Sociology
REID, J. J., Jr, Anthropology
ROHRBAUGH, M. J., Psychology; Family and Consumer Sciences
ROWE, D. C., Family and Consumer Sciences; Psychology
SALES, B. D., Psychology; Psychiatry; Law
SCHIFFER, M. B., Anthropology
SCHLEGEL, A. E., Anthropology
SCHMIDTZ, D. J., Philosophy; Economics
SCHWARTZ, G. E., Psychology; Psychiatry; Neurology; Medicine
SCHWARTZ, J. E., Political Science
SECHREST, L., Psychology
SHARKEY, J. E., Journalism
SHELDON, B. E., Information Resources and Library Science
SHERIDAN, T. E., Anthropology
SHOHAM, V., Psychology
SILVERS, A. L., Public Administration and Policy
SMITH, C. D., Jr, Near Eastern Studies
SMITH-LOVIN, D. L., Sociology
SNOW, D. A., Sociology
STEVENS, S. J., Research Professor
STINI, W. A., Anthropology; Family and Community Medicine; Public Health
SULLIVAN, M. P., Political Science
VOLGY, T. J., Political Science
WALKER, H. A., Sociology
WEINER, D. R., History

WELSH, W. A., Political Science; Family and Consumer Medicine
WENK, G. L., Psychology; Neurology
WILLIAMS, E. J., Political Science
WILLIAMS, J. M., Psychology
ZEGURA, S. L., Anthropology
ZEPEDA, O., Linguistics

Arizona International College:

AMEGAGO, M. M. K.
BIXBY, B. R.
BUKHARDT, P. E.
BURGESS, K. H.
CONTERIS, H. J.
DURAN-CERDA, D. M.
FERNANDO, J. L.
GRIJALVA, M. A.
HELGERT, J. P.
PELTIER, J.
POPE, E. R.
SCOTT, A. G.
SHERMAN, P. M.
SPATARO, L. P.
TAL, K.

Optical Sciences Center:

DERENIAK, E. L., Optical Sciences; Electrical and Computer Engineering
FALCO, C. M., Optical Sciences; Arizona Research Laboratories
FRIEDEN, B. R., Optical Sciences
GIBBS, H. M., Optical Sciences
MANSURIPUR, M., Optical Sciences
MARATHAY, A. S., Optical Sciences
MEYSTRE, P., Optical Sciences; Physics
PEYGHAMBARIAN, N. N., Optical Sciences; Materials Science and Engineering
POWELL, R. C., Optical Sciences; Materials Science and Engineering
SARGENT, M., III, Optical Sciences
SARID, D., Optical Sciences; Arizona Research Laboratories
SASIAN, J. M., Optical Sciences; Astronomy
SHACK, R. V., Optical Sciences
SHOEMAKER, R. L., Optical Sciences; Chemistry; Radiology
WRIGHT, E. M., Optical Sciences; Physics
WYANT, J. C., Optical Sciences; Electrical and Computer Engineering

Other academic units:

ACOSTA, J. J., Military Science Tactics
CHRISTMAN, W. E., Naval Science
DYCHE, D. D., Military Aerospace Studies
WILKINSON, R. H., Humanities Program

ATTACHED RESEARCH INSTITUTE

Mount Graham International Observatory: operated by Steward Observatory, the research arm of the Dept of Astronomy; see separate entry under Research Institutes.

UNIVERSITY OF PHOENIX

4615 East Elwood, Phoenix, AZ 85040
Telephone: (480) 966-9577
Internet: www.phoenix.edu
Founded 1976
Private control
President: Dr LAURA PALMER NOONE
Provost and Senior Vice-President, Academic Affairs: CRAIG SWENSON
Senior Vice-President, Public Affairs: TERRI HEDEGAARD-BISHOP
Executive Vice-President: BOB BARKER
Vice-President, Finance: LARRY FLEISCHER
Vice-President, University Services: NINA OMELCHENKO
CEO, Online Campus: BRIAN MUELLER

Number of teachers: 9,758
Number of students: 125,364

163 Campuses and learning centres in the USA, Canada and Puerto Rico; also Internet-based degree courses.

WESTERN INTERNATIONAL UNIVERSITY

9215 North Black Canyon Highway, Phoenix, AZ 85021
Telephone: (602) 943-2311
Fax: (602) 371-8637
E-mail: wiuinfo@apollogrp.edu
Internet: www.wintu.edu
Founded 1978
Private control
Registrar: HUE HASLIM

Campuses in China, India and Netherlands; undergraduate courses in: behavioural science, business, human resource management, accounting, business admin., information technology, int. business, management; graduate courses in: finance, information technology, int. business, management, marketing, information systems engineering.

BRANCH CAMPUSES

Chandler East Valley Campus: Suite 101, 55 North Arizona Place, Chandler, AZ 85225; tel. (602) 943-2311; fax (480) 726-3068.

Peoria Campus: Suite 100, 14100 North 83rd Ave, Peoria, AZ 85381; tel. (602) 943-2311; fax (623) 486-9030.

Fort Huachuca Campus: Buffalo Soldier Training and Education Center/Rascon Building #52104. ATZS-HRH-E, Fort Huachuca, AZ 85613-6000; tel. (520) 459-5040; fax (520) 459-7571.

Scottsdale Campus: Suite 120, 8860 East Chaparral Rd, Scottsdale, AZ 85250; tel. (602) 943-2311; fax (480) 850-1338.

ARKANSAS

ARKANSAS BAPTIST COLLEGE

1621 Dr Martin Luther King Dr., Little Rock, AR 72202
Telephone: (501) 370-4000
Internet: www.arkansasbaptist.edu
Private control
Founded 1885
Pres.: FITZ HILL
Vice-Pres.: JOHNNY JONES
Registrar: FREDDIE FOX
Librarian: SONYA BELL

DEANS

Scholars College: Dr MIRON BILLINGSLEY
School of Liberal Arts and Social Sciences: Dr NANCY GREER-WILLIAMS
School of Business and Applied Science: CONSTANCE MEADORS

ARKANSAS STATE UNIVERSITY

State University, AR 72467
Telephone: (870) 972-2030
Fax: (870) 972-2036
Internet: www.astate.edu
Founded 1909
Academic year: August to July
Pres.: Dr J. LESLIE WYATT
Vice-Pres. for Finance and Admin.: JENNUS L. BURTON
Vice-Pres. for Univ. Advancement: STEVE OWENS
Chancellor: Dr ROBERT POTTS
Vice-Chancellor for Research and Academic Affairs: Dr GLEN JONES
Vice-Chancellor for Student Affairs: Dr WILLIAM R. STRIPLING
Registrar: TRACY FINCH
Dir Library: CAROLYN HENDERSON

Library of 586,176 vols, 573,870 govt documents, 578,473 microform items, 14,508 audio-visual items, 1,675 periodicals, 117,328 journals

Number of teachers: 628

Number of students: 16,653 (ASU System)

Main campus in Jonesboro, also campuses in Beebe, Mountain Home, Newport, Heber Springs, Paragould; Technical Center at Marked Tree

DEANS

College of Agriculture: Dr GREGORY C. PHILLIPS

College of Business: Dr LEN FREY

College of Communications: Dr RUSSELL E. SHAIN

College of Education: Dr JOHN BEINEKE

College of Engineering: Dr GREG PHILLIPS

College of Fine Arts: Dr DANIEL REEVES

College of Humanities and Social Sciences: Dr GLORIA GIBSON

College of Nursing and Health Professions: Dr SUSAN N. HANRAHAN

College of Sciences and Mathematics: Dr GREG PHILLIPS

University College: Dr HERMAN W. STRICKLAND

Graduate School: Dr ANDREW SUSTICH

Independent Department of Military Science: Lt-Col LARRY AIKMAN (Chair)

ARKANSAS TECH UNIVERSITY

1605 Coliseum Dr, Russellville, AR 72801

Telephone: (479) 968-0389

Fax: (479) 964-0839

Internet: www.atu.edu

Founded 1909, present name and status 1976

Pres.: ROBERT CHARLES BROWN

Vice-Pres. for Academic Affairs: Dr JACK HAMM

Vice-Pres. for Admin. and Finance: DAVID MOSELEY

Vice-Pres. for Devt: JAYNE W. JONES

Vice-Pres. for Student Services: GARY M. BILLER

Chancellor of Ozark Campus: Dr JO ALICE BLONDIN

Registrar: C. GLENN SHEETS

Dir of Library: BILL PARTON

Library of 142,000 vols, 810,000 microforms, 88,000 govt documents and 1,245 current periodicals

Number of teachers: 300

Number of students: 5,855

DEANS

School of Business: THOMAS P. TYLER

School of Community Education and Professional Devt: MARY ANN ROLLINS

School of Education: GLENN SHEETS

School of Liberal and Fine Arts: GEORGENA D. DUNCAN

School of Physical and Life Sciences: RICHARD R. COHOON

School of Systems Science: JOHN W. WATSON

Graduate Studies: ELDON G. CLARY, Jr

CENTRAL BAPTIST COLLEGE

1501 College Ave, Conway, AR 72034

Telephone: (501) 329-6872

Fax: (501) 329-2941

E-mail: info@cbc.edu

Internet: www.cbc.edu

Founded 1952 as Conway Baptist College; present name 1962

Private control

Pres.: TERRY KIMBROW

Vice-Pres. for Academic Affairs: Dr GARY McALLISTER

Vice-Pres. for Financial Affairs: DON JONES

Vice-Pres. for Student Services: SANCY FAULK

Registrar: PHYLIS HOFFMANN

Librarian: ANNE CLEMENTS

Library of 40,000 books, periodicals, tapes, CDs, videos and microforms

Number of teachers: 50 full and part time

Number of students: 400

Depts of Behavioral Sciences, Bible, Business, Fine Arts, Health and Physical Education, Literature and Language Arts, Maths and Science, Social Studies.

HARDING UNIVERSITY

915 East Market Ave, Searcy, AR 72149

Telephone: (501) 279-4000

Fax: (501) 279-4865

E-mail: admissions@harding.edu

Internet: www.harding.edu

Founded 1924

Pres.: DAVID B. BURKS

Vice-Pres. for Academic Affairs: NEALE T. PRYOR

Registrar: JANICE HURD

Librarian: ANN DIXON

Library of 444,382 vols, 1,397 current periodicals, maps, audio-visual items, etc.

Number of teachers: 217

Number of students: 6,100

DEANS

College of Arts and Humanities: Dr DENNIS ORGAN

College of Bible and Religion: BRUCE McLARTY

College of Business Admin.: Dr BRYAN D. BURKS

College of Education: Dr LEWIS 'TONY' FINLEY

College of Nursing: Dr CATHLEEN M. SCULTZ

College of Sciences: Dr TRAVIS THOMPSON

HENDERSON STATE UNIVERSITY

1100 Henderson St, Arkadelphia, AR 71999-0001

Telephone: (870) 230-5000

Fax: (870) 230-5147

Internet: www.hsu.edu

Founded 1890 as church-related college; became a state institution in 1929

Academic year: August to May

Pres.: Dr CHARLES D. DUNN

Vice-Pres. for Academic Affairs: Dr ROBERT E. HOUSTON

Vice-Pres. for Finance and Admin.: BOBBY G. JONES

Vice-Pres. for Student Services: GAIL STEPHENS

Vice-Pres. for Univ. and Community Relations: DORIS N. WRIGHT

Registrar: TOM GATTIN

Dir of Learning Resources: ROBERT YEHL

Library of 250,000 vols

Number of teachers: 175

Number of students: 3,636

DEANS

School of Business: PAUL HUO

Ellis College of Arts and Sciences: Dr MARALYN SOMMER

Teachers College: JUDY HARRISON

Graduate School: Dr MARCK L. BEGGS

HENDRIX COLLEGE

1600 Washington Ave., Conway, AR 72032

Telephone: (501) 329-6811

Fax: (501) 450-1200

Internet: www.hendrix.edu

Founded 1876

Pres.: Dr J. TIMOTHY CLOYD

Provost: Dr ROBERT ENTZMINGER

Exec. Vice-Pres.: ROCK JONES

Vice-Pres. for Business and Finance: ROB YOUNG

Vice-Pres. for Enrolment: KAREN FOUST

Vice-Pres. for Student Affairs: JOYCE M. HARDIN

Registrar: XINYING WANG

Library Director: AMANDA MOORE

Depts of Biology, Chemistry, Mathematics and Computer Science, Physics, Art, English, Foreign Languages, Music, Philosophy, Religion, Theatre Arts and Dance, Economics and Business, Education, History, Kinesiology, Politics and Int. Relations, Psychology, Sociology

Library of 190,000 vols

Number of teachers: 85

Number of students: 1,094.

JOHN BROWN UNIVERSITY

2000 West University St, Siloam Springs, AR 72761

Telephone: (479) 5249500

E-mail: jbuinfo@jbu.edu

Internet: www.jbu.edu

Founded 1919 as Southwestern Collegiate Institute; name changed to John E. Brown College 1920; present name 1934

Private control

Pres.: Dr CHARLES POLLARD

Vice-Pres. for Academic Affairs: Dr ED ERICSON, III

Vice-Pres. for Enrollment Management: DON CRANDALL

Vice-Pres. for Finance and Administration: PATRICIA GUSTAVSON

Vice-Pres. for Student Development: Dr STEPHEN BEERS

Vice-Pres. for Univ. Advancement: Dr JAMES KRALL

Dean of Graduate Studies: Dr RICHARD ELLIS

Dean of Undergraduate Studies: Dr RICHARD OSTRANDER

Registrar: PAUL HINES

Library Director: MARY HABERMAS

Library of 120,000 items, incl. 4,000 periodicals

Number of teachers: 187 (92 full-time, 95 part-time)

Number of students: 2,000

Undergraduate academic divs: Biblical Studies, Business, Communication and Fine Arts, Education, Engineering and Construction Management, General Studies, Humanities and Social Sciences, Natural Sciences; depts in the Graduate Studies Division: Christian Ministry, Counselling, Leadership and Ethics.

LYON COLLEGE

POB 2317, Batesville, AR 72503-2317

Telephone: (870) 793-9813

Fax: (870) 698-4622

Internet: www.lyon.edu

Founded 1872; name changed from Arkansas College 1994

Academic year: September to May

President: WALTER B. ROETTGER

Vice-Pres. for Academic Services: JOHN M. PEEK

Vice-Pres. for Institutional Advancement: TIMOTHY L. BRUNER

Vice-Pres. for Enrolment Services: DENNY G. BARDOS

Vice-Pres. for Student Life and Dean of Students: Dr F. BRUCE JOHNSTON

Vice-Pres. for Business and Finance: KENNETH J. RUETER

Library Dir: DEAN COVINGTON

Library of 150,000 vols

Number of teachers: 45

Number of students: 540

Depts of: Accounting, Anthropology, Art, Biochemistry, Biology, Business Administration, Chemistry, Computer Science, Economics, Education, English, French, History, Mathematics, Music, Philosophy and Religion, Physics, Political Science, Psychology, Spanish, Theatre.

OUACHITA BAPTIST UNIVERSITY

410 Ouachita St, Arkadelphia, AR 71998
Telephone: (870) 245-5000
Fax: (870) 245-5412
Internet: www.obu.edu
Founded 1886 as Ouachita Baptist College; present name 1965
Private control
Academic year: August to July
Pres.: REX M. HORNE, Jr
Vice-Pres. for Academic Affairs: STAN POOLE
Chancellor: BEN ELROD
Vice-Pres. for Institutional Advancement: WESLEY KLUCK
Dean of Students: KELDON HENLEY
Registrar: JUDY JONES
Dir. of Library Services: Dr RAY GRANADE
Number of teachers: 108 full-time
Number of students: 1,452

DEANS

School of Business: PHILIP F. RICE
School of Christian Studies: J. SCOTT DUVALL
School of Education: MERRIBETH BRUNING
School of Fine Arts: CHARLES L. FULLER
School of Humanities: JEFF ROOT
School of Natural Sciences: JOE JEFFERS

PHILANDER SMITH COLLEGE

1 Trudie Kibbe Reed Dr., Little Rock, AR 72202
Telephone: (501) 375-9845
Fax: (501) 370-5277
Internet: www.philander.edu
Founded 1877 as Walden Seminary; present name 1882
Private control
Academic year: August to July
Pres.. Dr WALTER KIMBROUGH
Vice-Pres. for Institutional Advancement: Dr DELIA ANDERSON
Vice-Pres. for Student Affairs: Dr JULIANA MOSELEY ANDERSON
Vice-Pres. for Academic Affairs: Dr JOHN SIMPSON
Vice-Pres. for Fiscal Affairs and Chief Financial Officer: GERALD B. COLEMAN
Registrar: BERTHA OWENS
Dir Library Services: CHARLES ROGERS

Divs of: Humanities, Education, Business and economics, Natural and Physical Sciences, Social Sciences.

SOUTHERN ARKANSAS UNIVERSITY

100 East University, Magnolia, AR 71753-5000
Telephone: (870) 235-4000
Internet: www.saumag.edu
Founded 1911 as Third District Agricultural School; present name 1976
Academic year: August to July
Pres.: Dr DAVID RANKIN
Vice-Pres. for Academic Affairs: Dr CORBET J. LAMKIN
Vice-Pres. for Administration and General Counsel: ROGER GILES
Vice-Pres. for Student Affairs: Dr DONNA ALLEN
Vice-Pres. for Finance: DARRELL MORRISON
Dean of Students: BRIAN BERRY
Dean of Enrollment Services: SARA JENNINGS
Registrar: ED NIPPER
Library Dir: PEGGY WALTERS
Library of 150,000 vols
Number of students: 3,035

DEANS

College of Business: EARL STENNIS
School of Education: Dr RUBY BURGESS
College of Liberal and Performing Arts: DAVID L. CROUSE
School of Science and Technology: Dr JOE WINSTEAD
School of Graduate Studies: Dr KIM BLOSS-BERNARD

UNIVERSITY OF ARKANSAS

Fayetteville, AR 72701
Telephone: (479) 575-2000
Fax: (479) 575-7515
E-mail: uofa@uark.edu
Internet: www.uark.edu
Founded 1871
Academic year: August to May
Chancellor: Dr JOHN A. WHITE
Provost and Vice-Chancellor for Academic Affairs: Dr BOB SMITH
Vice-Chancellor for Finance and Administration: Dr DONALD PETERSON
Vice-Chancellor for Student Affairs: Dr JOHNETTA CROSS BRAZZELL
Vice-Chancellor for Univ. Advancement: Dr G. DAVID GEARHART
Vice-Chancellor for Government and Community Relations: RICHARD B. HUDSON
Dean of Students: Dr DANNY PUGH
Dir of Libraries: CAROLYN HENDERSON
Library of 1,656,907 vols
Number of teachers: 839 (main campus; 792 full-time, 47 part-time)
Number of students: 16,499 (main campus)

DEANS

Dale Bumpers College of Agricultural, Food and Life Sciences: GREG WEIDEMANN
J. W. Fulbright College of Arts and Sciences: Dr DON BOBBITT
College of Business Administration: DAN L. WORRELL
College of Education and Health Professions: Dr REED GREENWOOD
College of Engineering: ASHOK SAXENA
Graduate School: Dr COLLIS R. GEREN
School of Law: CYNDI NANCE
School of Architecture: JEFF SHANNON
School of Continuing Education: DONNIE DUTTON
Clinton School of Public Service: JAMES L. RUTHERFORD

UNIVERSITY OF ARKANSAS AT LITTLE ROCK

2801 South University Ave, Little Rock, AR 72204
Telephone: (501) 569-3000
Internet: www.ualr.edu
Founded 1927
Chancellor: Dr JOEL E. ANDERSON
Provost and Vice-Chancellor for Academic Affairs: DAVID BELCHER
Vice-Chancellor for Educational and Student Services: Dr CHARLES W. DONALDSON
Vice-Chancellor for Finance and Administration: LUCIAN SHOCKEY
Vice-Chancellor for Univ. Advancement: BILL WALKER
Dir Ottenheimer Library: BILL TRAYLOR
Dir Law Library: A. MICHAEL BEAIRD
Library of 500,000 vols, 11,000 and 28,000 electronic books and journals, 3,600 periodicals,
Number of teachers: 1,202 (675 full-time, 527 part-time)
Number of students: 10,889

DEANS

College of Arts, Humanities and Social Sciences: Dr DEBORAH BALDWIN

College of Business Administration: Dr WILLIAM C. GOOLSBY
College of Education: Dr ANGELA MAYNARD SEWALL
Donaghey College of Information Science and Systems Engineering: Dr MARY L. GOOD
College of Science and Mathematics: Dr MICHAEL LEDBETTER
Graduate Institute of Technology: Dr M. KEITH HUDSON (Dir)
College of Professional Studies: Dr ANGELA BRENTON
Graduate School: Dr RICHARD H. HANSON
School of Law: CHARLES W. GOLDNER, Jr

UNIVERSITY OF ARKANSAS AT MONTICELLO

Monticello, AR 71655
Telephone: (870) 460-1026
Fax: (870) 460-1933
Internet: www.uamont.edu
Founded 1909
Chancellor: H. JACK LASSITER
Vice-Chancellor for Academic Affairs: Dr R. DAVID RAY
Vice-Chancellor for Finance and Administration: JAY JONES
Vice-Chancellor for Student Affairs: Dr CLAY E. BROWN
Registrar: Dr DEBBIE K. BRYANT
Library Dir: SANDRA CAMPBELL
Library of 500,000 items incl. books, bound periodicals, govt documents, and 1,200 current periodicals
Number of teachers: 100
Number of students: 1,900

CHAIRS

Div. of Agriculture: Dr KELLY BRYANT
Div. of Computer Information Systems: Dr JIM ROIGER
Div. of Music: J. ANNETTE HALL
Div. of Nursing: Dr LARRY EUSTACE
General Studies: Dr RANELLE EUBANKS

DEANS

School of Arts and Humanities: Dr ERIN O'NEILL
School of Business: Dr LOUIS JAMES
School of Education: Dr PEGGY DOSS
School of Forest Resources: Dr RICHARD A. KLUENDER
School of Mathematics and Natural Sciences: Dr JOHN T. ANNULIS
School of Social and Behavioral Sciences: Dr VANNEISE COLLINS

UNIVERSITY OF ARKANSAS AT PINE BLUFF

1200 North University Dr., Pine Bluff, AR 71601
Telephone: (870) 575-8000
Internet: www.uapb.edu
Founded 1873
Liberal arts and land-grant institution
Chancellor: LAWRENCE A. DAVIS, Jr
Vice-Chancellor for Academic Affairs: Dr MARY E. BENJAMIN
Vice-Chancellor for Finance and Administration: JOSÉ R. ARJONA
Vice-Chancellor for Student Affairs: Dr BOBBIE A. IRVINS
Dir Library: EDWARD J. FONTENETTE
Library of 220,000 vols
Number of students: 3,710

DEANS

School of Agriculture, Fisheries and Human Sciences: Dr JACQUELINE W. McCRAY
School of Business and Management: Dr ANDREW HONEYCUTT
School of Education: Dr CALVIN JOHNSON

UNIVERSITY OF ARKANSAS FOR MEDICAL SCIENCES

4301 West Markham St, Little Rock, AR 72205

Telephone: (501) 686-7000
Internet: www.uams.edu

Pres.: B. ALAN SUGG
Chancellor: Dr I. DODD WILSON
Exec. Vice-Chancellor: JOHN SHOCK
Vice-Chancellor for Academic Affairs and Research Admin.: Dr LARRY D. MILNE
Vice-Chancellor for Admin. and Governmental Affairs: TOM S. BUTLER
Vice-Chancellor for Clinical Programs: RICHARD PIERSON
Vice-Chancellor for Devt and Alumni Affairs: JOHN I. BLOHM
Vice-Chancellor for Campus Operations: LEO GEHRING
Vice-Chancellor for Finance: MELONY GOODHAND
Vice-Chancellor for Regional Programs: Dr CHARLES O. CRANFORD
Vice-Chancellor for Institutional Compliance: ROBERT BISHOP
Library Dir: MARY L. RYAN

Library of 46,120 vols
Number of teachers: 1,031
Number of students: 2,320

DEANS

College of Health Related Professions: Dr RONALD H. WINTERS
College of Medicine: Dr DEBRA FISER
College of Nursing: Dr CLAUDIA P. BARONE
College of Pharmacy: Dr STEPHANIE GARDNER
College of Public Health: Dr JAMES M. RACZYNSKI
Graduate School: Dr ROBERT E. McGEHEE

UNIVERSITY OF CENTRAL ARKANSAS

201 Donaghey Ave, Conway, AR 72035

Telephone: (501) 450-5000
Fax: (501) 450-5734
E-mail: admissions@uca.edu
Internet: www.uca.edu

Founded 1907 as Arkansas State Normal School; name changed to Arkansas State Teachers College 1925, State College of Arkansas 1967; present name 1975
Academic year: August to August

Pres.: LU HARDIN
Executive Vice-Pres.: BARBARA ANDERSON
Vice-Pres. for Admin.: JACK GILLEAN
Vice-Pres. for Institutional Advancement and Development: KELLEY ERSTIN
Vice-Pres. for Financial Services: PAUL McLENDON
Vice-Pres. for Student Services: RONNIE WILLIAMS
Provost and Dean of the Faculty: Dr A. GABRIEL ESTEBAN
Dean of Students: Dr GARY ROBERTS
Registrar: ANTHONY D. SITZ
Library Dir: ART LICHTENSTEIN

Library of 400,000 vols
Number of teachers: 382 (full-time)
Number of students: 8,481

DEANS

College of Business Administration: Dr PATRICIA CANTRELL
College of Education: Dr LARRY ROBINSON
College of Fine Arts and Communication: Dr ROLLIN POTTER
College of Health and Applied Sciences: Dr NEIL W. HATTLESTAD
College of Liberal Arts: Dr MAURICE LEE
College of Natural Science and Mathematics: Dr STEPHEN SEIDMAN
Undergraduate Studies: Dr SALLY A. RODEN
Graduate School: Dr ELAINE McNIECE

UNIVERSITY OF THE OZARKS

415 North College Ave, Clarksville, AR 72830-2880

Telephone: (501) 979-1000
Fax: (501) 979-1355
E-mail: admiss@ozarks.edu
Internet: www.ozarks.edu

Founded 1834 as Cane Hill School; current name since 1987

Pres.: Dr RICK NIECE
Exec. Vice-Pres.: STEVE EDMISTEN
Vice-Pres. for Academic Affairs: Dr DANIEL TADDIE
Dean of Admissions and Financial Aid: JANA HART
Dean of Enrollment Management: KIM MYRICK
Dean of Students: JOE HOING
Registrar: WILMA HARRIS
Library Dir: STUART STELZER

Divs of: Business, Communications and Govt; Education; Humanities and Fine Arts; Sciences and Mathematics

Library of 80,000 vols, 40,000 govt documents, 10,000 microfilms, 12,000 bound periodicals, 480 current periodicals
Number of teachers: 49
Number of students: 622.

WILLIAMS BAPTIST COLLEGE

60 West Fulbright Ave, Walnut Ridge, AR 72476

Telephone: (870) 886-6741
Fax: (870) 886-3924
E-mail: admissions@wbcoll.edu
Internet: www.wbcoll.edu

Founded 1941 as Southern Baptist College; present name 1991
Private control

Pres.: Dr JEROL B. SWAIM
Academic Dean: Dr KENNETH STARTUP
Registrar: TONYA BOLTON
Dir Library: MARILYN GOODWIN

Library of 75,000 vols
Number of students: 691

Areas of study: Art, Education, Biblical Studies, Biology, Business Administration, Church Music, Computer Information Science, English, Psychology, History, Liberal Arts, Physical Education, Youth Ministry.

CALIFORNIA

ACADEMY OF ART UNIVERSITY

79 New Montgomery St, San Francisco, CA 94105

Telephone: (415) 274-2200
E-mail: info@academyart.edu
Internet: www.academyart.edu

Founded 1929
Private control

Pres.: ELISA STEPHENS
Library Dir: KERRI SHAFFER CARTER (acting)

Library of 30,000 vols
Number of students: 6,500

Schools of Advertising, Animation and visual effects, Architecture, Computer erts: new media, Digital arts and communication, Fashion, Fine art, Graphic design, Illustration, Industrial design, Interior architecture and design, Motion pictures and television, Photography.

AFI CONSERVATORY

2021 North Western Ave, Los Angeles, CA 90027-1657

Telephone: (323) 856-7628

Fax: (323) 467-4578
Internet: www.afi.com

Founded 1969
Private control

Dir and CEO: JEAN PICKER FIRSTENBERG
Chair: HOWARD STRINGER
Dean: ROBERT MANDEL
Artistic Dirs: ROGER BIRNBAUM, FRANK PIERSON
Exec. Vice-Dean: JOE PETRICCA
Vice-Dean for Production and Post-Production: PHILLIP LINSON
Vice-Dean for Fellow Affairs: SHEILA SULLIVAN

Library of 14,000 vols, 100 journals, 5,000 film scripts, 4,000 television scripts; spec. collns Martin Scorsese, Fritz Lang, Robert Aldrich, Charles Feldman

Depts of Cinematography, Directing, Editing, Producing, Production Design, Screenwriting; sound stage and post-production facilities.

ALLIANT INTERNATIONAL UNIVERSITY

10455 Pomerado Rd, San Diego, CA 92131-1799

Telephone: (858) 635-4000
E-mail: admissions@alliant.edu
Internet: www.alliant.edu

Founded 2001 following the merger of California School of Professional Psychology and United States Int. Univ.
Private control
Academic year: August to May

6 Campuses in Fresno, Irvine, Los Angeles, Sacramento, San Diego, San Francisco; also in Mexico (Mexico City)

Pres.: Dr GEOFFREY COX
Provost and Vice-Pres. for Academic Affairs: Dr RODNEY LOWMAN
Vice-Pres. for Devt and Univ. Relations: JOHN DE MICHELE
Vice-Pres. for Undergraduates: Dr ERIC GRAVENBERG
Vice-Pres. for Finance: TARUN BHATIA
Vice-Pres. for Int. Relations: TERENCE BARBER
Vice-Pres. for Legal Affairs: JENNIFER TREESE WILSON
Vice-Pres. for Student Affairs: JENNIFER TREESE WILSON
Chief Human Resources Officer: DENISE HANSON
Dir of Communications: NICOLETTE TOUSSAINT
Dir of Students: CRAIG BREWER
Univ. Librarian: TOBEYLYNN BIRCH

Library of 160,000 vols, 1,150 current journals, 12 electronic databases, 995 psychological test titles, 1,700 audiotapes, 1,200 videotapes
Number of students: 3,621 (3,508 in the USA, 113 in Mexico City, Mexico)

SYSTEM-WIDE DEANS

California School of Professional Psychology: Dr STEVEN BUCKY
School of Management: Dr JAY FINKELMAN
Graduate School of Education: Dr KAREN SCHUSTER WEBB

AMERICAN BAPTIST SEMINARY OF THE WEST

2606 Dwight Way, Berkeley, CA 94704

Telephone: (510) 841-1905
Fax: (510) 841-2446
E-mail: admissions@absw.edu
Internet: www.absw.edu

Founded 1968
Private control (part of the Graduate Theological Union)

Pres.: Dr KEITH A. RUSSELL
Vice-Pres: MICHELLE M. HOLMES
Dean of Faculty: JUDY YATES SIKER
Registrar: ANNIE RUSSELL
Graduate areas of study: Biblical studies, Theology, Ethics, Church history, Arts of ministry, History, Social sciences, Foreign languages, Social theory, Psychology, Art, Liturgical studies, Christian spirituality.

AMERICAN CONSERVATORY THEATER

6th Floor, 30 Grant Ave, San Francisco, CA 94108-5800
Telephone: (415) 834-3200
Internet: www.act-sfbay.org
Founded 1965
Private control
Artistic Dir: CAREY PERLOFF
Conservatory Dir: MELISSA SMITH
Exec. Dir: HEATHER KITCHEN
Producing Dir: JAMES HAIRE
Number of students: 1,900
Graduate area of study: fine arts.

ARMSTRONG UNIVERSITY

1608 Webster St, Oakland, CA 94612
Telephone: (510) 835-7900
Fax: (510) 835-1670
E-mail: au@armstrong-u.edu
Internet: www.armstrong-u.edu
Founded 1918
President: MICHAEL T. C. HWANG
Registrar: OWAIS QURESHI
Librarian: SARA O'KEEFE

Library of 15,000 vols
Number of teachers: 28
Number of students: 200
Graduate and undergraduate courses in accounting, international business, marketing, finance, management and computer management science.

ART CENTER COLLEGE OF DESIGN

1700 Lida St, Pasadena, CA 91103
Telephone: (626) 396-2200
Fax: (626) 405-9104
E-mail: mktngcomm@artcenter.edu
Internet: www.artcenter.edu
Founded 1930
Academic year: January to December
Pres. and CEO: RICHARD KOSHALEK
Exec. Vice-Pres. and Chief Academic Officer: NATE YOUNG
Sr Vice-Pres. and CFO: RICHARD HALUSCHAK
Sr Vice-Pres. for Int. Initiatives: ERICA CLARK
Sr Vice-Pres. for Real Estate and Operations: GEORGE FALARDEAU
Sr Vice-Pres. and Chief Human Resources Officer: JEAN L. FORD
Sr Vice-Pres. for Marketing and Communications: IRIS GELT
Sr Vice-Pres. for Institutional Advancement: EMILY LASKIN
Sr Vice-Pres. for Educational Planning and Architecture: PATRICIA BELTON OLIVER
Vice-Pres. and Chief Technology Officer: A. MICHAEL BERMAN
Vice-Pres. of Student Gallery: STEPHEN L. NOWLIN
Vice-Pres. for Educational Inititiatives: DAVE MUYRES
Vice-Pres. for Student Affairs: TRACY POON TAMBASCIA
Vice-Pres. for Admissions: KIT BARON
Registrar: JEFF ROAMES
Vice-Pres. and Library Dir: ELIZABETH GALLOWAY
Number of teachers: 300

Number of students: 1,522
Undergraduate courses in Advertising, Environmental design, Film, Fine art media, Graphic design, Illustration, Photography and imaging, Product design, Transportation design; graduate courses in Film, Art, Industrial design, Media design, Criticism and theory.

AZUSA PACIFIC UNIVERSITY

901 East Alosta Ave, POB 700, Azusa, CA 91702-700
Telephone: (626) 815-6000
Internet: www.apu.edu
Founded 1899
Private Christian univ.
Pres. and CEO: Dr JON R. WALLACE
Exec. Vice-Pres.and CDO: DAVID E. BIXBY
Exec. Vice-Pres. and CIO: JOHN C. REYNOLDS
Vice-Pres. for Legal Affairs and Community Relations: MARK S. DICKERSON
Sr Vice-Pres. for Student Life and Dean of Students: TERRY A. FRANSON
Vice-Pres. for Enrollment: DEANA L. PORTERFIELD
Provost: Dr MICHAEL M. WHITE
Vice-Provost for Undergraduate Programs: PAUL W. GRAY
Vice-Provost for Graduate and Adult Programs: PAUL W. GRAY
Vice-Provost for Academic Programs and Dean of Univ. Libraries: Dr PAUL W. GRAY
Library of 215,000 vols, media items, 630,000 microfilms, 1,800 serial titles, 100 online databases, 23,000 electronic titles
Number of teachers: 352
Number of students. 4,504

DEANS

Center for Adult and Professional Studies: FRED GARLETT
College of Liberal Arts and Sciences: DAVID L. WEEKS
School of Behavioural and Applied Sciences: MARK STANTON
School of Business and Management: ILENE L. SMITH-BEZJIAN
School of Education: HELEN EASTERLING WILLIAMS
School of Music: DUANE FUNDERBURK
School of Nursing: AJA TULLENERS LESH
Haggard School of Theology: DAVID WRIGHT

BETHANY COLLEGE

800 Bethany Dr, Scotts Valley, CA 95066
Telephone: (831) 438-3800
Fax: (831) 438-6104
E-mail: info@fc.bethany.edu
Internet: www.bethany.edu
Founded 1919
Private Christian college, affiliated to the Assemblies of God
Academic year: August to May
Pres.: Dr MÁXIMO ROSSI, Jr
Vice-Pres. for Academic Affairs: Dr RICHARD ISRAEL
Vice-Pres. for Business: JOHN JONES
Dean of Students: Dr SHARON ANDERSON
Registrar: WESLEY WICK
Librarian: ARNOLD MCLELLAN
Library of 65,000 vols, 800 magazine and journal titles
Number of teachers: 45 (incl. 23 part-time)
Number of students: 545

DEANS

School of Theological Studies: Dr TIMOTHY POWELL
School of Arts and Sciences: DON ADKINS
School of Professional Studies: SHARON ANDERSON

School of Distributed Learning: Dr JAMES W. STEWART

BIOLA UNIVERSITY

13800 Biola Ave, La Mirada, CA 90639-001
Telephone: (562) 903-6000
Fax: (562) 903-4761
Internet: www.biola.edu
Founded 1908
Pres.: Dr BARRY COREY
Provost and Sr Vice-Pres.: Dr GARY A. MILLER
Vice-Provost for Faculty Devt and Univ. Assessment: CHRIS GRACE
Vice-Provost for Undergraduate Education: CAROL TAYLOR
Vice-Pres. for Financial Affairs and Information Technology: CARL W. SCHREIBER
Vice-Pres. for Univ. Advancement: Dr WESLEY K. WILLMER
Vice-Pres. for Univ. Services: KEN BASCOM
Dean of Student Affairs: JOHN W. BACK
Sr Director for Enrollment Management: GREGORY VAUGHAN
Library of 270,000 vols, 1,100 current periodicals
Number of teachers: 252
Number of students: 3,447

DEANS

Crowell School of Business: LARRY D. STRAND
Fine Arts and Communication: DOUG TARPLEY
Humanities: TODD PICKETT
School of Intercultural Studies: Dr F. DOUGLAS PENNOYER
School of Professional Studies: Dr IRMA D. HILL
Rosemead School of Psychology: Dr PATRICIA L. PIKE
Science: WALT STANGL
Talbot School of Theology: Dr DAVID DIRKS

BROOKS INSTITUTE OF PHOTOGRAPHY

801 Alston Rd, Santa Barbara, CA 93108
Telephone: (805) 585-8000
E-mail: admissions@brooks.edu
Internet: www.brooks.edu
Founded 1945
Private control
Pres.: JOHN CALMAN
Areas of study: Photography, Visual communications, Visual journalism, Film and video production.

CALIFORNIA BAPTIST UNIVERSITY

8432 Magnolia Ave, Riverside, CA 92504
Telephone: (951) 689-5771
Fax: (951) 351-1808
E-mail: admissions@calbaptist.edu
Internet: www.calbaptist.edu
Founded 1950
Pres.: Dr RONALD L. ELLIS
Provost: Dr JONATHAN K. PARKER
Vice-Pres. for Finance and Admin.: MARK HOWE
Vice-Pres. for Institutional Advancement: BRUCE HITCHCOCK
Vice-Pres. for Marketing and Communication: Dr MARK A. WYATT
Vice-Pres. for Student Services: KENT DACUS
Dean of Students: ANTHONY LAMMONS
Registrar: SHAWNN KONING
Dir. of Library Services and Information Technology: ERICA MCLAUGHLIN
Library of 76,000 vols, 36,000 microfiches, 500 journals, 1,600 videotapes
Number of teachers: 51 full-time
Number of students: 3,400

DEANS

College of Arts and Sciences: Dr GAYNE ANACKER

School of Behavioural Sciences: Dr H. BRUCE STOKES

School of Business: Dr ANDREW HERRITY

School of Christian Ministries: Dr DAN WILSON

School of Education: Dr MARY CRIST

School of Eng.: Dr ANTHONY DONALDSON

School of Nursing: Dr CONSTANCE L. MILTON

School of Music: Dr GARY BONNER

CALIFORNIA COLLEGE OF THE ARTS

1111 Eighth St, San Francisco, CA 94107-2247

Telephone: (415) 703-9500
Fax: (415) 703-9539
E-mail: info@cca.edu
Internet: www.cca.edu

Founded 1907

Campuses in Oakland and San Francisco
Academic year: September to May

Founded 1907

Pres.: MICHAEL ROTH
Provost: STEPHEN BEAL
Vice-Pres. of Advancement: SUSAN AVILA
Vice-Pres. of Communications: CHRIS BLISS
Vice-Pres. of Enrollment Management: SHERI MCKENZIE
Dean of Students: LIZ POINTER
Dir of Libraries: JANICE WOO

Library of 73,000 vols, 2,500 online periodicals, 500,000 images and 150,000 slides
Number of teachers: 326
Number of students: 1,400

Publication: *Design Book Review* (quarterly).

ATTACHED INSTITUTE

Wattis Institute for Contemporary Arts: tel. (415) 551-9210; e-mail wattis@cca.edu; internet www.wattis.org; f. 1998; forum for presentation and discussion of local, nat., and int. contemporary culture; Dir JENS HOFFMAN.

Center for Art and Public Life: tel. (510) 594-3763; fax (510) 594-3769; internet center .cca.edu; f. 1998; Dir Dr SONIA BASSHEVA MAÑJON.

CALIFORNIA INSTITUTE OF INTEGRAL STUDIES

1453 Mission St, San Francisco, CA 94103
Telephone: (415) 575-6100
Fax: (415) 575-1628
Internet: www.ciis.edu

Founded 1968

Pres.: JOSEPH L. SUBBIONDO
Academic Vice-Pres.: JUDIE WEXLER
Dean of Students and Alumni: RICHARD BUGGS
Dir of Undergraduate Studies: MICHELLE ENG
Dir of Devt: DOROTEA REYNA
Dir of Communications and Marketing: VALERIE BUSH
Dir of Information Technology Services: SCOTT CILIBERTI
Dir of Financial Aid: MICHAEL SZKOTAK
Dir of Public Programs: KARIM BAER
Dir of Diversity and Human Resources: L'ESA GUILIAN
Dir of Finance: KEN ABIKO
Dir of Facilities and Operations: JONATHAN MILLS
Registrar: NANCY HAGER
Library Dir: LISE DYCKMAN

Library of 35,000 vols, 300 periodicals, 1,300 audio and video titles
Number of teachers: 55 full-time, 11 part-time
Number of students: 1,005

BA in Interdisciplinary Studies; School of Professional Psychology (1 PhD and 4 MA programmes) School of Consciousness and Transformation (7 MA and 6 PhD programmes).

CALIFORNIA INSTITUTE OF TECHNOLOGY

Mail Code 206-31, Pasadena, CA 91125
Located at: 1200 East California Blvd, Pasadena, CA 91125
Telephone: (626) 395-6811
Fax: (626) 795-1547
Internet: www.caltech.edu

Founded 1891
Private control
Academic year: September to June

Pres.: Dr JEAN-LOU CHAMEAU
Provost: PAUL C. JENNINGS
Vice-Provost: Dr DAVID L. GOODSTEIN
Vice-Pres. for Business and Finance: DEAN W. CURRIE
Vice-Pres. for Devt and Alumni Relations: GARY DICOVITSKY
Vice-Pres. for Public Relations: ROBERT L. O'ROURKE
Vice-Pres. for Student Affairs: JOHN F. HALL (acting)
Treasurer and Chief Investment Officer: SANDRA A. ELL (acting)
Dir of Admissions: RICHARD BISCHOFF
Dean of Students: JOHN FRANKLIN HALL
Controller: SHARON E. PATTERSON
Sec.: MARY L. WEBSTER
Registrar: MARY NEARY MOREY
Univ. Librarian: KIMBERLY DOUGLAS

Library of 729,128 vols
Number of teachers: 342
Number of students: 2,086

Publication: *Engineering and Science*

CHAIRMEN OF DIVISIONS

Biology: ELLIOTT MEYEROWITZ
Chemistry and Chemical Eng.: DAVID A. TIRRELL
Eng. and Applied Science: DAVID B. RUTLEDGE
Geological and Planetary Sciences: KENNETH A. FARLEY
Humanities and Social Sciences: PETER L. BOSSAERTS
Physics, Mathematics and Astronomy: THOMAS A. TOMBRELLO

PROFESSORS

ABU-MOSTAFA, Y. S., Electrical Eng. and Computer Science
ADOLPHS, R., Psychology and Neuroscience and Biology
ALLMAN, J. M., Neurobiology
ALVAREZ, R. M., Political Science
ANDERSEN, R. A., Neuroscience
ANDERSON, D. J., Biology
ANTONSSON, E. K., Mechanical Eng.
ARNOLD, F. H., Chemical Eng. and Biochemistry
ASCHBACHER, M., Mathematics
ATTARDI, G., Molecular Biology
ATWATER, H. A., Applied Physics and Materials Science
AVOUAC, J., Geology
BALTIMORE, D., Biology
BARR, A. H., Computer Science
BARTON, J. K., Chemistry
BEAUCHAMP, J. L., Chemistry
BECK, J. L., Eng. and Applied Science
BELLAN, P. M., Applied Physics
BERCAW, J. E., Chemistry
BHATTACHARYA, K., Mechanics and Materials Science
BJORKMAN, P., Biology
BLAKE, G. A., Cosmochemistry, Planetary Sciences, Chemistry

BORDER, K. C., Econ.
BORODIN, A., Mathematics
BOSSAERTS, P. L., Finance
BRADY, J. F., Chemical Eng. and Mechanical Eng.
BRENNEN, C. E., Mechanical Eng.
BREWER, J., History and Literature
BRONNER-FRASER, M., Biology
BROWN, M. E., Astronomy
BRUCK, J., Computation and Neural Systems and Electrical Eng.
BRUNO, O. P., Applied and Computational Mathematics
BUCHWALD, J., History
BURDICK, J. W., Mechanical Eng. and BioEng.
CAMERER, C. F., Econ.
CAMPBELL, J. L., Chemistry and Biology
CANDES, E. J. D., Applied and Computational Mathematics
CHANDY, K. M., Computer Science
CLAYTON, R. W., Geophysics
COHEN, J. G., Astronomy
COLONIUS, T. E., Mechanical Eng.
CROSS, M. C., Theoretical Physics
CVITANIC, J., Mathematical Finance
DAVIDSON, E. H., Cell Biology
DAVIS, M. E., Chemical Eng.
DERVAN, P. B., Chemistry
DESHAIES, R., Biology
DICKINSON, M. H., Bioengineering
DIMOTAKIS, P. E., Aeronautics, Applied Physics
DJORGOVSKI, S. G., Astronomy
DOUGHERTY, D. A., Chemistry
DOYLE, J. C., Control and Dynamical Systems, Electrical Eng. and Bioengineering
DUBIN, J. A., Econ.
DUNPHY, W. G., Biology
EFFROS, M., Electrical Eng.
EILER, J. M., Geochemistry
EISENSTEIN, J. P., Physics, Applied Physics
ELACHI, C., Electrical Eng. and Planetary Science
ELLIS, RICHARD, Astronomy
ENSMINGER, J. E., Anthropology
FARLEY, K. A., Geochemistry
FEINGOLD, M., History
FILIPPONE, B. W., Physics
FLACH, M., Mathematics
FLAGAN, R. C., Chemical Eng., Environmental Science and Eng.
FRASER, S. E., Biology, Bioengineering
FRAUTSCHI, S. C., Theoretical Physics
FULTZ, B. T., Materials Science and Applied Physics
GHARIB, M., Aeronautics and Bioengineering
GODDARD, W. A., III, Chemistry, Materials Science and Applied Physics
GOEREE, J. K., Econ.
GOODSTEIN, D. L., Physics and Applied Physics
GOODWIN, D. G., Mechanical Eng. and Applied Physics
GRAY, H. B., Chemistry
GRETHER, D. M., Econ.
GROTZINGER, J. P., Geology
GRUBBS, R. H., Chemistry
GURNIS, M. C., Geophysics
HAILE, S. M., Materials Science and Chemical Eng.
HALL, J. F., Civil Eng.
HARRISON, F. A., Physics and Astronomy
HEATH, J. R., Chemistry
HEATON, T. H., Eng. Seismology
HELMBERGER, D. V., Geophysics
HERING, J. G., Environmental Science and Eng.
HITCHCOCK, C. R., Philosophy
HITLIN, D. G., Physics
HOFFMAN, P. T., History and Social Science
HOFFMANN, M. R., Environmental Science
HOU, Y. T., Applied and Computational Mathematics
HUGHES, E. W., Physics
HUNT, M. L., Mechanical Eng.

INGERSOLL, A. P., Planetary Science
JACKSON, M. O., Econ.
JOHNSON, W. L., Eng. and Applied Science
KAMIONKOWSKI, M., Theoretical Physics and Astrophysics
KATZ, J. N., Political Science
KECHRIS, A. S., Mathematics
KENNEDY, M. B., Biology
KIEWIET, D. R., Political Science
KIMBLE, H. J., Physics
KIRSCHVINK, J. L., Geobiology
KITAEV, A., Theoretical Astrophysics and Computer Science
KOCH, C., Computation and Neural Systems
KONISHI, M., Behavioral Biology
KORMOS-BUCHWALD, D. L., History
KORNFIELD, J. A., Chemical Eng.
KOUSSER, J. M., History and Social Science
KULKARNI, S. R., Astronomy and Planetary Science
KUPPERMANN, A., Chemical Physics
LA BELLE, J., English
LANGE, A. E., Physics
LAURENT, G. J., Biology and Computation and Neural Systems
LEDYARD, J. O., Econ. and Social Sciences
LESTER, H. A., Biology
LEWIS, N. S., Chemistry
LIBBRECHT, K. G., Physics
LORDEN, G. A., Mathematics
LOW, S., Computer Science and Electrical Eng.
MCAFEE, R. P., Business Econ. and Management
MCELIECE, R. J., Electrical Eng.
MCGILL, T. C., Applied Physics
MCKEOWN, R. D., Physics
MCKOY, B. V., Theoretical Chemistry
MACMILLAN, D. W. C., Chemistry
MAKAROV, N. G., Mathematics
MARCUS, R. A., Chemistry
MARSDEN, J. E., Eng. and Control and Dynamical Systems
MARTIN, A. J., Computer Science
MARTIN, D. C., Physics
MAYO, S. L., Biology and Chemistry
MEIRON, D. I., Applied and Computational Mathematics and Computer Science
MEYEROWITZ, E. M., Biology
MURRAY, R. M., Control and Dynamical Systems
NEWMAN, H. B., Physics
NEWMAN, D. K., Geobiology and Biology
OGURI, H., Theoretical Physics
OH, H., Mathematics
OKUMURA, M., Chemical Physics
ORDESHOOK, P. C., Political Science
ORTIZ, M., Aeronautics and Mechanical Eng.
PALFREY, T. R., Econ. and Political Science
PARKER, C. S., Biochemistry
PATTERSON, P. H., Biology
PERONA, P., Electrical Eng.
PETERS, J. C., Chemistry
PHILLIPS, R., Applied Physics and Mechanical Eng.
PHILLIPS, T. G., Physics
PHINNEY, E. S., III, Theoretical Astrophysics
PIGMAN, G. W., English
PINE, J., Physics
PLOTT, C. R., Econ. and Political Science
POLITZER, H. D., Theoretical Physics
PORTER, FRANK C., Physics
PRESKILL, J. P., Theoretical Physics
PRINCE, T. A., Physics
PSALTIS, D., Electrical Eng.
PULLIN, D. I., Aeronautics
QUAKE, S. R., Applied Physics and Physics
RAMAKRISHNAN, D., Mathematics
RAVICHANDRAN, G., Aeronautics and Mechanical Eng.
READHEAD, A. C. S., Astronomy
REES, D. C., Chemistry
RICHARDS, J. H., Organic Chemistry and Biochemistry
ROSAKIS, A. J., Aeronautics and Mechanical Eng.

ROSENSTONE, R. A., History
ROSENTHAL, J., Econ.
ROSSMAN, G. R., Mineralogy
ROTHENBERG, E., Biology
ROUKES, M. L., Physics, Applied Physics and Bioengineering
RUTLEDGE, D. B., Electrical Eng.
SALEEBY, J. B., Geology
SARGENT, A. I., Astronomy
SARGENT, W. L. W., Astronomy
SCHERER, A., Electrical Eng., Applied Physics, and Physics
SCHLAG, W., Mathematics
SCHRODER, P., Computer Science and Applied and Computational Mathematics
SCHULMAN, L. J., Computer Science
SCHUMAN, E. M., Biology
SCHWARZ, J. H., Theoretical Physics
SCOVILLE, N. Z., Astronomy
SEINFELD, J. H., Chemical Eng.
SHEPHERD, J. E., Aeronautics and Mechanical Eng.
SHERMAN, R. P., Econ. and Statistics
SHIMOJO, S., Biology
SIEH, K. E., Geology
SIMON, B. M., Mathematics and Theoretical Physics
SOIFER, B. T., Physics
STEIDEL, C. C., Astronomy
STERNBERG, P. W., Biology
STEVENSON, D. J., Planetary Science
STOCK, J. M., Geology and Geophysics
STOLPER, E. M., Geology
STONE, E. C., Physics
STRAUSS, J. H., Biology
TAI, Y., Electrical Eng. and Mechanical Eng.
THORNE, K. S., Theoretical Physics
TIRRELL, D. A., Chemistry and Chemical Eng.
TOMBRELLO, T. A., Physics
TROMP, J., Geophysics
VAHALA, K. J., Applied Physics
VAIDYANATHAN, P. P., Electrical Eng.
VARSHAVSKY, A. J., Cell Biology
WALES, D. B., Mathematics
WANG, Z., Chemical Eng.
WEINSTEIN, A. J., Physics
WENNBERG, P. O., Atmospheric Chemistry and Environmental Science and Eng.
WERNICKE, B. P., Geology
WILSON, R. M., Mathematics
WISE, M. B., High Energy Physics
WOLD, B. J., Molecular Biology
WOODWARD, J. F., Philosophy
YARIV, A., Applied Physics and Electrical Eng.
YEH, N., Physics
YUNG, Y. L., Planetary Science
ZEWAIL, A. H., Chemical Physics, Physics
ZINN, K., Biology
ZMUIDZINAS, J., Physics
WEINSTEIN, C., English
WEITEKAMP, D. P., Chemical Physics

ATTACHED INSTITUTE

Jet Propulsion Laboratory: 4800 Oak Grove Dr., Pasadena, CA 91109; tel. (818) 354-4321; internet www.jpl.nasa.gov; planetary exploration and related research; Dir Dr CHARLES ELACHI.

CALIFORNIA INSTITUTE OF THE ARTS

24700 McBean Parkway, Valencia, CA 91355-2397

Telephone: (661) 255-1050
Fax: (661) 253-7710
E-mail: info@calarts.edu
Internet: www.calarts.edu

Founded 1961
Academic year: September to May
Pres.: STEVEN D. LAVINE
Vice-Pres. for Admin.: D. DEAN HOUCHIN
Vice-Pres. for Advancement: ARWIN DUFFY

Vice-Pres. for Spec. Projects: LYNN R. ROSENFELD
Provost: NANCY J. USCHER
Registrar: NANCY WHITTEMORE
Dean of Students: YVONNE GUY
Dean of Enrolment Management: CAROL KIM
Dean of Library: JEFFREY GATTEN
Library of 90,000 vols
Number of teachers: 201
Number of students: 1,300
Publications: *Afterall* (2 a year), *Trepan* (annual), *Black Clock* (2 a year)

DEANS

Art: THOMAS LAWSON
Critical Studies: NANCY WOOD
Dance: STEPHAN KOPLOWITZ
Film and Video: STEVEN ANKER
Music: DAVID ROSENBLOOM
Theatre: ERIK EHN

CALIFORNIA LUTHERAN UNIVERSITY

60 West Olsen Rd, Thousand Oaks, CA 91360-2787

Telephone: (805) 492-2411
Fax: (805) 493-3114
E-mail: cluadm@callutheran.edu
Internet: www.callutheran.edu

Founded 1959
Private control, affiliated with the Evangelical Lutheran Church in America

Pres.: Dr JOHN SLADEK
Provost and Vice-Pres. for Academic Affairs: CHRISTOPHER KIMBALL
Vice-Pres. for Admin. and Finance: ROBERT ALLISON
Vice-Pres. for Student Affairs and Dean of Students: WILLIAM ROSSER
Vice-Pres. for Marketing and Communications: RITCH EICH
Vice-Pres. for Univ. Advancement: STEPHEN WHEATLY
Registrar: MARIA KOHNKE
Dir of Library Operations and Systems: CYNTHIA CAMPBELL
Library of 110,416 vols
Number of teachers: 283 (134 full-time, 149 part-time)
Number of students: 3,298 (2,124 undergraduates, 1,174 graduates)

DEANS

College of Arts and Sciences: TIMOTHY HENGST
School of Business: Dr CHARLES MAXEY
School of Education: TERENCE CANNINGS

CALIFORNIA MARITIME ACADEMY

200 Maritime Academy Dr., Vallejo, CA 94590

Telephone: (707) 654-1000
Fax: (707) 654-1001
E-mail: admission@csum.edu
Internet: www.csum.edu

Founded 1929 as California Nautical School; present name 1938; attached to specialized campus of California State Univ.
Pres.: Dr WILLIAM B. EISENHARDT
Vice-Pres. for Academic Affairs: Dr DONALD ZINGALE
Vice-Pres. for Admin. and Finance: MARK NICKERSON
Vice-Pres. for Marine Programs and Student Devt: Capt. JOHN KEEVER
Academic Dean: STEVE KRETA
Degrees in Business admin., Facilities eng. technology, Global studies and maritime affairs, Marine eng. technology, Marine transportation, Mechanical eng.
Library of 35,000 vols, 270 periodicals.

CALIFORNIA STATE UNIVERSITY SYSTEM

401 Golden Shore, Long Beach, CA 90802-4210

Telephone: (562) 951-400
Internet: www.calstate.edu

Co-ordinating headquarters for 23 state univs

Number of teachers: 46,000
Number of students: 417,000
Chancellor: CHARLES B. REED.

CALIFORNIA POLYTECHNIC STATE UNIVERSITY

1 Grand Ave, San Luis Obispo, CA 93407
Telephone: (805) 756-1111
Fax: (805) 756-5400
E-mail: admissions@calpoly.edu
Internet: www.calpoly.edu
Founded 1901
Academic year: September to June
Pres.: WARREN J. BAKER
Provost and Vice-Pres. for Academic Affairs: LARRY KELLEY
Vice-Pres. for Student Affairs: CORNEL MORTON
Vice-Pres. for Univ. Advancement: SANDRA OGREN
Dean of Library Services: MICHAEL D. MILLER
Library of 769,180 vols and serials
Number of teachers: 1,203, incl. part-time
Number of students: 18,722
Publications: *Mustang Daily*, *Cal Poly Today* (quarterly)

DEANS

College of Agriculture: DAVID J. WEHNER
College of Architecture and Environmental Design: R. THOMAS JONES
College of Business: DAVE CHRISTY
College of Education: BONNIE KONOPAK
College of Eng. and Technology: MOHAMMAD NOORI
College of Liberal Arts: LINDA HALISKY
College of Science and Mathematics: PHILIP S. BAILEY

CALIFORNIA STATE POLYTECHNIC UNIVERSITY, POMONA

3801 West Temple Ave, Pomona, CA 91768
Telephone: (909) 869-7659
Internet: www.csupomona.edu
Founded 1938
Pres.: MICHAEL ORTIZ
Provost and Vice-Pres. for Academic Affairs: Dr TOMÁS D. MORALES
Vice-Pres. for Admin. Affairs: Dr EDWIN A. BARNES
Vice-Pres. for Instructional and Information Technology: DEBRA BRUM
Vice-Pres. for Student Affairs: Dr DOUGLAS R. FREER
Vice-Pres. for Univ. Advancement: SCOTT WARRINGTON
Registrar: JOANN M. PIERGALLINI
Library Dean: HAROLD B. SCHLEIFER
Library of 600,000 vols, 2m. microforms, 12,000 maps, 3,000 periodicals
Number of teachers: 958
Number of students: 18,424

DEANS

College of Agriculture: Dr WAYNE BIDLACK
College of Business Admin.: Dr DAVID KLOCK
College of Education and Integrative Studies: Dr BARBARA J. WAY
College of Eng.: Dr EDWARD C. HOHMANN
College of Environmental Design: Dr KAREN HANNA

Collins School of Hospitality Management: DAVID KLOCK
College of Letters, Arts and Social Sciences: Dr BARBARA J. WAY
College of Science: DONALD O. STRANEY
College of the Extended Univ.: GARY HAMILTON

CALIFORNIA STATE UNIVERSITY, BAKERSFIELD

9001 Stockdale Highway, Bakersfield, CA 93311-1022
Telephone: (661) 664-2011
Fax: (661) 664-3194
Internet: www.csub.edu
Founded 1970
Academic year: September to June
Pres.: Dr HORACE MITCHELL
Provost and Vice-Pres. for Academic Affairs: SORAYA M. COLEY
Vice-Pres. for Business and Admin. Services: MICHAEL A. NEAL
Vice-Pres. for Student Affairs: Dr SHELLEY RUELAS
Vice-Pres. for Univ. Advancement: W. MICHAEL CHERTOK
Deanr of Libraries: RODNEY M. HERBSBERGER
Library of 461,829 vols, 1,128 periodicals, 55,883 govt publs, 2,696 sound recordings, 5,555 films/videos
Number of teachers: 408
Number of students: 6,210

DEANS

School of Business and Public Admin.: Dr HENRY LOWENSTEIN
School of Education: Dr CURT GUAGLIANONE
School of Humanities and Social Sciences: MARIA IYASERE
School of Natural Sciences, Mathematics and Eng.: (vacant)

CALIFORNIA STATE UNIVERSITY, CHICO

400 West First St, Chico, CA 95929
Telephone: (530) 898-6116
Internet: www.csuchico.edu
Founded 1887
Pres.: PAUL J. ZINGG
Provost and Vice-Pres. for Academic Affairs: SANDRA M. FLAKE
Vice-Pres. for Business and Finance: DENNIS GRAHAM
Vice-Provost for Information Resources: WILLIAM POST
Vice-Pres. for Student Affairs: DREW CALANDRELLA
Vice-Pres. for Univ. Advancement: RICHARD ELLISON
Library Services Dir: CAROLYN DUSENBURY
Library of 634,000 vols, 2m. documents
Number of teachers: 960
Number of students: 15,500

DEANS

College of Agriculture: JENNIFER RYDER FOX
College of Behavioral and Social Sciences: Dr BOB JACKSON
College of Business: Dr WILLIE HOPKINS
College of Communication and Education: Dr PHYLLIS FERNLUND
College of Eng., Computer Science and Construction Management: Dr KENNETH N. DERUCHER
College of Humanities and Fine Arts: SARAH BLACKSTONE (acting)
College of Natural Sciences: Dr JAMES L. J. HOUPIS
School of Graduate, Int. and Sponsored Programs: SUSAN PLACE
Graduate Studies: WILLIAM LOKER

CALIFORNIA STATE UNIVERSITY, DOMINGUEZ HILLS

1000 East Victoria St, Carson, CA 90747
Telephone: (310) 243-3696
Fax: (310) 243-3858
Internet: www.csudh.edu
Founded 1960
Pres.: Dr BOICE M. BOWMAN
Provost and Vice-Pres. for Academic Affairs: Dr ALLEN MORI
Vice-Pres. for Admin. and Finance: MARY ANN RODRIGUEZ
Vice-Pres. for Student Affairs: Dr BOICE BOWMAN
Vice-Pres. for Univ. Advancement: Dr JUSTINE BELL-WATERS (acting)
Registrar: GAYLE BALL (acting)
Dean of Univ. Library: SANDRA PARHAM
Library of 440,000 vols, 687,800 microforms and 2,200 current periodicals
Number of teachers: 267 full-time, 420 part-time
Number of students: 12,068

DEANS

College of Business and Public Policy: Dr JAMES STRONG
College of Education: Dr KATHLEEN TAIRA
College of Extended Education: MARGARET GORDON
College of Health and Human Services: ANGELA ALBRIGHT (acting)
College of Liberal Arts: Dr SELASE WILLIAMS
College of Natural Behavioural Sciences: Dr CHARLES HOLM

CALIFORNIA STATE UNIVERSITY, FRESNO

5241 North Maple Ave, Fresno, CA 93740-8027
Telephone: (559) 278-4240
Internet: www.csufresno.edu
Founded 1911 as Fresno State Normal School
Academic year: July to June
Pres.: JOHN D. WELTY
Provost and Vice Pres. for Academic Affairs: Dr JERONIMA (JERI) ECHEVERRIA
Vice Pres. for Admin. and CFO: CYNTHIA TENIENTE-MATSON
Vice Pres. for Student Affairs and Dean of Students: Dr PAUL M. OLIARO
Vice Pres. for Univ. Advancement: Dr PETER N. SMITS
Dean of Undergraduate Studies: Dr DENNIS NEF
Dean of Library Services: PETER MCDONALD
Library of 1,000,000 vols
Number of teachers: 1,250
Number of students: 20,013

DEANS

College of Agricultural Sciences and Technology: CHARLES BOYER
College of Arts and Humanities: VIDA SAMIIAN
Craig School of Business: DOUG HENSLER
Kremen School of Education and Human Development: PAUL BEARE
College of Eng.: Dr MICHAEL JENKINS
College of Health and Human Services: BENJAMIN CUELLAR
College of Science and Mathematics: Dr KAREN CAREY
College of Social Sciences: LUZ GONZALEZ
Div. of Graduate Studies: DIANE DICKERSON

CALIFORNIA STATE UNIVERSITY, FULLERTON

800 North College Blvd, Fullerton, CA 92831-3599

Telephone: (714) 287-2011
Internet: www.fullerton.edu
Founded 1957
Pres.: MILTON A. GORDON
Exec. Vice-Pres.: JUDITH A. ANDERSON
Vice-Pres. for Academic Affairs: EPHRAIM P. SMITH
Vice-Pres. for Admin.: WILLIE J. HAGAN
Vice-Pres. for Student Affairs: ROBERT L. PALMER, Jr
Chief Information/Technology Officer: AMIR DABIRIAN
Vice-Pres. for Univ. Advancement: PAMELA HILLMAN
Registrar (vacant)
Library Dir:
Library of 1,189,727 vols, 3,690 serials, 1,144,117 microform titles, 5,715 films and videos
Number of teachers: 1,900
Number of students: 34,927

DEANS

School of the Arts: JERRY SAMUELSON
College of Business and Econ.: ANIL K. PURI
College of Communications: RICK D. PULLEN
College of Education: CLAIRE C. CAVALLARO (acting)
College of Eng. and Computer Science: RAMAN UNNIKRISHNAN
College of Health and Human Devt: Dr ROBERTA E. RIKLI
College of Humanities and Social Sciences: Dr THOMAS P. KLAMMER
College of Natural Sciences and Mathematics: STEVEN N. MURRAY

CALIFORNIA STATE UNIVERSITY, EAST BAY

25800 Carlos Bee Blvd, Hayward, CA 94542-3000

Telephone: (510) 885-3000
Fax: (510) 885-3808
Internet: www.csuhayward.edu
Founded 1957
Pres.: MO QAYOUMI
Provost and Vice-Pres. for Academic Affairs: Dr MICHAEL MAHONEY
Vice-Pres. for Admin. and Finance: SHAWN BIBB
Vice-Pres. for Student Affairs: Dr SONJA REDMOND
Vice-Pres. for Univ. Advancement: ROBERT BURT
Vice-Pres. for Planning and Enrollment Management: Dr LINDA DALTON
Chief Information Officer: JOHN CHARLES
Univ. Librarian: MYOUNG-JA LEE KWON
Library of 700,000 vols
Number of teachers: 506
Number of students: 12,706

DEANS

School of Arts, Letters and Social Sciences: BENJAMIN BOWSER
School of Business and Econ.: JOHN KOHL
School of Education and Allied Studies: EMILY BRIZENDINE
School of Science: MICHAEL LEUNG

CALIFORNIA STATE UNIVERSITY, LONG BEACH

1250 Bellflower Blvd, Long Beach, CA 90840-0115

Telephone: (562) 985-4111
Internet: www.csulb.edu
Founded 1949

Pres.: F. KING ALEXANDER
Provost and Sr Vice-Pres. for Academic Affairs: KAREN GOULD
Vice-Pres. for Admin. and Finance: WILLIAM H. GRIFFITH
Vice-Pres. for Univ. Relations and Devt: ANDREA TAYLOR
Vice Pres. for Student Services: DOUGLAS W. ROBINSON
Dean of Library Services: ROMAN KOCHAN
Library of 1,137,582 vols, 1,623,602 microforms, 35,080 non-book materials, 3,981 current periodicals
Number of teachers: 1,924 (1,011 full-time, 913 part-time)
Number of students: 32,126

DEANS

College of the Arts: DON PARA
College of Business Admin.: MO KHAN
College of Education: JEAN HOUCK
College of Eng.: MICHAEL MAHONEY
College of Health and Human Sciences: RONALD VOGEL
College of Liberal Arts: GERRY RIPOSA
College of Natural Sciences and Mathematics: LAURA KINGSFORD
Univ. College and Extension Services: MARILYN CREGO

CALIFORNIA STATE UNIVERSITY, LOS ANGELES

5151 State Univ. Dr., Los Angeles, CA 90032-8530

Telephone: (323) 343-3901
Fax: (323) 343-6306
E-mail: admission@calstatela.edu
Internet: www.calstatela.edu
Founded 1947
Pres.: JAMES M. ROSSER
Provost and Vice-Pres. for Academic Affairs: HERMAN D. LUJAN
Vice-Pres. for Admin. and Finance: STEVEN N. GARCIA
Vice-Pres. for Institutional Advancement: KYLE C. BUTTON
Vice-Pres. for Student Affairs: ANTHONY R. ROSS
Vice-Pres. for Information Technology Services: PETER QUAN
Dean of Graduate Studies and Research: JOSE L. GALVAN (acting)
Dean of Undergraduate Studies: ALFREDO G. GONZALEZ (acting)
Univ. Librarian: ALICE KAWAKAMI (acting)
Library of 1,000,000 vols
Number of teachers: 888
Number of students: 18,000

DEANS

College of Arts and Letters: TERRY L. ALLISON
College of Business and Econ.: DONG-WOO LEE (acting)
Charter College of Education: MARY FALVEY
College of Eng., Computer Science and Technology: Dr KEITH MOO-YOUNG
College of Health and Human Sciences: BEATRICE YORKER (acting)
College of Natural and Social Sciences: DESDEMONA CARDOZA

CALIFORNIA STATE UNIVERSITY, MONTEREY BAY

100 Campus Center, Seaside, CA 93955-8001
Telephone: (831) 582-3000
E-mail: moreinfo_prospective@csumb.edu
Internet: csumb.edu
Founded 1994
Academic year: August to May
Pres.: Dr DIANE F. HARRISON
Provost and Vice-Pres. for Academic Affairs: Dr KATHRYN CRUZ-URIBE

Vice-Pres. for Admin. and Finance: DAN KUBIAK
Vice-Pres. for Student Affairs: Dr SUSAN E. BORREGA
Vice-Pres. for Devt: Dr CHRIS HASEGAWA
Vice-Pres. for Univ. Advancement: STEVE REED
Dir of the Library: BILL ROBNETT
Library of 65,000 vols
Number of teachers: 280
Number of students: 4,000

DEANS

College of Arts, Humanities, and Social Sciences: RENÉE R. CURRY
College of Professional Studies: Dr MARTIN TADLOCK
College of Science, Media Arts, and Technology: Dr MARSHA MOROH
College of Univ. Studies and Programs: Dr DAVID ANDERSON

CALIFORNIA STATE UNIVERSITY, NORTHRIDGE

18111 Nordhoff St, Northridge, CA 91330

Telephone: (818) 677-1200
Fax: (818) 677-3766
E-mail: admissions@csun.edu
Internet: www.csun.edu
Founded 1958
Pres.: JOLENE KOESTER
Provost and Vice-Pres. for Faculty Affairs: LINDA BAIN
Vice-Pres. for Admin. and Finance: MOHAMMAD H. QAYOUMI
Vice-Pres. for Student Affairs: TERRY B. PIPER
Vice-Pres. for Univ. Advancement: JUDY C. KNUDSON
Vice-Pres. for Operations: JULIE WANKE
Director of Admissions and Records: ERIC FORBES
Dean of Univ. Library: SUSAN C. CURZON
Library of 1,200,000 vols, 8,000 periodicals, 3m. microforms, 60,000 pictures, 10,000 sound recordings, 6,000 films and video recordings
Number of teachers: 1,900
Number of students: 34,000

DEANS

College of Arts, Media and Communication: DAVE MOON
College of Business and Econ.: MICHAEL FRONMUELLER
Michael D. Eisner College of Education: PHILIP J. RUSCHE
College of Eng. and Computer Science: S.T. MAU
College of Health and Human Devt: HELEN CASTILLO
College of Humanities: ELIZABETH SAY
College of Science and Mathematics: EDWARD CARROLL
College of Social and Behavioural Sciences: STELLA THEODOULOU
College of Extended Learning: JOYCE FEUCHT-HAVIAR

CALIFORNIA STATE UNIVERSITY, SACRAMENTO

6000 J St, Sacramento, CA 95819-6056
Telephone: (916) 278-6011
Fax: (916) 278-6664
E-mail: infodesk@csus.edu
Internet: www.csus.edu
Founded 1947
Academic year: September to May
Pres.: ALEXANDER GONZALEZ
Provost and Vice-Pres. for Academic Affairs: JOSEPH F. SHELEY
Vice-Pres. for Admin.: STEPHEN G. GARCIA

Vice-Pres. for Student Affairs: LORI VARLOTTA
Vice-Pres. for Univ. Affairs: CAROLE HAYA-SHINO
Dir of Library Systems: CARLOS RODRIGUEZ
Library of 2,000,000 vols
Number of teachers: 1,647 (877 full-time, 770 part-time)
Number of students: 28,558
Publications: *Calaveras Station* (quarterly), *Capitol University Journal* (2 a year)

DEANS

College of Arts and Letters: JEFFREY MASON (acting)
College of Business Admin.: SANJAY VARSH-NEY
College of Education: Dr VANESSA SHEARED
College of Eng. and Computer Science: EMIR JOSÉ MACARI
College of Health and Human Services: Dr MARILYN HOPKINS
College of Natural Sciences and Mathematics: LAUREL HEFFERNAN
College of Social Sciences and Interdisciplinary Studies: OTIS L. SCOTT

CALIFORNIA STATE UNIVERSITY, SAN BERNARDINO

5500 University Parkway, San Bernardino, CA 92407

Telephone: (909) 880-5000
Fax: (909) 880-5903
E-mail: moreinfo@csusb.edu
Internet: www.csusb.edu

Founded 1960

Liberal Arts college with several applied programmes offering a broad range of first degrees, several teaching credentials and master degrees in selected fields

Pres.: Albert K. KARNIG
Provost and Vice-Pres. for Academic Affairs: Dr LOUIS A. FERNÁNDEZ
Vice-Pres. for Admin. and Finance: DAVID DEMAURO
Vice-Pres. for Information Resources and Technology: LORAINE M. FROST
Vice-Pres. for Student Affairs: Dr FRANK RINCÓN
Vice-Pres. for Univ. Advancement: WILLIAM AGUILAR
Univ. Librarian: JOHNNIE ANN RALPH
Library of 720,000 vols, 2,400 current periodicals and serial publications, also maps, microforms, musical scores, CD-ROMs; depository for CA state and Fed. Govt documents
Number of teachers: 454
Number of students: 16,341

DEANS

College of Arts and Letters: Dr ERI YASUHARA
College of Business and Public Admin.: KAREN DILL BOWERMAN
College of Education: Dr PATRICIA ARLIN
College of Natural Sciences: Dr B. ROBERT CARLSON
College of Social and Behavioral Sciences: Dr JOHN CONLEY

CALIFORNIA STATE UNIVERSITY, SAN MARCOS

333 South Twin Oaks Valley Rd, San Marcos, CA 92096

Telephone: (760) 750-4000
E-mail: apply@csusm.edu
Internet: www.csusm.edu

Founded 1989
Academic year: September to May

Pres.: Dr KAREN D. HAYNES
Chancellor: CHARLES B. REED

Provost and Vice-Pres. for Academic Affairs: EMILY F. CUTRER
Vice-Pres. for Univ. Advancement: RICK D. KEITH
Vice-Pres. for Finance and Admin.: NEIL HOSS
Vice-Pres. for Student Affairs: Dr PAT WORDEN
Dean of Library: MARION REID
Library of 250,000 vols, 800 periodicals
Number of teachers: 190
Number of students: 7,627

DEANS

College of Arts and Sciences: Dr VICKI GOLICH
College of Business Admin.: Dr DENNIS GUSEMAN
College of Education: Dr MARK BALDWIN
School of Nursing: JUDY PAPENHAUSEN
Extended Studies: JAN JACKSON
Graduate Studies: GERARDO M. GONZÁLEZ

CALIFORNIA STATE UNIVERSITY, STANISLAUS

801 West Monte Vista Ave, Turlock, CA 95382

Telephone: (209) 667-3122
Fax: (209) 667-3333
Internet: www.csustan.edu

Founded 1957

Pres.: HAMID SHIRVANI
Provost and Vice-Pres. for Academic Affairs: WILLIAM COVINO
Vice-Pres. for Business and Finance: MARY STEPHENS
Vice-Pres. for Univ. Advancement (vacant)
Vice-Pres. for Student Affairs: STACEY MORGAN-FOSTER
Assoc. Vice-Pres., Enrollment Management: ROGER PUGH
Dean of Admissions and Registrar: LISA BERNARDO
Dean of Library Services: CARL E. BENGSTON
Library of 361,000 vols, 2,000, current periodicals, 1.3m. microforms, 4,700 sound and video recordings, govt documents, special colln of children's literature
Number of teachers: 495 (285 full-time; 210 part-time)
Number of students: 8,137 (6,424 undergraduate; 1,713 postgraduate)

DEANS

College of Arts, Letters and Sciences: STEPHEN THOMAS
College of Business Admin.: AMIN A. ELMALLAH
College of Education: CARL BROWN
College of Human and Health Sciences: GARY NOVAK
College of Humanities and Social Sciences: MARJORIE JAASMA
College of Natural Sciences: JANE BRUNER

CALIFORNIA WESTERN SCHOOL OF LAW

225 Cedar St, San Diego, CA 92101

Telephone: (619) 239-0391
Fax: (619) 525-7092
E-mail: admissions@cwsl.edu
Internet: www.cwsl.edu

Founded 1924 as Balboa Law College; present name 1975
Private control
Academic year: August to August

Dean: Prof. STEVEN R. SMITH
Assoc. Dean for Academic Affairs: Prof. JANET M. BOWERMASTER
Assoc. Dean for Admin.: Prof. MARK I. WEINSTEIN
Asst Dean for Academic Support: MARILYN SCHEININGER

Asst Dean for Career Services: Dr LOUIS W. HELMUTH
Assoc. Dir of Marketing and Communications: FRANKI FITTERER
Assoc. Dir for Diversity Services: MARION CLOETE
Registrar: DIANE SHRAGG
Dir of Law Library: Prof. PHYLLIS C. MARION
Number of teachers: 40 (full-time)
Number of students: 1,002
Publication: *Law Review/International Law Journal* (2 a year).

CHAPMAN UNIVERSITY

1 University Dr., Orange, CA 92866

Telephone: (714) 997-6815
Internet: www.chapman.edu

Founded 1861
Private (Disciples of Christ) Liberal Arts

Pres.: Dr JAMES L. DOTI
Provost and Exec. Vice-Pres.: Dr HARRY HAMILTON
Exec. Vice-Pres. for Finance and Admin.: GARY BRAHM
Vice-Pres. and Dean for Enrollment Services: SASKIA KNIGHT
Vice-Pres. and Dean of Students: Dr JOSEPH KERTES
Vice-Pres. for Univ. Advancement: SHERYL BOURGEOIS
Registrar: JOHN SNODGRASS
Dean of the Libraries: CHARLENE BALDWIN
Library of 200,000 vols, 2,200 periodicals
Number of teachers: 581 (264 full-time, 317 part-time)
Number of students: 5,134

DEANS

Argyros School of Business and Econ.: Dr ARTHUR KRAFT
School of Arts and Communication: Dr MYRON YEAGER
School of Education: Dr DON CARDINAL
College of Film and Media Arts: BOB BASSETT
School of Law: Dr PARHAM WILLIAMS
School of Music: WILLIAM HALL
Univ. College: Dr KAREN GRAHAM
Wilkinson College of Letters and Sciences: Dr ROBERTA LESSOR

CHURCH DIVINITY SCHOOL OF THE PACIFIC

2451 Ridge Rd, Berkeley, CA 94709-1217

Telephone: (510) 204-0700
Fax: (510) 644-0712
E-mail: info@cdsp.edu
Internet: www.cdsp.edu

Founded 1839
Private control (part of the Graduate Theological Union)
Academic year: August to May

Pres. and Dean: Dr DONN F. MORGAN
Vice-Pres. for Admin.: N. DAVID LAWSON
Vice-Pres. for Advancement: JERRY CAMPBELL
Dean of Students: JAN WOOD
Dean of School for Deacons: RODERICK DUGLISS
Registrar: MARGO WEBSTER
Areas of study: Divinity, Theological Studies, Arts, Ministry.

CLAREMONT GRADUATE UNIVERSITY

171 East 10th St, Claremont, CA 91711

Telephone: (909) 621-8028
Fax: (909) 621-8390
Internet: www.cgu.edu

Founded 1925

Pres.: ROBERT KLITGAARD

Provost and Vice-Pres. for Academic Affairs: YI FENG

Vice-Pres. for Finance and Admin.: WILLIAM L. EVERHART

Vice-Pres. for Advancement: GRANTLAND RICE

Library: Claremont Colleges share 4 libraries with combined holdings of 2,000,000 vols

Number of teachers: 169 (81 full-time, 88 part-time; augmented by faculty members from The Claremont Colleges)

Number of students: 2,033

Masters and doctoral degrees in 22 professional and academic disciplines

DEANS

School of Behavioral and Organizational Sciences: STEWART DONALDSON

School of Mathematical Sciences: JOHN ANGUS

School of Politics and Econ.: THOMAS D. WILLETT

School of Information Systems and Technology: LORNE OLFMAN

School of the Arts and Humanities: PATRICIA EASTON

School of Religion: KAREN J. TORJESEN

Peter F. Drucker Graduate School of Management: IRA JACKSON

CLAREMONT MCKENNA COLLEGE

Claremont, CA 91711-6400

Telephone: (909) 621-8000

Internet: www.claremontmckenna.edu

Founded 1946

Liberal arts college with emphasis on business and public affairs; member of the Claremont Colleges

Pres.: Prof. PAMELA BROOKS GANN

Dean of the Faculty and Vice-Pres. for Academic Affairs: GREGORY HESS

Dean of Students and Vice-Pres. for Student Affairs: JEFFERSON HUANG

Vice-Pres. for Business and Admin./Treas.: ROBIN ASPINALL

Chief Technology Officer: CYNTHIA HUMES

Vice-Pres. for Devt and External Relations: WILLIAM LOWERY

Registrar and Dir of Institutional Research: ELIZABETH MORGAN

Number of teachers: 124

Number of students: 1,153.

CLAREMONT SCHOOL OF THEOLOGY

1325 North College Ave, Claremont, CA 91711-3199

Telephone: (909) 447-2500

Fax: (909) 626-7062

E-mail: admission@cst.edu

Internet: www.cst.edu

Founded 1885 as Maclay College of Theology; present name 1957

Private control

Academic year: September to May

Pres.: Dr JERRY D. CAMPBELL

Vice-Pres. for Academic Affairs and Dean: SUSAN NELSON

Vice-Pres. for Devt: BRONNIE MCNABB

Chief Financial Officer: JOAN FROST

Dean of Student Life: SOOMEE KIM

Registrar: JENNIE J. ALLEN

Library and IT Dir: JOHN DICKASON.

CLEVELAND CHIROPRACTIC COLLEGE

590 North Vermont Ave, Los Angeles, CA 90004

Telephone: (323) 660-6166

Fax: (323) 906-2094

E-mail: la.admissions@cleveland.edu

Internet: www.clevelandchiropractic.edu

Founded 1911 as Los Angeles branch of Ratledge System of Chiropractic Schools; present name 1955

Private control

Located on 2 campuses: Kansas City and Los Angeles

Pres.: Dr CARL S. CLEVELAND, III

Sr Vice-Pres. for Institutional Outreach: Dr MATTHEW M. GIVRAD

Vice-Pres. for Research and Scholarship: Dr CHERYL HAWK

Vice-Pres. for Academic Services: Dr RUTH SANDEFUR

Vice-Pres. for Enrollment Management: DENNIS L. GIACOMINO

Vice-Pres. for Finance and Admin.: JOHN J. SOPINSKI

Vice-Pres. for Institutional Planning and Assessment: GARY GLOBE

Library of 22,000 vols

Number of students: 568

Depts of Basic sciences, Diagnostic sciences, Chiropractic sciences, Clinical sciences, Humanities and social sciences, Physical and life sciences.

COGSWELL POLYTECHNICAL COLLEGE

1175 Bordeaux Drive, Sunnyvale, CA 94089-9772

Telephone: (408) 541-0100

Fax: (408) 747-0764

E-mail: info@cogswell.edu

Internet: www.cogswell.edu

Founded 1887

Private control

Academic year: September to August

Pres.: Dr CHESTER D. HASKELL

Vice-Pres. for Finance and Admin.: REJINO CASTANEDA

Dean of Institutional Advancement: BONNIE PHELPS

Dean of Student Life: BARB BLOOM

Dean of College: Dr TIMOTHY DUNCAN

Registrar: CATE CORGILL

Librarian: BRUCE DAHMS

Number of teachers: 48 incl. 36 part-time

Number of students: 185 (144 full-time, 141 part-time)

Library of 12,000 vols, 100 periodicals

Areas of study: 3D Animation, 3D Modeling, Game Design, Entertainment Design, Digital Audio, Digital Motion Picture, Software Eng., Electrical Eng., Digital Arts Eng.

COLEMAN COLLEGE

8888 Balboa Ave, San Diego, CA 92123-1506

Telephone: (858) 499-0202

Fax: (858) 499-0233

Internet: www.coleman.edu

Founded 1963

Private control

Pres.: PAUL PANESAR

Vice-Pres. for Academics: JIM FARMER

Vice-Pres. for Marketing: DARLENE ANKTON

Librarian (San Diego): MANNY BERNAD

Librarian (San Marcos): DONNA LONGSTREET

Number of students: 1,000

Depts of Bioinformatics, Graphic design, Information systems, Networks and security.

BRANCH CAMPUS

San Marcos Campus: 1284 West San Marcos Blvd, San Marcos, CA 92078-4073; tel. (760) 747-3990; fax (760) 752-9808.

COLUMBIA COLLEGE HOLLYWOOD

18618 Oxnard St, Tarzana, CA 91356

Telephone: (818) 345-8414

Fax: (818) 345-9053

E-mail: info@columbiacollege.edu

Internet: www.columbiacollege.edu

Founded 1951

Private control

Pres. and CEO: RICHARD KOBRITZ

Dean of Academics: Dr JAMES C. LUNDSTROM

Dean of Students: ANDREW H. KESLER

Dir of Admissions: CARMEN MUNOZ

Dir of Education Services and Registrar: STEVE MARTINEZ

Librarian: MARA BURNS

Areas of study: Television/video production, Cinema

Library of 10,000 vols.

CONCORDIA UNIVERSITY IRVINE

1530 Concordia West, Irvine, CA 92612-3203

Telephone: (949) 854-8002

Fax: (949) 854-6894

E-mail: admission@cui.edu

Internet: www.cui.edu

Founded 1973 as Christ College Irvine; present name 1993

Private control

Academic year: August to May

Pres.: Rev. Dr JACOB A. O. PREUS

Provost: Dr KURT J. KRUEGER

Exec. Vice-Pres. for Community and Church Relations: STEPHEN CHRISTENSEN

Exec. Vice-Pres. for Univ. Advancement: STEPHEN CHRISTENSEN

Vice-Pres. for Admin. Services: Dr MARY K. SCOTT

Vice-Pres. for Business Operations and Information Technology: ALAN K. RUDI

Vice-Pres. for Student Services: Dr GARY R. MCDANIEL

Dean of Students: Dr JOHN HOFFMAN

Registrar: KENNETH CLAVIR

Dir of Library Services: CAROLINA BARTON

Number of teachers: 74 (full-time)

Number of students: 1,650

Library of 92,000

DEANS

School of Arts and Sciences: Dr KENNETH MANGELS

School of Business: Dr JOHN ROONEY (acting)

Christ College: Dr STEVEN P. MUELLER

School of Education: BARBARA MORTON

School of Theology: Rev. Dr JAMES BACHMAN

School of Adult Studies: Dr TIMOTHY PETERS

DOMINICAN SCHOOL OF PHILOSOPHY AND THEOLOGY

2301 Vine St, Berkeley, CA 94708

Telephone: (510) 849-2030

Fax: (510) 849-1372

E-mail: info@dspt.edu

Internet: www.dspt.edu

Founded 1850s; present name 1978

Part of the Graduate Theological Union

Pres.: MICHAEL SWEENEY

Vice-Pres. for Admin. and Student Services: SCOTT CONNOLLY

Academic Dean: CHRISTOPHER RENZ

Registrar: TERESA OLSON

Masters programmes in Philosophy and Theology.

DOMINICAN UNIVERSITY OF CALIFORNIA

50 Acacia Ave, San Rafael, CA 94901-2298

Telephone: (415) 457-4440

Fax: (415) 485-3205

E-mail: enroll@dominican.edu

Internet: www.dominican.edu

Founded 1890 as a women's college; name changed to Dominican College of San Rafael 1917; present name 2000

Private control

Academic year: August to May

Pres.: Dr JOSEPH R. FINK

Provost: Dr KENNETH J. PORADA

Vice-Pres: DAVID BEHRS, ROGER ONO, VERN UMMEL

Dir of Library Services: CAL KURZMAN

Library of 100,000 vols, 375 periodicals

Number of teachers: 223

Number of students: 1,937 (1,391 undergraduate, 546 graduate)

DEANS

School of Arts and Sciences: MARTHA NELSON

School of Business and Leadership and School of Education: LUIS MARIA CALINGO

BRANCH CAMPUS

Ukiah Center: 2240 Old River Rd, Ukiah, CA 95482; tel. (707) 463-4800; fax (707) 463-5525; e-mail ukiah@dominican.edu; serves Lake, Mendocino and Sonoma counties; BA in Strategic Management, MSc in Education.

FIELDING GRADUATE INSTITUTE

2112 Santa Barbara St, Santa Barbara, CA 93105

Telephone: (805) 687-1099

E-mail: admissions@fielding.edu

Internet: www.fielding.edu

Founded 1974

Private control

Pres.: Dr JUDITH L. KUIPERS

Provost: Dr ANNA DiSTEFANO

Exec. Vice-Pres. for Institutional Partnerships: Dr BERNARD J. LUSKIN

Vice-Pres. for Advancement: Dr JAMES MURPHY

Vice-Pres. for Human Resources and Admin.: JOHN NELSON

Number of students: 1,400

DEANS

School of Psychology: Dr RONALD A. GIANNETTI

School of Educational Leadership and Change: Dr JUDY WITT

School of Human and Organization Development: Dr CHARLES McCLINTOCK

FIVE BRANCHES INSTITUTE

200 Seventh Ave, Santa Cruz, CA 95062

Telephone: (831) 476-9424

Fax: (831) 476-8928

E-mail: tcm@fivebranches.edu

Internet: www.fivebranches.edu

Founded 1984

Academic year: Programme begins in August and February

Private control

Pres. and CEO: RON ZAIDMAN

Academic Dean: Prof. JOANNA ZHAO

Dir of Admissions: ELEONOR MENDELSON

Registrar: JUDY CAVIN BROWN

Library of 2,000 vols

Number of teachers: 35

Number of students: 200

Areas of study: traditional Chinese medicine, Western medicine and natural sciences, acupuncture, Chinese herbology.

BRANCH CAMPUS

San Jose Campus: Suite 5PW, 3031 Tisch Way, San Jose, CA 95128; tel. (408) 260-0208; fax (408) 261-3166; e-mail sjcampus@fivebranches.edu; Dir LYNN ABLONDI; Clinic Dir GINA HUANG.

FRANCISCAN SCHOOL OF THEOLOGY

1712 Euclid Ave, Berkeley, CA 94709-1294

Telephone: (510) 848-5232

Fax: (510) 549-9466

E-mail: info@fst.edu

Internet: www.fst.edu

Run by Province of Saint Barbara of the Order of Friars Minor; part of the Graduate Theological Union

Pres. and Rector: MARIO DiCICCO

Academic Dean: Prof. JOSEPH P. CHINNICI

Number of students: 100

MAs in Theology, Divinity, Ministry, Arts; continuing education program.

FRESNO PACIFIC UNIVERSITY

1717 South Chestnut Ave, Fresno, CA 93702-4709

Telephone: (209) 453-2000

Fax: (209) 453-2007

Internet: www.fresno.edu

Founded 1944

Academic year: August to May

Pres.: Dr D. MERRILL EWERT

Provost and Vice-Pres. for Academic Affairs: Dr HERMA B. WILLIAMS

Vice-Pres. for Finance and Business Affairs: JOHN WARD

Vice-President for Advancement and Univ. Relations: MARK DEFFENBACHER

Vice-Pres. and Chief Information Officer: ALAN OURS

Library Dir: RICHARD RAWLS

Library of 145,000 vols

Number of teachers: 70

Number of students: 1,453

DEANS

School of Business: JANITA RAWLS

School of Education: JO ELLEN MISAKIAN

School of Humanities, Religion and Social Sciences: WILL FRIESEN

School of Natural Sciences: LORIN NEUFELD

BRANCH CAMPUSES

Bakersfield Center: Suite A, 1330 Truxtun Ave, Bakersfield, CA 93301; tel. (661) 864-1515; internet www.fresno.edu/bakersfield.

North Fresno Center: Suite 201, 5 River Place West, Fresno, CA 93720; tel. (559) 453-3440; internet www.fresno.edu/northfresno.

Visilia Center: 5429 West Cypress Ave, Visilia, CA 93277; tel. (866) 837-8648; fax (559) 622-9958; internet www.fresno.edu/visilia.

FULLER THEOLOGICAL SEMINARY

135 North Oakland Ave, Pasadena, CA 91182

Telephone: (626) 584-5498

E-mail: admiss@fuller.edu

Internet: www.fuller.edu

Founded 1947

Private control

Pres.: Dr RICHARD J. MOUW

Registrar: DAVID E. KIEFER

Library Dir.: DAVID BUNDY

Library of 400,000 vols, 3,400 print and 10,000 electronic periodicals

Number of teachers: 80

Number of students: 4,300

DEANS

School of Psychology: Dr WINSTON E. GOODEN

School of Theology: HOWARD LOEWEN

School of Intercultural Studies: Dr C. DOUGLAS McCONNELL

EXTENSION SITES

Fuller Colorado: Suite 202, 525 North Cascade Ave, Colorado Springs, CO 80903; tel. (719) 385-0085; fax (719) 385-0089; e-mail fullerco@fuller.edu; internet www.fuller.edu/cll/fco; Dir WILL STOLLER-LEE.

Fuller Northern California: POB 906, 320 Middlefield Rd, Menlo Park, CA 94026-0906; tel. (650) 321-7444; fax (650) 321-8606; e-mail fts.nca@fuller.edu; internet www.fuller.edu/cll/fnc; Dir Dr CURT LONGACRE.

Fuller Northwest: Suite 330, Nickerson Business Park, 101 Nickerson St, Seattle, WA 98109-1621; tel. (206) 284-9000; fax (206) 284-4735; e-mail fts.nw@fuller.edu; internet www.fuller.edu/cll/fnw; Dir KIM ANDERSON.

Fuller Southern California: Suite 102, 2061 Business Center Dr., Irvine, CA 92612; tel. (949) 975-0775; fax (949) 975-0787; e-mail fts.sca@fuller.edu; internet www.fuller.edu/cll/fsc; Dir PATRICIA REXROAT.

Fuller Southwest: Suite 185, 4636 East Van Buren St, Phoenix, AZ 85008; tel. (602) 220-0400; fax (602) 220-0444; e-mail fts.sw@fuller.edu; internet www.fuller.edu/cll/fsw; Dir THOMAS PARKER.

GOLDEN GATE BAPTIST THEOLOGICAL SEMINARY

201 Seminary Dr., Mill Valley, CA 94941-3197

Telephone: (415) 380-1300

Fax: (415) 380-1302

E-mail: admissions@ggbts.edu

Internet: www.ggbts.edu

Founded 1944

Private control

Academic year: August to August

Pres.: Dr JEFF IORG

Vice-Pres. for Academic Affairs: D. MICHAEL MARTIN

Vice-Pres. for Business and Finance: GARY GROAT

Vice-Pres. for Institutional Advancement: THOMAS O. JONES

Vice-Pres. for Student Services: MARK A. TICHENOR

Registrar: WAYNE WOMACK

Dir of Library Services: KELLY CAMPBELL

Number of students: 752

DIRECTORS

Bill and Pat Dixon School of Church Music: (vacant)

David and Faith Kim School of Intercultural Studies: Dr RAY TALLMAN

BRANCH CAMPUSES

Arizona Campus: Suite 101, 2240 North Hayden Rd, Scottsdale, AZ 852572840; tel. (480) 941-1993; fax (480) 945-4199; e-mail arc-info@ggbts.edu; Dir DAVID W. JOHNSON.

Pacific Northwest Campus: 3200 North East 109th Ave, Vancouver, WA 98682-7749; tel. (360) 882-2200; fax (360) 882-2270; e-mail pnwc-info@ggbts.edu; Dir CHRIS TURNER.

Rocky Mountain Campus: 7393 South Alton Way, Centennial, CO 80112-2372; tel. (303) 779-6431; fax (303) 779-6432; e-mail rmc-info@ggbts.edu; Dir STEPHEN G. VETETO.

Southern California Campus: Suite A, 251 South Randolph Ave, Brea, CA 92821-5705; tel. (714) 256-1311; fax (714) 256-9284; e-mail scc-info@ggbts.edu; Dir J. SAM SIMMONS.

GOLDEN GATE UNIVERSITY

536 Mission St, San Francisco, CA 94105

Telephone: (415) 442-7000

Fax: (415) 442-7807

Internet: www.ggu.edu
Founded 1901
Pres.: Dan Angel
Vice-Pres. for Academic Affairs: Dr Barbara H. Karlin
Vice-Pres. for Operations: Jeffrey V. Bialik
Dir of Univ. Library: Janice Carter
Dirs of Law Library: Michael Daw, Mohamed Nasralla
Library of 340,000 vols, 1,200 periodicals in the Law library
Number of teachers: 750
Number of students: 6,617

DEANS

School of Business: Terry Connelly
School of Law: Dr Frederic White
School of Taxation: Dr Mary Canning
School of Accounting: Dr Mary Canning

HARVEY MUDD COLLEGE

301 Platt Blvd, Claremont, CA 91711-5990
Telephone: (909) 621-8120
Fax: (909) 621-8360
E-mail: admissions@hmc.edu
Internet: www.hmc.edu
Founded 1955
Academic year: August to May
Mem. of the Claremont Colleges; depts of Biology, Chemistry, Computer science, Eng., Humanities and social sciences, Mathematics, Physics
Pres.: Maria Klawe
Vice-Pres. for Academic Affairs and Dean of Faculty: Daniel Goroff
Vice-Pres. for College Advancement: Marc Archambault
Vice-Pres. for Admin. and Finance/ Treasurer: Andrew Dorantes
Vice-Pres. for Admission and Financial Aid: Peter Osgood
Vice-Pres. and Dean of Students: Jeanne M. Noda
Chief Information Officer: Richard Parker
Registrar: Michael Hearon
Librarian: Yee Wah Chow
Library of 1,000,000 vols (shared with the Claremont Colleges)
Number of teachers: 80
Number of students: 730.

HEBREW UNION COLLEGE – JEWISH INSTITUTE OF RELIGION

3077 University Ave, Los Angeles, CA 90007
Telephone: (213) 749-3424
Fax: (213) 747-6128
Internet: www.huc.edu
Founded 1954
Private control
Academic year: September to May
Teaching centres in Cincinnati, New York and Jerusalem
Pres.: Rabbi David Ellenson
Provost: Norman J. Cohen Ellenson
Vice-Pres. Chief Admin. Officer: Gregory N. Brown
Vice-Pres. for Admin.: Gary G. Bokelman
Vice-Pres. for Spec. Projects: Rabbi Charles A. Kroloff
Vice-Pres. for Devt: Erica S. Frederick
Vice-Pres. for Finance: Michael A. Cheney
Dean and Vice-Pres. for Strategic Initiatives: Rabbi Aaron D. Panken
Registrar: Carol L. Sofer
Dir of Libraries: David J. Gilner
Library of 100,000 vols

DEANS

Cincinnati: Rabbi Kenneth E. Ehrlich
Los Angeles: Dr Steven F. Windmueller
New York: Rabbi Aaron D. Panken

Jerusalem: Rabbi Michael Marmur

HOLY NAMES UNIVERSITY

3500 Mountain Blvd, Oakland, CA 94619-1699
Telephone: (510) 436-1000
Fax: (510) 436-1199
Internet: www.hnu.edu
Founded 1868
Four-year, co-educational liberal arts college
Pres.: Dr Rosemarie Nassif (acting)
Vice-Pres. for Academic Affairs and Dean of Faculty: Lizbeth Martin
Vice-Pres. for Enrollment Management (vacant)
Vice-Pres. for Finance and Admin.: Stuart Koop
Vice-Pres. for Institutional Advancement: Dav Cvitkovic
Vice-Pres. for Mission Effectiveness: Dr Carol Sellman
Vice-Pres. for Student Affairs: Michael Miller
Dir of Library Services: Joyce McLean
Library of 111,000 vols
Number of teachers: 121
Number of students: 985.

HOPE INTERNATIONAL UNIVERSITY

2500 East Nutwood Ave, Fullerton, CA 92831
Telephone: (714) 879-3901
Fax: (714) 681-7451
Internet: www.hiu.edu
Founded 1928 as Pacific Bible Seminary; current name 1997
Private control
Pres.: Dr John Derry
Vice-Pres. for Institutional Advancement: David L. Poole
Vice-Pres. for Business and Finance: Laure Close
Vice-Pres. for Academic Affairs: Steve Eddington
Vice-Pres. for Student Affairs: Mark Comeaux
Registrar: Michael R. Boon
Dir of Library Services: Robin Hartman
Library of 65,000 vols
Number of teachers: 165
Number of students: 1,077

DEANS

School of Professional Studies: Dr Christopher A. Davis
School of Graduate Studies: Dr Alan Rabe
Pacific Christian College: Dr Steve Edgington

HUMBOLDT STATE UNIVERSITY

1 Harpst St, Arcata, CA 95521-8299
Telephone: (707) 826-3011
E-mail: welcome@humboldt.edu
Internet: www.humboldt.edu
Founded 1913
Academic year: August to May
Pres.: Rollin C. Richmond
Provost and Vice-Pres. for Academic Affairs: Richard Vrem
Vice-Pres. for Student Affairs: Steven Butler
Vice-Pres. for Admin. Affairs: Carl Coffey
Vice-Pres. for Univ. Advancement: Robert Gunsalus
Dean of Enrollment Management: Jean Butler
Registrar: Hilary Dashiell
Dean of the Library: Sharmon Kenyon
Library of 560,000 vols
Number of teachers: 563
Number of students: 7,550

DEANS

College of Arts, Humanities and Social Sciences: Robert A. Snyder
College of Natural Resources and Sciences: James Howard
College of Professional Studies: Susan Higgins

HUMPHREYS COLLEGE

6650 Inglewood Ave, Stockton, CA 95207
Telephone: (209) 478-0800
Fax: (209) 478-8721
Internet: www.humphreys.edu
Founded 1896 as Stockton Business College; present name 1947
Private control
Academic year: September to September
Pres.: Dr Robert G. Humphreys
Dean of Law School: L. Patrick Piggott
Dean of Admin.: Wilma Okamoto-Vaughn
Dean of Instruction: Jess Bonds
Registrar: Maria J. Garcia-Miller
Librarian: Stanislav Perkner
Areas of study: Accounting, Administrative Management, Business Admin., Community Studies, Court Reporting, Early Childhood Education, Liberal Arts, Paralegal Studies.

BRANCH CAMPUS

Modesto campus: Suite 3A, 3600 Sisk Rd, Modesto, CA 95356; tel. (209) 543-9411; fax (209) 543-9413.

ITT TECHNICAL INSTITUTE

9680 Granite Ridge Dr., San Diego, CA 922123
Telephone: (858) 571-8500
Internet: itt-tech.edu
Founded 1981
Private control (ITT Educational Services, Inc.)
85 Technical institutes in 30 states; Schools of Information Technology, Drafting and Design, Electronics Technology, Business, School of Criminal Justice, Health Sciences
Academic year: September to September
Dir: John A. Byers
Dean: Cornell R. Hoke
Registrar: Colleen Hebding.

JESUIT SCHOOL OF THEOLOGY AT BERKELEY

1735 LeRoy Ave, Berkeley, CA 94709
Telephone: (510) 549-5000
Fax: (510) 841-8536
E-mail: admissions@jstb.edu
Internet: www.jstb.edu
Founded 1934 as Alma College; present name 1969
Private control (part of the Graduate Theological Union)
Academic year: September to May
Pres.: Dr Joseph P. Daoust
Academic Dean: Kevin Burke
Dean of Students: Jill Marshall
Registrar: Sharon-Gay Smith
Dir of the Library: Bonnie Hardwick
Library of 684,000 holdings.

JOHN F. KENNEDY UNIVERSITY

100 Ellinwood Way, Pleasant Hill, CA 94563
Telephone: (510) 254-0200
Fax: (510) 254-6964
Internet: www.jfku.edu
Founded 1964
Pres.: Dr Steven Stargardter
Academic Vice-Pres.: Irving Berkowitz

Vice-Pres. for Enrollment Services: K. SUE DUNCAN
Vice-Pres. for Human Resources: PAULA L. SWAIN
Provost: DIANA PAQUE
Registrar: ADAM J. STONE
Librarians: ANN BUCHALTER (Campbell Campus), JOHN TAYLOR (Berkeley Campus)
Dir of Law Library: STEVEN R. FELLER
Library of 68,300 vols
Number of teachers: 687
Number of students: 1,900

DEANS

School of Education and Liberal Arts: SUSAN KWOCK
School of Law: GEOFFREY BROWN
School of Management: CARLOS GUTIERREZ
School of Holistic Studies: Dr PETER ROJCE-WICZ
Graduate School of Professional Psychology: Dr WILLIAM D. PARHAM

BRANCH CAMPUSES

Berkeley Campus: 2956 San Pablo Ave, Berkeley, CA 94702–2471; tel. (510) 649-0499.

Campbell Campus: 1 West Campbell Ave, Campbell, CA 95008; e-mail camp1@jfku.edu.

LA SIERRA UNIVERSITY

4500 Riverwalk Parkway, Riverside, CA 92515

Telephone: (951) 785-2000
Fax: (951) 785-2901
E-mail: info@lasierra.edu
Internet: www.lasierra.edu
Founded 1922
Academic year: September to June
Pres.: Dr LAWRENCE GERATY
Provost and Vice-Pres. for Academic Admin.: Dr WARREN C. TRENCHARD
Vice-Pres. for Advancement/Univ. Relations: JEFFRY M. KAATZ
Vice-Pres. for Enrollment Services: GENE EDELBACH
Vice-Pres. for Financial Admin.: DAVID GERIGUIS
Vice-Pres. for Student Life: JENNIFER TYNER
Registrar: FAYE SWAYZE
Library Dir: KITTY SIMMONS

Number of teachers: 110 (full-time)
Number of students: 1,400

Graduate and undergraduate curricula in Applied and Liberal Arts and Sciences, Business and Management, Education, Religion
Publication: *Adventist Heritage* (quarterly)

DEANS

College of Arts and Sciences: JAMES W. BEACH
School of Business and Management: Dr JOHN THOMAS
School of Education: Dr ED BOYATT
School of Religion: Dr JOHN WEBSTER

LIFE CHIROPRACTIC COLLEGE WEST

25001 Industrial Blvd, Hayward, CA 94545
Telephone: (510) 788-4467
Fax: (510) 780-4525
Internet: www.lifewest.edu
Founded 1976 as Pacific States Chiropractic College; present name 1981
Private control
Academic year: September to June
Offers Doctor's degree in Chiropractic
Pres.: Dr GERARD CLUM
Dean of College: Dr JOSEPH FERGUSON

Dean of Health Center: Dr SCOTT DONALDSON
Registrar: ARLENE BASILICO
Library Dir: ANNETTE OSENGA.

LIFE PACIFIC COLLEGE

1100 West Covina Blvd, San Dimas, CA 91773

Telephone: (909) 599-5433
Fax: (909) 599-6690
E-mail: info@lifepacific.edu
Internet: www.lifepacific.edu
Founded 1923
Private control
Academic year: August to May
Pres.: DAN R. STEWART
Vice-Pres. for Academic Affairs: Dr TERRY SAMPLES
Dir of Advancement: CARMEN QUEVEDO
Dir of Institutional Research: JASON SHIPMAN
Chief Financial Officer: JARROD KULA
Dean of Students: TIM CLARKE
Registrar: BRUCE PRIMROSE
Librarian: KEITH DAWSON

Biblical Exegesis, Children's Ministry, Counselling Ministry, Cross-Cultural Ministry, Education, Music and Worship Ministry, Pastoral Ministry, Youth Ministry.

LOMA LINDA UNIVERSITY

Loma Linda, CA 92350
Telephone: (909) 558-8161
Fax: (909) 558-0242
E-mail: admissions.app@llu.edu
Internet: www.llu.edu
Founded 1905
Pres. and CEO: B. LYN BEHRENS
Exec. Vice-Pres. for Finance and Admin./ Chief Financial Officer: KEVIN J. LANG
Exec. Vice-Pres. for Hospital Affairs: RUTHITA J. FIKE
Exec. Vice-Pres. for Medical Affairs: H. ROGER HADLEY
Exec. Vice-Pres. for Univ. Affairs: RICHARD H. HART
Sr Vice-Pres. for Educational Affairs: RONALD L. CARTER
Sr Vice-Pres. for Health Administration: DANIEL FONTOURA
Sr Vice-Pres. for Human Resource Management and Risk Management: MARK L. HUBBARD
Sr Vice-Pres. for Strategic Planning (vacant)
Exec. Vice-Pres. for Medical Affairs: MICHAEL H. JACKSON
Sr Vice-Pres. for Finance: STEVEN MOHR
Sr Vice-Pres. for Clinical Faculty: RICARDO PEVERINI
Sr Vice-Pres. for Managed Care: ZAREH SARRAFIAN
Sr Vice-Pres. for Faculty Practice: DAVID WREN
Vice-Pres. for Public Affairs: W. AUGUSTUS CHEATHAM
Vice-Pres. for Patient Care Services: ELIZABETH J. DICKINSON
Vice-Pres. for Graduate Medical Education: DANIEL W. GIANG
Vice-Pres. for Dentistry: CHARLES J. GOODACRE
Vice Pres./CIO for Academia: DAVID P. HARRIS
Vice Pres./CIO for Health Ministries: RICHARD HERGERT
Vice-Pres. for Nursing Education: MARILYN M. HERMANN
Vice-Pres. for Allied Health Professions Education: CRAIG R. JACKSON
Vice-Pres. for Quality: JAMES PAPPAS
Vice-Pres. for Religion Education: JON PAULIEN
Vice-Pres. for Diversity: LESLIE N. POLLARD

Vice-Pres. for Healthcare Business Devt/ Govt Relations: MEL SAUDER
Vice-Pres. for Finance: VERLON STRAUSS
Vice-Pres. for Spiritual Life and Wholeness: GERALD R. WINSLOW
Vice-Pres. for Graduate Studies Education: ANTHONY J. ZUCCARELLI
Dir of Libraries: CARLENE DRAKE
Library: Libraries with 317,368 vols and periodicals
Number of teachers: 1,068 (full-time)
Number of students: 3,427

DEANS

School of Allied Health Professions: CRAIG R. JACKSON
School of Dentistry: Dr CHARLES J. GOODACRE
School of Medicine: Dr ROGER HADLEY
School of Nursing: Dr MARILYN HERMANN
School of Pharmacy: Dr AVIS J. ERICSON
School of Public Health: Dr JAMES KYLE
Faculty of Religion: Dr DAVID L. TAYLOR
Faculty of Science and Technology: RONALD L. CARTER
Graduate School: ANTHONY J. ZUCCARELLI

LOYOLA MARYMOUNT UNIVERSITY

1 LMU Dr., Los Angeles, CA 90045-2659
Telephone: (310) 338-2700
Internet: www.lmu.edu
Founded 1911 by Jesuit Fathers; present name 1973
Academic year: August to May
Pres.: Rev. ROBERT B. LAWTON
Chancellor: PATRICK J. CAHALAN
Sr Vice-Pres. for Student Affairs: Dr LANE BOVE
Sr Vice-Pres.: DAVID W. BURCHAM
Sr Vice-Pres. for Business and Finance: THOMAS FLEMING
Sr Vice-Pres. for Admin.: LYNN SCARBOROUGH
Sr Vice-Pres. for Univ. Relations: DENNIS SLON
Sr Vice-Pres. for Academic Affairs: Dr ERNEST T. ROSE
Vice-Pres. for Communications and Govt Relations: KATHLEEN FLANAGAN
Vice-Pres. for Devt and Alumni Relations: BEDFORD MCINTOSH
Dir of Graduate Admissions: CHAKÉ KOUYOUMJIAN
Dean of Univ. Libraries: KRISTINE BRANCOLINI
Library of 561,498 vols (289,201 main campus; 272,297 Law School)
Number of teachers: 805 (692 main campus, 113 Law School)
Number of students: 8,215 (6,804 main campus, 1,411 Law School)

DEANS

College of Business Admin.: Dr JOHN T. WHOLIHAN
Frank R. Seaver College of Science and Eng.: Dr RICHARD G. PLUMB
Loyola Law School: Dr DAVID W. BURCHAM
Bellarmine College of Liberal Arts: Dr MICHAEL E. ENG
College of Communication and Fine Arts: Prof. BARBARA BUSSE
School of Education: SHANE MARTIN
School of Film and Television: TERRI SCHWARTZ

MASTER'S COLLEGE

21726 Placerita Canyon Rd, Santa Clarita, CA 91321
Telephone: (661) 259-3540
Fax: (661) 288-1037
E-mail: enrollment@masters.edu
Internet: www.masters.edu

Founded 1927 as Los Angeles Baptist Theological Seminary; present name 1985

Private control

Pres.: Dr JOHN MACARTHUR

Sr Vice-Pres. and Provost: Dr RICHARD MAYHUE

Vice-Pres. for Academic Affairs: Dr JOHN HUGHES

Vice-Pres. for Enrollment Management: Dr PAUL BERRY

Chief Financial Officer: BRADLEY G. WETHERELL

Vice-Pres. for Operations: ROBERT L. HOTTON

Vice-Pres. for Student Life: Dr MARK TATLOCK

Dir of Library Services: JOHN STONE

Library of 143,000 vols

Number of teachers: 70

Number of students: 1,100

Areas of study: Biblical Studies, Biological and Physical Science, Business, Communication, Computer and Information Sciences, English, History and Political Studies, Home Economics, Liberal Studies, Mathematics, Music, Physical Education, Teacher Education, Biblical Counselling, Divinity, Theology.

MENLO COLLEGE

1000 El Camino Real, Atherton, CA 94027-4301

Telephone: (650) 543-3753

E-mail: admissions@menlo.edu

Internet: www.menlo.edu

Founded 1927 as Menlo Junior College; present name 1949

Private control

Depts of Communication, Liberal Arts and Management

Pres.: TIMOTHY HAIGHT

Provost: JAMES J. KELLY

Academic Dean: LOWELL PRATT

Dean of Library and Information Services: C. BRIGID WELCH

Number of students: 550.

MENNONITE BRETHREN BIBLICAL SEMINARY

4824 East Butler Ave, Fresno, CA 93727-5097

Telephone: (559) 251-8628

Fax: (559) 251-7212

E-mail: fresno@mbseminary.edu

Internet: www.mbseminary.edu

Founded 1955

Private control

Academic year: August to August

Pres.: JIM HOLM

Academic Dean: LYNN JOST

Dean of Students: RICK BARTLETT

Chief Financial Officer: LINDA BOWMAN

Registrar: LORI JAMES

Librarian: RICHARD RAWLS

Library of 150,000 vols

Number of teachers: 11

Number of students: 140

MAs in Christian Ministry, Divinity, Intercultural Mission, Marriage, Family and Child Counselling, New Testament, Old Testament, Theology; diplomas in Anglican Studies, Christian Studies, Congregational Care, Evangelism and Church Planting, Integration, Presbyterian Studies, Women in Ministry.

CANADA CAMPUSES

Langley Campus: MBBS, 7600 Glover Rd, Langley, BC V2Y 1Y1, Canada; tel. (604) 513-2019; fax (604) 513-2045; e-mail langley@mbseminary.edu; internet www.acts.twu.ca.

Winnipeg Campus: MBBS, Canadian Mennonite Univ., 500 Shaftesbury Blvd, Winnipeg, MB R3P 2N5, Canada; tel. (204) 487-3300; fax (204) 487-3858; e-mail winnipeg@mbseminary.edu; internet www.ministrystudies.ca.

MILLS COLLEGE

5000 MacArthur Blvd, Oakland, CA 94613

Telephone: (510) 430-2255

Fax: (510) 430-3314

E-mail: admission@mills.edu

Internet: www.mills.edu

Founded as a Seminary 1852, as a College 1885

Academic year: June to May

Liberal arts college; women only at undergraduate level; mixed at graduate level

Pres.: JANET HOLMGREN

Provost and Dean of the Faculty: MARY-ANN MILFORD

Vice-Pres. for Admin. and Finance and Treasurer: ELIZABETH BURWELL

Vice-Pres. for Information Resources: RENÉE JADUSHLEVER

Exec. Vice-Pres. for Institutional Advancement: RAMON TORRECILHA

Dean of Student Life: KENNEDY GOLDEN (acting)

Dean of Admission: GIULIETTA AQUINO

Library of 225,000 vols; spec. collns 12,000 vols and 10,000 MSS, incl. Shakespeare's First Folio, a Mozart manuscript, and edn of *Alice in Wonderland* illustrated by Salvador Dali

Number of teachers: 94

Number of students: 1,400

Publications: *580 Split* (annual), *The Walrus* (annual)

DEANS

Fine Arts: MARY-ANN MILFORD

Letters: RUTH SAXTON

Natural Sciences and Education: LINDA KROLL

Social Sciences: LAURA NATHAN

MONTEREY INSTITUTE OF INTERNATIONAL STUDIES

460 Pierce St, Monterey, CA 93940

Telephone: (831) 647-4100

Fax: (831) 647-4199

E-mail: admit@miis.edu

Internet: www.miis.edu

Founded 1955

Academic year: September to June

Ind. int. graduate school

Pres.: CLARA YU

Vice-Pres. for Academic Affairs and Provost (vacant)

Vice-Pres. for Enrollment Management: DENNIS R. JOHNSON

Vice-Pres. for Finance and Admin. (vacant)

Vice-Pres. for Institutional Advancement: ANN JONES-WEINSTOCK

Library Dir: PETER LIU

Library of 90,000 vols, 500 periodical titles; incl. all UN publs since 1993, and dictionaries and translation resources (one-third of whole colln is in languages other than English)

Number of students: 699

DEANS

Fisher Graduate School of Int. Business: Dr ERNEST SCALBERG

Graduate School of Int. Policy Studies: EDWARD J. LAURANCE

Graduate School of Language and Educational Linguistics: RUTH LARIMER

Graduate School of Translation and Interpretation: CHUANYUN BAO

MOUNT ST MARY'S COLLEGE

Chalon Campus, 12001 Chalon Rd, Los Angeles, CA 90049-1599

Telephone: (310) 954-4000

Fax: (310) 954-4379

Internet: www.msmc.la.edu

Doheny Campus, 10 Chester Pl., Los Angeles, CA 9007

Telephone: (213) 477-2500

Founded 1925

Pres.: Dr JACQUELINE POWERS DOUD

Provost and Academic Vice-Pres.: Dr ELEANOR SIEBERT

Vice-Pres. for Admin. and Finance: CHRIS K. MCALARY

Vice-Pres. for Information Support Service: LARRY SMITH

Vice-Pres. for Institutional Advancement: STEPHANIE CUBBA

Vice-Pres. for Student Affairs: JANE LINGUA

Dir of Libraries: CLAUDIA REED

Library of 140,000 vols

Number of teachers: 185

Number of students: 2,480 (1,980 undergraduates, 500 graduates)

Depts of American studies, Art, Biological sciences, Business admin., Education, English, Film and social justice, Gerontology, History, Humanities, Language and culture, Music, Nursing, Philosophy, Physical sciences and mathematics, Physical therapy, Political science, Psychology, Religious studies, Social work, Sociology.

NATIONAL UNIVERSITY

11255 North Torrey Pines Rd, La Jolla, CA 92037-1011

Telephone: (858) 642-8000

Fax: (858) 642-8708

Internet: www.nu.edu

Founded 1971

Private control

26 Learning centres throughout California; campuses at Carlsbad, La Mesa, Mission Valley, Rancho Bernardo, South Bay, Spectrum Business Park

Chancellor: Dr JERRY C. LEE

Vice-Chancellor for Organizational Devt: Dr GARY FROST

Provost and Vice-Pres. for Academic Affairs: Dr SHARON P. SMITH

Vice-Pres. for Strategic Planning: RICHARD C. JOY

Vice-Pres. for Admin and Business: KEVIN CASEY

Vice-Pres. for Advancement and Alumni Relations: MAGGIE T. WATKINS

Vice-Pres. for Regional Operations and Marketing: VIRGINIA BENEKE

Vice-Pres. for Student Services: Dr DOUGLAS SLAWSON

Exec. Vice-Pres.: Dr JOHN F. CADY

Dean of Graduate Studies (vacant)

Library Dir: ANNE MARIE SECORD

Library of 200,000 vols

Number of teachers: 996 (140 full-time, 85 assoc., 871 adjunct)

Number of students: 17,090 (full-time)

DEANS

School of Business and Management: Dr WALI MONDAL

School of Education: Dr GLORIA JOHNSTON

School of Eng. and Technology: Dr HOWARD EVANS

School of Health and Human Sciences: (vacant)

College of Letters and Sciences: Dr DEBRA SCHNEIGER
School of Media and Communication: Dr MICHAEL MCANEAR

NAVAL POSTGRADUATE SCHOOL

1 University Circle, Monterey, CA 93943-5001
Telephone: (831) 656-2023
Fax: (831) 656-3238
Internet: www.nps.edu
Founded 1909
Pres.: Vice-Admiral DANIEL T. OLIVER
Provost and Academic Dean: Dr LEONARD A. FERRARI
Univ. Librarian: ELEANOR UHLINGER
Library of 1,063,696 vols (incl. microform)
Number of teachers: 359
Number of students: 1,500

Courses in Aeronautical Eng., Applied Mathematics, Applied Physics, Applied Science, Astronautical Eng., Computer Science, Contract Management, Defence Analysis, Electrical Eng., Eng. Acoustics, Eng. Science, Information Technology Management, Int. Resource Planning and Management, Leadership and Human Resource Devt, Management, Materials Science and Eng., Mechanical Eng., Meteorology, Meteorology and Physical Oceanography, Modelling, Operations Research, Physical Oceanography, Physics, Programme Management, Software Eng., Systems Eng., Systems Eng. Management, Systems Technology, Virtual Environments and Simulation

DEANS

Graduate School of Business and Public Policy: Dr ROBERT N. BECK
Graduate School of Eng. and Applied Sciences: Dr JAMES L. KAYS
Graduate School of Operational and Information Sciences: PETER PURDUE
School of Int. Graduate Studies: ROBERT L. ORD

NOTRE DAME DE NAMUR UNIVERSITY

1500 Ralston Ave, Belmont, CA 94002
Telephone: (650) 508-3500
Fax: (650) 508-3736
Internet: www.ndnu.edu
Founded 1851; chartered 1868
Pres.: Dr JOHN B. OBLAK
Provost: Dr JUDITH MAXWELL GREIG
Registrar: SANDRA LEE
Vice-Pres. for Institutional Advancement: DAVID CATHERMAN
Vice-Pres. for Campus Life: RAYMOND JONES
Dean of Enrollment: JARRID WHITNEY
Librarian: Dr KLAUS MUSMANN
Library of 105,910 vols
Number of teachers: 100
Number of students: 1,652

DEANS

School of Arts and Humanities: Dr GREGORY B. WHITE
School of Business and Management: GEORGE KLEMIC
School of Education and Leadership: Dr JOANNE ROSSI
School of Sciences: Dr GREGORY B. WHITE

OCCIDENTAL COLLEGE

1600 Campus Rd, Los Angeles, CA 90041
Telephone: (323) 259-2500
Fax: (323) 259-2958
Internet: www.oxy.edu

Founded 1887
Pres.: SUSAN WESTERBERG PRAGER
Vice-Pres. for Admin. and Finance: MICHAEL GROENER
Vice-Pres. for Admission and Financial Aid: WILLIAM D. TINGLEY
Vice-Pres. for Institutional Advancement: JON KEATES
Vice-Pres. for Legal Affairs and General Counsel: Dr SANDRA COOPER
Dean of Admission: VINCE CUSEO
Dean of the College: ERIC FRANK
Dean of Students: Dr LOUANNE KENNEDY,
Registrar: VICTOR T. EGITTO
Librarian: EMILY BERGMAN
Library of 500,000 items (books, video and audio recordings and microforms) and 1,255 current periodicals
Number of teachers: 140
Number of students: 1,534

Courses in American Studies, Art History and Visual Arts, Asian Studies, Biochemistry, Biology, Chemistry, Cognitive Science, Critical Theory and Social Justice, Diplomacy and World Affairs, Econ., Education, English and Comparative Literary Studies, English Writing, Environmental Programs, Geology, German, Russian, and Classical Studies, Global Affairs, History, Kinesiology, Mathematics, Music, Philosophy, Physics, Politics, Psychobiology, Psychology, Religious Studies, Sociology, Spanish and French Literary Studies, Theater, Women's Studies/Gender Studies.

OTIS COLLEGE OF ART AND DESIGN

9045 Lincoln Blvd, Los Angeles, CA 90045
Telephone: (310) 665-6800
Fax: (310) 665-6821
E-mail: admissions@otis.edu
Internet: www.otis.edu
Founded 1918
Pres.: SAMUEL HOI
Provost: JOHN S. GORDON
Vice-Pres. for Admin. and Finance: CHRIS ALFORD
Vice-Pres. for Enrollment Management: SAMUEL HOI
Dean of Admissions: MARC MEREDITH
Dean of Student Affairs: MARY WARDELL
Gallery Dir.: MEG LINTON
Registrar: ANNA MANZANO
Dir of Library: SUE MABERRY
Library of 25,000 vols
Number of teachers: 200
Number of students: 940

BAs in Architecture/Landscape/Interiors, Communication Arts, Digital Media, Fashion Design, Fine Arts, Interactive Product Design, Toy Design; MAs in Fine Arts, Public Practice, Writing.

PACIFIC GRADUATE SCHOOL OF PSYCHOLOGY

940 East Meadow Drive, Palo Alto, CA 94303
Telephone: (650) 843-3419
Fax: (650) 493-6147
E-mail: admissions@pgsp.edu
Internet: www.pgsp.edu
Founded 1975
Private control
Academic year: September to August
Pres.: Dr ALLEN CALVIN
Vice-Pres. for Business Affairs: JUNE KLEIN
Vice-Pres. for Information Resources: CHRISTINE DASSOFF KIDD
Vice-Pres. for Student Services: LIZ HILT
Dir of Admissions: DACIEN SIMS
Dir of Clinical Training: Dr PETER GOLDBLUM
Registrar: NORA MARQUEZ

Library of 8,000 vols, 450 journals, 500 audio cassettes, 150 videotapes
Number of teachers: 27
Number of students: 304.

PACIFIC LUTHERAN THEOLOGICAL SEMINARY

2770 Marin Ave, Berkeley, CA 94708
Telephone: (510) 524-5264
Fax: (510) 524-2408
E-mail: reception@plts.edu
Internet: plts.edu
Founded 1950
Private control (part of the Graduate Theological Union)
Academic year: September to May
Pres.: Dr PHYLIS ANDERSON
Vice-Pres. for Advancement: CINDY CARROLL
Dir of Admissions: GREG SCHAEFER
Dean of Faculty: MICHAEL B. AULNE
Dean of Students and Registrar: CHERYL HEUER
Library Dir: BONNIE HARDWICK
Library of 648,163 items, 382,523 bound vols, 301,640 audiovisual materials, 18,426 reference vols, 2,559 current subscriptions
Number of teachers: 15
Number of students: 186

MAs in Christian Ministry, Divinity, Theological Studies.

PACIFIC OAKS COLLEGE AND CHILDREN'S SCHOOL

5 Westmoreland Pl., Pasadena, CA 91103-3592
Telephone: (626) 397-1300
Fax: (626) 577-3502
Internet: www.pacificoaks.edu
Founded 1945
Pres.: CAROLYN DENHAM
Vice-Pres. for Advancement: ARRISTIDE J. COLLINS
Registrar: MARSHA FRANKER
Provost: LESLIE JOHNSON
Librarian: NERMINE HANNA
Library of 17,000 items
Number of teachers: 71
Number of students: 1,281

Courses in Human Devt, Marital and Family Therapy, Teacher Education programs.

PACIFIC SCHOOL OF RELIGION

1798 Scenic Ave, Berkeley, CA 94709-1323
Telephone: (510) 848-0528
Fax: (510) 845-8948
E-mail: psrinfo@psr.edu
Internet: www.psr.edu
Founded 1866 as Pacific Theological Seminary; present name 1916
Private control (part of the Graduate Theological Union)
Academic year: September to May
Pres.: Rev. Dr WILLIAM MCKINNEY
Vice-Pres. for Academic Affairs and Dean: Dr MARY DONOVAN TURNER
Registrar: DELPHINE HWANG
Dir of Badè Museum: AARON BRODY
Library Dir: ROBERT BENETTO
Library of 700,000 vols
Number of teachers: 57 (17 core, 40 adjunct)
Number of students: 241.

PACIFIC UNION COLLEGE

1 Angwin Ave, Angwin, CA 94508
Telephone: (707) 965-6311
Fax: (707) 965-6506
E-mail: enroll@puc.edu
Internet: www.puc.edu

Founded 1882
Private control, affiliated with the Seventh-day Adventist Church
Academic year: September to June

Pres.: Dr RICHARD C. OSBORN
Vice-Pres. for Academic Admin. and Academic Dean: NANCY LECOURT
Vice-Pres. for Financial Admin.: JOHN COLLINS
Vice-Pres. for Student Services: Dr LISA BISSELL PAULSON
Vice-Pres. for Advancement: PAM SADLER
Registrar: H. SUSI MUNDY
Chair of Library Services: ADUGNAW WORKU

Library of 240,000 vols
Number of teachers: 115
Number of students: 1,700

Depts of Aviation, Biology, Business admin. and econ., Chemistry, Communication, Computer science, Education, English, Exercise science, Health and nutrition, History, Honors, Mathematics, Modern languages, Music, Nursing, Psychology and social work, Physics, Religion, Visual arts

Publications: *College Bulletin*, *PUC Viewpoint* (quarterly).

PACIFICA GRADUATE INSTITUTE

249 Lambert Rd, Carpinteria, CA 93013
Telephone: (805) 969-3626
Fax: (805) 565-1932
E mail: admissions@pacifica.edu
Internet: www.pacifica.edu

Pres.: Dr STEPHEN AIZENSTAT
Provost: CHARLES ASHER
Chief Financial Officer: CATHY WALKER
Dean of Academic Affairs: Dr CINDY CARTER
Dir of Admissions: WENDY OVEREND
Registrar: FRANCINE MATAS
Dir of Library Services: ERIN BARTA

Depts of Clinical psychology, Counselling psychology, Depth psychology, Depth psychotherapy, Humanities, Mythological studies.

PARDEE RAND GRADUATE SCHOOL

1776 Main St, Santa Monica, CA 90407-3208
Telephone: (310) 393-0411
Fax: (310) 451-6978
E-mail: prgs@prgs.edu
Internet: www.prgs.edu

Founded 1970
Private control

Dean: JOHN GRAHAM

Number of teachers: 100
Number of students: 92

Areas of study: Policy analysis, Social and behavioural sciences, Science and technology, Modelling and computational methods, Empirical analysis, Econ.

PATTEN COLLEGE

2433 Coolidge Ave, Oakland, CA 94601
Telephone: (510) 261-8500
Fax: (510) 534-4344
E-mail: admissions@patten.edu
Internet: www.patten.edu

Founded 1944
Private control

Pres.: Dr GARY MONCHER
Academic Vice-Pres. and Provost: Dr KENNETH ROMINES
Dean of Enrollment Services: ROBERT OLIVERA
Dean of Student Services: SHARON BARTA
Library Dir: ANN ZEMENS

Library of 33,000 vols, 180 periodicals

Depts of Art, Biblical studies, Christian leadership, Church ministries, Communica-

tions, Education, Liberal studies for teaching, Music, Organizational management, Pastoral studies, Psychology, Urban missions, Youth ministry.

PEPPERDINE UNIVERSITY

24255 Pacific Coast Highway, Malibu, CA 90263
Telephone: (310) 506-4000
Internet: www.pepperdine.edu

Founded 1937 as college, attained univ. status 1970

Pres.: ANDREW K. BENTON
Chancellor: Dr CHARLES B. RUNNELS
Provost and Chief Academic Officer: Dr DARRYL TIPPENS
Exec. Vice-Pres. and Chief Operating Officer: GARY HANSON
Sr Vice-Pres. for Planning, Information and Technology: Dr NANCY MAGNUSSON
Sr Vice-Pres. for Investments: JEFF PIPPIN
Vice-Pres. for Advancement and Public Affairs: KEITH HINKLE
Dean of Student Affairs: MARK DAVIS
Dean of Admission and Enrolment Management: PAUL A. LONG
Dean of Int. Programs: CHARLES HALL
Dean of Libraries: MARK S. ROOSA

Library: 8 libraries with a combined colln of 650,000
Number of teachers: 300 full-time
Number of students: 8,000

Publication: *Pepperdine People* (quarterly)

DEANS

Seaver College: W. DAVID BAIRD
Graduate School of Education and Psychology: MARGARET WEBER
Graziadio School of Business and Management: LINDA A. LIVINGSTONE
School of Law: KENNETH W. STARR
School of Public Policy: JAMES R. WILBURN

PROFESSORS

Seaver College:
ADJEMIAN, C., Mathematics
ADLER, R., Marketing
ARDOIN, B., Communication
BAIM, D., Econ. and Finance
BAIRD, D., History
BANKS, J., Management and Organizational Behaviour
BATCHELDER, R., Econ.
BUCHANAN, R. W., Communication
CALDWELL, D. E., Social Sciences
CARROLL, L. A., English
CASEY, M. W., Communication
CHANDLER, R., Communication
CHESNUTT, R. D., Religion
CLEGG, C., English
CLOUD, D. C., Accounting
COBB, G., Music
COLLINGS, M. R., English
DAVIS, S., Biology
DOWDEY, D., German
DUNPHY, M., Physical Education
FALKNER, A., Art
FELTNER, M., Sports Medicine
GAMBILL, K., English
GANSKE, J., Chemistry
GIBONEY, S., Education
GIBSON, D., Philosophy
GOSE, M. D., Education
GREEN, D. B., Chemistry
HANCOCK, D. L., Mathematics
HART, G. W., English
HENDERSON, J., Theatre
HUGHES, R. T., Religion
KATS, L., Biology
LANGFORD, M., French
LOVE, S., Religion
LOWRY, D. N., Communication
MACRAE, H., Sports Medicine

MACRAE, P., Sports Medicine
MADDOX, R. B., Mathematics
MARRS, R. R., Religion
MARTIN, K. L., Biology
MONSMA, S., Political Science
MURRIE, M., Telecommunications
MYERS, V., English
NEILSON, G., Theatre
PARKENING, C., Music
PAYNE-PALACIO, J., Nutritional Science
PHILLIPS, W., Physics
PIASENTIN, J., Art
PULLEN, M., Music
REINECK, L., English
SESHAN, V., Management
SEXTON, R. L., Social Sciences
SHATZER, M., Communication
SHORES, D., Broadcasting
STRACHE, C. V., Physical Education
SUMMERS, M. R., Business Administration
SWARTZENDRUBER, D., Biology
THOMAS, J., English
THOMASON, P. B., Spanish
THOMPSON, D., Mathematics
TYLER, R. L., Religion
WARFORD, S., Computer Science
WEBB, G. T., Japanese Cultural History
WHITE, J. B., Chemistry
WILSON, J. F., New Testament
YATES, J. E., Organizational Behaviour and Management

School of Business and Management:
BLEUEL, W. H., Quantitative Methods
BUSKIRK, B. D., Marketing
DARDEN, C. E., Organization and Management
DUDLEY, T. J., Quantitative Methods
FLIEGE, S., Quantitative Methods
FOJTIK, C. W., Marketing
GERTMENIAN, W., Econ.
GOODRICH, J., Int. Business
HAGAN, A. J., Econ.
HALL Jr, O. P., Quantitative Methods
HESSE, R., Quantitative Methods
HITCHIN, D. E., Management
HOISMAN, A. J., Behavioural Science
HUNT Jr, C. J., Business Law
LARSON, W. G., Business Law
MALLINGER, M., Organization Behaviour
MARTINOFF, J. T., Finance
MOTAMEDI, K. K., Organization and Management
NICKLES, M. D., Econ.
PENDERGHAST, T. F., Quantitative Methods
PETRO, F. A., Accounting
REISMAN, G., Econ.
RICHARDSON, J. E., Marketing
RIERDAN, R. C., Behavioural Science
ROCKEY, E., Behavioural Science
SAMUELSON, B. A., Accounting
SANFORD, E., Econ.
SHAFER, W., Accounting
SIEGEL, S., Technology Management
STANLEY, D. J., Finance and Accounting
STROM, W. L., Behavioural Science
VARDIABASIS, D., Econ.
YOUNG, T. W., Econ.

School of Education and Psychology:
ASAMEN, J. K., Psychology
COZOLINO, L. J., Psychology
FOY, D., Psychology
GARCIA, C. L., Education
HARRELL, S. P., Psychology
HEDGESPETH, J., Psychology
HIATT-MICHAEL, D., Education
HIBBS, C., Psychology
INGRAM, B., Psychology
LEVY, D. A., Psychology
LOWE, D. W., Psychology
MARTINEZ, T., Psychology
McCALL, C., Research Methods
McMANUS, J. F., Education
NEELY, F. W., Psychology
PAULL, R., Education
POLIN, L. G., Education

ROWE, D., Psychology
SÁNCHEZ, M., Education
SCHMIEDER-RAMIREZ, J., Education
SHAFRANSKE, E. P., Psychology
STEPHENS, R., Education
School of Law:
ALFORD, R. P.
BOST, T. G.
BOYD, K. L.
BUCHAN, L.
CALDWELL, H. M.
CHASE, C. A.
COCHRAN Jr, R. F.
COE Jr, J. J.
GAFFNEY Jr, E. M.
GASH, J. A.
GOODMAN, C. C.
GRADISHER, M. R.
GRAFFY, C. P.
JAMES, B.
KERR, C. L.
KERR, J. E.
KNAPLUND, K. S.
LEVINE, S. J.
LOWRY, L. R.
MARTIN, D. W.
MCCRORY, J. P.
MCDERMOTT, A. X.
MCDONALD, B. P.
MCGOLDRICK Jr, J. M.
MENDOZA, A.
MILLER, A.
NELSON, C. I.
OGDEN, G. L.
PERRIN, L. T.
POPOVICH, R.
PUSHAW, R. J.
ROBINSON, P.
SAXER, S. R.
SCARBERRY, M. S.
SEYMOUR, A. D.
SMITH, M. L.
WENDEL, P. T.
WESTON, M. A.
School of Public Policy:
LLOYD, G., Public Policy
MCALLISTER, E., Public Policy
MONSMA, S. V., Political Science
SEXTON, R., Econ.
VAN EATON, C., Public Policy
VARDIABASIS, D., Econ.
WILSON, J. Q., Public Policy

PITZER COLLEGE

1050 North Mills Ave, Claremont, CA 91711-6110
Telephone: (909) 621-8000
E-mail: admission@pitzer.edu
Internet: www.pitzer.edu
Founded 1963
Private control, member of the Claremont Colleges
Pres.: LAURA SKANDERA TROMBLEY
Vice-Pres. for Admin. and Treasurer: VICKE SELK
Vice-Pres. of Admission and Financial Aid: ARNALDO RODRIGUEZ
Vice-Pres. of College Advancement (vacant)
Vice-Pres. of Academic Affairs and Dean of Faculty: ALAN JONES
Vice-Pres. of Student Affairs and Dean of Students: JIM MARCHANT
Vice-Pres. of Marketing and Public Relations: SUSAN ANDREWS
Registrar: CHERYL MORALES
Librarian: ALBERTA WALKER

Library of 2,000,000 vols
Number of teachers: 65
Number of students: 900.

POINT LOMA NAZARENE UNIVERSITY

3900 Lomaland Dr., San Diego, CA 92106-2899
Telephone: (619) 849-2200
Fax: (619) 849-2579
E-mail: admissions@ptloma.edu
Internet: www.pointloma.edu
Founded 1902 as Pacific Bible College; present name 1998
Private control
Academic year: August to May
Pres.: Dr BOB BROWER
Vice-Pres. for Financial Affairs: GEORGE LATTER
Vice-Pres. for Spiritual Devt: MICHAEL A. PITTS
Vice-Pres. for Student Devt: W. GORDON GOLSAN
Vice-Pres. for Univ. Advancement: DANIEL J. MARTIN
Provost and Chief Academic Officer: Dr JOHN W. HAWTHORNE
Dir of Admissions: SCOTT SHOEMAKER
Dir of Learning Services: Dr FRANK QUINN
Number of students: 2,000

Depts of Art and design, Biology, Chemistry, Communication and theatre, Family and consumer sciences, History and political science, Kinesiology, Literature, Journalism and modern languages, Mathematics, Information and computer sciences, Music, Physics and eng., Psychology, Sociology and social work

DEANS

Arts and Sciences: Dr DAVID L. STRAWN
Social Science and Professional Studies: Dr REBECCA A. HAVENS
Graduate and Continuing Education: Dr DARREL R. FALK

BRANCH CAMPUSES

Arcadia Campus: 225 East Santa Clara St, Arcadia, CA 91006; tel. (626) 821-8240; fax (626) 821-8249.

Bakersfield Campus: Suite 100, 2100 Chester Ave, Bakersfield, CA 93301; tel. (661) 321-3480; fax (661) 321-3489.

Mission Valley Campus: 4007 Camino Del Rio South, San Diego, CA 92108; tel. (619) 563-2818.

POMONA COLLEGE

Alexander Hall, 550 North College Ave, Claremont, CA 91711
Telephone: (909) 621-8000
Internet: www.pomona.edu
Founded 1887
Private control, mem. of the Claremont Colleges
Pres.: DAVID W. OXTOBY
Vice-Pres. for Academic Affairs and Dean of the College: GARY KATES
Vice-Pres. for Devt: CHRIS PONCE
Vice-Pres. and Dean of Students: ANN G. QUINLEY
Vice-Pres. and Treas.: CARLENE MILLER
Dean of Admissions: BRUCE POCH
Registrar: MARGARET ADORNO

Library of 1,900,000 vols
Number of teachers: 186
Number of students: 1,500
Publication: *Pomona College Magazine* (quarterly).

ST MARY'S COLLEGE OF CALIFORNIA

Moraga, CA 94575
Telephone: (925) 631-4000

Internet: www.stmarys-ca.edu
Founded 1863
Pres.: Bro. RONALD GALLAGHER
Vice-Pres. for Academic Affairs and Provost: Prof. SARA STAMPP
Vice-Pres. for Advancement and Planning: Bro. STANISLAUS SOBCZYK
Vice-Pres. for Finance: PETER MICHELL
Vice-Pres. for College Communications and Vice-Provost for Enrolment: MICHAEL BESEDA
Dean of Academic Resources: THOMAS CARTER
Vice-Provost for Academic Affairs: FRANCES SWEENEY
Vice-Provost for Student Life: SCOTT KIER
Library of 200,000 vols, 1,100 current periodicals
Number of teachers: 274
Number of students: 4,378

DEANS

School of Econ. and Business Admin.: Dr ROY ALLEN
School of Education: Dr NANCY L. SORENSON
School of Extended Education: Dr DEAN ELIAS
School of Nursing: Dr ARLENE SARGENT
School of Liberal Arts: Dr STEPHEN WOOLPERT
School of Science: Dr JUDD CASE

ST PATRICK'S SEMINARY AND UNIVERSITY

320 Middlefield Rd, Menlo Park, CA 94025
Telephone: (650) 325-5621
Fax: (650) 323-5447
E-mail: info@stpatricksseminary.org
Internet: www.stpatricksseminary.org
Founded 1898
Private control
Academic year: September to May
Pres. and Chancellor: Rev. GEORGE H. NIEDERAUER
Vice-Pres. and Sec.: Rev. JOHN C. WESTER
Vice-Pres. for Advancement: CHRISTOPHER GRASSO
Pres., Rector and Vice-Chancellor: Rev. GERALD S. S. BROWN
Academic Dean: DOROTHY TULLY
Dean of Students: Rev. VINCENT D. BUI
Registrar: NURIA ORTIZ
Dir of Library: Dr CECIL R. WHITE
Library of 101,400 vols, 286 periodicals.

ATTACHED INSTITUTE

Vatican II Institute for Continuing Formation: tel. (650) 325-9122; fax (650) 325-6765; e-mail vat2ins@aol.com; internet www.stpatricksseminary.org/vatican2; f. 1972; Dir Rev. JIM MYERS.

SAMRA UNIVERSITY OF ORIENTAL MEDICINE

4th Floor, 3000 South Robertson Blvd, Los Angeles, CA 90034
Telephone: (310) 202-6444
Fax: (310) 202-6007
E-mail: info@samra.edu
Internet: www.samra.edu
Private control
Languages of instruction: English, Chinese, Korean
Academic year: October to September
Pres.: Dr HYUNG JOO PARK
Vice-Pres.: Dr BYUNG S. HONG
Provost: Dr KAATSUYUKI SAKAMOTO
Registrar: Dr ELIZABETH GOMEZ
Librarian: GAN YE

Library of 7,000 items
Areas of study: Chinese Medical Theory, Acupuncture Theory, Chinese Herbology, Basic Sciences, Anatomy, Physiology.

SAMUEL MERRITT COLLEGE

370 Hawthorne Ave, Oakland, CA 94609
Telephone: (510) 869-6511
E-mail: information@samuelmerritt.edu
Internet: www.samuelmerritt.edu
Founded 1909, merged with California College of Podiatric Medicine (f. 1914) in 2002
Pres. and CEO: SHARON DIAZ
Academic Vice-Pres. and Provost: Dr SCOT FOSTER
Vice-Pres. for Finance and Admin.: GREGORY GINGRAS
Vice-Pres. for Enrolment and Student Services: JOHN GARTEN-SHUMAN
Library Dir: BARBARA RYKEN
Library of 15,000 vols, 7,740 bound periodicals, 474 current periodicals
Number of teachers: 42 (full time)
Number of students: 650
Depts of Nursing, Occupational Therapy, Physical Therapy, Physician Assistant Training, Podiatric Medicine

DEANS

Nursing: AUDREY BERMAN
Podiatric Medicine: AL BURNS

SAN DIEGO CHRISTIAN COLLEGE

2100 Greenfield Dr., El Cajon, CA 92019
Telephone: (619) 441-2200
Fax: (619) 590-1739
E-mail: admissions@sdcc.cdu
Internet: www.sdcc.edu
Founded 1971
Private control
Academic year: September to May
Pres.: Dr ALBERT LETTING
Vice-Pres. of Academic Affairs: LUNDIE CARSTENSEN
Dean of Students: STEVE JENKINS
Registrar: SUSIE PARKS
Dir of Library Services: RUTH MARTIN
Library of 60,000 vols, videos, CD-ROMs and periodicals
Number of students: 565
Depts of Aviation, Biblical studies, Business, Communication, Education, English, History and social science, Kinesiology, Mathematics, Music, Psychology, Biological science.

SAN DIEGO STATE UNIVERSITY

5500 Campanile Dr., San Diego, CA 92182-8000
Telephone: (619) 594-5200
Internet: www.sdsu.edu
Founded 1897
Academic year: August to May
Pres.: STEPHEN L. WEBER
Provost, Academic Affairs: NANCY A. MARLIN
Vice-Pres. for Research: THOMAS R. SCOTT
Vice-Pres. for Student Affairs: JAMES R. KITCHEN
Vice-Pres. for Univ. Relations and Advancement: MARY RUTH CARLETON
Exec. Dir of Enrollment Services: SANDRA COOK
Dean of Library: CONNIE V. DOWELL
Library of 1,342,735 vols, 644,028 govt documents
Number of teachers: 1,795 (985 full-time; 810 part-time)
Number of students: 38,567 (31,665 undergraduate; 6,566 graduate; 345 doctoral)
Publications: *Fiction International* (annual), *Poetry International* (annual), *Journal of Borderlands Studies* (2 a year), *Pacific Review: A West Coast Arts Review Annual*, *Mobilization* (3 a year), *Pacific Coast Council on Latin-American Studies* (2 a year)

DEANS

Business Admin.: GAIL K. NAUGHTON
Eng.: DAVID T. HAYHURST
Arts and Letters: PAUL WONG
Education: LIONEL R. MENO
Extended Studies: WILLIAM E. BYXBEE
Health and Human Services: MARILYN NEWHOFF
Professional Studies and Fine Arts: JOYCE M. GATTAS
Sciences: STANLEY MALOY
Graduate Studies: STEVEN KRAMER
Undergraduate Studies: GEOFFREY W. CHASE
Imperial Valley Campus: STEPHEN ROEDER

SAN FRANCISCO ART INSTITUTE

800 Chestnut St, San Francisco, CA 94133
Telephone: (415) 771-7020
E-mail: sfaiinfo@sfai.edu
Internet: www.sanfranciscoart.edu
Founded 1871 as San Francisco Art Asscn; present name 1961
Private control
Academic year: August to May
Pres.: CHRIS BRATTON
Sr Vice-Pres. for Finance and Admin.: JUDY LOGAN
Dean of Academic Affairs, Sr Vice-Pres.: OKWUI ENWEZOR
Vice-Pres. for Academic Planning and Facilities: JENNIFER STEIN
Vice-Pres. for Advancement: KATHY LOWRY
Library of 26,000 vols
Areas of study: Design and Technology, Filmmaking, Liberal Arts, New Genres, Painting, Photography, Printmaking, Sculpture.

SAN FRANCISCO CONSERVATORY OF MUSIC

50 Oak St, San Francisco, CA 94102-6011
Telephone: (415) 864-7326
Fax: (415) 503-6299
Internet: www.sfcm.edu
Founded 1917
Pres.: COLIN MURDOCH
Vice-Pres. for Advancement: NANCY SACKSON
Dean: MARY ELLEN POOLE
Dir, Office of Admission: ALEX BROSE
Registrar: RUBY PLEASURE
Chief Librarian: CARISSA CREED
Library of 60,000 items and 38,000 scores and parts, 15,000 audio-visual items, 12,500 vols, 77 periodicals
Number of teachers: 80
Number of students: 300
Depts of Brass, Chamber Music, Conducting, Composition, Guitar, Keyboards, Percussion, Strings, Voice, Woodwinds.

SAN FRANCISCO STATE UNIVERSITY

1600 Holloway Ave, San Francisco, CA 94132
Telephone: (415) 338-1111
Fax: (415) 338-2514
Internet: www.sfsu.edu
Founded 1899
Pres.: Dr ROBERT A. CORRIGAN
Vice-Pres. and Provost: JOHN M. GEMELLO
Vice-Pres. for Admin. and Finance: LEROY M. MORISHITA
Vice-Pres. for Academic Program Devt: GAIL WHITAKER (acting)
Vice-Pres. for Student Affairs and Dean of Students: J. E. (PENNY) SAFFOLD
Vice-Pres. for Univ. Advancement: DON SCOBLE (acting)
Registrar: SUZANNE DMYTRENKO
Univ. Librarian: DEBORAH MASTERS
Library of 4,000,000 items

Number of teachers: 1,783
Number of students: 29,628

DEANS

College of Behavioral and Social Sciences: JOEL KASSIOLA
College of Business: NANCY K. HAYES (acting)
College of Creative Arts: WAN-LEE CHENG (acting)
College of Education: JACOB E. PEREA
College of Ethnic Studies: KENNETH P. MONTEIRO
College of Extended Learning: GAIL WHITAKER
College of Health and Human Services: DON TAYLOR (acting)
College of Humanities: PAUL SHERWIN
College of Science and Eng.: SHELDON AXLER
Graduate Div.: ANN HALLUM

SAN FRANCISCO THEOLOGICAL SEMINARY

105 Seminary Rd, San Anselmo, CA 94960
Telephone: (415) 451-2800
Fax: (415) 451-2851
E-mail: jperry@sfts.edu
Internet: www.sfts.edu
Private control (part of the Graduate Theological Union)
Pres.: Dr PHILIP W. BUTIN
Vice-Pres. for Academic Affairs and Dean of the Seminary: Dr JANA L. CHILDERS
Vice-Pres. for Finance and Admin.: BARBARA BRENNER BUDER
Vice-Pres. for Seminary and Church Relations: PETER CROUCH
Vice-Pres. for Southern California Campus: Dr DAVID TOMLINSON
Registrar: Dr POLLY COOTE
Library Dir (GTU): ROBERT BENETTO
Librarian (SFTS): MICHAEL PETERSON
Library of 365,000 vols.

BRANCH CAMPUS

Southern California Campus: 54 North Oakland Ave, Pasadena, CA 91101; tel. (626) 397-9004; fax (626) 397-9011; internet www.sfts.edu/sc.

SAN JOSÉ STATE UNIVERSITY

San José, CA 95192
Telephone: (408) 924-1000
Internet: www.sjsu.edu
Founded 1857
Pres.: DON W. KASSING
Provost and Vice-Pres. for Academic Affairs: CARMEN SIGLER
Vice-Pres. for Administration and Finance: ROSE LEE
Vice-Pres. for Student Affairs: VERIL PHILLIPS
Vice-Pres. for Univ. Advancement: FRED NAJJAR
Dean of the Univ. Library: RUTH E. KIFER
Library of 900,000 vols, 3,500 periodical titles
Number of teachers: 704 (full-time)
Number of students: 30,000

DEANS

College of Applied Sciences and Arts: BARBARA CONRY
College of Business: BRUCE MAGID
College of Education: Prof. SUSAN MEYERS
College of Eng.: BELLE WEI
College of Humanities and the Arts: KARL TOEPFER
College of Science: MICHAEL PARRISH
College of Social Sciences: TIM HEGSTROM
Continuing Education: MARK NOVAK

SANTA CLARA UNIVERSITY

Santa Clara, CA 95053
Telephone: (408) 554-4000
Internet: www.scu.edu
Founded 1851
Private control
Academic year: September to June
Pres.: PAUL L. LOCATELLI
Provost: LUCIA ALBINO GILBERT
Vice-Pres. for Admin. and Finance: ROBERT WARREN
Vice-Pres. for Univ. Relations: JAMES PURCELL
Registrar: MONICA AUGUSTIN
Univ. Librarian: ELIZABETH SALZER
Library of 736,302 vols; Law library of 148,087 vols
Number of teachers: 721 (434 full-time, 287 part-time)
Number of students: 7,368
Publications: *Explore* (journal of the Bannan Center for Jesuit Education, quarterly), *STS Nexus* (journal of the Center for Science, Technology and Society, 2 a year)

DEANS

College of Arts and Sciences: YEE W. ATOM (acting)
School of Business: BARRY Z. POSNER
School of Eng.: JIM KOCH
School of Law: DONALD J. POLDEN
School of Education, Counselling Psychology and Pastoral Ministries: LESTER GOODCHILD

SAYBROOK GRADUATE SCHOOL AND RESEARCH CENTER

3rd Floor, 747 Front St, San Francisco, CA 94111-1920
Telephone: (415) 433-9200
Fax: (415) 433-9271
E-mail: admissions@saybrook.edu
Internet: www.saybrook.edu
Founded 1971
Academic year: September to July
Pres.: Dr LORNE M. BUCHMAN
Exec. Vice-Pres.: Dr ARTHUR C. BOHART, Jr
Vice-Pres. of Academic Affairs: DENISE SCATENA
Vice-Pres. of Marketing and Enrollment Management: SIGRID BADINELLI
Vice-Pres. of Operations, Treasurer and CFO: JOHN W. REHO
Dir of Admissions: ANN MCGEADY
Dir of Research and Library Services: ANNEMARIE WELTEKE
Number of teachers: 114 (20 executive, 22 consulting, 72 part-time)
Number of students: 525
Publication: *International Journal of Transpersonal Studies* (annual)
MA and PhD programs in Psychology, Human Science, and Organizational Systems; areas of study are Humanistic, Transpersonal Clinical Inquiry and Health Studies, Consciousness and Spirituality Studies, Peace, Conflict Resolution and Community Development, Organizational Systems.

SCRIPPS COLLEGE

1030 Columbia Ave, Claremont, CA 91711
Telephone: (909) 621-8000
Internet: www.scrippscol.edu
Founded 1926
Private control, mem. of the Claremont Colleges
Pres.: FREDERICK WEIS
Vice-Pres. of Business Affairs: JAMES MANIFOLD

Vice-Pres. for Devt and College Relations: MARTHA H. KEATES
Vice-Pres. and Dean of Faculty: MICHAEL D. LAMKIN
Vice-Pres. and Dean of Students: DEBRA CARLSON WOOD
Vice-Pres. and Dean of Admission and Financial Aid: PATRICIA F. GOLDSMITH
Librarian: JUDY HARVEY SAHAK
Library: Library: 110,000 vols in Denison Library and 10,000 in Rare Book Room
Number of teachers: 95 (69 full-time and 26 part-time)
Number of students: 859.

SIMPSON UNIVERSITY

2211 College View Dr., Redding, CA 96003
Telephone: (530) 226-4606
Fax: (530) 226-4861
E-mail: registrar@simpsonuniversity.edu
Internet: www.simpsonuniversity.edu
Founded 1921 as Simpson Bible Institute; Simpson College 1971; present name
Private control
Academic year: September to July
Pres.: LARRY J. MCKINNEY
Exec. Vice-Pres. and Vice-Pres. for Business Services: BRADLEY E. WILLIAMS
Vice-Pres. for Financial Affairs: THOMAS L. DAVIS
Vice-Pres. for Academic Affairs: Dr JUDITH A. FORTUNE
Vice-Pres. for Student Devt: LARRY D. POLVOGT
Vice-Pres. for Spiritual Formation: SARAH L. HERRING
Vice-Pres. for Marketing and Devt/Foundation: GORDON B. FLINN
Provost: Dr STANLEY A. CLARK
Dean of Education: GLEE R. BROOKS
Dir ASPIRE Program: PATTY TAYLOR
Registrar: LAURA MCKENZIE
Dir of Library Services: LARRY L. HAIGHT
Library of 70,000 vols
Number of students: 1,100.

SONOMA STATE UNIVERSITY

1801 East Cotati Ave, Rohnert Park, CA 94928
Telephone: (707) 664-2880
Fax: (707) 664-2505
Internet: www.sonoma.edu
Founded 1960
Academic year: August to June
Pres.: Dr RUBEN ARMIÑANA
CFO and Vice-Pres. for Admin. and Finance: Dr LAURENCE FURUKAWA-SCHLERETH
Vice-Pres. for Devt: BUCKY PETERSON
Vice-Pres. for Student Affairs and Enrollment Management: KATHARYN CRABBE
Vice-Pres. for Univ. Affairs: DAN CONDRON
Library Dean: Dr BARBARA BUTLER
Library of 636,613 vols, 21,115 periodicals, 1,708,201 microforms, 29,529 audio-visual items
Number of teachers: 610 (277 full-time, 333 part-time)
Number of students: 8,100

DEANS

School of Arts and Humanities: Dr WILLIAM BABULA
School of Business and Econ.: Dr JAMES ROBERTSON
School of Education: Dr MARY GENDERNALIK-COOPER
School of Science and Technology: Dr SAEID RAHIMI
School of Social Sciences: Dr ELAINE LEEDER

SOUTHERN CALIFORNIA COLLEGE OF OPTOMETRY

2575 Yorba Linda Blvd, Fullerton, CA 92831-1699
Telephone: (714) 449-7440
Fax: (714) 879-0481
Internet: www.scco.edu
Founded 1904
Pres.: Prof. LESLEY L. WALLS
Vice-Pres. for Student Affairs: LORRAINE I. VOORHEES
Vice-Pres. for Financial Affairs and CFO: LISA K. ALBERS
Vice-Pres. and Dean of Academic Affairs: Prof. MORRIS S. BERMAN
Vice-Pres. for Advancement: WILLIAM E. HEATON, Jr
Vice-Pres. and Dean of Clinical Affairs: Dr JOHN H. NISHIMOTO
Librarian: DONNAJEAN MATTHEWS
Library of 10,000 vols, 6,500 bound journals and 300 current periodicals
Number of teachers: 80 full- and part-time
Number of students: 381
Publications: *The Alumniscope* (quarterly), *The Reflex* (annual), *SCCO Admissions Catalog* (every 2 years).

SOUTHERN CALIFORNIA UNIVERSITY OF HEALTH SCIENCES

16200 East Amber Valley Dr., Whittier, CA 90604-4051
Telephone: (562) 947-8755
E-mail: admissions@scuhs.edu
Internet: www.scuhs.edu
Pres.: Dr REED B. PHILLIPS
Exec. Vice-Pres.: JOHN SCARINGE
CFO: ROGER JENKINS
Assoc. Vice-Pres. for Student Services: GEOFFREY HOWETT
Assoc. Vice-Pres. for Institutional Research and Accreditations: TRACEY RAMIREZ
Librarian: NEHMAT SAAB

DEANS

Acupuncture and Oriental Medicine: WENSHUO WU
Chiropractic: TODD KNUDSEN
Postgraduates: MELEA FIELDS

SOUTHWESTERN UNIVERSITY SCHOOL OF LAW

3050 Wilshire Blvd, Los Angeles, CA 90001
Telephone: (213) 738-6700
Fax: (213) 383-1688
E-mail: admissions@swlaw.edu
Internet: www.swlaw.edu
Founded 1911
Private control
Academic year: August to July
Dean and CEO: BRYANT G. GARTH
Assoc. Dean for Academic Affairs: Dr CHRISTOPHER D. RUIZ CAMERON
Assoc. Dean for Research: MICHAEL B. DORFF
Asst Dean for Academic Support: DOREEN E. HEYER
Asst Dean of Career Services: GARY G. GREENER
Dir of Admin. Services: JANICE A. MANIS
Dir of Admissions: LISA M. GEAR
Dir of Devt: DEBRA L. LEATHERS
Dir of Financial Aid: WAYNE MAHONEY
Dir of Public Information: LESLIE STEINBERG
Dir of Management Information Systems: BO SUZOW
Dir of Law Library: Dr LINDA WHISMAN
Dir of Registration and Academic Records: CAROLYN HAITH
CFO: PAUL KALUSH
Dean of Students: JANE POWELL (acting)
Library of 429,000 vols and vol. equivalents

Number of teachers: 53 (full-time)
Number of students: 900.

STANFORD UNIVERSITY

Stanford, CA 94305
Telephone: (650) 723-2300
Internet: www.stanford.edu
Founded 1885
Academic year: September to June
Pres.: JOHN HENNESSY
Provost: JOHN ETCHEMENDY
Vice-Pres. for Business Affairs and CFO: RANDALL S. LIVINGSTON
Vice-Pres. for Devt: MARTIN SHELL
Vice-Pres. for Land, Bldgs and Real Estate: ROBERT REIDY
Vice-Pres. for Public Affairs: DAVID DEMAREST
Vice-Pres. for Alumni Affairs: HOWARD WOLF
Vice-Pres. and General Counsel: DEBRA ZUMWALT
Sr Vice-Pres. for Univ. Resources: JOHN FORD
Registrar: ROGER PRINTUP
Vice-Provost for Graduate Education: PATRICIA GUMPORT
Univ. Librarian: MICHAEL KELLER
Library: see Libraries
Number of teachers: 1,749
Number of students: 14,454
Publications: *Stanford Law Review* (6 a year), *Stanford Journal of International Law* (2 a year), *Stanford Humanities Review* (2 a year), *Stanford Environmental Law Journal* (2 a year), *Journal of Law, Business and Finance* (2 a year), *Stanford Social Innovation Review* (quarterly)

DEANS

Graduate School of Business: ROBERT JOSS
School of Earth Sciences: PAMELA MATSON
School of Education: DEBORAH STIPEK
School of Eng.: JAMES PLUMMER
School of Humanities and Sciences: SHARON LONG
School of Law: LARRY KRAMER
School of Medicine: PHILIP PIZZO
Research: ANN ARVIN

DIRECTORS

Hoover Institution. JOHN RAISIAN
Stanford Linear Accelerator Center: JONATHAN DORFAN

PROFESSORS

AAKER, J. L., Graduate School of Business
ADLER, J. R., Jr, Neurosurgery
ADMATI, A. R., Graduate School of Business
ALBANESE, C., Surgery
ALBERS, G. W., Neurology
ALDRICH, R. W., Molecular and Cell Physiology
ALEXANDER, J. C., Law
ALEXANDER, S. R., Paediatrics
AMEMIYA, T., Econ.
ANDERSEN, H., Chemistry
ANDERSON, R. U., Jr, Urology
ANDRIACCHI, T. P., Mechanical Eng.
APOSTOLIDES, J.-M., French and Italian
ARBER, D., Pathology
ARIAGNO, R. L., Paediatrics
ARVIN, A. M., Paediatrics
ATHEY, S. C., Econ.
ATLAS, S. W., Radiology
ATTANASAIO, O., Econ.
AYDIN, A., Geology and Environmental Sciences
AZIZ, K., Petroleum Eng.
BABCOCK, B., Law
BACHRACH, L. K., Paediatrics
BAER, U., German Studies
BAKER, B. S., Biological Sciences
BAKER, K., History
BAMBOS, N., Management Science and Eng.

BANDURA, A., Psychology
BANKMAN, A. J., Law
BARCHIESI, A., Classics
BARLEY, S., Management Science and Eng.
BARNETT, D., Materials Science and Eng.
BARNETT, W., Graduate School of Business
BARON, D. P., Graduate School of Business
BARON, E. J., Pathology
BARON, J. N., Graduate School of Business
BARRES, B. A., Neurobiology
BARSH, G. S., Paediatrics
BARTH, M. E., Graduate School of Business
BARTH, R. A., Radiology
BAUGH, J., Education
BEACH, D., Mechanical Eng.
BEASLEY, M., Applied Physics
BEAVER, W. H., Graduate School of Business
BEININ, J. S., History
BENDER, J., English
BENDOR, J., Graduate School of Business
BENITZ, W. E., Paediatrics
BERGER, K., Music
BERMAN, R. A., German Studies
BERNHARDT, E., German Studies
BERNHEIM, B. D., Econ.
BERNSTEIN, B., History
BERNSTEIN, D., Paediatrics
BEROZA, G. C., Geophysics
BETTINGER, J. R., Communication
BIELEFELDT, C. W., Religious Studies
BIENENSTOCK, A. I., Stanford Synchrotron Radiation Laboratory
BIRD, D. K., Geological and Environmental Sciences
BLACK, B. S., Law
BLAND, R. D., Paediatrics
BLANDFORD, R., Stanford Linear Acceleration Center
BLASCHKE, T., Medicine
BLAU, H. M., Molecular Pharmacology
BLOCH, D. A., Health Research and Policy
BLOCK, S. M., Applied Physics
BLOOM, E., Stanford Linear Accelerator Center
BLUMENKRANZ, M. S., Ophthalmology
BOBO, L., Sociology
BOOTHROYD, J. C., Microbiology and Immunology
BORJA, R. I., Civil and Environmental Eng.
BOSKIN, M., Econ.
BOWER, G. H., Psychology
BOWMAN, C., Mechanical Eng.
BOXER, S., Chemistry
BOYD, S. P., Electrical Eng.
BOYER, A. L., Radiation Oncology
BRADY, D., Graduate School of Business
BRANDEAU, M. L., Management Science and Eng.
BRATMAN, M., Philosophy
BRAUMAN, J. J., Chemistry
BRAUND, S., Classics
BRAVMAN, J. C., Materials Science and Eng.
BREIDENBACH, M., Stanford Linear Accelerator Center
BRESNAHAN, T., Econ.
BRESNAN, J., Linguistics
BROCK-UTNE, J. G., Anaesthesia
BRODSKY, J. B., Anaesthesia
BRODSKY, S., Stanford Linear Accelerator Center
BROTHERSTON, J. G., Spanish and Portuguese
BROWN, G. H., English
BROWN, J. M., Radiation Oncology
BROWN, P. O., Biochemistry
BRUMFIEL, G., Mathematics
BRUNGER, A. T., Molecular and Cellular Physiology
BRUTLAG, D. L., Biochemistry
BRYK, A., Education
BUC, P. C., History
BULOW, J., Graduate School of Business
BUMP, D. W., Mathematics
BURCHAT, P. R., Physics
BURGELMAN, R. A., Graduate School of Business

BURKE, D. L., Stanford Linear Accelerator Center
BUTCHER, E. C., Pathology
BYER, R., Applied Physics
BYERS, T. H., Management Science and Eng.
CABRERA, B., Physics
CALLAN, E., Education
CAMARILLO, A. M., History
CAMPBELL, A. M., Biological Sciences
CANTWELL, B., Aeronautics, Astronautics
CARLSON, R., Management Science and Eng.
CARLSON, R. W., Medicine
CARLSSON, G., Mathematics
CARNOY, M., Education
CARRAGEE, E. J., Orthopaedic Surgery
CARROLL, G. R., Graduate School of Business
CARSON, C., History
CARSTENSEN, L. L., Psychology
CARTER, D., Mechanical Eng.
CARTER, S., Asian Languages
CASEY, E. B., English
CASPER, G., Law
CASPER, R., Psychiatry
CASTLE, T., English
CHAFE, C. D., Music
CHAMBERLAIN, C. P., Geological and Environmental Sciences
CHAN, P. H., Neurosurgery
CHANG, F. K., Aeronautics and Astronautics
CHAO, A. W., Stanford Linear Accelerator Center
CHERITON, D. R., Computer Science
CHIEN, Y. K., Microbiology and Immunology
CHRISTENSEN, R. M., Aeronautics and Astronautics
CHU, G., Medicine
CHU, S., Physics
CIOFFI, J. M., Electrical Eng.
CLAERBOUT, J. F., Geophysics
CLARK, E., Linguistics
CLARK, H. H., Psychology
CLAYBERGER, C. A., Paediatrics
CLEARY, M. L., Pathology
CLEMENS, B. M., Materials Science and Eng.
COHEN, H. J., Paediatrics
COHEN, M., French and Italian
COHEN, P. J., Mathematics
COHEN, R. L., Mathematics
COHEN, S. E., Anaesthesia
COHEN, S. N., Genetics
COLE, G. M., Law
COLLMAN, J. P., Chemistry
CONTI, M., Gynaecology and Obstetrics
COOK, K. S., Sociology
COOKE, J. P., Medicine
COOPER, A., Medicine
CORK, L., Comparative Medicine
CORN, W., Art, Art History
CORNELL, C. A., Civil and Environmental Eng.
COTTLE, R. W., Management Science and Eng.
COVER, T. M., Electrical Eng.
COX, D., Electrical Eng.
COX, K. L., Paediatrics
CRABTREE, G., Pathology
CRASWELL, R., Law
CROSS, P. C., Structural Biology
CUTKOSKY, M. R., Mechanical Eng.
DAHL, G. V. H., Paediatrics
DAINES, R., Law
DALLY, W. J., Electrical Eng.
DAMON, W., Education
DARLING-HAMMOND, L., Education
DAUSKARDT, R. H., Materials Science and Eng.
DAVID, P. A., Econ.
DAVIS, M. M., Microbiology and Immunology
DAVIS, R., Biochemistry
DE MICHELI, G., Electrical Eng.
DEIERLEIN, G. G., Civil and Environmental Eng.
DEKRUYFF, R. H., Paediatrics
DEMARZO, P. M., Graduate School of Business
DEMBO, A., Mathematics

KENDIG, J., Anaesthesia
KENNEDY, D. M., History
KERCKHOFF, S. P., Mathematics
KERNER, J. A., Paediatrics
KESSLER, D. P., Graduate School of Business
KESSLER, R., Urology
KHATIB, O., Computer Science
KHAVARI, P. A., Dermatology
KHOSLA, C. S., Chemical Eng.
KILLEN, J. D., Medicine
KIM, S. K., Developmental Biology
KING, A. C., Health Research and Policy
KINGSLEY, D. M., Developmental Biology
KIPARSKY, P., Linguistics
KIREMIDJIAN, A. S., Civil and Environmental Eng.
KIRKEGAARD, K, Microbiology and Immunology
KIRST, M., Education
KITANIDIS, P. K., Civil and Environmental Eng.
KLAUSNER, M., Law
KLEIN, R. G., Anthropological Studies
KLENOW, P., Econ.
KNIGHT, R., Geophysics
KNUDSEN, E. I., Neurobiology
KOBILKA, B. K., Medicine
KOCHERLAKOTA, N., Econ.
KOLLMAN, N. S., History
KOOL, E. T., Chemistry
KOPITO, R. R., Biological Sciences
KORAN, L. M., Psychiatry
KORNBERG, R. D., Structural Biology
KOSEFF, J. R., Civil and Environmental Eng.
KOSEK, J., Pathology
KOVACH, R. L., Geophysics
KRAEMER, F. B., Medicine
KRAEMER, H., Psychiatry
KRAMER, R. M., Graduate School of Business
KRANE, E. J., Anaesthesia
KRASNER, S., Political Science
KRASNOW, M. A., Biochemistry
KRAWINKLER, H., Civil and Environmental Eng.
KRAWITZ, J., Communication
KREHBIEL, K., Graduate School of Business
KRENSKY, A. M., Paediatrics
KREPS, D., Graduate School of Business
KROO, I. M., Aeronautics and Astronautics
KROSNICK, J. A., Communication
KRUGER, C. H., Mechanical Eng.
KRUMBOLTZ, J. D., Education
KRUMMEL, T. M., Surgery
KURZ, M., Econ.
LABAREE, D., Education
LAI, T. L., Statistics
LAITIN, D., Political Science
LAM, M. S., Computer Science
LANE, A. T., Dermatology
LANE, B., Radiology
LATOMBE, J.-C., Computer Science
LATTIN, J. M., Graduate School of Business
LAU, L. J., Econ.
LAUGHLIN, R., Physics
LAVORI, P. W., Health Research and Policy
LAW, K. H., Civil and Environmental Eng.
LAZEAR, E. P., Graduate School of Business
LECKIE, J., Civil and Environmental Eng.
LEE, H. L., Graduate School of Business
LEHMAN, I. R., Biochemistry
LEIFER, L., Mechanical Eng.
LEITH, D., Stanford Linear Accelerator Center
LEIVICK, J. R., Art and Art History
LELE, S. K., Aeronautics and Astronautics
LEMLEY, M., Law
LENOIR, T., History
LEPPER, M., Psychology
LERER, S., English
LESSIG, L., Law
LEUNG, L. L., Medicine
LEVIN, B., Linguistics
LEVITT, L. J., Medicine
LEVITT, M., Structural Biology
LEVITT, R. E., Civil and Environmental Eng.
LEVY, R., Medicine

LEVY, S., Medicine
LEWIS, M. E., Asian Languages
LI, J., Mathematics
LINDE, A., Physics
LINK, M., Paediatrics
LIOU, J., Geological and Environmental Sciences
LIPSICK, J., Pathology
LITT, I., Paediatrics
LIU, T.-P., Mathematics
LOAGUE, K., Geological and Environmental Sciences
LOEW, G. A., Stanford Linear Accelerator Center
LONG, S., Biological Sciences
LONGAKER, M. T., Surgery
LORIG, K., Medicine
LOUGEE CHAPPELL, C., History
LOWE, D. R., Geological and Environmental Sciences
LUENBERGER, D. G., Management Science and Eng.
LUNSFORD, A., English
LUTH, V., Stanford Linear Acceleration Center
LUTHY, R. G., Civil and Environmental Eng.
MCADAM, D., Sociology
MCCALL, M., Classics
MCCLUSKEY, E. J., Electrical Eng.
MCCONNELL, S. K., Biological Sciences
MACCORMACK, R., Aeronautics and Astronautics
MCDERMOTT, R., Education
MCDEVITT, H. O., Microbiology and Immunology
MCDONALD, J. G., Graduate School of Business
MCDOUGALL, I. R., Radiology
MCGINN, R. E., Management Science and Eng.
MCGUIRE, J., Dermatology
MCKAY, D., Structural Biology
MCKINNON, R. I., Econ.
MCLAUGHLIN, M. W., Education
MCMAHAN, U. J., Neurobiology
MCMILLAN, R. J., Graduate School of Business
MCNICHOLS, M., Graduate School of Business
MCNUTT, M. K., Geophysics
MACURDY, T., Econ.
MADIX, R. J., Chemical Eng.
MAHOOD, G. A., Geological and Environmental Sciences
MALENKA, R. C., Psychiatry
MANCALL, M., History
MANNA, Z., Computer Science
MARINA, N., Paediatrics
MARKMAN, E., Psychology
MARKUS, H., Psychology
MARMOR, M., Ophthalmology
MARTIN, J., Graduate School of Business
MARTIN, R. P., Classics
MATHESON, G. O., Orthopaedic Surgery
MATHEWS, M. V., Music
MATIN, A., Microbiology and Immunology
MATSON, P. A., Geological and Environmental Sciences
MAVKO, G. M., Geophysics
MAZZEO, R. R., Mathematics
MENDELSON, H., Graduate School of Business
MENDEZ, M. A., Law
MENDOZA, F. S., Paediatrics
MENG, T. H.-Y., Electrical Eng.
MERIGAN, T., Medicine
MEYER, T. W., Medicine
MICHELSON, P. F., Physics
MIGNOT, E., Psychiatry
MIHM, F. G., Anaesthesia
MILGRAM, R. J., Mathematics
MILGROM, P., Econ.
MILLER, D. A. B., Electrical Eng.
MILLER, D. C., Cardiothoracic Surgery
MILLER, D. T., Graduate School of Business
MILLER, E., Geological and Environmental Sciences
MINTS, G., Philosophy

MITCHELL, J. C., Computer Science
MITCHELL, R. S., Cardiothoracic Surgery
MOBLEY, W. C., Neurology
MOCARSKI, E. S., Microbiology and Immunology
MOCHLY-ROSEN, D., Molecular Pharmacology
MOE, T. M., Political Science
MOERNER, W. E., Chemistry
MOIN, P., Mechanical Eng.
MOLDOWAN, J. M., Geological and Environmental Sciences
MONISMITH, S. G., Civil and Environmental Eng.
MOONEY, H. A., Biological Sciences
MOOS, R. H., Psychiatry
MORA-MANGANO, C., Anaesthesia
MORAVCSIK, J. M., Philosophy
MORETTI, F., English
MORRIS, I., Classics
MORRIS, R. E., Cardiothoracic Surgery
MOSS, R. B., Paediatrics
MOTWANI, R., Computer Science
MUNGAL, M. G., Mechanical Eng.
MURRAY, W., Management Science and Eng.
MUSEN, M. A., Medicine
MYERS, B., Medicine
MYERS, R. M., Genetics
NAIMARK, N., History
NAPEL, S. A., Radiology
NASS, C. I., Communications
NEALE, M. A., Graduate School of Business
NELSON, D. V., Mechanical Eng.
NELSON, W. J., Molecular and Cell Physiology
NETZ, R., Classics
NEWSOME, W. T., III, Neurobiology
NISHI, Y., Electrical Eng.
NISHIMURA, D. G., Electrical Eng.
NOLL, R., Econ.
NUR, A., Geophysics
NUSSE, R., Developmental Biology
OAKES, D. D., Surgery
OI, J., Political Science
OKIMOTO, D. I., Political Science
OLCOTT, C., IV, Surgery
OLKIN, I., Statistics
OLSHEN, R., Health Research and Policy
OLZAK, S., Sociology
OMARY, M. R., Medicine
O'REILLY, C. A., III, Graduate School of Business
ORGEL, S., English
ORNSTEIN, D., Mathematics
ORR, F., Petroleum Eng.
ORTOLANO, L., Civil and Environmental Eng.
OSGOOD, B. G., Electrical Eng.
OSHEROFF, D., Physics
OWEN, A. B., Statistics
OYER, P. E., Cardiothoracic Surgery
PADILLA, A., Education
PALUMBI, S., Biological Sciences
PALUMBO-LIU, D. J., Comparative Literature
PAPANICOLAOU, G. C., Mathematics
PARHAM, P., Structural Biology
PARKER, G. G. C., Graduate School of Business
PARKER, P., English
PARNES, J. R., Medicine
PATE-CORNELL, E., Management Science and Eng.
PATELL, J., Graduate School of Business
PATERSON, J., Stanford Linear Accelerator Center
PAULRAJ, A., Electrical Eng.
PAULSON, B., Civil and Environmental Eng.
PEA, R., Education
PEARL, R., Anaesthesia
PEASE, R., Electrical Eng.
PECORA, R., Chemistry
PELC, N. J., Radiology
PENCAVEL, J., Econ.
PERKASH, I., Urology
PERLROTH, M. G., Medicine
PERRY, J., Philosophy
PERRY, W., Management Science and Eng.
PESKIN, M., Stanford Linear Accelerator Center

PETERS, P. S., Linguistics
PETERSEN, J., Medicine
PETROSIAN, V., Physics
PFEFFER, J., Graduate School of Business
PFEFFER, S. R., Biochemistry
PFEFFERBAUM, A., Psychiatry
PFLEIDERER, P., Graduate School of Business
PHELAN, P., Drama
PHILIP, A. G. S., Paediatrics
PHILLIPS, D., Education
PHIZACKERLEY, R. P., Stanford Synchrotron Radiation Laboratory
PIANETTA, P., Stanford Synchrotron Radiation Laboratory
PINSKY, P. M., Mechanical Eng.
PIZZO, P. A., Paediatrics
PLUMMER, J., Electrical Eng.
POLAN, M., Obstetrics and Gynaecology
POLHEMUS, R., English
POLINSKY, A., Law
POLLARD, D. D., Geological and Environmental Sciences
POPP, R., Medicine
PORTEUS, E., Graduate School of Business
POWELL, W. W., Education
PRATT, M., Spanish and Portuguese
PREDMORE, M., Spanish and Portuguese
PRESCOTT, C., Stanford Linear Accelerator Center
PRINCE, D. A., Neurology
PRINZ, F. B., Mechanical Eng.
PROBER, C. G., Paediatrics
PROCTOR, R., History
QUERTERMOUS, T., Medicine
QUINN, H., Stanford Linear Accelerator Center
RABIN, R. L., Law
RABINOVITCH, M., Paediatrics
RADIN, M., Law
RAJAN, M. V., Graduate School of Business
RAKOVE, J., History
RAMIREZ, F., Education
RAMPERSAD, A., English
RAMSAUR, M. F., Drama
RECHT, L., Neurology
REEVES, B., Communication
REHM, M. R., Drama
REICHELSTEIN, S. J., Graduate School of Business
REINHARD, M., Civil and Environmental Eng.
REISS, A. L., Psychiatry
REISS, P. C., Graduate School of Business
REITZ, B., Cardiothoracic Surgery
REMINGTON, J. S., Medicine
RHINE, W. D., Paediatrics
RHODE, D. L., Law
RICE, C., Political Science
RICHTER, B., Stanford Linear Accelerator Center
RICKFORD, J., Linguistics
RIDGEWAY, C., Sociology
RIGGS, D., English
RINSKY, L. A., Orthopaedic Surgery
RISCH, N. J., Genetics
RIVERS, D., Political Science
RIZK, N. W., Medicine
ROBERTS, D. F., Communication
ROBERTS, D. J., Graduate School of Business
ROBERTS, E. S., Computer Science
ROBERTS, R. L., Medicine
ROBERTSON, C. R., Chemical Eng.
ROBINSON, J. A., Political Science
ROBINSON, O. W., III, German Studies
ROBINSON, P., History
ROCK, S. M., Aeronautics and Astronautics
RODRIGUE, A., History
ROMANO, J., Statistics
ROMER, P., Graduate School of Business
RORTY, R., Comparative Literature
ROSALDO, R. I., Jr, Cultural and Social Anthropology
ROSENTHAL, M. H., Anaesthesia
ROSS, L., Psychology
ROTH, B., Mechanical Eng.
ROTH, R. A., Molecular Pharmacology
ROTH, W., Psychiatry

ROUGHGARDEN, J., Biological Sciences
ROUSE, R. V., Pathology
RUBIN, K., Mathematics
RUDD, P., Medicine
RUFFINELLI-ALTESOR, J., Spanish and Portuguese
RUMELHART, D. E., Psychology
RUTH, R. D., Stanford Linear Accelerator Center
SAG, I. A., Linguistics
SAGAN, S. D., Political Science
SAIDMAN, L. J., Anaesthesia
SALDIVAR, R., English
SALISBURY, J. K., Computer Science
SALONER, G., Graduate School of Business
SALVATIERRA, O., Jr, Surgery
SAMUELSON, K., Communication
SAPOLSKY, R. M., Biological Sciences
SARASWAT, K., Electrical Eng.
SARGENT, T. J., Econ.
SARNOW, P., Microbiology and Immunology
SAUNDERS, M. A., Management Science and Eng.
SAUSSY, C. P. H., Comparative Literature
SCANDLING, J., Medicine
SCHATZBERG, A., Psychiatry
SCHEIDEL, W., Classics
SCHENDEL, S. A., Surgery
SCHERRER, P. H., Physics
SCHIEBERGER, L., History
SCHINDLER, R., Stanford Linear Accelerator Center
SCHNAPP, J. T., French and Italian
SCHNEIDER, S., Biological Sciences
SCHNITTGER, I., Medicine
SCHOEN, R., Mathematics
SCHOOLNIK, G. K., Medicine
SCHROEDER, J. S., Medicine
SCHUPBACH, Slavic Languages and Literatures
SCHURMAN, D., Functional Restoration
SCOTT, M. P., Developmental Biology
SEGAL, I. R., Econ.
SEGALL, P., Geophysics
SELLS, P., Linguistics
SERRES, M., French and Italian
SHAFER, S. L., Anaesthesia
SHANKS, M., Classics
SHAPIRO, L., Developmental Biology
SHAQFEH, E. S. G., Chemical Eng.
SHAVELSON, R., Education
SHAW, K., Graduate School of Business
SHEEHAN, J. J., History
SHEEHAN, T., Religious Studies
SHEIKH, J. T., Psychiatry
SHEN, Z.-X., Applied Physics
SHENKER, S. H., Physics
SHORTLIFFE, L., Urology
SHOVEN, J., Econ.
SHUER, L. M., Neurosurgery
SIBLEY, R. K., Pathology
SIEGMUND, D. O., Statistics
SIEMANN, R., Stanford Linear Accelerator Center
SIKIC, B. I., Medicine
SILVERBERG, G. D., Neurosurgery
SILVERMAN, N., Paediatrics
SIMON, L., Mathematics
SIMONI, R., Biological Sciences
SIMONSON, I., Graduate School of Business
SINCLAIR, R., Materials Science and Eng.
SINGH, K., Ophthalmology
SINGLETON, K., Graduate School of Business
SKEFF, K. M., Medicine
SLEEP, N., Geophysics
SMITH, S. J., Molecular and Cell Physiology
SMITH, T. I., Physics
SNIDERMAN, P., Political Science
SNIPP, C. M., Sociology
So, S. K. S., Surgery
SOLOMON, E., Chemistry
SOMERO, G., Biological Sciences
SOMERVILLE, C., Biological Sciences
SOMMER, F. G., Radiology
SPAIN, D., Surgery
SPIEGEL, D., Psychiatry

SPRINGER, G., Aeronautics and Astronautics
SPUDICH, J. A., Biochemistry
SRINIVASAN, V., Graduate School of Business
STAMEY, T. A., Urology
STANSKI, D. R., Anaesthesia
STANSKY, P. D. L., History
STEBBINS, J., Geological and Environmental Sciences
STEELE, C. M., Psychology
STEFANICK, M., Medicine
STEINBERG, G. K., Neurosurgery
STEINER, H., Psychiatry
STEINMAN, L., Neurology
STEPHENS, S., Classics
STEVENS, D., Medicine
STEVENSON, D., Paediatrics
STIPEK, D. J., Education
STOHR, J., Stanford Synchrotron Radiation Laboratory
STREET, R. L., Civil and Environmental Eng.
STRNAD, J. F., Law
STROBER, M., Education
STROBER, S., Medicine
SULLIVAN, K., Law
SUSSKIND, L., Physics
SUSSMAN, H., Pathology
SUTTON, R. I., Management Science and Eng.
SWAIN, J., Medicine
SWARTZ, J. R., Chemical Eng.
SWEENEY, J., Management Science and Eng.
SWITZER, P., Statistics
TAKEUCHI, M. R., Art and Art History
TALLENT, E., English
TATUM, C. B., Civil and Environmental Eng.
TAYLOR, C., Psychiatry
TAYLOR, J. B., Econ.
TAYLOR, K. A., Philosophy
TESSIER-LAVIGNE, M., Biological Sciences
THOMAS, E. A. C., Psychology
THOMPSON, B. H., Jr, Law
THOMPSON, D. G., Psychiatry
THOMPSON, S., Biological Sciences
TIBSHIRANI, R. J., Health Research and Policy
TINKLENBERG, J., Psychiatry
TOBAGI, F., Electrical Eng.
TOMPKINS, L., Medicine
TRIADAFILOPOULOS, G., Medicine
TROST, B., Chemistry
TRUDELL, J. R., Anaesthesia
TSIEN, R., Molecular and Cellular Physiology
TULJAPURKAR, S., Biological Sciences
TUMA, N., Sociology
TURNER, P., Art and Art History
TVERSKY, B., Psychology
TYLER, G., Electrical Eng.
UMETSU, D. T., Paediatrics
VALANTINE, H. A., Medicine
VALDES, G., Education
VAN BENTHEM, J. F., Philosophy
VAN DAM, J., Medicine
VAN HORNE, J. C., Graduate School of Business
VAN MEURS, K. P., Paediatrics
VEINOTT, A. F., Jr, Management Science and Eng.
VINOGRAD, R. E., Art and Art History
VITOUSEK, P., Biological Sciences
WAGONER, R. V., Physics
WALBOT, V., Biological Sciences
WALD, M. S., Law
WALDER, A. G., Sociology
WALDRON, K. J., Mechanical Eng.
WALKER, D., Education
WANDELL, B. A., Psychology
WANG, J., Asian Languages
WANG, P., Medicine
WANG, T. S.-F., Pathology
WARNKE, R., Pathology
WASOW, T., Linguistics
WATT, W., Biological Sciences
WAYMOUTH, R. M., Chemistry
WEBER, C., Drama
WEIN, L. M., Graduate School of Business
WEINGAST, B. R., Political Science
WEISBERG, R., Law
WEISSMAN, I., Pathology

WENDER, P., Chemistry
WEYANT, J. P., Management Science and Eng.
WHANG, S., Graduate School of Business
WHITE, B., Mathematics
WHITE, R., History
WHITMORE, I., Surgery
WHITTEMORE, A., Health Research and Policy
WHYTE, R. I., Cardiothoracic Surgery
WIDROW, B., Electrical Eng.
WILSON, D. M., Paediatrics
WINE, J., Psychology
WINEBERG, S., Education
WINOGRAD, T., Computer Sciences
WOJCICKI, S. G., Physics
WOLAK, F. A., Econ.
WOLF, A., Anthropological Sciences
WOLF, B. J., Art and Art History
WOLFF, T., English
WONG, H.-S., Electrical Eng.
WONG, S.-W. S., Electrical Eng.
WOOD, A. W., Philosophy
WOOD, R., Philosophy
WOOLEY, B. A., Electrical Eng.
WRIGHT, G., Econ.
XIE, Y., Sociology
YAMAMOTO, Y., Electrical Eng.
YANAGISAKO, S. J., Cultural and Social Anthropology
YARBRO-BEJARANO, Y., Spanish and Portuguese
YAU, H.-T., Mathematics
YE, Y., Management Science and Eng.
YEARLEY, L., Religious Studies
YESAVAGE, J., Psychiatry
YOCK, P. G., Medicine
ZARE, R. N., Chemistry
ZARINS, C. K., Surgery
ZHANG, S., Physics
ZIPPERSTEIN, S. J., History
ZOBACK, M., Geophysics

STARR KING SCHOOL FOR THE MINISTRY

2441 LeConte Ave, Berkeley, CA 94709-1209
Telephone: (510) 845-6232
Fax: (510) 845-6273
E-mail: starrking@sksm.edu
Internet: www.sksm.edu
Founded 1904 as Pacific Unitarian School for the Ministry; present name 1941
Private control (part of the Graduate Theological Union)
Academic year: September to May
Pres.: Rev. Dr REBECCA A. PARKER
Vice-Pres. for Finance and Admin.: THOMAS SMITH
Vice-Pres. for Academic Affairs and Dean of Faculty: Rev. Dr IBRAHIM FARAJAJÉ
Vice-Pres. for Advancement: KELLY FLOOD
Dean of Students: BECKY LEYSER
Director of Continuing and Online Education: CATHLEEN YOUNG
Library Dir: BONNIE HARDWICK
Library of 365,000 vols.

THOMAS AQUINAS COLLEGE

10000 North Ojai Rd, Santa Paula, CA 93060
Telephone: (805) 525-4417
Fax: (805) 525-0620
E-mail: admissions@thomasaquinas.edu
Internet: www.thomasaquinas.edu
Founded 1971
Private control
Academic year: September to June
Pres.: Dr THOMAS E. DILLON
Dean: Dr MICHAEL MCLEAN
Asst Dean for Student Affairs: Dr MICHAEL LETTENEY
Vice-President for Devt and General Counsel: JOHN QUINCY MASTELLER
Registrar: SEAN COLLINS

Librarian: VILTIS JATULIS
Library of 50,000 vols
Number of teachers: 32
Number of students: 331
Publication: *The Aquinas Review* (2 a year).

THOMAS JEFFERSON SCHOOL OF LAW

2121 San Diego Ave, San Diego, CA 92110
Telephone: (619) 297-9700
Fax: (619) 294-4713
E-mail: info@tjsl.edu
Internet: www.tjsl.edu
Private control
Pres. and Dean: RUDY HASL
Library Dir: Prof. KARLA M. CASTETTER
Library of 116,537 vols.

UNIVERSITY OF CALIFORNIA

Office of the Pres., 12th Floor, 1111 Franklin St, Oakland, CA 94607-5200
Internet: www.universityofcalifornia.edu
Founded 1868
Campuses at Berkeley, Davis, Irvine, Los Angeles, Merced, Riverside, San Diego, San Francisco, Santa Barbara, and Santa Cruz
Library: see Libraries and Archives
Number of teachers: 8,776
Number of students: 208,000

UNIVERSITY-WIDE OFFICERS

Pres.: ROBERT DYNES
Provost and Exec. Vice-Pres. for Academic Affairs: Dr WYATT R. HUME
Exec. Vice-Pres. for Univ. Affairs: BRUCE B. DARLING
Vice-Pres. for Investments: MARIE N. BERGREN
Vice-Pres. for Financial Management: ANNE BROOME
Vice-Pres. for Laboratory Admin.: S. ROBERT FOLEY
Vice-Pres. for Agriculture and Natural Resources: W. R. GOMES
Vice-Pres. for Clinical Services Devt: WILLIAM H. GURTNER
Vice-Pres. for Budget: LARRY HERSHMAN
Vice-Pres. for Health Affairs: RORY HUME
Vice-Pres. for Legal Affairs: CHARLES F. ROBINSON
Vice-Pres. for Student Affairs: JUDY K. SAKAKI

OFFICERS OF THE REGENTS

General Counsel of the Regents and Vice-Pres. for Legal Affairs: CHARLES F. ROBINSON
Sec. of the Regents: ANNE SHAW (acting)
Treas. of the Regents: MARIE N. BERGREN (acting)

CONSTITUENT CAMPUSES

University of California, Berkeley

Berkeley, CA 94720
Telephone: (510) 642-6000
Internet: www.berkeley.edu
Founded 1868
130 Depts divided into 14 colleges and schools
Chancellor: ROBERT J. BIRGENEAU
Exec. Vice-Chancellor and Provost: GEORGE W. BRESLAUER
Vice-Chancellor for Admin.: NATHAN BROSTROM
Vice-Chancellor for Facilities Services: EDWARD J. DENTON
Vice-Chancellor for Research: BETH BURNSIDE

Vice-Chancellor for Student Affairs: HARRY LE GRANDE
Vice-Chancellor for Univ. Relations: SCOTT BIDDY
Univ. Librarian: THOMAS C. LEONARD
Number of teachers: 1,852
Number of students: 32,128

DEANS

Walter A. Haas School of Business: TOM CAMPBELL
College of Chemistry: CHARLES B. HARRIS
Graduate School of Education: P. DAVID PEARSON
College of Eng.: A. RICHARD NEWTON
College of Environmental Design: HARRISON F. FRAKER
Graduate Div.: MARY ANN MASON
School of Information: ANNA LEE SAXENIAN
Int. and Area Studies: JOHN LIE
Graduate School of Journalism: ORVILLE H. SCHELL
Boalt School of Law: CHRISTOPHER F. EDLEY
College of Letters and Science: MARK RICHARDS (Exec. Dean)
Div. of Arts and Humanities: JANET BROUGHTON
Div. of Biological Sciences: GEOFFREY OWEN
Div. of Physical Sciences: MARK RICHARDS
Div. of Social Sciences: JON GJERDE
Undergraduate Div.: CHRISTINA MASLACH
College of Natural Resources: PAUL LUDDEN
School of Optometry: DENNIS LEVI
School of Public Health: ROBERT SPEAR (acting)
Richard and Rhoda Goldman School of Public Policy: MICHAEL NACHT
School of Social Welfare: LORRAINE MIDANIK
Univ. Extension: JAMES SHERWOOD

CHAIRMEN OF DEPARTMENTS

College of Letters and Science:
African American Studies: Prof. PERCY HINTZEN
Anthropology: WILLIAM F. HANKS
Art Practice: LOREN PARTRIDGE
Astronomy: Prof. DONALD BACKER
Classics: Prof. ROBERT C. KNAPP (acting)
Comparative Literature: Dr ERIC NAIMAN
Demography: Dr KENNETH W. WACHTER
Earth and Planetary Science: Dr BARBARA ROMANOWICZ
Econ: Dr RICHARD J. GILBERT
English: JANET ADELMAN
Ethnic Studies: Dr JOSÉ DAVID SALDIVAR
French: Dr DAVID HULT
Geography: Dr MICHAEL JOHNS
German: Dr ANTON KAES
History: JON GJERDE
History of Art: Prof. WHITNEY DAVIS
Integrative Biology: Dr ROY CALDWELL
Italian: Prof. ALBERT RUSSELL ASCOLI
Linguistics: Dr LEANNE HINTON
Mathematics: HUGH WOODEN (acting)
Molecular and Cell Biology: LEE ROSENBERG
Music: Dr WYE ALLENBROOK
Near Eastern Studies: DANIEL BOYARIN
Philosophy: ALAN CODE
Physics: Dr CHRISTOPHER F. MCKEE
Political Science: JUDITH E. GRUBER
Psychology: Dr KAREN K. DEVALOIS
Rhetoric: Dr JUDITH BUTLER
Scandinavian: ELAINE C. TENNANT
Slavic Languages and Literatures: IRINA PAPERNO (First half of academic year: ALAN TIMBERLAKE (Second half of academic year)
Sociology: PETER EVANS
South and Southeast Asian Studies: Dr VASUDA DALMIA
Spanish and Portuguese: INGACIO NAVARRETE (acting)
Statistics: Dr JOHN RICE
Women's Studies: JUDITH BUTLER

College of Chemistry:
Chemical Eng.: ARUP K. CHAKRABORTY

College of Engineering:
Bioengineering: THOMAS BUDINGER
Civil and Environmental Eng.: GREGORY FENVES
Electrical Eng. and Computer Sciences: Dr S. SHANKAR SASTRY
Industrial Eng. and Operations Research: Dr LEE W. SCHRUBEN
Materials Science and Eng.: FIONA DOYLE
Mechanical Eng.: Dr J. KARL HEDRICK
Nuclear Eng.: Dr PER F. PETERSON

College of Environmental Design:
Architecture: CHARLES C. BENTON
City and Regional Planning: JOHN LANDIS
Landscape Architecture and Environmental Planning: PETER BOSSELMAN

College of Natural Resources:
Agricultural and Resource Econ.: Dr ANTHONY C. FISHER
Environment Science, Policy and Management: STEVE BEISSINGER
Nutritional Sciences and Toxicology: Dr LEONARD BJELDANES
Plant and Microbial Biology: Dr ANDREW D. JACKSON

University of California, Davis

1 Shields Ave, Davis, CA 95616
Telephone: (530) 752-1011
Fax: (530) 752-6363
Internet: www.ucdavis.edu
Founded 1905
State control
Academic year: September to June
Chancellor: LARRY N. VANDERHOEF
Provost and Exec. Vice-Chancellor: VIRGINIA S. HINSHAW
CEO: ANN MADDEN RICE
Vice-Chancellor for Admin.: STAN NOSEK
Vice-Chancellor for Univ. Relations: BEVERLEY SANDEEN
Vice-Chancellor for Research: BARRY M. KLEIN
Vice-Chancellor for Student Affairs: JANET GONG
Vice-Chancellor for Resource Management and Planning: JOHN MEYER
Vice-Chancellor for Human Health Sciences: CLAIRE POMEROY
Vice-Provost for Academic Personnel: BARBARA HORWITZ
Vice-Provost for Information and Educational Technology: PETER SIEGEL
Vice-Provost for Undergraduate Studies: FRED. E. WOOD
Vice-Provost for Univ. Outreach: WILLIAM LACY
Librarian: MARILYN SHARROW
Library: see Libraries
Number of teachers: 1,944
Number of students: 28,236
Publications: *UC Davis Law Review* (quarterly), *The Horse Report* (quarterly), *Environs* (2 a year), *Journal of International Law Policy* (2 a year), *Journal of Juvenile Law and Policy* (2 a year), *Migration News* (monthly), *BizLawJournal.com* (online), *CA&ES Outlook* (2 a year)

DEANS
College of Agricultural and Environmental Sciences: NEAL VAN ALFEN
Div. of Biological Sciences: KENNETH C. BURTIS
College of Education: HAROLD LEVINE
College of Eng.: ENRIQUE J. LAVERNIA (acting)
School of Law: REX PERSCHBACHER
Graduate School of Management: NICOLE BIGGART

Div. of Humanities, Arts and Cultural Studies: JESSIE ANN OWENS
Div. of Mathematics and Physical Sciences: WINSTON KO
Div. of Social Sciences: STEVEN M. SHEFFRIN
School of Medicine: CLAIRE POMEROY
School of Veterinary Medicine: BENNIE OSBURN
Graduate Studies: JEFF GIBELING
Univ. Extension: DENNIS PENDLETON

CHAIRPERSONS AND DIRECTORS OF FACULTY
College of Agricultural and Environmental Sciences (150 Mrak Hall, 1 Shields Ave, Davis, CA 95616; tel. (530) 752-0108; fax (530) 752-9049; internet www.aes.ucdavis.edu):
Agricultural and Resource Econ.: RICHARD HOWITT (Chair.)
Agronomy and Range Science: CHRIS VAN KESSEL (Chair.)
Animal Science: GARY ANDERSON (Chair.)
Biological and Agricultural Eng.: BRUCE HARTSOUGH (Chair.)
Entomology: ROBERT PAGE (Chair.)
Environmental Design – Landscape Architecture: HEATH SCHENKER
Environmental Design – Design: PATRICIA HARRISON (Chair.)
Environmental Horticulture: J. HEINER LIETH (Chair.)
Environmental Science and Policy: ANDREW SIH (Chair.)
Environmental Toxicology: MARION MILLER (Chair.)
Food Science and Technology: CHARLES SHOEMAKER (Chair.)
Human and Community Devt: BETH OBER (Chair.)
Land, Water and Air Resources: MICHAEL SINGER (Chair.)
Nematology: EDWARD P. CASWELL-CHEN (Chair.)
Nutrition: CARL L. KEEN (Chair.)
Plant Pathology: RICHARD M. BOSTOCK (Chair.)
Pomology: VITO POLITO (Chair.)
Division of Textiles and Clothing: SUSAN KAISER (Chair.)
Vegetable Crops: JOHN YODER (Chair.)
Viticulture and Oenology: ANDREW WATERHOUSE (Chair.)
Wildlife, Fish and Conservation Biology: DIRK VAN VUREN (Chair.)

School of Education (2077 Academic Surge Bldg, 1 Shields Ave, Davis, CA 95616; tel. (530) 752-8019; fax (530) 752-5411):
Education: HAROLD LEVIN (Dean)

College of Engineering (1050 Engineering Unit II, 1 Shields Ave, Davis, CA 95616; tel. (530) 752-0553; fax (530) 752-8058; internet www.engr.ucdavis.edu):
Applied Science: RICHARD FREEMAN (Chair.)
Biological and Agricultural Eng.: BRUCE HARTSOUGH (Chair.)
Division of Biomedical Eng.: KATHERINE FERRARA
Chemical Eng. and Materials Science: ROBERT POWELL
Civil and Environmental Eng.: DEBBIE NIEMEIER (Chair.)
Computer Science: DAN GUSFIELD (Chair.)
Electrical Eng. and Computer Eng.: JONATHAN HERITAGE (Chair.)
Mechanical and Aeronautical Eng.: RIDA FAROUKI (Chair.)

School of Law (1013 King Hall, 1 Shields Ave, Davis, CA 95616; tel. (530) 752-0243; fax (530) 752-4704; internet kinghall.ucdavis.edu):
Law: REX PERSCHBACHER (Dean)

College of Letters and Science (200 Social Sciences and Humanities Bldg, 1 Shields Ave, Davis, CA 95616; tel. (530) 752-0392; fax (530) 752-3490; internet www.ls.ucdavis.edu):
African-American and African Studies: JACOB K. OLUPONA (Dir)
American Studies: MICHAEL SMITH (Dir)
Anthropology: CAROL SMITH (Chair.)
Art: GINA WERFEL (Chair.)
Asian American Studies: WENDY HO (Dir)
Chemistry: WILLIAM JACKSON (Chair.)
Chicano/a Studies: ADELA DE LA TORRE (Dir)
Classics: LYNN E. ROLLER (Dir)
Communications: ROBERT BELL (Chair.)
Comparative Literature: GAIL FINNEY (Dir)
East Asian Languages and Cultures: ROBERT BORGEN (Chair.)
East Asian Studies: ROBERT BORGEN (Dir)
Econ.: KEVIN HOOVER (Chair.)
English: DAVID SIMPSON (Chair.)
French and Italian: JOANN CANNON (Chair.)
Geology: LOUISE KELLOGG (Chair.)
German and Russian: WINDER MCCONNELL (Chair.)
History: DANIEL R. BROWER (Chair.)
Humanities: MICHELE YEH (Dir)
Integrated Studies: JAMES SHACKELFORD (Dir)
Int. Relations: JEANETTE MONEY (Dir)
Italian: JOANN CANNON (Dir)
Linguistics: LENORA TIMM (Dir)
Mathematics: JOHN HUNTER (Chair.)
Medieval Studies: WINDER MCCONNELL (Dir)
Military Science: DONALD HILL
Music: ROSS BAUER (Chair.)
Native American Studies: VICTOR MONTEJO (Chair.)
Philosophy: GERALD DWORKIN (Chair.)
Physical Education: SUZANNE WILLIAMS (Dir)
Physics: WINSTON KO (Chair.)
Political Science: WALTER STONE (Chair.)
Psychology: PHILLIP SHAVER (Chair.)
Religious Studies: NAOMI JANOWITZ (Dir)
Russian: DANIEL RANCOUR-LAFERRIERE (Dir)
Sociology: MARY JACKMAN (acting) (Chair.)
Spanish and Classics: SAMUEL ARMISTEAD (Co-Chair.: ROBERT BLAKE (Co-Chair.)
Statistics: JANE-LING WANG (Chair.)
Theatre and Dance: SARAH PIA ANDERSON (Chair.)
Women and Gender Studies: JUDITH NEWTON (Dir)

Division of Biological Sciences (202 Life Sciences Addition, 1 Shields Ave, Davis, CA 95616; tel. (530) 752-0410; fax (530) 752-2604; internet www.dbs.ucdavis.edu):
Evolution and Ecology: MICHAEL TURELLI (Chair.)
Exercise Biology: CHARLES FULLER (Chair.)
Microbiology: DOUGLAS C. NELSON (Chair.)
Molecular and Cellular Biology: MICHAEL DAHMUS (Chair.)
Neurobiology, Physiology and Behaviour: LEO CHALUPA (Chair.)
Plant Biology: VENKATESAN SUNDARESAN (Chair.)

Graduate School of Management (106 AOB4, 1 Shields Ave, Davis, CA 95616; tel. (530) 752-7399; fax (530) 752-2924; e-mail gsm@ucdavis.edu; internet www.gsm.ucdavis.edu):
Management: ELIZABETH BIGGART (Dean)

School of Medicine (Med Sci 1C, Room 102 Campus, 1 Shields Ave, Davis, CA 95616; tel. (530) 752-4028; fax (530) 752-1532; internet www.med.ucdavis.edu):
Anaesthesiology: PETER MOORE (Chair.)
Biological Chemistry: LARRY HJELMELAND (Chair.)
Dermatology: FU-TONG LIU (Chair.)
Epidemiology and Preventive Medicine: MARC SCHENKER (Chair.)

Family Practice and Community Medicine: KLEA BERTAKIS (Chair.)

Cell Biology and Human Anatomy: KENT ERICKSON (Chair.)

Human Physiology: PETER CALA (Chair.)

Internal Medicine: FRED MEYERS (Chair.)

Medical Microbiology and Immunology: SATYA DANDEKAR (Chair.)

Medical Pharmacology and Toxicology: ANN BONHAM (Chair.)

Neurology: WILLIAM JAGUST (Chair.)

Neurological Surgery: J. PAUL MUIZELAAR (Chair.)

Obstetrics and Gynaecology: LLOYD H. SMITH (Chair.)

Ophthalmology: JOHN KELTNER (Chair.)

Orthopaedic Surgery: GEORGE RAB (Chair.)

Otolaryngology: HILARY BRODIE (acting) (Chair.)

Paediatrics: ANTHONY PHILLIPS (Chair.)

Pathology: RALPH GREEN (Chair.)

Physical Medicine and Rehabilitation: DAVID KILMER (Chair.)

Psychiatry: ROBERT HALES (Chair.)

Radiation Oncology: JANICE RYU (Chair.)

Radiology: JAMES BRUNBERG (Chair.)

Surgery: JAMES GOODNIGHT, Jr (Chair.)

Urology: RALPH DEVERE WHITE (Chair.)

School of Veterinary Medicine (1 Shields Ave, Davis, CA 95616; tel. (530) 752-1360; fax (530) 752-2801; internet www.vetmed.ucdavis.edu):

Anatomy, Physiology and Cell Biology: CHARLES PLOPPER (Chair.)

Medicine and Epidemiology: RICHARD W. NELSON (Chair.)

Molecular Biosciences: ALAN BUCKPITT (Chair.)

Pathology, Microbiology and Immunology: N. JAMES MACLACHLAN (Chair.)

Population Health and Reproduction: ROBERT BONDURANT (Chair.)

Surgical and Radiological Sciences: RICHARD A. LECOUTEUR (Chair.)

PROFESSORS

College of Agricultural and Environmental Sciences (150 Mrak Hall, 1 Shields Ave, Davis, CA 95616; tel. (530) 752-0107; fax (530) 752-9049; internet www.aes.ucdavis.edu):

Faculty of Agricultural and Resource Economics:

ALSTON, J. M.
CAPUTO, M. R.
CARMAN, H.
CARTER, C. A.
CHALFANT, J. A.
FARZIN, Y. H.
GREEN, R. D.
HAVENNER, A.
HEIEN, D. M.
HOWITT, R. E.
JARVIS, L. S.
MARTIN, P. L.
MORRISON PAUL, C. J.
PARIS, Q.
ROZELLE, S.
SEXTON, R. J.
SUMNER, D. A.
TAYLOR, J. E.
VOSTI, S. A.
WILEN, J. E.
WILLIAMS, J.

Faculty of Agronomy and Range Science:

DEMMENT, M. W.
DENISON, R. F.
DVORAK, J.
FOIN, T. C.
GENG, S.
GEPTS, P. L.
JERNSTEDT, J.
PHILLIPS, D. A.
PLANT, R. E.

RAINS, D. W.
RICE, K. J.
TEUBER, L. R.
TRAVIS, R. L.
VAN KESSEL, C.
WILKENS, T.

Faculty of Animal Science:

ADAMS, T. E.
ANDERSON, G. B.
BERGER, T. J.
CALVERT, C. C.
DE PETERS, E. J.
DOROSHOV, S. I.
FADEL, J. G.
FAMULA, T. R.
GALL, G. A.
HUNG, S. S.
KING, A. J.
KLASING, K. C.
LEE, Y. B.
MEDRANO, J. F.
OBERBAUER, A. M.
MENCH, J. A.
MILLAM, J. R.
PRICE, E. O.
ROSER, J. F.
WEATHERS, W. W.
WILSON, B. W.
ZINN, R. A.

Faculty of Biological and Agricultural Engineering under the College of Agricultural and Environmental Sciences:

PIEDRAHITA, R. H.
UPADHYAYA, S. K.

Faculty of Entomology:

CAREY, J. R.
CRANSTON, P. S.
DINGLE, H.
EDMAN, J. D.
EHLER, L. E.
GRANETT, J.
GULLAN, P. J.
HAMMOCK, B. D.
KARBAN, R.
KAYA, H. K.
KIMSEY, L. S.
LEAL, W. S.
PAGE, R. E.
PARRELA, M. P.
PENG, Y. S. C.
ROSENHEIM, J. A.
SCOTT, T. W.
ULLMAN, D. E.
WARD, P. S.

Faculty of Environmental Design:

GOTELLI, D. E.
HARRISON, P.
LAKY, G.
RIVERS, V. Z.
SHAWCROFT-GUARINO, B.

Faculty of Environmental Horticulture:

BARBOUR, M. G.
BERRY, A. M.
BURGER, D. W.
DURZAN, D. J.
HARDING, J. A.
LIETH, J. H.
REID, M. S.
WU, L. L.

Faculty of Environmental Science and Policy:

GOLDMAN, C. R.
HARRISON, S. P.
HASTINGS, A. M.
JOHNSTON, R. A.
ORLOVE, B. S.
QUINN, J. F.
REJMANKOVA, E.
RICHERSON, P. J.
SABATIER, P. A.
SIH, A.
WILLIAMS, S. L.

Faculty of Environmental Toxicology:

CHERR, G. N.
DENISON, M. S.
KADO, N. Y.
KNEZOVICH, J. P.
MATSUMURA, F.
MILLER-SEARS, M. G.
RICE, R. H.
SHIBAMOTO, T.
TJEERDEMA, R. S.

Faculty of Food Science and Technology:

BAMFORTH, C. W.
BANDMAN, E.
DUNGAN, S. R.
GERMAN, J. B.
GUINARD, J.
HAARD, N. F.
KROCHTA, J. M.
McCARTHY, M. J.
OGRYDZIAK, D. M.
O'MAHONY, M. A.
PRICE, C. W.
REID, D. S.
SHOEMAKER, C. F.
SINGH, R. P.
SMITH, G. M.

Faculty of Human and Community Development:

ALDWIN, C.
BARTON, K.
BRUSH, S. B.
BRYANT, B. K.
CONGER, R. D.
GE, X.
HARPER, L. V.
KENNEY, M. F.
LACY, W. B.
MOMSEN, J.
OBER, B. A.
SMITH, M. P.
WELLS, M. J.

Faculty of Land, Air and Water Resources:

BAHRE, C. J.
BLEDSOE, C. S.
CARROLL, J. J.
CASEY, W. H.
DAHLGREN, R. A.
FLOCCHINI, R. G.
FOGG, G. E.
GRISMER, M. E.
GROTJAHN, R.
HOPMANS, J. W.
HSIAO, T. C.
LAUCHLI, A. E.
NATHAN, T. R.
PAW U, K. T.
RECK, R. A.
RICHARDS, J. M.
ROLSTON, D. E.
SCOW, K. M.
SHELTON, M. L.
SILK, M. W.
SINGER, M. J.
SOUTHARD, R. J.
USTIN, S. L.
WEARE, B. C.
ZASOSKI, R. J.

Faculty of Landscape Architecture:

ALLAN, N.
FRANCIS, M.
MACCANNELL, E. D.

Faculty of Nematology:

CASWELL-CHAN, E. P.
FERRIS, H.
JAFFEE, B. A.
NADLER, S. A.
WILLIAMSON, V. M.

Faculty of Nutrition:

ALLEN, L. H.
BROWN, K. G.
CLIFFORD, A. J.
DEWEY, K. G.

GRIVETTI, L. E.
KEEN, C. L.
LONNERDAL, B. L.
McDONALD, R. B.
RUCKER, R. B.
SCHNEEMAN, B. O.
STERN, J. S.

Faculty of Plant Pathology:

BOSTOCK, R. M.
BRUENING, G.
COOK, D. R.
DAVIS, R. M.
DUNIWAY, J. M.
FALK, B. W.
GILBERTSON, R. L.
GILCHRIST, D. G.
GORDON, T. R.
KADO, C. I.
KIRKPATRICK, B. C.
MACDONALD, J. D.
RONALD, P. C.
TYLER, B. M.
VAN ALFEN, N.
WEBSTER, R. K.

Faculty of Pomology:

BLUMWALD, E.
BROWN, P. H.
DANDEKAR, A. M.
DEJONG, T. M.
GRADZIEL, T. M.
KADER, A. A.
LABAVITCH, J. M.
POLITO, V. S.
SHACKEL, K. A.
SHAW, D. V.
SUTTER, E. G.
WEINBAUM, S.

Faculty of Textiles and Clothing:

HSIEH, Y.
KAISER, S. B.
PAN, N.
RUCKER, M. H.

Faculty of Vegetable Crops:

BAYER, D. E.
BLOOM, A. J.
BRADFORD, K. J.
JACKSON, L. E.
MICHELMORE, R. W.
NEVINS, D. J.
QUIROS, C. F.
SALTVEIT, M. E.
YODER, J. I.

Faculty of Viticulture and Oenology:

BISSON, L. F.
BOULTON, R. B.
HEYMANN, H.
MATTHEWS, M. A.
MEREDITH, C. P.
NOBLE, A. C.
WALKER, M. A.
WATERHOUSE, A. L.
WILLIAMS, L. E.

Faculty of Wildlife, Fish and Conservation Biology:

ANDERSON, D. W.
BOTSFORD, L. W.
CARO, T. M.
CECH, J. J.
EADIE, J. M.
ELLIOTT-FISK, D. L.
MOYLE, P. B.
VAN VUREN, D.

School of Education (2077 Academic Surge Bldg, 1 Shields Ave, Davis, CA 95616; tel. (530) 752-8019; fax (530) 752-5411):

DUGDALE, S. S.
FIGUEROA, R. A.
GANDARA, P.
LEVINE, H. G.
MERINO, B. J.
MURPHY, S.
SANDOVAL, J. H.

WAGNER, J. C.
WATSON-GEGEO, K. A.
YOUNG, I. P.

College of Engineering (1050 Engineering Unit II, 1 Shields Ave, Davis, CA 95616; tel. (530) 752-0553; fax (530) 752-8058; internet www.engr.ucdavis.edu):

Faculty of Biological and Agricultural Engineering under the College of Engineering:

DELWICHE, M. J.
GILES, D. K.
HARTSOUGH, B. R.
HILLS, D. J.
JENKINS, B. M.
McCARTHY, K. L.
MILES, J. A.
RUMSEY, T. R.
SLAUGHTER, D. C.
UPADHYAYA, S. K.
WALLENDER, W. W.

Faculty of Biomedical Engineering:

BENHAM, C. J.
CHERRY, S. R.
FERRARA, K. W.
INSANA, M. F.
SAVAGEAU, M. A.
SIMON, I.

Faculty of Engineering: Applied Science:

BALDIS, H. A.
CRAMER, S. P.
FREEMAN, R. R.
HWANG, D. Q.
JENSEN, N. G.
KOLNER, B. H.
KROL, D.
LAUB, A. J.
LUHMANN, N. C.
MAX, N. L.
McCURDY, W. C.
MILLER, G. H.
OREL, A. E.
ROCKE, D. M.
RODRIGUE, G.
VEMURI, V.
YEH, Y.

Faculty of Engineering:

MUNIR, Z. A.

Faculty of Chemical Engineering and Materials Science:

BROWNING, N. D.
GATES, B. C.
GIBELING, J. C.
GROZA, J. R.
HIGGINS, B. G.
HOWITT, D. G.
JACKMAN, A. P.
McCOY, B. J.
McDONALD, K. A.
MUKHERJEE, A. K.
NAVROTSKY, A.
PALAZOGLU, A. N.
PHILLIPS, R. J.
POWELL, R. L.
RISBUD, S. H.
RYU, D. D. Y.
SHACKELFORD, J. F.
STROEVE, P.
WHITAKER, S.

Faculty of Civil and Environmental Engineering:

ARULANANDAN, K.
BOULANGER, R.
CHANG, D. P.
DAFALIAS, Y. F.
DARBY, J. L.
GINN, T.
IDRISS, I. M.
KAVVAS, M. L.
KUTTER, B. L.
LAROCK, B. E.
LUND, J. R.

MARINO, M. A.
MOKHTARIAN, P. L.
NIEMEIER, D. A.
RAMEY, M. R.
RUNDLE, J. B.
SPERLING, D.
YOUNIS, B.

Faculty of Computer Science:

BAI, Z.
BRUNO, J.
FARRENS, M. K.
GUSFIELD, D.
HAMANN, B.
JOY, K. I.
LEVITT, K. N.
MARTEL, C. U.
MATLOFF, N. S.
MUKHERJEE, B.
OLSSON, R. A.
ROGAWAY, P. W.
RUSCHITZKA, M. G.

Faculty of Electrical and Computer Engineering:

ABDEL-GHAFFAR, K. A.
BRANNER, G. R.
CHANG, T. S.
COLINGE, J. P.
CURRENT, K. W.
DING, Z.
FEHER, K.
FORD, G. E.
HALEY, S. B.
HERITAGE, J. P.
HUNT, C. E.
HURST, P. J.
KNOESEN, A.
LEVY, B. C.
LEWIS, S. H.
OKLOBDZIJA, V. G.
REDINBO, G. R.
REED, T. R.
SMITH, R. L.
SPENCER, R. R.
TIEN, N. C.
WANG, S.
YOO, S. B.

Faculty of Mechanical and Aeronautical Engineering:

BAUGHN, J. W.
CHATTOT, J. J.
DAVIS, R. J.
DWYER, H. A.
FAROUKI, R. T.
FRANK, A. A.
HAFEZ, M. M.
HESS, R. A.
HUBBARD, M.
HULL, M. L.
KARNOPP, D. C.
KENNEDY, I. M.
KOLLMANN, W.
MARGOLIS, D. L.
RAVANI, B.
REHFIELD, L. W.
SARIGUL-KLIJN, N.
SHAW, B. D.
VAN DAM, C. P.
VELINSKY, S. A.
WEXLER, A. S.
WHITE, B. R.
YAMAZAKI, K.

School of Law (1013 King Hall, 1 Shields Ave, Davis, CA 95616; tel. (530) 752-0243; fax (530) 752-4704; internet www.kinghall .ucdavis.edu):

AMANN, D. M.
AYER, J. D.
BROWNSTEIN, A. E.
DOBRIS, J. C.
DOREMUS, H.
FEENEY, F. F.
GANDARA, A.
GLENNON, M. J.
GROSSMAN, G. S.

HILLMAN, R. W.
IMWINKELRIED, E. J.
JOHNSON, K. R.
JOO, T. W.
KURTZ, L. A.
LEWIS, E. A.
OAKLEY, J. B.
PERSCHBACHER, R. R.
POULOS, J. W.
REYNOSO, C.
SIMMONS, D. L.
WEST, M. S.
WOLK, B. A.
WYDICK, R. C.

College of Letters and Science (200 Social Sciences and Humanities Bldg, 1 Shields Ave, Davis, CA 95616; tel. (530) 752-0392; fax (530) 752-3440; internet www-lsdo.ucdavis.edu):

Faculty of African American and African Studies:
OLUPONA, J. K.
STEWART, J. O.
TURNER, P. A.

Faculty of American Studies:
BLAIR, C.
FRANKENBERG, R.
MECHLING, J. E.
SMITH, M.

Faculty of Anthropology:
BETTINGER, R. L.
BORGERHOFF-MULDER, M.
DUNHAM, D. L.
HARCOURT, A. H.
JOSEPH, S.
MCHENRY, H. M.
RODMAN, P. S.
SMITH, C. A.
SMITH, D. G.
SMITH, J. S.
SRINIVAS, S.
WINTERHALDER, B. P.
YENGOYAN, A. A.

Faculty of Art Studio and Art History:
ATKINSON, C.
BILLS, T. B.
COLLINS, H. M.
HENDERSON, W.
HERSHMAN, L.
HOLLOWELL, D.
MACLEOD, D. S.
PULS, L. A.
RUDA, J.
WERFEL, G. S.

Faculty of Asian American Studies:
HAMAMOTO, D. Y.
HING, B. O.
SUE, S.

Faculty of Chemistry:
BALCH, A. L.
BRITT, R. D.
FAWCETT, W. R.
FINK, W. H.
GERVAY HAGUE, J.
JACKSON, W. M.
KAUZLARICH, S.
KELLY, P. B.
KURTH, M. J.
LAMAR, G. N.
LEBRILLA, C. B.
MEARES, C. F.
MOLINSKI, T.
NANTZ, M
NG, C. Y.
POWER, P. P.
ROCK, P. A.
SCHORE, N. E.
STUCHEBRUKHOV, A.
TINTI, D. S.
TRUE, N. S.
TUCKER, S. C.

Faculty of Chicano Studies:
CHABRAM-DERNE, A.
DE LA TORRE, A.
MONTOYA, M.

Faculty of Comparative Research:
SKINNER, G. W.

Faculty of East Asian Languages and Culture:
BORGEN, R.
YEH, M.

Faculty of Comparative Literature:
BLANCHARD, M. E.
FINNEY, G.
LARSEN, N. A.
LU, S. H.
MURAV, H. L.
SCHEIN, S. L.
SCHIESARI, J.
SCHILDGEN, B. P.
TORRANCE, R. M.

Faculty of Theatre and Dance:
ANDERSON, S. P.
IACOVELLI, J. C.
SELLERS-YOUNG, B. A.
SHANNON, P.

Faculty of Economics:
BONANNO, G.
CAMERON, A.
CLARK, G.
FEENSTRA, R. C.
HOOVER, K. D.
LINDERT, P. H.
MAKOWSKI, L.
OLMSTEAD, A. L.
QUINZII, M.
SHEFFRIN, S. M.
SILVESTRE, J.
WALTON, G. M.
WOO, W. T.

Faculty of English:
ABBOTT, D. P.
BYRD, W. M.
DALE, P. A.
DIEHL, J. F.
FERGUSON, M. W.
FREED, L. R.
GILBERT, S. M.
HAYS, P. L.
LANGLAND, E.
LEVIN, R. A.
LOKKE, K.
MAJOR, C.
MCPHERSON, S. J.
MORRIS, L. A.
OSBORN, M.
OWENS, L. D.
ROBERTSON, D. A.
SCHLEINER, W.
SIMMONS, S.
SIMPSON, D. E.
SNYDER, G. S.
VAN LEER, D. M.
WADDINGTON, R. B.
WATKINS, E. P.
WILLIAMSON, A. B.
ZENDER, K. F.

Faculty of French and Italian:
BLANCHARD, M. E.
CANNON, J.
DUTSCHKE, D. J.
MANOLIU, M. I.
VAN DEN ABBEELE, G.

Faculty of Geology:
CARLSON, S. J.
DAY, H. W.
DEWEY, J. F.
KELLOGG, L. H.
LESHER, C. E.
MONTAÑEZ, I. P.
MOORES, E. M.
MOUNT, J. F.

SCHIFFMAN, P.
SPERO, H. J.
TURCOTTE, D. L.
TWISS, R. J.
VERMEIJ, G.
VEROSUB, K. L.
ZIERENBERG, R. A.

Faculty of German and Russian:
BERND, C. A.
DRUZHNIKOV, Y.
MCCONNELL, W.
MENGES, K. R.
RANCOUR-LAFERRIERE, D.
SCHAEFFER, P. M.

Faculty of History:
BAUER, A. J.
BIALE, D.
BRANTLEY, C. L.
BROWER, D. R.
CADDEN, J.
HAGEN, W. W.
HALTTUNEN, K.
HOLLOWAY, T. H.
KUDLICK, C. J.
LANDAU, N. B.
MANN, S. L.
MARGADANT, T. W.
METCALF, B. O.
PRICE, D. C.
ROSEN, R. E.
SMITH, M.
SPYRIDAKIS, S.
TAYLOR, A. S.
WALKER, C. E.

Faculty of Linguistics:
BENWARE, W. A.
OJEDA, A. E.
TIMM, L. A.

Faculty of Mathematics:
BRAMSON, M. D.
BORGES, C. R.
CHEER, A. Y.
DIEDERICH, J. R.
EDELSON, A. L.
FUCHS, D. B.
GRAVNER, J.
HAAS, J.
HUNTER, J. K.
KRENER, A. J.
KUPERBERG, G. J.
MILTON, E. O.
MOGILNER, A.
MULASE, M.
NACHTERGAELE, B.
PUCKETT, E. G.
SAITO, N.
SALLEE, G. T.
SCHWARZ, A.
SHKOLLER, S.
SILVIA, E. M.
TEMPLE, J. B.
THOMPSON, A. A.
THURSTON, W. P.
TRACY, C. A.
WETS, R. J.

Faculty of Music:
BAUER, R.
BUSSE BERGER, A. M.
FRANK, A. D.
HOLOMAN, D. K.
NUTTER, D. A.
ORTIZ, P. V.
REYNOLDS, C. A.

Faculty of Native American Studies:
HERNANDEZ-AVILA, I.
LONGFISH, G. C.
MACRI, M. J.
MONTEJO, V. D.
VARESE, S.

Faculty of Philosophy:
CUMMINS, R. C.
DWORKIN, G.

GRIESEMER, J. R.
JUBIEN, M.
KING, J. C.
NEANDER, K. L.
TELLER, P.
WEDIN, M. V.
WILSON, G. M.

Faculty of Physics:

ALBRECHT, A. J.
BECKER, R. H.
CARLIP, S.
CHAU, L.
CHIANG, S.
CORRUCCINI, L. R.
COX, D. L.
FADLEY, C. S.
FONG, C.
GUNION, J. F.
KISKIS, J. E.
KLEIN, B. M.
KO, W. T.
LANDER, R.
PELLETT, D. E.
PICKETT, W. E.
SCALETTAR, R. T.
SINGH, R. R.
TRIPATHI, S. M.
YAGER, P. M.
ZHU, X.
ZIMANYI, G.

Faculty of Political Science:

HUCKFELDT, R. R.
JACKMAN, R. W.
NINCIC, M.
PETERMAN, L. I.
ROTHCHILD, D. S.
SIVERSON, R. M.
STONE, W. J.
WADE, L. L.

Faculty of Psychology:

ACREDOLO, L. P.
CAPITANIO, J. P.
COSS, R. G.
ELMS, A. C.
EMMONS, R. A.
ERICKSEN, K. P.
GOODMAN, G. S.
HARRISON, A. A.
HENRY, K. R.
HEREK, G. M.
JOHNSON, J. T.
KROLL, N. E.
KRUBITZER, L. A.
LONG, D. L.
MANGUN, G. R.
MENDOZA, S. P.
OWINGS, D. H.
PARKS, T. E.
POST, R. B.
SHAVER, P. R.
SIMONTON, D. K.
SOMMER, R.
WIDAMAN, K. F.

Faculty of Religious Studies:

JANOWITZ, N.
LAI, W. W.

Faculty of Communication:

BELL, R. A.
BERGER, C. R.
MOTLEY, M. T.

Faculty of Sociology:

BLOCK, F.
COHEN, L. E.
CRAMER, J. C.
FELMLEE, D. H.
GOLDSTONE, J. A.
HALL, J. R.
JACKMAN, M. R.
JOFFE, C.
LOFLAND, L. H.
MCCARTHY, W. D.
SMITH, V. A.
WALTON, J. T.

WOLF, D. L.

Faculty of Spanish and Classics:

ARMISTEAD, S. G.
BLAKE, R. J.
GONZÁLEZ, C.
LARSEN, N. A.
ROLLER, L. E.
SCARI, R. M.
TRAILL, D. A.
VERANI, H. J.

Faculty of Statistics:

BERAN, R. J.
BURMAN, P.
JOHNSON, W. O.
MACK, Y. P.
MUELLER, H. G.
ROUSSAS, G. G.
SAMANIEGO, F. J.
SHUMWAY, R. H.
UTTS, J. M.
WANG, J.-L.

Faculty of Women Studies:

KUHN, A. K.
NEWTON, J.
RABINE, L. W.

Division of Biological Sciences (202 Life Sciences Addition, 1 Shields Ave, Davis, CA 95616; tel. (530) 752-0410; fax (530) 752-2604; internet www.dbs.ucdavis.edu):

Biological Science:

CHANG, E. S.

Evolution and Ecology:

CHESSON, P. L.
DOYLE, J. A.
GILLESPIE, J. H.
GOTTLIEB, L. D.
GREY, R. D.
GROSBERG, R. K.
LANGLEY, C. H.
PEARCY, R. W.
REJMANEK, M.
SANDERSON, M. J.
SCHOENER, T. W.
SHAFFER, H. B.
SHAPIRO, A. M.
STAMPS, J. A.
STANTON, M. L.
STRONG, D. R.
TOFT, C. A.
TURELLI, M.
WAINWRIGHT, P. C.

Microbiology:

ARTZ, S. W.
BAUMANN, P.
HEYER, W. D.
KOWALCZYKOWSKI, S. C.
MANNING, J. S.
MEEKS, J. C.
NELSON, D. C.
PRIVALSKY, M. L.
STEWART, V. J.
ROTH, J. R.

Molecular and Cellular Biology:

ARMSTRONG, P. B.
BASKIN, R. J.
BURTIS, K. C.
CALLIS, J.
CLEGG, J. S.
CROWE, J. H.
DAHMUS, M. E.
DOI, R. H.
ERICKSON, C. A.
ETZLER, M. E.
GASSER, C. S.
HEDRICK, J. L.
HJELMELAND, L. M.
KIGER, J. A.
LAGARIAS, J. C.
MYLES, D.
RODRIGUEZ, R. L.
SCHMID, C. W.
SHOLEY, J. M.

SEGEL, I. H.

Neurobiology, Physiology and Behaviour:

CARSTENS, E. E.
FULLER, C. A.
HORWITZ, B. A.
ISHIDA, A. T.
MULLONEY, B.
PAPPONE, P. A.
SILLMAN, A. J.
WEIDNER, W. J.
WILSON, M. C.
WOOLLEY, D. E.

Plant Biology:

DELMER, D. P.
HARADA, J. J.
LUCAS, W. J.
MURPHY, T. M.
O'NEILL, S. D.
ROST, T. L.
SINHA, N.
STEMLER, A. J.
SUNDARESEN, V.
THEG, S. M.
VANDERHOEF, L. N.

Graduate School of Management (106 AOB4, 1 Shields Ave, Davis, CA 95616; tel. (530) 752-7399; fax (530) 752-2924; e-mail gsm@ucdavis .edu; internet www.gsm.ucdacvis.edu):

BARBER, B.
BIGGART, N. W.
BUNCH, D. S.
CLARK, P. K.
GERSTNER, E.
GRIFFIN, P. A.
MAHER, M.
PALMER, D.
SMILEY, R. H.
SWAMINATHAN, A.
TOPKIS, D. M.
TSAI, C.-L.
WOODRUFF, D.

School of Medicine (Med Sci 1C, Room 102 Campus, 1 Shields Ave, Davis, CA 95616; tel. (530) 752-4028; fax (530) 752-1532; internet www-med.ucdavis.edu):

Department of Anaesthesiology and Pain Medicine:

ANTOGNINI, J. F.

Department of Biological Chemistry:

BRADBURY, E. M.
HAGERMAN, P. J.
HERSHEY, J. W.
HJELMELAND, L. M.
HOLLAND, M. J.
JUE, T.
KUNG, H.-J.
TROY LI, F. A.

Department of Epidemiology and Preventive Medicine:

BECKETT, L. A.
CHEN, M. S.
GOLD, E. B.
LEIGH, J. P.
SCHENKER, M. B.
WINTEMUTE, G. J.

Department of Dermatology:

GRANDO, S. A.
HUNTLEY, A. C.
ISSEROFF, R. R.
LIU, F.-T.
ZIBOH, V. A.

Department of Family and Community Medicine:

BERTAKIS, K. D.
CALLAHAN, E. J.
FRANKS, P.
MELNIKOW, J.
NESBITT, T. S.
NUOVO, J.

Department of Cell Biology and Human Anatomy:
ERICKSON, K. L.
FITZGERALD, P.
KUMARI, V.
MEIZEL, S.
PRIMAKOFF, P.
TUCKER, R. P.

Department of Human Physiology:
CALA, P. M.
CARLSEN, R. C.
CURRY, F. E.
O'DONNELL, M. E.
TURGEON, J. L.
WIDDICOMBE, J.
WISE, P.

Department of Internal Medicine:
ALBERTSON, T. E.
AMSTERDAM, E. A.
AOKI, T.
BERGLUND, L.
BONHAM, A. C.
COHEN, S. H.
CROSS, C. E.
DEGREGORIO, M.
DENARDO, S. J.
DEPNER, T. A.
FITZGERALD, F. T.
GANDARA, D. R.
GERSHWIN, M. E.
HALSTED, C. H.
HINSHAW, V. S.
KAPPAGODA, C. T.
KARAKAS, S. E.
KAUFMAN, M. P.
KAYSEN, G.
KRAVITZ, R.
LAM, K.
LAST, J. A.
LEUNG, J.
LOEWY, E.
MARTIN, R. B.
MATTHEWS, H. R.
MEYERS, F. J.
PARSONS, G. H.
PIMSTONE, N. R.
POLLARD, R. B.
POWELL, J. S.
PRINDIVILLE, T. P.
REDDI, A. H.
RICHMAN, C. M.
ROBBINS, J. A.
ROBBINS, R. L.
RUTLEDGE, J. C.
SCHAEFER, S.
SIEGEL, D.
SILVA, J.
STEBBINS, C. L.
ZERN, M.

Department of Medical Microbiology and Immunology:
BEAMAN, B. L.
DANDEKAR, S.
PAPPAGIANIS, D.
SYVANEN, M.
THEIS, J. H.

Medicine:
ANDERS, T. F.
SELDIN, M. F.

Department of Neurology:
DE CARLI, C.
GORIN, F. A.
JAGUST, W. J.
KWEE, I.
MANGUN, G. R.
MASELLI, R. A.
REMLER, M. P.
RICHMAN, D. P.
SEYAL, M.

Department of Neurological Surgery:
BOGGAN, J. E.
BERMAN, R. F.

LYETH, B. G.
MATTHEWS, D. L.
MUIZELAAR, J. P.
SCHWARTZKROIN, P. A.

Department of Obstetrics and Gynaecology:
BOYERS, S.
GILBERT, W. M.
OVERSTREET, J. W.
SMITH, L. H.

Department of Ophthalmology:
CHALUPA, L. M.
KELTNER, J. L.
MANNIS, M. J.
WERNER, J. S.

Department of Orthopaedic Surgery:
BENSON, D. R.
RAB, G. T.
RODRIGO, J. J.
SZABO, R. M.

Department of Otolaryngology:
DONALD, P. J.

Department of Paediatrics:
HAGERMAN, R. J.
JOAD, J. P.
MAKKER, S. P.
PHILIPPS, A. F.
SHERMAN, M. P.
STYNE, D. M.
TARANTAL, A. F.
WENMAN, W. M.

Department of Pathology:
CARDIFF, R. D.
ELLIS, W. G.
GREEN, R.
JIALAL, I.
KOST, G. J.
LARKIN, E. C.
LUCIW, P. A.

Department of Pharmacology and Toxicology:
BONHAM, A. C.
CHUANG, R. Y.
HENDERSON, G. L.

Department of Plastic Surgery:
STEVENSON, T. R.

Department of Psychiatry:
AMARAL, D. G.
JONES, E. G.
HENDREN, R. L.
KNAPP, P. K.
MADDOCK, R. J.
MORRISON, T. L.
ROGERS, S. J.

Department of Radiology and Radiation Oncology:
BOGREN, H. G.
BOONE, J. M.
BRUNBERG, J. A.
BUONOCORE, M. H.
KATZBERG, R. W.
KUBO, H.
LATCHAW, R. E.
LINK, D. P.
MCGAHAN, J. P.
MOORE, E. H.
ROSENQUIST, C. J.
SEIBERT, J. A.
STADAINIK, R. C.
VIJAYAKUMAR, S.

Department of Surgery:
FOLLETTE, D. M.
GREENHALGH, D. G.
HOLCROFT, J. W.
SEGEL, L. D.
WISNER, D. H.
WOLFE, B. M.

Department of Urology:
DE VERE WHITE, R. W.
STONE, A. R.

School of Veterinary Medicine (tel. (530) 752-1360; fax (530) 752-2801; internet www.vetmed.ucdavis.edu):

Faculty of Anatomy, Physiology and Cell Biology:
BRUSS, M. L.
GIETZEN, D. W.
HART, B. L.
HYDE, D. M.
PINKERTON, K. E.
PLOPPER, C. G.
RAYBOULD, M. J.
STOVER, S. M.
TABLIN, F.
WU, R.

Faculty of Medicine and Epidemiology:
ARDANS, A. A.
CARLSON, G. P.
CARPENTER, T. E.
COWGILL, L. D.
FELDMAN, E. C.
GARDNER, I.
GEORGE, L. W.
HEDRICK, R. P.
HIRD, D. W.
IHRKE, P. J.
KITTLESON, M. D.
LING, G. V.
MADIGAN, J. E.
NELSON, R. W.
PEDERSEN, N. C.
SMITH, B. P.
THOMAS, W. P.
THURMOND, M. C.
WALSH, D. A.
WHITE, S. D.
WILSON, W. D.

Faculty of Population Health and Reproduction:
BALL, B. A.
BONDURANT, R. H.
CHOMEL, B. B.
CLIVER, D. O.
CULLOR, J. S.
FARVER, T. B.
HART, L. A.
LAM, K. M.
LASLEY, W. L.
LIU, I. K.
MURRAY, J. D.
TANNENBAUM, J.

Faculty of Surgical and Radiological Sciences:
BUYUKMIHCI, N. C.
GREGORY, C. R.
HASKINS, S. C.
HILDEBRAND, S. V.
HORNOF, W. J.
ILKIW, J.
JONES, J. H.
LECOUTEUR, R. A.
MADEWELL, B. R.
NYLAND, T. G.
O'BRIEN, T. R.
PASCOE, J. R.
PASCOE, P. J.
SNYDER, J. R.
STEFFEY, E. P.
THEON, A. P.
VASSEUR, P.
VERSTRAETE, F. J. M.
WISNER, E. R.

Faculty of Pathology, Microbiology and Immunology:
BARTHOLD, S. W.
BOYCE, W. M.
CHRISTOPHER, M. W.
CONRAD, P. A.
GERSHWIN, L. J.
HIGGINS, R. J.
LEFEBVRE, R. B.
LOWENSTINE, L. J.
MACLACHLAN, N. J.

MILLER, C. J.
MOORE, P. F.
MUNSON, L.
MURPHY, F. A.
OSBURN, B. I.
STOTT, J. L.
WILSON, D. W.
YILMA, T.
ZINKL, J. G.

Faculty of Molecular Biosciences:

BUCKPITT, A. R.
CORTOPASSI, G. I.
GIRI, S. N.
HANSEN, R. J.
PESSAH, I. N.
ROGERS, Q. R.
SEGALL, H. J.
VULLIET, P. R.

University of California, Irvine

Irvine, CA 92697
Telephone: (949) 824-5011
Internet: www.uci.edu
Founded 1965
State control
Chancellor: MICHAEL V. DRAKE
Exec. Vice-Chancellor and Provost: MICHAEL R. GOTTFREDSON
Vice-Chancellor for Student Affairs: MANUEL N. GÓMEZ
Vice-Chancellor (Admin. and Business Services): WENDELL C. BRASE
Vice-Chancellor for Planning and Budget: ROY E. DORMAIER
Vice-Chancellor for Research and Dean of Graduate Studies: WILLIAM H. PARKER
Vice-Chancellor (University Advancement): THOMAS J. MITCHELL
CEO: MAUREEN ZEHNTNER
Univ. Librarian: GERALD J. MUNOFF
Library of 2,250,000 vols and 22,000 current periodicals
Number of teachers: 1,800
Number of students: 25,000
Publications: *UCI General Catalogue* (annually), *UCI Journal* (newspaper, quarterly), *UCI News Paper* (monthly), *New University* (weekly student newspaper), and numerous student publications

DEANS

Claire Trevor School of the Arts: NOHEMA FERNÁNDEZ
School of Biological Sciences: SUSAN V. BRYANT
School of Eng.: NICOLAOS G. ALEXOPOULOS
School of Humanities: KAREN R. LAWRENCE
Donald Bren School of Information and Computer Sciences: DEBRA J. RICHARDSON (acting)
Paul Merage School of Business: ANDREW J. POLICANO (acting)
School of Physical Sciences: RONALD J. STERN
School of Social Ecology: C. RONALD HUFF
School of Social Sciences: BARBARA A. DOSHER
College of Health Sciences: THOMAS C. CESARIO
School of Medicine: THOMAS C. CESARIO
Continuing Education: GARY W. MATKIN
Graduate Studies: WILLIAM H. PARKER
Div. of Undergraduate Education: SHARON V. SALINGER

DIRECTORS AND DEPARTMENT CHAIRPERSONS

Biological Sciences:

Anatomy and Neurology: Prof. HERBERT P. KILLACKEY
Developmental and Cell Biology: Prof. ARTHUR D. LANDER
Ecology and Evolutionary Biology: Prof. ARTHUR F. BENNETT
Molecular Biology and Biochemistry: Prof. JERRY E. MANNING

College of Medicine:

Anaesthesiology: CYNTHIA ANDERSON
Anatomy and Neurobiology: Dr RICHARD T. ROBERTSON
Biological Chemistry: Prof. SUZANNE B. SANDMEYER
C and E Medicine: DANIEL MENZEL
Dermatology: Dr JERRY L. MCCULLOUGH
Emergency Medicine: Dr MARK I. LANGDORF
Family Medicine: JOSEPH E. SCHERGER (acting)
Medicine: ALLAN HUBBELL (acting)
Microbiology and Molecular Genetics: Dr BERT L. SEMLER
Neurological Surgery: MARIO AMMIRATI (acting)
Neurology: Dr MARK FISHER
Obstetrics and Gynaecology: Prof. THOMAS J. GARITE
Ophthalmology: Dr PETER J. MCDONNELL (acting)
Orthopaedic Surgery: Dr HARRY B. SKINNER
Otolaryngology, Head and Neck Surgery: Prof. ROGER L. CRUMLEY
Pathology: Prof. MICHAEL E. SELSTED
Paediatrics: Dr FEIZAL WAFFARN
Pharmacology: Prof. SUE PIPER DUCKLES
Physical Medicine and Rehabilitation: Prof. JEN YU
Physiology and Biophysics: Prof. JANOS LANYI
Psychiatry and Human Behaviour: SIU TANG
Radiation Oncology: NILAM RAMSINGHANI
Radiological Sciences: Prof. FONG Y. TSAI
Surgery: Prof. SAMUEL E. WILSON

Education:

DAVID BRANT (interim chair)

Engineering:

Biomedical Eng.: Dr STEVE C. GEORGE
Chemical Eng. and Materials Science: Prof. STANLEY B. GRANT
Civil and Environmental Eng.: Prof. MASANOBU SHINOZUKA
Electrical and Computer Eng.: Prof. ENDER AYANOGLU
Mechanical and Aerospace Eng.: Prof. DIMITRI PAPAMOSCHOU

Clare Trevor School of the Arts:

Dance: ALAN TERRICCIANO
Drama: CAMERON HARVEY
Music: CAMERON HARVEY (Co-Chair: ALAN TERRICCIANO (Co-Chair)
Studio Art: YONG SOON MIN

Humanities:

African American Studies: Dr BELINDA ROBNETT (acting)
Art History: Prof. JAMES D. HERBERT
Asian American Studies: Prof. KETU H. KATRAK
Classics: LYNN MALLY
East Asian Language and Literatures: Prof. STEVEN D. CARTER
English and Comparative Literature: Prof. STEVE MAILLOUX
English as a Second Language: ROBIN SCARCELLA
Film Studies: (vacant)
French and Italian: Prof. DAVID CARROLL
German: Prof. JENS RIECKMANN
History: Prof. KENNETH L. POMERANZ
Humanities Core Course: JOHN SMITH
Latin American Studies: JAIME E. RODRÍGUEZ
Philosophy: Prof. NICHOLAS P. WHITE
Russian Studies: Dr DRAGAN KUJUNDIZIC
Spanish and Portuguese: Dr ANA PAULA FERREIRA
Women's Studies: Prof. INDERPAL GREWAL

Information and Computer Science: Dr DEBRA J. RICHARDSON

Physical Sciences:

Chemistry: Prof. KENNETH J. SHEA
Earth System Science: Dr WILLIAM REEBURGH
Mathematics: Prof. BERNARD RUSSO
Physics and Astronomy: Prof. ANDREW LANKFORD

Social Ecology:

Criminology, Law and Society: Dr VALERIE JENNEESS
Environmental Analysis and Design: Prof. JONATHON E. ERICSON (acting)
Psychology and Social Behaviour: Dr CHUANSHENG CHEN
Urban Planning: Dr SCOTT BOLLENS

Social Sciences:

Anthropology: Prof. JAMES G. FERGUSON
Chicano and Latino Studies Programme: LEO CHÁVEZ
Cognitive Sciences: TED WRIGHT
Econ.: MICHELLE GARFINKEL
Global Peace and Conflict Studies: WAYNE SANDHOLTZ (acting)
Linguistics: Prof. NAOKO FUKUI
Logic and Philosophy of Science: JEFFREY BARRETT
Political Science: KATHERINE TATE
Sociology: CALVIN MORRILL
Transportation Studies: MICHAEL MCNALLY (acting)

Statistics:

Prof. HAL S. STERN

ATTACHED INSTITUTES

Beckman Laser Institute: Chair and CEO Prof. MICHAEL W. BERNS.

California Institute for Telecommunications and Information Technology (UC Irvine Division): Dir WILLIAM H. PARKER.

Cancer Research Institute: Dir HUNG Y. FAN.

Center for Arts Research in Education.

Center for Asian Studies: Dir R. BIN WONG.

Center for Embedded Computer Systems: Dir DANIEL D. GAJSKI.

Center for Global Peace and Conflict Studies: Dir WAYNE SANDHOLTZ.

Center for Interdiscipliniary Chemical Synthesis: Dir RICHARD CHAMBERLIN.

Center for the Neurobiology of Learning and Memory: Dir Dr JAMES L. MCGAUGH.

Center for Research in Educational Assessment and Measurement: Dir Dr RICHARD S. BROWN.

Center for Research on Latinos in a Global Society: Dir Prof. LEO CHÁVEZ.

Center for Research on Information Technology and Organizations: Dir Prof. KENNETH L. KRAEMER.

Center for the Study of Democracy: Dir Prof. RUSSEL J. DALTON.

Center for Virus Research: Dir Dr LUIS P. VILLARREAL.

Critical Theory Institute: Dir Prof. JAMES FERGUSON.

Developmental Biology Centre: Dir PETER J. BRYANT.

EpiCenter (Epilepsy Research Center): Dir TALLIE Z. BARAM.

Focused Research Program in Southern California Labor Studies: Dir GILBERT GONZALES.

Humanities Research Institute: Dir DAVID THEO GOLDBERG.

Institute for Brain Aging and Dementia: Dir Dr CARL W. COTMAN.

Institute for Genomics and Bioinformatics: Dir Prof. PIERRE BALDI.

Institute for Geophysics and Planetary Physics (incorporating Center for Global Environment Change Research): Dir SUSAN TRUMBORE.

Institute for Mathematical Behavioral Sciences: Dir WILLIAM H. BATCHELDER.

Institute for Research in the Arts (UCIRA): Dir DAVID TREND.

Institute for Software Research: Dir Prof. RICHARD N. TAYLOR.

Institute of Transportation Studies: Dir MICHAEL MCNALLY.

Institute for Surface and Interface Science: Dir ALEX MARADUDIN.

International Center for Writing and Translation: Dir NGUGI WA THIONG'O.

Irvine Research Unit on Health Policy and Research: Dir F. ALAN HUBBELL.

Irvine Research Unit on Hearing and Speech Sciences: Dir LEONARD KITZES.

National Fuel Cell Research Center: Dir Prof. SCOTT SAMUELSEN.

Reeve-Irvine Research Center: Dir Prof. OSWALD STEWARD.

Susan Samueli Center for Complementary and Alternative Medicine: Exec. Dir Dr DAVID FELTEN.

Thesaurus Linguae Graecae: Dir Prof. MARIA C. PANTELIA.

Transdisciplinary Tobacco Use Research Center: Dir Prof. FRANCES LESLIE.

University of California, Los Angeles (UCLA)

405 Hilgard Ave, Los Angeles, CA 90095
Telephone: (310) 825-4321
Internet: www.ucla.edu

Founded 1919

Chancellor: NORMAN ABRAMS (acting)
Exec. Vice-Chancellor and Provost: SCOTT WAUGH (acting)
Admin. Vice-Chancellor: SAM J. MORABITO
Vice-Chancellor for External Affairs: RHEA TURTELTAUB
Vice-Chancellor for Finance, Budget and Capital Programs: STEVEN A. OLSEN
Vice-Chancellor for Legal Affairs: JOSEPH D. MANDEL
Vice-Chancellor for Research Programs: ROBERTO PECCEI
Vice-Chancellor for Student Affairs: JANINA MONTERO
Vice-Chancellor (Graduate Studies) and Dean of Graduate Division: CLAUDIA MITCHELL-KERNAN
Exec. Dean: PATRICIA O'BRIEN
Univ. Librarian: GARY STRONG

Library of 8,000,000 vols, 90,000 periodicals
Number of teachers: 4,016
Number of students: 36,611

DEANS

Div. of Humanities: TIMOTHY STOWELL
Div. of Life Sciences: EMIL REISLER
Div. of Physical Sciences: JOSEPH RUDNICK
Div. of Social Sciences: REYNALDO F. MACIAS (acting)
Div. of Undergraduate Education: JUDITH L. SMITH
Int. Institute: RONALD ROGOWSKI
School of the Arts and Architecture: CHRISTOPHER WATERMAN
School of Dentistry: NO-HEE PARK
Graduate School of Education and Information Studies: AIMEE DORR
Henry Samueli School of Eng. and Applied Science: VIJAY DHIR
School of Law: MICHAEL SCHILL
Anderson School of Management: JUDY OLIAN
David Geffen School of Medicine: GERALD S. LEVEY

School of Nursing: MARIE J. COWAN
School of Public Affairs: BARBARA NELSON
School of Public Health: LINDA ROSENSTOCK
School of Theater, Film and Television: ROBERT ROSEN
Continuing Education and UCLA Extension: CATHY SANDEEN
Graduate Div.: CLAUDIA MITCHELL-KERNAN

CHAIRPERSONS OF DEPARTMENTS

Arts and Architecture (303 East Melnitz, Box 951427, Los Angeles, CA 90095-1427; tel. (310) 206-6465; fax (310) 206-8504; e-mail webmaster@arts.ucla.edu; internet www.arts.ucla.edu):

Architecture and Urban Design: Prof. RICHARD WEINSTEIN (acting)
Art: BARBARA DRUCKER
Design: VICTORIA VESNA
Ethnomusicology and Systematic Musicology: TIM RICE
Music: IAN KROUSE
World Arts and Cultures: DAVID GERE

Education and Information Studies (Moore Hall, Box 951521, 405 Hilgard Ave, Los Angeles, CA 90095-1521; tel. (310) 825-8326; fax (310) 794-4732; e-mail info@gseis.ucla.edu; internet www.gseis.ucla.edu):

Education: SANDRA GRAHAM
Information Studies: VIRGINIA WALTER

Engineering and Applied Science (7400 Boelter Hall, Box 951600, Los Angeles, CA 90095-1600; tel. (310) 825-2938; fax (310) 206-4061; e-mail mori@ea.ucla.edu; internet www.engineer.ucla.edu):

Bioengineering: Prof. CARLO D. MONTEMAGNO
Chemical Eng.: Prof. VASILOS MANOUSIOUTHAKIS
Civil and Environmental Eng.: Prof. WILLIAM W-G. YEH
Computer Science: Prof. MILOS D. ERCEGOVAC
Electrical Eng.: Prof. YAHYA RAHMAT-SAMII
Materials Science and Eng.: Prof. MARK GOORSKY
Mechanical and Aerospace Eng.: Prof. H. THOMAS HAHN

Letters and Science (1312 Murphy Hall, Box 143801, Los Angeles, CA 90095-1438; tel. (310) 825-9009; fax (310) 825-9368; e-mail webadmin@college.ucla.edu; internet www.college.ucla.edu):

Aerospace Studies: Lt Col ANTHONY LEPPELLERE
Anthropology: DOUGLAS HOLLAN
Applied Linguistics and TESL: LYLE BACHMAN
Art History: CECELIA KLEIN
Asian Languages and Cultures: GREGORY SCHOPEN
Atmospheric Sciences: LARRY LYONS
Cesar Chavez Center: REYNALDO MACIAS
Chemistry and Biochemistry: HAROLD MARTINSON
Classics: ROBERT GURVAL
Earth and Space Sciences: DAVID JACKSON
Ecology and Evolution: VICTORIA SORK
Econ.: DAVID LEVINE
English: THOMAS WORTHAM
French: FRANÇOISE LIONNET
Geography: GLEN MACDONALD
Germanic Languages: ANDREW HEWITT
History: TEOFILO RUIZ
Italian: MASSIMO CIAVOLELLA
Linguistics: TIMOTHY STOWELL
Mathematics: JAMES RALSTON
Microbiology and Molecular Genetics: JEFFREY MILLER
Military Science: Maj. SHAUN BUCK
Molecular, Cell and Developmental Biology: UTPAL BANERJEE
Musicology: ROBERT A. WALSER
Naval Science: Col STEPHEN HUBBLE

Near Eastern Languages and Cultures: WILLIAM SCHNIEDEWIND
Philosophy: CALVIN NORMORE
Physics and Astronomy: JOSEPH RUDNICK
Physiological Science: ART ARNOLD
Political Science: MICHAEL LOFCHIE
Psychology: ROBERT BJORK
Slavic Languages and Literatures: RONALD VROON
Sociology: DAVID LOPEZ
Spanish and Portuguese: JOHN DAGENAIS
Speech: NEIL MALAMUTH
Statistics: JAN DE LEEUW

Medicine (12-138 CHS, Box 951722, Los Angeles, CA 90095-1722; tel. (310) 825-6373; fax (310) 206-5046; e-mail trelease@ucla.edu; internet www.medsch.ucla.edu):

Anaesthesiology: PATRICIA KAPUR
Biological Chemistry: S. LAWRENCE ZIPURSKY
Biomathematics: ELLIOT LANDAW
Family Medicine: PATRICK DOWLING
Human Genetics: KENNETH LANGE
Medicine: ALAN FOGELMAN
Microbiology and Immunology: JEFFERY F. MILLER
Molecular and Medical Pharmacology: MICHAEL PHELPS
Neurobiology: MARIE-FRANÇOISE CHESSELET
Neurology: JOHN MAZZIOTTA
Obstetrics and Gynaecology: GAUTAM CHAUDHURI
Ophthalmology: BARTLY MONDINO
Orthopaedic Surgery: GERALD FINERMAN
Pathology and Laboratory Medicine: JONATHAN BRAUN
Paediatrics: EDWARD MCCABE
Physiology: KENNETH PHILIPSON
Psychiatry and Biobehavioural Sciences: PETER WHYBROW
Radiation Oncology: H. RODNEY WITHERS
Radiological Sciences: DIETER ENZMANN
Surgery: RONALD BUSUTTIL
Urology: JEAN DE KERNION

Public Health (16-071 CHS, Box 951772, Los Angeles, CA 90095-1772; tel. (310) 825-5524; fax (310) 825-8440; internet www.ph.ucla.edu):

Biostatistics: WILLIAM G. CUMBERLAND
Community Health Sciences: DONALD MORISKY
Environmental Health Sciences: CURTIS ECKHERT
Epidemiology: ROGER DETELS
Health Services: ROBERT KAPLAN

Public Policy and Social Research (3250 Public Policy Building, Box 951656, Los Angeles, CA 90095-1656; tel. (310) 825-3792; fax (310) 206-5773; e-mail emooreb@ucla.edu; internet www.sppsr.ucla.edu):

Policy Studies: MARK A. PETERSON
Social Welfare: STUART KIRK
Urban Planning: A. LOUKAITOU-SIDERIS

Theatre, Film and Television (Student Services, 103 E. Melnitz, Box 951622, Los Angeles, CA 90095-1622; tel. (310) 825-8787; fax (310) 825-3383; e-mail frontoffice@emelnitz.ucla.edu; internet www.tft.ucla.edu):

Film and Television: BARBARA BOYLE
Theatre: WILLIAM WARD

DIRECTORS OF ORGANIZED RESEARCH INSTITUTES

School of the Arts and Architecture:

Center for Intercultural Performance: Prof. JUDY MITOMA
Fowler Museum of Arts and Cultures: MARLA C. BERNS
Grunwald Center for the Graphic Arts: DAVID RODES
UCLA Hammer Museum: ANN PHILBIN

School of Dentistry:

Dental Research Institute: Dr DAVID WONG

Graduate School of Education and Information Studies:

Center for Entrepreneurial Leadership Clearinghouse on Entrepreneurship Education: Dr ARTHUR M. COHEN
Center for Int. and Devt Education: Prof. JOHN N. HAWKINS
Center for the Study of Evaluation (member of National Center for Research on Evaluation, Standards and Student Testing): Prof. EVA BAKER, Dr JOAN L. HERMAN (co-directors)
CONNECT: Center for Research and Innovation in Elementary Education: FREDERICK ERICKSON
Corrine A. Seeds University Elementary School: DONNA L. ELDER
Higher Education Research Institute: Dr ALEXANDER W. ASTIN
Teacher Education Program: ELOISE LOPEZ METCALFE

Henry Samuel School of Engineering and Applied Science:

California NanoSystems Institute (operated in collaboration with UC Santa Barbara): Prof. EVELYN HU (acting director, from UCSB: Prof. J. FRASER STODDART (acting co-director, from UCLA)
Center for Embedded Network Sensing: Prof. DEBORAH ESTIN
Fusion Science and Technology Center: Prof. MOHAMED ABDOU

College of Letters and Sciences:

Basic Plasma Science Facility: WALTER GEKELMAN
California Center for Population Research: DUNCAN THOMAS
Center for American Politics and Public Policy: Prof. JOEL D. ABERBACH
Center for Communications and Community: Prof. FRANKLIN D. GILLIAM, Jr
Center for Comparative Social Analysis: REBECCA EMIGH
Center for Digital Humanities: (vacant)
Center for Jewish Studies: DAVID MYERS
Center for Language, Interaction and Culture: Prof. ALESSANDRO DURANTI
Center for Medieval and Renaissance Studies: HENRY ANSGAR KELLY
Center for Modern and Contemporary Studies: Prof. VINCENT P. PECORA
Center for 17th- and 18th-Century Studies: PETER H. REILL
Center for Research in Society and Politics: MARTIN GILENS
Center for Social Theory and Comparative History: Prof. ROBERT P. BRENNER
Center for the Study of Religion: Prof. SCOTT BARTCHY
Center for the Study of Urban Poverty: Prof. ABEL VALENZUELA
Center for the Study of Women: CHRISTINE LITTLETON
Clark Library: PETER H. REILL
Cognitive Science Research Program: Prof. PHIL KELLMAN
Cotsen Institute of Archaeology: Prof. CHARLES S. STANISH
Humanities Consortium: Prof. VINCENT P. PECORA
Institute for Pure and Applied Mathematics: Dr MARK GREEN
Institute for Social Science Research: DAVID O. SEARS
Institute of Geophysics and Planetary Physics: JOHN VIDALE
Institute of Radiation and Remote Sensing: Prof. K. N. LIOU
Marine Science Center: Dr WILLIAM HAMNER
Molecular Biology Institute: Prof. STEVEN G. CLARKE
National Center for History in the Schools: Prof. GARY B. NASH

Plasma Science and Technology Institute: Prof. GEORGE J. MORALES
Stunt Ranch Santa Monica Mountains Reserve: Prof. PHILIP RUNDEL
Survey Research Center: EVE FIELDER

Anderson School of Management:

Center for Health Services Management: Prof. PAUL TORRENS
Center for Int. Business Education and Research: Prof. BHAGWAN CHOWDHRY
Center for Management in the Information Economy: Prof. UDAY KARMARKAR
Harold Price Center for Entrepreneurial Studies: ALFRED E. OSBOURNE, Jr
Information Systems Research Program: Prof. E. BURTON SWANSON
Richard S. Ziman Center for Real Estate: Prof. WALTER N. TOROUS
UCLA Anderson Forecast Center: Prof. EDWARD E. LEARNER

School of Medicine:

AIDS Institute: Prof. IRVIN CHEN
Brain Research Institute: Dr CHRISTOPHER EVANS
Crump Institute for Molecular Imaging: Dr MICHAEL PHELPS
CURE: Digestive Diseases Research Center: Prof. JUAN ENRIQUE ROZENGURT
Jonsson Comprehensive Cancer Center: Prof. PATRICIA GANZ
Jules Stein Eye Institute: Prof BARTLY J. MONDINO
Neuropsychiatric Institute: Dr PETER C. WHYBROW

School of Public Affairs:

Center for Communication Policy: JEFFREY COLE
Center for Globalization and Policy Research: HELMUT ANHEIER
Center for Health Policy Research: Prof. E. RICHARD BROWN
Center for Int. Science, Technology and Cultural Policy: LYNNE G. ZUCKER
Center for Policy Research on Aging: Dr FERNANDO TORRES-GIL
Institute of Industrial Relations: RUTH MILKMAN
Institute of Transportation Studies: Dr BRIAN TAYLOR
North American Integration and Devt Center: Dr LEO F. ESTRADA
Ralph and Goldy Lewis Center for Regional Policy Studies: Prof. PAUL ONG

DIRECTORS OF INDEPENDENT UNITS

American Indian Studies Center: Prof. HANAY GEIOGAMAH
Asian-American Studies Center: Prof. DON T. NAKANISHI
Center for African-American Studies: Prof. DARNELL M. HUNT
Chicano Studies Research Center: Prof. REYNALDO MACIAS

DIRECTORS OF INTERNATIONAL STUDIES AND OVERSEAS PROGRAMMES

Asia Institute: R. BIN WONG
James C. Coleman African Studies Center: Prof. ALLEN F. ROBERTS
Center for Chinese Studies: Prof. RICHARD BAUM
Center for European and Eurasian Studies: Prof. IVAN BEREND
Gustave Von Grunebaum Center for Near Eastern Studies: LEONARD BINDER
Center for Japanese Studies: Prof. FRED NOTEHELFER
Ronald W. Burkle Center for Int. Relations: Prof. GEOFFREY GARRETT
Education Abroad Program: Prof. VAL RUST
Center for Korean Studies: JOHN DUNCAN
Language Resource Center: OLGA KAGAN
Latin American Center: Prof. CARLOS TORRES

University of California, Merced

POB 2039, Merced, CA 95344

Telephone: (209) 228-4400

Internet: www.ucmerced.edu

Founded 2005

Chancellor: SUNG-MO (STEVE) KANG (acting)
Exec. Vice-Chancellor and Provost: KEITH E. ALLEY (acting)
Vice-Chancellor for Admin.: MARY E. MILLER
Vice-Chancellor for Research: SAMUEL TRAINA
Vice-Chancellor for Student Affairs: JANE FIORI LAWRENCE
Vice-Chancellor for Univ. Relations: JOHN GARAMENDI
Chief Information Officer: RICHARD M. KOGUT
Univ. Librarian: R. BRUCE MILLER

Number of teachers: 80
Number of students: 1,200

DEANS

School of Eng.: JEFF R. WRIGHT
School of Natural Sciences: MARIA G. PALLAVICINI
School of Social Sciences, Humanities and Arts: HANS BJÖRNSSON
Graduate Studies: SAMUEL TRAINA (acting)

School of Engineering: POB 2039, Merced, CA 95343; tel. (209) 228-4411; e-mail engineering@ucmerced.edu; internet eng.ucmerced.edu.

School of Natural Sciences: POB 2039, Los Angeles, CA 95344; tel. (209) 228-4309; e-mail naturalsciences@ucmerced.edu; internet naturalsciences.ucmerced.edu.

School of Social Sciences, Humanities and Arts: tel. (209) 228-7742; fax (209) 228-4007; internet ssha.ucmerced.edu.

ATTACHED RESEARCH INSTITUTES

Sierra Nevada Research Institute (SNRI): tel. (209) 724-4311; e-mail straina@ucmerced.edu; internet www.ucmerced.edu/research/snri.asp; interdisciplinary research in natural sciences, Eng. and policy sciences; Dir Dr SAMUEL TRAINA.

World Cultures Institute: tel. (209) 724-4335; e-mail ssha@ucmerced.edu; internet www.ucmerced.edu/research/wci.asp; combines humanities, arts and social sciences to research migration and impact on established peoples and resources.

University of California, Riverside

900 University Ave, Riverside, CA 92521

Telephone: (909) 787-1012

Fax: (909) 787-3866

Internet: www.ucr.edu

Founded 1954

State control

Academic year: September to June

Chancellor: Dr FRANCE A. CÓRDOVA
Exec. Vice-Chancellor and Provost: Dr ELLEN WARTELLA
Vice-Chancellor for Public Service and Int. Programs: JOHN F. AZZARETTO
Vice-Chancellor for Research: Dr CHARLES F. LOUIS
Vice-Chancellor for Academic Planning and Budget: GRETCHEN BOLAR
Vice-Chancellor for Admin.: AL DIAZ
Vice-Chancellor for Student Affairs: JAMES W. SANDOVAL
Vice-Chancellor for University Advancement: Dr WILLIAM G. BOLT
Registrar: ELIZABETH C. BENNETT
Univ. Librarian: Dr RUTH JACKSON

Library: see Libraries
Number of teachers: 615 f.t.e.
Number of students: 15,934

DEANS

College of Natural and Agricultural Sciences: DONALD COOKSEY

College of Humanities, Arts and Social Science: STEPHEN CULLENBERG

A. Gary Anderson Graduate School of Management: ANIL DEOLALIKAR

Graduate School of Education: STEVEN BOSSERT

Marlan and Rosemary Burns College of Eng.: REZA ABBASCHIAN

Div. of Biomedical Sciences: CRAIG V. BYUS

Graduate Div.: DALLAS L. RABENSTEIN

University Extension: SHEILA DWIGHT

University of California, San Diego

9500 Gilman Drive, MC 0001, La Jolla, CA 92093-0001

Telephone: (858) 534-2230

Fax: (858) 534-5355

Internet: ucsd.edu

Became part of the University of California system 1960

Academic year: September to June

Chancellor: MARYE ANNE FOX

Sr Vice-Chancellor for Academic Affairs: MARSHA CHANDLER

Vice-Chancellor for Business Affairs: STEVEN W. RELYEA

Vice-Chancellor for External Relations: V. WAYNE KENNEDY

Vice-Chancellor for Health Sciences and Dean of the School of Medicine: DAVID BRENNER

Vice-Chancellor for Marine Sciences and Director of Scripps Institution of Oceanography: TONY HAYMET

Vice-Chancellor for Research: ARTHUR ELLIS

Vice-Chancellor for Resource Management and Planning: GARY MATTHEWS

Vice-Chancellor for Student Affairs: JOSEPH WATSON

Provost of Revelle College: DANIEL WULBERT

Provost of John Muir College: SUSAN SMITH (acting)

Provost of Thurgood Marshall College: ALLAN HAVIS

Provost of Earl Warren College: STEVEN ADLER

Provost of Eleanor Roosevelt College: ANN CRAIG

Provost of Sixth College: GABRIELE WIENHAUSEN

Registrar and Admissions Officer: FRED ATCHISON (acting)

Librarian: BRIAN SCHOTTLAENDER

Number of teachers: 1,611

Number of students: 26,876

Publication: *USCD Perspectives*

DEANS

Arts and Humanities: MICHAEL A. BERNSTEIN (acting)

Biological Sciences: SURESH SUBRAMANI

Physical Sciences: MARK H. THIEMENS

Social Sciences: PAUL DRAKE

Natural Sciences: MARK THIEMENS

Graduate School of Int. Relations and Pacific Studies: PETER COWHEY

Graduate Studies: KIM BARRETT

Jacobs School of Eng.: FRIEDER SEIBLE

Preuss School: DORIS ALVAREZ

Rady Graduate School of Management: ROBERT SULLIVAN

School of Medicine: DAVID A. BRENNER

Skaggs School of Pharmacy and Pharmaceutical Sciences: PALMER TAYLOR

UCSD Extension: MARY LINDENSTEIN WALSHOK

CHAIRPERSONS OF DEPARTMENTS

Anthropology: M. SHOENINGER

Bioengineering: S. CHIEN

Cell and Developmental Biology: R. FIRTEL

Chemistry and Biochemistry: C. KUBIAK

Cognitive Science: R. BELEW

Communication: R. HORWITZ

Computer Science and Eng.: R. PATURI

Ecology, Behaviour and Evolution Biology: L. CHAO

Econ.: R. CARSON

Electrical and Computer Eng.: P. YU

Ethnic Studies: R. ALVAREZ

History: D. VICKERS

Linguistics: R. KLUENDER

Literature: T. KONTJE

Mathematics: B. DRIVER

Mechanics and Aerospace Eng.: P. LINDEN

Molecular Biology: J. KADONAGA

Music: J. FONVILLE

Neurobiology: W. KRISTAN

Philosophy: P. CHURCHLAND

Physics: B. MAPLE

Political Science: G. COX

Psychology: J. WIXTED

Scripps Institution of Oceanography: M. HENDERSHOTT

Sociology: A. SCULL

Structural Eng.: A. ELGAMAL

Theatre and Dance: C. OATES

Visual Arts: S. FAGIN

School of Medicine:

Anaesthesiology: J. DRUMMOND

Family and Medicine: R. KAPLAN

Medicine: K. KAUSHANSKY

Neurosciences: L. THAL

Ophthalmology: S. BROWN

Orthopaedics: S. GARFIN

Paediatrics: S. MENDOZA

Pathology: D. BAILEY

Pharmacology: P. TAYLOR

Psychiatry: L. JUDD

Radiology: G. LEOPOLD

Reproductive Medicine: T. MOORE

Surgery: A. MOOSSA

University of California, San Francisco

3rd and Parnassus Aves, San Francisco, CA 94143

Telephone: (415) 476-9000

Fax: (415) 476-9634

Internet: www.ucsf.edu

Founded 1873

Chancellor: J. MICHAEL BISHOP

Exec. Vice-Chancellor and Provost: A. EUGENE WASHINGTON

Sr Vice-Chancellor for Finance and Admin.: STEVE BARCLAY

Sr Vice-Chancellor for Univ. Advancement and Planning: BRUCE SPAULDING

Vice-Chancellor for Medical Affairs: DAVID KESSLER

Exec. Dir Institute for Biomedical Research: REGIS KELLY

Registrar: DOUGLAS CARLSON

Librarian: KAREN BUTTER

Library of 821,492 vols

Number of teachers: 2,051

Number of students: 4,051

DEANS

School of Dentistry: CHARLES BERTOLAMI

School of Medicine: DAVID KESSLER

School of Nursing: KATHLEEN DRACUP

School of Pharmacy: MARY-ANNE KODA-KIMBLE

Graduate Division: PATRICIA CALARCO

DIRECTORS

LPPI: CRAIG VAN DYKE

Center for Bioentrepreneurship and Industry Partnerships: GAIL SCHECHTER

Proctor Foundation: TODD MARGOLIS

University of California, Santa Barbara

Santa Barbara, CA 93106

Telephone: (805) 893-8000

Internet: www.ucsb.edu

Founded 1909; became part of the University of California 1944

Academic year: September to June

Chancellor: HENRY T. YANG

Exec. Vice-Chancellor: GLENN E. LUCAS

Vice-Chancellor for Admin. Services: DONNA J. CARPENTER (acting)

Vice-Chancellor for Institutional Advancement: JOHN WIEMANN

Vice-Chancellor (Research): STEVEN D. GAINES (acting)

Vice-Chancellor (Student Affairs): MICHAEL D. YOUNG

Assistant Chancellor (Budget and Planning): TODD G. LEE

Associate Vice-Chancellor (Academic Personnel): ARTHUR GOSSARD

Associate Vice-Chancellor for Academic Programs: RONALD W. TOBIN

Associate Vice-Chancellor for Diversity, Equity and Academic Policy: MARIA HERRERA-SOBEK

Associate Vice-Chancellor for Academic Affairs: JODY KAUFMAN

Registrar: VIRGINIA K. JOHNS (acting)

Univ. Librarian: SARAH M. PRITCHARD

Library of 3,228,557 vols, serial backfiles and govt documents, 3,753,711 microforms, 23,218 current periodicals, 306,334 audio recordings, 5,529 video recordings

Number of teachers: 1,033

Number of students: 21,026

DEANS

College of Creative Studies: BRUCE TIFFNEY

Gevirtz Graduate School of Education: JANE CONOLEY (acting)

College of Eng.: MATTHEW V. TIRRELL

Donald Bren School of Environmental Science and Management: ERNST VON WEIXSÄCKER

Graduate Division: (vacant)

Humanities and Fine Arts: Dr DAVID MARSHALL

Mathematical, Life and Physical Sciences: MARTIN MOSKOVITS

Social Sciences: Dr MELVIN OLIVER

Undergraduate Studies: ALAN WYNER

HEADS OF DEPARTMENTS

Graduate School of Education (tel. (805) 893-2137; internet www.education.ucsb.edu):

Education: CHUCK BAZERMAN (Chair.)

College of Engineering (tel. (805) 893-2809; fax (805) 893-8124; internet www.engineering.ucsb.edu):

Chemical Eng.: GARY LEAL (Chair.)

Electrical and Computer Eng.: UMESH MISHRA (acting) (Chair.)

Materials: FRED LANGE (Chair.)

Mechanical and Environmental Eng.: ECKART MELBURG (Chair.)

Computer Science: LINDA PETZOLD (Chair.)

College of Letters and Science (tel. (805) 893-2038; fax (805) 893-7654; internet www.ltsc.ucsb.edu):

Anthropology: MICHAEL GLASSOW (Chair.)

Art Museum: Dr BONNIE G. KELM (Dir)

Art Studio: KIP FULBECK (Chair.)

Asian American Studies: DOUGLAS DANIELS (Chair.)

Biomolecular Science and Eng.: PHILIP PINCUS (Chair.)

Black Studies: FRANCISCO LOMELI (Chair.)

Chemistry and Biochemistry: ALEC WODTKE (Chair.)

Chicano Studies: CHELA SANDOVAL (Chair.)

Classics: ROBERT MORSTEIN-MARX (Chair.)

Communication: MICHAEL STOHL (Chair.)

Comparative Literature: SUSAN DERWIN (Dir)

Computer Eng.: MALGORZATA MAREK-SADOWSKA (Dir)

Dramatic Art/Dance: SIMON WILLIAMS (Chair.)

East Asian Languages and Cultural Studies: RON EGAN (Chair.)

Ecology, Evolution and Marine Biology: ROGER NISBIT (Chair.)

Econ.: PETER KUHN (Chair.)

English: WILLIAM WARNER (Chair.)

Environmental Studies: SUSAN STONICH (Chair.)

Film Studies: JANET WALKER (Chair.)

French and Italian: CATHERINE NESCI (Chair.)

Geography: KEITH CLARKE (Chair.)

Geological Sciences: JAMES MATTINSON (Chair.)

Germanic, Slavic and Semitic Languages: ELISABETH WEBER (Chair.)

Global and Int. Studies: MARK JUERGENSMEYER (Dir)

History: PAT COHEN (Chair.)

History of Art and Architecture: PETER STURMAN (Chair.)

Latin American and Iberian Studies: SARAH CLINE (Dir)

Law and Society: KATHLEEN MOORE (Chair.)

Linguistics: CAROL GENETTI (Chair.)

Mathematics: JOHN DOUGLAS MOORE (Chair.)

Media Arts and Technology: JOANN KUCHERA-MORIN (Chair.)

Medieval Studies: HARVEY SHARRER (Dir)

Military Science: LTC JOHN B. SIMPSON, III (Chair.)

Molecular, Cellular and Developmental Biology: CHARLES SAMUEL (Chair.)

Music: LEE ROTHFARB (Chair.)

Philosophy: ANTHONY ANDERSON (Chair.)

Physical Activities and Recreation: JON SPAVENTU (Dir)

Physics: S. JAMES ALLEN (Chair.)

Political Science: PETER DIGESER (Chair.)

Psychology: DIANE MACKIE (Chair.)

Religious Studies: DAVID WHITE (Chair.)

Renaissance Studies: MICHAEL O'CONNELL (Chair.)

Sociology: NOAH FRIEDKIN (Chair.)

Spanish and Portuguese: EDUARDO RAPOSO (Chair.)

Speech and Hearing Sciences: JEFFREY DANHAUER (Chair.)

Statistics and Applied Probability: RAISA FELDMAN (Chair.)

Women's Studies: LEILA RUPP (Chair.)

Writing Program: SUSAN MCLEOD (Dir)

ATTACHED RESEARCH INSTITUTES

Alzheimer's Disease Research Center: Dir Dr LESLIE WILSON.

Autism Research Center: Co-Dirs Prof. ROBERT KOEGEL, LYNN KOEGEL.

California NanoSystems Institute (CNSI): Dir EVELYN HU.

Center for Advanced Studies of Individual Differences: Dir MICHAEL GERBER.

Center for Biologically Inspired Nanocomposite Materials: Dir DANIEL MORSE.

Center for Black Studies: Dir ANNA EVERETT (acting).

Center for Chicano Studies: Dir Prof. CARLOS MORTON.

Center for Cold War Studies: Dir TSUYOSHI HASEGAWA.

Center for Communication and Social Policy: Dir EDWARD DONNERSTEIN.

Center for Control Engineering and Computation: Dir Prof. ANDREW TEAL.

Center for Educational Change in Mathematics and Science (CECIMS): Dir JULIAN WEISSGLASS.

Center for Equity in Mathematics and Science Education: Dir JULIE BIANCHINI.

Center for Evolutionary Psychology: Co-Dirs Prof. LEDA COSMIDES, Prof. JOHN TOOBY.

Center for Global Studies: Co-Dirs RICHARD APPELBAUM, BARBARA HARTHORN.

Center for Information Processing Research (CIPR): Dir ALLEN GERSHO.

Center for Information Technology and Society (CITS): Co-Dirs Prof. BRUCE BIMBER, KEVIN ALMEROTH.

Center for Middle East Studies: Co-Dirs Prof. STEPHEN HUMPHREYS, Prof. JUAN CAMPO.

Center for Multifunctional Materials and Structures: Dir ANTONY G. EVANS.

Center for Nonlinear Sciences: Dir BJORN BIRNIR.

Center for Polymers and Organic Solids: Dir Prof. GUILLERMO BAZAN.

Center for Portuguese Studies (CPS): Dir JOÃO CAMILO-DOS-SANTOS.

Center for Research in Electronic Art Technology (CREATE): Dir Prof. JOANN KUCHERA-MORIN.

Center for Risk Studies and Safety: Dir Prof. THEOFANIS G. THEOFANOUS.

Center for Spatially Integrated Social Science (CSISS): Program Dirs MICHAEL GOODCHILD, RICHARD APPELBAUM.

Center for the Study of Macular Degeneration (CSMD): Dir Dr DON H. ANDERSON.

Center for the Study of Neurodegenerative Disorders (CSND): Dir Dr CYNTHIA HUSTED.

Center for Spintronics and Quantum Computation: Dir Prof. DAVID D. AWSCHALOM.

Center for the Study of Religion: Dir WADE CLARK ROOF.

Center for the Study of Sexual Minorities in the Military (CSSMM): Chair, Board of Advisors AARON BELKIN.

Center for Teaching for Social Justice: Dir JUDITH GREEN.

Center for Terahertz Science and Technology: Dir MARK SHERWIN.

Center on Police Practices and Community (COPPAC): Exec. Dirs Dr HOWARD GILES, DANIEL LINZ.

Coastal Research Center: Dir RUSSELL SCHMITT.

Cultures Project: Dir WILLIAM WARNER.

East Asia Center: Co-Dirs MARK ELIOT, LUKE ROBERTS.

Geography Remote Sensing Unit: Dir KEITH CLARKE.

Gevirtz Research Center (Gevirtz Graduate School of Education): Exec. Dir Dr VISHNA A. HERRITY.

Automated Vital Statistics System (AVSS): Dir RONALD WILLIAMS.

High-Performance Composites Center (HPCC): Dir Prof. FRANK ZOK.

Institute for Computational Earth Systems Science (ICESS): Dir Prof. DAVID SIEGEL.

Institute for Crustal Studies (ICS): Dir Prof. DOUGLAS W. BURBANK.

Institute for Quantum Engineering, Science and Technology (iQUEST): Dir MARK SHERWIN.

Institute for Social, Behavioural and Economic Research (ISBER): Dir Dr RICHARD P. APPELBAUM.

Interdisciplinary Center for Wide Bandgap Semiconductors: Dir Prof. JAMES SPECK.

Interdisciplinary Humanities Center (IHC): Dir Prof. RICHARD HEBDIGE.

Kavli Institute for Theoretical Physics (KITP): Dir Prof. DAVID GROSS.

Marine Biotechnology Center: Dir DANIEL MORSE.

Marine Science Institute (MSI): Dir Prof. STEVEN D. GAINES.

Materials Research Laboratory (MRL): Dir Prof. CRAIG HAWKER.

MesoAmerican Research Center (MARC): Dir ANABEL FORD.

Mitsubishi Chemical Center for Advanced Materials (MC-CAM): Dir Prof. GLENN H. FREDRICKSON.

National Nanotechnology Infrastructure Network (NINN): Dir MARK RODWELL.

National Center for Ecological Analysis and Synthesis (NCEAS): Dir Prof. O. JAMES REICHMAN.

National Center for Geographic Information and Analysis (NCGIA): Dir, UCSB Dr KEITH C. CLARKE.

Neuroscience Research Institute (NRI): Dir Dr STUART FEINSTEIN.

Ocean and Coastal Policy Center: Deputy Dir MICHAEL MCGINNIS.

Ocean Physics Laboratory (OPL): Dir Prof. TOMMY D. DICKEY.

Optoelectronics Technology Center (OTC): Dir Prof. LARRY A. COLDREN.

Research Center for Virtual Environments and Behavior (RECVEB): Co-Dirs Dr JAMES BLASCOVICH, Prof. ANDREW BEALL.

Research Unit on Spatial Cognition and Choice (RUSSC): Dir Prof. REGINALD G. GOLLEDGE.

Social Science Survey Center (SSSC): Dir Dr JON SONSTELIE.

Solid State Lighting and Display Center: Dir Prof. SHUJI NAKAMURA.

Southern California Earthquake Center (SC/EC): Board Representative, UCSB DOUG BURBANK (Dir).

University of California Linguistic Minority Research Institute (UC/LMRI): Dir Prof. RUSSELL RUMBERGER.

UCSB Natural Reserve System: Dir WILLIAM MURDOCH.

University of California Digital Cultures Project (UC/MRG): Dir Prof. WILLIAM BEATTY WARNER.

Walter Capps Center for the Study of Religion and Public Life: Dir WADE CLARKE ROOF.

University of California, Santa Cruz

1156 High St, Santa Cruz, CA 95064

Telephone: (831) 459-0111
Fax: (831) 459-0146
Internet: www.ucsc.edu

Founded 1962

Academic year: September to June

Chancellor: GEORGE BLUMENTHAL (acting)

Campus Provost and Exec. Vice-Chancellor: DAVID S. KLIGER

Vice-Provost for Academic Affairs: ALISON GALLOWAY

Vice-Provost and Dean of Undergraduate Education: WILLIAM A. LADUSAW

Vice-Provost and Dean of University Extension: CARL E. WALSH

Vice-Chancellor for Business and Admin. Services: THOMAS M. VANI

Vice-Chancellor for Planning and Budget: MEREDITH MICHAELS

Vice-Chancellor for Research: BRUCE MARGON

Vice-Chancellor for Student Affairs: SUSAN HANSEN (acting)

Vice-Chancellor for Univ. Relations: DONNA M. MURPHY

Exec. Director of Admissions and University Registrar: KEVIN BROWNE

Univ. Librarian: VIRGINIA STEEL

Library of 1,350,000 vols, 15,000 periodicals, 800,000 microforms, 500 other items (maps, slides, audio and visual recordings)

Number of teachers: 542 (ladder-rank faculty)

Number of students: 15,013

Publication: *The Cultivar* (2 a year)

DEANS

Arts: EDWARD F. HOUGHTON

Eng.: SUNG MO (STEVE) KANG

Humanities: GEORGE VAN DEN ABBEELE

Physical and Biological Sciences: STEPHEN THORSETT

Social Sciences: SHELDON KAMIENIECKI

Graduate Studies: LISA C. SLOAN

DIRECTORS OF INSTITUTES

Particle Physics: ABRAHAM SEIDEN

Marine Sciences: GARY B. GRIGGS

Geophysics and Planetary Physics: A. CHRISTINA RAVELO

UCO/Lick Observatory: MICHAEL J. BOLTE

PROVOSTS

Cowell College: Prof. WILLIAM LADUSAW

Stevenson College: MARGO HENDRICKS

Crown College: F. JOEL FERGUSON

Merrill College: JOHN SCHECHTER

Porter College: DAVID EVAN JONES

Kresge College: CONN HALLINAN

Oakes College: PEDRO CASTILLO

College Eight: ANDREW SZASZ

College Nine: CAMPBELL LEAPER

College Ten: CAMPBELL LEAPER

RESEARCH UNITS

Center for Adaptive Optics: Dir Prof. JERRY NELSON.

Center for Agroecology and Sustainable Food Systems: Dir CAROL SHENNAN.

Centre for Biomedical Science and Engineering: Dir Prof. DAVID HAUSSLER.

Center for Cultural Studies: Co-Dirs CHRIS CONNERY, GAIL HERSHATTER.

Center for Global, International and Regional Studies: Dir PAUL LUBECK.

Center for Information Technology Research in the Interest of Society: Dirs Prof. RUZENA BAJCSY (UCB), PATRICK MANTEY (CITRIS Affiliate Dir).

Center for Justice, Tolerance and Community: Dir Prof. MANUEL PASTOR.

Center for Research on Education, Diversity and Excellence: Dir ROLAND THARP.

Chicano/Latino Research Center: Co-Dirs PATRICIA ZAVELLA, OLGA NÁJERA-RAMÍREZ.

Institute of Geophysics and Planetary Physics: Dir A. CHRISTINA RAVELO.

Institute of Marine Sciences: Dir GARY B. GRIGGS.

Lick Observatory: Dir Prof. MICHAEL J. BOLTE.

Santa Cruz Institute for Particle Physics: Dir Prof. ABRAHAM SEIDEN.

UNIVERSITY OF JUDAISM

15600 Mulholland Dr., Bel Air, CA 90077

Telephone: (310) 476-9777

E-mail: admissions@uj.edu

Internet: www.uj.edu

Founded 1947

Private control

Academic year: August to May

Pres.: Dr ROBERT WEXLER

Vice-Pres. for Academic Affairs: Dr LOIS HECHT OPPENHEIM

Sr Vice-Pres. and Provost: Dr MARK BOOKMAN

Vice-Pres. for Business, Admin. and Technology: ZOFIA YALOVSKY

Vice-Pres. for Continuing Education and Extended Univ.: GLADY LEVY

Vice-Pres. for Devt: Rabbi JAY LEAR

Rector: Rabbi Dr ELLIOT DORFF

Registrar: JHONE DANIELS

Library Dir: PAUL MILLER

Library of 120,000 vols

DEANS

College of Arts and Sciences: Dr LOIS HECHT OPPENHEIM

Department of Continuing Education: GADY LEVY

Graduate Programs: NINA LIEBERMAN-GILADI

Fingerhut School of Education: RAMI WERNIK (acting)

Ziegler School of Rabbinic Studies: Rabbi BRADLEY SHAVIT ARTSON

DIRECTORS

Graduate Programs in Nonprofit Management: Dr BERYL GEBER

Whizin Center: Dr RONALD WOLFSON

UNIVERSITY OF LA VERNE

1950 Third St, La Verne, CA 91750

Telephone: (909) 593-3511

Fax: (909) 953-0965

Internet: www.ulv.edu

Founded 1891 as Lordsburg College; became La Verne College in 1917; present name 1977

9 Regional campuses

Private control

Academic year: September to June

Pres.: Dr STEPHEN MORGAN

Provost and Vice-Pres. for Academic Affairs: ROBERT NEHER

Exec. Vice-Pres.: PHILIP A. HAWKEY

Vice-Pres. for Enrollment Management: HOMA SHABAHANG

Vice-Pres. for Univ. Relations: JEAN BJERKE

Registrar: MARILYN DAVIES

Dean of Student Affairs: LORETTA RAHMANI

Librarian: TAYLOR RUHL

Library of 337,000 vols

Number of teachers: 220 (85 full-time, 135 part-time)

Number of students: 3,004

DEANS

College of Arts and Sciences: Prof. FRED YAFFE

School of Business and Public Management: GORDON J. BADOVICK

School of Education and Organization Leadership: LEONARD PELLICER

College of Law: Prof. DONALD DUNN

UNIVERSITY OF REDLANDS

1200 East Colton Ave, POB 3080, Redlands, CA 92373-0999

Telephone: (909) 793-2121

Fax: (909) 793-2029

Internet: www.redlands.edu

Founded 1907

Private

Pres.: STUART DORSEY

Chancellor: JAMES R. APPLETON

Vice-Pres. for Academic Affairs: Dr NANCY CARRICK

Sr Vice-Pres. for Finance and Admin.: PHILLIP DOOLITTLE

Vice-Pres. for Univ. Relations: RONALD STEPHANY

Registrar: CHARLOTTE LUCEY

Library Dir: JEAN SWANSON

Library of 233,882 vols

Number of teachers: 551

Number of students: 4,080

Publication: *Redlands*

DEANS

College of Arts and Sciences: Dr BARBARA JEAN MORRIS

School of Business: Dr STUART NOBLE-GOODMAN

School of Education: Dr PAM DWORAK

AFFILIATED CENTRES

Alfred North Whitehead College for Lifelong Learning: f. 1976; 2,150 students; Dean MARY BOYCE.

Johnston Center for Integrative Studies: tel. (909) 748-8615; f. 1969; 200 students; Dir Prof. KATHY OGREN.

UNIVERSITY OF SAN DIEGO

5998 Alcala Park, San Diego, CA 92110

Telephone: (619) 260-4600

E-mail: admissions@sandiego.edu

Internet: www.sandiego.edu

Founded 1949

Pres.: Dr MARY E. LYONS

Vice-Pres. and Provost: Dr JULIE SULLIVAN

Vice-Pres. for Finance and Admin.: PAUL E. BISSONNETTE

Vice-Pres. for Mission and Ministry: DANIEL DILLABOUGH

Vice-Pres. for Univ. Relations: Dr TIMOTHY O'MALLEY

Vice-Pres. for Student Affairs: CARMEN VAZQUEZ

Librarian: EDWARD STARKEY

Library of 300,000 vols and 2,200 current periodicals

Number of teachers: 508

Number of students: 7,000

Publications: *Law Review* (quarterly), *Contemporary Legal Issues* (1 or 2 a year), *Journal of International Law* (annual)

DEANS

School of Business Admin.: ANDREW ALLEN

School of Law: KEVIN COLE

School of Leadership and Education Sciences: Dr PAULA A. CORDEIRO

School of Nursing and Health Sciences: Prof. SALLY BROSZ HARDIN

School of Peace Studies: WILLIAM HEADLEY

College of Arts and Sciences: NICHOLAS M. HEALY

UNIVERSITY OF SAN FRANCISCO

2130 Fulton St, San Francisco, CA 94117-1080

Telephone: (415) 422-5555

Fax: (415) 422-2303

Internet: www.usfca.edu

Founded 1855

Private; Jesuit

Academic year: September to May

Pres.: STEPHEN A. PRIVETT

Provost and Vice-Pres. for Academic Affairs: Dr JAMES L. WISER

Chancellor: Rev. JOHN LO SCHIAVO

Vice-Pres. for Univ. Life: Dr MARGARET M. HIGGINS

Vice-Pres. for Int. Relations: STANLEY D. NEL

Vice-Pres. for Information Technology: TRACY SCHROEDER

Vice-Pres. for Univ. Advancement: DAVID F. MACMILLAN

Vice-Pres. for Business and Finance: CHARLIE CROSS

Dean of Students: FELICIA J. LEE

Dean of the Univ. Library: TYRONE H. CANNON

Library of 593,543 vols

Number of teachers: 290

Number of students: 8,568

Publication: *USF Law Review* (quarterly)

DEANS

Colleges of Arts and Sciences: Dr JENNIFER E. TURPIN

School of Business and Management: MICHAEL L. DUFFY

School of Law: Dr JEFFREY S. BRAND

School of Nursing: JUDITH F. KARSHNER

School of Education: Dr WALTER GMELCH

College of Professional Studies: Dr LARRY G. BREWSTER

UNIVERSITY OF SOUTHERN CALIFORNIA

University Park Campus, Los Angeles, CA 90089

Telephone: (213) 740-2311

Internet: www.usc.edu

Founded 1880

Academic year: August to May

Pres.: STEVEN B. SAMPLE

Provost and Sr Vice-Pres. for Academic Affairs: C. L. MAX NIKIAS

Sr Vice-Pres. for Admin.: TODD R. DICKEY

Sr Vice-Pres. for Finance: DENNIS F. DOUGHERTY

Sr Vice-Pres. for Univ. Relations: MARTHA HARRIS

Sr Vice-Pres. for Univ. Advancement: ALAN KREDITOR

Vice-Pres. for Capital Construction: CURT WILLIAMS

Vice-Pres. for External Relations: CAROLYN WEBB DE MACIAS

Vice-Pres. for Student Affairs: MICHAEL L. JACKSON

Vice-Pres. for Academic Planning and Budget: ELIZABETH GARRETT

Treas.: RUTH WERNIG

Univ. Sec.: CAROL MUNCH AMIR

Colleges of Letters, Arts and Sciences and Graduate School; 17 professional schools

Library: see Libraries and Archives

Number of teachers: 3,200 (full-time)

Number of students: 33,000

Publications: *USC Chronicle, USC Trojan Family* (quarterly)

DEANS

Leventhal School of Accounting: RANDOLPH P. BEATTY

Annenberg School for Communication: GEOFFREY COWAN

Thornton School of Music: ROBERT A. CUTIETTA

School of Cinematic Arts: ELIZABETH M. DALEY

Davis School of Gerontology: GERALD C. DAVISON

Marshall School of Business: JAMES G. ELLIS

School of Social Work: MARILYN FLYNN

Rossier School of Education: KAREN SYMMS GALLAGHER

Keck School of Medicine: BRIAN E. HENDERSON

School of Policy, Planning, and Devt: JACK H. KNOTT

School of Architecture: QUINGYUN MA

Gould School of Law: EDWARD J. MCCAFFERY

School of Theatre: MADELAINE PUZO

School of Dentistry: HAROLD C. SLAVKIN

College of Letters, Arts and Sciences: PETER STARR

School of Pharmacy: R. PETE VANDERVEEN

Roski School of Fine Arts: RUTH E. WEISBERG

Viterbi School of Eng.: YANNIS C. YORTSOS

PROFESSORS

Distinguished and University Professors:

ARBIB, MICHAEL A., Biological Sciences and Biomedical Eng.

ARMSTRONG, JR., LLOYD, Physics and Education

BENNIS, WARREN, Business Admin.

BRAUDY, LEO B., English and American Literature

CAPRON, ALEXANDER M., Law and Medicine

COHEN, MARSHALL, Emeritus of Philosophy and Law

COWAN, GEOFFREY, Communication Leadership

EASTERLIN, RICHARD A., Econ.

FINCH, CALEB, Gerontology and Biological Sciences

GOLOMB, SOLOMON W., Electrical Eng. and Mathematics

HELLWARTH, ROBERT W., Physics

JORDAN, THOMAS, Geophysics and Earth Sciences

KINDER, MARSHA, Comparative Literature

PIKE, MALCOLM CECIL, Preventive Medicine

SHIH, JEAN C., Cell and Neurobiology

STARR, KEVIN O., History and Policy, Planning and Devt

TIERNEY, WILLIAM G., Higher Education

TOULMIN, STEPHEN E., Anthropology, Int. Relations and Religion

WATERMAN, MICHAEL S., Biological Sciences and Mathematics

ARNHEIM, NORMAN, Biological Sciences

BENNIS, WARREN, English

CORAGHESSAN BOYLE, T., English

EVERETT, PERCIVAL, Cinematic Arts

HARRIS, MARK JONATHAN, Theory and Composition

HARTKE, STEPHEN, Preventive Medicine

HENDERSON, BRIAN E., Biochemistry and Molecular Biology

JONES, PETER A., Pediatrics

KAUFMAN, FRANCINE R., Molecular Microbiology and Immunology

LAI, MICHAEL M. C., Business

LAWLER, III, EDWARD E., Medicine

LEVINE, ALEXANDRA M., Chemistry

OLAH, GEORGE A., Medicine

RAHIMTOOLA, SHAHBUDIN H., Cardiothoracic Surgery

STARNES, VAUGHN A., Pharmaceutical Sciences

WOLF, MICHAEL A., Biological Sciences and Biomedical Eng.

School of Law:

ALTMAN, S. A.

ARMOUR, J. D.

BICE, S. H.

BRECHT, A. O.

CAPRON, A. M.

COWAN, G.

CRUZ, D. B.

DUDZIAK, M. L.

ESTRICH, S.

FINEGAN, E. J.

GARET, R. R.

GARRETT, E.

GILLMAN, H.

GRIFFITH, T. D.

GROSS, A. J.

HADFIELD, G.

KEATING, G. C.

KLERMAN, D. M.

KURAN, T.

LEFCOE, G.

LEVINE, M. L.

LYON, T. D.

MCCAFFERY, E. J.

MARMOR, A.

MURPHY, K. J.

SAKS, E. R.

SCHOR, H. M.

SHAPIRO, M. H.

SIMON, L. G.

SLAWSON, W. D.

SMITH, E. M.

SPITZER, M. L.

STOLZENBERG, N. M.

STONE, C. D.

TALLEY, E. L.

WHITEBREAD, C. H.

School of Medicine:

ADLER, R.

AHMADI, J.

AKMAL, M.

ALKANA, R.

ANDERSON, W.

ANN, D.

APUZZO, M.

ASKANAS, V.

AZEN, S.

BAEHNER, R.

BALLARD, C.

BEART JR, R.

BERGMAN, R.

BERNE, T.

BERNSTEIN, L.

BEYDOUN, S.

BONDAREFF, W.

BOYD, S.

BREMNER, C.

BRENNER, P.

BRINTON, R.

BROEK, D.

BUCHANAN, T.

CADENAS, E.

CAMPESE, V.

CHANDRASOMA, P.

CHUI, H.

CHUONG, C.-M.

CLARK, F.

COLLETTI, P.

CONTI, P.

COSTIN, G.

COTE, R.

CRAFT, C.

CRANDALL, E.

DANENBERG, P.

DE JUAN JR, E.

DE MEESTER, T.

DECLERCK, Y.

DEMETRIADES, D.

DENNERT, G.

DIZEREGA, G.

DUBEAU, L.

DWYER, J.

ELKAYAM, U.

EL-SHAHAWY, M.

ENGEL, W.

EPSTEIN, A.

FARLEY, R.

FEINSTEIN, D.

FRANK, G.

GAYNON, P.

GEFFNER, M.

GIANNOTTA, S.

GILL, P.

GILLES, F.

GILLILAND, F.

GILSANZ, V.

GOMER, C.
GONG JR, H.
GOODWIN, T.
GORAN, M.
GOVINDARAJAN, S.
GRANT, E.
GROFFEN, J.
GRUSHKIN, C.
HAHN, R.
HAILE, R.
HALLS, J.
HAMMOND, G.
HAYS, D.
HAYWOOD, L.
HEISTERKAMP, N.
HENDERSON, B.
HILL, A.
HINTON, D.
HODGMAN, J.
HODIS, H.
HOFMAN, F.
HOHN, A.
HORWITZ, D.
HSIEH, C.-L.
HUANG, H.
HUMAYUN, M.
HURVITZ, R.
ISRAEL, R.
IWAKI, Y.
JACOBS, R.
JELLIFFE, R.
JOHNSON, C.
JOHNSON, C.
JOHNSON, D.
JONES, P.
KALRA, V.
KAPLOWITZ, N.
KAPTEIN, E.
KAST, W. M.
KATKHOUDA, N.
KAUFMAN, F.
KEANE, J.
KEDES, L.
KEENS, T.
KILBURN, K.
KLONER, R.
KOHN, D.
KORSCH, B.
KOSS, M.
LAINE, L.
LAMB, H.
LAUG, W.
LAWLOR, M.
LEE, A.
LEVINE, A.
LEVY, D.
LEWIS, A.
LIEBER, M.
LIESKOVSKY, G.
LU, S.
LUMB, P.
MACK, T.
MAHOUR, G.
MARKLAND, F.
MARTIN, W.
MATTINGLY, C.
MAXSON, R.
McCOMB, J.
McDONOUGH, A.
McMILLAN, M.
McNEILL, T.
MEISELMAN, H.
MENDEZ, R.
MILLER, C.
MINCKLER, D.
MIRCHEFF, A.
MISHELL JR, D.
MISHRA, S.
MORROW, C.
MULL, J.
MURPHREE, A.
NATHWANI, B.
NELSON, M.
NEWTH, C.
NICOLOFF, J.
NIMNI, M.

O'LEARY, D.
OU, J.-H.
PARKMAN, R.
PATTENGALE, P.
PATZAKIS, M.
PAULSON, R.
PENTZ, M.
PETERS, J. M.
PIKE, M.
PLATZKER, A.
PORTNOY, B.
POWARS, D.
PRESS, M.
PRESTON-MARTIN, S.
QUISMORIO, F.
RADIN, D.
RAHIMTOOLA, S.
RALLS, P.
RAO, N.
RASHEED, S.
REYNOLDS, C.
RICE, D.
RICHARDSON, J.
ROSS, R.
ROY, S.
ROY-BURMAN, P.
RUDE, R.
RYAN JR, S.
SADUN, A.
SATTLER, F.
SCHECHTER, J.
SCHNEIDER, L.
SEEGER, R.
SEGALL, H.
SELBY, R.
SHARMA, O.
SHERWIN, R.
SHIBATA, D.
SHIH, J.
SHOUPE, D.
SHRIVASTAVA, P.
SHULMAN, I.
SIEGEL, M.
SIEGEL, S.
SILBERMAN, H.
SILKA, M.
SILVERSTEIN, M.
SINATRA, F.
SINGH, M.
SKINNER, D.
SMITH, R.
SOHAL, R.
SOKOL, R.
STALLCUP, M.
STANLEY, P.
STARNES, V.
STELLWAGEN, R.
STOHL, W.
STOHLMAN, S.
STRAM, D.
SUSSMAN, S.
TAKAHASHI, M.
TAYLOR, C.
TENG, E.
THOMAS, D.
THORDARSON, D.
TOKES, Z.
TOLO, V.
TRICHE, T.
TSUKAMOTO, H.
VANGSNESS JR, T.
VARMA, R.
VESELY, L.
WARBURTON, D.
WEAVER, F.
WEBER, J.
WEINBERG, K.
WEINER, L.
WEISS, M.
WETZEL, R.
WILLIAMS, R.
WOOD, B.
WOODLEY, D.
WU, P.
WU-WILLIAMS, A.
YELLIN, A.

YING, S.-Y.
YU, M.
ZEE, C.-S.
ZEIDLER, A.
ZELMAN, V.

School of Music:

BEER, H., Conducting
BERG, S., Jazz Studies
BROWN, B. A., Music History
CRAVENS, T., Winds and Percussion
CROCKETT, D., Composition
DEHNING, W., Choral and Sacred Music
GLAZE, G., Vocal Arts
GORDON, S., Keyboard Studies
HARTKE, S. N., Composition
HOPKINS, J. F., Composition
LAURIDSEN, II, M., Composition
LEONARD, R., Strings
LESEMANN, F., Composition
LIVINGSTON, L., Conducting
MASON, T. D., Jazz Studies
McCURDY, R. C., Jazz Studies
McINNES, D., Strings
PERRY, J., Keyboard Studies
POLLACK, D., Keyboard Studies
SCHOENFELD, E., Strings
SIMMS, B., Music History
THOMAS, W. E. L., Electro-Acoustic Media
TICHELI, IV, F., Composition
TYLER, J., Early Music Performance, Music
  History

School of Pharmacy:

ALKANA, R. L.
ANN, D.
BRINTON, R.
BURCKHART, G.
CADENAS, E.
CHAN, T. M.
JOHNSON, D.
SHEN, W.-C.
SHIH, J. C.
SOHAL, R.
STIMMEL, G. L.
WOLF, W.

School of Policy, Planning and Development:

BANERJEE, T.
CAIDEN, G.
COOPER, T.
FERRIS, J. M.
GABRIEL, S. A.
GIULIANO, G.
GORDON, P.
GRADDY, E.
GREENWALD, H.
HEIKKILA, E.
KREIGER, M. H.
LOPEZ-LEE, D.
MAZMANIAN, D.
MELNICK, G.
MYERS, D.
MYRTLE, R.
NEWLAND, C.
PACHON, H.
PETAK, W.
RICHARDSON, H.
SLOANE, D.
SUNDEEN, Jr, R.
TANG, S.-Y.
VON WINTERFELDT, D.
WHOLEY, J. S.

School of Social Work:

BREKKE, J.
CHI, I.
ELL, K.
FLYNN, M.
JANSSON, B.
McCROSKEY, J.
MONDROS, J.
MOR-BARAK, M.
STONER, M.
TRICKETT, P.

School of Theatre:

CARNICKE, S. M.

HOUSTON, V.
PUZO, M.
School of Gerontology:
BENGTSON, V. L.
BONDAREFF, W.
CRIMMINS, E.
DAVIES, K.
FINCH, C.
GATZ, M.
KNIGHT, R.
PYNOOS, J.
SCHNEIDER, E. L.
SCHNEIDER, L.
SILVERSTEIN, M.
WILBER, K.
ZELINSKI, E.

UNIVERSITY OF THE PACIFIC

3601 Pacific Ave, Stockton, CA 95211
Telephone: (209) 946-2344
E-mail: admissions@pacific.edu
Internet: www.uop.edu
Founded as California Wesleyan College
1851; name changed to Univ. of the Pacific
1852; consolidated with Napa College
1896; name changed to College of the
Pacific 1911; name changed to Univ. of
the Pacific 1961
Private control
Main campus in Stockton; McGeorge School
of Law in Sacramento; School of Dentistry
in San Francisco
Pres.: DONALD V. DEROSA
Provost: PHILIP N. GILBERTSON
Vice-Pres. for Business and Finance: PATRICK
CAVANAUGH
Vice-Pres. of Student Life: ELIZABETH GRIEGO
Vice-Pres. of Univ. Advancement: TED
LELAND
Assoc. Provost for Enrollment: THOMAS M.
RAJALA
Assoc. Provost and CIO: LAWRENCE FREDER-
ICK
Dean of the Library (vacant)
Library of 281,769 vols, 1,361 periodicals,
689,462 microforms
Number of teachers: 444 (all campuses)
Number of students: 6,000 (all campuses)
Publications: *Pacific Review*, *Pacific Histor-
ian*, *Pacifican*, *Contact Point* (Dental
School), *De Minimus* (School of Law)

DEANS

Eberhardt School of Business: CHUCK WIL-
LIAMS
School of Dentistry: PATRICK FERRILLO
Benerd School of Education: LYNN BECK
School of Eng. and Computer Science: RAVI
JAIN
School of Int. Studies: MARGEE ENSIGN
McGeorge School of Law: ELIZABETH RINDS-
KOPF PARKER
Conservatory of Music: STEPHEN ANDERSON
College of the Pacific: ROBERT COX
Thomas J. Long School of Pharmacy and
Health Sciences: PHILIP OPPENHEIMER
Graduate School: PHILIP OPPENHEIMER

UNIVERSITY OF WEST LOS ANGELES

9920 South La Cienega Blvd, Inglewood, CA
90301-4423
Telephone: (310) 342-5200
Fax: (310) 342-5295
Internet: www.uwla.edu
Founded 1966
Private control
Campuses in West Los Angeles and the San
Fernando Valley
Pres.: ROBERT W. BROWN
Vice-Pres. for Student Affairs: Dr ROBERT W.
ADAMS

Dean: GEORGE DEZES
Dir of Operations (San Fernando Valley
Campus): PAT GALASSO
Dir of Student Services: PAT MYERS
Dir of Facilities: RON BEATTY
Dir of Library Services: JIMMY RIMONTE
Library of 34,000 vols
Number of teachers: 40 (3 full-time, 37
adjunct)
Number of students: 350
Publication: *UWLA Law Review* (2 a year)

DEANS

School of Law: BASIL GEORGE DEZES
School of Paralegal Studies: MARLENE AMERA
ALHANDY

VANGUARD UNIVERSITY OF SOUTHERN CALIFORNIA

55 Fair Dr., Costa Mesa, CA 92626-9601
Telephone: (714) 556-3610
Fax: (714) 957-9317
Internet: www.vanguard.edu
Founded 1920
Pres.: MURRAY W. DEMPSTER
Provost: RUSSELL SPITTLER
Vice-Pres. for Business and Finance (vacant)
Vice-Pres. for Univ. Advancement: RICK
HARDY
Vice-Pres. for Enrollment Management: JES-
SICA MIRELESS
Vice-Pres. for Student Affairs: ED WEST-
BROOK
Dean of Students: LINDA HARTZELL
Registrar: JUDY HAMILTON
Head Librarian: ALISON ENGLISH
Library of 135,500 vols, 1,053 periodicals
Number of teachers: 162 (75 full-time, 87
part-time)
Number of students: 2,300

DEANS

School of Business and Management: DAVID
ALFORD
School of Communication and the Arts:
JAMES L. MELTON
School of Education: JERRY TERNES
School of Humanities and Social Sciences: Dr
MICHAEL D. WILSON
School of Natural Sciences and Mathematics:
Dr CECIL MILLER
School of Psychology: JERRE L. WHITE
School of Religion: APRIL WESTBROOK
School for Professional Studies: Dr PAUL COX

WESTERN STATE UNIVERSITY COLLEGE OF LAW

1111 North State College Blvd, Fullerton, CA
92831
Telephone: (714) 738-1000
Fax: (714) 441-1748
E-mail: adm@wsulaw.edu
Internet: www.wsulaw.edu
Founded 1966
Private control
Academic year: August to May
Dean and Pres.: MARYANN JONES
Dean of Academic Affairs: SUSAN KELLER
Dir of Criminal Law Practice Center: DAVID
FRAKT
Dir of Legal Clinic: TERENCE W. ROBERTS
Library Dir: PATRICIA HARRIS O'CONNOR (act-
ing)
Number of teachers: 48 (21 full-time, 27
adjunct)
Number of students: 1,157.

WESTERN UNIVERSITY OF HEALTH SCIENCES

309 East Second St, Pomona, CA 91766-1854
Telephone: (909) 6236116
E-mail: admissions@westernu.edu
Internet: www.westernu.edu
Founded 1977 as College of Osteopathic
Medicine of the Pacific; present name 1996
Private control
Pres.: Dr PHILIP PUMERANTZ
Provost and Chief Operating Officer: BENJA-
MIN L. COHEN
Treas. and Chief Financial Officer: KEVIN D.
SHAW
Sr Vice-Pres. for Executive Affairs: Dr GARY
M. GUGELCHUK
Vice-Pres. for Student Affairs: BEVERLY A.
GUIDRY
Vice-Pres. for Human Resources: HOWARD M.
PARDUE
Vice-Pres. for Research and Biotechnology:
STEVEN J. HENRIKSEN
Library Dir: PATRICIA VADER
Number of students: 1,425

DEANS

College of Allied Health Professions: Dr
STEPHANIE D. BOWLIN
College of Graduate Nursing: KAREN HAN-
FORD
College of Osteopathic Medicine of the Paci-
fic: CLINT ADAMS
College of Pharmacy: Dr DANIEL ROBINSON
College of Veterinary Medicine: Dr SHIRLEY
D. JOHNSTON

WESTMINSTER SEMINARY CALIFORNIA

1725 Bear Valley Parkway, Escondido, CA
92027
Telephone: (760) 480-8474
Fax: (760) 480-0252
E-mail: info@wscal.edu
Internet: www.wscal.edu
Founded 1980
Private control
Academic year: September to May
Pres.: Dr W. ROBERT GODFREY
Exec. Vice-Pres.: STEVEN OEVERMAN
Vice-Pres. for Advancement: DAWN G. DOORN
Academic Dean: Dr DENNIS E. JOHNSON
Dean of Students: Dr JULIUS J. KIM
Registrar: BRIAN J. MILLS
Library Dir: ELIZABETH E. MEHNE (acting)
Library of 120,000 vols, 260 periodicals
Number of teachers: 25
Number of students: 150
Areas of study: MDiv and MA in Biblical
Studies, Theological Studies, Historical
Theology or Christian Studies.

WESTMONT COLLEGE

955 La Paz Rd, Santa Barbara, CA 93108
Telephone: (805) 565-6000
Fax: (805) 565-6234
E-mail: president@westmont.edu
Internet: www.westmont.edu
Founded 1937
Academic year: September to May
Pres.: DAVID K. WINTER
Chancellor: Dr DAVID K. WINTER
Executive Vice-Pres.: J. CLIFTON LUNDBERG
Vice-Pres. for Admin.: CHRISTOPHER D. CALL
Vice-Pres. for Advancement: STEPHEN C.
BAKER
Vice-Pres. for Finance: ROD BROWN
Vice-Pres. for Student Life and Dean of
Students: JANE HIGA
Provost: Dr SHIRLEY MULLEN
Dir of Library and Information Services:
JOHN D. MURRAY

Library of 150,000 vols
Number of teachers: 90 full-time
Number of students: 1,328.

WHITTIER COLLEGE

13406 East Philadelphia, Whittier, CA 90608-4413

Telephone: (562) 907-4200
Fax: (562) 698-4067
E-mail: president@whittier.edu
Internet: www.whittier.edu

Founded 1887

Liberal Arts, Business and Law

Pres.: SHARON HERZBERGER
Vice-Pres. for Academic Affairs and Dean of the Faculty: SUSAN D. GOTSCH
Vice-Pres. for Advancement: ELIZABETH POWER
Vice-Pres. for Finance and Admin.: JANICE A. LEGOZA
Vice-Pres. for Enrolment: LISA MEYER
Dean of Whittier Law School: NEIL H. COGAN
Registrar: WILLIAM GARTRELL
Librarian: KATHERINE GILL

Library of 302,000 vols, 44,000 microfilms, 715 current periodicals; spec. collns: John Greenleaf Whittier, Quakers
Number of teachers: 96 full-time
Number of students: 1,427

Publications: *Cornerstone* (6 a year), *The Rock* (quarterly), *Whittier Law Review*

WILLIAM JESSUP UNIVERSITY

333 Sunset Blvd, Rocklin, CA 95765

Telephone: (916) 577-2200
Fax: (916) 577-2203
E-mail: information@jessup.edu
Internet: www.jessup.edu

Founded 1939 as San José Bible College; San José Christian College 1989; present name and status 2004

Private control

Academic year: September to May

Pres.: BRYCE JESSUP
Vice-Pres. for Finance and Admin.: GENE DE YOUNG
Vice-Pres. for Academic Affairs: Dr DAVID NYSTROM
Vice-Pres. for Advancement: JOSEPH D. WOMACK
Vice-Pres. for Student Devt and Dean of Students: PAUL BLEZIEN
Registrar: TINA PETERSEN
Library Dir: MAY WU

Library of 34,000 vols

Areas of study: Bible and Theology, Business Administration, Christian Education, Intercultural Studies, Liberal Studies, Music, Pastoral Ministry, Psychology, Public Policy, Youth Ministry.

BRANCH CAMPUS
San Jose Extension: Suite 210, 1190 Saratoga Ave, San Jose, CA 95129; tel. (408) 278-4343; fax (408) 278-4342; e-mail dcp-sj@jessup.edu.

WOODBURY UNIVERSITY

7500 Glenoaks Blvd, Burbank, CA 91510-7846

Telephone: (818) 767-0888
E-mail: info@woodbury.edu
Internet: www.woodbury.edu

Founded 1884 as Woodbury Business College; present name 1974

Private control

Academic year: August to August

Pres.: Dr KENNETH R. NIELSEN

Vice-Pres. for Academic Affairs: DAVID M. ROSEN
Vice-Pres. for Enrollment Management and Univ. Marketing: DON E. ST. CLAIR
Vice-Pres. for Finance and Admin.: KEN JONES
Vice-Pres. for Univ. Advancement: RICHARD M. NORDIN
Vice-Pres. for IT and Planning: STEVE DYER
Dir of Library Services: NEDRA PETERSON
Number of students: 1,500

DEANS
School of Architecture: NORMAN MILLAR
School of Media, Culture and Design: (vacant)
School of Business: ANDRÉ B. VAN NIEKERK
Transdisciplinary Studies: DOUGLAS J. CREMER

BRANCH CAMPUS
San Diego Campus: Suite 200, 1060 Eighth Ave, San Diego, CA 92101; tel. (619) 235-2900; e-mail san.diego@woodbury.edu; Admin. Dir DEBRA ABEL.

WRIGHT INSTITUTE

2728 Durant Ave, Berkeley, CA 94704

Telephone: (510) 841-9230
Fax: (510) 841-0167
E-mail: info@wrightinst.edu
Internet: www.wrightinst.edu

Founded 1968

Private control

Academic year: September to June

Pres.: PETER DYBWAD
Dean: Dr CHARLES ALEXANDER
Registrar: GINNY MORGAN
Librarian: JASON STRAUSS

Library of 10,000 items, 125 periodicals

Area of study: clinical psychology.

COLORADO

ADAMS STATE COLLEGE OF COLORADO

208 Edgemont Blvd, Alamosa, CO 81102

Telephone: (719) 587-7011
E-mail: ascadmit@adams.edu
Internet: www.adams.edu

Founded 1923

Pres.: DAVID SVALDI
Provost: FRANK NOVOTNY
Vice-Provost for Academic Affairs: MARGARET DOELL
Vice-Pres. for Enrollment Management: GORGIA GRANTHAM
Vice-Pres. for Finance and Administration: BILL MANSHEIM
Dean of Student Affairs: KEN MARQUEZ
Registrar: M. BELEN MAESTAS
Dir of Luther Bean Museum: KATHERINE OLANCE
Dir of Nielsen Library: DIANNE MACHADO

Library of 132,615 vols, 34,651 bound periodicals, 1,005 current periodicals, 488,675 govt publications, 1,334 maps, 2,493 audiovisual items, 732,387 microforms, 13,294 microfilms
Number of teachers: 123
Number of students: 1,455 full-time and 319 part time

Depts of Art, Biology, Business Administration, Chemistry, Communications, Computer Science, Earth Sciences, English, History/Government/Philosophy, Human Performance and Physical Education, Interdisciplinary Studies, Mathematics, Music, Nursing, Physics, Psychology, Sociology, Spanish, Teacher Education, Theatre.

COLORADO CHRISTIAN UNIVERSITY

8787 West Alameda Ave, Lakewood, CO 80226

Telephone: (303) 963-3000
Fax: (303) 963-3001
E-mail: admission@ccu.edu
Internet: www.ccu.edu

Founded 1989 following merger of Colorado Christian College and Colorado Baptist Univ.

Private control

Academic year: August to August

Pres.: BILL ARMSTRONG
Vice-Pres. for Business Affairs and Chief Financial Officer: BRIAN T. BISSELL
Vice-Pres. for Student Development: JAMES S. McCORMICK
Vice-Pres. for Adult and Graduate Studies: RICHARD D. CROMBIE
Vice-Pres. for Academic Affairs: Dr CHERRI PARKS
Vice-Pres. for Univ. Advancement: RONALD REX
Registrar: WENDY WIBBENS
Library Dir: GAYLE GUNDERSON

Library of 64,855 vols
Number of teachers: 334
Number of students: 2,200

DEANS
School of Business and Leadership: CHARLES KING
School of Education: SARA DALLMAN
School of Theology: JEFF MALLINSON
School of Humanities and Sciences: Dr WILLIAM R. SAXBY
School of Music: STEVEN T. TAYLOR

BRANCH CAMPUSES
Colorado Springs Center: Suite 150, 1125 Kelly Johnson Blvd, Colorado Springs, CO 80920; tel. (719) 528-5080.

Denver Metro Center: Suite 100, Financial Plaza II, 225 Union Blvd, Lakewood, CO 80228; tel. (303) 963-3300.

Northern Colorado Center: Suite 100, 1750 Foxtrail Dr., Loveland, CO 80538; tel. (970) 669-8700.

Western Colorado Center: Suite 220, 743 Horizon Court, Grand Junction, CO 81506; tel. (970) 242-1811.

COLORADO COLLEGE

14 East Cache La Poudre St, Colorado Springs, CO 80903

Telephone: (719) 389-6000
Fax: (719) 389-6933
E-mail: communications@coloradocollege.edu
Internet: www.coloradocollege.edu

Founded 1874

Pres.: RICHARD F. CELESTE
Vice-Pres. for Advancement: STEPHEN ELDER
Vice-Pres. for Enrollment Management: MARK HATCH
Vice-Pres. for Business/Finance and Treasurer: THOMAS NYCUM
Vice-Pres. for Information Management: RANDALL STILES
Vice-Pres. for Student Life: MIKE EDMONDS
Registrar: PHIL APODOCA
Library Dir: CAROL DICKERSON

Number of teachers: 140
Number of students: 1,850

American Cultural Studies, Anthropology, Art, Asian Studies, Biology, Chemistry, Classics, Comparative Literature, Drama and Dance, East Asian Languages, Economics and Business, Education, English, Environmental Science, Feminist and Gender Studies, Geology, German, History, Mathematics and Computer Science, Music, Philosophy, Physics, Political Science, Psychology, Religion, Romance Languages, Russian, Sociology, Sport Science, Southwest Studies

DEANS

College and Faculty: SUSAN A. ASHLEY
Summer Session: LIBBY RITTENBERG

COLORADO SCHOOL OF MINES

1500 Illinois St, Golden, CO 80401-1887
Telephone: (303) 273-3000
Fax: (303) 273-3278
E-mail: presoffice@mines.edu
Internet: www.mines.edu

Founded 1874

Engineering education and applied science related to Earth, Energy, Materials and Environment

Pres.: BILL SCOGGINS
Exec. Vice-Pres. for Academic Affairs and Dean of the Faculty: NIGEL T. MIDDLETON
Exec. Vice-Pres. for Research and Technology Transfer: Dr JOHN POATE
Vice-Pres. for Finance and Operations: ROBERT G. MOORE
Vice-Pres. for Institutional Advancement: PETER HAN
Vice-Pres. for Student Life and Dean of Students: HAROLD R. CHEUVRONT
Dean of Graduate Studies: Dr THOMAS M. BOYD
Dir of Admissions: BRUCE P. GOETZ
Dir of Information Services: GEORGE FUNKEY
Registrar: SUSAN A. SMITH
Dir of Library: JOANNE LERUD HECK

Library of 145,000 vols, 2,000 journals, 260,000 govt publications, 400,000 microforms and 189,300 maps, 6,100 monographs
Number of teachers: 200
Number of students: 3,200

Publications: *Mineral Industries Bulletin*, *Quarterly of the Colorado School of Mines*.

COLORADO STATE UNIVERSITY

Fort Collins, CO 80523
Telephone: (970) 491-1101
Fax: (970) 491-0501
Internet: www.colostate.edu

Founded 1870 as The Agricultural College of Colorado, became a State institution in 1876, a land-grant college in 1879

Pres.: LARRY EDWARD PENLEY
Provost and Sr Vice-Pres.: Dr TONY FRANK
Vice-Pres. for Administrative Services: BOB RIZZUTO
Vice-Pres. for Research: WILLIAM H. FARLAND
Vice-Pres. for Student Affairs: Dr BLANCHE HUGHES
Vice-Pres. for Advancement: JOYCE BERRY
Exec. Dir of Admissions: MARY R. ONTIVEROS
Dean of Libraries: CATHERINE MURRAY-RUST

Library of 2,000,000 vols
Number of teachers: 1,400
Number of students: 23,934

DEANS

College of Agricultural Sciences: Dr MARC JOHNSON
College of Applied Human Sciences: Dr APRIL MASON
College of Business: Dr AJAY MENON
College of Engineering: Dr SANDRA WOODS
College of Liberal Arts: Dr ANN GILL
College of Natural Resources: JOSEPH T. O'LEARY
College of Natural Sciences: Dr RICK MIRANDA
College of Veterinary Medicine and Biomedical Sciences: Dr LANCE E. PERRYMAN

ASSOCIATED INSTITUTIONS

Colorado Agricultural Experiment Station: Dir LEE E. SOMMERS.

Co-operative Extension: Dir MILAN A. REWARTS.

Colorado State Forest Service: Dir JAMES E. HUBBARD.

Colorado Cooperative Fish and Wildlife Research Unit: Unit Leader Prof. DAVID R. ANDERSON.

COLORADO STATE UNIVERSITY–PUEBLO

2200 Bonforte Blvd, Pueblo, CO 81001-4901
Telephone: (719) 549-2100
Fax: (719) 549-2419
E-mail: info@colostate-pueblo.edu
Internet: www.colostate-pueblo.edu

Founded as Junior College 1933, Southern Colorado State College 1961, Univ. of Southern Colorado 1975
State control, mem. of Colorado State Univ. system

Pres.: JOSEPH A. GARCIA
Provost and Vice-Pres. for Academic Affairs: Dr RUSS MEYER
Dean of Student Life and Devt: ARROW KENNEDY
Dean of Univ. Library: RHONDA GONZALES

Library of 171,000 vols, 1,600 periodical titles, 275,000 govt documents, 21,000 audio-visual items
Number of teachers: 200
Number of students: 4,000

DEANS

Hasan School of Business: SUE HANKS
Education, Engineering and Professional Studies: Prof. HECTOR R. CARRASCO
College of Humanities and Social Sciences: ROY B. SONNEMA
College of Science and Mathematics: Prof. KRISTINA PROCTOR

COLORADO TECHNICAL UNIVERSITY

4435 North Chestnut St, Colorado Springs, CO 80907
Telephone: (719) 598-0200
Fax: (719) 598-3740
E-mail: ctucos@coloradotech.edu
Internet: www.coloradotech.edu
Private control
Academic year: October to September

Pres.: GREG MITCHELL
CEO: Dr MARIJANE AXTELL PAULSEN
Chancellor: Dr RICHARD KETTNER-POLLEY
Vice-Pres. for Academic Affairs: Dr SCOTT VAN TONNINGEN
Dir of Education: Dr CHARLES SCHROEDER
Vice-Pres. for Admissions: ROBERT LEE
Librarian: KAY BURMAN

DEANS

Computer Science, Information Technology, and Management Information Systems: Dr MARY JANE WILLSHIRE
Engineering, Technology, Mathematics, and Sciences: ALEX DWELIS
Management: Dr ERIC GOODMAN
Nursing: Dr DEB BANIK

BRANCH CAMPUSES

Denver Campus: 5775 Denver Tech Center Blvd, Greenwood Village, CO 80111-3201; tel. (303) 694-6600; fax (303) 694-6673; e-mail ctudenver@coloradotech.edu; internet www.ctudenver.com.

North Kansas City Campus: 520 East 19th Ave, North Kansas City, CO 64116; tel. (816) 472-7400; internet kc.coloradotech.edu.

Colorado Technical University - Pueblo: 1025 West Sixth Street, Pueblo, CO 81003; tel. (877) 676-0200; internet pueblo .coloradotech.edu.

Sioux Falls Campus: 3901 West 59th Street, Sioux Falls, SD 57108; tel. (605) 361-0200; fax (605) 361-5954; e-mail ctusf@ coloradotech.edu; internet www.ctusiouxfalls .com.

DENVER SEMINARY

POB 100000, Denver, CO 80250-0100
Located at: 6399 South Santa Fe Dr., Littleton, CO 80120
Telephone: (303) 761-2482
Fax: (303) 761-8060
E-mail: info@denverseminary.edu
Internet: www.denverseminary.edu

Founded 1950
Private control; mem. of Institute of Theological Studies
Academic year: September to May

Pres.: Dr G. CRAIG WILLIFORD
Vice-Pres. and Academic Dean: Dr RANDY MACFARLAND
Vice-Pres. for Finance: JACK C. HEIMBICHNER
Vice-Pres. for Advancement: GARY HOAG
Vice-Pres. for Enrollment Management: BOB FOMER
Chancellor: Dr VERNON C. GROUNDS
Dean of Student Services: VANESSA ANDERSON
Registrar: PAM BETKER
Dir of Library: Dr P. KEITH WELLS

Library of 166,000 vols
Number of teachers: 57
Number of students: 700

MA in Counseling and Doctor of Ministry.

FORT LEWIS COLLEGE

1000 Rim Dr., Durango, CO 81301-3999
Telephone: (970) 247-7010
E-mail: admission@fortlewis.edu
Internet: www.fortlewis.edu

Founded 1911
State control, mem. of Colorado State Univ. system

Pres.: Dr BRAD BARTEL
Provost and Vice-Pres. for Academic Affairs: Dr STEPHEN A. RODERICK
Vice-Pres. for Finance and Admin.: STEVEN SCHWARTZ
Vice-Pres. for Student Affairs: Dr GLENNA WITT SEXTON
Dean of Admission and Devt: SHERI R. ROCHFORD
Registrar: EDWIN JOHNSON
Dir of the Library: CHANDLER JACKSON

Library of 175,000 vols
Number of teachers: 187
Number of students: 4,441

DEANS

School of Arts, Humanities and Social Sciences: RICHARD SAX
School of Business Administration: Dr TOM HARRINGTON
School of Natural and Behavioral Sciences: Dr JOHN NIMMEMANN
General and Exploratory Studies: Dr CAROL SMITH

ILIFF SCHOOL OF THEOLOGY

2201 South Univ. Blvd, Denver, CO 80210-4798
Telephone: (303) 744-1287
Fax: (303) 777-0164
E-mail: info@iliff.edu
Internet: www.iliff.edu
Private control
Academic year: September to August

Pres.: DAVID TRICKETT
Vice-Pres. for Student Services: JOAN VANBE-
CELAERE
Vice-Pres. for Business and Chief Fiscal
Officer: KELLY MCCORMICK
Academic Vice-Pres. and Dean of Faculty:
JEFFREY MAHAN
Vice-Pres. for Institutional Advancement:
MARY UNDERWOOD
Library Dir: DEBORAH CREAMER
Library of 202,250 vols, 700 periodicals
Number of teachers: 22
Number of students: 300.

ITT TECHNICAL INSTITUTE

500 East 84th Ave, Thornton, CO 80229-5338
learning site: 12500 East Iliff Ave, Aurora,
CO 80014
Telephone: (303) 695-6317
Internet: www.itt-tech.edu
Founded 1984
Private control (ITT Educational Services,
Inc.)
Academic year: September to September
Dir: RICHARD F. HANSEN
Dean: Dr PETER M. LINZMAIER
Registrar: LISA MEYERDIERKS

Depts of Computer and Electronics Engineering, Computer Drafting and Design, Data
Communication Systems Technology, Electronics and Communications Eng., Electronics Eng. and Technology, Information
Systems Security, Information Technology,
Technical Project Management for Electronic Commerce, General Education.

MESA STATE COLLEGE

1100 North Ave, Grand Junction, CO 81501
Telephone: (970) 248-1020
Fax: (970) 248-1973
Internet: www.mesastate.edu
Founded 1925 as Grand Junction Junior
College; present name 1988
Academic year: August to May
Pres.: TIM FOSTER
Vice-Pres. for Academic and Student Affairs:
CAROL FUTHEY
Vice-Pres. for Financial and Admin. Services:
PATRICK DOYLE
Dean of Students: ANDREW BRECKEL
Registrar: PATRICK HAMPTON
Dir of Library: ELIZABETH BRODAK (acting)
Library of 178,409 vols, 919 current journals,
82,375 govt docs, 12,248 audiovisual items,
17,390 maps
Number of teachers: 207
Number of students: 5,346 (3,983 full-time,
1,363 part-time)

Depts of Accounting and Information Tech-
nology, Applied Technology, Biological
Sciences, Business Admin., Computer
Sciences, Mathematics and Statistics,
Fine and Performing Arts (Art), Fine and
Performing Arts (Music), Fine and Per-
forming Arts (Theatre), Human Perfor-
mance and Wellness, Languages,
Literature and Communications, Nursing
and Radiologic Sciences, Physical and
Environmental Sciences, Social and Beha-
vioural Sciences.

BRANCH CAMPUSES

Montrose Campus: 234 S Cascade Ave,
Montrose, CO 81401; tel. (970) 249-7009; fax
(970) 249-2579; Dir BEN KEEFER.

Unified Technical Education Campus:
School of Applied Technology, 2508 Blich-
mann, Grand Junction, CO 81505; tel. (970)
255-2600.

METROPOLITAN STATE COLLEGE OF DENVER

POB 173362, Denver, CO 80217-3362
Telephone: (303) 556-2400
Internet: www.mscd.edu
Private control
Academic year: August to May
Pres.: Dr STEPHEN M. JORDAN
Provost and Vice-Pres. for Academic Affairs:
Dr RODOLFO ROCHA
Vice-Pres. for Admin. and Finance: NATALIE
LUTES
Vice-Pres. for Institutional Advancement:
GEORGE ENGDAHL
Vice-Pres. for Student Services: Dr DOUGLAS
SAMUELS
Vice-Pres. for Information Technology:
GEORGE MIDDLEMIST
Registrar: THOMAS R. GRAY
Dean of Library: ALIRE CAMILA
Library of 1,000,000 traditional print and
media items
Number of teachers: 402
Number of students: 18,432

DEANS

School of Business: Dr JOHN P. COCHRAN
School of Letters, Arts and Sciences: Dr JOAN
L. FOSTER
School of Professional Studies: Dr SANDRA D.
HAYNES

BRANCH CAMPUSES

Metro North Campus: Suite 102, 11990
Grant St, Northglenn, CO 80233; tel. (303)
450-5111.

Metro South Campus: Suite L100, 5660
Greenwood Plaza Blvd, Greenwood Village,
CO 80111; tel. (303) 721-1313.

NAROPA UNIVERSITY

2130 Arapahoe Ave, Boulder, CO 80302
Telephone: (303) 444-0202
Fax: (303) 444-0410
E-mail: infodesk@naropa.edu
Internet: www.naropa.edu
Founded 1974 by Chogyam Trungpa to
combine Buddhist studies with traditional
Western scholastic and artistic disciplines;
based on Nalanda Univ. (5th–12th cen-
tury), India
Pres.: THOMAS B. COBURN
Library Dir: MARK KILLE
Library of 26,000 vols, 100 periodicals; spec.
collns incl. 15,000 original Tibetan texts in
2,200 vols, 6,000 audiocassette recordings
of events held at Naropa Univ., psychology
Number of students: 1,000

BAs in Contemplative Psychology, Early
Childhood Education, Environmental Stu-
dies, Interdisciplinary Studies, Music, Reli-
gious Studies, Traditional Eastern Arts,
Visual Arts and Writing and Literature,
Fine Arts in Performance; MAs in Contem-
plative Education, Creative Writing, Divi-
nity, Environmental Leadership, Fine Arts,
Indo-Tibetan Buddhism, Religious Studies,
Counseling Psychology (Contemplative,
Somatic Transpersonal), Writing and Poe-
tics.

NATIONAL THEATRE CONSERVATORY

1050 13th Street, Denver, CO 80204-2154
E-mail: ntc@dcpa.org
Internet: www.denvercenter.org
Pres. of Denver Center for the Performing
Arts: RANDY WEEKS
Dir of Education: DANIEL RENNER
Registrar: KATE AMBERG
Librarian: LINDA ELLER

Library of 30,000 single scripts and antholo-
gies
Area of study: fine arts.

NAZARENE BIBLE COLLEGE

1111 Academy Park Loop, Colorado Springs,
CO 80910
Telephone: (719) 884-5000
Fax: (719) 884-5199
E-mail: info@nbc.edu
Internet: www.nbc.edu
Founded 1967
Private control
Academic year: September to May
Pres.: Dr HAROLD B. GRAVES
Vice-Pres. for Academic Affairs and Exten-
sion Education: Dr DONALD E. STELTING, Sr
Vice-Pres. for Online Education: Dr DAVID M.
PHILLIPS
Vice-Pres. for Enrollment and Student
Development: Dr LAUREL L. MATSON
Vice-Pres. for Finance: J. MIKE ARRAMBIDE
Registrar: Dr MIKE A. WORRELL
Library Dir: ANN M. ATTIG

BAs in Christian Counseling, Christian Educational Ministries, Christian School Education, Ministry, Music Ministries, Pastoral
Ministries.

REGIS UNIVERSITY

3333 Regis Blvd, Denver, CO 80221-1099
Telephone: (303) 458-4100
Fax: (303) 964-5473
E-mail: publicaffairs@regis.edu
Internet: www.regis.edu
Founded 1877
Private control (Society of Jesuits)
Academic year: August to August
Pres.: MICHAEL J. SHEERAN
Director of Admissions: VIC DAVOLT
Dean of Libraries: IVAN GAETZ
Library of 260,000 vols, 2,500 periodicals
Number of students: 16,128

Areas of study: Accounting, Biochemistry,
Biology, Business Admin., Catholic Studies,
Chemistry, Christian Leadership, Communi-
cation, Computer Science, Core Studies,
Economics Education, English, Environmen-
tal Studies, Exercise Science, French, His-
tory, Leadership, Mathematics, Music,
Neuroscience, Nursing, Peace and Justice
Philosophy, Political Economy, Politics, Pre-
Med/Health, Pre-Law, Psychology, Religious
Studies, Sociology, Spanish, Visual Arts,
Women's Studies
Publication: *Human Development* (2 a year).

BRANCH CAMPUSES

Aurora Campus: Suite 200, Abilene St,
Boulder, CO 80011; tel. (303) 458-7420; fax
(303) 964-5765.

Colorado Springs Campus: Suite 100,
7450 Campus Dr., Colorado Springs, CO
80920; tel. (303) 458-7420; fax (719) 264-
7095.

Denver Tech Center Campus: Suite 100N,
7600 East Orchard Rd, Englewood, CO
80111; tel. (303) 458-7420; fax (303) 964-
5053.

Fort Collins Campus: 1501 Academy
Court, Fort Collins, CO 80524; tel. (970)
472-2208; fax (970) 472-2201.

Interlocken at Broomfield Campus: Suite
150, 11001 West 120th Ave, Broomfield, CO
80021; tel. (303) 458-7420; fax (303) 635-
1363.

Las Vegas Campus: Suite 100, 1401 North
Green Valley Parkway, Henderson, NV
89074; tel. (702) 990-0375; e-mail vegas@
regis.edu.

Longmont Campus: 2101 Ken Pratt Blvd, Longmont, CO 80501; tel. (303) 458-7420.

UNITED STATES AIR FORCE ACADEMY

HQ USAFA/RRS, Suite 200, 2304 Cadet Dr., Colorado Springs, CO 80840

Telephone: (719) 333-1110
E-mail: webmaster@usafa.af.mil
Internet: www.usafa.edu

Founded 1954

Superintendent: Lieutenant Gen. JOHN F. REGNI

Dean of Faculty: Brigadier Gen. DANA H. BORN

Library of 387,000 vols
Number of teachers: 531.

UNIVERSITY OF COLORADO

System Admin., Boulder, CO 80309

Telephone: (303) 492-6201
Internet: www.cu.edu

Inc. 1861, opened 1877

Pres.: HANK BROWN
Vice-Pres. for Academic Affairs and Research: MICHAEL POLIAKOFF
Vice-Pres. for Human Relations and Risk Management and Univ. Counsel: CHARLES SWEET
Vice-Pres. for Budget and Finance: ROBERT MOORE
Vice-Pres. for Admin. and Chief of Staff: LEONARD DINEGAR

Library: see Libraries and Archives
Number of teachers: 3,500
Number of students: 50,000

Publications: *Colorado Alumnus* (monthly for 10 months), *College Catalog* (annual), *Colorado Business Review* (monthly), *Colorado Quarterly*, *English Language Notes*, *East European Quarterly*, *University of Colorado Law Review*, *Colorado Engineer*, *Arctic and Alpine Research* (quarterly), *Computer Newsletter* (9 a year), *and University of Colorado Studies series covering various subjects.*

CONSTITUENT CAMPUSES

University of Colorado at Boulder

Boulder, CO 80309

Telephone: (303) 492-1411
Internet: www.colorado.edu

Chancellor: G. P. PETERSON
Provost and Exec. Vice-Chancellor for Academic Affairs: PHILIP DISTEFANO
Sr Vice-Chancellor and Chief Financial Officer: RIC PORRECA
Vice-Chancellor for Admin.: PAUL TABOLT
Vice Chancellor for Research and Dean of the Graduate School: SUSAN AVERY
Vice-Chancellor for Student Affairs: RONALD STUMP
Dean of Libraries: JAMES WILLIAMS, II

Number of teachers: 1,375 full-time, 842 temporary and part-time
Number of students: 29,258

DEANS

College of Architecture and Planning: MARK GELERNTER
College of Arts and Sciences: TODD GLEESON
Leeds School of Business: DENNIS AHLBURG
School of Education: LORRIE SHEPARD
College of Engineering and Applied Science: ROBERT DAVIS
School of Journalism and Mass Communication: PAUL VOAKES
School of Law: DAVID H. GETCHES
College of Music: DANIEL SHER
Graduate School: SUSAN AVERY

Continuing Education: ANNE HEINZ

University of Colorado at Colorado Springs

1420 Austin Bluffs Pkwy, Colorado Springs, CO 80918

Telephone: (719) 262-3000
Internet: www.uccs.edu

Chancellor: Prof. PAMELA S. SHOCKLEY-ZALABAK
Vice-Chancellor for Academic Affairs: MARGARET BACON
Vice-Chancellor for Admin. and Finance: BRIAN D. BURNETT
Vice-Chancellor for Student Success: Prof. JAMES P. HENDERSON
Dean of Students: TAMARA MOORE
Dean of the Library: Prof. LESLIE A. MANNING

Library of 351,359 vols, 451,257 microforms, 358,019 govt docs/maps, 6,791 audio/visual items, 1,441 current journals in print, and c. 21,000 journals online
Number of teachers: 514
Number of students: 7,600

DEANS

College of Business and Administration: Dr VENKAT K. REDDY
College of Education: MARK MALONE
College of Engineering and Applied Science: JEREMY HAEFNER
College of Letters, Arts and Sciences: Dr THOMAS M. CHRISTIENSEN
Beth-El College of Nursing and Health Sciences: Prof. CAROLE SCHOFFSTALL
Graduate School of Public Affairs: Prof. KATHLEEN M. BEATTY

University of Colorado at Denver and Health Sciences Center

POB 173364, Denver, CO 80217-3364

Telephone: (303) 556-2400
Internet: www.cudenver.edu

Chancellor: M. ROY WILSON (acting)
Vice-Chancellor for Admin. and Finance: TERESA BERRYMAN
Vice-Chancellor for Student Affairs: MARGARET B. COZZENS
Provost and Vice-Chancellor for Academic and Student Affairs: MARK ALAN HECKLER
Dean of Faculty: J. C. BOSCH
Dean of the Library: DAVID GLEIM

Number of teachers: 437 (full-time)
Number of students: 27,000

DEANS

College of Architecture and Planning: MARK GELERNTER
College of Arts and Media: KATHY MAES
Business School: SUEANN AMBRON
College of Engineering and Applied Science: Dr RENJENG SU
College of Liberal Arts and Sciences: JON HARBOR
Graduate School: TOM CLARK
Graduate School: JIM HAGEMAN
Graduate School of Public Affairs: Prof. KATHLEEN BEATTY
School of Education and Human Development: LYNN RHODES

UNIVERSITY OF DENVER

2199 South Univ. Blvd, Denver, CO 80208

Telephone: (303) 871-2000
Fax: (303) 871-4000
Internet: www.du.edu

Founded 1864
Private control
Academic year: September to May

Chancellor: ROBERT COOMBE
Provost: GREGG KVISTAD

Vice-Chancellor for Business and Financial Affairs: CRAIG WOODY
Vice-Chancellor for Communications and Marketing: CAROL E. FARNSWORTH
Vice-Provost for Undergraduate Studies: SHEILA WRIGHT
Vice-Chancellor for Univ. Advancement: ED HARRIS
Vice-Provost for Graduate Studies and Research: Dr JAMES MORAN
Registrar: DENNIS BECKER
Dean and Dir of the Library: NANCY ALLEN

Library of 1,897,000 vols
Number of teachers: 500
Number of students: 4,850 undergraduates and 5,500 graduates

Arts, Humanities and Social Sciences: depts of Anthropology, Art and Art History, Economics, English, History, Human Communications, Judaic Study, Languages and Literature, Music (Lamont School of), Mass Communications and Journalism Studies, Philosophy, Political Sciences, Psychology, Public Policy Studies, Religious Studies, Sociology, Theatre. Natural Sciences, Mathematics and Engineering: depts of Biological Sciences, Chemistry and Biochemistry, Computer Science, Eng., Geography, Mathematics, Physics and Astronomy. Daniels College of Business: depts of Accountancy, Ethics and Legal Studies, Finance (Renman School of), Hotel, Restaurant and Tourism Management, Information Technology and Electronic Commerce, Management, Marketing, Real Estate and Construction Management, Statistics and Operations Technology

Publications: *Denver Law Journal of International Law and Policy*, *Denver Law Journal* (quarterly), *Transportation Law Journal*, *The University of Denver Law Review*, *Family Law Quarterly*, *The Centre Report* (quarterly)

DEANS

Arts, Humanities and Social Sciences: GEORGE POTTS
Daniels College of Business: KAREN NEWMAN
College of Education: Dr VIRGINIA MALONEY
School of Engineering and Computer Science: RAHMAT A. SHOURESHI
Graduate School of International Studies: TOM J. FARER
College of Law: JOSÉ ROBERTO JUÁREZ, Jr
Natural Sciences and Mathematics: JIM FOGLEMAN
Graduate School of Professional Psychology: Prof. PETER BUIRSKI
Graduate School of Social Work: CHRISTIAN E. MOLIDOR
Univ. College of Professional and Continuing Education: JAMES R. DAVIS
Women's College: LYNN M. GANGONE

ATTACHED INSTITUTE

University of Denver Research Institute.

UNIVERSITY OF NORTHERN COLORADO

Greeley, CO 80639

Telephone: (970) 351-1890
Fax: (970) 351-1837
E-mail: unc@mail.unco.edu
Internet: www.unco.edu

Founded 1889 as the State Normal School; name changed to Colorado State Teachers' College 1911, to Colorado State College of Education in 1935, to Colorado State College in 1957; present name adopted in 1970

Academic year: August to May

Pres.: KAY NORTON
Sr Vice-Pres. and Provost: Dr ABE HARRAF
Sr Vice-Pres. for Finance and Administration: RANDAL HAACK
Vice-Pres. and General Counsel: RON LAMBDEN
Registrar: REBECCA BARNES
Dean of Students: Dr SAMANTHA ORTIZ SCHRIVER
Dean of Libraries: Dr GARY PITKIN
Number of teachers: 547
Number of students: 13,932

DEANS

College of Arts and Science: DAVID CALDWELL
Kenneth W. Montfort College of Business: Dr JOE F. ALEXANDER
College of Education and Behavioral Sciences: Dr EUGENE SHEEHAN
Graduate School: (vacant)
College of Health and Human Sciences: DENISE BATTLES
College of Performing and Visual Arts: ANDREW SVEDLOW

WESTERN STATE COLLEGE OF COLORADO

600 North Adams St, Gunnison, CO 81231
Telephone: (970) 943-0120
Fax: (970) 943-7069
Internet: www.western.edu
Founded 1911
Pres.: Dr JAY W. HELMAN
Vice-Pres. for Academic Affairs: Prof. JOHN B. SOWELL
Vice-Pres. for Finance and Admin.: BRAD BACA
Vice-Pres. for Student Affairs and Dean of Students: SHERRYL HALL-PETERSON
Vice-Pres. for Devt: THOMAS F. BURGGRAF
Registrar: MARYETTE ROGERS
Dir of Library Services: ELIZABETH AVERY
Library of 435,000 vols, 700 periodicals, 1,461 videos; spec. colln of books and govt docs about Colorado
Number of teachers: 143
Number of students: 2,514
Depts of Art, Behavioural and social sciences, Business, accounting and economics, Communication arts, languages and literature, Environmental studies, Mathematics and computer information science, Music, Natural and environmental sciences, Recreation and exercise and sport science.

CONNECTICUT

ALBERTUS MAGNUS COLLEGE

700 Prospect St, New Haven, CT 06511
Telephone: (203) 777-8550
E-mail: registrar@albertus.edu
Internet: www.albertus.edu
Co-educational liberal arts college
Founded 1925
Pres.: Dr JULIA M. MCNAMARA
Vice Pres. for Academic Affairs: JOHN J. DONOHUE
Vice Pres. for Finance and Treas.: JEANNE MANN
Vice-Pres. for Institutional Advancement and Planning: ROBERT J. BUCCINO
Dean for Admissions and Financial Aid: RICHARD J. LOLATTE
Dean for Student Services: MAUREEN V. MORRISON
Registrar: EILEEN S. PERILLO
Dir of Library and Information Services: ANNE LECNEY-PANAGROSSI
Library of 100,000 vols, 650 periodical titles, 2,000 audiovisual titles

Number of teachers: 202
Number of students: 2,400.

CENTRAL CONNECTICUT STATE UNIVERSITY

1615 Stanley St, New Britain, CT 06050
Telephone: (860) 832-3200
Fax: (860) 832-2522
E-mail: admissions@ccsu.edu
Internet: www.ccsu.edu
Founded 1849
State control, mem. of Connecticut State Univ. system
Academic year: September to May
Pres.: JOHN W. MILLER
Provost and Vice-Pres. for Academic Affairs: Dr CARL R. LOVITT
Chief Financial Officer: LARRY WILDER
Chief Information Officer: ROBERT E. CERNOCK
Dean of Students: JANE M. HIGGINS
Registrar: SUSAN PETROSINO
Dir of Library Services: JEANNE SOHN
Library of 665,605 vols, 3,000 current periodicals, govt docs, Polish Heritage Colln of 17,000 vols
Number of teachers: 885 (417 full-time, 468 part-time)
Number of students: 11,418 (7,427 full-time, 3,991 part-time)
BAs and MAs in a wide variety of disciplines and Sixth-Year Certificate in Reading; Doctoral degree (EdD) in Educational Leadership

DEANS

School of Arts and Sciences: SUSAN PEASE
School of Business: CHRIS GALLIGAN (acting)
School of Education and Professional Studies: MITCHELL SAKOFS (acting)
School of Technology: ZDZISLAW KREMENS
School of Graduate Studies: PAULETTE LEMMA

CHARTER OAK STATE COLLEGE

55 Paul J. Manafort Dr., New Britain, CT 06053-2150
Telephone: (860) 832-3800
Fax: (860) 832-3999
E-mail: info@charteroak.edu
Internet: www.cosc.edu
Founded 1973
Pres.: Dr MERLE W. HARRIS
Vice-Pres. for Academic Affairs: Dr SHIRLEY M. ADAMS
Chief Financial and Admin. Officer: CLIFFOR S. WILLIAMS
Dean, Marketing and Enrollment Services: HARRY E. WHITE
Dean, Chief Information Officer: GEORGE F. CLAFFEY, Jr
Registrar: PATRICIA R. DERECH
Number of students: 2,000
Offers 4 general studies degrees in arts and sciences; professional certificates in Project Management, Computer Security, Public Safety Admin.

CONNECTICUT COLLEGE

270 Mohegan Ave, New London, CT 06320-4196
Telephone: (860) 447-1911
Internet: www.conncoll.edu
Founded 1911
Academic year: August to May
Pres.: LEO I. HIGDON, Jr
Vice-Pres. for College Relations: PATRICIA CAREY
Vice-Pres. for Advancement: GREG WALDRON
Vice-Pres. for Finance: PAUL MARONEY

Provost and Dean of the Faculty: FRANCES L. HOFFMAN
Dean of Admissions and Financial Aid: MARTHA MERRILL
Dean of Freshmen: ANDREA ROSSI-REDER
Dean of Student Life: DAVID MILSTONE
Dean of College Community: ARMANDO BENGOCHEA
Dean of Religious and Spiritual Life: CLAUDIA HIGHBAUGH
Registrar: AILEEN BURDICK
College Librarian: W. LEE HISLE
Library of 555,578 vols
Number of teachers: 162 full-time
Number of students: 1,912
Co-educational liberal arts college.

EASTERN CONNECTICUT STATE UNIVERSITY

83 Windham St, Willimantic, CT 06226-2295
Telephone: (860) 465-5000
Fax: (860) 465-4485
E-mail: webmaster@easternct.edu
Internet: www.easternct.edu
Founded 1889, re-f. as Willimantic State College 1959, present name 1983
Academic year: September to May
Pres.: Dr ELSA NUÑEZ
Exec. Vice-Pres.: Dr MICHAEL PERNAL
Vice-Pres. for Academic Affairs: Dr DIMITROIS S. PACHIS
Vice-Pres. for Finance and Admin.: DENNIS A. HANNON
Vice-Pres. for Institutional Advancement: KENNETH DeLISA
Vice-Pres. for Student Affairs: Dr LAURA TORDENTI
Dir of Admissions and Enrollment Management: KIMBERLY CRONE
Dean of Arts and Sciences: Dr CARMEN CID
Dean of Educational and Professional Studies: Dr PATRICIA A. KLEINE
Dean of Students: Dr PAUL BRYANT
Registrar: KATHLEEN B. FABIAN
Dir of Library Services: PATRICIA S. BANACH
Library of 311,320 vols
Number of teachers: 361 (184 full-time, 177 part-time)
Number of students: 5,095.

FAIRFIELD UNIVERSITY

1073 North Benson Rd, Fairfield, CT 06824-5195
Telephone: (203) 254-4000
Fax: (203) 254-4199
Internet: www.fairfield.edu
Founded 1942
Academic year: September to May
Pres.: Rev. JEFFREY P. VON ARX
Academic Vice-Pres.: Dr ORIN L. GROSSMAN
Vice-Pres. for Finance and Treas.: WILLIAM J. LUCAS
Vice-Pres. for Student Affairs: MARK C. REED
Vice-Pres. for Univ. Advancement: STEPHANIE FROST
Dean of Students: THOMAS C. PELLEGRINO
Univ. Registrar: ROBERT C. RUSSO
Vice-Pres. for Information Services and Univ. Librarian: JAMES A. ESTRADA
Library of 325,166 vols, 888,554 microforms, 9,615 audiovisual items, 4,478 e-books, 1,796 periodicals
Number of teachers: 424 (222 full-time, 204 part-time)
Number of students: 4,008 (and 1,083 graduates

DEANS

College of Arts and Sciences: Dr TIMOTHY SNYDER

Dolan School of Business: Dr NORMAN SOLOMON
Graduate School of Education and Allied Professions: SUSAN D. FRANZOSA
School of Eng.: Dr E. VAGOS HADJIMICHAEL
School of Continuing Education: Dr EDNA F. WILSON
School of Nursing: Dr JEANNE MARIE L. NOVOTNY

HARTFORD SEMINARY

77 Sherman St, Hartford, CT 06105-2260
Telephone: (860) 509-9500
Fax: (860) 509-9509
E-mail: info@hartsem.edu
Internet: www.hartsem.edu
Founded 1913 by merger of Hartford Theological Seminary, Hartford School of Religious Education and Kennedy School of Missions; present name 1981
Private control
3 Academic centres: Center for Faith in Practice, Hartford Institute for Religion Research, Duncan Black Macdonald Center for the Study of Islam and Christian–Muslim Relations
Academic year: September to June
Pres.: Dr HEIDI HADSELL
Dean: Dr IAN MARKHAM
Registrar: KAREN ROLLINS
Library Dir: Dr STEVEN BLACKBURN
Library of 83,000 vols, 312 periodicals
Publications: *Conversations in Religion and Theology* (quarterly), *The Muslim World* (quarterly), *Reviews in Religion and Theology* (quarterly).

HOLY APOSTLES COLLEGE

33 Prospect Hill Rd, Cromwell, CT 06416-2005
Telephone: (860) 632-3010
Fax: (860) 632-3030
E-mail: rector@holyapostles.edu
Internet: www.holyapostles.edu
Founded 1956 as Holy Apostles Seminary; present name 1972
Private control
Catholic liberal arts college
Academic year: September to May
Chancellor: Most Rev. MICHAEL R. COTE
Pres. and Rector: Very Rev. DOUGLAS L. MOSEY
Academic Dean: Rev. MAURICE SHEEHAN
Vice-Pres.: Rev. JOHN HILLIER
Registrar: Dr CYNTHIA TOOLIN
Library Dir: CLARE ADAMO
Library of 60,000 vols, 200 periodicals.

PAIER COLLEGE OF ART, INC.

20 Gorham Ave Hamden, CT 06514
Telephone: (203) 287-3031
Fax: (203) 287-3021
E-mail: paier.admin@snet.net
Internet: www.paierart.com
Founded 1946
Private control
Fine Arts, Graphic Design, Illustration, Interior Design, Photography.

POST UNIVERSITY

POB 2540, 800 Country Club Rd, Waterbury, CT 06723-2540
Telephone: (203) 596-4520
Fax: (203) 756-5810
E-mail: registrar@post.edu
Internet: www.post.edu
Founded 1890
Private control

Academic year: September to May
Pres.: Dr PATRICIA SANDERS
Vice-Pres. for Academic Affairs: Dr JEFFREY HAND
Vice-Pres. for Finance and Admin.: SCOTT T. ALLEN
Dean of Students: JOHN WALLACE
Library Dir: TRACY A. RALSTON
Library of 125,000 vols
Divs of Business, Arts and Science.

QUINNIPIAC UNIVERSITY

275 Mount Carmel Ave, Hamden, CT 06518-1908
Telephone: (203) 282-8200
Fax: (203) 281-8906
E-mail: admissions@quinnipiac.edu
Internet: www.quinnipiac.edu
Founded 1929
Independent
Pres.: JOHN L. LAHEY
Sr Vice-Pres. for Academic and Student Affairs: KATHLEEN McCOURT
Sr Vice-Pres. for Finance and Admin.: PATRICK HEALY
Vice-Pres. and Dean of Student Affairs: MANUEL CARREIRO
Vice-Pres. for Public Affairs: LYNN BUSHNELL
Vice-Pres. and Chief Information and Technology Officer: RICHARD FERGUSON
Vice-Pres. for Athletic Marketing and External Relations: VAL BELMONTE
Vice-Pres. and Dean of Admissions: JOHN ISAAC MOHR
Vice-Pres. for Devt and Alumni Affairs: DONALD WEINBACH
Registrar: DOROTHY LAURIA
Library Dir: CHARLES M. GETCHELL, Jr
Library of 466,000 vols
Number of teachers: 569 (248 full-time, 321 part-time)
Number of students: 7,400

DEANS

School of Business: Dr MARK A. THOMPSON
School of Communications: DAVID DONNELLY
School of Health Sciences: Dr EDWARD R. O'CONNOR
College of Liberal Arts: HANS BERGMANN
School of Law: Dr BRAD SAXTON

ATTACHED INSTITUTES

Albert Schweitzer Institute: tel. (203) 582-3144; fax (203) 582-8478; e-mail schweitzer@quinnipiac.edu; f. 1984 as Albert Schweitzer Memorial Foundation; affiliated with Quinnipiac Univ. in 2002; Dir DAVID T. IVES.

Bioanthropology Research Institute: f. 1998; research in biology, archeology, anthropology and paleopathology through diagnostic imaging, video endoscopy and laboratory analysis; Dirs RONALD BECKETT, WILLIAM HENNESSY.

RENSSELAER AT HARTFORD

275 Windsor St, Hartford, CT 06120-2991
Telephone: (860) 548-2400
Fax: (860) 548-7823
E-mail: info@ewp.rpi.edu
Internet: www.rh.edu
Founded 1955; attached to Rensselaer Polytechnic Institute, New York
Vice-Provost and Dean: LESTER GERHARDT
Registrar: DORIS M. MATSIKAS
Library Dir: MARY S. DIXEY
Library of 30,000 vols, 490 periodicals
Number of teachers: 135 (35 full-time, 100 part-time)
Number of students: 2,100

MAs in Computer Science, Management, Eng., and Information Technology; Computer Science and Eng. graduate certificate programs.

SACRED HEART UNIVERSITY

5151 Park Ave, Fairfield, CT 06825-1000
Telephone: (203) 371-7999
Internet: www.sacredheart.edu
Founded 1963
Private control
Pres.: Dr ANTHONY J. CERNERA
Provost and Vice-Pres. for Academic Affairs: Dr THOMAS V. FORGET
Vice-Pres. for Enrollment Planning and Student Affairs: JAMES M. BARQUINERO
Vice-Pres. for Finance and Admin.: Dr PAUL K. MADONNA
Vice-Pres. for Human Resources: ROB HARDY
Vice-Pres. for Institutional Advancement: MARY P. YOUNG
Dean of Students: LARRY WIELK
Registrar: DOUGLAS J. BOHN
Univ. Librarian: DENNIS C. BENAMATI
Library of 180,000 vols
Number of teachers: 153 (full-time)
Number of students: 5,800 (3,400 full-time undergraduates, 800 part-time undergraduates and 1,600 graduates)

DEANS

College of Arts and Sciences: Dr CLAIRE J. PAOLINI
John F. Welch College of Business: Dr STEPHEN BROWN
College of Education and Health Professions: Dr PATRICIA WALKER
Univ. College: NANCY SIDOTI

CAMPUSES

Sacred Heart University at Griswold: Griswold High School, 267 Slater Ave, POB 399, Griswold, CT 06351; tel. (860) 376-8408.

Sacred Heart University Ireland: Diseart Institute of Education and Celtic Culture, Green St, Dingle, Ireland; e-mail irishstudies@sacredheart.edu; internet shuireland.sacredheart.edu; Irish Linguistics and Culture (incl. Archaeology, Customs, Folklore, History, Language, Literature, Music, Spirituality, Theology); Dir of Admissions for SHU DEANNA FIORENTINO; Academic Dir of Diseart Institute Prof. PADRAIG O FIANNACHTA.

Sacred Heart University Luxembourg: see separate entry in Luxembourg chapter.

Sacred Heart University at Trumbull: 101 Oakview Dr., Trumbull, CT 06611; tel. (203) 371-7941.

Sacred Heart University at Stamford: Stamford Campus, 12 Omega Dr., Stamford, CT 06907; tel. (203) 323-4959; fax (203) 323-4974.

Sacred Heart University in the Valley: Derby Campus, Derby High School, 8 Nutmeg Ave, Derby, CT 06418; tel. (203) 371-7831.

SAINT JOSEPH COLLEGE

1678 Asylum Ave, West Hartford, CT 06117-2791
Telephone: (860) 232-4571
Fax: (860) 231-8396
E-mail: info@sjc.edu
Internet: www.sjc.edu
Founded 1932
Pres.: Dr CAROL J. GUARDO
Vice-Pres. for Finance and Admin.: CHUCK MANN
Registrar: BRENDA R. SEBASTIANELLI
Library Dir: LINDA GEFFNER

Library of 133,700 vols
Number of teachers: 119
Number of students: 1,794

Depts of Biology, Chemistry, Child Study, Counsellor Education, Education, English, Fine and Performing Arts, Gerontology, History and Political Science, Human Devt and Family Studies, Int. Studies, Languages, Liberal Studies, Management Sciences, Marriage and Family Therapy, Mathematical Sciences, Nursing, Nutrition and Dietetics, Philosophy, Pre-Med, Psychology, Religious Studies, Social Work, Sociology and Econ.

SOUTHERN CONNECTICUT STATE UNIVERSITY

501 Crescent St, New Haven, CT 06515

Telephone: (203) 392-5200
Fax: (203) 392-5705
Internet: www.southernct.edu

Founded 1893
State control, mem. of the Connecticut State Univ. system

Pres.: CHERYL J. NORTON
Provost: SELASE W. WILLIAMS
Exec. Vice-Pres.: JAMES E. BLAKE
Vice-Pres. for Institutional Advancement: MEGAN A. ROCK
Vice-Pres. for Student and Univ. Affairs: RONALD HERRON
Dean of Student and Univ. Affairs: RICHARD V. FARRICIELLI
Registrar: LYNN KOHRN
Dir of Library Services: EDWARD C. HARRIS

Library of 300,000 vols
Number of teachers: 786 (403 full-time, 383 part-time)
Number of students: 12,100 (incl. 6,010 full-time undergraduates, 992 full-time graduates)

Depts of Accounting, Anthropology, Art, Biology, Chemistry, Communication, Communication Disorders, Computer Science, Counselling and School Psychology, Earth Science, Econ. and Finance, Educational Leadership, Elementary Education, English, Ethnic Studies, Exercise Science, Foreign Languages, Geography, History, Information and Library Science, Journalism, Management and Management Information Systems, Marketing, Marriage and Family Therapy, Mathematics, Media Studies, Music, Nursing, Philosophy, Physics, Political Science, Psychology, Public Health, Recreation and Leisure Studies, School Health, Science Education and Environmental Studies, Social Work, Sociology, Special Education and Reading, Theatre, Urban Studies, Women's Studies

DEANS

School of Arts and Sciences: DONNA JEAN FREDEEN
School of Business: HENRY H. HEIN
School of Communication, Information and Library Sciences: Dr EDWARD C. HARRIS
School of Education: JAMES GRANFIELD
School of Graduate Studies: SANDRA C. HOLLEY
School of Health and Human Services: GEORGE APPLEBY

TRINITY COLLEGE

300 Summit St, Hartford, CT 06106

Telephone: (860) 297-2000
Fax: (860) 297-2257
Internet: www.trincoll.edu

Founded 1823
Independent

Pres.: JAMES F. JONES, Jr
Dean of the Faculty and Vice-Pres. for Academic Affairs: RENA FRADEN

Vice-Pres. of College Advancement: RONALD A. JOYCE
Vice-Pres. for Alumni Relations and Communications: KATHLEEN O'CONNOR BOELHOUWER
Vice-Pres. of Finance and Treas.: EARLY REESE
Vice-Pres. for Strategic Planning, Admin. and Affirmative Action: PAULA A. RUSSO
Dean of Students: FREDERICK ALFORD
Dean of Admissions and Financial Aid: LARRY DOW
Dean of Multicultural Affairs: KARLA SPURLOCK-EVANS
Librarian: RICHARD ROSS

Library of 100,000 vols, 13,000 current periodicals, 250,000 audiovisual materials, govt documents
Number of teachers: 174 (full-time)
Number of students: 2,203 (undergraduate)

Areas of study: American Studies, Anthropology, Art History, Biology, Chemistry/Biochemistry, Classics, Computer Science, Econ., Educational Studies, Eng., English, Environmental Science, History, Int. Studies, Jewish Studies, Mathematics, Modern Languages and Literature, Music, Neuroscience, Philosophy, Physics, Political Science, Psychology, Public Policy and Law, Religion, Sociology, Studio Arts, Theater and Dance, Women, Gender and Sexuality

Publications: *Reporter*, *Review*, *Tripod*, *Trinity Papers*.

UNITED STATES COAST GUARD ACADEMY

31 Mohegan Ave, New London, CT 06320-8103

Telephone: (860) 444-8444
E-mail: admissions@cga.uscg.mil
Internet: www.cga.edu

Founded 1876 as School of Instruction for the Revenue Marine; present name 1915

Superintendent: Rear Admiral J. SCOTT BURHOE
Dean of Academics: Dr KURT J. COLELLA
Registrar: DONALD E. DYKEE
Library Dir: PATRICIA DARAGAN

Library of 130,000 vols, 600 periodicals
Number of students: 950

Depts of Eng., Homeland Security, Humanities, Management, Mathematics, Natural science, Science.

UNIVERSITY OF BRIDGEPORT

126 Park Ave, Bridgeport, CT 06604

Telephone: (203) 576-4552
Fax: (203) 576-4941
E-mail: admit@bridgeport.edu
Internet: www.bridgeport.edu

Founded 1927
Academic year: September to May

Pres.: NEIL ALBERT SALONEN
Provost and Sr Vice-Pres. for Academic Affairs: LAURENCE CORNER
Vice-Pres. for Admin. and Finance and Treasurer: THOMAS R. OATES
Vice-Pres. for Institutional Advancement (vacant)
Vice-Pres. for Int. Programs: Dr THOMAS J. WARD
Vice-Pres. for Enrollment Management: AUDREY ASHTON SAVAGE
Dean of Admissions: BARBARA L. MARYAK
Dean of Student Affairs: Dr JOSEPH J. ORAVECZ
Univ. Registrar: VALERIE E. POWELL BALDWIN
Univ. Librarian: DIANE MIRVIS

Library of 215,000 vols, 1,082,000 microforms, 870 current periodicals
Number of teachers: 102 full-time

Number of students: 3,300

DEANS

School of Arts and Sciences: Dr HANS VAN DER GIESSEN
School of Business: Dr GLENN BASSETT
College of Chiropractice: FRANK A. ZOLLI
School of Continuing and Professional Studies: MICHAEL J. GIAMPAOLI
School of Education and Human Resources: (vacant)
School of Eng.: Dr TAREK M. SOBH
Int. College: Dr THOMAS J. WARD
College of Naturopathic Medicine: GURU SANDESH SINGH KHALSA

UNIVERSITY OF CONNECTICUT

Storrs, CT 06269

Telephone: (860) 486-2000
Internet: www.uconn.edu

Founded 1881 as The Storrs Agricultural School, present name 1939
State control
Language of instruction: English
Academic year: September to May

Pres.: PHILIP E. AUSTIN
Vice-Pres. and Chief Operating Officer: BARRY M. FELDMAN
Provost and Exec. Vice-Pres. for Academic Affairs: PETER J. NICHOLLS
Exec. Vice-Pres. for Health Affairs: PETER J. DECKERS
Vice-Pres. and Chief Financial Officer: LORRAINE ARONSON
Vice-Chancellor for Student Affairs: JOHN SADDLEMIRE
Vice-Pres. for Operations and Admissions: THOMAS CALLAHAN
Vice-Provost or Undergraduate Education and Regional Campus Admin.: VERONICA MAKOWSKY
Vice-Provost for Academic Programs: SUMAN SINGHA
Vice-Provost for Enrollment Management: DOLAN EVANOVICH
Vice-Provost for Multicultural and Int. Affairs: RONALD L. TAYLOR
Vice-Provost for Univ. Libraries: BRINLEY FRANKLIN
Vice-Provost for Research: GREGORY ANDERSON
Vice-Pres. for Institutional Advancement: JOHN K. MARTIN

Library: see Libraries
Number of teachers: 1,200 (full-time)
Number of students: 28,481

Publications: *UConn Traditions* (3 a year), *College of Agriculture and Natural Resources Journal* (quarterly), *Connecticut Insurance Law Journal* (2 a year), *University Advance* (weekly during academic year), *Connecticut Law Review* (quarterly), *Connecticut Journal of International Law* (2 a year), *Connecticut Public Interest Law Journal* (online), *The Connecticut Economy* (quarterly), *MELUS* (quarterly)

DEANS

College of Agriculture and Natural Resources: KIRKLYN M. KERR
College of Liberal Arts and Sciences: ROSS D. MACKINNON
School of Business: MOHAMMED HUSSEIN
School of Dental Medicine: PETER ROBINSON
School of Education: RICHARD L. SCHWAB
School of Eng.: ERLING SMITH
School of Fine Arts: DAVID G. WOODS
School of Law: JEREMY R. PAUL
School of Medicine: PETER J. DECKERS
School of Nursing: E. CAROL POLIFRONI
School of Pharmacy: ROBERT L. MCCARTHY
School of Social Work: KAY DAVIDSON
Graduate School: GREGORY ANDERSON

DIRECTORS

Marine Science and Technology Center: ANN BUCKLIN

Institute of Materials Science: HARRIS MARCUS

Institute for Social Inquiry: DAVID WEAKLIEM

Center for Academic Programs: MARIA MARTINEZ

Centre for Instructional Media and Technology: STEVEN M. MCDERMOTT

Int. Services and Programs: MARK WENTZEL

Institute for Teaching and Learning: KEITH BARKER

Urban Semester Program: LOUISE SIMMONS

Study Abroad Programs: ROSS LEWIN

Office of Institutional Research: PAM ROELFS

PROFESSORS

College of Agriculture and Natural Resources (1376 Storrs Rd, Unit 4066, Storrs, CT 06269-4066; tel. (860) 486-2917; fax (860) 486-5113; internet www.canr.uconn.edu):

ADAMS Jr, R. G., Entomology
BERKOWITZ, G., Plant Science
BLASIAK, M. M., Plant Science
BRAND, M. H., Plant Science
BRAVO-URETA, B. E., Agricultural Econ.
BULL, N. H., Co-operative Extension
CIVCO, D. L., Natural Resources Management
CLARK, R. M., Nutritional Sciences
COTTERILL, R. W., Agricultural Econ.
DARRE, M. J., Animal Science
FERRIS, A. G., Nutritional Sciences
FAUSTMAN, L. C., Animal Science
FERNANDEZ, M. L., Nutritional Sciences
FREAKE, H. C., Nutritional Sciences
GEARY, S. J., Pathobiology
GREGER, J., Nutritional Sciences
GUILLARD, K., Plant Science
HART, I. C., Animal Science
HOAGLUND, T. A., Animal Science
KERR, K. M., Pathobiology
KHAN, M. I., Pathology
KOO, S. I., Nutritional Sciences
LAMMI-KEEFE, C. J., Nutritional Sciences
LEE, L. K., Agriculture and Resource Econ.
LOPEZ, R. A., Agricultural Econ.
LOVE, C., Co-operative Extension
McAVOY, R. J., Plant Science
MILLER, D. R., Natural Resources
PAGOULATOS, E., Agricultural Econ.
ROBBINS, G. A., Natural Resources
SCHROEDER, D. B., Natural Resources
SILBART, L. K., Animal Science
SINGHA, S., Horticulture
VAN KRUININGEN, H. J., Pathobiology
YANG, X., Animal Science
YANG, X. (H.), Natural Resources Management and Eng.
ZINN, S. A., Animal Science

Ratcliffe Hicks School of Agriculture (1376 Storrs Rd, Unit 90, Storrs, CT 06269-4090; tel. (860) 486-2920; e-mail acadprog@canr.uconn.edu; internet www.canr.uconn.edu/rh):

School of Business (2100 Hillside Rd, Unit 1041, Storrs, CT 06269-1041; tel. (860) 486-2314; fax 486-0889; internet www.sba.uconn.edu):

BIGGS, S. F., Accounting
CARRAFIELLO, V. A., Business Law
CLAPP, J. M., Finance
FLOYD, S. W., Management
FOX, K. H., Business Law
GARFINKEL, R. S., Operations Research and Information Management
GHOSH, C., Finance
GIACOTTO, C., Finance
GOES, P. B., Operations and Information Management
GOPAL, R., Operations Research and Information Management

HEGDE, S. P., Finance
HUNTER, W. C., Finance
HUSSEIN, M. E., Accounting
JAIN, S. C., Marketing
KUMAR, V., Marketing
LUBATKIN, M. J., Management
MARSDEN, J. R., Operations Research and Information Management
MATHIEU, J. E., Management
NAIR, S. K., Operations Research and Information Management
O'BRIEN, T. J., Finance
POWELL, G. N., Management
SANTERRE, R., Finance
SCOTT, G. M., Operations Research and Information Management
SEWALL, M. A., Marketing
SIRMANS, C. F., Finance and Real Estate
SUTTON, S. G., Accounting
VEIGA, J. F., Management

School of Dental Medicine (263 Farmington Ave, Farmington, CT 06030; tel. (860) 679-2000; internet sdm.uchc.edu):

BEAZOGLOU, T., Paediatric Dentistry
EISENBERG, E., Oral Diagnosis
FRANK, M. E., Oral Diagnosis
FREILICH, M., Prosthodontics and Operative Dentistry
GOLDBERG, A. J., Prosthodontics and Operative Dentistry
HAND, A., Paediatric Dentistry
KELLY, J. R., Prostodontics and Operative Dentistry
LITT, M. D., Behavioural Science and Community Health
LURIE, A. G., Oral Diagnosis
MacNEIL, R., Periodontology
MINA, M., Paediatric Dentistry
NANDA, R., Orthodontics
NICHOLS, F., Periodontology
PETERSON, D. E., Oral Diagnosis
REISINE, S., Behavioural Sciences and Community Health
ROBINSON, P., Periodontology
ROSSOMANDO, E. P., Biostructure and Function
SAFAVI, K., Endodontology
SPANGBERG, L. S. W., Endodontology
TANZER, J. M., Oral Diagnosis
TAYLOR, T., Prosthodontics and Operative Dentistry
TONETTI, M., Periodontology
TRUMMEL, C. L., Periodontology
UPHOLT, W., Biostructure and Function

Neag School of Education (249 Glenbrook Rd, Unit 2064, Storrs, CT 06269-2064; tel. (860) 486-3813; fax (860) 486-0210; internet www.education.uconn.edu):

ARMSTRONG, L. E., Kinesiology
BROWN, S. W., Educational Psychology
DEFRANCO, T., Curriculum and Instruction
DOYLE, M. A., Curriculum and Instruction
GOODKIND, T. B., Curriculum and Instruction
IRWIN, J. W., Curriculum and Instruction
KARAN, O. C., Educational Psychology
KEHLE, T. J., Educational Psychology
KRAEMER, W. J., Kinesiology
LEU, D. J., Curriculum and Instruction
McGUIRE, J. M., Educational Psychology
MARESH, C. M., Kinesiology
RALLIS, S. F., Educational Leadership
REAGAN, T., Curriculum and Instruction
REIS, S. M., Educational Psychology
SCHWAB, R. L., Educational Leadership
SHAW, S. F., Educational Psychology
SHECKLEY, B. G., Educational Leadership
SWAMINATHAN, H., Educational Psychology
YIANNAKIS, A., Kinesiology

School of Engineering (261 Glenbrook Rd, Unit 2237, Storrs, CT 06269-2237; tel. (860) 486-2221; fax (860) 486-0318; internet www.enga.uconn.edu):

ACCORSI, M. L., Civil and Environmental Eng.
ACHENIE, L. E., Chemical Eng.
AMMAR, R. A., Computer Science and Eng.
ANWAR, A. F. M., Electrical and Computer Eng.
BANSAL, R., Electrical and Systems Eng.
BAR-SHALOM, Y., Electrical and Computer Eng.
BARKER, K., Computer Science and Eng.
BERGMAN, T. L., Mechanical Eng.
BRODY, H. D., Materials Science and Eng.
CETEGEN, B., Mechanical Eng.
COOPER, D. J., Chemical Eng.
DAVIS, C. F., Civil and Environmental Eng.
DEMURJIAN, S. A., Computer Science and Eng.
DEWOLF, J. T., Civil and Environmental Eng.
ENDERLE, J. D., Electrical and Computer Eng.
ENGEL, G. L., Computer Science and Eng. and Electrical and Systems Eng.
EPSTEIN, H. I., Civil and Environmental Eng.
FAGHIRI, A., Mechanical Eng.
FOX, M. D., Electrical and Computer Eng.
FRANTZ, G. C., Civil and Environmental Eng.
HELBLE, J., Chemical Eng.
HOAG, G. E., Civil Eng.
JAIN, F. C., Electrical and Computer Eng.
JAVIDI, B., Electrical and Computer Eng.
JORDAN, E. H., Mechanical Eng.
KATTAMIS, T. Z., Materials Science and Eng.
KAZEROUNIAN, K., Mechanical Eng.
LIPSKY, L., Computer Science and Eng.
LUH, P. B., Electrical and Computer Eng.
MAGNUSSON, R., Electrical and Computer Eng.
MARCUS, H. L., Materials Science and Eng.
MURTHA-SMITH, E., Civil and Environmental Eng.
OLGAC, N., Mechanical Eng.
OR, D., Civil and Electrical Eng.
PATTIPATI, K. R., Electrical and Computer Eng.
PITCHUMANI, R., Mechanical Eng.
RAJASEKARAN, S., Computer Science and Eng.
REIFSNIDER, K. L., Mechanical Eng.
SAMMES, N. M., Mechanical Eng.
SHAW, L. L., Materials Science and Eng.
SHAW, M. T., Chemical Eng.
SHIN, D. G., Computer Science and Eng.
TAYLOR, G. W., Electrical and Computer Eng.
WEISS, R. A., Chemical Eng.
WILLETT, P. K., Electrical and Computer Eng.
WOOD, T. K., Chemical Eng.
ZHANG, B., Mechanical Eng.

Whetten Graduate Center (438 Whitney Rd Ext, Unit 1006, Storrs, CT 06269-1006; tel. (860) 486-3617; fax (860) 486-6739; e-mail gradschool@uconn.edu; internet www.grad.uconn.edu):

School of Fine Arts (875 Coventry Rd, Unit 1128, Storrs, CT 06269-1128; tel. (860) 486-3016; fax (860) 486-5845; internet www.sfa.uconn.edu):

ARM, T. E., Music
BASS, W. R., Music
CROW, L. J., Dramatic Arts
ENGLISH, G. M., Dramatic Arts
FRANKLIN, J. F., Dramatic Arts
FROGLEY, A., Music
JUNDA, M. E., Music
McDONALD, R. A., Dramatic Arts
MARTINEZ, A., Art
MAZZOCCA, A. N., Art
MILLER, R. F., Music
MOLETTE, C. W., Dramatic Arts

MUIRHEAD, D. D., Art
MYERS, K. M., Art and Art History
RENSHAW, J. H., Music
ROCCOBERTON, B. P. Jr, Dramatic Arts
RYKER, K., Dramatic Arts
SABATINE, J. A., Dramatic Arts
STANLEY, G., Music
STEPHENS, R. W., Music
STERN, A. S., Dramatic Arts
TALVACCHIA, B. L., Art
THORPE, J. K., Art
WOODS, D. G., Music

School of Law (55 Elizabeth St, Hartford, CT 06105-2296; tel. (860) 570-5000; fax (860) 570-5128; internet www.law.uconn.edu):

BAKER, T. E.
BARNES, R. D.
BECKER, L. E., Jr
BERMAN, P. S.
BIRMINGHAM, R. L.
CALLOWAY, D. A.
DAILEY, A. C.
FERNOW, T. O.
GUSTAFSON, K.
JANIS, M. W.
KAY, R. S.
KIRK, D.
KURLANTZICK, L. S.
LEVIN, L. C.
MACGILL, H. C.
McCOY, P.
McLEAN, W. E.
MORAWETZ, T. H.
NEWTON, N. J.
OQUENDO, A. R.
ORLAND, L.
PARKER, R. W.
PAUL, J.
POMP, R. D.
SIEGELMAN, P.
SILVERSTEIN, E.
STARK, J. H.
STRASSER, K. A.
TONDRO, T. J.
UTZ, S. G.
WEISBROD, C. A.
WHITMAN, R.
WILF, S.

College of Liberal Arts and Sciences (215 Glenbrook Rd, Unit 4098, Storrs, CT 06269-4098; tel. (860) 486-2713; fax (860) 486-0304; internet www.clas.uconn.edu):

ABE, K., Mathematics
ABIKOFF, W., Mathematics
ABRAHAMSON, M., Sociology
ALBERT, A. D., Molecular and Cell Biology
ANDERSON, G. J., Ecology and Evolutionary Biology
ANDERSON, S. L., Philosophy
ANSELMENT, R. A., English
AUSTIN, P. E., Econ.
BAILEY, W. F., Chemistry
BARRECA, R. R., English
BASS, R., Mathematics
BASU, A. K., Chemistry
BAXTER, D. L., Philosophy
BENSON, C. D., English
BENSON, D. R., Molecular and Cell Biology
BERENTSON, W., Geography
BERTHELOT, A., Modern and Classical Languages (French)
BEST, P. E., Physics
BIGGS, F., English
BIRGE, R. R., Physics
BLEI, R. C., Mathematics
BLOOM, L. Z., English
BOHLEN, W. F., Marine Sciences
BOHN, R. K., Chemistry
BOSKOVIC, Z., Linguistics
BOSTER, J. S., Anthropology
BOYER, M. A., Political Science
BRADFIELD, S., English
BROADHEAD, R. S., Sociology
BROWN, R. D., History
BUCK, R. W., Communication Sciences

BUCKLEY, R. N., History
BUCKLIN, A., Marine Sciences
CAIRA, J. N., Ecology and Evolutionary Biology
CARELLO, C. A., Psychology
CARSTENSEN, F. V., Econ.
CHAFFIN, R., Psychology
CHAPPLE, W. D., Physiology and Neurobiology
CHARTERS, A. D., English
CHAZDON, R. L., Ecology and Environmental Biology
CHEN, M. H., Statistics
CHEN, T. T., Molecular and Cell Biology
CHOI, Y. S., Mathematics
CLARK, A., Philosophy
CLIFFORD, J. G., Political Science
COELHO, C. A., Communication Sciences
COLWELL, R. K., Ecology and Evolutionary Biology
COMPRONE, J. J., English
CORMIER, V. F., Physics
COSGEL, M. M., Econ.
COSTIGLIOLA, F., History
CRAWFORD, M., Psychology
CRIVELLO, J. F., Physiology and Neurobiology
CROMLEY, E. K., Geography
CROMLEY, R. G., Geography
CROTEAU, M. E., Journalism
D'ANDRELE, R., Anthropology
DALMOLIN, E. F., Modern and Classical Language (French)
DAM, H. G., Marine Sciences
DASHEFSKY, A. M., Sociology
DAVID, C. W., Chemistry
DAVIS, J. A., History
DEBLAS, A. L., Physiology and Neurobiology
DESCH Jr, C. E., Ecology and Evolutionary Biology
DEY, D. K., Statistics
DOVIDIO, J. T., Psychology
DULACK, T., English
DUNNE, G. V., Physics
DUTTA, N. K., Physics
ELDER, C. L., Philosophy
EBY, C. V., English
EYLER, E. E., Physics
FARNEN, R. F., Political Science
FEIN, D. A., Psychology
FISHER, J. D., Psychology
FITZGERALD, W. F., Marine Sciences
FOWLER, C. A., Psychology
FRANK, H. A., Chemistry
FRANKLIN, W., English
GAI, M., Physics
GALLO, R. V., Physiology and Neurobiology
GARRO, L. C., Anthropology
GIBSON, G. N., Physics
GILBERT, H. R., Communication Sciences
GILBERT, M. P., Philosophy
GINE, E., Mathematics
GLASBERG, D. S., Sociology
GLAZ, J., Statistics
GLAZ, S., Mathematics
GOGARTEN, J. P., Molecular and Cell Biology
GOODHEART, L. B., History
GOODSTEIN, L., Sociology
GORDON, R. B., Modern and Classical Languages (French)
GOULD, P. L., Physics
GREEN, J. A., Psychology
GROSS, R. A., History
GUENOUN, S., Modern and Classical Languages (French)
GUERRERO, H. D., Marine Sciences
HAAS, A. H., Mathematics
HALLWOOD, C. P., Econ.
HAMILTON, D. S., Physics
HANDWERKER, W. P., Anthropology
HANINK, D. M., Geography
HANSON, B. C., Political Science
HARRIS, S., English
HEFFLEY, D. R., Econ.

HENRY, C. S., Ecology and Evolutionary Biology
HERZBERGER, D. K., Modern and Classical Languages (Spanish)
HIGHTOWER, L. E., Molecular and Cell Biology
HIGONETT, M. R., English
HISER, C., Aerospace Studies
HISKES, R. P., Political Science
HOGAN, P. C., English
HOLLENBERG, D. C., English
HOLSINGER, K. E., Ecology and Evolutionary Biology
HOLZWORTH, J., Psychology
HOWELL, A. R., Chemistry
ISLAM, M. M., Physics
JAVANAINEN, J. M., Physics
JOESTEN, R. L., Chemistry
JOHNSON, B. T., Psychology
JONES, S. P., English
KALICHMAN, S., Psychology
KAPPERS, L. A., Physics
KATZ, L., Psychology
KENDALL, D. A., Molecular and Cell Biology
KENNY, D. A., Psychology
KNECHT, D. A., Molecular and Cell Biology
KNOBLAUCH, V. L., Econ.
KOLTRACIIT, I., Mathematics
KORN, S. J., Physiology and Neurobiology
KREMER, J. N., Marine Sciences
KUMAR, C. V., Chemistry
KUO, L., Statistics
KUPPERMAN, J. J., Philosophy
LANGLOIS, R. N., Econ.
LEADBETTER, E. R., Molecular and Cell Biology
LERMAN, M., Mathematics
LES, D. H., Ecology and Environmental Biology
LEWIS, C. W., Public Policy
LILLO-MARTIN, D. C., Linguistics
LIN, C. A., Communication Sciences
LINNEKIN, J. S., Anthropology
LoTURCO, J. J., Physiology and Neurobiology
LOWE, C. A., Psychology
LUYSTER, R. W., Philosophy
LYNES, M. A., Molecular and Cell Biology
McBREATY, S. A., Anthropology
McKENNA, P. J., Mathematics
MACKINNON, R. D., Geography
MACLEOD, G. G., English
MADYCH, W. R., Mathematics
MAKOWSKY, V. A., English
MALLETT, R. L., Physics
MANNHEIM, P. O., Physics
MARCUS, P. I., Molecular and Cell Biology
MARSDEN, J., English
MASCIANDARO, F., Modern and Classical Languages (Italian)
MAXSON, S. C., Psychology
MEYER, M., English
MEYERS, D. T., Philosophy
MICELI, T. J., Econ.
MICHEL, R. G., Chemistry
MILLER, D. B., Psychology
MILLER, R. L., English
MILLER, S. S., Modern and Classical Languages (Classics and Hebrew)
MOISEFF, A., Physiology and Neurobiology
MONAHAN, E. C., Marine Sciences
MUKHOPADHYAY, N., Statistics
MURPHY, B., English
MUSIEK, F., Communication Sciences
NAPLES, N., Sociology
NEUMANN, M., Mathematics
O'DONNELL, J., Marine Sciences
OLSHEVASKY, V., Mathematics
OSLEEB, J. P., Geography
PAPADIMITRAKOPOULOUS, F., Chemistry
PEASE, D. M., Physics
PETERSON, C. W., Physics
PETERSON, R. S., English
PHILLIPS, R. L., Philosophy
PICKERING, S. F., English
PRATTO, F., Psychology

RAVISHANKER, N., Statistics
RAWITSCHER, G. H., Physics
RAY, S. C., Econ.
REITER, H. L., Political Science
RENFRO, J. L., Physiology and Neurobiology
RICKARDS, J. P., Psychology
RIGGIO, T. P., English
ROCKWELL, R. C., Sociology
ROE, S. A., History
RUSLING, J. F., Chemistry
SALAMONE, J. D., Psychology
SANDERS, C. R., Sociology
SCHAEFER, C. W., Ecology and Evolutionary Biology
SCHLICHTING, C. D., Ecology and Environmental Biology
SCHWENK, K., Ecology and Environmental Biology
SEGERSON, K., Econ.
SEHULSTER, J. R., Psychology
SHOEMAKER, N., History
SIDNEY, S. J., Mathematics
SILANDER, J. A., Ecology and Evolutionary Biology
SILVESTRINI, B. G., History
SIMON, C. M., Ecology and Environmental Biology
SIMONSEN, W., Public Policy
SMITH, M. B., Chemistry
SMITH, W. W., Physics
SNYDER, L. B., Communication Sciences
SONSTROEM, D. A., English
SPALDING, K., History
SPIEGEL, E. S., Mathematics
STRAUSBAUGH, L. D., Molecular and Cell Biology
STWALLEY, W. C., Physics
SUIB, S. L., Chemistry
SUNG, C. S. P., Chemistry
SWADLOW, H. A., Psychology
SWANSON, M. S., Physics
TANAKA, J., Chemistry
TAYLOR, R. L., Sociology
THORSON, R. M., Ecology and Evolutionary Biology
TOLLEFSON, J. L., Mathematics
TORGERSEN, T. L., Marine Sciences
TUCHMAN, G., Sociology
TURCHIN, P., Ecology and Environmental Biology
TURVEY, M. T., Psychology
VAN DER HULST, H. G., Linguistics
VEILLEUX, P. C., Military Science
VENGROFF, R., Political Science
VILLEMEZ, W. J., Sociology
VINSONHALER, C., Mathematics
VITALE, R. A., Statistics
WALLACE, M., Sociology
WALLER, A. L., History
WANG, Y., Statistics
WEAKLIEM, D. L., Sociology
WELLS, K. D., Ecology and Evolutionary Biology
WHEELER, S. C., Philosophy
WHITLATCH, R. B., Marine Sciences
WILKENFELD, R. B., English
WILSON, R. A., Anthropology
WORCESTER, W. A., Journalism
YARISH, C., Ecology and Evolutionary Biology
YEAGLE, P. L., Molecular and Cell Biology
ZIRAKZADEH, C. E., Political Science

School of Medicine (263 Farmington Ave, Farmington, CT 06030-1920; tel. (860) 679-2413; fax (860) 679-1371; internet medicine .uchc.edu):

ALBERTSON, P. C., Surgery
ALTMAN, A. J., Paediatrics
ARNOLD, A., Medicine
BABOR, T. F., Community Medicine and Health Care
BARBARESE, E., Neuroscience
BAUER, L. O., Psychiatry

BENN, P. A., Genetics and Developmental Biology
BERLIN, R. D., Cell Biology
BIGAZZI, P. E., Pathology
BONKOVSKY, H. L., Medicine
BROWNER, B. O., Orthopaedic Surgery
BRUDER, M. E., Paediatrics
CAMPBELL, W. A., Obstetrics and Gynaecology
CARMICHAEL, G. G., Genetics and Developmental Biology
CARSON, J. H., Molecular, Microbial and Structural Biology
CHERNIAK, M. G., Medicine
CINTI, D. L., Pharmacology
CIVETTA, J. M., Surgery
CLOUTIER, M., Paediatrics
CONE, R. E., Pathology
CUSHMAN, R. A., Family Medicine
DAS, A. K., Molecular, Microbial and Structural Biology
DAS, D. K., Surgery
DECKERS, P. J., Surgery
DONALDSON III, J. O., Neurology
EIPPER, E. A., Molecular, Microbial and Structural Biology
EISENBERG, S., Molecular, Microbial and Structural Biology
FEDER Jr, H. M., Family Medicine
FEIN, A., Cell Biology
FEINSTEIN, M. B., Pharmacology
FIFIELD, J., Family Medicine
FOROUHAR, F., Pathology
FORTINSKY, R. H., Medicine
GARIBALDI, R., Medicine
GOLDSCHNEIDER, I., Pathology
GRANT-KELS, J. M., Dermatology
GRASSO, J. A., Cell Biology
GREENSTEIN, R. M., Genetics and Developmental Biology
GRONOWICZ, G. F., Orthopaedic Surgery
GROSS, J. B., Anaesthesiology
HANSEN, M., Medicine
HELFAND, S., Genetics and Developmental Biology
HESSELBROCK, V. M., Psychiatry
HLA, T. R., Cell Biology
HUEY, L., Psychiatry
HURLEY, M. M., Medicine
JAFFE, L., Cell Biology
KADDEN, R. M., Psychiatry
KIM, D. O., Neuroscience
KING, G. F., Molecular, Microbial and Structural Biology
KING, S. M., Molecular, Microbial and Structural Biology
KLOBUTCHER, L. A., Molecular, Microbial and Structural Biology
KOEPPEN, B. M., Medicine
KOPPEL, D. E., Molecular, Microbial and Structural Biology
KRANZLER, H. R., Psychiatry
KREAM, B., Medicine
KREUTZER, D. L., Pathology
KUWADA, S., Neuroscience
LALANDE, M., Genetics and Developmental Biology
LE FRANCOIS, L., Medicine
LEVINE, J. B., Medicine
LIANG, B. T., Medicine
LORENZO, J. A., Medicine
LOEW, L. M., Cell Biology
MAINS, R. E., Neuroscience
MAXWELL, G. D., Neuroscience
MOREST, D. K., Neuroscience
MUKHERJI, B., Medicine
OLIVER, D. L., Neuroscience
O'ROURKE, J. T., Pathology
OZOLS, J., Molecular, Microbial and Structural Biology
PAPERMASTER, D. S., Neuroscience
PAPPANO, A. J., Pharmacology
PELUSO, J. J., Cell Biology
PETRY, N., Psychiatry
PFEIFFER, S. E., Neuroscience
POTASHNER, S. J., Neuroscience

RADOLF, J. D., Medicine
RAISZ, L. G., Medicine
RAJAN, T. V., Pathology
RATZAN, S. K., Paediatrics
ROSENBERG, D., Medicine
ROWE, D. W., Genetics and Developmental Biology
RUNOWICZ, C. D., Obstetrics and Gynaecology
SANDERS, M. M., Pathology
SARFARAZI, M., Surgery
SETLOW, P., Molecular, Microbial and Structural Biology
SHANLEY, J. D., Medicine
SIMON, R. H., Surgery
SRIVASTAVA, P. K., Medicine
TENNEN, H., Community Medicine and Health Care
TRAHIOTIS, C., Neuroscience
WELLER, S. K., Molecular, Microbial and Structural Biology
WHITE, B. A., Cell Biology
WHITE, W. B., Medicine
WIKEL, S. K., Cell Biology
WINOKUR, A., Psychiatry
WOLFSON, L. I., Neurology
WU, C. H., Medicine
WU, D., Genetics and Developmental Biology
WU, G. Y., Medicine

School of Nursing (231 Glenbrook Rd, Unit 2026, Storrs, CT 06269-2026; tel. (860) 486-3716; fax (860) 486-0001; internet www .nursing.uconn.edu):

BECK, C. L., Nursing
CUSSON, R., Nursing
DZUREC, L., Nursing
KOERNER, B. L., Nursing
NEAFSEY, P. J., Nursing

School of Pharmacy (372 Fairfield Rd, Unit 2092, Storrs, CT 06269-2092; tel. (860) 486-2129; fax (860) 486-4998; internet pharmacy .uconn.edu):

BURGESS, D. J., Pharmaceutics
GERALD, M. C., Pharmacology
LANGNER, R. O., Pharmacology
McCARTHY, R. L., Pharmacy Practice
MORRIS, J. B., Toxicology
PIKAL, M. J., Pharmaceutics

School of Social Work (1798 Asylum Ave, West Hartford, CT 06117; tel. (860) 570-9141; fax (860) 570-9264; internet www.ssw.uconn .edu):

BLOOM, M.
DAVIDSON, K. W.
FISHER, R.
GITTERMAN, A.
HEALY, L. M.
HESSELBROCK, M. N.
HUMPHREYS, N. A.
JOHNSON, H. C.
KLEIN, W. C.
PINE, B. A.

ATTACHED INSTITUTES

Center for Contemporary African Studies: Dir ELIZABETH MAHAN.

Center for Applied Genetics and Technology: Dir LINDA D. STRAUSBAUGH.

Alcohol Research Center: Dir VICTOR HESSELBROCK.

Center for Biochemical Toxicology: Dir JOHN MORRIS.

Biotechnology Center: Dir PHILIP MARCUS.

Booth Engineering Center for Advanced Technology: Dir SANGUTHEVAR RAJASE-KARAN.

Center for International Business and Education Research: Dir SUBHASH JAIN.

Connecticut Center for Economic Analysis: Dir FRED CARSTENSEN.

Connecticut Small Business Development Center: Dir RICHARD CHENEY.

Center for Conservation and Biodiversity: Co-Dirs JOHN SILANDER, DAVID WAGNER.

Center for Economic Education: Chair. FRED CARSTENSEN.

Center for Environmental Health: Dir CAMERON FAUSTMAN.

Electrical Insulation Research Center: Dir STEVEN BOGGS.

Center for European Studies: Dir JOHN A. DAVIS.

Food Marketing Policy Center: Dir RONALD COTTERILL.

Connecticut Global Fuel Cell Center: Dir KENNETH REIFSNIDER.

Center for Judaic Studies and Contemporary Jewish Life: Dir ARNOLD DASHEFSKY.

Labor Education Center: Dir MARK SULLIVAN.

Center for Latin American and Caribbean Studies: Dir PETER KINGSTONE.

Center for Materials Simulation: Dir PHILIP C. CLAPP.

National Research Center on the Gifted and Talented: Dir JOSEPH RENZULLI.

National Undersea Research Center: Dir IVAR BABB.

Center for Oral History: Dir BRUCE STAVE.

Pappanikou Center for Developmental Disabilities: Dir MARY BETH BRUDER.

Center for Real Estate and Urban Economic Studies: Dir C. F. SIRMANS.

Center for International Social Work Studies: Dir LYNN HEALY.

Center for the Study of Parental Acceptance and Rejection: Dir RONALD P. ROHNER.

Northeastern Research Center for Wildlife Diseases: Dir HERBERT VAN KRUININGEN.

Insurance Law Center: Dir TOM BAKER.

Institute for African-American Studies: Dir JEFFREY OGBAR.

Asian American Studies Institute: Dir ROGER BUCKLEY.

Environmental Research Institute: Dir JOHN C. CLAUSEN.

Center for Healthcare and Insurance Studies: Dir JEFFREY KRAMER.

Marine Science and Technology Center: Dir ANN BUCKLIN.

Institute of Materials Science: Dir HARRIS MARCUS.

Institute of Public Affairs: Dir KENNETH DAUTRICH.

Institute for the Advancement of Political Social Work Practice: Dir NANCY A. HUMPHREYS.

Institute of Public Service International: Dir MARIA-TERESA LEPELEY.

Puerto Rican and Latino Studies Institute: Dir BLANCA SILVESTRINI (acting).

Small Business Institute: Dir JOHN F. VEIGA.

Institute for Social Inquiry (and The Roper Center for Public Opinion Research): Dir DAVID WEAKLIEM.

Connecticut Transportation Institute: Dir LISA AULTMAN-HALL.

Institute for Violence Reduction: Dir (vacant).

Institute of Water Resources: Dir GLEN WARNER.

Center for Immunotherapy of Cancer and Infectious Diseases: Dir PRAMOD SRIVASTAVA.

Center for Molecular Medicine: Dir Dr ANDREW ARNOLD.

Health Policy and Primary Care Research Center: Dir Dr HOWARD L. BAILIT.

Center for Microbial Pathogenesis: Dir Dr STEPHEN WIKEL.

UNIVERSITY OF HARTFORD

200 Bloomfield Ave, West Hartford, CT 06117

Telephone: (860) 768-4100
Fax: (860) 768-5417
Internet: www.hartford.edu
Founded 1877
Private control
Academic year: July to June
Pres.: Dr WALTER HARRISON
Provost: JOSEPH C. VOELKER
Asst Provost and Dean of Faculty Devt: KATHERINE A. BLACK
Vice-Pres. for Finance and Admin.: BEVERLY P. MAKSIN
Vice-Pres. for Institutional Advancement: DONALD RIZZO
Vice-Pres. for Univ. Relations: JOHN J. CARSON
Vice-Pres. for Student Affairs: J. LEE PETERS
Registrar: DOREEN LAY
Dean of Graduate Studies: PETER DIFFLEY
Assoc. Provost and Dean of Undergraduate Studies: GUY C. COLARULLI
Dean of Admissions: RICHARD ZEISER
Dir of Libraries and Learning Resources: RANDI ASHTON-PRITTING
Library of 606,154 vols
Number of teachers: 319 full-time, 425 part-time
Number of students: 7,200 (5,500 undergraduate, 1,700 postgraduate)

DEANS

Hartford Art School: Dr POWER BOOTHE
College of Arts and Sciences: Dr JOSEPH VOELKER
Barney School of Business: JAMES W. FAIRFIELD-SONN
Hillyer College: Dr DAVID GOLDENBERG
College of Education, Nursing and Health Professions: Dr DOROTHY ZEISER
College of Eng., Technology and Architecture: LOUIS T. MANZIONE
Hartt School: MALCOLM MORRISON

UNIVERSITY OF NEW HAVEN

300 Boston Post Rd, West Haven, CT 06516
Telephone: (203) 932-7000
Fax: (203) 932-3060
E-mail: adminfo@newhaven.edu
Internet: www.newhaven.edu
Founded 1920
Pres.: STEVEN H. KAPLAN
Provost and Sr Vice-Pres. for Academic and Student Affairs: Dr DAVID P. DAUWALDER
Vice-Pres. for Facilities: WILLIAM M. LEETE
Vice-Pres. for Univ. Advancement: CATHERINE SPINELLI
Vice-Pres. for Finance: GEORGE SYNODI
Vice-Pres. for Enrollment Management: DENNIS NOSTRAND
Librarian: HANKO DOBI
Library of 300,000 vols, 423,000 documents
Number of teachers: 599 (170 full-time, 429 part-time)
Number of students: 5,113
Publication: *Essays in Arts and Sciences*

DEANS

College of Arts and Sciences: Dr RONALD H. NOWACZYK
School of Business: JESS BORONICO

Tagliatela College of Eng.: Dr BARRY FARBROTHER
Henry C. Lee College of Criminal Justice and Forensic Sciences: THOMAS A. JOHNSON

WESLEYAN UNIVERSITY

229 High St, Middletown, CT 06459
Telephone: (860) 685-3500
Fax: (860) 685-3501
Internet: www.wesleyan.edu
Founded 1831
Academic year: September to May
Pres.: Dr DOUGLAS J. BENNET
Vice-Pres. for Academic Affairs and Provost: JOE BRUNO
Vice-Pres. for Finance and Admin.: MARCIA BROMBERG
Vice-Pres. and Sec.: JUDITH C. BROWN
Vice-Pres. for Univ. Relations: BARBARA-JAN WILSON
Dean of Admissions and Financial Aid: NANCY HARGRAVE MEISLAHN
Univ. Librarian: BARBARA JONES
Library of 1,000,000 vols
Number of teachers: 341
Number of students: 3,685 (2,700 undergraduate, 985 postgraduate)
Publication: *Catalog Annual*

DEANS

Arts and Humanities: LILY MILROY
Natural Sciences, Mathematics and Computer Science: DAVID BRODZNICK
Social Sciences and Interdisciplinary Programs: DONALD MOON

WESTERN CONNECTICUT STATE UNIVERSITY

181 White St, Danbury, CT 06810
Telephone: (203) 837-8210
Internet: www.wcsu.edu
Founded 1903
State control, mem. of Connecticut State Univ. System
Academic year: August to May
Pres.: JAMES W. ROACH
Provost and Vice-Pres. for Academic Affairs: Dr LINDA RINKER
Vice-Pres. for Student Affairs: WALTER B. BERNSTEIN
Dean of Students: WALTER CRAMER
Registrar: IRENE DUFFY
Dir of Library Services: RALPH HOLIBAUGH
Number of teachers: 518 (200 full-time and 318 part-time)
Number of students: 6,086 (4,208 full-time and 1,878 part-time)

DEANS

Ancell School of Business: ALLEN MORTON
School of Arts and Sciences: LINDA VANDENGOAD
School of Professional Studies: LYNNE CLARK
School of Visual and Performing Arts: CAROL A. HAWKES
Graduate Studies: Dr ELLEN D. DURNIN

BRANCH CAMPUS

WestConn at Waterbury: Founders Hall 129, 750 Chase Parkway, Waterbury, CT 06708; tel. (203) 596-8777; fax (203) 596-8793; e-mail durninc@wcsu.edu; programmes in Management and Nursing; Dean Dr ELLEN DURNIN.

YALE UNIVERSITY

New Haven, CT 06520
Telephone: (203) 432-1333
Internet: www.yale.edu

Founded 1701; named Yale College 1718; transition to univ. status took place from 1810 to 1861

Private control

Pres.: Dr RICHARD CHARLES LEVIN

Provost: ANDREW DAVID HAMILTON

Vice-Pres. and Gen. Counsel: Dr DOROTHY K. ROBINSON

Vice-Pres. and Sec.: Dr LINDA KOCH LORIMER

Vice-Pres. for Devt: INGEBORG THERESIA REICHENBACH

Vice-Pres. for Finance and Admin.: SHAUNA RYAN KING

Vice Pres. for New Haven and State Affairs and Campus Devt: Dr BRUCE D. ALEXANDER

Librarian: ALICE PROCHASKA

Library: see Libraries and Archives

Number of teachers: 3,333

Number of students: 11,250

Publications: *Yale Review, Yale Human Rights and Development Law Journal, Yale Journal of Biology and Medicine, Yale Journal of Ethics, Journal of Industrial Ecology, Yale Journal of Law and Feminism, Yale Journal of Law and the Humanities, Yale Law Journal, Yale Alumni Magazine, American Journal of Science, Library Gazette, Bulletin of Art Gallery Associates, American Scientist, Journal of American Oriental Society, Journal of Biological Chemistry, Yale Divinity News, Journal of the History of Medicine and Allied Sciences, Journal of Music Theory, Yale Forest School News, Yale Scientific Magazine, Yale French Studies, Yale Literary Magazine, Yale Journal of Criticism, Yale Journal of International Law, Yale Journal on Regulation, Yale Law & Policy Review, Technical Brief (Drama School), Theatre Magazine*

DEANS

School of Architecture: ROBERT A. M. STERN

School of Art: ROBERT STORR

Divinity School: HAROLD W. ATTRIDGE

School of Drama: JAMES BUNDY

Faculty of Eng.: PAUL A. FLEURY

School of Forestry and Environmental Studies: JAMES G. SPETH

Law School: HAROLD HONGJU KOH

School of Management: JOEL M. PODOLNY

School of Medicine: ROBERT J. ALPERN

School of Music: ROBERT BLOCKER

School of Nursing: MARGARET GREY

Graduate School of Arts and Sciences: JOHN BUTLER

Yale College: PETER SALOVEY

PROFESSORS

(Some staff serve in more than one faculty)

School of Architecture:

ALEXLEY, J. W.

BEEBY, T. H. (Architectural Design)

BLOOMER, K. C. (Architectural Design)

GARVIN, A., Urban Planning and Devt

HAYDEN, D., Architecture and Urbanism

KOETTER, F. H.

PLATTUS, A. J.

PURVES, A., Architectural Design

STERN, R. A. M.

School of Art:

BARTH, F., Painting and Printmaking

BENSON, R. M., Photography

DE BRETTEVILLE, S. L., Graphic Design

LYTLE, W. R., Painting

PAPAGEORGE, T., Photography

REED, R. J., Jr, Painting and Printmaking

STOCKHOLDER, J., Sculpture

Faculty of Arts and Sciences (Yale College and Graduate School):

ACKERMAN, B., Law and Political Science

ADAIR, R. K., Physics

ADORNO, R., Spanish

ALHASSID, Y., Physics

ADAMS, M. McC., Philosophy, Religious Studies

ADAMS, R. M., Philosophy

AGNEW, J.-C., American Studies and History

ALEXANDER, J. C., Sociology

ALEXANDROV, V. E., Slavic Languages and Literatures

ALHASSID, Y., Physics

ALTMAN, S., Biology

ALTONJI, J., Econ.

AMANAT, A., History

ANDERSON, S. R., Linguistics

ANDREW, D., Comparative Literature, Film Studies

ANDREWS, D. W. K., Econ. and Statistics

ANGULIN, D., Computer Science

APPADURAI, A., Int. Studies

APPELQUIST, T. W., Physics

AUSTIN, D. J., Chemistry

AVNI, O., French

BAILYN, C., Astronomy, Physics

BALTAY, C., Physics and Astronomy

BANAC, I., History

BARRON, A., Statistics

BATISTA, V. S., Chemistry

BEALS, R. W., Mathematics

BENHABIB, S., Philosophy, Political Science

BERCOVICI, D., Geology and Geophysics

BERNER, R. A., Geology and Geophysics

BERNSTEIN, I. B., Mechanical Eng. and Physics

BERRY, S. T., Econ.

BERS, V., Classics

BEWLEY, T. F., Econ.

BLOCH, R. H., French

BLOOM, H. I., English Language and Literature

BLOOM, P., Psychology and Linguistics

BOBZIEN, S., Philosophy

BOORMAN, S. A., Sociology

BÖWERING, G. H., Religious Studies

BRACKEN, P., Management and Political Science

BRAINARD, W. C., Econ.

BRAUND, S. M., Classics

BRISMAN, L., English Language and Literature

BRODHEAD, R. H., American Studies, English Language and Literature

BROMLEY, D. A., Physics

BROMWICH, D., English Language and Literature

BROOKS, P., Comparative Literature and French

BROWN, D. J., Econ.

BROWN, T. H., Psychology and Physiology

BROWNELL, K. D., Psychology

BRUDVIG, G., Chemistry

BURGER, R. L., Anthropology

BUSHKOVITCH, P. A., History

BUSS, L. W., Ecology and Evolutionary Biology, Geology and Geophysics

BUTLER, J., History and American Studies, Religious Studies

CAMERON, D. R., Political Science

CAMPBELL, J., English Language and Literature

CARBY, H. V., African American Studies and American Studies

CASSON, A. W., Mathematics

CASTEN, R., Physics

CHANG, J. T., Statistics

CHANG, K.-I. S., East Asian Languages and Literatures

CHANG, R. K., Applied Physics, Physics and Electrical Eng.

CHU, B.-T., Mechanical Eng.

CLARK, K., Comparative Literature and Slavic Languages and Literatures

COIFMAN, R. R., Mathematics and Computer Science

COLEMAN, J., Philosophy

CRABTREE, R. H., Chemistry

CROSS, R. J., Jr, Chemistry

CROTHERS, D. M., Chemical Eng., Chemistry and Molecular Physics and Biochemistry

DAVIS, D., Sociology

DE LA MORA, J. F., Mechanical Eng.

DELLAPORTA, S., Biology

DEMOS, J. P., Religious Studies, Near Eastern Languages and Civilizations, and History

DENNING, M., American Studies

DE ROSE, K., Philosophy

DEVORET, M., Applied Physics and Physics

DIMOCK, W. C., American Studies, English Language and Literature

DONOGHUE, M. J., Ecology and Environmental Biology

DORSEY, J., Computer Science

DOUDNA, J., Molecular Biophysics and Biochemistry

DUDLEY, K., American Studies

DUNCAN, J., Diagnostic Radiology, Electrical Eng.

DUVAL, E. M., French

EIRE, C. M. N., History and Religious Studies

EISENSTAT, S. C., Computer Science

ELIMELECH, M., Chemical Eng.

ENGEL, E., Econ.

ENGELMAN, D. M., Molecular Biophysics and Biochemistry

ENGELSTEIN, L., History

ERRINGTON, J. J., Anthropology, East Asian Languages and Literatures

EVENSON, R. E., Econ.

FAIR, R. C., Econ.

FALLER, J. W., Jr, Chemistry

FARAGHER, J. M., American Studies, History

FEIGELBAUM, J., Computer Science

FEIT, W., Mathematics

FELMAN, S., French and Comparative Literature

FISCHER, M. J., Computer Science

FLAVELL, R. A., Immunobiology and Biology

FLEURY, P., Eng. and Applied Physics, Physics

FOLTZ, W. J., African Studies and Political Science

FOSTER, B. R., Near Eastern Languages and Civilizations

FRAADE, S. D., Religious Studies

FRANK, R., English Language and Literature

FREEDMAN, P. H., History

FRENKEL, I. B., Mathematics

FRY, P. H., English Language and Literature

GADDIS, J. L., History

GAREN, A., Molecular Biophysics and Biochemistry

GARLAND, H., Mathematics

GAUTHIER, J. A., Geology and Geophysics

GEANAKOPLOS, J., Econ.

GELERNTNER, D., Computer Science

GERBER, A., Political Science

GHOSH, S., Molecular Biophysics and Biochemistry

GILMORE, G., African American Studies, History

GILROY, P., Sociology and African American Studies

GIRVIN, S. M., Physics and Applied Physics

GLIER, I., Germanic Languages and Literatures

GOLDBERG, P., Econ.

GOLDBLATT, H., Medieval Slavic Languages and Literatures

GOLDSMITH, M. H., Biology

GOLDSMITH, T. H., Biology

GOLDSTEIN, L. M., Linguistics

GOMEZ, A., Mechanical Eng.

GONZÁLEZ ECHEVERRÍA, R. O., Hispanic and Comparative Literatures

GOODYEAR, S. S., English Language and Literature
GORDON, R. B., Geology and Geophysics
GORDON, R. W., History, Law
GRAEDEL, T., Geology and Geophysics
GREEN, D., Political Science
GRIFFITH, E. H., African and African American Studies
GRINDLEY, N. D. F., Molecular Biophysics and Biochemistry
GROBER, R., Applied Physics and Physics
GRUENDLER, B., Near Eastern Languages and Civilizations
GUICHARNAUD, J. E., French
GUINNANE, T., Econ. and History
GUTAS, D., Near Eastern Languages and Civilizations
HALLER, G. L., Chemical Eng. and Chemistry
HAMADA, K., Econ.
HAMILTON, A. D., Chemistry
HAMLIN, C., Germanic Languages and Literatures and Comparative Literature
HAMMER, L., English Language and Literature
HANSEN, V., History
HARMS, R. W., African Studies, History
HARRIES, K., Philosophy
HARRIS, J., Physics
HARSHAV, B., Comparative Literature
HARTIGAN, J. A., Statistics
HARTWIG, J. F., Chemistry
HAYDEN, D., American Studies
HAYES, C., Religious Studies
HENRICH, V. E., Applied Sciences, Physics
HERSEY, G. L., History of Art
HICKEY, L. J., Geology and Geophysics
HILL, A., Anthropology
HOLE, F., Anthropology
HOLFORD, T., Public Health and Statistics
HOLLOWAY, J. S., History
HOLMES, F. L., History
HOMANS, M. B., English, Women's and Gender Studies
HORN, L. R., Linguistics
HORVÁTH, C. G., Chemical Eng.
HUDAK, P., Computer Science
HYMAN, P. E., Modern Jewish History
IACHELLO, F., Physics and Chemistry
INSLER, S., Linguistics
JACKSON, K. D., Spanish and Portuguese
JACOBS, C., Comparative Literature
JACOBSON, M. F., African American Studies, American Studies, History
JAYNES, G. D., Econ., African Studies and African American Studies
JESHION, R., Philosophy
JOHNSON, M. A., Chemistry
JOHNSON, M. K., Psychology
JONES, P. W., Mathematics
JORGENSEN, W. L., Chemistry
JOSEPH, G. M., History
KAGAN, D., Classics and History
KAGAN, S., Classics, Philosophy
KAMENS, E., East Asian Languages and Literatures
KANKEL, D. R., Biology
KARATO, S., Geology and Geophysics
KAVANAGH, T., French
KAZDIN, A. E., Psychology
KEANE, M., Econ.
KEIL, F. C., Psychology and Linguistics
KELLY, W. W., Anthropology
KENNEDY, P. M., History
KENNEY, J., Astronomy
KEVLES, D. J., History
KIERNAN, B. F., History
KLEIN, M. J., History of Science and Physics
KLEINER, D. E. E., Classics and History of Art
KLEVORICK, A. K., Econ.
KONIGSBERG, W., Molecular Biophysics and Biochemistry

KUTZINSKY, V. M., English Language and Literature, African American Studies and American Studies
LAFRANCE, M., Psychology, Women's and Gender Studies
LANG, S., Mathematics
LARSON, R. B., Astronomy
LAWLER, T., English Language and Literature
LAYTON, B. R., Religious Studies and Near Eastern Languages and Civilizations
LEE, R., Mathematics
LEVIN, R. C., Econ.
LIFTON, R., Medicine, Genetics, Molecular Biophysics and Biochemistry
LONG, M. B., Mechanical Eng. and Applied Physics
MA, T.-P., Electrical Eng. and Applied Physics
MACDOWELL, S. W., Physics
MACNAB, R. M., Molecular Biophysics and Biochemistry
MCDERMOTT, D. V., Computer Science
MANDELBROT, B. B., Mathematics
MANLEY, L. G., English Language and Literature
MARCUS, I. G., Jewish History
MARGULIS, G. A., Mathematics
MARMOR, T., Public Management and Political Science
MARTIN, D., Religious Studies
MATTHEWS, J. F., History and Classics
MAYER, E., Anthropology
MAYHEW, D. R., Political Science
MAZZOTTA, G., Italian
MENDELSOHN, R., Econ., Forestry and Enviromental Studies, Management
MENOCAL, M. R., Spanish
MERRIMAN, J. M., History
MILLER, C. L., French, and African and African American Studies
MILLER, G., Molecular Bophysics and Biochemistry
MOCHRIE, S., Physics and Applied Physics
MONTGOMERY, D., History
MOORE, P. B., Chemistry and Molecular Biophysics and Biochemistry
MOOSEKER, M. S., Biology and Cell Biology
MORGAN, R. P., Theory of Music
MORRIS, S., Econ.
MORSE, A. S., Computer Science, Electrical Eng.
MUSSER, C., American Studies, Film Studies
NALEBUFF, B., Econ.
NARENDRA, K. S., Electrical Eng.
NOVICK, A., Ecology and Environmental Biology
ORNSTON, L. N., Biology
ORSZAG, S. A., Mathematics
OUTKA, G., Philosophy and Christian Ethics
PARK, J., Geology and Geophysics
PARKER, P. D. M., Physics
PATTERSON, A., English Language and Literature
PATTERSON, L., English Language and Literature
PEARCE, D. G., Econ.
PETERSON, L. H., English Language and Literature
PEUCKER, B., Germanic Languages and Literatures
PFEFFERLE, L. D., Chemical Eng.
PHILLIPS, P. C. B., Econ. and Statistics
PIATETSKI-SHAPIRO, I., Mathematics
PLANTINGA, L. B., History of Music
POLAK, B., Econ.
POLLARD, D. B., Statistics and Mathematics
POWELL, J. R., Ecology and Environmental Biology
PROBER, D. E., Applied Physics, Physics
QUINT, D. L., English and Comparative Literature
RAE, D. W., Political Science and Management

RANIS, G., Int. Econ.
RAWSON, C., English Language and Literature
READ, N., Physics and Applied Physics
REED, M. A., Electrical Eng. and Applied Physics
REGAN, L. J., Molecular Biophysics and Biochemistry
RILEY, M. A., Ecology and Environmental Biology
ROACH, J. R., Theatre and English
ROBINSON, F. C., English
ROEDER, S., Biology
ROEMER, J. E., Econ., Political Science
ROGERS, J., English Language and Literature
ROKHLIN, V., Computer Science and Mathematics
ROSE-ACKERMAN, S., Jurisprudence, Law and Political Science
ROSENBAUM, J. L., Biology
ROSENBLUTH, F. M., Political Science
ROSNER, D. E., Chemical Eng.
RUDDLE, F. H., Biology and Genetics
RUSSETT, B. M., Political Science and Int. Relations
RUSSETT, C. E., History
RYE, D. M., Geology and Geophysics
SACHDEV, S., Physics and Applied Physics
SALOVEY, P., Epidemology and Public Health, Psychology
SALTZMAN, W. M., Chemical Eng.
SAMMONS, J. L., Germanic Languages and Literatures
SANDWEISS, J., Physics
SANNEH, L., History, Divinity
SAUNDERS, M., Chemistry
SCARF, H. E., Econ.
SCHEFFLER, H. W., Anthropology
SCHEPARTZ, A., Chemistry
SCHMIDT, M. P., Physics
SCHULTZ, M. H., Computer Science
SCHULZ, T. P., Econ. and Demography
SCHWARTZ, S. B., History
SCOTT, J. C., Political Science and Anthropology
SEILACHER, A., Geology and Geophysics
SHANKAR, R., Physics and Applied Physics
SHAPIRO, I., Political Science
SHIN, S.-J., Philosophy
SHUBIK, M., Econ.
SHULMAN, R. G., Chemistry, Molecular Biophysics and Biochemistry
SILBERSCHATZ, A., Computer Science
SIMPSON, W. K., Near Eastern Languages and Civilizations
SINGER, J. L., Psychology
SIU, H. F., Anthropology
SKINNER, B. J., Geology and Geophysics
SKOWRONEK, S., Political Science and Social Science
SMITH, R. B., Geology and Geophysics
SMITH, S. B., Political Science
SMOOKE, M. D., Mechanical Eng.
SNYDER, M., Molecular Biophysics and Biochemistry
SOFIA, S., Astronomy
SÖLL, D. G., Molecular Biophysics and Biochemistry, Biology and Chemistry
SOMMERFIELD, C. M., Physics
SPENCE, J. D., History
SREENIVASAN, K. R., Mechanical Eng., Physics and Applied Physics
SRINIVASAN, T. N., Econ.
STEITZ, T. A., Chemistry, Molecular Biophysics and Biochemistry
STEPTO, R. B., English, African American Studies, American Studies
STERNBERG, R. J., Psychology and Education
STIMSON, H. M., Linguistics, East Asian Languages and Literatures
STONE, A. D., Physics and Applied Physics
STOUT, H. S., History, Religious Studies and American Studies, American Christianity

STROBEL, S., Molecular Biophysics and Biochemistry

SUMMERS, W. C., History of Medicine and Science, Molecular Biophysics and Biochemistry, Therapeutic Radiology

SUNDER, SH., Accounting, Econ. and Finance

SZELENYI, I., Sociology

SZWED, J. F., Anthropology, African and African American Studies and American Studies

THOMPSON, R. F., African American Studies and History of Art

TREAT, J., East Asian Languages and Literatures

TRUMPENER, K., English and Comparative Literature

TULLY, J. C., Chemistry, Physics and Applied Physics

TUREKIAN, K. K., Geology and Geophysics

TURNER, F. M., History

TURNER, H. A., Jr, History

UDRY, C., Econ.

URRY, C. M., Physics and Astrophysics

VACCARO, P. H., Chemistry

VAISNYS, J. R., Ecology and Environmental Biology, Electrical Eng.

VALENTINE, A. M., Chemistry

VALESIO, P., Italian

VALIS, N., Spanish and Portuguese

VAN ALTENA, W. F., Astronomy

VENCLOVA, T., Slavic Languages and Literatures

VERONIS, G., Geology and Geophysics

VRBA, E. S., Geology and Geophysics

WAGNER, A. R., Psychology

WAGNER, G. P., Ecology and Environmental Biology

WALZ, J. Y., Chemical Eng.

WARD, D. C., Genetics, Molecular Biophysics and Biochemistry

WARNER, J. H., American Studies, History, History of Medicine

WATTS, D. P., Anthropology

WEINSTEIN, S., Religious Studies, Buddhist Studies and East Asian Languages and Literatures

WEISS, H., Near Eastern Archaeology, Near Eastern Languages and Civilizations, and Anthropology

WELSH, A., English Language and Literature

WETTLAUFER, J., Geology and Geophysics, Physics

WEXLER, L., American Studies

WHEELER, S., Law and the Social Sciences

WIKSTROM, L. L., Chemical Eng.

WILSON, R., Religious Studies

WINTER, J., History

WOOD, J. L., Chemistry

WOODALL, J. M., Electrical Eng.

WRIGHT, C. M., History of Music

WRIGHTSON, K., History

WYMAN, R. J., Biology

WYNN, K., Psychology

YEAZELL, R. B., English Language and Literature

ZELLER, M. E., Physics

ZIEGLER, F. E., Chemistry

ZIGLER, E. F., Psychology

ZILM, K. W., Chemistry

ZINN, R. J., Astronomy

ZUCKER, S. W., Computer Science and Electrical Eng.

ZUCKERMAN, G. J., Mathematics

Divinity School:

ADAMS, M. MC., Historical Theology

ATTRIDGE, H. W., New Testament

BARTLETT, D. L., Preaching and Christian Communication

COLLINS, A. Y., Old Testament Interpretation and Criticism

DITTES, J. E., Pastoral Theology and Psychology

FARLEY, M. A., Christian Ethics

FASSLER, M. E., Music History and Liturgy

KELSEY, D. H., Theology

MURRAY, T., Organ

OGLETREE, T. W., Theological Ethics

OUTKA, G., Philosophy and Christian Ethics

SANNEH, L. O., Missions and World Christianity and History

SPINKS, B. D., Liturgical Studies

STOUT, H. S., American Religious History

VOLF, M., Systematic Theology

WILSON, R. R., Old Testament and Religious Studies

School of Drama:

BUNDY, J.

School of Forestry and Environmental Studies:

ASHTON, M. S., Silviculture and Forest Ecology

BERLYN, G. P., Anatomy and Physiology of Trees

BREWER, G. D., Resource Policy and Management

BURCH, W. R., Jr, Natural Resource Management

DOVE, M. R., Social Ecology

ESTY, D. C., Environmental Law and Policy

GRAEDEL, T. E., Industrial Ecology

GREGOIRE, T. G., Forest Management

KELLERT, S. R., Social Ecology

LYONS, J. R., Natural Resource Management

MENDELSOHN, R., Forest Policy

MONTAGNINI, F., Tropical Forestry

OLIVER, C. D., Forest Policy

REPETTO, R., Econ. and Sustainable Devt

SCHMITZ, O. J., Population and Community Ecology

SICCIAMA, T. G., Forest Ecology

SPETH, J. G., Environmental Policy and Sustainable Devt

WARGO, J. P., Environmental Risk Analysis, Political Science

School of Law:

ACKERMAN, B. A., Law and Political Science

AMAR, A. R., Law

AYRES, I., Law

BALKIN, J. M., Constitutional Law and the First Amendment

BRILMAYER, L., Int. Law

BURT, R. A., Law

CARTER, S. L., Law

CHUA, A. L., Law

COLEMAN, J. L., Jurisprudence and Philosophy

CURTIS, D. E., Law

DALTON, H. L., Law

DAMASKA, M. R., Law

DAYS, D. S., III, Law

DEUTSCH, J. G., Law

DIGNAM, B., Law

DUKE, S. B., Law

ELLICKSON, R. C., Property and Urban Law

ESTY, D. C., Environmental Law and Policy

FISS, O. M., Law

GEWIRTZ, P. D., Constitutional Law

GOLDSTEIN, A. S., Law

GORDON, R. W., Law and Legal History

GRAETZ, M. J., Law

HANSMANN, H. B., Law

KAHAN, D. M., Law

KAHN, P. W., Law and the Humanities

KLEVORICK, A. K., Law and Econ.

KOH, H. H., Int. Law

LANGBEIN, J. H., Law and Legal History

LUCHT, C. L., Law

MASHAW, J. L., Law

PETERS, J. K., Law

POTTENGER, J. L., Law

PRIEST, G. L., Law and Econ.

REISMAN, W. M., Int. Law

RESNIK, J., Law

ROMANO, R., Law

ROSE, C. M., Law and Organization

ROSE-ACKERMAN, S., Jurisprudence (Law School and Dept of Political Science)

RUBENFELD, J., Law

SCHUCK, P. H., Law

SCHULTZ, V., Law and Social Sciences

SIEGEL, R., Law

SIMON, J. G., Law

SOLOMON, R. A., Law

STITH, K., Law

WEDGWOOD, R., Law

WHITMAN, J. Q., Comparative and Foreign Law

WIZNER, S., Law

YOSHINO, K., Law

Yale School of Management:

BRACKEN, P., Management and Political Science

BREWER, G. D., Resource Policy and Management

CHEN, ZH., Finance

CHEVALIER, J. A., Finance and Econ.

DHAR, R., Marketing

FEINSTEIN, J., Econ.

GARSTKA, S., Practice of Management

GARTEN, J. E., Practice of Int. Trade and Finance

GOETZMANN, W., Management and Finance Studies

IBBOTSON, R., Practice of Finance

INGERSOLL, J. E., Jr, Int. Trade and Finance

KAPLAN, E., Management Sciences, Public Health

LI, Production Management

LÓPEZ-DE-SILANES, F., Finance and Econ.

MACAVOY, P., Management Studies

MARMOR, T. R., Public Policy and Management

NALEBUFF, B., Econ. and Management

OSTER, S. M., Management and Entrepreneurship

POLAK, B., Econ. and Management

RAE, D. W., Management

ROUWENHORST, K. G., Finance

SCOTT MORTON, F. M., Econ.

SEN, S. K., Organization, Management and Marketing

SHUBIK, M. S., Mathematical Institutional Econ.

SPIEGEL, M., Finance

SUNDER, S. (Accounting, Econ. and Finance)

SWERSEY, A. J., Operations Research

VROOM, V. H., Organization and Management, Psychology

WELCH, I., Finance

WITTINK, D. R., Management and Marketing

School of Medicine:

AGHAJANIAN, G. K., Psychiatry and Pharmacology

ANDERSON, K. S., Pharmacology

ANDIMAN, W. A., Paediatrics and Epidemiology and Public Health

ANDREWS, N. W., Cell Biology, Microbial Pathogenesis

ANDRIOLE, V. T., Internal Medicine

ANYAN, W. R., Paediatrics

ARONSON, P. S., Internal Medicine and Cellular and Molecular Physiology

ASKENASE, P. W., Internal Medicine

BAKER, M. D., Emergency Medicine, Paediatrics

BALTIMORE, R. S., Paediatrics, Infectious Diseases and Epidemiology and Public Health

BARASH, P. G., Anaesthesiology

BARNSTABLE, C. J., Neurobiology, Ophthalmology and Visual Science

BARON, R., Orthopaedics and Rehabilitation, Internal Medicine and Cell Biology

BARTOSHUK, L. M., Surgery

BATSFORD, W. P., Internal Medicine

BEARDSLEY, G. P., Paediatric Haematology and Pharmacology

BEHRMAN, H. R., Obstetrics and Gynaecology
BELSKY, J. L., Internal Medicine
BERLINER, N., Genetics and Internal Medicine
BIA, F. J., Medicine and Laboratory Medicine
BIA, M. J., Medicine
BINDER, H. J., Cellular and Molecular Physiology, Digestive Diseases and Internal Medicine
BLATT, S. J., Psychiatry and Psychology
BOLOGNIA, J. L., Dermatology
BOOSS, J., Neurology and Laboratory Medicine
BORON, W. F., Cellular and Molecular Physiology
BOTHWELL, A., Immunobiology
BOTTOMLY, H. K., Immunobiology and Molecular, Cellular and Developmental Biology
BOULPAEP, E. L., Cellular and Molecular Physiology
BOWERS, M. B., Jr, Psychiatry
BOYER, J. L., Digestive Diseases, Internal Medicine
BRACKEN, M. B., Epidemiology and Public Health, Chronic Disease Epidemology, Neurology
BRASH, D. E., Genetics, Therapeutic Radiology
BRAVERMAN, I. M., Dermatology
BROADUS, A. E., Internal Medicine and Cellular and Molecular Physiology
BROWN, T. H., Cellular and Molecular Physiology, Psychology
BUCALA, R., Medicine
BUNNEY, B. S., Psychiatry and Pharmacology
BURRELL, M. I., Diagnostic Radiology
BURROW, G. N., Obstetrics and Gynaecology
BYRNE, T. N., Neurology and Medicine
CABIN, H., Internal Medicine
CADMAN, E. C., Internal Medicine
CAPLAN, M., Cellular and Molecular Physiology
CARPENTER, T. O., Endocrinology, Paediatrics
CARTER, D., Pathology
CENTRELLA, M., Surgery
CHAMBERS, S. K., Obstetrics and Gynaecology
CHANDLER, W. K., Cellular and Molecular Physiology
CHASE, H. S., Jr, Medicine
CHENG, Y.-C., Pharmacology
CHOI, Y., Laboratory Medicine, Pathology
CLEARY, J. P., Internal Medicine
CLEMAN, M., Internal Medicine
COCA-PRADOS, M., Ophthalmology and Visual Science
COHEN, L. B., Cellular and Molecular Physiology
COHEN, L. S., Internal Medicine
COLEMAN, D., Medicine
COLLINS, J. G., Anaesthesiology
COOLEY, L., Cell Biology, Genetics
COONEY, L. M., Jr, Internal Medicine
COSTA, J. C., Pathology
CRAFT, J., Immunobiology, Medicine
CRESSWELL, P., Immunobiology
CULLEN, M. R., Medicine, Occupational and Environmental Medicine, Public Health
CURTIS, A. M., Diagnostic Radiology
DANNIES, P. S., Pharmacology
DAW, N. W., Ophthalmology and Visual Science
DE CAMILLI, P. V., Cell Biology
DEISSEROTH, A. B., Internal Medicine
DELUCA, V. A., Internal Medicine
D'ESCOPO, N. D., Internal Medicine
DEVITA, V. T., Internal Medicine
DIMAIO, D., Genetics
DOBBINS, J. W., Internal Medicine
DONABEDIAN, R. K., Laboratory Medicine

DUBOIS, A. B., Epidemiology and Public Health, and Cellular and Molecular Physiology
DUFFY, T. P., Internal Medicine
DUNCAN, C. C., Neurosurgery and Paediatrics
DUNCAN, J., Diagnostic Radiology
EDBERG, S. C., Internal Medicine, Laboratory Medicine
EHRENKRANZ, R. A., Neonatology, Obstetrics and Gynaecology, Paediatrics
EHRENWERTH, J., Anaesthesiology
EHRLICH, B., Pharmacology and Cellular and Molecular Biology
ELEFTERIADES, J. A., Surgery
ELIAS, J. A., Medicine
FARBER, L. R., Internal Medicine
FERRO-NOVICK, S., Cell Biology
FINKELSTEIN, F. O., Internal Medicine
FISCH, D., Epidemiology of Microbial Diseases
FISCHER, D. S., Internal Medicine
FISCHER, J. J., Therapeutic Radiology
FLAVELL, R., Immunobiology, Molecular, Cellular and Developmental Biology
FLOCH, M. H., Internal Medicine
FLYNN, S. D., Pathology, Surgery
FORBUSH, B., III, Cellular and Molecular Physiology
FORGET, B. G., Medicine and Genetics
FORMAN, B. H., Internal Medicine
FORREST, J. N., Jr, Medicine
FRIEDLAENDER, G. E., Orthopaedics and Rehabilitation
FRIEDLAND, G. H., Epidemology, Medicine
GALÁN, J., Cell Biology, Microbial Pathogenesis
GEIBEL, J. P., Surgery
GENEL, M., Paediatrics
GHOSH, S., Immunobiology, Molecular Biophysics and Biochemistry, Molecular, Cellular and Developmental Biology
GIEBISCH, G. H., Cellular and Molecular Physiology
GIFFORD, R. H., Internal Medicine
GLAZER, P. M., Therapeutic Radiology and Genetics
GLICKMAN, M. G., Diagnostic Radiology and Surgery
GOLDMAN-RAKIC, P., Neurobiology, Neurology
GOLDSTEIN, S. A. N., Cellular and Molecular Physiology, Paediatrics
GONZALEZ, C., Ophthalmology and Visual Science, Paediatrics
GORE, J. C., Diagnostic Radiology
GORELICK, F., Internal Medicine, Digestive Diseases and Cell Biology
GREEN, B., Surgery
GREENFELD, D. G., Psychiatry
GREER, C., Neurobiology, Neurosurgery
GRIFFITH, B., Laboratory Medicine
GRIFFITH, E. E. H., Psychiatry
GROSS, I., Neonatology, Obstetrics and Gynaecology, Paediatrics
GROSZMANN, R. J., Digestive Diseases, Internal Medicine
GUSBERG, R. J., Surgery
HAFFTY, B. G., Therapeutic Radiology
HAYSLETT, J. P., Medicine
HEALD, P. W., Dermatology
HEBERT, S. C., Cellular and Molecular Physiology, Medicine
HENDLER, E. D., Internal Medicine
HENINGER, G. R., Psychiatry
HERBERT, P. N., Internal Medicine
HIERHOLZER, W. J., Internal Medicine and Epidemiology
HINES, R. L., Anaesthesiology
HOCKFIELD, S., Neurology
HOFFER, P. B., Diagnostic Radiology
HOFFMAN, J. F., Cellular and Molecular Physiology
HOLBROOK, N. J., Geriatrics
HOLFORD, T. R., Epidemiology and Public Health

HORWICH, A. L., Genetics and Paediatrics
HOSTETTER, M. K., Paediatrics
IANNINI, P. B., Internal Medicine
INNIS, R. B., Psychiatry and Pharmacology
INOUYE, S. K., Geriatrics
INSOGNA, K. L., Internal Medicine
JACOBS, S. C., Psychiatry
JACOBY, R. O., Comparative Medicine
JAFFE, C. C., Diagnostic Radiology and Internal Medicine
JAMIESON, J. D., Cell Biology
JANEWAY, C., Immunobiology and Molecular, Cellular and Developmental Biology
JATLOW, P. I., Laboratory Medicine and Psychiatry
JOINER, K. A., Internal Medicine, Cell Biology and Infectious Diseases
JOKL, P., Orthopaedics and Rehabilitation
KACZMAREK, L. K., Cellular and Molecular Physiology and Pharmacology
KAETZ, H. W., Internal Medicine
KAIN, Z., Anaesthesiology, Paediatrics
KANTOR, F. S., Internal Medicine
KAPADIA, C. R., Internal Medicine
KASHGARIAN, M., Pathology and Molecular, Cellular and Developmental Biology
KASL, S. V., Chronic Disease Epidemiology
KAVATHAS, P., Genetics, Immunobiology, Laboratory Medicine
KELLER, M. S., Diagnostic Radiology and Paediatrics
KENNEY, J. D., Internal Medicine
KICKBUSCH, I. S., Epidemology and Public Health
KIDD, K. K., Genetics, Molecular, Cellular and Developmental Biology, and Psychiatry
KIER, E. L., Diagnostic Radiology
KIM, J. H., Pathology
KINDER, B. K., Surgery
KLIGER, A. S., Internal Medicine
KOCSIS, J. D., Neurology
KOPF, G. S., Surgery
KOSTEN, T. R., Psychiatry
KRUMHOLZ, H. M., Epidemiology and Public Health, Internal Medicine
KRYSTAL, J. H., Psychiatry
LAMOTTE, R. H., Anaesthesiology
LANDRY, M., Laboratory Medicine
LANNIN, D. R., Surgery
LAWSON, J. P., Diagnostic Radiology, Orthopaedics and Rehabilitation
LEADERER, B. P., Public Health, Environmental Studies
LEDER, S. B., Surgery
LEFFELL, D. J., Dermatology
LENTZ, T. L., Cell Biology
LESSER, R. L., Neurology, Ophthalmology and Visual Science
LEVANTHAL, J. M., Nursing, Paediatrics and Child Study Center
LEVINE, R. A., Laboratory Medicine
LEVINE, R. J., Internal Medicine
LEVITIN, H., Internal Medicine
LEVY, L. L., Neurology
LEVY, S. R., Neurology
LIFTON, R. P., Medicine and Genetics
LISTER, G., Jr, Paediatrics and Anaesthesiology
LORBER, M. I., Surgery
LYTTON, B., Surgery, Urology
MCCARTHY, P., Paediatrics, Nursing
MCCARTHY, S., Diagnostic Radiology
MCCLENNAN, B. L., Diagnostic Radiology
MCCORMICK, D., Neurology
MCGLASHAN, T. H., Psychiatry
MCMAHON-PRATT, D., Epidemiology of Microbial Diseases
MCPHEDRAN, P., Laboratory Medicine and Internal Medicine
MADRI, J. A., Pathology
MAHNENSMITH, R., Medicine
MAHONEY, M. J., Genetics, and Obstetrics and Gynaecology, and Paediatrics
MAKUCH, R. W., Epidemiology and Public Health

MALAWISTA, S. E., Medicine
MARCHESI, S. L., Pathology and Laboratory Medicine
MARCHESI, V. T., Pathology, Cell Biology
MARIEB, N. J., Internal Medicine
MARKS, L. E., Environmental Health Sciences
MARSH, J. C., Internal Medicine
MATTHAY, R. A., Medicine
MAZURE, C. M., Psychiatry
MELLMAN, I. S., Cell Biology and Immunobiology
MENT, L. R., Paediatrics and Neurology
MERIKANGAS, K. R., Chronic Disease Epidemiology, Psychiatry
MERSON, M. H., Epidemiology and Public Health
MILLER, I. G., Jr, Epidemiology and Public Health, Molecular Biophysics and Biochemistry, Paediatrics
MILLER, P. L., Anaesthesiology
MILSTONE, L. M., Dermatology
MOCZYDLOWSKI, E. G., Cellular and Molecular Physiology, Pharmacology
MODLIN, I. M., Surgery
MOGHADDAM, B., Neurobiology, Psychiatry
MOOSEKER, M., Cell Biology
MORROW, J. S., Molecular, Cellular and Developmental Biology, Pathology
MOSER, M., Internal Medicine
MOYER, M. S., Paediatrics
NAIM, A., Psychiatry
NAIR, S., Internal Medicine
NATH, R., Therapeutic Radiology
NOVICK, P., Cell Biology
O'MALLEY, S. S., Psychiatry
PATTON, C. L., Epidemiology of Microbial Diseases
PELKER, R. R., Orthopaedics and Rehabilitation
PERILLIE, P. E., Internal Medicine
PERSING, J. A., Surgery and Neurosurgery
PESCHEL, R. E., Therapeutic Radiology
PEZZIMENTI, J. F., Internal Medicine
PIEPMEIER, J. M., Neurosurgery
POBER, J. S., Pathology, Dermatology and Immunobiology
QUAGLIARELLO, V. J., Medicine
RABINOVICI, R., Surgery
RADDING, C. M., Genetics and Molecular Biophysics and Biochemistry
RAFFERTY, T. D., Anaesthesiology
RAKIC, P., Neurology and Neurobiology
RAPPEPORT, J., Internal Medicine
RASTEGAR, A., Medicine
REDMOND, D. E., Jr, Psychiatry and Neurosurgery
RENSHAW, T., Orthopaedics and Rehabilitation
RICHARDS, F. F., Internal Medicine
RISCH, H. A., Chronic Disease Epidemiology
RITCHIE, J. M., Pharmacology
ROCKWELL, S. C., Pharmacology, Therapeutic Radiology
ROEDER, S., Genetics, Molecular, Cellular and Developmental Biology
ROSE, J. K., Pathology and Cell Biology
ROSENBAUM, S., Anaesthesiology
ROSENFIELD, A. T., Diagnostic Radiology
ROSENHECK, R. A., Epidemiology and Public Health, Psychiatry
ROTH, R. H., Jr, Psychiatry and Pharmacology
ROUNSAVILLE, B. J., Psychiatry
RUDDLE, F., Genetics, Molecular, Cellular and Developmental Biology
RUDDLE, N. H., Epidemiology of Microbial Diseases, Immunobiology
RUDNICK, G., Pharmacology
SACKS, F. L., Internal Medicine
SANTOS-SACCHI, J., Surgery
SARTORELLI, A. C., Pharmacology
SASAKI, C. T., Surgery
SCHATZ, D., Immunobiology
SCHLESSINGER, J., Pharmacology

SCHOEN, R., Internal Medicine
SCHOTTENFELD, R. S., Psychiatry
SCHWARTZ, I. R., Surgery
SCHWARTZ, P. E., Obstetrics and Gynaecology
SEASHORE, J. H., Surgery
SEASHORE, M. R., Genetics, Paediatrics
SEGAL, S. S., Cellular and Molecular Physiology
SESSA, W. C., Pharmacology
SHAPIRO, E. D., Epidemiology and Public Health, Paediatrics, Nursing
SHAW, C., Diagnostic Radiology
SHAYWITZ, A. E., Neurology, Paediatrics
SHAYWITZ, S. E., Paediatrics
SHERTER, C. B., Internal Medicine
SHERWIN, R. S., Internal Medicine
SHULMAN, G. I., Internal Medicine, and Cellular and Molecular Physiology
SIEGEL, N. J., Medicine, Paediatrics
SIGWORTH, F. J., Cellular and Molecular Physiology
SILVERMAN, D., Anaesthesiology
SINATRA, R., Anaesthesiology
SIVARAJAN, M., Anaesthesiology
SLAYMAN, C. L., Cellular and Molecular Physiology
SLAYMAN, C. W., Genetics and Cellular and Molecular Physiology
SLEDGE, W. H., Psychiatry
SMITH, B. R., Internal Medicine, Laboratory Medicine, Paediatrics
SNOW, D. L., Psychiatry
SNYDER, E. L., Laboratory Medicine
SPENCER, D. D., Neurosurgery
SPENCER, S. S., Neurology
SPIRO, H. M., Internal Medicine
STERN, D. F., Pathology
STITT, J. T., Cellular and Molecular Physiology, Epidemiology and Environmental Health Sciences
STRITTMATTER, S. M., Neurobiology, Neurology
SULAVIK, S. B., Internal Medicine
SUMMERS, W. C., Therapeutic Radiology, Molecular Biophysics and Biochemistry, and Genetics
SUMPIO, B. E., Surgery
TAMBORLANE, W. V., Paediatrics
TATTERSALL, P., Laboratory Medicine and Genetics
TAYLOR, K. J., Diagnostic Radiology
TIGELAAR, R. E., Dermatology and Immunobiology
TINETTI, M., Medicine, Epidemiology and Public Health
TOULOUKIAN, R. J., Paediatrics, Surgery
TRAUBE, M., Digestive Diseases, Internal Medicine
UDELSMAN, R., Surgery
ULLU, E., Cell Biology, Medicine
VAN DEN POL, A., Neurosurgery
WACKERS, F. J., Diagnostic Radiology and Medicine
WALSH, T. J., Neurology, Ophthalmology and Visual Science
WARD, D. C., Genetics, Molecular Biophysics and Biochemistry
WARDLAW, S. C., Laboratory Medicine
WARREN, G., Cell Biology
WAXMAN, S. G., Neurology, Neurobiology
WEISS, R. M., Surgery, Urology
WEISSMAN, S. M., Genetics and Internal Medicine
WESTCOTT, J. A., Diagnostic Radiology
WHITE, R. I., Jr, Diagnostic Radiology
WRIGHT, F. S., Internal Medicine and Cellular and Molecular Physiology
ZARET, B. L., Diagnostic Radiology, Medicine
ZELTERMAN, D., Epidemiology and Public Health
ZONANA, H. V., Psychiatry

School of Music:

AGAWU, K., Theory of Music

AKI, S., Violin
BERMAN, B., Piano
BRESNICK, M. I., Composition
CHOOKASIAN, L., Voice and Opera
DUFFY, T. C.
FASSLER, M. E.
FORTE, A., Theory of Music
FRANK, C., Piano
GOTTLIEB, G., Percussion
HARTH, S., Violin
HAWKSHAW, P., History of Music
LADERMAN, E., Composition
LEVINE, J., Viola
MURRAY, T., Organ
OUNDJIAN, P., Violin
PARISOT, A. S.
REPHANN, R.
ROSAND, E., History of Music
ROSEMAN, R., Oboe
RUFF, W. H., Jr
SHIFRIN, D., Clarinet
SMITH, L. L.
SWALLOW, J. W., Brass and Ensemble Performance
TIRRO, F. P.
YARICK-CROSS, D., Voice

School of Nursing:

BURST, H. V., Nursing
DIERS, D. K., Nursing
DIXON, J. K., Nursing
FUNK, M., Nursing
GILLISS, C. L., Nursing
GREY, M., Nursing
KNAFL, K. A., Nursing
KNOPF, M. T., Oncology Nursing
KRAUSS, J. B., Nursing
MILONE-NUZZO, P., Nursing
MINARKI, P., Nursing
WILLIAMS, A., Nursing

DELAWARE

DELAWARE STATE UNIVERSITY

1200 N. Dupont Highway, Dover, DE 19901-2277

Telephone: (302) 857-6290
Internet: www.desu.edu

Founded 1891

Pres.: Dr ALLEN L. SESSOMS
Provost and Vice-Pres. for Academic Affairs: Dr KENNETH W. BELL (acting)
Vice-Pres. for Business and Finance: DONALD L. HENRY
Vice-Pres. for Devt and Univ. Relations: CAROLYN S. CURRY
Vice-Pres. for Enrollment Management and Student Affairs (vacant)
Dean of Graduate Studies and Research: Dr HAZELL REED
Registrar: GLENN T. PARKER
Dir of Admissions: LAWITA G. CHEATHAM
Head Librarian: VIVIAN H. ROYSTER
Library of 205,400 vols, 22,000 microbooks, 12,635 microform reels, 14,871 audio-visual items, 3,367 bound periodicals
Number of teachers: 168
Number of students: 3,200

DEANS

College of Agriculture and Related Sciences: Dr KENNETH W. BELL
College of Education and Sport Sciences: Prof. DORIS E. WOOLEDGE (acting)
College of Humanities and Social Sciences: Prof. BRADLEY SKELCHER
School of Management: Prof. PATRICK R. LIVERPOOL
School of Professional Studies: Dr JACQUELYNE W. GORUM

GOLDEY-BEACOM COLLEGE

4701 Limestone Rd, Wilmington, DE 19808

Telephone: (302) 998-8814

E-mail: admissions@gbc.edu

Internet: www.gbc.edu

Founded 1886 as Wilmington Commercial College; present name 1951

Private control

Academic year: August to August

Pres.: MOHAMMAD ILYAS

Dean of Admissions (vacant)

Dean of Information Technology: EMILY JACKSON

Areas of study: accounting, accounting and information systems, business admin., computer information systems.

UNIVERSITY OF DELAWARE

Newark, DE 19716

Telephone: (302) 831-2000

Internet: www.udel.edu

Founded 1833 from the Newark Acad. founded in 1765; chartered 1769

Pres.: Dr DAVID P. ROSELLE

Provost: Dr DANIEL RICH (acting)

Exec. Vice-Pres. and Univ. Treas.: DAVID E. HOLLOWELL

Vice-Pres. and Univ. Sec.: PIERRE D. HAYWARD

Vice-Pres. for Admin.: Dr MAXINE COLM

Vice-Pres. for Devt and Alumni Relations: ROBERT R. DAVIS

Vice-Pres. for Information Technologies: SUSAN J. FOSTER

Vice-Pres. and Univ. Treas.: STEPHEN M. GRIMBLE

Dir of Libraries: SUSAN BRYNTESON

Library of 2,600,000 vols, 3,300,000 microforms

Number of teachers: 1,089

Number of students: 21,289

DEANS

College of Agriculture and Natural Resources: Prof. ROBIN MORGAN

College of Arts and Science: Prof. TOM APPLE

College of Business and Economics: Prof. MICHAEL J. GINZBERG

College of Eng.: Prof. ERIC W. KALER

College of Health and Nursing Sciences: Prof. BETTY J. PAULANKA

College of Human Services, Education and Public Policy: Prof. TIMOTHY K. BARENKOV (acting)

College of Marine Studies: Dr NANCY M. TARGETT

PROFESSORS

ABRAMS, B. A., Economics

ACKERMAN, B. P., Psychology, Linguistics

ADAMS, F., Philosophy

ADVANI, S. G., Mechanical Eng.

AGARWAL, S. K., Mechanical Eng.

AGUIRRE, B. E., Sociology and Criminal Justice

ALCHON, S. A., History

ALLEN, H. E., Civil Eng.

ALLMENDINGER, D. F., Jr, History

AMER, P. D., Computer and Information Sciences, Electrical and Computer Eng.

AMES, D. L., Urban Affairs and Public Policy, Geography

ANDERSEN, M. L., Sociology and Criminal Justice, Women's Studies

ANDERSON, L. G., Marine Studies, Economics

ANDREWS, D. C., English

ANGELL, T. S., Mathematical Sciences

ARCE, G. R., Electrical and Computer Eng., Marine Studies

ARDIS, A. L., English

ARENSON, M. A., Music

ATHANASSOGLOU-KALLMYER, N., Art History

BACH, R. D., Chemistry and Biochemistry

BACHMAN, R, Sociology and Criminal Justice

BADIEY, M., Marine Studies

BARNEKOV, T. K., Urban Affairs and Public Policy

BAROUDI, J., Accounting and Management Information Systems

BARR, S. M., Bartol Research Institute

BARTEAU, M. A., Chemical Eng., Chemistry and Biochemistry

BEAR, G. G., Education

BEASLEY, J. C., English

BEEBE, T. P., Jr, Chemistry and Biochemistry

BELLAMY, D. P., Mathematical Sciences

BENNETT, J., English

BENNETT, R. B., English

BERIS, A. N., Chemical Eng.

BERNHARDT, S. A., Writing

BERNSTEIN, J. A., History

BEST, J., Sociology and Criminal Justice

BIEBER, J. W., Bartol Research Institute

BIEDERMAN, K., Finance

BILINSKY, Y., Political Science and International Relations

BINDER-MACLEOD, S. A., Physical Therapy

BLITS, J. H., Education, Political Science and Int. Relations

BOLTON, R. C., Art

BONCELET, C. G., Electrical and Computer Eng.

BOULD, S., Sociology and Criminal Justice, Individual and Family Studies, Women's Studies

BOYER, J. S., Marine Biochemistry and Biophysics, Plant and Soil Sciences

BOYLAN, A. M., History, Women's Studies

BRAUN, T. E. D., Comparative Literature, Foreign Languages and Literatures

BRICKHOUSE, N., Education

BRILL, T. B., Chemistry and Biochemistry

BROADBRIDGE, P., Mathematical Sciences

BROCK, D. H., English

BROCKMANN, R. J., English

BROWN, F., English

BROWN, H. E., Art, Art Conservation, Art History, Museum Studies

BROWN, J. L., Foreign Languages and Literatures

BROWN, R. F., Philosophy

BROWN, R. P., Theatre

BROWN, S. D., Chemistry and Biochemistry

BROWNING, J. E., Theatre

BROWNING, W. L., Theatre

BUCHANAN, T. S., Mechanical Eng.

BUCKMASTER, D. A., Accounting and Management Information Systems

BURMEISTER, J. L., Chemistry and Biochemistry

BURNSIDE, J., Animal and Food Sciences, Biological Sciences

BUTKIEWICZ, J. L., Economics

BYRNE, J. M., Urban Affairs and Public Policy, Marine Studies

CALLAHAN, D. F., History

CALLAHAN, R. A., History

CAMPBELL, L. L., Biological Sciences

CARBERRY, M. S., Computer and Information Sciences, Linguistics

CARON, D. M., Entomology and Applied Ecology

CAROTHERS, M. L., Art

CARR, C. L., Music

CARROLL, R. B., Plant and Soil Sciences

CARSON, D., Biological Sciences

CASE, J., Computer and Information Sciences

CAVINESS, B. F., Computer and Information Sciences, Mathematical Sciences

CHAJES, M. J., Civil and Environmental Eng.

CHAPMAN, H. P., Art History

CHEN, J. G., Chemical Eng., Materials Science and Eng.

CHOU, T. W., Mechanical Eng.

CHUI, S.-T., Bartol Research Institute

CHURCH, T. M., Marine Studies, Chemistry and Biochemistry

CICALA, G. A., Psychology

CINCIN-SAIN, B., Marine Studies, Political Science and International Relations, Urban Affairs and Public Policy

COGBURN, L. A., Animal and Food Sciences

COHEN, L. H., Psychology

COLE, P., Linguistics

COLLINS, G. E., Computer and Information Sciences

COLLINS, N. E., Bioresources Eng.

COLMAN, R. F., Chemistry and Biochemistry

COLTON, D. L., Mathematical Sciences

COOK-IOANNIDIS, P., Mathematical Sciences

CORNELL, H. V., Biological Sciences

COURTRIGHT, J. A., Communications

COTUNGA, N., Nutrition and Dietetics

CURTIS, J. C., History

CURTIS, L. A., Biological Sciences, Marine Studies

CUSTER, J. F., Anthropology

DAVIS, S., Political Science and International Relations

DAVISON, R. A., English

DAWSON, C., English

DEAN, J. M., English

DEBESSAY, A., Accounting and Management Information Systems

DEINER, P. L., Individual and Family Studies

DELEON, P. A., Biological Sciences

DELFATTORE, J., English, Legal Studies

DEMICCIO, F. J., Hotel, Restaurant and Institutional Management

DENSON, C. D., Chemical Eng.

DENTEL, S. K., Civil and Environmental Eng.

DEXTER, S. C., Marine Studies, Materials Science and Eng.

DHURJATI, P., Chemical Eng.

DILORENZO, T. M., Psychology

DIRENZO, G., Sociology and Criminal Justice

DOHMS, J. E., Immunology and Microbiology

DONALDSON-EVANS, M. P., Foreign Languages and Literatures

DOREN, D. J., Chemistry and Biochemistry

DUGGAN, L. G. J., History

DURBIN, P. T., Philosophy, Urban Affairs and Public Policy

DYBOWSKI, C. R., Chemistry and Biochemistry

EBERT, G. L., Mathematical Sciences

EISENBERGER, R. W., Psychology

ELIAS, J. G., Electrical and Computer Eng.

ELSON, C. M., Legal Studies, Corporate Governance

EPIFANIO, C., Marine Studies

ERMANN, M. D., Sociology and Criminal Justice

EVANS, D. H., Chemistry and Biochemistry

EVENSON, P. A., Bartol Research Institute

FAGHRI, A., Civil and Environmental Eng.

FANELLI-KUCZMARSKI, M. T., Nutrition and Dietetics

FARACH-CARSON, M. C., Biological Sciences

FERRETTI, R., Education, Psychology

FITZMAURICE, C., Theatre

FLYNN, P. D., English

FOU, C.-M., Physics and Astronomy

FRETT, J. J., Plant and Soil Sciences

FUHRMANN, J. J., Plant and Soil Sciences

GAERTNER, S. L., Psychology

GAFFNEY, P. M., Marine Studies

GAISSER, T. K., Bartol Research Institute

GALLAGHER, J. L., Marine Studies

GALVIN, M. E., Materials Science and Eng.

GAO, G.-R., Electrical and Computer Eng.

GARLAND, H., Business Administration

GARVINE, R. W., Marine Studies, Civil and Environmental Eng.

GATES, B. T., English, Women's Studies

GEHRLEIN, W. V., Business Administration

GELB, J., Jr, Animal and Food Sciences

GEMPESHAW, C. M., II, Economics, Food and Resource Economics

GIBSON, A. E., Art History

GILBERT, R. P., Mathematical Sciences, Marine Studies, Computer and Information Sciences

GILLESPIE, J. W., Jr, Materials Science and Eng.
GINZBERG, M. J., Accounting and Management Information Systems, Business Administration
GLASS, B. P., Geology, Marine Studies
GLUTTING, J. J., Education
GLYDE, H. R., Physics and Astronomy
GOLDSTEIN, L. F., Political Science and Int. Relations
GOLINKOFF, R. M., Education, Linguistics, Psychology
GOODMAN, S., English
GREEN, P., Plant and Soil Sciences
GREENBERG, M. D., Mechanical Eng.
GRIFFITHS, L., Animal and Food Sciences
GRUBB, F., Economics, History
HAAS, K. C., Sociology and Criminal Justice
HABER, C., History
HADJIPANAYIS, G., Physics and Astronomy
HALIO, J. L., Communications, Comparative Literature, English, Theatre
HALL, H. B., Philosophy
HALL, S. J., Health and Exercise Sciences
HALLENBECK, D. J., Mathematical Sciences
HALPRIN, A., Physics and Astronomy
HAMILTON, C., Nutrition and Diatetics
HAMPEL, R., Education
HANEY, M. H., Electrical and Computer Eng.
HANS, V. P., Sociology and Criminal Justice
HAREVEN, T. K., Individual and Family Studies, History
HASLETT, B. J., Communications, Psychology, Women's Studies
HASLETT, D. W., Philosophy
HASTINGS, S. E., Food and Resource Economics
HAUS, H.-U., Theatre
HAWK, J. A., Plant and Soil Sciences
HAYES, E. R., Nursing
HELMLING, S., English
HERMAN, B. L., Art History, History
HERMAN, D., Music
HEWITT, K. H., Military Science
HEYRMAN, C. L., History
HIEBERT, J., Education
HIGGINBOTHAM, E., Sociology and Criminal Justice
HILDEBRANDT, D. J., Music
HOFFECKER, C. E., History
HOFFMAN, J. E., Psychology
HOFFMAN, S. D., Economics, Women's Studies
HOFSTETTER, F., Education
HOLMES, L. W., Art
HOOVER, D. G., Animal and Food Sciences
HOUGH-GOLDSTEIN, J. A., Entomology and Applied Ecology
HSIAO, G. C., Mathematical Sciences
HUANG, C. P., Civil and Environmental Eng., Marine Studies
HUDDLESTON, M. W., Political Science and Interntional Relations, Urban Affairs and Public Policy
HUNSPERGER, R. G., Electrical and Computer Eng.
HURT, J. J., History
IH, C. S., Electrical and Computer Eng., Marine Studies
ILVENTO, T. W., Food and Resource Economics
INCIARDI, J. A., Sociology and Criminal Justice
INGERSOLL, D. E., Political Science and International Relations
INTRAUB, H., Psychology
IZARD, C., Psychology
JACKSON, M. D., English
JAIN, M. K., Chemistry and Biochemistry
JOHNSON, H. B., Black American Studies, History
JOHNSON, M. V., Chemistry and Biochemistry
JONES, J. M., Psychology
JONES, S. K., Accounting and Management Information Systems
JORDAN, R. R., Geology
KALER, E. W., Chemical Eng.

KALKSTEIN, L. S., Geography
KALLAL, M. J., Consumer Studies
KAPLAN, D. W., Education
KARLSON, R. H., Biological Sciences
KEELER, C., Animal and Food Sciences
KENNEDY, J. A., Mathematical Sciences
KERR, A. D., Civil and Environmental Eng.
KERRANE, K., English
KIKUCHI, S., Civil and Environmental Eng.
KIRBY, J. T., Civil and Environmental Eng., Marine Studies
KIRCHMAN, D. L., Marine Studies
KIRWAN, A. D., Jr, Marine Studies
KITTO, S. L., Plant and Soil Sciences
KLEMAS, V. V., Marine Studies, Electrical and Computer Eng.
KLINZING, D. G., Individual and Family Studies
KLOCKARS, C. B., Sociology and Criminal Justice
KMIEC, E. B., Biological Sciences
KOBAYASHI, N., Civil and Environmental Eng., Marine Studies
KOFORD, K. J., History, Economics, Political Science and International Relations
KOLCHIN, P. R., History
KOLODZEY, J., Electrical and Computer Eng.
KRAFT, J. C., Geology, Marine Studies
KUNG, L., Animal and Food Sciences
KUSHMAN, J. E., Consumer Studies
LAMBRECHT, M., Nursing
LANE, R., Art
LATHROP, T. A., Foreign Languages and Literatures
LAZENBIK, F., Mathematical Sciences
LEATHERS, D. J., Geography
LEAVENS, P. B., Geology
LEITCH, T. M., English
LEJA, M., English
LEMIEUX, B., Plant and Soil Sciences
LENHOFF, A. M., Chemical Eng.
LESHCHINSKY, P. E., Civil and Environmental Eng.
LEUNG, C. N., Physics and Astronomy
LEWIS, K. A., Business
LI, W., Mathematical Sciences
LINK, C. R., Economics
LLOYD, E. L., Computer and Information Sciences
LUTHER, G. W., Marine Studies, Chemistry and Biochemistry, Civil and Environmental Eng.
MACDONALD, J., Physics and Astronomy
MCINNIS, J. B., Comparative Literature, Foreign Languages and Literatures, Women's Studies
MAGEE, J., Political Science and International Relations
MANGONE, G. J., Legal Studies, Marine Studies
MANRAI, A. K., Business Administration
MANRAI, L., Business Administration
MARKS, C. C., Black American Studies, Sociology and Criminal Justice
MARTIN, R. E., Geology
MASON, C. E., Entomology and Applied Ecology
MASON, D. M., Food and Resource Economics
MASTERSON, F. A., Psychology
MATTHAEUS, W. H., Bartol Research Institute
MAY, G., History
MELL, D. C., English
MEYER, D. H., History
MEYER, W. H., Political Science and International Relations
MILLER, G. E., English
MILLER, J. B., Economics
MILLER, M. J., Political Science and International Relations
MILLER, S., Sociology and Criminal Justice, Women's Studies
MILLS, D. L., Electrical and Computer Eng.
MONK, P. B., Mathematics
MOODY, W. B., Education, Mathematical Sciences

MORGAN, R. W., Agriculture and Food Sciences, Biology, Chemistry and Biochemistry
MORRISON, J. L., Consumer Studies
MULLAN, D. J., Bartol Research Institute
MULLIGAN, J., Economics
MUNSON, M. S. B., Chemistry and Biochemistry
MURRAY, F. B., Education, Psychology
NANDAKUMAR, R., Education
NASHED, M. Z., Mathematical Sciences, Electrical Eng.
NEES, L. P., Art History
NEEVES, R. E., Health and Exercise Science
NELSON, F. E., Geography
NELSON, M., English
NELSON, P., Food and Resource Economics
NESS, N. F., Bartol Research Institute
NEWTON, J. E., Black American Studies
NICHOLS, R. D., Art
NIGG, J. M., Sociology and Criminal Justice
NORTHMORE, D. P. M., Psychology
OLIVER, J. K., Political Science and International Relations, Marine Studies
O'NEILL, J. B., Economics
OPILA, R. L., Materials Science and Eng.
OWOCKI, S. P., Bartol Research Institute
PALKOVITZ, R. J., Individual and Family Studies
PALLEY, M. L., Political Science and International Relations, Women's Studies
PALMER, L. M., Philosophy, Women's Studies
PARSONS, G. R., Marine Studies, Economics
PAULANKA, B. J., Nursing
PAULY, T. H., English
PERSE, E. M., Communications
PETERS, D. L., Individual and Family Studies, Urban Affairs and Public Policy
PETERSON, L. W., Music
PFAELZER, J., English
PIFER, E. I., Communications, Comparative Literature, English
PIKA, J. A., Political Science and International Relations
PILL, W. G., Plant and Soil Sciences
PITTEL, S., Bartol Research Institute
PIZZOLATO, T. D., Plant and Soil Sciences
PIZZUTO, J. E., Geology
PONG, D., History
POPE, C. R., Animal and Food Sciences
POTTER, L. D., English
PRODAN, J. C., Music
PURNELL, L., Nursing
RABOLT, J. F., Materials Science and Eng.
RAFFEL, J. A., Urban Affairs and Public Policy, Political Science and International Relations
RATHS, J., Education
REEDY, C. L., Museum Studies, Art History, Urban Affairs and Public Policy
REIDEL, L., Theatre
REYNOLDS, H. T., Political Science and International Relations, Urban Affairs and Public Policy
RHEINGOLD, A. L., Chemistry and Biochemistry
RICH, D., Urban Affairs and Public Policy, Political Science and International Relations
RICHARDS, J. G., Health and Exercise Sciences
RICHARDS, M. P., English
RIDGE, D., Chemistry and Biochemistry
RITTER, W. F., Bioresources Eng.
ROBBINS, C., Sociology and Criminal Justice
ROBBINS, S. L., Theatre
ROBINSON, C. E., English
ROE, P. G., Anthropology
ROSELLE, D. P., Mathematics
ROSENBERGER, J. K., Microbiology
ROTH, R. R., Entomology and Applied Ecology
RUARK, G., English
RUSSELL, T. W. F., Chemical Eng.
SAFER, E. B., English
SANDLER, S. I., Chemical Eng., Chemistry and Biochemistry

SANIGA, E. M., Business Administration
SATINOFF, E., Psychology
SAUNDERS, B. D., Computer and Information Sciences, Mathematical Sciences
SAYDAM, T., Computer and Information Sciences
SCARPITTI, F. R., Sociology and Crimonal Justice
SCHWARTZ, L. W., Mechanical Eng., Mathematical Sciences
SCHWARTZ, N. B., Anthropology
SCHWEDA-NICHOLSON, N. L., Legal Studies, Linguistics
SCHWEITZER, R. L., Economics
SEIDMAN, L. S., Economics
SELEKMAN, J. A., Nursing
SETHI, A. S., Computer and Information Sciences
SETTLE, R. F., Economics
SETTLES, B. H., Individual and Family Studies
SHAFI, M., Foreign Languages and Literatures
SHAFI, Q., Bartol Research Institute
SHARNOFF, M., Physics and Astronomy
SHARP, J. H., Marine Studies
SHIPMAN, H. L., Physics and Astronomy
SIDEBOTHAM, S. E., History
SIGNORIELLI, N., Communications
SIMMONS, D. T., Biological Sciences
SIMONS, R.F., Psychology
SIMS, J. T., Plant and Soil Sciences
SKOPIK, S. D., Biological Sciences
SLOYER, C. W., Jr, Mathematical Sciences
SMITH, J. L., Nutrition and Dietetics
SNIDER, O. S., Animal and Food Sciences
SNYDER-MACKLER, L., Physical Therapy, Philosophy
SOLES, J. R., Political Science and International Relations
SPARKS, D. L., Civil and Environmental Eng., Chemistry and Biochemistry, Plant and Soil Sciences
SPINSKI, V., Art
STANEV, T., Bartol Research Institute
STARK, C., English
STARK, R. M., Mathematical Sciences, Civil and Environmental Eng.
STETSON, M. H., Biological Sciences
STONER, J. H., Art Conservation
ST PIERRE, E. K., Accounting and Management Information Systems
STRAIGHT, R., Arts
STRASSER, S., History
STRECKFUSS, R. J., Music
SVENDSEN, I. A., Civil and Environmental Eng., Marine Studies
SWASEY, J. E., Plant and Soil Sciences
SWEENEY, S. R., Theatre
SYLVES, R. T., Political Science and Int. Relations, Marine Studies, Urban Affairs and Public Policy
SZALEWICZ, K., Physics and Astronomy
SZERI, A. Z., Mechanical Eng.
TABER, D. F., Chemistry and Biochemistry
TALLAMY, D. W., Entomology and Applied Ecology
TARGETT, N. M., Marine Studies
TARGETT, T. E., Marine Studies
THEOPOLD, K. H., Chemistry and Biochemistry
THIBAULT, B., Foreign Languages and Literatures
THORPE, C., Chemistry and Biochemistry
TIERNEY, K. J., Sociology and Criminal Justice
TILMON, H. D., Food and Resource Economics
TOENSMEYER, U. C., Food and Resource Economics
TOLLES, B. F., Jr, Art History, History, Museum Studies
TURKEL, G. M., Sociology and Criminal Justice
ULLMAN, W. J., Marine Studies, Geology
UNGER, D. G., Individual and Family Studies
UNRUH, K., Physics and Astronomy

VARMA, R. D., Economics
VASILAS, B. L., Plant and Soil Sciences
VENEZKY, R., Education, Computer and Information Sciences, Linguistics
VICKERY, C. E., Nutrition and Dietetics
VINSON, J. R., Mechanical Eng.; Marine Studies
VUKELICH, C., Individual and Family Studies
WAGNER, N. J., Chemical Eng.
WAGNER, R. C., Biological Sciences
WALKER, J. H., Theatre
WALKER, J. M., English
WARREN, R., Urban Affairs and Public Policy; Political Science and International Relations
WATSON, G. H., Physics and Astronomy
WEBSTER, F., Marine Studies
WEDEL, A. R., Communications, Linguistics, Foreign Languages and Literatures
WEHMILLER, J. F., Geology, Marine Studies
WEISS, J. J., Art
WHITE, C. E., Jr, Accounting and Management Information Systems
WHITE, H. B., III, Chemistry and Biochemistry
WILDER, M. S., Urban Affairs and Public Policy
WILKINS, D. J., Mechanical Eng.
WILLMOTT, C. J., Geography, Marine Studies
WIRTH, M. J., Chemistry and Biochemistry
WOLTERS, R. B., History
WONG, K.-C., Marine Studies
WOOD, T. K., Entomology and Applied Ecology
WOOL, R. P., Chemical Eng.
YAGODA, B., English
YAN, X.-H., Marine Studies
ZINN, M. A., Music
ZIPSER, R. A., Foreign Languages and Literatures
ZUCKERMAN, M., Psychology

WESLEY COLLEGE

120 North State St, Dover, DE 19901
Telephone: (302) 736-2300
E-mail: info@wesley.edu
Internet: www.wesley.edu
Founded 1873 as Wilmington Conference Acad.; present name 1978
Private control
Academic year: August to May
Pres.: Dr SCOTT D. MILLER
Exec. Vice-Pres. and Provost: Dr BETTE S. COPLAN
Vice-Pres. for Institutional Advancement: KEVIN J. LOFTUS
Dean of Students: Dr KENNETH C. WALDROP
Registrar: PETER MEDWICK
Library Dir: SUSAN MATUSAK
Library of 460,000 vols
Number of students: 2,400

DEANS

School of Arts and Sciences: Dr PAUL J. DEGATEGNO
School of Professional Studies: Dr CHRISTOPHER MALONE

WIDENER UNIVERSITY SCHOOL OF LAW

Delaware Campus: POB 7474, 4601 Concord Pike, Wilmington, DE 19803-0474
Harrisburg Campus: POB 69381, 3800 Vartan Way, Harrisburg, PA 17106-9381
Telephone: (302) 477-2100 (Delaware); (717) 541-3900 (Harrisburg)
E-mail: meanderson@mail.widener.edu
Internet: www.law.widener.edu
Founded 1971
Academic year: August to May
Pres.: JAMES HARRIS
Dean: LINDA L. AMMONS

Number of teachers: 198 (78 full-time, 120 part-time)
Number of students: 1,600
Publications: *Delaware Journal of Corporate Law* (2 a year), *Widener Law Review* (annual), *Widener Law Journal* (annual).

DISTRICT OF COLUMBIA

AMERICAN UNIVERSITY

4400 Massachusetts Ave, NW, Washington, DC 20016
Telephone: (202) 885-1000
Fax: (202) 885-3265
E-mail: president@american.edu
Internet: www.american.edu
Chartered 1893
Pres.: CORNELIUS KERWIN
Provost: IVY E. BRODER
Vice-Pres. of Campus Life: GAIL SHORT HANSON
Vice-Pres. of Enrollment Services: CHERYL STORIE (acting)
Vice-Pres. of Finance and Treas.: DONALD L. MYERS
Vice-Pres. of Int. Affairs: ROBERT A. PASTOR
Vice-Pres. and Univ. Counsel: MARY E. KENNARD
Vice-Pres. of Univ. Relations: ALBERT R. CHECCIO
Dean of Academic Affairs: HAIG MARDIROSIAN
Dean of Students: FAITH C. LEONARD
Registrar: LINDA BOLDEN-PITCHER
Univ. Librarian: DIANA VOGELSONG (acting)
Library of 763,000 vols, 3,300 print periodicals, 1m. microforms, 8,759 films and videos, 34,000 sound recordings, 12,850 musical scores
Number of teachers: 594 full-time
Number of students: 11,224

DEANS

College of Arts and Sciences: KAY J. MUSSELL (acting)
Kogod College of Business Admin.: Dr RICHARD DURAND
Washington College of Law: CLAUDIO GROSSMAN
School of Public Affairs: WILLIAM M. LEOGRANDE (acting)
School of Communication: LARRY KIRKMAN
School of Int. Service: LOUIS GOODMAN

CATHOLIC UNIVERSITY OF AMERICA

620 Michigan Ave, NE, Washington, DC 20064
Telephone: (202) 319-5000
Internet: www.cua.edu
Founded 1887
Academic year: September to August
Chancellor: Most Rev. THEODORE E. McCARRICK
Pres.: Very Rev. DAVID M. O'CONNELL
Provost: Dr JOHN J. CONVEY
Vice-Pres. for Univ. Relations and Chief of Staff: FRANK G. PERSICO
Vice-Pres. for Enrollment Management: W. MICHAEL HENDRICKS
Vice-Pres. for Finance and Admin., Treas.: JULIE ENGLUND
Vice-Pres. for Student Life: SUSAN D. PERVI
Vice-Pres. for Univ. Devt: ROBERT SULLIVAN ROBERT M. SULLIVAN
Registrar (vacant)
Dir of Libraries: MICHAEL McLANE
Library of 1,500,000 vols.
Number of teachers: 672
Number of students: 5,510
Publications: *The Anthropological Quarterly*, *The Catholic Historical Review* (quarterly), *Catholic Biblical Quarterly*, *Catholic Uni-*

versity Law Review, Image: The Journal of Nursing Scholarship, Journal of Chinese Philosophy, Review of Metaphysics, Review of Religious Research

DEANS

School of Architecture and Planning: RANDALL OTT
School of Arts and Sciences: Dr L. R. POOS
School of Eng.: Dr CHARLES C. NGUYEN
Columbus School of Law: Dr WILLIAM F. FOX
School of Library and Information Science: MARTHA HALE
Benjamin T. Rome School of Music: MURRY SIDLIN
School of Nursing: Dr NALINI JAIRATH
School of Philosophy: Rev. Dr KURT PRITZL
School of Theology and Religious Studies: Rev. Dr FRANCIS J. MALONEY
Nat. Catholic School of Social Service: JAMES R. ZABORA
Metropolitan College: Dr SARA THOMPSON

CORCORAN COLLEGE OF ART AND DESIGN

500 17th St, NW, Washington, DC 20006-4804
Telephone: (202) 639-1801
E-mail: admissions@corcoran.org
Internet: www.corcoran.edu
Private control

Dean: CHRISTINA DEPAUL
Library of 26,000 vols.

OTHER CAMPUSES

Georgetown Campus: 1801 35th St, NW, Washington DC 20007; tel. (202) 298-2541.

H St Campus: 1705 H St, NW, Washington DC 20006.

DOMINICAN HOUSE OF STUDIES

487 Michigan Ave, NE, Washington, DC 20017-1585
Telephone: (202) 529-5300
Fax: (202) 636-1700
Internet: www.dhs.edu
Founded 1905
Private control
Academic year: August to May

Chancellor: Very Rev. CARLOS AZPIROZ
Vice-Chancellor: Very Rev. DOMINIC IZZO
Pres.: Very Rev. REGINALD WHITT
Vice-Pres. and Academic Dean: Fr GABRIEL O'DONNELL
Registrar: TOBIAS NATHE
Dir of Library: Rev. KEVIN MCGRATH

Library of 79,000 vols
Number of teachers: 19
Number of students: 67.

GALLAUDET UNIVERSITY

800 Florida Ave, NE, Washington, DC 20002
Telephone: (202) 651-5000
E-mail: public.relations@gallaudet.edu
Internet: www.gallaudet.edu
Academic year: August to May
Founded 1864

Pres.: Dr ROBERT R. DAVILA
Provost: Dr STEPHEN WEINER
Vice-Pres., Admin. and Finance: PAUL KELLY
Dean, Pre-College (vacant)
Dean of Student Affairs: CARL PRAMUK
Librarian (vacant)

Library of 200,000 vols
Number of teachers: 253
Number of students: 2,000

Publications: *Gallaudet Today* (2 a year), *Perspectives in Education and Deafness* (quarterly), *World Around You* (quarterly)

DEANS

College of Arts and Sciences: Dr JANE DILLEHAY
Graduate School and Professional Programs: Dr THOMAS ALLEN

ATTACHED INSTITUTE

Gallaudet Research Institute: research into deafness; Dir MICHAEL KARCHMER.

GEORGE WASHINGTON UNIVERSITY

2121 I St, NW, Washington, DC 20052
Telephone: (202) 994-1000
Fax: (202) 994-9025
Internet: www.gwu.edu
Founded 1821
Private control
Academic year: September to May

Pres.: STEPHEN JOEL TRACHTENBERG
Sr Vice-Pres. for Student and Academic Support Services: ROBERT A. CHERNAK
Exec. Vice-Pres. and Treas.: LOUIS H. KATZ
Exec. Vice-Pres. for Academic Affairs: DONALD R. LEHMAN
Vice-Pres. for Advancement: LAUREL PRICE JONES
Vice-Pres. for Communications: MICHAEL G. FREEDMAN
Vice-Pres. for Govt, Int. and Corporate Affairs: RICHARD N. SAWAYA
Provost and Vice-Pres. for Health Affairs: JOHN FRANKLIN WILLIAMS, Jr
Vice-Pres. and Gen. Counsel: DENNIS H. BLUMER
Assoc. Vice-Pres. for Academic Planning and Devt: CRAIG LINEBAUGH
Registrar: ELIZABETH ADMUNDSON
Univ. Librarian: JACK A. SIGGINS

Library of 2,000,000 vols
Number of teachers: 4,233
Number of students: 23,019

DEANS

Columbian College of Arts and Sciences: WILLIAM FRAWLEY
School of Business and Public Management: SUSAN PHILLIPS (acting)
School of Eng. and Applied Science: TIMOTHY TONG (acting)
Elliott School of Int. Affairs: HARRY HARDING
Law School: ROGER TRANGSRUD
School of Medicine and Health Sciences: JIM SCOTT, Jr
School of Public Health and Health Services: RUTH KATZ
College of Professional Studies: ROGER WHITAKER
Graduate School of Education and Human Devt: MARY FUTRELL

PROFESSORS

(some professors serve in more than one school)

Columbian School of Arts and Sciences and Elliott School of International Affairs:

ABRAMSON, F. P., Pharmacology, Chemistry
ABRAVANEL, E., Psychology
ADAMS, G. M., Int. Affairs
ALBRIGHT, J. W., Microbiology and Immunology
ALLEN, C. J., Anthropology, Int. Affairs
ANDERSON, J. C., Art
ARNDT, R. A., Physics
ARTERTON, F. C., Political Management
ASKARI, H. G., Business, Int. Affairs
ATKIN, M. A., History
AUSTIN, J. F., Sociology
AZAR, I., Spanish and Human Sciences
BAGINSKI, F. E., Mathematics
BAILEY, J. M., Biochemistry and Molecular Biology
BECKER, W. H., History, Int. Affairs
BELL, D., Anthropology

BERKOWITZ, E. D., History
BERMAN, B. L., Physics
BHALA, R., Law, Int. Affairs
BLACK, A. M., History and Int. Affairs
BLOSSOM, N. H., Interior Design
BORRIELLO, J., Psychology
BOULIER, B. L., Economics
BRADLEY, M. D., Economics, Int. Affairs
BRISCOE, W. J., Physics
BROCK, G. W., Telecommunications
BROWN, N. J., Political Science, Int. Affairs
BURNS, J. R., Zoology
CARESS, E. A., Chemistry
CAWS, P. J., Philosophy
CHAVES, J., Chinese
CHIAPPINELLI, V. A., Basic Science, Pharmacology, Neurological Surgery
CHURCHILL, R. P., Philosophy
CORDES, J. J., Economics and Int. Affairs
COSTIGAN, C. C., Design
COTTROL, R. J., Law, History, Sociology
DAVIS, H., Strategic Management and Int. Affairs
DEERING, C. J., Political Science
DONALDSON, R. P., Biology
DUNNING, R. M., Jr, Economics
EAST, M. A., Int. Affairs and Political Science
ETZIONI, A., Sociology
FALK, J. E., Operations Research
FEIGELBAUM, H. B., Political Science, Int. Affairs
FERRER, J., Jr, Business, Int. Affairs
FISHER, E. A., Classics
FRIEDLER, G., Eng. and Applied Science, Statistics
FUERTH, L., Int. Affairs
GALLO, L. L., Biochemistry and Molecular Biology
GANZ, R. N., Jr, English
GARNER, N. C., Theatre
GASTWIRTH, J. L., Statistics and Economics
GLICK, I. I., Mathematics
GOLDFARB, R. S., Economics
GOLDSTEIN, A. L., Biochemistry and Molecular Biology
GOW, D. D., Anthropology, Int. Affairs
GRIFFITH, W. B., Philosophy
GRINKER, R. R., Anthropology, Int. Affairs, Human Sciences
GUENTHER, R. J., Music
GUPTA, M. M., Mathematics
HARDING, H., Int. Affairs, Political Science
HARTMANN, H., Women's Studies
HENIG, J. R., Political Science
HILTEBEITEL, A. J., Religion, Human Sciences
HOLMES, D. E., Clinical Psychology
HORTON, J. O., American Civilization and History
HOTEZ, P. J., Microbiology, Tropical Medicine, Global Health, Int. Affairs
HOWE, G. W., Psychology
INDERFURTH, K. F., Int. Affairs
JACOBSON, L. B., Theatre
JOHNSON, K. E., Anatomy
JUDSON, H. F., History
JUNGHENN, H. D., Mathematics
KAMINSKI, G. L., Economics, Int. Affairs
KATZ, I. J., Mathematics
KENNEDY, D. K., History, Int. Affairs
KENNEDY, K. A., Pharmacology and Genetics
KENNEDY, R. E., Jr, European History
KIM-RENAUD, Y. K., Korean Language and Culture, Int. Affairs
KING, M. M., Chemistry
KLAMER, A., Economics, Int. Affairs
KLARÉAN, P. F., History, Int. Affairs
KNOWLTON, R. E., Biology
KUIPERS, J. C., Anthropology, Int. Affairs, Human Sciences
KUMAR, A., Biochemistry, Molecular Biology and Genetics
KWOKA, J. E., Jr, Economics
LABADIE, P. A., Economics

LACHIN, J. M., III, Statistics, Biostatistics
LADER, M. P., Art
LADISCH, S., Paediatrics, Biochemistry and Molecular Biochemistry
LAKE, J. L., Photography
LEHMAN, D. R., Physics
LENGERMANN, P. M., Sociology
LEWIS, J. F., Geology
LILLIEFORS, H. W., Statistics
LINEBAUGH, C. W., Speech and Hearing, Medicine
LIPSCOMB, D. L., Biology
LOGSDON, J. M., Political Science, Int. Affairs
LONGSTRETH, R. W., American Civilization
LUDLOW, G., French, Int. Affairs
McALEAVEY, D. W., English
McCLINTOCK, C., Political Science, Int. Affairs
McGRATH, D. C., Jr, Geography, Urban and Regional Planning
MADDOX, J. H., English
MAHMOUD, H. M., Statistics
MANDEL, H. G., Pharmacology
MANHEIM, J. B., Political Communications and Political Science
MAXIMON, L. C., Physics
MAZZUCHI, T. A., Operations Research, Eng. Management
MERGEN, B. M., American Civilization
MILLAR, J. R., Economics and Int. Affairs
MILLER, B. D., Anthropology, Int. Affairs
MILLER, J. A., English, American Studies
MILLER, J. C., Psychology
MILLER, J. H., Chemistry
MOLINA, S. B., Art
MUFTIC, S., Computer Science
NASR, S. H., Islamic Studies
NAU, H. R., Political Science and Int. Affairs
NAYAK, T. K., Statistics
OFFERMAN, L. R., Psychology
OZDOGAN, T., Ceramics
PACKER, R. K., Biology
PALMER, P. M., American Civilization, Women's Studies
PARKE, W. C., Physics
PARSONS, D. O., Economics
PASTER, G. K., English
PATIERNO, S. R., Pharmacology, Genetics
PECK, L. L., History
PELZMAN, J., Economics and Int. Affairs
PERRY, D. C., Pharmacology
PETERSON, R. A., Psychology, Psychiatry and Behavioural Sciences
PEUSNER, K. D., Anatomy
PLOTZ, J. A., English, Human Sciences
POPPEN, P. J., Psychology
POST, J. M., Psychiatry, Political Psychology, Int. Affairs
PRZYTYCKI, J. H., Mathematics
RAMAKER, D. E., Chemistry
RASKIN, M., Policy Studies
REDDAWAY, P., Political Science and Int. Affairs
REICH, B., Political Science and Int. Affairs
REICH, W., Int. Affairs, Ethics and Human Behaviour
REISS, D., Psychiatry and Behavioural Science, Medicine, Psychology
RIBUFFO, L. P., History
ROBINSON, E. A., Jr, Mathematics
ROBINSON, L. F., Art
ROBLES, F., Int. Marketing, Int. Affairs
ROSENAU, J. N., Int. Affairs
ROTHBLAT, L. A., Psychology, Anatomy
ROWE, W. F., Forensic Sciences
ROWLEY, D. A., Chemistry
RYCROFT, R. W., Int. Science and Technology Policy, Int. Affairs
SACHAR, H. M., History, Int. Affairs
SALAMON, L. B., English, Human Sciences
SAPERSTEIN, M. E., Jewish History
SASHKIN, M., Human Resource Devt
SCHAFFNER, R. F., Medical Humanities, Philosophy

SCHWANDT, D. R., Human Resource Devt
SCOTT, D. W., Microbiology and Immunology, Anatomy and Cell Biology
SEAVEY, O. A., English
SHAMBAUGH, D. L., Political Science and Int. Affairs
SHAO, X.-Q., Anthropology
SIGELMAN, C. K., Psychology
SIGELMAN, L., Political Science
SINGPURWALLA, N. D., Operations Research, Statistics
SMITH, S. C., Economics, Int. Affairs
SODARO, M. J., Political Science and Int. Affairs
SOLAND, R. M., Operations Research
SPECTOR, R. H., History and Int. Affairs
SQUIRES, G. D., Sociology
STEINHARDT, R., Law, Int. Affairs
STEN, C. W., English
STEPHENS, G. C., Geology
STERLING, C. H., Media and Public Affairs, Telecommunication
THIBAULT, J. F., French, Human Sciences
THORNTON, R. C., History and Int. Affairs
TROPEA, J. L., Sociology
TROST, R. P., Economics
TUCH, S. A., Sociology
ULLMAN, D. H., Mathematics
VANDERHOEK, J. Y., Biochemistry and Molecular Biology
VERTER, J. L., Statistics
VLACH, J. M., American Civilization, Anthropology
VON BARGHAHN-CALVETTI, B. A., Art
WADE, A. G., Theatre
WALLACE, S. D., Jr, Religion
WALLACE, R. A., Sociology
WALSH, R. J., Anatomy and Cell Biology
WARREN, C., Communication
WATSON, H. S., Economics
WEGLICKI, W. B., Medicine, Physiology
WEINER, R. J., Int. Business, Int. Affairs
WEITZER, R., Sociology
WERLING, L. L., Pharmacology
WILLIAMS, R. L., Naval Science
WINSLOW, E. K., Behavioural Sciences
WIRTZ, P. W., Management Science, Psychology
WITHERS, M. R., Dance
WOLCHIK, S. L., Political Science and Int. Affairs
WOOD, B., Human Origins, Human Evolutionary Anatomy
WOODWARD, W. T., Painting
WRIGHT, J. F., Jr, Drawing and Graphics
YEIDE, H. E., Jr, Religion
YEZER, A., Economics
ZIOLKOWSKI, J. E., Classics

School of Business and Public Management:
ACHROL, R. S., Marketing
ADAMS, W. C., Public Admin.
ARTERTON, F. C., Political Management
BABER, W. R., Accountancy
BAGCHI, P. K., Business Admin.
BARNHILL, T. M., Finance
CARSON, J. H., Management Science
CHERIAN, E. J., Information Systems
CHITWOOD, S. R., Public Admin.
COYNE, J. P., Management Science
DAVIS, H. J., Strategic Management
DIVITA, S. F., Marketing
DYER, R. F., Business Admin.
FOLKERTS, J., Media and Public Affairs
FORMAN, E. H., Management Science
GLASCOCK, J. L., Finance
GRANGER, M. J., Management Science
HALAL, W. E., Management Science
HANDORF, W. C., Finance
HARMON, M. M., Public Admin.
HARVEY, J. B., Management Science
HAWKINS, D. E., Tourism Studies, Tourism Policy, Medicine
HILMY, J., Accountancy
INFELD, D. L., Public Admin., Health Services Management and Policy

JAQUES, E., Management Science
KEE, J. E., Public Admin.
KLOCK, M. S., Finance
KUMAR, K. R., Accountancy
LAUTER, G. P., Int. Business
LENN, D. J., Strategic Management and Public Policy
LOBUTS, J. F., Jr, Management Science
MADDOX, L. M., Business Admin.
MANHEIM, J. B., Media and Public Affairs, Political Science
McSWAIN, C. J., Public Admin.
NEWCOMER, K. E., Public Admin.
PAIK, C.-M., Accountancy and Quantitative Methods
PARK, Y. S., International Business
PERRY, J. H., Jr, Business Admin.
PHILLIPS, S. M., Finance
RAU, P. A., Business Admin.
ROBERTS, S. V., Media and Public Affairs
ROBLES, F., Int. Marketing and Int. Affairs
SHELDON, D. R., Accountancy
SOYER, R., Management Science
STERLING, C. H., Media and Public Affairs, Telecommunication
STERN, C., Media and Public Affairs
TRACHTENBERG, S. J., Public Admin.
UMPLEBY, S. A., Management Science
UMPLEBY, S. A., Management Science
WEINER, R. J., Int. Business and Int. Affairs
WIRTZ, P. W., Management Science, Psychology
WORTH, M. J., Nonprofit Management

School of Engineering and Applied Science:
BERKOVICH, S. Y., Eng. and Applied Science
BOCK, P. S., Eng.
BRIER, G. R., Eng. Management
CARROLL, R. L., Jr, Eng. and Applied Science
CHOI, H.-A., Eng. and Applied Science
COOPER, P. A., Eng.
DEASON, J. P., Eng. Management, Systems Eng.
DELLA TORRE, E., Eng. and Applied Science
DIGGES, K. H., Eng. and Applied Science
EDELSON, B. L., Eng.
EISNER, H., Eng. Management
FELDMAN, M. B., Eng. and Applied Science
FRIEDER, G., Eng. and Applied Science, Statistics
GARRIS, C. A., Eng.
GILMORE, C. M., Eng. and Applied Science
HAQUE, M. I., Eng. and Applied Science
HARRALD, J. R., Eng. Management
HARRINGTON, R. J., Eng. and Applied Science
HELGERT, H. J., Eng. and Applied Science
HELLER, R. S., Eng. and Applied Science
HOFFMAN, L. J., Eng. and Applied Science
JONES, D. L., Eng.
KAHN, W. K., Eng. and Applied Science
KAUFMAN, R. E., Eng.
KYRIAKOPOULOS, N., Eng.
LANG, R. H., Eng. and Applied Science
LEE, J. D.-Y., Eng. and Applied Science
LIEBOWITZ, H., Eng. and Applied Science
LOEW, M. H., Eng.
MAHMOOD, K., Eng.
MARTIN, C. D., Eng. and Applied Science
MAURER, W. D., Eng. and Applied Science
MAZZUCHI, T. A., Operations Research, Eng. Management
MELTZER, A. C., Eng. and Applied Science
MURPHREE, E. L., Jr, Eng. Management, Systems Eng.
MYERS, M. K., Eng. and Applied Science
NAGEL, D. J., Eng.
NARAHARI, B., Eng. and Applied Science
PARDAVI-HORVATH, M., Eng. and Applied Science
PELTON, J. N., Eng.
PICKHOLTZ, R. L., Eng. and Applied Science

POST, J. M., Eng. Management, Political Psychology, Int. Affairs, Psychiatry and Behavioural Sciences
ROPER, W. E., Eng. and Applied Science
SANDUSKY, R. R., Jr, Eng. and Applied Science
SARKANI, S., Eng. Management, Systems Eng.
SIBERT, J. L., Eng. and Applied Science
SZU, H., Eng.
TOLSON, R. H., Eng. and Applied Science
TONG, T. W., Mechanical Eng.
VOJCIC, B. R., Eng. and Applied Science
WASYLKIWSKYJ, W., Eng. and Applied Science
WATERS, R. C., Eng. Management
YOUSSEF, A., Eng. and Applied Science
ZAGHLOUL, M. E., Eng. and Applied Science

Law School:

ADELMAN, M. J.
BANZHAF, J. F. III
BARRON, J. A.
BENITEZ, A. M.
BHALA, R.
BLOCK, C. D.
BRATTON, W. W.
BROWN, K. B.
BUTLER, P.
CAHN, N. R.
CARTER, W. B.
CHEH, M. M.
CLARK, B. R.
CRAVER, C. B.
CUNNINGHAM, L. E.
DIENES, C. T.
FRIEDENTHAL, J. H.
GABALDON, T. A.
GUTMAN, J. S.
IZUMU, C. L.
JOHNSTON, G. P.
JONES, S. R.
KOVACIC, W. E.
LEE, C.
LEES, F. J.
LERNER, R. L.
LUPU, I. C.
LYMAN, J. P.
MAGGS, G. E.
MEIER, J. S.
MEYER, P. H.
MITCHELL, L. E.
MORGAN, T. D.
PAGEL, S. B.
PARK, R. E.
PERONI, R. J.
PETERSON, T. D.
PIERCE, R. J., Jr
RAVEN-HANSEN, P.
REITZE, A. W., Jr
ROBINSON, D., Jr
SALTZBURG, S. A.
SCHECHTER, R. E.
SCHWARTZ, J. I.
SELMI, M.
SIEGEL, J. R.
SIRULNIK, E. S.
SOHN, L. B.
SOLOMON, L. D.
SPANOGLE, J. A.
STEINHARDT, R. G.
STRAND, J. H.
TRANGSRUD, R. H.
TURLEY, J. R.
TUTTLE, R.
WILMARTH, A. E., Jr
YOUNG, M. K.
ZUBROW, L. E.

School of Medicine and Health Sciences:

ABRAMSON, F. P., Pharmacology, Chemistry
ADELSON, E., Medicine
ADVANI, M., Psychiatry and Behavioural Sciences
AHLGREN, J. D., Medicine, Pharmacology
ALBERT, M., Medicine

ALBRIGHT, J., Microbiology and Tropical Medicine
AMIRI, S., Paediatrics
AMMERMAN, B., Neurological Surgery
APUD, J., Psychiatry and Behavioural Sciences
ARLING, B., Medicine
ARONS, B., Psychiatry and Behavioural Sciences
ASCENSAO, J., Medicine
AUGUST, G. P., Paediatrics
BACHMAN, L., Anaesthesiology, Critical Care Medicine, Paediatrics
BAILEY, J. M., Biochemistry and Molecular Biology
BANK, W. O., Radiology and Neurological Surgery
BARAF, H., Medicine
BARNHILL, R., Dermatology, Pathology
BARR, N., Surgery, Health Care Sciences
BARRY, P., Medicine, Health Care Sciences
BARTH, W. F., Medicine
BATSHAW, M., Paediatrics
BATTEY, J., Surgery
BATTLE, C., Paediatrics
BECKER, A., Obstetrics and Gynaecology
BECKER, K. L., Medicine and Physiology, Experimental Medicine
BELMAN, A. B., Urology and Paediatrics
BENNETT, H., Paediatrics
BERBERIAN, B. J., Dermatology
BERENSON, R., Health Care Sciences
BERNAD, P., Neurology
BERNSTEIN, L., Medicine
BERRY, G., Paediatrics
BIGELOW, L., Psychiatry and Behavioural Sciences
BLANK, A., Psychiatry and Behavioural Sciences
BORENSTEIN, D., Medicine
BORUM, M., Medicine
BOWLES, L. T., Surgery
BRAUN, M., Dermatology
BRILL, D., Medicine
BRILL, W., Medicine
BRONSTHER, O., Surgery
BROWN, B., Psychiatry and Behavioural Sciences
BROWN, H., Ophthalmology
BUKRINSKY, M., Microbiology and Tropical Medicine
BULAS, D., Radiology, Paediatrics
BURMAN, K., Medicine
BURNS, W., Pathology
BURRIS, B., Psychiatry
BYRNE, J., Paediatrics, Epidemology and Biostatistics
BYRON, H., Opthalmology
CAHAN, J., Surgery, Health Care Sciences
CALLENDER, C., Surgery
CAMPOS, J. M., Paediatrics, Pathology, Microbiology and Tropical Medicine
CANTER, J., Surgery
CAPUTY, A., Neurological Surgery
CARLSON, D., Obstetrics and Gynaecology
CAWLEY, J., Prevention and Community Health, Health Care Sciences
CHAMBERLAIN, J., Paediatrics
CHANDRA, R., Pathology, Paediatrics
CHANG, P., Medicine
CHATOOR-KOCH, I. M., Psychiatry and Behavioural Sciences and Paediatrics
CHENG, T. O., Medicine
CHERTOFF, J., Psychiatry and Behavioural Sciences
CHIAPPINELLI, V., Pharmacology and Neurological Surgery
CHIN, M., Anaesthesiology and Critical Care Medicine
CHODOFF, P., Psychiatry and Behavioural Sciences
CHUSED, J., Psychiatry and Behavioural Sciences, Paediatrics
COGEN, P., Neurological Surgery, Paediatrics

COHEN, G. D., Health Care Sciences, Psychiatry and Behavioural Sciences
COHEN, L., Paediatrics
COHEN, M., Surgery
COHEN-MANSFIELD, J., Health Care Sciences, Prevention and Community Health
COLBERG-POLEY, A., Paediatrics, Biochemistry and Molecular Biology
COLEMAN, R., Paediatrics
COLEMAN, R., Psychiatry and Behavioural Sciences
COLICE, G., Medicine
COMAS-DIAZ, L., Psychiatry and Behavioural Sciences
COOK, C., Pathology
COONEY, F., Neurological Surgery
COOPER, B., Medicine
CORSO, P., Surgery
COTLOVE, E., Psychiatry and Behavioural Sciences
COWAN, C., Ophthalmology
COX, G., Emergency Medicine
CYTRYN, L., Psychiatry and Behavioural Sciences
D'ANGELO, L. J., Paediatrics, Prevention and Community Health, Medicine
DANIEL, D., Psychiatry and Behavioural Sciences
DANOVITCH, S., Medicine
DAVIS, D., Psychiatry and Behavioural Sciences
DAVIS, D. O., Radiology, Neurology and Neurological Surgery
DAVIS, G., Microbiology and Tropical Medicine
DENNIS, M., Neurological Surgery
DePALMA, L., Pathology, Anatomy and Cell Biology
DIAMOND, D., Psychiatry and Behavioural Sciences
DIAMOND, R., Medicine
DLUHY, J., Psychiatry and Behavioural Sciences
DOMAN, D., Medicine
DOPPELHEUER, J., Obstetrics and Gynaecology
DOSA, S., Medicine
DRUY, E. M., Radiology
DUBEY, A., Obstetrics and Gynaecology
DUFOUR, D. R., Pathology
DYER, C., Psychiatry and Behavioural Sciences
EATON, J., Psychiatry and Behavioural Sciences
ECONOMOPOULOS, B., Anaesthesiology and Critical Care Medicine
EDELSON, R., Neurology
EDELSTEIN, S., Emergency Medicine, Anaesthesiology and Critical Care Medicine
EICHELBERGER, M. R., Surgery and Paediatrics
EIG, B., Paediatrics
EIN, D., Medicine
EIN, T., Obstetrics and Gynaecology
EIST, H., Psychiatry and Behavioural Sciences
ELLWOOD, L., Health Care Sciences
EL-MOHANDES, A., Prevention and Community Health, Paediatrics, Obstetrics and Gynaecology
ERSHLER, W., Medicine
EVANS, F. B., Psychiatry and Behavioural Sciences
FAIRBANKS, D., Surgery
FALK, N., Medicine, Health Care Sciences
FALK, R., Obstetrics and Gynaecology
FEIGIN, D., Radiology
FELDMAN, B., Surgery, Health Care Sciences, Paediatrics
FELDMAN, I., Surgery
FIELDS, A., Anaesthesiology and Critical Care Medicine
FINKELSTEIN, J. D., Medicine
FISCHER, R., Medicine

FRAM, D., Psychiatry and Behavioural Sciences
FRANK, J., Psychiatry and Behavioural Sciences
FRASER, C., Pharmacology, Microbiology and Tropical Medicine
FUCHS, M., Medicine
GAARDER, K., Psychiatry and Behavioural Sciences
GAASTERLAND, D., Ophthalmology
GAHRES, E., Obstetrics and Gynaecology
GALLO, L., Biochemistry and Molecular Biology
GALLO, V., Paediatrics, Pharmacology
GEELHOED, G. W., International Medicine and Surgery
GEORGE, D., Psychiatry and Behavioural Sciences
GERSHEN, B., Medicine
GIAUME, C., Anatomy and Cell Biology
GILBERT, C., Obstetrics and Gynaecology
GILLANDERS, R., Obstetrics and Gynaecology
GILLMAN, R., Psychiatry and Behavioural Sciences
GINDOFF, P. R., Obstetrics and Gynaecology
GINSBERG, A. L., Medicine
GIORDANO, J. M., Surgery
GLASER, B., Ophthalmology
GLASSMAN, L., Radiology
GLATT, M., Paediatrics, Psychiatry and Behavioural Sciences
GOLD, M., Medicine
GOLDSTEIN, A., Biochemistry and Molecular Biology
GOLDSTEIN, H., Medicine
GOLDSTEIN, K., Medicine
GOLDSTEIN, S., Medicine
GOODENOUGH, D. J., Radiology
GOODMAN, S., Psychiatry and Behavioural Sciences
GOODWIN, F., Psychiatry and Behavioural Sciences
GORDIN, F., Medicine
GORDON, G., Psychiatry and Behavioural Sciences
GORELICK, K., Psychiatry and Behavioural Sciences
GRAETER, J., Orthopaedic Surgery
GRANATIR, W., Psychiatry and Behavioural Sciences
GRAVITZ, M., Psychiatry and Behavioural Sciences
GREENBERG, L. W., Paediatrics
GREENE, C., Paediatrics
GREENSPAN, S., Psychiatry and Behavioural Sciences, Paediatrics
GRIFFITH, J. L., Psychiatry and Behavioural Sciences, Neurology
GROSS, P., Urology
GROSS, R., Psychiatry and Behavioural Sciences
GROSSMAN, J. H., Obstetrics and Gynaecology, Microbiology and Tropical Medicine, Prevention and Community Health
GUIDOTTI, T., Environmental Occupational Health, Medicine
GULYA, A., Surgery
GUNTHER, S. F., Orthopaedic Surgery
GUTIERREZ, G., Medicine, Anaesthesiology and Critical Care Medicine
HAAS, M., Psychiatry and Behavioural Sciences
HAAS, S., Orthopaedic Surgery
HAIDER, R., Medicine
HANNALLAH, R. S., Anaesthesiology and Critical Care Medicine, Paediatrics
HARSHBARGER, J., Pathology
HARISIADIS, L. A., Radiology
HARTMAN, G., Surgery, Paediatrics
HASSAN, M., Obstetrics and Gynaecology
HAUDENSCHILD, C. C., Pathology and Medicine
HAWLEY, R., Anatomy and Cell Biology
HECKMAN, B., Medicine

HEINTZE, A., Obstetrics and Gynaecology
HELLER, N., Psychiatry and Behavioural Sciences
HELMKAMP, B., Obstetrics and Gynaecology
HENSON, D., Pathology
HERER, G. R., Paediatrics
HERSH, S., Psychiatry and Behavioural Sciences, Paediatrics
HILL, M. C., Radiology
HOFFMAN, D., Epidemology and Biostatistics, Global Health
HOFFMAN, E., Paediatrics, Biochemistry and Molecular Biology
HOLBROOK, P. R., Anaesthesiology and Critical Care Medicine, Paediatrics
HOLLAND, C. A., Paediatrics
HOPPING, S., Surgery
HOTEZ, P., Microbiology and Tropical Medicine, Global Health, Epidemology and Biostatistics
HOWARD, W. J., Medicine
HOWE, G., Psychiatry and Behavioural Sciences
HSIA, J., Medicine
HURLEY, J., Paediatrics
HUTTON, J., Surgery
ISSA, F., Psychiatry and Behavioural Sciences
JAAFAR, M., Ophthalmology, Paediatrics
JACOBSEN, F., Psychiatry and Behavioural Sciences
JACOBSON, J., Neurological Surgery
JAFFE, E., Pathology
JANATI, A., Neurology
JEROME, M., Obstetrics and Gynaecology
JOHNSON, F., Pathology
JOHNSON, K., Anatomy and Cell Biology, Obstetrics and Gynaecology
JOSEPH, D., Psychiatry and Behavioural Sciences
JOSEPH, J., Paediatrics, Epidemology and Biostatistics
JOSHI, P., Psychiatry and Behavioural Sciences, Paediatrics
KAFKA, J., Psychiatry and Behavioural Sciences
KALINER, M., Medicine
KAMANI, N., Paediatrics
KAO, G., Dermatology
KAPIKIAN, A., Paediatrics
KAPLAN, K., Psychiatry and Behavioural Sciences, Paediatrics
KAPLAN, R., Anaesthesiology and Critical Care Medicine, Paediatrics
KARCHER, D., Pathology
KATZ, A., Pathology
KATZ, B., Ophthalmology
KATZ, N., Surgery
KATZ, R. J., Medicine and Emergency Medicine
KATZ, R., Dermatology, Paediatrics
KATZ, S., Urology
KAUFMAN, R., Medicine
KAUFMAN, R., Eng., Anatomy and Cell Biology
KELLEHER, J., Physiology and Experimental Medicine
KELLY, J. J., Neurology and Neurological Surgery
KENNEDY, K., Pharmacology, Genetics
KESHISHIAN, J., Surgery
KHOURY, A., Obstetrics and Gynaecology
KIMMEL, P. L., Medicine
KIRBY, E., Psychiatry and Behavioural Sciences
KIRKPATRICK, J., Surgery
KLINE, P., Medicine
KNELLER, M., Radiology
KNOLL, S., Surgery
KOBRINE, A., Neurological Surgery
KOCH, E., Obstetrics and Gynaecology
KOENIG, K., Emergency Medicine
KOVAL, N., Medicine
KOZLOFF, L., Surgery
KREBS, H., Obstetrics and Gynaecology
KRESSEL, B., Medicine

KUEHL, K., Paediatrics
KUMAR, A., Biochemistry and Molecular Biology, Genetics
KUSHNER, D. C., Radiology and Paediatrics
KUSHNER, E., Psychiatry and Behavioural Sciences
LACHER, D., Pathology
LADISCH, S., Paediatrics, Biochemistry and Molecular Biology
LAKSHMAN, R., Medicine, Biochemistry and Molecular Biology
LANDAU, B., Psychiatry and Behavioural Sciences, Paediatrics
LANDO, H., Medicine
LANE, H., Medicine
LARSEN, J. W., Jr, Obstetrics and Gynaecology
LAURENO, R., Neurology
LAWS, E., Neurological Surgery
LAZAR, S., Psychiatry and Behavioural Sciences
LAZARUS, A., Obstetrics and Gynaecology
LE GOLVAN, P., Pathology
LEATHERBURY, L., Paediatrics
LEFKOWITZ, L., Paediatrics, Health Care Sciences
LEMP, M., Ophthalmology
LEVI, L., Psychiatry and Behavioural Sciences
LEVINE, P., Epidemology and Biostatistics, Medicine
LEVITT, R., Obstetrics and Gynaecology
LEVY, L., Radiology
LEW, S., Medicine
LEWIS, J., Medicine
LEWIS, R., Orthopaedic Surgery
LIEBERMAN, E., Psychiatry and Behavioural Sciences
LIEBERMAN, M., Medicine
LINDSAY, J., Medicine
LIOTTA, L., Pathology
LIPSIUS, S., Psychiatry and Behavioural Sciences, Obstetrics and Gynaecology
LIPSON, A., Medicine
LITOVITZ, T., Emergency Medicine
LITTMAN, B., Obstetrics and Gynaecology
LOO, T., Pharmacology
LOWE, J., Paediatrics
LUBAN, N. C., Paediatrics and Pathology
LUKE, J., Pathology
LURIE, N., Medicine
LYNN, D. J., Health Care Sciences and Medicine
MCAFEE, J., Radiology
MACDONALD-GINZBURG, M. G., Paediatrics
MCDOWELL, R., Paediatrics
MCGILL, W. A., Anaesthesiology and Critical Care Medicine, Paediatrics
MACHT, S., Surgery
MCKNEW, D., Paediatrics
MADDOX, J., Obstetrics and Gynaecology
MAHDAVI, I., Paediatrics
MAJD, M., Radiology and Paediatrics
MALAWER, M. M., Orthopaedic Surgery
MANDEL, H. G., Pharmocology
MANDLER, R., Neurology and Neurological Surgery
MANYAK, M. J., Urology, Microbiology and Tropical Medicine
MARINOFF, S., Obstetrics and Gynaecology
MARLOW, M., Obstetrics and Gynaecology
MARTIN, D., Obstetrics and Gynaecology
MARTIN, G. R., Paediatrics
MASTERS, E. C., Obstetrics and Gynaecology
MASTROYANNIS, C., Obstetrics and Gynaecology
MASUR, H., Medicine
MAYER, T., Emergency Medicine
MECKLENBURG, F., Obstetrics and Gynaecology
MERIKANGAS, J., Psychiatry and Behavioural Science
MEYER, J., Medicine
MELVILLE, R., Pathology
MIDGLEY, F. M., Surgery and Paediatrics

MILLER, G., Psychiatry and Behavioural Sciences
MILOWE, I., Paediatrics
MOAK, J. P., Paediatrics
MONDZAC, A., Medicine
MOODY, S., Anatomy and Cell Biology
MOSKOVITZ, P., Orthopaedic Surgery, Neurological Surgery
MUFARRIJ, I., Obstetrics and Gynaecology
MULLAN, F., Health Care Sciences, Paediatrics, Prevention and Community Health
MURPHY, R., Ophthalmology
NACHNANI, G., Medicine
NASHEL, D., Medicine
NASR, M., Psychiatry and Behavioural Sciences
NAWAB, E., Obstetrics and Gynaecology
NEVIASER, R. J., Orthopaedic Surgery
NEWMAN, K., Surgery, Paediatrics
NEWMAN, M., Medicine
NG, L., Neurology
NICKLAS, R., Medicine
NICOLAS, J., Paediatrics, Pharmacology
NIERMAN, W., Biochemistry and Molecular Biology
NIGRA, T., Dermatology, Paediatrics
NOWAK, J., Psychiatry and Behavioural Sciences
OBOLER, A., Medicine
OCHSENSCHLAGER, D. W., Paediatrics and Emergency Medicine
O'KIEEFE, D., Medicine
OLDFIELD, E., Neurological Surgery
OMMAYA, A., Neurological Surgery
O'NEILL, J., Ophthalmology
ORENSTEIN, J., Pathology
ORKIN, B., Surgery
PACKER, R. J., Neurology and Paediatrics
PALOMBI, J., Psychiatry and Behavioural Sciences, Paediatrics
PAN, J., Obstetrics and Gynaecology
PARENTI, D., Medicine, Microbiology and Tropical Medicine
PARKER, P., Paediatrics
PARKS, M., Ophthalmology, Paediatrics
PATEL, R. I., Anaesthiology and Critical Care Medicine, Paediatrics
PATIERNO, S., Pharmacology, Genetics, Environmental Occupational Health
PAWLSON, L. G., Healthcare Sciences, Medicine, Health Services Management and Policy
PEDREIRA, F., Paediatrics
PEEBLES, P., Paediatrics
PEELE, R., Psychiatry and Behavioural Sciences
PERMAN, G., Psychiatry and Behavioural Sciences
PERRY, D., Pharmacology
PETROVITCH, C., Anaesthesiology and Critical Care Medicine
PEUSNER, K., Anatomy and Cell Biology
PHILLIPS, M., Medicine
PILLAI, M., Medicine
PLATIA, E. V., Medicine
POLIS, M., Emergency Medicine
POLLACK, M. M., Anaesthesiology and Critical Care Medicine, Paediatrics
POST, J., Psychiatry and Behavioural Sciences
POTOLICCHIO, S. J., Neurology and Neurological Surgery
POTTER, B. M., Radiology and Paediatrics
POVAR, G., Health Care Sciences, Medicine
POWERS, D., Obstetrics and Gynaecology
PRINCIPATO, J., Surgery
PROTOS, P., Obstetrics and Gynaecology
PULASKI, P., Neurology
PUMPHREY, R., Surgery
PUTNAM, J., Medicine
PYATT, R., Radiology
RABSON, A., Pathology
RAIS-BAHRMANI, K., Paediatrics
RANKIN, J., Psychiatry and Behavioural Sciences

RANKIN, R., Psychiatry and Behavioural Sciences
RAPOPORT, J., Psychiatry and Behavioural Sciences, Paediatrics
RATNER, R., Psychiatry and Behavioural Sciences
REAMAN, G. H., Paediatrics
REICH, W., Psychiatry and Behavioural Sciences
REISS, D., Psychiatry and Behavioural Sciences, Medicine and Psychology
RESTAK, R., Neurology
RICKLES, F., Medicine, Paediatrics
RIEGELMAN, R., Epidemiology and Biostatistics, Medicine, Health Care Sciences
RIEGER, R., Paediatrics, Psychiatry and Behavioural Sciences
ROBBINS, D. C., Medicine
ROBERTSON, W. W., Orthopaedic Surgery
ROBINOWITZ, C., Psychiatry and Behavioural Sciences
ROBINSON, L., Psychiatry and Behavioural Sciences
RODRIGUEZ-GARCIA, R., Global Health, Prevention and Community Health, International Affairs
ROSENBAUM, S., Health Policy, Health Services Management and Leadership, Health Care Sciences
ROSENBERG, J., Medicine
ROSENBLUM, S., Psychiatry and Behavioural Sciences
ROSENQUIST, G. C., Paediatrics
ROSENSTEIN, J., Anatomy and Cell Biology, Neurological Surgery
ROSS, M., Obstetrics and Gynaecology
ROTHMAN, B., Obstetrics and Gynaecology
ROTSZTAIN, A., Medicine
RUBOVITS-SEITZ, P., Psychiatry and Behavioural Sciences
RUCKMAN, R. N., Paediatrics
RUDZKI, C., Medicine
RUSHTON, H. G., Urology and Paediatrics
SADIN, H., Medicine
SARIN, P., Environmental Occupational Heath, Biochemistry and Molecular Biology
SCALETTAR, R., Medicine
SCHECHTER, G. P., Medicine
SCHEER, J., Health Care Sciences
SCHLEIN, P., Medicine
SCHNEIDER, M., Medicine
SCHWARTZ, A., Pathology
SCHWARTZ, R., Paediatrics, Health Care Sciences
SCOTT, D., Immunology, Anatomy and Cell Biology
SCOTT, J., Emergency Medicine
SCOTT, S., Medicine
SEIBEL, N., Paediatrics
SEIDES, S., Medicine
SEKHAR, L. N., Neurological Surgery
SEMERJIAN, H., Urology
SEVER, J. L., Paediatrics, Microbiology and Tropical Medicine, Obstetrics and Gynaecology
SHARGEL, M., Medicine
SHESSER, R. F., Emergency Medicine, Medicine, Environmental Occupational Health
SHORE, M., Paediatrics
SHORT, B. L., Paediatrics
SHRIER, D., Psychiatry and Behavioural Sciences, Paediatrics
SIDAWY, A. N., Surgery
SIDAWY, M., Pathology
SILBER, T. J., Paediatrics, Global Health, Prevention and Community Health
SILVA, C., Surgery
SILVER, S., Pathology, Prevention and Community Health, Medicine
SIMON, D., Medicine
SIMON, G. L., Medicine, Biochemistry and Molecular Biology, Microbiology and Tropical Medicine
SIMON, J., Obstetrics and Gynaecology

SINGH, N., Paediatrics, Health Care Sciences, Global Health
SLUZKI, C., Psychiatry and Behavioural Sciences
SLY, R. M., Paediatrics
SMITH, L., Surgery
SMITH, M., Emergency Medicine
SMOLLER, B., Psychiatry and Behavioural Sciences
SOLDIN, S. J., Paediatrics, Pathology
SOLOMON, F., Psychiatry and Behavioural Sciences
SOREL, E., Psychiatry and Behavioural Sciences
SOUTHBY, R., Global Health, Health Care Sciences, Health Policy
SPAGNOLO, S. V., Medicine
STAR, R., Medicine
STARK, W., Psychiatry and Behavioural Sciences, Paediatrics
STEIN, M., Psychiatry and Behavioural Sciences, Paediatrics
STEINBERG, W. M., Medicine
STEINFELD, H., Medicine
STERN, M., Psychiatry and Behavioural Sciences
STEVENS, C., Psychiatry and Behavioural Sciences
STOCK, M., Medicine and Health Care Sciences
STOCKTON, W., Psychiatry and Behavioural Sciences
STONE, A., Health Care Sciences, Medicine
STOPAK, B., Neurological Surgery
STOPAK, S., Ophthalmology
STRASSBURGER, F., Paediatrics
STRICKLAND, D., Biochemistry and Molecular Biology
TAUBER, L., Neurological Surgery
TAUBIN, J., Medicine, Health Care Sciences
TAVASSOLI, F., Pathology
TAYLOR, D., Psychiatry and Behavioural Sciences
TETTE, A., Surgery
THOMAS, J., Psychiatry and Behavioural Sciences
THOMPSON, A., Medicine
TIEVSKY, G., Radiology
TRAMONT, E., Medicine
TROUT, H., Surgery
TRUJILLO, N., Medicine
TSOKOS, G., Paediatrics
TUAZON, C. U., Medicine
TUCHMAN, M., Paediatrics, Biochemistry and Molecular Biology
TURNER, M., Dermatology
USHER, M., Psychiatry and Behavioural Sciences
VAN BREDA, A., Radiology
VANDERHOEK, J., Biochemistry and Molecular Biology
VARGHESE, P. J., Medicine and Paediatrics
VELASQUEZ, M. T., Medicine
VENBRUX, A., Radiology, Surgery
VIRMANI, R., Pathology
WALETZKY, J., Psychiatry and Behavioural Sciences
WALKER, G., Biochemistry and Molecular Biology
WALSH, R., Anatomy and Cell Biology, Neurological Surgery
WARGOTZ, E., Pathology
WARREN, N., Dermatology
WARTOFSKY, L., Medicine
WATKIN, D., Medicine
WEGLICKI, W. B., Medicine, Physiology and Experimental Medicine
WEINBERGER, D., Psychiatry and Behavioural Sciences
WEINSTEIN, S., Neurology, Paediatrics
WEISS, H., Medicine
WEISS, L., Medicine
WELBORN, L. G., Anaesthesiology and Critical Care Medicine, Paediatrics
WERLING, L., Pharmacology, Neurological Surgery

WHERRY, D., Surgery
WHITE, P. H., Medicine and Paediatrics
WILKINSON, R., Medicine
WILLIAMS, C. M., Dermatology and Pathology
WILLIAMS, J. F., Anaesthesiology and Critical Care Medicine, Health Services Management and Policy
WILLIAMS, M., Pathology
WILLIAMS, S., Obstetrics and Gynaecology
WINKLES, J., Biochemistry and Molecular Biology
WISNESKI, L., Medicine
WITTENBERG, R., Psychiatry and Behavioural Sciences
WOLFE, M., Medicine
WOLIN, S., Psychiatry and Behavioural Sciences
WOLMAN, S., Pathology
WOOD, B., Anthropology, Anatomy and Cell Biology
WRIGHT, D. C., Neurological Surgery
YODAIKEN, R., Pathology, Health Care Sciences
YOO, D., Medicine
YU, G., Urology
ZAJTCHUK, R., Surgery
ZALESKE, D., Orthopaedic Surgery, Paediatrics
ZALAL, G. H., Surgery and Paediatrics
ZEMAN, R., Radiology
ZIMMERMAN, M., Ophthalmology
ZINNER, J., Psychiatry and Behavioural Sciences

School of Public Health and Health Services:

BILES, B., Health Policy
BORZI, P., Health Policy
BOYD, N. R., Prevention and Community Health
CAWLEY, J. F., Prevention and Community Health
D'ANGELO, L. J., Prevention and Community Medicine
DARR, K. J., Health Services Management and Leadership
EASTAUGH, S. R., Health Services Management and Leadership
EL-MOHANDES, A., Prevention and Community Medicine
GREENBERG, W., Health Economics
GUIDOTTI, T. L., Environmental and Occupational Health
HIDALGO, J., Health Policy
HIRSCH, R. P., Epidemiology and Biostatistics
LACHIN, J., Epidemology and Biostatistics
LEVINE, P. H., Epidemiology and Biostatistics, Environmental and Occupational Health
MICHAELS, D., Environmental and Occupational Health
MILLER, W. C., Exercise Science
PAUP, D. C., Exercise Science
RIEGELMAN, R. K., Epidemiology and Biostatistics
RODRIGUEZ-GARCIA, R., Center for International Health
ROSSELLO, P., Global Health
SARIN, P., Environmental and Occupational Health
SOUTHBY, R. M. F., Global Health, Health Policy
SULLIVAN, P. A., Exercise Science
WINDSOR, R. A., Prevention and Community Medicine

Graduate School of Education and Human Development:

CASTLEBERRY, M. S., Special Education
CONFESSORE, G. J., Higher Education Administration
CUMMINGS, W. K., International Education
DEW, D. W., Counselling, Psychiatry and Behavioural Sciences
EL-KHAWAS, E. H., Education Policy
FERRANTE, R., Education

FREUND, M. B., Special Education
FUTRELL, M. H., Education
HEDDESHEIMER, J. C., Counselling, Psychiatry and Behavioural Sciences
HOARE, C. H., Human Devt and Human Resource Devt
HOLMES, D. H., Education
HOWERTON, E. B., Jr, Education
IANACONE, R. N., Special Education
KOCHHAR-BRYANT, C. A., Special Education
LINKOWSKI, D. C., Counselling, Psychology and Behavioural Sciences
LYNCH, S. H., Teacher Preparation, Special Education
MAZUR, A. J., Special Education
MULLER, R. O., Educational Research
PALEY, N. B., Elementary Education
PARATORE, S. R., Education
ROTBERG, I. C., Education Policy
SASHKIN, M., Human Resource Devt
SCHWANDT, D. R., Human Resource Devt
SHOTEL, J. R., Special Education
TAYMANS, J. H., Special Education
WATSON, A., Higher Education Admin.
WEST, L. L., Special Education
WHITAKER, R., Higher Education

GEORGETOWN UNIVERSITY

37th and O Sts, NW, Washington, DC 20057

Telephone: (202) 687-0100

Internet: www.georgetown.edu

Founded in 1789 as the first Catholic University in the USA

Pres.: JOHN J. DEGIOIA

Provost: Dr JAMES J. O'DONNELL

Sr Vice-Pres. and Chief Admin. Officer: SPIROS DIMOLITSAS

Sr Vice-Pres., Chief Financial Officer, and Treas.: CHRIS AUGOSTINI

Exec. Vice-Pres. for Law Center Affairs: T. ALEXANDER ALEINIKOFF

Vice-Pres. and Chief Human Resources Officer: MARY ANN MAHIN

Vice-Pres. for Facilities and Student Housing: KAREN S. FRANK

Vice-Pres. and Gen. Univ. Counsel: JANE E. GENSTER

Vice-Pres. for Information Services and Chief Information Officer: H. DAVID LAMBERT

Vice-Pres. for Mission and Ministry: Fr PHILIP L. BOROUGHS

Vice-Pres. for Public Affairs and Strategic Devt: DANIEL R. PORTERFIELD

Vice-Pres. for Student Affairs and Dean of Students: TODD A. OLSON

Vice-Pres. of Technology Licensing: CARLA D. DEMARIA

Vice-Pres. for Univ. Safety (vacant)

Librarian: ARTEMIS G. KIRK

Library of 2,123,000 vols

Number of teachers: 2,085 (1576 full-time, 509 part-time)

Number of students: 12,629

Publications: *American Criminal Law Review, Domesday Book, Entrecaminos, Georgetown Immigration Law Journal, Georgetown International Environmental Law Review, Georgetown Journal of Gender and the Law, Georgetown Journal of International Affairs, Georgetown Journal of Legal Ethics, Georgetown Journal on Poverty Law & Policy, Georgetown Law Journal (every 2 months), Georgetown Magazine (quarterly), Georgetown Medical Bulletin (3 a year), Georgetown Public Policy Review, Gnovis, Hoya Review, The Blue and Gray (fortnightly), Law and Policy in International Business (3 a year), The Hoya (2 a week), The Voice (weekly), The Anthem, The Tax Lawyer*

DEANS

Georgetown College: JANE DAMMEN MCAULIFFE
School of Nursing and Health Studies: BETTE KELTNER
Edmund A. Walsh School of Foreign Service: ROBERT L. GALLUCCI
McDonough School of Business: Prof. REENA AGGARWAL
School for Summer and Continuing Education: ROBERT J. THOMAS
Graduate School of Arts and Sciences: DAVID W. LIGHTFOOT
Law School: T. ALEXANDER ALEINIKOFF
School of Medicine: STEPHEN RAY MITCHELL

PROFESSORS

School of Business:

AGGARWAL, R.
ANDREASEN, A. R.
BIES, R. J.
BRENKERT, G. G.
COOKE, T. B.
DROMS, W. G.
POWERS, J. J., Jr
ERNST, R.
FEKRAT, M. A.
FERDOWS, K.
GRANT, R.
JOHANSSON, J. K.
LEVY, M. R.
MAYO, J. W.
MAZZOLA, J. B.
MCCABE, D. M.
MICELI, M. P.
NOLLEN, S. D.
ORD, J. K.
PARKER, R. S.
QUINN, D. P.
REINSCH, L.
STATEN, M. E.
THOMAS, R. J.
WALKER, D. A.

School of Foreign Service:

ALBRIGHT, M.
ANDERSON, J.
BAILEY, J.
CANZONERI, M.
CHICKERING, R.
CROCKER, C.
CUDDINGTON, J.
CUMBY, R. E.
ESPOSITO, J. L.
GALLUCCI, R. L.
HADDAD, Y. Y.
HOWE, H. M.
HUDSON, M. C.
IKENBERRY, G. J.
KEELY, C. B.
KLINE, J. M.
KROGH, P. F.
LAKE, A.
LANGAN, J.
LIEBER, R.
MCHENRY, D.
MCNEILL, J. R.
MIKELL, G.
MORAN, T. H.
PIRTLE, C. E.
RAMO, F.
REARDON-ANDERSON, J.
STENT, A.
STITES, R.
STOWASSER, B.
SUBIRATS, J.
TABAK, F.
TILLMAN, S. P.
TUCKER, N. B.
VALENZUELA, A.
VIKSNINS, G. J.
VOLL, J.
WEISS, C.
WINTERS, F. X.
YOST, C.

School of Law:

ABERNATHY, C. F.
ALEINIKOFF, T. A.
AREEN, J. C.
BABCOCK, H.
BAUMAN, J. D.
BLOCH, S. L.
BLOCHE, M. G.
BYRNE, J. P.
CAMPBELL, A. J.
CARTER, B. E.
CASHIN, S. D.
CHUSED, R. H.
COHEN, J. E.
COHEN, S. B.
COHN, S. L.
COLE, D. D.
COOK, A. E.
COPACINO, J. M.
DASH, S.
DIAMOND, R. D.
DINH, V. D.
DONAHOE, D. R.
DRINAN, R. F.
EDELMAN, P. B.
ERNST, D. R.
FEINERMAN, J. V.
FELDBLUM, C. R.
FELDMAN, H. L.
GINSBURG, M. D.
GOLDBERG, S. P.
GOLDBLATT, S. H.
GOSTIN, L. O.
GOTTESMAN, M. H.
GULATI, G. M.
GUSTAFSON, C. H.
HAFT, R. J.
HAY, A. M.
HEINZERLING, L.
JACKSON, J. H.
JACKSON, V. C.
JORDAN, E. C.
KATYAL, N. K.
KING, P. A.
KOPLOW, D. A.
LANGEVOORT, D. C.
LAWRENCE, C. R., III
LAZARUS, R. J.
LUBAN, D. J.
MACKLIN, L. W. S.
MATSUDA, M. J.
MENKEL-MEADOW, C. J.
MLYNIEC, W. J.
MURPHY, J. G., Jr
NORTON, E. H.
OAKLEY, R. L.
OLDHAM, J. C.
O'SULLIVAN, J. R.
PAGE, J. A.
PEARLMAN, R. A.
PELLER, G.
PERDUE, W. C.
PITOFSKY, R.
QUINN, K. P.
RAMSFIELD, J. J.
REGAN, M. C., Jr
ROE, R. L.
ROSS, S. D.
ROTHSTEIN, P. F.
SALOP, S. C.
SCHOTLAND, R. A.
SCHRAG, P. G.
SCHWARTZ, W. F.
SEIDMAN, L. M.
SPANN, G. A.
STROMSETH, J. E.
STUMBERG, R. K.
TAGUE, P. W.
TARULLO, D. K.
THOMAS, J. R.
TUSHNET, M. V.
VÁZQUEZ, C. M.
VUKOWICH, W. T.
WASSERSTROM, S. J.
WEIDENBRUCH, P. P., Jr

WEISS, E. B.
WERRO, F.
WEST, R. L.
WILLIAMS, W. W.

School of Nursing and Health Studies:

BAIGIS, J.
EVANS, C.
FILERMAN, G.
RAMEY, C.
RAMEY, S.

Undergraduate School:

AGGARWAL, R., School of Business
ALATIS, J. E., Linguistics and Modern Greek
ALBRECHT, J. W., Economics
ALBRIGHT, M. K., Practice of Diplomacy
ANDERLINI, L., Economics
ANDREASEN, A. R., School of Business
ASTARITA, T., History
BABB, V., English
BAILEY, J. J., Government and School of Foreign Service
BAIGIS, J., Nursing
BARNES, S. H., Govt and School of Foreign Service
BARROWS, E. M., Biology
BATES, R. D., Jr, Chemistry
BEAUCHAMP, T. L., Philosophy
BENKE, G., Mathematics
BENSKY, R. D., French
BETZ, P. F., English
BIES, R. J., School of Business
Rev. BRADLEY, D. J. M., Philosophy
BRENKERT, G. G., School of Business
BROUGH, J. B., Philosophy
BROWN, D. M., History
BYRNES, A. S., German
CALVERT, S., Psychology
CALVEZ, J.-Y., Government
CANZONERI, M. B., Economics and School of Foreign Service
CAREY, G. W., Government
CHANG, D.-C., Mathematics
CHAPMAN, G. B., Biology
CHAPMAN, T., School of Nursing and Health Studies
CHICKERING, R., History and School of Foreign Service
CIMA, G. G., English
COLLINS, J. B., History
COLLINS, S. M., Economics
COOKE, T. B., School of Business
CROCKER, C. A., Strategic Studies in School of Foreign Service
CUDDINGTON, J. T., Economics and School of Foreign Service
CUMBY, R. E., International Business Diplomacy
CURRAN, R. E., History
CURRIE, J. F., Physics
DAVIS, W., Philosophy
DENNING, D. E., Computer Science
DROMS, W.M G., School of Business
ENGLER, H., Mathematics
ERNST, R., School of Business
ESPOSITO, J. L., Center for Muslim–Christian Understanding
EVANS, M. D., Economics
FASOLD, R. H W., Linguistics
FEKRAT, M. A., School of Business
FERDOWS, K.A, School of Business
FILERMAN, G., Health Studies
FINKEL, N. J., Psychology
GALE, I., Economics
GALLUCCI, R. L., School of Foreign Service
GIBERT, S. P., Government
GLAVIN, J. J., English
GODSON, R., Government
GOLDFRANK, D. M., History
GOMEZ-LOBO, A., Philosophy
GOODMAN, A. E., School of Foreign Service
GORMLEY, W. T., Government and Public Policy
GRANT, R. M., School of Business
GUSTAFSON, T., Government

HADDAD, Y. Y., School of Foreign Service
HALL, C. M., Sociology
HAUGHT, J. F., Theology
HEELAN, P. A., Philosophy
HENDERSON, E. J., Biology
HILTON, A. H., Art
HIRSH, J. C., English
HOLMER, J. M., English
HOWARD, D. V., Psychology
HUDSON, M. C., Arab Studies
IKENBERRY, G. J., School of Foreign Service
IRIZARRY, E. D., Spanish
JANKOWSKY, K. R., German
JOHANSSON, J. K., School of Business
JOHNSON, R. M., History
JOYNER, C. C., Government
KALYANASUNDARAM, B., Computer Science
KAZIN, M., History
KELTNER, B., School of Nursing and Health Studies
KERTESZ, M., Chemistry
KING, T. M., Theology
KIRKPATRICK, J. J.
KLINE, J. M., School of Foreign Service
KONÉ, A., French
KORD, S. T., German
KROGH, P. F., School of Foreign Service
KUHN, S. T., Philosophy
LAGNESE, J. E., Mathematics
LAKE, A., School of Foreign Service
LARUBIA-PRADO, F., Spanish
LEVY, M. B., School of Business
LIEBER, R. J., Govt
MCAULIFFE, J. D., Georgetown College
MCCABE, D. M., School of Business
MCDONALD, W. F., Sociology
MCHENRY, D. F., School of Foreign Service
MCKEOWN, E., Theology
MCNAMARA, D., Sociology
MCNEILL, J. R., School of Foreign Service and History
MCNELIS, P. D., Economics and School of Foreign Service
MADDOX, L. B., English
MARTIRE, D. E., Chemistry
MARULLO, S., Sociology
MASSOUD-MOGHADDAM, F., Psychology
MAZZOLA, J. B., School of Business
MICELI, M. P., School of Business
MIKELL, G., Sociology and School of Foreign Service
MORAN, T. H., Int. Business Diplomacy
MORRIS, M. A., Slavic Languages
MUJICA, B. L., Spanish
MURPHY, G. R., German
NEALE, J. H., Biology
NISHIOKA, D. J., Biology
NOLLEN, S. D., School of Business
O'BRIEN, G., English
ORD, J. K., School of Business
PARKER, R. S., School of Business
PARROTT, W. G., Psychology
PFORDRESHER, J. C., English
PHILLIPS, D. A., Psychology
POPE, M. T., Chemistry
PRELINGER, E. A., Art
PUTO, C. P., School of Business
QUINN, D., School of Business
RAGUSSIS, M., English
RAMEY, C. T., School of Nursing and Health Studies
RAMEY, S. L., School of Nursing and Health Studies
RAPPAPORT, J., Spanish and School of Foreign Service
REARDON-ANDERSON, J., School of Foreign Service
REINSCH, N. LAMAR, Jr, School of Business
ROBINSON, D. N., Psychology
ROSENBLATT, J. P., English
ROSHWALD, A., History
RUEDY, J. D., History
RYDING, K. C., Arabic
SANDEFUR, J. T., Jr, Mathematics
SCHALL, J. V., Govt

SCHIFFRIN, D., Linguistics
SCHURER, W., School of Business
SCHWARTZ, M., Economics
SCOLLON, R. T., Linguistics
SERENE, J. W., Physics
SEVERINO, R., Italian
SHAHID, I., Arabic
SHERMAN, N.
SITTERSON, J. C., Jr, English
SLEVIN, J. F., English
SMITH, B. R., English
STEINBERG, D. I., School of Foreign Service
STENT, A., Govt
STITES, R., History and School of Foreign Service
STOWASSER, B., Arabic and School of Foreign Service
SWEENEY, R. J., School of Business
SZITTYA, P. R., English
TAMBASCO, A. J., Theology
TANNEN, D.
TAYLOR, D. W., Biology
THOMAS, R. J., School of Business
TUCKER, J. E., History
TUCKER, N. B., School of Foreign Service and History
VALENZUELA, A., Government
VEATCH, R. M., Philosophy
VELAUTHAPILLAI, M., Computer Science
VERECKE, W., Philosophy
VIKSNINS, G. J., Economics and School of Foreign Service
VOLL, J. O., School of Foreign Service and History
VROMAN, S., Economics
WALKER, D. A., School of Business
WALTERS, L. B., Jr, Philosophy
WAYNE, S. J., Govt
WEISS, C., School of Foreign Service
WEISS, R. G., Chemistry
WILCOX, W. C., Govt
WINTERS, F. X., School of Foreign Service
YANG, D. C., Chemistry
YOST, C. A., School of Foreign Service

ATTACHED INSTITUTES

Center for Applied Research in the Apostolate: Dir GERALD EARLY.

Center for Australian and New Zealand Studies: Dir ALAN C. TIDWELL.

Center for Business and Public Policy: Dir Prof. JOHN MAYO

Center for Clinical Bioethics: Dir CAROL R. TAYLOR.

Center for Contemporary Arab Studies: Dir MICHAEL C. HUDSON.

Center for Democracy and the Third Sector: Dir STEPHEN HEYDEMANN.

Center for Electronic Projects in American Culture Studies: Dir RANDY BASS.

Center for Eurasian, Russian and East European Studies: Dir MARCIA MORRIS (acting).

Center for Hypertension and Renal Disease Research: Dir CHRISTOPHER S. WILCOX.

Center for Intercultural Education and Devt: Dir CHRISTOPHER SHIRLEY.

Center for Latin American Studies: Dir ARTURO VALENZUELA.

Center for Liturgy: Dir LAWRENCE J. MADDEN.

Center for Minority Educational Affairs: Dir DENNIS A. WILLIAMS.

Center for Muslim–Christian Understanding: Dir JOHN VOLL.

Center for Neural Injury and Recovery: Dir JEAN WRATHALL.

Center for New Designs in Learning and Scholarship: Dir RANDALL BASS.

Center for Peace and Security Studies: Dir MICHAEL E. BROWN.

Center for Peace Studies: Dir HENRY SCHWARZ.

Center for Professional Devt: Dir ROBERT THOMAS.

Center for Public and Non-Profit Leadership: Dir KATHY POSTEL KRETMAN.

Center for Research on Children in the United States: Dirs DEBORAH A. PHILLIPS, WILLIAM T. GORMLEY.

Center for Social Justice: Dir PETER-HANS KOLVENBACH.

Center for the Brain Basis of Cognition: Dirs DARLENE HOWARD, MICHAEL ULLMAN.

Center for the Environment: Dir BILL BUTLER.

Center for the Study of Learning: Dir LIZ CRIGLER.

Center for the Study of Sex Differences in Health, Aging, and Disease: Dir KATHRYN SANDBERG.

Center on an Aging Society: Dir ROBERT B. FRIEDLAND.

Institute for the Study of Diplomacy: Dir CASIMIR A. YOST.

Joseph and Rose Kennedy Institute of Ethics: Dir LEROY WALTERS.

HOWARD UNIVERSITY

2400 Sixth St, NW, Washington, DC 20059

Telephone: (202) 806-6100

Fax: (202) 806-5934

Internet: www.howard.edu

Founded 1867

Private control

Academic year: August to May (2 terms)

Pres.: Dr H. PATRICK SWYGERT (acting)
Sr Vice-Pres.: Dr HASSAN MINOR
Sr Vice-Pres. and Chief Financial Officer: SIDNEY H. EVANS, Jr (acting)
Sr Vice-Pres. for Health Services: Dr VICTOR F. SCOTT
Vice-Pres. for Human Resource Management and Sec. of the Univ. Board of Trustees: ARTIS G. HAMPSHIRE-COWAN
Vice-Pres. for Univ. Advancement: VIRGIL ECTON
Vice-Provost for Student Affairs: Dr FRANKLIN CHAMBERS
Provost and Chief Academic Officer: Dr RICHARD ALLYN ENGLISH
Gen. Counsel (vacant)
Dir of Libraries: MOHAMED MEKKAWI

Library of 1,900,000 vols
Number of teachers: 2,051
Number of students: 10,987

Publications: *The Capstone* (weekly during academic terms), *Howard Journal of Communications* (quarterly), *Howard Law Review* (quarterly), *Journal of Negro Education* (quarterly), *Journal of Religious Thought* (2 a year)

DEANS

College of Arts and Sciences: Dr JAMES DONALDSON
College of Dentistry: Dr LEO E. ROUSE
College of Medicine: Dr FLOYD MALVEAUX
College of Pharmacy, Nursing and Allied Health Sciences: Dr PEDRO LECCA
School of Business: Dr BARRON HARVEY
School of Communications: Dr JANNETTE DATES (acting)
School of Divinity: Dr BERTRAM MELBOURNE
School of Education: Dr VINETTA JONES
School of Eng., Architecture and Computer Sciences: Dr JAMES JOHNSON
School of Law: Dr KURT L. SCHMOKE
School of Social Work: Dr CUDORE L. SNELL
Graduate School: Dr ORLANDO TAYLOR

NATIONAL DEFENSE INTELLIGENCE COLLEGE

200 MacDill Blvd, Washington, DC 20340-5100

Telephone: (202) 231-3319

E-mail: jmic@dia.mil;

Internet: www.dia.mil/college

Founded 1962 as Defense Intelligence School; renamed Joint Military Intelligence College 1993; present name 2006

Pres.: A. DENIS CLIFT
Provost: Dr TERESA J. DOMZAL
Dir, Office of Institutional Research: Dr TARA E. MCNEALY

Library of 2,500,000 items.

SOUTHEASTERN UNIVERSITY

501 I St, SW, Washington, DC 20024

Telephone: (202) 265-5343

Fax: (202) 488-8093

E-mail: admissions@seu.edu

Internet: www.seu.edu

Founded 1879

Assoc., Bachelors and Masters degrees in Business and Govt Man.

Pres.: Dr CHARLENE DREW JARVIS (acting)
Dean of Faculty and Academic Affairs: Dr GUGU MOCHE
Dir of Human Resources: TRACEY PRINCE
Chief Financial Officer: PETER CANINE
Dir of Devt and Alumni Relations: SHANA YOUNG
Registrar: PATRICIA V. MITCHELL

Library of 46,000 vols
Number of teachers: 92
Number of students: 1,057.

STRAYER UNIVERSITY

Suite 300, 1133 15th St, NW, Washington, DC 20005

Telephone: (202) 408-2400

Fax: (202) 289-1831

E-mail: washington@strayer.edu

Internet: www.strayer.edu

Founded 1892 as Strayer Business College; present name 1998

Private control (Strayer Education, Inc.)

Academic year: September to September

Pres. and CEO: ROBERT S. SILBERMAN
Provost and Academic Dean: Dr J. CHRIS TOE
Campus Man.: ED DOBSON

Library of 32,000 vols (combined holdings)
Number of teachers: 575 (125 full-time, 450 adjunct)
Number of students: 16,500

Areas of study: accounting, business admin., information technology.

BRANCH CAMPUSES

Alexandria Campus: 2730 Eisenhower Ave, Alexandria, VA 22314; tel. (703) 329-9100; fax (703) 3299602; e-mail alexandria@strayer.edu; Campus Man. OSCAR MAMARIL.

Anne Arundel Campus: 1520 Jabez Run, Suite 100, Millersville, MD 21108; tel. (410) 923-4500; e-mail annearundel@strayer.edu; Campus Man. JAMES DERDOCK.

Arlington Campus: 2121 15th St, North, Arlington, VA 22201; tel. (703) 892-5100; fax (703) 769-2677; e-mail arlington@strayer.edu; Campus Man. DAN JACKSON.

Cary Campus: Suite 105, 3200 Gateway Centre Blvd, Morrisville, NC 27560; tel. (919) 466-1150; e-mail cary@strayer.edu; Campus Man. DIANNA ANDERSON.

Chamblee Campus: Suite 100, 3355 Northeast Expressway, Atlanta, GA 30341; tel. (770) 454-9270; fax (770) 457-6958; e-mail chamblee@strayer.edu; Campus Man. AYANNA MARTIN.

Chesapeake Campus: Suite 400, 700 Independence Parkway, Chesapeake, VA 23320; tel. (757) 382-9900; e-mail chesapeake@strayer.edu; Campus Man. MICHAEL CAMDEN.

Chesterfield Campus: Suite 100, 2820 Waterford Lake Dr., Midlothian, VA 23112; tel. (804) 763-6300; fax (804) 763-6304; e-mail chesterfield@strayer.edu.

Cobb County Campus: Suite 700, 3101 Towercreek Parkway, Atlanta, GA 30339; tel. (770) 612-2170; fax (770) 956-7241; e-mail cobbcounty@strayer.edu; Campus Man. HAROON MOKEL.

Fredericksburg Campus: 4500 Plank Rd, Fredericksburg, VA 22407; fax (540) 785-8808; e-mail fredericksburg@strayer.edu; Campus Man. CLARY ORSBOURNE.

Greensboro Campus: Suite 400, 4900 Koger Blvd, Greensboro, NC 27404; tel. (336) 315-7800; fax (336) 315-7830; e-mail greensboro@strayer.edu; Campus Man. TONYA WILLIAMS.

Greenville Campus: Suite 300, 555 North Pleasantburg Dr., Greenville, SC 29607; tel. (864) 232-4700; fax (864) 235-5739; e-mail greenville@strayer.edu; Campus Man. KRISTA LIMER.

Henrico Campus: 11501 Nuckols Rd, Glen Allen, VA 23059; tel. (804) 527-1000; e-mail henrico@strayer.edu.

King of Prussia Campus: Suite G 50, 234 Mall Blvd, King of Prussia, PA 19406; tel. (610) 992-1700; fax (610) 992-9777; e-mail kingofprussia@strayer.edu; Campus Man. CHARLES BAUKMAN.

Loudoun Campus: Suite 200, 45150 Russell Branch Parkway, Ashburn, VA 20147; tel. (703) 729-8800; fax (703) 729-8820; e-mail loudoun@strayer.edu; Campus Man. BRENDA EVANS.

Lower Bucks County Campus: Suite 100, 3600 Horizon Blvd, Trevose, PA 19453; tel. (215) 953-5999; fax (215) 953-9464; e-mail bucks@strayer.edu; Campus Man. FATIMA ARUKWE.

Manassas Campus: 9990 Battleview Parkway, Manassas, VA 20109; tel. (703) 330-8400; fax (703) 330-8135; e-mail manassas@strayer.edu; Campus Man. MARLON PRINCE.

Montgomery Campus: Suite 300, 20030 Century Blvd, Germantown, MD 20874; tel. (301) 540-8066; e-mail montgomery@strayer.edu; Campus Man. ROBERT SCHULTZ.

Nashville Campus: Suite 200, 30 Rachel Dr., Nashville, TN 37214; tel. (615) 871-2260; fax (615) 391-5330; e-mail nashville@strayer.edu; Campus Man. TONYA YANCY.

Newport News Campus: Suite 100, 813 Diligence Dr., Newport News, VA 23606; tel. (757) 873-3100; e-mail newportnews@strayer.edu; Campus Man. CONSTANCE ARTER.

North Charlotte Campus: Suite 150, 8335 IBM Dr., Charlotte, NC 28262; tel. (704) 717-2380; e-mail northcharlotte@strayer.edu; Campus Man. CARTER SMITH.

North Raleigh Campus: Suite 3214, 3200 Spring Forest Rd, Raleigh, NC 27616; tel. (919) 878-9900; fax (919) 878-6625; e-mail northraleigh@strayer.edu; Campus Man. CHERRY CLARK.

Owings Mills Campus: Suite 100, 500 Redland Court, Owings Mills, MD 21117; tel. (443) 394-3339; e-mail owingsmills@strayer.edu; Campus Man. PAULA KHANAL.

Prince George's Campus: 4710 Auth Pl., 1st Floor, Suitland, MD 20746; tel. (301) 423-3600; fax (301) 423-3999; e-mail princegeorges@strayer.edu; Campus Man. SANA CHAUDRY.

Shelby Oaks Campus: Suite 100, 6211 Shelby Oaks Dr., Memphis, TN 38134; tel. (901) 383-6750; fax (901) 373-8700; e-mail shelbyoaks@strayer.edu; Campus Man. DARYL DANIELS.

South Charlotte Campus: Suite 700, 2430 Whitehall Park Dr., Charlotte, NC 28273; tel. (704) 587-5360; e-mail southcharlotte@strayer.edu; Campus Man. HELEN HOUSER.

Takoma Park Campus: 6830 Laurel St, NW, Washington, DC 20012; tel. (202) 722-8100; fax (202) 722-8108; e-mail takomapark@strayer.edu; Campus Man. KAVITA FREEMAN.

Tampa East Campus: Suite 450, 6302 East Martin Luther King Blvd, Tampa, FL 33619; tel. (813) 663-0100; fax (813) 626-2245; e-mail tampaeast@strayer.edu; Campus Man. ROBIN LEWIS-GAGE.

Tampa Westshore Campus: Suite 100, 4902 Eisenhower Blvd, Tampa, FL 33634; tel. (813) 882-0100; e-mail tampawestshore@strayer.edu; Campus Man. DEB SAWYER.

Thousand Oaks Campus: Suite 1100, 2620 Thousand Oaks Blvd, Memphis, TN 38118; tel. (901) 369-0835; fax (901) 565-9400; e-mail thousandoaks@strayer.edu; Campus Man. MARK WILLIAMS.

White Marsh Campus: 9409 Philadelphia Rd, Baltimore, MD 21237; tel. (410) 238-9000; fax (410) 238-9099; e-mail whitemarsh@strayer.edu; Campus Man. RUTH BUTLER.

Woodbridge Campus: 13385 Minnieville Rd, Woodbridge, VA 22192; tel. (703) 878-2800; fax (703) 878-2993; e-mail woodbridge@strayer.edu; Campus Man. FRANK HANCOCK.

TRINITY COLLEGE

125 Michigan Ave, NE, Washington, DC 20017

Telephone: (202) 884-9000
Fax: (202) 884-9229
E-mail: president@trinitydc.edu
Internet: www.trinitydc.edu

Founded 1897

Roman Catholic liberal arts college for women, sponsored by Sisters of Notre Dame de Namur

Pres.: Dr PATRICIA MCGUIRE
Exec. Vice-Pres. and Chief Financial Officer: RAYMOND V. BARBIC
Vice-Pres. for Institutional Advancement: ANN PAULEY
Vice-Pres. for Academic Affairs: SUE BLANSHAN
Dean of Student Services: MICHELE BOWIE
Dean of Education: SUELLEN MEARA
Registrar: MARVA BOSWELL
Dir of Library: KAYE GAPEN

Library: over 200,000 vols
Number of teachers: 59 full-time
Number of students: 1,500

Publications: *Trinity College Record, Trinity Times, Trinilogue, Alumnae Journal, Trinity Today*

DEANS

College of Arts and Sciences: Dr LORETTA MAY SHPUNT
School of Education: Dr GLORIA GRANTHAM
School of Professional Studies: Dr SARA MURRAY THOMPSON

UNIVERSITY OF THE DISTRICT OF COLUMBIA

4200 Connecticut Ave, NW, Washington, DC 20008

Telephone: (202) 274-5000
Internet: www.udc.edu

Founded 1851; a public urban land-grant univ. organized on 3 campuses from existing colleges; first degree programmes

Pres.: Dr WILLIAM LAWRENCE POLLARD
Provost and Vice-Pres. for Academic Affairs: WILHELMINA REUBEN-COOKE
Vice-Pres. for Student Affairs: CLEMMIE SOLOMON
Vice-Pres. for Univ. Relations: BOBBY W. AUSTIN
Chief of Staff and Vice-Pres. of Operations: STAN JACKSON
Number of students: 9,660

College of Arts and Sciences, and Schools of Business and Public Admin., Eng. and Applied Sciences, and Law

DEANS

School of Business and Public Admin.: Dr HERBERT QUIGLEY
David A. Clarke School of Law: Dr KATHERINE S. BRODERICK

WASHINGTON THEOLOGICAL UNION

6896 Laurel St, NW, Washington, DC 20012

Telephone: (202) 726-8800
Fax: (202) 726-1716
E-mail: pr@wtu.edu
Internet: www.wtu.edu

Founded 1968 as Coalition of Religious Seminaries; present name 1969
Private control
Academic year: August to May

Pres.: Rev. LOUIS V. IASIELLO
Vice-Pres. for Academic Affairs and Academic Dean: Rev. TOM REIST
Vice-Pres. for Institutional Advancement: KEVIN LOCKE
Registrar: Rev. BARTHOLOMEW MERELLA
Dir of Library: ALEXANDER MOYER

Library of 110,000 vols.

WESLEY THEOLOGICAL SEMINARY

4500 Massachusetts Ave, NW, Washington, DC 20016

Telephone: (202) 885-8600
Fax: (202) 885-8605
E-mail: admiss@wesleysem.edu
Internet: www.wesleyseminary.edu

Founded 1882 as Westminster Theological Seminary; present name 1958
Private control
Academic year: August to May

Pres.: Rev. Dr DAVID F. MCALLISTER-WILSON
Vice-Pres. for Int. Relations: KYUNGLIM SHIN LEE
Vice-Pres. for Devt: VOLLIE MELSON
Vice-Pres. for Finance and Admin.: JUNE R. STOWE
Dean: BRUCE C. BIRCH
Registrar: MITCHELL BOND
Dir of Library: BILL FAUPEL
Number of students: 660

ATTACHED RESEARCH INSTITUTES

Churches' Center for Theology and Public Policy: tel. (202) 885-8648; e-mail cctpp@wesleysem.edu; internet www.cctpp.org; Dir Rev. BARBARA G. GREEN.

G. Douglass Lewis Center for Church Leadership: tel. (202) 885-8757; e-mail lewiscenter@wesleyseminary.edu; internet www.churchleadership.com; Dir Dr LOVETT H. WEEMS, Jr.

Henry Luce III Center for Arts and Religion: tel. (202) 885-8608; e-mail artsandreligion@wesleysem.edu; internet www.luceartsandreligion.org; Dir CATHERINE ANDREWS KAPIKIAN.

FLORIDA

BAPTIST COLLEGE OF FLORIDA

5400 College Dr., Graceville, FL 32440-1898
Telephone: (850) 263-3261
E-mail: admissions@baptistcollege.edu
Internet: www.baptistcollege.edu
Founded 1943 as Baptist Bible Institute; present name 2000
Private control
Academic year: August to July
Pres.: Dr Thomas A. Kinchen
Sr Vice-Pres.: Dr R. C. Hammack
Vice-Pres. (Institutional Advancement): Charles R. Parker
Dir of Devt: Kyle S. Luke
Dir of Library Services: John E. Shaffett, Jr
Number of students: 600

Areas of study: theology, music, teacher education, child devt, residential child care.

BARRY UNIVERSITY

11300 North East Second Ave, Miami Shores, FL 33161-6695
Telephone: (305) 899-3000
Fax: (305) 899-3100
E-mail: admissions@mail.barry.edu
Internet: www.barry.edu
Founded 1940
Academic year: August to May
Pres.: Sister Linda Bevilacqua
Exec. Vice-Pres.: Sister Peggy Albert
Provost and Sr Vice-Pres. for Academic Affairs: Dr J. Patrick Lee
Sr Vice-Pres. for Business and Finance: Timothy H. Czerniec
Vice-Pres. for Planning and Assessment: Sister Candace Introcaso
Vice-Pres. for Enrollment and Academic Services: Dr G. Jean Cerra
Vice-Pres. for Institutional Advancement: Ann E. Paton
Vice-Pres. for Student Services: Dr Michael J. Griffin
Registrar: Debra D. Weyman
Library Dir (vacant): Estrella Iglesias
Library of 950,000 vols, 2,880 periodicals, 541,560 microforms
Number of teachers: 311 full-time
Number of students: 8,650

DEANS

School of Adult and Continuing Education: Dr Carol-Rae Sodano
School of Arts and Sciences: Dr Laura Armesto
School of Business: Dr Jack Scarborough
School of Education: Sister Evelyn Piché
School of Graduate Medical Science: Dr Chester Evans
School of Human Performance and Leisure Sciences: Dr G. Jean Cerra
School of Law: Dr Stanley Talcott
School of Natural and Health Sciences: Sister John Karen Frei
School of Nursing: Dr Pegge L. Bell
School of Social Work: Dr Stephen M. Holloway

BETHUNE-COOKMAN COLLEGE

640 Dr Mary McLeod Bethune Blvd, Daytona Beach, FL 32114-3099
Telephone: (386) 481-2000
Fax: (386) 481-2010
E-mail: bronson@cookman.edu
Internet: www.bethune.cookman.edu
Founded 1904
United Methodist Church
Academic year: August to April
Pres.: Dr Trudie Kibbe Reed

Provost/Vice-Pres. for Academic Affairs: William D. Lindsey
Vice-Pres. for Admin. and Finance: E. Dean Montgomery
Vice-Pres. for Institutional Advancement: Stephen Shafer
Vice-Pres. for Student Affairs: Ray Shackleford (acting)
Vice-Pres. Governmental Relations: Johnson Akinleye
Registrar: Ann Thomas
Dir of Library Learning: Tasha Lucas-Youmans
Library of 175,483 vols
Number of teachers: 192 (150 full-time, 42 part-time)
Number of students: 2,895 (2,677 full-time, 218 part-time)
Publication: *Undergraduate Research Journal* (annual)

DEANS OF SCHOOLS

Arts and Humanities: Dr Johnson O. Akinleye
Business: Dr Aubrey E. Long
Education: Dr Lorrain Daniels-Day
General Studies: Dr Lois S. Fennelly
Natural Sciences, Eng. and Mathematics: Dr Theodore R. Nicholson, Sr
Nursing: Dr Alma Y. Dixon
Social Sciences: Dr Sheila Y. Flemming

CLEARWATER CHRISTIAN COLLEGE

3400 Gulf-to-Bay Blvd, Clearwater, FL 33759
Telephone: (727) 726-1153
Fax: (727) 726-8597
E-mail: admissions@clearwater.edu
Internet: www.clearwater.edu
Founded 1966
Private control
Academic year: August to May
Pres.: Dr Richard A. Stratton
Chancellor: Dr Arthur E. Steele
Vice-Pres. (Academic Affairs): Dr Mary Draper
Vice-Pres. (Admin. Affairs): Dr Philip E. Larsen
Vice-Pres. (Financial Affairs): Randy T. Livingston
Vice-Pres. (Student Affairs): Robert Hodges
Registrar: Dr Roger C. Bradley
Dir of Library: Michael Clater
Library of 100,000 vols
Number of students: 628

Areas of study: biblical studies, business, education, fine arts, humanities, sciences.

ECKERD COLLEGE

4200 54th Ave, S, St Petersburg, FL 33711
Telephone: (727) 867-1166
Internet: www.eckerd.edu
Founded 1958 as Florida Presbyterian College
Academic year: August to May
Liberal arts college
Pres.: Dr Donald R. Eastman, III
Vice-Pres. and Dean of Faculty: Dr Lloyd W. Chapin
Chief Financial Officer: Chris Brennan
Vice-Pres. for Advancement: Matthew Bisset
Vice-Pres. for Church Relations: Benjamin J. Jacobson
Dean of Students: Dr James Annarelli
Dir of Admissions: John Sullivan
Dir of Library Services: Dr David Wenderson
Number of teachers: 102 (full-time)
Number of students: 1,631.

EDWARD WATERS COLLEGE

1658 Kings Rd, Jacksonville, FL 32209-6199
Telephone: (904) 470-8200
Fax: (904) 470-8048
Internet: www.ewc.edu
Private control
Pres.: Dr Oswald P. Bronson, Sr
Vice-Pres. for Academic Affairs: Dr Emmanuel O. Okafor
Registrar: Angela Freeman
Library Dir: Evelyn Brown

Areas of study: Biology, Business admin., Communications, Computer information systems, Criminal justice, Elementary education, Gerontology, Hotel, hospitality and tourism management, Mathematics, Music education, Physical education, Political science, Psychology, religion and philosophy, Sociology.

EMBRY-RIDDLE AERONAUTICAL UNIVERSITY

600 South Clyde Morris Blvd, Daytona Beach, FL 32114-3900
Telephone: (386) 226-6100
E-mail: dbadmit@erau.edu
Internet: www.embryriddle.edu
Founded 1926 as Embry-Riddle School of Aviation; present name 1970
Private control
Academic year: September to August
Pres.: Dr John P. Johnson
Provost and Chief Academic Officer: Dr John Johnson
Vice-Pres. and Chief Business Officer: Robert Jost
Vice-Pres. and Chief Financial Officer: Eric Weekes
Vice-Pres. for Devt: Pat Ramsey
Vice-Pres. for Global Planning and Program Devt: John Metzner
Vice-Pres. for Univ. Relations: Ken Stackpole
Chief Information Officer: Cindy Bixler
Chancellor of Daytona Beach Campus: Dr Tom Connolly
Chancellor of Prescott Campus: Daniel Carrell
Number of teachers: 227 (full-time)
Number of students: 4,776

Areas of study: Aviation, Arts and sciences, Business, Eng.

DEANS

College of Arts and Sciences: Dr Rodney Piercey
College of Aviation: Dr Tim Brady
College of Eng.: Dr Reda Mankbadi
College of Business: Dr Dan Petree

CAMPUSES

Embry-Riddle Aeronautical University–Prescott, Arizona Campus

3700 Willow Creek Rd, Prescott, AZ 86301-3720
Telephone: (928) 777-6600
Fax: (928) 777-6606
E-mail: pradmit@pr.erau.edu
Internet: www.erau.edu
Private control
Academic year: September to August
Chancellor: Dan Carrell
Number of teachers: 96 (full-time)
Number of students: 1,685 (1,653 undergraduate, 32 postgraduate)

DEANS

College of Arts and Sciences: Dr Richard Bloom
College of Aviation: Dr Jacky Luedtke

College of Eng.: Dr DON RABERN

Embry-Riddle Aeronautical University – Worldwide

600 South Clyde Morris Blvd, Daytona Beach, FL 32114-3900

Telephone: (386) 226-6910
E-mail: ecssc@erau.edu
Internet: www.embryriddle.edu

Chancellor: MARTIN SMITH
Eastern Regional Dean: Dr BERNARD CORDIAL
Central Regional Dean: Dr BRUCE ROTHWELL
Western Regional Dean: Dr KATHERINE MORAN
Int. Regional Dean: Dr DONNA ROBERTS

Number of teachers: 137 (full-time)
Number of students: 25,290 (19,527 undergraduate, 5,7631 undergraduate)

Comprises the Center for Distance Learning and the College of Career Education; operates in the USA and Europe.

FLAGLER COLLEGE

POB 1027, St Augustine, FL 32085-1027
74 King St, St Augustine, FL 32084

Telephone: (904) 829-6481
Fax: (904) 826-0094
Internet: www.flagler.edu

Founded 1968
Private control
Academic year: September to April

Chancellor: Dr WILLIAM L. PROCTOR
Pres.: Dr WILLIAM ABARE
Vice-Pres. of Business Services: KENNETH RUSSOM
Dean of Academic Affairs: PAULA MILLER
Dean of Student Services: DANIEL STEWART
Registrar: MIRIAM ROBERSON
Library Dir: MICHAEL GALLEN

Library of 193,729 holdings: 85,654 printed, 69,158 microform, 3,499 audiovisual, 34,940 electronic items, 470 periodicals
Number of students: 2,046.

FLORIDA AGRICULTURAL AND MECHANICAL UNIVERSITY

Tallahassee, FL 32307

Telephone: (904) 599-3000
Internet: www.famu.edu

Founded 1887

Pres.: JAMES AMMONS
Provost and Vice-Pres. for Academic Affairs: Dr DEBRA AUSTIN
Vice-Pres. for Admin.: Dr ROBERT D. CAROLL
Vice-Pres. for Research: Dr KEITH H. JACKSON
Vice-Pres. for Univ. Devt and Public Affairs: Col (Retd) RONALD JOE
Librarian: LAUREN B. SAPP

Library of 505,490 vols, 6,000 current periodicals, 131,500 microforms, 73,000 nonprint items; depository for US govt publications; consists of the main library and 4 br. libraries in the fields of Architecture, Eng., Journalism and Graphic Communication, and Science
Number of teachers: 532
Number of students: 12,161

DEANS

College of Arts and Sciences: Dr ARTHUR C. WASHINGTON
College of Education: Dr MELVIN GADSON
College of Eng. Sciences, Technology and Agriculture: Dr BOBBY R. PHILLS
FAMU/FSU College of Eng.: CHING-JEN CHENG
College of Pharmacy and Pharmaceutical Sciences: HENRY LEWIS, III
School of Architecture: RODNER WRIGHT

School of Allied Health Sciences: Dr JACQUELINE B. BECK
School of Business and Industry: Dr SYBIL C. MOBLEY
School of General Studies: Dr BARBARA BARNES
School of Graduate Studies, Research and Continuing Education: Dr THEODORE HEMMINGWAY
School of Journalism, Media and Graphic Arts: ROBERT RUGGLES
School of Nursing: Dr MARGARET W. LEWIS

FLORIDA ATLANTIC UNIVERSITY

Boca Raton, FL 33431

Telephone: (561) 297-3000
Internet: www.fau.edu

Founded 1961
State control

Campuses in Boca Raton, Davie, Fort Lauderdale, Jupiter and Port St. Lucie; also Open University and Continuing Education Division (Fort Lauderdale) and Sea-Tech (ocean engineering research and graduate education centre, Dania Beach)

Pres.: FRANK T. BROGAN
Univ. Provost and Chief Academic Officer: Dr JOHN PRITCHETT
Sr Vice-Pres. (Student Affairs): Dr EMANUEL NEWSOME
Sr Vice-Pres. (Finance) and Chief Operating Officer: Dr KENNETH A. JESSELL
Vice-Pres. (Univ. Advancement): ANN PATON
Vice-Pres. (Research): Dr LARRY LEMANSKI
Univ. Architect and Vice-Pres.: ROBERT FRIEDMAN
Campus Vice-Pres., Broward Campuses: Dr JOYANNE C. STEPHENS
Campus Vice-Pres., Jupiter: Dr KRISTEN O. MURTAUGH
Campus Vice-Pres., Treasure Coast: Dr GERALD F. LAFFERTY
Registrar: HARRY E. DeMIK
Dir of Libraries: Dr WILLIAM MILLER

Library of 665,000 volumes
Number of teachers: 778
Number of students: 25,000

Publication: *Journal of the Fantastic in the Arts*

DEANS

College of Architecture, Urban and Public Affairs: Dr ROSALYN CARTER
Dorothy F. Schmidt College of Arts and Letters: Dr WILLIAM CORVINO
College of Business: Dr BRUCE MALLEN
College of Education: Dr GREGORY F. ALOIA
College of Engineering: Dr KARL K. STEVENS (acting)
Harriet L. Wilkes Honors College: Dr WILLIAM P. MECH
Christine E. Lynn College of Nursing: Dr ANNE BOYKIN
Charles E. Schmidt College of Science: Dr NATHAN W. DEAN
Open Univ. and Continuing Education: Dr ELY MEYERSON

FLORIDA CHRISTIAN COLLEGE

1011 Bill Beck Blvd, Kissimmee, FL 34744

Telephone: (407) 847-8966
Fax: (407) 847-3925
E-mail: fcc@fcc.edu
Internet: www.fcc.edu

Founded 1975
Private control
Academic year: August to May

Pres.: HAROLD ARMSTRONG
Exec. Vice-Pres.: J. R. (TONY) BUCHANAN
Vice-Pres. (Student Life): TERRY ALLCORN
Vice-Pres. (Finance): DAVID L. McNEELY

Vice-Pres. (Institutional Advancement): WILLIAM K. BEHRMAN
Librarian: LINDA STARK
Number of teachers: 28
Number of students: 250

DEANS

Management Enrollment: PHILIP VINCENT

FLORIDA GULF COAST UNIVERSITY

10501 FGCU Blvd S, Fort Myers, FL 33965-6565

Telephone: (239) 590-1000
Fax: (239) 590-1059
E-mail: oar@fgcu.edu
Internet: www.fgcu.edu

Founded 1991
Academic year: August to May

Pres.: DICK PEGNETTER
Provost and Vice-Pres. for Academic Affairs: BONNIE L. YEGEDIS
Vice-President for Admin. Services: CURTIS BULLOCK
Vice-Pres. for Univ. Advancement: TOM HEALY
Dean of Graduate Studies and Continual Learning: W. JACK CROCKER
Dean of Instructional Technology: KATHLEEN DAVEY
Dean of Planning and Evaluation: JOSEPH L. RAVELLI
Dean of Student Affairs: JOE SHEPARD
Dir of Library Services: KATHLEEN HOETH
Number of students: 5,300

DEANS

College of Arts and Sciences: JOSE BARRETO
College of Business: RICHARD PEGNETTER
College of Education: LAWRENCE W. BYRNES
College of Health Professions: DENISE HEINEMAN
College of Professional Studies: JOHN McGAHA

FLORIDA INSTITUTE OF TECHNOLOGY

150 West University Blvd, Melbourne, FL 32901-6975

Telephone: (321) 674-8000
Fax: (321) 984-8461
E-mail: admission@fit.edu
Internet: www.fit.edu

Founded 1958
Academic year: August to April

Pres.: ANTHONY JAMES CATANESE
Sr Vice-Pres. for Advancement: THOMAS G. FOX
Vice-Pres. for Financial Affairs and Chief Financial Officer: JACK ARMUL
Vice-Pres. for Student Affairs and Assoc. Provost: MARSHA A. DUNCAN
Provost and Chief Academic Officer: T. DWAYNE McCAY
Vice Provost for Research and Information Technology: Dr ROBERT L. SULLIVAN
Asst Provost and Registrar: CHARLOTTE YOUNG
Dir of Admission: JUDITH A. MARINO
Dir of Libraries: CELINE ALVEY

Number of teachers: 261 (204 full-time, 57 part-time)
Number of students: 4,683

DEANS

College of Eng.: Dr J. RONALD BAILEY
College of Science and Liberal Arts: Dr GORDON NELSON
School of Aeronautics: Dr MICHAEL K. KARIM
School of Business: Dr A. THOMAS HOLLINGSWORTH
School of Psychology: Dr MARY BETH KENKEL

School of Extended Graduate Studies: Dr
RONALDO L. MARSHALL

FLORIDA INTERNATIONAL UNIVERSITY

University Park, Miami, FL 33199

Telephone: (305) 348-2000

Internet: www.fiu.edu

Founded 1965; part of the State Univ.
System of Florida

Pres.: MODESTO A. MAIDIQUE

Provost and Exec. Vice-Pres. for Academic
Affairs: RONALD M. BERKMAN

Vice-Provost for Academic Affairs at Biscayne Bay Campus: DAMIAN FERNANDEZ

Vice-Pres. for Research: GEORGE WALKER

Sr Vice-Pres.: PAUL GALLAGHER (acting)

Vice-Pres. for Advancement: HOWARD R. LIPMAN

Vice-Pres. for Student Affairs and Undergraduate Education (vacant)

Vice-Pres. for Univ. Technology Services and
Chief Information Officer (vacant)

Vice-Pres. for External Relations: DALE
CHAPMAN WEBB

Exec. Dir: ANTONIE DOWNS

Library of 1,500,000 vols, 9,700 current
periodicals, maps, microforms, govt documents, archives, rare books

Number of teachers: 1,100 (full-time)

Number of students: 34,000

DEANS

College of Arts and Sciences: Dr ARTHUR W.
HERRIOTT

College of Business Admin.: JOYCE J. ELAM
(Exec. Dean)

College of Education: LINDA P. BLANTON

College of Eng.: VISH PRASAD

College of Health and Urban Affairs: Prof.
RONALD BERKMAN

School of Journalism and Mass Communication: J. ARTHUR HEISE

FLORIDA MEMORIAL UNIVERSITY

15800 North West 42nd Ave, Miami, FL
33054

Telephone: (305) 626-3600

Internet: www.fmuniv.edu

Founded 1879

Pres.: Dr KARL S. WRIGHT

Provost: Dr SANDRA THOMPSON

Vice-Pres. for Business and Fiscal Affairs:
WILLIE KEMP

Vice-Pres. for Office of Institutional Advancement: Dr BARBARA EDWARDS

Dir of Information Management and Technology: PAMELA TENNELL

Vice-Pres. for Student Affairs: Dr HAROLD R.
CLARKE, Jr

Librarian

Library of 116,678 vols, 700 current periodicals

Number of teachers: 100

Number of students: 2,242.

FLORIDA METROPOLITAN UNIVERSITY

Suite 400, 6 Hutton Centre Dr., Santa Ana,
FL 92707

Telephone: (714) 427-3000

Fax: (714) 427-5111

Internet: fmu.edu

Founded 1995

Private control (Corinthian Colleges, Inc.)

Chair. and CEO: DAVID G. MOORE

Pres. and Chief Operating Officer: ANTHONY
DIGIOVANNI

Sr Vice-Pres. for Academic Affairs: Dr MARY
H. BARRY

Number of students: 11,000 (all campuses)

Areas of study: accounting, business admin.,
commercial art, computers, criminal justice,
film and video, heathcare, hospitality, int.
business, legal assistant/paralegal, management, marketing, network admin..

BRANCH CAMPUSES

Brandon Campus

3924 Coconut Palm Dr., Tampa, FL 33619

Telephone: (813) 621-0041

Fax: (813) 623-5769

Academic Dean: NEIL WERTLEY

Dean of Students: DOLLY BROWN

Registrar: INGRID ZEKAN

Library Dir: MADELINE LOCK.

Jacksonville Campus: 8226 Phillips Highway, Jacksonville, FL 32256; tel. (904) 731-4949; fax (904) 731-0599; f. 2000.

Lakeland Campus: Suite 110, 995 East
Memorial Blvd, Lakeland, FL 33801; tel.
(863) 686-1444; fax (863) 688-9881.

Melbourne Campus: 2401 North Harbor
City Blvd, Melbourne, FL 32935; tel. (321)
253-2929; fax (321) 255-2017.

North Orlando Campus: 5421 Diplomat
Circle, Orlando, FL 32810; tel. (407) 628-5870; fax (407) 628-1344; f. 1953 as Jones
College.

Orange Park Campus: 805 Wells Rd,
Orange Park, FL 32073; tel. (904) 264-9122;
f. 2003.

Pinellas Campus: Suite 200, 2471 McMullen Booth Rd, Clearwater, FL 33759; tel.
(727) 725-2688; fax (727) 796-3722.

Pompano Beach Campus: 225 North Federal Highway, Pompano Beach, FL 33062;
tel. (954) 783-7339; fax (954) 568-2008.

South Orlando Campus: 2411 Sand Lake
Rd, Orlando, FL 32809; tel. (407) 851-2525;
fax (407) 851-1477.

Tampa Campus: 3319 West Hillsborough
Ave, Tampa, FL 33614; tel. (813) 879-6000;
fax (813) 871-2483.

FLORIDA SOUTHERN COLLEGE

111 Lake Hollingsworth Dr., Lakeland, FL
33801-5698

Telephone: (863) 680-4111

Internet: www.flsouthern.edu

Founded 1885

Private control

Academic year: August to May

Pres.: Dr ANNE B. KERR

Vice-Pres. and Dean of the College: Dr SUSAN
P. CONNER

Vice-Pres. of Finance: V. TERRY DENNIS

Vice-Pres. for Student Life: Dr CAROLE R.
OBERMEYER

Vice-Pres. for Advancement: Dr ROBERT H.
TATE

Vice-Pres. and Dean of Enrollment Management: Dr ROBERT B. PALMER

Library Dir: ANDREW L. PEARSON

Library of 192,684 vols

Number of teachers: 109

Number of students: 2,487 (1,841 full-time,
646 part-time).

FLORIDA STATE UNIVERSITY

Tallahassee, FL 32306

Telephone: (904) 644-1234

Internet: www.fsu.edu

Founded 1851 as the Seminary W of the
Suwannee River, and later became the
Florida State College, became the Florida
State College for Women 1905, became co-

educational again and attained univ. status 1947

Academic year: August to April (2 semesters)

Chancellor of the State Univ. System:
CHARLES REED

Pres.: T. K. WETHERELL

Provost and Vice-Pres. for Academic Affairs:
LAWRENCE ABELE

Dean of the Faculties and Deputy Provost:
STEVE EDWARDS

Sr Vice-Pres. for Finance and Admin.: JOHN
R. CARNAGHI

Vice-Pres. for Student Affairs: WINSTON E.
SCOTT

Vice-Pres. for Research: RAYMOND E. BYE, Jr

Vice-Pres. for Univ. Relations: BEVERLEY B.
SPENCER

Dean, Undergraduate Studies: SANDRA RACKLEY

Dean, Graduate Studies: DIANNE F. HARRISON
(acting)

Dean, Panama City Campus: EDWARD
WRIGHT

Registrar: MAXWELL CARRAWAY

Dir of Univ. Libraries: RANDALL M. MACDONALD

Library: see Libraries and Archives

Number of teachers: 1,956

Number of students: 36,683

Publication: *Bulletin*

DEANS

College of Arts and Sciences: DONALD FOSS

College of Business: MELVIN T. STITH

College of Communication: JOHN K. MAYO

School of Criminology and Criminal Justice:
DANIEL MAIER-KATKIN

College of Education: RICHARD C. KUNKEL

FAMU-FSU College of Eng.: CHING-JEN CHEN

College of Human Sciences: PENNY A. RALSTON

School of Information Studies: JANE B.
ROBBINS

College of Law: DONALD J. WEIDNER

College of Medicine: JOSEPH E. SCHERGER

School of Motion Picture, Television and
Recording Arts: RAYMOND FIELDING

School of Music: JON R. PIERSOL

School of Nursing: KATHERINE P. MASON

College of Social Sciences: MARIE COWART

School of Social Work: BRUCE THYER

School of Theatre: STEVEN W. WALLACE

School of Visual Arts and Dance: JERRY L.
DRAPER

HOBE SOUND BIBLE COLLEGE

POB 1065, Hobe Sound, FL 33475

Telephone: (772) 546-5534

Fax: (772) 545-1422

E-mail: hobesoundbiblecollege@hsbc.edu

Internet: www.hsbc.edu

Founded 1960

Private control

Academic year: August to June

Pres.: P. DANIEL STETLER

Academic Dean: Dr CLIFFORD W. CHURCHILL

Dir of Admissions: JUDY FAY

Dir of Finance: KEN LITZINGER

Dean of Men: JOHN S. JONES, GEORGE VERNON

Dean of Women: LOUISE CROUSE

Registrar: ANN FRENCH

Librarian: WILLIAM SNIDER.

HODGES UNIVERSITY

2655 Northbrooke Dr., Naples, FL 34119

Telephone: (239) 513-1122

E-mail: admit@internationalcollege.edu

Internet: www.hodges.edu

Founded 1990 as International College, present name and status 2007

Private control

Academic year: September to August

Pres.: TERRY P. MCMAHAN
Exec. Vice-Pres. for Academic Affairs: JEAN-ETTE BROCK
Vice-Pres. for Student Devt: RON BOWMAN
Vice-Pres. for Information Technology: DAVE RICE
Vice-Pres. for Institutional Advancement: LOUIS TRAINA
Vice-Pres. for Student Enrollment Management: RITA LAMPUS
Vice-Pres. for Student Records Management: CAROL MORRISON
Registrar: LYDIA PORTER
Dir of Library: CAROLYNN VOLZ
Number of students: 1,300.

BRANCH CAMPUS

Fort Myers Campus: 4501 Colonial Blvd, Fort Myers, FL 33966; tel. (239) 482-0019.

JACKSONVILLE UNIVERSITY

2800 University Blvd, N, Jacksonville, FL 32211-3394

Telephone: (904) 256-8000
Internet: www.ju.edu

Founded 1934

Pres.: KERRY D. ROMESBURG
Sr Vice-Pres. for Academic Affairs: Dr LOIS S. BECKER
Sr Vice-Pres. for Enrollment Management: MIRIAM KING
Vice-Pres. for Finance and Admin.: Dr WILLIAM CROSBY
Registrar: CAROLYN A. BARRETT
Librarian: THOMAS H. GUNN

Library of 572,000 vols
Number of teachers: 233 (116 full-time, 117 part-time)
Number of students: 2,123.

JONES COLLEGE

5353 Arlington Expressway, Jacksonville, FL 32211-5588

Telephone: (904) 743-1122
E-mail: info@jones.edu
Internet: www.jones.edu

Founded 1918
Private control
Academic year: September to August

Pres.: Dr DAVID SWANN
Dean: CALVIN SLATTER

Areas of study: allied health management, business admin., computer information systems, interdisciplinary studies, legal asst (paralegal), medical asst.

BRANCH CAMPUSES

Miami Campus: Suite 200, 11430 North Kendall Dr., Kendall Summit, Miami, FL 33176; tel. (305) 275-9996; Dir and Dean SARAH FRIDAY.

West Campus: 1195 Edgewood Ave, S, Jacksonville, FL 32205; tel. (904) 743-1122; Dir and Dean DEE THORNTON.

LYNN UNIVERSITY

3601 North Military Trail, Boca Raton, FL 33431

Telephone: (561) 237-7000
E-mail: admission@lynn.edu
Internet: www.lynn.edu

Founded 1962 as Marymount College; present name 1991
Private control
Academic year: September to May

Pres. and CEO: Dr KEVIN M. ROSS
Chief of Staff: Dr JASON WALTON
Senior Vice-President for Institutional Advancement: Dr LANSING BAKER
Dean of Admin.: THOMAS HEFFERMAN

Sr Vice-Pres. for Enrollment Management: Dr KARLA STEIN
Vice-Pres. and Exec. Asst to the Pres.: ANTHONY J. CASALE
Vice-Pres. for Academic Affairs: Dr KATHLEEN CHEEK-MILBY
Vice-Pres. for Business and Finance: LAURIE LEVINE
Vice-Pres. for Endowment and Planned Giving: JOHN J. GALLO
Vice-Pres. for Corporate Devt: Dr ROBERT LEVINSON
Library Dir: CHARLES L. KUHN
Library of 235,648 items (incl. books, periodicals, videos and microforms)

DEANS

College of Arts and Sciences: Dr GREGG COX
College of Business and Management: Dr RALPH NORCIO
College of Education, Health and Human Services: Dr RICHARD B. COHEN
College of Hospitality Management: Dr JOSEPH A. ROONEY
College of Int. Communication: Dr IRVING R. LEVINE
College of Professional, Adult and Continuing Education: Dr CINDY L. SKARUPPA
School of Aeronautics: Major JEFFREY C. JOHNSON
Conservatory of Music: Dr CLAUDIO JAFFÉ

NEW COLLEGE OF FLORIDA

5800 Bay Shore Rd, Sarasota, FL 34243-2109

Telephone: (941) 487-5000
E-mail: admissions@ncf.edu
Internet: www.ncf.edu

Founded 1960

Pres.: Dr GORDON E. MICHALSON, Jr
Provost and Vice-Pres. of Academic Affairs: SAMUEL M. SAVIN
Vice-Pres. for Admin. and Finance: JOHN U. MARTIN
Dean of Student Affairs: WENDY BASHANT
Dean of Admissions and Financial Aid: KATHLEEN KILLION
Registrar: KATHY ALLEN
Dean of the Library: JOAN M. PELLAND

Library of 258,799 vols, 1,852 current periodicals, 533,984 microforms, 4,553 audio-visual items
Number of teachers: 81
Number of students: 750

DIVISIONAL CHAIRS

Humanities: Dr MARIBETH CLARK
Natural Sciences: Dr SANDRA GILCHRIST
Social Sciences: Dr RICHARD E. COE

PROFESSORS

Division of Humanities:

CARRASCO, M. E., Art History
CUOMO, G. R., German Language and Literature
EDIDIN, A. Z., Philosophy
HASSOLD, C., Art History
LANGSTON, D. C., Philosophy and Religion
MICHALSON, G. E., Humanities

Division of Natural Sciences:

BEULIG, A., Biology
DEMSKI, L. S., Biology
GILCHRIST, S., Biology
LOWMAN, M., Biology and Environmental Studies
RUPPEINER, G., Physics
SCUDDER, P., Chemistry

Division of Social Sciences:

ANTHONY, A. P., Art History
DOENECKE, J., History
ELLIOTT, C., Econ.
LEWIS, E., Political Science
STROBEL, F., Econ.

VESPERI, M. D., Anthroplogy

NOVA SOUTHEASTERN UNIVERSITY

3301 College Ave, Fort Lauderdale-Davie, FL 33314-7796

Telephone: (954) 262-7300
Fax: (954) 262-3800
E-mail: ron@nova.edu
Internet: www.nova.edu

Founded 1964
Academic year: July to June

Pres.: RAY FERRERO, Jr
Chancellor, Health Professions Division: Dr FREDERICK LIPPMAN
Vice-Pres. for Academic Affairs: FRANK DE PIANO
Exec. Vice-Pres. for Admin.: Dr GEORGE L. HANBURY, II
Vice-Pres. for Financial Operations: W. DAVID HERON
Vice-Pres. for Institutional Advancement (vacant)
Vice-Pres. for Legal Affairs: JOEL BERMAN
Vice-Pres. for Community and Govt Affairs: Dr LARRY A. CALDERON
Vice-Pres. for Information Services and Univ. Librarian: Dr DONALD RIGGS
Dean for Student Affairs: Dr BRAD WILLIAMS
Registrar: ELAINE POFF
Number of teachers: 503 full-time
Number of students: 21,619 (9,572 full-time, 12,047 part-time)

Publications: *The Qualitative Report* (quarterly), *International Travel Law Journal* (3 a year), *Internet Journal of Allied Health Sciences and Practice* (quarterly), *Peace and Conflict Studies* (2 a year), *Nova Law Review* (3 a year), *ILSA Journal of International and Comparative Law* (3 a year)

DEANS

Fischler Graduate School for the Advancement of Education and Human Services: Dr H. WELLS SINGLETON (Dean and Provost)
Graduate School of Computer and Information Sciences: Dr EDWARD LIEBLEIN
Mailman Segal Institute for Early Childhood Studies: Dr WENDY MASI
Farquhar College for Arts and Sciences: Dr NORMA GOONEN
Oceanographic Center: Dr RICHARD DODGE
Center for Psychological Studies: Dr RONALD F. LEVANT
Graduate School of Humanities and Social Sciences: Dr HONGGANG YANG
Wayne Huizenga School of Business and Entrepreneurship: Dr RANDOLPH A. POHLMAN
Shepard Broad Law Center: JOSEPH HARBAUGH
College of Allied Health: Dr RICHARD DAVIS
College of Pharmacy: Dr WILLIAM HARDIGAN
College of Medical Sciences: Dr HAROLD LAUBACH
College of Optometry: Dr DAVID LOSHIN
College of Dental Medicine: Dr ROBERT UCHIN
College of Osteopathic Medicine: Dr ANTHONY S. SILVAGNI
Univ. School: Dr JEROME CHERMAK

PALM BEACH ATLANTIC UNIVERSITY

POB 24708, West Palm Beach, FL 33416-4708
901 South Flagler Dr., West Palm Beach, FL 33401

Telephone: (561) 803-2000
E-mail: admit@pba.edu
Internet: www.pba.edu

Founded 1968
Private control

Academic year: August to May
Pres.: Dr DAVID W. CLARK
Provost: Dr JOSEPH A. KLOBA
Vice-Pres. and Chief Financial Officer: GEORGE GALL
Vice-Pres. for Devt: WILLIAM M. B. FLEMING, Jr
Vice-Pres. for Student Devt: Dr MARY ANN SEARLE
Vice-Pres. for Enrollment Services: BUCKLEY A. JAMES
Library Dean: Dr J. RAY DOERKSEN

Library of 259,877 vols
Number of teachers: 253
Number of students: 3,066

DEANS

School of Arts and Sciences: Dr JEFFREY W. STOUT
School of Business: Dr ROBERT MYERS
School of Communication and Media: Dr JOSEPH WEBB
School of Continuing Education: Dr PAM SIGAFOOSE
School of Education and Behavioral Studies: Dr DONA THORNTON
School of Ministry: Dr KENNETH L. MAHANES
School of Music and Fine Arts: Dr LLOYD MIMS
School of Nursing: Dr LINDA MILLER
School of Pharmacy: Dr SCOTT A. SWIGART

RINGLING COLLEGE OF ART AND DESIGN

2700 North Tamiami Trail, Sarasota, FL 342345895

Telephone: (941) 3515100
Fax: (941) 3597517
E-mail: info@ringling.edu
Internet: www.ringling.edu
Founded 1931 by John Ringling
Private control
Academic year: August to April
Pres.: Dr LARRY R. THOMPSON
Vice-Pres. for Devt and Alumni Relations: LANCE BURCHETT
Vice-Pres. for Finance and Admin.: TRACY WAGNER
Vice-Pres. for Institutional Advancement (vacant)
Dean of Admissions: AMY FISHER
Dean of Students: Dr TAMMY S. WALSH
Dir of Library Services: KATHLEEN LIST
Library: Verman Kimbrough Memorial Library of 43,000 print and media items, colln of 100,000 35mm slides
Number of teachers: 100
Number of students: 1,000.

ROLLINS COLLEGE

1000 Holt Ave, Winter Park, FL 32789

Telephone: (407) 646-2000
Fax: (407) 646-2600
E-mail: contact@rollins.edu
Internet: www.rollins.edu
Founded 1885
Academic year: September to May
Pres.: LEWIS M. DUNCAN
Vice-Pres. for Academic Affairs and Provost: Dr ROGER N. CASEY
Vice-Pres. for Business and Finance and Treas.: GEORGE H. HERBST
Vice-Pres. for Institutional Advancement: CYNTHIA R. WOOD
Dean of Admissions and Enrollment: DAVID G. ERDMANN
Dean of Faculty: HOYT EDGE
Dean of Student Affairs: DONNA A. LEE
Dean of the Hamilton Holt School: SHARRON CARRIER
Dir of Libraries: JONATHAN MILLER

Library of 303,000 vols, 1600 current periodicals
Number of teachers: 195
Number of students: 3,835.
Publications: *Alumni Record* (quarterly), *Brushing* (annual), *Sandspur* (weekly).

ST JOHN VIANNEY COLLEGE SEMINARY

2900 South West 87th Ave, Miami, FL 33165-3244

Telephone: (305) 223-4561
Fax: (305) 223-0650
E-mail: info@sjvcs.edu
Internet: www.sjvcs.edu
Founded 1959 as St John Vianney Seminary; present name 1977
Rector and Pres.: Very Rev. MICHAEL G. CARRUTHERS
Dean of Students: Rev. JOSÉ ALVAREZ
Academic Dean: Dr RAMON J. SANTOS
Registrar: BONNIE DE ANGULO
Library Dir: MARIA RODRIGUEZ

Library of 50,000 vols
Number of teachers: 22.

ST LEO UNIVERSITY

POB 6665, Saint Leo, FL 33574-6665

Telephone: (352) 588-8200
Fax: (352) 588-8654
Internet: www.saintleo.edu
Founded 1889
Private control, Catholic
Academic year: August to May
Pres.: Dr ARTHUR F. KIRK, Jr
Sr Exec. Asst to the Pres.: MARCIA MALIA
Vice-Pres. for Academic Affairs: MARIBETH DURST
Vice-Pres. for Student Affairs: Dr EDWARD DADEZ
Vice-Pres. for Business Affairs and Chief Financial Officer: FRANK MEZZANINI
Vice-Pres. for Enrollment: GARY BRACKEN
Dir of Univ. Advancement: SUSAN BARRETO
Registrar: KAREN HATFIELD
Librarian: BRENT SHORT

Library of 152,584 vols
Number of teachers: 107 (full-time)
Number of students: 12,000

DEANS

School of Arts and Sciences: (vacant)
School of Business: Dr THOMAS W. ZIMMERER
School of Education and Social Services: Dr MARIBETH DURST

ST THOMAS UNIVERSITY

16401 North West 37th Ave, Miami Gardens Miami, FL 33054

Telephone: (305) 628-2546
Fax: (305) 628-6591
E-mail: signup@stu.edu
Internet: www.stu.edu
Founded 1947 in Cuba, moved to present location 1961
Private control (Roman Catholic church)
Academic year: August to May
Pres.: Mgr FRANKLYN M. CASALE
Provost and Chief Academic Officer: Dr GREGORY CHAN
Asst Vice-Pres. for Academic Affairs: Dr SUSAN ANGULO
Vice-Pres. for Admin. Affairs and Treas.: TERRENCE O'CONNOR
Vice-Pres. for Univ. Advancement: BEVERLY S. BACHRACH
Vice-Pres. for Student Affairs: Dr SARAH SHUMATE
Dean of Undergraduate Studies: Dr GUIYOU HUANG

Dean of Graduate Studies: Dr JOSEPH A. IANNONE
Dean of Law School: ALFREDO GARCIA
Dean of Academic Support: BARBARA SINGER
Registrar: IRAIDA ACEBO
Library Dir: Dr L. BRYAN COOPER

Library of 215,000 vols
Number of teachers: 131 (72 full-time, 59 part-time)
Number of students: 2,500
Publication: *St Thomas Law Review* (annual).

ATTACHED RESEARCH INSTITUTES

Institute of Pastoral Ministries.
Human Rights Institute.

ST VINCENT DE PAUL REGIONAL SEMINARY

10701 South Military Trail, Boynton Beach, FL 33436-4899

Telephone: (561) 732-4424
Fax: (561) 737-2205
E-mail: seminary@svdp.edu
Internet: www.svdp.edu
Founded 1963
Academic year: August to May
Rector, Pres. and Dean of Formation: Rev. Mgr KEITH BRENNAN
Vice-Rector and Dean of Academic Formation: Rev. STEVEN O'HALA
Dean of Spiritual Formation: Rev. MICHAEL MUHR
Dean of Pastoral Formation: Rev. Mgr MICHAEL MCGRAW
Treas. and Dir of Office of Institutional Research and Evaluation: KEITH PARKER
Library Dir: ARTHUR G. QUINN

Library of 72,000
Number of teachers: 30.

SCHILLER INTERNATIONAL UNIVERSITY – FLORIDA

(For general information, see entry for Schiller International University in Germany chapter)

300 East Bay Dr., Largo, FL 33770

Telephone: (727) 736-5082
Fax: (727) 736-2623
E-mail: admissions@schiller.edu
Internet: www.schiller.edu
Academic year: September to June
Vice-Pres. and Dir: Dr CHRISTOPH LEIBRECHT

Number of teachers: 40
Number of students: 250.

SOUTHEASTERN UNIVERSITY OF THE ASSEMBLIES OF GOD

1000 Longfellow Blvd, Lakeland, FL 33801

Telephone: (863) 667-5000
Fax: (863) 667-5200
E-mail: info@secollege.edu
Internet: www.secollege.edu
Founded 1935
Private control
Academic year: August to May
Pres.: Dr MARK RUTLAND
Vice-Pres. for Academic Affairs: Dr ROBERT W. HERRON, Jr
Vice-Pres. for Finance and Admin.: JOHN KAUTZ, III
Vice-Pres. for Student Devt: Dr ROBERT CROSBY
Vice-Pres. for Devt: Dr JAMES L. DAVIS
Student Worship and Ministry Arts Dir: Dr WAYNE H. LEE, Jr
Registrar: Rev. GLENN PEARL
Dir of Library Services: GRACE VEACH

Library of 100,000 vols

Number of teachers: 52
Number of students: 1,076.

STETSON UNIVERSITY

421 North Woodland Blvd, DeLand, FL 32723

Telephone: (904) 822-7000
Fax: (904) 822-8925
E-mail: jward@stetson.edu
Internet: www.stetson.edu

Founded 1883 as DeLand Academy; became DeLand Univ. 1887; present name 1889
Academic year: August to May

Pres.: Dr H. DOUGLAS LEE
Chancellor: Dr POPE A. DUNCAN
Sr Vice-Pres. and Chief Operating Officer: Dr JAMES R. BEASLEY
Vice-Pres. of Finance: SALLY A. DOWLING
Vice-Pres. and Dean of College of Law: Dr W. GARY VAUSE
Vice-Pres. of Univ. Relations: F. MARK WHITTAKER
Vice-Pres. of Enrollment Growth: DEBORAH THOMPSON
Vice-Pres. of Information Technology: Dr SHAHRAM AMIRI
Vice-Pres. of Facilities Management: DAVID S. NOYES
Library of 330,000 vols and 245,000 govt documents
Number of teachers: 196 (excl. College of Law)
Number of students: 3,255 (2,505 in DeLand, 750 at College of Law in St Petersburg)
Publications: *The Stetson University Bulletin* (annual), *The Cupola* (quarterly), *Stetson University Magazine* (2 a year), *Commons* (2 a year)

DEANS

College of Arts and Sciences: Dr GRADY W. BALLENGER
School of Business Admin.: Dr PAUL E. DASCHER
College of Law: Dr W. GARY VAUSE
School of Music: Dr JAMES E. WOODWARD

UNIVERSITY OF CENTRAL FLORIDA

4000 Central Blvd Orlando, FL 32816

Telephone: (407) 823-2000
Internet: www.ucf.edu

Founded 1963 as Florida Technological Univ., present name 1978

Pres.: JOHN C. HITT
Provost and Exec. Vice-Pres.: Dr TERRY L. HICKEY
Vice-Provost and Dean of Graduate Studies: PATRICIA J. BISHOP
Vice-Pres. for Admin. and Finance: WILLIAM F. MERCK, II
Vice-Pres. and Chief of Staff: Dr BETH BARNES
Vice-Pres. for Student Devt and Enrollment Services: MARIBETH EHASZ
Vice-Pres. for Univ. Relations: Dr DANIEL C. HOLSENBECK
Vice-Pres. for Research: Dr M. J. SOILEAU
Vice-Pres. for Devt and Alumni Relations: ROBERT J. HOLMES, Jr
Registrar: Dr DENNIS J. DULNIAK
Dir of Univ. Libraries: BARRY B. BAKER
Library of 1,459,775 vols, 9,866 current periodicals, 2,372,416 microforms, 35,233 audio-visual items
Number of teachers: 1,308 (1,050 full-time, 258 part-time)
Number of students: 38,598

DEANS

College of Arts and Sciences: Dr KATHRYN SEIDEL

Burnett Honors College: Dr ALLYN MACLEAN STEARMAN
College of Business Admin.: Dr THOMAS KEON
College of Education: Dr SANDRA ROBINSON
College of Eng. and Computer Science: Dr MARTIN P. WANIELISTA
College of Health and Public Affairs: Dr BELINDA MCCARTHY

UNIVERSITY OF FLORIDA

Gainesville, FL 32611

Telephone: (904) 392-3261
Internet: www.ufl.edu

Founded 1853

Pres.: Dr JAMES BERNARD MACHEN
Provost and Sr Vice-Pre. for Academic Affairs: JUDITH RUSSELL
Sr Vice-Pres. for Agricultural and Natural Resources: Dr JIMMY G. CHEEK
Sr Vice-Pres. for Health Affairs: Dr DOUGLAS J. BARRETT
Vice-Pres. for Human Resource Services: KYLE CAVANAUGH
Vice-Pres. for Devt and Alumni Affairs: PAUL A. ROBELL
Vice-Pres. for Research: WINFRED M. PHILLIPS
Vice-Pres. for Student Affairs: PATRICIA TELLES-IRVIN
Vice-Pres. for Univ. Relations: JANE ADAMS
Vice-Pres. and Gen. Counsel: JAMIE LEWIS KEITH
Univ. Registrar: STEPHEN J. PRITZ, Jr
Dean of Univ. Libraries: JUDITH RUSSELL
Library: see Libraries
Number of teachers: 1,654
Number of students: 47,993

Publications: *Journal of Politics, Southern Folklore Quarterly, University of Florida Law Review, Florida Historical Quarterly, Latin American Studies Association Newsletter*

DEANS

College of Agricultural and Life Sciences: WAYNE SMITH
Warrington College of Business: JOHN KRAFT
Continuing Education: JAMES W. KNIGHT
College of Dentistry: TERESA DOLAN
College of Design, Construction and Planning: JAY M. STEIN
College of Education: CATHERINE EMIHOVICH
College of Eng.: PRAMOD KHARGONEKAR
College of Fine Arts: DONALD E. MCGLOTHLIN
Institute of Food and Agricultural Sciences: LARRY ARRINGTON (acting) (Extension: RICHARD L. JONES (Research)
Graduate School: KENNETH GERHARDT
College of Health and Human Performance: JILL VARNES
College of Health Professions: Prof. ROBERT G. FRANK
College of Journalism and Communications: TERRY HYNES
Levin College of Law: ROBERT JERRY
College of Liberal Arts and Sciences: NEIL SULLIVAN
College of Medicine: C. CRAIG TISHER
School of Natural Resources and Environment: NANCY PETERSON
College of Nursing: KATHLEEN A. LONG
College of Veterinary Medicine: JOSEPH A. DIPIETRO

UNIVERSITY OF MIAMI

Coral Gables, FL 33124

Telephone: (305) 284-2211
Internet: www.miami.edu

Founded 1925 (chartered)
Private control
Academic year: September to May (2 terms)

Pres.: DONNA E. SHALALA

Provost and Exec. Vice-Pres.: THOMAS J. LEBLANC
Sr Vice-Pres. for Business and Finance: JOE NATOLI
Sr Vice-Pres. for Medical Affairs: PASCAL J. GOLDSCHMIDT
Vice-Pres. and Gen. Counsel and Sec. of the Univ.: AILEEN M. UGALDE
Vice-Pres. and Treas.: DIANE COOK DIANE M. COOK
Vice-Pres. for Business Services: ALAN J. FISH
Vice-Pres. for Medical Admin.: WILLIAM J. DONELAN
Vice-Pres. for Enrollment Management and Continuing Studies: PAUL M. OREHOVEC
Vice-Pres. for Govt Affairs: RUDY FERNANDEZ
Vice-Pres. for Human Resources: ROOSEVELT THOMAS, Jr
Vice-Pres. for Information Technology: M. LEWIS TEMARES
Vice-Pres. for Student Affairs: PATRICIA A. WHITELY
Vice-Pres. for Univ. Advancement: SERGIO M. GONZALEZ
Univ. Librarian: WILLIAM D. WALKER
Library of 2,500,000 vols
Number of teachers: 2,466 (2,049 full-time, 417 part-time)
Number of students: 15,000
Publications: *The Miami Hurricane* (student fortnightly newspaper), *Ibis* (annual), *Journal of Inter-American Studies* (quarterly), *World Affairs* (quarterly)

DEANS

School of Architecture: ELIZABETH PLATER-ZYBERK
College of Arts and Sciences: MICHAEL HALLERAN
School of Business Admin.: Dr PAUL K. SUGRUE
School of Communication: SAM L. GROGG
School of Education: Dr SAMUEL J. YARGER
College of Eng.: Dr M. LEWIS TEMARES
School of Law: DENNIS LYNCH
School of Medicine: Dr JOHN G. CLARKSON
School of Music: Dr WILLIAM HIPP
School of Nursing: NILDA P. PERAGALLO
Rosenstiel School of Marine and Atmospheric Sciences: Dr OTIS BROWN
Graduate School: Dr STEVEN ULLMAN (acting)

UNIVERSITY OF NORTH FLORIDA

4567 St Johns Bluff Rd, S, Jacksonville, FL 32224-2645

Telephone: (904) 620-1000
Internet: www.unf.edu

Pres.: Prof. JOHN A. DELANEY
Provost: Dr GERARD GIORDANO
Vice-Pres. for Institutional Advancement: Dr PIERRE N. ALLAIRE
Vice-Pres. for Student Affairs: Dr MAURICIO GONZALEZ
Vice-Pres. for Admin. and Finance: SHARI SHUMAN (acting)
Vice-Pres. and Chief of Staff: Dr THOMAS S. SERWATKA
Dean of the Div. of Continuing Education: ROBERT WOOD
Dean of Library: SHIRLEY HALLBLADE
Library of 761,595 vols, 3,271 current periodicals, 69,180 audio-visual items, 7,067 maps, 1.3m. microforms
Number of teachers: 520 (full-time)
Number of students: 14,666

DEANS

College of Arts and Sciences: Prof. MARK E. WORKMAN
College of Business Admin.: Prof. EARLE C. TRAYNHAM

College of Computing Sciences and Eng.: Prof. NEAL S. COULTER
College of Education and Human Services: Dr LARRY DANIEL
College of Health: Prof. PAMELA S. CHALLY

UNIVERSITY OF SOUTH FLORIDA

4202 East Fowler Ave, SVC 1034, Tampa, FL 33620
Telephone: (813) 974-2000
E-mail: info@admin.usf.edu
Internet: www.usf.edu
Founded 1956, classes commenced 1960
State control
Academic year: September to April (semester system) and summer sessions
Pres.: Dr JUDY LYNN GENSHAFT
Provost and Vice-Pres. for Academic Affairs: Dr RENU KHATOR
Exec. Vice-Pres. and Chief Financial Officer: CARL CARLUCCI
Vice-Pres. of Student Affairs: Dr JUDITH MENINGALL
Vice-Pres. for Public Affairs: Dr MARK LONO
Vice-Pres. for Admin. Affairs: RICKARD C. FENDER
Vice-Pres. for Univ. Advancement: JO ANN ALESSANDRINI
Vice-Pres. for Research: Dr ROBERT CHANG
Vice-Pres. for Health Sciences: Dr ROBERT M. DAUGHERTY
Vice-Pres. and Campus Chief Exec. Officer, St Petersburg: Dr RALPH C. WILCOX
Vice-Pres. and Campus Chief Exec. Officer, Sarasota/Manatee: Dr LAUREY STRIKER
Vice-Pres. and Campus Chief Exec. Officer, Lakeland: Dr L. PRESTON MERCER
Registrar: LINDA ERICKSON
Library of 1,698,386 vols, 15,263 current periodicals, 4,194,897 microforms
Number of teachers: 1,754 (1594 full-time, 160 part-time)
Number of students: 39,262

DEANS

School of Architecture and Community Design: STEPHEN D. SCHREIBER (Dir)
College of Arts and Sciences: Dr RENU KHATOR
College of Business Admin.: ROBERT L. ANDERSON
College of Education: Dr HAROLD R. KELLER
College of Eng.: Dr LOUIS MARTIN-VEGA
College of Marine Science: Dr PETER R. BETZER
College of Medicine: Dr ROBERT DAUGHERTY (acting)
College of Nursing: Dr PATRICIA BURNS
College of Public Health: Dr LAURENCE BRANCH
College of Visual and Performing Arts: RON JONES

UNIVERSITY OF TAMPA

401 West Kennedy Blvd, Tampa, FL 33606-1490
Telephone: (813) 253-3333
Fax: (813) 258-7398
E-mail: admissions@ut.edu
Internet: www.utampa.edu
Founded 1931
Academic year: June to May
Pres.: Dr RONALD L. VAUGHN
Vice-Pres. for Admin. and Finance: ROBERT E. FORSCHNER, Jr
Vice-Pres. for Devt and Univ. Relations: DANIEL GURA
Vice-Pres. for Enrollment: BARBARA P. STRICKLER
Vice-Pres. for Operations and Planning: Dr LINDA W. DEVINE
Dean of Students: ROBERT M. RUDAY

Dir of Macdonald-Kelce Library: MARLYN R. PETHE
Library of 253,610 vols, 23,120 periodicals, 25,337 microforms, 7,909 audiovisual items, partial depository for US govt documents
Number of teachers: 201 full-time
Number of students: 4,879 full-time
Publication: *Tampa Review* (2 a year)

DEANS

John H. Sykes College of Business and Graduate Studies: Dr JOSEPH E. McCANN, III
College of Liberal Arts and Sciences: Dr JOE SCLAFORI

UNIVERSITY OF WEST FLORIDA

11000 University Parkway, Pensacola, FL 32514
Telephone: (850) 474-2000
E-mail: admissions@uwf.edu
Internet: www.uwf.edu
Founded 1963
Private control
Academic year: August to August
Pres.: Dr JOHN C. CAVANAUGH
Provost: SANDRA FLAKE
Exec. Vice-Pres.: HAROLD M. WHITE, Jr
Vice-Pres. for Admin. Affairs: Dr ALBERT HARTLEY
Vice-Pres. for Devt: DEAN VAN GALEN
Vice-Pres. for Student Affairs: DEBORAH LYNN FORD
Registrar: ANN DZIADON
Dean of Libraries: DANA SALLY
Library of 645,511 vols
Number of students: 9,136

DEANS

College of Arts and Sciences: Dr JANE HALONEN
College of Business: Prof. EDWARD RANELLI
College of Professional Studies: Dr DON CHU

BRANCH CAMPUS

Fort Walton Beach Campus: 1170 Martin Luther King Blvd, Fort Walton Beach, FL 32547; tel. (850) 863-6569; Vice-Provost Dr WESLEY LITTLE.

WARNER SOUTHERN COLLEGE

13895 Highway 27, Lake Wales, FL 33859
Telephone: (863) 638-1426
Fax: (863) 638-1472
E-mail: admissions@warner.edu
Internet: www.warner.edu
Founded 1968
Private control
Academic year: August to May
Pres.: Dr GREGORY V. HALL
Exec. Vice-Pres. and Chief Academic Officer: Dr WILLIAM M. RIGEL, Jr
Vice-Pres. for Advancement: DORIS B. GUKICH
Vice-Pres. for Church Relations: Dr DAVID REAMES
Dean of Enrolment Management: DAWN RAFOOL
Dean of Students: JANICE L. ROBILLARD
Library Dir: SHERILL HRRIGER
Library of 100,000 vols
Number of students: 1,040

DEANS

School of Arts and Science: Dr JAMES R. CHRISTOPH
School of Business: Dr CYNTHIA ROBINSON

WEBBER INTERNATIONAL UNIVERSITY

POB 96, 1201 North Scenic Highway, Babson Park, FL 33827
Telephone: (836) 638-1431
Fax: (836) 638-2823
E-mail: admissions@webber.edu
Internet: www.webber.edu
Founded 1927
Private control
Pres.: Dr WILLIAM B. LOGAN
Exec. Vice-Pres. and Chief Academic Officer: Dr H. KEITH WADE
Dean of Students: Dr FREDERICK ATHERTON
Registrar and Financial Aid Dir: KATHY WILSON
Number of teachers: 44 (19 full-time, 25 adjunct)
Number of students: 650
Offers BSc courses in accounting, business admin., finance, marketing, management, hospitality, sport management and pre-law; other courses include general MBAs and MBAs with a sport management major.

GEORGIA

AGNES SCOTT COLLEGE

141 East College Ave, Decatur, GA 30030
Telephone: (404) 471-6000
Fax: (404) 471-6067
E-mail: info@agnesscott.edu
Internet: www.agnesscott.edu
Founded 1889
Academic year: August to May
Liberal arts college for women
Pres.: ELIZABETH KISS
Vice-Pres. for Academic Affairs and Dean of College: Prof. ROSEMARY LÉVY ZUMWALT
Vice-Pres. for Business and Finance: JOHN P. HEGMAN
Vice-Pres. for Institutional Advancement: Dr MARY G. ACKERLY (acting)
Vice-Pres. for Student Life and Community Relations: GUÉ PARDUE HUDSON
Assoc. Vice-Pres. for Enrollment and Dean of Admissions: STEPHANIE S. BALMER
Registrar: NANCY ALBERT
Dir of Library Services: ELIZABETH BAGLEY
Library of 220,041 vols, 15,505 audio-visual items, 32,677 microforms, 1,264 current periodicals
Number of teachers: 74 full-time, 29 part-time
Number of students: 1,027.

ALBANY STATE UNIVERSITY

504 College Dr., Albany, GA 31705
Telephone: (229) 430-4600
Internet: asuweb.asurams.edu/asu
Founded 1903
Pres.: Dr EVERETTE J. FREEMAN
Dir of Admissions and Financial Aid: FRED SUTTLES
Vice-Pres. for Academic Affairs: Dr ELLIS SYKES
Librarian: Dr LAVERNE L. McLAUGHLIN
Library of 161,000 vols
Number of teachers: 150
Number of students: 2,405.

AMERICAN INTERCONTINENTAL UNIVERSITY

3330 Peachtree Rd, NE, Atlanta, GA 30326-1016
Telephone: (404) 965-5712
Fax: (404) 965-5701
Internet: www.aiuniv.edu

Multi-campus, nat. and int. (see www.aiustudyabroad.com) instn offering residential, correspondence and online (see www.aiuonline.edu) assoc., Bachelors and graduate degrees

Pres.: Dr GREG WASHINGTON.

NATIONAL CAMPUSES

AIU–Buckhead

3330 Peachtree Rd, NE, Atlanta, GA 30326-1016

Telephone: (404) 965-5712
Fax: (404) 965-5701
Internet: www.aiubuckhead.com

Undergraduate degree programmes: int. business, interior design, fashion, media production, visual communication.

AIU–Dunwoody

6600 Peachtree Rd, 500 Embassy Row, Atlanta, GA 30328
Internet: www.aiudunwoody.com

Assoc. degree programmes: business admin., visual communications; Bachelors degree programmes: information technology, enterprise management, visual communications; graduate degree programmes: global technology management, information technology.

AIU–Fort Lauderdale

8151 West Peters Rd, Suite 1000, Plantation, FL 33324
Internet: www.aiufortlauderdale.com

Assoc. degree programmes: business admin., int. business; Bachelors degree programmes: information technology, enterprise management, visual communication; graduate degree programmes: global technology, management information technology.

AIU–Los Angeles

12655 West Jefferson Blvd, Los Angeles, CA 90066

Telephone: (310) 302-2000
Fax: (310) 302-2002
Internet: www.aiula.com

Founded 1970

Number of teachers: 137
Number of students: 1,800

Assoc. degree programmes: business admin., int. business, fashion design, fashion marketing, media production, visual communication; Bachelors degree programmes: information technology, criminal justice, business admin., int. business, fashion design, fashion marketing, fashion marketing and design, interior design, visual communication; graduate programmes: information technology, global technology management, instructional technology..

INTERNATIONAL CAMPUSES

AIU–London: see separate entry in UK chapter.

The American University in Dubai: see separate entry in UAE chapter

ARMSTRONG ATLANTIC STATE UNIVERSITY

11935 Abercorn St, Savannah, GA 31419

Telephone: (912) 927-5277
E-mail: adm-info@armstrong.edu
Internet: www.armstrong.edu

Founded 1935
Academic year: August to May

Pres.: Dr THOMAS Z. JONES
Vice-Pres. and Dean of Faculty: ELLEN V. WHITFORD

Vice-Pres. (Business and Finance): JAMES BRIGNATI
Vice-Pres. (Student Affairs): VICKI L. McNEIL
Registrar: KIM WEST
Librarian: BEN LEE

Library of 800,000 items
Number of teachers: 250
Number of students: 5,700

DEANS

College of Arts and Sciences: Dr ED WHEELER
College of Education: Dr JANE McHANEY
College of Health Professions: Dr BARRY ECKERT
School of Computing: Dr RAYMOND GREENLAW
School of Graduate Studies: MICHAEL E. PRICE

ART INSTITUTE OF ATLANTA

6600 Peachtree Dunwoody Rd, 100 Embassy Row, Atlanta, GA 30328-1649

Telephone: (770) 394-8300
Fax: (770) 394-0008
E-mail: aiaadm@aii.edu
Internet: www.aia.artinstitute.edu

Founded 1949 as Massey Business College; present name 1975
Private control
Academic year: October to September

Pres.: JANET S. DAY
Vice-Pres. of Admin. and Financial Services: CHRISTOPHER J. FERRELL
Vice-Pres. of Admissions: DONNA SCOTT
Vice-Pres. of Human Resources: JOSELYN C. CASSIDY
Dean of Academic Affairs: Dr SALLY PARSONSON
Dean of Student Affairs: JAMES PETTY
Registrar: MARDI RICHARDSON
Library Dir: GAYLE MEIER

Number of teachers: 150
Number of students: 2,650

DIRECTORS

Culinary Arts: JAMES W. PAUL
Gen. Education: Dr HEATHER OLSON
Graphic Design: LARRY STULTZ
Illustration and Design: DAN L. HENDERSON
Interactive Media Design: Dr AMEETA JADAV
Interior Design: PAUL M. BLACK
Media Arts and Animation: LEE CROWE
Photographic Imaging: (vacant)
Video Production and Digital Media Production: ROB ALBERTSON

ATLANTA CHRISTIAN COLLEGE

2605 Ben Hill Rd, East Point, GA 30344

Telephone: (404) 761-8861
E-mail: kwagner@acc.edu
Internet: www.acc.edu

Founded 1928
Private control
Academic year: August to May

Pres.: DEAN COLLINS
Vice-Pres. (Academic Affairs): Dr DENNIS E. GLENN
Vice-Pres. (Admin.): S. TODD WEAVER
Vice-Pres. (Devt) (vacant)
Vice-Pres. (Student Devt): R. SIDNEY TILLER, Jr
Registrar: KATHLEEN D. DAVID
Library Dir: MICHAEL L. BAIN

Library of 55,500 vols

Depts of Biblical Studies, Business, Education, Human Relations, Humanities and General Studies, Music.

AUGUSTA STATE UNIVERSITY

2500 Walton Way, Augusta, GA 30904-2200

Telephone: (706) 737-1444

E-mail: admissions@aug.edu
Internet: www.aug.edu

Founded 1783 as Academy of Richmond County; present name 1996
Academic year: August to July

Pres.: Dr WILLIAM A. BLOODWORTH, Jr
Vice-Pres. (Academic Affairs): Dr SAMUEL SULLLIVAN
Vice-Pres. (Business Operations): DAN WHITFIELD
Vice-Pres. (Univ. Advancement): ELIZABETH B. HOUSE DEAN (acting)
Vice-Pres. (Student Services) and Dean of Students: Dr JOYCE A. JONES
Registrar and Dir of Admissions: KATHERINE H. SWEENEY
Library Dir: Dr WILLIAM N. NELSON

Library of 475,000 vols
Number of teachers: 200
Number of students: 5,000

DEANS

Pamplin College of Arts and Sciences: Dr M. E. PETTIT (acting)
College of Business Admin.: JACKSON K. WIDENER, Jr
College of Education: Dr THOMAS E. DEERING (acting)

BERRY COLLEGE

2277 Martha Berry Highway, NW, Mount Berry, GA 30149

Telephone: (706) 232-5374
Internet: www.berry.edu

Founded 1902

Pres.: Dr STEPHEN R. BRIGGS
Provost: Dr THOMAS E. DASHER
Vice-Pres. for Student Affairs and Dean of Students: DEBBIE E. HEIDA
Vice-Pres. for Finance: BRIAN ERB
Vice-Pres. for Institutional Advancement: BETTYANN M. O'NEILL
Dean of Admissions: RICHARD DANA PAUL
Registrar: LINDA A. TENNANT
Library Dir: MAUREEN K. MORGAN

Library of 184,829 vols, 495,679 microfiche vols, 104,871 govt documents, 507 compact discs, 1,365 current periodicals
Number of teachers: 126
Number of students: 2,038 (1846 undergraduate, 229 graduate)

DEANS

Campbell School of Business: Dr KRISHNA S. DHIR
Charter School of Education and Human Sciences: Dr JACQUELINE M. McDOWELL

BEULAH HEIGHTS BIBLE COLLEGE

POB 18145, 892 Berne Street, SE, Atlanta, GA 30316

Telephone: (404) 627-2681
Fax: (404) 627-0702
E-mail: admissionsinfo@beulah.org
Internet: www.beulah.org

Founded 1918
Private control
Academic year: August to May

Pres.: Dr BENSON M. KARANJA
Vice-Pres. (Finance): MAXINE MARKS
Vice-President and Dean of Academics: Dr JAMES B. KEILLER
Vice-President (Student Devt): WESLEY B. WILSON
Vice-President (Institutional Effectiveness and Operations): MONIQUE BAUCHAM
Registrar and Dean of Admissions: JACQUELYN B. ARMSTRONG
Dir of Library Service: PRADEEP K. DAS

Number of teachers: 35
Number of students: 677.

BREWTON-PARKER COLLEGE

Highway 280, 201 David-Eliza Fountain Circle, POB 197, Mount Vernon, GA 30445

Telephone: (912) 583-2241
Fax: (912) 583-4498
E-mail: admissions@bpc.edu
Internet: www.bpc.edu

Founded 1904 as Union Baptist Institute; present name 1978
Private control
Academic year: August to June

Pres.: Dr DAVID R. SMITH
Provost: Dr RON MELTON
Vice-Pres. (College Advancement): PAMELA DAVIS
Vice-Pres. (Enrollment Services): Dr CINDY SKARUPPA
Chief Financial Officer: SAMUEL T. MOORE
Dean of Students: SHERRIE HELMS
Registrar
Library Dir: ANN C. TURNER

Number of teachers: 52
Number of students: 1,136

Depts of Business, Education, Humanities, Intercollegiate Athletics, Mathematics and Natural Sciences, Music, Religion and Philosophy, Social and Behavioural Sciences

Publication: *Oracle* (annual).

CLARK ATLANTA UNIVERSITY

223 James P. Brawley Dr., SW, Atlanta, GA 30314-4389

Telephone: (404) 880-8000
Internet: www.cau.edu

Founded 1988, following consolidation of Atlanta Univ. (founded 1865) and Clark College (founded 1869); member of Atlanta Univ. Center

Pres.: Dr WALTER D. BROADNAX
Provost and Vice-Pres. for Academic Affairs: Dr DORCAS D. BOWLES
Exec. Vice-Pres.: Dr GEORGE E. ROSS
Vice-Pres. for Finance and Admin.: BOBBY E. YOUNG
Vice-Pres. for Enrollment Services and Student Affairs: DARRIN RANKIN
Gen. Counsel: LANCE DUNNINGS
Dean of the School of Arts and Sciences: Dr SHIRLEY WILLIAMS-KIRKSEY
Dean of Graduate Studies: Dr WILLIAM BOONE
Dean of Undergraduate Studies: Dr ALEXIA HENDERSON
Dir of Library Services (Atlanta Univ. Center): Dr ELAINE SLOAN

Library of 500,000 vols, 800,000 microforms, 300,000 govt documents, 50,000 bound periodicals, 5,000 compact discs
Number of teachers: 300
Number of students: 4,813 (3,864 undergraduate, 949 graduate)

DEANS

School of Arts and Sciences: Dr CHARLES W. WASHINGTON
School of Business: Dr EDWARD DAVIS
School of Education: Dr ERNEST J. MIDDLETON
School of Library and Information Studies: Dr ARTHUR C. GUNN
School of Social Work: Dr DORCAS D. BOWLES

CLAYTON COLLEGE AND STATE UNIVERSITY

2000 Clayton State Blvd, Morrow, GA 30260
Telephone: (678) 466-4000
E-mail: csu-info@clayton.edu
Internet: www.clayton.edu

Founded 1969 as Clayton Junior College; present name 1996
Academic year: August to May

Pres.: Dr THOMAS K. HARDEN
Provost and Vice-Pres. (Academic Affairs): Dr SHARON E. HOFFMAN
Vice-Pres. (Business and Operations) (vacant): DAVID HEFLIN
Vice-Pres. (Student Affairs): Dr BRIAN HAYNES
Vice-Pres. (External Relations): ROBERT L. STEPHENS, Jr
Vice-Pres. (Information Technology and Services): Dr JOHN BRYAN (acting)
Registrar: REBECCA GMEINER
Library Dir: GORDON BAKER

Number of teachers: 130
Number of students: 5,000

DEANS

School of Arts and Sciences: Dr RAY WALLACE
School of Business: Dr JUDITH PLANECKI
School of Health Sciences: Dr LINDA F. SAMSON
School of Technology: Dr ART ROSSNER (acting)
College of Information and Mathematical Sciences: Dr CHARLES FORD (acting)

COLUMBIA THEOLOGICAL SEMINARY

701 S Columbia Dr., Decatur, GA 30031
Telephone: (404) 378-8821
Fax: (404) 377-9696
Internet: www.ctsnet.edu

Founded 1828
Academic year: September to May

Pres.: LAURA S. MENDENHALL
Exec. Vice-Pres. and Dean of Faculty: D. CAMERON MURCHISON
Vice-Pres. (Advancement Services): C. J. DRYMON
Vice-Pres. (Business and Finance): MARTIN SADLER
Vice-Pres. (Institutional Advancement): RICHARD DuBOSE
Dean and Vice-Pres. (Lifelong Learning): DENT C. DAVIS
Dean of Students and Vice-Pres. (Student Services): JOHN E. WHITE
Registrar: LINDA SABO
Library Dir: SARA MYERS

Number of teachers: 36
Number of students: 500.

COLUMBUS STATE UNIVERSITY

4225 University Ave, Columbus, GA 31907
Telephone: (706) 568-2001
E-mail: academic_affairs@colstate.edu
Internet: www.colstate.edu

Founded 1958
Academic year: August to June

Pres.: Dr FRANK DOUGLAS BROWN
Vice-Pres. (Academic Affairs): Dr GEORGE STANTON
Vice-Pres. (Business and Finance): TOM HELTON
Vice-Pres. (Univ. Advancement): Dr KAYRON LASKA
Dean of Students: J. LARRY KEES
Registrar: BEVERLY LEAN
Dir of Libraries: CALLIE B. McGINNIS

Library of 240,000 vols
Number of teachers: 234
Number of students: 7,000

DEANS

College of Arts and Letters: Dr WILLIAM L. CHAPPELL, Jr (acting)
Abbott Turner College of Business: Dr LINDA HADLEY

College of Education: Dr THOMAS E. HARRISON
College of Science: Dr ARTHUR G. CLEVELAND
Univ. College: BEVERLY M. DAVIS (acting)

EMMANUEL COLLEGE

POB 129, Franklin Springs, GA 30639
Located at: 181 Springs St, Franklin Springs, GA 30639

Telephone: (706) 245-7226
Fax: (706) 245-4424
E-mail: mail@emmanuelcollege.edu
Internet: www.emmanuelcollege.edu

Founded 1919 as Franklin Springs Institute; present name 1939
Private control
Academic year: August to May

Pres.: Dr DAVID R. HOPKINS
Vice-Pres. and Academic Dean: CRAIG EDWARDS
Dean of Students: TIM HARRISON
Registrar: DEBRA F. GRIZZLE
Head Librarian: RICHARD DUPONT

Library of 50,000 vols
Number of students: 800

Schools of Business, Christian Ministries, Developmental Studies, Education, Humanities, Natural Sciences and Mathematics, Social and Behavioural Sciences.

EMORY UNIVERSITY

Atlanta, GA 30322
Telephone: (404) 727-6123
Internet: www.emory.edu

Founded 1836 as Emory College; became Univ. 1915
Related to the United Methodist Church
Academic year: August to May

Pres.: JAMES W. WAGNER
Provost and Exec. Vice-Pres. for Academic Affairs: EARL LEWIS
Exec. Vice-Pres. for Health Affairs and Dir of the Robert W. Woodruff Health Sciences Center: MICHAEL M. E. JOHNS
Dean of Emory College: ROBERT A. PAUL
Vice-Provost and Dean of the Graduate School: LISA A. TEDESCO
Exec. Vice-Pres. for Finance and Admin.: MICHAEL J. MANDL
Sr Vice-Pres. and Gen. Counsel: KENT B. ALEXANDER
Sr Vice-Pres. and Dean for Campus Life: JOHN L. FORD
Vice-Pres. and Sec. of the Univ.: ROSEMARY MAGEE
Vice-Pres. for Govt Affairs: JOHN ENGLEDON
Registrar: CHARLES R. NICOLAYSEN
Vice-Provost and Dir of Libraries: RICHARD E. LUCE

Library: Libraries with 2,591,912 vols
Number of teachers: 2,047 (full-time)
Number of students: 10,762

Publications: *Emory Magazine* (quarterly), *Emory Law Journal* (quarterly), *Emory Medicine* (3 a year), *Public Health Magazine* (2 a year), *New Vico Studies* (annual), *Emory International Law Review* (2 a year), *Emory Nursing* (2 a year), *Goizueta Business Magazine* (3 a year), *Bankruptcy Developments Journal* (2 a year)

DEANS

Emory College: ROBERT A. PAUL
Oxford College (Oxford): DANA KATHERINE GREENE
Business: THOMAS S. ROBERTSON
Graduate School: DONALD G. STEIN
School of Law: THOMAS C. ARTHUR
School of Medicine: THOMAS J. LAWLEY
School of Nursing: MARLA E. SALMON
School of Public Health: JAMES W. CURRAN

School of Theology: RUSSELL E. RICHEY

PROFESSORS

AABERG, T. M., Ophthalmology
ABRAMOWITZ, A., Political Science
ABRAMOWSKY, C. R., Pathology
ABRAMS, H. E., Law
ADAMSON, W. L., History
AGNEW, R. S., Sociology
ALARCON, R., Psychiatry/Behavioural Sciences
ALAVI, M., Information Strategy
ALBRECHT, T. E., Music
ALDRIDGE, D. P., Sociology
ALEXANDER, F. S., Law
ALEXANDER, G. E., Neurology
ALEXANDER, R. W., Medicine
ALLITT, P., History
AN-NA'IM, A., Law
ANSARI, A. A., Pathology
ANSEL, J. C., Dermatology
ARMELAGOS, G., Anthropology
ARTHUR, T. C., Law
AUSTIN, H., Epidemiology
BAJAJ, K., Physics
BARLETT, P., Anthropology
BARON, M., Radiology
BARROW, D., Neurosurgery
BARSALOU, L., Psychology
BAUERLEIN, M., English
BAUMGARTNER, B. R., Radiology
BEARD, L., Accounting
BECKER, E. R., Health Policy and Management
BEDERMAN, D. J., Law
BEIK, W., History
BENSTON, G. J., Finance
BERMAN, H. J., Law
BERNSTEIN, A., Law
BERNSTEIN, K. E., Pathology
BERRY, A. J., Anaesthesiology
BESSEMBINDER, H., Finance
BLACK, M., Political Science
BLAKE, D. A., Pharmacology
BLUMENTHAL, D. R., Judaic Studies
BONDI, R. C., Church History
BONNEFIS, P., French and Italian
BOOTHE, R., Psychology
BORING, J. R., III, Epidemiology
BOSS, J., Microbiology/Immunology
BOSTWICK, J., III, Plastic Surgery
BOSWELL, T. E., Sociology
BRACHMAN, P., International Health
BRAITHWAITE, R., Behavioural Science and Health Education
BRANCH, W. T., General Medicine
BRANN, A. W., Neurology, Paediatrics
BRIGHT, D. F., Classics and Comparative Literature
BROGAN, D. J., Biostatistics
BROWN, P. J., Anthropology
BROWN, W. V., Medicine (Lipids)
BROWNLEY, M. W., English
BRYAN, J. A., Pathology
BUGGE, J. M., English
BUSS, M. J., Religion
BUZBEE, W., Law
CALABRESE, R., Biology
CARNEY, W. J., Law
CARPENTER, L., English
CARR, D., Philosophy
CARTER, E. B., Biology
CARUTH, C., English
CASARELLA, W. J., Radiology
CATLIN, P. A., Rehabilitation Medicine
CAUGHMAN, S. W., Dermatology
CHAKRABORTY, H., Biostatistics
CHEN, R. L., Physics
CHENG, X., Biochemistry
CHIMOWITZ, M. I., Neurology
CHIRINKO, R., Economics
CHOPP, R., Systematic Theology
CHURCH, R., Ophthalmology
CLEMENTS, S. D., Cardiology
CLOUD, A. M., Law
COHEN, C., Pathology

COLE, J. A., Anthropology
COMPANS, R. W., Microbiology/Immunology
CONN, D. L., Rheumatology
CONN, P. J., Pharmacology
COOK, D. A., Film Studies
COOPER, R., Practice of Cost Management, Accounting
COPE, T., Physiology
CORNISH, J. D., Paediatrics
COURTRIGHT, P., Asian Studies
CRAVER, J. M., Cardiothoracic Surgery
CURRAN, J. M., Public Health
DANNER, D. J., Genetics
DAVIS, D. C., Medicine
DAVIS, L. W., Oncology
DAVIS, M., Psychiatry/Behavioural Sciences
DAVIS, P., Radiology
DE WAAL, F. B. M., Psychology, Primate Behaviour
DEANGRADE, J. R., Orthopaedics
DECONCINI, B., Religion
DELONG, M. R., Neurology
DICLEMENTE, R. J., Behavioural Science and Health Education
DIGIROLAMO, M., Medicine (Geriatrics)
DILORIO, C., Behavioural Science and Health Education
DINGLEDINE, R. J., Pharmacology
DOERNBERG, R. L., International Legal Studies
DOETSCH, P., Biochemistry
DONHAM, D. L., Anthropology
DOUGLAS, J. S., Medicine (Cardiology)
DUFFUS, D. A., Mathematic and Computer Science
DUKE, M., Psychology
DUNBAR, S., Adult and Elder Health
DUNCAN, M., Law
EATON, D. C., Physiology
ECKMAN, J. R., Haematology/Oncology
EDELHAUSER, H., Ophthalmology
EDMONDSON, D. E., Biochemistry
ELMER, W. A., Biology
ELSAS, L. J. II, Medical Genetics, Paediatrics
EMORY, E., Psychology
ENGELHARD, G., Educational Studies
ENGLAND, P., Physical Education
ENGLISH, A. W., Cell Biology
EPSTEIN, M., Russian and East Asian Languages and Culture
FALEK, A., Psychiatry/Behavioural Sciences
FAMILY, F., Physics
FARLEY, M. M., Infectious Diseases
FELICIANO, D. V., Surgery, Trauma/Critical Care
FELNER, J. M., Medicine (Cardiology)
FINK, A. S., General Surgery
FINNERTY, V. M., Biology
FIVUSH, R., Psychology
FLANDERS, W. D., Epidemiology
FLANNERY, J., Performing Arts
FLEMING, L. L., Orthopaedics
FLYNN, T. R., Philosophy
FONG, P., Physics
FOSTER, F. S., English
FOTION, N., Philosophy
FOWLER, J., Theology
FOX-GENOVESE, E., History
FRANCH, R., Medicine (Cardiology)
FRANKEL, B., Psychiatry/Behavioural Sciences
FREER, R. D., Law
FYFE, D., Paediatrics
GARCIA, E. V., Radiology
GARROW, D. J., Law
GELLER, R. J., Paediatrics
GIDDENS, D., Medical School Administration
GILES, M. W., Political Science
GOLDSMITH, D., Chemistry
GOODING, L. R., Microbiology/Immunology
GOODMAN, M., Radiology
GOULD, K., Primate Research
GOULD, R., Mathematic and Computer Science
GOUZOULES, H., Psychology
GOZANSKY, N. E., Law

GRAVANIS, M. B., Pathology
GREENAMYRE, T. J., Neurology
GREENE, D. K., History
GRIFFIN, J. B., Psychiatry/Behavioural Sciences
GRINDON, A. J., Pathology
GROSSNIKLAUS, H., Ophthalmology
GRUBER, W., English
GUNN, R. B., Physiology
GUNNEMANN, J., Social Ethics, Theology
GUTTERMAN, M., Law
GUTTIERREZ-MOUAT, R., Spanish
GUYTON, R., Cardiothoracic Surgery
HABER, M. J., Biostatistics
HAHN, C., Educational Studies
HALLORAN, M. E., Biostatistics
HANSON, S. R., Biomedical Engineering
HARARI, J., French and Italian
HARTGRAVES, A., Accounting
HARTLE, A., Philosophy
HARTZELL, H. C., Cell Biology
HATCHER, R. A., Gynaecology/Obstetrics
HAY, P., Law
HAYES, J. H., Theology (Old Testament)
HEAVEN, M., Chemistry
HERMAN, C., Pathology
HERRON, C., French and Italian
HICKS, A., Sociology
HILL, C. L., Chemistry
HOGUE, C., Epidemiology
HOLIFIELD, E. B., Theology
HOLLADAY, C. R., Theology (New Testament)
HOLLAND, B., Psychiatry/Behavioural Sciences
HOLTZMAN, S. G., Pharmacology
HOPKINS, L. C., Neurology
HOROWITZ, I. R., Gynaecology/Obstetrics
HUDSON, T., Radiology
HUG, C. C., Academic Affairs
HUMPHREY, D. R., Physiology
HUNTER, H. O., Law
HUNTER, R. J., Theology
HUTTON, W. C., Orthopaedics
HUYNH, B. H., Physics
INSEL, T. R., Psychiatry/Behavioural Sciences
IRVINE, J., Educational Studies
IUVONE, P. M., Pharmacology
JAFFE, S. L., Psychiatry/Behavioural Sciences
JENSEN, P., Pathology
JINKS-ROBERTSON, S., Biology
JOHNSON, L. T., Theology
JOHNSON, R., Chemistry
JOHNSON, T. C., Health, Physical Education and Dance
JOHNSTON, J. H., English
JONES, D. P., Biochemistry
JONES, E., Cardiothoracic Surgery
JONES, G., Biology
JORDAN, M., Religion
JOSEPH, R., Political Science
JOYNER, R. W., Paediatrics
JUDOVITZ, D., French and Italian
JUSTICE, J. B., Chemistry
KAHN, R. A., Biochemistry
KALAIDJIAN, W., English
KANTER, K. R., Cardiothoracic Surgery
KAPP, J., Ophthalmology
KARP, I., Liberal Arts, African Studies
KASLOW, N., Psychiatry/Behavioural Sciences
KAUFMAN, M. J., Chemistry
KAUFMAN, S., Radiology
KELLER, J. W., Radiation Oncology
KELLERMANN, A., Emergency Medicine
KERTZ, C. L., Accounting
KINKADE, J. M., Biochemistry
KLEHR, H., Politics and History
KLEIN, L., Gynaecology/Obstetrics
KLEINBAUM, D., Epidemiology
KLUGMAN, K. P., International Health
KNAUFT, B. M., Anthropology
KOHLI, A., Marketing
KONNER, M. J., Anthropology
KONSYNSKI, B., Business
KOVAC, S. R., Gynaecology/Obstetrics
KUHAR, M. J., Pharmacology
KULL, A., Law

KUSHNER, H., Science and Society
KUTNER, M., Biostatistics
KUTNER, N., Rehabilitation Medicine
LAMBETH, J. D., Biochemistry
LANGBERG, J. J., Cardiology, Electrophysiology
LAUER, S., Oncology, Paediatrics
LAWLEY, T. J., Medical School Administration
LAWRENCE, E. C., Medicine
LESSER, J., History, Latin American and Caribbean Studies
LETZ, R., Behavioural Science and Health Education
LEVEY, A. I., Neurology
LEVIN, B., Biology
LEVINSON, R. M., Medicine
LEVY, R., Psychiatry/Behavioural Sciences
LEWIS, W., Pathology
LIEBESKIND, L. S., Chemistry
LIN, M. C., Physical Chemistry
LINVILLE, K. B., Academic Affairs
LIOTTA, D. C., Chemistry
LIPSTADT, D., Judaic Studies
LIVINGSTON, D., Philosophy
LOLLAR, J. S., Haematology/Oncology
LONG, R. A., African Studies
LONG, T., Theology
LONGINI, I. M., Biostatistics
LOWE, W. J., Theology
LUCCHESI, J., Biology
LUSKIN, M. B., Cell Biology
LUTZ, L. J., Family and Preventive Medicine
LYNN, D., Chemistry
MABERLY, G., International Health
McCAREY, B. E., Ophthalmology
McCAULEY, R., Philosophy
McDOWELL, J. J., Psychology
McGINLEY, P. H., Radiation/Oncology
McGOWAN, J. E., Epidemiology
MACON, E. J., Medicine
McQUAIDE, M. M., Sociology
MADARA, J. L., Pathology
MAHAVIER, W. S., Mathematics and Computer Science
MAJMUDAR, B., Pathology
MAKKREEL, R. A., Philosophy
MANDELL, A. J., Psychiatry/Behavioural Sciences
MANSOUR, K., Cardiothoracic Surgery
MARSHALL, F. F., Urology
MARTIN, L. G., Radiology
MARTIN, R. C., Religion
MARTORELL, R., International Health
MARZILLI, L. G., Chemistry
MATTOX, D. E., Otolaryngology
MAYTON, W. T., Law
MEINERT, W. J., Family and Preventive Medicine
MERRILL, A. H., Biochemistry
MILLER, J. I., Cardiothoracic Surgery
MILLER, M., Law
MILLER, S. B., General Medicine
MINNEMAN, K. P., Pharmacology
MITCH, W. E., Medicine (Renal)
MOHANTY, J. N., Philosophy
MORAN, C., Microbiology/Immunology
MORGAN, E. T., Pharmacology
MOROKUMA, K., Chemistry
MORRIS, D. C., Cardiology
MURRAY, J., Adult and Elder Health
MUTH, R. D., Economics
NAHMIAS, A. J., Infectious Diseases, Paediatrics
NASSAR, V. H., Pathology
NAURIGHT, L. P., Adult and Elder Health
NEILL, D. B., Psychology
NEMEROFF, C., Psychiatry/Behavioural Sciences
NEWBY, G., Middle Eastern Studies
NEWSOM, C. A., Old Testament
NEYLAN, J. F., Medicine
NICHOLS, T. R., Physiology
NOE, B., Cell Biology
NOWICKI, S., Psychology
O'DAY, G. R., Theology

OLIKER, V., Mathematics and Computer Science
OLIVER, H. P., Religion
O'SHEA, H. S., Adult and Elder Health
OUSLANDER, J. G., Geriatric Medicine
PACKARD, R., International Health, History
PADWA, A., Chemistry
PARTIN, C., Health, Physical Education and Dance
PASCAL, R. R., Pathology
PASTOR, R., International Relations/Political Science
PATTERSON, R. E., Cardiology
PATTERSON, R., Philosophy
PEDERSON, L., English
PENNELL, J. N., Law
PERKOWITZ, S., Physics
PESKOWITZ, M., Religion
PETERSEN, K. W., Cell Biology
PETTIGREW, R., Radiology
PHILLIPS, L. S., Endocrinology
PINTER, M., Physiology
PLOTSKY, P. M., Psychiatry/Behavioural Sciences
PLUMMER, A., Medicine
POHL, J., Medicine
POLING, C. V., Art History
POLLET, R. J., Medicine
POMERANTZ, G., Journalism
POWELL, M. L., Nursing
POWNALL, G., Accounting
RAMBUSS, R., English
RAMOS, H. S., General Medicine
RANDALL, H. W., Gynaecology/Obstetrics
REAL, L., Biology
RECTOR, A. M., Law
REED, W. L., Law
REMINGTON, T. F., Political Science
RICHEY, R., Theology
RICKETTS, R., Surgery, Paediatrics
RIMLAND, D., Infectious Diseases
ROARK, J., History
ROBBINS, V., Religion
ROCHAT, P., Psychology
ROCK, J. A., Gynaecology/Obstetrics
RODL, V., Mathematics and Computer Science
ROSENBERG, A., Psychiatry/Behavioural Sciences
ROTHENBERG, R. B., Family and Preventive Medicine
RUBIN, P. H., Economics
RUBINSON, R., Sociology
RUSCHE, H., English
RYAN, P. B., Environmental and Occupational Health
SALAM, A., Surgery (Vascular)
SALE, W. S., Cell Biology
SALIERS, D. E., Theology
SALMON, M. E., Nursing
SALTMAN, R. B., Health Policy and Management
SANDS, J. M., Medicine
SARAL, R., Medicine
SCHAFFER, B. K., Economics
SCHINAZI, R. F., Paediatrics
SCHISLER, C., Music History
SCHMID, R., Mathematics and Computer Science
SCHUCHARD, R., English
SCOTT, J., Cell Biology
SCOTT, J. R., Microbiology/Immunology
SEBEL, P., Anaesthesiology
SEWELL, C. W., Pathology
SHAFER, W. M., Microbiology/Immunology
SHANOR, C. A., Law
SHAPIRO, M. M., Psychology
SHAPIRO, W., Political Science
SHAPPELL, R., Physical Education
SHARP, E., Nursing
SHERMAN, S., Genetics
SHETH, J., Marketing
SHORE, B., Anthropology
SHULMAN, J. A., Medicine
SHURE, D., Biology
SIDELL, N., Gynaecology/Obstetrics

SILVERMAN, M. E., Medicine
SIMONS, J. W., Medicine
SITTER, J. E., English
SKANDALAKIS, J. E., Surgical Anatomy and Technique
SLATER, N. W., Classics
SMITH, G. R., Law
SMITH, K., Haematology/Oncology
SMITH, L. E., Theology
SMITH, R. B. III, Surgery
SNAREY, J., Human Development and Ethics, Psychology
SOCOLOW, S. M., History, Latin American and Caribbean Studies
SOLOMON, A. R., Dermatology
SPITZNAGEL, J. K., Microbiology/Immunology
SPRAWLS, P., Radiological Services
SRIVASTAVA, R., Marketing
STEIN, D., Emergency Medicine
STEIN, D. G., Psychology
STEIN, K. W., Middle East Research
STERK, C. E., Behavioural Science and Health Education
STERN, B. J., Neurology
STERNBERG, P., Ophthalmology
STOKES, D., Biology
STONE, J., Medicine
STRICKLAND, O., Nursing
STULTING, R. D., Ophthalmology
SUNDERAM, V. S., Mathematics and Computer Science
SUNG, Y. F., Anaesthesiology
SYBERS, R. G., Radiology
SYMBAS, P., Cardiothoracic Surgery
TARCAN, Y., Radiology
TAYLOR, A., Nuclear Medicine, Radiology
TERRELL, T. P., Law
THOMAS, L.-G. III, Business Organization and Management
THORPE, K. E., Health Policy and Management
TIPTON, S. M., Theology
TORRES, W. E., Radiology
TUNE, L., Psychiatry/Behavioural Sciences
TUSA, R., Neurology
VAN DER VYVER, J., International Law
VANDALL, F. J., Law
VARADY, T., Law
VERENE, D. P. III, Philosophy
VINTEN-JOHANSEN, J., Cardiothoracic Surgery
VON WURTTEMBERG, A., Sanskrit
WAINER, B. E., Pathology, Geriatric Medicine
WALKER, E., Psychology
WALKER, H. K., Medicine
WALKER, T. G., Political Science
WALLEN, K., Psychology, Primate Research
WALLER, J. L., Anaesthesiology
WALTER, P. F., Medicine
WALTMAN, P., Mathematics and Computer Science
WARING, G. O., Ophthalmology
WARREN, K., Genetics
WATTS, N. B., Endocrinology
WATTS, R. L., Neurology
WAYMIRE, G., Marketing
WEATHERS, D. R., Pathology
WEBER, C. J., General Surgery
WEINTRAUB, W. S., Medicine
WEISS, B., Pathology
WEISS, J., Psychiatry/Behavioural Sciences
WEISS, S. A., Pathology
WENGER, N. K., Medicine
WHITE, D. F., Liberal Arts
WHITE, S., History
WHITESIDES, T. E., Orthopaedics
WILCOX, W. D., Paediatrics
WILKINSON, K. D., Biochemistry
WILLIAMS, W. H., Cardiothoracic Surgery
WILSON, M., Primate Research
WINOGRAD, E., Psychology
WITTE, J., Law
WOLF, S. L., Rehabilitation Medicine
WOOD, J. G., Cell Biology
WOOD, W. C., Surgical Oncology
WORKOWSKI, K. A., Infectious Diseases
WORTHMAN, C., Anthropology

YOUNG, J., Epidemiology
YOUNG, L., Physiology
ZAIDAN, J. R., Anaesthesiology
ZIEGLER, H. K., Microbiology/Immunology
ZUMPE, D., Psychiatry/Behavioural Sciences

FORT VALLEY STATE UNIVERSITY

1005 State University Dr., Fort Valley, GA
31030-4313
Telephone: (478) 825-6211
Fax: (478) 825-6394
Internet: www.fvsu.edu
Founded 1895
Academic year: July to June
Pres.: KOFI LOMOTEY
Vice-Pres. for Academic Affairs: Dr DOROTHY
CONTEH
Vice-Pres. for Business and Finance: E.
THOMAS OLIVER
Registrar: SHAREE LAWRENCE
Librarian: Dr CAROLE R. TAYLOR
Library of 191,806 vols
Number of teachers: 147
Number of students: 3,000

DEANS

Arts and Sciences: Dr LAWRENCE WANG
Education, Graduate and Special Academic
Programs: Dr CURTIS MARTIN
Agriculture and Allied Programs: Dr FRED
HARRISON

GEORGIA COLLEGE AND STATE UNIVERSITY

Milledgeville, GA 31061
Telephone: (478) 445-5004
Internet: www.gcsu.edu
Chartered in 1889 as Georgia Normal and
Industrial College; name changed 1922 to
Georgia State College for Women and 1961
to The Woman's College of Georgia;
became co-educational instn in 1967 under
the name of Georgia College; assumed
present name when designated as Geor-
gia's public liberal arts univ. in 1996
Pres.: Dr DOROTHY LELAND
Vice-Pres. for Academic Affairs and Dean of
Faculties: Dr ANNE V. GORMLY
Vice-Pres. for Institutional Research and
Enrollment Management: Dr PAUL JONES
Vice-Pres. for Student Affairs and Dean of
Students: Dr BRUCE HARSBARGER
Vice-Pres. for Univ. Advancement: AMY
NITSCHE
Dean of School of Health Sciences: Dr SANDRA
GANGSTEAD
Dean of School of Liberal Arts and Sciences:
Dr BETH RUSHING
Univ. Librarian: WILLIAM A. RICHARDS
Library of 190,000 vols, 23,500 print and
electronic periodicals, partial depository
for US govt documents
Number of teachers: 277
Number of students: 5,800

DEANS

School of Business: Dr JO ANN JONES
School of Education: Dr JANET FIELDS
School of Health Sciences: Dr JIMMY H. ISHEE
School of Liberal Arts and Sciences: Dr BETH
RUSHING

GEORGIA INSTITUTE OF TECHNOLOGY

225 North Ave, NW, Atlanta, GA 30332
Telephone: (404) 894-2000
Fax: (404) 894-5520
Internet: www.gatech.edu
Chartered 1885
Pres.: G. WAYNE CLOUGH

Provost and Vice-Pres. for Academic Affairs:
GARY SCHUSTER
Vice-Provost of Research and Dean of Grad-
uate Studies: Dr CHARLES L. LIOTTA
Sr Vice-Pres. for Admin. and Finance:
ROBERT K. THOMPSON
Vice-Provost for Institutional Devt: JACK R.
LOHMANN
Registrar: RITA PIKOWSKY
Dean of Library: RICHARD W. MEYER
Library of 4,286,595 vols
Number of teachers: 911
Number of students: 16,841
Publications: *Blue Print, Georgia Tech Fact
Book, Research Horizons, The Technique*

DEANS

College of Architecture: Prof. THOMAS D.
GALLOWAY
College of Computing: RICHARD A. DEMILLO
College of Engineering: Dr DON P. GIDDENS
Ivan Allen College of Liberal Arts: Dr SUE
ROSSER
College of Management: Dr TERRY C. BLUM
College of Sciences: Prof. GARY B. SCHUSTER

SCHOOL DIRECTORS

Aerospace Engineering: ROBERT G. LOEWY
Applied Physiology: Dr ROBERT J. GREGOR
Biology: JOHN MCDONALD
Chemical Engineering: Prof. RONALD W.
ROUSSEAU
Chemistry and Biochemistry: Prof. THOMAS
ORLANDO
Civil and Environmental Engineering:
JOSEPH B. HUGHES
Earth and Atmospheric Sciences: Dr JUDITH
A. CURRY
Economics: Prof. PATRICK S. MCCARTHY
Electrical and Computer Engineering: Prof.
ROGER P. WEBB
Industrial and Systems Engineering: Prof.
WILLIAM B. ROUSE
History, Technology and Society: Prof.
WILLIE PEARSON, Jr
International Affairs: Prof. WILLIAM J. LONG
Literature, Communication and Culture:
Prof. KENNETH KNOESPEL
Materials Science and Engineering: Prof.
ROBERT L. SNYDER
Mathematics: WILLIAM T. TROTTER
Mechanical Engineering: Dr WARD O. WINER
Modern Languages: PHILLIP MCKNIGHT
Physics: Prof. RONALD F. FOX
Psychology: Prof. RANDALL W. ENGLE
Public Policy: DIANA HICKS
Textile and Fibre Engineering: Prof. ANSELM
GRIFFIN, III

ACADEMIC DEPARTMENT DIRECTORS

Aerospace Studies (US Air Force ROTC): Col
TERRANCE J. MCCARTHY
Architecture Program: ELLEN DUNHAM-JONES
(acting)
Building Construction Program: Prof. ROOZ-
BEH KANGARI
City and Regional Planning Program: Prof.
CHERYL K. CONTANT
Industrial Design Program: WAYNE CHUNG
Military Science (US Army ROTC): Lt-Col
ALFRED SCOTT
Music: Prof. FRANK CLARK
Naval Science (US Navy ROTC): Capt. ROY
L. HOLBROOK

ATTACHED CENTRES AND INSTITUTES

**Advanced Technology Development
Center:** Dir WAYNE HODGES.
**Biomedical Interactive Technology Cen-
ter:** Dir JOHN W. PEIFER.
**Center for Assistive Technology and
Environmental Access:** Dir STEPHEN
SPRINGLE.

**Center for Computational Materials
Science:** Dir Prof. UZI LANDMAN.
**Center for Dynamical Systems and Non-
linear Studies (CDSNS):** Dir KONSTANTIN
MISCHAIKOW.
**Center for Emergency Response Tech-
nology, Instruction and Policy (CER-
TIP):** Dir Dr THOMAS BEVAN.
Center for Enterprise Systems: Dir Dr
GARY TJADEN.
**Center for Experimental Research in
Computer Systems (CERCS):** Dir Prof.
KARSTEN SCHWAN.
**Center for Geographic Information Sys-
tems:** Dir Dr STEVEN P. FRENCH.
**Center for Human-Machine Systems
Research (CHMSR).**
**Center for Innovative Fuel Cell and
Battery Technologies:** Dir Dr TOM FULLER,
Dr MEILIN LIU.
**Center for International Development
and Cooperation (affiliated to Sensors
and Electromagentic Applications
Laboratory):** Co-Dirs MELVIN L. BELCHER,
Jr, RICKY B. COTTON.
**Center for International Strategy, Tech-
nology and Policy:** Dir Dr JOHN E. END-
ICOTT.
**Center for Nanoscience and Nanotech-
nology:** Dir Prof. ZHONG L. WANG.
Center for Non-Linear Sciences: Dir
PREDRAG CVITANOVIC.
**Center for Paper Business and Industry
Studies:** Exec. Dir JIM MCNUTT.
Center for Polymer Processing.
Center for Public Buildings.
Center for Signal and Image Processing.
**Center for the Study of Women, Science
and Technology:** Co-Dirs Prof. MARY FRANK
FOX, Dr CAROL COLATRELLA, Dr MARY LYNN
REALFF.
**Center of Excellence in Rotorcraft Tech-
nology:** Dir Dr DANIEL P. SCHRAGE.
**Composites Education and Research
Center:** Dir Prof. STEVE JOHNSON.
Economic Development Institute: Dir
RICK DUKE.
European Union Center: Co-Dirs Dr
BRIAN MURPHY, Dr KATJA WEBER.
Georgia Electronic Design Center: Dir
JOY LASKAR, RICKY B. COTTON.
**Georgia Tech Broadband Institute
(GTBI).**
**Georgia Tech/Emory Center for the
Engineering of Living Tissues:** Dir Prof.
ROBERT M. NEREM.
**Georgia Tech Information Security Cen-
ter:** Dir Dr RALPH MERKLE.
**Graphics Visualization and Usability
(GVU) Center:** Dir Prof. AARON BOBICK.
Health Systems Research Center.
**Institute of Paper Science and Technol-
ogy:** Pres. W. J. FREDERICK, Jr.
**Institute for Sustainable Technology
and Development (ISTD):** Dir CHARLES L.
LIOTTA.
Interactive Media Technology Center:
Research Dir ED PRICE.
**Interactive Media Architecture Group
in Education (IMAGINE).**
Logistics Institute: Exec. Dir Dr CHELSEA
WHITE; Dir HARVEY DONALDSON.
**Logistics and Maintenance Applied
Research Center (LandMARC):** Co-Dirs
GARY O'NEILL, NEIL W. LAREAU, WILLIAM
ROBINSON.

Manufacturing Research Center: Dir Prof. STEVEN DANYLUK.

Mechanical Properties Research Laboratory (MPRL): Dir Dr D. L. McDO-WELL.

Microelectronics Research Center: Dir Dr JAMES D. MEINDL.

Microsystems Packaging Research Center (PRC).

Molecular Design Institute: Dir Prof. WILLIAM S. REES, Jr.

Multimedia Environmental Simulation Laboratory: Dir Prof. MUSTAFA M. ARAL.

MultiUniversity Center for Integrated Diagnostics: Principal Investigator Dr WARD O. WINER; Program Manager RICHARD S. COWAN.

National Electric Energy Testing Research and Application Center (NEE-TRAC): Dir Dr HANS BJÖRN PÜTTGEN.

Parker H. Petit Institute for Bioengineering and Bioscience (IBB): Dir ROBERT NEREM.

Phosphor Technology Center of Excellence (PTCOE): Dir Dr CHRISTOPHER J. SUMMERS.

Rapid Prototyping and Manufacturing Institution (RPMI): Dir Dr DAVID ROSEN.

Space Technology Advanced Research Center (STAR).

Technology Policy and Assessment Center: Dir Dr SAMUEL M. BLANKENSHIP.

University Center of Excellence for Photovoltaics Research and Education (UCEP): Dir Prof. AJEET ROHATGI.

Wireless Systems Laboratory: Dir Dr GORDON STÜBER.

GEORGIA SOUTHERN UNIVERSITY

Statesboro, GA 30460
Telephone: (912) 681-5611
Internet: www.georgiasouthern.edu
Founded 1906
Academic year: August to July
Pres.: Dr BRUCE GRUBE
Provost and Vice-Pres. for Academic Affairs: Dr LINDA M. BLEICKEN (acting)
Vice-Pres. for Business and Finance: JOSEPH W. FRANKLIN
Vice-Pres. for Student Affairs and Enrollment Management: Dr TERESA ELAINE THOMPSON
Vice-Pres. for Univ. Advancement: WILLIAM I. GRIFFIS
Registrar: MIKE DEAL
Dean of the Library: W. BEDE MITCHELL
Library of 541,535 vols
Number of teachers: 720 (626 full-time, 94 part-time)
Number of students: 14,371.

GEORGIA SOUTHWESTERN STATE UNIVERSITY

800 Wheatley St, Americus, GA 31709
E-mail: gswapps@canes.gsw.edu
Internet: www.gsw.edu
Founded 1906 as Third Agricultural and Mechanical School; present name 1996
Academic year: August to May
Pres.: Dr KENDALL BLANCHARD
Vice-Pres. (Academic Affairs) and Dean of Faculty: Dr CATHY L. ROZMUS
Vice-Pres. (Business and Finance): Dr C. ALAN PARKS
Vice-Pres. (Student Affairs): Dr SAMUEL T. MILLER
Vice-Pres. (Dir of Univ. Relations) (vacant): STEPHEN SNYDER
Dean of Students: GAYE S. HAYES

Registrar: DONJA TRIPP
Dean of the Library: VERA WEISSKOPF
Library of 190,000 vols
Number of teachers: 108
Number of students: 2,237 (1,969 undergraduate, 270 graduate)

DEANS

School of Arts and Sciences: Dr WILLIAM WYSOCHANSKY
School of Business Admin.: Dr JOHN G. KOOTI
School of Computer and Information Sciences: Dr BORIS V. PELTSVERGER
School of Education: Dr MARY GENDERNALIK COOPER
School of Nursing: Dr MARIA R. WARDA

GEORGIA STATE UNIVERSITY

University Plaza, POB 2000, Atlanta, GA 30303
Telephone: (404) 651-2000
Internet: www.gsu.edu
Founded 1913
Academic year: August to May
Pres.: CARL V. PATTON
Provost and Vice-Pres. for Academic Affairs: Dr RONALD J. HENRY
Vice-Pres. for Devt: NANCY E. PETERMAN
Vice-Pres. for External Affairs: THOMAS C. LEWIS
Vice-Pres. for Finance and Admin.: JERRY J. RACKLIFFE
Vice-Pres. for Research: Dr ROBIN MORRIS
Vice-Pres. for Student Services: DOUGLASS COVEY
Dir of Admissions: DIANE M. WEBER
Registrar: CHERISE Y. PETERS (acting)
Dean of Libraries: CHARLENE S. HURT
Library of 1,397,629 vols, 4,788 current periodicals, 21,772 audio-visual items, 807,224 US govt documents
Number of teachers: 1,027
Number of students: 27,267

Publications: *South Atlantic Review* (quarterly), *Eudora Welty Newsletter* (2 a year), *International Journal of High Performance and Computer Networking* (6 a year), *International Journal of Bioinformatics Research* (quarterly), *Medicinal Research Reviews* (6 a year), *The Forecast for the Nation* (quarterly), *RMI Report Newsletter* (6 a year), *State of Business Magazine* (3 a year), *The Briefing* (3 a year), *COE Update* (monthly), *Studies in Literary Imagination* (2 a year), *GSU Review* (2 a year), *Journal of Advanced Composition* (quarterly), *CHHS E-Newsletter* (monthly), *Health and Human Review* (annual), *5 Points: A Journal of Literature and Art* (3 a year)

DEANS

College of Arts and Sciences: Dr LAUREN B. ADAMSON
Dean J. Mack Robinson College of Business: Dr H. FENWICK HUSS
College of Education: Dr RONALD P. COLARUSSO
College of Health and Human Sciences: Dr SUSAN J. KELLEY
College of Law: Dr STEVEN J. KAMINSHINE (acting)
Andrew Young School of Policy Studies: Dr ROY W. BAHL Jr (acting)

ATTACHED RESEARCH INSTITUTES

Institute of Gerontology: Dir FRANK WHITTINGTON.

Institute of International Business: Dir KAREN LOCH.

Institute of Public Health: Dir MICHAEL ERIKSON.

Ron Brown Institute: Co-Dirs ROY BAHL, JOHN HICKS.

INTERDENOMINATIONAL THEOLOGICAL CENTER

700 Martin Luther King, Jr Dr., Atlanta, GA 303144143
Telephone: (404) 527-7700
E-mail: info@itc.edu
Internet: www.itc.edu
Founded 1958
Academic year: September to May
Pres.: Dr MICHAEL A. BATTLE.

KENNESAW STATE UNIVERSITY

1000 Chastain Rd, Kennesaw, GA 30144
Telephone: (770) 423-6300
E-mail: ksuadmit@kennesaw.edu
Internet: www.kennesaw.edu
Founded 1963 as Kennesaw Junior College; present name 1996
Academic year: August to May
Pres.: Dr DANIEL S. PAPP
Provost and Vice-Pres. (Academic Affairs): Dr LENDLEY C. BLACK
Vice-Pres. (Operations): RANDY C. HINDS
Vice-Pres. (Student Success and Enrollment Services): Dr NANCY S. KING
Vice-Pres. (Univ. Advancement): WESLEY K. WICKER
Dean of Graduate Studies: Dr TERESA M. JOYCE
Dean of Undergraduate and Univ. College: Dr MARY LOU FRANK
Dean, Division of Continuing Education: BARBARA S. CALHOUN
Registrar: WILLIAM L. HAMRICK
Library Dir: DAVID EVANS
Library of 600,000 vols and govt publs)
Number of teachers: 537
Number of students: 18,000

DEANS

College of the Arts: JOSEPH MEEKS
Coles College of Business: Dr TIM MESCON
Bagwell College of Education: Dr YIPING WAN
College of Health and Human Services: Dr RICHARD SOWELL
College of Humanities and Social Sciences: Dr HELEN S. RIDLEY
College of Science and Mathematics: Dr LAURENCE I. PETERSON

LAGRANGE COLLEGE

601 Broad St, LaGrange, GA 30240
Telephone: (706) 880-8005
Fax: (706) 880-8358
Internet: www.lagrange.edu
Founded 1831
Academic year: September to May
Pres.: Dr FRANK STUART GULLEY
Exec. Vice-Pres. (Admin.): PHYLLIS D. WHITNEY
Vice-Pres. (Academic Affairs) and Dean: Dr JAY K. SIMMONS
Vice-Pres. and Dean for Student Life and Retention: Dr LINDA R. BUCHANAN
Vice-Pres. (Advancement): Rev. B. DAVID ROWE
Dir (Enrollment Management and Admissions): WELLS SHEPARD
Registrar: JIMMY HERRING
Library Dir: LOREN PINKERMAN
Library of 138,000 vols
Number of teachers: 70
Number of students: 1,000.

LIFE UNIVERSITY

1269 Barclay Circle, Marietta, GA 30060
Telephone: (770) 426-2884
Fax: (770) 426-2895
E-mail: admissions@life.edu
Internet: www.life.edu
Founded 1974 as Life Chiropractic College; present name 1997
Private control
Pres.: Dr GUY F. RIEKEMAN
Provost: Dr BRIAN MCAULAY
Vice-Pres. (Univ. Advancement): BARRY NICKELSBERG
Vice-Pres. (Operations and Finance): BILL JARR
Dean (College of Arts and Sciences): Dr JERRY HARDEE
Registrar: BRIAN SHERES
Number of teachers: 126
Number of students: 1,242

DEANS

College of Arts and Sciences: Dr SAM DEMONS (acting)
College of Chiropractic Science: Dr ROBERT M. SCOTT

MEDICAL COLLEGE OF GEORGIA

1120 15th St, Augusta, GA 30912
Telephone: (706) 721-0211
Internet: www.mcg.edu
Founded 1828 as Medical Academy of Georgia
Part of Univ. System of Georgia
Pres.: Dr DANIEL W. RAHN
Provost: Dr BARRY D. GOLDSTEIN
Vice-Pres. for Admin.: Dr J. MICHAEL ASH
Vice-Pres. for Enrollment and Student Services: Dr MICHAEL H. MILLER
Vice-Pres. for Univ. Advancement: BRIAN R. GINN, Jr
Vice-Pres. for Finance: DIANE C. WRAY
Vice-Pres. for Information Technology (vacant): BETH BRIGDON
Vice-Pres. for Legal Affairs: ANDREW R. H. NEWTON
Vice-Pres. for Research: FRANK A. TREIBER
Vice-Pres. for Decision Support: DEB BARSHAFSKY
Registrar: Dr MIKE MILLER, RITA GARNER
Dir of Libraries: TAMERA LEE
Library of 219,984 vols, 1,232 current periodicals, 980 audio-visual titles
Number of teachers: 2,023 (590 full-time, 119 part-time, 1,314 volunteer)
Number of students: 1,939
Publication: Scope

DEANS

Allied Health Sciences: Dr SHELLEY MISHOE
Dentistry: Dr BRAD J. POTTER
Medicine: Dr DAVID M. STERN
Nursing: Dr MARLENE ROSENKOETTER
Graduate Studies: Dr MATTHEW J. KLUGER

MERCER UNIVERSITY

1400 Coleman Ave, Macon, GA 31207-0001
Telephone: (912) 752-2700
Fax: (912) 752-4124
Internet: www.mercer.edu
Chartered 1833
Private control (Baptist)
Pres.: WILLIAM D. UNDERWOOD
Exec. Vice-Pres. for Finance and Admin.: Dr JAMES S. NETHERTON
Sr Vice-Pres. for Univ. Advancement and External Affairs: EMILY P. MYERS
Vice-Pres. and Dean of Students: Dr DOUGLAS R. PEARSON

Exec. Vice-Pres. and Provost: HORACE W. FLEMING
Library of 243,000 vols, 1,000 current periodicals, 4,400 audio items, US govt documents
Number of teachers: 1,291
Number of students: 7,300
Publications: The Mercerian, Discoveries, Inside Mercer, The Business Advisor, The Mercer Engineer, TIFToday, The Law Letter

DEANS

Stetson School of Business and Economics: Prof. WILLIAM CARL JOINER
Tift College of Education: Prof. RICHARD T. SIETSEMA
School of Engineering: Prof. M. DAYNE ALDRIDGE
Law: Prof. MICHAEL SABBATH
College of Liberal Arts: Prof. RICHARD C. FALLIS
Medicine: Dr ANN JOBE
Georgia Baptist College of Nursing: Dr SUSAN S. GUNBY
Pharmacy (Atlanta): Prof. HEWITT W. 'TED' MATTHEWS
McAfee School of Theology: Prof. R. ALAN CULPEPPER

MOREHOUSE COLLEGE

830 Westview Dr., SW, Atlanta, GA 30314
Telephone: (404) 681-2800
Internet: www.morehouse.edu
Founded 1867; member of Atlanta Univ. Center
Pres.: Dr WALTER E. MASSEY
Provost and Sr Vice-Pres. for Academic Affairs: DAVID V. TAYLOR
Vice-Pres. for Business and Finance: KEITH APPLETON
Vice-Pres. for Campus Operations: ANDRÉ BERTRAND
Vice-Pres. for Institutional Advancement: PHILLIP HOWARD
Library Dir: LORETTA PARHAM
Library of 650,000 vols
Number of teachers: 238 (176 full-time, 62 part-time)
Number of students: 3,000
Publication: Journal of Negro History.

MOREHOUSE SCHOOL OF MEDICINE

720 Westview Dr., SW, Atlanta, GA 30310-1495
Telephone: (404) 752-1500
Internet: www.msm.edu
Founded 1975 as School of Medicine at Morehouse College; present name 1981
Private control
Academic year: July to May
Pres.: Dr JOHN E. MAUPIN
Dean and Sr Vice-Pres. (Academic Affairs): Dr EVE J. HIGGINBOTHAM
Vice-Pres. (Finance): ELI H. PHILLIPS
Vice-Pres. (Human Resources): SYLVIA D. NEALY
Exec. Dir (Marketing and Communications): CHERIE A. RICHARDSON
Chief Information Officer: ERIC L. JACKSON
Registrar: RODDRICK JONES
Library of 73,572 vols
Number of teachers: 204
Number of students: 217.

MORRIS BROWN COLLEGE

634 Martin Luther King Dr., SW, Atlanta, GA 30314
Telephone: (404) 220-0270
Fax: (404) 659-4315

Internet: www.morrisbrown.edu
Founded 1881; member of Atlanta Univ. Center and United Negro College Fund
Pres.: Dr CHARLES E. TAYLOR (acting)
Vice-Pres. for Academic Affairs: Dr REGINALD LINDSEY (acting)
Vice-Pres. for Devt: OLIVER DELK
Vice-Pres. for Student Affairs: Dr LeVITA SMALL
Vice-Pres. for Fiscal Affairs: DENISE SMITH-MOORE
Vice-Pres. for Legal Affairs: DIONYSIA JOHNSON-MASSIE
Vice-Pres. for Admin. and Operations: JIM MARING
Registrar: LUCILE WILLIAMS
Library of 797,684 vols
Number of teachers: 143
Number of students: 2,154
Publications: Bulletin, Wolverine Observer (monthly).

NORTH GEORGIA COLLEGE AND STATE UNIVERSITY

82 College Circle, Dahlonega, GA 30597
Telephone: (706) 864-1400
Fax: (706) 864-1478
E-mail: admissions@ngcsu.edu
Internet: www.ngcsu.edu
Founded 1873
Academic year: August to May
Pres.: DAVID POTTER
Vice-Pres. for Business and Finance: FRANK J. McCONNELL
Vice-Pres. for Academic Affairs: Dr LINDA ROBERTS-BETSCH
Vice-Pres. for Student Affairs: Dr CHARLES SCHRODER
Vice-Pres. for Institutional Advancement: BRUCE HOWERTON
Registrar: JASON K. PRUITT
Dir of Library Services: SHAWN TONNER
Library of 175,330 vols (incl. old periodicals, electronic documents and govt documents), 550 paper periodicals, 100 microform periodicals, 15,978 electronic periodicals, 1,487 audio-visual items, 92 CD-ROMs
Number of teachers: 362
Number of students: 4,552
Publication: Honores: The NGCSU Journal of Undergraduate Research (2 a year)

DEANS

Arts and Letters: Dr ROBERT LYMAN
Business and Govt: Dr GERALD SKELLY
Education: Dr BOB MICHAEL
Natural and Health Sciences: Dr THOMAS FOX

OGLETHORPE UNIVERSITY

4484 Peachtree Rd, NE, Atlanta, GA 30319
Telephone: (404) 261-1441
Fax: (404) 364-8500
E-mail: admission@oglethorpe.edu
Internet: www.oglethorpe.edu
Founded 1835
Academic year: September to May
Pres.: LAWRENCE SCHALL
Registrar: TANYA CRUMP
Provost: WILLIAM O. SHROPSHIRE
Vice-Pres. for Business and Finance: MARILYN FOWLÉ
Vice-Pres. for Devt: PETER A. ROONEY
Dir of the Library: ANNE A. SALTER
Library of 150,000 bound vols
Number of teachers: 116
Number of students: 1,230
Publications: The Flying Petrel (quarterly), The Stormy Petrel (fortnightly), The Tower (2 a year), Yamacraw (annual).

PAINE COLLEGE

1235 15th St, Augusta, GA 30901-3182
Telephone: (706) 821-8200
Internet: www.paine.edu
Founded 1882
Pres.: Dr SHIRLEY A. R. LEWIS
Vice-Pres. of Academic Affairs: Dr CURTIS E. MARTIN
Vice-Pres. of Admin. and Fiscal Affairs: FREDDIE L. JOHNSON
Vice-Pres. for Institutional Devt: JUDITH LITTLE
Registrar: CAROLYN MARTIN
Dir of Library: SUZETTE HOLLINS

Library of 73,000 vols
Number of teachers: 74
Number of students: 900

Publications: *The Paine Magazine* (quarterly), *The Windowpaine* (monthly), *The Lion* (annual), *The Paineite* (2 to 4 a year).

PIEDMONT COLLEGE

Demorest, GA 30535
Telephone: (706) 778-3000
Internet: www.piedmont.edu
Founded 1897
Pres.: Dr W. RAY CLEERE
Vice-Pres. for Academic Affairs: Dr JAMES MELLICHAMP
Admissions: JEM CLEMENT
Registrar: LINDA WOFFORD
Librarian: ROBERT GLASS

Library of 100,000 vols
Number of teachers: 50
Number of students: 1,700.

REINHARDT COLLEGE

7300 Reinhardt College Circle, Waleska, GA 30183-2981
Telephone: (770) 720-5600
Fax: (770) 720-5602
E-mail: admissions@reinhardt.edu
Internet: www.reinhardt.edu
Founded 1883 as Reinhardt Academy; present name 1911
Private control
Academic year: August to May
Pres.: Dr J. THOMAS ISHERWOOD
Vice-Pres. (Academic Affairs) and Dean of the College: Dr ROBERT L. DRISCOLL
Vice-Pres. (Institutional Advancement and External Affairs): JOELLEN WILSON
Vice-Pres. (Finance and Admin.) (vacant): JAMES T. HAKES
Vice-Pres. (Student Affairs) and Dean of Students (vacant): Dr ROGER R. LEE
Library Dir: MICHAEL MARTINEZ

Library of 49,507 vols and bound periodicals
Number of teachers: 56 full-time
Number of students: 1,086

DEANS

School of Arts and Humanities: Dr CURTIS G. LINDQUIST
McCamish School of Business: Dr DAVID W. CHOWN
School of Communication Arts and Music: PEG O'CONNOR
Price School of Education: Dr ROBERT L. DRISCOLL
School of Mathematics and Sciences: ANDY M. EDWARDS

BRANCH CAMPUS

N Fulton Center: 4100 Old Milton Parkway, Suite 250, Alpharetta, GA 30005-4442; tel. (770) 7209191; fax (770) 4750263; e-mail nfmail@reinhardt.edu; Asst Dean for Extended Academic Studies Dr DONALD D. WILSON, Jr.

SAVANNAH COLLEGE OF ART AND DESIGN

POB 77300, Atlanta, GA 30357-1300
Telephone: (404) 253-2700
Fax: (404) 253-3466
E-mail: scadatl@scad.edu
Internet: www.scad.edu
Founded 1905
Incorporates the Atlanta College of Art and Design; additional campus in Lacoste, France
Private control
Academic year: August to May
Pres.: PAULA S. WALLACE
Vice-Pres. (Academic Services) and Asst Vice-Pres. for SCAD-Atalanta: TERESA GRIFFIS
Vice-Pres. (Business and Finance): TIMOTHY A. SPAETH
Vice-Pres. (Enrollment Management): LUCY LEUSCH
Vice-Pres. (Institutional Advancement): ELIZABETH CHAPMAN
Vice-Pres. (Student Services): DAVID PUGH
Head Librarian: MELISSA MCDONALD

Library of 25,000 vols, 180 periodicals, 90,000 slides
Number of teachers: 73
Number of students: 425.

SAVANNAH STATE UNIVERSITY

3219 College St, Savannah, GA 31404
Telephone: (912) 356-2240
Fax: (912) 356-2998
E-mail: ssu.inquiries@tigerpaw.savstate.edu
Internet: www.savstate.edu
Founded 1890
Academic year: August to May
Pres.: Dr JULIUS S. SCOTT, Jr
Vice-Pres. for Academic Affairs: Dr JANE MCBRIDE-GATES
Vice-Pres. for Business and Finance: ELAINE CAMPBELLE
Vice-Pres. for Institutional Advancement: LARION WILLIAMS
Vice-Pres. for Student Affairs: Dr RANDY GUNTER
Library Dir: MARY JO FAYOYIN

Library of 188,068 items
Number of teachers: 160
Number of students: 2,300.

SHORTER COLLEGE

315 Shorter Ave, Rome, GA 30165-4298
Telephone: (706) 291-2121
Fax: (706) 236-1515
E-mail: els@shorter.edu
Internet: www.shorter.edu
Founded 1873
Academic year: August to May
Pres.: HAROLD E. NEWMAN
Provost: Dr HAROLD E. NEWMAN
Exec. Vice-Pres. and Chief Financial Officer: STEPHANIE OWENS
Vice-Pres. for Student Affairs (vacant)
Dir of Institutional Advancement: SUZANNE SCOTT
Registrar: KATHERINE LOVVORN
Dir of Admissions: WENDY SUTTON
Dean of Libraries: KIM HERNDON

Library of 126,483 vols
Number of teachers: 62
Number of students: 1,849.

SOUTHERN POLYTECHNIC STATE UNIVERSITY

1100 S Marietta Parkway, Marietta, GA 30060-2896
Telephone: (678) 915-7778

Fax: (678) 915-7483
E-mail: admissions@spsu.edu
Internet: www.spsu.edu
Founded 1948 as The Technical Institute; present name 1996
Part of Univ. System of Georgia
Academic year: August to August
Pres.: Dr LISA A. ROSSBACHER
Vice-Pres. (Academic Affairs): Dr ZVI SZAFRAN
Vice-Pres. (Business and Finance): PATRICK R. MCCORD
Vice-Pres. (Student and Enrollment Services): Dr RON R. KOGER
Library Dir: Dr JOYCE WHITE MILLS

Library of 105,000 vols
Number of teachers: 150
Number of students: 4,000

DEANS

School of Architecture, Civil Engineering Technology, and Construction: Dr WILSON BARNES
School of Arts and Sciences: Dr ALAN GABRIELLI
School of Computing and Software Engineering: Dr MICHAEL MURPHY
School of Engineering Technology and Management: Dr C. WAYNE UNSELL
Extended Univ.: DAWN RAMSEY

SPELMAN COLLEGE

350 Spelman Lane, SW, Atlanta, GA 30314-4399
Telephone: (404) 681-3643
Fax: (404) 223-1428
Internet: www.spelman.edu
Founded 1881; member of Atlanta Univ. Center
Pres.: Dr BEVERLEY DANIEL TATUM
Provost: Dr JOHNNELLA BUTLER
Vice-Pres. for Business and Financial Affairs and Treasurer: ROBERT D. FLANAGAN, Jr
Vice-Pres. for Institutional Advancement: A. TRISA LONG PASCHAL
Vice-Pres. for Student Affairs: Dr SHERRY L. TURNER
Vice-Pres. for Media and Informaton Technology: ELLIS RAINEY
Assoc. Provost for Liberal Arts and Education: Dr RONNIE TRIBBLE
Assoc. Provost for Science Programs and Mathematics: Dr SYLVIA T. BOZEMAN
Academic Dean: Dr CYNTHIA NEAL SPENCE
Registrar: Dr FRED BUDDY

Number of teachers: 156
Number of students: 2,139.

STATE UNIVERSITY OF WEST GEORGIA

1601 Maple St, Carrollton, GA 30118
Telephone: (678) 839-5000
Internet: www.westga.edu
Founded 1933; sr college status 1957, univ. status 1995
Academic year: August to July
Pres.: Dr BEHERUZ N. SETHNA
Vice-Pres. for Academic Affairs: Dr THOMAS J. HYNES
Vice-Pres. for Business and Finance: WILLIAM GAUTHIER, JEROME MOCK
Vice-Pres. for Univ. Advancement: TARA SINGER
Vice-Pres. for Student Services: Dr MELANIE MCCLELLAN
Registrar: BONITA B. STEVENS
Dir of Admissions: ROBERT S. JOHNSON
Dir of Libraries: CHARLES E. BEARD LORENE FLANDERS

Library of 370,896 vols, 23,706 microfilm reels, 1,040,266 microforms, 19,362 maps

and charts, 208,215 US govt documents, 28,498 manuscript vols
Number of teachers: 366 (269 full-time, 98 part-time)
Number of students: 9,030
Publications: *Under Graduate Catalog, Graduate Catalog, West Georgia Fact Book, Studies in the Social Sciences, West Georgia College Faculty Research Review* (all annual)

DEANS

College of Arts and Sciences: Dr RICHARD MILLER
Richards College of Business: Dr JACK JOHNSON
College of Education: Dr KENT LAYTON
Honors College: Dr DON WAGNER
Graduate School: Dr JACK JENKINS

THOMAS UNIVERSITY

1501 Millpond Rd, Thomasville, GA 31792
Telephone: (229) 226-1621
Fax: (229) 226-1653
E-mail: admissions@thomasu.edu
Internet: www.thomasu.edu
Founded 1950 as Birdwood Junior College; present name 2000
Private control
Academic year: August to May
Pres.: Dr GARY BONVILLIAN
Vice-Pres. for Academic Affairs: KIM ESTEP
Vice-Pres. for Finance and Admin. (vacant): ALLEN TOWNS
Vice-Pres. for Institutional Advancement: RICHARD MUNROE
Academic Dean: ANN M. LANDIS
Registrar: DEBBIE WHITE
Dir of Library Services: GARY COOPER

Library of 49,153 vols
Number of teachers: 61
Number of students: 5,509
Depts of Arts and Sciences, Business, Counselling and Rehabilitation, Education, Human Services, Justice Studies, Nursing, Social Work.

TOCCOA FALLS COLLEGE

325 Chapel Dr., POB 800777, Toccoa Falls, GA 30598
Telephone: (706) 886-6831
Fax: (706) 282-6005
E-mail: president@tfc.edu
Internet: www.tfc.edu
Founded 1907
Private control
Academic year: August to May
Pres.: WAYNE GARDNER
Vice-Pres. (Academic Affairs): BARBARA BELLEFEUILLE
Vice-Pres. (Institutional Advancement): JOHN HOWELL
Vice-Pres. (Spiritual Formation): JEFFREY GANGEL
Vice-Pres. (Student Affairs): KEN SANDERS
Dir for Finance: DAVID GRUEN
Registrar: KELLY VICKERS
Dir of Library Services: PATRICIA FISHER
Number of teachers: 67
Number of students: 827
Schools of Arts and Sciences, Bible and Theology, Business Admin., Christian Education, Communication, Counselling, Music, Teacher Education, World Missions.

UNIVERSITY OF GEORGIA

Athens, GA 30602
Telephone: (706) 542-3000
Internet: www.uga.edu

Founded 1785
Pres.: MICHAEL F. ADAMS
Sr Vice-Pres. for Finance and Admin.: TIM BURGESS
Sr Vice-Pres. for Academic Affairs and Provost: ARNETT C. MACE, Jr
Sr Vice-Pres. for External Affairs: TOM S. LANDRUM
Vice-Pres. for Research: DAVID LEE
Vice-Pres. for Instruction: DELMER D. DUNN, JERE W. MOREHEAD
Vice-Pres. for Public Service and Outreach: ARTHUR DUNNING
Vice-Pres. for Student Affairs: RODNEY BENNETT
Registrar: REBECCA MACON
Univ. Librarian: Dr WILLIAM G. POTTER

Library of 3,955,004 vols
Number of teachers: 2,984
Number of students: 33,878
Publications: *The Georgia Review* (quarterly), *Georgia Magazine* (quarterly), *State and Local Government Review* (3 a year), *Teaching Georgia Government* (3 a year), *Fact Book* (annual), *Georgia Journal of Ecological Anthropology* (annual), *Journal of Public Service and Outreach* (3 a year), *Journal of Agribusiness* (2 a year), *Environmental Ethics* (quarterly), *Journal of Business Research* (monthly), *Journal of Research and Development in Education* (quarterly), *Georgia Journal of College Student Affairs* (2 a year), *Georgia Economic Outlook* (annual), *Environmental Ethics* (quarterly), *The Aesculapian* (quarterly), *Georgia Science Teacher* (3 a year), *Georgia Historical Quarterly* (quarterly), *The Georgia Advocate* (3 a year), *Georgia Journal of International and Comprative Law* (3 a year), *Georgia Pharmacist Quarterly* (quarterly), *Georgia Pharmacist Magazine* (annual), *Georgia Preceptor* (quarterly), *Toxicology Digest* (quarterly), *Impact Interactive* (a service-learning magazine project, annual), *Georgia Museum of Art Bulletin* (annual)

DEANS

Graduate School: Dr MAUREEN GRASSO
College of Agricultural and Environmental Sciences: Dr GALE A. BUCHANAN
Franklin College of Arts and Sciences: Dr WYATT W. ANDERSON
C. Herman and Mary Virginia Terry College of Business: Dr P. GEORGE BENSON
College of Education: Dr LOUIS A. CASTENELL, Jr
College of Environment and Design: Dr JOHN F. CROWLEY
College of Family and Consumer Sciences: Dr SHARON Y. NICKOLS
Daniel B. Warnell School of Forest Resources: Dr JAMES SWEENEY (acting)
Henry W. Grady College of Journalism and Mass Communication: Dr JOHN SOLOSKI
School of Law: Dr DAVID E. SHIPLEY
College of Pharmacy: Dr SVEIN OIE
School of Public and Int. Affairs: Dr THOMAS P. LAUTH
School of Social Work: Dr LARRY NAKERUD
School of Veterinary Medicine: Dr KEITH W. PRASSEE

VALDOSTA STATE UNIVERSITY

1500 North Patterson St, Valdosta, GA 31698
Telephone: (912) 333-5952
Internet: www.valdosta.edu
Founded 1906
Pres.: Dr RONALD M. ZACCARI
Vice-Pres. for Academic Affairs: Dr LOUIS H. LEVY
Vice-Pres. for Student Affairs: Dr KURT J. KEPPLER

Vice-Pres. for Finance and Admin.: JAMES L. BLACK
Vice-Pres. for Univ. Advancement: SCOTT H. SYKES (acting)
Dir of Human Resources and Employee Devt: Dr DENISE BOGART
Registrar: GERALD B. WRIGHT
Librarian: Dr GEORGE R. GAUMOND

Library of 395,000 vols
Number of teachers: 500
Number of students: 10,000
Publication: *The Journal of Southwest Georgia History* (quarterly)

DEANS

College of the Arts: Dr JOHN GASTON (acting)
College of Arts and Sciences: Dr SHARON GRAVETT (acting)
Harley Labgdale, Jr College of Business Admin.: Dr KENNETH A. STANLEY
College of Education: Dr THOMAS REED, III (acting)
College of Nursing: Dr MARYANN REICHENBACH
Division of Social Work: Dr MARTHA M. GIDDINGS
Graduate School: Dr ERNESTINE CLARK

WESLEYAN COLLEGE

4760 Forsyth Rd, Macon, GA 31210
Telephone: (478) 477-1110
Fax: (478) 757-4030
Internet: www.wesleyancollege.edu
Founded 1836
Academic year: August to May
Pres.: RUTH A. KNOX
Vice-Pres. for Academic Affairs and Dean of the College: DELMAS S. CRISP, Jr
Vice-President for Admin. and Marketing: C. STEPHEN FARR
Vice-Pres. for Enrollment Services and Student Affairs: PATRICIA M. GIBBS
Vice-Pres. for Finance and Treas.: RICHARD P. MAIER
Vice-Pres. for Institutional Advancement: DEBORAH JONES SMITH
Librarian: CATHERINE LEE
Library of 142,579 vols
Number of teachers: 79
Number of students: 715.

HAWAII

BRIGHAM YOUNG UNIVERSITY, HAWAII CAMPUS

55–220 Kulanui St, Laie, Oahu, HI 96762
Telephone: (808) 293-3211
Internet: www.byuh.edu
Founded 1955
Pres.: Dr ERIC B. SHUMWAY
Vice-Pres. for Academics: KEITH J. ROBERTS
Vice-Pres. for Admin. Services: MICHAEL B. BLISS
Vice-Pres. for Student Affairs: ILILELI T. KONGAIKA
Vice-Pres. for Univ. Advancement: V. NAPUA BAKER
Chief Information Officer: JIM NILSON
Asst to Pres.: WILLIAM G. NEAL
Registrar: VERNELLE LAKATANI
Librarian: DOUGLAS BATES
Library of 163,000 vols
Number of teachers: 109
Number of students: 2,400

DEANS

College of Arts and Sciences: W. JEFFERY BURROUGHS
School of Business: CLAYTON HUBNER
School of Computing: BRET ELLIS
School of Education: JOHN BAILEY

Center for Instructional Technology and Outreach: ROBERT HAYDEN

ATTACHED RESEARCH INSTITUTE

Institute of Polynesian Studies: Dir Dr VERNICE WINEERA; publ. *Pacific Studies* (quarterly).

CHAMINADE UNIVERSITY OF HONOLULU

3140 Waialae Ave, Honolulu, HI 96816-1578
Telephone: (808) 735-4711
Fax: (808) 735-4870
E-mail: admissions@chaminade.edu
Internet: www.chaminade.edu
Founded 1955
Academic year: August to May
Pres.: SUE WESSELKAMPER
Exec. Vice-Pres. and Provost: Bro. BERNARD PLOEGER
Vice-Pres. for Finance and Facilities: DANIEL GILMORE
Dean of Enrollment Management: JOY BOUEY
Dean of Students: GRISSEL BENITEZ-HODGE
Registrar: JOHN MORRIS
Dean of Information Services and Library: LARRY OSBORNE
Library of 75,000 vols
Number of teachers: 245
Number of students: 2,800

Publications: *Aulama, Chaminade Literary Review* (2 a year)

DEANS

Behavioral Science: ROBERT SANTEE
Education: DAVID JELINEK
Humanities and Fine Arts: DAVID L. COLEMAN
Natural Sciences and Mathematics: LEE M. GOFF
Professional Studies: SCOTT SCHROEDER

HAWAII PACIFIC UNIVERSITY

1164 Bishop St, Honolulu, HI 96813
Telephone: (808) 544-0200
Fax: (808) 544-9323
E-mail: admissions@hpu.edu
Internet: www.hpu.edu
Founded 1965
Academic year: September to June
Pres.: CHATT G. WRIGHT
Sr Vice-Pres. for Academic Affairs: JOHN FLECKLES
Vice-Pres. for Research: ALISSA ARP
Vice-Pres. for Student Support Services: JEFFREY PHILPOTT
Vice-Pres. for Human Resources: LINDA KAWAMURA
Vice-Pres. for Community Relations: NANCY ELLIS
Vice-Pres. for Enrollment Management: SCOTT STENSRUD
Registrar: KELLY NASHIRO-YOSHIDA
Librarian: KATHLEEN CHEE
Library of 180,000 vols and 11,000 periodicals
Number of teachers: 587
Number of students: 7,800
Colleges of Business, Communication, Int. Studies, Liberal Arts, Natural Sciences, Professional Studies, School of Nursing
Publications: *Hawaii Pacific Review* (annual), *Kalamalama* (monthly), *The Voice* (2 a year), *Wanderlust* (annual).

BRANCH CAMPUS

Windward Campus: 45–045 Kamehameha Highway, Kaneohe, HI 96744-5297.

UNIVERSITY OF HAWAII

2444 Dole St, Honolulu, HI 96822
Telephone: (808) 956-8207
Fax: (808) 956-5286
Internet: www.hawaii.edu
Founded 1907, Univ. of Hawaii 1920
Central admin. for Univ. of Hawaii System
Academic year: August to May
10 Campuses: 3 univs and 7 community colleges in Hawaii, Honolulu, Kapiolani, Kauai, Leeward, Maui, Windward
Pres.: DAVID MCCLAIN
Vice-Pres. for Legal Affairs and Univ. General Counsel: DAROLYN LENDIO
Vice-Pres. for Research: JAMES GAINES
Vice-Pres. for Admin.: SAM CALLEJO
Vice-Pres. for Academic Planning and Policy: LINDA JOHNSRUD
Vice-Pres. for Community Colleges: JOHN MORTON
Vice-Pres. for Budget and Finance: HOWARD TODO
Vice-Pres. for Information Technology: DAVID LASSNER
Librarian: DIANE PERUSHEK
Library of 3,000,000 vols
Number of teachers: 3,310
Number of students: 45,994
Publications: *Asian Perspectives* (archaeology for Asia and the Pacific, 2 a year), *Asian Theatre Journal* (journal of the Association for Asian Performance, 2 a year), *Buddhist–Christian Studies* (journal of the Society for Buddhist–Christian Studies, annual), *Biography* (interdisciplinary biographical scholarship, quarterly), *The Contemporary Pacific* (island affairs, 2 a year), *China Review International* (reviews of scholarly literature in Chinese studies, 2 a year), *Journal of World History* (journal of the World History Association, quarterly), *Ka Ho'oilina* (journal of Hawaiian language sources, 2 a year), *Korean Studies* (multidisciplinary journal on Korea and Koreans abroad, 2 a year), *Manoa* (new writing from America, the Pacific and Asia, 2 a year), *Oceanic Linguistics* (current research on languages of the Oceanic area, 2 a year), *Pacific Science* (biological and physical sciences of the Pacific region, quarterly), *Philosophy East & West* (comparative philosophy, quarterly), *Journal of Modern Literature in Chinese* (bilingual, 2 a year), *Yearbook of the Association of Pacific Coast Geographers* (annual), *Yishu* (contemporary Chinese art, quarterly).

CONSTITUENT CAMPUSES

University of Hawaii at Hilo

200 West Kawili St, Hilo, HI 96720-4091
Telephone: (808) 974-7414
Fax: (808) 933-0861
E-mail: uhhadm@hawaii.edu
Internet: www.uhh.hawaii.edu
Founded 1941 as Hawaii Vocational School; present name 1970
Academic year: August to May
Chancellor: Dr ROSE Y. TSENG
Number of teachers: 230
Number of students: 3,457

DEANS

College of Agriculture, Forestry and Natural Resource Management: WILLIAM MOKAHI STEINER
College of Arts and Sciences: RANDY HIROKAWA
College of Business and Econ.: MARCIA SAKAI
College of Pharmacy: JOHN M. PEZZUTO

Ka Haka 'Ula O Ke'elikolani (College of Hawaiian Language): KALENA SILVA (Dir)

University of Hawaii at Manoa

2500 Campus Rd, Honolulu, HI 96822
Telephone: (808) 956-8111
Internet: manoa.hawaii.edu
Founded 1907
Academic year: August to May
Chancellor: DENISE KONAN
Number of teachers: 1,695
Number of students: 20,600

DEANS

School of Architecture: RAYMOND YEH
College of Arts and Humanities: JUDITH R. HUGHES
College of Business Administration: DAVID MCCLAIN
College of Education: Dr RANDY A. HITZ
College of Eng.: Dr WAI-FAH CHEN
School of Hawaiian, Asian and Pacific Studies: EDGAR A. PORTER
College of Languages, Linguistics and Literature: JOSEPH H. O'MEALY
School of Law: LAWRENCE FOSTER
School of Medicine: Dr EDWIN C. CADMAN
College of Natural Sciences: CHARLES HAYES
School of Nursing and Dental Hygiene: BARBARA MOLINA KOOKER
School of Ocean and Earth Science and Technology: C. BARRY RALEIGH
College of Social Sciences: RICHARD DUDA NOSKI
School of Social Work: Dr JON K. MATSUOKA
School of Travel Industry Management: Dr PAULINE J. SHELDON
College of Tropical Agriculture and Human Resources: ANDREW HASHIMOTO
Graduate Division: ALAN TERAMURA
Outreach College: PETER TANAKA

University of Hawaii – West O'ahu

96-129 Ala Ike, Pearl City, HI 96782
Telephone: (808) 454-4700
Fax: (808) 453-6075
Internet: westoahu.hawaii.edu
Founded 1976
Academic year: August to May
Divs of Humanities, Professional Studies, Social Sciences
Chancellor: GENE AWAKUNI
Number of teachers: 41
Number of students: 740.

IDAHO

ALBERTSON COLLEGE OF IDAHO

2112 Cleveland Blvd, Caldwell, ID 83605
Telephone: (208) 459-5011
Fax: (208) 454-2077
E-mail: admissions@albertson.edu
Internet: www.albertson.edu
Founded 1891
Academic year: September to June
Pres.: Dr ROBERT HOOVER
Vice-Pres. for Academic Affairs: Dr MARK SMITH
Vice-Pres. for Advancement: ROBERT HOOVER
Dir of Admissions: CHARLENE BROWN
Dean of Student Affairs: PAUL BENNION
Vice-Pres. for Admin. and Finance: CHRIS ANTON
Exec. Dir of Devt: MICHAEL VANDERVELDEN
Library Dir: CHRISTINE SCHUTZ
Library of 183,756 vols, 75,000 govt documents, 27,535 microforms, 797 current periodicals, 1,117 audio-visual items
Number of teachers: 60 (full-time)
Number of students: 761 (undergraduate)

Publications: *Quest* (3 a year), *Catalog* (annual).

BOISE BIBLE COLLEGE

8695 West Marigold St, Boise, ID 83714

Telephone: (208) 376-7731
Fax: (208) 376-7743
E-mail: rknudsen@boisebible.edu
Internet: www.boisebible.edu

Founded 1945
Private control
Academic year: July to June

Pres.: Dr CHARLES A. CRANE
Academic Dean: CHARLES H. FABER
Student Dean: NEIL KLUCKOW
Dir of Admissions: MARTIN FLAHERTY
Dir of Devt: DAVID DAVOLT
Librarian: NADENE MACK

Library of 32,500 vols
Number of teachers: 15
Number of students: 175.

BOISE STATE UNIVERSITY

1910 University Dr., Boise, ID 83725

Telephone: (208) 385-1011
Internet: www.boisestate.edu

Founded 1932

Pres.: ROBERT W. KUSTRA
Provost and Vice-Pres. for Academic Affairs: SONA ANDREWS
Vice-Pres. for Finance and Admin.: STACY A. PEARSON
Vice-Pres. for Student Affairs: MICHAEL LALIBERTE
Registrar: KRIS MARIE COLLINS
Dean of Univ. Libraries: MARILYN MOODY

Library of 583,955 vols, 1.4m. microforms, 4,513 current periodicals, 79,421 bound periodicals, 116,021 maps, 94,409 US govt documents, 5,211 linear ft of MSS, 57,929 non-print materials
Number of teachers: 987 (577 full-time, 410 adjunct)
Number of students: 17,814

DEANS

College of Applied Technology: Dr LARRY BARNHART
College of Arts and Sciences: Dr PHILLIP M. EASTERMAN
College of Business and Econ.: Dr WILLIAM LATHEN
College of Education: Dr JOYCE LYNN GARRETT
College of Eng.: Dr LYNN RUSSELL
College of Health Science: Dr JAMES TAYLOR
College of Social Sciences and Public Affairs: Dr MICHAEL B. BLANKENSHIP
Graduate College: Dr JACK PELTON
Honors College: Dr GREGORY A. RAYMOND (Dir)

IDAHO STATE UNIVERSITY

921 South Eighth Ave, Pocatello, ID 83209

Telephone: (208) 236-0211
Fax: (208) 236-4000
Internet: www.isu.edu

Founded 1901

Pres.: ARTHUR C. VAILAS
Provost and Vice-Pres. for Academic Affairs: ROBERT A. WHARTON
Vice-Pres. for Financial Services: KEN PROLO
Vice-Pres. for Institutional Advancement: Dr KENT TINGLEY
Vice-Pres. for Student Affairs: Dr LEE E. KREHBIEL
Registrar: ROSS RUCHTI
Librarian: KAY FLOWERS

Library of 995,525 vols (incl. books, bound periodicals and govt documents), 34,428

microfilms, 1,847,083 microfiches and microcards, 44,257 maps and 2,938 current periodicals
Number of teachers: 770
Number of students: 12,739

DEANS

College of Arts and Sciences: JAMES R. 'DICK' PRATT
College of Business: WILLIAM E. STRATTON
College of Education: LARRY B. HARRIS
College of Eng.: JAU KUNZE
College of Health Professions: LINDA C. HATZENBUEHLER
College of Pharmacy: JOSEPH STEINER
College of Technology: RAYANE J. MARSH
Graduate Studies: PAUL TATE

LEWIS-CLARK STATE COLLEGE

500 Eighth Ave, Lewiston, ID 83501

Telephone: (208) 792-5272
Fax: (208) 792-2822
E-mail: admissions@lcsc.edu
Internet: www.lcsc.edu

Founded 1893 as Lewiston State Normal School; present name 1971
Academic year: August to May

Offers academic, professional-technical and community college support programmes

Pres.: Dr DENE KAY THOMAS
Provost and Vice-Pres. for Academic Affairs: Dr J. ANTHONY FERNANDEZ
Vice-Pres. for Admin. Services: CHET HERBST
Dean of Student Services: ANDREW HANSON
Registrar: LEILANI ANDERSON
Dir of Library Services: SUSAN NIEWENHOUS

Library of 251,000 vols
Number of teachers: 180
Number of students: 3,325

DEANS

Academic Programmes: Dr CHRISTINE PHARR
Community Programmes: KATHY MARTIN
School of Technology: Dr ROB LOHRMEYER

NORTHWEST NAZARENE COLLEGE

623 Holly St Nampa, ID 83686-5897

Telephone: (208) 467-8011
Fax: (208) 467-8645
Internet: www.nnu.edu

Founded 1913

Pres.: Dr RICHARD A. HAGOOD
Vice-Pres. for Academic Affairs: MARK PITTS
Registrar: NANCY AYERS
Vice-Pres. for Enrollment and Marketing: ERIC FORSETH
Dir of Library Services: SHARON BULL

Library of 120,000 vols, 850 current periodicals, 600,000 vols of microforms, non-print materials and govt documents
Number of teachers: 105 (full-time)
Number of students: 1,700 (c. 1200 undergraduate, 500 graduate).

UNIVERSITY OF IDAHO

Moscow, ID 83843

Telephone: (208) 885-6111
E-mail: info@uidaho.edu
Internet: www.uidaho.edu

Chartered 1889

Pres.: TIMOTHY WHITE
Provost: DOUGLAS D. BAKER
Vice-Provost for Student Affairs: BRUCE M. PITMAN
Vice-Pres. for Research: JOHN TRACY
Vice-Pres. for Finance and Admin.: LLOYD MUES
Vice-Pres. for Univ. Advancement: CHRIS MURRAY
Registrar: RETA PIKOWSKY

Dean of the Library: LYNN BAIRD
Library of 936,738 vols, 105,493 microforms, 642,199 govt documents, 786,882 govt documents on microfiche, 207,087 maps and 5,305 current periodicals
Number of teachers: 814
Number of students: 11,027

DEANS

College of Agriculture and Life Sciences: Dr LARRY BRANEN
College of Business and Econ.: BYRON DANGERFIELD
College of Education: JEANNE CHRISTIANSEN
College of Eng.: DAVE THOMPSON
College of Forestry, Wildlife and Range Sciences: STEVEN DALEY LAURSEN
College of Law: Dr DONALD L. BURNETT, Jr
College of Letters, Arts and Social Sciences: JOE ZELLER
College of Science: EARL BENNETT

ILLINOIS

ADLER SCHOOL OF PROFESSIONAL PSYCHOLOGY

Suite 2100, 65 East Wacker Place, Chicago, IL 60601-7298

Telephone: (312) 201-5900
Fax: (312) 201-5917
E-mail: information@adler.edu
Internet: www.adler.edu

Founded 1952 as Alfred Adler Institute of Chicago; present name 1991
Private control
Academic year: June to June

Campus in Vancouver, Canada

Pres.: RAYMOND E. CROSSMAN
Vice-Pres. for Academic Affairs: Dr FRANK GRUBA-McCALLISTER
Vice-Pres. for IT and Finance: JOEL POMERENK
Vice-Pres. for Admin.: JO BETH CUP
Dir of Psychological Services Centre: Dr DAN BARNES
Dir of Institute on Social Exclusion: Dr LINDA TODMAN
Dir of Library Services: KERRY COCHRANE

Library of 10,000 vols
Number of teachers: 30.

ARGOSY UNIVERSITY

3rd Floor, 20 South Clark St, Chicago, IL 60603

Telephone: (312) 899-9900
Fax: (312) 899-1938
Internet: www.argosyu.edu

Campuses: Atlanta, Georgia; Chicago, Illinois; Dallas, Texas; Denver, Honolulu, Hawaii; Inland Empire, Nashville, Tennessee; Orange County, California; Phoenix, Arizona; San Diego, San Francisco Bay Area, California; Santa Monica, Sarasota, Florida; Schaumburg, Illinois, Seattle, Washington; Tampa, Florida; Twin Cities (Minneapolis and St Paul), Minnesota; Washington, DC

Founded 2001 following merger of American Schools of Professional Psychology, Medical Institute of Minnesota and Univ. of Sarasota
Private control

Pres.: Dr JIM OTTEN

Colleges of Business and Information Technology, Education and Human Devt, Health Sciences, Psychology and Behavioral Sciences.

AUGUSTANA COLLEGE

639 38th St, Rock Island, IL 61201

Telephone: (309) 794-7000
Fax: (309) 794-7422
Internet: www.augustana.edu

Founded 1860
Academic year: September to May

Pres.: STEVEN C. BAHLS
Dean of the College: JEFF ABERNATHY
Dean of Students: EVELYN S. CAMPBELL
Dean of Enrollment (vacant)
Registrar: LIESL FOWLER
Dir of the Library: CARLA TRACY

Library of 244,368 vols
Number of teachers: 184 (135 full-time, 49 part-time)
Number of students: 2,300

Courses in Accounting, Art, Art Education, Art History, Biochemistry, Biology, Business Admin., Chemistry, Classics, Computer Science/Mathematics, Earth Science Teaching, Econ., Elementary and Secondary Education, English, French, Geography, Geology, German, History, Mathematics, Pre-Medicine, Music, Music Education, Music Performance, Philosophy, Physics, Political Science, Psychology, Religion, Scandinavian, Sociology, Spanish, Speech Communication, Communication Sciences and Disorders, Studio Art, and Theatre.

AURORA UNIVERSITY

347 South Gladstone Ave, Aurora, IL 60506-4892

Telephone: (630) 892-6431
Fax: (630) 844-5463
E-mail: admission@aurora.edu
Internet: www.aurora.edu

Founded 1893 as Mendota Seminary; present name 1985
Private control
Academic year: September to May

Pres.: REBECCA L. SHERRICK
Vice-Pres. for Admin.: THOMAS HAMMOND
Vice-Pres. for Finance: DAVE EISINGER
Vice-Pres. for Enrollment: CAROL R. DUNN
Vice-Pres. for Student Life: MICHAEL MOSER
Vice-Pres. for Advancement: THEODORE PARGE
Vice-Pres. for George Williams Campus: WILLIAM B. DUNCAN
Provost: ANDREW P. MANION
Registrar: LYNN HAYES
Library Dir: JOHN LAW

Library of 110,000 vols and multimedia materials
Number of teachers: 155
Number of students: 4,300

DEANS

College of Arts and Sciences: Dr LORA DeLACEY
College of Professional Studies: MICK CARROLL
College of Education: DONALD WOLD
School of Experiential Leadership: Dr RITA YERKES

BRANCH CAMPUS

George Williams College of Aurora University: 350 Constance Blvd, POB 210, Williams Bay, WI 53191-0210; tel. (262) 245-5531; fax (262) 245-8505; Academic Dean LINDA OLBINSKI.

BENEDICTINE UNIVERSITY

5700 College Rd., Lisle, IL 60532-0900
Telephone: (630) 829-6000
Internet: www.ben.edu

Founded 1887 as St Procopius College

Pres.: Dr WILLIAM J. CARROLL
Provost and Vice-Pres. for Academic Affairs: DANIEL J. JULIUS (acting)
Exec. Vice-Pres.: CHARLES GREGORY
Vice-Pres. for Finance and Admin.: ROBERT HEAD
Vice-Pres. for Advancement: MICHAEL WALL
Dir of Library Services: JACK FRITTS

Library of 164,079 vols
Number of teachers: 251
Number of students: 3,000 (2,000 undergraduate, 1,000 graduate)

Publication: *Benedictine Voices Magazine* (quarterly and annual)

DEANS

Margaret and Harold Moser College of Adult and Professional Studies: Dr EILEEN KOLICH
College of Business: Dr SANDRA GILL
College of Education and Health Services: Dr ALAN GORR
College of Liberal Arts: Dr MARÍA DE LA CÁMARA
College of Science: Dr DONALD TAYLOR

BLACKBURN COLLEGE

700 College Ave, Carlinville, IL 62626
Telephone: (217) 854-3231
Fax: (217) 854-3713
Internet: www.blackburn.edu

Founded 1837
Academic year: August to May

Pres.: MIRIAM R. PRIDE
Provost: JEFFERY APER
Dean of Enrollment Management: JOHN MALIN
Dean of Students: HEIDI HEINZ
Registrar: DIANNA RUYLE
Head Librarian: CAROL SCHAEFER

Library of 81,250 vols
Number of teachers: 46 (31 full-time, 15 part-time)
Number of students: 600

Depts of Accounting, Art, Biology, Business and Econ., Chemistry, Communications, Computer Science, Criminal Justice, Education, Eng., English, History, Mathematics, Medical Technology, Performing Arts, Philosophy and Religion, Physical Education, Physics, Political Science, Pre-Law, Pre-Professional, Psychology, Spanish.

BRADLEY UNIVERSITY

1501 West Bradley Ave, Peoria, IL 61625
Telephone: (309) 676-7611
Internet: www.bradley.edu

Founded 1897
Ind. comprehensive univ.

Pres.: Dr DAVID C. BRODSKI
Provost and Vice-Pres. for Academic Affairs: Dr PETER BERGHSEY JOHNSEN
Vice-Pres. for Advancement: WILLIAM D. ENGELBRECHT
Vice-Pres. for Business Affairs: GARY ANNA
Assoc. Provost for Student Affairs: Dr ALAN GALSKY
Registrar: KATHERINE M. BEATY
Exec. Dir of Library: BARBARA A. GALIK

Library of 1.2m. items, incl. 521,000 books, bound periodicals and govt documents; 737,000 microforms
Number of teachers: 300
Number of students: 6,090 (5,271 undergraduate, 908 graduate)

DEANS

Foster College of Business Admin.: Dr ROB BAER
Slane College of Communications and Fine Arts: Dr JEFFREY H. HUBERMAN

College of Education and Health Sciences: Dr JOAN SATTLER
College of Eng. and Technology: Dr RICHARD T. JOHNSON
College of Liberal Arts and Sciences: Dr CLAIRE ETAUGH
Graduate School: Dr CONLEY STUTZ

CATHOLIC THEOLOGICAL UNION

5401 South Cornell Ave, Chicago, IL 60615-5698

Telephone: (773) 324-8000
E-mail: admissions@ctu.edu
Internet: www.ctu.edu

Founded 1968
Private control
Academic year: September to June

Pres.: DONALD SENIOR
Vice-Pres. and Academic Dean: GARY RIEBE-ESTRELLA
Vice-Pres. for Admin. and Finance: MICHAEL W. CONNORS
Registrar: MARÍA DE JESÚS LEMUS
Library Dir: MARY H. OCASEK

Library of 150,000 vols, 500 periodicals

Depts of Biblical Literature and Languages, Cross-Cultural Ministries, Historical and Doctrinal Studies, Spirituality and Pastoral Care, Word and Worship

Publication: *New Theology Review*.

CHICAGO SCHOOL OF PROFESSIONAL PSYCHOLOGY

2nd Floor, 47 West Polk Street, Chicago, IL 60605

Telephone: (312) 329-6600
Fax: (312) 644-3333
E-mail: admissions@thechicagoschool.edu
Internet: www.thechicagoschool.edu

Founded 1979
Private control
Academic year: October to August

Pres.: Dr MICHAEL HOROWITZ
Vice-Pres. for Admin.: TAMARA ROZHON
Vice-Pres. for Finance: JEFF KEITH
Vice-Pres. for Academic Affairs: Dr PAT BREEN
Registrar: ANA DEL CASTILLO
Dir of Library Services: INDU AGGARWAL

Applied Behavior Analysis, Clinical Psychology Graduate Program, Counseling Psychology Graduate Programs, Forensic Psychology Graduate Programs, Industrial Organizational and Business Psychology Programs, School Psychology, Continuing Professional Education.

CHICAGO STATE UNIVERSITY

9501 South King Dr., Chicago, IL 60628-1598
Telephone: (773) 995-2000
Internet: www.csu.edu

Founded 1867
State control
Academic year: August to May (2 terms)

Pres.: ELNORA DANIEL
Provost and Vice-Pres. for Academic Affairs: BEVERLEY J. ANDERSON
Sr Vice-Pres. for Admin. and External Affairs: SYLVIUS S. MOORE, Jr
Vice-Pres. for Student Affairs: MICHAEL BATTLE
Vice-Pres. for Planning, Research and Sponsored Programs: LINDA PETTY
Asst Vice-Pres. for Academic Personnel: DEBRAH H. JEFFERSON
Registrar: LOIS M. DAVIS
Dean of Library and Learning Resources: LAWRENCE MCCRANK

Number of teachers: 282

Number of students: 9,500

Publications: *Illinois Schools Journal, Tempo* (fortnightly), *Reflections* (monthly), *CSU Excellence Magazine* (2 a year)

DEANS

College of Arts and Sciences: RACHEL LINDSEY
College of Business: FARHAD SIMYAR
College of Education: SANDRA WESTBROOKS
College of Health Sciences: JOSEPH BALOGUN
Continuing Education and Non-Traditional Degree Programs: CECILIA BOWIE
Graduate Studies: ANITRA WARD
Honors College: RICHARD G. MILO

CHICAGO THEOLOGICAL SEMINARY

5757 South University Ave, Chicago, IL 60637
1164 East 58th St, Chicago, IL 60637
Telephone: (773) 752-5757
Fax: (773) 752-0905
E-mail: info@ctschicago.edu
Internet: www.chgosem.edu

Founded 1855
Private control

Pres.: Rev. Dr SUSAN THISTLETHWAITE
Vice-Pres. for Finance and Admin.: TERRY CORCORAN
Vice-Pres. for Devt: ED PRATT
Academic Dean: Dr W. DOW EDGERTON
Registrar: CHERYL MILLER
Library Dir: Dr NEIL GERDES

Library of 110,000 vols

Programmes of study for Master of Arts, Master of Divinity, Master of Sacred Theology, Doctor of Ministry, Doctor of Philosophy.

COLUMBIA COLLEGE

600 South Michigan Ave, Chicago, IL 60605
Telephone: (312) 663-1600
E-mail: admissions@colum.edu
Internet: www.colum.edu

Founded 1890

Pres.: Dr WARWICK L. CARTER
Assoc. Vice-Pres. and Chief of Staff: PAUL CHIARAVALLE
Provost and Sr Vice-Pres. for Academic Affairs: Dr STEVEN KAPELKE
Vice-Pres. for Academic Affairs: LOUISE LOVE
Vice-Pres. for Business Affairs and Chief Financial Officer: R. MICHAEL DeSALLE
Vice-Pres. for Student Affairs: MARK KELLY
Vice-Pres. for Campus Environment: ALICIA BERG
Vice-Pres. for Institutional Advancement: ERIC WINSTON
Vice-Pres. and General Counsel: ANNICE M. KELLY
Dean of Students: SHARON WILSON-TAYLOR
Library Dir: CONRAD WINKIE (acting)

Library of 225,000 vols, 2,000 current periodicals, 13,000 films and videos, 12,000 slides, CDs; spec. collns incl. artists' books, history of black music, history of photography, film and television scripts, music scores and pop-up and spec. format books
Number of teachers: 1,167
Number of students: 10,850 (10,200 undergraduate, 650 graduate)

DEANS

School of Liberal Arts and Sciences: DOMINIC PACYGA (acting)
School of Fine and Performing Arts: LEONARD LEHRER (acting)
School of Media Arts: DOREEN BARTONI (acting)
School of Graduate and Continuing Education: KEITH CLEVELAND (acting)

CONCORDIA UNIVERSITY

7400 Augusta St, River Forest, IL 60305-1499
Telephone: (708) 771-8300
Internet: www.cuchicago.edu

Founded 1864
Private control
Academic year: August to May

Pres.: Dr JOHN F. JOHNSON
Sr Vice-Pres. for Academics: Dr MANFRED B. BOOS
Sr Vice-Pres. for Univ. Planning: ALAN E. MEYER
Sr Vice-Pres. for Univ. Advancement: Dr ALAN C. KLAAS
Vice-Pres. for Enrollment and Marketing: EVELYN BURDICK
Vice-Pres. for Admin.: Dr DENNIS WITTE
Vice-Pres. for Finance and Chief Financial Officer: TOM W. HALLETT
Vice-Pres. for Student Life and Leadership: JEFFREY C. HYNES
Registrar: CONSTANCE K. PETTINGER
Dir of Library Services: YANA V. SERDYUK

Library of 160,000 vols, 237 periodicals, 480,000 ERIC microfiche documents
Number of students: 3,710 (1,074 undergraduate, 2,636 graduate)

DEANS

College of Arts and Sciences: Dr GARY E. WENZEL
College of Education: Dr JANE BUERGER
College of Graduate and Innovative Programs: Dr THOMAS JANDRIS

ATTACHED COLLEGE

West Suburban College of Nursing: 3 Erie Court, Oak Park, IL 60302; tel. (708) 763-6530; internet www.wscn.edu/; Chancellor Dr REBECCA A. JONES.

DEPAUL UNIVERSITY

Chicago, IL 60604
Telephone: (312) 362-8000
Internet: www.depaul.edu

Chartered as Saint Vincent's College 1898, as DePaul Univ. 1907

Campuses at Lincoln Park, Loop, Naperville, O'Hare, Oak Forest, Rolling Meadows

Pres.: Rev. DENNIS H. HOLTSCHNEIDER
Chancellor: Rev. JOHN T. RICHARDSON
Provost: Dr HELMUT P. EPP
Exec. Vice-Pres.: Dr SCOTT L. SCARBOROUGH
Sr Vice-Pres. for Advancement: MARY C. FINGER
Sr Vice-Pres. for Enrollment Management and Marketing: Dr DAVID H. KALSBEEK
Sr Exec. for Presidential Operations: JAY BRAATZ (acting)
Sec. of the Univ.: Rev. EDWARD R. UDOVIC
Vice-Pres. for Devt: JOHN BERGHOLZ
Vice-Pres. for Community, Govt and Int. Affairs: J. D. BINDENAGEL
Vice-Pres. for Student Affairs: JAMES R. DOYLE
Treas.: DAVID O. DABNEY
Vice-Pres. and Gen. Counsel: JOSÉ D. PADILLA
Vice-Pres. for Human Resources: WILLIAM SEITHEL
Vice-Pres. for Information Services: VINCENT J. KELLEN
Vice-Pres. for Facility Operations: ROBERT JANIS
Vice-Pres. for Finance: ROBERT L. KOZOMAN
Vice-Pres. for Institutional Diversity and Equity: ELIZABETH F. ORTIZ
Registrar: NANCY GALL
Dir of Libraries: LINDA MORRISSETT

Library of 906,794 vols
Number of teachers: 1,521

Number of students: 23,149

Publications: *De Paul Magazine* (quarterly), *De Paulia* (weekly), *Law Review* (2 a year), *Newsline* (monthly), *Journal of Health and Hospital Law* (monthly), *Philosophy Today* (quarterly), *Journal of Art and Entertainment* (2 a year), *Business Law Journal* (2 a year)

DEANS

College of Commerce: Dr RAY WHITTINGTON
School of Computer Science, Telecommunications and Information Systems: Dr DAVID MILLER
School of Education: Dr CLARA M. JENNINGS
College of Law: Dr GLEN WEISSENBERGER
College of Liberal Arts and Sciences: Dr CHARLES S. SUCHAR
School of Music: Dr DONALD E. CASEY
School for New Learning: Dr SUSANNE DUMBLETON
Theatre School: JOHN CULBERT

DEVRY UNIVERSITY

1 Tower Lane, Oakbrook Terrace, IL 60181
Telephone: (630) 571-7700
E-mail: info@devry.edu
Internet: www.devry.edu

Founded 2002 following merger of DeVry Institutes (f. 1931 as DeForest Training School) and Keller Graduate School of Management (f. 1973 as CBA Institute)
Private control (a division of DeVry Inc.)
Academic year: November to October

Chairman: DENNIS J. KELLER
President: DAVID J. PAULDINE
Chief Exec. Officer: DANIEL HAMBURGER
Number of students: 47,000 (incl. online)

11 Campuses in Illinois, 23 in the United States and 1 in Canada.

Areas of undergraduate study: Business Admin., Computer Eng. Technology, Computer Information Systems, Electronics and Computer Technology, Electronics Eng. Technology, Information Technology, Network Systems Admin., Technical Management, Telecommunications Management.

GRADUATE SCHOOL

Keller Graduate School of Management

1 Tower Lane, Oakbrook Terrace, IL 60181-4624
Telephone: (630) 574-1960
Fax: (630) 574-1969
Internet: www.keller.edu
Academic year: September to June

53 Centres in 16 states

Chair. and CEO: DENNIS J. KELLER
Pres. and Chief Operating Officer: RONALD L. TAYLOR
Vice-Pres. for Enrollment Management and Dean: Dr TIMOTHY H. RICORDATI
Academic Dean of Admin. and Accreditation: Dr SHERRIL HOEL
Dean of Curriculum: DAVID OVERBYE
Registrar: SANDRA BRANICK
Dir of Libraries: MARIS ROZE
Number of students: 9,000 (incl. online)

DIRECTORS

Business Admin.: JOHN HEINEMANN
Accounting and Financial Management: SETH LEVINE
Human Resource Management: Dr ROMUALD A. STONE
Information Systems Management: AMITA SUHRID
Project Management: Dr FRANK CESARIO
Public Admin.: Dr FRANK CESARIO
Telecommunications Management: AMITA SUHRID

DOMINICAN UNIVERSITY

River Forest, IL 60305
Telephone: (708) 366-2490
Fax: (708) 366-5360
Internet: www.dom.edu

Founded 1901
Academic year: May to April

Pres.: DONNA M CARROLL
Sr Vice-Pres. for Admin.: AMY MCCORMACK
Vice-Pres. for Academic Affairs: CHERYL JOHNSON-OLIM
Vice-Pres. for Institutional Advancement: STEPHEN KUHN
Vice-Pres. for Mission and Ministry: DIANE KENNEDY
Vice-Pres. for Enrollment: PAMELA JOHNSON
Registrar: MARILYN GERKEN BENAKIS
Academic Dean: MOLLY BURKE
Dean of Students: TRUDI GOGGIN
Assoc. Dean for Information Services: INEZ RINGLAND

Library of 320,000 vols
Number of teachers: 201
Number of students: 2,500

Publication: *World Libraries* (2 a year)

DEANS

College of Arts and Sciences: Dr JEFFREY CARLSON
School of Education: Sister COLLEEN MCNICHOLAS
Brennan School of Business: MOLLY BURKE
Graduate School of Library and Information Science: Prof. SUSAN ROMAN
Graduate School of Social Work: MARK RODGERS
Institute for Adult Learning: BRIAN J. WATKINS (Exec. Dir)

EAST-WEST UNIVERSITY

816 South Michigan Ave, Chicago, IL 60605
Telephone: (312) 939-0111
Fax: (312) 939-0083
E-mail: info@eastwest.edu
Internet: www.eastwest.edu

Founded 1978
Private control
Academic year: September to August

Chancellor: Dr M. WASIULLAH KHAN
Provost: Dr MADHU JAIN
Dean of Enrollment Management: MAZIN SAFAR
Registrar: AMAL MATARI
Librarian: Dr EKKEHARD-TEJA WILKE

Number of teachers: 43 full-time
Number of students: 1,128

Depts of Behavioral and Social Sciences, Biology and Physical Science, Business Admin., Computer and Information Science, Criminal Justice, Electronics and Eng. Technology, English and Communications, Mathematics, Pre-Medical, Pre-Nursing

Publication: *Eastwest Newsletter* (2 a year)

DIRECTORS

Behavioral Sciences: Dr FARID MUHAMMED
Biological and Physical Sciences Program and Electroneurodiagnostic Technology Program: Dr VERONICA DRANTZ
Business Admin.: Dr ROBERT GOODMAN
Computer Science: Dr INJOO JEONG
Electronics Eng.: BADRINATH MIRMIRA
English and Communications: Dr LARRY GORMAN
History: Dr EKKEHARD-TEJA WILKE
Mathematics: Dr SUPHA PHINAITRUP

EASTERN ILLINOIS UNIVERSITY

600 Lincoln Ave, Charleston, IL 61920-3099
Telephone: (217) 581-5000

Internet: www.eiu.edu
Founded 1895
Academic year: August to June

Pres.: LOUIS V. HENCKEN
Provost and Vice-Pres. for Academic Affairs: Dr BLAIR M. LORD
Vice-Pres. for Student Affairs: Dr DANIEL P. ADLER
Vice-Pres. for Business Affairs: JEFF COOLEY
Vice-Pres. for External Relations: Dr JILL F. NILSEN
Dean of Enrollment Management: FRANK HOHENGARTEN
Dean of Library Services: Dr ALLEN LANHAM
Number of teachers: 659 (585 full-time, 74 part-time)
Number of students: 10,963

DEANS

College of Arts and Humanities: JAMES JOHNSON
Lumpkin College of Business and Applied Sciences: DIANE HOADLEY
College of Education and Professional Studies: DIANE H. JACKMAN
College of Sciences: Dr MARY ANNE HANNER
Graduate School, Research and Int. Programs: Dr ROBERT AUGUSTINE
School of Continuing Education: Dr WILLIAM C. HINE
Honors College: Dr BONNIE IRWIN

ELMHURST COLLEGE

190 Prospect Ave, Elmhurst, IL 60126
Telephone: (630) 617-3500
Fax: (630) 617-3282
E-mail: admit@elmhurst.edu
Internet: elmhurst.edu

Founded 1871

Pres.: BRYANT L. CURETON
Exec. Vice-Pres.: JAMES KULICH
Vice-Pres. for College Relations: KENNETH E. BARTELS
Vice-Pres. of Academic Affairs and Dean of the Faculty: ALZADA J. TIPTON
Vice-Pres. for Devt: PEGGY SANDGREN
Vice-Pres. for Financial Affairs: DENISE P. JONES
Dean of Students: KATHLEEN MACKAY
Dean of Admission and Financial Aid: GARY ROLD
Librarian: SUSAN SWORDS STEFFEN

Library of 320,000 vols
Number of teachers: 121 (full-time)
Number of students: 2,681

Depts of Art, Biology, Business and Econ., Chemistry, Communication Arts and Sciences, Computer Science and Information Systems, Education, English, Foreign Languages and Literatures, Geography and Geosciences, History, Kinesiology, Mathematics, Music, Nursing, Philosophy, Physics, Political Science, Psychology, Sociology, Theology and Religion, Urban Studies.

EUREKA COLLEGE

300 East College Ave, Eureka, IL 61530
Telephone: (309) 467-3721
Fax: (309) 467-6386
Internet: www.eureka.edu

Founded 1855
Academic year: August to May

Pres.: DAVID J. ARNOLD
Vice-Pres. for Student Services: KENNETH BAXTER
Vice-Pres. for Finance and Facilities: MARC PASTERIS
Vice-Pres. for Admissions and Marketing and Dean of Admissions and Financial Aid: BRIAN SAJKO

Assoc. Academic Dean and Provost: IRENE BURGESS
Asst Dean for Records: SCOTT WIGNALL
Library Dir: VIRGINIA MCCOY
Library of 75,000 vols, 330 current periodicals
Number of teachers: 44
Number of students: 520

Divs of Business, Education, Fine and Performing Arts, Humanities, Science and Mathematics, Social Sciences.

GARRETT-EVANGELICAL THEOLOGICAL SEMINARY

2121 Sheridan Rd, Evanston, IL 60201
Telephone: (847) 866-3900
Fax: (847) 866-3957
E-mail: seminary@northwestern.edu
Internet: www.garrett.edu

Founded 1853 as Garrett Biblical Institute; present name 1974
Private control (United Methodist Church)
Academic year: September to July

Pres.: PHILIP AMERSON
Vice-Pres. for Devt: DAVID HEETLAND
Vice-Pres. for Business and Financial Affairs: TOM PETTY
Vice-Pres. for Vocation in Ministry: MARK FOWLER
Academic Dean: LALLENE RECTOR
Dean of Students: PAMELA LIGHTSEY
Dir of Academic Studies and Registrar: PEGGY MAGEE
Librarian: Dr ALVA CALDWELL

Library of 300,000 vols
Number of teachers: 36

Programmes of study for Master of Arts, Master of Divinity, Master of Theological Studies, Doctor of Ministry, Doctor of Philosophy.

GOVERNORS STATE UNIVERSITY

1 University Parkway, University Park, IL 60466-0975
Telephone: (708) 534-5000
Fax: (708) 534-8399
E-mail: gsunow@govst.edu
Internet: www.govst.edu

Founded 1969

Pres.: STUART I. FAGAN
Provost: PEGGY WOODWARD
Exec Vice-Pres.: GEBEYEHU EJIGU
Vice-Pres. for Institutional Advancement: JAMES BRITT
Registrar: ADRIENNA TROTTER
Dean of Library Services: DIANE DATES CASEY

Library of 375,000 vols.
Number of teachers: 300
Number of students: 6,200

DEANS

College of Arts and Sciences: ERIC V. MARTIN
College of Business and Public Admin.: Dr WILLIAM A. NOWLIN
College of Education: STEVEN RUSSELL
College of Health Professions: Dr LINDA SAMSON

ATTACHED INSTITUTE

Institute for Public Policy and Administration: Dir JOHN W. SWAIN.

GREENVILLE COLLEGE

315 East College Ave, Greenville, IL 62246-0159
Telephone: (618) 664-2800
Internet: www.greenville.edu

Founded 1892

Pres.: Dr V. JAMES MANNOIA, Jr

Sr Vice-Pres. for College Advancement: DAVID A. HOEG
Vice-Pres. for Enrollment Management: PEPPER DILL
Vice-Pres. and Dean of Student Devt: NORMAN HALL
Vice-Pres. for Technology and Planning: WILL KRAUSE
Vice-Pres. for Finance and Admin.: RICK RIEDER
Dean of College/Academic Affairs: PAM DAVIS
Registrar: KAY PAULSEN
Library of 114,059 vols
Number of teachers: 68 (53 full-time, 15 part-time)
Number of students: 1,230

Depts of Art, Biology, Chemistry, Communication, Digital Media, Education, English, Health, Physical Education and Recreation, History and Political Science, Language, Literature and Culture, Management, Mathematics, Modern Languages, Music, Philosophy, Religion, Physics, Psychology, Science, Sociology, Theatre
Publication: *Record* (quarterly).

HARRINGTON INSTITUTE OF INTERIOR DESIGN

2nd Floor, 200 West Madison St, Chicago, IL 60606-3433
Telephone: (877) 939-4975
Fax: (312) 939-8005
Internet: www.interiordesign.edu
Founded 1931
Private control
Pres.: PATRICK W. COMSTOCK

Library of 22,000 vols
Number of teachers: 70
Number of students: 508

Courses in Communication Design, Digital Photography, Interior Design.

ILLINOIS COLLEGE

1101 West College Ave, Jacksonville, IL 62650
Telephone: (217) 245-3030
Fax: (217) 245-3034
Internet: www.ic.edu
Founded 1829
Pres.: Dr AXEL D. STEUER
Vice-Pres. for Academic Affairs and Dean of the College: Dr ELIZABETH TOBIN
Vice-Pres. for Enrollment: SCOTT BELOBRAJDIC
Vice-Pres. for Business Affairs: FRANK G. WILLIAMS
Vice-Pres. for Advancement: ROBERT J. LANE
Vice-Pres. for Student Affairs: Dr MALINDA L. CARLSON
Registrar: Dr GLEN W. CLATTERBUCK
Librarian: MARTIN H. GALLAS

Library of 164,000 vols
Number of teachers: 52
Number of students: 975

Divs of Humanities, Natural Science, Social Sciences.

ILLINOIS COLLEGE OF OPTOMETRY

3241 South Michigan Ave, Chicago, IL 60616
Telephone: (312) 949-7400
E-mail: admissions@eyecare.ico.edu
Internet: www.ico.edu
Founded 1872
Private control
Academic year: August to May
Pres.: Dr AROL AUGSBURGER
Vice-Pres. and Dean for Academic Affairs: Dr KENT DAUM

Vice-Pres. for Patient Care Services: Dr LEONARD V. MESSNER
Vice-Pres. for Business and Finance: JOHN W. BUDZYNSKI
Vice-Pres. for Devt: DAVID KORAJCZYK
Vice-Pres. for Compliance and Risk Management: VALERIE LYNN CONRAD
Vice-Pres. for Human and Physical Resources: LAURA ROUNCE
Registrar: LAVERN YOUNG
Dir of Learning Resources: GERALD DUJSIK
Library of 22,000 vols
Number of teachers: 87 (54 full-time, 33 part-time)
Number of students: 600

Degrees offered: Doctor of Optometry, Bachelor of Science in Visual Science; in conjunction with the Univ. of Chicago, Master of Science, Doctor of Philosophy.

ILLINOIS INSTITUTE OF TECHNOLOGY

3300 South Federal St, Chicago, IL 60616-3793
Telephone: (312) 567-3000
Internet: www.iit.edu
Formed 1940 by consolidation of Armour Institute of Technology (founded 1892), Lewis Institute (founded 1896)
Pres.: Dr JOHN L. ANDERSON
Sr Vice-Pres. and Provost: Dr ALLEN S. MYERSON
Vice-Pres. for Int. Affairs: Prof. DARSH WASAN
Vice-Pres. for Enrollment and General Counsel: MARY ANN ROWAN
Vice-Pres. for Institutional Advancement: BETSY HUGHES
Dean of Student Affairs: DOUG GEIGER
Registrar: REBECCA NICHOLES
Dean of Libraries: CHRISTOPHER STEWART

4 Libraries with 522,000 vols
Number of teachers: 551 (295 full-time, 256 part-time)
Number of students: 6,199

Publications: *Employee Rights and Employment Policy, Seventh Circuit Review* (2 a year)

DEANS

College of Architecture: DONNA ROBERTSON
Armour College of Eng.: HAMID ARASTOOPOUR
College of Science and Letters: F. R. McMORRIS
Graduate College: Dr ALI CINAR
Institute of Design: PATRICK WHITNEY (Dir)
Chicago-Kent College of Law: Prof. HARLD J. KRENT
Institute of Psychology: Dr M. ELLEN MITCHELL (Dir)
Stuart School of Business: Dr HARVEY KAHALAS
Center for Professional Devt: ROBERT CARLSON (Dir)

AFFILIATED INSTITUTES

IIT Research Institute: f. 1936.
Institute of Gas Technology: f. 1941.
Center for Law and Financial Markets: Chair. Dr JOHN A. WING.
Institute for Science, Law and Technology: Dir Prof. LORI B. ANDREWS.
Center for the Study of Ethics in the Professions: Dir Dr VIVIAN WEIL.
Pritzker Institute of Biomedical Science and Engineering: Dir Dr VINCENT TURITTO.

ILLINOIS STATE UNIVERSITY

Normal, IL 61790
Telephone: (309) 438-5677
E-mail: admissions@ilstu.edu

Internet: www.ilstu.edu
Founded 1857
Pres.: Dr AL BOWMAN
Vice-Pres. and Provost: Dr JOHN PRESLEY
Vice-Pres. for Finance and Planning: Dr STEPHEN BRAGG
Vice-Pres. for Univ. Advancement: Dr DIANNE ASHBY
Vice-Pres. for Student Affairs: STEVE ADAMS
Dean of Univ. Libraries: CHERYL ELZY
Library of 1,500,000 vols, 12,200 current periodicals (printed and electronic)
Number of teachers: 1,101
Number of students: 20,975 (on-campus)

DEANS

College of Applied Science and Technology: Dr JEFF WOOD
College of Arts and Sciences: GARY A. OLSON
College of Business: Prof. DIXIE MILLS
College of Education: DEBORAH J. CURTIS
College of Fine Arts: JAMES MAJOR (acting)
Mennonite College of Nursing: Dr NANCY RIDENOUR

ILLINOIS WESLEYAN UNIVERSITY

1312 Part St, Bloomington, IL 61702
Telephone: (309) 556-1000
Fax: (309) 556-3411
Internet: www.iwu.edu
Founded 1850
Private control
Academic year: August to May
Pres.: RICHARD F. WILSON
Provost and Dean of the Faculty: BETH CUNNINGHAM
Assoc. Provost: ROGER H. SCHNAITTER
Vice-Pres. for Univ. Advancement: RICHARD WHITLOCK
Vice-Pres. for Business and Finance: KENNETH C. BROWNING
Dean of Admissions: J. R. RUOTI
Dean of Student Affairs: JAMES MATTHEWS
Assoc. Dean of the Faculty: FRANK BOYD
Registrar and Asst Provost: JACK FRICK
Librarian: KRISTIN VOGEL (acting)

Number of teachers: 143
Number of students: 2,100

Publication: *Illinois Wesleyan University Quarterly*

Schools of Music, Theatre, Art and Nursing.

JOHN MARSHALL LAW SCHOOL

315 South Plymouth Court, Chicago, IL 60604
Telephone: (312) 427-2737
E-mail: admission@jmls.edu
Internet: www.jmls.edu
Founded 1899
Private control
Academic year: August to May
Dean: JOHN E. CORKERY (acting)
Assoc. Dean for Academic Affairs: WILLIAM B. T. MOCK, Jr
Assoc. Dean for Admin.: JAMES J. KREMINSKI
Assoc. Dean for Admission and Student Affairs: Dr WILLIAM B. POWERS
Asst Dean for InstitutionalAffairs: JOHN M. McNAMARA
Assoc. Dean for Advanced Studies and Research: GERALD BERENDT
Assoc. Dean for Faculty Devt: LINDA R. CRANE
Assoc. Dean for Outreach and Planning: RORY DEAN SMITH
Registrar: JODIE PANARIELLO NEEDHAM
Library Dir: CLAIRE DURKIN (acting)

Library of 360,000 vols
Number of teachers: 57
Number of students: 1,444 (1,234 undergraduate, 210 graduate)

Advocacy and Dispute Resolution, Global Legal Studies, Tax, Employee Benefits, Fair Housing, Information Technology and Privacy, Intellectual Property, Int. Business and Trade, Real Estate.

JUDSON COLLEGE

1151 North State St, Elgin, IL 60123-1498
Telephone: (847) 628-2500
Fax: (847) 695-0712
Internet: www.judsoncollege.edu
Founded 1963

Pres.: Dr JERRY B. CAIN
Chancellor: Dr HARM A. WEBER
Provost and Vice-Pres. for Academic Affairs: Dr DALE H. SIMMONS
Vice-Pres. for Business Affairs: LAINE MALMQUIST
Senior Vice-Pres. for Advancement and Marketing: Dr C. NEAL DAVIS
Vice-Pres. for Enrollment Services: PHILIP C. GUTH
Vice-Pres. for Student Devt: LeANN PAULEY HEARD
Vice-Pres. and Sr Dean for Graduate, Adult and Continuing Education: Dr C. JIM ROHE
Registrar: ELAINE SUITTS
Library Dir: LARRY C. WILD

Library of 91,000 vols
Number of teachers: 103 (40 full-time, 63 part-time)
Number of students: 883

Programmes in Art, Design and Architecture, Business, Christian Religion, Philosophy, and Ministry, Communication Arts, Education, Exercise and Sports Sciences, Music, Science and Mathematics, Social Sciences.

KENDALL COLLEGE

900 North North Branch St, Chicago, IL 60662
Telephone: (312) 752-2000
Fax: (312) 752-2057
E-mail: admissions@kendall.edu
Internet: www.kendall.edu
Founded 1934 as Evanston Collegiate Institute; present name 1950
Private control
Academic year: November to October

Pres.: Dr NIVINE MEGAHED
Registrar: BRAD BERGERON
Dir of Devt: CHARLES JONES
Dir of Enrollment Management: KATIE KILLIAN
Dir of Finance and Business Services: DAVID DONENBERG
Dir of Library Services: IVA FREEMAN

Library of 35,000 vols
Number of teachers: 32
Number of students: 560

DEANS

School of Culinary Arts: CHRIS KOETKE
School of Business: SASCHA COCRON
Education: Dr MARTI WATSON GARLETT
Hospitality Management: JEFFREY CATRETT

KNOX COLLEGE

2 East South St, Galesburg, IL 61401-4999
Telephone: (309) 341-7000
Fax: (309) 341-7090
E-mail: admission@knox.edu
Internet: www.knox.edu/knox
Founded 1837

Pres.: ROGER L. TAYLOR
Vice-Pres. for Finance and Treasurer: THOMAS B. AXTELL
Vice-Pres. for Advancement: BEVERLY HOLMES

Vice-Pres. for Enrollment and Dean of Admission: PAUL STEENIS
Vice-Pres. for Student Devt and Dean of Students: XAVIER ROMANO
Dean of College and Vice-Pres. for Academic Affairs: LAWRENCE B. BREITBORDE
Librarian: JEFFREY DOUGLAS

Library of 295,922 vols
Number of teachers: 94
Number of students: 1,351

Publications: *Knox Bulletin*, *Knox Magazine* (quarterly), *Catch*.

LAKE FOREST COLLEGE

555 North Sheridan Rd, Lake Forest, IL 60045
Telephone: (847) 234-3100
Fax: (847) 735-6291
Internet: www.lakeforest.edu
Founded 1857
Academic year: August to May

Pres.: STEPHEN D. SCHUTT
Provost and Dean of the Faculty: JANET McCRACKEN
Vice-Pres. for Business Affairs: LESLIE T. CHAPMAN
Vice Pres. for Alumni and Devt: JAMES P. THOMPSON
Vice Pres. for Admissions and Career Services: WILLIAM J. MOTZER, Jr
Registrar: RUTHANE BOPP
Dean of Students: BETH TYLER
Librarian: JAMES R. CUBIT

Library of 265,000 vols, incl. 40,000 rare and spec. collns
Number of teachers: 117
Number of students: 1,413

4-Year liberal arts college.

LAKE FOREST GRADUATE SCHOOL OF MANAGEMENT

1905 West Field Court, Lake Forest, IL 60045-4824
Telephone: (847) 234-5005
Fax: (847) 295-3656
Internet: www.lfgsm.edu
Founded 1946
Private control
Academic year: August to June

Pres. and CEO: JOHN N. POPOLI
Exec. Vice-Pres. and Dean for Degree Programs: BRUCE J. SUCH
Exec. Vice-Pres. for Corporate Education Programs: KATHLEEN M. LECK
Vice-Pres. for Enterprise Advancement: JOAN M. STELTMANN
Vice-Pres. for Finance, Technology and Admin.: MALCOLM C. DOUGLAS
Vice-Pres. for Marketing and Communications: CURTIS P. WANG
Vice-Pres. for Alumni Relations: JOAN STELTMANN
Registrar: CHRISTINE L. PERLSTROM

Number of teachers: 120 (all adjunct faculty)
Number of students: 825.

BRANCH CAMPUSES

Chicago Campus: Federal Reserve Bank of Chicago, Suite 100, 230 South LaSalle St, Chicago, IL 60604; tel. (312) 435-5330; fax (312) 435-5333.

Schaumburg Campus: Motorola Galvin Center, 1295 East Algonquin Rd, Schaumburg, IL 60196; tel. (847) 576-1212; fax (847) 576-1213.

LEWIS UNIVERSITY

1 University Parkway, Romeoville, IL 60446-2200
Telephone: (815) 838-0500

Fax: (815) 838-9456
Internet: www.lewisu.edu
Founded 1932

Pres.: Br JAMES GAFFNEY
Provost: STEPHANY SCHLACHTER
Exec. Vice-Pres.: WAYNE DRAUDT
Vice-Pres. for Enrollment Management: RAYMOND KENNELLY
Vice-Pres. for Business and Finance: ROBERT C. DeROSE
Vice-Pres. for Univ. Advancement: DANIEL J. ALLEN
Vice-Pres. for Student Services: JOSEPH FALESE
Dean of Admissions: ANDREW SISON
Registrar: ROBERT KEMPIAK
Library Dir: LAURA PATTERSON

Library of 145,000 vols, 600 current periodicals, 2,500 videos
Number of teachers: 140 (full-time)
Number of students: 4,400 (3,400 undergraduate, 1,000 graduate)

DEANS

College of Arts and Sciences: Dr ANGELA DURANTE
College of Business: Dr RAMI KHASAWNEH
College of Education: Dr JEANETTE M. MINES
College of Nursing and Health Professions: Dr PEGGY RICE

LINCOLN CHRISTIAN COLLEGE

100 Campus View Dr., Lincoln, IL 62656
Telephone: (217) 732-3168
Fax: (217) 732-4078
E-mail: coladmis@lccs.edu
Internet: www.lccs.edu
Founded 1944
Private control
Academic year: August to May

Pres.: Dr KEITH H. RAY
Vice-Pres. for Academics: Dr TOM TANNER
Vice-Pres. for Finance: KEVIN CRAWFORD
Vice-Pres. for Stewardship Devt: GARY EDWARDS
Vice-Pres. for Church Devt: DON GREEN
Vice-Pres. for Alumni Devt: LYNN LAUGHLIN
Vice-Pres. for Student Devt: Dr MARK SCARDY
Registrar: ALAN KLINE
Library Dir: NANCY OLSON

Library of 135,000 vols
Number of students: 1,200.

LOYOLA UNIVERSITY CHICAGO

6525 North Sheridan Rd, Chicago, IL 60626
Telephone: (312) 915-6000
Internet: www.luc.edu

Founded 1870 as St Ignatius College; incorporated as Loyola Univ. 1909
Academic year: August to May

Pres.: Rev. MICHAEL J. GARANZINI
Pres. for the Medical Center: Dr ANTHONY L. BARBATO
Provost: Dr JOHN FRENDREIS
Vice-Pres. for Finance: WILLIAM G. LAIRD
Vice-Pres. for Admin.: Dr MARJORIE BEANE
Vice-Pres. for Strategic Planning: WAYNE MAGDZIARZ
Vice-Pres. for Student Services: Rev. RICHARD P. SALMIE
Vice-Pres. for Univ. Ministry: LUCIEN ROY
Vice-Pres. for Advancement: JONATHAN HEINTZELMAN
Vice-Pres. for Human Resources: THOMAS KELLY
Vice-Pres. and General Counsel: ELLEN KANE MUNRO
Vice-Pres. for Facilities: PHILIP KOSIBA
Vice-Pres. for Public Affairs: PHILIP D. HALE
Vice-Pres. and Chief Information Officer: SUSAN M. MALISCH

Dean of Libraries: ROBERT SEAL
Library of 1,400,000 vols
Number of teachers: 1,600
Number of students: 13,759

Publications: *Stritch M.D.*, *Loyola Law*, *Loyola World*, *Loyola Magazine*

DEANS

College of Arts and Sciences: Dr ISIAAH CRAWFORD (acting)
School of Business Admin.: Dr ABOL JALLIVAND
Graduate School: Dr SAMUEL ATTOH
School of Law: DAVID YELLEN
School of Social Work: Dr JACK WALL
School of Education: Dr DAVID PRASSE

LUTHERAN SCHOOL OF THEOLOGY AT CHICAGO

1100 East 55th St, Chicago, IL 60615
Telephone: (773) 256-0700
Fax: (773) 256-0782
E-mail: admissions@lstc.edu
Internet: www.lstc.edu

Founded 1962 from merger of 4 seminaries
Private control
Academic year: September to May
Pres.: JAMES KENNETH ECHOLS
Vice-Pres. for Operations: BOB BERRIDGE
Vice-Pres. for Advancement: MARK VAN SCHARREL
Registrar: PATRICIA A. BARTLEY
Dir of Library: CHRISTINE WENDEROTH

Library of 400,000 items

Publication: *Currents in Theology and Mission* (quarterly)

Areas of study incl. Biblical Studies, Environmental Ministry and Interfaith, Religion and Science, Urban Ministry.

MCCORMICK THEOLOGICAL SEMINARY

5460 South University Ave, Chicago, IL 60615
Telephone: (773) 947-6300
Fax: (773) 947-6273
E-mail: info@mccormick.edu
Internet: www.mccormick.edu

Founded 1829 as Indiana Seminary; present name 1884
Private control (associated with the Presbyterian Church)
Academic year: September to June
Pres.: Rev. Dr CYNTHIA M. CAMPBELL
Vice-Pres. for Academic Affairs and Dean of Faculty: DAVID ESTERLINE
Vice-Pres. for Seminary Relations and Devt: WALTER VERDOOREN
Vice-Pres. for Finance and Operations: DANA PETERSON
Vice-Pres. for Student Affairs: MARY PAIK
Registrar: JANE BRAWLEY
Dir of Library: CHRISTINE WENDEROTH

Library of 400,000 items
Number of teachers: 28.

MCKENDREE COLLEGE

701 College Rd, Lebanon, IL 62254
Telephone: (618) 537-4481
E-mail: colrel@mckendree.edu
Internet: www.mckendree.edu

Founded 1828 as Lebanon Seminary; present name 1830
Private control
Academic year: August to May
Pres.: Dr JAMES M. DENNIS
Provost and Dean of the College: Dr GERALD A. DUFF

Vice-Pres. for Admin. and Finance: ROBERT G. MCKINNON
Vice-Pres. for Student Affairs: Dr TODD A. REYNOLDS
Vice-Pres. for Devt: VICTORIA DOWLING
Vice-Pres. for College Relations: Dr SUSAN S. SCRIBNER
Vice-Pres. for Admissions: MARK CAMPBELL
Academic Dean, Kentucky Centers: Dr ROBERT A. GERVASI
Registrar: GRETCHEN D. FRICKE
Librarian: LIZ VOGT

Library of 70,000 vols
Number of teachers: 66
Number of students: 2,000

Divs of Business, Education, Computer Science, Humanities, Language, Literature and Communications, Nursing, Science and Mathematics, Social Science.

BRANCH CAMPUSES

Louisville Campus: 11850 Commonwealth Dr., Louisville, KY 40299; tel. (502) 266-6696; fax (502) 267-4340.

Radcliff Campus: 1635 West Lincoln Trail Blvd. Radcliff, KY 40160; tel. (270) 351-5003; fax (502) 267-4340.

Center at Scott AFB: 375 MSS/DPE, 604 Tyler St (Room 73), Scott AFB, IL 622255420; tel. (618) 256-2006; fax (618) 744-0635.

MACMURRAY COLLEGE

447 East College Ave, Jacksonville, IL 62650
Telephone: (217) 479-7000
Fax: (217) 245-0405
Internet: www.mac.edu

Founded 1846
Pres.: Dr LAWRENCE D. BRYAN
Vice-Pres. for Academic Affairs and Dean of College: DAVID FITZ
Vice-Pres. and Chief Financial Officer: WENDY LITTLE
Vice-Pres. and Chief Information Officer: MORRIS RANG III
Vice-Pres. for Enrollment Management: RHONDA CORS
Vice-Pres. for Institutional Advancment: ERIC J. GREEN
Vice-Pres. for Student Affairs: SALLY CAYAN
Library Dir: SUSAN EILERING

Library of 130,000 vols, 200 periodicals
Number of teachers: 53
Number of students: 715

Publications: *MacMurray College News*, *Montage*

Depts of Art, Biology, Business and Accounting, Chemistry, Criminal Justice, Education, English and Theatre, History and Political Science, Modern Languages, Music, Nursing, Philosophy and Religion, Physics and Mathematics, Psychology, Social Work.

MEADVILLE LOMBARD THEOLOGICAL SCHOOL

5701 South Woodlawn Ave, Chicago, IL 60637
Telephone: (773) 753-1323
Fax: (773) 256-3006
Internet: www.meadville.edu

Founded 1844
Private control (affiliated with the Unitarian Universalist Asscn)
Academic year: September to June
Pres.: LEE BARKER
Vice-Pres. for Finance and Admin.: DEBORAH BIEBER
Vice-Pres. for Institutional Advancement: JOAN WHITE
Vice-Pres. for Enrollment and Student Services: JOHN TOLLEY

Registrar (vacant)
Librarian: Rev. Dr NEIL W. GERDES
Library of 100,000 vols
Number of teachers: 9
Number of students: 101.

MIDWESTERN UNIVERSITY

555 31st St, Downers Grove, IL 60515
Telephone: (630) 969-4400
E-mail: admissil@midwestern.edu
Internet: www.midwestern.edu

Founded 1993 following merger of 3 colleges
Private control
Academic year: September to May

Pres. and CEO: Dr KATHLEEN H. GOEPPINGER
Exec. Vice-Pres. and Chief Operating Officer: Dr ARTHUR G. DOBBELEARE
Sr Vice-Pres. and Chief Financial Officer: GREGORY J. GAUS
Vice-Pres. for Clinical Education: GEORGE T. CALEEL
Vice-Pres. for Univ. Relations: KAREN D. JOHNSON
Vice-Pres. for Business Services: DEAN P. MALONE
Vice-Pres. for Human Resources and Admin.: ANGEL L. MARTY
Dean of Students: Dr TERESA DOMBROWSKI

DEANS

Basic Sciences: Dr JOHN R. BURDICK
College of Pharmacy: Dr MARY W.L. LEE
College of Health Sciences: Dr DENNIS J. PAULSON
College of Dental Medicine: RICHARD J. SIMONSEN

BRANCH CAMPUS

Glendale, Arizona Campus: 19555 North 59th Ave, Glendale, AZ 85308; tel. (623) 572-3200; e-mail admissaz@midwestern.edu; Dean of Students Dr ROSS J. KOSINSKI

DEANS

College of Pharmacy: Dr ANNE Y.F. LIN
College of Osteopathic Medicine: JAMES W. COLE

MILLIKIN UNIVERSITY

1184 West Main St, Decatur, IL 62522-2084
Telephone: (217) 424-6211
Fax: (217) 424-3993
Internet: www.millikin.edu

Founded 1901
Academic year: August to May
Pres.: DOUGLAS E. ZEMKE
Vice-Pres. for Academic Affairs: JAMIE CORNSTOCK
Vice-Pres. for Business Affairs: RONALD RECK
Vice-Pres. for Univ. Devt: PEGGY S. LUY
Vice-Pres. of Enrollment: RICH DUNSWORTH
Registrar: WALTER WESSEL
Dean of Student Life and Academic Devt: DAVID WOMACK
Dir of the Library: KARIN BOREI

Number of teachers: 249
Number of students: 2,499

Publications: *Millikin University Quarterly*, *The Decaturian* (fortnightly), *Quarterly Economic and Financial Forecast*, *Collage* (annual)

DEANS

College of Arts and Sciences: Dr RALPH CZERWINSKI
College of Fine Arts: BARRY PEARSON
Tabor School of Business: Dr JAMES DAHL
College of Professional Studies: Dr KATHY BOOKER

MONMOUTH COLLEGE

700 East Broadway, Monmouth, IL 61462
Telephone: (309) 457-2131
Fax: (309) 457-2310
E-mail: info@monm.edu
Internet: www.monm.edu

Founded 1853

Pres.: Dr MAURI DITZLER
Vice-Pres. for Academic Affairs and Dean of the Faculty: JANE JAKOUBEK
Vice-Pres. for Student Life and Dean of Students: JACQUELYN CONDON
Vice-Pres. for Finance and Business: DONALD GLADFELTER
Vice-Pres. for Advancement: J. LANCE CAVANAUGH
Registrar: SUSAN DAGIT
Library Dir: J. RICHARD SAYRE

Library of 300,000 vols
Number of teachers: 82 (full-time)
Number of students: 1,097.

MOODY BIBLE INSTITUTE

820 North LaSalle Blvd, Chicago, IL 60610
Telephone: (312) 329-4000
E-mail: pr@moody.edu
Internet: www.moody.edu

Founded 1886 as Chicago Evangelization Society; present name 1900
Private control
Academic year: August to May

Pres.: Dr MICHAEL J. EASLEY
Exec. Vice-Pres. and Chief Operating Officer: EDWARD CANNON
Vice-Pres. and General Counsel: ROBERT GUNTER
Vice-Pres. for Educational Resources: BILL BLOCKER
Vice-Pres. and Dean of Undergraduate School: THOMAS H. L. CORNMAN
Vice-Pres. and Dean of Graduate School: JOSEPH HENRIQUES
Vice-Pres. of Student Services: THOMAS SHAW
Registrar: TIMOTHY C. WIEGUT
Library Dir: JAMES PRESTON.

NAES COLLEGE/NATIVE AMERICAN EDUCATIONAL SERVICES

2838 West Peterson, Chicago, IL 60659
Telephone: (773) 761-5000
Internet: www.naes.edu

Founded 1974
Private control
Academic year: September to July

Campuses in Twin Cities in Minnesota, Fort Peck in Montana, Santa Domingo Pueblo, Leech Lake Reservation, Menominee Reservation in Wisconsin

Pres.: DORENE WIESE
Dean: LOLA HILL
Registrar: CHRISTINE REDCLOUD
Head Librarian: MELANIE CLOUD

Library of 10,000 items

Areas of study: public policy, with emphasis on tribal knowledge, community service, community devt and leadership.

NATIONAL–LOUIS UNIVERSITY

Chicago Campus, 122 South Michigan Ave, Chicago, IL 60603
Telephone: (312) 621-9650
Fax: (312) 621-3057
E-mail: nluinfo@nl.edu
Internet: www.nl.edu

Founded 1886

Campuses in Skokie, Lisle, Wheeling and Elgin (Illinois), Milwaukee and Beloit (Wisconsin), Tampa (Florida), Washington, McLean (Virginia) and Nowy Sacz (Poland)

Pres.: RICHARD J. PAPPAS
Provost: KATHRYN J. TOORDEMAN
Vice-Pres. for Enrollment and Student Services: LARRY POLSELLI
Vice-Pres. for Devt: REBECCA STIMSON
Vice-Pres. for Communications: CHRISTIAN ANDERSON
Vice-Pres. for Human Resources: THOMAS BERGMANN
Vice-Pres. for Operational Services: WILLIAM ROBERTS
Registrar: KENNETH GILSON
Dean of Library: KATHLEEN WALSH

Library of 125,000 vols
Number of teachers: 745 (320 full-time, 425 part-time)
Number of students: 14,166 (4,057 undergraduate, 10,109 graduate)

DEANS

Nat. College of Education: Dr ALISON HILSABECK
College of Arts and Sciences: Dr MARTHA CASAZZA
College of Management and Business: Dr RICHARD MAGNER

NATIONAL UNIVERSITY OF HEALTH SCIENCES

200 East Roosevelt Rd, Lombard, IL 60148
Telephone: (630) 629-2000
Internet: www.nuhs.edu

Founded 1906 as Nat. School of Chiropractic; present name 2000
Private control

Pres.: Dr JAMES WINTERSTEIN
Vice-Pres. for Academic Services: Dr CHRISTINA NICHOLSON
Vice-Pres. for Business Services: RON MENSHING
Registrar: KEITH WEROSH
Librarian: JOYCE WHITEHEAD

Library of 15,000 vols

DEANS

College of Professional Studies: Dr KEITH SMITH
College of Allied Health Sciences: Dr RANDY SWENSON
Lincoln College of Post-Professional, Graduate and Continuing Education: Dr JONATHAN SOLTYS

NORTH CENTRAL COLLEGE

30 North Brainard St, Naperville, IL 60540
Telephone: (630) 637-5100
Fax: (630) 637-5121
Internet: www.noctrl.edu

Founded 1861
Academic year: September to June

Liberal arts college

Pres.: Dr HAROLD WILDE
Vice-Pres. for Academic Affairs and Dean of Faculty: Dr R. DEVADOSS PANDIAN
Vice-Pres. for Business Affairs: PAUL H. LOSCHEIDER
Vice-Pres. for Enrollment Management and Student Affairs: LAURIE HAMEN
Vice-Pres. for Institutional Advancement: RICK SPENCER
Librarian: CAROLYN SHEEHY

Library of 150,777 vols
Number of teachers: 125 (full-time)
Number of students: 2,550.

NORTH PARK UNIVERSITY

3225 West Foster Ave, Chicago, IL 60625-4895
Telephone: (773) 244-6200
Internet: www.northpark.edu

Founded 1891

Pres.: Dr DAVID L. PARKYN
Exec. Vice-Pres. of Academic Affairs and Dean of Seminary: Dr JOHN E. PHELAN, Jr
Vice-Pres. for Univ. Relations, Communications and Devt: DANIEL TEPKE
Vice-Pres. for Estate Planning Services: LEROY M. JOHNSON
Academic Dean: CHARLES PETERSON
Dean of Enrollment: MARK OLSON
Registrar: AARON SCHOOF
Library Dir: SARAH ANDERSON

Library of 443,665 vols
Number of teachers: 125 full-time
Number of students: 2,900.

NORTHEASTERN ILLINOIS UNIVERSITY

5500 North St Louis Ave, Chicago, IL 60625-4699
Telephone: (773) 583-4050
Fax: (773) 442-4900
Internet: www.neiu.edu

Founded 1961

Pres.: Dr SALME H. STEINBERG
Provost and Vice-Pres. for Academic Affairs: LAWRENCE P. FRANK
Vice-Pres. for Finance and Admin.: MARK D. WILCOCKSON
Vice-Pres. for Student Affairs: Dr MELVIN C. TERRELL
Exec. Dir of Marketing and Communications: TERRY M. BUSH
Dir of Devt and Alumni Affairs: LEONARD IAQUINTA
Dean of Students: Dr MICHAEL T. KELLY
Dir for Admissions and Records: MIRIAM RIVERA
Univ. Librarian: BRADLEY BAKER

Library of 651,005 vols (and Regional Archives Depository)
Number of teachers: 488 (325 full-time, 163 part-time)
Number of students: 12,000

DEANS

College of Arts and Sciences: KATIE L. FORHAN
College of Business and Management: Dr VARKEY K. TITUS
College of Education: MAUREEN D. GILLETTE
Graduate College: Dr JANET FREDERICKS (acting)

NORTHERN BAPTIST THEOLOGICAL SEMINARY

660 East Butterfield Rd, Lombard, IL 60148
Telephone: (630) 620-2100
E-mail: admissions@northern.seminary.edu
Internet: www.seminary.edu

Founded 1913
Private control

Pres.: JOHN KIRN
Vice-Pres. for Advancement: TOM FOOTE
Vice-Pres. for Operations: GARY GREEN
Vice-Pres. for Academic Affairs: CHARLES HAMBRICK-STOWE
Registrar: MARILYN MAST HEWITT
Library Dir: BLAKE WALTER

Library of 50,000 vols
Number of teachers: 15
Number of students: 493.

NORTHERN ILLINOIS UNIVERSITY

1425 West Lincoln Highway, DeKalb, IL 60115-2854
Telephone: (815) 753-1000
Fax: (815) 753-8686
E-mail: admissions@niu.edu
Internet: www.niu.edu

Founded 1895
Academic year: August to May
Pres.: JOHN G. PETERS
Vice-Pres. for Admin. and Univ. Outreach: ANNE C. KAPLAN
Exec. Vice-Pres. and Provost: RAYMOND W. ALDEN III
Vice-Pres. for Research and Dean of Graduate School: RATHINDRA N. BOSE
Vice-Pres. for Student Affairs: BRIAN HEMPHILL
Exec. Vice-Pres. for Finance and Facilities: EDDIE R. WILLIAMS
Vice-Pres. for Devt and Univ. Relations: MICHAEL P. MALONE
Dean of Univ. Libraries: MARY MUNROE
Library of 2,000,000 vols, 1,343,933 govt documents, 21,267 current periodicals, 3,000,087 microfilm units
Number of teachers: 1,292
Number of students: 24,948 (incl. 2,704 extension)
Publications: *Applied and Computational Control, Signals, and Circuits* (annual), *International Economic Journal* (quarterly), *International Review of Modern Sociology* (2 a year), *Journal of Political and Military Sociology* (2 a year), *Popular Music and Society* (quarterly), *Crossroads: An Interdisciplinary Journal of Southeast Asian Studies* (2 a year), *George Eliot – George Henry Lewes Studies* (1 or 2 a year), *International Journal of Sociology of the Family* (2 a year), *The Journal of Burma Studies* (annual), *Names: A Journal of Onomastics* (quarterly), *Style* (quarterly), *Thresholds in Education* (quarterly)

DEANS

Graduate School: RATHINDRA N. BOSE
College of Business: DENISE D. SCHOENBACHLER
College of Education: CHRISTINE K. SORENSEN
College of Health and Human Sciences: SHIRLEY A. RICHMOND
College of Visual and Performing Arts: HAROLD A. KAFER
College of Eng. and Eng. Technology: PROMOD VOHRA (acting)
College of Liberal Arts and Sciences: CHRISTOPHER MCCORD
College of Law: LEROY PERNELL

NORTHWESTERN UNIVERSITY

633 Clark St, Evanston, IL 60208
Telephone: (847) 491-3741
Internet: www.northwestern.edu
Founded 1851
Private control
Academic year: September to June
Pres.: HENRY S. BIENEN
Provost: LAWRENCE B. DUMAS
Sr Vice-Pres. for Business and Finance: EUGENE S. SUNSHINE
Vice-Pres. for Admin. and Planning: MARILYN MCCOY
Vice-Pres. for Information Technology: MORTEZA A. RAHIMI
Vice-Pres. for Research: C. BRADLEY MOORE
Vice-Pres. for Student Affairs: WILLIAM J. BANIS
Vice-Pres. for Alumni Relations and Devnt: SARAH PEARSON
Vice-Pres. for Univ. Relations: ALAN K. CUBBAGE
Vice-Pres. and Chief Investment Officer: WILLIAM H. MCLEAN
Vice-Pres. and Gen. Counsel: THOMAS G. CLINE
Registrar: SUZANNE M. W. ANDERSON
Librarian: SARAH M. PRITCHARD
Library: see Libraries and Archives
Number of teachers: 2,500 full-time

Number of students: 14,108 full-time
Publications: *Tri-Quarterly* (3 a year), *Northwestern Perspective* (quarterly), *Journal of Criminal Law and Criminology* (quarterly), *Northwestern University Journal of International Law and Business* (3 a year), *The Reporter* (quarterly), *Northwestern University Law Review* (quarterly), *Northwestern Observer* (weekly)

DEANS

Weinberg College of Arts and Sciences: DANIEL I. LINZER
School of Communication: BARBARA J. O'KEEFE
School of Education and Social Policy: PENELOPE L. PETERSON
McCormick School of Eng. and Applied Science: JULIO OTTINO
Medill School of Journalism: JOHN LAVINE
School of Law: DAVID E. VAN ZANDT
Kellogg School of Management: DIPAK JAIN
Feinberg School of Medicine: LEWIS LANDSBERG
School of Music: TONI-MARIE MONTGOMERY
School of Continuing Studies: THOMAS F. GIBBONS
Graduate School: ANDREW WACHTEL

OLIVET NAZARENE UNIVERSITY

1 University St, Bourbonnais, IL 60914-2345
Telephone: (815) 939-5011
Internet: www.olivet.edu
Founded 1907
Pres.: Dr JOHN C. BOWLING
Vice-Pres. for Institutional Advancement: BRIAN ALLEN
Vice-Pres. for Finance: Dr DOUGLAS PERRY
Vice-Pres. for Academic Affairs and Academic Dean: Dr GARY STREIT
Vice-Pres. for Student Devt and Dean of Students: Rev. WALTER (WOODY) WEBB
Registrar: JIM KNIGHT
Dean of Admissions: JOHN MONGERSON
Library Dir: KATHY BOYENS
Library of 160,000 vols, 900 current periodicals, 100,000 other items (maps, pamphlets, sheet-music, microforms, govt documents)
Number of teachers: 100
Number of students: 4,400

DEANS

College of Arts and Sciences: Dr GREGG CHENOWETH
School of Professional Studies: Dr FRAN REED
School of Theology and Christian Ministry: Dr CARL LETH
School of Education: Dr JAMES UPCHURCH
School of Graduate and Continuing Studies: Dr CAROL MAXSON

PRINCIPIA COLLEGE

Elsah, IL 62028-9799
Telephone: (618) 374-2131
Fax: (618) 374-5122
E-mail: registrar@prin.edu
Internet: www.prin.edu/college
Founded 1910
Pres.: Dr GEORGE D. MOFFETT
Dean of Faculty: Dr G. CURTIS MARTIN
Registrar: PATRICIA W. LANGTON
Dir of Admissions and Enrollment: MARTHA QUIRK
Librarian: CAROL STOOKEY
Library of 125,000 vols
Number of teachers: 95
Number of students: 550.

QUINCY UNIVERSITY

1800 College Ave, Quincy, IL 62301-2699
Telephone: (217) 222-8020
Fax: (217) 228-5257
Internet: www.quincy.edu
Founded 1860; chartered 1873
Pres.: Dr DAVID SCHACHTSIEK (acting)
Exec. Vice-Pres.: PATRICIA LAYTHAM
Vice-Pres. for Business and Finance: CHARLES DAVIS
Vice-Pres. for Student Affairs: GREG WARREN
Vice-Pres. for Univ. Advancement: MICHAEL WHELAN
Vice-Pres. for Mission and Ministry: Fr JOSEPH ZIMMERMAN
Registrar: ROBERTA L. PAUL
Dean of Library and Information Resources: PAT TOMCZAK
Library of 250,000 vols
Number of teachers: 111
Number of students: 1,243

DEANS

School of Business: Dr MELISSA THOMAS
School of Education: Dr ELLEN CROWE
School of Professional Studies: Dr DAVID SCHACHTSIEK
Div. Behavioral and Social Sciences: Dr WENDY BELLER (Chair.)
Div. Fine Arts and Communication: Dr BARBARA SCHLEPPENBACH (Chair.)
Div. Humanities: Dr ROBERT MANNING (Chair.)
Div. Science and Technology: Dr E. JOSEPH EMEKA (Chair.)

ROBERT MORRIS COLLEGE

401 South State St, Chicago, IL 60605
Telephone: (312) 935-6800
Fax: (312) 935-6819
E-mail: enroll@robertmorris.edu
Internet: www.robertmorris.edu
Founded 1965
Private control
Pres.: MICHAEL P. VIOLLT
Sr Vice-Pres. for Advancement: DEBORAH DAHLEN-ZELECHOWSKI
Sr Vice-Pres. for Academics: MABLENE KRUEGER
Sr Vice-Pres. for Resource Admin.: DEBORAH BRODZINSKI
Sr Vice-Pres. for Enrollment: CANDACE GOODWIN
Vice-Pres. for Academic Admin.: LAUREN K. MILLER
Vice-Pres. for Business Affairs: RONALD M. ARNOLD
Vice-Pres. for Human Resources: NICOLE R. SKALUBA
Vice-Pres. for Information Systems: LISA CONTRERAS
Vice-Pres. for Marketing: CONNIE ESPARZA
Vice-Pres. for External Affairs: MARIE GIACOMELLI
Vice-Pres. for Student Affairs: ANGELA JORDAN
Registrar: ANEDRA BOWENS
Institutional Library Dir: SUE DUTLER
Library of 105,098 vols in 5 campus libraries
Number of students: 6,037

DEANS

Institute of Art and Design: JANICE KAUSHAL
School of Business Admin.: SHARON BRABSON
School of Computer Studies: Dr KAYED AKKAWI
Div. of Science and Humanities: PAULA DIAZ
School of Health Studies: Dr JANET HAGGERTY DAVIS

BRANCH CAMPUSES

DuPage Campus: 905 Meridian Lake Dr., Aurora, IL 60504; tel. (630) 375-8020; fax (630) 375-8000.

Bensenville Campus: 1000 Tower Lane, Bensenville, IL 60106; tel. (630) 787-7800; fax (630) 787-7802.

Orland Park Campus: 43 Orland Sq. and 82 Orland Sq., Orland Park, IL 60462; tel. (708) 226-3800; fax (708) 226-3873.

Peoria Campus: 211 Fulton St, Peoria, IL 61602; tel. (309) 636-8600; fax (309) 636-8602.

Springfield Campus: 3101 Montvale Dr., Springfield, IL 62704; tel. (217) 793-2500; fax (217) 793-4210.

Lake County Campus: 1507 Waukegan Rd, Waukegan, IL 60085; tel. (847) 578-6000; fax (847) 578-7110.

ROCKFORD COLLEGE

5050 East State St, Rockford, IL 61108

Telephone: (815) 226-4000
Fax: (815) 226-4119
Internet: www.rockford.edu

Co-educational college founded 1847

Pres.: Dr RICHARD KNEEDLER
Exec. Vice-Pres. and Dean of College: Dr STEPHANIE QUINN
Vice-Pres. for College Devt: JOHN MCNAMARA
Vice-Pres. for Student Life: HENRY ESPENSEN
Library Dir: KAREN TIBBETTS

Library of 130,000 vols and 500 current periodicals
Number of teachers: 133 (83 full-time, 50 part-time)
Number of students: 1,100

Depts of Anthropology and Sociology, Art and Art History, Biology, Chemistry/Biochemistry, Computer Science: MIS, Economics, Business and Accounting, Education, English, History, Mathematics, Modern and Classical Languages, Nursing, Performing Arts, Philosophy, Physical Education, Physics, Political Science, Psychology

Publications: *Rockford Report* (quarterly), *Decus* (3 a year).

ROOSEVELT UNIVERSITY

430 South Michigan Ave, Chicago, IL 60605

Telephone: (312) 341-3800
Internet: www.roosevelt.edu

Founded 1945
Private control

Pres.: Dr CHARLES R. MIDDLETON
Provost and Exec. Vice-Pres.: PAMELA TROTMAN REID
Vice-Pres. for Governmental Relations: J. MICHAEL DURNIL
Graduate Dean and Vice-Provost for Research: JANETT TRUBATCH
Sr Vice-Pres. for Finance and Operations: JOHN ALLERSON
Vice-Pres. and Dean of Albert A. Robin Campus: Dr ANTONIA POTENZA
Vice-Pres. for Enrollment and Student Services: MARY E. HENDRY
Vice-Pres. for Institutional Advancement: THOMAS MINAR
Vice-Pres. for Technology and Chief Information Officer: J. BRADLEY REESE
Vice-Pres. for Human Resources: GRETCHEN VAN NATTA
Registrar: MICHAEL D. FORD
Librarian: MARY BETH RIEDNER

Library of 374,000 vols
Number of teachers: 500
Number of students: 7,400

Publications: *Business and Society*, *Roosevelt University Magazine*

DEANS

Chicago College of Performing Arts: Dr JAMES GANDRE
College of Arts and Science: Dr LYNN Y. WEINER
Walter E. Heller College of Business Administration: Dr GORDON L. PATZER
College of Education: Dr JAMES GANDRA
Evelyn T. Stone Univ. College: Dr DOUGLAS G. KNERR

ROSALIND FRANKLIN UNIVERSITY OF MEDICINE AND SCIENCE

3333 Green Bay Rd, North Chicago, IL 60064

Telephone: (847) 578-3000
Internet: www.rosalindfranklin.edu

Founded 1967 as Univ. of Health Sciences/The Chicago Medical School following the merger of Chicago Medical School (f. 1912), School of Graduate and Postdoctoral Studies (f. 1968) and School of Related Health Sciences (f. 1970); renamed Finch Univ. of Health Sciences/The Chicago Medical School 1994; incorporated Dr William M. Scholl College of Podiatric Medicine (f. 1912) 2001; present name 2004
Private control
Academic year: July to June

Pres.: K. MICHAEL WELCH
Exec. Vice-Pres. and Chief Operating Officer: MARGOT SURRIDGE
Vice-Pres. for Academic Affairs: TIMOTHY HANSEN
Vice-Pres. for Institutional Advancement: PRISCILLA KHOURY
Vice-Pres. for Medical Affairs: ARTHUR J. ROSS, III
Vice-Pres. for Strategic Devt: NABIH RAMADAN
Vice-Pres. for Univ. Relations: NANCY GARN
Vice-Pres. for Research: Dr MICHAEL P. SARRAS, Jr
Registrar: CINDY FRIESEN
Dir of Library: BONNIE WATSON

Library of 119,000 vols

DEANS

Chicago Medical School: Dr ARTHUR J. ROSS
School of Graduate and Postdoctoral Studies: Dr MICHAEL P. SARRAS, Jr
College of Health Professions: Dr WENDY RHEAULT
Dr William M. Scholl College of Podiatric Medicine: Dr TERENCE ALBRIGHT

RUSH UNIVERSITY

Suite 440, 600 South Paulina St, Chicago, IL 60612

Telephone: (312) 942-5000
Internet: www.rushu.rush.edu

Founded 1972
Private control
Academic year: September to June (3 terms)

Pres.: Dr LARRY J. GOODMAN
Vice-Pres. for Academic Resources: Dr JOHN E. TRUFANT
Registrar: WILLIAM F. KARNOSCAK
Library Dir: Dr TRUDY GARDNER

Library of 59,451 vols, 2,003 periodicals
Number of teachers: 2,900
Number of students: 1,452

DEANS

Rush Medical College: THOMAS A. DEUTSCH (acting)
College of Nursing: Dr MELANIE C. DREHER
Graduate College: Dr PAUL M. CARVEY
College of Health Sciences: Dr HERB MILLER (acting)

SAINT ANTHONY COLLEGE OF NURSING

5658 East State Street, Rockford, IL 61108-2468

Telephone: (815) 395-5091
Fax: (815) 227-2730
E-mail: webmaster@sacn.edu
Internet: www.sacn.edu

Founded 1915 as Saint Anthony School of Nursing; present name 1990
Private control
Academic year: August to May

Dean and CEO: Dr TERESE ANN BURCH
Asst Dean for Admission and Student Affairs: NANCY SANDERS
Dir of Learning Resource Center: TABITHA BILYEU

Library of 1,500 vols
Number of teachers: 11.

SAINT FRANCIS MEDICAL CENTER COLLEGE OF NURSING

511 Northeast Greenleaf St, Peoria, IL 61603-3783

Telephone: (309) 655-2596
Internet: www.sfmccon.edu

Founded 1905 as Saint Francis Hospital School of Nursing; present name 1985
Private control
Academic year: August to May

Dean: Dr LOIS J. HAMILTON
Registrar: JANICE FARQUHARSON
Librarian: KARL GIBSON

Library of 6,300 vols
Number of teachers: 18
Number of students: 181 (154 undergraduate, 27 graduate)

Offers BSc and MSc in Nursing and RN accelerated path to BscN.

ST JOHN'S COLLEGE

421 North Ninth St, Springfield, IL 62702

Telephone: (217) 525-5628
Fax: (217) 757-6870
E-mail: college@st-johns.org
Internet: www.st-johns.org/education/schools/nursing

Founded 1886
Private control

Pres.: Dr JANE SCHACHTSIEK
Number of teachers: 18
Number of students: 93.

SAINT XAVIER UNIVERSITY

3700 West 103rd St, Chicago, IL 60655

Telephone: (773) 298-3000
Fax: (773) 779-9061
E-mail: admission@sxu.edu
Internet: www.sxu.edu

Founded 1846
Academic year: August to May

Pres.: Dr JUDITH A. DWYER
Provost: Dr DOMINICK HART
Vice-Pres. for Univ. Research: Dr KATHLEEN CARLSON
Vice-Pres. for Univ. Advancement: Dr STEVEN J. MURPHY
Vice-Pres. for Univ. Mission and Heritage: Dr SUSAN M. SANDERS
Vice-Pres. for Univ. Relations: ROBERT C. TENCZAR
Vice-Pres. for Business and Finance: SUSAN L. PIROS
Vice-Pres. for Student Affairs: JOHN P. PELRINE, Jr
Librarian: MARK VARGAS

Library of 123,325 vols
Number of teachers: 187

Number of students: 5,648

DEANS

College of Arts and Sciences: Dr KATHLEEN ALAIMO
School of Education: Dr BEVERLY GULLEY
School for Continuing and Professional Studies: Dr LESLIE M. PETTY
Graham School of Management: Dr JOHN E. EBER
School of Nursing: Dr ANNE R. BAVIER

BRANCH CAMPUS

Orlando Park Campus: Orlando Park, IL 60467; tel. (708) 802-6200.

SCHOOL OF THE ART INSTITUTE OF CHICAGO

37 South Wabash, Chicago, IL 60603
Telephone: (312) 629-6100
Fax: (312) 263-0141
E-mail: admiss@saic.edu
Internet: www.saic.edu
Founded 1866
Academic year: September to May
Pres.: TONY JONES
Dean: CAROL BECKER
Library: libraries with 325,000 vols, 450,000 slides, 4,000 video tapes, films, sound recordings
Number of teachers: 160 full-time and 400 part-time
Number of students: 2,588 (2,008 undergraduate, 580 graduate)
Depts of Architecture, Art Education, Art History, Art and Technology Studies, Ceramics, Design for Emerging Technologies, Fashion Design, Fiber and Material Studies, Film, Video and New Media, Liberal Arts, Painting and Drawing, Performance, Photography, Printmedia, Sculpture, Sound, Visual Communication, Visual and Critical Studies, Writing.

SEABURY-WESTERN THEOLOGICAL SEMINARY

2122 Sheridan Rd, Evanston, IL 60201
Telephone: (847) 328-9300
Fax: (847) 328-9624
E-mail: seabury@seabury.edu
Internet: www.seabury.edu
Founded 1933 following merger of Seabury Divinity School (f. 1858) and Western Theological Seminary (f. 1883)
Private control (Episcopal Church)
Academic year: September to June
Dean and Pres.: GARY HALL
Vice-Pres. for Advancement and Admin.: ELIZABETH BUTLER
Academic Dean: RUTH A. MYERS
Registrar: PEGGY PEARSON
Librarian: NEWLAND F. SMITH, 3RD
Library of 300,000 vols
Number of students: 92
Degrees in Congregational Devt, Divinity, Theological Studies, Preaching.

SOUTHERN ILLINOIS UNIVERSITY CARBONDALE

Carbondale, IL 62901
Telephone: (618) 453-2341
Fax: (618) 453-5362
E-mail: sferry@siu.edu
Internet: www.siuc.edu
Founded 1869
State control
Chancellor: Dr JOHN M. DUNN
Provost and Vice-Chancellor: Dr DON S. RICE
Vice-Chancellor for Institutional Advancement: RICKEY N. McCURRY

Vice-Chancellor for Research and Graduate Dean: JOHN A. KOROPCHAK
Vice-Chancellor for Student Affairs: LARRY H. DIETZ
Pres.: Dr GLENN POSHARD
Exec. Dir for Admin.: CATHERINE A. HAGLER
Exec. Dir for Finance: KEVIN D. BAME
Library of 2,866,748 vols, 4,566,453 microforms, 43,083 periodicals
Number of students: 21,441
Publication: *The Daily Egyptian*

DEANS

College of Agricultural Sciences: GARY L. MINISH
College of Applied Sciences and Arts: PAUL D. SARVELA
College of Business and Admin.: J. DENNIS CRADIT
College of Education and Human Services: PATRICIA ELMORE
College of Eng.: WILLIAM P. OSBORNE
College of Liberal Arts: ALAN VAUX
College of Mass Communication and Media Arts: MANJUNATH PENDAKUR
College of Science: JAMES TYRELL

SOUTHERN ILLINOIS UNIVERSITY EDWARDSVILLE

Edwardsville, IL 62026-1151
Telephone: (618) 650-2000
Fax: (618) 650-3837
E-mail: president@notes.siu.edu
Internet: www.siue.edu
Founded 1957
State control
Academic year: August to May
Chancellor: VAUGHN VANDEGRIFT
Provost and Vice-Chancellor for Academic Affairs: PAUL W. FERGUSON
Vice-Chancellor for Admin.: KENNETH NEHER
Vice-Chancellor for Student Affairs: NARBETH EMMANUEL
Vice-Chancellor for Univ. Relations and Chief Exec. Officer of the SIUE Foundation: GARY A. GIAMARTINO
Dean of the Lovejoy Library: JAY STARRATT
Library of 827,403 vols, 1,676,670 microforms, 13,472 current periodicals, 30,379 audio-visual items
Number of teachers: 770 (528 full-time, 242 part-time)
Number of students: 13,493
Publications: *Papers on Language and Literature*, *Sou'wester*

DEANS

College of Arts and Sciences: Dr KENT NEELY
School of Business: TIM SCHOENECKER
School of Dental Medicine: Dr ANN M. BOYLE
School of Education: BILL SEARCY
School of Eng.: HASAN SEVIM
School of Nursing: Dr MARCIA MAURER
School of Pharmacy: Dr PHILIP MEDON
Graduate College: Dr STEVE HANSEN

SPERTUS INSTITUTE OF JEWISH STUDIES

618 South Michigan Ave, Chicago, IL 60605
Telephone: (312) 322-1700
E-mail: college@spertus.edu
Internet: www.spertus.edu
Founded 1924
Private control
Dean of Spertus College: Dr DEAN BELL
Library of 110,000 vols; spec. colln 1,500 rare books dating from 15th–20th centuries; Chicago Jewish Archives.

TELSHE YESHIVA–CHICAGO

3535 West Foster Ave, Chicago, IL 60625
Telephone: (312) 463-7738
Private control
Pres.: Rabbi AVRAHAM LEVIN
Number of students: 74
Areas of study: rabbinical and Talmudic education.

TRINITY CHRISTIAN COLLEGE

6601 West College Dr., Palos Heights, IL 60463-0929
Telephone: (708) 597-3000
E-mail: admissions@trnty.edu
Internet: www.trnty.edu
Founded 1959
Private control
Academic year: August to May
Pres.: Dr STEVEN TIMMERMANS
Vice-Pres. for Finance and Admin.: EUN AHN
Vice-Pres. for Admissions and Marketing: PETER HAMSTRA
Vice-Pres. for Devt: LARRYL HUMME
Vice-Pres. for Student Devt: GINNY CARPENTER
Provost: Dr ELIZABETH A. RUDENGA
Dean of Academic Services: Dr BURTON J. ROZEMA
Registrar: S. DEAN ELLENS
Library Dir: MARCILLE FREDERICK
Library of 68,000 vols
Number of students: 1,310
Programmes of study in Accounting, Art and Design, Biology, Business, Business Communication, Chemistry, Church and Ministry Leadership, Communication Arts, Computer Science, Econ., Education English, Exercise Science, Geology, Greek, History, Information Systems, Mathematics, Music, Nursing, Philosophy, Physical Education, Physics, Political Science, Psychology, Science, Social Work, Sociology, Spanish, Special Education, Theology.

TRINITY INTERNATIONAL UNIVERSITY

2065 Half Day Rd, Deerfield, IL 60015
Telephone: (847) 945-8800
Fax: (847) 317-8097
Internet: www.tiu.edu
Founded 1995 following merger of Trinity Evangelical Divinity School and Trinity College; Trinity Graduate School formed 1997; Trinity Law School (formerly Simon Greenleaf School of Law) joined 1998
Campuses in California, Illinois and Florida
Chancellor: KENNETH L. MEYER
Pres.: GREGORY L. WAYBRIGHT
Exec. Vice-Pres.: JEANETTE L. HSIEH
Sr Vice-Pres. for Academic Affairs: JAMES STAMOOLIS
Sr Vice-Pres. for Education: TITE TIÉNOU
Sr Vice-Pres. for Enrollment: ROGER L. KIEFFER
Sr Vice-Pres. for Institutional Advancement: PAUL MAURER
Sr Vice-Pres. for Student Affairs: WILLIAM O. WASHINGTON
Sr Vice-Pres. for Business and Finance: MIKE PICHA
Sr Vice-Pres. for Information Technology: STEVE GEGGIE
Sr Vice-Pres. for Planning and Enrollment: ROGER L. KIEFFER
Vice-Pres. for Communications and Marketing: GARY CANTWELL
Vice-Pres. for Institutional and Auxiliary Services: LYLE ERSTAD
Registrar: ROBERT M. BOSANAC
Univ. Librarian: ROBERT H. KRAPOHL

Library of 233,000 bound vols, 170,000 microform vols, 2,000 current periodicals; 2 major microform collns of English literature from 15th–17th centuries; items from collns of Dr Carl F. H. Hentry and Dr Wilbur Smith

Publication: *Trinity Journal* (2 a year).

CONSTITUENT COLLEGES

Trinity College

E-mail: tcadmissions@tiu.edu
Internet: www.tiu.edu/college

Depts of Athletic Training, Biblical and Religious Studies, Bioethics, Business, Education, History, Human Performance and Wellness, Interdisciplinary Studies, Language, Literature and Communication, Music, Philosophy, Psychology and Sociology, Science

Dean: Dr JEANETTE L. HSIEH

DIRECTORS

School of Biblical and Religious Studies: Assoc. Prof. JAMES W. MOHLER
School of Human Performance and Well-being: Assoc. Prof. TIMOTHY J. VOSS
School of Humanities: Assoc. Prof. STEVEN D. FRATT
School of Language, Literature and Communications: Assoc. Prof. LOIS C. FLEMING
School of Science and Technology: Assoc. Prof. ANGELO G. RENTAS
School of Social Sciences: Prof. PAUL A. TWELKER

PROFESSORS

GRADDY, W. E., English
MOULDER, W. J., Biblical Studies
POINTER, S. R., History
SATRE, P. J., Music

Trinity Evangelical Divinity School

E-mail: tedsadm@tiu.edu
Internet: www.tiu.edu/divinity

Dean: TITE TIÉNOU
Theological Librarian: KEITH P. WELLS
Number of students: 1,800 (post-graduate)

PROFESSORS

AVERBECK, R. E., Old Testament and Semitic Languages
BEITZEL, B. J., Old Testament and Semitic Languages
CANNELL, L. M., Educational Ministries
CARSON, D. A., New Testament
COLE, G. A., Biblical and Systematic Theology
ELMER, D. H., Educational Ministries
FEINBERG, P. D., Biblical and Systematic Theology
HIEBERT, P. G., Mission and Anthropology
HOFFMEIER, J. K., Old Testament and Ancient Near Eastern History and Archaeology
KILNER, J. F., Bioethics and Contemporary Culture
NETLAND, H. A., Mission and Evangelism
NYQUIST, J. W., Mission and Evangelism
OSBORNE, G. R., New Testament
SENTER, M. H., Educational Ministries
VanGEMEREN, W. A., Old Testament and Semitic Languages
WOODBRIDGE, J. D., Church History and the History of Christian Thought
YOUNGER, K. L., Jr, Old Testament, Semitic Languages and Near Eastern History

Trinity Law School/Trinity California Campus

2200 North Grand Av, Santa Ana, CA 92705
Telephone: (714) 636-7500
Fax: (714) 796-7190
Internet: www.tiu.edu/law

Dean: DONALD R. MCCONNELL
Law and Humanities Librarian: Asst Prof. MICHAEL E. BRYANT
Library: Law library incl. primary sources of Federal and California law, also int. human rights colln of 3,000 vols and periodocals
Number of students: 158.

Trinity Graduate School

E-mail: tgsadm@tiu.edu
Internet: www.tiu.edu/graduate

Dean: JOYCE A. SHELTON
Number of teachers: 46
Number of students: 163 (Deerfield, California and South Florida campuses)

PROFESSORS

KILNER, J. F., Bioethics and Contemporary Culture
TIÉNOU, T., Theology of Mission.

ATTACHED INSTITUTE

Bannockburn Institute for Christianity and Contemporary Culture.

Constituent centres:

Center for Bioethics and Human Dignity: Dir Dr JOHN F. KILNER.
Center for Family Life: Dir Dr CHARLES SELL.
Center for Human Rights and Freedom: Dir WINSTON FROST.
Center of the Foundations of the Law: Dir MYRON STEEVES.
Center for Theological Understanding: Dir Dr DOUG SWEENEY.

UNIVERSITY OF CHICAGO

5801 South Ellis Ave, Chicago, IL 60637
Telephone: (773) 702-1234
Internet: www.uchicago.cdu

Founded 1890
Academic year: September to June

Pres.: ROBERT J. ZIMMER
Provost: THOMAS F. ROSENBAUM
Sr Vice-Pres. for Univ. Resources: RANDY L. HOLGATE
Vice-Pres. and Dean for College Enrollment: MICHAEL BEHNKE
Vice-Pres. and Chief Financial Officer: GREGORY A. JACKSON
Vice-Pres. for Community and Govt Affairs: HENRY S. WEBBER
Vice-Pres. and Chief Investment Officer: PETER D.A. STEIN
Vice-Pres. for Medical Affairs, and Dean of the Biological Sciences Division: Dr JAMES MADARA
Vice-Pres. for Devt and Alumni Relations: RONALD J. SCHILLER
Vice-Pres. and Dean of Students in the Univ.: KIMBERLY GOFF-CREWS
Vice-Pres. for Communication: JULIE PETERSON
Vice-Pres. and Gen. Counsel: BETH HARRIS
Vice-Pres. for Research: DONALD H. LEVY
Vice-Pres. and Chief Information Officer: GREGORY JACKSON
Registrar: THOMAS BLACK
Dir of Libraries: JUDITH NADLER
Library: see Libraries

Number of teachers: 2,159
Number of students: 12,989

Publications: *American Art: Smithsonian American Art Museum* (3 a year), *American Journal of Education* (quarterly), *American Journal of Human Genetics* (monthly), *American Journal of Sociology* (6 a year), *American Naturalist* (monthly), *Astronomical Journal* (monthly), *Astrophysical Journal* (3 a month and a monthly supplement), *Classical Philology* (quarterly), *Clinical Infectious Diseases* (2 a month), *Comparative Education Review* (quarterly), *Crime and Justice* (annual), *Critical Inquiry* (quarterly), *Current Anthropology* (5 a year), *Economic Development and Cultural Change* (quarterly), *Elementary School Journal* (5 a year), *Ethics: An International Journal of Social, Political, and Legal Philosophy* (quarterly), *History of Religions* (quarterly), *International Journal of American Linguistics* (quarterly), *International Journal of Plant Sciences* (6 a year), *Isis* (quarterly, plus *Current Bibliography* as 5th issue), *Journal of the American Musicological Society* (3 a year), *Journal of British Studies* (quarterly), *Journal of Business* (quarterly), *Journal of Consumer Research: An Interdisciplinary Quarterly*, *Journal of Geology* (6 a year), *Journal of Infectious Diseases* (2 a month), *Journal of Labor Economics* (quarterly), *Journal of Law & Economics* (2 a year), *Journal of Legal Studies* (2 a year), *Journal of Modern History* (quarterly), *Journal of Near Eastern Studies* (quarterly), *Journal of Political Economy* (6 a year), *Journal of Religion* (quarterly), *Law & Social Inquiry* (quarterly), *Library Quarterly*, *Modern Philology* (quarterly), *Ocean Yearbook* (annual), *Osiris* (annual), *Philosophy of Science* (5 a year), *Physiological and Biochemical Zoology* (6 a year), *Publications of the Astronomical Society of the Pacific* (monthly), *Quarterly Review of Biology*, *Signs: Journal of Women in Culture and Society* (quarterly), *Social Service Review* (quarterly), *Supreme Court Economic Review* (annual), *Supreme Court Review* (annual), *Winterthur Portfolio: A Journal of American Material Culture* (3 a year)

DEANS

The College: JOHN W. BOYER
School of Business: EDWARD A. SNYDER
Divinity School: RICHARD ROSENGARTEN
Law School: SAUL LEVMORE
School of Social Service Admin.: JEANNE C. MARSH
Biological Sciences Div.: Dr JAMES MADARA (acting)
Humanities: DANIELLE ALLEN
Physical Sciences: ROBERT A. FEFFERMAN
Social Sciences: JOHN MARK HANSEN
Irving B. Harris School of Public Policy Studies: SUSAN MAYER
Graham School of General Studies: DANIEL SHANNON

UNIVERSITY OF ILLINOIS

Urbana, IL 61801
Telephone: (217) 333-1000
Fax: (217) 333-9758
E-mail: presidentwhite@uillinois.edu
Internet: www.uillinois.edu

Founded 1867 (Chartered)
State control

Pres.: B. JOSEPH WHITE
Vice-Pres. for Academic Affairs: MRINALINI CHATTA RAO
Chief Financial Officer and Comptroller: WALTER KNORR

Vice-Pres. for Technology and Economic Devt: JAMES WEYHENMEYER
Vice-Pres. for Planning and Admin.: STEPHEN K. RUGG
Library: see Libraries and Archives
Number of teachers: 5,460 (full-time)
Number of students: 65,800.

CONSTITUENT CAMPUSES

University of Illinois at Chicago

601 South Morgan St, Chicago, IL 60607-7128
Telephone: (312) 413-3350
Fax: (312) 413-3393
Internet: www.uic.edu

Founded 1894

Chancellor: SYLVIA MANNING
Provost and Vice-Chancellor for Academic Affairs: R. MICHAEL TANNER
Vice-Chancellor for Admin.: JOSEPH MUSCARELLA
Vice-Chancellor for Research: ERIC A. GISLASON
Vice-Chancellor for Student Affairs: BARBARA HENLEY
Vice-Chancellor for External Affairs: WARREN CHAPMAN
Vice-Chancellor for Human Resources: JOHN LOYA
Vice-Chancellor for Devt: PENELOPE HUNT
Univ. Librarian: MARY CASE (acting)
Library of 1,900,000 vols
Number of teachers: 2,413
Number of students: 24,530

DEANS

College of Applied Health Sciences: CHARLOTTE (TOBY) TATE
College of Architecture and the Arts: JUDITH R. KIRSHNER
College of Business Admin.: STEFANIE LENWAY
College of Dentistry: BRUCE GRAHAM
College of Education: VICTORIA CHOU
College of Eng.: PRITH BANNERJEE
Graduate College: CLARK HULSE
Honors College: LON KAUFMAN
College of Liberal Arts and Sciences: CHRISTOPHER M. COMER (acting)
College of Medicine: JOSEPH A. FLAHERTY
College of Medicine at Peoria: RODNEY LORENZ (Regional Dean)
College of Medicine at Rockford: MARTIN LIPSKY (Regional Dean)
College of Medicine at Urbana-Champaign: BRADFORD S. SCHWARTZ (acting) (Regional Dean)
College of Nursing: JOAN SHAVER
College of Pharmacy: JERRY L. BAUMAN ROSALIE SAGRAVES
School of Public Health: SYLVIA FURNER SUSAN C. M. SCRIMSHAW
Jane Addams College of Social Work: CREASIE FINNEY HAIRSTON
College of Urban Planning and Public Affairs: ROBIN HAMBLETON

ATTACHED CENTRES AND INSTITUTES

Advanced Materials Research Laboratory: Dir Prof. CHRISTOS G. TAKOUDIS.
Artificial Intelligence Laboratory: Dir Prof. PETER NELSON.
Biomedical Function Imaging and Computation Laboratory: Dir Prof. BIN HE.
Cancer Center: Dir Dr RONALD HOFFMAN.
Center for Molecular Biology of Oral Diseases: Dir Prof. DONALD A. CHAMBERS.
Center for Narcolepsy Research (CNR): Dir Dr SHARON MERRITT.
Center for Pharmaceutical Biotechnology: Dir Prof. MICHAEL JOHNSON.

Center for Pharmacoeconomic Research: Dir GLEN T. SCHUMOCK.
Center for Research on Cardiovascular and Respiratory Health (CRCRH): Dir Dr JANET L. LARSON.
Center for Research in Law and Justice: Dir Dr DENNIS ROSENBAUM.
Center for Research in Periodontal Diseases and Oral Molecular Biology: Dir Dr DONALD CHAMBERS.
Center for Research on Women and Gender: Dir Dr ALICE DAN.
Center for Urban Economic Development: Dir Dr WILLIAM HOWARD.
Center for Urban Education Research and Development: Dir Prof. LASCELLES ANDERSON.
City Design Center: Dirs Dr ROBERTA FELDMAN BRENT RYAN.
Collaborative for Academic, Social and Emotional Learning (CASEL): Exec. Dir Prof. ROGER P. WEISSBERG.
Concurrent Software Systems Laboratory: Dir Prof. TAD MURATA.
Craniofacial Center: Dir Dr JOHN W. POLLEY.
Electronic Visualization Laboratory: Dirs Dr THOMAS DEFANTI, DANIEL SADIN.
Energy Resources Center: Dir Dr WILLIAM WOREK.
Fracture Mechanics and Materials Durability Laboratory: Dir Dr ALEXANDER CHUDNOVSKY.
Gerontology Center: Dir Dr DONNA COHEN.
Great Lakes Addiction Technology Transfer Center (GLATTC): Project Dir LONNETTA ALBRIGHT.
Institute for Tuberculosis Research: Dir Dr MICHAEL GROVES.
Institute on Disability and Human Development: Dir Dr DAVID BRADDOCK.
Integrated Systems Laboratory: Dir RAFFI TURIAN.
IVHS Laboratory: Dir Dr PETER NELSON.
Jane Addams Center for Social Policy and Research: Dir Dr DONALD BRIELAND.
Laboratory for Product and Process Design: Dir Prof. ANDREAS A. LINNINGER.
Manufacturing Research Center: Dir Dr SABRI CETINKUNT.
Microfabrication Applications Laboratory: Dir Prof. ALAN FEINERMAN.
MicroSystems Research Center: Dir Prof. KRISHNA SHENAI.
Midwest AIDS Training and Education Center (MATEC).
Midwest Latino Health Research, Training and Policy Center: Dir Dr AIDA GIACHELLO.
Nathalie P. Voorhees Center for Neighborhood and Community Improvement: Dir Dr PATRICIA WRIGHT.
Power Electronics Research Laboratory: Dir Prof. KRISHNA SHENAI.
Program for Collaborative Research in the Pharmaceutical Sciences: Dir Dr JOHN PEZZUTO.
Rheology Laboratory: Dir Prof. LEWIS WEDGEWOOD.
Robotics and Automation Laboratory: Dir Dr JAMES LIN.
Thermodynamics Research Laboratory: Dir Prof. G. A. MANSOORI.
Urban Transportation Center: Dir Dr ASHISH SEN.
Virtual Reality Manufacturing Institute: Dir Dr PRASHANT BANERJEE.

University of Illinois at Springfield

1 University Plaza, Springfield, IL 62703
Telephone: (217) 206-6600
Internet: www.uis.edu

Chancellor: RICHARD RINGEISEN
Provost and Vice-Chancellor for Academic Affairs: HARRY J. BERMAN
Vice-Chancellor for Student Affairs: L. CHRISTOPHER MILLER
Librarian: JANE TREADWELL
Number of students: 4,500

DEANS

College of Business and Management: RONALD MCNEIL
College of Education and Human Services: Dr LARRY STONECIPHER
College of Liberal Arts and Sciences: MARGOT I. DULY
College of Public Affairs and Admin.: (vacant)

University of Illinois at Urbana-Champaign

Urbana, IL 61801
Telephone: (217) 333-1000
E-mail: comeseeus@uiuc.edu
Internet: www.uiuc.edu

Chancellor: RICHARD HERMAN
Provost and Vice-Chancellor for Academic Affairs: LINDA KATEHI
Vice-Chancellor for Student Affairs: RENEE ROMANO
Vice-Chancellor for Research: CHARLES ZUKOWSKI

Number of teachers: 2,848
Number of students: 37,743

More than 80 centres, laboratories, and institutes on the Urbana-Champaign campus that perform research for govt agencies and industry

DEANS

College of Agricultural, Consumer and Environmental Sciences: R. A. EASTER
College of Liberal Arts and Sciences: (vacant)
College of Business: AVJIT GHOSH
College of Eng.: ILSANMI ADESIDA
College of Education: S. KALANTIS
College of Fine and Applied Arts: ROBERT B. GRAVES
College of Law: HEIDI M. HURD
College of Communications: RON YATES
College of Applied Health Sciences: T. M. GALLAGHER
School of Social Work: WYNNE KORR
Graduate College: R. P. WHEELER
College of Veterinary Medicine: H. E. WHITELY
College of Medicine at Urbana-Champaign: B. S. SCHWARTZ
Graduate School of Library and Information Science: JOHN UNSWORTH
Institute of Aviation: TOM W. EMANUEL (Dir)
Institute of Labor and Industrial Relations: NELL MADIGAN

PROFESSORS

College of Agricultural, Consumer and Environmental Sciences:
AHERIN, R. A., Farm Safety
ANSELIN, L. E., Econometrics, Regional Econ.
BAHR, J. M., Reproductive Physiology
BAIANU, I. C., Food Chemistry
BANWART, W. L., Soil Chemistry
BARRICK, R. K., Human and Community Devt
BARRY, P. J., Agricultural Finance
BELLER, A. H., Family Econ.
BELOW, F. E., Plant Physiology
BERENBAUM, M. R., Insect Ecology
BERGER, L. L., Ruminant Nutrition

MONAHAN, G. E., Business Admin., Management Science/Process Management
MONROE, K. B., Marketing
NEAL, L. D., Econ.
NEUMANN, F. L., Accountancy Executive Leadership
NORTHCRAFT, G., Organizational Behaviour
OLDHAM, G., Organizational Behaviour
PEARSON, N. D., Finance
PENNACCHI, G. G., Finance
QUALLS, W. J., Business Admin., Marketing
RASHID, S., Econ.
RESEK, R. W., Econ.
ROSZKOWSKI, M. E., Business Admin., Business Law
SETH, A., Business Admin., Strategic Management
SHAFER, W. J., Econ.
SHAVITT, S., Business Admin., Marketing
SHAW, M. J., Commerce and Business Admin., Marketing
SOLOMON, I., Accountancy
SUDHARSHAN, D., Business Admin., Marketing
TAUB, B., Econ.
VILLAMIL, A. P., Econ.
WANSINK, B., Marketing
WEISBACH, M. S., Finance
WILLIAMS, S. R., Econ.
WON, Y., Accountancy
YANNELIS, N. C., Econ.
ZIEBART, D. A., Accountancy

College of Education:
ALEXANDER, K.
ANDERSON, R.
ANDERSON, T.
ARMBRUSTER, B.
BAROODY, A.
BARRERA, R.
BRAGG, D.
BRESLER, L.
BURBULES, N.
CHADSEY, J.
CLIFT, R.
CORDOVA-WENTLING, R. M.
CZIKO, G.
FEINBERG, W.
GARCIA, G.
GREENE, J.
HALLE, J.
HARRIS, V.
HUNTER, R.
IKENBERRY, S. R.
JOHNSON, S.
LEVIN, J.
LOEB, J.
MCCLURE, E.
MCCOLLUM, J.
MCCONKIE, G.
MIRON, L.
PERRY, M.
RENZAGLIA, A.
RIZVI, F.
ROUNDS, J.
RUSCH, F.
SCHWANDT, T.
STAHL, S.
TRAVERS, K.
TRENT, W.
WARD, J.
WESTBURY, I.
WILLIS, A.

College of Engineering:
ABELSON, J. R., Materials Science and Eng.
ADRIAN, R. J., Mechanical and Industrial Eng., Theoretical and Applied Mechanics
AGHA, G., Computer Science
AHERIN, R., Agricultural Eng.
AHUJA, N., Eng.
ALKIRE, R. C., Chemical and Biomolecular Eng.
AREF, H., Physics, Theoretical and Applied Mechanics

AVERBACK, R. S., Materials Science and Eng.
AXFORD, R., Nuclear, Plasma and Radiological Eng.
BALACHANDAR, S. B., Theoretical and Applied Mechanics
BASAR, T., Electrical and Computer Eng.
BAYM, G. A., Physics
BECK, D. H., Physics
BERGMAN, L. A., Aeronautical and Astronautical Eng.
BLAHUT, R., Electrical and Computer Eng.
BRAATZ, R. D., Chemical and Biomolecular Eng.
BRAGG, M. B., Aeronautical and Astronautical Eng.
BREWSTER, M. Q., Mechanical and Industrial Eng.
BUCKIUS, R. O., Mechanical and Industrial Eng.
BUCKMASTER, J. D., Aeronautical and Astronautical Eng., Theoretical and Applied Mechanics
BULLARD, C. W., Mechanical and Industrial Eng.
BURIAK, P., Agricultural Eng.
BURTON, R. L., Aeronautical and Astronautical Eng.
CAHILL, D. G., Materials Science and Eng.
CAMPBELL, E., Computer Science
CARLSON, D. E., Theoretical and Applied Mechanics
CEPERLEY, D. M., Physics
CHANG, Y.-C., Physics
CHEW, W., Eng.
CHIANG, T.-C., Physics
CHRISTIANSON, L., Agricultural Eng.
CLEGG, R. M., Physics
COLEMAN, J., Electrical and Computer Eng.
CONRY, T. F., General Eng.
CONWAY, B. A., Aeronautical and Astronautical Eng.
COOK, H. E., Gen. Eng.
COOPER, S. L., Physics
CRAIG, J., Mechanical and Industrial Eng.
DANTZIG, J. A., Mechanical and Industrial Eng.
DAVIS, W. J., Gen. Eng.
DEBEVEC, P. T., Physics
DEJONG, G., Computer Science
DEVOR, R. E., Mechanical and Industrial Eng.
ECKHOFF, S., Agricultural Eng.
ECKSTEIN, J. N., Physics
ECONOMY, J., Materials Science and Eng.
EHRLICH, G., Materials Science and Eng.
ERREDE, S. M., Physics
FENG, M., Electrical and Computer Eng.
FERREIRA, P. M., Mechanical and Industrial Eng.
FLYNN, C.P., Physics
FRADKIN, E. H., Physics
GEIL, P. H., Materials Science and Eng.
GEORGIADIS, J. G., Mechanical and Industrial Eng.
GLADDING, G. E., Physics
GOLDBART, P. M., Physics, Gen. Eng.
GOLDENFELD, N. D., Physics
GOLLIN, G. D., Physics
GRANICK, S., Chemical and Biomolecular Eng., Materials Science and Eng., Physics
GRATTON, E., Physics
GREENE, J. E., Materials Science and Eng., Physics
GREENE, L. H., Physics
GRUEBELE, M. H., Physics
HABER, R. B., Theoretical and Applied Mechanics
HAJEK, B., Eng.
HAN, J., Computer Science
HEATH, M. T., Computer Science
HERTZOG, D. W., Physics
HESS, K., Physics
HIGDON, J. J. L, Chemical and Biomolecular Eng.

HIRSCHI, M., Agricultural Eng.
HODDESON, L., Physics
HOLONYAK, N., Physics
HRNJAK, P. S., Mechanical and Industrial Eng.
HUANG, T., Electrical Eng.
HUANG, Y. Y., Mechanical and Industrial Eng., Theoretical and Applied Mechanics
HWU, W.-M., Electrical and Computer Eng.
IYER, R., Eng.
JACOBI, A. M., Mechanical and Industrial Eng.
JACOBSON, S. H., Mechanical and Industrial Eng.
JAMISON, R. D., Materials Science and Eng.
JONES, B. G., Nuclear, Plasma and Radiological Eng., Mechanical and Industrial Eng.
KALE, L., Computer Science
KAPOOR, S. G., Mechanical and Industrial Eng.
KATZ, S., Physics
KERKHOVEN, T., Computer Science
KIM, K., Nuclear, Plasma and Radiological Eng.
KLEIN, M. V., Physics
KOGUT, J. B., Physics
KRIER, H., Mechanical and Industrial Eng.
KRIVEN, W. M., Materials Science and Eng.
KUMAR, P., Electrical and Computer Eng.
KUSHNER, M., Eng.
KUSHNER, M. J., Physics
KUSHNER, M. K., Chemical and Biomolecular Eng.
KWIAT, P. G., Physics
LAMB, F. K., Physics
LAWRENCE, F. V., Jr, Materials Science and Eng.
LECKBAND, D. E., Chemical and Biomolecular Eng.
LEE, K. D., Aeronautical and Astronautical Eng.
LEGGETT, A. J., Physics
LISS, TONY M., Physics
LOTH, E., Aeronautical and Astronautical Eng.
MAKRI, N., Physics
MARTIN, R. M., Physics
MASEL, R. I., Chemical and Biomolecular Eng.
MEDANIC, J. V., Gen. Eng.
MESEGUER, J., Computer Science
MILEY, G. H., Nuclear, Plasma and Radiological Eng.
MOSER, R. D., Theoretical and Applied Mechanics
MOUSCHOVIAS, T. C., Physics
MUNSON, D., Jr, Electrical and Computer Eng.
NAHRSTEDT, K., Computer Science
NAMACHCHIVAYA, N. S., Aeronautical and Astronautical Eng.
NAYFEH, M. H., Physics
NEWELL, T. A., Mechanical and Industrial Eng.
OONO, Y., Physics
PADUA, D., Computer Science
PANDHARIPANDE, V. R., Physics
PATEL, J., Eng.
PAULSEN, M., Agricultural Eng.
PAYNE, D. A., Materials Science and Eng.
PEARLSTEIN, A. J., Mechanical and Industrial Eng., Theoretical and Applied Mechanics
PENG, J.-C., Physics
PHILLIPS, J. W., Theoretical and Applied Mechanics
PHILLIPS, P. W., Physics
PHILLIPS, W. R. C., Theoretical and Applied Mechanics
PINES, D., Physics
PITT, L., Computer Science
PONCE, J., Computer Science
PRICE, R. L., Gen. Eng.

PRUSSING, J. E., Aeronautical and Astronautical Eng.
REED, D., Computer Science
REIS, H. L. M., Gen. Eng.
RIAHI, D. N., Theoretical and Applied Mechanics
ROBERTSON, I. M., Materials Science and Eng.
ROBINSON, I. K., Physics
ROCKETT, A., Materials Science and Eng.
ROGERS, J. A., Materials Science and Eng.
RUZIC, D. N., Nuclear, Plasma and Radiological Eng.
SALAMON, M. B., Physics
SCHULTEN, K. J., Physics
SCHWEIZER, K. S., Chemical and Biomolecular Eng., Materials Science and Eng.
SEEBAUER, E. G., Chemical and Biomolecular Eng.
SEHITOGLU, H., Mechanical and Industrial Eng.
SELEN, M. A., Physics
SENTMAN, L. H., Aeronautical and Astronautical Eng.
SHA, L., Computer Science
SHAPIRO, S. L., Physics
SINGER, C., Nuclear, Plasma and Radiological Eng.
SKEEL, R. D., Computer Science
SLICHTER, C. P., Physics
SNIR, M., Computer Science
SOCIE, D. F., Mechanical and Industrial Eng.
SOTTOS, N. R., Theoretical and Applied Mechanics
SPONG, M. W., Gen. Eng.
STACK, J. D., Physics
STEWART, D. S., Theoretical and Applied Mechanics
STONE, M., Physics
STUBBINS, J. F., Nuclear, Plasma and Radiological Eng.
SULLIVAN, J. D., Physics
THALER, J. J., Physics
THOMAS, B. G., Mechanical and Industrial Eng.
THURSTON, D. L., Gen. Eng.
TORRELLAS, J., Computer Science
TORTORELLI, D. A., Mechanical and Industrial Eng., Theoretical and Applied Mechanics
TUCKER, C. L., III, Mechanical and Industrial Eng.
VAN HARLINGEN, D. J., Physics
VANKA, S. P., Mechanical and Industrial Eng.
WAH, B., Electrical and Computer Eng.
WALKER, J. S., Mechanical and Industrial Eng.
WATSON, W. D., Physics
WEAVER, J. H., Materials Science and Eng., Physics
WEAVER, R. L., Theoretical and Applied Mechanics
WEISSMAN, M. B., Physics
WHITE, S. R., Aeronautical and Astronautical Eng.
WILTZIUS, P., Materials Science and Eng., Physics
WISS, J. E., Physics
WOLFE, J. P., Physics
ZUKOSKI, C. F., Chemical and Biomolecular Eng.

College of Fine and Applied Arts:
ALBRECHT, J. G., Architecture
ALEXANDER, R., Music
ALI, M. M., Architecture
ANDERSON, J. R., Architecture
ANTHONY, K. H., Architecture
ARENDS, M., Industrial Design
BASKINGER, M., Graphic Design
BELLAFIORE, V., Landscape Architecture
BOGNAR, B., Architecture
BULLOCK, W., Industrial Design
CAMERON, M., Music

CARLSON, W., Glass
CONLIN, K. F., Theatre
DALHEIM, E., Music
DI VIRGILIO, N., Music
DRY, C., Architecture
EWALD, M., Music
FINEBERG, J., Art History
FORREST, C. W., Urban and Regional Planning
GARNER, J. S., Architecture
GOGGIN, N., Narrative Media
GRAVES, R., Theatre
GRUCZA, L., Painting
HARKNESS, T., Landscape Architecture
HARRIS, J. B., Theatre
HEDEMAN, A. D., Art History
HEDLUND, R., Music
HEILES, W., Music
HILL, J. W., Music
HOBSON, I., Music
HOPKINS, L., Landscape Architecture
HOPKINS, L. D., Urban and Regional Planning
HOSTETTER, E., Art History
ISSERMAN, A., Urban and Regional Planning
JAKLE, J., Landscape Architecture
KEENE, J. F., Music
KENDRICK, B., Painting
KEYS, H., Theatre
KIM, M. K., Architecture
KIM, T. J., Urban and Regional Planning
KINDERMAN, W., Music
KNAAP, G. J., Urban and Regional Planning
KOVATCH, R., Ceramics
KRAMER, R., Music
MACHALA, K., Music
MARTENS, C., Foundation
McFARQUHAR, R., Theatre
METTEM, A., Foundation
NETTLES, B., Photography
OUSTERHOUT, R. G., Architecture
PERKINS, K. A., Theatre
PLUMMER, H. S., Architecture
RICHTMEYER, D., Music
ROMM, R., Music
ROWAN, D., Printmaking
SCHAFFER, P., Music
SCHWARTZ, R., Painting
SIENA, J., Music
SILVER, C., Urban and Regional Planning
SOCHA, D., Printmaking
SQUIERM, J., Narrative Media
STOLTZFUS, F., Music
STONE, S., Music
SULLIVAN, D., Theatre
THEIDE, B. J., Metals
TIPEI, S., Music
TURINO, T., Music
VAN LAARM, T., Painting
WADLEIGH, R., Dance
WARD, T. R., Music
WARFIELD, J. P., Architecture
WESCOAT, J. L., Landscape Architecture
WILLIAMS, B., Urban and Regional Planning
WYATT, S. A., Music

College of Communications:
BREWER, W. F., Psychology
CHRISTIANS, C., Communications
DASH, L., Journalism
DAVIS, S., Folklore and Folklife
DELIA, J. G., Communication and Human Relations
DENZIN, N., Sociology
DESSER, D., Cinema Studies, Speech Communication
GAINES, W., Journalism
HARRINGTON, W., Journalism
HELLE, S., Advertising and Journalism
LIEBOVICH, L. W., Mass Communications
McCARTHY, C., Education, Curriculum Theory

McCHESNEY, R. W., Library and Information Science
MERRITT, R. L., Int. Relations, Political Science
NERONE, J., Media Studies
O'GUINN, T., Advertising and Business Admin.
PRESS, A., Media Studies, Speech Communication
RICH, R., Law, Political Science
ROTZOLL, K., Advertising
SCHILLER, D., Communication, Library and Information Science
SRULL, T., Advertising
TREICHLER, P. A., Linguistics, Criticism and Interpretive Theory
WILLIAMS, B., Political Science
YATES, R., Journalism

College of Liberal Arts and Sciences:
ACCAD, E., French
ADELMAN, G., English
ALEXANDER, S., Mathematics
ALKIRE, R. C., Chemical and Biomolecular Eng.
ANGIONE, R. J., Astronomy
AUGSPURGER, C., Animal Biology, Plant Biology
BAILLARGEON, R., Psychology
BARON, D., English
BASS, J. D., Geology
BASSETT, T. J., Geography
BATZLI, G. O., Animal Biology
BAYM, G. A., Physics
BAYM, N., English
BEAK, P., Chemistry
BEARD, K., Atmospheric Sciences
BELFORD, R. L., Chemistry
BELMONT, A. S., Cell and Structural Biology, Biophysics
BERENBAUM, M. R., Entomology
BERNDT, B. C., Mathematics
BEST, P. M., Molecular and Integrative Physiology, Biophysics, Neuroscience and Bioengineering
BETHKE, C. M., Geology
BLAKE, D. B., Geology
BLAKE, N., Comparative Literature, Slavic Languages and Literature
BOCK, J. K., Psychology
BOHN, P. W., Chemistry
BOHNERT, H., Plant Biology and Crop Sciences
BOURGAIN, J., Mathematics
BRAATZ, R. D., Chemical and Biomolecular Eng.
BRECHIN, S., Sociology
BREWER, D. J., Anthropology
BREWER, W. F., Psychology
BRISKIN, D., Natural Resources and Environmental Sciences, Plant Biology
BRISTOL, E., Slavic Languages and Literature
BROWNE, G. M., Classics
BUDESCU, D., Psychology
BUSH, D. R., Plant Biology
CALDER, W. M., III, Classics
CAPWELL, C., Music
CARMEN, I. H., Political Science
CARRINGER, R. L., Cinema Studies, English
CASSELL, A. K., Italian and Comparative Literature
CHAI, L., English
CHEESEMAN, J., Plant Biology
CHEN, W.-P., Geology
CHENG, C-C., East Asian Languages and Culture
CHU, Y.-H., Astronomy
CLARK, R. A., Speech Communication
CLEGG, R. M., Physics and Biophysics
COATES, R. M., Chemistry
COHEN, N. J., Psychology
CONLEY, T. M., Speech Communication
CONTRACTOR, N., Speech Communication
CROFTS, A. R., Biochemistry
CRONAN, J. E., Microbiology, Biochemistry

DADE, E. C., Mathematics
D'ANGELO, J. P., Mathematics
DELCOMYN, F., Entomology
DELEY, H., French
DELIA, J. G., Speech Communication
DELL, G. S., Psychology
DeLUCIA, E., Plant Biology
DENMARK, S. E., Chemistry
DENZIN, N., Cinema Studies
DESSER, D., Cinema Studies
DeVRIES, A. L., Animal Biology
DIENER, E. F., Psychology
DLOTT, D. D., Chemistry
DRASGOW, F., Psychology
DUTTA, S., Mathematics
FAGYAL, Z., French
FENG, A. S., Molecular and Integrative Physiology, Biophysics, Bioengineering, and Neuroscience
FITZGERALD, L., Psychology
FOSSUM, R. M., Mathematics
FRANCIS, G. K., Mathematics
FRAZZETTA, T. H., Animal Biology
FRIEDMAN, P., English
FRITZSCHE, P., History
FÜREDI, Z., Mathematics
GABRIEL, M., Psychology
GARBER, P. A., Anthropology
GARCIA, P., Agricultural Econ.
GARRETT, P., English
GENNIS, R. B., Biochemistry, Chemistry, Biophysics
GERLACH, U. H., Germanic Languages and Literature
GERLT, J. A., Biochemistry, Chemistry and Biophysics, Basic Medical Science
GEWIRTH, A. A., Chemistry
GIROLAMI, G. S., Chemistry
GLASER, M., Biochemistry, Basic Medical Sciences
GOLATO, P., French
GOLD, P. E., Psychology
GOODMAN, D. G., East Asian Languages and Culture
GOTTLIEB, A., Anthropology
GRAHAM, P., English
GRANICK, S., Chemical and Biomolecular Eng.
GRAY, M. E., Entomology
GRAYSON, D. R., Mathematics
GREENOUGH, W. T., Psychology
GROVE, D., Anthropology
GRUEBELE, M., Chemistry
GUIBBOR, A., English
GUMPORT, R. I., Biochemistry, Basic Medical Sciences
HABOUSH, W., Mathematics
HADLEY, A. O., French
HANNON, B. M., Geography
HAWISHER, G. E., English
HE, X., Statistics
HELLER, W., Psychology
HELMAN, S. I., Molecular and Integrative Physiology, Biophysics, and Bioengineering
HENSON, C. W., Mathematics
HEWINGS, G. J. D., Geography
HIGDON, J. J. L., Chemical and Biomolecular Eng.
HILDEBRAND, A. J., Mathematics
HINKKANEN, A., Mathematics
HITCHINS, K., History
HOCK, H. H., Linguistics
HSUI, A. T., Geology
HUALDE, J. I., Linguistics and Spanish, Italian, and Portuguese
HUBERT, L., Psychology
IBEN, I., Jr, Physics
IMREY, P., Statistics
IRWIN, D., Psychology
IRWIN, M. E., Entomology
IVANOV, S. V., Mathematics
JACOBSON, H., Classics
JAEGER, C. S., Cinema Studies
JAEGER, S., Comparative Literature
JAHER, F. C., Cinema Studies

JAHIEL, E., Cinema Studies, French
JAKLE, J. A., Geography
JAKOBSSON, E., Molecular and Integrative Physiology, Biochemistry, Biophysics, Bioengineering, and Neuroscience
JOCKUSCH, C. G., Mathematics
JOHNSON, D. L., Geography
JURASKA, J., Psychology
KALINKE, M. E., Germanic Languages and Literature
KATZ, S., Mathematics
KATZENELLENBOGEN, B. S., Molecular and Integrative Physiology
KATZENELLENBOGEN, J. A., Chemistry
KELLER, J. D., Anthropology
KELLY, B., English
KEMPER, B. W., Molecular and Integrative Physiology, Cell and Structural Biology
KIBBEE, D., French
KIM, C. W., Linguistics, East Asian Languages and Culture
KIRKPATRICK, R. J., Geology
KLEMPERER, W. G., Chemistry
KLEPINGER, L. L., Anthropology
KLUEGEL, J., Sociology
KNOTT, J. H., Political Science
KOENKER, D. P., History
KOSTOCHKA, A. V., Mathematics
KRAMER, A., Psychology
KRANZ, D. M., Biochemistry
KUKLINSKI, J. H., Political Science
LAMB, F. K., Physics
LAUGHLIN, P. R., Psychology
LAUTERBUR, P. C., Chemistry
LECKBAND, D. E., Chemistry, Chemical and Biomolecular Engineering
LEHMAN, F. K., Anthropology
LEWIS, R. B., Anthropology
LIEBERMAN, L., English
LISY, J. M., Chemistry
LOEB, P. A., Mathematics
LOTZ, H. P., Mathematics
LOVE, J. L., History
MAHER, P., Philosophy
MAK, M., Atmospheric Sciences
MAKRI, N., Chemistry
MALL, L., French
MALPELI, J. G., Psychology
MANGELSDORF, S., Psychology
MARDEN, J., Statistics
MARSHAK, S., Geology
MARTINSEK, A., Statistics
MASEL,R.I.,ChemicalandBiomolecularEng.
MATHY, J.-P., French, Comparative Literature
McCARTHY, T., Philosophy
McDONALD, J. D., Chemistry
McDONALD, R., Psychology
McKIM, R., Religious Studies, Philosophy
McLAFFERTY, S., Geography
McLINDEN, L., Mathematics
McMAHAN, J., Philosophy
MICHELSON, B., English
MILES, J. B., Mathematics
MILLER, G., Psychology
MILLER, P., Psychology
MILLER, P. J., Speech Communication
MOHR, R., Philosophy
MOORE, J. S., Chemistry
MORGAN, J. L., Linguistics
MORRISSEY, J. H., Biochemistry
MORTIMER, A., French
MOUSCHOVIAS, T., Physics and Astrophysics
MURAV, H., Slavic Languages and Literature, Comparative Literature
MUSUMECCI, A., Italian
NARDULLI, P. F., Political Science
NEDERVEEN-PIETERSE, J., Sociology
NEELY, C., English
NIKOLAEV, I., Mathematics
NUZZO, R., Chemistry
O'KEEFE, D. J., Speech Communication
OLDFIELD, E., Chemistry
ONO, K., Asian American Studies
ORDAL, G. W., Biochemistry, Basic Medical Science

ORT, D. R., Plant Biology
PACKARD, J., East Asian Languages and Culture
PAHRE, R., Political Science
PAIGE, K. N., Animal Biology
PALENCIA-ROTH, M., Comparative Literature
PALMORE, J. I., Mathematics
PANDHARIPANDE, R., Linguistics, Religious Studies, Sanskrit, Comparative Literature
PANDHARIPANDE, V., Physics
PARK, D., Psychology
PARKER, R. D., English
PHILLIPS, P. W., Physics
PHILLIPS, T. L., Plant Biology
PILLAY, A., Mathematics
PINDERHUGHES, D. M., Political Science, Afro-American Studies
PINES, D., Physics and Electrical and Computer Eng.
PITARD, W. T., Religious Studies
PORTON, G. G., Religious Studies, History, Comparative Literature
POWERS, R., English
PRESS, A., Speech Communication
QUIRK, P. J., Political Science
RAPPAPORT, J., Psychology
RAUBER, R., Atmospheric Sciences
RAUCHFUSS, T. B., Chemistry
REZNICK, B., Mathematics
RHOADS, B. L., Geography
RICH, R. F., Political Science
ROBERTSON, H. M., Entomology
ROBINSON, D. J. S., Mathematics
ROBINSON, G. E., Entomology, Political Science
ROBINSON, S. K., Animal Biology
ROBINSON, W., Atmospheric Sciences
ROEDIGER, D., Afro-American studies
ROGERS, J. A., Chemistry
RONCADOR, S. M., Brazilian, Portuguese and Lusophone Literatures
ROSENBLATT, J., Mathematics
ROSS, B., Psychology
ROTMAN, J., Mathematics
ROY, E., Psychology
RUAN, Z.-J., Mathematics
SAHINIDIS, N. V., Chemical and Biomolecular Eng.
SANSONE, D., Classics
SCHACHT, R., Philosophy
SCHEELINE, A., Chemistry
SCHEHR, L., French
SCHLESINGER, M., Atmospheric Sciences
SCHULER, M. A., Cell and Structural Biology, Biochemistry
SCHULTEN, K., Chemistry
SCHUPP, P., Mathematics
SCHWEIZER, K. S., Chemistry, Chemical and Biomolecular Eng.
SEEBAUER, E. G., Chemical and Biomolecular Eng.
SEIGLER, D. S., Plant Biology
SHAFTER, A. W., Astronomy
SHAPIRO, M., English
SHAPIRO, S. L., Physics and Astronomy
SHAPLEY, J. R., Chemistry
SHAPLEY, P. A., Chemistry
SHEARER, C. A., Plant Biology
SHERWOOD, O. D., Molecular and Integrative Physiology
SHOBEN, E. J., Psychology
SIMPSON, D., Statistics
SLIGAR, S. G., Chemistry
SMITH, S. G., Chemistry
SNIEZEK, J. A., Psychology
SOFFER, O., Anthropology
SOUSA, R., Portuguese, Spanish and Comparative Literature
SRULL, T. K., Psychology
STEFFEY, K. L., Entomology
STILLINGER, N. B., English
STOLARSKY, K. B., Mathematics
SULLIVAN, Z., English
SUSLICK, K. S., Chemistry

SWANSON, D. L., Political Science, Speech Communication
SWEEDLER, J. V., Chemistry
TALBOT, E. J., French
TEARE, S., Electrical Eng.
THOMPSON, L. A., Astronomy
THOMPSON, J., English
TOBY, R. P., East Asian Languages and Culture
TODOROVA, M., History
TUMANOV, A. E., Mathematics
ULLOM, S. V., Mathematics
UNNEVEHR, L., Agricultural and Consumer Econ.
VALENTE, J., English
VAN DEN DRIES, L., Mathematics
WALLACE, J., Philosophy
WALSH, J., Atmospheric Sciences
WASSERMAN, S., Psychology, Statistics
WATSON, W. D., Physics and Astronomy
WATTS, E., English
WEATHERHEAD, P. J., Animal Biology, Natural Resources, Environmental Sciences
WEBBINK, R. F., Astronomy
WEINZIERL, R. A., Entomology
WEISSBERG, R., Political Science
WEST, D. B., Mathematics
WHITT, G. S., Animal Biology
WHITTEN, N. E., Jr, Anthropology
WICKENS, C., Psychology
WIECKOWSKI, A., Chemistry
WILCOX, J., Spanish
WILHELMSON, R., Atmospheric Sciences
WILSON, B. J., Speech Communication
WOESE, C. I., Microbiology and Animal Biology
WRAIGHT, C. A., Biochemistry and Plant Biology
WRIGHT, D., English
WRIGHT, R., Germanic Languages and Literature, Cinema Studies
WU, J.-M., Mathematics
WUEBBLES, D. J., Atmospheric Sciences
YU, G. T., Political Science
ZIMMERMAN, S. C., Chemistry
ZINNES, D., Political Science
ZUKOSKI, C. F., Chemical and Biomolecular Eng.

College of Applied Life Studies:
BOILEAU, R. A., Kinesiology
CHAMBERS, R. D., Speech and Hearing Science
CHODZKO-ZAJKO, W., Kinesiology
FESENMAIER, D. R., Leisure Studies
GALLAGHER, T. M., Speech and Hearing Science
GOOLER, D. M., Speech and Hearing Science
HENGST, J., Speech and Hearing Science
IWAMOTO, G., Kinesiology
JOHNSON, C. J., Speech and Hearing Science
KUEHN, D. P., Speech and Hearing Science
LANSING, C. R., Speech and Hearing Science
MCAULEY, E., Kinesiology
O'ROURKE, T., Community Health
PERLMAN, A. L., Speech and Hearing Science
PROCTOR, F. A., Speech and Hearing Science
REIS, J., Community Health
SCHIRO-GEIST, C., Community Health
WATKIN, K. L., Speech and Hearing Science
WATKINS, R. V., Speech and Hearing Science
YAIRI, E., Speech and Hearing Science

College of Veterinary Medicine:
ANDREWS, J. J., Veterinary Pathobiology
ARDEN, W. A., Veterinary Clinical Medicine
BEASLEY, V. R., Veterinary Biosciences
BENSON, G. J., Veterinary Clinical Medicine, Veterinary Anesthesiology and Comparative Medicine

CAMPBELL, K. L., Veterinary Clinical Medicine
CLARKSON, R. B., Veterinary Clinical Medicine, Veterinary Biosciences
COOKE, P. S., Veterinary Biosciences
DOCAMPO, R., Veterinary Pathobiology
GOETZ, T. E., Veterinary Clinical Medicine
GROSS, D. R., Veterinary Biosciences
HANSEN, L. G., Veterinary Biosciences
HASCHEK-HOCK, W. M., Veterinary Pathobiology
HESS, R. A., Veterinary Biosciences
JOHNSON, A. L., Veterinary Clinical Medicine
KITRON, U. D., Veterinary Pathobiology
KUHLENSCHMIDT, M. S., Veterinary Pathobiology
LOCK, T. F., Veterinary Clinical Medicine
MANOHAR, M., Veterinary Biosciences
MARRETTA, S. M., Veterinary Clinical Medicine
MEERDINK, G. L., Toxicology
MILLER, G. Y., Veterinary Pathobiology, Veterinary Clinical Medicine
OTT, R. S., Veterinary Clinical Medicine, Veterinary Medicine Administration
PAUL, A. J., Veterinary Pathobiology
RAFFE, M. R., Veterinary Clinical Medicine
SCHANTZ, S. L., Veterinary Biosciences
SEGRE, M., Veterinary Pathobiology
SISSON, D. D., Veterinary Clinical Medicine
SMITH, R. D., Veterinary Pathobiology
TRANQUILLI, W. J., Veterinary Clinical Medicine
TROUTT, H. F., Veterinary Clinical Medicine
VALLI, V. E. O., Veterinary Pathobiology
VIMR, E. R., Veterinary Pathobiology
WALLIG, M. A., Veterinary Pathobiology
WEIGEL, R. M., Veterinary Pathobiology
WHITELEY, H. E., Veterinary Pathobiology
ZACHARY, J. F., Veterinary Pathobiology

College of Law:
BALL, C. A.
BELL, G.
BOYLE, F. A.
COLOMBO, J. D.
DAVEY, W. J.
FINKIN, M. W.
FREYFOGLE, E. T.
GEERDES, C. E.
HARRIS, O. F., Jr
HURD, H. M.
KAPLAN, R. L.
KINPORTS, K.
LEIPOLD, A. D.
MAGGS, P. B.
MCADAMS, R. H.
MEYER, D. D.
PAINTER, R. W.
PFANDER, J. E.
REYNOLDS, L. A.
RIBSTEIN, L. E.
RICH, R. F.
ROSS, S. F.
SHOBEN, E. W.
TABB, C. J.
TARR, N. W.
TERRY, C. T.
ULEN, T. S.

College of Medicine:
BAKER, D. H., Internal Medicine
BELMONT, A. S., Cell and Structural Biology
BEST, P. M., Molecular and Integrative Physiology, Physiology, Biophysics, Bioengineering and Neuroscience
BOILEAU, R. A., Internal Medicine
BUETOW, M. K., Paediatrics and Adolescent Health
CLEGG, R. M., Physics and Biophysics
CRASS, J. R., Internal Medicine
CROFTS, A. R., Biochemistry and Biophysics

CRONAN, J. E., Microbiology, Biochemistry and Microbiology
DONCHIN, E., Internal Medicine
ENSRUD, E. R., Internal Medicine
ERDMAN, Jr, J. W., Internal Medicine
ESSEX-SORLIE, D. L., Internal Medicine
FARRAND, S., Microbiology and Plant Pathology
FENG, A. S., Physiology, Biophysics, Bioengineering and Neuroscience
FREEDMAN, P., Internal Medicine
GARDNER, J. F., Microbiology
GELFAND, V. I., Cell and Structural Biology
GENNIS, R. B., Biochemistry, Chemistry, Biophysics
GERLT, J. A., Biochemistry, Chemistry and Biophysics, Basic Medical Sciences
GILLETTE, M. U., Cell and Structural Biology, Cell and Structural Biology
GILLETTE, R., Molecular and Integrative Physiology, Biophysics
GLASER, M., Biochemistry and Biophysics
GREENOUGH, W. T., Psychiatry, Cell and Structural Biology, Psychology and Psychiatry
GUMPORT, R. I., Biochemistry, Basic Medical Sciences
HELMAN, S. I., Physiology, Biophysics and Bioengineering
JAKOBSSON, E., Physiology, Biochemistry, Biophysics
JEFFERY, E., Pharmacology
KATZENELLENBOGEN, B. S., Cell and Structural Biology, Molecular and Integrative Physiology
KAUFMAN, S. J., Cell and Structural Biology
KEMPER, B. W., Cell and Structural Biology, Pharmacology, Molecular and Integrative Physiology
KIRBY, R. W., Internal Medicine
KRANZ, D. M., Biochemistry
LAYMAN, D. K., Internal Medicine
LEVY, A., Pathology
MARSHALL, W. P., Internal Medicine
MILLER, C. G., Microbiology
MILLER, G. A., Psychiatry
MORRISSEY, J. H., Biochemistry
NELSON, R. A., Internal Medicine
OLSEN, G., Microbiology and Biophysics
ORDAL, G. W., Biochemistry, Basic Medical Science
POLLARD, J. W., Internal Medicine
PRABHUDESAI, M., Pathology
RAMIREZ, V. D., Physiology and Neuroscience
ROBBINS, A. W., Internal Medicine
ROBERTSON, H. M., Cell and Structural Biology, Entomology
ROBINSON, G. E., Cell and Structural Biology, Entomology
RUEDA, J. L., Psychiatry
SALYERS, A., Microbiology
SCHULER, M. A., Cell and Structural Biology, Biochemistry, Plant Biology
SCHWARTZ, B. S., Biochemistry
SHAPIRO, D. J., Biochemistry
SHERWOOD, O. D., Physiology
SIEGEL, I. A.
SLIGAR, S. G., Biochemistry, Chemistry, Physiology and Biophysics, Medicine
SWITZER, R. L., Biochemistry, Basic Medical Sciences
WEYHENMEYER, J., Pathology
WILLIAMS, B., Pathology
WOESE, C. R., Microbiology
WRAIGHT, C. A., Biochemistry, Biophysics, Plant Biology

Institute of Labor and Industrial Relations:
DRASGOW, F.
FEUILLE, P.
LAWLER, J.
LEROY, M.
MARTOCCHIO, J.
NORTHCRAFT, G.

OLDHAM, G.
OLSON, C.

UNIVERSITY OF ST FRANCIS

500 Wilcox St, Joliet, IL 60435
Telephone: (815) 740-3360
Fax: (815) 740-5032
E-mail: information@stfrancis.edu
Internet: www.stfrancis.edu
Founded 1920
Private
Academic year: August to May
Pres.: Dr MICHAEL J. VINCIGUERRA
Provost and Vice-Pres. for Academic Affairs:
Dr CONSTANCE BAUER
Vice-Pres. for Admin. and Finance: DAVID
EATON
Vice-Pres. for Univ. Advancement: WILLIAM
A. BIEBUYCK
Vice-Pres. for Mission Integration and Ministry: ROSEMARY SMALL
Vice-Pres. for Admission and Enrollment
Services: CHARLES M. BEUTEL
Dir of Libraries: TERRY COTTRELL

Library of 105,000 vols
Number of teachers: 351
Number of students: 3,958

DEANS

College of Arts and Sciences: Dr FRANK
PASCOE
College of Business: Dr MIKE LaRocco
College of Education: Dr JOHN GAMBRO
College of Nursing and Allied Health: Dr
MARIA CONNOLLY
College of Professional Studies: MARY LOU
NUGENT

UNIVERSITY OF ST MARY OF THE LAKE – MUNDELEIN SEMINARY

1000 East Maple Ave, Mundelein, IL 60060
Telephone: (847) 566-6401
E-mail: info@usml.edu
Internet: www.vocations.org
Private control

Rector and Pres.: Very Rev. DENNIS LYLE
Vice-Pres. for Facilities: STAN RYS
Vice-Pres. for Finance): JOHN LEHOCKY
Library Dir: LORRAINE OLLEY

Library of 180,000 vols

Publication: *Chicago Studies* (3 a year).

VANDERCOOK COLLEGE OF MUSIC

3140 South Federal St, Chicago, IL 60616
Telephone: (312) 225-6288
Fax: (312) 225-5211
Internet: www.vandercook.edu
Private control
Pres.: Dr CHARLES MENGHINI
Dean of Undergraduate Studies: KAYE CLEMENTS
Dean of Graduate Studies: RUTH RHODES
Registrar: CAROLYN BERGHOFF
Library Dir: DON WIDMER

Number of teachers: 6
Number of students: 230.

WESTERN ILLINOIS UNIVERSITY

710 West University Dr., Macomb, IL 61455-1380
Telephone: (309) 295-1414
Fax: (309) 298-2400
E-mail: info@wiu.edu
Internet: www.wiu.edu
Founded 1899
Academic year: August to May
Pres.: Dr AL GOLDFARB
Provost and Academic Vice-Pres.: Dr JOE
RALLO

Vice-Pres. for Student Services: Dr W. GARRY
JOHNSON
Vice-Pres. for Admin. Services: JACQUELINE
THOMPSON
Vice-Pres. for Advancement and Public Services: Dr DAN HENDRICKS
Dean of Univ. Libraries: Dr PHYLIS C. SELF

Library of 1,150,000 vols
Number of teachers: 648
Number of students: 13,206

Publication: *Essays in Literature*

DEANS

College of Arts and Sciences: Dr INESSA LEVI
College of Business and Technology: Dr TOM
EREKSON
College of Education and Human Services:
Dr BONNIE SMITH-SKRIPPS
College of Fine Arts and Communication: Dr
PAUL KREIDER
School of Graduate Studies: Dr BARBARA A.
BAILY

WHEATON COLLEGE

501 College Ave, Wheaton, IL 60187-5593
Telephone: (630) 752-5000
Fax: (630) 752-5555
Internet: www.wheaton.edu
Founded 1860
Private interdenominational Christian college
Academic year: August to May
Pres.: Dr DUANE LITFIN
Provost: Dr STANTON JONES
Sr Vice-Pres. for Finance: Dr DAVID JOHNSTON
Vice-Pres. for Student Devt: Dr SAMUEL A.
SHELLHAMER
Vice-Pres. for Advancement and Alumni
Relations: Dr R. MARK DILLON
Dean of Student Life: Dr EDEE SCHULZE
Dean of Students: Dr RICH POWERS
Registrar: PAUL E. JOHNSON
Librarian: LISA RICHMOND

Library of 978,290 items, 1,562 current
periodicals
Number of teachers: 275 (186 full-time, 89
part-time)
Number of students: 2,897 (2,439 undergraduate, 458 graduate)

Publications: *InForm* (5 a year), *Kodon
Literary Magazine* (3 a year), *Record*
(weekly), *Tower* (year book)

DEANS

Graduate School: Dr STANTON L. JONES
Arts, Media and Communications: Dr
GEORGE ARASIMOWICZ
Humanities and Theological Studies: Dr JILL
PELÁEZ BAUMGAERTNER
Natural and Social Sciences: Dr DOROTHY F.
CHAPPELL

INDIANA

ANDERSON UNIVERSITY

Anderson, IN 46012
Telephone: (765) 649-9071
Fax: (765) 641-3851
E-mail: matas@anderson.edu
Internet: www.anderson.edu
Founded 1917
Academic year: August to May
President: Dr JAMES L. EDWARDS
Senior Vice-President: RONALD W. MOORE
Vice-President for Academic Affairs and
Dean: Dr CARL H. CALDWELL
Vice-President for Enrollment Management
and Information Systems: Dr MICHAEL
COLLETTE

Vice-President for Finance and Treasurer:
SENA LANDEY
Vice-President for Student Life and Dean of
Students: BRENT BAKER
Registrar: ARTHUR LEAK
Director of University Libraries: RICHARD
SNYDER

Library of 210,000 vols
Number of teachers: 140
Number of students: 2,250

DEANS

College of the Arts: JEFFREY E. WRIGHT
Falls School of Business: KENNETH D. ARMSTRONG
School of Education: DIANA N. ROSS (Chair)
College of Science and Humanities: D. BLAKE
JANUTOLO
School of Theology: Dr DAVID SEBASTIAN

ASSOCIATED MENNONITE BIBLICAL SEMINARY

3003 Benham Ave, Elkhart, IN 46517-1999
Telephone: (574) 295-3726
Fax: (574) 295-0092
E-mail: admissions@ambs.edu
Internet: www.ambs.edu
Private control
President: Dr J. NELSON KRAYBILL
Vice-President: MARK WEIDNER
Dean: Dr LOREN L. JOHNS
Registrar: NISHA SPRINGER
Librarian: EILEEN K. SANER

Library of 109,000 vols
Number of teachers: 35
Number of students: 180.

BRANCH CAMPUS

Great Plains Campus: 2517 Main Street,
POB 306, North Newton, KS 67117; tel. (316)
283-6300; Director Dr LOIS Y. BARRETT.

BALL STATE UNIVERSITY

Muncie, IN 47306
Telephone: (765) 289-1241
E-mail: askbsu@bsu.edu
Internet: www.bsu.edu
Founded 1918
Academic year: August to May
President: Dr BLAINE A. BROWNELL
Provost and Vice-President for Academic
Affairs: BEVERLY J. PITTS
Vice-President for Business Affairs: THOMAS
J. KINGHORN
Vice-President for Student Affairs and
Enrollment Management: Dr DOUGLAS F.
McCONKEY
Vice-President for University Advancement:
Dr DON L. PARK
Vice-President for Informational Technology:
Dr H. O'NEAL SMITHERMAN
Registrar: THOMAS BILGER
Dean of University Libraries: ARTHUR W.
HAFNER

Library of 1,500,000 items (inc. microfilms
and audio-visual items), 4,000 current
periodicals
Number of teachers: 836 (full-time)
Number of students: 18,000

Publications: *International Journal of Social
Education*, *Teacher Educator* (4 a year),
*Proceedings of the Indiana Academy of
Social Sciences* (annually), *Odyssey*
(annually), *Indiana Mathematics Teacher*
(2 a year), *Ball State Monographs* (irregular)

DEANS

College of Applied Sciences and Technology:
Dr NANCY KINGSBURY
College of Architecture and Planning: Prof.
JOSEPH BILELLO

College of Business: Prof. LYNNE RICHARDSON
College of Communication, Information, and Media: Prof. SCOTT R. OLSON
College of Fine Arts: Prof. ROBERT A. KVAM
College of Sciences and the Humanities: Prof. DONALD E. VAN METER
Teachers College: ROY A. WEAVER
University College: Dr B. THOMAS LOWE

BETHANY THEOLOGICAL SEMINARY

615 National Rd West, Richmond, IN 47374-4019
Telephone: (765) 983-1800
Fax: (765) 983-1840
E-mail: bethanysem@aol.com
Internet: www.brethren.org/bethany
Founded 1905 as Bethany Bible School; present name 1963
Private control
Academic year: August to May
President: EUGENE F. ROOP
Academic Dean: RICHARD B. GARDNER
Number of teachers: 17
Number of students: 64.

BRANCH CAMPUS
Susquehanna Valley Satellite: 1 Alpha Dr., Elizabethtown College, Elizabethtown, PA 17022-2298; tel. (717) 361-1450.

BETHEL COLLEGE

1001 W McKinley Avenue, Mishawaka, IN 46545
Telephone: (219) 259-8511
Fax: (219) 257-3326
E-mail: info@bethelcollege.edu
Internet: www.bethel-in.edu
Founded 1947
Private control
Academic year: August to May
President: Dr NORMAN V. BRIDGES
Senior Vice-President: Dr DENNIS D. ENGBRECHT
Vice-President (Academic Services) and Dean: Dr MICHAEL L. HOLTGREN
Vice-President and Dean of Graduate Studies: Dr C. ROBERT LAURENT
Vice-President (Institutional Advancement): STEVEN R. CRAMER
Vice-President and Chief Fiscal Officer: JOHN R. MYERS
Registrar: SHARON M. SNYDER
Director of Library Services: Dr CLYDE R. ROOT
Number of teachers: 149
Number of students: 1,600

HEADS OF DEPARTMENTS
Business: JOHN R. MOW
Education: Dr JEFFREY W. PECK
Fine Arts: ROBERT N. HAM
Language and Literature: Dr CHRISTIAN R. DAVIS
Mathematics and Computer Science: (vacant)
Natural Sciences: Dr BRYAN J. ISAAC
Nursing: Dr RUTH E. DAVIDHIZAR (Dean)
Religion and Philosophy: Dr EUGENE E. CARPENTER
Social Sciences: Dr ELIZABETH A. HOSSLER

BUTLER UNIVERSITY

4600 Sunset Ave, Indianapolis, IN 46208
Telephone: (317) 940-8000
Fax: (317) 940-9930
Internet: www.butler.edu
Founded 1855
Private control
President: BOBBY FONG

Provost and Senior Vice-President for Academic Affairs: BILL BERRY
Vice-President for University Advancement: CAMERON A. McGUIRE
Registrar: SONDREA OZOLINS
Dean, Libraries: LEWIS MILLER
Number of teachers: 255 (full-time)
Number of students: 4,326

DEANS
College of Business Administration: Dr RICHARD FETTER
College of Education: Dr BOB RIDER
Jordan College of Fine Arts: Dr PETER ALEXANDER
College of Liberal Arts and Sciences: Dr PAUL HANSON
College of Pharmacy and Health Sciences: Dr PATRICIA A. CHASE

CALUMET COLLEGE OF ST JOSEPH

2400 New York Ave, Whiting, IN 46394
Telephone: (219) 473-7770
Fax: (219) 473-4259
E-mail: admissions@ccsj.edu
Internet: www.ccsj.edu
Founded 1951
Academic year: September to August
President: Dr DENNIS C. RITTENMEYER
Registrar: DIANA FRANCIS
Librarian: JoANN ARNOLD
Library of 115,874 vols
Number of teachers: 60
Number of students: 1,300.

CHRISTIAN THEOLOGICAL SEMINARY

1000 W 42nd Street, Indianapolis, IN 46208
Telephone: (317) 924-1331
Fax: (317) 923-1961
E-mail: communications@cts.edu
Internet: www.cts.edu
Private control
Academic year: September to May
President: Dr EDWARD L. WHEELER
Vice-President and Dean for Academic Affairs: Dr CAROLYN HIGGINBOTHAM
Vice-President (Seminary Development): AUSTIN W. GREENE
Vice-President (Finance): DEAN RAMGA
Librarian: LORNA SHOEMAKER
Number of teachers: 44
Number of students: 300.

CONCORDIA THEOLOGICAL SEMINARY

6600 N Clinton Street, Fort Wayne, IN 46825-4996
Telephone: (260) 452-2100
Fax: (260) 452-2121
Internet: www.ctsfw.edu
Founded 1847
Private control
Academic year: September to May
President: DEAN O. WENTHE
Academic Dean: WILLIAM C. WEINRICH
Director of Library and Information Services: ROBERT ROETHEMEYER
Library of 150,000 items
Number of teachers: 29
Number of students: 389
Publication: *Concordia Theological Quarterly* (4 a year).

DEPAUW UNIVERSITY

313 S. Locust St, Greencastle, IN 46135
Telephone: (765) 658-4800
Fax: (317) 658-4177
Internet: www.depauw.edu

Founded 1837 as Indiana Asbury University; present name 1884
Academic year: August to May
President: Dr ROBERT G. BOTTOMS
Executive Vice-President and Dean of the Faculty: Dr NEAL ABRAHAM
Vice-President for Finance and Administration: RICHARD SPELLER
Vice-President for Development and Alumni Relations: LISA HOLLANDER
Vice-President for Admission and Financial Aid: MADELEINE R. EAGON
Vice-President for Student Services: JAMES L. LINCOLN
Registrar: Dr KENNETH J. YKirkpatrick
Secretary: Dr PAUL HARTMAN
Director of Libraries: RICK PROVINE
Library of 318,427 vols
Number of teachers: 254 (213 full-time, 441 part-time)
Number of students: 2,370.

EARLHAM COLLEGE

Richmond, IN 47374
Telephone: (765) 983-1200
Fax: (765) 983-1560
E-mail: admissions@earlham.edu
Internet: www.earlham.edu
Academic year: August to May
Founded 1847
President: DOUGLAS BENNETT
Vice-President for Business Affairs: RICHARD K. SMITH
Vice-President for Institutional Advancement: JAMES McKEY
Provost and Dean of Academic Affairs: LEN CLARK
Librarian: TOM KIRK
Number of teachers: 96
Number of students: 1,187

DEANS
College: LEN CLARK
Earlham School of Religion: JAY MARSHALL

FRANKLIN COLLEGE

Franklin, IN 46131
Telephone: (317) 738-8000
Fax: (317) 736-6030
Internet: www.franklincollege.edu
Founded 1834
Academic year: August to May
Chancellor (vacant)
President: JAMES MOSELEY
Vice-President for Academic Affairs and Dean of the College: DAVID BRAILOW
Vice-President for Business and Finance: LARRY GRIFFITH
Vice-President for Enrollment and Student Affairs: ALAN HILL
Vice-President for Institutional Advancement: MYRON DAVIS
Dean of Students: ELLIS HALL
Head Librarian: RONALD SCHUETZ
Library of 126,345 vols
Number of teachers: 100
Number of students: 994.

GOSHEN COLLEGE

Goshen, IN 46526
Telephone: (219) 535-7000
Fax: (219) 535-7660
E-mail: admission@goshen.edu
Internet: www.goshen.edu
Founded 1894
President: SHIRLEY H. SHOWALTER
Provost and Executive Vice-President: JOHN D. YORDY
Vice-President for Academic Affairs and Dean: ANITA STALTER

Vice-President for Multicultural Education: ZENABE ABEBE
Vice-President for Student Life and Dean of Students: BILL BORN
Vice-President for Institutional Advancement: ANDREA COOK
Registrar: STANLEY MILLER
Library Director: LISA GUEDEA CARREÑO
Library of 155,000 vols
Number of teachers: 112 (82 full-time, 30 part-time)
Number of students: 1,000
Publication: *Mennonite Quarterly Review* (quarterly).

GRACE COLLEGE AND SEMINARY

200 Seminary Drive, Winona Lake, IN 46590
Telephone: (574) 372-5100
Fax: (574) 372-5263
Internet: www.grace.edu
Private control
President: Dr RONALD E. MANAHAN
Vice-President (Academic Affairs): Dr DAVID R. PLASTER
Registrar: ANECIA MILLER
Director of Library Services: WILLIAM DARR
Library of 140,000 vols
Number of teachers: 33
Number of students: 1,300 (incl. distance education)

HEADS OF DEPARTMENTS

Art: ARTHUR W. DAVIS
Behavioral Science: Dr GEORGE SLAUGHTER
Biblical Studies: Dr BRENT SANDY
Biological Science: Dr RICHARD JEFFREYS
Business: WILLIAM GORDON
Communication: FRANK BENYOUSKY
Education: Dr SHARA B. CURRY
English: Dr PAULETTE G. SAUDERS
History: R. WAYNE SNIDER
Languages and Cultures: JACQUELINE SCHRAM
Management of Information Technology: RICHARD KOONTZ
Mathematics: Dr JIM LESKO
Music: Dr PETER GANO
Physical Education: Dr DARRELL JOHNSON
Physical Science: Dr DONALD B. DEYOUNG
Religious Studies: Dr BRENT SANDY
Social Work: CARRIE YOCUM

HANOVER COLLEGE

Hanover, IN 47243
Telephone: (812) 866-2151
Internet: www.hanover.edu
First instruction 1827; chartered 1829
Private control (Presbyterian)
President: RUSSELL L. NICHOLS
Vice-President and Dean of Academic Affairs: JANE JAKOUBEK
Vice-President for Administrative Affairs: TERRY A. PHILLIPS
Vice-President for Business Affairs: FRANK G. WILLIAMS
Vice-President for Development: RICK HASKINS
Vice-President for Student Life: DENNIS McDONALD
Associate Dean of Academic Affairs and Registrar: JON ENRIQUEZ
Director of Duggan Library: KENNETH E. GIBSON
Library of 215,000 vols, 284,000 documents, 4,500 audio-visual items
Number of teachers: 71
Number of students: 1,050.

HUNTINGTON COLLEGE

2303 College Ave, Huntington, IN 46750
Telephone: (219) 356-6000
Fax: (219) 359-4086
Internet: www.huntington.edu
Founded 1897
Academic year: September to May
President: Dr G. BLAIR DOWDEN
Vice-President and Dean of the College: Dr RONALD J. WEBB
Vice-President for Advancement: NED J. KISER
Vice-President for Business and Finance: THOMAS W. AYERS
Vice-President for Student Development: Dr A. NORRIS FRIESEN
Dean of Enrollment: JEFF BERGGREN
Registrar: SARAH J. HARVEY
Director of Library Services: ROBERT E. KAEHR
Library of 164,000 items, 550 current periodicals, 14,000 bound periodical vols, 50,000 govt documents
Number of teachers: 68
Number of students: 942.

INDIANA INSTITUTE OF TECHNOLOGY

1600 E. Washington, Fort Wayne, IN 46803
Telephone: (219) 422-5561
Fax: (219) 422-7696
Internet: www.indianatech.edu
Founded 1930
President: Dr ARTHUR E. SNYDER
Library of 33,000 volumes
Number of teachers: 50
Number of students: 2,700
Schools of engineering, business and computer science.

INDIANA STATE UNIVERSITY

Terre Haute, IN 47809
Telephone: (812) 237-6311
Fax: (812) 237-2291
Internet: web.indstate.edu
Founded 1865
Academic year: August to May
President: Dr LLOYD W. BENJAMIN III
Provost and Vice-President for Academic Affairs: Dr C. JACK MAYNARD
Vice-President for Administration and Secretary of the University: ROBERT E. SCHAFER
Vice-President for Business Affairs and Finance: GREGG S. FLOYD
Vice-President for University Advancement: GARY A. BOUSE
Vice-President for Student Affairs and Dean of Students: D. THOMAS RAMEY
Associate Vice-President for Enrollment Services: REBECCA W. LIBLER
Registrar: STACEY J. THOMAS
Dean of Library Services: MYRNA McCALLISTER
Library of 2,000,000 vols
Number of teachers: 536 full-time
Number of students: 11,714
Publications: *Midwestern Folklore* (2 a year), *The Hoosier Science Teacher* (4 a year), *Indiana English* (3 a year), *Folklore Historian* (2 a year), *Cognitive Technology*, *The Indiana Council of Teachers of Mathematics Journal—Mathematics Teacher* (2 a year)

DEANS

College of Arts and Sciences: DIANA P. MICHELFELDER
School of Business: RONALD GREEN
School of Education: ROBERT WILLIAMS
School of Graduate Studies: KWEKU BENTL

School of Health and Human Performance: BARBARA PASSMORE
School of Nursing: BONNIE SAUCIER
School of Technology: W. TAD FOSTER

INDIANA UNIVERSITY

Bloomington, IN 47405
Telephone: (812) 855-4848
Internet: www.indiana.edu
Founded 1820 as a State Seminary, opened 1824, became Indiana College 1828, attained university status 1838, became State University 1852
President: GERALD L. BEPKO
Vice-President for Academic Affairs: SHARON S. BREHM
Vice-President for Long-Range Planning: GERALD L. BEPKO
Vice-President and Chief Administrative Officer: J. TERRY CLAPACS
Vice-President and Chief Financial Officer: JUDITH G. PALMER
Vice-President for Research and Dean of the Graduate School: GEORGE E. WALKER
Vice-President for Public Affairs and Government Relations: WILLIAM STEPHAN
Vice-President for Information Technology: MICHAEL A. McROBBIE
Vice-President for Student Development and Diversity: CHARLIE HELMS
Dean of University Libraries: SUZANNE THORIN
Number of students: 98,710 (all campuses).

CONSTITUENT CAMPUSES

Indiana University Bloomington

107 S. Indiana Ave, Bloomington, IN 47405-7000
Telephone: (812) 855-4848
Internet: www.iub.edu
Chancellor: SHARON S. BREHM
Vice-Chancellor for Academic Support and Diversity: CHARLIE NELMS
Vice-Chancellor for Student Affairs and Dean of Students: RICHARD McKAIG
Registrar: ROLAND COTE
Director of Admissions: DON HOSSLER
Librarian: SUZANNE THORIN
Library: see Libraries and Archives
Number of teachers: 1,539
Number of students: 38,903 (33,540 full-time, 5,363 part-time)
Publications: *American Historical Review* (5 a year), *American Journal of Semiotics* (quarterly), *Anthropological Linguistics* (quarterly), *Business Horizons* (every 2 months), *Folklore Research Journal* (3 a year), *Indiana Business Review* (every 2 months), *Indiana Law Journal* (quarterly), *Indiana Magazine of History* (quarterly), *Indiana Slavic Studies* (annually), *Indiana University Mathematics Journal* (quarterly), *Journal of American History* (quarterly), *Journal of Asian History*, *Journal of Chemical Physics* (weekly), *Journal of Mathematical Physics* (monthly), *Journal of Slavic Linguistics* (2 a year), *Journal of the Experimental Analysis of Behavior* (every 2 months), *Phi Delta Kappan* (10 a year), *University Bulletin* (30 a year), *Victorian Studies* (quarterly)

DEANS

Graduate School: GEORGE E. WALKER
College of Arts and Sciences: KUMBLE R. SUBBASWAMY
Kelley School of Business: DAN DALTON
School of Continuing Studies: JEREMY DUNNING
School of Education: Prof. GERARDO GONZÁLEZ

School of Health, Physical Education and Recreation: DAVID L. GALLAHUE
School of Journalism: Dr TREVOR R. BROWN
School of Law: Prof. LAUREN ROBEL (acting)
School of Library and Information Science: (vacant)
School of Music: GWYN RICHARDS
School of Optometry: Prof. GERALD E. LOWTHER
School for Public Affairs and Environmental Sciences: ASTRID MERGET

CHAIRPERSONS OF DEPARTMENTS

College of Arts and Sciences:

African American and African Diaspora Studies: Prof. JOHN H. STANFIELD, II (acting)
Anthropology: Dr RICHARD R. WILK
Apparel Merchandising and Interior Design: Prof. REED BENHAMOU
Astronomy: Prof. RICHARD H. DURISEN
Biology: JEFFREY D. PALMER
Central Eurasian Studies: Dr ELLIOT H. SPERLING
Chemistry: Prof. DAVID E. CLEMMER
Classical Studies: Prof. WILLIAM HANSEN (acting)
Communication and Culture: Prof. ROBERT L. IVIE
Comparative Literature: Prof. OSCAR S. KENSHUR
Criminal Justice: Dr KIP SCHLEGEL
East Asian Languages and Cultures: Prof. RICHARD RUBINGER
Economics: Prof. JAMES A. WALKER
English: Prof. STEPHEN MYERS WATT
Folklore and Ethnomusicology: Prof. JOHN H. McDOWELL
French and Italian: Dr ANDREA CICCARELLI
Geography: Prof. DANIEL C. KNUDSEN
Geological Sciences: Prof. CHRISTOPHER G. MAPLES
Germanic Studies: Prof. KARI ELLEN GADE
History: Prof. JOHN BODNAR (acting)
History and Philosophy of Science: WILLIAM ROYALL NEWMAN (acting)
Linguistics: Prof. STEVEN L. FRANKS
Mathematics: Prof. DANIEL P. MAKI
Near Eastern Languages and Cultures: Prof. M. NAZIF SHAHRANI
Philosophy: Prof. MARK KAPLAN
Physics: Prof. STEVEN E. VIGADOR
Political Science: Prof. JEFFREY A. HART
Psychology: Prof. JOSEPH E. STEINMETZ
Religious Studies: RICHARD B. MILLER
Slavic Languages and Literatures: Prof. RONALD FELDSTEIN
Sociology: Prof. ROBERT VICTOR ROBINSON
Spanish and Portuguese: Prof. CONSUELO LOPEZ-MORILLAS
Speech and Hearing Sciences: Prof. PHIL J. CONNELL
Telecommunications: Prof. WALTER GANTZ
Theatre and Drama: Prof. RONALD WAINSCOTT
West European Studies: PETER BONDANELLA

School of Business:

Accounting and Information Systems: Prof. JAMIE PRATT
Business Communication: Dr SUE VARGO
Business Economics and Public Policy: Prof. MICHELE FRATIANNI
Business Law: Prof. ARLEN W. LANGVARDT
Finance: Prof. ROBERT C. KLEMKOSKY
Management: Prof. PATRICIA P. McDOUGALL
Marketing: Prof. DAN SMITH
Operations and Decision Technology: Prof. MUNIRPALLAM A. VENKATARAMANAN

School of Education:

Counselling and Educational Psychology: Prof. DANIEL J. MUELLER

Curriculum and Instruction: Prof. SUSAN M. KLEIN
Educational Leadership and Policy Studies: Prof. BARRY BULL
Instructional Systems Technology: ELIZABETH BOLING
Language Education: Dr MARTHA NYIKOS

School of Health, Physical Education and Recreation:

Applied Health Science: Prof. MOHAMMAD RAHIM TORABI
Kinesiology: Prof. JOHN B. SHEA
Recreation and Park Adminstration: Dr LYNN MARIE JAMIESON

School of Music:

Ballet: VIRGINIA CESBRON
Bands: RAY E. CRAMER
Brass: F. MICHAEL HATFIELD
Choral Conducting: JAN. D. HARRINGTON
Composition: Prof. CLAUDE BAKER
Early Music Institute: PAUL D. HILLIER
Harp: SUSANN McDONALD
Instrumental Conducting: IMRE ZOLTAN PALLO
Jazz: DAVID N. BAKER
Music Education: Prof. MICHAEL SCHWARTZKOPF
Music (in General Studies): Prof. MARY GOETZE
Musicology: Prof. A. PETER BROWN
Music Theory: Dr ERIC J. ISAACSON
Organ: CHRISTOPHER YOUNG
Percussion: GERALD CARLYSS
Strings: LAWRENCE P. HURST
Theory: MARY H. WENNERSTROM
Woodwinds: HOWARD KLUG

DIRECTORS OF RESEARCH INSTITUTES

Institute for Advanced Study: Prof. MARY ELLEN BROWN
African American Arts Institute: Dr CHARLES E. SYKES
Center on Aging and Aged: BARBARA A. HAWKINS
American Indian Studies Research Institute: Prof. RAYMOND J. DeMALLIE
Anthropological Center for Training & Research on Global Environmental Change (ACT): Prof. EMILIO MORAN
Indiana University Art Museum: ADELHEID GEALT
Glenn A. Black Laboratory of Archaeology: Prof. CHRIS PEEBLES
Borish Center for Ophthalmic Research: Prof. B. SARITA SONI, Prof. GERALD E. LOWTHER
School of Business Division of Research: MORTON MARCUS
School of Business Institute for Research on the Management of Information Systems: JO BASEY
Center for Postsecondary Research and Planning: ASHTON ALEY HALL
Center for Research into the Anthropological Foundations of Technology (CRAFT): NICHOLAS TOTH, KATHY SCHICK
Center for Research on Concepts and Cognition: Prof. DOUGLAS HOFSTADTER
Chemical Informatics Center: GARY WIGGINS
Institute for Child Study: RUSSELL SKIBA
Center for the Study of the College Fraternity: RICHARD N. McKAIG
Committee for Research and Development in Language Instruction: ALBERT VALDMAN
Computational Fluid Dynamics Laboratory: Prof. AKIN ECER
Creole Institute: Albert VALDMAN
Indiana University Cyclotron Facility: Prof. JOHN M. CAMERON
Center for Design Process: C. THOMAS MITCHELL
Institute for Study of Developmental Disabilities: DAVID MANK
Early Music Institute: PAUL HILLIER (acting)

East Asian Studies Center: GEORGE M. WILSON
East Asian Summer Language Institute: YASUKO ITO WATT
Center for Econometric Model Research: R. JEFFREY GREEN, MORTON MARCUS
Center for Economic Education: (vacant)
Center for Electronic and Computer Music: Prof. JEFFREY HASS
Center for English Language Training: MARLIN HOWARD
Environmental Systems Applications Center: WILLIAM W. JONES
ERIC Clearinghouse for Social Studies/Social Science Education: JOHN PATRICK
Indiana Center for Evaluation: Dr KIM K. METCALF
Folklore Institute: JOHN McDOWELL
Center for Genomics and Bioinformatics: PETER CHERBAS
Indiana Geological Survey: JOHN STEINMETZ
Center for Geospatial Data Analysis: EDWIN HARTKE
Institute of German Studies: MARC WEINER
Center for Health and Safety Studies: JAMES W. CROWE
High School Journalism Institute: Prof. JACK DVORAK
Center for the History of Medicine: ANN G. CARMICHAEL, ELLEN DWYER
Howard Hughes Medical Institute Research Laboratory: THOMAS C. KAUFMAN
Center for Human Growth: Dr THOMAS L. SEXTON
Indiana Business Research Center: MORTON J. MARCUS
Indiana Education Policy Center: JONATHAN PLUCKER
Indiana Institute on Disability and Community: Dr DAVID M. MANK
Indiana Molecular Biology Institute: Dr RUDOLF A. RAFF
Indiana University Molecular Structure Center: JOHN C. HUFFMAN
Inner Asian and Uralic National Resource Center: WILLIAM FIERMAN
Institute for Development Strategies: DAVID B. AUDRETSCH
Institute for Drug Abuse Prevention: WILLIAM J. BAILEY, Prof. MOHAMMAD R. TORABI
Institute for Family and Social Responsibility: Prof. MAUREEN A. PIROG, Dr KATHARINE V. BYERS
Institute for Neural Systems and Plasticity: GEORGE V. REBEC
Insititute for Scientific Computing and Applied Mathematics: ROGER TEMAM
Institute for Study of Human Capabilities: Prof. CHARLES WATSON
Center for the Study of Institutions, Populations and Environmental Change (CIPEC): Dr EMILIO MORAN, Dr ELINOR OSTROM
Institute for the Study of Labor in Society (ISLS): JEFF VINCENT
Institute for the Study of Russian and Eurasian Education: BEN EKLOF, HOWARD MEHLINGER
Center for the Integrative Study of Animal Behavior (CISAB): EMILIA P. MARTINS
International Development Institute: CHARLES RAEFSNYDER
Center for Italian Studies: ANDREA CICCARELLI
Center for Research and Development in Language Instruction: ALBERT VALDMAN
Jewish Studies Center: ALVIN H. ROSENFELD
Johnson Center for Entrepreneurship and Innovation: ELIZABETH J. GATEWOOD
Kinsey Institute for Research in Sex, Gender, and Reproduction: Prof. JOHN BANCROFT
Laboratory Animal Resources: RUSSELL L. SCHMIDT
Latin American Music Center: CARMEN TÉLLEZ
Center for Latin American and Caribbean Studies: JEFFREY GOULD

Center for Studies of Law in Action: Prof. KIP SCHLEGEL, Dr BARRY K. LOGAN
Center for the Study of Law and Society: LEE LUSKIN
Leisure Research Institute: LYNN M. JAMIESON
William Hammond Mathers Museum: GEOFFREY W. CONRAD
Mathematics Education Development Center: FRANK K. LESTER, Jr
Medieval Studies Institute: LAWRENCE M. CLOPPER
National Center on Accessibility: GARY ROBB
National Center for Recreation Resources: BRUCE HRONEK
National Clearinghouse for United States–Japan Studies: C. FREDERICK RISINGER
National Institute on Global Environment Change – Midwest Regional Center: J. C. RANDOLPH
Nuclear Theory Center: J. TIMOTHY LONDERGAN
Philanthropy and Americans Outdoors Program: BRUCE HRONEK
Polish Studies Center: BILL JOHNSTON
Population Institute for Research and Training: Prof. GEORGE ALTER
Poynter Center for the Study of Ethics and American Instutitions: DAVID H. SMITH
Center for Public Sector Labor Relations: RICHARD S. RUBIN
Center for Reading and Language Studies: ROGER C. FARR
Reading Practicum Center: ANNABEL NEWMAN
Research Institute for Inner Asian Studies (RIFIAS): DEVIN DeWEESE
Rural Center for AIDS/STD Prevention (RCAP): Prof. WILLIAM L. YARBER
Russian and East European Institute: Prof. DAVID RANSEL
Seismic Laboratory: MICHAEL W. HAMBURGER
Center for Social Informatics: Prof. ROB KLING
Institute of Social Research: DAVID JAMES
Social Studies Development Center: JOHN J. PATRICK
Center for the Study of Global Change: BRIAN WINCHESTER
Center for Survey Research: JOHN M. KENNEDY
Telecommunications Management Inst- itution: BOB AFFE
Transportation Research Center: STEPHEN McDONALD
Institute for Urban Transportation: GEORGE M. SMERK
Underwater Science: CHARLES BEEKER
Workshop in Political Theory and Policy Analysis: ELINOR OSTROM, VINCENT OSTROM
West European National Resource Center: PETER BONDANELLA

Indiana University East

Richmond, IN 47374
Telephone: (317) 966-8261
Internet: www.iue.edu

Chancellor: DAVID J. FULTON
Library Director: GORDON LYNN HUFFORD
Number of students: 2,480.

Indiana University at Kokomo

Kokomo, IN 46902
Telephone: (317) 453-2000
Internet: www.iuk.edu

Chancellor: RUTH J. PERSON
Vice-Chancellor for Academic Affairs: STUART GREEN
Number of students: 2,772.

Indiana University Northwest

Gary, IN 46408
Telephone: (219) 980-6700
Internet: www.iun.edu

Chancellor: BRUCE BERGLAND
Executive Vice-Chancellor for Academic Affairs: MARILYN VASQUEZ
Vice-Chancellor for Student Affairs: ERNEST SMITH
Library Director: ROBERT MORAN
Library of 200,000 vols, 200,000 govt documents
Number of students: 5,149.

Indiana University at South Bend

South Bend, IN 46634
Telephone: (219) 237-4220
Internet: www.iusb.edu

Chancellor: UNA RAE MECK
Library Director: MICHELE RUSSO
Number of students: 7,457

DEANS

School of the Arts: TOM MILLER
School of Business and Economics: BILL N. SCHWARTZ
School of Education: Dr GWYNN METTETAL
College of Liberal Arts and Sciences: MIRIAM SHILLINGSBURG
Division of Nursing and Health Professions: Dr LAWRENCE GERBER
School of Public and Environmental Affairs: Dr LEDA McINTYRE HALL
School of Social Work: Dr PAUL R. NEWCOMB (Dir)

Indiana University Southeast

New Albany, IN 47150
Telephone: (812) 945-2731
Internet: www.ius.edu

Chancellor: SANDRA R. PATTERSON-RANDLES
Vice-Chancellor of Academic Affairs: GILBERT ATNIP
Vice-Chancellor for Administrative Affairs: STEPHEN J. TAKSAR
Vice-Chancellor for Student Affairs: Dr RUTH C. GARVEY-NIX
Director of Library Services: C. MARTIN ROSEN
Library of 585,000 vols and microforms, 1,200 current periodicals
Number of students: 6,716

DEANS

School of Education: GLORIA MURRAY
School of Natural Sciences: Prof. BAHMAN (BEN) E. NASSIM
Division of Nursing: Dr LILLIAN E. YEAGER
School of Social Sciences: CLIFF STATEN

Indiana University — Purdue University at Fort Wayne

Fort Wayne, IN 46805
Telephone: (219) 482-5356
Internet: www.ipfw.edu

Chancellor: MICHAEL A. WARTELL
Vice-Chancellor for Academic Affairs: SUSAN B. HANNAH
Vice-Chancellor for Financial Affairs: WALTER J. BRANSON
Vice-Chancellor for Student Affairs: FRANK L. BORELLI
Registrar: KEVIN M. BROWNE
Library Director: JUDITH L. VIOLETTE
Library of 300,000 vols, 1,700 current periodicals, 150,000 govt publications, microforms, audio-visual items
Number of students: 6,463

DEANS

School of Arts and Sciences: Prof. EVANGELOS COUFOUDAKIS
School of Business and Management Studies: Prof. JOHN WELLINGTON
Division of Continuing Studies: Dr MICHAEL STOCKSTILL (Exec. Dir)

School of Education: Prof. ROBERTA B. WIENER
School of Engineering, Technology and Computer Science: Prof. G. ALLEN PUGH
School of Health Sciences: Prof. JAMES E. JONES
Division of Labour Studies: MARK A. CROUCH (Dir)
Medical Education: Prof. BARTH H. RAGATZ (Dir)
Division of Organizational Leadership and Supervision: Dr KIMBERLY S. McDONALD (Co-ordinator)
Division of Public and Environmental Affairs: Dr WILLIAM G. LUDWIN
School of Visual and Performing Arts: Prof. BENJAMIN CHRISTY

Indiana University — Purdue University at Indianapolis

Indianapolis, IN 46202
Telephone: (317) 274-4417
Internet: www.iupui.edu

Chancellor: Dr WILLIAM M. PLATER (acting)
Executive Vice-Chancellor and Dean of the Faculties: Dr WILLIAM M. PLATER
Vice-Chancellor for Administration and Finance: ROBERT E. MARTIN
Vice-Chancellor for External Affairs: CHERYL G. SULLIVAN
Vice-Chancellor for Planning and Institutional Improvement: Dr TRUDY W. BANTA
Vice-Chancellor for Research and Graduate Education: Dr MARK L. BRENNER
Vice-Chancellor for Student Life and Diversity: KAREN WHITNEY
Number of students: 29,025

DEANS

School of Allied Health Sciences: Prof. MARK SOTHMANN
Herron School of Art: VALERIE EICKMEIER
Kelley School of Business: Prof. JOHN M. HASSELL (Acting Assoc. Dean)
School of Dentistry: Prof. LAWRENCE I. GOLDBLATT
School of Education: GERARDO GONZALES
School of Engineering and Technology: H. ONER YURTSEVEN
School of Informatics: Dr DARRELL L. BAILEY
School of Journalism: Prof. JAMES W. BROWN
School of Law: Prof. ANTHONY A. TARR
School of Liberal Arts: Prof. HERMAN J. SAATKAMP, Jr
School of Library and Information Science: Prof. BLAISE CRONIN
School of Medicine: Prof. D. CRAIG BRATER
School of Nursing: Prof. ANGELA BARRON McBRIDE
School of Physical Education and Tourism Management: Prof. P. NICHOLAS. KELLUM
School of Science: Prof. DAVID L. STOCUM
School of Social Work: MICHAEL PATCHNER

CHAIRS OF DEPARTMENTS

School of Allied Health Sciences:

Clinical Laboratory Science: LINDA M. KASPER (Dir)
Cytotechnology: WILLIAM N. CRABTREE (Dir)
Health Information Administration: DANITA FORGEY (Dir)
Health Sciences Education: Dr KAREN E. GABLE (Dir)
Histotechnology: GLENDA F. HOYE (Dir)
Nutrition and Dietetics: Prof. JACQUELYNN M. O'PALKA (Dir)
Occupational Therapy: CELESTINE HAMANT (Dir)
Paramedic Sciences: LEON H. BELL (Dir)
Physical Therapy: Dr WILLIAM S. QUILLEN (Dir)
Radiation Therapy: DONNA K. DUNN (Dir)
Radiologic Sciences: EMILY M. HERNANDEZ (Dir)

Respiratory Therapy: Prof. DEBORAH L. CULLEN (Dir)

Therapeutic Outcomes Research: Prof. NEIL OLDRIDGE

School of Business:

Accounting and Information Systems: JAMES H. PRATT

Business Economics and Public Policy: MICHELE FRATIANNI

Business Law: TERRY M. DWORKIN

Distance Education: RICHARD J. MAGJUKA

Finance: ROBERT H. JENNINGS

Management: HARVEY HEGARTY

Marketing: FRANKLIN ACITO

Masters of Professional Accountancy: WILLIAM R. KULSRUD

Operations and Decision Technologies: MUNIRPALLAM A. VENKATARAMANAN

Undergraduate Program: GLEN A. LARSEN

School of Dentistry:

Endodontics: CECIL E. BROWN, Jr (acting)

Oral Biology: Prof. ARDEN G. CHRISTEN (acting)

Oral Facial Development: Prof. JAMES K. HARTSFIELD

Oral Pathology, Medicine and Radiology: Prof. SUSAN L. ZUNT (acting)

Oral Surgery and Hospital Dentistry: Dr WILLIAM C. HINE, Jr (acting)

Periodontics and Allied Dental Programs: Prof. E. BRADY HANCOCK

Preventative and Community Dentistry: Prof. DOMENICK T. ZERO

Restorative Dentistry: Prof. E. STEVEN DUKE

School of Engineering and Technology:

Biomedical Engineering Program: Prof. EDWARD J. BERBARI (Dir)

Computer Technology: Prof. THOMAS HO

Construction Technology: Prof. ERDOGAN SENER

Electrical and Computer Engineering: Prof. RUSSEL C. EBERHART (acting)

Electrical and Computer Engineering Technology: Prof. MARVIN NEEDLER

Mechanical Engineering: Prof. HASAN AKAY

Mechanical Engineering Technology: Prof. JACK ZECHER

Organizational Leadership and Supervision: CLIFFORD GOODWIN

School of Liberal Arts:

Anthropology: JEANETTE DICKERSON-PUTMAN

Communication Studies: Prof. JOHN PARRISH-SPROWL

Economics: Dr ROBERT SANDY

English: Prof. CHRISTIAN KLOESEL

Foreign Languages and Cultures: Prof. GABRIELLE BERSIER

Geography: Dr TIMOTHY S. BROTHERS

History: Dr PHILIP V. SCARPINO

Medical Humanities: Prof. WILLIAM H. SCHNEIDER (Dir)

Museum Studies: Dr ELIZABETH KRYDER-REID

Philanthropic Studies: EUGENE TEMPEL (Exec. Dir, Center on Philanthropy)

Philosophy: Prof. MICHAEL B. BURKE

Political Science: Prof. JOHN McCORMICK

Religious Studies: Prof. ROWLAND A. SHERRILL

Sociology: Dr DAVID A. FORD

School of Medicine:

Anaesthesia: Dr ROBERT K. STOELTING

Anatomy and Cell Biology: Prof. DAVID B. BURR

Biochemistry and Molecular Biology: Prof. ROBERT A. HARRIS

Cellular and Integrative Physiology: Dr RODNEY RHOADES

Dermatology: Dr JEFFREY B. TRAVERS

Emergency Medicine: Prof. ROLAND B. McGRATH

Experimental Oncology Laboratory: GEORGE WEBER (Dir)

Family Medicine: Prof. DOUGLAS B. McKEAG

Medical and Molecular Genetics: Dr GAIL HABEGGER VANCE

Medicine: Prof. DAVID W. CRABB

Microbiology and Immunology: Prof. HAL E. BROXMEYER

Neurology: Prof. JOSÉ BILLER

Obstetrics and Gynaecology: Prof. FREDERICK B. STEHMAN

Ophthalmology: Prof. ROBERT D. YEE

Orthopaedic Surgery: Prof. STEPHEN B. TRIPPEL

Otolaryngology–Head and Neck Surgery: Prof. RICHARD T. MIYAMOTO

Paediatrics: Prof. RICHARD L. SCHREINER

Pathology and Laboratory Medicine: Prof. JOHN N. EBLE

Pharmacology and Toxicology: Prof. MICHAEL R. VASKO

Physical Medicine and Rehabilitation: RALPH M. BUSCHBACHER (acting)

Physiology and Biophysics: RODNEY A. RHOADES

Psychiatry: Dr CHRISTOPHER McDOUGLE

Public Health: Dr STEPHEN J. JAY

Radiation Oncology: Prof. MARCUS E. RANDALL

Radiology: Prof. VALERIE P. JACKSON

Surgery: Prof. JAY L. GROSFELD

Urology: Prof. MICHAEL O. KOCH

School of Nursing:

Adult Health: JUANITA KECK

Environments for Health: Prof. DANIEL J. PESUT

Family Health: Prof. SHARON SIMS

School of Physical Education and Tourism Management:

Physical Education: BETTY JONES

Tourism, Conventions and Events Management: LINDA R. BROTHERS

School of Science:

Biology: NORMAN D. LEES

Chemistry: Prof. FRANKLIN A. SCHULTZ

Computer Science: Prof. MATHEW J. PALAKAL

Geology: ANDREW P. BARTH

Mathematical Sciences: Prof. BENZION BOUKAI

Physics: Prof. GAUTAM VEMURI

Psychology: Prof. JOHN GREGOR FETTERMAN

INDIANA WESLEYAN UNIVERSITY

4201 S Washington St, Marion, IN 46953

Telephone: (765) 674-6901

Fax: (765) 677-2499

Internet: www.indwes.edu

Founded 1920

Academic year: September to April

President: Dr JAMES BARNES

Vice-President for Financial Affairs: ELVIN WEINMANN

Vice-President for Academic Affairs: Dr HENRY SMITH

Librarian: SHEILA CARLBLOM

Library of 133,396 vols

Number of teachers: 121

Number of students: 3,027.

ITT TECHNICAL INSTITUTE

9511 Angola Court, Indianapolis, IN 46268-1119

Telephone: (317) 875-8640

Internet: www.itt-tech.edu

Private control

President: Dr LARRY L. GRAPHMAN

Number of students: 1,690

Areas of study: automated manufacturing technology, computer and electronics engineering technology, computer drafting and design, computer visualization technology, computer-aided drafting and design technology, electronics engineering technology, information systems security, information technology – computer network systems, information technology – multimedia, information technology – software applications and programming, information technology – web development, technical project management for electronic commerce.

MANCHESTER COLLEGE

604 College Ave, North Manchester, IN 46962

Telephone: (219) 982-5000

Internet: www.manchester.edu

Founded 1889

Four-year liberal arts and professional studies

President: Dr PARKER G. MARDEN

Vice-President for Academic Affairs: Dr JO YOUNG SWITZER

Vice-President and Dean of Student Development: WILLIAM RHUDY

Vice-President and Treasurer: NANCY E. KIN

Vice-President of Enrollment and Planning: Dr DAVID F. McFADDEN

Registrar: LILA D. HAMMER

Director of the Library: ROBIN J. GRATZ

Library of 160,000 vols

Number of teachers: 72 full-time

Number of students: 1,054

Publications: Manchester Magazine (quarterly), The Oak Leaves (every 2 weeks), The Aurora (annually).

MARIAN COLLEGE

3200 Cold Spring Rd, Indianapolis, IN 46222-1997

Telephone: (317) 955-6000

Fax: (317) 955-6448

E-mail: regis@marian.edu

Internet: www.marian.edu

Founded 1851

Baccalaureate liberal arts college

Academic year: August to May

President: DANIEL J. ELSENER

Chief Advancement Officer: ANN RUNYON

Dean for Academic Affairs: Dr C. EDWARD BALOG

Dean for Student Affairs: WILLIAM H. WOODMAN

Chief Financial Officer: RUSSELL GLASSBURN

Librarian: KELLEY GRIFFITH

Library of 135,000 vols

Number of teachers: 77 (full-time)

Number of students: 1,427.

MARTIN UNIVERSITY

2171 Avondale Place, Indianapolis, IN 46218

Telephone: (317) 543-3237

Fax: (317) 543-4790

Internet: www.martin.edu

Founded 1977

Private control

President: Rev. Fr BONIFACE HARDIN

Number of teachers: 33

Number of students: 1,000

Academic divisions: business and management, human sciences, liberal arts, religious studies, science and mathematics.

OAKLAND CITY UNIVERSITY

143 N Lucretia Street, Oakland City, IN 47660

Telephone: (812) 749-1222
Fax: (812) 749-1233
E-mail: ocuadmit@oak.edu
Internet: www.oak.edu
Private control

President: Dr JAMES W. MURRAY
Vice-President (Academic Affairs): Dr BERNARD MARLEY
Vice-President (Administration): Dr ORA JOHNSON
Vice-President (Development): Dr JACK TICHENOR
Vice-President (Personnel): RANEL ESKEW
Registrar: BETTY BURNS
Library Director: DENISE J. PINNICK
Number of teachers: 32
Number of students: 1,789 (1,492 undergraduate, 297 graduate)

DEANS

School of Arts and Sciences: Dr MICHAEL ATKINSON
School of Business: Dr VICKY BLACK
School of Education: Dr PATRICIA SWAILS
Chapman School of Religion: Dr RAY BARBER
School of Technology: DAVID SWAILS

PURDUE UNIVERSITY

West Lafayette, IN 47907

Telephone: (765) 494-4600
Fax: (765) 494-7875
E-mail: webmaster@purdue.edu
Internet: www.purdue.edu
Founded 1869; instruction commenced 1874
State control
Academic year: August to May

President: MARTIN C. JISCHKE
Provost: SALLY FROST MASON
Executive Vice-President and Treasurer: KENNETH P. BURNS
Vice-Provost for Academic Affairs: MARGARET M. ROWE
Vice-Provost for Research: CHARLES O. RUTLEDGE
Vice President for Government Relations: TERRY D. STRUEH
Vice-President for Physical Facilities: WAYNE W. KJONAAS
Vice-President for Student Services: THOMAS B. ROBINSON
Vice-President for Housing and Food Services: JOHN A. SAUTTER
Vice-President for University Relations: JOSEPH L. BENNETT
Vice-President for Human Relations: ALYSA C. ROLLOCK (acting)
Vice-President for Business Services and Assistant Treasurer: JAMES S. ALMOND
Vice-President for Engagement: DON K. GENTRY
Chancellor of Indiana University–Purdue University Fort Wayne: MICHAEL A. WARTELL
Chancellor of Indiana University–Purdue University Indianapolis: GERALD L. BEPKO
Registrar: MARLESA A. RONEY
Director of Admissions: DOUGLAS L. CHRISTIANSEN
Dean of Libraries: EMILY R. MOBLEY
Dean of Students: L. TONY HAWKINS
Dean of the Graduate School: JOHN J. CONTRENI
Dean of International Programmes: MICHAEL J. STOHL
Library: see Libraries and Archives
Number of teachers: 3,811
Number of students: 68,046 (38,564 at West Lafayette campus, 29,482 at regional campuses

Publications: *University Bulletins, Inside Purdue, Perspective*

DEANS

School of Agriculture (West Lafayette): VICTOR L. LECHTENBERG
School of Arts and Sciences (Fort Wayne): MARC J. LIPMAN
School of Business and Management Sciences (Fort Wayne): JOHN F. WELLINGTON
School of Consumer and Family Sciences (West Lafayette): DENNIS A. SAVAIANO
School of Education (West Lafayette): JERRY L. PETERS
School of Education (Fort Wayne): ROBERTA B. WIENER
Schools of Engineering (West Lafayette): LINDA P. B. KATEHI
School of Engineering, Technology and Computer Science (Fort Wayne): C. WAYNE UNSELL
School of Engineering and Technology (Indianapolis): H. ONER YURTSEVEN
School of Fine and Performing Arts (Fort Wayne): BENJAMIN C. CHRISTY
School of Health Sciences (Fort Wayne): JAMES E. JONES
School of Liberal Arts (West Lafayette): TOBY L. PARCEL
School of Management and Krannert Graduate School of Management (West Lafayette): RICHARD A. COSIER
Schools of Pharmacy, Nursing and Health Sciences (West Lafayette): JOHN M. PEZZUTO
School of Physical Education and Tourism Management (Indianapolis): P. NICHOLAS KELLUM
School of Science (West Lafayette): JEFFREY S. VITTER
School of Science (Indianapolis): DAVID L. STOCUM
School of Technology (West Lafayette): DON K. GENTRY
School of Veterinary Medicine (West Lafayette): ALAN H. REBAR
Continuing Studies (Fort Wayne): DEBORAH M. CONKLIN (Exec. Dir)

HEADS OF DEPARTMENTS

School of Agriculture (West Lafayette):

Agricultural and Biological Engineering: Prof. VINCENT F. BRALTS
Agricultural Communication: CHRIS SIGURDSON
Agricultural Economics: Prof. THOMAS HERTEL
Agronomy: Prof. CRAIG A. BEYROUTY
Animal Sciences: Prof. ALAN L. GRANT
Biochemistry: Prof. JAMES D. FORNEY
Botany and Plant Pathology: Prof. RAYMOND D. MARTYN
Entomology: Prof. PETER E. DUNN
Food Science: Prof. PHILIP E. NELSON
Forestry and Natural Resources: DENNIS C. LE MASTER
Horticulture and Landscape Architecture: EDWARD N. ASHWORTH

School of Consumer and Family Sciences (West Lafayette):

Child Development and Family Studies: DOUGLAS R. POWELL
Consumer Sciences and Retailing: Prof. RICHARD WIDDOWS
Foods and Nutrition: Prof. CONNIE M. WEAVER
Restaurant, Hotel, Institutional and Tourism Management: Prof. RAPHAEL R. KAVANAUGH

School of Education (West Lafayette):

Curriculum and Instruction: JAMES D. LEHMAN
Educational Studies: KEVIN KELLY

Schools of Engineering (West Lafayette):

Aeronautics and Astronautics: Prof. THOMAS N. FARRIS
Chemical Engineering: Prof. GINTARAS V. REKLAITIS
Civil Engineering: Prof. FRED L. MANNERING
Construction Engineering and Management: Prof. DANIEL W. HALPIN
Electrical and Computer Engineering: Prof. MARK J. T. SMITH
Freshman Engineering: Prof. JENNFIER S. CURTIS
Industrial Engineering: Prof. DENNIS ENGI (acting)
Interdisciplinary Engineering Studies: Dr PHILLIP C. WANKAT
Materials Engineering: Dr ALEXANDER H. KING
Mechanical Engineering: Prof. E. DANIEL HIRLEMAN
Nuclear Engineering: Prof. LEFTERI H. TSOUKALAS

School of Liberal Arts (West Lafayette):

Audiology and Speech Sciences: Prof. ANNE SMITH
Communication: (vacant)
English: THOMAS P. ADLER
Foreign Languages and Literatures: Prof. PAUL DIXON
Health, Kinesiology and Leisure Studies: Prof. THOMAS J. TEMPLIN
History: Prof. GORDON R. MORK
Philosophy: Prof. ROD BERTOLET
Political Science: Prof. WILLIAM R. SHAFFER
Psychological Sciences: Prof. THOMAS J. BERNDT
Sociology and Anthropology: CAROLYN CUMMINGS PERUCCI
Visual and Performing Arts: Prof. DAVID L. SIGMAN (acting)

School of Management:

Accounting: ROBERT K. ESKEW, III
Business Law: PHILLIP J. SCALETTA
Economics: Prof. JOHN R. UMBECK
Finance: JOHN J. McCONNELL
Management Information Systems: KEMAL ALTINKEMER
Marketing: MANOHAR U. KALWANI
Organizational Behaviour/Human Resources: DAVID SCHOORMAN
Operations Management: JAMES E. WARD
Quantitative Methods: GORDON P. WRIGHT
Strategic Management: DAN E. SCHENDEL

Schools of Pharmacy, Nursing, and Health Sciences (West Lafayette):

Health Sciences: PAUL L. ZIEMER
Industrial and Physical Pharmacy: Prof. STEPHEN R. BYRN
Medicinal Chemistry and Molecular Pharmacology: Prof. RICHARD F. BORCH
Nursing: Dr LINDA AGUSTIN SIMUNEK
Pharmacy Practice: Prof. STEVEN R. ABEL

School of Science (West Lafayette):

Biological Sciences: Prof. LOUIS A. SHERMAN
Chemistry: Prof. IAN P. ROTHWELL
Computer Sciences: Prof. SUSANNE E. HAMBRUSCH
Earth and Atmospheric Science: Prof. HARSHVARDHAN
Mathematics: Prof. LEONARD LIPSCHITZ
Physics: Prof. ANDREW S. HIRSCH
Statistics: Prof. MARY ELLEN BOCK

School of Technology (West Lafayette):

Aviation Technology: Prof. THOMAS Q. CARNEY
Building Construction Management: Prof. STEPHEN D. SCHUETTE
Computer Graphics Technology: Prof. MARK W. BALLANTYNE
Computer Technology: Prof. LONNIE D. BENTLEY

Electrical Engineering Technology: Prof. ROBERT J. HERRICK
Industrial Technology: Prof. M. NIAZ LATIF
Mechanical Engineering Technology: Prof. NANCY L. DENTON
Organizational Leadership and Supervision: Prof. CYNTHIA L. TOMOVIC

School of Veterinary Medicine:

Basic Medical Sciences: Prof. GORDON L. COPPOC
Veterinary Clinical Sciences: L. KIRK CLARK
Veterinary Pathobiology: Prof. HARM HOGENESCH

UNIVERSITY BRANCHES

Purdue University Calumet

2200 169th Street, Hammond, IN 463232094
Telephone: (219) 989-2400
Fax: (219) 989-2775
E-mail: adms@calumet.purdue.edu
Internet: www.calumet.purdue.edu

Chancellor: HOWARD COHEN
Vice-Chancellor (Academic Affairs): NABIL A. IBRAHIM
Vice-Chancellor (Student Services)/Dean of Students: LEO A. BRYANT
Vice-Chancellor (Administrative Services): GARY H. NEWSOM
Vice-Chancellor (Advancement): DOLORES M. STEUER-WAGNER
Executive Dean, Graduate School: DANIEL DUNN
Registrar: ANNE AGOSTO-SEVERA
Library Director: KATHRYN H. CARPENTER
Library of 264,000 vols
Number of teachers: 247
Number of students: 8,863 (7,920 undergraduate, 943 graduate)

DEANS

School of Education: Dr ROBERT RIVERS
School of Engineering, Mathematics and Science: Dr MICHAEL GEALT
School of Liberal Arts and Social Sciences: Dr DANIEL DUNN
School of Management: Dr SHOMIR SIL
School of Nursing: Dr PEGGY GERARD
School of Technology: DENNIS KORCHEK

Purdue University North Central

1401 S U.S. 421, Westville, IN 46391
Telephone: (219) 8720527
Fax: (219) 7855355
E-mail: admissions@pnc.edu
Internet: www.purduenc.edu

Founded 1967

Chancellor: Dr JAMES B. DWORKIN
Vice-Chancellor (Academic Affairs): Dr L. EDWARD BEDNAR
Vice-Chancellor (Administration): Dr G. WILLIAM BACK
Vice-Chancellor (Development): JOSEPH K. GOEPFRICH
Registrar: GEORGE ROYSTER
Library Director: K. R. JOHNSON
Number of teachers: 244
Number of students: 3,657 (3,635 undergraduate, 22 graduate)

HEADS OF DEPARTMENTS

Behavioral Sciences, Social Sciences and Humanities: Dr HOWARD JABLON
Biology and Chemistry: Dr JOSEPH W. CAMP, Jr (acting)
Business: Dr ANDREW R. WEISS
Computer Technology: RICHARD M. SCROGGIN (acting)
Developmental Studies: Dr LINDA DUTTLINGER
Elementary Education: Dr CYNTHIA J. PULVER FONTAINE (acting)

Engineering Technology: RICHARD L. TAYLOR
Letters and Languages: Dr THOMAS E. YOUNG
Mathematics, Statistics and Physics: Dr KEITH E. SCHWINGENDORF (acting)
Nursing: Dr L. EDWARD BEDNAR (acting)

ROSE-HULMAN INSTITUTE OF TECHNOLOGY

5500 Wabash Ave, Terre Haute, IN 47803
Telephone: (812) 877-1511
Fax: (812) 877-9925
E-mail: webmaster@rose-hulman.edu
Internet: www.rose-hulman.edu

Founded 1874

President: Dr SAMUEL F. HULBERT
Vice-President for Academic Affairs and Dean of the Faculty: Prof. ARTHUR B. WESTERN
Associate Vice-President, Business and Finance: ROBERT A. COONS
Registrar: TIMOTHY PRICKEL
Director of the Library: JOHN ROBSON
Library of 70,000 vols, 22,000 vols of periodicals, 1,500 NASA and NATO documents
Number of teachers: 120
Number of students: 1,812

Publication: Bulletin (every 2 years).

SAINT JOSEPH'S COLLEGE

Rensselaer, IN 47978
Telephone: (219) 866-6000
E-mail: admissions@saintjoe.edu
Internet: www.saintjoe.edu

Founded 1889

President: Dr ERNEST R. MILLS, III
Registrar: CAROL BURNS
Librarian: CATHERINE SAYLERS
Library of 150,000 vols
Number of teachers: 64
Number of students: 974.

SAINT MARY-OF-THE-WOODS COLLEGE

Saint Mary-of-the-Woods, IN 47876
Telephone: (812) 535-5151
Fax: (812) 535-5010
E-mail: smeier@smwc.edu
Internet: www.smwc.edu

Founded 1840

Academic year: August to May

President: Dr JOAN LESCINSKI
Co-Chancellors: Dr BARBARA DOHERTY, Dr JEANNE KNOERLE
Chief Academic Officer: Dr CHRIS BAHR
Director of Academic Records and Institutional Research: SUSAN MEIER
Librarian: JUDITH TRIBBLE
Library of 151,000 vols
Number of teachers: 67
Number of students: 881 full-time

Publication: Aurora (Literary Journal 2 a year)

CHAIRS OF DEPARTMENTS

Business: Dr JENNIE MITCHELL
Education: DEBRA HARDIN
English, Journalism and Language: TERRY McCAMMON
Mark Hulman George School of Equine Studies: Dr CHRISTINE STEWART MARKS
Performing and Visual Arts: PAT JANCOSEK
Science, Mathematics and Computer Information Systems: Dr ELLEN CUNNINGHAM
Social and Behavioural Science: Dr GLENNA SIMONS
Theology and Philosophy: Dr ROBERT WATTS

SAINT MARY'S COLLEGE

Notre Dame, IN 46556
Telephone: (219) 284-4000
E-mail: admission@saintmarys.edu
Internet: www.saintmarys.edu

Founded 1844

President: Dr MARILOU ELDRED
Vice-President and Dean of Faculty: Dr DOROTHY M. FEIGL
Vice-President for College Relations (vacant)
Vice-President for Student Affairs: Dr LINDA L. TIMM
Vice-President for Fiscal Affairs: DANIEL F. OSBERGER
Registrar: LORRAINE A. KITCHENER
Library of 195,424 vols
Number of students: 1,435 full-time

Publications: Courier, Blue Mantle, Chimes (annually).

SAINT MEINRAD SCHOOL OF THEOLOGY

200 Hill Drive, St Meinrad, IN 47577
Telephone: (812) 357-6611
Fax: (812) 357-6964
E-mail: theology@saintmeinrad.edu
Internet: www.saintmeinrad.edu
Private control

President and Rector: Rev. MARK O'KEEFE
Academic Dean: Dr THOMAS P. WALTERS
Library of 166,000 items
Number of teachers: 28
Number of students: 117.

TAYLOR UNIVERSITY

236 W. Reade Ave, Upland, IN 46989-1001
Telephone: (317) 998-2751
Fax: (317) 998-4925
E-mail: admissions_u@taylor.edu
Internet: www.tayloru.edu

Founded 1846

Private interdenominational Christian liberal arts college; campuses in Upland and Fort Wayne

Academic year: September to May (three terms)

President: Dr DAVID J. GYERTSON
Chancellor: Dr JAY KESLER
Executive Vice-President and Provost: Dr DARYL YOST
Vice-President, Administration and Planning: STEVE BEDI
Registrar: LAGATHA ADKISON
Director of Admissions: STEPHEN MORTLAND
Librarian: DAN BOWELL
Library of 235,114 vols
Number of teachers: 153
Number of students: 2,400 (Upland campus 1,900, Fort Wayne campus 500)

Publications: Profile, Taylor University Magazine, Taylor Club News.

TRI-STATE UNIVERSITY

1 University Ave, Angola, IN 46703-1764
Telephone: (260) 665-4100
Fax: (260) 665-4292
E-mail: admit@tristate.edu
Internet: www.tristate.edu

Founded 1884 as Tri-State Normal College; present name 1975
Private control

President: Dr EARL D. BROOKS, II
Vice-President (Academic Affairs): Dr THOMAS J. ENNEKING
Vice-President (Finance and Administration): JOHN LYNCH
Vice-President (Student Life): Dr JEAN DELLER
Registrar: DEBBIE HELMSING

Library Director: KRISTINA BREWER
Number of teachers: 65
Number of students: 1,480

DEANS

Allen School of Engineering and Technology: Dr DAVID FINLEY
Ketner School of Business: Dr JEFFERY SHERLOCK
School of Education: Dr SUZANNE VANWAGNER
School of Arts and Sciences: Dr DOLORES TICHENOR

BRANCH CAMPUSES

Fort Wayne Campus: 328 Ley Rd, Suite 200, Fort Wayne, IN 46825; tel. (260) 483-4949; fax (260) 482-8553; e-mail tsufw@tristate.edu; Dir CLIFF GJERTSON, Sr.

South Bend Campus and Merrillville Site: 215 S St Joseph St, Suite 201, South Bend, IN 46601; tel. (574) 234-4810; fax (574) 234-4854; e-mail tsusb@tristate.edu; Dir DENNIS BANAS.

UNIVERSITY OF EVANSVILLE

1800 Lincoln Ave, Evansville, IN 47722
Telephone: (812) 479-2000
Fax: (812) 479-2320
E-mail: webmaster@evansville.edu
Internet: www.evansville.edu
Founded 1854
Academic year: August to May
President: Dr STEPHEN G. JENNINGS
Vice-President for Academic Affairs: Dr STEPHEN GREINER
Vice-President for Fiscal Affairs: ROBERT E. GALLMAN
Vice-President for Development: W. SCOTT SHRODE
Dean of Students: DANA CLAYTON
Director of University Relations: MARCIA DOWELL
Director of Continuing Education: LYNN R. PENLAND
Registrar: KEITH M. KUTZLER
University Librarian: WILLIAM LOUDEN
Number of teachers: 192
Number of students: 2,400

DEANS

School of Business Administration: Dr DAVID B. REEDER
College of Arts and Sciences: Dr STEPHEN G. GREINER
College of Engineering and Computer Science: Dr PHILIP GERHART
College of Education and Health Sciences: Dr LYNN R. PENLAND

UNIVERSITY OF INDIANAPOLIS

1400 East Hanna Ave, Indianapolis, IN 46227
Telephone: (317) 788-3368
Internet: www.uindy.edu
Founded 1902
President: Dr JERRY ISRAEL
Senior Vice-President and Provost: Dr EVERETTE FREEMAN
Vice-President for Institutional Advancement: MICHAEL J. FERIN
Vice-President for Business and Treasurer: KENDALL L. HOTTELL
Vice-President for Student Affairs: DAVID W. WANTZ
Vice-President for Enrollment: MARK T. WEIGAND
Registrar: Dr MARY BETH BAGG
Dean of Extended Programs: Dr PAT JEFFERSON BIBLY
Co-ordinator of Graduate Business Programs: Dr RENEE WACHTER

Director of Admissions: RON WILKS
Librarian: Dr PHILIP H. YOUNG
Library of 180,000 vols
Number of teachers: 165 full-time
Number of students: 4,300.

UNIVERSITY OF NOTRE DAME

Notre Dame, IN 46556
Telephone: (574) 631-5000
E-mail: admissions@nd.edu
Internet: www.nd.edu
Founded 1842
Academic year: August to May
President: Rev. EDWARD A. MALLOY
Provost: NATHAN O. HATCH
Executive Vice-President: Rev. TIMOTHY R. SCULLY
Vice-President and Associate Provost: Rev. JOHN I. JENKINS
Vice-President and Associate Provost: JOHN AFFLECK-GRAVES
Vice-President and Associate Provost: CAROL A. MOONEY
Vice-President for Graduate Studies and Research: Dr JEFFREY C. KANTOR
Vice-President for Student Affairs: Rev. MARK L. POORMAN
Vice-President for University Relations: LOUIS M. NANNI
Vice-President for Public Affairs and Communication: J. ROBERTO GUTIERREZ
Registrar: HAROLD L. PACE
Director of Admissions: DANIEL J. SARACINO
Librarian: JENNIFER YOUNGER
Archivist: WENDY C. SCHLERETH
Library: see Libraries
Number of teachers: 1,171
Number of students: 11,311
Publications: *Academy of Management Review, American Midland Naturalist, Review of Politics, Bullán, Notre Dame Law Review, Technical Review, Journal of College and University Law, Notre Dame Journal of Formal Logic, Journal of Legislation, Journal of Multicultural Counseling and Development, Nineteenth-Century Contexts, The American Journal of Jurisprudence, Notre Dame Philosophical Review, Notre Dame Review, Religion and Literature, Notre Dame Journal of Law, Ethics and Public Policy*

DEANS

Freshman Year of Studies: Dr EILEEN M. KOLMAN
College of Arts and Letters: Dr MARK W. ROCHE
Mendoza College of Business: Dr CAROLYN Y. WOO
College of Engineering: Dr FRANK P. INCROPERA
Law School: PATRICIA A. O'HARA
College of Science: Dr JOSEPH P. MARINO

PROFESSORS

College of Arts and Letters:
  ALDOUS, J., Sociology
  AMERIKS, K., Philosophy
  ANADON, J., Romance Languages and Literatures
  APPLEBY, R. S., History
  ARNOLD, P., Political Science
  AUNE, D. E., Theology
  AYO, N., Liberal Studies
  BARBER, S. A., Political Science
  BARTELL, E., Economics
  BIDDICK, K., History
  BLACHLY, A., Music
  BLANTZ, T. E., History
  BOBIK, J., Philosophy
  BORKOWSKI, J. G., Psychology
  BOULTON, M. B., Romance Languages and Literatures

BOWER, C., Music
BRADLEY, K. R., Classics
BRADSHAW, P. F., Theology
BROGAN, J. V., English
BRUNS, G. L., English
BURRELL, D. B., Philosophy
BUSTAMANTE, J. A., Psychology, Sociology
BUTTIGIEG, J. A., English
CACHEY, T., Romance Languages and Literatures
CARDENAS, G., Psychology
CRAFTON, D., Film, Television, and Theatre
CRAMER, C., Music
CUMMINGS, E. M., Psychology
CUNNINGHAM, L. S., Theology
DALEY, S. J., Theology
DALLMAYR, F., Political Theory
DAMATTA, R., Anthropology
DAVID, M., Philosophy
DAY, J. D., Psychology
DELANEY, C. F., Philosophy
DEPAUL, M., Philosophy
DETLEFSEN, M., Philosophy
DOODY, M. A., English Literature
DOUGHERTY, J. P., English
DOUTHWAITE, J., Romance Languages and Literatures
DOWTY, A., Political Science
DUNNE, J. S., Theology
DUTT, A., Economics
DYE, K., Music
EMERY, K., Jr, Program of Liberal Studies
FLINT, T., Philosophy
FOX, C. B., English
FRANCIS, M. J., Political Science
FREDDOSO, A. J., Philosophy
FREDMAN, S., English
FRESE, D., English
GERNES, S. G., English
GERSH, S., Medieval Studies
GIBBONS, L., English, Film, Television, and Theatre
GODMILOW, J., Film, Television, and Theatre
GUTTING, G., Philosophy
HAIMO, E. T., Music
HALLINAN, M. W., Sociology
HALTON, E., Sociology
HAMBURG, G., History
HAMLIN, C., History
HART, K., English
HERO, R. E., Political Science
HIGGINS, P., Music
HOLLAND, P. D., Film, Television, and Theatre
HÖSLE, V., German and Russian Languages and Literatures
HOWARD, D. A., Philosophy
HOWARD, G. S., Psychology
JAKSIC, I., History
JEMIELITY, T. J., English
JENSEN, R., Economics
JOHANSEN, R. C., Political Science
JOHNSON, M., Theology
JOY, L. S., Philosophy
KAVENY, M., Theology
KIM, K., Economics
KLINE, E. A., English
KOMMERS, D. P., Political Science
KREMER, W. J., Art, Art History, and Design
KRIEG, R. A., Theology
KSELMAN, T., History
LAPIDGE, M., English
LEAHY, W. H., Economics
LOPEZ, G., Political Science
LOUX, M. J., Philosophy
McADAMS, A. J., Political Science
McBRIEN, R. P., Theology
McINERNY, R., Philosophy
McKENNA, J. J., Anthropology
MAINWARING, S., Political Science
MANIER, E., Philosophy
MANN, G. L., English
MARSDEN, G. M., History

MARULLO, T., German and Russian Languages and Literature
MATTHIAS, J. E., English
MAXWELL, S. E., Psychology
MEIER, J. P., Theology
MOODY, P., Political Science
MURRAY, D., History
NEYREY, S. J., Theology
NICGORSKI, W. J., Political Science, Program of Liberal Studies
NOBLE, T., Medieval Institute
NORTON, R. E., German and Russian Languages and Literatures
O'BRIEN O'KEEFFE, K., English
O'DONNELL, G., Political Science
O'REGAN, C., Theology
O'ROURKE, W. A., English
PILKINTON, M. C., Film, Television, and Theatre
PLANTINGA, A., Philosophy
POPE-DAVIS, D., Psychology
POWER, F. C., Liberal Studies, Psychology
PROFIT, V. B., German and Russian Languages and Literatures
ROCHE, M., German Language and Literature, Philosophy
ROOS, J., Political Science
ROS, J., Economics
ROSENBERG, C., Art, Art History and Design
SAYERS, V., English
SAYRE, K. M., Philosophy
SCHLERETH, T. J., American Studies
SCHMUHL, R., American Studies
SCULLY, T. R., Political Science
SEIDENSPINNER-NÚÑEZ, D., Romance Languages and Literatures
SHEERIN, D., Classics, Theology
SHRADER-FRECHETTE, K., Philosophy, Biological Sciences
SKURSKI, R., Economics
SLAUGHTER, T., History
SLOAN, P. R., Liberal Studies
SMYTH, J., History
STERBA, J., Philosophy
STERLING, G. E., Theology
SWARTZ, T., Economics
TURNER, J., History
ULRICH, E., Theology
VALENZUELA, J. S., Sociology
VANDEN BOSSCHE, C., English
VANDERKAM, J. C., Theology
VAYRYNEN, R., Political Science
WALSHE, A. P., Political Science
WALTON, J., English
WATSON, S., Philosophy
WEGS, R., History
WEIGERT, A., Sociology
WEITHMAN, P., Philosophy
WELLE, J., Romance Languages and Literatures
WERGE, T., English
WHITMAN, T., Psychology
YOUENS, S., Music
ZIAREK, E., English

Mendoza College of Business:
AFFLECK-GRAVES, J., Finance and Business Economics
BRETZ, R., Management and Administrative Sciences
CONLON, E. J., Management and Administrative Sciences
COSIMANO, T. F., Finance and Business Economics
ENDERLE, G., Marketing
ETZEL, M. J., Marketing
FRECKA, T. J., Accountancy
GRESIK, T., Finance and Business Economics
GUILTINAN, J. P., Marketing
GUNDLACH, G. T., Marketing
HARTVIGSEN, D. B., Management and Administrative Sciences
HUANG, R. D., Finance and Business Economics

KEANE, J. G., Management and Administrative Sciences
KEATING, B. P., Finance and Business Economics
KENNEDY, J. J., Marketing
KRAJEWSKI, L., Management and Administrative Sciences
McDONALD, W. D., Finance and Business Economics
MATTA, K. F., Management and Administrative Sciences
MILANI, K. W., Accountancy
MITTELSTAEDT, H. F., Accountancy
MORRIS, M. H., Accountancy
MURPHY, P. E., Marketing
NICHOLS, W. D., Accountancy
RAMANAN, R., Accountancy
REILLY, F. K., Finance and Business Economics
RICCHIUTE, D. N., Accountancy
RUESCHHOFF, N. G., Accountancy
SCHAEFER, T., Accountancy
SCHULTZ, P., Finance and Business Economics
SHEEHAN, R. G., Finance and Business Economics
SIMON, D. T., Accountancy
TAVIS, L. A., Finance and Business Economics
URBANY, J., Marketing
VECCHIO, R. P., Management and Administrative Sciences
WILKIE, W. L., Marketing
WITTENBACH, J. L., Accountancy

College of Engineering
Department of Aerospace and Mechanical Engineering:
ATASSI, H. M., Aero-acoustics
BATILL, S. M., Design
CORKE, T. C., Fluid Mechanics
DUNN, P. F., Particle Dynamics
INCROPERA, F. P., Heat Transfer
JUMPER, E. J., Aerodynamics
MUELLER, T. J., Fluid Mechanics
NELSON, R. C., Aerodynamics
OVAERT, T., Manufacturing
PAOLUCCI, S., Fluid Mechanics
RENAUD, J. E., Design
SEN, M., Heat Transfer
SKAAR, S. B., Control
THOMAS, F. O., Fluid Mechanics

Department of Chemical Engineering:
BRENNECKE, J. F.
CHANG, H.-C.
KANTOR, J. C.
LEIGHTON, D. T.
McCREADY, M. J.
McGINN, P. J.
MILLER, A. E.
STADTHERR, M. A.
STRIEDER, W. C.
VARMA, A.
SCHMITZ, R. A.
WOLF, E. E.

Department of Civil Engineering and Geological Sciences:
BURNS, P. C.
KAREEM, A.
SILLIMAN, S. E.
TAYLOR, J. I.

Department of Computer Science and Engineering:
BOWYER, K.
CHEN, D. Z.
KOGGE, P. M.
UHRAN, J., Jr

Department of Electrical Engineering:
ANTSAKLIS, P. J.
BAUER, P. H.
BERNSTEIN, G. H.
COLLINS, O.
COSTELLO, D. J.
FUJA, T. E.

HUANG, Y.-F.
LENT, C. S.
MERZ, J. L.
POROD, W.
ROSENTHAL, J.
SAIN, M. K.
SEABAUGH, A. C.
STEVENSON, R. L.

Law School:
BARRETT, M.
BAUER, J. P.
BENNETT, G.
BLAKEY, G. R.
BRADLEY, G. V.
DUTILE, F. N.
GUNN, A.
GURULE, J.
JACOBS, R. F.
KAVENY, M. C.
KELLENBERG, C. L.
KOMMERS, D. P.
MENDEZ, J. E.
MOONEY, C. A.
O'HARA, P.
PHELPS, T. G.
PRATT, W. F., Jr
RODES, R. E., Jr
SECKINGER, J. H.
SHELTON, D. L.
SMITHBURN, E.
TIDMARSH, J.

College of Science:
ALBER, M. S., Mathematics
APRAHAMIAN, A., Physics
ARNOLD, G. B., Physics
ASMUS, K.-D., Chemistry and Biochemistry
BARABASI, A.-L., Physics
BASU, S. C., Chemistry and Biochemistry
BELOVSKY, G. E., Biological Sciences
BENDER, H. A., Biological Sciences
BERRY, H. G., Physics
BESANSKY, N. J., Biological Sciences
BIGI, I. I., Physics
BLACKSTEAD, H. A., Physics
BOTTEI, R. S., Chemistry and Biochemistry
BUECHLER, S. A., Mathematics
BUNKER, B. A., Physics
CAO, J., Mathematics
CASON, N. M., Physics
COLLINS, F. H., Biological Sciences
CONNOLLY, F. X., Mathematics
CREARY, X., Chemistry and Biochemistry
DOBROWOLSKA-FURDYNA, M., Physics
DUMAN, J., Biological Sciences
DWYER, W. G., Mathematics
FAYBUSOVICH, L. E., Mathematics
FEHLNER, T. P., Chemistry and Biochemistry
FRASER, M. J., Jr, Biological Sciences
FRAUENDORF, S. G., Physics
FURDYNA, J. K., Physics
GARG, U., Physics
GOERRES, J., Physics
HAHN, A. J., Mathematics
HELLENTHAL, R., Biological Sciences
HELQUIST, P., Chemistry and Biochemistry
HIMONAS, A. A., Mathematics
HOWARD, A., Mathematics
HU, B., Mathematics
HYDE, D. R., Biological Sciences
HYDER, A. K., Research Physics
JACOBS, D. C., Chemistry and Biochemistry
JOHNSON, A. L., Biological Sciences
JOHNSON, W. R., Physics
JONES, G. L., Physics
KNIGHT, J. F., Mathematics
KOLATA, J. J., Physics
KULPA, C. F., Biological Sciences
LAMBERTI, G. A., Biological Sciences
LAPPIN, A. G., Chemistry and Biochemistry
LEPRAPPIER, F., Mathematics
LIVINGSTON, A. E., Physics
LODGE, D. M., Biological Sciences
LoSECCO, J. M., Physics
MARINO, J. P., Chemistry and Biochemistry

MATHEWS, G. J., Physics
MEISEL, D., Chemistry and Biochemistry
MERZ, J. L., Physics
MIGLIORE, J. C., Mathematics
MILLER, M. J., Chemistry and Biochemistry
NEWMAN, K. E., Physics
NOWAK, T. L., Chemistry and Biochemistry
O'TOUSA, J. E., Biological Sciences
PAONI, N., Chemistry and Biochemistry
RETTIG, T. W., Physics
ROSENTHAL, J. J., Mathematics
RUCHTI, R. C., Physics
SAPIRSTEIN, J. R., Physics
SCHEIDT, W. R., Chemistry and Biochemistry
SERIANNI, A. S., Chemistry and Biochemistry
SEVERSON, D. W., Biological Sciences
SEVOV, S., Chemistry and Biochemistry
SHAW, M.-C., Mathematics
SHEPHARD, W. D., Physics
SHRADER-FRECHETTE, K., Biological Sciences
SMITH, B. D., Chemistry and Biochemistry
SMYTH, B., Mathematics
SNOW, D. M., Mathematics
SOMMESE, A. J., Mathematics
STANTON, N. K., Mathematics
STOLZ, S. A., Mathematics
TAYLOR, L. R., Mathematics
TENNISWOOD, M. P., Biological Sciences
WARCHOL, J., Physics
WAYNE, M. R., Physics
WELSH, J. E. J., Biological Sciences
WIESCHER, M. C. F., Physics
WILLIAMS, E. B., Mathematics
WONG, P.-M., Mathematics
XAVIER, F., Mathematics

School of Architecture:
AMICO, R.
CROWE, N.
LYKOUDIS, M.
SMITH, T. G.
WESTFALL, C. W.

UNIVERSITY OF SAINT FRANCIS

2701 Spring St, Fort Wayne, IN 46808-3994
Telephone: (219) 434-3100
Fax: (219) 434-3183
E-mail: admis@sf.edu
Internet: www.sf.edu

Founded 1890
Academic year: August to May

President: Sister M. ELISE KRISS
Vice-President for Academic Affairs: Dr MARCIA SAUTER
Vice-President for University Advancement: Dr WILLIAM J. SHUSTOWSKI, Jr
Vice-President for Student Life: SHARON MEJEUR
Vice-President for Finance: DONALD SIMMONS
Vice-President for Operations: KENNETH WILLIAMS
Vice-President for Enrollment Management: RONALD SCHUMACHER
Registrar: FRANK CONNOR
Director of Library Services: LAURALEE AVEN
Number of teachers: 125
Number of students: 1,883.

UNIVERSITY OF SOUTHERN INDIANA

8600 University Blvd, Evansville, IN 47712-3596
Telephone: (812) 464-8600
Fax: (812) 465-7154
E-mail: enroll@usi.edu
Internet: www.usi.edu

Founded 1965 as the Evansville Campus of Indiana State University, current name and independent status 1985
State control

Academic year: August to May

President: Dr H. RAY HOOPS
Provost and Vice-President (Academic Affairs): ROBERT L. REID
Vice-President (Student Affairs): ROBERT W. PARRENT
Vice-President (Governmental Relations): CYNTHIA S. BRINKER
Vice-President (Business Affairs): ROBERT W. RUBLE
Vice-President (Advancement): SHERRIANNE M. STANDLEY

Number of teachers: 255
Number of students: 9,675

DEANS

School of Business: Dr PHIL FISHER
Bower-Suhrheinrich School of Education and Human Services: Dr THOMAS PICKERING
School of Liberal Arts: IAIN L. CRAWFORD
School of Nursing and Health Professions: Dr NADINE COUDRET
Pott School of Science and Engineering: Dr JEROME R. CAIN

VALPARAISO UNIVERSITY

Valparaiso, IN 46383
Telephone: (219) 464-5000
Fax: (219) 464-5381
E-mail: university.relations@valpo.edu
Internet: www.valpo.edu

Founded 1859

President: ALAN F. HARRE
Provost and Vice-President for Academic Affairs: Dr ROY AUSTENSEN
Vice-President for Administration and Finance: CHARLEY GILLESPIE
Vice-President for Admissions, Financial Aid and Marketing: KATHARINE WEHLING
Vice-President for Institutional Advancement: RICHARD MADDOX
Dean of Students: TIMOTHY JENKINS
Dean of Graduate and Continuing Education: DAVID ROWLAND
Registrar: ANN TROST
Librarian: RICHARD A. AMRHEIN

Library of 451,000 vols
Number of teachers: 228
Number of students: 3,603

DEANS

College of Arts and Sciences: ALBERT TROST
College of Business Administration: KARL REICHARDT (acting)
Christ College: MARK SCHWEIHN
College of Engineering: KRAIG J. OLEJNICZAK
College of Nursing: JANET BROWN

WABASH COLLEGE

Crawfordsville, IN 47933
Telephone: (317) 362-1400
E-mail: admissions@wabash.edu
Internet: www.wabash.edu

Founded 1832

President: Dr ANDREW T. FORD
Treasurer and Chief Financial Officer: DEANNA MCCORMICK
Dean of the College: MAURI DITZLER
Dean of Students: TOM BAMBREY
Dean of College Advancement: MARK W. JONES
Director of Admissions: STEVE KLEIN
Registrar: LESTER L. HEARSON
Librarian: LARRY J. FRYE

Library of 260,000 vols, 1,234 current periodicals, 155,000 govt documents, 9,300 audiovisual items
Number of teachers: 80
Number of students: 860.

ALLEN COLLEGE

1825 Logan Ave, Waterloo, IA 50703
Telephone: (319) 226-2000
Fax: (319) 226-2020
E-mail: allencollegeadmissions@ihs.org
Internet: www.allencollege.edu

Founded 1925 as Allen Memorial Hospital Nurses Training School; present name 1989
Private control

Chancellor: Dr JERRY D. DURHAM
Dean of Academic Affairs: Dr SUSAN DAWSON
Dir of Student Services: JOANNA RAMSDEN-MEIER
Library/Media Services Coordinator: MELISSA KANE

Number of teachers: 23
Number of students: 220

Faculties of nursing and radiography

CHAIRMEN OF ACADEMIC PROGRAMMES
Radiography: PEGGY FORTSCH
Nursing: Dr NANCY KRAMER (BSc), Dr DIANE YOUNG (MSc)

ASHFORD UNIVERSITY

400 North Bluff Blvd, Clinton, IA 52732
Telephone: (563) 242-4023
E-mail: admissions@ashford.edu
Internet: www.ashford.edu

Founded 1918 as Mount St Clare College; Franciscan Univ. 2002; present name 2005
Private control

Pres.: Dr MICHAEL E. KAELKE
Chancellor: Dr JANE MCAULIFFE
Exec. Vice-Pres. for College Relations and Mission Effectiveness: MARY ANN PHELAN
Academic Dean: Dr WILLIAM C. LOWE
Dean of Student Affairs: GARY COOPER
Library Dir: FLORA S. LOWE

Library of 101,000 vols, 650 periodicals, 70,000 microforms, 700 audiovisual titles
Number of teachers: 52 (26 full-time, 26 part-time)
Number of students: 495 (461 undergraduate, 34 graduate)

BAs in Accounting, Art (visual), Biology, Business Admin., Business Education, Clinical Laborary Science, Computer Graphic Design, Computer Science, Criminal Justice, Clinical Cytotechnology, Elementary Education, Health and Human Services Management, Information Systems, Liberal Arts, Nuclear Medicine Technology, Psychology, Social Justice, Social Science, Sports and Recreation Management

DEANS

School of Arts and Sciences: Dr WILLIAM LOWE
College of Education: Dr JOEN ROTTLER

DIVISION CHAIRS

Business Div.: Dr M. DIANE CORNILSEN
Fine Arts Div.: Dr ROBERT A. ENGELSON
Social Science Div.: Dr GARY HEATH
Humanities Div.: THERESA JUDGE
Education Div.: Dr LOIS J. YOCUM
Science Div.: Dr JOHN W. ZIMMERMAN

BRIAR CLIFF UNIVERSITY

POB 2100, Sioux City, IA 51104-0100
3303 Rebecca St, Sioux City, IA 51104-2324
Telephone: (712) 279-5200
Fax: (712) 279-1632

E-mail: admissions@briarcliff.edu
Internet: www.briarcliff.edu

Founded 1930 as Briar Cliff College; present name 2001
Private control
Academic year: September to May
Pres.: BEVERLY A. WHARTON
Provost/Vice-Pres. and Academic Dean: Dr THOMAS V. BOEKE
Vice-Pres. for Institutional Advancement: PHYLLIS M. CONNER
Vice-Pres. for Finance: RUTH BITTNER
Vice-Pres. for Enrollment Management: SHARISUE WILCOXON
Dean of Students: CALVIN J. BRINKERHOFF
Registrar: BEV AHRENS
Library Dir: RACHEL CROWLEY

Number of teachers: 51
Number of students: 1,000

Programmes in Accounting, Art, Biology, Business Administration, Chemistry, Computer Science, Criminal Justice, Elementary Education, English, Environmental Science, Graphic Design, Health, Physical Education, and Recreation, History, Human Resource Management, Mass Communications, Management Information Systems, Mathematics, Medical Technology, Music, New Media, Nursing, Political Science, Psychology, Radiologic Technology, Secondary Education, Social Research, Social Work, Spanish, Sports Science, Theatre, Theology, Writing.

BUENA VISTA UNIVERSITY

610 West Fourth St, Storm Lake, IA 50588
Telephone: (712) 749-2351
Fax: (712) 749-2037
E-mail: library@bvu.edu
Internet: www.bvu.edu

Founded 1891
Academic year: September to May
Pres.: FREDERICK V. MOORE
Vice-Pres. for Academic Affairs and Dean of Faculty: Dr MICHAEL WHITLATCH
Vice-Pres. for Business Services: RANDOLPH FEHR
Vice-Pres. for Institutional Advancement: KENNETH CONVERSE
Vice-Pres. for Student Services and Dean of Students: KEITH BETTS
Univ. Librarian: JAMES R. KENNEDY

Library of 146,000 vols
Number of teachers: 80 full-time
Number of students: 2,607

Programmes in Accounting, Art, Arts Management, Athletic Training, Biology, Business Economics, Business Education, Chemistry, Communication and Graphic Design, Communication and Performance Studies, Corporate Communication, Computer Science, Computer Science/Mathematics, Criminology and Criminal Justice, Elementary Education, English, Exercise Science (Teaching Emphasis), Finance and Banking, General Science, History, Int. Business, Management, Management Information Systems, Marketing, Mathematics, Media Studies, Music, Philosophy and Religion, Physics, Political Science, Psychology, Public Admin., Social Science, Social Work, Spanish.

CENTRAL COLLEGE

812 University, Pella, IA 50219
Telephone: (515) 628-9000
Fax: (515) 628-5316
E-mail: admission@central.edu
Internet: www.central.edu

Founded 1853
4-Year liberal arts college; attached to Reformed Church

Academic year: August to May
Pres.: Dr DAVID ROE
Vice-Pres. for Business and Finance: B. BOWZER
Vice-Pres. for Academic Affairs: PAUL NAOUR
Library Dir: ROBIN MARTIN

Library of 220,000 vols
Number of teachers: 93
Number of students: 1,700

Programmes in Accounting, Anthropology, Art, Biology, Business Management, Chemistry, Communication Studies, Computer Science, Econ., Elementary Education, English, Eng., Environmental Studies, Exercise Science, French, General Studies, German Studies, History, Information Systems, International Management, International Studies, Law, Linguistics, Mathematics, Mathematics/Computer Science, Music, Music Education, Natural Science, Philosophy, Physics, Political Science, Psychology, Religion, Secondary Education, Social Science, Sociology, Spanish, Theatre

Publications: *The Central Bulletin*, *The Central Ray*, *The Pelican*.

CLARKE COLLEGE

1550 Clarke Dr., Dubuque, IA 52001-3198
Telephone: (563) 588-6300
Fax: (563) 588-6789
E-mail: clarke-info@clarke.edu
Internet: www.clarke.edu

Founded 1843
Academic year: August to May
Pres.: Dr JOANNE M. BURROWS
Provost and Vice-Pres. for Academic Affairs: JOAN LINGEN
Vice-Pres. for Student Life and Enrollment Management: KATHLEEN ZANGER
Vice-Pres. for Institutional Advancement: MELBA RODRIGUEZ
Vice-Pres. for Business and Finance and Treasurer: DEANNA McCORMICK
Vice-Pres. for Information Technology: PAT MADDUX
Registrar: KRISTI DROESSLER
Library Dir: NANCY CARROLL

Library of 121,000 vols
Number of teachers: 120
Number of students: 1,201

Depts of Accounting and Business Admin., Art and Art History, Athletic Training, Biology, Chemistry, Communication, Computer Science, Drama and Speech, Education, History/Political Science, Language and Literature, Mathematics, Music, Nursing, Philosophy, Physical Therapy, Psychology, Religious Studies, Social Work.

COE COLLEGE

1200 First Ave, NE, Cedar Rapids, IA 52402
Telephone: (319) 399-8500
Fax: (319) 399-8816
E-mail: admission@coe.edu
Internet: www.coe.edu

Founded 1851
Academic year: August to May
Pres.: JAMES R. PHIFER
Vice-Pres. for Academic Affairs and Dean of Faculty: MARC ROY
Vice-Pres. for Admin. Services: MICHAEL WHITE
Vice-Pres. for Advancement: RICHARD MEISTERLING
Vice-Pres. for Student Affairs: LOU STARK
Vice-Pres. for Enrollment and Admin.: MICHAEL WHITE
Registrar: Dr EVELYN MOORE
Dir of Library Services: RICHARD DOYLE

Library of 202,000 vols, 1,100 current periodicals, 10,000 microforms, 9,000 audiovisual items
Number of teachers: 80
Number of students: 1,300

Majors in Accounting, African-American Studies, American Studies, Art, Asian Studies, Athletic Training, Biochemistry, Biology, Business Admin., Chemistry, Computer Science, Econ., Education, English, English as a Second Language, Environmental Science, French, French Studies, Gender Studies, General Science, German, German Studies, History, Historical Studies, Interdisciplinary, Literature, Mathematics, Molecular Biology, Music, Nursing, Philosophy, Physical Education, Physics, Political Science, Pre-Professional Programs, Psychology, Public Relations, Religion, Sociology, Spanish, Spanish Studies, Speech, Theatre Arts, Writing

Publication: *Courier* (quarterly).

CORNELL COLLEGE

600 First St, SW, Mount Vernon, IA 52314-1098
Telephone: (319) 895-4477
Fax: (319) 895-4492
E-mail: admission@cornellcollege.edu
Internet: www.cornellcollege.edu

Founded 1853
Pres.: Dr LESLIE H. GARNER, Jr
Vice-Pres. for Academic Affairs and Dean of the College: BRENDA TOOLEY
Sr Vice-Pres. for Alumni and College Advancement: TERRY GIBSON
Vice-Pres. for Business Affairs and Treasurer: MARK ZINKULA
Vice-Pres. for Student Affairs: JOHN HARP
Vice-Pres. for Enrollment and Dean of Admissions: JONATHAN STROUD
Registrar: JACKIE WALLACE
Librarian: Dr JEAN DONHAM

Library of 190,000 vols
Number of teachers: 82
Number of students: 1,000

Depts of Art, Biology, Chemistry, Computer Science, Econ. and Business, Education, English, Geology, History, Kinesiology, Languages, Mathematics, Music, Philosophy, Physics, Politics, Psychology, Religion, Sociology and Anthropology, Theatre and Communications Studies.

DES MOINES UNIVERSITY

3200 Grand Ave, Des Moines, IA 50312-4198
Telephone: (515) 271-1400
Fax: (515) 271-1578
E-mail: webmaster@dmu.edu
Internet: www.dmu.edu

Founded 1898 as Dr S. S. Still College of Osteopathy
Private control

Pres. and CEO: TERRY BRANSTAD
Exec. Vice-Pres. and Chief Operating Officer: STEPHEN DENGLE
Vice-Pres. for Academic Admin.: Dr ROBERT M. YOHO
Vice-Pres. for Planning and Technology: Dr WILLIAM APPELGATE
Vice-Pres. for Student Services: MARY ANN ZUG
Registrar: KATHY L. SCAGLIONE
Library Dir: LARRY D. MARQUARDT

Library of 23,000 medical vols, 29,000 bound journals
Number of students: 1,306

DEANS

Univ. Research: Dr BRYAN LARSEN

College of Health Sciences: Dr JODI L. CAHALAN

College of Osteopathic Medicine and Surgery: Dr KENDALL REED

College of Podiatric Medicine and Surgery: Dr ROBERT M. YOHO

DIVINE WORD COLLEGE

102 Jacoby Drive, POB 380, Epworth, IA 52045-0380

Telephone: (319) 876-3353

E-mail: dwcinfo@dwci.edu

Internet: www.dwci.edu

Founded 1931 as St Paul's Mission House; present name 1964

Private control

Academic year: August to May

Pres.: Rev. MICHAEL HUTCHINS

Vice-Pres. for Academic Affairs: Dr JAMES RUSSETT

Vice-Pres. for Formation and Dean of Students: Rev. KHIEN MAI LUU

Vice-Pres. (Devt): MARK SINGSANK

Vice-Pres. for Finance: LINDA WEIDEMANN

Vice-Pres. for Recruitment and Admissions: LEN UHAL

Registrar: DEBORAH HIRSCH

Library Dir: DANIEL BOICE

BAs in Philosophy and Cross Cultural Studies.

DORDT COLLEGE

498 Fourth Ave, NE, Sioux Center, IA 51250

Telephone: (712) 722-6000

Fax: (712) 722-1185

E-mail: public-relations@dordt.edu

Internet: www.dordt.edu

Founded 1955

Languages of instruction: English, Dutch

Languages of instruction: Spanish, Latin

Academic year: August to May

Pres.: Dr CARL ZYLSTRA

Vice-Pres. for Academic Affairs: Dr ROCKNE MCCARTHY

Vice-Pres. for Business: ARLAN NEDERHOFF

Vice-Pres. for College Advancement: JOHN BAAS

Vice-Pres. for Student Services: KEN BOERSMA

Exec. Dir of Admissions: QUENTIN VAN ESSEN

Registrar: JIM BOS

Dir of Library Services: SHERYL TAYLOR

Library of 306,000 vols

Number of teachers: 80 full-time

Number of students: 1,250

Publication: *Pro Rege* (quarterly).

DRAKE UNIVERSITY

2507 University Ave, Des Moines, IA 50311

Telephone: (515) 271-2011

Fax: (515) 271-3977

Internet: www.drake.edu

Founded 1881

Private control

Academic year: September to May (2 semesters)

Pres.: Dr DAVID E. MAXWELL

Provost: RONALD J. TROYER

Vice-Pres. for Admission and Financial Aid: TOM DELAHUNT

Vice-Pres. for Business and Finance: VICTORIA PAYSEUR

Vice-Pres. for Alumni and Devt: JOHN SMITH

Dean of Students: Dr SENTWALI BAKARI

Registrar: NANCY GEIGER

Dean of Cowles Library: RODNEY HENSHAW

Dir of Law Library: JOHN EDWARDS

Library of 471,209 vols, 2,000 periodicals, 96,147 govt documents, 855 audio-visual items

Number of teachers: 417 (237 full-time, 180 part-time)

Number of students: 5,150 (3,577 undergraduate, 1,573 postgraduate)

Publications: *Drake Law Review, Drake Update*

DEANS

College of Arts and Sciences: Dr JOHN M. BURNEY

College of Business and Public Admin.: CHARLIE EDWARDS

School of Education: JAN MCHILL

School of Journalism and Mass Communication: CHARLES EDWARDS

Law School: Prof. C. PETER GOPLERUD, III

College of Pharmacy and Health Sciences: RAYLENE ROSPOND

EMMAUS BIBLE COLLEGE

2570 Asbury Rd, Dubuque, IA 52001

Telephone: (563) 588-8000

Fax: (563) 588-1216

E-mail: info@emmaus.edu

Internet: www.emmaus.edu

Private control

Academic year: August to May

Pres.: KENNETH A. DAUGHTERS

Chancellor: Dr DANIEL H. SMITH

Vice-Pres. for Admin,: KENNETH W. MURRAY

Dean for Academic Affairs: LISA L. BEATTY

Dean for Student Affairs: JONATHAN W. GLOCK

Dean for Biblical Studies: DAVID J. MACLEOD

Registrar: KATHRYN L. VAN DINE

Librarian: JOHN H. RUSH

Number of teachers: 25

Number of students: 283

Programmes in Biblical Studies, Ministry Studies, Professional Studies.

FAITH BAPTIST BIBLE COLLEGE AND THEOLOGICAL SEMINARY

1900 Northwest Fourth St, Ankeny, IA 50023

Telephone: (515) 964-0601

Fax: (515) 964-1638

E-mail: admissions@faith.edu

Internet: www.faith.edu

Private control

Academic year: August to May

Pres.: Dr JAMES MAXWELL

Vice-Pres. for Academic Services and Dean of College: Dr GEORGE G. HOUGHTON

Vice-Pres. for Enrollment and Constituent Services: TIMOTHY NILIUS

Vice-Pres. for Student Enrichment and Services: TIMOTHY A. CROWN

Vice-Pres. for Institutional Advancement: DAN DARK

Dean of Seminary: Dr ERNIE SCHMIDT (acting)

Registrar: DAVID STOUT

Head Librarian: JEFFERY GATES

Library of 67,000 vols, 430 periodicals

Number of teachers: 21

Number of students: 378

Divs of Christian Studies, Bible and Theology, Gen. Education.

GRACELAND UNIVERSITY

1 University Pl., Lamoni, IA 50140

Telephone: (641) 784-5000

Fax: (641) 784-5480

E-mail: admissions@graceland.edu

Internet: www.graceland.edu

Founded 1895

Pres.: Dr STEVEN L. ANDERS (acting)

Vice-Provost for Academic Affairs and Dean of Faculty: STEVEN L. ANDERS

Vice-Pres. for Business and Admin. Services: KAREN L. MERCER

Vice-Provost for Enrollment and New Business Devt: JAMES R. SIMPSON

Vice-Pres. for Institutional Advancement: SHARON M. KIRKPATRICK

Vice-Pres. for Student Life and Dean of Students: THOMAS L. POWELL

Exec. Dir for Information Technology Services: KAM MAHI

Dean of Admissions: BRIAN SHANTZ

Registrar: JOYCE LIGHTHILL

Librarian: DIANE E. SHELTON

Library of 114,249 vols

Number of teachers: 93 (full-time)

Number of students: 2,351 (undergraduate and graduate)

DEANS

School of Education: Dr WILLIAM L. ARMSTRONG

School of Nursing: Dr PATRICIA K. TRACHSEL

Seminary: Dr DON COMPIER

BRANCH CAMPUS

Independence Campus: 1401 West Truman Rd, Independence, MO 64050-3434; tel. (816) 833-0524; School of Nursing; Business Admin., Education and Religion courses.

GRAND VIEW COLLEGE

1200 Grandview Ave, Des Moines, IA 50316

Telephone: (515) 263-2800

Fax: (515) 263-6095

E-mail: admissions@gvc.edu

Internet: www.gvc.edu

Founded 1896

Private control

Academic year: August to May

Pres.: KENT L. HENNING

Provost and Vice-Pres. for Academic Affairs: Dr RONALD L. TAYLOR

Vice-Pres. for Admin. and Finance: SCOTT BOCK

Vice-Pres. for Enrollment Management: DEBBIE M. BARGER

Vice-Pres. for Advancement: WILLIAM BURMA

Dean, College for Professional and Adult Learning: KAREN ANDERSON

Dir of Admissions: DIANE JOHNSON

Registrar: ELLEN M. STRACHOTA

Library Dir: SANDRA H. KEIST

Number of teachers: 180 (incl. 95 part-time)

Number of students: 1,750

HEADS OF ACADEMIC DIVISIONS

Natural Sciences: Dr DIANE DOIDGE

Nursing: Dr JEAN LOGAN

Social Sciences: Dr A. KATHLEEN PETERSON

Humanities: KAYLENE RUBY

GRINNELL COLLEGE

Grinnell, IA 50112-1690

Telephone: (641) 269-4000

Fax: (641) 269-3408

E-mail: askgrin@grinnell.edu

Internet: www.grinnell.edu

Founded 1846

Pres.: RUSSELL K. OSGOOD

Vice-Pres. for Academic Affairs and Dean of the College: Dr JIM SWARTZ

Vice-Pres. and Treas. of the College: DAVID S. CLAY

Vice-Pres. of Institutional Planning: MARCI SORTOR

Vice-Pres. for College Services: JOHN W. KALKBRENNER

Vice-Pres. for College and Alumni Relations: MICKEY MUNLEY

Vice-Pres. for Student Services: THOMAS CRADY

Dean of Admission and Financial Aid: JAMES M. SUMNER

Registrar: GERALD S. ADAMS

Librarian: RICHARD FYFFE

Library of 1,000,000 vols, 5,100 current periodicals, govt documents

Number of teachers: 141

Number of students: 1,460

Depts of Anthropology, Art, Biology, Chemistry, Chinese/Japanese, Classics, Computer Science, Econ., Education, English, French, German, History, Mathematics and Statistics, Music, Philosophy, Physical Education, Physics, Political Science, Psychology, Religious Studies, Russian, Sociology, Spanish, Theatre.

IOWA STATE UNIVERSITY

Ames, IA 50011

Telephone: (515) 294-4111

E-mail: admissions@iastate.edu

Internet: www.iastate.edu

Founded 1858

Pres.: Prof. GREGORY GEOFFROY

Exec. Vice-Pres. and Provost: ELIZABETH HOFFMAN

Vice-Pres. for Research and Economic Devt: JOHN A. BRIGHTON

Vice-Pres. for Extension and Outreach: JACK M. PAYNE

Vice-Pres. for Business and Finance: WARREN R. MADDEN

Vice-Pres. for Student Affairs: THOMAS L. HILL

Dean of Library Services: OLIVIA MADISON

Library of 2,348,646 vols, 29,681 current periodicals, 3,380,573 microforms, 780,839 photographs and slides, 46,493 films and videos, 11,562 audio items, 130,008 maps and aerial photographs, 14,042 linear ft of manuscripts and archives

Number of teachers: 1,709

Number of students: 26,000

Publications: *The Agriculturist, The Iowa Engineer, Outlook, Ethos, Iowa State Daily, Iowa Stater, Inside Iowa State, Visions, Inquiry, Marston Muses, The Gentle Doctor, Iowa State University Veterinarian*

DEANS

Agriculture: WENDY WINTERSTEEN

Business: Prof. LABH S. HIRA

Design: MARK ENGELBRECHT

Eng.: MARK J. KUSHNER

Graduate College: DAVID K. HOLGER

Human Sciences: CHERYL L. ACHTERBERG

Liberal Arts and Sciences: MICHAEL B. WHITEFORD

Veterinary Medicine: JOHN U. THOMSON

ATTACHED RESEARCH INSTITUTES AND CENTRES

Ames Laboratory of US Department of Energy: Dir Prof. THOMAS J. BARTON.

Analog and Mixed-Signal VLSI Design Center: Dir Prof. ROBERT J. WEBER.

Carrie Chapman Catt Center for Women and Politics: Dir Dr DIANNE G. BYSTROM.

Center for Advanced Technology Development: Dir MARK LAURENZANO.

Center for Agricultural and Rural Development: Dir Prof. BRUCE BABCOCK.

Center for Agricultural History: Dir Prof. R. DOUGLAS HURT.

Center for Crops Utilization Research: Prof. LAWRENCE A. JOHNSON.

Center for Designer Crops: Dir BASIL J. NIKOLAU.

Center for Designing Foods to Improve Nutrition: Dir Prof. DIANE BIRT.

Center for Family Policy.

Center for Historical Studies of Technology and Science: Dir ALAN MARCUS.

Center for Indigenous Knowledge for Agricultural and Rural Development: Dir MIKE WARREN.

Center for Industrial Research and Service: Dir RONALD A. COX.

Center for International Agricultural Finance: Dir Prof. NEIL E. HARL.

Center for Nondestructive Evaluation: Dir R. BRUCE THOMPSON.

Center for Physical and Computational Mathematics: Dir BRUCE N. HARMON (acting).

Center for Plant Genomics: Dir Prof. PATRICK S. SCHNABLE.

Center for Plant Responses to Environmental Stresses: Dir CHARLOTTE R. BRONSON.

Center for Plant Transformation and Gene Expression: Dir Prof. PATRICK S. SCHNABLE.

Center for Survey Statistics and Methodology: Dir SARAH NUSSER.

Center for Sustainable Environmental Technologies: Dir Prof. ROBERT C. BROWN.

Center for Teaching Excellence: Dir CORLY BROOKE.

Center for Technology in Learning and Teaching: Dir ANN THOMPSON.

Center for Transportation Research and Education: Dir STEVE ANDRLE.

Computational Fluid Dynamics Center: Man. Prof. JOHN TANNEHILL.

Electric Power Research Center: Dir VIJAY VITTAL.

Food and Agricultural Policy Research Institute: Dir JOHN C. BEGHIN.

Food Safety Consortium.

Industrial Relations Center: Dir Prof. PETER F. ORAZEM.

Institute for Design Research and Outreach: Dir MARK ENGELBRECHT.

Institute for International Cooperation in Animal Biologics (IICAB): Exec. Dir Dr JAMES ROTH.

Institute for Physical Research and Technology: Dir Prof. THOMAS J. BARTON.

Institute for Social and Behavioral Research: Dir CAROLYN CUTRONA.

Interdisciplinary Research Institute for Social Science (IRISS): Dir KIRK WOLTER.

Iowa Energy Center: Dir FLOYD E. BARWIG (acting).

Iowa Lakeside Laboratory: Dir Dr ARNOLD VAN DER VALK.

Iowa Pork Industry Center: Dir JOHN MABRY.

Iowa Space Grant Consortium: Dir WILLIAM J. BYRD.

Laurence H. Baker Center for Bioinformatics and Biological Statistics: Dir ROBERT L. JERNIGAN.

Leopold Center for Sustainable Agriculture: Dir Prof. FREDERICK L. KIRSCHENMANN.

Microanalytical Instrumentation Center: Dir MARC PORTER.

Microelectronics Research Center: Dir Prof. VIKRAM L. DALAL.

Midwest Agribusiness Trade Research and Information Center (MATRIC): Exec Dir BRUCE A. BABCOCK.

NASA Food Technology Commercial Space Center: Dir Dr TONY POMETTO, III.

National Soil Tilth Laboratory: Dir Dr JERRY HATFIELD.

North Central Regional Aquaculture Center.

North Central Regional Center for Rural Development: Dir Dr CORNELIA BUTLER FLORA.

Raymond F. Baker Center for Plant Breeding: Dir KENDALL R. LAMKEY.

Research Institute for Studies in Education: Dir Dr JACKIE BLOUNT.

Seed Science Center: Dir MANJIT K. MISRA.

Veterinary Medical Research Institute: Dir RICHARD F. ROSS.

Water Resources Research Institute: Dir STEVE MELVIN.

IOWA WESLEYAN COLLEGE

601 North Main, Mount Pleasant, IA 52641

Telephone: (319) 385-8021

E-mail: wnj@iwc.edu

Internet: www.iwc.edu

Founded 1842

Pres.: WILLIAM JOHNSTON

Vice-Pres. for Academic Affairs: NANCY ERICKSON

Vice-Pres. of Devt: JOHN HELD

Registrar: ED KROPA

Dean of Enrollment Management: CARY OWENS

Library Dir: PAULA KINNEY

Library of 108,427 vols

Number of teachers: 42

Number of students: 849

Divs of Business, Education, Fine Arts, Human Studies, Language and Literature, Nursing, Science, Mathematics and Computer Studies.

LORAS COLLEGE

1450 Alta Vista, POB 178, Dubuque, IA 52004-0178

Telephone: (563) 588-7100

E-mail: admissions@loras.edu

Internet: www.loras.edu

Founded 1839

Pres.: JAMES E. COLLINS

Provost: CHERYL R. JACOBSEN

Vice-Pres. for Institutional Advancement: DANIEL J. ALLEN

Vice-Pres. for Finance and Admin. Services: STEVE SCHMALL

Vice-Pres. for Enrollment Management: LISA BUNDERS

Dean of Students: ARTHUR W. SUNLEAF

Dean of Campus Spiritual Life: Fr JOHN HAUGEN

Registrar: MARY K. WECK

Librarian: ROBERT F. KLEIN

Library of 440,000 vols, 8,000 current periodicals

Number of teachers: 141

Number of students: 1,683

Courses in Accounting, Art-Studio, Athletic Training, Archaeology/Cultural Interpretation, Biochemistry, Biology, Business, Business Finance, Business Management, Business Marketing, Catholic Studies, Chemistry, Computer Science, Criminal Justice, Econ., Electromechanical Eng., Elementary Education, English Literature, English Writing, Greek and Roman Studies, Gender Studies, History, Integrated Visual Arts, Int. Studies, Irish Studies, Management Information Systems, Mathematics, Media Studies, Music/Music Education, Philosophy, Physics-Applied, Politics, Psychology, Public Relations, Publishing, Religious Studies, Social Work, Sociology, Spanish, Sport Management, Sport Science, Theatre, World Literature.

LUTHER COLLEGE

700 College Dr., Decorah, IA 52101-1045

Telephone: (563) 387-2000

Fax: (563) 387-2158

Internet: www.luther.edu

Founded 1861

Pres.: Dr RICHARD L. TORGERSON

Vice-Pres. for Academic Affairs and Dean of the College: WILLIAM CRAFT

Vice-Pres. for Devt: KEITH CHRISTENSEN

Vice-Pres. for Finance and Admin.: DIANE TACKE

Vice-Pres. and Dean for Student Life: ANN HIGHUM

Vice-Pres. for Enrollment and Marketing (vacant)

Registrar: LIANG CHEE WEE

Librarian: JANE KEMP

Library of 340,000 vols

Number of teachers: 191 full-time

Number of students: 2,600

Majors/minors in Accounting, African Studies, Anthropology, Art, Arts Management, Athletic Training, Biblical Languages, Biology, Business (Management), Chemistry, Classics, Classical Studies, Communication Studies, Computer Science, Econ., Education, English, Environmental Studies, French, German, Greek, Health, History, Int. Management Studies, Latin, Latin American Studies, Management, Management Information Systems, Mathematics, Mathematics/Statistics, Museum Studies, Music, Music Management, Nursing, Philosophy, Physical Education, Physics, Political Science, Psychology, Religion, Resource Management, Russian Studies, Scandinavian Studies, Social Work, Sociology, Spanish, Speech/Theatre, Sports Management, Theatre/Dance Management, Women's and Gender Studies.

MAHARISHI UNIVERSITY OF MANAGEMENT

Fairfield, IA 52557

Telephone: (641) 472-7000

Fax: (641) 472-1179

E-mail: admissions@mum.edu

Internet: www.mum.edu

Founded 1971 as Maharishi International Univ.; present name 1995

Private control

Academic year: August to July

Pres.: Dr BEVAN MORRIS,

Exec. Vice-Pres.: Dr CRAIG PEARSON

Chief Admin. Officer: DAVID STREID

Exec. Dir of Institutional Advancement: BRADFORD MYLETT

Dean of Faculty: CATHERINE GORINI

Dean of Women: SUSAN RUNKLE

Dean of Men: DAVID POHLMAN

Dean of Admissions: RON BARNETT

Registrar: TOM ROWE

Library Dir: MARTIN SCHMIDT

Library of 144,000 vols

Number of teachers: 102

Number of students: 901

DEANS

College of Arts and Sciences: SAM BOOTHBY

College of Computer Science and Mathematics: GREGORY GUTHRIE

Graduate School: Dr FRED TRAVIS

MORNINGSIDE COLLEGE

1501 Morningside Ave, Sioux City, IA 51106

Telephone: (712) 274-5000

Fax: (712) 274-5101

E-mail: msadm@morningside.edu

Internet: www.morningside.edu

Founded 1894

Pres.: JOHN C. REYNDERS

Vice-Pres. for Academic Affairs and Dean of the College: WILLIAM C. DEEDS

Vice-Pres. for Business and Finance: RONALD A. JORGENSEN

Vice-Pres. for Student Services: TERRI CURRY

Vice-Pres. for Institutional Advancement: TOM RICE

Registrar: MARY PESHEK

Dean of Enrollment: ROBBIE ROHLENA

Dir of Library Services: DARIA BOSSMAN

Library of 117,330 vols, 3,575 sound recordings, 8,869 micofilm, 76,285 microfiche

Number of teachers: 75

Number of students: 1,122

Depts of Art, Biology, Business Admin., Chemistry, Computer Science, Computer and Application Programming, Corporate Communication, Education, Eng. Physics, English, History, Mass Communication, Mathematics, Music, Nursing, Philosophy, Political Science, Psychology, Religious Studies, Spanish, Theatre

CHAIRPERSONS OF ACADEMIC DIVISIONS

Behavioural and Health Science: CAROL SEARLS

Business Admin. and Communication: DOUGLAS LIVERMORE

Education: GLENNA TREVIS

Fine Arts: LANCE LEHMBERG

Humanities: GAIL AMENT

Natural Sciences and Mathematics: DOUG SWAN

MOUNT MERCY COLLEGE

1330 Elmhurst Dr., NE, Cedar Rapids, IA 52402-4798

Telephone: (319) 363-1323

Fax: (319) 363-5270

Internet: www.mtmercy.edu

Founded 1928

Private Control

Academic year: August to May

Pres.: Dr CHRISTOPHER R.L BLAKE

Vice-Pres. for Academic Affairs: A. BUELANE DAUGHERTY

Vice-Pres. for Finance: BARBARA PARKS POOLEY

Vice-Pres. for Enrollment and Student Services: PHILIP C. ADAMS, III

Vice-Pres. for Institutional Advancement: DEBORAH K. GREEN

Registrar: LORI HEYING

Dir of Library Services: MARILYN MURPHY

Library of 128,000 vols

Number of teachers: 142

Number of students: 1,486

Depts of Applied Philosophy, Art, Biology, Business Admin. (Accounting, Management, Marketing, Interdisciplinary), Communication, Computer Information Systems, Computer Science, Criminal Justice, Education, English, Health Services, History, Int. Studies, Mathematics, Medical Technology, Music, Nursing, Political Science, Pre-Professional Programs, Psychology, Religious Studies, Social Work, Sociology, Speech/Drama, Urban and Community Services.

NORTHWESTERN COLLEGE

101 Seventh St, SW, Orange City, IA 51041-1996

Telephone: (712) 707-7100

Fax: (712) 707-7247

E-mail: postmaster@nwciowa.edu

Internet: www.nwciowa.edu

Founded 1882

Academic year: August to May

Pres.: Dr BRUCE G. MURPHY

Vice-Pres. for Academic Affairs: Dr JASPER LESAGE

Vice-Pres. for Financial Affairs: DOUG BEUKELMAN

Vice-Pres. for Student Devt: JOHN G. BROGAN

Vice-Pres. for External Relations: RON DE JONG

Vice-Pres. for Advancement: JOHN GRELLER

Dean of Spiritual Formation: Dr SUSAN REESE

Registrar: CHARLIE COUCH

Dir of Library: DANIEL DAILY

Library of 185,000 items

Number of teachers: 78 full-time and 53 part-time

Number of students: 1,342

Depts of Art, Biology, Business/Economics, Chemistry, Communications, Computer Science, Education, English/Writing and Rhetoric, Foreign Languages, History, Humanities, Kinesiology, Mathematics, Music, Nursing, Philosophy, Physics, Political Science, Psychology, Religion/Christian Education, Social Work, Sociology, Theatre and Speech.

PALMER CHIROPRACTIC UNIVERSITY SYSTEM

723 Brady St, Davenport, IA 52803

Telephone: (563) 884-5500

Fax: (563) 884-5505

Internet: www.palmer.edu

Founded 1897 as Palmer School and Cure; present name 1991

Private control

Chair. Board of Trustees: VICKIE A. PALMER

Vice-Chair.: TREVOR V. IRELAND

Sec.: KENT M. FORNEY.

CONSTITUENT COLLEGES

Palmer College of Chiropractic

1000 Brady St, Davenport, IA 52803

Telephone: (563) 884-5656

Fax: (563) 884-5414

E-mail: pcadmit@palmer.edu

Internet: www.palmer.edu

Chancellor: Dr GUY F. RIEKEMAN

Pres.: Dr DONALD KERN

Vice-Pres. for Academic Affairs: Dr BRIAN J. MCAULAY

Vice-Pres. for Education and Research Devt: Dr KEVIN MCCARTHY

Vice-Pres. for Alumni, Devt and Student Affairs: GARY M. MOHR

Vice-Pres. for Professional and Int. Affairs: Dr DAVID B. KOCH

Vice-Pres. for Research: Dr WILLIAM MEEKER

Vice-Pres. for Marketing and Recruitment: C. RANDALL HEUSTON

Vice-Pres. for Operations and Finance: WILLIAM JARR

Registrar: MINDY LEAHY

Dir of Libraries: DENNIS PETERSON

Library of 50,000 vols

Publication: *Streams from the Fountainhead* (2 a year).

Palmer College of Chiropractic–West

90 East Tasman Dr., San Jose, CA 95134

Telephone: (408) 944-6000

Fax: (408) 944-6032

E-mail: pccw_admiss@palmer.edu

Internet: www.palmer.edu

Founded 1978 as Northern California College of Chiropractic; present name 1980

Academic Dean: Dr KEVIN MCCARTHY.

Palmer College of Chiropractic–Florida
4777 City Centre Parkway, Port Orange, FL 32129

Telephone: (386) 763-2709
Fax: (386) 763-2620
E-mail: pccf_admiss@palmer.edu
Internet: www.palmer.edu
Academic Dean: Dr GLORIA NILES.

ST AMBROSE UNIVERSITY

518 West Locust St, Davenport, IA 52803-2898

Telephone: (319) 333-6000
Fax: (319) 333-6243
Internet: www.sau.edu
Founded 1882
Private control (Roman Catholic church)
Pres.: Dr EDWARD J. ROGALSKI
Vice-Pres. for Academic Affairs: Dr LORRAINE RODRIGUES-FISHER
Vice-Pres. for Advancement: Dr EDWARD LITTIG
Vice-Pres. for Enrollment Management and Student Services: Dr JAMES LOFTUS
Vice-Pres. for Finance: Dr EDWARD HENKHAUS
Library Dir: MARY HEINZMAN
Library of 143,334 vols
Number of teachers: 299
Number of students: 3,780 (2,829 undergraduate, 951 graduate)

DEANS

College of Arts and Sciences: Dr ARON R. AJI
College of Business: Dr RICHARD DIENESCH
College of Education and Health Sciences: Dr ROBERT RISTOW
College of Professional Studies: Dr LEWIS SANBORNE

SIMPSON COLLEGE

701 North C St, Indianola, IA 50125-1297
Telephone: (515) 961-6251
Fax: (515) 961-1498
E-mail: admiss@simpson.edu
Internet: www.simpson.edu
Founded 1860
Academic year: August to May
Pres.: JOHN W. BYRD
Vice-Pres. for Student Devt and Dean of Students: JIM THORIUS
Vice-Pres. and Dean for Academic Affairs: STEVE GRIFFITHS
Vice-Pres. for College Advancement: BOB LANE
Vice-Pres. for Business and Finance: KEN BIRKENHOLTZ
Vice-Pres. for Enrollment: DEB TIERNEY
Vice-Pres. for Information Services and Chief Information Officer: KELLEY BRADDER
Registrar: JOHN BOLAN
Librarian: CYD DYER
Library of 155,761 vols
Number of teachers: 87
Number of students: 1,950
Depts of Art, Biology and Environmental Science, Business Admin. and Econ., Chemistry and Physics, Communication Studies, Computer Science, Dunn Library, Education, English, Foreign Languages, Hawley Academic Resource Center, History, Mathematics, Music, Philosophy and Religion, Physical Education, Political Science, Psychology, Social Sciences, Student Support Services, Theatre Arts, Women's Studies
Publications: *The Simpson Magazine* (quarterly), *Viewbook* (annual), *Admissions Newsletter* (3 a year).

BRANCH CAMPUSES

West Des Moines Campus: Suite 2E, 3737 Westown Parkway, West Des Moines, IA 50265; tel. (515) 223-8842; fax (515) 961-1887.

Ankeny Campus: Suite 800, Southeast Tones Dr., West Des Moines, IA 50021; tel. (515) 965-9355; fax (515) 286-6195.

UNIVERSITY OF DUBUQUE

2000 University Ave, Dubuque, IA 52001
Telephone: (319) 589-3000
Internet: www.dbq.edu
Founded 1852
Pres.: Rev. Dr JEFFREY F. BULLOCK
Sr Vice-Pres. for Advancement: JOHN PUOTINEN
Vice-Pres. Academic Affairs: JOHN STEWART
Vice-Pres for Enrollment Management, Marketing, and Univ. Relations: SUSAN SMITH, PETER SMITH
Sr Vice-Pres. for Finance and Auxiliary Services: RENNIE ROOT
Vice-Pres. and Dean of the Seminary: BRADLEY LONGFIELD
Dean of Student Life: Dr PETER GITAU
Library Dir: MARY ANN KNEFEL
Library of 165,000 vols, 25,000 microtext items, 9,000 vols in spec collns, 700 current periodicals
Number of students: 1,000
Schools of Business, Liberal Arts, Professional Programmes, Theological Seminary.

UNIVERSITY OF IOWA

2222 Old Highway 218 South, Iowa City, IA 52242-1602

Telephone: (319) 335-3549
Fax: (319) 335-0807
Internet: www.uiowa.edu
Founded 1847
State control
Academic year: August to May (2 terms and summer session)
Pres.: GARY FETHKE
Exec. Vice-Pres. and Provost: MICHAEL J. HOGAN
Sr Vice-Pres. and Treas.: DOUGLAS K. TRUE
Vice-Pres. for Research: MEREDITH HAY
Vice-Pres. of Student Services and Dean of Students: PHILLIP E. JONES
Vice-Pres. for Legal Affairs and General Counsel: MARCUS MILLS
Vice-Pres. for Medical Affairs: JEAN E. ROBILLARD
Registrar: LAWRENCE LOCKWOOD
Univ. Librarian: NANCY L. BAKER
Library of 4,626,626 vols, also manuscript and special collns
Number of teachers: 1,679 (tenured and tenure-track faculty)
Number of students: 29,979 (20,738 undergraduate, 5,388 graduate, 3,853 professional)
Publications: *Walt Whitman Quarterly Review* (quarterly), *Syllecta Classica* (annual), *Iowa Law Review* (5 a year), *The Iowa Review* (3 a year), *Journal of Communication Inquiry* (quarterly)

DEANS

Henry B. Tippie College of Business: WILLIAM C. HUNTER
College of Dentistry: DAVID C. JOHNSEN
College of Education: SANDRA BOWMAN DAMICO
College of Eng.: P. BARRY BUTLER
College of Law: CAROLYN JONES
College of Liberal Arts and Sciences: LINDA MAXSON

Roy J. and Lucille A. Carver College of Medicine: JEAN E. ROBILLARD
College of Nursing: MARTHA CRAFT-ROSENBERG
College of Pharmacy: JORDAN L. COHEN
College of Public Health: JAMES A. MERCHANT
Graduate College: JOHN C. KELLER

UNIVERSITY OF NORTHERN IOWA

1227 West 27th St, Cedar Falls, IA 50614
Telephone: (319) 273-2311
Fax: (319) 273-3509
Internet: www.uni.edu
Founded 1876
Academic year: July to June
Pres.: Dr BEN ALLEN
Provost and Vice-Pres. for Academic Affairs: Dr JAMES LUBKER
Vice-Pres. for Admin. and Finance: TOM SCHELLHARDT
Vice-Pres. for Advancement: WILLIAM CALHOUN
Vice-Pres. for Educational and Student Services: Dr JAN HANISH
Assoc. Vice-Pres. and Dean of Students: Dr EDGAR BERRY
Dir of Institutional Research: Dr THULASI KUMAR
Dir of Admissions: ROLAND CARRILLO
Registrar: PHILIP PATTON
Library of 887,000 vols, 575,000 govt docs, 760,000 microforms, 40,700 maps, 14,200 sound recordings, 3,300 journals, 50 newspapers
Number of teachers: 829 (641 full-time, 188 part-time)
Number of students: 12,513
Publications: *Business and Society* (quarterly), *Journal of Economics* (2 a year), *Journal of Religion and Education* (3 a year), *Journal of Social Studies Research* (2 a year), *The North American Review* (5 a year)

DEANS

College of Business Admin.: Dr FARZAD MOUSSAVI
College of Education: Dr WILLIAM CALLAHAN
College of Humanities and Fine Arts: Dr REINHOLD BUBSER
College of Natural Sciences: Dr JOEL HAACK
College of Social and Behavioural Science: Dr JULIA WALLACE
Graduate College: Dr SUSAN KOCH
Library: Ms MARILYN MERCADO

UPPER IOWA UNIVERSITY

605 Washington, POB 1857, Fayette, IA 52142
Telephone: (563) 425-5200
Fax: (563) 425-5271
E-mail: admissions@uiu.edu
Internet: www.uiu.edu
Founded 1857
Academic year: August to May
Pres.: Dr ALAN WALKER
Sr Vice-Pres. for Residential Univ.: Dr EDWARD OGLE
Sr Vice-Pres. for Business Services: DONALD AUNGST
Registrar: HOLLY STREETER
Library Dir: BECKY WADIAN
Library of 155,108 vols
Number of teachers: 574
Number of students: 5,799
BAs in Arts and Science; MAs in Business Admin., Education, Public Admin.

VENNARD COLLEGE

POB 29, University Park, IA 52595
2300 Eighth Ave East, University Park, IA 52595
Telephone: (641) 673-8391
Fax: (641) 673-8365
E-mail: admiss@vennard.edu
Internet: www.vennard.edu
Founded 1910 as Chicago Evangelistic Institute; present name 1959
Private control
Academic year: August to May
Pres.: Dr BRUCE MOYER
Vice-Pres. for Academic Affairs and Academic Dean: Dr ROBERT W. BAGLEY
Vice-Pres. for Business: JEFF STRONG
Vice-Pres for Student Affairs and Dean of Students: LARRY OLSON
Registrar: DEANNE DOLL
Librarian (vacant)
Number of teachers: 12
Number of students: 100
Areas of study: Business Management, Christian Ministries, Christian Education, Pastoral Ministries, World Missions, Youth Ministries, Computer Technology and Communications, Multidisciplinary Studies, Psychology and Human Relations, Elementary Education, Secondary Education, Bible/Theology, General Education, Professional Education, Music.

WARTBURG COLLEGE

100 Wartburg Blvd, Waverly, IA 50677
Telephone: (319) 352-8200
Fax: (319) 352-8514
Internet: www.wartburg.edu
Founded 1852
Academic year: September to June
Pres.: Dr JACK R. OHLE
Vice-Pres. for Academic Affairs and Dean of Faculty: Dr FEROL MENZEL
Vice-Pres. for Enrollment Management: Dr EDITH J. WALDSTEIN
Vice-Pres. for Institutional Advancement: SCOTT LEISINGER
Vice-Pres. for Student Life and Dean of Students: Dr ALEXANDER SMITH
Dir of Financial Aid: JENNIFER SASSMAN
Registrar: SHEREE COVERT
Librarian: KAREN LEHMAN
Library of 130,000 vols
Number of teachers: 160
Number of students: 1,769
Depts of Accounting, Art, Art Education, Biochemistry, Biology, Business Admin., Chemistry, Church Music, Communication Arts, Communication Studies, Communication Design, Community Sociology, Computer Information Systems, Computer Science, Econ., Education, Eng. Science, English, Exploring, Fitness Management, History, Interdepartmental Major, Int. Relations, Mathematics, Medical Technology, Modern Languages, Music Education, Music Performance, Music Therapy, Philosophy, Physical Education, Physics, Political Science, Psychology, Religion, Social Work, Sociology, Writing.

WARTBURG THEOLOGICAL SEMINARY

333 Wartburg Pl., POB 5004, Dubuque, IA 52004-5004
Telephone: (563) 589-0200
Fax: (563) 589-0333
E-mail: admissions@wartburgseminary.edu
Internet: www.wartburgseminary.edu
Founded 1854
Private control

Pres.: DUANE LARSON
Vice-Pres. Finance and Operations: ANDREW WILLENBORG
Vice-Pres. for Mission Support: Rev. KEN GIBSON
Dean of Students and Enrollment Services: Rev. M DEWAYNE TEIG
Registrar: KEVIN ANDERSON
Dir of Libraries: SUSAN EBERTZ
Library of 84,500 vols
Number of teachers: 21
Number of students: 190
MAs in Arts, Diaconal Ministry, Divinity, Sacred Theology, Theology, Devt and Evangelism.

WILLIAM PENN UNIVERSITY

201 Trueblood Ave, Oskaloosa, IA 52577
Telephone: (641) 673-1076
Fax: (641) 673-1385
E-mail: admissions@wmpenn.edu
Internet: www.wmpenn.edu
Founded 1873 as Penn College; present name 2000
Private control
Academic year: August to May
Pres.: Dr RICHARD E. SOURS
Vice-Pres. for Advancement: STEPHEN NOAH
Vice-Pres. for Enrollment Management: JOHN OTTOSSON
Dean of Students: GARY GARVIS
Registrar: PATRICK MCADAMS
Librarian: JULIE HANSEN
Number of teachers: 55
Number of students: 1,400

DEANS

College of Arts, Sciences and Professional Studies: Dr FREDERICK ALLEN
College for Working Adults: Dr LEE BASH

CHAIRMEN OF ACADEMIC DIVISIONS

Applied Technology: JIM DROST
Business Admin.: LONNY L. WILSON
Education: PAMELA MARTIN
Health and Life Sciences: JAMES NORTH
Humanities: DAVID L. MAJOR
Social and Behavioral Sciences: L. FREDERICK ALLEN

KANSAS

BAKER UNIVERSITY

POB 65, Baldwin City, KS 66006-0065
Telephone: (785) 594-6451
Fax: (785) 594-8425
E-mail: admission@bakeru.edu
Internet: www.bakeru.edu
Founded 1858 (Chartered)
United Methodist
Academic year: August to May
Pres.: PATRICIA N. LONG
Vice-Pres. for Univ. Advancement: LYN LAKIN
Vice- Pres. for Financial Services: JO ADAMS
Vice-Pres. for Enrollment Management: JO ADAMS
Vice-Pres. for Marketing: ANNETTE GALLUZZI
Assoc. Dean of Student Affairs: SHELBY COXON
Vice-Pres.: RAND ZIEGLER
Chief Operating Officer: STEVE COHEN
Vice-Pres.: Dr KATHLEEN HARR
Dir of Library Services: KAY BRADT
Library of 66,000 vols
Number of teachers: 140
Number of students: 2,947

DEANS

College of Arts and Sciences: RAND ZIEGLER
Education: WILLIAM NEUENSWANDER
Nursing: KATHLEEN HARR

School of Professional and Graduate Studies: STEVE COHEN

BARCLAY COLLEGE

607 North Kingman, Haviland, KS 67059
Telephone: (620) 862-5252
Fax: (620) 862-5242
E-mail: admission@barclaycollege.edu
Internet: www.barclaycollege.edu
Founded 1917 as Kansas Central Bible Training School; present name 1990
Private control
Pres.: HERB FRAZIER
Librarian: EMILY HARKNESS
Library of 50,000 vols
Number of teachers: 30
Number of students: 171
Divs of Biblical Studies, General Studies, Liberal Arts.

BENEDICTINE COLLEGE

1020 North Second St, Atchison, KS 66002-1499
Telephone: (913) 367-5340
Fax: (913) 367-6566
Internet: www.benedictine.edu
Founded 1858, name changed 1971 as result of merger of College of St Benedict's and Mount St Scholastica College
Pres.: STEPHEN D. MINNIS
Vice-Pres. for Academic Affairs and Dean of College: KIMBERLY J. SHANKMAN
Dean of Students: LINDA HENRY (acting)
Vice-Pres. for Institutional Advancement and Enrollment: KELLY J. VOWELS
Treas.: JOHN C. MCCLAFLIN
Library Dir: STEVEN GROMATZKY
Library of 320,000 vols, 340 current periodicals
Number of teachers: 52
Number of students: 730 full-time
Depts of Arts and Communication, Business and Public Policy, Education, Health, Science and Mathematics, Humanities, Social and Behavioral Science.

BETHANY COLLEGE

421 North First St, Lindsborg, KS 67456
Telephone: (785) 227-3311
Fax: (785) 227-2860
Internet: www.bethanylb.edu
Founded 1881
Academic year: September to June
Pres.: Dr ROBERT L. VOGEL
Vice-Pres. for Academic Affairs and Dean: Dr EUGENE BALES
Registrar: BETTE ZEHNDER
Librarian: DENISE CARSON
Library of 115,000 vols
Number of teachers: 54
Number of students: 622
Depts of Accounting, Anthropology, Art, Biology, Business, Chemistry, Communication, Criminal Justice, Computer Science, Econ., Education, English, Geography, German, History, Health Physical Education/Athletic Training, Mathematics, Music, Philosophy, Physics, Political Science, Psychology, Religion, Social Work, Spanish, Spec. Education, Swedish, Theatre.

BETHEL COLLEGE

300 East 27th St, North Newton, KS 67117
Telephone: (316) 283-2500
E-mail: admissions@bethelks.edu
Internet: www.bethelks.edu
Founded 1887
Liberal arts college

Pres.: Barry C. Bartel
Vice-Pres. for Admissions: Alan Bartel
Vice-Pres. for Academic Affairs: Brad Born
Vice-Pres. for Student Life: Aaron Deckert
Vice-Pres. for Business Affairs: Gregg Dick
Vice-Pres. for Advancement: Sondra Koontz
Exec. Vice-Pres. for Institutional Devt: John Sheriff
Registrar: Rodney Frey
Co-Dirs of Libraries: Gail Niles Stucky, Barbara Thiesen, John Thiesen
Library of 125,000 vols
Number of teachers: 72 (59 full-time, 13 part-time)
Number of students: 610

Publications: *Bulletin*, *Mennonite Life*.

EMPORIA STATE UNIVERSITY

1200 Commercial St, Emporia, KS 66801-5087
Telephone: (620) 341-1200
Fax: (316) 341-5073
Internet: www.emporia.edu
Founded 1863, univ. status 1976
Pres.: Michael R. Lane
Vice-Pres. for Academic Affairs: Dr John O. Schwenn
Vice-Pres. for Student Affairs: James E. Williams
Dean of Graduates: Robert Grover
Dean of the Library: Joyce Davis
Library of 711,000 vols
Number of students: 6,006 (4,476 under-graduate, 1,530 postgraduate)
Publications: *ESU Business World* (quarterly), *Kansas School Naturalist* (quarterly), *Spotlight* (quarterly), *Flint Hills Review*

DEANS

School of Business: Robert Hite
College of Liberal Arts and Sciences: Rodney Sobieski
School of Library and Information Management: Ann O'Neill
Teacher's College: Teresa Mehring

FORT HAYS STATE UNIVERSITY

600 Park St, Hays, KS 67601-4099
Telephone: (785) 628-4000
Internet: www.fhsu.edu
Founded 1902
Pres.: Dr Edward H. Hammond
Provost: Lawrence V. Gould (acting)
Vice-Pres. for Admin.: Mike Barnett
Vice-Pres. for Student Affairs: Dr Herbert Songer
Asst Vice-Pres. for Student Affairs and Registrar: Joey Linn
Library Dir: John Ross
Library of 300,000 vols, 500,000 vols in govt document section,
Number of teachers: 278
Number of students: 5,620

Publications: *Leader*, *Reveille*

DEANS

College of Arts and Sciences: Paul W. Faber
College of Business and Leadership: Steve Williams
College of Education and Technology: Debbie Mercer
College of Health and Life Sciences: Jeff Briggs
Virtual College: Cynthia Elliot
Graduate Studies and Research: Steven Trout

FRIENDS UNIVERSITY

2100 West University St, Wichita, KS 67213
Telephone: (316) 295-5000
Fax: (316) 295-5060
E-mail: learn@friends.edu
Internet: www.friends.edu
Founded 1898
Academic year: July to June
Pres.: Dr Biff Green
Vice-Pres. for Academic Affairs: Dr John Yoder
Vice-Pres. for Admin. and Finance: Randall C. Doerksen
Vice-Pres. for Univ. Advancement: Hervey Wright, III
Associate Vice-Pres. for Student Affairs: Cynthia Jacobson
Registrar: Marcia Morton
Librarian: David Pappas
Library of 100,000 vols
Number of teachers: 79
Number of students: 2,749

Publication: *Focus* (quarterly)

DEANS

Graduate School: Dr Al Saber
College of Adult and Professional Studies: Dr Vicki Bergkamp
College of Business, Arts, Sciences, and Education: Dr Wayne Howdeshell

KANSAS STATE UNIVERSITY

Manhattan, KS 66506
Telephone: (785) 532-6151
Fax: (785) 532-6393
E-mail: kstateag@ksu.edu
Internet: www.ksu.edu
Founded 1863
Pres.: Dr Jon Wefald
Provost: M. Duane Nellis
Vice-Provost for Research: Prof. R. W. Trewyn
Vice-Provost for Academic Services and Technology: Elizabeth A. Unger
Vice-Pres. for Admin. and Finance: Dr Thomas M. Rawson
Vice-Pres. for Institutional Advancement: Robert Krause
Dean of Libraries: Lori A. Goetsch
Library: see Libraries
Number of teachers: 1,197
Number of students: 23,000

Publications: *K-Stater* (5 a year), *K-State Engineer Magazine* (2 a year)

DEANS

College of Agriculture: Fred Cholick
College of Architecture: Dennis Law
College of Arts and Sciences: Stephen White
College of Business Admin.: Prof. Yar Ebadi
College of Education: Michael C. Holen
College of Eng.: Richard R. Gallagher
College of Human Ecology: Virginia Moxley
College of Technology and Aviation: Dennis Kuhlman
College of Veterinary Medicine: Ralph C. Richardson
Graduate School: Prof. R. W. Trewyn
Continuing Education: Elizabeth A. Unger

KANSAS WESLEYAN UNIVERSITY

100 East Claflin Ave, Salina, KS 67401-6196
Telephone: (785) 827-5541
Fax: (785) 827-0927
E-mail: admissions@kwu.edu
Internet: www.kwu.edu
Founded 1886
Private control, affiliated with the United Methodist Church
Pres.: Philip Kerstetter

Vice-Pres. and Academic Dean: Dr Mike Mitchell
Vice-Pres. for Finance and Admin.: Wayne Schneider
Vice-Pres. for Institutional Advancement: Darin Russell
Dir of Admissions: Jim Allen
Dir of Enrollment and Financial Services: Glenna Alexander
Registrar: Denise Hoeffner
Dir of Library Services: Ruth Cox
Library of 75,938 vols
Number of teachers: 45 (40 full-time, 5 part-time)
Number of students: 800.

McPHERSON COLLEGE

1600 East Euclid, POB 1402, McPherson, KS 67460
Telephone: (620) 241-0731
Fax: (620) 241-8443
E-mail: admiss@mcpherson.edu
Internet: www.mcpherson.edu
Founded 1887 as McPherson College and Institute; present name 1898
Private control
Academic year: September to May
Pres.: Ron Hovis
Vice-Pres. for Advancement: Michael P. Schneider
Provost and Dean of Faculty: Dr Laura Eells
Dean of Students: LaMonte Rothrock
Dir of Library and Media Services: Dr Susan Taylor
Number of teachers: 42
Number of students: 440

Depts of Art, Behavioral Science, Business, English, Health, PE and Recreation, History, Mathematics and Information Technology, Modern Language, Music, Natural Sciences, Philosophy and Religion, Teacher Education, Technology, Theatre.

MANHATTAN CHRISTIAN COLLEGE

1415 Anderson Ave, Manhattan, KS 66502
Telephone: (785) 539-3571
Fax: (785) 539-0832
E-mail: admit@mccks.edu
Internet: www.mccks.edu
Founded 1927 as Christian Workers Univ.; present name 1971
Private control
Academic year: August to May
Pres.: Kevin Ingram
Vice-Pres. for Student Life: Dr Rick L. Wright
Vice-Pres. for Business Affairs: Lori Jo Stanfield
Vice-Pres. for Academic Affairs: Randy Ingmire
Vice-Pres. for Institutional Advancement: Vern Henricks
Librarian: Mary Ann Littrell
Library of 40,000 vols
Number of teachers: 24
Number of students: 406

Depts of Bible and Theology, General Studies, Practical Ministries.

MID-AMERICA NAZARENE UNIVERSITY

2030 East College Way, Olathe, KS 66062-1899
Telephone: (913) 782-3750
Fax: (913) 791-3290
E-mail: info@mnu.edu
Internet: www.mnu.edu
Founded 1966
Private control
Academic year: August to April

Pres.: ED ROBINSON
Vice-Pres. for Academic Affairs and Dean: Dr
  FRANK MOORE
Vice-Pres. for Student Devt: MARGARET E.
  GILLILAND
Vice-Pres. for Institutional Advancement:
  DWIGHT E. DOUGLAS
Vice-Pres. for Enrollment Devt: RONALD J.
  HYSON
Vice-Pres. for Finance: BILL CLAIR
Registrar: PATRICIA J. WALSH
Librarian: Dr RAY L. MORRISON

Library of 400,000 items
Number of teachers: 123
Number of students: 1,900

Depts of Behavioral Sciences, Business
Admin., Education, Fine Arts, Humanities,
Innovative Adult Education, Nursing, Religion and Philosophy, Science and Mathematics

CHAIRMEN OF ACADEMIC DIVISIONS

Behavioral Sciences and Physical Education:
  Dr DOUG HENNING
Business Admin.: Dr MARK FORD
Education: Dr VERLA POWERS
Fine Arts: Dr DENNIS CROCKER
Humanities: Dr MARK A. HAMILTON
Nursing: Dr PAM SMITH
Religion and Philosophy: Dr JIM EDLIN
Science and Mathematics: Dr RICK BADLEY

NEWMAN UNIVERSITY

3100 McCormick Ave, Wichita, KS 67213-
  2097

Telephone: (316) 942-4291
Fax: (316) 942-4483
E-mail: admissions@newmanu.edu
Internet: www.newmanu.edu

Founded 1933 as Sacred Heart Junior College; present name 1998
Private control

Pres.: Dr NOREEN M. CARROCCI
Provost and Vice-Pres. for Academic Affairs:
  Dr B. LEE COOPER
Vice-Pres. for Finance and Admin.: MARK B.
  DRESSELHAUS
Vice-Pres. for Enrollment Management: KIM
  MILLER JACOBS
Vice-Pres. for Institutional Advancement:
  THOMAS E. BORREGO
Registrar: SHIRLEY RUEB
Library Dir: JOSEPH FORTE
Number of teachers: 191
Number of students: 2,071

DEANS

School of Applied Social Sciences: Dr
  MICHAEL SMITH
School of Arts and Humanities: NYALLS
  HARTMAN
School of Business: Dr JOSEPH GOETZ
School of Education: Dr GREGORY MOSS
School of Science, Nursing and Allied Health:
  Dr JOAN FELTS

OTTAWA UNIVERSITY

1001 South Cedar St, Ottawa, KS 66067
Telephone: (785) 242-5200
Fax: (785) 229-1020
E-mail: admiss@ottawa.edu
Internet: www.ottawa.edu

Founded 1865
Academic year: June to May
Mesa, Phoenix and Tempus campuses in
Arizona; Indiana, Kansas City and Wisconsin
campuses

Pres.: Dr FREDERICK R. SNOW
Exec. Vice-Pres.: Dr JAMES BILLICK
Vice-Pres. for Enrollment Management:
  SUSAN BACKOFEN

Provost: Dr BARBARA DINEEN
Provost, Kansas City: Dr TERREL W. HAINES
Provost, Arizona: Dr DONNA LEVENE
Dir, Milwaukee: Dr DONALD CLAUSER
Registrar: KAREN ADAMS
Dir of Library Services: GLORIA CREED-
  DIKEOGU

Library of 84,000 vols, 186 periodicals
Number of teachers: 65
Number of students: 2,503 full-time.

PITTSBURG STATE UNIVERSITY

1701 South Broadway, Pittsburg, KS 66762
Telephone: (620) 231-7000
Fax: (620) 235-6192
Internet: www.pittstate.edu

Founded 1903

Pres.: TOM W. BRYANT
Vice-Pres. for Academic Affairs: STEVEN A.
  SCOTT
Vice-Pres. for Admin. and Campus Life: JOHN
  D. PATTERSON
Vice-Pres. for Univ. Advancement: J. BRAD-
  FORD HODSON
Registrar: DEBBIE GREVE
Dean of Learning Resources: ROBERT WALTER

Library of 545,000 vols
Number of teachers: 325
Number of students: 6,500

DEANS

College of Arts and Sciences: Dr LYNETTE
  OLSON
Kelce College of Business: Dr J. RUSSELL
  HARDIN
College of Education: Dr JAMES C. CHRISTMAN
College of Technology: Dr BRUCE DALLMAN
Graduate Studies: Dr OLIVER HENSLEY

SAINT MARY COLLEGE

4100 South Fourth St, Leavenworth, KS
  66048-5082

Telephone: (913) 682-5151
Fax: (913) 758-6140
E-mail: admiss@stmary.edu
Internet: www.stmary.edu

Founded 1923
Private control (Roman Catholic church)
Academic year: August to July

Pres.: Dr DIANE STEELE
Vice-Pres. and Dean for Academic Affairs: Dr
  SANDRA VAN HOOSE
Vice-Pres. for Finance and Admin. Services:
  DALE L. CULVER
Vice-Pres. for Student Life: KEITH R. HANSEN
Vice-Pres. and Dean of Overland Park:
  RONALD LOGAN
Registrar: WANDA OWEN
Dean of Students: KEITH HANSEN
Librarian: PENELOPE LONERGAN

Library of 118,195 vols
Number of teachers: 43
Number of students: 826.

SOUTHWESTERN COLLEGE

100 College St, Winfield, KS 67156-2499
Telephone: (620) 229-6000
Fax: (620) 229-6224
Internet: www.sckans.edu

Founded 1885
Academic year: August to May

Pres.: Dr W. RICHARD MERRIMAN, Jr
Vice-Pres. for Academic Affairs and Dean of
  Faculty: J. ANDREW SHEPPARD
Vice-Pres. for Institutional Advancement:
  PAUL M. BEAN
Registrar: STACY TOWNSLEY
Dir of Admission: TODD N. MOORE
Library Dir: VERONICA MCASEY

Library of 70,000 vols, 11,000 e-books

Number of teachers: 50 full-time
Number of students: 1,401 (691 full-time, 710
  part-time)

Professional, Liberal Arts and General, Teacher Preparatory College.

STERLING COLLEGE

125 West Cooper, Sterling, KS 67579
Telephone: (620) 278-2173
Fax: (620) 278-3188
Internet: www.sterling.edu

Founded 1887

Pres.: Dr DOUGLAS BRUCE
Vice-Pres. of Academic Affairs: TROY PETERS
Vice-Pres. for Institutional Advancement:
  MARK SARVER
Vice-Pres. for Student Life: TINA WOHLER
Registrar: JANET CAYWOOD
Library Dir: BETTY CALDERWOOD

Library of 85,000 vols
Number of teachers: 32
Number of students: 490

Majors incl. Art and Graphic Design, Athletic
Training, Biology, Business Admin., Chemistry, Christian Ministries, Communication
and Theatre Arts, Culinary Arts, Elementary
Education, English, Exercise Science, Graphic Design and Effects, History, Ind. Interdisciplinary, Mathematics, Music, Music
Education, Psychology, Religious and Philosophical Studies.

TABOR COLLEGE

400 South Jefferson, Hillsboro, KS 67063
Telephone: (620) 947-3121
Fax: (620) 947-2676
E-mail: admissions@tabor.edu
Internet: www.tabor.edu

Founded 1908
Academic year: August to May

Pres.: LARRY NIKKEL
Vice-Pres. of Academics and Student Devt:
  Dr LAWRENCE RESSLER
Vice-Pres. for Advancement: JIM ELLIOTT
Vice-Pres. for Business and Finance: KIRBY
  FADENRECHT
Dean of Enrolment Management (vacant):
  RUSTY ALLEN
Registrar: DEANNE DUERKSEN
Dean of Student Devt: ERIC CODDING
Dir of Library Services: ROBIN OTTOSON

Library of 80,000 vols
Number of teachers: 65
Number of students: 586

Liberal arts college.

UNITED STATES ARMY COMMAND
AND GENERAL STAFF COLLEGE

1 Reynolds Ave, Fort Leavenworth, KS
  66027-1352
E-mail: leav-cgscregistrar@conus.army.mil
Internet: www.cgsc.army.mil

Founded 1882 as School of Application for
  Cavalry and Infantry; present name 1947
Academic year: August to June

Deputy Commandant: Brig.-Gen. JAMES
  HIRAI
Librarian: EDWIN B. BURGESS.

UNIVERSITY OF KANSAS

Room 230, 1450 Jayhawk Blvd, Lawrence,
  KS 66045
Telephone: (785) 864-2700
Fax: (785) 864-4120
E-mail: chancellor@ku.edu
Internet: www.ku.edu

Founded 1864

State Univ., under the Kansas Board of Regents

Academic year: August to May

Chancellor: ROBERT E. HEMENWAY

Provost and Exec. Vice-Chancellor: RICHARD LARIVIERE

Sr Vice-Provost for Academic Affairs: KATHLEEN MCCLUSKEY-FAWCETT

Vice-Provost for Admin. and Finance: WILLIAM L. (LINDY) EAKIN

Vice-Provost for Faculty Devt: MARY LEE HUMMERT

Vice-Provost for Facilities Planning and Management: JAMES A. LONG

Vice-Provost for Scholarly Support: DON STEEPLES

Vice-Provost for Student Success: MARLESA RONEY

Vice-Provost for Information Services and Chief Information Officer: DENISE STEPHENS

Vice-Chancellor of Research: JAMES ROBERTS

Vice-Chancellor and Dean of Edwards Campus: Dr ROBERT M. CLARK

Assoc. Vice-Provost and Dean of Students: RICHARD JOHNSON

Registrar: CINDY DERRITT

Dean of Libraries: LORRAINE HARICOMBE

Library of 3,908,979 vols, 33,874 periodicals, 3,489,807 microforms

Number of teachers: 2,165

Number of students: 28,849

Publications: *American Studies Journal, Auslegung, Chimères, Indigenous Nations Studies Journal, Journal of Applied Behavior Analysis, Journal of Dramatic Theory and Criticism, Journal of Kansas Entomological Society, Journal of Public Administration Research and Theory, Journal of Social and Clinical Psychology, Kansas Academy of Science Transactions, Kansas Journal of Law and Public Policy, Kansas Law Review, La Coronica: A Journal of Medieval Spanish Language and Literature, Latin American Theatre Review, Middle School Journal, The Nabokovian, Paleontological Contributions, Research Opportunities in Renaissance Drama, Russkii Tekst, Slovene Linguistic Studies, Social Thought and Research, Treatise on Invertebrate Paleontology, Yearbook of German-American Studies*

DEANS

School of Architecture and Urban Design: Prof. JOHN GAUNT

School of Business: WILLIAM FUERST

College of Liberal Arts and Sciences: JOSEPH STEINMETZ

School of Education: RICK GINSBERG

School of Eng.: Dr STUART R. BELL

School of Fine Arts: STEVEN K. HEDDEN

School of Journalism and Mass Communications: ANN M. BRILL

School of Law: GAIL B. AGRAWAL

School of Pharmacy: KENNETH L. AUDUS

School of Social Welfare: MARY ELLEN KONDRAT

Graduate School and Int. Programs: DIANA CARLIN

ATTACHED MEDICAL CENTRE

Kansas University Medical Center

3901 Rainbow Blvd, Kansas City, KS 66160

Telephone: (913) 588-5000

Fax: (913) 588-1412

Internet: www.kumc.edu

Founded 1905

Exec. Vice-Chancellor: Dr BARBARA ATKINSON

Sr Vice-Chancellor for Academic and Student Affairs: KAREN MILLER

Vice-Chancellor for Admin.: EDWARD PHILLIPS

Vice-Chancellor for Academic Affairs: Dr ALLEN B RAWITCH

Vice-Chancellor for Research: Dr JAMES VOGT

Vice-Chancellor for External Affairs: Dr DAVID ADKINS

Number of teachers: 739

Number of students: 2,409

DEANS

School of Allied Health: Prof. KAREN MILLER

Graduate Studies: Dr ALLEN B RAWITCH

School of Medicine: Dr BARBARA F. ATKINSON (Exec. Dean)

School of Nursing: Dr KAREN MILLER

WASHBURN UNIVERSITY

1700 Southwest College, Topeka, KS 66621

Telephone: (785) 670-1010

Fax: (785) 670-1048

E-mail: webmaster@washburn.edu

Internet: www.washburn.edu

Founded 1865

Academic year: August to May

Pres.: Dr JERRY B. FARLEY

Vice-Pres. for Academic Affairs and Provost: Dr RON WASSERSTEIN

Vice-Pres. for Admin. and Treas.: WANDA HILL

Vice-Pres. for Student Life: Dr WANDA HILL

Dean of Univ. Library: Dr GARY SCHMIDT

Registrar: Dr WANDA DOLE

Library of 315,293 vols

Number of teachers: 300

Number of students: 6,626

Publications: *Alumni Magazine, Circuit Rider, KAW, Washburn Review, Washburn Update*

DEANS

Law: WILLIAM RICH

School of Business: Dr DAVID SOLLARS

School of Applied Studies: Dr WILLIAM S. DUNLAP

College of Arts and Sciences: Dr GORDON MCQUERE

School of Nursing: Dr CYNTHIA HORNBERGER

Division of Continuing Education: Dr TIM PETERSON

WICHITA STATE UNIVERSITY

1845 Fairmont St, Wichita, KS 67260

Telephone: (316) 978-3456

Fax: (316) 978-3174

Internet: www.wichita.edu

Founded 1894 as Fairmount College (Congregational), control transferred to City of Wichita 1926, added to the Kansas state higher education system 1964

Pres.: Dr DONALD L. BEGGS

Vice-Pres. for Academic Affairs and Research: Dr GARY L. MILLER

Vice-Pres. for Campus Life and Univ. Relations: Dr RON R. KOPITA

Vice-Pres. for Admin. and Finance: ROBERT D. LOWE

Vice-Pres. and Gen. Counsel: TED D. AYRES

Dean of Univ. Libraries: PAL RAO

Library of 1,085,000 vols, 1,096,000 microforms, 14,270 current periodicals, 495,000 govt documents, 4,000 linear ft of archives and MSS

Number of teachers: 520 (479 full-time, 41 part-time)

Number of students: 15,000

Publications: *Sunflower, Wichita State Alumni News, Wichita State University Magazine*

DEANS

Barton School of Business: Dr JOHN M. BEEHLER

College of Education: JON ENGELHARDT

College of Eng.: ZULMA TORO-RAMOS

College of Fine Arts: RODNEY E. MILLER

College of Health Professions: Prof. PETER A. COHEN

College of Liberal Arts and Sciences: WILLIAM D. BISCHOFF

Graduate School: SUSAN KOVAR

KENTUCKY

ALICE LLOYD COLLEGE

100 Purpose Rd, Pippa Passes, KY 41844

Telephone: (606) 368-2101

Fax: (606) 368-2125

E-mail: enrolments@alc.edu

Internet: www.alc.edu

Founded 1923

Private control

Academic year: August to May

Pres.: JOE A. STEPP

Vice-Pres. for Academic Affairs: MARYLEE JAMES

Vice-Pres. for Admin.: JAMES STEPP

Vice-Pres. for Business Affairs: DAVID JOHNSON

Registrar: THELMARIE THORNSBERRY

Library Dir: ANDREW BUSROE

Number of teachers: 32

Number of students: 508

CHAIRS OF ACADEMIC DIVISIONS

Humanities: RICHARD KENNEDY

Natural Science and Mathematics: Dr PAUL YEARY

ASBURY COLLEGE

1 Macklem Dr., Wilmore, KY 40390

Telephone: (859) 858-3511

E-mail: pr@asbury.edu

Internet: www.asbury.edu

Founded 1890

Private control

Academic year: August to May

Pres.: Dr WILLIAM C. CROTHERS

Provost: Dr JOHN S. KULAGA

Vice-Pres. for Business Affairs: Dr CHARLIE D. FISKEAUX

Vice-Pres. for Student Devt: Dr W. JOSEPH BROCKINTON

Vice-Pres. for Institutional Advancement: ROBERT T. BRIDGES

Registrar: Dr TIMOTHY L. THOMAS

Dir of Library Services: DOUGLAS J. BUTLER

Library of 155,000 vols

Number of teachers: 155

Number of students: 1,218 (1,155 undergraduate, 63 graduate).

ASBURY THEOLOGICAL SEMINARY

204 North Lexington Ave, Wilmore, KY 40390

Telephone: (859) 858-3581

Internet: www.asburyseminary.edu

Founded 1923

Private control

Academic year: September to May

Pres.: ELLSWORTH KALAS

Vice-Pres. for Academic Affairs and Provost: Dr BILL ARNOLD

Vice-Pres. for Finance and Admin.: BRYAN BLANKENSHIP

Vice-Pres. for Seminary Advancement: RONNIE JONES

Vice-Pres. for Community Life: Rev. JOHN DAVID WALT

Vice-Pres. for Florida Campus: Dr J. STEVEN HARPER

Exec. Dir of Libraries: PAUL TIPPEY

Library of 247,000 items
Number of teachers: 62
Number of students: 1,778.

BRANCH CAMPUS
Florida Campus: 8401 Valencia College Lane, Orlando, FL 32825; tel. (407) 482-7564.

BELLARMINE UNIVERSITY

2001 Newburg Rd, Louisville, KY 40205-0671
Telephone: (502) 452-8000
Fax: (502) 452-8033
E-mail: admissions@bellarmine.edu
Internet: www.bellarmine.edu
Founded 1950
Academic year: August to May
Pres.: Dr JOSEPH J. McGOWAN
Provost: PETER CIMBOLIC
Sr Vice-Pres. for Academic Affairs: Dr DORIS TEGART
Vice-Pres. for Enrollment Management: SEAN J. RYAN
Vice-Pres. for Institutional Advancement: VINCE MANIACI
Vice-Pres. for Student Affairs and Dean of Students: Dr FRED RHODES
Chair of Business Affairs Dept: JOHN T. BYRD, III
Dean of Undergraduate Admissions: TIMOTHY STURGEON
Library Dir: JOHN STEMMER
Library of 93,000 vols
Number of teachers: 204 (114 full-time, 90 part-time)
Number of students: 2,200

DEANS
Bellarmine College of Arts and Sciences: Dr MARY JO VESPER
Rubel School of Business: Dr DANIEL L. BAUER
Annsley Frazier Thornton School of Education: Dr MAUREEN R. NORRIS
Allan and Donna Lansing School of Nursing and Health Sciences: Dr SUSAN H. DAVIS

BEREA COLLEGE

101 Chestnut St, Berea, KY 40404
Telephone: (859) 985-3000
Fax: (859) 985-3915
Internet: www.berea.edu
Founded 1855
Academic year: September–May
Pres.: Dr LARRY D. SHINN
Academic Vice-Pres. and Provost: CAROLYN NEWTON
Vice-Pres. for Business and Admin.: DIANE KERBY
Vice-Pres. for College Relations and Devt: WILLIAM LARAMEE
Vice-Pres. for Finance: JEFFREY AMBURGEY
Vice-Pres. for Labor and Student Life: GAIL WOLFORD
Dean of the Faculty: STEPHANIE P. BROWNER
Dir of Library Services: ANNE CHASE
Library of 358,566 vols
Number of teachers: 131
Number of students: 1,500.

BRESCIA UNIVERSITY

717 Frederica St, Owensboro, KY 42301-3023
Telephone: (270) 685-3131
E-mail: admissions@brescia.edu
Internet: www.brescia.edu
Founded 1925 as Mount Saint Joseph Jr College for Women; present name 1998
Private control
Academic year: August to May
Pres.: Sr VIVIAN M. BOWLES

Vice-Pres. for Academic Affairs and Academic Dean: JAMES AHERN
Dir of Library Services: Sr JUDITH NELL RINEY
Number of teachers: 60
Number of students: 840

CHAIRMEN OF ACADEMIC DIVISIONS
Educational Studies: Sr SHARON SULLIVAN
Fine Arts: Sr MARY DIANE TAYLOR
Humanities: Dr ELLEN DUGAN-BARRETTE
Mathematics and Natural Sciences: Sr MICHELE MOREK
Social and Behavioral Sciences: (vacant)
William H. Thompson School of Business: Dr JULIE JOHNSON

CAMPBELLSVILLE COLLEGE

1 University Dr., Campbellsville, KY 42718-2799
Telephone: (800) 264-6014
Fax: (800) 789-5020
E-mail: admissions@campbellsville.edu
Internet: www.campbellsville.edu
Founded 1906
Affiliated with the Kentucky Baptist Convention
Pres.: Dr MICHAEL V. CARTER
Vice-Pres. for Academic Affairs: Dr FRANKLIN D. CHEATHAM
Vice-Pres. for Church and External Relations: JOHN E. CHOWNING
Vice-Pres. for Devt: Dr ALAN MEDDERS
Vice-Pres. for Finance and Admin.: OTTO TENNANT, Jr
Vice-Pres. for Communications and Marketing: MARCUS C. WHITT
Dir of Library Services: Dr JOHN RUSSELL BIRCH, Jr
Library of 95,000 vols
Number of teachers: 45
Number of students: 1,800.

CENTRE COLLEGE

Danville, KY 40422
Telephone: (606) 238-5200
Fax: (606) 236-9610
Internet: www.centre.edu
Founded 1819
Pres.: JOHN ROUSH
Vice-Pres. and Dean of Student Life: RANDY HAYS
Vice-Pres. and Treas.: JOHN CUNY
Registrar: TIM CULHAN
Library Dir: STAN CAMPBELL
Library of 200,000 vols and 850 periodicals
Number of teachers: 90
Number of students: 1,000.

CLEAR CREEK BAPTIST BIBLE COLLEGE

300 Clear Creek Rd, Pineville, KY 40977
Telephone: (606) 337-3196
Fax: (606) 337-2372
E-mail: ccbbc@ccbbc.edu
Internet: www.ccbbc.edu
Founded 1926 as Clear Creek Mountain Springs, Inc.; present name 1986
Private control
Academic year: August to May
Pres.: Dr DONNIE FOX
Academic Dean: Dr MALCOLM HESTER
Registrar: MARY LOU WALZER
Dir of Library Services: MARGE CUMMINGS
Library of 37,000 vols
Number of teachers: 22
Number of students: 174.

EASTERN KENTUCKY UNIVERSITY

521 Lancaster Ave, Richmond, KY 40475-3102
Telephone: (859) 622-1000
Fax: (859) 622-1020
Internet: www.eku.edu
Founded 1906
Academic year: August to May
Pres.: JOANNE K. GLASSER
Provost and Vice-Pres. for Academic Affairs and Research: Dr RODNEY PIERCEY
Vice-Pres. for Financial Affairs and Treas.: DEBORAH NEWSOM
Dir of Govt Relations: Dr PAUL BLANCHARD
Vice-Pres. for Student Affairs: Dr JAMES CONNEELY (acting)
Vice-Pres. for Univ. Advancement: JOSEPH FOSTER (acting)
Registrar: JILL ALLGIER
Dean of Libraries: CARRIE COOPER
Library of 837,945 vols, 3,565 current periodicals, 1,410,522 current periodicals
Number of teachers: 575 (full-time)
Number of students: 15,061

DEANS
Arts and Sciences: Dr DOMINIC HART
Business and Technology: Dr ROBERT ROGOW
Education: Dr LARRY SEXTON (acting)
Graduate Studies: Dr BANKOLE THOMPSON
Health Sciences: Dr DAVID GALE
Law Enforcement: Dr GARY CORDNER

GEORGETOWN COLLEGE

Georgetown, KY 40324-1696
Telephone: (502) 863-8011
Fax: (502) 868-8891
E-mail: pr@georgetowncollege.edu
Internet: www.georgetowncollege.edu
Founded 1829
Pres.: Dr WILLIAM H. CROUCH, Jr
Vice-Pres. for Leadership and Ethics: Dr JUDY R. ROGERS
Provost and Academic Dean: Dr ROSEMARY ALLEN
Vice-Pres. for Student Life and Dean of Students: TODD GAMBILL
Vice-Pres. for Institutional Advancement: DAN MILLER
Vice-Pres. for Enrollment Management and Institutional Research: GARVEL KINDRICK
Library Dir: MARY MARGARET LOWE
Library of 152,531 vols, 733 current periodicals, 4064 audio-visual items
Number of teachers: 105
Number of students: 1,514.

KENTUCKY CHRISTIAN UNIVERSITY

100 Academic Parkway, Grayson, KY 41143-2205
Telephone: (606) 474-3000
Fax: (606) 474-3154
Internet: www.kcu.edu
Founded 1919 as Christian Normal Institute; as Kentucky Christian College 1944; present name 2004
Private control
Academic year: August to May
Pres.: Dr KEITH P. KEERAN
Chancellor: Dr L. PALMER YOUNG
Exec. Vice-Pres.: JOHN L. DUNDON
Sr Vice-Pres. and Provost: Dr JEFF METCALF
Vice-Pres. for Student Life: Dr SHERRY L. CURTIS
Vice-Pres. for Enrollment Management: SANDRA DEAKINS
Vice-Pres. for Business and Finance: Dr TIM NISCHIN
Vice-Pres. for Academic Afairs: Dr JEFF METCALF
Registrar: GEORGE W. WAGGONER, III

Library Dir: THOMAS SCOTT
Library of 80,000
Number of teachers: 32
Number of students: 580.

KENTUCKY MOUNTAIN BIBLE COLLEGE

POB 10, Vancleve, KY 41385-0010
855 Kentucky Highway 541, Vancleve, KY 41385-0010
Telephone: (606) 693-5000
Fax: (606) 693-4844
E-mail: kmbc@kmbc.edu
Internet: www.kmbc.edu
Founded 1931 as Kentucky Mountain Bible Institute; present name 1989
Private control
Pres.: Dr PHILIP SPEAS
Exec. Vice-Pres. and Vice-Pres. for Academic Affairs: THOMAS LORIMER
Business Man.: DOUG DUNN
Vice-Pres. for Student Affairs and Devt: JOHN NEIHOF
Registrar: CATY NELSON
Librarian: PAT BOWEN
Library of 26,000 vols
Number of teachers: 14
Number of students: 54.

KENTUCKY STATE UNIVERSITY

400 East Main St, Frankfort, KY 40601
Telephone: (502) 597-6000
E-mail: admissions@kysu.edu
Internet: www.kysu.edu
Founded 1886
Academic year: August to May
Pres.: Dr MARY EVANS SIAS
Vice-Pres. for Academic Affairs and Provost: STEFANIE WATSON
Vice-Pres. for Student Affairs: Dr RUBYE JONES
Vice-Pres. for External Relations and Devt: HINFRED MCDUFFIE
Vice-Pres. for Finance and Admin. (vacant): KATHY WILSON
Dir of Records, Registration and Admissions: JAMES BURRELL
Dir of Libraries: SHEILA A. STUCKEY
Library of 304,000 vols
Number of teachers: 149
Number of students: 2,315.

KENTUCKY WESLEYAN COLLEGE

3000 Frederica St, Owensboro, KY 42301
Telephone: (270) 926-3111
Fax: (270) 926-3196
E-mail: admitme@kwc.edu
Internet: www.kwc.edu
Founded 1858
Academic year: August to May
Pres.: Dr ANNE CAIRNS FEDERLEIN
Vice-Pres. of Finance: CINDRA K. STIFF
Vice-Pres.for Advancement: RONALD S. MCCRACKEN
Dean of the College: Dr M. MICHAEL FAGAN
Dean of Admission and Financial Aid: CLAUDE M. BACON
Dean of Student Life: SCOTT E. KRAMER
Dir of Library: PATRICIA MCFARLING
Library of 85,085 vols, 315 periodicals
Number of teachers: 69
Number of students: 679 (606 full-time, 30 part-time).

LEXINGTON THEOLOGICAL SEMINARY

631 South Limestone St, Lexington, KY 40508
Telephone: (859) 252-0361

Fax: (859) 281-6042
E-mail: admissions@lextheo.edu
Internet: www.lextheo.edu
Founded 1865 as College of the Bible; present name 1965
Private control
Pres.: R. ROBERT CUENI
Vice-Pres for Advancement: DAISY L. MACHADO, JAMES M. WRAY, Jr
Registrar: DABNEY PARKER
Librarian: TIM BROWNING
Number of teachers: 12
Number of students: 141.

LINDSEY WILSON COLLEGE

210 Lindsey Wilson St, Columbia, KY 42728
Telephone: (270) 384-2126
Fax: (270) 384-8200
E-mail: info@lindsey.edu
Internet: www.lindsey.edu
Founded 1903 as Lindsey Wilson Training School; present name 1923
Private control
Academic year: August to May
Pres.: WILLIAM T. LUCKEY, Jr
Chancellor: JOHN B. BEGLEY
Vice-Pres. for Advancement: RON HEATH
Vice-Pres. (Admin. and Finance): ROGER DRAKE
Vice-Pres. for Student Services and Enrollment Management: DEAN ADAMS
Provost and Dean of Faculty: JOHN RIGNEY
Registrar: SUE COOMER
Library Dir: PHILIP HANNA
Library of 496,000 items
Number of teachers: 58
Number of students: 1,585.

CHAIRMEN OF ACADEMIC DIVISIONS

Business and Computer Information Systems: JOHN HOWERY
Education: ROBERT BROWN
Human Services and Counseling: JOHN RIGNEY
Humanities and Fine Arts: TIM SMITH
Mathematics and Natural Sciences: ROBERT SHUFFETT
Social and Behavioral Sciences: (vacant)

LOUISVILLE PRESBYTERIAN THEOLOGICAL SEMINARY

1044 Alta Vista Rd, Louisville, KY 40205
Telephone: (502) 895-3411
Fax: (502) 895-1096
E-mail: admissions@lpts.edu
Internet: www.lpts.edu
Private control
Pres.: DEAN K. THOMPSON
Dean: DONNA MELLOAN
Library Dir: DOUGLAS GRAGG
Library of 130,000 vols
Number of teachers: 22
Number of students: 250.

MID-CONTINENT COLLEGE

99 Powell Rd, E, Mayfield, KY 42066-9007
Telephone: (270) 247-8521
Fax: (270) 247-3115
E-mail: mcc@midcontinent.edu
Internet: www.midcontinent.edu
Founded 1949
Private control
Pres.: Dr ROBERT IMHOFF
Provost and Vice-Pres. for Academic Affairs: Dr ALLAN L. BEANE
Exec. Vice-Pres. for Admin. and Student Affairs: CHARLES W. FORD
Vice-Pres. for Business Operations: ANDY STRATTON
Vice-Pres. for Devt: Dr LARRY STEWART

Registrar: YVONNE YATES
Library Dir: Dr RAYMOND E. CARROLL
Number of students: 786

DEANS

Baptist College of Arts and Sciences: Dr STEPHEN WILSON
Baptist College of the Bible: Dr JAMES CECIL

MIDWAY COLLEGE

512 East Stephens St, Midway, KY 40347
Telephone: (859) 846-4421
Fax: (859) 846-5817
Internet: www.midway.edu
Founded 1847 as Kentucky Female Orphan School; present name 1978
Private control
Academic year: August to May
Pres.: Dr WILLIAM B. DRAKE, Jr
Vice-Pres. for Academic Affairs (vacant)
Vice-Pres. for Business Affairs: LYEN CREWS
Vice-Pres. for College Relations and Devt: JUDY MARCUM
Vice-Pres. and Dean of Enrollment Management: Dr JAMES WOMBLES
Vice-Pres. and Assoc. Dean, School for Career Devt: Dr WILLIAM BROWN
Provost and Dean of Women's College: SARAH H. LAWS
Registrar: P. EDWARD PRESLER
Dir of Library Services: CATHY REILENDER
Number of teachers: 18 full time, 112 assoc staff
Number of students: 1,200

CHAIRMEN OF ACADEMIC DIVISIONS

Business Studies and Organizational Management: Dr FRANK FLETCHER
Equine Studies: Dr SALLY REYAN
Liberal Studies: Dr JUDITH HATCHETT
Mathematics and Science: Dr JOHN SASSER
Nursing: Dr PATTY RYAN
Teacher Education: (vacant)

MOREHEAD STATE UNIVERSITY

150 University Blvd, Morehead, KY 40351
Telephone: (606) 783-2221
Fax: (606) 783-2678
E-mail: webmaster@moreheadstate.edu
Internet: www.moreheadstate.edu
Founded 1922
Academic year: August to May
Pres.: Dr WAYNE D. ANDREWS
Provost and Exec. Vice-Pres. for Academic Affairs: MICHAEL MOORE
Vice-Pres. for Admin. and Fiscal Services: MICHAEL WALTERS
Vice-Pres. for Student Life: MADONNA WEATHERS
Vice-Pres. for Univ. Relations: KEITH KAPPES
Vice-Pres. for Planning, Budgets and Technology: BETH G. PATRICK
Vice-Pres. for Devt: BARBARA A. ENDER
Vice-Pres. for Student Life: MADONNA WEATHERS
Registrar: LORETTA B. LYKINS
Dean of Library Services: ELSIE PRITCHARD
Library of 441,203 vols, 2,546 periodicals
Number of teachers: 440 (320 full-time, 120 part-time)
Number of students: 8,171 (5,849 full-time, 2,322 part-time)

DEANS

Caudill College of Humanities: Dr MICHAEL SEELIG
College of Business: Dr ROBERT ALBERT
College of Education: Dr DAN BRANHAM
College of Science and Technology: Dr GERALD DEMOSS
Institute for Regional Analysis and Public Policy: Dr DAVID RUDY

MURRAY STATE UNIVERSITY

13 Sparks Hall, Murray, KY 42071-3318

Telephone: (270) 762-3011

Fax: (270) 762-3413

E-mail: admissions@murraystate.edu

Internet: www.murraystate.edu

Founded 1922

Academic year: August to May

Pres.: RANDY J. DUNN

Provost and Vice-Pres. for Academic Affairs: Dr GARY BROCKWAY

Vice-Pres. for Finance and Admin. Services: THOMAS W. DENTON

Assoc. Vice-Pres. for Devt and Govt Relations: BOB JACKSON

Vice-Pres. for Student Affairs: Dr DONALD ROBERTSON

Dean of Libraries: Dr LAURENE ZAPOROZHETS

Library of 964,894 vols

Number of teachers: 539 (380 full-time, 159 part-time)

Number of students: 10,128 (7,535 full-time, 2,593 part-time)

DEANS

College of Business and Public Affairs: Dr DANNIE HARRISON

College of Education: Dr RUSS WALL

College of Health Sciences and Human Services: Dr BETTY BLODGETT

College of Humanities and Fine Arts: Dr TED BROWN

College of Science, Eng. and Technology: Dr NEIL WEBER

School of Agriculture: Dr TONY BRANNON

Academic Outreach and Continuing Education: Dr JOHN YATES

NORTHERN KENTUCKY UNIVERSITY

Nunn Dr., Highland Heights, KY 41099

Telephone: (859) 572-5220

Fax: (859) 572-5566

E-mail: admitnku@nku.edu

Internet: www.nku.edu

Founded 1968 as Northern Kentucky State College; present name 1976

State control

Academic year: August to May

Pres.: Dr JAMES C. VOTRUBA

Vice-Pres. for Academic Affairs and Provost: Dr GAIL W. WELLS

Vice-Pres. for Admin. and Finance: W. MICHAEL BAKER

Vice-Pres. for Student Affairs: Dr MARK G. SHANLEY

Vice-Pres. for Planning, Policy and Budget: SUE HODGES MOORE

Vice-Pres. for Govt and Community Relations: JOSEPH E. WIND

Vice-Pres. for Univ. Advancement: GERARD A. ST AMAND

Vice-Pres. for Legal Affairs and Gen. Counsel: SARA L. SIDEBOTTOM

Registrar: KIMBERLY K. TAYLOR

Assoc. Provost of Libraries: ARNE ALMQUIST

Library of 342,642 vols

Number of teachers: 648 (full-time)

Number of students: 13,743

DEANS

College of Arts and Sciences: Dr PHILLIP SCHMIDT

College of Business: Dr MICHAEL R. CARRELL

College of Education: RACHELLE BRUNO

Chase College of Law: Dr GERARD A. ST AMAND

College of Professional Studies: J. PATRICK MOYNAHAN

PIKEVILLE COLLEGE

147 Sycamore St, Pikeville, KY 41501

Telephone: (606) 218-5250

Fax: (606) 218-5269

Internet: www.pc.edu

Founded 1889

Academic year: August to July

Pres.: HAROLD H. SMITH

Vice-Pres. for Academic Affairs and Dean of the College: WALLACE CAMPBELL

Librarian: LEE ROBBINS

Library of 72,673 vols

Number of teachers: 57

Number of students: 1,013 (762 undergraduate, 251 postgraduate).

SOUTHERN BAPTIST THEOLOGICAL SEMINARY

2825 Lexington Rd, Louisville, KY 40280

Telephone: (502) 897-4011

Fax: (502) 899-1770

E-mail: admissions@sbts.edu

Internet: www.sbts.edu

Founded 1859

Private control

Academic year: August to May

Pres.: Dr R. ALBERT MOHLER, Jr

Sr Vice-Pres. for Academic Admin.: Dr RUSSELL D. MOORE

Sr Vice-Pres. for Institutional Admin.: R. CLARK LOGAN

Sr Vice-Pres. for Institutional Relations: DOUGLAS C. WALKER, III

Vice-Pres. for Student Services: DANIEL E. HATFIELD

Registrar: NORMAN CHUNG

Librarian and Assoc. Vice-Pres. for Academic Resources: BRUCE L. KEISLING

Library of 900,000 items

Number of teachers: 130

Number of students: 2,890

Publication: *Southern Baptist Journal of Theology* (quarterly).

SPALDING UNIVERSITY

851 South Fourth St, Louisville, KY 40203

Telephone: (502) 585-9911

Fax: (502) 585-7158

E-mail: info@spalding.edu

Internet: www.spalding.edu

Founded 1814

Pres.: Dr JO ANN ROONEY

Sr Vice-Pres. for Academic Affairs: RANDY L. STRICKLAND

Vice-Pres. for Finance: LARRY ROMINE

Vice-Pres. for Univ. Advancement: JEFFREY L. ASHLEY

Dean of Students: RICHARD HUDSON

Dir of Admissions: CHRIS HART

Asst Dir of Financial Aid: KRYSTAN LIVELY

Library Dir: JACKIE LENARZ

Library of 200,000 vols, 22,000 bound journals, 450 current periodical subscriptions

Number of teachers: 147 (81 full-time, 66 part-time)

Number of students: 1,585

DEANS

College of Arts and Sciences: (vacant)

College of Professional Studies: Dr JUDITH PLAWECKI

SULLIVAN UNIVERSITY

3101 Bardstown Rd, Louisville, KY 40205

Telephone: (502) 456-6505

Fax: (502) 454-4880

E-mail: admissions@sullivan.edu

Internet: www.sullivan.edu

Founded 1962 as Sullivan Business College; present name 2000

Private control

Academic year: September to September (4 quarters)

Pres.: Dr THOMAS F. DAVISSON

Exec. Vice-Pres. and CEO: Dr STEPHEN COPPOCK

Dean of Graduate School: Dr JEFFREY JOHNSON

Library Dir: CHARLES BROWN

Library of 20,000 vols

Number of teachers: 38

Number of students: 2,001

Areas of study: business, childhood education, computer technology, legal studies, office admin., hospitality.

BRANCH CAMPUSES

Lexington Campus: 2355 Harrodsburg Rd, Lexington, KY 40504; tel. (859) 276-4357; fax (859) 276-1153.

Fort Knox Campus: 63 Quartermaster St, Fort Knox, KY 40121-0998; tel. (502) 942-8500; fax (502) 942-3640.

THOMAS MORE COLLEGE

333 Thomas More Parkway, Crestview Hills, KY 41017-3495

Telephone: (859) 341-5800

Fax: (859) 344-3345

E-mail: admissions@thomasmore.edu

Internet: www.thomasmore.edu

Founded 1921

Private control

Pres.: Sister MARGARET A. STALLMEYER

Vice-Pres. for Academic Affairs: Dr BRADLEY BIELSKI

Vice-Pres. for Enrollment Management: ANGELA GRIFFIN-JONES

Vice-Pres. for Finance: PEG BRADNER HANCOCK

Vice-Pres. for Institutional Advancement (vacant): CATHY SILVERS

Registrar: KELLY GOYETTE

Librarian: JIM McKELLOGG

Library of 113,056 vols

Number of teachers: 129 (72 full-time, 57 part-time)

Number of students: 1,465.

TRANSYLVANIA UNIVERSITY

300 North Broadway, Lexington, KY 40508-1797

Telephone: (859) 233-8111

E-mail: admissions@transy.edu

Internet: www.transy.edu

Founded 1780 as Transylvania Seminary, inc. as Transylvania Univ. 1799

Pres.: CHARLES L. SHEARER

Vice-Pres. and Dean of the College: WILLIAM F. POLLARD

Vice-Pres. for Devt: RICHARD D. VALENTINE

Chief Financial Officer: GERALD E. RAY

Dean of Students: MICHAEL K. VETTER

Dir of Admissions: BRADLEY L. GOAN

Registrar: JAMES M. MILLS

Librarian: SUSAN M. BROWN

Library of 115,000 vols

Number of teachers: 64

Number of students: 1,075.

UNION COLLEGE

310 College St, Barbourville, KY 40906-1499

Telephone: (606) 546-4151

Fax: (606) 546-1217

Internet: www.unionky.edu

Founded 1879

Academic year: July to June

Pres.: EDWARD DE ROSSET
Vice-Pres. for Academic Affairs: Dr THOMAS J. McFARLAND
Vice-Pres. for Advancement: DENISE WAINSCOTT
Dean of Admissions and Financial Aid: ANDRE WASHINGTON
Athletics Dir: DARIN WILSON
Dean of Education: Dr ROBERT SWANSON
Dean of Student Life: DEBBIE D'ANNA
Registrar: KATHY WEBB
Head Librarian: TARA L. COOPER
Library of 162,646 vols, 439,794 microforms
Number of teachers: 54
Number of students: 1,069 (637 undergraduate, 432 postgraduate).

UNIVERSITY OF THE CUMBERLANDS

6191 College Station Dr., Williamsburg, KY 40769
Telephone: (606) 549-2200
E-mail: admiss@ucumberlands.edu
Internet: www.ucumberlands.edu
Founded 1889
Pres.: JIM TAYLOR
Vice-Pres. for Academic Affairs: Dr LARRY COCKRUM
Vice-Pres. for Business Affairs and Treas.: BARRY POYNTER
Vice-Pres. for Institutional Advancement: SUE WAKE
Vice-Pres. for Student Services: MICHAEL COLGROVE
Registrar: EMILY MEADORS
Dir of the Library: JANICE WREN
Library of 155,000 vols
Number of teachers: 112
Number of students: 1,743.

UNIVERSITY OF KENTUCKY

Lexington, KY 40506
Telephone: (606) 257-9000
Fax: (606) 257-4000
Internet: www.uky.edu
Founded 1865
Academic year: August to May
Pres.: Dr LEE T. TODD, Jr
Provost: KUMBLE R. SUBBASWAMY (acting)
Exec. Vice-Pres. for Finance and Admin.: FRANK A. BUTLER
Exec. Vice-Pres. for Health Affairs: MICHAEL KARPF
Vice-Pres. for Information Technology: EUGENE R. WILLIAMS
Vice-Pres. for Institutional Advancement: TERRY B. MOBLEY
Vice-Pres. for Institutional Research, Planning and Effectiveness: Dr CONNIE A. RAY
Vice-Pres. for Student Affairs: Dr PATRICIA S. TERRELL
Vice-Pres. for Facilities Management: BOB WISEMAN
Vice-Pres. for Commercialization and Economic Devt: LEN HELLER
Vice-Pres. for Planning, Budget and Policy: ANGELA S. MARTIN
Gen. Counsel: BARBARA W. JONES (acting)
Assoc. Provost for Academic Affairs: Dr DAVID WATT
Assoc. Provost for Undergraduate Education: Dr PHILIP J. KRAEMER
Assoc. Provost for Multicultural and Academic Affairs: Dr LAURETTA BYARS
Assoc. Provost for Int. Affairs: Dr DAVID BETTEZ (acting)
Dean of the Graduate School: Dr JEANNINE BLACKWELL (acting)
Dir of Admissions and Univ. Registrar: DONALD E. WITT
Dir, UK Art Museum: KATHY WALSH-PIPER
Dean of Libraries: CAROL PITTS DIEDRICHS
Library: see Libraries and Archives

Number of teachers: 1,209 full-time
Number of students: 25,397
Publications: *Retiarius: commentarii periodici Latini* (annual), *Alzheimer's Disease Review* (quarterly), *Disclosure (Lexington)* (annual), *Kentucky Review* (2 a year), *Esprit Createur* (quarterly), *Growth and Change* (urban and regional policy, quarterly), *Colloquia Germanica* (quarterly), *Kentucky Law Journal* (quarterly)

DEANS

College of Agriculture: Dr M. SCOTT SMITH
College of Arts and Sciences: Dr STEVEN L. HOCH
College of Business and Econ.: Dr DEVANTHAN SUDHARSHAN
College of Communications and Information Studies: Dr J. DAVID JOHNSON
College of Design: DAVID MOHNEY
College of Education: Dr JAMES G. CIBULKA (acting)
College of Eng.: Dr THOMAS W. LESTER
College of Fine Arts: Dr ROBERT SHAY
College of Law: ALLAN WALKER VESTAL
College of Social Work: Dr KAY S. HOFFMAN
College of Dentistry: Dr SHARON P. TURNER
College of Health Sciences: Dr THOMAS C. ROBINSON
College of Medicine: Dr JAY A. PERMAN
College of Nursing: Dr CAROLYN A. WILLIAMS
College of Pharmacy: Dr KENNETH B. ROBERTS

UNIVERSITY OF LOUISVILLE

Louisville, KY 40292
Telephone: (502) 852-5555
E-mail: admitme@louisville.edu
Internet: www.louisville.edu
Founded 1798
Pres.: Dr JAMES RAMSEY
Univ. Provost: Dr SHIRLEY C. WILLIHNGANZ (acting)
Vice-Pres. for Finance: MICHAEL J. CURTIN
Vice-Pres. for Student Affairs: TOM JACKSON, Jr (acting)
Vice-Pres. for Advancement: KEITH INMAN
Vice-Pres. for Health Affairs: LARRY N. COOK
Vice-Pres. for Information Technology: RONALD MOORE
Vice-Pres. for Research: MANUEL MARTINEZ
Vice-Pres. for External Affairs: Dr DAN HALL
Registrar: KATHLEEN OTTO
Dean of Univ. Libraries: Prof. HANNELORE RADER (acting)
Library of 2,000,000 vols
Number of teachers: 1,154
Number of students: 21,089
Publications: *The Cardinal, Inside U of L*

DEANS

College of Arts and Sciences: JAMES F. BRENNAN
College of Business and Public Admin.: ROBERT L. TAYLOR
School of Dentistry: Dr JOHN N. WILLIAMS
College of Education and Human Devt: Dr JOHN F. WELSH (acting)
Louis D. Brandeis School of Law: Prof. LAURA F. ROTHSTEIN
School of Medicine: Dr JOEL A. KAPLAN
School of Music: Dr CHRISTOPHER DOANE
School of Nursing: Dr MARY MUNDT (acting)
School of Public Health and Information Sciences: Dr RICHARD D. CLOVER (acting)
Speed Scientific School (Eng.): Dr THOMAS HANLEY
Kent School of Social Work: TERRY SINGER (acting)
Graduate School: RONALD M. ATLAS

WESTERN KENTUCKY UNIVERSITY

1906 College Heights Blvd, Bowling Green, KY 42101
Telephone: (270) 745-0111
E-mail: western@wku.edu
Internet: www.wku.edu
Founded 1906
Pres.: Dr GARY A. RANSDELL
Provost and Vice-Pres. for Academic Affairs: Dr BARBARA G. BURCH
Vice-Pres. for Finance and Admin.: Dr JAMES RAMSEY
Vice-Pres. for Student Affairs and Campus Services: Dr GERALD E. TICE
Vice-Pres. for Institutional Advancement: THOMAS S. HILES
Vice-Pres. for Information Technology: Dr RICHARD H. KIRCHMEYER
Registrar: FREIDA EGGLETON
Dean of Libraries: Dr MICHAEL BINDER
Library of 1,060,000 vols
Number of teachers: 599
Number of students: 16,579

DEANS

College of Arts, Humanities and Social Sciences: Dr DAVID LEE
Gordon Ford College of Business: Dr ROBERT W. JEFFERSON
College of Education and Behavioural Sciences: Dr KAREN I. ADAMS
College of Science, Technology and Health: Dr MARTIN HOUSTON
Bowling Green Community College: Dr FRANK D. CONLEY
Graduate Studies, Research and Extended Programs: Dr ELMER GRAY

LOUISIANA

CENTENARY COLLEGE OF LOUISIANA

POB 41188, Shreveport, LA 71134-1188
Telephone: (318) 869-5011
Internet: www.centenary.edu
Founded 1825
Academic year: June to May
Pres.: KENNETH L. SCHWAB
Provost and Dean of College (vacant): DARRELL COLSON
Dean of Student Life: LORI BRADSHAW
Registrar: GARY YOUNG
Dir of Library Services: CHRISTY WRENN
Number of teachers: 74
Number of students: 1,017.

DILLARD UNIVERSITY

1555 Poydras St, 12th Floor New Orleans, LA 70112
Telephone: (504) 571-2160
E-mail: admissions@dillard.edu
Internet: www.dillard.edu
Founded 1869
Pres.: Dr MARVALENE HUGHES
Dean of Academic Affairs: Dr KASSIE FREEMAN
Vice-Pres. for Business and Finance: SIDNEY H. EVANS, Jr
Vice-Pres. for Institutional Advancement and Devt: LOVE COLLINS, III
Vice-Pres. for Student Affairs: JANICE L. BARTLEY
Vice-Pres. for Enrollment Management: DARRIN RANKIN
Registrar: CHARLES SAUNDERS
Dean of Library: TOMMY S. HOLTON
Library of 105,128 vols, 295 current periodicals, 1,150 microfilms, 320 audio-visual items
Number of teachers: 139 full-time

Number of students: 1,953.

ATTACHED CENTRE
National Center for Black–Jewish Relations.

LOUISIANA COLLEGE

1140 College Dr., Pineville, LA 71359
Telephone: (318) 487-7011
E-mail: admissions@lacollege.edu
Internet: www.lacollege.edu

Founded 1906

College of liberal arts and sciences under auspices of the Louisiana Baptist Convention

Pres.: Dr JOE AQUILLARD
Vice-Pres. for Academic Affairs: Dr GLENN SUMRALL
Vice-Pres. for Business Affairs and Chief Financial Officer: RANDALL HARGIS
Vice-Pres. for Student Devt: Dr PEGGY PACK
Registrar: ALAN MOBLEY
Dean of Students: LORI THAMES
Dir of Library: W. TERRY MARTIN

Library of 135,000 vols, 199,000 govt documents, music scores, audio-visual items
Number of teachers: 109
Number of students: 1,204.

LOUISIANA STATE UNIVERSITY SYSTEM

3810 West Lakeshore Dr., Baton Rouge, LA 70808
Telephone: (225) 388-2111
Internet: www.lsusystem.lsu.edu

Founded 1860

Academic year: August to July

Pres.: Dr WILLIAM L. JENKINS.

CONSTITUENT UNIVERSITIES

Louisiana State Univ.

Baton Rouge, LA 70803
Telephone: (504) 388-3202
Fax: (504) 388-5982
E-mail: admissions@lsu.edu
Internet: www.lsu.edu

Founded 1860

Chancellor: Dr SEAN O'KEEFE
Exec. Vice-Chancellor and Provost: Dr HAROLD SILVERMAN
Vice-Provost for Academics and Planning: FRANK K. CARTLEDGE
Vice-Provost for Equity, Diversity and Community Outreach: KATRICE ALBERT
Vice-Chancellor for Finance and Admin. Services: Dr JERRY BAUDIN
Vice-Chancellor for Research and Economic Devt: BROOKS KEEL
Vice-Chancellor for Strategic Initiatives: Dr ISIAH M. WARNER
Vice-Chancellor for Student Life and Academic Services: Dr F. NEIL MATHEWS
Chancellor of Law Center: JOHN J. COSTONIS
Chancellor of LSU Agriculture Center: Dr PAUL COREIL
Dean of Students: Dr KEVIN S. PRICE
Dean of Univ. Libraries: JAMES G. NEAL
Registrar: ROBERT K. DOOLOS

Library of 2,900,000 vols
Number of teachers: 1,300 (full-time)
Number of students: 30,000

DEANS

College of Agriculture: Dr KENNETH KOONCE
College of Art and Design: KENNETH E. CARPENTER
College of Arts and Sciences: Dr M. JANE COLLINS
College of Basic Sciences: Dr HAROLD SILVERMAN

E. J. Ourso College of Business Admin.: THOMAS D. CLARK, Jr
School of the Coast and Environment: Dr RUSSELL L. CHAPMAN
College of Education: Dr BARBARA FUHRMANN
College of Eng.: Dr PIUS J. EGBELU
College of Music and Dramatic Arts: Dr RONALD ROSS
School of Library and Information Science: Dr BETH M. PASKOFF
Manship School of Mass Communication: Dr JOHN M. HAMILTON
School of Social Work: Dr STEVEN R. ROSE (Interim Dir)
School of Veterinary Medicine: Dr MICHAEL GROVES
Honors College: Dr BILLY M. SEAY
Univ. College: Dr CAROLYN C. COLLINS
Graduate School: Dr KEVIN M. SMITH
Division of Continuing Education: Dr DANIEL C. WALSH

Louisiana State University. at Alexandria

8100 Highway 71, S, Alexandria, LA 71302-9633
Telephone: (318) 473-6444
E-mail: info@lsua.edu
Internet: www.lsua.edu

Founded 1960

Chancellor: Dr ROBERT CAVANAUGH
Provost and Vice-Chancellor for Academic and Student Affairs: Dr THOMAS ARMSTRONG
Vice-Chancellor for Business Affairs: VIRGIL STANFORD
Dir of the Library: ALBERT TATE

Library of 120,000 vols
Number of students: 2,404

HEADS OF DIVISIONS

Div. of Business Admin.: Dr JAMES K. BREYLEY
Div. of Liberal Arts: Dr GREG GORMANOUS
Div. of Nursing and Health Sciences: Dr SANDRA TUCKER
Div. of Sciences: Dr FRED BECKERDITE

Louisiana State University at Eunice

POB 1129, Eunice, LA 70535
Telephone: (337) 457-7311
Fax: (337) 546-6620
Internet: www.lsue.edu

Founded 1964

Academic year: August to July

Chancellor: Dr WILLIAM J. NUNEZ, III
Vice-Chancellor for Academic Affairs and Technology Transfer: CAROLYN H. HARGRAVE
Vice-Chancellor for Business Affairs: ARLENE C. TUCKER
Vice-Chancellor for Student Affairs: Dr JOHN L. COUVILLION
Dir of Continuing Education: DAVID PULLING
Dir of the Library: JUD COPELAND

Library of 100,000 vols
Number of teachers: 85
Number of students: 3,000

HEADS OF DIVISIONS

Business and Technology: Dr FRED LANDRY
Liberal Arts: Dr DOUGLAS NARBY
Nursing and Allied Health: THERESA A. DEBECHE
Sciences: Dr GRACE COSCIO-HOUSTON

Louisiana State University Shreveport

One University Pl., Shreveport, LA 71115
Telephone: (318) 797-5000
Internet: www.lsus.edu

Founded 1965

Chancellor: Dr VINCENT J. MARSALA

Provost and Vice-Chancellor for Academic Affairs: Dr STUART MILLS (acting)
Vice-Chancellor for Business Affairs: MICHAEL T. FERRELL
Vice-Chancellor for Univ. Devt (vacant): GLENDA ERWIN
Vice-Chancellor for Student Affairs: Dr GLORIA RAINES
Registrar and Dir of Admissions: MICKY P. DIEZ (acting)
Dean of the Library: Dr ALAN D. GABEHART

Library of 250,000 vols, 2,000 periodicals
Number of students: 4,100

Publications: *Bulletin of the Museum of Life Sciences* (2 a year), *North Louisiana Historical Journal* (quarterly)

DEANS

College of Business Admin.: Dr CHARLOTTE A. JONES
College of Education: (vacant)
College of Liberal Arts: Dr MERRELL KNIGHTEN
College of Sciences: Dr WILLIAM A. VEKOVIUS
Graduate Studies: Dr PATRICIA F. DOERR
Continuing Education and Public Service: Dr DONNA AUSTIN

University of New Orleans

2000 Lakeshore Dr., New Orleans, LA 70148
Telephone: (504) 280-6000
Fax: (504) 280-6872
E-mail: pr@uno.edu
Internet: www.uno.edu

Metropolitan campus of the Louisiana State Univ. System; founded 1956 by Act 60 of Louisiana State Legislature

Chancellor: Dr TIMOTHY P. RYAN
Vice-Chancellor for Academic and Student Affairs and Provost: FREDERICK BARTON
Vice-Chancellor for Financial Services, Comptroller and Chief Financial Officer: LINDA K. ROBISON
Vice-Chancellor for Governmental Affairs and Athletic Dir: ROBERT W. BROWN
Vice-Chancellor for Campus Services: JOEL CHAITLIN
Vice-Chancellor for Research and Sponsored Programs: Dr ROBERT C. CASHNER
Vice-Chancellor for Univ. Advancement: SHARON WHITE GRUBER
Univ. Registrar (vacant): KATHLEEN PLANTE
Dean of Admissions: RONALD MAGIORE
Dean of Library Services: Dr SHARON MADER

Library of 800,000 vols, 3,000 current periodicals, 2m. microforms, govt documents
Number of teachers: 455
Number of students: 16,262

Publications: *Metropolitan Report* (quarterly), *New Orleans Real Estate Market Survey* (2 a year), *Review of Business and Economics Research* (2 a year), *Statistical Abstract of Louisiana* (3 a year)

DEANS

College of Business Admin.: Dr JOHN C. GARDNER
College of Education and Human Devt: Dr JAMES MEZA, Jr
College of Eng.: JOHN N. CRISP
College of Liberal Arts: Prof. FREDERICK BARTON
College of Sciences: Dr JOE M. KING
College of Urban and Public Affairs: Prof. ALAN F. J. ARTIBISE
Graduate School: Dr ROBERT C. CASHNER
Metropolitan College: ROBERT L. DUPONT.

OTHER CONSTITUENT INSTITUTIONS

Louisiana State University Agricultural Center

101 Efferson Hall, Baton Rouge, LA 70803
Telephone: (225) 578-4161
Fax: (225) 578-4143
Internet: www.lsuagcenter.com
Chancellor: WILLIAM B. RICHARDSON.

Louisiana State University Health Sciences Center, New Orleans

New Orleans, LA 70112-2784
Telephone: (504) 568-4800
Internet: www.lsuhsc.edu
Chancellor: Dr LARRY H. HOLLIER
Number of students: 2,500

DEANS

School of Allied Health: Dr JOHN R. SNYDER
School of Dentistry: Dr ERIC J. HOVLAND
School of Graduate Studies: Prof. JOSEPH M. MOERSCHBAECHER, III
School of Medicine: Prof. JAMES P. O'LEARY (acting)
School of Nursing: Dr ELIZABETH A. HUMPHREY

Louisiana State University Health Sciences Center, Shreveport

1501 Kings Highway, Shreveport, LA 71103-4228
Telephone: (318) 675-5000
Internet: www.sh.lsuhsc.edu
Chancellor: Dr JOHN C. MCDONALD.

Paul M. Hebert Law Center

202 Law Center, Baton Rouge, LA 70803-1000
Telephone: (225) 578-8646
Fax: (225) 578-8647
E-mail: admissions@law.lsu.edu
Internet: www.law.lsu.edu
Chancellor: JOHN COSTONIS.

Pennington Biomedical Research Center

6400 Perkins Rd, Baton Rouge, LA 70808
Telephone: (225) 763-2500
Internet: www.pbrc.edu
Exec. Dir: Dr CLAUDE BOUCHARD.

LOYOLA UNIVERSITY

6363 St Charles Ave, New Orleans, LA 70118
Telephone: (504) 865-2011
E-mail: publaff@loyno.edu
Internet: www.loyno.edu
Founded 1905 as Loyola College; chartered as Univ. 1912
Pres.: Rev. KEVIN WM. WILDES
Provost and Vice-Pres. for Academic Affairs: Dr WALTER HARRIS, Jr
Vice-Pres. for Finance and Admin.: RHONDA DELRIE CARTWRIGHT
Vice-Pres. for Institutional Advancement: VICTORIA A. FRANK
Vice-Pres. for Student Affairs: Dr M. L. (CISSY) PETTY
Dean of Univ. Ministry: KURT BINDEWALD
Dean of Admissions and Enrollment Management: DEBORAH STIEFFEL
Dean of Libraries: MARY LEE SWEAT
Library of 255,000 vols; Law library of 123,000 vols
Number of teachers: 275
Number of students: 5,500
Publications: *New Orleans Review, Loyola Law Review, Loyola Magazine*

DEANS

College of Arts and Sciences: Dr FRANK E. SCULLY Jr
College of Business Admin.: Dr J. PATRICK O'BRIEN
School of Law: Dr JAMES M. KLEBBA (acting)
College of Music: Dr EDWARD J. KVET
City College: Dr MARCEL DUMESTRE

NEW ORLEANS BAPTIST THEOLOGICAL SEMINARY

3939 Gentilly Blvd, New Orleans, LA 70126
Telephone: (504) 282-4455
Fax: (504) 816-8023
Internet: www.nobts.edu
Private control
Pres.: Dr CHARLES S. KELLEY, Jr
Vice-Pres. for Business Affairs: L. CLAY CORVIN
Provost: Dr STEVE W. LEMKE
Dean of Libraries: Dr JEFF GRIFFIN
Library of 266,000 vols
Number of teachers: 102
Number of students: 1,926 (full-time).

NOTRE DAME SEMINARY

2901 South Carrolton Ave, New Orleans, LA 70118 4391
Telephone: (504) 866-7426
Fax: (504) 866-3119
E-mail: registrar@nds.edu
Internet: www.nds.edu
Founded 1923
Private control
Chancellor: THE ARCHBISHOP OF NEW ORLEANS
Pres. and Rector: Very Rev. PATRICK J. WILLIAMS
Academic Dean: Rev. JOSE I. LAVASTIDA
Registrar: MARGARET BREAUX
Library Dir: GEORGE DANSKER
Library of 94,000 vols
Number of teachers: 30
Number of students: 154 (full time).

OUR LADY OF HOLY CROSS COLLEGE

4123 Woodland Dr., New Orleans, LA 70131-7399
Telephone: (504) 394-7744
Fax: (504) 391-2421
E-mail: admissions@olhcc.edu
Internet: www.olhcc.edu
Founded 1916
Academic year: August to July
Pres.: Rev. ANTHONY J. DE CONCILIIS
Vice-Pres. of Academic Affairs: Dr EDWARD J. DUPAY
Registrar: Sister ANN MARTINEZ
Librarian: Sister HELEN FONTENOT
Library of 201,807 vols
Number of teachers: 116 (45 full-time, 71 part-time)
Number of students: 1,450.

SAINT JOSEPH SEMINARY COLLEGE

St Benedict, LA 70457
Telephone: (985) 867-2225
Fax: (985) 867-2270
E-mail: acdean@sjasc.edu
Internet: www.sjasc.edu
Private control
Pres.-Rector: Rev. GREGORY BOQUET
Library Dir: BONNIE BESS WOOD
Number of teachers: 26
Number of students: 194.

SOUTHERN UNIVERSITY SYSTEM

J. S. Clark Admin. Bldg, Baton Rouge, LA 70813
Telephone: (225) 771-4500
Internet: www.sus.edu
Founded 1880
Pres.: Dr RALPH SLAUGHTER
Vice-Pres. for Finance and Business Affairs: TOLOR E. WHITE
Vice-Pres. for Academic and Student Affairs: PRESS L. ROBINSON.

CONSTITUENT INSTITUTIONS

Southern Univ. and A & M College

Baton Rouge, LA 70813
Telephone: (225) 771-4500
Internet: www.subr.edu
Chancellor: EDWARD R. JACKSON
Vice-Chancellor for Academic Affairs: Dr JOHNNY TOLLIVER
Vice-Chancellor for Student Affairs: LYNN DICKERSON
Vice-Chancellor for Finance and Admin.: FLANDUS McCLINTON, Jr
Number of students: 9,172.

Southern University. at New Orleans

6801 Press Dr. New Orleans, LA 70126
Telephone: (225) 286-5314
Internet: www.suno.edu
Chancellor: Dr VICTOR UKPOLO
Number of students: 4,000.

Southern University. at Shreveport

3050 Martin Luther King, Jr Dr. Shreveport, LA 71107
Telephone: (318) 674-3300
E-mail: admissions@susla.edu
Internet: www.susla.edu
Chancellor: Dr RAY L. BELTON
Vice-Chancellor for Student Affairs: Dr SHARON F. GREEN
Vice-Chancellor for Academic Affairs: Dr RUBY EVANS
Vice-Chancellor for Fiscal Affairs: BENJAMIN W. PUGH
Vice-Chancellor for Community and Workforce Devt: JANICE R. STEED
Librarian: Dr ORELLA BRAZILE
Number of students: 1,229

CHAIRS OF DIV.

Allied Health Sciences: HAYWOOD JOINER
Behavioural Sciences: ROSALYN HOLT
Business Studies: GEORGE LEWIS III
Humanities: JUNE PHILLIPS
Science and Technology: Dr BARRY HESTER
Academic Outreach Programs: GWENDOLYN LEWIS

TULANE UNIVERSITY OF LOUISIANA

6823 St Charles Ave, New Orleans, LA 70118
Telephone: (504) 865-5000
E-mail: pr@tulane.edu
Internet: www2.tulane.edu
Founded 1834 as Medical College of Louisiana, became Tulane Univ. of Louisiana 1884
Pres.: SCOTT S. COWEN
Sr Vice-Pres. for Academic Affairs, Provost and Chief Information Officer: PAUL BARRON
Sr Vice-Pres. for External Affairs: YVETTE M. JONES
Sr Vice-Pres. for Operations and Chief Financial Officer: ANTHONY P. LORINO
Sr Vice-Pres. for the Health Sciences: ALAN MILLER
Vice-Pres., Tulane Univ. Health Sciences Center: JAMES J. CORRIGAN

Vice-Pres. for Clinical Affairs, Tulane Univ. Health Sciences Center: ALAN M. MILLER
Vice-Pres. for Student Affairs and Dean of Students: CYNTHIA CHERREY
Vice-Pres. for Enrollment Management and Institutional Research and Registrar: EARL RETIF
Vice-Pres. of Human Resources: ANDREW HICK
Gen. Counsel: VICTORIA JOHNSON
Vice-Pres. and Chief of Staff: ANNE P. BAÑOS
Dean of Libraries and Academic Information Resources: LANCE QUERY

Library: see Libraries
Number of teachers: 1,988
Number of students: 12,381

DEANS

School of Architecture: DONALD GATZKE
A. B. Freeman School of Business: JAMES W. MCFARLAND
School of Eng.: NICHOLAS J. ALTIERO
Graduate School: MICHAEL HERMAN
Law School: LAWRENCE PONOROFF
School of Medicine: IAN LOGAN TAYLOR
Newcomb College: CYNTHIA J. LOWENTHAL
School of Public Health and Tropical Medicine: PIERRE BUEKENS (acting)
School of Social Work: RON MARKS
Tulane College: T. R. KIDDER
Univ. College: RICHARD A. MARKSBURY
Faculty of the Liberal Arts and Sciences: TERESA S. SOUFAS (acting)

UNIVERSITY OF LOUISIANA SYSTEM

Suite 7-300, 1201 North Third St, Baton Rouge, LA 70802
Telephone: (225) 342-6950
E-mail: sclausen@uls.state.la.us
Internet: www.uls.state.la.us
Founded 1974
Number of students: 83,000 at 8 univs
Pres.: Dr SALLY CLAUSEN.

CONSTITUENT INSTITUTIONS

Grambling State University

403 Main St Grambling, LA 71245
Telephone: (318) 247-3811
Fax: (318) 274-6172
E-mail: admissions@gram.edu
Internet: www.gram.edu
Founded 1901
Academic year: August to May
Pres.: Dr HORACE A. JUDSON (acting)
Provost and Vice-Pres. for Academic Affairs: Dr ROBERT M. DIXON
Vice-Pres. of Finance: BILLY OWENS
Registrar and Exec. Dir: KAREN C; LEWIS
Dir of Library Services: Dr ROSEMARY N. MOKIA (acting)
Library of 294,000 vols
Number of teachers: 250
Number of students: 4,716.

Louisiana Tech University

Ruston, LA 71272
Telephone: (318) 257-0211
Internet: www.latech.edu
Chartered 1894 as Louisiana Industrial Institute and College; name changed to Louisiana Industrial Institute 1898; became Louisiana Polytechnic Institute 1921; present name and status 1970
Pres.: DANIEL D. RENEAU
Vice-Pres. for Academic Affairs: KENNETH REA
Vice-Pres. for Admin. Services: JERRY DREWETT
Vice-Pres. for Finance and Admin.: JOSEPH R. THOMAS, Jr

Vice-Pres. for Student Affairs: Dr JAMES M. KING
Vice-Pres. for Univ. Advancement: CORRE STEGALL
Registrar: BOB VENTO
Dean of Library Services: WALTER WICKER
Library of 400,000 vols, 500,000 microforms, 2,250,000 govt documents
Number of teachers: 400
Number of students: 10,000

DEANS

College of Admin. and Business: Dr SHIRLEY P. REAGAN
College of Applied and Natural Sciences: Dr JAMES D. LIBERATOS
College of Education: Dr JO ANN DAUZAT
College of Eng. and Science: Dr LESLIE GUICE, Jr
College of Liberal Arts: Dr EDWARD C. JACOBS
Graduate School and Univ. Research: TERRY MCCONATHY

McNeese State University

4205 Ryan St, Lake Charles, LA 70609
Telephone: (337) 475-5000
Fax: (337) 475-5012
Internet: www.mcneese.edu
Founded 1939
Academic year: August to May
Pres.: Dr ROBERT D. HEBERT
Registrar: STEPHANIE B. TARVER
Librarian: NANCY L. KHOURY
Number of teachers: 285
Number of students: 8,000
Publications: The Log (annual), The McNeese Arena (annual), The McNeese Review (annual), The McNeese Update (3 a year)

DEANS

College of Business: Dr BRENDA BIRKETT
College of Education: Dr WAYNE FETTER
College of Eng. and Technology: Dr CARROLL KARKALITS
College of Liberal Arts: Dr RAY MILES
College of Nursing: Dr PEGGY L. WOLFE
College of Science: Dr GEORGE F. MEAD, Jr
Graduate School: Dr GEORGE MEAD

Nicholls State University

Thibodaux, LA 70310
Telephone: (985) 446-8111
Internet: www.nicholls.edu
Founded 1948 as a junior college of Louisiana State Univ.; became Francis T. Nicholls State College 1956; univ. status 1970
Pres.: Dr STEPHEN T. HULBERT
Provost and Vice-Pres. for Academic Affairs: Dr CARROLL J. FALCON (acting)
Vice-Pres. for Finance and Admin.: LIONEL O. NAQUIN, Jr
Vice-Pres. for Institutional Advancement: Dr DAVID E. BOUDREAUX
Vice-Pres. for Student Affairs and Enrollment Services: Dr EUGENE A. DIAL Jr
Library Dir: CAROL A. MATHIAS
Library of 400,000 vols and periodicals and 380,000 microforms
Number of teachers: 278 (full-time)
Number of students: 7,262

DEANS

College of Arts and Sciences: Dr THOMAS MORTILLARO
College of Business Admin.: Dr RIDLEY GROS
College of Education: Dr O. CLEVELAND HILL
College of Life Sciences and Technology: Dr SUE WESTBROOK
Chef John Folse Culinary Institute: Dr ROBERT HARRINGTON
Jr Div.: Dr PETER B. STRAWITZ

Northwestern State University

Natchitoches, LA 71497
Telephone: (318) 357-6441
Fax: (318) 357-4223
Internet: www.nsula.edu
Founded 1884 as State Normal School; univ. status 1970
Academic year: June to June
Pres.: Dr RANDALL J. WEBB
Provost and Vice-Pres. for Academic Affairs: Dr TOM HANSON
Vice-Pres. for Business Affairs and Controller: CARL JONES
Vice-Pres. for External Affairs: JERRY D. PIERCE
Vice-Pres. for Student Affairs: Dr PATRICE MOULTON (acting)
Vice-Pres. for Univ. Affairs: JOHN DILWORTH
Registrar: LILLIE BELL
Librarian: THOMAS FLEMING
Library of 320,000 vols
Number of teachers: 300
Number of students: 8,600
Publication: Southern Studies (quarterly)

DEANS

College of Business: Dr STEPHEN ELLIOTT (acting)
College of Education: Dr VICKIE GENTRY (acting)
College of Liberal Arts: Dr DONALD HATLEY
College of Nursing: Dr NORMAN PLANCHOCK
College of Science and Technology: Dr AUSTIN TEMPLE
Graduate Studies and Research: Dr STEVEN HORTON
Univ. College: Dr SUE WEAVER

Southeastern Louisiana University.

SLU 10752, Hammond, LA 70402
Telephone: (985) 549-2000
Fax: (985) 549-2061
Internet: www.selu.edu
Founded 1925 as college, attained univ. status 1970
Academic year: June to May
Pres.: Dr RANDY MOFFETT
Provost: Dr JOHN CRAIN
Vice-Pres. for Admin. and Finance: STEPHEN SMITH
Vice-Pres. for Student Affairs: Dr MARVIN L. YATES
Vice-Pres. for Univ. Advancement: Dr JOSEPH H. MILLER, Jr
Dir of Records and Registration: PAULETTE M. POCHÉ
Library Dir: ERIC JOHNSON
Library of 382,877 bound vols
Number of teachers: 497 full-time, 233 part-time
Number of students: 15,472
Publications: Louisiana Literature (2 a year), The Southeastern Outlook (2 a year).

University of Louisiana at Lafayette

104 Univ. Circle, Lafayette, LA 70504-1732
Telephone: (337) 482-1000
Fax: (337) 482-6195
Internet: www.louisiana.edu
Founded 1898 as Southwestern Louisiana Industrial Institute; became Southwestern Louisiana Institute 1921 and Univ. of Southwestern Louisiana 1960; present name 1999
Academic year: June to May
Pres.: Dr RAY
Registrar: DeWAYNE BOWIE
Librarian: Dr CHARLES TRICHE
Library of 976,202 vols
Number of teachers: 699
Number of students: 16,561

Publications: *Attakapas Gazette* (quarterly), *Louisiana History* (quarterly), *Southwestern Review* (annualy).

University of Louisiana at Monroe

700 University Ave, Monroe, LA 71209
Telephone: (318) 342-1000
Fax: (318) 342-5161
Internet: www.ulm.edu

Founded 1931 as college, attained univ. status 1970

Pres.: Dr JAMES E. COFER, Sr
Provost and Vice-Pres. for Academic Affairs: Dr STEPHEN RICHTERS
Vice-Pres. for Business Affairs: DAVE NICKLAS
Vice-Pres. for Student Affairs: Dr WAYNE BRUMFIELD
Vice-Pres. for Univ. Advancement: Dr DON SKELTON
Registrar: CARLETTE M. BROWDER
Dean of the Library: DONALD R. SMITH

Library of 633,818 vols, incl. 193,935 govt documents, 2,939 current periodicals, 555,603 microformat vols
Number of teachers: 521
Number of students: 9,400

DEANS

College of Arts and Sciences: Dr CARLOS FANDAL
College of Business Admin.: Dr RONALD BERRY
College of Education and Human Devt: Dr LUKE THOMAS
College of Health Sciences: Dr JAN CORDER
College of Pharmacy: Dr F. LAMAR PRITCHARD
Graduate Studies and Research: Dr VIRGINIA EATON (Dir)

XAVIER UNIVERSITY OF LOUISIANA

1 Drexel Dr., New Orleans, LA 70125
Telephone: (504) 486-7411
Internet: www.xula.edu

Founded 1915

Pres.: NORMAN C. FRANCIS
Sr Vice-Pres. for Admin.: CALVIN TREGRE
Sr Vice-Pres. for Sponsored Programs: Dr GENE D'AMOUR
Vice-Pres. for Academic Affairs: ELIZABETH A. BARRON
Vice-Pres. for Institutional Advancement: KENNETH ANTHONY ST CHARLES
Vice-Pres. for Student Services: JOSEPH K. BYRD
Vice-Pres. for Fiscal Affairs: EDWARD J. PHILLIPS
Dean of Admissions: WINSTON D. BROWN
Librarian: ROBERT E. SKINNER

Library of 120,000 vols
Number of teachers: 226 (full-time)
Number of students: 3,994

DEANS

College of Arts and Sciences: Dr KENNETH G. BOUTTE
College of Pharmacy: Dr WAYNE HARRIS
Graduate School: Dr ALVIN J. RICHARD

MAINE

BANGOR THEOLOGICAL SEMINARY

300 Union St, Bangor, ME 04401
Telephone: (207) 942-6781
Fax: (207) 990-1267
E-mail: wimes@bts.edu
Internet: www.bts.edu

Founded 1814
Private control
Academic year: September to May

Pres.: Dr WILLIAM C. IMES
Vice-Pres. for Advancement and Dir of Portland Campus: REBECCA WRIGHT
Registrar: BRIAN MOODY
Librarian: Dr BETH BIDLACK

Library of 124,000 vols
Number of teachers: 50
Number of students: 70 (full-time).

BRANCH CAMPUS

Portland Campus: 159 State St, Portland, ME 04101; tel. (207) 774-5212; fax (207) 874-2214.

BATES COLLEGE

Lewiston, ME 04240
Telephone: (207) 786-6000
Fax: (207) 786-6025
E-mail: president@bates.edu
Internet: www.bates.edu

Founded 1855
Academic year: September to May

Pres.: ELAINE TUTTLE HANSEN
Dean of Faculty: Dr JILL REICH
Dean of Admissions: WYLIE L. MITCHELL
Librarian: EUGENE WIEMERS

Library of 568,750 vols
Number of teachers: 203
Number of students: 1,738.

BOWDOIN COLLEGE

Brunswick, ME 04011
Telephone. (207) 725-3000
Fax: (207) 725-3123
Internet: www.bowdoin.edu

Founded 1794

Pres.: BARRY MILLS
Sr Vice-Pres. for Finance and Admin. and Treas.: S. CATHERINE LONGLEY
Sr Vice-Pres. for Planning and Devt and Chief Devt Officer: WILLIAM A. TORREY
Vice-Pres. for Investments: PAULA J. VOLENT
Vice-Pres. for Finance and Controller: NIGEL BEARMAN
Vice-Pres. for Communications and Public Affairs: SCOTT W. HOOD
Dean for Academic Affairs: CRAIG A. MCEWAN
Dean of Student Life: CRAIG W. BRADLEY
Dean of Admissions and Financial Aid: JAMES S. MILLER
Dir of Research and Records: CHRISTINE BROOKS
Librarian: SHERRIE BERGMAN

Library of 940,000 vols
Number of teachers: 158
Number of students: 1,629

Publications: *Bowdoin Magazine* (quarterly), *Bowdoin Forum* (int. affairs, annual).

COLBY COLLEGE

Waterville, ME 04901
Telephone: (207) 872-3000
Fax: (207) 872-3555
E-mail: admissions@colby.edu
Internet: www.colby.edu

Undergraduate college of liberal arts
Founded 1813
Academic year: September to May

Pres.: WILLIAM D. ADAMS
Vice-Pres., Academic Affairs and Dean of Faculty: EDWARD H. YETERIAN
Admin. Vice-Pres.: W. ARNOLD YASINSKI
Vice-Pres. for Devt and Alumni Relations: PEYTON RANDOLPH HELM
Vice-Pres. of Student Affairs and Dean of Students: JANICE A. KASSMAN
Dean of Admissions and Financial Aid: PARKER J. BEVERAGE
Registrar: GEORGE L. COLEMAN II

Librarian: SUANNE MUEHLNER
Library of 500,000 vols
Number of teachers: 160
Number of students: 1,800

Publications: *Colby, President's Report, Report of Contributions, Colby Perspective, Colby Library Quarterly.*

COLLEGE OF THE ATLANTIC

105 Eden Street, Bar Harbor, ME 04609
Telephone: (207) 288-5015
Fax: (207) 288-4126
E-mail: inquiry@ecology.coa.edu
Internet: www.coa.edu

Founded 1969
Private control
Academic year: September to June

President: Dr STEVEN KATONA
Academic Dean: Dr RICHARD BORDEN
Registrar: LYMAN FEERO
Library Director: MARCIA DWORAK

Number of teachers: 34
Number of students: 283

Areas of study: environmental science, arts and design, human studies.

HUSSON COLLEGE

1 College Circle, Bangor, ME 04401
Telephone: (207) 941-7100
Fax: (207) 941-7935
E-mail: admit@husson.edu
Internet: www.husson.edu

Private control
Academic year: September to May

President: Dr WILLIAM H. BEARDSLEY
Dean: JOHN RUBINO
Librarian: AMY AVERRE

Number of teachers: 53
Number of students: 2,000 (1,600 undergraduate, 400 graduate)

Areas of study: accounting, business administration, computer information systems, hospitality management, paralegal studies, physical education, nursing, occupational therapy, physical therapy, biology, education, psychology, science and humanities, broadcast communications.

MAINE COLLEGE OF ART

97 Spring St, Portland, ME 04101
Telephone: (207) 775-3052
Fax: (207) 772-5069
E-mail: info@meca.edu
Internet: www.meca.edu
Private control

President: CHRISTINE J. VINCENT
Vice-President (Academic Affairs) and Dean of the College: GREG MURPHY
Vice-President (Administration and Finance): BETH ELICKER
Vice-President (Advancement and College Relations): TIM KANE
Vice-President (Enrollment): RICK LONGO
Registrar: ANNE DENNISON
Library Director: MARGARET BOYLAN

Library of 20,000 vols
Number of teachers: 53
Number of students: 314.

ATTACHED RESEARCH INSTITUTES

Institute of Contemporary Art: Porteous Building, 522 Congress St, Portland, ME 04101; tel. (207) 879 5742; e-mail ica@meca.edu; Dir TOBY KAMPS.

MAINE MARITIME ACADEMY

Castine, ME 04420-5000
Telephone: (207) 326-2206

E-mail: admissions@mma.edu
Internet: www.mainemaritime.edu
Founded 1941
State control
Academic year: September to April
President: LEONARD H. TYLER
Provost and Academic Dean: Dr JOHN BAR-LOW
Vice-President (Finance, Administration and Governmental Affairs): RICHARD R. ERICSON
Registrar: TOM SAWYER
Director of Library Services: BRENT HALL
Number of teachers: 53
Number of students: 750

CHAIRS OF DEPARTMENT

Corning School of Ocean Studies: Dr STEPHEN FEGLEY
Loeb-Sullivan School of International Business and Logistics: Dr SHASHNI N. KUMAR
Thompson School of Marine Transportation: J. SAMUEL TEEL
Arts and Sciences: SUSAN K. LOOMIS
Engineering: Dr GROVES E. HERRICK
Physical Education: WILLIAM J. MOTTOLA

THOMAS COLLEGE

180 W River Rd, Waterville, ME 04901-5097
Telephone: (207) 859-1111
Fax: (207) 859-1114
E-mail: admissions@thomas.edu
Internet: www.thomas.edu
Founded 1894
Private control
Academic year: September to May
President: Dr GEORGE SPANN
Vice-President (Academic Affairs): Dr THOMAS EDWARDS
Vice-President (Enrollment Management): ROBERT CALLAHAN
Vice-President (Information Technology): CHRISTOPHER RHODA
Vice-President (Financial Affairs): BETH GIBBS
Vice-President (Institutional Advancement): ERIC ROLFSON
Registrar: VALERIE SIROIS
Library Director: STEPHEN LaROCHELLE
Library of 30,000 vols
Number of students: 594

CHAIRS OF DEPARTMENT

Arts and Sciences: JUDY HANSEN-CHILDERS
Business: TOM LARGAY

SAINT JOSEPH'S COLLEGE

Standish, ME 04084-5263
Telephone: (207) 893-7746
Fax: (207) 893-7862
E-mail: marketing@sjcme.edu
Internet: www.sjcme.edu
Founded 1912
President: Dr DAVID B. HOUSE
Registrar: TOM SAWYER
Vice-President of Academic Affairs: Dr DANIEL P. SHERIDAN
Librarian: Sister FLEURETTE KENNON
Library: over 50,000 vols
Number of teachers: 53 full-time
Number of teachers: 43 part-time
Number of students: 750 full-time
Number of students: 446 part-time (external 3,932).

UNITY COLLEGE

90 Quaker Hill Rd, Unity, ME 04988
Telephone: (207) 948-3131
Fax: (207) 948-6277
E-mail: admissions@unity.edu

Internet: www.unity.edu
Founded 1965
Private control
Academic year: September to May
President: Dr DAVID C. GLENN-LEWIN
Vice-President (Finance): ROGER R. JOLIN
Director of College Advancement and Vice-President: MARTHA NORDSTROM
Dean for Student Affairs: GARY ZANE
Registrar: HOLLY A. HEIN
Library Director: ROBERT DOAN
Library of 40,000 vols
Number of teachers: 33
Number of students: 508

CHAIRMEN OF ACADEMIC DIVISIONS

Environmental Programs: Dr JERRY CINNAMON
Liberal Studies: PATRICIA CLARK (acting)

UNIVERSITY OF MAINE SYSTEM

16 Central St, Bangor, ME 04401
Telephone: (207) 973-3240
Fax: (207) 973-3296
E-mail: gshaw@maine.edu
Internet: www.maine.edu
Number of students: 34,700 total across seven universities
Chancellor: Dr JOSEPH W. WESTPHAL.

CONSTITUENT INSTITUTIONS

University of Maine

Orono, ME 04469
Telephone: (207) 581-1110
E-mail: umainetoday@umaine.edu
Internet: www.umaine.edu
Founded 1865
President: ROBERT A. KENNEDY
Vice-President for Academic Affairs and Provost: Dr JOHN MAHON
Vice-President for Administration and Finance: JANET E. WALDRON
Vice-President for Research: Dr MICHAEL J. ECKARDT
Dean of Students: ROBERT DANA
Number of teachers: 608
Number of students: 9,213
Publications: *Agricultural Experimental Station Publications, Bulletin, Co-operative Extension Bulletins, Maine Studies, Technology Experiment Station Publications*

DEANS

College of Education and Human Development: ROBERT COBB
College of Engineering: Dr JOHN FIELD (acting)
College of Liberal Arts and Sciences: Dr REBECCA EILERS
College of Natural Sciences, Forestry and Agriculture: Dr G. BRUCE WIERSMA
College of Public Policy and Health: Dr VIRGINIA GIBSON (acting)

University of Maine at Augusta

46 University Drive, Augusta, ME 04330-9410
Telephone: (207) 621-3000
Fax: (207) 621-3116
E-mail: umaar@maine.edu
Internet: www.uma.edu
Founded 1965
President: Dr RICHARD RANDALL
Executive Vice-President and Provost: JOSHUA NADEL
Vice-President for Administration: SHERI STEVENS
Vice-President for Finance: RICHARD CAMPBELL
Dean of Students: KATHLEEN DEXTER

Dean, University College of Bangor: TRACY R. GRAN
Dean of Libraries and Dean, Lewiston-Auburn College: Dr THOMAS E. ABBOTT
Number of teachers: 100 (full-time)
Number of students: 6,000

DEANS

College of Arts and Humanities: MARGARET DANIELSON
College of Mathematics and Professional Studies: FRANK B. BEAN
College of Natural and Social Sciences: GRACE M. LEONARD

BRANCH CAMPUSES

Lewiston-Auburn College: 51–55 Westminster St, Lewiston, ME 04240; tel. (207) 753-6600.

University College of Bangor: 216 Texas Ave, Bangor, ME 04401-4367; tel. (207) 262-7800.

University of Maine at Farmington

224 Main St, Farmington, ME 04938
Telephone: (207) 778-7000
Fax: (207) 778-7247
E-mail: umfadmit@maine.edu
Internet: www.umf.maine.edu
Founded 1864 as college, university status 1970
President: THEODORA J. KALIKOW
Vice-President for Academic Affairs and Provost: ALLEN H. BERGER
Vice President for Administration: ROGER G. SPEAR
Vice-President for Student and Community Services: WILLIAM W. GELLER
Director of Admissions: SHARON M. OLIVER
Director of Library: FRANKLIN D. ROBERTS
Library of 105,000 vols
Number of teachers: 125
Number of students: 2,000

DEANS

College of Arts and Sciences: ROBERT L. LIVELY
College of Education, Health and Rehabilitation: KATHERINE W. YARDLEY

University of Maine at Fort Kent

23 University Drive, Fort Kent, ME 04743
Telephone: (207) 834-7500
Fax: (207) 834-7503
E-mail: umfkadm@maine.edu
Internet: www.umfk.maine.edu
Academic year: September to May
President: CHARLES M. LYONS
Vice-President (Academic Affairs): CAROL S. BROWNE
Vice-President (Administration): JOHN D. MURPHY
Registrar: DONALD M. RAYMOND
Dean of Information Services: SHARON M. JOHNSON
Library of 64,000 vols
Number of teachers: 59
Number of students: 850

CHAIRMEN OF ACADEMIC DIVISIONS

Arts and Humanities: CHARLES E. CLOSSER, Jr
Education: BRUNO HICKS
Natural and Behavioral Sciences: BRADLEY G. RITZ
Nursing: Dr RACHEL E. ALBERT

University of Maine at Machias

9 O'Brien Ave, Machias, ME 04654-1397
Telephone: (207) 255-1200
Fax: (207) 255-4864
Internet: www.umm.maine.edu
Founded 1909

Academic year: September to May

President: Dr CYNTHIA E. HUGGINS

Vice-President (Academic Affairs): STUART SWAIN (acting)

Registrar: MARY STOVER

Librarian: BERT PHIPPS

Library of 89,000 vols

Number of teachers: 52

Number of students: 1,300

CHAIRMEN OF ACADEMIC DIVISIONS

Arts and Letters: Dr RANDALL KINDLEBERGER

Environmental and Biological Science: SHERRIE SPRANGERS

Professional Studies: Dr WILLIAM J. ECKHART, Jr

University of Maine at Presque Isle

181 Main Street, Presque Isle, ME 04769-2888

Telephone: (207) 768-9400

Fax: (207) 768-9608

E-mail: adventure@umpi.maine.edu

Internet: www.umpi.maine.edu

Academic year: September to May

President: Dr KARL E. BURGHER

Vice-President (Academic Affairs): Dr RICHARD KIMBALL

Vice-President (Administration and Finance): CHARLES BONIN

Vice-President (Enrollment Management and Student Services): Dr KURT HOFMANN

Registrar: SHARON ROIX

Library Director: GREG CURTIS

Library of 458,500 items

Number of students: 1,367

Departments: Business and International Studies; English, Communication and Fine Art; Exercise Science/Physical Education, Recreation/Leisure Services, Athletic Training, and Health; Psychology, Social Work, and Criminal Justice; Teacher Education; Science and Mathematics.

University of New England

11 Hills Beach Rd, Biddeford, ME 04005

Telephone: (207) 283-0171

Fax: (207) 282-6379

E-mail: admissions@une.edu

Internet: www.une.edu

Founded 1939 as College Séraphique; present name 1978; merged with Westbrook College (f. 1831) 1996

Private control

Academic year: September to May

President: Dr SANDRA FEATHERMAN

Vice-President (Academic Affairs): Dr LEMUEL BERRY, Jr

Vice-President (Business and Finance): BERNARD G. CHRETIEN

Vice-President (Information Services): ANDREW J. GOLUB

Vice-President (University Relations): Dr EDWARD P. LEGG

Registrar: STEVE KELLY

Number of teachers: 148

Number of students: 3,800

DEANS

College of Arts and Sciences: Dr JACQUE CARTER

College of Health Professions: Dr VERNON L. MOORE

College of Osteopathic Medicine: Dr STEPHEN C. SHANNON

BRANCH CAMPUS

Westbrook College Campus: 716 Stevens Ave, Portland, ME 04103; tel. (207) 797-7261.

University of Southern Maine

POB 9300, Portland, ME 04104-9300

Telephone: (207) 780-4141

Fax: (207) 780-4933

Internet: www.usm.maine.edu

Founded 1878

Academic year: September to May

President: Dr RICHARD L. PATTENAUDE

Provost: Dr JOSEPH WOOD

Vice-President for Student Affairs: JUDITH RYAN

Vice-President for University Advancement: ELIZABETH SHORR

Registrar: STEVEN RAND

Director of Admission: DAVID PIRANI

Librarian: STEVEN C. BLOOM

Library of 484,000 volumes

Number of teachers: 351

Number of students: 10,820.

MARYLAND

BALTIMORE HEBREW UNIVERSITY

5800 Park Heights Ave, Baltimore, MD 21215

Telephone: (410) 578-6900

Fax: (410) 578-6940

E-mail: bhu@bhu.edu

Internet: www.bhu.edu

Founded 1919

Private control

Academic year: September to May

Pres.: Dr BARRY M. GITTLEN

Dean for Academic Admin. and Chief Academic Officer: Dr BARBARA G. ZIRKIN

Registrar: ZELDA RACHBACH

Library Dir: LIBBY KRAMER WHITE

Number of teachers: 10

Number of students: 164 (108 undergraduate, 56 graduate)

Areas of study: Jewish studies, Jewish education, Jewish communal service, English language, continuing education.

BALTIMORE INTERNATIONAL COLLEGE

Commerce Exchange, 17 Commerce St, Baltimore, MD 21202-3230

Telephone: (410) 752-4710

Fax: (410) 752-3730

E-mail: admissions@bic.edu

Internet: www.bic.edu

Founded 1972

Private control

Pres.: Dr ROGER CHYLINSKI

Library of 11,000 vols

Number of students: 800

Areas of study: Business and management, Culinary arts.

CAPITOL COLLEGE

11301 Springfield Rd, Laurel, MD 20708

Telephone: (301) 369-2800

Fax: (301) 953-1442

E-mail: admissions@capitol-college.edu

Internet: www.capitol-college.edu

Private control

Pres.: Dr MICHAEL T. WOOD

Dir of Library Services: RICK A. SAMPLE

Library of 10,000 vols

Number of teachers: 57

Number of students: 801 (630 undergraduate, 171 graduate)

Areas of study: Computer eng., Computer eng. technology, Computer science, Electrical eng., Electronics eng. technology, Management of information technology, Management of telecommunication systems, Software eng., Software and internet applications, Telecommunications eng. technology, Electronic commerce management, Network security, Information systems management, Information architecture.

COLLEGE OF NOTRE DAME OF MARYLAND

4701 North Charles St, Baltimore, MD 21210

Telephone: (410) 435-0100

Fax: (410) 532-6287

E-mail: admiss@ndm.edu

Internet: www.ndm.edu

Founded 1873

Private control

Pres.: Dr MARY PAT SEURKAMP

Number of teachers: 90

Number of students: 3,178 (1,930 undergraduate, 1,248 graduate).

COLUMBIA UNION COLLEGE

7600 Flower Ave, Takoma Park, MD 20912

Telephone: (301) 891-4000

Fax: (301) 891-4167

E-mail: info@cuc.edu

Internet: www.cuc.edu

Founded 1904

Private (Seventh-Day Adventist) liberal arts college

Pres.: Dr RANDAL WISBEY

Dean: GINA BROWN

Vice-Pres., Finance: PATRICK FARLEY

Dir of Admissions: EMILE JOHN

Registrar: Dr ANTHONY FUTCHER

Librarian: MARGARET VON HAKE

Library of 127,000 vols

Number of teachers: 53

Number of students: 1,212

Publications: *Reunion* (quarterly), *The Bulletin*, *Columbia Perspectives* (2 a year), *Golden Memories*, *Montage* (annual).

GOUCHER COLLEGE

1021 Dulaney Valley Rd, Baltimore, MD 21204

Telephone: (410) 337-6000

E-mail: communications@goucher.edu

Internet: www.goucher.edu

Founded 1885

Pres.: SANFORD J. UNGAR

Vice-Pres. and Dean of Students: GAIL EDMONDS

Registrar: PATRICIA KELLY

Vice-Pres. for Finance: TOM PHIZACKLEA

Librarian: NANCY MAGNUSON

Number of teachers: 173

Number of students: 2,350

Publications: *Quindecim, Donnybrook Fair, Preface, The Goucher Quarterly, Goucher College Catalog, President's Bulletin.*

HOOD COLLEGE

401 Rosemont Ave, Frederick, MD 21701-8575

Telephone: (301) 663-3131

Fax: (301) 694-7653

Internet: www.hood.edu

Founded 1893

Academic year: August to May

Pres.: Dr RONALD VOLPE

Provost and Dean of the Faculty (vacant): Dr ROBERT FUNK

Sr Vice-Pres. for Finance and Admin and Treas.: WILLIAM GEARHART

Vice-Pres. for Institutional Advancement: NANCY GILLECE

Vice-Pres. for Student Life and Dean of Students: OLIVIA WHITE

Registrar: NANETTE MARKEY

Library Dir: JAN SAMET O'LEARY

Library of 175,000 vols

Number of teachers: 143 (73 full-time, 70 adjunct)

Publications: *Hood Magazine* (quarterly), *Graduate Bulletin*

DEANS

Academic Affairs: TOM SAMET

Graduate School: ANN BOYD

JOHNS HOPKINS UNIVERSITY

3400 North Charles St, Baltimore, MD 21218

Telephone: (410) 516-8000

Internet: www.jhu.edu

Founded 1876

Private control

Academic year: September to June

Pres.: WILLIAM R. BRODY

Provost and Vice-Pres. for Academic Affairs: STEVEN KNAPP

Sr Vice-Pres. for Finance and Admin.: JAMES T. McGILL

Vice-Pres. for Medicine: EDWARD D. MILLER, Jr

Vice-Pres. for Devt and Alumni Relations: MICHAEL C. EICHER

Vice-Pres. and Gen. Counsel: STEPHEN S. DUNHAM

Registrar: HEDY SCHAEDEL

Library: see Libraries

Number of teachers: 6,670 full-time

Number of students: 17,967

DEANS

Zanvyl Krieger School of Arts and Sciences: RICHARD E. McCARTY

G. W. C. Whiting School of Eng.: ILENE BUSCH-VISHNIAC

Faculty of Medicine: EDWARD D. MILLER, Jr

Bloomberg School of Public Health: ALFRED SOMMER

School of Nursing: MARTHA HILL (acting)

School of Professional Studies in Business and Education: RALPH FESSLER

Paul H. Nitze School of Advanced Int. Studies: STEPHEN SZABO (acting)

Peabody Institute (Affiliated Instn): ROBERT SIROTA (Dir)

Applied Physics Laboratory: EUGENE T. ROCA (Dir)

PROFESSORS

Zanvyl Krieger School of Arts and Sciences:

ACHINSTEIN, P., Philosophy

ALEXANDER, K., Sociology

ANDERSON, A., English

ANDERSON, W., Romance Languages and Literatures

ARRIGHI, G., Sociology

BAGGER, J., Physics and Astronomy

BALL, G., Psychology

BALL, L., Econ.

BARNETT, B., Physics and Astronomy

BECKWITH, S., Physics and Astronomy

BEEMON, K., Biology

BELL, D., History

BERRY, S., History

BESSMAN, M., Biology

BETT, R., Philosophy

BLUMENFELD, B. J., Physics and Astronomy

BOARDMAN, J. M., Mathematics

BOWEN, K., Chemistry

BRAND, L., Biology

BRIEGER, G., History of Science, Medicine and Technology

BROHOLM, C., Physics and Astronomy

BROOKS, J., History

BRYAN, B. M., Near Eastern Studies

BURZIO, L., Cognitive Science

CAMERON, S., English

CAMPE, R., German

CARROLL, C., Econ.

CASTRO-KLARÉN, S., Romance Languages and Literatures

CHERLIN, A., Sociology

CHIEN, C.-L., Physics and Astronomy

CHIEN, C.-Y., Physics and Astronomy

CONE, R. A., Biophysics

CONNOLLY, W., Political Science

COOPER, J., Political Science

COOPER, J. S., Near Eastern Studies

CORCES, V., Biology

CRENSON, M., Political Science

CUMMINGS, M., Political Science

DAGDIGIAN, P., Chemistry

DAS, V., Anthropology

DAVID, S., Political Science

DAVIDSEN, A., Physics and Astronomy

DEFAUX, G., Romance Languages and Literatures

DEMPSEY, C., History of Art

DETIENNE, M., Classics

DIETZE, G., Political Science

DITZ, T., History

DIXON, S., Writing Seminars

DOERING, J., Chemistry

DOMOKOS, G., Physics and Astronomy

DRAPER, D., Chemistry

DRAPER, D., Biophysics and Chemistry

EBERT, J. D., Biology

EDIDIN, M., Biology

EGETH, H., Psychology

FALK, A., Physics and Astronomy

FAMBROUGH, D., Biology

FELDMAN, G., Physics and Astronomy

FELDMAN, P., Physics and Astronomy

FERGUSON, F., English

FERRY, J., Earth and Planetary Sciences

FISHER, G. W., Earth and Planetary Sciences

FLATHMAN, R. C., Political Science

FORD, H., Physics and Astronomy

FORNI, P., Romance Languages and Literatures

FORSTER, E., Humanities Center

FREIRE, E., Biology, Biophysics

FRIED, M., Humanities Center, History of Art

GALAMBOS, L. P., History

GALLAGHER, M., Psychology

GARVEN, G., Earth and Planetary Sciences

GERSOVITZ, M., Econ.

GINSBERG, B., Political Science

GOLDBERG, J., English

GONZÁLEZ, E., Romance Languages and Literatures

GORDON, R., Sociology

GREENE, J., History

GROSSMAN, A., English

GROSSMAN, J., Political Science

HARDIE, L. A., Earth and Planetary Sciences

HARRINGTON, J., Econ.

HECKMAN, T., Physics and Astronomy

HEDGECOCK, E., Biology

HENRY, R., Physics and Astronomy

HERTZ, N., Humanities Center

HOLLAND, P., Psychology

HOYT, M. A., Biology

HUANG, R. C., Biology

IRWIN, J., Writing Seminars

JOHNSON, M., History

JUSCZYK, P., Psychology

KAGAN, R., History

KARGON, R. H., History of Science, Medicine and Technology

KARLIN, K., Chemistry

KARNI, E., Econ.

KATZ, R., Political Science

KECK, M., Political Science

KESSLER, H., History of Art

KHAN, M. A., Econ.

KINGSLAND, S., History of Science, Medicine and Technology

KNIGHT, F., History

KOHN, M., Sociology

KOLYVAGIN, V., Mathematics

KOVESI-DOMOKOS, S., Physics and Astronomy

KROLIK, J., Physics and Astronomy

LANDAU, B., Cognitive Science

LATTMAN, E., Biophysics

LEE, Y. C., Biology

LEE, Y. K., Physics and Astronomy

LEGENDRE, G., Cognitive Science

LESLIE, S., History of Science, Medicine and Technology

LEYS, R., Humanities Center

LYKKEN, J., Physics and Astronomy

MACCINI, L., Econ.

MACKSEY, R., Humanities Center

MAGUIRE, H., History of Art

MARSH, B., Earth and Planetary Sciences

McCARTER, P. K., Jr, Near Eastern Studies

McCARTY, R., Biology

McCLOSKEY, M., Cognitive Science

McGARRY, J., Writing Seminars

MELION, W., History of Art

MEYER, G., Chemistry

MINICOZZI, W. P., Mathematics

MOFFITT, R., Econ.

MOON, M., English

MOOS, H. W., Physics and Astronomy

MORAVA, J., Mathematics

MORGAN, P., History

MOUDRIANAKIS, E., Biology

NÄGELE, R., German

NEUFELD, D., Physics and Astronomy

NEWMAN, S., Introduction to Policy Analysis (Policy Studies)

NICHOLS, S., Romance Languages and Literature

NICHOLS, S., Humanities Center

NIRENBERG, D., History

NORMAN, C., Physics and Astronomy

OLSON, P. L., Earth and Planetary Sciences

ONO, T., Mathematics

OSBORN, T., Earth and Planetary Sciences

PAGDEN, A., History

PANDEY, G., Anthropology

PAULSON, R., English

PEVSNER, A., Physics and Astronomy

POLAND, D., Chemistry

POSNER, G. H., Chemistry

PRIVALOV, P., Biology

REICH, D., Physics and Astronomy

ROBBINS, M., Physics and Astronomy

ROSEMAN, S., Biology

ROSS, D., History

ROWE, W., History

RUSSELL-WOOD, A. J. R., History

RUSSO, E., Romance Languages and Literature

RYNASIEWICZ, R., Philosophy

SALAMON, L., Political Science

SCHLEIF, R., Biology

SCHROER, T., Biology

SCHWARTZ, G. M., Near Eastern Studies

SHALIKA, J., Mathematics

SHAPIRO, A., Classics

SHEARN, A., Biology

SHIFFMAN, B., Mathematics

SHOKUROV, V. A., Mathematics

SIEBER, H., Romance Languages and Literatures

SILVERSTONE, H. J., Chemistry

SISSA, G., Classics

SMOLENSKY, P., Cognitive Science

SOGGE, C., Mathematics

SPIEGEL, G., History

SPRUCK, J., Mathematics

STANLEY, S., Earth and Planetary Sciences

STEPHENS, W., Romance Languages and Literatures

STROBEL, D., Earth and Planetary Sciences

SVERJENSKY, D., Earth and Planetary Sciences

SWARTZ, M., Physics and Astronomy

SZALAY, A., Physics and Astronomy

TESANOVIC, Z., Physics and Astronomy

TOWNSEND, C., Chemistry

VEBLEN, D., Earth and Planetary Sciences
VISHNIAC, E., Physics and Astronomy
WALKER, J. C., Physics and Astronomy
WALKOWITZ, J., History
WALTERS, R., History
WEISS, D., History of Art
WENTWORTH, R., Mathematics
WESTBROOK, R., Near Eastern Studies
WILLIAMS, M., Philosophy
WILSON, G., Philosophy
WILSON, W. S., Mathematics
WOLF, S., Philosophy
WOODSON, S. A., Biophysics
WYSE, R., Physics and Astronomy
YANTIS, S., Psychology
YARKONY, D., Chemistry
YOUNG, H. P., Econ.
ZELDICH, S., Mathematics
ZUCKER, S., Mathematics

GWC Whiting School of Engineering:

ANANDARAJAH, A., Civil Eng.
ANDREOU, A. G., Electrical and Computer Eng.
AWERBUCH, B., Computer Science
BALL, W. P., Geography and Environmental Eng.
BETENBAUGH, M. J., Chemical Eng.
BOLAND, J., Geography and Environmental Eng.
BOUWER, E. J., Geography and Environmental Eng.
BRUSH, G. S., Geography and Environmental Eng.
BUSCH-VISHNIAC, I. J., Mechanical Eng.
CAMMARATA, R., Materials Science and Eng.
CHEN, S., Mechanical Eng.
CHIRIKJAN, G., Mechanical Eng.
DAVIDSON, F. M., Electrical and Computer Eng.
DONOHUE, M., Chemical Eng.
DOUGLAS, A. S., Mechanical Eng.
ELLIS, J. H., Geography and Environmental Eng.
FILL, J. A., Mathematical Sciences
GERMAN, D., Mathematical Sciences
GOODRICH, M. T., Computer Science
GOUTSIAS, J. I., Electrical and Computer Eng.
GREEN, R. E., Jr, Materials Science and Eng.
HAGER, G. D., Computer Science
HAN, S.-P., Mathematical Sciences
HANKE, S., Geography and Environmental Eng.
HEMKER, K. J., Mechanical Eng.
HOBBS, B. F., Geography and Environmental Eng.
IGUSA, T., Civil Eng.
JELINEK, F., Electrical and Computer Eng.
JONES, N. P., Civil Eng.
JOSEPH, R. I., Electrical and Computer Eng.
KAPLAN, A. E., Electrical and Computer Eng.
KATZ, J., Mechanical Eng.
KATZ, J. L., Chemical Eng.
KHURGIN, J. B., Electrical and Computer Eng.
KNIO, O., Mechanical Eng.
KOSARAJU, S. R., Computer Science
MASSON, G. M., Computer Science
MENEVEAU, C. V., Mechanical Eng.
MEYER, G. G. L., Electrical and Computer Eng.
MILLER, M., Biomedical Eng.
MILLER, M. I., Electrical and Computer Eng.
NAIMAN, D. Q., Mathematical Sciences
O'MELIA, C. R., Geography and Environmental Eng.
PANG, J.-S., Mathematical Sciences
PARLANGE, M. B., Geography and Environmental Eng.
PAULAITIS, M. E., Chemical Eng.

PRIEBE, C. E., Mathematical Sciences
PRINCE, J. L., Electrical and Computer Eng.
PROSPERETTI, A., Mechanical Eng.
RAMESH, K. T., Mechanical Eng.
REVELLE, C., Geography and Environmental Eng.
RUGH, W. J., Electrical and Computer Eng.
SCHEINERMAN, E. R., Mathematical Sciences
SCHOENBERGER, E. J., Geography and Environmental Eng.
SEARSON, P. C., Materials Science and Eng.
SHARPE, W. N., JR, Mechanical Eng.
SMITH, S. F., Computer Science
STEBE, K., Chemical Eng.
STONE, A. T., Geography and Environmental Eng.
TAYLOR, R. H., Computer Science
WEINERT, H. L., Electrical and Computer Eng.
WIERMAN, J. C., Mathematical Sciences
WILCOCK, P. R., Geography and Environmental Eng.
WOLFF, L. B., Computer Science
WOLMAN, M. G., Geography and Environmental Eng.

Faculty of Medicine:

ABELOFF, M. D., Oncology, Medicine
ACHUFF, S. C., Medicine
ADKINSON, N. F., Jr, Medicine
ADLER, R., Ophthalmology and Neuroscience
AGNEW, W. S., Physiology and Neuroscience
AGRE, P. C., Biological Chemistry and Medicine
AMBINDER, R. F., Oncology, Pathology, Pharmacology and Molecular Science
AMZEL, L. M., Biophysics and Biophysical Chemistry
ANHALT, G. J., Dermatology and Pathology
ASKIN, F. B., Pathology
ATOR, N. A., Psychiatry
AUGUST, J. T., Pharmacology and Molecular Sciences, Oncology
BARBARAN, J. M., Neuroscience, Psychiatry
BARKER, L. R., Medicine
BARTLETT, J. G., Medicine
BAUGHMAN, K. L., Medicine
BAUMGARTNER, W. A., Surgery and Cardiac Surgery
BAYLESS, T. M., Medicine
BAYLIN, S. B., Oncology and Medicine
BEACHY, P. A., Molecular Biology and Genetics
BECKER, D. M., Medicine
BECKER, L. C., Medicine
BELL, W. R., Medicine
BERG, J. M., Biophysics and Biophysical Chemistry
BIGELOW, G. E., Psychiatry and Behavioural Sciences
BOCHNER, B. S., Medicine
BOEKE, J. D., Molecular Biology and Genetics
BOITNOTT, J. K., Pathology
BOROWITZ, M. J., Pathology, Oncology
BOTTOMLEY, P. A., Radiology and Radiological Science, Nuclear Magnetic Resonance Research, Biomedical Eng. and Medicine
BRANDT, J., Psychiatry
BREAKEY, W. R., Psychiatry
BREM, H., Neurological Surgery, Oncology
BRESSLER, N. M., Ophthalmology
BRESSLER, S. B., Ophthalmology
BRIEGER, G. H., History of Science, Medicine and Technology
BRINKER, J. A., Medicine
BROONER, R. K., Psychiatry
BRUSHART, T. M., Orthopaedic Surgery, Surgery, Plastic Surgery and Neurology
BULKLEY, G. B., Surgery
BURDICK, J. F., Surgery

BURGER, P. C., Pathology, Oncology Center, Neurological Surgery
BURKE, P. J., Oncology Center, Medicine
BURTON, J. R., Medicine
CALKINS, H. G., Medicine and Paediatrics
CAMERON, J. L., Surgery, Oncology
CAMPBELL, J. N., Neurological Surgery
CAMPOCHIARO, P. A., Ophthalmology and Neuroscience
CAPUTE, A. J., Paediatrics
CARSON, B. S., Neurological Surgery, Oncology, Paediatrics and Plastic Surgery
CARTER, H. B., Urology and Oncology
CASELLA, J. F., Paediatrics, Oncology Center
CASERO, R. J., Jr, Oncology
CATALDO, M. F., Psychiatry and Paediatrics
CHAISSON, R. E., Medicine
CHAKRAVARTI, A., Medicine and Paediatrics
CHAN, D. W., Pathology, Oncology, Radiology and Radiological Science, Urology
CHANDRA, N., Medicine
CHANG, A. Y., Oncology
CHAO, E. Y., Orthopaedic Surgery and Biomedical Eng.
CHARACHE, P., Pathology, Oncology, Medicine
CHATTERJEE, S. B., Paediatrics
CIVIN, C. I., Oncology, Paediatrics
CLEMENTS, J. E., Comparative Medicine, Neurology and Pathology
COFFEY, D. S., Urology, Oncology, Pharmacology and Molecular Sciences
COLE, P. A., Pharmacology and Molecular Sciences
COLOMBANI, P. M., Surgery, Paediatric Surgery, Oncology
CORDEN, J. L., Molecular Biology and Genetics
CORNBLATH, D. R., Neurology
COTTER, R. J., Pharmacology and Molecular Sciences, Biophysics and Biophysical Chemistry
CRAIG, N. L., Molecular Biology and Genetics
CRAIG, S. W., Biological Chemistry and Pathology
CUMMINGS, C. W., Otolaryngology, Head and Neck Surgery, Oncology
CUTTING, G. R., Paediatrics and Medicine
DANG, C. V., Medicine, Oncology, Pathology
DANNALS, R. F., Radiology, Radiological Science and Nuclear Medicine
DAVIDSON, N. E., Oncology
DAWSON, T., Neurology and Neuroscience
DE JUAN, E., Jr, Ophthalmology
DELATEUR, B. J., Physical Medicine and Rehabilitation
DENCKLA, M. B., Neurology and Paediatrics
DEPAULO, J. R., Psychiatry
DESIDERIO, S. V., Molecular Biology and Genetics
DEVREOTES, P. N., Biological Chemistry, Cell Biology and Anatomy
DICELLO, J. F., Oncology
DIEHL, A. M., Medicine
DIETZ, H. C., Paediatrics
DONEHOWER, R. C., Oncology and Medicine
DONOWITZ, M., Medicine
DOVER, G. J., Paediatrics and Oncology
DRACHMAN, D. B., Neurology and Neuroscience
EGGLESTON, P. A., Paediatrics
EISELE, D. W., Otolaryngology, Head and Neck Surgery, Anaesthesiology, Critical Care Medicine, Oncology and Urology
ENGLUND, P. T., Biological Chemistry
EPSTEIN, J. I., Pathology, Oncology, Urology
EROZAN, Y. S., Pathology
ETTINGER, D. S., Oncology, Medicine
FAJARDO, L. L., Radiology and Radiological Science, Diagnostic Radiology and Oncology

FEINBERG, A. P., Medicine and Oncology
FINKELSTEIN, D., Ophthalmology
FISHMAN, E. K., Radiology and Radiological Science, Diagnostic Radiology, Oncology
FORASTIERE, A. A., Oncology, Otolaryngology – Head and Neck Surgery
FORTUIN, N. J., Medicine
FOX, H. E., Gynaecology and Obstetrics
FRASSICA, F. J., Orthopaedic Surgery and Oncology
FREEMAN, J. M., Neurology and Paediatrics
FRIED, L. P., Medicine
FROST, J. J., Radiology and Radiological Science, and Nuclear Medicine and Neuroscience
FUCHS, P. A., Otolaryngology – Head and Neck Surgery, Biomedical Eng. and Neuroscience
GARCIA, J. G., Medicine
GEARHART, J. D., Gynaecology and Obstetrics, Comparative Medicine and Physiology
GEARHART, J. P., Urology and Paediatrics
GERSTENBLITH, G., Medicine
GIARDIELLO, F. M., Medicine, Oncology, Pathology
GIBSON, D. W., Pharmacology and Molecular Sciences
GOLDBERG, M. F., Ophthalmology
GOLDSTEIN, G. W., Neurology and Paediatrics
GORDIS, L., Paediatrics
GORDON, B., Neurology
GOTTSCH, J. D., Ophthalmology
GREEN, W. R., Ophthalmology and Pathology
GREENOUGH, W. B., III, Medicine
GREIDER, C. W., Molecular Biology and Genetics, Oncology
GRIFFIN, J. W., Neurology, Neuroscience and Pathology
GRIFFITH, L. S., Medicine
GRIFFITHS, R. R., Psychiatry and Neuroscience
GROSSMAN, S. A., Oncology, Medicine and Neurological Surgery
GUGGINO, W. B., Physiology and Paediatrics
GUYTON, D. L., Ophthalmology
HALPERIN, H. R., Medicine, Biomedical Eng.
HAMILTON, R. G., Medicine
HANDLER, J. S., Medicine
HANLEY, D. F., Neurology, Anaesthesiology and Critical Care Medicine
HAPONIK, E. F., Medicine
HARMON, J. W., Surgery
HARRIS, J. C., Jr, Psychiatry and Paediatrics
HART, G. W., Biological Chemistry
HAWKINS, B. S., Ophthalmology
HAYWARD, G. S., Pharmacology and Molecular Sciences, Oncology and Pathology
HAYWARD, S. D., Pharmacology and Molecular Sciences, Oncology and Pathology
HELLMAN, D. B., Medicine
HENDRY, S. H., Neuroscience
HEPTINSTALL, R. H., Pathology
HESS, A. D., Oncology and Pathology
HOLTZMAN, N. A., Paediatrics
HRUBAN, R. H., Pathology, Oncology
HUBBARD, A. L., Cell Biology, Anatomy and Physiology
HUGANIR, R. L., Neuroscience
HUGGINS, G. R., Gynaecology and Obstetrics
HUNGERFORD, D. S., Orthopaedic Surgery
HUTCHINS, G. M., Pathology
ISAACS, J. T., Oncology and Urology
ISAACS, W. B., Urology, Oncology
JABS, D. A., Ophthalmology and Medicine
JABS, E. W., Paediatrics, Medicine, Surgery and Plastic Surgery
JACKSON, J. B., Pathology
JASINSKI, D. R., Medicine

JOHNS, R. A., Anaesthesiology and Critical Care Medicine
JOHNS, R. J., Medicine
JOHNSON, K. O., Neuroscience and Biomedical Eng.
JOHNSON, R. T., Neurology, Molecular Biology, Genetics and Neuroscience
JOHNSTON, M. V., Neurology and Paediatrics
JONES, B., Radiology and Radiological Sciences, Diagnostic Radiology
JONES, R. J., Oncology
KAN, J. S., Paediatrics
KASHIMA, H. K., Otolaryngology – Head and Neck Surgery, Oncology
KASS, D. A., Medicine and Biomedical Eng.
KAVOUSSI, L. R., Urology
KELEN, G. D., Emergency Medicine
KELLY, T. J., Jr, Molecular Biology and Genetics
KICKLER, T. S., Pathology, Oncology and Medicine
KIM, K. S., Paediatrics
KINZLER, K. W., Oncology
KIRSCH, J. R., Anaesthesiology and Critical Care Medicine
KLAG, M. J., Medicine
KLEIN, A. S., Surgery
KOCH, W., Otolaryngology, Oncology
KOEHLER, R. C., Anaesthesiology and Critical Care Medicine
KOSTUIK, J., Orthopaedic Surgery and Neurological Surgery
KUNCL, R. W., Neurology
KURMAN, R. J., Gynaecology and Obstetrics, Pathology
KWITEROVICH, P. O., Jr, Paediatrics and Medicine
LADENSON, P. W., Medicine, Oncology and Pathology
LANE, M. D., Biological Chemistry
LAWSON, E. E., Paediatrics
LEDERMAN, H. M., Paediatrics
LEE, S., Molecular Biology and Genetics
LENZ, F. A., Neurological Surgery
LEONG, K. W., Biomedical Eng.
LESSER, R. P., Neurology, Neurological Surgery
LEVINE, D. M., Medicine
LEVINE, M. A., Paediatrics and Medicine
LI, G., Emergency Medicine
LICHTENSTEIN, L. M., Medicine
LIETMAN, P. S., Medicine, Paediatrics, Pharmacology and Molecular Sciences
LILLEMOE, K. D., Surgery
LIU, J., Pharmacology and Molecular Sciences, Neuroscience
LONG, D. M., Neurological Surgery
LOUGHLIN, G. M., Paediatrics
LYKETSOS, C. G., Psychiatry
MacGLASHAN, D. W., Medicine
MALONEY, P. C., Physiology
MANN, R. B., Pathology, Oncology
MANSON, P. N., Surgery and Plastic Surgery
MARBAN, E., Medicine and Physiology
MASSOF, R. W., Ophthalmology
MAUGHAN, W. L., Medicine and Biomedical Eng.
MAUMENEE, I. E., Ophthalmology
MCARTHUR, J. C., Neurology
MCCARTHY, E. F., Jr, Pathology, Orthopaedic Surgery
MCCAUL, M. E., Psychiatry
MCHUGH, P. R., Psychiatry
MCKHANN, G. M., Neurology and Neuroscience
MCKUSICK, V. A., Medicine
MCMILLAN, J. A., Paediatrics
MERZ, W. G., Pathology
MEYER, R. A., Neurological Surgery and Biomedical Eng.
MEZEY, E., Medicine
MIGEON, B. R., Paediatrics
MIGEON, C. J., Paediatrics
MILDVAN, A. S., Biological Chemistry

MILLER, E. D., Anaesthesiology and Critical Care Medicine
MILLER, N. R., Ophthalmology and Neurology, Neurological Surgery
MINOR, L. B., Otolaryngology – Head and Neck Surgery, Biomedical Eng., Neuroscience
MOLLIVER, M. E., Neuroscience and Neurology
MONTELL, C., Biological Chemistry and Neuroscience
MONTZ, F. J., Gynaecology and Obstetrics, Oncology
MOORE, T. H., Medicine
MORAN, T. H., Psychiatry
MOSER, H. W., Neurology and Paediatrics
MOSTWIN, J. L., Urology
MUNSTER, A. M., Surgery and Plastic Surgery
MURPHY, D. B., Cell Biology and Anatomy
MURPHY, P. A., Medicine and Molecular Biology and Genetics
NAIDU, S., Neurology, Paediatrics
NATARAJAN, V., Medicine
NATHANS, J., Molecular Biology and Genetics, Neuroscience and Ophthalmology
NESS, P. M., Pathology and Medicine
NICHOLS, D. G., Anaesthesiology, Critical Care Medicine
NIPARKO, J. K., Otolaryngology – Head and Neck Surgery
NORTH, R., Neurological Surgery, Anesthesiology and Critical Care Medicine
PARDOLL, D. M., Oncology, Medicine and Pathology
PARTIN, A., Urology
PEARLSON, G. D., Psychiatry
PEDERSEN, P. L., Biological Chemistry
PERLER, B. A., Surgery
PERMUTT, S., Medicine
PETRI, M., Medicine
PIANTADOSI, S., Oncology
PITHA-ROWE, P. M., Oncology
PLOTNICK, L., Paediatrics
POPEL, A. S., Biomedical Eng.
POWE, N. R, Medicine
PRICE, D. L., Pathology, Neurology and Neuroscience
QUIGLEY, H. A., Ophthalmology
QUINN, T. C., Medicine
RABINS, P. V., Psychiatry
RACUSEN, L., Pathology
RAJA, S. N., Anaesthesiology and Critical Care Medicine
REED, R. R., Molecular Biology and Genetics and Neuroscience
REEVES, R. H., Physiology
REPKA, M. X., Ophthalmology, Paediatrics
RICHARDSON, M. A., Otolaryngology – Head and Neck Surgery
RIGAMONTI, D., Neurological Surgery, Radiology and Radiological Science, Neuroradiology
RONNETT, G. V., Neuroscience, Neurology
ROSE, G. D., Biophysics and Biophysical Chemistry
ROSE, K. D., Cell Biology and Anatomy
ROSENSTEIN, B. J., Paediatrics
ROSENTHAL, D. L., Pathology, Gynaecology and Obstetrics, Oncology
ROSS, C. A., Psychiatry and Neuroscience
ROTHSTEIN, J. D., Neurology and Neuroscience
ROWE, P. C., Paediatrics
RUFF, C. B., Cell Biology, Anatomy and Orthopaedic Surgery
RYUGO, D. K., Otolaryngology – Head and Neck Surgery, Neuroscience
SACHS, M. B., Biomedical Eng. and Neuroscience, Otolaryngology – Head and Neck Surgery
SAUDEK, C. D., Medicine
SAUDER, D. N., Dermatology
SCHACHAT, A. P., Ophthalmology and Oncology
SCHEIN, O. D., Ophthalmology

SCHLEIMER, R. P., Medicine
SCHMIDT, C. W., Jr, Psychiatry
SCHNAAR, R. L., Pharmacology, Molecular Sciences and Neuroscience
SCHNECK, J., Pathology
SCHRAMM, L. P., Biomedical Eng. and Neuroscience
SCHWARZ, K., Paediatrics
SCIUBBA, J. J., Otolaryngology – Head and Neck Surgery, Dermatology, Pathology
SEMENZA, G. L., Paediatrics
SHAPER, J. H., Oncology
SHAPIRO, E. P., Medicine
SHAPIRO, T. A., Medicine
SHARKIS, S. J., Oncology
SHORTLE, D. R., Biological Chemistry, Biophysics and Biophysical Chemistry
SHOUKAS, A. A., Biomedical Eng.
SIDRANSKY, D., Otolaryngology – Head and Neck Surgery, Urology, Oncology, Pathology
SIEGELMAN, S. S., Radiology and Radiological Science
SILICIANO, R. F., Medicine
SINGER, H. S., Neurology and Paediatrics
SLAVNEY, P. R., Psychiatry and Medicine
SMITH, K. D., Paediatrics
SMITH, P. L., Medicine
SNYDER, S. H., Neuroscience, Pharmacology, Molecular Sciences and Psychiatry
SOLLNER-WEBB, B. T., Biological Chemistry
SOMMER, A., Ophthalmology
SPIVAK, J. L., Medicine and Oncology
SPONSELLER, P. D., Orthopaedic Surgery
STARK, W. J., Jr, Ophthalmology
STITZER, M. L., Psychiatry
STRAIN, E. C., Psychiatry
SYLVESTER, J. T., Medicine
TALALAY, P., Pharmacology and Molecular Sciences
TEAFORD, M. F., Cell Biology and Anatomy
TERRY, P. B., Medicine
THAKOR, N. V., Biomedical Eng.
THOMAS, G. H., Paediatrics and Pathology
TOMASELLI, G. F., Medicine
TRAILL, T. A., Medicine
TRAYSTMAN, R. J., Anaesthesiology and Critical Care Medicine
TSO, M. D., Ophthalmology and Pathology
UNDEM, B. J., Medicine
VALLE, D. L., Paediatrics and Ophthalmology
VAN ZIJL, P. C., Radiology and Radiological Sciences, Nuclear Magnetic Resonance, Biophysics and Biophysical Chemistry
VOGELSANG, G. B., Oncology
VOGELSTEIN, B., Oncology and Pathology
VON DER HEYDT, R., Neuroscience
WALLACH, E. E., Gynaecology and Obstetrics
WALSER, M., Pharmacology and Molecular Sciences and Medicine
WALSH, P.C., Urology
WAND, G. S., Medicine, Psychiatry
WATKINS, L., Jr, Surgery and Cardiac Surgery
WEISHAMPEL, D. B., Cell Biology and Anatomy
WEISS, J. L., Medicine
WEST, S., Ophthalmology
WHARAM, M. D., Jr, Oncology, Paediatrics, Radiology and Radiological Science and Neurological Surgery
WIGLEY, F. M., Medicine
WILLIAMS, G. M., Surgery
WINCHURCH, R. A., Surgery
WINKELSTEIN, J. A., Paediatrics, Medicine and Pathology
WINSLOW, R. L., Biomedical Eng.
WISE, R. A., Medicine
WOLBERGER, C., Biophysics and Biophysical Chemistry
WONG, D. F., Radiology and Radiological Science, and Nuclear Medicine
WORLEY, P. F., Neuroscience and Neurology

YARDLEY, J. H., Pathology
YASTER, M., Anaesthesiology and Critical Care Medicine
YAU, K., Neuroscience and Ophthalmology
YEO, C. J., Surgery and Oncology
YOLKEN, R. H., Paediatrics
YOUNG, E. D., Biomedical Eng. and Neuroscience, Otolaryngology – Head and Neck Surgery
YOUSEM, D. M., Radiology and Radiological Science, Neuroradiology
YUE, I. D., Biomedical Eng. and Neuroscience
ZACUR, H. A., Gynaecology and Obstetrics
ZEE, D. S., Neurology and Neuroscience, Ophthalmology and Otolaryngology – Head and Neck Surgery
ZEIMER, R., Ophthalmology
ZEITLIN, P. L., Paediatrics
ZERHOUNI, E. A., Radiology and Radiological Science, Diagnostic Radiology and Biomedical Eng.
ZIEVE, P. D., Medicine
ZINK, C., Comparative Medicine and Pathology
ZWEIER, J. L., Medicine

Bloomberg School of Public Health:

ALEXANDER, C. S., Population and Family Health Sciences
ANDERSON, G. F., Health Policy and Management
ANTHONY, J. C., Mental Hygiene
ARMENIAN, H. K., Epidemiology
BAKER, S. P., Health Policy and Management
BAKER, T. D., Int. Health
BEATY, T. H., Epidemiology
BECKER, S., Population and Family Health Sciences
BERTRAND, J. T., Population and Family Health Sciences
BLACK, R., Int. Health
BREITNER, J. C. S., M2ental Hygiene
BRENNER, M. H., Health Policy and Management
BREYSSE, P., Environmental Health Sciences
BROOKMEYER, R., Biostatistics
BROWN, T. R., Biochemistry and Molecular Biology
BRYANT, F. R., Biochemistry and Molecular Biology
BURKE, D. S., Int. Health
CABALLERO, B., Int. Health
CELENTANO, D., Epidemiology
CHANDRASEGARAN, S., Environmental Health Sciences
CHOW, L., Population and Family Health Sciences
COHEN, B. H., Epidemiology
COMSTOCK, G. W., Epidemiology
CULOTTA, V., Environmental Health Sciences
DANNENBERG, A. M., Environmental Health Sciences
DIENER-WEST, M., Biostatics
EATON, W. W., Mental Hygiene
ENSMINGER, M. E., Health Policy and Management
FADEN, R., Health Policy and Management
FEINLEIB, M., Epidemiology
FITZGERALD, R. S., Environmental Health Sciences
GIELEN, A., Health Policy and Management
GILMAN, R., Int. Health
GOLDBERG, A. M., Environmental Health Sciences
GOLDMAN, L., Environmental Health Sciences
GORDIS, L., Epidemiology
GOSTIN, L., Health Policy and Management
GRAY, R. H., Population and Family Health Sciences

GRIFFIN, D. E., Molecular Microbiology and Immunology
GROOPMAN, J. D., Environmental Health Sciences
GROSSMAN, L., Biochemistry and Molecular Biology
GUILARTE, T. R., Environmental Health Sciences
GUYER, B., Population and Family Health Sciences
HALSEY, N., Int. Health
HARDWICK, J. M., Molecular Microbiology and Immunology
HELZLSOUER, K., Epidemiology
HENDERSON, D. A., Int. Health
HILL, K. H., Population and Family Health Sciences
HUANG, P. C., Biochemistry
JAKAB, G. J., Environmental Health Sciences
KASPER, J. A., Health Policy and Management
KATZ, J., Int. Health
KENSLER, T. W., Environmental Health Sciences
KETNER, G. W., Molecular Microbiology and Immunology
KIM, Y. J., Population and Family Health Sciences
KLEEBURGER, S., Environmental Health Sciences
KRAG, S. S., Biochemistry and Molecular Biology
KUMAR, N., Molecular Microbiology and Immunology
LAWRENCE, R. S., Health Policy and Management
LEAF, P. J., Mental Hygiene
LEVIN, D. E., Biochemistry
LIANG, K. Y., Biostatistics
LINKS, J. M., Environmental Health Sciences
MACKENZIE, E. J., Health Policy and Management
MARGOLIK, J., Molecular Microbiology and Immunology
MARKHAM, R., Molecular Microbiology and Immunology
MATANOSKI, G. M., Epidemiology
McMACKEN, R., Biochemistry and Molecular Biology
MEINERT, C. L., Epidemiology
MILLER, P. S., Biochemistry and Molecular Biology
MITZNER, W. A., Environmental Health Sciences
MORLOCK, L., Health Policy and Management
MORROW, R., Int. Health
MOSLEY, W. H., Population and Family Health Sciences
MUÑOZ, A., Epidemiology
NATHANSON, C. A., Population and Family Health Sciences
NAVARRO, V., Health Policy and Management
NELSON, K., Epidemiology
PAIGE, D. M., Population and Family Health Sciences
PICKART, C. M., Biochemistry
PIERCE, N. F., Int. Health
PIOTROW, P. T., Population and Family Health Sciences
POWE, N. R., Epidemiology
REINKE, W. A., Int. Health
RISBY, T., Environmental Health Sciences
ROHDE, C. A., Biostatistics
ROSE, N. R., Molecular Microbiology and Immunology
ROTER, D., Health Policy and Management
ROYALL, R. M., Biostatistics
SACK, D., Int. Health
SACK, R. B., Int. Health
SALKEVER, D. S., Health Policy and Management
SAMET, J., Epidemiology

SANTOSHAM, M., Int. Health
SCHOENRICH, E. H., Health Policy and Management
SCHWARTZ, B., Environmental Health Sciences
SCOCCA, J. J., Biochemistry
SCOTT, A. L., Molecular Microbiology and Immunology
SHAH, K. V.2, Molecular Microbiology and Immunology
SOMMER, A., Epidemiology
SPANNHAKE, E., Environmental Health Sciences
STARFIELD, B., Health Policy and Management
STEINHOFF, M., Int. Health
STEINWACHS, D. M., Health Policy and Management
STRICKLAND, P. T., Environmental Health Sciences
STROBINO, D. M., Population and Family Health Sciences
SZKLO, M., Epidemiology
TERET, S. P., Health Policy and Management
TIELSCH, J. M., Int. Health
TONASCIA, J., Biostatistics
TRPIS, M., Molecular Microbiology and Immunology
TRUSH, M. A., Environmental Health Sciences
TS'O, P. O. P., Biochemistry and Molecular Biology
TSUI, A. O., Population and Family Health Sciences
WAGNER, H. N., Environmental Health Sciences
WANG, M., Biostatistics
WEINER, J. P., Health Policy and Management
WEST, K., Int. Health
WRIGHT, W. W., Biochemistry and Molecular Biology
YAGER, J., Environmental Health Sciences
ZABIN, L. S., Population and Family Health Sciences
ZEGER, S., Biostatistics
ZIRKIN, B., Biochemistry and Molecular Biology

Paul H. Nitze School of Advanced Int. Studies (1730 Massachusetts Ave, Washington, DC 20036):

AJAMI, F., Middle East Studies
BARRET, S., Int. Relations
BODNAR, G., Int. Finance
CALLEO, D. P., European Studies
COHEN, E. A., Strategic Studies
CORDEN, W. M., Int. Econ.
DORAN, C. F., Canadian Studies and Int. Relations
FRANK, I., Int. Econ.
FUKUYAMA, F., Political Economy
GLEIJESES, P., US Foreign Policy and Latin American Studies
GOODELL, G. E., Int. Devt
GRILLI, E., Int. Econ.
JACKSON, K. D., Asian and South East Asia Studies
LAMPTON, D. M., Asian Studies
MANDELBAUM, M., US Foreign Policy
PARROTT, B., Russian and Eurasian Studies
PEARSON, C. S., Int. Econ.
RIEDEL, J. C., Int. Econ.
ROETT, R., Latin American Studies and Western Hemisphere Programs
THAYER, N. B., Asian Studies
WEDGEWOOD, J. D., Int. Law and Organization
ZARTMAN, I. W., African Studies

School of Nursing:

ALLEN, J., Preventive Cardiology
BERK, R. A., Psychometrics and Statistics
CAMPBELL, J., Community Health
DONALDSON, S., Physiology and Biophysics
FRALIC, M., Nursing Management

GASTON-JOHANSSON, F., Research Utilization and Pain
HILL, M., Adult Health

LOYOLA COLLEGE IN MARYLAND

4501 North Charles St, Baltimore, MD 21210-2699

Telephone: (410) 617-2000
Fax: (410) 617-2176
Internet: www.loyola.edu

Founded 1852
Private control
Academic year: August to May
Pres.: Rev. BRIAN S. J. LINNANE
Vice-Pres. for Academic Affairs: TIMOTHY SNYDER
Vice-Pres. for Student Devt and Dean of Students: Dr SUSAN M. DONOVAN
Vice-Pres. for Admin.: TERRENCE SAWYER
Vice-Pres. for Devt and College Relations: Dr MICHAEL GOFF

Number of teachers: 520
Number of students: 6,144 (3,488 undergraduate, 2,656 postgraduate)

DEANS

College of Arts and Sciences: Dr JAMES BUCKLEY
Sellinger School of Business and Management: Dr LEE DAHRINGER

MCDANIEL COLLEGE

2 College Hill, Westminster, MD 21157-4390

Telephone: (410) 848-7000
Fax: (410) 857-2729
E-mail: pio@mcdaniel.edu
Internet: www.mcdaniel.edu

Founded 1867 as Western Maryland College; present name 2002
Academic year: August to June
Pres.: JOAN DEVELIN COLEY
Provost and Dean of the Faculty: THOMAS M. FALKNER
Vice-Pres. for Admin. and Finance: ETHAN A. SEIDEL
Vice-Pres. for Institutional Advancement: RICHARD G. KIEF
Dean and Vice-Pres. for Student Affairs: BETH R. GERL
Vice-Pres. for Enrollment Management and Dean of Admissions: FLORENCE W. HINES
Registrar: JAN KIPHART
Chief Information Officer and Library Dir: MICHELE M. REID

Library of 203,351 vols
Number of teachers: 306
Number of students: 3,304

Liberal arts; first and masters degrees; training for teachers of the deaf.

MARYLAND INSTITUTE, COLLEGE OF ART

1300 Mt Royal Ave, Baltimore, MD 21217

Telephone: (410) 669-9200
Fax: (410) 669-9206
E-mail: pr@mica.edu
Internet: www.mica.edu

Founded 1826
Pres.: FRED LAZARUS, IV
Vice-Pres. and Dean for Admission and Financial Aid: THERESA LYNCH BEDOYA
Provost and Vice-Pres. for Academic Affairs: RAYMOND V. ALLEN
Vice-Pres. for Advancement: MICHAEL FRANCO
Librarian: MARJORIE CHENOWETH

Library of 51,000 vols
Number of teachers: 178
Number of students: 1,143.

MORGAN STATE UNIVERSITY

1700 East Coldspring Lane, Baltimore, MD 21251

Telephone: (443) 885-3333
E-mail: info@morgan.edu
Internet: www.morgan.edu

Founded 1867
Pres.: Dr EARL S. RICHARDSON
Vice-Pres. for Academic Affairs: Dr T. JOAN ROBINSON
Vice-Pres. for Finance and Management: ABRAHAM MOORE
Vice-Pres. for Institutional Advancement: CHERYL Y. HITCHCOCK
Vice-Pres. for Planning and Evaluation: Dr JOSEPH POPOVICH
Vice-Pres. for Student Services: A. RECARDO PERRY
Dir of Library: KAREN A. ROBERTSON

Library of 350,042 vols
Number of teachers: 278
Number of students: 5,034

DEANS

College of Arts and Sciences: Dr BURNEY HOLLIS
School of Education and Urban Studies: Dr PATRICIA MORRIS (acting)
School of Eng.: Dr EUGENE M. DeLOATCH
School of Graduate Studies: Dr FRANK MORRIS
School of Business and Management: Dr OTIS THOMAS

MOUNT SAINT MARY'S UNIVERSITY

Emmitsburg, MD 21727

Telephone: (410) 447-6122
Fax: (301) 447-5755
E-mail: postmaster@msmary.edu
Internet: www.msmary.edu

Founded 1808
Pres.: THOMAS H. POWELL
Vice-Pres. for Academic Affairs: Dr DAVID REHM
Registrar: JOHN C. GILL
Dir of Library: Dr D. STEPHEN ROCKWOOD

Library of 200,000 vols
Number of teachers: 98 full-time
Number of teachers: 22 part-time
Number of students: 1,798

Publication: *Mountaineer Briefing* (quarterly).

ST JOHN'S COLLEGE

60 College Ave, Annapolis, MD 21401

Telephone: (410) 263-2371
Fax: (410) 626-2886
E-mail: admissions@sjca.edu
Internet: www.sjca.edu

Founded as King William's School 1696
Academic year: September to May
Pres.: CHRISTOPHER B. NELSON
Vice-Pres. for Advancement: JEFFREY A. BISHOP
Dean: MICHAEL DINK
Treas.: FRED H. BILLUPS, Jr
Registrar: JON ENRIQUEZ
Dir of Alumni Relations: JO ANN MATTSON
Dir of Admissions: JOHN CHRISTENSEN
College Librarian: ANDREA LAMB

Library of 93,000 vols
Number of teachers: 69
Number of students: 450

Publication: *The Review* (3 a year)

For Santa Fe campus see under New Mexico.

ST MARY'S COLLEGE OF MARYLAND

18952 East Fisher Rd, St Mary's City, MD 20686-3001

Telephone: (240) 895-2000
Fax: (240) 895-5001
E-mail: admissions@smcm.edu
Internet: www.smcm.edu

Founded 1840
Academic year: August to May

Pres.: JANE MARGARET O'BRIEN
Provost: LARRY E. VOTE (acting)
Vice-Pres. for Business and Finance: Dr TOM BOTZMAN (acting)
Vice-Pres. for Devt: SALVATORE M. MERRINGOLO (acting)
Dean of Students: MARK W. HEIDRICH
Dean of Admissions and Financial Aid: Dr WESLEY JORDAN
Dir of Library (vacant): CELIA RABINOWITZ

Library of 200,000 vols
Number of teachers: 143
Number of students: 1,939

Publication: *The Mulberry Tree* (2 a year).

ST MARY'S SEMINARY AND UNIVERSITY

5400 Roland Ave, Baltimore, MD 21210-1994

Telephone: (410) 864-4000
E-mail: admissions@stmarys.edu
Internet: www.stmarys.edu

Founded 1791

Pres. and Rector: Father TOM HURST
Vice-Rector: Rev. GLADSTONE STEVENS
Vice-Pres. for Finance: RICHARD G. CHILDS
Vice-Pres. for Advancement and Admin.: ELIZABETH L. VISCONAGE
Registrar and Dir of Information Services: PATRICIA GREGA

Libraries of 95,281 vols

Number of teachers: 21 full-time
Number of teachers: 24 part-time
Number of students: 75 full-time
Number of students: 201 part-time

Publications: *St Mary's Bulletin* (quarterly), *Catalogues*.

SOJOURNER-DOUGLASS COLLEGE

200 North Central Ave, Baltimore, MD 21202

Telephone: (410) 276-0306
Fax: (410) 276-1810
Internet: www.sdc.edu
Private control

Pres.: Dr CHARLES W. SIMMONS
Provost and Vice-Pres. for Academic and Student Affairs: Dr MARIAN STANTON
Vice-Pres. for Admin. and Fiscal Affairs: DONALD HUTCHINS

Number of teachers: 44
Number of students: 444

Areas of study: admin., human and social resources, human growth and devt.

BRANCH CAMPUSES

Annapolis Campus: Suite 302, 49 Old Solomons Island Rd, Annapolis, MD 21401; tel. (410) 897-1244; fax (410) 897-1245; Dir Dr CHARLESTINE FAIRLEY.

Bahamas Campus: Gold Circle House, 2nd Floor, East Bay St, Nassau; tel. (242) 394-8570; fax (242) 394-8623; Dir DORIS CARROLL.

Cambridge Campus: 824 Fairmount Ave, Cambridge, MD 21613; tel. (410) 943-1171; fax (410) 943-1976; Dir ENEZ GRUBB.

Prince George's County Campus: Suite 11, 8200 Professional Pl., Lanham, MD 20785; tel. (301) 459-8686; fax (301) 459-2023; Dir Dr BERNARD GROSS.

Salisbury Campus: Salisbury Mall, 351 Civic Ave, Unit B-17, Salisbury, MD 21804; tel. (410) 572-5640; fax (410) 572-5642; Dir (vacant).

UNIFORMED SERVICES UNIVERSITY OF THE HEALTH SCIENCES

4301 Jones Bridge Rd, Bethesda, MD 20814

Telephone: (301) 295-3101
E-mail: admissions@mxa.usuhs.mil
Internet: www.usuhs.mil

Founded 1972

Pres.: Dr CHARLES S. RICE
Vice-Pres. for Exec. Affairs: CHARLES R. MANNIX
Vice-Pres. for Teaching and Research Support: Dr VERNON D. SCHINSKI
Vice-Pres. for Research: Dr STEVEN KAMINSKY
Assoc. Registrar: LINDA A. PORTER

Number of teachers: 332 (on campus)
Number of students: 896

DEANS

F. Edward Hébert School of Medicine: Dr LARRY W. LAUGHLIN
Graduate School of Nursing: Dr PATRICIA HINTON WALKER
Graduate Education: Dr CINDA J. HELKE (Assoc. Dean)

UNITED STATES NAVAL ACADEMY

Annapolis, MD 21402-5000

Telephone: (410) 293-1000
Fax: (410) 293-3734
Internet: www.usna.edu

Founded 1845
Academic year: August to May

Superintendent: Vice Admiral JEFFREY L. FOWLER
Commandant of Midshipmen: Capt. MARGARET D. KLEIN
Academic Dean and Provost: WILLIAM C. MILLER
Vice Academic Dean: MICHAEL C. HALBIG
Dean of Admissions: BRUCE LATTA
Registrar: Dr MICHAEL CHAMBERLAIN
Dir of Museum: Dr J. SCOTT HARMON
Librarian: RICHARD HUME WERKING

Library of 653,600 vols
Number of teachers: 600
Number of students: 4,265 midshipmen

Publications: *Lucky Bag*, *Shipmate* (online), *Trident*

DIVISION DIRECTORS

Eng. and Weapons: Capt. DOUGLAS H. RAU
Humanities and Social Sciences: Col. KENNETH A. INMAN
Mathematics and Science: Capt. SCOTT S. PUGH
Professional Devt: Capt. RICHARD THAYER
Athletics: CHET GLADCHUK

UNIVERSITY OF MARYLAND SYSTEM

3300 Metzerott Rd, Adelphi, MD 20783-1690

Telephone: (301) 445-2740
Fax: (301) 445-4761
E-mail: webnotes@usmd.edu
Internet: www.usmd.edu

Founded 1988 by the merger of the 5 Univ. of Maryland instns and 6 mems of the State Univ. and College System of Maryland
Number of students: 130,000 across 13 instns

Chancellor: Dr WILLIAM ENGLISH KIRWAN.

CONSTITUENT UNIVERSITIES

Bowie State University

14000 Jericho Park Rd, Bowie, MD 20715

Telephone: (301) 860-4000
Internet: www.bowiestate.edu

Founded 1865
Academic year: September to May

Pres.: Dr MICKEY L. BURNIM
Provost and Vice-Pres. for Academic Affairs: Dr PATRICIA P. RAMSEY
Vice-Pres. for Finance and Admin.: Dr KARL B. BROCKENBROUGH
Vice-Pres. for External Relations: MAITLAND DADE

Library of 352,795 vols
Number of teachers: 346 (190 full-time, 156 part-time)
Number of students: 5,415

DEANS

School of Arts and Sciences: Dr COSMAS NWOKEAFOR
School of Business: Dr MATHIAS MBAH
School of Education: Dr VERNON POLITE
School of Professional Studies: Dr JOYCE BOWLES
School of Graduate Studies and Continuing Education: Dr DIANNE KRECHMAR (acting)

CHAIRS OF DEPARTMENTS

School of Arts and Sciences (New Sciences Bldg, Dean's Office 315, 14000 Jericho Park Rd, Bowie, MD 20715; tel. (301) 860-3320; fax (301) 860-3325):

Communications: Dr CHUCKA ONWUMECHILLI
Computer Science: Dr SADANAND SRIVASTAVA
English and Modern Languages: Dr SIDNEY WALKER
Fine and Performing Arts: Dr CLARENCE KNIGHT
History and Govt: Dr WILLIAM LEWIS
Mathematics: Dr NELSON PETULANTE
Natural Sciences: Dr ELAINE DAVIS

School of Business (Milk Bldg, Dean's Office, Room 301, 14000 Jericho Park Rd, Bowie, MD 20715; tel. (301) 860-3502; fax (301) 860-3644):

Financial and Economic Accounting: Dr SAMUEL DUAL
Management Information System: Dr DAVID ANYIWO
Management, Marketing and Public Admin.: Dr SHELTON RHODES

School of Education (CLT Bldg, Dean's Office, Room 226, 14000 Jericho Park Rd, Bowie, MD 20715; tel. (301) 860-3230; fax (301) 860-3234):

Counselling: Dr RHONDA JETER
Educational Leadership: Dr BARBARA JACKSON
Teaching, Learning and Professional Devt: Dr BARBARA SMITH

School of Professional Studies (CLT Bldg, Dean's Office, Room 321, 14000 Jericho Park Rd, Bowie, MD 20715; tel. (301) 860-4700; fax (301) 860-4702):

Behavioural Sciences and Human Services: Dr ELLIOTT PARRIS
Nursing: Dr JOSEPHINE MCCASKELL
Psychology: Dr CHERYL BLACKMAN
Social Work: Dr DORIS POLSTON

Coppin State University

2500 West North Ave, Baltimore, MD 21216-3698

Telephone: (410) 951-3000
Fax: (410) 523-7351
E-mail: admissions@coppin.edu
Internet: www.coppin.edu

Founded 1900; part of Univ. of Maryland System

Academic year: August to May

Pres.: Dr STANLEY F. BATTLE

Provost and Vice-Pres. for Academic Affairs: Dr SADIE GREGORY

Vice-Pres. for Admin. and Finance: WILLIAM H. FEATHERSTONE

Vice-Pres. for Student Life: Dr EARL JENKINS

Dir, Institutional Research: Dr OYEBANJO LAJUBUTU

Registrar: Dr MARGARET W. TURNER

Dir of Library: Dr MARY E. WANZA

Library of 81,742 vols, 286,929 microform titles, 705 current periodicals

Number of teachers: 238

Number of students: 3,875

Publication: *Journal of Minority Affairs* (annual).

Frostburg State University

101 Braddock Rd, Frostburg, MD 21532

Telephone: (301) 687-4000

Fax: (301) 687-4737

Internet: www.frostburg.edu

Founded 1898

Pres.: Dr JONATHAN C. GIBRALTER

Vice-Pres. for Economic Devt: STEPHEN SPAHR

Vice-Pres. for Admin. and Finance: DAVID ROSE

Provost and Vice-Pres. for Academic Affairs: Dr STEPHEN J. SIMPSON

Vice-Pres. for Student and Educational Services: Dr THOMAS L. BOWLING

Registrar: MORRIS H. WILLEY

Dir of Admissions: PATRICIA E. GREGORY

Dir of the Library: DAVID M. GILLESPIE

Library of 423,782 vols

Number of teachers: 305

Number of students: 5,295.

Salisbury University

1101 Camden Ave, Salisbury, MD 21801

Telephone: (410) 543-6000

Fax: (410) 677-5025

Internet: www.salisbury.edu

Founded 1925

Academic year: August to May

Pres.: Dr JANET DUDLEY-ESHBACH

Provost: Dr TOM JONES

Registrar: JACQUELINE M. MAISEL

Vice-Pres. of Business and Finance: GREIG MITCHELL

Vice-Pres. for Univ. Advancement: Dr ROSEMARY THOMAS

Vice-Pres. of Student Affairs: Dr ELLEN NEUFELDT

Dean of Enrollment Management: JANE DANÉ

Dean of Libraries and Instructional Resources: Dr ALICE H. BAHR

Library of 254,151 vols, 4,467 audiovisual items

Number of teachers: 494 (314 full-time, 180 part-time)

Number of students: 6,942

Publication: *Literature/Film Quarterly* (quarterly).

Towson University

8000 York Rd, Towson, MD 21252-0001

Telephone: (410) 704-2000

E-mail: admissions@towson.edu

Internet: www.towson.edu

Founded 1866

Academic year: September to May

Pres.: BOB CARET

Registrar: DAVID DECKER

Dir of Admissions: LOUISE SHULACK (acting)

Provost and Vice-Pres. for Academic Affairs: JAMES CLEMENTS

Vice-Pres. for Admin. and Finance: JAMES SHEEHAN

Vice-Pres. for Univ. Advancement: Dr GARY RUBIN

Vice-Pres. for Student Affairs: DEB MORIARTY

Univ. Librarian: DEBORAH NOLAN

Library of 573,000 vols

Number of teachers: 678

Number of students: 15,105

Publications: *Metropolitan Universities: an International Forum* (quarterly), *Tower Echoes* (annual), *Towson Journal of International Affairs*, *Transitions* (annual).

University of Baltimore

1420 North Charles St, Baltimore, MD 21201

Telephone: (410) 837-4200

E-mail: intladms@ubalt.edu

Internet: www.ubalt.edu

Founded 1925

Pres.: ROBERT L. BOGOMOLNY

Provost and Sr Vice-Pres. for Academic Affairs: WIM WIEWEL

Sr Vice-Pres. for Admin. and Finance: HARRY SCHUCKEL

Vice-Pres. for Institutional Advancement: THERESA SILANSKIS

Dir of Library: STEVE LaBASH

Library of 400,000 vols

Number of teachers: 167

Number of students: 5,000

DEANS

Robert G. Merrick School of Business: JOHN HATFIELD

School of Law: JOHN SEBENT

Yale Gordon College of Liberal Arts: CARL STENBENG

DEPARTMENT CHAIRS

Robert G. Merrick School of Business:

  Accounting: Dr KAREN FOR TIN

  Econ. and Finance: Dr SINAN CEBENOYAN

  Information and Quantitative Sciences: Dr MARILYN OBLAK

  Management: Dr SUSAN ZACUR

  Marketing: Dr R. STIFF

Yale Gordon College of Liberal Arts:

  Criminal Justice: Dr JEFFERY SENSE

  English and Communications Design: Dr STEPHEN MATANLE

  Govt and Public Admin.: Dr L. THOMAS

  History and Philosophy: Dr JEFFERY SAWYER

  Psychology: Dr BILL CLEWELL

University of Maryland, Baltimore

522 West Lombard St, Baltimore, MD 21201

Telephone: (410) 706-3100

Internet: www.umaryland.edu

Founded 1807

Pres.: Dr DAVID J. RAMSAY

Vice-Pres. for Admin. and Finance: JAMES HILL

Library of 613,407 vols

Number of students: 5,975

Schools of dentistry, law, medicine, nursing, pharmacy, social work, Univ. of Maryland Medical System, Univ. of Maryland Graduate School.

University of Maryland, Baltimore County

1000 Hilltop Circle, Baltimore, MD 21250

Telephone: (410) 455-1000

Internet: www.umbc.edu

Founded 1963

Academic year: September to May

Pres.: FREEMAN A. HRAQBOWSKI, III

Provost and Sr Vice-Pres. for Academic Affairs: ARTHUR T. JOHNSON

Vice-Pres. for Research and Dean of the Graduate School: SCOTT A. BASS

Vice-Pres. for Institutional Advancement: SHELDON K. CAPLIS

Vice-Pres. for Student Affairs: CHARLES J. FEY

Vice-Pres. for Admin. and Finance: LYNNE SCHAEFER

Gen. Counsel: DAVID GLEASON

Dean of Art, Humanities and Sciences: JOHN W. JEFFRIES

Library of 763,045 vols and 4,108 journals

Number of teachers: 835

Number of students: 10,265

Publications: *Undergraduate Catalog, Graduate Catalog* (every 2 years).

University of Maryland, College Park

College Park, MD 20742-5260

Telephone: (301) 405-1000

Internet: www.umd.edu

Founded 1856

State control

Academic year: September to May

Pres.: Dr C. D. (DAN) MOTE Jr

Provost and Sr Vice-Pres. for Academic Affairs: Dr WILLIAM W. DESTLER

Vice-Pres. for Admin. Affairs: DOUGLAS M. DUNCAN

Vice-Pres. for Student Affairs: Dr LINDA M. CLEMENT

Dean of Graduate School: Dr J. DENNIS O'CONNOR

Registrar: DAVID ROBB

Dean of Libraries: CHARLES LOWRY

Library of 2,956,648 vols

Number of students: 35,329

Colleges: Agriculture and Natural Resources; Arts and Humanities; Behavioural and Social Sciences; Computer, Mathematical and Physical Sciences; Education; Journalism; Information Studies; Life Sciences; Health and Human Performance. Schools: Architecture; Business; Eng.; Public Policy.

University of Maryland Eastern Shore

1 Backbone Rd, Princess Anne, MD 21853

Telephone: (410) 651-2200

Fax: (410) 651-6105

Internet: www.umes.edu

Founded 1886

Pres.: Dr THELMA B. THOMPSON

Vice-Pres. for Academic Affairs: Dr EMMANUEL ACQUAH

Vice-Pres. for Admin. Affairs: Dr RONNIE HOLDEN

Vice-Pres. for Student Life and Enrollment Management: Dr RONALD H. BROWN

Vice-Pres. for Planning: Dr RONALD G. FORSYTHE

Dir of Library: MARTHA C. ZIMMERMAN

Library of 161,000 vols

Number of teachers: 212

Number of students: 3,166.

University of Maryland University College

3501 University Blvd, E, Adelphi, MD 20783

Telephone: (301) 985-7000

Fax: (301) 985-7678

E-mail: umucinfo@info.umuc.edu

Internet: www.umuc.edu

Founded 1947

Pres.: Dr SUSAN C. ALDRIDGE

Provost and Chief Academic Officer: Dr LAWRENCE E. LEAK

Vice-Pres. for the Office of Planning: JAVIER MIYARES

Vice-Pres. for the Dept of Defense Relations: JOHN F. JONES, Jr

Vice-Pres. and Dir of UMUC Asia: Dr LORRAINE R. SUZUKI
Vice-Pres. and Dir of UMUC Europe: Dr ALLEN J. BERG
Vice-Pres. for Information Technology and Chief Information Officer: J. ROBERT SAPP
Vice-Pres. and Gen. Counsel: RACHEL E. ZELKIND
Vice-Pres. for Admin.: M. TERESA COOK
Vice-Pres. for Strategy and Business Devt: MARK W. CARTER
Number of teachers: 1,446 world-wide
Number of students: 71,303 world-wide

DEANS

Graduate Studies: CHRISTINA HANNAH
Undergraduate Programs: MARY ELLEN HRUTKA.

OTHER CONSTITUENT INSTITUTIONS

University of Maryland Biotechnology Institute

9600 Gudelsky Dr., Rockville, MD 20850
Telephone: (240) 314-6000
Fax: (240) 314-6255
Internet: www.umbi.umd.edu
Pres.: JENNIE C. HUNTER-CEVERA.

University of Maryland Center for Environmental Science

POB 775, Cambridge, MD 21613
Telephone: (410) 228-9250
Internet: www.ca.umces.edu
Pres.: Prof. DONALD F. BOESCH.

VILLA JULIE COLLEGE

1525 Greenspring Valley Rd, Stevenson, MD 21153-0641
Telephone: (410) 486-7001
E-mail: admissions@mail.vjc.edu
Internet: www.vjc.edu
Founded 1947
Private control
Academic year: August to May
Pres.: Dr KEVIN J. MANNING
Exec. Vice-Pres. and Chief Financial Officer: TIMOTHY M. CAMPBELL
Vice-Pres. for Academic Affairs and Dean: Dr PAUL D. LACK
Vice-Pres. for Institutional Advancement: STEVENSON W. CLOSE, Jr
Registrar: TRACY R. BOLT
Dir of Library Services: PATTI RICKERT-WILBUR

Library of 100,000 vols
Number of students: 2,410

DIRECTORS

Arts and Humanities: (vacant)
Business and Paralegal Studies: PATRICIA M. TURNBAUGH
Education and Social Sciences: Dr DEBORAH S. KRAFT
Information Technology: STEVEN R. ENGHORN
Nursing and Allied Health: Dr JUDITH A. FEUSTLE
Science and Mathematics: Dr SUSAN T. GORMAN
School of Graduate and Professional Studies (Baltimore): Dr JEAN BLOSSER

WASHINGTON BIBLE COLLEGE/ CAPITAL BIBLE SEMINARY

6511 Princess Garden Parkway, Lanham, MD 20706
Telephone: (301) 552-1400
Fax: (301) 552-2775
E-mail: admissions@bible.edu
Internet: www.bible.edu

Founded 1938 by merger of 3 Bible institutes; present name 1956
Private control
Pres.: Dr LARRY A. MERCER
Library Dir: JAMES S. STAMBAUGH
Library of 92,000 items
Number of teachers: 26
Number of students: 670.

WASHINGTON COLLEGE

300 Washington Ave, Chestertown, MD 21620-1197
Telephone: (410) 778-2800
Fax: (410) 778-7850
Internet: www.washcoll.edu
Founded 1782
Pres.: BAIRD TIPSON
Provost and Dean of the College: CHRISTOPHER AMES
Sr Vice-Pres. for Finance and Management: JAMES MANARO
Vice-Pres. for College Advancement: BETH HERMAN
Vice-Pres. for Admissions and Enrollment Management: KEVIN COVENEY
Vice-Pres. for College Relations and Marketing: MEREDITH DAVIES HADAWAY
Exec. Vice-Pres.: JOSEPH L. HOLT
Vice-Pres. for Student Affairs and Dean of Students: MELA DUTKA
Registrar: JENNIFER BERSHON
Dir of Library: RUTH SHOGE
Library of 200,000 vols
Number of teachers: 75
Number of students: 1,053.

MASSACHUSETTS

AMERICAN INTERNATIONAL COLLEGE

100 State St, Springfield, MA 01109
Telephone: (413) 737-7000
E-mail: inquiry@aic.edu
Internet: www.aic.edu
Founded 1885
Pres.: VINCENT M. MANIACI
Exec. Vice-Pres. for Admin.: RICHARD BEDARD
Vice-Pres for Institutional Advancement: JOHN T. SHORT, Dr GREGORY T. SCHMUTTE
Vice-Pres. for Admissions: PETER J. MILLER
Registrar: JUDITH SYNER
Librarian: F. KNOWLTON UTLEY
Library of 189,000 vols
Number of teachers: 84 full-time
Number of teachers: 83 part-time
Number of students: 1,350 undergraduates, 539 graduates

DEANS

Arts and Sciences: Dr VICKIE L. HESS
Business Admini.: Dr JOHN W. ROGERS
Graduate and Continuing Education: Dr ROLAND E. HOLSTEAD
Health Sciences: Dr CAROL JOBE
Psychology and Education: Dr GREGORY T. SCHMUTTE

AMHERST COLLEGE

Amherst, MA 01002-5000
Telephone: (413) 542-2000
E-mail: info@amherst.edu
Internet: www.amherst.edu
Founded 1821; chartered 1825
Academic year: September to May
Pres.: ANTHONY W. MARX
Dir of Public Affairs: STACEY SCHMEIDEL
Registrar: GERALD M. MAGER
Dean of the Faculty: GREGORY S. CALL
Dean of Students: BENSON LIEBER

Dean of Admissions: SHERRE HARRINGTON
Library of 1,000,000 vols, 12,000 videos/DVDs, 5,000 online and 2,500 print journals
Number of teachers: 177
Number of students: 1,668

Depts of American Studies, Anthropology and Sociology, Asian Languages and Civilizations, Astronomy, Biology, Black Studies, Chemistry, Classics, Econ., English, European Studies, Fine Arts, French, Geology, German, History, Law, Jurisprudence, and Social Thought, Mathematics and Computer Science, Music, Neuroscience, Philosophy, Physical Education and Athletics, Physics, Political Science, Psychology, Religion, Russian, Spanish, Theater and Dance, Women's and Gender Studies.

ANDOVER NEWTON THEOLOGICAL SCHOOL

210 Herrick Rd, Newton Centre, MA 02459
Telephone: (617) 964-1100
Fax: (617) 965-9756
E-mail: admissions@ants.edu
Internet: www.ants.edu
Private control
Academic year: September to May
Founded 1807; attached to Boston Theological Institute
Pres.: Rev. NICK CARTER
Vice-Pres. for Academic Affairs and Dean of the Faculty: WILLIAM R. HERZOG
Vice-Pres. for Institutional Advancement: PRISCILLA DECK
Vice-Pres. for Finance and Operations: ROBERT MACDONALD
Registrar: NAYDA AQUILA
Dirs: S. DIANA YOUNT, JEFFREY L. BRIGHAM
Library of 230,000 vols
Number of teachers: 91
Number of students: 480.

ANNA MARIA COLLEGE

50 Sunset Lane Paxton, MA 01612
Telephone: (800) 344-4586
E-mail: admissions@annamaria.edu
Internet: www.annamaria.edu
Founded 1946
Pres.: JACK P. CALARESO
Academic Dean: Dr CYNTHIA M. PATTERSON
Dean of Students: Dr JOSEPH FARRAGHER
Dir of Institutional Advancement: BRIDGET HAVARD
Registrar: Sister ROLLANDE QUINTAL
Library Dir: RUTH PYNE
Library of 95,000 vols
Number of teachers: 150
Number of students: 1,915

Divs of Business, Law and Public Policy, Environmental, Natural and Technological Sciences, Fine Arts, Humanities and Int. Studies, Human Devt and Human Services.

ASSUMPTION COLLEGE

500 Salisbury St, Worcester, MA 01609-1296
Telephone: (508) 767-7000
Fax: (508) 756-1780
E-mail: admiss@assumption.edu
Internet: www.assumption.edu
Founded 1904
Augustinians of the Assumption (Roman Catholic)
Academic year: September to May
Pres.: THOMAS R. PLOUGH
Vice-Pres. for Mission: Fr DENNNIS GALLAGHER
Dir of Public Affairs: NANCY MCBRIDE
Provost: ELLEN BEADLE

Dean of College: MARY LOU ANDERSON
Registrar: DAVID W. AALTO
Dir of Library Services: DAWN THISTLE
Library of 201,000 vols
Number of teachers: 260
Number of students: 2,814

Divs of Art and Music, Business Studies, Econ. and Global Studies, Education, English, Modern and Classical Languages and Cultures, History, Human Services and Rehabilitation Studies, Mathematics and Computer Science, Natural Sciences, Philosophy, Political Science, Psychology, Social and Rehabilitation Services, Sociology and Anthropology, Theology

Publication: *Assumption College Magazine* (quarterly).

ATLANTIC UNION COLLEGE

338 Main St, POB 1000, South Lancaster, MA 01561-1000

Telephone: (978) 368-2000
Fax: (978) 368-2015
E-mail: enrolment@auc.edu
Internet: enrolment@auc.edu
Founded 1882

Pres.: GEORGE BABCOCK
Sr Vice-Pres. for Academic Admin.: BORDES HENRY-SATURNE
Vice-Pres. for Finance: JAMES SEGAR
Vice-Pres. for Student Services: JOHN F. MENTGES
Vice-Pres. for Enrollment Services: WAYNE DUNBAR
Vice-Pres. for Advancement: HEBE SOARES
Registrar: ROGER BOTHWELL
Dir of Library Services: MONICA K. McCARTER

Library of 119,000 vols
Number of teachers: 53
Number of students: 623

Depts of Art, Business, Computer Science and Mathematics, Education, English, History, Music, Natural Science, Nursing, Physical Education, Religion and Theology, Social Work, Vegetarian Culinary Arts.

BABSON COLLEGE

231 Forest St, Babson Park, Wellesley, MA 02457-0310

Telephone: (781) 235-1200
Fax: (617) 239-5614
E-mail: ugradadmission@babson.edu
Internet: www.babson.edu
Founded 1919

Pres.: BRIAN M. BAREFOOT
Provost: PATRICIA GREENE
Vice-Provost: HENRY DENEAULT
Vice-Pres. for Devt: ERIC GRAAGE
Vice-Pres. for Finance: PHILIP SHAPIRO
Vice-Pres. for Admin.: MARY ROSE
Vice-Pres. for Advancement: RICHARD VOOS
Vice-Pres. for College Marketing: E. SCOTT TIMMINS
Dean of Faculty: FRITZ FLEISCHMANN
Dir of Libraries: HOPE N. TILLMAN

Library of 132,024 vols
Number of teachers: 151
Number of students: 3,342

DEANS

Babson Executive Education: ELAINE EISENMAN
Undergraduate School: DENNIS HANNO
F. W. Olin Graduate School of Business: MARK RICE

BAY PATH COLLEGE

588 Longmeadow St, Longmeadow, MA 01106

Telephone: (413) 565-1000
Fax: (413) 565-1103
E-mail: contact@baypath.edu
Internet: www.baypath.edu
Founded 1897
Private control

Pres.: Dr CAROL A. LEARY
Provost and Vice-Pres. for Academic Affairs: Dr WILLIAM SIPPLE
Vice-Pres. for Finance and Admin. Services: MICHAEL GIAMPIETRO
Vice-Pres. for Institutional Advancement: KATHY BOURQUE
Registrar: CHARLES J. BERTOLINO
Dir of Library and Information Services: MAUREEN HORAK

Library of 42,300 vols, 150 periodicals, 3,400 items of video, audio, microfilm and CD-ROM
Number of teachers: 68
Number of students: 1,200

Accounting, Biology, Biotechnology, Business Administration, Child Psychology, Communications, Criminal Justice, Early Childhood Education, Elementary Education, Forensic Psychology, Forensic Science, Interior Design, Legal Studies, Liberal Studies, Management, Marketing, Occupational Therapy, Paralegal, Psychology.

BENTLEY COLLEGE

175 Forest St, Waltham, MA 02154

Telephone: (781) 891-2000
Fax: (781) 891-2569
Internet: www.bentley.edu
Founded 1917

Pres.: GLORIA LARSON
Provost and Vice-Pres. for Academic Affairs: ROBERT D. GALLIERS
Vice-Pres. for Marketing, Communication and Enrollment: SANDRA T. KING
Vice-Pres. for Business and Finance, and Treas.: PAUL CLEMENTE
Vice-Pres. for Information Technology: TRACI A. LOGAN
Vice-Pres. for Devt, Corporate and Alumni Affairs: ROBERT H. MINETTI
Vice-Pres. for Student Affairs: KATHLEEN L. YORKIS
Library Dir: PHIL KNUTEL

Library of 192,566 vols
Number of teachers: 271 full-time
Number of students: 3,994 undergraduate, 1,256 graduate

Publication: *Business in the Contemporary World* (quarterly)

DEANS

Business and the McCallum Graduate School: MARGRETHE H. OLSON
Arts and Sciences: CATHERINE A. DAVY

BERKLEE COLLEGE OF MUSIC

1140 Boylston St, Boston, MA 02215-3695

Telephone: (617) 266-1400
Fax: (617) 536-2632
E-mail: admissions@berklee.edu
Internet: www.berklee.edu
Founded 1945 as Schillinger House of Music; present name 1973
Ind. control
Academic year: September to May

Pres.: ROGER BROWN
Sr Vice-Pres. for Institutional Advancement: DEBORAH GROZEN BIERI
Sr Vice-Pres. for Academic Affairs: LAWRENCE J. SIMPSON
Sr Vice-Pres. for Admin. and Finance and Secretary/Treasurer: DAVID R. HORNFISCHER
Vice-Pres. for Student Affairs and Dean of Students: LAWRENCE E. BETHUNE
Vice-Pres. for Cultural Diversity: MYRA HINDUS
Vice-Pres. for Finance: AMELIA KOCH
Vice-Pres. for Academic Affairs: LARRY A. MONROE
Vice-Pres. for Admin.: JOHN ELDERT
Vice-Pres. for Berklee Media: DAVID KUSEK
Vice-Pres. for External Affairs: TOM RILEY
Vice-Pres. for Information Technology: DAVID S. MASH
Vice-Pres. for Institutional Advancement: DAVID M. McKAY
Library Dir: GARY HAGGERTY

Library of 20,000 vols, 11,500 recordings, 17,000 musical scores, 6,000 lead sheets
Number of teachers: 460
Number of students: 3,800

DEANS

Music Technology Div.: STEPHEN CROES
Professional Education Div.: LAWRENCE McCLELLAN, Jr
Professional Performance Div.: MATT MARAVUGLIO
Professional Writing Div.: KARI H. JUUSELA

BLESSED JOHN XXIII NATIONAL SEMINARY

558 South Ave, Weston, MA 02493-2699

Telephone: (781) 899-5500
Fax: (781) 899-9057
E-mail: seminary@blessedjohnxxiii.edu
Internet: www.blessedjohnxxiii.edu
Founded 1964
Private control
Academic year: September to May
Roman Catholic professional and graduate theological instn

Rector and Pres.: Rev. PETER J. UGLIETTO
Academic Dean and Registrar: Rev. WILLIAM B. PALARDY
Dean of Students: Rev. THOMAS F. SCHMITT
Library Dir: Sister JACQUELINE MILLER

Library of 53,000 vols
Number of teachers: 20
Number of students: 73.

BOSTON ARCHITECTURAL CENTER

320 Newbury St, Boston, MA 02115

Telephone: (617) 262-5000
Fax: (617) 585-0121
E-mail: info@the-bac.edu
Internet: www.the-bac.edu
Founded 1889 as Boston Architectural Club; present name 1944
Private control

Pres.: Dr THEODORE LANDSMARK
Provost: EDMUND C. TOOMEY
Exec. Vice-Pres.: JAMES T. DUNN
Vice-Pres. for Finance and Admin.: KATHY ROOD
Vice-Pres. for Student Affairs: BARBARA MORGAN
Registrar: RICHARD MOYER
Library Dir: SUSAN LEWIS

Library of 27,000 vols, 40,000 slides
Number of teachers: 330
Number of students: 1,175 (797 undergraduate, 378 graduate)

Areas of study incl. Architecture, Interior Design, Landscape Architecture.

BOSTON COLLEGE

140 Commonwealth Ave, Chestnut Hill, MA 02467

Newton Campus, 885 Centre St, Newton Centre, MA 02459

Telephone: (617) 552-3100
Fax: (617) 552-0798
Internet: www.bc.edu

Founded 1863 by the Soc. of Jesus
Academic year: September to May

Pres.: Rev. WILLIAM P. LEAHY
Provost and Dean of Faculty: CUTBERTO GARZA
Exec. Vice-Pres.: P. KEATING
Vice-Pres. for Human Resources: L. SULLIVAN
Vice-Pres. for Student Affairs: C. PRESLEY
Vice-Pres. for Information Technology: M. MOORE
Financial Vice-Pres. and Treasurer: PETER C. MCKENZIE
Vice-Pres. for Facilities Management: T. DEVINE
Dir of Libraries: JEROME YAVARKOVSKY

Library of 1,981,254 vols
Number of teachers: 939
Number of students: 14,297

Publications: *Boston College Law Review* (5 a year), *Boston College Environmental Affairs Law Review* (quarterly), *Boston College International and Comparative Law Review* (2 a year), *Philosophy and Social Criticism* (6 a year), *Boston College Third World Law Journal* (2 a year), *Uniform Commercial Code Reporter-Digest* (quarterly), *Religion and the Arts* (quarterly), *Études Phénoménologiques* (2 a year), *Lonergan Workshop Journal* (annual), *Method: Journal of Lonergan Studies* (2 a year), *Proceedings of the Boston Area Colloquium in Ancient Philosophy* (annual)

DEANS

College of Arts and Sciences: PATRICK MANEY
Graduate School of Arts and Sciences: PATRICK MANEY
School of Management: ANDREW C. BOYNTON
School of Education: JOSEPH O'KEEFE
School of Nursing: BARBARA HAZARD
Law School: JOHN H. GARVEY
Graduate School of Social Work: ALBERTO GODENZI
College of Advancing Studies: ALBERTO GODENZI

PROFESSORS

College of Arts and Sciences (140 Commonwealth Ave, Chestnut Hill, MA 02467; tel. (617) 552-3270; fax (617) 552-1383):

ANDERSON, J., Econ.
ANNUNZIATO, A., Biology
ARNOTT, R., Econ.
ASH, A., Mathematics
BAGLIVO, J., Mathematics
BANUAZIZI, A., Psychology
BARTH, J. R., English
BEDELL, K., Physics
BELSLEY, D., Econ.
BERGER, P., Fine Arts
BERNAUER, J. W., Philosophy
BLAKE, R., Fine Arts
BLANCHETTE, O., Philosophy
BODENHEIMER, R., English
BOMBOLAKIS, E. G., Geology and Geophysics
BROIDO, D. A., Physics
BROWN, S., Theology
BROWNELL, H., Psychology
BRUCKNER, M. T., Romance Languages
BRUELL, C., Political Science
BUCKLEY, M., Theology
BUNIE, A., History
BURGESS, D., Biology
BYRNE, P. H., Philosophy

CAHILL, L., Theology
CARPENTER, D. E., Romance Languages
CLARKE, M. J., Chemistry
CLEARY, J. J., Philosophy
CLOONEY, F. X., Theology
CLOTE, P., Biology
COBB-STEVENS, R., Philosophy
COX, D., Econ.
CRANE, M., English
CRONIN, J., History
DAVIDOVITS, P., Chemistry
DERBER, C., Sociology
DI BARTOLO, B., Physics
DIETRICH, D., Theology
EASTON, R., Psychology
EBEL, J. E., Geology and Geophysics
EGAN, H., Theology
EYKMAN, C., German Studies
FAULKNER, R. K., Political Science
FLANAGAN, J. F., Philosophy
FLEMING, R., History
FOURKAS, J. T., Chemistry
FRIEDBERG, S., Mathematics
GARCIA, J., Philosophy
GOIZUETA, R., Theology
GOLLOP, F. M., Econ.
GOTTSCHALK, P., Econ.
GRAY, P., Psychology
GROOME, T. H., Theology
GUILLEMIN, J., Sociology
HACHEY, T. E., History
HAFNER, D. L., Political Science
HASKIN, D., English
HEINEMAN, J., History
HEPBURN, J. C., Geology and Geophysics
HERBECK, D., Communications
HESSE-BIBER, S., Sociology
HIBBS, T., Philosophy
HIMES, M., Theology
HOFFMAN, C., Biology
HOLLENBACH, D., Theology
HOLMSTROM, L. L., Sociology
HOVEYDA, A. H., Chemistry
IRELAND, P., Econ.
KANTROWITZ, E. R., Chemistry
KARP, D. A., Sociology
KEARNEY, R., Philosophy
KELLY, C. J., Political Science
KELLY, T. R., Chemistry
KEMPA, K., Physics
KENNEDY, T. F., Music
KENNEY, M., Mathematics
KIRSCHNER, D. A., Biology
KRAUS, M., Econ.
KREEFT, P. J., Philosophy
LAMB, M., Theology
LANDY, M., Political Science
LEE, T. O., Music
LEWBEL, A., Econ.
LEWIS, P., English
LIEM, R., Psychology
LOWRY, R., Sociology
LYDENBERG, R., English
MADIGAN, A., Philosophy
MANNING, R., History
MARIANI, P., English
MATELSKI, M., Communications
MATSON, S., English
McFADDEN, D. L., Chemistry
McLAUGHLIN, L. W., Chemistry
MEISSNER, W., Theology
MELNICK, R. S., Political Science
MEYERHOFF, G. R., Mathematics
MICHALCZYK, J., Fine Arts
MILLER, S. J., Chemistry
MUNNELL, A. H., Finance
MUSKAVITCH, M., Biology
NAUGHTON, M., Physics
NETZER, N., Fine Arts
NORTHRUP, D., History
NUMAN, M., Psychology
PARIS, J. J., Theology
PERKINS, P., Theology
PFOHL, S. J., Sociology
PHILIPPIDES, D. M. L., Classics
QUINN, J., Econ.

RASMUSSEN, D. M., Philosophy
REEDER, M., Mathematics
REINERMAN, A. J., History
RESLER, M., German Studies
RESTUCCIA, F., English
RICHARDSON, A., English
RICHARDSON, W. J., Philosophy
RINTALA, M., Political Science
ROBERTS, M. F., Chemistry
ROSS, R. S., Political Science
ROY, D. C., Geology and Geophysics
RUSSELL, J. A., Psychology
SARDELLA, D. J., Chemistry
SCHERVISH, P. G., Sociology
SCHIANTARELLI, F., Econ.
SCHLOZMAN, K. L., Political Science
SCHOR, J., Sociology
SCHRADER, R., English
SCOTT, L. T., Chemistry
SCOTT-JONES, D., Psychology
SEGAL, U., Econ.
SEYFRIED, T., Biology
SHELL, S., Political Science
SHOLL, M. J., Psychology
SMITH, J. H., Mathematics
SMYER, M., Psychology
SNAPPER, M. L., Chemistry
TAMINIAUX, J., Philosophy
TAYLOR, D., English
THIE, P. R., Mathematics
VALETTE, R. M., Romance Languages
VAUGHAN, D., Sociology
WEILER, P., History
WILLIAMSON, J. B., Sociology
WILSON, C. P., English
WILT, J., English
WINNER, E., Psychology
WOLFE, A., Political Science
WOLFF, L., History

School of Management (140 Commonwealth Ave, Chestnut Hill, MA 02467; tel. (617) 552-8420; fax (617) 552-2593):

BARTUNEK, J., Organization Studies
CAMPANELLA, F. B., Finance
CLOTE, P., Computer Science
CRONIN, M., Operations and Strategic Management
FERSON, W. E., Finance
GIPS, J., Computer Science
GRAVES, S., Operations and Strategic Management
HOLDERNESS, C. G., Finance
KANE, E. J., Finance
MARCUS, A., Finance
NIELSEN, R., Organization Studies
O'BRIEN, C., Business Law
PARKER, F. J., Business Law
RAELIN, J., Operations and Strategic Management
RINGUEST, J., Operations and Strategic Management
RITZMAN, L., Operations and Strategic Management
SAFIZADEH, M. H., Operations and Strategic Management
STRAUBING, H., Computer Science
TAGGART, R., Finance
TEHRANIAN, H., Finance
TORBERT, W. R., Organization Studies
TWOMEY, D. P., Business Law
WADDOCK, S., Operations and Strategic Management
WILSON, G. P., Accounting
WOODSIDE, A., Marketing
WRIGHT, A., Accounting

School of Education (140 Commonwealth Ave, Chestnut Hill, MA 02467; tel. (617) 552-4200; fax (617) 552-0812):

AIRASIAN, P. W.
ALTBACH, P. G.
BLUSTEIN, D.
BRABECK, M. M.
BRISK, M. E.
CASEY, M. B.
COCHRAN-SMITH, M.

DACEY, J. S.
DUDLEY-MARLING, C.
HANEY, W. M.
HARGREAVES, A.
HAUSER-CRAM, P.
HELMS, J. E.
LADD, G. T.
LERNER, J. V.
LYKES, M. B.
MADAUS, G. F.
MULLIS, I. V. S.
PINE, G. J.
PULLIN, D. C.
SHIRLEY, D. L.
STARRATT, R. J.
TWOMEY, E.
WALSH, M. E.
YOUN, E. I. K.

School of Nursing (140 Commonwealth Ave,
Chestnut Hill, MA 02467; tel. (617) 552-4250;
fax (617) 552-0745):

BURGESS, A. W.
DUFFY, M. E.
FRY, S. T.
HAWKINS, J. W.
JONES, D. A.
MUNRO, B. H.
ROY, Sr, C.
VESSEY, J. A.
WARDLE, M. G.

Law School (885 Centre Street, Newton
Center, MA 02459; tel. (617) 552-4340; fax
(617) 552-2851):

AULT, H. J.
BARON, C. H.
BLOOM, R. M.
BRODIN, M. S.
BROWN, G. D.
COQUILLETTE, D. R.
CUNNINGHAM, L.
FITZGIBBON, S. T.
GOLDFARB, P.
HILLINGER, I. M.
HOWE, R.-A. W.
KATZ, S. N.
KOHLER, T. C.
McMORROW, J. A.
PLATER, Z. J..B.
REPETTI, J. R.
ROGERS, J. S.
SOIFER, A.
SPIEGEL, M.
WELLS, C.
WIRTH, D. A.
YEN, A. C.-C.

School of Social Work (140 Commonwealth
Ave, Chestnut Hill, MA 02467; tel. (617) 552-
4020; fax (617) 552-2374):

BLYTHE, B.
GODENZI, A.
IATRIDIS, D. S.
KAYSER, K.
MALUCCIO, A. N.

BOSTON CONSERVATORY

8 The Fenway, Boston, MA 02215
Telephone: (617) 536-6340
Fax: (617) 912-9101
E-mail: admissions@bostonconservatory.edu
Internet: www.bostonconservatory.edu
Founded 1867
Private control
Academic year: September to May
Pres.: RICHARD ORTNER
Dean of the Conservatory: MICHAEL NASH
Vice-Pres. for Admin. Services and Dean of
Students: CARMEN GRIGGS
Registrar: GREGORY KARAS
Library Dir: JENNIFER HUNT

Library of 40,000 vols
Number of teachers: 160
Number of students: 500

DIRECTORS
Dance Div.: YASUKO TOKUNAGA
Liberal Arts Dept: JUDSON EVANS
Music Div.: KARL PAULNACK
Theater Div.: NEIL DONOHOE

BOSTON UNIVERSITY

1 Sherborn St, Boston, MA 02215
Telephone: (617) 353-2000
Fax: (617) 353-2053
Internet: www.bu.edu
Founded 1839, chartered 1869
Private control
Academic year: September to May (2 seme-
sters), June to August (summer session)
Pres.: ROBERT A. BROWN
Provost: DAVID K. CAMPBELL
Exec. Vice-Pres.: JOSEPH P. MERCURIO
Vice-Pres. for Admin. Services: PETER FIE-
DLER
Vice-Pres. for Auxiliary Services: PETER
CUSATO
Vice-Pres. for Financial Affairs: KENNETH
CONDON
Vice-Pres. for Govt and Community Affairs:
EDWARD KING
Vice-Pres. for Operations: GARY NICKSA
Registrar: FLORENCE BERGERON
Dir of Library: ROBERT HUDSON
Library: see Libraries
Number of teachers: 3,130
Number of students: 29,544
Publications: *Journal of Education, Boston
University Law Review, Arion, Journal of
Field Archaeology*

DEANS
College of General Studies: LINDA WELLS
College of Communication: TOBE BERKOVITZ
College of Eng.: KENNETH LUTCHEN
College of Arts and Sciences: JEFFREY HEN-
DERSON
Graduate School: JEFFREY HENDERSON
Sargent College of Health and Rehabilitation
Sciences: GLORIA S. WATERS
College of Fine Arts: WALT MEISSNER
School of Education: CHARLES GLENN
School of Dental Medicine: SPENCER FRANKL
School of Law: MAUREEN O'ROURKE
School of Management: LOUIS LATAIF
School of Medicine: JOHN McCAHAN
School of Social Work: GAIL STEKETEE
School of Theology: RAY HART
School of Hospitality Admin.: JAMES STAMAS
School of Public Health: ROBERT MEENAN

BRANDEIS UNIVERSITY

415 South St, Waltham, MA 02454-9110
Telephone: (781) 736-2000
Fax: (781) 736-8699
E-mail: sendinfo@brandeis.edu
Internet: www.brandeis.edu
Founded 1948
Academic year: September to May
Pres.: Dr JEHUDA REINHARZ
Provost and Sr Vice-Pres. for Academic
Affairs: MARTY WYNEGARDEN KRAUSS
Exec. Vice-Pres. and Chief Operating Officer:
PETER FRENCH
Sr Vice-Pres. for Devt and Alumni Relations:
NANCY K. WINSHIP
Vice-Pres. for Students and Enrollments:
JEAN EDDY
Vice-Pres. for Research: MARIA PELLEGRINI
Vice-Pres. and Vice-Provost for Libraries and
Information Technology: PERRY HANSON
Library of 1,000,000 vols, 880,000 micro-
forms, 385,000 US docs, 16,000 periodicals
Number of teachers: 499 (355 full-time, 144
part-time)

Number of students: 5,313 (3,304 undergraduate, 2,009 postgraduate)

DEANS
School of Arts and Sciences: Dr ADAM JAFFE
Florence Heller School for Social Policy and
Management: Prof. STUART ALTMAN
Int. Business School: Prof. F. TRENERY DOL-
BEAR, JR
Raab School of Summer, Special and Con-
tinuing Studies: SYBIL SMITH

BRIDGEWATER STATE COLLEGE

131 Summer St, Bridgewater, MA 02325
Telephone: (508) 531-1000
Fax: (508) 697-1707
Internet: www.bridgew.edu
Founded 1840
Pres.: Dr DANA MOHLER-FARIA
Provost and Vice-Pres. for Academic Affairs:
NANCY KLENIEWSKI
Dir of Libraries: MICHAEL A. SOMMERS
Library of 352,500 vols
Number of teachers: 259
Number of students: 8,400

DEANS
School of Arts and Sciences: Dr HOWARD B.
LONDON
School of Business: CATHERINE MORGAN
School of Education and Allied Studies: Dr
ANNA BRADFIELD
School of Graduate Studies: Dr WILLIAM S.
SMITH (acting)

CAMBRIDGE COLLEGE

1000 Massachusetts Ave, Cambridge, MA
02138-5304
Telephone: (617) 868-1000
Fax: (617) 349-3561
E-mail: admit@cambridgecollege.edu
Internet: www.cambridgecollege.edu
Founded 1971
Private control
Academic year: September to August
Founder and Chancellor: EILEEN M. BROWN
Pres.: MAHESH C. SHARMA
Exec. Vice-Pres.: Dr EZAT PARNIA
Vice-Pres. for Academic Affairs: Dr JOSEPH C.
REED
Vice-Pres. for Finance, Admin. and Student
Services: JENNIFER TONNESON
Vice-Pres. for College Affairs: Dr JOSEPH
DAISY
Number of teachers: 718
Number of students: 8,300

DEANS OF GRADUATE STUDIES
School of Education: Dr ANTHONY DeMATTEO
School of Management: Dr EZAT PARNIA
Counselling Psychology: Dr NITI SETH

BRANCH CAMPUSES
Chesapeake Campus: Suite 300, 1403
Greenbrier Parkway, Chesapeake, VA
23320; tel. (757) 424-0333; fax (757) 424-
1140; e-mail chesapeake@cambridgecollege
.edu; Dir JIM WALDMAN.
Springfield Campus: 570 Cottage St,
Springfield, MA 01104; tel. (413) 747-0204;
fax (413) 747-0613; e-mail springfield@
cambridgecollege.edu; Dir PATRICIA CRUTCH-
FIELD.
Lawrence Campus: Lawrence Center, 60
Island St, Lawrence, MA 01840-1835; tel.
(978) 738-0502; fax (978) 738-9655; e-mail
lawrence@cambridgecollege.edu; Dir
DOLORES C. CALAF.
Puerto Rico Center: Suite 1400, Hato Rey
Center Building, 268 Ponce de Leon Ave, San

Juan, PR 00918; tel. (787) 296-1101; e-mail puertorico@cambridgecollege.edu.

Cambridge College Georgia: Suite 1000, Lamar Bldg, 753 Broad St, Augusta, GA 30901; tel. (706) 821-3965; fax (706) 821-3793; Dir SHARLOTTE EVANS.

Cambridge College California: Suite 100, 337 North Vineyard Ave, Ontario, CA 91764; tel. (909) 635-0250; fax (909) 635-0253; Dir GREGORY WHITE.

CLARK UNIVERSITY

950 Main St, Worcester, MA 01610-1477
Telephone: (508) 793-7711
E-mail: admissions@clarku.edu
Internet: www.clarku.edu
Founded 1887
Academic year: September to May
Pres.: JOHN E. BASSETT
Provost and Vice-Pres. for Academic Affairs: DAVID ANGEL
Exec. Vice-Pres.: JAMES E. COLLINS
Vice-Pres. for Govt and Community Affairs: JOHN FOLEY
Vice-Pres. for Univ. Advancement: C. ANDREW MCGADNEY
Vice-Pres. for Planning and Budget: ANDREA MICHAELS
Assoc. Provost and Dean of College: WALTER WRIGHT
Dean of Admissions: HAROLD WINGOOD
Dean of Graduate Studies and Research: NANCY BUDWIG
Registrar: JANE RENO
Librarian: GWENDOLYNE ARTHUR

Library of 584,350 vols
Number of teachers: 172 full-time
Number of students: 2,115

Publications: *Clark University News, Economic Geography, Idealistic Studies*.

COLLEGE OF THE HOLY CROSS

1 College St, Worcester, MA 01610
Telephone: (508) 793-2011
Fax: (508) 793-3030
Internet: www.holycross.edu
Founded 1843
Pres.: Rev. MICHAEL MCFARLAND
Sr Vice-Pres.: FRANK VELLACCIO
Vice-Pres. for Academic Affairs and Dean of the College: TIMOTHY R. AUSTIN
Vice-Pres. for Student Affairs and Dean of Students: JACQUELINE D. PETERSON
Vice-Pres. for Devt and Alumni Relations: PAUL E. SHEFF
Dir of Library Services: JAMES E. HOGAN

Library of 550,000 vols
Number of teachers: 239
Number of students: 2,790

Depts of African Studies, American Sign Language/Deaf Studies, Asian Studies, Biochemistry, Biological Psychology, Biology, Chemistry, Chinese, Classics, Econ. and Accounting, Education, Eng., English, Environmental Studies, French, German, Gerontology Studies, Graduate Studies, History, Italian, Latin American and Latino Studies, Mathematics and Computer Science, Medieval and Renaissance Studies, Modern Languages and Literatures, Music, Naval Science (NROTC), Peace and Conflict Studies, Philosophy, Physics, Political Science, Prebusiness, Prelaw, Premedical and Predental Studies, Psychology, Religious Studies, Russian, Russian and Eastern European Studies, Science Coordinator, Sociology and Anthropology, Spanish, Studies in World Literature, Theatre, Visual Arts, Women's and Gender Studies.

CURRY COLLEGE

1071 Blue Hill Ave, Milton, MA 02186
Telephone: (617) 333-0500
Fax: (617) 333-6860
E-mail: curryadm@curry.edu
Internet: www.curry.edu
Founded 1879 as School of Elocution and Expression; present name 1943
Private control
Academic year: September to May
Pres.: Dr KENNETH K. QUIGLEY, Jr
Vice-Pres. of Academic Affairs: SUSAN W. PENNINI
Dean of Academic Affairs: LISA IJIRI
Registrar: SALLY A. BUCKLEY
Library Dir: JANE LAWLESS

Number of teachers: 76
Number of students: 3,880

Depts of Applied Technology Communication, Education, Fine and Applied Arts, Humanities, Interdisciplinary Studies, Management, Natural Sciences and Mathematics, Nursing, Politics and History, Psychology, Sociology and Criminal Justice.

EASTERN NAZARENE COLLEGE

23 East Elm Ave, Quincy, MA 02170
Telephone: (617) 745-3000
Fax: (617) 745-3910
E-mail: admissions@enc.edu
Internet: www.enc.edu
Founded 1900
Pres.: Dr CORLIS MCGEE
Vice-Pres. for Academic Affairs: Dr NANCY ROSS
Vice-Pres. for Enrollment: JEFFREY A. WELLS
Vice-Pres. for Student Devt: VERNON WESLEY
Registrar: MEREDITH BAKER
Dir of Library Services: SUSAN WATKINS

Library of 126,465 vols
Number of teachers: 52
Number of students: 1,260

Depts of Biology, Business, Chemistry, Communication Arts, Computer Sciences, Criminal Justice, Education, Eng., English, Environmental Science, General Studies, Govt, Health Sciences, History, Int. Studies, Liberal Arts, Mathematics, Movement Arts, Music, Philosophy, Physics, Prelaw, Premedical, Prenursing, Prephysical Therapy, Psychology, Religion, Social Work, Sociology.

ELMS COLLEGE

291 Springfield St, Chicopee, MA 01013-2839
Telephone: (413) 594-2761
Fax: (413) 592-4871
Internet: www.elms.edu
Founded 1928
Liberal arts college
Pres.: Dr JAMES H. MULLEN, Jr
Vice-Pres. for Academic Affairs: Dr WALTER C. BREAU
Vice-Pres. for Finance and Admin.: BRIAN DOHERTY
Vice-Pres. for Institutional Advancement: MARYANNE ROONEY
Vice-Pres. for Student Affairs: DAWN M. ELLINWOOD
Registrar: LAURA LANDER
Dir of Library: PATRICIA BOMBARDIES

Library of 103,000 vols, 684 periodicals
Number of teachers: 68
Number of students: 1,191

Divs of Business and Law, Education, Health Sciences, Humanities and Fine Arts, Natural Sciences and Mathematics, Social Sciences.

EMERSON COLLEGE

120 Boylston St, Boston, MA 02116-4624
Telephone: (617) 824-8500
Internet: www.emerson.edu
Founded 1880
Pres.: Dr JACQUELINE W. LIEBERGOTT (acting)
Vice-Pres. for Admin. and Finance: DAVID A. ELLIS
Vice-Pres. for Information Technology: WILLIAM GILLIGAN
Vice-Pres. for Academic Affairs: LINDA MOORE
Vice-Pres. for Public Affairs: DAVID ROSEN
Vice-Pres. and General Counsel: CHRISTINE HUGHES
Vice-Pres. for Institutional Advancement: DONALD C. MAIN
Registrar: WILLIAM F. DEWOLF
Dir of Library: ROBERT FLEMING

Library of 125,000 vols
Number of teachers: 225
Number of students: 3,900

Publications: *Emerson Review* (2 a year), *Omnivore* (2 a year), *Berkeley Beacon* (2 a week)

DEANS

School of Arts: GRAFTON NUNES
School of Communication: JANIS ANDERSEN
Graduate Studies: DONNA SCHROTH (Dir)
Institute for Liberal Arts and Interdisciplinary Studies: DAVID BOGEN (Dir)
Professional Studies and Spec. Programs: HANK W. ZAPPALA (Dir)

EMMANUEL COLLEGE

400 The Fenway, Boston, MA 02115
Telephone: (617) 735-9715
Fax: (617) 735-9801
E-mail: enroll@emmanuel.edu
Internet: www.emmanuel.edu
Founded 1919
Pres.: Sister JANET EISNER
Vice-Pres. for Finance and Admin.: NEIL BUCKLEY
Vice-Pres. for Programs and Partnerships in Education: SALLY DIAS
Vice-Pres. for Govt and Community Relations: SARAH WELSH
Vice-Pres. for Operations and Information Technology: JOHN AVERSA
Vice-Pres. for Devt and Alumnae Relations: Sister ANNE DONOVAN (acting)
Vice-Pres. of Student Affairs: PATRICIA RISSMEYER
Library Dir: Dr SUSAN VON DAUM THOLL (acting)

Library of 134,000 vols
Number of teachers: 80
Number of students: 1,800

Depts of American Studies, Art, Biology, Chemistry and Physics, Econ., Education, English, Environmental Science, Foreign Languages, Global Studies, Graduate Studies, History, Individualized Major, Information Technology, Management, Mathematics, Nursing, Performance Arts, Philosophy, Physics, Political Science, Psychology, Religious Studies, Sociology, Women's Studies

DEANS

Arts and Sciences: Dr NANCY NORTHRUP

EPISCOPAL DIVINITY SCHOOL

99 Brattle St, Cambridge, MA 02138
Telephone: (617) 868-3450
Fax: (617) 864-5385
E-mail: admissions@eds.edu
Internet: www.eds.edu
Private control
Academic year: September to May

Pres. and Dean: Rt Rev. STEVEN CHARLESTON
Academic Dean: SHERYL KUJAWA-HOLBROOK
Registrar: LISA HOWELL
Library Dir: ESTHER A. GRISWOLD

Library of 232,000 vols
Number of teachers: 22
Number of students: 68 (full-time)

Master of Divinity, MA in Theological Studies, Doctor of Ministry, Certificates in Theological Studies.

FITCHBURG STATE COLLEGE

160 Pearl St, Fitchburg, MA 01420-2697
Telephone: (978) 345-2151
Fax: (978) 665-3693
E-mail: mriccards@fsc.edu
Internet: www.fsc.edu
Founded 1894
Academic year: September to June
Pres.: Dr ROBERT V. ANTONUCCI
Vice-Pres. for Academic Affairs: Dr MICHAEL FIORENTINO, JR
Vice-Pres. for Finance and Admin.: SHEILA SYKES
Library Dir: ROBERT FOLEY

Library of 229,000 vols, 478,000 microforms, 1,000 periodicals
Number of teachers: 171
Number of students: 7,000

Depts of Behavioral Sciences, Biology/Chemistry, Business Admin., Communications Media, Computer Science, Education, English/Speech/Theater, Exercise and Sport Science, Geo/Physical Sciences, Industrial Technology, Interdisciplinary Studies/Humanities/Music, Mathematics, Nursing, Social Science

DEANS

Education: ELAINE E. FRANCIS
Graduate and Continuing Education: CATHERINE CANNEY

FRAMINGHAM STATE COLLEGE

100 State St, Framingham, MA 01701-9101
Telephone: (508) 620-1220
Fax: (508) 626-4592
E-mail: fscfeedback@frc.mass.edu
Internet: www.framingham.edu
Founded 1839
Pres.: Dr TIMOTHY J. FLANAGAN
Vice-Pres. for Academic Affairs: Dr ROBERT A. MARTIN
Vice-Pres. for Admin. and Finance: JOHN J. HORRIGAN
Dean of Students: SUSANNE H. CONLEY
Librarian: BONNIE MITCHELL (acting)

Library of 344,185 vols
Number of teachers: 290
Number of students: 6,093

Depts of Art and Music, Biology, Chemistry and Food Science, Communication Arts, Computer Science, Consumer Sciences, Econ. and Business Admin., Education, English, Geography, Govt, History, Mathematics, Modern Languages, Nursing, Physics and Earth Science, Psychology and Philosophy, Sociology.

GORDON COLLEGE

255 Grapevine Rd, Wenham, MA 01984
Telephone: (978) 927-2300
Fax: (978) 524-3704
E-mail: info@gordon.edu
Internet: www.gordon.edu
Founded 1889; merged with Barrington College, RI, 1985
Pres.: R. JUDSON CARLBERG
Provost: MARK L. SARGENT

Sr Vice-Pres. for Finance and Admin.: JAMES R. MACDONALD
Vice-Pres. for Advancement, Communications and Technology: DAN TYMANN
Vice-Pres. for Devt: ROBERT GRINNELL
Vice-Pres. for Enrollment: SILVIO VAZQUEZ
Dean of Students: BARRY J. LOY
Registrar: CAROL HERRICK
Dir of Library Services: MYRON SCHIRER-SUTER

Library of 190,000 vols
Number of teachers: 75
Number of students: 1,375

Divs of Fine Arts, Education, Humanities, Natural Sciences, Mathematics and Computer Science, Social and Behavioral Sciences.

GORDON-CONWELL THEOLOGICAL SEMINARY

130 Essex St, South Hamilton, MA 01982
Telephone: (978) 646-4300
Fax: (978) 468-6691
E-mail: info@gcts.edu
Internet: www.gordonconwell.edu
Founded 1969 following merger of Conwell School of Theology (f. 1884) and Gordon Divinity School (f. 1889)
Private control
Academic year: September to May
Pres.: Dr HADDON W. GORDON-CONWELL
Exec. Vice-Pres.: ROBERT S. LANDREBE
Academic Dean: BARRY H. COREY
Dean of Enrollment Management and Registrar: WILLIAM B. LEVIN
Dean of Students: LISE SCHLUETER
Head Librarian: FREEMAN BARTON

Library of 250,000 vols
Number of teachers: 48
Number of students: 986.

BRANCH CAMPUSES

Center for Urban Ministerial Education, Boston Campus: 90 Warren St, Roxbury, MA 02119; tel. (617) 427-7293; fax (617) 541-3432; e-mail cumeinfo@gcts.edu; Dean Dr ALVIN PADILLA.

Charlotte Campus: 14542 Choate Circle, Charlotte, NC 28273-5596; tel. (704) 527-9909; fax (704) 527-8577; e-mail charinfo@gcts.edu; Dean Dr SIDNEY L. BRADLEY.

HAMPSHIRE COLLEGE

893 West St, Amherst, MA 01002
Telephone: (413) 549-5471
Fax: (413) 582-5584
E-mail: admissions@hampshire.edu
Internet: www.hampshire.edu
Founded 1965
Private control
Pres.: RALPH J. HEXTER
Vice-Pres. and Dean of Faculty: AARON BERMAN
Vice-Pres. for Finance and Admin.: JOHAN BRONGERS
Dean of Student Services: R. MICHELLE GREEN
Dir of Admissions: KAREN S. PARKER
Librarian: GAI CARPENTER

Library of 111,000 vols
Number of teachers: 100
Number of students: 1,100

DEANS

Interdisciplinary Arts: WILLIAM BRAYTON
Cognitive Science: NEIL STILLINGS
Humanities, Arts and Cultural Studies: SUSAN TRACY
Natural Science: CHARLENE D'AVANZO
Social Science: BARBARA YNGVESSON

HARVARD UNIVERSITY

Cambridge, MA 02138
Telephone: (617) 495-1000
Internet: www.harvard.edu
Founded 1636; charter signed 1650
Academic year: September to June
Pres.: DREW GILPIN FAUST
Provost: STEPHEN E. HYMAN FAUST
Vice-Pres. for Administration: SALLY ZECKHAUSER
Vice-Pres. for Alumni Affairs and Development: ROBERT CASHION (acting)
Vice-Pres. for Finance: ELIZABETH MORA
Vice-Pres. and General Counsel: ROBERT IULIANO (acting)
Vice-Pres. for Government, Community and Public Affairs: ALAN STONE
Vice-Pres. for Human Resources: MARILYN HAUSAMMANN
Vice-Pres. for Policy: A. CLAYTON SPENCER
Dir of Univ. Library: SIDNEY VERBA

Number of teachers: 11,022 (1,997 non-medical, 9,025 medical)
Number of students: 19,638

DEANS

Faculty of Arts and Sciences: MICHAEL D. SMITH
Graduate School of Arts: THEDA SKOCPOL
Harvard Business School: JAY O. LIGHT
Harvard College: BENEDICT H. GROSS
Continuing Education and Univ. Extension: MICHAEL SHINAGEL
Faculty of Medicine: JOSEPH B. MARTIN
Harvard School of Dental Medicine: R. BRUCE DONOFF
Graduate School of Design: ALAN ALTSHULER
Harvard Divinity School: WILLIAM A. GRAHAM
Harvard Graduate School of Education: KATHLEEN MCCARTNEY
Division of Engineering and Applied Sciences: VENKATESH NARAYANAMURTI
Kennedy School of Government: DAVID T. ELLWOOD
Harvard Law School: ELENA KAGAN
Harvard School of Public Health: BARRY R. BLOOM
Radcliffe Institute for Advanced Study: BARBARA J. GROSZ

PROFESSORS

Divinity School (Office of Admissions and Financial Aid, Room 214, 14 Divinity Ave, Cambridge, MA 02138; tel. (617) 495-5796; e-mail admissions@hds.harvard.edu; internet www.hds.harvard.edu):

AHMED, L., Women's Studies in Religion
BOVON, F., New Testament
COAKLEY, S., Theology
COX, H. G., Theology
CURRASCO, D., Religion, America and Anthropology
DYCK, A., Ethics
ECK, D., Comparative Religion
FIORENZA, F. S., Roman Catholic Theological Studies
GOMES, P. J., Christian Morals
GRAHAM, W., Middle Eastern Studies
GYATSO, J., Comparative Religion
HALL, D. D., American Religious History
HANSON, P. D., Hebrew Bible/Old Testament
KING, K. L., New Testament Studies and Gnosticism
LEVENSON, J. D., Jewish Studies
ORSI, R., History of Religion
SCHÜSSLER FIORENZA, E., New Testament and Ministerial Studies
SULLIVAN, L., History of Religion
THIEMANN, R. F., Theology

Faculty of Arts and Sciences (University Hall, Cambridge, MA 02138; tel. (617) 495-1566; internet www.fas.harvard.edu):

ABERNATHY, F. H., Mechanical Engineering
ALESINA, A., Economics and Government
ALEXIOU, M., Modern Greek Studies, Comparative Literature
ALT, J. E., Government
ANDERSON, D., Applied Mathematics
ANDERSON, J. G., Atmospheric Chemistry
ASHTON, P. S., Forestry
AZIZ, M., Materials Science
BAR-YOSEF, O., Prehistoric Archaeology
BARANCZAK, S., Polish Language and Literature
BATES, R. H., Government
BAZZAZ, F. A., Biology
BENHABIB, S., Government
BENSON, L. D., English Literature
BERCOVITCH, S., English and American Literature and Language, Comparative Literature
BERG, H. C., Molecular and Cellular Biology, Physics
BIAGIOLI, M., History of Science
BIEWENER, A., Biology
BISSON, T. N., Medieval History
BLACKBOURN, D., History
BLIER, S., History of Art and Architecture
BLOXHAM, J., Geophysics
BOBO, L., Sociology and Afro-American Studies
BOIS, Y.-A., Modern Art
BOL, P., Chinese History
BOLITHO, H., Japanese History
BOSS, K. J., Biology
BOSSERT, W. H., Science
BOTT, R., Mathematics
BOYM, S., Slavic Languages and Literatures, Comparative Literature
BRANDT, A., History of Science
BRANTON, D., Biology
BRINKMANN, R., Music
BROCKETT, R. W., Electrical Engineering and Computer Science
BRYSON, W., History of Art and Architecture
BUELL, L., English
BURGARD, P., German
BUTLER, J. N., Applied Chemistry
CAMERON, A., Astrophysics
CAMPBELL, J. Y., Applied Economics
CARAMAZZA, A., Psychology
CATON, S., Contemporary Arab Studies
CAVANAGH, P., Psychology
CAVANAUGH, C., Biology
CAVES, R. E., Political Economy
CHAMBERLAIN, G., Economics
CHANDRA, P., Indian and South Asian Art
CHEATHAM, T. E., Computer Science
COATSWORTH, J., Latin American Affairs
COELHO, J.-F., Portuguese Language and Literature, Comparative Literature
COHEN, L., History
COLEMAN, K., Latin
COLEMAN, S. R., Science
COLTON, T., Government and Russian Studies
CONLEY, T., Romance Languages and Literature
COOPER, R., International Economics
COREY, E. J., Organic Chemistry
COTT, N. F., History
CRAIG, A. M., History
CRANSTON, E. A., Japanese Literature
CROMPTON, A. W., Natural History
CUTLER, D., Economics
DAMROSCH, L., Literature
DAVIDOVSKY, M., Music
DAWSON, M., Government
DEMPSTER, A. P., Theoretical Statistics
DeVORE, B. I., Biological Anthropology
DOMINGUEZ, J. I., International Affairs
DONOGHUE, D., English and American Literature and Language
DONOGHUE, M., Biology
DOWLING, J., Natural Sciences
DUFFY, J., Byzantine Philology and Literature

DZIEWONSKI, A. M., Science
ECK, D. L., Comparative Religion and Indian Studies
ECKERT, C., Korean History
EHRENREICH, H., Science
EKSTROM, G., Geology and Geophysics
ELKIES, N., Mathematics
ELLISON, P., Anthropology
ENGELL, J., English and Comparative Literature
EPPS, B., Romance Languages and Literature
ERIKSON, R. L., Cellular and Developmental Biology
EVANS, A., Materials Engineering
EVANS, D. A., Chemistry
FANGER, D. L., Literature
FARRELL, B., Meteorology
FASH, W., Central American and Mexican Archaeology and Ethnology
FELDMAN, G., Science
FELDSTEIN, M. S., Economics
FERNANDEZ-CIFUENTE, L., Romance Languages and Literatures
FIDO, F., Romance Languages and Literatures
FIELD, G. B., Applied Astronomy
FISHER, D., Physics
FISHER, P. J., English and American Literatures
FLEMING, D. H., American History
FLIER, M., Ukrainian Philology
FORD, P., Celtic Languages and Literatures
FRANKLIN, M., Physics
FREEMAN, R. B., Economics
FRIEDEN, J., Government
FRIEDMAN, B. M., Political Economy
FRIEND, C., Chemistry
FUDENBERG, D., Economics
GABRIELSE, G., Physics
GALISON, P., History of Science and of Physics
GARBER, M., English
GATES, H., Humanities
GAYLORD, M., Romance Languages and Literatures
GELBART, W. M., Molecular and Cellular Biology
GEORGI, H. M., Physics
GIENAPP, W., History
GILBERT, D., Psychology
GILBERT, W.
GLASHOW, S. L., Physics
GLAUBER, R. J., Physics
GOLDFARB, W., Modern Mathematics and Mathematical Logic
GOLDIN, C., Economics
GOLOVCHENKO, J., Physics
GORDON, A., History
GORDON, R. G., Chemistry
GRABOWICZ, G. G., Ukrainian Literature
GRAHAM, W. A., History of Religion and Islamic Studies
GREEN, J. R., Political Economy
GREENBLATT, S., English and American Literature and Language
GRILICHES, Z., Economics
GRINDLAY, J. E., Astronomy
GROSS, B. H., Mathematics
GROSZ, B., Computer Science
GUIDOTTI, G., Biochemistry
GUILLORY, J., English
GUTHKE, K. S., German Art and Culture
GUZZETTI, A. F., Visual Arts
HACKMAN, J., Social and Organizational Psychology
HALL, P., Government
HALPERIN, B. I., Mathematics and Natural Philosophy
HANKINS, J., History
HARDACRE, H., Japanese Religions and Society
HARRINGTON, A., History of Science
HARRINGTON, J. J., Environmental Engineering
HARRIS, J. C., English and Folklore

HARRIS, J. D., Mathematics
HARRIS, J. M., Jewish Studies
HARRISON, S. C., Biochemistry and Molecular Biology
HART, O., Economics
HARTL, D., Biology
HASTINGS, J., Natural Sciences
HEIMERT, A. E., American Literature
HEINRICHS, W. P., Arabic
HELLER, E., Physics
HELPMAN, E., Economics
HENRICHS, A. M., Greek Literature
HERSCHBACH, D. R., Science
HERZFELD, M., Anthropology
HIGGINBOTHAM, E. B., Afro-American Studies, History
HIGONNET, P. L.-R., French History
HO, Y. C., Engineering and Applied Mathematics
HOFFMAN, P., Geology
HOFFMANN, S. H.
HOLLAND, H. D., Geology
HOLM, R. H., Chemistry
HOOLEY, J., Psychology
HOROWITZ, P., Physics
HOWE, R., Engineering
HUEHNERGARD, J. D., Semitic Philology
HUNTINGTON, S. P.
HUTCHINSON, J. W., Applied Mechanics
HUTH, J., Physics
IRIYE, A., American History
JACOB, D., Atmospheric Chemistry, Environmental Engineering
JACOBSEN, E., Chemistry
JACOBSEN, S. B., Geochemistry
JAFFE, A. M., Mathematics and Theoretical Science
JARDINE, A., Romance Languages and Literatures
JASANOFF, J., Linguistics
JENKINS, F., Zoology and Biology
JOHNSON, B., Law and Psychiatry in Society
JONES, C. P., Classics and History
JONES, R. V., Applied Physics
JORGENSON, D. W., Economics
KAFADAR, C., Turkish Studies
KAGAN, J., Psychology
KAISER, W. J., English and Comparative Literature
KALAVREZOU, I., Byzantine Art
KATZ, L., Economics
KAZHDAN, D., Mathematics
KEENAN, E. L., History
KELLY, T., Music
KELMAN, H. C., Social Ethics
KIELY, R. J., English
KILLIP, C., Visual and Environmental Studies
KILSON, M. L., Government
KING, G., Government
KIRBY, W., History
KIRSHNER, R. P., Astronomy
KISHLANSKY, M., History
KLECKNER, N., Biochemistry and Molecular Biology
KLEINMAN, A. M., Medical Anthropology
KLEMPERER, W. A., Chemistry
KNOLL, A., Biology
KNOWLES, J. R., Chemistry
KOERNER, J., History of Art and Architecture
KORNAI, J., Economics
KORSGAARD, C., Philosophy
KOSSLYN, S. M., Psychology
KRONAUER, R. E., Mechanical Engineering
KRONHEIMER, P., Mathematics
KUGEL, J. L., Classical and Modern Jewish and Hebrew Literature and Comparative Literature
KUHN, P. A., History and East Asian Languages and Civilizations
KUNG, H., Electrical Engineering and Computer Science
KUNO, S., Linguistics
LAIOU, A. E., Byzantine History

LAMBERG-KARLOVSKY, C. C., Archaeology and Ethnology
LANGER, E. J., Psychology
LEE, L., Chinese Literature
LEVIN, R., Music
LEVINE, N., History of Art and Architecture
LEWALSKI, B., History and Literature, English Literature
LEWIN, D. B., Music
LEWIS, H. R., Computer Science
LEWONTIN, R. C., Biology
LIEBER, C., Chemistry
LIEBERSON, S., Sociology
LIEM, K., Ichthyology
LOCKWOOD, L. H., Music
LOEB, A., Astronomy
LOSICK, R. M., Biology
MacFARQUHAR, R., History and Political Science
MACHINIST, P., Hebrew and Other Oriental Languages
MAHER, B. A., Psychology of Personality
MAIER, C. S., European Studies
MALMSTAD, J., Slavic Languages and Literatures
MANIATIS, T. P., Molecular and Cellular Biology
MANKIW, N. G., Economics
MANSFIELD, H. C., Government
MARGLIN, S. A., Economics
MARSDEN, P. V., Sociology
MARTIN, L., Government
MARTIN, P. C., Pure and Applied Physics
MASKIN, E. S., Economics
MAY, E. R., American History
MAYBURY-LEWIS, D. H., Anthropology
MAZUR, B., Mathematics
MAZUR, E., Physics
McCANN, D., Korean Literature
McCARTHY, J. J., Biological Oceanography
McCORMICK, M., History
McDONALD, C., Romance Languages and Literatures
McELROY, M. B., Environmental Studies
McMAHON, A., Molecular and Cellular Biology
McMAHON, T. A., Applied Mechanics and Biology
McMULLEN, C., Mathematics
McNALLY, R., Personality Psychology
MEDOFF, J. L., Labour and Industry
MEISTER, M., Molecular and Cellular Biology
MELTON, D. A., Molecular and Cellular Biology
MENDELSOHN, E. I., History of Science
MESELSON, M. S., Natural Sciences
MITCHELL, R., Applied Biology
MITCHELL, S. A., Scandinavian and Folklore
MITTEN, D. G., Classical Art and Archaeology
MORALEJO, S., Fine Arts
MORAN, R., Philosophy
MORRIS, C., Statistics
MOTTAHEDEH, R., History
MURDOCH, J. E., History of Science
MYERS, A., Chemistry and Chemical Biology
NAGY, G. J., Classical Greek Literature and Comparative Literature
NAKAYAMA, K., Psychology
NARAYAN, R., Astronomy
NECIPOGLU, G., Islamic Art
NELSON, D. R., Physics
NOZICK, R., Philosophy
O'CATHASAIGH, T., Irish Studies
O'CONNELL, R. J., Geophysics
OETTINGER, A., Applied Mathematics, Information Resources Policy
OWEN, E., Middle East History
OWEN, S.
OZMENT, S. E., Ancient and Modern History
PALUMBI, S., Biology

PARK, K., History of Science, Women's Studies
PARSONS, C., Philosophy
PATTERSON, O., Sociology
PAUL, W., Applied Physics
PEARSALL, D. A., English Literature
PEDERSON, S., History
PERALTA, E., Molecular Neurobiology
PERKINS, D. H., Political Economy
PERRY, E., Government
PERSHAN, P. S., Applied Physics
PERTILE, L., Romance Languages and Literature, Comparative Literature
PETERSON, P., Government
PFISTER, D. H., Systematic Botany
PHARR, S. J., Japanese Politics
PIERCE, N., Biology
PIERSON, P., Government
PILBEAM, D. R., Social Sciences
PINNEY, G., Classical Archaeology and Art
PRENTISS, M., Physics
PRESS, W. H., Astronomy, Physics
PUTNAM, H. W.
PUTNAM, R. D., Political Science
RABIN, M. O., Computer Science
RANDS, B., Music
RENTSCHLER, E., German
RESKIN, B., Sociology
RICE, J. R., Engineering Sciences and Geophysics
ROBERTSON, E., Molecular and Cellular Biology
ROBINSON, A. R., Geophysical Fluid Dynamics
ROGERS, P. P., Environmental Engineering
ROSEN, S., National Security and Military Affairs
ROSENTHAL, R., Social Psychology
RUBIN, D. B., Statistics
RUBIN, J., Japanese Humanities
RUDENSTINE, N., English and American Literature and Language
RUSSELL, J., Armenian Studies
RUVOLO, M., Anthropology
RYAN, J. L., German and Comparative Literature
SACKS, G. E., Mathematical Logic
SACKS, P., English and American Literature and Language
SANDEL, M. J., Government
SCANLON, T., Natural Religion, Moral Philosophy and Civil Policy
SCARRY, E., Aesthetics and the General Theory of Value
SCHACTER, D., Psychology
SCHMID, W., Mathematics
SCHOR, N., Romance Languages and Literature
SCHREIBER, S. L., Chemistry
SEGAL, C., Classics
SEN, A., Economics, Philosophy
SEPTIMUS, B., Jewish History and Sephardic Civilization
SHAKHNOVICH, E., Chemistry and Chemical Biology
SHAPIRO, I. I.
SHEARMAN, J.
SHELEMAY, K., Music
SHELL, M., English and Comparative Literature
SHEPSLE, K., Government
SHIEBER, S., Computer Science
SHLEIFER, A., Economics
SILVERA, I. F., Natural Sciences
SIMON, E., Germanic Languages and Literature
SIU, Y. T., Mathematics
SKJAERVO, P., Iranian
SKOCPOL, T. R., Government, Sociology
SOLBRIG, O. T., Biology
SOLLORS, W., English Literature, Afro-American Studies
SOMMER, D., Romance Languages and Literatures
SØRENSEN, A. B., Sociology
SPAEPEN, F. A., Applied Sciences

STAGER, L., Archaeology of Israel
STEINKELLER, P., Assyriology
STERNBERG, S. Z., Mathematics
STEVENS, P. F., Biology
STILGOE, J. R., History of Landscape
STONE, H. A., Applied Mathematics, Chemical Engineering
STONE, P. J., Psychology
STROMINGER, J. L., Biochemistry
SULEIMAN, S. R., Civilization of France, Comparative Literature
SZPORLUK, R., Ukrainian History
TAI, H., Sino-Vietnamese History
TAMBIAH, S. J., Anthropology
TARRANT, R. J., Latin Language and Literature
TATAR, M. M., German
TAUBES, C. H., Mathematics
TAYLOR, R. L., Mathematics
THERNSTROM, S., History
THOMAS, R., Greek and Latin
THOMPSON, D., Political Philosophy
TINKHAM, M., Physics
TODD, W. M., Slavic Languages and Literatures, Comparative Literature
TOMLINSON, P. B., Biology
TROMP, J., Geophysics
TU, W.-M., Chinese History and Philosophy
TUCK, R., Government
ULRICH, L., Early American History
VAFA, C., Physics
VAIL, H., History
VALIANT, L. G., Computer Science and Applied Mathematics
VAN DER KUIJP, L., Tibetan and Himalayan Studies
VAN DER MERWE, N. J., Scientific Archaeology
VENDLER, H.
VERBA, S.
VERDINE, G., Bio- and Organic Chemistry
VOGEL, E. F., Social Sciences
WANG, J. C., Biochemistry and Molecular Biology
WARREN, K., Anthropology
WATERS, M., Sociology
WATKINS, C. W., Linguistics and Classics
WATSON, J., Chinese Society
WEITZMAN, M., Economics
WESTERVELT, R., Physics
WHITE, S. H., Psychology
WHITESIDES, G. M., Chemistry
WILLIAMSON, J. G., Economics
WILSON, R., Physics
WINSHIP, C., Sociology
WINTER, I. J., Fine Arts
WISSE, R., Yiddish Literature and Comparative Literature
WITZEL, E., Sanskrit
WOFSEY, S., Atmospheric and Environmental Studies
WOLFF, C., Music
WOMACK, J., Latin American History and Economics
WOOLLACOTT, R. M., Biology
WRANGHAM, R., Anthropology
WU, T. T., Applied Physics
YALMAN, N. O., Social Anthropology and Middle Eastern Studies
YANG, W., Electrical Engineering and Computer Science
YAU, S., Mathematics
ZIOLKOWSKI, J., Medieval Latin and Comparative Literature

Graduate School of Design (Office of Admissions, 419 Gund Hall, 48 Quincy St, Cambridge, MA 02138; tel. (617) 495-5453; e-mail admissions@gsd.harvard.edu; internet www.gsd.harvard.edu):

ALTSHULER, A., Urban Policy and Planning
BAIRD, G., Architecture
FORMAN, R. T. T., Landscape Ecology
GOMEZ-IBAÑEZ, J. A., Urban Planning and Public Policy

HARGREAVES, G., Landscape Architecture
HAYS, M., Architectural Theory
KOOLHAAS, R., Architecture and Urban Design
KRIEGER, A., Urban Design
MACHADO, R., Architecture and Urban Design
MONEO, J. R., Architecture
MORI, T., Architecture
PEISER, R., Real Estate Development
POLLALIS, S. N., Design Technology and Management
ROWE, P. G., Architecture and Urban Design
SCHODEK, D. L., Architectural Technology
SILVETTI, J. S., Architecture
SMITH, C., Architectural History
STEINITZ, C. F., Landscape Architecture and Planning
STILGOE, J. R., History of Landscape Development
VAN VALKENBURGH, M., Landscape Architecture
VIGIER, F. C., Regional Planning

Law School (1563 Massachusetts Avenue, Cambridge, MA 02138; tel. (617) 495-3100; e-mail jdadmiss@law.harvard.edu; internet www.law.harvard.edu):

ALFORD, W.
ANDREWS, W. D.
BARTHOLET, E., Public Interest
BEBCHUK, L. A., Law, Economics, Finance
BELLOW, G.
BREWER, S.
CHARNY, D.
CLARK, R. C.
DERSHOWITZ, A. M.
DESAN, C.
DONAHUE, C.
EDLEY, C. F.
ELHAUGE, E.
FALLON, R. H.
FIELD, M.
FISHER, W.
FRUG, G. E.
GLENDON, M. A.
GUINIER, L.
HALPERIN, D. I.
HANSON, J.
HAY, B. L.
HERWITZ, D. R.
HEYMANN, P. B.
HORWITZ, M. J., Legal History
JACKSON, H.
KAPLOW, L.
KAUFMAN, A. L.
KENNEDY, D. M.
KENNEDY, D. W., General Jurisprudence
KENNEDY, R. L.
KRAAKMAN, R. H.
LESSIG, L.
MANSFIELD, J. H.
MARTIN, H. S.
MELTZER, D. J.
MICHELMAN, F. I.
MILLER, A. R.
MINOW, M.
MNOOKIN, R.
NESSON, C. R.
OGLETREE, C., Jr
PARKER, R. D.
RAKOFF, T. D., Administrative Law
RAMSEYER, M.
ROSENBERG, M. D.
SANDER, F. E. A.
SARGENTICH, L. D.
SCOTT, H. S., International Financial Systems
SHAPIRO, D. L.
SHAVELL, S. M., Law and Economics
SINGER, J. W.
SLAUGHTER, A.-M.
STEIHER, C.
STEINER, H. J.
STONE, A. A., Law and Psychiatry

TRIBE, L. H., Constitutional Law
UNGER, R. M.
VAGTS, D. F., International Law
VISCUSI, W. K.
VORENBERG, J.
WARREN, A. C.
WARREN, E.
WEILER, J. H. H.
WEILER, P. C.
WEINREB, L. L.
WESTFALL, D.
WHITE, L.
WILKINS, D. B.
WOLFMAN, B.

Medical School (Office of the Committee on Admissions, 25 Shattuck St, Boston, MA 02115; tel. (617) 432-1550; e-mail admissions_office@hms.harvard.edu; internet www.hms.harvard.edu):

ABBAS, A. K., Pathology
ABBOTT, W. M., Surgery
ADAMS, D. F., Radiology
ADELSTEIN, S. J., Medical Biophysics
AISENBERG, A. C., Medicine
AKINS, C. W., Surgery
ALBERT, M. S., Psychiatry
ALI, H. H., Anaesthesia
ALONSO, A. W., Psychiatry
ALPER, C., Paediatrics
ALT, F. W., Genetics
ANDERSON, E., Comparative Anatomy
APPLEBURY, M. L., Ophthalmology
ARKY, R., Medicine
ARNAOUT, M. A., Medicine
ARNDT, K. A., Dermatology
ATHANASOULIS, C. A., Radiology
AUSIELLO, D. A., Medicine
AUSTEN, K. F., Medicine
AUSTEN, W. G., Surgery
AUSUBEL, F., Genetics
AVRUCH, J., Medicine
BACH, F., Surgery
BADEN, H., Dermatology
BAIM, D., Medicine
BALDESSARINI, R. J., Psychiatry
BARBIERI, R., Obstetrics, Gynaecology and Reproductive Biology
BARLOW, C. F., Neurology
BARNETT, G. O., Medicine
BARSAMIAN, E. M., Surgery
BARSKY, A. J., III, Psychiatry
BEAL, M. F., Neurology
BEAN, B. P., Neurobiology
BEARDSLEE, W., Psychiatry
BECKWITH, J. R., Microbiology and Molecular Genetics
BELFER, M. L., Psychiatry
BENACERRAF, B. R., Obstetrics, Gynaecology and Reproductive Biology
BENDER, W. W., Biological Chemistry, Molecular Pharmacology
BENES, F. M., Psychiatry
BENJAMIN, T. L., Pathology
BERKOWITZ, R. S., Obstetrics, Gynaecology and Reproductive Biology
BERNFIELD, M., Paediatrics
BERSON, E. L., Ophthalmology
BIEDERMAN, J., Psychiatry
BIGGERS, J., Cell Biology
BIRD, E. D., Neuropathology
BISTRIAN, B. R., Medicine
BLACK, P. M., Neurosurgery
BLENIS, J., Cell Biology
BLOCH, K. J., Medicine
BONVENTRE, J. V., Medicine
BORUS, J. F., Psychiatry
BRADY, T., Radiology
BRANDT, A. M., History of Medicine
BRAUNWALD, E., Medicine
BREAKEFIELD, X. O., Neurology
BRENNAN, T., Medicine
BRENNER, B., Medicine
BRENNER, M. B., Medicine
BREWSTER, D., Surgery
BROTMAN, A. W., Psychiatry

BROWN, E. M., Medicine
BRUGGE, J. S., Cell Biology
BUCHANAN, J. R., Medicine
BUCKLEY, M. J., Surgery
BUNN, H. F., Medicine
BURAKOFF, S. J., Paediatrics
BURGESON, R. E., Dermatology
BURROWS, P. E., Radiology
CANELLOS, G. P., Medicine
CANTLEY, L. C., Medicine
CANTOR, H. I., Pathology
CAPLAN, D. N., Neurology
CAREY, M. C., Medicine
CARPENTER, C. B., Medicine
CASSEM, E. H., Psychiatry
CAVINESS, V. S., Jr, Child Neurology and Mental Retardation
CEPKO, C. L., Genetics
CHABNER, B., Medicine
CHEN, L. B., Pathology
CHIN, W. W., Medicine
CHRISTIANI, D. C., Medicine
CHURCH, G. H., Genetics
CHYLACK, L. T., Jr, Ophthalmology
CLAPHAM, D. E., Neurobiology
CLEARY, P. D., Medical Sociology
CLEVELAND, R. H., Radiology
CLOUSE, R., Medicine
COEN, D. M., Biological Chemistry, Molecular Pharmacology
COHEN, B. M., Psychiatry
COHEN, J. B., Neurobiology
COHN, L. H., Surgery
COLDITZ, G. A., Medicine
COLE, J. O., Psychiatry
COLEMAN, C. N., Radiation Oncology
COLES, R., Psychiatry and Medical Humanities
COLLIER, R. J., Microbiology and Molecular Genetics
COLLINS, J. J., Surgery
COLLINS, P., Pathology
COLODNY, A. H., Surgery
COLVIN, R. B., Pathology
COMPTON, C. C., Pathology
COOPER, G. M., Pathology
COREY, D. P., Neurobiology
CORSON, J. M., Pathology
COSIMI, A. B., Surgery
COTRAN, R., Pathology
COYLE, J. T., Psychiatry
CRONE, R., Anaesthesia
CROWLEY, W. F., Jr, Medicine
CRUM, C. P., Pathology
CRUMPACKER, C., Medicine
DAGGETT, W. M., Surgery
D'AMORE, P. A., Ophthalmology
DATTA, S., Anaesthesiology
DAVID, J. R., Medicine
DAVIDOVITCH, Z., Orthodontics
DAVIS, K. R., Radiology
DAWSON, D. M., Neurology
DELBANCO, T., Medicine
DEMLING, R. H., Surgery
DESANCTIS, R. W., Medicine
DESROSIERS, R. C., Microbiology, Molecular Genetics
DEUEL, T. F., Medicine
DEWOLF, W. C., Surgery
DIAMANDOPOULOS, G. T., Pathology
DOGON, I. L., Operative Dentistry
DONAHOE, P. K., Surgery
DONOFF, R. B., Oral and Maxillofacial Surgery
DORF, M. E., Pathology
DORSEY, J. L., Medicine
DORWART, R., Psychiatry
DOUGLASS, C. W., Dental Care Administration
DOWLING, J. E., Ophthalmology
DRAZEN, J. M., Medicine
DRETLER, S. P., Surgery
DRYJA, T. P., Jr, Ophthalmology
DVORAK, A. M., Pathology
DVORAK, H. F., Pathology
DZAU, V. J., Medicine

EARLS, F. J., III, Child Psychiatry
EBERLEIN, T. J., Surgery
EDELMAN, R., Radiology
EISENSTEIN, B., Medicine
EPSTEIN, A., Medicine
EPSTEIN, F., Medicine
ERIKSSON, E., Surgery
EZEKOWITZ, R. A. B., Paediatrics
FEDERMAN, D. D., Medicine and Medical Education
FEIN, R., Medical Economics
FINBERG, R. W., Medicine
FINK, M., Surgery
FISCHBACH, G. D., Neurobiology
FISHMAN, M. C., Medicine
FLEISHER, G. R., Paediatrics
FLETCHER, C., Pathology
FLETCHER, R., Ambulatory Care and Prevention
FLETCHER, S., Ambulatory Care and Prevention
FLIER, J. S., Medicine
FOLKMAN, M. J., Paediatric Surgery
FOSTER, C. S., Ophthalmology
FOX, I. H., Medicine
FRAENKEL, D. G., Microbiology
FRANK, R., Health Economics in Health Care Policy
FREI, E., III, Medicine
FRIED, M. P., Otology and Laryngology
FRIEDMAN, E., Ophthalmology
FRIGOLETTO, F. D., Jr, Obstetrics and Gynaecology
FURIE, B., Medicine
FURSHPAN, E. J., Neurobiology
GALABURDA, A., Neurology and Neuroscience
GALLI, J. J., Pathology
GARNICK, M. B., Medicine
GEHA, R. S., Paediatrics
GELBER, R. D., Paediatrics
GELMAN, S., Anaesthesia
GIMBRONE, M. A., Pathology
GIPSON, I. K., Ophthalmology
GLICKMAN, R. M., Medicine
GLIMCHER, L. H., Medicine
GLIMCHER, M. J., Orthopaedic Surgery
GOETINCK, P. F., Dermatology
GOITEIN, M., Radiation Therapy
GOLDBERG, A. L., Cell Biology
GOLDBERG, I. H., Pharmacology
GOLDHABER, P., Periodontology
GOLDMAN, H., Pathology
GOLDMAN, P., Biological Chemistry and Molecular Pharmacology
GOLDMANN, D. A., Paediatrics
GOLDSTEIN, D. P., Obstetrics, Gynaecology and Reproduction
GOLDWYN, R. M., Surgery
GOOD, B. J., Medical Anthropology
GOOD, M. J. D., Social Medicine
GOODENOUGH, D. A., Anatomy and Cell Biology
GOODMAN, H. M., Genetics
GOYAL, R. K., Medicine
GRAGOUDAS, E., Ophthalmology
GREEN, H., Cell Biology
GREENBERG, M. E., Neurology, Neuroscience
GREENBERG, R. M., Psychiatry
GREENE, R. E., Radiology
GREENES, R. A., Radiology
GRIFFIN, J., Medicine
GRILLO, H. C., Surgery
GRISCOM, N. T., Radiology
GROOPMAN, J. E., Medicine
GROWDON, J. H., Neurology
GRUNEBAM, H. U., Psychiatry
GUNDERSON, J. G., Psychiatry
GUREWICH, V., Medicine
GUSELLA, J. F., Genetics
GUTHEIL, T. G., Psychiatry
HABENER, J. F., Medicine
HABER, E., Medicine
HALES, C. A., Medicine
HALL, F. M., Radiology

HALL, J. E., Orthopaedic Surgery
HANDIN, R. I., Medicine
HARLOW, E. E., Genetics
HARRIS, J. R., Radiation Oncology
HARRIS, N. L., Pathology
HARRIS, W. H., Orthopaedic Surgery
HARRISON, S. C., Biological Chemistry and Molecular Biology
HAUSER, S. T., Psychiatry
HAVENS, L. L., Psychiatry
HAY, D. I., Oral Biology
HAY, E. D., Embryology
HAYES, W. C., Biomechanics
HAYNES, H. A., Dermatology
HEALY, G. B., Otolaryngology
HECHTMAN, H. B., Surgery
HEDLEY-WHITE, E. T., Pathology
HEDLEY-WHITE, J., Anaesthesia and Respiratory Therapy
HEMLER, M., Pathology
HENDREN, W. H., III, Paediatric Surgery
HENNEKENS, C. H., Ambulatory Care and Prevention
HERNDON, J. H., Orthopaedic Surgery
HERZOG, D. B., Psychiatry
HIATT, H. H., Medicine
HICKEY, P. R., Anaesthesia
HIROSE, T., Ophthalmology
HIRSCH, M. S., Medicine
HOBSON, J. A., Psychiatry
HOGLE, J. M., Biological Chemistry and Molecular Pharmacology
HOLLENBERG, N. K., Radiology
HOLMES, G. L., Neurology
HOLMES, L. B., Paediatrics
HORTON, J. E., Medicine
HOWLEY, P. M., Comparative Pathology
HUBEL, D. H., Neurophysiology
HUNT, R. D., Comparative Pathology
IEZZONI, L. I., Medicine
INGWALL, J. S., Medicine
INUI, T. S., Ambulatory Care and Prevention
ISSELBACHER, K. J., Medicine
IZUMO, S., Medicine
JACOBSON, A. M., Psychiatry
JAIN, R. K., Radiation Oncology
JAKOBIEC, F. A., Ophthalmology
JANDL, J. H., Medicine
JELLINCK, M. S., Paediatrics
JENIKE, M. A., Psychiatry
JOHNSON-POWELL, G., Child Psychiatry
JOLESZ, F. A., Radiology
JONAS, R., Surgery
JONES, H. R., Neurobiology
JOSEPHSON, M., Medicine
KABAN, L. B., Oral and Maxillofacial Surgery
KAHN, C. R., Medicine
KARCHMER, A. W., Medicine
KARNOVSKY, M. J., Pathological Anatomy
KASPER, D. L., Medicine
KASSER, J. R., Orthopaedic Surgery
KAUFMAN, D. S., Medicine
KAZEMI, H., Medicine
KESSLER, R., Health Care Policy
KHANTZIAN, E., Psychiatry
KHURI, S. F., Surgery
KIEFF, E. D., Medicine
KINET, J. P., Pathology
KING, G. L.
KINGSTON, R., Genetics
KIRSCHNER, M. W., Medicine and Cell Biology
KISSIN, I., Anaesthesia
KITZ, R. J., Research and Teaching in Anaesthetics and Anaesthesia
KLAGSBRUN, M., Surgery
KLEINMAN, A. M., Medical Anthropology
KLIBANSKI, A., Medicine
KNIPE, D. M., Microbiology and Molecular Genetics
KOLODNER, R. D., Biological Chemistry and Molecular Pharmacology
KOLTER, R. G., Microbiology and Molecular Genetics

KOMAROFF, A. L., Medicine
KOSIK, K. S., Neurology
KRANE, S. M., Clinical Medicine
KRAVITZ, E. A., Neurobiology
KRESSEL, H. Y., Radiology
KRIS, A., Psychiatry
KRONENBERG, H. M., Medicine
KUFE, D. W., Medicine
KUNKEL, L. M., Genetics
KUPPER, T., Dermatology
LAING, F. C.
LAMONT, J. T., Medicine
LARSEN, P. R., Medicine
LEBOWITZ, R. L., Radiology
LEDER, P., Genetics
LEFFERT, R. D., Orthopaedic Surgery
LESSELL, S., Ophthalmology
LETVIN, N., Medicine
LEVITON, A., Neurology
LEVITSKY, S., Surgery
LI, F. P., Medicine
LIANG, M., Medicine
LIBBY, P., Medicine
LIBERMAN, M. C., Physiology
LIN, E. C. C., Microbiology and Molecular Genetics
LIPSITT, D. R., Psychiatry
LIVINGSTON, D. M., Medicine
LIVINGSTONE, M. S., Neurobiology
LOCK, J. E., Paediatrics
LOEFFLER, J. S., Radiation Oncology
LOGERFO, F. W., Surgery
LOVEJOY, F. H. Jr, Paediatrics
LOWENSTEIN, E., Anaesthesia
LUX, S. E., IV, Paediatrics
MACK, J. E., Psychiatry
MANKIN, H. J., Orthopaedic Surgery
MANNICK, J. A., Surgery
MANSCHRECK, T. C., Psychiatry
MARGOLIES, M. N., Surgery
MARTIN, J. B., Neurology
MARTYN, J. A. J., Anaesthesia
MASLAND, R. H., Neuroscience
MATTHYSSE, S., Psychiatry
MAY, J., Surgery
MAYER, J. E., Jr, Surgery
MAYER, R. J., Medicine
McCARLEY, R. W., Psychiatry
McCORMICK, M. C., Paediatrics
McDOUGAL, W. S., Surgery
McINTOSH, K., Paediatrics
McKEON, F. D., Cell Biology
McLOUD, T. C., Radiology
McNEIL, B. J., Health Care Policy
MEKALANOS, J. J., Microbiology and Molecular Genetics
MELLO, N. K., Psychology
MENDELSON, J. H., Psychiatry
MEYER, J. E., Radiology
MIHM, M. C., Jr, Dermatopathology
MILLER, K. W., Anaesthesiology
MIRIN, S. M., Psychiatry
MISHLER, E. G., Social Psychology
MITCHISON, T. J., Cell Biology
MODELL, A. H., Psychiatry
MOELLERING, R. C. Jr, Medical Research
MONACO, A. P., Surgery
MONGAN, J., Health Care Policy
MONTGOMERY, W. W., Otolaryngology
MONTMINY, M., Cell Biology
MOORE, G. T., Ambulatory Care and Prevention
MORGAN, J. P., Medicine
MORRIS, C. N., Health Care Policy
MORSE, W. H., Psychobiology
MORTON, C. C., Obstetrics and Gynaecology
MOSKOWITZ, M. A., Neurology
MULLIGAN, R., Genetics
MURPHY, J. M., Psychiatry
NADELSON, C., Psychiatry
NADLER, L. M., Medicine
NADOL, J. B. Jr, Otolaryngology
NATHAN, D. G., Paediatrics
NEEDLEMAN, H. L., Paediatric Dentistry
NEER, E. J., Medicine
NESSON, H. R., Medicine

NEUTRA, M. R., Paediatrics
NEWBURGER, J. W., Paediatrics
NEWHOUSE, J. P., Health Care Policy
NOTMAN, M. T., Psychiatry
NOVELLINE, R. A., Radiology
OJEMANN, R. G., Surgery
OLSEN, B. R., Anatomy
ORKIN, S. H., Paediatrics
PALFREY, J. S., Paediatrics
PARRISH, J. A., Dermatology
PAUL, D. L., Neurobiology
PENNEY, J. B., Jr, Neurology
PEPPERCORN, M. A., Medicine
PERRIMON, N., Genetics
PFEFFER, M. A., Medicine
PIER, G. B., Pathology
PINKUS, G. S., Pathology
PIZZO, P., Paediatrics
PLATT, O., Paediatrics
PLOEGH, H. L., Pathology
PODOLSKY, D. K., Medicine
POSS, R., Orthopaedic Surgery
POTTER, D. D., Neurobiology
POTTS, J. T., Jr, Clinical Medicine
POUSSAINT, A. F., Psychiatry
RABKIN, M. T., Medicine
RANDO, R. R., Biological Chemistry and
    Molecular Pharmacology
RAO, A., Pathology
RAPOPORT, T. A., Cell Biology
RAVIOLA, E., Neurobiology
REICH, P., Psychiatry
REID, L., Pathology
REINHERZ, E. L., Medicine
REMOLD, H. G., Medicine
REPPERT, S. M., Paediatrics
RETIK, A. B., Surgery
RICHARDSON, C. C., Biological Chemistry
    and Molecular Pharmacology
RICHIE, J. P., Surgery
RIORDAN, J. F., Biochemistry
RITZ, J., Medicine
ROBERTS, T. M., Pathology
ROBINSON, D. R., Medicine
ROSEN, F. S., Paediatrics
ROSEN, S. S., Pathology
ROSENBERG, R. D., Medicine
ROSENBLATT, M., Molecular Medicine
ROSENTHAL, D. I., Radiology
ROSENTHAL, D. S., Medicine
ROSNER, B. A., Medicine
ROTHENBERG, A., Psychiatry
RUDERMAN, J. V., Anatomy and Cell Biol-
    ogy
RUSSELL, P. S., Surgery
RUVKUN, G. B., Genetics
SACHS, B. P., Obstetrics, Gynaecology and
    Reproductive Medicine
SACHS, D. H., Surgery
SAITO, H., Biological Chemistry and Mole-
    cular Pharmacology
SALLAN, S. E., Paediatrics
SALZMAN, C., Psychiatry
SAMUELS, M. A., Neurology
SAPER, C. B., Neurology
SCHIFF, I., Gynaecology
SCHILDKRAUT, J. J., Psychiatry
SCHLOLLSMAN, S. F., Medicine
SCHNEEBERGER, E. E., Pathology
SCHNIPPER, L. E., Medicine
SCHOEN, F. J., Pathology
SCHUR, P. H., Medicine
SCOTT, R. M., Surgery
SEED, B., Genetics
SEIDMAN, C. E., Medicine
SEIDMAN, J. G., Genetics
SELKOE, D. J., Neurology
SELMAN, R. L., Psychology
SELTZER, S. E., Radiology
SELWYN, A., Medicine
SERHAN, C. N., Anaesthesia
SHANNON, D. C., Paediatrics
SHEFFER, A. L., Medicine
SHIPLEY, W. U., Radiation Therapy
SHKLAR, G., Oral Pathology
SHORE, M. F., Psychiatry

SIDMAN, R. L., Neuropathology
SILBERT, J. E., Medicine
SILEN, W., Surgery
SILVER, P. A., Biological Chemistry and
    Molecular Pharmacology
SIMEONE, J. F., Radiology
SIMON, B., Psychiatry
SKILLMAN, J. J., Surgery
SKLAR, J. L., Pathology
SLEDGE, C. B., Orthopaedic Surgery
SMITH, A. R., Radiation Oncology
SOBER, A. J., Dermatology
SODROSKI, J. G., Pathology
SONIS, S. T., Oral Medicine and Oral
    Pathology
SOUBA, W. W., Surgery
SPEALMAN, R. D., Psychobiology
SPECTOR, M., Orthopaedic Surgery
SPEIZER, F. E., Medicine
SPIEGELMAN, B. M., Biological Chemistry
    and Molecular Pharmacology
SPIRO, R. G., Biological Chemistry
SPRINGER, T. A., Pathology
STEER, M. L., Surgery
STEINMAN, T. I., Medicine
STERN, R. S., Dermatology
STILES, C. D., Microbiology and Molecular
    Genetics
STONE, A. A., Law and Psychiatry
STOSSEL, T. P., Medicine
STREILEIN, J. W., Ophthalmology
STREWLER, G. J., Medicine
STRICHARTZ, G. R., Anaesthesia
STROM, T. B., Medicine
STRUHL, K., Biological Chemistry and
    Molecular Pharmacology
SUIT, H. D., Radiation Oncology
SUKHATME, V. P., Medicine
SWARTZ, M. N., Medicine
SZOSTAK, J. W., Genetics
TABIN, C. J., Genetics
TASHJIAN, A. H. Jr, Biological Chemistry
    and Molecular Pharmacology
TAUBMAN, M. A., Oral Biology
TAYLOR, G. A., Radiology
TERHORST, C. P., Medicine
THIBAULT, G. E., Medicine
THIER, S. O., Medicine and Health Care
    Policy
THRALL, J. H., Radiology
TILNEY, N. L., Surgery
TOMKINS, R. G., Surgery
TOSTESON, D. C., Cell Biology
TREVES, S. T., Radiology
TSUANG, M. T., Psychiatry
TYLER, H. R., Neurology
UTIGER, R. D., Medicine
VACANTI, J. P., Surgery
VAILLANT, G. E., Psychiatry
VAN PRAAGH, R., Pathology
VOLPE, J. J., Neurology
WAGNER, G., Biological Chemistry and
    Molecular Pharmacology
WALKER, W. A., Nutrition and Paediatrics
WALSH, C. T., Biological Chemistry and
    Molecular Pharmacology
WARSHAW, A. L., Surgery
WEINBERG, A. N., Medicine
WEINBERGER, S. E., Medicine
WEINBLATT, M. E., Medicine
WEINER, H. L., Neurology
WEINSTEIN, H. J., Paediatrics
WEINSTEIN, M. C., Medicine
WEISS, S. T., Medicine
WEISSMAN, B. N., Radiology
WEIR, G. C., Medicine
WELLER, P. F., Medicine
WEYMAN, A. E., Medicine
WHITE, A. A. III, Orthopaedic Surgery
WHITTEMORE, A., Surgery
WILLETT, W. C., Medicine
WILLIAMS, G. H., Medicine
WILMORE, D. W., Surgery
WILSON, T. H., Cell Biology
WINKELMAN, J. W., Pathology
WINSTON, F. M., Genetics

WITTENBERG, J., Radiology
WOHL, M. E., Paediatrics
WOLF, G. L., Radiology
WOLF, M. A., Medicine
WOLFF, C., Anaesthesia
WOLFF, P. H., Psychiatry
WRAY, S. H., Neurology
YARMUSH, M., Surgery
YOUNG, A. B., Neurology
YOUNG, R. H., Pathology
YUNIS, E. J., Pathology
ZAPOL, W. M., Anaesthesia
ZERVAS, N. T., Neurosurgery
ZETTER, B. R., Surgery
ZINNER, M., Surgery

Graduate School of Public Health (Harvard
School of Public Health, Admissions Office,
677 Huntington Ave, Boston, MA 02115; tel.
(617) 432-1031; e-mail admisofc@haph
.harvard.edu; internet www.hsph.harvard
.edu):

ALONSO, W., Population and International
    Health
BERKMAN, L. F., Health and Social Beha-
    viour
BLENDON, R. J., Health Policy and Manage-
    ment
BLOOM, D. E., Population and Interna-
    tional Health
BRAIN, J. D., Environmental Health
BRENNAN, T. A., Health Policy and Man-
    agement
CHEN, L. C., Population and International
    Health
CHRISTIANI, D. C., Environmental Health
COOK, E. F., Epidemiology
DAVID, J. R., Tropical Public Health
DeGRUTTOLA, V. G., Biostatistics
DEMPLE, B. F., Toxicology
DYCK, A. J., Population and International
    Health
EARLS, F. J., Maternal and Child Health
EPSTEIN, A. M., Health Policy and Manage-
    ment
ESSEX, M. E., Cancer Biology
FINEBERG, H. V., Administration
FREDBERG, J. J., Environmental Health
GLIMCHER, L. H., Cancer Biology
GOLDMAN, P., Nutrition
GRAHAM, J. D., Health Policy and Manage-
    ment
HARN, D. A., Tropical Public Health
HARRINGTON, D. P., Biostatistics
HARRINGTON, J. J., Environmental Health
HEMENWAY, D., Health Policy and Manage-
    ment
HILL, A. G., Population and International
    Health
HSIAO, W. C., Health Policy and Manage-
    ment
KELSEY, K. T., Environmental Health
KOUTRAKIS, P., Environmental Health
LAGAKOS, S. W., Biostatistics
LAIRD, N. M., Biostatistics
LEE, T., Immunology and Infectious Dis-
    eases
LEVINS, R., Population and International
    Health
LI, F. P., Epidemiology
LITTLE, J. B., Cancer Biology
McCORMICK, M. C., Maternal and Child
    Health
MONSON, R. R., Epidemiology and Environ-
    mental Health
MUELLER, N. E., Epidemiology
MURRAY, C., Population and International
    Health
NEWHOUSE, J. P., Health Policy and Man-
    agement
PAGANO, M., Biostatistics
PIESSENS, W. F., Tropical Public Health
PROTHROW-STITH, D. B., Health Policy and
    Management

REICH, M. R., Population and International Health, and Health Policy and Management

ROBERTS, M. J., Health Policy and Management

ROBINS, J. M., Epidemiology and Biostatistics

RYAN, L. M., Biostatistics

SAMSON, L. D., Molecular and Cellular Toxicology

SMITH, T. J., Environmental Health

SORENSON, G., Health and Social Behaviour

SPEIZER, F. E., Environmental Health

SPENGLER, J. D., Environmental Health

SPIELMAN, A., Tropical Public Health

STAMPFER, M. J., Nutrition and Epidemiology

TARLOV, A., Health Policy and Management

TASHJIAN, A. H., Jr, Toxicology

TRICHOPOULOS, D. V., Epidemiology

WALKER, A. M., Epidemiology

WARE, J. H., Biostatistics

WEI, L. J., Biostatistics

WEINSTEIN, M. C., Health Policy, Management and Biostatistics

WILLETT, W. C., Epidemiology and Nutrition

WIRTH, D. F., Tropical Public Health

ZELEN, M., Biostatistics

Graduate School of Education (Admissions, 111 Longfellow Hall, Cambridge, MA 021388; tel. (617) 495-3414; e-mail gseadmissions@harvard.edu; internet www.gse.harvard.edu/admissions):

CHAIT, R.

DUCKWORTH, E. R.

ELGIN, C. Z.

ELMORE, R. F.

FISCHER, K. W.

GARDNER, H. E.

HARRIS, P.

JOHNSON, S. M.

JUEL, C.

KORETZ, D.

LAWRENCE-LIGHTFOOT, S.

LIGHT, R. J.

MCCARTNEY, K.

MURNANE, R.

MURPHY, J. T.

ORFIELD, G., Education and Social Policy

PERKINS, D.

REUBEN, J.

SELMAN, R. L.

SINGER, J. D.

SNOW, C. E.

SUÁREZ-OROZCO, M.

WILLETT, J. B.

Graduate School of Business Administration (Communications Office, Harvard Business School, Soldiers Field, Boston, MA 02163; tel. (617) 495-6000; e-mail news@hbs.edu; internet www.hbs.edu):

AMABILE, T. M., Entrepreneurial Management

APPLEGATE, L. M., General Management

AUSTIN, J. E., Business, Government and International Economy

BADARACCO, J. L., General Management

BAKER, G. P., III, Organizations and Markets

BALDWIN, C. Y., Organizations and Markets

BARTLETT, C. A., General Management

BARTON, D. A., Technology and Operations Management

BEER, M., Organizational Behaviour

BELL, D. E., Marketing

BOWEN, H. K., Technology and Operations Management

BOWER, J. L., General Management

BRADLEY, S. P., Competition and Strategy

BRANDENBERGER, A. M., Competition and Strategy

BRUNS, W. J., Jr, Accounting and Control

CASH, J. I., Jr, Service Management

CAVES, R. E., Competition and Strategy

CHRISTENSEN, C. J., Control

CLARK, K. B., Dean of the Faculty

CRANE, D. B., Finance

CRUM, M. C., Finance

DATAR, S., Accounting and Control

DEIGHTON, J. A., Marketing

DESHPANDÉ, R., Marketing

FROOT, K. A., Finance

FRUHAN, W. E., Jr, Finance

GABARRO, J. J., Organizational Behaviour

GARVIN, D. A., General Management

GHEMAWAT, P., Competition and Strategy

GREYSER, S. A., Marketing

HAMMOND, J. H., Technology and Operations Management

HAWKINS, D. F., Accounting and Control

HAYES, R. H., Technology and Operations Management

HEALY, P. M., Accounting and Control

HERZLINGER, R. E., Accounting and Control

HILL, L. A., Organizational Behaviour

IANSITI, M., Technology and Operations Management

IBARRA, H., Organizational Behaviour

JENSEN, M. C., Organizations and Markets

KANTER, R. M., General Management

KAPLAN, R. S., Accounting and Control

KESTER, W. C., Finance

KOHLBERG, E., Competition and Strategy

KOTTER, J. P., Organizational Behaviour

LIGHT, J. O., Finance

LORSCH, J. W., Organizational Behaviour

MASON, S. P., Finance

McCRAW, T. K., Business, Government and International Economy

McFARLAN, F. W., General Management

McKENNEY, J. L., Management Information Systems

MERTON, R. C., Finance

MEYER, R. F., Managerial Economics

MILLS, D. Q., Human Resource Management

MONTGOMERY, C. A., Competition and Strategy

NOHRIA, N., Organizational Behaviour

NOLAN, R. L., General Management

PAINE, L. S., General Management

PALEPU, K. G., Accounting and Control

PEROLD, A. F., Finance

PIPER, T. R., Finance

PISANO, G., Technology and Operations Management

PODOLNY, J.

PORTER, M. E., Competition and Strategy

QUELCH, J.

RANGAN, V. K., Marketing

REILING, H. B., Finance

ROTEMBERG, J. J., Business, Government and International Economy

ROTH, A. E., Negotiation and Decision Making.

RUBACK, R. S., Finance

SAHLMAN, W. A., Entrepreneurial Management

SALTER, M. S., Organizations and Markets

SASSER, W. E. Jr, Service Management

SCHLESINGER, L. A., Service Management

SCOTT, B. R., Business, Government and International Economy

SEBENIUS, J. K., Negotiation and Decision Making

SHAPIRO, R. D., Technology and Operations Management

SILK, A. J., Marketing

SIMONS, R. L., Accounting and Control

SLOANE, C. S., Organizational Behaviour

STEVENSON, H. H., Entrepreneurial Management

STOBAUGH, R. B., Production and Operations Management

TEDLOW, R. S., Business, Government and International Economy

TUFANO, P., Finance

TUSHMAN, M. L., Organizational Behaviour

UPTON, D. M., Technology and Operations Management

VIETOR, R. H. K., Business, Government and International Economy

WELLS, L. T., Jr, Business, Government and International Economy

WHEELWRIGHT, S. C., Technology and Operations Management

YOFFIE, D. B., Competition and Strategy

YOSHINO, M. Y., General Management

ZALTMAN, G., Marketing

ZUBOFF, S., Organizational Behaviour

J. F. Kennedy School of Government (Admissions, Harvard University, 119 Belfer, Cambridge, MA 2138; tel. (617) 495-1155; e-mail ksg_admissions@harvard.edu; internet www.ksg.harvard.edu/apply):

ALLISON, G. T., Government

ALTSHULER, A., Urban Policy and Planning

APPLBAUM, A., Ethics and Public Policy

AVERY, C., Public Policy

BANE, M. J., Domestic Social Policy

BORJAS, G., Immigration

CARTER, A. B., International and National Security

CLARK, W. C., International Science, Public Policy and Human Development

DOTY, P. M., Public Policy

ELLWOOD, D., Income Support and Social Welfare Policy

FRANKEL, J., Capital Formation and Growth

GERGEN, D., Public Management and Leadership

GOLDSMITH, S., Practice of Public Management

GOMEZ-IBANEZ, J. A., Public Policy and Urban Policy

GRINDLE, M. S., International Development

HAUSMANN, R., Practice of Economic Development

HOGAN, W., Public Policy and Management

HOLDREN, J., Science and Energy Policy

IGNATIEFF, M., Human Rights Practice

JASANOFF, S., Science and Public Policy

JENCKS, C., US Domestic Social Policy

JUMA, C., Practice of International Development

KALT, J., International Political Economy

KELMAN, S. J., Public Management

KEYSSAR, A., History and Social Policy

LAWRENCE, R. Z., International Trade

LEONARD, H., Public Management

LIGHT, R., Education

MANSBRIDGE, J., Democratic Governance

MOORE, M. H., Criminal Justice Policy and Management

NEWHOUSE, J. P., Health Policy and Management

NEWMAN, K., Sociology of Labour Markets

NYE, J., International Affairs and Democratic Governance

ORREN, G. R., Public Policy

PATTERSON, T., Press and Politics

PORTER, R., Business and Government

PUTNAM, R., Democratic Governance

RODRIK, D., International Trade and Development

ROSENSWEIG, M., Public Policy

RUGGIE, J., International Affairs

SAICH, A., International Affairs

SCHAUER, F., First Amendment

SPARROW, M., Practice of Public Management

STAVINS, R. N., Environmental Economics

THOMPSON, D., Political Philosophy

VELASCO, A., International Finance and Development

WILSON, W. J., Urban Sociology

WISE, D., Political Economy

ZECKHAUSER, R. J., Political Economy

School of Dental Medicine (Office of Admissions, DMD, 188 Longwood Ave, Boston, MA 02115; tel. (617) 432-1443; e-mail hsdm_admissions@hsdm.harvard.edu; internet www.hsdm.harvard.edu):

DOGON, I. L., Restorative Dentistry
DONOFF, R. B., Oral and Maxillofacial Surgery
DOUGLASS, C. W., Oral Health Policy and Epidemiology
GOLDHABER, P., Periodontology
HAY, D. I., Oral Biology
KABAN, L. B., Oral and Maxillofacial Surgery
OLSEN, B. R., Oral Biology
SHKLAR, G., Oral Pathology
SONIS, S. S., Oral Medicine and Diagnostic Sciences
TAUBMAN, M. A., Oral Biology

HEBREW COLLEGE

160 Herrick Rd, Newton Centre, MA 02459
Telephone: (617) 559-8600
Fax: (617) 559-8601
E-mail: admissions@hebrewcollege.edu
Internet: www.hebrewcollege.edu
Founded 1921

Pres.: Dr DAVID GORDIS
Sr Vice-Pres.: ROBERT LEIKIND
Vice-Pres. for Devt: MICHAEL GILBERT
Provost: Dr BARRY MESCH
Dean of Students: INA REGOSIN
Registrar: MARILYN JAYE
Library Dir: JUDITH SEGAL

Library of 100,000 vols
Number of teachers: 43
Number of students: 730

Publication: *Hebrew College Today* (quarterly)

DEANS

Educational Planning and Devt: AVI BERNSTEIN-NAHAR
Hebrew College Online: NATHAN EHRLICH
Jewish Music Institute: SCOTT SOKOL
Me'ah: DAVID STARR
Rabbinical School: SHARON ANISFELD-COHEN
Shoolman Graduate School of Jewish Education: HARVEY SHAPIRO

HELLENIC COLLEGE–HOLY CROSS GREEK ORTHODOX SCHOOL OF THEOLOGY

50 Goddard Ave, Brookline, MA 02445-7496
Telephone: (617) 731-3500
Fax: (617) 850-1460
E-mail: admissions@hchc.edu
Internet: www.hchc.edu
Private control

Pres.: Rev. NICHOLAS C. TRIANTAFILOU
Chief Operating Officer: JAMES D. KARLOUTSOS
Dean of Holy Cross: Fr EMMANUEL CLAPSIS
Dean of Hellenic College: LILY MACRAKIS
Registrar: ALBA PAGAN
Library Dir: Very Rev. Dr Archimandrite JOACHIM COTSONIS

Library of 120,000 vols
Number of teachers: 18
Number of students: 204 (104 undergraduate, 100 graduate).

HULT INTERNATIONAL BUSINESS SCHOOL

1 Education St, Cambridge, MA 02141
Telephone: (617) 746-1990
Fax: (617) 746-1991
E-mail: admissions@hult.edu
Internet: www.hult.edu
Founded 1964 as Arthur D. Little School of Management
Private control

Pres. and Chair.: STEPHEN HODGES

Dean of Academic Affairs: RICHARD JOSEPH
Registrar: NICOLE GREGOIRE
Librarian: JOHN WALSH
Number of teachers: 38
Number of students: 59.

LASELL COLLEGE

1844 Commonwealth Ave, Newton, MA 02466
Telephone: (617) 243-2000
Fax: (617) 796-4343
E-mail: info@lasell.edu
Internet: www.lasell.edu
Founded 1851
Private control
Academic year: September to May

Pres.: MICHAEL B. ALEXANDER
Vice-Pres. for Academic Affairs: JAMES OSTROW
Vice-Pres. for Enrollment Management: KATHLEEN M. O'CONNOR
Library Dir: ALLYSON GRAY

Library of 55,000 vols
Number of teachers: 331
Number of students: 1,200

DEANS

School of Allied Health and Sports Studies: Dr LISA BORTMAN
School of Arts and Sciences: Dr STEVEN BLOOM
School of Business and Information Technology: Dr K. BREWER DORAN
Graduate and Professional Studies: MARK SCIEGAI
Undergraduate Education: STEVEN BLOOM

LESLEY UNIVERSITY

29 Everett St, Cambridge, MA 02138-2790
Telephone: (617) 868-9600
Fax: (617) 349-8717
E-mail: info@lesley.edu
Internet: www.lesley.edu
Founded 1909
Academic year: September to May

Pres. and Provost: MARGARET A. MCKENNA
Vice-Pres. for Finance): BERNICE BRADIN
Vice-Pres. for Urban Initiatives: WILLIAM DANDRIDGE
Vice-Pres. for Budgeting and Financial Planning: ML DYMSKI
Vice-Pres. for Admin.: MARY LOU BATT
Dean of Faculty: WILLIAM STOKES
Registrar: MELISSA JANOT
Dir of Libraries: PATRICIA PAYNE

Library of 100,000 vols
Number of teachers: 500
Number of students: 12,344 (1,702 undergraduate, 9,557 postgraduate)

Publication: *Journal of Pedagogy, Pluralism and Practice* (irreg.)

DEANS

Art Institute of Boston: TERRENCE KEENEY
Graduate School of Arts and Social Sciences: JULIA HALEVY
School of Education: MARIO BORUNDA
Lesley College: SHAUN MCNIFF

MASSACHUSETTS COLLEGE OF ART

621 Huntington Ave, Boston, MA 02215
Telephone: (617) 232-1555
Fax: (617) 232-0050
Internet: www.massart.edu
Founded 1873

Pres.: Dr KATHERINE SLOAN
Sr Vice-Pres. for Academic Affairs: Dr JOHANNA BRANSON
Vice-Pres. for Admin. and Finance: KURT STEINBERG

Vice-Pres.for Student Devt: MAUREEN KEEFE
Vice-Pres. for Institutional Advancement: RICAHRD MACMILLAN
Library Dir: PAUL DOBBS

Library of 95,000 vols
Number of teachers: 216
Number of students: 1,432 and 617 continuing education students.

MASSACHUSETTS COLLEGE OF LIBERAL ARTS

375 Church St, North Adams, MA 01247
Telephone: (413) 662-5000
Fax: (413) 662-5580
Internet: www.mcla.mass.edu
Founded 1894

Pres.: Dr MARY K. GRANT
Vice-Pres. for Academic Affairs: Dr STEVE GREEN
Vice-Pres. for Enrollment and External Relations: DENISE RICHARDELLO
Vice-Pres. for Admin. and Finance: Dr JAMES STAKENAS
Dean of Academic Affairs: Dr MONICA NESET JOSLIN
Dir of Career Services: SHARRON ZAVATTARO
Registrar: ANDREA DEMAYO (acting)
Library Dir: LINDA M. KAUFMANN (acting)

Library of 172,000 vols, 500 print periodicals, 300,000 microforms, 4,000 online journals

Depts of Arts Management, Biology, Business Admin., Chemistry, Computer Science and Information Systems, Education, English/Communications, Environmental Studies, Fine and Performing Arts, History, Political Science and Geography, Interdisciplinary Studies, Mathematics, Modern Languages, Philosophy, Physical Education, Physics, Psychology, Sociology, Anthropology and Social Work, Women's Studies.

MASSACHUSETTS COLLEGE OF PHARMACY AND HEALTH SCIENCES

179 Longwood Ave, Boston, MA 02115-5896
Telephone: (617) 732-2800
Fax: (617) 732-2801
Internet: www.mcphs.edu
Founded 1823
Private control

Pres.: CHARLES F. MONAHAN, Jr
Vice-Pres. for Academic Affairs and Provost: Dr MICHELLE M. KALIS (acting)
Assoc. Vice-Pres. for External Relations: Dr GEORGE E. HUMPHREY
Vice-Pres. for Finance and Admin.: RICHARD J. LESSARD
Vice-Pres. for Legal Affairs: Dr ROBERT W. HOLMES, Jr
Registrar: MARJORIE MCMAHON
Dean of Students: JEAN JOYCE-BRADY
Dean of Library: RICHARD KAPLAN

Library of 30,000 vols, 800 periodicals
Number of teachers: 157
Number of students: 3,200

DEANS

School of Arts and Sciences: Dr DAVID E. TANNER
Forsyth School of Dental Hygiene: (vacant)
School of Health Sciences: Dr JAMES BLAGG
School of Nursing: (vacant)
School of Pharmacy, Boston: Dr DOUGLAS J. PISANO
School of Pharmacy, Worcester/Manchester: Dr MICHAEL J. MALLOY
School of Radiologic Sciences: Dr K. CYRUS WHALEY (acting)

BRANCH CAMPUSES

Manchester Campus: 1260 Elm St, Manchester, NH 03101-1305; tel. (603) 314-0210; fax (603) 314-0303.

Worcester Campus: 19 Foster St, Worcester, MA 01608-1715; tel. (508) 890-8855; fax (508) 890-8515.

MASSACHUSETTS INSTITUTE OF TECHNOLOGY

77 Massachusetts Ave, Cambridge, MA 02139-4307

Telephone: (617) 253-1000

Fax: (617) 253-8000

Internet: web.mit.edu

Founded 1861

Private Institution

Academic year: September to May

Pres.: SUSAN HOCKFIELD

Chancellor: PHILLIP L. CLAY

Provost: L. RAFAEL REIF

Exec. Vice-Pres. and Treas.: THERESA STONE

Vice-Pres. for Human Resources: ALISON ALDEN

Vice-Pres. for Information Services and Technology: JERROLD M. GROCHOW

Vice-Pres. for Research and Associate Provost: CLAUDE CANIZARES

Vice-Pres. for Resource Devt: JEFFREY NEWTON

Vice-Pres. for Institute Affairs and Corporation Sec.: KIRK KOLENBRANDER

Vice-Pres. for External Affairs: DEBORAH BOHREN

Vice-Pres. and Gen. Counsel: R. GREGORY MORGAN

Dir of Lincoln Laboratory: ERIC EVANS

Assoc. Vice-Provosts: LORNA GIBSON, PHILIP S. KHOURY

Dean of Graduate Students: STEVEN LERMAN

Dean of Undergraduate Education: DANIEL HASTINGS

Dean of Student Life: LARRY BENEDICT

Registrar: MARY R. CALLAHAN

Dir of Libraries: ANN J. WOLPERT

Library of 5,000,000 vols

Number of teachers: 998

Number of students: 10,320

Publications: *MIT Bulletin* (annual), *Sloan Management Review* (quarterly), *Technology Review* (monthly), *Tech Talk* (30 a year)

DEANS

School of Architecture and Planning: ADÈLE NAUDÉ SANTOS

School of Eng.: THOMAS L. MAGANTI

School of Humanities, Arts and Social Sciences: DEBORAH FITZGERALD

Sloan School of Management: STEVEN EPPINGER

School of Science: MARC KASTNER

PROFESSORS

(Some professors serve in more than one department)

School of Architecture and Planning (77 Massachusetts Ave, Room 7-231, Cambridge, MA 02139-4307; tel. (617) 253-4401; fax (617) 253-9417; internet sap.mit.edu):

Department of Architecture:

ANDERSON, S., History and Architecture (Head)

BEINART, J., Architecture

CHANG, Y. H., Architecture (Head)

DE MONCHAUX, J., Architecture and Urban Planning

DENNIS, M., Architecture

GLICKSMAN, L. R., Building Technology and Mechanical Eng.

JARZOMBEK, M., History and Architecture

JONAS, J., Visual Arts

KNIGHT, T., Design and Computation

MITCHELL, W. J., Architecture, Media Arts and Sciences

NORFORD, L., Building Technology

SANTOS, A. N., Architecture

SPIRN, A. W., Landscape Architecture and Planning

STINY, G., Design and Computation

WAMPLER, J., Architecture

WODICZKO, K., Visual Arts

Program in Media Arts and Sciences:

MACHOVER, T., Music and Media

MITCHELL, W. J., Media Arts and Sciences (Head)

NEGROPONTE, N. P., Media Technology

PENTLAND, A. P., Media Arts and Sciences

PICARD, R. W., Media Arts and Sciences

VERCOE, B., Media Arts and Sciences

Department of Urban Studies and Planning:

AMSDEN, A., Political Economy

CIOCHETTI, B. A., Practice of Real Estate

CLAY, P., Urban Studies and Planning

DAVIS, D., Political Sociology

DE MONCHAUX, J., Architecture and Urban Planning

FERREIRA, J., Urban Studies and Operations Research

FOGELSON, R. M., History and Urban Studies

FRENCHMAN, D., Practice of Urban Design

GAKENHEIMER, R., Urban Planning

GELTNER, D., Real Estate Finance

KEYES, L. C., City and Regional Planning

LEVY, F. S., Urban Econ.

OSTERMAN, P., Human Resources and Management

POLENSKE, K. R., Regional Political Economy and Planning

REIN, M., Social Policy

SANYAL, B., Urban and Regional Planning

SCHUSTER, J. M., Urban Cultural Policy

SPIRN, A., Landscape Architecture and Planning

SUSSKIND, L. E., Urban and Environmental Planning

TENDLER, J., Political Economy

VALE, L. J., Urban Design and Planning (Head)

WHEATON, W. C., Urban Econ.

School of Engineering (77 Massachusetts Ave, Room 1-206, Cambridge, MA 02139-4307; tel. (617) 253-3291; fax (617) 253-8549; internet web.mit.edu/engineering):

Department of Aeronautics and Astronautics:

CHAN, V. W. S., Aeronautics and Astronautics, Electrical Eng. and Computer Science

CRAWLEY, E. F., Aeronautics and Astronautics

DEYST, J. J., Aeronautics and Astronautics

DRELA, M., Aeronautics and Astronautics

EPSTEIN, A. H., Aeronautics and Astronautics

GREITZER, E. M., Aeronautics and Astronautics

HALL, S. R., Aeronautics and Astronautics

HANSMAN, R. J., Aeronautics and Astronautics

HARRIS, W. L., Aeronautics and Astronautics (Head)

HASTINGS, D. E., Aeronautics and Astronautics, Eng. Systems

HOFFMAN, J. A., Practice of Astronautics

LAGACE, P. A., Aeronautics and Astronautics, Eng. Systems

LEVESON, N. G., Aeronautics and Astronautics, Eng. Systems

LIEBECK, R., Practice of Aerospace Eng.

MARTINEZ-SANCHEZ, M., Aeronautics and Astronautics

MURMAN, E. M., Aeronautics and Astronautics, Eng. Systems

NEWMAN, D. J., Aeronautics and Astronautics, Eng. Systems

NIGHTINGALE, D. J., Practice of Aeronautics and Astronautics and Eng. Systems

ODONI, A. R., Aeronautics and Astronautics

PERAIRE, J., Aeronautics and Astronautics

VANDER VELDE, W. E., Aeronautics and Astronautics

WAITZ, I. A., Aeronautics and Astronautics

WIDNALL, S. E., Aeronautics and Astronautics

YOUNG, L. R., Astronautics

Biological Engineering Division:

BELCHER, A. M., Materials Science and Biological Eng.

DEDON, P. C., Toxicology and Biological Eng.

DEEN, W. M., Chemical and Biological Eng.

DELONG, E. F., Environmental and Biological Eng.

DEWEY, C. F., Jr, Mechanical Eng. and Biological Eng.

ESSIGMAN, J. M., Chemistry, Toxicology and Biological Eng.

FOX, J. G., Div. of Comparative Medicine and Biological Eng.

GRIFFITH, L. G., Mechanical and Biological Eng.

GRODZINSKY, A. J., Electrical, Mechanical and Biological Eng.

HUNTER, I. W., Mechanical Eng. and Bioengineering

KLIBANOV, A. M., Chemistry and Biological Eng.

LANGER, R. S., Chemical and Biolmedical Eng.

LAUFFENBURGER, D. A., Biological Eng., Chemical Eng. and Biology (Dir)

LODISH, H. F., Biology and Biological Eng.

MATSUDAIRA, P. T., Biology and Biological Eng.

SAMSON, L. D., Toxicology and Biological Eng.

SASISEKHARAN, R., Biological Eng.

SCHAUER, D. B., Biological Eng. and Comparative Medicine

SO, P. T., Mechanical and Biological Eng.

SORGER, P. K., Biology and Biological Eng.

SURESH, S., Materials Science and Eng.

TANNENBAUM, S. R., Toxicology and Chemistry

THILLY, W. G., Biological Eng.

TIDOR, B., Bioengineering and Computer Science

WITTRUP, K. D., Chemical Eng. and Biological Eng.

WOGAN, G. N., Chemistry and Biological Eng.

YANNAS, I. V., Polymer Science and Eng.

Department of Chemical Engineering:

ARMSTRONG, R. C., Chemical Eng. (Head)

BLANKSCHTEIN, E. D., Chemical Eng.

BRENNER, H., Chemical Eng.

BROWN, R. A., Chemical Eng.

COHEN, R. E., Chemical Eng.

COLTON, C. K., Chemical Eng.

COONEY, C. L., Chemical and Biochemical Eng.

DEEN, W. M., Chemical Eng. and Biological Eng.

GAST, A. P., Chemical Eng.

GLEASON, K. K., Chemical Eng.

HATTON, T. A., Chemical Eng. Practice

JENSEN, K. F., Chemical Eng.

LANGER, R. S., Chemical and Biomedical Eng.

LAUFFENBURGER, D. A., Chemical Eng. and Biological Eng.

McRAE, G. J., Chemical Eng.

RUTLEDGE, G. C., Chemical Eng.

SAWIN, H. H., Chemical Eng. and Electrical Eng.

SMITH, K. A., Chemical Eng.

STEPHANOPOULOS, G., Chemical Eng.

STEPHANOPOULOS, GRE., Chemical Eng.

TESTER, J. W., Chemical Eng.

WANG, D. I. C., Chemical Eng.

WITTRUP, K. D., Chemical Eng. and Biological Eng.

YING, J. Y.-R., Chemical Eng.

Department of Civil Engineering and Environmental Engineering:

BARNHART, C., Civil and Environmental Eng.

BEN-AKIVA, M., Civil and Environmental Eng.

BRAS, R. L., Civil and Environmental Eng. and Earth, Atmospheric and Planetary Sciences

BUYUKOZTURK, O., Civil and Environmental Eng.

CHISHOLM, S., Civil and Environmental Eng. and Biology

CONNOR, J. J., Jr, Civil and Environmental Eng.

DeLONG, E., Civil and Environmental Eng., Biological Eng. Div.

DE NEUFVILLE, R. L., Civil and Environmental Eng., Eng. Systems

EINSTEIN, H. H., Civil and Environmental Eng.

ELTAHIR, E., Civil and Environmental Eng.

ENTEKHABI, D., Civil and Environmental Eng.

GIBSON, L., Mechanical Eng., Materials Science and Eng., Civil and Environmental Eng.

GSCHWEND, P., Civil and Environmental Eng.

HEMOND, H. F., Civil and Environmental Eng.

JAILLET, P., Civil and Environmental Eng. (Head)

KAUSEL, E., Civil and Environmental Eng.

LARSON, R. C., Civil and Environmental Eng.

LERMAN, S. R., Civil and Environmental Eng.

MADSEN, O. S., Civil and Environmental Eng.

MARKS, D. H., Civil and Environmental Eng., Eng. Systems

McLAUGHLIN, D. B., Civil and Environmental Eng.

MEI, C. C., Civil and Environmental Eng.

MOAVENZADEH, F., Civil and Environmental Eng., Eng. Systems

NEPF, H., Civil and Environmental Eng.

ODONI, A. R., Aeronautics and Astronautics and Civil and Environmental Eng.

SHEFFI, Y., Civil and Environmental Eng., Eng. Systems

SIMCHI-LEVI, D., Civil and Environmental Eng., Eng. Systems

SUSSMAN, J. M., Civil and Environmental Eng., Eng. Systems

VENEZIANO, D., Civil and Environmental Eng.

WHITTLE, A. J., Civil and Environmental Eng.

WILSON, N. H. M., Civil and Environmental Eng.

Department of Electrical Engineering and Computer Science:

ABELSON, H., Computer Science and Eng.

AGARWAL, A., Computer Science and Eng.

AKINWANDE, A., Electrical Eng.

ANTONIADIS, D., Electrical Eng.

ARVIND, Computer Science and Eng.

BAGGEROER, A. B., Eng. and Mechanical Eng.

BERS, A., Electrical Eng.

BERTSEKAS, D. P., Electrical Eng.

BERWICK, R. C., Computer Science and Eng. and Computational Linguistics

BONING, D., Computer Science and Eng.

BRAIDA, L. B. D., Electrical Eng. and Health Sciences and Technology

BROOKS, R. A., Computer Science and Eng.

CHAN, V. W. S., Electrical Eng. and Aeronautics and Astronautics

CHANDRAKASAN, A., Electrical Eng.

DAHLEH, M. A., Electrical Eng.

DAVIS, R., Computer Science and Eng.

DEL ALAMO, J. A., Electrical Eng.

DEVADAS, S., Electrical Eng.

DRESSELHAUS, M. S., Electrical Eng. and Physics

FONSTAD, C. G., Jr, Electrical Eng.

FREEMAN, D. M., Electrical Eng.

FUJIMOTO, J. G., Electrical Eng.

GALLAGER, R. G., Electrical Eng.

GIFFORD, D. K., Computer Science and Eng.

GOLDWASSER, S., Computer Science and Eng.

GRAY, M. L., Medical and Electrical Eng.

GRAY, P. E., Electrical Eng.

GRIMSON, W. E. L., Medical Eng.

GRODZINSKY, A. J., Electrical, Mechanical and Biological Eng.

GUTTAG, J. V., Computer Science and Eng.

HENNIE, F. C, III, Computer Science and Eng.

HORN, B. K., Computer Science and Eng.

HOYT, J. L., Electrical Eng.

HU, Q., Electrical Eng.

IPPEN, E. P., Electrical Eng. and Physics

JACKSON, D. N., Computer Science and Eng.

KAASHOEK, M. F., Computer Science and Eng.

KAEBLING, L. P., Computer Science and Eng.

KAERTNER, F. X., Electrical Eng.

KARGER, D. R., Computer Science and Eng.

KASSAKIAN, J. G., Electrical Eng.

KIRTLEY, J. L., Jr, Electrical Eng.

KOLODZIEJSKI, L. A., Electrical Eng.

KONG, J. A., Electrical Eng.

LANG, J. H., Electrical Eng.

LEE, H.-S., Electrical Eng.

LEEB, S. B., Electrical Eng.

LEISERSON, C. E., Computer Science and Eng.

LIM, J. S., Electrical Eng.

LISKOV, B. H., Computer Science and Eng.

LOZANO-PÉREZ, T., Computer Science and Eng.

LYNCH, N. A., Computer Science and Eng.

MAGNANTI, T. L., Management Science and Electrical Eng.

MARK, R. G., Health Sciences and Technology and Electrical Eng.

MEYER, A. R., Computer Science and Eng.

MICALI, S., Computer Science and Eng.

MINSKY, M. L., Media Arts and Sciences and Computer Science and Eng.

MITTER, S. K., Electrical Eng. and Eng. Systems

MOSES, J., Computer Science and Eng. and Eng. Systems

OPPENHEIM, A. V., Electrical Eng.

ORLANDO, T. P., Electrical Eng.

PARKER, R. R., Electrical Eng. and Nuclear Eng.

PEAKE, W.T ., Electrical and Bioengineering

PENFIELD, P. L., Jr, Electrical Eng.

REIF, L. R., Electrical Eng. (Head)

RIVEST, R. L., Computer Science and Eng.

ROBERGE, J. K., Electrical Eng.

RUBINFELD, R., Computer Science and Eng.

SALTZER, J. H., Computer Science and Eng.

SAWIN, H. H., Chemical Eng. and Electrical Eng.

SCHMIDT, M. A., Electrical Eng.

SHAPIRO, J. H., Electrical Eng.

SMITH, A. C., Electrical Eng.

SMITH, H. I., Electrical Eng.

SODINI, C. G., Electrical Eng.

STAELIN, D. H., Electrical Eng.

STEVENS, K. N., Electrical Eng. and Health Sciences and Technology

SUDAN, M., Computer Science and Eng.

SUSSMAN, G. J., Electrical Eng.

SZOLOVITS, P., Computer Science and Eng. and Health Sciences and Technology

TIDOR, B., Electrical Eng., Bioengineering and Computer Science

TROXEL, D. E., Electrical Eng.

TSITSIKLIS, J. N., Electrical Eng. and Computer Science

VERGHESE, G. C., Electrical Eng.

WARD, S. A., Computer Science and Eng.

WARDE, C., Electrical Eng.

WHITE, J. K., Electrical Eng.

WILLSKY, A. S., Electrical Eng.

WILSON, G. L., Electrical and Mechanical Eng.

WINSTON, P. H., Computer Science

WORNELL, G. W., Electrical Eng.

WYATT, J. L., Electrical Eng.

ZAHN, M., Electrical Eng.

ZUE, V. M., Electrical Eng. and Computer Science

Engineering Systems Division:

ALLEN, T. J., Management and Eng. Systems

APOSTOLAKIS, G., Nuclear Eng. and Eng. Systems

BARNHART, C., Civil and Environmental Eng. and Eng. Systems

CARROLL, J., Behavioural and Policy Sciences and Eng. Systems

CLARK, J. P., Eng. Systems and Materials Systems

CRAWLEY, E. F., Aeronautics and Astronautics and Eng. Systems

DE NEUFVILLE, R., Eng. Systems and Civil and Environmental Eng.

EAGAR, T. W., Materials Eng. and Eng. Systems

EPPINGER, S. D., Management Science and Eng. Systems

FINE, C., Management and Eng. Systems

GRAVES, S. C., Management and Eng. Systems

HANSMAN, J., Aeronautics and Astronautics and Eng. Systems

HARDT, D. E., Mechanical Eng. and Eng. Systems

HASTINGS, D., Aeronautics and Astronautics and Eng. Systems (Co-Dir)

KOCHAN, T. A., Management and Eng. Systems

LAGACE, P. A., Aeronautics and Astronautics and Eng. Systems

LARSON, R., Civil and Environmental Eng. and Eng. Systems

LEVESON, N., Aeronautics and Astronautics and Eng. Systems

LLOYD, S., Mechanical Eng. and Eng. Systems

MADNICK, S., Information Technology and Eng. Systems

MARKS, D. H., Eng. Systems and Civil and Environmental Eng.

MINDELL, D., History of Eng. and Manufacturing and Eng. Systems

MITTER, S., Electrical Eng. and Computer Science and Eng. Systems

MOAVENZADEH, F., Eng. Systems and Civil and Environmental Eng.

MONIZ, E., Physics and Eng. System Environmental Eng.

MOSES, J., Computer Science and Eng. Systems

MURMAN, E. M., Aeronautics and Astronautics and Eng. Systems

NEWMAN, D. J., Aeronautics and Astronautics and Eng. Systems

ROOS, D., Eng. Systems and Civil and Environmental Eng. (Co-Dir)

SEERING, W. P., Mechanical Eng. and Eng. Systems

SHEFFI, Y., Eng. Systems and Civil and Environmental Eng.

SIMCHI-LEVI, D., Civil and Environmental Eng. and Eng. Systems

STERMAN, J., Management and Eng. Systems
SUSSMAN, J. M., Eng. Systems and Civil and Environmental Eng.
UTTERBACK, J., Management and Innovation and Eng. Systems
WELSCH, R., Statistics and Management Science and Eng. Systems
WIDNALL, S., Aeronautics and Astronautics and Eng. Systems

Department of Materials Science and Engineering:

ALLEN, S. M., Physical Metallurgy
BELCHER, A. M., Materials Science and Eng. and Biomedical Eng.
CARTER, W. C., Materials Science and Eng.
CEDER, G., Materials Science and Eng.
CHIANG, Y.-M., Ceramics
CIMA, M., Ceramic Processing
CLARK, J. P., Materials Systems
EAGAR, T. W., Materials Eng. and Materials Systems
FITZGERALD, E. A., Electronic and Optoelectronic Materials
GIBSON, L., Materials Science and Eng., Mechanical Eng. and Civil and Environmental Eng.
HOBBS, L. W., Materials and Nuclear Eng.
HOSLER, D., Archaeology and Ancient Technology
JENSEN, K. F., Chemical Eng., Materials Science and Eng.
KIMERLING, L. C., Materials Science and Eng.
LECHTMAN, H., Archaeology and Ancient Technology
MAYES, A. M., Polymer Physics
ROSS, C., Materials Science and Eng.
RUBNER, M. F., Polymer Materials Science and Eng.
SADOWAY, D. R., Electrochemical Processes in Nanoqueous Media
SURESH, S., Materials Science and Eng. and Mechanical Eng. (Head)
THOMAS, E. L., Materials Science and Eng.
THOMPSON, C. V., Materials Science and Eng.
TULLER, H. L., Ceramics and Electronic Materials
WUENSCH, B. J., Ceramics
YIP, S., Nuclear and Materials Science Eng.

Department of Mechanical Engineering:

ABEYARATNE, R., Mechanical Eng. (Head)
AKYLAS, T. R., Mechanical Eng.
ANAND, L., Mechanical Eng.
ASADA, H., Mechanical Eng.
BAGGEROER, A., Mechanical, Ocean and Electrical Eng.
BATHE, K.-J., Mechanical Eng.
BOYCE, M. C., Mechanical Eng.
CHEN, G., Mechanical Eng.
CHENG, W. K., Mechanical Eng.
CHRYSSOSTOMIDIS, C., Mechanical and Ocean Eng.
CHUN, J. H., Mechanical Eng.
CRAVALHO, E. G., Mechanical Eng.
D'ARBELOFF, A., Mechanical Eng. and Management
DEWEY, C. F., Jr, Mechanical Eng. and Bioengineering
DUBOWSKY, S., Mechanical Eng.
FLOWERS, W. C., Mechanical Eng.
GHONIEM, A. F., Mechanical Eng.
GIBSON, L., Materials Science and Mechanical Eng.
GLICKSMAN, L., Architecture and Mechanical Eng.
GOSSARD, D. C., Mechanical Eng.
GRIFFITH, L., Mechanical Eng. and Bioengineering
GRODZINSKY, A. J., Electrical, Mechanical and Biological Eng.
GUTOWSKI, T. G., Mechanical Eng.
HALLER, G., Mechanical Eng.

HARDT, D. E., Mechanical Eng.
HART, D., Mechanical Eng.
HEYWOOD, J. B., Mechanical Eng.
HOGAN, N. J., Mechanical Eng. and Brain and Cognitive Science
HUNTER, I. W., Mechanical Eng.
KAMM, R. D., Mechanical Eng.
KAZIMI, M. S., Mechanical and Nuclear Eng.
KEENAN, P. J., Naval Construction and Eng.
LIEHARD, J., Mechanical Eng.
LLOYD, S., Mechanical Eng.
MAGEE, C. L., Practice of Eng. Systems and Mechanical Eng.
MARCUS, H., Marine Systems
McKINLEY, G. H., Mechanical Eng.
MEI, C. C., Civil and Environmental Eng. and Mechanical Eng.
MIKIC, B. B., Mechanical Eng.
MILGRAM, J., Mechanical Eng. and Marine Technology
PARKS, D. M., Mechanical Eng.
PATERA, A. T., Mechanical Eng. and Teaching Innovation
PATRIKALAKIS, N. M., Ocean Eng. and Mechanical Eng.
ROWELL, D., Mechanical Eng.
SACHS, E. M., Mechanical Eng.
SCHMIDT, H., Ocean Eng. and Mechanical Eng.
SCLAVOUNOS, P., Mechanical Eng. and Naval Architecture
SEERING, W. P., Mechanical Eng.
SLOCUM, A., Mechanical Eng.
SLOTINE, J.-J. E., Mechanical Eng. and Information Sciences
SMITH, J. L., Jr, Mechanical Eng.
SO, P. T., Mechanical and Biological Eng.
SONIN, A. A., Mechanical Eng.
SUH, N. P., Mechanical Eng.
SURESH, S., Materials Science, Mechanical Eng. and Eng.
TODREAS, N., Nuclear and Mechanical Eng.
TRIANTAFYLLOU, M., Mechanical and Ocean Eng.
TRUMPER, D. L., Mechanical Eng.
VANDIVER, J. K., Mechanical and Ocean Eng.
VEST, C. M., Mechanical Eng.
WIERZBICKI, T., Mechanical and Ocean Eng.
WILLIAMS, J. H., Jr, Eng.
WILSON, G. L., Electrical and Mechanical Eng.
YANNAS, I. V., Mechanical Eng., Polymer Science and Biological Eng.
YOUCEF-TOUMI, K., Mechanical Eng.
YUE, D. K.-P., Mechanical and Ocean Eng.

Department of Nuclear Science and Engineering:

APOSTOLAKIS, G., Nuclear Science and Eng. and Eng. Systems Div.
BALLINGER, R. G., Nuclear Science and Eng. and Materials Science and Eng.
CHEN, S.-H., Nuclear Science and Eng.
CORY, D. G., Nuclear Science and Eng.
FREIDBERG, J. P., Nuclear Science and Eng.
GOLAY, M. W., Nuclear Science and Eng.
HANSEN, K. F., Nuclear Science and Eng.
HARLING, O. K., Nuclear Science and Eng.
HOBBS, L. W., Materials and Nuclear Science and Eng.
HUTCHINSON, I. H., Nuclear Science and Eng. (Head)
KADAK, A. C., Practice, Nuclear Science and Eng.
KAZIMI, M. S., Nuclear Science and Eng. and Mechanical Eng.
LESTER, R. K., Nuclear Science and Eng.
PARKER, R. R., Electrical Eng. and Computer Science and Nuclear Science and Eng.
TODREAS, N. E., Nuclear Science and Eng. and Mechanical Eng.

YANCH, J. C., Nuclear Science and Eng.
YIP, S., Nuclear Science and Eng. and Materials Science and Eng.

School of Humanities, Arts and Social Sciences (77 Massachusetts Ave, Room E51-255, Cambridge, MA 02139-4307; tel. (617) 253-3470; e-mail www-shss@mit.edu; internet web.mit.edu/shass):

Program in Anthropology:

FISCHER, M. M. J., Anthropology and Science and Technology Studies
HOWE, J., Anthropology
JACKSON, J. E., Anthropology
SILBEY, S., Sociology and Anthropology
SLYMOVICS, S., Anthropology

Program in Comparative Media Studies:

JENKINS, H., III, Comparative Media Studies and Literature
URICCHIO, W., Comparative Media Studies

Department of Economics:

ACEMOGLU, K. D., Econ.
ANGRIST, J., Econ.
BANERJEE, A., Econ.
BLANCHARD, O. J., Econ.
CABALLERO, R., Econ.
COSTA, D., Econ.
DIAMOND, P. A., Econ.
DUFLO, E., Econ.
ELLISON, G., Econ.
GIBBONS, R. S., Management and Econ.
GRUBER, J., Econ.
HARRIS, J. E., Econ.
HAUSMAN, J. A., Econ.
HOLMSTRÖM, B. R., Econ. (Head)
JOSKOW, P. L., Econ. and Management
NEWEY, W. K., Econ.
PIORE, M. J., Political Economy
POTERBA, J. M., Econ.
ROSE, N., Econ.
ROSS, S., Finance and Econ.
SCHMALENSEE, R. L., Management and Econ.
SNYDER, J., Political Science and Econ.
TEMIN, P., Econ.
THUROW, L. C., Econ. and Management
WHEATON, W. C., Econ. and Urban Studies

Foreign Languages and Literatures Section:

DE COURTIVRON, I., French Studies
GARRELS, E., Spanish and Latin American Studies
MIYAGAWA, S., Japanese and Linguistics
TURK, E. B., French and Film Studies
WANG, J., Chinese Languages and Culture

History Section:

DOWER, J. W., History
FOGELSON, R. M., History and Urban Studies
KHOURY, P. S., History
MAIER, P., History
PERDUE, P., Asian Civilizations
RITVO, H., History (Head)
SMITH, M. R., History of Technology

Department of Linguistics and Philosophy:

CHOMSKY, N. A., Linguistics
COHEN, J., Philosophy and Humanities
FLYNN, S., Second Language Acquisition
HASLANGER, S., Philosophy
HEIM, I., Linguistics
HOLTON, R., Philosophy
IATRIDOU, S., Linguistics
KENSTOWICZ, M., Linguistics
LANGTON, R., Philosophy
MARANTZ, A., Linguistics
McGEE, V., Philosophy
MIYAGAWA, S., Linguistics and Japanese
O'NEIL, W., Linguistics
PESETSKY, D., Linguistics
SINGER, I., Philosophy
STALNAKER, R., Philosophy
STERIADE, D., Linguistics
WEXLER, K. N., Linguistics and Psychology
YABLO, S., Philosophy (Head)

Literature Section:

BUZARD, P. S., Literature (Head)
DONALDSON, P. S., Literature
HILDEBIDLE, J., Literature
JENKINS, H., III, Comparative Media Studies and Literature
KIBEL, A. C., Literature
PERRY, R., Literature and Women's Studies
TAPSCOTT, S. J., Literature
THORBURN, D., Literature
URICCHIO, W., Comparative Media Studies

Music and Theater Arts Section:

BRODY, A., Theatre Arts
CHILD, P., Music
HARBISON, J., Music
HARRIS, E. T., Music
LINDGREN, L., Music
THOMPSON, M. A., Music
ZIPORYN, E., Music (Head)

Department of Political Science:

ANSOLABEHERE, S. D., Political Science
BERGER, S., Political Science
CHOUCRI, N., Political Science
COHEN, J., Philosophy and Political Science and Humanities
LOCKE, R. M., Entrepreneurship and Political Science
MEYER, S. M., Political Science
PIORE, M. J., Political Economy and Political Science
POSEN, B. R., Political Science
SAMUELS, R. J., Political Science
SAPOLSKY, H. M., Public Policy and Organization
SNYDER, J. R., Political Science and Econ.
STEWART, C., III, Political Science (Head)
VAN EVERA, S. W., Political Science

Program in Science, Technology and Society:

FISCHER, M. M. J., Anthropology and Science and Technology Studies
FITZGERALD, D. K., History of Technology
GRAHAM, L. R., History of Science
KELLER, E. F., History and Philosophy of Science
MANNING, K. R., Rhetoric and the History of Science
MINDELL, D. A., History of Technology and Eng. Systems
POSTOL, T. A., Science, Technology and Nat. Security Policy
SMITH, M. R., History of Technology
TURKLE, S. R., Sociology of Science
WILLIAMS, R. H., History of Technology (Dir)

Program in Writing and Humanistic Studies:

KANIGEL, R., Science Writing
MANNING, K. R., Rhetoric, Writing Biography and Autobiography, and the History of Science
PARADIS, J., Victorian Cultural Studies, Scientific and Technical Communication
WILLIAMS, J. H., Writing and Humanistic Studies
WILLIAMS, R. H., Writing

Sloan School of Management (50 Memorial Dr., Cambridge, MA 02142; tel. (617) 253-2659; internet mitsloan.mit.edu):

ALLEN, T. J., Jr, Management
ANCONA, D. G., Management
ARIELY, D., Management
ASQUITH, K. P., Accounting
BAILYN, L. L., Management
BARNETT, A. I., Operations Research and Management and Management Science
BERNDT, E. R., Applied Econ.
BERTSIMAS, D., Management
BITRAN, G. R., Management
BRYNJOLFSSON, E., Management
CARROLL, J. S., Behavioural and Policy Sciences
COX, J. C., Finance
CUSUMANO, M. A., Management
EPPINGER, S. D., Management

FERNANDEZ, R. M., Organization Studies
FINE, C. H., Management
FREUND, R. M., Management Science
GIBBONS, R. S., Management
GRAVES, S. C., Management
HAUSER, J. R., Marketing
HAX, A. C., Management
HENDERSON, R. M., Management
HOLMSTROM, B. R., Econ. and Management
JACOBY, H. D., Applied Econ.
JOHNSON, S., Entrepreneurship
JOSKOW, P. L., Econ. and Management
KAUFMAN, G. M., Operations Research and Management
KOCHAN, T. A., Management
KOTHARI, S. P., Accounting
LESSARD, D. R., Int. Management
LITTLE, J. D. C., Marketing
LO, A. W., Finance
LOCKE, R., Management and Political Science
MADNICK, S. E., Information Technology
MAGNANTI, T. L., Management Science and Electrical Eng.
MALONE, T. W., Information Systems
MYERS, S. C., Finance
ORLIKOWSKI, W. J., Communication Sciences
ORLIN, J. B., Management Science and Operations Research
OSTERMAN, P., Human Resources and Management
PINDYCK, R. S., Finance and Econ.
PRELEC, D., Management Science
ROBERTS, E. B., Management of Technology
ROSS, S. A., Finance
SCHMALENSEE, R. L., Management and Econ.
SCOTT MORTON, M. S., Behavioural and Policy Sciences
SIMESTER, D., Marketing
STERMAN, J., Management Science
STOKER, T. M., Applied Econ.
THUROW, L. C., Management and Econ.
URBAN, G. L., Marketing
UTTERBACK, J., Management
VAN MAANEN, J. E., Organizational Studies
VON HIPPEL, E. A., Management
WANG, J., Finance
WATTS, R. L., Accounting
WELSCH, R. E., Statistics and Management Science
WERNERFELT, B., Management Science
WESTNEY, D. E., Int. Management
YATES, J., Management Communications

School of Science (77 Massachusetts Ave, Room 6-123, Cambridge, MA 02139; tel. (617) 253-8900; fax (617) 253-8901; internet web .mit.edu/science):

Department of Biology:

BAKER, T., Biology
BARTEL, D. P., Biology
BELL, S., Biology
CHEN, J., Biology
CHISHOLM, S. W., Civil and Environmental Eng. and Biology
CONSTANTINE-PATON, M., Biology
FINK, G. R., Genetics
GROSSMAN, A. D., Biology
GUARENTE, L. P., Biology
HOPKINS, N. H., Biology
HORVITZ, H. R., Biology
HOUSMAN, D. E., Cancer Research
HYNES, R. O., Cancer Research
IMPERIALI, B., Biochemistry
INGRAM, V. M., Biochemistry
JACKS, T. E., Biology
JAENISCH, R., Biology
KAISER, C., Genetics (Head)
KING, J. A., Biology
KRIEGER, M., Molecular Genetics
LANDER, E., Biology
LAUFFENBURGER, D., Biological Eng.
LEES, J. A., Biology
LINDQUIST, S., Plant Molecular Biology

LODISH, H. F., Biology and Bioengineering
MATSUDAIRA, P., Biology and Eng.
ORR-WEAVER, T., Biology
PAGE, D., Biology
PARDUE, M. L., Biology
QUINN, W., Neurobiology
RAJBHANDARY, U. L., Biochemistry
RICH, A., Biophysics
SAMSON, L., Biological Eng.
SAUER, R. T., Biology
SHARP, P. A., Biology
SHENG, M., Neuroscience
SINSKEY, A. J., Microbiology
SIVE, H. L., Biology
SOLOMON, F., Biology
SORGER, P. K., Biology and Biological Eng.
STEINER, L. A., Immunology
STUBBE, J. D., Chemistry and Biology
TONEGAWA, S., Biology and Neuroscience
WALKER, G. C., Biology
WEINBERG, R. A., Cancer Research
YOUNG, R. A., Biology

Department of Brain and Cognitive Sciences:

ADELSON, E. H., Visual Sciences
BEAR, M., Neuroscience
BERWICK, R. C., Computational Linguistics
BIZZI, E., Brain Sciences and Human Behaviour
CHOROVER, S. L., Psychology
CONSTANTINE-PATON, M., Biology
CORKIN, S. H., Behavioural Neuroscience
DESIMONE, R., Neuroscience
GABRIELI, J., Health Sciences and Technology and Cognitive Neuroscience
GIBSON, E., Cognitive Sciences
GRAYBIEL, A. M., Neuroanatomy
HEIN, A., Experimental Psychology
HOCKFIELD, S., Neuroscience
HOGAN, N., Mechanical Eng.
KANWISHER, N. G., Cognitive Neuroscience
MILLER, E. K., Visual Neuroscience
POGGIO, T. A., Vision Sciences and Biophysics
POTTER, M. C., Psychology
QUINN, W. G., Neurobiology
RICHARDS, W. A., Psychophysics
SCHILLER, P. H., Medical Eng. and Medical Physics
SCHNEIDER, G. E., Neuroscience
SCHULTZ, W., Neuroscience
SEUNG, H. S., Computational Neuroscience
SHENG, M. H-T., Neurobiology
SLOTINE, J.-J. E., Mechanical Eng. and Information Sciences
SUR, M., Neuroscience (Head)
TONEGAWA, S., Biology and Neuroscience
WEXLER, K. N., Psychology and Linguistics
WILSON, M., Neuroscience
WURTMAN, R. J., Neuropharmacology

Department of Chemistry:

BAWENDI, M. G., Chemistry
BUCHWALD, S. L., Chemistry
CEYER, S. T., Chemistry
CUMMINS, C. C., Chemistry
DANHEISER, R. L., Chemistry
DEUTCH, J. M., Chemistry
ESSIGMANN, J. M., Chemistry, Toxicology and Biological Eng.
FIELD, R. W., Chemistry
FU, G. C., Chemistry
GRIFFIN, R. G., Chemistry
IMPERIALI, B., Chemistry and Biology
KEMP, D. S., Chemistry
KLIBANOV, A. M., Chemistry and Bioengineering
LIPPARD, S. J., Chemistry
NELSON, K. A., Chemistry
NOCERA, D. G., Chemistry
SCHROCK, R. R., Chemistry
SILBEY, R. J., Chemistry
STEINFELD, J. I., Chemistry
STUBBE, J., Chemistry and Biology
SWAGER, T. M., Chemistry (Head)
TANNENBAUM, S. R., Chemistry and Toxicology

Department of Earth, Atmospheric and Planetary Sciences:

BINZEL, R. P., Planetary Science
BOWRING, S. A., Geology
BOYLE, E. A., Ocean Geochemistry
BRAS, R. L., Civil and Environmental Eng. and Earth, Atmospheric and Planetary Science
BURCHFIEL, B. C., Geology
ELLIOT, J. L., Planetary Astronomy and Physics
EMANUEL, K. A., Atmospheric Science
ENTEKHABI, D., Civil and Environmental Eng. and Earth, Atmospheric and Planetary Sciences
EVANS, J. B., Geophysics
FLIERL, G. R., Oceanography
FREY, F. A., Geochemistry
GROTZINGER, J. P., Geology
GROVE, T. L., Geology
HAGER, B. H., Earth Sciences
HERRING, T. A., Geophysics
HODGES, K., Geology
LINDZEN, R. S., Meteorology
MARSHALL, J., Atmospheric and Oceanic Sciences
MOLINA, M. J., Atmospheric Chemistry and Environmental Studies
MORGAN, F. D., Geophysics
PLUMB, R. A., Meteorology
PRINN, R. G., Atmospheric Chemistry (Head)
RIZZOLI, P. M., Physical Oceanography
ROTHMAN, D. H., Geophysics
ROYDEN, L., Geology and Geophysics
STONE, P. H., Climate Dynamics
SUMMONS, R. E., Geobiology
TOKSÖZ, M. N., Geophysics
VAN DER HILST, R., Geophysics
WHIPPLE, K., Process Geomorphology
WISDOM, J., Planetary Sciences
WUNSCH, C. I., Physical Oceanography
ZUBER, M. T., Planetary Sciences and Geophysics (Head)

Department of Mathematics:

ARTIN, M., Mathematics
BENNEY, D. J., Applied Mathematics
BERGER, B., Applied Mathematics
BEZRUKANNIKOV, R., Mathematics
CHENG, H., Applied Mathematics
COLDING, T. H., Mathematics
DE JONG, A. J., Mathematics
DUDLEY, R. M., Mathematics
EDELMAN, A., Applied Mathematics
ETINGOF, P. I., Mathematics
FREEDMAN, D. Z., Applied Mathematics
GOEMANS, M., Applied Mathematics
GUILLEMIN, V. W., Mathematics
HELGASON, S., Mathematics
JERISON, D. S., Mathematics
KAČ, V., Mathematics
KLEIMAN, S., Mathematics
KLEITMAN, D. J., Applied Mathematics
LEIGHTON, F. T., Applied Mathematics
LUSZTIG, G., Mathematics
MATTUCK, A. P., Mathematics
MELROSE, R. B., Mathematics
MILLER, H. R., Mathematics
MROWKA, T., Mathematics
ROGERS, H., Jr, Mathematics
ROSALES, R. R., Applied Mathematics
SACKS, G. E., Mathematical Logic
SHOR, P., Applied Mathematics
SINGER, I. M., Mathematics
SIPSER, M., Applied Mathematics (Head)
STANLEY, R. P., Applied Mathematics
STRANG, W. G., Mathematics
STROOCK, D. W., Mathematics
TIAN, G., Mathematics
TOOMRE, A., Applied Mathematics
VOGAN, D. A., Jr, Mathematics

Department of Physics:

ASHOORI, R., Physics
BECKER, U. J., Physics

BELCHER, J. W., Physics
BENEDEK, G. B., Physics and Biological Physics
BERTOZZI, W., Physics
BERTSCHINGER, E., Physics
BUSZA, M. S., Physics
CANIZARES, C. R., Physics
CHEN, M., Physics
COPPI, B., Physics
DRESSELHAUS, M. S., Physics and Electrical Eng.
ELLIOT, J. L., Physics and Astronomy
FARHI, E., Physics
FELD, M. S., Physics
FISHER, P. H., Physics
FREEDMAN, D., Mathematics and Physics
GREYTAK, T. J., Physics
GUTH, A. H., Physics
HEWITT, J. N., Physics
IPPEN, E. P., Electrical Eng. and Physics
JACKIW, R. W., Physics
JAFFE, R. L., Physics and Science
JOANNOPOULOS, J. D., Physics
JOSS, P. C., Physics
KARDAR, M., Physics
KASTNER, M., Physics (Head)
KETTERLE, W., Physics
KOWALSKI, S. B., Physics
LEE, P. A., Physics
LEVITOV, L., Physics
LEWIN, W. H. G., Physics
LITSTER, J. D., Physics
MATTHEWS, J. L., Physics
MILNER, R. G., Physics
MONIZ, E. J., Physics
NEGELE, J. W., Physics
PORKOLAB, M., Physics
PRITCHARD, D. E., Physics
RAJAGOPAL, K., Physics
RAPPAPORT, S. A., Physics
REDWINE, R. P., Physics
SCHECHTER, P., Astrophysics
SEUNG, H. S., Life Sciences and Physics
TAYLOR, W., Physics
TING, S. C. C., Physics
WEN, X.-G., Physics
WILCZEK, F., Physics
WYSLOUCH, B., Physics
YAMAMOTO, R. K., Physics
ZWIEBACH, B., Physics

Whitaker College of Health Sciences and Technology (77 Massachusetts Ave, Room E25-519, Cambridge, MA 02139; tel. (617) 258-8974; fax (617) 253-7498; internet http://hst.mit.edu):

BENEDEK, G. B., Physics and Health Sciences and Technology
BRAIDA, L. D., Electrical Eng. and Health Sciences and Technology
COHEN, R. J., Health Sciences and Technology
CRAVALHO, E. G., Mechanical Eng. and Health Sciences and Technology
EDELMAN, E. R., Health Sciences and Technology
GABRIELI, J., Health Sciences and Technology, Brain and Cognitive Sciences
GEHRKE, L., Health Sciences and Technology
GRAY, M. L., Medical Eng.
HOUSMAN, D. D., Biology
LANGER, R. S., Chemical and Biomedical Eng. and Health Sciences and Technology
LEES, R. S., Health Sciences and Technology
MARK, R. G., Health Sciences and Technology and Electrical Eng.
SINSKEY, A. J., Biology and Health Sciences and Technology
STEVENS, K. N., Electrical Eng.
SZOLOVITS, P., Electrical Eng. and Computer Science
WURTMAN, R. J., Neuropharmacology and Health Sciences and Technology

YOUNG, L. R., Astronautics and Health Sciences and Technology

HEADS OF OTHER ACADEMIC ACTIVITIES

Biotechnology Process Eng. Center: L. G. GRIFFITH
Cambridge–MIT Institute: E. CRAWLEY
Center for Advanced Visual Studies: K. WODICZKO
Center for Archaeological Materials: H. LECHTMAN
Center for Biomedical Eng.: A. J. GRODZINSKY
Center for Cancer Research: T. JACKS
Center for Computational Research in Econ. and Management Science: R. E. WELSCH
Center for Co-ordination Science: T. W. MALONE
Center for ebusiness @ MIT: E. BRYNJOLFSSON
Center for Energy and Environmental Policy Research: P. JOSKOW
Center for Environmental Health Sciences: L. SAMSON, P. DEDON
Center for Information Systems Research: P. WEILL
Center for Int. Studies: R. SAMUELS
Center for Materials Science and Eng.: M. F. RUBNER
Center for Real Estate: D. GELTNER
Center for Space Research: JACQUELINE HEWITT
Center for Transportation and Logistics: Y. SHEFFI
Clinical Research Center: R. J. WURTMAN
Computer Science and Artificial Intelligence Laboratory: R. BROOKS
Deshpande Center for Technological Innovation: K. HOLLY, C. L. COONEY
Edgerton Center: J. K. VANDIVER
Francis Bitter Magnet Laboratory: R. G. GRIFFIN
Harvard–MIT Div. of Health Sciences and Technology: M. L. GRAY, J. V. BONVENTRE
Haystack Observatory: J. E. SALAH
Institute for Soldier Nanotechnologies: E. L. THOMAS
Institute for Work and Employment Research: T. KOCHAN, P. OSTERMAN
Kavli Institute for Astrophysics and Space Research: J. HEWITT
Knight Science Journalism Fellows Program: B. RENSBERGER
Laboratory for Electromagnetic and Electronic Systems: J. KASSAKIAN
Laboratory for Energy and the Environment: DAVID H. MARKS
Laboratory for Financial Eng.: D. H. MARKS, E. MONIZ
Laboratory for Information and Decision Systems: V. W. S. CHAN
Laboratory for Manufacturing and Productivity: T. G. GUTOWSKI
Laboratory for Nuclear Science: J. MATTHEWS
Leaders for Manufacturing Program: T. J. ALLEN, D. SIMCHI-LEVI
Lincoln Laboratory: D. L. BRIGGS
Management of Technology Program: J. M. UTTERBACK
Materials Processing Center: L. C. KIMERLING
McGovern Institute for Brain Research: P. A. SHARP
Media Laboratory: N. P. NEGROPONTE W. BENDER
Microsystems Technology Laboratories: M. A. SCHMIDT
MIT Entrepreneurship Center: K. P. MORSE E. B. ROBERTS
MIT–WHOI Joint Program in Oceanography: P. MALANOTTE-RIZZOLI
Nuclear Reactor Laboratory: D. MONCTON
Office of Professional Education Program: J. STINE
Operations Research Center: J. B. ORLIN J. N. TSITSIKLIS

Picower Center for Learning and Memory: S. TONEGAWA

Plasma Science and Fusion Center: M. PORKOLAB

Productivity from Information Technology Initiative: M. D. SIEGEL, S. MADNICK

Program in Polymer Science and Technology: G. C. RUTLEDGE

Program on the Pharmaceutical Industry: T. J. ALLEN, C. L. COONEY, S. N. FINKELSTEIN, A. J. SINSKEY

Research Laboratory of Electronics: J. H. SHAPIRO

Sea Grant College Program: C. CHRYSSOSTOMIDIS

Singapore-MIT Alliance: A. T. PATERA

George Russell Harrison Spectroscopy Laboratory: M. S. FELD

System Design and Management Program: T. J. ALLEN, D. SIMCHI-LEVI

System Dynamics Group: J. STERMAN

Technology and Devt Program: F. MOAVENZADEH

Undergraduate Research Opportunities Program: J. K. VANDIVER

Whitehead Institute for Biomedical Research: D. PAGE

Women's Studies: E. WOOD

ATTACHED INSTITUTES

Research Institutes: Broad Institute, Cambridge–MIT Institute, Center for Advanced Visual Studies, Center for Archaeological Materials, Center for Biomedical Eng., Center for Biomedical Innovation, Center for Cancer Research, Center for Computational Research in Econ. and Management Science, Center for Collective Intelligence, Center for Digital Business, Center for Energy and Environmental Policy Research, Center for Environmental Health Sciences, Center for Global Change Science, Center for Int. Studies, Center for Materials Science and Eng., Center for Real Estate, Center for Technology, Policy, and Industrial Devt, Center for Transportation and Logistics, Clinical Research Center, Computer Science and Artificial Intelligence Laboratory, Deshpande Center for Technological Innovation, Div. of Comparative Medicine, Francis Bitter Magnet Laboratory, Haystack Observatory, Institute for Soldier Nanotechnologies, Institute for Work and Employment Research, Joint Program on the Science and Policy of Global Change, Knight Science Journalism Fellows Program, Laboratory for Electromagnetic and Electronic Systems, Laboratory for Energy and the Environment, Laboratory for Financial Eng., Laboratory for Information and Decision Systems, Laboratory for Manufacturing and Productivity, Laboratory for Nuclear Science, Lean Aerospace Initiative, Lincoln Laboratory, Materials Processing Center, McGovern Institute for Brain Research, Media Laboratory, Microsystems Technology Laboratories, MIT Entrepreneurship Center, MIT Kavli Institute for Astrophysics and Space Research, Nuclear Reactor Laboratory, Office of Professional Education Programs, Operations Research Center, Picower Institute for Learning and Memory, Plasma Science and Fusion Center, Productivity from Information Technology Initiative, Research Laboratory of Electronics, Sea Grant College Program, Singapore–MIT Alliance, Spectroscopy Laboratory, System Dynamics Group, Technology and Devt Program, Whitaker College of Health Sciences and Technology, Women's Studies Program.

MASSACHUSETTS MARITIME ACADEMY

101 Academy Dr., Buzzards Bay, MA 02532

Telephone: (508) 830-5000

Fax: (508) 830-5077

E-mail: admissions@maritime.edu

Internet: www.maritime.edu

Founded 1891 as Massachusetts Nautical Training School; present name 1942

Pres. (vacant)

Vice-Pres. for Academic Affairs: BRADLEY LIMA

Vice-Pres. for Admin. and Finance: MICHAEL A. JOYCE

Vice-Pres. for Student Services: ALLEN HANSEN

Dir of Admissions: ROY FULGUERAS

Library Dir: SUSAN BERTEAUX

Number of teachers: 52

Number of students: 770

Depts of Eng., Humanities, Int. Maritime Business, Marine Safety and Environmental Protection, Marine Transportation, Science and Mathematics, Social Science.

MERRIMACK COLLEGE

315 Turnpike St, North Andover, MA 01845

Telephone: (978) 837-5000

Fax: (978) 837-5222

Internet: www.merrimack.edu

Founded 1947

Academic year: September to May

Pres.: RICHARD J. SANTAGATI

Registrar: JENNIFER DISTEFFANO

Dir of Library: BARBARA LACHANCE

Library of 118,083 vols, 1,069 current periodicals

Number of teachers: 139

Number of students: 2,000

DEANS

Girard School of Business and Int. Commerce: ROBERT CUOMO

Science and Eng.: RUSSELL PINIZZOTTO

MGH INSTITUTE OF HEALTH PROFESSIONS

Charleston Navy Yard, 36 First Ave, Boston, MA 02129-4557

Telephone: (617) 726-2947

Fax: (617) 726-3716

E-mail: admissions@mghihp.edu

Internet: www.mghihp.edu

Founded 1980

Academic year: September to August

Pres.: ANN W. CALDWELL

Academic Dean: KEVIN KEARNS

Library of 50,000 vols

Number of teachers: 79

Number of students: 665 (498 full-time)

Divs of Clinical Investigation, Communication Sciences and Disorders, Medical Imaging, Nursing, Physical Therapy

DIRECTORS OF GRADUATE PROGRAMS

Clinical Investigation: Dr PAUL BOEPPLE

Communication Sciences and Disorders: Dr KEVIN P. KEARNS

Medical Imaging: Dr RICHARD TERRASS

Nursing: Dr MARGERY CHISHOLM

Physical Therapy: Dr LESLIE PORTNEY

MONTSERRAT COLLEGE OF ART

23 Essex St, POB 26, Beverly, MA 01915

Telephone: (978) 922-8222

Fax: (978) 921-4241

E-mail: admiss@montserrat.edu

Internet: www.montserrat.edu

Private control

Academic year: September to May

Pres.: Dr HELENA J. STURNICK

Vice-Pres. for Admin. and Finance: LOREN LOOMIS-HUBBELL

Dean of Student Services: BRIAN BICKNELL

Dean of Faculty and Academic Affairs: LAURA TONELLI

Registrar: THERESA SKELLY

Library Dir: CHERI COE

Library of 12,000

Number of teachers: 60

Number of students: 403

Divs of Art Education, Foundation, Graphic Design, Illustration, Interdisciplinary, Liberal Arts, Painting and Drawing, Photo and Video, Printmaking, Sculpture.

MOUNT HOLYOKE COLLEGE

50 College St, South Hadley, MA 01072

Telephone: (413) 538-2000

Fax: (413) 538-2391

E-mail: admission@mtholyoke.edu

Internet: www.mtholyoke.edu

Founded 1837

Academic year: September to May

Pres.: JOANNE V. CREIGHTON

Treas.: MARY JO MAYDEW

Dean of Faculty: DONAL O'SHEA

Dean of College: LEE BOWIE

Assoc. Dean of College and Dean of Students: H. ELIZABETH BRAUN

Dean of Studies: JOSEPH COHEN

Registrar: MONICA AUGUSTIN

Chief Information Officer and Dir of Library, Information and Technology Services: PATRICIA ALBANESE

Library of 700,000 vols

Number of teachers: 206

Number of students: 2,100

Divs of Humanities, Science and Mathematics, Social Sciences

Publication: *Alumnae Quarterly*.

MOUNT IDA COLLEGE

777 Dedham St, Newton Centre, MA 02459

Telephone: (617) 928-4500

Fax: (617) 928-4760

E-mail: admissions@mountida.edu

Internet: www.mountida.edu

Founded 1899

Private control

Academic year: August to May

Pres.: CAROL J. MATTESON

Vice-Pres. for Devt: CHRISTOPHER S. MOSHER

Vice-Pres. for Enrollment Management and Marketing: PHILIP A. CONROY, JR

Vice-Pres. for Academic Affairs: Dr LANCE W. CARLUCCIO

Vice-Pres. for Finance and Admin.: DAVID HEALY

Vice-Pres. for Student Affairs: Dr ELIZABETH TRUE

Registrar: MAUREEN MORIARTY

Dean of Academic Services: ALYCE CURTIS

Dean of Information Technology and Learning Resources: MARGE LIPPINCOTT

Library of 60,000 titles

Number of teachers: 100

Number of students: 1,370

Schools of Animal Science, Arts and Sciences, Business, Design.

NEW ENGLAND COLLEGE OF OPTOMETRY

424 Beacon St, Boston, MA 02115

Telephone: (617) 266-2030

E-mail: admissions@neco.edu

Internet: www.neco.edu

Founded 1894 as Klein School of Optics; present name 1976
Private control
Academic year: September to May
Pres.: ELIZABETH CHEN
Vice-Pres. for Devt: LARRY RAFF
Vice-Pres. for Clinical Care and Services: Dr BARRY J. BARRESI
Vice-Pres. and Dean of Academic Affairs: Dr STEVEN KOEVARY
Vice-Pres. for Finance and Admin.: CAROL DECOURCEY
Vice-Pres. for Professional Services: ROGER WILSON
Vice-Pres. and Dean of Students, Admin. and Alumni: Dr TERRANCE B. NEYLON
Dir of Admissions: TALINE FARRA
Registrar: GLENDA UNDERWOOD
Dir of Library Services: CINDY HUTCHISON
Number of teachers: 77
Number of students: 425

Depts of Biomedical Science and Disease, Community Care, Specialty and Advanced Care, Vision Science.

NEW ENGLAND CONSERVATORY OF MUSIC

290 Huntington Ave, Boston, MA 02115
Telephone: (617) 585-1101
Fax: (617) 585-1115
E-mail: admission@newenglandconservatory.edu
Internet: www.newenglandconservatory.edu
Founded 1867
Academic year: September to May
Pres.: TONY WOODCOCK
Provost: ROBERT DODSON
Dean of College: TOM NOVAK
Registrar: ROBERT WINKLEY
Dir of Libraries: JEAN MORROW
Library: Spaulding Library contains 85,000 vols (books, scores, periodicals); the Firestone Library contains 60,000 sound and video recordings
Number of teachers: 216
Number of students: 770

Publications: *Notes* (2 a year), *Journal for Learning through Music* (annual).

NEW ENGLAND SCHOOL OF LAW

154 Stuart St, Boston, MA 02116
Telephone: (617) 451-0010
E-mail: admit@admin.nesl.edu
Internet: www.nesl.edu
Founded 1908 as Portia Law School; present name 1969
Private control
Academic year: August to May
Dean: JOHN F. O'BRIEN
Assoc. Dean for Academic Affairs: JUDITH G. GREENBERG
Assoc. Dean for Admin.: SUSAN CALAMARE
Chief Financial Officer: FRANK A. SCIOLI
Library Dir: ANNE M. ACTON
Library of 351,000 vols
Number of teachers: 41 full-time, 70 part-time
Number of students: 700 full-time, 400 part-time
Publications: *New England Journal of Comparative and International Law*, *New England Journal on Criminal and Civil Confinement*, *New England Law Review*.

ATTACHED RESEARCH INSTITUTES
Center for Business Law.
Center for International Law and Policy.
Center for Law and Social Responsibility.

NICHOLS COLLEGE

POB 5000, Dudley, MA 01571
Telephone: (508) 213-1560
Fax: (508) 213-2225
E-mail: admissions@nichols.edu
Internet: www.nichols.edu
Founded 1815
Business Admin. and Liberal Arts
Pres.: Dr DEBRA M. MURPHY
Exec. Vice-Pres. and Provost: EZAT PARNIA
Vice-Pres. and Dean: ALAN REINHARDT
Vice-Pres. for Admissions: SUE TELLER
Vice-Pres. for Enrollment and Marketing: TOM CAFARO
Vice-Pres. for College Advancement: JOE COFIELD
Vice-Pres. for Information Technology: KEVIN BRASSARD
Vice-Pres. and Dean of Student Services: BRIAN McCOY
Registrar: BETIN ROBICHAUD
Dir of Library: JIM DOUGLAS
Library of 67,000 vols
Number of teachers: 50
Number of students: 1,532 undergraduates, 415 graduates.

NORTHEASTERN UNIVERSITY

360 Huntington Ave, Boston, MA 02115
Telephone: (617) 373-2000
Internet: www.neu.edu
Founded 1898
Pres.: Dr JOSEPH AOUN
Sr Vice-Pres. for Exec. Affairs: MARK PUTNAM
Vice-Pres. for Student Affairs: E. EDWARD KLOTZBIER
Vice-Pres. for Marketing and Communications: BRIAN KENNY
Provost: AHMED ABDELAL
Dean of Admissions: RONNE PATRICK
Dean of Library: EDWARD A. WARRO
Library of 915,342 vols, 2,152,277 microforms, 8,590 serial titles, 19,279 audio and video items, 167,893 govt documents
Number of teachers: 1,949 (769 full-time, 1,180 part-time)
Number of students: 24,009 (16,456 full-time, 7,553 part-time)

DEANS
College of Business Admin.: Prof. TOM MOORE
College of Criminal Justice: JACK R. GREENE
College of Eng.: ALLEN L. SOYSTER
College of Arts and Sciences: JAMES R. STELLAR
School of Law: EMILY SPIELER
Bouvé College of Health Sciences: STEPHEN R. ZOLOTH
School of Technological Entrepreneurship: PAUL ZAVRACKY
College of Computer and Information Science: LARRY FINKELSTEIN

OLIN COLLEGE OF ENGINEERING

Olin Way, Needham, MA 02492-1200
Telephone: (781) 292-2300
E-mail: info@olin.edu
Internet: www.olin.edu
Founded 1997
Private control; funded by F. W. Olin Foundation
Academic year: August to May
Pres.: RICHARD K. MILLER
Vice-Pres. for Admin. and Finance: STEPHEN P. HANNABURY
Vice-Pres. for External Relations and Enrollment and Dean of Admission: CHARLES S. NOLAN
Vice-Pres. for Innovation and Research: SHERRA E. KERNS

Provost and Dean of Faculty: MICHAEL MOODY (acting)
Dean of Student Life: ROGER C. CRAFTS
Registrar: LINDA CANAVAN
Library Dir: DIANNA MAGNONI
Number of teachers: 28
Number of students: 304
Publication: *Journal of Asynchronous Learning Networks* (2–4 a year).

PINE MANOR COLLEGE

400 Heath St, Chestnut Hill, MA 02467
Telephone: (617) 731-7000
Fax: (617) 731-7199
E-mail: admission@pmc.edu
Internet: www.pmc.edu
Founded 1911 as a post-secondary div. of Dana Hall School; present name and status 1977
Private control
Academic year: September to May
Pres.: Dr GLORIA NEMEROWICZ
Dean of the College: Dr NIA LANE CHESTER
Vice-Pres. for Finance and Business: BETSY ESPE
Vice-Pres. for Institutional Advancement: SUSAN WEBBER
Registrar: KERRY BOYD
Dean of Student Life: DENISE ALLEYNE
Library Dir: MARILYN SMITH BREGOLI
Library of 70,000 vols
Number of teachers: 66
Number of students: 491

Majors in Biology, Business Admin., Communication, Economic and Financial Systems, English, History, Liberal Studies, Management, Psychology, Social and Political Systems, Visual Arts.

REGIS COLLEGE

235 Wellesley St, Weston, MA 02493-1571
Telephone: (781) 768-7000
Fax: (781) 768-8339
Internet: www.regiscollege.edu
Founded 1927
Academic year: September to June
Pres.: MARY JANE ENGLAND
Vice-Pres. for Academic Affairs: PAULA HARBECKE
Vice-Pres. for Student Affairs: LYNN TRIPP COLEMAN
Vice-Pres. for Enrollment and Marketing: R. JOSEPH BELLEVANCE, JR
Vice-Pres. for Finance and Business: THOMAS G. PISTORINO
Registrar: Sister PATRICIA McDONOUGH
Dir of Library: LYNN TRIPLETT
Library of 133,000 vols
Number of teachers: 145
Number of students: 1,138
Publications: *Regis Today*, *Hemetera*, *Alumnae Bulletin*.

ST JOHN'S SEMINARY

127 Lake Street, Brighton, MA 02135
Telephone: (617) 254-2610
Fax: (617) 787-2336
E-mail: rjsullivan@rcab.org
Internet: www.sjs.edu
Founded 1884
Private control
Academic year: September to May
Rector: Rev. JOHN A. FARREN
Vice-Rector: Rev. STEPHEN DONOHOE
Dean of Students: Rev. CHRISTOPHER K. O'CONNOR
Dean of Faculty: Rev. STEPHEN SALOCKS
Librarian: Rev. Mgr LAURENCE W. McGRATH
Library of 159,000 vols

Number of teachers: 22
Number of students: 80 (full-time).

SALEM STATE COLLEGE

352 Lafayette St, Salem, MA 01970
Telephone: (978) 542-6000
E-mail: college.relations@salemstate.edu
Internet: www.salemstate.edu
Founded 1854
Pres.: Dr NANCY D. HARRINGTON
Vice-Pres. for Academic Affairs: Dr DIANE R. LAPKIN
Vice-Pres. for Admin. and Finance: JOSEPH DONOVAN
Vice-Pres. for Institutional Advancement: CYNTHIA McGURREN
Exec. Vice-Pres. for Student Life: STANLEY P. CAHILL
Dean of Students: JAMES G. STOLL
Dean of Library: SUSAN E. CIRILLO

Library of 225,000 vols
Number of teachers: 301
Number of students: 5,400

Depts of Accounting and Finance, Art, Biology, Business, Cartography and GIS, Chemistry, Communications, Computer Science, Criminal Justice, Econ., Education, English, Fire Science, Foreign Languages, Geography, Geology, History, Interdisciplinary Studies, Management, Marketing and Decision Sciences, Mathematics, Music, Nursing, Occupational Therapy, Philosophy, Physics, Political Science, Psychology, Speech Communication, Social Work, Spanish, Sociology, Sport, Fitness and Leisure Studies, Theatre

DEANS

School of Arts and Sciences: ANITA SHEA
School of Business: K. BREWER DORAN
Schools of Human Services: NEAL DeCHILLO

SCHOOL OF THE MUSEUM OF FINE ARTS

230 The Fenway, Boston, MA 02115
Telephone: (617) 267-6100
Fax: (617) 424-6271
E-mail: admissions@smfa.edu
Internet: www.smfa.edu
Academic year: September to May
Dean of the School: DEBORAH H. DLUHY
Dean of Faculty: LORNE FALK
Dean of Admissions: SUSAN CLAIN
Provost and Dir of Devt: DAN POTEET
Library of 130,000 vols
Number of teachers: 140
Number of students: 1,124.

SIMON'S ROCK COLLEGE OF BARD

84 Alford Rd, Great Barrington, MA 01230
Telephone: (413) 528-0771
Fax: (413) 528-7365
E-mail: admin@simons-rock.edu
Internet: www.simons-rock.edu
Founded 1966
Private control
Academic year: August to May
Pres.: LEON BOTSTEIN
Provost and Vice-Pres.: MARY MARCY
Exec. Vice-Pres.: DIMITRI PAPADIMITRIOU
Vice-Pres. for Early College Policies and Programs: U BA WIN
Registrar: ROCHELLE DUFFY
Library Dir: JOAN GOODKIND
Library of 71,000 items
Number of teachers: 40
Number of students: 390

Divs of Arts, Languages and Literature, Science, Mathematics and Computing, Social Studies.

SIMMONS COLLEGE

300 The Fenway, Boston, MA 02115
Telephone: (617) 521-2000
Fax: (617) 521-3199
E-mail: ugadm@simmons.edu
Internet: www.simmons.edu
Founded 1899
Pres.: SUSAN SCRIMSHAW
Sr Vice-Pres. for Admin. and Planning: LISA CHAPNICK
Vice-Pres. for Advancement: KRISTINA SCHAEFFER
Sr Vice-Pres. and Treasurer: HUMBERTO GONÇALVES
Registrar: DONNA DOLAN
Dir of Libraries: DAPHNE HARRINGTON
Number of teachers: 403 (184 full-time, 219 part-time)
Number of students: 3,334
Publications: *Simmons Review*, *Now*, *Simmons News*, *Essays and Studies*, *Abafazi*

DEANS

College of Arts and Sciences: DIANE RAYMOND (acting)
School of Management: DEBORAH MERRILL-SANDS
Graduate School of Library and Information Sciences: MICHELE CLOONAN
School of Social Work: STEFAN KRUG
School of Health Studies: GERALD KOOCHER

SMITH COLLEGE

Northampton, MA 01063
Telephone: (413) 584-2700
Fax: (413) 585-2123
E-mail: admission@smith.edu
Internet: www.smith.edu
Founded 1871
Academic year: September to May
Pres.: CAROL CHRIST
Provost and Dean of the Faculty: SUSAN BOURQUE
Vice-Pres. for Advancement: PATRICIA JACKSON
Dean of the College: MAUREEN A. MAHONEY
Dean of Students: JULIANNE OHOTNICKY
Registrar: TRICIA O'NEILL
Dir of Libraries: CHRISTOPHER LORING
Library of 1,200,000 vols
Number of teachers: 303 (287 full-time, 16 part-time)
Number of students: 2,781students (2,682 undergraduate women, 99 postgraduate men and women)
Publications: *Bulletin of the Museum of Art* (irreg.), *Alumnae Quarterly*, *Meridians*.

SOUTHERN NEW ENGLAND SCHOOL OF LAW

333 Faunce Corner Rd, North Dartmouth, MA 02747
Telephone: (508) 998-9600
E-mail: admissions@snesl.edu
Internet: www.snesl.edu
Private control
Academic year: August to May
Chancellor: Hon. FRANCIS J. LARKIN
Dean: Dr ROBERT V. WARD, Jr
Registrar: CAROL VIDAL
Library Director: LOIS KANE
Number of students: 227.

SPRINGFIELD COLLEGE

263 Alden St, Springfield, MA 01109-3797
Telephone: (413) 748-3000
Fax: (413) 748-3746
Internet: www.spfldcol.edu
Founded 1885

Academic year: August to May
Pres.: Dr RICHARD B. FLYNN
Vice-Pres. for Academic Affairs: Dr JEAN WYLD
Vice-Pres. for Finance and Admin.: JOHN MAILHOT
Vice-Pres. for Institutional Advancement: DAVID FRABONI
Vice-Pres. for Student Affairs: Dr DAVID G. BRAVERMAN
Registrar: IRENE RIOS
Librarian: ANDREA TAUPIER
Library of 187,358 vols, 25,586 bound periodicals
Number of teachers: 205 full-time
Number of students: 5,090 (incl. satellite campuses)

DEANS

School of Arts, Science and Professional Studies: Dr MARY HEALEY
School of Health, Physical Education, and Recreation: Dr WILLIAM J. CONSIDINE
School of Health Sciences and Rehabilitation Studies: Dr WILLIAM M. SUSMAN
School of Human Services: Dr ROBERT WILLEY
School of Social Work: Dr FRANCINE J. VECCHIOLLA

STONEHILL COLLEGE

320 Washington St, Easton, MA 02357
Telephone: (508) 565-1000
Fax: (508) 565-1500
Internet: www.stonehill.edu
Founded 1948
Academic year: September to May
Pres.: Rev. MARK T. CREGAN
Vice-Pres. for Academic Affairs: KATIE CONBOY
Vice-Pres. for Student Affairs: Rev. GEORGE B. MULLIGAN
Vice-Pres. for Advancement: FRANCIS X. DILLON
Vice-Pres. for Finance: JEANNE FINLAYSON
Vice-Pres. for Mission: Rev. JOHN DENNING
Dean of Faculty: KAREN TALENTINO
Registrar: JOHN PESTANA
Dir of Library: ED HYNES
Library of 194,587 vols
Number of teachers: 230 (126 full-time, 104 part-time)
Number of students: 2,617

Depts of Admin., History, History and Philosophy of Science, Int. Studies, Irish Studies, Labor Studies, Mathematics, Middle Eastern/Asian Studies, Military Science, Philosophy, Physics, Political Science, Psychology, Public Admin., Religious Studies, Sociology and Criminology, Theatre Arts, Writing Program.

SUFFOLK UNIVERSITY

8 Ashburton Place, Boston, MA 02108-2770
Telephone: (617) 573-8000
Fax: (617) 573-8353
Internet: www.suffolk.edu
Founded 1906
Pres.: DAVID J. SARGENT
Provost and Academic Vice-Pres.: PATRICIA MAGUIRE MESERVEY
Vice-Pres. for Enrollment and Int. Programs: MARGUERITE DENNIS
Vice-Pres. for Advancement: KATHRYN M. BATTILLO
Vice-Pres. for Govt and Community Affairs: JOHN A. NUCCI
Vice-Pres. and Treasurer: FRANCIS X. FLANNERY
Dean of Students: NANCY C. STOLL
Dean of College: KENNETH S. GREENBERG

Registrar of Colleges: MARY M. LALLY
Registrar of Law School: LORRAINE D. COVE
Dir of Libraries: EDMUND HAMANN

Libraries of 241,000 vols, 2,070 periodicals, 396,250 microform units

Number of teachers: c. 400
Number of students: 6,203

Publications: *Suffolk Journal, Suffolk Law Review, The Advocate, Venture, Transnational Law Journal*

DEANS

Colleges of Arts and Sciences: KENNETH S. GREENBERG
Sawyer Business School: WILLIAM J. O'NEILL, Jr
Law School: ALFRED C. AMAN, Jr

TUFTS UNIVERSITY

Admin. Bldg, 169 Holland St, Somerville, MA 02144

Telephone: (617) 628-5000
Internet: www.tufts.edu

Founded 1852

Academic year: September to May

Pres.: LAWRENCE S. BACOW
Provost and Sr Vice-Pres.: JAMSHED BHARU-CHA
Exec. Vice-Pres.: STEVEN S. MANOS
Vice-Pres. for Operations: JOHN M. ROBERTO
Vice-Pres. for Operations: THOMAS S. McGURTY
Vice-Pres. for Human Resources: KATHE CRONIN
Vice-Pres. for Univ. Advancement: BRIAN LEE
Vice-Pres. for Univ. Relations: MARY R. JAKE
Dean of Undergraduate Admissions: LEE COFFIN
Dean of Students: BRUCE REITMAN
Dir of Tisch Library: JO-ANN MICHALAK

Library of 1,134,519 vols

Number of teachers: 1,143 (739 full-time, 404 part-time)

Number of students: 8,500

Attached research institutes and centres: Institute for Global Leadership; Talloires European Center; Int. Food and Nutrition Center; Alan Shawn Feinstein Int. Famine Center; Fares Center for Eastern Mediterranean Studies; Center for South Asian and Indian Ocean Studies; Center for Int. Environmental and Resource Policy; Int. Food and Nutrition Center; Alan Shawn Feinstein Int. Famine Center; Jean Mayer USDA Human Nutrition Research Center on Aging (HNRCA); Center for Physical Fitness; Matthew and Brenda B. Ross Initiative on Aging; Center on Nutrition Communication; Center on Hunger, Poverty and Nutrition Policy; Tufts Univ. Nutrition and HIV Research Program; Center on Agriculture, Food, and Environment; Institute for Applied Research in Youth Devt; Tufts Univ. Center for Children; Center for Applied Child Devt; Eliot-Pearson Children's School; Tufts Educational Day Care Center; Center for Academic Excellence; Center for Interdisciplinary Studies; Center for Eng. Educational Outreach; Center for Reading and Language Research; Tufts Institute for Lifelong Learning; Gordon Institute; Center for Science and Mathematics Teaching; Wright Center for Innovative Science Education; Tissue Eng. Resource Center (TERC); Tufts Center for the Study of Drug Devt; Eng. Project Devt Center; Cancer Center; Center for Adaptation Genetics and Drug Resistance; Center for Gastroenterology Research on Absorptive and Secretory Processes; Molecular Cardiology Research Institute; Center for Cognitive Studies; Thermal Analysis of Materials Processing Laboratory; Institute for Applied Research in Youth Devt;

Center for Vision Research; Center on Agriculture, Food, and Environment; Center for Conservation Medicine; Center for Animals and Public Policy; Global Devt and Environment Institute; Tufts Institute of the Environment; Water: Systems, Science, and Society (WSSS) Research and Graduate Education Program; Water and Environmental Research, Education and Applications Solutions Network (WE REASoN); Tufts Univ. Center for Children; Talloires European Center; Fares Center for Eastern Mediterranean Studies; Tufts Institute of the Environment; Institute for Global Leadership; Matthew and Brenda B. Ross Initiative on Aging; Univ. Council on Graduate Education

Publications: *Tufts Journal, Tufts Health and Nutrition Letter, International Journal of Middle East Studies, Tufts Medicine, Tufts Veterinary Medicine* (2 a year)

DEANS

School of Arts and Sciences (Medford): ROBERT J. STERNBERG
Graduate School of Arts and Sciences (Medford): LYNNE PEPALL
School of Eng. (Medford): LINDA ABRIOLA
Cummings School of Veterinary Medicine (Grafton): DEBORAH T. KOCHEVAR
Fletcher School of Law and Diplomacy (Medford): STEPHEN BOSWORTH
Friedman School of Nutrition Science and Policy (Boston): EILEEN KENNEDY
School of Dental Medicine (Boston): LONNIE NORRIS
School of Medicine (Boston): MICHAEL ROSENBLATT
Sackler School of Graduate Biomedical Sciences (Boston): NAOMI ROSENBERG
Jonathan M. Tisch College of Citizenship and Public Service (Medford): ROB HOLLISTER

PROFESSORS

ADELMAN, L., Pathology
ADLER, D., Psychiatry
AFSAR, M. N., Electrical Eng. and Computer Science
ALONSO, J. M., Romance Languages
AMMONS, E. M., English
ANWER, S., Biomedical Sciences
ARIAS, I., Physiology
ARMON, C., Neurology
AUSMAN, L., Nutrition
BACHOVCHIN, W. W., Biochemistry
BAND, V., Radiation Oncology
BANKOFF, M., Radiology
BANKS, H., Orthopaedic Surgery
BARRETT, D. M., Neurology
BARZA, M., Medicine
BEINFELD, M. C., Pharmacology
BERG, J., Clinical Sciences
BERNSTEIN, J. A., Music
BERNSTEIN, M., Arts and Sciences
BERRY, J., Political Science
BIANCHI, D. W., Paediatrics
BLACHER, R., Psychiatry
BLOOMQUIST, E., Physiology
BOGHOSIAN, B., Mathematics
BORGERS, C., Mathematics
BOTSARIS, G. D., Chemical Eng.
BOUDRIEAU, R. J., Clinical Sciences
BOYER, M., Public Health and Family Medicine
BRATT, R. G., Urban and Environmental Policy and Planning
BRENNER, B., Civil and Environmental Eng.
BRIDGES, R., Biomedical Sciences
BRODER, M. I., Medical Admin.
BRONSON, R. T., Biomedical Sciences
BROWN, L. C., Civil and Environmental Eng.
BROWN, R. B., Medicine
BROWN, W., Neurology
BULLOCK, P. A., Biochemistry
BURKMAN, R. T., Obstetrics and Gynaecology

BUSHNELL, E. W., Psychology
CANTOR, A. J., English
CARR, D., Anaesthesiology
CARTER, B., Radiology
CASSADY, J., Radiation Oncology
CASTELLOT, J., Anatomy
CAVAZOS, L., Public Health and Family Medicine
CAVE, D. R., Medicine
CAVINESS, M., Art and Art History
CEBE, P., Physics
CELLI, B., Medicine
CETRULO, C., Obstetrics and Gynaecology
CHAPMAN, R., Dental Health
CHAPRA, S., Civil and Environmental Eng.
CHECHILE, R. A., Psychology
CHEN, J., General Dentistry
CHEW, F., Biology
CHOI, I. S., Radiology
CIRAULO, D., Psychiatry
COCHRAN, B., Physiology
COCHRANE, D. E., Biology
COE, N., Surgery
COFFIN, J. M., Microbiology
CONKLIN, J. E., Sociology
CONNELLY, N., Anaesthesiology
COOK, R. G., Psychology
COTTER, S., Clinical Sciences
CRANE, G., Classics
CRAVEN, D. E., Medicine
CROCHETIERE, W. J., Mechanical Eng.
CULLEN, D. J., Anaesthesiology
DAMASSA, D., Anatomy
DARLING, D. B., Radiology
DAWSON-HUGHES, B., Medicine
DEBOLD, J. F, Psychology
DENNETT, D. C., Philosophy
DEWALD, R. R., Chemistry
DICE, J. F., Jr, Physiology
DIGGES, D., English
DODMAN, N. H., Clinical Sciences
DRACHMAN, V., History
DRAPKIN, M. S., Medicine
DUCIBELLA, T., Obstetrics and Gynaecology
DUKER, J. S., Ophthalmology
DUNLAP, K., Neuroscience
DWYER, J., Nutrition
EASTERBROOKS, A., Child Devt
EDELMAN, L. C., English
EDGERS, L., Civil and Environmental Eng.
ELKIND, D., Child Devt
ENGELKING, L., Biomedical Sciences
EPSTEIN, S. K., Medicine
ESTES, N. A. M., Medicine
FANBURG, B. L., Medicine
FAWAZ, K., Medicine
FAWAZ, L., Diplomacy
FEIG, L. A., Biochemistry
FEINGOLD, D., Dermatology
FELDMAN, D. H., Child Devt
FLYNN, C., English
FLYTZANI-STEPHANOPOULOS, M., Chemical Eng.
FOLSTEIN, M. F., Biological Science
FORCE, T. L., Medicine
FORD, L. H., Physics
FORGAC, M., Physiology
FRANK, E., Physiology
FRANTZ, III, I. D., Paediatrics
FRIEDBERG, R. C., Pathology
FRISKEN, S., Computer Science
FYLER, J., English
GAASCH, W. H., Medicine
GALBURT, E. B., Restorative Dentistry
GALPER, J. R., Medicine
GANDA, K., General Dentistry
GANG, D. L., Pathology
GELFAND, J. A., Medicine
GEORGAKIS, C., Chemical Eng.
GHEEWALLA, R., Orthodontics
GITTLEMAN, S., German, Russian and Asian Languages
GLENNON, M. J., Instruction – Fletcher School
GOLDBERG, E. B., Microbiology
GOLDBERG, J., Nutrition

GOLDBERG, J. R., Orthopaedic Surgery
GOLDENBERG, D., Medicine
GOLDIN, B., Public Health and Family Medicine
GOLDIN, B. R., Nutrition, Infection Unit
GOLDNER, R. B., Electrical Eng. and Computer Science
GOLDSTEIN, G. R., Physics
GONSALVES, R. A., Electrical Eng. and Computer Science
GOODE, R. K., Oral Pathology
GORBACH, S. L., Public Health and Family Medicine
GRACE, N., Medicine
GREEN, D. B., Endodontics
GREENBLATT, D. J., Pharmacology
GREENFIELD, S., Family Medicine/Community Health
GREIF, R., Mechanical Eng.
GUERTIN, R. P., Physics
GUNTHER, L., Physics
GUTIERREZ, M. A., Mathematics
HAAS, T. E., Chemistry
HAFFAJEE, C., Medicine
HAHN, M. G., Mathematics
HAMMER, R. P., Psychiatry
HANNUM, H., Instruction - Fletcher School
HARDER, D. W., Psychology
HARTNELL, G., Radiology
HASSELBLATT, B., Mathematics
HEDGES, III, T., Ophthalmology
HENEIN, E., Romance Languages
HENNEMAN, P., Emergency Medicine
HERMAN, I. M., Physiology
HESKETH, P., Medicine
HESS, A., Instruction - Fletcher School
HIBBERD, P., Medicine
HIGBY, D. J., Medicine
HILL, N. S., Medicine
HOLCOMB, P., Psychology
HOMER, M. J., Medicine
HOWE, E. T., Romance Languages
HSU, L. K. G., Psychiatry
HUBER, B., Pathology
HUDEC, R., Instruction - Fletcher School
IOANNIDES, Y., Econ.
ISBERG, R., Microbiology
ISLAM, S., Civil and Environmental Eng.
JACKSON, F. R., Neuroscience
JACOB, M. H., Neuroscience
JACOBSON, S., Anatomy
JACQUE, L., Instruction - Fletcher School
JALAL, A., History
JAY, D. G., Physiology
JENKINS, R., Surgery
JENNINGS, J., Urban and Environmental Policy and Planning
JOHNSON, V. T., German, Russian and Asian Languages
JOSEPH, P., Sociology
KACHANOV, M. L., Mechanical Eng.
KAFKA, T., Physics
KAHN, M., Oral Pathology
KAPLAN, D., Biomedical Eng.
KAPLAN, D., Chemical Eng.
KAPLAN, M., Medicine
KASSIRER, J. P., Medical Admin.
KAUER, J., Neuroscience
KENNISON, R. D., Obstetrics and Gynaecology
KENNY, J. E., Chemistry
KIRSHEN, P., Civil and Environmental Eng.
KLAUBER, G., Urology
KLEIN, M., Instruction - Fletcher School
KONSTAM, M. A., Medicine
KOPELMAN, R. I., Medicine
KOPIN, A. S., Medicine
KOSOWSKY, B. D., Medicine
KRAUS, K. H., Clinical Sciences
KRIMSKY, S., Urban and Environmental Policy and Planning
KUGEL, G., Dental Admin.
KULIG, J. W., Paediatrics
KUMAR, M.S.A., Biomedical Sciences
LANG, K. R., Physics
LAU, J., Medicine
LEAV, I., Biomedical Sciences

LEBOWITZ, A. L., English
LECHAN, R. M., Medicine
LEITER, A. R., Medicine
LERNER, R. M., Child Devt
LEVEY, A. S., Medicine
LEVINE, H. J., Medicine
LINSENMAYER, T. F., Anatomy
LIPTZIN, B., Psychiatry
LISCUM, L., Physiology
LITVAK, J. D., English
LOCKERETZ, W., Instruction – Nutrition
LOPEZ, M. J., Surgery
LOSORDO, D. W., Medicine
LYNCH, L. M., Teaching at Fletcher School
MCCAULEY, R., Radiology
MACDONNELL, K. F., Medicine
MACKEY, W. C., Surgery
MADIAS, N. E., Medicine
MADOFF, M. A., Public Health and Family Medicine
MALAMY, M., Microbiology
MALCHOW, H., History
MANN, W. A., Physics
MANNO, V., Mechanical Eng.
MARCOPOULOS, G. J., History
MARRONE, S. P., History
MEHTA, N. R., General Dentistry
MEIRI, K., Anatomy
MENDELSOHN, M. E., Medicine
METCALF, G. E., Econ.
MICZEK, K. A., Psychology
MOOMAW, W., Instruction – Fletcher School
MOORE, A. S., Clinical Sciences
MOORE, C., Microbiology
MULHOLLAND, D. M., History
MURPHY, R., Medicine
NAIMI, S., Medicine
NAPIER, A., Physics
NAVAB, V., Medicine
NELSON, C. G., German, Russian and Asian Languages
NELSON, F. C., Mechanical Eng.
NEWBERG, A. H., Radiology
NIELSEN, H. C., Paediatrics
NITECKI, Z. H., Mathematics
NOLLER, K. L., Obstetrics and Gynaecology
NOONAN, J. P., Electrical Eng. and Computer Science
NORMAN, G., Econ.
O'CONNELL, B., Citizenship and Public Service
O'CONNELL, B., Lincoln Filene Centre
O'DONNELL, T. F., Surgery
O'GRADY, J., Obstetrics and Gynaecology
OLIVER, W. P., Physics
OSTRANDER, S. A., Sociology
OXENKRUG, G. F., Psychiatry
PAGE, D. W., Surgery
PALMER, C., Preventive Dentistry
PANJWANI, N., Ophthalmology
PAPAGEORGE, M., Oral and Maxillofacial Surgery
PAPAS, A., General Dentistry
PAUKER, S. G., Medicine
PAYNE, D. D., Surgery
PECHENIK, J., Biology
PENNINCK, D. G., Clinical Sciences
PEREIRA, B., Medicine
PERLMAN, B., Mechanical Eng.
PERRIN, M. A., Pathology
PERRONE, R. D., Medicine
PERRY, J., Instruction – Fletcher School
PFALTZGRAFF, R., Instruction – Fletcher School
PLAUT, A. G., Medicine
PORTNEY, K. E., Political Science
PREIS, D., Electrical Eng. and Computer Science
PREVELAKIS, G., Fletcher School
QUINTO, E. T., Mathematics
RABSON, A., Pathology
RAND, W., Public Health and Family Medicine
REBEIZ, E., Otolaryngology, Head and Neck Surgery
REID, P. L. D., Classics

REITER, E., Paediatrics
REUBEN, S., Anaesthiology
REUTER, K., Radiology
RICHARD, M., Philosophy
RICHMOND, J., Lincoln Filene Centre
RIDGE, J. C., Geology
ROBBINS, A., Public Health and Family Medicine
ROFFLER TARLOV, S., Neuroscience
ROGERS, B. L., Nutrition
ROGERS, C., Mechanical Eng.
ROHRER, R. J., Surgery
ROMERO, C. Z., German, Russian and Asian Languages
ROPPER, A., Neurology
ROSE, D. N., Medicine
ROSENBERG, I., Physiology
ROSENBERG, M., Oral and Maxillofacial Surgery
ROSENBERG, N., Medical Pathology
ROSS, J., Jr, Clinical Sciences
ROTHBAUM, F. M., Child Devt
ROWLAND, T. W., Paediatrics
RUBY, L., Orthopaedic Surgery
RUSH, J. E., Clinical Sciences
RUSSELL, R., Medicine
SABIN, T. D., Neurology
SADEGHI-NEJAD, A., Paediatrics
SAHAGIAN, G., Physiology
SAIGAL, A., Mechanical Eng.
SALACUSE, J. W., Instruction – Fletcher School
SALEM, D., Medicine
SALTER, R., German, Russian and Asian Languages
SANAYEI, M., Civil and Environmental Eng.
SAPERSTEIN, G., Environmental and Population Health
SARNO, R. C., Radiology
SBARRA, A. J., Obstetrics and Gynaecology
SCHAEFER, E., Medicine
SCHAFFHAUSEN, B. S., Biochemistry
SCHALLER, J., Paediatrics
SCHLIEMANN, A. D., Education
SCHNEPS, J., Physics
SCHOETZ, D. J., Surgery
SCHWARTZ, A., Clinical Sciences
SCHWARTZ, R. S., Medicine
SCHWARTZBERG, S., Occupational Therapy
SCHWOB, J., Anatomy
SELKER, H. P., Medicine
SENELICK, L., Drama
SHADER, R. I., Pharmacology
SHAPIRA, Y., Physics
SHERWIN, M. J., History
SHULTZ, M. J., Chemistry
SHULTZ, R., Instruction – Fletcher School
SIEGEL, E. C., Biology
SLIWA, K., Physics
SMITH, G. E., Philosophy
SMITH, T., Political Science
SNYDMAN, D. R., Medicine
SOLOMON, H. M., History
SONENSHEIN, A. L., Microbiology
SONNENSCHEIN, C., Anatomy
SORBERA, R., Oral and Maxillofacial Surgery
SOTO, A., Anatomy
SOUVAINE, D. L., Electrical Eng. and Computer Science
SPIVAK, H., Paediatrics
SQUIRES, C., Microbiology
STADECKER, M., Pathology
STEARNS, N., Medicine
STECHENBERG, B. W., Paediatrics
STOLLAR, B. D., Biochemistry
STOLOW, R. D., Chemistry
STROM, J. A., Medicine
SUMMERGRAD, P., Psychiatry
SUNG, N. H., Chemical Eng.
SWAP, W., Psychology
SYMES, J. F., Surgery
TALAMO, B., Neuroscience
TARLOV, S. R., Neuroscience
TERES, D., Medicine
THEOHARIDES, T.C., Pharmacology
THORLEY-LAWSON, D. A, Medical Pathology

TILLMAN, H., Geriatrics (Dental)
TILLOTSON, J., Nutrition
TISCHLER, A. S., Pathology
TOBIN, R., Physics
TRACHTMAN, J. P., Instruction – Fletcher School
TRIMMER, B. A., Biology
TSAMTSOURIS, A., Paediatric Dentistry
TSICHLIS, P., Medicine
TZIPORI, S., Biomedical Sciences
UEDA, R., History
VAN ETTEN, R. A., Medicine
VAN WORMER, K. A., Chemical Eng.
VILENKIN, A., Physics
VOGEL, R. M., Civil and Environmental Eng.
WALT, D. R., Chemistry
WAZER, D. E., Radiation Oncology
WEAVER, D., Physics
WECHSLER, J., Art and Art History
WEILER, K., Education
WEINER, A., Oral Diagnostic (Dental)
WEINSTEIN, R., Medicine
WEISS, R. M., Mathematics
WERTLIEB, D., Child Devt
WHITE, G., Paediatric Dentistry
WILSON, J., English
WINN, P. E., History
WOLF, M., Child Devt
WONG, J. B., Medicine
WORTIS, H. H., Medical Pathology
WRIGHT, A., Microbiology
ZISSI, V., Continuing Education (Dental)

CAMPUSES

Medford/Somerville Campus: Medford, MA 02155; School of Arts and Sciences, School of Eng., Fletcher School, Gerald J. and Dorothy R. Friedman School of Nutrition Science and Policy, Jonathan M. Tisch College of Citizenship and Public Service.

North Grafton Campus: 22 Westboro Rd, North Grafton, MA 01536; Cummings School of Veterinary Medicine.

Boston Campus: 136 Harrison Ave, Boston, MA 02111; Schools of Medicine, Dental Medicine, Sackler School of Graduate Biomedical Services, Jean Mayer USDA Human Nutrition Research Center on Aging.

UNIVERSITY OF MASSACHUSETTS

225 Franklin St, Boston, MA 02110
Telephone: (617) 287-7000
Internet: www.massachusetts.edu

Founded 1863
Number of students: 60,000 across 5 campuses
Pres.: JACK WILSON
Exec. Vice-Pres.: JAMES JULIAN
Vice-Pres. for Economic Devt: THOMAS CHMURA
Vice-Pres. for Information Services, Chief Information Officer and CEO, UMassOnline: DAVID GRAY
Vice-Pres. for Management and Fiscal Affairs and Treasurer: STEPHEN LENHARDT
Vice-Pres. for Univ. Advancement: KATHERINE V. SMITH
Sec. to the Board of Trustees: BARBARA DEVICO

Comprises campuses at Amherst, Boston, Dartmouth and Lowell, University of Massachusetts Medical School and UMassOnline (online undergraduate and graduate degree programmes).

CONSTITUENT UNIVERSITIES

University of Massachusetts Amherst
Amherst, MA 01003
Telephone: (413) 545-0111
Fax: (413) 545-2328
Internet: www.umass.edu

Chartered as Massachusetts Agricultural College 1863; name changed to Massachusetts State College 1931; university status 1947
Academic year: September to June
Chancellor: JOHN V. LOMBARDI
Provost and Sr Vice-Chancellor for Academic Affairs: CHARLENA SEYMOUR
Vice-Chancellor for Admin. and Finance: JOYCE HATCH
Vice-Provost for Research: PAUL KOSTECKI
Vice-Provost for Outreach: SHARON L. FROSS
Vice-Chancellor for Student Affairs: MIKE GARGANO
Dean of Students: JO-ANNE T. VANIN
Dir of Libraries: JAY SCHAFER
Library of 5,800,000 vols
Number of teachers: 1,169
Number of students: 25,593
Publication: *The Massachusetts Review* (quarterly)

DEANS

Commonwealth College: PRISCILLA CLARKSON
School of Education: CHRISTINE B. McCORMICK
College of Eng.: MICHAEL F. MALONE
Graduate School: SANDY PETERSON
College of Humanities and Fine Arts: JOEL MARTIN
Isenberg School of Management: SOREN BISGAARD
College of Natural Resources and the Environment: CLEVE E. WILLIS
College of Natural Sciences and Mathematics: GEORGE M. LANGFORD
School of Nursing: EILEEN T. BRESLIN
School of Public Health and Health Sciences: JOHN CUNNINGHAM
College of Social and Behavioral Sciences: JANET RIFKIN

ASSOCIATED INSTITUTE

Stockbridge School of Agriculture: Amherst, MA 01003; tel. (413) 545-2222; fax (413) 577-0242; e-mail stockbridgeschool@nre.umass.edu; internet www.umass.edu/stockbridge; f. 1918; Dir MARTHA G. BAKER.

University of Massachusetts Boston

100 Morrissey Blvd, Boston, MA 02125-3393
Telephone: (617) 287-5000
Fax: (617) 265-7173
Internet: www.umb.edu

Founded 1964
Chancellor: J. KEITH MOTLEY
Provost and Sr Vice-Chancellor for Academic Affairs: PAUL J. FONTEYN
Vice-Chancellor for Admin. and Finance: ELLEN M. O'CONNOR
Vice-Chancellor for Athletics and Recreation, Special Projects and Programs: CHARLIE TITUS
Vice-Chancellor for Enrollment Management: KATHLEEN S. TEEHAN
Vice-Chancellor for Student Affairs: PATRICK K. DAY
Vice-Chancellor for Univ. Advancement: DARRELL C. BYERS
Vice-Provost for Information Technology: ANNE SCRIVENER AGEE
Library of 547,846 vols
Number of teachers: 842
Number of students: 12,142

DEANS

College of Liberal Arts: DONNA KUIZENGA
College of Management: PHILIP L. QUAGLIERI
College of Nursing and Health Sciences: GREER GLAZER
College of Public and Community Service: ADONRELE AWOTONA

College of Science and Mathematics: WILLIAM HAGAR
Graduate College of Education: CAROL L. COLBECK
John W. McCormack Graduate School of Policy Studies: STEPHEN CROSBY

University of Massachusetts Dartmouth

285 Old Westport Rd, North Dartmouth, MA 02747-2300
Telephone: (508) 999-8000
Fax: (508) 999-8901
Internet: www.umassd.edu

Founded 1895
Academic year: September to May
Chancellor: Dr JEAN F. MacCORMACK
Provost and Vice-Chancellor for Academic Affairs: ANTHONY J. GARRO, Dr LOUIS ESPOSITO
Vice-Chancellor for Student Affairs: Dr SUSAN T. COSTA
Vice-Chancellor for Library Services, Information Resources and Technology: Dr ROBERT GREEN
Registrar: ANN M. WELSH
Dean of Library Services: SHARON WEINER
Library of 455,245 vols
Number of teachers: 543 (340 full-time, 203 part-time)
Number of students: 8,500
Publication: *Portuguese Literary and Cultural Studies* (annually)

DEANS

College of Arts and Sciences: Dr WILLIAM HOGAN
College of Eng.: Dr ANTONIO H. COSTA
College of Nursing: Dr JAMES A. FAIN
College of Visual and Performing Arts: Dr MICHAEL D. TAYLOR
Charlton College of Business: Dr EILEEN PEACOCK
School of Marine Science and Technology: Dr BRIAN J. ROTHSCHILD

University of Massachusetts Lowell

1 University Ave, Lowell, MA 01854
Telephone: (978) 934-4000
Fax: (978) 934-3000
Internet: www.uml.edu

Founded 1975 by merger of Lowell State College and Lowell Technological Institute; present name 1991
Academic year: September to June
Chancellor: MARTY MEEHAN
Provost: DONALD E. PIERSON
Vice Chancellor for Univ. Advancement and Chief Devt Officer: JOHN DAVIS
Vice Chancellor for Enrollment and Student Affairs: JOYCE TAYLOR GIBSON
Vice Chancellor for Admin. and Finance: LOUISE GRIFFIN
Vice Chancellor for Facilities: DIANA PRIDEAUX-BRUNE
Library of 440,500 titles
Number of teachers: 664
Number of students: 11,208
Publication: *New Solutions* (environmental and occupational health policy, 4 a year)

DEANS

Education: Dr ANITA GREENWOOD
College of Eng.: Dr JOHN TING
College of Health and Environment: Dr DAVID WEGMAN
College of Arts and Sciences, Fine Arts, Humanities and Social Sciences: Dr CHARLES CARROLL
College of Management: Dr KATHRYN VERREAULT
College of Marine Sciences: Dr ROBERT GAMACHE
Arts and Sciences: Dr ROBERT TAMARIN

University of Massachusetts Medical School

55 Lake Avenue North, Worcester, MA 01655
Telephone: (508) 856-2000
E-mail: publicaffairs@umassmed.edu
Internet: www.umassmed.edu
Founded 1962
Chancellor: Dr MICHAEL F. COLLINS
Dean and Exec. Deputy Chancellor: TERRY R. FLOTTE
Vice-Chancellor for Operations: ROBERT E. JENAL
Vice-Chancellor for Research: JOHN L. SULLIVAN
Vice-Chancellor and Chief Operating Officer: JOYCE A. MURPHY
Vice-Chancellor for Faculty Admin.: Dr JUDITH K. OCKENE
Vice-Chancellor for Devt: CHARLIE J. PAGNAM
Vice-Chancellor for Univ. Relations: ALBERT SHERMAN
Dir, Library Services: ELAINE R. MARTIN
Number of teachers: 810
Number of students: 741

DEANS

School of Medicine: Dr TERRY R. FLOTTE
Graduate School of Biomedical Sciences: Dr ANTHONY CARRUTHERS (acting)
Graduate School of Nursing: Dr PAULETTE SEYMOUR ROUTE

WELLESLEY COLLEGE

106 Central St, Wellesley, MA 02481
Telephone: (781) 283-1000
Fax: (781) 283-3650
E-mail: publicinfo@wellesley.edu
Internet: www.wellesley.edu
Chartered 1870; opened 1875
Pres.: KIM BOTTOMLY
Vice-Pres. for Admin. and Planning: PATRICIA M. BYRNE
Asst Vice-Pres. for Public Affairs: MARY ANN HILL
Dean of the College: ANDREW SHERMAN
Dean of Students: MICHELLE M. LEPORE (acting)
Vice-Pres for Information Services and College Librarian: MICHELINE JEDREY
Library of 687,000 vols
Number of teachers: 241 full-time
Number of teachers: 72 part-time
Number of students: 2,136 full-time
Number of students: 204 part-time.

WENTWORTH INSTITUTE OF TECHNOLOGY

550 Huntington Ave, Boston, MA 02115-5998
Telephone: (617) 989-4590
Fax: (617) 989-4591
E-mail: admissions@wit.edu
Internet: www.wit.edu
Private control
Academic year: August to May
Founded 1904
Pres.: Dr ZORICA PANTIC
Vice-Pres. of Academic Affairs and Provost: KUEI-WU TSAI
Vice-Pres. for Business and Finance: JOHN P. HEINSTADT
Registrar: MATTHEW BURKE
Library Dir: WALTER PUNCH
Number of teachers: 134
Number of students: 3,636
Depts of Architecture, Civil, Construction and Environment, Computer Science and Systems, Design and Facilities, Electronics and Mechanics, Humanities, Social Sciences, and Management.

WESTERN NEW ENGLAND COLLEGE

1215 Wilbraham Rd, Springfield, MA 01119
Telephone: (413) 782-3111
Fax: (413) 782-1746
E-mail: ugradmis@wnec.edu
Internet: www.wnec.edu
Founded 1919
Pres.: ANTHONY S. CAPRIO
Provost and Vice-Pres. for Academic Affairs: JERRY A. HIRSCH
Vice-Pres. for Finance and Admin.: DAVID P. KRUGER
Vice-Pres. for Marketing and External Affairs: BARBARA A. CAMPANELLA
Vice-Pres. for Devt and Alumni Relations: BEVERLY DWIGHT
Vice-Pres. for Enrollment Management: CHARLES R. POLLOCK
Vice-Pres. for Student Affairs and Dean of Students: RICHARD M. DIRUZZA
Assoc. Dean for Library and Information Resources: BARBARA WEST
Library of 510,000 vols
Number of teachers: 164 full-time
Number of students: 4,000

DEANS

School of Arts and Sciences: SAEED GHAHRAMANI
School of Business: JULIE SICILIANO
School of Eng.: CARL RATHMANN
School of Law Admin.: ARTHUR R. GAUDIO

WESTON JESUIT SCHOOL OF THEOLOGY

3 Phillips Place, Cambridge, MA 02138
Telephone: (617) 492-1960
Fax: (617) 492-5833
E-mail: admissionsinfo@wjst.edu
Internet: www.wjst.edu
Private control
Academic year: September to May
Pres.: ROBERT MANNING
Vice-Pres.: JOHN P. STACHNIEWICZ
Academic Dean: Dr JOHN R. SACHS
Dean of Students: JACQUELINE REGAN
Library Dir: ESTHER GRISWOLD
Library of 232,000 vols
Number of teachers: 31
Number of students: 186 (full-time).

WESTFIELD STATE COLLEGE

POB 1630, Westfield, MA 01086-1630
577 Western Ave, Westfield, MA 01086
Telephone: (413) 572-5300
E-mail: admissions@wsc.ma.edu
Internet: www.wsc.ma.edu
Founded 1838
Pres.: BARRY MALONEY
Sr Vice-Pres. for Academic Affairs: Dr JOAN A. RASOOL
Vice-Pres. for Student Affairs: Dr ARTHUR J. JACKSON
Vice-Pres. for Admin. and Finance: NICK A. WOJTOWICZ
Vice-Pres. for Advancement and College Relations: ROBERT ZIOMEK
Library Dir: CATHERINE DOYLE
Library of 136,000 vols
Number of teachers: 170
Number of students: 3,200
Majors in Art, Biology, Business Management, Computer Information Systems, Computer Science, Criminal Justice, Econ., Education, English, Environmental Sciences, French, General Science, History, Mass Communication, Mathematics, Movement Science, Multicultural and Ethnic Studies, Music, Philosophy, Political Science, Psychology, Regional Planning, Social Work, Sociology, Spanish, Theatre Arts, Women's Studies.

WHEATON COLLEGE

26 East Main St, Norton, MA 02766
Telephone: (508) 286-8200
Fax: (508) 285-8270
E-mail: info@wheatoncollege.edu
Internet: www.wheatoncollege.edu
Founded 1834
Pres.: RONALD A. CRUTCHER
Provost: MOLLY EASO SMITH
Vice-Pres. for Enrollment and Marketing: GAIL BERSON
Vice-Pres. for Finance and Operations: RODERICK G. WALLICK
Vice-Pres. for Library and Information Services: TERRY METZ
Dean of Students: SUE ALEXANDER
Library of 352,700 vols
Number of teachers: 140
Number of students: 1,550
Depts of Africana Studies, American Studies, Ancient Studies, Anthropology, Art History, Studio Art, Asian Studies, Astronomy, Biochemistry, Biology, Chemistry, Classics, Computer Science, Devt Studies, Economics, Education, English, Environmental Science, Environmental Studies, Family Studies, French, German, Greek, Hispanic Studies, History, Int. Relations, Italian Studies, Latin, Latin American Studies, Legal Studies, Management, Mathematics, Mathematics and Computer Science, Mathematics and Econ., Music, Philosophy, Physics and Astronomy, Political Science, Psychobiology, Psychology, Public Policy Studies, Religion, Russian and Russian Studies, Sociology, Statistics, Theatre Studies and Dance, Urban Studies, Women's Studies
Publications: *Quarterly Magazine*, *Wheaton Matters*.

WHEELOCK COLLEGE

200 The Riverway, Boston, MA 02215
Telephone: (617) 879-2000
Internet: www.wheelock.edu
Founded 1888
Pres.: JACKIE JENKINS-SCOTT
Vice-Pres. for Academic Affairs: SUZANNE PASCH
Vice-Pres. and Chief Financial Officer: ANNE MARIE MARTORANA
Vice-Pres. for Institutional Advancement and Devt: LINDA WELTER
Dean of Students: SUSAN ANTONELLI
Assoc. Vice-Pres. for Academic Resources and Library Dir: ALBIE JOHNSON
Library of 85,000 vols
Number of teachers: 65 (full-time)
Number of students: 1,640
Academic programmes in Arts and Sciences, Child Life, Child and Family Studies, Education, Juvenile Justice and Youth Advocacy, Social Work
Publications: *Bulletin*, *Magazine*.

WILLIAMS COLLEGE

Williamstown, MA 01267
Telephone: (413) 597-3131
E-mail: admission@williams.edu
Internet: www.williams.edu
Chartered as Free School 1791; college charter granted 1793
Pres.: MORTON OWEN SCHAPIRO
Vice-Pres. for Operations: STEPHEN P. KLASS
Vice-Pres. for Strategic Planning and Institutional Diversity: MIKE REED
Provost: WILLIAM J. LENHART

Dean of the Faculty: WILLIAM G. WAGNER
Dean of the College: NANCY ROSEMAN
Dir of Admission: DICK NESBITT
Registrar: CHARLES R. TOOMAJIAN, Jr
Librarian: DAVID M. PILACHOWSKI

Library of 885,000 vols, 50,000 rare books, 13,500 paper and electronic periodicals, 492,000 microtexts, 30,000 sound recordings, 9,500 videos, 430,000 govt documents
Number of teachers: 173
Number of students: 2,021

Depts of American Studies, Anthropology, Art, Asian Studies, Astronomy, Astrophysics, Biology, Chemistry, Chinese, Classics, Comparative Literature, Computer Science, Econ., English, French, Geosciences, German, History, Japanese, Literary Studies, Mathematics and Statistics, Music, Philosophy, Physics, Political Economy, Political Science, Psychology, Religion, Russian, Sociology, Spanish, Theatre, Women's and Gender Studies.

WORCESTER POLYTECHNIC INSTITUTE

100 Institute Rd, Worcester, MA 01609-2280
Telephone: (508) 831-5000
Fax: (508) 831-5753
Internet: www.wpi.edu
Founded 1865
Academic year: August to May
Pres.: DENNIS D. BERKEY
Exec. Vice-Pres.: JEFFREY S. SOLOMON
Provost and Vice-Pres. for Academic Affairs: JOHN A. ORR
Vice-Pres. for Student Affairs: JANET BEGIN RICHARDSON
Vice-Pres. for Enrollment Management: KRISTIN RUTH TICHENOR
Vice-Pres. for Information Technology: THOMAS J. LYNCH
Vice-Pres. for Marketing and Communications: CHRISTOPHER HARDWICK
Registrar: ALAINA WIEHN
Librarian: HELEN M. SHUSTER

Library of 225,000 vols
Number of teachers: 324
Number of students: 3,903

Areas of study incl. Eng. and Computer Science, Liberal Arts, Management, Sciences, Pre-Professional Studies.

WORCESTER STATE COLLEGE

486 Chandler St, Worcester, MA 01602-2597
Telephone: (508) 929-8000
Fax: (508) 929-8191
E-mail: admissions@worcester.edu
Internet: www.worcester.edu
Founded 1874
Academic year: September to May
Pres.: JANELLE C. ASHLEY
Vice-Pres. of Academic Affairs: DOROTHY ESCRIBANO
Library Dir: DONALD HOCHSTETLER

Library of 149,662 vols
Number of teachers: 170
Number of students: 5,369

Depts of Biology, Business Admin./Econ., Communication, Computer Science, Criminal Justice, Education, Health Sciences, History/Political Science, Languages and Literature, Mathematics, Nursing, Philosophy, Physical and Earth Sciences, Psychology, Sociology, Visual and Performing Arts

Publication: *Journal of Graduate Research* (annual).

ATTACHED RESEARCH INSTITUTES
Center for Effective Instruction.
Center for Health Professions.

Intergenerational Urban Institute.

MICHIGAN

ADRIAN COLLEGE

110 S. Madison, Adrian, MI 49221-2575
Telephone: (517) 265-5161
Fax: (517) 264-3331
Internet: www.adrian.edu
Founded 1859
Academic year: September to May
President: STANLEY P. CAINE
Vice-President, Business Affairs: MICHAEL J. AYRE
Vice-President, Institutional Advancement: WILLIAM S. KENYON
Vice-President and Dean, Student Affairs: PAMELA M. BOERSIG
Vice-President and Dean, Academic Affairs: JAMES B. BORLAND
Admissions Director: JANEL A. SUTKUS
Registrar: MICHAEL H. JACOBITZ
Librarian: NOELLE KELLER

Library of 147,080 vols
Number of teachers: 71
Number of students: 1,028.

ALBION COLLEGE

Albion, MI 49224
Telephone: (517) 629-1000
Fax: (517) 629-0509
Internet: www.albion.edu
Founded 1835
President: Dr PETER T. MITCHELL
Vice-President for Academic Affairs: Dr JEFFREY C. CARRIER
Vice-President for Enrollment Management: Dr ROBERT E. JOHNSON
Librarian: JOHN KONDELIK

Library of 562,000 vols
Number of teachers: 113
Number of students: 1,487.

ALMA COLLEGE

614 W. Superior St Alma, MI 48801
Telephone: (517) 463-7111
Fax: (517) 463-7277
E-mail: admissions@alma.edu
Internet: www.alma.edu
Founded 1886
President: ALAN J. STONE
Registrar: KAREN KLUMPP
Director of Admissions (vacant)
Librarian: PETER DOLLARD

Library of 212,000 vols
Number of teachers: 86 full-time
Number of teachers: 20 part-time
Number of students: 1,350.

ANDREWS UNIVERSITY

Berrien Springs, MI 49104
Telephone: (800) 253-2874
Fax: (269) 471-3228
E-mail: enroll@andrews.edu
Internet: www.andrews.edu
Founded 1874
Academic year: August to May
President: NIELS-ERIK ANDREASEN
Registrar: Dr EMILIO GARCIA-MARENKO
Librarian: LARRY ONSAGER

Library of 1,513,179 vols
Number of teachers: 227
Number of students: 3,017

Publication: *Andrews University Seminary Studies* (2 a year)

DEANS
College of Arts and Sciences: Dr WILLIAM RICHARDSON
College of Technology: Dr VERLYN BENSON
Division of Architecture: CAREY CARSCALLEN
Graduate Studies: Dr LYNDON G. FURST
School of Business: Dr ANNE GIBSON
School of Education: Dr JAMES JEFFERY
SDA Theological Seminary: Dr JOHN McVAY

AQUINAS COLLEGE

1607 Robinson Rd, SE, Grand Rapids, MI 49506
Telephone: (616) 632-8900
Internet: www.aquinas.edu
Founded 1886
President: HARRY J. KNOPKE
Vice-Presidents: JULIE RIDENOUR (Development), WILLIAM SHEFFERLY (Finance and Operations), MICHAEL KELLER (Planning and Enrollment)
Chancellor: Sister MARY AQUINAS WEBER
Provost: C. EDWARD BALOG
Registrar: CECELIA MESLER

Library of 100,000 vols, 991 periodicals and over 16,000 non-print items
Number of teachers: 187
Number of students: 2,500

Publications: *Aquinas Magazine* (quarterly), *Presidential Perspectives* (2 a year).

AVE MARIA COLLEGE

300 W Forest Ave, Ypsilanti, MI 48197
Telephone: (734) 337-4100
Fax: (734) 337-4140
E-mail: admissions@avemaria.edu
Internet: www.avemaria.edu
Founded 1998
Private control
Academic year: September to April
President: Dr R. P. MULLER
Academic Dean: Fr NEIL J. ROY
Vice-President (Administration): MATTHEW S. LEONARD
Vice-President (Institutional Advancement): DAVE KELLEY
Vice-President (University Relations): Dr CAROLE CARPENTER
Dean of Student Life: Dr. CHRISTOPHER BEITING
Registrar: MARIA HERBEL
Librarian: SARAH BEITING
Number of teachers: 28 (12 full-time, 16 adjunct)
Number of students: 109

Areas of study: classics and early Christian literature, economics, history, literature, mathematics, philosophy, political science, theology, natural sciences.

AVE MARIA SCHOOL OF LAW

3475 Plymouth Rd, Ann Arbor, MI 48105-2550
Telephone: (734) 827-8040
Fax: (734) 622-0123
E-mail: info@avemarialaw.edu
Internet: www.avemarialaw.edu
Founded 1999
Private control
Academic year: August to May
Dean and President: Dr BERNARD DOBRANSKI
Associate Dean for Academic Affairs: Dr JOSEPH L. FALVEY, Jr
Registrar: CHEZARAE ROSE
Library Director: Dr MITCHELL E. COUNTS
Library of 400,000 vols and other items.

CALVIN COLLEGE

3201 Burton SE, Grand Rapids, MI 49546
Telephone: (616) 957-6000
Fax: (616) 957-8551
E-mail: info@calvin.edu
Internet: www.calvin.edu
Founded 1876
Academic year: September to May

President: Dr GAYLEN J. BYKER
Vice-Presidents: SHIRLEY HOOGSTRA (Student Life), Dr HENRY E. DEVRIES II (Information Services and Administration and Finance), THOMAS MCWHERTOR (Enrollment and External Relations), ROBERT BERKHOF (Development)
Provost: Dr JOEL CARPENTER
Registrar: THOMAS STEENWYK
Academic Dean for the Social Sciences and for Languages, Literature and the Arts: Dr DAVID DIEPHOUSE
Academic Dean for the Contextual Disciplines and for the Natural Sciences and Mathematics: Dr MICHAEL STOB
Director of the Library: GLENN A. REMELTS
Library of 700,000 vols
Number of teachers: 349 (284 full-time, 65 part-time)
Number of students: 4,162
Publications: *Fides et Historia* (2 a year), *Turkish Studies Association Bulletin* (2 a year).

AFFILIATED RESEARCH CENTRES

Calvin Center for Christian Scholarship: Dir. Dr JAMES BRATT.

H. H. Meeter Center for Calvin Studies: Dir Dr KARIN MAAG.

Institute of Christian Worship: Dir Dr JOHN WITVLIET.

Paul Henry Institute for Christianity and Politics: Dir Dr CORWIN SMIDT.

Social Research Center: Dir Dr MARK REGNERUS.

CALVIN THEOLOGICAL SEMINARY

3233 Burton St SE, Grand Rapids, MI 49546
Telephone: (616) 957-6006
Fax: (616) 957-8621
E-mail: admissions@calvinseminary.edu
Internet: www.calvinseminary.edu
Private control (Christian Reformed Church in North America)

President: Dr CORNELIUS PLANTINGA, Jr
Vice-President (Academic Affairs): Dr HENRY DE MOOR
Vice-President (Administration): Dr DUANE KELDERMAN
Librarian: PAUL FIELDS
Number of teachers: 28
Number of students: 222 (full-time).

CENTRAL MICHIGAN UNIVERSITY

Mount Pleasant, MI 48859
Telephone: (989) 774-4000
E-mail: cmuline@cmich.edu
Internet: www.cmich.edu
Academic year: August to May
Founded 1892

President: MICHAEL RAO
Provost and Vice-President for Academic Affairs: THOMAS STORCH
Vice-President (Advancement): MICHAEL LETO
Vice-President (Business and Finance): GEORGE ROSS
Registrar: KAREN HUTSLAR
Dean of Students: BRUCE ROSCOE
Dean of Libraries: THOMAS J. MOORE
Number of teachers: 1,015

Number of students: 28,159
Publication: *Michigan Historical Review* (2 a year)

DEANS

College of Health Professions: MARVIS LARY
College of Communication and Fine Arts: SUE ANN MARTIN
College of Science and Technology: ROBERT KOHRMAN
College of Humanities and Social and Behavioural Sciences: GARY SHAPIRO
College of Graduate Studies: JAMES HAGEMAN
College of Business Administration: DANIEL VETTER
College of Education and Human Services: KAREN ADAMS

CLEARY UNIVERSITY

3601 Plymouth Rd, Ann Arbor, MI 48105
Telephone: (734) 332-4477
Fax: (734) 332-8694
E-mail: admissions@cleary.edu
Internet: www.cleary.edu
Founded 1883 as The Cleary School of Penmanship; present name 2002
Private control
Academic year: September to June

President: THOMAS P. SULLIVAN
Vice-President (Academic Affairs): Dr VINCE LINDER
Vice-President (Administration and Finance): JUDITH WALKER
Number of teachers: 33
Number of students: 1,000
Area of study: business administration.

COLLEGE FOR CREATIVE STUDIES

201 E Kirby, Detroit, MI 48202-4034
Telephone: (313) 664-7400
Fax: (313) 827-2739
E-mail: admissions@ccscad.edu
Internet: www.ccscad.edu
Founded 1906 as Detroit Society of Arts and Crafts; present name 2001
Private control
Academic year: September to May

President: RICHARD L. ROGERS
Dean: IMRE MOLNAR
Vice-President (Administration and Finance): ANNE BECK
Vice-President (Institutional Advancement): NANCY J. NELSON
Registrar: NADINE HAGOORT
Librarian: BETH WALKER
Library of 30,000 vols, 86,000 slides, 188,000 current periodicals
Number of teachers: 212
Number of students: 1,218

HEADS OF DEPARTMENTS

Animation and Digital Media: ROBERT ANDERSON
Art Education: CHRISTINE SEGUIN
Communication Design: DOUGLAS R. KISOR
Crafts: HERBERT BABCOCK
Fine Arts: ZDZISLAW SIKORA
Foundation: ROBERT SCHEFMAN
Illustration: GIL ASHBY
Industrial Design: BYRON FITZPATRICK
Interior Design: SANDRA SABBAGH
Liberal Arts: Dr DOROTHY KOSTUCH
Photography: JOHN GANIS

CONCORDIA UNIVERSITY – ANN ARBOR

4090 Geddes Rd, Ann Arbor, MI 48105
Telephone: (734) 995-7300
Fax: (734) 995-4610
E-mail: admission@cuaa.edu

Internet: www.cuaa.edu
Founded 1963 as Concordia Lutheran Junior College
Private control
Academic year: September to May

President: Dr JAMES KOERSCHEN
Executive Vice-President and Vice-President (External Relations): STEVE DEBOER
Registrar: TIM TAYLOR
Library Director: KEVIN J. BRANDON
Number of teachers: 47
Number of students: 770

DEANS

School of Adult and Continuing Education: Dr JEANETTE SPRIK
School of Arts and Sciences: Dr ROBERT MCCORMICK
Haab School of Business and Management: Dr F. K. MARSH
School of Education: Dr TIMOTHY FRUSTI

CORNERSTONE UNIVERSITY

1001 E Beltline NE, Grand Rapids, MI 49525
Telephone: (616) 949-5300
E-mail: admissions@cornerstone.edu
Internet: www.cornerstone.edu
Private control

President: Dr REX M. ROGERS
Executive Vice-President: ROBERT NIENHUIS
Vice-President (Student Development): TOM EMIGH
Vice-President (Business): MARC FOWLER
Vice-President and Chief Financial Officer: MICHAEL GOAD
Vice-President (Broadcasting): LEE GEYSBEEK
Vice-President (Information Systems): MIKE ROHWER
Number of teachers: 64
Number of students: 1,848 (1,592 undergraduate, 256 graduate)

DEANS

School of Arts and Sciences: Dr TIMOTHY DETWILER
School of Professional Studies: DAVIS BERRYMAN

CRANBROOK ACADEMY OF ART

39221 Woodward Ave, POB 801, Bloomfield Hills, MI 48303-0801
Telephone: (248) 645-3300
Fax: (248) 646-0046
E-mail: caainfo@cranbrook.edu
Internet: www.cranbrookart.edu
Founded 1932

Director: GERHARDT KNODEL
Dean of Admissions: KATHARINE WILLMAN
Registrar: KATHARINE WILLMAN
Librarian: JUDITH DYKI
Library of 25,000 vols
Number of teachers: 10 full-time
Number of students: 150.

DAVENPORT UNIVERSITY

415 E Fulton, Grand Rapids, MI 49503
Telephone: (616) 451-3511
Fax: (616) 732-1142
Internet: www.davenport.edu
Founded 1866 as Grand Rapids Business College; present name 2000
Private control
Academic year: September to August

President: RANDOLPH K. FLECHSIG
Executive Vice-President (Academics) and Provost: Dr ROBERT L. FUNARO
Executive Vice-President (Operations): Dr MATTHEW CAWOOD
Executive Vice-President (Advancement): Dr BARBARA A. MIERAS

Executive Vice-President (Finance): MICHAEL VOLK

Senior Vice-President (Project Development): Dr THOMAS H. BROWN

Vice-President (Marketing): NANCY FRENCH

Vice-President (University Communications): CATHY YARED

Vice-President (Human Resources and Organizational Development): BRIAN L. MORTIMORE

Number of teachers: 1,200

Number of students: 13,048 (all campuses; 12,956 undergraduate, 92 graduate)

Areas of study: business, health professions, technology.

30 Campuses throughout Michigan and northern Indiana.

EASTERN MICHIGAN UNIVERSITY

Ypsilanti, MI 48197

Telephone: (734) 487-1849

Fax: (734) 487-7170

Internet: www.emich.edu

Founded 1849

Academic year: September to April

Pres.: DON LOPPNOW

Provost and Vice-Pres. for Academic Affairs: DON LOPPNOW

Vice-Pres. for Student Affairs: JIM VICK

Vice-Pres. for Business and Finance: PATRICK DOYLE

Vice-Pres. for Enrollment Services: COURTNEY MCANUFF

Vice-Pres. for Univ. Relations: JUANITA REID

Dean of Students: GREG PEOPLES

Registrar: JOY GARRETT

Univ. Librarian (vacant)

Library of 600,000 vols, 129,847 periodicals

Number of teachers: 675

Number of students: 25,000

DEANS

Business: EARL POTTER

Education: JERRY ROBBINS

Graduate School: ROBERT HOLKEBEER

Arts and Science: LINDA PRITCHARD

Human Services: ELIZABETH C. KING

Technology: JOHN DUGGER

Continuing Education: DAVID CLIFFORD

FERRIS STATE UNIVERSITY

1201 South State St, CSS 301, Big Rapids, MI 49307

Telephone: (616) 592-2000

E-mail: international@ferris.edu

Internet: www.ferris.edu

Founded 1884

Academic year: August to May

President: WILLIAM A. SEDERBURG

Vice-Presidents: RICHARD DUFFETT (Administration and Finance), DANIEL BURCHAM (Student Affairs), TOM OLDFIELD (Academic Affairs, acting)

Dean of Enrollment Services: RONNIE HIGGS

Dean of Instructional Services and Library: RICHARD COCHRAN

Library of 350,000 books and periodicals

Number of teachers: 530

Number of students: 11,074.

GRACE BIBLE COLLEGE

POB 910, 1011 Aldon SW, Grand Rapids, MI 49509

Telephone: (616) 538-2330

Fax: (616) 538-0599

E-mail: info@gbcol.edu

Internet: www.gbcol.edu

Founded 1939 as Milwaukee Bible Institute; present name 1961

Private control

President: KEN KEMPER

Executive Vice-President and Academic Dean: Dr TIMOTHY F. CONKLIN

Vice-President (Business and Finance): BRUCE A. HOEKER

Vice-President (Advancement): KEITH D. MEYERING

Vice-President (Community Life): BRIAN SHERSTEAD

Number of teachers: 29

Number of students: 149.

GRAND VALLEY STATE UNIVERSITY

1 Campus Drive, Allendale, MI 49401-9403

Telephone: (616) 331-5000

Internet: www.gvsu.edu

State control

Academic year: August to April

President (vacant)

Provost and Vice-President (Academic Affairs): Dr GAYLE R. DAVIS

Vice-President (Development): MARIBETH G. WARDROP

Vice-President (Finance and Administration): Dr TIMOTHY O. SCHAD

Vice-President (Planning and Equity): Dr PATRICIA OLDT

Vice-President (University Relations): MATTHEW E. MCLOGAN

Registrar: LYNN BLUE

Library Director: LEROY LEBBIN

Library of 627,000 vols

Number of teachers: 574

Number of students: 19,762

DEANS

Arts and Humanities: JON JELLEMA

Seidman School of Business: Dr DAVID MIELKE

School of Education: Dr ANNE MULDER

Kirkhof School of Nursing: Dr PHYLLIS E. GENDLER

Science and Mathematics: Dr P. DOUGLAS KINDSCHI

Social Sciences: Dr ERIKA KING

School of Social Work: Dr RODNEY MULDER

BRANCH CAMPUSES

Meijer Campus: 515 S Waverly Rd, Holland, MI 49423; tel. (616) 394-4848.

Muskegon Center: 221 S Quaterline Rd, Muskegon, MI 49442; tel. (231) 777-0505.

Pew Campus: 401 W Fulton St, Grand Rapids, MI 49504; tel. (616) 895-6611.

Traverse City Center: 2200 Dendrinos Drive, Suite 101, Traverse City, MI 49684; tel. (231) 995-1785.

GREAT LAKES CHRISTIAN COLLEGE

6211 W Willow Highway, Lansing, MI 48917

Telephone: (517) 321-0242

Fax: (517) 321-5902

E-mail: glcc@glcc.edu

Internet: www.glcc.edu

Founded 1949 as Great Lakes Bible College; present name 1992

Private control

Academic year: August to May

President: LAWRENCE L. CARTER

Vice-President (Academic Affairs): Dr PAUL J. KISSLING

Vice-President (Finance and Operations): WILLIAM D. BROSSMANN

Vice-President (Institutional Advancement): PHILIP E. BEAVERS

Registrar: JUDITH M. SAUNDERS

Librarian: KEITH UPTON

Library of 52,000 vols

Number of teachers: 14

Number of students: 192

Areas of study: Christian ministries, youth ministries, psychology/counselling, music, Christian education, cross-cultural ministries, Bible theology.

HILLSDALE COLLEGE

Hillsdale, MI 49242

Telephone: (517) 437-7341

Fax: (517) 437-0190

E-mail: admissions@hillsdale.edu

Internet: www.hillsdale.edu

Founded 1844

President: Dr GEORGE ROCHE

Provost: Dr ROBERT BLACKSTOCK

Vice-President for Administration: F. LAMAR FOWLER

Vice-President for Student Affairs: CAROLANN BARKER

Vice-President for Development: JOHN CERVINI

Vice-President for External Programs and Communications: Dr RONALD L. TROWBRIDGE

Vice-President for Financial Affairs: H. KENNETH COLE

Registrar: KAY COSGROVE

Librarian: DANIEL JOLDERSMA

Library of 209,000 vols

Number of teachers: 89

Number of students: 1,170

Publication: *Imprimis* (monthly).

HOPE COLLEGE

POB 9000, Holland, MI 49422-9000

Telephone: (616) 395-7000

Fax: (616) 395-7922

Internet: www.hope.edu

Founded 1866

Academic year: August to May

President: Dr JAMES E. BULTMAN

Vice-President for Admissions: Dr JAMES A. BEKKERING

Vice-President of Student Development and Dean of Students: Dr RICHARD FROST

Provost: Dr JAMES N. BOELKINS

Director of Admissions: GARY CAMP

Director of Libraries: DAVID P. JENSEN

Library of 359,825 vols

Number of teachers: 300 (208 full-time, 92 part-time)

Number of students: 3,112.

KALAMAZOO COLLEGE

Kalamazoo, MI 49006-3295

Telephone: (269) 337-7000

Fax: (269) 337-7251

Internet: www.kzoo.edu

Founded 1833 as Michigan and Huron Institute; name changed to Kalamazoo Literary Institute 1837, to Kalamazoo College 1855

Academic year: September to June

President: EILEEN WILSON-OYELARAN (acting)

Provost: GREGORY S. MAHLER

Vice-President for Advancement: BERNARD PALCHICK

Vice-President for Business and Finance: THOMAS PONTO

Director, Information Services: LISA PALCHICK

Dean of Enrollment: JOELLEN SILBERMAN

Dean of Students: VAUGHN MAATMAN

Library of 330,000 vols

Number of teachers: 89

Number of students: 1,280.

KETTERING UNIVERSITY

1700 West Third Ave, Flint, MI 48504-4898

Telephone: (810) 762-9500

Internet: www.gmi.edu
Founded 1919
President: JAMES E. A. JOHN
Vice-President for International and Governmental Activities: DAVID J. DOHERTY
Vice-President for Business: SUSAN BOLT
Vice-President and Provost: JOHN D. LORENZ
Dean of Students: PATRICK DEESE

Library of 80,000 vols
Number of teachers: 135
Number of students: 3,200.

LAKE SUPERIOR STATE UNIVERSITY

650 W Easterday Avenue, Sault Ste. Marie, MI 49783

Telephone: (906) 635-2231
Fax: (906) 635-2111
E-mail: admissions@lssu.edu
Internet: www.lssu.edu

Founded 1946 as Sault Ste. Marie Branch of Michigan College of Mining and Technology; present name 1987
State control
Academic year: September to May

President: Dr BETTY J. YOUNGBLOOD
Executive Vice-President and Provost: Dr DONALD J. McCRIMMON
Vice-President (Student Affairs): THOMAS R. BUGBEE
Vice-President (Institutional Advancement): MARK A. JASTORFF
Vice-President (Business and Financial Operations): SCOTT W. SMART
Vice-President (Information Technology): Dr OMER E. PREWETT
Registrar: ARLENE K. MacPHERSON
Dean of Library: Dr FREDRICK A. MICHELS

Library of 130,000 vols
Number of teachers: 112
Number of students: 3,077

DEANS

College of Arts, Letters and Social Sciences: JAMES R. BLASHILL
College of Business and Economics: Dr VARKEY K. TITUS
College of Engineering and Mathematics: RAY L. ADAMS
College of Natural and Health Sciences: Dr MICHAEL P. DONOVAN
Great Lakes Academy: Dr MELVIN L. WAISANEN

LAWRENCE TECHNOLOGICAL UNIVERSITY

21000 W Ten Mile Rd, Southfield, MI 48075-1058

Telephone: (248) 204-4000
Fax: (248) 204-3727
E-mail: admissions@ltu.edu
Internet: www.ltu.edu

Founded 1932
Private control
Academic year: August to May

President and CEO: Dr CHARLES M. CHAMBERS
Provost: Dr LEWIS N. WALKER
Vice-President (Finance and Administration): LINDA L. HEIGHT
Vice-President (University Advancement): STEPHEN C. RAGAN
Registrar: HOLLY A. DIAMOND
Dean of Students: Dr JEROME E. WEBSTER
Admissions Director: JANE T. ROHRBACK
Library Director: GARY R. COCOZZOLI

Number of teachers: 452
Number of students: 5,000

Publication: *Prism* (Annually)

DEANS

College of Architecture and Design: GLEN S. LEROY
College of Arts and Sciences: Dr HSIAO-PING MOORE
College of Engineering: Dr LAIRD E. JOHNSTON
College of Management: Dr LOUIS A. DeGENNARO

ATTACHED RESEARCH INSTITUTE

Center for Innovative Materials Research: f. 2005; Dir Dr NABIL F. GRACE.

MADONNA UNIVERSITY

36600 Schoolcraft Rd, Livonia, MI 48150

Telephone: (734) 432-5300
Fax: (734) 432-5393
E-mail: muinfo@madonna.edu
Internet: www.madonna.edu

Founded 1947
Academic year: September to July

President: Sister Dr ROSE MARIE KUJAWA
Vice-President for Academic Administration: ERNEST NOLAN
Vice-President for Student Life: Sister NANCY MARIE
Director for Enrollment Management: FRANK HRIBAR
Director of Financial Aid: CHRIS ZIEGLER
Director, Center for International Studies: Dr JONATHAN SWIFT
Registrar: KATHY GRENDA
Director of Library Services: JOANNE LUMMETTA

Library of 163,678 vols
Number of teachers: 274
Number of students: 4,000

Publication: *Madonna Mind* (2 a year).

MARYGROVE COLLEGE

8425 West McNichols Rd, Detroit, MI 48221

Telephone: (313) 927-1200
Fax: (313) 927-1345
E-mail: info@marygrove.edu
Internet: www.marygrove.edu

Founded 1905
Academic year: September to April

President: Dr GLENDA PRICE
Provost (vacant)
Vice-President for Finance and Administration: VINCE ABATEMARCO
Vice-President for Institutional Advancement: JoANN CUSMANO
Associate Provost for Student Affairs: Dr LISA JONES-BROWN
Director of Graduate Admission: Dr PAMELA LLOYD
Director of Institutional Research and Assessment: Dr BIN NING
Director of Undergraduate Admissions: SALLY JANECEK
Registrar: Dr GAYLE REYNOLDS

Library of 78,196 vols
Number of teachers: 65 full-time, 6 part-time, 70 adjuncts, 150 mentors
Number of students: 4,610 (738 undergraduate, 3,872 postgraduate)

Publication: *Maxis Review* (annually)

Liberal arts college; two- and four-year undergraduate courses; master's courses; continuing education programme.

DEANS

Arts and Sciences: Dr JUDITH HEINEN
Education: Dr ALFRED COOKE
Fine Arts: ROSE DE SLOOVER
Professional Studies: Dr KURT SMITH
Continuing Education: SHERRY LEFTON (Assistant Dean: MARTHA SOLEAU (Assistant Dean)

MICHIGAN JEWISH INSTITUTE

25401 Coolidge Highway, Oak Park, 48237-1304

Telephone: (248) 414-6900
Fax: (248) 414-6907
E-mail: info@mji.edu
Internet: www.mji.edu

Founded 1994
Private control
Academic year: September to August

President: Rabbi DAVID KAGAN
Vice-President, Institutional Advancement, and Dean of Academic Affairs: Dr T. HERSHEL GARDIN
Chief Financial Officer and Vice-President, Financial Affairs: KASRIEL SHEMTOV
Registrar: FRAN HERMAN

Areas of study: communication, mathematics/science, social sciences, ethics/philosophy/religion, language and literature, aesthetics, computer information systems, business and information systems.

MICHIGAN STATE UNIVERSITY

East Lansing, MI 48824

Telephone: (517) 355-6560
Fax: (517) 355-4670
E-mail: presmail@msu.edu
Internet: www.msu.edu

Founded 1855; the first college for teaching scientific agriculture and the forerunner of the American system of land-grant colleges
State control
Academic year: August to May (2 terms)

Pres.: LOU ANN K. SIMON
Provost and Vice-Pres. for Academic Affairs: KIM A. WILCOX
Vice-Pres. for Finance and Operations and Treas.: FRED POSTON
Vice-Pres. for Univ. Devt: CHARLES WEBB
Vice Pres. for Research and Graduate Studies: J. IAN GRAY
Vice-Pres. for Student Affairs and Services: LEE JUNE
Vice-Pres. for Univ. Relations: TERRY DENBOW
Vice-Pres. for Legal Affairs and Gen. Counsel: ROBERT NOTO
Vice-Pres. for Governmental Affairs: STEVEN WEBSTER
Vice-Pres. for Global Engagement and Strategic Projects: JOHN HUDZIK
Registrar: DUGALD McMILLAN LINDA STANFORD (acting)
Dir of Libraries: CLIFFORD H. HAKA
Library: see Libraries
Number of teachers: 4,500
Number of students: 45,520

Publications: *Centennial Review, MSU News Bulletin, MSU Alumni Magazine*

DEANS

Agriculture and Natural Resources: JEFFREY D. ARMSTRONG
Arts and Letters: KAREN A. WURST
Eli Broad College of Business and Eli Broad Graduate School of Management: ROBERT B. DUNCAN
Communication Arts and Sciences: CHARLES SALMON
Education: CAROLE AMES
Eng.: SATISH UDPA
Human Medicine: MARSHA D. RAPPLEY (acting)
James Madison College: SHERMAN GARNETT
Law: CLIFF F. THOMSON (acting)
Lyman Briggs College: ELIZABETH SIMMONS
Music: JAMES FORGER
Natural Science: ESTELLE McGROARTY
Nursing: MARY MUNDT
Osteopathic Medicine: WILLIAM D. STRAMPEL
Social Science: MARIETTA BABA

Veterinary Medicine: CHRISTOPHER M. BROWN
Honors College: RONALD FISHER
Residential College in Arts and Humanities:
STEPHEN L. ESQUITH (acting)

PROFESSORS

(C = Chairman of Department)

(Departments may be attached to more than one college)

Department of Accounting:
ARENS, A. A. (C)
BUZBY, S. L.
DILLEY, S. C.
GRAY, J.
HAKA, S.
McCARTHY, W. E.
MEAD, G. C.
O'CONNOR, M. C.
OUTSLAY, E.
SHIELDS, M. D.
SOLLENBERGER, H. M.
WARD, D. D.

Department of Advertising:
PRATT, C.
REECE, B. B.
SALMON, C.
VANDENBERGH, B. G. (C)

Department of Agricultural Economics:
BATIE, S. S.
BERNSTEN, R. H.
BLACK, J. R.
CRAWFORD, E.
HAMM, L. G. (C)
HARSH, S. B.
HARVEY, L. R.
HILKER, J. H.
HOEHN, J.
KELSEY, M. P.
LEHOLM, A. G.
MOSER, C. H.
MYERS, R. J.
NOTT, S. B.
PIERSON, T. R.
RICKS, D. J.
ROBISON, L. J.
SCHMID, A. A.
SCHWAB, G.
STAATZ, J. M.
VAN RAVENSWAAY, E.
WEBER, M.

Department of Agricultural Engineering:
BAKKER-ARKEMA, F. W.
BICKERT, W. G.
BROOK, R.
GERRISH, J.
LOUDON, T. L.
MROZOWSKI, T.
SEGERLIND, L. J.
SRIVASTAVA, A. (C)
STEFFE, J. F.
SURBROOK, T. C.
VAN EE, G. R.
VON BERNUTH, R.

Department of American Thought and Language:
ABRAHAMS, E. C.
BECKWITH, G. M.
BRATZEL, J. N.
BRESNAHAN, R. J.
BUNGE, N. L.
CHAMBERLAIN, W.
COOPER, D. D.
D'ITRI, P. A.
ELLISTON, S. F.
HOPPENSTAND, G. C.
LADENSON, J. R.
LUNDE, E.
McKINLEY, B. E.
NOVERR, D. A. (acting C)
ROUT, K.
SOMERS, P. P., Jr
STEINBERG, M.
THOMAS, F. R.

ZIEWACZ, L. E.

Department of Animal Science:
ALLEN, M. S.
AULERICH, R. J.
BEEDE, D. K.
BENSON, M. E.
BUCHOLTZ, H. F.
BURSIAN, S.
DENNIS BANKS, B.
ERICKSON, R. W.
FERRIS, T. A.
FOGWELL, R. L.
HAWKINS, D. R.
HOGBERG, M. G. (C)
IRELAND, J.
MELLENBERGER, R. W.
RAHN, A. P.
RITCHIE, H. D.
RUST, S. R.
SHELLE, J. E.
VARGHESE, S. K.
YOKOYAMA, M. T.

Department of Anthropology:
CHARTKOFF, J.
CLELAND, C. E.
CLIMO, J.
DERMAN, W.
DWYER, D.
GALLIN, B.
GOLDSTEIN, L. G. (C)
LOVIS, W. A.
POLLARD, H. P.
ROBBINS, L. H.
SAUER, N.
SPIELBERG, J.
WHITEFORD, S.

Department of Art:
BANDES, S. J.
DEUSSEN, P. W.
FAGAN, J. E.
FUNK, R.
GLENDINNING, P.
KILBOURNE, W. G.
KUSZAI, J. J.
LAWTON, J. L.
MacDOWELL
STANFORD, L. O.
TARAN, I. Z.
VANLIERE, E. N.
WOLTER, K. H.

Department of Audiology and Speech Sciences:
CASBY, M.
EULENBERG, J. B.
MOORE, E. J.
PUNCH, J. L. (C)
RAKERD, B. S.
SMITH, L. L.
STOCKMAN, I. G.

Department of Biochemistry and Molecular Biology:
BIEBER, L. L.
FERGUSON-MILLER, S.
FRAKER, P. J.
GREEN, P. G.
HOLLINGSWORTH, R. I.
KAGUNI, J. M.
KAGUNI, L. S.
KINDEL, P. K.
KROOS, L. R.
McCORMICK, J. J.
McGROARTY, E. J.
McINTOSH, L.
MAHER, V. M.
PREISS, J.
RAIKHEL, N. V.
REVZIN, A.
SCHINDLER, M. S.
SMITH, W. L. (C)
TRIEZENBERG, S. J.
WANG, J. L.
WATSON, J. T.
WILSON, J. E.

Department of Botany and Plant Pathology:
DeZOETEN, G. A.
EKERN, F. F.
EWERS, F. W.
FULBRIGHT, D. W.
HAMMERSCHMIDT, R. (C)
HART, L. P.
HOLLENSEN, R.
JONES, A. L.
KEEGSTRA, K. G.
KENDE, H.
KLOMPARENS, K. L.
MURPHY, P. G.
NADLER, K. D.
OHLROGGE, J. B.
POFF, K. L.
SAFIR, G. R.
SEARS, B.
TAGGART, R.
VARGAS, J. M., Jr
WALTON, J. D.
WEBBER, P. J.
WOLK, C. P.
ZEEVAART, J. A. D.

Department of Chemical Engineering:
BERGLUND, K.
DALE, B. (C)
DRZAL, L. T.
HAWLEY, M. C.
JAYARAMAN, K.
MILLER, D. J.
NARAYAN, R.
PETTY, C. A.
WORDEN, R. M.

Department of Chemistry:
ALLISON, J.
BABCOCK, G. T.
CHANG, C. K.
CROUCH, S. R.
CUKIER, R. I.
DUNBAR, K.
FROST, J.
HARRISON, J. F.
HUNT, K. C.
HUNT, P. M.
KANATZIDES, M. G.
LEROI, G. E.
McGUFFIN, V. L.
McHARRIS, W. C.
MORRISSEY, D. J.
PINNAVAIA, T. J.
RATHKE, M. W.
REUSCH, W. H.
WAGNER, P. J.
WULFF, W. D.

Department of Civil and Environmental Engineering:
BALADI, G.
DAVIS, M. L.
HARICHANDRAN, R. S. (C)
HATFIELD, F.
LYLES, R. W.
McKELVEY, F.
SOROUSHIAN, P.
TAYLOR, W. C.
VOICE, T. C.

Department of Communication:
ATKIN, C. K. (C)
BOSTER, F. J.
DONOHUE, W.
SMITH, S. W.

Department of Computer Science and Engineering:
CHUNG, M.-J.
DILLON, L. K.
GREENBERG, L.
HUGHES, H. D.
JAIN, A. K. (C)
NI, L. M.
PRAMANIK, S.
STOCKMAN, G. C. (acting C)
WEINSHANK, D. J.
WOJCIK, A. S.

Department of Counseling, Educational Psychology and Special Education:

AMES, C.
BECKER, B. J.
CLARK, C. M.
CREWE, N. M.
DICKSON, W. P.
ENGLERT, C. S.
FLODEN, R. E.
HAPKIEWICZ, W. C.
JUNE, L. N.
LEAHY, M. J.
LOPEZ, F. G.
MEHRENS, W. A.
PALAS, A. M.
PERNELL, E.
PHILLIPS, S. E.
PRAWAT, R. (C)
RECKASE, M. D.
SCHMIDT, W. H.
SMITH, G.
SPIRO, R. J.
STEWART, D. A.
YELON, S. L.

School of Criminal Justice:

BONNER, R. W.
BYNUM, T. S.
CARTER, D. L.
HORVATH, F. S.
HUDZIK, J. K.
MASTROFSKI
MORASH, M. A. (Dir)
NALLA, M. K.
SIEGEL, J.
SMITH, C. E.
STEWART, C. S.

Department of Crop and Soil Sciences:

BOYD, S. A.
CHRISTENSON, D. R.
CRUM, J. R.
FOSTER, E. F.
FREED, R. D.
GOODMAN, E.
HARWOOD, R. R.
JACOBS, L. W.
JOHNSTON, T. J. (acting C)
KELLS, J. D.
KELLY, J. D.
LEEP, R. H.
LEMME, G. D.
LENSKI, R. E.
MOKMA, D. L.
PAUL, E. A.
PENNER, D.
PIERCE, F. J.
RENNER, K. A.
RITCHIE, J. T.
ROBERTSON, G. P.
SMUCKER, A. J. M.
THOMASHOW, M.
TIEDJE, J. M.
WARNCKE, D. D.

Department of Economics:

ALLEN, B. T.
BAILLIE, R. T.
BALLARD, C. L.
BIDDLE, J. E.
BOYER, K. D.
BROWN, B. W.
CHOI, J. P.
DAVIDSON, C.
FISHER, R. C.
GODDEERIS, J. H. (C)
HOLZER, H. J.
KREININ, M. E.
LIEDHOLM, C. E.
LINZ, S. J.
MACKEY, M. C.
MARTIN, L. W.
MATUSZ, S. J.
MENCHIK, P. L.
MEYER, J.
NEUMARK, D. B.
OBST, N. P.

PECCHENINO, R. A.
SCHMIDT, P. J.
SEGERSTROM, P. S.
STRAUSS, J. A.
WILSON, J. D.
WOODBURY, S. A.
WOOLDRIDGE, J.

Department of Educational Administration:

CHURCH, R. L.
CUSICK, P. A. (C)
DAVIS, M.
FAIRWEATHER, J.
GRANDSTAFF, M. E.
IGNATOVICH, F. R.
KAAGAN, S. S.
MOORE, K. M.
PLANK, D. N.
ROMANO, L. G.
SIMON, L. A. K.
SYKES, G.
TURNER, M.
WEILAND, S.

Department of Electrical and Computer Engineering:

ASMUSSEN, J., Jr (C)
DELLER, J.
FISHER, P. D.
FOUKE, J. M.
KHALIL, H.
NYQUIST, D. P.
PIERRE, P. A.
REINHARD, D. K.
ROTHWELL, E. J.
SALAM, F. M.
SCHLUETER, R. A.
SHANBLATT, M.
SIEGEL, M.
TUMMALA, R. L.
WEY, C.-L.

Department of English:

ATHANASON, A. N.
BANKS, J. S.
BRUNNER, D. D.
CRANE, M.
DEWHURST, C. K.
DULAI, S. S.
FISHBURN, K. R.
GASS, S. M.
GOCHBERG, D. S.
GOODSON, A. C.
GROSS, B. E.
HARROW, K.
HILL, J. L.
JOHNSEN, W.
LANDRUM, L. N.
LUDWIG, J. B.
MARTIN, R. A.
MATHESON, I. M.
McCLINTOCK, J. I.
McGUIRE, P. C.
MEINERS, R. K.
O'DONNELL, P. J. (C)
PAANANEN, V. N.
PENN, W. S.
POGEL, N.
ROBINSON, R. F.
ROSENBERG, D. M.
SEATON, J.
SKEEN, A. C.
SMITHERMAN, G.
STALKER, J. C.
STOCK, P. L.
TAVORMINA, M. T.
UPHAUS, R. W.
VINCENT, W. A.
WAKOSKI, D.
WHALLON, W.
WILSON, M.

Department of Entomology:

AYERS, G. S.
BESAW, L. C.
BIRD, G. W.
GAGE, S.
GRAFIUS, E. J. (C)

HOLLINGWORTH, R. M.
MERRITT, R. W.
MILLER, J. R.
POSTON, F. L.
RAIKHEL, A.
SCRIBER, J. M. (C)
SMITLEY, D. R.
STEHR, F. W.
VanTASSELL, E.
WHALON, M. E.
ZABIK, M. J.

Department of Epidemiology:

PARETH, N. (C)
PATHAK, P. K.

Department of Family and Child Ecology:

AMES, B. D.
BARRATT, M. S.
BOBBITT, N.
BOGER, R.
GRIFFORE, R.
IMIG, D. R.
IMIG, G. L.
JOHNSON, D. J.
KEITH, J. G.
KOSTELNIK, M. (C)
LUSTER, T. J.
McADOO, H. P.
MILLER, J. R.
PHENICE, L.
SCHIAMBERG, L. B.
SODERMAN, A. K.
TAYLOR, C. S.
WALKER, R.
WHIREN, A. P.
YOUATT, J. P.

Department of Family and Community Medicine:

AGUWA, M. I. (C)
BORDINAT, S. M.
CUMMINGS, M.
KURTZ, M.
PAPSIDERO, J.

Department of Family Practice:

ALEXANDER, E.
BRODY, H.
GERARD, R.
GIVEN, C. W.
HICKNER, J.
OGLE, K. S.
PATHAK, D. R.
WHITTIER, H. L.

Department of Finance:

BOOTH, G. G. (C)
GRUNEWALD, A. E.
HENRY, J. B.
KHANNA, N.
LASHBROOKE, E. C., Jr
O'DONNELL, J. L.
RAINEY, J. F.
SIMONDS, R. R.
STENZEL, P.

Department of Fisheries and Wildlife:

BATIE, R. E.
D'ITRI, F.
DOBSON, T. A.
GARLING, D. L.
JOHNSON, D. I.
PEYTON, R. B.
PRINCE, H. H.
TAYLOR, W. W. (C)

Department of Food Science and Human Nutrition:

BENNINK, M. R.
BOND, J. T.
BOOREN, A. M.
CASH, J. N.
CHENOWETH, W. L.
GRAY, I. J.
HEGARTY, P. V.
HOERR, S. M.
LINZ, J. E.
PESTKA, J. J.

ROMSOS, D. R.
SMITH, D. M.
SONG, W. O.
UEBERSAX, M. A. (C)
ZABIK, M.
ZILE, M. H.

Department of Forestry:

DICKMANN, D. I.
KEATHLEY, D. E. (C)
KIELBASO, J. J.
KOELLING, M. R.
MCDONOUGH, M.
POTTER-WITTER, K. L.

Department of Geography:

CAMPBELL, D. J.
CHUBB, M.
COREY, K. E.
GROOP, R. E. (C)
HAMLIN, R.
HARMAN, J. R.
HINOJOSA, R.
LIM, G.-C.
MANSON, G. A.
MEHRETU, A.
OLSON, J. M.
SCHAETZL, R. J.
SKOLE, D. L.
THOMAS, J.
WILLIAMS, J.
WITTICK, R. I.

Department of Geological Sciences:

ANSTEY, R. L.
CAMBRAY, F. W.
FUJITA, K.
LARSON, G. J.
LONG, D. T.
SIBLEY, D. F.
TROW, J. W.
VELBEL, M. A. (C)
VOGEL, T. A.

Department of History:

ANDERSON, J. R.
EADIE, J. W.
FISHER, A.
GLIOZZO, C. A.
HINE, D. C.
LAURENCE, R. R.
LEVINE, P. D.
MARCUS, H. G.
MOCH, L. P.
RADDING, C. M.
REED, H. A.
ROBINSON, D. W.
SCHOENL, W. J.
SIEGELBAUM, L. H. (C)
SILVERMAN, H.
STEWART, G. T.
SWEENEY, J. M.
THOMAS, R. W.
THOMAS, S. J.
VIETH, J. K.
WILBUR, E.

Department of Horticulture:

BIERNBAUM, J. A.
CAMERON, A. C.
CARLSON, W. H.
DILLEY, D. R.
FLORE, J. A.
HANCOCK, J. F.
HANSON, E. J.
HEINS, R. D.
HERNER, R. C.
HOWELL, G. S.
IEZZONI, A. F.
NAIR, M.
LOESCHER, W. H. (C)
PERRY, R. L.
SINK, K. C.
WIDDERS, I. E.
ZANDSTRA, B. H.

School of Hospitality Business:

CICHY, R. (Dir)
KASAVANA, M. L.

KNUTSON, B. J.
NINEMEIER, J. D.
SCHMIDGALL, B. H.

Department of Human Environment and Design:

SONTAG, M. S.
STERNQUIST, B.
STEWART, D. G. (C)

Division of Human Pathology:

JONES, M.
KUMAR, K.
SANDER, C. M.
SIEW, S.

Department of Internal Medicine:

HUGHES, M. J.
OTTEN, R. F.
PYSH, J. J.
RISTOW, G. E.

James Madison College:

AYOOB, M.
BANKS, R. F.
DORR, R. F.
GARNETT, S. W. (Dean)
GRAHAM, N. A.
HOEKSTRA, D. J.
RUBNER, M.
SCHECHTER, M.
SEE, K. O.
WALTZER, K.
ZINMAN, M. R.

School of Journalism:

BOSSEN, H. S.
COTE, W. E.
DAVENPORT, L. D.
DETJEN, J. T.
FICO, F.
LACY, S. R. (acting Dir)
MOLLOY, J. D.
SOFFIN, S. I.
SPANIOLO, J. D.

W. K. Kellogg Biological Station:

GROSS, K. L.
KLUG, M. J. (Dir)
KNEZEK, B. D.
MITTELBACH, G. G.
TESSIER, A. J.

Department of Kinesiology:

DUMMER, G.
FELTZ, D. L. (C)
HAUBENSTRICKER, J. L.
MALINA, R. M.
PIVARNIK, J. M.

School of Labor and Industrial Relations:

BLOCK, R. N.
CURRY, T. H. (Dir)
KOSSEK, E. E.
KRUGER, D. H.
MOORE, M. L. (Dir)
REVITTE, J.
SMITH, P. R.
TOBEY, S. H.
VANDE VORD, N.
WOLKINSON, B. W.

Department of Large Animal Clinical Sciences:

AMES, N. K.
BAKER, J. C.
BARTLETT, P. C.
CARON, J. P.
DERKSEN, F. J. (C)
HERDT, T.
HOLLAND, R. E.
KANEENE, J. B.
KING, L. J.
LLOYD, J. W.
MATHER, E. C.
NACHREINER, R. F.
NICKELS, F. A.
ROBINSON, N. E.
ROOK, J. S.
SEARS, P. M.

SPRECHER, D. J.
STICK, J. A.
STRAW, B. E.

Department of Linguistics and Germanic, Slavic, Asian and African Languages:

ABBOTT, B. K.
BELGARDT, R.
FALK, J. S.
HUDSON, G.
JUNTUNE, T. W.
LIN, Y.-H.
LOCKWOOD, D. G.
MCCONEGHY, P.
PAULSELL, P.
PETERS, G. F. (C)
PRESTON, D.
SENDICH, M.
WILKINS, W. K.
WURST, K. A.

Lyman Briggs School:

EBERT-MAY, D. (Dir)
INGRAHAM, E. C.
MERCURO, N.
SAYED, M. M. A.
SIMPSON, W. A.
SPEES, S. T.

Department of Management:

BARRICK, M.
HOLLENBECK, J. R.
MOCH, M. K.
RUBIN, P. A.
WAGNER III, J. A. (C)

Department of Marketing and Supply Chain Management:

ALLEN, J. W.
BOWERSOX, D. J.
CALANTONE, R. J.
CAVUSGIL, S. T.
CLOSS, D.
DROGE, C. L.
HARRELL, G. D.
MELNYK, S. A.
NARASIMHAN, R.
NASON, R. W. (C)
SONG, X.-X. M.
VICKERY, S. K.
WILSON, R. D.

Department of Materials Science and Mechanics:

ALTIERO, N. J. (C)
CASE, E. D.
CLOUD, G. L.
GRUMMON, D. S.
HUBBARD, R. P.
LIU, D.
MUKHERJEE, K.
PENCE, T. J.
SOUTAS-LITTLE, R. W.
SUBRAMANIAN, K. N.

Department of Mathematics:

AKBULUT, S.
BAO, P.
BLAIR, D. E.
BROWN, W. C.
CHEN, B.-Y.
DRACHMAN, B.
DUNNINGER, D. R.
FINTUSHEL, R. A.
FRAZIER, M. W.
HALL, J. I.
HESTENES, M.
HILL, R. O.
IVANOV, N.
KUAN, W. E.
KURTZ, J. C.
LAMM, P. K.
LAPPAN, G.
LAPPAN, P. A. (C)
LI, T. Y.
LO, C. Y.
LUDDEN, G. D.
MACCLUER, C. R.
MASTERSON, J. J.

McCarthy, J. D.
Meierfrankenfeld, U.
Moran, D. A.
Newhouse, S. E.
Ow, W. H.
Palmer, E. M.
Parker, T. H.
Plotkin, J. M.
Rotthaus, C.
Sagan, B. E.
Schuur, J. D.
Seebeck, C. L.
Senk, S. L.
Shapiro, J. H.
Sledd, W. T.
Sonneborn, L. M.
Sreedharan, V. P.
Treil, S.
Ulrich, B.
Volberg, A.
Wald, J. W.
Wang, C.-Y.
Weil, C. E.
Winter, D. L.
Winter, M. J. K.
Wolfson, J. G.
Wong, P. K.
Zeidan, V. M.
Zhou, Z.

Department of Mechanical Engineering:
Foss, J. F.
Lloyd, J. R.
McGrath, J.
Medick, M. A.
Radcliffe, C. J.
Rosenberg, R. C. (C)
Schock, H. J.
Shaw, S. W.
Shik, T.
Thompson, B. S.
Wichman, I. S.

Office of Medical Education Research and Development:
Abbett, W. S.
Anderson, W. A. (Dir)
Farquar, L. J.
Henry, R. C.
Molidor, J. B.

Medical Technology Program:
Davis, G. L.

Department of Medicine:
Abela, G. S.
Dimitrov, N. V.
DiPette, D. J. (C)
Gossain, V. V.
Hassouna, H. I.
Holmes-Rovner, M.
Hoppe, R.
Jones, J. W.
Mayle, J. E.
Neiberg, A. D.
Penner, J. A.
Rosenman, K. D.
Schwartz, K. A.
Smith, R. C.
Stein, G. E.
Swanson, G. M.
Wang, D. H.

Department of Microbiology and Molecular Genetics:
Bagdasarian, M.
Bertrand, H.
Breznak, J. A.
Brubaker, R. R.
Conrad, S. E.
Corner, T.
Dazzo, F.
DeBruijn, F. J.
Dodgson, J. B. (C)
Esselman, W.
Fluck, M. M.
Garrity, G. M.
Haug, A.

Hausinger, R. P.
Jackson, J. H.
Kierszenbaum, F.
Maes, R. K.
Mulks, M. H.
Oriel, P. J.
Patterson, M. J.
Patterson, R.
Reddy, C. A.
Reusch, R. N.
Snyder, L. R.
Velicer, L. F.
Walker, R. D.

School of Music:
Carman, O. W.
Catron, D. L.
Dan, R. M.
Donakowski, C.
Ell, F. W.
Forger, D. M.
Forger, J. B. (Dir)
Gregorian, L.
Hutcheson, J. T.
Johnson, M. E.
Johnson, T. O.
Kratus, J. K.
LeBlanc, A.
Lulloff, J. P.
Moon, Y. H.
Newman, R.
Olson, C.
Ruggiero, C. H.
Sinder, P. N.
Smith, C. K.
Stolper, D.
Tims, F. C.
Verdebr, E. L.
Verdebr, W.
Votapek, R. J.
Ward, B. W.
Whitwell, J. L.
Zara, M.

National Superconducting Cyclotron Laboratory:
Blosser, H. G.
Gelbke, C. K. (Dir)
Hansen, P. G.
York, R. C.

College of Nursing:
Allen, G. D.
Collins, C.
Gift, A. G.
Given, B. A.
Rothert, M. L. (Dean)

Department of Obstetrics, Gynecology and Reproductive Biology:
Marshall, J. F. (C)
Vasilenko, P.

Department of Osteopathic Manipulative Medicine:
Rechtien, J. J. (acting C)
Reynolds, H.
Ward, R. C.

Department of Osteopathic Surgical Specialties:
Beckmeyer, H. E.
Haut, R. C.
Hogan, M. J.
Jacobs, A. W.

School of Packaging:
Burgess, C. J.
Downes, T. W.
Giacin, J. R.
Harte, B. (Dir)
Hughes, H. A.
Lockhart, H. E.
Selke, S. E. M.

Department of Park, Recreation and Tourism Resources:
Bristor, J. L.
Fridgen, J. (C)
Holecek, D. F.

Rasmussen, G. A.
Stynes, D. J.
Van Der Smissen, B.

Department of Pathology:
Bell, T. G.
Harkema, J. R.
Krehbiel, J.
Lovell, K. L.
MacKenzie, C.
Mullaney, T. P.
Padgett, G. A.
Reed, W. M. (acting C)
Rheuben, M. B.
Tvedten, H.
Williams, C. S. F.
Yamini, B.

Department of Pediatrics:
Breitzer, G. M.
Magen, M.
Schneiderman, D. O.

Department of Pediatrics and Human Development:
Chang, C. C.
Fisher, R.
Gordon, R.
Kallen, D. J.
Kaufman, D. B.
Kulkarni, R.
Kumar, A.
Murray, D. L.
Netzloff, M. L.
Scott-Emuakpor, A.
Seagull, E. A.
Sparrow, A. W. (C)
Trosko, J. E.

Department of Pharmacology and Toxicology:
Atchison, W. D.
Barman, S.
Bennett, J. L.
Braselton, W. E., Jr
Fink, G. D.
Fischer, L. J.
Galligan, J. J.
Gebber, G. L.
Goodman, J. I.
Kaminski, N. E.
Moore, K. E. (C)
Roth, R. A.
Thornburg, J.

Department of Philosophy:
Andre, J. A.
Asquith, P. D. (C)
Benjamin, M.
Esquith, S. L.
Fleck, L. M.
Frye, M.
Garelick, H. M.
Hall, R. J.
Hanna, J. F.
Koch, D. F.
Kotzin, R. H.
McCracken, C. J.
Lawson, B. E.
Miller, B.
Peterson, R. T.
Tomlinson, T.

Department of Physical Medicine and Rehabilitation:
Hallgren, R.
Hinds, W. C.
Kaufman, D.
Stanton, D. F.

Department of Physics and Astronomy:
Abolins, M. A.
Austin, S. M.
Baldwin, J. A.
Bass, J.
Bauer, W. W.
Benenson, W.
Berz, M. M.
Borysowicz, J.

BROCK, R. L. (C)
BROMBERG, C. M.
BROWN, B. A.
DANIELEWICZ, P.
DUXBURY, P. M.
DYKMAN, M. I.
GALONSKY, A. I.
GOLDING, B.
HARRISON, M. J.
HARTMANN, W. M.
HUSTON, J. W.
KASHY, E.
LINNEMAN, J. T.
LYNCH, W. G.
MAHANTI, S. D.
POLLACK, G. L.
POPE, B. G.
PRATT, W. P., Jr
PUMPLIN, J. C.
REPKO, W. W.
SHERRILL, B. M.
SIGNELL, P. S.
SIMKIN, S. M.
SMITH, H. A.
STEIN, R. F.
THOENNESSEN, M.
THORPE, M. F.
TOMANEK, D.
TUNG, W. K.
WEERTS, H. J.
WESTFALL, G. D.
ZELENVINSKY, V.

Department of Physiology:
ADAMS, T.
HASLAM, S. Z.
HEIDEMANN, S.
HOOTMAN, S. R.
JUMP, D. B.
KREULEN, D. L.
MEYER, R. A.
PETROPOULOS, E. A.
RIEGLE, G. D.
ROOT-BERNSTEIN, R. S.
SPARKS, H.
SPIELMAN, W. S. (C)
TIEN, H. T.
ZIPSER, B.

Department of Political Science:
ABRAMSON, P. R.
ALLEN, W. B.
BRATTON, M.
FINIFTER, A. W.
HALL, M. G.
HAMMOND, T. H.
HULA, R. C.
KNOTT, J. H.
MELZER, A.
OSTROM, C. W., Jr
ROHDE, D. W.
SILVER, B. D.
STEIN, B. N.
WAGMAN, J.
WEINBERGER, J. W. (C)

Department of Psychiatry:
BIELSKI, R. J.
COLENDA, C. (C)
OSBORN, G. G.
ROSEN, L. W.
STOFFELMAYR, B.
VAN EGEREN, L. F.
WERNER, A.
WILLIAMS, D. H.

Department of Psychology:
ABELES, N.
BARCLAY, A. M.
BOGAT, G. A.
CALDWELL, R. A.
CARR, T. H.
DAVIDSON, W., II
FERREIRA, M. F.
FITZGERALD, H. E.
FORD, J. K.
HARRIS, L. J.
HENDERSON, J. M.

HUNTER, J. E.
ILGEN, D. R.
JACKSON, L. A.
KARON, B. P.
KERR, N. L.
KOSLOWSKI, S. W.
LEVINE, R. L.
LOMBARDI, V. L.
MESSE, L. A.
NUNEZ, A. A.
PAULUS, G. S.
SCHMITT, N. W. (C)
SISK, C. L.
STOLLAK, G. E.
VON EYE, A. A.
WOOD, G. (C)
ZACKS, J. L.
ZACKS, R. T.

Department of Radiology:
FALLS, W. M.
GOTTSCHALK, A.
HALPERT, R. D.
JOHNSON, J. I.
POTCHEN, E. J. (C)
ROSS, L. M.
WALKER, B. E.

Department of Religious Studies:
GREENE, J. T.
WELCH, A. T.

Department of Resource Development:
BARNES-MCCONNELL, P.
BRONSTEIN, D. A.
DERSCH, E.
FEAR, F. A.
KAKELA, P. J.
KAMRIN, M. A.
NICKEL, P. E.
ROWAN, G.
SCHULTINK, G.
WRIGHT, D.

Department of Romance and Classical Languages:
COLMEIRO, J. F.
DONOHOE, J. I.
FIORE, R. L.
FRANCESE, J.
GRAY, E. F.
JOSEPHS, H.
KOPPISCH, M.
MANSOUR, G. P.
MARINO, N. F.
PORTER, L. M. (acting C)
SNOW, J. T.
TYRRELL, W. B.

Department of Small Animal Clinical Sciences:
ARNOCZKY, S. P.
BRADEN, T. D.
DECAMP, C. E.
EVANS, A. T.
EYSTER, G. E.
FLO, G. L.
HAUPTMAN, J.
JOHNSON, C.
MOSTOSKY, U. V.
PROBST, C. W. (C)
ROSSER, E. J.
SCHALL, W. D.
WALSHAW, R.

School of Social Work:
ANDERSON, G. R. (Dir)
DUANE, E. A.
FREDDOLINO, P. P.
HAROLD, R. D.
HERRICK, J. M.
LEVANDE, D. I.
WHITEMAN, V. L.

Department of Sociology:
BOKEMEIER, J.
BROMAN, C. L.
BUSCH, L. M.
CONNER, T. L. (C)

GALLIN, R. S.
GOLD, S. J.
HAMILTON, R. S.
HILL, R. C.
JOHNSON, N. E.
KAPLOWITZ, S.
MANNING, P. K.
PERLSTADT, H.
RUMBAUT, R. G.
SHLAPENTOKH, V.
VANDERPOOL, C. K.
WILEY, D.
ZINN, M. B.

Department of Statistics and Probability:
ERICKSON, R. V.
FABIAN, V.
FELDMAN, D.
GARDINER, J. C.
GILLILAND, D. C.
HANNAN, J. F.
KOUL, H. L.
LEPAGE, R. D.
MANDREKAR, V.
PAGE, C. F.
RAMAMOORTHI, R. V.
SALEHI, H. (C)
STAPLETON, J.

Department of Surgery:
DEAN, R. E. (C)
HARKEMA, J.
OSUCH, J. R.
TOLEDO, L. H.

Department of Teacher Education:
ALLEMAN, J. E.
ANDERSON, C. W.
ANDERSON, K.
ANDERSON, L. M.
BADER, L. A.
BARNES, H. L.
BOOK, C.
BROPHY, J. E.
CHERRYHOLMES, C.
EDWARDS, P. A.
FEATHERSTONE, J.
FERRINI-MUNDY, J.
FLORIO-RUANE, S.
GALLAGHER, J. J.
JOYCE, W. W.
KENNEDY, M. M.
KOZIOL, S. M. (C)
LABAREE, D. F.
LANIER, J. E.
LANIER, P. E.
LITTLE, T.
NEMSER, S. F.
PEARSON, P. D.
PURCELL-GATES, V.
PUTNAM, J. G.
RIETHMILLER, P. L.
ROEHLER, L. R.
SCHWILLE, J. R.
SEDLAK, M. W.
WEST, B. B.
WHEELER, C.

Department of Telecommunication:
BIOCCA, F. A.
GREENBERG, B. S.
HEETER, C. J.
LA ROSE, R. J.
LEVY, M. R. (C)
LITMAN, B. R.
MODY, B.
MUTH, T. A.
STEINFIELD, C.
WILDMAN, S. S.
WILLIAMS, G. A.

Department of Theatre:
DURR, D. L. (C)
RUTLEDGE, F. C.
RUTLEDGE, G.
SCHUTTLER, G.

Undergraduate University Division:
CURRY, B. P. (Dir)

Urban Affairs Programs:
DARDEN, J. T. (Dean)
LANG, M.
SCHWEITZER, J. H.
THORNTON, D. (acting Dean)
Department of Zoology:
AGGARWAL, S. K.
ATKINSON, J. W.
BAND, R. N.
BEAVER, D. L.
BROMLEY, S. C.
BURTON, T. M. (C)
BUSH, G. L.
CATHEY, B.
CLEMENS, L. G.
COOPER, W. E.
DYER, F. C.
EILAND, L. C.
GIESY, J. P.
HALL, D. J.
HILL, R. W.
HOLEKAMP, K. E.
HUGGETT, R. J.
MUZZALL, P. M.
PEEBLES, C.
ROBBINS, L. G.
SNIDER, R. J.
STEVENSON, R. J.
STRANEY, D.
WEBBER, M. M.

Centers and Other Administrative Units:
BLINN, L. V.
BOWMAN, H. E.
CARROLL, T. W.
KAUFMAN, G.
LOPUSHINSKY, T.
NERENZ, D. R.
NOVICKI, D. J.
ROSENTHAL, W. H.
SIERRA, L.
VORRO, J.
WILLIAMS, J. G.

MICHIGAN TECHNOLOGICAL UNIVERSITY

1400 Townsend Dr., Houghton, MI 49931
Telephone: (906) 487-1885
Internet: www.mtu.edu
Founded 1885; formerly Michigan College of Mining and Technology
Academic year: August to April
President: Dr GLENN D. MROZ
Provost and Senior Vice-President for Academic Affairs: Dr DAVID D. REED
Vice-President for Governmental Relations and Secretary, Board of Control: Dr DALE TAHTINEN
Vice-President of Michigan Tech Fund: SHEA McGRAW
Chief Financial Officer: DANIEL GREENLEE
Director of Library: PHYLLIS JOHNSON
Number of teachers: 400
Number of students: 6,540
Publication: Catalog

DEANS

Engineering: Dr ROBERT O. WARRINGTON
Forestry: Dr MARGARET GALE
Sciences and Arts: Dr MAX J. SEEL
Graduate School: Dr MARTYN SMITH
School of Business: Dr KEITH LANTZ
School of Technology: SCOTT AMOS

HEADS OF DEPARTMENTS

Materials Science and Engineering: Dr MARK PLITCHA
Physical Education: Prof. CHERYL DEPUYDT
Mathematics: Dr ALPHONSE H. BAARTMANS
Computer Sciences: Dr LINDA OTT
Electrical and Computer Engineering: Dr TIM SCHULZ

Mechanical Engineering: Dr WILLIAM PREDEBON
Humanities: Dr ROBERT JOHNSON
Social Sciences: Dr BRUCE SEELY
Chemical Engineering: Dr MICHAEL MULLINS
Forestry: Dr MARGARET GALE
Geology and Geological Engineering: Dr WAYNE PENNINGTON
Biological Sciences: Dr JOHN ADLER
Physics: RAVI PANDEY
Civil Engineering: Dr C. ROBERT BAILLOD
Chemistry: Dr PUSHPA MURTHY
Fine Arts: Dr MILT OLSSON

HEAD OF RESEARCH AGENCY

Keweenaw Research Center: Dr JAY MELDRUM

NORTHERN MICHIGAN UNIVERSITY

Marquette, MI 49855
Telephone: (906) 227-1000
Fax: (906) 227-2204
Internet: www.nmu.edu
Founded 1899
Academic year: August to May
President: LESLIE E. WONG
Provost and Vice-President for Academic Affairs: Dr FRED JOYAL
Dean of Academic Information Services: DARLENE PIERCE
Director of Admissions: GERRI DANIELS
Library of 520,945 vols
Number of teachers: 399
Number of students: 8,577

DEANS

College of Arts and Sciences: Dr TERRANCE SEETHOFF
College of Business: Dr JAMES SCHEINER
College of Professional Studies: Dr M. CAMERON HOWES
College of Technology and Applied Sciences: Dr MARK CURTIS

NORTHWOOD UNIVERSITY

4000 Whiting Drive, Midland, MI 48640-2398
Telephone: (989) 837-4200
Fax: (989) 837-4490
E-mail: admissions@northwood.edu
Internet: www.northwood.edu
Founded 1959
Private control
Academic year: September to May
President and CEO: Dr DAVID E. FRY
Provost: Dr CATHERINE W. CHEN
Vice-President (Academic Affairs): Dr ROBERT W. SERUM
Vice-President (Finance): DONALD E. HUNKINS
Vice-President (Operations and Enrollment Management): Dr DAVID D. LONG
Vice-President (University Advancement): SHERRIE GRAHAM
Library Director: SANDRA POTTS
Library of 50,000 vols
Number of teachers: 61
Number of students: 1,775
Areas of study: arts, business administration..

BRANCH CAMPUSES

Florida Campus: 2600 N Military Trail, West Palm Beach, FL 33409-2911; tel. (561) 478-5500; fax (561) 697-9495; e-mail fladmit@northwood.edu; Provost JOHN H. HAYNIE; 661 students.
Texas Campus: 1114 W FM 1382, Cedar Hill, TX 75104-1204; tel. (972) 291-1541; fax (972) 291-3824; e-mail txadmit@northwood.edu; Provost Dr WILLIAM C. OLIVER; 681 students.

OAKLAND UNIVERSITY

Rochester, MI 48309-4401
Telephone: (248) 370-2100
Internet: www.oakland.edu
Founded 1957
State control
Academic year: September to August (2 semesters, 2 sessions)
President: Dr GARY D. RUSSI
Vice-Presidents: VIRINDER MOUDGIL (Academic Affairs), VICTOR ZAMBARDI (General Counsel and Sec. to the Board of Trustees), JOHN W. BEAGHAN (Finance and Administration), MARY BETH SNYDER (Student Affairs), SUSAN GOEPP (University Relations)
Librarian: JULIE VOELCK
Number of teachers: 434 full-time
Number of students: 16,902
Publication: Oakland University Magazine (quarterly)

DEANS

School of Business Administration: JOHN TOWER
School of Educational and Human Service: MARY L. OTTO
School of Engineering and Computer Science: PIETER FRICK
School of Health Sciences: KENNETH HIGHTOWER
School of Nursing: LINDA THOMPSON-ADAMS
College of Arts and Sciences: DAVID J. DOWNING
Graduate Study and Research: RONALD OLSON

OLIVET COLLEGE

Olivet, MI 49076
Telephone: (616) 749 7000
Fax: (616) 749-7121
Internet: www.olivetcollege.edu
Founded 1844
President: MICHAEL S. BASSIS
Vice-President and Dean of the College: JAMES A. HALSETH
Vice-President for Finance and Administration: TIMOTHY J. NELSON
Vice-President for Institutional Advancement (vacant)
Vice-President for Facilities, Planning, Operations and Technological Services: LARRY COLVIN
Vice-President for Enrollment Management (vacant)
Director of Libraries (vacant)
Number of students: 825.

REFORMED BIBLE COLLEGE

3333 E Beltline NE, Grand Rapids, MI 49525
Telephone: (616) 222-3000
E-mail: admissions@reformed.edu
Internet: www.reformed.edu
Founded 1939 as Reformed Bible Institute; present name 1971
Private control
Academic year: August to April
President: Dr NICHOLAS V. KROEZE
Vice-President (Academic Administration): Dr MELVIN J. FLIKKEMA
Academic Dean and Registrar: Dr BEN A. MEYER
Director of Library Services: DIANNE ZANDBERGEN
Library of 55,000 vols
Number of teachers: 38
Number of students: 299
Areas of study: cross-cultural studies, educational ministries. pre-seminary studies, social work, youth ministry, Bible and theol-

ogy, liberal arts, professional education, general education, physical education.

ROCHESTER COLLEGE

800 W Avon Rd, Rochester Hills, MI 48307
Telephone: (248) 218-2000
Fax: (248) 650-6060
E-mail: admissions@rc.edu
Internet: www.rc.edu

Founded 1959 as North Central Christian College; present name 1997
Private control
Academic year: August to May

President: Dr KENNETH L. JOHNSON
Executive Vice-President: C. MARK VAN-RHEENEN
Provost: Dr MICHAEL W. WESTERFIELD
Vice-President (Human Resources and Special Projects): GARY CARSON
Vice-President (Institutional Advancement): DOUGLAS P. EDWARDS
Vice-President (Extended Learning: TRACEY HEBERT
Vice-President (Enrollment Services): LARRY D. NORMAN
Registrar: KEITH HUEY
Library Director: STEVEN K. BOWERS

Number of teachers: 37
Number of students: 600

HEADS OF DEPARTMENTS
Business: JEFF G. COHU
English: (vacant)
Professional Studies: Dr BRIAN L. STOGNER
Mathematics and Science: DAVID L. BRACKNEY
Music: JOE R. BENTLEY
Religion and Bible: Dr MELVIN R. STORM

SACRED HEART MAJOR SEMINARY

2701 Chicago Boulevard, Detroit, MI 48206
Telephone: (313) 883-8500
Fax: (313) 868-6440
E-mail: information@shms.edu
Internet: www.aodonline.org/SHMS

Founded 1919 as Sacred Heart Seminary; present name 1988
Private control

Rector and President: Rev. PATRICK F. HALFPENNY
Dean of Studies: Rev. STEVEN BOGUSLAWSKI
Dean of Administration and Advancement: ANNE-MARIE FREY
Library Director: KAREN RAE MEHAFFEY

Library of 110,000 vols
Number of teachers: 39
Number of students: 428 (300 undergraduate, 128 graduate).

SAGINAW VALLEY STATE UNIVERSITY

7400 Bay Rd, University Center, MI 48710
Telephone: (989) 964-4000
E-mail: admissions@svsu.edu
Internet: www.svsu.edu

Founded 1963
State control
Academic year: August to August

President: Dr ERIC R. GILBERTSON
Vice-President (Academic Affairs): ROBERT S. P. YIEN
Vice-President (Administration and Business Affairs): JIM MULADORE
Vice-President (Public Affairs): GENE HAMILTON
Vice-President (Student Services and Enrollment Management): ROBERT MAUROVICH
Library Director: LINDA FARYNK

Library of 621,113 items, 370,000 microforms
Number of teachers: 186

Number of students: 7,336 (6,406 undergraduate, 930 graduate)

DEANS
College of Arts and Behavioral Sciences: DONALD BACHAND
College of Business and Management: PAUL USELDING
College of Education: STEVE BARBUS
Crystal M. Lange College of Nursing and Health Sciences: CHERYL EASLEY
College of Science, Engineering and Technology: TOM KULLGREN

SAINT MARY'S COLLEGE OF MADONNA UNIVERSITY

3535 Indian Trail, Orchard Lake, MI 48324
Telephone: (248) 683-1757
E-mail: muinfo@madonna.edu
Internet: www.madonna.edu

Founded 1885 as Saints Cyril and Methodius Seminary; present name 1929
Private control

President: ROSE MARIE KUJAWA
Vice-President (Academics): Dr ERNEST NOLAN
Vice-President (Institutional Affairs) (vacant)
Registrar: STEVEN GRENUS
Library Director: PATRICIA HUGO

Library of 78,000 vols

HEADS OF DEPARTMENTS
Business Administration and Computer Information Systems: STUART ARENDS
Humanities: Dr KATHLEEN O'DOWD
Natural Science and Mathematics: Dr THEODORE BIERMANN
Philosophy and Theology: Dr MONICA MILLER
Polish Studies and East Central European Studies: Dr JANUSZ WROBEL
Social Sciences: Dr GERALD CHARBONNEAU

SIENA HEIGHTS UNIVERSITY

Adrian, MI 49221-1796
Telephone: (517) 263-0731
Fax: (517) 264-7702
Internet: www.sienahts.edu

Founded 1919
Academic year: August to May

President: Dr RICHARD B. ARTMAN
Academic Dean: Dr SHARON WEBER
Dean of Graduate Studies and Lifelong Learning: Dr ROBERT W. GORDON
Dean of Students: TRUDY McSORLEY
Dean of College for Professional Studies: DEBORAH CLARKE
Director of Admissions and Enrollment: KEVIN KUCERA
Vice-President for Advancement: THOMAS KAVANAGH, Jr
Chief Financial Officer: J. LEE JOHNSON
Registrar: AMY SMITH
Librarian (vacant)

Library of 136,082 vols
Number of teachers: 220
Number of students: 2,161
Publications: *Reflections* (3 a year), *Spectra* (6 a year).

SPRING ARBOR UNIVERSITY

Spring Arbor, MI 49283
Telephone: (517) 750-1200
Fax: (517) 750-2108
Internet: www.arbor.edu

Founded 1873

President: Dr GAYLE D. BEEBE
Vice-Presidents: Dr BETTY OVERTON-ADKINS (Academic Affairs), JAY MANSUR (Advancement), DOUGLAS JONES (Business Affairs),

MATTHEW OSBORNE (Program Development and Enrollment), DAMON SEACOTT (Student Development)
Library of 120,300 vols
Number of students: 2,623.

THOMAS M. COOLEY LAW SCHOOL

POB 13038, Lansing, MI 48901
Located at: 300 S Capitol Ave, Lansing, MI 48933
Telephone: (517) 371-5140
Fax: (517) 334-5718
E-mail: admissions@cooley.edu
Internet: www.cooley.edu

Founded 1972
Private control

President and Dean: DON LEDUC
Vice-President (Finance) and Chief Operating Officer: WILLIAM SCHOETTLE
Associate Dean (Enrollment and Student Services): Dr PAUL ZELENSKI
Associate Dean (Faculty): CHARLES CERCONE
Associate Dean (Library and Instructional Support): DUANE STROJNY
Associate Dean (Students and Professionalism): AMY TIMMER
Associate Dean (Grand Rapids/Western Michigan University Campus): MARION HILLIGAN
Associate Dean (Rochester/Oakland University Campus: JOHN NUSSBAUMER

Number of teachers: 160
Number of students: 2,807.

UNIVERSITY OF DETROIT MERCY

POB 19900, 4001 W. McNichols Rd, Detroit, MI 48219-0900
Telephone: (313) 993-1000
Internet: www.udmercy.edu

Founded 1877 as Detroit College and chartered as such 1881; chartered as a University 1911; merged with Mercy College of Detroit in 1990

President: GERARD L. STOCKHAUSEN
Vice-President for Academic Affairs: GEORGE F. LUNDY
Vice-President for Business and Finance: WILLIAM L. JOHNSON
Vice-President for University Advancement and Contract Learning: ADRIAN V. KERRIGAN
Vice-President for Enrollment and Student Affairs: MICHAEL JOSEPH
Dean of Admissions: DENISE WILLIAMS
Registrar: DIANE M. PRAET
Librarian: MARGARET AUER

Library of 508,000 vols
Number of full-time teachers: 360
Number of students: 5,600

DEANS
College of Liberal Arts: CHARLES E. MARSKE
College of Business Administration: BAHMAN MIRSHAB
College of Engineering and Science: LEO C. HANIFIN
College of Education and Human Services: (vacant)
College of Health Professions: SUZANNE MELLON
School of Architecture: STEPHEN VOGEL
School of Law: STEPHEN A. MAZURAK
School of Dentistry: H. ROBERT STEIMAN

UNIVERSITY OF MICHIGAN

Ann Arbor, MI 48109
Telephone: (734) 764-1817
Internet: www.umich.edu

Founded 1817
Academic year: September to April

President: MARY SUE COLEMAN

Provost and Executive Vice-President for Academic Affairs: Dr PAUL N. COURANT

Executive Vice-President and Chief Financial Officer: TIMOTHY P. SLOTTON

Vice-President for Student Affairs: E. ROYSTER HARPER

Vice-President for Development: JERRY A. MAY

Vice-President for Government Relations: CYNTHIA H. WILBANKS

Vice-President for Research: Dr FAWWAZ T. ULABY

Vice-President and General Counsel: MARVIN KRISLOV

Associate Provost for Academic and Multicultural Affairs: Dr LESTER MONTS

University Registrar: PAUL ROBINSON

Director of Admissions: THEODORE L. SPENCER

Library: see Libraries

Number of teachers: 4,447

Number of students: 39,031

Publications: *Michigan Quarterly Review*, *The University of Michigan Today* (4 a year), *Research News* (monthly), *Michigan Alumnus* (4 a year)

DEANS

College of Architecture and Urban Planning: DOUGLAS S. KELBAUGH

School of Art and Design: BRYAN V. ROGERS

School of Business Administration: ROBERT J. DOLAN

School of Dentistry: PETER J. POLVERINI

School of Education: KAREN K. WIXSON (acting)

College of Engineering: STEPHEN W. DIRECTOR

Graduate School: STEVEN L. KUNKEL

Law School: EVAN H. CAMIKER

School of Information: JOHN L. KING

College of Literature, Science and the Arts: TERRENCE J. MCDONALD

Medical School: ALLEN S. LICHTER

School of Music: KAREN L. WOLF

School of Natural Resources: ROSINA M. BIERBAUM

School of Nursing: ADA SUE HINSHAW

College of Pharmacy: FRANK J ASCIONE

School of Public Health: NOREEN M. CLARK

School of Public Policy: REBECCA M. BLANK

School of Social Work: PAULA ALLEN-MEARES

University Library: WILLIAM GOSLING (Director)

Division of Kinesiology: BEVERLEY D. ULRICH

PROFESSORS

College of Architecture and Urban Planning (tel. (734) 764-1300; fax (734) 763-2322; internet www.tcaup.umich.edu):

BORKIN, H.
BURESH, T.
CHAFFERS, J.
DEWAR, M.
FISHMAN, R. L.
GROAT, L.
KELBAUGH, D. S.
MARANS, R.
SNYDER, J.
TURNER, J.

School of Art and Design (tel. (734) 764-0397; fax (734) 936-0463; internet www.art-design.umich.edu):

CASTAGNACCI, V. E.
HERWITZ, D.
HINTON, A.
OVERMEYER, D.
ROGERS, B.
RUSH, J.
SAMUELS, A.
SMITH, S.
TAKAHARA, T.
WEST, E.

ZIRBES, G.

School of Business Administration (tel. (734) 763-5796; fax (734) 763-7804):

ANDERSON, E. W.
ASHFORD, S.
BAKER, W. E.
BATRA, R.
BLAIR, D. C.
CAMERON, G.
CAMERON, K. S.
CAPOZZA, D.
DAVIS, G.
DECHOW, P.
DOLAN, R. J.
DUTTON, J.
DVENYAS, I.
FORNELL, C.
GLADWIN, T.
GORDON, M.
HINES, JR, J. R.
IMHOFF, E.
INDJEJKIAN, R. J.
JACKSON, J.
JOHNSON, M. D.
KAUL, G.
KIM, H.
KINNEAR, T.
KOHRS, K. K.
KRISHNA, A. J.
LAFONTAINE
LANEN, W.
LEWIS, D.
LIEBERTHAL, K.
LIM, L. Y.
LOVEJOY, W.
LUNDHOLM, R.
MASTEN, S.
NARAYANAN, M. P.
OLSON, J.
OSWALD, L. J.
PRAHALAD, C.
PRICE, R.
QUINN, R.
RAMASWAMY, V.
REECE, J.
REILLY, R.
RYAN, M.
SANDELANDS, L.
SCHIPANI, C.
SCHRIBER, T.
SEVERANCE, D.
SEYHUN, N.
SIEDEL, G.
SKINNER, D.
SLEMROD, J.
SLOAN, R.
SVEJNAR, J.
TALBOT, B.
TERRELL, K.
TICHY, N.
ULRICH, D.
WALSH, J.
WEICK, K.
WEISS, J.
WHITE, B.
WHITMAN, M.
YATES, F.

School of Dentistry (tel. (734) 763-6933; internet www.dent.mich.edu):

BAGRAMIAN, R. A.
BRADLEY, R. M.
BROOKS, S. L.
BURGETT, F. G.
CLARKSON, B. H.
CLEWELL, D. B.
DENNISON, J. D.
DRACH, J. C.
FRANCESCHI, R.
GOBETTI, J. P.
HANKS, C. T.
HEYS, D. R.
HOLLAND, G. R.
ISMAIL, A.
JOHNSTON, L. E., Jr
KOTOWICZ, W. E.

KOWALSKI, C. J.
LOPATIN, D. E.
MCCAULEY, L.
MCNAMARA, J. A.
MISTRETTA, C. M.
MOONEY, D. J.
O'BRIEN, W. J.
PETERS, M.
POLVERINI, P. J.
RAZZOOG, M. E.
ROBINSON, E.
STOHLER, C. S.
STRAFFON, L. H.
TEDESCO, L.
UPTON, L. G.
WANG, H. L.
WOOLFOLK, M.

School of Education (tel. (734) 764-7563; internet www.soe.umich.edu):

ALLEN-MEARES, P.
BALL, D.
BASS, A.
BATES, P.
BLUMENFELD, P.
BURKHARDT, J.
CAMERON, K.
COHEN, D.
ECCLES, J.
FENSTERMACHER, G.
GERE, A. R.
GOODMAN, F. L.
HIEBERT, E.
KELLER-COHEN, D.
KING, PAT
KRAJCIK, J.
LEMKE, J.
LAMPERT, M.
LEE, V.
MAEHR, M.
MARX, R. W.
MIREL, J.
MISKEL, C. G.
MORRISON, F.
NETTLES, M.
NEUMAM, S.
PALINSCAR, A.
PARIS, S. G.
PETERS, C. W.
PETERSON, M. W.
RAUDENBUSH, S.
REID, P.
RICHARDSON, V.
ROWAN, B.
SOLOWAY, E.
SILVER, E.
STONE III, C.
SULZBY, E. F.
TO, C.
WAGAW, T.
WIXSON, K. K.

College of Engineering (tel. (734) 647-7000; fax (734) 647-7001; internet www.engine.umich.edu):

Aerospace Engineering:

BERNSTEIN, D.
BOYD, I.
DAHM, W.
DRISCOLL, J. F.
FAETH, G. M.
FRIEDMANN, P.
HYLAND, D.
KABAMBA, P. T.
KAUFFMAN, C. W.
MCCLAMROCH, N. H.
POWELL, K. G.
ROE, P. L.
TRIANTAFYLLIDIS, N.
VAN LEER, B.
WAAS, A. M.

Atmospheric, Oceanic and Space Sciences:

ATREYA, S.
BANKS, P.
BARKER, J. R.
BOYD, J.

CARROLL, M.
DRAKE, R.
ENGLAND, A.
FISK, L.
GILCHRIST, B.
GOMBOSI, T.
KEELER, G.
KUHN, W. R.
NAGY, A. F.
PENNER, J.
SAMSON, P.
WAITE, Jr, J. H.

Biomedical Engineering:

ANDERSON, D.
ARMSTRONG, T.
BAKER, Jr, J.
BURNS, M.
CAIN, C.
CARSON, P.
CHAFFIN, D.
FAULKNER, J.
GOLDSTEIN, S.
GROTBERG, J.
HERO, A.
KEARFOTT, K.
LEVINE, S.
MEYER, C.
MOONEY, D.
NAJATI, J.
O'DONNELL, M.
WANG, H.
WINEMAN, A.
WISE, K.

Chemical Engineering:

BURNS, M. A.
FOGLER, H. S.
GLAND, J.
GULARI, E.
LARSON, R.
LINDERMAN, J.
MOONEY, D.
SAVAGE, P.
SCHWANK, J. W.
THOMPSON , Jr, L. T.
WANG, H. Y.
WEBER, W.
YANG, R. T.
ZIFF, R.

Civil and Environmental Engineering:

ABRIOLA, L.
ADRIAENS, P.
BULKLEY, J.
CARR, R.
GOEL, S.
HAYES, K. F.
HRYCIW, R.
IOANNOU, P.
KATOPODES, N.
LI, V. C.
MICHALOWSKI, R. L.
NAAMAN, A. E.
NOWAK, A. S.
WEBER, W. J., Jr
WIGHT, J. K.
WRIGHT, S. J.

Electrical Engineering and Computer Science:

ANDERSON, D. J.
ATKINS, D. E.
BHATTACHARYA, P.
BROWN, R.
CAIN, C. A.
DIRECTOR, S.
DURFEE, E.
ENGLAND, A.
FREUDENBERG, J.
FURNAS, G.
GILCHRIST, B.
GRIZZLE, J. W.
HADDAD, G. I.
HAYES, J.
HOLLAND, J.
ISLAM, M.
JAGADISH, H.

JAHANIAN, F.
KABAMBA, P. T.
KANICKI, J.
KAPLAN, S.
KATEHI, P. B.
KIERAS, D.
KODITSCHEK, D.
LAFORTUNE, S.
LAIRD, J.
LEITH, E. N.
McCLAMROCH, N. H.
MAZUMDER, P.
MEERKOV, S. M.
MERLIN, R.
MOUROU, G.
MUDGE, T. N.
MUNSON, D.
NAGY, A. F.
NAJAFI, K.
NEUHOFF, D. L.
O'DONNELL, M.
PANG, S.
PAVLIDIS, D.
POLLACK, M.
PRAKASH, A.
RAND, S.
REBEIZ, G.
ROUNDS, W. C.
SAKALLAH, K.
SARABUNDI, K.
SHIN, K.
SINGH, J.
SOLOWAY, E.
STARK, W.
STEEL, D. G.
STOUT, Q. F.
TENEKETZIS, D.
TEOREY, T. J.
THOMASON, R.
VOLAKIS, J. L.
WELLMAN, M.
WINFUL, H. G.
WISE, K. D.
YAGLE, A.

Center for Ergonomics:

ARMSTRONG, T. J.
CHAFFIN, D. B.
HERRIN, G. D.
KEYSERLING, W. M.

Industrial and Operations Engineering:

ARMSTRONG, T.
BEAN, J.
BOZER, Y.
CHAFFIN, D.
DUENYAS, I.
HERRIN, G.
KEYSERLING, W.
LIKER, J.
MURTY, K.
NAIR, V.
POLLOCK, S.
SAIGAL, R.
SEIFORD, L. M.
SHI, J.
SMITH, R. L.
WU, C.

Materials Science and Engineering:

BILELLO, J.
EWING, R.
FILISKO, F. E.
GHOSH, A.
GIBALA, R.
HALLORAN, J. W.
HOSFORD, W. F.
JONES, J. W.
LAINE, R.
MAZUMDER, J.
POLLOCK, T.
ROBERTSON, R. E.
WAS, G. S.
YEE, A. F.

Mechanical Engineering and Applied Mechanics:

ASSANIS, D.

ATREYA, A.
BARBER, J. R.
CECCIO, S.
CHEN, M. M.
DUTTA, D.
GHOSH, A.
GOLDSTEIN, S.
HU, S.
HULBERT, G.
JACOBS, S.
KANNATEY-ASIBU, E.
KAVIANY, M.
KIKUCHI, N.
KOREN, Y.
KOTA, S.
MAZUMDER, J.
NI, J.
PAN, J.
PAPALAMBROS, P. Y.
PIERRE, C.
SCHULTZ, W.
SCOTT, R. A.
STEIN, J.
ULSOY, A. G.
WINEMAN, A. S.
YANG, W. H.

Naval Architecture and Marine Engineering:

BECK, R. F.
BERNITSAS, M. M.
MEADOWS, G.
PARSONS, M. G.
TROESCH, A. W.

Nuclear Engineering and Radiological Sciences:

BIELAJEW, A.
EWING, R.
FLEMING, R.
GILGENBACH, R.
KEARFOTT, K.
LARSEN, E. W.
LAU, Y.
LEE, J.
MARTIN, W.
WAS, G.

Space Physics:

CARROLL, M.
DRAKE, R.
ENGLAND, A.
FISK, L.
GILCHRIST, B.
GOMBOSI, T.
NAGY, A.
WAITE, J.

Law School (tel. (734) 764-0514; fax (734) 763-9375; internet www.law.umich.edu):

ALLEN, L. E.
AVI-YOHAH, R.
BEN-SHAHAR, O.
CAMINKER, E.
CHAMBERS, D. L.
CLARK, S.
COOPER, E. H.
CROLEY, S.
EISENBERG, R. S.
ELLSWORTH, P.
FRIEDMAN, R.
FRIER, B. W.
GREEN, T. A.
GROSS, S. R.
HATHAWAY, J.
HERZOG, D. J.
HILLS, R.
HOWSE, R.
KAHN, D. A.
KAMISAR, Y.
KAUPER, T. E.
KRIER, J. E.
LEHMAN, J. S.
LEMPERT, R. O.
LOGUE, K.
MacKINNON, C. A.
MALAMUD, D.
MILLER, W. I.
PARSON, E.

PAYTON, S.
PRITCHARD, A.
REGAN, D. H.
REIMANN, M. W.
SCHNEIDER, C.
SCOTT, R.
SIMPSON, A.
SOPER, P.
VINING, J.
WAGGONER, L. W.
WESTEN, P. K.
WHITE, J. B.
WHITE, J. J.
WHITMAN, C. B.

School of Information (tel. (734) 964-9376; fax (734) 764-2475; internet www.si.umich .edu):

ATKINS, D. E.
BLOUIN, F. X.
COHEN, M.
DRABENSTOTT, K.
DURFEE, E.
DURRANCE, J.
FROST, C. O.
FURNAS, G.
KING, J.
MACKIE-MASON, J.
OLSON, G.
OLSON, J.
SOLOWAY, E.
VanHOUWELING, D.

College of Literature, Science and the Arts (tel. (734) 764-0322; fax (734) 764-2697; internet www.lsa.umich.edu):

American Culture:

DOWD, G. E.
ELLISON, J.
FREEDMAN, J.
HOWARD, J.
KELLEY, M.
SMITH-ROSENBERG, C.
WALD, A.

Anthropology:

BEHAR, R.
BRACE, C. L.
COHEN, D.
FEELEY-HARNIK, G.
FLANNERY, K. V.
FORD, R. I.
FRICKE, T.
FRISANCHO, A. R.
GINGERICH, P. D.
HOLL, A. F. C.
IRVINE, J. T.
KELLY, R. C.
KOTTAK, C. P.
MANNHEIM, B.
MARCUS, J. P.
MITANI, J. C.
O'SHEA, J.
OWUSU, M.
PARSONS, J. R.
ROBERTSON, J.
SINOPOLI, C.
SPETH, J. D.
STOLER, A.
TRAUTMAN, T.
VERDERY, K.
WHALLON, R. W.
WILLIAMS, M.
WOLPOFF, M. H.
WRIGHT, H. T., III
YOFFEE, N.

Applied Physics:

ALLEN, J.
BERMAN, P.
BHATTACHARYA, P. K.
BILELLO, J.
BUCKSBAUM, P.
CARSON, P.
CLARKE, R.
DIERKER, S.
DRAYSON, S.

EVANS, B.
GAFNI, A.
GILCHRIST, B.
GILGENBACH, R.
GLAND, J. L.
HADDAD, G.
ISLAM, M.
KANICKI, J.
KOPELMAN, R.
LAU, Y. Y.
LEIGH, R.
MERLIN, R.
MOUROU, G.
O'DONNELL, M.
ORR, B.
PAVLIDIS, D.
RAND, S.
ROSS, M.
SANDER, L. M.
SINGH, J.
SROLOVITZ, D.
STEEL, D.
UHER, C.
WINFUL, H.
ZORN, J.

Astronomy:

ALLER, H.
BREGMAN, J.
COWLEY, A.
RICHSTONE, D.

Biological Station:

DIANA, J.
FORD, R.
HAZLETT, B.
NADELHOFFER, K.
WEBB, P.
WITTER, J.

Biology:

ADAMS, J. P.
BENDER, R. A.
EASTER, S. S., Jr
ESTABROOK, G. F.
FINK, W.
FISHER, D.
FOGEL, R.
FORD, R.
FOSTER, D.
FUTUYMA, D. J.
GINGERICH, P.
GOLDBERG, D.
HAZLETT, B. A.
HUME, R.
KLEINSMITH, L. J.
KLING, G.
KLIONSKY, D. J.
KUWADA, J. Y.
LEHMAN, J.
NADELHOFFER, K.
NOODEN, L. D.
NUSSBAUM, R. A.
O'CONNOR, B.
PAYNE, R. B.
PICHERSKY, E.
SCHIEFELBEIN , Jr, J. W.
SMITH, G. R.
TOSNEY, K.
VANDERMEER, J. H.
WEBB, P.
WERNER, E. E.
WYNNE, M. J.
YOCUM, C. F.

Chemistry:

ASHE, A. J.
BARKER, J.
CARROLL, M.
COLEMAN, M.
COPPOLA, B. R.
COUCOUVANIS, D.
COWARD, J.
CURTIS, M. D.
FIERKE, C. A.
FRANCIS, A. H.
GLAND, J.
GLICK, G. D.

GRIFFIN, H. C.
KENNEDY, R. J.
KOPELMAN, R.
KOREEDA, M.
LUBMAN, D. M.
MATTHEWS, R.
MEYERHOFF, M. E.
MORRIS, M. D.
PEARSON, W.
PECORARO, V. L.
PENNER-HAHN, J.
RASMUSSEN, P. G.
ROUSH, W.
SACKS, R. D.
SHARP, R.
VEDEJS, E.
YAGHI, O. M.
YOCUM, C.
ZELLERS, E.
ZUIDERWEG, E.

Classical Studies:

ALCOCK, S. E.
CAMERON, H. D.
CARSON, A.
CHERRY, J. F.
FRIER, B. W.
GARBRAH, K.
HERBERT, S.
JANKO, R.
LAMBROPOULOS
OBBINK, D.
PORTER, J. I.
POTTER, D.
SCODEL, R.

Communication Studies:

ALLEN, R. L.
BUSHMAN, B.
DOUGLAS, S.
HUESMANN, L.
NEUMAM, W. R.
TRAUGOTT, M.

Comparative Literature:

CARSON, A.
GIKANDI, S.
LAMBROPOULOS, V.
LIU, L.
PORTER, J.
SHAMMAS, A.
SIEBERS, T.

Economics:

ADAMS, W.
BARSKY, R. B.
BASU, S.
BOUND, J.
BROWN, C.
COURANT, P.
DEARDORFF, A.
GRAMLICH, E.
HINES, J.
HOWREY, E. P.
HYMANS, S.
JOHNSON, G.
LAITNER, J.
LARN, D.
LEVINSOHN, J. A.
SALANT, S. W.
SAXONHOUSE, G.
SHAPIRO, M.
SLEMROD, J.
SMITH, L.
SOLON, G.
STACCHETTI, E.
STAFFORD, F.
SVEJNAR, S.
TESAR, L. L.
WEISSKOPF, T.
WHATLEY, W.

English Language and Literature:

ALEXANDER, W.
BAILEY, R.
BORNSTEIN, G.
BRATER, E.
DELBANCO, N.

FALLER, L.
FREEDMAN, J.
GERE, A.
GIKANDI, S.
GOLDSTEIN, L.
GREGERSON, L. K.
HALPERIN, D. M.
HERRMAN, A. C.
HOWARD, J. M.
JENSEN, E.
KNOTT, J.
KUCICH, J.
LEVINSON, M.
LEWIS, R.
MOSS, T.
RABKIN, E.
SCHOENFELDT, M.
SIEBERS, T.
SMITH, S.
STUDLER, G.
TILLINGHAST, R.
TRAUB, V. J.
VICINUS, M.
WALD, A.
WHITE, J.
WILLIAMS, R.

Film and Video Studies:

ABEL, R.
BEAVER, F.
COHEN, H.
STUDLAR, G.

Geological Sciences:

BLUM, J. D.
ESSENE, E. J.
EWING, R. C.
FISHER, D. C.
GINGERICH, P. D.
KESLER, S. E.
LOHMANN, K. C.
MEYERS, P. A.
MOORE, T. C.
MUKASA, S. B.
OWEN, R. M.
POLLACK, H. N.
POULSEN, C.
REA, D. K.
RUFF, L J.
SMITH, G. R.
VAN DER PLUIJM, B. A.
VAN DER VOO, R.
WALTER, L. M.
WILKINSON, B. H.

Germanic Languages and Literatures:

KYES, R. L.
MARKOVITS, A.

History:

BLOUIN, F. X.
BRIGHT, C.
CHANG, C. S.
COHEN, D. W.
COLE, J. R.
DANN, J.
DIOUF, M.
DOWD, G.
ELEY, G. H.
ENDELMAN, T.
FINE, J. V. A.
GOODMAN, D.
KELLY, M. C.
LEE, J.
LEWIS, E.
LIEBERMAN, V. B.
LINDNER, R. P.
MACDONALD, M.
MARKEL, H.
METCALF, B.
MIREL, J.
MORANTZ-SANCHEZ, R.
PERNICK, M. S.
ROSE, S. O.
ROSENBERG, W. G.
SCOTT, R. J.
SMITH-ROSENBERG, C.
STENECK, N. H.

STOLER, A.
THORNTON, J. M.
TRAUTMANN, T. R.
VAN DAM, R. H.
VICINUS, M.
VINOVSKIS, M. A.

History of Art:

BISSELL, R. W.
BRUSATI, C. A.
GAZDA, E.
HERWITZ, D. A.
POTTS, A. D.
POWERS, M. J.
ROOT, M. C.
SEARS, E. L.
SIEGFRIED, S. L.
SILVERMAN, R. A.
STEWARD, J.

Linguistics:

BEDDOR, P. S.
DWORKIN, S.
EPSTEIN, S. O.
HEATH, J.
HOOK, P. E.
KELLER-COHEN, D.
LUDLOW, P.
MILROY, L.
MORLEY, J.
SHATZ, M.
SHEVOROSHKIN, V.
SWALES, J.
THOMASON, R.
THOMASON, S.

Mathematics:

BARRETT, D. E.
BARVINOK, A. I.
BASS, H.
BLASS, A. R.
BONK, M.
BROWN, M.
BURNS, D. M., Jr
CONLON, J.
DOERING, C.
DOLGACHEV, I. V.
DUREN, P. L.
FEDERBUSH, P. G.
FORNAESS, J. E.
FULTON, W.
GRIESS, R. L., Jr
HANLON, P. J.
HEINONEN, J.
HINMAN, P. G.
HOCHSTER, M.
HUNTINGTON, C. E.
KARNI, S.
KLEINER, B.
KRASNY, R.
KRIZ, I.
LAZARSFELD, R.
LOTT, J.
MEGGINSON, R. E.
MONTGOMERY, H. L.
MOY, A.
PRASAD, G.
RAUCH, J. B.
SCOTT, G. P.
SIMON, C.
SMEREKA, P.
SMILA, K.
SMOLLER, J. A.
SPATZIER, R. J.
STAFFORD, J.
STEMBRIDGE, J. R.
STENSONES, B.
TAYLOR, B. A.
URIBE, A.
WASSERMAN, A. G.
WINTER, D. J.
WOOLEY, T.

Near Eastern Studies:

BARDAKJIAN, K.
BECKMAN, G.
KNYSH, A.
KRAHMALKOV, C. R.

LEGASSICK, T. J.
MICHALOWSKI, P.
RAMMUNY, R. M.
SHAMMAS, A.
WINDFUHR, G. L.
YOFFEE, N.

Philosophy:

ANDERSON, E. S.
CURLEY, E.
DARWALL, S.
GIBBARD, A.
HERWITZ, D.
LOEB, L.
LUDLOW, P.
RAILTON, P.
REGAN, D.
SKLAR, L.
THOMASON, R.
VELLEMAN, D.
WALTON, K.

Physics:

ADAMS, F. C.
AKERLOF, C. W.
AKHOURY, R.
ALLEN, J.
AMIDEI, D. E.
ARONSON, M. C.
AXELROD, D.
BECCHETTI, F. D.
BERMAN, P.
BRETZ, M.
BUCKSBAUM, P.
CAMPBELL, M.
CHAPMAN, J. W.
CHUPP, T.
CLARKE, R.
DUFF, M.
EINHORN, M. B.
EVRARD, A.
FREESE, K.
GIDLEY, D.
HEGYI, D.
KANE, G. L.
KRISCH, A. D.
KRISCH, J.
LONGO, M. J.
MERLIN, R.
MONROE, C.
NEAL, H.
ORR, B.
RAND, S.
RILES, J.
ROE, B. P.
SANDER, L. M.
SAVIT, R.
STEEL, D. G.
TARLE, G.
THUN, R. P.
TOMOZAWA, Y.
UHER, C.
YAO, Y.-P. E.
ZHOU, B.
ZORN, J. C.

Political Science:

AXELROD, S.
CAMPBELL, J.
CHAMBERLIN, J.
CORCORAN, M.
GITELMAN, Z.
GOLDENBERG, E. N.
HALL, R.
HERZOG, D.
HUTH, P. K.
INGLEHART, R.
JACKSON, J.
KINDER, D.
LEVINE, D.
LIEBERTHAL, K.
LUPIA, A.
MARKUS, G.
MORROW, J. D.
PAGE, S.
SAXONHOUSE, A.
TESSLER, M. A.

VARSHNEY, A.
WALTON, H., Jr
WIDNER, J. A.
WOO-CUMMINGS, M.
ZIMMERMAN, W.

Psychology:

ADAMS, K.
ANTONUCCI, T.
BECKER, J.
BERENT, S.
BERRIDGE, K.
CAIN, A.
CROCKER, J.
ECCLES, J.
ELLSWORTH, P.
FEATHERMAN, D.
GELMAN, S.
GOMEZ, L.
GONZALEZ, R.
GUTIERREZ, L.
HAGEN, J.
HOLLAND, J.
HUESMANN, R.
JACKSON, J.
JONIDES, J.
KANTOWITZ, B.
KAPLAN, R.
KAPLAN, S.
KINDER, D.
LEE, T.
LINDSAY, R.
LORD, C.
MCLOYD, V.
MAEHR, M.
MEYER, D.
MOODY, D.
MORRISON, F.
NAGATA, D.
NESSE, R.
NISBETT, R.
NOLAN-HOEKSEMA, S. K.
OLSEN, S.
OLSON, G.
OLSON, J.
PACHELLA, R.
PARIS, S.
PERLMUTTER, M.
PETERSON, C.
PINTNINCH, P.
PRICE, R.
REID, P.
REUTER-LORENZ, P. A.
ROBINSON, T.
SAMEROFF, A.
SANDELANDS, L. E.
SCHULENBERG, J.
SCHWARZ, N.
SEIFERT, C. M.
SELLERS, R. M.
SHATZ, M.
SHEVRIN, H.
SMITH, E.
SMUTS, B.
STEWART, A.
WEICK, K.
WELLMAN, H.
WINTER, D.
WOODS, J.
YATES, F.
ZUCKER, R.

Program on Studies in Religion:

BECK, A.
BOCCACCINI, G.
BONNER, M.
COLE, J.
COLLINS, D.
CURLEY, E.
DESHPANDE, M.
FEELEY-HARNIK, G.
FINE, J.
FREEDMAN, J.
GINSBERG, E.
GOMEZ, L.
HERBERT, S.
JACKSON, S.

KNYSH, A.
KOENEN, L.
KRAHMALKOV, C.
LEVINE, D.
LOEB, L.
LOPEZ, D.
MACCORMACK, S.
MICHALOWSKI, P.
POTTER, D.
SCHMIDT, B.
SCHRAMM, G.
SHARF, R.
SINGH, P.
TENTLER, T.
WILLIAMS, R.
WINDFUHR, G.
YOFFEE, N.

Residential College:

BRIGHT, C. C.
COHEN, C.
COHEN, H.
WEISSKOPF, T.

Romance Languages and Literatures:

CASA, F. P.
DWORKIN, S. N.
PAULSON, W.

Slavic Languages and Literatures:

CARPENTER, B.
RONEN, O.
SHEVOROSHKIN, V.
TOMAN, J.

Sociology:

ANDERSON, B.
AXINN, W.
BAKER, W.
CHESLER, M.
DAVIS, G.
FARLEY, R.
FEATHERMAN, D.
GROVES, R.
HOUSE, J.
KENNEDY, M.
KIMELDORF, H.
KNODEL, J.
LEE, J.
LEMPERT, R.
MIZRUCHI, M.
PAIGE, J.
RAUDENBUSH, S.
ROSE, S.
THORNTON, A.
WILLIAMS, D.
XIE, Y.

Southeast Asian Languages:

DESHPANDE, M.
GOMEZ, L.
HOOK, P.
LIN, S.
LOPEZ, D.

Statistics:

FARAWAY, J. J.
GONZALEZ, R.
HERO, A.
HOWREY, E. P.
KALBFLEISCH, J.
KEENER, R. W.
LITTLE, R.
MUIRHEAD, R. J.
MURPHY, S. A.
NAIR, V.
RAUDENBUSH, S.
ROTHMAN, E.
WOODROOFE, M.
WU, C. F. J.
XIE, Y.

Theatre and Drama:

DICKERSON, G.
FREDRICKSEN, E.
KERR, P.
NEVILLE-ANDREWS, J.
WOODS, L.

Women's Studies:

ANDERSON, E.
BEHAR, R.
BOYD, C.
BRUSATI, C.
CORCORAN, M.
ECCLES, J.
GOODMAN, D.
GUTEK, B.
HALPUIN, D.
HERRMANN, A.
HOWARD, J.
JOHNSON, T.
KELLER-COHEN, D.
KELLEY, M.
LARIMORE, A.
LEONARD, J.
MCCRACKEN, P.
REID, P.
ROBERTSON, J.
ROSE, S.
SAMPSELLE, L.
SAXONHOUSE, A.
SIEGFRIED, S.
SMITH, S.
SMITH-ROSENBERG, C.
STEWART, A.
STOLER, A.
STUDLAR, G.
TRAUB, V.
VICINUS, M.
WHITMAN, C.
YAEGER, P.

Medical School (tel. (734) 763-9600; fax (734) 763-4936; internet www.med.umich.edu/medschool):

Anaesthesiology:

BAGHDOYAN, H.
BROWN, A.
LYDIC, R.
SANFORD, T.
SATWANT, S.
TREMPER, K.
WASKELL, L.

Biological Chemistry:

ANDREWS, P.
AGRANOFF, B. W.
BALLOU, P.
ENGELKE, D.
FIERKE, C.
FRANCESCHI, R.
FULLER, R.
GAFNI, A.
GLICK, G.
GOLDMAN, D.
GUAN, K. L.
HAJRA, A. K.
KAUFMAN, R.
KENT, C.
KLIONSKY, D.
LUDWIG, M. L.
MATTHEWS, R. G.
MENON, K. M. J.
NINFA, A.
ROSS, B.
SCHACHT, J. H.
SEAHOLTZ, A.
SMITH, W.
THIELE, D.
WEINHOLD, P. A.
WILLIAMS, C. H., Jr
ZAND, R.
ZUIDERWEG, E.

Cardiology:

ARMSTRONG, W.
BATES, E.
CODY, R.
DAS, S.
EAGLE, K.
MORADY, F.
PITT, B.
RUBENFIRE, M.
SHEA, M.
STARLING, M.

Cell and Developmental Biology:

ALTSCHULER, R. A.
CARLSON, B. M.
CLARKE, M.
ENGEL, J.
ERNST, S. A.
GUMUCIO, D.
HOLLAND, G.
MACCALLUM, D. K.
MCNAMARA, J. A.
RAYMOND, P. A.
WELSH, M. J.

Dermatology:

ELLIS, C. N.
RASMUSSEN, J. E.
VOORHEES, J. J.

Endocrinology and Metabolism:

ARVAN, P.
BARKAN, A. L.
GREKIN, R. J.
HERMAN, W.
KOENIG, R.
SCHTEINGART, D. F.

Family Medicine:

APGAR, B.
PEGGS, J.
REED, B.
SCHWENK, T. L.
ZAZOVE, P.

Gastroenterology:

DEL VALLE, J.
ELTA, G.
GUMUCIO, J. J.
HENLEY, K.
LOK, A.
MERCHANT, J.
MOSELEY, R.
NOSTRANT, T.
OWYANG, C.
SCHEIMAN, J.
VAN DYKE, R.

General Medicine:

HAYWARD, R.
HOWELL, J.
MCMAHON, L.
STROSS, J.
WOOLLISCROFT, J.

Geriatric Medicine:

HALTER, J.
SUPIANO, M.

Haematology:

ENSMINGER, W. D.
SCHMAIER, A.
WICHA, M.

Human Genetics:

BREWER, G. J.
CAMPER, S.
FEARON, E.
GELEHRTER, T. D.
GINSBURG, D.
GLOVER, T.
GORSKI, J.
KURACHI, K.
LONG, J.
MEISLER, M. H.
OMENN, G.
ROBINS, D.
STATES, D.

Hypertension:

JULIUS, S.
WEDER, A. B.

Infectious Diseases:

ENGELBERG, C.
KAUFFMAN, C.
MARKOVITZ, D.

Medical Education:

ANDERSON, R.
GRUPPEN, L.
SCHWENK, T.
VAN HARRISON, R.

Microbiology and Immunology:

CLEWELL, D. B.
COOPER, S.
DIRITA, V.
DUNNICK, W.
ENGLEBERG, N.
FRIEDMAN, D.
IMPERIALE, M.
KIRSCH, D.
LOESCHE, W.
MOBLEY, H.
NEIDHARDT, F. C.
SHERMAN, D.
SWANSON, J.

Molecular Medicine and Genetics:

BREWER, G.
CAMPER, S.
CHO, K.
COLLINS, F.
FEARON, E.
GELEHRTER, T.
GINSBURG, D.
OMENN, G.
SALTIEL, A.

Neurology:

ALBERS, J. W.
ALBIN, R.
BERENT, S.
CASEY, K. L.
FELDMAN, E.
FINK, J.
FOSTER, N.
FREY, K.
GILMAN, S.
GREENBERG, H. S.
JINCK, L.
PARENT, J.
SILVERSTEIN, F.
TROBE, J.

Neurosurgery:

CHANDLER, W.
FARHAT, S.
HOFF, J.
MCGILLICUDDY, J.

Nuclear Medicine:

CORBETT, J. R.
FREY, K.
GROSS, M.
KILBOURN, M. R.
KOEPPE, R.
KUHL, D. E.
SHAPIRO, B.
SHULKIN, B.
WIELAND, D. M.

Obstetrics and Gynaecology:

ANSBACHER, R.
DELANCEY, J.
FOSTER, D.
HAYASHI, R.
JOHNSON, T.
LUKE, B.
MENON, K. M. J.
PEARLMAN, M.

Ophthalmology:

BERGSTROM, T. J.
DEL MONTE, M.
ELNER, V.
FRUEH, B. R.
GREEN, D. G.
JOHNSON, M.
LICHTER, P. R.
PURO, D. G.
SUGAR, A.
SWAROOP, A.
TROBE, J.
VINE, A. K.

Orthopaedic Surgery:

GOLDSTEIN, S. A.
GOULET, J.
HENSINGER, R. N.
LOUIS, D. S.
MATTHEWS, L. S.

WOJTYS, E.

Otolaryngology:

BAKER, S.
KILENY, P. R.
KING, M.
KOOPMANN, C. F.
TEKNOS, T.
TELIAN, S.
TERRELL, J.
WOLF, G.

Pharmacology:

BAGHDOYEN, H.
BRENNER, D.
CAREY, T.
ENSMINGER, W.
FISHER, S.
GNEGY, M. E.
HOLLENBERG, P. F.
HOLZ, R. W.
LUCCHESI, B. R.
MAYBAUM, J.
NEUBIG, R. R.
PRATT, W. B.
SHAYMAN, J.
SHEWACH, D.
SHLAFER, M.
SIMPSON, R.
SMITH, C. B.
UEDA, T.
WOODS, J. H.

Physiology:

CARTER-SU, C.
D'ALECY, L. G.
FAULKNER, J. A.
KARSCH, F. J.
KEYES, P. L.
LOGSDON, C.
LYDIC, R.
MCREYNOLDS, J. S.
METZGER, J.
MOISES, H. C.
SAMUELSON, L.
SCHWARTZ, J.
STUENKEL, E.
WEBB, R. C.
WILLIAMS, J.

Psychiatry:

ADAMS, K.
AGRANOFF, B.
AKIL, H.
ALBERS, J.
ALESSI, N.
ARMITAGE, R.
BERENT, S.
GREDEN, J.
GUYER, M.
MEADOR-WOODRUFF, J.
NESSE, R.
POMERLEAU, O.
RIBA, M.
SHEVRIN, H.
SILK, K.
TANDON, R.
TSAI, L.
UEDA, T.
WATSON, S.
YOUNG, E.
ZUBIETA, J.
ZUCKER, R.

Pulmonary and Critical Care Medicine:

GRUM, C.
MARTINEZ, F.
PAINE, R.
PETERS-GOLDEN, F.
SIMON, R.
SITRIN, R.
STANDIFORD, T.
TOEWS, G. B.

Radiology:

ADLER, D.
BLANE, C. E.
CARSON, P. L.
CASCADE, P.

CHAN, H. P.
CHENEVERT, T.
CHO, K.
COHAN, R.
DIPIETRO, M.
DUNNICK, N. R.
ELLIS, J.
FRANCIS, I. F.
GEBARSKI, S.
GOODSITT, M.
GROSS, B. H.
HELVIE, M.
HERNANDEZ, R.
KOROBKIN, M.
KUHL, D. E.
KUHNS, L. R.
MEYER, C.
NOLL, D.
PLATT, J.
QUINT, D.
QUINT, L.
ROSS, B.
RUBIN, J. M.
SILVER, T. M.
WILLIAMS, D.

Surgery:
BARLETT, R., General Surgery
BARSAN, W., Emergency Medicine
BEER, D., Thoracic Surgery
BIRKMEYER, J., General Surgery
BOLLING, S., Cardiac Surgery
BORE, E., Cardiac Surgery
BURNEY, R., General Surgery
CAMPBELL, D., General Surgery
CHANDLER, S., Neurosurgery
CHANG, A., General Surgery
CORAN, A. G., Paediatric Surgery
DEEB, G., Cardiac Surgery
DOHERTY, G., General Surgery
FEINBERG, S., Oral and Maxillofacial Surgery
GREENFIELD, L., Vascular Surgery
HENSINGER, R., Orthopaedic Surgery
HINSHAW, D., General Surgery
HIRSCHL, R., Paediatric Surgery
HOFF, J. T., Neurosurgery
KIRSCH, M., Cardiac and Thoracic Surgery
KUZON, W., Plastic Surgery
MERION, R., General Surgery
MONTIE, J., Urology
MULHOLLAND, M., General Surgery
ORRINGER, M., Thoracic Surgery
PARHAT, S., Neurosurgery
REES, R., Plastic Surgery
STANLEY, J., Vascular Surgery
WAKEFIELD, T., Vascular Surgery

School of Music
Dance:
DELANGHE, G.
DEYOUNG, Jr, G. W.
FOGEL, J. K.
SPARLING, P.

Music:
ASPNES, L.
BECKER, J. A.
BENGTSSON, E.
BOARDMAN, E.
BOLCOM, W. E.
BORDERS, J.
CRAWFORD, R.
CULVER, R.
DAPOGNY, J.
DAUGHERTY, M.
DERR, E.
ELLIOTT, A.
GANNETT, D.
GILLAS, J.
GLASGOW, R. E.
GREENE, A.
GUCK, M.
HAITHCOCK, M.
JENNINGS, A.
KAENZIG, F.
KATZ, M.

KIBBIE, J.
KIESLER, K.
LAM, J.
MASON, M.
MEAD, A.
MONTS, L.
NAGEL, L.
ORMAND, F.
PARMENTIER, E.
SARAH, E.
SCHOTTEN, Y.
SHENG, B.
SHIPPS, S.
SHIRLEY, G.
SINTA, D. J.
STEIN, L.
UDOW, M.
VERRETT, S.
WILEY, R. J.

Division of Kinesiology:
BORER, K. T.
CARTEE, C.
EDINGTON, D. W.
KATCH, V. L.
ULRICH, B.
ULRICH, D.

School of Natural Resources and Environment (tel. (734) 764-6453; fax (734) 936-2195; internet www.snre.umich.edu):
ALLAN, D.
BARNES, B. V.
BROWN, T.
BRYANT, B.
BULKLEY, J. W.
BURCH, J. B.
DIANA, J.
GLADWIN, T.
KAPLAN, R.
LANSING, J.
LOW, B. S.
NASSAUER, J.
PARSONS, E.
RABE, B.
STOERMER, E.
TILTON, D. L.
WEBB, P. W.
WILEY, M.
WITTER, J. A.
YAFFEE, S. L.
ZAK, D.

School of Nursing (tel. (734) 764-7185; fax (734) 936-3644; internet www.nursing.umich.edu):
ALGASE, P. L.
BOYD, C.
HINSHAW, A. S.
KALISCH, B.
KALISCH, P.
KETEFIAN, S.
LOVELAND-CHERRY, C.
METZGER, B. L.
NORTHHOUSE, L.
REAME, N.
SAMPSELLE, C. M.
WHALL, A.
WILLIAMS, R. A.

College of Pharmacy (tel. (734) 764-7312; fax (734) 763-2022; internet www.umich.edu/~pharmacy):
AMIDON, G. L.
ASCIONE, F.
BERARDI, R. R.
COWARD, J. K.
CRESSWELL, R.
CRIPPEN, M.
DRACH, J. C.
JOHNSON, C.
KENYON, G.
KIRKING, D.
KOREEDA, M.
MOSBERG, H. I.
MUELLER, B.
SHERMAN, D.
SHIMP, L.

SMITH, D.
STEVENSON, J.
TOPLISS, J. G.
WOODARD, R.
YANG, V.

School of Public Health (tel. (734) 763-5454; internet www.sph.umich.edu):
Biostatistics:
BECKER, M.
BOEHNKE, M. L.
BROWN, M. B.
JOHNSON, V.
KALBFLEISCH, J.
KSHIRSAGAR, A. M.
LIN, X.
LITTLE, R. J. A.
RAGHUMTHAN, T.
SCHORK, M. A.
TAYLOR, J.
WOLFE, R. A.

Environmental and Industrial Health:
ALBERS, J. A.
ARMSTRONG, T. J.
BATTERMAN, S.
BERENT, S.
CARUSO, R. L.
CHAFFIN, D. B.
DEININGER, R. A.
ETHIER, S.
FRANBLAU, A.
GARABRANT, D.
GOODSTITT, M.
KEELER, G.
KEYSERLING, M.
LAWRENCE, T.
LEVINE, S. P.
LOZOFF, B.
MAIO, R.
NRIAGU, J.
PIPER, W.
RICHARDSON, R. J.
ROBINS, T. G.
VICENT, J.
ZELLORS, E. T.

Epidemiology:
BARLOW, R.
BURT, B. A.
FAXMAN, B.
GARABRANT, D.
GILSDORF, J.
ISMAIL, A.
KAPLAN, G.
KOOPMAN, J. S.
MAASSAB, H. F.
MONTO, A. S.
MORGANSTERN, H.
PEYSER, P. A.
SCHOTTENFELD, D.
SOWERS, M.
WILLIAMS, D.

Health Behaviour and Health Education:
CLARK, N. M.
CONNELL, C.
GERONIMUS, A. T.
ISRAEL, B. A.
JACKSON, J.
KRAUSE, N. M.
RESNICOW, K.
SIMMONS, R.
STRECHER, V.
ZIMMERMAN, M.

Health Services Management and Policy:
ALEXANDER, J.
BASHUR, R.
FREED, G.
FRIES, B. E.
GRIFFITH, J. R.
HAYWARD, R.
HOWELL, J.
LIANG, J.
MCLAUGHLIN, C. G.
MCMAHON, L.
SMITH, D. G.

WARNER, K. E.
WEISMAN, C.
WEISSERT, W. G.
WHEELER, J. R. C.

School of Public Policy (tel. (734) 764-3490; fax (734) 763-9181; internet www.fordschool.umich.edu):

AXELROD, R.
BLANK, R.
CHAMBERLIN, J.
COHEN, D.
COHEN, M.
CORCORAN, M.
COURANT, P.
DANZIGER, S.
DEARDORFF, A.
DINARDO, J. E.
GERBER, E.
GOLDENBERG, E.
GRAMLICH, E.
HALL, R.
HINES, Jr, J. R.
LEVISOHN, J. A.
RABE, B.
SIMON, C.
TERRELL, K.
VINOVSKIS, M.
WALTZ, S.
WEISS, J.
WHITMAN, M.

School of Social Work (tel. (734) 764-3309; fax (734) 936-1961; internet www.ssw.umich.edu):

ALLEN-MEARES, P.
BARBARIN, O.
CHECKOWAY, B.
CORCORAN, M.
DANZIGER, S.
DUNKLE, R.
FALLER, K.
GUTIERREZ, L. M.
INGERSOLL-DAYTON, B.
JAYARATNE, S.
MAPLE, F.
MEEZAN, C.
MOWBRAY, C. T.
POWELL, T.
REISCH, M. S.
ROOT, L.
SAUNDERS, D.
SIEFERT, K.
TAYLOR, R.
TOLMAN, R.
TROPMAN, J.
TUCKER, D.

SELECTED ATTACHED INSTITUTIONS

English Language Institute, Kresge Hearing Research Institute, Simpson Memorial Institute, Mental Health Research Institute, Institute for Human Adjustment, Institute for Social Research, Institute of Gerontology, Institute of Labor and Industrial Relations, Institute of Continuing Legal Education, Institute of Environmental and Industrial Health, Transportation Research Institute, Tauber Manufacturing Institute, Center for Chinese Studies, Center for Japanese Studies, Center for Near Eastern and North African Studies, Center for Russian and East European Studies, Center for South and Southeast Asian Studies, Lawrence D. Buhl Genetics Research Center for Human Genetics, Center for Great Lakes and Aquatic Science, Center for Ergonomics, Center for Human Growth and Development, Center for the Study of Higher Education, Center for Research on Learning and Teaching, Automotive Research Center, Cancer Center, National Pollution Prevention Center, Information Technology Division, Biological Station, Botanical Gardens, University Herbarium, Museum of Anthropology, Museum of Paleontology, Museum of Zool-

ogy, University Observatories, Middle English Dictionary, Clinical Research Unit, Center for the Education of Women, Communicative Disorder Clinic, Michigan Memorial Phoenix Project, Center for Population Planning and Population Studies, Laboratory for Scientific Computation, Nuclear Resonance Laboratory, Mass Spectroscopy Laboratory, DNA Sequencing Laboratory, Electron Microbeam Analysis Laboratory.

There are more than one hundred other research units attached to the schools, colleges and departments.

BRANCH CAMPUSES

University of Michigan–Dearborn

4901 Evergreen Rd, Dearborn, MI 48128-1491
Telephone: (313) 593-5000
Fax: (313) 593-5452
Internet: www.umd.umich.edu
Founded 1959
Academic year: September to August
Chancellor: DANIEL LITTLE
Provost: ROBERT L. SIMPSON
Vice-Chancellor for Business Affairs: ROBERT G. BEHRENS
Vice-Chancellor for Institutional Advancement: SUSAN L. MCCLANAHAN
Vice-Chancellor for Government Relations: EDWARD J. BAGALE
Vice-Chancellor for Student Affairs: DONNA L. MCKINLEY
Number of students: 8,215

DEANS

Arts, Sciences and Letters: PAUL WONG
Education: JOHN B. POSTER
Engineering: SUBRATA SENGUPTA
Management: GARY WAISSI

University of Michigan–Flint

302 E. Kearsley Flint, MI 48502-1950
Telephone: (313) 762-3000
Fax: (313) 762-3687
E-mail: admissions@umflint.edu
Internet: www.umflint.edu
Founded 1956
61 Bachelor programmes, 7 Masters programmes
State control
Academic year: July to June
Chancellor: JUAN MESTAS
Provost and Vice-Chancellor for Academic Affairs: RENATE MCLAUGHLIN
Vice-Chancellor for Administration: DAVID BARTHELMES
Vice-Chancellor for Institutional Advancement: Dr KRISTEN SKIVINGTON
Vice-Chancellor for Student Services and Enrollment Management: MARY-JO SEKELSKY
Librarian: ROBERT L. HOUBECK, Jr
Library of 865,795 vols
Number of teachers: 372 full-time
Number of students: 6,188

DEANS AND DIRECTORS

College of Arts and Sciences: D. J. TRELA (acting)
School of Education and Human Services: SUSANNE CHANDLER
School of Health Professions and Studies: AUSTIN AGHO
School of Management: Dr I. DOUGLAS MOON
College of Nursing: ELLEN A. WOODMAN
Graduate Programs: DEAN VAHID

WALSH COLLEGE OF ACCOUNTANCY AND BUSINESS ADMINISTRATION

POB 7006, 3838 Livernois Rd, Troy, MI 48007-7006
Telephone: (248) 689-8282
Fax: (248) 689-0938
E-mail: admissions@walshcollege.edu
Internet: www.walshcollege.edu
Founded 1922 as Walsh Institute of Accountancy; present name 1968
Private control
Academic year: September to September
President and CEO: Dr KEITH A. PRETTY
Vice-President (Human Resources and Administration): ELIZABETH A. BARNES
Vice-President (Finance): HELEN C. KIEBA-TOLKSDORF
Vice-President (Academic Affairs) and Dean: Dr MICHAEL T. WOOD
Vice-President (External Affairs and Marketing): JOHN O. YOUNG
Registrar: VICTORIA R. SCAVONE
Library Director: H. DAVID MURPHY
Library of 30,000 vols
Number of students: 3,046 (1,161 undergraduate, 1,885 graduate)

HEADS OF DEPARTMENTS

Accounting: CHRISTINE LEWANDOWSKI
Master of Science in Business Information and Technology Program: W. DON GOTTWALD (Dir)
Business Law and Taxation: Dr MARK SOLOMON
Communications: Dr BARBARA ALPERN
Economics and Finance: HARRY VERYSER, Jr
Management, Marketing, MBA and Quantitative Methods: Dr DAVID ODETT

BRANCH CAMPUSES

Novi Campus: 41500 Gardenbrook Rd, Novi, MI 48375-1313; tel. (248) 349-5454; fax (248) 349-7449.

University Center at Macomb Community College: 44575 Garfield Rd, Clinton Township, MI 48038-1139; tel. (586) 723-1500; fax (586) 723-1501.

WAYNE STATE UNIVERSITY

Detroit, MI 48202
Telephone: (313) 577-5743
Fax: (313) 577-2198
E-mail: emoen@oia.wayne.edu
Internet: www.wayne.edu
Founded as university 1933; oldest antecedent college 1868
State control
Academic year: August to May
President: IRVIN D. REID
Vice-President for Finance and Administrative Services: JOHN L. DAVIS
Provost and Vice-President for Academic Affairs: NANCY BARRETT
Chief of Staff: MEREDITH GIBBS
Number of teachers: 2,636
Number of students: 33,091

DEANS

College of Education: PAULA WOOD
College of Engineering: RALPH KUMMLER
College of Liberal Arts: ROBERT THOMAS
College of Nursing: BARBARA REDMAN
College of Pharmacy and Health Sciences: BEVERLEY SCHMOLL
College of Science: ROBERT THOMAS
School of Social Work: PHYLLIS VROOM
School of Medicine: JOHN CRISSMAN
Law School: FREDERICA LOMBARD
School of Business Administration: HARVEY KAHALAS
College of Lifelong Learning: ROBERT L. CARTER

College of Fine and Performing Arts: JACK KAY
Graduate School: HILARY RATNER
College of Urban, Labor and Metropolitan Affairs: ROBIN BOYLE

PROFESSORS
(H = Head of Department)

School of Business Administration
Accounting:
BILLINGS, B.
REINSTEIN, A.
SPAULDING, A. (H)
VOLZ, W.

Finance and Business Economics:
HAMILTON, J.
SOMERS, T. (H)
SPENCER, M.

Management:
MARTIN, J. E.
OSBORN, R. N.

Marketing:
BELTRAMINI, R.
CANNON, H.
JACKSON, G. (H)
KELLY, J.
RIORDAN, E.
RYMER, J.
YAPRAK, A.

College of Education
Administrative and Organizational Studies:
BRANDENBURG, D.
DEMONT, R.
GIPSON, J. H.
MORRISON, G.
RICHEY, R.

Teacher Education:
BALE, J.
KAPLAN, L.
PETERSON, J. M.
RONEY, R.
SMITH, G.
WHITIN, D.

Theoretical and Behavioural Foundations:
HILLMAN, S.
MARCOTTE, D.
MARKMAN, D. S.
PIETROFESA, J.
SAWILOWSKY, S.

College of Engineering
Chemical Engineering:
GULARI, E.
HUANG, Y.
NG, K.
PUTATUDNA, S.
ROTHE, E. W.

Civil Engineering:
AKTAN, H. M.
DATTA, T. K.
FU, G.
MILLER, C.

Electrical and Computer Engineering:
AUNER, G.
ERLANDSON, R.
HASSOUN, M.
HUANG, C.
LIN, F.
SILVERSMITH, D.
SINGH, H.
SIY, P.
WANG, L.
YING, H.

Industrial and Manufacturing Engineering:
PLONKA, F.
SINGH, N.

Mechanical Engineering:
BERDICHEVSKY, V.
GIBSON, R.
IBRAHIM, R.

MAI, M.-C.
RIVIN, E.
SINGH, T.
TAN, C.-A.
TARAZA, D.
WHITMAN, A. B.
WU, S.
YANG, K.-H.

Fine and Performing Arts
Art and Art History:
HEGARTY, J.
JACKSON, M.
MARTIN, R.
NAWARA, J.
ROBARE, D.
ROSAS, M.
WILLIAMS, P.
ZAJAC, J.

Music:
MARKOU, K.

Communication:
SEEGER, M.

Theatre:
CALARCO, J.
KAUSHANSKY, L.
MAGIDSON, D.
PULLIN, N.
SCHRAEDER, T.
THOMAS, J. (H)

Law School:
BROWN, R.
BURNHAM, W.
CALKINS, S.
DANNIN, E.
FRIEDMAN, J. M.
HENNING, P.
LITMAN, J.
MCINTYRE, M. J.
MOGK, J.
SCHENK, A.

College of Liberal Arts
Africana Studies:
BOYD, M. (H)
HUTCHFUL, E.

Anthropology:
MONTILUS, G.
SANKAR, A.

Classics, Greek and Latin:
MCNAMEE, K. (H)

Criminal Justice:
STACK, S. (H)
ZALMAN, M.

Economics:
BRAID, R.
LEE, L.
ROSSANA, A. (H)
SPURR, S.

English:
BARTON, E.
BRILL, L.
BURGOYNE, R. (H)
COLEMBA, H.
HARRIS, W.
LANDRY, D.
LELAND, C.
LINDBERG, K.
MAROTTI, A.
RAY, R.
SCRIVENER, M.
SKLAR, E.
VLASOPOLOS, A.
WASSERMAN, R.

History:
BUKOWCZYK, J.
FAUE, E.
HYDE, C.
RAUCHER, A.
SMALL, M.

Humanities:
COGAN, M.

Philosophy:
GRANGER, H.
LOMBARD, L. (H)
MCKINSEY, T.
YANAL, R.

Political Science:
ABBOTT, P. R.
BLEDSOE, T.
DOWNING, R. G.
ELDER, C. (H)
FINO, S.
PARRISH, C.

Romance Languages and Literatures:
DITOMMASO, A.
HIGUERO, F.
STIVALE, C. (H)

Sociology:
ESHLEMAN, J. R.
GELFAND, D. (H)
HANKIN, J.
SENGSTOCK, M.
WARSHAY, L.

College of Science
Biology:
ARKING, R.
FREEMAN, D.
GREENBERG, M.
HEBERLEIN, G.
HOUGH, R.
MIZUKAMI, H.
MOORE, W. S.
SMITH, P. D.
TAYLOR, J.

Chemistry:
BHAGWAT, A.
CHA, J.-K.
LINVELDT, R. (H)
MCCLAIN, W.
MONTGOMERY, J.
POOLE, C.
RABAN, J. P.
ROMANO, L.
RORABCHER, D.
SCHLEGEL, H.

Computer Science:
GOEL, N.
REYNOLDS, R.

Mathematics:
BACHELIS, G. F.
BRENTON, L.
CHOW, P.-L. (H)
COHN, W.
GLUCK, D. H.
HANDEL, D.
KHAN, S.
KHASMINSKII, R.
KLEIN, J.
KOROSTELEV, A.
LIANG, T.
MAGAARD, K.
MAKAR-LIMANOV, L.
MALCOLMSON, P.
MENALDI, J. L.
MORDUKHOVICH, B.
OKOH, F.
RHEE, C.
SCHOCHET, C. L.
SCHREIBER, B. H.
SUN, T.-C.
YIN, G.
ZHANG, Z.

Nutrition and Food Science:
JEN, C.
KLURFELD, D. M. (H)
SHELEF, L.

Physics:
BELLWIED, R.
CHANG, J. J.

CORMIER, T. (H)
DUNIFER, G.
KARCHIN, P.
KAUPPILA, W. E.
KEYES, P. H.
KUO, P. K.
MORGAN, C.
NAIK, R.
SAPERSTEIN, A. M.
STEIN, T. S.

Psychology:

ALEXANDER, S.
COSCINA, D. (H)
FIRESTONE, I. J.
FITZGERALD, J.
KAPLAN, K.
KILBEY, M. M.
LABOUVIE-VIEF, G.
LEVY, S.
URBERG, K.
WEISFELD, G.

College of Lifelong Learning

Interdisciplinary Studies Program:

ARONSON, A. R.
BAILS, J. G.
GLABERMAN, M.
KLEIN, J.
MAIER, C. L.
RASPA, R. N.
SCHINDLER, R. (H)
WRIGHT, R. H.

School of Medicine

Anatomy:

BERNSTEIN, M.
GOODMAN, M.
GOSHGARIAN, H.
HAZLETT, L.
LASKER, G.
MAISEL, H. (H)
MEYER, D.
MITCHELL, J. A.
MIZERES, N. J.
POURCHO, R.
RAFOLS, J.
ROHER, A.
SKOFF, R.

Anaesthesiology:

BROWN, E. (H)

Audiology:

RINTELMANN, W. F. (H)

Biochemistry:

BROOKS, S.
BROWN, R. K.
EDWARDS, B.
EVANS, D.
JOHNSON, R.
LEE, C. P.
ROSEN, B. (H)
ROWND, R.
VINOGRADOV, S.

Cardiology:

KLONER, R.
WYNNE, J.

Community Medicine:

WALLER, J. (H)

Dermatology and Syphilology:

BIRMINGHAM, D.
HASHIMOTO, K. (H)

Family Medicine:

DALLMAN, J.
GALLAGHER, R. E.
WERNER, P. (H)

Immunology and Microbiology:

BERK, R.
BOROS, D. L.
BROWN, W. J.
DEGUISTI, D.
HAZLEH, L.
JEFFRIES, C.
KAPLAN, J.

KONG, Y.-C.
LEFFORD, M.
LEON, M.
LEVIN, S.
LISAK, R.
MONTGOMERY, P. C. (H)
PALCHAUDHURI, S.
SOBEL, J.
SUNDICK, R.
SWANBORG, R. H.
WEINER, L. M.

Internal Medicine:

AL-SARRAF, M.
BAGCHI, N.
BERGSMAN, K. L.
BISHOP, C. R.
BRENNAN, M.
CLAPPER, I.
CORBETT, T.
FERNÁNDEZ-MADRID, F. B.
GRUNBERGER, G.
HEILBRUN, L.
HEPPNER, G.
KESSEL, D.
LERNER, S.
LEWIS, B. M.
LUM, L.
LYNNE-DAVIS, P.
McDONALD, F.
MACK, R.
MAJUMDAR, A.
MARSH, J.
MIGDAL, S.
MILLER, R.
MUTCHNICK, M.
NAKEFF, A.
PRASAD, A. S.
PURI, P.
RESNICK, L.
SAMSON, M. (H)
SANTEN, R.
SENSENBRENNER, L.
SOBEL, J.
SOWERS, J.
SPEARS, J.
TALMERS, F.
TRANCHIDA, L.
VAITKEVICIUS, V.
VALDIVIESO, M.
VALERIOTE, F.
WYNNE, J.

Neurology:

BENJAMINS, J. A.
CHUGANI, H.
DORE-DUFFY, P.
LeWITT, P.
LISAK, R. (H)
NIGRO, M.

Neurosurgery:

DIAZ, F. G. (H)
THOMAS, L. M.

Obstetrics and Gynaecology:

ABEL, E.
AGER, J.
BEHRMAN, S. J.
BERMAN, R.
COTTON, D. (H)
DEPPE, G.
EVANS, M.
FREEDMAN, R.
LANCASTER, W.
MAMMEN, E.
MARIONA, F.
MILLER, O.
MOGHISSI, K.
POLAND, M.
ROMERO, R.
SACCO, A. G.
SHERMAN, A.
SOBEL, J.
SOKOL, R.
STRYKER, J.
SUBRAMANIAN, M.

Ophthalmology:

ESSNER, E.
FRANK, R. N.
JAMPEL, R. S. (H)
PUKLIN, J.
SHICHI, H.
SHIN, D.
SPOOR, T.

Orthopaedic Surgery:

FITZGERALD, R. (H)
MANOLI II, A.
RYAN, J.

Otolaryngology:

COHN, A. M.
DRESCHER, D.
DWORKIN, J.
JACOBS, J.
MATHOG, R. H. (H)

Paediatrics:

BEN-YOSEPH, Y.
BRANS, Y. W.
CASH, R.
CHUGANI, H.
COHEN, S.
COLLINS, J.
DAJANI, A. S.
EPSTEIN, M.
FAROOKI, Z.
FLEISCHMANN, L.
GRUSKIN, A. (H)
GUTAI, J.
KAPLAN, J.
KAUFFMAN, R.
LUM, L.
LUSHER, J.
NIGRO, M.
OSTREA, E.
PINSKY, W. W.
RAUMDRANATH, Y.
ROBIN, A.
SAMAIK, A.
SARNAIK, A.
SENSENBRENNER, L.
SHANKARIAN, G.
SLOVIS, T.

Pathology:

BEDROSSIAN, C.
BROWN, W.
CRISSMAN, J. (H)
DALE, E.
EVANS, M.
GIACOMELLI, F. E.
HONN, K.
KURKINEN, M.
MAMMEN, E.
MILLER, D.
PALUTKE, M.
PERRIN, E. V.
RAZ, A.
SHEAHAN, D.
SPITZ, W. U.
THIBERT, R.
WEINER, L.
WIENER, J.
ZAK, B.

Pharmacology:

ANDERSON, G.
BANNON, M.
CHOPRA, D.
DUTTA, S.
GOLDMAN, H.
HIRATA, F.
HOLLENBERG, P. F. (H)
KESSEL, D.
MARKS, B.
NOVAK, R.
SLOANE, B.
WAKADE, A.

Physiology:

BARRACO, R.
CHURCHILL, P. C.
DUNBAR, J. C.

FOA, P.
GALA, R.
HONG, F. T.
LAWSON, D.
McCOY, L. E.
MAMMEN, E.
NYBOER, J.
PENNEY, D.
PHILLIS, J. W. (H)
RAM, J.
RILLEMA, J. A.
SEEGERS, W.
WALZ, D. A. (H)

Psychiatry:

BANNON, M.
FISCHHOFF, J.
FREEDMAN, R.
GALLOWAY, M.
KAPATOS, G.
KUHN, D.
LeWITT, P.
LUBY, E.
LYCAKI, H.
POHL, R.
ROSENBAUM, A.
ROSENZWEIG, N.
SARWER-FONER, G.
SCHORER, C.
SITARAM, N.
UHDE, T. (H)

Radiation Oncology:

HERSKOVIC, A. M.
HONN, K. V.
MARUYAMA, Y.
ORTON, C. G.
PORTER, A. (H)

Radiology:

KLING, G. (H)
SOULEN, R.
WOLLSCHLAEGER, G.

Surgery:

BERGUER, R.
FROMM, D. (H)
KLEIN, M.
LEDGERWOOD, A. M.
LUCAS, C.
PHILIPPART, A.
ROSENBERG, J. C.
SILVA, Y. J.
STEPHENSON, L.
SUGAWA, C.
WALT, A. J.
WEAVER, A. W.
WILSON, R. F.

Urology:

JAFFER, D.
MONTIE, J.
PERLMUTTER, A. D.
PONTES, J. (H)

College of Nursing:

AROIAN, K.
HOUGH, E.
NIES, M.
OERMANN, M.
PIPER, B. A.
RICE, V.

Pharmacy and Health Sciences

Anaesthesia:

COOK, K. A.
CRAWFORTH, K. L.
HAGLUND, V. L.
MANGAHAS, P.
WALCZYK, M. L.
WORTH, P. A. (H)

Clinical Laboratory Science:

ALDRIGE, G. (H)
CASTILLO, J. B.
HARAKE, B.
WALLACE, A. M.

Mortuary Science:

BURDA-MASTROGIANIS, L.

FRADE, P.
FRITTS-WILLIAMS, M. L. (H)
HUNTOON, R.

Occupational and Environmental Health Sciences:

BASSETT, D. (H)
BHALLA, D.
KERFOOT, E. J.
TAFFE, B.
WARNER, P. O.

Occupational Therapy:

BROWN, K.
ESDAILE, S. (H)
LUBORSKY, M.
LYSACK, C.
POWELL, N.

Physical Therapy:

AMUNDSEN, L. (H)
CARLSON, C.
DROVIN, J.
DUNLEAVY, K.
McNEVIN, N.
TALLEY, S.

Physician Assistant Studies:

FRICK, J.
NORMILE, H.
SIDDIQUE, M.
TODD, K.
WORMSER, H. (H)

Radiation Therapy Technology:

CHADWELL, D. (H)
KEMPA, A.

Pharmaceutical Sciences:

ABRAMSON, H.
BOLARIN, D.
COMMISSARIS, R.
CORCORAN, G. B. (H)
FULLER, G. C.
GIBBS, R.
HIRATA, F.
LINDBLAD, W.
LOUIS-FERDINAND, R. T.
PITTS, D. K.
SVENSSON, C. K.
WORMSER, H.
WOSTER, P. M.

Pharmacy Practice:

CAPPELLETTY, D.
EDWARDS, D. J.
FAGAN, S.
JABER, L. A.
KALE-PRADHAN, P. B.
KEYS, P.
MILLER, M.
MOSER, L. R.
MUNZENBERGER, P. J.
RHONEY, D.
RYBAK, M. J.
SCHUMANN, W.
SINGH, R.
SLAUGHTER, R. L. (H)
SMITH, G. B.
SMYTHE, M. A.
STEVENSON, J. G.
TISDALE, J. E.
VIVIAN, J. C.
WILSON, J.

College of Urban, Labor and Metropolitan Affairs

Urban and Labor Studies:

BATES, T.
BROWN, D. R.
COOKE, W.
MASON, P.
SMOCK, S. M. (H)
WOLMAN, H.
YOUNG, H.

Clarence Hillberry Prof. of Urban Affairs:

GALSTER, G.

Coleman A. Young Prof. of Urban Affairs:

YOUNG, A. H.

Geography and Urban Planning:

BOYLE, R. M.
RESSE, L.
SINCLAIR, R.

School of Social Work:

BEVERLY, C.
BRANDALL, J.
MOXLEY, D.

University Libraries

Library and Information Science:

ALBRITTON, R. L.
BAKER, L. M.
BROWN-SYED, C. L.
EZELL, C. L.
FIELD, J. J.
HOLLEY, R. (H)
JOHNSON, N. B.
MIKA, J.
NEAVILL, G. B.
POWELL, R.
SPITERI, L. F.

ATTACHED RESEARCH INSTITUTES

Addiction Research Institute: attached to Department of Community Medicine; Dir Dr CHARLES SCHUSTER.

African American Film Institute: Dirs Dr MICHAEL MARTIN, Dr ROBERT BURGOYNE.

Asthma and Related Lung Disorders Research Center: Dir Dr GEORGE FULLER.

Bioengineering Center: attached to College of Engineering; Dir Dr ALBERT KING.

Barbara Anne Karmanos Cancer Institute: Dir JOHN C. RUCKDESCHEL.

Center for Academic Ethics: Dir (vacant).

Center for Automotive Research: attached to College of Engineering; Dir Dr NAEIM HENEIN.

Center for Chicano-Boricua Studies: attached to College of Urban, Labor and Metropolitan Affairs; Dir Dr JORGE CHINEA.

Center for Health Research: attached to College of Nursing; Dir JUDITH FLOYD.

Center for International Business Studies: attached to School of Business Administration; Dir Dr ATTILA YAPRAK.

Center for Legal Studies: attached to Law School; Dir STEVEN WINTER.

Center for Molecular Medicine and Genetics: attached to School of Medicine; Dir LAWRENCE I. GROSSMAN.

Center for Peace and Conflict Studies: attached to College of Urban, Labor and Metropolitan Affairs; Dir Dr FREDERIC PEARSON.

Center for the Study of Arts and Public Policy: Dirs DAVID MAGIDSON, Dr BERNARD BROCK.

Center for the Study of Citizenship: Dir MARC W. KRUMAN.

Center for Urban Studies: Dir THOMAS LYKE THOMPSON.

Cohn-Haddow Center for Judaic Studies: Dir Dr DAVID WEINBERG.

C. S. Mott Center for Human Growth and Development: Dir ROBERT J. SOKOL.

Developmental Disabilities Institute: Dir Dr BARBARA LeROY.

Douglas A. Fraser Center for Workplace Issues: Dir WILLIAM COOKE.

Humanities Center: Dir Dr WALTER EDWARDS.

Igon Research Center of Vision: attached to Eresge Eye Institute; Dir GARY ABRAMS.

Institute of Chemical Toxicology: Dir Dr RAYMOND F. NOVAK.

Institute of Environmental Health Science: Dir RAYMOND NOVAK.

Institute of Gerontology: attached to Graduate School; Dir PETER LICHTENBERG.

Institute for Information Technology and Culture: Dir ALLEN BATTEAU.

Institute for Learning and Performance Improvement: attached to College of Education; Dir DALE BRANDENBURG.

Institute for Manufacturing Research: Dir LAWRENCE FAVRO.

Institute of Maternal and Child Health: Dir Dr JOHN B. WALLER, Jr.

Institute for Organizational and Industrial Competitiveness: attached to School of Business Administration; Dir LARRY L. FOBES.

Institute for Scientific Computing: attached to College of Science; Dir VIPIN CHAUDHARY.

Labor Studies Center: attached to College of Urban, Labour and Metropolitan Affairs; Dir HAL STACK.

Manufacturing Information Systems Center: attached to School of Business Administration; Dir ARIK RAGOWSKY.

Merill-Palmer Institute: Dir GERALDINE BROOKINS.

Skillman Center for Children: Dir KRISTINE MIRANNE.

Small Business Development Center—WSU: Dir RONALD HALL.

State Policy Center: Dir PETER EISINGER.

WESTERN MICHIGAN UNIVERSITY

1903 West Michigan, Kalamazoo, MI 49008

Telephone: (269) 387-1000

E-mail: ask-wmu@wmich.edu

Internet: www.wmich.edu

Founded 1903

Academic year: August to April

President: DANIEL M. LITYNSKI

Provost and Vice-President for Academic Affairs: ELISE JORGENS

Vice-President for Business and Finance: ROBERT M. BEAM

Vice-President for Student Affairs: DIANE SWARTZ

Vice-President for Research: JACK R. LUDERER

General Counsel: CAROL L. J. HUSTOLES

Executive Director for International Affairs: HOWARD J. DOOLEY

Executive Director of Student Services: SUSAN O'FLAHERTY

Librarian: JOSEPH G. REISH

Number of teachers: 985

Number of students: 29,732

Publications: *Research Magazine* (2 a year), *Medieval Prosopography* (2 a year), *Studies in Iconography* (annually), *Studies in Medieval Culture* (series of vols, annually), *Yearbook of Langland Studies* (annually), *Old English Newsletter* (4 a year), *Medieval Review* (online), *Journal of Comparative Religion* (online), *Caribe* (Jointly with Marquette University of Milwaukee, 2 a year), *Comparative Drama* (4 a year), *Sociology and Social Welfare* (4 a year), *Behavior Analyst* (2 a year), *Analysis of Verbal Behavior* (annually), *Third Coast* (2 a year), *Proceedings of the Heraclitean Society* (annually), *Old English Newsletter – Subsidia* (annually), *Mid-American Journal of Business* (4 a year)

DEANS

Business: J. SCHMOTTER

Engineering and Applied Sciences: MICHAEL ATKINS

Arts and Sciences: LEONARD GINSBERG

Education: GARY WEGENKE

Graduate: WILLIAM WIENER

Fine Arts: M. MERRION

Health and Human Services: J. PISANESCHI

Aviation: ROBERT AARDEMA

WESTERN THEOLOGICAL SEMINARY

101 E 13th St, Holland, MI 49423

Telephone: (616) 392-8555

Fax: (616) 392-2072

Internet: www.westernsem.org

Founded 1866

Private control

Academic year: September to May

President: Dr DENNIS VOSKUIL

Academic Dean: Dr LEANNE VAN DYK

Registrar: PAT DYKHUIS

Librarian: PAUL M. SMITH

Library of 100,000 vols

Number of teachers: 18

Number of students: 119 (full-time).

MINNESOTA

AUGSBURG COLLEGE

2211 Riverside Ave, Minneapolis, MN 55454

Telephone: (612) 330-1000

Fax: (612) 330-1649

Internet: www.augsburg.edu

Founded 1869

President: WILLIAM V. FRAME

Registrar: WAYNE KALLERSTAD

Director of Library: JANE ANN NELSON

Library of 175,000 vols

Number of teachers: 125 full-time

Number of teachers: 180 part-time

Number of students: 3,023

Publication: *Augsburg College Now* (quarterly).

BEMIDJI STATE UNIVERSITY

1500 Birchmont Drive NE, Bemidji, MN 56601-2699

Telephone: (218) 755-2000

E-mail: admissions@bemidjistate.edu

Internet: www.bemidjistate.edu

Founded 1919

Part of Minnesota State Colleges and Universities system

President: Dr M. JAMES BENSEN

Dean of Graduate Studies, Library and Special Programs: Dr JON QUISTGAARD

Library of 184,000 vols

Number of teachers: 220 full-time

Number of students: 4,991.

BETHEL UNIVERSITY

3900 Bethel Drive, St Paul, MN 55112

Telephone: (651) 638-6230

Fax: (651) 638-6008

E-mail: caps@bethel.edu

Internet: www.bethel.edu

Founded 1871

School of the churches of the Baptist General Conference

Liberal arts co-educational Christian college, offering baccalaureate and master's degree, and graduate theological seminary

President: GEORGE K. BRUSHABER

Provost (Seminary): LELAND ELIASON

Provost (College): JAMES H. BARNES

College Librarian: ROBERT C. SUDERMAN

Seminary Librarian: MARIEL VOTH

Library: Libraries with 267,000 vols (College Library: 132,000 vols, 675 periodicals;

Seminary Library: 135,000 vols, 2,400 periodicals)

Number of teachers: 219 (190 at College, 29 at Seminary)

Number of students: 3,900 (2,962 at College, 938 at Seminary).

CARLETON COLLEGE

1 North College St, Northfield, MN 55057

Telephone: (507) 646-4000

Fax: (507) 646-4204

Internet: www.carleton.edu

Founded 1866 by Board of Trustees appointed by the Minnesota Conference of Congregational Churches

Independent

Academic year: September to June

President: STEPHEN R. LEWIS, Jr

Vice-President and Treasurer: BARBARA JOHNSON

Dean of the College: ELIZABETH McKINSEY

Dean of Students: MARK W. GOVONI

Dean for Budget and Planning: Dr STEVEN KELLY

Registrar: ROGER LASLEY

Library of 510,000 vols of books and journals, 480,000 vols of government documents

Number of teachers: 185

Number of students: 1,850.

COLLEGE OF SAINT BENEDICT

37 S. College Ave, Saint Joseph, MN 56374-2099

Telephone: (612) 363-5011

Fax: (612) 363-6099

Internet: www.csbsju.edu

Chartered 1887

A Catholic liberal arts college for women partnered with Saint John's University for men; co-educational classes and social activities available to students on both campuses

President: MARY E. LYONS

Provost for Academic Affairs: Dr CLARK HENDLEY

Dean and Rector of Benedictine University: Dr CHARLES VILLETTE

Vice-President for Institutional Advancement: BARBARA CARLSON

Vice-President for Finance: S. MIRIAM ARDOLF

Vice-President for Student Development: Dr KATHLEEN ALLEN

Dean of the College: Dr RITA KNUESEL

Dean of Admissions: MARY MILBERT

Librarian: MICHAEL KATHMAN

Library of 535,400 vols

Number of teachers: 129 full-time

Number of teachers: 29 part-time

Number of students: 1,940

Publications: *Saint Benedict's Today, Diotima, Studio I, Independent.*

COLLEGE OF ST CATHERINE

2004 Randolph Ave, St Paul, MN 55105

Telephone: (612) 690-6000

Fax: (612) 690-6024

Internet: www.stkate.edu

Founded 1905

Roman Catholic liberal arts college for women

President: ANDREA J. LEE

Senior Vice-President: COLLEEN HARGREAVES (acting)

Vice-President for Institutional Advancement: PAT HUIDSTON

Vice-President for Business and Finance: TOMMY McGEE

Librarian: CAROL JOHNSON

Library of 252,107 vols
Number of students: 4,800.

COLLEGE OF ST SCHOLASTICA

1200 Kenwood Ave, Duluth, MN 55811-4199
Telephone: (218) 723-6000
Fax: (218) 723-6290
E-mail: admissions@css.edu
Internet: www.css.edu

Founded 1912

Private (Roman Catholic) liberal arts college; graduate programs in nursing, physical therapy, management, educational media, occupational therapy, science and mathematics education, exercise physiology and education

President: Dr LARRY GOODWIN
Dean of Faculty: Dr ELIZABETH DOMHOLDT
Registrar: GEORGE BEATTIE
Librarian: KEVIN McGREW

Library of 127,400 vols
Number of teachers: 126 full-time
Number of teachers: 40 part-time
Number of students: 2,030

HEADS OF DEPARTMENTS

American-Indian Studies: Dr BARB KING
Biology: Dr DOUGLAS WALTON
Catholic Studies: Dr WILLIAM GRAHAM
Computer Science/Information Systems: Dr THOMAS GIBBONS
Education: Dr MARIE KELSEY
English: Dr BILL HODAPP
Exercise Physiology: Dr TOMMY BOONE
Healthcare Informatics/Information Management: KATHLEEN LaTOUR
Languages and International Studies: Dr DIANE KESSLER
Physical Therapy: Dr DENISE WISE

COLLEGE OF VISUAL ARTS

344 Summit Avenue, St Paul, MN 55102
Telephone: (651) 224-3416
Fax: (651) 224-8854
E mail: info@cva.edu
Internet: www.cva.edu
Private control

President: JOHN LENERTZ
Academic Dean: JOHN DuFRESNE
Registrar: LOIS CANEDAY
Library Director: KATHRYN HEUER

Library of 5,000 vols, 27,500 slides
Number of teachers: 65
Number of students: 250

HEADS OF DEPARTMENTS

Fine Arts/Foundation Studies: KAREN WIRTH
Liberal Arts: JULIE L'ENFANT
Visual Communications: JOHN DuFRESNE

CONCORDIA COLLEGE

901 S 8th St, Moorhead, MN 56560
Telephone: (218) 299-4000
Fax: (218) 299-3947
Internet: www.cord.edu

Founded 1891

President: Dr PAMELA M. JOLICOEUR
Vice-President for Academic Affairs: Dr MARK KREJCI
Registrar: CAROLE STALHEIM
Dean of Admissions: LEE E. JOHNSON
Librarian: SHARON HOVERSON

Library of 328,349 vols
Number of teachers: 225
Number of students: 2,814

Four-year liberal arts college, granting bachelor of arts and bachelor of music degrees.

CONCORDIA UNIVERSITY, ST PAUL

275 Syndicate St North, St Paul, MN 55104-5494
Telephone: (651) 641-8278
Fax: (651) 659-0207
Internet: www.csp.edu

Founded 1893
Academic year: August to May

President: Dr ROBERT HOLST
Executive Vice-President: Dr CHERYL CHATMAN
Vice-President (Academic Affairs): Dr CARL SCHOENBECK
Vice-President (Advancement): DOUGLAS HARTFORD
Vice-President (Student Affairs): Dr EDITH JONES
Vice-President (Information Technology and Operations): Dr ERIC LaMOTT
Chief Financial Officer: MICHAEL DORNER
Librarian: Dr CHARLOTTE KNOCHE

Library of 136,000 vols
Number of teachers: 466 (81 full-time, 385 part-time)
Number of students: 2,051.

CROSSROADS COLLEGE

920 Mayowood Rd SW, Rochester, MN 55902
Telephone: (507) 288-4563
Fax: (507) 288-9046
E-mail: info@crossroadscollege.edu
Internet: www.crossroadscollege.edu

Founded 1913 as International Christian Bible College Association; present name 2002
Private control
Academic year: August to May

President: BILL LUCE
Vice-President (Academics): RICK D. WALSTON
Vice-President (Student Development): R. MARK COMEAUX
Vice-President (Admissions): RANDALL MUNSON
Vice-President (Institutional Advancement): ROBERT P. BARNES
Registrar: MELINDA F. SARGENT
Director of Library: HAROLD MAHAN

Library of 32,000 vols
Number of teachers: 21
Number of students: 120

Areas of study: Christian education, general ministry, intercultural studies, music ministry, pastoral leadership, youth and family studies, counselling psychology, general studies, music, youth and family ministries, spiritual formation, professional studies.

CROWN COLLEGE

6425 County Rd 30, St Bonifacius, MN 55375
Telephone: (952) 446-4142
Fax: (952) 446-4149
E-mail: info@crown.edu
Internet: www.crown.edu
Private control

President: GARY BENEDICT
Provost and Vice-President (Academic Affairs): RICK MANN
Vice-President (Student Development): TIM McKINNEY
Vice-President (Finance and Operations): TIM SAVALOJA
Vice-President (Enrollment Services): PAUL AGUE
Vice-President (Advancement): RANDY DIRKS
Registrar: STEVE MILLS
Director of Library and Media Services: DENNIS INGOLGSLAND

Library of 80,000 vols
Number of teachers: 57

Number of students: 950

HEADS OF DEPARTMENTS

Biblical and Theological Studies: Dr GLENN MYERS
Business, Science, and Information Technology: Dr DONALD G. HARDY
Christian Ministry: RONALD L. GRIFFITHS
Human and Social Science: Dr WILLIAM B. BEDFORD
Intercultural Studies: WILLIAM F. MANGHAM
Music: Dr DAVID DONELSON
Teacher Education: Dr SCOTT H. MOATS

GUSTAVUS ADOLPHUS COLLEGE

800 West College Ave, St Peter, MN 56082
Telephone: (507) 933-8000
Fax: (507) 933-7041
Internet: www.gustavus.edu

Founded 1862
Academic year: September to June

President: JAMES L. PETERSON
Registrar: DAVID WICKLUND
Dean of the Faculty: JOHN A. MOSBO
Librarian: DAN MOLLNER

Library of 245,000 vols
Number of teachers: 200
Number of students: 2,500.

HAMLINE UNIVERSITY

St Paul, MN 55104
Telephone: (612) 523-2202
Internet: www.hamline.edu

Founded 1854
Related to the United Methodist Church

President: LARRY G. OSNES
Vice-Presidents: DAN LORITZ (University Relations), ORWIN CARTER (Finance and Administration)
Registrars: STEVE BJORK (Liberal Arts), JOYCE TRAYNOR (Law), DIANNE STIFFLER (Graduate)
Directors of Admissions: THERESA DECKER, SHELLEY HARKER (Law), LOUISE CUMMINGS (Liberal Arts)
Librarians: JULIE ROCHAT (Liberal Arts College), SUSAN KIEFER (School of Law)

Library of 230,000 vols
Number of teachers: 152
Number of students: 2,228

DEANS

College of Liberal Arts: JERRY GREINER
School of Law: RAYMOND KRAUSE
Graduate School: JOE GRABA
Students: MARILYN DEPPE

LUTHER SEMINARY

2481 Como Avenue, St Paul, MN 55108
Telephone: (651) 641-3456
Fax: (651) 523-1609
Internet: www.luthersem.edu
Private control
Academic year: September to May

President: DAVID L. TIEDE
Academic Dean: MARC KOLDEN
Vice-President (Administration and Finance): HOWARD OSTREM
Registrar: DIANE DONCITS
Director of Library Services: DITA LEININGER

Number of teachers: 42
Number of students: 760.

MACALESTER COLLEGE

The Office of the President, 1600 Grand Ave, St Paul, MN 55105-1899
Telephone: (612) 696-6000
Fax: (612) 696-6689
E-mail: lundin@macalester.edu

Internet: www.macalester.edu
Founded 1874
Liberal arts college
President: BRIAN C. ROSENBERG
Vice-Presidents: MARK KRONHOLM (College Advancement), JOEL G. KLEMMER (Library and Information Services), LAURIE B. HAMRIE (Student Affairs and Dean of Students), DAVID WHEATON (Administration and Treasurer)
Dean of the Faculty and Provost: DANIEL J. HORNBACH
Chief Investment Officer: CRAIG H. AASE
Director, Athletics, Physical Education and Recreation: IRV CROSS
Dean of Admissions and Financial Aid: LORNE T. ROBINSON
Library of 400,000 vols
Number of teachers: 143 (full-time)
Number of students: 1,850
Publications: *College Catalog* (annually), *Prospectus* (annually), *Macalester Today* (4 a year).

MARTIN LUTHER COLLEGE

1995 Luther Court, New Ulm, MN 56073-3300
Telephone: (507) 354-8221
Fax: (507) 354-8225
E-mail: mlcadmit@mlc-wels.edu
Internet: www.mlc-wels.edu
Founded 1995 following merger of Dr Martin Luther College (f. 1884) and Northwestern College (f. 1865)
Private control (Wisconsin Evangelical Lutheran Synod)
Academic year: August to May
President: THEODORE B. OLSEN
Vice-President (Academics): DAVID O. WENDLER
Vice-President (Student Life): JEFFREY L. SCHONE
Vice-President (Administration): STEVEN R. THIESFELDT
Vice-President (Enrollment Management): PHILIP M. LEYRER
Library Director: DAVID M. GOSDECK
Number of teachers: 88
Number of students: 1,021
Publication: *The Lutheran Educator* (4 a year)

HEADS OF DEPARTMENTS

Education: Dr JOHN R. ISCH
English: THOMAS N. HUNTER
Foreign Languages: THOMAS P. NASS
Mathematics and Science: Dr ROGER C. KLOCKZIEM
Music: KERMIT G. MOLDENHAUER
Physical Education: DREW M. BUCK
Religion: MARK J. LENZ
Social Studies: PAUL E. KOELPIN

METROPOLITAN STATE UNIVERSITY

700 E. 7th St, St Paul, MN 55106
Telephone: (616) 772-7777
Fax: (616) 772-7738
Internet: www.metrostate.edu
Founded 1971
Part of Minnesota State Colleges and Universities system
President (vacant)
Admissions Director: JANICE HARRING-HENDON
Librarian: DAVID BARTON
Number of teachers: 610 (110 full-time, 500 part-time)
Number of students: 8,600.

MINNEAPOLIS COLLEGE OF ART AND DESIGN

2501 Stevens Ave, Minneapolis, MN 55404
Telephone: (612) 874-3700
Fax: (612) 874-3704
E-mail: admissions@mcad.edu
Internet: www.mcad.edu
Founded 1886
Academic year: September to May
President: JOHN S. SLORP
Director of Admissions: BRAD NUORALA
Director of Continuing Studies: BRENDA GRACHER
Treasurer: JAMES HOSETH
Dean of Student Affairs: SUSAN CALMENSON
Dean of Studio Programs: TOM DE BIASO
Dean of Liberal Studies: MARY MCDUNN
Library Director: SUZANNE DEGLER
Library of 60,000 vols
Number of teachers: 65
Number of students: 600.

MINNESOTA STATE COLLEGES AND UNIVERSITIES

501 World Trade Center, 30 E. 7th St, St Paul, MN 55101
Telephone: (612) 296-8012
Fax: (612) 297-5550
Internet: www.mnscu.edu
Founded 1995
Academic year: August to May
Chancellor: JAMES H. MCCORMICK
Senior Vice-Chancellor for Academic and Student Affairs: LINDA BAER
Vice-Chancellor and Chief Financial Officer: LAURA M. KING
Vice-Chancellor for Human Resources: BILL TSCHIDA
Deputy to the Chancellor (Government Relations): JOHN OSTREM
Deputy to the Chancellor and Chief of Staff: JANICE FITZGERALD
Number of students: 225,000 (system-wide)
Incorporates 34 colleges and universities and 53 campuses.

MINNESOTA STATE UNIVERSITY, MANKATO

228 Wiecking Center, Mankato, MN 56001
Telephone: (507) 389-1866
Fax: (507) 389-2227
E-mail: thehub@mnsu.edu
Internet: www.mnsu.edu
Part of Minnesota State Colleges and Universities system
Founded 1868
Academic year: August to May
President: Dr RICHARD R. RUSH
Vice-President for Academic Affairs: Dr KAREN BOUBEL
Vice-President for Fiscal Affairs: H. DEAN TRAUGER
Vice-President for Student Affairs: Dr MARGARET HEALY
Registrar: DAVE GJERDE
Director of Library Services and Information Technology: Dr SYLVERNA FORD
Library of 693,973 vols
Number of teachers: 700
Number of students: 12,316
Publications: *Today at Minnesota State*, *The Reporter*, *Campus Buzz*.

MINNESOTA STATE UNIVERSITY, MOORHEAD

1104 7th Ave S., Moorhead, MN 56563
Telephone: (218) 236-2011
Fax: (218) 236-2168
E-mail: adminaff@mnstate.edu

Internet: www.mnstate.edu
Founded 1887
Part of Minnesota State Colleges and Universities system
Academic year: August to May
President: Dr ROLAND E. BARDEN
Vice-President for Academic Affairs: Dr BETTE G. MIDGARDEN
Vice-President for Administrative Affairs: Dr DAVID CROCKETT
Vice-President for Student Affairs: WARREN WIESE
Registrar: JOHN TANDBERG
Library of 595,000 books and periodicals
Number of teachers: 547
Number of students: 7,400.

NORTH CENTRAL UNIVERSITY

910 Elliot Avenue, Minneapolis, MN 55404
Telephone: (612) 343-4400
E-mail: info@northcentral.edu
Internet: www.northcentral.edu
Founded 1930 as North Central Bible Institute; present name 1998
Private control
President: Dr GORDON ANDERSON
Vice-President (Academic Affairs): Dr THOMAS BURKMAN
Vice-President (Student Development): MIKE NOSSER
Vice-President (University Relations): DAN CALL
Vice-President (Business and Finance): CHERYL BOOK
Registrar: Dr RON JEWETT
Librarian: Dr JOHN DAVENPORT
Library of 70,000 vols
Number of teachers: 88
Number of students: 1,220

HEADS OF DEPARTMENTS

Arts and Sciences: Dr ROGER SORBO
Carlstrom Deaf Studies: Dr JoANN SMITH
Cross Cultural Studies: Dr BOB BRENNEMAN
Education: Dr MARGO LLOYD
Fine Arts: Dr LARRY BACH
Psychology: Dr DANIEL NELSON

NORTHWESTERN COLLEGE

3003 Snelling Avenue North, St Paul, MN 55113-1598
Telephone: (651) 631-5100
E-mail: admissions@nwc.edu
Internet: www.nwc.edu
Private control
Academic year: August to May
President: Dr ALAN CURETON
Library Director: DALE W. SOLBERG
Library of 90,000 vols
Number of teachers: 117
Number of students: 1,600
Areas of study: art and graphic design, Bible, business administration, Christian ministries, communication, education, English and literature, history and related fields, modern languages and cultures, music, psychology, science and mathematics.

NORTHWESTERN HEALTH SCIENCES UNIVERSITY

2501 W 84th Street, Bloomington, MN 55431
Telephone: (952) 888-4777
E-mail: admit@nwhealth.edu
Internet: www.nwhealth.edu
Private control
President: Dr ALFRED TRAINA
Registrar: PAUL SIMMONS
Director of Library Services: DELLA SHUPE
Number of students: 1,000.

OAK HILLS CHRISTIAN COLLEGE

1600 Oak Hills Rd SW, Bemidji, MN 56601
Telephone: (218) 751-8670
Fax: (218) 751-8825
E-mail: admissions@oakhills.edu
Internet: www.oakhills.edu
Founded 1946 as Oak Hills Christian Training School; present name 1998
Private control
President and Academic Dean: DAN CLAUSEN
Dean of Student Life: JIM HODGSON
Registrar: MARY HANNAH
Librarian: KEITH BUSH
Library of 23,000
Number of teachers: 20
Number of students: 152
Areas of study: Biblical studies, general education, Christian ministries.

ST CLOUD STATE UNIVERSITY

St Cloud, MN 56301
Telephone: (612) 255-2122
Internet: www.mnstate.edu/home
Founded 1869
Part of Minnesota State Colleges and Universities system
President: ROBERT O. BESS
Vice-President for Academic Affairs: BARBARA GRACHEK
Dean of Learning Resources: JOHN G. BERLING
Library of 569,000 vols
Number of teachers: 650
Number of students: 16,000.

SAINT JOHN'S UNIVERSITY

Collegeville, MN 56321
Telephone: (612) 363-2011
Internet: www.csbsju.edu
Founded 1857
Private liberal arts college for men; co-operates with the College of Saint Benedict
President: Bro. DIETRICH REINHART
Director of Admissions: MARY MILBERT
Librarian: MICHAEL KATHMAN
Library of 310,000 vols, 17,000 microforms, 123,000 government documents, over 1,200 periodicals
Number of teachers: 165
Number of students: 2,025.

SAINT MARY'S UNIVERSITY

Winona, MN 55987
Telephone: (507) 452-4430
Fax: (507) 457-1633
Internet: www.smumn.edu
Founded 1912
President: Bro. LOUIS DE THOMASIS
Vice-President for Student Development: SHARYN GOO
Vice-President for Academic Affairs: Dr JEFFREY HIGHLAND
Vice-President for Graduate and Special Programs: Dr DANIEL MALONY
Executive Vice-President for Admission: TONY M. PISCITIELLO
Vice-President for Corporate and Community Relations: LORAS SIEVE
Vice-President for Financial Affairs: CYNTHIA MAREK
Vice-President for University Relations: MARY FOX
Librarian: Bro. RICHARD LEMBERG
Library of 140,000 vols
Number of teachers: 440
Number of students: 8,000.

ST OLAF COLLEGE

1520 St Olaf Avenue, Northfield, MN 55057-1098
Telephone: (507) 646-2222
Fax: (507) 646-3549
Internet: www.stolaf.edu
Founded 1874
Academic year: September to May
President: CHRISTOPHER M. THOMFORDE
Vice-President and Dean of Faculty: JAMES MAY
Vice-Presidents: JOHN KILBRIDE, MICHAEL KYLE, JAN McDANIEL, ALAN NORTON
Dean of Students: GREG KNESER
Director of College Relations: JAN McDANIEL
Director of the Library: BRYN GEFFERT
Library of 685,000 vols
Number of teachers: 327
Number of students: 3,046
Publication: *St. Olaf.*

SOUTHWEST MINNESOTA STATE UNIVERSITY

1501 State St, Marshall, MN 56258-1598
Telephone: (507) 537-7021
Fax: (507) 537-7154
Internet: www.southwestmsu.edu
Part of Minnesota State Colleges and Universities system
Founded 1963
Academic year: August to May
President: Dr DAVID C. DANAHAR
Provost: Dr RAYMOND LOU
Vice-President (Student Affairs): SCOTT CROWELL
Vice-President (Advancement): Dr VINCENT PELLEGRINO
Vice-President (Finance and Administration): DOUG FRAUNFELDER
Registrar: PHIL COLTART
Library Director: JOHN BOWDEN
Library of 160,000 vols
Number of teachers: 162
Number of students: 5,500

DEANS

College of Arts, Letters and Sciences: Dr BETH WEATHERBY
College of Business, Education, Professional and Graduate Studies: GEORGE MITCHELL

UNITED THEOLOGICAL SEMINARY OF THE TWIN CITIES

3000 Fifth St NW, New Brighton, MN 55112
Telephone: (651) 633-4311
Fax: (651) 633-4315
Internet: www.unitedseminary-mn.org
Private control
President: WILSON YATES
Dean: RICHARD D. WEIS
Vice-President (Finance and Administration): JUDY LANGE
Vice-President (Development and Stewardship): JONATHAN MORGAN
Registrar: SHERYL ABBOTT
Library Director: SUSAN K. EBBERS
Library of 83,000 vols
Number of teachers: 27
Number of students: 112 (full-time).

UNIVERSITY OF MINNESOTA

100 Church St, SE, Minneapolis, MN 55455
Telephone: (612) 625-5000
Fax: (612) 624-6369
E-mail: feedback@tc.umn.edu
Internet: www.umn.edu
Founded 1851
State control
Academic year: September to May

Pres.: ROBERT H. BRUININKS
Senior Vice-Pres. for Academic Affairs and Provost: E. THOMAS SULLIVAN
Senior Vice-Pres. for Health Sciences: FRANK B. CERRA
Senior Vice-Pres. for System Admin.: ROBERT J. JONES
Vice-Pres. and Chief of Staff: KATHRYN BROWN
Vice-Pres. for Human Resources: CAROL CARRIER (acting)
Vice-Pres. for Research: R. TIMOTHY MULCAHY
Vice-Pres. for Univ. Relations: KAREN HIMLE
Vice-Pres. for Univ. Services: KATHLEEN O'BRIEN
Vice-Pres. and Chief Financial Officer: RICHARD PFUTZENREUTER
Gen. Counsel: MARK ROTENBERG
Dir of Libraries: WENDY P. LOUGEE
Library: see Libraries
Number of teachers: 3,483 system-wide (2,874 Twin Cities campus)
Number of students: 65,247 system-wide (50,954 Twin Cities campus)

DEANS

College of Biological Sciences: ROBERT ELDE
College of Continuing Education: MARY NICHOLS
School of Dentistry: PATRICK LLOYD
College of Design: KATHERINE SOLOMONSON
College of Education and Human Devt: DARLYNE BAILEY
Graduate School: GAIL DUBROW
College of Food, Agricultural and Natural Resource Sciences: JAY BELL
Law School: (vacant)
College of Liberal Arts: STEVEN ROSENSTONE
Carlson School of Management: ALISON DAVIS-BURKE
Medical School: DEBORAH POWELL
School of Nursing: CONNIE DELANEY
College of Pharmacy: MARILYN K. SPEEDIE
Humphrey (Hubert H.) Institute of Public Affairs: J. BRIAN ATWOOD
School of Public Health: JOHN FINNEGAN
Institute of Technology: STEVEN L. CROUCH
College of Veterinary Medicine: JEFFREY KLAUSNER (acting)

PROFESSORS

(Some staff serve in more than one capacity, C = Chair of Department, Co-ord. = Co-ordinator, D = Director of Department, H = Head of Department)

Accounting (3-122 Carlson School of Management, 321 19th Ave, S, Minneapolis, MN 55455; tel. (612) 624-6506; fax (612) 626-1335; e-mail balston@esom.umn.edu; internet www.csom.umn.edu/facultydepartments/departments/accounting/welcometoaccounting/welcometoaccounting.cfm):

AMERSHI, A.
DICKHAUT, J. (C)
JOYCE, E.
KANODIA, C.
RAYBURN, J. (C)

Adult Psychiatry (F-282/2a West, 2450 Riverside Ave, Minneapolis, MN 55455; tel. (612) 273-9800; fax (612) 273-9779):

CARROLL, M.
ECKERT, E.
EL-FAKAHANY, E.
HARTMAN, B.
HATSUKAMI, D.
KROLL, J.
MACKENZIE, T.
SCHULTZ, C.

Aerospace Engineering and Mechanics (107 Akerman Hall, 110 Union St, SE, Minneapolis, MN 55455; tel. (612) 625-8000; fax (612)

626-1558; e-mail dept@aem.umn.edu; internet www.aem.umn.edu):

BALAS, G.
BEAVERS, G. S.
CANDLER, G. V.
FOSDICK, R. L.
GARRARD, W. L. (H)
LEO, P.
WILSON, T. A.

African-American and African Studies (808 Social Sciences Bldg, 267 19th Ave, S, Minneapolis, MN 55455; tel. (612) 624-9847; internet www.afroam.umn.edu):

FARAH, C.
ISAACMAN, A. F.
MCCURDY, R.
NIMTZ, A.
PORTER, P. W.
SCOTT, E.

Agricultural, Food and Environmental Education (320 Vocational and Technical Education Bldg, 1954 Buford Ave, St Paul, MN 55108; tel. (612) 624-2221; fax (612) 625-2798; internet education.umn.edu/wcfe/afee):

KRUEGER, R.
PETERSON, R. (H)

Agronomy and Plant Genetics (411 Borlang Hall, 1991 Upper Burford Circle, St Paul, MN 55108; tel. (612) 625-7773; fax (612) 625-1268; e-mail agro@coates.umn.edu; internet www.agro.agri.umn.edu):

BECKER, R. L.
CARDWELL, V. B.
DURGAN, B. R.
EHLKE, N. J.
GENGENBACH, B. G. (H)
GRONWALD, J. W.
GUNSOLUS, J. L.
HARDMAN, L. L.
HICKS, D. R.
JONES, R. J.
JUNG, H. J.
LUESCHEN, W. E.
ORF, J. H.
PHILLIPS, R. L.
RINES, H. W.
SHEAFFER, C. C.
SIMMONS, S. R.
SOMERS, D. A.
STUTHMAN, D. D.
VANCE, C. P.
WYSE, D. L.

American Studies (104 Scott Hall, 72 Pleasant St, SE, Minneapolis, MN 55455; tel. (612) 624-4190; fax (612) 624-3858; e-mail amstdy@umn.edu; internet cla.umn.edu/american/american.html):

MAY, E. T.
MAY, L. (D)
NOBLE, D.
PRELL, R. E.
YATES, G. G.

Anaesthesiology (B-515 Mayo Memorial Bldg (MMC 294), 420 Delaware St, SE, Minneapolis, MN 55455; tel. (612) 624-9990; fax (612) 624-2363; internet www.anesthesiology.umn.edu):

BEEBE, D. S.
BELANI, K. G. (H)
IAIZZO, P. A.
PALAHNIUK, R. J.

Animal Science (305 Haecker Hall, 1364 Eckles Ave, St Paul, MN 55108; tel. (612) 624-9752; fax (612) 625-5789; internet www.ansci.umn.edu):

CROOKER, B. A.
DAYTON, W. R.
EL HALAWANI, M. E.
FOSTER, D. N.
HANSEN, L. B.
HATHAWAY, M. R.
HAWTON, J. D.

HUNTER, A. G.
JOHNSON, D. G.
JOHNSTON, L. J.
LINN, J. G.
MARX, G. D.
NOLL, S. N.
O'GRADY, S. M.
OSBORN, J. W.
PONCE DE LEÓN, F. A. (H)
RENEAU, J. K.
SEYKORA, A.
SHURSON, G. C.
STERN, M. D.
WHEATON, J. E.
WHITE, M. E.

Anthropology (395 Hubert H. Humphrey Center, 301 19th Ave, S, Minneapolis, MN 55453; tel. (612) 625-3400; fax (612) 625-3095; internet www.cla.umn.edu/anthropology):

GIBBON, G.
GUDEMAN, S.
INGHAM, J. M. (C)
MILLER, F. C.
RAHEJA, G. G.
WELLS, P.

Applied Economics (231 Classroom-Office Bldg, 1994 Buford Ave, St Paul, MN 55108; tel. (612) 625-1222; fax (612) 625-6245; e-mail depthead@dept.agecon.umn.edu; internet www.apec.umn.edu):

APLAND, J. D.
EASTER, K. W.
EIDMAN, V. R. (H)
GARTNER, W. C.
KING, R. P.
KINSEY, J. L.
LEVINS, R. L.
MORSE, G. W.
OLSEN, K. D.
PARLIAMENT, C. D.
PEDERSON, E. D.
POLASKY, S.
ROE, T. L.
RUNGE, C. F.
RUTTEN, V. W.
SCHUH, G. E.
SENAUER, B. H.

Architecture (89 Church St, SE, Minneapolis, MN 55455; tel. (612) 626-9068; fax (612) 625-7525; e-mail calainfo@tc.umn.edu; internet www.cala.umn.edu/architecture.html):

FISHER, T.
LaVINE, L.
ROBINSON, J. W.
ROCKCASTLE, G.
SATKOWSKI, L.

Art (208 Art Bldg, 216 21st Ave, Minneapolis, MN 55455; tel. (612) 625-8096; fax (612) 625-7881; e-mail artdept@tc.umn.edu; internet artdept.umn.edu):

BETHKE, K. E.
HOARD, C. C.
KATSIAFICAS, D.
MORGAN, C.
PHARIS, M. (C)
PORTRATZ, W. E.
ROSE, T. A.

Art History (338 Heller Hall, 271 19th Ave, S, Minneapolis, MN 55455; tel. (612) 624-4500; fax (612) 626-8679; internet www.arthist.umn.edu):

ASHER, F. M. (C)
COOPER, F.
MCNALLY, S.
MARLING, K. A. R.
POOR, R. J.
WEISBERG, G.

Astronomy (356 Tate Lab of Physics, 116 Church St, SE, Minneapolis, MN 53455; tel. (612) 624-0211; fax (612) 626-2029; internet www.astro.umn.edu):

DAVIDSON, K. D.

DICKEY, J. M.
GEHRZ, R. D.
HUMPHREYS, R. M.
JONES, T.
JONES, T. W.
KUHI, L. (C)
RUDNICK, L.
SKILLMAN, E.
WOODWARD, P. R.

Biochemistry, Molecular Biology and Biophysics (6-155 Jackson Hall, 321 Church St, SE, Minneapolis, MN 55455; tel. (612) 625-6100; fax (612) 625-2163; e-mail bmbb@biosci.cbs.umn.edu; internet www.cbs.umn.edu/bmbb):

ALLEWELL, N. M.
ANDERSON, J. S.
ARMITAGE, I. M.
BANASZAK, L. J.
BARRY, B. A.
BERNLOHR, D. A.
BLOOMFIELD, V. A.
CONTI-FINE, B. M.
DAS, A.
DEMPSEY, M. E.
FLICKINGER, M. C.
FUCHS, J. A.
HOGENKAMP, H. P. C.
HOOPER, A. B.
HOWARD, J. B.
KOERNER, J. F.
La PORTE, D. C.
LIPSCOMB, J. D.
LIVINGSTON, D. M.
LOUIS, C. F. (H)
LOVRIEN, R. E.
MAYO, K. H.
NELSESTUEN, G. L.
OEGEMA, T. R.
OHLENDORF, D. H.
SANDERS, M. M.
SCHOTTEL, J. S.
THOMAS, D. D.
TOWLE, H. C.
TSONG, T.
VAN NESS, B. G.
WACKETT, L. P.

Bioethics (N-504 Boynton, 410 Church St, SE, Minneapolis, MN 55455; tel. (612) 624-9440; fax (612) 624-9108; e-mail bioethx@umn.edu; internet www.bioethicsd.umn.edu):

BEBEAU, M.
BURK, D.
CRANFORD, R.
KANE, R.
MAYO, D.

Biotechnology Institute (240 Gortner Lab of Biochemistry, 1479 Gortner Ave, St Paul, MN 55108; tel. (612) 624-6774; fax (612) 625-1700; e-mail bti@biosci.cbs.umn.edu; internet biosci.cbs.umn.edu/bti):

BROOKER, R.
FLICKINGER, M.
SADOWSKY, M.
SHERMAN, D.
SRIENC, F.
URRY, D.
WACKETT, L.

Biomedical Engineering (7-105 Basic Sciences and Biomedical Engineering, 312 Church St, SE, Minneapolis, MN 55455; tel. (612) 626-3332; fax (612) 626-6583; internet www1.umn.edu/bme):

POLLA, D.
SIEGEL, R.
TRANQUILLO, R. (H)

Biostatistics (A-460 Mayo Bldg (MMC 303), 420 Delaware St, Minneapolis, MN 55455; tel. (612) 624-4655; fax (612) 626-0660; internet www.biostat.umn.edu):

CARLIN, B.
CONNETT, J.
DUNSMUIR, W.

GOLDMAN, A.
LE, C.
LOUIS, T.
NEATON, J.
TWEEDIE, R. (H)

Biosystems and Agricultural Engineering (213 Biosystems and Agricultural Eng., 1390 Eckles Ave, St Paul, MN 55108; tel. (612) 625-7733; fax (612) 624-3005; e-mail bae@gaia.bae.umn.edu; internet www.bae .umn.edu):

BHATTACHARYA, M.
CLAYTON, C. J.
JACOBSEN, L. D.
JANNI, K. A.
MOREY, R. V. (H)
NIEBER, J. L.
RUAN, R.
WILCKE, W. F.

Business and Industry Education (425 Vocational and Technical Education Bldg, 1954 Buford Ave, St Paul, MN 55108; tel. (612) 624-3004; fax (612) 624-4720; internet education.umn.edu/wcfe/BIE):

BROWN, J.
LAMBRECH, J.
LEWIS, T.
MCLEAN, G.
PUCEL, D.

Chemical Engineering and Materials Science (151 Amundson Hall, 421 Washington Ave, SE, Minneapolis, MN 55455; tel. (612) 625-1010, fax (612) 626-7246, e-mail jjmurphy@tc .umn.edu; internet www.cems.umn.edu):

BATES, F. (H)
CARETTA, R.
CARR, R. W.
CARTER, B.
CHELIKOWSKY, J. R.
CUSSLER, E. L.
DAVIS, H. T.
DERBY, J.
EVANS, D. F.
GEANKOPLIS, C. J.
GERBERICH, W. W.
HU, W. S.
KELLER, K. H.
MCCORMICK, A.
MACOSKO, C. W.
PALMSTROM, C.
SCHMIDT, L. D.
SCRIVEN, L. E.
SEIDEL, R.
SHORES, D. A.
SMYRL, W. H.
SRIENC, F.
TRANQUILLO, R.
WARD, M. D.

Chemistry (139 Smith Hall, 207 Pleasant St, SE, Minneapolis, MN 55455; tel. (612) 624-6000; fax (612) 6626-7541; internet www .chem.umn.edu):

BARANY, G.
BLOOMFIELD, V. A.
CARR, P. W.
CRAMER, C. J.
DAVIS, H. T.
ELLIS, J. E.
GENTRY, W. R.
GLADFELTER, W. L. (C)
GRAY, G. R.
HOYE, T.
KASS, S.
LEOPOLD, K.
LIPSKY, S.
LODGE, T.
MANN, K. R.
MILLER, L. L.
NOLAND, W. E.
PIGNOLET, L. H.
QUE, L.
RAFTERY, M.
STANKOVICII, M. T.
TOLMAN, W.

TRUHLAR, D. G.

Child Development (51 East River Rd, Minneapolis, MN 55455; tel. (612) 624-0526; fax 612 624-6373; e-mail icd@umn.edu; internet education.umn.edu/icd):

BAUER, P.
COLLINS, W. A.
CRICK, N.
EGELAND, B. R.
GUNNAR, M. R.
MARATSOS, M. P.
MASTEN, A. S. (D)
NELSON, C.
PICK, A. D.
PICK, H. L., Jr
SROUFE, L. A.
WEINBERG, R. A.
YONAS, A.

Civil Engineering (122 Civil Eng. Bldg, 500 Pillsbury Dr., SE, Minneapolis, MN 55455; tel. (612) 625-5522; fax (612) 626-7750; e-mail cive@umn.edu; internet www.ce.umn .edu):

ARNDT, R. E. A.
BREZONIK, P. L.
CROUCH, S. L.
DETOURNAY, E.
DRESCHER, A.
FOUFOULA-GEORGIOU, E.
FRENCH, C. W.
GULLIVER, J. S. (H)
MICHALOPOULOS, P.
PARKER, G. N.
SEMMENS, M. J.
STEFAN, G.
STOLARSKI, H. K.
STRACK, O. D. L.
VOLLER, V. R.

Classical and Near Eastern Studies (305 Folwell Hall, 9 Pleasant St, SE, Minneapolis, MN 55455; tel. (612) 625-5353; fax (612) 624-4894; e-mail cnes@umn.edu; internet cnes .cla.umn.edu):

BELFIORE, E.
CLAYTON, T.
COOPER, F.
DOUGLAS, S.
MCNALLY, S.
OLSON, T.
SONKOWSKY, R. P.
STAVROU, T.

Classical Civilization Program (330 Folwell Hall, 9 Pleasant St, SE, Minneapolis, MN 55455; tel. (612) 625-7565):

AKEHURST, F. R.
BELFIORE, E.
CLAYTON, T. (C and D)
COOPER, F.
LIBERMAN, A.
SONKOWSKY, R.
TRACY, J.
WILSON, L.

Clinical and Population Sciences (225 Veterinary Teaching Hospitals, 1352 Boyd Ave/ 1365 Gortner Ave, St Paul, MN 55108; tel. (612) 625-7755; fax (612) 625-6241; e-mail amesx001@tc.umn.edu; internet www.cvm .umn.edu):

AMES, T. R. (C)
BLAHA, T. C.
FAHNING, M. L.
FARNSWORTH, R. J.
FETROW, J. P.
JOO, H. S.
MOLITOR, T. M.
MORRISON, R. B.
PIJOQAN, C. J.
PULLEN, M. M.
SEGUIN, B. E.
TURNER, T. A.

Clinical Pharmacology (6-120 Jackson Hall, 321 Church St, SE, Minneapolis, MN 55455;

tel. (612) 625-9997; fax (612) 625-8408; internet www.pharmacology.med.umn.edu):

HOLZMAN, J. L. (D)
HUNNINGHAKE, D.
PENTEL, P.
YEE, D.

Cognitive Sciences (205 Elliot Hall, 75 East River Rd, Minneapolis, MN 55455; tel. (612) 625-9367; fax (612) 626-7253; e-mail ccs@ cogsci.umn.edu; internet www.cogsci.umn .edu):

CHILDERS, T.
GEORGOPOULOS, A.
GINI, M.
GUNDEL, J.
JOHNSON, P.
KERSTEN, D.
LEGGE, G. (D)
MARATSOS, M.
NELSON, C.
OVERMIER, B.
PICK, A.
PICK, H.
SAMUELS, J.
SPEAKS, C.
UGURBIL, K.
VAN DEN BROEK, P.
VIEMEISTER, N.
WADE, M.
YONAS, A.

Communication Disorders (115 Shevlin Hall, 164 Pillsbury Dr., SE, Minneapolis, MN 55455, tel. (612) 624-3322, fax (612) 624-7586; e-mail cdis@tc.umn.edu; internet www .cdis.umn.edu):

CARNEY, A. E. (C)
REICHLE, J. E.
SPEAKS, C. E.
WINDSOR, J.

Communication Studies (225 Ford Hall, 221 Church St, SE, Minneapolis, MN 55455; tel. (612) 624-5800; internet www.comm.umn .edu):

BROWNE, D. R.
CAMPBELL, K. (C)
HEWES, D.
SCHIAPPA, E.

Community Health Education (300 West Bank Office Bldg, 1300 52nd St, Minneapolis, MN 55455; tel. (612) 624-1878; fax (612) 624-0315; internet www.epi.umn.edu):

FORSTER, J.
GARRAD, J.
JEFFREY, R. W.
LANDO, H. A.
LYTLE, P.
LUEPKER, R. V.
MCGOVERN, P.
PERRY, C. L.
PIRIE, P. L.
VENMGA, R.
WAGENAAR, A. C.

Computer Science and Engineering (4-192 Electrical Eng./Computer Sicence, 200 Union St, SE, Minneapolis, MN 55455; tel. (612) 625-4002; fax (612) 625-0572; internet www .cs.umn.edu):

BOLEY, D. L.
DU, D.
DU, D. Z.
FOX, D.
GINI, M. L.
JANARDAN, R.
KUMAR, V.
NORBERG, A. L.
PAPANIKOLOPOULOUS, W.
PARK, H.
SAAD, Y.
SHEKHAR, S.
SHRAGOWITZ, E.
SRIVASTAVA, J.
TRIPATHI, A. R.
YEW, P. (H)

Counselling and Student Personnel Psychology (129 Burton Hall, 178 Pittsburgh Dr., SE, Minneapolis, MN 55455; tel. (612) 624-6827; fax (612) 625-4063; e-mail cspp-adm@umn.edu; internet www.education.umn.edu/edpsych/cspp):

HUMMEL, T.
ROMANO, J.
SKOVHOLT, T. (Co-ord.)
VEACH, P.

Cultural Studies and Comparative Literature (350 Folwell Hall, 9 Pleasant St, SE, Minneapolis, MN 55455; tel. (612) 624-8099; fax (612) 626-0228; internet cscl.cla.umn.edu):

BRENNAN, T.
LEPPERT, R. (C)
MOWITT, J.
SARLES, H. B.
SCHULTE-SASSE, J.

Curriculum and Instruction (125 Peik Hall, 159 Pillsbury Dri., SE, Minneapolis, MN 55455; tel. (612) 625-6372; fax (612) 624-8277; e-mail ciinfo@umn.edu; internet www.education.umn.edu/ci):

AVERY, P.
BEACH, R. W.
COGAN, J.
DILLON, D (C)
GRAVES, M.
JOHNSON, R.
LAMBRECHT, J.
LAWRENZ, F.
MANNING, J. C.
O'BRIEN, D.
POST, T.
TAYLOR, B.

Dental Research Center for Biomaterials and Biomechanics (16-212 Malcolm Moos Health Sciences Tower, 515 Delaware St, SE, Minneapolis, MN 55455; tel. (612) 625-0950; fax (612) 626-1484):

COMBE, E.
DOUGLAS, W. (D)

Dermatology (4-240 Phillips-Wangensteen Bldg, 516 Delaware St, SE, Minneapolis, MN 55455; tel. (612) 625-8625; fax (612) 624-6678; internet www.dermatology.umn.edu):

HORDINSKY, M. (H)
KING, R.

Design, Housing, and Apparel (240 McNeal Hall of Home Econ., 1985 Buford Ave, St Paul, MN 55108; tel. (612) 624-9700; fax (612) 624-2750; internet dha.che.umn.edu):

ANGELL, W.
DELONG, M.
EICHER, J.
GUERIN, D.
JOHNSON, K.

Ecology, Evolution, and Behaviour (100 Ecology Bldg, 1987 Upper Buford Circle, St Paul, MN 55108; tel. (612) 625-5200; fax (612) 624-6777; internet www.cbs.umn.edu/eeb):

ALSTAD, D.
BARNWELL, F.
BEATTY, J.
CORBIN, K.
CURTSINGER, J.
CUSHING, E.
LANYON, S.
MEGARD, R.
MORROW, P.
NEUHAUSER, C.
PACKER, C.
PUSEY, A.
REGAL, P.
SHAW, R.
SINIFF, D.
STARFIELD, A.
STERNER, R. W. (H)

TILMAN, G. D.
ZINK, R.

Economics (1035 Walter West Heller Hall, 271 19th Ave, S, Minneapolis, MN 55455; tel. (612) 625-6353; fax (612) 624-0209; e-mail econdept@econ.umn.edu; internet www.econ.umn.edu):

ALLEN, B.
BOLDRIN, M.
CHARI, V. V.
CHIPMAN, J. S.
ECKSTEIN, Z.
FELDMAN, R. D.
FOSTER, E. (C)
HOLMES, T.
HURWICZ, L.
JONES, L.
KEHOE, T.
KOCHERLAKOTA, N.
MCLENNAN, A.
PRESCOTT, E. C.
RICHTER, M. K.
RUSTICHOTRI, A.
RUTTAN, V.
SCHUH, G. E.
SWAN, C.
WERNER, J.

Education for Work and Community (425 Vocational and Technical Education Bldg, 1954 Buford Ave, St Paul, MN 55108; tel. (612) 624-3004; fax (612) 624-4720; internet education.umn.edu/wcfe/wcfe):

BROWN, J.
KRUEGER, R.
LEWIS, T.
PETERSON, R.
THOMAS, R.

Educational Policy and Administration (330 Wulling Hall, 86 Pleasant St, SE, Minneapolis, MN 55455; tel. (612) 624-1006; fax (612) 624-3377; e-mail edpagrad@umn.edu; internet www.education.umn.edu/edpa):

AMMENTORP, W. M.
CHAPMAN, D. W.
COGAN, J. J.
FRY, G. W.
HEARN, J. C. (C)
LEWIS, D. R.
LEWIS, T.
SEASHORE, R.

Educational Psychology (204 Burton Hall, 178 Pillsbury Dr., SE, Minneapolis, MN 55455; tel. (612) 624-1698; fax (612) 624-8241; e-mail epsy-adm@umn.edu; internet www.education.umn.edu/edpsych):

BART, W. M.
BRUININKS, R.
CHRISTENSON, S.
DAVISON, M. L.
DENO, S.
HARWELL, M.
HUMMEL, T.
HUPP, S.
JOHNSON, D. W.
LAWRENZ, F.
MCCONNELL, S.
MCEVOY, M.
MARUYAMA, G.
PELLEGRINI, A.
ROMANO, J.
SAMUELS, S. J. (D)
SKOVHOLT, T. M.
TENNYSON, R.
VAN DEN BROEK, P.
VEACH, P. M.
YSSELDYKE, J.

Electrical and Computer Engineering (4-178 Electrical Eng./Computer Science, 200 Union St, SE, Minneapolis, MN 55455; tel. (612) 625-3300; fax (612) 625-4583; internet www.ece.umn.edu):

COHEN, P. I.
GEORGIOU, T.

GIANNAKIS, G.
GOPINATH, A.
KAVEH, M. (H)
KIEFFER, J. C.
KIEHL, R.
KINNEY, L. L.
KUMAR, K. S. P.
LEE, E. B.
LEGER, J.
LILJA, D.
MAZIAR, C.
MOHAN, N.
MOON, J.
NATHAN, M.
PARHI, K.
PERIA, W. T.
POLLA, D.
ROBBINS, W. P.
RUDEN, P.
TANNENBAUM, A.
TEWFIK, A.
WOLLENBERG, B. F.

Emergency Medicine (A-624 Mayo Memorial Bldg (MMC 911), 420 Delaware St, SE, Minneapolis, 55455; tel. (612) 626-6911; fax (612) 626-2352):

AMSTERDAM, J.
CLINTON, J.
KNOPP, R.
LING, L. (D)
RUIZ, E.

English (207 Lind Hall, 207 Church St, SE, Minneapolis, MN 55455; tel. (612) 625-3363; fax (612) 624-8228; internet english.cla.umn.edu):

BALES, K. (C)
BRENNAN, T.
BRIDWELL-BOWLES, L.
BROWNE, M. D.
CLAYTON, T.
ELFENBEIN, A.
ESCURE, G.
FIRCHOW, P. E.
GARNER, S.
GRIFFIN, E. M.
HALEY, D.
HAMPL, P. M.
HANCHER, M.
HIRSCH, G.
KENDALL, C.
MINER, V.
MOWITT, J.
RABINOWITZ, P.
REED, P. J.
ROSS, D.
ROTH, M.
SOLOTAROFF, R.
SPRENGNETHER, M.
WEINSHEIMER, J.

English as a Second Language (214 Nolte Center for Continuing Education, 315 Pillsbury Dr., SE, Minneapolis, MN 55455; tel. (612) 624-3331; fax (612) 624-4579; e-mail eatarone@tc.umn.edu; internet www.iles.umn.edu/esl.htm):

COHEN, A.
TARONE, E. (C and D)

Entomology (219 Hodson Hall, 1980 Folwell Ave, St Paul, MN 55108; tel. (612) 624-3636; fax (612) 625-5299; e-mail entodept@tc.umn.edu):

ANDOW, D. A.
ASCERNO, M. E. (H)
HIEMPEL, G. E.
HOLZENTHAL, R. W.
HUTCHINSON, W. G.
KURTTI, T. J.
MESCE, R. D.
MOON, R. D.
OSTLIE, K. R.
RADCLIFFE, E. B.
RAGSDALE, D. W.
WALGENBACH, D. D.

Environmental and Occupational Health (1260 Mayo Memorial Bldg (MMC 807), 420 Delaware St, SE, Minneapolis, MN 55455; tel. (612) 626-0900; fax (612) 626-4837; internet www.umn.edu/eoh):

GERBERICH, S.
SEXTON, K.
SWACKHAMER, D.
TOSCANO, W. (H)
VESLEY, D.

Epidemiology (300 West Bank Office Bldg, 1300 52nd St, Minneapolis, MN 55455; tel. (612) 624-1878; fax (612) 624-0315; internet www.epi.umn.edu):

BROWN, J. E.
CROW, R. S.
FINNEGAN, J. R.
FOLSOM, A. R.
FORSTER, J. L.
GARRAD, J.
GLASSER, S. P.
HIMES, J. M.
JACOBS, D. R.
JEFFEREY, R. W.
LANDO, H. A.
LUEPKER, R. V. (H)
McGOVERN, P.
MENOTTI, A.
PERRY, C. L.
PIRIE, P. L.
SHAHAR, E.
STORY, M. T.
VENINGA, R.
WAGENAAR, A. C.

Experimental and Clinical Pharmacology (7-159 Weaver-Densford Hall, 308 Harvard St, SE, Minneapolis, MN 55455; tel. (612) 626-9937; fax (612) 625-9931; internet www.pharmacy.umn.edu):

CLOYD, J. C.
FLETCHER, C. V.
GROSS, C. (H)
GUAY, D. R.
HANLON, J. T.
LACKNER, J. E.
MANN, K. J.
ROTSCHAFER, J. C.
ZASKE, D. E.

Family Education (325 Vocational and Technical Education Bldg, 1954 Buford Ave, St Paul, MN 53708; tel. (612) 624-3010; fax (612) 625-6798; internet education.umn.edu/wcfe/FE):

THOMAS, R.

Family Practice and Community Health (6-240 Phillips-Wangensteen Bldg, 516 Delaware St, SE, Minneapolis, MN 55455; tel. (612) 624-2622; fax (612) 624-5930; internet www.med.umn.edu/fp):

BLAND, C. J.
COLEMAN, E.
GJEROINGEN, D.
KEENAN, J. (H)
SIMON ROSSER, B. R.

Family Social Science (290 McNeal Hall of Home Econ., 1985 Buford Ave, St Paul, MN 55108; tel. (612) 625-1900; fax (612) 625-4227; internet fsos.che.umn.edu):

BAUER, J.
BOSS, P.
DANES, S.
DETZNER, D.
DOHERTY, W.
GROTEVANT, H. D. (H)
HOGAN, M. J.
MADDOCK, J.
RETTIG, K.
ROSENBLATT, P.
TURNER, W.

Finance (3-122 Carlson School of Management, 321 19th Ave, S, Minneapolis, MN 55455; tel. (612) 624-2888; fax (612) 626-1335; internet www.csom.umn.edu):

ALEXANDER, G.
BENVENISTE, L.
BOYD, J. (C)
LEVINE, R.
NANTELL, T.

Fisheries and Wildlife (200 Hodson Hall, 1980 Folwell Ave, St Paul, MN 55455; tel. (612) 624-3600; fax (612) 625-5299; internet www.fw.umn.edu):

ADELMAN, I.
ANDERSON, D.
COHEN, Y.
COOPER, J.
CUTHBERT, F.
KAPUSCINSKI, A.
PERRY, J.
SMITH, D.
SORENSEN, P.
SPANGLER, G.

Food Science and Nutrition (225 Food Science and Nutrition, 1334 Eckles Ave, St Paul, MN 55108; tel. (612) 624-1290; fax (612) 625-5272; e-mail fscn@mail.coafes.umn.edu; internet fscn.che.umn.edu):

ADDIS, P. B.
BRADY, L. J.
CSALLANY, A. S.
FULCHER, R. G.
LABUZA, T. P.
McKAY, L. L.
REINECCIUS, G. A.
SLAVIN, J. L.
SMITH, D. E.
TATINI, S. R.
VICKERS, Z. M.
WARTHESEN, J. J. (H)

Forest Resources (115 Green Hall, 1530 North Cleveland Ave, St Paul, MN 53108; tel. (612) 624-3400; fax (612) 625-5212; e-mail fr@forestry.umn.edu; internet www.cnr.umn.edu/FR):

ANDERSON, D. H.
BAUER, M. E.
BAUGHMAN, M. J.
BLINN, C. R.
BROOKS, K. N.
BURK, T. E.
EK, A. R. (H)
ELLEFSON, P. B.
PERRY, J. A., II
REICH, P. B.
ROSE, D. W.

French and Italian (260 Folwell Hall, 9 Pleasant St, SE, Minneapolis, MN 55455; tel. (612) 624-4308; fax (612) 624-6021; e-mail frit@umn.edu; internet cla.umn.edu/frit):

AKEHURST, F. R. P.
NOAKES, S.
PAGANINI, M.

General College (25 Appleby Hall, 128 Pleasant St, SE, Minneapolis, MN 55455; tel. (612) 625-3339; fax (612) 625-0704; internet www.gen.umn.edu):

BROTHEN, T. F.
COLLINS, T. G.
GIDMARK, J. B.
HIGHBEE, J. H.
MOORE, R. C.
ROBERTSON, D. F.
YAHNKE, R. E.

Genetics, Cell Biology and Development (6-160 Jackson Hall, 321 Church St, SE, Minneapolis, MN 55455; tel. (612) 624-3110; fax (612) 626-6140; e-mail gcd@mail.med.umn.edu; internet www.gcd.med.umn.edu):

BAUER, G. E.
BERMAN, J. G.
BERRY, S.
BROOKER, R. J.
ERLANDSEN, S. L.
FAN, D. P.
FARAS, A. H.

GOLDSTEIN, S. F.
HACKETT, P. B.
HAMILTON, D. W.
HERMAN, R. K.
HERMAN, W. S.
JOHNSON, R. G.
KING, R. A.
KURIYAMA, P. A.
LEFEBVRE, P. A.
LINCK, R. W.
MAGEE, P. T.
MOIVOR, R. S.
O'CONNOR, M. B.
ORR, H. T.
SILFLOW, C. D.
SIMMONS, M. J.
SNUSTAD, D. P.
SORENSON, R. L.
VANNESS, B. G. (H)

Geography (414 Social Sciences Bldg, 267 19th Ave, S, Minneapolis, MN 55455; tel. (612) 625-6080; fax (612) 624-1044; e-mail geog@geog.umn.edu; internet www.geog.umn.edu):

ADAMS, J. S. (C)
BROWN, D. A.
GERSMEHL, P. J.
HART, J. F.
HSU, M. L.
LEITNER, H.
McMASTER, R. B.
MARTIN, J. A.
SAMATOR, A. I.
SCOTT, E. P.
SHEPPARD, E. S.
SKAGGS, R. H.

Geology and Geophysics (108 Pilsbury Hall, 310 Pilsbury Dr., SE, Minneapolis, MN 55455; tel. (612) 624-1333; fax (612) 625-3819; e-mail geology@umn.edu; internet www.geo.umn.edu):

ALEXANDER, E. C., Jr
BANERJEE, S. K.
EDWARDS, R. L.
HUDLESTON, P.
ITO, E.
KOHLSTEDT, D.
KOHLSTEDT, S. G.
MOREY, G. B.
MOSHOWITZ, B.
MURTHY, V. R.
PAOLA, C.
PFANNKUCH, H. O.
SEYFRIED, W. E., Jr (H)
STOUT, J.
SOUTHWICK, D.
TEYSSIER, C.
YUEN, D.

German, Scandinavian, and Dutch (205 Folwell Hall, 9 Pleasant St, SE, Minneapolis, MN 55455; tel. (612) 625-2080; fax (612) 624-8297; internet www.folwell.umn.edu/gsd):

FIRCHOW, E. S.
HASSELMO, N.
HOUE, P.
JOERES, R. B.
LIBERMAN, A.
PARENTE, J., Jr
SCHULTE-SASSE, J.
STOCKENSTRÖM, G.
TERAOKA, A. (C)
ZIPES, J.

Gerontology (D-312 Mayo Memorial Bldg (MMC 197), 420 Delaware St, SE, Minneapolis, MN 55455; tel. (612) 624-3904; fax (612) 624-8448; e-mail coa@tc.umn.edu; internet www.umn.edu/coa):

AHLBURG, D.
BORN, D.
BOSS, P.
BOULT, C.
CLOYD, J.
CURTSONGER, J.
DETZNER, D.

DiFabio, R.
Durfee, W.
Dysken, M.
Eustis, N.
Feldman, B.
Garrard, J.
Gersheenson, C.
Guay, D.
Hancock, P.
Hanlon, J.
Heller, L.
Kane, R.
Kane, R. (D)
Keller, L.
Kivnick, H.
Lackner, T.
Larson, A.
Le, C.
McGue, M.
Meyers, S.
Miles, S.
Park, R.
Quam, J.
Schondemeyer, S.
Seybold, V.
Snyder, M.
Swiontkowski, M.
Thomas, D.
Wade, M.
Wyman, J.
Zimmerman, S.

Health Ecology (15-136 Malcolm Moos Health Sciences Tower, 515 Delaware St, SE, Minneapolis, MN 55455; tel. (612) 625-1191; fax (612) 626-6096; e-mail tlpash@maroon.tc.umn.edu; internet www.umn.edu/dental/department/prevsei/div_hecology.html):

Bebeau, M.
Born, D. (D)
DiAngelis, A.
Martens, L.

Health Informatics (777 Mayo Memorial Bldg (MMC 511), 420 Delaware St, SE, Minneapolis, MN 55455; tel. (612) 625-8440; fax (612) 625-7166; e-mail grad@email.labmed.umn.edu; internet www.hinf.umn.edu):

Connelly, D. (D)
Finkelstein, S.
Gatewood, L.
Speedie, S.

Health Informatics Graduate Program (777 Mayo Memorial Bldg (MMC 511), 420 Delaware St, SE, Minneapolis, MN 55455; tel. (612) 625-8440; fax (612) 625-7166; e-mail grad@email.labmed.umn.edu; internet www.hinf.umn.edu):

Connelly, D.
Ellis, L.
Fan, J.
Finkelstein, S.
Fricton, J.
Gatewood, L.
Harris, I.
Johnson, P.
McQuarrie, D.
Patterson, R.
Speedie, S. (D)
Wholey, D.
Wilcox, G.

Health Services Research and Policy, Division of (15-200 Phillips-Wangensteen Bldg, 516 Delaware St, SE, Minneapolis, MN 55455; tel. (612) 624-6151; fax (612) 624-2196; e-mail ihsr@umn.edu; internet www.hsr.umn.edu):

Christianson, J.
Dowd, B.
Feldman, R.
Garrard, J.
Hanlon, J.
Kane, R.
Kane, R.

Kralewski, J.
Lurie, N.
McBean, M.
Moscovice, I.
Nyman, J.
Swiontkowski, M.
Venniga, R.

Healthcare Management (3-140 Carlson School of Management, 321 19th Ave, S, Minneapolis, MN 55455; tel. (612) 624-8814; internet www.csom.umn.edu/facultydepartments/departments/healthcaremgmt/healthcaremgmt.cfm):

Begun, J. (C and D)
Christianson, J.
Weckwerth, V.

History (614 Social Sciences Bldg, 267 19th Ave, S, Minneapolis, MN 55455; tel. (612) 624-2800; fax (612) 624-7096; internet www.hist.umn.edu):

Altholz, J. L.
Bachrach, B. S.
Berman, H.
Evans, J.
Evans, S.
Farmer, E. L.
Good, D. (C)
Isaacman, A. F.
McCaa, R.
Maynes, M. J.
Menard, R. R.
Munholland, J. K.
Noonan, T. S.
Phillips, C.
Phillips, W.
Reyerson, K.
Ruggles, S.
Samaha, J.
Stavrou, T. G.
Thayer, J. A.
Tracy, J. D.
Vecoli, R. J.
Waltner, A.

History of Medicine (511A Diehl Hall, 505 Essex St, SE, Minneapolis, MN 55455; tel. (612) 624-4416; fax (612) 625-7938; internet www.med.umn.edu/history/home.htm):

Eyler, J. M. (D)

History of Science and Technology (381 Tate Lab of Physics, 116 Church St, SE, Minneapolis, MN 55455; tel. (612) 624-7069; fax (612) 624-4578; internet www.physics.umn.edu):

Beatty, J.
Kohlstedt, S. G.
Norberg, A. L.
Seidel, R. W.
Shapiro, A. E. (D)

Hormel Institute (801 16th Avenue, NE, Austin, MN 55912; tel. (507) 433-8804; fax (507) 437-9606; internet www.smig.net/hi):

Brockman, H. L.
Brown, R. E.
Dong, Z. (D)
Kiss, Z.
Schmid, H. H. O. (D)

Horticultural Science (305 Alderman Hall, 1970 Rolwell Ave, St Paul, MN 55108; tel. (612) 624-5300; fax (612) 624-4941; internet www.hort.agri.umn.edu):

Becker, R. L.
Brown, D. L.
Cohen, J. D.
Gardner, G. M. (H)
Hoover, E. E.
Li, P. H.
Luby, J. J.
Markhart, A. H., III
Olin, P. J.
Pellett, H. M.
Preston, D.
Rosen, C. J.
Sowokinos, J. R.

White, D. B.
Wildung, D. K.

Human Genetics (4-122 Malcolm Moos Health Sciences Tower, 515 Delaware St, SE, Minneapolis, MN 55455; tel. (612) 624-8111; fax (612) 626-7031; internet www.ihg.med.umn.edu):

Berry, S.
Conklin, K.
Hackett, P.
Kersey, J.
King, R.
McIvor, R. S.
Moser, K.
Orr, H. (D)
Somia, M.
VanNess, B.
Whitley, C.

Human Resource Development and Adult Education (425 Vocational and Technical Education Bldg, 1954 Buford Ave, St Paul, MN 55108; tel. (612) 624-3004; fax (612) 624-4720; internet education.umn.edu/wcfe/hrd/default.html):

Brown, J.
Lewis, T.
McLean, G. (Co-ord.)
Pucel, D.
Swanson, R.

Human Sexuality (180 West Bank Office Bldg, 1300 52nd St, Minneapolis, MN 55455; tel. (612) 625-1500; fax (612) 626-8311):

Coleman, E. (D)
Rosser, S.

Humphrey (Hubert H.) Institute of Public Affairs (300 Hubert H. Humphrey Center, 301 19th Ave, S, Minneapolis, MN 55455; tel. (612) 625-9505; fax (612) 625-3513; internet www.hhh.umn.edu):

Adams, J.
Archibald, S.
Brandl, J. (Dean)
Bryson, J.
Eustis, N.
Fennelly, K.
Hoenack, S.
Kapstein, E.
Keller, K.
Kenney, S.
Kleiner, M.
Kudrle, R.
Markusen, A.
Myers, S. L., Jr
Schuh, G. E.

Industrial Relations (3-300 Carlson School of Management, 321 19th Ave, S, Minneapolis, MN 55455; tel. (612) 624-2500; fax (612) 624-8360; internet www.irc.csom.umn.edu):

Ahlburg, D.
Arvey, R.
Ben-Ner, A. (C)
Bognanno, M.
Fossum, J.
Remington, J.
Scoville, J.
Whitman, A.
Zaidi, M.

Information and Decision Sciences (3-365 Carlson School of Management, 321 19th Ave, S, Minneapolis, MN 55455; tel. (612) 624-8030; fax (612) 626-1316; internet www.csom.umn.edu):

Adams, C. R.
Chervany, N. L.
Curley, S.
Davis, G. B.
Johnson, P. E.
Kauffman, R. J. (C)

Jewish Studies Center (339 Folwell Hall, 9 Pleasant St, SE, Minneapolis, MN 55455; tel. (612) 624-4914):

BACHRACH, B.
BERMAN, H.
BRUSTEIN, W.
PRELL, R. V.-E.
ZIPES, J.

Journalism and Mass Communication (111 Murphy Hall, 206 Church St, SE, Minneapolis, MN 55455; tel. (612) 625-9824; fax (612) 626-8251; internet sjmc.umn.edu):

DICKEN-GARCIA, H.
FABER, R. J.
FANG, I. E.
HANSEN, K. A.
KIRTLEY, J. E.
LEE, C. C.
ROBERTS, N. L.
SULLIVAN, D.
WACKMAN, D. B.

Kinesiology (220 Cooke Hall, 1900 University Ave, SE, Minneapolis, MN 55455; tel. (612) 625-5300; fax (612) 625-7700; internet education.umn.edu/kls/kinesiology/default .html):

KANE, J.
LEON, A.
WADE, M. (D)

Laboratory Medicine and Pathology (D-242 Mayo Memorial Bldg (MMC 609), 420 Delaware St, SE, Minneapolis, MN 55455; tel. (612) 625-9171; fax (612) 625-0617; internet www.borg.labmed.umn.edu/ateam .html):

AHMED, K.
APPLE, F.
BALFOUR, H. J.
BROWN, D. M.
CLARK, B.
ECKFELDT, J.
ELLIS, L.
FERRIERI, P.
FINKELSTEIN, S.
FURCHT, L. T. (H)
GARRY, V.
GATEWOOD, L. C.
HALBERG, F.
HAUS, E.
HECHT, S.
HORWITZ, C.
JESSURUN, J.
KERSEY, J. H.
LEBIEN, T.
MCCARTHY, J.
MCCULLOUGH, J. J.
MCIVOR, S.
MALEJKA-GIGANTI, D.
MANIVEL, C.
MESCHER, M.
ORR, H.
RAO, G.
ROSE, A.
SHIMIZU, Y.
STANLEY, M.
TSAI, M.
WATTENBERG, L.
WELLS, C.
WHITE, J.
WILSON, M.

Landscape Architecture (1425 University Ave, SE, Minneapolis, MN 55455; tel. (612) 625-6860; fax (612) 625-0710; internet www .cala.umn.edu/landscape_architecture/land-scape.html):

NECKAR, L.
PITT, D.

Law (285 Mondale Hall, 229 19th Ave, S, Minneapolis, MN 55455; tel. (612) 625-1000; fax (612) 625-2011; internet www.law.umn .edu):

ADAMS, E.
BEFORT, S.
BURK, P.
BURKHART, A.
CHEN, J.

COOPER, L. J.
DRIPPS, D.
ERICKSON, M.
FARBER, D. A.
FELD, B. C.
FELLOWS, M. L.
FRASE, R. S.
GIFFORD, D. J.
KELLY, B.
KOEPPEN, B.
MARSHALL, D. P.
MATHESON, J.
MORRISON, F. L.
MUNDSTOCK, G.
OKEDIJI, R.
PAULSEN, M.
POWELL, J.
SAMAHA, A.
SCHOETTLE, F.
SHARPE, C.
STEIN, R. A.
TONRY, M. H.
WEISS, F.
WEISSBRODT, D. S.
WOLF, S.
YOUNGER, J.
YUDOF, M.

Life Course Center (1014 Social Sciences Bldg, 267 19th Ave, S, Minneapolis, MN 55455; tel. (612) 624-6333; fax (612) 624-7020; internet www.soc.umn.edu/research/aboutlcc.htm):

KRUTTSCHNITT, C.
LASLETT, B.
MALMQUIST, C.
MORTIMER, J. (D)
STRYKER, R.

Limnological Research Center (220 Pillsbury Hall, 310 Pillsbury Dr., SE, Minneapolis, MN 55455; tel. (612) 624-7005; fax (612) 625-3819; internet lrc.geo.umn.edu):

BANERJEE, S. K.
CUSHING, E. J.
EDWARDS, L.
ITO, E. (D)
JOHNSON, T. C.
MEGARD, R. O.

Linguistics (214 Nolte Center for Continuing Education, 315 Pillsbury Dr., SE, Minneapolis, MN 55455; tel. (612) 624-3331; fax (612) 624-4579; e-mail umling@tc.umn.edu):

GUNDEL, J. (C)

Marketing and Logistics Management (3-150 Carlson School of Managment, 321 19th Ave, S, Minneapolis, MN 55455; tel. (612) 624-5055; fax (612) 624-8804; internet www.csom .umn.edu/wwwpages/depts/mktg/mktgdept .htm):

HOUSTON, M. (C)
JOHN, D.
JOHN, G.
LOKEN, B.
MEYERS-LEVY, J.
ROERING, K.
RUEKERT, R.
WALKER, O.

Mathematics (127 Vincent Hall, 206 Church St, SE, Minneapolis, MN 55455; tel. (612) 625-2004; fax (612) 626-2017; e-mail dpt@ math.umn.edu; internet www.math.umn .edu):

ADAMS, S.
AGARD, S.
ANDERSON, G.
ARNOLD, D.
ARONSON, D.
BAXTER, J.
BOBKOV, S.
BRAMSON, M.
CALDERER, M. C.
COCKBURN, B.
FESHBACH, M.
FRISTEDT, B.

GARRETT, P.
GOLDMAN, J.
GRAY, L.
GULLIVER, R.
HARRIS, M.
HEJHAL, D.
JAIN, N. (H)
JODEIT, M.
KAHN, D.
KEYNES, H.
KRYLOV, N.
LITTMAN, W.
LOWENGRUB, J.
LUSKIN, M.
LYUBEZNIK, G.
MCCARTHY, C.
MCGEHEE, R.
MARDEN, A.
MESSING, W.
MEYERS, N.
MILLER, W., Jr
MOECKEL, R.
NI, W.-M.
ODLYZKO, A.
OLVER, P.
OTHMER, H.
POLACIK, P.
PRIKRY, K.
REINER, V.
REITICH, F.
REJTO, P.
ROBERTS, J.
SAFONOV, M.
SANTOSA, F.
SELL, G.
SPERBER, S.
STANTON, D.
STORVICK, D.
WEBB, P.
WHITE, D.

Mechanical Engineering (1100 Mechanical Eng., 111 Church St, SE, Minneapolis, MN 55455; tel. (612) 625-0705; fax (612) 626-1854; e-mail mech-eng-info@me.umn.edu; internet www.me.umn.edu):

ARORA, S. R.
BAR-COHEN, A.
DAVIDSON, J.
DONATH, M.
DURFEE, W.
ERDMAN, A. G.
GIRSHICK, S.
HEBERLEIN, J.
KITTLESON, D. B.
KLAMECHI, B.
KUEHN, T. H.
KULACKI, F.
KVÅLSETH, T. O.
LEWIS, J.
MCMURRY, P. H. (H)
MARPLE, V. A.
PUI, D.
RAMALINGAM, S.
RAMSEY, J. W.
SIMON, T. W.
SPARROW, E. M.
STARR, P.
STELSON, K.
STRYKOWSKI, P.
TAMMA, K.

Medical Biotechnology (7-105 Basic Sciences and Biomedical Eng., 312 Church St, SE, Minneapolis, MN 55455; tel. (612) 626-2366; fax (612) 625-1121; internet www.med.umn .edu/imb):

FURCHT, L. (D)
MCCARTHY, J.
MCCULLOUGH, J.
RAO, G.

Medical Technology (15-170 Phillips-Wangensteen Bldg, 516 Delaware St, SE, Minneapolis, MN 55455; tel. (612) 625-9490; fax (612) 625-5901; e-mail medtech@tc.umn .edu):

TSAI, M.
WELLS, C.

Medicinal Chemistry (8-101 Weaver-Densford Hall, 308 Harvard St, SE, Minneapolis, MN 55455; tel. (612) 624-9919; fax (612) 624-0139; internet www.pharmacy.umn.edu):

ABUL-HAJJ, Y. J.
HANNA, P. E.
HECHT, S. S.
JOHNSON, R. L. (D)
NAGASAWA, H. T.
PORTOGHESE, P. S.
REMMEL, R. P.
SHIER, W. T.
SPEEDIE, M. K.
VINCE, R.

Medicine (100 Philips-Wangensteen Bldg, 516 Delaware St, SE, Minneapolis, MN 55455; tel. (612) 625-7140):

ANAND, I.
ASINGER, R.
BACHE, R.
BANTLE, J.
BEHRENS, T.
BENDITT, D.
BILLINGTON, C.
BITTERMAN, P.
BLUMENTHAL, M.
BOND, J.
CHESLER, E.
CHRISTIANSON, J.
COHN, J. N.
COLLINS, A.
CROSSLEY, K.
DANIELS, B.
DAVIES, S.
DUANE, W.
FROHNERT, P.
FROM, A.
GEORGOPOULOS, A.
GLASSER, S.
GOLDSMITH, S.
GOODMAN, J.
GRAY, R.
GRIMM, R.
HAASE, A.
HEBBEL, R.
HERTZ, M.
HOLTZMAN, J.
HOSTETTER, T.
HOWE, R.
HUNNINGHAKE, D.
INGBAR, D.
JANOFF, E.
JOHNSON, G.
JOHNSON, J.
KAHN, J.
KASISKE, B.
KEANE, W.
KENNEDY, H.
KING, R.
KUBO, S.
LAKE, J.
LEDERLE, F.
LEVINE, A.
LEVITT, M. D.
LUEPKER, R.
LUIKART, S.
LURIE, N.
MCCLAVE, P.
MAHOWALD, M.
MARIASH, C.
MARINI, J.
MESSNER, R.
MILES, S.
MILLER, J.
MILLER, L.
MILLER, W.
MOLDOW, C.
MUELLER, D.
NICHOL, K.
NIEWOEHNER, D.
NUTTALL, F. O.
PALLER, M.
PENTEL, P.

PETERSON, B.
PETERSON, P. K.
PIERACH, C.
POPKIN, M.
RALJ, L.
RAO, K.
RAVDIN, J. (C)
ROSENBERG, A.
ROSENBERG, M.
RUBINS, H.
SABATH, L. D.
SIMON, G.
SKUBITZ, K.
STEER, C.
TAYLOR, A.
UGURBIL, K.
VERCELLOTTI, G.
VERFAILLIE, C.
WEIR, E. K.
WEISDORF, D.
WHITE, C.
WILLIAMS, D.
WILSON, R.
WOLF, S.
YEE, D.

Microbial Biochemistry and Biotechnology (156 Gortner Laboratory, 1479 Gortner Ave, St Paul, MN 55108; tel. (612) 625-3785; fax (612) 625-5780; internet www.cbs.umn.edu/bmbb):

ANDERSON, J. S.
FLICKINGER, M. C.
HOOPER, A. B.
SCHOTTEL, J. L.

Microbiology (1460 Mayo Memorial Bldg (MMC 196), 420 Delaware St, SE, Minneapolis, MN 55455; tel. (612) 624-6190; fax (612) 626-0623; e-mail micro@lenti.med.umn.edu; internet www.microbiology.med.umn.edu):

BERMAN, J.
CLEARY, P. P.
DUNNY, G.
DWORKIN, M.
FARAS, A. J.
HAASE, A. (H)
HANSON, R.
JENKINS, M.
JOHNSON, R. C.
MAGEE, P. T.
PLAGEMANN, P. G. W.
SCHLIEVERT, P. M.
SHERMAN, D.

Molecular and Cellular Therapy (D-242 Mayo Memorial Bldg (MMC 609), 420 Delaware St, SE, Minneapolis, MN 55455; tel. (612) 626-3272; fax (612) 625-0617; internet www.mbbnet.umn.edu/institutes/cmct):

MCCULLOUGH, J. (D)
MILLER, J.

Molecular Biology (6-155 Jackson Hall, 321 Church St, SE, Minneapolis, MN 55455; tel. (612) 625-6100; fax (612) 625-2163; internet www.cbs.umn.edu/bmbb):

DAS, A.
FUCHS, J. A.
LAPORTE, D. C.
LIVINGSTON, D. M. (D)
SANDERS, M. M.
TOWLE, H. C.
VANNESS, B. G.

Music (100 Donald N. Ferguson Hall, 2106 4th St, S, Minneapolis, MN 55455; tel. (612) 624-5740; fax (612) 626-2200; internet www.music.umn.edu):

ANDERSON, J.
ASHWORTH, T.
BALDWIN, D.
BRAGINSKY, A.
CHERLIN, M.
GARRETT, M.
GRAYSON, D.

HAACK, P.
JACKSON, D.
KIRCHHOFF, C.
KONKOLL, K.
LANCASTER, T.
LUBET, A.
MCCURDY, R.
MAURICE, J.
O'REILLY, S.
REMENIKOVA, T.
SHOCKLEY, R.
SUTTON, V.
WARE, D. C.
WELLER, L.
ZAIMONT, J. L.

Naval Science (203 Armory Bldg, 15 Church St, SE, Minneapolis, MN 55455; tel. (612) 625-6677; fax (612) 624-5030; e-mail nrotc@umn.edu; internet www.umn.edu/nrotc):

FREY, W.

Neurology (12-100 Phillips-Wangensteen Bldg (MMC 295), 516 Delaware St, SE, Minneapolis, MN 55455; tel. (612) 625-9900; fax (612) 625-7950; internet www.neurology.umn.edu):

ANSARI, K.
ASHE, K.
CRANFORD, R.
ETTINGER, M.
GEORGOPOULOS, A.
IADECOLA, C.
KENNEDY, W. R.
KLASSEN, A. C.
KNOPMAN, D.
KRIEL, R.
LOCKMAN, L.
MAHOWALD, M.
MORIARTY, G.
NELSON, C.
PARRY, G. (H)
RAMIREZ-LASSEPAS, M.
ROSS, E. M.
ROTTENBERG, D.
SHAPIRO, E.
TRUWITT, C.
WIRTSCHAFTER, J.

Neuroscience (6-145 Jackson Hall, 321 Church St, SE, Minneapolis, MN 55455; tel. (612) 626-6800; fax (612) 626-5009; internet www.neurosci.umn.edu):

CARROLL, M.
ELDE, R.
EL-FAKAHANY, E.
ENGELAND, W.
FLANDERS, M.
GEORGOPOULOS, A.
GIESLER, G., Jr
JUHN, S.
IADECOLA, C.
LARSON, A.
LETOURNEAU, P.
LEVINE, A.
MANTYH, P.
MCLOON, S.
MILLER, R.
NEWMAN, E.
POPPELE, R.
SANTI, P.
SEYBOLD, V.
SOECHTING, J.
SORENSON, P.
SPARBER, S.
UGURBIL, K.
WILCOX, G.

Neurosurgery (D-429 Mayo Memorial Bldg (MMC 96), 420 Delaware St, SE, Minneapolis, MN 55455; tel. (612) 624-6666; fax (612) 624-0644; internet www.neuro.umn.edu):

EFANGE, S. M. N.
HALL, W. A.
KUCHARCZYK, J.
LOW, W. C.
MAXWELL, R. E. (H)
ROCKSWOLD, G. L.

WIRTSCHAFTER, J. D.

Nuclear Medicine (2-449 Fairview Univ. Medical Center (MMC 292), 420 Delaware St, SE, Minneapolis, MN 55455; tel. (612) 273-4092; fax (612) 273-1950; internet www .med.umn.edu/radiology):

ANDERSON, Q. (D)
EFRANGE, S.
GOMES, M.

Nursing (6-101 Weaver-Densford Hall, 308 Harvard St, SE, Minneapolis, MN 55455; tel. (612) 624-9600; fax (612) 626-2359; internet www.nursing.umn.edu):

BEARINGER, L.
DISCH, J.
EDWARDSON, S. (Dean)
GROSS, C.
HODGE, F.
LEONARD, B.
WYMAN, J.

Obstetrics, Gynaecology, and Women's Health (12-211 Malcolm Moos Health Sciences Tower, 515 Delaware St, SE, Minneapolis, MN 55455; tel. (612) 626-3111; fax (612) 626-0665; internet www.med.umn./obgyn):

CARSON, L. (H)
DE JONGE, C.
GAZIANO, E. P.
KNOX, G. E.
LEUNG, B. S.
MARTENS, M. G.
OKAGAKI, T.
POTISH, R.
RAMAKRISHAN, S.
THOMPSON, T. R.
TROFATTER, K. F.
TWIGGS, L. B.

Operations and Management Science (3-150 Carlson School of Management, 321 19th Ave, S, Minneapolis, MN 55455; tel. (612) 624-7010; fax (612) 624-8804; internet carlsonschool.umn.edu/csom/deptinfo.html.):

ANDERSON, J. C. (C)
CHERVANY, N.
HILL, A. V.
NACHTSHEIM, C.
SCHROEDER, R. G.

Ophthalmology (9th Floor, Phillips-Wangensteen Bldg, 516 Delaware St, SE, Minneapolis, MN 55455; tel. (612) 625-4400; fax (612) 626-3119; internet www.med.umn.edu/ophthalmology):

DOUGHMAN, D. J.
GREGERSON, D. S.
KRACHMER, J. H. (H)
NELSON, J. D.
SUMMERS, C. G.
WIRTSCHAFTER, J. D.

Oral Sciences (17-252 Malcolm Moos Health Sciences Tower, 515 Delaware St, SE, Minneapolis, MN 55455; tel. (612) 624-9123; fax (612) 626-2651; internet www1.umn.edu/dental/department/oralsci/dep_oral.html):

ANDERSON, D. L.
COMBE, E.
DELONG, R.
DOUGLAS, W. H. (acting C)
GERMAINE, G. R.
LILJEMARK, W. F.
ROHRER, M.
SCHACHTELE, C. F.
SHAPIRO, B. L.

Orthodontics (6-320 Malcolm Moos Health Sciences Tower, 515 Delaware St, SE, Minneapolis, MN 55455; tel. (612) 625-5110; fax (612) 626-2571):

SPEIDEL, T. M. (D)

Orthopaedic Surgery (350 Variety Club Research Center, 401 East River Rd, Minneapolis, MN 55455; tel. (612) 625-1177; fax (612) 625-6032):

LEWIS, J. L.
OEGEMA, T., Jr
OGILVIE, J.
SWIONTKOWSKI, M. (H)
THOMPSON, R. C., Jr

Otolaryngology (8-240 Phillips-Wangensteen Bldg (MMC 396), 516 Delaware St, SE, Minneapolis, MN 55455; tel. (612) 625-3200; fax (612) 625-2101):

ADAMS, G. (H)
GIEBINK, G. S.
JUHN, S. K.
MAISEL, R.
MARGOLIS, R.
NELSON, D.
SANTI, P.

Paediatrics (13-118 Phillips-Wangensteen Bldg, 516 Delaware St, SE, Minneapolis, MN 55455; tel. (612) 624-3113; fax (612) 626-6601):

BALFOUR, H.
BELANI, K.
BERRY, S.
BLAZAR, B.
BLUM, R.
BLUMENTHAL, M.
BROWN, D. M.
CHAVERS, B.
CLAWSON, C. C.
FERRIERI, P.
FISH, A.
GEORGIEFF, M
GIEBINK, G. S.
HULL, H.
INGBAR, D.
JOHNSON, D.
KAPLAN, E.
KASHTAN, C.
KERSEY, J.
KIM, Y.
KING, R.
KOHEN, D.
KRIEL, R.
LOCKMAN, L.
MAMMEL, M.
MAUER, S. M.
MOLLER, J (H)
NELSON, C.
NEVINS, T.
OGILVIE, J.
RAMSAY, N.
REMAFEDI, G.
RESNICK, M.
ROBISON, L.
SHAPIRO, E.
SHARP, H.
SINAIKO, A.
STORY, M.
SUMMERS, G.
THOMPSON, T.
TRUWIT, C.
WAGNER, J.
WANGENSTEEN, O. D.
WARWICK, W.
WHITE, J.
WHITLEY, C.

Paediatric Dentistry (6-150 Malcolm Moos Health Sciences Tower, 515 Delaware St, SE, Minneapolis, MN 55455; tel. (612) 624-1985; fax (612) 629-2900; internet www.umn.edu/dental/department/prevsci/div_pediatric .html):

BEIRAGHI, S. (D)
MOLLER, K.
TILL, M.

Periodontology (7-368 Malcolm Moos Health Sciences Tower, 515 Delaware St, SE, Minneapolis, MN 55455; tel. (612) 625-5400; fax (612) 626-2652; internet www.umn.edu/dental/department/prevsci/div_perio.html):

BAKDASH, B. (D)
HERZBERG, M. C.
PHILSTROM, B. L.
WOLFF, L. F.

Pharmaceutical Care and Health Systems (7-159 Weaver-Densford Hall, 308 Harvard St, SE, Minneapolis, MN 55455; tel. (612) 626-9938; e-mail tesda001@tc.umn.edu; internet www.pharmacy.umn.edu):

CIPOLLE, R. J.
MORLEY, P. C.
SCHONDELMEYER, S. W. (H)
STRAND, I. M.
WEAVER, L. C.

Pharmaceutics (9-177 Weaver-Densford Hall, 308 Harvard St, SE, Minneapolis, MN 55455; tel. (612) 624-5151; fax (612) 626-2125; internet www.pharmacy.umn.edu/resgrad/pceutics/pharmaceuticshome.html):

BRAECKMAN, R.
FREY II, W. H.
GRANT, D. J. W.
RESCIGNO, A.
SAWCHUK, R. J.
SIEGEL, R. A. (H)
SURYANARAYANAN, R. G.

Pharmacology (6-120 Jackson Hall, 321 Church St, SE, Minneapolis, MN 55455; tel. (612) 625-9997; fax (612) 625-8408; internet www.pharmacology.med.umn.edu):

BEATTIE, C. W.
CONTI-FINE, B.
EL-ZAKAHANY, E.
HANNA, P. E.
HOLTZMAN, J. L.
HUNNINGHAKE, D. B.
LAW, P.
LEE, H. C.
LOH, H. H. (H)
PENTEL, P. R.
SINAIKO, A. R.
SLADEK, N. E.
SPARBER, S. B.
THAYER, A.
WILCOX, G. L.
WOOD, W. G.
YEE, D.
ZIMMERMAN, B. G.

Philosophy (831 Walter W. Heller Hall, 271 19th Ave, S, Minneapolis, MN 55455; tel. (612) 625-6563; fax (612) 624-8380; internet philosophy.umn.edu):

BOWIE, N.
DAHL, N. O.
EATON, M. M.
GIERE, R.
GUNDERSON, K.
HANSON, W. H.
HELLMAN, G.
HOPKINS, J. S.
KAC, M.
LEWIS, D. (C)
LONGINO, H.
OWENS, J.
PETERSON, S.
SAVAGE, C. W.
SCHEMAN, N.
WALLACE, J. R.

Philosophy of Science (746 Walter W. Heller Hall, 271 19th Ave, S, Minneapolis, MN 55455; tel. (612) 625-6635; fax (612) 626-8380; internet www.mcps.umn.edu):

GIERE, R.
GUNDERSON, K.
HANSON, W.
HELLMAN, G.
LONGINO, H.
SAVAGE, C. W.
SHAPIRO, A.
STUEWER, R.

Physical Medicine and Rehabilitation (500 Boynton (MMC), Minneapolis, MN 55455; tel. (612) 626-4050; fax (612) 624-6686; internet www.mcps.umn.edu):

DI FABIO., R.
PATTERSON, R.

Physics and Astronomy (148 Tate Lab of Physics, 116 Church St, SE, Minneapolis, MN 55455; tel. (612) 624-7375; fax (612) 624-4578; internet www.physics.umn.edu):

BROADHURST, J. H.
CAMPBELL, C. E.
CATTELL, C.
CUSHMAN, P.
DAHLBERG, E. D.
ELLIS, P. J.
GOLDMAN, A. M. (H)
GROSBERG, A.
HALLEY, J. W.
HELLER, K. J.
HUANG, C. C.
KAKALIOS, J.
KAPUSTA, J. I.
LARKIN, A.
LYSAK, R. L.
MARSHAK, M. L.
PEPIN, R. O.
PETERSON, E. A.
POLING, K.
RUDAZ, S.
RUDDICK, K.
RUSACK, R.
SHIFMAN, M.
SHKLOVSKII, B.
VAINSHTEIN, A.
VALLS, O. T.
VOLOSHIN, M.
WALSH, T. F.

Physiology (6-125 Jackson Hall, 321 Church St, SE, Minneapolis, MN 55455; tel. (612) 625-5902; fax (612) 625-5149; internet physiology.med.umn.edu):

DI SALVO, J. (H)
IAIZZO, P.
LEVITT, D.
LOW, W.
O'GRADY, S.
OSBORN, J.
WANGENSTEEN, O. D.
WEIR, K. E.

Plant Biology (220 Biological Sciences Center, 1445 Gortner Ave, St Paul, MN 55108; tel. (612) 625-1234; fax (612) 625-1738; e-mail pbio@ux.acs.umn.edu; internet www.cbs.umn.edu/plantbio/pbio):

BIESBOER, D. D.
BRAMBL, R.
CHARVAT, L.
GLEASON, F. K.
KOUKKARI, W. L.
MCLAUGHLIN, D. J.
OLSZEWSKI, N. E.
SNUSTAD, P. D.
VANDENBOSCH, K. (H)
WETMORE, C. M.
WICK, S.

Plant Pathology (495 Borlaug Hall, 1991 Upper Buford Circle, St Paul, MN 55108; tel. (612) 625-8200; fax (612) 625-9728; internet www.plpa.agri.umn.edu):

BLANCHETTE, R. A.
GROTH, J. V.
JONES, R. K.
KINKEL, L. L.
KRUPA, S. V.
LARSEN, P. O.
LOCKHART, B. E.
MACDONALD, D. H.
NYVALL, R. F.
PERCICH, J. A.
PFLEGER, F. L. (H)
WINDELS, C. E.
YOUNG, N. D.
ZEYEN, R. J.

Political Science (1414 Social Sciences Bldg, 267 19th Ave, S, Minneapolis, MN 55455; tel. (612) 624-4144; fax (612) 626-7599; internet www.polisci.umn.edu):

DIETZ, M.

DUVALL, R.
FARR, J.
FLANIGAN, W. H.
FOGELMAN, E.
JACOBS, L.
KVAVIK, R.
NIMITZ, A.
ROSENSTONE, S.
SCOTT, T. M.
SHIVELY, W. P.

Psychiatry Research (628 Diehl Hall (MMC 392), 505 Essex St, SE, Minneapolis, MN 55455; tel. (612) 626-4034; fax (612) 624-8939):

CARROLL, M. E.
EL-FAKAHANY, E.
HATSUKAMI, D.

Psychological Foundations of Education (206 Burton Hall, 178 Pillsbury Drive, SE, Minneapolis, MN 55455; tel. (612) 624-6083; fax (612) 624-8241; internet www.coled.umn.edu/edpsych/default.html):

BART, W.
DAVISON, M.
HARWELL, H.
JOHNSON, D.
LAWRENZ, F.
MARUYAMA, G.
PELLEGRINI, A.
SAMUELS, S. J.
TENNYSON, R.
VAN DEN BROEK, P.

Psychology (N-218 Elliot Hall, 75 East River Rd, Minneapolis, MN 55455; tel. (612) 625-4042; fax (612) 626-2079; internet www.psych.umn.edu):

BORGIDA, E.
BOUCHARD, T. J.
BURKHARDT, D. A.
BUTCHER, J. N.
CAMPBELL, J. P. (C)
CUDECK, R.
DAVIS, E. R.
DUNETTE, M.
FOX, P.
GARMEZY, N.
HANSEN, J. I.
KERSTEN, D.
LEON, G. R.
LYKKEN, D.
MCGUE, M.
MATOWIDLOS, S.
MOTOWIDLO, S.
OVERMIER, J. B.
PATRICK, C.
SACKETT, D.
SNYDER, M.
TELLEGEN, A.
VIEMEISTER, N. F.
WEISS, D. J.

Public Health Administration (D-359 Mayo Memorial Bldg (MMC 97), 420 Delaware St, SE, Minneapolis, MN 55455; tel. (612) 625-9480; fax (612) 624-5920; internet www.hsr.umn.edu):

MCBEAN, M.
VENINGA, R.

Public Health Nutrition (300 West Bank Office Bldg, 1300 52nd St, Minneapolis, MN 55455; tel. (612) 624-1818; fax (612) 624-0315; internet www.epi.umn.edu):

BROWN, J. E.
HIMES, J. H.
JEFFERY, R. W.
LUEPKER, R. V.
PERRY, C.
STORY, M. T.

Radiology (2-300 Fairview Univ. Medical Center (MMC 292), 420 Delaware St, SE, Minneapolis, MN 55455; tel. (612) 273-6004; fax (612) 273-1470; internet www.med.umn.edu/radiology):

EFANGE, S.

GARWOOD, M.
HU, X.
HUNTER, D.
JEROSCH-HERALD, M.
KIEFFER, S.
KIM, S.
KUCHARCZYK, J.
REINKE, D.
RITENOUR, E. R.
STEENSON, C.
STILLMAN, A.
TRUWIT, C.
UGURBIL, K.

Recreation and Sports Studies (220 Cooke Hall, 1900 University Ave, SE, Minneapolis, MN 55455; tel. (612) 625-5300; fax (612) 626-7700; internet www.kls.umn.edu):

KANE, M. J.
MCAVOY, L.

Regulatory Biochemistry (374 Gortner Lab, 1479 Gortner Ave, St Paul, MN 55108; tel. (612) 624-3622; internet www.cbs.umn.edu/bmbb):

BERNLOHR, D. A.
CONTI-FINE, B. M.
DEMPSEY, M. E.
KOERNER, J. F.
LOUIS, C. F.
NELSESTUEN, G. L. (D)
OEGEMA, T. G.
RAFTERY, M. A.

Rhetoric (4 Classroom Office Bldg, 1994 Buford Ave, St Paul, MN 55108; tel. (612) 624-3445; fax (612) 624-3617; internet www.rhetoric.umn.edu):

BECKER, S.
BERKEKOTTER
GROSS, A. G.
LAY, M. M.
MARCHAND, W. M.
MCDOWELL, E. E.
MIKELONIS, V. M.
WAHLSTROM, B. J.
WHARTON, W. K.

Rural Sociology and Community Analysis (230 Peters Hall, 1404 Gortner Ave, St Paul, MN 55108; tel. (612) 625-4779; fax (612) 625-3746; internet ssw.che.umn.edu/centers.htm#crsca):

MCTAVISH, D.
MENANTEAU, D. (D)
MEYERS, S. S.

St Anthony Falls Laboratory (2 Third Ave, SE, Minneapolis, MN 55414; tel. (612) 627-4010; fax (612) 627-4609; internet www.umn.edu/safl):

ARNDT, R.
FARELL, C.
FOUFOULA-GEORGIOU, E. (D)
GULLIVER, J.
PAOLA, C.
PARKER, G.
SONG, C.
STEFAN, H.
VOLLER, V.

School Psychology (344 Elliot Hall, 75 East River Rd, Minneapolis, MN 55455; tel. (612) 624-4156; fax (612) 624-0879; internet education.umn.edu/edpsych):

CHRISTENSON, S.
MCCONNELL, S.
YSSELDYKE, J.

Scientific Computation (Graduate Program) (7-125 Weaver Densford Hall, 308 Harvard St, SE, Minneapolis, MN 55455; tel. (612) 626-2601; fax (612) 626-4429):

ANDERSON, R.
BOLEY, D.
CANDLER, G.
CHELIKOWSKY, J.
COCKBURN, B.
CRAMER, C.

DERBY, J.
EBNER, T.
FONTOULA-GEORGIO, E. F.
FRIEDMAN, A.
KERSTEN, D.
KUMAR, V.
LOWENGRUB, J.
LUSKIN, M.
NIEBER, J.
OTHMER, H.
PARK, H.
PATANKAR, S.
SAAD, Y.
SCRIVEN, L. E.
SELL, G.
SONG, C.
SRIVASTAVA, J.
STECH, H.
THOMAS, D.
TIERNEY, L.
TRUHLAR, D.
TWETIK, A. H.
VOLLER, V.
WILCOX, G.
WOODWARD, P.
YUEN, D.

Slavic and Central Asian Languages and Literatures (214 Nolte Center for Continuing Education, 315 Pillsbury Dr., SE, Minneapolis, MN 55455; tel. (612) 624-3331; fax (612) 624-4579; e-mail iles@umn.edu):

BASHIRI, I.
JAHN, G.

Small Animal Clinical Sciences (C-339 Veterinary Teaching Hospitals, 1352 Boyd Ave and 1365 Gortner Ave, St Paul, MN 55108; tel. (612) 625-7744; fax (612) 624-0751):

ARMSTRONG, P. J.
BISTNER, S.
FEENEY, D.
HARDY, R.
JESSEN, C.
KLAUSNER, J.
LIPOWITZ, A.
OSBORNE, C.
POLZIN, D.
REDIG, P.
WALLACE, L.

Social Administrative and Clinical Pharmacy (7-155 Weaver-Densford Hall, 308 Harvard St, SE, Minneapolis, MN 55455; tel. (612) 624-2973; fax (612) 625-9931; internet www .pharmacy.umn.edu):

CIPOLLE, R. J.
GARRARD, J. M.
GATEWOOD, L. C.
LANGLEY, P. C.
MORLEY, P. C.
SCHONDELMEYER, S. W.
SPEEDIE, S. M.
STRAND, L. M.
WEAVER, L. C.
WECKWERTH, V. E.
ZASKE, D. E.

Social Work (105 Peters Hall, 1404 Gortner Ave, St Paul, MN 55108; tel. (612) 625-1220; fax (612) 624-3744; internet ssw.che.umn .edu):

BAIZERMAN, M.
BEKER, J.
EDLESON, J.
GILGUN, J.
HOLLISTER, D.
KIVNICK, H.
MENANTEAU, D.
MEYERS, S.
QUAM, J. (D)
ROONEY, R.
UMBREIT, M.
WELLS, S.

Sociology (909 Social Sciences Bldg, 267 19th Ave, S, Minneapolis, MN 55455; tel. (612) 624-4300; fax (612) 624-7020; internet www .soc.umn.edu):

AMINZADE, R. (C)
ANDERSON, J.
ANDERSON, R. E.
GALASKIEWICZ, J.
KNOKE, D.
KRUTTSCHNITT, C.
LASLETT, B.
LEIK, R. K.
MALMQUIST, C.
MARINI, M.
MORTIMER, J.
NELSON, J. I.
STRYKER, R.

Soil, Water, and Climate (439 Borlaug Hall, 1991 Upper Buford Circle, St Paul, MN 55108; tel. (612) 625-1244; fax (612) 625-2208; internet www.soils.agri.umn.edu):

ALLAN, D. L.
ANDERSON, J. L.
BAKER, J. M.
BLOOM, P. R.
CLAPP, C.
COOPER, T. H.
DOWDY, R. H.
GRAHAM, P. H.
GUPTA, S. C.
HALBACH, T. R.
KOSKINEN, W. C.
LAMB, J. A.
MALZER, G.
MOLINA, J. A.
MONCRIEF, J. F.
MULLA, D. J.
NATER, E. A.
RANDALL, G. W.
REHM, G. W.
REICOSKY, D. C.
ROBERT, P. C.
ROSEN, C. J.
RUSSELLE, M. P.
SADOWSKI, M. J.
SCHMITT, M. A.
SEELEY, M. W.

Spanish and Portuguese (34 Folwell Hall, 9 Pleasant St, SE, Minneapolis, MN 55455; tel. (612) 625-5858; fax (612) 625-3549; internet spansport.cla.umn.edu):

JARA, R.
SPADACCINI, N.
VIDAL, H.

Special Education Programs (227 Burton Hall, 178 Pillsbury Drive, SE, Minneapolis, MN 55455; tel. (612) 624-2342; fax (612) 626-9627; internet education.umn.edu/edpsych):

DENO, S.
HUPP, S.
McEVOY, M.

Statistics (313 Ford Hall, 224 Church St, SE, Minneapolis, MN 55455; tel. (612) 625-8046; fax (612) 624-8858; internet www.stat.umn .edu):

BINGHAM, C.
CHALONER, K.
COOK, R. D.
DICKEY, J.
EATON, M. L.
GEISSER, S.
GEYER, C.
HAWKINS, D.
MEEDEN, G. (D)
OEHLERT, G.
SUDDERTH, W. D.
TIERNEY, L.
WEISBERG, S.

Strategic Management and Organization (3-353 Carlson School of Management, 321 19th Ave, S, Minneapolis, MN 55455; tel. (612) 624-5232; fax (612) 626-1316; internet www .csom.umn.edu/wwwpages/depts/smo):

BROMILEY, P.
ERICKSON, W. B.

LENWAY, S. (C)
MAITLAND, I.
MARCUS, A.
NICHOLS, M.
SAPIENZA, H.
VAN DE VEN, A.

Structural Biology and Biophysics (140 Gortner Laboratory, 1479 Gortner Ave, St Paul, MN 55108; tel. (612) 625-6100; e-mail bmbb@ biosci.cbs.umn.edu; internet www.cbs.umn .edu/bmbb):

ARMITAGE, I. M.
BANASZAK, L. J.
BARRY, B. A.
BLOOMFIELD, V. A.
HOGENKAMP, H. P.
HOWARD, J. B.
LIPSCOMB, J. D.
LOVRIEN, R. E.
MAYO, K. H.
OHLENDORF, D. H.
THOMAS, D. D. (D)
TSONG, T. Y.

Surgery (11-100 Phillips-Wangensteen Bldg (MMC 195), 516 Delaware St, SE, Minneapolis, MN 55455; tel. (612) 625-1400; fax (612) 625-8496; internet www.surg.umn .edu):

BOLMAN, R. M., III
BUCHWALD, H.
CERRA, F.
CUNNINGHAM, B.
DALMASSO, A.
DRIES, D.
DUNN, D. (H)
ENGELAND, W.
EYLER, J.
FOKER, J.
GOODALE, R. L.
GRUESSNER, R.
LAKE, J.
LEE, J. T.
LEVINE, A.
LYTE, M.
McQUARRIE, D. G.
MATAS, A.
MILLER, L.
MOLINA, E.
PARK, S.
PAYNE, W.
RODRIGUEZ, J.
ROTHENBERGER, D. A.
SAKO, Y.
SHUMWAY, S.
SUTHERLAND, D.
WARD, H.
WELLS, C.

Surgical Sciences (11-100 Phillips-Wangensteen (MMC 195), 516 Delaware St, SE, Minneapolis, MN 55455; tel. (612) 625-1400):

DALMASSO, A.
ENGELAND, W.
EYLER, J.
WELLS, C.

Theatre Arts and Dance (580 Rarig Center, 330 21st Ave, S, Minneapolis, MN 55455; tel. (612) 625-6699; fax (612) 625-6334; e-mail theatre@umn.edu; internet cla.umn.edu/ theater):

BROCKMAN, C. L.
KOBIALKA, M. (C)
REID, B.

Therapeutic Radiology/Radiation Oncology (M-26 Masonic Cancer Center (MMC 494), 424 Harvard St, SE, Minneapolis, MN 55455; tel. (612) 626-6146; fax (612) 624-5445; internet www.ahc.umn.edu):

LEE, C. K.
LEVITT, S. H.
POTISH, R. A.
SONG, C. W.
VALLERA, D.

TMJ/Orofacial Pain (6-320 Malcolm Moos Health Sciences Tower, 515 Delaware St, SE, Minneapolis, MN 55455; tel. (612) 624-3130; fax (612) 626-0138):

FRICTON, J.

Toxicology Graduate Program (244 Veterinary Diagnostic Lab, 1333 Gortner Ave, St Paul, MN 55108; tel. (612) 625-8787; fax (612) 624-8707; internet www.mvdl.umn .edu):

ABUL-HAJJ, Y.
BROWN, D.
CARLSON, R.
DISALVO, J.
DREWES, L.
HANNA, P.
MURPHY, M. (D)
NAGASAWA, H.
NIEMI, G.
PROHASKA, J.
SCHOOK, L.
SPARBER, S.
WALLACE, K.

Urban Studies (348 Social Sciences Bldg, 267 19th Ave, S, Minneapolis, MN 55455; tel. (612) 626-1626; fax (612) 624-1044; internet urbanstudies.cla.umn.edu):

ADAMS, J. S.
FISHER, T.
GALASKIEWICZ, J.
LEITNER, H.
RUNGE, C. F.
SCOTT, T.
SHEPPARD, E.

Urologic Surgery (A-597 Mayo Memorial Bldg (MMC 394), 420 Delaware St, SE, Minneapolis, MN 55455; tel. (612) 625-9933):

HULBERT, J.

Veterinary Diagnostic Medicine (277 Veterinary Diagnostic Lab, 1333 Gortner Ave, St Paul, MN 55108; tel. (612) 625-8787; internet www.mvdl.umn.edu):

COLLINS, J.
GOYAL, S. (C)
HAYDEN, D.
KURTZ, H.
O'BRIEN, T.
WALSER, M.

Veterinary Pathobiology (205 Veterinary Science, 1971 Commonwealth Ave, St Paul, MN 55108; tel. (612) 625-5255; fax (612) 625-5203; internet www.cvm.umn.edu):

BEITZ, A. J.
BEY, R. F.
BROWN, D. R.
FLETCHER, T. F.
GALLANT, E. M.
HALVORSON, D. A.
LARSON, A. A.
MAHESWARAN, S. K.
MURTAUGH, M. M.
NAGARAJA, K. V.
SHARMA, J. M.
STROMBERG, B. E.
WEISS, D. J.

Women's Studies (425 Ford Hall, 277 Church St, SE, Minneapolis, MN 55455; tel. (612) 624-6006; fax (612) 624-3573; internet womenstudy.cla.umn.edu):

KAMINSKY, A. (C)
LONGINO, H.
SCHEMAN, N.

Wood and Paper Science (203 Kaufert Lab of Forest Products and Wood Science, 2004 Folwell Ave, St Paul, MN 55108; tel. (612) 625-5200; fax (612) 625-6286; internet www .cnr.umn.edu/wps):

BOWYER, J.
MASSEY, J. (H)
SARKANEN, S.
SCHMIDT, E.

Work, Community, and Family Education (Adm 210 Vocational and Technical Education Bldg, 1954 Buford Ave, St Paul, MN 55108; tel. (612) 625-3757; fax (612) 624-2231; e-mail wcfe@umn.edu; internet education.umn.edu/wcfe):

BROWN, J.
LAMBRECHT, J.
LEWIS, T.
MCLEAN, G.
PETERSON, R.
PUCEL, D.
SWANSON, R.
THOMAS, R.

OTHER CAMPUSES

University of Minnesota, Crookston

2900 University Ave, Crookston, MN 56716
Telephone: (218) 281-6510
Fax: (218) 281-8050
E-mail: umcinfo@umn.edu
Internet: www.crk.umn.edu

Founded 1966
Academic year: August to May

Chancellor: CHARLES H. CASEY
Sr Vice-Chancellor for Academic Affairs: THOMAS BALDWIN
Vice-Chancellor for Finance and Univ. Services: JOHN JOHNSTON-ORTIZ
Registrar: BOB NELSON
Dir of Library Services: OWEN WILLIAMS

Number of teachers: 53
Number of students: 2,320

PROFESSORS

BRORSON, S., Marketing and Management
KNOWLTON, D., Art and Sciences
MARX, G., Agricultural, Food, and Environmental Sciences
NEET, S., Art and Sciences
PETERSON, W. C., Art and Sciences
SARGEANT, D., Agriculture and Natural Resources
SELZLER, B., Art and Sciences
SVEDARSKY, W. D., Agricultural Management
WINDELS, C., Agricultural, Food and Environmental Sciences

University of Minnesota, Duluth

1049 University Dr., Duluth, MN 55812
Telephone: (218) 726-8000
Fax: (218) 726-6186
E-mail: sknill@d.umn.edu
Internet: www.d.umn.edu

Founded 1895
Academic year: September to May

Chancellor: KATHRYN A. MARTIN
Vice-Chancellor for Academic Admin.: VINCENT MAGNUSON
Vice-Chancellor for Academic Support and Student Life: BRUCE GILDSETH
Vice-Chancellor for Finance and Operations: GREGORY FOX
Vice-Chancellor for Univ. Relations: WILLIAM WADE

Number of teachers: 431
Number of students: 10,366

DEANS

Labovitz School of Business and Econ.: KJELL R. KNUDSEN (acting)
College of Education and Human Service Professions: PAUL N. DEPUTY
School of Fine Arts: JACK BOWMAN
College of Liberal Arts: LINDA KRUG
College of Science Eng.: JAMES P. RIEHL
Duluth School of Medicine: RICHARD ZIEGLER

PROFESSORS

ADAMS, S. J., English
ANDERSON, A. C., Music
ANDERSON, C., Econ.

ANDREWS, I. T., Biology
BACIG, T., Sociology—Anthropology
BARTLETT, E., Women's Studies
BELOTE, L., Sociology—Anthropology
BRUSH, G., Art
BRUSH, L., Art
BURNS, S. G., Electrical and Computer Eng.
CAPLE, R., Chemistry
CARLSON, H., Education
CARLSON, R. M., Chemistry
CASTLEBERRY, S., Management Studies
CROUCH, D., Computer Science
DAS, A., Psychology
DEPUTY, P. N., Communication Sciences and Disorders
DREWES, L., Biochemistry and Molecular Biology
DUFF, T., Finance and Management Information Sciences
DURGUNOGLA, A. Y., Psychology
EISENBERG, R. M., Pharmacology
ELLIOT, B. A., Behavioural Sciences
ELLIOT, B. A., Family Medicine
EVANS, J., Chemistry
FALK, D., Social Work
FEROZ, E., Accounting
FETZER, J., Philosophy
FIRLING, C., Biology
FLEISCHMAN, W., Sociology—Anthropology
FUGELSO, M., Industrial Eng.
FULKROD, J., Chemistry
GALLIAN, J. A., Mathematics and Statistics
GORDON, R., Psychology
GRANT, J. A., Geological Sciences
GREEN, R., Mathematics and Statistics
HAFFERTY, F., Behavioural Science
HARRISS, D. K., Chemistry
HEDIN, T., Art
HEDMAN, S., Biology
HELLER, L. J., Medical and Molecular Physiology
HILLER, J., Physics
HOLST, T., Geological Sciences
JAMES, B., Mathematics and Statistics
JAMES, K. L., Mathematics and Statistics
JANKOFSKY, K. P., English
JESSWEIN, W. A., Econ.
JOHNSON, T., Industrial Eng.
JOHNSON, T. C., Geological Sciences
JORDAN, T. F., Physics
KARIM, M. R., Biology
KENDALL, L. A., Industrial Eng., MSc in Eng. Management
KLEMER, A., Biology
KLUEG, J., Art
KNOPP, L. M., Jr, Geography
KRAMER, J., Social Work
KRITZMIRE, J., Music
LAUNDERGAN, J. C., Sociology—Anthropology
LETTENSTROM, D., Art
LEY, E., Health, Physical Education and Recreation
LICHTY, R. W., Econ.
LIEVANO, R., Finance and Management Information Sciences
LINDEKE, R., Industrial Eng.
LINN, M. D., Composition
LIU, Z, Mathematics and Statistics
MCCARTHY, D. A., Education
MCCLURE, B., Psychology
MAGNUSON, V. R., Chemistry
MAIOLO, J. C., English
MARCHESE, R., Sociology—Anthropology
MARTIN, K. A., Theatre
MAYO, D., Philosophy
MERRIER, P., Finance and Management Information Sciences
MILLER, K., Psychology
MILLER-CLEARY, L., English
MIZUKO, M. I., Communications Sciences and Disorders
MORTON, R., Geological Sciences
NEWSTROM, J. W., Management Studies
OJAKANGAS, R. W., Geological Sciences
PASTOR, J., Biology
PETERSON, J. M., Econ.

PIERCE, J. L., Management Studies
POE, D., Chemistry
PROHASKA, J., Biochemistry and Molecular Biology
RAAB, R. L., Econ.
RED HORSE, J. G., American Indian Studies
REGAL, J., Pharmacology
REGAL, R., Mathematics and Statistics
RICHARDS, C., Biology
RIEHL, J. P., Chemistry
RILEY, K., Composition
ROUFS, T. G., Sociology—Anthropology
RUBENFELD, S., Management Studies
SEVERSON, A. R., Anatomy and Cell Biology
SEYBOLT, R., Foreign Languages and Literatures
SHARP, P., Political Science
SHEHADEH, N., Electrical and Computer Eng.
SHEPHARD, M., Social Work
SMITH, D., Sociology—Anthropology
STACHOWITZ, M., Electrical and Computer Eng.
STECH, H., Mathematics and Statistics
STEINNES, D. N., Econ.
STORCH, N. T., History
STUECHER, U., Psychology
SUNNAFRANK, M., Communication
SYDOR, M., Physics
THOMPSON, L. C., Chemistry
TRACHTE, G., Pharmacology
TROLANDER, J., Women's Studies
TROLANDER, J. A., History
TSAI, B., Chemistry
WALLACE, K., Biochemistry and Molecular Biology
WARD, P., Pathology and Laboratory Medicine
WEGREN, T., Music
WOLD, S., Music
WONG, S., Finance and Management Information Sciences
ZEITZ, E., Foreign Languages and Literatures
ZHDANKIN, V., Chemistry
ZIEGLER, R., Medical Microbiology and Immunology

University of Minnesota, Morris

600 East Fourth St, Morris, MN 56267
Telephone: (320) 589-6035
Fax: (320) 589-6051
E-mail: petersdk@mrs.umn.edu
Internet: www.morris.umn.edu
Founded 1959
Academic year: August to May

Chancellor: JACQUELINE JOHNSON
Vice-Chancellor for Academic Affairs: JUDY A. KUECHLE
Vice-Chancellor for Finance: GARY STREI
Vice-Chancellor for Student Affairs: SANDRA OLSON-LOY
Library Dir: LEANN DEAN

Number of teachers: 128
Number of students: 1,927

Divs of Education, Humanities, Science and Mathematics, Social Sciences

PROFESSORS
AHERN, W. H., History
CABRERA, V., Modern Languages
CARLSON, J. A., Music
COTTER, J., Geology
DEMOS, V. P., Sociology
FRENIER, M. D., History
GARARASO, P., Philosophy
GOOCH, V., Biology
GUYOTTE, R., History
HINDS, H. E., Jr, History
HOPPE, D. M., Biology
INGLE, J. S., Art Studio
KISSOCK, C. M., Education
KLINGER, E., Psychology
LEE, J., Political Science
LEE, M.-L., Modern Languages
LOPEZ, A. A., Computer Science

NELLIS, J. G., Art Studio
O'REILLY, M. F., Mathematics
PAYNE, T. R., Theatre Arts
PETERSON, F. W., Art History
PURDY, D. H., English
SCHUMAN, S., English
SUNGUR, E., Mathematics
TOGEAS, J. B., Chemistry
VAN ALSTINE, J. B., Geology

University of Minnesota, Rochester

855 30th Ave, SE, Rochester, MN 55904
Fax: (507) 280-2820
Internet: www.r.umn.edu
Founded 1959
Academic year: August to May
Provost: DAVID L. CARL
Vice-Provost for Health Sciences: CHUCK CHRISTIANSEN

PhD, MA and BA in Business, Education, Fine Arts, Health Sciences, Adult Education/Human Resource Devt, Interpreting, Nursing, Public Health, Social Work, Technology.

UNIVERSITY OF ST THOMAS

2115 Summit Ave, St Paul, MN 55105
Telephone: (651) 962-5000
Fax: (651) 962-6504
E-mail: admissions@stthomas.edu
Internet: www.stthomas.edu
Founded 1885
Academic year: September to May
President: Rev. DENNIS DEASE
Executive Vice-Presidents: Dr MARK DIENHART, Dr THOMAS ROCHON
Director of Admissions: MARLA FRIEDERICHS
Librarian: DANIEL GJELTEN

Library of 458,000 vols, 2,200 periodicals
Number of teachers: 782
Number of students: 11,079

Publications: *Logos: A Journal of Catholic Thought and Culture* (4 a year), *New Hibernia Review* (4 a year)

WILLIAM MITCHELL COLLEGE OF LAW

875 Summit Ave, St Paul, MN 55105
Telephone: (651) 227-9171
Fax: (651) 290-6414
E-mail: admissions@wmitchell.edu
Internet: www.wmitchell.edu
Founded 1900
Private control
Academic year: August to May
President and Dean: ALLEN K. EASLEY
Chief Administrative Officer: MAUREEN E. WARREN
Vice-President (Development and Alumni Relations): MARK J. MARSHALL
Vice-President (Human Resources): MARY GALE
Vice-President (Information Technology Services): JAMES VILLARS
Vice-President (Strategic Marketing): JOHN STEMPER
Dean (Student Affairs and Student Life): DANIEL THOMPSON
Vice-Dean (Academic Affairs): ERIC S. JANUS
Associate Dean, Library Director: ANN L. BATESON
Associate Dean, Multicultural Affairs: ANDRIEL DEES

Number of teachers: 40 full-time faculty, 50 adjunct faculty
Number of students: 1,100

Publication: *William Mitchell Law Review* (4 a year).

ATTACHED INSTITUTE

Tobacco Law Center: 875 Summit Ave, Saint Paul, MN 55105; Exec. Dir DOUG BLANKE

PROFESSORS
BYRNE, A.
COLBERT, B.
DUBE, D.
EASLEY, A.
ERLINDER, P.
HAUGEN, P.
HAYDOCK, R.
HAYNSWORTH, H.
HEIDENREICH, D.
HOGG, J.
IIJIMA, A.
JANUS, E.
JORDAN, M.
JUERGENS, A.
KIRWIN, K.
KLASS, A.
KLEINBERGER, D.
KNAPP, P.
KRISHNAN, J.
KUNZ, C.
LEVINE, R.
LOGAN, W.
MOY, C.
MURPHY, R.
OH, P.
OLIPHANT, R.
PANNIER, R.
PORT, K.
PRINCE, D.
RADSAN, J.
ROBERTS, E.
ROY, D.
SCALLEN, E.
SCHAUMANN, N.
SCHMEDMAN, D.
SONSTENG, J.
STEENSON, M.
VER PLOEG, C.
VER STEEGH, N.
WINER, A.

WINONA STATE UNIVERSITY

Winona, MN 55987
Telephone: (507) 457-5000
Fax: (507) 457-5586
Internet: www.winona.edu
Founded 1858
Academic year: August to May
Part of Minnesota State Colleges and Universities system
President: Dr DARRELL KRUEGER
Vice-Presidents: Dr STEVEN RICHARDSON (Academic), JAMES SCHMIDT (University Relations)
Dean of Library: CHRISTINE CLEMENTS
Library of 262,692 vols, 772,500 microforms
Number of teachers: 350
Number of students: 7,925.

MISSISSIPPI

ALCORN STATE UNIVERSITY

1000 ASU Dr., Alcorn State, MS 39096-7500
Telephone: (601) 877-6100
Fax: (601) 877-2975
Internet: www.alcorn.edu
Founded 1871
Academic year: August to May
Pres.: Dr MALVIN WILLIAMS, Sr
Vice-Pres. for Academic Affairs: Dr NAPOLEON MOSES
Vice-Pres. for Business Affairs: CLAUDINE GEE
Vice-Pres. for Student Affairs: LAPLOSE JACKSON

Vice-Pres. for Institutional Advancement: Dr
FRANKIN JACKSON
Registrar: Dr ALICE GILL
Librarian: JESSIE ARNOLD
Library of 269,858 vols
Number of teachers: 2,237
Number of students: 3,100
Publications: *Alcorn State University Catalogue* (every 2 years), *Weekly Bulletin*, *Alcornite* (annual), *The Alcorn Report* (quarterly).

BELHAVEN COLLEGE

1500 Peachtree St, Jackson, MS 39202
Telephone: (601) 968-5928
Fax: (601) 968-9998
E-mail: admissions@belhaven.edu
Internet: www.belhaven.edu
Founded 1883
Academic year: August to May
Pres.: Dr ROGER PARROTT
Sr Vice-Pres. and Provost: Dr DANIEL C.
FREDERICKS
Vice-Provost and Dean of the Graduate
School (vacant)
Vice-Pres. for Institutional Advancement
and Admin.: KEVIN RUSSELL
Vice-Pres. for Campus Operations: TOM
PHILLIPS
Vice-Pres. for Student Learning: Dr PAMELA
JONES
Chief Financial Officer: VIRGINIA HENDERSON
Dir of Admissions: SUZANNE SULLIVAN
Dir of Library: CRYSTAL STAMPS-ETHERIDGE
Library of 108,042 vols
Number of teachers: 195 (51 full-time, 144
adjunct)
Number of students: 1,883.

BLUE MOUNTAIN COLLEGE

POB 160, Blue Mountain, MS 38610
Telephone: (662) 685-4771
Fax: (662) 685-4776
Internet: www.bmc.edu
Sr liberal arts college for women, with co-
ordinate programme for men in church-
related vocations
Founded 1873
Academic year: August to May
Pres.: BETTYE R. COWARD
Vice-Pres. for Academic Affairs: SHARON
ENZOR
Academic Dean: GARTH E. RUNION
Dir of Admissions: MARIA TEEL
Dean of Students: REBECCA BENNETT
Business Manager: PAM PHARR
Registrar: SHEILA FREEMAN
Dir of Library Services: SUE ETHERIDGE
Library of 60,500 vols
Number of teachers: 30
Number of students: 438.

DELTA STATE UNIVERSITY

Highway 8, Cleveland, MS 38733
Telephone: (662) 846-3000
E-mail: president@deltastate.edu
Internet: www.deltastate.edu
Founded 1924
Pres.: Dr JOHN M. HILPERT
Vice-Pres. for Univ. Relations: Dr MICHELLE
ROBERTS
Provost and Vice-Pres. for Academic Affairs:
Dr BILLY MOREHEAD
Registrar: JOHN ELLIOTT
Dir of Library Services: JEFF SLAGELL
Library of 360,000 vols
Number of teachers: 270
Number of students: 4,000.

JACKSON STATE UNIVERSITY

1400 J. R. Lynch St, Jackson, MS 39217
Telephone: (601) 968-2121
E-mail: jsumedia@jsums.edu
Internet: www.jsums.edu
Founded 1877
Pres.: Dr RONALD MASON, Jr
Chief of Staff: EVOLA BATES
Vice-Pres. for Academic Affairs and Student
Life: VELVELYN B. FOSTER
Sr Vice-Pres. for Finance and Operations:
TROY A. STOVALL
Vice-President for Research and Federal
Relations: Dr FELIX A. OKOJIE
Vice-Pres. for Information Management: Dr
WILLIE G. BROWN
Dir of Libraries: Dr LOU H. SANDERS
Library of 376,566 vols
Number of students: 6,224
Publications: *Blue and White Flash* (quarterly), *Alumni Newsletter* (quarterly)

DEANS

Graduate Dean: Dr BETTYE FLETCHER
School of Education: Dr JOHNNIE MILLS-
JONES
Liberal Arts: Dr DOLLYE ROBINSON
School of Business: Dr GLENDA GLOVER
School of Science and Technology: Dr ABDUL
MOHOMED
School of Social Work: Dr GWENDOLYN PRATER

MAGNOLIA BIBLE COLLEGE

822 S Huntington St, Kosciusko, MS 39090
Telephone: (662) 289-2896
Fax: (662) 289-1850
Internet: www.magnolia.edu
Founded 1976
Private control
Academic year: August to July
Pres.: Dr GARVIS SEMORE
Academic Dean: JOHN F. GARDNER
Dean of Students: SHAWN L. HARDIN
Dir of Admissions: TRAVIS BROWN
Number of teachers: 8
Number of students: 55.

MILLSAPS COLLEGE

1701 North State St, Jackson, MS 39210-
0001
Telephone: (601) 974-1000
E-mail: communications@millsaps.edu
Internet: www.millsaps.edu
Founded 1890
Pres.: Dr FRANCES LUCAS
Dean of Faculty: Dr RICHARD SMITH
Librarian: THOMAS HENDERSON
Library of 209,900 vols
Number of teachers: 92
Number of students: 1,154.

MISSISSIPPI COLLEGE

200 South Capitol St, Clinton, MS 39058
Telephone: (601) 925-3000
Internet: www.mc.edu
Founded 1826
Pres.: Dr LEE ROYCE
Vice-Pres. for Academic Affairs: Dr RON
HOWARD
Vice-Pres. for Admin. and Govt Relations: Dr
STEVE STANFORD
Vice-President for Advancement: DANNY RUT-
LAND
Vice-Pres. for Enrollment Management and
Student Affairs: Dr JIM TURCOTTE
Vice-Pres. for Planning and Assessment: Dr
DEBBIE NORRIS
Chief Financial Officer: DONNA LEWIS
Library Dir: KATHLEEN HUTCHISON

Library of 234,000 vols
Number of teachers: 150 (incl. 75 part-time)
Number of students: 3,800.

MISSISSIPPI STATE UNIVERSITY

POB 5325, Mississippi State, MS 39762
Telephone: (662) 325-2323
Internet: www.msstate.edu
Founded 1878
Pres.: ROBERT H. FOGLESONG
Vice-Pres. for Academic Affairs and Provost:
PETER RABIDEAU
Vice-Pres. for Agriculture, Forestry and
Veterinary Medicine: VANCE WATSON
Vice-Pres. for Student Affairs: WILLIAM
KIBLER
Vice-Pres. for Research and Economic Devt:
KIRK SCHULZ (acting)
Vice-Pres. for Devt and Alumni: JOHN RUSH
Chief of Staff and Chief Financial Officer:
MICHAEL J. MCGREVEY
Registrar: BUTCH STOKES
Dean of Libraries: FRANCES COLEMAN
Library of 873,000 vols, 2,108,000 micro-
forms, 8,464 records and tapes, 7,500
periodicals
Number of teachers: 1,032
Number of students: 16,206

DEANS

Agriculture and Home Econ.: WILLIAM R. FOX
Architecture: JOHN MCRAE
Arts and Sciences: FRANK E. SAAL
Business and Industry: HARVEY S. LEWIS
Continuing Education: BILL SMITH
Education: WILLIAM H. GRAVES
Eng.: WAYNE BENNETT
Forestry: JOHN E. GUNTER
Veterinary Medicine: DWIGHT MERCER

MISSISSIPPI UNIVERSITY FOR WOMEN

Columbus, MS 39701
Telephone: (662) 329-4750
Fax: (662) 329-7297
Internet: www.muw.edu
Founded 1884
First State-supported college exclusively for
women to be founded in the US
Academic year: August to May
Pres.: Dr CLAUDIA LIMBERT (acting)
Provost and Vice-Pres. for Academic Affairs:
TOM RICHARDSON
Vice-Pres. for Student Services: BUCKY WES-
LEY
Vice-Pres. for Finance and Admin.: NORA
MILLER
Vice-Pres. for Institutional Advancement:
GARY BOUSE
Asst to the Pres.: PERRY SANSING
Dir of Library: GAIL GUNTER
Library of 426,900 vols
Number of teachers: 128
Number of students: 3,314

HEADS OF DIVISIONS

Fine and Performing Arts: MICHAEL GARRETT
Business and Communications: ANNE BALAZS
Education and Human Sciences: HAL JEN-
KINS
Health and Kinesiology: JO SPEARMAN
Humanities: BRIDGET PIESCHEL
Nursing: SHEILA ADAMS
Science and Mathematics: NANCY BRYSON
Culinary Arts Institute: SARAH LABENSKY

MISSISSIPPI VALLEY STATE UNIVERSITY

14000 Highway 82, W, Itta Bena, MS 38941-1400

Telephone: (662) 254-9041
E-mail: admsn@mvsu.edu
Internet: www.mvsu.edu

Founded 1946

Pres.: Dr LESTER C. NEWMAN
Vice-Pres. for Academic Affairs: W. ERIC THOMAS
Registrar: DARRELL L. JAMES
Library Dir: Dr ANNIE PAYTON

Library of 125,000 vols
Number of teachers: 112
Number of students: 2,168.

REFORMED THEOLOGICAL SEMINARY

5422 Clinton Blvd, Jackson, MS 39209

Telephone: (601) 923-1600
Fax: (601) 923-1654
E-mail: rts.jackson@rts.edu
Internet: www.rts.edu

Founded 1966
Private control

Chancellor: Dr ROBERT C. CANNADA, Jr
Pres. (Jackson Campus): Dr GUY RICHARDSON
Chief Devt Officer: Rev. LYN PEREZ
Registrar: Dr PAUL LONG, Jr
Library Dir: Rev. KENNETH ELLIOTT

Library of 150,000 vols
Number of teachers: 105
Number of students: 600.

BRANCH CAMPUSES

Atlanta Campus

3585 Northside Parkway, NW, Atlanta, GA 30327-2309

Telephone: (404) 995-8484
Fax: (404) 995-8997
E-mail: admissions.atlanta@rts.edu

Founded 1906

Exec. Vice-Pres. of Extensions: JOHN T. SOWELL.

Boca Raton Campus

2400 Yamato Rd, Boca Raton, FL 33431

Telephone: (561) 994-5000
Fax: (561) 995-5005
E-mail: admissions.boca@rts.edu

Exec. Dir: Dr BUZ McNUTT.

Charlotte Campus

2101 Carmel Rd, Charlotte, NC 28226-6399

Telephone: (704) 366-5066
Fax: (704) 366-9295
E-mail: rts.charlotte@rts.edu

Founded 1992

Pres.: Dr RIC CANNADA
Vice-Pres. for Devt: CHARLIE DUNN
Registrar: ANGELA BOYD
Library Dir: Rev. KENNETH McMULLEN

Library of 46,000 vols.

Orlando Campus

1231 Reformation Dr., Oviedo, FL 32765

Telephone: (407) 366-9493
Fax: (407) 366-9425
E-mail: rts.orlando@rts.edu

Founded 1989

Pres.: Dr FRANK A. JAMES, III
Vice-Pres. for Devt: JOHNNY MASTRY
Registrar: LANNY CONLEY
Library Dir: JOHN MUETHER

Library of 75,000 vols.

Virtual Campus

2101 Carmel Rd, Charlotte, NC 28226

Telephone: (704) 366-4853
Fax: (704) 366-9295
E-mail: distance.education@rts.edu

Founded 1998

Pres.: Dr ANDREW J. PETERSON.

Washington DC Campus

12500 Fairlakes Circle, Suite 325, Fairfax, VA 22033

Telephone: (703) 222-7871
Fax: (703) 738-7389
E-mail: admissions.washington@rts.edu

Founded 1997

Exec. Dir: Dr FRANK E. YOUNG, HUGH WHELCHEL
Number of students: 250.

RUST COLLEGE

150 Rust Ave, Holly Springs, MS 38635

Telephone: (662) 252-8000
Fax: (662) 252-6107
E-mail: admissions@rustcollege.edu
Internet: www.rustcollege.edu

Founded 1866
Private control
Academic year: August to April

Pres.: Dr DAVID L. BECKLEY
Vice-Pres.: Dr ISHMELL H. EDWARDS
Academic Dean: Dr MARIAN Y. TALLEY
Dean for Student Affairs: ERIC W. JACKSON
Registrar: CLARENCE E. SMITH
Head Librarian: ANITA W. MOORE

Library of 120,000 vols
Number of teachers: 59
Number of students: 1,029.

SOUTHEASTERN BAPTIST COLLEGE

4229 Highway 15, N, Laurel, MS 39440

Telephone: (601) 426-6346
Fax: (601) 426-6347
E-mail: info@southeasternbaptist.edu
Internet: www.southeasternbaptist.edu

Founded 1948
Private control
Academic year: August to July

Pres.: MEDRISK SAVELL
Librarian: AMY HINTON
Number of students: 63

Areas of study: business admin. and management, gen. studies, Bible studies.

TOUGALOO COLLEGE

500 West Country Line Rd, Tougaloo, MS 39174

Telephone: (601) 977-7700
Fax: (601) 977-7739
Internet: www.tougaloo.edu

Founded 1869

Private liberal arts college, affiliated with Disciples of Christ and United Church of Christ

Pres.: Dr BEVERLEY WADE HOGAN
Vice-Pres. for Academic Affairs, and Provost: Dr ABDUL TURAY
Vice-Pres. for Facilities Management: KELLE MENOGAN, Sr
Vice-Pres. for Institutional Advancement: EDWINA HARRIS HAMBY
Vice-Pres. for Finance and Admin.: Dr CYNTHIA MELVIN

Library of 139,600 vols
Number of teachers: 73
Number of students: 916

Publications: *Tougaloo News* (3 a year), *The Harambee* (monthly).

UNIVERSITY OF MISSISSIPPI

POB 1848, University, MS 38677-1848

Telephone: (662) 915-7211
Fax: (662) 915-7486
E-mail: ipdebt@olemiss.edu
Internet: www.olemiss.edu

The School of Medicine, the School of Dentistry, the School of Nursing and the School of Health Related Professions are constituents of the Univ. of Mississippi Medical Center, located in Jackson, Mississippi

Founded 1844

Chancellor: ROBERT C. KHAYAT
Pres. and Chief Exec. Officer of the Univ. Foundation: WENDELL WEAKLEY
Provost, and Vice-Chancellor for Academic Affairs: CAROLYN STATON
Vice-Chancellor for Research and Sponsored Programs: ALICE M. CLARK
Vice-Chancellor for Finance and Admin.: LARRY SPARKS
Vice-Chancellor for Student Life: Dr THOMAS D. WALLACE (acting)
Registrar: CHARLOTTE FANT (acting)
Dean of Libraries: JULIA ROLES

Library of 1,268,000 vols
Number of teachers: 595
Number of students: 11,000

Publications: *Catalogues* (Graduate School), *Law School, Medical Center, Summer Session, Undergraduate*

DEANS

Accountancy: Dr JAMES W. DAVIS
Business Admin.: Dr RANDY BOXX
Education: Dr JIM CHAMBLESS
Eng.: Dr ALLIE M. SMITH
Graduate School: Dr MICHAEL R. DINGERSON
Law School: Dr SAMUEL M. DAVIS
Liberal Arts: Dr H. DALE ABADIE
Pharmacy: Dr KENNETH B. ROBERTS

UNIVERSITY OF MISSISSIPPI MEDICAL CENTER

2500 North State St, Jackson, MS 39216

Telephone: (601) 984-1080
Fax: (601) 984-1079
E-mail: bbishop@registrar.umsmed.edu
Internet: www.umc.edu

Founded 1955
State control

Chancellor: ROBERT KHAYAT
Vice-Chancellor for Health Affairs: DANIEL W. JONES
Assoc. Vice-Chancellor for Admin. Affairs: DAVID POWE
Associate Vice-Chancellor for Academic Affairs: Dr HELEN TURNER
Assoc. Vice-Chancellor for Research: Dr JOHN E. HALL
Registrar: BARBARA WESTERFIELD
Library Dir: ADA M. SELTZER

Number of teachers: 587
Number of students: 1,778 (603 undergraduate, 1,175 graduate)

DEANS

School of Dentistry: Dr JAMES R. HUPP
School of Health Related Professions: JACK R. GORDY
School of Medicine: Dr A. WALLACE CONERLY, Sr
School of Nursing: Dr ANNE PEIRCE
School of Graduate Studies: Dr ING K. HO

UNIVERSITY OF SOUTHERN MISSISSIPPI

118 College Dr., POB 5001, Hattiesburg, MS 39406-0001

Telephone: (601) 266-5001

Fax: (602) 266-5756
E-mail: shelby.f.thames@usm.edu
Internet: www.usm.edu
Founded 1910

Pres.: Dr SHELBY F. THAMES
Provost of Hattiesburg Campus: DARRELL JAY
Provost of Gulf Coast Campus
Vice-President for Research and Economic Devt: Dr CECIL D. BURGE
Assoc. Vice-Pres. for Research and Economic Devt: JULIAN ALLEN
Vice-Pres. for Student Affairs: JOSEPH S. PAUL
Chief Financial Officer: JOE MORGAN
Dean of Univ. Admissions: Dr KRISTI MOTTER
Univ. Librarian: EDWARD MCCORMACK

Library of 1,327,628 vols
Number of teachers: 687
Number of students: 14,810

Publications: *Journal of Mississippi History, Mississippi Review, Southern Quarterly*

DEANS

Arts and Letters: Dr ELLIOTT A. POOD
Business and Economic Devt: Dr HAROLD DOTY
Education and Psychology: Dr W. LEE PIERCE
Health: Dr PETER FOS
Science and Technology: Dr REX FRANKLIN GANDY
Honors College: Dr KENNETH PANTON
Graduate Studies: Dr BRADLEY G. BOND

WESLEY COLLEGE

POB 1070, 111 Wesley Circle, Florence, MS 39073
Telephone: (601) 845-2265
Fax: (601) 845-2266
E-mail: admissions@wesleycollege.edu
Internet: www.wesleycollege.com

Founded 1944 as Congregational Methodist Bible School; present name 1975
Private control

Pres.: LANCE SHERER

Number of teachers: 4
Number of students: 105

Areas of study: pastoral ministries, youth ministries, Christian education, missions, Christian ministries, biblical literature, gen. education.

WILLIAM CAREY COLLEGE

498 Tuscan Ave, Hattiesburg, MS 39401-5499
Telephone: (601) 318-6051
Fax: (601) 318-6454
Internet: www.wmcarey.edu
Founded 1906

Chancellor: JAMES W. EDWARDS
Pres. and Chief Exec.: R. TOMMY KING
Vice-Pres. for Academic Affairs: CLOYD L. EZELL, Jr
Vice-Pres. for Institutional Effectiveness and Planning: BENNIE R. CROCKETT, Jr
Vice-Pres. for Business Affairs: JOE RILEY
Vice-Pres. for Advancement: ARGILE A. SMITH, Jr
Vice-Pres. for Student Services: BRENDA F. WALDRIP
Dean of Enrollment Management: WILLIAM N. CURRY
Registrar: GAYLE KNIGHT
Dir of Library Services (vacant): PATRICIA H. FURR

Library of 127,000 resources
Number of teachers: 80 full-time
Number of students: 2,172.

MISSOURI

AQUINAS INSTITUTE OF THEOLOGY

3642 Lindell Blvd, St Louis, MO 63108
Telephone: (314) 977-3869
Fax: (314) 977-7225
E-mail: aquinas@slu.edu
Internet: www.ai.edu
Founded 1925
Private control
Academic year: August to May

President: Dr CHARLES E. BOUCHARD
Vice-President and Academic Dean: Dr DIANE KENNEDY
Registrar: SHEILA BRENNAN
Librarian: SALLY GUNTER

Number of teachers: 35
Number of students: 145 (full-time).

ASSEMBLIES OF GOD THEOLOGICAL SEMINARY

1435 N Glenstone Ave, Springfield, MO 65802
Telephone: (417) 268-1000
Fax: (417) 268-1001
E-mail: agts@agts.edu
Internet: www.agts.edu

Founded 1972 as Assemblies of God Graduate School; present name 1984
Private control
Academic year: September to July

Number of teachers: 15
Number of students: 550

President: Dr BYRON D. KLAUS.

A. T. STILL UNIVERSITY OF HEALTH SCIENCES

800 W Jefferson St, Kirksville, MO 63501
Telephone: (660) 626-2391
Fax: (660) 626-2672
E-mail: admissions@atsu.edu
Internet: www.atsu.edu

Founded 1892 as Kirksville College of Osteopathic Medicine; present name 1993
Private control
Academic year: August to June

President: Dr JAMES J. MCGOVERN
Vice-President and Dean of Students: RONALD R. GABER
Vice-President and General Counsel: HENRY R. SETSER
Vice-President (Institutional Advancement): RANDY ROGERS (acting)
Vice-President (Medical Affairs) and Dean: Dr PHILIP C. SLOCUM
Vice-President (Research, Grants, and Information Systems): Dr JOHN HEARD
Provost, ATSU Mesa: Dr CRAIG M. PHELPS
Dean, Arizona School of Dentistry and Oral Health: Dr JACK DILLENBERG
Dean, Arizona School of Health Sciences: Dr RANDY DANIELSEN
Dean, School of Health Management: Dr JON PERSAVICH
Library Director: JEAN SIDWELL

Library of 80,000 vols
Number of teachers: 100
Number of students: 1,328.

AVILA COLLEGE

11901 Wornall Rd, Kansas City, MO 64145
Telephone: (816) 942-8400
Fax: (816) 942-3362
E-mail: admissions@mail.avila.edu
Internet: www.avila.edu
Founded 1916

President: THOMAS F. GORDON
Registrar: TONI BINK
Librarian: KATHLEEN FINEGAN

Library of 74,658 vols
Number of teachers: 160 (full- and part-time)
Number of students: 1,600

Publication: *The Scop.*

BAPTIST BIBLE COLLEGE AND GRADUATE SCHOOL

628 E Kearney, Springfield, MO 65803
Telephone: (417) 268-6000
Fax: (417) 268-6694
Internet: www.baptist.edu
Founded 1950
Private control
Academic year: August to May

President: Dr MIKE RANDALL
Vice-President: Dr RICK CARTER
Academic Dean: Dr RUSSELL DELL
Dean of Students: RAY ADAMS
Registrar: Dr JOSEPH GLEASON

Library of 52,000 vols
Number of teachers: 28
Number of students: 805 (746 undergraduate, 59 graduate)

HEADS OF DEPARTMENTS

Business: JULIE BECK
Church Ministries: Dr STEVE LAWRENCE
Elementary Education: Dr CYNTHIA EVANS
Missions: DAVID LINGO
Music: Dr JACK HENRY
Pastoral Studies: Dr WILLIAM DOWELL

CALVARY BIBLE COLLEGE AND THEOLOGICAL SEMINARY

15800 Calvary Rd, Kansas City, MO 64147-1341
Telephone: (816) 322-0110
Fax: (816) 331-4474
E-mail: admissions@calvary.edu
Internet: www.calvary.edu

Founded 1961 following merger of Kansas City Bible College (f. 1932) and Midwest Bible College (f. 1938); Calvary Theological Seminary f. 1966 as Graduate Division of Calvary Bible College; present name 1992
Private control
Academic year: August to May

President: Dr ELWOOD CHIPCHASE
Vice-President and College Academic Dean: Dr JAMES CLARK
Seminary Academic Dean: Dr THOMAS BAURAIN
Registrar: STAN DERKSEN
Librarian: SUZANNE GUINN

Library of 53,500 vols
Number of teachers: 28
Number of students: 289 (214 undergraduate, 75 graduate)

HEADS OF DEPARTMENTS

Biblical Counseling: Rev. JAMES BRADEN, Dr JAMES CLARK (Seminary)
Biblical Education: TIMOTHY SMITH
Education: Dr TOM BONINE
Missions: LEM MORGAN
Music: PAUL VANDER MEY
Pastoral Studies: Dr KEITH MILLER

CENTRAL BIBLE COLLEGE

3000 N Grant Avenue, Springfield, MO 65803
Telephone: (417) 833-2551
Fax: (417) 833-0854
E-mail: info@cbcag.edu
Internet: www.cbcag.edu
Founded 1922
Private control (General Council of the Assemblies of God)
Academic year: August to April

President: Rev. M. WAYNE BENSON

Vice-President (Academic Affairs): Dr CHARLES A. ESTRIDGE

Vice-President (Student Development): Rev. GARY R. BRUEGMAN

Vice-President (Operations): ROBERT W. P. PATTERSON

Vice-President (College Advancement): Rev. RICHARD L. HARDY

Librarian: LYNN ANDERSON

Library of 156,000 vols
Number of teachers: 39
Number of students: 805

HEADS OF DEPARTMENTS

Biblical Education: Dr FRED HALTOM
Church Ministries: Rev. JIM P. VIGIL
General Education: SHARON ROONEY
Music: Rev. ROGER C. THOMASSEN

CENTRAL CHRISTIAN COLLEGE OF THE BIBLE

911 E Urbandale Drive, Moberly, MO 65270
Telephone: (660) 263-3900
Fax: (660) 263-3936
E-mail: iwant2be@cccb.edu
Internet: www.cccb.edu

Founded 1957
Private control

President: Dr RUSSELL N. JAMES, III
Chancellor: LLOYD M. PELFREY
Academic Dean: DAVID B. FINCHER
Dean of Students: WILLIAM P. WALTON
Registrar: CHERYL RATZLAFF
Librarian: PATTY AGEE

Number of teachers: 24
Number of students: 150

Areas of study: biblical studies, general studies, professional studies.

CENTRAL METHODIST UNIVERSITY

Fayette, MO 65248
Telephone: (660) 248-3391
Internet: www.centralmethodist.edu

Founded 1854
Academic year: August to May

President: Dr MARIANNE INMAN
Dean of the College: Dr ROGER KUGLER
Librarian: RITA GULSTAD

Library of 85,000 vols
Number of teachers: 60
Number of students: 1,400

Publications: *Inscape, The Talon, Collegian.*

CENTRAL MISSOURI STATE UNIVERSITY

Warrensburg, MO 64093
Telephone: (660) 543-4111
Fax: (660) 543-8517
Internet: www.cmsu.edu
Academic year: August to May

Founded 1871

President: Dr AARON PODOLEFSKY
Provost: Dr GEORGE WILSON
Vice-Presidents: Dr PAUL PAGE (University Advancement), WALT HICKLIN (Student Affairs)
Director of Administration: MARTHA ALBIN
Librarian: MOLLIE DINWIDDIE

Library of 1,300,000 vols, 2,500 newspaper and periodical subscriptions, 829,100 microforms
Number of teachers: 430
Number of students: 10,100

DEANS

College of Arts and Sciences: Dr VIRGINIA WHEELESS
College of Applied Science and Technology: Dr ALICE GREIFE

Harmon College of Business Administration: Dr JACK ELFRINK
College of Education and Human Services: Dr RICK SLUDER
School of Graduate Studies: Dr NOVELLA PERRIN
Honors College: Dr PETER VISCUSI

CLEVELAND CHIROPRACTIC COLLEGE

6401 Rockhill Rd, Kansas City, MO 64131
Telephone: (816) 501-0100
Fax: (816) 361-0272
E-mail: kc.admissions@cleveland.edu
Internet: www.cleveland.edu

Founded 1922 as Central Chiropractic College; present name 1924
Private control
Academic year: September to August

President: Dr CARL S. CLEVELAND, III
Executive Vice-President and Chief Academic Officer: Dr DONNA BROADSTREET
Dean of Instruction: Dr RUTH SANDEFUR
Registrar (vacant)
Library Director: MARCIA M. THOMAS

Library of 14,800 vols
Number of students: 502

HEADS OF DEPARTMENTS

Basic Sciences: Dr DAVID L. DEUPREE
Chiropractic Sciences: Dr THOMAS K. NICHOLS
Clinical Sciences: Dr MURIEL M. PERILLAT
Diagnostic Sciences: Dr BRYAN M. BOND

COLLEGE OF THE OZARKS

Point Lookout, MO 65726
Telephone: (417) 334-6411
Fax: (417) 335-2618
E-mail: admiss4@cofo.edu
Internet: www.cofo.edu

Founded 1906
Academic year: August to May

President: Dr JERRY C. DAVIS
Vice-President: Dr HOWELL KEETER
Dean of the Work Program: Dr MAYBURN DAVIDSON
Dean of Institutional Advancement: Dr RODNEY ARNOLD
Dean of the College: Dr MARILYN GRAVES
Dean of Students: Dr CHRIS LARSEN

Library of 119,000 vols
Number of teachers: 115
Number of students: 1,348

Publication: *Ozark Visitor* (quarterly).

COLUMBIA COLLEGE

1001 Rogers Street, Columbia, MO 65216
Telephone: (573) 875-8700
Fax: (573) 875-7209
E-mail: admissions@ccis.edu
Internet: www.ccis.edu

Founded 1851 as Christian Female College; present name 1970
Private control
Academic year: August to July

President: Dr GERALD T. BROUDER
Vice-President and Dean for Academic Affairs: Dr TERRY B. SMITH
Library Director: JANET CARUTHERS

Library of 80,000 vols
Number of teachers: 51
Number of students: 2,100

Areas of study: art, business administration, computer and mathematical sciences, criminal justice administration and social work education, history and social sciences, humanities, science.

23 Extension campuses throughout the United States.

CONCEPTION SEMINARY COLLEGE

POB 502, 37174 State Highway V V, Conception, MO 64433-0502
Telephone: (660) 944-3105
Fax: (660) 944-2800
E-mail: communications@conception.edu
Internet: www.conception.edu

Founded 1886 as College of New Engelberg; present name 1972
Private control (Conception Abbey)

President/Rector: Rev. BENEDICT NEENAN
Library Director: Bro. THOMAS SULLIVAN

Number of teachers: 32
Number of students: 80.

CONCORDIA SEMINARY

801 DeMun Ave, St Louis, MO 63105
Telephone: (314) 505-7000
Fax: (314) 505-7001
E-mail: csladmis@aol.com
Internet: www.csl.edu

Founded 1839
Private control (Lutheran Church—Missouri Synod)
Academic year: September to May

President: Dr JOHN F. JOHNSON
Vice-President (Academic Affairs): Dr ANDREW H. BARTELT
Vice-President (Student Life): LARRY W. ROCKEMANN
Registrar: WILLIAM W. CARR, Jr
Director of Library Services: DAVID O. BERGER

Library of 230,000 vols
Number of teachers: 55
Number of students: 534 (full-time)

HEADS OF DEPARTMENTS

Exegetical Theology: Dr ANDREW H. BARTELT
Historical Theology: Dr ROBERT L. ROSIN
Practical Theology: Dr RICHARD H. WARNECK
Systematic Theology: Dr CHARLES P. ARAND

COVENANT THEOLOGICAL SEMINARY

12330 Conway Rd, St Louis, MO 63141
Telephone: (314) 434-4044
Fax: (314) 434-4819
Internet: www.covenantseminary.edu

Founded 1956
Private control (Presbyterian Church in America)
Academic year: September to May

President: Dr BRYAN CHAPELL
Vice-President (Academics): Dr DONALD GUTHRIE
Dean of Students: Dr MARK DALBEY
Dean of Faculty: Dr DANIEL M. DORIANI
Library Director: JAMES C. PAKALA

Library of 68,000 vols
Number of teachers: 42
Number of students: 435 (full-time).

CULVER-STOCKTON COLLEGE

One College Hill, Canton, MO 63435
Telephone: (573) 288-6541
Fax: (573) 288-6616
Internet: www.culver.edu

Founded 1853
Academic year: August to May

President: Dr WILLIAM L. FOX
Registrar: MARJORIE ELLISON
Dean of Academic Affairs: Dr R. JOSEPH DIEKER
Librarian: SHARON UPCHURCH

Library of 164,266 vols
Number of teachers: 50
Number of students: 855
Publications: *Catalog* (annually), *Chronicle* (4 a year), *Ex Scientia* (annually), *Harmony* (literary magazine, annually).

DRURY UNIVERSITY

Springfield, MO 65802
Telephone: (417) 873-7879
Fax: (417) 873-7821
E-mail: drury@drury.edu
Internet: www.drury.edu
Founded 1873
President: Dr JOHN SELLARS
Dean of the College: Dr STEPHEN H. GOOD
Registrar: GALE BOUTWELL
Librarian: STEVE STOAN
Library of 160,000 vols
Number of teachers: 118 full-time equivalent
Number of students: 2,467 full-time equivalent.

EDEN THEOLOGICAL SEMINARY

475 E Lockwood Ave, St Louis, MO 63119-3192
Telephone: (314) 961-3627
Fax: (314) 918-2535
E-mail: dwindler@eden.edu
Internet: www.eden.edu
Private control
President: Rev. Dr DAVID M. GREENHAW
Vice-President (Administration): MILTON W. MATTHEWS
Vice-President (Development): DAVID P. HARKINS
Academic Dean: Rev. Dr JORETTA L. MARSHALL
Dean of Students: Rev. Dr HOLLY S. NELSON
Registrar: CHRIS DAVIS
Library Director: LAURA REIN
Library of 86,000 vols
Number of teachers: 24
Number of students: 131 (full-time).

EVANGEL UNIVERSITY OF THE ASSEMBLIES OF GOD

1111 N. Glenstone, Springfield, MO 65802
Telephone: (417) 865-2811
Fax: (417) 865-9599
Internet: www.evangel.edu
Founded 1955
Academic year: September to May
President: Dr ROBERT H. SPENCE
Vice-Presidents: Dr GLENN BERNET (Academic Affairs), GEORGE CRAWFORD (Business), DAVID BUNDRICK (Student Development), JIM WILLIAMS (Institutional Advancement)
Library of 120,000 vols
Number of students: 1,525
Publication: *Vision* (College magazine, 4 a year).

FONTBONNE UNIVERSITY

6800 Wydown Blvd, St Louis, MO 63105
Telephone: (314) 862-3456
Fax: (314) 889-1451
Internet: www.fontbonne.edu
Founded 1917
President: DENNIS GOLDEN
Vice-President for Academic and Student Affairs: JUDITH MEYER
Associate Vice-President for Student Affairs: RANDI WILSON
Vice-President for Advancement: VICKI FRANK

Vice-President for Finance and Administration: GARY ZACK
Vice-President for Enrollment and Management: JOHN SEVELAND
Registrar: MAZIE MOORE
Librarian: JOHN GRESHAM
Library of 90,020 vols, 510 periodicals
Number of teachers: 105 (45 full-time, 60 part-time)
Number of students: 1,990
Publication: *Fontbonne University Magazine* (3 a year)

HEADS OF DEPARTMENTS
Fine Arts: CATHERINE CONNOR-TALASEK
Business Administration: GREG TAYLOR
Communication Disorders: GALE RICE
Education/Special Education: BILL FREEMAN
Literature and Language Arts: BEN MOORE
Human and Environmental Sciences: JANET CRITES
Mathematics and Computer Science: BETH NEWTON
Biological and Physical Sciences: TOMMIE FRISON
Philosophy, Religion and Social Science: DONALD P. BURGO

HANNIBAL-LAGRANGE COLLEGE

2800 Palmyra Rd, Hannibal, MO 63401
Telephone: (573) 221-3675
Fax: (573) 221-6594
Internet: www.hlg.edu
Private control
President: Dr WOODROW W. BURT
Vice-President (Academic Affairs): Dr GARRY M. BRELAND
Vice-President (Business and Student Affairs): TOM R. DUGGER
Vice-President (Collegiate Affairs): Dr L. THOMAS HUFTY
Vice-President (Enrollment Management): RAYMOND W. CARTY
Vice-President (Institutional Advancement): Dr CHARLES W. STEWART, III
Registrar: DARLA THOMASON
Library Director: JULIE A. ANDRESEN
Library of 118,000 vols
Number of teachers: 46
Number of students: 1,150

HEADS OF DEPARTMENTS
Christian Studies: Dr ROBERT D. BERGEN
Education: B. JANE SCHAFER
Humanities: Dr JOHN D. BOOTH
Natural Science and Mathematics: Dr DAVID C. ZIEGLER
Nursing and Allied Health: SENDA C. GUERTZGEN
Social Science: BETTY S. RHOADS

HARRIS-STOWE STATE UNIVERSITY

3026 Laclede Ave, St Louis, MO 63103
Telephone: (314) 340-3380
Fax: (314) 340-3399
E-mail: admissions@hssu.edu
Internet: www.hssu.edu
Founded 1857; present name and status 2005
President: Dr HENRY GIVENS, Jr
Director of Admissions: Mrs VALERIE BEESON
Vice-President for Academic Affairs: Dr PATRICIA NICHOLS
Vice-President for Business and Financial Services: ROCHELLE TILGHMAN
Vice-President for Institutional Support and Enrollment Management: Dr JAMES GORHAM
Vice-President for Student Affairs: Dr PATRICIA NICHOLS
Registrar: Mrs MARY K. JONES
Librarian: MARTIN KNORR
Library of 87,000 vols

Number of teachers: 82
Number of students: 1,980
Publication: *The Harris-Stowe Vision* (every 6 months).

KANSAS CITY ART INSTITUTE

4415 Warwick Blvd, Kansas City, MO 64111-1874
Telephone: (816) 472-4852
E-mail: info@kcai.edu
Internet: www.kcai.edu
Founded 1885
Academic year: August to May
Four-year college of art and design
President: KATHLEEN COLLINS
Executive Vice-President for Administration: RON CATTELINO
Vice-President for Enrollment Management: LARRY STONE
Vice-President for Planning and Strategic Initiatives: LANCE CARLSON
Library of 33,000 vols and 60,000 slides
Number of students: 600.

KANSAS CITY UNIVERSITY OF MEDICINE AND BIOSCIENCES

1750 Independence Ave, Kansas City, MO 64106-1453
Telephone: (816) 283-2000
Fax: (816) 283-2484
E-mail: admissions@kcumb.edu
Internet: www.kcumb.edu
Founded 1916 as Kansas City College of Osteopathy and Surgery; as University of Health Sciences 1980; present name and structure 2004
Private control
Academic year: August to July
President and CEO: Dr KAREN L. PLETZ
Vice-President (Academic Affairs) and Dean: Dr SANDRA K. WILLSIE
Director of Library Information Center: MARILYN J. DeGEUS
Number of teachers: 48
Number of students: 900.

KENRICK GLENNON SEMINARY

5200 Glennon Drive, St Louis, MO 63119
Telephone: (314) 644-0266
Fax: (314) 644-3079
E-mail: frrice@kenrick.edu
Internet: www.kenrick.edu
Founded 1931
Liberal arts college exclusively for candidates for Roman Catholic priesthood
Academic year: August to May
President: Rev. Msgr GEORGE J. LUCAS
Director: Rev. EDWARD M. RICE
Librarian: Dr ANDREW J. SOPKO
Library of 75,000 vols
Number of students: 24.

LINCOLN UNIVERSITY

820 Chestnut St, Jefferson City, MO 65102
Telephone: (573) 681-5000
Fax: (573) 681-5566
E-mail: president@lincolnu.edu
Internet: www.lincolnu.edu
Founded 1866
Academic year: August to July
President: Dr CAROLYN R. MAHONEY
Vice-President for Academic Affairs and Provost: Dr JOE L. SIMMONS
Vice-President for Administration and Finance: CURTIS CREAGH
Vice-President for Student Affairs and Enrollment Management: CONSTANCE WILLIAMS

Vice-President for University Advancement: IDA SIMON
Director of University Relations: BRIAN GRAVES
Librarian: ELIZABETH WILSON
Library of 164,800 vols
Number of teachers: 179
Number of students: 3,347
Publications: *Lincoln Clarion* (6 a year), *Alumni-Line* (3 a year)

DEANS

School of Agriculture and Natural Sciences: Dr MICHAEL HEARD
College of Business and Professional Studies: Dr KOJO QUARTEY
College of Liberal Arts, Education and Journalism: Dr PATRICK HENRY
School of Graduate Studies and Continuing Education: Dr LINDA BICKEL

LINDENWOOD UNIVERSITY

209 S. Kingshighway, St Charles, MO 63301
Telephone: (314) 949-2000
E-mail: admissions@lindenwood.edu
Internet: www.lindenwood.edu
President: DENNIS C. SPELLMANN
Provost: ARLENE TAICH
Dean of the College and Dean of Admissions and Financial Aid: DAVID R. WILLIAMS
Dean of Students: JOHN CREER
Librarian: JAN CZAPLA
Library of 132,000 books and pamphlets
Number of teachers: 100
Number of students: 5,000
Publication: *LindenWorld*.

LOGAN COLLEGE OF CHIROPRACTIC

1851 Schoettler Rd, POB 1065, Chesterfield, MO 63006-1065
Telephone: (636) 227-2100
Fax: (636) 207-2424
E-mail: loganadm@logan.edu
Internet: www.logan.edu
Founded 1935
Private control
Academic year: September to April
President: Dr GEORGE A. GOODMAN
Vice-President (Academic Affairs): Dr WILLIAM L. RAMSEY
Vice-President (Administrative Affairs): SHARON K. KEHRER
Vice-President (Institutional Advancement): MICHAEL J. REILLY
Vice-President (Student Enrollment): Dr PATRICK M. BROWNE
Library of 16,000 vols
Number of students: 854

HEADS OF DEPARTMENTS

Basic Science: Dr VINOD K. ANAND
Chiropractic Science: Dr GARY P. CASPER
Clinical Science: Dr RICHARD W. CRANWELL
Health Center: Dr GLENN BUB (Chief of Staff)
Research: Dr DENNIS NOSCO (Director)

MARYVILLE UNIVERSITY OF SAINT LOUIS

13550 Conway Rd, St Louis, MO 63141-7299
Telephone: (800) 627-9855
Fax: (314) 542-9085
E-mail: admissions@maryville.edu
Internet: www.maryville.edu
Founded 1872
Academic year: August to May
President: Dr KEITH LOVIN
Vice-President for Planning, Information and Institutional Research and Special Assistant to the President: Dr EDGAR RASCH

Vice-President for Academic and Student Affairs and Dean of the Faculty: Dr LORRAINE RODRIGUES-FISHER
Vice-President for Institutional Advancement: LARRY WILLIAMSON
Vice-President for Administration and Finance: Dr LARRY HAYS
Vice-President for Enrollment: Dr BETH TRIPLETT
Registrar: MICHELLE ZIOLKOWSKI
Librarian: Dr EUGENIA McKEE
Library of 269,764 items
Number of teachers: 283
Number of students: 3,055

DEANS

School of Liberal Arts and Professional Programs: Dr EDWARD PALM
John E. Simon School of Business: Dr PAMELA HORWITZ
School of Education: Dr KATHE RASCH
School of Health Professions: Dr LANCE CARLUCCIO

MIDWESTERN BAPTIST THEOLOGICAL SEMINARY

5001 N Oak Trafficway, Kansas City, MO 64118-4697
Telephone: (816) 414-3700
Fax: (816) 414-3799
E-mail: admissions@mbts.edu
Internet: www.mbts.edu
Founded 1957
Private control (Southern Baptist Convention)
Academic year: August to July
President: Dr R. PHILIP ROBERTS
Vice-President (Academic Affairs) and Academic Dean of the Faculty: Dr MALCOLM B. YARNELL, III
Vice-President (Student Development): Dr ALAN BRANCH
Vice-President (Institutional Advancement): W. MICHAEL WILSON
Librarian: J. CRAIG KUBIC
Library of 115,000 vols
Number of teachers: 30
Number of students: 253 (full-time).

MISSOURI BAPTIST UNIVERSITY

1 College Park Drive, Creve Coeur, MO 63141
Telephone: (314) 434-1115
Fax: (314) 434-7596
E-mail: admissions@mobap.edu
Internet: www.mobap.edu
Founded 1957 as campus extension of Hannibal-LaGrange College; present name 1999
Private control
Academic year: August to April
President: Dr R. ALTON LACEY
Provost/Vice-President (Academic Affairs): Dr ARLEN R. DYKSTRA
Vice-President (Institutional Advancement): KEITH ROSS
Dean of Students: Dr ANDY CHAMBERS (acting)
Director of Admissions: THOMAS SMITH
Director of Library Services: NITSA HINDELEH
Number of teachers: 151
Number of students: 2,740 (all campuses)

HEADS OF DEPARTMENTS

Business: BRENDA D. BRADFORD
Education: JAMES FRENCH
Fine Arts: Dr LADD FASZOLD
Humanities: Dr CURTIS K. McCLAIN, Jr
Natural and Health Sciences: Dr J. B. BOREN
Social and Behavioral Sciences: Dr CORDELL SCHULTEN

BRANCH CAMPUSES

Franklin County Extension: 960H St Clair Plaza Drive, St Clair, MO 63077; tel. (636) 629-4111; fax (636) 629-8055; e-mail fc@mobap.edu; Dean Dr ROBERTA ROSS-FISHER.

Jefferson College Extension: 1000 Viking Drive, Hillsboro, MO 63050; tel. (636) 797-3000 ext. 242; fax (636) 789-5103; e-mail jc@mobap.edu.

Troy/Wentzville Campus: 75 College Campus Drive, Moscow Mills, MO 63362; tel. (636) 366-4363; fax (636) 356-4119; e-mail tw@mobap.edu; Dean MARY SUE THOMPSON.

MISSOURI SOUTHERN STATE UNIVERSITY–JOPLIN

3950 E Newman Rd, Joplin, MO 64801-1595
Telephone: (417) 625-9399
Fax: (417) 659-4497
E-mail: admissions@mssu.edu
Internet: www.mssu.edu
Founded 1937 as Joplin Junior College; as Missouri Southern State College 1965; present name and status 2003
State control
Academic year: June to May
President: Dr JULIO S. LEÓN
Vice-President (Academic Affairs): Dr J LARRY MARTIN
Vice-President (Business Affairs): Dr THERESA A. AGEE
Vice-President (Lifelong Learning): Dr JACK G. SPURLIN
Registrar: SANDRA GIESON
Library Director: WENDY L. McGRANE
Number of teachers: 289
Number of students: 5,899

DEANS

School of Arts and Sciences: Dr JOHN P. MESSICK
School of Business Administration: JAMES M. GRAY
School of Education: Dr MICHAEL J. HORVATH
School of Technology: Dr TIA M. STRAIT

MISSOURI STATE UNIVERSITY

901 South National, Springfield, MO 65804
Telephone: (417) 836-5000
Fax: (417) 836-6777
E-mail: president@missouristate.edu
Internet: www.missouristate.edu
Founded 1905
President: JOHN H. KEISER
Director of Admissions (vacant)
Dean of Library Services: KAREN HORNY
Library of 609,852 vols, 827,099 government documents, 871,618 units of microform, 29,373 audio-visual titles, 184,580 maps, 4,750 current periodicals
Number of teachers: 649 full-time
Number of teachers: 167 part-time
Number of students: 16,439.

MISSOURI VALLEY COLLEGE

500 East College, Marshall, MO 65340
Telephone: (660) 831-4108
Fax: (660) 831-4039
Internet: www.moval.edu
Founded 1889
President: Dr CHAD FREEMAN
Registrar: MARSHA LASHLEY
Vice-President for Operations/Admissions: MIKE KENAGY
Librarian: PAMELA REEDER
Library of 70,000 vols
Number of teachers: 85
Number of students: 1,351.

MISSOURI WESTERN STATE UNIVERSITY

4525 Downs Drive, St Joseph, MO 64507
Telephone: (816) 271-4200
E-mail: admission@missouriwestern.edu
Internet: www.missouriwestern.edu

Founded 1915 as St Joseph Junior College; present name 1969
State control
President: Dr JAMES SCANLON
Vice-President (Academic and Student Affairs): Dr J. DAVID ARNOLD
Vice-President (Financial Planning and Administration): RON OLINGER
Vice-President (Institutional Advancement): Dr JAMES E. ROEVER
Registrar: Dr GENE EULINGER
Library Director: JULIA SCHNEIDER
Library of 202,000 vols
Number of teachers: 190
Number of students: 5,100

DEANS

Liberal Arts and Sciences: Dr MARTIN A. JOHNSON
Professional Studies: Dr JEANNE M. DAFFRON

NAZARENE THEOLOGICAL SEMINARY

1700 E Meyer Boulevard, Kansas City, MO 64131
Telephone: (816) 333-6254
Fax: (816) 333-6271
E-mail: enroll@nts.edu
Internet: www.nts.edu

Founded 1945
Private control
Academic year: August to May
President: Dr RON BENEFIEL
Dean of Administration: Dr MARTY BUTLER
Dean of the Faculty: Dr ROGER HAHN
Librarian: Prof. DEBRA L. BRADSHAW
Library of 99,000 vols
Number of teachers: 27
Number of students: 350 (full-time)
Publication: The Tower.

NORTHWEST MISSOURI STATE UNIVERSITY

Maryville, MO 64468
Telephone: (660) 562-1212
Fax: (660) 562-1900
E-mail: admissions@nwmissouri.edu
Internet: www.nwmissouri.edu

Founded 1905
President: Dr DEAN L. HUBBARD
Provost: Dr JOSEPH E. (TIM) GILMOUR
Vice-President for Finance and Support Services: RAY COURTER
Vice-President for Student Affairs: KENT PORTERFIELD
Dean of Graduate School: Dr FRANCES SHIPLEY
Dean of Libraries: Dr PATRICIA VANDYKE
Library of 221,200 vols
Number of teachers: 227
Number of students: 6,280
Publications: Northwest Missourian (weekly newspaper), Tower (student yearbook).

PARK UNIVERSITY

Parkville, MO 64152
Telephone: (816) 741-2000
Fax: (816) 741-4911
Internet: www.park.edu
Founded 1875
President: Dr DONALD J. BRECKON
Registrar: EILEEN WEST

Vice-President of Academic Affairs: Dr Z. CLARA BRENNAN
Vice-President of Enrollment Management and Student Services: CLARINDA CREIGHTON
Director of Admissions: Dr RON CARRUTH
Librarian: ANN SCHULTIS
Library of 130,900 vols
Number of teachers: 100
Number of students: 1,194
Publications: The Park Alumniad, Park College Partners (both quarterly).

ROCKHURST UNIVERSITY

1100 Rockhurst Rd, Kansas City, MO 64110
Telephone: (816) 501-4000
Fax: (816) 501-4588
Internet: www.rockhurst.edu
Founded 1910
Academic year: August to May
President: Rev. EDWARD KINERK
Vice-President for Enrollment Management (vacant)
Vice-President for Business Affairs: GUY SWANSON
Vice-President for Student Development: Dr LIZ BRENT
Vice-President for Institutional Advancement: Dr NAN EVANSON
Vice-President for Academic Programs: Dr WILLIAM HAEFELE
Registrar: MINDA WHITESIDE
Librarian: JEANNE LANGDON
Library of 115,615 vols
Number of teachers: 208
Number of students: 2,765

DEANS

Arts and Sciences: Dr SHIRLEY SCRITCHFIELD
School of Management: Dr JAMES DALEY
School of Graduate and Professional Studies: Dr ROBIN BOWEN
Research College of Nursing: Dr NANCY O. DEBASIO

SAINT LOUIS CHRISTIAN COLLEGE

1360 Grandview Dr, Florissant, MO 63033
Telephone: (314) 837-6777
Fax: (314) 837-8291
E-mail: admissions@slcconline.edu
Internet: www.slcconline.edu
Founded 1956
Private control
Academic year: August to May
President: Dr KENNETH L. BECK
Chancellor: THOMAS W. MCGEE
Vice-President: TOM WALLACE
Academic Dean: Dr RONALD L. OAKES
Dean of Students: CHRISTINE CABLE
Registrar: Prof. RICHARD A. FORDYCE
Library Director: TERRY DAY
Library of 40,298 vols
Number of teachers: 9
Number of students: 195

HEADS OF DEPARTMENTS

Biblical Education: Dr BILLY W. JONES
General Education: Dr JUDITH A. LINCOLN

ST LOUIS COLLEGE OF PHARMACY

4588 Parkview Place, St Louis, MO 63110-1088
Telephone: (314) 367-8700
E-mail: admissions@stlcop.edu
Internet: www.stlcop.edu
Founded 1864
Private control
President: Dr THOMAS F. PATTON
Vice-President (Academic Affairs) and Dean of the College: Dr KENNETH W. KIRK

Vice-President (Information Technology): F. CHAD SHEPHERD
Vice-President (Advancement): JAMES G. SALMO
Vice-President (Finance): GARY G. TORRENCE
Vice-President (Enrollment Services): GLORIA J. VERTREES
Registrar: PENELOPE MYERS BRYANT
Library Director: JILL NISSEN
Library of 54,000 vols
Number of teachers: 108
Number of students: 854 (788 undergraduate, 66 graduate)

DIRECTORS

Division of Administrative Sciences and Liberal Arts: Dr PETER HURD
Division of Pharmaceutical Sciences: Dr JOHN BEALE
Division of Pharmacy Practice: Dr MICHAEL MADDUX

SAINT LOUIS UNIVERSITY

221 North Grand Blvd, St Louis, MO 63103
Telephone: (314) 977-2222
Fax: (314) 977-3874
Internet: www.slu.edu
Founded 1818; chartered 1832
Private control
Academic year: September to May (two terms)
President: Rev. LAWRENCE H. BIONDI
Provost: JOE WEIXLMANN
Vice-President for Business and Finance: ROBERT ALTHOLZ
Vice-President for Student Development: KATHY W. HUMPHREY
Vice-President and General Counsel: WILLIAM KAUFFMAN
Vice-President for Human Resource Management: KATHY G. HAGEDORN
Vice-President for Development and University Relations: DONALD WHELAN, Jr
Vice-President and Dean for Madrid Campus: RICK L. CHANEY
Vice-President for Facilities Management and Civic Affairs: KATHLEEN BRADY
Vice-President for University Mission and Ministry: CARL F. STARKLOFF
Vice-President and Chief Information Officer: THOMAS MOBERG
Registrar: JOHN-HERBERT JAFFRY
Undergraduate Admissions Director: SCOTT BELOBRAJDIC
Controller: MARK C. SCHMOTZER
Director of Pius XII Memorial Library: FRANCES BENHAM
Library: see Libraries
Number of teachers: 3,121 (1,301 full-time, 1,820 part-time)
Number of students: 11,112
Publications: The Modern Schoolman, Review for Religious, Theology Digest, Saint Louis University Law Journal, Manuscripta, Boulevard, Forum for Social Economics, Warsaw Trans Atlantic Law Journal, Journal of Health Law, Policy History, Gerontology: Social Science, Pageoph, Institute of Jesuit Sources, Studies in the Spirituality of Jesuits, Journal of Herpetology, Public Law Review, Journal of Urban Affairs, African American Review

DEANS

College of Arts and Sciences: JOE WEIXLMANN
Graduate School: DONALD G. BRENNAN
School of Medicine: PATRICIA L. MONTELEONE
School of Law: JEFFREY LEWIS
College of Philosophy and Letters: GARTH L. HALLETT
John Cook School of Business: NEIL SEITZ
School of Nursing: JOAN M. HRUBETZ

School of Public Health: RICHARD S. KURZ
School of Allied Health Professions: JOAN M. HRUBETZ (acting)
School of Social Service: SUSAN C. TEBB
Madrid Campus: RICK L. CHANEY
Parks College of Engineering and Aviation: CHARLES KIRKPATRICK
College of Public Service: JAMES GILSINAN
School for Professional Studies: ROBERT HASENSTAB

PROFESSORS
ABELL, B. F., Meteorology
AL-JUREIDINI, S. B., Paediatrics
ALBERT, S. G., Internal Medicine
ALDRIDGE, R. D., Biology
AMINE, L. S., Marketing
AMON, E., Obstetrics and Gynaecology
ANDERSON, E. L., Internal Medicine
ANDERSON, R. O., Communication
ARMBRECHT, H. J., Internal Medicine
ARTAL, R., Obstetrics and Gynaecology
ASPINWALL, N., Biology
AZZAM, F. J., Anaesthesiology
BACON, B. R., Internal Medicine
BAJAJ, S. P., Internal Medicine
BALDASSARE, J. J., Pharmacological and Physiological Sciences
BALFOUR, I. C., Paediatrics
BANKS, W. A., Internal Medicine
BARBER, M. D., Philosophy
BARENKAMP, S. J., Paediatrics
BARMANN, L. F., American Studies
BARRY, R. C., Paediatrics
BASTANI, B., Internal Medicine
BAUDENDISTEL, L. J., Anaesthesiology
BELLONE, C. J., Molecular Microbiology and Immunology
BELSHE, R. B., Internal Medicine
BENOFY, L. P., Physics
BENOIT, R. P., English
BENTLEY, D. W., Internal Medicine
BERNHARDT, P., Biology
BIONDI, L. H., Modern Languages
BJERREGAARD, P., Internal Medicine
BLASKIEWICZ, R. J., Obstetrics and Gynaecology
BOHMAN, J. P., Philosophy
BOLLA, R. I., Biology
BRENNAN, D. G., Communication Sciences and Disorders
BRENNAN, W. C., Social Work
BRESLIN, R. D., Educational Leadership and Higher Education
BROCKHAUS, R. H., Management
BROWN, W. W., Internal Medicine
BROWNSON, R. C., Community Health
BUCHOLZ, R. D., Surgery
BULLER, R. M., Molecular Microbiology and Immunology
BURDGE, R. E., Orthopaedic Surgery
BURGIN, R. W., Communication
BURKE, W. J., Neurology
BURTON, F. R., Internal Medicine
CANTWELL, J. C., Mathematics and Mathematical Computer Science
CASE, M. E., Pathology
CERVENKA, P. A., Law
CHAITMAN, B. R., Internal Medicine
CHAPNICK, B. M., Pharmacological and Physiological Sciences
CHARRON, W. C., Philosophy
CHEN, S.-C., Paediatrics
CHINNADURAI, G., Molecular Virology
CHOATE, J. W., Obstetrics, Gynaecology and Women's Health
CHU, J.-Y., Paediatrics
CHUNG, H. D., Pathology
COHEN, J. D., Internal Medicine
COOPER, M. H., Anatomy and Neurobiology
COSCIA, C., Biochemistry and Molecular Biology
COUNTE, M. A., Health Administration
CREER, M. H., Pathology
CRITCHLOW, D. T., History
CROSSLEY, D. J., Geophysics

CUMMINGS, S. B., Public Policy Studies
CZYSZ, P. A., Aerospace Engineering
DAHMS, T. E., Anaesthesiology
DAVENPORT, G., Psychology
DELESPESSE, J. B., Aerospace Studies (ROTC)
DEMELLO, D. E., Pathology
DEUEL, R. K., Neurology
DiBISCEGLIE, A., Internal Medicine
DIECK, H. A., Chemistry
DIXIT, V. V., Physics
DORE, I. I., Law
DORSETT, D., Biochemistry and Molecular Biology
DOWDY, J., Mathematics and Mathematical Computer Science
DOYLE, J. P., Philosophy
DOYLE, R. E., Comparative Medicine
DUCKRO, P. N., Community and Family Medicine
DUNSFORD, J. E., Law
ELICEIRI, G. L., Pathology
ELLSWORTH, M. L., Pharmacological and Physiological Sciences
FARRIS, B. E., Jr, Sociology
FEMAN, S. S., Ophthalmology
FERGUSON, D. J., Orthodontics
FERMAN, M. A., Aerospace and Mechanical Engineering
FETE, T. J., Paediatrics
FIORE, A. C., Surgery
FISHER, J. T., Theological Studies
FITCH, C. D., Internal Medicine
FITZGIBBON, S. A., Law
FLETCHER, J. W., Internal Medicine
FLICK, L. H., Community Health
FLIESLER, S. J., Ophthalmology
FORD, C. E., Mathematics and Mathematical Computer Science
FORRESTER, T., Pharmacological and Physiological Science
FRANKOWSKI, S., Law
FREESE, R. W., Mathematics and Mathematical Computer Science
GALE, J. B., Paediatrics
GANNON, P., Psychiatry and Human Behaviour
GARCIA, P., Modern Languages
GARVIN, P. J., Surgery
GIBBONS, J. L., Psychology
GILNER, F. H., Psychology
GILSINAN, J. F., Public Policy Studies
GOLDMAN, R. L., Law
GOLDNER, J. A., Law
GOLDSTEIN, J. K., Law
GORSE, G. J., Internal Medicine
GRADY, M. P., Educational Studies
GRAFF, R. J., Surgery
GRAHAM, M. A., Pathology
GRANDGENETT, D. P., Molecular Virology
GREANEY, T. L., Law
GREEN, MAURICE, Molecular Virology
GREEN, MICHAEL, Molecular Microbiology and Immunology
GRIFFING, G. T., Internal Medicine
GROSSBERG, G. T., Psychiatry and Human Behaviour
GUITHUES, H. J., Finance
HAIRE-JOSHU, D. L., Community Health
HALLETT, G. L., Philosophy
HAMRICK, L. C., Modern Languages
HANDAL, P. J., Psychology
HARRIS, S. G., Mathematics and Mathematical Computer Science
HEANEY, R. M., Internal Medicine
HEBDA, J. J., Mathematics and Mathematical Computer Science
HEIBERG, E., Radiology
HERRMANN, R. B., Geophysics, Earth and Atmospheric Sciences
HITCHCOCK, J. F., History
HOMAN, S. M., Community Health
HOOVER, R. G., Pathology
HORVATH, F. L., Physician Assistant Education
HOWARD, A. J., Law
HRUBETZ, J., Nursing

HUANG, J. S., Biochemistry and Molecular Biology
HUGHES, H. M., Psychology
JANNEY, C. G., Pathology
JENNINGS, J. P., Accounting
JOHNSON, F. E., Surgery
JOHNSON, R. G., Surgery
JOHNSON, S. H., Law
JOHNSON, T. H., Modern Languages
JOIST, J. H., Pathology
JOS, C. J., Psychiatry and Human Behaviour
KALLIONGIS, J. E., Mathematics and Mathematical Computer Science
KAMINSKI, D. L., Surgery
KAO, M. S., Obstetrics and Gynaecology
KARUNAMOORTHY, S. N., Aerospace and Mechanical Engineering
KATZ, B. M., Research Methodology
KATZ, J. A., Management
KAUFMAN, N. H., Law
KAVANAUGH, J. F., Philosophy
KEENAN, W. J., Paediatrics
KEITHLEY, J. P., Accounting
KELLOGG, R. T., Psychology
KENNEDY, D. J., Internal Medicine
KERN, M. J., Internal Medicine
KIM, S. H., Finance
KIM, Y. S., Pharmacological and Physiological Sciences
KIMMEY, J. R., Community Health
KLEIN, C., Biochemistry and Molecular Biology
KNUEPFER, M. M., Pharmacological and Physiological Sciences
KNUTSEN, A. P., Paediatrics
KOLMER, E., American Studies
KORN, J. H., Psychology
KORNBLUTH, J., Pathology
KOWERT, B. A., Chemistry
KRAMER, T. J., Psychology
KURZ, R. S., Health Administration
KWAK, N. K., Decision Sciences and MIS
KWON, I. W., Decision Sciences and MIS
LABOVITZ, A. J., Internal Medicine
LAGUNOFF, D., Pathology
LANE, B. C., Theological Studies
LANG, J. M., Psychiatry and Human Behaviour
LECHNER, A. J., Pharmacological and Physiological Sciences
LEGUEY-FEILLEUX, J. R., Political Science
LEIPPE, M. R., Psychology
LEVARY, R. R., Decision Sciences and MIS
LEWIS, J. E., Law
LIN, Y. J., Meteorology, Earth and Atmospheric Sciences
LIU, M.-S., Pharmacological and Physiological Sciences
LOMPERIS, T. J., Political Science
LONGO, W. E., Surgery
LONIGRO, A. J., Internal Medicine
LUISIRI, A., Radiology
LYNCH, R. E., Paediatrics
MAGILL, G., Health Care Ethics
MALONE, L. J., Jr, Chemistry
MANCINI, M. J., American Studies
MANOR, D., Aerospace and Mechanical Engineering
MARGOLIS, R. B., Psychiatry and Human Behaviour
MARSKE, C. E., Sociology
MARTIN, D. S., Radiology
MARTIN, K. J., Internal Medicine
MATTFELDT-BEMAN, M., Nutrition and Dietetics
MATUSCHAK, G. M., Internal Medicine
MAYDEN, R. L., Biology
McCLURE, H. L., Aviation Science
McGOWAN, J. R., Accounting
McGUIRE, R. A., Communication Sciences and Disorders
McLEOD, F. G., Theological Studies
McSWEENEY, M., Nursing Research
MEDOFF, J., Biology
MENGEL, M. B., Community and Family Medicine

METHENY, N. A., Adult and Gerontological Nursing
MEYER, A. E., Communication
MILLER, D. D., Internal Medicine
MILLER, D. K., Internal Medicine
MILLER, S. W., Marketing
MITCHELL, B. J., Geophysics, Earth and Atmospheric Sciences
MOBERG, T. F., Research Methodology
MODRAS, R. E., Theological Studies
MOISAN, T. E., English
MONTELEONE, J. A., Paediatrics
MONTELEONE, P. L., Paediatrics
MOORADIAN, A. D., Internal Medicine
MOORE, J. T., Meteorology, Earth and Atmospheric Sciences
MOORE, T. L., Internal Medicine
MORLEY, J. E., Internal Medicine
MURDICK, N. L., Educational Studies
MUNZ, D. C., Psychology
MURPHY, D. T., Modern Languages
MURRAY, R. L. E., Mental Health, Family, Community, and Systems Nursing
NAGABHUSHAN, B. L., Aerospace and Mechanical Engineering
NAUNHEIM, K. S., Surgery
NEEDHAM, C. A., Law
NEVINS, F. M., Law
NIKOLAI, R. J., Orthodontics
NOFFSINGER, J. E., Paediatrics
NOGUCHI, A., Paediatrics
O'BRIEN, J. C., Law
O'CONNOR, D. M., Paediatrics
OHAR, J. A., Internal Medicine
O'TOOLE, M. L., Obstetrics and Gynaecology
OLIVER, J. M., Psychology
ORDOWER, H. M., Law
PADBERG, W. H., Social Work
PALETTA, C. E., Surgery
PANNETON, W. M., Anatomy and Neurobiology
PARKER, G. E., Management
PAULY, J. J., Communication
PERMAN, W. H., Radiology
PERRY, E. I., History
PERRY, H. M., Internal Medicine
PERRY, L. C., History
PERRY, S. A., Adult and Gerontological Nursing
PETERSON, G. J., Surgery
PETRUSKA, P. J., Internal Medicine
PIERRON, R. L., Orthopaedic Surgery
POLLARD, C. A., Community and Family Medicine
PUNZO, V. C., Philosophy
PURO, S., Political Science
RAHMAN, H., Electrical Engineering
RANA, W.-U.-Z., Anatomy and Neurobiology
RAO, G. V., Earth and Atmospheric Sciences
RAO, P. S., Paediatrics
RAVINDRA, K., Aerospace and Mechanical Engineering
RAY, R., Internal Medicine
REBORE, R. W., Educational Leadership and Higher Education
REESE, C., Mental Health, Family, Community and Systems Nursing
REIMERS, H. J., Internal Medicine
RENARD, G. J., Jr, Theological Studies
ROHLIK, J., Law
ROMEIS, J. C., Health Services Research
ROSS, M. J., Psychology
ROY, T. S., Radiation Oncology
RUCKDESCHEL, R. A., Social Work
RUDDY, T. M., History
RUH, M. F., Pharmacological and Physiological Sciences
RUH, T. S., Pharmacological and Physiological Sciences
RYERSE, J. S., Pathology
SALIMI, Z., Radiology
SALINAS-MADRIGAL, L., Pathology
SALSICH, P. W., Jr, Law
SAMSON, W. K., Pharmacological and Physiological Sciences
SANCHEZ, J. M., History

SANTHANAM, T. S., Physics
SCALZO, A. J., Paediatrics
SCHLAFLY, D. L., Jr, History
SCHMITZ, H. H., Health Administration
SCHMITZ, P. G., Internal Medicine
SCHULZE, I. T., Molecular Microbiology and Immunology
SCOTT, J. F., English
SEITZ, N. E., Finance
SELHORST, J. B., Neurology
SEVERSON, J. G., Jr, Biology
SHANER, M. C., Management
SHAPIRO, M. J., Surgery
SHEA, W. M., Theological Studies
SHIELDS, J. B., Radiology
SHIPPEY, T. A., English
SILBERSTEIN, M. J., Radiology
SILVERBERG, A. B., Internal Medicine
SLAVIN, R. G., Internal Medicine
SLY, W. S., Biochemistry and Molecular Biology
SMITH, G. S., Surgery
SMITH, K., Jr, Surgery
SOTELO-AVILA, C., Pathology
SPAZIANO, V. T., Chemistry
SPRAGUE, R. S., Internal Medicine
STACEY, L. M., Physics
STANTON, C. M., Educational Leadership and Higher Education
STARK, W., Biology
STEINHARDT, G. F., Urology, Surgery
STEVENS, T. C., Mathematics and Mathematical Computer Science
STOEBERL, P. A., Management
STOLZER, A. J., Aviation Science
STRATMAN, H. G., Internal Medicine
STRETCH, J. J., Social Work
STUMP, D. V., English
STUMP, E. A., Philosophy
SWANSTROM, T., Public Policy Studies
SWIERKOSZ, E. M., Pathology
TAIT, R. C., Psychiatry and Human Behaviour
TAN, Y., Anatomy and Neurobiology
TERRY, N., Law
THACKER, W. D., Physics
THOMAS, C. W., Biomedical Engineering
THOMAS, D. R., Internal Medicine
TOCE, S. S., Paediatrics
TOLBERT, D. L., Anatomy and Neurobiology
TOMAZIC, T. J., Research Methodology
TREADGOLD, W., History
TRUE, W. R., Community Health
TSAU, C. M., Mathematics and Mathematical Computer Science
TUCHLER, D. J., Law
ULTMANN, M. H., Paediatrics
VAGO, S., Sociology
VAN DER BERG, S., English
VIRGO, K. S., Surgery
VOGLER, C. A., Pathology
VOGLER, G. A., Comparative Medicine
WACKER, W. D., Mathematics and Mathematical Computer Science
WALENTIK, C. A., Paediatrics
WARREN, K. F., Political Science
WATSON, S., Law
WEBB, K., Community and Family Medicine
WEBER, T. R., Surgery
WEBSTER, R. O., Internal Medicine
WEINBERGER, A. M., Law
WEIXLMANN, J., English
WELCH, P. J., Economics
WERNET, S. P., Social Work
WESTFALL, T. C., Pharmacological and Physiological Sciences
WHITING, R. B., Internal Medicine
WHITMAN, B., Paediatrics
WILLIAMS, D. R., Law
WILLMORE, L. J., Jr, Neurology
WINN, H. N., Obstetrics and Gynaecology
WOLD, W. S. M., Molecular Microbiology and Immunology
WOLINSKY, F. D., Health Administration
WOLVERSON, M. K., Radiology
WONGSURAWAT, N., Internal Medicine

WOOD, E. G., Paediatrics
WOOD, T. T., Art and Art History
YEAGER, F., Finance
YOUNG, P. A., Anatomy and Neurobiology
ZAHM, D. S., Anatomy and Neurobiology
ZASSENHAUS, H. P., Molecular Microbiology and Immunology
ZENSER, T. V., Internal Medicine

SAINT PAUL SCHOOL OF THEOLOGY

5123 Truman Rd, Kansas City, MO 64127

Telephone: (816) 483-9600
Fax: (816) 483-9605
E-mail: spst@spst.edu
Internet: www.spst.edu
Private control

President: LOVETT H. WEEMS, Jr
Academic Dean: JANE E. MCAVOY
Registrar: NICOLE SCHOENHALS
Director of Library and Information Services: LOGAN S. WRIGHT

Library of 81,000 vols
Number of teachers: 41
Number of students: 340.

SOUTHEAST MISSOURI STATE UNIVERSITY

Cape Girardeau, MO 63701

Telephone: (314) 651-2000
Fax: (314) 651-5061
Internet: www.semo.edu
Founded 1873

President: Dr KENNETH W. DOBBINS
Provost: Dr JANE STEPHENS
Director of Admissions: DEBORAH BELOW
Registrar: SANDRA HINKLE
Director of Library: Dr SARAH CRON

Library of 409,000 vols, 287,000 government documents and 1,174,000 microforms
Number of teachers: 401
Number of students: 9,534.

SOUTHWEST BAPTIST UNIVERSITY

1600 University Avenue, Bolivar, MO 65613

Telephone: (417) 326-5281
Fax: (417) 326-1514
E-mail: admitme@sbuniv.edu
Internet: www.sbuniv.edu

Founded 1878 as Southwest Baptist College; present name 1981
Private control

President: Dr C. PAT TAYLOR
Provost: Dr GORDON DUTILE
Vice-President (Administration): RON MAUPIN
Vice-President (Student Development): STEVE MORROW
Vice-President (Estate Planning): Dr ROBERT G. INGOLD
Vice-President (Enrollment Management): Dr STEPHANIE MILLER
Vice-President (Development): Dr CARL SINGER
Registrar: JOHN CREDILLE
Director of Library Services: ED WALTON

Library of 129,000 vols
Number of teachers: 106
Number of students: 3,700 (all campuses – 2,700 undergraduate, 1,000 graduate)

DEANS

College of Business and Computer Science: Dr DAVID WHITLOCK
Courts Redford College of Theology and Church Vocations: (vacant)
Lewis E. Schollian College of Education and Social Science: Dr LINDA WOODERSON
Geneva Casebolt College of Music, Arts and Letters: (vacant)

College of Science and Mathematics: Dr GARY O. GRAY

BRANCH CAMPUSES

SBU-Mountain View: POB 489, Mountain View, MO 65548; located at: 209 W First Street, Mountain View, MO 65548; tel. (417) 934-2999; Director LARRY PRICE.

SBU-Salem: 501 S Grand, Salem, MO 65560; tel. (573) 729-7071; Director MIKE SHELTON.

SBU-Springfield: 4431 S Fremont, Springfield, MO 65804; tel. (417) 841-5049.

STEPHENS COLLEGE

Columbia, MO 65215

Telephone: (573) 442-2211
Fax: (573) 876-7248
E-mail: apply@stephens.edu
Internet: www.stephens.edu
Founded 1833
Academic year: August to May

President: MARCIA S. KIERSCHT
Vice-President for Academic and Student Affairs: ROBERT S. BADAL
Director of Admissions: PATRICIA GIBBS
Librarian: JONI BLAKE

Library of 120,000 vols
Number of teachers: 53 full-time
Number of students: 800.

TRUMAN STATE UNIVERSITY

Kirksville, MO 63501

Telephone: (660) 785-4000
Fax: (660) 785-7456
E-mail: webmaster@truman.edu
Internet: www.truman.edu

Founded 1867; formerly Northeast Missouri State University (until 1996)
Academic year: August to May

President: Dr BARBARA DIXON
Vice-President for Academic Affairs: GARRY GORDON
Co-Directors of Admission: BRAD CHAMBERS, MELODY CHAMBERS
Registrar: KAY ANDERSON

Library of 455,971 vols
Number of teachers: 347
Number of students: 5,862

Publications: *Truman Review* (3 a year), *Detours Magazine* (4 a year).

UNIVERSITY OF MISSOURI SYSTEM

Columbia, MO 65211

Telephone: (573) 882-2011
Fax: (573) 882-2721
E-mail: mu4u@missouri.edu
Internet: www.umsystem.edu
Founded 1839

President: ELSON S. FLOYD
Senior Vice-President for Academic Affairs: STEPHEN W. LEHMKUHLE
Vice-President for Human Resources: R. KENNETH HUTCHINSON
Vice-President for Finance and Administration: NATALIE KRAWITZ
Vice-President for Government Relations: STEVE KNORR
Vice-President for Information Systems: RALPH H. CARUSO, Jr
Libraries and Archives: see University Libraries.

CONSTITUENT CAMPUSES

University of Missouri—Columbia

Columbia, MO 65211

Telephone: (573) 882-2121
E-mail: mu4u@missouri.edu

Internet: www.missouri.edu
Founded 1839
State control
Academic year: August to May

Chancellor: BRADY DEATON
Provost: LORI FRANZ
Vice-Chancellor for Student Affairs: CATHY SCROGGS
Vice-Chancellor for Administrative Services: JACQUELYN JONES
Vice-Chancellor for Development and Alumni Relations: DAVID HOUSH
Registrar: BRENDA SELMAN
Director of Admissions: BARBARA RUPP

Number of teachers: 1,364
Number of students: 27,003

DEANS AND DIRECTORS

College of Agriculture, Food and Natural Resources: THOMAS PAYNE
College of Arts and Sciences: RICHARD SCHWARTZ
College of Business: BRUCE J. WALKER
College of Education: RICHARD L. ANDREWS
College of Engineering: JAMES E. THOMPSON
College of Human and Environmental Sciences: STEPHEN JORGENSEN
College of Veterinary Medicine: JOE KORNEGAY
Graduate School: PAM BENOIT
School of Accountancy: THOMAS HOWARD
School of Fine Arts: MELVIN PLATT
School of Health Professions: RICHARD OLIVER
School of Journalism: R. DEAN MILLS
School of Law: R. LAWRENCE DESSEM (acting)
School of Information Science and Learning Technologies: JOHN WEDMAN
School of Medicine: WILLIAM CRIST
School of Natural Resources: MARK RYAN
School of Nursing: ROSE PORTER
School of Social Work: COLLEEN GALAMBOS
Harry S. Truman School of Public Affairs: BARTON WECHSLER

University of Missouri—Kansas City

5100 Rockhill Rd, Kansas City, MO 64110

Telephone: (816) 235-1000
E-mail: admit@umkc.edu
Internet: www.umkc.edu

Founded 1929
State control
Academic year: August to July

Chancellor: ELEANOR BRANTLEY SCHWARTZ
Executive Vice-Provost/Executive Dean: MARVIN R. QUERRY
Vice-Chancellor for Administrative Affairs: J. JOSEPH DOERR
Vice-Chancellor for University Advancement: WILLIAM J. FRENCH
Vice-Chancellor for Student Affairs: LARRY DIETZ
Registrar: WILSON BERRY
Director, Admissions: MELVIN TYLER
Director, University Libraries: TED SHELDON

Library of 868,000 vols, 1,537,912 microforms
Number of teachers: 850
Number of students: 12,000

DEANS

College of Arts and Sciences: JAMES DURIG
Henry W. Bloch School of Business and Public Administration: WILLIAM B. EDDY
School of Dentistry: MICHAEL J. REED
School of Education: BERNARD OLIVER
School of Law: BURNELE V. POWELL
Conservatory of Music: TERRY APPLEBAUM
School of Pharmacy: ROBERT W. PIEPHO
School of Nursing: NANCY MILLS
School of Medicine: MARJORIE SIRRIDGE
School of Biological Sciences: MARINO MARTINEZ-CARRION
Extended Programs: JANET STRATTON (Dir)

Coordinated Undergraduate Engineering Programs: QUINTON BOWLES (Assoc. Dean)
Computer Science/Telecommunications Program: RICHARD HETHERINGTON (Dir)

University of Missouri—Rolla

1870 Miner Circle, Rolla, MO 65401

Telephone: (314) 341-4114
Fax: (314) 341-6306
Internet: www.umr.edu

Founded 1870
State control
Academic year: August to July

Chancellor: GARY THOMAS
Provost: Y. T. SHAH
Vice-Chancellor for Administrative Affairs: STEVE MALOTT
Vice-Chancellor for University Advancement: CONNIE EGGERT
Vice-Chancellor for Student Affairs: DEBRA ROBINSON
Registrar: LAURA STOLL
Dean of Enrollment Management: JAY GOFF
Librarian: ANDREW STEWART

Library of 388,000 vols
Number of teachers: 474
Number of students: 5,504

DEANS AND DIRECTORS

School of Engineering: O. ROBERT MITCHELL
School of Mines and Metallurgy: MARIESA CROW
College of Arts and Sciences: PAULA LUTZ

University of Missouri—St Louis

One University Boulevard, St Louis, MO 63121-4400

Telephone: (314) 516-5000
Fax: (314) 516-5378
Internet: www.umsl.edu

Founded 1963
State control
Academic year: August to July

Chancellor: THOMAS F. GEORGE
Provost and Vice-Chancellor for Academic Affairs: GLEN H. COPE
Vice-Chancellor for Administrative Services: REINHARD M. SCHUSTER
Vice-Chancellor for Development: THOMAS M. ESCHEN
Vice-Chancellor for Managerial and Technological Services: JAMES M. KRUEGER
Vice-Chancellor for University Relations: DIXIE A. KOHN
Vice-Provost for Research Administration: NASSER ARSHADI
Vice-Provost for Student Affairs: CURTIS C. COONROD
Assistant to the Chancellor for Public Affairs and Economic Development: ELIZABETH VAN UUM
Director, Office of Equal Opportunity: DEBORAH J. BURRIS
Registrar: LINDA C. SILMAN (acting)
Director of Admissions: MELISSA HATTMAN

Library of 1,105,983 vols, 1,204,239 government documents, 1,319,004 microfilm units, 3,878 audiovisual units
Number of teachers: 1,113 (489 full-time, 624 part-time)
Number of students: 15,498 (11,867 on-campus, 3,631 off-campus)

DEANS AND DIRECTORS

College of Arts and Sciences: MARK A. BURKHOLDER
College of Business Administration: N. KEITH WOMER
College of Education: CHARLES D. SCHMITZ
College of Fine Arts and Communication: JOHN B. HYLTON
College of Optometry: LARRY J. DAVIS
College of Nursing: LUCILLE L. TRAVIS

Graduate School: JUDITH WALKER DE FELIX
Continuing Education and Outreach: DAVID N. KLOSTERMANN
Honors College: ROBERT M. BLISS
UMSL/WU Joint Engineering Program: WILLIAM P. DARBY

PROFESSORS
ANDERSON, K. C., Art and Art History
BARTON, L., Chemistry
BEATTY, M., Communication
BERKOWITZ, M. W., Education
BIRD, A., Business Administration
BREAUGH, J., Business Administration
BURSIK, R. J., Criminology and Criminal Justice
CALSYN, R. J., Psychology
CAMPBELL, J. F., Business Administration
CARROLL, J. C., English
CHENG, T., Physics and Astronomy
CHICKOS, J., Chemistry
CHRISTENSEN, J. L., Optometry
CHUI, C., Mathematics and Computer Science
COCHRAN, J. A., Education
COOK, S., English
COREY, J. Y., Chemistry
COSMOPOULOS, M., Anthropology
COTTONE, R. R., Counselling (College of Education)
CURRY, G. D., Criminology and Criminal Justice
DECKER, S. H., Criminology and Criminal Justice
DURHAM, J. D., Nursing
ESBENSEN, F. A., Criminology and Criminal Justice
EVEN, Y., Art and Art History
FEIGENBAUM, S. K., Economics
FERGUSON, P., Education
FLORES, R. A., Physics and Astronomy
FRIEDLANDER, R. J., Mathematics and Computer Science
FUNG, H. G., Business Administration
GERTEIS, L. S., History
GILLINGHAM, J. R., History
GRANGER, C. R., Biology
HANDEL, P. H., Physics and Astronomy
HARBACH, B. C., Music
HARRIS, W. R., Chemistry
HARRIS, M. M., Business Administration
HENSON, B. L., Physics and Astronomy
HUNT, J. H., Biology
HURLEY, A., History
JANSON, M. A., Business Administration
JONES, E., Political Science
JOSHI, K., Business Administration
KELLOGG, E. A., Biology
KYLE, W. C., Science Education
LACITY, M. C., Business Administration
LANKFORD, E. L., Art and Art History
LAURITSEN, J. L., Criminology and Criminal Justice
LAWRENCE, E. C., Business Administration
LEE, R. K., Nursing
LEVENTHAL, J. J., Physics and Astronomy
MARQUIS, R. J., Biology
MARTINICH, J. S., Business Administration
MARWIT, S. J., Psychology
MITCHELL, R. H., History
MOSS, F. E., Physics and Astronomy
MUNSON, R., Philosophy
MUSHABEN, J. M., Political Science
NAUSS, R. M., Business Administration
O'BRIEN, J. J., Chemistry
OHALLMHURAIN, G., Music
PARKER, P. G., Biology
PATTERSON, M. L., Psychology
PECK, C. K., Optometry
RAO, A. P., Mathematics and Computer Science
RAY, R. J., Music
RICHARDS, J., Music
RICHARDSON, L. I., Educational Leadership and Policy
RICKLEFS, R. E., Biology

RICKS, D. A., Business Administration
ROBERTSON, D. B., Political Science
ROCHESTER, J. M., Political Science
RONEN, D., Business Administration
ROSE, D. C., Economics
ROSENFELD, R. B., Criminology and Criminal Justice
ROSS, S. A., Philosophy
ROWAN, S. W., History
SABHERWAL, R., Business Administration
SARGENT, L. T., Political Science
SAUTER, V. L., Business Administration
SCHWANTES, C. A., History
SCHWARTZ, H. E., English
SILVA, G. E., Political Science
SORENSEN, R. L., Economics
SPILLING, C., Chemistry
STAKE, J. E., Psychology
STEIN, L., Political Science
STEVENS, P. F., Biology
TANG, M. Z., Biology
TAYLOR, G. T., Psychology
TURPIN, D., Music
VANDENBERG, B. R., Psychology
WANG, X., Biology
WHITE, L. H., Economics
WILKENS, L. A., Biology
WILKING, B. A., Physics and Astronomy
WILLIAMS, L. V., Foreign Languages and Literature
WILLMAN, F., Music
WINKLER, A. E., Economics
WOLFE, P., English
WRIGHT, R. T., Criminology and Criminal Justice
YOUNGER, D., Art and Art History
ZARUCCHI, J. M., Foreign Languages and Literature
ZENI, J. E., English.

ATTACHED RESEARCH INSTITUTES
Center for Business and Industrial Studies.
Center for Emerging Technologies.
Center for Entrepreneurship and Economic Education.
Center for Eye Care and Vision Research.
Center for Human Origin and Cultural Diversity.
Center for the Humanities.
Center for International Studies.
Center for Molecular Electronics.
Center for Neurodynamics.
Center for Teaching and Learning.
Center for Transportation Studies.
Center for Trauma Recovery.
E. Desmond Lee Technology & Learning Center.
Institute for Women's and Gender Studies.
International Center for Tropical Ecology.
Kathy J. Weinman Children's Advocacy Centre.
Missouri Research Park.
Public Policy Research Center.
Regional Center for Education and Work.
Sue Shear Institute for Women in Public Life.

WASHINGTON UNIVERSITY IN SAINT LOUIS

Saint Louis, MO 63130-4899
Telephone: (314) 935-5000
Fax: (314) 935-5799
E-mail: admissions@wustl.edu
Internet: www.wustl.edu

Founded 1853 as Eliot Seminary; charter altered to Washington University 1857
Private control
Academic year: August to May

Chancellor: MARK S. WRIGHTON
Executive Vice-Chancellors: EDWARD S. MACIAS, RICHARD A. ROLOFF DAVID T. BLASINGAME, JOHN E. KLEIN MICHAEL R. CANNON (General Counsel), LARRY J. SHAPIRO (Medical Affairs)
Vice-Chancellors: M. FREDRIC VOLKMANN (Public Affairs), THEODORE J. CICERO (Research), BARBARA A. FEINER (Finance), JAMES E. McLEOD (Students), ANN B. PRENATT (Human Resources)
Director of Community and Governmental Relations: PAMELA S. LOKKEN
Special Assistant to the Chancellor for Academic Affairs: GERHILD S. WILLIAMS
Director of Student Records: SUSAN E. HOSACK
Dean of Libraries: SHIRLEY K. BAKER
Number of teachers: 2,955 (1,782 full-time, 466 part-time)
Number of students: 10,641 full-time, 2,700 part-time

DEANS
Faculty of Arts and Sciences: EDWARD S. MACIAS
School of Architecture: CYNTHIA WEESE
School of Art: JEFFREY C. PIKE
John M. Olin School of Business: STUART I. GREENBAUM
School of Engineering and Applied Science (includes the Sever Institute of Graduate Engineering): CHRISTOPHER I. BYRNES
School of Law: JOEL SELIGMAN
School of Medicine: LARRY J. SHAPIRO
George Warren Brown School of Social Work: EDWARD F. LAWLOR
College of Arts and Sciences: JAMES E. McLEOD
Graduate School of Arts and Sciences: ROBERT E. THACH

WEBSTER UNIVERSITY

470 East Lockwood Ave, St Louis, MO 63119
Telephone: (314) 968-6900
Fax: (314) 968-7117
E-mail: admit@webster.edu
Internet: www.webster.edu

Founded 1915
Academic year: August to May
President: Dr RICHARD S. MEYERS
Registrar: DON MORRIS
Librarian: LAURA REIN
Library of 299,000 vols
Number of teachers: 2,273 (173 full-time, 2,100 part-time)
Number of students: 20,964
Publications: *Annual Report*, *Webster World* (4 a year).

WESTMINSTER COLLEGE

Fulton, MO 65251
Telephone: (573) 642-3361
Fax: (573) 642-6356
E-mail: admissions@jaynet.wcmo.edu
Internet: www.westminster-mo.edu

Founded 1851
Academic year: August to May
President: FLETCHER M. LAMKIN
Dean of Faculty and Vice-President: ROBERT A. SEELINGER
Vice-President for Development: DAN DIEDRICH
Registrar: PHYLLIS MASEK
Librarian: LORNA MITCHELL
Library of 121,073 vols
Number of teachers: 60
Number of students: 700.

WILLIAM JEWELL COLLEGE

500 College Hill, Liberty, MO 64068
Telephone: (816) 781-7700
Fax: (816) 415-5027
Internet: www.jewell.edu
Founded 1849
Academic year: September to May
President: DAVID L. SALLEE
Registrar: STEVE SCHWEGLER
Director of Admissions: EDWIN HARRIS
Librarian: J. P. YOUNG
Library of 260,119 vols
Number of teachers: 128
Number of students: 1,500.

WILLIAM WOODS UNIVERSITY

One University Ave, Fulton, MO 65251
Telephone: (573) 642-2251
Fax: (573) 592-1146
E-mail: admissions@williamwoods.edu
Internet: www.williamwoods.edu
Founded 1870
Academic year: August to May
President: Prof. Dr JAHNAE H. BARNETT
Vice-Presidents: Prof. Dr BETSY TUTT, Dr BOB
 FESSLER, SCOTT GALLAGHER
Director of Admissions: JIMMY CLAY
Director of University Relations: MARY ANN
 BEAHON
Director of Athletics: LARRY YORK
Academic Dean: Dr SHERRY MCCARTHY
Dean of Student Life: VENITA MITCHELL
Library of 160,000 vols
Number of teachers: 52 full-time, 300 part-
 time
Number of students: 3,000
Publication: *The Woods Magazine* (alumni
 magazine, 2 a year)

DEANS

Business: DAVID FORSTER
Education and Social Science: Dr TOM FRANK-
 MAN
Equestrian Studies: LAURA WARD
Human Performance, Science and Mathe-
 matics: MARSHALL ROBB
Visual, Performing and Communication
 Arts: Prof. PAUL CLERVI

MONTANA

CARROLL COLLEGE

1601 North Benton Ave, Helena, MT 59625
Telephone: (406) 447-4300
Fax: (406) 447-4533
Internet: www.carroll.edu
Founded 1909
Academic year: August to May
Pres.: Dr THOMAS TREBON
Vice-Pres. for Student Life: LYNN C. ETCHART,
 Dr JIM D. HARDWICK
Vice-Pres. for Institutional Advancement: Dr
 RICHARD ORTEGA
Academic Dean: JOHN SCHARF
Registrar: MARY PAT DUTTON
Librarian: LOIS FITZPATRICK
Library of 94,000 vols
Number of teachers: 85
Number of students: 1,400.

MONTANA STATE UNIVERSITY

Bozeman, MT 59717
Telephone: (406) 994-0211
Fax: (406) 994-2893
Internet: www.montana.edu
Founded 1893
Pres.: Dr GEOFFREY GAMBLE

Provost and Vice-Pres. for Academic Affairs:
 DAVID DOOLEY
Vice-Pres. for Research, Creativity and Tech-
 nology Transfer: THOMAS McCOY
Vice-Pres. for Admin. and Finance: CRAIG
 ROLOFF
Vice-Pres. for Student Affairs and Dean of
 Students: Dr ALLEN YARNELL
Registrar and Dir of Admissions: CHARLES
 NELSON
Dean of Library: BRUCE MORTON
Number of students: 10,700

DEANS OF COLLEGES

Letters and Science: JAMES McMILLAN
Agriculture: THOMAS McCOY
Education, Health and Human Devt: LARRY
 BAKER
Eng.: DAVID F. GIBSON
Arts and Architecture: JERRY BANCROFT
Graduate Studies: JOSEPH FEDOCK
Nursing: LEA ACORD
Business: MICHAEL OWEN

MONTANA STATE UNIVERSITY – BILLINGS

Billings, MT 59101
Telephone: (406) 657-2011
Fax: (406) 657-2299
E-mail: admissions@msubillings.edu
Internet: www.msubillings.edu
Founded 1927
Academic year: September to May
Chancellor: RONALD P. SEXTON
Provost and Vice-Chancellor for Academic
 Affairs: Dr GEORGE WHITE
Vice-Chancellor for Admin. Affairs: TERRIE
 IVERSON
Vice-Chancellor for Student Affairs: STACY
 KLIPPENSTEIN
Library Dir: JANE HOWELL
Library of 281,258 vols
Number of teachers: 226
Number of students: 4,300.

MONTANA STATE UNIVERSITY— NORTHERN

POB 7751 Havre, MT 59501
Telephone: (406) 265-3700
E-mail: admissions@msun.edu
Internet: www.msun.edu
Founded 1929
Chancellor: ALEX CAPDEVILLE
Registrar: STEVE JAMRUSZKA
Library Dir: VICKI GIST
Library of 84,000 vols
Number of teachers: 80
Number of students: 1,800

Baccalaureate courses in arts and sciences,
teacher education, technology, business, nursing. Masters courses in education.

MONTANA TECH OF THE UNIVERSITY OF MONTANA

1300 West Park St, Butte, MT 59701-8997
Telephone: (406) 496-4101
Fax: (406) 496-4133
E-mail: admissions@mtech.edu
Internet: www.mtech.edu
Founded 1893
Academic year: August to May
Chancellor: FRANK GILMORE
Vice-Chancellor of Academic Affairs and
 Research: Dr SUSAN PATTON
Dean of Students (vacant): PAUL BEATTY
Vice-Chancellor of Research and Graduate
 Studies: JOSEPH F. FIGUEIRA
Registrar: EDWIN JOHNSON
Dir of Admissions: TONY CAMPEAU
Dir of Library: ANN ST. CLAIR

Number of teachers: 90
Number of students: 2,067
Publications: *Catalog, The Technocrat.*

ROCKY MOUNTAIN COLLEGE

1511 Poly Dr., Billings, MT 59102
Telephone: (406) 657-1000
Fax: (406) 259-9751
E-mail: admissions@rocky.edu
Internet: www.rocky.edu
Founded 1878
Academic year: August to May
Pres.: Dr MICHAEL MACE (acting)
Vice-Pres. for Academic Affairs: ANTHONY
 PILTZ
Dir of Library: WILLIAM KEHLER
Library of 86,600 vols
Number of teachers: 83 (45 full-time, 38 part-
 time)
Number of students: 800.

UNIVERSITY OF GREAT FALLS

1301 20th St, S, Great Falls, MT 59405
Telephone: (406) 761-8210
Fax: (406) 791-5393
Internet: www.ugf.edu
Founded 1932
Liberal arts college; 4-year and 2-year degree
 courses in Human Services, Professional
 Counselling, and Education
Pres.: EUGENE J. McALLISTER
Provost and Academic Vice-Pres.: Dr
 RICHARD McDOWELL
Dir of Admissions and Records: R. HENSLEY
Dir of Library: DAVID BIBB
Library of 97,353 vols
Number of teachers: 80
Number of students: 1,400.

UNIVERSITY OF MONTANA

32 Campus Dr., Missoula, MT 59812
Telephone: (406) 243-0211
Fax: (406) 243-2797
Internet: www.umt.edu
Founded 1893
Pres. and Provost: GEORGE M. DENNISON
Vice-Pres. for Admin and Finance: ROBERT
 DURINGER
Assoc. Vice-Pres. for Research and Devt:
 DANIEL J. DWYER
Vice-Pres. for Student Affairs: TERESA
 BRANCH
Registrar: DAVID MICUS
Dean of Students: Dr CHARLES COUTURE
Dean of Libraries: BONNIE ALLEN
Library: *c.* 700,000 vols, plus 77,600 US Govt
 documents
Number of teachers: 450
Number of students: 13,019

DEANS

College of Arts and Sciences: GERALD FETZ
College of Technology: PAUL WILLIAMSON
School of Business Admin.: LARRY D. GIAN-
 CHETTA
School of Education: PAUL ROWLAND
School of Fine Arts: SHIRLEY HOWELL
School of Forestry: PERRY BROWN
School of Journalism: JERRY BROWN (acting)
School of Law: EDWARD ECK
School of Pharmacy and Allied Health Ser-
 vices: DAVID FORBES
Graduate School: DAVID STROBEL
Div. of Continuing Education: SHARON ALEX-
 ANDER

UNIVERSITY OF MONTANA–WESTERN

710 South Atlantic St, Dillon, MT 59725

Telephone: (406) 683-7331
Fax: (406) 683-7493
E-mail: admissions@umwestern.edu
Internet: www.umwestern.edu

Founded 1893
State control
Academic year: September to June

Chancellor: Dr RICHARD STOREY
Provost and Vice-Chancellor for Academic Affairs: Dr KARL ULRICH
Vice-Chancellor for Admin. and Finance: SUSAN BRIGGS
Vice-Chancellor for Institutional Advancement: TOM YAHRAES
Registrar: JASON KARCH
Library Dir: MICHAEL SCHULZ

Number of teachers: 50
Number of students: 1,100.

NEBRASKA

BELLEVUE UNIVERSITY

1000 Galvin Rd South, Bellevue, NE 68005

Telephone: (402) 293-2000
Fax: (402) 293-2020
E-mail: pr@bellevue.edu
Internet: www.bellevue.edu

Founded 1966
Private control

President: Dr JOHN B. MULLER
Provost: MARY HAWKINS
Vice-President (Administration): GERALD BLASIG
Vice-President (Development Programs): DOROTHY D. MORROW
Vice-President (Marketing and Enrollment): MIKE ECHOLS
Registrar: PHILLIP E. CHAPMAN
Library Director: ROBIN BERNSTEIN

Library of 90,000 vols
Number of teachers: 62
Number of students: 3,913

DEANS

College of Arts and Sciences: Dr JOSEPH J. WYDEVEN
College of Business: Dr DOUGLAS A. FROST
College of Professional Studies: JOHN C. LEBER

CHADRON STATE COLLEGE

Chadron, NE 69337

Telephone: (308) 432-6000
Fax: (308) 432-6464
Internet: www.csc.edu

Founded 1911
Academic year: August to May

President: THOMAS L. KREPEL
Registrar: DALE WILLIAMSON
Librarian: TERRY BRENNAN

Library of 190,666 vols
Number of teachers: 101 full-time
Number of students: 3,206.

CLARKSON COLLEGE

101 S 42nd Street, Omaha, NE 68131-2739

Telephone: (402) 552-3100
Fax: (402) 552-6057
E-mail: admiss@clarksoncollege.edu
Internet: www.clarksoncollege.edu
Private control

President: Dr J. W. UPRIGHT

Number of teachers: 26
Number of students: 496 (379 undergraduate, 117 graduate)

DIRECTORS

Health Related Business: JODY WOODWORTH
Medical Imaging Program: JOEY BATTLES
Nursing: Dr LINDA CHRISTENSEN (Dean)
Occupational Therapy Assistant Program: CRISTY SCHAEFER
Physical Therapist Assistant Program: KIRK PECK
Radiologic Technology Program: ELLEN COLLINS

COLLEGE OF SAINT MARY

7000 Mercy Rd, Omaha, NE 68106

Telephone: (402) 399-2405
Fax: (402) 399-2341
E-mail: enroll@csm.edu
Internet: www.csm.edu

Founded 1923
Private control
Academic year: August to August

President: Dr MARYANNE STEVENS
Registrar: DEBBIE NUGEN
Graduate Studies and Continuing Education: Dr MARTIN LARREY
Library Director: SUSAN PAYNE

Number of teachers: 54
Number of students: 1,000
Areas of study: arts and sciences, health care professions, professional studies.

BRANCH CAMPUS

Lincoln Campus: 4600 Valley Rd, Suite 403, Lincoln, NE 68510; tel. (402) 489-2900; e-mail lincoln@csm.edu.

CONCORDIA UNIVERSITY—NEBRASKA

800 North Columbia Ave, Seward, NE 68434

Telephone: (402) 643-3651
Fax: (402) 643-4073
Internet: www.cune.edu

Founded 1894
Academic year: August to May

President: Rev. BRIAN L. FRIEDRICH
Provost: Dr DAVID DOLAK
Registrar: EDWIN SIFFRING
Director of Admissions: CHAD THIERS
Librarian: BASIL WEHRMANN

Library of 230,000 vols
Number of teachers: 65
Number of students: 1,311

Publication: *Issues in Christian Education* (3 a year).

CREIGHTON UNIVERSITY

Omaha, NE 68178

Telephone: (402) 280-2700
Internet: www.creighton.edu

Founded 1878; chartered 1879
Private independent, associated with the Society of Jesus
Academic year: August to May

President: Rev. JOHN P. SCHLEGEL
Vice-President (Academic Affairs): Dr CHRISTINE WISEMAN
Vice-President (Administration and Finance): DANIEL E. BURKEY
Vice-President (Health Sciences): Dr CAM E. ENARSON
Vice-President (Information Systems): BRIAN A. YOUNG
Vice-President (Student Services): Dr JOHN CERNECH
Vice-President (University Ministry): Rev. ANDREW F. ALEXANDER
Vice-President (University Relations): LISA D. CALVERT
Dean of Students: JOHN CERNECH
Director of Admissions: MARY E. CHASE

Registrar: JOHN A. KRECEK
Director of Alumni Memorial Library: MICHAEL LaCROIX

Library of 909,634 vols
Number of teachers: 1,527
Number of students: 6,723

Publications: *Creighton University Bulletin*, *The Creightonian*, *Bluejay*, *Creighton Law Review*, *Creighton University Magazine*

DEANS

Arts and Sciences: Dr TIMOTHY AUSTIN
Business Administration: Dr DEBORAH WELLS
Dentistry: Dr STEPHEN FRIEDRICHSEN
Graduate: BARBARA BRADEN
Law: PATRICK BORCHERS
Medicine: CAM E. ENARSON
Nursing: ELEANOR HOWELL
Pharmacy and Health Professions: CHRIS J. BRADBURY
University College and Summer Sessions: BARBARA BRADEN

DANA COLLEGE

Blair, NE 68008

Telephone: (402) 426-9000
Fax: (402) 426-7332
E-mail: admissions@dana.edu
Internet: www.dana.edu

Founded 1884
Academic year: September to May

President: Dr JANET S. PHILIPP
Registrar: MELINDA STONER
Dean: Dr BRIAN VIETS
Librarian: THOMAS NIELSEN

Library of 152,028 vols
Number of teachers: 75
Number of students: 582.

DOANE COLLEGE

Crete, NE 68333

Telephone: (402) 826-2161
E-mail: admissions@doane.edu
Internet: www.doane.edu

Founded 1872

President: JONATHAN BRAND
Dean of Business: DAN KUNZMAN
Dean of the College: GLEN DAVIDSON
Registrar: PAULA VALENTA
Librarian: PEGGY BROOKS SMITH

Library of 221,435 vols
Number of teachers: 104
Number of students: 885 (Crete Campus).

ATTACHED INSTITUTE

Midwest Institute for International Studies: Dir MAUREEN FRANKLIN.

GRACE UNIVERSITY

1311 S 9th Street, Omaha, NE 68108-3629

Telephone: (402) 449-2800
Fax: (402) 341-9587
E-mail: info@graceuniversity.edu
Internet: www.graceuniversity.edu

Founded 1943 as Grace Bible Institute; present name 1995
Private control

President: Dr JAMES P. ECKMAN
Vice-President (Academic Affairs): Dr PATRICK A. BLEWETT
Vice-President (Student Services): Dr JARED BURKHOLDER
Vice-President (Business and Finance): TIMOTHY HURLEY
Vice-President (University Advancement): KATHY LARSEN
Registrar: BENHAIMANOT YOSIEF
Library Director: GARY SHOOK

Number of teachers: 15

Number of students: 578 (509 undergraduate, 69 graduate)

HEADS OF DEPARTMENTS
Biblical Studies: Dr KARL E. PAGENKEMPER
General Studies: Dr STANLEY V. UDD
Professional Studies: DAVID M. SHRADER

HASTINGS COLLEGE

710 N. Turner, Hastings, NE 68902-0269
Telephone: (402) 463-2402
Internet: www.hastings.edu
Founded 1882
President: Dr PHILLIP DUDLEY
Academic Dean: Dr DWAYNE STRASHEIM
Registrar: JAMES SMITH
Librarian: ROBERT NEDDERMAN
Library of 115,000 vols
Number of teachers: 69
Number of students: 1,060
Publication: *Hastings College Today* (2 a year).

MIDLAND LUTHERAN COLLEGE

900 N. Clarkson St, Fremont, NE 68025
Telephone: (402) 721-5480
Fax: (402) 721-0250
E-mail: braaten@admin.mlc.edu
Internet: www.mlc.edu
Founded 1883
Academic year: August to May
President: Dr STEVEN E. TITUS
Executive Vice-President: Dr GENE CRUME
Vice-President for Business and Finance: SARAH KOTTICH
Vice-President for Academic Affairs: Dr JAMES REYNOLDS
Vice-President for Student Development: Dr TARA KNUDSON CARL
Associate Vice-President for Enrollment Management and Financial Aid: DOUG WATSON
Registrar: JENNIFER VERHEIN
Director of Library: Dr THOMAS E. BOYLE
Library of 114,000 vols
Number of teachers: 55
Number of students: 1,025
Publications: *The Midland* (every 2 weeks), *MLC Magazine* (4 a year).

NEBRASKA CHRISTIAN COLLEGE

1800 Syracuse Avenue, Norfolk, NE 68701
Telephone: (402) 379-5000
Fax: (402) 379-5100
E-mail: admissions@nechristian.edu
Internet: www.nechristian.edu
Founded 1944
Private control
President: RICHARD MILLIKEN
Academic Dean: Dr DAN DONALDSON
Registrar: JUNE PIEPER
Librarian: LINDA LU LLOYD
Number of teachers: 24
Number of students: 162
Areas of study: biblical studies, Christian education, family life ministry, church music, deaf ministries, general studies, missions, pastoral ministries, youth ministries.

NEBRASKA WESLEYAN UNIVERSITY

5000 St Paul Ave, Lincoln, NE 68504-2796
Telephone: (402) 466-2371
Fax: (402) 465-2179
Internet: www.nebrwesleyan.edu
Founded 1887
President: Dr JEANIE WATSON
Vice-President for Academic Affairs: Dr NORVAL KNETEN

Registrar: PATRICIA HALL
Director of Admissions: KEN SIEG
Library of 200,000 vols
Number of teachers: 166 (86 full-time, 80 part-time)
Number of students: 1,583.

PERU STATE COLLEGE

600 Hoyt St, POB 10, Peru, NE 68421
Telephone: (402) 872-3815
E-mail: admissions@oakmail.peru.edu
Internet: www.peru.edu
Founded 1867
President: Dr BEN E. JOHNSON
Vice-President, Administration and Finance: LINDA JACOBSEN
Vice-President, Academic Affairs: Dr JEROME MARTIN
Vice-President, Student Affairs: TED HARSHBARGER
Registrar: Dr DIANNA EASON
Director of Continuing Education: Dr CARL ELLIS
Librarian: PEG O'ROURKE
Library of 100,000 vols
Number of teachers: 47
Number of students: 1,745.

UNION COLLEGE

3800 South 48th St, Lincoln, NE 68506
Telephone: (402) 488-2331
Fax: (402) 486-2895
E-mail: ucinfo@ucollege.edu
Internet: www.ucollege.edu
Founded 1891
Academic year: August to May
President: DAVID SMITH
Vice-President and Dean: MALCOLM RUSSELL
Vice-President for Finance: GARY BOLLINGER
Vice-President for Enrollment: BUELL FOGG
Registrar: OSA BERG
Director of Institutional Advancement: LuANN DAVIS
Librarian: SABRINA RILEY
Library of 112,283 vols
Number of teachers: 73
Number of students: 951.

UNIVERSITY OF NEBRASKA

Lincoln, NE 68583-0745
Telephone: (402) 472-2111
Fax: (402) 472-1237
Internet: www.nebraska.edu
Founded 1869
President: JAMES B. MILLIKEN
Executive Vice-President and Provost: Dr JAY NOREN
Vice-President for Business and Finance: DAVID LECHNER
Vice-President and General Counsel: RICHARD R. WOOD.

CONSTITUENT CAMPUSES

University of Nebraska at Kearney

905 West 25th St, Kearney, NE 68849-0601
Telephone: (308) 865-8441
Fax: (308) 865-8157
Internet: www.unk.edu
Founded 1903
Chancellor: DOUGLAS A. KRISTENSEN
Senior Vice-Chancellor for Academic Affairs: Dr FINNIE MURRAY
Vice-Chancellor for Business and Finance: Dr RANDAL HAACK
Vice-Chancellor for University Relations: KATHLEEN SMITH
Dean of Student Life: Dr LOIS FLAGSTAD
Director of Libraries: LARRY HARDESTY

Library of 228,625 vols
Number of teachers: 360 (full-time)
Number of students: 8,045

DEANS
College of Business and Technology: Dr GALEN D. HADLEY
College of Education: Dr MARILYN HADLEY
College of Fine Arts and Humanities: Dr WILLIAM JURMA
College of Natural and Social Sciences: Dr FRANCIS HARROLD
College of Graduate Studies and Research: Dr KEN NIKELS

University of Nebraska at Lincoln

201 Canfield Administration Bldg, Lincoln, NE 68588-0419
Telephone: (402) 472-2116
Fax: (402) 472-5110
Internet: www.unl.edu
Founded 1869
Chancellor: HARVEY PERLMAN
Senior Vice-Chancellor for Academic Affairs: Dr BARBARA COUTURE
Vice-Chancellor for Business and Finance: CHRISTINE M. JACKSON
Vice-Chancellor for Student Affairs: Dr JAMES V. GRIESEN
Vice-President and Vice-Chancellor for Agriculture and Natural Resources: Dr JOHN OWENS
Director of Admissions: ALAN CERVENY
Dean of Libraries: JOAN R. GIESECKE
Library: see Libraries and Archives
Number of teachers: 1,732 (full-time)
Number of students: 24,491
Publications: *Nebraska Law Review, University of Nebraska Studies, Nebraska Journal of Economics and Business, Prairie Schooner, University of Nebraska—Lincoln Daily Nebraskan*

DEANS
College of Agricultural Sciences and Natural Resources: Dr STEVEN S. WALLER
College of Architecture: Dr WAYNE DRUMMOND
College of Arts and Sciences: Dr RICHARD J. HOFFMANN
College of Business Administration: CYNTHIA H. MILLIGAN
College of Engineering and Technology: Dr DAVID H. ALLEN
College of Human Resources and Family Sciences: Dr MARJORIE KOSTELNIK
Graduate Studies: Dr PREM S. PAUL
College of Law: Dr STEVE WILLBORN
Teachers' College: Dr JAMES P. O'HANLON
College of Journalism: Dr WILL NORTON, Jr
College of Fine and Performing Arts: Dr GIACOMO M. OLIVA

University of Nebraska at Omaha

6001 Dodge St, Omaha, NE 68182
Telephone: (402) 554-2200
Fax: (402) 554-3555
Internet: www.unomaha.edu
Founded 1908
Chancellor: Dr NANCY BELCK
Vice-Chancellor for Academic and Student Affairs: Dr JOHN CHRISTENSEN
Vice-Chancellor for Administration: WADE ROBINSON
Associate Vice-Chancellor for Business and Finance: JULIE TOTTEN
Associate Vice-Chancellor for Student Affairs: Dr WADE ROBINSON
Director of Admissions: JOLENE ADAMS
Librarian: JANICE S. BOYER
Library of 623,000 vols, 1,700,000 micromaterial items
Number of teachers: 519

Number of students: 15,899
Publication: *Gateway* (weekly)

DEANS

College of Arts and Sciences: Dr SHELTON
  HENDRICKS
College of Business Administration: Dr LOU
  POL
College of Education: Dr JOHN LANGAN
College of Fine Arts: ROBERT WELK
College of Human Resources and Family
  Sciences: Dr MARJORIE KOSTELNIK
College of Public Affairs and Community
  Service: Dr B. J. REED
Graduate Studies and Research: Dr THOMAS
  BRAGG
International Studies and Programs: THOMAS
  E. GOUTTIERRE

University of Nebraska Medical Center

600 South 42nd St, Omaha, NE 68198

Telephone: (402) 559-4200
Fax: (402) 559-4396
Internet: www.unmc.edu

Founded 1880

Chancellor: Dr HAROLD M. MAURER
Vice-Chancellor for Academic Affairs: Dr
  RUBENS J. PAMIES
Vice-Chancellor for Business and Finance:
  DONALD S. LEUENBERGER
Library Director: Dr NANCY N. WOELFL

Library of 196,313 vols
Number of teachers: 689
Number of students: 2,703

DEANS

College of Dentistry: Dr JOHN REINHARDT
College of Medicine: Dr JOHN J. GOLLAN
College of Nursing: Dr VIRGINIA TILDEN
College of Pharmacy: Dr CLARENCE UEDA
Graduate Studies and Research: Dr RUBENS
  J. PAMIES

ATTACHED INSTITUTIONS

**Eppley Institute for Research in Cancer
and Allied Diseases:** Dir Dr KENNETH
COWAN.

Meyer Rehabilitation Institute: Dir Dr
BRUCE A. BUEHLER..

WAYNE STATE COLLEGE

1111 Main St, Wayne, NE 68787

Telephone: (402) 375-7000
E-mail: admit1@wsc.edu
Internet: www.wsc.edu

Founded 1910

President: Dr RICHARD J. COLLINGS
Enrollment and Admissions: R. LINE MORRIS
Librarian: STAN GARDNER

Library of 243,848 vols
Number of teachers: 199
Number of students: 3,500.

YORK COLLEGE

1125 E 8th Street, York, NE 68467

Telephone: (402) 363-5600
Fax: (402) 363-5623
E-mail: enroll@york.edu
Internet: www.york.edu

Founded 1890
Private control
Academic year: August to May

President: Dr WAYNE BAKER
Vice-President (Academic Affairs) and Dean
  of College: MARY WALLER
Vice-President (Enrollment Management):
  Dr JIM WHITE
Director of Student Records and Registra-
  tion: STEWART SIKES
Library Director: KEN GUNSELMAN

Number of teachers: 49
Number of students: 488

HEADS OF DEPARTMENTS

Division of Biblical Studies and Behavioral
  Sciences: Dr FRANK WHEELER
E. A. Levitt School of Business: JAMES M.
  GERHARDT
Division of Education: Dr KATHLEEN B.
  WHEELER
Division of Humanities: JOHN I. BAKER, III
Division of Natural Sciences and Mathe-
  matics: Dr L. RAY MILLER, II

NEVADA

SIERRA NEVADA COLLEGE

999 Tahoe Blvd, Incline Village, NV 89451-
9500

Telephone: (775) 831-1314
Fax: (775) 831-1347
E-mail: admissions@sierranevada.edu
Internet: www.sierranevada.edu

Founded 1969
Private control
Academic year: September to May

Pres.: LARRY LARGE
Vice-Pres. for Academic Affairs: RAY RYAN
Vice-Pres. for Finance and Chief Operating
  Officer: SCOTT GOODIN
Registrar: SHANNON BEETS
Library Dir: ANNALI KIERS

Number of teachers: 27
Number of students: 504 (400 undergraduate, 104 graduate).

**NEVADA SYSTEM OF HIGHER
EDUCATION**

2601 Enterprise Rd, Reno, NV 89512

Telephone: (775) 784-4905
Fax: (775) 784-5049
Internet: www.nevada.edu

Chancellor: JAMES E. ROGERS.

CONSTITUENT INSTITUTIONS

Nevada State College

1125 Nevada State Dr., Henderson, NV
89002

Telephone: (775) 992-2000
Fax: (775) 992-2226
E-mail: students@nsc.nevada.edu
Internet: www.nsc.nevada.edu

Founded 2002

Pres.: Dr FRED J. MARYANSKI.

University of Nevada, Las Vegas

4505 Maryland Parkway, Las Vegas, NV
89154-9900

Telephone: (775) 895-3011
Fax: (775) 895-3850
Internet: www.unlv.edu

Founded 1957
Academic year: August to May

Pres.: DAVID B. ASHLEY
Exec. Vice-Pres. and Provost: Dr NEAL J.
  SMATRESK
Vice-Pres. for Finance: GERRY BOMOTTI
Vice-Pres. for Student Life: Dr REBECCA
  MILLS
Assoc. Vice-Pres. for Community Relations:
  SCHYLER RICHARDS
Sr Assoc. Vice-Pres. for Devt: NANCY STROUSE
Registrar: JEFF HALVERSON
Dean of Libraries: PATRICIA A. IANNUZZI

Library of 2,966,000 vols
Number of teachers: 1,199 (752 full-time, 447
  part-time)
Number of students: 28,000

DEANS

College of Business: Dr RICHARD FLAHERTY
College of Hotel Admin.: Dr STUART MANN
College of Education: Dr GENE HALL
College of Health Sciences: Dr CAROLYN SABO
College of Law: Dr RICHARD MORGAN
College of Urban Affairs: Dr MARTHA WATSON
College of Liberal Arts: Dr JAMES FREY
College of Sciences: Dr PETER STARKWEATHER
College of Eng.: Dr RONALD SACK
College of Fine Arts: Dr JEFF KOEP
College of Graduate Studies: Dr PAUL FERGU-
  SON
Honors College: Dr SUE REIMOND
College of Extended Studies: Dr PAUL AIZLEY

ATTACHED INSTITUTE

Desert Research Institute: 2215 Raggio
Parkway, Reno, NV 89512; tel. (775) 673-
7300; internet www.dri.edu; offices and
laboratories in Reno, Boulder City, Las
Vegas and Boulder City; research in energy,
atmospheric environment, water resources,
ecology, anthropology, socio-economics and
demography; Pres. Dr STEPHEN G. WELLS.

University of Nevada, Reno

Reno, NV 89557

Telephone: (775) 784-1110
Fax: (775) 784-1300
E-mail: asknevada@unr.edu
Internet: www.unr.edu

Founded 1874
Academic year: August to May

Pres.: MILTON D. GLICK
Exec. Vice-Pres. and Provost: JOHN FREDER-
  ICK
Vice-Pres. for Admin. and Finance: RONALD
  ZUREK
Vice-Pres. for Devt and Alumni Relations:
  JOHN CARUTHERS
Vice-Pres. for Information Technology and
  Dean of Libraries: STEVEN D. ZINK
Vice-Pres. for Marketing and Communica-
  tions: CINDY POLLARD
Vice-Pres. for Research: MARSHA READ
Vice-Pres. for Student Services: SHANNON
  ELLIS
Registrar: MELISSA N. CHOROSZY

Library of 1,128,954 vols
Number of teachers: 985
Number of students: 15,950

Publication: *Electronic Journal of Science
  Education* (quarterly)

DEANS

College of Agriculture: DAVID THAWLEY
College of Business Admin.: H. MIKE REED
College of Education: WILLIAM SPARKMAN
College of Eng.: TED E. BATCHMAN
Graduate School: MARSHA READ
College of Human and Community Sciences:
  JEAN PERRY
School of Journalism: COLE CAMPBELL
College of Liberal Arts: ERIC HERZIK
Mackay School of Mines: ROBERT TARANIK
  (Dir)
School of Medicine: JOHN MCDONALD
Orvis School of Nursing: PATSY RUCHALA
  (Dir)
College of Science: DAVID WESTFALL

NEW HAMPSHIRE

COLBY-SAWYER COLLEGE

541 Main St, New London, NH 03257

Telephone: (603) 526-3000
Fax: (603) 526-3452
Internet: www.colby-sawyer.edu

Founded 1837 as New London Academy;
  present name 1975

Private control
Academic year: September to May
President: Dr ANNE PONDER
Vice-President (Academic) and Dean of Faculty: Dr JUDITH A. MUYSKENS
Vice-President (Administration): DOUGLAS C. ATKINS
Vice-President (Advancement): Dr DONALD A. HASSELTINE
Vice-President (Enrollment Management) and Dean of Admissions (vacant)
Registrar: CAROLE H. PARSONS
Librarian: CARRIE THOMAS
Number of teachers: 118
Number of students: 986

HEADS OF DEPARTMENTS
Business Adminstration: ANTHONY N. QUINN
Institute for Community and Environmental Studies: Dr JOHN H. CALLENWAERT (Dir)
Exercise and Sport Sciences: Dr JEAN ECK-RICH
Fine and Performing Arts: JON P. KEENAN
Humanities: Dr AMY L. KNISLEY
Natural Sciences: Dr BENJAMIN B. STEELE
Nursing: (vacant)
Social Sciences and Education: Dr JANICE K. EWING

DANIEL WEBSTER COLLEGE

20 University Dr., Nashua, NH 03063-1300
Telephone: (603) 577-6000
Fax: (603) 577-6001
E-mail: info@dwc.edu
Internet: www.dwc.edu
Founded 1965
Private control
Academic year: August to May
President: HANNAH M. MCCARTHY
Vice-President (Academic Affairs) and Dean of the Faculty: Dr SUZAN H. SCHAFER
Vice-President (Finance and Operations): TODD C. EMMONS
Dean of Students: SUSAN C. ELSASS
Registrar: JEAN P. ANDERSON
Library Director: FRANCHESCA DENTON
Library of 34,000 vols
Number of teachers: 60
Number of students: 1,200

HEADS OF DEPARTMENTS
Aviation: ROGER D. BACCHIERI
Business and Management: Dr A. REZA HOSHMAND
Computer Sciences: FRANK MURGIDA
Engineering, Mathematics, and Science: NICHOLAS BERTOZZI
Social Science and Humanities: Dr JAMES P. O'DONNELL

DARTMOUTH COLLEGE

Hanover, NH 03755
Telephone: (603) 646-1110
Fax: (603) 646-2850
E-mail: contact@dartmouth.edu
Internet: www.dartmouth.edu
Founded 1769
Private control
Pres.: JAMES WRIGHT
Provost: BARRY P. SCHERR
Exec. Vice-Pres. for Finance and Admin.: ADAM KELLER
Vice-Pres. for Public Affairs: SHEILA CULBERT
Exec. Vice-Pres. for Information Technology: ELLEN J. WAITE-FRANZEN
Vice-Pres. for Alumni Affairs: DAVID P. SPALDING
Registrar: MEREDITH H. BRAZ
Dean of Admissions and Financial Aid: MARIA LASKARIS
Dean of Libraries: JEFFREY L. HORRELL (acting)

Number of teachers: 922
Number of students: 5,704
Publications: *Linguistic Discovery* (online), *Encrucijada* (online)

DEANS
College: DAN NELSON (acting)
Faculty: CAROL L. FOLT (acting)
Graduate Studies: CHARLES K. BARLOWE
Medical School: STEPHEN SPIELBERG (acting)
Thayer School of Eng.: JOSEPH H. HELBLE (acting)
Tuck School of Business Admin.: PAUL DANOS

PROFESSORS
Note: some professors serve in more than one department

Humanities
Department of African and African American Studies:
ALVERSON, H. S., Anthropology
AMADIUMI, I., Religion
COOK, W., English
HALL, R. L., Sociology
KASFIR, N. M., Govt
LANGFORD, G. M., Biology
PEASE, D. L., English
SPITZER, L., History
WALKER, K., French and Italian
WILDER, C., History

Department of Art History:
JORDAN, J., Modern Art
KENSETH, J., Renaissance and Baroque Art

Department of Asian and Middle Eastern Languages and Literatures:
ALLAN, S., Chinese
GLINERT, L., Hebrew

Department of Classics:
BRADLEY, E. M., Greek and Latin Literature, Roman and Early Christian Art and Architecture
RUTTER, J. B., Classical Art and Archaeology, Archaeology of the Aegean
SCOTT, W. C., Greek and Latin Literature, Classical Drama, Homer
TATUM, J., Greek and Latin Literature, Ancient Fiction, The Classical Tradition, Roman Comedy

Department of Comparative Literature:
COOK, W., English
CREWE, J., English
GAYLORD, A. T., English
GEMUNDEN, G., German
GLINERT, J. A., Asian, Middle Eastern Languages and Literature
GREEN, M. J., French and Italian
HEFFERNAN, J. W., English
HIGGINS, L. A., French and Italian
HIRSCH, M., French and Italian
JEWELL, K. J., French and Italian
KOPPER, J. M., Russian
KRITZMAN, L. D., French and Italian
LAWRENCE, A., Film

Department of English:
BOOSE, L., English
COOK, W., English
CREWE, J., English and Comparative Literature
GAYLORD, A., English
HEBERT, E., English
HEFFERNAN, J. A. W., English
HUNTINGDON, C., English
McKEE, P., English
MATHIS, C., English and Creative Writing
RENZA, L., English
SACCIO, P., English and Shakespearean Studies
SILVER, B. R., English
SLEIGH, T., English
TRAVIS, P. W., English
WYKES, P., English

Department of Film and Television Studies:
LAWRENCE, A.
Department of French and Italian:
GREEN, M.
HIGGINS, L.
HIRSCH, M.
JEWELL, K.
KRITZMAN, L. D.
RASSIAS, J.
WALKER, K. L.

Department of German:
DUNCAN, B., German Language
GEMÜNDEN, G., German, Comparative Literature
SCHER, S. P., German, Comparative Literature

Department of Linguistics and Cognitive Science:
ALVERSON, H. S., Anthropology
DUNBAR, K., Education and Psychology
DUNCAN, B., German
GLINERT, L. H., AMELL
GRENOBLE, L., Russian
HUGHES, H. C., Psychology
JAHNER, E. A., English and Native American Studies
MOOR, J. H., Philosophy
PETTITO, L. A., Education and Psychology
SCHERR, B. P., Russian
SINNOTT-ARMSTRONG, W. P., Philosophy
SORENSEN, R. A., Philosophy
TAUBE, J., Psychology
TRAVIS, P. W., English
WALKER, K. L., French and Italian
WOLFORD, G. L., Psychology

Department of Music:
APPLETON, J. H.
O'NEAL, M.
PINKAS, S.

Department of Philosophy:
DRIVER, J.
GERT, B.
MOOR, J. H.
SINNOTT-ARMSTRONG, W.
SORENSEN, R.

Department of Religion:
ACKERMAN, S.
AMADIUME, I., African Religions
FRANKENBERRY, N., Philosophy of Religion, Women and Religion, Science and Religion
GREEN, R. M., Religious Ethics, Business Ethics
HENRICKS, R. G., Religions of China

Department of Russian:
GRENOBLE, L.
KOPPER, J.
LOSEFF, L.
SCHERR, B.

Department of Spanish and Portuguese:
BUENO-CHAVEZ, R.
PASTOR, B.

Department of Studio Art:
FRANK MOSS, IIII, B.
RANDALL, C.
THOMPSON, E.

Department of Theatre:
CRICKARD, L.
GAFFNEY, P.
GRENOBLE, L.
SPICER, M.

Women and Gender Studies:
ACKERMAN, S., Religion
AMADIUMI, I., Religion
BOOSE, L. E., English
DARROW, M. H., History
DOMOSH, M., Geography
FOWLER, L. L., Govt
FRANKENBERRY, N. K., Religion
GARROD, A. G., Education

GREEN, M. J., French and Italian
HIGGINS, L. A., French and Italian
HIRSCH, M., French and Italian
JEWELL, K. J., French and Italian
LAWRENCE, A., Film
SILVER, B. R., English
SPITZER, L., History

Science

Department of Biological Sciences:

BERGER, E. M., Molecular Genetics, Cell
  Biology
FOLT, C. L., Aquatic Ecology
GILBERT, J. J., Ecology, Aquatic Biology
GUERINOT, M. L., Molecular Genetics,
  Microbiology
HOLMES, R. T., Animal Behaviour, Ecology
LANGFORD, G. M., Cell Biology
McCLUNG, C. R., Molecular Genetics
McPEEK, M. A., Community Ecology, Evo-
  lution
PEART, D. R., Population and Community
  Ecology, Forest Ecology
SLOBODA, R. D., Cell Biology, Neurobiology
WITTERS, L. A., Human Biology, Endocri-
  nology/Metabolism

Department of Chemistry:

BELBRUNO, J. J.
BRAUN, C. L.
CANTOR, R. S.
DITCHFIELD, R.
GRIBBLE, G. W.
HUGHES, R. P.
JACOBI, P. A.
LEMAL, D. M.
LIPSON, J. E. G.
SODERBERG, R. H.
SPENCER, T. A.
WILCOX, D. E.
WINN, J. S.

Department of Environmental Studies:

FRIEDLAND, A.
HOWARTH, R.
SHEPHERD, J.
VIRGINIA, R.

Department of Computer Science:

DONALD, B. R.
DRYSDALE, III, R. L.
KOTZ, D. F.
MAKEDON, F. S.
ROCKMORE, D.

Department of Mathematics:

ARKOWITZ, M. A.
BAUMGARTNER, J. E.
BICKEL, T. F.
BOGART, K. P.
DOYLE, P.
GORDON, C. S.
GROSZEK, M.
LAHR, C. D.
POMERANCE, C. B.
ROCKMORE, D. N.
SHEMANSKE, T. R.
WALLACE, D. I.
WEBB, D. L.
WILLIAMS, D. P.

Department of Physics and Astronomy:

FESEN, C. G.
FESEN, R. A.
GLEISER, M.
HUDSON, M. K.
LABELLE, J. W.
LAWRENCE, W. E.
MONTGOMERY, D. C.
MOOK, D. E.
THORSTENSEN, J. R.
WEGNER, G. A.
WYBOURNE, M. N.

Social Sciences

Department of Anthropology:

ALVERSON, H.
EICKELMAN, D. F.
ENDICOTT, K.

KAN, S.
NICHOLS, D. L.

Department of Economics:

BLANCHFLOWER, D. G.
FISCHEL, W. A.
GUSTMAN, A. L.
IRWIN, D. A.
KOHN, M.
MARION, N. P.
SAMWICK, A. A.
SCOTT, J. T.
SKINNER, J.
STAIGER, D. O.
VENTI, S. F.

Department of Education:

DUNBAR, K.
GARROD, A.
PETITTO, L. A.

Department of Geography:

DOMOSH, M.
MAGILLIGAN, F. J.
WRIGHT, R. A.

Department of Government:

FOWLER, L. L.
FREEDMAN, J. O.
KASFIR, N. M.
LEBOW, R. N.
MASTANDUNO, M.
SA'ADAH, M. A.
WINTERS, R. F.

Department of History:

CALLOWAY, C.
CROSSLEY, P. K.
DARROW, M.
ERMARTH, H. M.
GARTHWAITE, G. R.
NAVARRO, M.
NELSON, J. B.
SHEWMAKER, K. E.
SPITZER, L.
WHELAN, H. W.
WILDER, C. S.
WRIGHT, J.

Department of Latin American, Latino and Caribbean Studies:

BUENO-CHAVEZ, R., Spanish and Portu-
  guese
NAVARRO, M., History
NICHOLS, D. L., Anthropology
PASTOR, B., Spanish and Portuguese
WALKER, K. L., French and Italian
WRIGHT, R., Geography

Department of Native American Studies:

CALLOWAY, C. G.
KAN, S.
NICHOLS, D. L.

Department of Psychological and Brain Sciences:

DUNBAR, K., Cognitive Psychology
GAZZANIGA, M. S., Cognitive Neuroscience
GRAFTON, S., Functional Brain Imaging
HEATHERTON, T. F., Experimental Social
  Neuroscience, Personality and Motiva-
  tion
HUGHES, H. C., Electrophysiological and
  Psychophysical Studies of Sensory Pro-
  cessing in Humans
HULL, J. G., Structure of Self-Knowledge
  and Function of Self-Regulatory Systems
JERNSTEDT, G. C., Learning, Instructional
  Design Theory, Evaluation Research
KLECK, R. E., Experimental Social Com-
  munication Processes
MACRAE, C. N., Social Cognition
MORRIS, W. N., Mood and Emotion
PETITTO, L. A., Cognitive Psychology and
  Psycholinguistics
TAUBE, J. S.
WOLFORD, G. L.

Department of Sociology:

CAMPBELL, J. L.

HALL, R. L.
PARSA, M.

Dartmouth Medical School (1 Rope Ferry Rd,
Hanover, NH 03755-1404; tel. (603) 650-
1200; fax (603) 650-1202; internet www
.dartmouth.edu/dms):

ADDANTE, R. R., Oral-Maxillofacial Surgery
  and Anaesthesiology
AHLES, T. A., Psychiatry
ALTO, W. A., Community and Family
  Medicine
AMBROS, V. R., Genetics
AUBUCHON, J. P., Pathology and Hematol-
  ogy-Oncology
BALDWIN, J. C., Surgery
BANKER, B. Q., Pathology
BARLOWE, C. K., Biochemistry
BARON, J. A., General Internal Medicine
  and Community and Family Medicine
BARTELS, S. J., Psychiatry
BARTLETT, D., Physiology
BATALDEN, P. B., Paediatrics and Commu-
  nity and Family Medicine
BAUGHMAN, R. D., Dermatology
BEISSWENGER, P. J., Medicine
BERGER, B. J., Psychiatry
BERMAN, S. A., Medicine
BERNAT, J. L., Neurology
BERNINI, P. M., Surgery (Orthopaedics)
BIRD, H. H., Anaesthiology
BLACK, W. C., Radiology
BOYLE, W. E., Paediatrics and Community
  and Family Medicine
BRINCKERHOFF, C. E., Medicine and Bio-
  chemistry
BRINCK-JOHNSER, T., Pathology
BROOKS, J. G., Paediatrics
BROWN, F. E., Plastic Surgery
BURCHARD, K. W., Surgery and Anaesthe-
  siology
BYOCK, I. R., Anaesthiology
BZIK, D. J., Microbiology and Immunology
CAMPBELL, D. G., Surgery (Ophthalmology)
CARPENTER, S. J., Anatomy
CENDRON, M., Surgery
CHAMBERS, W. F., Anatomy
CHANG, T. Y., Biochemistry
CHEUNG, A., Microbiology and Immunology
CLENDENNING, W. E., Medicine
COHEN, J. A., Medicine
COLACCHIO, T. A., Surgery
COLE, C. N., Biochemistry and Genetics
COLE, M. D., Pharmacology and Toxicology
COMPTON, D. A., Biochemistry
CORNELL, C. J., Hematology-Oncology and
  Paediatrics
CORNELL, G. G., Medicine
CORSON, J. A., Psychiatry
CORWIN, H. L., Medicine and Anaesthesiol-
  ogy
CRAIG, R. W., Pharmacology, Toxicology
CRICHLOW, R. W., Surgerys
CROMWELL, L. D., Radiology and Neurosur-
  gery
CRONENWETT, J. L., Surgery
CROW, H. C., Radiology
DARNALL, R. A., Paediatrics and Physiology
DAUBENSPECK, A., Physiology
DELEO, J. A., Anaesthesiology
DIETRICH, A. J., Community and Family
  Medicine
DMITROVSKY, E., Pharmacology and Toxi-
  cology
DONEGAN, J. O., Otolaryngology
DOW, R. W., Surgery
DRAKE, R. E., Psychiatry; Community and
  Family Medicine
DUHAIME, A.-C., Surgery
DUNLAP, J. C., Genetics and Biochemistry
EASTMAN, A., Pharmacology and Toxicology
EDWARDS, W. H., Paediatrics
EISENBERG, B. L., Surgery
ERNSTOFF, L. T., Hematology-Oncology
ERNSTOFF, M. S., Hematology-Oncology

FANGER, M. W., Microbiology and Immunology
FEJES-TOTH, A. N., Physiology
FEJES-TOTH, G., Physiology
FERM, V. H., Anatomy
FISHER, E. S., Community and Family Medicine
FLOOD, A. B., Community and Family Medicine
FRANK, J. E., Paediatrics
FREY, W. G., Medicine
FRIEDMAN, M. J., Psychiatry, Pharmacology and Toxicology
FROMM, H., Gastroenterology
GALLAGHER, J. D., Anaesthesiology
GALTON, V. A., Physiology
GLASS, D. D., Anaesthesiology
GOODMAN, D. C., Paediatrics
GORMLEY, E. A., Surgery
GOSSELIN, R. E., Pharmacology and Toxicology
GRAFTON, S. T., Medicine
GREEN, A. I., Psychiatry
GREEN, R. L., Psychiatry
GREEN, W. R., Microbiology and Immunology
GREENBERG, R., Community and Family Medicine
GUYRE, P. M., Physiology
HAMILTON, J. W., Pharmacology, Toxicology
HARBAUGH, R. E., Surgery (Neurosurgery) and Radiology
HARBURY, H. A., Biochemistry
HARTMAN, G. S., Anaesthiology
HAZARD, R. G., Orthopaedics
HEAD, J. M., Surgery
HEANEY, J. A., Surgery
HENDERSON, J. V., Community and Family Medicine
HENDERSON, L. P., Physiology
HICKEY, W. F., Pathology
HOFNAGEL, D., Paediatrics
HOLMES, G. L., Medicine
HUG, E. B., Medicine
INSELBURG, J. W., Microbiology
ISRAEL, M. A., Paediatrics and Genetics
JACOBS, N. J., Microbiology
KARAGAS, M., Community and Family Medicine
KARL, R. C., Surgery
KASPER, L. H., Medicine
KELLEY, M. L., Medicine
KERRIGAN, C. L., Surgery
KING, B. H., Psychiatry
KLAUS, S. N., Medicine
KLEIN, R. Z., Paediatrics
KOOP, C. E., Surgery
KORC, M., Medicine
KOVAL, K. J., Orthopaedics
LANE, F. W., Surgery
LAYTON, W. M., Anatomy
LEITER, J. C., Physiology and Medicine
LEVIN, D. L., Paediatrics and Anaesthesiology
LEVINE, G. M., Community and Family Medicine
LEWIS, L. D., Medicine
LIENHARD, G. E., Biochemistry
LITTLE, G. A., Paediatrics; Obstetrics and Gynaecology
LLEWELLYN-THOMAS, H. A., Community and Family Medicine
LONGNECKER, D. S., Pathology
LOROS, J. J., Biochemistry and Genetics
LUBIN, M., Microbiology
MAHLER, D. A., Medicine
MANGANIELLI, P. D., Obstetrics and Gynaecology
MARON-PADILLA, M., Pathology
MARRIN, C. A. S., Surgery
MAUE, R. A., Medicine
MAURER, L. H., Medicine
MAYOR, M. B., Surgery (Orthopaedics)
MCALLISTER, T. W., Psychiatry
MCCANN, F. V., Physiology

MCCOLLUM, R. W., Community and Family Medicine
MCDANIEL, M. D., Anatomy
MCINTYRE, D. R., Medicine
MEMOLI, V. A., Pathology
MODLIN, J. F., Paediatrics
MOESHLER, J. B., Paediatrics
MOGIELNICKI, R. P., General Internal Medicine
MOHANDAS, T. K., Pathology
MUESER, K. T., Psychiatry; Community and Family Medicine
MUNCK, A. U., Physiology
NAITOVE, A., Surgery
NATTIE, E. E., Physiology
NELSON, E. C., Community and Family Medicine
NELSON, W. H., Psychiatry
NEMIAH, J. C., Psychiatry
NIERENBERG, D. W., Pharmacology and Toxicology
NODA, L. H., Biochemistry
NOELLE, R. J., Microbiology and Immunology
NOLL, W. W., Paediatrics
NORDGREN, R. E., Paediatrics
NORTH, W. G., Physiology
NUGENT, W.C., Surgery
NYE, R. E., Physiology
O'CONNOR, G. T., Community and Family Medicine
O'DONNELL, J. F., Medicine
ONION, D. K., Community and Family Medicine
OXMAN, T. E., Psychiatry; Community and Family Medicine
PAYSON, H. E., Psychiatry
PEARLMAN, J. D., Medicine
PFEFFERKORN, E. R., Microbiology
PLUME, S. K., Surgery
QUILL, T. J., Anaesthesiology
RAVARIS, C. L., Psychiatry
REGAN-SMITH, M. G., Rheumatology; Community and Family Medicine
REEVES, A. G., Medicine
RIGBY, W. F. C., Microbiology and Immunology;
ROBERTS, D. W., Surgery (Neurosurgery)
ROEBUCK, W. D., Pharmacology and Toxicology
ROGERS, C. C., Medicine
ROLETT, E. L., Medicine
ROSENBERG, S. D., Psychiatry
ROTHSTEIN, R. I., Medicine
ROUS, S. N., Surgery
ROZYCKI, A. A., Paediatrics
RUECKERT, F., Surgery
ST GERMAIN, D. L., Medicine
ST JOHN, W. M., Physiology
SANDERS, J. H., Surgery
SARGENT, J. D., Paediatrics
SATEIA, M. J., Psychiatry
SAUNDERS, R. L., Surgery
SAYKIN, A. J., Psychiatry
SCHNED, A. R., Pathology
SCHWARTZMAN, J. D., Pathology
SCORNIK, O. A., Biochemistry
SILBERFARB, P. M., Psychiatry and Medicine
SIMONS, M., Cardiology; Pharmacology and Toxicology
SKINNER, J. S., Community and Family Medicine
SMITH, B. D., Obstetrics and Gynaecology
SMITH, R. P., Pharmacology and Toxicology
SOBEL, R., Psychiatry
SOKOL, H. W., Physiology
SOLOW, C., Psychiatry
SORENSON, G. D., Pathology
SPECK, N. A., Biochemistry
SPENCER, S. K., Dermatology and Surgery (Dermatology)
SPIEGEL, P. K., Radiology
SPIELBERG, S. P., Paediatrics
STANTON, B. A., Physiology
STAUFFER, M. W., Pathology

STOKES, D. C., Paediatrics
STRICKLER, J. C., Medicine
STYS, S. J., Obstetrics and Gynaecology (Maternal-Foetal Medicine)
SUTTON, J. E., Surgery
SWARTZ, H. M., Radiology; Community and Family Medicine; Physiology
TOSTESON, A. N., Community and Family Medicine
TOSTESON, T. D., Community and Family Medicine
TRUMPOWER, B. L., Biochemistry
VALTIN, H., Physiology
VAN LEEUWIN, D. J., Medicine
VARNUM, J. W., Hospital Administration
VIDAVER, R. M., Psychiatry
VON REYN, C. F., Medicine
WADE, W. F., Microbiology
WALLACE, A. G., Medicine
WALSH, D. B., Surgery
WASSON, J. H., Community and Family Medicine
WEINSTEIN, J. N., Surgery (Orthopaedics); Community and Family Medicine
WELCH, H. G., Community and Family Medicine
WENNBERG, J. E., Community and Family Medicine
WICKNER, W. T., Biochemistry
WILKINSON, R. H., Radiology
WILLIAMSON, P. D., Medicine
WIRA, C. R., Physiology
YEAGER, M. P., Anaesthiology
YEO, K.-T. J., Pathology
YOUNG, R. D., Obstetrics and Gynaecology
ZACHARSKI, L. R., Medicine
ZUBKOFF, M., Community and Family Medicine
ZWOLAK, R. M., Surgery

Thayer School of Engineering (internet engineering.dartmouth.edu/thayer):

BAKER, I.
CUSHMAN-ROISIN, B.
CYBENKO, G.
GARMIRE, E.
GRAEVE, R. J.
HUTCHINSON, C. E.
KANTROWITZ, A. R.
KENNEDY, F. E.
LOTKO, W
LYNCH, D. R.
PAULSEN, K. D.
PETRENKO, V. F.
RICHTER, H. J.
SCHULSON, E. M.
STRATTON, W. D.
TAYLOR, S.
WYMAN, C. E.

Tuck School of Business Administration (fax (603) 646-1308; e-mail tuck.school@dartmouth.edu; internet www.tuck.dartmouth.edu):

ARGENTI, P.A., Management and Corporate Communication
BAKER, K. R., Management
BERNARD, A., Int. Econ.
BLAYDON, C. C., Management
DANOS, P., Business Admin.
DAVENI, R. A., Strategic Management
ECKBO, B. E., Finance
FINKELSTEIN, S., Management
FRENCH, K. R., Finance
GOVINDARAJAN, V., Int. Business
GREENHALGH, L., Management
HANSEN, R. G., Business Admin.
HELFAT, C. E., Strategy and Technology
JOHNSON, M. E., Operations Management
JOYCE, W. F., Strategy and Organizational Theory
KELLER, K. L., Marketing
KELLER, P.A., Management
LAPORTA, R., Finance
MASSEY, J. A., Int. Business
MUNTER, M. M., Management Communication

NESLIN, S. A., Marketing
POWELL, S. G., Business Admin.
PYKE, D. F., Business Admin.
ROGALSKI, R. J., Investments
SHANK, J. K., Managerial Accounting and Management Control
STICKNEY, C. P., Management
ZUBKOFF, M., Health Econ. and Management

ATTACHED RESEARCH INSTITUTES

Institute for Security Technology Studies: e-mail info@ists.dartmouth.edu; internet www.ists.dartmouth.edu; f. 2000; Dir DAVID KOTZ.

Nelson A. Rockefeller Center for the Social Services: internet www.dartmouth.edu/~rocky; Dir ANDREW SAMWICK.

Institute of Arctic Studies: internet www.dartmouth.edu/~arctic; Dir ROSS VIRGINIA.

FRANKLIN PIERCE COLLEGE

20 College Rd, Rindge, NH 03461-0060

Telephone: (603) 899-4000
Fax: (603) 899-4394
E-mail: admissions@fpc.edu
Internet: www.fpc.edu

Founded 1962
Private control
Academic year: September to May

President: Dr GEORGE J. HAGERTY
Senior Vice-President (College Relations and Enrollment Services): ROBERT J CONDON, Jr
Provost and Vice-President (Academic Affairs): Dr SUZANNE C. BUCKLEY
Vice-President (Finance): Dr JAMES KRAAI
Vice-President (Student Affairs): Dr JAMES P. EARLE
Registrar: Dr SUSAN R. CHAMBERLIN
Director of Library Services: MARY E. LEDOUX

Library of 120,000 vols
Number of teachers: 65
Number of students: 1,489

HEADS OF DEPARTMENTS

Behavioral Sciences: Dr CRAIG W. PLATT
Business Administration: Dr KELLY M. KILCREASE
Humanities: Dr DOUGLAS A. LEY
Natural Sciences: Dr FREDERICK S. ROGERS (acting)
Visual and Performing Arts: ROBERT E. DIERCKS

BRANCH CAMPUSES

Concord Campus: 130 Pembroke Rd, Concord, NH 03301-5753; tel. (603) 228-1155; fax (603) 229-4580; Dir MAJOR W. WHEELOCK, III.

Keene Campus: 17 Bradco St, Keene, NH 03431-3900; tel. (603) 357-0079; fax (603) 899-1062; Dir ANDREA M. BRODE.

Lebanon Campus: 24 Airport Rd, West Lebanon, NH 03784; tel. (603) 298-5549; fax (603) 899-1065; Dir KAREN STEWART.

Nashua Campus: 20 Cotton Rd, Nashua, NH 03063-1213; tel. (603) 889-4143; fax (603) 889-1063; Dir KAREN GRANT.

Portsmouth Campus: 73 Corporate Dr., Portsmouth, NH 03801-2847; tel. (603) 433-2000; fax (603) 899-1067; Dir M. DERMOT O'BRIEN.

Salem Campus: 12 Industrial Way, Salem, NH 03079-2837; tel. (603) 898-1263; fax (603) 899-1064; Dir LORAINE HOBAUSZ.

FRANKLIN PIERCE LAW CENTER

2 White Street, Concord, NH 03301

Telephone: (603) 228-1541
Fax: (603) 228-1074
E-mail: admissions@piercelaw.edu
Internet: www.piercelaw.edu

Founded 1973
Private control
Academic year: August to April

Dean: JOHN D. HUTSON
Vice-Dean: Dr KEITH M. HARRISON
Vice-President (Financial Affairs) and Treasurer: LIZ BRUEN
Assistant Dean for Registration and Records: LORY ATTALLA
Law Librarian: Dr JUDITH GIRE
Number of students: 450

HEADS OF DEPARTMENTS

Commerce and Technology Graduate Programs: Dr WILLIAM J. MURPHY
Education Law Graduate Programs: Dr SARAH E. REDFIELD
Intellectual Property Graduate Programs: Dr WILLIAM O. HENNESSEY

NEW ENGLAND COLLEGE

24 Bridge St, Henniker, NH 03242

Telephone: (603) 428-2000
Fax: (603) 428-7230
E-mail: admission@nec.edu
Internet: www.nec.edu

Founded 1946
Academic year: September to May

President: Dr STEPHEN E. FRITZ
Vice-President for Academic Affairs and Dean of Faculty: ZVI SZAFRAN
Registrar: FRANK L. HALL
Vice-President for Development: KARL SALATHÉ
Vice-President for Finance and Treasurer: VINCENT MASSARO
Vice-President for Student Development and Dean of Student Affairs: E. JOSEPH PETRICK
Vice-President for Enrollment: MICHELE PERKINS
Director of Admissions: LISA PARTRIDGE
Librarian: JOSEPH D. CONSIDINE

Library of 103,000 vols
Number of teachers: 76 (51 full-time, 25 part-time)
Number of students: 1,000.

RIVIER COLLEGE

420 Main St, Nashua, NH 03060

Telephone: (603) 888-1311
Fax: (603) 897-8883
E-mail: rivadmit@rivier.edu
Internet: www.rivier.edu

Founded 1933
Academic year: September to May

President: WILLIAM FARRELL
Vice-President for Academic Affairs: Sister THERESE LAROCHELLE
Vice-President for Student Development: LINDA JANSKY
Vice-President for Finance and Operations: JOSEPH A. FAGAN
Vice-President for Institutional Advancement: KENNETH P. BINDER
Academic Dean: Dr ALBERT DECICCIO
Librarian: BRIAN COURTEMANCHE

Library of 128,473 vols
Number of teachers: 172 (65 full-time, 107 part-time)
Number of students: 2,375 (905 full-time, 1,470 part-time).

SAINT ANSELM COLLEGE

100 St Anselm Drive, Manchester, NH 03102-1310

Telephone: (603) 641-7000
Fax: (603) 641-7116
E-mail: admission@anselm.edu
Internet: www.anselm.edu

Founded 1889

A liberal arts college with a baccalaureate program in nursing

President: Rev. JONATHAN DEFELICE
Dean of the College: Rev. PETER J. GUERIN
Registrar: MARY ANN ERICSON
Librarian: JOSEPH W. CONSTANCE, Jr

Library of 190,000 vols
Number of teachers: 117 full-time
Number of teachers: 38 part-time
Number of students: 2,019.

SOUTHERN NEW HAMPSHIRE UNIVERSITY

2500 N River Rd, Manchester, NH 03106

Telephone: (603) 668-2211
E-mail: info@snhu.edu
Internet: www.snhu.edu
Private control

President: Dr RICHARD GUSTAFSON
Vice-President (Academic Affairs): Dr ELISABETH NOYES
Vice-President (Student Affairs): Dr GEORGE J. LARKIN
Vice-President (Operations and Finance): JOHN C. MILES
Vice-President (Institutional Advancement): MICHAEL MACNEIL
Executive Director of Continuing Education/Distance Education: KAREN L. MUNCASTER
Registrar: Dr RICHARD OUELLETTE
Library Director: RONALD EPP

Number of teachers: 100
Number of students: 5,611

DEANS

School of Business: Dr PAUL SCHNEIDERMAN
School of Hospitality, Tourism and Culinary Management: WILLIAM PETERSEN
School of Liberal Arts: Dr ROBERTA SALPA

THOMAS MORE COLLEGE OF LIBERAL ARTS

6 Manchester St, Merrimack, NH 03054

Telephone: (603) 880-8308
Fax: (603) 880-9280
E-mail: admissions@thomasmorecollege.edu
Internet: www.thomasmorecollege.edu

Founded 1978
Private control
Academic year: September to May

President: Dr PETER V. SAMPO
Dean of the College: Dr MARY K. MUMBACH
Registrar: BRIAN P. SHEA
Librarian: THOMAS SYSESKEY

Number of teachers: 9
Number of students: 61

Areas of study: literature, philosophy, political science, history, writing, theology, fine arts, Latin, Greek, mathematics, biology, chemistry.

UNIVERSITY SYSTEM OF NEW HAMPSHIRE

Dunlap Center, 25 Concord Rd, Durham, NH 03824-3545

Telephone: (603) 862-1800
Fax: (603) 862-0908
E-mail: usnh.chancellor@unh.edu
Internet: www.usnh.unh.edu

Chancellor: Dr STEPHEN J. RENO
Number of students: 30,000 at four constituent institutions.

CONSTITUENT INSTITUTIONS

Granite State College

18 Old Suncook Rd, Concord, NH 03301

Telephone: (603) 228-3000
Fax: (603) 229-0964

E-mail: ask.granite@granite.edu
Internet: www.granite.edu

Founded 1972 as School of Continuing Studies; later named the College for Lifelong Learning; present name 2005

State control

Academic year: July to June

President: Dr KAROL LACROIX

Vice-President (Academic Affairs): MARJORIE W. LAVIN

Vice-President (Administration and Finance): ERIC BLUMENTHAL

Registrar: KAREN KING

Director of Information Resources and Services (vacant)

Number of teachers: 600
Number of students: 4,000

Areas of study: adult learning and development, behavioural science, criminal justice, computing and information technology, early childhood education, health care, management.

Courses offered at more than 50 locations across New Hampshire.

Keene State College

229 Main St, Keene, NH 03435

Telephone: (603) 352-1909
Internet: www.keene.edu

Founded 1909

Academic year: September to May

President: STANLEY J. YAROSEWICK

Vice-President for Academic Affairs: ROBERT GOLDEN

Vice-President for Finance and Planning: JAY V. KAHN

Vice-President for Student Affairs: CORINNE KOWPAK

Librarian: THOMAS WARGER (acting)

Library of 258,181 vols
Number of teachers: 181
Number of students: 4,081.

Plymouth State University

Plymouth, NH 03264

Telephone: (603) 535-5000
Fax: (603) 535-2654
E-mail: pscadmit@psc.plymouth.edu
Internet: www.plymouth.edu

Founded 1871

Academic year: September to May

President (vacant)

Vice-President of Academic Affairs: VIRGINIA BARRY

Vice-President of Financial Management: WILLIAM R. CRANGLE

Vice-President for Institutional Advancement: RETHA L. FIELDING

Vice-President of Student Affairs: RICHARD T. HAGE

Senior Associate Director of Admissions: EUGENE FAHEY

Dean of Students: TIMOTHY C. KEEFE

Registrar: MATTHEW BURKHART

Librarian: TODD TREVORROW

Library of 306,314 vols
Number of teachers: 170 full-time
Number of students: 5,151

Publications: Anthology of Teachers' Writing (annually), Centripetal (2 a year), The New Hampshire Journal of Education (annually), Writing across the Curriculum (annually).

University of New Hampshire

Durham, NH 03824

Telephone: (603) 862-1234
Fax: (603) 862-2030
E-mail: telecom@unh.edu
Internet: www.unh.edu

Founded 1866 as New Hampshire College of Agriculture and the Mechanic Arts; present name 1923; in 1963, the State Colleges at Plymouth and Keene were added as separate campuses of the University System of New Hampshire. In 1985 Merrimack Valley College (f. 1967) became the University of New Hampshire at Manchester, a branch campus

Academic year: September to May

President (vacant)

Provost and Executive Vice-President for Academic Affairs: BRUCE MALLORY

Vice-President for Finance and Administration: CANDACE CORVEY

Vice-President for Research and Public Service: JOHN ABER

Vice-President for Student Affairs: MARK RUBINSTEIN

Director of Admissions: ROBERT McGANN

Dean of Co-operative Extension: JOHN PIKE

Registrar: KATHRYN P. FORBES

Librarian: CLAUDIA MORNER

Library of 1,771,477 vols
Number of teachers: 607 (full-time)
Number of students: 14,405

Publications: Portuguese Studies Review, Seafare (jointly with Univ. of Maine)

DEANS

College of Engineering and Physical Sciences: ARTHUR GREENBERG

College of Liberal Arts: MARILYN HOSKIN

College of Life Sciences and Agriculture: WILLIAM TRIMBLE

Arthur Greenberg Graduate School: HARRY RICHARDS

The Whittemore School of Business and Economics: STEVEN BOLANDER

Harry Richards School of Health and Human Services: JAMES McCARTHY

University of New Hampshire at Manchester: ROBERT JOLLEY (acting)

NEW JERSEY

CALDWELL COLLEGE

9 Ryerson Ave, Caldwell, NJ 07006

Telephone: (973) 618-3000
Fax: (973) 618-3600
E-mail: admissions@caldwell.edu
Internet: www.caldwell.edu

Founded 1939

Academic year: August to May

Pres.: Sister PATRICE WERNER

Vice-Pres. and Dean for Academic Affairs: Dr PAUL R. DOUILLARD

Vice-Pres. for Enrollment Management: JOSEPH L. POSILLICO

Exex. Dir of Library: PETER PANOS

Library of 142,356 vols
Number of teachers: 184
Number of students: 2,219 (1,599 full-time).

CENTENARY COLLEGE

400 Jefferson St, Hackettstown, NJ 07840-9930

Telephone: (908) 852-1400
Fax: (908) 979-4359
E-mail: admissions@centenarycollege.edu
Internet: www.centenarycollege.edu

Founded 1867

Private control

Pres.: Dr KENNETH L. HOYT

Vice-Pres. for College Relations: DEBRA ALBANESE

Vice-Pres. for Academic Affairs: BARBARA-JAYNE LEWTHWAITE

Vice-Pres. for Business and Finance: JOHN SOMMER

Vice-Pres. for Enrollment Management: DIANE P. FINNAN

Vice-Pres. for Information Systems: NORMAN W. RANKIS

Vice-Pres. for Admin.: Dr JOHN A. SHAYNER

Dean of Students: Rev. DAVID JONES

Registrar: ELISE BAYSE

Library Dir: NANCY MADACSI

Number of teachers: 40
Number of students: 970.

COLLEGE OF NEW JERSEY

2000 Pennington Rd, POB 7718, Ewing, NJ 08628-0718

Telephone: (609) 771-1855
Internet: www.tcnj.edu

Founded 1855

Pres.: R. BARBARA GITENSTEIN

Provost and Vice-Pres. for Academic Affairs: BETH PAUL

Vice-Pres. for Admin. and Finance: PETER L. MILLS

Vice-Pres. for Devt and Alumni Affairs: JOHN MARCY

Vice-Pres. for Student Life (vacant): JAMES M. NORFLEET

Registrar: DONALD WORTHINGTON

Dean of the Library and Information Services: TARAS PAVLOVSKY

Library of 450,000 vols
Number of teachers: 619
Number of students: 5,239
Number of students: 6,706 (5,239 full-time; 1,467 part-time)

DEANS

Arts and Sciences: Dr RICHARD KAMBER

Education: Dr SUZANNE PASCH

School of Business: Dr THOMAS BRESLIN (acting)

School of Technology: Dr ROBERT BITTNER

School of Nursing: Dr LAURIE SHERWEN

Graduate Studies: Dr SUZANNE PASCH

COLLEGE OF SAINT ELIZABETH

2 Convent Rd, Morristown, NJ 07960-6989

Telephone: (973) 290-4000
E-mail: apply@cse.edu
Internet: www.cse.edu

Founded 1899

Pres.: Sister FRANCIS RAFTERY

Vice-Pres. and Dean for Academic Affairs: JAMES S. DLUGOS

Vice-Pres. for Finance and Admin. and Treasurer: MARIA CAMMARATA

Vice-Pres. for Institutional Advancement: JEANINE HIRSCH

Librarian: Bro. PAUL CHERVENIE

Library of 188,000 vols
Number of teachers: 171
Number of students: 1,791.

DREW UNIVERSITY

36 Madison Ave, Madison, NJ 07940

Telephone: (973) 408-3000
Fax: (973) 408-3080
Internet: www.drew.edu

Founded 1867

Academic year: September to May

Pres.: ROBERT WEISBUCH

Provost and Academic Vice-Pres.: PAMELA GUNTER-SMITH

Vice-Pres. for Admin.: MARGARET E. L. HOWARD

Vice-Pres. for Finance and Business Affairs: MICHAEL B. McKITISH

Vice-Pres. for Devt: RONALD ROSS

Registrar: HORACE TATE HORACE TATE

Dean of Libraries: ANDREW D. SCRIMGEOUR

Number of teachers: 157 (full-time faculty)

Number of students: 2,675

Publication: *Drew Magazine* (alumni magazine, quarterly)

DEANS

College of Liberal Arts: PAOLO M. CUCCHI
Theological School: MAXINE C. BEACH
Graduate School: JAMES PAIN

FAIRLEIGH DICKINSON UNIVERSITY

Teaneck, NJ 07666

Telephone: (201) 692-2000
E-mail: global@fdu.edu
Internet: www.fdu.edu

Founded 1942

Campuses at Madison, NJ 07940 (tel. (973) 443-8500); Teaneck, NJ 07666 (tel. (201) 692-2000); and Wroxton, Oxon., England

Pres.: Dr J. MICHAEL ADAMS
Exec. Vice-Pres.: CARL VIOLA
Sr Vice-Pres. for Academic Affairs: Dr WILLARD GINGERICH
Vice-Pres. for Institutional Advancement and Enrollment Management: BERNADETTE MILLONDE
Univ. Librarian: JAMES MARCUM

Library of 650,000 vols
Number of teachers: 669
Number of students: 11,000

Publications: *The Literary Review, FDU Magazine, Journal of Psychology and the Behavioral Sciences*

DEANS

Becton College of Arts and Sciences (Florham-Madison Campus): Dr BARBARA SALMORE
Univ. College (Teaneck-Hackensack Campus): Dr JOHN SNYDER
Silberman College of Business Admin.: Dr LEO ROGERS
Edward Williams College (Teaneck-Hackensack Campus): KENNETH T. VEHRKENS

FELICIAN COLLEGE

262 South Main St, Lodi, NJ 07644-2117

Telephone: (201) 559-6000
Fax: (201) 559-6188
E-mail: admissions@inet.felician.edu
Internet: www.felician.edu

Campuses at Lodi and Rutherford

Founded 1923 as Immaculate Conception Normal School; present name 1967
Private control

Pres.: Sister THERESA MARY MARTIN
Registrar: JUNE FINN

Number of teachers: 30
Number of students: 1,790

Divs of arts and sciences, nursing and allied health, teacher education.

GEORGIAN COURT UNIVERSITY

900 Lakewood Ave, Lakewood, NJ 08701-2697

Telephone: (732) 364-2700
Fax: (732) 987-2000
E-mail: admissions@georgian.edu
Internet: www.georgian.edu

Founded 1908 as Mount Saint Mary College and Academy; present name 1924
Private control
Academic year: September to May

Pres.: Dr ROSEMARY E. JEFFRIES

Number of teachers: 261
Number of students: 2,976

Schools of arts and humanities, sciences and mathematics, business, education.

INSTITUTE FOR ADVANCED STUDY

Einstein Dr., Princeton, NJ 08540

Telephone: (609) 734-8000
Fax: (609) 924-8399
Internet: www.ias.edu

Founded 1930 for post-doctoral research in the fields of mathematics, natural sciences, historical studies and social sciences
Private control
Academic year: September to April (2 terms)
Chair. of the Board of Trustees: JAMES D. WOLFENSOHN
Dir: PETER GODDARD
Librarians: MARCIA TUCKER, MOMOTA GANGULI

Library of 130,000 volsc.
Number of teachers: 190 (46 permanent)

PROFESSORS

School of Historical Studies:
  BOWERSOCK, G.
  BYNUM, C.
  CRONE, P.
  DI COSMO, N.
  ISRAEL, J.
  VON STADEN, H.

School of Mathematics:
  BOMBIERI, E.
  BOURGAIN, J.
  DELIGNE, P.
  GRIFFITHS, P. A.
  LANGLANDS, R.
  MacPHERSON, R.
  SPENCER, T.
  VOEVODSKY, V.
  WIGDERSON, A.

School of Natural Sciences:
  ADLER, S.
  BAHCALL, J.
  GOLDREICH, P.
  LEVINE, A. J.
  MALDACENA, J.
  SEIBERG, N.
  WITTEN, E.

School of Social Science:
  MASKIN, E.
  SCOTT, J.
  WALZER, M.

KEAN UNIVERSITY

1000 Morris Ave, Union NJ 07083

Telephone: (908) 527-2000
E-mail: admitme@kean.edu
Internet: www.kean.edu

Founded 1855, present name 1997
Academic year: September to June

Pres.: Dr DAWOOD FARAHI
Vice-Pres. of Academic Affairs: Dr JOSÉ QUILES (acting)
Vice-Pres. of Student Services: JANICE MURRAY-LAURY (acting)

Library of 350,000 vols
Number of teachers: 1,047 (372 full-time, 11 part-time, 664 adjunct)
Number of students: 13,050

Colleges of: Arts, Humanities and Social Sciences; Business and Public Admin.; Education; Natural, Applied and Health Sciences; Nathan Weiss Graduate Studies.

MONMOUTH UNIVERSITY

400 Cedar Ave, West Long Branch, NJ 07764-1898

Telephone: (732) 571-3400
E-mail: gradadm@monmouth.edu
Internet: www.monmouth.edu

Founded 1933

Ind., co-educational, non-sectarian, comprehensive univ.

Pres.: PAUL G. GAFFNEY, II
Provost and Vice-Pres. for Academic Affairs: THOMAS PEARSON
Vice-Pres. for Enrollment Management: ROBERT D. McCAIG
Librarian: SUSAN KUYHENDALL

Library of 252,500 vols, 1,250 periodicals
Number of teachers: 397 full-time and part-time
Number of students: 5,311 (4,037 undergraduate; 1,274 graduate).

MONTCLAIR STATE UNIVERSITY

Upper Montclair, NJ 07043

Telephone: (973) 655-4000
Fax: (973) 655-5455
E-mail: undergraduate.admissions@montclair.edu
Internet: www.montclair.edu

Founded 1908

Liberal arts and professional studies
Academic year: September to May

Pres.: Dr SUSAN A. COLE
Vice-Pres. for Academic Affairs and Provost: RICHARD A. LYNDE
Sr Vice-Pres. for Admin. (vacant)
Asst Vice-Pres. for Facilities Operations: WALTER WATKINS
Vice-Pres. for Univ. Advancement: Dr THOMAS J. HAYNES
Vice-Pres. for Student Devt and Campus Life: Dr KAREN PENNINGTON
Vice-Pres. for Finance and Treas.: DONALD C. CIPULLO
Vice-Pres. for Human Resources: JUDITH T. HAIN
Dean of Library Services: JUDITH LIN HUNT

Library of 455,185 vols
Number of teachers: 846 (415 full-time, 431 part-time)
Number of students: 16,063.

NEW BRUNSWICK THEOLOGICAL SEMINARY

17 Seminary Pl., New Brunswick, NJ 08901-1196

Telephone: (732) 247-5241
Fax: (732) 249-5412
E-mail: info@nbts.edu
Internet: www.nbts.edu

Founded 1784
Private control
Academic year: September to May

Pres.: GREG A. MAST
Dean: VIRGINIA WILES
Dir of Library: CHRISTOPHER BRENNAN

Library of 150,000 vols, 300 periodicals
Number of teachers: 40
Number of students: 280.

ATTACHED RESEARCH INSTITUTE

Center for Reformed Church Studies: Dir Rev. Dr JOHN W. COAKLEY.

NEW JERSEY CITY UNIVERSITY

2039 Kennedy Blvd, Jersey City, NJ 07305-1597

Telephone: (201) 200-2000
Fax: (201) 200-2044
E-mail: admissions@njcu.edu
Internet: www.njcu.edu

Founded 1927 as New Jersey State Normal School; present name and status 1998
Academic year: September to May

Pres.: Dr CARLOS HERNÁNDEZ
Library Dir: GRACE F. BULAONG

Number of teachers: 170
Number of students: 7,700

DEANS

College of Professional Studies: Dr SANDRA BLOOMBERG
College of Education: Dr MURIEL RAND
College of Arts and Sciences: (vacant)

NEW JERSEY INSTITUTE OF TECHNOLOGY

University Heights, Newark, NJ 07102-1982
Telephone: (973) 596-3000
Fax: (973) 642-4380
E-mail: information@njit.edu
Internet: www.njit.edu

Founded 1881

Pres.: ROBERT A. ALLENKIRCH
Provost and Sr Vice-Pres. for Academic Affairs: PRISCILLA P. NELSON
Sr Vice-Pres. for Admin. and Treas.: HENRY A. MAUERMEYER
Vice-Pres. for Academic and Student Services: JOEL BLOOM
Vice-Pres. for Univ. Advancement: CHARLES R. DEES, Jr
Sr Vice-Pres. for Research and Devt: Dr DONALD H. SEBASTIAN
Gen. Counsel: HOLLY STERN
Librarian: RICHARD T. SWEENEY

Library of 181,000 vols
Number of teachers: 354, part-time 233
Number of students: 7,837

DEANS

School of Architecture: URS GAUCHAT
College of Computing Sciences: STEPHEN SEIDMAN
College of Eng.: ANGELO PERNA (acting)
School of Management: MARK SOMERS
College of Science and Liberal Arts: Dr G. MÜLLER JONAKAIT
Albert Dorman Honors College: JOEL BLOOM
Graduate Studies: RONALD KANE

PRINCETON THEOLOGICAL SEMINARY

64 Mercer St, POB 821, Princeton, NJ 08542-0803
Telephone: (609) 921-8300
Fax: (609) 924-2973
E-mail: admissions@ptsem.edu
Internet: www.ptsem.edu

Founded 1812
Private control

Pres.: IAIN R. TORRANCE
Sr Vice-Pres., Chief Operating Officer and Treas.: JOHN W. GILMORE
Vice-Pres. for Information Technology: ADRIAN BACKUS
Vice-Pres. for Investment and Chief Investment Office: JUDITH W. HEAGSTEDT
Vice-Pres. for Seminary Relations: ROSEMAY MITCHELL
Dean of Academic Affairs: Prof. DARRELL L. GULDER
Dean of Continuing Education: JOYCE C. TUCKER
Dean of Student Affairs: NANCY LAMMERS GROSS
Registrar: DAVID WALL
Librarian: Dr STEPHEN D. CROCCO

Number of teachers: 50
Number of students: 746.

PRINCETON UNIVERSITY

Princeton, NJ 08544
Telephone: (609) 258-3000
Internet: www.princeton.edu

Founded 1746 as the College of New Jersey, became Princeton Univ. 1896
Academic year: September to May
President: SHIRLEY M. TILGHMAN

Provost: CHRISTOPHER EISGRUBER
Vice-President and Secretary: ROBERT K. DURKEE
Vice-President for Development: BRIAN McDONALD
Vice-President for Facilities: MICHAEL E. McKAY
Vice-President for Human Resources: MAUREEN E. NASH
Vice-President for Information Technology: BETTY LEYDON
Controller: HENRY J. MORPHY
Treasurer: CHRISTOPHER McCRUDDEN
General Counsel: PETER G. McDONOUGH
Librarian: KARIN TRAINER

Library: see Libraries
Number of teachers: 720 full-time
Number of students: 7,115

Publications: *Annals of Mathematics* (every 2 months), *Library Chronicle, Population Index* (quarterly), *Princeton Weekly Bulletin, Record of the Art Museum* (2 a year), *World Politics* (quarterly). Publ. by Princeton University Press: *Philosophy and Public Affairs* (quarterly), *Princeton Alumni Weekly*.

DEANS

Faculty: JOSEPH TAYLOR
College: NANCY MALKIEL
Undergraduates: KATHLEEN DEIGNAN
Graduate School: JOHN F. WILSON
School of Engineering and Applied Science: MARIA M. KLAWE
Admission: FRED HARGADON
Woodrow Wilson School of Public and International Affairs: ANNE-MARIE SLAUGHTER
School of Architecture: STANLEY T. ALLEN
Religious Life and Chapel: JOSEPH C. WILLIAMSON

DEPARTMENT CHAIRS

Anthropology: JAMES A. BOON
Art and Archaeology: PATRICIA FORTINI BROWN
Astrophysical Sciences: SCOTT D. TREMAINE
Chemistry: STEVEN L. BERNASEK (acting)
Classics: DENIS C. FEENEY
Comparative Literature: SANDRA L. BERMANN
East Asian Studies: SUSAN NAQUIN
Ecology and Evolutionary Biology: DANIEL I. RUBENSTEIN
Economics: GENE M. GROSSMAN
Chemical Engineering: PABLO G. DEBENEDETTI
Civil and Environmental Engineering: PETER R. JAFFÉ
Computer Science: LARRY L. PETERSON
Electrical Engineering: PETER J. RAMADGE
English: MICHAEL G. WOOD
French and Italian: MARIE-HÉLÈNE HUET
Geosciences: F. ANTHONY DAHLEN, Jr
Germanic Languages and Literatures: MICHAEL W. JENNINGS
History: ROBERT L. TIGNOR
Mathematics: NICHOLAS M. KATZ
Molecular Biology: THOMAS E. SHENK
Music: SCOTT G. BURNHAM
Near Eastern Studies: ANDRAS P. HAMORI
Philosophy: MARK JOHNSTON
Physics: DANIEL R. MARLOW
Politics: JEFFREY I. HERBST
Psychology: DEBORAH A. PRENTICE
Religion: MARTHA HIMMELFARB
Slavic Languages and Literatures: CARYL G. EMERSON
Sociology: ALEJANDRO PORTES
Spanish and Portuguese Languages and Cultures: ANGEL G. LOUREIRO

PROGRAMME DIRECTORS

African-American Studies: VALERIE A. SMITH
Applied and Computational Mathematics: BJORN ENGQUIST
Astrophysical Sciences/Plasma Physics: NATHANIEL J. FISCH

Creative Writing: EDMUND V. WHITE
Hellenic Studies: PETER R. BROWN
Judaic Studies: FROMA I. ZENITH
Latin American Studies: JEREMY ADELMAN
Linguistics: LEONARD H. BABBY
Princeton Writing Program: KERRY WALK
Study of Women and Gener: CHRISTINE STANSELL (acting)
Theater and Dance: MICHAEL W. CADDEN
Visual Arts: EVE MICHELE ASCHHEIM

PROFESSORS

ABBATE, C., Music
ABREU, D. J., Economics
ACTON, F. S., Electrical Engineering and Computer Science
ADELMAN, J. I., Latin American Studies
AGAWU, V. K., African Studies
AIT-SAHALIA, Y., Economics
AIZENMAN, M., Physics
AKSAY, I., Chemical Engineering
ALLEN, L. C., Chemistry
ALTMANN, J., Ecology and Evolutionary Biology
APPIAH, K., Afro-American Studies
ARMSTRONG, C. M., Art and Archaeology
ARNOLD, R. D., Politics and Public Affairs
ASHENFELTER, O. C., Economics
ATKINS, S. D., Classics
AUSTIN, R. H., Physics
AXTMANN, R. C., Chemical Engineering
BABBITT, M. B., Music
BABBY, L. H., Slavic Language and Literature
BAGLEY, R. W., Art and Archaeology
BAHCALL, N., Astrophysical Science
BARTELS, L. M., Public and International Affairs
BAUMOL, W. J., Economics
BELLOS, D. M., Romance Languages and Literatures
BENABOU, R. J.-M., Economics and Public Affairs
BENACERRAF, P., Philosophy
BENDER, M. L., Geosciences
BENTLEY, G. E., English Literature
BENZIGER, J. B., Chemical Engineering
BERMAN, S. L., Comparative Literature
BERNANKE, B., Economics and Public Affairs
BERNASEK, S. L., Chemistry
BERNHEIM, B. D., Economics
BERRY, C. H., Economics and Public Affairs
BHATT, R. N., Electrical Engineering
BILLINGTON, D. P., Civil Engineering
BLINDER, A. S., Economics
BOCARSLY, A. B., Chemistry
BOGDONOFF, S. M., Aeronautical, Mechanical and Aerospace Engineering
BOLTON, P., Finance, Economics
BONINI, W. E., Geophysics and Geological Engineering, Civil Engineering
BOON, J. A., Anthropology
BOYER, M. C., Architecture
BRACCO, F., Mechanical and Aerospace Engineering
BRADFORD, D. F., Economics and Public Affairs
BRANSON, W. H., Economics and International Affairs
BROACH, J. R., Molecular Biology
BROADIE, S. W., Philosophy
BRODSKY LACOUR, C. J., Comparative Literature
BROMBERT, V. H., Romance Languages and Literatures and Comparative Literature
BROWDER, W., Mathematics
BROWN, C. F., Jr, Comparative Literature
BROWN, G. L., Mechanical and Aerospace Engineering
BROWN, P. F., Art and Archaeology
BROWN, P. R., History
BUNNELL, P. C., History of Photography and Modern Art; Art and Archaeology
BURGESS, J. P., Philosophy
CALAPRICE, F. P., Physics
CALLAN, C. G., Jr, Physics

CAMPBELL, B. A., Psychology
CAR, R., Chemistry
CARMONA, R. A., Operations Research and Financial Engineering
CARRASACO, D., Religion
CASE, A. C., Economics and Public Affairs
CATES, G. D. , Jr, Physics
CAVA, R. J., Chemistry
CELIA, M. A., Civil and Environmental Engineering
CHAIKIN, P. M., Physics
CHAMPLIN, E. J., Humanities; Classics
CHANCES, E. B., Slavic Languages and Literatures
CHANG, S.-Y. A., Mathematics
CHASE, A. M., Biology
CHAZELLE, B. M., Computer Science
CHENG, S. I., Aeronautical Engineering
CHILDS, W. A. P., Art and Archaeology
CHOU, C.-P., East Asian Studies
CHOU, S. Y., Engineering
CHOW, G. C., Economics, Political Economy
CHRISTODOULOU, D., Mathematics
CINLAR, E., Civil Engineering
CLARK, D., Computer Sciences
CLINTON, J. W., Near Eastern Studies
COALE, A. J., Economics and Public Affairs
COFFIN, D. R., Art and Archaeology
COHEN, M. R., Near Eastern Studies
COLE, M. D., Molecular Biology
COLLCUTT, M. C., East Asian Studies
CONWAY, J. H., Applied and Computational Mathematics
COOPER, J., Psychology
COOPER, J. M., Philosophy
CORNGOLD, S. A., Germanic Languages
COX, E. C., Biology
ČURČIĆ, S., Art and Archaeology
CURSCHMANN, M. J. H., Germanic Languages
DAHLEN, F. A., Geological and Geophysical Sciences
DANIELSON, M. N., Politics and Public Affairs
DANSON, L. N., English
DARLEY, J. M., Psychology
DARNTON, R. C., History
DAUBECHIES, I. C., Mathematics
DAVIDSON, R. C., Astrophysical Sciences
DAVIES, H. M., Religion
DEATON, A. S., Economics and International Affairs
DEBENEDETTI, P. G., Engineering
DIAMOND, M. L., Religion
DÍAZ-QUIÑONES, A., Romance Languages and Literatures
DI BATTISTA, M. A., English and Comparative Literature
DICKINSON, B. W., Electrical Engineering
DIIULIO, J. J., Politics and Public Affairs
DILLIARD, I., Journalism and Public Relations
DIMAGGIO, P. J., Sociology
DISMUKES, G. C., Chemistry
DIXIT, A. K., Economics and International Affairs
DOBBIN, F. R., Sociology
DOBKIN, D. P., Electrical Engineering and Computer Science
DOIG, J. W., Politics and Public Affairs
DOYLE, M. W., Public and International Affairs
DRAINE, B. T., Astrophysical Sciences
DRYER, F. L., Mechanical and Aerospace Engineering
EBERT, R. P., Germanic Languages and Literatures
EMERSON, C. G., Slavic Languages and Literatures
ENGELSTEIN, L., History
ENQUIST, L. W., Molecular Biology
ERMOLAEV, H., Slavic Languages and Literatures
ESPENSHADE, T. J., Sociology
EVANS, A. G., Engineering
FAGLES, R., Comparative Literature
FALK, R. A., International Law, Politics, and International Affairs
FALTINGS, G., Mathematics

FARBER, H. S., Economics
FEENEY, D. C., Classics
FEFFERMAN, C., Mathematics
FISCH, N. J., Astrophysical Sciences
FISKE, S. T., Psychology
FITCH, V. L., Physics
FLEMING, J. V., English and Comparative Literature
FLINT, S. J., Molecular Biology
FLOUDAS, C. A., Chemical Engineering
FORCIONI, A., Comparative Literature
FORD, A. L., Classics
FORREST, S. R., Electrical Engineering
FOSTER, H. F., Art and Archaeology
FRANKFURT, H. G., Philosophy
FRASSICA, P., Romance Languages and Literatures
FREEDMAN, R. W. B., Comparative Literature
FREIDIN, R. A., Council of the Humanities
FRESCO, J. R., Life Sciences
FRIEDBERG, A. L., Politics and International Affairs
GAGER, J. G., Jr, Religion
GANDELSONAS, M. I., Architecture
GARON, S. M., History and East Asian Studies
GARVEY, G., Politics
GEDDES, R. L., Architecture
GEISON, G. L., History and History of Science
GEORGE, R. P., Jurisprudence
GIBBS, N., Journalism and Council of Humanities
GIRGUS, J. S., Psychology
GLASSMAN, I., Mechanical and Aerospace Engineering
GLUCKSBERG, S., Psychology
GOLDMAN, M. P., English
GOLDMAN, N. J., Demography and Public Affairs
GOLDSTON, R. J., Astrophysical Sciences
GOODMAN, J., Astrophysical Sciences
GOSSMAN, J. L., Romance Languages and Literatures
GOTT, J. R., III, Astrophysical Sciences
GOULD, E., Psychology
GOULD, J. L., Biology
GOWA, J., Politics
GOWIN, E. W., Council of the Humanities and Visual Arts
GRAF, F., Classics
GRAFTON, A. T., History
GRANT, P., Biology
GRAVES, M., Architecture
GREENSTEIN, F. I., Politics
GROSS, C. G., Psychology
GROSSMAN, G. M., Economics and Business Policy
GROTH, E. J., III, Physics
GROVES, J. T., Chemistry
GRUNER, S. M., Physics
GUL, F. R., Economics
GUNN, J. E., Astronomy
GUNNING, R. C.
GUTMANN, A., Politics
HAHN, B., Germanic Languages and Literatures
HALDANE, F. D. M., Physics
HAMMOUDI, A., Anthropology and Near East Studies
HAMORI, A. P., Near Eastern Studies
HANIOGLU, M. S., Near Eastern Studies
HAPPER, W., Physics
HARMAN, G. H., Philosophy
HARTOG, H. A., History
HELD, I. M., Geological and Geophysical Sciences, Atmospheric and Oceanic Sciences
HERBST, J. I., Politics and International Affairs
HIMMELFARB, M., Religion
HINDERER, W., Germanic Languages and Literatures
HOCHSCHILD, J. L., Politics and Public Affairs
HOEBEL, B. G., Psychology
HOFFMANN, L.-F., Romance Languages

HOLLANDER, R. B., Jr, European and Comparative Literature
HOLLISTER, L. S., Geological and Geophysical Sciences
HOLMES, P. J., Mechanical and Aerospace Engineering
HONORE, B. E., Economics
HOPFIELD, J. J., Molecular Biology
HORN, H. S., Biology
HOWARTH, W. L., English
HSIANG, W.-C., Mathematics
HUET, M.-H., Romance Languages and Literatures
ISSAWI, C., Near Eastern Studies
ITZKOWITZ, N., Near Eastern Studies
JACOBS, B. L., Psychology
JAFFE, P. R., Civil and Environmental Engineering
JAHN, R. G., Aerospace Sciences
JAMES, H., History
JAMESON, A., Mechanical and Aerospace Engineering
JEFFREY, P., Music
JENNINGS, M. W., Germanic Languages and Literatures
JHA, N. K., Electrical Engineering
JOHNSON, C. L., English
JOHNSON, M., Psychology
JOHNSON-LAIRD, P. N., Psychology
JOHNSTON, M., Philosophy
JONES, M., Chemistry
JORDON, W. C., History
KAHN, A., Electrical Engineering
KAHN, V. A., English and Comparative Literature
KAHNEMAN, D., Psychology
KASTER, R. A., Latin Language and Literature
KATEB, G., Politics
KATZ, N. M., Mathematics
KAUFMANN, T. D., Art and Archaeology
KELLER, G., Geological and Geophysical Sciences
KELLER, S., Sociology
KELLEY, S., Politics
KENEN, P. B., Economics and International Finance
KEVREKIDIS, Y. G., Chemical Engineering
KINCHLA, R. A., Psychology
KING, E. L., Language, Literature, and Civilization of Spain
KLAINERMAN, S., Mathematics
KLEBANOV, I. R., Mathematical Physics
KNAPP, G. R., Astrophysical Sciences
KNOEPFLMACHER, U. C., English
KOBAYASHI, H., Electrical Engineering and Computer Science
KOCHEN, S. B., Mathematics
KOHLI, A., Politics and International Affairs
KOHN, J. J., Mathematics
KOLLAR, J., Mathematics
KOMUNYAKAA, Y., Council of the Humanities and Creative Writing
KORNHAUSER, A. L., Civil Engineering
KOSTIN, M. D., Chemical Engineering
KRIPKE, S., Philosophy
KROMMES, J. A., Astrophysical Sciences
KUNG, S.-Y., Electrical Engineering
LAKE, P. G., History
LAM, S.-H., Mechanical and Aerospace Engineering
LAMB, J., English
LAMONT, M., Sociology
LANGE, V., Modern Languages
LANGLOIS, J. D. , Jr, East Asian Studies
LANSKY, P., Music
LA PAUGH, A. S., Computer Science
LAU, N.-C., Geosciences and Atmospheric and Oceanic Sciences
LAW, C. K., Mechanical and Aerospace Engineering
LEE, P. C. Y., Civil Engineering
LEE, R. B.-L., Engineering
LEHMANN, K. K., Chemistry
LEIBLER, S., Physics and Molecular Biology
LERNER, R., Architecture

LEVIN, S. A., Ecology and Evolutionary Biology
LEWIS, D. K., Philosophy
LEWIS, J. P., Economics and International Affairs
LI, K., Computer Science
LIEB, E. H., Mathematical Physics
LINK, E. P., East Asian Studies
LIPTON, R. J., Computer Science
LITTMAN, M. G., Mechanical and Aerospace Engineering
LIU, B., Electrical Engineering
LONGUENESSE, B. M., Philosophy
LOWRY, H. N., Ottoman and Modern Turkish Studies
LYON, S. A., Electrical Engineering
MACEDO, S. J., Politics
MACKEY, S., Music
MAHLMAN, J. D., Geological and Geophysical Sciences and Atmospheric and Oceanic Sciences
MAHONEY, M. S., History and History of Science
MAKINO, S., East Asian Studies
MALIK, S., Electrical Engineering
MALKIEL, B. G., Economics
MALKIEL, N. W., History
MAMAN, A., French, Romance Languages and Literatures
MARLOW, D. R., Physics
MARTIN, E., Anthropology
MARTIN, R. B., English
MATHER, J. N., Mathematics
McDONALD, K. T., Physics
McLANAHAN, S. S., Sociology and Public Affairs
McLENDON, G. L., Chemistry
McPHERSON, J. M., History
MEYER, H., Art and Archaeology
MEYERS, P. D., Physics
MILES, R. B., Mechanical and Aerospace Engineering
MILLER, D. T., Psychology
MILLER, G. A., Psychology
MILLER, H. K., English
MITCHELL, L. C., English
MODARRESSI, H., Near Eastern Studies
MOREL, F. M., Geosciences
MORGAN, W. J., Geophysics
MULDOON, P. B., Humanities
MULVEY, J. M., Civil Engineering
MURRIN, J. M., History
NAQUIN, S., History
NASH, S. C., Romance Languages and Literature
NEHAMAS, A., Humanities, Philosophy and Comparative Literature
NELSON, J., Mathematics
NEWTON, A., Molecular Biology
NOLET, A. M., Geological and Geophysical Sciences
NORD, D. E., English
NORD, P. G., History
OBER, J., Classics
ONG, N.-P., Physics
ORLANSKI, I., Geological and Geophysical Sciences and Atmospheric and Oceanic Sciences
OSTRIKER, J. P., Astrophysical Sciences
PACALA, S., Ecology
PACZYNSKI, B., Astrophysical Sciences
PAGE, L. A., Jr, Physics
PAGELS, E. H., Religion
PAINTER, N. I., History
PANAGIOTOPOULOS, A. Z., Chemical Engineering
PAVEL, T., Comparative Literature and Romance Languages and Literatures
PAXSON, C. H., Economics and Public Affairs
PEEBLES, P. J. E., Physics
PETERSON, L. I., Computer Science
PETERSON, W. J., East Asian Studies
PHILANDER, S. G. H., Geological and Geophysical Sciences
PHINNEY, R. A., Geological and Geophysical Sciences

PINTO, J. A., Art and Archaeology
PIROUÉ, P. A., Physics
PLAKS, A. H., East Asian Studies
POLYAKOV, A., Physics
POOR, H. V., Electrical Engineering
PORTES, A., Sociology
POWELL, W. B., Civil Engineering
POWERS, H. S., Music
PRAKASH, G., History
PRENTICE, D. A., Psychology
PREVOST, J.-H., Civil Engineering
PRUCNAL, P. R., Electrical Engineering
PRUDHOMME, P. R., Chemical and Electrical Engineering
RABB, T. K., History
RABINBACH, A. G., History
RABITZ, H. A., Chemistry
RABOTEAU, A. J., Religion
REINHARDT, U. E., Economics and Public Affairs, Political Economy
RICHARDSON, J., English
RIGOLOT, F., Romance Languages and Literatures
ROCHE, T. P., Jr, English
RODGERS, D. T., History
RODRIGUEZ-ITURBE, I., Civil and Environmental Engineering
ROMER, T., Politics and Public Affairs
ROSE, M. D., Molecular Biology
ROSEN, H. S., Economics
ROSEN, L., Anthropology
ROSENTHAL, H., Social Sciences
ROTHSCHILD, M., Economics and Public Affairs
ROYCE, B. S. H., Mechanical and Aerospace Engineering
ROZMAN, G. F., Sociology
RUBENSTEIN, A., Economics
RUBENSTEIN, D. I., Ecology and Evolutionary Biology
RUSSEL, W. B., Chemical Engineering
RYSKAMP, C. A., English
SARMIENTO, J. L., Geological and Geophysical Sciences
SARNAK, P. C., Mathematics
SAVILLE, D. A., Chemical Engineering
SCANLON, R. H., Civil Engineering
SCHAFER, P., Jewish Studies
SCHEDL, P. D., Molecular Biology
SCHEINKMAN, J. A., Economics
SCHERER, C. W., Civil and Environmental Engineering
SCHMIDT, L. E., Religion
SCHOWALTER, W. R., Engineering and Applied Science
SCHUPBACH, G. M., Molecular Biology
SCHUTT, C. E., Chemistry
SCHWARTZ, J., Chemistry
SCHWARTZ, S. C., Electrical Engineering
SCOLES, G., Chemistry
SEAWRIGHT, J. L., Council of Humanities
SEDGEWICK, R., Computer Science
SEMMELHACK, M. F., Chemistry
SEYMOUR, P. D., Mathematics and Applied and Computational Mathematics
SHAFIR, E. B., Psychology
SHAPIRO, H. T., Economics and Public Affairs
SHAYEGAN, M., Electrical Engineering
SHEAR, T. L., Jr, Classical Archaeology
SHENK, T. E., Molecular Biology
SHIMIZU, Y., Art and Archaeology
SHOWALTER, E., English
SIGMUND, P. E., Politics
SILHAVY, T. J., Molecular Biology
SILVER, L. M., Molecular Biology
SIMS, C. A., Economics
SINAI, Y. G., Mathematics
SINGER, B. H., Public and International Affairs
SINGER, P. A. D., Bioethics
SITNEY, P. A., Council of Humanities
SLABY, S. M., Civil Engineering
SMITH, A. J., Physics
SMITH, J. A., Civil and Environmental Engineering
SMITH, J. C. O., Humanities

SMITH, J. W., Philosophy
SMITH, N., English
SMITS, A., Mechanical and Aerospace Engineering
SMOLUCHOWSKI, R., Solid State Sciences
SOANES, S., Philosophy
SOBOYEJO, W. O., Mechanical and Aerospace Engineering
SOCOLOW, R. H., Mechanical and Aerospace Engineering
SONER, H. M., Engineering and Finance
SOOS, Z. G., Chemistry
SPIRO, T. G., Chemistry
SPITZER, L., Jr, Astronomy
SROLOVITZ, D. J., Mechanical and Aerospace Engineering
STANSELL, M. C., History
STARR, P., Sociology
STEIGLITZ, K., Computer Science
STEIN, E. M., Mathematics
STEIN, S. J., History
STEINBERG, M., Biology
STEINHARDT, P. J., Physics
STENGEL, R. F., Mechanical and Aerospace Engineering
STOCK, J. B., Molecular Biology
STOUT, J. L., Religion
STURM, J. C., Electrical Engineering
SUCKEWER, S., Mechanical and Aerospace Engineering
SULEIMAN, E. N., Politics
SUNDARESAN, S., Chemical Engineering
SUO, Z., Mechanical and Aerospace Engineering
SUPPE, J. E., Geological and Geophysical Sciences
SURTZ, R. E., Romance Languages and Literatures
TARJAN, R. E., Computer Science
TATE, C. C., English
TAYLOR, H. F., Sociology
TAYLOR, J. H., Physics
TEISER, S. F., Buddhist Studies
TEYSSOT, G. M., Architecture
TIENDA, M., Demographic Studies
TIGNOR, R. L., History
TORQUATO, S., Civil Engineering
TOWNSEND, C. E., Slavic Languages and Literatures
TREISMAN, A., Psychology
TREMAINE, S. D., Astrophysical Sciences
TROTTER, H. F., Mathematics
TRUSSELL, T. J., Economics and Public Affairs
TSUI, D. C., Electrical Engineering
TUKEY, J. W., Science, Statistics
TURNER, E. L., Astrophysical Sciences
UDOVITCH, A. L., Near Eastern Studies
UITTI, K. D., Modern Languages, Romance Languages and Literatures
ULLMAN, R., International Affairs
VAN FRAASSEN, B. C., Philosophy
VAN HOUTEN, F. B., Geological and Geophysical Sciences
VANMARCKE, E., Civil Engineering
VERDU, S., Electrical Engineering
VERLINDE, H. L., Physics
VOLKER, P. A., International and Economic Policy
VON GOELER, S. E., Astrophysical Sciences
VON HIPPEL, F. N., Public and International Affairs
WACHTEL, M. A., Slavic Languages and Literatures
WAGNER, S., Electrical Engineering
WALLACE, W. L., Sociology
WARD, B. B., Geosciences
WARREN, S., Chemistry
WATSON, G. S., Statistics
WATSON, M. W., Economics and Public Affairs
WEI, J., Chemical Engineering
WEIGERT, M., Molecular Biology
WEINAN, E., Mathematics
WEISS, T. R., English and Creative Writing
WEITZMANN, K., Art and Archaeology
WEST, C., Afro-American Studies

WEST, C. R., Religion
WESTERGAARD, P. T., Music
WESTERN, B., Sociology
WHITE, L. T., Politics
WHITWELL, J. C., Chemical Engineering
WIESCHAUS, E. F., Biology
WIGHTMAN, A. S., Mathematical Physics
WILENTZ, R. S., History
WILES, A. J., Mathematics
WILKINSON, D. T., Physics
WILLIAMS, E. S., Humanities
WILLIG, R. D., Economics and Public Affairs
WILLIS, J. R., Near Eastern Studies
WILMERDING, J., American Art; Art and Archaeology
WILSON, J. F., Religion
WOLFSON, S. J., English
WOLPERT, J., Geography, Public Affairs and Urban Planning
WOOD, E. F., Civil Engineering
WOOD, M. G., English
WOODFORD, M. D., Economics and Banking
WUTHNOW, R. J., Sociology
YAO, A. L.-L., Computer Science
YU, Y. S., East Asian Studies
ZAKIAN, V. A., Molecular Biology
ZEITLIN, F. I., Classics
ZELIZER, V. A., Sociology
ZIOLKOWSKI, T. J., Germanic Languages and Literatures and Comparative Literature

ATTACHED INSTITUTES

Center of Domestic and Comparative Policy Studies: Dir JENNIFER HOCHSCHILD (acting).

Center for Economic Policy Studies: Dirs ALAN S. BLINDER, HARVEY S. ROSEN.

Center for Energy and Environmental Studies: Dir IGNACIO RODRIGUEZ-ITURBE.

Princeton Environmental Institute: Dir FRANCOIS MOREL.

Bendheim Center for Finance: Dir YACINE AIT-SAHALIA.

Institute for Genomic Analysis: Dir SHIRLEY TILGHMAN.

Shelby Cullom Davis Center for Historical Studies: Dir ANTHONY T. GRAFTON.

University Center for Human Values: Dir STEVEN MACEDO (acting).

Center of International Studies: Dir MICHAEL DOYLE.

Plasma Physics Laboratory: Dir ROBERT J. GOLDSTON.

Office of Population Research: Dir JAMES TRUSSELL.

Center for the Study of Religion: Dir ROBERT WUTHNOW.

Center for the Study of American Religion: Dir ROBERT WUTHNOW.

Princeton Institute for the Science and Technology of Materials: Dir JAMES C. STURM.

RAMAPO COLLEGE OF NEW JERSEY

505 Ramapo Valley Rd, Mahwah, NJ 07430-1680

Telephone: (201) 684-7500
Internet: www.ramapo.edu

Founded 1969
Academic year: September to May

Pres: Dr PETER PHILIP MERCER
Provost and Vice-Pres. for Academic Affairs: Dr BETH E. BARNETT
Vice-Pres. for Institutional Advancement: CATHLEEN DAVEY
Vice-Pres. for Student Affairs: Dr PAMELA M. BISCHOFF
Dean of Students: NANCY MACKIN
Registrar: CYNTHIA BRENNAN
Librarian: ELIZABETH SIECKE

Number of teachers: 187
Number of students: 5,459 (5,148 undergraduate, 311 postgraduate)

DEANS

School of Admin. and Business: Dr FREDERIC CHAMPLIN
School of Social Science and Human Services: Dr HENRY VANCE DAVIS
School of Theoretical and Applied Science: Dr ERIC KARLIN
School of American and Int. Studies: Dr JENNEFER MAZZA
School of Contemporary Arts: STEVE PERRY

RICHARD STOCKTON COLLEGE OF NEW JERSEY

POB 195, Pomona, NJ 08240

Telephone: (609) 652-1776
Internet: www.stockton.edu

Founded 1969 as Richard Stockton State College; present name 1993
Academic year: September to May

Pres.: Dr HERMAN J. SAATKAMP, Jr
Provost and Exec. Vice-Pres. for Academic Affairs: DAVID CARR
Vice-Pres. for Admin. and Finance: CHARLES E. KLEIN
Vice-Pres. for Student Affairs: Dr JOSEPH J. MARCHETTI
Dean of Students: THOMASA GONZALEZ
Registrar: JOSEPH J. LoSASSO
Library Dir: DAVID PINTO

Number of teachers: 343 (216 full-time, 127 part-time)
Number of students: 6,459

DEANS

Arts and Humanities: KENNETH J. DOLLARHIDE
General Studies: G JAN COLIJN
Natural Sciences and Mathematics: DENNIS WEISS
Professional Studies: MARC LOWENSTEIN
Social and Behavioural Sciences: WILLIAM C. JAYNES, IV
Graduate and Continuing Professional Education: DEBRA ISRAEL

RIDER UNIVERSITY

2083 Lawrenceville Rd, Lawrenceville, NJ 08648-3099

Telephone: (609) 896-5000
Fax: (609) 896-8029
Internet: www.rider.edu

Founded 1865

Pres.: Dr MORDECHAI ROZANSKI
Vice-Pres. for Academic Affairs and Provost: Dr DONALD A. STEVEN
Assoc. Vice-Pres. for Student Affairs: Dr ANTHONY CAMPBELL
Vice-Pres. for Univ. Advancement: JONATHAN MEER
Dean of Univ. Libraries: F. WILLIAM CHICKERING

Library of 417,000 vols
Number of teachers: 200
Number of students: 5,790.

ROWAN UNIVERSITY

201 Mullica Hill Rd, Glassboro, NJ 08028

Telephone: (856) 256-4000
Fax: (856) 256-4929
E-mail: webmaster@rowan.edu
Internet: www.rowan.edu

Founded 1923 as Glassboro Normal School; became New Jersey State Teachers' College at Glassboro 1937, Glassboro State College 1958 and Rowan College of New Jersey 1992; present name and status 1997

Academic year: July to June

Pres.: Dr DONALD J. FARISH
Exec. Vice-Pres. and Provost: Dr ALI A. HOUSHMAND
Registrar: MURIEL A. J. FRIERSON
Dean of Library Services: GREGORY POTTER

Library of 339,000 vols
Number of teachers: 350
Number of students: 9,368.

RUTGERS, THE STATE UNIVERSITY OF NEW JERSEY

Old Queens Bldg, 83 Somerset St, New Brunswick, NJ 08901

Telephone: (732) 932-4636
Internet: www.rutgers.edu

Founded as Queen's College by Royal Charter 1766, name changed to Rutgers College 1825, Rutgers Univ. 1924. Designated by legislature as State Univ. of New Jersey 1945 and 1956
Academic year: September to May

Pres.: RICHARD L. McCORMICK
Exec. Vice-Pres. for Academic Affairs: Dr PHILIP FURMANSKI
Sr Vice-Pres. for Admin. and Chief Financial Officer: BRUCE C. FEHN
Exec. Dir, Univ. Relations: KIMBERLY MANNING-LEWIS
Vice-Pres. for Univ. Budgeting: NANCY S. WINTERBAUER
Vice-Pres. for Undergraduate Education: BARRY QUALLS
Vice-Pres. for Student Affairs (vacant): GREGORY S. BLIMLING
Vice-Pres. for Research and Graduate and Professional Education: MICHAEL J. PAZZANI
Vice-Pres. for Continuing Education and Outreach: RACHEL CAPRIO
Exec. Asst to the Pres.: CAROL KONCSOL
Newark Campus Provost: Dr STEVEN DINER
Camden Campus Provost: Dr ROGER DENNIS
Univ. Librarian: MARIANNE GAUNT

Library: see Libraries
Number of teachers: 2,661
Number of students: 50,016 (incl. 12,944 postgraduate students)

Publications: *Journal for International Law*, *Raritan Review*, *Journal for the History of Ideas*, *Public Productivity and Management Review*, *Journal of Research in Crime and Delinquency*, *Academic Questions*, *The American Sociologist*, *Child Welfare*, *Labor Studies Journal*, *Society*, *Women Studies* (quarterly), *North–South*, *Plant Molecular Biology Reporter*, *Public Budgeting and Finance*

DEANS

New Brunswick Campus:

Rutgers Business School (Newark and New Brunswick): HOWARD P. TUCKMAN
Rutgers College: CARL KIRSCHNER
Cook College: KEITH COOPER
Douglass College: CARMEN TWILLI AMBAR
Graduate School of Education: RICHARD DELISI
Graduate School: HOLLY SMITH
Livingston College: ARNOLD G. HYNDMAN
Ernest Mario School of Pharmacy: JOHN COLAIZZI
Social Work: MARY E. DAVIDSON
Univ. College: EMMET DENNIS
Applied Professional Psychology: STANLEY B. MESSER
Mason Gross School of the Arts: GEORGE B. STAUFFER
School of Communications, Information and Library Studies: GUSTAV W. FRIEDRICH
Edward J. Bloustein School of Planning and Public Policy: JAMES W. HUGHES

School of Management and Labor Relations: BARBARA LEE

Camden Campus:
Arts and Sciences: MARGARET MARSH
Law: RAYMAN SOLOMON
Graduate School: MARGARET MARSH
School of Business: MILTON LEONTIADES

Newark Campus:
Arts and Sciences: EDWARD KIRBY
Rutgers Business School (Newark and New Brunswick): HOWARD P. TUCKMAN
Law: STUART DEUTSCH
Nursing: FELISSA LASHLEY
Criminal Justice: LESLIE W. KENNEDY
Graduate School: STEVEN DINER

SAINT PETER'S COLLEGE

2641 Kennedy Blvd, Jersey City, NJ 07306-5997

Telephone: (201) 761-6000
Internet: www.spc.edu

Founded 1872

Pres.: Dr EUGENE J. CORNACCHIA
Assoc. Vice-Pres. for Enrollment and Academic Admin.: Dr VIRGINIA BENDER
Academic Dean: MARYLOU LAM
Dir of Admissions: JOE GIGLIO
Registrar and Dir of Enrollment Services: STEVEN E. SMITH
Library Dir: CHARLES J. MYERS

Library of 282,000 vols
Number of teachers: 118 full-time
Number of teachers: 242 part-time
Number of students: 3,477 full-time
Number of students: 1,221 part-time

Undergraduate courses in the humanities, nursing, sciences, business studies; masters courses in education, int. business, accountancy, management, management information systems, nursing.

SETON HALL UNIVERSITY

South Orange, NJ 07079

Telephone: (973) 761-9000
Fax: (973) 275-2040
E-mail: thehall@shu.edu
Internet: www.shu.edu

Founded 1856
Academic year: September to May

Pres.: Mgr ROBERT SHEERAN
Exec. Vice-Pres. and Provost for Academic Affairs: Dr FREDERICK F. TRAVIS
Exec. Vice-Pres. for Admin.: Sr PAULA M. BULEY
Vice-Pres. for Finance and Technology: DENNIS GARBINI
Vice-Pres. for Human Resources: SUSAN BASSO
Vice-Pres. for Mission and Ministry: Rev. PAUL A. HOLMES
Vice-Pres. for Student Affairs and Enrollment Services: Dr LAURA WANKEL
Vice-Pres. for Univ. Advancement: JOSEPH G. SANDMAN
Vice-Pres. and Gen. Counsel: CATHERINE KIERNAN

Number of teachers: 908 (426 full-time, 482 part-time)
Number of students: 10,000

Publications: *Mid-Atlantic Journal of Business* (3 a year), *Journal of Diplomacy and International Relations* (2 a year)

DEANS
College of Arts and Sciences: Dr MOLLY EASO SMITH
School of Business: Dr KAREN BOROFF
School of Diplomacy and Int. Relations: Amb. CLAY CONSTANTINOU

School of Education and Human Services: Dr JOSEPH DE PIERRO (acting)
School of Law (in Newark): Dr PATRICK HOBBS
College of Nursing: Dr PHYLLIS HANSELL (acting)
Immaculate Conception School of Theology: Mgr ROBERT COLEMAN
School of Graduate Medical Education: Dr DAVID FELTEN

STEVENS INSTITUTE OF TECHNOLOGY

Castle Point on Hudson, Hoboken, NJ 07030-5991

Telephone: (201) 216-5000
Internet: www.stevens-tech.edu

Founded 1870

Pres.: HAL RAVECHE
Provost and Univ. Vice-Pres.: GEORGE KORFIATIS
Vice-Pres. for Univ. Enrollment and Admin.: MAUREEN WEATHERALL
Vice-Pres. for Devt and Univ. Communications: MARJORIE J. EVERITT
Vice-Pres. for Univ. Research and Enterprise Devt: HELENA S. WISNIEWSKI
Vice-Pres. for Finance, Chief Financial Officer and Treas.: STEFANO FALCONI
Dean of Admissions and Financial Aid: DANIEL S. GALLAGHER
Dean of Graduate Studies: CHARLES L. SUFFEL

Library of 105,000 vols
Number of teachers: 230
Number of students: 1,700 (1,200 undergraduates, 500 full-time graduate).

THOMAS EDISON STATE COLLEGE

101 West State St, Trenton, NJ 08608-1176

Telephone: (888) 442-8372
Fax: (609) 984-8447
E-mail: info@tesc.edu
Internet: www.tesc.edu

Founded 1972

Pres.: Dr GEORGE A. PRUITT
Vice-Pres. and Provost: WILLIAM J. SEATON
Number of students: 10,233

Areas of study: arts, applied science and technology, business admin., health sciences, human services, nursing.

WESTMINSTER CHOIR COLLEGE OF RIDER UNIVERSITY

101 Walnut Lane, Princeton, NJ 08540-3899

Telephone: (609) 921-7100
Internet: westminster.rider.edu

Founded 1926

Pres.: Dr J. BARTON LUEDEKE
Vice-Pres. and Provost: Dr HELEN L. STEWART
Dir and Dean: ROBERT L. ANNIS
Registrar: PETER D. WRIGHT
Librarian: JANE NOWAKOWSKI

Library of 55,000 vols; there is also a choral library with 5,000 titles and 300,000 copies
Number of teachers: 50
Number of students: 350.

WILLIAM PATERSON UNIVERSITY OF NEW JERSEY

300 Pompton Rd, Wayne, NJ 07470

Telephone: (973) 720-2000
Internet: www.wpunj.edu

Founded 1855
Academic year: September to June

Pres.: Dr ARNOLD SPEERT
Exec. Vice-Pres. and Provost: Dr CHERNOH SESAY

Vice-Pres. for Admin. and Finance: STEPHEN BOLYAI
Vice-Pres. for Institutional Advancement: SANDRA DELLER
Dean of Student Devt: GLEN SHERMAN
Registrar: MARK EVANGELISTA
Librarian: Dr JOHN GABOURY

Library of 303,545 vols
Number of teachers: 358
Number of students: 9,945

DEANS
College of Humanities and Social Science: Dr ISABEL TIRADO
College of Arts and Communication: OFELIA GARCIA
College of Education: Dr LESLIE AGARD-JONES
College of Science and Health: Dr ESWAR PHADIA
College of Business: Dr JESS BORONICO

NEW MEXICO

COLLEGE OF SANTA FE

1600 St Michael's Drive, Santa Fe, NM 87505

Telephone: (505) 473-6133
Fax: (505) 473-6127
E-mail: admissions@csf.edu
Internet: www.csf.edu

Founded 1947

President: Dr JAMES A. FRIES
Registrar: GERALD VINTHER
Librarian: SUSAN MYERS

Library of 135,000 vols
Number of teachers: 51 full-time
Number of teachers: 117 part-time
Number of students: 1,518.

COLLEGE OF THE SOUTHWEST

6610 Lovington Highway, Hobbs, NM 88240

Telephone: (505) 392-6561
E-mail: admissions@csw.edu
Internet: www.csw.edu

Campuses at Hobbs and Carlsbad
Founded 1962
Private control

President: Dr GARY A. DILL

Number of teachers: 50
Number of students: 900

Depts of: arts and sciences, business administration, education.

EASTERN NEW MEXICO UNIVERSITY

Portales, NM 88130

Telephone: (505) 562-1011
E-mail: enrollment.services@enmu.edu
Internet: www.enmu.edu

Founded 1934

President: EVERETT L. FROST
Vice-President for Academic Affairs: Dr GEORGE MEHAFFY
Registrar: LARRY FUQUA
Librarian: C. EDWIN DOWLIN

Library of 699,847 vols
Number of teachers: 262
Number of students: 3,632.

NEW MEXICO HIGHLANDS UNIVERSITY

Box 9000, Las Vegas, NM 87701

Telephone: (505) 425-7511
Internet: www.nmhu.edu

Founded 1893
Academic year: August to May

President: Dr SHARON CABALLERO
Chief Fiscal Officer: JACK SHERMAN

Academic Dean: Dr CLARENCE SANCHEZ (acting)
Registrar: JOHN COCA
Dean of Students: Dr BETSY YOST
Librarian: RUBEN ARAGON

Number of teachers: 120
Number of students: 2,300.

NEW MEXICO STATE UNIVERSITY

Las Cruces, NM 88003-8001

Telephone: (505) 646-0111
Fax: (505) 646-1517
Internet: www.nmsu.edu

Founded 1888 as Las Cruces College;as New Mexico College of Agriculture and Mechanic Arts 1899; present name and status 1960

Academic year: August to May

President: G. JAY GOGUE
Executive Vice-President: JOHN C. OWENS
Vice-President–Business and Finance: JAMES MCDONOUGH
Vice-President–Student Affairs: PATRICIA R. WOLF
Vice-President–University Advancement: JOE CREED
Vice-President–Research: GARY CUNNINGHAM
Vice-President–Administration: JUAN N. FRANCO
Library Dean: ELIZABETH TITUS

Library of 1,032,970 vols, plus 431,225 bound and unbound government documents and 1,337,979 microforms

Number of teachers: 963
Number of students: 15,409

Publications: *Graduate Catalog, Undergraduate Catalog, Panorama*

DEANS

Graduate School: TIMOTHY J. PETTIBONE
College of Agriculture and Home Economics: JERRY SCHICKEDANZ
College of Arts and Sciences: RENÉ CASILLAS
College of Business Administration and Economics: DANNY R. ARNOLD
College of Education: ROBERT MOULTON
College of Engineering: JAY JORDAN
College of Health and Social Services: (vacant)

ATTACHED RESEARCH INSTITUTES

Agricultural Experiment Station: Dir GARY CUNNINGHAM.

Arts and Science Research Center: Dir REED DASENBROCK.

Business Research and Services: Dir KATHLEEN BROOK.

Computing Research Laboratory: Dir SERGEI NIRENBURG.

Educational Research Center: Dir ANNE GALLEGOS.

Engineering Research Center: Dir KENNETH WHITE.

Physical Science Laboratory: Dir DONALD BIRX.

Plant Genetic Engineering Laboratory: Dir JOHN D. KEMP.

Southwest Technical Development Institute: Dir RUDI SCHOENMACKERS.

Water Resources Research Institute: Dir KARL WOOD.

NEW MEXICO TECH

Socorro, NM 87801

Telephone: (505) 835-5011
Internet: www.nmt.edu

Founded 1889

President: DANIEL H. LOPEZ

Vice-President for Administration and Finance: W. DENNIS PETERSON
Vice-President for Academic Affairs: CARL J. POPP
Vice-President for Research and Economic Development: VAN D. ROMERO
Vice-President for Institutional Development: HERBERT M. FERNANDEZ
Librarian: KAY KREHBIEL

Library of 115,000 vols
Number of students: 1,500

DIRECTORS

New Mexico Bureau of Mines and Mineral Resources: CHARLES E. CHAPIN
New Mexico Petroleum Recovery Research Center: ROBERT L. LEE

ST JOHN'S COLLEGE

Santa Fe, NM 87501

Telephone: (505) 984-6000
Fax: (505) 984-6003
Internet: www.sjcsf.edu

Founded 1964

President: MIKE PETERS
Dean: A. JAMES CAREY
Registrar: DIANE MARTINEZ
Librarian: INGA M. WAITE

Library of 55,000 vols
Number of teachers: 61
Number of students: 400

For Annapolis branch see under Maryland.

SOUTHWESTERN COLLEGE

POB 4788, Santa Fe, NM 87502

Telephone: (877) 471-5756
E-mail: info@swc.edu
Internet: www.swc.edu

Founded 1976 as Quimby College

President: Dr BRADFORD KEENEY
Academic Dean: Dr LARRY DETTWEILER
Registrar: ANDREA PACHECO
Librarian: SANDRA HARELD

Masters programmes: Counselling, Art Therapy. Certificate programs: Art Therapy, Grief Counselling, Action Methods, School Counselling.

UNIVERSITY OF NEW MEXICO

Albuquerque, NM 87131
Internet: www.unm.edu

Founded 1889
State control

Academic year: August to May

President: Dr WILLIAM C. GORDON
Provost/Vice-President for Academic Affairs: WILLIAM C. GORDON
Vice-President for Student Affairs: ELISIO TORRES
Vice President for Business and Finance: DAVID MCKINNEY
Director of the Medical Centre: JANE E. HENNEY
Dean of Library Services: CAMILA A. ALIRE

Library of 1,000,000 vols
Number of teachers: 1,250
Number of students: 25,009

Publication: various departmental publs

DEANS

Graduate School: NASIR AHMED
Continuing Education: JERONIMO DOMINGUEZ
School of Architecture and Planning: RICHARD ERIBES
Students: KAREN M. GLASER
College of Arts and Sciences: MICHAEL FISCHER (acting)
College of Education: PEGGY BLACKWELL
College of Engineering: PAUL FLEURY

College of Fine Arts: THOMAS DODSON
School of Law: LEO ROMERO
Anderson Schools of Management: HOWARD L. SMITH
School of Medicine: PAUL B. ROTH
College of Nursing: KATHLEEN BOND
College of Pharmacy: WILLIAM M. HADLEY
Office of Undergraduate Studies: JANET ROEBUCK
Division of Dental Programs: JOSEPH SCALETTI (acting)

PROFESSORS

(C = Chairman of Department)

ABDALLA, R. N., Art and Art History
ABRAMS, J., Medicine
ADAMSON, G. W., Special Education
AHLUWALIA, H. S., Physics and Astronomy
AHMED, N., Electrical and Computer Engineering
ALLEN, F. S., Chemistry (C)
ALTENBACH, J. S., Biology
ALVERSON, D. C., Paediatrics
ANGEL, E. S., Electrical and Computer Engineering
ANGEL, R. M., Music
ANSPACH, J. F., Law
ATENCIO, A. C., Physiology
ATTERBOM, H. A., Health Promotion, Physical Education and Leisure Programmes
AVASTHI, P., Medicine
BACA, O. G., Biology
BAKER, W. E., Mechanical Engineering
BANKHURST, A. D., Medicine
BARBO, D. M., Obstetrics and Gynaecology
BARROW, T. F., Art and Art History
BARTLETT, L. A., English
BARTON, L. M., Biology
BASSALLECK, B., Physics and Astronomy
BASSO, K. H., Anthropology
BAWDEN, G. L., Anthropology
BEAR, D. G., Cell Biology
BEENE, L., English
BENNAHUM, D. A., Medicine
BENNAHUM, J., Theatre and Dance
BENNETT, M. D., Family and Community Medicine
BENZEL, E. C., Surgery
BERGEN, J. J., Spanish and Portuguese
BERGMAN, B. E., Law
BICKNELL, J. M., Neurology
BILLS, G. D., Linguistics
BIRKHOLZ, G. A., Nursing
BLACK, W. C., III, Pathology
BLACKWELL, P. J., Educational Foundations
BORDEN, T. A., Surgery
BORN, J. L., Pharmacy
BOWES, S., Educational Administration
BOYER, C. P., Mathematics and Statistics
BROGAN, J., Civil Engineering
BROOKSHIRE, D. S., Economics
BROWDE, M. B., Law
BROWN, F. L., Jr, Public Administration
BROWN, J., Biology
BRUECK, S. R. J., Electrical and Computer Engineering
BRYANT, H. C., Physics and Astronomy
BUCHNER, M. A., Mathematics and Statistics
BULLERS, W. I., Jr, Management
BURCHIEL, S. W., Pharmacy
BURNESS, H. S., Economics
BURR, S. L., Law
BURRIS, B. H., Sociology
BUSS, W., Pharmacology (C)
BYBEE, J. L., Linguistics
CAHILL, K. E., Physics and Astronomy
CAPUTI, J. E., American Studies
CARDENAS, A. J., Spanish and Portuguese
CARLOW, T. J., Neurology
CAVES, C. M., Physics and Astronomy
CECCHI, J. L., Chemical and Nuclear Engineering (C)
CHAMPOUX, J. E., Management
CHANDLER, C., Physics and Astronomy
CHANG, B. K., Medicine

CHAPDELAINE, M., Music
CHENG, J., Electrical and Computer Engineering
CHRISTENSEN, R. R., Mathematics and Statistics
CIVIKLY-POWELL, J. M., Communications and Journalism
CLARK, J. M., Music
CLOUGH, D. H., Nursing
COES, D. V., Management
COFER, L. F., Psychology
COHEN, E. B., Law Library
COLTON, D. L., Educational Administration
CONDON, J. C., Communication and Journalism
CONNELL-SZASZ, M., History
CORCORAN, G. B., Pharmacy
CORDOVA, I. R., Educational Administration
COUGHLIN, R., Sociology (C)
COUTSIAS, E. A., Mathematics and Statistics
CRAVEN, D. L., Art and Art History
CRAWFORD, M. H., Medicine
CURET, L. B., Obstetrics and Gynaecology
DAIL, W. G., Jr, Anatomy
DAMICO, H., English
DATYE, A. K., Chemical and Nuclear Engineering
DAVIDSON, R., Librarianship
DAVIS, G. L., American Studies
DAVIS, L., Neurology
DAVIS, M., Radiology
DeKEYSER, J., Music
DELANEY, H. D., Psychology
DESIDERIO, R. J., Law
DeVRIES, R. C., Electrical and Computer Engineering
DICKINSON, W. E., Surgery
DIELS, J.-C. M., Physics and Astronomy
DIETERLE, B., Physics and Astronomy
DILLARD, J. F., Management
DINIUS, A., Dental Program
DODSON, T. A., Music
DORATO, P., Electrical and Computer Engineering
DOUGHER, M. J., Psychology (C)
DRENNAN, J., Orthopaedics
DUBAN, S. L., Pediatrics
DuMARS, C., Law
DUNCAN, M. H., Paediatrics
DURYEA, P. J., Education
DUSZYNSKI, D. W., Biology
EATON, R. P., Medicine
EFROMOVICH, S., Mathematics and Statistics
EL-GENK, M. S., Chemical and Nuclear Engineering
ELIAS, L., Medicine
ELLIOTT, P. C., Management
ELLIS, J. W., Law
ELLISON, J. A., Mathematics and Statistics
ENGELBRECHT, G. A., Counselling and Family Studies
ENKE, C. G., Chemistry
ERIBES, R. A., Architecture and Planning
ESTRIN, J. A., Anaesthesiology (C)
ETULAIN, R., History
EVANS, W., Theatre and Dance
EWING, R. C., Earth Sciences
FEENEY, D., Psychology
FEINBERG, E. A., Art and Art History (C)
FELBERG, L., Music
FIELD, F. R., Training and Learning Technologies (C)
FINLEY, D., Physics and Astronomy
FISCHER, M. R., English
FISHBURN, W. R., Counselling and Family Studies
FLEMING, R. E., English
FLETCHER, M. P., General Library
FLEURY, P. A., Electrical and Computer Engineering
FORMAN, W. B., Medicine
FOUCAR, M. K., Pathology
FRANDSEN, K. D., Communication and Journalism
FRITZ, C. G., Law
FROELICH, J. W., Anthropology

FRONECH, D. K., Electrical and Computer Engineering
FRY, D., Surgery (C)
GAINES, B., English
GALEY, W. R., Jr, Physiology
GALLAGHER, P. J., English
GARCIA, F. C., Political Science
GARRY, P. J., Pathology
GEISSMAN, J. W., Earth Sciences
GELL-MAN, M., Physics and Astronomy
GERDES, D. C., Modern and Classical Languages (C)
GIBSON, A. G., Mathematics and Statistics
GILFEATHER, F., Mathematics and Statistics
GISSER, M., Economics
GLEW, R. H., Biochemistry (C)
GLUCK, J. P., Psychology (acting C)
GOMEZ-PALACIO, I., Law
GONZALES-BERRY, E., Modern and Classical Languages
GONZALES, R. A., Law
GOODMAN, R., Philosophy (C)
GORDON, W. C., Psychology
GOSZ, J. R., Biology
GRANT, D., Management
GREENBERG, R. E., Paediatrics
GRIFFIN, L. E., Health Promotion, Physical Education and Leisure Programmes
GWIN, M. C., English
HAALAND, K. Y., Psychiatry
HADLEY, W. M., Pharmacy
HAHN, B., Art and Art History
HAIMAN, F. S., General Honours
HALL, G. E., Law
HALL, J., Civil Engineering (C)
HALL, L. B., History
HARJO, J., Engineering
HARRIS, F., Political Science
HARRIS, M., Educational Foundations
HARRIS, R. J., Psychology
HART, F. M., Law
HARTSHORNE, M. F., Radiology
HASHIMOTO, F., Medicine
HAWKINS, C., Electrical and Computer Engineering
HEFFRON, W. A., Family and Community Medicine
HEGGEN, R. J., Civil Engineering
HENNEY, J. E., Medicine
HERMANN, M. S. G., Law
HERZON, F. S., Surgery
HEYWARD, V., Health Promotion, Physical Education and Leisure Programmes
HIGGINS, P. A., Nursing
HINTERBICHLER, K., Music
HOLDER, R. W., Chemistry
HOLLAN, J. D., Computer Science
HUACO, G. A., Sociology
HUMPHRIES, S., Jr, Electrical and Computer Engineering
JAFFE, I. S., Theatre and Dance
JAIN, R., Electrical and Computer Engineering
JAMSHIDI, M., Electrical and Computer Engineering
JEWELL, P. F., Surgery
JOHN-STEINER, V. P., Education
JOHNSON, D. M., English
JOHNSON, G. V., Biology
JOHNSON, J. D., Paediatrics
JOHNSON, P. J., Psychology
JONES, D., English
JOOST-GAUGIER, C., Art and Art History
JORDAN, S. W., Pathology
JUNGLING, K. C., Electrical and Computer Engineering (C)
KARLSTROM, K. E., Earth Sciences
KARNI, S., Electrical and Computer Engineering
KASSICIEH, S. K., Management
KAUFFMAN, D., Chemical and Nuclear Engineering
KAUFMAN, A., Family, Community and Emergency Medicine (C)
KEITH, S. J., Psychiatry (C)
KELLEY, R. O., Anatomy (C)

KELLY, H. W., Pharmacy
KELLY, S. G., Law
KELSEY, C. A., Radiology
KELSEY, C. W., Education
KENDALL, D. L., Electrical and Computer Engineering
KENKRE, V. M., Physics and Astronomy
KERN, R. W., History
KEY, C. R., Pathology
KISIEL, W., Pathology
KLEIN, C., Geology
KLEPPER, D. J., Medicine
KLINE, W., Education
KODRIC-BROWN, A., Biology
KOGOMA, T., Cell Biology
KORNFELD, M., Pathology
KOSTER, F. T., Medicine
KOVNAT, R., Law
KUCHARZ, W., Mathematics and Statistics
KUDO, A. M., Geology
KUES, B. S., Earth Sciences
LaFREE, G., Sociology (C)
LAMPHERE, L., Anthropology
LANCASTER, J. B., Anthropology
LEWIS, S. L., Nursing
LIGON, J. D., Biology (C)
LINDEMAN, R. D., Medicine
LINNELL, J., Theatre and Dance (C)
LIPSCOMB, M. F., Pathology (C)
LIPSKI, J., Modern Languages (C)
LONG, V., Counselling and Family Studies
LOPEZ, A. S., Law
LORENZ, J., Mathematics and Statistics
LOTFIELD, R. B., Biochemistry
LOVE, E. B., Librarianship
LUCKASSON, R. A., Special Education
LUGER, G. F., Computer Science
LUMIA, R., Mechanical Engineering
LUTZ, W., Chemical and Nuclear Engineering
MACIEL, D. R., History
McCARTHY, D. M., Medicine
McCLELLAND, C. E., III, History
McCONNELL, T. S., Pathology
McCULLOUGH-BRABSON, E., Music
McDANIEL, M., Psychology
McFARLANE, D. R., Public Administration
McGRAW, J., Physics and Astronomy
McGUFFEE, L. J., Pharmacology
McIVER, J. K., Physics and Astronomy
McLAUGHLIN, J. C., Pathology
McNAMARA, P. A., Sociology
McNEIL, J., Electrical and Computer Engineering
McPHERSON, D., English
MacPHERSON, W. T., Law
MAKI, G., Electrical and Computer Engineering
MALOLEPSY, J., Theatre and Dance
MANN, B. M., Mathematics and Statistics
MARTINEZ, J. G. R., Special Education
MATTHEWS, J. A. J., Physics and Astronomy
MATTHEWS, O. P., Geography (C)
MATHEWSON, A. D., Law
MATWIYOFF, N. A., Cell Biology (C)
MAY, G. W., Civil Engineering
MAY, P. A., Sociology
MEIZE-GROCHOWSKI, R., Nursing
MELADA, I. P., English
MENNIN, S. P., Anatomy
MERKX, G. W., Sociology
METTLER, F. A., Jr, Radiology (C)
MIGNEAULT, R., Librarianship
MILLER, W. R., Psychology
MILSTEIN, M. M., Educational Administration
MOLD, C., Microbiology (C)
MONEIM, M. S., Orthopaedics (C)
MORAIN, S. A., Geography (C)
MORET, B. M., Computer Science
MORRIS, D. M., Surgery
MORRIS, M. M., Education
MORROW, C., Chemistry (C)
MOSELEY, P. L., Medicine
MURATA, G. H., Medicine
MURPHY, S. J., Paediatrics
NIEMCZYK, T. M., Chemistry
NORDHAUS, R. S., Architecture and Planning

NORWOOD, J. M., Law
NORWOOD, V. L., American Studies (C)
NURNBERG, H. G., Psychiatry
NUTTALL, H. E., Jr, Chemical and Nuclear Engineering
OBENSHAIN, S. S., Paediatrics
OCCHIALINO, M., Law
OGILBY, P. R., Chemistry
OLIVER, J. M., Pathology
OLLER, J. W., Jr, Linguistics
OMDAHL, J. L., Biochemistry
OMER, G., Jr, Orthopaedics
ONDRIAS, M. R., Chemistry
ONNEWEER, C., Mathematics and Statistics
ORRISON, W. W., Radiology
ORTIZ, A. A., Anthropology
ORTIZ, J. V., Chemistry
OVERTURF, G. D., Paediatrics
OWENS, L. D., English
PABISCH, P. K., Foreign Languages and Literature
PADILLA, R. S., Dermatology
PAINE, R. T., Jr, Chemistry
PANITZ, J. A., Physics and Astronomy
PAPADOPOULOS, E. P., Chemistry
PAPIKE, J. J., Geology
PAPILE, L. A., Paediatrics
PARK, S. M., Chemistry
PARKMAN, A. M., Management
PARNALL, T., Law
PARTRIDGE, L. D., Physiology
PATHAK, P. T., Mathematics and Statistics
PEABODY, D. S., Cell Biology
PECK, R. E., English
PEREZ-GOMEZ, J. R., Music
PETERSON, S. L., Pharmacy
PHAM, C., Economics
PIPER, J., Music
PORTER, J., History
PREDOCK-LINNELL, J., Theatre and Dance
PRICE, R. M., Physics and Astronomy
PRINJA, A. K., Chemical and Nuclear Engineering
PRIOLA, D. V., Physiology (C)
PYLE, R. R., Medicine
QUENZER, R. W., Medicine
RABINOWITZ, H., History
RADOSEVICH, R. R., Management
RAIZADA, V., Medicine
RAZANI, A., Mechanical Engineering
REBOLLEDO, T. D., Modern Languages
REED, W. D., Medicine
REES, B. L., Nursing
REEVES, T. Z., Public Administration
REHDER, R. R., Management
REID, R. A., Management
REMMER, K. L., Political Science
REYES, P., Biochemistry
RICHARDS, C. G., Mechanical Engineering
RIENSCHE, L. L., Comm. Disorders (C)
ROBBINS, R. G., History
ROBIN, D. M., Foreign Languages and Literature
RODERICK, N. F., Chemical and Nuclear Engineering
RODRIGUEZ, A., Modern and Classical Languages
ROEBUCK, J., History
ROGERS, E. M., Communication and Journalism
ROLL, S., Psychology
ROMERO, L. M., Law
ROSENBERG, G. A., Neurology (C)
ROSS, H. L., Sociology
ROSS, T. J., Civil Engineering
ROTH, P. B., Emergency Medicine
RUEBUSH, B. K., Psychiatry and Psychology
RUYBAL, S. E., Nursing
SAIERS, J. H., Medicine
SAIKI, J. H., Medicine
SALAND, L. C., Anatomy
SALVAGGIO, R., American Studies
SANTLEY, R. S., Anthropology
SARTO, G. E., Obstetrics and Gynaecology (C)
SAVAGE, D. D., II, Pharmacology
SCALES, A. C., Law

SCALETTI, J. V., Microbiology
SCALLEN, T. J., Biochemistry
SCHADE, D. S., Medicine
SCHARNHORST, G. F., English and American Studies
SCHAU, C. G., Educational Foundations
SCHREYER, H. L., Mechanical Engineering
SCHUELER, G. F., Philosophy (C)
SCHUETZ, J. E., Communication
SCHULTZ, C., Management
SCHUYLER, M. R., Medicine
SCHWARTZ, R. L., Law
SCHWERIN, K. H., Anthropology
SCOTT, P. B., Curriculum and Instruction in Multicultural Teacher Education
SEARLES, R. P., Medicine
SEMO, E., History
SEVERINO, S. K., Psychiatry
SHAHINPOOR, M., Mechanical Engineering
SHAMA, A., Management
SHANE, D. L., Nursing
SHELTON, S. P., Civil Engineering
SHIPMAN, V. C., Counselling and Family Studies
SHOMAKER, D. J., Nursing
SHULTIS, C. L., Music
SIBBITT, W. L., Jr, Medicine
SIEMBIEDA, W. J., Architecture and Planning
SIMONSON, D. G., Management
SKIPPER, B. J., Family, Community and Emergency Medicine
SKLAR, D. P., Emergency Medicine (C)
SKLAR, L. A., Pathology
SMITH, B. T., Computer Science
SMITH, D. D., Special Education
SMITH, D. M., Chemical and Nuclear Engineering
SMITH, H. L., Management
SMITH, M. M., Counselling and Family Studies
SMITH, P. J., Special Education
SMITH, W. S., Jr, Foreign Languages and Literature
SNYDER, R. D., Neurology
SONNENBERG, A., Medicine
SOUTHALL, T. W., Art and Art History
SRUBEK, J., Art Education
STARR, G. P., Mechanical Engineering
STEINBERG, S. L., Mathematics and Statistics
STONE, A. P., Mathematics and Statistics (C)
STRAUS, L. G., Anthropology
STRICKLAND, R. G., Medicine (C)
STURM, F. G., Philosophy
SUMMERS, J. W., Cell Biology
SUTHERLAND, R. J., Psychology
SWINSON, D., Physics and Astronomy
SZASZ, F. M., History
TANDBERG, W. D., Emergency Medicine
TAYLOR, A. P., Architecture and Planning
TAYLOR, S. A., Law
THOMPSON, D. E., Mechanical Engineering (C)
THOMSON, B. M., Civil Engineering
THORNHILL, A. R., Biology
THORSON, J. L., English
TIANO, S. B., Sociology
TOLMAN, J. M., Modern and Classical Languages
TOOLSON, E. C., Biology
TRINKAUS, E., Anthropology
TROTTER, J. A., Anatomy
TROUP, G. M., Pathology
TROUTMAN, W. G., Pharmacy
TUASON, V. B., Psychiatry
TURAN, M., Architecture and Planning
TURNER, P. H., Counselling and Family Studies (C)
TYLER, M., Music
TZAMALOUKAS, A., Medicine
UHLENHUTH, E. H., Psychiatry
USCHER, N. J., Music
USEEM, B., Sociology
UTTON, A. E., Law
VALDES, N., Sociology
VANDERJAGT, D., Biochemistry

VAN DONGEN, R. D., Curriculum and Instruction in Multicultural Teacher Education
VOGEL, K. G., Biology
WALDMAN, J. D., Paediatrics
WALKER, B. R., Physiology
WALTERS, E. A., Chemistry
WANG, M.-L., Civil Engineering
WATERMAN, R. E., Anatomy
WEIGLE, M. M., Anthropology (C)
WEISS, G. K., Physiology
WEISS, J. R., Nursing
WERNLEY, J. A., Surgery
WHEELAND, R. G., Dermatology (C)
WHIDDEN, M. B., English
WHITE, P., English
WIESE, W., Family, Community and Emergency Medicine
WILDIN, M. W., Mechanical Engineering
WILKINS, E. S., Chemical and Nuclear Engineering
WILLIAMS, R. H., Electrical and Computer Engineering
WILLIAMSON, M. R., Radiology
WILLIAMSON, S. L., Radiology
WILLMAN, C. L., Pathology
WINOGRAD, P., Law
WITEMEYER, H., English
WOFSY, C., Mathematics and Statistics
WOLF, S. S., Law
WOLFE, D. M., Physics and Astronomy (C)
WOLFE, J. D., Theatre and Dance
WOOD, C. J., Education Administration
WOOD, J. E., Mechanical Engineering
WOOD, W. F., Music
WOODWARD, L. A., Geology
WORRELL, R. V., Orthopaedics
WRIGHT, J. B., Library
YAGER, J., Psychiatry
YATES, T. L., Biology (C)
ZAGER, P. G., Medicine
ZANNES, E., Communication and Journalism
ZEILIK, M., II, Physics and Astronomy
ZIMMER, W. J., Mathematics and Statistics
ZONGOLOWICZ, H. M.
ZUMWALT, R. E., Pathology

WESTERN NEW MEXICO UNIVERSITY

Box 680, Silver City, NM 88062
Telephone: (505) 538-6011
E-mail: admissions@wnmu.edu
Internet: www.wnmu.edu

Founded 1893

President: Dr JOHN COUNTS
Provost and Vice-President for Academic Affairs: Dr FAYE VOWELL
Vice-President for Business Affairs: CHRISTINE CASEY
Vice-President for Student Affairs: Dr PHILLIP J. FARREN
Registrar: BETSY MILLER
Librarian: BEN WAKASHIGE

Library of 388,193 vols
Number of teachers: 65
Number of students: 1,600.

NEW YORK

ADELPHI UNIVERSITY

Garden City, NY 11530
Telephone: (516) 877-3000
Internet: www.adelphi.edu

Founded 1896
Academic year: August to May

Pres.: Dr ROBERT A. SCOTT
Provost and Sr Vice-Pres. for Academic Affairs: MARCIA G. WELSH
Vice-Pres. for Enrollment and Student Affairs: ANGELA B. PROTO
Vice-Pres. for Univ. Advancement: CHRISTIAN P. VAUPEL
Dean of Univ. Libraries: CHARLES SIMPSON

Library of 650,000 vols, 805,000 microforms
Number of teachers: 706 (239 full-time, 467 part-time)
Number of students: 7,932

DEANS

Arts and Sciences, Graduate and Undergraduate: GAYLE INSLER
School of Social Work: ANDREW SAFYER
School of Nursing: PATRICK COONAN
Schools of Business: ANTHONY LIBERTELLA
Institute of Advanced Psychological Studies: LOUIS PRIMAVERA
School of Education: RONALD FEINGOLD
Honors College: RICHARD GARNER

ALBANY COLLEGE OF PHARMACY

106 New Scotland Ave, Albany, NY 12208-3492
Telephone: (518) 445-7200
E-mail: info@acp.edu
Internet: www.acp.edu
Founded 1881
Pres. and Dean: JAMES J. GOZZO
Assoc. Dean for Academic Affairs: HOWARD D. COLBY
Asst Dean for Student Affairs: PACKY McGRAW
Director of Finance and Business Affairs: WILLIAM M. CRONIN
Dir of Admissions: CARLY T. CONNERS
Dir of Library Services: SUE IWANOWICZ
Number of teachers: 95
Number of students: 1,240.

ALBANY LAW SCHOOL

80 New Scotland Ave, Albany, NY 12208-3494
Telephone: (518) 445-2311
Fax: (518) 445-2315
E-mail: admissions@albanylaw.edu
Internet: www.albanylaw.edu
Founded 1851
Academic year: July to June
Chair. of Board of Trustees: HARRY L. ROBINSON
Pres. and Dean: THOMAS F. GUERNSEY
Registrar: JOANN FITZSIMMONS
Assoc. Dean and Dir of Library: ROBERT T. BEGG
Library of 620,000 vols
Number of teachers: 71 (42 full-time, 29 adjunct)
Number of students: 755.

ALBANY MEDICAL COLLEGE

43 New Scotland Ave, Albany, NY 12208
Telephone: (518) 445-5544
Internet: www.amc.edu
Founded 1839
Dean: Dr VINCENT VERDILE
Dir of Admissions: JOANNE H. NANOS
Librarian: SHERRY HARTMAN
Library of 150,000 vols
Number of teachers: 111
Number of students: 542 medical, 198 graduate.

ALFRED UNIVERSITY

1 Saxon Dr., Alfred, NY 14802-1232
Telephone: (607) 871-2111
E-mail: admwww@alfred.edu
Internet: www.alfred.edu
Founded 1836
Pres.: CHARLES M. EDMONDSON
Provost and Vice-Pres. for Academic Affairs: SUZANNE C. BUCKLEY

Vice-Pres. for Business and Finance: IRENE M. MOSZER
Vice-Pres. for Univ. Relations: SYLVIA BRYANT
Dir of Admissions: JEREMY C. SPENCER
Library Dir: STEPHEN S. CRANDALL
Library of 234,466 vols
Number of teachers: 165
Number of students: 2,400
Publications: *Fiat Lux, Alfred Reporter, Kanakadea, University Catalogue*

DEANS

College of Liberal Arts and Sciences: CHRISTINE GRONTKOWSKI
School of Ceramic Eng. and Sciences: ALASTAIR CORMACK
College of Business: DAVID SZCZERBACKI
College of Eng. and Professional Studies: W. RICHARD OTT
School of Art and Design: KATHLEEN COLLINS
Graduate Studies: W. RICHARD OTT (Dir)

BANK STREET COLLEGE OF EDUCATION

610 West 112th St, New York, NY 10025-1898
Telephone: (212) 875-4400
Fax: (212) 875-4759
E-mail: collegepubs@bankstreet.edu
Internet: www.bnkst.edu
Founded 1916
Academic year: September to July
Pres.: Dr AUGUSTA SOUZA KAPPNER
Vice-Pres. for Finance and Admin.: FRANK NUARA
Vice-Pres. for Institutional Advancement (vacant): JOHN BORDEN
Dean of Children's Programmes Div.: REUEL M. JORDAN
Dean of Graduate School: JON SNYDER
Dean of Continuing Education: FERN KHAN
Dir of Library: LINDA GREENGRASS
Library of 123,215 vols
Number of teachers: 125
Number of students: 1,052.

BARD COLLEGE

POB 5000, Annandale-on-Hudson, NY 12504
Telephone: (845) 758-6822
E-mail: admission@bard.edu
Internet: www.bard.edu
Founded 1860
Pres.: LEON BOTSTEIN
Registrar: PETER GADSBY
Dean: DAVID SHEIN
Dir of Admissions: MARY BACKLUND
Dir of Libraries: JEFFREY KATZ
Library of 280,000 vols
Number of teachers: 224
Number of students: 1,681.

BORICUA COLLEGE

3755 Broadway, New York, NY 10032
Telephone: (212) 694-1000
E-mail: acruz@boricuacollege.edu
Internet: www.boricuacollege.edu
Campuses in Manhattan and Brooklyn
Founded 1974
Private control
Pres.: VICTOR G. ALICEA
Vice-Pres. and Dean of Academic Affairs, Manhattan Campus: SHIVAJI SENGUPTA
Vice-Pres. and Dean of Academic Affairs, Brooklyn Campus: MARIA MONTES MORALES
Library Dir: LIZA RIVERA
Number of teachers: 40
Number of students: 1,190.

BROOKLYN LAW SCHOOL

250 Joralemon St, Brooklyn, NY 11201
Telephone: (718) 625-2200
E-mail: admitq@brooklaw.edu
Internet: www.brooklaw.edu
Founded 1901
Private control
Academic year: August to May
Dean: JOAN G. WEXLER
Assoc. Dean for Academic Affairs: LAWRENCE M. SOLAN
Assoc. Dean for Devt: MICHAEL A. GERBER
Assoc. Dean for Student Affairs: BERYL R. JONES-WOODIN
Registrar: SUZANNE M. DENNIS
Number of students: 1,510.

CANISIUS COLLEGE

2001 Main St, Buffalo, NY 14208-1098
Telephone: (716) 888-2200
Fax: (716) 888-3230
E-mail: admissions@canisius.edu
Internet: www.canisius.edu
Founded 1870
Pres.: Rev. VINCENT M. COOKE
Chancellor: Rev. JAMES M. DEMSKE
Vice-Pres. for Academic Affairs: Dr HERBERT J. NELSON
Vice-Pres. for Business and Finance: LAURENCE W. FRANZ
Vice-Pres. for College Relations: JOHN J. HURLEY
Vice-Pres. for Student Affairs: THOMAS E. MILLER
Assoc. Vice-Pres for Library Services: Dr JOEL COHEN
Library of 350,361 vols
Number of teachers: 358 (198 full-time; 160 part-time)
Number of students: 4,944.

CAZENOVIA COLLEGE

22 Sullivan St, Cazenovia, NY 13035
Telephone: (315) 655-7000
E-mail: admissions@cazenovia.edu
Internet: www.cazcollege.edu
Founded 1824 as Seminary of the Genesee Conference; present name 1982
Private control
Academic year: September to May
Pres.: Dr MARK JOHN TIERNO
Exec. Vice-Pres.: SUSAN A. BERGER
Vice-Pres. for Academic Affairs: DONALD McCRIMMON
Vice-Pres. for Student Devt: C. JOSEPH BEHAN
Vice-Pres. for Enrollment Management: ROBERT A. CROOT
Vice-Pres. for Institutional Advancement: CAROL M. SATCHWELL
Registrar: J. ZACHARY KELLEY
Library Dir: STANLEY KOZACZKA
Library of 90,000
Number of teachers: 123 (52 full-time, 71 part-time)
Number of students: 817 full-time
Areas of study: art and design, business and management, humanities, natural sciences, education, social and behavioural sciences.

CHRIST THE KING SEMINARY

711 Knox Rd, East Aurora, NY 14052
Telephone: (716) 652-8900
Fax: (716) 652-8903
E-mail: cksacad@cks.edu
Internet: www.cks.edu
Founded 1857
Private control
Pres. and Rector: Rev. RICHARD W. SIEPKA

Vice-Rector: Rev. GREGORY M. FAULHABER
Academic Dean: Rev. EDWARD J. SHEEDY
Library Dir: TERESA LUBIENECKI

Library of 160,000 vols
Number of teachers: 25 (18 full-time, 7 adjunct)
Number of students: 45 full-time.

CITY UNIVERSITY OF NEW YORK

535 East 80th St, New York, NY 10021
Telephone: (212) 794-5555
Internet: www.cuny.edu
Founded 1847

Public instn comprising 10 sr colleges, listed below, a Graduate School and Univ. Center, a law school, a medical school, a technical college and 6 community colleges: Borough of Manhattan Community College, Bronx Community College, Hostos Community College, Kingsborough Community College, Fiorello H. La Guardia Community College and Queensborough Community College

Chancellor: MATTHEW GOLDSTEIN

Library: Combined libraries of 6,000,000 vols.

CONSTITUENT COLLEGES AND SCHOOLS

Baruch College

1 Bernard Baruch Way, New York, NY 10010
Telephone: (646) 312-1000
Internet: www.baruch.cuny.edu
Founded 1919
Pres.: KATHLEEN M. WALDRON
Number of teachers: 500 (full-time)
Number of students: 15,500.

Brooklyn College

2900 Bedford Ave, Brooklyn, NY 11210
Telephone: (718) 951-1000
Internet: www.brooklyn.cuny.edu
Founded 1930
Pres.: CHRISTOPHER M. KIMMICH
Number of teachers: 496 (full-time)
Number of students: 14,964.

City College

Convent Ave and 138th St, New York, NY 10031
Telephone: (212) 650-7000
Internet: www.ccny.cuny.edu
Founded 1847
Pres.: GREGORY H. WILLIAMS
Number of teachers: 457 (full-time)
Number of students: 12,083.

City University School of Law at Queens College

65-21 Main St, Flushing, NY 11367
Telephone: (718) 575-4200
Internet: www.law.cuny.edu
Founded 1973
Dean: MICHELLE J. ANDERSON
Number of teachers: 28 (full-time)
Number of students: 467.

College of Staten Island

2800 Victory Blvd, Staten Island, NY 10314
Telephone: (718) 982-2000
Internet: www.csi.cuny.edu
Founded 1976 by amalgamation of Staten Island Community College and Richmond College
Pres.: Dr TOMAS D. MORALES
Number of teachers: 266 (full-time)

Number of students: 12,023.

Graduate School and University Center

365 Fifth Ave, New York, NY 10016-4309
Telephone: (212) 817-7000
Internet: www.gc.cuny.edu
Founded 1961
Pres.: WILLIAM P. KELLY
Number of teachers: 334 (full-time)
Number of students: 3,813.

Hunter College

695 Park Ave, New York, NY 10021
Telephone: (212) 772-4000
Internet: www.hunter.cuny.edu
Founded 1870
Pres.: JENNIFER J. RAAB
Number of teachers: 488 (full-time)
Number of students: 19,689.

John Jay College of Criminal Justice

899 10th Ave, New York, NY 10019
Telephone: (212) 237-8000
Internet: www.jjay.cuny.edu
Founded 1964
Pres.: JEREMY TRAVIS
Number of teachers: 256 (full-time)
Number of students: 10,834.

Lehman College

Bedford Park Blvd, W, Bronx, NY 10468
Telephone: (212) 960-8000
Internet: www.lehman.cuny.edu
Founded 1931
Pres.: RICARDO R. FERNANDEZ
Number of teachers: 266 (full-time)
Number of students: 9,283.

Medgar Evers College

1650 Bedford Ave, Brooklyn, NY 11225
Telephone: (718) 951-5000
Internet: www.mec.cuny.edu
Founded 1969
Pres.: EDISON O. JACKSON
Number of teachers: 127 (full-time)
Number of students: 5,063.

New York City Technical College

300 Jay St, Brooklyn, NY 11201
Telephone: (718) 260-5500
E-mail: connect@citytech.cuny.edu
Internet: www.citytech.cuny.edu
Pres.: Dr RUSSELL K. HOTZLER (acting)
Number of teachers: 276 (full-time)
Number of students: 11,124.

Queens College

65-30 Kissena Blvd, Flushing, NY 11367
Telephone: (718) 997-5000
Internet: www.qc.edu
Founded 1937
Pres.: JAMES L. MUYSKENS
Number of teachers: 514 (full-time)
Number of students: 16,381.

Sophie Davis School of Biomedical Education

160 Convent Ave, Room H-107, New York, NY 10031
Telephone: (212) 650-5275
Fax: (212) 650-6696
Internet: med.cuny.edu
Founded 1984
Dean: STANFORD A. ROMAN, Jr.

York College

94-20 Guy R. Brewer Blvd, Jamaica, NY 11451
Telephone: (718) 262-2000
Internet: www.york.cuny.edu
Founded 1966
Pres.: Dr MARCIA C. KEIZS
Number of teachers: 144 (full-time)
Number of students: 6,030.

CLARKSON UNIVERSITY

8 Clarkson Ave, Potsdam, NY 13699-5500
Telephone: (315) 268-6400
Fax: (315) 268-7993
E-mail: admission@clarkson.edu
Internet: www.clarkson.edu
Founded 1896
Pres.: TONY COLLINS
Vice-Pres for Business and Financial Affairs/Treas.: BRUCE T. H. KNILL
Dean of Admissions: SUZANNE A. LIBERTY
Registrar: LYNN BROWN
Library Dir: NATALIA STAHL
Library of 229,000 vols, 272,000 microforms
Number of teachers: 172, incl. 48 full professors
Number of students: 2,670
Publication: Clarkson

DEANS

Graduate School: (vacant)
School of Eng.: ANTHONY G. COLLINS
School of Science: JAMES H. THORP, III
School of Business: VICTOR P. PEASE
Summer Session and Spec. Programmes: STEPHEN NEWKOFSKY
Student Life: MICHAEL E. COOPER
Liberal Studies: JERRY GRAVANDER

COLGATE ROCHESTER CROZER DIVINITY SCHOOL

1100 South Goodman St, Rochester, NY 14620-2589
Telephone: (585) 271-1320
Fax: (585) 340-9644
E-mail: admissions@crcds.edu
Internet: www.crds.edu
Founded 1970 by merger of 3 theological seminaries, 1 missionary training school and 1 theological school
Private control
Academic year: September to May
Pres.: Dr EUGENE C. BLAY
Vice-Pres. for Institutional Advancemen): PATRICK HANLEY
Vice-Pres. for Enrollment Services: MELISSA MORRAL
Vice-Pres. for Academic Life and Dean of Faculty: MELANIE MAY
Registrar: GORDON CHAPMAN
Library Dir: MARGE NEAD
Library of 300,000 vols
Number of teachers: 11.

COLGATE UNIVERSITY

13 Oak Dr., Hamilton, NY 13346
Telephone: (315) 228-1000
Fax: (315) 228-7798
Internet: www.colgate.edu
Founded 1819; chartered as Madison Univ. 1846, name changed to Colgate Univ. 1890
Academic year: August to May
Pres.: REBECCA S. CHOPP
Vice-Pres. for Business and Finance: DAVID HALE
Controller: THOMAS O'NEILL
Registrar: GRETCHEN B. HERRINGER
Vice-Pres. for Communications and Public Relations: CHARLIE MELICHAR

Dean of the College: DEAN JOHNSON
Dean of Faculty: LYLE ROELOFS
Dir of Graduate Programs: SUSAN KAPLAN
Librarian: JUDITH NOYES
Library of 700,102 vols
Number of teachers: 343 (267 full-time; 76 part-time)
Number of students: 2,750.

VAUGHN COLLEGE OF AERONAUTICS AND TECHNOLOGY

86-01 23rd Ave, Flushing, NY 11369
Telephone: (718) 429-6600
Fax: (718) 429-0256
E-mail: admissions@vaughn.edu
Internet: www.vaughn.edu

Founded 1932 as Casey Jones School of Aeronautics; present name 1986
Private control

Pres.: Dr JOHN C. FITZPATRICK

Number of teachers: 119
Number of students: 1,308.

COLLEGE OF MOUNT SAINT VINCENT

6301 Riverdale Ave, Riverdale, NY 10471
Telephone: (718) 405-3267
E-mail: admissions.office@mountsaintvincent.edu
Internet: www.mountsaintvincent.edu

Founded 1847

Pres.: CHARLES L. FLYNN, Jr
Vice-Pres. for Student Affairs and Dean of Students: ADELE GATENS
Dir of Library: EDWARD O'HARA

Library of 149,000 vols
Number of teachers: 80
Number of students: 1,150.

COLLEGE OF NEW ROCHELLE

29 Castle Pl., New Rochelle, NY 10805
Telephone: (914) 654-5000
Fax. (914) 654-5980
E-mail: admission@cnr.edu
Internet: www.cnr.edu

Founded 1904

Pres.: Dr STEPHEN J. SWEENEY
Sr Vice-Pres, for Academic Affairs: Dr JOAN E. BAILEY
Vice-Pres. for Financial Affairs: JUDITH A. HUNTINGTON
Vice-Pres. for College Advancement: BRENNA SHEENAN MAYER
Dean of the Library: Dr JAMES T. SCHLIEFER

Library of 200,000 vols
Number of teachers: 774
Number of students: 6,475

DEANS

School of Arts and Sciences: Dr C. J. DENNE
School of New Resources: BESSIE BLAKE
Graduate School: LAURA ELLIS
School of Nursing: CONNIE VANCE

COLLEGE OF SAINT ROSE

432 Western Ave, Albany, NY 12203-1490
Telephone: (518) 454-5111
Fax: (518) 454-2013
E-mail: admit@mail.strose.edu
Internet: www.strose.edu

Founded 1920
Academic year: September to May

Pres.: R. MARK SULLIVAN
Registrar: JUDITH KELLY
Provost and Vice-Pres. for Academic Affairs: Dr DAVID SZCZERBACKI
Vice-Pres. of Institutional Advancement: KARIN CARR

Vice-Pres. of Finance and Admin.: MARCUS BUCKLEY
Vice-Pres; for Enrollment Management: MARY M. GRONDAHL
Dir of Library Services: PETER KOONZ
Library of 209,899 vols
Number of teachers: 452
Number of students: 4,980.

COLUMBIA UNIVERSITY

Morningside Heights, New York, NY 10027
Telephone: (212) 854-1754
Fax: (212) 932-0418
Internet: www.columbia.edu

Founded as King's College 1754; inc. in 1784 and name changed to Columbia College. By order of the Supreme Court of State of New York, in 1912, title changed to Columbia Univ.
Private control
Academic year: September to May

Pres.: LEE C. BOLLINGER
Provost: JONATHAN R. COLE
Exec. Vice-Pres. for Admin.: EMILY C. LLOYD
Exec. Vice-Pres. for Finance: JOHN MASTEN
Vice-Pres. for Facilities Management (vacant)
Vice-Pres. for Arts and Sciences: DAVID H. COHEN
Vice-Pres. for Devt and Alumni Relations: RICHARD K. NAUM
Vice-President for Public Affairs: ALAN J. STONE
Vice-President for Information Services and University Librarian: JAMES G. NEAL
Vice-President for Health Sciences: HERBERT PARDES
Vice-President for Human Resources: COLLEEN CROOKER
Secretary: KEITH WALTON
Treasurer and Controller: PATRICIA L. FRANCY

Library: see Libraries
Number of teachers: 3,219
Number of students: 20,504 (7,530 undergraduate, 12,974 postgraduate and professional)

Publications: *Journal of the Ancient Near Eastern Society, The Astronomical Journal, Current Musicology, Germanic Review, Columbia Human Rights Law Review, Journal of International Affairs, Johnsonian News Letter, Columbia Journalism Review, Columbia Law Review, Journal of Philosophy, Renaissance Quarterly, Revista Hispánica Moderna, Romanic Review, Columbia Journal of Transnational Law, Columbia Journal of World Business, Chemical Highlights, Columbia Journal of Environmental Law, Columbia Studies in the Classical Tradition, Critical Texts, Global Political Assessment, Journal of Art and the Law, Prospects: The Annual for American Cultural Studies, Semiotext(e), Studies in American Indian Literature, Translation*

DEANS

Columbia College: AUSTIN E. QUIGLEY
Graduate School of Arts and Sciences: EDUARDO MACAGNO
School of Law: LANCE LIEBMAN
School of Medicine: HERBERT PARDES
School of Eng. and Applied Science: ZVI GALIL
Graduate School of Architecture, Planning and Preservation: BERNARD TSCHUMI
Graduate School of Journalism: DAVID A. KLATELL (acting)
Graduate School of Business: MEYER FELDBERG
School of Dental and Oral Surgery: ALLAN J. FORMICOLA

School of Public Health: ALLAN G. ROSENFIELD
School of Nursing: MARY O. MUNDINGER
General Studies: PETER AWN
School of International and Public Affairs: LISA ANDERSON
School of Social Work: RONALD A. FELDMAN
School of the Arts: (vacant)

PROFESSORS

Anaesthesiology:
FINCK, A. D.
FINSTER, M.
HILLEL, Z.
HYMAN, A. I.
MORISHIMA, H. O.
ORNSTEIN, E.
PANG, L.
PANTUCK, E. J.
SMILEY, R. M.
STONE, J. G.
THYS, D. M.
TRINER, L.
WEISSMAN, C.
YOUNG, W. L.

Anatomy and Cell Biology:
AMBRON, R.
APRIL, E. W.
BELLVE, A. R.
BRANDT, P.
BULINSKI, J. C.
GERSHON, M. D.
KESSIN, R. H.
ROLE, L. W.
SILVERMAN, A.-J.
TENNYSON, V. M. S.
TORAN-ALLERAND, C. D.

Anthropology:
ALLAND, A., Jr
COHEN, M. L.
COMBS-SCHILLING, M. E.
D'ALTROY, T.
HOLLOWAY, R. L.
MELNICK, D.
NEWMAN, K.
SKINNER, E. P.
TAUSSIG, M.

Applied Physics:
BOOZER, A. H.
CHU, C. K.
HERMAN, I. P.
MARSHALL, T. C.
MAUEL, M.
NAVRATIL, G.

Architecture, Planning and Preservation:
FRAMPTON, K.
GRAVA, S.
HERDEG, K.
HOLL, S.
MARCUSE, P.
McINTYRE, L.
McLEOD, M.
PLUNZ, R.
POLSHEK, J. S.
SASSEN, S. J.
SCLAR, E.
STERN, R. A. M.
TSCHUMI, B.
WRIGHT, G.

Art History and Archaeology:
BALLON, H. M.
BECK, J. H.
MYCK, A.
BERGDOLL, B. G.
BRILLIANT, R.
CONNORS, J.
FREEDBERG, D.
KRAUSS, R.
MIDDLETON, R.
MURASE, M. C.
MURRAY, S.
PASZTORY, E.
REFF, T.

ROSAND, D.
STALEY, A.

Arts:

FORMAN, M., Film
INSDORF, A., Film
SARRIS, A., Film

Astronomy:

APPLEGATE, J.
BAKER, N.
HALPERN, J. P.
HELFAND, D.
PATTERSON, J.
PRENDERGAST, K. H.
SPIEGEL, E. A.
VAN GORKOM, J.

Biochemistry and Molecular Biophysics:

FEIGELSON, P.
GOFF, S.
GOLD, A. M.
GOLDBERGER, R. F.
GOTTESMAN, M. E.
GREENWALD, I. S.
HENDRICKSON, W. A.
HIRSH, D. I.
HONIG, B.
JESSELL, T.
KRASNA, A. I.
SRINIVASAN, P. R.

Biological Sciences:

BOCK, W. J.
CHALFIE, M.
CHASIN, L. A.
COHEN, D. H.
KELLEY, D. B.
MACAGNO, E. R.
MANCINELLI, A.
MANLEY, J.
POLLACK, R.
POO, M.
PRIVES, C. L.
TZAGOLOFF, A.
ZUBAY, G. L.

Business:

ADLER, M.
ARZAC, E. R.
BARTEL, A.
BROCKNER, J.
BURTON, J. C.
CAPON, N.
DONALDSON, J.
EDWARDS, F.
FEDERGRUEN, A.
GIOVANNINI, A.
GLASSERMAN, P.
GLOSTEN, L. R.
GREEN, L.
GREENWALD, B. C. N.
GUPTA, S.
HARRIGAN, K.
HARRIS, T.
HEAL, G.
HOLBROOK, M.
HORTON, R.
HUBBARD, R. G.
HUBERMAN, G.
HULBERT, J. M.
ICHNIOWSKI, B. E.
KOHLI, R.
KOLESAR, P.
LEFF, N.
LEHMANN, D.
LICHTENBERG, F. R.
MELUMAD, N. D.
MISHKIN, F.
NOAM, E.
OHLSON, J.
PATRICK, H.
SELDEN, L.
SEXTON, R.
STARR, M.
SUNDARESAN, S.
THOMAS, J. K.
TUSHMAN, M.

WARREN, E. K.
WILKINSON, M.
ZIPKIN, P.

Chemical Engineering and Applied Chemistry:

CHEH, H. Y.
DURNING, C.
GRYTE, C.
LEONARD, E. F.
O'SHAUGHNESSY, B.
SPENCER, J.

Chemistry:

BENT, B. E.
BERNE, B. J.
BERSOHN, R.
BRESLOW, R.
DANISHEFSKY, S. J.
EISENTHAL, K. B.
FLYNN, G. W.
FRIESNER, R.
KATZ, T. J.
NAKANISHI, K.
PARKIN, G. F. R.
PECHUKAS, P.
STILL, W. C.
TURRO, N. J.
VALENTINI, J.

Civil Engineering and Engineering Mechanics:

DASGUPTA, G.
DIMAGGIO, F. L.
FRIEDMAN, M. B.
GJELSVIK, A.
GRIFFIS, F. H.
MEYER, C.
STOLL, R. D.
TESTA, R. B.
VAICAITIS, R.

Classics:

BAGNALL, R. S.
CAMERON, A.
COULTER, J. A.
SAID, S.
TARÁN, L.
ZETZEL, J.

Computer Science:

AHO, A. V.
ALLEN, P. K.
FEINER, S. K.
GALIL, Z.
GROSS, J. L.
KAISER, G.
KENDER, J.
McKEOWN, K.
STOLFO, S.
TRAUB, J. F.
UNGER, S.
WOZNIAKOWSKI, M.
YEMINI, Y.

Dental and Oral Surgery:

CANGIALOSI, T. J.
DAVIS, M. J.
EFSTRATIADIS, S. S.
FORMICOLA, A. J.
HASSELGREN, B. G.
HILLS, H. L.
ISRAEL, H. A.
KAHN, N.
KLYVERT, M.
LAMSTER, I. B.
MOSS-SALENTIJN, L.
MYERS, R.
ODRICH, J.
ROSER, S. M.
TROUTMAN, K. C.
ZEGARELLI, D. J.

Dermatology:

BICKERS, D. R.

East Asian Languages and Cultures:

ANDERER, P.
HYMES, R.
LEDYARD, G. K.

SHIRANE, H.
SMITH, H. D., II
WANG, D. D.-W.
ZELIN, M.

Economics:

BHAGWATI, J.
BLOOM, D.
CHICHILNISKY, G.
CLARIDA, R.
DESAI, P.
DHRYMES, P.
DUTTA, P. K.
ERICSON, R.
FINDLAY, R.
HAYASHI, F.
LANCASTER, K.
MUNDELL, R.
PHELPS, E.
SACHS, J. D.
WATTS, H.
WELLISZ, S. H.

Electrical Engineering:

ACAMPORA, A.
ANASTASSIOU, D.
DIAMENT, P.
HEINZ, T.
LAZAR, A.
MEADOWS, H. E.
OSGOOD, R.
SCHWARTZ, M.
SEN, A. K.
STERN, T. E.
TEICH, M. C.
TSIVIDIS, Y.
WANG, W.
YANG, E. S.
ZUKOWSKI, C. A.

English and Comparative Literature:

BLOUNT, M.
DAMROSCH, D.
DELBANCO, A.
DOUGLAS, A.
EDEN, K.
FERGUSON, R.
FERRANTE, J.
HANNING, R.
HOWARD, J.
KASTAN, D.
KOCH, J. K.
KROEBER, K.
MARCUS, S.
MEISEL, M.
MENDELSON, E.
MILLER, D. A.
MIROLLO, J. V.
MORETTI, F.
O'MEALLY, R. G.
PETERS, J. S.
QUIGLEY, A.
ROSENBERG, J. D.
ROSENTHAL, M.
SEIDEL, M.
SHAPIRO, J.
SPIVACK, G. C.
STADE, G.
TAYLER, E. W.
YERKES, D.

French and Romance Philology:

BLOCH, R. H.
COMPAGNON, A.
CONDE, M.
FORCE, P.
LOTRINGER, S.
MAY, G.
MITTERAND, H.
RIFFATERRE, M.

Genetics and Development:

BESTOR, T.
CARLSON, M.
COSTANTINI, F.
EFSTRATIADIS, A.
GILLIAM, T. C.
OTT, J.

PAPAIOANNOU, V.
ROTHSTEIN, R. J.
SCHON, E. A.
STERN, C. D.
STRUHL, G.
WARBURTON, D.
WOLGEMUTH, D.

Geological Sciences:
BROECKER, W. S.
CHRISTIE-BLICK, N.
FAIRBANKS, R. G.
GORDON, A. L.
HAYES, D. E.
HAYS, J. O.
LANGMUIR, C.
MENKE, W.
MUTTER, J.
OLSEN, P.
RICHARDS, P. G.
SCHLOSSER, P.
SCHOLZ, C.
SIMPSON, H. J.
SYKES, L. R.
WALKER, D.

Germanic Languages:
ANDERSON, M. M.
HUYSSEN, A.
MULLER, H.
VON MUCKE, D. E.

History:
BILLOWS, R.
BLACKMAR, E.
BRINKLEY, A.
BULLIET, R.
BUSHMAN, R.
BYNUM, C.
CANNADINE, D.
DE GRAZIA, V.
DEAK, I.
FIELDS, B.
FONER, E.
GLUCK, C.
GOREN, A. A.
HAIMSON, L.
HARRIS, W. V.
HOWELL, M.
JACKSON, K. T.
KLEIN, H. S.
LYNCH, H. R.
MALEFAKIS, E. E.
MARABLE, M.
PAXTON, R.
ROTHMAN, D.
SCHAMA, S.
SHENTON, J. P.
SMIT, J. W.
STANISLAWSKI, M.
STEPAN, N.
STERN, F.
VON HAGEN, M. L.
WOLOCH, I.
WORTMAN, R.
WRIGHT, M.
YERUSHALMI, Y. H.

Industrial Engineering and Operations Research:
BIENSTOCK, D.
GALLEGO, G.
GOLDFARB, D.
KLEIN, M.
PINEDO, M.
SIGMAN, K.
YAO, D. D.-W.

International and Public Affairs:
MOLZ, R. K.
NELSON, R. R.
RODRIK, D.

Italian:
BAROLINI, T.
REBAY, L.

Journalism:
BELFORD, B.

BENEDICT, H.
CAREY, J. W.
GARLAND, P.
GOLDSTEIN, K. K.
ISAACS, S. D.
KONNER, J.

Krumb School of Mines:
BESHERS, D. N.
DUBY, P. F.
HARRIS, C. C.
SOMASUNDARAN, P.
THEMELIS, N. J.
YEGULALP, T. M.

Law:
BARENBERG, M.
BERGER, C. J.
BERGER, V.
BERMANN, G.
BLACK, B. A.
BLACK, B. S.
BLASI, V.
BRIFFAULT, R.
CHIRELSTEIN, M.
COFFEE, J. C.
CRENSHAW, K. W.
DAMROSCH, L.
EDGAR, H. S. H.
EDWARDS, R.
FARNSWORTH, E. A.
FINEMAN, M.
FLETCHER, G.
GARDNER, R.
GILSON, R. J.
GINSBURG, J. C.
GOLDBERG, V. P.
GOLDSCHMID, H. J.
GORDON, J. N.
GREENAWALT, R. K.
GREENBERG, J.
HOOVER, J.
JONES, W. K.
KORN, H. L.
LEEBRON, D. W.
LIEBMAN, J.
LIEBMAN, L.
LYNCH, G.
MOGLEN, E.
MONAGHAN, H.
NARASIMHAN, S.
NEUMAN, G. L.
PARKER, K. E.
RABB, H. S.
RAPACZYNSKI, A.
ROE, M. J.
SABEL, C. F.
SMIT, H.
SOVERN, M.
STONE, R.
STRAUSS, P. L.
THOMAS, K.
UVILLER, H. R.
WILLIAMS, P. J.
YOUNG, M.
YOUNG, W. F., Jr

Mathematics:
BASS, H.
FRIEDMAN, R.
GALLAGHER, P. X.
GOLDFELD, D.
JACQUET, H. M.
JORGENSEN, T.
KARATZAS, I.
KURANISHI, M.
MORGAN, J.
PHONG, D.
PINKHAM, H. C.

Mechanical Engineering:
CHEVRAY, R.
FREUDENSTEIN, F.
LONGMAN, R. W.
MODI, V.

Medicine:
AL-AWQATI, Q.

APPEL, G. B.
BAER, L. R.
BANK, A.
BIGGER, J. T.
BILEZIKIAN, J. P.
BUTLER, V. P., Jr
CALDWELL, L. P.
CANFIELD, R. E.
CANNON, P. J.
CHESS, L.
CIMINO, J. J.
CLAYTON, P. D.
CORTELL, S.
FIELD, M.
FRANCIS, C. K.
FRANTZ, A. G.
GIARDINA, E.-G.
GINSBURG, H. N.
GOLDBERG, I. J.
GRIECO, M. H.
HOLT, P. R.
JACOBS, T. P.
KEMP, H., Jr
LEGATO, M. J.
LEIFER, E.
LINDENBAUM, J.
LOEB, J.
MELCHER, G.
MORRIS, T. Q.
MORSE, J. E.
NEU, H. C.
PHILLIPS, G. B.
PI SUNYER, F. X.
ROSNER, W.
SCHWARTZ, M. J.
TABAS, I. A.
TALL, A.
TAPLEY, D. F.
TAUB, R. N.
THOMSON, G. E.
TURINO, G. M.
WARDLAW, S.
WEINSTEIN, I. B.
WEISFELDT, M. L.
WEISS, H. J.

Microbiology:
CALAME, K. L.
FIGURSKI, D.
MITCHELL, A. P.
RACANIELLO, V. R.
SHORE, D. M.
SHUMAN, H. A.
SILVERSTEIN, S. J.
YOUNG, C.

Middle East and Asian Languages and Cultures:
BURRILL, K. R. F.
MADINA, M.
MIRON, D.
PRITCHETT, F.
RICCARDI, T.
SALIBA, G.
VAN DE MIEROOP, M.

Music:
BENT, I.
CHRISTENSEN, D.
EDWARDS, G.
FRISCH, W.
KRAMER, J.
LERDAHL, A. W.
PERKINS, L.
SISMAN, E.
TUCKER, M. T.

Neurological Surgery:
BRISMAN, R.
HOUSEPIAN, E. M.
MCMURTRY, J.
QUEST, D. O.
STEIN, B. M.

Neurology:
BRUST, J. C. M., Jr
COTE, L. J.
DE VIVO, D. C.

DI MAURO, S.
EMERSON, R. G.
FAHN, S.
GHEZ, C.
GOLD, A. P.
HALSEY, J., Jr
HAUSER, W. A.
KARLIN, A.
LATOV, N.
LOVELACE, R. E.
MAYEUX, R.
MOHR, J. P.
PEDLEY, T.
PENN, A. S.
ROWLAND, L. P.
SCHWARTZ, J.
SCIARRA, D.
STERN, Y.
WEXLER, N.

Nursing:

FULMER, T. T.
MUNDINGER, M. O.

Obstetrics and Gynaecology:

BOWE, E. T.
FERIN, M.
HEMBREE, W. C.
JAGIELLO, G.
LOBO, R. A.
NEUWIRTH, R. S.
TIMOR, I. E.
WILLIAMS, S. B.

Ophthalmology:

BEHRENS, M.
BITO, L.
DONN, A.
FARRIS, R. L.
FORBES, M.
GOURAS, P.
L'ESPERANCE, F., Jr
MOORE, S.
SPALTER, H.
SPECTOR, A.
SRINIVASAN, B.
TROKEL, S.
WORGUL, B. V.
YANNUZZI, L. A.

Orthopaedic Surgery:

DICK, H.
EFTEKHAR, N.
FIELDING, J. W.
GRANTHAM, S. A.
LAI, W. M.
MOW, V. C.
RATCLIFFE, A.
SHELTON, M. L.

Otolaryngology:

BLITZER, A.
CLOSE, L. G.
KHANNA, S. M.

Pathology:

AXEL, R.
DALLA-FAVERA, R.
GELLER, L. M.
GOLDMAN, J. E.
GREENE, L. A.
KAUFMAN, M.
KOHN, D. F.
LEFKOWITCH, J. H.
LIEM, R. K. H.
MASON, C. A.
PERZIN, K. H.
RICHART, R. M.
SHELANSKI, M. L.
SUCIU-FOCA, N.

Paediatrics:

COOPER, L. Z.
CUNNINGHAM, N.
DECKELBAUM, R. J.
DELL, R. B.
DRISCOLL, J. M.
GERSHON, A. A.
GERSONY, W. M.

HEAGARTY, M.
JACOBS, J.
KRONGRAD, E.
LEBLANC, W.
LEVINE, L.
MELLIN, G. W.
MELLINS, R. B.
NICHOLSON, J. F.
PIOMELLI, S.
SITARZ, A.
STARK, R.
WETHERS, D. L.
WINCHESTER, R. J.

Pharmacology:

BOYDEN, P.
GOLDBERG, D. J.
GRAZIANO, J. H.
HOFFMAN, B. F.
ROBINSON, R. B.
ROSEN, M. R.
SIEGELBAUM, S. A.
WIT, A. L.

Philosophy:

ALBERT, D.
BEROFSKY, B.
BILGRAMI, A.
GAIFMAN, H.
GOEHR, L. D.
LARMORE, C.
LEVI, I.
POGGE, T.
SIDORSKY, D.

Physical Education and Intercollegiate Athletics:

ROHAN, J. P.

Physics:

APRILE, E.
CHRIST, N. H.
GYULASSY, M.
HAILEY, C. J.
HARTMANN, S.
KAHN, S. M.
LEE, T. D.
LEE, W.
MUELLER, A.
NAGAMIYA, S.
RUDERMAN, M. A.
SCHWARTZ, M.
SCIULLI, F.
SHAEVITZ, M. H.
TUTS, P. M.
UEMURA, Y.
WEINBERG, E.
WILLIS, W. J.
ZAJC, W. A.

Physiology and Cellular Biophysics:

BLANK, M.
DODD, J.
FISCHBARG, J.
KANDEL, E. R.
LOW, M. G.
SCHACHTER, D.
SILVERSTEIN, S. C.
STERN, D.

Political Science:

ANDERSON, L.
BALDWIN, D.
BERNSTEIN, T. P.
BETTS, R. K.
BIALER, S.
CHALMERS, D. A.
COHEN, J. L.
CURTIS, G. L.
ELSTER, J.
FRANKLIN, J. H.
HAMILTON, C. V.
JERVIS, R. L.
JOHNSTON, D. C.
KATZNELSON, I. I.
KESSELMAN, M. J.
LEGVOLD, R.
MILNER, H.
NATHAN, A. N.

ROTHSCHILD, J.
RUGGIE, J.
SCHILLING, W. R.
SHAPIRO, R. Y.
SNYDER, J.
WESTIN, A. F.

Psychiatry:

BENNETT, R.
DEVANAND, D.
DOHRENWEND, B.
DUNTON, H. D.
EHRHARDT, A. A.
ENDICOTT, J.
ERLENMEYER-KIMLING, L.
FIEVE, R. R.
FISCHMAN, M. W.
FOLEY, A. R.
GLASSMAN, A. H.
GORMAN, J. M.
GURLAND, B. J.
HOFER, M.
JAFFE, J.
KLEBER, H. D.
KLEIN, D. F.
KLEIN, R. G.
KUPFERMANN, I.
PARDES, H.
PROHOVNIK, I.
RAINER, J.
RYAN, J.
SACKEIM, H. A.
SHAFFER, D.
SPITZER, R.
TAMIR, H.
WEISSMAN, M. M.

Psychology:

COOPER, L. A.
DWECK, C. S.
GALANTER, E. H.
GIBBON, J.
GRAHAM, N.
HIGGINS, E. T.
HOOD, D. C.
KRANTZ, D.
KRAUSS, R.
MATIN, L.
METCALFE, J.
MISCHEL, W.
TERRACE, H. S.

Public Health:

BAYER, R.
BRANDT-RAUF, P. W.
BROWN, L.
CHALLENOR, B. D.
COLOMBOTOS, J. L.
DAVIDSON, A.
DESPOMMIER, D. D.
FLEISS, J. L.
HASHIM, S. A.
HOWE, G. R.
KANDEL, D.
LEVIN, B.
LINK, B. G.
LO, S.-H.
MCCARTHY, J.
OTTMAN, R.
PEARSON, T. A.
PERERA, F. P.
ROSENFIELD, A. G.
SANTELLA, R. P.
SISK, J. E.
STRUENING, E. L.
TSAI, W.-Y.

Radiation Oncology:

AMOLS, H. I.
BRENNER, D. J.
GEARD, C.
HALL, E.
HEI, T. K.
SCHIFF, P. B.

Radiology:

ABLOW, R. C.
ALDERSON, P. O.

BERDON, W.
ESSER, P.
FELDMAN, F.
HILAL, S.
KING, D. L.
NEWHOUSE, J. H.
NICKOLOFF, E. L.
SILVER, A. J.

Rehabilitation Medicine:

DOWNEY, J. A.
EDELSTEIN, J. E.
LIEBERMAN, J. S.
MYERS, S. J.
NEUHAUS, B. E.
THORNHILL, H.

Religion:

AWN, J.
LINDT, G.
PROUDFOOT, W.
RUPP, G.
SOMERVILLE, R.
THURMAN, R.
WEISS-HALIVNI, D.

Slavic Languages:

BELKNAP, R. L.
GASPAROV, B.
MAGUIRE, R. A.
MILLER, F. J.
POPKIN, C.
REYFMAN, I.

Social Work:

AKABAS, S.
BLACK, R. B.
CLOWARD, R. A.
FELDMAN, R.
GARFINKEL, I.
GITTERMAN, A.
HESS, M. M.
IVANOFF, A.
KAMERMAN, S. B.
KIRK, S.
McGOWAN, B.
MEYER, C. H.
MONK, A.
MULLEN, E. J.
POLSKY, H.
SCHILLING, R. F.
SCHINKE, S.
SIMON, B. L.
SOLOMON, R.

Sociology:

COLE, J. R.
GANS, H.
LITWAK, E.
RUGGIE, M.
SILVER, A. A.
SPILERMAN, S.
WHITE, H.

Spanish and Portuguese:

ALAZRAKI, J.
GRIEVE, P. E.
MARTINEZ-BONATI, F.
SILVER, P. W.
SOBEJANO, G.

Statistics:

DE LA PENA, V.
HEYDE, C. C.

Surgery:

ALTMAN, R. P.
CHIU, D. T. W.
FORDE, K.
HARDY, M. A.
HUGO, N.
LO GERFO, P.
MARKOWITZ, A.
NOWYGROD, R.
QUAEGEBEUR, J. M.
REEMTSMA, K.
ROSE, E. A.
SMITH, C. R.
SPOTNITZ, H. M.
STOLAR, C. J. H.

TILSON, M. D.

Urology:

BUTTYAN, R.
HENSLE, T. W.
OLSSON, C. A.
PUCHNER, P. J.
ROMAS, N. S.

AFFILIATED COLLEGES

Barnard College: 606 W. 120th St, New York, NY 10027; private liberal arts for women; Pres. JUDITH R. SHAPIRO.

Teachers College, Columbia University: 525 W. 120th St, New York, NY 10027; private, professional, graduate only; Pres. ARTHUR ELLIOTT LEVINE.

ATTACHED INSTITUTES AND CENTRES

Accounting Research Center: Dirs TREVOR HARRIS, NAHUM MELUMAD.

Center for Chinese Business Studies: Dir HOKE SIMPSON.

Center for Chinese Legal Studies: Dir R. RANDLE EDWARDS.

Center for Climate Research: Dir WALLACE BROECKER.

Center for Human Resource Management Studies: Dir ANN BARTEL.

Center for International Business Education: Dir KATHRYN HARRIGAN.

Center for Israel and Jewish Studies: Dir YOSEF H. YERUSHALMI.

Center for Japanese Economy and Business: Dir HUGH PATRICK.

Center for Japanese Legal Studies: Dir MICHAEL K. YOUNG.

Center for Law and the Arts: Dir JOHN M. KERNOCHAN.

Center for Law and Economic Studies: Dirs VICTOR P. GOLDBERG, JEFFREY N. GORDON.

Center for Molecular Recognition: Dir ARTHUR KARLIN.

Center for Neurobiology and Behavior: Dir JOHN KOESTER (acting).

Center for the Study of Operations: Dir MARTIN K. STARR.

Center for Population and Family Health: Dir JAMES McCARTHY.

Center for Preservation Research: Dir MARTIN WEAVER.

Center for Psychoanalytic Training and Research: Dir ROGER MacKINNON.

Center for Radiological Research: Dir ERIC J. HALL.

Center for Research in Arts and Culture: Dir JOAN JEFFRI.

Center for Telecommunications Research: Dir ANTHONY ACAMPORA.

Center for the Social Sciences: Dir HARRISON WHITE.

Center for the Study of Futures Markets: Dir FRANKLIN R. EDWARDS.

Center for the Study of Geriatrics and Gerontology: Dir BARRY J. GURLAND.

Center for the Study of Human Rights: Dir J. PAUL MARTIN.

Center for the Study of Innovation and Entrepreneurship: Dir MICHAEL TUSHMAN.

Center for the Study of Society and Medicine: Dir DAVID J. ROTHMAN.

Columbia Institute for Tele-Information: Dir ELI NOAM.

Columbia-Presbyterian Cancer Center: Dir I. BERNARD WEINSTEIN.

Donald Keene Center of Japanese Culture: Dir HARUO SHIRANE.

East Asian Institute: Dir MADELEINE ZELIN.

Executive Leadership Research Center: Dir DONALD HAMBRICK.

Fritz Reiner Center: Dir ALFRED LERDAHL.

George T. Delacorte Center for Magazine Journalism: Dir (vacant).

Gertrude H. Sergievsky Center: Dir RICHARD P. MAYEUX.

Harriman Institute: Dir MARK VON HAGEN.

Herbert and Florence Irving Center for Clinical Research: Dir HENRY N. GINSBERG.

Institute for Marketing: Dir DONALD LEHMANN.

Institute for Not-for-Profit Management: Dir RAYMOND D. HORTON.

Institute of African Studies: Dir GEORGE C. BOND.

Institute of Cancer Research: Dir MAXWELL E. GOTTESMAN.

Institute of Comparative Medicine: Dir DENNIS S. KOHN.

Institute of Human Nutrition: Dir RICHARD J. DECKELBAUM.

Institute of Latin American and Iberian Studies: Dir DOUGLAS CHALMERS.

Institute of War and Peace Studies: Dir JACK L. SNYDER.

Institute for Research on Women and Gender: Dir VICTORIA DE GRAZIA.

Institute on Aging: Dir ABRAHAM MONK.

Institute on East Central Europe: Dir JOHN S. MICGIEL.

Institute on Western Europe: Dir GLENDA G. ROSENTHAL.

International Institute for the Study of Human Reproduction: Dir GEORGIANA JAGIELLO.

Lamont-Doherty Earth Observatory: Dir JOHN C. MUTTER (acting).

Legislative Drafting Research Fund: Dir RICHARD BRIFFAULT.

Management Institute: Dir E. KIRBY WARREN.

Middle East Institute: Dir RICHARD W. BULLIET.

Parker School of Foreign and Comparative Law: Dir HANS SMIT.

Southern Asian Institute: Dir PHILIP K. OLDENBURG.

Temple Hoyne Buell Center for the Study of American Architecture: Dir JOAN OCKMAN.

CONCORDIA COLLEGE

171 White Plains Rd, Bronxville, NY 10708

Telephone: (914) 337-9300
Fax: (914) 395-4500
E-mail: admission@concordia-ny.edu
Internet: www.concordia-ny.edu

Founded 1881
Private control
Academic year: August to May

Pres;: Dr VIJI GEORGE
Chief Financial Office: DENNIS LONNERGAN
Vice-Pres. for Institutional Advancement: PAUL GRAND PRÉ
Chief Academic Officer: SHERRY J. FRASER
Dean of Students: JOHN M. BAHR
Registrar: MARK E. BLANCO
Library Dir: BRENDA BURROUGHS

Number of teachers: 30
Number of students: 635

Areas of study: arts management, behavioural sciences, biology, business admin., education, educational services, English, environmental science, history, interdisciplinary studies, int. studies, mathematics, music, religious studies, social work.

COOPER UNION FOR THE ADVANCEMENT OF SCIENCE AND ART

30 Cooper Sq., New York, NY 10003-7120
Telephone: (212) 353-4100
Internet: www.cooper.edu

Founded 1859
Academic year: September to May

Pres.: GEORGE CAMPBELL, Jr
Chair. of Trustees: RONALD W. DRUCKER
Vice-Pres. for Business Affairs and Treas.: ROBERT E. HAWKS
Vice-Pres. for External Affairs: RONNI DENES
Dean of Admissions: MITCHELL LIPTON
Library Dir: ULLA VOLK

Library of 88,900 vols
Number of teachers: 212
Number of students: 956

Publication: *At Cooper Union*

DEANS

School of Art: ROBERT RINDLER
School of Architecture: ANTHONY VIDLER
School of Eng.: ELEANOR BAUM
Faculty of Humanities and Social Sciences: DAVID WEIR

CORNELL UNIVERSITY

Ithaca, NY 14853
Telephone: (607) 255-2000
Internet: www.cornell.edu

Founded 1865
State and private control
Academic year: September to May

Pres.: DAVID J. SKORTON
Provost: CAROLYN (BIDDY) MARTIN
Provost for Medical Affairs: ANTONIO M. GOTTO, Jr
Exec. Vice-Pres. for Finance and Admin.: STEPHEN T. GOLDING
Vice-Pres. for Alumni Affairs and Devt: CHARLES T. PHLEGAR
Vice-Pres. for Student and Academic Services: SUSAN H. MURPHY
Vice-Pres. for Information Technologies: POLLEY ANN McCLURE
Vice-Pres. for Budget and Planning: CAROLYN N. AINSLIE
Vice-Pres. for Financial Affairs and Univ. Controller: JOANNE M. DeSTEFANO
Vice-Pres. for Human Resources: MARY G. OPPERMAN
Vice-Pres. for Communications: THOMAS W. BRUCE
Vice-Pres. for Govt and Community Relations: STEPHEN PHILIP JOHNSON
Vice-Provosts: JOHN A. SICILIANO, ROBERT C. RICHARDSON (Research), STEPHEN KRESOVICH (Life Sciences), STEVEN P. ROSALIE (Medical Affairs), JOSEPH A. BURNS (Physical Sciences and Eng.), ROBERT L. HARRIS, Jr (Diversity and Faculty Devt), CHARLES FAY (Research Admin.), MICHELE M. MOODY-ADAMS (Undergraduate Education), RONALD SEEBER (Land Grant Affairs)
Dean of Univ. Faculty: CHARLES WALCOTT
Dean of Students: KENT L. HUBBELL
Univ. Librarian: ANNE R. KENNEY

Library: see Libraries
Number of teachers: 2,722
Number of students: 20,638

Publications: *Administrative Science Quarterly* (academic), *Agricultural Finance Review* (academic), *Andean Past* (academic), *Animal Life* (newspaper), *Bird Scope* (newsletter), *Cat Watch* (newsletter), *Colloqui: Cornell Journal of Planning and Urban Issues* (academic), *Communique (Ithaca)* (academic), *Cornell Alumni* (magazine), *Cornell Biennial Electrical Engineering Conference* (academic), *Cornell Chronicle* (newspaper), *Cornell Daily Sun* (newspaper), *Cornell East Asia Series* (academic), *Cornell Engineering* (magazine), *Cornell Enterprise* (magazine), *Cornell Field Crops and Soils Handbook* (bulletin), *Cornell Focus* (academic), *Cornell Hotel and Restaurant Administration Quarterly* (academic), *Cornell Hotel School* (magazine), *Cornell International Industrial and Labor Relations Reports* (monograph), *Cornell International Law Journal* (academic), *Cornell Journal of Architecture* (academic), *Cornell Journal of Law and Public Policy* (academic), *Cornell Law Forum* (academic), *Cornell Law Review* (academic), *Cornell Linguistic Contributions* (monograph), *Cornell Linguistic Dissertations* (monograph), *Cornell Lunatic* (magazine), *Cornell Medicine* (bulletin), *Cornell Modern Indonesia Project Publications* (academic), *Cornell Nutrition Conference for Feed Manufacturers* (proceedings), *Cornell Phonetics Laboratory* (working papers), *Cornell Plantations Magazine* (academic), *Cornell Recommendations for Commercial Florist Crops* (bulletin), *Cornell Recommendations for Commercial Turfgrass Management* (academic), *Cornell Recommendations for Field Crops* (bulletin), *Cornell Recommendations for Pest Control for Commercial Production and Maintenance of Trees andShrubs* (bulletin), *Cornell Science and Technology Magazine* (academic), *Cornell Studies in Industrial and Labor Relations* (monograph), *Cornell Working Papers in Linguistics* (academic), *Cornellian* (newspaper), *Dog Watch* (academic), *Epoch (Icatha)* (contemporary literature), *Feline Health Topics* (newsletter), *Food and Fitness Advisor* (newsletter), *Human Ecology (Ithaca)* (magazine), *Indonesia* (academic), *Industrial and Labor Relations Review* (academic), *Journal of Empirical Legal Studies* (academic), *Living Bird* (academic), *N K A* (contemporary African art), *Pest Management Recommendations for Commercial Vegetable and Potato Production* (bulletin), *Philosophical Review* (academic), *RLG DigiNews* (newsletter), *Traces (Ithaca)* (cultural theory and translation), *Window (New York)* (newspaper), *Women's Health Advisor* (newsletter), *Working Papers in Planning* (working papers)

DEANS

College of Architecture, Art and Planning: M. MOSTAFAVI
College of Arts and Sciences: G. P. LEPAGE
Law School: S. J. SCHWAB
Medical College: ANTONIO M. GOTTO, Jr
Graduate School of Medical Sciences: DAVID P. HAJJAR
College of Eng.: W. KENT FUCHS
Graduate School: ALISON POWER
Faculty of Computing and Information Science: ROBERT CONSTABLE
School of Continuing Education and Summer Sessions: GLENN C. ALTSCHULER
New York State College of Veterinary Medicine: DONALD SMITH
New York State College of Agriculture and Life Sciences: SUSAN A. HENRY
New York State College of Human Ecology: L. STAIANO-CAICO
Johnson Graduate School of Management: ROBERT SWIERINGA
School of Hotel Admin.: DAVID W. BUTLER
New York State School of Industrial and Labor Relations: EDWARD LAWLER

PROFESSORS

Law School (Myron Taylor Hall, Ithaca, NY 14853-4901; tel. (607) 255-0565; e-mail lawadmit@law.mail.cornell.edu; internet www.lawschool.cornell.edu):

ALEXANDER, G.
BARCELO, J., III
CLERMONT, K. M.
CLYMER, S.
EISENBERG, T.
FARINA, C.
GARVEY, S.
GERMAIN, C.
GREEN, R.
HAY, G. A.
HEISE, M.
HENDERSON, J., Jr
HILLMAN, R.
HOLDEN-SMITH, B.
JOHNSON, S. L.
LASSER, M.
LEHMAN, J.
MARTIN, P. W.
NDULO, M.
RACHLINSKI, J.
RILES, A.
ROSSI, F. F.
SCHWAB, S.
SHERWIN, E.
SHIFFRIN, S.
SILICIANO, J.
SIMSON, G. J.
SUMMERS, R. S.
TAYLOR, W.
WIPPMAN, D.

Joan and Sanford I. Weill Medical Division (1300 York Ave, New York, NY 10021; tel. (212) 821-0560; fax (212) 821-0576; e-mail cumc_admissions@med.cornell.edu; internet www.med.cornell.edu):

University Professors:

MICHELS, R. T.

Anaesthesiology:

AMAR, D., Anaesthesiology
DESIDERIO, D., Anaesthesiology
DINNER, M., Anaesthesiology (Clinical)
HALPERN, N. A., Anaesthesiology (Clinical)
HARRISON, N., Anaesthesiology (Pharmacology)
HEMMINGS, H. C., Jr, Anaesthesiology
KELLY, R. E., Anaesthesiology (Clinical)
LIEN, C. A., Anaesthesiology (Clinical)
MALHOTRA, V., Anaesthesiology (Clinical)
SAVARESE, J., Anaesthesiology
THOMAS, S. J., Anaesthesiology
THORNE, A. C., Anaesthesiology (Clinical)
WILSON, R. S., Anaesthesiology
YAO, F.-S. F., Anaesthesiology (Clinical)

Biochemistry:

BOSKEY, A. L., Biochemistry
BRESLOW, E. M. G., Biochemistry
COOPER, A. J. L., Biochemistry
McGRAW, T. E., Biochemistry
MAXFIELD, F. R., Biochemistry
MENON, A. K., Biochemistry
NOVOGRODSKY, A., Biochemistry
ROBERTSON, H. D., Biochemistry
RUBIN, A. L., Biochemistry
RYAN, T. A., Biochemistry
STENZEL, K. H., Biochemistry
TATE, S. S., Biochemistry
WU, H., Biochemistry

Cardiothoracic Surgery:

ADKINS, M. S., Cardiothoracic Surgery (Clinical)
ALTORKI, N. K., Cardiothoracic Surgery
ISOM, O. W., Cardiothoracic Surgery
KRIEGER, K. H., Cardiothoracic Surgery
LARAGH, J. H., Medicine
TORTOLANI, A. J., Cardiothoracic Surgery (Clinical)

Cell and Developmental Biology:

BACHVAROVA, R. F., Cell and Developmental Biology
FISCHMAN, D. A., Cell and Developmental Biology
HAJJAR, K. A., Cell and Developmental Biology

MIKAWA, T., Cell and Developmental Biology
SATO, T. N., Cell and Developmental Biology

Dermatology:

GRANSTEIN, R. D., Dermatology
HALPERN, A. C., Dermatology
VARGHESE, M. C., Dermatology

Genetic Medicine:

RAFII, S., Genetic Medicine

Medicine:

ALLISON, J. P., Medicine (Immunology)
AUGUST, P., Medicine
BAJORIN, D. F., Medicine
BARDES, C. L., Medicine (Clinical)
BASSON, C. T., Medicine
BERMAN, E., Medicine (Clinical)
BOCKMAN, R. S., Medicine
BORER, J. S., Medicine
BOSL, G. J., Medicine
BROWN, A. E., Medicine
CARMEL, R., Medicine
CASPER, E. S., Medicine
CHANDRA, P., Medicine (Clinical)
CHARLSON, M. E., Medicine
CHEIGH, H., Medicine (Clinical)
CLARKSON, B. D., Medicine
CROW, M. K., Medicine
CRYSTAL, R. G., Medicine
DANNENBERG, A. J., Medicine
DEVEREUX, R. B., Medicine
DOSIK, H., Medicine
ETINGIN, O. R., Medicine
FAHEY, T. J., Jr, Medicine (Clinical)
FEIN, O. T., Medicine (Clinical)
FELDMAN, E. J., Medicine
FINNS, J. J., Medicine
FLOMENBAUM, N. E., Medicine (Clinical)
FUKS, Z. Y., Medicine (Radiation Oncology)
GIBOFSKY, A., Medicine (Clinical)
GOLDE, D. W., Medicine
GORDON, B., Medicine (Clinical)
GOTTO, A. M., Jr, Medicine
GROEGER, J. S., Medicine (Clinical)
HAYES, J. G., Medicine
HEMPSTEAD, B. L., Medicine
HOUGHTON, A. N., Medicine
IMPERATO-MCGINLEY, J. L., Medicine
IVANSHKIV, L. B., Medicine
JACOBS, J. L., Medicine (Clinical)
JACOBSON, I. M., Medicine (Clinical)
JOHNSON, W. D., Medicine
KAGEN, L. J. A., Medicine
KELSEN, D. P., Medicine
KEMENY, N. E., Medicine
KIEHN, T. E., Medicine (Clinical and Clinical Microbiology)
KLEIN, H., Medicine
KLIGFIELD, P. D., Medicine
KOLESNICK, R. N., Medicine
KRIS, M. G., Medicine
KROWN, S. E., Medicine
KURTZ, R. C., Medicine (Clinical)
LACHS, M. S., Medicine
LAURENCE, J. C., Medicine
LERMAN, B. B., Medicine
LIPKIN, M., Medicine
LIVINGSTON, P. O., Medicine
LOCKSHIN, M. D., Medicine
McCORMICK, B., Medicine (Radiation Oncology)
MARCUS, A. J., Medicine
MARKENSON, J. A., Medicine (Clinical)
MARKS, P. A., Medicine
MAYER, K., Medicine (Clinical)
MESSINEO, F., Medicine (Clinical)
MEYER, B. R., Medicine (Clinical)
MINSKY, B., Medicine (Radiation Oncology)
MOORE, A., Medicine (Clinical)
MOTZER, R. J., Medicine
MURRAY, H. W., Medicine
NACHMAN, R. L., Medicine
NANUS, D. M., Medicine (Haematology, Oncology)

NIMER, S. D., Medicine
NORTON, L., Medicine
OETTGEN, H. F., Medicine
OFFIT, K., Medicine
OKIN, P. M., Medicine
PAGET, S. A., Medicine
PAMER, E. G., Medicine
PAPE, J. W., Medicine
PECKER, M. S., Medicine (Clinical)
PFISTER, D. G., Medicine
PORTLOCK, C. S., Medicine (Clinical)
POSNET, D. N., Medicine
PRITCHETT, R. A. R., Medicine (Clinical)
RAHAL, J. J., Medicine
RIGGIO, R. R., Medicine (Clinical)
RIVLIN, R. S., Medicine
ROBBINS, R. J., Medicine
ROBERTS, R. B., Medicine
ROMAN, M. J., Medicine
ROSEN, N., Medicine
ROSENFELD, I., Medicine (Clinical)
SAAL, S. D., Medicine (Clinical)
SALMON, J. E., Medicine
SALTZ, L. B., Medicine
SCHEIDT, S., Medicine (Clinical)
SCHEINBERG, D. A., Medicine
SCHER, H. I., Medicine
SCHUSTER, M. W., Medicine (Clinical)
SEPKOWITZ, K. A., Medicine
SHIKE, M., Medicine
SILVER, R. T., Medicine
SMITH, K. A., Medicine
SPRIGGS, D. R., Medicine
STEINBERG, C. R., Medicine (Clinical)
STEINGART, R. M., Medicine
STOVER, D. E., Medicine (Clinical)
STRAUS, D. J., Medicine (Clinical)
SUTHANTHIRAN, M., Medicine
THOMAS, H. M., III, Medicine (Clinical)
WADLER, S., Medicine
WEINSTEIN, A. M., Medicine
WEKSLER, B. B., Medicine
WEKSLER, M. E., Medicine
WHITE, D. A., Medicine
WINAWER, S. J., Medicine
WITTES, R., Medicine
WUEST, D. L., Medicine (Pathology in Clinical)
YAHALOM, J., Medicine (Radiation Oncology)

Microbiology and Immunology:

BARANY, F., Microbiology and Immunology
BROT, N., Microbiology and Immunology
COICO, R., Microbiology and Immunology (Education)
DING, A, Microbiology and Immunology
FALCK-PEDERSEN, E., Microbiology and Immunology
HOLLOMAN, W. K., Microbiology and Immunology
MOORE, J. P., Microbiology and Immunology
NAQI, S. A., Microbiology and Immunology (Education)
NATHAN, C., Microbiology and Immunology

Neurology and Neuroscience:

APPEL, S. H., Neurology
BAKER, H., Neuroscience
BEAL, M. F., Neurology and Neuroscience
BLASBERG, R. G., Neurology
BLASS, J., Neurology and Neuroscience
BROOKS, D. C., Neurology and Neuroscience (Anatomy)
CARONNA, J. J., Neurology (Clinical)
DANNON, M. J., Neurology (Clinical)
DeANGELIS, L. M., Neurology (Clinical)
FOLEY, K. M., Neurology and Neuroscience
GIBSON, G. E., Neuroscience
IADECOLA, C., Neurology and Neuroscience
LABAR, D. R., Neurology and Neuroscience
LATOV, N., Neurology and Neuroscience
McDOWELL, F. H., Neurology and Neuroscience
MILNER, T. A., Neuroscience

PASTERNAK, G. W., Neurology and Neuroscience
PETITO, F. A., Neurology (Clinical)
PICKEL, V. M., Neuroscience
POLLACK, C. P., Neurology (Clinical)
POSNER, J. B., Neurology and Neuroscience
RATAN, R. R., Neurology and Neuroscience
ROSS, M. E., Neurology and Neuroscience
RUBIN, M., Neurology (Clinical)
VICTOR, J. D., Neurology and Neuroscience
VOLPE, B. T., Neurology and Neuroscience
WAGNER, J. A., Neurology and Neuroscience

Neurological Surgery:

GUTIN, P. H., Neurological Surgery
STEIG, P. E., Neurological Surgery

Obstetrics and Gynaecology:

CAPUTO, T. A., Obstetrics and Gynaecology (Clinical)
CHERVENAK, F. A., Obstetrics and Gynaecology
GOSDEN, R. G., Obstetrics and Gynaecology
LIU, H.-C., Obstetrics and Gynaecology (Reproductive Medicine)
POST, R. C., Obstetrics and Gynaecology (Clinical)
ROSENWAKS, Z., Obstetrics and Gynaecology
SAXENA, B. B., Obstetrics and Gynaecology (Endocrinology)
SPITZER, M., Obstetrics and Gynaecology (Clinical)
WITKIN, S. S., Obstetrics and Gynaecology (Immunology)

Ophthalmology:

ABRAMSON, D. H., Ophthalmology
COLEMAN, D. J., Ophthalmology
RODRIGUEZ-BOULAN, E. J., Ophthalmology (Cell and Developmental Biology)
SILVERMAN, R. H., Ophthalmology (Computer Science)

Orthopaedic Surgery:

BURKE, G. W., Orthopaedic Surgery (Clinical)
CORNELL, C. N., Orthopaedic Surgery (Clinical)
CRAIG, E. V., Orthopaedic Surgery (Clinical)
HEALEY, J. H., Orthopaedic Surgery
HELFET, D. L., Orthopaedic Surgery
LANE, J. M., Orthopaedic Surgery
LASKIN, R. S., Orthopaedic Surgery (Clinical)
PELLICI, P. M., Orthopaedic Surgery (Clinical)
ROOT, L., Orthopaedic Surgery (Clinical)
SALVATI, E. A., Orthopaedic Surgery (Clinical)
SCULCO, T. P., Orthopaedic Surgery (Clinical)
TORZILLI, P. A., Orthopaedic Surgery (Applied Biomechanics)
WARREN, R. F., Orthopaedic Surgery
WEILAND, A. J., Orthopaedic Surgery (Plastic)
WICKIEWICZ, T. L., Orthopaedic Surgery (Clinical)
WILSON, P. D., Jr, Orthopaedic Surgery
WINDSOR, R. E., Orthopaedic Surgery (Clinical)
WOLFE, S. W., Orthopaedic Surgery
WRIGHT, T. M., Orthopaedic Surgery (Applied Biomechanics)

Otorhinolaryngology:

SELESNICK, S. H., Otorhinolaryngology

Paediatrics:

BROMBERG, K., Paediatrics
BUSSEL, J. B., Paediatrics
CHUTORIAN, A. B., Paediatrics
COOPER, R. S., Ophthalmology
CUNNINGHAM-RUNDLES, S., Paediatrics (Immunology)
GERMAN, J. L., Paediatrics

GERSONY, W. M., Paediatrics
GIARDINA, P. V., Paediatrics (Clinical)
GLASS, L., Paediatrics
GREENWALD, B. M., Paediatrics (Clinical)
HILGARTNER, M. W., Paediatrics
KLEIN, A. A., Paediatrics (Clinical)
KOSOFSKY, B., Paediatrics
KRAUSS, A. N., Paediatrics (Clinical)
LEHMAN, T. J. A., Paediatrics (Clinical)
LOUGHLIN, G. M., Paediatrics
MENDEZ, H. A., Paediatrics (Clinical)
MOSCONA, A., Paediatrics
O'REILLY, R. J., Paediatrics
PERLMAN, J. M., Paediatrics
RAJEGOWDA, B., Paediatrics (Clinical)
RUBIN, D. H., Paediatrics (Clinical)
SOLOMON, G. E., Paediatrics (Clinical/Neurology)
STEINHERZ, P. G., Paediatrics

Pathology and Laboratory Medicine:
AKHTAR, M., Pathology and Laboratory Medicine
ALONSO, D. R., Pathology and Laboratory Medicine
BAERGEN, R., Pathology and Laboratory Medicine (Clinical)
BARRIOS, R., Pathology and Laboratory Medicine
BULLOUGH, P. G., Pathology and Laboratory Medicine
BURKE, M. D., Pathology and Laboratory Medicine
CAGLE, P. T., Pathology and Laboratory Medicine
CHADBURN, A., Pathology and Laboratory Medicine
CHAGANTI, R. S. K., Pathology and Laboratory Medicine (Genetics)
CHEN, Y. T., Pathology and Laboratory Medicine
CHEN-KIANG, S., Pathology and Laboratory Medicine
ELLENSON, L. H., Pathology and Laboratory Medicine
HAJJAR, D. P., Pathology and Laboratory Medicine
HODA, S. A. F., Pathology and Laboratory Medicine (Clinical)
HUVOS, A. G., Pathology and Laboratory Medicine
JONES, J. G., Pathology and Laboratory Medicine
KLIMSTRA, D. S., Pathology and Laboratory Medicine
KNOWLES, D. M., Pathology and Laboratory Medicine
LAND, G. A., Pathology and Laboratory Medicine (Clinical)
LAVI, E., Pathology and Laboratory Medicine
LEONARD, D. G. B., Pathology and Laboratory Medicine
LIEBERMAN, M. W., Pathology and Laboratory Medicine
LIPMAN, N. S., Pathology and Laboratory Medicine (Veterinary Medicine)
McNUTT, N. S., Pathology and Laboratory Medicine
MODY, D. R., Pathology and Laboratory Medicine
MULLER, W. A., Pathology and Laboratory Medicine
PEERSCHKE, E. I. B., Pathology and Laboratory Medicine
PETROVIC, L. M., Pathology and Laboratory Medicine
REUTER, V. E., Pathology and Laboratory Medicine
ROSEN, P. P., Pathology and Laboratory Medicine
ROSENBLUM, M., Pathology and Laboratory Medicine
SALEEM, A., Pathology and Laboratory Medicine (Clinical)

SESHAN, S. V., Pathology and Laboratory Medicine (Clinical)
TRUONG, L. D., Pathology and Laboratory Medicine (Clinical)
WOLF, C. F. W., Pathology and Laboratory Medicine (Clinical)

Pharmacology:
BUCK, J., Pharmacology
GROSS, S. S., Pharmacology
GUDAS, L. J., Pharmacology
INTURRISI, C., Pharmacology
LEVI, R., Pharmacology
OKAMOTO, M., Pharmacology
REIDENBERG, M. M., Pharmacology
RIFKIND, A. B., Pharmacology
SZETO, H. H., Pharmacology
TOTH, M., Pharmacology

Physiology and Biophysics:
ANDERSEN, O. S., Physiology and Biophysics
GARDNER, D., Physiology and Biophysics
GRAFSTEIN, B., Physiology and Biophysics
HUANG, X., Physiology and Biophysics
MAACK, T., Physiology and Biophysics
MEHLER, E. L., Physiology and Biophysics
PALMER, L. G., Physiology and Biophysics
RAMIREZ, F., Physiology and Biophysics
ROUX, B., Physiology and Biophysics
WEINSTEIN, H., Physiology and Biophysics
WINDHAGER, E. E., Physiology and Biophysics

Psychiatry:
ADDONIZIO, G. C., Psychiatry (Clinical)
ALEXOPOULOS, G. S., Psychiatry
AUCHINCLOSS, E. L., Psychiatry (Clinical)
BARCHAS, J. D., Psychiatry
BREITBART, W., Psychiatry
BRUCE, M. L., Psychiatry (Sociology)
CAMPBELL, S. S., Psychiatry (Psychology)
CASEY, B. J., Psychiatry (Developmental Psychobiology)
CLARKIN, J. F., Psychiatry (Clinical Psychology)
FERRANDO, S. J., Psychiatry (Clinical)
FRIEDMAN, R. A., Psychiatry (Clinical)
GEARY, N. D., Psychiatry (Psychology)
GIBBS, J. A., Jr, Psychiatry
HALMI, K. A., Psychiatry
HERTZIG, M. E., Psychiatry
HOLLAND, J. C. B., Psychiatry
KERNBERG, O. F., Psychiatry
KERNBERG, P. F., Psychiatry
KOCSIS, J. H., Psychiatry
LEDERBERG, M. S., Psychiatry (Clinical)
LEON, A. C., Psychiatry (Biostatistics)
MATTSON, M. R. A., Psychiatry (Clinical)
MEYERS, B. S., Psychiatry
PARDES, H., Psychiatry
PFEFFER, C. R., Psychiatry
POSNER, M. I., Psychiatry (Psychology)
SACKS, M. H., Psychiatry
SCHULBERG, H. C., Psychiatry (Psychology)
SHAMOIAN, C. A., Psychiatry (Clinical)
TARDIFF, K., Psychiatry
WILSON, P. G., Psychiatry (Clinical)
YOUNG, R. C., Psychiatry

Public Health:
BEGG, C. B., Public Health (Biostatistics)
BOTVIN, G. J., Public Health (Psychology)
DRUSIN, L. M., Public Health (Clinical)
FINKEL, M. L., Public Health (Clinical)
MILLMAN, R. B., Public Health
MUSHLIN, A. I., Public Health
RUCHLIN, H. S., Public Health (Economics)

Radiology:
ABRAMSON, S. J., Radiology (Clinical)
ADLER, R., Radiology
AMOLS, H. I., Radiology (Physics)
ANDERSON, L. L., Radiology (Physics)
AUH, Y. H., Radiology
BECKER, D. V., Radiology
BRILL, P., Radiology
CARAVELLI, J. F., Radiology (Clinical)

COHEN, M. A., Radiology (Clinical)
DECK, M. D. F., Radiology
DERSHAW, D. D., Radiology
DIVGI, C. R., Radiology
FINN, R. D., Radiology (Physics)
GAMSU, G., Radiology
GOBIN, Y. P., Radiology
GOLDSMITH, S. J., Radiology
HANN, L. E., Radiology
HEELAN, R. T., Radiology
HEIER, L. A., Radiology (Clinical)
HENSCHKE, C. I., Radiology
HERZOG, R. J., Radiology
HRICAK, H., Radiology
KOUTCHER, J. A., Radiology
KROL, G., Radiology (Clinical)
LARSON, S., Radiology
LI, G. C., Radiology (Biophysics)
LIBERMAN, L., Radiology
LING, C. C., Radiology (Physics)
McCAULEY, D., Radiology (Clinical)
NORI, D., Radiology (Clinical)
PANICEK, D. M., Radiology
PAVLOV, H., Radiology
POTTER, M. R., Radiology
PRINCE, M. R., Radiology
ROSEN, N. S., Radiology (Clinical)
ROSENBLATT, R., Radiology (Clinical)
SOS, T. A., Radiology
SOSTMAN, H. D., Radiology
STRAUSS, H. W., Radiology
VALLABHAJOSULA, S., Radiology (Radiopharmacy)
WINCHESTER, P., Radiology
YANKELEVITZ, D. F., Radiology
ZAIDER, M., Radiology (Physics)
ZIMMERMAN, R. D., Radiology

Rehabilitation Medicine:
LIEBERMAN, J. S., Rehabilitation Medicine
O'DELL, M. W., Rehabilitation Medicine (Clinical)

Surgery:
BAINS, M. S., Surgery (Clinical)
BARIE, P. S., Surgery
BARONE, J. E., Surgery (Clinical)
BESSEY, P. Q., Surgery
BLUMGART, L. H., Surgery
BRENNAN, M. F., Surgery
CHASSIN, J. L., Surgery (Clinical)
CODY, H. S., III, Surgery (Clinical)
CORDEIRO, P.G., Surgery
EISENBERG, M. M., Surgery
FONG, Y., Surgery
GAGNER, M., Surgery
HURYN, J. M., Surgery (Clinical Oral and Maxillofacial Surgery)
ISRAEL, H. A., Surgery (Clinical)
KENT, K. C., Surgery
LAQUAGLIA, M. P., Surgery
MICHELASSI, F., Surgery
MILSOM, J. W., Surgery
OSBORNE, M. P., Surgery
PETREK, J. A., Surgery
PIZZI, W. F., Surgery (Clinical)
RUSCH, V. W., Surgery
SHAH, J. P., Surgery (Clinical)
SHAHA, A. R., Surgery
SMITH, B. H., Surgery (Clinical)
STAIANO-COICO, L., Surgery (Microbiology)
STOLAR, C. J., Surgery
STUBENBORD, W. T., Surgery
WISE, L., Surgery
WONG, G. Y., Surgery (Statistics)
WONG, W. D., Surgery
YURT, R. W., Surgery

Urology:
BANDER, N. H., Urology
GUILLONNEAU, B., Urology
GOLDSTEIN, M., Urology
HERR, H. W., Urology
SCARDINO, P. T., Urology
SCHLEGEL, P. N., Urology
SHEINFELD, J., Urology
SOGANI, P. C., Urology (Clinical)

VAUGHAN, E. D., Urology

College of Architecture, Art and Planning
(129 Sibley Dome, Ithaca, NY 14853; tel.
(607) 255-9110; e-mail aapdean@cornell.edu;
internet www.aap.cornell.edu):

Architecture:

GOEHNER, W.
GREENBERG, D. P.
HASCUP, G.
HUBBELL, K.
MOSTAFAVI, M.
OTTO, C. F.
RICHARDSON, H.
WELLS, J.

Art:

KORD, V.
LOCEY, J.
SPECTOR, F.
SQUIER, J. L.
WALKINGSTICK, K.

City and Regional Planning:

AZIS, I.
BENERIA, L.
BOOTH, R.
CHRISOPHERSON, S.
CLAVEL, P.
DRENNAN, M.
FORESTER, J.
GOLDSMITH, W.
LEWIS, D.
OLPADWALA, P.
REARDON, K.

College of Arts and Sciences (172 Golden
Smith Hall, Ithaca, NY 14853; tel. (607) 255-
4833; e-mail as_admissions@cornell.edu;
internet www.arts.cornell.edu):

Anthropology:

GREENWOOD, D.
HENDERSON, J.
HOLMBERG, D.
MARCH, K.
SANGREN, P.
SIEGEL, J.
SMALL, M.

Asian Studies:

DE BARY, B.
GOLD, D.
GUNN, E.
MINKOWSKI, C.
SAKAI, N.
TAYLOR, K.

Astronomy:

CAMPBELL, D.
CHERNOFF, D.
CORDES, J.
GIERASCH, P.
GIOVANELLI, R.
GOLDSMITH, P.
HAYNES, M.
HERTER, T.
HOUCK, J.
NICHOLSON, P.
SQUYRES, S.
STACEY, G.
TERZIAN, Y.
VEVERKA, J.
WASSERMAN, I.

Chemistry and Chemical Biology:

ABRUNA, H.
BAIRD, B.
BEGLEY, T.
BURLITCH, J.
CARPENTER, B.
COATES, G.
COLLUM, D.
DAVIS, H.
DISALVO, F.
EALICK, S.
EZRA, G.
FAY, R.
FREED, J.
GANEM, B.

HINES, M.
HOFFMANN, R.
HOUSTON, P.
LEE, S.
LORING, R.
MEINWALD, J.
SOGAH, D.
WIDOM, B.
WOLCZANSKI, P.

Classics:

AHL, F.
CLINTON, K.
COLEMAN, J.
NUSSBAUM, A.
PELLICCIA, H.
PUCCI, P.
RAWLINGS, H., III
RUSTEN, J.

Comparative Literature:

CARMICHAEL, C.
COHEN, W.
KENNEDY, W.
MONROE, J.

Ecology and Systematics:

ELLNER, S.
GREENE, H.
HAIRSTON, N., Jr
KENNEDY, K.
POWER, A.
PROVINE, W.

Economics:

BASU, K.
BLUME, L.
COATE, S.
DAVIS, T.
EASLEY, D.
HONG, Y.
KIEFER, N.
LYONS, T.
MAJUMDAR, M.
MASSON, R.
MITRA, T.
POSSEN, U.
SHELL, K.
VOGELSANG, T.
WAN, H., Jr

English:

BOGEL, F.
BROWN, L.
CHASE, C.
CHEYFITZ, E.
CULLER, J.
FULTON, A.
GILBERT, R.
HERRIN, W.
HILL, T.
HITE, M.
JANOWITZ, P.
JEYIFO, B.
MCCALL, D.
MCCLANE, K., Jr
MCMILLIN, H.
MOHANTY, S.
MORGAN, R.
MURRAY, T.
PARKER, A.
SAMUELS, S.
SAWYER, P.
SCHWARZ, D.
SHAW, H.
SIEGEL, S.
SPILLERS, H.
VAUGHN, S.
WETHERBEE, W., III

German Studies:

ADELSON, L.
GROOS, A., Jr
HOHENDAHL, P.
KITTLER, W.
MARTIN, C.

Government:

BENSEL, R.

BUCK-MORSS, S.
BUNCE, V.
EVANGELISTA, M.
HERRING, R.
KATZENSTEIN, M.
KATZENSTEIN, P.
KRAMNICK, I.
LOWI, T.
MEBANE, W.
PONTUSSON, J.
RABKIN, J.
RUBENSTEIN, D.
SANDERS, M.
SHEFTER, M.
TARROW, S.
VANDEWALLE, N.

History:

ALTSCHULER, G.
BLUMIN, S.
CARON, V.
COCHRAN, S.
DEAR, P.
GREENE, S.
HULL, I.
HYAMS, P.
KAMMEN, M.
KAPLAN, S.
KOSCHMANN, J.
LACAPRA, D.
LOGEVALL, F.
MOORE, R.
NAJEMY, J.
NORTON, M.
PETERSON, C.
POLENBERG, R.
STEINBERG, M.
STRAUSS, B.
WASHINGTON, M.

History of Art:

KUNIHOLM, P.
LAZZARO, C.
RAMAGE, A.

Linguistics:

BOWERS, J.
COLLINS, C.
DIESING, M.
HARBERT, W.
MCCONNELL-GINET, S.
ROOTH, M.
ROSEN, C.
WHITMAN, J.
ZEC, D.

Mathematics:

BARBASCH, D.
BILLERA, L.
BROWN, K.
CHASE, S.
CONNELLY, R.
DENNIS, R. K.
DURRETT, R.
DYNKIN, E.
GROSS, L.
GUCKENHEIMER, J.
HATCHER, A.
HENDERSON, D.
HUBBARD, J.
HWANG, J. T.
ILIACHENKO, I.
KAHN, P.
LAWLER, G.
NERODE, A.
NUSSBAUM, M.
SALOFF-COSTE, L.
SCHATZ, A.
SEN, S.
SHORE, R.
SMILLIE, J.
SPEH, B.
STILLMAN, M.
STRICHARTZ, R.
THURSTON, W.
VOGTMANN, K.
WAHLBIN, L.
WEST, J.

Molecular Biology and Genetics:

AGUADRO, C.
BRETSCHER, A.
BROWN, W.
CLARK, A.
FEIGENSON, G.
HESS, G.
HINKLE, P.
HUFFAKER, T.
WILSON, D.
WOLFNER, M.

Music:

BILSON, M.
HARRIS-WARRICLE, R.
HSU, J.
ROSEN, D.
SIERRA, R.
STUCKY, S.
WEBSTER, J., Jr
ZASLAW, N.

Near Eastern Studies:

BRANN, R.
OWEN, D.
POWERS, D.

Neurobiology and Behaviour:

BASS, A.
FETCHO, J.
HOWLAND, H.
HOY, R.
SEELEY, T.
SHERMAN, P.

Philosophy:

BOYD, R.
FINE, G.
IRWIN, T.
MACDONALD, S.
MILLER, R.
MOODY-ADAMS, M.
STURGEON, N.

Physics:

ALEXANDER, J.
AMBEGAOKAR, V.
ASHCROFT, N.
BERKELMAN, K.
BODENSCHATZ, E.
CASSEL, D.
DAVIS, J.
DUGAN, G.
ELSER, V.
FITCHEN, D.
GALIK, R.
GINSPARG, P.
GRUNER, S.
HAND, L.
HARTILL, D.
HENLEY, C.
HOFFSTAETTER, G.
LECLAIR, A.
LEE, D.
LEPAGE, G.
MCEUEN, P.
MERMIN, N.
NEUBERT, M.
PARPIA, J.
PATTERSON, J.
RALPH, D.
RICHARDSON, R.
RUBIN, D.
SETHNA, J.
SIEVERS III, A.
STEIN, P.
TALMAN, R.
TEUKOLSKY, S.
THORNE, R.
TYE, S.-H.
YAN, T.-M.
YORK, J.

Plant Biology:

TURGEON, E. G.

Program on Ethics and Public Life:

SHUE, H.

Psychology:

BEM, D.
BEM, S.
CUTTING, J.
DARLINGTON, R.
DEVOOGD, T.
DUNNING, D.
EDELMAN, S.
FINLAY, B.
GILOVICH, T.
HALPERN, B.
JOHNSTON, R.
KRUMHANSL, C.
MAAS, J.
NEISSER, U.
REGAN, E.

Romance Studies:

BERGER, A.
CASTILLO, D.
GREENBERG, M.
KLEIN, R.
LEWIS, P.
LONG, K.
MIGIEL, M.
RESINA, J.

Russian Literature:

CARDEN, P.
POLLACK, N.
SENDEROVICH, S.
SHAPIRO, G.

Science and Technology Studies:

LYNCH, M.
PINCH, T.
REPPY, J.
ROSSITER, M.

Sociology:

HARRIS, D.
HECKATHORN, D.
MACY, M.
NEE, V.
STRANG, D.
SWEDBERG, R.

Theatre, Film and Dance:

BATHRICK, D.
FELDSHUH, D.
GAINOR, J.
GOETZ, K.
LEVITT, B.

College of Engineering (Engineering-Swanson Center, 102 Hollister Hall, Ithaca, NY 14853-3501; tel. (607) 255-5008; fax (607) 255-0971; e-mail engr_admissions@cornell .edu; internet www.engineering.cornell.edu):

Applied and Engineering Physics:

BROCK, J.
BUHRMAN, R.
COOL, T.
CRAIGHEAD, H.
GAETA, A.
KUSSE, B.
LINDAU, M.
LOVELACE, R.
SILCOX, J.
WEBB, W.
WISE, F.

Chemical Engineering:

ARCHER, L.
CLANCY, P.
COHEN, C.
KOCH, D.
OLBRICHT, W.
SHULER, M.
STEEN, P.

Civil and Environmental Engineering:

BRUTSAERT, W.
GOSSETT, J.
GRIGORIU, M.
HOVER, K.
INGRAFFEA, A.
KULHAWY, F.
LION, L.

LIU, P.
LOUCKS, D.
MEYBURG, A.
NOZICK, L.
O'ROURKE, T.
PEKOZ, T.
SANSALONE, M.
SCHULER, R.
SHOEMAKER, C.
STEDINGER, J.
TURNQUIST, M.

Computer Sciences:

ARMS, W.
BAILEY, G.
BIRMAN, K.
COLEMAN, T.
CONSTABLE, R.
ELBER, R.
GRIES, D.
HALPERN, J.
HOPCROFT, J.
HUTTENLOCHER, D.
KEDEM, K.
KOZEN, D.
PINGALI, K.
SCHNEIDER, F.
TARDOS, E.
VAN LOAN, C.
VAVASIS, S.

Earth and Atmospheric Sciences:

ALLMENDINGER, R.
BARAZANGI, M.
BROWN, L.
CATHLES, L.
CISNE, J.
GREENE, C.
ISACKS, B.
JORDAN, T.
KAY, R.
KAY, S.
PHIPPS MORGAN, J.
RHODES, F.
WHITE, W.

Electrical Engineering:

BERGER, T.
CHIANG, H.-D.
EASTMAN, L.
FARLEY, D., Jr
FINE, T.
FUCHS, W.
HAAS, Z.
HAMMER, D.
JOHNSON, C., Jr
KELLEY, M.
KINTNER, P., Jr
KLINE, R.
PARKS, T.
POLLOCK, C.
SEYLER, C.
SHEALY, J.
SPENCER, M.
TANG, C.-L.
THOMAS, H.
TIWARI, S.
TONG, L.
WICKER, S.

Materials Science and Engineering:

AST, D.
BLAKELY, J.
DIECKMANN, R.
GIANNELIS, E.
OBER, C.
RUOFF, A.
SASS, S.
VAN DOVER, R.

Mechanical and Aerospace Engineering:

AVEDISIAN, C.
BARTEL, D.
CAUGHEY, D.
COLLINS, L.
DAWSON, P.
GEORGE, A.
GOULDIN, F.

LEIBOVICH, S.
LOUGE, M.
MOON, F.
POPE, S.
TORRANCE, K.
WARHAFT, Z.
WILLIAMSON, C.
ZABARAS, N.

Operations Research and Industrial Engineering:

BLAND, R.
JACKSON, P.
LEWIS, A.
MUCKSTADT, J.
PROTTER, P.
RENEGAR, J.
RESNICK, S.
ROUNDY, R.
RUPPERT, D.
SAMORODNITSKY, G.
SHMOYS, D.
TODD, M.
TROTTER, L., Jr
TURNBULL, B.
WILLIAMSON, D.

Theoretical and Applied Mechanics:

BURNS, J.
CADY, K.
HEALEY, T.
HUI, CH.-Y.
JENKINS, J.
MUKHERJEE, S.
PHOENIX, S.
RAND, R.
RUINA, A.
SACHSE, W.
STROGATZ, S.
ZEHNDER, A.

New York State College of Agriculture and Life Sciences (260 Roberts Hall, Ithaca, NY 14853-4203; tel. (607) 255-2241; e-mail als_admissions@cornell.edu; internet www.cals.cornell.edu):

Animal Science:

AUSTIC, R.
BAUMAN, D.
BELL, A.
BLAKE, R.
BUTLER, W.
CHASE, L.
CURRIE, W.
EVERETT, R.
FOX, D.
GALTON, D.
GOREWIT, R.
HINTZ, H.
JOHNSON, P.
OLTENACU, P.
PARKS, J.
PELL, A.
POLLAK, E.
QUAAS, R.
THONNEY, M.

Applied Economics and Management:

BARRETT, C.
BILLS, N.
BOISVERT, R.
CHAPMAN, L.
CHRISTY, R.
CONRAD, J.
KAISER, H.
KANBUR, R.
KNOBLAUCH, W.
LADUE, E.
LEE, D.
LESSER, W.
MCLAUGHLIN, E.
MOUNT, T.
NOVAKOVIC, A.
RAJ, S.
SCHULZE, W.
STREETER, D.
TAUER, L.

WANSINK, B.
WHITE, G.

Biological and Environmental Engineering:

ALBRIGHT, L.
ANESHANSLEY, D.
COOKE, J.
DATTA, A.
GEBREMEDHIN, K.
HAITH, D.
JEWELL, W.
PARLANGE, J.-Y.
SCOTT, N.
SPANSWICK, R.
STEENHUIS, T.
TIMMONS, M.
WALKER, L.
WALTER, M.

Communication:

BOOTH, J.
GAY, G.
OSTMAN, R.
WALTHER, J.

Crop and Soil Sciences:

CHERNEY, J.
COX, W.
DEGLORIA, S.
DUXBURY, J.
FICK, G.
MCBRIDE, M.
OBENDORF, R.
SETTER, T.
VAN ES, H.

Developmental Sociology:

BROWN, D.
EBERTS, P.
FELDMAN, S.
GEISLER, C.
GURAK, D.
HIRSCHL, T.
LYSON, T.
MCMICHAEL, P.
PFEFFER, M.

Earth and Atmospheric Sciences:

COLUCCI, S.
COOK, K.
RIHA, S.
WILKS, D.

Ecology and Evolutionary Biology:

CHABOT, B.
DHONDT, A.
FEENY, P.
FITZPATRICK, J.
HARRISON, R.
HARVELL, C.
HOWARTH, R.
MARKS, P.
MCCLURE, P.
MORIN, J.
ROOT, R.
WINKLER, D.

Education:

CAFFARELLA, R.
CAMP, W.

Entomology:

AGNELLO, A.
HOFFMANN, M.
LIEBHERR, J.
NYROP, J.
PECKARSKY, B.
REISSIG, W.
ROELOFS, W.
RUTZ, D.
SCOTT, J.
SHELTON, A.
SHIELDS, E.
SODERLUND, D.
STRAUB, R.
TINGEY, W.

Food Science:

ACREE, T.
BARBANO, D.

BATT, C.
BRADY, J., Jr
DURST, R.
GRAVANI, R.
HANG, Y.
HOTCHKISS, J.
HRADZINA, G.
LAWLESS, H.
LEE, C.
MILLER, D.
REGENSTEIN, J.
RIZVI, S.
SIEBERT, K.

Horticultural Sciences:

BROWN, S.
HARMAN, G.
LAKSO, A.
POOL, R.
REISCH, B.
TAYLOR, A.

Horticulture:

BASSUK, N.
BELLINDER, R.
BRIDGEN, M.
GOOD, G.
MILLER, W.
PETROVIC, A.
PRITTS, M.
WAKKINS, C.
WEILER, T.
WIEN, H.
WOLFE, D.

International Programs:

UPHOFF, N.

Landscape Architecture:

ADLEMAN, M.
GLEASON, K.
GOTTFRIED, H.
TRANCIK, R.
TROWBRIDGE, P.

Microbiology:

GHIORSE, W.
HELMANN, J.
WINANS, S.
ZINDER, S.

Molecular Biology and Genetics:

CALVO, J.
FOX, T.
GOLDBERG, M.
HANSON, M.
HENRY, S.
KEMPHUES, K.
LIS, J.
MACINTYRE, R.
ROBERTS, J.
SHALLOWAY, D.
TYE, B.
VOGT, V.
WU, R.

Natural Resources:

DECKER, D.
FAHEY, T.
GILLETT, J.
HULLAR, T.
KNUTH, B.
KRASNY, M.
LASSOIE, J.
MILLS, E.

Neurobiology and Behaviour:

ADLER, K.
BRADBURY, J.
EISNER, T.
EMLEN, S.
HARRIS-WARRICK, R.
HOPKINS, C.
VEHRENCAMP, S.
WALCOTT, C.

Nutrition:

BENSADOUN, A.
LEVITSKY, D.
NOY, N.

PINSTRUP-ANDERSON, P.

Plant Biology:

BATES, D.
CREPET, W.
DAVIES, P.
DOYLE, J.
NASRALLAH, J.
NASRALLAH, M.
NIKLAS, K.
RODRIGUEZ, E.

Plant Breeding:

COFFMAN, W. R.
EARLE, E.
JOHN, M.
KRESOVICH, S.
McCOUCH, S.
MUTSCHLER, M.
SORRELLS, M.
TANKSLEY, S.
VIANDS, D.

Plant Pathology:

ABAWI, G.
ALDWINCKLE, H.
BEER, S.
BERGSTROM, G.
BURR, T.
COLLMER, A.
DILLARD, H.
FRY, W.
HOCH, H.
HUDLER, G.
KOELLER, W.
LAZAROWITZ, S.
LORBEER, J.
LORIA, R.
MARTIN, G.
MILGROOM, M.
ROSENBERGER, D.
SEEM, R.
WILCOX, W.
ZITTER, T.

New York State College of Human Ecology (Martha Van Rensselaer Hall, Ithaca, NY 14853; tel. (607) 255-2216; fax (607) 255-3794; e-mail humec_admissions@cornell.edu; internet www.human.cornell.edu):

Design and Environmental Analysis:

BECKER, F.
ESHELMAN, P.
EVANS, G.
HEDGE, A.
JENNINGS, J.
LAQUATRA, J., Jr
SIMS, W.

Human Development and Family Studies:

BRUMBERG, J.
CECI, S.
COCHRAN, M.
DEPUE, R.
ECKENRODE, J.
GABARINO, J.
HAMILTON, S.
LUST, B.
PILLEMER, K.
ROBERTSON, S.
SAVIN-WILLIAMS, R.
WILLIAMS, W.

Nutrition:

BISOGNI, C.
BRANNON, P.
BRENNA, J.
GARZA, C.
HAAS, J.
HABICHT, J.-P.
OLSON, C.
PELTO, G.
RASMUSSEN, K.
SAHN, D.
STIPANUK, M.

Policy Analysis and Management:

AVERY, R.
BATTISTELLA, R.

BURKHAUSER, R.
GERNER, J.
KENTEL, D.
MATHIOS, A.
PARROT, A.
PETERS, H.
TROCHIM, W.
WHITE, W.

Textiles and Apparel:

CHU, CH.-CH.
LEMLEY, A.
LOKER, S.
NETRAVALI, A.
OBENDORF, S.

New York State College of Industrial and Labor Relations

Collective Bargaining:

DANIEL, C.
GROSS, J.
HURD, R.
KAHN, L.
KATZ, H.
KURUVILLA, S.
LIPSKY, D.
SALVATORE, N.
TURNER, L.

Employment and Disability Institute:

BRUYERE, S.

Human Resource Studies:

BRIGGS, V., Jr
DYER, L.
SNELL, S.
WRIGHT, P.

Labor Economics:

ABOWD, J.
BLAU, F.
BOYER, G.
EHRENBERG, R.
FIELDS, G.
HUTCHENS, R.
SMITH, R.

Organizational Behavior:

BACHARACH, S.
HAMMER, T.
LAWLER, E.
TOLBERT, P.

Social Statistics:

DICICCIO, T.
WELLS, M.

New York State College of Veterinary Medicine (Ithaca, NY 14853-6401; tel. (607) 253-3000; fax (607) 253-3709; e-mail vet_admissions@cornell.edu; internet www.vet.cornell.edu):

Biomedical Sciences:

BEYENBACH, K.
DELAHUNTA, A.
FARNUM, C.
FORTUNE, J.
GILMOUR, R. Jr
HOUPT, K.
KOTLIKOFF, M.
LOEW, E.
MINOR, R.
NODEN, D.
QUARONI, A.
SCHIMENTI, J.
SCHLAFER, D.
SUAREZ, S.
SUMMERS, B.
YEN, A.

Clinical Sciences:

AINSWORTH, D.
BARR, S.
CENTER, S.
DIVERS, T.
DUCHARME, N.
FUBINI, S.
GILBERT, R.
GLEED, R.
HACKETT, R.

HORNBUCKLE, W.
KALLFELZ, F.
KOLLIAS, G., Jr
LUDDERS, J.
MILLER, W.
MOISE, N.
NIXON, A.
PAGE, R.
RANDOLPH, J.
SCOTT, D.
SMITH, D.
TENNANT, B.

Microbiology, Immunology and Parasitology:

ANTCZAK, D.
APPLETON, J.
BAINES, J.
BLOOM, S.
BOWMAN, D.
BOWSER, P.
DIETERT, R.
LUST, G.
McGREGOR, D.
MARSH, J.
PARRISH, C.
RUSSELL, D.
SCHAT, K.

Molecular Medicine:

CERIONE, R.
GUAN, J.
OSWALD, R.
PAULI, B.
SCHWARK, W.
SHARP, G.
WEILAND, G.

Population Medicine and Diagnostic Services:

CHANG, Y.-F.
ERB, H.
GROHN, Y.
MOHAMMED, H.
SCHUKKEN, Y.
TORRES, A.
WHITE, M.

Johnson Graduate School of Management (Sage Hall, Ithaca, NY 14853; tel. (607) 255-4526; fax (607) 255-0065; e-mail mba@cornell.edu; internet www.johnson.cornell.edu):

BENDANIEL, D.
BIERMAN, H., Jr
BLOOMFIELD, R.
DYCKMAN, T.
FRANK, R.
HART, S.
HASS, J.
HILTON, R.
ISEN, A.
JARROW, R.
LEE, C.
LIBBY, R.
McADAMS, A.
McCLAIN, J.
MICHAELY, R.
NELSON, M.
O'HARA, M.
ORMAN, L.
RAO, V.
RUSSO, J.
SMIDT, S.
SWAMINATHAN, B.
SWIERINGA, R.
THOMAS, L.
WALDMAN, M.

School of Hotel Administration (Statler Hall, Ithaca, NY 14853; tel. (607) 255-9393; fax (607) 255-4179; e-mail sha_student_svcs@cornell.edu; internet www.hotelschool.cornell.edu):

BROWNELL, J.
CORGEL, J.
DITTMAN, D.
ENZ, C.
GELLER, A.
HINKIN, T.

KIMES, S.
MUTKOSKI, S.
PENNER, R.
REDLIN, M.
SIGUAW, J.
THOMPSON, G.

Africana Studies and Research Center (310 Triphammer Rd, Cornell Univ., Ithaca, NY 14853; tel. (607) 255-4625; fax (607) 255-0784; internet www.asrc.cornell.edu):

EDMONDSON, L.
HARRIS, R.
HASSAN, S.
TURNER, J.

CULINARY INSTITUTE OF AMERICA

1946 Campus Dr., Hyde Park, NY 12538-1499

Telephone: (845) 452-9600
Internet: www.ciachef.edu

Campuses at: Hyde Park, NY, and St Helena, CA.

Founded 1946 as New Haven Restaurant Institute; present name 1951
Private control

Pres.: Dr L. TIMOTHY RYAN
Sr Vice-Pres. for Finance and Admin.: CHARLES A. O'MARA
Vice-Pres. for Greystone and Continuing Education: MARK ERICKSON
Vice-Pres. for Marketing and Strategy: BRUCE D. HILLENBRAND
Vice-Pres. for Advancement: VANCE T. PETERSON
Dean of Student Affairs: ALICE-ANN SCHUSTER

Number of teachers: 115
Number of students: 2,285.

DAEMEN COLLEGE

4380 Main St, Amherst, NY 14226

Telephone: (716) 839-3600
Fax: (716) 839-8516
E-mail: admissions@daemen.edu
Internet: www.daemen.edu

Founded 1947 as Rosary Hill College; name changed 1976
Liberal arts and sciences

Pres.: Dr MARTIN J. ANISMAN
Dean: EDWIN CLAUSEN

Library of 135,000 vols
Number of teachers: 120
Number of students: 1,900.

DAVIS COLLEGE

400 Riverside Dr, Johnson City, NY 13790

Telephone: (607) 729-1581
Fax: (607) 729-2962
E-mail: info@davisny.edu
Internet: www.davisny.edu

Founded 1900 as a Bible institute; Practical Bible College 1993; present name 2004
Private control
Academic year: August to May

Pres.: Dr GEORGE D. MILLER, III
Exec. Vice-Pres.: Dr GARY SMITH
Vice-Pres. for Academic Affairs: Dr GILBERT PARKER
Vice-Pres. for Business Affairs: SPENCER KEY
Vice-President for Institutional Advancement: MARSHALL SORBER
Vice-Pres. for Student Devt: RICK CRAMER
Librarian: Dr GERALD FRANZ

Number of teachers: 16
Number of students: 300.

DOMINICAN COLLEGE

470 Western Highway, Orangeburg, NY 10962

Telephone: (845) 359-7800
Fax: (845) 359-2313
E-mail: admissions@dc.edu
Internet: www.dc.edu

Founded 1952
Private control
Academic year: August to May

Pres.: Sister MARY EILEEN O'BRIEN
Chancellor for External Affairs: Sister KATHLEEN SULLIVAN
Vice-Pres. for Academic Affairs and Academic Dean: JOHN F. M. FLYNN
Vice-Pres. for Enrollment Management: BRIAN G. FERNANDES
Vice-Pres. for Financial Affairs: CATHLEEN KENNY
Vice-Pres. for Student Devt and Dean of Students: DOHN E. HARSHBARGER
Vice-Pres. for Institutional Advancement: DOROTHY CHRISTINE FILORAMO
Registrar: MARY McFADDEN
Head Librarian: JOHN BARRIE

Library of 102,000 vols
Number of teachers: 40
Number of students: 1,855

DIRECTORS

Arts and Sciences Div.: Dr WILLIAM HURST
Business Admin. Div.: JOHN SPILLNER
Nursing Div.: Dr MAUREEN CREEGAN
Social Sciences Div.: Dr BARBARA SOCOR
Teacher Education Div.: Dr MARIE PAGLIARO
Allied Health Div.: Dr Sister BERYL HERDT

DOWLING COLLEGE

Idle Hour Blvd, Oakdale, NY 11769

Telephone: (631) 244-3000
Fax: (631) 563-9681
E-mail: admissions@dowling.edu
Internet: www.dowling.edu

Founded 1968
Private control

Pres.: ROBERT J. GAFFNEY
Provost: Dr LINDA ARDITO

Number of teachers: 450
Number of students: 7,000 (undergraduate and postgraduate)

Schools of Arts and Science, Aviation, Business, Education.

D'YOUVILLE COLLEGE

320 Porter Ave, Buffalo, NY 14201-9985

Telephone: (716) 829-8000
Internet: www.dyc.edu

Founded 1908 by the Grey Nuns of the Sacred Heart

Pres.: Sister DENISE A. ROCHE
Sr Vice-Pres.: RICHARD WIESEN
Vice-Pres. for Student Affairs: ROBERT P. MURPHY
Registrar: DION DALY
Dir of Admissions: RONALD H. DANNECKER
Librarian: MARC BAYER

Library of 127,000 vols
Number of teachers: 85
Number of students: 1,900

First degree courses in business, education, humanities, management, natural sciences, nursing, occupational therapy, pre-professional programs, social sciences; graduate degrees in community health, nursing, physical therapy, physician assistance, occupational therapy.

ELMIRA COLLEGE

1 Park Pl., Elmira, NY 14901

Telephone: (607) 735-1800
E-mail: admissions@elmira.edu
Internet: www.elmira.edu

Founded 1855
Private control
Academic year: September to June

Pres.: Dr THOMAS K. MEIER
Academic Vice-Pres.: Dr BRYAN D. REDDICK
Vice-Pres. and Dean of Student Life: JULIANNE BAUMANN
Vice-Pres. for Devt and Dean: SHERRI TROCINO
Vice-Pres. and Dir of Athletics and Health Services and Dean: PATRICIA THOMPSON
Dir of Library: ELIZABETH WAVLE

Library of 335,506 vols
Number of teachers: 78
Number of students: 1,200 full-time

Publications: *New Novel Review* (annual), *Quarry Farm Papers* (irreg.).

EXCELSIOR COLLEGE

7 Columbia Circle, Albany, NY 12203-5159

Telephone: (518) 464-8500
E-mail: admissions@excelsior.edu
Internet: www.excelsior.edu

Pres.: JOHN F. EBERSOLE
Provost and Chief Academic Officer: DANA OFFERMAN

Number of students: 20,485.

FIVE TOWNS COLLEGE

305 North Service Rd, Dix Hills, NY 11746-5871

Telephone: (631) 424-7000 ext 110
E-mail: info@ftc.edu
Internet: www.fivetowns.edu

Founded 1972
Private control

Pres.: Dr STANLEY G. COHEN
Vice-Pres. and Provost: DAVID M. COHEN

Number of teachers: 83
Number of students: 1,038.

FORDHAM UNIVERSITY

Fordham Rd, Bronx, NY 10458

Telephone: (718) 817-1000
Fax: (718) 817-4925
E-mail: publicaff@fordham.edu
Internet: www.fordham.edu

Founded 1841 by Rt Rev. John Hughes, first Roman Catholic Archbishop of New York, as St. John's College. Inc. as a univ. 1846. Name changed to Fordham Univ. 1907
Academic year: July to June

Pres.: Rev. JOSEPH M. McSHANE
Sr Vice-Pres. and Chief Financial Officer: JOHN J. LORDAN
Vice-Pres. for Admin.: BRIAN J. BYRNE
Vice-Pres. for Academic Affairs: JUDITH MILLS
Vice-Pres. for Student Affairs: JEFFREY L. GRAY
Vice-Pres. for Finance: FRANK SIMIO
Vice-Pres. for Devt and Univ. Relations: ALBERT R. CHECCIO
Vice-Pres. for Enrollment: PETER A. STACE
Vice-Pres. for Technology: FRANK SIRIANNI
Registrar: KENNETH POKROWSKI
Dir of Libraries: Dr JAMES McCABE

Library of 2,000,000 vols
Number of teachers: 1,064
Number of students: 15,253

Publications: *International Philosophical Quarterly*, *Traditio* (annual)

DEANS

College of Business Admin.: Dr SHARON SMITH
School of Law: WILLIAM TREANOR
Graduate School of Arts and Sciences: Dr NANCY BUSCH
Graduate School of Business Admin.: Dr SHARON SMITH
Graduate School of Religion and Religious Education: Rev. VINCENT M. NOVAK
Graduate School of Social Service: Dr PETER VAUGHAN
Graduate School of Education: Dr REGIS BERNHARDT
Fordham College: Rev. JEFFREY P. VON ARX
Fordham College of Liberal Studies: Dr MICHAEL GILLAN
Fordham College at Lincoln Center: Rev. ROBERT GRIMES
Fordham College at Rose Hill: Dr BRENNAN O'DONNELL

HAMILTON COLLEGE

198 College Hill Rd, Clinton, NY 13323

Telephone: (315) 859-4011
Fax: (315) 859-4648
E-mail: admission@hamilton.edu
Internet: www.hamilton.edu

Founded 1793 as Hamilton-Oneida Academy; chartered as Hamilton College 1812
Academic year: September to May

Pres.: JOAN HINDE STEWART
Dean of Students: NANCY THOMPSON (acting)

Library of 500,000 vols
Number of teachers: 180
Number of students: 1,775.

HARTWICK COLLEGE

1 Hartwick Dr, Oneonta, NY 13820-4020

Telephone: (607) 431-4000
Fax: (607) 431-4154
E-mail: admissions@hartwick.edu
Internet: www.hartwick.edu

Founded 1797
Private liberal arts college
Academic year: September to May

Pres.: RICHARD P. MILLER, Jr
Vice-Pres. of Academic Affairs: JOHN ANDERSON (acting)
Vice-Pres. for Student Life: GREGORY H. KRIKORIAN (acting)
Vice Pres. for Institutional Advancement: ROBERT J. KALLIN
Vice-Pres. and Chief Financial Officer: WILLIAM WOOD
Dean of Enrollment Management: PATRICIA MABEN
Dean of Student Life: GREGORY K. KRIKORIAN
Dir of Libraries: MARILYN DUNN

Library of 355,776 vols
Number of teachers: 178
Number of students: 1,480.

HOBART AND WILLIAM SMITH COLLEGES

Geneva, NY 14456-3397

Telephone: (315) 781-3000
Fax: (315) 781-3400
E-mail: admissions@hws.edu
Internet: www.hws.edu

Liberal arts colleges
Founded 1822 (Hobart), 1908 (William Smith)
Academic year: September to May

Pres.: MARK D. GEARAN
Provost: TERESA AMOTT
Treas.: PETER POLINAK
Librarian: P. W. CRUMLISH

Library of 387,650 vols

Number of teachers: 207
Number of students: 1,928
Publications: *The Pulteney St. Survey, The Seneca Review*

DEANS

Hobart: CLARENCE BUTLER
William Smith: DEBRA K. DEMEIS

HOFSTRA UNIVERSITY

144 Hofstra Univ., Hempstead, NY 11549-1000

Telephone: (516) 463-6800
Fax: (516) 463-6096
Internet: www.hofstra.edu

Founded 1935

Pres.: STUART RABINOWITZ
Provost and Sr Vice-Pres. for Academic Affairs: Dr HERMAN A. BERLINER
Sr Vice-Pres. for Planning and Admin.: Dr M. PATRICIA ADAMSKI
Vice-Pres. for Financial Affairs and Treas.: CATHY HENNESSY
Vice-Pres. for Business Devt: RICHARD V. GUARDINO, Jr
Vice-Pres. for Student Affairs: SANDRA S. JOHNSON
Vice-Pres. for Devt: ALAN J. KELLY
Vice-Pres. for Information Technology: ROBERT W. JUCKIEWICZ
Vice-Pres. for Legal Affairs: DOLORES FREDRICH
Vice-Pres. for Univ. Relations: MELISSA KANE CONNOLLY
Assoc. Dean of Students: LYNDA O'MALLEY
Dean of Library and Information Services: Dr DANIEL R. RUBEY (acting)
Dir of Intercollegiate Athletics: JACK HAYES

Library of 1,100,000 vols
Number of teachers: 1,256
Number of students: 13,000

DEANS

Frank G. Zarb School of Business: Dr RALPH POLIMENI
School of Communication: Dr SYBIL DELGAUDIO
School of Education and Allied Human Services: Dr JAMES R. JOHNSON
College of Liberal Arts and Sciences: Dr BERNARD J. FIRESTONE (acting)
School of Law: AARON TWERSKI
New College and School for Univ. Studies: DAVID C. CHRISTMAN
Univ. College of Continuing Education: ROSANN KELLY

HOUGHTON COLLEGE

1 Willard Ave, Houghton, NY 14744

Telephone: (585) 567-9200
E-mail: admission@houghton.edu
Internet: www.houghton.edu

Founded 1883

Pres.: SHIRLEY MULLIN
Academic Dean: DARLENE BRESSLER
Vice-Pres. for Student Life: WAYNE MACBETH
Vice-Pres. for Finance: DALE WRIGHT
Dir of Records: MARGE AVERY
Dir of Library: BRAD WILBER

Library of 246,000 vols
Number of teachers: 95
Number of students: 1,250.

BRANCH CAMPUS

Houghton College Suburban Campus: 910 Union Rd, West Seneca, NY 14224; tel. (716) 674-6363; Co-ordinator JOHN DURBIN.

IONA COLLEGE

715 North Ave, New Rochelle, NY 10801-1890

Telephone: (914) 633-2000
Fax: (914) 633-2018
E-mail: admissions@iona.edu
Internet: www.iona.edu

Founded 1940

Pres.: JAMES A. LIGOURI
Provost and Vice-Pres. for Academic Affairs: WARREN ROSENBERG
Vice-Pres. for Finance and Admin.: MARIE THORNTON
Vice Provost for Student Devt: CHARLES CARLSON
Dir of Libraries: RICK PALLADINO

Library of 309,518 vols, 1,760 periodicals
Number of students: 4,303

DEANS

School of Arts and Sciences: WARREN ROSENBERG
School of Business: NICHOLAUS BEUTELL
Dean of Columba School: Dr GLORIA MOLDOW

ITHACA COLLEGE

100 Job Hall, Ithaca, NY 14850

Telephone: (607) 274-3124
Fax: (607) 274-1900
E-mail: admission@ithaca.edu
Internet: www.ithaca.edu

Founded 1892

Pres.: PEGGY R. WILLIAMS
Provost and Vice-Pres. for Academic Affairs: KATHLEEN ROUNTREE
Registrar: CHRISTOPHER KNAUER
Dean of Admissions: LARRY METZGER
College Librarian: LISABETH CHABOT

Library of 611,176 bound vols, and microforms, 2,541 periodical serial subscriptions
Number of teachers: 460 full-time
Number of teachers: 210 part-time
Number of students: 6,409

Publications: *Admissions Prospectus, Undergraduate Catalog, Graduate Catalog, Ithaca College Quarterly*

DEANS

School of Business: ROBERT ULLRICH
Roy H. Park School of Communications: THOMAS BOHN
School of Health Sciences and Human Performance: RICHARD MILLER
School of Music: ARTHUR OSTRANDER
School of Humanities and Sciences: HOWARD ERLICH
Athletics: ELIZABETH A. ALDEN

JEWISH THEOLOGICAL SEMINARY

3080 Broadway, New York, NY 10027

Telephone: (212) 678-8000
Fax: (212) 678-8947
Internet: www.jtsa.edu

Founded 1886
Private control

Chancellor and Pres. of the Faculties: ARNOLD EISEN
Vice-Chancellor and Chief Operating Oficer: Dr MICHAEL B. GREENBAUM
Vice-Chancellor for Rabbinic Devt: Rabbi WILLIAM H. LEBEAU
Vice-Chancellor for Institutional Advancement: CAROL DAVIDSON
Provost: Dr ALAN COOPER
Vice-Pres. for Student Affairs: JOSEPH A. BRODIE
Dean of Academic Affairs: Dr STEPHEN GARFINKEL
Library Dir: NAOMI M. STEINBERGER (acting).

JUILLIARD SCHOOL

60 Lincoln Center Plaza, New York, NY 10023
Telephone: (212) 799-5000
E-mail: admissions@juilliard.edu
Internet: www.juilliard.edu
Founded 1905
Pres.: JOSEPH W. POLISI
Provost and Dean: ARA GUZELIMIAN
Registrar: ELIZABETH BRUMMETT
Library of 68,000 music scores and 20,000 vols; record library: 25,000 long-playing records, CDs and tape recordings, 1,200 video cassettes
Number of teachers: 305 (incl. pre-college and evening div.)
Number of students: 1,425 (incl. pre-college and evening div.).

KEUKA COLLEGE

Keuka Park, NY 14478
Telephone: (315) 279-5000
Fax: (315) 279-5216
E-mail: admissions@mail.keuka.edu
Internet: www.kcuka.edu
Founded 1890
Academic year: August to May
Pres.: Dr JOSEPH G. BURKE
Exec. Vice-Pres.: CAROLANNE MARQUIS
Dean of Admissions and Financial Aid: CLAUDINE NINESTINE
Dir of Library: DEBORAH COOVER
Library of 85,000 vols
Number of teachers: 64
Number of students: 1,521
4-Year liberal arts college.

LABORATORY INSTITUTE OF MERCHANDISING

12 East 53rd St, New York, NY 10022
Telephone: (212) 752-1530
Fax: (212) 750-3432
E-mail: info@limcollege.edu
Internet: www.limcollege.edu
Founded 1939
Private control
Academic year: August to July
Pres.: ELIZABETH S. MARCUSE
Exec. Vice-Pres.: LINDA HARRIS PAOLILLO
Dean of Academic Affairs: Dr JACQUELINE LEBLANC
Dean of Enrollment Management: ADAM ROSEN
Sr Vice-Pres. of Finance and Operation and Treas.: MICHAEL DONOHUE
Asst Dean of Students: LORI MICKENBERG
Dir of Admissions: KRISTINA GIBSON
Dir of Library Services: GEORGE SANCHEZ
Number of teachers: 55
Number of students: 500.

LE MOYNE COLLEGE

1419 Salt Springs Rd, Syracuse, NY 13214-1399
Telephone: (315) 445-4100
Fax: (315) 445-4540
Internet: www.lemoyne.edu
Founded 1946
Academic year: August to May
President: Rev. CHARLES J. BEIRNE
Provost and Academic Vice-President: Dr JOHN SMARRELLI, Jr
Director of Admissions: DENNIS NICHOLSON
Director of Library: JAMES SIMONIS
Library of 242,293 vols
Number of teachers: 300
Number of students: 3,487.

LONG ISLAND UNIVERSITY

Brookville, Long Island, NY 11548
Telephone: (516) 299-2000
Fax: (516) 299-2072
E-mail: attend@liu.edu
Internet: www.liu.edu
Founded 1926
President: Dr DAVID J. STEINBERG
Vice-President for Academic Affairs: Dr MICHAEL ARONS
Vice-President for Finance and Treasurer: MARY M. LAI
Vice-President for University Relations: JEROME A. KLEINMAN
Campus Provost, LIU-Brooklyn: GALE STEVENS HAYNES
Campus Provost, LIU-C.W. Post: Dr JOSEPH SCHENKER
Campus Provost, LIU-Westchester: Dr DENNIS PAYETTE
Campus Provost, LIU-Southampton: TIMOTHY BISHOP
Campus Provost, LIU-Brentwood: DENNIS PAYETTE
Campus Provost, LIU-Rockland: DENNIS PAYETTE
Library: Libraries with 2,297,679 vols
Number of teachers: 1,205 full-time
Number of students: 23,540.

MANHATTAN COLLEGE

Manhattan College Parkway, Riverdale, NY 10471
Telephone: (718) 862-8000
Fax: (718) 862-8014
Internet: www.manhattan.edu
Founded as Academy of the Holy Infancy 1853; chartered as Manhattan College 1863
Private, co-educational
President and Treasurer: Bro. Dr THOMAS J. SCANLAN
Provost and Executive Vice-President: Dr WELDON JACKSON
Vice-President for Student Services: Bro. Dr ROBERT C. BERGER
Vice-President for Finance: JOHN DALY
Bursar: MARIA T. BREWSTER
Vice-President for Advancement: JAMES H. HEISEY
Director of Institutional Research: Dr SUSANNE M. TUMELTY
Registrar: PHYLLIS T. BAGLEY
Director of Library: HARRY WELSH
Library of 240,000 vols
Number of teachers: 390
Number of students: 3,070
Publications: *Humanist* (annually), *Engineer*, *Vistas*

DEANS

Arts: Dr MARY ANN O'DONNELL
Science: Dr EDWARD BROWN
Engineering: Dr RICHARD HEIST
Business: Dr JAMES SUAREZ
Education: Dr WILLIAM MERRIMAN
Graduate Division: Dr JAMES SUAREZ

MANHATTAN SCHOOL OF MUSIC

120 Claremont Ave, New York, NY 10027
Telephone: (212) 749-2802
E-mail: administration@msmnyc.edu
Internet: www.msmnyc.edu
Founded 1917
President: MARTA ISTOMIN
Vice-President and Dean: RICHARD ADAMS
Library: Libraries with 95,000 vols
Number of teachers: 250
Number of students: 850.

MANHATTANVILLE COLLEGE

Purchase, NY 10577
Telephone: (914) 323-5464
Fax: (914) 694-1732
E-mail: admissions@mville.edu
Internet: www.manhattanville.edu
Founded 1841
Academic year: September to May
President: RICHARD A. BERMAN
Provost (vacant)
Number of teachers: 75 (full-time)
Number of students: 2,600 (1,600 full-time undergraduates, 1,000 graduates)
Publication: *Inkwell* (annually).

MARIST COLLEGE

290 North Rd, Poughkeepsie, NY 12601
Telephone: (914) 575-3000
E-mail: admissions@marist.edu
Internet: www.marist.edu
Founded 1929
President: DENNIS J. MURRAY
Executive Vice-President: Dr R. MARK SULLIVAN
Vice-President for Student Affairs: GERARD COX
Vice-President for Academic Affairs: Dr MARC VAN DER HEYDEN
Vice-President for Admissions and Enrollment: HARRY WOOD
Vice-President for College Advancement: SHAILEEN KOPEC
Vice-President for Information Services: CARL GERBERICH
Vice-President for Business Affairs: ANTHONY CAMPILII
Registrar: JUDY IVANKOVIC
Librarian: JOHN McGINTY
Library of 120,000 vols
Number of teachers: 250
Number of students: 4,025.

MARYMOUNT MANHATTAN COLLEGE

221 East 71st St, New York, NY 10021
Telephone: (212) 517-0400
Internet: marymount.mmm.edu
Founded 1936, chartered 1961
President: Dr JUDSON SHAVER
Vice-Presidents: DAWN R. WEBER (Academic Affairs and Dean of the College), PAUL CIRAULO (Finance and Administration), JIM HUNDREISER (Student Affairs and Enrollment Management), MARGARET MINSON (Institutional Advancement)
Library of 85,000 vols
Number of teachers: 142
Number of students: 2,185 (1,500 full-time, 685 part-time).

MEDAILLE COLLEGE

18 Agassiz Circle, Buffalo, NY 14214
Telephone: (716) 884-3281
Fax: (716) 884-0291
E-mail: lkaveney@medaille.edu
Internet: www.medaille.edu
Founded 1875 as Sisters of St Joseph Institute; present name 1967
Private control
Academic year: September to June
President: Dr JOSEPH W. BASCUAS
Academic Dean: JOSEPH E. SAVARESE
Registrar: KATHLEEN LAZAR
Library Director: ILONA MIDDLETON
Number of teachers: 175
Number of students: 1,401.

MERCY COLLEGE

555 Broadway, Dobbs Ferry, NY 10522
Internet: www.mercy.edu
Campuses in: Dobbs Ferry, Bronx, Manhattan, White Plains, Yorktown Heights
Founded 1950
Private control
Academic year: September to May
President: Dr LAPOVSKY
Provost: Dr LOUISE H. FEROE
Library Director: Prof. W. BRUCE FULTON
Number of students: 10,400.

METROPOLITAN COLLEGE OF NEW YORK

75 Varick St, New York, NY 10013
Telephone: (212) 343-1234
Fax: (212) 343-7399
E-mail: admissions@metropolitan.edu
Internet: www.metropolitan.edu
Campuses in New York, Bronx, Staten Island and Flushing
Founded 1964 as Women's Talent Corps; present name 2002
Academic year: September to August
President: STEPHEN GREENWALD
Executive Vice-President and Provost: PAUL LERMAN
Senior Vice-President (Finance): VINCENT MASSARO
Vice-President (Finance): LINCOLN RONEY
Vice-President (Student Affairs): MARCIA Y. CANTARELLA
Vice-President (Institutional Advancement): MARY BALABAN
Vice-President (Schools Project): JANITH JORDAN
Vice-President (Governmental and Public Affairs): RAE ALEXANDER-MINTER
Dean of Students: DONA SOSA
Registrar: ANITA O'BRIEN
Library Director: ROBERT DORN
Number of teachers: 190
Number of students: 1,650

DEANS

Audrey Cohen School for Human Services and Education: Dr RUTH LUGO
School for Public Affairs and Administration: Dr HUMPHREY CROOKENDALE
School for Business: RALPH LEAL
Graduate School for Business: Dr FAYE RAN

MOLLOY COLLEGE

1000 Hempstead Ave, Rockville Centre, NY 11571-5002
Telephone: (516) 678-5000
Internet: www.molloy.edu
Founded 1955
Private control
President: Dr DREW BOGNER
Vice-President (Academic Affairs) and Dean of Faculty: Dr VALERIE COLLINS
Vice-President (Student Affairs): ROBERT HOULIHAN
Vice-President (Finance): MICHAEL McGOVERN
Vice-President (Planning, Research and Information Technology): Dr JOAN MERLO
Vice-President (Mission): Sr DOROTHY FITZGIBBONS
Vice-President (Enrollment Management): LINDA ALBANESE
Vice-President (Advancement): EDWARD THOMPSON
Library Director: ROBERT MARTIN
Number of teachers: 209
Number of students: 2,500.

MOUNT SAINT MARY COLLEGE

330 Powell Avenue, Newburgh, NY 12550
Telephone: (914) 569-3259
Fax: (914) 562-6762
Internet: www.msmc.edu
Founded 1960
Private control
President: Sister ANN SAKAC
Registrar: GERALD JILBERT
Head Librarian: MARY REED McTAMANY
Library of 113,000 vols
Number of teachers: 60 full-time, 45 adjunct
Number of students: 1,920

CHAIRPERSONS

Division of Arts and Letters: JAMES BEARD
Division of Business: Dr JEROME PICARD
Division of Education: Dr LUCY DIPAOLA
Division of Mathematics and Computer Science: VINCENT KAYES
Division of Natural Sciences: Dr IRIS TURKENKOPF
Division of Nursing: Dr NANCY ZWEIG
Division of Religion and Philosophy: Dr KATE LINDEMANN
Division of Social Sciences: Dr JOHN REILLY

NAZARETH COLLEGE

4245 East Ave, Rochester, NY 14618-3790
Telephone: (716) 389-2525
Fax: (716) 586-2452
Internet: www.naz.edu
Founded 1924
President: ROBERT A. MILLER
Vice-President (Academic Affairs): DENNIS SILVA
Registrar: NANCY GREAR
Library Director: SCOTT SMITH (acting)
Library of 266,000 vols, 2,004 serials
Number of teachers: 143
Number of students: 3,062
Publication: *Verity*

DEANS

College of Arts and Sciences: MICHAEL RENNER
College of Health and Human Services: SHIRLEY SZEKERES

ATTACHED RESEARCH INSTITUTES

Center for Teaching Excellence: Dir DIANE ENERSON.

Center for International Study: Executive Dir GEORGE EISEN.

NEW SCHOOL UNIVERSITY

66 West 12th St, New York, NY 10011
Telephone: (212) 229-5600
Fax: (212) 229-5330
Internet: www.newschool.edu
Founded 1919
President: BOB KERREY
Provost: ARJUN APPADURAI
Executive Vice-President: JAMES MURTHA
Vice-President for Communications and External Affairs: NANCY DONNER
Vice-President for Development: KRISTIN SORENSON
Vice-President and General Counsel: GREGORY K. SPENCE
Secretary of the Corporation: ROBERT A. GATES
Library of 4,130,688 vols
Number of teachers: 1,818
Number of students: 23,000 (8,000 undergraduates, 15,000 students in continuing education)
Publications: *Philosophy Journal*, *Social Research*, *World Policy Journal*

DEANS

Graduate Faculty of Political and Social Science: BENJAMIN LEE
New School Adult Division: ANN-LOUISE SHAPIRO
Parsons School of Design: FRED P. HOCHBERG
New School University Jazz and Contemporary Music Program: MARTIN MUELLER
Milano Graduate School: FRED P. HOCHBERGER
Eugene Lang College: JONATHAN VEITCH
Mannes College of Music: JOEL LESTER

NEW YORK CHIROPRACTIC COLLEGE

2360 State Route 89, Seneca Falls, NY 13148
E-mail: camsonline@nycc.edu
Internet: www.nycc.edu
Private control
President: Dr FRANK J. NICCHI
Number of students: 720.

NEW YORK COLLEGE OF PODIATRIC MEDICINE

1800 Park Ave, New York, NY 10035
Telephone: (212) 410-8000
Fax: (212) 722-4918
E-mail: admissions@nycpm.edu
Internet: www.nycpm.edu
Founded 1911 as New York School of Chiropody; present name 1972
Private control
Academic year: July/August to May
President and CEO: LOUIS L. LEVINE
Dean and Vice-President (Academic Affairs): Dr MICHAEL J. TREPAL
Vice-President (Administration): JOEL A. STURM
Vice-President (Finance): ALAN SHOIOCK
Vice-President (Information Technology and Operations): WILLIAM H. GRAHAM
Vice-President (Medical and Professional Affairs): Dr MARK H. SWARTZ
Librarian: THOMAS P. WALKER
Number of teachers: 119
Number of students: 283.

NEW YORK INSTITUTE OF TECHNOLOGY

POB 8000, Old Westbury, NY 11568-0800
Telephone: (516) 686-7516
Fax: (516) 686-7613
E-mail: admissions@nyit.edu
Internet: www.nyit.edu
Founded 1955
Academic year: September to May
President: EDWARD GUILIANO
Chief Financial Officer and Treasurer: JOSEPH COOK III
Vice-President for Academic Affairs and Dean of Faculty: ALEXANDRA W. LOGUE
Vice-President for Health Sciences and Medical Affairs: BARBARA ROSS-LEE
Vice-President for Development: THOMAS MAURIELLO
Vice-President for Student Affairs: JOSEPH FORD
Vice-President for Campus Operations: RAJENDRA SINGH
Library of 206,758 vols, 2,745 periodicals
Number of teachers: 847 (283 full-time, 564 part-time)
Number of students: 9,629 (5,718 undergraduate, 2,764 postgraduate, 1,147 first-time professionals).

NEW YORK LAW SCHOOL

57 Worth St, New York, NY 10013
Telephone: (212) 431-2100

E-mail: admissions@nyls.edu
Internet: www.nyls.edu
Founded 1891
Private control
Academic year: August to May
Dean and President: Dr RICHARD A. MATASAR
Associate Dean (Academic Affairs): Dr JETHRO K. LIEBERMAN
Associate Dean (Professional Development): Dr CAROL BUCKLER
Associate Dean (Faculty Development): Dr STEPHEN ELLMANN
Associate Dean (Finance and Administration): Dr FRED DeJOHN
Associate Dean (Institutional Advancement): BARBARA I. LESHINSKY
Associate Dean (Public Affairs): ALTAGRACIA LEVAT
Associate Dean (Special Projects): JOAN FISHMAN
Library Director: Dr JOYCE SALTALAMACHIA
Number of teachers: 155 (62 full-time, 93 adjunct)
Number of students: 1,400.

NEW YORK MEDICAL COLLEGE

Valhalla, NY 10595
Telephone: (914) 594-4000
Internet: www.nymc.edu
Founded 1860
Private control
President: Rev. Mgr HARRY C. BARRETT
Registrar: BARBARA WINES
Librarian: DIANA CUNNINGHAM
Library of 149,000 vols, 2,100 journal titles
Number of teachers: 2,800 (1350 full-time; 1450 part-time and voluntary)
Number of students: 1,650

DEANS

School of Medicine: RALPH A. O'CONNELL
Graduate School of Health Sciences: SHEILA M. SMYTHE
Graduate School of Basic Medical Sciences: FRANCIS L. BELLONI

NEW YORK SCHOOL OF INTERIOR DESIGN

170 E 70th St, New York, NY 10021
Telephone: (212) 472-1500
Fax: (212) 472-3800
E-mail: admissions@nysid.edu
Internet: www.nysid.edu
Founded 1916
Private control
Academic year: June to May
Number of teachers: 90
Number of students: 750.

NEW YORK THEOLOGICAL SEMINARY

475 Riverside Drive, Suite 500, New York, NY 10115
Telephone: (212) 870-1211
Fax: (212) 870-1236
E-mail: online@nyts.edu
Internet: www.nyts.edu
Founded 1900 as Bible Teachers' College; present name 1965
Private control
President: Dr HILLARY GASTON, Sr
Vice-President: Dr LAURA PIRES-HESTER
Academic Dean: Dr DALE T. IRVIN
Registrar: SU KANG
Librarian: ELEANOR SOLER
Number of teachers: 35
Number of students: 287.

NEW YORK UNIVERSITY

Washington Square, New York, NY 10003
Telephone: (212) 998-1212
Internet: www.nyu.edu
Founded 1831
Private
Academic year: September to May
President: JOHN SEXTON
Provost: DAVID W. McLAUGHLIN
Executive Vice-President: JACOB J. LEW
Senior Vice-President (Health): ROBERT BERNE
Chair of Faculty Advisory Committee on Academic Priorities: RICHARD FOLEY
Chief of Staff and Deputy to the President: DIANE C. YU
Senior Vice-President (University Relations and Public Affairs): LYNNE P. BROWN
Counselor to the President: NORMAN DORSEN
Senior Vice-Provost (Research): PIERRE HOHENBERG
Senior Vice-Provost (Planning): FRANK C. HOPPENSTEADT
Senior Vice-President (Development and Alumni Relations): DEBRA A. LaMORTE
Senior Vice-President (Operations and Administration): CHERYL MILLS
Senior Vice-President, General Counsel and Secretary of the University: S. ANDREW SCHAFFER
Senior Vice-President (Finance and Budget): JEANNEMARIE SMITH
Vice-President (Public Affairs): JOHN BECKMAN
Vice-President (Public Resource Administration and Development): RICHARD N. BING
Associate Provost (Admissions and Financial Aid): BARBARA F. HALL
Associate Vice-President (Student Affairs): JUDY JACKSON
Vice-President (Auxiliary Services): ROBERT S. KIVETZ
Vice-President (Public Safety): JULES MARTIN
Associate Provost and Chief Information Technology Officer: MARILYN McMILLAN
Vice-Provost (University Life and Interdisciplinary Initiatives): LINDA G. MILLS
Vice-Provost (Globalization and Multicultural Affairs): YAW NYARKO
Associate Provost and Executive Director of Faculty Housing: CAROLYN SARGENT
Vice-President (Student Affairs): MARC L. WAIS
Vice-Provost (Faculty Affairs): SHARON L. WEINBERG
Dean of Libraries: CAROL A. MANDEL
Library: see Libraries
Number of teachers: 5,602
Number of students: 38,188
Publications: *Annual Survey of American Law* (4 a year), *Environmental Law Journal* (3 a year), *Inquiry* (annually), *Journal of Accounting, Auditing and Finance* (4 a year), *Journal of International Financial Management and Accounting* (3 a year), *Journal of International Law and Politics* (4 a year), *Journal of Legislation and Public Policy* (2 a year), *Law Review* (6 a year), *Moot Court Casebook* (annually), *Review of Law and Social Change* (6 a year), *TDR: a Journal of Performance Studies* (4 a year), *Victorian Literature and Culture* (2 a year), *Women and Performance: a Journal of Feminist Theory* (2 a year), *Wordsworth Circle* (4 a year), *Washington Square* (2 a year)

DEANS

Faculty of Arts and Science: RICHARD FOLEY, PETER LENNIE (Science: MARY J. CARRUTHERS (Humanities: GEORGE W. DOWNS (Social Sciences)
Graduate School of Arts and Science: CATHARINE R. STIMPSON

College of Arts and Science: MATTHEW S. SANTIROCCO
School of Law: RICHARD L. REVESZ
New York School of Medicine and Post-Graduate Medical Center: ROBERT M. GLICKMAN
College of Dentistry: MICHAEL C. ALFANO
Steinhardt School of Education: MARY M. BRABECK
Leonard N. Stern School of Business: THOMAS F. COOLEY
Leonard N. Stern School of Business Undergraduate College: SALLY BLOUNT-LYON
School of Continuing and Professional Studies: DAVID F. FINNEY
Robert F. Wagner Graduate School of Public Service: ELLEN SCHALL
Shirley M. Ehrenkrantz School of Social Work: SUZANNE E. ENGLAND
Tisch School of the Arts: MARY SCHMIDT CAMPBELL
Gallatin School of Individualized Study: E. FRANCES WHITE
Mount Sinai School of Medicine (affiliated): KENNETH L. DAVIS
Institute of Fine Arts: MARIËT WESTERMANN (Dir)
Courant Institute of Mathematical Science: CHARLES M. NEWMAN (Dir)

PROFESSORS

College of Arts and Science (100 Washington Square East, New York, NY 10003; internet www.nyu.edu/cas):

AARONSON, D., Psychology
AFFRON, C., French
ALEXANDER, J. J. G., Fine Arts
ALLEN, L. R., Psychology
AMENTA, E., Sociology
ANDERSEN, S. M., Psychology
ANDERSON, H. M., Spanish and Portuguese Languages and Literatures
AVELLANEDA, M., Mathematics
AVERILL, G., Music
AZMITIA, E. C., Biology, Neural Science
BACIC, Z., Chemistry
BAER, N. S., Conservation, Fine Arts
BAILEY, R., Music
BAKER, P. R., History
BALTIN, M. R., Linguistics
BARGH, J. A., Psychology
BAUMOL, W. J., Economics
BEAUJOUR, M., French
BEIDELMAN, T. O., Anthropology
BENDER, T., History
BENHABIB, J., Political Economy, Economics
BERENSON, E., History, French Studies
BERGER, M., Computer Science
BERMAN, S. M., Mathematics
BISHOP, T., French Literature, Comparative Literature
BLOCK, N., Philosophy, Psychology
BLOOM, H., English and American Literature, English
BOGHOSSIAN, P., Philosophy
BOGOMOLOV, F. A., Mathematics
BONFANTE, L., Classics
BOORMAN, S. H., Music
BRAMS, S. J., Politics
BRANDT, K. W.-G., Fine Arts
BRANDT, R. A., Physics
BRATHWAITE, K., Comparative Literature
BROWN, JR, H. H., Physics
BROWN, J., Fine Arts
BROYDE, S., Biology
BRUNER, J., Psychology
BUDICK, B., Physics
BUENO DE MESQUITA, B., Politics
BURNS, F. J., Environmental Science
BURROWS, D. L., Music
BURROWS, W. E., Journalism and Mass Communication
CALHOUN, C. J., Sociology
CANARY, J. W., Chemistry

CANTOR, N. F., History, Comparative Literature, Sociology
CAPLIN, A., Economics
CAPPELL, S., Mathematics
CARNEVALE, P., Psychology
CARRASCO, M., Psychology and Neuroscience
CARRUTHERS, M. J., Literature
CHAIKEN, S., Psychology
CHAUDHURI, U., English
CHAZAN, R., Modern Jewish History
CHEEGER, J., Mathematics
CHELKOWSKI, P. J., Middle Eastern Studies
CHILDRESS, W. S., Mathematics
CHIOLES, J., Comparative Literature
CHUSID, M., Music
CLASTER, J. N., History
COHEN, B. S., Environmental Medicine
COHEN, J.-L., History of Architecture
COHEN, S. F., Russian Studies and History
COLE, R., Computer Science
COLLINS, C., English
COONS, E. E., Psychology, Neural Science
CORRADI, J. E., Sociology
CORUZZI, G. M., Biology
COSTA, M., Environmental Science
COSTELLO, J. R., Linguistics
DASH, J. M., French
DEIFT, P., Mathematics
DESPLAN, C., Biology
DEWAR, R. B. K., Computer Science
DIAWARA, M., Comparative Literature
DINER, H. R., American Jewish History, Hebrew and Judaic Studies, History
DINSHAW, C., English
DJEBAR, A., French
DOCTOROW, E. L., American Letters, English
DONOGHUE, D., English and American Letters
DOUBROVSKY, S., French
DOWNS JR, G. W., Politics
DUSTER, T., Sociology
DWORKIN, R., Law, Philosophy
EISLER, C., Fine Arts
ELBOURNE, P. D., Linguistics
ELLIS, M. H., Fine Arts
ENGEL, D., Holocaust Studies, Hebrew and Judaic Studies, and History
EVANS, H. L., Environmental Science
FAIRCHILD, S., Conservation
FARRAR, G., Physics
FELDMAN, S. M., Neural Science, Psychology
FELDMAN, Y. S., Hebrew Culture and Education
FERNANDEZ, R., Economics
FIELD, H. H., Philosophy
FINE, K., Philosophy
FLINN, C. J., Economics
FRECCERO, J., Italian, Comparative Literature
FRYDMAN, R., Economics
FURMANSKI, P., Biology
GALE, D., Economics
GANS, P. J., Chemistry
GARABEDIAN, P. R., Mathematics
GARLAND, D., Sociology
GATELY, D., Economics
GEACINTOV, N. E., Chemistry
GERSON, K., Sociology
GERSON, S., French
GERTLER, M., Economics
GILMAN, E. B., English
GILSENAN, M., Humanities, Middle Eastern Studies, Anthropology
GINSBURG, F., Anthropology
GITLIN, T., Journalism and Mass Communication, Education, Sociology
GOLDSTEIN, G. R., Dental Materials Science
GOLLWITZER, P. M., Psychology
GOODMAN, J., Mathematics
GOTTLIEB, A., Computer Science
GREENBERG, D. F., Sociology
GREENGARD, L., Mathematics
GREENLEAF, F. P., Mathematics

GRIFFIN, D., English
GRISHMAN, R., Computer Science
GROMOV, M., Mathematics
GROSS, J. T., Politics
GUILLORY, J., English
GURLAND, R. H., Philosophy
GUY, G. R., Linguistics
HAMEIRI, E., Mathematics
HANSEN, D., Ancient Middle Eastern Art and Archaeology
HARDIN, R., Politics
HARLEY, N. H., Environmental Science
HAROOTUNIAN, H., History
HARPER, P. B., English, American Studies
HARRINGTON, C., Politics
HARRISON, T., Anthropology
HAUSNER, M., Mathematics
HAVERKAMP, A., English
HAWKEN, M. J., Neural Science, Psychology
HEEGER, D. J., Psychology and Neural Science
HEILMAN, M., Psychology
HENDIN, J. G., English
HEYDEBRAND, W., Sociology
HEYNS, B., Sociology
HOFER, H., Mathematics
HOFFERT, M. I., Physics
HOFFMAN, M., Psychology
HOLLIER, D., French
HOROWITZ, R., Sociology
HOY, P. C., English
HSIUNG, J. C., Politics
HUGGINS, P., Physics
HULL, R. W., History
HÜPPAUF, B. R., German
HYMAN, I., Fine Arts
IVRY, A. L., Modern Jewish Thought, Hebrew and Judaic Studies, Middle Eastern Studies
JACOBY, L., Psychology
JAEGER, R. J., Environmental Science
JASSO, G., Sociology
JAVITCH, D., Comparative Literature, Italian
JOHNSON, P., History
JOLLY, C. J., Anthropology
JOVANOVIC, B., Economics
JUDT, A., European Studies, History
KALLENBACH, N. R., Chemistry
KAMM, F. M., Philosophy, Law
KAPLAN, F. E. S., Museum Studies
KAPLAN, M. A., Hebrew and Judaic Studies
KARCHIN, L., Music
KAYNE, R. S., Linguistics
KAZEMI, F., Politics, Middle Eastern Studies
KEDEM, Z. M., Computer Science
KELLEY, R. D. G., History
KINNELL, G., Creative Writing, English
KIRSHENBLATT-GIMBLETT, B., Performance Studies, Hebrew and Judaic Studies
KOHN, R. V., Mathematics
KOPCKE, G., Humanities
KRABBENHOFT, K., Spanish and Portuguese Languages and Literatures
KRAUSKOPF, J., Neural Science, Psychology
KRINSKY, C., Fine Arts
KRISER, D. B., Anthropology
KULICK, D., Anthropology
KUPPERMAN, K., History
LANDAU, S., Fine Arts
LANDY, M. S., Psychology, Neural Science
LAX, P. D., Mathematics
LEDOUX, J. E., Neural Science and Psychology
LEGEROS, R. Z., Dental Materials Science
LEHMAN, E. W., Sociology
LENNIE, P., Neural Science
LEVINE, B. A., Bible and Ancient Near Eastern Studies, Hebrew and Judaic Studies
LEVY, P. M., Physics
LIN, F.-H., Mathematics
LIPPMANN, M., Environmental Science
LOCKMAN, Z., Middle Eastern Studies, History

LOCKRIDGE, L. S., English
LOW, A., English
LOWENSTEIN, J. H., Physics
LUKES, S. M., Sociology
LYNCH, O. M., Urban Anthropology
MAGNUSON, P. A., English
MAJDA, A. J., Mathematics
MANIN, B., Politics
MANOFF, R. K., Journalism and Mass Communication
MARINCOLA, M. D., Conservation
MARMOR, M., Environmental Medicine
MARSHALL, P., English
MARTIN, E., Anthropology
MARTÍNEZ, H. S., Spanish and Portuguese Languages and Literatures
MATHEWS, T. F., History of Art
MATTHEWS, T. J., Psychology, Neural Science
MATTINGLY, P., History
MAYNARD, J., English
MCCHESNEY, R. D., Middle Eastern Studies
MCKEAN, H. P., Mathematics
MCLAUGHLIN, D. W., Mathematics
MCNELIS, E. J., Chemistry
MEAD, L. M., Politics
MEISEL, P., English
MICHELSON, A., Cinema Studies
MINCER, A., Physics
MISHRA, B., Computer Science
MITCHELL, C., Politics
MITCHELL, T., Politics, Middle Eastern Studies
MITSIS, P., Hellenic Culture and Civilization, Classics
MOLLOY, S., Spanish and Portuguese Languages and Literatures, Comparative Literature
MORTON, R. B., Politics
MOVSHON, J. A., Neural Science, Psychology
MURPHY, G. L., Psychology
MURPHY, L. B., Law, Philosophy
MYERS, F. R., Anthropology
NADIRI, M. I., Economics
NAGEL, T., Philosophy
NELKIN, D., Sociology
NEMETHY, P., Physics
NEWMAN, C. M., Mathematics
NICOLE, E., French
NIRENBERG, L., Mathematics
NOCHLIN, L., Modern Art
NOLAN, M., History
NYARKO, Y., Economics
O'CONNOR, D., Ancient Egyptian Art
OLDS, S., English
OLIVA, L. J., European Studies, History
OLLMAN, B., Politics
ORDOVER, J. A., Economics
OVERTON, M., Computer Science
PEACHIN, M., Classics
PEACOCKE, C., Philosophy
PELLI, D. G., Psychology, Neural Science
PERCUS, J. K., Mathematics, Physics
PERSELL, C. H., Sociology
PESKIN, C. S., Mathematics
PETERS, F. E., Middle Eastern Studies, Religious Studies, History
PINES, M. S., Dental Materials Science
PNUELI, A., Computer Science
POLLACK, R., Mathematics
POOVEY, M., English
PORRATI, M., Physics
POSNER, D., Fine Arts
POSNOCK, R., English
POSTAL, P. M., Linguistics
PRATT, M. L., Spanish and Portuguese
PRZEWORSKI, A., Politics
RAMSEY, J. B., Economics
RANDALL, R. S., Politics
RAPP, R., Anthropology
RAY, D., Economics
REGALADO, N. F., French
REIMERS, D. E., History
REISS, C. S., Biology
REISS, T. J., Comparative Literature

RICHARDSON, J., Philosophy
RICHARDSON, R. W., Physics
RINZEL, J., Neural Science, Mathematics
ROBINSON, E. J., Physics
ROELOFS, H. M., Politics
ROESNER, E. H., Music
RONELL, A., Germanic Languages and Literatures, Comparative Literature
ROSENBERG, L., Physics
ROSENBLUM, R., Modern European Art
ROSS, A., Comparative Literature
ROSS, K., Comparative Literature
ROSSMAN, T. G., Environmental Science
RUBLE, D. N., Psychology
RUDDICK, W., Philosophy
SAMMONS, J. T., History
SANDLER, L., Art History
SANTIROCCO, M. S., Classics
SARNAK, P., Mathematics
SCALLY, R. J., History, Classics
SCHAIN, M., Politics, French Studies
SCHECHNER, R., Performance Studies
SCHIEFFELIN, B. B., Anthropology
SCHIFFER, S., Philosophy
SCHIFFMAN, L. H., Hebrew and Judaic Studies
SCHLESINGER, R. B., Environmental Science
SCHLICK, T., Chemistry, Mathematics
SCHONBERG, E., Computer Science
SCHOTTER, A., Economics
SCHUCKING, E. L., Physics
SCHULMAN, A., Dental Materials Science
SCHUSTER, D. I., Chemistry
SCHWARTZ, J. T., Computer Science
SCHWEITZER, A., Humanities, Spanish and Portuguese Languages and Literatures, Comparative Literature
SCOTT, W., Biology
SCULLI, J., Physics
SEEMAN, N. C., Chemistry
SEIDMAN, E., Psychology
SEIGEL, J., History
SENNETT, R., Sociology, History
SHAPLEY, R. M., Sciences, Neural Science, Biology, Psychology
SHASHA, D., Computer Science
SHATAH, J., Mathematics
SHELLEY, M., Mathematics
SHINN, M., Psychology
SHOHAT, E., Art and Public Policy, Middle Eastern Studies
SHORE, R. E., Environmental Science
SHROUT, P., Psychology
SIDER, D., Classics
SIEBURTH, R., Comparative Literature, French
SIFAKIS, G. M., Hellenic Culture and Civilization, Classics
SILVER, K., Fine Arts, French Studies
SINGLER, J. V., Linguistics
SIRLIN, A., Physics
SKLAR, R., Cinema Studies
SMITH, M. S., Hebrew and Judaic Studies
SNODGRASS, J. G., Psychology
SOKAL, A. D., Physics
SOLOMON, S. D., Journalism and Mass Communication
SORENSEN, R. A., Philosophy
SOUCEK, P., Islamic Art
SPENCER, J. H., Computer Science, Mathematics
STAM, R., Cinema Studies
STEHLIN, S. A., History
STEPHENS, M., Journalism and Mass Communication
STIMPSON, C. R., Arts and Science
STOTZKY, G., Biology
STROKE, H. H., Physics
SUBIRATS, E., Spanish and Portuguese Languages and Literatures
SULLIVAN, E., Fine Arts
SZABOLCSI, A., Linguistics
TAYLOR, D., Performance Studies, Spanish
TING, L., Mathematics
TRACHTENBERG, M., History of Fine Arts
TROPE, Y., Psychology

TURNER, R., Art and Humanities
TYLER, T. R., Psychology
ULEMAN, J. S., Psychology
UNGER, I., History
UNGER, P., Philosophy
VARADHAN, S. R. S., Science, Mathematics
VITZ, E. B., French
VITZ, P. C., Psychology
VOLOGODSKII, A. V., Chemistry
WALEY-COHEN, J., History
WALKOWITZ, D., History
WEITZNER, H., Mathematics
WELKOWITZ, J., Psychology
WEINEN, E., Mathematics
WHITE, D., Anthropology
WIDLUND, O. B., Computer Science
WILSON, C. A., Economics
WILSON, S. R., Chemistry
WOLFF, E. N., Economics
WOLFSON, E., Hebrew Studies, Religious Studies
WRIGHT, M. H., Computer Science
XIN, Z., Mathematics
YAP, C. K., Computer Science
YAU, H.-T., Mathematics
YELLIN, V. F., Music
YOUNG, M. B., History
YÚDICE, G., Spanish and Portuguese and American Studies
ZASLAVSKY, G. M., Physics, Mathematics
ZHANG, J. Z. H., Chemistry
ZWANZIGER, D., Physics, Mathematics

College of Dentistry (345 East 24th St, New York, NY 10010; tel. (212) 998-9800; internet www.nyu.edu/dental):

BAHN, S., Biological Sciences, Medicine and Surgery
BRAL, M., Periodontics
CALAMIA, J., Restorative and Prosthodontics
CAUFIELD, P. W., Cariology and Operative Dentistry
GLICKMAN, R., Oral Maxillofacial Surgery
GOLDSTEIN, G., Prosthodontics
GUTTENPLAN, J., Basic Sciences (Biochemistry)
KATZ, R., Epidemiology and Health Promotion
KINNALLY, K., Basic Sciences
KIREMIDJIAN-SCHUMACHER, L., Basic Sciences
KUFTINEC, M., Orthodontics
LeGEROS, R., Implant Dentistry and Restorative and Prosthodontic Sciences
PINES, M., Biomaterials
REKOW, D., Basic Sciences and Craniofacial Biology and Orthodontics
ROSENBERG, P., Endodontics
ROT, M., Basic Sciences
SCHERER, W., Reconstructive and Comprehensive Care
SHIP, J. A., Oral Medicine
SINGH, I., Basic Sciences
SPIELMAN, A., Basic Science and Craniofacial Biology
TARNOW, D., Implant Dentistry
TERRACIO, L., Basic Sciences and Craniofacial Biology
VERNILLO, A., Oral Pathology

Courant Institute of Mathematical Sciences (251 Mercer St, New York, NY 10012; tel. (212) 998-3000; internet www.cims.nyu.edu):

AVELLANEDA, M. M., Mathematics
AROUS, G. B., Mathematics
BERGER, M. J., Computer Science and Mathematics
BERMAN, S. M., Mathematics
BOGOMOLOV, F. A., Mathematics
CAPPELL, S. E., Mathematics
CHANG, C.-S., Research Mathematics
CHILDRESS, W. S., Mathematics
COLDING, T. H., Mathematics
COLE, R. J., Computer Science
DEIFT, P. A., Mathematics
DEWAR, R. B. K., Computer Science

GARABEDIAN, P. R., Mathematics
GOODMAN, J. B., Mathematics
GOTTLIEB, A., Computer Science
GREENGARD, L., Mathematics and Computer Science
GREENLEAF, F. P., Mathematics
GRISHMAN, R., Computer Science
GROMOV, M., Mathematics
HAMEIRI, E., Mathematics
HAUSNER, M., Mathematics
HOFER, H., Mathematics
KEDEM, Z. M., Computer Science
KOHN, R. V., Mathematics
LIN, F.-H., Mathematics
MAJDA, A. J., Mathematics
McKEAN, H. P., Mathematics
McLAUGHLIN, D. W., Mathematics and Neural Science
MISHRA, B., Computer Science and Mathematics
NEWMAN, C. M., Mathematics
NOVIKOFF, A. B. J., Mathematics
OVERTON, M. L., Computer Science and Mathematics
PERCUS, J. K., Mathematics and Physics
PERLIN, K., Computer Science
PESKIN, C. S., Mathematics
PNUELI, A., Computer Science
POLLACK, R., Mathematics and Computer Science
RINZEL, J., Neural Science and Mathematics
SAGER, N., Natural Language Processing
SARNAK, P., Mathematics
SCHLICK, T., Chemistry, Mathematics, and Computer Science
SCHONBERG, E., Computer Science
SCHWARTZ, J. T., Computer Science and Mathematics
SHASHA, D. E., Computer Science
SHATAH, J. M. I., Mathematics
SHELLEY, M. J., Mathematics and Neural Science
SOKAL, A., Physics and Mathematics
SPENCER, J. H., Mathematics and Computer Science
STRAUSS, H. R., Computational Plasma Physics
TERZOPOULOS, D., Computer Science and Mathematics, Science
VARADHAN, S. R. S., Mathematics, Science
WEITZNER, H., Mathematics
WIDLUND, O. B., Computer Science and Mathematics
WRIGHT, M. H., Computer Science
YAP, C. K., Computer Science
YAU, H.-T., Mathematics
YOUNG, L.-S., Mathematics
ZASLAVSKY, G., Physics and Mathematics

Institute of Fine Arts (1 East 78th St, New York, NY 10021; tel. (212) 992-5800; fax (212) 992-5807; e-mail ifa.program@nyu.edu; internet www.nyu.edu/gsas/dept/fineart):

ALEXANDER, J. J. G., Fine Arts
BAER, N. S., Conservation
BROWN, J., Fine Arts
COHEN, J.-L., History of Architecture
EISLER, C., Fine Arts
ELLIS, M. H., Conservation
FAIRCHILD, S., Fine Arts
HANSEN, D. P., Fine Arts
KOPCKE, G. H., Humanities
MARINCOLA, M., Conservation
MATHEWS, T. F., History of Art
NOCHLIN, L., Modern Art
O'CONNOR, D., Ancient Egyptian Art
POSNER, D., Fine Arts
ROSENBLUM, R., Modern European Art, Fine Arts
SANDLER, L. F., Fine Arts
SOUCEK, P. P., Islamic Art
STORR, R., Modern Art
SULLIVAN, E. J., Fine Arts
TRACHTENBERG, M., History of Fine Arts
VARNEDOE, J. K. T., History of Art

WALLACE, L. A., Ancient Egyptian Art
WEIL-GARRIS BRANDT, K., Fine Arts
WESTERMANN, M., Fine Arts

Shirley M. Ehrenkranz School of Social Work (1 Washington Square North, New York, NY 10003; internet www.nyu.edu/socialwork):

ANASTAS, J. W.
DANE, B.
ENGLAND, S.
FESTINGER, T. B.
GOLDSTEIN, E. G.
HOLDEN, G.
LANDSBERG, G.
MEENAGHAN, T. M.
MILLS, L. G.
MISHNE, J.
PADGETT, D.
SEINFELD, J.
STRAUSSNER, S. L.

School of Law (110 West 3rd St, New York, NY 10012; internet www.law.nyu.edu):

ADLER, A. M., Law
ADLER, B. E., Law
ALLEN, W. T., Law and Business
ALSTON, P., Law
AMSTERDAM, A. G., Law
ANGELOS, C., Law
ARLEN, J., Law
BEEN, V. L., Law
BENKLER, Y., Law
BILLMAN, B. D., Law
BURNS, S. E., Clinical Law
CALDWELL, P. M., Law
CHASE, O. G., Law
CHEVIGNY, P. G., Law
COHEN, J. A., Law
CUNNINGHAM, N. B., Law
DAINES, R. M., Law
DALE, H. P., Philanthropy and the Law
DAVIS, P. C., Lawyering and Ethics
DORSEN, N., Law
DREYFUSS, R. C., Law
DWORKIN, R. M., Law
ESTREICHER, S., Law
EUSTICE, J. S., Taxation
FIRST, H., Law
FOX, E. M., Trade Regulation
FRIEDMAN, B., Law
GALOWITZ, P., Law
GARLAND, D. W., Law
GEISTFELD, M., Law
GILLERS, S., Law
GILLETTE, C. P., Contract Law
GOLOVE, D. M., Law
GUGGENHEIM, M. F., Clinical Law
HERSHKOFF, H., Law
HERTZ, R. A., Clinical Law
HOLMES, S. T., Law
JACOBS, J. B., Constitutional Law and the Courts
KAHAN, M., Law
KINGSBURY, B., Law
KORNHAUSER, L. A., Law
LAW, S. A., Law
LEVINSON, D., Law
LÓPEZ, G., Clinical Law
LOWENFELD, A. F., International Law
MAGUIGAN, H., Clinical Law
MALMAN, L. L., Law
MARTELL, L. A., Law
MERON, T., Law
MILLER, G. P., Law
MORAWETZ, N., Clinical Law
MURPHY, L., Law
NAGEL, T., Law
NELSON, W. E., Law
NEUBORNE, B., Law
NOBLE, R. K., Law
PILDES, R. H., Law
PRICE, M. K., Law
REID, J. P., Law
REVESZ, R. L., Law
RICHARDS, D. A. J., Law
SAGER, L., Law
SCHENK, D. H., Taxation

SCHILL, M. H., Law and Urban Planning
SCHMOLKA, L. L., Law
SCHULHOFER, S. J., Law
SCOTT, H. S., Law
SEXTON, J., Law
SHAVIRO, D. N., Law
SIEGEL, S., Law
SILBERMAN, L. J., Law
SORTER, G. H., Law
STEINES Jr, J. P., Law
STEWART, R. B., Law
TAYLOR-THOMPSON, K. A., Clinical Law
THOMPSON, A. C., Law
UPHAM, F. K., Law
WEILER, J. H. H., Law
ZIMMERMAN, D. L., Law

School of Medicine (550 First Ave, New York, NY 10016; tel. (212) 263-7300; internet www.med.nyu.edu):

ABADIR, A. R., Anaesthesiology
ABELE, M. G., Radiology
ABRAMS, S., Psychiatry
ABRAMSON, S. B., Medicine, Rheumatology, Pathology
ADESNIK, M. B., Cell Biology
AIGES, H. W., Paediatrics
AL-ASKARI, S., Urology
ALBANO, A. M., Psychiatry
ALBOM, M. J., Dermatology
AMELAR, R. D., Urology
ANGRIST, B. M., Psychiatry
ARGYROS, T. G., Medicine
ARKEL, Y. S., Obstetrics and Gynaecology
ARLOW, J. A., Psychiatry
ARONOFF, M. S., Psychiatry
ARTMAN, M., Paediatric Surgery, Pharmacology
ASTON, S. J., Surgery
AUERBACH, R., Dermatology
AXEL, P. L., Radiology
AXELROD, F. B., Dysautonomia Treatment, Neurology
AYVAZIAN, L. F., Medicine
BAKER, R. G., Physiology, Neuroscience
BALDWIN, D. S., Medicine, Nephrology
BALLARD, H. S., Medicine
BARKIN, L., Psychiatry
BARRON, B. A., Obstetrics and Gynaecology
BASCH, R. S., Pathology
BASILICO, C., Microbiology
BAUMANN, F. G., Surgery
BEASLEY, R. W., Surgery, Plastic and Reconstructive Surgery
BEATTIE, C. N., Anaesthesiology
BECKER, J. A., Radiology
BELASCO, J. G., Microbiology
BELMAN, S., Environmental Medicine
BEN-YISHAY, Y., Rehabilitation Medicine
BENJAMIN, V., Neurosurgery
BERANBAUM, S. L., Radiology
BERCZELLER, P. H., Medicine
BERG, P., Medicine
BERGER, M. M., Psychiatry
BERKELEY, A. S., Obstetrics and Gynaecology
BERNSTEIN, R. L., Anaesthesiology
BHANOT, O. S., Environmental Medicine
BHARDWAJ, N., Medicine Physiology, Neuroscience Pharmacology
BIRNBAUM, B. A., Radiology
BLANCK, T. J. J., Anaesthesiology, Physiology, Neuroscience
BLASER, M., Internal Medicine, Microbiology
BLAUGRUND, S. M., Otolaryngology
BLOCK, J. M., Neurology
BLUM, H. P., Psychiatry
BLUM, M., Medicine, Endocrinology Radiology
BODIAN, E. L., Dermatology
BOGART, B. I., Cell Biology
BORKOWSKY, W., Paediatrics
BOSLAND, M. C., Environmental Medicine, Urology
BOUFFORD, J. I., Paediatrics

BOXER, R. A., Paediatrics
BOYD, A. D., Surgery, Cardiothoracic Surgery
BRANCACCIO, R. R., Dermatology
BRODIE, J. D., Psychiatry
BROOME, J. D., Pathology
BROTMAN, A. W., Psychiatry
BROWN, E. R., Neurosurgery
BROWN, J. W., Neurology
BRUNO, M. S., Clinical Medicine
BUDMAN, D. R., Medicine, Oncology
BURAKOFF, S. J., Medicine, Oncology
BURDEN, S. J., Pharmacology
BURDOCK, E. I., Psychiatry
BURNS, F. J., Environmental Medicine
BUYON, J. P., Medicine, Rheumatology
BYSTRYN, J.-C., Dermatology
CAHILL, K. M., Medicine
CALANOG, A. M., Obstetrics and Gynaecology
CANCRO, R., Psychiatry
CAPAN, L., Anaesthesiology
CARR, R. E., Ophthalmology
CASTELLANOS, F. X., Child and Adolescent Psychiatry, Clinical Radiology
CHALFIN, L. S., Psychiatry
CHANDRA, M. M., Paediatrics
CHANDRA, R., Radiology
CHAO, M. V., Cell Biology
CHARAP, M. H., Medicine, General Medicine
CHARLES, N. C., Ophthalmology
CHARNEY, A. N., Medicine, Nephrology
CHASSIN, J. L., Surgery
CHESLER, M., Neurosurgery, Physiology and Neuroscience
CHESS, S., Psychiatry
CHIORAZZI, N., Medicine, Infectious Diseases and Immunology Pathology
CHIU, D. T., Surgery, Plastic and Reconstructive Surgery
CITROME, L. L., Psychiatry
CLAPS, A. A., Paediatrics
COBRINIK, R., Paediatrics
COHEN, B. S., Environmental Medicine
COHEN, I. J., Ophthalmology
COHEN, N. L., Otolaryngology
COHEN, T., Medicine
COLLINS, A. H., Psychiatry
COLOMBO, A., Medicine
COLTRERA, J. T., Psychiatry
COOPER, J. S., Radiation Oncology
COOPER, N. S., Pathology
COOPER, P. R., Neurosurgery, Orthopaedic Surgery
COPLAN, N. L., Medicine
COSTA E SILVA, J. A., Psychiatry
COSTA, M., Environmental Medicine, Pharmacology
COWAN, N. J., Biochemistry
CRONSTEIN, B. N., Medicine, Rheumatology, Pathology, Pharmacology
CULLIFORD, A. T., Surgery, Cardiothoracic Surgery
CURTIN, J. P., Obstetrics and Gynaecology
D'AMICO, R. A., Ophthalmology
DANCIS, J., Paediatrics
DANILOWICZ, D. A., Paediatrics
DANTUONO, L. M., Obstetrics and Gynaecology
DAUM, F., Paediatrics
DAVID, R., Paediatrics
DAVIES, E. A., Paediatrics
DAVIS, J. E., Urology
DE LEON, M. J., Psychiatry
DEBROVNER, C. H., Obstetrics and Gynaecology
DEFENDI, V., Oncology, Pathology
DEGNAN, T. J., Medicine, Oncology
DELISI, L. E., Psychiatry
DELPHIN, E. S., Anaesthesiology
DEMOPOULOS, R. I., Pathology
DePASQUALE, N. P., Medicine
DEUTSCH, B. G., Psychiatry
DEVINSKY, O., Neurology
DEWEY, S. L., Psychiatry

DHAWAN, V., Neurology
DILLER, L., Rehabilitation Medicine
DODICK, J. M., Ophthalmology
DOLGIN, M., Medicine, Cardiology
DRLICA, K. A., Microbiology
DUBIN, L., Urology
DUBNAU, D., Microbiology
DUBOIS, M. Y., Anaesthesiology
DUSTIN, M. L., Pathology
EBERSTEIN, A., Rehabilitation Medicine
EIDELBERG, D., Neurology, Neurosurgery
ELSBACH, P., Medicine
ENG, K., Surgery
EVANS, H. L., Environmental Medicine
FANTL, J. A., Obstetrics and Gynaecology
FARBER, S. J., Medicine, Nephrology
FARCON, E. M., Urology
FARCY, J.-P. C., Orthopaedic Surgery
FEINBERG, A. W., Medicine, Geriatrics
FEINER, H. D., Pathology
FERRIS, S. H., Psychiatry
FINGER, P. T., Ophthalmology
FINLAY, J. L., Paediatrics, Neurosurgery
FINLAY, J. R., Ophthalmology
FIRESTEIN, S. K., Psychiatry
FISCHEL, R. E., Psychiatry
FISHER, A. A., Dermatology
FISHER, M. M., Paediatrics
FISHER, Y. L., Ophthalmology
FISHMAN, G. I., Medicine, Cardiology Physiology and Neuroscience Pharmacology
FLOWER, R. W., Ophthalmology
FORMENTI, S. C., Medical Oncology
FOSTER, J. R., Psychiatry
FOX, A. C., Medicine, Cardiology
FRANCES, R. J., Psychiatry
FRANGIONE, B., Pathology, Psychiatry
FRANK, J., Cell Biology
FRANKEL, V. H., Orthopaedic Surgery
FRANKS JR, A. G., Dermatology
FREEDBERG, I. M., Dermatology, Cell Biology
FREEDMAN, M. L., Medicine, Geriatrics
FRENKEL, K., Environmental Medicine, Pathology
FRIEDMAN, H. S., Medicine
FRIEDMAN-KIEN, A. E., Dermatology
FROST, J. O., Otolaryngology
FURMANSKI, P., Pathology
GABRIEL, H. P., Psychiatry
GALANTER, M., Psychiatry
GALLOWAY, A. C., Surgery, Cardiothoracic Surgery
GARAY, S. M., Medicine, Pulmonary and Critical Care
GARDNER, E. P., Physiology and Neuroscience
GENIESER, N. B., Radiology
GEORGE, A. E., Radiology
GERONEMUS, R. G., Dermatology
GITTELMAN, M. I., Psychiatry
GLENN, J., Psychiatry
GLICKMAN, R. M., Medicine
GODSON, G. N., Biochemistry
GOLDBERG, E., Neurology
GOLDBERG, J. D., Environmental Medicine
GOLDBERGER, M., Psychiatry
GOLDFRANK, L. R., Medicine, Emergency Medicine Surgery
GOLDRING, R. M., Medicine, Pulmonary and Critical Care
GOLDSTEIN, N., Psychiatry
GOLDSTEIN, S. R., Obstetrics and Gynaecology
GOLIMBU, C. N., Radiology
GOLIMBU, M. N., Urology
GOLOMB, F. M., Surgery, Surgical Oncology
GONEN, O., Radiology
GOODGOLD, A. L., Neurology, Radiology
GOPINATHAN, G., Neurology
GOUGE, T. H., Surgery
GRANT, A. D., Orthopaedic Surgery
GREBB, J. A., Psychiatry
GRECO, G. J., Ophthalmology
GREEN, M. R., Psychiatry
GREENE, J. B., Medicine

GREENSTEIN, V. C., Ophthalmology
GREGERSEN, P. K., Medicine, Rheumatology, Pathology
GRIECO, A. J., Medicine, General Medicine
GRIFO, J. A., Obstetrics and Gynaecology
GROSSI, E. A., Surgery, Cardiothoracic Surgery
GROSSMAN, R. I., Radiology, Neurosurgery, Neurology, and Physiology and Neuroscience
GROSSMAN, S., Psychiatry
GRUEN, P. H., Psychiatry
GUYER, D. R., Ophthalmology
HAGIN, R. A., Psychiatry
HAJDU, S. I., Pathology
HALPERIN, J. J., Neurology
HALPERT, E., Psychiatry
HARIN, A., Paediatrics
HARLAP, S., Obstetrics and Gynaecology
HARLEY, N. H., Environmental Medicine
HARPER, R. G., Paediatrics, Obstetrics and Gynaecology
HARRIS, H. W., Medicine, Pulmonary and Critical Care
HARRIS, M. N., Surgery, Surgical Oncology
HARRISON, R. M., Ophthalmology
HAZZI, C. G., Medicine
HEITLER, M. S., Paediatrics
HELPERN, J. A., Radiology, Psychiatry, Physiology and Neuroscience
HILLER, J. M., Psychiatry
HILLMAN, D. E., Physiology and Biophysics
HILZ, M. J., Neurology, Medicine
HIRSCH, C. S., Forensic Medicine Pathology
HIRSCHHORN, R., Medicine, Genetics, Cell Biology, Paediatrics
HOFFMAN, I. R., Medicine
HOLZMAN, R. S., Medicine, Infectious Diseases and Immunology, Environmental Medicine
HOOD, R. M., Surgery
HORNBLASS, A., Ophthalmology
HOROWITZ, L., Medicine
HOROWITZ, M. H., Psychiatry
HOROWITZ, S. T., Obstetrics and Gynaecology
HSU, L. Y.-F., Paediatrics, Obstetrics and Gynaecology
IOACHIM, H. L., Pathology
ISRAEL, J. S., Anaesthesiology
ITIL, T., Psychiatry
ITOH, M., Rehabilitation Medicine
JACOBS, A. J., Obstetrics and Gynaecology
JACOBS, D. R., Medicine
JACOBS, J. B., Otolaryngology
JACOBS, T. J., Psychiatry
JAFAR, J. J., Neurosurgery
JAFFE, W. L., Orthopaedic Surgery
JAHSS, M. H., Orthopaedic Surgery
JAVITT, D. C., Psychiatry
JAVITT, N. B., Medicine, Gastroenterology, Paediatrics
JELINEK, J. E., Dermatology
JELINEK, W. R., Biochemistry
JIMENEZ, A. C., Rehabilitation Medicine
JOHANSON, K.-E., Urology
JOHN, E. R., Psychiatry
JONAS, S., Neurology
JONG, A. Y., Psychiatry
JOYNER, A. L., Cell Biology, Physiology and Neuroscience
KAHN, E. I., Surgical Pathology, Clinical Paediatrics
KAHN, M. L., Cardiology
KALOGERAKIS, M. G., Psychiatry
KAMHOLZ, S. L., Medicine
KAMM, F. M., Medicine
KANOF, N. B., Dermatology
KANTOR, T. G., Medicine
KAPLAN, L. A., Pathology
KAPLAN, M. H., Medicine, Infectious Diseases and Immunology
KAPLAN, S. J., Clinical Psychiatry
KARPATKIN, M. H., Paediatrics
KARPATKIN, S., Medicine, Haematology
KATZ, J. L., Clinical Psychiatry

KATZ, L. A., Medicine, Nephrology
KATZ, S., Medicine
KATZ, S. E., Psychiatry
KEEGAN, A. F., Radiology
KEILL, S. L., Psychiatry
KELLY, P. J., Neurosurgery
KENAN, S., Orthopaedic Surgery
KENNEDY, J. T., Medicine
KERMANI, E. J., Psychiatry
KESSLER, R. E., Surgery
KHATAMEE, M. A., Obstetrics and Gynaecology
KING, S. A., Psychiatry
KITTREDGE, R. D., Radiology
KLEIN, H. L., Biochemistry, Medicine
KLEIN, I. L., Medicine, Endocrinology, Cell Biology
KLEIN, R. G., Psychiatry
KLEINBERG, D. L, Medicine, Endocrinology
KOCHEN, J. A., Paediatrics
KOHAN, S. L., Obstetrics and Gynaecology
KOLODNY, E. H., Neurology
KOMISAR, A., Otolaryngology
KOPF, A. W., Dermatology
KOPLEWICZ, H. S., Child and Adolescent Psychiatry, Clinical Paediatrics
KORELITZ, B. I., Medicine
KOVAL, K. J., Orthopaedic Surgery
KOZ, G., Psychiatry
KRAMER, E. L., Radiology
KRAMER, F. R., Microbiology
KRAMER, M., Psychiatry
KRASINSKI, K. M., Paediatrics, Environmental Medicine
KRASNER, R. C. J., Medicine
KREIBICH, G., Cell Biology
KREIS, W., Medicine, Oncology
KREY, L. C., Obstetrics and Gynaecology, Cell Biology
KRONZON, I., Medicine, Cardiology
KUHNS, T. R., Ophthalmology
KUMMER, F., Orthopaedic Surgery
KUPERSMITH, M. J., Neurology, Ophthalmology
KUSCHNER, M., Pathology, Environmental Medicine
LAJTHA, A. L., Psychiatry
LANE, M. E., Rehabilitation Medicine
LANYI, V. F., Rehabilitation Medicine
LASKA, E. M., Psychiatry
LASKIN, M., Psychiatry
LAVKER, R. M., Dermatology
LEE, M. H. M., Rehabilitation Medicine
LEE-HUANG, S., Biochemistry
LEGGIADRO, R. J., Paediatrics
LEHMAN, W. B., Orthopaedic Surgery
LEHMANN, R., Cell Biology
LEHNEIS, H. R., Rehabilitation Medicine
LEITMAN, B. S., Radiology
LEPOR, H., Urology, Pharmacology
LESSER, G. T., Medicine
LEVIN, R. I., Medicine, Cardiology
LEVINE, B. B., Medicine, Infectious Diseases and Immunology
LEVINE, D. N., Neurology
LEVINE, I. S., Psychiatry
LEVITZ, M., Obstetrics and Gynaecology
LEVY, D. E., Molecular Pathology
LEW, A., Psychiatry
LEWIS, D. O., Psychiatry
LIFSHITZ, K., Psychiatry
LIFSHITZ, M. S., Pathology
LILLESKOV, R. K., Psychiatry
LINDENMAYER, J.-P., Psychiatry
LIPKIN, G., Dermatology
LIPKIN JR, M., Medicine, Primary Care
LIPPMANN, M., Environmental Medicine
LISMAN, R., Ophthalmology
LITTMAN, D. R., Molecular Immunology, Pathology and Microbiology
LLINAS, R., Physiology and Neuroscience
LOCKWOOD, C. J., Obstetrics and Gynaecology
LOFTUS, T. A., Psychiatry
LOVECCHIO, J. L., Obstetrics and Gynaecology

LOWENSTEIN, J., Medicine, Nephrology
LUNTZ, M. H., Ophthalmology
LUSSKIN, R., Orthopaedic Surgery
LYNFIELD, J., Paediatrics
MA, D. M., Rehabilitation Medicine
MAGRAMM, I., Ophthalmology
MAHONEY, C. J., Forensic Medicine
MALACH, M., Medicine
MANGER, W. M., Medicine
MANGIARDI, J. R., Neurosurgery
MANHEIMER, E. D., Medicine
MANNUZZA, S., Psychiatry
MARCOS, L. R., Psychiatry
MARGOULEFF, D., Medicine, Nuclear Medicine
MARGOLIS, R. U., Pharmacology
MARKOWITZ, J. F., Paediatrics
MARMOR, M., Environmental Medicine, Medicine, Pulmonary and Critical Care
MARSHALL, C. H., Radiology
MAS, F. G., Psychiatry
MASDEU, J. C., Neurology
MATTSSON, A., Psychiatry
McCARTHY, J. G., Plastic Surgery
MEGIBOW, A. J., Radiology
MEHL, S. J., Medicine
MEISELAS, L. E., Medicine, General Medicine
MEISLIN, A. G., Paediatrics
MERLINO, J. P., Psychiatry
MERUELO, D., Pathology
MESSITE, J., Environmental Medicine
MEYERSON, A. T., Psychiatry
MICHELIS, M. F., Medicine
MILANO, A. M., Medicine
MINDICH, L., Microbiology
MINUCHIN, P. P., Psychiatry
MINUCHIN, S., Psychiatry
MITNICK, H. J., Medicine
MONTEAGUDO, A., Obstetrics and Gynaecology
MORALES, P. A., Urology
MOSCATELLI, D. A., Cell Biology
MOSES, J. W., Medicine
MOSKOWITZ, P. K., Internal Medicine
MUGGIA, F. M., Oncology
NACHTIGALL, L. E., Obstetrics and Gynaecology
NACHTIGALL, R. H., Medicine
NAFTCHI, N. E., Rehabilitation Medicine
NAIDICH, D. P., Radiology
NAIDICH, J. B., Radiology
NARINS, R. S., Dermatology
NASS, R. D., Neurology
NEOPHYTIDES, A. N., Neurology
NEUBAUER, P. B., Psychiatry
NEWMAN, D., Psychiatry
NEZIROGLU, F. A., Psychiatry
NICHOLSON, C., Physiology and Neuroscience
NIXON, R. A., Psychiatry, Cell Biology
NORDIN, M., Orthopaedic Surgery, Environmental Medicine
NOVICK, R. P., Microbiology Medicine, Pulmonary and Critical Care
NOZ, M. E., Radiology
NUSSENZWEIG, R. S., Medical and Molecular Parasitology
NUSSENZWEIG, V., Pathology
O'HARE, D. B., Paediatrics
OBSTBAUM, S. A., Ophthalmology
OLIVA-LOPEZ, E., Environmental Medicine
OPLER, L. A., Psychiatry
ORENTREICH, N., Dermatology
ORGEL, S., Psychiatry
ORLOW, S. J., Paediatric Dermatology
ORRIS, L., Environmental Medicine
ORT, P. J., Orthopaedic Surgery
OSTRER, H., Paediatrics, Pathology, Medicine
OVARY, Z., Pathology
PACHTER, H. L., Surgery
PACKER, S., Ophthalmology
PAHWA, S., Paediatrics
PANKOVICH, A. M., Orthopaedic Surgery
PAPERNIK, D. S., Psychiatry

PARISIEN, J. S., Orthopaedic Surgery
PARKS, W. P., Paediatrics, Microbiology
PASTERNACK, B. S., Environmental Medicine
PEARSON, J., Pathology
PELCOVITZ, D., Psychiatry
PELLICER, A. G., Pathology
PEPPER, B., Psychiatry
PERRY, R. I., Psychiatry
PESELOW, E. D., Psychiatry
PHILLIPS, R. A., Medicine
PHILLIPS-QUAGLIATA, J. M., Pathology
PINE, D. S., Psychiatry
PINTER, A., Microbiology
PLAINE, L., Urology
POMARA, N., Psychiatry
PORGES, R. F., Obstetrics and Gynaecology
PORTNOW, S. L., Psychiatry
POSNER, M. A., Orthopaedic Surgery
POST, R. C., Obstetrics and Gynaecology
POTMESIL, M., Radiology
POTTASH, A. C., Psychiatry
PRINCE, A. M., Pathology
QUARTERMAIN, D., Neurology, Physiology and Neuroscience
RACKOW, E., Medicine, Cardiology
RAFII, M., Radiology
RAICHT, R. F., Medicine, Gastroenterology
RAMSAY, D. L., Clinical Dermatology
RAUSEN, A. R., Paediatrics
RAYNOR, R. B., Neurosurgery
REEM, G. H., Pharmacology
REES, T. D., Surgery, Plastic and Reconstructive Surgery
REICH, T., Experimental Surgery
REISBERG, B., Psychiatry
RICHARDSON, M. A., Psychiatry
RIFKIN, D. B., Medicine and Cell Biology
RIGEL, D. S., Dermatology
RILES, T. S., Surgery
ROBBINS, E. S., Psychiatry
ROBBINS, H., Orthopaedic Surgery
ROBINS, P., Dermatology
ROGERS, B. O., Surgery
ROM, Jr, W. N., Medicine and Environmental Medicine
RON, D., Medicine, Endocrinology
ROSENBLUTH, J., Physiology and Neuroscience
ROSENBERG, Z. S., Radiology
ROSENFELD, D. L., Obstetrics and Gynaecology
ROSES, D. F., Surgery
ROSNER, R., Psychiatry
ROSSMAN, T. G., Environmental Medicine
ROTHSTEIN, A. A., Psychiatry
ROTROSEN, J. P., Psychiatry
ROUBIN, G. S., Medicine
ROVIT, R. L., Neurosurgery
ROWAN, R. L., Urology
ROY, A., Psychiatry
RUBERMAN, W., Environmental Medicine
RUBIN, S. E., Ophthalmology
RUDY, B., Physiology and Neuroscience, Biochemistry
RUOFF, M. J., Medicine
SABATINI, D. D., Cell Biology
SADOCK, B. J., Psychiatry
SADOCK, V. A., Psychiatry
SALZER, J. L., Neurology, Cell Biology
SAMUELS, H. H., Pharmacology and Medicine
SARNO, Jr, J. E., Rehabilitation Medicine
SARNO, M. T., Rehabilitation Medicine
SAXE, D. H., Surgery
SCHACHNE, L., Ophthalmology
SCHACHT, R. G., Paediatrics
SCHARFMAN, M. A., Psychiatry
SCHERR, L., Medicine, General Medicine
SCHLOSSMAN, A., Ophthalmology
SCHMIDT-SAROSI, C. L., Obstetrics and Gynaecology
SCHNEIDER, R. J., Microbiology
SCHOENFELD, M., Psychiatry
SCHREIBER, S. S., Clinical Medicine
SCHWARTZ, S., Medicine

SEDLIS, E., Paediatrics
SEIPLE, W. H., Ophthalmology
SHAPIRO, E., Urology
SHAW, L. N., Psychiatry
SHENGOLD, L. L., Psychiatry
SHORE, R. E., Environmental Medicine
SHUPACK, J. L., Dermatology
SIDTIS, J. J., Psychiatry
SIEGEL, C., Psychiatry
SIEGEL, I. M., Experimental Ophthalmology
SILBER, A., Psychiatry
SILVER, J., Medicine, Molecular Medicine, Pathology
SILVER, J. M., Psychiatry
SILVERBERG, M., Paediatrics
SILVERMAN, M. A., Psychiatry
SIMMS, H. H., Surgery
SIMON, E. J., Psychiatry, Pharmacology
SIMPSON, J. I., Physiology and Neuroscience
SINGER, M. H., Psychiatry
SKOLNICK, P., Psychiatry
SLABY, A. E., Psychiatry
SLAKTER, J. S., Ophthalmology
SLIPP, S., Psychiatry
SMALL, A. M., Psychiatry
SMITH, B. F., Ophthalmology
SMITH, I., Microbiology
SMITH, R. C., Psychiatry
SNYDER, C. A., Environmental Medicine
SOBERMAN, R. J., Medicine, Nephrology
SOLOMON, J. J., Environmental Medicine
SOLOWEY, A. C., Surgery
SOTER, N. A., Dermatology
SPATZ, M., Urology
SPEISER, P. W., Clinical Paediatrics
SPENCER, F. C., Surgery
SPEYER, J. L., Medicine, Oncology
SPITZER, M., Clinical Obstetrics and Gynaecology
SPRITZ, N., Medicine, Endocrinology
STEIGBIGEL, N. H., Medicine
STEINETZ, B. G., Environmental Medicine
STENSON, S. M., Ophthalmology
STERN, A., Pharmacology
STONE, E. A., Psychiatry
STONE, S. M., Paediatrics
SUGIMORI, M., Physiology and Neuroscience
SUN, T.-T., Dermatology
SUNSHINE, A., Medicine
SUSSMAN, N., Psychiatry
SVERDLIK, S. S., Rehabilitation Medicine
TAINTOR, Z. C., Psychiatry
TANCREDI, L. R., Psychiatry
TANG, M.-S., Environmental Medicine, Pathology Medicine
TAPPER, M. L., Medicine
TEEBOR, G. W., Pathology, Environmental Medicine
TESSLER, A. N., Urology
TESTA, N. N., Orthopaedic Surgery
THOMAS, A., Psychiatry
TICE, D. A., Surgery
TIMOR, I. E., Obstetrics and Gynaecology
TOBIAS, H., Medicine
TOLK, C. S., Psychiatry
TOMATIS, L., Environmental Medicine
TONIOLO, P. G., Environmental Medicine, Obstetrics and Gynaecology
TRUJILLO, M., Psychiatry
TUCHMAN, M., Medicine
TUNICK, P. A., Medicine, Cardiology
TZIMAS, N. A., Orthopaedic Surgery
VADASZ, C., Psychiatry
VALENTINE, F. T., Medicine, Infectious Diseases and Immunology
VANDERBERG, J. P., Medical and Molecular Parasitology
VAZQUEZ, C. I., Psychiatry
VILCEK, J. T., Microbiology
VINCIGUERRA, V. P., Medicine, Oncology
VOGEL, S. A., Psychiatry
VOLAVKA, J., Psychiatry

VORONTSOV, M. A., Physiology and Neuroscience
WAISMAN, J., Pathology
WALKER, P. S., Orthopaedic Surgery
WALLACH, R. C., Obstetrics and Gynaecology
WALLACH, S., Medicine
WALTZMAN, S. B., Otolaryngology
WAN, L. S., Obstetrics and Gynaecology
WANG, B. C., Anaesthesiology
WAPNIR, R. A., Paediatrics, Biochemistry
WARNER, R. S., Urology
WARSHAW, L. J., Environmental Medicine
WEINBERG, H. J., Neurology
WEINBERG, S., Dermatology
WEINSTEIN, H. C., Psychiatry
WEISSMANN, G., Medicine, Rheumatology
WELSH, H. K., Psychiatry
WEST, A. B., Pathology
WIKLER, N. S., Clinical Medicine
WILKES, B. M., Medicine, Nephrology
WISHNICK, M. M., Paediatrics
WITKOVSKY, P., Experimental Ophthalmology, Physiology and Neuroscience
WOLFF, B. B., Psychiatry
YANNUZZI, L. A., Ophthalmology
YARYURA-TOBIAS, J. A., Psychiatry
YOUNG, B. K., Obstetrics and Gynaecology
YOUNG, L. Y., Environmental Medicine
YUVIENCO, F. P., Urology
ZAVALA, F., Medical and Molecular Parasitology
ZELIKOVSKY, G., Urology
ZIDE, B. M., Surgery, Plastic and Reconstructive Surgery
ZIFF, E. B., Biochemistry
ZIMMON, D. S., Medicine, Gastroenterology
ZOLLA-PAZNER, S. B., Pathology
ZUCKER-FRANKLIN, D., Medicine, Haematology
ZUCKERMAN, J. D., Orthopaedic Surgery

Steinhardt School of Education (82 Washington Square East, New York, NY 10003; tel. (212) 998-5030; internet www.nyu.edu/education):

CAROTHERS, S. C., Teaching and Learning
KOVNER, C., Nursing
MAYHER, J. S., English Education
McCLOWRY, S., Nursing
MILLER, M. C., Culture and Communication
NORMAN, E., Nursing
RICHARDSON, R., Higher Education
STAGE, F., Higher Education

Leonard N. Stern School of Business (Henry Kaufman Management Center, 44 West Fourth St, New York, NY 10012; tel. (212) 998-0100; internet www.stern.nyu.edu):

BALACHANDRAN, K. R., Accounting and Operations Management
BARDES, P., Accounting and Finance
BARTOV, E., Accounting, Business Ethics
BILDERSEE, J. S., Accounting
BRIEF, R., Statistics and Accounting
HIPSCHER, A., Accounting, Taxation and Business Law
JONES, S., Accounting, Taxation and Business Law
LIVNAT, J., Accounting
MORAN, M. J., Accounting
NICHOLS, C. W., Business Ethics
RONEN, J., Accounting
SORTER, G. H., Accounting and Law
WIESEN, J., Accounting, Taxation and Business Law
ZICKLIN, L., Accounting

Tisch School of Arts (721 Broadway, New York, NY 10003; internet www.nyu.edu/tisch):

CAMPBELL, M. S., Art and Public Policy
CANEMAKER, J., Film and Television
COOPER, P., Film and Television
DANCYGER, K., Film and Television
FROST, E. C., Film, Television, and Radio

JENKIN, L., Dramatic Writing
KIMBRELL, M. A., Acting and Directing Studies
KIRSHENBLATT-GIMBLETT, B., Performance Studies
MARTIN, R., Art and Public Policy
MICHELSON, A., Cinema Studies
MILLER, T., Cinema Studies
NEIPRIS, J., Dramatic Writing
SCHECHNER, R., Performance Studies
SHOHAT, E., Art and Public Policy
SKLAR, R., Cinema Studies
SMITH, A. D., Performance Studies
SMITH, A. D., Performance Studies
STAM, R., Cinema Studies
STONEY, G. C., Film
TAYLOR, D., Performance Studies
WILLIS, D., Photography and Imaging

Robert F. Wagner Graduate School of Public Service (4 Washington Square North, New York, NY 10003; tel. (212) 998-7400; internet www.nyu.edu/wagner):

BERNE, R., Public Policy and Financial Management
BOISE, W. B., Public Administration
BOUFFORD, J. I., Health Policy and Public Service
BRECHER, C. M., Public and Health Administration
CHERKASKY, M., Health Policy and Management
FINKLER, S. A., Public and Health Administration, Accounting, and Financial Management
KOVNER, A., Public and Health Management
KROPF, R., Health Management
LEW, J. J., Public Administration
LIGHT, P., Public Service
MOSS, M., Urban Policy and Planning
RODWIN, V. G., Health Policy and Management
SCHALL, E., Health Policy and Management
SCHILL, M. H., Law and Urban Planning
SPARROW, R. L., Public Management
STAFFORD, W. W., Public Policy and Planning
STIEFEL, L., Economics
ZIMMERMAN, R., Planning and Public Administration

NIAGARA UNIVERSITY

NY 14109
Telephone: (716) 285-1212
Internet: www.niagara.edu
Founded 1856
President: Rev. JOSEPH L. LEVESQUE
Executive Vice-President and Vice-President for Academic Affairs: Dr BONNIE ROSE
Dean of Admissions and Records: GEORGE C. PACHTER
Dean of Student Affairs: JOSEPH H. CUDA
Director of Libraries: DAVID SCHOEN
Library of 279,793 vols
Number of teachers: 323
Number of students: 3,689
Publications: *Index* (monthly), *Niagaran* (annually)

DEANS

Arts and Sciences: Dr NANCY McGLEN
Business Administration: Dr JOHN A. HELMUTH (acting)
Education: Dr DEBRA COLLEY
Hospitality and Tourism Management: Dr GARY D. PRATZEL

NYACK COLLEGE

Nyack, NY 10960-3698
Telephone: (845) 358-1710
Fax: (845) 358-1751

E-mail: admissions@nyack.edu
Internet: www.nyack.edu
Founded 1882
Academic year: September to May
President: Dr DAVID E. SCHROEDER
Provost and Vice-President for Academic Affairs: DAVID F. TURK
Executive Vice-President and Treasurer: DAVID C. JENNINGS
Vice-President for Advancement: SHINO JOHN
Vice-President for Student Development: EARL MILLER
Registrar: SUE HO
Librarian: LINDA POSTON
Library of 133,000 vols
Number of teachers: 288 (107 part-time, 181 full-time)
Number of students: 2,908.

PACE UNIVERSITY

Pace Plaza, New York, NY 10038
Telephone: (212) 346-1200
Internet: www.pace.edu
Founded 1906
Campuses at New York, Pleasantville and White Plains
President: Dr PATRICIA EWERS
University Registrar: MARCIA JACQUES
University Librarian: WILLIAM MURDOCK (acting)
Library of 938,158 vols, 5,100 periodicals
Number of teachers: 1,200
Number of students: 15,000.

POLYTECHNIC UNIVERSITY

6 MetroTech Center, Brooklyn, NY 11201
Telephone: (718) 260-3600
Fax: (718) 260-3136
Internet: www.poly.edu
Founded 1854
Campuses at Brooklyn, Farmingdale and Westchester
President: Dr DAVID C. CHANG
Executive Vice-President and Provost: IVAN T. FRISCH
Senior Vice-President for Finance and Administration: LEONARD CUGICK
Senior Vice-President for Institutional and Alumni Relations: Dr RICHARD THORSEN
Vice-President for Academic Operations: ROGER ROESS
Vice-Provost for Academic Development: DEANE YANG
Vice-Provost for Research and Strategic Initiatives: DONALD HOCKNEY
Director of Library Services: JANA STEVENS-RICHMAN
Number of teachers: 185 full-time
Number of students: 3,282

DEANS

Engineering: R. ROESS (Associate Provost for Academic Affairs)
Research and Graduate Studies: R. THORSEN

PRATT INSTITUTE

200 Willoughby Ave, Brooklyn, NY 11205
Telephone: (718) 636-3600
Fax: (718) 636-3785
Internet: www.pratt.edu
Founded 1887
Academic year: September to May
President: Dr THOMAS F. SCHUTTE
Vice-President for Finance: EDMUND RUTKOWSKI
Vice-President for Student Life: Dr HELEN MATUSOUR-AYRES
Vice-President for Institutional Advancement: PATRICIA HYNES

Provost: PETER BARNA
Registrar: PATRICIA CIAVALRELLI
Director of Libraries: PATRICIA CUTRIGHT

Library of 177,198 vols
Number of teachers: 867
Number of students: 4,280

Publications: *Pratt Institute Bulletin*, *Pratt-folio* (4 a year), *Gateway* (every 2 weeks), *Prattler* (every 2 weeks), *Prattonia* (annually)

DEANS

School of Art and Design: FRANK LIND
School of Architecture: TOM HANRAHAN
School of Liberal Arts and Sciences: Dr TONI OLIVIERO
Center for Professional and Continuing Education: CHARLES MUNSTER
Graduate School of Information and Library Science: Dr TULA GIANNINI (acting)

RENSSELAER POLYTECHNIC INSTITUTE

110 8th St, Troy, NY 12180-3590
Telephone: (518) 276-6000
Fax: (518) 276-6003
E-mail: admissions@rpi.edu
Internet: www.rpi.edu

Founded 1824

President: SHIRLEY ANN JACKSON
Vice-President for Administration: TOM YUR-KEWECZ
Vice-President for Finance: VIRGINIA GREGG
Vice-President for Student Life: DAVID HAVI-LAND
Vice-President for Institute Advancement: ROBBEE KOSAK
Vice-President for Government Relations: LARRY SNAVLEY
Vice-President for Human Resources and Institute Diversity (vacant)
Provost: G. DOYLE DAVES (acting)
Director, Office of Contracts and Grants: RICHARD SCAMMELL
Registrar: SHARON KUNKEL
Librarian: H. LORETTA EBERT

Library of 475,000 vols, 3,117 periodicals
Number of teachers: 374 full-time
Number of students: 6,509 (5,920 full-time, 589 part-time)

Publications: *Graduate Catalogue*, *Undergraduate Catalogue* (annually)

DEANS AND DIRECTORS

Science: G. DOYLE DAVES
Engineering: JAMES TIEN (acting)
Humanities and Social Sciences: FAYE DUCHIN
Architecture: ALAN BALFOUR
Undergraduate and Continuing Education: JACK WILSON
Management: JOSEPH ECKER

ROBERTS WESLEYAN COLLEGE

Rochester, NY 14624-1997
Telephone: (585) 594-6000
Fax: (585) 594-6371
E-mail: admissions2@roberts.edu
Internet: www.roberts.edu

Founded 1866
Academic year: September to May

President: JOHN A. MARTIN
Vice-President for Development: PETER L. MCCOWN
Vice-President and Treasurer: JAMES E. CUTHBERT
Vice-President for Admissions and Marketing: LINDA KURTZ
Vice-President for Academic Development: BURTON R. JONES
Registrar: WESLEY VANDERHOOF

Director of Financial Aid: STEPHEN FIELD
Librarian: ALFRED C. KROBER

Library of 115,921 vols
Number of teachers: 76
Number of students: 1,428

Publication: *Roberts Today* (quarterly).

ROCHESTER INSTITUTE OF TECHNOLOGY

1 Lomb Memorial Dr., Rochester, NY 14623
Telephone: (585) 475-2411
Internet: www.rit.edu

Founded 1829 as the Rochester Athenaeum

President: Dr ALBERT J. SIMONE
Provost and Vice-President for Academic Affairs: Dr STANLEY MCKENZIE
Vice-President for Development and Alumni Relations: LAUREL PRICE JONES
Vice-President for Enrollment Management and Career Services: Dr JAMES MILLER
Vice-President for Finance and Administration: Dr JAMES WATTERS
Vice-President for Student Affairs: Dr MARY-BETH COOPER
Secretary of the Institute and Assistant to the President: Dr FRED W. SMITH
Librarian: CHANDRA MCKENZIE

Library of 400,000 vols
Number of teachers: 1,347
Number of students: 15,300

Publications: *Undergraduate Bulletin* (annually), *Graduate Bulletin* (annually), *Admissions Bulletin* (annually), *Application*, *The University Magazine* (3 a year)

DEANS

College of Applied Science and Technology: WILEY R. MCKINZIE
College of Business: Dr THOMAS HOPKINS
Kate Gleason College of Engineering: Dr HARVEY PALMER
College of Imaging Arts and Sciences: Dr JOAN STONE
College of Liberal Arts: Dr ANDREW MOORE
College of Science: Dr IAN GATLEY
B. Thomas Golisano College of Computing and Information Sciences: Dr JORGE DIAZ-HERRERA
National Technical Institute for the Deaf: Dr T. ALAN HURWITZ

ROCKEFELLER UNIVERSITY

1230 York Ave, New York, NY 10021-6399
Telephone: (212) 327-8000
Internet: www.rockefeller.edu

Founded 1901; became a graduate university in 1954; name changed from Rockefeller Institute to The Rockefeller University in 1965

President: Sir PAUL NURSE
Corporate Secretary: FRED M. BOHEN (acting)
Vice-Presidents: FRED M. BOHEN (Executive), WILLIAM H. GRIESAR (and General Counsel)
Librarian: PATRICIA E. MACKEY

Library of 230,000 vols

Number of teachers: 250 professors, 69 heads of laboratories
Number of students: 398 (148 graduates, 250 research fellows)

Publications: *Journal of Experimental Medicine*, *Journal of General Physiology*, *Journal of Cell Biology*, *Journal of Clinical Investigation* (all monthly), *Scientific and Educational Programs* (annually) and occasional publications.

SAGE COLLEGES

45 Ferry St, Troy, NY 12180
Telephone: (518) 270-2000

Fax: (518) 244-6880
Internet: www.sage.edu

Founded 1916

President: Dr JEANNE H. NEFF
Vice-Presidents: WILLIAM BECKMAN (Finance and Administration), Dr DAVID MARCELL (External Relations), Dr D'ANN CAMPBELL (Academic Affairs)
Assistant Vice-President for Admissions: MICHAEL SPOSILI
Director of Libraries: KINGSLEY GREENE

Library of 350,000 vols, 1,200 periodicals
Number of teachers: 139 (92 full-time; 47 part-time)
Number of students: 1,000 full-time

Comprised of Russell Sage College, Sage College of Albany and Sage Graduate School.

ST BONAVENTURE UNIVERSITY

St Bonaventure, NY 14778
Telephone: (716) 375-2000
Fax: (716) 375-2005
Internet: www.sbu.edu

Founded 1858

Chair, Board of Trustees: SUSAN R. GREEN
President: Sr MARGARET CARNEY
Vice-President (Academic Affairs): Dr FRANK E. SAAL
Vice-President (Business): BRENDA MCGEE SNOW
Vice-President (Student Life): GEORGE F. SOLAN
Vice-President (University Relations): DAVID P. FERGUSON
Registrar: HEATHER L. JACKSON
Librarian: PAUL SPAETH

Number of teachers: 160
Number of students: 2,552

Publications: *Cithara*, *Laurel*, *Bonadieu*, *Bonaventure*, *Cord*, *Franciscan Studies*, *The Works of William of Ockham*

DEANS

School of Arts and Sciences: Dr STEPHEN STAHL
School of Business: Dr MICHAEL J. FISCHER
School of Journalism and Mass Communication: Dr LEE COPPOLA
School of Education: Dr PEGGY Y. BURKE
School of Graduate Studies: Dr MICHAEL J. FISCHER
School of Franciscan Studies: Sr MARGARET CARNEY
Clare College: Dr MICHAEL V. CHIARELLO

ST FRANCIS COLLEGE

180 Remsen St, Brooklyn, NY 11201
Telephone: (212) 522-2300
Internet: www.stfranciscollege.edu

Chartered 1884

President: Dr FRANK J. MACCHIAROLA
Registrar (vacant)
Librarian: WENDELL GUY

Library of 177,000 vols
Number of teachers: 155
Number of students: 2,136 (1,633 full-time; 503 part-time).

ST JOHN FISHER COLLEGE

3690 East Ave, Rochester, NY 14618
Telephone: (585) 385-8000
Fax: (585) 385-8386
E-mail: admissions@sjfc.edu
Internet: www.sjfc.edu

Founded 1948
Private control

President: Dr KATHERINE E. KEOUGH
Provost and Dean: Dr DONALD E. BAIN

Vice-President (Financial Affairs): JOHN P. PECCHIA
Vice-President (Enrollment Management and External Relations): GERARD J. ROONEY
Registrar: JULIE THOMAS
Librarian: KAREN JUNKER
Number of students: 3,100.

ST JOHN'S UNIVERSITY, NEW YORK

8000 Utopia Parkway, Jamaica, NY 11439
Telephone: (718) 990-6161
Fax: (718) 990-5723
Internet: www.stjohns.edu

Campuses at Queens, Staten Island, Eastern Long Island (New York) and Rome (Italy)

Founded 1870 chartered 1871; re-chartered by Regents of the University of the State of New York 1906

Academic year: September to May

President: Rev. DONALD J. HARRINGTON
Executive Vice-President and Treasurer: JAMES PELLOW
Provost: Dr JULIE UPTON
Senior Vice-President for Student Life: Dr SUSAN L. EBBS
Vice-President and Secretary to the University: Dr DOROTHY E. HABBEN
Executive Vice-President for Student Service: Rev. MICHAEL J. CARROLL
Vice-President for International Relations: Dr CECILIA CHANG
Vice-President for Administrative Services: JOHN P. CONNOLLY, Jr
Vice-President for Human Resources: MARY T. HARPER
Vice-President for Government and Community Relations: JOSEPH SCIAME
Vice-President for Institutional Advancement: Rev. BERNARD TRACEY
Vice-President for Academic Support Services: Dr ANDRÉ MCKENZIE
Vice-President for University Ministry: Rev. JAMES J. MAHER
Vice-President for Planning and Information Technology: Dr FRANK SIRIANNI
Vice-President for Property Management: CLARE T. CROSSLEY
Vice-President for Enrollment Management: GLENN SKLARIN
Vice-President for University Services: DENNIS P. MCAULIFFE
Vice-President, Office of Student Service: JOHN P. CONNOLLY, Jr
Dean of Libraries: Dr JAMES BENSON

Library of 1,700,000 vols, 6,000 periodical subscriptions
Number of teachers: 1,111
Number of students: 18,478

Publications: *Bankruptcy Law Review, The Forum, Law Review/Catholic Lawyer, Journal of Legal Commentary, New York International Law Review, Recipe, Res Gestae, Sequoya Art and Literary Magazine, The Spectator, St. John's Today, Vincentian, The Torch, The Stormfront, The Mission Yearbook*

DEANS

St John's College of Liberal Arts and Sciences: Dr JEFFERY FAGEN (acting)
School of Education and Human Services: Dr JERROLD ROSS
Peter J. Tobin College of Business: PETER J. TOBIN
College of Pharmacy and Allied Health Professions: Dr ROBERT MANGIONE
Metropolitan College: Dr MARY MULVIHILL (acting)
College of Professional Studies: Dr KATHLEEN VOUTÉ MACDONALD
School of Law: Judge JOSEPH W. BELLACOSA

BRANCH CAMPUSES

Staten Island Campus: 300 Howard Ave, Staten Island, NY 10301; Senior Vice-President for the Staten Island Campus Rev. JAMES F. KIERNAN.
Eastern Long Island Campus: 500 Montauk Highway, Oakdale, NY 11769; Director BRIAN BROWNE.
Rome Campus (Italy): Graduate Center, Pontificio Oratorio San Pietro, Via Santa Maria Mediatrice 24, 00165 Rome, Italy; Vice-President for Rome Campus Rev. MICHAEL J. CARROLL.

ST JOSEPH'S COLLEGE

245 Clinton Ave, Brooklyn, NY 11205
Telephone: (718) 636-6800
Internet: www.sjcny.edu

Campuses in: Brooklyn and Patchogue.

Founded 1916 as St Joseph's College for Women; present name 1970
Private control

President: Sr ELIZABETH A. HILL
Librarian: Sr TERESA RYAN.

SAINT JOSEPH'S SEMINARY

201 Seminary Ave, Yonkers, NY 10704-1896
Internet: www.ny-archdiocese.org/pastoral/seminary.cfm

Founded 1896
Private control

Rector: Rev. Mgr PETER G. FINN
Academic Dean: Rev. Mgr WILLIAM B. SMITH
Registrar: Sr MARY FRANCES MILLS
Library Director: Sr MONICA WOOD
Number of teachers: 22 (12 full-time, 10 part-time).

ST LAWRENCE UNIVERSITY

Canton, NY 13617
Telephone: (315) 229-5011
Internet: www.stlawu.edu

Founded 1856
Academic year: August to May

President: DANIEL F. SULLIVAN
Vice-President and Dean: THOMAS COBURN
Vice-President for University Advancement: MICHAEL ARCHIBALD
Vice-President for Business Affairs: KATHRYN MULLANEY
Vice-President for Student Affairs: MARCIA LOU PETTY
Vice-President for Finance: KATHRYN MULLANEY
Vice-President for Administrative Operations: THOMAS COAKLEY
Secretary: ANGELA M. JOHNSTON
Registrar: CAROLYN FILIPPI
Librarian: BART HARLOE

Library of 522,722 vols
Number of teachers: 192
Number of students: 1,958 (undergraduate)

Publications: *St Lawrence Magazine* (quarterly), *Hill News* (weekly), *Laurentian* (annually), *Gridiron* (annually).

ST THOMAS AQUINAS COLLEGE

125 Route 340, Sparkill, NY 10976-1050
Telephone: (845) 398-4000
E-mail: admissions@stac.edu
Internet: www.stac.edu

Founded 1952
Private control

President: Dr MARGARET MARY FITZPATRICK
Senior Vice-President: Dr L. JOHN DURNEY, III
Vice-President: ANNE DONINI

Provost and Vice-President (Academic Affairs): Dr LEE D. BADGETT
Vice-President (Financial Affairs): MANUEL D. FERNANDES
Vice-President and Dean of Student Affairs: Dr WALTER SCHNEIDER
Registrar: MILDRED ALEXIOU
Library Director: SUZANN M. WEEKLY
Number of students: 2,200

HEADS OF DEPARTMENTS

Business Administration: MICHAEL MURPHY
Humanities: Dr BARBARA WARD KLEIN
Natural Sciences and Mathematics: Dr MARY ELLEN FERRARO
Social Sciences: Dr JOSEPH COYNE
Teacher Education: Dr MEENAKSHI GAJRIA

ST VLADIMIR'S ORTHODOX THEOLOGICAL SEMINARY

575 Scarsdale Rd, Crestwood, NY 10707-1699
Telephone: (914) 961-8313
Fax: (914) 961-4507
E-mail: info@svots.edu
Internet: www.svots.edu

Founded 1938
Academic year: September to May

Dean and Chairman: JOHN H. ERICKSON
Vice-Chairman: PETER PRUZINSKY
Associate Dean (Academic Affairs): PAUL MEYENDORFF
Associate Dean (Student Affairs): Very Rev. PAUL LAZOR
Librarian: ELEANA SONNIE SILK
Number of teachers: 16
Number of students: 105
Publication: *The Quarterly*.

SARAH LAWRENCE COLLEGE

Bronxville, NY 10708
Telephone: (914) 337-0700
E-mail: admin@mail.slc.edu
Internet: www.slc.edu

Provisional charter 1926; absolute charter 1931

President: MICHELE TOLELA MYERS
Vice-President for Finance and Planning: DENNIS CROSS
Dean of College: BARBARA KAPLAN
Dean of Studies: ROBERT CAMERON (acting)
Dean of Admissions: THYRA BRIGGS
Director of Public Relations: DIANE FUSILLI
Registrar: MARY DRISCOLL

Library of 200,000 vols
Number of teachers: 238
Number of students: 1,111

Publications: *Sarah Lawrence Tribune, Sarah Lawrence Magazine, Sarah Lawrence Literary Review*.

SCHOOL OF VISUAL ARTS

209 E 23rd St, New York, NY 10010
Telephone: (212) 592-2100
Fax: (212) 592-2116
E-mail: admissions@sva.edu
Internet: www.schoolofvisualarts.edu

Founded 1947
Private control
Academic year: September to May

President: DAVID RHODES
Executive Vice-President: ANTHONY P. RHODES
Provost: CHRISTOPHER CYPHERS
Registrar: JON TODD
Library Director: ROBERT LOBE
Number of students: 7,047 (3,189 undergraduate, 358 postgraduate, 3,500 continuing education).

SEMINARY OF THE IMMACULATE CONCEPTION

440 W Neck Rd, Huntington, NY 11743
Telephone: (631) 423-0483
Fax: (631) 423-2346
Internet: www.icseminary.edu
Founded 1930
Private control
Number of teachers: 14.

SIENA COLLEGE

Loudonville, NY 12211
Telephone: (518) 783-2300
Fax: (518) 783-4293
Internet: www.siena.edu
Founded 1937
Independent liberal arts college
President: Rev. KEVIN E. MACKIN
Vice-President for Academic Affairs: Dr DOUGLAS ASTOLFI
Vice-President for Finance and Administration: ANTHONY G. PONDILLO
Vice-President for Development: Dr GREGORY J. STAHL
Vice-President for Student Affairs: Rev. JOHN FRAMBES
Dean of Residential and Judicial Services: JEANNE OBERMAYER
Director of Admissions: EDWARD J. JONES
Library Director: TIMOTHY G. BURKE
Library of 244,564 vols, 33,206 other items
Number of teachers: 255 (171 full-time; 84 part-time)
Number of students: 3,436 (2,669 full-time; 767 part-time).

SKIDMORE COLLEGE

Saratoga Springs, NY 12866
Telephone: (518) 580-5000
Internet: www.skidmore.edu
Founded 1903, chartered 1922
President: Dr DAVID H. PORTER
Vice-President for Business Affairs and Treasurer: KARL W. BROEKHUIZEN
Vice-President for Development and Alumni Affairs: CHRISTINE R. HOEK
Dean of the Faculty: PHYLLIS A. ROTH
Dean of Student Affairs: JOSEPH A. TOLLIVER
Dean of Special Programs: DONALD J. McCORMACK
Dean of Enrollment and College Relations: KENT H. JONES
Director of Admissions: MARY LOU BATES
Director, Skidmore University Without Walls: CORNEL J. REINHART
Librarian: PEGGY SEIDEN
Library of 420,000 vols
Number of teachers: 200 (184 full-time; 16 part-time)
Number of students: 2,189.

STATE UNIVERSITY OF NEW YORK

System Administration, State University Plaza, Albany, NY 12246
Telephone: (518) 443-5355
Internet: www.suny.edu
Founded 1948
Chancellor: ROBERT L. KING
Provost and Vice-Chancellor for Academic Affairs: PETER D. SALINS
University Counsel and Vice-Chancellor for Legal Affairs: D. ANDREW EDWARDS
Senior Vice-Chancellor for Finance and Business: BRIAN T. STENSON
Vice-Chancellor, and Secretary of the University: JOHN J. O'CONNOR
Vice-Chancellor for Business and Industry Relations: WAYNE DIESEL

Vice-Chancellor for Community Colleges: CAROL EATON
Vice-Chancellor and Chief of Staff: ELIZABETH CAPALDI
Vice-Chancellor and Chief Financial Officer: DAVID RICHTER
Chief Operating Officer: RICHARD P. MILLER
Number of teachers: 29,922 full-time.
Number of students: 409,886 full-time.

UNIVERSITY CENTRES

University at Albany

Albany, NY 12222
Telephone: (518) 442-3300
Internet: www.albany.edu
Founded 1844
Academic year: August to May
President: JOHN R. RYAN
Provost and Vice-President for Academic Affairs: JERYL L. MUMPOWER
Vice-President for Finance and Business: KATHRYN LOWERY
Vice-President for University Advancement: ROBERT ASHTON
Vice-President for Research and Dean of Graduate Studies: JERYL L. MUMPOWER
Vice-President for Student Affairs: JAMES P. DOELLEFELD
Number of teachers: 964
Number of students: 16,751.

Binghamton University

POB 6000, Binghamton, NY 13902-6000
Telephone: (607) 777-2000
Fax: (607) 777-4000
E-mail: webmaster@binghamton.edu
Internet: www.binghamton.edu
Founded 1946
Academic year: August to May
President: LOIS B. DeFLEUR
Provost and Vice-President for Academic Affairs: MARY ANN SWAIN
Vice-President for Administration: ANTHONY A. FERRARA
Vice-President for Student Affairs: RODGER SUMMERS
Vice-President for External Affairs: THOMAS F. KELLY
Number of teachers: 658
Number of students: 12,473.

University at Buffalo

Buffalo, NY 14260
Telephone: (716) 645-2400
Fax: (716) 645-2895
Internet: www.buffalo.edu
Founded 1846
Academic year: August to May
President: JOHN BARCLAY SIMPSON
Provost: ROBERT J. GENCO
Vice-President for Research: DALE M. LANDI
Vice-President for Student Affairs: DENNIS R. BLACK
Senior Vice-President: ROBERT J. WAGNER
Vice-President for Health Affairs: MICHAEL BERNARDINO
Vice-President for University Advancement and Development: JENNIFER McDONOUGH
Vice-President for Public Service and Urban Affairs: MARY H. GRESHAM
Number of teachers: 2,149
Number of students: 24,830.

Stony Brook University

Stony Brook, NY 11794
Telephone: (516) 632-6000
Internet: www.sunysb.edu
Founded 1957
Academic year: August to May
President: SHIRLEY STRUM KENNY

Provost: ROBERT L. McGRATH
Vice-President for Student Affairs: FREDERICK R. PRESTON
Vice-President for Administration: RICHARD MANN
Vice-President, Health Sciences Center: NORMAN EDELMAN
Vice-President for Research: GAIL HABICHT
Vice-President for Hospital Affairs: LEONARD A. ACBEIT
Vice-President for Brookhaven Affairs: ROBERT McGRATH
Number of teachers: 1,778
Number of students: 19,924.

HEALTH SCIENCE CENTERS

Health Science Center at Brooklyn: 450 Clarkson Ave, Brooklyn, NY 11203; Pres. JOHN C. LA ROSA.

Health Science Center at Syracuse: Syracuse, NY 13210; Pres. GREGORY L. EASTWOOD.

UNIVERSITY COLLEGES

State University College at Brockport: NY 14420; Officer-in-Charge TIMOTHY J. FLANAGAN.

State University College at Buffalo: NY 14222; Pres. MURIEL A. HOWARD.

State University College at Cortland: NY 13045; Pres. ERIK J. BITTERBAUM.

State University College at Fredonia: NY 14063; Pres. DENNIS L. HEFNER.

State University College at Geneseo: NY 14454; Pres. CHRISTOPHER C. DAHL.

State University College at New Paltz: NY 12561; Pres. STEVEN POSKANZER.

State University College at Old Westbury: NY 11568; Pres. CALVIN O. BUTTS, III.

State University College at Oneonta: NY 13820; Pres. ALAN B. DONOVAN.

State University College at Oswego: NY 13126; Pres. DEBORAH FLEMMA STANLEY.

State University College at Plattsburgh: NY 12901; Pres. JOHN ETTLING.

State University College at Potsdam: NY 13676; Pres. JOHN A. FALLON III.

State University College at Purchase: NY 10577; Pres. THOMAS J. SCHWARZ.

State University Empire State College: Saratoga Springs, NY 12866; Pres. JOSEPH B. MOORE.

COLLEGES OF TECHNOLOGY

State University of New York College of Technology at Alfred: Alfred, NY 14802; Pres. UMA GUPTA.

State University of New York College of Technology at Canton: Canton, NY 13617; Pres. JOSEPH L. KENNEDY.

State University of New York College of Agriculture and Technology at Cobleskill: Cobleskill, NY 12043; Pres. THOMAS J. HAAS.

State University of New York College of Technology at Delhi: Delhi, NY 13753-1190; Pres. CANDACE S. VANCKO.

State University of New York College of Technology at Farmingdale: Farmingdale, NY 11735; Pres. Dr JONATHAN GIBRALTER.

State University of New York College of Agriculture and Technology at Morrisville: Morrisville, NY 13408-0636; Pres. RAYMOND W. CROSS.

SPECIALIZED COLLEGES

State University of New York College of Environmental Science and Forestry: Syracuse, NY 13210; Pres. CORNELIUS B. MURPHY.

State University of New York College of Optometry at New York City: 100 E 24th St, New York, NY 10010; Pres. ALDEN N. HAFFNER.

State University Institute of Technology at Utica/Rome: POB 3050, Utica, NY 13504-3050; Pres. MASON H. SOMERVILLE.

State University of New York Maritime College: Fort Schuyler, Bronx, NY 10465; Pres. JOHN R. RYAN.

SYRACUSE UNIVERSITY

Syracuse, NY 13244

Telephone: (315) 443-1870

E-mail: gradinfo@syr.edu

Internet: www.syr.edu

Founded 1870

Chancellor and President: Dr KENNETH A. SHAW

Vice-Chancellor for Academic Affairs: Dr DEBORAH FREUND

Executive Assistant to the Chancellor: GRETCHEN GOLDSTEIN

Senior Vice-President for Institutional Advancement: Dr JOHN SELLARS

Senior Vice-President, Business and Finance: LOUIS MARCOCCIA

Senior Vice-President, Giving Programs: Dr THOMAS HARBLIN

Senior Vice-President, Human Services and Government Relations: ELEANOR WARE

Senior Vice-President and Dean for Student Affairs: BARRY L. WELLS

Vice-President, Enrollment Management and Continuing Education: DAVID SMITH

Vice-President for Research and Computing: Dr BEN WARE

Executive Director of Government Relations: ELIZABETH ROUGEUX

Dean of Admissions and Financial Aid: SUSAN DONOVAN

Registrar: MAUREEN BREED

University Librarian: PETER GRAHAM

Library: see Libraries

Number of teachers: 1,386

Number of students: 18,600

Publications: *Symposium* (on foreign languages and literature, 4 a year), *Syracuse Law Review* (4 a year), *Syracuse University Record* (weekly), *Syracuse University Magazine* (3 a year)

DEANS

School of Architecture: Dr MARK ROBBINS

College of Arts and Sciences. Dr CATHRYN NEWTON

Maxwell Graduate School of Citizenship and Public Affairs: Dr MITCHELL WALLERSTEIN

School of Education: Dr LOUISE WILKINSON

College of Engineering and Computer Science: Dr ERIC SPINA

Graduate School: Dr JOHN MERCER

Hendricks Memorial Chapel: THOMAS WOLFE

School of Information Studies: Dr RAYMOND F. VON DRAN

College of Law: Prof. DAAN BRAVEMAN

School of Management: SANDY HURD

S. I. Newhouse School of Public Communications: Dr DAVID RUBIN

Summer Sessions: CHARLES BARLETTA

University College: CHARLES BARLETTA

Utica College: Dr MICHAEL SIMPSON

College of Visual and Performing Arts: CAROLE BRZOZOWSKI

College of Human Services and Health Professionals: BRUCE LAGAY

AFFILIATED INSTITUTIONS

Center of Hispanic Studies: f. 1945; co-operates closely with the faculties of geography and history.

Center on Human Policy.

Communications Research Center.

Institute for Energy Research.

Institute for Sensory Research.

All-University Gerontology Center.

Division of International Programs Abroad.

Center for Northeast Parallel Architectures.

Center for Computer Applications and Software Engineering.

Center for Membrane Science.

Global Affairs Institute.

TOURO COLLEGE

27–33 W 23rd St, New York, NY 10010

Telephone: (212) 463-0400

Internet: www.touro.edu

Campuses in: Manhattan, Brooklyn, Queens, Long Island, California and Israel.

Founded 1970

Private control

President: Dr BERNARD LANDER

Library Director: JACQUELINE A. MAXIN

Number of teachers: 247

Number of students: 8,950.

UNIFICATION THEOLOGICAL SEMINARY

30 Seminary Drive, Barrytown, NY 12507

Telephone: (845) 752-3000

Fax: (845) 752-3016

E-mail: admissions@uts.edu

Internet: www.uts.edu

Founded 1975

Private control

Academic year: September to June

President: Dr TYLER O. HENDRICKS

Vice-President: Dr MICHAEL L. MICKLER

Academic Dean: Dr ANDREW WILSON

Dean of Students: SUNHEE DAVIES

Dean, New York City Extension Center: Dr KATHY WININGS

Registrar: UTE DELANEY

Library Director: Dr KEISUKE NODA

Publication: *Journal of Unification Studies* (annually).

UNION COLLEGE

Schenectady, NY 12308

Telephone: (518) 388-6000

Internet: www.union.edu

Founded 1795; oldest non-denominational college in US

President: ROGER H. HULL

Vice-President (Academic Affairs) and Dean of Faculty: LINDA E. COOL

Vice-President (Admissions and Financial Aid): DANIEL M. LUNDQUIST

Vice-President (Alumni Affairs): JOSEPH L. MAMMOLA

Vice-President (College Relations): DAN C. WEST

Vice-President (Finance and Administration): DIANE T. BLAKE

Registrar: PENELOPE S. ADEY

Library Director: THOMAS McFADDEN

Library of 515,000 vols

Number of teachers: 184 (full-time)

Number of students: 2,000 (full-time day)

Publications: *Catalogue*, *Chronicle* (college weekly), *Concordiensis* (student weekly), *Idol* (student literary magazine), *Sentinel* (political magazine), *Union Book* (Senior Year Book), *Union College* (Alumni)

DEANS

Faculty: LINDA COOL

Students: FREDERICK ALFORD

UNION THEOLOGICAL SEMINARY

3041 Broadway, New York, NY 10027

Telephone: (212) 662-7100

E-mail: contactus@uts.columbia.edu

Internet: www.uts.columbia.edu

Founded 1836

Private control

Academic year: September to May

President: Rev. JOSEPH C. HOUGH, Jr

Executive Vice-President: MARY E. McNAMARA

Academic Dean: ROSEMARY SKINNER KELLER

Dean of Academic Administration: JAMES A. HAYES

Director of Admissions and Registrar: DAVID L. McDONAGH

Library Director: SARA J. MYERS

Number of teachers: 46

Number of students: 245.

UNITED STATES MERCHANT MARINE ACADEMY

Kings Point, NY 11024-1699

Telephone: (516) 773-5000

Fax: (516) 773-5509

E-mail: admissions@usmma.edu

Internet: www.usmma.edu

Founded 1943

Academic year: July to June

Superintendent: Vice-Admiral JOSEPH D. STEWART

Chief of Staff: Capt. ROBERT SAFARIK

Academic Dean: Dr WARREN F. MAZEK

Commandant of Midshipmen: Capt. ROBERT ALLEE

Director, Office of External Affairs: Capt. DONALD FERGUSON

Library: Dr GEORGE BILLY

Number of teachers: 81 instructors

Number of students: 950 midshipmen

HEADS OF ACADEMIC DEPARTMENTS

Engineering: Prof. JOSÉ FEMENIA

Humanities: Dr JANE BRICKMAN

Marine Transportation: Capt. GEORGE SANDBERG

Mathematics and Science: Dr HOWARD BEIM

Naval Science: Cdr THOMAS HODGSON

Physical Education: Prof. SUSAN PETERSEN-LUBOW

UNITED STATES MILITARY ACADEMY

West Point, NY 10996

Telephone: (914) 938-4011

E-mail: webmail@usma.edu

Internet: www.usma.edu

Founded 1802

Superintendent: Lt.-Gen. WILLIAM J. LENNOX, Jr

Commandant of Cadets: Brig.-Gen. ROBERT J. ST ONGE, Jr

Dean of the Academic Board: Brig.-Gen. FLETCHER M. LAMKIN, Jr

Director of Admissions: Col. MICHAEL L. JONES

Librarian: JOSEPH BARTH

Library of 500,000 vols

Number of instructors: 562

Number of cadets: 4,112

HEADS OF DEPARTMENTS

Behavioral Science and Leadership: Col. CHARLES F. BROWER, IV

Chemistry: Col. DAVID C. ALLBEE

Civil and Mechanical Engineering: Col. KIP P. NYGREN

Mathematical Sciences: Col. DAVID C. ARNEY
Geography and Environmental Engineering:
Col. JOHN GRUBBS
Foreign Languages: Col. WILLIAM G. HELD
Law: Col. DENNIS R. HUNT
English: Col. PETER L. STROMBERG
Social Sciences: Col. JAMES R. GOLDEN
Physics: Col. RAYMOND J. WINKEL
Electrical Engineering and Computer
Science: Col. DANIEL M. LITYNSKI
Systems Engineering: Col. JAMES L. KAYS
History: Col. ROBERT A. DOUGHTY
Military Instruction: Col. GREGORY K. WADE
Physical Education: Col. JAMES L. ANDERSON

UNIVERSITY OF ROCHESTER

Wilson Blvd, Rochester, NY 14627
Telephone: (716) 275-2121
Fax: (716) 275-0359
Internet: www.rochester.edu

Founded 1850
Private control
Academic year: September to May (two terms).

President: THOMAS JACKSON
Provost: CHARLES PHELPS
Executive Vice-President and Treasurer (vacant)
Vice-President for Development: HOLLIS BUDD
Dean for Enrollment Policy and Management: NEILL F. SANDERS
Registrar: NANCY SPECK
Director of River Campus Libraries: RONALD DOW

Library: see Libraries
Number of teachers: 1,000
Number of students: 7,885

DEANS

The College: THOMAS J. LeBLANC
Graduate Studies: B. JACOBS
School of Medicine and Dentistry: E. HINDERT
Eastman School of Music: J. UNDERCOFLER
School of Nursing: P. CHIVERTON
Graduate School of Business Administration: CHARLES PLOSSER
Graduate School of Education and Human Development: R. BORASI (acting)
Memorial Art Gallery: GRANT HOLCOMB

CHAIRMEN OF DEPARTMENTS

Psychiatry: E. CAINE
Health Services: R. MANCHESTER
Modern Languages and Cultures: T. DIPIERO
Linguistics: (vacant)
Preventive Medicine and Community Health: T. PEARSON
Chemical Engineering: H. PALMER
Keyboard: N. TRUE, D. HIGGS
English: B. LONDON
Cancer Center: G. ABRAHAM
Surgery: J. SITZMAN
Orthopaedics: R. BURTON
Computer Science: M. OGIHARA
Radiology: A. ROBINSON
Theory: E. MARVIN
Optics: D. HALL
Anaesthesiology: D. WARD
Physics and Astronomy: A. BODEK
Musicology: J. THYM
Statistics: W. J. HALL
Anthropology: T. GIBSON
History: R. WESTBROOK
Biology: R. ANGERER
Conducting and Ensembles: D. HUNSBERGER
Medicine: M. UTELL
Physiology: M. ANDERS
Psychology: M. ZUCKERMAN
Neurology: R. GRIGGS
Chemistry: J. FARRAR
Animal Medicine: J. WYATT
Philosophy: D. MODRAK
Biophysics: R. BAMBARA

Pharmacology and Toxicology: M. ANDERS
String Department: N. GOLUSES
Geological Sciences: J. TARDUND
Voice: J. MALOY
Biochemistry: F. SHERMAN
Microbiology: B. IGLEWSKI
Electrical Engineering: P. FAUCHET
Naval Science: Capt. T. FEEKS
Ophthalmology: B. KATZ (acting)
Art and Art History: D. CRIMP (acting)
Political Science: G. GAMM
Biostatistics: D. OAKES
Economics: A. STOCKMAN
Pathology: S. SPITALNIK
Composition: R. MORRIS
Mathematics: D. RAVENEL
Humanities (Eastman School of Music): J. BALDO
Music Education: D. BRINK FOX
Mechanical Engineering: J. LAMBROPOULOS
Paediatrics: E. McANARNEY
Anatomy: G. PAIGE
Obstetrics and Gynaecology: D. GUZICK
Woodwind, Brass and Percussion: J. MARCELLYS
Music: K. KOWALKE
Dental Research: L. TABAK
Jazz Studies: F. STURM

VASSAR COLLEGE

Poughkeepsie, NY 12604
Telephone: (845) 437-7000
Internet: www.vassar.edu

Founded 1861
Academic year: September to May

President: FRANCES DALY FERGUSSON
Vice-President for Finance and Treasurer: ELIZABETH EISMEIER
Director of College Relations: SUSAN DeKREY
Vice-President for Development: CATHERINE BAER
Dean of the Faculty: RONALD SHARP
Dean of the College: JUDITH JACKSON
Dean of Students: DAVID H. BROWN
Director of Libraries: SABRINA PAPE

Library of 830,235 vols
Number of teachers: 267
Number of students: 2,475.

WAGNER COLLEGE

Grymes Hill, Staten Island, NY 10301
Telephone: (718) 390-3100
Fax: (718) 390-3105
Internet: www.wagner.edu

Founded 1883

President: Dr RICHARD GUARASCI
Dean of Admissions: ANGELO ARAIMO
Librarian: Y. JOHN AUH

Library of 285,000 vols
Number of teachers: 80 full-time
Number of teachers: 110 part-time
Number of students: 1,800.

WEBB INSTITUTE

Glen Cove, Long Island, NY 11542
Telephone: (516) 671-2213
Fax: (516) 674-9838
E-mail: admissions@webb-institute.edu
Internet: www.webb-institute.edu

Founded 1889
Academic year: August to June

President: Dr RONALD K. KISS
Registrar: WILLIAM G. MURRAY
Dean: Dr ROGER H. COMPTON
Librarian: PATRICIA PRESCOTT

Library of 50,000 vols
Number of teachers: 14 (10 full-time, 4 adjunct)
Number of students: 74.

WELLS COLLEGE

Aurora, NY 13026
Telephone: (315) 364-3266
Fax: (315) 364-3227
E-mail: admissions@wells.edu
Internet: www.wells.edu

Founded 1868
Women's liberal arts college
Academic year: August to May

President: LISA MARSH RYERSON
Vice-President and Treasurer: DIANE HUTCHINSON
Dean of Students: SUSAN RYAN
Dean of the College: ELLEN HALL
Director of Admissions: SUSAN SLOAN
Registrar: KARLA LEYBOLD-TAYLOR
Librarian: JERI VARGO

Library of 248,130 vols
Number of teachers: 55
Number of students: 352

Publication: *Wells College Express* (4 a year).

YESHIVA UNIVERSITY

500 West 185th St, New York, NY 10033-3201
Telephone: (212) 960-5400
Fax: (212) 960-0055
Internet: www.yu.edu

Founded 1886
Independent control
Languages of instruction: English, Hebrew

President: RICHARD M. JOEL
Vice-President for Academic Affairs: S. R. GELMAN
Vice-President for Medical Affairs: D. P. PURPURA
Vice-President for Business Affairs: S. E. SOCOL
Vice-President for Development: D. T. FORMAN
Vice-President for University Affairs: H. C. DOBRINSKY
Director of Public Relations: D. M. ROSEN
General Counsel: M. H. BOCKSTEIN
Dean of University Libraries: P. BERGER

Library: 6 libraries with 1,000,000 vols
Number of teachers: 1,100
Number of students: 6,335

Publications: *Yeshiva University Review*, *Yeshiva University Today*

DEANS

Yeshiva College: N. T. ADLER
Isaac Breuer College of Hebraic Studies: M. D. SHMIDMAN
James Striar School of General Jewish Studies: M. D. SHMIDMAN
Yeshiva Program and Mazer School of Talmudic Studies: Z. CHARLOP
Irving I. Stone Beit Midrash Program: M. D. SHMIDMAN
Stern College for Women: K. BACON
Sy Syms School of Business: H. NIERENBERG
Albert Einstein College of Medicine: D. P. PURPURA
Benjamin N. Cardozo School of Law: P. R. VERKUIL
Bernard Revel Graduate School and Harry Fischel School for Higher Jewish Studies: A. HYMAN
Ferkauf Graduate School of Psychology: L. J. SIEGEL
Wurzweiler School of Social Work: S. R. GELMAN
Azrieli Graduate School of Jewish Education and Administration: Y. S. HANDEL
Sue Golding Graduate Division of Medical Sciences: A. M. ETGEN

ATTACHED RESEARCH INSTITUTES

Irwin S. and Sylvia Chanin Institute for Cancer Research.

Rose F. Kennedy Center for Research in Mental Retardation and Human Development.

Jack and Pearl Resnick Gerontology Center.

Florence and Theodore Baumritter Kidney Dialysis and Research Center.

Marion Bessin Liver Research Center.

Ebrahim Ben Davood Eliahu Eshgaghian Transgenic Facility for Biomedical Research.

Samuel H. and Rachel Golding Center for Developmental Neurobiology.

Samuel H. and Rachel Golding Center for Molecular Genetics.

Cardiovascular Center.

Center for Diabetes Research.

Center for Research in Neuropsychopharmacology.

Institute for Human Communication Disorders.

NORTH CAROLINA

APPALACHIAN STATE UNIVERSITY

Boone, NC 28608

Telephone: (828) 262-2000
Internet: www.appstate.edu

Founded 1899; attached to Univ. of North Carolina

Chancellor: Dr KENNETH E. PEACOCK
Provost and Exec. Vice-Chancellor: Dr STANLEY R. AESCHLEMAN
Registrar: DON RANKINS
Univ. Librarian: MARY REICHEL

Library of 800,000 vols
Number of teachers: 619
Number of students: 15,117.

BARBER-SCOTIA COLLEGE

145 Cabarrus Ave, Wt, Concord, NC 28025

Telephone: (704) 789-2900
Fax: (704) 789-2958
Internet: www.b-sc.edu

Founded 1867

Pres.: CARL FLAMER
Vice-Pres. for Academic Affairs: ALEXANDER ERWIN
Vice-Pres. for Student Affairs: ERIC JACKSON
Vice-Pres. for Fiscal Affairs: NEMICHAND JAIN
Vice-Pres. for Institutional Advancement: EUGENE C. PERRY
Registrar: EMMA WITHERSPOON
Librarian: MINORA HICKS

Library of 68,374 vols
Number of teachers: 36
Number of students: 500.

BARTON COLLEGE

POB 5000, Wilson, NC 27893-7000

Telephone: (252) 399-6300
Fax: (252) 399-6571
Internet: www.barton.edu

Founded 1902
Private (Disciples of Christ)
Academic year: September to May

Pres.: Dr NORVAL C. KNETEN
Vice-Pres. for Academic Affairs: Dr TERRENCE M. GRIMES
Vice-Pres. for Admin. and Finance: RICHARD A. MARSHALL
Dir of Library: RODNEY LIPPARD

Library of 150,000 vols
Number of teachers: 82
Number of students: 1,300.

BELMONT ABBEY COLLEGE

100 Belmont-Mt Holly Rd, Belmont, NC 28012

Telephone: (704) 825-6700
Fax: (704) 825-6670
Internet: www.belmontabbeycollege.edu

Founded 1876
Academic year: August to May

Pres.: Dr WILLIAM K. THIERFELDER
Vice-Pres. for Academic Affairs: Dr DEAN DE LA MOTTE
Vice-Pres. for Business Affairs: JAMES SCHUPPENHAUER
Vice-Pres. for Institutional Advancement: Dr JOHN MARSHALL
Vice-Pres. for Student Affairs: KAREN VAN NORMAN
Dean of Admissions and Dir of Financial Aid: ANNE STEVENS
Dir of Public Relations: THERESA SOWERS MCKINNEY

Library of 150,000 vols
Number of teachers: 50
Number of students: 1,000

Publications: *Agora*, *Crossroads*.

BENNETT COLLEGE

Greensboro, NC 27401-3239

Telephone: (336) 273-4431
Internet: www.bennett.edu

Founded 1873 (reorganized 1926)

Pres.: Dr JOHNNETTA BETSCH COLE
Dir of Admissions: LINDA TORRENCE
Vice-Pres. for Academic Affairs and Student Devt: Dr DONNA H. OLIVER
Library Dir: JOAN WILLIAMS

Library of 100,000 vols
Number of teachers: 46
Number of students: 607.

CAMPBELL UNIVERSITY

POB 488, Buie's Creek, NC 27506

Telephone: (910) 893-1200
Fax: (910) 893-1424
Internet: www.campbell.edu

Founded 1887

Pres.: Dr JEREMY M. WALLACE
Chancellor: Dr NORMAN ADRIAN WIGGINS
Vice-Pres. for Business and Treas.: JIM ROBERTS
Vice-Pres. for Academic Affairs and Provost: Dr DWAINE GREENE
Vice-Pres. for Student Life: Dr DENNIS BAZEMORE
Vice-Pres. for Institutional Advancement: Dr JACK BRITT
Dir of Library Services: Dr RONNIE W. FAULKNER

Library of 478,772 vols
Number of teachers: 428 (175 full-time, 253 part-time)
Number of students: 9,220

Publication: *Pine Burr* (year book)

DEANS

School of Arts and Sciences: Dr MARK L. HAMMOND
School of Law: WILLIS P. WHICHARD
School of Pharmacy: Dr RONALD W. MADDOX
School of Business: Dr CHRISTIAN ZINKHAN
School of Education: Dr KAREN P. NERY
Divinity School: Dr MICHAEL G. COGDILL

CATAWBA COLLEGE

2300 West Innes St, Salisbury, NC 28144

Telephone: (704) 637-4111
Internet: www.catawba.edu

Founded 1851

Pres.: Dr ROBERT E. KNOTT
Registrar: P. CAROL GAMBLE
Vice-Pres. and Dean of Admissions: Dr L. RUSSELL WATJEN
Librarian: STEVEN MCKINZIE

Library of 200,000 vols
Number of teachers: 67
Number of students: 950.

CHOWAN UNIVERSITY

1 Univ. Pl., Murfreesboro, NC 27855

Telephone: (252) 398-6500
Fax: (252) 398-1190
E-mail: admissions@chowan.edu
Internet: www.chowan.edu

Founded 1848 as Chowan Baptist Female Institute; present name 1910
Private control

Pres.: M. CHRISTOPHER WHITE
Vice-Pres. for Academic Affairs: Dr DANNY B. MOORE
Registrar: LLOYD LEE WILSON

Number of teachers: 68 (full-time)
Number of students: 900.

DAVIDSON COLLEGE

209 Ridge Rd, Davidson, NC 28036

Telephone: (704) 894-2000
Fax: (704) 894-2005
Internet: www.davidson.edu

Founded 1837
Academic year: August to May

Pres.: THOMAS W. ROSS, Sr
Vice-Pres. for Academic Affairs and Dean of the Faculty: CLARK G. ROSS
Vice-Pres. for Institutional Advancement: JAMES W. MAY, Jr
Vice-President for Business and Finance: ROBERT C. NORFLEET
Vice-Pres. for College Relations: EILEEN KEELEY
Dir of Alumni Relations (vacant): PETER WAGNER
Dean of Admissions and Financial Aid: CHRISTOPHER J. GRUBER
Registrar: Dr HANSFORD M. EPES
Dir of Library: JILL GREMMELS

Library of 600,000 vols
Number of teachers: 152
Number of students: 1,700

Publications: *Davidson Journal* (quarterly), *Oak Row Report* (monthly), *The Davidsonian* (weekly student newspaper), *Quips and Cranks* (year book), *Hobart Park* (literary, annual).

DUKE UNIVERSITY

Durham, NC 27708

Telephone: (919) 684-8111
Internet: www.duke.edu

Founded 1838 as Union Institute Society in Randolph County, NC; became Trinity College 1851; moved to Durham 1892; present name 1924
Academic year: September to August

Pres.: RICHARD H. BRODHEAD
Provost: PETER LANGE
Chancellor for Health Affairs: RALPH SNYDERMAN
Exec. Vice-Pres.: TALLMAN TRASK, III
Provost: PETER LANGE
Vice-Pres. and Chief Information Officer: TRACY FUTHEY
Sr Vice-Pres. for Public Affirs: JOHN F. BURNESS
Vice-Pres. for Human Resources: H. CLINT DAVIDSON
Vice-Pres. for Alumni Affairs and Devt: BOB SHEPARD
Vice-Pres. for Finance: HOF MILAM

Vice-Pres. for Campus Services: KEMEL DAW-
KINS
Vice-Pres. for Student Affairs: LARRY MONETA
Registrar: BRUCE CUNNINGHAM
Vice-Provost for Library Affairs: DAVID FER-
RIERO

Number of teachers: 2,179 full-time
Number of students: 12,192

Publications: *American Literary Scholarship*
(annual), *American Literature* (quarterly),
American Speech (quarterly), *boundary 2*
(3 a year), *Camera Obscura* (3 a year),
Common Knowledge (2 a year), *Comparative Studies of South Asia, Africa and the
Middle East* (2 a year), *Duke Gifted Letter*
(quarterly), *Duke Mathematical Journal*
(15 a year), *Eighteenth-Century Life* (3 a
year), *Environmental History* (quarterly),
Ethnohistory (quarterly), *French Historical Studies* (quarterly), *GLQ: A Journal of
Lesbian and Gay Studies* (quarterly), *Hispanic American Historical Review* (quarterly), *History of Political Economy*
(quarterly), *Journal of Health Politics,
Policy and Law* (6 a year), *Journal of
Medieval and Early Modern Studies* (3 a
year), *Lesbian and Gay Studies Newsletter*
(3 a year), *Mediterranean Quarterly* (quarterly), *Modern Language Quarterly* (quarterly), *Nepantla: Views from the South* (3 a
year), *Pedagogy* (3 a year), *Poetics Today*
(quarterly), *positions* (3 a year), *Public
Culture* (3 a year), *Radical History Review*
(3 a year), *Social Science History* (quarterly), *Social Text* (quarterly), *South Atlantic Quarterly* (quarterly), *Theater* (3 a
year), *Transition* (quarterly)

DEANS

Faculty of Arts and Sciences: WILLIAM H.
CHAFE
Divinity School: L. GREGORY JONES
Medical Education: R. SANDERS WILLIAMS
School of Eng.: KRISTINA M. JOHNSON
School of the Environment and Earth
Sciences: WILLIAM H. SCHLESINGER
School of Law: KATHERINE BARTLETT
Fuqua School of Business: DOUGLAS T. BREE-
DEN
School of Nursing: MARY CHAMPAGNE
Graduate School: LEWIS SIEGEL

PROFESSORS

ABOU-DONIA, M. B., Pharmacology and Can-
cer Biology
ADDISON, W. A., Obstetrics and Gynaecology
AERS, D., English
AGARWAL, P. K., Computer Science
AKWARI, O. E., Surgery
ALBALA, D. M., Surgery
ALDRICH, J., Political Science
ALLARD, W. K., Mathematics
ALLEN, N. B., Medicine
ANDERSON, E. E., Surgery
ANDERSON, P. A. W., Paediatrics
ANDERSON, R. W., Surgery
ANDERSON, W. B., Ophthalmology
ANDREWS, E., Slavic Languages and Litera-
ture
ANLYAN, W. G., Surgery
ANSCHER, M. S., Radiation Oncology
APPLEWHITE, J. W., English
ASHER, S. R., Psychology, Social and Health
Sciences
ASHTON, R. H., Business Admin.
AUGUSTINE, Jr, G. J., Neurobiology
AVISSAR, R., Civil and Environmental Eng.
BAILLIE, J., Medicine
BAKER, H. A., English
BAKER, P. A., Earth and Ocean Sciences
BALDWIN, S. W., Chemistry
BARANGER, H. U., Physics
BARBER, R. T., Marine Sciences
BARR, R. C., Biomedical Eng.
BARTLETT, J. A., Medicine

BARTLETT, K., Law
BASHORE, T. M., Medicine
BASSETT, III, F. H., Surgery
BEALE, J. T., Mathematics
BEALE, S. S., Law
BECKWITH, S., English
BEEN, M. D., Biochemistry
BEHAR, V. S., Medicine
BEHRINGER, R. P., Physics
BEJAN, A., Mechanical Eng.
BELL, D. F., Romance Studies
BENFEY, P. N., Biology
BENNETT, G. V., Cell Biology
BENNETT, P. B., Anaesthesiology
BERATAN, D. N., Chemistry
BERCHUCK, A., Obstetrics and Gynaecology
BERGER, J. O., Statistics
BERTOZZI, A. L., Mathematics
BETTMAN, J. R., Business Admin.
BIERMANN, A. W., Computer Science
BIGNER, D. D., Pathology
BISSET, III, G. S., Radiology
BLAND, K. P., Religion
BLAZER, D. G., Psychiatry and Behavioural
Sciences
BLUMENTHAL, J. A., Psychiatry and Beha-
vioural Sciences
BOATWRIGHT, M. T., Classical Studies
BOLLERSLEV, T., Econ.
BOLLINGER, R. R., Surgery
BOLOGNESI, D. P., Surgery
BONAVENTURA, C. J., Marine Sciences
BONAVENTURA, J., Marine Sciences
BONK, J. F., Chemistry
BORCHARDT, F. L., Germanic Languages
BOSSEN, E. H., Pathology
BOULDING, W. F., Business Admin.
BOWIE, J. D., Radiology
BOYLE, J. D. A., Law
BRADFORD, W. D., Pathology
BRADLEY, M., Business Admin.
BRADY, D. J., Electrical and Computer Eng.
BRANDON, R. N., Philosophy
BREEDEN, D. T., Business Admin.
BRIZEL, D. M., Radiation Oncology
BRODIE, H. K. H., Psychiatry and Beha-
vioural Sciences
BROWN, A. S., Electrical and Computer Eng.
BROWN, H. L., Obstetrics and Gynaecology
BRUZELIUS, C., Art and Art History
BRYANT, R., Mathematics
BUCKLEY, E. G., Ophthalmology
BUCKLEY, P. J., Pathology
BUCKLEY, R. H., Paediatrics
BUEHLER, A., Health, Physical Education and
Recreation
BURCH, Jr, W. M., Medicine
BURIAN, P. H., Classical Studies
BURNS, B. J., Psychiatry and Behavioural
Sciences
BURTON, R. M., Business Admin.
BUTTERS, R. R., English
CALIFF, R. M., Medicine
CARIN, L., Electrical and Computer Eng.
CARON, M. G., Cell Biology
CARRINGTON, P. D., Law
CARROLL, B. A., Radiology
CARTER, J. H., Psychiatry and Behavioural
Sciences
CARTMILL, M., Biological Anthropology and
Anatomy
CASEY, P. J., Pharmacology and Cancer
Biology
CHAFE, W. H., History
CHAO, N. J., Medicine
CHEN, Y., Paediatrics
CHIKARAISHI, D. M., Neurobiology
CHRISTENSEN, N. L., Earth and Environmen-
tal Sciences
CHRISTIE, G. C., Law
CLARK, E. A., Religion
CLARK, J. S., Biology
CLARK, R. L., Mechanical Engi.
CLARKE-PEARSON, D. L., Obstetrics and
Gynaecology
CLAY, D., Classical Studies

CLEMENTS, III, D. A., Paediatrics
CLIPP, E. C., Nursing
CLOTFELTER, C., Public Policy Studies
CLUM, J. M., Theatre Studies
COBB, F. R., Medicine
COCKS, F. H., Mechanical Eng.
COFFMAN, T. M., Medicine
COHEN, H. J., Medicine
COHEN, W. M., Business Admin.
COHN, J. A., Medicine
COIE, J. D., Psychology, Social and Health
Sciences
COLEMAN, R. E., Radiology
COLEMAN, W. J., Business Admin.
COLVIN, O. M., Medicine
COOK, D. R., Anaesthesiology
COOK, P. J., Public Policy Studies
COOKE, M., Asian and African Language and
Literature
COREY, G. R., Medicine
CORLISS, B., Earth and Ocean Sciences
COSTANZO, P. R., Psychology, Social and
Health Sciences
COSTELLO, E. J., Psychiatry and Behavioural
Sciences
COX, J. D., Law
CRAWFORD, J., Medicine
CRENSHAW, J. L., Divinity
CROVITZ, H. F., Psychiatry and Behavioural
Sciences
CROWDER, L. B., Marine Sciences
CROWLEY, T. J., Earth and Ocean Sciences
CRUMBLISS, A. L., Chemistry
CULLEN, B. R., Molecular Genetics and
Microbiology
CULP, J. M., Law
DAVIDSON, C. N., English
DAVIDSON, J. R., Psychiatry and Behavioural
Sciences
DAVIS, N. G., Classical Studies
DAWSON, J. R., Immunology
DE BELLIS, M. D., Psychiatry and Beha-
vioural Sciences
de MARCHI, N., Econ.
DELLINGER, W. E., Law
DELONG, G. R., Paediatrics
DeMOTT, D., Law
DeNEEF, A. L., English
DESANCTIS, G., Business Admin.
DEWHIRST, M. W., Radiation Oncology
Di GIULIO, R. T., Earth and Environmental
Sciences
DiPRETE, T. A., Sociology
DODGE, K. A., Public Policy Studies
DOWELL, E. H., Mechanical Eng.
ECKERMAN, C. O., Psychological and Brain
Sciences
EDELSBRUNNER, H., Computer Science
EDWARDS, G. S., Physics
EFIRD, J. M., Divinity
ELLINWOOD, Jr, E. H., Psychiatry and Beha-
vioural Sciences
ELLIS, C. S., Computer Science
ENDOW, S. A., Cell Biology
ENGLISH, P. C., History
EPSTEIN, D. L., Ophthalmology
ERICKSON, C. J., Psychological and Brain
Sciences
ERICKSON, H. P., Cell Biology
EVERETT, R. O., Law
FAIR, R. B., Electrical and Computer Eng.
FALLETTA, J. M., Paediatrics
FARMER, J. C., Surgery
FEINGLOS, M. N., Medicine
FISCHER, G. W., Business Admin.
FISH, P. G., Political Science
FISHER, S. R., Surgery
FITZPATRICK, D., Neurobiology
FLANAGAN, O., Philosophy
FLEISHMAN, J., Law
FLOYD, Jr, C. E., Radiology
FOREMAN, J. W., Paediatrics
FORWARD, R. B., Marine Sciences
FRANCES, A. J., Psychiatry and Behavioural
Sciences
FRANCIS, J., Business Admin.

FRANK, M. M., Paediatrics
FREEMARK, M. S., Paediatrics
FRIEDMAN, A. H., Surgery
FRIEDMAN, H. S., Paediatrics
FRIEDMAN, M., Biomedical Eng.
FULKERSON, Jr, W. J., Medicine
GAINES, J. M., Literature
GARCIA-BLANCO, M. A., Molecular Genetics and Microbiology
GARCI-GOMEZ, M., Romance Studies
GARG, D. P., Mechanical Eng.
GASPAR, B., History
GAVINS, R., History
GELFAND, A., Statistics
GEORGE, L. K., Sociology
GEORGE, S. L., Biostatistics and Bioinformatics
GEORGIADE, G. S., Surgery
GEREFFI, G., Sociology
GILBOA, E., Surgery
GILLESPIE, M. A., Political Science
GILLIAM, B., Music
GLANDER, K. E., Biological Anthropology and Anatomy
GLOWER, Jr, D. D., Surgery
GOCKERMAN, J. P., Medicine
GOLDBERG, R. N., Paediatrics
GOLDING, M. P., Philosophy
GOLDSCHMIDT, P. J., Medicine
GOLDSTEIN, L. B., Medicine
GOODMAN, P. C., Radiology
GOODWIN, C. D., Econ.
GOODWYN, L. C., History
GOSHAW, A. T., Physics
GRABOWSKI, H. G., Econ.
GRAHAM, D. A., Econ.
GRANT, A. O., Medicine
GRANT, J. P., Surgery
GRANT, R. W., Political Science
GREENBERG, C. S., Medicine
GREENFIELD, Jr, J. C., Medicine
GREENLEAF, A. L., Biochemistry
GREENSIDE, H., Physics
GREER, M. R., Romance Studies
GRIECO, J., Political Science
GRIFFITHS, P. A., Mathematics
HAAGEN, P. H., Law
HAFF, P. K., Earth and Ocean Sciences
HAIN, R., Mathematics
HALL, K. C., Mechanical Eng.
HALL, III, R. P., Medicine
HALL, W. C., Neurobiology
HALL, W. G., Psychological and Brain Sciences
HALPERIN, E. C., Radiation Oncology
HAMILTON, J. A., Psychology, Social and Health Sciences
HAMILTON, J. D., Medicine
HAMMES, G. G., Biochemistry
HAMMOND, C. B., Obstetrics and Gynaecology
HAN, M. Y., Physics
HANEY, A. F., Obstetrics and Gynaecology
HARER, J., Mathematics
HARMAN, C. M., Mechanical Eng.
HARRELSON, J. M., Surgery
HARVEY, C. R., Business Admin.
HAUERWAS, S. M., Divinity
HAVIGHURST, C. C., Law
HAYNES, B. F., Medicine
HAYS, R. B., Divinity
HEALY, R. G., Earth and Environmental Sciences
HEINZ, E. R., Radiology
HEITMAN, J. B., Molecular Genetics and Microbiology
HEITZENRATER, R. P., Divinity
HELMS, C. A., Radiology
HERRUP, C. B., History
HERSHFIELD, M. S., Medicine
HERTZBERG, B. S., Radiology
HILL, G. B., Obstetrics and Gynaecology
HILL, R. L., Biochemistry
HILLERBRAND, H. J., Religion
HINTON, D. E., Earth and Environmental Sciences
HOCHMUTH, R. M., Mechanical Eng.

HOFFMAN, M. R., Pathology
HOLLOWAY, K., English
HOROWITZ, D. L., Law
HOUGH, J. F., Political Science
HOWELL, C. R., Physics
HSIEH, D. A., Business Admin.
HSIEH, T., Biochemistry
HUANG, A. T., Medicine
HUBER, J. C., Business Admin.
HYLANDER, W. L., Biological Anthropology and Anatomy
JAFFE, G. J., Ophthalmology
JAFFE, S., Music
JAMESON, F., Literature
JASZCZAK, R. J., Radiology
JENNINGS, R. B., Pathology
JENTLESON, B. W., Public Policy Studies
JIRTLE, R. L., Radiation Oncology
JOHNSON, G. A., Radiology
JOHNSON, K. M., Eng.
JOHNSON, V. E., Statistics
JOINES, W. T., Electrical and Computer Eng.
JONES, L. G., Divinity
JONES, R. H., Surgery
JONES, T., Law
KAMAKURA, W. A., Business Admin.
KANE, W. H., Medicine
KAPLAN, A., Romance Studies
KARSON, J. A., Earth and Ocean Sciences
KATUL, G. G., Earth and Environmental Sciences
KATZ, D. F., Biomedical Eng.
KATZ, L. C., Neurobiology
KAY, R. F., Biological Anthropology and Anatomy
KEEFE, F. J., Psychiatry and Behavioural Sciences
KEENE, J. D., Molecular Genetics and Microbiology
KELLER, T. F., Business Admin.
KELLEY, A. C., Econ.
KELSOE, G. H., Immunology
KEOHANE, N. O., Political Science
KEOHANE, R., Political Science
KERN, F. H., Anaesthesiology
KIEHART, D. P., Biology
KILLENBERG, P. G., Medicine
KIMBROUGH, K. P., Econ.
KINNEY, T. R., Paediatrics
KIRBY, M. L., Paediatrics
KISSLO, J. A., Medicine
KITSCHELT, H. P., Political Science
KLINTWORTH, G. K., Pathology
KOCH, W. J., Surgery
KOONZ, C., History
KORNBERG, A., Political Science
KORT, W. A., Religion
KRAMER, R. A., Earth and Environmental Sciences
KREDICH, N. M., Medicine
KREUZER, K. N., Biochemistry
KRISHNAN, K. R. R., Psychiatry and Behavioural Sciences
KROLIK, J. L., Electrical and Computer Eng.
KUHN, C. M., Pharmacology and Cancer Biology
KUNIHOLM, B. R., Public Policy Studies
KUO, P. C., Surgery
KURTZBERG, J., Paediatrics
KYLE, A. S., Business Admin.
LADD, H., Public Policy Studies
LAHUSEN, T., Literature
LAND, K. C., Sociology
LANGE, D. L., Law
LANGE, P., Political Science
LAUGHHUNN, D. J., Business Admin.
LAVINE, M. L., Statistics
LAWLER, G. F., Mathematics
LAWRENCE, B. B., Religion
LAYTON, H., Mathematics
LEE, P. P., Ophthalmology
LEFKOWITZ, R. J., Medicine
LEIGHT, G. S., Surgery
LEIGHTEN, P., Art and Art History
LENTRICCHIA, F., Literature
LEVIN, L. S., Surgery

LEWIN, A. Y., Business Admin.
LEWIS, D. V., Paediatrics
LIDDLE, R. A., Medicine
LIN, N., Sociology
LIND, E. A., Business Admin.
LINNEY, E. A., Molecular Genetics and Microbiology
LISCHER, R., Divinity
LIVINGSTONE, D. A., Biology
LOCHMULLER, C. H., Chemistry
LOCKHEAD, G. R., Psychological and Brain Sciences
LOGUE, P. E., Psychiatry and Behavioural Sciences
LONGINO, M., Romance Studies
LOONEY, J. G., Psychiatry and Behavioural Sciences
LOWE, J. E., Surgery
LYERLY, H. K., Surgery
LYLES, K. W., Medicine
LYNCH, J. G., Business Admin.
MacINTYRE, N. R., Medicine
MADDEN, D. J., Psychiatry and Behavioural Sciences
MAHONEY, E. P., Philosophy
MALIN, P. E., Earth and Environmental Sciences
MARCH, J. S., Psychiatry and Behavioural Sciences
MARCUS, J., Divinity
MARINOS, P. N., Electrical and Computer Eng.
MARK, D. B., Medicine
MARK, J. B., Anaesthesiology
MARKS, L. B., Radiation Oncology
MARTINEZ, S., Radiology
MASON, R. M., Surgery
MASSEY, J. M., Medicine
MASSOUD, H. Z., Electrical and Computer Eng.
MATCHAR, D. B., Medicine
MAUSKOPF, S., History
McCANN, R. L., Surgery
McCARTHY, G., Radiology
McCLAIN, P. D., Political Science
McCLAY, D. R., Biology
McCUEN, B. W., Ophthalmology
McDONNELL, D. P., Pharmacology and Cancer Biology
McELROY, M. B., Econ.
McGOVERN, F. E., Law
McGOWN, L., Chemistry
McINTOSH, T. J., Cell Biology
McLENDON, R. E., Pathology
McNAMARA, Sr, J. O., Neurobiology
McPHAIL, A. T., Chemistry
MEANS, A. R., Pharmacology and Cancer Biology
MECK, W. H., Psychological and Brain Sciences
MEDINA, M. A., Civil and Environmental Eng.
METZLOFF, T. B., Law
MEYERS, C. L., Religion
MEYERS, E. M., Religion
MICKIEWICZ, E., Public Policy Studies
MIGNOLO, W., Literature
MILLER, M. A., History
MILLS, E., Pharmacology and Cancer Biology
MITCHELL, W. G., Business Admin.
MODRICH, P. L., Biochemistry
MOI, T., Literature
MOON, R. E., Anaesthesiology
MOORE, J. O., Medicine
MOORMAN, C., Business Admin.
MOREIRAS, A., Romance Studies
MORGAN, S. P., Sociology
MORRIS, J. J., Medicine
MORRIS, M., Law
MORRISON, D. R., Mathematics
MOSTELLER, R. P., Law
MUDIMBE, V., Literature
MUELLER, B., Physics
MUNGER, M. C., Political Science
NADLER, J. V., Pharmacology and Cancer Biology
NEEDHAM, D., Mechanical Eng.

NELSON, R. C., Radiology
NEVINS, J. R., Molecular Genetics and Microbiology
NEWGARD, C. B., Pharmacology and Cancer Biology
NEWMAN, M. F., Anaesthesiology
NICKLAS, R. B., Biology
NICOLELIS, M. A., Neurobiology
NIJHOUT, H. F., Biology
NIOU, E. S., Political Science
NOLTE, L. W., Electrical and Computer Eng.
NOWICKI, S., Biology
NUNLEY, II, J. A., Surgery
O'BARR, W. M., Cultural Anthropology
OH, S., Physics
OLSEN, E. A., Medicine
O'RAND, A. M., Sociology
OREN, R., Earth and Environmental Sciences
ORR, L., Romance Studies
OSTBYE, T., Community and Family Medicine
PALETZ, D. L., Political Science
PALMER, R. A., Chemistry
PALMER, R. G., Physics
PAPPAS, T. N., Surgery
PARDON, W. L., Mathematics
PARKERSON, G. R., Community and Family Medicine
PATZ, E. F., Radiology
PAULSON, D. F., Surgery
PAULSON, E. K., Radiology
PAYNE, C. M., History
PAYNE, J. W., Business Admin.
PERFECT, J. R., Medicine
PERICAK-VANCE, M. A., Medicine
PETER, R. H., Medicine
PETROSKI, H., Civil and Environmental Eng.
PHILLIPS, III, H. R., Medicine
PIANTADOSI, C. A., Medicine
PIMM, S. L., Earth and Environmental Sciences
PIRRUNG, M. C., Chemistry
PISETSKY, D. S., Medicine
PIZZO, S. V., Pathology
POPE, D., English
PORTER, J. A., English
POWELL, H. J., Law
POWELL, R. J., Art and Art History
PREMINGER, G. M., Surgery
PRICE, D. E., Political Science
PRICE, E. R., English
PROSNITZ, L. R., Radiation Oncology
PROVENZALE, J. M., Radiology
PUROHIT, D., Business Admin.
PURVES, D., Neurobiology
PUTALLAZ, M., Psychology, Social and Health Sciences
QUARLES, L. D., Medicine
QUILLIGAN, M., English
QUINN, N., Cultural Anthropology
RADTKE, R. A., Medicine
RADWAY, J. A., Literature
RAETZ, C. R. H., Biochemistry
RAJAGOPALAN, K. V., Biochemistry
RAMUS, J. S., Marine Sciences
RAUSHER, M. D., Biology
RAVIN, C. E., Radiology
RECKHOW, K. H., Earth and Environmental Sciences
REDDY, W. M., History
REED, M. C., Mathematics
REEDY, M. K., Cell Biology
REICHERT, W. M., Biomedical Eng.
REICHMAN, J. H., Law
REIF, J. H., Computer Science
REINSMOEN, N. L., Pathology
RELLER, L. B., Pathology
REMMER, K. L., Political Science
REPPY, W. A., Law
REYNOLDS, J. F., Biology
RICHARDS, J. F., History
RICHARDSON, C. J., Earth and Environmental Sciences
RICHARDSON, D. C., Biochemistry
RICHARDSON, J. S., Biochemistry
RICHTER, D. D., Earth and Environmental Sciences

RIGSBY, K. J., Classical Studies
ROBBOY, S. J., Pathology
ROCKEY, D. C., Medicine
ROCKMAN, H. A., Medicine
ROGGLI, V. L., Pathology
ROLAND, A., History
ROLLESTON, J. L., Germanic Languages
ROSE, D., Computer Science
ROSENBERG, A., Philosophy
ROTH, S., Psychology, Social and Health Sciences
ROWE, T. D., Law
RUBIN, D. C., Psychological and Brain Sciences
RYAN, T. J., Medicine
SABISTON, D. C., Surgery
SACKS, J., Statistics
SAMULSKI, T. V., Radiation Oncology
SANDERS, D. B., Medicine
SANDERS, E. P., Religion
SANDERS, S. P., Paediatrics
SANFORD, D. H., Philosophy
SCHAEFFER, D. G., Mathematics
SCHANBERG, S. M., Pharmacology and Cancer Biology
SCHIFFMAN, S. S., Psychiatry and Behavioural Sciences
SCHLESINGER, W. H., Biology
SCHMALBECK, R. L., Law
SCHMECHEL, D. E., Medicine
SCHOEN, C. L., Mathematics
SCHOMBERG, D. W., Obstetrics and Gynaecology
SCHROEDER, C., Law
SCHULMAN, K. A., Medicine
SCHWAB, S. J., Medicine
SCHWARCZ, S. L., Law
SCHWARTZ, D. A., Medicine
SCHWARTZ-BLOOM, R. D., Pharmacology and Cancer Biology
SCHWINN, D. A., Anaesthesiology
SEIGLER, H. F., Surgery
SEXTON, D. J., Medicine
SHATZMILLER, J., History
SHAUGHNESSY, E. J., Mechanical Eng.
SHAW, A. J., Biology
SHAW, B. R., Chemistry
SHELBURNE, J. D., Pathology
SHENOLIKAR, S., Pharmacology and Cancer Biology
SHEPPARD, B. H., Business Admin.
SHERWOOD, A., Psychiatry and Behavioural Sciences
SIEDOW, J. N., Biology
SIEGEL, L. M., Biochemistry
SIEGLER, I. C., Psychiatry and Behavioural Sciences
SIMEL, D. L., Medicine
SIMON, J. D., Chemistry
SIMON, S. A., Neurobiology
SIMONS, E. L., Biological Anthropology and Anatomy
SIMPSON, I. H., Sociology
SLOAN, F. A., Economics
SLOTKIN, T. A., Pharmacology and Cancer Biology
SMITH, B. C., Philosophy
SMITH, B. H., Literature
SMITH, K. K., Biology
SMITH, P. K., Surgery
SMITH, S. W., Biomedical Eng.
SMITH, T. P., Radiology
SNYDERMAN, R., Medicine
SOPER, J. T., Obstetrics and Gynaecology
SPENNER, K. I., Sociology
SPICER, L. D., Radiology
SPRAGENS, T. A., Political Science
SPRITZER, C. E., Radiology
ST CLAIR, E. W., Medicine
STADDON, J. E. R., Psychological and Brain Sciences
STAELIN, R., Business Admin.
STAMLER, J. S., Medicine
STANLEY, D. K., Classical Studies
STEEGE, D. A., Biochemistry
STEINMETZ, D. C., Divinity

STERN, M. A., Mathematics
STEWART, P., Romance Studies
STILES, G. L., Medicine
STRANDBERG, V. H., English
STRAUMAN, T. J., Psychology, Social and Health Sciences
STRITTMATTER, W. J., Medicine
STROHBEHN, J. W., Biomedical Eng.
SUGARMAN, J., Medicine
SULLENGER, B. A., Surgery
SULLIVAN, K. M., Medicine
SURIN, K. J., Literature
SURWIT, R. S., Psychiatry and Behavioural Sciences
SVETKEY, L. P., Medicine
SWARTZ, M. S., Psychiatry and Behavioural Sciences
TAN, T. Y., Mechanical Eng.
TAUCHEN, G. E., Econ.
TAYLOR, C. R., Econ.
TEDDER, T. F., Immunology
TELEN, M. J., Medicine
TERBORGH, J. W., Earth and Environmental Sciences
THOMAS, J., Romance Studies
THOMAS, J. E., Physics
THOMPSON, J. H., History
THOMPSON, R. J., Psychology, Social and Health Sciences
THOMPSON, W. M., Radiology
TIRYAKIAN, E. A., Sociology
TODD, R. L., Music
TOONE, E. J., Chemistry
TORGOVNICK, M., English
TORNOW, W., Physics
TOWER, E., Econ.
TRAHEY, G. E., Biomedical Eng.
TRANGENSTEIN, J. A., Mathematics
TREEM, W. R., Paediatrics
TRIVEDI, K. S., Electrical and Computer Eng.
TRUSKEY, G. A., Biomedical Eng.
TURNER, B. S., Nursing
TURNER, D. A., Surgery
TYREY, E. L., Obstetrics and Gynaecology
ULSHEN, M. H., Paediatrics
UNDERKUFFLER, L. S., Law
URBANIAK, J. R., Surgery
UYENOYAMA, M. K., Biology
VAN ALSTYNE, W. W., Law
VAN ROMPAY, L., Religion
VAN SCHAIK, C., Biological Anthropology and Anatomy
VANCE, J. M., Medicine
VENAKIDES, S., Mathematics
VERNON, J. M., Econ.
VIDMAR, N. J., Law
VILGALYS, R. J., Biology
VISWANATHAN, S., Business Admin.
VOGEL, S., Biology
VON RAMM, O. T., Biomedical Eng.
WACKER, G. A., Divinity
WAINWRIGHT, G., Divinity
WALLACH, M. A., Psychological and Brain Sciences
WALTER, R. L., Physics
WALTHER, P. J., Surgery
WANG, P. P., Electrical and Computer Eng.
WARE, R. E., Paediatrics
WARNER, D. S., Anaesthesiology
WEBSTER, G. D., Surgery
WEBSTER, R. E., Biochemistry
WEINBERG, J. B., Medicine
WEINER, R. D., Psychiatry and Behavioural Sciences
WEINERTH, J. L., Surgery
WEINHOLD, K. J., Surgery
WEINTRAUB, E. R., Econo.
WEISTART, J. C., Law
WELLER, H. R., Physics
WELLS, S. A., Surgery
WEST, M., Statistics
WHALEY, R. E., Business Admin.
WHARTON, A. W., Art and Art History
WHITE, R. A., Biology
WIENER, J. B., Law
WILBUR, R. L., Biology

WILKINS, R. H., Surgery
WILKINSON, W. E., Biostatistics and Bioinformatics
WILLIAMS, C. L., Psychological and Brain Sciences
WILLIAMS, K. J., English
WILLIAMS, R. B., Psychiatry and Behavioural Sciences
WILLIAMS, R. S., Medicine
WILLIMON, W. H., Divinity
WILSON, J., Sociology
WILSON, J. A. P., Medicine
WILSON, K. H., Medicine
WILSON, R. L., Nursing
WINKLER, R. L., Business Admin.
WITT, R. G., History
WOLBARSHT, M. L., Psychological and Brain Sciences
WOLFE, W. G., Surgery
WOLPERT, R. L., Statistics
WONG, D. B., Philosophy
WOOD, P. H., History
WRIGHT, J. R., Cell Biology
YANG, W., Chemistry
YARGER, W. E., Medicine
YOUNG, S. L., Medicine
ZALUTSKY, M. R., Radiology
ZHOU, X., Mathematics
ZHOU, X., Sociology
ZIPKIN, P. H., Business Admin.

EAST CAROLINA UNIVERSITY

East Fifth St, Greenville, NC 27858-4353

Telephone: (252) 328-6131
Internet: www.ecu.edu
Founded 1907
Constituent instn of the Univ. of North Carolina system
Chancellor: STEVE BALLARD
Provost and Vice-Chancellor for Academic Affairs: JAMES L. SMITH
Vice-Chancellor for Admin. and Finance: KEVIN SEITZ
Vice-Chancellor for Univ. Advancement: MICHAEL B. DOWDY
Registrar: ANGELA R. ANDERSON
Dir of Admissions: DONALD C. JOYNER
Dir of Academic Library Services: LARRY BOYER

Library of 1,339,345 vols
Number of teachers: 1,529
Number of students: 22,767

Publications: *The Children's Folklore Review* (2 a year), *The North Carolina Literary Review* (annual), *The North Carolina Folklore Journal* (2 a year), *Technical Communication* (quarterly), *Tar River Poetry* (2 a year).

ELIZABETH CITY STATE UNIVERSITY

1704 Weeksville Rd, Elizabeth City, NC 27909

Telephone: (252) 335-3400
Fax: (252) 335-3731
E-mail: infoline@mail.ecsu.edu
Internet: www.ecsu.edu
Founded 1891 as a Normal School; present name 1969
Academic year: August to May
Chancellor: WILLIE J. GILCHRIST
Provost and Vice-Chancellor for Academic Affairs: RONALD BLACKMON
Vice-Chancellor for Student Affairs: Dr ANTHONY BROWN
Vice-Chancellor for Business and Finance: GREGORY DAVID
Vice-Chancellor for Institutional Advancement: RICHARD LUCAS, Jr
Number of teachers: 99
Number of students: 2,330.

ELON UNIVERSITY

Elon, NC 27244
Telephone: (336) 278-2000
Fax: (336) 278-7699
E-mail: interadm@elon.edu
Internet: www.elon.edu
Founded 1889
Related to the United Church of Christ
Academic year: September to May
Pres.: LEO M. LAMBERT
Provost: GERALD L. FRANCIS
Dean and Univ. Librarian: KATE D. HICKEY
Library of 240,000 vols
Number of teachers: 270 (201 full-time, 69 part-time)
Number of students: 4,138.

FAYETTEVILLE STATE UNIVERSITY

1200 Murchison Rd, Fayetteville, NC 28301-4298

Telephone: (919) 672-1111
Internet: www.uncfsu.edu
Founded 1867 as the Howard School, attained Univ. status 1969
Part of Univ. of North Carolina System
Chancellor: T. J. BRYAN
Provost and Vice-Chancellor for Academic Affairs: JULIETTE BELL
Vice-Chancellor for Business and Finance: LATONYA HANKINS
Vice-Chancellor for Intitutional Advancement: STEPHEN MCDANIEL
Vice-Chancellor for Student Affairs: OLIVIA CHAVIS
Registrar: SARAH BAKER
Librarian: BOBBY WYNN
Library of 500,000 vols
Number of teachers: 210 full-time
Number of students: 5,307.

GARDNER-WEBB UNIVERSITY

POB 997, Boiling Springs, NC 28017
Located at: 110 South Main St, Boiling Springs, NC 28017
Telephone: (704) 406-4000
E-mail: admissions@gardner-webb.edu
Internet: www.gardner-webb.edu
Founded 1905 as Boiling Springs High School; present name 1993
Private control
Academic year: August to May
Pres.: Dr A. FRANK BONNER
Vice-Pres. and Provost of Academics: Dr BEN C. LESLIE
Vice-Pres. and Dean of Student Devt: BRUCE MOORE
Vice-Pres. for Business and Finance: MIKE W. HARDIN
Vice-Pres. for Enrollment Management: JACK BUCHANAN
Vice-Pres. for Advancement: RALPH DIXON Jr
Vice-Pres. for Athletics: CHUCK BURCH
Registrar: STEPHEN SAIN
Library Dir: VALERIE PARRY
Number of teachers: 133 full-time
Number of students: 4,000.

GREENSBORO COLLEGE

815 West Market St, Greensboro, NC 27401-1875

Telephone: (336) 272-7102
Fax: (336) 271-6634
E-mail: admissions@gborocollege.edu
Internet: www.gborocollege.edu
Founded 1838
Academic year: August to May
Pres.: Dr CRAVEN E. WILLIAMS
Exec. Vice-Pres.: Dr TIFFANY MCKILLIP FRANKS

Vice-Pres. for Academic Affairs: PAUL LESLIE
Assoc. Vice-Pres. for Technology: PAMELA MCKIRDY
Dir of Admissions: TIMOTHY JACKSON
Library of 100,000 vols
Number of teachers: 103
Number of students: 950.

GUILFORD COLLEGE

5800 West Friendly Ave, Greensboro, NC 27410

Telephone: (336) 316-2000
Fax: (336) 316-2949
Internet: www.guilford.edu
Founded 1837
Private (Society of Friends) co-educational liberal arts college
Academic year: August to May
Pres.: KENT JOHN CHABOTAR
Vice-Pres. for Academic Affairs and Academic Dean: MARTHA H. COOLEY
Vice-Pres. for Enrollment and Campus Life: RANDY DOSS
Vice-Pres. for Finance and Admin.: JERRY BOOTHBY
Vice-President for Advancement: MIKE POSTON
Dean for Campus Life: AARON FETROW
Library Dir: MARY ELLEN CHIJIOKE
Library of 220,000 vols
Number of teachers: 132
Number of students: 1,400

Publications: *Journal of Undergraduate Mathematics* (2 a year), *Journal of Undergraduate Research in Physics* (2 a year), *The Southern Friend* (2 a year).

HIGH POINT UNIVERSITY

833 Montlieu Ave, High Point, NC 27262-3598

Telephone: (336) 841-9000
Fax: (336) 841-4599
Internet: www.highpoint.edu
Founded 1924
Pres.: NIDO R. QUBEIN
Vice-Pres. for Academic Affairs and Dean of Arts and Sciences: DENNIS G. CARROLL
Vice-Pres. for Enrollment: ANDY BILLS
Registrar: DIANA LEE ESTEY
Dir of Library Services: DAVID L. BRYDEN
Library of 170,000 vols
Number of teachers: 210
Number of students: 2,800.

JOHN WESLEY COLLEGE

2314 North Centennial St, High Point, NC 27265

Telephone: (336) 889-2262
Fax: (336) 889-2261
E-mail: admissions@johnwesley.edu
Internet: www.johnwesley.edu
Founded 1903 as Greensboro Bible and Literary School; closed 1931; re-opened 1932 as People's Bible School; present name 1956
Private control
Academic year: August to May
Pres.: Dr BRIAN DONLEY
Registrar: STEVE QUESENBERRY
Academic Dean: Dr JOHN LINDSEY
Director of Library Services: APRIL LINDSEY
Number of teachers: 18 (6 full-time, 12 part-time)
Number of students: 145.

JOHNSON C. SMITH UNIVERSITY

100–152 Beatties Ford Rd, Charlotte, NC 28216

Telephone: (704) 378-1000
Fax: (704) 372-5746
Internet: www.jcsu.edu

Founded 1867

Pres.: Dr DOROTHY COWSER YANCY
Vice-Pres. for Academic Affairs: Dr MARILYN SUTTON-HAYWOOD
Vice-Pres. for Finance: GERALD HECTOR
Vice-Pres. for Student Affairs: JEFFREY SMITH
Vice-Pres. for Institutional Advancementt: KENNETH WESTARY
Dir of Admissions: JOCELYN BIGGS
Dir of Honors College: Dr SHANNA BENJAMIN
Registrar: MOSES JONES
Dir of Library: FAYE PRIESTLY

Library of 113,000 vols
Number of teachers: 80, incl. 10 professors
Number of students: 1,427.

LEES-MCRAE COLLEGE

POB 128, Banner Elk, NC 28604

Telephone: (828) 898-5241
Fax: (828) 898-8814
E-mail: admissions@lmc.edu
Internet: www.lmc.edu

Founded 1900 as a girls' school; present name 1931
Private control
Academic year: August to May

Pres.: Dr DAVID W. BUSHMAN
Provost and Dean of the Faculty: Dr DEBRA THATCHER
Sr Vice-Pres. for Academic Affairs and Dean of Faculty: GENE SPEARS
Sr Vice-Pres. for Finance and Admin.: DAVID A. BROWNING
Vice-Pres. for Advancement (vacant): MERRITT YACKEY
Dir of Libraries (vacant)

Library of 99,138 print vols, 22,750 electronic books, 484 print periodicals, 9,364 electronic periodicals
Number of teachers: 73
Number of students: 700 (undergraduate)

CHAIRS OF ACADEMIC DIVISIONS

Science and Mathematics: Dr GENE SPEARS
Business and Social Sciences: Dr KATHERINE LOGAN
Education and Physical Education: Dr PETE CAMPBELL
Performing Arts: Dr JANET BARTON SPEER
Humanities: Dr JOHN F. KEENER

LENOIR-RHYNE COLLEGE

Hickory, NC 28603

Telephone: (828) 328-1741
Fax: (828) 328-7368
E-mail: admissions@lrc.edu
Internet: www.lrc.edu

Founded 1891
Private control (Evangelical Lutheran Church in America)
Academic year: August to May

Pres.: WAYNE B. POWELL
Academic Dean: JOHN D. SORENSON
Dean of Students: ANITA JOHNSON GWIN
Admissions Dir: RACHEL NICHOLS

Library of 124,000 vols
Number of teachers: 111
Number of students: 1,492.

LIVINGSTONE COLLEGE

701 West Monroe St, Salisbury, NC 28144

Telephone: (704) 638-5500
Internet: www.livingstone.edu

Founded 1879
Academic year: August to May

Pres.: Dr JIMMY R. JENKINS, Sr (acting)
Vice-Pres. for Academic Affairs: Dr BERTHA TAYLOR ESCOFFERY
Vice-Pres. for Institutional Advancement: Rev. ANTHONY DAVIS
Vice-Pres. for Business and Finance: PETA-GAYE SHAW
Vice-Pres. for Student Affairs: Dr STANLEY ELLIOTT
Librarian: MELISSA SMITH

Library of 80,000 vols
Number of teachers: 71
Number of students: 1,000

Publications: *Alumni Bulletin* (quarterly), *Bears' Tale* (annual), *College Catalog* (annual), *The Livingstonian* (annual).

MARS HILL COLLEGE

100 Athletic St, Mars Hill, NC 18754

Telephone: (828) 689-1208
E-mail: admissions@mhc.edu
Internet: www.mhc.edu

Founded 1856

Pres.: Dr DAN LUNSFORD
Vice-Pres. for Academic and Student Affairs: Dr NINA POLLARD
Vice-Pres. for Institutional Advancement: ALEX MILLER (acting)

Library of 90,000 vols
Number of teachers: 85
Number of students: 1,200

First degree courses in arts, science, music and social work.

MEREDITH COLLEGE

3800 Hillsborough St, Raleigh, NC 27607-5298

Telephone: (919) 760-8600
Fax: (919) 760-2874
Internet: www.meredith.edu

Founded 1891

Pres.: MAUREEN A. HARTFORD
Registrar: JODY HAMILTON-DAVIS
Dir of Admissions: HEIDI FLETCHER
Dean of Library Information Services: LAURA DAVIDSON

Library of 137,000 vols
Number of teachers: 261 (112 full-time, 149 part-time)
Number of students: 1,991.

METHODIST COLLEGE

5400 Ramsey St, Fayetteville, NC 28311-1498

Telephone: (910) 630-7000
Fax: (910) 630-7317
Internet: www.methodist.edu

Founded 1956
Academic year: September to May

Pres.: Dr M. ELTON HENDRICKS
Vice-Pres. for Academic Affairs and Dean of Univ.: DELMAS S. CRISP, Jr
Vice-Pres. for Business Affairs: GENE T. CLAYTON
Vice-Pres. for Devt: ROBIN DAVENPORT

Library of 88,133 vols, 45,000 non-book holdings
Number of teachers: 115 full-time
Number of students: 2,255 (1,700 full-time, 555 part-time).

MONTREAT COLLEGE

310 Gaither Circle, POB 1267, Montreat, NC 28757

Telephone: (828) 669-8012
Fax: (828) 669-0120

E-mail: admissions@montreat.edu
Internet: www.montreat.edu

Campuses at Asheville, Black Mountain, Charlotte

Founded 1916
Private control
Academic year: August to May

Pres.: Dr DAN STRUBLE
Vice-Pres. and Dean of Academics: Dr ABBY FAPETU
Vice-Pres. for Finance and Information Technology: Dr DIRK WILMOTH
Vice-Pres. for Institutional Advancement: Dr JERRY BOBILYA
Dean of Admissions and Financial Aid: LISA LANKFORD
Dean of Students: CHARLES LANCE
Registrar: KEITH KARRIKER
Library Dir: ELIZABETH PEARSON

Number of teachers: 89
Number of students: 1,036.

MOUNT OLIVE COLLEGE

634 Henderson St, Mount Olive, NC 28365

Telephone: (919) 658-2502
Fax: (919) 658-7180
Internet: www.mountolivecollege.edu

Campuses at Mount Olive, Goldsboro, New Bern, Research Triangle Park, Wilmington

Founded 1951 as Mount Allen Junior College; present name 1970
Private control
Academic year: August to May

Pres.: J. WILLIAM BYRD

Number of teachers: 199 (66 full-time, 133 part-time)
Number of students: 2,582 (2,245 full-time, 718 part-time).

NORTH CAROLINA AGRICULTURAL AND TECHNICAL STATE UNIVERSITY

1601 East Market St, Greensboro, NC 27411

Telephone: (919) 334-7500
Internet: www.ncat.edu

Founded 1891; attached to Univ. of North Carolina

Chancellor: STANLEY F. BATTLE
Vice-Chancellor for Academic Affairs: HAROLD MARTIN
Vice-Chancellor for Business/Finance: CHARLES MCINTYRE
Vice-Chancellor for Student Affairs: SULLIVAN WELBORNE
Vice-Chancellor for Devt and Univ. Relations: ROBERT P. JENNINGS
Registrar: DORIS GRAHAM
Librarian: WALTRENE CANADA

Library of 416,000 vols
Number of teachers: 813
Number of students: 11,103.

NORTH CAROLINA CENTRAL UNIVERSITY

Durham, NC 27707

Telephone: (919) 530-6100
Fax: (919) 530-7976
Internet: www.nccu.edu

Founded 1910
State control, linked to the Univ.y of N Carolina
Academic year: August to May

Chancellor: CHARLIE NELMS
Vice-Chancellor for Financial Affairs: CHARLES O'DUOR
Provost and Vice-Chancellor for Academic Affairs: BEVERLY JONES
Vice-Chancellor for Institutional Advancement: SUSAN L. HESTER

Vice-Chancellor for Student Affairs: ROLAND GAINES
Registrar: Dr JEROME GOODWIN
Dir of Library Services: Dr THEODOSIA SHIELDS
Library of 850,000 vols
Number of teachers: 388
Number of students: 6,521
Publications: *Ex Umbra, Campus Echo, Bulletins*

DEANS

College of Arts and Sciences: Dr BERNICE JOHNSON
School of Graduate Studies: Dr PERCY MURRAY
School of Library and Information Science: Dr BENJAMIN F. SPELLER
School of Law: JANICE MILLS
School of Business: Dr H. JAMES WILLIAMS
Univ. College: Dr BEVERLY W. JONES
School of Education: Dr CECELIA STEPPE-JONES

NORTH CAROLINA WESLEYAN COLLEGE

3400 North Wesleyan Blvd, Rocky Mount, NC 27804-9906
Telephone: (252) 985-5100
Fax: (252) 977 3701
Internet: www.ncwc.edu
Founded 1956
Co-educational, church-related liberal arts college
Pres.: IAN D. C. NEWBOULD
Vice-Pres. for Academic Affairs and Dean of the College: Dr JAMES F. TRAER
Library of 81,000 vols
Number of teachers: 70
Number of students: 1,900
Publication: *Bulletin* (quarterly).

PFEIFFER UNIVERSITY

Misenheimer, NC 28109
Telephone: (704) 463-1360
Fax: (704) 463-1363
E-mail: admis@pfeiffer.edu
Internet: www.pfeiffer.edu
Founded 1885
Private (Methodist) Control
Academic year: August to May
Pres.: Dr CHARLES M. AMBROSE
Chief Operating Officer and Exec. Vice-Pres.: DAVID OLIVE
Vice-Pres. for Academic Affairs: Dr PHILIP OTT
Vice-Pres. for Advancement: SHON HERRICK
Vice-Pres. for Enrollment Management: DAVID M. SMITH
Vice-Pres. for Finance: ROBIN LESLIE
Library Coordinator: LARA LITTLE
Library of 129,000 vols
Number of teachers: 65 full-time
Number of students: 2,027.

QUEENS UNIVERSITY OF CHARLOTTE

1900 Selwyn Ave, Charlotte, NC 28274
Telephone: (704) 337-2200
Fax: (704) 337-2517
Internet: www.queens.edu
Founded 1857 as Charlotte Female Institute; re-named Seminary for Girls 1891; became part of new Presbyterian Female College 1896; re-named Queens College 1912; present name and status 2002
Academic year: August to May

Liberal arts college, undergraduate and postgraduate programmes; Presbyterian (USA) affiliation
Pres.: Dr PAMELA L. DAVIES
Vice-Pres. for Academic Affairs: Dr J. NORRIS FREDERICK
Vice-Pres. for Enrollment Management: Dr BRIAN RALPH (acting)
Vice-Pres. for Univ. Advancement: PATTON McDOWELL, III
Vice-Pres. for Admin. and Operations: LAURIE GUY
Librarian: Dr CAROL W. JORDAN
Library of 150,000 vols
Number of teachers: 85 (61 full-time, 24 part-time)
Number of students: 1,550
Publication: *Odyssey* (quarterlyr).

ROANOKE BIBLE COLLEGE

715 North Poindexter St, Elizabeth City, NC 27909
Telephone: (252) 334-2000
Fax: (252) 334-2071
E-mail: admissions@roanokebible.edu
Internet: www.roanokebible.edu
Founded 1948
Private control
Pres.: WILLIAM A. GRIFFIN
Vice-Pres. for Academic Affairs: S. ELIZABETH BONDURANT
Vice-Pres. for Devt: E. HOWARD AMLAND
Vice-Pres. for Finance: JAMES R. CORMODE
Vice-Pres. for Student Life: GARRETT D. LEWIS
Registrar: JOAN U. SAWYER
Dir of Library Services: L. FRANK DODSON
Number of teachers: 17
Number of students: 194.

ST ANDREWS PRESBYTERIAN COLLEGE

1700 Dogwood Mile, Laurinburg, NC 28352
Telephone: (910) 277-5555
Fax: (910) 277-5020
E-mail: info@sapc.edu
Internet: www.sapc.edu
Founded 1896
Private control
Academic year: August to May
Pres.: PAUL BALDASARE
Vice-Pres. for Academic Affairs and Dean of the College: Dr ROBERT J. HOPKINS
Vice-Pres. (for Admin. and Finance: JOHN HARLAN
Vice-Pres. for Enrollment and Student Services: Rev. GLENN T. BATTEN
Registrar: DEBORAH A. SMITH
Library Dir: RITA DURSI JOHNSON
Library of 111,064 vols
Number of teachers: 45
Number of students: 741
Publication: *Cairn* (annual).

SAINT AUGUSTINE'S COLLEGE

1315 Oakwood Ave, Raleigh, NC 27610
Telephone: (919) 516-4000
Internet: www.st-aug.edu
Founded 1867
Private control
Academic year: August to May
Pres.: Dr DIANNE BOARDLEY SUBER
Vice-Pres. of Institutional Advancement: MARC A. NEWMAN
Library Dir: LINDA SIMMONS-HENRY
Number of teachers: 100
Number of students: 1,600.

SALEM ACADEMY AND COLLEGE

601 South Church St, Winston-Salem, NC 27108-0548
Telephone: (336) 721-2600
Fax: (336) 917-5339
Internet: www.salem.edu
Founded 1772
Private control
Pres.: Dr SUSAN E. PAULY
Vice-Pres. for Academic Affairs: ANN McELANEY-JOHNSON
Dir of Admin.: ANNA BECK GALLIMORE
Dean of Students: KRISPIN W. BARR
Dir of Libraries: Dr ROSE A. SIMON
Library of 128,500 vols
Number of teachers: 84
Number of students: 1,002.

SHAW UNIVERSITY

118 East South St, Raleigh, NC 27601
Telephone: (919) 546-8200
Fax: (919) 546-8301
E-mail: admissions@shawu.edu
Internet: www.shawu.edu
Founded 1865
Pres.: Dr CLARENCE G. NEWSOME
Academic Dean: JAMES TERRY ROBERSON, Jr
Exec. Vice-Pres.: MARTEL PERRY
Registrar: GENE PAGE
Librarian: TOM CLARK
Library of 122,413 vols
Number of teachers: 242
Number of students: 2,565.

SOUTHEASTERN BAPTIST THEOLOGICAL SEMINARY

POB 1889, Wake Forest, NC 27588
Located at: 120 South Wingate St, Wake Forest, NC 27587
Telephone: (919) 761-2100
E-mail: president@sebts.edu
Internet: www.sebts.edu
Founded 1950
Private control
Academic year: August to May
Pres.: Dr DANIEL AKIN
Sr Vice-Pres. for Academic Admin. and Dean of the Faculty: DAVID NELSON
Vice-Pres. for Student Services: Dr N. ALLAN MOSELEY
Vice-Pres. for Institutional Advancement: ANTHONY ALLEN
Vice-Pres. for Institutional Effectiveness and Assessment: Dr WAYLAN OWENS
Vice-Pres. for Admin.: RYAN R. HUTCHINSON
Registrar: SHELDON H. ALEXANDER
Library Dir: SHAWN C. MADDEN
Number of teachers: 80
Number of students: 1,500.

UNIVERSITY OF NORTH CAROLINA

POB 2688, Chapel Hill, NC 27515-2688
Telephone: (919) 962-1000
Fax: (919) 962-2751
Internet: www.northcarolina.edu
Pres.: ERSKINE BOWLES
Sr Vice-Pres. for Academic Affairs: HAROLD L. MARTIN
Vice-Pres. for Fed. Relations: KIMREY RHINEHARDT
Vice-Pres. for Govt Relations: ANDY WILLS
Vice-Pres. for Finance: ROBERT NELSON
Vice-Pres. for Academic Planning: ALAN R. MABE
Vice-Pres. for Institutional Research: SCOTT JENKINS
Vice-Pres. for Information Resources and Chief Information Officer: ROBYN R. RENDER

Vice-Pres. and Gen. Counsel: LESLIE J. WINNER

Sec. of the Univ.: BART CORGNATI

The Univ. of North Carolina is a multi-campus univ. composed of 16 instns: Univ. of North Carolina at Asheville, Univ. of North Carolina at Chapel Hill, Univ. of North Carolina at Greensboro, Univ. of North Carolina at Charlotte, Univ. of North Carolina at Wilmington, and North Carolina State Univ. at Raleigh. Also Appalachian State Univ., East Carolina Univ., Elizabeth City State Univ., Fayetteville State Univ., North Carolina Agricultural and Technical State Univ., North Carolina Central Univ., North Carolina School of the Arts, Univ. of North Carolina at Pembroke, Western Carolina Univ., Winston-Salem State Univ. (*q.v.*).

CONSTITUENT UNIVERSITIES

University of North Carolina at Asheville

1 Univ. Heights, Asheville, NC 28804-3299

Telephone: (828) 251-6600

E-mail: admissions@unca.edu

Internet: www.unca.edu

Established as Buncombe County Junior College 1927; later as Asheville-Biltmore College; made a unit of the Univ. in 1969

Chancellor: ANNE PONDER

Vice-Chancellor for Academic Affairs: Dr KATHERINE M. WHATLEY

Vice-Chancellor for Finance and Operations: Dr PAT W. HUNT

Vice-Chancellor for Student Affairs: Dr BILL HAGGARD

Vice-Chancellor for Alumni and Devt: WILLIAM P. MASSEY

Registrar: REBECCA SENSABAUGH

Univ. Librarian: JAMES R. KUHLMAN

Library of 243,800 vols

Number of teachers: 269

Number of students: 3,179

Publication: *Images*

CHAIRMEN OF DEPARTMENTS

Art: COOKE, T.
Atmospheric Sciences: HUANG, A.
Biology: KORMANIK, G.
Chemistry: GUPTON, J.
Computer Science: DAUGHTERTY, J.
Drama: WALTERS, S.
Econ.: LARSON, B.
Education: MCGLINN, J.
Environmental Studies: MAAS, R.
Foreign Languages: MCDONALD, P.
Health and Fitness: RAY, K.
History: SPELLMAN, W.
Humanities: DOWNES, M.
Literature: CAULFIELD, J.
Management: MCKENZIE, C.
Mass Communication: MITCHELL, C.
Mathematics: GALE, S.
Music: MCKNIGHT, C.
Political Science: MULLEN, D.
Philosophy: WILSON, G.
Physics: RUIZ, M.
Psychology: FRIEDENBERG, L.
Sociology: HAAS, W.

University of North Carolina at Chapel Hill

Chapel Hill, NC 27599

Telephone: (919) 962-2211

E-mail: uadm@email.unc.edu

Internet: www.unc.edu

Chartered 1789, opened 1795; since 1931 a unit of the Univ. of North Carolina

Academic year: August to May

Chancellor: JAMES MOESER

Provost and Exec. Vice-Chancellor: BERNADETTE GRAY-LITTLE

Exec. Assoc. Provost: STEPHEN ALLRED

Vice-Chancellor for Admin.: JANE DELANO BROWN

Vice-Chancellor for Univ. Advancement: MATTHEW KUPEC

Vice-Chancellor for Student Affairs: MARGARET JABLONSKI

Gen. Counsel: LESLIE CHAMBERS STROHM

Registrar: ALICE C. POEHLS

Asst Provost for Institutional Research and Assessment: Dr LYNN E. WILLIFORD

Sec. of the Faculty: JOSEPH FERRELL

Dir of Undergraduate Admissions: TERRY RHODES

Univ. Librarian: SARAH C. MICHALAK

Library: see Libraries

Number of teachers: 2,421

Number of students: 24,189

Publications: *Southern Economic Journal* (quarterly), *Social Science Newsletter* (quarterly), *The High School Journal* (quarterly), *Current Contents* (quarterly), *Centerpieces* (monthly), *Baseline* (3 a year), *Dear Colleague* (2 a year), *and numerous other faculty publications*

DEANS

College of Arts and Sciences and General College: RISA PALM
Kenan-Flagler Business School: JULIE COLLINS
School of Education: MADELEINE GRUMET
School of Law: JUDITH W. WEGNER
School of Medicine: JEFFREY HOUPT
School of Pharmacy: WILLIAM CAMPBELL
School of Public Health: WILLIAM ROPER
School of Information and Library Science: BARBARA B. MORAN
School of Dentistry: JOHN W. STAMM
School of Journalism: RICHARD R. COLE
School of Nursing: CYNTHIA FREUND
School of Social Work: RICHARD EDWARDS
Graduate School: LINDA DYKSTRA
Summer School: JAMES L. MURPHY

PROFESSORS

Allied Medical Programs:
MITCHELL, M. M.
MITCHELL, R. U.
PETERS, R. W.
SAKATA, R.
YODER, D. E.

American Studies Curriculum:
ALLEN, R. C.
KASSON, J. S.

Anaesthesiology:
BOYSEN, P. G.
GHIA, J. N.
KAFER, E. R.
MUELLER, R. A.
NORFLEET, E. A.
SPIELMAN, F. J.
SPRAGUE, D. H.
VAUGHAN, R. W.

Anthropology:
CRUMLEY, C. L.
EVENS, T. M.
FINKLER, K.
HOLLAND, D. C.
JOHNSON, N. B.
LARSEN, C. S.
LUTZ, C. A.
PEACOCK, J. L., III
STEPONAITIS, V. P.
WINTERHALDER, B.

Art:
FOLDA, J. T., III
GRABOWSKI, S. E.
KINNAIRD, R. W.
MARKS, A. S.
NOE, J. L.

SHERIFF, M. D.
STURGEON, C.
ZABOROWSKI, D. J.

Biochemistry:
CAPLOW, M.
CARTER, C. W., Jr
CHANEY, S. G.
ERREDE, B. J.
HERMANS, J.
LEE, D. C.
LENTZ, B. R.
MARZLUFF, W. F.
MEISSNER, G. W.
MORELL, P.
NAYFEH, S. N.
SANCAR, A.
SWANSTROM, R. I.
TIDWELL, P. F.
TRAUT, T. W.
VAN DYKE, T. A.
WOLFENDEN, R. V.

Biomedical Engineering Programme:
LUCAS, C. N.
TSUI, B. M.

Biostatistics:
DAVIS, C. E.
HELMS, R. W.
KALSBEEK, W. D.
KOCH, G. G.
KUPPER, L. L.
MARGOLIN, B. H.
QUADE, D. E.
SEN, P. K.
SUCHINDRAN, C. M.
SYMONS, M. J.

Biology:
BLOOM, K. S.
BOLLENBACHER, W. E.
DICKISON, W. C.
FEDUCCIA, J. A.
GENSEL, P. G.
GILBERT, L. I.
HARRIS, A. K., Jr
MATSON, S. W.
MATTHYSSE, A. G.
PARKS, C. R.
PEET, R. K.
PETES, T. D.
PRINGLE, J. R.
QUATRANO, R. S.
SALMON, E. D.
SCOTT, T. K.
STAFFORD, D. W.
STIVEN, A. E.
WHITE, P. S.
WILEY, R. H., Jr

Business Administration:
ALDER, R. S.
ANDERSON, C. R.
ARMSTRONG, G. M.
BATEMAN, T. S.
BAYUS, B. L.
BETTIS, R. A.
BLOCHER, E. J.
BLOOM, P. N.
COLLINS, J. H.
CONRAD, J. S.
EDWARDS, J. R.
ELVERS, D. A.
EVANS, J. P.
FISCHER, W. A.
HARTZELL, D. J.
KASARDA, J. D.
KLOMPMAKER, J. E.
LANDSMAN, W. R.
MCENALLY, R. W.
MANN, R. A.
MARUCHECK, A. E.
NEEBE, A. W.
PEIRCE, E. R.
PERREAULT, W. D., Jr
PRINGLE, J. J.
RAVENSCRAFT, D. J.

RENDLEMAN, R. J.
ROBERTS, B. S.
RONDINELLI, D. A.
ROSEN, B.
RUBIN, D. S.
SHAPIRO, D. L.
SULLIVAN, R. S.
TILLMAN, R.
WAGNER, H. M.
WHYBARK, D. C.

Cell Biology and Anatomy:
BURRIDGE, K. W. T.
GRANGER, N. A.
HACKENBROCK, C. R.
HENSON, O. W., Jr
HERMAN, B.
JACOBSON, K. A.
KOCH, W. E.
LAUDER, J. M.
LeMASTERS, J. J.
MONTGOMERY, R. L.
O'RAND, M. G.
PENG, H. B.
PETRUSZ, P.
RUSTIONI, A.
SADLER, T. W.
SULIK, K. K.

Chemistry:
BAER, T.
BROOKHART, M. S.
BUCK, R. P.
COKE, J. L.
CRIMMINS, M. T.
DESIMONE, J. M.
ERICKSON, B. W.
EVANS, S. A., Jr
IRENE, E. A.
JICHA, D. C.
JOHNSON, C. S., Jr
JORGENSON, J. W.
KROPP, P. J.
MEYER, T. J.
MILLER, R. E.
MURRAY, R. W.
PEDERSEN, L. G.
SAMULSKI, E. T.
SORRELL, T. N.
SPREMULLI, L. L.
TEMPLETON, J. L.
THOMPSON, N. L.
WIGHTMAN, R. M.

City and Regional Planning:
GODSCHALK, D. R.
GOLDSTEIN, H. A.
KAISER, E. J.
LACEY, L.
LUGER, M. I.
MALIZIA, E. E.
MOREAU, D. H.
ROHE, W. M.

Classics:
BROWN, E. L.
HOUSTON, G. W.
LINDERSKI, J.
MACK, S.
RACE, W. H.
RECKFORD, K. J.
SAMS, G. K.
STADTER, P. A.
WEST, W. C., III
WOOTEN, C. W.

Communication Studies:
BALTHROP, V. W.
COX, J. R., Jr
DYSON, M. E.
GROSSBERG, L.
HORNE, G. C.
KINDEM, G. A.
LONG, B. W.
ROSENFELD, L. B.
WOOD, J. T.

Comparative Literature:
FURST, L. R.

Computer Science:
BROOKS, F. P., Jr
FUCHS, H.
HALTON, J. H.
MAGO, G. A.
PIZER, S. M.
PLAISTED, D. A.
SMITH, J. B.
WEISS, S. F.

Curriculum, African and Afro-American Study:
NYANG'ORO, J. E.
SELASSIE, B. H.

Curriculum, Asian Studies:
SEATON, J. P.

Curriculum, Linguistics and Non-West Languages:
HENDRICK, R. J.
MELCHERT, H. C.
TSIAPERA, M.

Curriculum, Public Policy Analysis:
DILL, D. D.
STEGMAN, M. A.

Dentistry:
ARNOLD, R. R.
AUKHIL, I.
BAWDEN, J. W.
BAYNE, S. C.
BECK, J. D.
BURKES, E. J.
CRENSHAW, M. A.
HANKER, J. S.
HERSHEY, H. G.
HEYMANN, H. O.
HUNT, R. J.
HUTCHENS, L. H., Jr
JENZANO, J. W.
KUSY, R. P.
McIVER, F. T.
MURRAH, V. A.
OFFENBACHER, S.
OLDENBURG, T. R.
PROFFIT, W. R.
ROBERSON, T. M.
SHUGARS, D. A.
SIMPSON, D. M.
STAMM, J. W.
STRAUSS, R. P.
TROPE, M.
TULLOCH, J. F. C.
TURVEY, T. A.
VANN, W. F., Jr
WARREN, D. W.
WHITE, R. P.
WHITE, R. P., Jr
WILLIAMS, R. C.
WRIGHT, J. T.
YAMAUCHI, M.
WOOD, M. T.

Dermatology:
BRIGGAMAN, R. A.
FINE, J. D.
O'KEEFE, E. J.

Developmental Disabilities Training Institute:
BAROFF, G. S.

Dramatic Art:
BARRANGER, M. S.
HAMMOND, D. A.
OWEN, R. A.
RAPHAEL, B. N.
TURNER, C. W.

Economics:
AKIN, J. S.
BENAVIE, A.
BLACK, S. W., III
BLAU, D. M.
CONWAY, P. J.
DARITY, W. A., Jr
FIELD, A. J., Jr
FRIEDMAN, J. W.

FROYEN, R. T.
GALLANT, A. R.
GALLMAN, R. E.
GUILKEY, D. K.
MROZ, T. A.
MURPHY, J. L.
ROSEFIELDE, S. S.
SALEMI, M. K.
STEWART, J. F.
TARASCIO, V. J.
TAUCHEN, H. V.

Education:
BALLEW, J. H.
BRANTLEY, J. C.
BROWN, D.
BROWN, F.
BURKE, W. I.
COOP, R. H.
CUNNINGHAM, J.
DAY, B. D.
FITZGERALD, W. J.
FRIERSON, H. T.
GALASSI, J. P.
GALLAGHER, J. J.
HENNIS, R. S.
HUNTER, R. C.
LILLIE, D. L.
MARSHALL, C.
MORRISON, J. L.
NOBLIT, G. W.
ODOM, S. L., Jr
PALMER, W.
PRYZWANSKY, W. B.
SIMEONSON, R. J.
SPIEGEL, D. L.
STEDMAN, D. J.
STUCK, G. B.
TOM, A. R.
UNKS, G.
WARE, W. B.
WASIK, B. H.
WHITE, K. P.

Emergency Medicine:
TINTINALLI, J. E.

English:
ANDREWS, W. L.
AVERY, L. G
BETTS, D. W.
DESSEN, A. C.
EBLE, C. C.
FLORA, J. M.
GLESS, D. J.
GREENE, J. L.
GURA, P. F.
HARMON, W. R.
HARRIS, T.
HENDERSON, M. G.
HOBSON, F. C., Jr
KENNEDY, E. D.
KING, J. K.
LENSING, G. S., Jr
LINDEMANN, E.
LUDINGTON, C. T., Jr
McGOWAN, J. P.
MOSKAL, J.
O'NEILL, P. P.
PATTERSON, D. W.
RAPER, J. R.
RUST, R. D.
SHAPIRO, A. R.
TAYLOR, B. W.
THOMPSON, J. P.
THORNTON, W.
WAGNER-MARTIN, L. C.
WHISNANT, D. E.
WITTING, J. S.
ZUG, C. G., III

Environmental Science and Engineering:
ANDREWS, R. N.
CHRISTAKOS, G.
CHRISTMAN, R. F.
CRAWFORD-BROWN, D. J.
DIGIANO, F. A.
FOX, D. L.

GLAZE, W. H.
GOLD, A.
JEFFRIES, H.
KAMENS, R. M.
LAURIA, D. T.
LEITH, D.
MILLER, C. T.
PFAENDER, F.
RAPAPORT, S. M.
REIST, P. C.
SINGER, P. C.
SOBSEY, M. D.
SWENBERG, J. A.
WATSON, J. E., Jr
WHITTINGTON, D.

Epidemiology:
HEISS, G.
HULKA, B.
IBRAHIM, M. A.
SAVITZ, D. A.
SEED, J. R.

Family Medicine:
CURTIS, P.
FIELDS, K. B.
GWYTHER, R. E.
LEA, J. W.
OLSON, P. R.
REEB, K. G.
SLOANE, P. D.

Geography:
BAND, L. E.
BIRDSALL, S. S.
FLORIN, J. W.
GESLER, W. M.
GREENLAND, D. E.
JOHNSON, J. H., Jr
MEADE, M.
MORIARTY, B. M.
PALM, R. I.
ROBINSON, P. J.
WALSH, S. J.
ZONN, L. E.

Geology:
BENNINGER, L. K.
CARTER, J. G.
DENNISON, J. M.
FULLAGAR, P. D.
POWELL, C. A.
TEXTORIS, D. A.

German:
KOELB, C. T.
MEWS, S. E.
PIKE, D. C.
ROBERGE, P. T.

History:
BARNEY, W. L.
BULLARD, M. M.
CHOJNACKI, S. J.
FILENE, P. G.
FINK, L. R.
FLETCHER, W. M.
GRIFFITHS, D. M.
HALL, J. D.
HARRIS, B. J.
HEADLEY, J. M.
HIGGINBOTHAM, R. D.
HUNT, M. H.
JARAUSCH, K. H.
KASSON, J. F.
KESSLER, L. D.
KOHN, R. H.
KRAMER, L. S.
LOTCHIN, R. W.
MATHEWS, D. G.
MCNEIL, G. R.
MCVAUGH, M. R.
NELSON, J. K.
PEREZ, L. A.
PFAFF, R. W.
SEMONCHE, J. E.
SOLOWAY, R. A.
TALBERT, R. J.
WATSON, H. L.

WILLIAMSON, J. R.

Information and Library Science:
CHATMAN, E. A.
DANIEL, E. H.
MORAN, B. B.
SHAW, W. M., Jr

Institute of Government:
ALLRED, S.
BELL, A. F. II
BRANNON, J. G.
CAMPBELL, W. A.
CLARKE, S. H.
DELLINGER, A. M.
DRENNAN, J. C.
FARB, R. L.
FERRELL, J. S.
JOYCE, R. P.
LAWRENCE, D. M.
LINER, C. D.
LOEB, B. F., Jr
MASON, J.
MESIBOV, L. L.
OWENS, D. W.
SMITH, M. R.
VOGT, A. J.
WHITAKER, G. P.

Journalism:
BLANCHARD, M. A.
BOWERS, T. A.
BROWN, J. D.
COLE, R. R.
ELAM, A. R.
LAUTERBORN, R. F.
LINDEN, T. R.
MEYER, P. E.
SHAVER, M. A.
SHAW, D. L.
SIMPSON, R. H.
STEVENSON, R. L.
STONE, C. S., Jr
WALDEN, R. C.

Law:
BILIONIS, L. D.
BLAKEY, W.
BOGER, J. C.
BROOME, L. L.
BROUN, K. S.
BROWN, C. N.
BRYAN, P. L.
BYRD, R. G.
CALMORE, J. O.
CLIFFORD, D. F., Jr
CONLEY, J. M.
CORRADO, M. L.
CRAIN, M. G.
DAYE, C. E.
GIBSON, S. E.
HASKELL, P. G.
HAZEN, T. L.
HORNSTEIN, D. T.
KALO, J. J.
LINK, R. C.
LOEWY, A. H.
MARKHAM, J. W.
MCUSIC, M. S.
ORTH, J. V.
ROSEN, R. A.
SHARP, S. B.
TURNIER, W. J.
WEGNER, J. W.
WEISBURD, A. M.
YARBROUGH, M. V.
ZELENAK, L. A.

Law Library:
GASAWAY, L. N.

Leisure Studies and Recreation Administration:
HENDERSON, K. A.

Marine Sciences:
BANE, J. M., Jr
FRANKENBERG, D.
HAY, M. E.

KOHLMEYER, J. J.
MARTENS, C. S.
NEUMANN, A. C.
PAERL, H. W.
PETERSON, C. H.
SCHWARTZ, F. J.
WELLS, J. T.
WERNER, P. E.

Maternal and Child Health Care:
BUEXENS, P.
KOTCH, J. B.
KOTELCHUCK, M.
TSUI, A. O.
UDRY, J. R.

Mathematics:
ASSANI, I.
BRYLAWSKI, T. H.
CIMA, J. A.
DAMON, J. N.
EBERLEIN, P. B.
FOREST, M. G.
GEISSINGER, L. D.
GOODMAN, S. E.
GRAVES, W. H.
HAWKINS, J. M.
KERZMAN, N.
KUMAR, S.
PETERSEN, K. E.
PFALTZGRAFF, J. A.
PLANTE, J. F.
PROCTOR, R. A.
SCHLESSINGER, M.
SMITH, W. W.
STASHEFF, J.
TAYLOR, M. E.
VARCHENKO, A.
WAHL, J. M.
WILLIAMS, M.
WOGEN, W. R.

Medical Allied Health Prof.:
BAILEY, D.
LEGRYS, V. A.
SAKATA, R.
YODER, D. E.

Medicine:
BERKOWITZ, L. R.
BERNARD, S. A.
BONDURANT, S.
BOUCHER, R. C., Jr
BOZYMSKI, E. M.
BRENNER, D. A.
BROMBERG, P. A.
CAREY, T. S.
CLEMMONS, D. R.
COHEN, M. S.
COHEN, P. L.
COLINDRES, R. E.
DEHMER, G. J.
DONOHUE, J. F.
DROSSMAN, D. A.
EARP, H. S., III
FALK, R. J.
FINN, W. F.
GABRIEL, D. A.
GETTES, L. S.
GONZALEZ, J. J.
GREGANTI, M. A.
GRIGGS, T. R.
HEIZER, W. D.
HOOLE, A. J.
HUANG, E. S.
KIZER, J. S.
KNOWLES, M. R.
LANE, T. W.
LIU, E. T.
MATTERN, W. D.
MITCHELL, B. S.
NUZUM, C. T.
ONTJES, D. A.
ORRINGER, E. P.
PAGANO, J. S.
RANSOHOFF, D. F.
ROBERTS, H.
ROGERS, C. S.

RUTALA, W. A.
SANDLER, R. S.
SARTOR, R. B.
SHEA, T. C.
SIMPSON, R. J., Jr
SMITH, S. C., Jr
SPARLING, P. F.
UNGARO, P. C.
WHITE, G. C., II
WILLIAMS, M. E.
WILLIS, P. W.
WINFIELD, J. B.
YOUNT, W. J.

Microbiology and Immunology:

BACHENHEIMER, S. L.
BOTT, K. F.
CANNON, J. G.
CLARKE, S. H.
EDGELL, M. H.
FRELINGER, J. A.
GILLIGAN, P. H.
GRIFFITH, J.
HAUGHTON, G.
HUTCHISON, C. A.
JOHNSTON, R. E.
KLAPPER, D. G.
NEWBOLD, J. E.
RAAB-TRAUB, N.
TING, J. P.
WYRICK, P. B.

Microelectronics—Chemistry:

IRENE, E. A.

Music:

BONDS, M. E.
FINSON, J. W.
KETCH, J. E.
MCKINNON, J. W.
NADAS, J. L.
NEFF, S.
OEHLER, D. L.
SMITH, B.
WARBURTON, T. A.
ZENGE, M. W.

Neurology:

GREENWOOD, R. S.
HALL, C. D.
HOWARD, J. N.
MANN, J. D.
SUZUKI, K.

Nursing:

DALTON, J. B.
DAVIS, D. H.
DOUGHERTY, M. C.
FOGEL, C. I.
FREUND, C. M.
FUNK, S. G.
GOEFFINGER, J.
HARRELL, J. S.
KJERVIK, D. K.
MILES, M. S.
MILIO, N.
MISHEL, M. H.
SANDELOWSKI, M. J.

Obstetrics and Gynaecology:

DROEGEMUELLER, W.
FOWLER, W. C., Jr
FRITZ, M. A.
GRANADOS
HASKILL, J. S.
PARISI, Y. M.
STEEGE, J. F.
WALTON, L. A.

Operations Research:

FISHMAN, G.
PROVAN, J. S.
STIDHAM, S., Jr
TOLLE, J. W.

Ophthalmology:

COHEN, K. L.
EIFRIG, D. E.
GRIMSON, B. S.
PEIFFER, R. L., Jr

Paediatrics:

AYLSWORTH, A. S.
BOSE, C. L.
CARSON, J. L.
COLLIER, A. M.
COOPER, H. A.
D'ERCOLE, A. J.
FERNALD, G. W.
FRENCH, F. S.
HAMRICK, H.
HENDERSON, F. W.
HENRY, G. W.
INGRAM, D. L.
KRAYBILL, E. N.
LAWSON, E. E.
LEIGH, M. W.
LEVINE, M. D.
LODA, F. A.
LOHR, J. A.
ROBERTS, K. B.
SCHALL, S. A.
SIMMONS, M. A.
STILES, A. D.
UNDERWOOD, L. E.
WILLIAMS, R. G.
WILSON, E. M.
WOOD, R. E.

Pathology and Laboratory Medicine:

ANDERSON, N. N.
BELLINGER, D. A.
BENTLEY, S. A.
BOULDIN, T. W.
CHAPMAN, J. F.
CROSS, R. E.
FARBER, R. A.
FOLDS, J. D.
FORMAN, D. T.
GRISHAM, J. W.
HAMMOND, J. E.
JENNETTE, J. C.
KAUFMAN, D. G.
LORD, S. T.
MAEDA, N.
REISNER, H. M.
SILVERMAN, L. M.
SMITH, G. J.
SMITHIES, O.
SUZUKI, K. I.
TIDWELL, R. R.
TOPAL, M. D.
WEISSMAN, B. E.

Pharmacology:

CREWS, F. T.
DER, C. J.
DUDLEY, K. H.
GATZY, J. T., Jr
GOZ, B.
HARDEN, T. K.
JULIANO, R. L.
KOLE, R.
MCCARTHY, K. D.
SCARBOROUGH, G. A.
THURMAN, R. G.

Pharmacy:

BROUWER, K. R.
CAMPBELL, W. H.
COCOLAS, G. H.
ECKEL, F. M.
HADZIJA, B. W.
HALL, I. H.
HARTZEMA, A. G.
LEE, K. H.
PIEPER, J. A.
THAKKER, D. R.

Philosophy:

ANTONY, L. M.
BLACKBURN, S. W.
BOXILL, B. R.
HILL, T. E., Jr
HOOKER, M.
LONG, D. C.
LYCAN, W. G.
MUNSAT, S. M.

POSTEMA, G. J.
RESNIK, M. D.
ROSENBERG, J. F.
SAYRE-MCCORD, G. D.
SCHLESINGER, G.
SMYTH, R. A.

Physical Education, Exercise and Sport Science:

BILLING, J. E.
HYATT, R. W.
MCMURRAY, R. G.
MUELLER, F. O.
PRENTICE, W. E., Jr
SILVA, J. M.

Physics/Astronomy:

CARNEY, B. W.
CHRISTIANSEN, W. A.
CLEGG, T. B.
DOLAN, L. A.
DY, K. S.
FRAMPTON, P. H.
HERNANDEZ, J.
KARWOWSKI, H. J.
LUDWIG, E. J.
MCNEIL, L. E.
NG, Y. J.
ROSE, J. A.
ROWAN, L. G.
SCHROEER, D.
THOMPSON, W. J.
VAN DAM, H.
YORK, J. W., Jr

Physiology:

ARENDSHORST, W. J.
FABER, J. E.
FAREL, P. B.
FAUST, R. G.
FROEHNER, S. C.
LIGHT, A. R.
LUND, P. K.
MCILWAIN, D. L.
OXFORD, G. S.
PERL, E. R.
REID, L. M.
SEALOCK, R. W.
STUART, A. E.
WHITSEL, B. L.

Political Science:

BEYLE, T. L.
CONOVER, P. J.
HARTLYN, J.
HUBER, E. H.
LOWERY, D. L.
MARKS, G. W.
PHAY, R. E.
RABINOWITZ, G.
RICHARDSON, R. J
SCHOULTZ, L. G.
SCHWARTZ, J.
SEARING, D. D.
STEINER, J.
STEPHENS, J. D.
STIMSON, J. A.
WHITE, J. W.
WRIGHT, D. S.

Psychiatry:

BREESE, G. R., Jr
GOLDEN, R. N.
HOUPT, J. L.
JANOWSKY, D. S.
LIEBERMAN, J. A.
LIGHT, K. C.
MCCARTNEY, C. F.
MAILMAN, R. B.
MARCUS, L. M.
MESIBOV, G. B.
STABLER, B.
VAN BOURGONDIE, M. E.
WHITT, J. K.

Psychology:

BAUCOM, D. H.
CAIRNS, R. B.
CHAMBLESS, D. L.

DYKSTRA-HYLAND, L. A.
ECKERMAN, D. A.
FILLENBAUM, S.
GRAY-LITTLE, B.
HOLLINS, M.
INSKO, C. A.
JOHNSON, E. S.
ORNSTEIN, P.
SCHOPLER, J. H.
SHINKMAN, P. G.
THISSEN, D. M.
THOMPSON, V. D.
WALLSTEN, T. S.
YOUNG, F. W.

Public Health:
ROPER, W. L.

Public Health Nursing:
ATWOOD, J. R.
SALMON, M. E.

Health Policy and Administration:
JAIN, S.
KALUZNY, A. D.
KILPATRICK, K. E.
ROZIER, R. G.
VENEY, J. E.
ZELMAN, W. N.

Health Behaviour and Health Education:
BAUMAN, K. E.
DEVELLIS, B. M.
EARP, J. L.
MUTRAN, E.
SORENSON, J.
STECKLER, A. B.

Nutrition:
ANDERSON, J. J.
COLEMAN, R. A.
KOHLMEIER, L.
POPKIN, B. M.
ZEISEL, S. H.

Radiation Oncology:
CHANEY, E. L.
LEADON, S. A.
RALEIGH, J. A.
ROSENMAN, J. G.
TEPPER, J. E.
VARIA, M. A.

Radiology:
JAQUES, P. F.
JOHNSTON, R. E.
KWOCK, L.
LEE, J. K.
MAURO, M. A.
MCCARTNEY, W. H.
MITTELSTAEDT, C. A.

Religious Studies:
ERNST, C. W.
HALPERIN, D. J.
KAUFMAN, P. I.
SASSON, J. M.
TYSON, R. W., Jr
VAN SETERS, J.

Romance Languages:
BANDERA, C.
CASADO, P. G.
CERVIGNI, D. S.
CILVETI, A. L.
CLARK, F. M.
DOMINGUEZ, F. A.
HAIG, I. R. S., II
ILLIANO, A.
KING, L. D.
MALEY, C. A.
MASTERS, G. M.
RECTOR, M. P.
SALGADO, M. A.
SHERMAN, C. L.
VOGLER, F. W.

Slavic Languages:
DEBRECZENY, P.
JANDA, L. A.
LEVINE, M. G.

Social Medicine:
CHURCHILL, L. R.
CROSS, A. W.
DE FRIESE, G. H.
ESTROFF, S. E.
MADISON, D. L.
MORRISSEY, J. P.
RUNYAN, D. K.

Social Work:
BOWEN, G. L.
COOKE, P. W.
DOBELSTEIN, A. W.
EDWARDS, R. L.
FRASER, M. W.
GALINSKY, M. J.
HENLEY, H. C.
NELSON, G. M.
ORTHNER, D. K.
USHER, C. L.
WEIL, M. O.

Sociology:
ALDRICH, H. E.
BEARMAN, P. S.
BLAU, J. R.
ELDER, G. H.
ENTWISLE, B.
KALLEBERG, A. L.
KLEINMAN, S.
NEILSEN, F. D.
OBERSCHALL, A. R.
REED, J. S., Jr
RINDFUSS, R. R.
SIMPSON, R. L.
UHLENBERG, P.

Statistics:
ADLER, R.
CARLSTEIN, E.
CHAKRAVARTI, I. M.
KALLIANPUR, G.
KARR, A. F.
KELLY, D. G.
LEADBETTER, M. R.
MARRON, J. S.
SIMONS, G.
SMITH, R. L.

Surgery:
BAKER, C. C.
BLIGHT, A. R.
BUNZENDAHL, H.
BURNHAM, S. J.
CARSON, C. C., III
HALL, J. W., III
KEAGY, B. A.
MANDEL, S. R.
MAXWELL, J. G.
MEYER, A. A.
NAKAYAMA, D. K.
OLLER, D. W.
PECK, M. D.
PILLSBURY, H. C., III
PRAZMA, J.
SHELDON, G. F.
SHOCKLEY, W. M.
SLOAN, G. M.
STAREK, P. J.
WEISSLER, M. C.
WILCOX, B. R.

Women's Studies Program:
BURNS, E. J.
HOFFERT, S. D.

University of North Carolina at Charlotte

9201 University City Blvd, Charlotte, NC 28223-0001
Telephone: (704) 687-2000
Fax: (704) 687-6483
E-mail: unccadm@email.uncc.edu
Internet: www.uncc.edu
Founded 1946 as an extension centre of the Univ. of North Carolina; later Charlotte College; made a degree-granting instn in

1963; became part of UNC State System in 1965
Academic year: August to May
Chancellor: Dr PHILIP L. DUBOIS
Vice-Chancellor for Academic Affairs and Provost: Dr JOAN F. LORDEN
Vice-Chancellor for Student Affairs: CHARLES F. LYNCH
Vice-Chancellor for Devt and Alumni Relations: NILES F. SORENSON
Vice-Chancellor for Business Affairs: ELIZABETH A. HARDIN
Registrar: RICHARD YOUNT
Univ. Librarian: CAROLE RUNNION
Library of 916,218 vols, 10,599 periodicals
Number of teachers: 810
Number of students: 19,846 (15,875 undergraduates, 3,971 graduates)

DEANS
College of Architecture: KENNETH A. LAMBLA
College of Arts and Sciences: Dr NANCY GUTIERREZ
College of Business Admin.: Dr CLAUDE C. LILLEY, III
College of Education: Dr MARY LYNNE CALHOUN
College of Eng.: Dr ROBERT E. JOHNSON
College of Health and Human Services: Dr KAREN SCHAMLING
College of Information Technology: Dr MIRSAD HADZIKADIC

University of North Carolina at Greensboro

1000 Spring Garden St, Greensboro, NC 27403
Telephone: (336) 334-5000
Internet: www.uncg.edu
Founded 1891 as a Normal College; since 1931 a unit of the Univ. of North Carolina; 1963 name changed to the Univ. of North Carolina at Greensboro
Academic year: August to May
Chancellor: PATRICIA A. SULLIVAN
Vice-Chancellor for Business Affairs: READE TAYLOR
Vice-Chancellor for Information Technology: Dr JAMES H. CLOTFELTER
Vice-Chancellor for Univ. Advancement: Dr PATRICIA W. STEWART
Vice-Chancellor for Student Affairs: Dr CAROL DISQUE
Provost and Vice-Chancellor for Academic Affairs: Dr A. EDWARD UPRICHARD
Registrar: ELLEN H. ROBBINS
Dir of Library: DORIS D. HULBERT
Library of 2,525,000 vols
Number of teachers: 812 (631 full-time, 181 part-time)
Number of students: 12,731

DEANS
College of Arts and Sciences: Dr TIMOTHY D. JOHNSTON
Bryan School of Business and Econo.: Dr JAMES K. WEEKS
School of Education: Dr DALE H. SCHUNK
School of Health and Human Performance: Dr DAVID H. PERRIN
School of Human Environmental Sciences: Dr LAURA S. SIMS
School of Music: Dr JOHN J. DEAL
School of Nursing: Dr LYNNE G. PEARCEY

University of North Carolina at Pembroke

POB 1510, Pembroke, NC 28372-1510
Telephone: (910) 521-6000
Internet: www.uncp.edu
Founded 1887 as College, attained Univ. status 1969
Part of the Univ. of North Carolina

Academic year: August to May

Chancellor: Dr ALLEN C. MEADORS

Provost and Vice-Chancellor for Academic Affairs: Dr CHARLES F. HARRINGTON

Vice-Chancellor for Advancement: SANDRA WATERKOTTE

Vice-Chancellor for Business Affairs: R. NEIL HAWK

Vice-Chancellor for Enrollment Management: JACKIE CLARK

Vice-Chancellor for Student Affairs: Dr DIANE JONES

Vice-Chancellor for Univ. and Community Relations: Dr GLEN BURNETTE

Registrar: SARA BRACKIN

Dir of Athletics: DANIEL KENNEY

Dean of Library Services: Dr ELINOR FOSTER

Library of 300,000 vols

Number of teachers: 345 (204 full-time, 82 part-time)

Number of students: 5,132

DEANS

School of Arts and Sciences: Dr THOMAS LEACH

School of Business: Dr ERIC DENT

School of Education: Dr ZOE LOCKLEAR (acting)

Graduate Studies: Dr KATHLEEN HILTON

North Carolina State University at Raleigh

Raleigh, NC 27695

Telephone: (919) 515-2191

Fax: (919) 515-2556

E-mail: undergrad_admissions@ncsu.edu

Internet: www.ncsu.edu

Founded 1887 as North Carolina College of Agriculture and Mechanic Arts; present name 1965

State control

Language of instruction: English

Academic year: August to May

Chancellor: Dr JAMES L. OBLINGER

Provost and Exec. Vice Chancellor: LARRY A. NIELSEN

Vice-Chancellor for Research and Graduate Studies: Dr JOHN G. GILLIGAN

Vice-Chancellor and Gen. Counsel: MARY ELIZABETH KURZ

Vice-Chancellor for Student Affairs: THOMAS H. STAFFORD, Jr

Vice-Chancellor for Univ. Advancement: TERRY G. WOOD

Vice-Chancellor for Finance and Business: CHARLES D. LEFFLER

Registrar: Dr LOUIS D. HUNT

Vice-Provost and Dir of Libraries: SUSAN K. NUTTER

Library of 2,900,000 vols, bound journals and fed. govt publs

Number of teachers: 1,685

Number of students: 29,637

DEANS

College of Agriculture and Life Sciences: Dr JAMES L. OBLINGER

College of Design: MARVIN J. MALECHA

College of Education: Dr KATHRYN M. MOORE

College of Eng.: NINO A. MASNARI

College of Humanities and Social Sciences: LINDA P. BRADY

College of Management: Dr JON W. BARTLEY

College of Natural Resources: Dr LARRY A. NIELSEN

College of Physical and Mathematical Sciences: Dr DANIEL L. SOLOMON

College of Textiles: Dr A. BLANTON GODFREY

College of Veterinary Medicine: OSCAR J. FLETCHER

University of North Carolina at Wilmington

Wilmington, NC 28403-5931

Telephone: (910) 962-3000

Fax: (910) 962-4050

Internet: www.uncw.edu

Founded 1947 as Wilmington College, a county instn under the control of the New Hanover County Board of Education; in 1969 made a campus of the Univ. of North Carolina, with emphasis on undergraduate teaching

Academic year: August to May

Chancellor: ROSEMARY DePAOLO

Provost and Vice-Chancellor for Academic Affairs: PAUL E. HOSIER

Vice-Chancellor for Student Affairs: PATRICIA LYNN LEONARD

Vice-Chancellor for Business Affairs: KAY M. WARD

Vice-Chancellor for Univ. Advancement: MARY M. GORNTO

Librarian: SHERMAN HAYES

Library of 517,046 vols

Number of teachers: 650

Number of students: 10,929.

WAKE FOREST UNIVERSITY

1834 Wake Forest Rd, Winston-Salem, NC 27106

Telephone: (336) 758-5000

Fax: (336) 758-6074

E-mail: admissions@wfu.edu

Internet: www.wfu.edu

Founded 1834

Private control

Pres.: Dr NATHAN O. HATCH

Provost: WILLIAM C. GORDAN

Sr Vice-Pres. and Chief Financial Officer: NANCY D. SUTTENFIELD

Vice-Pres. for Univ. Advancement: JAMES R. BULLOCK

Vice-Pres. for Admin.: MATTHEW S. CULLINAN

Librarian: RHODA K. CHANNING

Library of over 1 million vols

Number of teachers: 1,740 (1,158 full-time, 582 part-time)

Number of students: 6,504

DEANS

Wayne Calloway School of Business and Accountancy: JACK E. WILKERSON, Jr

College: DEBBIE L. BEST

Divinity School: BILL J. LEONARD

Graduate School of Arts and Sciences: GORDON A. MELSON

Babcock Graduate School of Management: AJAY PATEL

School of Law: ROBERT K. WALSH

School of Medicine: WILLIAM B. APPLEGATE

International Center for Computer Enhanced Learning: DAVID G. BROWN

PROFESSORS

Graduate School of Management:

BALIGA, B. R., Management

FLYNN, B. B., Operations Management

HARRIS, F. H. deB., Managerial Econ. and Finance

MEREDITH, J. R., Management

NARUS, J. A., Business Marketing

PATEL, A., Finance

RESNICK, B. G., Banking and Finance

SHOESMITH, G. L., Econ.

SMUNT, T. L., Management

Divinity School:

KIMBALL, C. A., Religion

LEONARD, W. J., Church History

TRIBLE, P., Religion

TUPPER, E. F., Theology

Graduate School of Arts and Sciences:

ABRAMSON, J. S., Pediatrics

ADAMS, M. R., Comparative Medicine

AKMAN, S. A., Cancer Biology, Internal Medicine

ALTMAN, D. G., Public Health Sciences

ANDERSON, J. P., Education

ASCHNER, M., Physiology and Pharmacology

BAREFIELD, J. P., History

BASS, D. A., Medicine

BAXLEY, J. V., Mathematics

BECK, R. C., Psychology

BERRY, M. J., Health and Exercise Science

BEST, D. L., Psychology

BO, W. J., Neurobiology and Anatomy

BOND, M. G., Neurobiology and Anatomy

BORWICK, S. H., Music

BOWDEN, D. W., Biochemistry

BOYD, S. B., Religion

BROSNIHAN, K. B., Physiology and Pharmacology

BROWN, D. G., Econ.

BROWNE, C. L., Biology

BROWNE, R. A., Biology

BRUNSO-BECHTOLD, J. K., Neurobiology and Anatomy

BUCKALEW, V. M., Jr, Medicine (Nephrology)

BURKE, G. L., Public Health Sciences

BUSIJA, D. W., Physiology and Pharmacology

BYINGTON, R. P., Public Health Sciences

CARMICHAEL, R. D., Mathematics

CHILDERS, S. R., Physiology and Pharmacology

CHILTON, F. H., Internal Medicine

CLAIBORNE, H. A., Jr, Biochemistry

CLARKSON, T. B., Jr, Comparative Medicine

COLLINS, J. E., Religion

CONNER, W. E., Biology

COTTON, N., English

CRAMER, S. D., Cancer Biology, Internal Medicine

CROUSE, J. R., III, Medicine (Endocrinology and Metabolism)

CUNNINGHAM, C. C., Biochemistry

CUNNINGHAM, P. M., Education

CURRAN, J. F., Biology

DANIEL, L. W., Biochemistry

DEADWYLER, S. A., Physiology

DeSHAZER, M. K., English

DIMOCK, R. V., Jr, Biology

DuRANT, R. H., Paediatrics and Public Health Sciences

EISENACH, J. C., Anaesthesia

ESCH, G. W., Biology

ESCOTT, P. D., History

ESPELAND, M. A., Public Health Sciences (Biostatistics)

ETTIN, A. V., English

EURE, H. E., Biology

FELDMAN, S. R., Dermatology, Pathology

FERRARIO, C. M., Surgical Sciences

FRANKEL, A. E., Medicine and Cancer Biology

FREY, D. E., Econ.

FURBERG, C. D., Medicine and Public Health Sciences

GLADDING, S. T., Education

GRANT, K. A., Physiology and Pharmacology, Comparative Medicine

HALL, M. A., Law and Public Health Sciences

HAMILTON, W. S., Russian

HANS, J. S., English

HAYASHI, E. K., Mathematics and Computer Science

HAZEN, M. D., Communication

HEARN, T. K., Jr, Philosophy

HENDRICKS, J. E., Jr, History

HINZE, W. L., Chemistry

HOLZWARTH, G. M., Physics

HOLZWARTH, N. A. W., Physics

HOWARD, F. T., Mathematics

HUGHES, M. L., History
HUTSON, S. M., Biochemistry
HYDE, M. J., Communication Ethics
JARRETT, D. B., Physiology and Pharmacology
JOHNSTON, W. D., English
KAMMER, G. M., Internal Medicine
KAPLAN, J. R., Comparative Medicine, Anthropology
KERR, W. C., Physics
KIMBALL, C. A., Religion
KIRKMAN, E. E., Mathematics
KOMAN, L. A., Orthopaedics
KONDEPUDI, D. K., Chemistry
KUBERSKI, P., English
KUCERA, L. S., Microbiology
KUHN, R. E., Biology
KUZMANOVICH, J., Mathematics
LANE, H. C., Biology
LEARY, M. R., Psychology
LEONARD, W. J., Divinity School
LITCHER, J. H., Education
LIVELY, M. O., Biochemistry
LONGINO, C. F., Sociology, Public Health Sciences
LORENTZ, W. B., Jr, Paediatrics
LYLES, D. S., Microbiology and Immunology
McCALL, C. E., Medicine (Infectious Disease), Microbiology and Immunology
McMILLAN, J. J., Communication
McPHAIL, L. C., Biochemistry
MAINE, B. G., English
MARGITIC, M. R., Romance Languages
MARTIN, D. R., Accountancy
MARTIN, J. A., Jr, Religion
MATTHEWS, G. E., Physics
MAY, J. G., Mathematics
MEIS, P. J., Obstetrics and Gynaecology
MELSON, G. A., Chemistry
MESSIER, S. P., Health and Exercise Science
MILLER, H. S., Medicine
MILNER, J. O., Education
MIZEL, S. B., Microbiology and Immunology
MORAN, P. R., Radiology
MORGAN, T. M., Public Health Sciences
MOSS, W. M., English
NADER, M. A., Physiology and Pharmacology
NIELSEN, L. N., Education
NOFTLE, R. E., Chemistry
O'FLAHERTY, J. T., Medicine
OPPENHEIM, R. W., Anatomy
OVERING, G. R., English
OWEN, J., Medicine
PARKS, J. S., Pathology
PLEMMONS, R. J., Mathematics and Computer Science
PORRINO, L. J., Physiology and Pharmacology
PRINEAS, R., Public Health Sciences
REIFLER, B. V., Psychiatry
REJESKI, W. J., Health and Exercise Science
RIBISL, P. M., Health and Exercise Science
RICH, S. S., Public Health Sciences
RICHMAN, C. L., Psychology
ROBERTS, D. C. S., Physiology and Pharmacology
ROSE, J. C., Physiology, Obstetrics and Gynaecology
RUBIN, B. K., Paediatrics, Physiology, and Pharmacology
RUDEL, L. L., Comparative Medicine, Biochemistry
ST CLAIR, R. W., Pathology (Physiology)
SAMSON, H. H., III, Physiology and Pharmacology, Comparative Medicine
SHAPERE, D., Philosophy and History of Science
SHERERTZ, R. J., Medicine
SHIHABI, Z. K., Pathology (Clinical Chemistry)

SHIVELY, C. A., Comparative Medicine, Psychology
SHUMAKER, S. A., Public Health Sciences
SIGAL, G., English
SILVER, W. L., Biology
SIMONELLI, J. M., Anthropology
SINCLAIR, M. L., History
SMITH, E., Sociology, American Ethnic Studies
SMITH, J. H., History
SMITH, J. E., Physiology and Pharmacology
SMITH, M. S., Art
SMITH, P. B., Biochemistry
SONNTAG, W. E., Physiology
SORCI-THOMAS, M., Comparative Medicine
STEIN, B. E., Neurobiology and Anatomy
STRANDHOY, J. W., Pharmacology
SWOFFORD, R. L., Chemistry
TAYLOR, T. C., Accountancy
THOMAS, M. J., Biochemistry
TOOLE, J. F., Neurology
TORTI, F. M., Cancer Biology, Internal Medicine
TOWER, R. B., Jr, Taxation
TRIBLE, P., Religion
VALBUENA, O., English
VAN DE RIJN, I., Microbiology and Immunology
VELEZ, R., Internal Medicine
WAGNER, W. D., Comparative Medicine
WASILAUSKAS, B. L., Pathology (Clinical Microbiology)
WEAVER, D. S., Anthropology
WEBBER, R. L., Dentistry, Medical Eng.
WEIGL, P. D., Biology
WEINBERG, R. B., Internal Medicine
WELKER, M. E., Chemistry
WELLS, B. R., Romance Languages
WHEELER, K. T., Jr, Radiology
WILKERSON, J. E., Jr, Accounting
WILLIAMS, A. J., History
WILLIAMS, J. K., Comparative Medicine
WILLIAMS, R. T., Physics
WILLINGHAM, M. C., Pathology
WILSON, E. G., English
WOODALL, J. N., Anthropology
WOODWARD, D. J., Physiology and Pharmacology
WYKLE, R. L., Biochemistry

School of Law:
ANDERSON, C. B.
BILLINGS, R. B.
CASTLEMAN, D. R.
CORBETT, L. H., Jr
COVINGTON, I. B., III
CURTIS, M. K.
DAVIS, T.
FOY, H. M., III
GREBELDINGER, S. K.
HALL, M. A.
HERRING, B. O. H.
LOGAN, D. A.
MEWHINNEY, K.
MONTAQUILA, S. R.
NEWMAN, J. S.
PALMITER, A. R.
PARKER, D. L.
PARKER, J. W.
PARKER, M. F.
PEEPLES, R. A.
REYNOLDS, S.
ROBERTS, P. J.
ROBERTS, T. E.
ROSE, C. P., Jr
ROSE, S.
SCHNEIDER, R. C., Jr
SHORES, D. F.
STEELE, T. M.
TAYLOR, M. H.
WALKER, G. K.
WALSH, R. K.
WRIGHT, R. F., Jr
ZICK, K. A., II

School of Medicine:
ABRAMSON, J. S., Paediatrics

ADAMS, M. R., Comparative Medicine
ADAMS, P. L., Internal Medicine (Nephrology)
ADCOCK, E. W., III, Paediatrics
AKMAN, S. A., Cancer Biology, Internal Medicine (Haematology/Oncology)
ALTMANN, D. G., Public Health Sciences (Social Sciences and Health Policy)
APPLEGATE, R. J., Internal Medicine (Cardiology)
APPLEGATE, W. B., Internal Medicine
ARGENTA, L. C., Surgical Sciences (Plastic/Reconstructive)
ASCHNER, M., Physiology and Pharmacology
ASSIMOS, D. G., Surgical Sciences (Urology)
BASS, D. A., Internal Medicine (Pulmonary Critical Care Medicine)
BECHTOLD, R. E., Radiological Sciences (Radiology)
BLEECKER, E. R., Internal Medicine (Pulmonary Critical Care Medicine)
BO, W. J., Neurobiology and Anatomy
BOND, M. G., Neurobiology and Anatomy
BOWDEN, D. W., Biochemistry
BOWTON, D. L., Anaesthesiology, Internal Medicine (Pulmonary Critical Care Medicine)
BROSNIHAN, K. B., Surgical Sciences (General)
BRUNSO-BECHTOLD, J. K., Neurobiology and Anatomy
BUCKALEW, V. M., Jr, Internal Medicine (Nephrology)
BURKART, J. M., Internal Medicine (Nephrology)
BURKE, G. L., Public Health Sciences
BUSIJA, D. W., Physiology and Pharmacology
BUSS, D. H., Pathology
BUTTERWORTH, J. F., IV, Anaesthesiology
BYINGTON, R., Public Health Sciences (Epidemiology)
CHALLA, V. R., Pathology
CHENG, C.-P., Internal Medicine (Cardiology)
CHEW, F. S., Radiological Sciences (Radiology)
CHILDERS, S. R., Physiology and Pharmacology
CHILES, C., Radiological Sciences (Radiology)
CHILTON, F. L., Internal Medicine (Pulmonary Critical Care Medicine)
CLAIBORNE, A., Biochemistry
CLARKSON, T. B., Comparative Medicine
COATES, M. L., Family and Community Medicine
COOPER, M. R., Internal Medicine (Haematology/Oncology)
COVITZ, W., Paediatrics
CROUSE, J. R., III, Internal Medicine (Endocrinology/Metabolism)
CUNNINGHAM, C. C., Biochemistry
CURL, W. W., Surgical Sciences (Orthopaedics)
DANIEL, L. W., Biochemistry
DEAN, R. H., Surgical Sciences (General)
DENTON, W. H., Psychiatry and Behavioural Medicine
DEWAN, D. M., Obstetric Anaesthesiology
DILLARD, R. G., Paediatrics
DIXON, R. L., Radiological Sciences (Radiology)
DIZ, D. I., Surgical Sciences (General), Physiology and Pharmacology
DONOFRIO, P. D., Neurology (Neuromuscular Diseases)
DURANT, R. H., Paediatrics, Public Health Sciences
DYER, R. B., Radiological Sciences (Radiology)
EISENACH, J. E., Obstetric Anaesthesiology
ELSTER, A. D., Radiological Sciences (Radiology)

ERNEST, J. M., III, Obstetrics and Gynaecology (Maternal/Fetal Medicine)
ESPELAND, M. A., Public Health Sciences (Biostatistics)
FELDMAN, S. R., Pathology
FERRARIO, C.M., Surgical Sciences (General)
FERREE, C. R., Radiation Oncology
FLEISCHER, A. B., Jr, Dermatology
FRANKEL, A. E., Cancer Biology, Internal Medicine (Haematology/Oncology)
FURBERG, C. D., Public Health Sciences
GARRISON, R. S., Dentistry
GARVIN, A. J., Pathology
GEISINGER, K. R., Pathology
GELFAND, D. W., Radiological Sciences (Radiology)
GIVNER, L. G., Paediatrics
GMEINER, W. H., Biochemistry
GOOD, D. C., Neurology
GREVEN, C. M., Surgical Sciences (Orthopaedics)
GREVEN, K. M., Radiation Oncology
HALL, M., Public Health Sciences (Social Sciences and Health Policy)
HAMMON, J. W., Jr., Surgical Sciences (Cardiothoracic)
HANSEN, K. J., Surgical Sciences (General)
HARLE, T. S., Radiological Sciences (Radiology)
HARRIS, M. B., Surgical Sciences (Orthopaedics)
HENKEL, C. K., Neurobiology and Anatomy
HERRINGTON, D. M., Internal Medicine (Cardiology)
HILL, I. D., Paediatrics
HUDSPETH, A. S., Surgical Sciences (Cardiothoracic)
HURD, D. D., Internal Medicine (Haematology/Oncology)
HUTSON, S. M., Biochemistry
JANEWAY, R., Neurology
JOHNSON, C. A., Paediatrics
JORIZZO, J. L., Dermatology
KAMMER, G. M., Internal Medicine (Rheumatology)
KAPLAN, J. R., Comparative Medicine, Anthropology
KELLEY, A. E., Psychiatry and Behavioural Medicine (Child/Adolescent Psychiatry)
KELLY, D. L., Jr, Surgical Sciences (Ophthalmology)
KOMAN, L. A., Surgical Sciences (Orthopaedics)
KON, N., Surgical Sciences (Cardiothoracic)
KOUFMAN, J. A., Surgical Sciences (Otolaryngology)
KREMKAU, F. W., Medical Ultrasound
KROWCHUK, D. P., Paediatrics, Dermatology
KUCERA, L. S., Microbiology and Immunology
LAWLESS, M. R., Paediatrics
LICHSTEIN, P. R., Internal Medicine
LINK, K. M., Radiological Sciences (Radiology)
LITTLE, W. C., Internal Medicine (Cardiology)
LIVELY, M. O., III, Biochemistry
LONGINO, C. F., Jr, Public Health Sciences (Epidemiology)
LORENTZ, W. B., Paediatrics
LYLES, D. S., Microbiology and Immunology
McCALL, C. E., Microbiology and Immunology, Internal Medicine (Infectious Diseases)
McCALL, W. V., Psychiatry and Behavioural Medicine
McCULLOUGH, D. L., Surgical Sciences (Urology)
McGUIRT Sr, W. F., Surgical Sciences (Otolaryngology)
MACH, R. H., Radiological Sciences (Radiology), Physiology and Pharmacology
McPHAIL, L. C., Biochemistry

MARKS, M. W., Surgical Sciences (Plastic/Reconstructive)
MAYNARD, C. D., Radiological Sciences (Radiology)
MEIS, P. J., Obstetrics and Gynaecology (Maternal/Fetal Medicine), Family and Community Medicine
MEREDITH, J. Q., Surgical Sciences (General)
MEYERS, D. A., Paediatrics
MICHIELUTTE, R. L., Family and Community Medicine
MILLER, A. A., Internal Medicine (Haematology/Oncology)
MILLER, M. E., Public Health Sciences (Biostatistics)
MIZEL, S. B., Microbiology and Immunology
MOODY, D. M., Radiological Sciences (Radiology)
MORGAN, T. M., Public Health Sciences (Biostatistics)
MORTON, K. A., Radiological Sciences (Radiology)
MOSKOVITZ, J., Public Health Sciences
MUELLER-HEUBACH, E., Obstetrics and Gynaecology
NELSON, L. H., III, Obstetrics and Gynaecology (Maternal/Foetal Medicine)
NELSON, T. E., Anaesthesiology
OBER, K. P., Internal Medicine (Endocrinology/Metabolism)
O'FLAHERTY, J. T., Internal Medicine (Haematology/Oncology)
OPPENHEIM, R., Neurobiology and Anatomy
O'SHEA, T. M. D., Paediatrics
OTT, D. J., Radiological Sciences (Radiology)
OWEN, J., Internal Medicine (Haematology/Oncology)
PARKS, J. S., Comparative Medicine
PAUCA, A. L., Anaesthesiology
PEACOCK, J. E., Jr, Internal Medicine (Haematology/Oncology)
PEGRAM, P. S., Internal Medicine (Haematology/Oncology)
PENNELL, T. C., Surgical Sciences (General)
PETROZZA, P. H., Anaesthesiology
POEHLING, G. G., Surgical Sciences (Orthopaedics)
PONS, T., Surgical Sciences (Neurosurgery), Physiology and Pharmacology
POWELL, B. L., Internal Medicine (Haematology/Oncology)
PRIELIPP, R. C., Anaesthesiology
PRINEAS, R. J., Public Health Sciences (Epidemiology)
QUANDT, S. A., Public Health Sciences (Epidemiology)
RAPP, S. R., Psychiatry and Behavioural Medicine (Geriatric Medicine)
RAUTAHARJU, P. M., Public Health Sciences
REIFLER, B. V., Psychiatry and Behavioural Medicine
RICH, S. S., Public Health Sciences
RILEY, W. A., Neurology
ROGERS, L. F., Radiological Sciences (Radiology)
ROHR, M. S., Surgical Sciences (General)
ROSE, J.C., Obstetrics and Gynaecology (Maternal/Fetal Medicine)
ROUFAIL, W. M., Internal Medicine (Gastroenterology)
ROY, R. C., Anaesthesiology
ROYSTER, R. L., Anaesthesiology
RUBIN, B. K., Paediatrics, Physiology and Pharmacology
RUDEL, L. L., Comparative Medicine, Biochemistry
ST CLAIR, R. W., Pathology
SANGÜEZA, O. P., Pathology
SARTIANO, G. P., Internal Medicine (Haematology/Oncology)
SCUDERI, P. E., Anaesthesiology
SHAW, E. G., Radiation Oncology

SHERERTZ, R. J., Internal Medicine (Infectious Diseases), Microbiology and Immunology
SHIHABI, Z. K., Pathology
SHIVELY, C. A., Comparative Medicine
SHUMAKER, S. A., Public Health Sciences (Social Sciences and Health Policy)
SIMON, J. L., Paediatrics
SINAL, S. H., Paediatrics, Family and Community Medicine
SLUSHER, M. M., Surgical Sciences (Ophthalmology)
SMITH, J. E., Physiology and Pharmacology
SMITH, P. B., Biochemistry
STEIN, B. E., Neurobiology and Anatomy
STRANDHOY, J. W., Physiology and Pharmacology
SUMNER, T. E., Radiological Sciences (Radiology)
TEGELER, C. H., IV, Neurology
THOMAS, M. J., Biochemistry
THOMPSON, J. N., Surgical Sciences (Otolaryngology)
TOOLE, J. F., Neurology
TORTI, F. M., Cancer Biology, Internal Medicine (Haematology/Oncology)
TROOST, B. T., Neurology
TYTELL, M., Neurobiology and Anatomy
VAN DE RIJN, I., Microbiology and Immunology
VEILLE, J.-C., Obstetrics and Gynaecology (Maternal/Fetal Medicine)
VELEZ, R., Internal Medicine
WAGNER, W. D., Comparative Medicine
WALKER, F. O., Neurology (Neuromuscular Diseases)
WARD, W. G., Surgical Sciences (Orthopaedics)
WASILAUSKAS, B. L., Pathology
WEBB, L. X., Surgical Sciences (Otolaryngology)
WEBBER, R. L., Radiological Sciences (Medical Eng.), Dentistry
WEINBERG, R. B., Internal Medicine (Gastroenterology)
WHEELER, K. T., Jr, Radiological Sciences (Radiology)
WILLIAMS, J. K., Comparative Medicine
WILLINGHAM, M. C., Pathology
WOOD, F. B., Neurology (Neuropsychology)
WOODWARD, D. J., Physiology and Pharmacology
WYKLE, R. L., Biochemistry
ZAGORIA, R. J., Radiological Sciences (Radiology)
ZAMKOFF, K. W., Internal Medicine (Haematology/Oncology)

School of Business and Accountancy:

AKINC, U., Production and Operations Management
EWING, S., Management and Statistics
HARRISON, K., Management
JURAS, P., Academic Excellence
KNIGHT, L., Accounting
MARTIN, D., Financial Accounting
ROBIN, D., Business Ethics
TAYLOR, T., Accounting
TOWER, R., Taxation
WILKERSON, J., Accounting

WARREN WILSON COLLEGE

POB 9000, Asheville, NC 28815
701 Warren Wilson Rd, Swannanoa, NC 28778

Telephone: (828) 298-3325
Fax: (828) 298-1440
E-mail: admit@warren-wilson.edu
Internet: www.warren-wilson.edu
Private control
Academic year: August to May

Pres.: SANDY PFEIFFER

Vice-Pres. for Academic Affairs and Dean of the College: JOHN CASEY

Vice-Pres. for College Relations: CARLA E. SUTHERLAND
Vice-President for Business and Treas.: LARRY R. MODLIN
Registrar: CHRISTA BRIDGMAN
Library Dir: CHRISTINE RICHERT NUGENT
Number of teachers: 70
Number of students: 777 (full-time).

WESTERN CAROLINA UNIVERSITY

Cullowhee, NC 28723
Telephone: (828) 227-7211
Fax: (828) 227-7202
Internet: www.wcu.edu
Founded 1889
Linked to the Univ. of North Carolina
Chancellor: JOHN W. BARDO
Provost: KYLE CARTER
Vice-Chancellor for Advancement and External Affairs: CLIFTON METCALF
Vice-Chancellor for Student Affairs: ROBERT CARUSO
Sr Dir of Admissions: CHRIS PARRISH
Registrar: LARRY HAMMER (acting)
Assoc. Dir of Library: ELOISE HITCHCOCK
Library of 436,041 vols
Number of teachers: 335
Number of students: 6,619.

WINGATE UNIVERSITY

POB 159, Wingate, NC 28174
Telephone: (704) 233-8000
Fax: (704) 233-8110
E-mail: admit@wingate.edu
Internet: www.wingate.edu
Founded 1896
Private control
Academic year: August to May
Pres.: Dr JERRY E. MCGEE
Exec. Vice-Pres. and Chief Financial Officer: CHARLES TAYLOR
Vice-Pres. for Academic Affairs: Dr MARTHA S. ASTI
Vice-Pres. for Resource Devt: VINT TILSON
Vice-Pres. and Athletic Dir: STEVE POSTON
Registrar: LOURDES SILVA
Library Dir: AMEE ODOM
Number of teachers: 107
Number of students: 1,799

DEANS

College of Arts and Sciences: Dr DONALD MERRILL
School of Business and Econ.: JOSEPH GRAHAM
School of Education: Dr ROBERT SHAW
School of Pharmacy: Dr ROBERT SUPERNAW

WINSTON-SALEM STATE UNIVERSITY

601 South Martin Luther King, Jr. Dr., Winston-Salem, NC 27110
Telephone: (336) 750-2000
Fax: (336) 750-2049
E-mail: chancellorsoffice@wssu.edu
Internet: www.wssu.edu
Founded 1892
Academic year: August to May
Linked to the Univ. of North Carolina
Chancellor: Dr MICHELLE HOWARD-VITAL
Vice-Chancellor for Finance and Admin.: ROBERT L. BOTLEY
Vice-Chancellor for Student Affairs and Enrollment Services: Dr MELODY C. PIERCE
Vice-Chancellor for Univ. Advancement: LEE WEAVER RICHARDSON
Dir of Library Services: Dr MAE L. RODNEY
Library of 158,858 vols
Number of teachers: 199

Number of students: 6,000.

NORTH DAKOTA

JAMESTOWN COLLEGE

Jamestown, ND 58405
Telephone: (701) 252-3467
Fax: (701) 253-4318
E-mail: admissions@jc.edu
Internet: www.jc.edu
Founded 1884
Private control
Academic year: August to May
President: Dr JERRY COMBEE
Provost: Dr JIM STONE
Director of Admissions: CAROL SCHMEICHEL
Librarian: Mrs PHYLLIS BRATTON
Library of 117,000 vols
Number of teachers: 60
Number of students: 1,100.

NORTH DAKOTA UNIVERSITY SYSTEM

10th Floor, State Capitol 600 East Boulevard Ave, Dept 215, Bismarck, ND 58505-0230
Telephone: (701) 328-2960
Fax: (701) 328-2961
E-mail: ndus.office@ndus.nodak.edu
Internet: www.ndus.edu
Chancellor: Dr ROBERT POTTS
Number of teachers: 2,300.

CONSTITUENT UNIVERSITIES

Dickinson State University

Dickinson, ND 58601-4896
Telephone: (701) 227-2507
Fax: (701) 227-2006
E-mail: dsu.hawks@dsu.nodak.edu
Internet: www.dickinsonstate.edu
Founded 1918
President: PHILIP W. CONN
Registrar: MARSHALL MELBYE
Librarian: BERNNETT REINKE
Library of 82,000 vols
Number of teachers: 106
Number of students: 1,601
Publications: *Catalog* (every 2 years), *Prospective Student View Book* (annually), *Western Concept* (student newspaper), *Prairie Smoke* (student yearbook), *Impressions* (student creative writing), *Alumni News* (quarterly), *Departmental brochures* (annually), *DSU Digest* (weekly), *Parents Newsletter* (quarterly), *Views* (quarterly).

Mayville State University

330 Third St NE, Mayville, ND 58257
Telephone: (701) 786-2301
Fax: (701) 786-4748
E-mail: help_desk@mayvillestate.edu
Internet: www.mayvillestate.edu
Founded 1889
President: PAMELA M. BALCH
Vice-President for Academic Affairs: GARY HAGEN
Registrar: MARY IVERSON
Librarian: SARAH BATESEL
Library of 83,964 vols
Number of teachers: 52
Number of students: 756.

Minot State University

Minot, ND 58707
Telephone: (701) 858-3000
E-mail: msu@minotstateu.edu
Internet: www.minotstateu.edu
Founded 1913

President: Dr DAVID FULLER
Registrar: Dr NANCY HALL
Librarian: LARRY GREENWOOD
Library of 335,000 vols
Number of teachers: 220
Number of students: 3,200
Additional campus in Bottineau offers Associate in Science (AS), Associate in Arts (AA), and Associate of Applied Science (AAS) degrees.

North Dakota State University

12th Ave N., Fargo, ND 58105
Telephone: (701) 237-8011
Internet: www.ndsu.edu
Founded 1890
President: Dr JOSEPH A. CHAPMAN
Vice-President of Academic Affairs: CRAIG SCHNELL
Vice-President for Business and Finance: RICHARD RAYL
Vice-President for Student Affairs: GEORGE H. WALLMAN
Vice-President for Agricultural Affairs: PATRICIA JENSEN
Vice-President for Research, Creative Activities and Technology Transfer: PHILIP BOUDJOUK
Executive Director, University Relations: KEITH D. BJERKE
Registrar: DEANNA SELLNOW
Librarian: PAMELA DRAYSON
Library of 506,444 vols
Number of teachers: 550
Number of students: 10,000

DEANS

Faculty of Agriculture: PATRICIA JENSEN
Faculty of Arts, Humanities and Social Sciences: THOMAS RILEY
Faculty of Science and Mathematics: ALAN WHITE
Faculty of Engineering and Architecture: OTTO HELWEG
Faculty of Pharmacy: CHARLES D. PETERSON
Faculty of Graduate School: VELMER BURTON
Faculty of University Studies: CAROLYN SCHNELL (Dir)
Faculty of Business Administration: JAY LEITCH
Faculty of Human Development and Education: VIRGINIA CLARK

University of North Dakota

University Station, Grand Forks, ND 58202
Telephone: (701) 777-2011
Fax: (701) 777-3650
E-mail: university_relations@und.edu
Internet: www.und.edu
Founded 1883
Academic year: August to May
President: CHARLES KUPCHELLA
Vice-President (Academic Affairs): MARTHA POTVIN
Vice-President (Finance and Operation): ROBERT GALLAGER
Vice-President (Student and Outreach Services): ROBERT BOYD
Vice-President (Health Sciences): H. DAVID WILSON
Vice-President (Research): PETER ALFONSO
Registrar: NANCY KROGH
Librarian: WILBUR STOLT
Library of 1,118,419 vols, also e-books, microforms, audiovisual items
Number of teachers: 610
Number of students: 13,034
Publication: *North Dakota Quarterly*

DEANS

Graduate: JOSEPH BENOIT
Arts and Sciences: BRUCE DEARDEN

Business: DENNIS ELBERT
College of Education and Human Development: DAN RICE
Engineering: JOHN WATSON
Law: PAUL LE BEL
Medicine and Health Sciences: H. DAVID WILSON
Nursing: ELIZABETH NICHOLS
Outreach Services: JIM SHAEFFER
Odeguard School for Aerospace Sciences: BRUCE SMITH

Valley City State University

101 College St SW, Valley City, ND 58072
Telephone: (701) 845-7990
Fax: (701) 845-7245
Internet: www.vcsu.edu
Founded 1890
President: Dr ELLEN E. CHAFFEE
Academic Dean: Dr LESLIE E. WONG
Vice-President for Business Affairs: STEVE BENSEN
Vice-President for Student Affairs: GLEN SCHMALZ
Librarian: DARRYL B. PODOLL
Library of 80,000 vols
Number of teachers: 56
Number of students: 1,077
Publication: *The Bulletin*.

There are five two-year colleges offering associate and trade/technical degrees.

TRINITY BIBLE COLLEGE

50 S Sixth Ave, Ellendale, ND 58436
Telephone: (701) 349-3621
Fax: (701) 349-5443
E-mail: president@trinitybiblecollege.edu
Internet: www.trinitybiblecollege.edu
Founded 1948 as Lakewood Park Bible School; present name 1983
Private control
Academic year: August to May
President: Rev. DENNIS D. NILES
Vice-President (Academic Affairs): Dr MICHAEL DUSING
Vice-President (College Relations): Rev. STEVEN TVEDT
Number of teachers: 25
Number of students: 280.

UNIVERSITY OF MARY

7500 University Drive, Bismarck, ND 58504
Telephone: (701) 255-7500
Fax: (701) 255-7687
E-mail: marauder@umary.edu
Internet: www.umary.edu
Campuses at Bismarck and Fargo
Founded 1955 as Mary College; present name 1986
Private control
Academic year: August to May
President: Sr THOMAS WELDER
Vice-President (Academic Affairs): Dr DIANE FLADELAND
Vice-President (Enrollment Services): DAVID HERINGER
Vice-President (Financial Affairs): JERRY FISCHER
Vice-President (Public Affairs): NEAL KALBERER
Vice-President (Student Development): Dr TIM SEAWORTH
Library Director: CHERYL BAILEY
Number of teachers: 95
Number of students: 2,757.

OHIO

AIR FORCE INSTITUTE OF TECHNOLOGY

Wright-Patterson Air Force Base, OH 45433-7765
Telephone: (937) 255-2321
Fax: (937) 656-7600
Internet: www.afit.edu
Founded 1919
Commandant: Col JOHN H. RUSSELL
Director of Admissions: Maj. BARBARA E. JOSEPH
Director of Academic Affairs: Dr JAMES M. HORNER
Library Director: JAMES T. HELLING
Library of 120,000 vols
Number of teachers: 134 civilian, 126 military

DEANS

Graduate School of Engineering: Dr ROBERT A. CALICO, Jr
Graduate School of Logistics and Acquisition Management: Dr JAN P. MUCZYK
School of Systems and Logistics: Dr RICHARD L. MURPHY
Civil Engineering and Services School: Col JOSEPH H. AMEND
Civilian Institution Programs: Col PAUL D. COPP

ANTIOCH UNIVERSITY

150 E South College, Yellow Springs, OH 45387-1635
Telephone: (937) 769-1340
Fax: (937) 769-1350
Internet: www.antioch.edu
Founded 1852
Academic year: July to June
Chancellor: JAMES H. CRAIGLOW
Vice-Chancellor and Chief Financial Officer: DON TECKLENBURGH
Vice-Chancellor for Development and External Relations: LOIS A. MANN
Number of teachers: 495
Number of students: 4,230
Publications: *Antioch Review* (4 a year), *The Record* (weekly), *The Antiochian* (4 a year), *Antioch Notes* (irregular), *The McGregor News* (4 a year), *Whole Terrain* (annually), *Antioch* (4 a year), *Grapevine* (2 a year)

PRESIDENTS

Antioch College: STEVE LAWRY
Antioch New England Graduate School: NEIL KING
Antioch University–Southern California: LUCYANN GEISELMAN
Antioch University–Seattle: TONI MURDOCK
Antioch University–McGregor: BARBARA DANLEY

ART ACADEMY OF CINCINNATI

1125 St Gregory St, Cincinnati, OH 45202
Telephone: (513) 721-5202
E-mail: admissions@artacademy.edu
Internet: www.artacademy.edu
Founded 1869 as McMicken School of Design; present name 1887
Private control
Academic year: August to May
President: GREGORY ALLGIRE SMITH
Academic Dean: KEITH KUTCH
Registrar: DAVE JOHNSON
Number of teachers: 15
Number of students: 250.

ASHLAND UNIVERSITY

Ashland, OH 44805
Telephone: (419) 289-4142
Fax: (419) 289-5333
E-mail: auadmsn@ashland.edu
Internet: www.ashland.edu
Founded 1878
Academic year: August to May
President: G. WILLIAM BENZ
Provost: BOB SUGGS
Registrar: KAREN A. LITTLE
Director of Libraries: WILLIAM B. WEISS
Library of 265,000 vols
Number of teachers: 205
Number of students: 6,105
Publication: *River Teeth* (2 a year).

ATHENAEUM OF OHIO

6616 Beechmont Ave, Cincinnati, OH 45230
Telephone: (513) 231-2223
Fax: (513) 231-3254
E-mail: ath@mtsm.org
Internet: www.mtsm.org
Founded 1829
Private control (Roman Catholic)
Academic year: September to June
Chancellor: Archbishop DANIEL E. PILARCZYK
President: Rev. GERALD R. HAEMMERLE
Academic Dean: Dr TERRENCE CALLAN
Librarian: Sister DEBORAH HARMELING
Library of 77,000 volumes
Number of teachers: 58
Number of students: 252.

BALDWIN-WALLACE COLLEGE

275 Eastland Rd, Berea, OH 44017
Telephone: (216) 826-2900
Internet: www.bw.edu
Founded 1845
President: Dr NEAL MALICKY
Dean of Enrollment Services: J. EDWARD WARNER
Librarian: Dr PATRICK SCANLAN
Library of 210,000 vols
Number of teachers: 152 full-time
Number of students: 4,700.

BLUFFTON UNIVERSITY

1 University Drive, Bluffton, OH 45817-2104
Telephone: (419) 358-3000
Fax: (419) 358-3323
Internet: www.bluffton.edu
Founded 1899 as Bluffton College, present name and status August 2004
Private control
Academic year: August to May
President: LEE SNYDER
Vice-President for Fiscal Affairs: WILLIS J. SOMMER
Vice-President and Dean of Academic Affairs: WILLIAM TROLLINGER
Vice-President and Dean of Student Life: ERIC FULCOMER
Librarian: MARY JEAN JOHNSON
Library of 160,000 vols
Number of teachers: 70
Number of students: 1,191.

BOWLING GREEN STATE UNIVERSITY

Bowling Green, OH 43403
Telephone: (419) 372-2531
Internet: www.bgsu.edu
Founded 1910
Academic year: August to May
President: SIDNEY A. RIBEAU

Provost, and Vice-President for Academic Affairs: LINDA DOBB (acting)
Vice-President for University Advancement: J. DOUGLAS SMITH
Vice-President for Student Affairs: EDWARD G. WHIPPLE
Senior Vice-President for Finance and Administration: CHRISTOPHER DALTON
Library: Library of 6,000,000 vols, recordings, documents and other materials
Number of teachers: 690
Number of students: 18,200
Publications: *Philosopher's Index* (4 a year), *Journal of Popular Culture* (4 a year), *Key* (annually)

DEANS

Arts and Sciences: CHARLES J. CRANNY
Education and Human Development: LES STERNBERG
Business Administration: JAMES SULLIVAN
Graduate College: STEVEN BALLARD
Health and Human Services: CLYDE WILLIS
Musical Arts: H. LEE RIGGINS
Firelands: WILLIAM BALZER (acting)
Continuing Education, International and Summer Programs: SUZANNE CRAWFORD
Libraries and Learning Resources: CHRISTOPHER MIKO (acting)
College of Technology: ERNEST SAVAGE (acting)

CAPITAL UNIVERSITY

Columbus, OH 43209-2394
Telephone: (614) 236-6011
Fax: (614) 236-6147
Internet: www.capital.edu

Founded 1850
A Lutheran institution
Academic year: August to May (two terms)
President: Dr DANIEL A. FELICETTI
Vice-President for Academic Affairs: RONALD J. VOLPE
Vice-President for University Relations: SHEA MCGREW
Vice-President for Resource Management: VERNON TRUESDALE
Registrar: AMY BUCKINGHAM
Librarian: ALBERT MAAG
Number of teachers: 473
Number of students: 4,047
Publications: *Chimes* (newspaper), *Capital Literary Arts Magazine* (2 a year), *Alumni Magazine* (4 a year)

DEANS

Arts and Sciences: DAINA MCGARY
Conservatory of Music: WILLIAM DEDERER
School of Nursing: DORIS EDWARDS
Capital Law School: STEVEN BAHLS
Graduate School of Administration: (vacant)
Student Affairs: STEPHEN BELLER
Adult Learning and Assessment: (vacant)

CASE WESTERN RESERVE UNIVERSITY

10900 Euclid Ave, Cleveland, OH 44106
Telephone: (216) 368-2000
Fax: (216) 368-4325
Internet: www.case.edu

Founded 1967 from the Western Reserve Univ. (f. 1826 as College) and the Case Institute of Technology (f. 1880 as Case School of Applied Science)
Private control
Academic year: August to May
Pres.: BARBARA R. SNYDER
Sr Vice-Pres. for Univ. Relations and Devt: BRUCE LOESSIN
Provost and Univ. Vice-Pres.: JOHN L. ANDERSON

Deputy Provost and Vice-Pres. for Academic Programs: LYNN T. SINGER
Chief Financial and Admin. Officer: HOSSEIN SADID
Vice-Pres. and Gen. Counsel: JEANINE ARDEN ORNT
Vice-Pres. for Campus Planning and Operations: KENNETH A. BASCH
Vice-Pres. for Cleveland and Regional Affairs: JOHN WHEELER
Vice-Pres. for Human Resources: CAROLYN GREGORY
Vice-Pres. for Information Technology Services: LEV S. GONICK
Vice-Pres. for Planning and Budget: CHRISTINE ASH
Vice-Pres. for Commercial Devt: RUSSELL BERUSCH
Vice-Pres. for Research and Technology Management: MARK COTICCHIA
Vice-Pres. for Student Affairs: GLENN NICHOLLS
Vice-Pres. for Univ. Relations: LARA KALAFATIS
Chief Devt Officer: SALLY J. STALEY
Vice-Pres. for Campus Services: DICK JAMIESON
Univ. Registrar: AMY HAMMETT
Dir of Univ. Library: JOANNE D. EUSTIS

Number of teachers: 2,521
Number of students: 9,927

DEANS

Arts and Sciences: CYRUS TAYLOR
Case School of En.: NORMAN TIEN
School of Dentistry: JEROLD S. GOLDBERG
Graduate Studies: CHARLES ROZEK
Undergraduate Studies: JEFFREY WOLCOWITZ
School of Law: GARY J. SIMSON
Weatherhead School of Management: MOHAN REDDY
School of Medicine: PAMELA BOWES DAVIS
Frances Payne Bolton School of Nursing: MAY L. WYKLE
Mandel School of Applied Social Sciences: GROVER C. GIMORE

PROFESSORS

Arts and Sciences (tel. (216) 368-4413; internet www.case.edu/artsci):

ADAMS, H., Art History and Art
AKERIB, D., Physics
ALEXANDER, J., Mathematics
ANDERSON, A. B., Chemistry
BARKLEY, M. D., Chemistry
BEAL, T., Religion
BEALL, C. M., Anthropology
BROWN, R., Physics
BURKE, M., Biology
CALVETTI, D., Mathematics
CAPLAN, A. I., Biology
CARRIER, D., Art History and Art
CHIEL, H. J., Biology
CHOTTINER, G. S., Physics
CULLIS, C. A., Biology
DANNEFER, W. D., Sociology
DEACOSTA, A. D., Mathematics
DEIMLING, G. T., Sociology
DETTERMAN, D. K., Psychology
DUFFIN, R. W., Music
DUNBAR, R. C., Chemistry
FAGAN III, J. F., Psychology
FARRELL, D. E., Physics
GAINES, A. D., Anthropology
GARNER, P. P., Chemistry
GILMORE, G. C., Psychology
GOLDSTEIN, M. C., Anthropology
GREENE, R. L., Psychology
GREKSA, L. P., Anthropology
GRUNDY, K. W., Political Science
GUP, T. S., English
GURARIE, D., Mathematics
HAAS, P. J., Religion
HAMMACK, D. C., History
HEFLING, S. E., Music

HELZE, M., Classics
HURLEY, M. G., Mathematics
IKELS, C., Anthropology
JENKINS, J. H., Anthropology
KAHANA, E., Sociology
KASH, K., Physics
KENNEY, M. E., Chemistry
KIM, C.-T., Philosophy
KOONCE, J. F., Biology
KORBIN, J. E., Anthropology
KOTELENEZ, P., Mathematics
KOWALSKI, K. L., Physics
KRAUSS, L. M., Physics
LAMBRECHT, W., Physics
LANDAU, E. G., Art History and Art
LANGER, J., Mathematics
LATHERS, M., Modern Languages and Literature
LEE, D. H., Mathematics
LEITMAN, M. J., Mathematics
LOADER, C., Statistics
LUCK, R. E., Astronomy
MARLING, W. H., English
MATEESCU, G. D., Chemistry
MATISOFF, G., Geological Sciences
MCCALL, P. L., Geological Sciences
MCHALE, V. E., Political Science
NEILS, J., Art History and Art
OLSZEWSKI, E. J., Art History and Art
ORLOCK, J. M., Theatre Arts
OVERHOLSER, J. C., Psychology
PEARSON, A. J., Chemistry
PETSCHEK, R. G., Physics
PROTASIEWICZ, J., Chemistry
RITZMANN, R. E., Biology
ROCKE, A. J., History
ROSENBLATT, C. S., Physics
RUHL, J. E., Physics
RUSS, S. W., Psychology
SALOMON, R. G., Chemistry
SAVIN, S. M., Geological Sciences
SAYRE, L. M., Chemistry
SCHERSON, D. A., Chemistry
SCHUELE, D. E., Physics
SEDRANSK, J., Statistics
SIEBENSCHUH, W. R., English
SETTERSTEN Jr, R., Sociology
SINGER, D. A., Mathematics
SINGER, K. D., Physics
STARKMAN, G. D., Physics
STEINBERG, T. L., History
STOLLER, E. P., Sociology
STONUM, G. L., English
STRAUSS, M. E., Psychology
STUEHR, J. E., Chemistry
SUN, J., Statistics
SZAREK, S. J., Mathematics
TAYLOR, C. C., Physics
TAYLOR, P., Physics
TURNER, M., Cognitive Science
URBACH, F. L., Chemistry
VACHASPATI, T., Physics
WERNER, E., Mathematics
WHITBECK, C., Philosophy
WHITE, J., Political Science
WILSON, R. G., Theatre Arts
WOODMANSEE, M. A., English
WOYCZYNSKI, W. A., Statistics
WU, T.-S., Mathematics
ZULL, J. E., Biology

School of Dentistry (tel. (216) 368-3200; internet dental.case.edu):

BISSADA, N., Periodontics
GOLDBERG, J. S., Oral and Maxillofacial Surgery
OCCHIONERO, R. L., Dentistry
SAWYER, D. R., Oral Diagnosis and Radiology
WOTMAN, S., Community Dentistry

Case School of Engineering (tel. (216) 368-4436; internet www.engineering.case.edu):

ADAMS, M. L., Mechanical and Aerospace Engineering
ALEXANDER, J. I. D., Mechanical and Aerospace Engineering

BAER, E., Macromolecular Science and Engineering
BALLARINI, R., Engineering Mechanics
BEER, R., Electrical Engineering and Computer Science
BLACKWELL, J., Macromolecular Science and Engineering
CAWLEY, J. D., Materials Science and Engineering
CRAGO, P. E., Biomedical Engineering
DAVY, D. T., Mechanical and Aerospace Engineering
DURAND, D. M., Biomedical Engineering
EDWARDS, R. V., Chemical Engineering
ERNST, F., Materials Science and Engineering
FEKE, D. L., Chemical Engineering
GASPARINI, D. A., Structural Engineering
GREBER, I., Mechanical and Aerospace Engineering
HEUER, A. H., Materials Science and Engineering
HILTNER, A., Macromolecular Science and Engineering
ISHIDA, H., Macromolecular Science and Engineering
JAMIESON, A. M., Macromolecular Science and Engineering
JENNINGS, A. A., Environmental Engineering
KADAMBI, J. R., Mechanical and Aerospace Engineering
KAMOTANI, Y., Mechanical and Aerospace Engineering
LACKS, D. J., Chemical Engineering
LANDAU, U., Chemical Engineering
LANDO, J. B., Macromolecular Science and Engineering
LEWANDOWSKI, J. J., Materials Science and Engineering
LITT, M., Macromolecular Science and Engineering
LIU, C.-C., Chemical Engineering
LOPARO, K. A., Electrical Engineering and Computer Science
MALAKOOTI, B., Electrical Engineering and Computer Science
MANAS-ZLOCZOWER, I., Macromolecular Science and Engineering
MANN Jr, J. A., Chemical Engineering
MANSOUR, J. M., Mechanical and Aerospace Engineering
MARCHANT, R. E., Biomedical Engineering
MEHREGANY, M., Electrical Engineering and Computer Science
MESAROVIC, M. D., Electrical Engineering and Computer Science
MICHAL, G. M., Materials Science and Engineering
MULLEN, R. L., Engineering Mechanics
NEWMAN, W. S., Electrical Engineering and Computer Science
OSTRACH, S., Mechanical and Aerospace Engineering
OZSOYOGLU, G., Electrical Engineering and Computer Science
OZSOYOGLU, Z. M., Electrical Engineering and Computer Science
PAPACHRISTOU, C. A., Electrical Engineering and Computer Science
PAYER, J. H., Materials Science and Engineering
PECKHAM, P. H., Biomedical Engineering
PINTAURO, P. N., Chemical Engineering
PIROUZ, P., Materials Science and Engineering
PRAHL, J. M., Mechanical and Aerospace Engineering
QUINN, R. D., Mechanical and Aerospace Engineering
QUTUBUDDIN, S., Chemical Engineering
SAADA, A. S., Geotechnical Engineering
SAIDEL, G. M., Biomedical Engineering
SAVINELL, R. F., Chemical Engineering
TABIB-AZAR, M., Electrical Engineering and Computer Science

T'IEN, J. S., Mechanical and Aerospace Engineering
WELSCH, G. E., Materials Science and Engineering
WHITE, L., Electrical Engineering and Computer Science
WILSON, D., Biomedical Engineering
ZAWODZINSKI, T., Chemical Engineering

School of Law (11075 East Blvd, Cleveland, OH 44106; tel. (216) 368-3600; fax (216) 368-1042; e-mail lawadmissions@case.edu; internet law.case.edu):

AUSTIN II, A. D.
CHISOLM, L. B.
CHODOSH, H. E.
COFFEY, R. J.
DENT Jr, G. W.
DURCHSLAG, M. R.
ENTIN, J. L.
GABINET, L.
GERHART, P. M.
GIANNELLI, P. C.
HESSLER, K.
JENSEN, E. M.
KATZ, L. R.
KING Jr, H. T.
KORNGOLD, G.
KOSTRITSKY, J. P.
KU, R. S. R.
LAWRY, R. P.
LEATHERBERRY, W. C.
LIPTON, J. P.
McKINNEY, L. W.
McMUNIGAL, K. C.
MARGOLIS, K. R.
MEHLMAN, M. J.
MORRISS, A. P.
NANCE, D. A.
NARD, C. A.
NETH, S.
SCHARF, M. P.
SHANKER, M. G.
SHARPE, C. W.
SOUTHWORTH, A.
STRASSFELD, R. N.

Weatherhead School of Management (tel. (216) 368-2030; internet weatherhead.case.edu):

ANVARI, M., Finance
ARAM, J. D., Management Policy
BALLOU, R. H., Operations
BOLAND, R., Information Systems
BOYATZIS, R. E., Organizational Behaviour
BRICKER, R., Accountancy
CARLSSON, B., Econ.
CHATTERJEE, S., Management Policy
COLLOPY, F., Information Systems
COOPERRIDER, D., Organizational Behaviour
ERDILEK, A., Econ.
FINE, S., Banking and Finance
FOGARTY, T., Accountancy
GERHART, P. F., Labour and Human Resource Policy
HELPER, S., Econ.
HISRICH, R. D., Entrepreneurial Studies
KOLB, D. A., Organizational Behaviour
LYNN, L. H., Management Policy
LYYTINEN, K., Information Systems
NEILSEN, E. H., Organizational Behaviour
OSBORNE, R. L., Practice of Management
PEARSON, D., Practice of Accountancy
POZA, E. J., Practice of Family Business
PREVITS, G. J., Accountancy
REBITZER, J. B., Econ.
RITCHKEN, P. H., Banking and Finance
ROOMKIN, M., Labour and Human Resource Policy
SALIPANTE Jr, P. F., Labour and Human Resource Policy
SALKIN, H. M., Operations
SHANE, S. A., Econ.
SILVERS, J. B., Banking and Finance
SINGH, J., Marketing
SOBEL, M. J., Operations

VANDENBOSCH, B., Information Systems
VONK, T., Labour and Human Resource Policy

School of Medicine (tel. (216) 368-2820; e-mail casemed@case.edu; internet casemed.case.edu):

AACH, R. D., Medicine
ABDUL-KARIM, F., Pathology
ADLER, D., Cardiology
AGARWAL, A., Surgery
AGICH, G. J., Medicine
AGLE, D., Psychiatry
ALTHOF, S., Urology
ALTOSE, M. D., Medicine
ANDERSON, J. M., Pathology
ANDERSON, V., Biochemistry and Chemistry
ARAFAH, B., Molecular Endocrinology
ARNOLD, J. E., Otolaryngology
ARON, D. C., Endocrinology and Hypertension
ARROLIGA, A., Medicine
ASKARI, A. D., Medicine
ATAYA, K., Reproductive Biology
BAHLER, R. C., Medicine
BALEY, J. E., Paediatrics
BANERJEE, A., Virology
BARNETT, G., Surgery
BERGER, M., Paediatrics
BERGER, N., Medicine, Biochemistry
BERMAN, B., Paediatrics
BINDER, L. S., Emergency Medicine
BINSTOCK, R. H., Bioethics, Ageing, Health and Society
BLUMER, J. L., Paediatrics and Pharmacology
BODNAR, D., Urology
BOHLMAN, H., Orthopaedics
BOOM, W. H., Infectious Disease
BOOTHMAN, D. A., Radiation Oncology
BORDEN, E., Molecular Medicine
BROUHARD, B. H., Paediatrics
BROZOVICH, F. V., Medicine and Physiology
BRUNENGRABER, H., Nutrition
BUCKLEY, P., Psychiatry
BUDD, G., Medicine
BUKOWSKI, R., Medicine
BURNEY, E., Ophthalmology
CALABRASE, J. R., Psychiatry
CAMPBELL, J., Family Medicine
CAREY, P., Biochemistry
CAREY, W. D., Medicine
CARLIN, C., Physiology and Biophysics
CARLSON, M. D., Cardiology
CARTER, S. G., Medicine
CASCORBI, H. F., Anaesthesiology
CATALANO, P. M., Reproductive Biology
CATHCART, M., Molecular Medicine
CAVANAUGH, P., Molecular Medicine
CEBUL, R. D., Medicine
CHAO, J., Family Medicine
CHISHOLM, G., Molecular Medicine
CHWALS, W. J., Surgery
CLARK, G. S., Medicine
COHEN, A. R., Neurosurgery
COHEN, M. L., Pathology
COLE-KELLY, K., Family Medicine
CONNORS, A., Medicine
COOPER, K. D., Dermatology
COOPERMAN, D. R., Orthopaedics
CRABB, J. W., Molecular Medicine
CROMER, B. A., Paediatrics
CULP, L. A., Molecular Biology and Microbiology
CUTTLER, L., Paediatrics and Pharmacology
CZINN, S. J., Paediatrics
DAHMS, B. B., Pathology
DAHMS, W., Paediatrics
DAROFF, R., Neurology
DAVIS, B. R., Dermatology
DAVIS, P. B., Paediatrics, Physiology and Biophysics, Molecular Biology and Microbiology
DAWSON, N. V., Medicine

DEARBORN, D., Paediatrics
DEBANNE, S., Epidemiology and Biostatistics
DEHASETH, P., Biochemistry
DELANEY, C., Surgery
DELGARDO, P. L., Psychiatry
DELL'OSSO, L., Neurology
DENERIS, E., Neuroscience
DENNIS, V. W., Medicine
DEVEREAUX, M., Neurology
DICORLETO, P. E., Physiology and Biophysics
DIMARCO, A. F., Physiology and Biophysics
DIERKER, L. J., Reproductive Biology
DISTELHORST, C. W., Haematology, Oncology
DOERSCHUK, C., Paediatrics
DRAKE, R., Surgery
DREICER, R., Medicine
DRISCOLL, D., Molecular Medicine
DROTAR, D., Paediatrics
DUBYAK, G. R., Physiology, Biophysics
DUERK, J. L., Radiology
ECKERT, R., Physiology
ELDER, J. S., Urology
ELLIS, S., Medicine
ELSTON, R. C., Epidemiology and Biostatistics
EMANCIPATOR, S. N., Pathology
EMERMAN, C. L., Emergency Medicine
ERNHART, C., Psychiatry
ERZURUM, S. C., Medicine
ESCLAMADO, R., Surgery
ESTAFANOUS, F., Anaesthesiology
EVANS, H., Radiation Oncology
FAIRCHILD, R. L., Surgery
FALCONE, T., Surgery
FANAROFF, A. A., Paediatrics
FARAH, M. G., Cardiology
FINDLING, R., Psychiatry
FINKE, J., Molecular Medicine
FIOCCHI, C., Gastroenterology Medicine
FOX, J. E. B., Physiology and Biophysics
FOX, P., Molecular Medicine
FRANCIS, G., Medicine
FRATIANNE, R. B., Surgery
FRIEDLAND, R., Neurology
GAMBETTI, P., Pathology
GANAPATHI, R., Medicine
GENUTH, S. M., Endocrinology and Hypertension
GERSON, S. L., Haematology and Oncology
GHANNOUM, M. A., Dermatology
GILL, I., Surgery
GOLDBERG, V. M., Orthopaedics
GOLDBLUM, J., Pathology
GOLDING, L., Molecular Medicine
GOLDSTONE, J., Surgery
GORDON, N. H., Bioethics
GORODESKI, G. I., Reproductive Biology
GRAHAM, A. V., Family Medicine
GRAHAM, L., Surgery
GRAHAM, R. C., Medicine
GREENFIELD, E., Orthopaedics
GREENSPAN, N. S., Pathology
GUDKOV, A. V., Biochemistry
HAAGA, J. R., Radiology
HACK, M., Paediatrics
HALL, G., Pathology
HAMILTON, T., Molecular Medicine
HAMPEL, N., Surgery
HANSON, R. W., Biochemistry
HAQQI, T. M., Medicine
HARDING, C. V., III, Pathology
HARDY, R. W., Neurosurgery
HART, W. R., Pathology
HARTE, P., Genetics
HASCALL, V. C., Biochemistry
HATZOGLOU, M., Nutrition
HAUGHEL-DE-MOUZON, S., Reproductive Biology
HAXHIU, M., Paediatrics
HAZEN, S., Molecular Medicine
HENDERSON, J. M., Surgery
HENSON, L., Anaesthesiology
HERRUP, K., Alzheimer Centre

HESTON, W., Molecular Medicine
HINES, J. D., Medicine
HODGSON, J., Medicine
HOFFMAN, G. S., Medicine
HOIT, B., Cardiology
HOLLYFIELD, J., Molecular Medicine
HOPFER, U., Physiology and Biophysics
HOPPEL, C. H., Pharmacology
HORWITZ, R. I., Medicine
HORWITZ, S. M., Psychiatry
HOSKINS, L. C., Gastroenterology Medicine
HOWE, P., Physiology and Biophysics
HRICIK, D. E., Nephrology Medicine
HUANG, S., Ophthalmology
HUGHES, G., Surgery
HUNDERT, E., Bioethics
ISMAIL-BEIGI, F., Endocrinology, Hypertension
JACOBBERGER, J. W., Cancer Research Center
JACOBS, M. R., Pathology
JACOBSEN, D., Molecular Medicine
JENTOFT, J. E., Biochemistry
JONES, S. W., Physiology
JUNIGRO, D., Molecular Medicine
KAISERMAN-ABRAMOF, I., Anatomy
KALHAN, S. C., Paediatrics
KAMINSKI, H. J., Neurology
KAPLAN, D. R., Pathology
KARN, J., Molecular Biology and Microbiology
KARNIK, S., Molecular Medicine
KASHANI, J. H., Psychiatry
KASS, L., Pathology
KATIRJI, M. B., Neurology
KATZ, D. M., Neurosciences
KAZURA, J. W., International Health
KEITH, M. W., Orthopaedics
KERCSMAR, C. M., Paediatrics
KERN, J. A., Pulmonary and Critical Care
KERN, T. S., Clinical and Molecular Endocrinology
KERR, D., Paediatrics
KHAN, M. A., Medicine
KIKANO, G. E., Family Medicine
KINSELLA, T. J., Radiation Oncology
KLEIN, A., Medicine
KLEIN, E., Paediatrics
KODISH, E., Surgery
KOWAL, J., Geriatric Medicine
KUMAR, M. L., Paediatrics
KUNZE, D. L., Neurosciences
KURSH, E., Surgery
KUSHNER, I., Medicine
LAMANNA, J. C., Anatomy
LAMM, M. E., Pathology
LANDAU, B. R., Endocrinology and Hypertension
LANDIS, D. M., Neurology and Neurosciences
LANDMESSER, L., Neurosciences
LANDRETH, G., Neurology and Neurosciences
LANZIERI, C. F., Radiology
LARNER, A., Molecular Medicine
LASEK, R. J., Bio-architectonics
LASS, J. H., Ophthalmology
LATSON, L. A., Paediatrics
LAUER, M. S., Medicine
LAVERTU, P., Otolaryngology
LAZARUS, H., Haematology and Oncology
LEDERMAN, M., Infectious Disease
LEHMANN, P. V., Pathology
LEIGH, R. J., Neurology
LEVIN, K., Medicine
LEVINE, A. D., Gastroenterology Medicine
LEVITAN, N., Haematology and Oncology
LEWIS, H., Surgery
LIEBMAN, J., Paediatrics
LIEBERMAN, I., Surgery
LIEDKE, C. M., Paediatrics
LINCOFF, A., Medicine
LIU, J., Reproductive Biology
LOUE, S., Epidemiology and Biostatistics
LOWE, J., Pathology
LÜDERS, H. O., Medicine

LUSE, D., Biochemistry
LUST, W. D., Neurological Surgery
MACIUNAS, R. J., Neurosurgery
MACKLIN, W. B., Neurosciences
MACKNIN, M., Paediatrics
MACLIS, R., Medicine
MAGUIRE, M. E., Pharmacology
MALANGOLI, M., Surgery
MALEMUD, C. J., Rheumatology Medicine
MANSOUR, E. G., Surgery
MARCHANT, K., Pathology
MARCUS, R. E., Orthopaedics
MARKOWITZ, S., Haematology, Oncology
MARSOLAIS, E. B., Orthopaedics
MARTIN, P. J., Physiology and Biophysics
MARTIN, R. J., Paediatrics
MASARYK, T. J., Radiology
MAVISSAKALIAN, M., Psychiatry
MAYBERG, M. R., Surgery
MCCULLOUGH, A. J., Medicine
MCFADDEN, E. R., Jr, Pulmonary and Critical Care
MCHENRY, C. R., Surgery
MCLAIN, R., Surgery
MEDOF, M. E., Pathology
MENON, M., Urology
MERCER, B. M., Reproductive Medicine
MERRICK, W. C., Biochemistry
MIEYAL, J. J., Pharmacology
MILLER, C., Surgery
MILLER, R., Neurosciences
MILLER, R. T., Medicine
MODIC, M., Radiology
MONNIER, V. M., Pathology
MONTAGUE, D., Surgery
MONTENEGRO, H. D., Pulmonary and Critical Care
MOORE, J. J., Paediatrics
MORGAN, P. G., Anaesthesiology
MOSKOWITZ, R. W., Rheumatology Medicine
MULLEN, K. D., Medicine
MURRAY, P., Anaesthesiology
MUSCHLER, G., Surgery
NADEAU, J. H., Genetics
NAGARAJ, R., Ophthalmology
NAGY, L., Nutrition
NAIR, R., Cardiology
NEARMAN, H. S., Anaesthesiology
NEDRUD, J. G., Pathology
NEUHAUSER, D., Epidemiology and Biostatistics
NEWMAN, C., Surgery
NILSEN, T. W., Molecular Biology
NILSON, J. H., Pharmacology
NOSEK, T., Physiology and Biophysics
NOVIC, A. C., Surgery
O'HARA, P., Surgery
OLEINICK, N., Radiation Oncology
OLNESS, K. N., Paediatrics
OURIEL, K., Surgery
PEACHEY, N., Molecular Medicine
PEARLMAN, E., Ophthalmology
PELLETT, P., Molecular Medicine
PERRY, G., Pathology
PETOT, G., Nutrition
PIÑA, I. L., Medicine
PILAR, G., Neurosciences
PLOW, E. F., Molecular Medicine
PONSKY, J. L., Surgery
POST, S. G., Bioethics
PRABHAKAR, N. R., Physiology and Biophysics
PRAYSON, R. A., Pathology
PRESTON, D. C., Neurology
PRETLOW, T. G., II, Pathology
PRETLOW, T. P., Pathology
QIN, J., Pharmacology
RANSOHOFF, R., Molecular Medicine
RATCHESON, R. A., Neurosurgery
REDLINE, R. W., Pathology
REDLINE, S., Paediatrics
REED, M. D., Paediatrics
REINHART, W., Ophthalmology
REMICK, S. C., Medicine
RESNICK, M. I., Urology
RESNICK, P., Psychiatry

RICANATI, E. S., Medicine
RICE, L. B., Infectious Disease
RICE, T., Surgery
RIMM, A. A., Epidemiology and Biostatistics
RONIS, R., Psychiatry
ROSE, P. G., Reproductive Biology
ROSS, J., Radiology
ROTE, N. S., Reproductive Biology
ROTH, B. L., Biochemistry
RUDICK, R. A., Medicine
RUFF, R., Neurology
SAGAR, S., Neurology
SAHGAL, V., Medicine
SALATA, R. A., Infectious Disease
SALZ, H., Genetics
SAMOLS, D., Biochemistry
SCARPA, A., Physiology and Biophysics
SCHER, M., Paediatric Neurology
SCHILLING, W. P., Physiology and Biophysics
SCHLUCHTER, M. D., Paediatrics
SCHUBERT, A., Anaesthesiology
SCHULAK, J. A., Surgery
SCHWARTZ, S., Genetics
SEDENSKY, M. M., Anaesthesiology
SEDOR, J. R., Medicine
SEDWICK, W. D., Haematology and Oncology
SEFTEL, A., Urology
SEGRAVES, R. T., Psychiatry
SELMAN, W. R., Neurosurgery
SEN, G. C., Physiology and Biophysics
SEN, S., Molecular Medicine
SHAFFER, J. W., Orthopaedics
SHUCK, J., Anatomy, Surgery
SCHURIN, S., Paediatrics
SHU, S., Surgery
SIEGEL, R. E., Pharmacology
SILVER, J., Neurosciences
SILVERMAN, R. H., Biochemistry
SILVERSTEIN, R., Molecular Medicine
SIMINOFF, L. A., Bioethics
SINGER, L. T., Paediatrics
SIVAK, M. V., Gastroenterology Medicine
SIVIT, C. J., Radiology
SMITH, C. E., Anaesthesiology
SMITH, C. K., Family Medicine
SMITH, J., Molecular Medicine
SMITH, M. A., Pathology
SMITH, M. C., Nephrology Medicine
SODEE, D. B., Radiology
SPIRNAK, J. P., Surgery
STANCIN, T., Paediatrics
STANGE, K. C., Family Medicine
STANLEY, W., Physiology and Biophysics
STANTON-HICKS, M., Anaesthesiology
STARK, G. R., Genetics
STAVNEZER, E., Biochemistry
STELLATO, T. A., Surgery
STERN, R., Paediatrics
STOLLER, J. K., Medicine
STORK, E. K., Paediatrics
STRAUSS, M., Otolaryngology
STROHL, K. P., Anatomy, Pulmonary and Critical Care
STROME, M., Surgery
SUPER, D. M., Paediatrics
SUREWICZ, W. K., Physiology and Biophysics
SY, M.-S., Pathology
TAKAOKA, Y., Surgery
TARR, R. W., Radiology
TARTAKOFF, A. M., Pathology
TAVILL, A. S., Medicine
TAYLOR, H. G., Paediatrics
TETZLAFF, W., Anaesthesiology
THOMPSON, G. H., Orthopaedics
TOMASHEFSKI, J. F., Pathology
TOOSSI, Z., Infectious Disease
TOPOL, E. J., Medicine
TRAPP, B., Neurosciences
TUBBS, R. R., Pathology
TUCKER, H. M., Otolaryngology
TUOHY, V., Molecular Medicine
VERTES, V., Medicine

WALDO, A. L., Cardiology
WALSH, R. A., Medicine
WALSH-SUKYS, M. C., Paediatrics
WEBER, P., Surgery
WEISS, M., Biochemistry
WEISS, M. F., Medicine
WESSELS, B. W., Radiation Oncology
WHITE, R. J., Surgery
WHITEHOUSE, F. W., Medicine
WHITEHOUSE, P. J., Bioethics, Neurology, Neuroscience, and Psychiatry
WILBER, J. H., Orthopaedics
WILKOFF, B., Medicine
WILLIAMS, B. R. G., Genetics
WISE, J., Molecular Biology and Microbiology
WISH, J. B., Nephrology Medicine
WISNIESKI, J., Medicine
WOLPAW, D., General Internal Medicine
WRIGHT, J., Hypertension Medicine
YANG, Y.-C., Pharmacology
YEN-LIEBERMAN, B., Pathology
YOMTOVIAN, R. A., Pathology
YOUNG, J., Medicine
YOUNGNER, S. J., Bioethics
ZAHKA, K. G., Paediatrics
ZIGMOND, R. E., Neurosciences
ZINS, J., Surgery
ZOLLINGER, R. M., Surgery
ZYZANSKI, S. J., Family Medicine

Frances Payne Bolton School of Nursing (tel. (216) 368-4700; internet fpb.case.edu):

ANDERSON, G., Nursing
ANDREWS, C., Nursing
FITZPATRICK, J. J., Nursing
GARY, F. A., Nursing
GOOD, M., Nursing
LUDINGTON, S. M., Paediatric Nursing
MOORE, S., Nursing
ROBERTS, B. L., Gerontological Nursing
WYKLE, M. L., Gerontological Nursing

Mandel School of Applied Social Sciences (11235 Bellflower Rd, Cleveland, OH 44106; tel. (216) 368-2290; e-mail msassweb@case .edu; internet msass.case.edu):

BIEGEL, D. E., Social Work Practice, Psychiatry and Sociology
CHATTERJEE, P., Social Work
COULTON, C. J., Social Work and Urban Poverty
FLEISHER, M., Violence Prevention, Research and Education
GINGERICH, W. J., Social Work
GROZA, V., Social Work
HOKENSTAD Jr, M.C., International Social Work
MAHONEY, G., Families and Communities
SINGER, M. I., Social Work, Youth Violence
WELLS, K., Social Work, Child Welfare
YOUNG, D. R., Non-profit Management

RESEARCH CENTRES AND INSTITUTES

Center for Regional Economic Issues: Dir ED MORRISON.

Center on Aging and Health: Dir MAY L. WYKLE.

Center for Micro and Nano Processing: Dir C. C. LIU.

Mandel Center for Non-Profit Organizations: Dir SUSAN L. EAGAN.

Yeager Center for Electrochemical Sciences: Dir JOE H. PAYER.

Center for Applied Polymer Research: Dir ANNE HILTNER.

Center on Urban Poverty and Social Change: Dirs CLAUDIA J. COULTON SHARON E. MILLIGAN.

Western Reserve Geriatric Education Center: Dir JULIA H. ROSE.

Law–Medicine Center: Dir MAXWELL J. MEHLMAN.

Health Systems Management Center: Dir BARBARA J. BOLEK.

Center for Global Health and Diseases: Dir JAMES W. KAZURA.

University Memory and Aging Center: Dir KARL HERRUP.

Applied Neural Control Laboratory: Dir J. THOMAS MORTIMER.

Center for Adolescent Health: Dir BARBARA CROMER.

Center for Bio-architectonics: Dir RAYMOND J. LASEK.

Center for Cardiovascular Biomaterials: Co-Dirs ROGER E. MARCHANT KANDICE MARCHANT.

National Centre for Space Exploration Research on Fluids and Combustion: Dir SIMON OSTRACH.

Cancer Center: Dir STANTON L. GERSON.

Center for RNA Molecular Biology: Dir TIMOTHY NILSEN.

Frederick K. Cox International Law Center: Dir MICHAEL P. SCHARF.

Case Advanced Power Institute: Dir THOMAS ZAWODZINSKI.

Center for Computational Genomics: Co-Dirs JOSEPH NADEAU, YOH-HAN PAO.

Neural Engineering Center: Dir DOMINIQUE M. DURAND.

Cleveland Functional Electrical Stimulation Center: Dir P. HUNTER PECKHAM.

Center for Modeling Integrated Metabolic Systems: Dir GERALD M. SAIDEL.

Center for Research on Tibet: Co-Dirs CYNTHIA M. BEALL, MELVYN C. GOLDSTEIN.

Skeletal Research Center: Dir ARNOLD I. CAPLAN.

Laboratory for Neuromimetric and Neural Integrated Systems: Dir DUSTIN J. TYLER.

CEDARVILLE UNIVERSITY

251 N Main St, Cedarville, OH 45314

Telephone: (937) 766-7700
Fax: (937) 766 7575
E-mail: admissions@cedarville.edu
Internet: www.cedarville.edu

Founded 1887 as Cedarville College; present name 2000

Private control

Academic year: August to April

President: Dr WILLIAM E. BROWN
Chancellor: Dr PAUL H. DIXON
Vice-President (Academic): Dr DUANE R. WOOD
Vice-President (Business): JOHN C. ANGLEA
Vice-President (Christian Ministries): ROBERT K. ROHM
Vice-President (Development): Dr DAVID M. ORMSBEE
Vice-President (Enrollment Management) (vacant)
Vice-President (Student Services): Dr CARL A. RUBY
Registrar: FRAN CAMPBELL
Library Director: LYNN A. BROCK

Number of teachers: 208 (full-time)
Number of students: 2,931 (full-time)

Publication: *Journal of Biblical Integration in Business* (annually).

CENTRAL STATE UNIVERSITY

Wilberforce, OH 45384

Telephone: (216) 376-6332
Fax: (513) 376-6318
E-mail: info@centralstate.edu
Internet: www.centralstate.edu

Founded 1887

President: JOHN W. GARLAND
Registrar: LARRY CANNON
Director of Admissions: Dr ERIC HILTON
Librarian: JOHNNY JACKSON

Library of 130,000 vols
Number of teachers: 80
Number of students: 1,400

Publications: *Catalog, Alumni Journal* (quarterly)

DEANS

College of Arts and Sciences: Dr WILLIE HOUSTON
College of Business Administration: Dr C. H. SHOWELL
College of Education: Dr KAYE JETER

CINCINNATI CHRISTIAN UNIVERSITY

POB 04320, 2700 Glenway Ave, Cincinnati, OH 45204

Telephone: (513) 244-8100
Fax: (513) 244-8140
E-mail: ccuadmissions@ccuniveristy.edu
Internet: www.ccuniversity.edu

Founded 1924 as Cincinnati Bible Seminary by merger of McGarvey Bible College (f. 1923) and Cincinnati Bible Institute (f. 1923); Cincinnati Bible College and Seminary 1987; present name and status 2004
Private control
Academic year: August to May
President: Dr DAVID FAUST
Chief Operating Officer and Executive Vice-President: J. EDWARD RAUCH
Vice-President (Academic Affairs): Dr WILLIAM C. WEBER
Academic Dean: Dr JON A. WEATHERLY
Registrar: DON THOMASON
Library Director: JAMES H. LLOYD

Number of teachers: 40
Number of students: 920.

CINCINNATI COLLEGE OF MORTUARY SCIENCE

645 W North Bend Rd, Cincinnati, OH 45224-1462

Telephone: (513) 761-2020
E-mail: generalinfo@ccms.edu
Internet: www.ccms.edu

Founded 1882 as Cincinnati School of Embalming; present name 1966
Private control
President: Dr DAN L. FLORY
Academic Dean: DAVID W. TACKETT
Registrar: PATRICIA JENNINGS
Library Director: BRIAN EASTERLING

Number of teachers: 6
Number of students: 120.

CIRCLEVILLE BIBLE COLLEGE

1476 Lancaster Pike, Circleville, OH 43113

Telephone: (740) 474-8896
Fax: (740) 477-7755
E-mail: enroll@biblecollege.edu
Internet: www.biblecollege.edu

Founded 1948
Private control
Academic year: September to May
President: Dr JOHN W. CONLEY
Academic Dean: JOE BROWN
Director of Institutional Advancement: JAMES SCHROEDER
Dean of Students: LARRY OLSON
Registrar: SHIRLEY POLLARD
Librarian: DAVID TIPTON

Number of teachers: 25
Number of students: 350.

CLEVELAND INSTITUTE OF ART

11141 East Blvd, Cleveland, OH 44106-1710

Telephone: (216) 421-7000
Fax: (216) 421-7438
E-mail: admiss@gate.cia.edu
Internet: www.cia.edu

Founded 1882
Private control
Academic year: August to May
President: DAVID L. DEMING
Provost: NANCY M. STUART
Senior Vice-President (Institutional Advancement): R. MICHAEL COLE
Vice-President (Academic Affairs): Dr HARVEY L. HIX
Vice-President (Business Affairs): ALMUT ZVOSEC
Vice-President (Enrollment and Student Affairs): WILLIAM EDMONDSON
Vice-President (Marketing and Public Relations): TED SHERRON
Registrar: KAREN HUDY
Library Director: CRISTINE ROM

Number of teachers: 62
Number of students: 607.

CLEVELAND INSTITUTE OF MUSIC

11021 East Blvd, Cleveland, OH 44106

Telephone: (216) 791-5000
Fax: (216) 791-3063
E-mail: cimadmission@case.edu
Internet: www.cim.edu

Founded 1920
Academic year: August to May
President: DAVID CERONE
CEO: A. MALACHI MIXON III
Dean: JEFFREY SHARKEY
Registrar: HALLIE MOORE
Library Director: JEAN TOOMBS

Number of teachers: 100
Number of students: 400.

CLEVELAND STATE UNIVERSITY

Euclid Ave at East 24th St, Cleveland, OH 44115

Telephone: (216) 687-2000
Fax: (216) 687-9366
E-mail: admissions@csuohio.edu
Internet: www.csuohio.edu

Founded 1964
President: Dr MICHAEL SCHWARTZ
Provost and Senior Vice-President for Academic and Student Affairs (vacant)
Vice-President for Finance and Administration: CHRISTINE A. JACKSON
Vice-President for Minority Affairs and Human Relations: NJERI NURU
Executive Director for Development and University Relations: ROBERT GORDON
Director of Libraries (vacant)
Library of 856,978 vols, 4,005 periodicals, 625,191 microforms
Number of teachers: 808 (531 full-time, 277 part-time)
Number of students: 17,137

DEANS

College of Business Administration: ROBERT MINTER
College of Engineering: KENNETH KEYES
College of Arts and Sciences: KAREN STECKOL
College of Education: JAY MCLOUGHLIN
College of Graduate Studies: A. HARRY ANDRIST
Cleveland-Marshall College of Law: STEVEN STEINGLASS
Levin College of Urban Affairs: DAVID C. SWEET
Continuing Education: FERRIS F. ANTHONY

COLLEGE OF MOUNT ST JOSEPH

5701 Delhi Rd, Cincinnati, OH 45233-1670

Telephone: (513) 244-4200
Internet: www.msj.edu

Founded 1920
President: Sr FRANCIS MARIE THRAILKILL
Registrar: LEW RITA MOORE
Academic Dean: Sr JOHN MIRIAM JONES
Director of Business and Finance: ANNE MARIE WAGNER
Director of Admissions: EDWARD ECKEL
Dean of Students: JEFF LONG
Librarian: PAUL JENKINS

Library of 87,000 vols
Number of teachers: 104 full-time equivalent
Number of students: 2,594

Publications: *Catalog, Mount Magazine* (3 a year).

COLLEGE OF WOOSTER

Wooster, OH 44691

Telephone: (330) 263-2311
Fax: (330) 263-2427
Internet: www.wooster.edu

Founded 1866
Independent, founded by the Presbyterian Church (USA)
Academic year: August to May
President: R. STANTON HALES
Vice-President for Academic Affairs: IAIN CRAWFORD
Vice-President for Development: SARA L. PATTON
Vice-President for Finance and Business: ROBERT WALTON
Secretary: ANNE GATES
Registrar: BOB BLAIR
Director of Admissions: RIC MARTINEZ (acting)
Dean of Faculty: SHILA GARG
Dean of Students: KURT HOLMES
Librarian: DAMON D. HICKEY

Library of 673,879 vols
Number of teachers: 133 full-time
Number of students: 1,827

Publication: *Wooster* (alumni magazine).

COLUMBUS COLLEGE OF ART AND DESIGN

107 N Ninth St, Columbus, OH 43215

Telephone: (614) 224-9101
Fax: (614) 224-4040
E-mail: contact@ccad.edu
Internet: www.ccad.edu

Founded 1879 as Columbus Art School; present name 1959
Private control
Academic year: August to August
Provost: Dr ANEDITH NASH

Number of teachers: 180
Number of students: 1,500

DEANS

Foundation Studies: JEFF LINK
Liberal Arts: Dr EDWARD LATHY
Fine Arts: LOWELL TOLSTEDT
Industrial/Interior Design: CARL GARANT
Media Studies: RIC PETRY
Visual Communications: RICHARD ASCHENBRAND

DEFIANCE COLLEGE

Defiance, OH 43512

Telephone: (419) 784-4010
Internet: www.defiance.edu

Founded 1850
President: JAMES T. HARRIS

Vice-President for Academic Affairs/Academic Dean: Dr RICHARD W. STROEDE
Librarian: SHELIA COLLINS
Library of 90,000 vols
Number of teachers: 55
Number of students: 1,030.

DENISON UNIVERSITY

Granville, OH 43023-0603
Telephone: (740) 587-0810
Fax: (740) 587-6417
E-mail: admissions@denison.edu
Internet: www.denison.edu
Founded 1831
Private control
Academic year: September to June
President: DALE T. KNOBEL
Provost: DAVID R. ANDERSON
Vice-President for Finance and Management: SETH PATTON
Vice-President for Student Affairs and Dean of Students: SAMUEL J. THIOS
Registrar: LARRY R. MURDOCK
Director of Admissions: PERRY ROBINSON
Director of Libraries: LYNN S. COCHRANE
Number of teachers: 187 (full-time)
Number of students: 2,094 (full-time)
Publications: *Denison Journal of Religion* (annually), *Denison Journal of Geosciences* (annually), *Denison Journal of Biological Science* (annually), *Articulate* (dept of English, annually).

FRANCISCAN UNIVERSITY OF STEUBENVILLE

1235 University Blvd, Steubenville, OH 43952-1763
Telephone: (740) 283-3771
Fax: (740) 284-5456
Internet: www.franciscan.edu
Founded 1946
Academic year: September to May
President: Rev. TERENCE HENRY
Dean of Faculty: Dr STEPHEN MILETIC
Director of Admissions: MARGARET WEBER
Director of Library and Information Services: WILLIAM JAKUB
Library of 232,013 vols
Number of teachers: 172 (103 full-time, 69 part-time)
Number of students: 2,281 (1,690 full-time, 154 part-time, 437 postgraduate)
Publication: *Fides Quaerens Intellectum* (4 a year).

FRANKLIN UNIVERSITY

201 South Grant Ave, Columbus, OH 43215
Telephone: (614) 797-4700
E-mail: helpdesk@franklin.edu
Internet: www.franklin.edu
Founded 1902 as School of Commerce under YMCA sponsorship; present name 1933
Private control
Pres.: Dr PAUL J. OTTE
Sr Vice-Pres. for Strategic Relationships and Initiatives: LINDA M. STEELE
Vice-Pres. for Academics and Curriculum Devt: Dr EDWARD W. HOLZAPFEL, Jr
Vice-Pres. for Academic Relations: Dr SHIRLEY PALUMBO
Vice-Pres. for Admin.: EVELYN LEVINO
Number of students: 8,200.

HEBREW UNION COLLEGE – JEWISH INSTITUTE OF RELIGION

3101 Clifton Ave, Cincinnati, OH 45220-2488
Schools at Cincinnati, Los Angeles and New York (USA) and Jerusalem (Israel)
Telephone: (513) 221-1875
Internet: www.huc.edu
Founded 1875
Academic year: August to June
President: Dr DAVID ELLENSON
Provost: Dr NORMAN COHEN
Dean of Cincinnati School: Rabbi KENNETH EHRLICH
Dean of Los Angeles School: Dr LEWIS M. BARTH
Dean of New York School: Rabbi AARON PANKEN
Dean of Jerusalem School: Rabbi MICHAEL MARMUR
Director of Libraries: Dr DAVID GILNER
Library of 425,000 vols and 3,000 codices
Number of teachers: 130
Number of students: 780
Publications: *American Jewish Archives*, *Hebrew Union College Annual*, *Studies in Bibliography and Booklore*.

HEIDELBERG COLLEGE

310 East Market St, Tiffin, OH 44883
Telephone: (419) 448-2000
Fax: (419) 448-2124
Internet: www.heidelberg.edu
Founded 1850
Academic year: August to May
President: Dr F. DOMINIC DOTTAVIO
Vice-President for Academic Affairs: LAURA DE ABRUNA
Vice-President for Enrollment and Student Affairs: Dr JAMES TROHA
Vice-President for Institutional Advancement: WILLIAM STEPP
Registrar: PAMELA FABER
Director of Library Services: EDWARD KRAKORA
Library of 200,000 vols
Number of teachers: 102 (72 full-time, 30 part-time)
Number of students: 1,500
Publications: *Heidelberg Alumni Magazine*, *Heidelberg College Catalogue*.

HIRAM COLLEGE

Office of Admission, POB 96, Hiram, OH 44234
Telephone: (330) 569-5169
Fax: (330) 569-5944
E-mail: interal@hiram.edu
Internet: www.hiram.edu
Founded 1850
Private control
Academic year: August to May
President: THOMAS V. CHAMA
Registrar: MARY ANN PAINLEY
Librarian: DAVID EVERETT
Library of 202,000 books; govt depository in receipt of approx. 7,000 federal documents annually; mem. of OhioLINK-Consortium of Ohio college, university, and state libraries with shared colln of 7m. vols
Number of teachers: 68
Number of students: 900
Publication: *Hiram Poetry Review* (2 a year).

JOHN CARROLL UNIVERSITY

Cleveland, OH 44118
Telephone: (216) 397-1886
Fax: (216) 397-4256
Internet: www.jcu.edu

Founded 1886
Private control (Roman Catholic affiliated)
Academic year: September to May
President: Rev. ROBERT NIEHOFF
Academic Vice-President: Dr DAVID LaGUARDIA
Associate Academic Vice-President (Enrollment Services) (vacant)
Dean of College of Arts and Sciences: Dr LINDA EISENMANN
Dean of School of Business (vacant)
Dean of Graduate School: Dr MARY E. BEADLE
Registrar: KATHLEEN DI FRANCO
Director of Library: Dr JEANNE SOMERS
Library of 720,000 vols
Number of teachers: 240 (full-time)
Number of students: 4,100.

KENT STATE UNIVERSITY

Kent, OH 44242
Telephone: (330) 672-3000
Internet: www.kent.edu
Founded 1910
Academic year: July to June
President: Dr CAROL A. CARTWRIGHT
Vice-President (Business and Finance): Dr DAVID K. CREAMER
Provost: Dr PAUL GASTON
Vice-President (University Relations and Development): Dr KATHY STAFFORD
Vice-President (Human Resources): CAROLYN PIZZUTO
Vice-President (Enrollment Management and Student Affairs): Dr HAROLD GOLDSMITH
Director of Admissions: NANCY DELLAVECCHIA
Dean of Libraries and Media Services: Dr MARK WEBER
Library of 2,270,690 vols
Number of teachers: 1,097
Number of students: 36,000
Publication: *Inside Kent*

DEANS AND DIRECTORS

Arts and Sciences: Dr JOSEPH H. DANKS
Business Administration: Dr GEORGE STEVENS
Communication and Information: Dr JAMES GAUDINO
Education: Dr DAVID ENGLAND
Fine and Professional Arts: RICHARD WORTHING
School of Nursing: Dr DAVINA J. GOSNELL
Technology: Dr RAJ CHOWDHURY

ATTACHED INSTITUTES

Liquid Crystal Institute: Dir Dr OLEG LAVRENTOVICH.

Biomedical Studies: Dir Dr JAMES BLANK.

Applied Linguistics Center: Dir Dr GREG SHREVE.

Center for International and Comparative Programs: Dir Dr MARK RUBIN.

Kent State University Museum: costume and decorative art; 20,000 items; Dir Dr JEAN DRUESEDOW.

KENYON COLLEGE

Gambier, OH 43022-9623
Telephone: (740) 427-5000
E-mail: admissions@kenyon.edu
Internet: www.kenyon.edu
Founded 1824
President: ROBERT A. ODEN Jr
Provost: KATHERINE H. WILL
Dean of Admissions: JOHN W. ANDERSON
Dean of Students: DONALD J. OMAHAN
Dean for Academic Advising: JANE MARTINDELL

Vice-President for Library and Information Services: DANIEL TEMPLE

Library of 977,846 items

Number of teachers: 176

Number of students: 1,467.

LAKE ERIE COLLEGE

Painesville, OH 44077

Telephone: (440) 352-3361

Fax: (440) 352-3533

E-mail: blee@lec.edu

Internet: www.lec.edu

Founded 1856

Private control

Academic year: August to May

President: Dr HAL LAYDON

Dean of College: Dr LYNNE SECHRIST

Registrar: BARB EMCH

Director of Admissions: MARY ANN NASO

Library of 100,000 vols

Number of teachers: 82

Number of students: 916

Publication: *Bulletin*.

MALONE COLLEGE

515 25th St, NW, Canton, OH 44709

Telephone: (330) 471-8100

Fax: (330) 454-8478

E-mail: admissions@malone.edu

Internet: www.malone.edu

Founded 1892

President: Dr RONALD G. JOHNSON

Provost: Dr ROBERT ZWIER

Library of 142,000 vols

Number of teachers: 89 (full-time)

Number of students: 2,239

Publication: *Horizon*.

MARIETTA COLLEGE

215 Fifth St, Marietta, OH 45750

Telephone: (740) 376-4643

Fax: (740) 376-4896

E-mail: admit@marietta.edu

Internet: www.marietta.edu

Founded 1797

Private control

Academic year: August to May

President: JEAN A. SCOTT

Provost and Dean: SUE DeWINE

Vice-President and Dean for Student Life and Leadership: STEPHEN SCHWARTZ

Librarian: SANDRA NEYMAN

Library of 287,493 vols

Number of teachers: 80 (full time)

Number of students: 1,108

Publications: *Marcolian, The BlueLine, The Navy Blue and White, The Blue and White*

Courses in liberal arts and sciences, fine arts, computer science, environmental science, economics, management and accounting, sports medicine, international business, Asian and international studies, petroleum engineering.

METHODIST THEOLOGICAL SCHOOL IN OHIO

3081 Columbus Pike, Delaware, OH 43015

Telephone: (740) 363-1146

E-mail: admit@mtso.edu

Internet: www.mtso.edu

Founded 1958

Private control

Academic year: August to May

President: Dr NORMAN DEWIRE

Executive Vice-President: COLLEEN HOGAN

Academic Dean: Dr JEFFREY JAYNES

Registrar: JON JUMP

Library Director: Dr PAUL SCHRODT

Number of teachers: 30

Number of students: 260.

MIAMI UNIVERSITY

Oxford, OH 45056

Telephone: (513) 529-1809

Fax: (513) 529-3841

Internet: www.muohio.edu

Founded 1809

State control

President: DAVID HODGE

Provost and Executive Vice-President for Academic Affairs: JEFFREY HERBST

Vice-President for Finance and University Services: RICHARD NORMAN

Vice-President for Information Technology: JOHN REID CHRISTENBERRY

Vice-President for Student Affairs: RICHARD NAULT

Vice-President for University Advancement: JAYNE WHITEHEAD

University Registrar: DAVE SAUTER

Secretary to the Board of Trustees and Executive Assistant to the President: STEPHEN SNYDER

University Librarian: JUDITH SESSIONS

Library of 2,700,000 vols, 110,000 maps, 26,000 recordings, 20,000 journals, magazines and newspapers and more than 3m. pieces of microfilm

Number of teachers: 849 full-time

Number of students: 16,900

DEANS

Applied Science: DAVID C. HADDAD

Arts and Science: STEVEN DeLUE (acting)

Business Administration: ROGER JENKINS

Education and Allied Professions: SALLY LLOYD (acting)

Fine Arts: ROBERT BENSON

Graduate School: JEFFREY POTTEIGER

MOUNT UNION COLLEGE

1972 Clark Ave, Alliance, OH 44601

Telephone: (330) 821-5320

E-mail: info@muc.edu

Internet: www.muc.edu

Founded 1846

President: Dr HAROLD M. KOLENBRANDER

Dean: TRUMAN TURNQUIST (acting)

Registrar: STUART TERRASS

Librarian: ROBERT R. GARLAND

Number of teachers: 90 (full-time)

Number of students: 1,847

Publications: *Mount Union Magazine, Catalogues*.

MOUNT VERNON NAZARENE UNIVERSITY

800 Martinsburg Rd, Mount Vernon, OH 43050

Telephone: (740) 392-6868

Fax: (740) 397-2769

Internet: www.mvnu.edu

Founded 1968

Private control

President: Dr E. LeBRON FAIRBANKS

Provost and Vice-President (Academic Affairs): RANDY L. TIMPE

Vice-President (Finance and Management): RICHARD H. RAYMOND

Vice-President (Enrollment Services and Student Development): DOUG K. MATTHEWS

Vice-President (University Advancement): J. KEITH NEWMAN

Vice-President (Campus Ministries): GARY M. SIVEWRIGHT

Library Director: EDYTHE FEAZEL

Number of teachers: 128 (full-time)

Number of students: 2,455.

MUSKINGUM COLLEGE

163 Stormont St, New Concord, OH 43762

Telephone: (614) 826-8211

Fax: (614) 826-8404

Internet: www.muskingum.edu

Founded 1837

Church related, liberal arts college

President: SAMUEL W. SPECK

Vice-President of Academic Affairs: DANIEL E. VAN TASSEL

Vice-President for Development: MATTHEW P. ELLI

Treasurer: F. B. THOMAS

Dean of Student Life: JANET HEETER-BASS

Dean of Enrollment: JEFF ZELLERS

Librarian: ROBIN HANSON

Library of 223,000 vols

Number of professors: 82 full-time

Number of students: 1,200

Publications: *Catalog, Alumni Bulletin, The Muskie Handbook, View Book*.

MYERS UNIVERSITY

112 Prospect Ave, Cleveland, OH 44115

Telephone: (216) 696-9000

Fax: (216) 696-6430

E-mail: admissions@dnmyers.edu

Internet: www.dnmyers.edu

Founded 1848 as Folsom's Business College; present name 2001

Private control

President: Dr PAUL FEINGOLD

Vice-President: ERIC W. DAMON

Vice-President (Academic Affairs): LEWIS JONES

Vice-President (Institutional Advancement): ELVING F. OTERO

Library Director: RICHARD BRHEL

Number of teachers: 15

Number of students: 1,150.

NORTHEASTERN OHIO UNIVERSITIES COLLEGE OF MEDICINE

4209 State Route 44, POB 95, Rootstown, OH 44272-0095

Telephone: (330) 325-2511

E-mail: admission@neoucom.edu

Internet: www.neoucom.edu

Founded 1973

President and Dean: Dr LOIS MARGARET NORA

Senior Vice-President for Academic Affairs: Dr MARK A. PENN

Vice-President (Administration and Finance): RICHARD J. EPLAWY

Vice-President (Institutional Advancement): M. SUE DREITZLER

Director of Information Center: THOMAS C. ATWOOD

Number of students: 420.

NOTRE DAME COLLEGE OF OHIO

4545 College Rd, Cleveland, OH 44120

Telephone: (216) 381-1680

Fax: (216) 381-3802

E-mail: admissions@ndc.edu

Internet: www.ndc.edu

Founded 1922

Academic year: September to May

President: ANNE L. DEMING

Vice-President for Academic Affairs: MARILYN JONES

Librarian: KAREN ZOLLER

Library of 88,159 vols

Number of teachers: 101 (37 full-time, 64 part-time)
Number of students: 843.

OBERLIN COLLEGE

Oberlin, OH 44074
Telephone: (216) 775-8121
Internet: www.oberlin.edu

Founded 1833
Academic year: September to May

President: NANCY S. DYE
Vice-President for Finance: ANDREW EVANS
Vice-President for Development and Alumni Affairs: KAY THOMSON
Director of Admissions for the College of Arts and Sciences: DEBRA CHERMONTE
Director of Admissions for the Conservatory of Music: MICHAEL MANDEREN
Secretary: ROBERT A. HASLUN
Director of Libraries: RAY ENGLISH

Library of 1,300,000 vols
Number of teachers: 250
Number of students: 2,900

DEANS

College of Arts and Sciences: CLAYTON KOPPES
Conservatory of Music: ROBERT K. DODSON

OHIO COLLEGE OF PODIATRIC MEDICINE

10515 Carnegie Ave, University Circle, Cleveland, OH 44106
Telephone: (216) 231-3300
Fax: (216) 231-0453
Internet: www.ocpm.edu

Founded 1916
Private control
Academic year: August to May

President: THOMAS MELILLO
Executive Vice-President: DAVID NICOLANTI
Vice-President and Dean of Academic Affairs: Dr VINCENT J. HETHERINGTON
Director of Student Affairs: LOIS LOTT
Librarian: DONNA PERZESKI

Number of students: 285.

OHIO DOMINICAN COLLEGE

1216 Sunbury Rd, Columbus, OH 43219
Telephone: (614) 251-4500
Fax: (614) 251-0156
E-mail: admissions@odc.edu
Internet: www.odc.edu

Four-year co-educational liberal arts college
Founded 1911 as College of St Mary of the Springs; name changed 1968
Academic year: September to May (two terms and a summer session)

President: Dr JACK P. CALARESO
Registrar: SHIRLEY MCBRAYER
Vice-President for Student Affairs and Admissions: JAMES SAGONA
Director of the Library: MICHELE SALFF

Library of 154,000 vols
Number of teachers: 130
Number of students: 2,100.

OHIO NORTHERN UNIVERSITY

Ada, OH 45810
Telephone: (419) 772-2000
Fax: (419) 772-1932
Internet: www.onu.edu

Founded 1871
Private (United Methodist)
Academic year: September to May

President: Dr KENDALL L. BAKER
Registrar: R. G. CARPENTER
Librarian: P. LOGSDON

Library of 500,000 vols
Number of teachers: 200
Number of students: 2,870

DEANS

Arts and Sciences: Dr BYRON L. HAWBECHER
Engineering: Dr BARRY FARBROTHER
Pharmacy: Dr BOBBY BRYANT
Law: Dr DAVID CRAGO
Business Administration: Dr TERRY L. MARIS

OHIO STATE UNIVERSITY

190 N. Oval Mall, Columbus, OH 43210
Telephone: (614) 292-6446
Internet: www.osu.edu

Founded 1870
Campuses at Lima, Mansfield, Marion and Newark

President: KAREN A. HOLBROOK
Executive Vice-President and Provost: BARBARA R. SNYDER
Senior Vice-President for Business and Finance: WILLIAM J. SHKURTI
Senior Vice-President for External Relations: CURT STEINER
Senior Vice-President for Health Sciences: Dr FRED SANFILIPPO
Senior Vice-President for Research: ROBERT McGRATH
Vice-President for Agricultural Administration: BOBBY D. MOSER
Vice-President for Development: JAMES SCHROEDER
Vice-President for Government Relations: R. ELLYN PERRONE
Vice-President for Student Affairs: WILLIAM H. HALL

Library: see Libraries and Archives
Number of teachers: 3,782 (main campus)
Number of students: 58,365 (of which 50,995 at the main campus)

Publications: *American Periodicals* (2 a year), *Journal of Higher Education* (every 2 months), *Journal of Money, Credit and Banking* (every 2 months), *The Leibniz Review* (Mansfield Campus, annually), *Narrative* (3 a year), *Ohio State Journal of Criminal Law* (2 a year), *Ohio State Journal on Dispute Resolution* (quarterly), *Ohio State Law Journal* (6 a year), *Theory into Practice* (quarterly)

DEANS

College of Arts: KAREN A. BELL
College of Biological Sciences: JOAN M. HERBERS
Fisher College of Business: JOSEPH A. ALUTTO
College of Dentistry: JAN E. KRONMILLER
College of Education: DONNA EVANS
College of Engineering: WILLIAM A. BAESLACK, III
College of Food, Agriculture and Environmental Sciences: BOBBY D. MOSER
College of Human Ecology: DAVID W. ANDREWS
College of Humanities: JOHN W. ROBERTS
College of Law: NANCY H. ROGERS
College of Mathematical and Physical Sciences: RICHARD R. FREEMAN
College of Medicine and Public Health: Dr FRED SANFILIPPO
College of Nursing: ELIZABETH R. LENZ
College of Optometry: MELVIN D. SHIPP
College of Pharmacy: ROBERT W. BRUEGGEMEIER
College of Social and Behavioural Sciences: PAUL A. BECK
College of Social Work: TONY TRIPODI
College of Veterinary Medicine: JOHN A. E. HUBBELL

ACADEMIC DIRECTORS

School of Allied Medical Professions: STEPHEN L. WILSON
School of Architecture: ROBERT S. LIVESEY
School of Biomedical Science: WOLFGANG SADEE
School of Communication: CARROLL J. GLYNN
School of Educational Policy and Leadership: ROBERT LAWSON
School of Music: MELLASENAH MORRIS
School of Natural Resources: JERRY M. BIGHAM
School of Physical Activities and Educational Services: DONNA L. PASTORE
School of Public Health: STANLEY A. LEMESHOW
School of Public Policy and Management: BERT A. ROCKMAN
School of Teaching and Learning: PETER V. PAUL

DEPARTMENTS, ACADEMIC FACULTIES, DIVISION DIRECTORS

Accounting and Management Information Systems: J. RICHARD DIETRICH
Aerospace Engineering: MEYER J. BENZAKEIN
African-American and African Studies: KENNETH W. GOINGS
Agricultural, Environmental and Development Economics: ALAN J. RANDALL
Air Force and Aerospace Studies: Col MICHAEL J. HUHN
Anaesthesiology: MICHAEL B. HOWIE
Animal Sciences: JAMES E. KINDER
Anthropology: CLARK S. LARSEN
Art: ARDINE K. NELSON
Art Education: PATRICIA L. STUHR
Astronomy: PATRICK S. OSMER
Aviation: NAWAL K. TANEJA
Biochemistry: RICHARD P. SWENSON
Biomedical Informatics: JOEL H. SALTZ
Chemical Engineering: STUART L. COOPER
Chemistry: PRABIR K. DUTTA
Civil and Environmental Engineering and Geodetic Science: OLIVER G. MCKEE, III
Comparative Studies: DAVID G. HORN
Computer Science and Engineering: STUART ZWEBEN
Consumer Sciences: GONG-SOOG HONG
Dance: L. SCOTT MARSH
East Asian Languages and Literatures: MARI NODA
Economics: MASANORI HASHIMOTO
Electrical and Computer Engineering: FUSUN OZGUNER
Emergency Medicine: DOUGLAS A. RUND
English: VALERIE B. LEE
Entomology: DAVID DENLINGER
Evolution, Ecology and Organismal Biology: RALPH E. J. BOERNER
Family Medicine: MARYJO WELKER
Finance: ANIL MAKHIJA
Food, Agricultural and Biological Engineering: THOMAS L. BEAN
Food Science and Technology: KENNETH LEE
French and Italian: DIANE W. BIRCKBICHLER
Geography: MORTON E. O'KELLY
Geological Sciences: E. SCOTT BAIR
Germanic Languages and Literature: ANNA A. GROTANS (acting)
Greek and Latin: DAVID A. HAHM
History: KENNETH J. ANDRIEN
History of Art: MARK D. FULLERTON (acting)
Horticulture and Crop Science: STEPHEN C. MYERS
Human and Community Resource Development: ROBERT J. BIRKENHOLZ
Human Development and Family Science: ALBERT J. DAVIS
Human Nutrition: MARK L. FAILLA
Industrial, Interior and Visual Communication Design: WAYNE E. CARLSON
Industrial, Welding and Systems Engineering: JOHN C. LIPPOLD
Internal Medicine: MICHAEL R. GREVER

Linguistics: PETER W. CULICOVER
Management and Human Resources: DAVID B. GREENBERGER
Management Sciences: PETER T. WARD
Marketing and Logistics: ROBERT E. BURNKRANT
Materials Science and Engineering: JOHN E. MORRAL
Mathematics: PETER D. MARCH
Mechanical Engineering: KRISHNASWAMY SRNIVASAN
Medieval and Renaissance Studies: BARBARA HANAWALT
Melton Center for Jewish Studies: TAMAR RUDAVSKY
Mershon Center for International Security Studies: RICHARD K. HERRMANN
Microbiology: JOHN N. REEVE
Molecular and Cellular Biochemistry: CHARLES R. HILLE
Molecular Genetics: LEE F. JOHNSON
Molecular Virology, Immunology and Medical Genetics: CARLO M. CROCE
Near-Eastern Languages and Cultures: RICHARD DAVIS
Neurological Surgery: ENNIO A. CHIOCCA
Neurology: JOHN T. KISSEL
Neuroscience: MICHAEL S. BEATTIE
Obstetrics and Gynaecology: LARRY J. COPELAND
Ohio State University Extension: BARBARA G. LUDWIG
Ophthalmology: THOMAS F. MAUGER
Orthopaedics: GARY D. BOS
Otolaryngology: DAVID E. SCHULLER
Paediatrics: THOMAS N. HANSEN
Pathology: MICHAEL G. BISSELL
Pharmacology: WOLFGANG SADEE
Philosophy: GEORGE S. PAPPAS
Physical Medicine and Rehabilitation: WILLIAM S. PEASE
Physics: WILLIAM F. SAAM
Physiology and Cell Biology: MUTHU PERIASAMY
Plant, Cellular and Molecular Biology: FRED D. SACK
Plant Pathology: RANDALL C. ROWE
Political Science: PAUL A. BECK
Psychiatry: RUDU SAVEANU
Psychology: GIFFORD WEARY
Radiology: MICHAEL KNOPP
Slavic and East European Languages and Literatures: DANIEL E. COLLINS
Sociology: ROBERT L. KAUFMAN
Spanish and Portuguese: FERNANDO UNZUETA
Speech and Hearing Science: ROBERT A. FOX
Statistics: DOUGLAS A. WOLFE
Surgery: E. CHRISTOPHER ELLISON
Theatre: LESLEY K. FERRIS
Veterinary Biosciences: MICHAEL D. LAIRMORE
Veterinary Clinical Sciences: ROBERT G. SHERDING
Veterinary Hospital: RICHARD BEDNARSKI
Veterinary Preventive Medicine: KENT H. HOBLET
Women's Studies: LINDA M. MIZEJEWSKI

BRANCH CAMPUSES

Agricultural Technical Institute: 1328 Dover Rd, Wooster, OH 44691; tel. (330) 264-3911; f. 1972; 2-year courses; Dir STEPHEN P. NAMETH.

Ohio State University, Lima: 4240 Campus Drive, Lima, OH 45804; tel. (419) 221-1641; f. 1959; 2- and 4-year courses; Dean and Dir JOHN R. SNYDER.

Ohio State University, Mansfield: 1680 University Drive, Mansfield, OH 44906; tel. (419) 755-4001; f. 1958; Dean and Dir EVELYN B. FREEMAN.

Ohio State University, Marion: 142A Morrill Hall, 1465 Mt Vernon Ave, Marion, OH 43302; tel. (614) 389-2361; f. 1957; 2- and 4-year courses; Dean and Dir GREGORY S. ROSE.

Ohio State University, Newark: 1170 University Drive, Newark, OH 43055; tel. (740) 366-3321; f. 1957; 2- and 4-year courses; Academic Dean WILLIAM L. MACDONALD.

OHIO UNIVERSITY

Athens, OH 45701

Telephone: (614) 593-1000
Fax: (614) 593-4229
Internet: www.ohiou.edu

Founded 1804; the first land-grant college in the US; main campus in Athens, regional campuses in Chillicothe, Ironton, Lancaster, St Clairsville, Zanesville

President: ROBERT GLIDDEN
Provost: SHARON STEPHENS BREHM
Director of Admissions: N. KIP HOWARD
Librarian (vacant)

Library of 2,044,000 vols
Number of teachers: 1,600
Number of students: 27,386

Publications: *Ohio Review*, *Milton Quarterly*

DEANS

Engineering and Technology: Dr W. KENT WRAY
Arts and Sciences: Dr LESLIE A. FLEMMING
Business Administration: GLENN CORLETT
Education: Dr KAREN J. VIECHNICKI (acting)
Fine Arts: Dr JAMES STEWART (acting)
University College: Dr PATRICIA RICHARD
Graduate Programs: Dr CAROL J. BLUM (acting)
Health and Human Services: Dr BARBARA K. CHAPMAN
Communications: Dr KATHY A. KRENDL
Osteopathic Medicine: Dr BARBARA ROSS-LEE
Honors Tutorial College: Dr JOSEPH H. BERMAN

OHIO WESLEYAN UNIVERSITY

61 S. Sandusky St, Delaware, OH 43015

Telephone: (740) 368-2000
Fax: (740) 368-3299
E-mail: owupr@owu.edu
Internet: www.owu.edu

Founded 1841 by Methodist Episcopal Church; chartered 1842
Academic year: August to May

President: THOMAS B. COURTICE
Provost: W. C. LOUTHAN
Vice-President (Business Affairs) and Treasurer: GEORGE J. ELSBECK
Vice-President (University Relations): AUDRY K. CARTER
Dean of Academic Affairs (vacant):
Chair, Division of Student Life: JOHN M. DELANEY
Registrar: SALLY A. SIKORSKI
Librarian: THERESA BYRD

Number of teachers: 138 full-time
Number of students: 1,885

Publications: *Civic Arts Review* (4 a year), *Alumni Magazine* (4 a year), *Zumari: a Journal of Black World Studies* (2 a year).

OTTERBEIN COLLEGE

Westerville, OH 43081

Telephone: (614) 890-3000
Fax: (614) 823-1200
E-mail: uotterb@otterbein.edu
Internet: www.otterbein.edu

Founded 1847
Private control
Academic year: September to August

President: C. BRENT DE VORE
Registrar: DONALD FOSTER

Dean of Admissions and Financial Aid: THOMAS STEIN
Academic Dean: PATRICIA FRICK
Director of the Library: LOIS SZUDY

Library of 200,000 vols
Number of teachers: 140
Number of students: 2,500

Publications: *Otterbein Miscellany*, *Quiz and Quill*.

SAINT MARY SEMINARY AND GRADUATE SCHOOL OF THEOLOGY

28700 Euclid Ave, Wickliffe, OH 44092-2585

Telephone: (440) 943-7600
Fax: (440) 943-7577
E-mail: mal@dioceseofcleveland.org
Internet: www.stmarysem.edu

Founded 1848 as a diocesan seminary; present name 1968
Private control
Academic year: August to May

President-Rector: Rev. THOMAS W. TIFFT
Vice-President, Vice-Rector and Academic Dean: Rev. MARK A. LATCOVICH
Dean of Students: Rev. DAVID J. WALKOWIAK
Registrar: KATHRYN C. SIMMONS

Number of teachers: 20
Number of students: 110.

SHAWNEE STATE UNIVERSITY

940 Second St, Portsmouth, OH 45662-4344

Telephone: (740) 351-3205
Fax: (740) 351-3416
E-mail: to_ssu@shawnee.edu
Internet: www.shawnee.edu

Founded 1986
Academic year: September to June

President: Dr RITA RICE MORRIS
Vice-President and General Counsel: Dr STEPHEN P. DONOHUE
Vice-President (Academic Affairs) and Provost: Dr MICHAEL FIELD
Vice-President (Student Affairs): Dr LARRY L. MANGUS
Vice-President (Business Affairs): ROGER T. MURPHY
Library Director: TESS MIDKIFF

Number of teachers: 120
Number of students: 3,600

DEANS

College of Professional Studies: Dr MARTHA C. RADER
College of Arts and Sciences: Dr JERRY G. HOLT

SIEGAL COLLEGE OF JUDAIC STUDIES

26500 Shaker Blvd, Cleveland, OH 44122

Telephone: (216) 464-4050
E-mail: info@siegalcollege.edu
Internet: www.siegalcollege.edu
Private control

President: Dr DAVID S. ARIEL
Dean: Dr SYLVIA F. ABRAMS
Dean: LINDA L. ROSEN
Library Director: JEAN LETTOFSKY

Number of teachers: 30
Number of students: 130.

TIFFIN UNIVERSITY

155 Miami St, Tiffin, OH 44883

Telephone: (419) 447-6443
Fax: (419) 443-5006
Internet: www.tiffin.edu

Founded 1888
Private control
Academic year: August to May

President: PAUL MARION
Vice-President and Dean of Faculty: Dr JOHN MILLAR
Vice-President (Admissions and Student Affairs): CAM CRUICKSHANK
Vice President (Business): DAVID BOYD
Vice-President (Campus Services and Athletics): IAN DAY
Vice-President (Development): MICHAEL GRANDILLO
Vice-President (Enrollment Services): JUDY GARDNER
Registrar: ALICE NICHOLS
Library Director: FRANCES A. FLEET
Number of teachers: 72
Number of students: 1,634

DEANS

School of Arts and Sciences: Dr TJANET HANNA
School of Business: Dr WALTER VERDON
School of Criminal Justice and Social Sciences: Dr CHARLES CHRISTENSEN
Graduate Sand Online Education: Dr SHAWN P. DALY

TRINITY LUTHERAN SEMINARY

2199 E Main St, Columbus, OH 43209-2334
Telephone: (614) 235-4136
E-mail: admissions@trinitylutheranseminary.edu
Internet: www.trinitylutheranseminary.edu
Founded 1830 as Evangelical Lutheran Theological Seminary; present name 1978
Private control
Academic year: September to May
President: MARK R. RAMSETH
Vice-President (Operations and Finance): JAMES T. CALDWELL
Vice-President (Development): KAY A. HELMAN
Dean of Academic Affairs: DONALD L. HUBER
Registrar: CAROL M. DIXON
Librarian: RAY A. OLSON
Number of teachers: 26
Number of students: 250.

UNION INSTITUTE & UNIVERSITY

440 E. McMillan St, Cincinnati, OH 45206-1925
Telephone: (800) 486-3116
Fax: (513) 861-4887
E-mail: admissions@tui.edu
Internet: www.tui.edu
Founded 1964
Private control
President: JUDITH A. STURNICK
Provost: ROGER SUBLETT
Vice-President and Dean of Graduate Studies: RICHARD GREEN
Vice-President and Dean of Undergraduate Studies: RICHARD HANSEN
Vice-President of Development and University Relations: KRISTINE HOWLAND
Chief Financial Officer: EDWARD WALTON
Chief Librarian: MATTHEW PAPPATHAN
Library of 50,000 books, 2,000 periodicals
Number of teachers: 230
Number of students: 2,741 (1,112 undergraduate, 1629 postgraduate).

CONSTITUENT COLLEGE

Vermont College

Montpelier Campus, 36 College St, Montpelier, VT 05602
Telephone: (802) 828-8500
Founded 1834 as the Vermont Seminary; acquired by Union Institute & University 2001.

UNITED THEOLOGICAL SEMINARY

1810 Harvard Blvd, Dayton, OH 45406
Telephone: (937) 278-5817
Fax: (937) 278-1218
E-mail: utscom@united.edu
Internet: www.united.edu
Campuses at Dayton and Buffalo (NY)
Private control
President: G. EDWIN ZEIDERS
Vice-President (Academic Affairs): KENDALL MCCABE
Vice-President (Administration): DICK DELON
Vice-President (Enrollment Management): THERESE A. LIMBERT
Vice-President (Institutional Advancement): MICHAEL WALTERS
Registrar: MARTHA M. ANDERSON
Library Director: SARAH D. BROOKS BLAIR
Number of teachers: 12
Number of students: 170 (full-time).

UNIVERSITY OF AKRON

302 E. Buchtel Ave, Akron, OH 44325
Telephone: (216) 375-7111
Internet: www.uakron.edu
Founded 1870 by Ohio Universalist Convention; became Municipal University of Akron 1913; present title 1926; became State University 1967
President: LUIS M. PROENZA
Senior Vice-President and Provost: TERRY L. HICKEY
Vice-President for Public Relations and Development: JOHN LA GUARDIA
Vice-President for Business and Finance: HENRY NETTLING
Registrar: Dr H. DON FOX, Jr
Dean, University Libraries: DELMUS WILLIAMS
Library of 2,817,426 vols
Number of teachers: 2,900
Number of students: 24,000
Publications: Bulletin (annually), UA News (every 2 weeks), Akron Magazine (quarterly)

DEANS

Graduate Studies: GEORGE R. NEWKOME
Buchtel College of Arts and Sciences: ROGER CREEL
College of Education: ELIZABETH STROBLE (acting)
College of Engineering: S. GRAHAM KELLY
College of Business Administration: STEPHEN F. HALLAM
College of Fine and Applied Arts: MARK S. AUBURN
School of Law: RICHARD L. AYNES
College of Nursing: CYNTHIA CAPERS
University College: KARLA MUGLER
Community and Technical College: WILLIAM H. BEISEL
Wayne General and Technical College: JOHN KRISTOFCO

UNIVERSITY OF CINCINNATI

2624 Clifton Ave, Cincinnati, OH 45221
Telephone: (513) 556-6000
Fax: (513) 556-2340
Internet: www.uc.edu
Founded 1819 as Cincinnati College; renamed University of Cincinnati (a municipal instn) 1870; became a municipally sponsored state-affiliated instn 1968; joined State of Ohio University system 1977
Academic year: September to June
President: NANCY ZIMPHER

Senior Vice-President for the Medical Center: JANE HENNEY
Senior Vice-President and Provost: ANTHONY PERZEGIAN
Vice-President and Dean for Graduate Studies and Research: HOWARD JACKSON
Vice-President for Public Affairs: GREGORY VEHR
Vice-President for Student Services: MITCHELL LIVINGSTON
Vice-President for Finance: DALE MCGIRR
Vice-President for Administrative and Business Services: JAMES TUCKER
University Registrar (vacant)
Director of Admissions: JAMES WILLIAMS
Dean and University Librarian: Dr VICTORIA MONTAVON
Library: see Libraries
Number of teachers: 3,481 (2,149 full-time, 1,332 part-time)
Number of students: 33,823 (26,165 undergraduate, 6,685 postgraduate, 973 professional)
Publications: Horizon (7 a year), University Currents (weekly during term), News record (3 a week during term), College Bulletins (every 2 years)

DEANS

McMicken College of Arts and Sciences: KAREN GOULD
College of Engineering: STEPHEN KOWEL
College of Education: LAWRENCE JOHNSON
College of Business Administration: FREDRICK RUSS
College of Medicine: WILLIAM MARTIN
College of Law: JOSEPH P. TOMAIN
College of Nursing: ANDREA R. LINDELL
College of Design, Architecture, Art and Planning: JUDITH KOROSCIK
College of Pharmacy: DAN ACOSTA
College-Conservatory of Music: DOUGLAS LOWRY
School of Social Work: PHILLIP JACKSON (Director)
Raymond Walters College: DOLORES STRAKER
OMI College of Applied Science: RICHARD NEWROCK
Clermont College: DAVID DEVIER
College of Allied Health Sciences: ELIZABETH KING

PROFESSORS

College of Arts and Sciences (POB 210037, Cincinnati, OH 45221-0037; tel. (513) 556-5860; fax (513) 556-0142; internet ucaswww.mcm.uc.edu):
ALEXANDER, J. J., Chemistry
ALEXANDER, J. K., History
ARDEN, H. M., Romance Languages and Literatures
ARNER, R., English
ATKINSON, M., English
AULT, B. S., Chemistry
BACON, S. M., Romance Languages
BEAVER, D., History
BECK, T. L., Chemistry
BENNETT, S., Political Science
BERRY, C. A., Economics
BERRYMAN-FINK, C. L., Communication Arts
BISHOP, G. F., Political Science
BOBST, A. M., Chemistry
BOGEN, D. H., English
BOWMAN, S., Judaic Studies
BRETT, C. E., Geology
BRISKIN, M., Geology
BRYC, W., Mathematical Sciences
BURLEW, A. K. H., Psychology
CAMERON, B. N., Biological Sciences
CARUSO, J., Biological Sciences
CHALKLEY, R., Mathematical Sciences
CHANG, T. C., Mathematical Sciences
CHIMEZIE, A., Afro-American Studies
COHEN, G., Classics

COLLINS, P. H., Afro-American Studies
DANIELS, R., History
DAVIS, J. L., Classics
DAY, R. A., Chemistry
DEDDENS, J. A., Mathematical Sciences
DRURY, J. P., English
DUMAS, H. S., Mathematical Sciences
DURST, R. K., English
ELDER, A. A., English
ELDER, R. C., Chemistry
ENDORF, R. J., Physics
ERWAY, L. C., Biological Sciences
ESPOSITO, F. P., Physics
FAIRHURST, G., Communication Arts
FEINBERG, W. E., Sociology
FENICHEL, H., Physics
FISHBEIN, H., Psychology
FISHER, J. W., Mathematical Sciences
FRENCH, D. A., Mathematical Sciences
FRIEDRICHSMEYER, S. L., Germanic Languages
GALLO, J., Economics
GAUKER, C. P., Philosophy
GERMAN, R., Biological Sciences
GLENN, J. H., Germanic Languages
GODDARD, H. C., Economics
GODSHALK, W. L., English
GOTOFF, H. C., Classics
GRASHA, A. F., Psychology
GROVER, J. E., Geology
GUTZWILLER, R. J., Classics
HALPERIN, R., Anthropology
HALPERN, H. P., Mathematical Sciences
HALSALL, B., Chemistry
HAMILTON, J. F., Romance Languages and Literatures
HEINEMAN, W., Chemistry
HERMAN, E., Economics
HERRON, D. A., Mathematical Sciences
HINKEL, J. M., Geography
HODGES, T., Mathematical Sciences
HONECK, R. P., Psychology
HORN, P. S., Mathematical Sciences
HUDGINS, A. L., English
HUETHER, C., Biological Sciences
HUFF, W. D., Geology
HUGHES, J., English
ISAAC, B. L., Anthropology
JAMISON-HALL, A., Afro-American Studies
JARRELL, M. S., Physics
JAYASIMHULU, K., Chemistry
JENSEN, W. B., Chemistry
JOHNSON, R. A., Physics
JOINER, W. C. H., Physics
JOST, L. J., Philosophy
KAFTAL, V., Mathematical Sciences
KANE, T. C., Biological Sciences
KANESHIRO, E., Biological Sciences
KAPLAN, F., Chemistry
KARP, R., Biological Sciences
KILINC, A. I., Geology
KING, T., Mathematical Sciences
KINOSHITA, K., Physics
KLEIN, E. B., Psychology
KORMAN, P., Mathematical Sciences
KREISHMAN, G., Chemistry
LANGMEYER, D., Psychology
LEAKE, L., Mathematical Science
LECLAIR, T. E., English
LEFTWICH, H. M., Economics
LEUNG, A., Mathematical Sciences
LOWELL, T. V., Geology
LUNDGREN, D., Sociology
MA, M., Physics
McCORD, C. K., Mathematical Sciences
McEVOY, J., Philosophy
MANSOURI, F., Physics
MARGOLIS, M. S., Political Science
MARK, H. B., Jr, Chemistry
MARK, J. E., Chemistry
MARTIN, J., Philosophy
MAUME, D. J., Sociology
MAYER, W., Economics
MAYNARD, J. B., Geology
MEADOWS, B. T., Physics
MEEKS, F., Chemistry

MELTON, R. S., Psychology
MEYER, D. L., Geology
MEYER, K. R., Mathematical Sciences
MEYER, R. R., Biological Sciences
MEYERS, W., Psychology
MICHELINI, A. N., Classics
MILLER, A., Political Science
MILLER, A. I., Geology
MILLER, M. C., Biological Sciences
MINDA, C. D., Mathematical Sciences
MITRO, J., Mathematical Sciences
MUKKADA, A. J., Biological Sciences
MURIO, D. A., Mathematical Sciences
MURRAY, J. M., History
NASH, D. B., Geology
NAVEH, G. O. S., Judaic Studies
NIGRO, K. V., Romance Languages
OSTERBURG, J., Mathematical Sciences
PELIGRAD, C., Mathematical Sciences
PELIGRAD, M., Mathematical Sciences
PELIKAN, S., Mathematical Sciences
PERSON, L. S., English
PINHAS, A. R., Chemistry
PINSKI, F., Physics
PORTE, M., Communication Arts
RALESCU, D., Mathematical Sciences
RAMUSACK, B. N., History
RAWLINGS, E. I., Psychology
RESNIK, D., Pharmacological Sciences
RICHARDSON, R., Philosophy
RIDGWAY, T. H., Chemistry
ROBINSON, J., Philosophy
RODER, W., Geography
ROLWING, R., Mathematical Sciences
ROMERO, A., Romance Languages and Literatures
RUBENSTEIN, J., English
RUSSELL, J., Physics
SABOURIN, T. C., Community Arts
SAGE, M. M., Classics
SAKMYSTER, T., History
SCARBOROUGH, V. L., Anthropology
SCHADE, R., Germanic Languages and Literature
SCHULTZ, L. M., English
SCHUMSKY, D. A., Psychology
SELISKAR, C., Chemistry
SELYA, R. M., Geography
SHAPIRO, H., History
SITKO, M. L., Physics
SIVAGANESAN, S., Mathematical Sciences
SLOTKIN, E., English
SMITH, H., History
SNIDER, J. A., Biological Sciences
SOKOLOFF, M. D., Physics
SPRAGUE, E. D., Chemistry
STAFFORD, H., Geography
STEVER, J. A., Political Science
STOJANOVIC, S., Mathematical Sciences
STUTZ, R. M., Psychology
SULLIVAN, A. P., Anthropology
SURANYI, P., Physics
TEPPERMAN-ELDER, K., Biological Sciences
THAYER, J., Chemistry
TOLLEY, H. B., Political Science
TUAN, T.-F., Physics
TWINAM, A., History
UETZ, G. W., Biological Sciences
UNGAR, G. S., Mathematical Sciences
VESPRANI, G. J., Psychology
VIALET, M. E., Romance Languages
VREDEVELD, G. M., Economics
WALBERG, G., Classics
WARM, J., Psychology
WEISS, G. M., Mathematical Sciences
WELLINGTON, D. C., Economics
WHITMORE, H. W., Economics
WIJEWARDHANA, L. C. R., Physics
WILSON, R. M., Chemistry
WINGET, G., Biological Sciences
WOLFE, J. D., Political Science
WRIGHT, D. J., Mathematical Sciences
YORK, A. D., English
ZANDVAKILI, S., Economics
ZHANG, B., Mathematical Sciences
ZHANG, F., Physics

ZHANG, S., Mathematical Sciences

College of Engineering (POB 210018, Cincinnati, OH 45221-0018; tel. (513) 556-5417; fax (513) 556-5007; internet www.eng.uc.edu):

ABDALLAH, S. A., Aerospace Engineering and Engineering Mechanics
AGRAWAL, D. P., Electrical and Computer Engineering and Computer Science
ALLEMANG, R. J., Mechanical and Industrial Engineering
BERMAN, K. A., Computer Science
BISHOP, P. L., Civil and Environmental Engineering
BOERIO, F. J., Materials Science and Engineering
BOOLCHAND, P., Electrical and Computer Engineering
BOYD, J. T., Electrical and Computer Engineering
BROWN, D. L., Mechanical and Industrial Engineering
BUCHANAN, R. C., Materials Science and Engineering
BUTLER, D. L., Aerospace Engineering and Engineering Mechanics
CAHAY, M. M., Electrical and Computer Engineering and Computer Science
CARTER, H. W., Electrical and Computer Engineering
CHRISTENSON, J., Mechanical and Industrial Engineering
CLARSON, S. J., Materials Science and Engineering
DEGOUVEA-PINTO, N. R., Chemical Engineering
FAN, H. H., Electrical and Computer Engineering
FRANCO, J. V., Electrical and Computer Engineering and Computer Science
FRIED, J. R., Chemical Engineering
GERNER, F. M., Mechanical, Industrial and Nuclear Engineering
GHIA, K. N., Aerospace Engineering and Engineering Mechanics
GHIA, U., Mechanical and Industrial Engineering
GOVIND, R., Chemical Engineering
GROOD, E. S., Aerospace Engineering and Engineering Mechanics
GUTMARK, E. J., Aerospace Engineering and Engineering Mechanics
HALL, E. L., Mechanical and Industrial Engineering
HAMED, A., Aerospace Engineering and Engineering Mechanics
HERSHEY, D., Chemical Engineering
HUSTON, R. L., Mechanical and Industrial Engineering
HWANG, S.-T., Chemical Engineering
JAYARAMAN, N., Materials Science and Engineering
JAIN, R. K., Civil and Environmental Engineering
JENG, S. M., Aerospace Engineering and Engineering Mechanics
KAO, Y. K., Chemical Engineering
KEENER, T. C., Civil and Environmental Engineering
KHANG, S. J., Chemical Engineering
KHOSLA, P. K., Aerospace Engineering and Engineering Mechanics
KINMAN, R. N., Civil and Environmental Engineering
KOSEL, P. B., Electrical and Computer Engineering
KRANTZ, W., Chemical Engineering
KROLL, R. J., Aerospace Engineering and Engineering Mechanics
KUKRETI, A. R., Civil and Environmental Engineering
LIN, R. Y., Materials Science and Engineering
MANTEI, T. D., Electrical and Computer Engineering

MITAL, A., Mechanical and Industrial Engineering
NAGY, P., Aerospace Engineering and Engineering Mechanics
NAYFEH, A. H., Aerospace Engineering and Engineering Mechanics
PANT, P. D., Civil and Environmental Engineering
PAUL, J. L., Computer Science
POOL, M. J., Materials Science and Engineering
PRATSINIS, S. E., Chemical Engineering
PURDY, G. B., Computer Science
QUO, P. C., Mechanical and Industrial Engineering
RALESCU, A. L., Electrical and Computer Engineering and Computer Science
RAMAMOORTHY, P., Electrical and Computer Engineering
RICHARDSON, D., Aerospace Engineering and Engineering Mechanics
ROENKER, K. P., Electrical and Computer Engineering
SCARPINO, P. V., Civil and Environmental Engineering
SCHAEFER, D. W., Materials Science and Engineering
SCHLIPF, J. S., Electrical and Computer Engineering and Computer Science
SCHMIDT, D. S., Computer Science
SEKHAR, J. A., Materials Science and Engineering
SHELL, R. L., Mechanical and Industrial Engineering
SINGH, R. N., Materials Science and Engineering
SLATER, G., Aerospace Engineering and Engineering Mechanics
STECKL, A., Electrical and Computer Engineering
SUIDAN, M. T., Civil and Environmental Engineering
VAN OOIJ, W. J., Materials Science and Engineering
VASUDEVAN, V. K., Materials Science and Engineering
VEMURI, R., Electrical and Computer Engineering and Computer Science
WEE, W. G., Electrical and Computer Engineering

College of Education (POB 210002, Cincinnati, OH 45221-0002; tel. (513) 556-2335; fax (513) 556-2483; internet www.education.uc.edu):

AMSPAUGH-CORSON, L. B., Curriculum and Instruction
BARNETT, D. W., School Psychology and Counselling
BAUER, A. M., Early Childhood and Special Education
BERLOWITZ, M. J., Educational Foundation
CHAMLIN, L. B., Criminal Justice
COLLINS, R. L., Educational Foundation
CONYNE, R. K., School Psychology and Counselling
COOK, E. P., School Psychology and Counselling
COTTRELL, R., Health and Nutrition Sciences
CULLEN, F. T., Criminal Justice
DORSEY, A., Early Childhood and Special Education
EKVALL, S., Health and Nutrition Sciences
EVERS, N. A., Educational Administration
FOWLER, T. W., Curriculum and Instruction
GORDON, J. S., Curriculum and Instruction
GRADEN, J. L., School Psychology and Counselling
KRETSCHMER, R., Early Childhood and Special Education
KRZYWKOWSKI, L. V., Educational Foundation
LATESSA, E. J., Criminal Justice

LENTZ, F. E., School Psychology and Counselling
MARKLE, G. C., Curriculum and Instruction
MATRIANO, E., Curriculum and Instruction
NAYLOR, D., Curriculum and Instruction
O'REILLY, P., Educational Foundation
STEVENS, J., Educational Foundation
SWAMI, P., Curriculum and Instruction
TRAVIS, L. F., Criminal Justice
TRUAX, R. R., Early Childhood and Special Education
VANVOORHIS, P., Criminal Justice
WAGNER, D. I., Health and Nutritional Sciences
WILSON, B., Health and Nutritional Sciences
WILSON, F. R., School Psychology and Counselling
YAGER, G. G., School Psychology and Counselling
ZINS, J., Early Childhood and Special Education

College of Business Administration (POB 210020, Cincinnati, OH 45221-0020; tel. (513) 556-7001; fax (513) 556-4891; internet www.cba.uc.edu):

ALLEN, C. T., Marketing
ANDERSON, D. R., Quantitative Analysis and Information Systems
ANGLE, H., Management
BAKER, N. R., Quantitative Analysis and Information Systems
BURNS, D., Accounting
CAMM, J. D., Quantitative Analysis and Information Systems
COMER, J., Marketing
CURRY, D. J., Marketing
DEAN, M., Marketing
DWYER, F. R., Marketing
EVANS, J. R., Quantitative Analysis and Information Systems
GELTNER, D. M., Finance
HENDERSON, G. V., Finance
KARDES, F., Marketing
KELTON, W. D., Quantitative Analysis and Information Systems
KIM, Y. H., Finance
LEVY, M. S., Quantitative Analysis and Information Systems
MACHLEIT, K., Marketing
MACKLIN, M. C. W., Marketing
MAGAZINE, M., Quantitative Analysis and Information Systems
MILLER, N. G., Finance
SALE, T., Accounting
SWEENEY, D. J., Quantitative Analysis and Information Systems
WALKER, M. C., Finance
WYATT, S. B., Finance

College of Medicine (POB 670555, Cincinnati, OH 45267-0555; tel. (513) 558-7391; fax (513) 558-1165; internet www.med.uc.edu):

ALEXANDER, J. W., Surgery
ALLOWAY, R. R., Internal Medicine
ASBURY, T., Ophthalmology
ASHRAF, M., Pathology and Laboratory Medicine
AZIZKHAN, R. G., Surgery
BALASUBRAMANIAM, A., Surgery
BANKS, R. O., Molecular and Cellular Physiology
BAUGHMAN, R. P., Internal Medicine
BEHBEHANI, M. M., Molecular and Cellular Physiology
BEN-JONATHAN, N., Cell Biology
BERNSTEIN, D. I., Internal Medicine
BHATTACHARYA, A., Environmental Health
BIBLER, M. R., Internal Medicine
BORNSCHEIN, R. L., Environmental Health
BOWER, R. H., Surgery
BRACKEN, R. B., Surgery
BRACKENBURY, R. W., Cell Biology
BRENEMAN, J. C., Radiology
BUNCHER, C. R., Environmental Health

CAVALLO, T., Pathology and Laboratory Medicine
CHATTERJEE, M., Internal Medicine
CHATTERJEE, S. K., Internal Medicine
CHERNUS, L., Psychiatry
CLARK, C. S., Environmental Health
CLARK, K. E., Obstetrics and Gynaecology
CLEMENS, T. L., Internal Medicine
COTTON, R., Otolaryngology
COX, J. A., Surgery
CRAWFORD, A. H., Orthopaedic Surgery
CROCKER, D. J., Surgery
CRUTCHER, K. A., Neurosurgery
CUPPOLETTI, J., Molecular and Cellular Physiology
DANIELS, A. S., Psychiatry
DECOURTEN-MYERS, G. M., Pathology
DEDMAN, J. R., Molecular and Cellular Physiology
DEEPE, G. S., Internal Medicine
DIETRICH, R. N., Environmental Health
DIXON, K., Environmental Health
DOETSCHMAN, T. C., Molecular Genetics and Biochemistry
DONOVAN, E. F., Paediatrics
DORN, G. W., Internal Medicine
DRAKE, R. L., Cell Biology
DUNSKER, S. B., Neurosurgery
ECKMAN, M. H., Internal Medicine
ELSON, H. R., Radiology
FAGIN, J. A., Internal Medicine
FEINBERG, J., Internal Medicine
FERNANDEZ-ALLOA, M., Radiology
FINKELMAN, F. D., Internal Medicine
FIRST, M. R., Internal Medicine
FISCHER, C. G., Anaesthesiology
FOON, K. A., Internal Medicine
FRAME, P. T., Internal Medicine
FRANCO, R. S., Internal Medicine
GALLA, J. H., Internal Medicine
GASS, M. L., Obstetrics and Gynaecology
GERSON, M. C., Internal Medicine
GHOSN, S., Pathology and Laboratory Medicine
GIANNELLA, R. A., Internal Medicine
GOTHELF, E. J., Family Medicine
GRERNER, A. L., Neurosurgery
GRUENSTEIN, E. I., Molecular Genetics and Biochemistry
GRUNENWALD, P. W., Internal Medicine
GRUPP, I. L., Pharmacology and Cell Biophysics
HANTO, D. W., Surgery
HASSELGREN, P., Surgery
HAWKINS, H. H., Radiology
HEATON, C. L., Radiology
HECK, J. E., Family Medicine
HENTHORN, R. W., Internal Medicine
HERMAN, J. P., Psychiatry
HILLARD, P. A., Obstetrics and Gynaecology
HORSEMAN, N., Molecular and Cellular Physiology
HOUR, J. L., Internal Medicine
HUI, D. Y., Pathology and Laboratory Medicine
HURST, J. M., Surgery
HUSSEINZADEH, N., Obstetrics and Gynaecology
IP, W. S., Cell Biology
IVEY, T. D., Surgery
JARRELL, J. L., Environmental Health
KANT, S., Internal Medicine
KAO, W. W. Y., Ophthalmology
KECK, P. E., Psychiatry
KEITH, R. W., Otolaryngology
KELLER, J. T., Neurosurgery
KHADADAD, G., Neurosurgery
KHAN, S. A., Cell Biology
KOTAGAL, U. R., Paediatrics
KRANIAS, E. G., Pharmacy and Cell Biophysics
LABARBERA, A. R., Obstetrics and Gynaecology
LEHMAN, M. N., Cell Biology
LEIKAUF, G. D., Environmental Health
LEMASTERS, G., Environmental Health

LEVY, R. C., Emerging Medicine
LIEBERMAN, M. A., Molecular Genetics and Biochemistry
LIGGETT, S. B., Internal Medicine
LIND, L. J., Anaesthesiology
LINGREL, J. B., Molecular Genetics and Biochemistry
LIU, J. H., Obstetrics and Gynaecology
LOCKEY, J. E., Environmental Health
LOWE, E. E., Anaesthesiology
LOWER, E., Internal Medicine
LUDKE, R. L., Family Medicine
MCCALL, J. E., Anaesthesiology
MCELROY, S. L., Psychiatry
MAGGIO, J. E., Pharmacology and Cell Biophysics
MALIK, I. A., Internal Medicine
MARCIANI, R. D., Surgery
MARGOLIS, C. F., Family Medicine
MATHIEU, A., Anaesthesiology
MATLIB, M. A., Pharmacology and Cell Biophysics
MICHAEL, J. G., Molecular Genetics and Biochemistry
MICKELSON, J. K., Internal Medicine
MILLARD, R., Pharmacology and Cell Biophysics
MILLHORN, D. E., Molecular and Cellular Physiology
MONTAUK, S. L., Family Medicine
MORRIS, R. E., Cell Biology
MOULTON, J. S., Radiology
MUHLEMAN, A. F., Internal Medicine
MUNDA, R., Surgery
MYATT, L., Obstetrics and Gynaecology
MYER, C., Otolaryngology
NEALE, H. W., Surgery
NEBERT, D. W., Environmental Health
NELSON, R. D., Pharmacology and Cell Biophysics
NEWMAN, S. L., Internal Medicine
NORLUND, J., Dermatology
NORMAN, A. B., Psychiatry
OGLE, C. K., Surgery
OPPENHEIMER, S., Paediatrics
OTTEN, E. J., Emergency Medicine
PAI, U. T., Anaesthesiology
PAUL, R. J., Molecular and Cellular Physiology
PENSAK, M. L., Otolaryngology
PERIASAMY, M., Internal Medicine
PESCE, A. J., Pathology and Laboratory Medicine
PHERO, J. C., Anaesthesiology
PIKE, J. W., Molecular and Cellular Physiology
POREMBKA, D. T., Anaesthesiology
PRIVITERA, M. D., Neurology
PUGA, A., Environmental Health
RASHKIN, M. C., Internal Medicine
RATNER, N., Cell Biology
REIF, M. C., Internal Medicine
RICE, C. H., Environmental Health
RICER, R. E., Family Medicine
ROUAN, G. W., Internal Medicine
SAELINGER, C., Molecular Genetics and Biochemistry
SAMAHA, F. J., Neurology
SCHWARTZ, A., Surgery
SEIDEN, A. M., Otolaryngology
SHARP, F. R., Neurology
SHELDON, C. A., Surgery
SHUKIA, R., Environmental Health
SHULL, B. E., Molecular Genetics and Biochemistry
SHUMRICK, D. A., Otolaryngology
SHUMRICK, K. A., Otolaryngology
SIDDIGI, T. A., Obstetrics and Gynaecology
SIDMAN, C. L., Molecular Genetics and Biochemistry
SIEGEL, E. G., Emergency Medicine
SINGH, S., Internal Medicine
SMITSON, W. S., Psychiatry
SOLEIMANI, M., Internal Medicine
SOLOMKIN, J. S., Surgery

SPINNATO, J. A., Obstetrics and Gynaecology
STAMBROOK, P. J., Cell Biology
STEICHEN, J. J., Paediatrics
STEMMERMAN, G. N., Pathology and Laboratory Medicine
STONE, W. N., Psychiatry
STRAKOWSKI, S. M., Psychiatry
STRIKER, T. W., Anaesthesiology
STRINGER, J. R., Molecular Genetics and Biochemistry
SUBBIAH, M. T. R., Internal Medicine
SUSZKIW, J. B., Molecular and Cellular Pathology
TABOR, M. W., Environmental Health
TAMI, T. A., Otolaryngology
TOMSICK, T. A., Radiology
TROTT, A., Emergency Medicine
TSO, P. P. W., Pathology and Laboratory Medicine
VANLOVEREN, H. R., Neurosurgery
WALZER, P. D., Internal Medicine
WANDER, A. H., Ophthalmology
WARDEN, G. D., Surgery
WARSHAW, G. A., Family Medicine
WARSHAWSKY, D., Environmental Health
WEISS, A. A., Molecular Genetics and Biochemistry
WEXLER, L., Internal Medicine
WHITSETT, J. A., Paediatrics
WILLEKE, K., Environmental Health
WONES, R. G., Internal Medicine
WOODLE, E. S., Surgery
WOODS, S. C., Psychiatry
YATANI, A., Pharmacology and Cell Biophysics
YEH, H.-S., Neurosurgery
YOUNKER, D., Anaesthesiology
YU, L, Cell Biology
ZEMLAN, F., Psychiatry

College of Law (POB 210040, Cincinnati, OH 45221-0040; tel. (513) 556-6805; fax (513) 556-2391; internet www.law.uc.edu):

BIANCALANA, J.
BROWN, D. A.
CARON, P.
CHIN, G. J.
EISELE, T. D.
LASSITER, C.
LETSOU, P. V.
LOCKWOOD, B. B.
MANK, B. C.
NAGY, D. M.
RANDS, W.
SCHNEIDER, R.
SOLIMINE, M. E.
VAN ALSTINE, M. P.
WEISSENBERGER, G.

College of Nursing (POB 670038, Cincinnati, OH 45267-0038; tel. (513) 558-5500; fax (513) 558-3600; internet www.nursing.uc.edu):

BUNYAN, R. M., Medical Surgical Nursing
DRISCOLL, R. A., Mental Health Nursing
DYEHOUSE, J. M., Physical and Mental Health Nursing
HERN, M. J., Parent-Child Nursing
KENNER, C. A., Parent-Child Nursing
MARTIN, M. T., Medical Surgical Nursing
MILLER, E. L., Medical Surgical Nursing
SOMMERS, M., Medical Surgical Nursing
WERNER, E. E., Medical Surgical Nursing
WILSON, C. R., Parent-Child Nursing

College of Allied Health Sciences (POB 670394, Cincinnati, OH 45267-0394; tel. (513) 558-7495; fax (513) 558-7494; internet www.uc.edu/cahs):

CREAGHEAD, N., Communication Sciences
FALCIGLIA, G., Health Sciences
KRETSCHMER, L. W., Rehabilitation Sciences
LEE, L., Communications Sciences and Disorders
NEILS-STRUNJAS, J., Communications Sciences and Disorders

WALLACE, G. J., Communications Sciences and Disorders
WEILER, E. M., Rehabilitation Sciences

College of Design, Architecture, Art and Planning (POB 210016, Cincinnati, OH 45221-0016; tel. (513) 556-1204; fax (513) 556-3288; internet www.daap.uc.edu):

BARRY, R. J., Planning
BOTTONI, J., Design
BURLEIGH, K., Art
BURNHAM, R., Architecture and Interior Design
CARTWRIGHT, R., Art
EDELMAN, D. J., Planning
ELLISON, C. E., Planning
ENGELBRECHT, L. C., Art
ENSTICE, W. E., Art
GOSLING, D., Planning
HANCOCK, J. E., Architecture and Interior Design
HERRMANN, F. H., Art
HILDEBRANDT, H. P., Architecture and Interior Design
MANN, D. A., Architecture and Interior Design
MEACHAM, G. M., Design
NILAND, D. L., Architecture and Interior Design
PREISER, W., Architecture and Interior Design
PROBST, R., Design
PUHALLA, D. M., Design
RIESS, J. B., Art
ROMANOS, M. C., School of Planning
SAILE, D., Architecture and Interior Design
SALCHOW, G. R., School of Design
SIMMONS, G. B., Architecture and Interior Design
SMITH, D. L., Architecture and Interior Design
STEVENS, J. A., Art
STEWART, J. P., Art
STRICEVIC, G., Art
TUCKER, M., Art
VARADY, D., Planning
WOODHAM, D., Art
WOOL, M., Design

College of Pharmacy (POB 670004, Cincinnati, OH 45267-0004; tel. (513) 558-3784; fax (513) 558-4372; internet pharmacy.uc.edu):

BOTTORFF, M. B.
CACINI, W.
CAPERELLI, C. A.
CONRAD, W. F.
JANG, R.
SAKR, A.
SHENOUDA, L. S.
SKAU, K. A.
WARNER, V. D.
WICKETT, R. R.
WUEST, J. R.

College-Conservatory of Music (POB 210003, Cincinnati, OH 45221-0003; tel. (513) 556-6638; fax (513) 556-3330; internet www.ccm.uc.edu):

ADAMS, D., Performance Studies
ANDERSON, S. V., History and Composition
BERG, A., Opera and Musical Theatre
BLACK, W. D., Keyboard
BOYER-ALEXANDER, R., Music Education
CALLAHAN, C., Performance Studies
CHILDS, S. G., Opera and Musical Theatre
DEKANT, R., Performance Studies
DOAN, G. R., Music Education
FAABORG, K. K., Opera and Musical Theatre
FINNEY, T., Opera and Musical Theatre
FISHER, L. W., Performance Studies
FRASER, M., Opera and Musical Theatre
GAGE, J. H., Opera and Musical Theatre
GARDNER, R. C., Performance Studies
GARNER, B. A., Performance Studies
GARY, R., Keyboard
GIESBRECHT, P. M. B., Performance Studies

GRIFFITHS, K., Keyboard
HALE, N. K., Opera and Musical Theatre
HANANI, Y., Performance Studies
HASHIMOTO, E., Keyboard
HOFFMAN, J., History and Composition
HONN, B., Performance Studies
IWASAKI, C. N., Dance
LEMAN, J. W., Ensembles and Conducting
McGRAW, W., Performance Studies
METZ, D., Music Education
MORRIS, R., Keyboard
OTTE, A. C., Performance Studies
PENDLE, K., History and Composition
PLYLER, S. J., Opera and Musical Theatre
PRIDONOFF, E. A., Keyboard
RIVERS, E., Ensembles and Conducting
SABLINE, O., Dance
SASSMANNSHAUS, K., Performance Studies
SHORTT, P., Opera and Musical Theatre
STUCKY, M. H., Performance Studies
TOCCO, J. V., Keyboard
UMFRID, T., Opera and Musical Theatre
WAXLER, S., Opera and Musical Theatre
WEINSTOCK, F. M., Keyboard
WING, L., Music Education
WINTHER, R. K., Ensembles and Conducting
WOLFRAM, M., Broadcasting
ZIEROLF, R. L., History and Composition

School of Social Work (POB 21018, Cincinnati, OH 45221-0108; tel. (513) 556 4615; fax (513) 556-2077; internet www.uc.edu/socialwork):

BORKIN, J.
SUNDERLAND, S. C.

College of Applied Science (2220 Victory Parkway, Cincinnati, OH 45206-2839, tel. (513) 556-6567; fax (513) 556-5056; internet www.uc.edu/cas):

BILL, H. L., Construction Science
BORONKAY, T. G., Mechanical Engineering Technology
BROWN, M. A., Humanities
DORSEY, R. W., Construction Science
DURBIN, D. J., Construction Science
GEONETTA, S. C., Humanities
GILLIGAN, L. G., Mathematics
KREPPEL, M. C., Humanities
MEAL, L., Chemical Technology
SUCKARIEH, G. G., Construction Science
SULLIVAN, J. F., Mathematics

Raymond Walters College (9555 Plainfield Rd, Blue Ash, OH 45236-1096; tel. (513) 745-5600; fax (513) 745-8300; internet www.rwc.uc.edu):

ALLYANG, G. C., Behavioural Science
BAUGHIN, J. H., Foreign Languages
BAUMAN, D. H., Administration
BROD, E. F., Foreign Languages
CALLAN, J., Business and Commerce
CEBULA, J. E., History
CHISKO, A. M., Mathematics and Physics
COOPER-FREYTAG, L., Biological Sciences
DAVIS, L. K., Mathematics and Physics
FLAVIN, L. A., English
GARNETT, W. B., Biological Sciences
GOODMAN, E., History
HAGERTY, R. E., Communications and Visual Art
HANSEN, B. L., English
HEHMAN, R. G., Business and Commerce
LEAKE, J. A., History
LUTHER, P. A., English
MARSH, C. W., Mathematics, Physics
RNO, J., Mathematics, Physics
ROOS, M. E., English
SCHIERLING, J. M., Dental Hygiene
SCHLECHT, P. A., Nursing
SCHULTZ, J. A., Biological Sciences
SULKES, S., English
TAYLOR, R. N., Business and Commerce
WEINGARTNER, E. L., Nursing
WHEELER, S. G., History
YAKALI, E., Chemistry

University College (POB 210047, Cincinnati, OH 45221-0047; tel. (513) 556-1646; fax (513) 556-3007; internet www.ucollege.uc.edu):

CROCKER-LAKNESS, J. W., Language Arts
DZIECH, B., Language Arts
GARRETT, M. P., Language Arts
GRIESINGER, W. S., Humanities and Social Science
KAHN, S. R., Business and Commerce
MEEM, D. T., Language Arts
MURDOCH, N. H., Humanities and Social Science
NAPOLI, D., Humanities and Social Science
RUSH, S., Humanities and Social Science
SUMMERLIN, L., Language Arts
WHITE, L. M., Language Arts

Clermont College (4200 Clermont College, Batavia, OH 45103-1749; tel. (513) 732-5200; fax (513) 732-5275; internet www.clc.uc.edu):

BENOIT, M., Academic Service
DEJONG, M. F., Art
FANKHAUSER, D. B., Biology and Chemistry
HEIMBOLD, B. L., English
LONG, L. L., Academic Service
MURDOCH, G., Academic Service
WOLFF, G., English

Collateral Department – Professional Practice (POB 210115, Cincinnati, OH 45221-0115; tel. (513) 556-4634; fax (513) 556-5061; internet www.uc.edu/proprractice):

ABEL, R. J., Professional Practice
EVANS, B. T., Professional Practice
KEELING, A. E., Professional Practice
SORILLA, E. S., Professional Practice

UNIVERSITY OF DAYTON

Dayton, OH 45469
Telephone: (513) 229-4122
Internet: www.udayton.edu
Founded 1850
President: Bro. RAYMOND L. FITZ
Senior Vice-President for Administration: Bro. BERNARD J. PLOEGER
Provost: Rev. JAMES L. HEFT
Registrar: DANIEL F. PALMERT
Vice-President for University Advancement: FRANCES E. ARY
Vice-President and Treasurer: THOMAS E. BURKHARDT
Vice-President for Student Development: Dr WILLIAM C. SCHUERMAN
Vice-President for Athletic Programs and Facilities: THEODORE KISSELL
Vice-President for Graduate Studies and Research: Dr GORDON A. SARGENT
Dean of Libraries: Dr EDWARD D. GARTEN
Library of 1,304,000 vols
Number of teachers: 781
Number of students: 9,906
Publications: *University of Dayton Review* (quarterly), *Dimensions* (5 a year), *Law Review*

DEANS

Arts and Sciences: PAUL J. HORMAN
Graduate Studies and Research: Dr GORDON A. SARGENT
School of Engineering: Dr JOSEPH LESTINGI
School of Business: Dr SAM B. GOULD
School of Education: Dr PATRICIA F. FIRST
School of Law: FRANCIS J. CONTE

DIRECTORS

Continuing Education: CAROL M. SHAW
Admissions: MYRON H. ACHBACH
Research Institute: Dr JOSEPH E. ROWE

UNIVERSITY OF FINDLAY

1000 North Main St, Findlay, OH 45840
Telephone: (419) 422-8313
Fax: (419) 424-4822

Internet: www.findlay.edu
Founded 1882
President: Dr KENNETH E. ZIRKLE
Vice-President for Academic Affairs: Dr EDWARD W. ERNER
Vice-President for Business Affairs: MARTIN L. TERRY
Vice-President for Institutional Advancement: WILLIAM C. TRIGG, Jr
Vice-President for Student Services: FRANKLIN J. SCHULTZ
Registrar: TONY G. GOEDDE
Librarian: ROBERT W. SCHIRMER
Library of 127,000 vols
Number of teachers: 128
Number of students: 4,018.

UNIVERSITY OF RIO GRANDE

218 N College Ave, Rio Grande, OH 45674-3131

Telephone: (740) 245-5353
E-mail: admissions@rio.edu
Internet: www.urgrgcc.edu
Private control
Academic year: August to May
President: Dr BARRY DORSEY
Provost and Vice-President (Academic Affairs): Dr GREGORY SOJKA
Vice-President (Finance): RANDY ELDRIDGE
Vice-President (Administrative Services): PAUL HARRISON
Vice-President (Enrollment Management and Institutional Advancement): DEAN BROWN
Library Director: J. DAVID MAUER
Number of teachers: 85
Number of students: 2,081

DEANS

College of Liberal Arts and Sciences: Dr BARBARA HATFIELD
College of Professional Studies: Dr DAVID FREITAS

UNIVERSITY OF TOLEDO

Toledo, OH 43606-3390
Telephone: (419) 530-2696
Fax: (419) 530-4504
Internet: www.utoledo.edu
Founded 1872 as Toledo University of Arts and Trades; became Municipal University 1883, State University 1967
President: WILLIAM R. DECATUR
Senior Vice-President for Academic Affairs: JUDY HAMPLE
Vice-President for Student Affairs: DAVID MEABON
Vice-President for Graduate Studies, Research and Economic Development: JAMES FRY
Vice-President for Administrative Affairs: THOMAS REPP
Director of Registration: JOSEPH DeCHRISTOFORO
Dean of Libraries: LESLIE W. SHERIDAN
Library of over 1,000,000 vols
Number of teachers: 1,316 (614 full-time; 702 part-time)
Number of students: 20,307
Publications: *The Alumnus* (quarterly), *The Collegian, and various departmental newsletters and journals*

DEANS

College of Arts and Sciences: Dr DAVID STERN
College of Business Administration: Dr SONNY ARISS
College of Education and Allied Professions: Dr CHARLENE CZERNIAK
College of Engineering: Dr RONALD FOURNIER
College of Law: PHILLIP J. CLOSIUS

College of Pharmacy: Dr JOHNNIE L. EARLY, II
University College Programs: MARY JO WALDOCK
Graduate School: JAMES FRY
University Community College: JERRY SULLIVAN
Dean of Enrollment Management: KENT HOPKINS

PROFESSORS
College of Arts and Sciences
Anthropology:
METRESS, S.

Art:
ATTIE, D.
BASTIAN, D.
BELL-AMES, L.
ELLOIAN, P.
GUIP, D.

Astronomy:
ANDERSON, L.
BOPP, B. W.
WITT, A. N.

Biology:
GOLDMAN, S. L.
JOHNSON, K.
KOMUNIECKI, P.
KOMUNIECKI, R. W.
LEE, H. H.
PRIBOR, D. B.
TRAMER, E. J.
WHEELOCK, M. J.

Chemistry:
CHRYSOCHOOS, J.
DAVIES, J. A.
DOLLIMORE, D.
EDWARDS, J. G.
FUNK, M. O., Jr
GANO, J. E.
PINKERTON, A. A.

Communications:
BENJAMIN, J. B.
KNECHT, R. J.
RUSSELL, C. G.
WILCOX, E. M.

Economics:
LESAGE, J.
MAGURA, M.
ROY, R.
WEISS, S. J.

English:
ABU-ABSI, S.
BARDEN, T.
BOENING, J.
DESSNER, L. J.
FREE, W. N.
LIPMAN, J.
REISING, R.
RUDOLPH, R. S.
SAUNDERS, J.
SZUBERLA, G. A.
WIKANDER, M. H.

Foreign Languages:
FEUSTLE, J. A.
NORMAND, G. M.
O'NEAL, W. J.
SCANLAN, T. M.
SCHAUB, U. T.

Geography:
FRANCKOWIAK, E. N.
MURACO, W. A.

Geology:
CAMP, M.
HARRELL, J.
HATFIELD, C.
PHILLIPS, M. W.

History:
BRITTON, D.
CAVE, A. A.
GLAAB, C. N.

HOOVER, W. D.
LINEBAUGH, P.
LONGTON, W. H.
LORA, R. G.
MENNING, C.
NATSOULAS, T.
O'NEAL, W.
RAY, R. D.
SMITH, R. F.
THOMPSON, G. E.
WILCOX, L. D.

Mathematics:
BENTLEY, H. L.
CARLSON, D.
KERTZ, G. J.
KUMMER, M.
LIN, E. B.
NAGISETTY, R. V.
PETTET, M. R.
SCHWARZ, F.
SHIELDS, P. C.
STEINBERG, S. A.
VAYO, H. W.
WENTE, H. C.
WHITE, D.
WOLFF, H. E.

Music:
DEYARMAN, R. M.
JEX, D.
KIHSLINGER, M. R.
RENZI, F. A.
RONDELLI, B.
VAN DER MERWE, R. A.
WEBSTER, R. M.

Nursing:
FABISZAK, A.

Philosophy:
BLATZ, C.
CAMPBELL, J.

Physics:
BOHN, R. G.
COMPAAN, A. D.
CURTIS, L. J.
ELLIS, D. G.
IWAMOTO, N.
JAMES, P. B.
KVALE, T.
LEE, S.
SIMON, H. J.
THEODOSIOU, C.
WILLIAMSON, W.

Political Science:
LINDEEN, J. W.
RANDALL, R.
WEISFELDER, R. F.

Psychology:
ARMUS, H.
ELLIOTT, R. K., Jr
HAAF, R. A.
HEFFNER, H.
HEFFNER, R.
HOROWITZ, I. A.
McKEEVER, W. F.
PALMER, A.
SLAK, S.

Sociology:
ALKALIMAT, A.
KART, C. S.
KING, J. A.
METRESS, S.
MORRISSEY, M.

Theater:
HILL, J.
WATERMEIER, D. J.

College of Business Administration
Accounting:
FINK, P. R.
GAFFNEY, D. J.
LAVERTY, B.
RAGUNATHAN, B.

SAFTNER, D.
SCHROEDER, N.
Information Systems and Operations Management:
AHMED, M. U.
KAMBUROWSKI, J.
KUNNATHUR, A.
MARCHAL, W. G.
RACHAMADUGU, R.
RAGHUNATHAN, T.
RAO, S. S.
SASS, C. J.
SMITH, A.
SUNDARARAGHAVAN, P. S.
VONDEREMBSE, M. A.

Finance:
SMOLEN, G. E.

Management:
BEEMAN, D. R.
BHATT, B. J.
DOLL, W. J.
KIM, K. I.
LONGNECKER, C.
NYKODYM, N.
SIMONETTI, J. L.
SPIRN, S.
TIMMINS, S. A.

Marketing:
DEKORTE, M. J.
FLASCHNER, A. B.
KOZLOWSKI, P. J.
LIM, J.
OKOROAFO, S.
THUONG, L.
ZALLOCCO, R.

College of Education
Educational Administration and Supervision:
BALDWIN, G.
MERRITT, D.
PIPER, J.
RUSCH, E.
SULLIVAN, R.

Educational Psychology, Research and Social Foundation:
DAVISON, D. C.
DUNN, T. G.
GRAY, W. M.
HUDSON, L. M.
HURST, J.
JURS, S.
LOPEZ, T.
ZIMMER, J.

Elementary and Early Childhood Education:
AHERN, J.
BALZER, D. M.
CARR, E.
COOKE, G. E.
CRYAN, J. R.
DEBRUIN, J. E.
GRESS, J. R.
KOONTZ, F.
McFARLAND, S. L.
SANDMAN, A.
SHIRK, G. B.

Counselor and Human Services Education:
PIAZZA, N.
RITCHIE, M.
WENDT, R. N.

Health Promotion and Human Performance:
ANDRES, F. F.
ARMSTRONG, C.
DROWATZKY, J.
FULTON, G. B.
GRENINGER, L. O.
METRESS, E.
OLSSON, R.
PRICE, J. H.
RANCK, S. L.

Educational Technology:
ELSIE, L. J.
PATTERSON, A. C.

Secondary Education:
DEMEDIO, D.
NATSOULAS, A.

Special Education:
BENJAMIN, B.
CARROLL, M. E.
MCINERNEY, W.

Vocational Education:
PIPER, J.

College of Engineering
Bio-engineering:
CIOS, K.
DHAWAN, A.
FARISON, J.
FOURNIER, R.
LU, S.-Y.
MIKHAIL, W. E.

Chemical Engineering:
ABRAHAM, M.
CHANG, L.
DISMUKES, J.
JABARIN, S.

Civil Engineering:
ANGELBECK, D. I.
FU, K. C.
GUPTA, J.
KUMAR, A.
MOSTAGHEL, N.

Electrical Engineering:
ALAM, M.
ELTIMSAHY, A. H.
GHANDAKLY, A. A.
KING, R.
KWATRA, S. C.
LEDGARD, H.
SALARI, E.
SELIGA, T.
SMITH, E.
STUART, T. A.

Mechanical Engineering:
AFJEH, A.
BENNETT, R.
CHEN, F.
FATEMI, A.
HEFZY, M.
IREY, R. K.
KEITH, T. G.
KRAMER, S. N.
MCNICHOLS, R.
NAGANATHAN, N.
NG TSUNG, M.
WHITE, P.
WOLFE, K. R.

College of Law:
ANDERSON, R. W.
BERKOWITZ, R. L.
BOURGUIGNON, H. J.
CAMPBELL, B. A.
CHAPMAN, D. K.
CLOSIUS, P. J.
CRANDALL, T.
FRIEDMAN, H.
HARRIS, D.
HOPPERTON, R. J.
KADENS, M.
KENNEDY, B.
KLEIN, J. M.
LEAFFER, M. A.
MARTYN, S. R.
MERRITT, F. S.
MORAN, G. P.
RAITT, R.
RAY, D. E.
RICHMAN, W. M.
RIPPS, S. R.
STEINBOCK, D. J.
TIERNEY, J.

Library
Library Administration:
BALDWIN, J. F.
HOGAN, A. D.
SHERIDAN, L.

Technological Media:
KALMBACH, J. A.

College of Pharmacy:
ALEXANDER, K.
BACHMANN, K. A.
BILLUPS, N. F.
BLACK, C. D.
DOLLIMORE, D.
ERHARDT, P.
HINKO, C.
HUDSON, R. A.
LIVELY, B. T.
MESSER, W.
PARKER, G.
SHERMAN, G. P.

University Community and Technical College
General Studies:
GERLACH, J.
GLEN, M.
KRAUSE, T. J.
MILLER, K. J.

Technical Science and Mathematics:
GRECO, D.
PALMER, J.
STEIN, R. D.

Business Technologies:
DETTINGER, J. F.
LAWSHE, C. J.
POSTA, B.
RUDDY, M.

Engineering Technologies:
GALLAGHER, R.
KAMM, J.
KIME, E.
SOLAREK, D.

Health and Human Services:
LEWTON, J.
SULLIVAN, J.
TRABAND, M.
WEDDING, M. E.

Law Enforcement Technologies:
ROSSI, R.
TELB, J.

URBANA UNIVERSITY

579 College Way, Urbana, OH 43078
Telephone: (937) 404-1400
E-mail: admiss@urbana.edu
Internet: www.urbana.edu
Founded 1850
Private control
President: ROBERT HEAD
Vice-President (Academic Affairs): THOMAS FAUQUET
Vice-President (Advancement): BOB KELLER
Vice-President (Administration): KAANNE M. MORRIS
Vice-President (Student and Enrollment Services): M. L. SMITH
Dean of Students: PAULA BROWN
Registrar: KATHY YODER
Library Director: BARBARA MACKE
Number of teachers: 81
Number of students: 1,300.

URSULINE COLLEGE

2550 Lander Rd, Pepper Pike, Cleveland, OH 44124
Telephone: (440) 449-4200
Fax: (440) 646-8318
E-mail: admission@ursuline.edu
Internet: www.ursuline.edu

Founded 1871
President: Sr DIANA STANO
Director of Admissions (vacant)
Vice-President for Academic Affairs: Dr JOANNE PODIS
Vice-President for Student Services (vacant)
Vice-President for Institutional Advancement: KEVIN GLADSTONE
Vice-President for Finance and Administration: VALERIE A. HUGHES
Registrar: ANN MARIE SICLARE
Librarian: BETSEY BELKIN
Library of 120,000 vols
Number of teachers: 125
Number of students: 1,220.

WALSH UNIVERSITY

2020 Easton St NW, North Canton, OH 44720
Internet: www.walsh.edu
Campuses at: North Canton, Akron and Medina
Private control
President: RICHARD JUSSEAUME
Vice-President (Academic Projects): NANCY BLACKFORD
Vice-President (Academic): LAURENCE F. BOVE
Vice-President (Student Affairs): DALE S. HOWARD
Vice-President (Development and University Relations): JOANNE MATIKA
Vice-President (Business and Finance): JOHN WRAY
Registrar: EDNA McCULLOH
Librarian: DAN SUVAK
Number of teachers: 65
Number of students: 1,522 (1,401 undergraduate, 121 graduate)

HEADS OF DEPARTMENTS
Business and Economics: Dr CAROLE MOUNT
Communication: Dr MARK C. ROGERS
Education: Dr CAROL F. SANDBRINK
Humanities: Dr JOHN G. TRAPANI, Jr
Language and Letters: Dr CYNTHIA WISE STAUDT
Nursing: Dr JANIS CAMPBELL
Physical Therapy: Dr SUSAN A. BEMIS
Social and Behavioural Sciences: Dr PENNY A. BOVE

WILBERFORCE UNIVERSITY

Wilberforce, OH 45384
Telephone: (937) 376-2911
Fax: (937) 376-2627
Internet: www.wilberforce.edu
Founded 1856
Academic year: August to May
President: Rev. Dr FLOYD H. FLAKE
Academic Dean: Dr ABHAY TRIVEDI
Registrar: GAIL LASH
Director, Learning Resources Center: JEAN MULHERN
Executive Assistant to the President: MOSES GRIFFIN
Library of 68,000 vols
Number of teachers: 72
Number of students: 998.

WILMINGTON COLLEGE

Wilmington, OH 45177
Telephone: (937) 382-6661
Fax: (937) 382-7077
E-mail: admission@wilmington.edu
Internet: www.wilmington.edu
Founded 1870
Private control
Academic year: August to May
President: DANIEL A. DiBIASIO

Vice-President for Academic Affairs and Dean of Faculty: KATHRYN SPRINGSTEEN
Vice-President for Business and Finance: ROBERT G. LEVIN
Dean of Students: KENNETH PERESS
Vice-President for Enrollment Management and Dean of Admissions and Financial Aid: LAWRENCE T. LESICK
Registrar: MAUREEN C. HEACOCK
Director of Library: DAVID GANSZ

Library of 110,000 vols
Number of teachers: 65 full-time
Number of students: 1,203.

WINEBRENNER THEOLOGICAL SEMINARY

701 E Melrose Ave, POB 478, Findlay, OH 45839

Telephone: (419) 422-4824
Fax: (419) 422-3999
E-mail: admissions@winebrenner.edu
Internet: www.winebrenner.edu

Founded 1942
Private control

President: Dr DAVID E. DRAPER
Academic Dean: Dr M. JOHN NISSLEY
Registrar: SHARI BRENDEBERRY
Assistant Library Director: MARGARET HIRSCHY

Number of teachers: 17
Number of students: 130.

WITTENBERG UNIVERSITY

POB 720, Ward St at North Wittenberg Ave, Springfield, OH 45501-0720

Telephone: (937) 327-6231
Fax: (937) 327-6340
E-mail: admission@wittenberg.edu
Internet: www.wittenberg.edu

Founded 1842
Private control
Academic year: August to May

President: MARK H. ERICKSON
Provost: KENNETH W. BLADH
Vice-President for Business and Finance: DARRELL KITCHEN
Dean of Admissions: LINDA BEALS
Registrar: JACK CAMPBELL
Director of Library: DOUGLAS LEHMAN

Library of 367,000 vols, 1,500 periodicals
Number of teachers: 239 (170 full-time, 69 part-time)
Number of students: 2,100

Publications: *The Wittenberg East Asian Studies Journal, Wittenberg Magazine* (3 a year), *The Wittenberg Review of Literature and Art, Pholeos: Journal of the Wittenberg Speleological Society, Spectrum, The Wittenberg History Journal.*

WRIGHT STATE UNIVERSITY

Dayton, OH 45435

Telephone: (937) 775-3333
Fax: (937) 775-3301
E-mail: registrar@wright.edu
Internet: www.wright.edu

Founded 1967

President: Dr KIM GOLDENBERG
Registrar: GAIL FRED
Librarian: Dr V. MONTEVON

Library of 696,000 vols
Number of teachers: 676 full-time
Number of students: 11,878 full-time

DEANS

College of Business and Administration: RISHI KUMAR
College of Education and Human Services: GREGORY BERNHARDT

College of Liberal Arts: WILLIAM E. RICKERT
College of Science and Mathematics: ROGER K. GILPIN
School of Graduate Studies: JOSEPH A. THOMAS
School of Medicine: HOWARD PART
School of Nursing: JANE SWART
School of Professional Psychology: LEON VANDECREEK
School of Engineering and Computer Service: JAMES E. BRANDEBERRY
Lake Campus: DAN L. EVANS

ATTACHED INSTITUTES

Bolinga Cultural Resources Center: Dir LILLIAN JOHNSON.
Center for Economic Education: Dir ROGER SYLVESTER.
Center for Ground Water Management: Dir ROBERT W. RITZI, Jr.
Center for Labor-Management Co-operation: Dir SANDRA KENNEDY.
Center for Small Business Assistance: Dir ROBERT SCHERER.
Center for Urban and Public Affairs: Dir MARY E. MAZEY.
Conferences and Events: Dir TERRI MILEO WEBB.
Division of Professional Practice and Research: Dir JAMES TRENT.
Statistical Consulting Center: Dir HARRY J. KHAMIS.
University Research Center: Dir DAVID LOOK.

XAVIER UNIVERSITY

3800 Victory Parkway, Cincinnati, OH 45207

Telephone: (513) 745-3000
Fax: (513) 745-4223
Internet: www.xu.edu

Founded 1831
Academic year: August to May

President: Rev. MICHAEL J. GRAHAM
Vice-President and Provost (Academic Affairs): Dr ROGER A. FORTIN
Vice-President (Administration): Dr JOHN F. KUCIA
Sr Vice-President (Financial Administration): Dr J. RICHARD HIRTÉ
Vice-President (Information Resources): Dr MARY WALKER (acting)
Vice-President (Spiritual Development): Rev. J. LEO KLEIN
Vice-President (Student Development): Dr RONALD A. SLEPITZA
Vice-President (University Relations): GARY R. MASSA
Dean of Admission: MARC CAMILLE
Librarian: Dr JOANNE L. YOUNG

Library of 355,000 vols
Number of teachers: 589 (290 full-time, 299 part-time)
Number of students: 6,668

Publications: *Preview, Xavier Magazine, Xavier University Newswire*

DEANS

College of Arts and Sciences: Dr JANICE B. WALKER
Williams College of Business: Dr ALI MALEKZADEH
College of Social Sciences: Dr NEIL R. HEIGHBERGER

YOUNGSTOWN STATE UNIVERSITY

One University Plaza, Youngstown, OH 44555

Telephone: (330) 742-3000
Fax: (330) 742-1998
Internet: www.ysu.edu

Founded 1908
State control
Academic year: September to August (four terms)

President: Dr DAVID C. SWEET
Provost: Dr JAMES J. SCANLON
Executive Vice-President: Dr G. L. MEARS
Vice-President, Student Affairs: Dr CYNTHIA E. ANDERSON
Vice-President, Development and Community Affairs: Dr GIL PETERSON
Executive Director, Administrative Services: PHILIP HIRSCH
Director, Public Relations and Marketing: LINDA LEWIS
Executive Director, Human Resources: JEAN R. WAINIO
Director of Library: THOMAS C. ATWOOD

Library of 492,300 titles
Number of teachers: 732
Number of students: 12,222

DEANS

College of Arts and Sciences: Dr BARBARA BROTHERS
College of Business Administration: Dr BETTY JO LICATA
College of Education: (vacant)
College of Engineering and Technology: Dr CHARLES A. STEVENS
College of Fine and Performing Arts: Dr GEORGE McCLOUD
College of Health and Human Services: Dr JOHN J. YEMMA
School of Graduate Studies: Dr PETER J. KASVINSKY

OKLAHOMA

EAST CENTRAL UNIVERSITY

Ada, OK 74820

Telephone: (405) 332-8000
Internet: www.ecok.edu

Founded 1909

President: BILL S. COLE
Registrar: PAMLA ARMSTRONG
Librarian: CHARLES PERRY

Library of 275,000 vols
Number of teachers: 168
Number of students: 4,378.

LANGSTON UNIVERSITY

Langston, OK 73050

Telephone: (405) 466-2231
Fax: (405) 466-3271
E-mail: admissions@lunet.edu
Internet: www.lunet.edu

Founded 1897
Academic year: August to May

President: Dr ERNEST L. HOLLOWAY
Vice-President for Academic Affairs: Dr JEAN B. MANNING
Vice-President for Fiscal Affairs: ANGELA KELSO-WATSON
Vice-President for Student Affairs: Dr ELBERT L. JONES
Vice-President for Institutional Advancement: Dr MAJOR MADISON
Provost for Oklahoma City campus: Dr WILBUR THOMAS

Number of teachers: 143
Number of students: 3,482

DEANS AND CHAIRMEN

School of Arts and Sciences: Dr CLYDE MONTGOMERY
Department of Music: Dr MARK DAVIS
Department of Natural Sciences: Dr ROSEMARY HARKINS
Department of English and Foreign Languages: Dr EDMUND KLOH

Department of Mathematics: Dr REZA POUR-DAVOOD
Department of Social Science: Dr LAWRENCE GREAR
Department of Physical Science: Dr JOHN K. COLEMAN
School of Business: Dr SOLOMON SMITH
School of Education and Behavioral Sciences: Dr DARLENE S. ABRAM
Department of Elementary Education: Dr LESTER CLARK
Department of Health, Physical Education and Recreation: ROZALYN L. WASHINGTON
School of Agriculture and Applied Sciences: Dr MARVIN BURNS
Department of Human Ecology: Dr EVIA DAVIS
Department of Technology: CLARENCE HEDGE
School of Nursing and Health Professions: Dr CAROLYN T. KORNEGAY
Honors Program: Dr JOANN CLARK
Graduate Program: Dr ALEX LEWIS

MID-AMERICA CHRISTIAN UNIVERSITY

3500 SW 119th St, Oklahoma City, OK 73170
Telephone: (405) 691-3800
E-mail: info@macu.edu
Internet: www.macu.edu

Founded 1953 as South Texas Bible Institute; present name 2003
Private control
Academic year: August to May
President: Dr JOHN FOZARD
Vice-President (Academic Affairs): Dr RON RODDY
Vice-President (Student Affairs): DERRY EBERT
Vice-President (Financial Affairs): STEVE GILLILAND
Registrar: DEBORAH SHOEMAKE
Library Director: PATSY RUTHERFORD
Number of teachers: 59
Number of students: 600.

NORTHEASTERN STATE UNIVERSITY (OKLAHOMA)

Tahlequah, OK 74464-2399
Telephone: (918) 456-5511
Fax: (918) 458-2015
E-mail: nsuinfo@nsuok.edu
Internet: www.nsuok.edu

Founded 1888 (state purchase 1909)
Academic year: August to July
President: Dr LARRY B. WILLIAMS
Vice-President for Academic Affairs: Dr JAMES PATE
Vice-President for Business and Development: JAMES HOWARD
Vice-President for Administration (vacant)
Registrar: BILL NOWLIN
Dean of Library: BÉLA FOLTIN , Jr
Library of 500,000 vols
Number of teachers: 290 full-time
Number of students: 8,750.

NORTHWESTERN OKLAHOMA STATE UNIVERSITY

709 Oklahoma Blvd, Alva, OK 73717-2799
Telephone: (580) 327-1700
Fax: (580) 327-1881
E-mail: pbberan@nwosu.edu
Internet: www.nwosu.edu

Founded 1897
Academic year: August to May
President: Dr PAUL B. BERAN
Registrar: SHIRLEY MURROW
Librarian: SUSAN JEFFRIES

Library of 500,000 vols (including microforms)

Number of teachers: 168
Number of students: 2,013.

OKLAHOMA BAPTIST UNIVERSITY

Shawnee, OK 74804
Telephone: (405) 275-2850
Fax: (405) 878-2069
E-mail: admissions@mail.okbu.edu
Internet: www.okbu.edu

Founded 1910
President: Dr MARK A. BRISTER
Vice-President for Academic Affairs: Dr JOE BOB WEAVER
Executive Vice-President: JOHN PARRISH
Dean of Admissions: MICHAEL CAPPO
Dean of Students: TODD REAM
Assistant Vice-President for Business Affairs: RANDY SMITH
Vice-President for Religious Life: Dr DICK RADER
Director of Academic Records: PEGGY ASKINS
Dean of Library Sciences: Dr JONATHON SPARKS
Library of 252,000 vols
Number of teachers: 140
Number of students: 2,000

DEANS

Arts and Sciences: Dr DEBORAH BLUE
Fine Arts: Dr PAUL HAMMOND
Business and Administration: Dr DAN REEDER
Christian Service: Dr DICK RADER
Nursing: Dr LARA BOLHOUSE

OKLAHOMA CHRISTIAN UNIVERSITY

Box 11000, Oklahoma City, OK 73136-1100
Telephone: (405) 425-5000
Fax: (405) 425-5090
Internet: www.oc.edu

Founded 1950
Campuses in Oklahoma City and Portland, OR
Private control
Academic year: August to April
President: Dr MIKE E. O'NEAL
Executive Vice-President and Chief Operating Officer: ALFRED BRANCH
Vice-President (Academic Affairs): Dr JEANINE VARNER
Vice-President (Advancement): Dr JOHN deSTEIGUER
Vice-President (Finance): JEFF BINGHAM
Vice-President (Enrollment and Marketing): KYLE WRAY
Dean of Students: NEIL ARTER
Registrar: MICKEY D. BANISTER
Library Director: TAMIE WILLIS
Number of teachers: 100
Number of students: 2,000

DEANS

College of Biblical Studies: Dr LYNN McMILLON
College of Arts and Sciences: Dr LARRY JURNEY
College of Professional Studies: Dr PHIL LEWIS

OKLAHOMA CITY UNIVERSITY

2501 North Blackwelder, Oklahoma City, OK 73106
Telephone: (405) 521-5000
Fax: (405) 521-5264
Internet: www.okcu.edu

Founded 1904
President: Dr JERALD C. WALKER
Vice-President for Academic Affairs: Dr C. B. CLARK (acting)

Vice-President for Institutional Advancement: RONALD BOGLE
Vice-President for Student and Administrative Services: MARY E. COFFEY
Vice-President for University/Church Relations: Dr GLEN O. MILLER
Vice-President for Fiscal Affairs: DEBORAH MILLS
Registrar: GAYLE ROBERTSON
Librarian: DANELLE HALL
Library of 362,500 vols, 195,000 government documents
Number of teachers: 276
Number of students: 4,400.

OKLAHOMA PANHANDLE STATE UNIVERSITY

Goodwell, OK 73939
Telephone: (580) 349-2611
Fax: (580) 349-2302
Internet: www.opsu.edu

Founded 1909
Academic year: August to May
President: JOHN GOODWIN
Vice-President for Academic Affairs: DALE GOLDSMITH
Vice-President for Business and Fiscal Affairs: CHUCK JORDAN
Director of Student Activities: ALESHA CRUZ
Registrar: VIC SCHROCK
Librarian: EVLYN SCHMIDT
Library of 91,000 vols
Number of teachers: 69
Number of students: 1,400.

OKLAHOMA STATE UNIVERSITY

Stillwater, OK 74078
Telephone: (405) 744-5000
Fax: (405) 744-5285
E-mail: admit@okstate.edu
Internet: www.okstate.edu

Founded 1890
Academic year: August to May
President: Dr DAVID J. SCHMIDLY
Provost and Senior Vice-President: Dr MARLENE STRATHE
Vice-President for Administration and Finance: Dr DAVID C. BOSSERMAN
Vice-President for Student Affairs: Dr LEE BIRD
Vice-President for Research and Technology Transfer: Dr STEPHEN W. McKEEVER
Vice-President for Enrollment Management and Marketing: Dr MICHAEL HEINTZE
Vice-President for Information Technology: Dr GARY WIGGINS
Registrar: JOAN PAYNE
Director of Admissions: GORDON REESE
Dean of Libraries: SHEILA JOHNSON
Library of 2,470,138 vols
Number of teachers: 1,060
Number of students: 23,571

Publications: Journal of Computer Information Systems (quarterly), The Review of Regional Studies (3 a year), International Fire Service Journal of Leadership and Management (quarterly)

DEANS

College of Agricultural Sciences and Natural Resources: Dr SAMUEL E. CURL
College of Arts and Sciences: Dr PETER SHERWOOD
College of Business Administration: Dr JAMES R. LUMPKIN
College of Education: Dr PAMELA FRY
College of Engineering, Architecture and Technology: Dr KARL N. REID, Jr
College of Human Environmental Sciences: Dr PATRICIA K. KNAUB
Graduate College: Dr GORDON EMSLIE

College of Veterinary Medicine: Dr MICHAEL D. LORENZ

OKLAHOMA WESLEYAN UNIVERSITY

2201 Silver Lake Rd, Bartlesville, OK 74006
Telephone: (918) 335-6200
Fax: (918) 335-6229
E-mail: info@okwu.edu
Internet: www.okwu.edu
Founded 1910 as Colorado Springs Bible College; present name 2001
Private control
Academic year: August to July
President: Dr EVERETT PIPER
Vice-President (Academic Affairs): Dr GRAHAM WALKER
Vice-President (Business Affairs): JIM GOINGS
Vice-President (Enrollment Services): JAMES WEIDMAN
Vice-President (Institutional Development): JONATHAN MORGAN
Dean of Student Life: EDDY SHIGLEY
Dean of Adult and Graduate Studies: Dr DAREK JARMOLA
Registrar: BECKY TUPPER
Library Director: WENDELL THOMPSON
Number of teachers: 70
Number of students: 700

HEADS OF DEPARTMENTS

Business: Dr BRETT ANDREWS
Education: Dr ROBERT BONNER
Science and Mathematics: Dr RICHARD DAAKE
Nursing: PAM GILES
Humanities: Dr RANDY THOMPSON
Religion and Philosophy: Dr MICHAEL THOMPSON
Social and Behavioural Science: Dr SPENCER WILSON

ORAL ROBERTS UNIVERSITY

7777 South Lewis, Tulsa, OK 74171
Telephone: (918) 495-6161
Fax: (918) 495-6033
E-mail: admissions@oru.edu
Internet: www.oru.edu
Founded 1965
Academic year: August to May
Chancellor: G. ORAL ROBERTS
President: Dr RICHARD L. ROBERTS
Vice-Presidents: Dr RALPH FAGIN (Academic Affairs), DAVE ELLSWORTH (Finance and Operations), MIKE BERNARD (Information and Communications), COLEEN BARKER (Partner Communications), Dr JEFF OGLE (Student Services), DAVID WAGNER (University Relations and Development)
Library of 1,000,000 vols
Number of teachers: 275
Number of students: 5,000

DEANS

Arts and Sciences: Dr GEORGE THYVELIKAKATH
Business: Dr MARK LEWANDOWSKI
Education: Dr DAVID HAND
Nursing: Dr KENDA JEZEK
Theology and Missions: Dr THOMSON MATHEW
School of Lifelong Education: Dr JEFF OGLE

PHILLIPS THEOLOGICAL SEMINARY

901 N Mingo Rd, Tulsa, OK 74116
Telephone: (918) 610-8303
Fax: (918) 610-8404
E-mail: myrna.jones@ptstulsa.edu
Internet: www.ptstulsa.edu
Founded 1906 as College of the Bible; present name 1995
Private control

President: Dr WILLIAM TABBERNEE
Executive Vice-President: Dr JOHN M. IMBLER
Dean: Dr DON A. PITTMAN
Registrar: LINDA ASHLOCK
Library Director: ROBERTA HAMBURGER
Number of teachers: 15
Number of students: 185.

SOUTHEASTERN OKLAHOMA STATE UNIVERSITY

Durant, OK 74701
Telephone: (580) 924-0121
Internet: www.sosu.edu
Founded 1909, refounded under present name 1974
Academic year: August to May (and summer session)
President: GLEN JOHNSON
Library Director: Dr DOROTHY DAVIS
Library of 180,000 vols
Number of students: 4,000.

SOUTHERN NAZARENE UNIVERSITY

6729 NW 39th Expressway, Bethany, OK 73008
Telephone: (405) 789-6400
Fax: (405) 491-6381
E-mail: admissions@snu.edu
Internet: www.snu.edu
Founded 1899
Church control
Academic year: August to June (two summer sessions and two terms)
President: Dr LOREN P. GRESHAM
Academic Dean: Dr DON DUNNINGTON
Registrar: GARY LANCE
Librarian: SHIRLEY PELLEY
Library of 105,000 vols, 13,000 periodicals, 339,000 microform items
Number of teachers: 70
Number of students: 1,499
Publication: *Southern Lights.*

SOUTHWESTERN CHRISTIAN UNIVERSITY

POB 340, Bethany, OK 73008
Located at: 7210 NW 39th Expressway, Bethany, OK 73008
Telephone: (405) 789-7661
Fax: (405) 495-0078
E-mail: admissions@swcu.edu
Internet: www.swcu.edu
Founded 1946 as Southwestern Bible College; present name 2001
Private control
President: BOB R. ELY
Number of teachers: 24
Number of students: 150.

SOUTHWESTERN OKLAHOMA STATE UNIVERSITY

Weatherford, OK 73096
Telephone: (405) 772-6611
Internet: www.swosu.edu
Founded 1901
President: JOE ANNA HIBLER
Registrar: BOB KLAASSEN
Librarian: BEVERLY JONES
Library of 242,406 vols
Number of teachers: 222
Number of students: 5,226.

UNIVERSITY OF CENTRAL OKLAHOMA

Edmond, OK 73034
Telephone: (405) 341-2980
Fax: (405) 359-5841
Internet: www.ucok.edu
Founded 1890
President: GEORGE NIGH
Assistant to the President: ED PUGH
Vice-President for Academic Affairs: Dr CLYDE JACOB
Vice-President for Administration: Dr CORNELIUS WOOTEN
Vice-President for Student Services: Dr DUDLEY RYAN
Director of Public Relations: LINDA JONES
Director of Library Services: Dr JOHN LOLLEY
Library of 706,000 vols
Number of teachers: 730
Number of students: 15,400
Publications: *Alumni Newsletter* (quarterly), *The Territory* (monthly), *Vista Newspaper* (twice weekly), *Bronze Catalog* (every two years), *Central State Review* (2 a year), *Tower Review* (2 a year), *CSU Alumni Newsletter* (quarterly)

DEANS

Graduate Studies and Research: Dr GEORGE AVELLANO
College of Business: Dr DAVID HARRIS (acting)
College of Education: Dr KEN ELSNER
College of Liberal Arts: Dr C. WARREN
College of Mathematics and Science: Dr GLENDA K. POWERS

UNIVERSITY OF OKLAHOMA

660 Parrington Oval, Norman, OK 73019-0390
Telephone: (405) 325-0311
E-mail: publicaffairs@ou.edu
Internet: www.ou.edu
Founded 1890; opened 1892
Campuses at Norman, Oklahoma City and Tulsa
State control
Academic year: August to May (summer session June and July)
President: DAVID L. BOREN
Vice-President for Administrative Affairs, Norman Campus: B. MADDY
Vice-President for University Affairs, Norman Campus: DAVID MALONEY
Vice-President for Administrative Affairs, Health Sciences Center: KEN ROWE
Associate Vice-President for Health Sciences, Health Sciences Center: MARCIA M. MORRIS
Number of teachers: 1,138 (920 full-time, 218 part-time)
Number of students: 24,887
Publications: *University of Oklahoma Bulletin* (2 a month), *World Literature Today* (quarterly), *Oklahoma Law Review* (quarterly), *Oklahoma Business Bulletin* (monthly), *American Indian Law Review* (2 a year), *Genre* (quarterly), *Papers on Anthropology* (2 a year), *Comparative Frontiers Studies: An Interdisciplinary Newsletter* (quarterly), *Oklahoma Dentistry Magazine* (2 a year), *Vector* (monthly), *Better Babies* (quarterly), *Oklahoma Geriatric Newsnet* (monthly), *Chronicle* (quarterly).

CAMPUSES

Norman Campus

Senior Vice-President and Provost: NANCY MERGLER
Registrar: MATT HAMILTON
Librarian: SUL LEE

DEANS

College of Architecture: BOB FILLPOT
College of Arts and Sciences: PAUL B. BULL, Jr
College of Business Administration: DENNIS LOGUE
College of Education: JOAN K. SMITH
College of Engineering: W. ARTHUR PORTER
College of Fine Arts: MARVIN M. LAMB
College of Geosciences: JOHN SNOW
Graduate College: T. H. LEE WILLIAMS
College of Journalism: CHARLES SELF
Honors College: STEVE GILLON
College of Law: ANDY COATS
College of Liberal Studies: JAMES PAPPAS
University College: ROSA CINTRON

University of Oklahoma Health Sciences Center

POB 26901, Oklahoma City, OK 73190

Telephone: (405) 271-4000
Fax: (405) 271-3151
Internet: www.ouhsc.edu

Founded 1900

Academic year: June to May

Senior Vice-President and Provost: JOSEPH SERRETTI
Registrar: WILLIE V. BRYAN
Librarian: MARTY M. THOMPSON

Number of teachers: 981 (781 full-time, 200 part-time)
Number of students: 2,817

DEANS

College of Allied Health: CAROLE A. SULLIVAN
College of Dentistry: STEPHEN K. YOUNG
Graduate College: O. RAY KLING
College of Medicine: JERRY B. VANNATTA
College of Nursing: PATRICIA R. FORNI
College of Public Health: ELISA LEE
College of Pharmacy: CARL BUCKNER
College of Medicine, Tulsa: M. DeWAYNE ANDREWS

UNIVERSITY OF SCIENCE AND ARTS OF OKLAHOMA

POB 82345, Chickasha, OK 73018-0001

Telephone: (405) 224-3140
Fax: (405) 521-6244
Internet: www.usao.edu

Founded 1908

State-supported college

President: Dr ROY TROUTT
Vice-President for Academic Affairs: Dr JOHN FEAVER
Vice-President for Fiscal Affairs: NICK WIDENER
Vice-President for Administrative Affairs: TERRY WINN
Librarian: MARTHA WOLTZ

Library of 97,000 vols
Number of teachers: 55
Number of students: 1,393

Publication: *Trend*.

UNIVERSITY OF TULSA

600 South College Ave, Tulsa, OK 74104

Telephone: (918) 631-2000
Fax: (918) 631-2622
E-mail: elisso@utulsa.edu
Internet: www.utulsa.edu

Founded as Henry Kendall College under Presbyterian control 1894, reorganized and name changed to University of Tulsa 1920; became non-denominational 1928

Independent control

Academic year: August to May

President: ROBERT W. LAWLESS
Provost and Vice-President for Academic Affairs: ROGER N. BLAIS

Vice-Presidents: KEVAN C. BUCK (Business and Finance), JANIS I. CAVIN (Institutional Advancement), ROGER W. SOROCHTY (Enrollment and Student Services)
Executive Director of Research, Sponsored Programs and Government Relations: ALLEN R. SOLTOW
Registrar: RUTH V. LANGSTON
Director of Libraries: FRANCINE J. FISK

Number of teachers: 406

Number of students: 4,072

Publications: *James Joyce Quarterly, University of Tulsa Magazine, Nimrod International Journal, Tulsa Studies in Women's Literature, Graduate Review, Lithic Technology*

DEANS

Henry Kendall College of Arts and Sciences: D. THOMAS BENEDIKTSON
College of Business Administration: A. GALE SULLENBERGER
College of Engineering and Applied Science: STEVEN J. BELLOVICH
College of Law: MARTIN H. BELSKY
Research and Graduate Studies: JANET A. HAGGERTY

PROFESSORS

ADAMS, C. W., Law
ALLISON, G. D., Law
ARNOLD, M. T., Law
ASHENAYI, K., Electrical Engineering
BAILEY, G. A., Anthropology
BELSKY, M. H., Law
BENEDIKTSON, D. T., Languages
BERRY, J. O., Psychology
BEY, R. P., Finance
BLAIR, D. M., Law
BRADLEY, J. C., History
BROWN, C. R., Biological Sciences
BUCHOLTZ, B. K., Law
BUCKLEY, T. H., History
BURGESS, R. C., Finance
BURSTEIN, A. M., History
CAGLEY, J. W., Management and Marketing
CAIRNS, T. W., Mathematics and Computer Science
CHIANG, W. C., Operations Management
COLLIER, G. E., Biological Science
COLLINS, J. M., Finance
CONSTANDA, C., Mathematics and Computer Science
COOK, D. B., Theatre
CRAVENS, K. S., Accounting
CULLEM, C. M., Law
DE ALMEIDA, H. B., English
DIAZ, J. C., Mathematics and Computer Science
DONALDSON, R. H., Political Science
DOTY, D. R., Mathematics and Computer Science
DUGGER, W. M., Economics
DURHAM, M. O., Electrical Engineering
EISENACH, E. J., Political Science
FINKELMAN, P., Law
GAMBLE, R. F., Computer Science
GASTON, S. K., Nursing
GILPIN, G. H., English
HAGGERTY, J. A., Geosciences
HANSSON, R. O., Psychology
HENNESSEE, P. A., Accounting
HENRY, D. O., Anthropology
HENSHAW, J. M., Mechanical Engineering
HICKS, J. F., Law
HIPSHER, W. L., Education
HITTINGER, F. R., Philosophy and Religion
HOLLAND, T. L., Law
HOLLINGSWORTH, W. G., Law
HORNE, T. A., Political Science
HOWARD, R. E., Chemistry
HOWLAND, J. A., Philosophy
HUIE, M. C., Law
HYATTE, R. L., Languages
JENSEN, J. K., Communication

KANE, G. R., Electrical Engineering
KELKAR, B. G., Petroleum Engineering
KESTNER, J. A., English
KRAIGER, K., Psychology
LACEY, L. J., Law
LAIRD, H. A., English
LAMPTON, J. D., Art
LANGENKAMP, R. D., Law
LAWLESS, R. W., Mathematical Sciences and Quantitative Methods
LEVETIN, E. A., Biological Science
LEWICKI, P., Psychology
LIMAS, V. J., Law
LINDSTROM, L. C., Anthropology
LUKS, K. D., Chemical Engineering
MANNING, F. S., Chemical Engineering
MANSFIELD, M. E., NELPI, Law
MARTIN, B. C., Nursing
MICHAEL, P. J., Geosciences
MILLER, G. P., Physics
MISKA, S. Z., Petroleum Engineering
MONCRIEF, D. L., Communication
MONROE, R. J., Finance
NEIDELL, L. A., Management and Marketing
NORBERG, A. H., Music
ODELL, G. H., Anthropology
PARKER, J. C., Law
PRICE, G. L., Chemical Engineering
RAHE, P. A., History
REDNER, R. A., Mathematics and Computer Science
REEDER, R. L., Biological Science
REYNOLDS, A. C., Petroleum Engineering
RONDA, J. P., History
ROYSTER, J. V., Law
RUSSELL, R. A., Management Information Systems
RYBICKI, E. F., Mechanical Engineering
SAMIEE, S., Management and Marketing
SARICA, C., Petroleum Engineering
SCHOENEFELD, D. A., Mathematics and Computer Science
SEN, S., Computer Science
SHADLEY, J. R., Mechanical Engineering
SHENOI, S., Mathematics and Computer Science
SHIRAZI, S. A., Mechanical Engineering
SHOHAM, O., Petroleum Engineering
SMITH, P. C., Management
SOREM, J. R., Mechanical Engineering
STEID, S., Economics
SUBLETTE, K. L., Chemical Engineering
SULLENBERGER, A. G., Management Information Systems and Operations Management
TAI, H. M., Electrical Engineering
TAKACH, N. E., Chemistry
TATUM, M. L., Law
TAYLOR, G. O., English
TEOTERE, D. C., Chemistry
THOMAS, J. C., Law
TIPTON, S. M., Mechanical Engineering
TOMLINS, C. B., Art
URBAN, T. L., Operation Management
VOZIKIS, G. S., Bovaird Chair
WAINWRIGHT, R. L., Mathematics and Computer Science
WAITS, K., Law
WATSON, J. G., English
WHALEN, M. E., Anthropology
WILSON, L. C., Theatre
YASSER, R. L., Law
YEVTUSHENKO, Y. A., English
ZEDALIS, R. J., NELPI

OREGON

ART INSTITUTE OF PORTLAND

1122 Northwest Davis St, Portland, OR 97209

Telephone: (503) 228-6528
E-mail: aipdadm@aii.edu
Internet: www.aipd.artinstitutes.edu
Private control
Academic year: October to June

Pres.: Dr STEVEN GOLDMAN
Dir of Admin.: ANGELA BOSTOCK
Dir Learning Resources: NANCY THURSTON
Registrar: ROBERT TUFTS

Number of teachers: 33 full-time, 60 adjunct per quarter
Number of students: 1,538.

CONCORDIA UNIVERSITY

2811 Northeast Holman St, Portland, OR 97211

Telephone: (503) 288-9371
E-mail: admissions@cu-portland.edu
Internet: www.cu-portland.edu

Founded 1905 as a 4-year academy; present name 1995
Private control
Academic year: August to May

Pres.: Dr CHARLES E. SCHLIMPERT
Provost and Chief Operating Officer: Dr MARK WAHLERS
Dean of Students: Dr GLENN SMITH
Registrar: MICKIE BUSH
Librarian: BRENT MAI

Number of teachers: 60
Number of students: 1,600

DEANS

College of Education: Dr JOSEPH MANNION
College of Theology, Arts and Sciences: Dr CHARLES J. KUNERT
School of Management: Dr ANN WIDMER

CORBAN COLLEGE

5000 Deer Park Dr., SE, Salem, OR 97317-9392

Internet: www.corban.edu

Founded 1935 as Bible Institute; Western Baptist College 1978; present name 2005
Private control
Academic year: August to April

Pres.: RENO R. HOFF
Provost: LINDA L. SAMEK
Vice-Pres. for Business: CHRIS D. ERICKSON
Vice-Pres. for Marketing: J. STEVEN HUNT
Vice-Pres. for Student Life: NANCY HEDBERG
Vice-Pres. for Advancement: MICHAEL BATES
Dean of Education: D. MATTHEW LUCAS

Number of teachers: 60
Number of students: 900

Publication: *Corban News* (quarterly).

EASTERN OREGON UNIVERSITY

1 University Blvd, La Grande, OR 97850

Telephone: (541) 962-3672
Fax: (541) 962-3113
E-mail: dheinzma@eou.edu
Internet: www.eou.edu

Founded 1929
Academic year: July to June

Pres.: Dr KHOSROW FATEMI
Provost and Vice-Pres. for Academic Affairs: JOHN MILLER
Vice-Pres. for Student Affairs: Dr SHELDON NORD
Vice-Pres. for Business, Finance and Facilities: VIRGINIA KEY
Dean of Colleges of Education and Business: MICHAEL JAEGER
Dean of Div. of Distance Education (vacant): MICHAEL CANNON
Dean of College of Arts and Sciences: MARILYN LEVINE
Dir of Libraries: KAREN CLAY

Library of 154,000 vols
Number of teachers: 170
Number of students: 3,338

DEANS

School of Arts and Sciences: SARAH WITTE

School of Education and Business Programs: MICHAEL JAEGER
Distance Education: Dr MICHAEL CANNON

EUGENE BIBLE COLLEGE

2155 Bailey Hill Rd, Eugene, OR 97405
E-mail: admissions@ebc.edu
Internet: www.ebc.edu
Private control
Academic year: September to June

Pres.: Dr DAVID COLE
Academic Dean: Dr LARRY BURKE
Registrar: Dr JAMES WICK
Librarian: N. PRISCILLA CAMERON

Number of teachers: 15
Number of students: 175.

GEORGE FOX UNIVERSITY

Newberg, OR 97132-2697

Telephone: (503) 538-8383
Fax: (503) 537-3830
Internet: www.georgefox.edu

Founded 1891
Academic year: September to April

Pres.: Dr H. DAVID BRANDT
Dir of Admissions: BRENDON CONNELLY
Provost and Vice-Pres. for Academic Affairs: ROBIN BAKER
Vice-Pres. for Finance: MICHAEL GOINS
Vice-Pres. for Marketing and Advancement: DANA MILLER
Vice-Pres. for Student Life: BRAD LAU
Librarian: CHARLIE KAMILOS

Library of 200,000 vols
Number of teachers: 151
Number of students: 3,185

Publication: *Life* (quarterly).

LEWIS AND CLARK COLLEGE

615 Southwest Palatine Hill Rd, Portland, OR 97219

Telephone: (503) 768-7000
Fax: (503) 768-7055
E-mail: collcomm@lclark.edu
Internet: www.lclark.edu

Founded 1867

Pres.: THOMAS J. HOCHSTETTLER
Dean of College of Arts and Sciences: JULIO DE PAULA
Dean of Law School: JAMES HUFFMAN
Dean of Graduate School (vacant): PETER COOKSON
Vice-Pres. for Business and Finance: CARL B. VANCE
Vice-Pres. for College Relations: SCOTT STAFF
Registrar: CURT LUTTRELL
Dir of Library: JAMES KOPP

Library of 477,010 vols
Number of teachers: 191
Number of students: 3,641

Publication: *Journal*.

LINFIELD COLLEGE

900 Southeast Baker St, McMinnville, OR 97128-6894

Telephone: (503) 883-2200
Fax: (503) 883-2630
E-mail: admission@linfield.edu
Internet: www.linfield.edu

Founded 1849
Academic year: September to May

Pres.: Dr THOMAS L. HELLIE
Vice-Pres. for Academic Affairs: Dr MARVIN HENBERG
Vice-Pres. (for College Relations: BRUCE WYATT
Vice-Pres. for Finance and Admin.: CARL VANCE

Dean of Students: DAVE HANSEN
Registrar: EILEEN BOURASSA

Library of 135,000 vols
Number of teachers: 273 (138 full-time, 135 part-time)
Number of students: 2,313 (full-time).

MARYLHURST UNIVERSITY

17600 Pacific Highway, POB 261, Marylhurst, OR 97036-0261

Telephone: (503) 636-8141
Fax: (503) 636-9526
E-mail: admissions@marylhurst.edu
Internet: www.marylhurst.edu
Private control

Pres.: Dr NANCY WILGENBUSCH
Vice-Pres. for Academic Affairs and Academic Dean: Dr DAVID PLOTKIN
Vice-Pres. for Devt: DAVID DICKSON
Vice-Pres. for Human Resourses: JANET WILLIAMS
Vice-Pres. for Finance and Facilities: MICHAEL LAMMERS

Number of teachers: 379
Number of students: 1,253.

MULTNOMAH BIBLE COLLEGE

8435 Northeast Glisan St, Portland, OR 97220

Telephone: (503) 255-0332
Fax: (503) 254-1268
E-mail: admiss@multnomah.edu
Internet: www.multnomah.edu

Founded 1936 as Mulnomah School of the Bible; present name 1994
Private control
Academic year: August to May

Pres.: Dr DANIEL R. LOCKWOOD
Academic Dean and Vice-Pres.: Dr WAYNE STRICKLAND
Vice-President, Director of Information Systems: Dr JOE WONG
Dean of Student Services: MATTHEW RYGG
Registrar: Prof. AMY STEPHENS
Dir of Library: Dr PHILIP JOHNSON

Number of teachers: 33
Number of students: 595.

NORTHWEST CHRISTIAN COLLEGE

828 East 11th Ave, Eugene, OR 97401

Telephone: (541) 343-1641
Fax: (541) 343-9159
E-mail: admissions@nwcc.edu
Internet: www.nwcc.edu

Founded 1895
Academic year: September to June

Pres.: DAVID W. WILSON
Vice-Pres. for Academic Affairs: DENNIS LINDSAY
Library Dir: STEVE SILVER

Library of 65,000 vols
Number of teachers: 21
Number of students: 500.

OREGON HEALTH SCIENCES UNIVERSITY

3181 Southwest Sam Jackson Park Rd, Portland, OR 97239-3098

Telephone: (503) 494-8311
Internet: www.ohsu.edu

Pres.: Dr PETER O. KOHLER
Chief Financial Officer: BRADLEY N. KING
Exec. Vice-Pres.: STEVEN D. STADUM
Dean, School of Dentistry: JACK CLINTON
Dean School of Medicine: MARK RICHARDSON (acting)
Dean, School of Nursing: SANDY THEIS

Library of 180,000 vols.

OREGON STATE UNIVERSITY

Corvallis, OR 97331
Telephone: (541) 737-0123
Fax: (541) 737-2400
E-mail: osuadmit@oregonstate.edu
Internet: oregonstate.edu
Founded 1858
State control
Academic year: September to June
Pres.: EDWARD J. RAY
Provost and Exec. Vice-Pres.: SABAH U. RANDHAWA
Vice-Provost for Student Affairs: LARRY D. ROPER
Vice-Pres. for Finance and Admin.: MARK E. MCCAMBRIDGE
Vice-Pres. for Research: JOHN M. CASSADY
Vice-Pres. for Univ. Advancement: LUANNE LAWRENCE
Vice-Provost for Academic Affairs and Int. Programmes: REBECCA L. JOHNSON
Registrar: BARBARA S. BALZ
Univ. Librarian: KARYLE BUTCHER
Library of 1,403,451 vols, 1,905,093 micro-films
Number of teachers: 1,231
Number of students: 19,162
Publications: *Oregon Stater* (3 a year), *Oregon Agricultural Progress* (3 a year), *OSU Fact Book* (annual), *OSU Facts-at-a-Glance* (annual), *OSU Enrollment Summary* (quarterly), *OSU Graduation Summary* (annual), *Beaver* (yearbook), *President's Report* (annual), *Prism* (literary magazine, annual), *The Daily Barometer* (newspaper), *Research OSU* (annual)

DEANS

College of Agricultural Sciences: THAYNE R. DUTSON
College of Business: ILLENE K. KLEINSORGE
School of Education: SAM STERN
College of Eng.: RONALD L. ADAMS
College of Forestry: HAL SALWASSER
College of Health and Human Sciences: TAMMY M. BRAY
College of Liberal Arts: KAY F. SCHAFFER
College of Oceanic and Atmospheric Sciences: MARK R. ABBOTT
College of Pharmacy: WAYNE A. KRADJAN
College of Science: SHERMAN H. BLOOMER
College of Veterinary Medicine: HOWARD P. GELBERG
Graduate School: SALLY K. FRANCIS
Univ. Honors College: JON A. HENDRICKS

PACIFIC NORTHWEST COLLEGE OF ART

1241 Northwest Johnson, Portland, OR 97209
Telephone: (503) 226-4391
Fax: (503) 226-3587
E-mail: admissions@pnca.edu
Internet: www.pnca.edu
Private control
Academic year: September to May
Pres.: Dr THOMAS MANLEY
Vice-Pres. for Academic Affairs): GREG WARE
Vice-President for Finance and Admin.: NANCY BARROWS
Dir of Advancement: SUZANNE HASHIM
Registrar: JENNIFER DeKALB
Library Dir: RACHEL MENDEZ
Number of teachers: 50
Number of students: 300.

PACIFIC UNIVERSITY

College Way, Forest Grove, OR 97116
Telephone: (503) 352-6151
Internet: www.pacificu.edu

Founded 1849
Pres.: PHILLIP D. CREIGHTON
Vice6Pres. for Academic Affairs: WILLARD M. KNIEP
Registrar: TANIA M. HAND
Dir of Admissions: JON-ERIK LARSEN
Library Management Team Co-ordinator: ALEX TOTH
Library of 135,360 vols, 130,086 US documents, 1,670 Oregon documents
Number of teachers: 79 (full-time)
Number of students: 1,750 (full-time).

PORTLAND STATE UNIVERSITY

POB 751, Portland, OR 97207-0751
Telephone: (503) 725-6411
Fax: (503) 725-4882
E-mail: askadm@mail_pdx.edu
Internet: www.pdx.edu
Founded 1946
Academic year: September to June
Pres.: Prof. MICHAEL REARDON
Provost and Vice-Pres. for Academic Affairs: ROY KOCH
Vice-Pres. for Finance and Admin.: LINDSAY DESROCHERS
Vice-Provost for Graduate Studies and Research: WILLIAM FEYERHERM
Vice-Provost and Dean of Extended Studies: MICHAEL BURTON
Vice-Provost for Student Affairs: DAN FORTMILLER
Dir of Financial Aid: PHILLIP RODGERS
Dir of Institutional Research and Planning: KATHI KETCHESON
Assoc. Vice-Pres. for Information Technology: MARK GREGORY
Dir of Library: HELEN SPALDING
Library of 1,805,336 vols
Number of teachers: 1,260
Number of students: 24,284

DEANS

School of Business Admin.: SCOTT DAWSON
School of Eng. and Applied Science: ROBERT DRYDEN
School of Extended Studies: MICHAEL BURTON
School of Fine and Performing Arts: ROBERT SYLVESTER
Graduate School of Education: PHYLLIS EDMUNDSON
Graduate School of Social Work: KRISTINE NELSON
College of Liberal Arts and Sciences: MARVIN KAISER
College of Urban and Public Affairs: LAWRENCE WALLACK

REED COLLEGE

3203 Southeast Woodstock Blvd, Portland, OR 97202-8199
Telephone: (503) 771-1112
Fax: (503) 777-7769
Internet: www.reed.edu
Founded 1908
Pres.: COLIN S. DIVER
Dean of the Faculty: PETER J. STEINBERGER
Vice-Pres. for College Relations: HUGH PORTER HUGH PORTER
Vice-Pres. and Treas.: EDWIN O. McFARLANE
Vice-Pres. and Dean of Student Services: MARY CATHERINE KING
Registrar: NORA McLAUGHLIN
Dir of Institutional Research: JON W. RIVENBURG
Dir of Computing and Information Systems: ETHAN J. BENATAN
Dean of Admissions: PAUL MARTHERS
Librarian: VICTORIA HANAWALT
Library of 490,000 vols
Number of teachers: 132

Number of students: 1,396.

SOUTHERN OREGON UNIVERSITY

1250 Siskiyou Blvd, Ashland, OR 97520
Telephone: (541) 552-6111
Fax: (541) 552-6337
Internet: www.sou.edu
Founded 1926
Academic year: September to June
Pres.: MARY CULLINAN
Registrar: MICHAEL CORCORAN
Provost: EDWIN L. BATTISTELLA
Library Dir: TERESA MONTGOMERY
Library of 375,000 vols incl. bound periodicals, 200,000 govt documents, 600,000 items on microfilm
Number of teachers: 288
Number of students: 5,478.

UNIVERSITY OF OREGON

Eugene, OR 97403-1242
Telephone: (541) 346-3111
Fax: (541) 346-2537
E-mail: fdyke@oregon.uoregon.edu
Internet: www.uoregon.edu
Founded 1872
State control
Academic year: September to June
Pres.: DAVE FROHNMAYER
Sr Vice-Pres. and Provost: LINDA P. BRADY
Vice-Pres. for Finance and Admin.: FRANCES DYKE
Vice-Pres. for Academic Affairs: RUSSELL S. TOMLIN
Vice-Pres. for Student Affairs: MICHAEL E. EYSTER
Vice-Pres. for Public and Govt Affairs: MICHAEL REDDING
Vice-Pres. for Research: RICHARD W. LINTON
Registrar: HERBERT R. CHERECK
Dean of Libraries: DEBORAH CARVER
Library: see Libraries
Number of teachers: 1,168
Number of students: 17,207
Publications: *University of Oregon Bulletine*, *University of Oregon Books*, *Comparative Literature*, *Oregon Law Review*, *Oregon Business Review* (quarterly), *Physical Education Microcards*, *Governmental Research Bulletins*, *Imprint Oregon*, *Northwest Review*, *Bulletin of the Museum of Natural History*

DEANS

Graduate School: MARIAN FRIESTAD
College of Arts and Sciences: JOE A. STONE
School of Architecture and Allied Arts: ROBERT MELNICK
College of Business Admin.: DALE MORSE
College of Education: MARTIN KAUFMAN
School of Journalism: TIMOTHY GLEASON
School of Law: RENNARD STRICKLAND
School of Music: ANNE DHU McLUCAS

PROFESSORS

ACRES, A. J., Art History
AGUIRRE, C. A., History
AIKENS, C. M., Anthropology
ALBAUM, G. S., Business
ALBERTGALTIER, A., Romance Languages
ALLEY, H. M., Honors College
ALPERT, L. J., Fine Arts
ALTMANN, B., Romance Languages
ANDERSON, F. W., Mathematics
ANDERSON, M. C., Psychology
ANDERSON, S. C., German
ANDERSON-INMAN, L., Education Policy and Management
AOKI, K., Law
ARIOLA, Z., Computer and Information Science
ASH, A. D., Political Science

AXLINE, M. D., Law
AYRES, W. S., Anthropology
BALDWIN, D. A., Psychology
BALDWIN, J. H., Planning Public Policy Management
BAMBURY, J. E., Architecture
BARACCHI, C., Philsophy
BARKAN, A., Biology
BARNES, B. A., Mathematics
BARNHARD, R. J., Chemistry
BARR, S. A., Dance
BARTLEIN, P., Geography
BARTON, R. F., Theatre Arts
BAUGH, W. H., Political Science
BAUMGOLD, D. J., Political Science
BAYLESS, M. J., English
BELITZ, D., Physics
BENDER, S. W., Law
BENGSTON, M. C., Fine Arts
BENNETT, R. W., Music
BENZ, M. R., Education Policy and Management
BERK, G. P., Political Science
BEST, R. J., Business
BEUDERT, M. C., Music
BIERSACK, A., Anthropology
BIRN, R. F., History
BIVINS, T. H., Journalism
BJERRE, C., Law
BLANDY, D. E., Arts and Admin.
BLONIGEN, B. A., Econ.
BOGEL, C. J., Art History
BOLTON, C. R., Recreation and Tourist Management
BONDS, A. B., Theatre Arts
BONINE, J. E., Law
BOREN, J. L., English
BOROVSKY, Z. P., German
BOSS, J. F., III, Music
BOTHUN, G. D., Physics
BOTVINNIK, B., Mathematics
BOUSH, D. M., Business
BOWDITCH, P. L., Classics
BOWERMAN, B. A., Biology
BOYNTON, S. L., Music
BRADSHAW, W. E., Biology
BRANCHAUD, B. P., Chemistry
BRAU, J. E., Physics
BRICK, H., History
BRICKER, D. D., Special Education
BRODIE, D. W., Law
BROKAW, C. J., History
BROWN, G. Z., Architecture
BROWN, S. T., East Asian Languages
BROWN, W. B., Business
BROX, R. M., Romance Languages
BULLIS, M. D., Education Policy and Management
BURRIS, V. L., Sociology
BUSTAMANTE, C. J., Chemistry
BYBEE, C. R., Journalism
BYRD, B. K., Labor Education Center
CALHOON, K. S., German
CALIN, F. G., Romance Languages
CAMPBELL, E. A., Music
CAPALDI, R. A., Biology
CARMICHAEL, H. J., Physics
CARNINE, D. W., Education Policy and Management
CARPENTER, G. M., Recreaction and Tourism Management
CARPENTER, K. L., Linguistics
CARROLL, G. C., Biology
CARTER, L. R., Sociology
CARTIER, C. L., Geography
CARTWRIGHT, V., Architecture
CASHMAN, K. V., Geological Sciences
CASTENHOLZ, R. W., Biology
CASTILLO, D., Romance Languages
CHALMERS, J. M., Business
CHANDLER, V. L., Biology
CHANEY, R. P., Anthropology
CHATFIELD, S. J., Dance
CHENG, N. YEN-WEN, Architecture
CINA, J., Chemistry
CLARK, R., Music

CLARK, S., English
COGAN, F. B., Honors College
COHEN, J. D., Physics
COHEN, S. E., Geography
COLEMAN, E. L., II, English
COLLIN, R. M., Law
COLLINS, P. F., Psychology
CONERY, J. S., Computer and Information Science
CONLEY, D. T., Education Policy and Management
CORNER, D. B., Architecture
CRAIG, J. P., Dance
CROSSWHITE, J. R., English
CRUMB, D. R., Music
CRUZ, J., Romance Languages
CSONKA, P. L., Physics
CUNY, J., Computer and Information Science
DAHLQUIST, F. W., Chemistry
DANN, L. Y., Business
DARST, R. G., Political Science
DAVIE, W. E., Philosophy
DAVIES, P. H., Creative Writing
DAVIS, H., Architecture
DAVIS, R. L., Romance Languages
DAWSON, J. I., Political Science
DEGGE, R. M., Arts and Admin.
DELANCEY, S. C., Linguistics
DELGUERCIO, D. G., Business
DENNIS, M., History
DESCUTNER, J. W., Dance
DESHPANDE, N. G., Physics
DEVRIES, P. J., Biology
DIAMOND, I., Political Science
DICKMAN, A. W., Biology
DIETHELM, J. K., Landscape Architecture
DISHION, T. J., Special Education
DOERKSEN, D. P., Music
DOERKSEN, P. F., Music
DOLEZAL, M.-L., Art History
DORSEY, R. J., Geological Science
DOUGLAS, S. A., Computer and Information Science
DOWD, C. R., Music
DOWNES, B. T., Planning Public Policy Management
DOXSEE, K. M., Chemistry
DREILING, M. C., Sociology
DUFEK, J. S., Exercise and Movement Sciences
DUFF, S. F., Architecture
DUGAW, D. M., English
DUNCAN, I. H., English
DURRANT, J., East Asian Languages
DYER, M. N., Mathematics
DYKE, T. R., Chemistry
EARL, J. W., English
EDSON, C. H., Education Policy and Management
EISEN, J. S., Biology
ELLIS, C. J., Econ.
EMLET, R. B., Biology
ENGELKING, P. C., Chemistry
EPPLE, J. A., Romance Languages
EPPS, G., Law
EPSTEIN, M., East Asian Languages
ERLANDSON, J. M., Anthropology
ETTINGER, L. F., Arts and Admin.
EVANS, G. W., Econ.
EXTON, D., Chemistry
FAGOT, B. I., Psychology
FAIR, L. J., History
FANG, Y., Business
FARLEY, A. M., Computer and Information Science
FARWELL, M. R., English
FICKAS, S. F., Computer and Information Science
FIGLIO, D. N., Econ.
FISHLEN, M. B., East Asian Languages
FLYNN, G. C., Chemistry
FORD, K. J., English
FORELL, C. A., Law
FOSTER, J. B., Sociology
FRACCHIA, J. G., Honors College
FRANK, D. A., Honors College

FRANKLIN, J. D., Journalism
FRAZIER, G. V., Business
FREINKEL, L. A., English
FREY, R. E., Physics
FREYD, J. J., Psychology
FRIESTAD, M. S., Business
FRISHKOFF, P., Business
FRY, G., International Studies
FUJII, N., East Asian Languages
FULLER, L. O., Sociology
GAGE, J. T., English
GALE, M. K., Planning Public Policy Management
GALL, M. D., Education Policy and Management
GARCIA-PABON, L., Romance Languages
GARY, S. N., Law
GASSAMA, I. J., Law
GAST, W. G., Architecture
GENASCI, D. B., Architecture
GEORGE, K. M., Anthropology
GEORGE, O., English
GERBER, T. P., Sociology
GERNON, H., Business
GERSTEN, R. M., Special Education
GILKEY, P. B., Mathematics
GILLAND, W. G., Architecture
GIRLING, C. L., Landscape Architecture
GIVON, T., Linguistics
GLADHART, A., Romance Languages
GLASER, S. R., Business
GLEASON-RICKER, M. M., Education Policy and Management
GLOVER, E., Special Education
GOBLE, A. E., History
GOLDMAN, M. S., Sociology
GOLDMAN, P., Education Policy and Management
GOLDRICH, D., Political Science
GOLDSCHMIDT, S. M., Education Policy and Management
GOLES, G. G., Geological Sciences
GOOD, R. H. III, Special Education
GOODMAN, B., History
GORDON-LICKEY, B., Psychology
GORDON-LICKEY, M., Psychology
GOULD, E., Romance Languages
GRAFF, R. J., Fine Arts
GRAY, J., Biology
GRAY, J. A., Econ.
GREENE, F. D., Law
GREENE, R. A., Comparative Literature
GREENLAND, D. E., Geography
GREGORY, S., Physics
GRIFFITH, O. H., Chemistry
GROSENICK, J. K., Education Policy and Management
GRUDIN, R., English
GWARTNEY, P., Sociology
HACKMAN, R. M., Academic Affairs
HALEY, M. M., Chemistry
HANES, J. E., History
HARBAUGH, W. T., Econ.
HARFORD, W. T., Business
HARRIS, L. J., Law
HARVEY, S. M., Anthropology
HASKETT, R. S., History
HATON, D. S., Music
HAUSHALTER, G. D., Business
HAWKINS, D. I., Business
HAWLEY, D. K., Chemistry
HAWN, A. W., Architecture
HAYDOCK, R., Physics
HAYNES, S. E., Econ.
HECKER, S. F., Labor Education Center
HELPHAND, K. I., Landscape Architecture
HERRICK, D. R., Chemistry
HESSLER, J. M., History
HIBBARD, J., Planning Public Policy Management
HIBBARD, M. J., Planning Public Policy Management
HICKMAN, R. C., Fine Arts
HILDRETH, R. G., Law
HINTZMAN, D. L., Psychology
HO, S., Architecture

HODGES, S. D., Psychology
HOKANSON, K. E., Comparative Literature
HOLCOMB, J. M., Fine Arts
HOLLAND, M. J., Law
HOLLANDER, J. A., Sociology
HONGO, G. K., Creative Writing
HORNER, R. H., Center on Human Devt
HOSAGRAHAR, J., Architecture
HOUSWORTH, E. A., Mathematics
HOWARD, D. R., Business
HUDSON, B. S., Chemistry
HUHNDORF, S. M., English
HULSE, D. W., Landscape Architecture
HUMMER, T. R., Creative Writing
HUMPHREYS, E. D., Geological Sciences
HURWIT, J. M., Art History
HURWITZ, R., Music
HUTCHINSON, J., Chemistry
HYMAN, R., Psychology
IMAMURA, J. N., Physics
ISENBERG, J., Mathematics
JACOBS, D., Political Science
JACOBSON, J. L., Law
JACOBSON-TEPFER, E., Art History
JAEGER, M. K., Classics
JEWETT, W. J., Architecture
JOHNSON, B. R., Landscape Architecture
JOHNSON, D. C., Chemistry
JOHNSON, L. B., Fine Arts
JOHNSON, L. T., Architecture
JOHNSON, M. L., Philosophy
JOHNSTON, A. D., Geological Sciences
JONES, B. J. K., Arts and Admin.
JONES, S. I., Landscape Architecture
KAHLE, L. R., Business
KAMEENUI, E. J., Education Policy and Management
KANAGY, R., East Asian Languages
KANTOR, W. M., Mathematics
KARLYN, K., English
KATAOKA, H. C., East Asian Languages
KAYS, M. A., Geological Sciences
KEANA, J. F. W., Chemistry
KELLETT, R. W., Architecture
KELLMAN, M. E., Chemistry
KELSKY, K. L., Anthropology
KEMPNER, K. M., Education Policy and Management
KESSLER, L. J., Journalism
KEVAN, S. D., Physics
KEYES, P. A., Architecture
KIMBALL, R. A., History
KIMBLE, D. P., Psychology
KIMMEL, C. B., Biology
KING, R. D., Business
KINTZ, L. C., English
KIRKPATRICK, L. C., Law
KLESHCHEV, A., Mathematics
KLOPPENBERG, L. A., Law
KLUG, G. A., Exercise and Movement Sciences
KOCH, R. M., Mathematics
KOHL, S. W., East Asian Languages
KOKIS, G., Fine Arts
KOLPIN, V. W., Econ.
KOREISHA, S. G., Business
KRAMER, D. F., Music
KRAUS, R. C., Political Science
KRUSOE, S., Fine Arts
KYR, R. H., Music
LAFER, G. C., Labour Education
LANDE, R., Biology
LARSON, S., Music
LARSON, S. J., English
LARSON, W. A., East Asian Languages
LASKAYA, C. A., English
LAUX, D. L., Creative Writing
LAVERY, R. M., Journalism
LAWRENCE, M. S., Law
LEAHY, J. V., Mathematics
LEE, C.-R., Creative Writing
LEES, C. A., English
LEFEVRE, H. W., Physics
LEONG, A., Russian
LESAGE, J. L., English
LEVI, D. S., Philosophy

LIBERMAN, K. B., Sociology
LIBESKIND, S., Mathematics
LIN, H., Mathematics
LIVELYBROOKS, D. W., Physics
LO, V. M., Computer and Information Science
LOCKERY, S. R., Biology
LONERGAN, M., Chemistry
LONG, J. W., Chemistry
LOVINGER, R. J., Landscape Architecture
LOWENSTAM, S. D., Classics
LUCKTENBERG, K., Music
LUEBKE, D. M., History
LUKACS, J. R., Anthropology
LUKS, E. M., Computer and Information Science
LYNCH, M. R., Biology
LYONS, R. M., Creative Writing
LYSAKER, J. T., Philosophy
MADDEX, J. P., Jr, History
MADRIGAL, R., Business
MAITLAND-GHOLSON, J. C., Arts and Admin.
MALLE, B. F., Psychology
MALLINCKRODT, B. S., Counselling Psychology
MALONY, A., Computer and Information Science
MALSCH, D. L., Linguistics
MANCE, A. M., English
MANGA, M., Geological Sciences
MARCUS, A. H., Chemistry
MARROCCO, R. T., Psychology
MARTIN, G. M., Music
MARTINS, E., Biology
MATE, M., History
MATHAS, A., German
MATSUNAGA, S. R., Business
MATTHEWS, B. W., Physics
MATTHEWS, K. M., Architecture
MAURO, R., Psychology
MAVES, L. C., Jr, Music
MAXWELL, A., Journalism
MAY, B. D., Romance Languages
MAY, G. A., History
McCOLE, J. J., History
McDOWELL, P. F., Geography
McGOWEN, R. E., History
McKERNIE, G., Theatre Arts
McLAUCHLAN, G., Sociology
McWHIRTER, B. T., Behaviour and Communication Sciences
McWHIRTER, E. H., Behaviour and Communication Sciences
MEDLER, J. F., Political Science
MEEKS-WAGNER, D. R., Biology
MELONE, N. P., Business
MERSKIN, D. L., Journalism
MEYER, A. D., Business
MEYER, G. W., Computer and Information Science
MIKKELSON, W. H., Business
MILLS, P. K., Business
MITCHELL, R. B., Political Science
MOHR, J. C., History
MONROE, S. M., Psychology
MOONEY, R. J., Law
MOORE, J. R., Music
MOORE, R. S., Music
MORENO-BLACK, G., Anthropology
MORGEN, S. L., Sociology
MORROGH, A., Art History
MORSE, D. C., Business
MOSES, L., Psychology
MOSS, M. L., Anthropology
MOSSBERG, T. W., Physics
MOURSUND, D. G., Education Policy and Management
MOURSUND, J. P., Counselling Psychology
MOWDAY, R. T., Business
MOYE, G. W., Architecture
MURPHY, A. B., Geography
MYAGKOV, M. G., Political Science
NATELLA, D. C., Fine Arts
NEAL, L. L., Recreation and Tourism Management
NEVILLE, H., Psychology
NICHOLSON, K., Art History

NICOLS, J., History
NIPPOLD, M. A., Special Education
NOVKOV, J. L., Political Science
O'BRIEN, R. M., Sociology
O'CONNELL, K. R., Fine Arts
O'FALLON, J. M., Law
O'KEEFE, T., Business
ORBELL, J. M., Political Science
OSTERNIG, L. R., Exercise and Movement Sciences
OSTLER, J., History
OVERLEY, J. C., Physics
OWEN, H. J., Music
OWEN, S. W., Music
PAGE, C. J., Chemistry
PAINTER, R. W., Law
PALMER, T. W., Mathematics
PAN, Y., Business
PARIS, M. L., Law
PARK, K., Physics
PARTCH, M. M., Business
PASCOE, P. A., History
PAUL, K. H., Fine Arts
PAYNE, D. L., Linguistics
PENA, R. B., Architecture
PEPPIS, P. W., English
PETING, D. L., Architecture
PETTINARI, J. A., Architecture
PHILLIPS, N. C., Mathematics
PICKETT, B. S., Fine Arts
PIELE, P. K., Education Policy and Management
POLOGE, S., Music
PONDER, S. E., Journalism
PONTO, R. D., Music
POPE, B. C., Women's Studies
POPE, D. A., History
POSNER, M. I., Psychology
POSTLETHWAIT, J. H., Biology
POVEY, D. C., Planning Public Policy Management
POWELL, D. T., Fine Arts
PRATT, S. L., Philosophy
PRENTICE, M. H., Fine Arts
PROSKUROWSKI, A., Computer and Information Science
PROUDFOOT, R. C., International Studies
PSAKI, F. R., Romance Languages
PYLE, F. B., III, English
RACETTE, G. A., Business
RAISKIN, J. L., Women's Studies
RAMIREZ, E. C., Theatre Arts
RAMSING, K. D., Business
RAVITS, M. A., Women's Studies
RAYFIELD, G. W., Physics
RAYMER, M. G., Physics
RECKER, G. W., Music
REED, M. H., Geological Sciences
REMINGTON, S. J., Physics
RETALLACK, G. J., Geological Sciences
REYNOLDS, J. S., Architecture
RIBE, R. G., Landscape Architecture
RICE, J. L., Russian
RICE, J. M., Geological Sciences
RICE, K. S., Physical Education and Recreation Services
RICHARDS, L. E., Business
RICHMOND, G. L., Chemistry
ROBERTS, W. M., Biology
ROBINSON, D. M., Journalism
ROCHA, E., Planning Public Policy Management
ROCKETT, G. W., English
RONDEAU, J. F., History
ROSE, J., Theatre Arts
ROSS, K. A., Mathematics
ROSSI, W. J., English
ROTH, L. M., Art History
ROTHBART, M. K., Psychology
ROTHBART, M., Psychology
ROWE, G. E., English
ROWELL, J., Architecture
RUSH, K. L., Behaviour and Communication Sciences
RUSSIAL, J. T., Journalism
RUSSO, M. V., Business

RYAN, C. C., Philosophy
RYAN, W. E., II, Journalism
SABRY, A., Computer and Information Science
SADOFSKY, H., Mathematics
SANG, T., East Asian Languages
SARANPA, K., German
SAUCIER, G. T., Psychology
SAYRE, G. M., English
SCHACHTER, J., Linguistics
SCHOMBERT, J. M., Physics
SCHULTZ, K. L., German
SCHUMAN, D., Law
SCHWARZ, I. E., Special Education
SEGALL, Z., Computer and Information Science
SEITZ, G. M., Mathematics
SELKER, E. U., Biology
SERCEL, P. C., Physics
SHANKMAN, S., English
SHANKS, A. L., Institute of Marine Biology
SHAO, Q. M., Mathematics
SHAPIRO, L., Biology
SHELTON, B. S., Mathematics
SHERER, P. D., Business
SHERIDAN, G. J., Jr, History
SHERMAN, S. R., English
SHINN, M. R., Special Education
SHURTZ, N. E., Law
SIERADSKI, A. J., Mathematics
SILVA, E. C., Econ.
SILVERMAN, C. T., Anthropology
SIMMONS, D. C., Education Policy and Management
SIMMONS, W. S., Art History
SIMONDS, P. E., Anthropology
SIMONS, A. D., Psychology
SIMONSEN, W. S., Planning Public Policy Management
SINGELL, L. D., Jr, Econ.
SISLEY, B. L., Physical Education and Recreation Services
SKALNES, L., Political Science
SLOVIC, P., Psychology
SMITH, J. R., Business
SMITH, M. E., Music
SOHLBERG, M. M., Behavioural and Communication Sciences
SOHLICH, W. F., Romance Languages
SOKOLOFF, D. R., Physics
SOPER, D. E., Physics
SOUTHWELL, P., Political Science
SPALTENSTEIN, J. N., Mathematics
SPRAGUE, G. F., Jr, Biology
SPRAGUE, K. U., Biology
STAHL, F. W., Biology
STAVITSKY, A. G., Journalism
STEEVES, H. L., Journalism
STEIN, A. J., Sociology
STEIN, R. L., English
STEINHARDT, V., Music
STEVENS, K. A., Computer and Information Science
STEVENS, T. H., Chemistry
STEVENSON, R. C., English
STOCKARD, A. J., Sociology
STOLET, J., Dance
STONE, J. A., Econ.
STORMSHAK, E. A., Behaviour and Communication Sciences
STRAKA, L. M., Music
STROM, D. M., Physics
SUGAI, G. M., Education Policy and Management
SUNDT, R. A., Art History
SUTTMEIER, R. P., Political Science
SWAN, P. N., Law
SZURMUK, M., Romance Languages
TAKAHASHI, T. T., Biology
TAN, Y., Fine Arts
TAYLOR, M. E., Psychology
TAYLOR, Q., Jr, History
TEDARDS, A. B., Music
TEICH, N., English
TERBORG, J. R., Business
TERWILLIGER, N. B., Biology

THALLON, R., Architecture
THEODOROPOULOS, C., Architecture
THOMA, M. A., Econ.
THOMAS, S., Mathematics
THOMPSON, A. C., Religious Studies
TICE, J. T., Architecure
TINDAL, G., Education Policy and Management
TIRAS, S. L., Business
TOKUNO, K., Religious Studies
TOMLIN, R., Linguistics
TONER, J., Physics
TOOMEY, D. R., Geological Sciences
TROMBLEY, R., Music
TUAN, M. H. C., Sociology
TUANA, N., Philosophy
TUBLITZ, N. J., Biology
TUCKER, D. M., Psychology
TYLER, D. R., Chemistry
UDOVIC, J. D., Biology
UNGSON, G. R., Business
UPSHAW, J. R., Journalism
UTSEY, G. F., Architecture
UTSEY, M. D., Architecture
VAKARELIYSKA, C., Russian
VANDENNOUWELAND, A., Econ.
VANHEECKEREN, J., Business
VAN HOUTEN, D. R., Sociology
VAN SCHEEUWIJCK, M., Music
VARGAS, M., Music
VERSACE, G. T., Music
VETRI, D. R., Law
VITULLI, M. A., Mathematics
VLATTEN, A., German
VONHIPPEL, P. H., Chemistry
WACHTER, C. L., Music
WAFF, H. S., Geological Sciences
WAGLE, K. E., Fine Arts
WALKER, H. M., Center on Human Devt
WALKER, P. A., Geography
WANG, H., Physics
WANTA, W. M., Journalism
WARPINSKI, T. L., Fine Arts
WASKO, J., Journalism
WATSON, J. C., Theatre Arts
WEEKS, E. C., Planning Public Policy Management
WEEKS, J. C., Biology
WEINSTEIN, M. G., Business
WEISS, A. M., International Studies
WEISS, J., Romance Languages
WEISS, M. R., Exercise and Movement Sciences
WEISS, R. L., Psychology
WELCH, M. C., Architecture
WELDON, R. J., Geological Sciences
WELKE, B. Y., History
WESTERFIELD, M., Biology
WESTLING, L. H., English
WESTLING, W. T., Law
WESTON, J. A., Biology
WHEELER, T. H., Journalism
WHITELAW, W. E., Econ.
WHITLOCK, C. L., Geography
WIDENOR, M. R., Labor Education Center
WILLIAMS, J. P., Music
WILLIAMS, J. R., Theatre Arts
WILLIS, J. H., III, Biology
WILSON, C. B., Computer and Information Science
WILSON, M. C., Classics
WILSON, W. W., Econ.
WIXMAN, R., Geography
WOJCIK, D. N., English
WOLFE, A. S., East Asian Languages
WOLFE, J. M., Mathematics
WONHAM, H. B., English
WOOD, A. M., Biology
WOOD, M. C., Law
WOOD, M. E., English
WOOLLACOTT, M. H., Exercise and Movement Sciences
WRIGHT, C. R. B., Mathematics
WRIGHT, P. L., Business
WYBOURNE, M. N., Physics
XU, D., Mathematics

XU, Y., Mathematics
YOUNG, J. E., Architecture
YOUNG, M. T., Computer Science
YOUNG, P. D., Anthropology
YUZVINSKY, S., Mathematics
ZILIAK, J. P., Econ.
ZIMMER, L. K., Architecture
ZIMMERMAN, R. L., Physics
ZINBARG, R., Psychology
ZUCK, O. V., German

ATTACHED INSTITUTES

Institute of Molecular Biology: Dir FREDERICK DAHLQUIST.

Institute of Neurosciences: Dir MONTE WESTERFIELD.

Institute of Theoretical Science: Dir DAVISON SOPER.

Oregon Institute of Marine Biology: Dir LYNDA SHAPIRO.

Solar Energy Center: Dir JOHN S. REYNOLDS.

Advanced Science and Technology Institute: Dir ROBERT McQUATE.

Oregon Humanities Center: Dir STEVEN SHANKMAN.

Center for the Study of Women in Society: Dir SANDRA MORGEN.

Chemical Physics Institute: Dir DAVID HERRICK.

Materials Science Institute: Dir DAVID JOHNSON.

Center for Asian and Pacific Studies: Dir STEPHAN DURRANT.

Institute of Cognitive and Decision Sciences: Dir SARAH DOUGLAS.

Center for Housing Innovation: Dir DONALD B. CORNER.

Center for the Study of Work, Economy and Community: Dir DONALD VAN HOUTEN.

Institute for Sustainable Environment: Dir JOHN BALDWIN.

Computational Intelligence Research Laboratory: Dir DAVID ETHERINGTON.

Computational Science Institute: Dirs JOHN S. CONERY, JANICE CLUNY.

International Institute for Sports and Human Performance: Dir HENRIETTE HEINY.

Institute on Violence and Destructive Behavior: Dir HILL WALKER.

Institute for Community Arts: Dir DOUG BRANDY.

Oregon Center for Optics: Dir MICHAEL RAYMER.

UNIVERSITY OF PORTLAND

5000 North Willamette Blvd, Portland, OR 97203

Telephone: (503) 943-8000
Fax: (503) 943-7399
Internet: www.up.edu

Founded 1901
Private control
Language of instruction: English
Academic year: August to May

Pres.: Rev. E. WILLIAM BEAUCHAMP
Provost: Brother DONALD J. STABROWSKI
Vice-Pres. for Financial Affairs: ROY F. HEYNDERICKX
Vice-Pres. for Student Services: JOHN T. GOLDRICK
Vice-Pres. for Univ. Relations: Rev. THOMAS P. DOYLE
Registrar: BOBBI LINDAHL
Univ. Librarian: DREW HARRINGTON

Library of 360,000 vols
Number of teachers: 175
Number of students: 3,263

DEANS

Graduate School: Dr PATRICIA L. CHADWICK
College of Arts and Sciences: Dr MARLENE MOORE
School of Business Admin.: Dr LAWRENCE LEWIS
School of Nursing: Dr TERRY MISENER
School of Eng.: Dr ZIA YAMAYEE
School of Education: Sr MARIA CIRIELLO

PROFESSORS

ADRANGI, B., Business Admin.
ALBRIGHT, R. J., Eng.
ARWOOD, E., Education
ASARNOW, H., English and Foreign Languages
ASKAY, R., Philosophy
BAILLIE, J., Philosophy
BOWEN, E., Drama
DOYLE, R. O., Music
DRAKE, B. H., Business Admin.
DUFF, R., Psychology and Social Science
FALLER, T., Philosophy
FAVERO, T., Biology
FREED, E., Business Admin.
GAYLE, B., Communication Studies
GRITTA, P. R., Business Admin.
HODDICK, J. P., Theater
HOSINSKI, T., Theology
HOUCK, B., Biology
INAN, A., Eng.
KHAN, K. H., Eng.
KLESYNSKI, K., Music
KOLMES, S., Biology
LINCOLN, S., Chemistry
LUM, L., Mathematics and Computer Science
MALE, J., Eng.
MASSON, L., English
MONTO, M., Sociology
MURTY, D., Eng.
RUTHERFORD, H. R., Theology
SHANK, T., Business
SHERRER, C., English and Foreign Languages
SNOW, M., Physics
UTLAUT, M., Physics
WYNNE, A., Nursing

WARNER PACIFIC COLLEGE

2219 Southeast 68th Ave, Portland, OR 97215
Telephone: (503) 517-1000
Fax: (503) 517-1350
E-mail: admiss@warnerpacific.edu
Internet: www.warnerpacific.edu
Founded 1937
Academic year: August to May
Pres.: Dr JAY A. BARBER, Jr
Vice-Pres. for Academic Affairs and Dean of Faculty (vacant): COLE DAWSON
Vice-Pres. for Institutional Advancement: ANDREA COOK
Vice-Pres., Chief Operating Officer and Treas.: WAYNE PEDERSON
Registrar: TORI CUMMINGS
Gen. Library Admin.: ALICE KIENBERGER
Library of 53,000 vols
Number of teachers: 35
Number of students: 740.

WESTERN OREGON UNIVERSITY

345 North Monmouth Ave, Monmouth, OR 97361
Telephone: (503) 838-8000
Fax: (503) 838-8474
E-mail: fultzk@wou.edu
Internet: www.wou.edu
Founded 1856 as Monmouth Univ.; present name 1997
Academic year: September to June
Pres.: Dr JOHN P. MINAHAN
Provost and Vice-Pres. for Academic Affairs: Dr JEM SPECTAR

Vice-Pres. for Student Affairs: Dr GARY L. DUKES
Registrar (vacant): NANCY FRANCE
Number of teachers: 150
Number of students: 4,850

DEANS

College of Education: Dr HILDA ROSSELLI
College of Liberal Arts and Sciences: Dr JAMES CHADNEY

WESTERN SEMINARY

5511 Southeast Hawthorne Blvd, Portland, OR 97215
Telephone: (503) 517-1800
E-mail: western@westernseminary.edu
Internet: www.westernseminary.edu
Campuses at Portland (OR) and San Jose (CA)
Private control
Academic year: September to April
Pres.: Dr BERT E. DOWNS
Academic Dean and Provost: Dr RANDAL R. ROBERTS
Vice-Pres. for Advancement: DUANE STOREY
Dean of Student Devt and Registrar: Dr ROBERT W. WIGGINS
Library Dir: Dr ROBERT A. KRUPP
Number of teachers: 40
Number of students: 675.

WESTERN STATES CHIROPRACTIC COLLEGE

2900 Northeast 132nd Ave, Portland, OR 97230-3099
Telephone: (503) 256-3180
Fax: (503) 251-5723
E-mail: admissions@wschiro.edu
Internet: www.wschiro.edu
Founded 1904 as Marshes' School and Cure; present name 1967
Private control
Academic year: September to June
Pres.: Dr JOSEPH E. BRIMHALL
Number of teachers: 35
Number of students: 400.

WILLAMETTE UNIVERSITY

900 State St, Salem, OR 97301
Telephone: (503) 370-6300
E-mail: communications@willamette.edu
Internet: www.willamette.edu
Founded 1842
Pres.: M. LEE PELTON
Registrar: THOMAS H. HIBBARD
Dir of Library: RICHARD BREEN
Library of 285,000 vols, 1,355 periodicals
Number of teachers: 145 (full-time)
Number of students: 2,300
Publications: *Willamette University Bulletin, College of Law Bulletin, Willamette Scene, Willamette College of Law Journal, Atkinson Graduate School of Management Bulletin*

DEANS

College of Liberal Arts: LAWRENCE D. CRESS
College of Law: ROBERT M. ACKERMAN
George H. Atkinson Graduate School of Management: DALE WEIGHT

PENNSYLVANIA

ALBRIGHT COLLEGE

POB 15234, Reading, PA 19612-5234
Telephone: (610) 921-2381
Fax: (610) 921-7530
Internet: www.albright.edu

Founded 1856
Pres.: LEX O. MCMILLAN, III
Dir of Admissions: GREGORY EICHHORN
Library Dir: ROSEMARY DEEGAN
Library of 240,000 vols
Number of teachers: 103
Number of students: 1,650.

ALLEGHENY COLLEGE

520 North Main St, Meadville, PA 16335
Telephone: (814) 332-3100
Internet: www.allegheny.edu
Founded 1815
Academic year: September to May
Pres.: RICHARD J. COOK
Dean: LINDA C. DEMERITT
Vice-Pres. for Devt: MARJORIE KLEIN
Vice-Pres. for Admin. and Treas.: MARCUS BUCKLEY
Registrar: BENJAMIN HAYTOCK
Sec.: DAVID W. MCINALLY
Dir of Library: LINDA BILLS
Library of 752,905 vols
Number of teachers: 132 full-time
Number of students: 1,850
Publications: *Campus, Allegheny Magazine, Kaldron, Literary Magazine, Literary Review.*

ALVERNIA COLLEGE

400 Saint Bernardine St, Reading, PA 19607-1799
Telephone: (610) 796-8220
Internet: www.alvernia.edu
Founded 1958
Private control
Academic year: August to May
Pres.: Dr THOMAS F. FLYNN
Provost: Dr SHIRLEY J. WILLIAMS
Registrar: BEKI STEIN
Dean of Library and Educational Services: Dr MARTHA M. SMITH
Number of teachers: 65
Number of students: 2,136.

AMERICAN COLLEGE

270 Bryn Mawr Ave, Bryn Mawr, PA 19010
Telephone: (610) 526-1000
Fax: (610) 526-1465
E-mail: studentservices@theamericancollege.edu
Internet: www.theamericancollege.edu
Founded 1927
Ind., non-traditional, distance-education instn; professional diplomas and designations, graduate degrees in the financial sciences and management
Private control (non-profit public charity)
Pres. and CEO: Dr LAURENCE BARTON
Sr Vice-Pres.: STEPHEN D. TARR
Exec. Vice-Pres.: Prof. H. KING MCGLAUGHON
Vice-Pres. for Academics and Dean: WALT J. WOERHEIDE
Vice-Pres. for Finance and Admin.: NEAL R. FEGELY
Vice-Pres. for Marketing: KEITH E. HICKERSON
Vice-Pres. for Sales: JACK C. HONDROS
Assoc. Vice-Pres. for Information Technology: EDWARD M. MCEVOY
Assoc. Vice-Pres. for Institutional Assessment: Dr JOHN W. BAJTELSMIT
Exec. Dir, Online Learning: BILLY L. WILLIAMS
Librarian: JUDITH L. HILL
Library of 13,000 vols, 600 periodicals
Number of teachers: 20
Number of students: 35,000 (part-time and non-resident).

ARCADIA UNIVERSITY

450 South Easton Rd, Glenside, PA 19038-3295
Telephone: (215) 572-2900
Fax: (215) 572-0240
E-mail: admiss@arcadia.edu
Internet: www.arcadia.edu

Founded 1853
Academic year: September to May
Pres.: Dr JERRY M. GREINER
Registrar: BILL ELNICK
Vice-Pres. for Technology and Chief Information Officer: PARAM BEDI

Library of 136,900 vols, 56,940 microforms
Number of teachers: 304
Number of students: 3,600
Publications: *Arcadia Bulletin, Arcadia Herald, Landmarks*.

BAPTIST BIBLE COLLEGE AND SEMINARY

538 Venard Rd, Clarks Summit, PA 18411
Telephone: (570) 586-2400
E-mail: info@bbc.edu
Internet: www.bbc.edu
Private control
Academic year: August to May
Pres.: JAMES JEFFERY
Seminary Dean and Vice-Pres. for Seminary Academics: HOWARD BIXBY
Vice-Pres. for College Academics: Dr BARRY PHILLIPS
Vice-Pres. for College and Graduate School Academics: JIM LYTLE
Vice-Pres. for Student Devt: Dr FRIEDIE LOESCHER
Vice-Pres. for Business and Finance: HAL CROSS
Vice-Pres. (for Institutional Advancement: Dr DENNIS TOCCI
Vice-Pres. for Communications: TOM GATTORNA
Vice-Pres. for Enrollment Management: GLENN AMOS
Vice-Pres. for Alumni Services and Summer Ministries: JIM HUCKABY

Number of teachers: 47
Number of students: 1,142 (983 undergraduate, 159 postgraduate).

BRYN ATHYN COLLEGE OF THE NEW CHURCH

2895 College Dr., POB 717, Bryn Athyn, PA 19009
Telephone: (215) 938-2543
E-mail: admissions@brynathyn.edu
Internet: www.brynathyn.edu
Private control
Academic year: August to May
Pres.: Rev. PRESCOTT A. ROGERS
Dean: Dr CHARLES W. LINDSAY
Library Dir: CARROLL C. ODHNER
Number of teachers: 39
Number of students: 150.

BRYN MAWR COLLEGE

Bryn Mawr, PA 19010-2899
Telephone: (610) 526-5000
E-mail: info@brynmawr.edu
Internet: www.brynmawr.edu
Founded 1885
Academic year: September to May
Pres.: NANCY J. VICKERS
Provost: KIMBERLY E. CASSIDY
Dean of Admissions: JENNIFER RICKARD
Chief Admin. Officer: JERRY BERENSON
Dir of Libraries: ELLIOTT SHORE
Library of 1,000,000 vols
Number of teachers: 158

Number of students: 1,701
Publications: *Bryn Mawr Classical Review* (online), *Bryn Mawr Review of Comparative Literature* (annual)

DEANS
Undergraduate College: KAREN TIDMARSH
Graduate School of Arts and Sciences: DALE KINNEY
School of Social Work and Social Research: MARCIA MARTIN, RAYMOND ALBERT

BUCKNELL UNIVERSITY

Lewisburg, PA 17837
Telephone: (570) 577-2000
Fax: (570) 577-3760
Internet: www.bucknell.edu
Founded 1846
Academic year: August to May
Pres.: Dr BRIAN C. MITCHELL
Provost (vacant): MARY A. DeCREDICO
Vice-Pres. for Finance: DENNIS SWANK
Vice-Pres. for Devt: SAMUEL T. LUNDQUIST
Vice-Pres. for Enrollment Management and Dean of Admissions: KURT THIEDE
Dean of Student Life: GERALD COMMERFORD
Dir of Information Services and Resources: JEANNIE ZAPPE

Library of 793,936 vols
Number of teachers: 322 (300 full-time, 22 part-time)
Number of students: 3,550 full-time
Publication: *Aperçus*

DEANS
College of Arts and Sciences: Dr EUGENIA GERDES
College of Eng.: Dr JAMES ORBISON

CABRINI COLLEGE

610 King of Prussia Rd, Radnor, PA 19087-3698
Telephone: (610) 902-8100
Fax: (610) 902-8539
E-mail: admit@cabrini.edu
Internet: www.cabrini.edu
Founded 1957 by the Missionary Sisters of the Sacred Heart
Academic year: September to May
Co-educational liberal arts and sciences college, offering undergraduate and graduate programs
Pres.: Dr ANTIONETTE IADAROLA
Dean for Graduate and Professional Studies: Dr MICHAEL MARKOWITZ
Vice-Pres.: Dr JONNIE GUERRA
Vice-Pres. for Institutional Advancement (vacant): MARGARET FOX-TULLY
Vice-Pres. for Student Devt: Dr CHRISTINE LYSIONEK
Dir of Admissions: CHARLES SPENCER
Dir of Admin. Services: HEATHER CARDAMONE
Library Dir: Dr ROBERTA JACQUET
Library of 189,760 vols
Number of teachers: 194 (56 full-time, 138 part-time)
Number of students: 2,300.

CARLOW COLLEGE

3333 Fifth Ave, Pittsburgh, PA 15213
Telephone: (412) 578-6000
E-mail: admissions@carlow.edu
Internet: www.carlow.edu
Founded 1929
Academic year: August to May
Pres.: Dr MARY HINES
Dir, Adult Degree Center and Graduate Admissions: SUSAN SHUTTER
Dir of Admissions: CHRISTINE DEVINE

Exec. Dir of Corporate and Foundation Relations: BRUCE SEILING
Provost and Vice-Pres. for Academic Affairs: Dr GARY SMITH
Vice-Pres. for Advancement: Dr PAT JOYCE
Vice-Pres. for Student Affairs: Dr CAROL A. GRUBER
Vice-Pres. for Institutional Relations: ANN RAGO
Dean, Enrollment Management: CAROL DESCAK
Librarian: ELAINE MISKO
Library of 123,927 vols
Number of teachers: 255
Number of students: 2,070.

CARNEGIE MELLON UNIVERSITY

5000 Forbes Ave, Pittsburgh, PA 15213
Telephone: (412) 268-2000
Fax: (412) 268-7838
Internet: www.cmu.edu
Founded 1900
Private control
Academic year: August to May
Pres.: JARED L. COHON
Provost: MARK SCOTT KAMLET
Vice-Pres. for Business and Planning, and Chief Financial Officer: JEFFREY W. BOLTON
Vice-Provost for Computing Services: ALEX HILLS
Vice-Pres. for Devt: ROBBEE BAKER-KOSAK
Vice-Pres. for Enrollment: WILLIAM F. ELLIOTT
Vice-Pres. for Univ. Relations (vacant)
Vice-Provost for Research: DUANE A. ADAMS
Dir of University Libraries: GLORIANA ST. CLAIR
Library of 961,507 vols
Number of teachers: 2,276
Number of students: 8,514

DEANS AND DIRECTORS
Carnegie Institute of Technology: JOHN L. ANDERSON
College of Fine Arts: MARTIN PREKOP
College of Humanities and Social Sciences: JOE W. TROTTER, Jr
Graduate School of Industrial Admin.: DOUGLAS M. DUNN
Mellon College of Science: WILLIAM O. WILLIAMS
School of Computer Science: JAMES H. MORRIS
H. J. Heinz School of Public Policy and Management: JEFFREY HUNKER
Hunt Institute for Botanical Documentation: ROBERT W. KIGER (Dir)
Carnegie Mellon Research Institute: THEODORE L. WILKE (Dir)
Software Eng. Institute: STEVE CROSS

PROFESSORS
Mellon College of Science (tel. (412) 268-5124; fax (412) 268-3268; internet www.cmu.edu/mcs):
ANDREWS, P. B., Mathematical Sciences
BERRY, G. C., Chemistry
BROWN, W. E., Biology
COLLINS, T., Chemistry
FEENSTRA, R., Physics
FERGUSON, T., Physics
FONSECA, I., Mathematical Sciences
FRANKLIN, G. B., Physics
FRIEZE, A., Physics
GAROFF, S., Physics
GILMAN, F., Physics
GREENBERG, J., Mathematical Sciences
GRIFFITHS, R. B., Physics
GRIFFITHS, R. E., Physics
GURTIN, M. E., Mathematical Sciences
HACKNEY, D., Biology
HEATH, D. C., Mathematical Sciences

Ho, C., Biology
HOLLINGER, J. O., Biology
HOLMAN, R. F., Physics
HRUSA, W. J., Mathematical Sciences
JONES, E. W., Biology
KAPLAN, M., Chemistry
KAROL, P., Chemistry
KINDERLEHRER, D., Mathematical Sciences
KISSLINGER, L. S., Physics
KRAEMER, R. W., Physics
LEVINE, M. J., Physics
LI, L.-F., Physics
LLINÁS, M., Chemistry
MCCLURE, W. R., Biology
MCCULLOUGH, R., Chemistry
MAJETICH, S., Physics
MATYJASZEWSKI, K., Chemistry
MIZEL, V. J., Mathematical Sciences
MÜNCH, E., Chemistry
NAGLE, J. F., Physics
NICOLAIDES, R. A., Mathematical Sciences
OWEN, D. R., Mathematical Sciences
PATTERSON, G. D., Chemistry
RUSS, J. S., Physics
SCHÄFFER, J. W., Mathematical Sciences
SCHUMACHER, R. A., Physics
SEKERKA, R. F., Physics
SHREVE, S. E., Mathematical Sciences
STALEY, S. W., Chemistry
STATMAN, R., Mathematical Sciences
STEWART, R. F., Chemistry
SUTER, R., Physics
SWENDSEN, R. H., Physics
TA'ASAN, S., Mathematical Sciences
TARTAR, L., Mathematical Sciences
VOGEL, H., Physics
WAGGONER, A., Biology
WALKINGTON, N. J., Mathematical Sciences
WIDOM, M., Physics
WILLIAMS, J. F., Biology
WILLIAMS, W. O., Mathematical Sciences
WOOLFORD, J., Biology
YOUNG, H., Physics

Carnegie Institute of Technology (tel. (412) 268-2481; fax (412) 268-6421; internet www.cit.cmu.edu):

AKAY, A., Mechanical Eng.
AMON, C., Mechanical Eng.
ANDERSON, J., Chemical Eng.
BAUMANN, D. M. B., Mechanical Eng.
BHAGAVATULA, V., Electrical and Computer Eng.
BIEGLER, L. T., Chemical Eng.
BIELAK, J., Civil Eng.
CAGAN, J., Mechanical Eng.
CARLEY, L. R., Electrical and Computer Eng.
CASASENT, D., Electrical and Computer Eng.
CHIGIER, N. A., Mechanical Eng.
CRAMB, A., Materials Science Eng.
DAVIDSON, C., Civil Eng.
DOMACH, M., Chemical Eng.
DZOMBAK, D. A., Civil Eng.
FRUEHAN, R. J., Materials Science Eng.
GABRIEL, K. S., Electrical and Computer Eng.
GARRETT, J. H., Civil Eng.
GARRISON, W. M., Jr, Materials Science Eng.
GELLMAN, A., Chemical Eng.
GREVE, D. W., Electrical and Computer Eng.
GRIFFIN, J. H., Mechanical Eng.
GROSSMANN, I. E., Chemical Eng.
HENDRICKSON, C. T., Civil Eng.
HOBURG, J. F., Electrical and Computer Eng.
JHON, M. S., Chemical Eng.
KHOSLA, P., Electrical and Computer Eng.
KIM, H. S., Electrical and Computer Eng.
KROGH, B., Electrical and Computer Eng.
KRYDER, M. H., Electrical and Computer Eng.
KUMTA, P., Material Science Eng.

LAMBETH, D. N., Electrical and Computer Eng.
LAUGHLIN, D. E., Materials Science Eng.
MCHENRY, M., Materials Science Eng.
MCMICHAEL, F. C., Civil Eng.
MALY, W., Electrical and Computer Eng.
MORGAN, M. G., Eng. and Public Policy
MOURA, J. M., Electrical and Computer Eng.
NEUMAN, C. P., Electrical and Computer Eng.
OPPENHEIM, I. J., Civil Eng.
PIEHLER, H. R., Materials Science Eng.
PILEGGI, L., Electrical and Computer Eng.
POWERS, G., Chemical Eng.
PRIEVE, D. G., Chemical Eng.
REHAK, D. R., Civil Eng.
ROHRER, G., Material Science Eng.
ROLLETT, T., Materials Science Eng.
RUBIN, E. S., Eng. and Public Policy
RUTENBAR, R., Electrical and Computer Eng.
SAIGAL, S., Civil Eng.
SCHLESINGER, E., Electrical and Computer Eng.
SHEN, J., Electrical and Computer Eng.
SIDES, P. J., Chemical Eng.
SINCLAIR, G. B., Mechanical Eng.
SIRBU, M. A., Eng. and Public Policy
SKOWRONSKI, M., Materials Science Eng.
SMALL, M. J., Civil Eng.
STANCIL, D. D., Electrical and Computer Eng.
STEIF, P. S., Mechanical Eng.
STERN, R., Electrical and Computer Eng.
STROJWAS, A., Electrical and Computer Eng.
TALUKDAR, S., Electrical and Computer Eng.
THOMAS, D. E., Jr, Electrical and Computer Eng.
WESTERBERG, A. W., Chemical Eng.
WHITE, L. R., Chemical Eng.
WHITE, R., Electrical and Computer Eng.
WICKERT, J., Mechanical Eng.
WYNBLATT, P., Materials Science Eng.
YAO, S.-C., Mechanical Eng.
YDSTIE, B. E., Chemical Eng.
ZHU, J., Electrical and Computer Eng.

College of Fine Arts (tel. (412) 268-2349; internet www.cmu.edu/cfa):

AKIN, O., Architecture
ANDERSON, B. J. B., Drama
ANDERSON, C. R., Drama
BALADA, L. I., Music
BALLAY, J. M., Design
BAXTRESSER, J., Music
BECKLEY, J., Art
BELLAN-GILLEN, P., Art
BENNETT, R., Art
BOYARSKI, D., Design
BUCHANAN, R., Design
BURGESS, L., Art
CARDENES, A., Music
COOPER, W. D., Architecture
FLEMMING, U., Architecture
FRISCH, P., Drama
HARTKOPF, V., Architecture
IZQUIERDO, J.-P., Music
JOHNSTON, B., Drama
JOSEPH, A., Music
KEELING, K., Sr, Music
KING, E., Art
KRISHNAMURTI, R., Architecture
KUMATA, C., Art
LEE, S., Architecture
LEHANE, G., Drama
LOFTNESS, V., Architecture
MAHDAVI, A., Architecture
MAIER, J., Art
MARINELLI, D., Drama
MENTZER, M., Design
MIDANI, A., Drama
OLDS, H. T., Art
PREKOP, M., Art

SLAVICK, S., Art
STITT, M., Drama
SWINEHART, R. O., Design
THOMAS, M., Music
VOGEL, C. M., Design
WADSWORTH, D. H., Drama
WEIDNER, M., Art

College of Humanities and Social Sciences (tel. (412) 268-2830; internet hss.cmu.edu):

ANDERSON, J. R., Psychology
BALAS, E., History
BICCHIERI, C., Philosophy
CARLEY, K. M., Social and Decision Sciences
CARPENTER, J., Psychology
CARRIER, D. S., Philosophy
CLARK, M., Psychology
COHEN, S. A., Psychology
COHEN, W., Social and Decision Sciences
COSTANZO, G., English
DANIELS, J., English
DAVIS, O. A., Social and Decision Sciences
DAWES, R., Social and Decision Sciences
EDDY, W. F., Statistics
FEINBERG, S. E., Statistics
FISCHHOFF, B., Social and Decision Sciences
FLOWER, L. S., English
FREED, B. F., Modern Languages
GLYMOUR, C., Philosophy
GREENHOUSE, J., Statistics
HAYES, A. L., English
HAYES, J. R., Psychology
HOPPER, P., English
HOUNSHELL, D. A., History and Social and Decision Sciences
JOHNSTONE, B., English
JUST, M. A., Psychology
KADANE, J. B., Statistics
KASS, R. E., Statistics
KAUFER, D., English
KEECH, W., Social and Decision Sciences
KELLY, K. T., Philosophy
KENNEDY, A., English
KLAHR, D., Psychology
KLATZKY, R., Psychology
KLEPPER, S., Social and Decision Sciences
KNAPP, P., English
KOTOVSKY, K., Psychology
LEHOCZKY, J. P., Statistics
LINDEMANN, M., History
LOEWENSTEIN, G., Social and Decision Sciences
LYNCH, K., History
MACWHINNEY, B., Psychology
MCCLELLAND, J., Psychology
MASTERS, H., English
MILLER, D. W., History
MILLER, J. H., Social and Decision Sciences
MODELL, J., History
REDER, L., Psychology
RESNICK, D. P., History
ROEDER, K., Statistics
SCHEIER, M. F., Psychology
SCHERVISH, M., Statistics
SCHLOSSMAN, B. F., Modern Languages
SCHLOSSMAN, S., History
SEIDENFELD, T., Philosophy
SHUMWAY, D., English
SIEG, W., Philosophy
SIEGLER, R. S., Psychology
SPIRTES, P. L., Philosophy
STEINBERG, E. R., English
SUTTON, D., History
TARR, J. A., History
TROTTER, J., History
TUCKER, G. R., Modern Languages
WASSERMAN, L., Statistics

Graduate School of Industrial Administration (tel. (412) 268-2266; internet www.gsia.cmu.edu):

ARGOTE, L., Organizational Behaviour
BALAS, E., Industrial Admin. and Mathematics
BAYBARS, I., Industrial Admin.

CORNUEJOLS, G. P., Operations Research and Mathematics
DUNN, D., Industrial Admin. and Statistics
EPPLE, D., Econ.
GOODMAN, P. S., Industrial Admin. and Psychology
GREEN, R. C., Financial Econ.
HOOKER, J., Jr, Industrial Admin.
IJIRI, Y., Industrial Admin.
KEKRE, S., Industrial Admin.
KYDLAND, F. E., Econ.
LAVE, L. B., Econ.
MCCALLUM, B. T., Econ.
MELTZER, A. H., Econ., Industrial Admin. and Public Policy
MILLER, R., Econ.
MUKHOPADHYAY, T., Information Systems
SHAW, K., Econ.
SPATT, C. S., Econ. and Finance
SPEAR, S., Econ.
SRINIVASAN, K., Industrial Admin.
SRIVASTAVA, S., Econ. and Finance
TAYUR, S.
THOMPSON, G. L., Industrial Admin. and Mathematics
WILLIAMS, J., Industrial Admin.
ZIN, S., Econ. and Finance

H. J. Heinz School of Public Policy and Management (tel. (412) 268-2164; fax (412) 268-7036; internet www.heinz.cmu.edu):
BABCOCK, L. C., Econ.
BLUMSTEIN, A., Urban Systems and Operations Research
CAULKINS, J. P., Operations Research
DUNCAN, G., Statistics
FLORIDA, R., Public Policy and Management
GAYNOR, M. S., Econ. and Health Policy
GORR, W., Public Policy and Management Information Systems
KRACKHARDT, D. M., Organizations and Public Policy
KRISHNAN, R., Management Science and Information Systems
LARKEY, P. D., Public Policy and Decision-making
NAGIN, D., Management
ROUSSEAU, D., Organization Behaviour
STEWMAN, S., Sociology and Demography
STRAUSS, R. P., Econ. and Public Policy
TAYLOR, L., Econ. and Public Policy

School of Computer Science (tel. (412) 268-8525; fax (412) 268-5576; e-mail scs@cs.cmu.edu; internet www.cs.cmu.edu):
BLELLOCH, G. E., Computer Science
BRYANT, R. E., Computer Science
CARBONELL, J. G., Computer Science
CLARK, E. M., Jr, Computer Science
FALOUTSOS, C. N., Computer Science
HARPER, R. W., Computer Science
HERBERT, M., Robotics
KANADE, T., Robotics
KIESLER, S., Human–Computer Interaction
KRAUT, R. E., Human–Computer Interaction
LEE, P., Computer Science
MASON, M. T., Computer Science
MILLER, G. L., Computer Science
MITCHELL, T. M., Computer Science
MORRIS, J., Computer Science
PAUSCH, R. F., Human–Computer Interaction
REDDY, R., Computer Science
REYNOLDS, J. C., Computer Science
SATYANARAYANEN, M., Computer Science
SCOTT, D. F., Computer Science, Mathematics and Philosophy
SHAW, M., Computer Science
SIEWIOREK, D., Human–Computer Interaction
SLEATOR, D. D., Computer Science
WAIBEL, A., Language Technologies
WING, J., Computer Science

ATTACHED INSTITUTES

Hunt Institute for Botanical Documentation: Dir Dr ROBERT W. KIGER.

Carnegie Mellon Research Institute: Dir Dr THEODORE L. WILLKE.

Carnegie Bosch Institute for Applied Studies in International Management: Pres Dr MICHAEL A. TRICK; Exec. Dir Dr HEINZ SCHULTE.

Information Networking Institute: Dir Dr PRADEEP K. KHOSLA (acting).

Robotics Institute: Dir CHUCK THORPE.

Software Engineering Institute: Dir Dr STEPHEN E. CROSS.

Centre for Economic Development: Dir Dr DONALD F. SMITH, Jr.

VOK Engineering Design Research Center: Dir Dr CRISTINA H. AMON.

Data Storage Systems Center: Dir Dr ROBERT M. WHITE.

Environmental Institute: Dir Dr CLIFF I. DAVIDSON.

Center for Integrated Study of the Human Dimensions of Global Change: Dir Dr HADI DOWLATABADI.

Center for Iron and Steelmaking Research: Dirs Dr RICHARD J. FRUEHAN, Dr ALAN W. CRAMB.

GUIde Consortium on the Forced Response of Bladed Disks: Dir Dr JERRY H. GRIFFIN.

Pittsburgh Supercomputing Center: Dir BEVERLY CLAYTON.

Center for Nonlinear Analysis: Dir Dr IRENE FONSECA.

Pittsburgh NMR Center for Biomedical Research: Dir Dr CHIEN HO.

NSF Science and Technology Center for Light Microscope Imaging and Biotechnology: Dir (vacant).

W. M. Keck Center for Advanced Training in Computational Biology: Dir WILLIAM E. BROWN.

Center for Integrated Manufacturing Decision Systems.

Field Robotics Center: Dir (vacant).

Center for Medical Robots and Computer-Assisted Surgery: Dir JAMES OSBORN.

Vision and Autonomous Systems Center.

Robotics Engineering Consortium: Dir (vacant).

Language Technology Institute: Dir JAIME CARBONELL.

Center for Machine Translation: Dir JAIME G. CARBONELL.

Human–Computer Interaction Institute: Dir DANIEL P. SIEWIOREK.

Information Technology Center: Dir Dr STEPHEN E. CROSS.

Studio for Creative Inquiry: Dirs BOB BINGHAM, JAMES DEUSING.

Center for Building Performance and Diagnostics: Dir VOLKER HARTKOPF.

Advanced Building Systems Integration Consortium: Dir VOLKER HARTKOPF.

Carnegie Mellon/Building Industry Computer-Aided Design Consortium.

Center for the Study of Writing and Literacy: Dirs LINDA FLOWER, JOHN HAYES.

Center for History and Policy: Dir Dr JOE W. TROTTER.

Pittsburgh Center for Social History: Dir DONALD SUTTON.

Center for Business, Technology and the Environment: Dir JOEL A. TARR.

Center for African American Studies and the Economy: Dir Dr JOE W. TROTTER.

Center for Historical Information Systems and Analysis: Dir DAVID MILLER.

Language Learning Research Center: Dir Dr CHRISTOPHER M. JONES.

Center for the Advancement of Applied Ethics: Dir Dr PRESTON K. COVEY, Jr.

Center for the Neural Basis of Cognition: Dirs Dr PETER L. STRICK, Dr JAMES L. MCCLELLAND.

Donald H. Jones Center for Entrepreneurship: Dir Dr THOMAS EMERSON.

Center for Financial Analysis and Securities Training: Dir Dr SANJAY SRIVASTAVA.

Center for the Management of Technology: Dir Dr PAUL S. GOODMAN.

Center for Risk Perception and Communication.

Center for the Study of Public Policy: Dir Dr ALLAN H. MELTZER.

Green Design Initiative: Dir Dr LESTER LAVE.

National Consortium on Violence Research: Dir Dr PATRICIA S. EDGAR.

National Census Data Research Center: Dir Dr JEFFREY E. DOMINITZ.

Center for Innovation in Learning: Dir JOHN R. HAYES.

Center for University Outreach.

Intelligent Systems: Dir ALAN F. MANDEL.

Advanced Devices and Materials Group: Dir Dr THEODORE L. WILLKE.

Biotechnology Group: Dir Dr THEODORE L. WILLKE.

ASTM Engine Test Monitoring Center: Dir Dr THEODORE L. WILLKE.

Center on the Materials of the Artist and Conservator: Dir Dr THEODORE L. WILLKE.

EPRI Center for Materials Production: Dir Dr THEODORE L. WILLKE.

CMU-ITESM Institute for Strategic Development: Dir Dr PAUL S. GOODMAN.

Andrew Consortium: Dir Dr WILFRED J. HANSEN.

Brownfields Center: Dir DEBORAH A. LANGE.

Center for Arts Management and Technology: Dir DAN J. MARTIN.

Center for Automated Learning and Discovery: Dir TOM MITCHELL.

Center for Cognitive Brain Imaging: Dir Dr MARCEL JUST.

Entertainment Technology Center: Dirs Dr DONALD MARINELLI, Dr RANDY PAUSCH.

Child Language Data Exchange System: Dir Dr BRIAN J. MACWHINNEY.

Center for Advanced Process Decision-Making/Computer-Aided Design Consortium: Dir Dr LORENZ T. BIEGLER.

Institute for Complex Engineered Systems: Dir Dr CRISTINA H. AMON.

CERT (Computer Emergency Response Team) Co-ordination Center.

Spray Systems Technology Center: Dir NORMAN CHIGIER.

Center for Changing Employment Relationships.

Center For Literacy and Cultural Analysis.

Center for the Study and Improvement of Regulation: Dir Dr SCOTT FARROW.

Automated Highway Systems Group.

Imaging Systems Laboratory.

Learning Robots Laboratory.

Manipulation Laboratory.

Measurement and Control Laboratory: Dir Dr MEL SIEGEL.

Microdynamic Systems Laboratory: Dir RALPH L. HOLLIS.

Mobile Robots Laboratory.

Shape Deposition Manufacturing Laboratory.

Carnegie Mellon Building Industry Computer-Aided Design Consortium: Dir Dr ULRICH FLEMING.

Computer, Automation and Robotics Group: Dir Dr THEODORE L. WILLKE.

Center for Arts in Society.

Center for Complex Fluids Engineering: Dir Dr LEE R. WHITE.

Center for Silicon System Implementation: Dir Dr LARRY PILEGGI.

Materials Research Science and Engineering Center: Dir Dr GREGORY S. ROHRER.

Pittsburgh Tissue Engineering Initiative: Dir Dr ALAN J. RUSSELL.

Software Industry Center: Dir Dr DONALD J. McGILLEN.

CEDAR CREST COLLEGE

100 College Dr., Allentown, PA 18055
Telephone: (610) 437-4471
Fax: (610) 437-5955
Internet: www.cedarcrest.edu
Founded 1867
Private control
Liberal arts college for women
Pres.: JILL LEAUBER SHERMAN
Library Dir: MARY BETH FREEH
Library of 133,763 vols
Number of teachers: 72
Number of students: 1,527

Publications: *Alumnae Magazine*, *Exchange* (quarterly), *Catalog and Promotional Brochures*.

CHATHAM COLLEGE

Woodland Rd, Pittsburgh, PA 15232
Telephone: (412) 365-1100
Fax: (412) 365-1505
Internet: www.chatham.edu
Founded 1869
Liberal arts undergraduate college for women; masters degree programmes open to women and men
Pres.: ESTHER L. BARAZZONE
Vice-Pres. for Devt and Alumni Affairs: ANNA DOERING
Vice-Pres. for Academic Affairs: LAURA ARMESTO
Vice-Pres for Student Affairs and Dean of Students: JANICE EDWARDS
Vice-Pres. for Admissions: MICHAEL POLL
Librarian (vacant)
Library of 120,000 vols
Number of teachers: 65
Number of students: 1,600.

CHESTNUT HILL COLLEGE

9601 Germantown Ave, Philadelphia, PA 19118
Telephone: (215) 248-7000
Fax: (215) 248-7056
Internet: www.chc.edu
Founded 1924
Pres.: CAROL JEAB VALE
Sr Vice-President and Vice-Pres. for Academic Affairs: WILLIAM T. WALKER

Vice-Pres. for Institutional Advancement: KENNETH M. HICKS
Librarian: MARY JO LARKIN
Library of 135,554 vols
Number of teachers: 120
Number of students: 1,543.

COLLEGE MISERICORDIA

301 Lake St, Dallas, PA 18612
Telephone: (570) 674-6400
E-mail: admiss@misericordia.edu
Internet: www.misericordia.edu
Founded 1924
Private control
Academic year: August to May
Pres.: Dr MICHAEL A. MacDOWELL
Dean of Students: JEAN MESSAROS
Registrar: EDWARD LAHART
Library Dir: BARBARA BURD
Number of teachers: 145
Number of students: 2,358.

CURTIS INSTITUTE OF MUSIC

1726 Locust St, Philadelphia, PA 19103
Telephone: (215) 893-5252
Fax: (215) 893-9065
E-mail: info@curtis.edu
Internet: www.curtis.edu
Founded 1924
Academic year: September to May
Pres. and Dir: ROBERTO DIAZ
Vice-Pres. for Devt: ELIZABETH A. WRIGHT
Exec. Vice-Pres. for Finance and Admin.: ELIZABETH WARSHAWER
Dean: ROBERT FITZPATRICK
Registrar: PAUL BRYAN
Head Librarian: ELIZABETH WALKER
Library of 60,000 vols, musical scores and recordings
Number of teachers: 82 (mainly part-time)
Number of students: 169.

DELAWARE VALLEY COLLEGE OF SCIENCE AND AGRICULTURE

Doylestown, PA 18901
Telephone: (215) 345-1500
Fax: (215) 345-8916
E-mail: leamer@devalcol.edu
Internet: www.devalcol.edu
Founded 1896
Academic year: August to May
Pres.: JOSEPH S. BROSNAN
Vice-Pres for Academic Affairs and Dean of Faculty: Dr DOROTHY A. PRISCO
Registrar: ROBERT P. MORAN
Vice-Pres. for Institutional Advancement: JASON KETTER
Library Dir: PETER KUPERSMITH
Library of 73,600 vols
Number of teachers: 81
Number of students: 1,380.

DESALES UNIVERSITY

2755 Station Ave, Center Valley, PA 18034-9568
Telephone: (610) 282-1100
E-mail: admiss@desales.edu
Internet: www.desales.edu
Founded 1964 as Allentown College of St Francis de Sales; present name 2001
Private control
Academic year: August to May
Pres.: Fr BERNARD O'CONNOR
Sr Vice-Pres.: Rev. ALEXANDER T. POCETTO
Provost and Vice-Pres. for Academic Affairs: Dr KAREN DOYLE WALTON
Vice-Pres. for Program and Strategic Devt: Dr MOHAMED LATIB

Vice-Pres. for Admin., Finance and Technology: WILLARD H. CRESSMAN
Vice-Pres. for Institutional Advancement: THOMAS L. CAMPBELL
Registrar: THOMAS MANTONI
Library Dir: DEBORAH MALONE
Number of teachers: 60
Number of students: 2,225 (1,445 undergraduate, 780 postgraduate and evening).

DICKINSON COLLEGE

POB 1773, Carlisle, PA 17013-2896
Telephone: (717) 243-5121
Fax: (717) 245-1899
Internet: www.dickinson.edu
Founded 1783
Academic year: August to May
Pres.: WILLIAM G. DURDEN
Dean of Students: APRIL VARI
Registrar: KAREN WEIKEL
Dir of Library: ELEANOR MITCHELL
Number of teachers: 210
Number of students: 2,321

Publications: *The Dickinson Review* (annual), *John & Mary's Journal* (published by Friends of the Library), *Frontiers* (annual), *Glossen* (3 or 4 a year and online).

DREXEL UNIVERSITY

3141 Chestnut St, Philadelphia, PA 19104
Telephone: (215) 895-2000
Fax: (215) 895-1414
E-mail: enroll@drexel.edu
Internet: www.drexel.edu
Founded 1891 as Drexel Institute of Art, Science and Industry; current name and status 1970; assumed full control of the collective instns formerly known as MCP Hahnemann Univ. (previously Allegheny Univ. of the Health Sciences) in 2002
Private control
Academic year: September to August
Pres.: Dr CONSTANTINE N. PAPADAKIS
Provost and Sr Vice-Pres. for Academic Affairs: STEPHEN W. DIRECTOR
Sr Vice-Pres. for Finance and Treas.: THOMAS J. ELZEY
Sr Vice-Pres. for Institutional Advancement: ELIZABETH A. DALE
Sr Vice-Pres. for Student Life and Admin. Services: JAMES R. TUCKER
Vice-Pres. for Govt and Community Relations: BRIAN KEECH
Vice-Pres. for Information Resources and Technology: Dr JOHN A. BIELEC
Vice-Pres. for Univ. Relations: PHILIP TERRANOVA
Vice-Provost for Research and Graduate Studies: KENNETH BLANK
Dir of Libraries: JANE G. BRYAN
Library of 570,335 vols
Number of teachers: 1,760 (1,044 full-time, 716 part-time)
Number of students: 17,000 (11,613 undergraduate, 5,387 postgraduate)

DEANS

College of Arts and Sciences: Dr DONNA MURASCO
Bennett S. LeBow College of Business: Dr GEORGE P. TSETSEKOS
College of Eng.: Dr SELCUK GUCERI
College of Information Science and Technology: Dr DAVID E. FENSKE
College of Media Arts and Design: JONATHAN ESTRIN
Drexel Univ. College of Medicine: Dr STEPHEN KLASKO
College of Nursing and Health Professions: Dr GLORIA F. DONNELLY
School of Public Health: Dr MARLA GOLD

Richard C. Goodwin College of Evening and Professional Studies: Dr HORACIO SOSA
Pennoni Honors College: Dr MARK GREEN-BURG

DIRECTORS

School of Biomedical Eng., Science and Health Systems: Dr BANU ONARAL
School of Education: Dr MARK GREENBURG
Athletics: Dr ERIC ZILLMER

DUQUESNE UNIVERSITY

600 Forbes Ave, Pittsburgh, PA 15282
Telephone: (412) 396-6000
E-mail: president@duq.edu
Internet: www.duq.edu
Founded 1878; chartered 1911
Private control
Language of instruction: English
Academic year: August to May
Pres.: Dr CHARLES J. DOUGHERTY
Vice-Pres. for Management and Business: STEPHEN A. SCHILLO
Provost and Academic Vice-Pres.: Dr RALPH L. PEARSON
Exec. Vice-Pres. for Student Life: Rev. SEAN M. HOGAN
Vice-Pres. for Institutional Advancement: JOHN PLANTE
Registrar: PATRICIA JAKUB
Librarian: Dr LAVERNA SAUNDERS
Library of 723,919 vols, 328,312 microforms
Number of teachers: 874 (414 full-time, 460 part-time)
Number of students: 9,722
Publications: *Classical World* (quarterly), *Duquesne Law Review* (quarterly)

DEANS

McAnulty College and Graduate School of Liberal Arts: Dr FRANCESCO C. CESAREO
Palumbo School of Business Admin.: JAMES C. STALDER
Bayer School of Natural and Environmental Sciences: Dr DAVID SEYBERT
School of Education: Dr RICK R. McCOWN
Rangos School of Health Sciences: Dr GREGORY H. FRAZER
School of Law: NICHOLAS P. CAFARDI
School of Music: Dr EDWARD KOCHER
School of Nursing: Dr EILEEN ZUNGOLO
Mylan School of Pharmacy: Dr R. PETE VANDERVEEN
School of Leadership and Professional Advancement: Dr BENJAMIN HODES

PALMER THEOLOGICAL SEMINARY

6 East Lancaster Ave, Wynnewood, PA 19096
Telephone: (610) 896-5000
Fax: (610) 649-3834
E-mail: semadmis@eastern.edu
Internet: www.palmerseminary.edu
Founded 1925
Founded as Eastern Baptist Theological Seminary; present name 2005
Private control
Seminary Pres.: WALLACE CHARLES SMITH
Univ. Pres.: DAVID R. BLACK
Vice-Pres. and Academic Dean: ELOUISE RENICH FRASER
Vice-Pres. of Finance and Chief Operating Officer: ANUP KAPUR
Registrar: CRAIG MILLER
Library Dir: MELODY MAZUK
Number of teachers: 55
Number of students: 700.

EASTERN UNIVERSITY

1300 Eagle Rd, St Davids, PA 19087-3696
Telephone: (610) 341-5800
Fax: (610) 341-1377
Internet: www.eastern.edu
Founded 1932 as a dept of Eastern Baptist Theological Seminary; became a separate instn as Eastern Baptist College 1952; renamed Eastern College 1972; present name and status 2001
Academic year: August to May
Pres.: BRYAN STEVENSON
Exec. Vice-Pres.: HAROLD HOWARD
Chief Operating Officer: A. WESLEY BRYAN
Chief Academic Officer, and Academic Dean (Undergraduate): DAVID FRASER
Academic Dean (Graduate and Professional): EFRAIN RAMIREZ
Academic Dean (Campolo School): VIVIAN NIX-EARLY
Academic Dean (Junior College): SARA MILES
Academic Dean (Honors College): ALLEN GUELZO
Vice-Pres. for Student Devt: THEODORE J. CHAMBERLAIN
Vice-Pres. for Enrollment Management: LEONARD JAMISON
Librarian: JAMES L. SAUER
Library of 260,000 vols, 6,000 online journals
Number of teachers: 335
Number of students: 3,700.

ELIZABETHTOWN COLLEGE

One Alpha Dr, Elizabethtown, PA 17022-2298
Telephone: (717) 361-1000
Internet: www.etown.edu
Founded 1899
Pres.: THEODORE E. LONG
Provost: SUSAN TRAVERSO
Vice-Pres. for Advancement: DAVID C. BEIDLEMAN
Library of 180,000 vols
Number of teachers: 125
Number of students: 1,900.

EVANGELICAL SCHOOL OF THEOLOGY

121 South College St, Myerstown, PA 17067
Telephone: (717) 866-5775
Fax: (717) 866-4667
E-mail: admissions@evangelical.edu
Internet: www.evangelical.edu
Private control
Pres.: Dr DENNIS P. HOLLINGER
Vice-Pres. (Institutional Advancement): ANN E. STEEL
Vice-Pres. for Academic Affairs and Dean of Faculty: JOHN V. TORNFELT
Head Librarian: TERRY M. HEISEY
Number of teachers: 15
Number of students: 150.

FRANKLIN AND MARSHALL COLLEGE

POB 3003, Lancaster, PA 17604-3003
Telephone: (717) 291-3911
Internet: www.fandm.edu
Franklin College founded in 1787, Marshall College founded in 1836; merged in 1853
Pres.: JOHN A. FRY
Dean: KENT TRACHTE
Provost: ANN STEINER
Librarian (vacant): PAMELA SNELSON
Library of 360,000 vols
Number of teachers: 152
Number of students: 1,853.

GANNON UNIVERSITY

109 University Sq.e, Erie, PA 16541-0001
Telephone: (814) 871-7000

Internet: www.gannon.edu
Founded 1925
Pres.: Dr ANTOINE M. GARIBALDI
Provost and Vice-Pres. for Academic Affairs: KEITH TAYLOR
Dean of Student Services: WARD McCRACKEN
Library Dir: MARION GALLIVAN
Library of 211,000 vols, 2,650 periodicals
Number of teachers: 202 full-time
Number of teachers: 143 part-time
Number of students: 3,500.

GENEVA COLLEGE

3200 College Ave, Beaver Falls, PA 15010
Telephone: (724) 846-5100
Fax: (724) 847-6687
E-mail: geneva@geneva.edu
Internet: www.geneva.edu
Founded 1848
Academic year: August to May
Pres.: KEN SMITH
Chief Financial Officer (vacant): MIKE FOX
Vice-Pres. for Academic Affairs: KEN CARSON
Registrar: ANN WOLLMAN
Library Dir: JOHN DONCEVIC
Library of 404,500 vols, incl. microforms
Number of teachers: 90
Number of students: 2,000.

GETTYSBURG COLLEGE

300 North Washington St, Gettysburg, PA 17325
Telephone: (717) 337-6000
Fax: (717) 337-6008
E-mail: admiss@gettysburg.edu
Internet: www.gettysburg.edu
Founded 1832 as Pennsylvania College; present name 1921
Academic year: August to May
Pres.: KATHERINE HALEY WILL
Provost: JANET MORGAN RIGGS
Vice-Pres. for College Life and Dean of Students: JULIE L. RAMSEY
Dir of Admissions: GAIL SWEEZEY
Library of 350,000 vols
Number of teachers: 174
Number of students: 2,200
Publication: *Gettysburg Review.*

GRATZ COLLEGE

7605 Old York Rd, Melrose Park, PA 19027
Telephone: (215) 635-7300
Fax: (215) 635-7399
E-mail: admissions@gratz.edu
Internet: www.gratzcollege.edu
Founded 1895
Private control
Pres.: Dr JONATHAN ROSENBAUM
Dean for Academic Affairs: Dr JERRY M. KUTNICK
Library Dir: ELIEZER M. WISE
Number of teachers: 15
Number of students: 150.

GROVE CITY COLLEGE

100 Campus Dr., Grove City, PA 16127
Telephone: (724) 458-2000
E-mail: admissions@gcc.edu
Internet: www.gcc.edu
Founded 1876
Private control
Academic year: August to May
Pres.: Dr RICHARD G. JEWELL
Provost and Vice-Pres. for Academic Affairs: Dr WILLIAM P. ANDERSON, Jr
Vice-Pres. for Operations: THOMAS W. GREGG

Vice-Pres. for Institutional Advancement: THOMAS J. PAPPALARDO
Vice-Pres. for Student Life: Dr JEAN-NOEL THOMPSON
Vice-Pres. for Financial Affairs: ROGER K. TOWLE
Dean of Int. Studies, Graduate Advancement and Faculty Devt: Dr CHARLES W. DUNN
Registrar: JOHN G. INMAN
Library Dir: DIANE H. GRUNDY
Number of teachers: 115
Number of students: 2,250

DEANS

School of Arts and Letters: Dr JOHN A. SPARKS
School of Science and Eng.: JOSEPH F. GONCZ, Jr

GWYNEDD-MERCY COLLEGE

1325 Sumneytown Pike, POB 901, Gwynedd Valley, PA 19437-0901
Telephone: (215) 646-7300
E-mail: admissions@gmc.edu
Internet: www.gmc.edu
Campuses at Gwynedd Valley and Fort Washington
Founded 1948 as Gwynedd-Mercy Junior College; present name 1963
Private control
Pres.: Dr KATHLEEN OWENS
Vice-Pres. for Student Services: Dr CHERYL LYNN HORSEY
Vice-Pres. for Institutional Advancement: GERALD MCLAUGHLIN
Vice-Pres. for Finance and Admin.: KEVIN O'FLAHERTY
Vice-Pres. for Enrollment Management: JAMES ABBUHL
Vice-Pres. for Academic Affairs: Dr DENISE WILBUR
Registrar: THERESA ANDERSON
Library Dir: KATHLEEN MULROY
Number of teachers: 193
Number of students: 2,429

DEANS

School of Allied Health Professions: LINDA REILLY
School of Arts and Sciences: (vacant)
School of Business and Computer Information Sciences: JOANNE TROTTER
School of Education: LORRAINE CAVALIERE
School of Nursing: ANDREA HOLLINGSWORTH

HAVERFORD COLLEGE

370 Lancaster Ave, Haverford, PA 19041-1392
Telephone: (610) 896-1000
Fax: (610) 896-1224
Internet: www.haverford.edu
An ind. co-educational liberal arts college
Founded 1833 by the Soc. of Friends
Academic year: September to May
Pres.: Dr THOMAS R. TRITTON
Vice-Pres. for Institutional Advancement: JILL SHERMAN
Treas. and Vice-Pres. for Admin. and Finance: G. RICHARD WYNN
Dean of Admissions: JESS H. LORD
Registrar: LEE WATKINS
Dean of College: GEORGE KANNERSTEIN
Librarian: ROBERT KIEFT
Library of 425,000 vols
Number of teachers: 109 (95 full-time, 14 part-time)
Number of students: 1,147
Publications: Haverford Newsletter (quarterly), Haverford Magazine (3 a year).

HOLY FAMILY UNIVERSITY

Grand and Frankford Aves, Philadelphia, PA 19114
Telephone: (215) 637-7700
Fax: (215) 824-2438
E-mail: admissions@holyfamily.edu
Internet: www.holyfamily.edu
Founded 1954
Academic year: August to May (2 semesters)
Pres.: Sister Dr FRANCESCA ONLEY
Exec. Dir of Undergraduate Admissions: ROBERTA NOLAN
Dir of Library Services: LORI SCHWABENBAUER
Library of 106,000 vols
Number of teachers: 256
Number of students: 2,100
Publications: Bulletin Shield, College Catalog, Familogue (annually), The Family Tree, Folio, Tri-Lite
Degree programs in the liberal arts, business admin., education, medical technology, nursing, fire science admin., interdisciplinary programs, medical imaging, science, mathematics. Masters programs in counselling psychology, education, nursing, human resources, computer communications management.

IMMACULATA UNIVERSITY

1145 King Rd, Immaculata, PA 19345
Telephone: (610) 647-4400
Fax: (610) 251-1668
Internet: www.immaculata.edu
Founded 1920 as Villa Maria College; became Immaculata College 1929; present name and status 2002
Pres.: Sister R. PATRICIA FADDEN
Registrar: JANICE BATES
Dir of Admissions: REBECCA BOWLBY
Library Dir: JEFFREY ROLLISON
Library of 115,000 vols
Number of teachers: 164
Number of students: 2,391.

JUNIATA COLLEGE

1700 Moore St, Huntingdon, PA 16652
Telephone: (814) 641-3000
Fax: (814) 641-3199
E-mail: info@juniata.edu
Internet: www.juniata.edu
Founded 1876
Private control
Academic year: August to May
Pres.: Dr THOMAS R. KEPPLE, Jr
Provost and Vice-Pres. for Student Devt: JAMES LAKSO
Vice-Pres. and Chief Information Officer: RAY CHAMBERS
Vice-Pres. for Finance and Operations: WILLIAM ALEXANDER
Vice-Pres. for Advancement and Marketing: JOHN HILLE
Registrar: ATHENA FREDERICK
Library Dir: JOHN MUMFORD
Number of teachers: 120
Number of students: 1,356 (full-time).

KING'S COLLEGE

Wilkes-Barre, PA 18711
Telephone: (570) 208-5900
Fax: (570) 825-9049
E-mail: admissions@kings.edu
Internet: www.kings.edu
Founded 1946
Academic year: August to May
Pres.: Rev. THOMAS J. O'HARA
Registrar: DANIEL CEBRICK

Dean of Enrollment Management: TERESA PECK
Library Dir: Dr TERRENCE MECH
Library of 168,793 vols
Number of teachers: 180 (108 full-time, 72 part-time)
Number of students: 2,200.

LA ROCHE COLLEGE

9000 Babcock Blvd, Pittsburgh, PA 15237-5898
Telephone: (412) 367-9300
E-mail: admsns@laroche.edu
Internet: www.laroche.edu
Private control
Pres.: Sister CANDACE INTROCASO
Vice-Pres. for Academic Affairs: Dr HOWARD ISHIYAMA
Vice-Pres. for Institutional Relations: KEN SERVICE
Vice-Pres. for Devt: JANET DENNIS
Vice-Pres. for Admin. Services: GEORGE ZAFFUTO
Registrar: LUCILLE ADKINS
Library Dir: LAVERNE P. COLLINS
Number of teachers: 155
Number of students: 1,280 (1,150 undergraduate, 130 postgraduate).

LA SALLE UNIVERSITY

1900 West Olney Ave, Philadelphia, PA 19141
Telephone: (215) 951-1000
Fax: (215) 951-1892
Internet: www.lasalle.edu
Founded 1863
Pres.: MICHAEL J. McGINNISS
Provost: RICHARD A. NIGRO
Dean of Admissions: ROBERT G. VOSS
Library Dir: JOHN BAKY
Library of 375,000 vols
Number of teachers: 478 (218 full-time; 260 part-time)
Number of students: 5,130 (3,200 Day Div.; 1,800 Evening Div.; 1,300 Graduate Div.)
Publications: La Salle Bulletin (quarterly), La Salle Magazine (quarterly), Four Quarters (quarterly).

LAFAYETTE COLLEGE

Easton, PA 18042
Telephone: (610) 330-5000
E-mail: admissions@lafayette.edu
Internet: www.lafayette.edu
Founded 1826
Pres.: DANIEL H. WEISS
Provost: ANTHONY M. CUMMINGS
Secretary, Board of Trustees: STEVIE O. DANIELS
Registrar: FRANCIS A. BENGINIA
Clerk of the Faculty: JAMES WOOLLEY
Dir of Libraries and Academic Information Resources: NEIL J. MCELROY
Library of 502,603 vols
Number of teachers: 198
Number of students: 2,381
Publications: Announcement (annual), Mélange (annual), The Lafayette (weekly), The Lafayette Magazine (3 a year), The Alumni News (3 a year).

LANCASTER BIBLE COLLEGE

901 Eden Rd, POB 83403, Lancaster, PA 17608-3403
Telephone: (717) 569-7071
E-mail: admissions@lbc.edu
Internet: www.lbc.edu
Private control

Pres.: Dr PETER W. TEAGUE
Vice-Pres. for Academic Affairs: Dr RAY A. NAUGLE
Library Dir: GERALD E. LINCOLN
Number of teachers: 80
Number of students: 1,126 (854 undergraduate, 272 postgraduate).

LEBANON VALLEY COLLEGE

Annville, PA 17003-1400
Telephone: (717) 867-6100
Fax: (717) 867-6018
Internet: www.lvc.edu

Founded 1866
Academic year: August to May

Pres.: STEPHEN C. MacDONALD
Registrar: PATRICIA A. KALEY
Vice-Pres. for Academic Affairs and Dean of Faculty: GARY GRIEVE-CARLSON (acting)
Vice-Pres. for Enrollment: BILL BROWN
Dir of Library: FRANK MOLS

Library of 178,288 vols, 23,709 microfilms and recordings
Number of teachers: 96 full-time
Number of students: 1,567 full-time.

LEHIGH UNIVERSITY

27 Memorial Dr., W, Bethlehem, PA 18015-3089
Telephone: (610) 758-3000
Fax: (610) 758-3154
Internet: www.lehigh.edu

Founded 1865
Language of instruction: English
Academic year: August to May

Pres.: ALICE P. GAST
Provost and Vice-Pres. for Academic Affairs: MOHAMMED S. EL-AASSER
Sr Vice-Provost for Institutional Research: STEPHEN J. DEVLIN
Vice-Pres. for Finance and Admin.: MARGARET F. PLYMPTON
Assoc. Vice-Pres. for Govt Relations: WILLIAM D. MICHALERYA
Vice-Pres. for Advancement: BONNIE N. DEVLIN
Vice-Pres. for Univ. Relations: BRADLEY M. DREXLER
Vice-Provost for Student Affairs: JOHN W. SMEATON
Vice-Provost for Library and Technology Services: BRUCE M. TAGGART
Registrar: BRUCE S. CORRELL

Library of 1,324,500 vols
Number of teachers: 393
Number of students: 6,479

DEANS

College of Arts and Sciences: Dr BOBB CARSON
College of Business and Econ.: RICHARD M. DURAND
College of Education: SALLY A. WHITE
College of Eng. and Applied Science: MOHAMED S. EL-AASSER

PROFESSORS

College of Arts and Sciences (tel. (610) 758-3300):

ABEL, J. H., Biological Sciences
ALHADEFF, J., Chemistry
BARKEY, H., Int. Relations
BAYLOR, M., History
BEARN, G., Philosophy
BEHE, M., Biological Sciences
BEIDLER, P., English
BICKHARD, M., Psychology
BORSE, G., Physics
BROSS, A., English
CARRELL-SMITH, K., History

CARSON, R., Earth and Environmental Sciences
CHABUT, M.-H., Modern Languages and Literature
COLON, F., Political Science
CUNDALL, D., Biological Sciences
DAVIS, D., Mathematics
DeLEO, G., Physics
DOBRIC, V., Mathematics
DOTY, A., English
DUFFY, I., History
EISENBERG, B., Mathematics
EVENSON, E., Earth and Environmental Sciences
FERGUS, J., English
FIFER, E., English
FOLK, R., Physics
FRIEDMAN, S., Journalism
GALLAGHER, E., English
GANS, L., Art and Architecture
GATEWOOD, J., Sociology and Anthropology
GHOSH, B. K., Mathematics
GIRARDOT, N., Religion
GOLDMAN, S., Philosophy
GORNEY, C., Journalism
GUNTON, J., Physics
HEINDEL, N. D., Chemistry
HERRENKOHL, R., Sociology and Anthropology
HICKMAN, P., Physics
HUANG, W.-M., Mathematics
HUENNEKENS, J., Physics
HYLAND, D., Psychology
ITZKOWITZ, M., Biological Sciences
KANOFSKY, A., Physics
KHABBAZ, S., Mathematics
KIM, Y., Physics
KING, J. P., Mathematics
KLIER, K., Chemistry
KODAMA, K., Earth and Environmental Sciences
KRAFT, K., Religion
KRAWIEC, S., Biological Sciences
KRITZ, A., Physics
KROLL, B., English
LARSEN, J., Chemistry
LASKER, J., Sociology and Anthropology
LULE, J. F., Journalism
MALT, B., Psychology
MARKLEY, N. G., Mathematics
MASON, D., Art and Architecture
MATTHEWS, R., Political Science
McCLUSKEY, G. E., Mathematics
McINTOSH, J., Sociology and Anthropology
MELTZER, A. S., Earth and Environmental Sciences
MENON, M. R., International Relations
MILET, J., Theatre
MOON, B., International Relations
MORGAN, E., Political Science
MUNDHENK, R., English
MYERS, P. B., Earth and Environmental Sciences
NYBY, J. G., Biological Sciences
OLSON, L., Political Science
OU-YANG, D., Physics
PANKENIER, D., Modern Languages and Literature
PETERS, T., Art and Architecture
PHILLIPS, C. R., History
RAPOSA, M., Religion
REGEN, S. L., Chemistry
RICHTER, M., Psychology
RIPA, A., Theatre
ROSENWEIN, R., Sociology and Anthropology
SAEGER, J. S., History
SALATHE, E., Mathematics
SALERNI, P., Music
SAMETZ, S., Music
SANDS, J., Biological Sciences
SCHRAY, K., Chemistry
SCOTT, W. R., History
SILBERSTEIN, L., Religion
SIMMONS, G. W., Chemistry
SIMON, N., Biological Sciences

SIMON, R., History
SINE, N., Music
SMALL, D., Sociology and Anthropology
SMOLANSKY, O., International Relations
SODERLUND, J., History
STANLEY, L., Mathematics
STAVOLA, M., Physics
STEFFEN, L., Religion
STENGLE, G. A., Mathematics
STEWART-GAMBINO, H., Political Science
TANNENBAUM, N., Sociology and Anthropology
TOULOUSE, J., Physics
TRAISTER, B., English
USSLER, C., Art and Architecture
VIERA, R., Art and Architecture
WEINTRAUB, S. H., Mathematics
WEISS, R., Philosophy
WEISSLER, L. E. C., Religion
WILLIAMSON, C., Earth and Environmental Sciences
WOLFGANG, L., Modern Languages and Literature
WRIGHT, B., Religion
WYLIE, R., International Relations
YUKICH, J., Mathematics
ZAKNIC, I., Art and Architecture
ZEITLER, P., Earth and Environmental Sciences
ZEROKA, D., Chemistry

College of Business and Economics (tel. (610) 758-3400):

ARONSON, J. R., Business and Econ.
BARSNESS, R. W., Management
BUELL, S. G., Finance
DEARDEN, J. A., Econ.
DURAND, R. M., Management and Marketing
FALCINELLI, D. F., Marketing and Management
HYCLAK, T. J., Econ.
KING, A. E., Econ.
KISH, R. J., Finance
KOLCHIN, M. G., Management
KUCHTA, R., Management and Marketing
LARGAY III, J. A., Accounting
MUNLEY, V. G., Econ.
NATION III, G. A., Law and Business
NAYAR, N., Finance
O'BRIEN, A. P., Econ.
PAUL, J. W., Accounting
SHERER, S. A., Management and Technology
SINCLAIR, K. P., Accounting
SIVAKUMAR, K., International Marketing and Logistics
SMACKEY, B. M., Marketing and Manufacturing Systems Eng.
STEVENS, J. E., Management
TAYLOR, L. W., Econ.
THORNTON, R. J., Econ.
ZIRKEL, P. A., Education and Law

College of Education (tel. (610) 758-3225):

BAMBARA, L. M., Special Education
CATES, W. M., Instructional Design and Devt
COLE, C., Psychology
DuPAUL, G., Psychology
JITENDRA, A., Special Education
MILLER, D. N., Psychology
SHAPIRO, E., Psychology
ZIRKEL, P., Education and Law

College of Engineering and Applied Science (tel. (610) 758-4025):

BLYTHE, P. A., Chemical Eng., Mechanical Eng. and Mechanics
BOULT, T. E., Computer Science and Eng.
BROWN, F. T., Mechanical Eng. and Mechanics
CARAM, H. S., Chemical Eng.
CARGILL III, G. S., Materials Science and Eng.
CHAN, H. M., Materials Science and Eng.
CHARLES, M., Chemical Eng.
CHAUDHURY, M. K., Chemical Eng.

CHEN, J. C., Chemical Eng.
CHRISTODOULIDES, D., Electrical and Computer Eng.
COULTER, J. P., Mechanical Eng. and Mechanics
DECKER, D. R., Electrical and Computer Eng.
DELPH, T. J., Mechanical Eng. and Mechanics
EADES, J. A., Materials Science and Eng.
EL-AASSER, M. S., Chemical Eng.
FARRINGTON, G. C., Chemical Eng.
FISHER, J. W., Civil and Environmental Eng.
FREY, D. R., Electrical and Computer Eng.
FRITCHMAN, B. D., Electrical and Computer Eng.
GARDINER, K. M., Industrial and Systems Eng.
GROOVER, M. P., Industrial and Systems Eng.
GULDEN, S. L., Computer Science and Eng.
HARLOW, D. G., Mechanical Eng. and Mechanics
HARMER, M. P., Materials Science and Eng.
HARTRANFT, R. J., Mechanical Eng. and Mechanics
HATALIS, M., Electrical and Computer Eng.
HEINDEL, N. D., Chemistry
HERTZBERG, R. W., Materials Science and Eng.
HILLMAN, D. J., Computer Science and Eng.
HSU, J. T., Chemical Eng.
HWANG, J. C. M., Electrical and Computer Eng.
JAIN, H., Materials Science and Eng.
JOHNSON, S. H., Mechanical Eng. and Mechanics
KALNINS, A., Mechanical Eng. and Mechanics
KAY, E. J., Computer Science and Eng.
KAZAKIA, J. Y., Mechanical Eng. and Mechanics
KLEIN, A., Chemical Eng.
KORTH, H., Computer Science and Eng.
KOSTEM, C. N., Civil and Environmental Eng.
LARSEN, J. W., Chemistry
LENNON, G. P., Civil and Environmental Eng.
LEVY, E. K., Mechanical Eng. and Mechanics
LU, L.-W., Civil and Environmental Eng.
LUCAS, R. A., Mechanical Eng. and Mechanics
LUTHER, W. L., Chemical Eng.
MACPHERSON, A. K., Mechanical Eng. and Mechanics
MARDER, A. R., Materials Science and Eng.
MCAULAY, A. D., Electrical and Computer Eng.
MCHUGH, A., Chemical Eng.
NAGEL, R. N., Computer Science and Eng.
NETI, S., Mechanical Eng. and Mechanics
NIED, H. F., Mechanical Eng. and Mechanics
NOTIS, M. R., Materials Science and Eng.
OCHS, J. B., Mechanical Eng. and Mechanics
ODREY, N. G., Industrial and Systems Eng.
OU-YANG, H. D., Physics
REGEN, S. L., Chemistry
ROBERTS, R., Mechanical Eng. and Mechanics
ROCKWELL, D. O., Mechanical Eng. and Mechanics
SAWYERS, K. N., Mechanical Eng. and Mechanics
SCHIESSER, W. E., Chemical Eng.
SCHRAY, K. J., Chemistry
SENGUPTA, A. K., Chemical Eng., Civil and Environmental Eng.
SILEBI, C. A., Chemical Eng.
SIMMONS, G. W., Chemistry

SMITH, C. R., Mechanical Eng. and Mechanics
SORENSEN, R. M., Civil and Environmental Eng.
SPERLING, L. H., Chemical Eng., Materials Science and Eng.
STENGER Jr, H. G., Chemical Eng.
TARBY, S. K., Materials Science and Eng.
TZENG, K. K., Electrical and Computer Eng.
VARLEY, E., Mechanical Eng. and Mechanics
VOLOSHIN, A. S., Mechanical Eng. and Mechanics
WACHS, I. E., Chemical Eng.
WALKER, J. D. A., Mechanical Eng. and Mechanics
WEI, R. P., Mechanical Eng. and Mechanics
WEISMAN, R. N., Civil and Environmental Eng.
WHITE, M. H., Electrical and Computer Eng.
WILLIAMS, D. B., Materials Science and Eng.
WILSON, J. L., Civil and Environmental Eng.
WU, S. D., Industrial and Systems Eng.
ZIMMERS Jr, E. W., Industrial and Systems Eng.

LINCOLN UNIVERSITY

1570 Baltimore Pike, POB 179, PA 19352
Telephone: (610) 932-8300
Fax: (610) 932-8316
Internet: www.lincoln.edu
Founded 1854
Academic year: August to April
Pres.: Dr IVORY V. NELSON
Vice-Pres. for Academic Affairs: Dr GRANT VENERABLE II
Vice-Pres. for Devt and External Relations: MICHAEL B. HILL
Vice-Pres. for Student Affairs and Enrollment Management: Dr WILLIAM BYNUM
Vice-Pres. for Fiscal Affairs: HOWARD MERLIN
Registrar: JAMES SIMINGTON
Library Dir: NEAL CARSON
Library of 185,000 vols
Number of teachers: 102 (full-time)
Number of students: 2,084.

LUTHERAN THEOLOGICAL SEMINARY AT GETTYSBURG

61 Seminary Ridge, Gettysburg, PA 17325
Telephone: (717) 334-6286
Fax: (717) 334-3469
E-mail: info@ltsg.edu
Internet: www.ltsg.edu
Founded 1826
Private control
Academic year: September to May
Pres.: Rev. MICHAEL L. COOPER-WHITE
Dean: Rev. Dr ROBIN J. STEINKE
Registrar: MARTY STEVENS
Library Dir: BRIANT BOHLEKE
Number of teachers: 22
Number of students: 225.

LUTHERAN THEOLOGICAL SEMINARY AT PHILADELPHIA

7301 Germantown Ave, Philadelphia, PA 19119-1794
Telephone: (215) 248-4616
Fax: (215) 248-4577
E-mail: admissions@ltsp.edu
Internet: www.ltsp.edu
Founded 1864
Private control
Pres.: Rev. Dr PHILIP D. W. KREY

Exec. Dir: GLENN MILLER
Dean: PAUL RAJASHEKAR
Registrar: RENÉ DIEMER
Library Dir: KARL KRUEGER
Number of teachers: 35
Number of students: 220 (full-time).

LYCOMING COLLEGE

700 College Pl., Williamsport, PA 17701
Telephone: (717) 321-4000
Fax: (717) 321-4337
Internet: www.lycoming.edu
Founded 1812
Pres.: JAMES E. DOUTHAT
Provost and Dean: THOMAS A. GRIFFITHS
Registrar: MARY SAVOY
Dir of Library Services: JANET MCNEIL HURLBERT
Library of 178,400 vols
Number of teachers: 92 (full-time)
Number of students: 1,546.

MARYWOOD UNIVERSITY

2300 Adams Ave, Scranton, PA 18509
Telephone: (570) 348-6211
Internet: www.marywood.edu
Founded 1915
Pres.: Sister ANNE MUNLEY
Vice-Pres. for Academic Affairs: PETER CIMBOLIC
Vice-Pres. for Student Life: RAYMOND P. HEATH
Vice-Pres. for Univ. Advancement: CLAYTON N. PHEASANT
Dir of Library: CATHY SCHAPPERT
Library of 216,191 vols
Number of teachers: 294
Number of students: 2,926.

MERCYHURST COLLEGE

501 East 38th St, Erie, PA 16546-0001
Telephone: (814) 824-2000
Internet: www.mercyhurst.edu
Founded 1926
Private control
Academic year: September to May
Pres.: Dr THOMAS J. GAMBLE
Exec. Vice-Pres. for Admin.: Dr HEIDI HOSEY
Vice-Pres. for Academic Affairs: Dr BARBARA A. BEHAN
Vice-Pres. for Institutional Advancement: GARY L. BUKOWSKI
Vice-Pres. for Finance: JANE M. KELSEY
Registrar: Sister PATRICIA WHALEN
Dean of Libraries: KENNETH BRUNDAGE
Number of teachers: 124
Number of students: 3,080.

MESSIAH COLLEGE

1 College Ave, Grantham, PA 17027
Telephone: (717) 766-2511
Fax: (717) 691-6025
Internet: www.messiah.edu
Founded 1909
Private control
Academic year: September to May
Pres.: Dr KIM S. PHIPPS
Provost: Dr RANDALL G. BASINGER
Vice-Pres. for Advancement: BARRY G. GOODLING
Vice-Pres. for Finances: Dr LOIS J. VOIGT
Vice-Pres. for Operations (vacant): KATHRYNNE G. SHAFER
Dean of Enrollment Management: Dr WILLIAM G. STRAUSBAUGH
Dean of Students: Dr KRISTIN M. HANSEN-KIEFFER
Library of 290,838 vols

Number of teachers: 310 (170 full-time, 140 part-time)
Number of students: 2,917 (2,860 full-time, 57 part-time)
Publication: *The Bridge* (quarterly).

MOORE COLLEGE OF ART AND DESIGN

20th St and The Parkway, Philadelphia, PA 19103-1179
Telephone: (215) 568-4515
Fax: (215) 568-8017
E-mail: info@moore.edu
Internet: www.moore.edu
Founded 1848
Private control
Academic year: August to May
Pres.: Dr HAPPY CRAVEN FERNANDEZ
Vice-Pres. for Finance and Admin.: WILLIAM L. HILL, II
Academic Dean: DONA LANTZ
Dean of Students: JOAN STEVENS
Registrar: DIANNE RUNYON
Library Dir: SHARON WATSON-MAURO
Number of teachers: 55
Number of students: 500.

MORAVIAN COLLEGE

1200 Main St, Bethlehem, PA 18018
Telephone: (610) 861-1300
Fax: (610) 861-1445
Internet: www.moravian.edu
Founded 1742; men first admitted 1807
Academic year: August to May
Pres.: Dr CHRISTOPHER M. THOMFORDE
Vice-Pres. for Admin.: DENNIS A. DOMCHEK
Vice-Pres. for Institutional Advancement: PETER CAPUTO
Vice-Pres. for Planning and Enrollment: BERNARD J. STORY
Vice-Pres. for Academic Affairs and Dean of Faculty: CURTIS A. KEIM
Dean of Student Life: ROBERT R. WINDOLPH
Vice-Pres. for Student Affairs and Dean of Students: BEVERLY J. KOCHARD
Library of 220,000 vols
Number of teachers: 88
Number of students: 1,234.

MUHLENBERG COLLEGE

2400 Chew St, Allentown, PA 18104
Telephone: (610) 821-3100
Fax: (610) 821-3234
Internet: www.muhlenberg.edu
Founded 1848
Pres.: PEYTON RANDOLPH HELM
Provost: Dr MARJORIE HASS
Dean of Students: KAREN GREEN
Dean of Admissions and Financial Aid: CHRIS HOOKER-HARING
Library Dir: JOYCE HOMMEL
Library of 290,000 vols
Number of teachers: 126
Number of students: 1,735.

NEUMANN COLLEGE

1 Neumann Dr., Aston, PA 19014-1298
Telephone: (610) 459-0905
Fax: (610) 459-1370
E-mail: neumann@neumann.edu
Internet: www.neumann.edu
Founded 1965 as Our Lady of Angels College; present name 1980
Private control
Pres.: Dr ROSALIE M. MIRENDA
Vice-Pres. for Academic Affairs: GERALD P. O'SULLIVAN

Vice-Pres. for Finance and Admin.: DAVID W. BROWNLEE
Vice-Pres. for Mission and Ministry Affairs: Sr MARGUERITE O'BEIRNE
Vice-Pres. for Institutional Advancement and College Relations: HENRY A. SUMNER
Vice-Pres. for Enrollment Management and Student Affairs: DENNIS MURPHY
Library Dir: JOHN MICHAEL POWELL
Number of teachers: 158
Number of students: 2,221 (1,853 undergraduate, 368 postgraduate).

PENNSYLVANIA COLLEGE OF OPTOMETRY

8360 Old York Rd, Elkins Park, PA 19027-1598
Telephone: (215) 780-1400
Fax: (215) 780-1336
Internet: www.pco.edu
Founded 1919
Academic year: August to May
Pres.: THOMAS L. LEWIS
Vice-Pres. and Dean of Academic Affairs: ANTHONY F. DI STEFANO
Vice-Pres. for Finance and Business Affairs: PATRICK J. SWEENEY
Vice-Pres., Dean of Student Affairs and Dir of Admissions: ROBERT E. HORNE
Dir of Devt: LYNNE C. CORBOY
Dir of Library: KEITH LAMMERS
Library of 21,000 vols
Number of teachers: 70 (46 full-time; 24 part-time)
Number of students: 700.

PENNSYLVANIA STATE SYSTEM OF HIGHER EDUCATION

Office of the Chancellor, Dixon Univ. Center, 2986 North Second St Harrisburg, PA 17110
Telephone: (717) 720-4010
Fax: (717) 720-4011
Internet: www.passhe.edu
Chancellor: Dr JUDY G. HAMPLE
Number of students: 107,000 total at 14 univs.

CONSTITUENT INSTITUTIONS

Bloomsburg University of Pennsylvania

400 East Second St, Bloomsburg, PA 17815
Telephone: (717) 389-4000
Internet: www.bloomu.edu
Founded 1839
Pres.: Dr JESSICA KOZLOFF
Provost: Dr WILSON BRADSHAW
Registrar: K. SCHNURE
Librarian: (vacant)
Library of 376,800 vols
Number of teachers: 396
Number of students: 7,500
Courses in arts and sciences, business, teacher education, nursing and medical imaging, computer and information science.

California University of Pennsylvania

250 University Ave, California, PA 15419-1394
Telephone: (412) 938-4000
Internet: www.cup.edu
Founded 1852
Pres.: Dr ANGELO ARMENTI, Jr
Dean of Admissions and Academic Records: NORMAN HASBROUCK
Dean of Library Services: WILLIAM L. BECK
Library of 739,395 vols (405,667 microforms)
Number of teachers: 311
Number of students: 5,850

Publications: *Contribution to Scholarship* (annual), *Graduate Catalog* (2 a year), *Undergraduate Catalog* (2 a year)

DEANS

College of Liberal Arts: JESSE CIGNETTI
College of Education and Human Services: Dr STEPHEN PAVLAK
School of Graduate Studies and Research: Dr GEORGE CRANE
School of Science and Technology: Dr RICHARD HART

Cheyney University of Pennsylvania

Cheyney and Creek Rds, Cheyney, PA 19319-0200
Telephone: (610) 399-2220
Fax: (610) 399-2415
E-mail: admissions@cheyney.edu
Internet: www.cheyney.edu
Founded 1837
Academic year: August to May
Pres.: W. CLINTON PETTUS
Dir of Enrollment Management: JAMES BROWN
Provost: TETA V. BANKS
Librarian: LUT NERO
Library of 238,699 vols
Number of teachers: 102
Number of students: 1,821.

Clarion University of Pennsylvania

Clarion, PA 16214
Telephone: (814) 393-2000
E-mail: info@clarion.edu
Internet: www.clarion.edu
Founded 1867
Academic year: August to May
Pres.: DIANE L. REINHARD
Provost: JOSEPH P. GRUNENWALD
Vice-Pres. for Devt and Student Affairs: HARRY E. TRIPP
Vice-Pres. for Finance and Admin.: W. PAUL BYLASKA
Dir of Admissions: WILLIAM D. BAILEY
Dir of Libraries: HOWARD F. McGINN
Library of 363,000 vols
Number of teachers: 364
Number of students: 6,300.

East Stroudsburg University of Pennsylvania

200 Prospect St, East Stroudsburg, PA 183301-2999
Telephone: (570) 422-3211
Internet: www.esu.edu
Founded 1893 as East Stroudsburg Normal School; present name 1983
Academic year: August to May
Pres.: Dr ROBERT J. DILLMAN
Provost and Vice-Pres. for Academic Affairs: Dr EVELYN C. LYNCH
Vice-Pres. for Finance and Admin.: RICHARD A. STANESKI
Vice-Pres. for Univ. Advancement: Dr ISAAC W. SANDERS
Vice-Pres. for Student Affairs: VALERIE M. HODGE
Registrar: GEORGIA PRELL
Library Dir: DAVID G. SCHAPPERT
Number of teachers: 274
Number of students: 6,291 (5,176 undergraduate, 1,115 postgraduate)

DEANS

School of Arts and Sciences: Dr BONNIE NEUMANN
School of Professional Studies: Dr SAM HAUSFATHER
School of Health Sciences and Human Performance: Dr MARK J. KILKER

School of Graduate Studies and Research: Dr JAMES A. FAGIN

Edinboro University of Pennsylvania

219 Meadville St, Edinboro, PA 16444
Telephone: (814) 732-2000
Fax: (814) 732-2880
E-mail: eup_admissions@edinboro.edu
Internet: www.edinboro.edu

Founded 1857
Academic year: August to May

Pres.: Dr FRANK G. POGUE
Provost and Vice-Pres. for Academic Affairs: Dr PEARL W. BARTELT
Vice-Pres. for Finance and Admin.: JAMES P. SHEEHAN
Vice-Pres. for Student Affairs and Student Success: Dr GERALD W. KIEL
Asst Vice-Pres. for Admissions: TERRENCE CARLIN
Assoc. Vice-Pres. for Univ. Libraries: Dr DONALD DILMORE

Library of 501,276 vols
Number of teachers: 374
Number of students: 7,773

DEANS

Graduate Studies and Research: Dr MARY MARGARET BEVEVINO
School of Education: Dr R. SCOTT BALDWIN
School of Liberal Arts: Dr TERRY L. SMITH
School of Science, Management and Technology: Dr ERIC A. RANDALL

Indiana University of Pennsylvania

Indiana, PA 15705
Telephone: (412) 357-2100
Internet: www.iup.edu

Founded 1875, as Indiana State Normal School
State control
Academic year: September to May (2 sessions)

Pres.: Dr LAWRENCE K. PETTIT
Provost and Vice-Pres. for Academic Affairs: Dr MARK J. STASZKIEWICZ
Vice-Pres. for Admin.: C. EDWARD RECESKI
Vice-Pres. for Finance: C. EDWARD RECESKI
Vice-Pres. for Student Affairs: Dr HAROLD GOLDSMITH
Vice-Pres. for Institutional Advancement: Dr JOAN FISHER
Dean of Graduate School: Dr JAMES PETERSON
Dean of Admissions: WILLIAM NUNN
Dir of Libraries and Media Resources: Dr RENA FOWLER

Library of 806,332 vols
Number of teachers: 738
Number of students: 13,410

DEANS

College of Business: Dr ROBERT C. CAMP
School of Continuing Education: Dr NICHOLAS E. KOLB
College of Education: Dr JOHN BUTZOW
College of Fine Arts: Dr MICHAEL J. HOOD
College of Human Ecology and Health Sciences: Dr CARLENE ZONI
College of Natural Sciences and Mathematics: Dr JOHN ECK
College of Humanities and Social Sciences: Dr BRENDA CARTER
Graduate School: Dr JAMES PETERSON
International Studies: Dr PATRICK CARONE

Kutztown University of Pennsylvania

POB 730, Kutztown, PA 19530
Telephone: (610) 683-4000
Fax: (610) 683-4010
E-mail: admission@kutztown.edu
Internet: www.kutztown.edu

Founded 1866
State control
Academic year: September to May

Pres.: Dr F. JAVIER CEVALLOS
Provost, and Vice-Pres. for Academic Affairs: Dr LINDA RINKER
Vice-Pres. for Information Technology: RICHARD ZERA
Vice-Pres. for Student Affairs: Dr CHARLES WOODARD
Vice-Pres. for Admin. and Finance: JAMES R. SUTHERLAND
Vice-Pres. for Univ. Advancement: WILLIAM J. SUTTON
Dir of Admissions: Dr WILLIAM STAHLER
Registrar: LAURA YOUTZ
Librarian: MARGARET DEVLIN

Library of 415,000 vols
Number of teachers: 350
Number of students: 9,100

DEANS

College of Visual and Performing Arts: Dr WILLIAM MOWDER
College of Liberal Arts and Sciences: Dr EDWARD SIMPSON (acting)
College of Education: REGIS BERNHARDT (acting)
College of Graduate Studies and Research: Dr CHARLES CULLUM
College of Business: Dr EILEEN HOGAN

Lock Haven University of Pennsylvania

Lock Haven, PA 17745
Telephone: (717) 893-2000
Fax: (717) 893-2432
Internet: www.lhup.edu

Founded 1870
Academic year: August to May

Pres.: Dr CRAIG D. WILLIS
Dir of Admissions: JAMES REESER
Dir of Library Services: TARA FULTON

Library of 352,369 vols
Number of teachers: 224
Number of students: 3,945

Publication: *Lock Haven International Review* (annual).

Mansfield University of Pennsylvania

Mansfield, PA 16933
Telephone: (717) 662-4000
Internet: www.mansfield.edu

Founded 1857
Academic year: September to May

Pres.: JOHN R. HALSTEAD
Dir of Student Records: CAROL ALEXANDER
Dir of Enrollment Services: BRIAN BARDEN
Dir of Library Service and Instructional Resources: LARRY NESBIT

Library of 222,650 vols
Number of teachers: 170
Number of students: 3,500.

Millersville University of Pennsylvania

POB 1002, Millersville, PA 17551-0302
Telephone: (717) 872-3011
Fax: (717) 871-2251
Internet: www.millersville.edu

Founded 1855
Academic year: September to August

Pres.: Dr FRANCINE G. MCNAIRY
Registrar: CANDACE A. DEEN
Dir of Admissions: DOUGLAS ZANDER
Librarian: Dr DAVID S. ZUBATSKY

Library of 1,106,025 vols incl. microfilm/microfiche
Number of teachers: 468
Number of students: 7,998 (6,991 undergraduate, 1,007 postgraduate)

Associate, baccalaureate and masters degree programs in the liberal arts and sciences, teacher education, business, and professional studies.

Shippensburg University of Pennsylvania

1871 Old Main Dr., Shippensburg, PA 17257-2299
Telephone: (717) 477-7447
Fax: (717) 477-1273
E-mail: admiss@ship.edu
Internet: www.ship.edu

Founded 1871
Academic year: August to May

Pres.: ANTHONY F. CEDDIA
Provost and Vice-Pres. for Academic Affairs: PATRICIA SPAKES
Assoc. Provost: JAMES COOLSEN
Vice-Pres. for Student Affairs: GEORGE F. HARPSTER Jr
Vice-Pres. for Admin. and Finance: DONALD WILKINSON
Dean of Academic Programs and Services: MARIAN SCHULTZ
Dean of Admissions: JOSEPH CRETELLA
Dean of Library and Media Services: HECTOR MAYMI-SUGRANES

Library of 1,804,005 items
Number of teachers: 393 (365 instructional)
Number of students: 7,607

Publication: *Proteus: A Journal of Ideas* (2 a year)

DEANS

College of Arts and Sciences: SARA GROVE
College of Business: STEPHEN HOLOVIAK
College of Education and Human Services: ROBERT B. BARTOS

Slippery Rock University of Pennsylvania

Slippery Rock, PA 16057
Telephone: (724) 738-9000
Fax: (724) 738-2098
E-mail: apply@sru.edu
Internet: www.sru.edu

Founded 1889
Academic year: June to May

Pres.: Dr ROBERT M. SMITH
Provost and Vice-Pres. for Academic Affairs: Dr WILLIAM F. WILLIAMS
Vice-Pres. for Finance and Admin. Affairs: Dr CHARLES CURRY
Vice-Pres. for Student Affairs and Dean of Students: Dr ROBERT WATSON
Vice-Pres. for Univ. Advancement: ROBERT J. MOLLENHAUER
Dir of Academic Records and Summer School: ELIOTT BAKER
Dir of Admissions: JAMES BARRETT
Dir of Graduate Admissions: DUNCAN SARGENT
Dir of Int. Initiatives: DONALD KERCHIS
Dir of Library Services: PHILIP TRAMDACK

Library of 501,228 vols, 586 periodicals, 1,505,304 microforms
Number of teachers: 404
Number of students: 7,789

Publications: *The Rock* (quarterly), *Saxigena* (annual), *Ginger Hill* (annual)

DEANS

College of Business, Information and Social Sciences: Dr BRUCE RUSSELL
College of Education: Dr C. JAY HERTZOG
College of Health, Environment and Sciences: Dr JANE FULTON
College of Humanities, Fine and Performing Arts: Dr WILLIAM MCKINNEY

West Chester University of Pennsylvania

West Chester, PA 19383

Telephone: (610) 436-1000

Internet: www.wcupa.edu

Founded 1871

Pres.: Dr MADELEINE WING ADLER

Dir of Admissions: Ms MARSHA HAUG

Librarian: F. Q. HELMS

Library of 500,000 vols

Number of teachers: 670 (539 full-time; 131 part-time)

Number of students: 11,344

Publications: *College Literature, Serpentine.*

PENNSYLVANIA STATE UNIVERSITY

University Park, PA 16802

Telephone: (814) 865-4700

Internet: www.psu.edu

Founded 1855

Academic year: August to May

Pres.: GRAHAM SPANIER

Executive Vice-Pres. and Provost: RODNEY A. ERICKSON

Vice-Provost for Information Technology: J. GARY AUGUSTSON

Vice-Provost and Dean for Undergraduate Education: JOHN J. CAHIR

Vice-Provost for Educational Equity: TERRELL JONES

Dean of the University Office of International Programs: BEVERLY LINDSAY

Vice-Provost and Dean for Enrollment Management and Admin.: JOHN J. ROMANO

Vice-Pres. for Outreach and Cooperative Extension: JAMES H. RYAN

Executive Director of the Center for Quality and Planning: LOUISE E. SANDMEYER

Vice-Provost for Academic Affairs: ROBERT SECOR

Assistant Vice-Provost for Enrollment Management and University Registrar: J. JAMES WAGER

Dean of Libraries: NANCY EATON

Number of teachers: 4,429 (full-time)

Number of students: 75,489 (all locations except Pennsylvania College of Technology)

Campuses: Abington, Altoona, Berks, Beaver, Delaware County, DuBois, Erie (Behrend College), Fayette, Harrisburg, Hazleton, Lehigh Valley, McKeesport, Mont Alto, New Kensington, Schuylkill, Shenango, Wilkes-Barre, Worthington Scranton, York.

DEANS

University Park Colleges:

College of Agricultural Sciences: ROBERT D. STEELE

College of Arts and Architecture: RICHARD W. DURST

The Mary Jean and Frank P. Smeal College of Business Admin.: JUDY OLIAN

College of Communications: DOUGLAS ANDERSON

College of Earth and Mineral Sciences: ERIC J. BARRON

College of Education: DAVID H. MONK

College of Engineering: DAVID N. WORMLEY

College of Health and Human Devt: RAYMOND T. COWARD

School of Information Sciences and Technology: JAMES B. THOMAS

College of the Liberal Arts: SUSAN WELCH

The Eberly College of Science: DANIEL J. LARSON

Graduate School: EVA J. PELL

Degree-conferring Colleges:

Abington College: KAREN W. SANDLER

Altoona College: WILLIAM G. CALE

Berks–Lehigh Valley College: SUSAN P. SPEECE

Behrend College, Penn State Erie: JACK BURKE (Provost and Dean)

Capital College, Harrisburg and Schuylkill: MADLYN L. HANES (Provost and Dean)

Commonwealth College: DIANE M. DISNEY

Dickinson School of Law, Carlisle: PHILIP J. McCONNAUGHEY

College of Medicine, Hershey: DARRELL G. KIRCH

Pennsylvania College of Technology, Penn College: DAVIE JANE GILMOUR (Pres.)

Schreyer Honors College: CHERYL ACHTERBERG

School of Graduate Professional Studies, Penn State Great Valley: WILLIAM MILHEIM (CEO)

PROFESSORS

(Some professors serve in more than one department)

College of Agricultural Sciences (201 Ag Admin, University Park, PA 16802; internet www.cas.psu.edu):

Agricultural and Biological Engineering:

BUFFINGTON, D. E., Agricultural Engineering

ELLIOT, H. A., Agricultural Engineering

GRAVES, R. E.

HEINEMANN, P. H., Systems Modelling

JARRETT, A. R.

MANBECK, H. B.

MURPHY, D. J., Agricultural Engineering

PURI, V. M., Agricultural Engineering

WALKER, P. N.

YOUNG, R. E.

Agricultural Economics and Rural Sociology:

ABLER, D. G., Agricultural, Environmental and Regional Economics and Demography

ALTER, T. R., Agricultural Economics

BAILEY, K. W., Agricultural Economics

BECKER, J. C., Agricultural Economics

BEIERLEIN, J. G., Agricultural Economics

BLANDFORD, D., Agricultural Economics

DUNN, J. W., Agricultural Economics

EPP, D. J., Agricultural Economics

FISHER, A. N. P., Agricultural and Environmental Economics

HANSON, G. D., Agricultural Economics

HARPER, J. K., Agricultural and Environmental Economics

HYMAN, D. W., Public Policy and Community Systems

JENSEN, L. I., Rural Sociology and Demography

LULOFF, A. E., Rural Sociology

MOORE, H. L., Agricultural Economics

SACHS, C., Rural Sociology

SHORTLE, J. S., Agricultural Economics

SMITH, S. M., Agricultural Economics

STEFANOU, S. E., Agricultural Economics

STOKES, C. S., Rural Sociology

VAN HORN, J. E., Rural Sociology

WEAVER, R. D., Agricultural Economics

WILLITS, F. K., Rural Sociology

ZOUMAS, B., Agribusiness

Agricultural and Extension Education:

BOWEN, B. E., Agricultural and Extension Education

CAREY, H. A., Extension Information

FLANAGAN, C. A., Agricultural and Extension Education

LEWIS, R. B., 4-H Youth

SCANLON, D. C., Agricultural and Extension Education

THOMSON, J. S., Agricultural Communications

YODER, E. P., Agricultural and Extension Education

Crop and Soil Sciences:

BEEGLE, D. B., Agronomy

CIOLKOSZ, E. J., Soil Genesis and Morphology

CURRAN, W. S., Weed Science

FRITTON, D. D., Soil Physics

HALL, M. H., Agronomy

HATLEY, O. E., Agronomy

KOMARNENI, S., Clay Mineralogy

KRUEGER, C. R., Agronomy

LANYON, L. E., Soil Science and Management

PENNYBACKER, B. W., Agronomy

PETERSEN, G. W., Soil and Land Resources

SYLVIA, D., Soil Microbiology

TURGEON, A. J., Turfgrass Management

WATSCHKE, T. L., Turfgrass Science

Dairy and Animal Science:

BAUMRUCKER, C. R., Animal Nutrition-Physiology

CASH, E. H., Animal Science

ETHERTON, T. D., Animal Nutrition

HAGEN, D. R., Animal Science

HEALD, C. W., Dairy Science

HEINRICHS, A. J., Dairy and Animal Science

HENNING, W. R., Animal Science

KEPHART, K. B., Animal Science

KILLIAN, G. J., Reproductive Physiology

MULLER, L. D., Dairy Science

O'CONNOR, M. L., Dairy Science

VARGA, G. A., Animal Science

VASILATOS-YOUNKEN, R., Endocrine Physiology and Nutrition

Entomology:

CALVIN, D.

FELTON, G.

FRAZIER, J. L., Entomology

HELLER, P. R., Entomology

HULL, L. A., Entomology

KIM, K. C., Entomology

McPHERON, B.

MULLIN, C. A., Entomology

SCHULTZ, J. C., Entomology

Food Science:

ANANTHESWARAN, R. C., Food Science

BEELMAN, R. B., Food Science

FLOROS, J. D., Food Science

HOOD, L. F., Food Science

MARETZKI, A. N., Food Science and Nutrition

THOMPSON, D. B., Food Science

School of Forest Resources:

ABRAMS, M. D., Forestry

BLANKENHORN, P. R., Wood Technology

BOWERSOX, T. W., Silviculture

BROOKS, R. P., Wildlife and Wetlands

DeWALLE, D. R., Forest Hydrology

GERHOLD, H. D., Forest Genetics

LYNCH, J. A., Forest Hydrology

McCORMICK, L. H., Forest Resources

McKINSTRY, R. B., Forestry and Environmental Resource Management

SAN JULIAN, G., Wildlife Resources

SHARPE, W. E., Forest Resources

SMITH, P. M., Wood Products Marketing

STAUFFER, J. R., Ichthyology

STEINER, K. C., Forest Biology

YAHNER, R. H., Wildlife Management

Horticulture:

ARTECA, R. N., Horticultural Physiology

BROWN (EVENSON), K. M., Post-harvest Physiology

CRAIG, R., Plant Breeding

CRASSWELLER, R. M., Tree Fruit

EISSENSTAT, D. M., Woody Plant Physiology

FERRETTI, P. A., Vegetable Crops

GUILTINAN, M. J., Plant Molecular Biology

HEUSER, C. W., Horticultural Physiology

HOLCOMB, E. J., Floriculture

KOIDE, R. T., Horticultural Ecology

KUHNS, L. J., Ornamental Horticulture

ORZOLEK, M. D., Horticulture

Plant Pathology:

AYERS, J. E.

CHRIST, B. J., Potato Breeding and Diseases
COLE, H., Jr, Agricultural Sciences
DAVIS, D. D.
GILDOW, F. E., Virus-vector Biology
FLORES, H. E.
LUKEZIC, F. L.
MACNAB, A. A.
MOORMAN, G. W., Plant Pathology
PELL, E. J., Agriculture
ROMAINE, C. P., Plant Viruses
ROYSE, D. J., Plant Pathology
SKELLY, J. M.
STEWART, E. L., Plant Pathology
TRAVIS, J. W.

Poultry Science:

ELKIN, R. G., Nutritional Biochemistry
LEACH, R. M., Jr, Poultry Science
VASILATOS-YOUNKEN, R., Metabolic Endocrinology

Veterinary Science:

GRIEL, L. C., Jr
HUTCHINSON, L. J.
OMIECINSKI, C.
PERDEW, G. H.
REDDY, C. C.
SHAW, D. P.
SORDILLO, L. M.
WOJCHOWSKI, D. M.

College of Arts and Architecture (Office of the Dean, 111 Arts Bldg, University Park, PA 16802; tel. (814) 865-2591; fax (814) 865-7140; internet www.artsandarchitecture.psu.edu):

Architecture:

HAIDER, J., Architecture
KALISPERIS, L. N., Architecture
LUCAS, J. P., Architecture

Art History:

CUTLER, A.

Integrative Arts:

HAMPTON, G., Art Education and Integrative Arts
LANG, G., Art and Integrative Arts

Landscape Architecture:

DICKIE, G.
JONES, D. R.
ORLAND, B.

School of Music:

ARMSTRONG, D. C., Music
BROYLES, M., Music and American History
CARR, M. A., Music
DOSSE, M., Music
SMITH, S. H., Music
THOMPSON, K. P., Music Education
TRINKLEY, W. B., Music
WILLIAMS, E. V., Music
YODER, M. D., Music

School of Theatre:

CARTER, D. H.
GIBSON, A. A.
LEONARD, R. E.
NICHOLS, R.

School of Visual Arts:

AMATEAU, M., Art and Women's Studies
GRAVES, K., Art
HAMPTON, G., Art and Art Education
LANG, G., Art
LEUPP, L. G., Art
MADDOX, J., Art
PORTER, S., Art
SOMMESE, L. B., Art
STEPHENSON, J. E., Art
WILSON, B. G., Art Education

The Mary Jean and Frank P. Smeal College of Business Administration (Dean's Office, 801H Business Admin. Bldg, University Park, PA 16802-3009; tel. (814) 867-0448; fax (814) 865-7064; e-mail deansoffice@smeal.psu.edu; internet www.smeal.psu.edu):

Accounting:

DIRSMITH, M. W.
GIVOLY, D.
MCKEOWN, J. C.
SMITH, C. H.

Business Logistics:

SPYCHALSKI, J. C., Business Logistics
STENGER, A. J., Business Logistics
TYWORTH, J. E., Business Logistics

Finance:

EZZELL, J. R.
GHADAR, F.
KRACAW, W. A.
MILES, J. A.
MUSCARELLA, C.
WOOLRIDGE, J. R.

Insurance and Real Estate:

BAGBY, J. W., Business Law
JAFFE, A. J., Business Admin.
LUSHT, K. M., Business Admin.
SHAPIRO, A. F., Business Admin.
YAVAS, A., Business Admin.

Management and Organization:

GIOIA, D. A., Organizational Behaviour
GRAY, B. L., Organizational Behaviour
HAMBRICK, D., Management
HARRISON, D. A., Management
KILDUFF, M., Organizational Behaviour
SNOW, C. C., Business Admin.
STEVENS, J. M.
SUSMAN, G. I., Management
TREVINO, L. K., Management

Management Science and Information Systems:

BALAKRISHNAN, A.
BARTON, R., Management Science
BHARGAVA, H., Management Information Systems
BOLTON, G. E., Management Science
CHATTERJEE, K., Management Science
FONG, D. K. H., Management Science and Statistics
HARRISON, T. P., Management Science
KELTON, W. D., Management Science and Information Systems
LILIEN, G. L., Management Science
LIN, D. K., Management Science
XU, S., Management Science

Marketing:

BAUMGARTNER, J.
DESARBO, W. S., Marketing
GOLDBERG, M. E., Marketing
OLIVA, R. A., Marketing
OLSON, J. C., Marketing
RANGASWANY, A., Marketing

College of Communications (Dean's Office, 201 Carnegie, University Park, PA 16802; internet www.psu.edu/dept/comm):

Advertising and Public Relations:

BAUKUS, R. A., Communications (non-professorial Head)

Film/Video and Media Studies:

BARTON, R. L., Media Studies
COHEN, J., Communications
DAVIS, D., Communications
NICHOLS, J. S., Communications

Journalism:

BERNER, R. T., Journalism and American Studies
CURLEY, J., Communications
FOREMAN, G., Communications
RICHARDS, R. D., Journalism and Law

Telecommunications:

FRIEDEN, R. M., Cable Telecommunications
SCHEMENT, J. R., Telecommunications
TAYLOR, R. D., Telecommunications Studies and Law

College of Earth and Mineral Sciences (; internet www.ems.psu.edu):

Energy and Geo-Environmental Engineering:

ADEWUMI, M., Petroleum and Natural Gas Engineering
BISE, C. J., Mining Engineering and Industrial Health and Safety
CHANDER, S., Mineral Processing and Geo-Environmental Engineering
ELSWORTH, D., Energy and Geo-Environmental Engineering
ERTEKIN, T., Petroleum and Natural Gas Engineering
GRADER, A., Petroleum and Natural Gas Engineering
OSSEO-ASARE, K., Metals Science and Engineering and Geo-Environmental Engineering
PARIZEK, R., Geosciences and Geo-Environmental Engineering
SCARONI, A., Energy and Geo-Environmental Engineering
SCHOBERT, H. H., Fuel Science
WYNGAARD, J. C., Meteorology, Mechanical Engineering, and Geo-Environmental Engineering
YOUNG, G., Meteorology and Geo-Environmental Engineering

Geography:

CARLETON, A. M.
DOWNS, R. M.
ERICKSON, R. A., Geography and Business Admin.
GLASMEIER, A. K., Geography and Regional Planning
HOLDSWORTH, D. W.
KNIGHT, C. G.
MACEACHREN, A. M., Geography
PEUQUET, D. J., Geography
YARNAL, B. M.

Geosciences:

ALEXANDER, S. S., Geophysics
ALLEY, R. B., Geosciences
ARTHUR, M. A., Geosciences
BARRON, E. J., Geosciences
BRANTLEY, S. L., Geosciences
CUFFEY, R. J., Palaeontology
DEINES, P., Geochemistry
EGGLER, D. H., Petrology
ENGELDER, T. E., Geosciences
FURLONG, K. P., Geosciences
GRAHAM, E. K., Geophysics
KASTING, J. F., Geosciences and Meteorology
KERRICK, D. M., Petrology
KUMP, L. R., Geosciences
OHMOTO, H., Geochemistry
PARIZEK, R. R., Geology
SLINGERLAND, R. L., Geology
VOIGHT, B., Geology
WHITE, W. B., Geochemistry

Materials Science and Engineering:

ADAIR, J. H., Materials Science and Engineering
ALLARA, D. L., Polymer Science and Chemistry
BROWN, P., Ceramic Science and Engineering
CHEN, L.-Q., Materials Science and Engineering
CHUNG, T.-C., Polymer Science
COLBY, R. H., Polymer Science
COLEMAN, M. M., Polymer Science
DEBROY, T., Metallurgy
GREEN, D. J., Ceramic Science and Engineering
HARRISON, I. R., Polymer Science
HOWELL, P. R., Metallurgy
KOSS, D. A., Metallurgy
KUMAR, S. K., Materials Science and Engineering
LANAGAN, M., Materials Science and Engineering

MacDonald, D. D., Materials Science and Engineering
Messing, G. L., Ceramic Science and Engineering
Osseo-Asare, K., Metallurgy
Painter, P. C., Polymer Science
Pantano, C. G., Materials Science and Engineering
Pickering, H. W., Metallurgy
Randall, C. A.,
Runt, J. P., Polymer Science
Ruzyllo, J., Electrical Engineering and Materials Science
Schlom, D. G., Materials Science and Engineering
Singh, J., Materials Science and Engineering
Spear, K. E., Ceramic Science
Tressler, R. E., Materials Science and Engineering
Trolier-McKinstry, S., Ceramic Science

Meteorology:

Bannon, P.
Brune, W. H.
Cahir, J. J.
Carlson, T. N.
Dutton, J. A.
Frank, W. M.
Kasting, J. F., Geosciences and Meteorology
Kleit, A. N., Economics
Fritsch, J. M.
Lamb, D.
Thomson, D. W.
Wyngaard, J. C.
Young, G. S., Meteorology and Geo-environmental Engineering

College of Education (tel. (814) 863-2216; e-mail jdeitrich@psu.edu; internet www.ed.psu.edu):

Adult Education, Instructional Systems, and Workforce Education and Development:

Askov, E. N., Education
Dwyer, F., Instructional Systems
Gray, K. C., Education
Passmore, D. L., Education
Rothwell, W. J., Workforce Education and Devt

Counselor Education, Counseling Psychology, and Rehabilitation Services:

Herbert, J. T., Counselor Education
Herr, E. L., Education
Keat, D. B., II, Education and Counseling Psychology
Niles, S. G., Counselor Education
Slaney, R. B., Counseling Psychology

Curriculum and Instruction:

Blume, G. W., Mathematics Education
Carlsen, W. S., Science Education
Giroux, H.
Heid, M. K., Mathematics Education
Johnson, J. E.
Nelson, M. R., Education and American Studies
Nolan, J. F., Jr, Curriculum and Supervision
Rubba, P. A., Jr
Shannon, P.
Simon, M. A., Mathematics Education
Soto, L., Language and Literacy
Yawkey, T. C.

Education Policy Studies:

Baker, D. P., Education
Boyd, W. L., Educational Admin.
Evensen, D., Education
Geiger, R., Education
Hartman, W., Education
Hendrickson, R. M., Education
Nicely, R., Jr, Education
Prakash, M. S., Education
Stefkovich, J. A., Education
Terenzin, P., Education
Tippeconnic, J., III, Education

Volkwein, J. F., Education

Educational and School Psychology and Special Education:

Gajar, A. H., Special Education
Hale, R. L., Education
Hughes, C. A., Education
Meyer, B. J. F., Educational Psychology
Roberts, D. M., Educational Psychology
Ruhl, K. L., Special Education
Salvia, J. A., Special Education
Suen, H. K., Educational Psychology
Watkins, M., Education (School Psychology)

College of Engineering (101 Hammond, University Park, PA 16802; internet www.engr.psu.edu):

Acoustics:

Atchley, A. A.
Blood, I. M., Communication Disorders
Brentner, K. S., Aerospace Engineering
Frank, T. A., Communication Disorders
Garrett, S. L.
Hettche, L. R., Engineering Research
Koopmann, G. H., Mechanical Engineering
Lamancusa, J. S., Mechanical Engineering
Lauchle, G. C.
Lesieutre, G. A., Aerospace Engineering
Long, L. N., Aerospace Engineering
Maynard, J. D., Physics
McLaughlin, D. K., Aerospace Engineering
Morris, P. J., Aerospace Engineering
Shung, K. K., Bioengineering
Stern, R., Applied Science and Mechanics
Thomson, D. W., Meteorology
Tittmann, B. R., Engineering Science and Mechanics

Aerospace Engineering:

Camci, C., Aerospace Engineering
Lesieutre, G. A., Aerospace Engineering
Long, L.
McLaughlin, D. K.
Maughmer, M. D., Aerospace Engineering
Melton, R. G., Aerospace Engineering
Micci, M. M.
Morris, P. J.

Agricultural and Biological Engineering:

Buffington, D. E., Agricultural Engineering
Elliot, H. A., Agricultural Engineering
Graves, R. E.
Heinemann, P. H., Systems Modelling
Jarrett, A. R.
Manbeck, H. B.
Murphy, D. J., Agricultural Engineering
Puri, V. M., Agricultural Engineering
Walker, P. N.
Young, R. E.

Architectural Engineering:

Behr, R. A.
Burnett, E. F. P., Architectural and Civil Engineering
Geschwinder, L. F.
Mumma, S. A.

Bioengineering:

Allcock, H. R., Chemistry
Brown, P. W., Materials Science and Engineering
Curtis, W. R., Chemical Engineering
Freivalds, A., Industrial and Manufacturing Engineering
Geselowitz, D. B., Bioengineering
Higgins, W. E., Electrical and Computer Engineering
Kenney, E. S., Nuclear Engineering
Lipowsky, H. H., Bioengineering and Engineering Science
Rose, J. L., Engineering Design and Manufacturing
Rosenberg, G., Bioengineering and Surgery
Runt, J. P., Polymer Sciences

Snyder, A. J., Surgery and Bioengineering
Tarbell, J. M., Chemical Engineering and Bioengineering
Ultman, J. S., Chemical Engineering
Zelis, R., Medicine and Cellular and Molecular Physiology

Chemical Engineering:

Ben-Jebria, A.
Borhan, A.
Curtis, W.
Danner, R. P.
Duda, J. L.
Fichthorn, K.
Foley, H. C.
Nagarajan, R.
Nedwick, R.
Tarbell, J. M.
Ultman, J. S.
Vannice, M. A.
Vrentas, J. S.
Zydney, A. L.

Civil and Environmental Engineering:

Anderson, D. A.
Burnett, E. F. P., Architectural and Civil Engineering
Goulias, K. G.
Jovanis, P. P.
Kilareski, W. P.
Krauthammer, T.
Logan, B. E.
Matson, J. V.
Miller, A. C.
Regan, R. W., Sr
Scanlon, A.
Thomas, H. R.
Wang, M. C.

Computer Science and Engineering
(joint department with the Eberly College of Science)

Acharya, R.
Barlow, J.
Das, C.
Feng, T.-Y.
Giles, C. L.
Higgins, W.
Hurson, A. R.
Irwin, M. J.
Kasturi, R.
Kumara, S.
La Porta, T.
Long, L. N.
Metzner, J. J.
Miller, D. A.
Miller, W. C.
Palamidessi, C.
Saraswat, V. A.
Yen, J.

Electrical Engineering:

Aydin, K., Electrical Engineering
Bose, N. K., Electrical Engineering
Breakall, J. K.
Burton, L. C., Electrical and Computer Engineering
Croskey, C. L.
Cross, L. E., Electrical Engineering
Ferraro, A. J., Electrical Engineering
Gildenblat, G., Electrical Engineering
Hall, D. L.
Higgins, W.
Jackson, T. N., Electrical Engineering
Jenkins, K., Electrical Engineering
Kavehrad, M.
Khoo, I. C., Electrical Engineering
Kurtz, S. K., Electrical Engineering
Lee, K. Y., Electrical Engineering
Luebbers, R. J., Electrical Engineering
Mathews, J. D., Electrical Engineering
Metzner, J., Electrical Engineering
Miller, D. L., Electrical Engineering
Mitchell, J. D., Electrical Engineering
Mittra, R., Electrical Engineering
Philbrick, C. R., Electrical Engineering

PHOHA, S., Electrical and Computer Engineering
RUSSELL, D., Electrical Engineering
RUZYLLO, J., Electrical Engineering and Materials Science and Engineering
SZNAIER, M., Electrical Engineering
UCHINO, K., Electrical Engineering
WRONSKI, C. R., Microelectronic Materials and Devices
YU, F. T. S., Electrical Engineering
ZHANG, Q., Electrical Engineering

Engineering Science and Mechanics:
AMATEAU, M. F., Engineering Science and Mechanics
ASHOK, S., Engineering Science
AWADLEKARIM, O. O., Engineering Science and Mechanics
BAKIS, C. E.
CONWAY, J. C., Engineering Mechanics
ENGEL, R. S.
FONASH, S. J., Engineering Sciences
GERMAN, R. M., Materials
HAYEK, S. I., Engineering Mechanics
LAKHTAKIA, A.
LENAHAN, P. M., Engineering Science and Mechanics
McGRATH, R. T.
McNITT, R. P., Engineering Science and Mechanics
MESSIER, R. F., Engineering Science and Mechanics
PANGBORN, R. N., Engineering Mechanics
QUEENEY, R. A., Engineering Mechanics
ROSE, J. L., Engineering Design and Manufacturing
SALAMON, N. L., Engineering Science and Mechanics
TITTMANN, B. R., Engineering
TODD, J. A., Engineering Science and Mechanics
URQUIDI-MACDONALD, M.
VARADAN, V. K., Engineering Science and Mechanics
VARADAN, V. V., Engineering Science and Mechanics, and Electrical Engineering
VENTSEL, E. S., Engineering Science
WRONSKI, C. R., Microelectronic Devices and Materials

Industrial and Manufacturing Engineering:
CAVALIER, T. M.
CHANDRA, M. J.
COHEN, P. H.
ENSCORE, E. E.
FREIVALDS, A.
JOSHI, S. B.
KUMARA, S.
RAVINDRAN, A.
RUUD, C. O.
VENTURA, J. A.
VOIGHT, R. C.
WYSK, R. A.

Mechanical and Nuclear Engineering:
BARATTA, A. J.
BELEGUNDU, A. D.
BRASSEUR, J. G.
CATCHEN, G. L.
CHEUNG, F. B.
CIMBALA, J. M.
HARRIS, T. A.
HOCHREITER, L.
JESTER, W. A.
KOOPMAN, G. H.
KULAKOWSKI, B. T.
KULKARNI, A. K.
KUO, K. K.
LAMANCUSA, J. S.
LITZINGER, T. A.
MODEST, M. F.
PEREZ-BLANCO, H.
RAY, A.
SANTAVICA, D. A.
SANTORO, R. J.
SETTLES, G. S.
SINHA, A.

SOMMER, H. J., III
THYNELL, S. T.
TRETHEWY, M. W.
TURNS, S. R.
WEBB, R. L.
YANG, V.
YAVUZKURT, S.

School of Engineering Technology and Commonwealth Engineering:
HAGER, W. R.

College of Health and Human Development (Office of the Dean, 201 Henderson Bldg, University Park, PA 16802-6501; tel. (814) 865-1428; fax (814) 865-3282; e-mail healthhd@psu.edu; internet www.hhdev.psu.edu):

Biobehavioural Health:
AHERN, F. M.
AIRHIHENBUWA, C. O., Biobehavioural Health
BEARD, J. L., Nutrition Science
BECHTEL, L. J., Biobehavioural Health
CAVANAGH, P. R., Locomotion Studies, Biobehavioural Health, Medicine and Orthopaedics
FINKELSTEIN, J. W.
GRAHAM, J. W., Biobehavioural Health and Human Devt
GRANGER, D. A., Biobehavioural Health, Human Devt and Family Studies
JONES, B. C., Biobehavioural Health and Pharmacology
KOZLOWSKI, L. T.
McCLEARN, G. E., Biobehavioural Health and Psychology
NEWELL, K. M., Biobehavioural Health and Kinesiology
NICHOLSON, M. E., Health Education and Biobehavioural Health
ROLLS, B. J., Biobehavioural Health
SUSMAN, E. J., Biobehavioural Health, Human Devt and Nursing
VICARY, J. R.
VOGLER, G. P., Biobehavioural Health

Communication Disorders:
BLOOD, G. W.
BLOOD, I. M.
FRANK, T A.
LIGHT, J. C.
PROSEK, R. A.

Health Policy and Administration:
BRANNON, D.
KEMPER, P.
SHEA, D. G.
SHORT, P. F.
YESALIS, C. E.
YU, L. C.

Hotel, Restaurant and Recreational Management:
CALDWELL, L., Leisure Studies
CHICK, G., Hotel, Restaurant and Recreation Management (Leisure Studies)
GODBEY, G. C., Leisure Studies
LEE, R. D., Public Admin.
SHAFER, E. L., Environmental Management and Tourism

Human Development and Family Studies:
BARRY, K., Human Devt
BIRCH, L. L.
BURGESS, R. L.
BURTON, L. M., Sociology and Human Devt
COLLINS, L. M.
CROUTER, A. C., Human Devt
D'AUGELLI, A. R., Human Devt
EDELBROCK, C. S., Behavioural Health
GREENBERG, M. T.
McHALE, S. M., Human Development
SCHAIE, K. W., Human Devt and Psychology
STIFTER, C. A.
VONDRACEK, F. W.
WILLIS, S. L.

ZARIT, S. H., Human Devt

Kinesiology:
BUCKLEY, W. E., Exercise and Sport Science and Health Education
CAVANAUGH, P. R., Locomotion Studies
ECKHARDT, R. B., Kinesiology
FARRELL, P. A., Physiology
GRAHAM, G. M., Kinesiology
KENNEY, W. L., Physiology and Kinesiology
KRETCHMAR, R. S., Exercise and Sport Science
LARSSON, L. G., Physiology and Clinical Neurophysiology
LATASH, M. L., Kinesiology
MARTIN, P. E., Kinesiology
NEWELL, K. M., Kinesiology and Biobehavioural Health
ZATSIORSKY, V., Kinesiology

Nursing:
BROWN, R.
PRESTON, D.

Nutrition:
ACHTERBERG, C. L.
BAUMRUCKER, C. R., Animal Nutrition, Physiology
BEARD, J. L.
BERLIN, C. M., Jr, Paediatrics, Pharmacology
BIRCH, L. L.
CONNOR, J. R.
ETHERTON, T. D., Animal Nutrition
GREEN, M. H., Nutrition Science
JEFFERSON, L. S., Jr
KRIS-ETHERTON, P. M., Nutrition Science
LEACH, R. M., Jr
MARETZKI, A. N., Food Science and Nutrition
ROLLS, B. J., Nutrition and Biobehavioural Health
MASTRO, A. M., Microbiology and Cell Biology
REDDY, C. C.
ROLLS, B. J.
ROSS, A. C., Nutrition and Veterinary Science
SMICIKLAS-WRIGHT, H.
THOMPSON, D. B.
VASILATOS-YOUNKEN, R.
YEH, Y.-Y.

School of Information Sciences and Technology (504 Rider I Bldg, 120 South Burrowes St, University Park, PA 16801-3857; tel. (814) 865-3528; fax (814) 865-5604; internet ist.psu.edu):

BAGBY, J. W., Information Sciences and Technology
GILES, C. L., Information Sciences and Technology, Computer Science and Engineering
TRAUTH, E. M., Information Sciences and Technology
YEN, J., Information Sciences and Technology, Computer Science and Engineering

College of the Liberal Arts (110 Sparks Bldg, University Park, PA 16802; tel. (814) 865-7691; internet www.la.psu.edu):

African and African American Studies:
McBRIDE, D., African American History
MENGISTEAB, K.
SPENCER, R. C., African American History

American Studies:
CLARKE, D. C.

Anthropology:
DURRENBERGER, E.
HIRTH, K. G.
MILNER, G. R.
RICHTSMEIER, J. T.
SANDERS, W. T.
SNOW, D. R.
WALKER, A.
WEBSTER, D. L.
WEISS, K. M., Anthropology and Genetics

WOOD, J. W.

Classics and Ancient Mediterranean Studies:
BALDI, P. H., Linguistics and Classics
HALPERN, B., Ancient History and Religious Studies
KNOPPERS, G.
PETERSEN, W., Religious Studies
REDFORD, D. B.

Communication Arts and Sciences (Speech Communication):
BENSON, T. W.
BROWNE, S. H.
GOURAN, D. S.
HECHT, M.
HOGAN, J.
NUSSBAUM, J. F.
PARROTT, R. L.

Comparative Literature:
BEEBEE, T. O., Comparative Literature and German
BEGNAL, M., English and Comparative Literature
CHENEY, P., English and Comparative Literature
ECKHARDT, C. D., English and Comparative Literature
EDWARDS, R. R., English and Comparative Literature
GROSSMAN, K., French
HALE, T. A., African, French, and Comparative Literature
KADIR, D., Comparative Literature
LIMA, R. F., Spanish and Comparative Literature
MAKWARD, C. P., French and Women's Studies
STOEKL, A., French and Comparative Literature
STRASSER, G. F., German and Comparative Literature

Crime, Law and Justice:
AUSTIN, R. L., Theory of Crime and Deviancy
BERNARD, T. J.
BLOCK, A. A.
FELSON, R., Crime
KRAMER, J. H., Sociology, and Admin. of Justice
MILLER, L. L.
OSGOOD, D. W.
RUBACK, R. B.
SILVER, E.
STEFFENSMEIER, D., Sociology, and Crime, Law and Justice
ULMER, J. T.

Economics:
BIERENS, H. J.
CHATTERJEE, K., Economics and Management Science
BOND, E. W.
CHATTERJEE, K., Economics and Management Science
FELLER, I.
ICKES, B. W.
JORDAN, J. S.
KLEIN, P. A.
KRISHNA, K.
KRISHNA, V.
LOMBRA, R. E.
MARSHALL, R. C.
NELSON, J. P.
ROBERTS, B.-Y.
ROBERTS, M. J.
SHAPIRO, D., Economics and Women's Studies
SJÖSTRÖM, J. T.
TYBOUT, J. R.
WALLACE, N.

English:
BECKER, R., English and Women's Studies
BEGNAL, M. H., English and Comparative Literature
BELL, B.

BIALOSTOSKY, D.
BUCKALEW, R.
CHENEY, P., English and Comparative Literature
CLAUSEN, C.
ECKHARDT, C. D., English and Comparative Literature
EDWARDS, R., English and Comparative Literature
GANNON, R.,
GILYARD, K.
HARRIS, S. K.
HUME, K.
HUME, R. D.
NEALON, J.
SELZER, J. L.
SQUIER, S. M., Women's Studies and English
WEST, J. L. W., III
WOODBRIDGE, L.

French:
BRAGGER, J. D.
GREENBERG, W. N.
GROSSMAN, K. M.
HALE, T. A., African, French and Comparative Literature
LACY, N. J.
MAKWARD, C. P., French, and Women's Studies
STOEKL, A., French and Comparative Literature

Germanic and Slavic Languages and Literature:
BEEBEE, O. B., Comparative Literature and German
GENTRY, F. G.
NAYDAN, M. M.
SCHURER, E.
STRASSER, G. F., German and Comparative Literature

History and Religious Studies:
CROSS, G. S., Modern European History
DERICKSON, A., Labour History
FINKE, R., Sociology and Religious Studies
HALPERN, B., Ancient History and Jewish Studies
HSIA, R., History and Religious Studies
JENKINS, P., Religious Studies and History
KNOPPERS, G., Religious Studies
LANDES, J. B., Women's Studies and History
McMURRY, S. A., American History
MOSES, W. J., American History
NEELY, M. E., American Civil War
PENCAK, W. A., American History
PETERSEN, W., Religious Studies
PREBISH, C., Religious Studies
PROCTOR, R. N., History of Science
ROEBER, A. G., Early Modern History and Religious Studies
ROSE, A. C., American History and Religious Studies
ROSE, P. L., European History, Jewish Studies
RUGGIERO, G., Renaissance History
SCHIEBINGER, L. L., History of Science
SWEENEY, J. R., Medieval European History

Jewish Studies:
BLOCK, A., Admin. of Justice
HALPERN, B., Ancient History and Religious Studies
KNOPPERS, G., Religious Studies
ROSE, P. L., European History, Jewish Studies

Labour Studies and Industrial Relations:
CLARK, P. F.
DERICKSON, A., Labour Studies and History
DRAGO, R.
GOURAN, D. S., Communications Arts and Sciences
FILIPPELI, R. L.
ROGERS, J. K.

STEWART, J. B.
Latin American Studies:
GONZALEZ-PEREZ, A., Spanish
HIRTH, K., Anthropology
LIMA, R., Spanish and Comparative Literature
NICHOLS, J. S., Communications
PEAVLER, T. J., Spanish
SNOW, D., Anthropology
WEBSTER, D., Anthropology

Linguistics and Applied Language Studies:
BALDI, P. H., Linguistics and Classics
GOLOMBEK, P., English as a Second Language
JOHNSON, K. E., Applied Linguistics
KROLL, J., Psychology and Applied Linguistics
LANTOLF, J. P., Spanish and Applied Linguistics
SAVIGNON, S. J., Applied Linguistics

Philosophy:
COLAPIETRO, V.
CONWAY, D. W.
GROSHOLZ, E. R.
JACQUETTE, D. L.
SALLIS, J.
SCOTT, C. E.
STUHR, J. J.
TUANA, N.

Political Science:
BAUMGARTNER, F.
BREMER, S.
EISENSTEIN, J.
HARKAVY, R. E.
LaPORTE, R., Jr, Public Admin. and Political Science
WELCH, S.

Psychology:
BERENBAUM, S.
BIERMAN, K. L.
BORKOVEC, T. D.
CARLSON, R.
CLEVELAND, J. N.
COLE, P. M.
CRNIC, K. A.
FARR, J. L.
JACOBS, R. R.
JOHNSON, E.
KROLL, J. F.
LIBEN, L. S.
MARK, M. M.
MURPHY, K. R.
NELSON, K. E.
RAY, W. J.
ROSENBAUM, D. A.
SHIELDS, S. A., Women's Studies and Psychology
STERN, R. M.
THOMAS, H.

Sociology:
BAKER, D. P., Education and Sociology
BOOTH, A.
BURTON, L., Human Devt and Sociology
CLEMENTE, F. A.
DE JONG, G. F.
FARKAS, G., Sociology and Demography
FELSON, R., Crime, Law, Justice and Sociology
FINKE, R., Sociology and Religious Studies
FIREBAUGH, G.
HAYWARD, M. D.
JOHNSON, D. R., Sociology and Human Devt and Family Studies
KRAMER, J., Sociology, Crime, Law and Justice
LANDALE, N. S., Sociology and Demography
LEE, B. A.
McCARTHY, J. D.
MORRIS, M. W.
NELSEN, H. M.
OSGOOD, D. W., Crime, Law, Justice and Sociology

RUBACK, R. B., Crime, Law, Justice and Sociology
SCHOEN, R., Family Sociology and Demography
SICA, A.
STEFFENSMEIER, D. J., Sociology, and Crime, Law and Justice

Spanish, Italian and Portuguese:

GONZALEZ-PEREZ, A., Spanish
LANTOLF, J., Spanish and Applied Linguistics
LIPSKI, J. M., Spanish and Linguistics

Women's Studies:

LANDES, J. B., Women's Studies and History
MANSFIELD, P. K., Women's Studies and Health Education
SQUIER, S. M., Women's Studies and English

The Eberly College of Science (Office of Public Information, 427 Thomas Bldg, University Park, PA 16802-2112; fax (814) 863-2246; internet www.science.psu.edu):

Astronomy and Astrophysics:

BEATTY, J. J.
FEIGELSON, E. D.
GARMIRE, G. P.
LAGUNA, P.
MESZAROS, P. I.
RAMSEY, L. W.
RICHARDS, M.
SCHNEIDER, D. P.
WOLSZCZAN, A.

Biochemistry and Molecular Biology:

BRENCHLEY, J. E., Microbiology and Biotechnology
BRYANT, D. A., Biotechnology
FERRY, J. G., Biochemistry and Molecular Biology
FRISQUE, R. J., Molecular Virology
GAY, C. V., Cell Biology and Poultry Science
GOLBECK, J. H., Biochemistry and Biophysics
HARDISON, R. C., Biochemistry
KAO, T.-H., Biochemistry and Molecular Biology
MASTRO, A. M., Microbiology and Cell Biology
SCHLEGEL, R. A., Biochemistry and Molecular Biology
SIMPSON, R. T., Biochemistry and Molecular Biology
TIEN, M., Biochemistry
TU, C. P. D., Biochemistry and Molecular Biology

Biology:

ASSMANN, S. M.
CAVENER, D. R.
COSGROVE, D. J.
CYR, R. J.
FEDOROFF, N. V.
FISHER, C. R.
HEDGES, B.
MA, H.
MITCHELL, R. B.
NEI, M.
STEPHENSON, A. G.
UHL, C.
WALKER, A., Anthropology and Biology

Chemistry:

ALLARA, D. L., Polymer Science and Chemistry
ALLCOCK, H. R.
ANDERSON, J. B.
BENKOVIC, S. J.
CASTLEMAN, A. W., Jr
ERNST, W. E., Physics and Chemistry
EWING, A. G.
FELDMAN, K.
FUNK, R. L.
GARRISON, B. J.

JURS, P. C.
MALLOUK, T. E.
MARONCELLI, M.
MERZ, K. M., Jr
SEN, A.
WEINREB, S. M., Natural Products Chemistry
WEISS, P. S.
WINOGRAD, N.

Mathematics:

ANDERSON, J. H.
ANDREWS, G. E.
BANYAGA, A.
BAUM, P.
BROWNAWELL, D.
DU, Q.
FORMANEK, E.
HAMMACK, J.
HUNTER, R. P.
JAMES, D. G.
KATOK, A.
KATOK, S.
LALLEMENT, G. J.
LEVI, M.
LI, W.-C.
MULLEN, G. L.
NISTOR, V.
NOURI, M.
OCNEANU, A.
PESIN, Y. B.
ROE, J.
SIMPSON, S.
SWIATEK, G.
VASERSTEIN, L.
VAUGHAN, R.
WARE, R. P.
WATERHOUSE, W. C.
XU, J.
ZARHIN, Y.
ZHENG, Y.

Physics:

BANAVAR, J. R.
CASTLEMAN, W., Jr,
CHAN, M. H. W.
COLE, M. W.
COLLINS, J. C.
COLLINS, R. W.
DIEHL, R.
ERNST, W. E.
FREED, N.
GUNAYDIN, M.
JAIN, J.
MAYNARD, J. D.
OH, B.
SOKOL, P. E.
STRIKMAN, M.
WEISS, D. S.
WHITMORE, J. J.

Statistics:

AKRITAS, M. G.
ARNOLD, S. F.
BABU, G. J.
CHINCHILLI, V., Biostatistics
FONG, D., Management Science and Statistics
HARKNESS, W. L.
HETTMANSPERGER, T. P.
LIN, D. K. J., Management Science and Statistics
LINDSAY, B. G.
PATIL, G. P.
RAO, C. R.
ROSENBERGER, J. L.
TEMPELMAN, A.

Abington College (1600 Woodland Rd, Abington, PA 19001; tel. (215) 881-7300; fax (215) 881-7317; internet www.abington.psu.edu):

Division of Arts and Humanities:

KLIGER, H., Communications and Jewish Studies
MILLER, L., English
MUSTAZZA, L., English and American Studies

SMITH, J. F., English and American Studies
STUTMAN, S., English

Division of Science and Engineering:

AYOUB, A., Mathematics
JOHNSON, K., Mathematics
MOORE, G., Chemistry
REDLIN, L., Mathematics
SCHUSTER, I., Chemistry

Division of Social and Behavioural Sciences:

SMITH, J., English and American Studies

Altoona College (3000 Ivyside Park, Altoona, PA 16601; tel. (814) 949-5000; internet www.aa.psu.edu):

Division of Arts and Humanities:

MARSHALL, I. S., English
MOORE, D. W., English
WOLFE, M., History

Division of Education, Human Development and Social Sciences:

BECHTEL, L. J., Biobehavioural Health

Berks–Lehigh Valley College (Berks campus: Tulpehocken Rd, POB 7009, Reading, PA 19610-6009
Lehigh Valley campus: 8380 Mohr Lane, Fogelsville, PA 18051-9999; tel. (610) 396-6000 (Berks), (610) 285-5220 (Lehigh Valley); fax (610) 285-5220 (Lehigh Valley); internet www.bklv.psu.edu):

BARTKOWIAK, R. A., Engineering
FIFER, K., English
GREENBERG, W., French
LITVIN, D. B., Physics
LODWICK, K. L., History
MILAKOFSKY, L., Chemistry
RILEY, M., English

Behrend College, Penn State Erie (5091 Station Rd, Erie, PA 16563; tel. (814) 898-6000; internet www.pserie.psu.edu):

School of Business:

PATTERSON, R., Accountancy
VOSS, J. A., Accountancy

School of Humanities and Social Sciences:

BALDWIN, D., English
FERNANDEZ-JIMENEZ, J., Spanish
FRANKFORTER, A. D., European History
GAMBLE, J. K., Political Science and International Law
GEORGE, D. H., English and Women's Studies
MORRIS, G. L., American Literature
PORAC, C., Psychology
WOLFE, K., French
WOLFORD, C., English, Business

School of Science:

LARSON, K., Mathematics (Calculus)

Capital College, Harrisburg and Schuylkill (Harrisburg campus: 777 W Harrisburg Pike, Middletown, PA 17057-4846
Schuylkill campus: 200 University Drive, Schuylkill Haven, PA 17972-2208; tel. (717) 948-6250 (Harrisburg), (570) 385-6000 (Schuylkill); fax (570) 385-3672 (Schuylkill); internet www.cl.psu.edu):

ANSARY, O., Engineering
ASWAD, A., Engineering
BLUMBERG, M., Management
BRONNER, S. J., American Studies and Folklore
CARDAMONE, M. J., Physics
CHEN, Y. F., Civil Engineering
CHISHOLM, R. F., Management
CIGLER, B. A., Public Policy and Admin.
COLE, C. A., Engineering
COUCH, S. R., Sociology
CULPAN, R., Management
DISHNER, E. K., Education
FOXX, R., Psychology
HANES, M. L., Education
KAYNAK, E., Marketing
MAHAR, W. J., Humanities and Music
MILLS, P., Business Admin.

PETERSON, S. A., Public Affairs
PLANT, J. F., Public Policy and Admin.
RABIN, J. M., Public Admin. and Public Policy
RAY, G., Engineering
RICHMAN, I., American Studies and History
SACHS, H. G., Biology
STEPHENS, J. L., Speech Communications
YAVERBAUM, G. J., Information Systems
ZIEGENFUSS, J. T., Management and Health Care Systems

Commonwealth College (111 Old Main, University Park, PA 16802-1501; tel. (814) 863-0327); internet www.cwc.psu.edu):

Arts and Humanities Division:

CLEMENT, P., History
GINSBERG, R., Philosophy
PLUHAR, E., Philosophy

Business and Economics Division:

KUCUKEMIROGLU, O., Accounting

English Division:

COLLISON, G.
FRUSHELL, R.
JARRETT, J.
MCCARTHY, W.
PRICE, R. A.
SORKIN, A.

Engineering Division:

WALTERS, R.
WEED, M.

Mathematics Division:

BARSHINGER, R.
DAWSON, J.
GOMEZ-CALDERON, J.
HELOU, C.
IVANOV, A.
HORWITZ, A.
NOURI, M.
ZEMYAN, S.

Science Division:

BITTNER, E., Chemistry
BLACK, R., Biology
BURSEY, C., Biology
CAMARDA, H., Physics
DE ROSA, M., Chemistry
FEHLNER, J., Chemistry
HARRISON, E., Chemistry
HOULIHAN, J., Physics
KHAN, A., Chemistry
MARICONDI, C., Chemistry
MILLER, D., Physics
MONROE, J., Physics
OBERMYER, R., Physics
SARAFIAN, H., Physics
SUBRAMANIAM, G., Chemistry
VISWANATHAN, N., Chemistry
WINTER, T., Physics
WOLFE, C., Biology

Social Sciences and Education Division:

BALL, R., AOJ
CIMBALA, S., Political Science
GERGEN, M., Psychology
GRESSON, A., Curriculum and Instruction
JOHNSON, J., Psychology

Dickinson School of Law, Carlisle (150 South College St, Carlisle, PA 17013; tel. (717) 240-5000; internet www.dsl.psu.edu):

ACKERMAN, R. M.
ALEXANDER, P. C.
BACKER, L. C.
BARKER, W. B.
DEL DUCA, L. F.
FARMER, S. B.
FARRIOR, S. T.
FELDMAN, H. A.
FOX, J. R.
GILDIN, G. S.
GLENN, P. G.
HAUGHNEY, E. W.
KEATING, W. J.
KELLETT, C. H.

MACRAE, L. M.
MARION, C.
MOGILL, M. A.
MOOTZ, F. J., III
MULLER-PETERSON, J.
NAIDES, P. H.
NAVIN, M. J.
PEARSON, K.
PLACE, T. M.
POLACHEK, M. K.
RAINS, R. E.
RIGLER, J.
ROMERO, V.
SCOTT, G. R.
TERRY, L. S.

College of Medicine, Hershey (Penn State Milton S. Hershey Medical Center, 500 University Drive, Hershey, PA 17033; tel. (717) 531-8521; internet www.hmc.psu.edu):

Behavioural Science:

JONES, M. B.
NORGREN, R.

Biochemistry and Molecular Biology:

BHAVANANDAN, V. P.
BOND, J. S.
GOWDA, D. C.
HOPPER, A. K.
HOPPER, J. E.
SCHENGRUND, C.-L.

Cellular and Molecular Physiology:

FLOROS, J.
JEFFERSON, L. S., Jr
LANG, C. H.
LANOUE, K. F.
PEGG, A. E.
QUINN, P. G.
RANNELS, D. E.
VARY, T. C.

Comparative Medicine:

LANG, C. M.
GRIFFITH, J. W.

Health Evaluation Sciences:

CHINCHILLI, V. M.
LLOYD, T.
ORKIN, F. K.
YOUNG, M. J.

Humanities:

BALLARD, J. O., Medicine and Humanities
HUFFORD, D., Humanities, Behavioural Science and Family and Community Medicine
HAWKINS, A. H., Humanities

Microbiology and Immunology:

CHORNEY, M. J., Microbiology and Immunology, Paediatrics
COURTNEY, R. J.
HOWETT, M. K.
ISOM, H. C.
MEYERS, C. M.
SUN, S.-C.
TEVETHIA, M. J.
TEVETHIA, S. S.
WIGDAHL, B.
WILLS, J. W.

Neuroscience and Anatomy:

CONNOR, J. R.
MILNER, R. J.
SIMPSON, I. A.
ZAGON, I. S.

Ophthalmology:

AMINLARI, A., Clinical Ophthalmology
GARDNER, T. W., Ophthalmology, Cellular and Molecular Physiology
SASSANI, J. W., Ophthalmology and Pathology

Pharmacology:

BERLIN, C. M., Jr, Paediatrics and Pharmacology
BILLINGSLEY, M. L., Pharmacology

BURKHART, K. K., Emergency Medicine and Pharmacology
JONES, B. C., Biobehavioural Health and Pharmacology
KESTER, M., Pharmacology
LAKOSKI, J. M., Pharmacology and Anaesthesiology
LEVENSON, R., Pharmacology
LLOYD, T. A., Health Evaluation Sciences
MULDER, K. M., Pharmacology
NAIDES, S. J., Medicine, Microbiology and Immunology, Pharmacology
PEGG, A. E., Cellular and Molecular Physiology and Pharmacology
SMITH, C. D., Pharmacology
SUMMY-LONG, J. Y., Pharmacology
VESELL, E. S., Pharmacology, Medicine, Genetics

School of Graduate Professional Studies, Penn State Great Valley (30 East Swedesford Rd, Malvern, PA 19355-1443; tel. (610) 648-3200; e-mail gvinfo@psu.edu; internet www.gv.psu.edu):

Education:

MILHEIM, W., Education

Engineering:

MCCOOL, J., Systems Engineering
RUSSELL, D., Electrical Engineering

Information Sciences:

RUSSELL, D., Electrical Engineering

Management:

FRITZSCHE, D. J., Management and Organisation

ATTACHED RESEARCH INSTITUTES

Applied Research Laboratory: POB 30, State College, PA 16804;Located at: N Atherton St, State College, PA 16801; tel. (814) 865-6343; internet www.arl.psu.edu; f. 1945 by the U.S. Navy; research and Devt in technical fields, especially underwater systems; Dir Dr EDWARD G. LISZKA.

Biotechnology Institute: internet www.lsc.psu.edu/biotech.html; f. 1984; Dir Dr NINA V. FEDOROFF.

Center for Applied Behavioural Sciences: Asst Dir Dr ROBERT J. VANCE.

Centre for Developmental and Health Genetics: Amy Gardner Hse, University Park, PA 16802-2317; tel. (814) 865-1717; fax (814) 863-4768; e-mail pvq@psu.edu; internet www.hhdev.psu.edu/old/centers/genetics.htm; f. 1988.

Particulate Materials Center: internet www.mri.psu.edu/centers/pmc; Dir Dr JAMES H. ADAIR.

Center for Locomotion Studies: Rm 29, Recreation Bldg, University Park, PA 16802; internet www.celos.psu.edu; Dir Dr PETER R. CAVANAGH.

Center for the Study of Higher Education: 400 Rackley Bldg, University Park, PA 16802; tel. (814) 865-6346; fax (814) 865-3638; e-mail cshe@psu.edu; internet www.ed.psu.edu/cshe; f. 1969; Dir Prof. J. FREDERICKS VOLKWEIN.

Environmental Resources Research Institute: tel. (814) 863-0291; fax (814) 865-3378; internet www.environment.erri.psu.edu; Dir Dr ARCHIE J. MCDONNELL.

Institute for the Arts and Humanistic Studies: 101 Ihlseng Cottage, University Park, PA 16802; tel. (814) 865-0495; fax (814) 863-8349; e-mail iah1@psu.edu; internet www.research.psu.edu/iah; attached to the Office of the Vice Pres. for Research; Dir Dr ROBERT R. EDWARDS.

Institute for Policy Research and Evaluation: 251 N Burrowes, University Park, PA 16802-6211; tel. (814) 865-9561; fax (814)

865-3098; e-mail dpb4@psu.edu; internet www.ssri.psu.edu/ipre; Dir DAVID BAKER.

Materials Research Institute: 199 MRI Bldg, University Park, PA 16802-7003; tel. (814) 863-8407; fax (814) 863-8561; internet www.mri.psu.edu; established to coordinate activities and provide leadership for interdisciplinary materials research throughout the Pennsylvania State University; Dir CARLO PANTANO (acting).

Pennsylvania Transportation Institute: Dir Dr JAMES MILLER.

Population Research Institute: 601 Oswald Tower, University Park, PA 16802-6211; tel. (814) 865-0486; fax (814) 863-8342; internet www.pop.psu.edu; Dir MARK D. HAYWARD.

PHILADELPHIA BIBLICAL UNIVERSITY

200 Manor Ave, Langhorne, PA 19047

Telephone: (215) 752-5800

E-mail: admissions@pbu.edu

Internet: www.pcb.edu

Founded 1913 as Bible Institute of Pennsylvania; present name 2001

Private control

Academic year: August to May

Pres.: Dr W. SHERRILL BABB

Sr Vice-Pres. for Finance and Admin.: JAN M. HAAS

Sr Vice-Pres. and Provost: TODD WILLIAMS

Sr Vice-Pres. for Univ. Advancement: SCOTT A. KEATING

Vice-Pres. for Research and Planning: MAE E. STEWART

Number of teachers: 130

Number of students: 1,410 (1,050 undergraduate, 360 postgraduate).

PHILADELPHIA COLLEGE OF OSTEOPATHIC MEDICINE

4170 City Ave, Philadelphia, PA 19131

Telephone: (215) 871-6100

E-mail: admissions@pcom.edu

Internet: www.pcom.edu

Pres.: Dr MATTHEW SCHURE

Vice-Pres. for Academic Affairs and Dean: Dr KENNETH J. VEIT

Vice-Pres. for Finance: PETER DOULIS

Vice-Pres. for Alumni Relations and Devt: FLORENCE D. ZELLER

Number of students: 1,410.

PHILADELPHIA UNIVERSITY

School House Lane and Henry Ave, Philadelphia, PA 19144

Telephone: (215) 951-2700

Fax: (215) 951-2615

E-mail: pr@philau.edu

Internet: www.philau.edu

Founded 1884

Academic year: September to August

President: JAMES P. GALLAGHER

Vice-President for Enrollment and Student Affairs: JANE H. ANTHEIL

Vice-President of Academic Affairs: CAROL S. FIXMAN

Vice-President for Business and Finance: RANDALL D. GENTZLER

Library of 88,000 vols, 16,000 periodicals, 5,500 microforms

Number of teachers: 90

Number of students: 3,600.

PITTSBURGH THEOLOGICAL SEMINARY

616 North Highland Ave, Pittsburgh, PA 15206-2525

Telephone: (412) 362-5610

Fax: (412) 363-3260

Internet: www.pts.edu

Founded 1794 by the merger of Pittsburgh-Xenia Theological Seminary and Western Theological Seminary

Private control

Pres.: WILLIAM CARL, III

Vice-Pres. for Academic Affairs: BRIAN JACKSON

Vice-Pres. for Finance and Admin.: PATRICK J. CUNNINGHAM

Library Dir: SHARON TAYLOR

Number of teachers: 30

Number of students: 385.

POINT PARK UNIVERSITY

201 Wood St, Pittsburgh, PA 15222

Telephone: (412) 391-4100

E-mail: enroll@ppc.edu

Internet: www.ppc.edu

Private control

Academic year: August to May

Fmrly Point Park College

Pres.: Dr PAUL HENNIGAN

Provost and Vice-Pres. for Academic Affairs: Dr CHARLES A. PERKINS

Vice-President for Finance and Admin.: BRIDGET MANCOSH

Registrar: JENNIFER FEDELE

Number of teachers: 70

Number of students: 3,123 (2,743 undergraduate, 380 postgraduate)

DEANS

School of Arts and Sciences: Dr STEPHEN FRITZ

School of Business: Dr BRUCE MURPHY

Conservatory of Performing Arts: RONALD LINDBLOM

ROBERT MORRIS UNIVERSITY

6001 University Blvd, Moon Township, PA 15108

Telephone: (412) 262-8200

E-mail: enrollmentoffice@rmu.edu

Internet: www.rmu.edu

Founded 1921

Private control

Academic year: August to May

Pres.: Dr GREGORY G. DELL'OMO

Senior Vice-Pres. for Academic and Student Affairs: Dr WILLIAM J. KATIP

Vice-Pres. for Institutional Advancement: JAY T. CARSON

Vice-Pres. and Gen. Counsel: SIDNEY ZONN

Vice-Pres. for Financial Operations: JEFFREY A. LISTWAK

Registrar: FRANCIS E. PERRY

Library Dir: Dr FRANCES J. CAPLAN

Number of teachers: 383

Number of students: 5,100

DEANS

School of Adult and Continuing Education: DARCY B. TANNEHILL

School of Business: Dr DERYA A. JACOBS

School of Communications and Information Systems: Dr DAVID L. JAMISON

School of Education and Social Sciences: Dr JOHN E. GRAHAM

School of English, Mathematics and Science: Dr YILDIRIM OMURTAG

School of Nursing and Allied Health: LYNDA J. DAVIDSON

ROSEMONT COLLEGE

1400 Montgomery Ave, Rosemont, PA 19010

Telephone: (215) 527-0200

Fax: (610) 527-1041

E-mail: webinfo@rosemont.edu

Internet: www.rosemont.edu

Founded 1921

Catholic liberal arts college

Pres.: SHARON LATCHAW HIRSH

Vice-Pres. for Academic Affairs: DEBRA G. KLINMAN

Registrar: JOSEPH T. ROGERS

Vice-Pres. for Student Affairs: MARILYN A. MOLLER

Vice-Pres. for Institutional Advancement: MADONNA MARION-LANDAIS

Vice-Pres. for Information Services: CATHERINE M. FENNELL

Library of 157,000 vols

Number of teachers: 141

Number of students: 9 (361 full-time; 434 part-time; 152 graduate).

SAINT CHARLES BORROMEO SEMINARY

100 Wynnewood Rd, Wynnewood, PA 19096

Telephone: (610) 667-3394

Fax: (610) 617-9267

E-mail: developmentscs@adphila.org

Internet: www.scs.edu

Founded 1832

Private control

Academic year: September to May

Rector: Rev. JOSEPH G. PRIOR

Vice-Rector: Rev. CHRISTOPHER J. SCHRECK

Vice-Pres. for Finance and Operations: ELAINE K. RICE

Registrar: LAWRENCE A. HEYMAN

Library Dir: CAIT KOKOLUS

Number of teachers: 32

Number of students: 160 (full-time).

SAINT FRANCIS UNIVERSITY

POB 600 Loretto, PA 15940

Telephone: (814) 472-3000

E-mail: admissions@francis.edu

Internet: www.francis.edu

Founded 1847

Academic year: August to May

Pres.: Rev. CHRISTIAN ORAVEC

Asst to the Pres.: RICHARD CRAWFORD

Vice-Pres. for Academic Affairs: Rev. ANTHONY DE CONCILIIS

Vice-Pres. for Finance: KEVIN O'FLAHERTY

Vice-Pres. for Student Affairs: DENNIS RIEGELNEGG

Dir of Devt: RAYMOND PONCHIONE

Dir of Library: SANDRA A. BALOUGH

Library of 199,000 vols

Number of teachers: 172

Number of students: 2,090.

SAINT JOSEPH'S UNIVERSITY

5600 City Ave, Philadelphia, PA 19131

Telephone: (610) 660-1000

Fax: (610) 660-3300

Internet: www.sju.edu

Founded 1851

Pres.: TIMOTHY R. LANNON

Asst Vice-Pres. for Enrollment Management: DAVID CONWAY

Vice-Pres. for Academic Affairs: DANIEL J. CURRAN

Registrar: GERARD DONAHUE

Librarian: EVELYN MINICK

Library of 335,000 vols

Number of teachers: 428 (189 full-time; 239 part-time)

Number of students: 7,027 (3,076 day; 1,128 evening; 2,823 graduate)

Degree courses in the liberal arts, science, business admin. and computer sciences.

SAINT VINCENT COLLEGE

300 Fraser Purchase Rd, Latrobe, PA 15650-2690

Telephone: (724) 539-9761
E-mail: pr@stvincent.edu
Internet: www.stvincent.edu

Founded 1846

Pres.: H. JAMES TOWEY
Exec. Vice-Pres.: Bro. NORMAN W. HIPPS
Vice-Pres. for Student Affairs: ALICE KAYLOR
Vice-Pres. for Finance and Admin.: DENNIS THIMONS (acting)
Vice-Pres. for Institutional Advancement: PAUL R. TAYLOR
Registrar: CELINE R. HAAS
Librarian: Rev. CHRYSOSTOM V. SCHLIMM

Library of 340,000 vols
Number of teachers: 100
Number of students: 1,200

Publication: *Saint Vincent Magazine* (quarterly).

SETON HILL COLLEGE

1 Seton Hill Dr., Greensburg, PA 15601

Telephone: (724) 834-2200
Fax: (724) 830-1294
Internet: www.setonhill.edu

Founded 1883

Academic year: August to May

Pres.: JoANNE W. BOYLE
Vice-Pres. for Enrollment Services: BARBARA HINKLE
Dir of Library: DAVID STANLEY

Library of 119,000 vols
Number of teachers: 114 (58 full-time, 56 part-time)
Number of students: 1,200.

SUSQUEHANNA UNIVERSITY

51 University Ave, Selinsgrove, PA 17870

Telephone: (574) 374-0101
Fax: (574) 372-4040
Internet: www.susqu.edu

Founded 1858

Pres.: L. JAY LEMONS
Provost and Dean of Faculty: Dr LINDA McMILLIN
Dir of Library: KATHLEEN GUNNING

Library of 244,000 vols
Number of teachers: 123
Number of students: 1,900

Publication: *Susquehanna University Studies*.

SWARTHMORE COLLEGE

500 College Ave, Swarthmore, PA 19081-1397

Telephone: (610) 328-8000
Fax: (610) 328-8673
Internet: www.swarthmore.edu

Founded 1864 by members of the Religious Soc. of Friends

Academic year: September to May

Pres.: ALFRED H. BLOOM
Vice-Pres.: MAURICE ELDRIDGE
Registrar: MARTIN O. WARNER
Provost: CONSTANCE CAIIN HUNGERFORD
Dean: JIM LARIMORE
Librarian: PEGGY SEIDEN

Library of 754,499 vols, 7,811 periodical subscriptions
Number of teachers: 171

Number of students: 1,474.

TEMPLE UNIVERSITY

1801 North Broad St, Philadelphia, PA 19122

Telephone: (215) 204-7000
Internet: www.temple.edu

Founded 1884

Pres.: ANN WEAVER HART
Vice Pres. for Research and Graduate Studies: Dr KENNETH SOPRANO
Provost: LISA STAIANO-COICO
Vice Provosts: Dr RON J. TALLARIDA (Faculty Affairs), STEPHEN ZELNICK (acting) (Undergraduate Studies)
Sec.: WILLIAM C. SEYLER
Vice Provost for Libraries: LARRY ALFORD

Library: c. 2,400,000 vols, 16,000 periodicalsc.
Number of teachers: 2,600
Number of students: 33,286

Publications: *Law Quarterly*, *The American Journal of Legal History*, *Temple Review*, *Journal of Economics and Business*

DEANS

College of Allied Health: RONALD BROWN
Ambler Campus: SOPHIA WISNIEWSKA
Tyler School of Art: HESTER STINNETT (acting)
Fox School of Business and Management: MOSHE PORAT
School of Communications and Theater: CONCETTA STEWART
School of Dentistry: F. MARTIN TANSY
College of Education: KENT McGUIRE
College of Eng.: KEYA SADEGHIPOUR
Graduate School: AQUILES IGLESIAS
Beasley School of Law: ROBERT REINSTEIN
College of Liberal Arts: SUSAN HERBST
School of Medicine: JOHN M. DALY
Esther Boyer College of Music and Dept of Dance: ROBERT STROKER
School of Pharmacy: PETER DOUKAS
School of Podiatric Medicine: JOHN MATTIACCI
College of Science and Technology: ALLEN NICHOLSON (acting)
School of Social Admin. and Dept of Health Studies: LARRY ICARD
School of Tourism and Hospitality Management: MOSHE PORAT

THIEL COLLEGE

Greenville, PA 16125

Telephone: (412) 589-2000
Internet: www.thiel.edu

Founded 1866

Pres.: ROBERT C. OLSON
Sr Vice Pres.: GARY J. WITOSKY
Vice-President for College Advancement: DAVID J. GROBER
Vice-Pres. for Student Life and Dean of Students: ROSEANNE GILL JACOBSON
Dir of Admissions: SONYA LAPIKAS
Dean of the Faculty: MERVIN E. NEWTON
Vice-Pres. for Finance: M. SCOTT HARTLE
Dir of Library: ALLEN S. MORRILL

Library of 135,000 vols
Number of teachers: 57
Number of students: 965.

THOMAS JEFFERSON UNIVERSITY

1020 Walnut St, Philadelphia, PA 19107

Telephone: (215) 955-6000
Internet: www.jefferson.edu

Founded 1824

Pres.: ROBERT L. BARCHI
Librarian: EDWARD N. TAWYEA

Library of 167,504 vols
Number of teachers: 761
Number of students: 2,596

DEANS

Jefferson Medical College: JOSEPH S. GONNELLA
College of Graduate Studies: JUSSI J. SAUKKONEN
College of Allied Health Sciences: LAWRENCE ABRAMS

TRINITY EPISCOPAL SCHOOL FOR MINISTRY

311 Eleventh St, Ambridge, PA 15003

Telephone: (724) 266-3838
Fax: (724) 266-4617
Internet: www.tesm.edu

Founded 1976
Private control

Dean and Pres.: PAUL ZAHL
Academic Dean: Rev. Dr GAVIN J. McGRATH
Registrar: SHIRLEY BRUCE
Library Dir: SUSANAH HANSON

Number of teachers: 40
Number of students: 110 (full-time).

UNIVERSITY OF PENNSYLVANIA

3451 Walnut St, Philadelphia, PA 19104

Telephone: (215) 898-5000
Internet: www.upenn.edu

Founded 1740
Private control
Academic year: September to May, and two six-week summer terms

President: AMY GUTMANN
Provost: RONALD DANIELS
Vice-Provost and Director of Libraries: CARTON ROGERS
Senior Vice-President for Facilities and Real Estate Services: OMAR BLAIK
Executive Vice-President for Finance: CRAIG CARNAROLI
Executive Vice-President, University of Pennsylvania Health System: ARTHUR RUBENSTEIN
Senior Vice-President and General Counsel: WENDY WHITE
Vice-President of Budget and Management Analysis and Executive Director for Administrative Affairs in the Office of the Provost: BONNIE GIBSON
Vice-President for Business Services: LEROY NUNERY
Vice-President and Chief of Staff: JOANN MITCHELL
Vice-President for Development and Alumni Relations: JOHN ZELLER
Vice-President for Division of Public Safety: MAUREEN RUSH
Vice-President for Finance and Treasurer: SCOTT DOUGLASS
Vice-President for Government, Community and Public Affairs: CAROL SCHEMAN
Vice-President of Human Resources: JOHN J. HEUER
Vice-President for Information Systems and Computing: ROBIN BECK
Vice-President for University Communications: LORI DOYLE
Comptroller: KENNETH CAMPBELL
Secretary: LESLIE KRUHLY
Chief Executive Officer, University of Pennsylvania Health System: RALPH MULLER
Registrar: RONALD SANDERS
Dean of Admissions: WILLIS STETSON

Library: see Libraries and Archives
Number of teachers: 4,238
Number of students: 23,305

Publications: *Almanac* (journal of record), *Arts at Penn*, *Daily Pennsylvanian* (student newspaper), *PENN Current*, *Pennsylvania Gazette* (for alumni), *Red and Blue*, *Research at PENN* (online)

DEANS AND DIRECTORS

Annenberg School for Communication: MICHAEL DELLI CARPINI
School of Arts and Sciences: REBECCA BUSHNELL
School of Dental Medicine: MARJORIE JEFFCOAT
School of Engineering and Applied Science: EDUARDO GLANDT
Law School: MICHAEL FITTS
School of Medicine: ARTHUR RUBENSTEIN
School of Nursing: AFAF MELEIS
School of Social Work: RICHARD GELLES
School of Veterinary Medicine: ALAN KELLY
PennDesign: GARY A. HACK
Graduate School of Education: SUSAN FUHRMAN
Wharton School: PATRICK HARKER

HEADS OF DEPARTMENTS

Annenberg School for Communication (3620 Walnut St, Philadelphia, PA 19104-6220; tel. (215) 898-7041; internet www.asc.upenn .edu):

Dean: Dr MICHAEL DELLI CARPINI

School of Arts and Sciences (116 College Hall, Philadelphia, PA 19104-6377; internet www .sas.upenn.edu):

Anthropology: GREG URBAN
Biology: RICHARD SCHULTZ
Chemistry: LARRY SNEDDON
Classical Studies: SHEILA MURNAGHAN
Criminology: LAURIE ROBINSON
Earth and Environmental Science: FREDERICK SCATENA
East Asian Languages and Cultures: (vacant)
Economics: KENNETH WOLPIN
English: JAMES ENGLISH
Germanic Languages and Literatures: FRANK TROMMLER
History: SHELDON HACKNEY
History and Sociology: RUTH SCHWARTZ COWAN
History of Art: DAVID BROWNLEE
Linguistics: DONALD RINGE
Mathematics: JULIUS SHANESON
Music: JEFFREY KALLBERG
Near Eastern Languages and Civilizations: DAVID SILVERMAN
Philosophy: SCOTT WEINSTEIN
Physics and Astronomy: TOM LUBENSKY
Political Science: ROGERS SMITH
Psychology: ROBERT DeRUBEIS
Religious Studies: E. ANN MATTER
Romance Languages: IGNACIO LOPEZ
Slavic Languages and Literatures: KEVIN PLATT
Sociology: PAUL ALLISON
South Asia Studies: ADITYA BEHL

School of Dental Medicine (The Robert Schattner Center, 240 South 40th St, Philadelphia, PA 19104-6030; tel. (215) 898-8961; internet www.dental.upenn.edu):

Anatomy and Cell Biology: EDWARD MACARAK
Biochemistry: SHERRILL ADAMS
Endodontics: SYNGCUK KIM
Microbiology: GARY COHEN
Oral Medicine: MARTIN GREENBERG
Oral Surgery/Pharmacology: PETER QUINN
Orthodontics: ROBERT VANARSDALL
Pathology: BRUCE SHENKER
Periodontics: CYRIL EVIAN
Preventative and Restorative Dentistry: ALAN ATLAS, NAJEED SALEH

School of Education (3700 Walnut St, Philadelphia, PA 19104-6216; tel. (877) 736-6473; internet www.gse.upenn.edu):

Dean: Dr SUSAN FUHRMAN

School of Engineering and Applied Science (111 Towne Building, 220 South 33rd St, Philadelphia, PA 19104-6391; tel. (215) 898-

7246; ; tel. apo@seas.upenn.edu; internet www.seas.upenn.edu):

Bioengineering: DANIEL HAMMER
Chemical and Biomolecular Engineering: JOHN VOHS
Computer and Information Science: FERNANDO PEREIRA
Electrical and Systems Engineering: DANIEL KODITSCHEK
Materials Science and Engineering: PETER DAVIES
Mechanical Engineering and Applied Mechanics: JOHN BASSANI

Law School (3400 Chestnut St, Philadelphia, PA 19104-6204; tel. (215) 898-7483; internet www.law.upenn.edu):

Dean: MICHAEL FITTS

School of Medicine (295 John Morgan, Philadelphia, PA 19104-6055; tel. (215) 898-6796; fax (215) 898-8030; e-mail ahrdean@ mail.med.upenn.edu; internet www.med .upenn.edu):

Anaesthesia: LEE FLEISCHER
Biochemistry and Biophysics: P. LESLIE DUTTON
Biostatistics and Epidemiology: BRIAN L. STROM
Cancer Biology: CRAIG THOMPSON
Cell and Developmental Biology: JOE SANGER
Dermatology: JOHN STANLEY
Emergency Medicine: WILLIAM G. BAXT
Family Practice and Community Medicine: MARJORIE BOWMAN
Genetics: HAIG KAZAZIAN
Medical Ethics: ARTHUR CAPLAN
Medicine: ANDREW SCHAFER
Microbiology: ROBERT DOMS
Neurology: FRANCISCO GONZALEZ-SCARANO
Neuroscience: IRWIN LEVITAN
Neurosurgery: M. SEAN GRADY
Obstetrics and Gynaecology: MICHAEL MENNUTI
Ophthalmology: STUART FINE
Orthopaedic Surgery: RICHARD LACKMAN
Otorhinolaryngology: BERT O'MALLEY
Paediatrics: ALAN COHEN
Pathology and Laboratory Medicine: MARK TYKOCINSKI
Pharmacology: GARRET FITZGERALD
Physical Medicine and Rehabilitation: RICHARD SALCIDO
Physiology: H. LEE SWEENEY
Psychiatry: DWIGHT EVANS
Radiation Oncology: W. GILLES McKENNA
Radiology: R. NICK BRYAN
Surgery: LARRY KAISER

School of Nursing (Nursing Education Building, 420 Guardian Drive, Philadelphia, PA 19104-6096; tel. (215) 898-8281; internet www.nursing.upenn.edu):

Dean: ALAF MELEIS

School of Social Work (3701 Locust Walk, Philadelphia, PA 19104-6214; tel. (215) 898-5511; internet www.ssw.upenn.edu):

Dean: RICHARD GELLES

School of Veterinary Medicine (3800 Spruce St, Philadelphia, PA 19104-6006; tel. (215) 898-5438; internet www.vet.upenn.edu):

Animal Biology: NARAYAN AVADHANI
Clinical Studies, New Bolten Center: DAVID NUNAMAKER
Clinical Studies, Philadelphia: GAIL SMITH
Pathobiology: PHILLIP SCOTT

PennDesign (102 Meyerson, Philadelphia, PA 19104-6311; tel. (215) 898-8321; internet www.design.upenn.edu):

Architecture: RICHARD WESLEY
City and Regional Planning: Prof. EUGENIE BIRCH
Fine Arts: JOHN MOORE
Historic Preservation: FRANK MATERO

Landscape Architecture: JAMES CORNER
Real Estate: WITOLD RYBCZYNSKI
Urban Design: JONATHAN BARNETT

Wharton School (1000 SH-DH, Philadelphia, PA 19104-6364; tel. (215) 898-3030; fax (215) 898-3031; internet www.wharton.upenn .edu):

Accounting: ROBERT HOLTHAUSEN
Business and Public Policy: ELIZABETH BAILEY
Finance: MICHAEL GIBBONS
Health Care Systems: PATRIZIA DANZON
Insurance and Risk Management: NEIL DOHERTY
Legal Studies: KENNETH SHROPSHIRE
Management: DANIEL LEVINTHAL
Marketing: STEPHEN HOCH
Operations and Information Management: KARL ULRICH
Real Estate: GEORGETTE CHAPMAN POINDEXTER
Statistics: ABBA M. KRIEGER

PROFESSORS

Annenberg School for Communication
Communications:

CAPPELLA, J.
DELLI CARPINI, M.
FISHBEIN, M.
GANDY, O. H.
GROSS, L.
HORNIK, R.
JAMIESON, K. H.
JEMMOTT, J.
KATZ, E.
KRIPPENDORFF, K.
LINEBARGER, D.
MARVIN, C.
MESSARIS, P.
PRICE, V.
TUROW, J.
ZELIZER, B.

School of Arts and Sciences
Anthropology:

DIBBLE, H. L.
KOPYTOFF, I.
LEVENTHAL, R.
POSSEHL, G.
SABLOFF, J.
SANDAY, P.
SHARER, R.
SILVERSTEIN, M.
SPOONER, B.
URBAN, G.

Biology:

BINNS, A.
CASHMORE, A.
CASPER, B.
CEBRA, J.
CHENEY, D.
DALDAL, M. F.
DUNHAM, A. E.
EWENS, W.
GUILD, G.
JANZEN, D.
KIM, J.
PETRAITIS, P.
POETHIG, R. S.
REA, P. A.
ROME, L.
ROOS, D. S.
SCHULTZ, R.
WALDRON, I.
WEINBERG, E.
ZIGMOND, S.

Chemistry:

BERRY, D.
BLASIE, J. K.
CHRISTIANSON, D.
COOPERMAN, B.
DAI, H.-L.
FITTS, D.
HOCHSTRASSER, R.

JOULLIE, M.
KLEIN, M.
LESTER, M. I.
LU, P.
MACDIARMID, A.
MOLANDER, G.
PERCEC, V.
SMITH, A. B.
SNEDDON, L.
THERIEN, M.
THORNTON, E.
TOPP, M. R.
WAYLAND, B.
WINKLER, J.

Classical Studies:

COPELAND, R.
FARRELL, Jr, J.
MURNAGHAN, S.
ROSEN, R.

Criminology:

SHERMAN, L.

Earth and Environmental Science:

GIEGENGACK, R.
JOHNSON, A.
PFEFFERKORN, H.
SCATENA, F.

East Asian Languages and Civilizations:

HURST, G.
LAFLEUR, W.
MAIR, V.
STEINHARDT, N.

Economics:

BEHRMAN, J. R.
BURDETT, K.
CASS, D.
DIEBOLD, F.
ETHIER, W.
LEVINE, H.
MAILATH, G.
MATTHEWS, S.
MERLO, A.
POSTLEWAITE, A.
RIOS-RULL, J.-V.
ROB, R.
WOLPIN, K.
WRIGHT, R.

English:

AUERBACH, N.
BERNSTEIN, C.
BUSHNELL, R.
CONN, P.
CORRIGAN, T.
CURRAN, S.
DAVIS, T.
ENGLISH, J.
FILREIS, A.
DE GRAZIA, M.
KAPLAN, A.
KAUL, S.
LOOMBA, A.
MAHAFFEY, V.
PERELMAN, R.
QUILLIGAN, M.
RABATE, J.
RICHETTI, J.
STALLYBRASS, P.
STEINER, W.
STEWART, S.
WALLACE, D.

Germanic Languages and Literatures:

TROMMLER, F.
WEISSBERG, L.

History:

BEEMAN, R.
BERRY, M. F.
CHILDERS, T.
ENGS, R. F.
FARRISS, N.
HACKNEY, S.
HAHN, S.
KATZ, M.
KORS, A.

KUKLICK, B.
LEES, L. H.
LICHT, W.
LUDDEN, D.
MCDOUGALL, W.
PEISS, K.
PETERS, E.
RICHTER, D.
RUDERMAN, D.
SAVAGE, B.
STEINBERG, J.
SUGRUE, T. J.
TODD, M.
WALDRON, A.
ZUCKERMAN, M.

History and Sociology of Science:

COWAN, R.
FEIERMAN, S.
KOHLER, R.
KUKLICK, H.
LINDEE, M.
SIVIN, N.

History of Art:

BROWNLEE, D.
HOLOD, R.
MEISTER, M.
PITTMAN, H.
SILVER, L.

Linguistics:

CARDONA, G.
KROCH, A.
LABOV, W.
LIBERMAN, M
PRINCE, E.
RINGE, D.
SANKOFF, G.

Mathematics:

CHAI, C.
CHINBURG, T.
CROKE, C.
DETURCK, D.
DONAGI, R.
EPSTEIN, C.
FREYD, P.
GERSTENHABER, M.
GLUCK, H.
HARBATER, D.
KADISON, R. V.
KAZDAN, J.
KIRILLOV, A.
MINSKY, Y.
PEMANTLE, R.
PIMSNER, M.
POP, F.
PORTER, G.
POWERS, R.
SCEDROV, A.
SHANESON, J.
SHATZ, S.
WILF, H.
ZILLER, W.

Music:

BERNSTEIN, L.
KALLBERG, J.
NARMOUR, E.
PRIMOSCH, J.
REISE, J.
TOMLINSON, G.

Near Eastern Languages and Civilizations:

ALLEN, R.
BEN-AMOS, D.
SILVERMAN, D.
STERN, D.
TIGAY, J. H.

Philosophy:

BICCHIERI, C.
DOMOTOR, Z.
FREEMAN, S.
GUYER, P.
HATFIELD, G.
KAHN, C.
ROSS, J.

WEINSTEIN, S.

Physics and Astronomy:

BALAMUTH, D.
BEIER, E.
CVETIC, M.
DURIAN, D.
FORTUNE, H.
HEINEY, P.
HOLLEBEEK, R.
KAMIEN, R.
LANDE, K.
LANGACKER, P. G.
LIU, A.
LOCKYER, N.
LUBENSKY, T.
MELE, E.
NELSON, P.
OVRUT, B.
SEGRE, G.
SOVEN, P.
WILLIAMS, H.
YODH, A.

Political Science:

CALLAGHY, T.
DIIULIO, J.
FRANKEL, F.
GOLDSTEIN, A.
GUMANN, A.
KENNEDY, E.
KETTI, D.
LUSTICK, I. S.
MANSFIELD, E.
MUTZ, D.
NAGEL, J.
NORTON, A.
SMITH, R.
O'LEARY, B.
REED, A.
TEUNE, H.

Psychology:

BARON, J.
BRAINARD, D.
CHAMBLESS, D.
DERUBEIS, R.
FARAH, M.
GRILL, H.
KAHANA, M.
NORMAN, M. F.
RESCORLA, R.
RICHARDS, V.
RODIN, J.
ROZIN, P.
SABINI, J. P.
SELIGMAN, M.
SEYFARTH, R.

Religious Studies:

DUNNING, S.
DYSON, M.
MATTER, E. A.

Romance Languages:

ALONSO, C.
BROWNLEE, K.
DEJEAN, J.
DONALDSON-EVANS, L.
KIRKHAM, V.
LOPEZ, I.
MARCUS, M.
PRINCE, G.

Slavic Languages:

STEINER, P.

Sociology:

ALLISON, P.
ANDERSON, E.
BERG, I.
BIELBY, W.
BOSK, C.
COLLINS, R.
ENGLAND, P.
FURSTENBERG, F.
JACOBS, J.
MADDEN, J. F.
PRESTON, S.

SMITH, H.
WATKINS, S.
ZUBERI, T.

South Asian Regional Studies:

ROCHER, R.
SCHIFFMAN, H.

School of Dental Medicine

Anatomy/Cell Biology:

MACARAK, E.
GIBSON, C.

Biochemistry:

ADAMS, S.
GOLUB, E. E.
LeBOY, P.
MALAMUD, D.

Endodontics:

KIM, S.

Microbiology:

COHEN, G.
DiRIENZO, J.
RICCIARDI, R.

Oral Medicine:

GREENBERG, M.

Oral Surgery:

FONSECA, R.
HERSH, E.
QUINN, P.

Orthodontics:

KATZ, S.
VANARSDALL, R.

Pathology:

LALLY, E.
SHENKER, B.

Periodontics:

EVIANS, C.
JEFFCOAT, M.
POLSON, A.

School of Education:

BOE, E.
BORUCH, R.
FANTUZZO, J.
FUHRMAN, S.
GOERTZ, M.
GOODMAN, J.
HORNBERGER, N.
INGERSOLL, R.
KURILOFF, P.
LAZERSON, M.
MAYNARD, R.
McDERMOTT, P.
PICA, T.
SLAUGHTER-DEFOE, D.
SPENCER, M. D.
WAGNER, D.
WORTHAM, S.
ZEMSKY, R. M.

School of Engineering and Applied Science:

ALUR, R.
AYYASWAMY, P.
BADLER, N.
BASSANI, J.
BAU, H.
BONNELL, D.
BORDOGNA, J.
BUCHSBAUM, G.
CASSEL, T.
CHEN, I.-W.
COHEN, I.
DAVIDSON, S.
DAVIES, P.
DIAMOND, S.
DUCHEYNE, P.
EGAMI, T.
ENGHETA, N.
FARHAT, N.
FINKEL, L.
FISCHER, J.
FOSTER, K.
GALLIER, J. H.

GIRIFALCO, L.
GLANDT, E.
GORTE, R.
GRAHAM, W.
GUERIN, R.
HAMMER, D.
JAGGARD, D.
JOSHI, A.
KANNAN, S.
KASSAM, S.
KEARNS, M.
KEENAN, J.
KUMAR, V.
LAIRD, C.
LAKER, K.
LEE, I.
LIOR, N.
LUZZI, D.
MACARAK, E.
MARCUS, M. P.
MARGULIES, S.
MEANEY, D.
MINTZ, M.
PEREIRA, F.
PIERCE, B.
PONTE-CASTANEDA, P.
POPE, D.
RABII, S.
SCHERER, P.
SEIDER, W.
SHIEH, W.
SILVERMAN, B.
SMITH, J. M.
SMITH, T.
SOSLOWSKY, L.
TANNEN, V. B.
ULRICH, K.
VAN DER SPEIGEL, J.
VITEK, V.
VOHS, J.
VUCHIC, V.

Law School:

ADLER, M.
ALLEN-CASTELLITO, A.
AUSTIN, R.
BAKER, C. E.
BURBANK, S.
CHANG, H.
DELISLE, J.
EWALD, W.
FINKELSTEIN, C.
FITTS, M.
GOODMAN, F.
GORDON, S.
JOHNSTON, J.
KATZ, L.
KNOLL, M.
KREIMER, S.
KUBLER, F.
LESNICK, H.
MANN, B.
MOONEY, C.
MORSE, S.
PARCHOMOVSKY, G.
PERRY, S.
REITZ, C.
ROBINSON, P.
ROCK, E.
RUBIN, E.
SANCHIRICO, C.
SCHEPPLE, K. L.
SHULDINER, R.
SKEEL, D.
WACHTER, M.
WAX, A.

School of Medicine (295 John Morgan, Philadelphia, PA 19104-6055; internet www.med.upenn.edu):

Anaesthesia:

DEUTSCHMANN, C.
ECKENDOFF, R.
FLEISHER, L.
LONGNECKER, D.

Biochemistry and Biophysics:

DEGRADO, W.
DREYFUSS, G.
DUTTON, P. L.
ENGLANDER, S. W.
KALLEN, R.
LEMMON, M.
LEWIS, M.
LIEBMAN, P.
MATSCHINSKY, F.
OHNISHI, T.
VAN DUYNE, G.
VANDERKOOI, J.
WAND, A. J.
WILSON, D.
YONETANI, T.

Biostatistics and Epidemiology:

HEITJAN, D.
KUMANYIKA, S.
LANDIS, J. R.
LEE, H.
REBBECK, T.
STROM, B.
TEN HAVE, T.

Cancer Biology:

ALWINE, J.

Cell and Developmental Biology:

DiNARDO, S.
FRANZINI-ARMSTRONG, C.
SANGER, J.
SIMON, M.
WEISEL, J.

Dermatology:

ROOK, A.
STANLEY, J.

Emergency Medicine:

BAXT, W. G.
THORN, S.

Family Practice and Community Medicine:

BOWMAN, M.

Genetics:

BUCAN, M.
GASSER, D.
KADESCH, T.
KAZAZIAN, H.
LIEBHABER, S.
SPIELMAN, R.

Medical Ethics:

CAPLAN, A.

Medicine:

ALBELDA, S.
ASCH, D.
BENNETT, J.
BIRNBAUM, M.
BLUMBERG, B.
BRASS, L.
COHEN, P.
COLLMAN, R.
COOKE, N.
DANIELE, R.
EISENBERG, R.
EMERSON, S. G.
EPSTEIN, J.
FELDMAN, H.
FITZGERALD, G.
FRIEDMAN, H. M.
GEWIRTZ, A.
GLICK, J.
HILLMAN, A.
HOXIE, J.
KELLEY, W.
LAZAR, M.
LEVINSON, A.
MacGREGOR, R. R.
MADAIO, M.
PACK, A.
PANETTIERI, R.
PARMACEK, M.
PHILLIPS, S.
PYERITZ, R.
RUBENSTEIN, A.

RUBIN, H.
RUSTGI, A.
SCHAFER, A.
SCHREIBER, A.
SCHUMACHER, H.
SCHWARTZ, J.
SNYDER, P.
TANNEN, R.
THOMPSON, C.
TURKA, L.
TURNER, B.
WEBER, B.
WILSON, J.
ZIYADEH, F.

Microbiology:
BOETTIGER, D.
BUSHMAN, F.
DAVIES, H. C.
FRANKEL, F.
FRASER, N.
GOLDFINE, H.
KAJI, A.
PATERSON, Y.
ROSS, S.
WEISS, S.

Neurology:
BARCHI, R.
BERMAN, P.
BROWN, M.
COSLETT, H. B.
DICHTER, M.
GONZALEZ-SCARANO, F.
PLEASURE, D.
SCHERER, S.
SELZER, M.
TENNEKOON, G. I.

Neuroscience:
HAYDON, P.
LEVITAN, I.
LINDSTROM, J.
NUSBAUM, M.
PALMER, L.
RAPER, J.
ROSENQUIST, A.
SALZBERG, B.
SEHGAL FIELD, A.
STERLING, P.

Neurosurgery:
GRADY, M. S.
WELSH, F.

Obstetrics and Gynaecology:
HECHT, N.
MASTROIANNI, L.
MENNUTI, M.
RUBIN, S.
STRAUSS, J.

Ophthalmology:
BENNETT, J.
FINE, S.
JACOBSON, S.
LATIES, A.
PUGH, E.
STONE, R.

Orthopaedic Surgery:
FITZGERALD, R.
HEPPENSTALL, R.
KAPLAN, F.
SOSLOWSKY, L.

Otorhinolaryngology:
DOTY, R.
KENNEDY, D.
O'MALLEY, B.
SAUNDERS, J.

Paediatrics:
ASAKURA, T.
BALLARD, P. L.
BRODEUR, G.
DOUGLAS, S.
EMANUEL, B.
FOX, W.
GRUNSTEIN, M.

HIGH, K.
HONIG, P.
HOYER, J.
JOHNSON, P.
LEVY, R.
OFFIT, P.
PONCZ, M.
SEGAL, S.
SILBER, J.
YUDKOFF, M.

Pathology and Laboratory Medicine:
ARGON, Y.
CANCRO, M.
CHOI, Y.
CINES, D.
DAVIES, P.
DOMS, R.
GAULTON, G.
GONATAS, N.
GREENE, M.
HANCOCK, W.
JARETT, L.
JUNE, C. H.
KAMOUN, M.
KORETZKY, G. A.
LAMBRIS, J.
LEE, V. M.-Y.
LIVOLSI, V.
MONROE, J.
MUSCHEL, R.
NOWELL, P.
SCHLAEPFER, W.
SHAW, L.
TROJANOWSKI, J.
TYKOCINSKI, M.
WOLF, B.
YOUNG, D.

Pharmacology:
ASSOIAN, R.
BLAIR, I.
EBERWINE, J.
MANNING, D.
PENNING, T.
PITTMAN, R.
WHITEHEAD, A. S.

Physiology:
BAYLOR, S. M.
CIVAN, M.
COBURN, R.
DE WEER, P.
DEUTSCH, C.
FISHER, A.
FOSKETT, J. K.
GOLDMAN, Y.
HOLZBAUR-HOWARD, E.
JAMMEY, P.
LAHIRI, S.
LU, Z.
SWEENEY, H. L.
WINEGRAD, S.

Psychiatry:
ASTON-JONES, G.
BERRETTINI, W.
COYNE, J.
CRITS-CHRISTOPH, P.
DINGES, D. F.
EVANS, D.
FOA, E.
GUR, R.
GUR, R.
KATZ, I.
LERMAN, C.
LUCKI, I.
NICHOLLS, R.
O'BRIEN, C.
PRICE, R.
RICKELS, K.
WADDEN, T.
WELLER, E.

Radiation Oncology:
BIAGLOW, J.
BLOCH, P.
GLATSTEIN, E.

KENNEDY, A.
KOCH, C.
MCKENNA, W.

Radiology:
BAUM, S.
BRYAN, R. N.
JOSEPH, P.
KARP, J.
KUNG, H.
LEIGH, J.
SCHNALL, M.
UDUPA, J.
WEHRLI, F.

Surgery:
ADZICK, N. S.
BARKER, C. F.
DREBIN, J.
EDMUNDS, L.
FLAKE, A.
KAISER, L.
NAJI, A.
NUSBAUM, M.
ROMBEAU, J.
ROSATO, E.
SHAKED, A.
SPRAY, T.
WEIN, A.
WHITAKER, L.

School of Nursing:
AIKEN, L.
BARNSTEINER, J.
BROWN, L. P.
BUHLER-WILKERSON, K.
EVANS, L.
GENNARO, S.
JEMMOTT, L.
LANG, N.
MCCAULEY, L.
MEDOFF-COOPER, B.
MELEIS, A.
NAYLOR, M.
O'SULLIVAN, A.
STRUMPF, N.

School of Social Work

Social Work:
CNAAN, R.
ESTES, R.
SANDS, R.
SELTZER, V.
SOLOMON, P.
SPIGNER, C.
STERN, M.

School of Veterinary Medicine:
AQUIRRE, G.
ATCHISON, M.
AVADHANI, N.
BEECH, J.
BELLO, L.
BENSON, C.
BOSTON, R.
BRINSTER, R.
CHACKO, S.
CHALUPA, W.
DAVIES, R.
DODSON, P.
DROBATZ, K.
EISENBERG, R.
FARRELL, J.
FERGUSON, J.
FERRER, J.
FLUHARTY, S.
GIGER, U.
GOLDSCHMIDT, M. H.
HARVEY, C.
HASKINS, M.
HENDRICKS, J. C.
KELLY, A.
KING, L.
KLIDE, A.
LASTER, L.
MISELIS, R.
NEWTON, C.
NUNAMAKER, D.

RAMBERG, C.
REEF, V.
RICHARDSON, D.
ROSS, M.
ROZMIAREK, H.
SCHAD, G.
SCOTT, P.
SERPELL, J.
SHAPIRO, B.
SMITH, G.
SOMA, L.
SPEAR, J.
SWEENEY, C.
WEBER, W.
WEISS, L.
WOLFE, J. H.

PennDesign:
GYOURKO, J.
LINNEMAN, P.
POINDEXTER, G.
RYBCZYNSKI, W.
SAGALYN, L.

Wharton School
Accounting:
BAIMAN, S.
GONEDES, N.
HOLTHAUSEN, R.
ITTNER, C.
LAMBERT, R. A.
LARCKER, D.
VERRECCHIA, R.

Business and Public Policy:
ALLEN, W. B.
BAILEY, E.
FAULHABER, G.
PACK, H.
PACK, J.
WALDFOGEL, J.

Finance:
ABEL, A.
ALLEN, H. F.
BLUME, M.
GIBBONS, M.
GORTON, G.
HERRING, R.
INMAN, R.
KEIM, D.
KIHLSTROM, R.
LEWIS, K. K.
MACKINLAY, A. C.
MARSTON, R.
RAMASWAMY, K.
SIEGEL, J.
STAMBAUGH, R.

Health Care Systems:
DURNS, L.
DANZON, P.
HARRINGTON, S.
PAULY, M.

Insurance and Risk Management:
BABBEL, D.
CUMMINS, J. D.
DOHERTY, N.
LEMAIRE, J.
MITCHELL, O.
ROSENBLOOM, J.

Legal Studies:
BELLACE, J.
DONALDSON, T.
DUNFEE, T.
ORTS, E.
ROSOFF, A.
SHELL, G. R.
SHROPSHIRE, K.

Management:
AMIT, R.
CAPPELI, P.
GERRITY, T.
GULLEN, M.
HAMILTON, W. F.
HOUSE, R.

KIMBERLY, J.
KLEIN, K.
KOBRIN, S.
LEVINTHAL, D.
MacMILLAN, I.
MEYER, M.
PENNINGS, J.
SINGH, H.
SINGH, J.
USEEM, M.
WEIGELT, K.
WINTER, S.

Marketing:
ARMSTRONG, J. S.
DAY, G.
ELIASHBERG, J.
FADER, P.
HOCH, S.
HUTCHISON, J.
IANOBUCCI, D.
KAHN, B.
LODISH, L.
MEYER, R.
RAJU, J. S.
REIBSTEIN, D.
SCHMITTLEIN, D.
WARD, S.
WIND, Y.

Operations and Information Management:
CLEMONS, E.
COHEN, M.
FISHER, M.
GUIGNARD-SPIELBERG, M.
HARKER, P.
HERSHEY, J.
KIMBROUGH, S.
KLEINDORFER, P.
KUNREUTHER, H.
ULRICH, K.
ZHENG, Y.

Real Estate:
GYOURKO, J.
LINNEMAN, P.
POINDEXTER, G.
WACHTER, S.

Statistics:
BROWN, L.
BUJA, A.
GEORGE, E.
KRIEGER, A.
LOW, M.
ROSENBAUM, P.
SHAMAN, P.
STEELE, J. M.
STINE, R.

ATTACHED INSTITUTIONS
Abramson Cancer Center.
Abramson Family Cancer Research Institute.
Ackoff Center for Advancement of Systematic Approaches (ACASA).
African Studies Center.
Alice Paul Research Center for Research on Women and Gender.
Alzheimer's Disease Center.
Ancient Studies Center.
Annenberg Public Policy Center.
Bioengineering Research Laboratories.
Boettner Center of Financial Gerontology.
Cartographic Modeling Laboratory.
Center for Advanced Judaic Studies.
Center for Advanced Study of India.
Center for Advancing Care in Serious Illness.
Center for AIDS Research.
Center for Analytic Research in Economics and Social Sciences (CARESS).

Center for Animal Health and Productivity.
Center for Animal Transgenesis and Germ Cell Research.
Center for Bioethics.
Center for Bioinformatics.
Center for Children's Policy Practice and Research.
Center for Clinical Epidemiology and Biostatistics.
Center for Cognitive Neuroscience.
Center for Cognitive Therapy.
Center for Communications and Information Science and Policy.
Center for Comparative Genetics.
Center for Computer Analysis of Texts (CCAT).
Center for Developmental Biology.
Center for East Asian Studies.
Center for Economic Studies in Technology.
Center for Equine Sports Medicine.
Center for Experimental Therapeutics.
Center for Folklore and Ethnography.
Center for Functional and Metabolic Imaging.
Center for Functional Neuroimaging.
Center for Gerontologic Nursing Science.
Center for Greater Philadelphia.
Center for Health Management and Economics.
Center for Health Outcomes and Policy Research.
Center for Health, Achievement, Neighborhood, Growth and Ethnic Studies (CHANGES).
Center for Hearing Science.
Center for Human Modeling and Simulation.
Center for Human Resources.
Center for the Interaction of Animals and Society.
Center for International Comparisons.
Center for Intervention and Practice Research.
Center for Leadership and Change Management.
Center for Mental Health Policy and Services Research.
Center for Neurodegenerative Disease Research (CNDR).
Center for Nursing Research.
Center for Programs in Contemporary Writing.
Center for Research on Religion and Urban Civil Society.
Center for Research on Reproduction and Women's Health.
Center for School Study Councils.
Center for Sensor Technologies.
Center for Sleep and Respiratory Neurobiology.
Center for the Study of Black Literature and Culture.
Center for the Study of Social Work Practice.
Center for the Study of the History of Nursing.
Center for the Study of Youth Policy.
Center for Teaching and Learning.
Center for the Treatment and Study of Anxiety.

Center for Undergraduate Research and Fellowships.

Center for Urban Ethnography.

Center for Urban Health Research.

Center for Veterinary Critical Care.

Cerebrovascular Research Center.

Chemical Heritage Foundation.

Christopher H. Browne Center for International Politics.

Computational Biology and Informatics Laboratory.

Consortium for Policy Research in Education (CPRE).

Data Mining Group.

David A. Mahoney Institute of Neurological Sciences.

Deafness and Family Communication Center.

Diabetes Center.

Digital Design Research Laboratory.

Distributed Systems Laboratory.

Dubois Collective Research Institute.

Economics Research Unit.

Emerging Economies Program.

Fels Center of Government.

Fishman-Davidson Center for Service and Operations Management.

French Institute for Culture and Technology.

General Clinical Research Center.

General Robotics, Automation, Sensing and Perception Lab (GRASP Lab).

George Weiss Center for International Financial Research.

Hartford Center for Geriatric Nursing Excellence.

Head Injury Center.

Human Genetics Center.

Institute on Aging.

Institute for Economic Research.

Institute for Environmental Medicine.

Institute for Environmental Studies.

Institute for Law and Economics.

Institute for Medicine and Engineering.

Institute for Research in Cognitive Science.

Institute for Research on Higher Education.

Institute for Strategic Threat Analysis and Response (ISTAR).

International Center of Research for Women, Children and Families.

International Literacy Institute (ILI).

Italian Studies Center.

Jerry Lee Center on Criminology.

Krogman Center for Research in Child Growth and Development.

Labor Relations Council.

Laboratory for Biological Research in Nursing.

Laboratory for Research on the Structure of Matter (LRSM).

Leonard Davis Institute of Health Economics.

Linguistic Data Consortium.

Logic and Computation Group.

Mari Lowe Center for Comparative Oncology Research.

McNeil Center for Early American Studies.

Metabolic Magnetic Resonance Research and Computing Center (MMRRCC).

Middle East Center.

Museum Applied Science Center for Archaeology.

Nano/Bio Interface Center.

National Center on Adult Literacy.

National Center on Educational Quality of the Workforce.

National Center on Fathers and Families.

National Scalable Cluster Project.

NIH Center for Molecular Studies in Digestive and Liver Diseases.

Penn Genomics Institute.

Penn Humanities Forum.

Penn Language Center.

Penn Lung Center.

Penn Regional Nanotechnology Facility.

PennGen Medical Genetics.

PennHIP (University of Pennsylvania Hip Improvement Program).

Pennsylvania Muscle Institute.

Pension Research Council.

PET (Positron Emission Tomography) Center.

Plant Science Institute.

Population Studies Center.

Premenstrual Syndrome Program.

Real-Time Systems Group.

Reginald H. Jones Center for Management Policy & Strategy Organization.

Regional Laser and Biotechnology Laboratory.

Research and Evaluation of Social Policy.

Research Center in Oral Biology.

Risk Management and Decision Processes Center.

Rodney L. White Center for Financial Research.

S. S. Huebner Foundation for Insurance Education.

Samuel Zell and Robert Lurie Real Estate Center.

School Change through Inquiry (SCI) Program.

SEI Center for Advanced Studies in Management.

Smell and Taste Center.

Social Science Data Center.

Social Work Mental Health Research Center.

Sol C. Snider Entrepreneurial Research Center.

Solomon Asch Center for Study of Ethnopolitical Conflict.

SwitchWare Project.

Systems Design Research Laboratory.

The Campbell Collaboration.

The Center of Neurobiology and Behavior (CNB).

The Eldridge Reeves Johnson Center for Molecular Biophysics.

The Joseph H. Lauder Institute of Management and International Studies.

The Knight Higher Education Collaborative.

Treebank Project.

WEBI–Wharton E-Business Initiative.

Wharton Center for Quantitative Finance.

Wharton Financial Institutions Center.

Wharton Small Business Development Center.

William and Phyllis Mack Center for Technological Innovation.

Zicklin Center for Business Ethics Research

UNIVERSITY OF PITTSBURGH

4200 Fifth Ave, Pittsburgh, PA 15260(412) 624-4141

Internet: www.pitt.edu

Founded 1787 as Pittsburgh Academy; in 1819 became Western University of Pennsylvania, and in 1908 University of Pittsburgh

State-related

Academic year: August to DecemberJanuary to April (two semesters) (summer sessions also available)

Chancellor: MARK A. NORDENBERG

Senior Vice Chancellor and Provost: JAMES V. MAHER

Senior Vice Chancellor for Health Sciences and Dean, School of Medicine: ARTHUR S. LEVINE

Executive Vice-Chancellor and Interim General Counsel: JEROME COCHRAN

Vice Chancellor, Budget, and Controller: ARTHUR G. RAMICONE

Vice Chancellor for Institutional Advancement: ALBERT J. NOVAK, Jr

Vice-Provost and Dean of Students: KATHY W. HUMPHREY

Secretary of the Board of Trustees and Assistant Chancellor: B. JEAN FERKETISH

University Registrar: SAMUEL D. CONTE

Director of University Library System: RUSH G. MILLER

Library: see Libraries and Archives

Number of teachers: 4,243 (Pittsburgh campus; 3,552 full-time, 691 part-time)

Number of students: 26,559 (Pittsburgh campus; 21,776 full-time, 4,783 part-time)

DEANS

School of Arts and Sciences: N. JOHN COOPER

School of Dental Medicine: T. W. BRAUN

School of Education: A. LESGOLD

School of Engineering: G. D. HOLDER

College of General Studies: S. R. KINSEY

School of Health and Rehabilitation Sciences: C. E. BRUBAKER

School of Law: MARY A. CROSSLEY

School of Information Sciences: R. L. LARSEN

School of Medicine: A. S. LEVINE

School of Nursing: J. DUNBAR-JACOB

School of Pharmacy: P. D. KROBOTH

School of Social Work: L. DAVIS

Joseph M. Katz Graduate School of Business: LAWRENCE F. FEICK

Graduate School of Public Health: DONALD S. BURKE

Graduate School of Public and International Affairs: DAVID MILLER

College of Business Administration: JOHN T. DELANEY

University Honors College: G. A. STEWART

CHAIRS OF DEPARTMENTS

Arts and Sciences:

Africana Studies: C. BLAKE

Anthropology: R. SCAGLION

Architectural Studies: M. F. HEARN Jr

Biological Sciences: G. HATFULL

Chemistry: D. WALDECK

Classics: M. POSSANZA

Communication: D. EGOLF

Computer Science: R. MELHEM

East Asian Languages and Literatures: H. NARA

Economics: J. F. RICHARD

English: S. CARR

Film Studies: M. LANDY

French and Italian: P. WATTS

Geology and Planetary Sciences: B. STEW-
ART
Germanic Languages and Literatures: C.
MUENZER
Hispanic Languages and Literatures: J.
BEVERLEY
History: W. CHASE
History and Philosophy of Science: S.
MITCHELL
History of Art and Architecture: K. SAVAGE
Intelligence Systems: J. WIEBE
Jewish Studies: A. ORBACH
Linguistics: A. JUFFS
Mathematics: J. M. CHADAM
Music: D. ROOT
Neuroscience: A. SVED
Philosophy: J. ALLEN
Physics and Astronomy: D. JASNOW
Political Science: B. AMES
Psychology: A. R. CAGGIULA
Religious Studies: L. PENKOWER
Slavic Languages and Literatures: D. J.
BIRNBAUM
Sociology: J. MARKOFF
Statistics: S. IYENGAR
Studio Arts: D. JENKINS
Theatre Arts: A. FAVORINI
Urban Studies: E. MULLER

Education:

Administrative and Policy Studies: M. W.
MCCLURE
Psychology in Education: C. JOHNSON
Instruction in Learning: G. ZIMMERMAN
Health, Physical and Recreation Educa-
tion: J. JAKICIC

Dental Medicine:

Dental Hygiene: A. RICCELLI
Endodontics: J. A. WALLACE
Orthodontics and Dentofacial Orthopae-
dics: J. SCIOTE
Paediatric Dentistry: D. STUDEN-PAVLO-
VICH
Periodontics: P. FAMILI
Prosthodontics: D. J. PIPKO

Engineering:

Bioengineering: H. BOROVETZ
Chemical and Petroleum: R. M. ENICK
Civil and Environmental: C. J. EARLS
Electrical and Computer Engineering: W.
STANCHINA
Industrial: B. BIDANDA
Materials Science and Engineering: J. A.
BARNARD
Mechanical: M. CHUYU

Health and Rehabilitation Sciences:

Clinical Dietetics and Nutrition: S. M.
LEFHART (acting)
Communication Science and Disorders: M.
R. MCNEIL
Emergency Medicine: W. STOY
Health Information Management: M.
ABDELHAK
Occupational Therapy: J. C. ROGERS
Physical Therapy: A. DELITTO
Rehabilitation Science and Technology: R.
COOPER

Information Sciences:

Information Science and Telecommunica-
tions: M. B. H. WEISS
Library and Information Science: M. M.
KIMMEL

Medicine:

Cell Biology and Physiology: S. C. WATKINS
Molecular Genetics and Biochemistry: J. C.
GLORIOSO
Neurobiology: S. G. AMARA
Pathology: G. MICHALOPOULOS
Pharmacology: P. A. FRIEDMAN

Nursing:

Acute/Tertiary Care: L. HOFFMAN
Health and Community Systems: E.
OLSHANSKY

Health Promotion and Development: S.
ENGBERG

Graduate School of Public Health:

Behavioural and Community Health Ser-
vices: R. M. GOODMAN
Biostatistics: H. E. ROCKETTE
Environmental and Occupational Health:
B. PITT
Epidemiology: R. B. NESS
Health Policy and Management: J. R. LAVE
Human Genetics: I. KAMBOH
Infectious Diseases and Microbiology: C. R.
RINALDO

Graduate School of Public and International
Affairs:

International Development: P. NELSON
Public and Urban Affairs Division: L.
HALEY
International Affairs Division: M. STANI-
LAND

RESEARCH CENTRES

**Learning Research and Development
Center:** Dir L. B. RESNICK.

**University Center for International Stu-
dies:** Dir W. BRUSTEIN.

**University Center for Social and Urban
Research:** Dir R. SCHULZ.

**University of Pittsburgh Cancer Insti-
tute:** Dir R. B. HERBERMAN.

REGIONAL CAMPUSES

University of Pittsburgh at Bradford:
President LIVINGSTON ALEXANDER; 76 teachers (69 full-time, 7 part-time); 1,427 students (1,076 full-time, 351 part-time).

University of Pittsburgh at Greensburg:
President FRANK A. CASSELL; 142 teachers (81
full-time, 61 part-time); 1,864 students
(1,656 full-time, 208 part-time).

University of Pittsburgh at Johnstown:
President ALBERT L. ETHERIDGE; 164 teachers
(144 full-time, 20 part-time); 3,209 students
(2,946 full-time, 263 part-time).

University of Pittsburgh at Titusville:
President WILLIAM A. SHIELDS; 60 teachers
(22 full-time, 38 part-time); 565 students
(422 full-time, 143 part-time).

UNIVERSITY OF SCRANTON

Scranton, PA 18510
Telephone: (570) 941-7400
Fax: (570) 941-6369
E-mail: admissions@scranton.edu
Internet: www.scranton.edu
Founded 1888
Academic year: August to May
Pres.: SCOTT R. PILARZ
Provost and Vice-Pres. for Academic Affairs:
HAROLD W. BAILLIE
Vice-Pres. for Finance and Treasurer: DAVID
E. CHRISTIANSEN
Vice-Pres. for Student Affairs: VINCENT CAR-
ILLI
Dean of Library: CHARLES E. KRATZ
Number of teachers: 251
Number of students: 4,615
Publications: *The Scranton Journal* (alumni
magazine, quarterly), *Windhover* (year-
book), *Aquinas* (student newspaper), *Dia-
konia* (eastern Christian studies)

DEANS

College of Arts and Sciences: Dr JOSEPH
DREISBACH
Graduate School: Dr ROSE SEBASTIAVELLI
(acting)
Dexter Hanley College: Dr SHIRLEY ADAMS
Arthur J. Kania School of Management: Dr
RONALD JOHNSON

Panuska College of Professional Studies: Dr
JAMES PALLANTE

UNIVERSITY OF THE ARTS

320 South Broad St, Philadelphia, PA 19102
Telephone: (215) 717-6000
Fax: (215) 717-6045
E-mail: admissions@uarts.edu
Internet: www.uarts.edu
Founded 1987 by merger of Philadelphia
College of Art and Design (f. 1876) and
Philadelphia College of Performing Arts (f.
1870)
Academic year: September to May
Pres.: WILLIAM E. MEA
Provost: RICHARD J. LAWN
Dean of Students: R. ALLEN LEFFERS
Dean of Enrollment Management: BARBARA
ELLIOTT
Dir of Libraries: CAROL GRANEY
Number of teachers: 329 (101 full-time, 228
part-time)
Number of students: 1,938

DEANS

Philadelphia College of Art and Design:
STEPHEN TARANTAL
Philadelphia College of Performing Arts:
RICHARD LAWN
College of Media and Communications: NEIL
KLEINMAN

UNIVERSITY OF THE SCIENCES IN PHILADELPHIA

600 South 43rd St, Philadelphia, PA 19104
Telephone: (215) 596-8800
Internet: www.pcps.edu
Founded 1821
President: PHILIP P. GERBINO
Vice-President for Academic Affairs: BARBARA
BYRNE
Dean of Students and Academic Support
Services: JUANA REINA-LEWIS
Dean of Arts and Sciences: CHARLES W.
GIBLEY, Jr
Dean of Pharmacy: GEORGE DOWNS
Financial Aid Officer: MICHAEL COLAHAN
Registrar: M. THERESE SCANLON
Librarian: MIGNON ADAMS
Library of 76,000 vols
Number of students: 2,000
Publication: *American Journal of Pharmacy*
(4 a year)

DIRECTORS

Biological Sciences: MARGARET KASSCHAU
Biomedical Writing: LILI FOX VELEZ
Chemistry: EDWARD BIRNBAUM
Humanities: BEVERLEY ALMGREN (acting)
Mathematics, Physics and Computer
Science: BERNARD BRUNNER
Medical Technology: MARGARET REINHART
Occupational Therapy: RUTH SCHEMM
Pharmaceutical Sciences: EDWIN T. SUGITA
Pharmacy Practice and Administration:
REBECCA FINLEY
Physical Education: ROBERT MORGAN
Physical Therapy: ANNETTE IGLARSH
Physician Assistants: KENNETH HARBERT
Social Sciences: JOSEPH LAMBERT

URSINUS COLLEGE

POB 1000, Collegeville, PA 19426-1000
Telephone: (610) 409-3000
Internet: www.ursinus.edu
Founded 1869
Pres.: Dr JOHN STRASSBURGER
Vice-Pres. for Enrollment: RICK DiFELICIAN-
TONIO
Librarian: CHARLIE JAMISON

Library of 200,000 vols
Number of teachers: 165
Number of students: 1,184 day, 1,300 evening.

VALLEY FORGE CHRISTIAN COLLEGE

1401 Charlestown Rd, Phoenixville, PA 19460
Telephone: (610) 935-0450
Fax: (610) 935-9353
E-mail: admissions@vfcc.edu
Internet: www.vfcc.edu

Founded 1932 as Maranatha Summer Bible School; present name 1977
Private control
Academic year: August to May

President: Dr DONALD G. MEYER
Vice-President (Academic Affairs): Dr PHILIP MCLEOD
Vice-President (Student Life): Dr DANIEL MORTENSEN
Vice-President (Institutional Advancement): CHARLES COLES
Head Librarian: DORSEY REYNOLDS

Number of teachers: 39
Number of students: 757.

VILLANOVA UNIVERSITY

Villanova, PA 19085
Telephone: (610) 519-4500
Fax: (610) 519-5000
Internet: www.villanova.edu

Founded 1842
Academic year: August to May

President: Rev. EDMUND J. DOBBIN
Vice-President for Academic Affairs: Dr JOHN JOHANNES
University Vice-President: Dr HELEN K. LAFFERTY
Vice-President for Institutional Advancement: JOHN M. ELIZANDRO
Vice-President for Student Life: Rev. JOHN STACK
Vice-President and General Counsel: DOROTHY MOLLOY
Senior Vice-President, Administration: Rev. WILLIAM MCGUIRE
Librarian: JOSEPH LUCIA

Library of 1,010,421 vols, 2,998 periodicals, 1,789,816 microforms
Number of teachers: 820 (511 full-time, 309 part-time)
Number of students: 9,833

Publications: *Horizons* (2 a year), *The Theology Institute Proceedings* (annually), *Journal for Peace and Justice Studies* (2 a year), *Journal of South Asian and Middle Eastern Studies* (4 a year), *Villanova Law Review* (4 a year), *Augustinian Studies* (2 a year), *Journal of Financial Education* (2 a year), *Concept: Graduate Journal of Interdisciplinary Research* (annually), *Concept* (2 a year), *Journal of Catholic Social Thought* (2 a year), *American Catholic Studies* (quarterly)

DEANS

Arts and Science: Rev. KAIL C. ELLIS
Commerce and Finance: Dr EDWARD MATHIS
Enrollment Management: STEPHEN MERRITT
Law: Dr MARK A. SARGENT
Engineering: BARRY C. JOHNSON
Nursing: Dr M. LOUISE FITZPATRICK
Graduate Studies for the College of Liberal Arts and Sciences: Dr GERALD LONG

WASHINGTON & JEFFERSON COLLEGE

60 South Lincoln St Washington, PA 15301
Telephone: (888) 926-3529
Fax: (724) 223-6534
Internet: www.washjeff.edu
Language of instruction: English

Founded 1781
Academic year: September to May

President: TORI HARING-SMITH
Special Assistant to the President: G. ANDREW REMBERT
Vice-President Academic Affairs and Dean of the Faculty: JAN CZECHOWSKI
Vice-President Business and Finance: DAVID CARSON
Vice-President Development and Alumni Relations: JOHN P. PLANTE
Vice-President Enrollment: ALTON E. NEWELL
Associate Vice-President for Business: DENNIS E. MCMASTER
Executive Director of Communications and Corporate Relations: MARY BETH FORD
Director of Admissions: ROBERT ADKINS
Director of Alumni Relations: MICHELE HUFNAGEL
Director of Career Services: ROBERTA CROSS
Director of Financial Aid: MICHELLE VETTOREL
Director of Foundation and Government Relations: LYNN I. BARGER
Director of Information and Technology Services: DANIEL FAULK
Director of Library Services: ALLEN C. BENSON
Director of Protection Service: EDWARD COCHRAN
Registrar: BRENT KOERBER

Library of 189,848 vols, 526 current serial subscriptions; 14,877 microforms; 9,159 audiovisual materials
Number of teachers: 130 (97 full-time, 33 part-time)
Number of students: 1,418 (1,400 full-time, 18 part-time)

Publication: *Topic* (The Washington & Jefferson College Review is published annually.)

DEANS

Assoc. Dean for Academic Affairs: DANA J. SHILLER
Asst Dean for Multicultural Affairs: CONSTINIA CHARBONNETTE
Dean of Student Life: SUSAN C. YUHASZ

WAYNESBURG COLLEGE

51 West College St, Waynesburg, PA 15370
Telephone: (724) 627-8191
E-mail: admissions@waynesburg.edu
Internet: www.waynesburg.edu

Founded 1849

Liberal arts and sciences

Pres.: TIMOTHY R. THYREEN
Vice-Pres. for Academic Affairs: A. J. ANGLIN
Assoc. Vice-Pres. for Institutional Advancement: KAREN E. GALENTINE
Sr Vice-Pres. for Institutional Planning, Research and Educational Services: RICHARD L. NOFTZGER, Jr
Vice-Pres. for Business and Finance: ROY R. BARNHART
Vice-Pres. of Student Devt: GERALD WOOD
Dir of College Relations: BETHANY DOYLE
Registrar: RONALD D. COLTRANE
Library Dir: SUZANNE WYLIE

Library of 126,098 vols
Number of teachers: 66 full-time
Number of teachers: 48 part-time
Number of students: 1,351.

WESTMINSTER COLLEGE

New Wilmington, PA 16172
Telephone: (724) 946-8761
Fax: (724) 946-7171
Internet: www.westminster.edu

Founded 1852
Academic year: August to May
Related to the Presbyterian Church (USA)

Pres.: R. THOMAS WILLIAMSON
Vice-Pres. for Academic Affairs and Dean of the College: JESSE T. MANN
Vice-Pres. for Finance: KENNETH J. ROMIG
Dean of Students: NEAL A. EDMAN
Dean of Admissions: BRADLEY P. TOKAR
Registrar: JUNE G. PIERCE
Head Librarian: DORITA F. BOLGER

Library of 224,000 vols
Number of teachers: 96
Number of students: 1,650 (1,450 undergraduate, 200 postgraduate)

Publications: *Holcad* (newspaper), *Scrawl* (literary), *Argo* (yearbook), *Westminster Magazine* (quarterly).

WESTMINSTER THEOLOGICAL SEMINARY

2960 West Church Rd, Glenside, PA 19038
Telephone: (215) 887-5511
Fax: (215) 887-5404
E-mail: admissions@wts.edu
Internet: www.wts.edu

Founded 1929
Private control
Academic year: September to May

Pres.: PETER A. LILLBACK
Chief Operating Officer: A. D. DABNEY
Vice-Pres. for Institutional Advancement: ALAN WHITE
Vice-Pres. for Finance: ERIK V. DAVIS
Vice-Pres. and Dean of Texas Campus: STEVEN T. VANDERHILL
Registrar: KAREN PRESTON
Library Dir: ALEXANDER FINLAYSON

Number of teachers: 50
Number of students: 450 (full-time).

WIDENER UNIVERSITY

1 University Pl., Chester, PA 19013-5792
Telephone: (610) 499-4000
Fax: (610) 876-9751
Internet: www.widener.edu

Founded 1821; formerly Widener College

Pres.: Dr ROBERT J. BRUCE, Dr JAMES T. HARRIS, III
Sr Vice-Pres. and Provost: JO ALLEN

Library of 845,762 vols
Number of teachers: 704 (310 full-time; 394 part-time)
Number of students: 7,355 (3,823 full-time; 3,532 part-time)

Publications: *Bulletin*, *Summer Sessions Bulletin*, *Alumni Magazines*, *Law Review*, *Corporate Law Journal*, *Widener Law Symposium Journal*

DEANS

College of Arts and Sciences: Dr LAWRENCE W. PANEK
School of Eng.: Dr FRED A. AKL
School of Hospitality Management: NICHOLAS J. HADGIS
School of Law: DOUGLAS E. RAY
School of Business Admin.: Dr JOSEPH A. DIANGELO, Jr
School of Nursing: Dr MARGUERITE M. BARBIERE
School of Human Service Professions: Dr STEPHEN C. WILHITE
Univ. College: Dr ARLENE DECOSMO

WILKES UNIVERSITY

84 West South St, Wilkes-Barre, PA 18766
Telephone: (570) 408-5000
Fax: (570) 408-7800
E-mail: info@wilkes.edu
Internet: www.wilkes.edu
Founded 1933
Academic year: August to May
Pres.: TIM GILMORE
Provost: BERNARD GRAHAM
Vice-Pres. for Human Resources: MAGGIE LUND
Vice-Pres. for Devt: MARTY WILLIAMS
Vice-Pres. for Enrollment Services: MICHAEL J. FRANTZ
Registrar: SUSAN A. HRITZAK
Library Dir: JON LINDGREN
Library of 233,709 vols
Number of teachers: 122 full-time
Number of students: 2,157 full-time

DEANS

Nesbit College of Pharmacy of Nursing: Dr BERNARD W. GRAHAM
Jay S. Sidhu School of Business and Leadership: Dr PAUL C. BROWNE
College of Science and Eng.: Dr DALE A. BURNS
College of Arts, Humanities and Social Sciences: Dr DARIN E. FIELDS

WILSON COLLEGE

Chambersburg, PA 17201
Telephone: (717) 264-4141
Fax: (717) 264-1578
E-mail: admissions@wilson.edu
Internet: www.wilson.edu
Founded 1869
Pres.: Dr LORNA DUPHINEY EDMUNDSON
Vice-Pres. for Enrollment: MARY ANN NASO
Librarian: KATHLEEN MURPHY
Library of 170,000 vols, 450 periodicals
Number of teachers: 77 (38 full-time, 39 part-time)
Number of students: 776 (370 full-time, 406 part-time)
Private liberal arts college.

YORK COLLEGE OF PENNSYLVANIA

York, PA 17405-7199
Telephone: (717) 846-7788
Fax: (717) 846-1607
E-mail: admissions@ycp.edu
Internet: www.ycp.edu
Founded 1787 as York County Academy; present name 1968
Private control
Academic year: August to May
Pres.: Dr GEORGE W. WALDNER
Dean of Academic Affairs: Dr WILLIAM T. BOGART (acting)
Dean of Student Affairs: JOSEPH F. MERKLE
Library Dir: SUSAN M. CAMPBELL
Number of teachers: 370
Number of students: 5,900 (4,400 full-time undergraduate, 1,500 part-time and post-graduate).

RHODE ISLAND

BROWN UNIVERSITY

POB 1920 Providence, RI 02912
Telephone: (401) 863-1000
Fax: (401) 863-7737
E-mail: postmaster@brown.edu
Internet: www.brown.edu
Founded 1764
Private

Academic year: September to May
Chancellor: STEPHEN ROBERT
Pres.: RUTH J. SIMMONS
Provost: DAVID KERTZER
Sr Vice-Pres. for Univ. Advancement: RONALD D. VANDEN DORPEL
Exec. Vice-Pres. for Planning: RICHARD R. SPIES
Exec. Vice-Pres. for Finance and Admin.: ELIZABETH HUIDEKOPER
Vice-Pres. for Public Affairs and Univ. Relations: MICHAEL CHAPMAN
Vice-Pres. and Chief Investment Officer: CYNTHIA E. FROST
Vice-Pres. for Admin.: WALTER C. HUNTER
Vice-Pres. and Gen. Counsel: BEVERLY E. LEDBETTER
Vice-Pres. for Int. Advancement: RONALD D. MARGOLIN
Vice-Pres. for Campus Life and Student Services: RUSSELL CAREY
Vice-Pres. for Alumni Relations: TODD ANDREWS
Vice-Pres. for Computing and Information Services: TERRI-LYNN THAYER (acting)
Vice-Pres. for Facilities Management: STEPHEN MAIORISI
Vice-Pres. for Devt: NEIL STEINBERG
Vice-Pres. for Research: CLYDE BRIANT
Dean of Admission: JAMES MILLER
Univ. Registrar: MICHAEL J. PESTA
Univ. Librarian: HARRIETTE HEMMASI
Library of 6,000,000 vols
Number of teachers: 658
Number of students: 7,744

DEANS

College: KATHERINE BERGERON
Faculty: RAJIV VOHRA
Graduate School: SHEILA BONDE
Medicine and Biological Sciences: ELI ADASHI

BRYANT COLLEGE

1150 Douglas Pike, Smithfield, RI 02917-1284
Telephone: (401) 232-6000
Fax: (401) 232-6319
E-mail: www@bryant.edu
Internet: www.bryant.edu
Founded 1863
President: RONALD K. MACHTLEY
Vice-President for University Advancement: LAURIE MUSGROVE
Vice-President for Student Affairs/Dean of Students: TOM EAKIN
Vice-President for Business Affairs/Treasurer: JOSEPH R. MEICHELBECK
Vice-President for Academic Affairs and Dean of Faculty: V. K. UNNI
Director of Undergraduate Programs: ELIZABETH A. POWERS
Director of Graduate Programs: W. DAYLE NATTRESS
Director of Library Services: MARY F. MORONEY
Library: over 127,000 vols
Number of students: 2,748 undergraduates, 584 graduates
Publication: *Bryant Review*.

JOHNSON AND WALES UNIVERSITY

8 Abbott Park Place, Providence, RI 02903
Telephone: (401) 598-1000
E-mail: admissions@jwu.edu
Internet: www.jwu.edu
Campuses at Providence (RI), Charleston (SC), Norfolk (VA), North Miami (FL), Denver (CO)
Founded 1914
Private control
University President: Dr JOHN A. YENA

Executive Vice-President and President, Providence Campus: Dr JOHN J. BOWEN
Vice-President: Dr IRVING SCHNEIDER
Vice-President (Administration): ROBIN KRAKOWSKY
Dean of Libraries: Dr HELENA RODRIGUES
Number of students: 9,635

DEANS

College of Business: Dr PAUL R. TRZNADEL
College of Culinary Arts: KARL GUGGENMOS
Hospitality College: RICHARD L. BRUSH
School of Technology: EVERETT V. ZURLINDEN
School of Arts and Sciences: Dr ANGELA R. RENAUD
Graduate School: Dr JOE GOLDBLATT

PROVIDENCE COLLEGE

Providence, RI 02918
Telephone: (401) 865-1000
Internet: www.providence.edu
Founded 1917
President: Rev. PHILIP A. SMITH
Dean of Enrollment Management: CHRISTOPHER P. LYDON
Associate Registrar: ANN A. LOOMIS
Librarian: EDGAR C. BAILEY, Jr
Library of 342,000 vols
Number of teachers: 338
Number of undergraduate students: 3,597.

RHODE ISLAND COLLEGE

600 Mount Pleasant Ave, Providence, RI 02908
Telephone: (401) 456-8000
Fax: (401) 456-8379
E-mail: theweb@ric.edu
Internet: www.ric.edu
Founded 1854
President: JOHN NAZARIAN
Vice-President for Academic Affairs: JOHN J. SALESSES
Vice-President for Student Affairs: GARY M. PENFIELD
Vice-President for Administration and Finance: LENORE DELUCIA
Vice-President for Development and College Relations (vacant)
Director of Records: BURT D. CROSS
Librarian: RICHARD A. OLSEN
Library of 360,000 vols
Number of teachers: 375
Number of students: 7,214 undergraduate, 1,852 graduate

DEANS

Arts and Sciences: RICHARD WEINER
Education and Human Development: DAVID E. NELSON
Graduate Studies: JAMES TURLEY
Social Work: GEORGE METREY
Student Affairs: GARY PENFIELD

RHODE ISLAND SCHOOL OF DESIGN

Providence, RI 02903
Telephone: (401) 454-6100
Fax: (401) 454-6420
E-mail: admissions@risd.edu
Internet: www.risd.edu
Founded 1877
Academic year: September to May
President: ROGER MANDLE
Executive Vice-President (Finance and Administration): JEFF APFEL
Provost: JOSEPH DEAL
Director (Planning and Research): FELICE BILLUPS
Dean (Student Affairs): EDWARD DWYER
Librarian: CAROL TERRY
Library of 107,000 vols

Museum of Art: 75,000 items
Number of teachers: 503 (146 full-time; 357 part-time)
Number of students: 2,294
Publications: *RISD Views*, *Portfolio* (Student Year Book), *Bulletin of Rhode Island School of Design, Museum Notes.*

ROGER WILLIAMS UNIVERSITY

1 Old Ferry Rd, Bristol, RI 02809
E-mail: admit@rwu.edu
Internet: www.rwu.edu
Private control
Academic year: September to May
President: Dr Roy J. Nirschel
Provost: Dr Edward J. Kavanagh
Vice-President (Finance and Administration): James C. Noonan
Vice-President (Enrollment Management and Retention): Lynn Fawthrop
Registrar: Peter Wilbur (acting)
Dean of Library: Peter Van Deekle
Number of teachers: 315
Number of students: 4,087 (3,361 full-time undergraduate, 726 postgraduate and professional)

DEANS

College of Arts and Sciences: Dr Ruth A. Koelle
School of Business: Dr Maling Ebrahimpour
School of Architecture, Art and Historic Preservation: Stephen White
School of Education: Dr Marie C. DiBiasio
School of Engineering, Computing and Construction Management: Robert A. Potter, Jr
School of Justice Studies: Dr Anthony M. Pesare

SALVE REGINA UNIVERSITY

Newport, RI 02840
Telephone: (401) 847-6650
Fax: (401) 847-0372
Internet: www.salve.edu
Founded 1947
Private control (Religious Sisters of Mercy)
President: Dr M. Therese Antone
Vice-President for Business and Financial Affairs: William B. Hall
Vice-President for Institutional Advancement: Michael Semenza
Vice-President for Academic Affairs and Dean of Faculty: Dr Judith M. Mills
Vice-President for Administrative Services and Community Relations: Thomas P. Flanagan
Vice-President for Student Development: John Rok
Executive Vice-President: Dominic C. Varisco
Registrar: Kathleen H. Willis
Dean of Students: John Quinn
Dean of Enrollment and Admissions: Laura McPhie

Library of 116,000 vols
Number of teachers: 120
Number of students: 2,100.

UNIVERSITY OF RHODE ISLAND

Kingston, RI 02881
Telephone: (401) 874-1000
E-mail: admissions@uri.edu
Internet: www.uri.edu
Founded 1892 as Rhode Island College of Agriculture and Mechanic Arts; attained university status 1951
President: Robert L. Carothers
Provost: M. Beverly Swan

Vice-President for Business and Finance: Kenneth N. Kermes
Vice-President for Student Affairs: John McCray
Vice-President for University Relations: Robert L. Beagle
Registrar: Robert Strobel
Dean of University Libraries: Paul Gandel
Library of 1,000,000 vols
Number of teachers: 721
Number of students: 13,698
Publications: *URI Commercial Fisheries Newsletter*, *URI Reporter* (Newsletter), *Pacer*

DEANS

College of Arts and Sciences: Winifred Brownell (acting)
College of Business Administration: Frank S. Budnick (acting)
College of Continuing Education: Walter A. Crocker, Jr
College of Engineering: Thomas J. Kim
College of Human Science and Services: Barbara Brittingham
University College: Diane W. Strommer
College of Pharmacy: Louis A. Luzzi
College of Resource Development: Margaret Leinen (acting)
College of Nursing: Dayle Joseph (acting)
Graduate School of Oceanography: Margaret Leinen
Graduate School: Thomas Rockett (acting)
Admissions and Student Financial Aid: David G. Taggart

ATTACHED RESEARCH PROGRAMS

Agricultural Experiment Station.
Biotechnology Center.
Center for Atmospheric Chemistry Studies.
Center for Energy Study.
Center for Ocean Management Studies.
Coastal Resources Center.
Consortium for the Development of Technology.
Co-operative Extension Service.
Division of Engineering Research and Development.
Institute for Advanced Manufacturing.
Institute in Human Science and Services.
International Center for Marine Resource Development.
Laboratories for Scientific Criminal Investigation.
Marine Experiment Station.
Marine Advisory Service.
National Sea Grant Depository.
Research Center in Business and Economics.
Rhode Island Teachers' Center.
RI Water Resources Center.
Robotics Research Center.

SOUTH CAROLINA

ALLEN UNIVERSITY

1530 Harden St, Columbia, SC 29204
Telephone: (803) 375-5700
Fax: (803) 375-5733
E-mail: admissions@allenuniversity.edu
Internet: www.allenuniversity.edu
Founded 1870
Private control
Pres.: Dr Charles E. Young
Vice-Pres. for Academic Affairs: Dr Walter C. Howard

Number of teachers: 35
Number of students: 350.

ANDERSON COLLEGE

316 Boulevard, Anderson, SC 29621
Telephone: (864) 231-2000
Fax: (864) 231-2004
E-mail: admissions@ac.edu
Internet: www.anderson-college.edu
Founded 1911
Private control
Academic year: August to May
Pres.: Dr Evans P. Whitaker
Vice-Pres. for Academic Affairs and Academic Dean: Dr Danny Parker
Vice-Pres. for Finance and Admin.: John M. Kunst
Vice-Pres. for Institutional Advancement: R. Dean Woods
Vice-Pres. for Student Services: Dr Bob L. Hanley
Vice-Pres. for Enrollment Services and Quality Initiatives: R. Mark Hughes
Registrar: Lisa M. Thompson
Library Dir: Kent Millwood
Number of teachers: 151
Number of students: 1,664.

BENEDICT COLLEGE

1600 Harden St, Columbia, SC 29204
Telephone: (803) 253-5143
Fax: (803) 253-5215
Internet: www.benedict.edu
Founded 1870 as Benedict Institute; present name 1894
Private control
Academic year: August to May
President: Dr David H. Swinton
Executive Vice-President: Dr Ruby W. Watts
Senior Vice-President (Academic Affairs): Dr Richard C. Miller
Vice-President (Institutional Advancement): Barbara C. Moore
Vice-President (Student Affairs): Dr David B. Whaley
Vice-President (Institutional Effectiveness): Gary E. Knight
Vice-President (Business Affairs): Claudine Gee
Vice-President (Community Development): Jabari Simama
Library Director: Darlene Zinnerman-Bethea
Number of teachers: 159 (126 full-time, 33 part-time)
Number of students: 2,770

DEANS

School of Business: Dr John Cole
School of Education: Dr Janeen Witty
School of Humanities, Arts and Social Sciences: Dr Peter Jackson
School of Science, Technology, Engineering and Mathematics: Dr Stacey Jones

CHARLESTON SOUTHERN UNIVERSITY

9200 University Blvd, POB 118087, Charleston, SC 29423-8087
Telephone: (843) 863-7004
Fax: (843) 863-8074
Internet: www.csuniv.edu
Founded 1964
Private control
Academic year: August to April
President: Dr Jairy C. Hunter, Jr
Provost: Dr A. Kennerley Bonnette
Vice-President (Business Affairs): Kent Brasher

Vice-President (Planning and Student Affairs): Dr RICK BREWER
Vice-President (Advancement and Marketing): JIM BRADLEY
Vice-President (Enrollment Management): DEBBIE WILLIAMSON
Registrar: REX NESTOR
Library Director: Dr ENID RUTHERFORTH CAUSEY

Number of teachers: 80
Number of students: 2,800

DEANS

College of Human and Social Sciences: Dr DON DOWLESS
College of Science and Mathematics: Dr JERYL JOHNSON
School of Business: Dr JOHN B. DUNCAN
School of Education: Dr SANDRA BOWDEN
School of Nursing: Dr MARIAN M. LARISEY

THE CITADEL

171 Moultrie St, Charleston, SC 29409
Telephone: (803) 953-5000
Internet: www.citadel.edu
Founded 1842
Controlled by State of South Carolina
President: JOHN GRINALDS
Executive Vice-President and Dean of the College: Brig.-Gen. R. CLIFTON POOLE
Vice-President for Facilities and Administration: Col DONALD M. TOMASIK
Commandant of Cadets: Col JOSEPH W. TREZ
Vice-President for Finance and Business Affairs: Col CALVIN G. LYONS
Director of Libraries: Lt-Col ANGIE S. W. LE CLERCQ
Registrar: Col ISAAC S. METTS, Jr (acting)
Library of 182,000 vols
Number of teachers: 163 full-time, 53 part-time, 28 ROTC
Number of students: 7,500
Publications: *Sphinx*, *Brigadier*, *Guidon*, *Shako*, *Citadel Monograph Series*, *Citadel Review*.

CLAFLIN UNIVERSITY

400 Magnolia St, Orangeburg, SC 29115-9970
Telephone: (803) 535-5000
E-mail: mzeigler@claflin.edu
Internet: www.claflin.edu
Founded 1869
Private control
Academic year: August to May
President: Dr HENRY N. TISDALE
Vice-President (Academic Affairs): Dr HOWARD D. HILL
Vice-President (Development and Alumni Affairs): Rev. W. V. MIDDLETON
Vice-President (Student Development and Services): Dr LEROY A. DURANT
Head Librarian: MARILYN PRINGLE
Number of teachers: 50
Number of students: 965

HEADS OF DEPARTMENTS

Division of Humanities and Social Sciences: Dr PEGGY S. RATLIFF
Division of Business Administration: Dr HARPAL S. GREWAL
Division of Natural Sciences and Mathematics: Dr VERLIE TISDALE
Division of Education: Dr BARBARA BOWMAN

CLEMSON UNIVERSITY

Clemson, SC 29634
Telephone: (864) 656-3311
Fax: (864) 656-4676
Internet: www.clemson.edu

Founded 1889 as Clemson Agricultural College
Language of instruction: English
Academic year: August to May
President: JAMES F. BARKER
Provost and Vice-President for Academic Affairs: DORIS R. HELMS
Vice-President for Student Affairs: ALMEDA R. JACKS
Vice-President for Advancement: NEILL CAMERON, Jr
Vice-President for Public Service and Agriculture: JOHN W. KELLY
Vice-President for Research: CHRISTIAN E. G. PRZIREMBEL
Executive Secretary of the Board: J. THORNTON KIRBY
Librarian: J. F. BOYKIN
Library of 1,437,333 vols
Number of teachers: 1,204 (1,057 full-time, 147 part-time)
Number of students: 16,980

DEANS

Vice-Provost and Dean of Graduate School: BONNIE HOLADAY
Vice-Provost and Dean of Undergraduate Studies: JEROME REEL
College of Agriculture, Forestry and Life Sciences: CALVIN SCHOUTTIES
College of Architecture, Arts and Humanities: JANICE SCHACH
College of Health, Education and Human Development: LAWRENCE R. ALLEN
College of Engineering and Science: THOMAS M. KEINATH
College of Business and Public Affairs: JERRY TRAPNELL

COASTAL CAROLINA UNIVERSITY

POB 261954, Conway, SC 29528-6054
Telephone: (843) 347-3161
E-mail: admissions@coastal.edu
Internet: www.coastal.edu
Founded 1954 as Coastal Carolina Junior College; present name 1993
Academic year: August to May
President: RONALD R. INGLE
Dean of Library Services: Dr LYNNE SMITH
Number of teachers: 353
Number of students: 5,980

DEANS

College of Business Administration: DAVID A. DeCENZO
College of Education: GILBERT H. HUNT
College of Humanities and Fine Art: LYNN FRANKEN
College of Natural and Applied Sciences: (vacant)
School of Continuing Studies: PETER B. BALSAMO

COKER COLLEGE

Hartsville, SC 29550
Telephone: (803) 383-8000
Fax: (803) 383-8129
Internet: www.coker.edu
Founded 1908
Academic year: September to May
President: JAMES D. DANIELS
Dean of the Faculty and College Provost: RONALD L. CARTER
Vice-President for Enrollment Management: Dr STEPHEN B. TERRY
Director of Financial Aid: BETTY WILLIAMS
Librarian: MINOO MONAKES
Library of 70,000 vols
Number of teachers: 51
Number of students: 975.

COLLEGE OF CHARLESTON

66 George St, Charleston, SC 29424
Telephone: (803) 953-5500
Fax: (843) 953-5811
Internet: www.cofc.edu
Founded 1770; chartered 1785
Public control
Academic year: August to May
President: LEO I. HIGDON, JR
Provost, and Senior Vice-President, Academic Affairs: ELISE B. JORGENS
Registrar: WILLIAM ANDERSON
Librarian: DAVID COHEN
Number of teachers: 467
Number of students: 11,356
Publications: *Chrestomathy* (undergraduate research in the humanities and social sciences, annually), *Crazyhorse* (literary magazine, 2 a year)

DEANS

School of Arts: VALERIE MORRIS
School of Business and Economics: ROBERT PITTS
School of Education: FRANCES WELCH
School of Humanities and Social Sciences: SAMUEL S. HINES, Jr
School of Sciences and Mathematics: NORINE NOONAN

COLUMBIA COLLEGE

Columbia, SC 29203
Telephone: (803) 754-3178
Internet: www.columbiacollegesc.edu
Founded 1854
President: Dr CAROLINE WHITSON
Provost: Dr LAURIE B. HOPKINS
Registrar: JACK HAMILTON
Librarian: JOHN C. PRITCHETT
Library of 176,018 vols
Number of teachers: 105
Number of students: 1,453.

COLUMBIA INTERNATIONAL UNIVERSITY

7435 Monticello Rd, Columbia, SC 29203
Telephone: (803) 754-4100
Fax: (803) 786-4209
E-mail: yesciu@ciu.edu
Internet: www.ciu.edu
Founded 1923 as Columbia Bible School; present name 1994
Private control
Academic year: August to May
President: Dr GEORGE W. MURRAY
Vice-President (Business and Finance): GREGG SCHULTE
Vice-President (Corporate Planning): BOB KALLGREN
Vice-President (Development): CHARLIE LAW
Provost: RALPH ENLOW
Registrar: JIM ROCHE
Dean of Information Sources and Services: DAVID MASH
Number of students: 1,082.

CONVERSE COLLEGE

Spartanburg, SC 29302
Telephone: (864) 596-9040
Fax: (864) 596-9225
E-mail: info@converse.edu
Internet: www.converse.edu
Founded 1889
Academic year: September to May
President: NANCY O. GRAY
Director of Admissions: WANDA MOORE McDOWELL
Librarian: WADE WOODWARD
Library of 200,000 vols

Number of teachers: 85
Number of students: 1,200
Arts, sciences, music.

ERSKINE COLLEGE

Due West, SC 29639
Telephone: (803) 379-8833
E-mail: admissions@erskine.edu
Internet: www.erskine.edu
Founded 1839
President: LUDER G. WHITLOCK, Jr
Director of Admissions: BART WALKER
Librarian: JOHN F. KENNERLY

Library of 150,000 vols
Number of teachers: 62
Number of students: 831.

FRANCIS MARION UNIVERSITY

POB 100547, Florence, SC 29501
Telephone: (843) 661-1231
E-mail: admissions@fmarion.edu
Internet: www.fmarion.edu
Founded 1970
State control
Academic year: August to May
President: Dr LUTHER F. CARTER
Provost: Dr RICHARD N. CHAPMAN
Vice-President (Administration): Dr GARY W. HANSON
Vice-President (Student Affairs): Dr JOSEPH E. HEYWARD
Vice-President (Business Affairs): JOHN J. KISPERT
Registrar: H. ELIZABETH McLEAN
Dean of Library: H. PAUL DOVE, Jr

Number of teachers: 210
Number of students: 3,360 (2,940 undergraduate, 420 postgraduate)

DEANS

College of Liberal Arts: Dr RICHARD N. CHAPMAN
School of Business: Dr M. BARRY O'BRIEN
School of Education: (vacant)

FURMAN UNIVERSITY

Greenville, SC 29613
Telephone: (864) 294-2000
Internet: www.furman.edu
Founded 1826
President: DAVID E. SHI
Vice-President for Academic Affairs and Dean: A. V. HUFF
Vice-President for Business Affairs: WENDY LIBBY
Vice-President for Development: DONALD J. LINEBACK
Vice-President for Enrollment: BENNY WALKER
Vice-President for Intercollegiate Athletics: JOHN BLOCK
Vice-President for Marketing and Public Relations: GREGORY A. CARROLL
Vice-President for Student Services: HARRY B. SHUCKER
Registrar: PAUL H. ANDERSON
Librarian: JANIS BANDELIN

Library of 390,000 vols
Number of teachers: 200
Number of students: 2,840
Publications: *Studies* (2 a year), *Paladin* (weekly), *The Echo* (literary, 2 a year), *Furman Magazine* (annually), *Furman Reports* (4 a year), *Humanities Review* (annually)

DEANS

Graduate Studies: HAZEL W. HARRIS
Continuing Education: JOHN H. DICKEY

LANDER UNIVERSITY

Greenwood, SC 29649
Telephone: (864) 388-8000
Fax: (864) 388-8890
Internet: www.lander.edu
Founded 1872
President: Dr DANIEL W. BALL
Vice-President for Academic Affairs: LEONARD E. LUNDQUIST
Vice-President for Business and Administration: DIANE NEWTON
Vice-President for Student Affairs: RANDY BOUKNIGHT
Vice-President for University Advancement: ELEANOR S. TEAL
Dean of Enrollment Services: R. THOMAS NELSON III
Director of Library: ANN T. HARE

Library of 379,300 vols
Number of teachers: 130
Number of students: 2,710.

LIMESTONE COLLEGE

Gaffney, SC 29340-3799
Telephone: (864) 489-7151
Fax: (864) 487-8706
E-mail: admiss@limestone.edu
Internet: www.limestone.edu
Founded 1845
Academic year: August to May
President: Dr WALT GRIFFIN
Vice-President (Academic Affairs): Dr CHARLES J. CUNNING
Vice-President (Institutional Advancement): Dr WILLIAM H. BAKER
Vice-President (Financial Affairs): DAVID S. RILLING
Vice-President (Enrollment Services): CHRISTOPHER N. PHENICIE
Vice-President (Information Technology): CARNEGIE R. HORTON
Vice-President (Student Services): ROBERT A. OVERTON
Librarian: CAROLYN T. HAYWARD

Library of 105,523 vols
Number of teachers: 50 (full-time)
Number of students: 3,024 (620 main campus, 2,404 off-campus).

LUTHERAN THEOLOGICAL SOUTHERN SEMINARY

4201 N Main St, Columbia, SC 29203-5898
Telephone: (803) 786-5150
Fax: (803) 786-6499
E-mail: thenderson@ltss.edu
Internet: www.ltss.edu
Private control
President: Rev.Dr H. FREDERICK REISZ, Jr
Vice-President (Academic Affairs) and Dean: MICHAEL ROOT
Vice-President (Business Affairs): RICHARD KENDRICK
Vice-President (Development and Seminary Relations): Dr MARY ANN W. SHEALY
Registrar: SANDRA RHYNE
Library Director: Dr LYNN A. FEIDER

Number of teachers: 20
Number of students: 140 (full-time).

MEDICAL UNIVERSITY OF SOUTH CAROLINA

171 Ashley Ave, Charleston, SC 29425
Telephone: (803) 792-2300
Fax: (803) 792-0392
Internet: www.musc.edu
Founded 1824
Language of instruction: English
Academic year: September to June
President: Dr RAYMOND S. GREENBERG

Vice-President (Academic Affairs): Dr JOHN R. RAYMOND
Vice-President (Finance and Administration): Dr LISA MONTGOMERY
Vice-President (Information Technology): Dr FRANK C. CLARK
Vice-President (Medical Affairs): Dr JOSEPH G. REVES
Librarian: Dr THOMAS P. BASLER
Number of teachers: 1,281
Number of students: 2,339
Publication: *Humanitas* (annually)

DEANS

College of Dental Medicine: JACK SANDERS
College of Health Professions: Dr DANIELLE RIPICH
College of Medicine: Dr JOSEPH G. REVES
College of Nursing: Dr GAIL W. STUART
College of Pharmacy: Dr JOSEPH DIPERO
College of Graduate Studies and University Research: Dr PERRY V. HALUSHKA

MORRIS COLLEGE

100 W College St, Sumter, SC 29150-3599
Telephone: (803) 934-3200
Fax: (803) 773-3687
E-mail: webcomment@morris.edu
Internet: www.morris.edu
Founded 1908
Private control
President: LUNS C. RICHARDSON
Dean of Student Affairs: MARION R. SANFORD

Number of teachers: 70
Number of students: 880

HEADS OF DEPARTMENTS

Division of Business Administration: Assoc. Prof. RICHARD L. SMITH
Division of Religion and Humanities: Assoc. Prof. LEROY STAGGERS
Division of General Studies: ALLTHEA J. TRUITT (acting)
Division of Education: Prof. BOBBY L. BRISBON
Division of Natural Sciences and Mathematics: Prof. RADMAN M. ALI
Division of Social Sciences: JACOB E. BUTLER, Jr

NEWBERRY COLLEGE

2100 College St, Newberry, SC 29108
Telephone: (803) 276-5010
Fax: (803) 321-5627
E-mail: admissions@newberry.edu
Internet: www.newberry.edu
Founded 1856
Private control (affiliated with the Evangelical Lutheran Church in America: South Carolina, Southeastern, Florida-Bahamas, and Caribbean Synods)
Academic year: August to May
President: Dr MITCHELL M. ZAIS
Dean of Academic Affairs: Dr L. FRANK McCOY
Librarian: LAWRENCE ELLIS

Library of 79,899 vols
Number of teachers: 70
Number of students: 760
Publications: *Dimensions* (2 a year), *The Indian* (2 a month), *Eklekta* (annually), *Kinnikinnick* (annually), *The Newberrian* (annually).

NORTH GREENVILLE COLLEGE

POB 1892, Tigerville, SC 29688
Telephone: (864) 977-7001
E-mail: admissions@ngc.edu
Internet: sharepoint.ngc.edu

Founded 1892 as North Greenville High School; present name 1972
Private control
Academic year: August to May
President: JAMES B. EPTING
Registrar: PAMELA FARMER
Number of teachers: 35
Number of students: 1,300.

PRESBYTERIAN COLLEGE

Clinton, SC 29325
Telephone: (864) 833-2820
Fax: (864) 833-8481
Internet: www.presby.edu
Founded 1880
Academic year: August to May
President: Dr JOHN V. GRIFFITH
Vice-President for Academic Affairs: Dr J. DAVID GILLESPIE
Vice-President for Enrollment: R. DANA PAUL
Dean of Students: TELESIA DAVIS
Director of Library: DAVID CHATHAM
Library of 166,110 vols
Number of teachers: 111 (79 full-time, 32 part-time)
Number of students: 1,182.

SOUTH CAROLINA STATE UNIVERSITY

Orangeburg, SC 29117
Telephone: (803) 536-7000
Fax: (803) 533-3622
Internet: www.scsu.edu
Founded 1896
Academic year: August to May
President: Dr LEROY DAVIS
Director of Admissions: LILLIAN ADDERSON (acting)
Library Director: MARY L. SMALLS
Library of 298,051 vols
Number of teachers: 311
Number of students: 4,500.

SOUTHERN WESLEYAN UNIVERSITY

907 Wesleyan Drive, Central, SC 29630-1020
Telephone: (864) 644-5000
Internet: www.swu.edu
Founded 1906
Private control
Academic year: August to May
President: DAVID J. SPITTAL
Number of teachers: 130
Number of students: 1,360 (1,310 undergraduate, 50 postgraduate).

UNIVERSITY OF SOUTH CAROLINA

Columbia, SC 29208
Telephone: (803) 777-2001
Fax: (803) 777-3264
Internet: www.sc.edu
Chartered 1801; opened 1805
President: Dr ANDREW A. SORENSEN
Vice-President for Academic Affairs and Provost: JEROME D. ODOM
Vice-President for Business and Finance and Treasurer: JOHN FINAN
Vice-Provost for Research: MARSHA TORR
Vice-President for Human Resources: JANE M. JAMESON
Vice-President for Development: CHARLES D. PHLEGAR
Vice-President for Student Affairs: DENNIS A. PRUITT
Vice-Provost for Regional Campuses and Continuing Education: JOHN J. DUFFY
Vice-Provost for Libraries and Information Systems: GEORGE D. TERRY
Registrar: RICHARD L. BAYER

Chancellor, USC Aiken: ROBERT E. ALEXANDER
Chancellor, USC Spartanburg: JOHN C. STOCKWELL
Library of over 7,000,000 vols
Number of teachers: 1,810 full-time (8 campuses)
Number of students: 36,717 (8 campuses)
Publication: *Annual Bulletins*

DEANS

College of Science and Mathematics: GERALD M. CRAWLEY
College of Business Administration: DAVID L. SHROCK
College of Education: HARVEY A. ALLEN (acting)
College of Engineering: CRAIG A. ROGERS
College of Liberal Arts: C. BLEASE GRAHAM (acting)
College of Journalism and Mass Communications: JUDY VANSLYKE TURK
College of Pharmacy: FARID SADIK (acting)
South Carolina Honors College: PETER C. SEDERBERG
School of Law: JOHN E. MONTGOMERY
School of Music: MANUEL ALVAREZ
College of Nursing: MARY ANN C. PARSONS
College of Applied Professional Sciences: JOHN J. DUFFY (acting)
College of Social Work: FRANK B. RAYMOND, III
College of Library and Information Science: FRED W. ROPER
College of Criminal Justice: C. BLEASE GRAHAM
Graduate School: CAROL Z. GARRISON
School of Medicine: LARRY R. FAULKNER
School of Public Health: HARRIS PASTIDES
USC Beaufort: CHRIS P. PLYLER
USC Lancaster: JOSEPH PAPPIN III
USC Salkehatchie: CARL A. CLAYTON
USC Sumter: C. LESLIE CARPENTER
USC Union: JAMES W. EDWARDS

VOORHEES COLLEGE

POB 678, Denmark, SC 29042
Telephone: (803) 793-3351
Fax: (803) 793-4584
Internet: www.voorhees.edu
Founded 1897
Private control
Academic year: August to May
President: Dr LEE E. MONROE, Jr
Vice-President (Academic Affairs): Dr JUDY CARTER
Vice-President (Student Affairs): WILLIE JEFFERSON
Vice-President (Business Affairs): GERALDINE JONES
Vice-President (Planning and Information Management): SAMUEL BLACKWELL
Vice-President (Institutional Advancement): GLORIA A. RICHARD
Registrar: FELICIA MAYES
Library Director: MARIE MARTIN
Number of teachers: 25
Number of students: 700

HEADS OF DEPARTMENTS

Division of Arts and Sciences: Dr CASSANDRA SMITH
Division of Business and Professional Studies: Dr CHEULHO LEE
Division of Education: COSTA LEMPESIS

WINTHROP UNIVERSITY

Rock Hill, SC 29733
Telephone: (803) 323-2236
Internet: www.winthrop.edu
Founded 1886

President: Dr ANTHONY DiGIORGIO
Vice-President for Academic Affairs: PATRICIA CORMIER
Vice-President for External Relations: BECKY McMILLAN
Vice-President for Finance and Business: J. P. McKEE
Vice-President for Student Life: FRANK P. ARDAIOLO
Registrar: KAREN C. JONES
Director of Admissions: DEBI BARBER
Library of 357,110 vols
Number of teachers: 401
Number of students: 5,107
Publications: *The Johnsonian* (weekly), *The Tatler*, *The Winthrop Anthology* (annually)

DEANS

Arts and Sciences: BETSY BROWN (acting)
Business Administration: JERRY H. PADGETT
Education: TOM POWELL
Library Services: PAUL DuBOIS
Visual and Performing Arts: BENNETT LENTCZNER
Admissions: JIM BLACK

WOFFORD COLLEGE

Spartanburg, SC 29303-3663
Telephone: (803) 597-4000
Fax: (803) 597-4019
Internet: www.wofford.edu
Founded 1854
President: JOAB M. LESESNE, Jr
Vice-President for Academic Affairs/Dean of the College: DAN B. MAULTSBY
Vice-Presidents: LARRY McGEHEE, B. G. STEPHENS
Vice-President for Business: EDWARD E. GREENE
Vice-President for Student Affairs: MICHAEL J. PRESTON
Executive Director of Development: DAVID BEACHAM
Director of Admissions: BRAND STILLE
Registrar: LUCY B. QUINN
Librarian: OAKLEY HERMAN COBURN
Library of 200,000 vols
Number of teachers: 70 (57 full-time; 13 part-time)
Number of students: 1,100
Publication: *Wofford Today* (newspaper).

SOUTH DAKOTA

AUGUSTANA COLLEGE

2001 So Summit, Sioux Falls, SD 57197
Telephone: (605) 274-0770
Fax: (605) 274-5299
E-mail: admission@augie.edu
Internet: www.augie.edu
Founded 1860
President: Dr BRUCE R. HALVERSON
Vice-President for Academic Services and Dean: Dr RICHARD A. HANSON
Vice-President for Administration and Finance (vacant)
Vice-President for Advancement: Rev. DOUG OLSON
Vice-President for Enrollment: ROBERT E. PRELOGER
Vice-President for Student Services: JAMES BIES
Registrar: GLENDA SEHESTED
Librarian: RONELLE THOMPSON
Library of 228,000 vols
Number of teachers: 121
Number of students: 1,750.

BLACK HILLS STATE UNIVERSITY

Spearfish, SD 57783
Telephone: (605) 642-6011
Fax: (605) 642-6214
Internet: www.bhsu.edu

Founded 1883
Academic year: August to May

President: THOMAS O. FLICKEMA
Director (Records): APRIL MEEKER
Director (Library and Learning Center): Dr
EDWIN ERICKSON

Library of 240,364 vols
Number of teachers: 183
Number of students: 3,846.

DAKOTA STATE UNIVERSITY

Madison, SD 57042
Telephone: (605) 256-5111
Fax: (605) 256-5316
Internet: www.dsu.edu

Founded 1881
Academic year: September to May

President: Dr DOUGLAS KNOWLTON
Academic Vice-President: Dr CECELIA M.
WITTMAYER
Vice-President for Student Affairs: STEVEN
W. SHIRLEY
Vice-President for Business and Administrative Services: MARILYN FOWLE
Registrar: SANDRA A. ANDERSON
Director of Admissions: AMY CRISSINGER
Librarian: ETHELLE BEAN

Library of 133,371 vols
Number of teachers: 110
Number of students: 2,295

Programmes in teacher training, business management, computer science, mathematics, sciences, respiratory care, medical record, information systems, liberal arts, web development and e-commerce; Master's programmes in information systems, information assurance and computer security and computer education technology

DEANS

College of Arts and Sciences: Dr KARI FORBES-BOYTE
College of Business and Information Systems: Dr TOM HALVERSON
College of Education: Dr TOM HAWLEY

DAKOTA WESLEYAN UNIVERSITY

1200 West University Ave, DWU Box 901
Mitchell, SD 57301
Telephone: (605) 995-2600
Fax: (605) 995-2699
Internet: www.dwu.edu

Founded 1885

President: Dr ROBERT G. DUFFETT
Registrar: SARA JORGENSEN
Vice-President (Academic Affairs): DONALD
WATT
Vice-President (Advancement): GREGORY
CHRISTY
Vice-President (Business and Finance):
BRYAN SLABA
Vice-President (Campus Life): GWENDA KOCH
Vice-President (University Relations): LORI
ESSIG

Library of 66,000 vols
Number of teachers: 45
Number of students: 651

PROFESSORS

ALMJELD, P., Music
CATALANO, M., Mathematics
DITTA, J., English
FARNEY, M. N., Mathematics
McGREEVY, M. J., Criminal Justice
MILLER, M. H., Religion and Philosophy

MITCHELL, D. B., Business Administration
and Economics
MULLICAN, T. R., Biology
NIELSON, G. E., Sociology
TATINA, R. E., Biology

HURON UNIVERSITY

333 9th St SW, Huron, SD 57350
Telephone: (605) 352-8721
Internet: www.huron.edu

Founded 1883
Academic year: September to June

President: DAVID D. O'DONNELL
Vice-President for Academic Affairs: Dr JOHN
ZINGG
Vice-President for Finance: TERESA HOFER
Registrar: CINDY ZINGG
Librarian: ROBERT BEHIKE

Library of 70,000 vols
Number of teachers: 120 (61 full-time, 59
adjunct)
Number of students: 650.

MOUNT MARTY COLLEGE

1105 West 8th, Yankton, SD 57078
Telephone: (605) 668-1011
Internet: www.mtmc.edu

Founded 1936

President: Dr JAMES T. BARRY
Registrar: GARY KLEIN
Librarian: SANDY BROWN

Library of 76,000 vols
Number of teachers: 65
Number of students: 1,000.

NORTH AMERICAN BAPTIST SEMINARY

1525 S Grange Ave, Sioux Falls, SD 57105
Fax: (605) 335-9090
E-mail: admissions@nabs.edu
Internet: www.nabs.edu
Private control

President: Dr G. MICHAEL HAGAN
Academic Vice-President and Dean: Dr BENJAMIN C. LESLIE
Registrar: LEEDEL HOWARD
Library Director: PAUL ROBERTS

Number of teachers: 35
Number of students: 125.

NORTHERN STATE UNIVERSITY

Aberdeen, SD 57401
Telephone: (605) 626-3011
Fax: (605) 626-3022
Internet: www.northern.edu

Founded 1901

President: JOHN HILPERT
Vice-President for Academic Affairs: DON
COZZETTO
Director of Graduate School: MARGARET COXWELL
Director of Libraries: J. PHILIP MULVANEY

Library of 250,000 vols
Number of teachers: 150
Number of students: 3,315.

OGLALA LAKOTA COLLEGE

Piya Wiconi, POB 490, Kyle, SD 57752
Telephone: (605) 455-6000
Fax: (605) 455-2787
Internet: www.olc.edu

Founded 1971
Private control
Academic year: August to May

President: THOMAS SHORT BULL
Registrar: BILLI K. HOMBECK
Library Director: ANN RUTHERFORD

Number of teachers: 15
Number of students: 650 (full-time).

PRESENTATION COLLEGE

1500 N Main St, Aberdeen, SD 57401
Telephone: (605) 225-1634
Fax: (605) 229-8518
E-mail: admit@presentation.edu
Internet: www.presentation.edu

Campuses at Aberdeen and Eagle Butte
(SD), and Fairmont (MN)

Founded 1922 as Notre Dame Junior College;
present name 1965
Private control
Academic year: August to May

President: Sr LORRAINE HALE
Library Director: ARVYCE BURNS

Number of teachers: 47
Number of students: 642.

SINTE GLESKA UNIVERSITY

POB 105, Mission, SD 57555
Telephone: (605) 856-5880
E-mail: admin@sinte.edu
Internet: www.sinte.edu

Founded 1970 as Sinte Gleska College;
present name 1992
Private control
Academic year: August to May

President: LIONEL R. BORDEAUX
Vice-President (Administration): MICHAEL H.
BENGE
Vice-President (Academic Affairs): LELAND
BORDEAUX
Vice-President (Institutional Relations and
Development): GEORGIA HACKETT
Vice-President (Community, Business and
Policy Development): STEVE EMERY
Registrar: JACK HERMAN
Librarian: RACHEL LINDVALL

Number of teachers: 36
Number of students: 1,080 (960 undergraduate, 120 postgraduate)

HEADS OF DEPARTMENTS

Art Institute: MARGARET MacKICHAN
Arts and Sciences: Dr GODFREY LOUDNER
Business Administration and Management:
NORA ANTOINE
Education and Graduate Education: CHERYL
MEDEARIS
Human Services: SHERYL KLEIN
Institute of Technologies: JIM POIGNEE
Lakota Studies: IONE QUIGLEY

SOUTH DAKOTA SCHOOL OF MINES AND TECHNOLOGY

501 E. St Joseph, Rapid City, SD 57701
Telephone: (605) 394-2411
Fax: (605) 394-3388
Internet: www.sdsmt.edu

Founded 1885
Academic year: September to May

President: CHARLES P. RUCH
Vice-President (Academic Affairs): KAREN L.
WHITEHEAD
Vice-President (Business and Administration): TIMOTHY G. HENDERSON
Vice-President (University Relations): JULIE
A. SMORAGIEWICZ
Vice-President (Student Affairs): PATRICIA G.
MAHON
Dean of Graduate Education and Research:
SHERRY O. FARWELL
Director of Library: PATRICIA M. ANDERSEN

Library of 220,224 vols
Number of teachers: 110 (full-time)
Number of students: 2,275.

SOUTH DAKOTA STATE UNIVERSITY

Box 2201, Brookings, SD 57007
Telephone: (605) 688-4151
Internet: www.sdstate.edu

Founded 1881 as Dakota Agricultural College; became University 1964
Academic year: August to May
President: Dr PEGGY GORDON MILLER
Executive Vice-President (Administration): Dr MICHAEL REGER
Assistant Vice-President (Finance and Budget): W. G. TSCHETTER
Vice-President of Student Affairs: Dr MARYSZ RAMES
Vice-President (Academic Affairs) and Provost: Dr CAROL PETERSON
Director of Library: Dr STEVE MARQUARDT

Library of 617,767 vols
Number of teachers: 657 (515 full-time, 142 part-time)
Number of students: 10,954.

UNIVERSITY OF SIOUX FALLS

1101 West 22nd St, Sioux Falls, SD 57105
Telephone: (800) 888-1047
Fax: (605) 331-6615
E-mail: admissions@usiouxfalls.edu
Internet: www.thecoo.edu

Founded 1883
Private (American Baptist)
Pre-professional liberal arts university
President: MARK BENEDETTO
Provost and Academic Dean: RICHARD MAYER
Registrar: PHYLLIS THOMPSON
Librarian: AILEEN MADDOX

Library of 75,000 vols
Number of teachers: 65 (37 full-time; 28 part-time)
Number of students: 950.

UNIVERSITY OF SOUTH DAKOTA

Vermillion, SD 57069-2390
Telephone: (605) 677-5011
Fax: (605) 677-5073
Internet: www.usd.edu

Founded 1862
Academic year: August to May
President: Dr DONALD DAHLIN (acting)

Library of 488,000 vols
Number of teachers: 463
Number of students: 7,317

DEANS

College of Arts and Sciences: Dr SUSAN J. WOLFE (acting)
School of Business: Dr DIANE B. HOADLEY (acting)
School of Education: Dr JERI ENGLEKING (acting)
College of Fine Arts: JOHN DAY
School of Law: BARRY VICKREY
School of Medicine: Dr ROBERT TALLEY
Graduate School: Dr ROYCE ENGSTROM
Continuing Education: Dr MARGOT HOOD-ROGERS

TENNESSEE

AMERICAN BAPTIST COLLEGE

1800 Baptist World Centre Dr., Nashville, TN 37207-4952
Telephone: (615) 256-1463
Fax: (615) 226-7855
Internet: www.abcnash.edu

Pres.: Dr FORREST ELLIOTT HARRIS, Sr
Vice-Pres. of Campus Operations: JOHN K. WRIGHT
Academic Dean: DOREEN W. McCALLA

Librarian (vacant).

AQUINAS COLLEGE

4210 Harding Rd, Nashville, TN 37205
Telephone: (615) 297-7545
E-mail: president@aquinas-tn.edu
Internet: www.aquinas-tn.edu

Founded 1961
Academic year: August to May
Pres.: Sister THOMAS AQUINAS
Head Librarian: J. MARK HALL.

AUSTIN PEAY STATE UNIVERSITY

601 College St, Clarksville, TN 37044
Telephone: (931) 221-7566
Fax: (931) 221-7297
E-mail: gov@apsu.edu
Internet: www.apsu.edu

Founded 1927
Academic year: August to May
Pres.: SHERRY L. HOPPE
Provost and Vice-Pres. for Academic and Student Services: Dr BRUCE SPECK
Vice-Pres. for Legal Affairs (vacant): RICHARD E. JACKSON
Vice-Pres. for Admin. and Finance: MITCH ROBINSON
Exec. Dir for Devt: ROY GREGORY
Registrar: TELAINA WRIGLEY
Dir of Library: JOE WEBER

Library of 328,523 vols
Number of teachers: 276
Number of students: 7,033.

BELMONT UNIVERSITY

1900 Belmont Blvd, Nashville, TN 37212-3757
Telephone: (615) 383-7001
Fax: (615) 385-6446
Internet: www.belmont.edu

Founded 1951
Pres.: BOB FISHER
Registrar: STEVEN REED
Library Dir: Dr ERNEST WILLIAM HEARD

Library of 127,600 vols
Number of teachers: 280 (141 full-time; 139 part-time)
Number of students: 4,500
Publications: *The Tower* (annual), *Vision* (6 a year), *Belmont Circle* (quarterly)

DEANS

Academic: JERRY WARREN
Students: SUZANNE MATHENY
Admissions: CLAUDE PRESSNELL

BETHEL COLLEGE

325 Cherry Ave, McKenzie, TN 38201
Telephone: (731) 352-4000
Internet: www.bethel-college.edu

Founded 1842
Pres.: ROBERT PROSSER
Academic Dean: MARIBETH McGUIRE
Registrar: SHIRLEY MARTIN
Dir of Library: HAROLD KELLY

Library of 53,000 vols
Number of teachers: 36
Number of students: 843
Publications: *Bethel Beacon* (weekly), *Log Cabin* (annual), *Bethel Captions* (quarterly).

CARSON-NEWMAN COLLEGE

1646 Russell Ave, Jefferson City, TN 37760
Telephone: (865) 471-2000
Fax: (865) 471-3502
Internet: www.cn.edu

Founded 1851
Academic year: August to May
Pres.: JOE BILL SLOAN
Vice-Pres. for Finance: ROBERT DRINNEN

Library of 200,000 vols
Number of teachers: 125
Number of students: 2,200
Publications: *CN Studies, NUA – Studies in Contemporary Irish Writing, Mossy Creek Reader, Baptist History and Heritage.*

CHRISTIAN BROTHERS UNIVERSITY

650 East Parkway, S, Memphis, TN 38104
Telephone: (901) 321-3000
Internet: www.cbu.edu

Founded 1871
Private (Roman Catholic) control
Pres.: VINCENT MALHAM
Academic Vice-Pres.: ANTHONY ARETZ
Registrar: BARBARA HAVEY
Librarian: MAYA BERRY

Library of 100,000 vols
Number of teachers: 150
Number of students: 1,800
Publication: *Catalog* (annual).

CRICHTON COLLEGE

255 North Highland, Memphis, TN 38111
Telephone: (901) 320-9725
Fax: (901) 320-9700
E-mail: info@crichton.edu
Internet: www.crichton.edu

Founded 1960 as Mid-South Bible College, present name 1987
Pres. (vacant): LARRY L. LLOYD
Vice-Pres. for Academic Affairs: ROBERT M. BRIAN
Vice-Pres. for Admissions: CAROLYN S. CATES (acting)

DEANS

Arts and Sciences: KEITH CALLIS
School of Bible and Theology: JAMES THORNE
Business Faculty: BOB WHARTON
Education and Behavioural Studies: (vacant)

CUMBERLAND UNIVERSITY

1 Cumberland Sq., Lebanon, TN 37087-3408
Telephone: (615) 444-2562
Fax: (615) 444-2569
Internet: www.cumberland.edu

Founded 1842
Academic year: August to May
Pres.: Dr HARVILL C. EATON
Vice-Pres. for Academic Affairs: WILBUR PETERSON

Number of teachers: 127
Number of students: 1,420

DIRECTORS OF SCHOOLS

Business and Econ.: Dr WILLIAM B. FOX
Arts and Humanities: Dr STEPHEN FARNSLEY
Educational Studies: Dr K. CHARLES COLLIER
Nursing: Dr LEANNE C. BUSBY
Mathematics, Natural and Social Sciences: Dr WILBUR L. PETERSON

EAST TENNESSEE STATE UNIVERSITY

Johnson City, TN 37614
Telephone: (423) 439-1000
Fax: (423) 439-5710
E-mail: saucenaf@etsu.edu
Internet: www.etsu.edu

Founded 1911
Academic year: August to May
President: Dr PAUL E. STANTON, Jr

Associate Vice-President for Admissions, Retention and Enrollment Management (vacant)

Associate Registrar: PAUL HAYES

Provost and Vice-President for Academic Affairs: Dr BERT C. BACH

Vice-President for University Advancement: Dr RICHARD MANAHAN

Vice-President for Health Affairs: Dr RONALD D. FRANKS

Vice-President for Business and Finance: JAMES BOWMAN

Vice-President for Administration and Student Affairs: Dr WAYNE ANDREWS

Dean of University Libraries: RITA SCHER

Library of 456,000 vols

Number of teachers: 650

Number of students: 12,000

Publications: *Aethlon: Journal of Sport Literature* (2 a year), *Storytelling World* (2 a year), *Science Educator* (2 a year), *The Tennessee Reading Educator* (2 a year)

DEANS

College of Arts and Sciences: Dr DONALD R. JOHNSON

College of Education: Dr MARTHA COLLINS

College of Business: Dr GLEN RIECKEN

College of Public and Allied Health: Dr WILSIE BISHOP

James H. Quillen College of Medicine: Dr RONALD D. FRANKS

School of Continuing Studies: Dr GLENN BETTIS

School of Graduate Studies: Dr WESLEY BROWN

College of Applied Science and Technology: Dr JAMES HALES

College of Nursing: Dr JOELLEN EDWARDS

FISK UNIVERSITY

17th Ave, N, Nashville, TN 37208-3051

Telephone: (615) 329-8500

Fax: (615) 329-8576

Internet: www.fisk.edu

Founded 1866 as Fisk School; univ. charter 1867

Academic year: August to May

Pres.: HAZEL R. O'LEARY

Provost: KOFI LOMOTEY

Librarian: JESSIE C. SMITH

Library of 210,000 vols

Number of teachers: 85 (63 full-time, 22 part-time)

Number of students: 845

Publications: *Fisk University Bulletin* (every 2 years), *Fisk News* (annual), *Fisk Reports* (quarterly), *Fisk Herald* (2 a year).

FREE WILL BAPTIST BIBLE COLLEGE

3606 West End College, Nashville, TN 37205

Telephone: (800) 763-9222

Fax: (615) 269-6028

Internet: www.fwbbc.edu

Pres.: J. MATHEW PINSON

Chancellor: Dr TOM MALONE

Registrar: Dr MILTON FIELDS

Librarian: CAROL REID (acting).

FREED-HARDEMAN UNIVERSITY

158 East Main St, Henderson, TN 38340

Telephone: (800) 348-3481

Internet: www.fhu.edu

Pres.: MILTON R. SEWELL

Vice-Pres. for Academic Affairs: Dr W. STEPHEN JOHNSON

DEANS

School of Education: Dr JOHN SWEENEY

School of Business: JIM EDMONDS

School of Sciences and Mathematics: Dr ALLEN WALKER

School of Arts and Humanities: Dr SAMUEL T. JONES

School of Biblical Studies: Dr BILLY R. SMITH

Honors College: ROLLAND W. PACK

HARDING UNIVERSITY GRADUATE SCHOOL OF RELIGION

1000 Cherry Rd, Memphis, TN 38117-5499

Telephone: (901) 761-1356

Fax: (901) 761-1358

E-mail: mparker@hugsr.edu

Internet: www.hugsr.edu

Dean and Exec. Dir: Dr EVERTT W. HUFFARD.

JOHNSON BIBLE COLLEGE

7900 Johnson Dr., Knoxville, TN 37998

Telephone: (865) 573-4517

Fax: (865) 251-2337

E-mail: jbc@jbc.edu

Internet: www.jbc.edu

Academic year: August to May

Pres.: Dr GARY E. WEEDMAN

Vice-Pres. for Academics: RICHARD BEAM

Vice-Pres. for Business: BEN LUTZ, SR

Vice-Pres. for Devt: PHILIP EUBANKS

Vice-Pres. for Student Services: DAVID LEGG

Number of teachers: 55

Number of students: 850.

KING COLLEGE

1350 King College Rd, Bristol, TN 37620

Telephone: (423) 652-4861

Fax: (423) 968-4456

E-mail: admissions@king.edu

Internet: www.king.edu

Founded 1867

Academic year: August to May

Pres.: GREGORY D. JORDAN

Dean of Academic Affairs: MATTHEW S. PELTIER

Vice-Pres. for Institutional Advancement: WILLIAM M. MCELROY

Vice-Pres. for Student Affairs: ROBERT A. LITTLETON

Vice-Pres. for Enrollment Management: MELINDA S. CLARK

Vice-Pres. for Business Operations: JAMES P. DONAHUE

Librarian: MATTHEW S. PELTIER

Library of 98,000 vols

Number of teachers: 70

Number of students: 608

Publication: *Tornado*.

KNOXVILLE COLLEGE

901 Knoxville College Dr., Knoxville, TN 37921

Telephone: (615) 524-6500

E-mail: admissions@knoxvillecollege.edu

Internet: www.knoxvillecollege.edu

Founded 1875

Liberal arts college

Pres.: Dr ROBERT H. HARVEY

Dean: Dr EVELYN HALLMAN

Registrar: BARBARA BOOKER

Librarian: PATTY COOPER

Library of 78,445 vols

Number of teachers: 51

Number of students: 633.

LAMBUTH UNIVERSITY

705 Lambuth Blvd, Jackson, TN 38301

Telephone: (901) 425-2500

Fax: (901) 423-1990

Internet: www.lambuth.edu

Founded 1843

Pres.: R. FRED ZUKER

Vice-Pres. for Academic Affairs and and Dean of the College: TREVOR MORRIS

Vice-Pres. for Devt: STEVE MALOAN

Vice-Pres. for Business Affairs: JAMES WOULFE

Vice-Pres. for Enrollment Management: CHERINE D. HECKMAN

Library Dir: PAM DENNIS

Library of 155,554 vols

Number of teachers: 65 (38 full-time; 27 part-time)

Number of students: 819.

LANE COLLEGE

545 Lane Ave, Jackson, TN 38301-4598

Telephone: (901) 426-7500

Fax: (901) 427-3987

Internet: www.lanecollege.edu

Founded 1882

Academic year: August to June

Pres.: WESLEY MCCLURE

Registrar: TERRY BLACKMON

Vice-Pres. for Academic Affairs: Dr VICKI VERNON LOTT

Vice-Pres.: MELVIN R. HAMLETT

Vice-Pres. for Admin.: NICOL EDWARDS

Exec. Vice-Pres.: SHARRON BURNETT

Librarian: SHIRLEY HUDSON

Library of 130,000 vols

Number of teachers: 42

Number of students: 627.

LEE UNIVERSITY

1120 North Ocoee St, Cleveland, TN 37320-3450

Internet: www.leeuniversity.edu

Pres.: Dr CHARLES PAUL CONN

Vice-Pres. for Academics: CAROLYN DIRKSEN

Vice-Pres. for Instiutional Advancement: DALE GOFF

Vice-Pres. for Student Life: WALT MAULDIN

Vice-Pres. for Business and Finance: DAVID PAINTER

Vice-Pres. of Enrollment Management: GARY RAY.

LE MOYNE-OWEN COLLEGE

807 Walker Ave, Memphis, TN 38126

Telephone: (901) 774-9090

E-mail: contact@nile.loc.edu

Internet: www.loc.edu

Founded 1862

Pres.: JOHNNIE B. WATSON

Dean of Academic Affairs: BARBARA FRANKLE

Librarian: ANNETTE BERHA

Library of 82,043 vols

Number of teachers: 41

Number of students: 1,212.

LINCOLN MEMORIAL UNIVERSITY

6965 Cumberland Gap Parkway, Harrogate, TN 37752

Telephone: (423) 869-3611

Fax: (423) 869-6250

E-mail: presidentsoffice@lmunet.edu

Internet: www.lmunet.edu

Founded 1897

Academic year: August to May

Pres.: NANCY B. MOODY

Vice-Pres. for Finance: RANDY ELDRIDGE

Vice-Pres. for Univ. Advancement: CYNTHIA WHITT

Vice-Pres. and Dean of the Faculty: Dr RAY E. STOWERS

Vice-Pres. for Student Affairs: Dr PAMELA MOON
Vice-Pres. for Academic Affairs: Dr SHERILYN EMBERTON
Dir of Admissions: CONRAD DANIELS
Head Librarian: DONNA BIBLE
Library of 120,000 vols
Number of teachers: 71
Number of students: 2,000
Publication: *The Lincoln Herald* (quarterly).

LIPSCOMB UNIVERSITY

3901 Granny White Pike, Nashville, TN 37204-3951
Telephone: (615) 269-1000
Internet: www.lipscomb.edu
Founded 1891
4-Year liberal arts college
Pres.: L. RANDOLPH LOWDRY
Exec. Vice-Pres.: WILLIAM TUCKER
Provost: Dr W. CRAIG BLEDSOE
Vice-Pres. for Univ. Relations: WALT LEAVER
Library Dir: CAROLYN T. WILSON
Library of 216,300 vols
Number of teachers: 194
Number of students: 2,555

DEANS

College of Arts and Humanities: Dr VALERY A. PRILL
College of Education and Professional Studies: JIM L. THOMAS
College of Natural and Applied Sciences: Dr LINDA ROBERSON
College of Bible and Ministry: Dr TERRY BRILEY

MARTIN METHODIST COLLEGE

433 West Madison St, Pulaski, TN 38478-2799
Telephone: (931) 363-9868
Fax: (931) 363-9811
E-mail: admit@martinmethodist.edu
Internet: www.martinmethodist.edu
Pres.: TED BROWN
Vice-Pres. for Enrollment Management: ROBBY SHELTON
Vice Pres. for Finance and Admin.: RON DOWDY
Academic Dean: JAMES T. MURRELL
Registrar: SHERRY YOKLEY
Library Dir: RICHARD MADDEN.

MARYVILLE COLLEGE

Maryville, TN 37804
Telephone: (865) 981-8000
Fax: (865) 981-8136
Internet: www.maryvillecollege.edu
Founded 1819
Academic year: September to May
Pres.: Dr GERALD W. GIBSON
Vice-Pres. and Treas.: NANCY PYANOE
Vice-Pres. and Dean of Students: VANDY KEMP
Vice-Pres. for Advancement: JASON MCNEAL
Vice-Pres. for Admin. Services: Dr WILLIAM SEYMOUR
Library Dir: ANGELA QUICK
Library of 128,022 vols
Number of teachers: 112 (72 full-time, 40 part-time)
Number of students: 1,080
Publications: *Laurels* (2 a year), *Impressions* (2 a year).

MEHARRY MEDICAL COLLEGE

1005 Dr D. B. Todd, Jr Boulevard, Nashville, TN 37208
Telephone: (615) 327-6000
Internet: www.mmc.edu
Pres.: WAYNE J. RILEY
Vice-Pres. of Finance: LAMEL BANDY-NEAL
Sr Vice-Pres. of Health Affairs: VALERIE MONTGOMERY RICE
Vice-Pres. for Student and Academic Affairs: PAMELA WILLIAMS

DEANS

School of Medicine: PONJOLA CONEY (acting)
School of Dentistry: WILLIAM B. BUTLER (acting)
School of Graduate Studies and Research: MARIA FATIMA LIMA (acting)
School of Allied Health: KATHLEEN MCENERNEY (acting)

MEMPHIS COLLEGE OF ART

Overton Park, 1930 Poplar Ave, Memphis, TN 38104-2764
Telephone: (901) 272-5100
Fax: (901) 272-5104
E-mail: info@mca.edu
Internet: www.mca.edu
Founded 1936
Academic year: August to May
Pres.: JEFFREY D. NASIN
Vice Pres. for Academic Affairs: KEN STRICKLAND
Vice-Pres. for College Advancement: KIM WILLIAMS
Vice-Pres. for Enrollment and Student Services: SUSAN MILLER SUSAN MILLER
Library of 19,000 vols
Number of teachers: 34 (19 full-time, 15 part-time)
Number of students: 297.

MEMPHIS THEOLOGICAL SEMINARY

168 East Parkway, S, Memphis, TN 38104
Telephone: (901) 458-8232
Fax: (901) 452-4051
E-mail: info@mtscampus.edu
Internet: www.mtscampus.edu
Pres.: Dr DANIEL J. EARHART-BROWN
Vice-Pres. for Academic Affairs and Dean: Dr BARBARA HOLMES
Library Dir: STEVE EDSCORN (acting).

MID-AMERICA BAPTIST THEOLOGICAL SEMINARY

2216 Germantown Rd, Germantown, TN 38138-3815
Telephone: (901) 751-8453
Fax: (901) 751-8454
E-mail: info@mabts.edu
Internet: www.mabts.edu
Pres.: MICHAEL R. SPRADLIN
Vice-Pres. for Admin.: JOHN FLOYD
Vice-Pres. of Institutional Assessment: BRADLEY C. THOMPSON.

MIDDLE TENNESSEE STATE UNIVERSITY

Murfreesboro, TN 37132
Telephone: (615) 898-2300
Fax: (615) 898-5906
Internet: www.mtsu.edu
Founded 1911
Academic year: August to May
Pres.: Dr SIDNEY A. MCPHEE
Vice-Pres. for Finance and Admin.: DUANE STUCKY

Provost and Exec. Vice-Pres.: Dr KAYLENE GEBERT
Sr Vice-Pres.: JOHN W. COTHERN
Vice-Pres. for Student Affairs: Dr ROBERT K. GLENN
Vice-Pres. for Devt and Univ. Relations: WILLIAM J. BALES
Librarian: DON CRAIG
Library of 564,000 vols
Number of teachers: 642
Number of students: 17,000

DEANS

College of Business: DWIGHT BULLARD (acting)
College of Basic and Applied Sciences: EARL KEESE
College of Education: ROBERT EAKER
College of Liberal Arts: JOHN MCDANIEL
Graduate School: DONALD CURRY
College of Mass Communication: DERYL LEAMING

MILLIGAN COLLEGE

Milligan College, TN 37682
Telephone: (615) 929-0116
E-mail: admissions@milligan.edu
Internet: www.milligan.edu
Founded 1866 (reorganized 1881)
Pres.: DONALD R. JEANES
Academic Dean: GARY E. WEEDMAN
Library Dir: STEVEN L. PRESTON
Library: c. 108,500 vols
Number of teachers: 46
Number of students: 811.

O'MORE COLLEGE OF DESIGN

423 South Margin St, Franklin, TN 37064
Telephone: (615) 794-4254
Fax: (615) 790-1662
E-mail: admissions@omorecollege.edu
Internet: www.omorecollege.edu
Pres.: Dr MARK HILLIARD.

RHODES COLLEGE

2000 North Parkway, Memphis, TN 38112
Telephone: (901) 843-3000
Fax: (901) 843-3718
Internet: www.rhodes.edu
Liberal arts college
Founded 1848
Library of 308,637 vols
Academic year: August to May
Pres.: WILLIAM E. TROUTT
Provost: CHARLOTTE G. BORST
Dean of Academic Affairs: JOHN S. OLSEN (acting)
Dean of Admissions: DAVID J. WOTTLE
Dean of Students: CAROL E. CASEY
Vice-Pres. for Finance and Admin.: JAMES ALLEN BOONE, Jr
Vice-Pres. for College Relations: RUSSELL T. WIGGINTON
Vice-Pres. for Information Services: ROBERT M. JOHNSON, Jr
Registrar: GLENN W. MUNSON
Dir of Library: LYNNE M. BLAIR
Library of 308,637 vols
Number of teachers: 154 full-time
Number of students: 1,699.

SOUTHERN ADVENTIST UNIVERSITY

POB 370, Collegedale, TN 37315-0370
Telephone: (423) 238-2111
Fax: (423) 238-3001
E-mail: postmaster@southern.edu
Internet: www.southern.edu
Founded 1892

Academic year: August to May
Pres.: GORDON BIETZ
Registrar: JONI ZIER
Librarian: GENEVIEVE STEYN
Library of 127,186 vols, 11,163 periodical subscriptions, 587,809 microforms
Number of teachers: 111 (108 full-time, 3 part-time)
Number of students: 2,200.

SOUTHERN COLLEGE OF OPTOMETRY

1245 Madison Ave, Memphis, TN 38104-2222
Telephone: (901) 722-3200
Internet: www.sco.edu

Pres.: RICHARD W. PHILLIPS
Vice-Pres. for Academic Affairs: CHARLES L. HAINE
Vice-Pres. for Clinical Programs: FRANK S. GIBSON
Vice-Pres. for Finance and Admin.: EUGENE J. BAGAGLIO
Vice-Pres. for Institutional Advancement: LISA R. WADE
Librarian: NANCY GATLIN.

TENNESSEE STATE UNIVERSITY

3500 John A. Merritt Blvd, Nashville, TN 37209-1561
Telephone: (615) 963-5000
Internet: www.tnstate.edu
Founded 1912
Pres.: MALVIN N. JOHNSON
Provost and Exec. Vice-Pres.: Dr ROBERT L. HAMPTON
Registrar: VICKIE HOLMES
Librarian: Dr YILDIZ BINKLEY
Library of 565,400 vols
Number of teachers: 518
Number of students: 8,625.

TENNESSEE TECHNOLOGICAL UNIVERSITY

Cookeville, TN 38505
Telephone: (615) 372-3101
Fax: (615) 372-3898
Internet: www.tntech.edu
Founded 1915
Academic year: August to May
Pres.: Dr ROBERT R. BELL
Provost: Dr MARVIN BARKER
Vice-Pre. for Student Affairs: MARC BURNETT
Vice-Pres. for Business and Fiscal Affairs: LINDA MAXWELL
Vice-Pres. for Univ. Advancement: MARK HUTCHINS
Dir of Library Services: WINSTON WALDEN
Library of 896,555 vols
Number of teachers: 400
Number of students: 9,107.

TENNESSEE TEMPLE UNIVERSITY

1815 Union Ave, Chattanooga, TN 37404-3587
Telephone: (423) 493-4378
Fax: (423) 493-4497
E-mail: ttuinfo@tntemple.edu
Internet: www.tntemple.edu

Pres.: Dr DANNY LOVETT
Chancellor: Dr LEE ROBERSON
Exec. Vice-Pres.: ROGER H. STILES
Sec. and Treasurer: JIMMY WILSON.

TENNESSEE WESLEYAN COLLEGE

POB 40, Athens, TN 37371-0040
Telephone: (423) 745-7504
Internet: www.twcnet.edu

Founded 1857
Pres.: Dr STEPHEN CONDON
Vice-Pres. for Academics: Dr SUZANNE HINE
Vice-Pres. for Student Life and Enrollment Management: Dr SCOTT MASHBURN
Library of 75,000 vols
Number of teachers: 29
Number of students: 633.

TREVECCA NAZARENE UNIVERSITY

333 Murfreesboro Rd, Nashville, TN 37210
Telephone: (615) 248-1200
Fax: (615) 248-1432
E-mail: admissions_und@trevecca.edu
Internet: www.trevecca.edu

Founded 1901 as Literary and Bible Training School for Christian Workers; became Trevecca College 1911 and Trevecca Nazarene College 1917; present name 1995
Private control
Pres.: DAN BOONE
Provost: STEPHEN M. PUSEY
Vice-President for Church Relations: JIM MAHAN
Exec. Vice-Pres. for Financial Services and Admin.: MARK MYERS
Vice-Pres. for External Relations: PEGGY COONING
Dean of Student Devt: STEPHEN HARRIS
Dean of Enrollment Management: SAM GREEN
Dir of Library Services: RUTH KINNERSLEY
Library of 103,571 vols, 507 print periodicals, 3,632 audiovisual items, 295,265 microforms, electronic periodicals
Number of teachers: 77
Number of students: 1,911

DEANS

School of Arts and Sciences: Div. of Communication, Language and Literature: Dr J. DOUGLAS LEPTER
School of Arts and Sciences: Div. of Music: Dr SAM GREEN
School of Arts and Sciences: Div. of Natural and Applied Sciences: Dr G. MICHAEL MOREDOCK
School of Arts and Sciences: Div. of Social and Behavioural Sciences: Dr PETER WILSON
School of Religion: Dr TIM GREEN
School of Education: Dr ESTHER SWINK
School of Business and Management: Dr JAMES HIATT

TUSCULUM COLLEGE

60 Shiloh Rd, Greeneville, TN 37743
Telephone: (423) 636-7300
Fax: (423) 798-1622
E-mail: admissions@tusculum.edu
Internet: www.tusculum.edu

Founded 1794
Academic year: August to May
Pres.: Dr RUSSELL L. NICHOLS
Provost and Academic Vice-Pres.: Dr KIMBERLY K. ESTEP
Vice-Pres. for Admin.: MARK A. STOKES
Vice-Pres. and Chief Financial Officer: FRANK G. WILLIAMS
Vice-Pre. for Enrollment Management: GEORGE WOLF
Dir of Admissions: TONY S. ENGLAND
Library of 192,000 vols
Number of teachers: 130
Number of students: 2,000.

UNION UNIVERSITY

1050 Union University Dr, Jackson, TN 38305
Telephone: (901) 668-1818

Fax: (901) 661-5187
E-mail: info@uu.edu
Internet: www.uu.edu
Founded 1823
Academic year: September to May
Pres.: Dr DAVID S. DOCKERY
Provost: STEVE BAKER
Vice-Pres. of Information Services and Academic Resources: Dr HAL POE
Dir of Student Enlistment: CARROLL GRIFFIN
Library of 167,629 vols
Number of teachers: 197
Number of students: 2,783.

UNIVERSITY OF MEMPHIS

Memphis, TN 38152
Telephone: (901) 678-2000
Fax: (901) 678-3299
Internet: www.memphis.edu
Founded 1912
Pres.: Dr SHIRLEY RAINES
Provost: Dr RALPH FAUDREE
Vice-Pres. for Advancement: JULIE JOHNSON
Vice-Pres. for Business and Finance: CHARLES SMITH
Vice-Pres. for Information Technology: Dr DOUGLAS HURLEY
Vice-Pres. for Student Affairs: Dr ROSIE PHILLIPS BINGHAM
Dean of Libraries: Dr SYLVERNA V. FORD
Library of 1,051,000 vols
Number of teachers: 1,207 (full-time and part-time)
Number of students: 20,100

Publications: *The Southern Journal of Philosophy* (quarterly), *Law Review*, *The University of Memphis Magazine* (quarterly), *Bulletin of the University of Memphis* (quarterly), *Mid-South Business Journal*, *Memphis Economy*.

UNIVERSITY OF TENNESSEE SYSTEM

Knoxville, TN 37996
Telephone: (615) 974-1000
Internet: www.tennessee.edu/system

Chartered 1794 as Blount College; name changed by legislature 1840 to E Tennessee Univ., and in 1879 to The Univ. of Tennessee
Major campuses at Chattanooga, Knoxville, Martin and Memphis
State control
Academic year: September to August
Pres.: Dr JOHN D. PETERSEN
Gen. Counsel and Sec. of Board of Trustees: BEAUCHAMP E. BROGAN
Sr Vice-Pres. and Chief Financial Officer: Dr GARY W. ROGERS
Vice Pres. for Devt: HENRY NEMCIK
Vice-Pres. for Agriculture: Dr JOSEPH A. DiPIETRO
Vice-Pres. for Public and Govt Relations: SAMMIE LYNN PUETT HANK DYE
Vice-Pres. for Academic Affairs: Dr ROBERT LEVY
Vice-Pres., Gen. Counsel and Sec.: CATHERINE S. MEZILL
Library: see Libraries
Number of teachers: 3,189
Number of students: 41,927

Publications: *The University Record*, *Extension Series* (4 to 6 a year), *Tennessee Alumnus* (quarterly), *Horizons* (quarterly).

MAJOR CAMPUSES

University of Tennessee at Chattanooga
Chattanooga, TN 37401
Telephone: (615) 755-4141

UNIVERSITIES AND COLLEGES—TENNESSEE

Internet: www.utc.edu
Chancellor: FREDERICK W. OBEAR
Asst to the Chancellor: SUSAN CARDWELL
Provost: GRAYSON H. WALKER
Assoc. Provost for Academic Services: JANE W. HARBAUGH
Assoc. Provost for Academic Admin.: WILLIAM AIKEN
Vice-Chancellor for Business and Finance: RALPH W. MOSER (acting)
Vice-Chancellor for Devt: VINCENT M. PELLEGRINO
Vice-Chancellor for Student Affairs: CHARLES RENNEISEN
Asst Vice-Chancellor for Admin.: RICHARD L. BROWN (acting)

DEANS

College of Arts and Sciences: CHARLES T. SUMMERLIN
Continuing Education: MARILYN WILLIS
School of Business Admin.: LINDA P. FLETCHER
School of Education: MARY N. TANNER (acting)
College of Health and Human Services: RANDY WALKER (acting)
School of Eng.: RONALD B. COX
Library: SHEILA DELACROIX

University of Tennessee, Knoxville

Knoxville, TN 37996
Telephone: (615) 974-1000
Internet: www.utk.edu
Chancellor: Dr WILLIAM T. SNYDER
Exec. Asst to the Chancellor: MARIANNE R. WOODSIDE
Vice-Chancellor for Student Affairs: PHILIP A. SCHEURER
Vice-Chancellor for Computing and Telecommunications: (vacant)
Vice-Chancellor for Business and Finance: RAYMOND L. HAMILTON
Vice-Chancellor for Devt and Alumni Affairs: JACK E. WILLIAMS

DEANS

Admissions and Records: SUSIE COLEMAN ARCHER
College of Agriculture: GERHARDT SCHNEIDER (acting)
School of Architecture: MARLEEN K. DAVIS
College of Business Admin.: C. WARREN NEEL
College of Communications: DWIGHT L. TEETER, Jr
College of Education: RICHARD WISNIEWSKI
College of Eng.: JERRY E. STONEKING
College of Human Ecology: JACQUELYN O. DEJONGE
College of Law: RICHARD S. WIRTZ
College of Liberal Arts: LORMAN A. RATNER
College of Veterinary Medicine: MICHAEL H. SHIRES
Division of Continuing Education: LAVERNE B. LINDSEY
Graduate School of Social Work: EUNICE O. SHATZ
Graduate Studies: CLARENCE W. MINKEL
Research: LEO RIEDINGER
College of Nursing: (vacant)
Institute of Agriculture: DON O. RICHARDSON (Agricultural Experiment Stations: BILLY G. HICKS (Admin.))
Graduate School of Library and Information Science: (vacant)
Space Institute: JOEL W. MUELHAUSER (Admin.: KAPULURU C. REDDY (Academic Affairs))
Library: PAULA T. KAUFMAN
Students: W. TIMOTHY ROGERS

PROFESSORS

College of Liberal Arts:
ADCOCK, J. L., Chemistry

AIKEN, C. S., Geography
ALEXANDRATOS, S. D., Chemistry
ALEXIADES, V., Mathematics
ALIKAKOS, N., Mathematics
ANDERSON, D. F., Mathematics
AQUILA, R. E., Philosophy
ASP, C. W., Audiology and Speech Pathology
BAGBY, R. M., Zoology
BAKER, D. C., Chemistry
BAKER, G. A., Mathematics
BALL, C. H., Music
BARRETTE, P., Romance and Asian Languages
BARTMESS, J. E., Chemistry
BECKER, J. M., Microbiology
BELL, T. L., Geography
BERGERON, P. H., History
BETZ, M., Sociology
BINGHAM, C. R., Physics
BITZAS, G. C., Music
BLACK, J. A., Sociology
BLAIN, S. J., Arts
BLASS, W. E., Physics
BRADY, P. S., Romance and Asian Languages
BRAKKE, P. M., Arts
BRATTON, E. W., English
BREINIG, M., Physics
BRENKERT, G. G., Philosophy
BROADHEAD, T., Geological Sciences
BROCK, J. P., Jr, Music
BUGG, W. M., Physics
BUHITE, R. D., History
BULL, W. E., Chemistry
BUNTING, D. L., II, Ecology
BURGDOERFER, J. E., Physics
BURGHARDT, G. M., Psychology
BURSTEIN, A. G., Psychology
CALHOUN, W. H., Psychology
CALLCOTT, T. A., Physics
CAPONETTI, J. D., Botany
CARNEY, P. J., Audiology and Speech Pathology
CARROLL, D. A., English
CARRUTH, J. H., Mathematics
CEBIK, L. B., Philosophy
CHAMBERS, J. Q., Chemistry
CHEN, T. T., Zoology
CHILDERS, R. W., Physics
CHMIELEWSKI, E. V., History
CHURCHICH, J. E., Biochemistry
CLARK, C. E., Mathematics
COBB, C. W., Romance and Asian Languages
COBB, J. C., History
COHEN, C. P., Psychology
COHN, H. O., Physics
COKER, J., Music
COMBS, F. M., Music
CONDO, G. T., Physics
CONWAY, J. B., Mathematics
COOK, K. D., Chemistry
COOKE, T. P., Theatre
COTHRAN, R. M., Jr, Theatre
COX, D. R., English
CUNNINGHAM, R. B., Political Science
CUSTER, M., Theatre
CUTLER, E. W., History
DAEHNERT, R. H., Arts
DAVERMAN, R. J., Mathematics
DOBBS, D. E., Mathematics
DONGARRA, J., Computer Science
DRAKE, R. Y., Jr, English
DUNGAN, D. L., Religious Studies
DYDAK, J., Mathematics
ECHTERNACHT, A. C., Zoology
EDWARDS, R. B., Philosophy
EGUILUZ, A. G., Physics
ELSTON, S. B., Physics
ENSOR, A. R., English
ETNIER, D. A., Zoology
FALSETTI, J. S., Arts
FARRIS, W. W., History
FAULKNER, C. H., Anthropology
FIELD, R. C., Theatre

UNITED STATES OF AMERICA

FINGER, J. R., History
FINNERAN, R. J., English
FITZGERALD, M. R., Political Science
FORESTA, R., Geography
FOX, K., Physics
FRANDSEN, H., Mathematics
GANT, M. M., Political Science
GEORGHIOU, S., Physics
GESELL, G. C., Classics
GOLDENSTEIN, M. B., Arts
GORMAN, R., Political Science
GOSLEE, N. M., English
GRABER, G. C., Philosophy
GRIMM, F. A., Chemistry
GROSS, L. J., Mathematics
GUIDRY, M. W., Physics
GUIOCHON, G. A., Chemistry
HAAS, A. G., History
HALLAM, T. G., Mathematics
HANDEL, M. A., Zoology
HANDEL, S. J., Psychology
HANDELSMAN, M. H., Romance and Asian Languages
HANDLER, L., Psychology
HANDLER, T., Physics
HAO, YEN-PING, History
HARRIS, W. F., Biology
HART, E. L., Physics
HASTINGS, D. W., Sociology
HATCHER, R. D., Zoology
HEFFERNAN, T. J., English
HEFLIN, W. H., Romance and Asian Languages
HICKOK, L. G., Botany
HINTON, D. B., Mathematics
HOLTON, R. W., Botany
HOOD, T. C., Sociology
HUGHES, K. W., Botany
HUSCH, L. S., Mathematics
JACKSON, C. O., Admin.
JACOBS, K. A., Music
JACOBSON, H. C., Admin.
JANTZ, R. L., Anthropology
JEON, K. W., Zoology
JOHANNSON, K., Mathematics
JONES, W. H., Psychology
JORDAN, G. S., Mathematics
JOSHI, J. G., Biochemistry
JOY, D. C., Zoology
JUMPER, S. R., Geography
KABALKA, G. W., Chemistry
KALLET, M., English
KAMYCHKOV, I. A., Physics
KARAKASHIAN, O., Mathematics
KEELING, K. A., Music
KEENE, M. L., English
KELLY, R. M., English
KENNEDY, J. R., Zoology
KENNEDY, W. C., Arts
KLEINFELTER, D. C., Chemistry
KLIPPEL, W. E., Anthropology
KOPP, O. C., Geology
KOVAC, J. D., Chemistry
LABOTKA, T. C., Geological Sciences
LANGSTON, M. A., Computer Science
LAWLER, J. E., Psychology
LAWLER, K., Psychology
LEE, B. S., Arts
LEGGETT, B. J., English
LEKI, I., English
LELAND, W. E., Arts
LENHART, S. M., Mathematics
LESTER, L. W., Admin.
LEVY, K. D., Romance and Asian Languages
LINGE, D. E., Religious Studies
LIVINGSTON, P. R., Arts
LOFARO, M. A., English
LUBAR, J., Psychology
LYONS, W., Political Science
MACCABE, J. A., Zoology
MCCLELLAND, D. K., Music
MCCONNEL, R. M., Mathematics
MCCORMICK, J. F., Ecology
MCCRACKEN, G. F., Zoology
MACEK, J. H., Physics

2681

MCSWEEN, H. Y., Geological Sciences
MAGDEN, N. E., Arts
MAGID, L. J., Chemistry
MAGID, R. M., Chemistry
MAHAN, G. D., Physics
MALAND, C., English
MALONE, J. C., Jr, Psychology
MARSH, F. H., Arts
MARTINSON, F. H., Arts
MASHBURN, R. R., Speech and Theatre
MATHEWS, H. T., Mathematics
MISRA, K. C., Geology
MONTIE, T. C., Microbiology
MONTY, K. J., Biochemistry
MOORE, M. C., Music
MOORE, R. N., Microbiology
MOSER, H. D., History
MULLIN, B. C., Botany
NABELEK, A. K., Audiology and Speech Pathology
NAZAREWICZ, W., Physics
NORMAN, R. V., Religious Studies
NORTHINGTON, D. B., Music
PAGNI, R. M., Chemistry
PAINTER, L. R., Physics
PEACOCK, D., Arts
PEDERSON, D. M., Music
PEGG, D. J., Physics
PENNER, A. R., English
PETERSEN, R. H., Botany
PETERSON, H. A., Audiology and Speech Pathology
PETERSON, J. R., Chemistry
PIMM, S. L., Zoology
PLAAS, H., Political Science
PLOCH, D. R., Sociology
PLUMMER, E. W., Physics
POLLIO, H. R., Psychology
POORE, J. H., Computer Science
POSTOW, B. C., Philosophy
PULSIPHER, L. M., Geography
QUINN, J. J., Physics
RAJPUT, B. S., Mathematics
RALSTON, B. A., Geography
REESE, J. E., English
REYNOLDS, C. H., Religious Studies
RIECHERT, S. E., Zoology
RIESING, T. J., Arts
RIGGSBY, W. S., Microbiology
RIVERA-RODAS, O., Romance and Asian Languages
ROMEISER, J. B., Romance and Asian Languages
ROSINSKI, J., Mathematics
ROTH, L. E., Zoology
RUTLEDGE, H. C., Classics
SAMEJIMA, F., Psychology
SANDERS, N. J., English
SAUDARGAS, R. S., Psychology
SAVAGE, D. C., Psychology
SAYLER, G. S., Microbiology
SCHAEFER, P. W., Mathematics
SCHEB, J. M., Political Science
SCHILLING, E., Botany
SCHMUDDE, T. H., Geography
SCHWEITZER, G. K., Chemistry
SCURA, D. M., English
SELLIN, I. A., Physics
SEPANIAK, M. J., Chemistry
SERBIN, S. M., Mathematics
SHIH, C. C., Physics
SHIVERS, C. A., Zoology
SHOVER, N. E., Sociology
SHURR, W. H., English
SILVERSTEIN, B., Audiology and Speech Pathology
SIMPSON, H. C., Mathematics
SMITH, T. A., Political Science
SMITH, W. O., Botany
SONI, K., Mathematics
SONI, R. P., Mathematics
SORENSEN, S. P., Physics
STACEY, G., Microbiology
STEPHENS, O. H., Jr, Political Science
STEPHENSON, K., Mathematics
STEWART, F. C., Arts

STUTZENBERGER, D. R., Music
SUNDBERG, C., Mathematics
SUNDELL, S. E., Physics
SUNDSTROM, E. D., Psychology
TAYLOR, L. A., Geology
THISTLETHWAITE, M. B., Mathematics
THOMAS, J. C., English
THOMASON, M. G., Computer Science
THOMPSON, J. R., Jr, Physics
THONNARD, N., Science Alliance
TIPPS, A. W., Music
TRAHERN, J. B., English
TRAVIS, C. B., Psychology
UNGS, T. D., Political Science
VAN DE VATE, D., Jr, Philosophy
VANHOOK, A., Chemistry
VAUGHN, G. L., Zoology
WADE, W. R., II, MATHEMATICS
WAGNER, C. G., Mathematics
WAHLER, R. G., Psychology
WALKER, K. R., Geology
WALLACE, S. E., Sociology
WALNE, P. L., Botany
WARD, B. F. L., Physics
WARD, R. C., Computer Science
WASHBURN, Y. M., Romance and Asian Languages
WEHRY, E. L., Chemistry
WEIR, A., English
WELBORN, D. M., Political Science
WHEELER, T. V., English
WHEELER, W. B., History
WHITE, D. C., Microbiology
WHITSON, G. L., Zoology
WICKS, W. D., Biochemistry
WILLIAMS, T. F., Chemistry
WOODS, C., Chemistry
WUNDERLICH, B., Chemistry
YATES, S. A., Arts
ZAK, T., Mathematics
ZHANG, J. Y., Physics

College of Human Ecology:
BLANTON, P. W., Child and Family Studies
CAMPBELL, C. P., Human Resources Devt
CARRUTH, B. R., Nutrition
CHEEK, G. D., Human Resources Devt
COAXLEY, C. B., Human Resources Devt
CRAIG, D. G., Human Resources Devt
CUNNINGHAM, J. L., Child and Family Studies
DELONG, A. J., Textiles, Retailing and Interior Design
DRAKE, M. F., Textiles, Retailing and Interior Design
DUCKETT, K. E., Textiles, Retailing and Interior Design
FOX, G. L., Child and Family Studies
GORSKI, J. D., Health, Leisure and Safety Sciences
HAMILTON, C. B., Health, Leisure and Safety Sciences
HANSON, R. R., Human Resources Devt
HASKELL, R. W., Human Resources Devt
HAYES, G. A., Health, Leisure and Safety Sciences
KIRK, R. H., Health, Leisure and Safety Sciences
MORAN, J. D., Admin.
NORDQUIST, V. M., Child and Family Studies
SACHAN, D. S., Nutrition
SKINNER, J. D., Nutrition
STEELE, C., Child and Family Studies
TWARDOSZ, S. L., Child and Family Studies
WADSWORTH, L. C., Textiles, Retailing and Interior Design
WALLACE, B. C., Health, Leisure and Safety Sciences
ZEMEL, M. B., Nutrition

College of Engineering:
ALEXEFF, I., Electrical Eng.
ARIMILLI, R. V., Mechanical and Aerospace Eng.
BAILEY, J. M., Electrical Eng.
BAKER, A. J., Eng. Science and Mechanics

BENNETT, R. M., Civil and Environmental Eng.
BIENKOWSKI, P. R., Chemical Eng.
BIRDWELL, J. D., Electrical Eng.
BISHOP, A. O., Jr, Electrical Eng.
BLALOCK, T. V., Electrical Eng.
BODENHEIMER, R. E., Electrical Eng.
BOGUE, D. C., Chemical Eng.
BONTADELLI, J. A., Industrial Eng.
BOSE, B. K., Electrical Eng.
BOULDIN, D. W., Electrical Eng.
BROOKS, C. R., Jr, Materials Science and Eng.
BUCHANAN, R. A., Materials Science and Eng.
BURDETTE, E. G., Civil and Environmental Eng.
CARLEY, T. G., Eng. Science and Mechanics
CHATTERJEE, A., Civil and Environmental Eng.
CLARK, E. S., Materials Science and Eng.
CLAYCOMBE, W. W., Industrial Eng.
COUNCE, R. M., Chemical Eng.
CUMMINGS, P. T., Chemical Eng.
DAVIS, W. T., Civil and Environmental Eng.
DEPORTER, E. L., Industrial Eng.
DODDS, H. L., Nuclear Eng.
DRUMM, E. C., Civil and Environmental Eng.
EDMONDSON, A. J., Mechanical and Aerospace Eng.
FELLERS, J. F., Materials Science and Eng.
FORRESTER, J. H., Eng. Science and Mechanics
FRAZIER, G. C., Chemical Eng.
GHOSH, M. M., Civil and Environmental Eng.
GONZALEZ, R. C., Electrical Eng.
GOODPASTURE, D. W., Civil and Environmental Eng.
GREEN, W. L., Electrical Eng.
HANSEN, M. G., Chemical Eng.
HODGSON, J. W., Mechanical and Aerospace Eng.
HOFFMAN, G. W., Electrical Eng.
HUNG, J. C., Electrical Eng.
JENDRUCKO, R. J., Eng. Science and Mechanics
JOHNSON, W. S., Mechanical and Aerospace Eng.
KENNEDY, E. J., Electrical Eng.
KERLIN, T. W., Jr, Nuclear Eng.
KIM, K. H., Eng. Science and Mechanics
KRANE, R. J., Mechanical and Aerospace Eng.
KRIEG, R. D., Eng. Science and Mechanics
LANDES, J. D., Eng. Science and Mechanics
LAWLER, J. S., Electrical Eng.
LIAW, P. K., Materials Science and Eng.
LUNDIN, C. D., Materials Science and Eng.
MILLER, L. F., Nuclear Eng.
MILLER, W. A., Civil and Environmental Eng.
MILLIGAN, M. W., Mechanical and Aerospace Eng.
MOORE, C. F., Chemical Eng.
NEFF, H. P., Jr, Electrical Eng.
OLIVER, B. F., Materials Science and Eng.
PACE, M. O., Electrical Eng.
PARANG, M., Mechanical and Aerospace Eng.
PARSONS, J. R., Mechanical and Aerospace Eng.
PEDRAZA, A. J., Materials Science and Eng.
PERONA, J. J., Chemical Eng.
PHILLIPS, P. J., Materials Science and Eng.
PITTS, D. R., Eng.—Admin.
PRADOS, J. W., Chemical Eng.
REED, G. D., Civil and Environmental Eng.
ROBERTS, M. J., Electrical Eng.
ROBINSON, R. B., Civil and Environmental Eng.
ROTH, J. R., Electrical Eng.
SCHMITT, H. W., Industrial Eng.
SCOTT, W. E., Eng. Science and Mechanics

SHANNON, T. E., Nuclear Eng.
SMITH, G. V., Mechanical and Aerospace Eng.
SNIDER, J. N., Industrial Eng.
SOLIMAN, O., Eng. Science and Mechanics
SPECKHART, F. H., Mechanical and Aerospace Eng.
SPRUIELL, J. E., Materials Science and Eng.
SYMONDS, F. W., Electrical Eng.
TOMPKINS, F. D., Eng. Academic
TRIVEDI, M. M., Electrical Eng.
TSCHANTZ, B. A., Civil and Environmental Eng.
UHRIG, R. E., Nuclear Eng.
UPADHYAYA, B. R., Nuclear Eng.
WASSERMAN, J. F., Eng. Science and Mechanics
WEGMANN, F. J., Civil and Environmental Eng.
WEITSMAN, Y. J., Center of Excellence
WILKERSON, H. J., Mechanical and Aerospace Eng.
WILSON, C. C., Mechanical and Aerospace Eng.

College of Business Administration:

BARNABY, D. J., Marketing and Transportation
BLACK, H. A., Finance
BOEHM, T. P., Finance
BOHM, R. A., Econ.
BOWLBY, R. L., Econ.
CADOTTE, E. R., Marketing and Transportation
CARROLL, S. L., Econ.
CHANG, H., Econ.
CLARK, D. P., Econ.
COLE, W. E., Econ.
DAVIDSON, P., Econ.
DAVIS, F. W., Jr, Marketing and Transportation
DEWHIRST, H. D., Management
DICER, G. N., Marketing and Transportation
FISHER, B. D., Accounting
FOX, W. F., Econ.
GARRISON, C. B., Econ.
HERRING, H. C., Accounting
HERZOG, H. W., Economics
JAMES, L. R., Management
KIGER, J. E., Accounting
LANGLEY, C. J., Jr, Marketing and Transportation
LEE, F.-Y., Econ.
MAYHEW, A., Econ.
MAYO, J. W., Econ.
MENTZER, J. T., Marketing Logistics and Transportation
MUNDY, R. A., Marketing and Transportation
PARR, W. C., Statistics
PATTON, E. P., Marketing and Transportation
PHILIPPATOS, G. C., Finance
PHILPOT, J. W., Statistics
REEVE, J. M., Accounting
ROTH, H. P., Accounting
RUSH, M. C., Management
SANDERS, R. D., Statistics
SCHLOTTMANN, A., Econ.
SHRIEVES, R. E., Finance
STAHL, M. J., Business Admin.
STANGA, K. G., Accounting
SYLWESTER, D. L., Statistics
WACHOWICZ, J. M., Finance
WANSLEY, J. W., Finance
WILLIAMS, J. R., Accounting
WOODRUFF, R. B., Marketing Logistics and Transportation

College of Education:

ALEXANDER, J. E., Holistic Teaching and Learning
ALLISON, C. B., Cultural Studies in Education
BENNER, S. M., Inclusive Early Childhood Education

BLANK, K. J., Inclusive Early Childhood Education
BOGUE, E. G., Leadership Studies
BUTEFISH, W. L., Education in Science and Mathematics
CAMERON, W., Psychoeducational Studies
COLEMAN, L. J., Inclusive Early Childhood Education
DAVIS, A. R., Holistic Teaching and Learning
DAVIS, K. L., Counsellor Education and Counselling Psychology
DESSART, D. J., Curriculum and Instruction
DICKINSON, D. J., Education in Science and Mathematics
DOAK, E. D., Education in Science and Mathematics
FRENCH, R. L., Education in Science and Mathematics
GEORGE, T. W., Educational Administration
HARGIS, C. H., Holistic Teaching and Learning
HARRIS, G., Leadership Studies
HECTOR, M. A., Counsellor Education and Counselling Psychology
HIPPLE, T. W., Holistic Teaching and Learning
HOWLEY, E. T., Exercise Science
HUCK, S. W., Counsellor Education and Counselling Psychology
HUFF, P F., Holistic Teaching and Learning
HULL, H. N., Language Communication and Humanities Education
JOST, K. J., Holistic Teaching and Learning
KASWORM, C. E., Bureau of Educational Research and Services
KNIGHT, L. N., Holistic Teaching and Learning
KOZAR, A. J., Exercise Science
KRONICK, R. F., Holistic Teaching and Learning
LIEMOHN, W. P., Exercise Science
McCALLUM, R. S., Psychoeducational Studies
McINTYRE, L. D., Education in Science and Mathematics
MALIK, A., Cultural Studies in Education
MEAD, B. J., Cultural Studies in Education
MERTZ, N. T., Leadership Studies
MILLER, J. H., Rehabilitation and Deafness Programs
MORGAN, W. J., Cultural Studies in Education
MYER, M. E., Jr, Education in Science and Mathematics
PAUL, M. J., Cultural Studies in Education
PETERS, J. M., Psychoeducational Studies
PETERSON, M. P., Counsellor Education and Counselling Psychology
POPPEN, W. A., Counsellor Education and Counselling Psychology
RAY, J. R., Education in Science and Mathematics
ROCKETT, I. R. H., Exercise Science
ROESKE, C. E., Education in Science and Mathematics
ROWELL, C. G., Educational Administration
SCHINDLER, W. J., Holistic Teaching and Learning
THOMPSON, C. L., Counsellor Education and Counselling Psychology
TURNER, T. N., Holistic Teaching and Learning
UBBEN, G. C., Leadership Studies
WELCH, O. M., Rehabilitation and Deafness Programs
WILEY, P. D., Language Communication and Humanities Education
WILLIAMS, R. L., Psychoeducational Studies
WOODRICK, W. E., Rehabilitation and Deafness Programs
WRISBERG, C. A., Cultural Studies in Education

College of Communications:

ASHDOWN, P. G., Journalism
BOWLES, D. A., Journalism
CROOK, J. A., Journalism
EVERETT, G. A., Journalism
HOWARD, H. H., Broadcasting
LITTMANN, M. E., Journalism
MILLER, M. M., Journalism
MOORE, B. A., Broadcasting
SINGLETARY, M. W., Journalism
SMYSER, R. D., Journalism
STANKEY, M. J., Advertising
SWAN, N. R., Jr, Broadcasting
TAYLOR, R. E., Advertising

College of Agriculture:

ALLEN, F. L., Plant and Soil Science
ASHBURN, E. L., Plant and Soil Science
BERNARD, E. C., Entomology and Plant Pathology
BLEDSOE, B. L., Agricultural Eng.
BOST, S. C., Entomology and Plant Pathology
BREKKE, C. J., Food Science and Technology
BROOKER, J. R., Agricultural Economics
BUCKNER, E. R., Forestry
BURGESS, E. E., Entomology and Plant Pathology
CALLAHAN, L. M., Ornamental Horticulture and Landscape Design
CARTER, C. E., Jr, Agricultural Extension Education
CHAMBERS, A. Y., Entomology and Plant Pathology
CLELAND, C. L., Agricultural Econ.
COFFEY, D. L., Plant and Soil Science
COLLINS, J. L., Food Technology and Science
CONATSER, G. E., Animal Science
CONGER, B. V., Plant and Soil Science
COOK, O. F., Four-H Club
CRATER, G. D., Ornamental Horticulture and Landscape Design
DALY, R. T., Home Econ.
DEARDEN, B. L., Forestry
DIMMICK, R. W., Forestry
DRAUGHON, F. A., Food Science and Technology
EASTWOOD, D. B., Agricultural Econ.
ENGLISH, B. C., Agricultural Econ.
FARMER, C. M., Agricultural Econ.
FLINCHUM, W. T., Plant and Soil Science
FOSS, J. E., Plant and Soil Science
FRIBOURG, H. A., Plant and Soil Science
GARLAND, C. D., Agricultural Econ.
GERHARDT, R. R., Entomology and Plant Pathology
GILL, W. W., Animal Science
GOAN, H. C., Animal Science
GODKIN, J. D., Animal Science
GRAHAM, E. T., Ornamental Horticulture and Landscape Design
GRAVES, C. R., Plant and Soil Science
GRESSHOFF, P. M., Ornamental Horticulture, Center of Excellence
HADDEN, C. H., Entomology and Plant Pathology
HALL, R. F., Extension Veterinary Medicine
HAYES, R. M., Plant and Soil Science
HENRY, Z. A., Agricultural Eng.
HILL, T. K., Forestry
HOPPER, G. M., Forestry
HOWARD, D. D., Plant and Soil Science
HUNTER, D. L., Agricultural Econ.
JENKINS, R. P., Agricultural Econ.
KIRKPATRICK, F. D., Animal Science
LAMBDIN, P. L., Entomology and Plant Pathology
LANE, C. D., Jr, Animal Science
LESSLY, R. R., Agricultural Extension Education
LEUTHOLD, F. O., Agricultural Econ.
LITTLE, R. L., Forestry
LOCKWOOD, D. W., Plant and Soil Science

McDaniel, G. L., Ornamental Horticulture and Landscape Design
McLemore, D. L., Agricultural Econ.
Mays, G. C., Communication
Meadows, D. G., Animal Science (Beef)
Melton, C. C., Food Technology
Melton, S. L., Food Technology and Science
Miller, J. K., Animal Science
Miller, R. D., Plant and Soil Science
Montgomery, M. J., Animal Science
Morris, W. C., Food Science and Technology
Mote, C. R., Agricultural Eng.
Mullins, C. A., Plant and Soil Science
Mundy, S. D., Agricultural Econ.
Neel, J. B., Animal Science
Newman, M. A., Entomology and Plant Pathology
Oliver, S. P., Animal Science
Ostermeier, D. M., Forestry
Park, W. M., Agricultural Econ.
Patrick, C. R., Entomology and Plant Pathology
Pelton, M. R., Forestry
Penfield, M. P., Food Technology and Science
Pless, C. D., Entomology and Plant Pathology
Powell, B. T., Four-H
Rawls, E. L., Agricultural Econ.
Ray, D. E., Agricultural Econ.
Reinhardt, C. A., Communication
Rennie, J. C., Forestry
Reynolds, J. H., Plant and Soil Science
Robbins, K. R., Animal Science
Roberts, R. K., Agricultural Econ.
Rutledge, A. D., Plant and Soil
Sams, C. E., Plant and Soil Science
Sams, D. W., Plant and Soil Science
Sanders, W. L., Statistics
Saxton, A. M., Statistics
Simms, R. H., Animal Science
Smith, G. F., Agricultural Econ.
Southards, C. J., Entomology and Plant Pathology
Strange, R. J., Forestry
Todd, J. D., Agricultural Extension and Education
Tyler, D. D., Plant and Soil Science
West, D. R., Plant and Soil Science
Westbrook, E. M., Home Economics and Family Economy
Wilhelm, L. R., Agricultural Eng.
Williams, D. B., Ornamental Horticulture and Landscape Design
Williamson, H., Agricultural Econ.
Wills, J. B., Agricultural Eng.
Wilson, J. L., Forestry

College of Veterinary Medicine:
Brace, J. J., Admin.
Brian, D. A., Microbiology and Veterinary Medicine
Bright, R. M., Small Animal Clinical Sciences
Dorn, A. S., Small Animal Clinical Sciences
Edwards, D. F., Pathology
Farkas, W. R., Comparative Medicine
Green, E. M., Large Animal Clinical Sciences
Henry, R. W., Animal Science
Hopkins, F. M., Large Animal Clinical Sciences
Krahwinkel, D. J., Jr, Small Animal Clinical Sciences
Legendre, A. M., Small Animal Clinical Sciences
McCord, S. P., Comparative Medicine
McDonald, T. P., Animal Science and Veterinary Medicine
McGavin, M. D., Pathology
Oliver, J. W., Comparative Medicine
Patton, C. S., Pathology
Potgieter, L. N. D., Comparative Medicine

Rouse, B. T., Microbiology and Veterinary Medicine
Schuller, H. M., Pathology
Shull, R. M., Pathology
Shultz, T. W., Animal Science and Veterinary Medicine
Sims, M. H., Animal Science and Veterinary Medicine
Slauson, D. O., Pathology

College of Law:
Blaze, D. A.
Cohen, N. P.
Cook, J. G.
Dessem, R. L.
Hardin, P.
Hess, A. M.
King, J. H., Jr
Leclercq, F. S.
Lloyd, R. M.
Phillips, J. J.
Rivkin, D. H.
Sobieski, J. L., Jr

School of Architecture:
Anderson, G.
Grieger, F.
Kelso, R. M.
Kersavage, J. A.
Kinzy, S. A.
Lauer, W. J.
Lester, A. J.
Lizon, P.
Robinson, M. A.
Rudd, J. W.
Shell, W. S.
Watson, J. S.
Wodehouse, L. M.

School of Nursing:
Alligood, M. R.
Goodfellow, D. H.
Mozingo, J.
Thomas, S. P.

Graduate School of Social Work:
Cetingok, M.
Faver, C. A.
Glisson, C. A.
Hirayama, H.
Nooe, R. M.
Rubinstein, H.

Graduate School of Bio-medical Sciences:
Olins, A. L.
Olins, D. E.
Popp, R. A.

Graduate School of Planning:
Johnson, D. A.
Prochaska, J. M.
Spencer, J. A.

Graduate School of Library and Information Science:
Estes, G. E.
Tenopir, C.

Space Institute:
Antar, B. N.
Collins, F. G.
Crater, H. W.
Crawford, L. W.
Crawford, R. A.
Flandro, G. A.
Garrison, G. W.
Keefer, D. R.
Kuperschmidt, B. A.
Lewis, J. W.
Lo, C.
McCay, M. H.
Paludan, C. T. N.
Peters, C. E.
Pujol, A.
Schulz, R. J.
Shahrokhi, F.
Sheth, A. C.
Wu, J. M.

Center for Assessment Research:
McGlasson, N.

Library:
Bayne, P. S.
Best, R. A., Law
Crawford, M. F.
Felder-Hoehne, F. H.
Grady, A. M.
Leclercq, A. W.
Phillips, L. L.
Piquet, D. C., Law
Rader, J. C.

Learning Research Center:
Walter L. Humphreys

Energy, Environment and Resources Center:
Colglazier, E. M.

University of Tennessee Health Sciences Center

Memphis, TN 38103
Telephone: (902) 528-5500
Internet: www.utmem.edu

Chancellor: William R. Rice
Exec. Asst to the Chancellor: Martha J. Young
Vice-Chancellor for Univ. Relations: Jesse F. McClure
Vice-Chancellor for Student Affairs: William C. Robinson
Vice-Chancellor for Devt: Glenda A. O'Connor
Vice-Chancellor for Business and Finance: Robert L. Blackwell
Vice-Chancellor for Admin.: Raymond H. Colson

DEANS

College of Allied Health Sciences: William G. Hinkle
College of Medicine: Robert L. Summitt
College of Dentistry: William F. Slagle
College of Pharmacy: Dick R. Gourley
College of Nursing: Michael A. Carter
College of Graduate Health Sciences: Robert Freeman

University of Tennessee at Martin

Martin, TN 38328
Telephone: (901) 587-7000
Internet: www.utm.edu

Chancellor: Margaret N. Perry
Vice-Chancellor for Academic Affairs: Frank S. Black
Vice-Chancellor for Financial Affairs: Phillip W. Dane
Vice-Chancellor for Student Affairs: Philip W. Watkins
Exec. Vice-Chancellor for Devt: Nick Dunagan

DEANS

School of Agriculture and Home Econ.: James L. Byford
School of Business Administration: Gary F. Young
School of Education: Gary Rush
School of Arts and Sciences: Robert M. Smith
School of Eng.: Troy F. Henson
Student Affairs: Donald G. Sexton
Intensive English Language Programs: John A. Eisterhold

UNIVERSITY OF THE SOUTH

Sewanee, TN 37383-1000
Telephone: (931) 598-1000
Internet: www.sewanee.edu
Founded 1858
Private control (Protestant Episcopal Church)
Language of instruction: English

Academic year: August to May
Pres.: Dr JOEL L. CUNNINGHAM
Provost: LINDA B. LANKEWICZ
Dir of Summer College: JESSE SPAULDING
Dean of Graduate School of Theology: WILLIAM STAFFORD
Dir of Admissions: DAVID LESESNE
Registrar: PAUL G. WILEY, II
Librarian: VICKI SELLS
Library of 469,000 vols
Number of teachers: 156 (127 full-time, 29 part-time)
Number of students: 1,559 (1,467 college, 92 seminary)
Publications: *Sewanee Review*, *Sewanee Theological Review*

DEANS

College of Arts and Sciences: THOMAS A. KAZEE
School of Theology: Very Rev. Dr GUY F. LYTLE, III

VANDERBILT UNIVERSITY

Nashville, TN 37235
Telephone: (615) 322-7311
Fax: (615) 343-7765
E-mail: admissions@vanderbilt.edu
Internet: www.vanderbilt.edu
Founded 1873
Academic year: August to April
Chancellor: GORDON GEE
Provost: NICHOLAS S. ZEPPOS
Vice-Chancellors: HARRY R. JACOBSON, MICHAEL J. SCHOENFELD, WILLIAM T. SPITZ, DAVID WILLIAMS, II, LAUREN J. BRISKEY, NICHOLAS S. ZEPPOS
Sec.: WILLIAM W. BAIN, Jr
Registrar: R. G. GIBSON
Librarian: PAUL GHERMAN
Number of teachers: 4,052 (2,346 full-time, 1,706 part-time)
Number of students: 11,092
Publications: *The Graduate Post* (annual), *The Nurse* (2 a year), *Peabody Reflector* (College of Education and Continuing Development, 2 a year), *The Engineer* (2 a year), *The Spire* (Divinity School, 3 a year), *Owen Manager* (Graduate School of Management, 2 a year), *The Lawyer* (2 a year), *The Cornerstone* (College of Arts and Science, 3 a year)

DEANS

College of Arts and Science: RICHARD MCCARTY
Graduate School: WILLIAM SMITH
Blair School of Music: MARK WAIT
Divinity: JAMES HUDNUT-BEUMLER
School of Eng.: KENNETH GALLOWAY
School of Law: KENT SYVERUD
Owen Graduate School of Management: WILLIAM CHRISTIE
School of Medicine: STEVEN GABBE
School of Nursing: COLLEEN CONWAY-WELCH
George Peabody College: CAMILLA BENBOW

PROFESSORS

ABKOWITZ, M. D., Civil and Environmental Eng.
ABUMRAD, N. N., Surgery
AHNER, J., Mathematics
ALBRIDGE, R. G., Physics and Astronomy
ALDROUBI, A., Mathematics
ALLEN, G. S., Neurological Surgery
ARMSTRONG, R. N., Biochemistry
ARTEAGA, C. L., Medicine
ATACK, J., Econ.
ATKINSON, J. B., III, Pathology
AURBACH, M. L., Art and Art History
AVISON, M. J., Radiology and Radiological Sciences

BADER, D. M., Medicine
BALDWIN, H. S., Paediatrics
BALDWIN, L. V., Religious Studies
BALL, C. A., Management
BALLARD, D. W., Microbiology and Immunology
BALSER, J. R., Anaesthesiology
BARRY, B., Management
BARSKY, R. F., French and Italian
BASU, P. K., Civil and Environmental Eng.
BEAUCHAMP, R. D., Surgery
BELL, V. M., English
BELTON, R., Law
BENBOW, C. P., Psychology and Human Devt
BERNARD, G. R., Medicine
BESS, F. H., Hearing and Speech Sciences
BETH, A. H., Molecular Physiology and Biophysics
BIAGGIONI, I. O., Medicine
BICKMAN, L., Psychology and Human Devt
BISCH, D., Mathematics
BLACKBURN, J. O., Management
BLACKETT, R., History
BLAKE, R., Psychology
BLAKELY, R. D., Pharmacology
BLANNING, R. W., Management
BLOCH, F. S., Law
BOEHM, F. H., Obstetrics and Gynaecology
BÖER, G. B., Management
BOLTON, R., Management
BOND, E., Econ.
BONDS, A. B., III, Electrical Eng. and Computer Science
BOOTH, W. J., Political Science
BORNHOP, D. J., Chemistry
BOYD, S. B., Oral and Maxillofacial Surgery
BRANDON, M. E., Law
BRANDT, S. J., Medicine
BRASH, A. R., Pharmacology
BRAU, C. A., Physics and Astronomy
BRAXTON, J., Leadership, Policy and Organizations
BRESSMAN, L. S., Law
BREYER, M. D., Medicine
BROADIE, K., Biological Sciences
BROWN, R. L., Law
BRUCE, J. W., Law
BUERHAUS, P. I., Nursing
BURK, R. F., Medicine
BURNETT, L. S., Obstetrics and Gynaecology
BURNS, J. P., Divinity
BURR, I. M., Paediatrics
BYRD, B. F., III, Medicine
CADZOW, J. A., Electrical Eng. and Computer Science
CAMARATA, S. M., Hearing and Speech Sciences
CAPDEVILA, J. H., Medicine
CAPRIOLI, R. M., Biochemistry
CARBONE, D. P., Medicine
CARPENTER, G. F., Biochemistry
CARROLL, F. E., Jr, Radiology and Radiological Sciences
CARTER, C. E., Biological Sciences
CASAGRANDE, V. A., Cell Biology
CHALKLEY, G. R., Molecular Physiology and Biophysics
CHANEY, P. K., Management
CHAZIN, W. J., Boichemistry
CHERRINGTON, A. D., Molecular Physiology and Biophysics
CHRISTIE, W. G., Management
CHRISTMAN, J. W., Medicine
CHURCHILL, L. R., Medicine
CLAYTON, E., Paediatrics
CLAYTON, J. B., English
COBB, P. A., Teaching and Learning
COFFEY, R. J., Jr, Medicine
COLE, D. A., Psychology and Human Devt
COLLINS, R. D., Pathology
COMPAS, B., Psychology and Human Devt
CONLEY, J., Econ.
CONN, P. J., Pharmacology
CONTURE, E. G., Hearing and Speech Sciences
CONWAY-WELCH, C. M., Nursing

COOK, G. E., Electrical Eng. and Computer Science
CORBIN, J. D., Molecular Physiology and Biophysics
CORDRAY, D. S., Psychology and Human Devt
CORN, A. L., Special Education
CORNFIELD, D. B., Sociology
COTTON, R. B., Paediatrics
COVINGTON, R. N., Law
CROOKE, P. S., III, Mathematics
CROWSON, R., Leadership, Policy and Organizations
CUMMINGS, P., Chemical Eng.
D'AQUILA, R. T., Medicine
DAFT, R. L., Management
DALLEY, A. F., Cell Biology
DAMON, W. W., Econ.
DANZO, B. J., Obstetrics and Gynaecology
DAUGHETY, A. F., Econ.
DAVIDSON, J. M., Pathology
DAVIDSON, J. L., Electrical Eng. and Computer Science
DAVIS, S. N., Medicine
DAVIS, T. M., English
DeFELICE, L. J., Pharmacology
DELBEKE, D., Radiology and Radiation Sciences
DEMAREST, A. A., Anthropology
DERMODY, T. S., Paediatrics
DESHPANDE, J. K., Paediatrics
DesPREZ, R. M., Nursing
DEUTCH, A. Y., Psychiatry
DEY, S. K., Paediatrics
DiBENEDETTO, E., Mathematics
DICKERSON, D. C., History
DILLEHAY, T. D., Anthropology
DILTS, D., Electrical Eng. and Computer Science
DITTUS, R. S., Medicine
DOKECKI, P. R., Human and Organizational Devt
DOWDY, L. W., Electrical Eng. and Computer Science
DOWNING, J. W., Anaesthesiology
DOYLE, D. H., History
DREWS, R., Classical Studies
DRINKWATER, D. C., Jr, Cardiac and Thoracic Surgery
DRISKILL, R. A., Econ.
DuBOIS, R. N., Jr, Medicine
DUNCAVAGE, J. A., Otolaryngology
DUPONT, W. D., Preventative Medicine
DYKENS, E. A., Psychology and Human Devt
EAKIN, M. C., History
EBNER, F. F., Psychology
EDELMAN, P. H., Mathematics
EDEN, B., Econ.
EDWARDS, K. M., Paediatrics
ELLEDGE, W. P., English
ELLIOTT, S. N., Special Education
ELY, J. W., History
ELY, J. W., Law
ENTERLINE, L., English
ENTMAN, S. S., Obstetrics and Gynaecology
EPSTEIN, J. A., History
ERNST, D. J., Physics and Astronomy
EXTON, J. H., Molecular Physiology and Biophysics
FAN, Y., Econ.
FANNING, E. H., Biological Sciences
FARRAN, D., Teaching and Learning
FAZIO, S., Medicine
FELDMAN, L. C., Physics and Astronomy
FELZMAN, L. C., Physics and Astronomy
FENICHEL, G. M., Neurology
FITZ, E. E., Spanish and Portuguese
FITZPATRICK, J. M., Electrical Eng. and Computer Science
FLEETWOOD, D. M., Electrical Eng. and Computer Science
FLEISCHER, A. C., Radiology and Radiological Sciences
FLEXNER, J. M., Medicine
FOGO, A. B., Pathology
FOLGARAIT, L., Art and Art History
FOSTER, J. E., Econ.

FOX, R., Psychology
FRANKS, J. J., Psychology
FREEMAN, M. L., Radiation Oncology
FREEMON, F. R., Neurology
FRIEDMAN, E. H., Spanish and Portuguese
FRIEDMAN, R. A., Management
FROMENT-MEURICE, M., French and Italian
FRYD, V. G., Art and Art History
FUCHS, D. H., Special Education
FUCHS, L. S., Special Education
FURBISH, D. J., Geology
GABBE, S. G., Obstetrics and Gynaecology
GAFFNEY, F. A., Medical Admin.
GALLOWAY, K. F., Electrical Eng. and Computer Science
GALLOWAY, R. L., Jr, Biomedical Eng.
GARBER, J., Psychology and Human Devt
GAY, V. P., Religious Studies
GEE, E. G., Law
GEER, J., Political Science
GEORGE, A. L., Jr, Medicine
GIRGUS, S. B., English
GIUSE, N. B., Biomedical Informatics
GOLDBERG, J. C., Law
GOLDENRING, J. R., Surgery
GOLDRING, E., Leadership, Policy and Organizations
GOODMAN, L. E., Philosophy
GORDON, J., Nursing
GORE, J. C., Radiology and Radiological Sciences
GOTTFRIED, R. K., English
GOULD, K. L., Cell and Developmental Biology
GOULD, M. I., Mathematics
GRAHAM, G. J., Jr, Political Science
GRAHAM, T. P., Jr, Paediatrics
GRANNER, D. K., Molecular Physiology and Biophysics
GRANTHAM, D. W., Hearing and Speech Sciences
GREEN, N. E., Orthopaedics and Rehabilitation
GREENE, J. W., Paediatrics
GREER, J. P., Medicine
GREGOR, T. A., Anthropology
GRIFFIN, L. J., Sociology and Political Science
GRIFFIN, M. R., Preventive Medicine
GUENGERICH, F. P., Biochemistry
GUTHRIE, C. P., Law
GUTHRIE, J. W., Leadership, Policy and Organizations
HAGLUND, R. F., Physics and Astronomy
HAHN, B., German and Slavic Language
HAINES, J. L., Molecular Physiology and Biophysics
HALL, D., Physics and Astronomy
HALL, D. J., Law
HALL, R., Teaching and Learning
HALLAHAN, D., Radiation Oncology
HALPERIN, J., English
HAMILTON, J. H., Physics and Astronomy
HAMM, H. E., Pharmacology
HANCOCK, M. D., Political Science
HANDE, K. R., Medicine
HANKS, S. K., Cell Biology
HANN, S. R., Cell Biology
HARRIS, R. C., Jr, Medicine
HARRIS, T. R., Biomedical Eng.
HAWIGER, J., Microbiology and Immunology
HAZINSKI, T. A., Paediatrics
HEAD, D. R., Pathology
HEARN, J., Leadership, Policy and Organizations
HELDERMAN, J. H., Medicine
HELFER, L. R., Law School
HELLER, R. M., Jr, Radiology and Radiological Sciences
HELLERQVIST, C. G., Biochemistry
HERCULES, D. M., Chemistry
HERNANZ-SCHULMAN, M., Radiology and Radiological Sciences
HESS, B. A., Jr, Chemistry
HETCHER, S. A., Law
HEYNEMAN, S., Leadership, Policy and Organizations

HICKSON, G. B., Paediatrics
HIEBERT, S. W., Biochemistry
HILL, G. C., Medical Admin.
HODAPP, R., Special Education
HODGES, M., Philosophy
HOFFMAN, D. L., Management
HOGGE, J. H., Psychology and Human Devt
HOLLON, S. D., Psychology
HOOVER, R. L., Pathology
HUDNET-BEUMLER, J., Divinity
HUDSON, D. J., Medicine
HUFFMAN, G. W., Econ.
HUGHES, C. B., Mathematics
ICHIKAWA, I., Paediatrics
INAGAMI, T., Biochemistry
ISAAC, L. W., Sociology
JACOBSON, G. P., Hearing and Speech Sciences
JACOBSON, H. R., Medicine
JARMAN, M. F., English
JENSEN, G. F., Sociology
JENSEN, R. M., Divinity
JOHNS, C. M. S., Art and Art History
JOHNSON, C. H., Biological Sciences
JOHNSON, D. A., Divinity
JOHNSON, D. H., Nursing
JONES, H. W., III, Obstetrics and Gynaecology
JRADE, C. L., Spanish and Portuguese
KAAS, J. H., Psychology
KAISER, A. B., Medicine
KAISER, A. P., Special Education
KANG, W. P., Electrical Eng. and Computer Science
KASPAROV, G., Mathematics
KAWAMURA, K., Electrical Eng. and Computer Science
KAYE, J. J., Radiology and Radiological Sciences
KESSLER, R. M., Radiology and Radiological Sciences
KING, L. E., Jr, Medicine
KING, N. J., Law
KINSER, D. L., Mechanical Eng.
KIRSHNER, H. S., Neurology
KNIGHT, D. A., Divinity
KOSSON, D. S., Civil and Environmental Eng.
KOURY, M. J., Medicine
KOVACS, W. J., Medicine
KREYLING, M. P., English
KUTZINSKI, V. M., Dean's Office
LACHS, J., Philosophy
LAMB, J., English
LaMONTAGNE, L. L., Nursing
LANCASTER, L. E., Nursing
LAPPIN, J. S., Psychology
LAWTON, A. R., III, Paediatrics
LE VAN, M., Chemical Eng.
LEBLANC, L. J., Management
LEGAN, H. L., Oral and Maxillofacial Surgery
LEHRER, R., Teaching and Learning
LeSTOURGEON, W. M., Biological Sciences
LeVAN, D. M., Chemical Eng.
LEVINE, A.-J., Divinity
LEVITT, P. R., Pharmacology
LEWIS, J. G., Medicine
LIEBLER, D. C., Biochemistry
LIGHT, R. W., Medicine
LIMBIRD, L. E., Pharmacology
LINTON, M. F., Medicine
LOGAN, G. D., Psychology
LOOSEN, P. T., Psychiatry
LORENZI, N. M., Biomedical Informatics
LOYD, J. E., Medicine
LUBINSKI, D., Psychology and Human Devt
LUIS, W., Spanish and Portuguese
LUKEHART, C. M., Chemistry
LYBRAND, T. P., Chemistry
McCARTHY, J. A., German and Slavic Languages
McCARTY, R., Psychology
McCAULEY, D. E., Biological Sciences
McCLURE, J. S., Divinity
McCOY, T. R., Law
MACDONALD, R. L., Neurology

McKENNA, S. J., Oral and Maxillofacial Surgery
McKENZIE, R. N., Mathematics
McLOED, R., Nursing
McMAHON, D. G., Biological Sciences
McNAMARA, T. P., Psychology
McWILLIAM, R. A., Paediatrics
MAGNUSON, M. A., Molecular Physiology and Biophysics
MAGUIRE, C. F., Physics and Astronomy
MAHADEVAN, S., Civil and Environmental Eng.
MAIER, H. G., Law
MANESCHI, A. E., Econ.
MARCH, S. T., Management
MARCUS, L. S., English
MARGO, R. A., Econ.
MARNETT, L. J., Biochemistry
MARTIN, P. R., Psychiatry
MASSENGILL, L.W., Electrical Eng. and Computer Science
MASULIS, R. W., Management
MATRISIAN, L. M., Cancer Biology
MATUSIK, R. J., Urologic Surgery
MAY, J. M., Medicine
MEEKS, M. D., Divinity
MEGIBBEN, C. K., Mathematics
MELLOR, A. M., Mechanical Eng.
MELNER, M. H., Obstetrics and Gynaecology
MELTZER, H. Y., Psychiatry
MEYRICK-CLARRY, B. O., Pathology
MIHALIK, M. L., Mathematics
MILLER, C. F., Geology
MILLER, G. G., Medicine
MILLER, M. F., Geology
MILLER, R. A., Biomedical Informatics
MILLER-McLEMORE, B. J., Divinity
MITCHELL, W. M., Pathology
MONGA, L., French and Italian
MOORE, R. A., Nursing
MORAN, B. I., Law
MORRIS, J. A., Jr, Surgery
MORROW, J. D., Medicine
MOSES, H. L., Cancer Biology
MURPHY, J. F., Leadership and Organizations
MURPHY, M. L., Art and Art History
NAGAREDA, R. A., Law
NANNEY, L. B., Plastic Surgery
NEILSON, E. G., Medicine
NELSON, D., Dean's Office
NETTERVILLE, J. L., Otolaryngology
NEWBROUGH, J. R., Human and Organization Devt
NEWMAN, J. H., Medicine
NORDEN, J. J., Cell and Devt Biology
NOVAK, T. P., Management
OATES, J. A., Medicine
OBERACKER, V. E., Physics and Astronomy
O'DAY, D. M., Ophthalmology and Visual Sciences
O'HARA, E. A., Law
OHDE, R. N., Hearing and Speech Sciences
OLIVER, K., Philosophy
OLIVER, R. L., Management
OLSEN, N. J., Medicine
OLSON, G. E., Cell and Developmental Biology
ONG, D. E., Biochemistry
OPPENHEIMER, B. I., Political Science
ORGEBIN-CRIST, M. C., Obstetrics and Gynaecology
OSHEROFF, N., Biochemistry
OSSOFF, R. H., Otolaryngology
OSTEEN, K. G., Obstetrics and Gynaecology
OUTLAW, L. T., Philosophy
OVERHOLSER, K. A., Biomedical Eng.
OZBOLT, J. G., Nursing
PACE, J., Nursing
PAGE, D. L., Pathology
PAGE, T. L., Biological Sciences
PANTELIDES, S. T., Physics and Astronomy
PARK, J. H., Molecular Physiology and Biophysics
PARKER, F. L., Civil and Environmental Eng.
PARL, F. F., Pathology

PARTAIN, C. L., Radiology and Radiological Sciences
PARTRIDGE, W., Human and Organizational Devt
PATTE, D. M., Religious Studies
PATTON, J. A., Radiology and Radiological Sciences
PENN, J. S., Ophthalmology and Visual Sciences
PHILLIPS, J. A, III, Paediatrics
PIETENPOL, J. A., Biochemistry
PILON, B. A., Nursing
PINCUS, T., Medicine
PISTON, D. W., Molecular Physiology and Biophysics
PITZ, R. W., Mechanical Eng.
PLUMMER, J. F., English
PLUMMER, M. D., Mathematics
POLAVARAPU, P. L., Chemistry
PORTER, A. C., Leadership and Organizations
PORTER, N. A., Chemistry
PRICE, R. R., Radiology and Radiological Sciences
PRIETO, R., Spanish and Portuguese
PRILLELTENSKY, I., Human and Organizational Devt
PUTNAM, J. B., Jr, Thoracic Surgery
QUARANTA, V., Cancer Biology
RAMAYYA, A. V., Physics and Astronomy
RASCH, R. F. R., Nursing
RASICO, P. D., Spanish and Portuguese
RASMUSSEN, R. K., Law
RATCLIFFE, J. G., Mathematics
RAY, J. L., Political Science
RAY, W. A., Preventive Medicine
REINGANUM, J. F., Econ.
RESCHLY, D. J., Special Education
REYNOLDS, A. B., Cancer Biology
RICHARDS, W. O., Surgery
RICHMOND, J. A., Cancer Biology
RIESER, J. J., Psychology and Human Devt
RISKO, V. J., Teaching and Learning
ROBACK, H. B., Psychiatry
ROBERTS, L. J., II, Pharmacology
ROBERTSON, D. H., Medicine
ROBERTSON, R. M., Medicine
RODEN, D. M., Medicine
ROSELLI, R. J., Biomedical Eng.
ROTH, B. J., Medicine
ROTH, J. A., Chemical Eng.
ROTHENBERG, M. L., Medicine
RUBIN, C. A., Mechanical Eng.
RUBIN, D. H., Medicine
RULEY, H. E., Microbiology and Immunology
SAFF, E. B., Mathematics
SANDERS-BUSH, E., Pharmacology
SANDLER, H. M., Psychology and Human Devt
SANDLER, M. P., Radiology and Radiological Sciences
SAPIR, M., Mathematics
SASSON, J., Divinity
SCHAFFNER, W., Preventative Medicine
SCHALL, J. D., Psychology
SCHAUBLE, L., Teaching and Learning
SCHERRER, R. J., Physics and Astronomy
SCHLUNK, H. J., Law
SCHMIDT, D., Electrical Eng. and Computer Science
SCHNELLE, K. B., Chemical Eng.
SCHOENBLUM, J. A., Law
SCHRIMPF, R., Electrical Eng. and Computer Science
SCHUENING, F. G., Medicine
SCHULMAN, G., Medicine
SCHUMAKER, L. L., Mathematics
SCHWARTZ, H. S., Orthopaedics and Rehabilitation
SCHWARTZ, T. A., History
SCUDDER, G. D., Management
SEGOVIA, F. F., Divinity
SELIGSON, M. A., Political Science
SERGENT, J. S., Medicine
SEVIN, D. H. O., German and Slavic Languages
SHACK, R. B., Plastic Surgery

SHELTON, R. C., Psychiatry
SHENAI, J., Paediatrics
SHEPHERD, V. L., Pathology
SHERRY, S., Law
SHIAVI, R. G., Biomedical Eng.
SHU, X. O., Medicine
SHYR, Y., Preventitive Medicine
SIAMI, G., Medicine
SIEGFRIED, J. J., Econ.
SINGLETON, C. K., Biological Sciences
SLOVIS, C. M., Emergency Medicine
SMITH, H. W., History
SMITH, J. A., Jr, Urologic Surgery
SMITH, W. P., Psychology
SNELL, J. D., Jr, Medicine
SODERQUIST, L. D., Law
SOSMAN, J. A., Medicine
SPENGLER, D. M., Orthopaedics and Rehabilitation
SPICKARD, W. A., Jr, Medicine
SPINDLER, K. P., Orthopaedics and Rehabilitation
SRIRAM, S., Neurology
STAHLMAN, M. T., Paediatrics
STEAD, W. W., Medicine
STEIGER, J. H., Psychology and Human Devt
STEIN, R. W., Molecular Physiology and Biophysics
STEINBERG, R., Sociology
STERNBERG, P., Ophthalmology and Visual Sciences
STOLL, H. R., Management
STONE, M. P., Chemistry
STONE, W. J., Medicine
STONE, W. L., Paediatrics
STRANGE, K., Anaesthesiology
STRAUSS, A. M., Mechanical Eng.
STRAUSS, A. W., Paediatrics
STRICKLIN, G. P., Medicine
STUBBS, G. J., Biological Sciences
STUHR, J. J., Philosophy
SUNDELL, H. W., Paediatrics
SWAIN, C. M., Law
SWIFT, L. L., Pathology
SYVERUD, J., Electrical Eng. and Computer Science
SZTIPANOVITS, J., Electrical and Computer Eng.
TAM, J. P., Microbiology and Immunology
TANNER, R. D., Chemical Eng.
TATE, C. N., Political Science
TELLINGHUISEN, J., Chemistry
TELOH, H. A., Philosophy
THOITS, P. A., Sociology
THOMAS, J. W., II, Medicine
THOMAS, R. S., Law
THOMPSON, P. W., Teaching and Learning
THOMPSON, R. B., Law
TICHI, C., English
TOLK, N. H., Physics and Astronomy
TRANGENSTEIN, P., Nursing
TULIPAN, N. B., Neurological Surgery
UMAR, S. A., Physics and Astronomy
USNER, D. H., History
VAN KAER, L., Microbiology and Immunology
VAUGHAN, D. E., Medicine
VICTOR, B., Management
WAGNER, C., Biochemistry
WALDEN, T. A., Psychology and Human Devt
WALKER, L. S., Paediatrics
WALLER, N., Psychology and Human Devt
WALLSTON, K. A., Nursing
WANG, P., Econ.
WANG, T. G., Mechanical Eng.
WARD, P. A., French and Italian
WASHINGTON, M. K., Pathology
WASSERMAN, D. H., Molecular Physiology and Biophysics
WASSERSTEIN, D. J., History
WATERMAN, M. R., Biochemistry
WEBB, G. F., Mathematics
WEBSTER, M. S., Physics and Astronomy
WEIL, P. A., Molecular Physiology and Biophysics
WEILER, T. J., Physics and Astronomy
WEINER, E. E., Nursing

WELLER, R. A., Electrical Eng. and Computer Science
WENTE, S. R., Cell and Devt Biology
WEYMARK, J. A., Econ.
WIKSWO, J. P., Physics and Astronomy
WIKSWO, J. P., Molecular Physiology and Biophysics
WILEY, R. G., Neurology
WILKINSON, G. R., Pharmacology
WILSON, J. R., Medicine
WILTSHIRE, S. F., Classical Studies
WOLERY, M., Special Education
WONG, K. K., Leadership, Policy and and Organizations
WOOD, A. J., Medicine
WOOD, D. C., Philosophy
WRENN, K. D., Emergency Medicine
WRIGHT, C. V., Cell and Developmental Biology
WRIGHT, P. F., Paediatrics
XIA, D., Mathematics
YODER, P. J., Special Education
YU, G., Mathematics
ZEPPOS, Jr, N. S., Law
ZHENG, W., Medicine
ZUTTER, M. M., Pathology

TEXAS

ABILENE CHRISTIAN UNIVERSITY

ACU Box 29100, Abilene, TX 79699-9105

Telephone: (325) 674-2000
Fax: (325) 674-2958
Internet: www.acu.edu

Founded 1906
Private (Church of Christ) liberal arts
Academic year: August to May

President: ROYCE L. MONEY
Executive Vice-President: JACK RICH
Provost: DWAYNE VAN RHEENEN
Librarian: MARK TUCKER

Library of 497,000 vols
Number of teachers: 347
Number of students: 4,761

DEANS

College of Arts and Sciences: COLLEEN DURRINGTON
College of Biblical Studies: JACK REESE
College of Business Administration: RICK LYTLE
Graduate School: CAROL WILLIAMS

ARLINGTON BAPTIST COLLEGE

3001 W. Division St, Arlington, TX 76012

Telephone: (817) 461-8741
Fax: (817) 274-1138
E-mail: info@abconline.org
Internet: www.abconline.edu

President: Dr DAVID BRYANT.

AUSTIN COLLEGE

900 North Grand Ave, Sherman, TX 75090-4400

Telephone: (903) 813-2000
Fax: (903) 813-3199
E-mail: admission@austincollege.edu
Internet: www.austincollege.edu

Founded 1849
Private control, affiliated to Presbyterian Church
Academic year: September to June

President: OSCAR C. PAGE
Vice-President for Academic Affairs and Dean of the Faculty: MICHAEL IMHOFF
Treasurer and Vice-President for Business Affairs: GEORGE ROWLAND
Vice-President for Institutional Advancement: JAMES LEWIS

Vice-President for Student Affairs: TIMOTHY P. MILLERICK

Vice-President for Institutional Enrollment: NAN DAVIS

Library of 206,324 vols

Number of teachers: 122 (92 full-time, 30 part-time)

Number of students: 1,332 (1,316 full-time, 16 part-time)

Four-year liberal arts co-educational Christian college.

AUSTIN PRESBYTERIAN THEOLOGICAL SEMINARY

100 East 27th St, Austin, TX 78705

Telephone: (512) 472-6736

Fax: (512) 479-0738

Internet: www.austinseminary.edu

Founded 1902

President: THEODORE J. WARDLAW

Vice-President (Business and Finance): LAWRENCE W. FOSTER

Vice-President (Institutional Advancement): TIMOTHY A. KUBATZKY

Vice-President (Student Affairs): ANN B. FIELDS

Academic Dean: MICHAEL JINKINS

Registrar: JACQUELINE D. HEFLEY

Publications: *Insights* (2 a year), *Horizons in Biblical Theology* (2 a year).

BAPTIST MISSIONARY ASSOCIATION THEOLOGICAL SEMINARY

1530 East Pine St, Jacksonville, TX 75766-5407

Telephone: (903) 586-2501

Fax: (903) 586-0378

E-mail: bmatsem@bmats.edu

Internet: www.bmats.edu

President: Dr CHARLEY HOLMES

Dean and Registrar: PHILIP ATTEBERY

Librarian: JAMES C. BLAYLOCK.

BAYLOR COLLEGE OF MEDICINE

1 Baylor Plaza, Houston, TX 77030

Telephone: (713) 798-4951

Fax: (713) 798-4951

E-mail: admissions@bcm.edu

Internet: www.bcm.edu

President: Dr PETER G. TRABER

Vice-President and Dean of Medicine: BOBBY R. ALFORD

Vice-President and Dean of Research: JAMES W. PATRICK

Vice-President for Graduate Sciences and Dean of Graduate School of Biomedical Sciences: WILLIAM R. BRINKLEY

CHAIRS OF DEPARTMENTS

Anaesthesiology: LYDIA ANN CONLAY

Biochemistry and Molecular Biology: SALIH J. WAKIL

Dermatology: JOHN E. WOLF

Family and Community Medicine: STEPHEN J. SPANN

Immunology: RICHARD G. COOK

Medicine: STEPHEN B. GREENBERG (acting)

Molecular Physiology and Biophysics: SUSAN L. HAMILTON

Molecular Virology and Microbiology: JANET S. BUTEL

Molecular and Cellular Biology: BERT W. O'MALLEY

Moecular and Human Genetics: ARTHUR L. BEAUDET

Neurology: STANLEY H. APPEL

Neuroscience: JAMES W. PATRICK

Neurosurgery: ROBERT G. GROSSMAN

Obstetrics and Gynaecology: JOE LEIGH SIMPSON

Ophthalmology: DAN B. JONES

Orthopaedic Surgery: MICHAEL H. HEGGENESS (acting)

Otorhinolaryngology and Communicative Sciences: BOBY R. ALFORD

Pathology: MICHAEL W. LIEBERMAN

Paediatrics: RALPH FEIGIN

Pharmacology: SUSAN M. BERGET (acting)

Physical Medicine and Rehabilitation: MARTIN GRABOIS

Psychiatry and Behavioural Sciences: STUART C. YUDOFSKY

Radiology: MICHAEL E. MAWAD

Surgery: F. CHARLES BRUNICARDI

Urology: TIMOTHY B. BOONE

BAYLOR UNIVERSITY

One Bear Place, Waco, TX 76798

Telephone: (254) 710-1011

Internet: www.baylor.edu

Chartered 1845 under Republic of Texas by Texas Baptist Educational Society at Independence, Texas; consolidated 1886 with Waco University and affiliated with Baptist General Convention of Texas

Academic year: August to May

President: Dr ROBERT B. SLOAN, Jr

Secretary: PAM EDENS

Director (Admissions): DIANA RAMEY

Librarian: Dr REAGAN M. RAMSOWER

Number of teachers: 775

Number of students: 14,000

Publications: *Law Review, Baylor Business Review, Baylor Line, Baylor Geological Studies, Journal of Church and State, Baylor News, The Lariat, Baylor Magazine* (every 2 months).

CONCORDIA UNIVERSITY, AUSTIN

3400 IH 35 North, Austin, TX 78705

Telephone: (512) 486-2000

Fax: (512) 459-8517

E-mail: admissions@concordia.edu

Internet: www.concordia.edu

Founded 1926

Academic year: July to June

President: Dr THOMAS CEDEL

Vice-President (Academic Services): JOEL HECK

Vice-President (Business and Finance): PAMELA LEE

Vice-President (University Services): DAVID KLUTH

Vice-President (Advancement): JOHN SCHOEDEL

Vice-President (Student Services): WILLIAM DRISKILL

Number of students: 1,160

DEANS

Liberal Arts and Sciences: Dr MICHAEL MOYER

Business: DAVID WHITE

Education: Dr SANDRA DOERING

Adult Education: Dr VICTORIA SCHOEDEL

CRISWELL COLLEGE

4010 Gaston Ave, Dallas, TX 75246

Telephone: (214) 821-5433

Fax: (214) 818-1310

Internet: www.criswell.edu

Founded 1970

Academic year: August to July

Chancellor: D. MCCALL BRUNSON

Executive Vice-President and Provost: LAMAR E. COOPER, SR

Vice-President for Development: MARK M. OVERSTREET

Vice-President for Enrollment and Academic Services: KATE FINLEY

Registrar: PATRICIA MCCLUNG

Library of 100,000 vols

Number of teachers: 18

Number of students: 460

Publication: *Criswell Theological Review* (2 a year).

DALLAS BAPTIST UNIVERSITY

3000 Mountain Creek Parkway, Dallas, TX 75211

Telephone: (214) 333-7100

Fax: (214) 333-5536

E-mail: admiss@dbu.edu

Internet: www.dbu.edu

President: Dr GARY COOK.

DALLAS CHRISTIAN COLLEGE

2700 Christian Parkway, Dallas, TX 75234-7299

Telephone: (972) 241-3371

E-mail: admin@dallas.edu

Internet: www.dallas.edu

Founded 1950

President: DUSTIN D. RUBECK

Vice-President (Academic Affairs): Dr RAY KELLEY

Registrar: CRYSTAL LAIDACKER

Library Director: SUSAN SPRINGER.

DALLAS THEOLOGICAL SEMINARY

3909 Swiss Avenue, Dallas, TX 75204

Telephone: (214) 824-3094

Fax: (214) 841-3664

Internet: www.dts.edu

President: MARK L. BAILEY.

EAST TEXAS BAPTIST UNIVERSITY

1209 N Grove St, Marshall, TX 75670-1498

Telephone: (903) 935-7963

Fax: (903) 938-1705

Internet: www.etbu.edu

Founded 1912

President: BOB E. RILEY

Registrar: DAVID MOHN

Librarian: Dr ROSE MARY MAGRILL

Library of 100,000 vols

Number of teachers: 55

Number of students: 1,200

Courses in the liberal arts.

EPISCOPAL THEOLOGICAL SEMINARY OF THE SOUTHWEST

POB 2247, Austin, TX 78768

Located at: 606 Rathervue Place, Austin, TX

Telephone: (512) 472-4133

Fax: (512) 472-3098

E-mail: seminary@etss.edu

Internet: www.etss.edu

President and Dean: TITUS PRESLER

Vice-President of Administration: JOHN BENNET WATERS

Vice-President of Development: NANCY SPRINGER-BALDWIN.

HARDIN-SIMMONS UNIVERSITY

Box 16000, HSU Station, Abilene, TX 79698

Telephone: (915) 670-1000

Fax: (915) 671-2157

Internet: www.hsutx.edu

Founded 1891

Academic year: August to May

President: Dr LANNY HALL

Executive Vice-President and Chief Academic Officer: Dr CRAIG TURNER

Associate Vice-President, Enrollment Services: SHANE DAVIDSON

Registrar: DOROTHY KISER
Director of University Libraries: ALICE W. SPECHT
Library of 415,752 vols
Number of teachers: 140
Number of students: 2,312.

HOUSTON BAPTIST UNIVERSITY

7502 Fondren Rd, Houston, TX 77074-3298
Telephone: (281) 649-3000
E-mail: admissions@hbu.edu
Internet: www.hbu.edu
President: EDWARD DOUGLAS HODO
Vice-President for Development: DON ANDERSON
Vice-President for Academic Affairs: DONALD W. LOOSER
Vice-President for Financial Affairs: RICHARD D. PARKER
Vice-President for Student Affairs: JACK PURCELL
Vice-President for Marketing: SHARON SAUNDERS.

HOWARD PAYNE UNIVERSITY

Brownwood, TX 76801
Telephone: (915) 646-2502
Fax: (915) 649-8905
E-mail: enroll@hputx.edu
Internet: www.hputx.edu
Founded 1889
Academic year: September to May
President: Dr LANNY HALL
Vice-President for Academic Affairs: Dr DONNIE AUVENSHINE
Registrar: LANA WAGNER
Librarian: NANCY ANDERSON
Library of 125,000 vols
Number of teachers: 124
Number of students: 1,424.

HUSTON-TILLOTSON UNIVERSITY

900 Chicon St, Austin, TX 78702
Telephone: (512) 505-3000
Fax: (512) 505-3190
E-mail: admission@htu.edu
Internet: www.htu.edu
Founded 1875
Academic year: August to May
President: Dr LARRY L. EARVIN
Vice-President for Academic and Student Affairs: Dr NADINE F. JENKINS
Dean of Academic Affairs: Dr JUDITH G. LOREDO
Dean of Enrollment Management (vacant)
Dean of Student Affairs (vacant)
Registrar: EARNESTINE STRICKLAND
Librarian: PATRICIA QUARTERMAN
Library of 88,000 vols
Number of teachers: 37
Number of students: 685.

JARVIS CHRISTIAN COLLEGE

POB 1470, Hawkins, TX 75765
Telephone: (903) 769-5700
Internet: www.jarvis.edu
Pres.: Dr SEBETHA JENKINS
Chairman of the Administrative Council: JOHN GLOVER.

LETOURNEAU UNIVERSITY

POB 7001, Longview, TX 75607
Located at: 2100 S Mobberly Ave, Longview, TX 75602
Telephone: (903) 388-5327
Fax: (903) 233-3411
E-mail: admissions@letu.edu
Internet: www.letu.edu

President: Dr ALVIN AUSTIN
Vice-President for Executive Affairs and Planning: MARILA PALMER
Provost and Vice-President for Academic Affairs: Dr H. GLENN SUMRALL
Vice-President for Business and Administration: Dr WILLIAM MCDOWELL
Vice-President for University Advancement: JIM HUGHEY
Vice-President for Student Affairs: DOUGLAS WILCOXSON
Vice-President for Enrollment Services: LINDA FITZHUGH
Vice-President for Graduate and Professional Studies: Dr ROBERT W. HUDSON
Registrar: BRENDA MCGHEE.

LUBBOCK CHRISTIAN UNIVERSITY

5601 19th Street, Lubbock, TX 79407
Telephone: (806) 796-8800
Fax: (806) 796-8917
Internet: www.lcu.edu
Founded 1957
President: L. KEN JONES
Executive Vice-President: ROD BLACKWOOD
Vice-President for Academic Affairs: DOYLE CARTER
Vice-President for Enrollment Management: RANDY SELLERS
Vice-President for Admissions: KEVIN ELMORE
Vice-President for Global Affairs: NAT COOPER.

MCMURRY UNIVERSITY

McMurry Station, Abilene, TX 79697
Telephone: (915) 691-6200
E-mail: admissions@mcm.edu
Internet: www.mcm.edu
Founded 1923
President: JOHN H. RUSSELL
Vice-President for Academic Affairs: PAUL LACK
Vice-President for Financial Affairs: CARL BROWN
Vice-President for Institutional Advancement: JAMES DOTHEROW
Vice-President for Enrollment Management and Student Relations: RUSSELL WATJEN
Director of Library: JOE W. SPECHT
Library of 200,000 vols
Number of teachers: 119
Number of students: 1,400.

MIDWESTERN STATE UNIVERSITY

3410 Taft Boulevard, Wichita Falls, TX 76308
Telephone: (940) 397-4000
Fax: (940) 397-4302
E-mail: information@mwsu.edu
Internet: www.mwsu.edu
Founded 1922
Academic year: September to August
President: Dr JESSE W. ROGERS
Provost: FRIEDERIKE WIEDEMANN
Vice-President (Business Affairs): JOHN H. ALEXANDER
Vice-President (University Development and Student Affairs): Dr HOWARD FARRELL
Registrar: DARLA INGLISH
Librarian: CLARA LATHAM
Number of teachers: 172
Number of students: 6,500
Publications: *The Wichitan* (weekly), *The Wai-Kun* (annually), *Voices* (annually), *Faculty Forum Papers* (annually).

OBLATE SCHOOL OF THEOLOGY

285 Oblate Drive, San Antonio, TX 78216-6693
Telephone: (210) 341-1366
Fax: (210) 341-4519
E-mail: info@ost.edu
Internet: www.ost.edu
Founded 1903
President: WILLIAM MORELL
Academic Dean: ELAINE BROTHERS.

OUR LADY OF THE LAKE UNIVERSITY OF SAN ANTONIO

411 SW 24th St, San Antonio, TX 78207-4689
Telephone: (210) 434-6711
Fax: (210) 436-0824
Internet: www.ollusa.edu
Founded 1883
Academic year: August to May
President: SALLY MAHONEY
Provost: JAMES L. GEARITY
Vice-President for Finance and Facilities: ALLEN R. KLAUS
Vice-President for Institutional Advancement: MICHAEL MULNIX
Vice-President and Dean of Student Life: MARY ELLEN SMITH
Dean of Enrollment and Management: LORETTA A. SCHLEGEL
Institutional Research Officer: FRED D. SCOTT
Library of 254,419 vols
Number of teachers: 140
Number of students: 3,564.

PAUL QUINN COLLEGE

3837 Simpson-Stuart Rd, Dallas, TX 75241
Telephone: (214) 376-1000
Internet: www.pqc.edu
Founded 1872
President: LEE MONROE
Vice-President for Academic Affairs: Dr CHARLES HUMPHREY
Registrar: J. D. HURD
Librarian: Ms. MACHIE
Number of teachers: 48
Number of students: 780
Publication: *Paul Quinn Gazette*.

RICE UNIVERSITY

POB 1892, Houston, TX 77251
Telephone: (713) 348-0000
Internet: www.rice.edu
Founded 1891
Private control
Language of instruction: English
President: MALCOLM GILLIS
Provost: EUGENE LEVY
Vice-President for Enrollment: ANN WRIGHT
Vice-President for Finance and Administration: DEAN W. CURRIE
Vice-President for Student Affairs: ZENAIDO CAMACHO
Vice-President for Public Affairs: TERRY SHEPARD
Vice-President for Investments and Treasurer: SCOTT WISE
Vice-President and Chief Information Officer: CHARLES HENRY
Vice-Provost and Vice-President for Resource Development: ERIC C. JOHNSON
Registrar: JERRY MONTAG
Library of 1,400,000 vols
Number of teachers: 476
Number of students: 4,274
Publications: *Journal of Southern History*, *Studies in English Literature 1500–1900*, *Rice University Studies* (4 a year)

DEANS

Humanities: GALE STOKES
Wiess School of Natural Sciences: KATHLEEN S. MATTHEWS
Social Sciences: ROBERT M. STEIN
Architecture: LARS LERUP
Shepherd School of Music: ANNE SCHNOEBELEN
George R. Brown School of Engineering: C. SIDNEY BURRUS
Jesse H. Jones School of Administration: GILBERT R. WHITAKER, Jr
Continuing Studies: MARY B. MCINTIRE

PROFESSORS

AAZHANG, B., Electrical and Computer Engineering
AKIN, J. E., Mechanical Engineering
ALCOVER, M., French
ALFORD, J. R., Political Science
AMBLER, J. S., Political Science
ANDERSON, J. B., Earth Science
ANTOULAS, A. C., Electrical and Computer Engineering
ARESU, B., French Studies
ARMENIADES, C. D., Chemical Engineering
ATHANASIOU, A., Bioengineering
AVE-LALLEMANT, H. G., Earth Science
BAGOZZI, R., Management
BAKER, S. D., Physics and Astronomy
BARRON, A., Chemistry
BAYAZITOGLU, Y., Mechanical Engineering and Materials Science
BECKINGHAM, K., Biochemistry and Cell Biology
BEDIENT, P. B., Civil and Environmental Engineering
BENNETT, G., Biochemistry and Cell Biology
BILLUPS, W. E., Chemistry
BLACK, E., Political Science
BOLES, J. B., History
BONNER, B. E., Physics and Astronomy
BOSHERNITZAN, M., Mathematics
BRACE, P., Political Science
BRITO, D. L., Economics
BRODY, B. A., Philosophy
BROKER, K. L., Art and Art History
BROOKS, P. R., Chemistry
BROWN, B. W., Economics and Statistics
BROWN, J. N., Economics
BRYANT, J., Economics
BURRUS, C. S., Electrical and Computer Engineering
BUYSE, L., Music
CAMFIELD, W. A., Art and Art History
CANNADY, W. T., Architecture
CARROLL, M. M., Computational and Applied Mathematics
CARTWRIGHT, R. S., Computer Science
CASBARIAN, J. J., Architecture
CASTAÑEDA, J. A., Hispanic and Classical Studies
CHANCE, J., English
CHAPMAN, W. G., Chemical Engineering
CITRON, M., Music
CLARK, J. W., Jr, Electrical and Computer Engineering
CLOUTIER, P. A., Physics and Astronomy
COCHRAN, T., Mathematics
COOPER, K. D., Computer Science
CORCORAN, M., Physics and Astronomy
COX, D., Statistics
COX, S. G., Philosophy
COX, S. J., Computational and Applied Mathematics
CROWELL, S. G., Philosophy
CURL, R. F., Jr, Chemistry
CUTHBERTSON, G. M., Political Science
DAVIDSON, C., Sociology
DAVIS, P. W., Linguistics
DHARAN, B. G., Management
DIPBOYE, R., Psychology
DOODY, T., English
DRISKILL, L., English
DUCK, I., Physics and Astronomy

DUFOUR, R. J., Physics and Astronomy
DUNHAM, J. F., Music
DUNNING, F. B., Physics and Astronomy
DURRANI, A. J., Civil and Environmental Engineering
EIFLER, M., German and Slavic Studies
EL-GAMAL, M., Economics
ELLISON, P., Music
ENGEL, P. S., Chemistry
ENGELHARDT, T., Philosophy
ENSOR, K. B., Statistics
FARWELL, J., Music
FELLEISEN, M., Computer Science
FEW, A., Physics and Astronomy
FISCHER, N., Music
FISHER, F. M., Jr, Ecology and Evolutionary Biology
FORMAN, R., Mathematics
GEORGE, J., Management
GLANTZ, R. M., Biochemistry and Cell Biology
GLASS, G. P., Chemistry
GOLDMAN, R. N., Computer Science
GOLDSMITH, K., Music
GOMER, R. H., Biochemistry and Cell Biology
GONZÁLEZ-STEPHEN, B., Hispanic and Classical Studies
GORDON, R., Earth Science
GORRY, G. A., Management
GOTTSCHALK, A. W., Music
GOUX, J., French
GRANDY, R. E., Philosophy
GROB, A., English
GRUBER, I. D., History
HALAS, N., Electrical and Computer Engineering
HAMM, K. E., Political Science
HANNON, J. P., Physics and Astronomy
HARCOMBE, P., Ecology and Environmental Biology
HARDT, R. M., Mathematics
HARTLEY, P. R., Economics
HARVEY, F. R., Mathematics
HASKELL, T., History
HEMPEL, J., Mathematics
HIGHTOWER, J. W., Chemical Engineering
HILL, T. W., Physics and Astronomy
HIRASAKI, G., Chemical Engineering
HOLLOWAY, C., Music
HUANG, H. W., Physics and Astronomy
HUFFER, L., French Studies
HUGHES, J. B., Civil and Environmental Engineering
HULET, R., Physics and Astronomy
HUSTON, J. D., English
HUTCHINSON, J. S., Chemistry
IAMMARINO, N., Kinesiology
ISLE, W., English
JOHNSON, D. H., Electrical and Computer Engineering
JONES, B. F., Mathematics
JUMP, J. R., Electrical and Computer Engineering
KANATAS, G., Administrative Science
KAUN, K., Music
KELBER, W. H., Religious Studies
KENNEDY, K. W., Jr, Computer Science
KIMMEL, M., Statistics
KINSEY, J. L., Chemistry
KLEIN, A., Religious Studies
KLINEBERG, S. L., Sociology
KONISKY, J., Biochemistry and Cell Biology
KULSTAD, M., Philosophy
LANE, N., Physics and Astronomy
LEVANDA, R. A., Music
LEE, B., Anthropology
LEEMAN, W. P., Earth Science
LEVANDER, A. R., Earth Science
LIANG, S., Physics and Astronomy
LUCA, S., Music
MCINTIRE, L. V., Chemical Engineering
MCINTOSH, R. J., Anthropology
MCINTOSH, S. K., Anthropology
MCLELLAN, R. B., Materials Science
MANCA, J., Art and Art History
MARCUS, G. E., Anthropology
MARGRAVE, J. L., Chemistry

MARTIN, R. C., Psychology
MARTIN, W. C., Sociology
MATUSOW, A., History
MICHIE, H., English
MIESZKOWSKI, P., Economics
MIETTINEN, H. E., Physics and Astronomy
MIKOS, A., Bioengineering
MILLER, C. A., Chemical Engineering
MORGAN, T. C., Political Science
MORRIS, W. A., English
MORRISON, D. R., Philosophy
MOULIN, H. M., Economics
MUTCHLER, G. S., Physics and Astronomy
NAPIER, H. A., Management
NELSON, D., French Studies
NORDLANDER, P., Physics and Astronomy
ODHIAMBO, A., History
OLSON, J. S., Biochemistry
ORCHARD, M. T., Electrical and Computer Engineering
OSHERSON, D., Psychology
PARKER, J. K., Music
PARRY, R. J., Chemistry
PATTEN, R. L., English
POLKING, J. C., Mathematics
POULOS, B., Art and Art History
QUELLER, D. C., Ecology and Evolutionary Biology
RACHLEFF, L., Music
RAU, C., Physics and Astronomy
REIFF, P., Physics and Astronomy
ROBERT, M., Chemical Engineering
ROBERTS, J. B., Physics and Astronomy
ROJO, J., Statistics
RUDOLPH, F. B., Biochemistry and Cell Biology
ROUX, R., Music
SAN, K. Y., Bioengineering
SASS, R. L., Ecology and Evolutionary Biology
SAWYER, D., Earth Science
SCHNEIDER, D. J., Psychology
SCHNOEBELEN, A. M., Music
SCOTT, D. W., Statistics
SCUSERIA, G., Chemistry
SEED, P., History
SEMMES, S. W., Mathematics
SHER, G., Philosophy
SHIBATANI, M., Linguistics
SICKLES, R., Economics
SKURA, M., English
SMALLEY, R. E., Chemistry
SMITH, G., Art and Art History
SMITH, G. W., Economics
SMITH, R. J., History
SNOW, E. A., English
SOLIGO, R., Economics
SORENSEN, D. C., Computational and Applied Mathematics
SPANOS, P. D., Mechanical Engineering and Materials Science
SPENCE, D. W., Kinesiology
STEIN, R., Political Science
STEVENSON, P. M., Physics and Astronomy
STEWART, C. R., Biochemistry and Cell Biology
STOKES, G., History
STOLL, R. J., Political Science
STONG, R., Mathematics
STRASSMAN, J., Ecology and Evolutionary Biology
STROUP, J. M., Religious Studies
SYMES, W. W., Computational and Applied Mathematics
TALWANI, M., Earth Science
TAPIA, R. A., Computational and Applied Mathematics
TAYLOR, J., Anthropology
TAYLOR, R. N., Management
TEZDUYAR, T. E., Mechanical Engineering and Materials Science
THOMPSON, E. M., German and Slavic Studies
THOMPSON, J. R., Statistics
TITTEL, F., Electrical and Computer Engineering
TOMSON, M. B., Civil and Environmental Engineering

TOUR, J., Chemistry
TYLER, S. A., Anthropology
UECKER, W. C., Management
VARDI, M. Y., Computer Science
VEECH, W. A., Mathematics
VELETSOS, A. S., Civil and Environmental Engineering
WARD, C. H., Civil and Environmental Engineering
WARREN, J. D., Computer Science
WATKINS, M. J., Psychology
WEISMAN, R. B., Chemistry
WEISSENBERGER, K. H., German and Slavic Studies
WESTBROOK, R. A., Management
WHITAKER, G., Management
WHITMIRE, K. H., Chemistry
WIENER, M. J., History
WIESNER, M., Civil and Environmental Engineering
WILLIAMS, E. E., Management
WILSON, L. J., Chemistry
WILSON, R. K., Political Science
WILSON, W. L., Electrical and Computer Engineering
WINDSOR, D., Management
WINKLER, K., Music
WINNINGHAM, G. L., Art and Art History
WITTENBERG, G., Architecture
WOLF, M., Mathematics
WOLF, R. A., Physics and Astronomy
WOOD, S., English
WYSCHOGROD, E., Religious Studies
YOUNG, J. F., Electrical and Computer Engineering
YUNIS, H., Hispanic and Classical Studies
ZAMMITO, J. H., History
ZEFF, S. A., Management
ZODROW, G., Economics
ZWAENEPOEL, W., Computer Science
ZYGOURAKIS, K., Chemical Engineering

ST EDWARDS UNIVERSITY

3001 South Congress Ave, Austin, TX 78704
Telephone: (512) 448-8400
Fax: (512) 448-8492
E-mail: seu.admit@admin.stedwards.edu
Internet: www.stedwards.edu
Founded 1885
Academic year: August to May
President: Dr GEORGE E. MARTIN
Executive Vice-President: Sr DONNA M. JURICK
Assistants to the President: JOSIE BARRETT CRISTINA BORDIN
Vice-President for Financial Affairs: DAVID A. DICKSON, Jr
Vice-President for Information Technology: BILL CAHILL
Vice-President for Marketing: PAIGE BOOTH
Vice-President for Student Affairs: Dr SANDRA PACHECO
Vice-President for University Advancement: MICHAEL LARKIN
Dean of Academic Standing: Dr MOLLY E. MINUS
Dean of Admissions: TRACY MANIER
Dean of Graduate and Adult Services: Dr THOMAS M. EVANS
Dean of Students: LISA KIRKPATRICK
Director of Student Financial Services: DORIS F. CONSTANTINE
Director, Campus Ministry: Fr RICHARD WILKINSON
Controller: PAUL R. SINTEF
Registrar: Dr LANCE HAYES
Director, Scarborough-Phillips Library: THOMAS LEONHARDT

Library of 122,403 titles
Number of teachers: 435
Number of students: 4,651

Private, co-educational; four-year liberal arts; graduate courses in business, human services, organizational leadership and ethics, counselling, computer information science, and liberal studies; also New College (non-traditional undergraduate courses).

DEANS

School of Behavioral and Social Sciences: BRENDA VALLENCE
School of Business and Management: MARSHA KELLIHER
School of Education: KAREN JENLINK
School of Humanities: Fr LOUIS BRUSATTI
School of Natural Sciences: CHARLES BICAK
New College: Dr RAMSEY FOWLER

ST MARY'S UNIVERSITY OF SAN ANTONIO

San Antonio, TX 78228-8572
Telephone: (210) 436-3011
Fax: (210) 436-3500
Internet: www.stmarytx.edu
Founded 1852
Academic year: August to May
President: Dr CHARLES L. COTRELL
Academic Vice-President: Dr DAVID MANUEL (acting)
Vice-President for Student Development: KATHERINE SISOIAN
Vice-President for University Advancement: THOMAS B. GALVIN
Vice-President for Financial Administration: DAVID SIMPSON
Assistant to President for Planning: Dr GERARD DIZINNO
Registrar: LOUISA AVITUA-TREVINO
Librarian: H. PALMER HALL

Library of 324,000 vols
Number of students: 4,166

DEANS

School of Humanities and Social Sciences: Dr JANET B. DIZINNO
School of Science, Engineering and Technology: Dr ANTHONY KAUFMANN
Graduate School: Dr RON MERRELL
Law School: ROBERT WILLIAM PIATT
School of Business Administration: Dr SUZANNE CORY (acting)

SCHREINER UNIVERSITY

2100 Memorial Boulevard, Kerrville, TX 78028
Telephone: (830) 896-5411
Fax: (830) 792-7226
Internet: www.schreiner.edu
President: TIM SUMMERLIN
Provost and Vice-President for Academic Affairs: Dr MICHAEL LOONEY
Vice-President for Administration: FRED GAMBLE
Vice-President for Advancement and Public Affairs: MARK TUSCHAK
Vice-President for Enrollment and Student Services: PEG LAYTON
Dean of Admissions and Financial Aid: SANDY SPEED

DEANS

The Trull School of Science and Mathematics: Dr DIANA COMUZZIE
School of Liberal Arts: Dr JOHN HUDDLESTON
Cailloux School of Professional Studies: Prof. JOHN JONES

SOUTH TEXAS COLLEGE OF LAW

1303 San Jacinto, Houston, TX 77002-7000
Telephone: (713) 659-8040
Fax: (713) 646-1780
Internet: www.stcl.edu
Library of 400,000 vols
President: JAMES J. ALFINI.

SOUTHERN METHODIST UNIVERSITY

6425 Boaz, Dallas, TX 75275
Telephone: (214) 768-2000
Fax: (214) 768-1001
E-mail: enrol_serv@mail.smu.edu
Internet: www.smu.edu
Founded 1911
Language of instruction: English
Academic year: August to May
President: Dr R. GERALD TURNER
Provost: Dr ROSS C. MURFIN
Vice-President for Student Affairs: Dr JAMES E. CASWELL
Vice-President for Business and Finance, and Treasurer: Dr MORGAN OLSEN
Vice-President for Development and External Affairs: JEANNE WHITMAN
Vice-President for Executive Affairs: Dr THOMAS BARRY
Vice-President for Legal Affairs and Government Relations, General Counsel, and University Secretary: S. LEON BENNETT
Admissions: RON MOSS
Registrar: JOHN A. HALL

Library of 4,111,460 vols
Number of teachers: 732 (520 full-time, 212 part-time)
Number of students: 10,266

Publications: Southwest Review (4 a year), Journal of Air Law and Commerce (4 a year), SMU Law Review (4 a year), The International Lawyer (4 a year)

DEANS

Dedman College: Dr JASPER NEEL
Arts: Dr CAROLE BRANDT
Business: Dr ALBERT W. NIEMI, Jr
Engineering: Dr STEPHEN SZYGENDA
Law: JOHN B. ATTANASIO
Theology: Dr ROBIN W. LOVIN

SOUTHWESTERN ADVENTIST UNIVERSITY

100 Hillcrest Drive, Keene, TX 76059
Telephone: (817) 645-3921
Fax: (817) 556-4744
E-mail: admissions@swau.edu
Internet: www.swau.edu
President: DON SAHLY
Secretary to the President: DICKIE MARTIN
Vice-President for Academics: Dr TOM BUNCH
Vice-President for Finance: LARRY GARRETT
Vice-President for Student Services: DAVID KNIGHT.

SOUTHWESTERN ASSEMBLIES OF GOD UNIVERSITY

1200 Sycamore St, Waxahachie, TX 75165-5735
Telephone: (972) 937-4010
Fax: (972) 923-0488
Internet: www.sagu.edu
President: KERMIT BRIDGES
Vice-President for Academics: PAUL BROOKS
Vice-President for Student Services: TERRY PHIPPS
Assistant to the President: EDDIE DAVIS.

SOUTHWESTERN BAPTIST THEOLOGICAL SEMINARY

POB 22000, Fort Worth, TX 76122
Located at: 2001 W. Seminary Drive, Fort Worth, TX 76115
Telephone: (817) 923-1921
Fax: (817) 921-8761
Internet: www.swbts.edu
Founded 1908
President: PAIGE PATTERSON

Executive Vice-President and Provost: CRAIG BLAISING
Vice-President for Institutional Advancement: JACK TERRY
Vice-President for Business Affairs: HUBERT MARTIN
Vice-President for Student Services: RUDY GONZALEZ
Publication: *Southwestern Journal of Theology* (4 a year).

SOUTHWESTERN CHRISTIAN COLLEGE

200 Bowser Circle, Terrell, TX 75160
Telephone: (972) 524-3341 ext. 142
Fax: (972) 563-7133
Internet: www.swcc.edu
Private control
Academic year: August to May
President: Dr JACK EVANS, Sr
Vice-President for Institutional Advancement: Dr JAMES MAXWELL
Vice-President of Student Affairs: Dr BEN FOSTER
Vice-President of Fiscal Affairs: DOUGLAS HOWIE
Vice-President of Academic Affairs: ZOAANN TURNER
Comptroller: JOYCE CATHEY
Assistant to the President for Development: GERALD LEE
Librarian: DORIS JOHNSON

Library of 30,870 books, 158 periodicals
Number of teachers: 21
Number of students: 220.

SOUTHWESTERN UNIVERSITY

Telephone: (512) 863-6511
Fax: (512) 863-5788
Internet: www.southwestern.edu
Founded 1873 by merging of Rutersville College (Chartered 1840), Wesleyan College (1844), McKenzie College (1848), and Soule University (1856)
Academic year: August to May
President: JAKE B. SCHRUM
Vice-President for Fiscal Affairs: RICHARD L. ANDERSON
Vice-President for Enrollment Services: THOMAS J. OLIVER
Vice-President for Institutional Advancement: C. RICHARD MCKELVEY
Associate Vice-President for University Relations: CINDY LOCKE
Provost and Dean of the Faculty: JAMES W. HUNT
Dean of the Sarofin School of Fine Arts: Dr PAUL GAFFNEY
Registrar: DAVID STONES
Dean of Library Services: LYNNE M. BRODY

Library of 292,756 vols
Number of teachers: 116
Number of students: 1,309
Publications: *Bulletin* (monthly), *The Megaphone* (weekly), *Southwestern Magazine* (4 a year), *The Sou' Wester* (annually).

STEPHEN F. AUSTIN STATE UNIVERSITY

Box 6078, Nacogdoches, TX 75962
Telephone: (713) 468-2011
Internet: www.sfasu.edu
Founded 1923
President: DANIEL D. ANGEL
Vice-President for Academic Affairs: JANELLE ASHLEY
Vice-President for Business Affairs: ROLAND SMITH

Vice-President for University Affairs: BAKER PATTILLO
Vice-President for University Advancement: JERRY HOLBERT
Library Director: ALVIN CAGE
Library of 1,465,322 vols
Number of teachers: 599
Number of students: 12,500 full-time

DEANS

College of Applied Arts and Sciences: JAMES STANDLEY
College of Business: MARLIN YOUNG
College of Education: THOMAS FRANKS
College of Fine Arts: RON JONES
College of Forestry: SCOTT BEASLEY
College of Liberal Arts: JIM SPEER (acting)
College of Sciences and Mathematics: THOMAS ATCHISON

TEXAS A & M UNIVERSITY SYSTEM

College Station, TX 77840-7896
Telephone: (409) 845-4331
Fax: (409) 845-2490
Internet: tamusystem.tamu.edu
Founded 1876
Academic year: September to August
Chancellor: Dr BARRY B. THOMPSON
Deputy Chancellor for Finance and Operations: RICHARD LINDSAY
Deputy Chancellor for Academic Institutions and Agencies: Dr LEO SAYAVEDRA
Vice-Chancellor for Agriculture: Dr EDWARD HILER
Vice-Chancellor for Engineering: Dr C. ROLAND HADEN
Vice-Chancellor for Business Services: TOM KALE
Vice-Chancellor for Research, Planning and Continuing Education: Dr J. CHARLES LEE
Vice-Chancellor for Facilities Planning and Construction: Gen. WESLEY PEEL.

CONSTITUENT UNIVERSITIES

Texas A & M International University

5201 University Blvd, Laredo, TX 78041-1900
Telephone: (956) 326-2001
Fax: (956) 326-2346
Internet: www.tamiu.edu
Founded 1969 as part of Texas A & I University
Upper level college, junior, senior and graduate courses
President: Dr RAY M. KECK
Director of Admissions and Advisement: MARÍA DEL REFUGIO ROSILLO
Vice-President for Finance and Administration: JOSÉ GARCÍA
Vice-President for Academic Affairs and Provost: DAN JONES
Vice-President for Institutional Advancement: CANDY WEIN
Dean of Student Affairs: Dr TOM CORTI
Registrar: BARBARA LUNCE
Librarian: RODNEY WEBB
Library of 200,000 vols
Number of students: 3,700

DEANS

College of Arts and Sciences: Dr NASSER MOMAYEZI
College of Business Administration: Dr JOHN P. KOLL
College of Education: Dr ROSA MARIA VIDA

Texas A & M University

College Station, TX 77843
Telephone: (409) 845-3211
Internet: www.tamu.edu

Founded 1876, University 1963
President: Dr RAY M. BOWEN
Vice-Presidents: Dr RONALD R. DOUGLAS (Academic Affairs), Dr JERRY GASTON (Administration), BILL KRUMM (Finance), ROBERT L. WALKER (Development), Dr J. MALON SOUTHERLAND (Student Affairs)
Executive Director, Admissions and Records: GARY ENGELGAU
Director of Library: Dr FRED M. HEATH
Library of 2,500,000 vols
Number of teachers: 2,327
Number of students: 41,461

DEANS

College of Engineering: Dr C. ROLAND HADEN
College of Agriculture and Life Sciences: Dr EDWARD A. HILER
College of Veterinary Medicine: Dr H. RICHARD ADAMS
College of Education: Dr JANE C. CONOLEY
College of Geosciences: Dr DAVID PRIOR
College of Science: Dr RICHARD E. EWING
College of Liberal Arts: Dr WOODROW JONES, Jr
College of Business Administration and Graduate School of Business: Dr A. BENTON COCANOUGHER
College of Architecture: WARD WELLS
College of Medicine: Dr MICHAEL L. FRIEDLAND

Texas A & M University—Commerce

Commerce, TX 75429
Telephone: (903) 886-5014
Internet: www.tamu-commerce.edu
Founded 1889
President: KEITH W. MCFARLAND
Vice-President for Academic Affairs: Dr DONNA ARLTON
Vice-President for Student and University Services: GENE LOCKHART
Library of 1,544,588 vols and microfilms
Number of teachers: 250 full-time
Number of students: 7,260.

Texas A & M University—Corpus Christi

6300 Ocean Drive, Corpus Christi, TX 78412
Telephone: (361) 825-5700
Fax: (361) 825-5810
Internet: www.tamucc.edu
Founded 1971; part of University System of South Texas
President: ROBERT R. FURGASON
Vice-President for Institutional Advancement: S. TRENT HILL
Provost/Vice-President for Academic Affairs: SANDRA S. HARPER
Executive Vice-President for Finance: KATHY FUNK-BAXTER
Executive Vice-President for Administration: PAUL ORSER
Librarian: CHRISTINE SHUPALA

DEANS

Arts and Humanities: RICHARD J. GIGLIOTTI
Science and Technology: DIANA I. MARINEZ
Teacher Education: DEE HOPKINS
Business Administration: MOUSTAFA ABDELSAMAD

Texas A & M University—Kingsville

700 University Blvd, MSC101 Kingsville, TX 78363
Telephone: (361) 593-2111
Internet: www.tamuk.edu
Founded 1917 as South Texas Normal School; name changed to South Texas State Teachers' College in 1923, to Texas College of Arts and Industries in 1929, to Texas A & I University by law in 1967, and

to Texas A & M University – Kingsville in 1993

President: RUMALDO Z. JUAREZ
Vice-President (Academic Affairs) and Provost: KAY CLAYTON
Vice-President (Finance and Administration): STEVE CRANDALL
Vice-President (Institutional Advancement): J. RANDY HUGHES
Vice-President (Student Affairs): TOM JACKSON, Jr
Director (Research): SANDRA REXROAT
Director (Continuing Education): TADEO REYNA
Registrar: MAGGIE WILLIAMS
Librarian: GILDEO B. ORTEGO

Library of 748,000 vols, 2,122 periodicals
Number of teachers: 329
Number of students: 5,876

DEANS

Agriculture: RON ROSATI
Arts and Sciences: RONN HY
Business Administration: ROBERT DIERSING
Engineering: WILLIAM HEENAN
Education: MIKE DANIEL
Graduate Studies: ALBERTO M. OLIVARES
King Ranch Institute of Range Management: BARRY DUNN
Pharmacy: INDRA REDDY
University College: GLADYS HINES

ATTACHED INSTITUTES

Texas A & M University Kingsville Citrus Center: Weslaco, Texas; Dir JOHN DA GRACA.

Caesar Kleberg Wildlife Research Institute: Kingsville, Texas; Dir Dr FRED BRYANT.

System Center: Palo Alto, San Antonio, Texas; Dir GARRY ROSS.

Prairie View A & M University

POB 188, Prairie View, TX 77446

Telephone: (409) 857-3311
Fax: (409) 857-3928
Internet: www.pvamu.edu

Founded 1876, University 1973

President: GEORGE C. WRIGHT
Registrar: ROBERT FORD
Provost and Vice-President for Academic Affairs: FLOSSIE M. BYRD
Vice-President for Administration and Finance: HAROLD S. BONNER
Director of Institutional Development: HARVEY G. DICKERSON
Vice-President for Student Affairs: JILES P. DANIELS
Director of Library: DUDLEY YATES
Director of Public Information Services: BRYAN BARROWS

Library of 260,000 vols
Number of teachers: 315
Number of students: 5,600

DEANS

Graduate School: WILLIE F. TROTTY
Banneker Honors College: JEWEL L. PRESTAGE
College of Arts and Sciences: EDWARD W. MARTIN
College of Engineering and Architecture: JOHN FOSTER
College of Applied Sciences and Engineering Technology: HAKUMAT ISRANI
College of Education: M. PAUL MEHTA
College of Nursing: DOLLIE BRATHWAITE
College of Business: BARBARA A. JONES

Tarleton State University

Stephenville, TX 76402

Telephone: (254) 968-9000
Fax: (254) 968-9920
E-mail: info@tarleton.edu

Internet: www.tarleton.edu

Founded 1899, University 1973
Academic year: September to August

President: Dr DENNIS P. MCCABE
Provost and Vice-President for Academic Affairs: Dr GARY G. PEER
Vice-President for Institutional Advancement: Dr KOY FLOYD
Vice-President for Student Services: Dr WANDA L. MERCER
Vice-President for Finance and Administration: JERRY GRAHAM
Executive Director (Tarleton – Central Texas): Dr JOHN IDOUX
Executive Director (Planning and Research): Dr BRAD CHILTON
Executive Director (TIAER): RON JONES
Director of Admissions: CYNTHIA HESS
Registrar: DENISE SILER GROVES
Librarian: Dr KENNETH W. JONES

Library of 328,989 vols
Number of teachers: 523
Number of students: 9,033

DEANS

College of Liberal and Fine Arts: Dr DONALD L. ZELMAN
College of Education: Dr JILL BURK
College of Agriculture and Human Sciences: Dr DON CAWTHON
College of Business Administration: Dr RUBY BARKER
College of Graduate Studies: Dr LINDA JONES
College of Science and Technology: Dr RUEBEN WALTER

Texas A & M University – Texarkana

2600 North Robison Rd, Texarkana, TX 75501

Internet: www.tamut.edu

Founded 1971 as East Texas State University at Texarkana; joined Texas A & M University System 1996

Academic year: August to May

President: Dr STEPHEN R. HENSLEY

Number of teachers: 53 full-time
Number of students: 1,369

DEANS

College of Arts and Sciences, and Education: Dr GENE MUELLER
College of Business and Behavioral Sciences: Dr ALFRED N. NTOKO
Department of Nursing: Dr JO KAHLER (Dir)

West Texas A & M University

West Texas Station, Canyon, TX 79016-0001

Telephone: (806) 651-2100
Fax: (806) 651-2126
E-mail: cbarnes@wtamu.edu
Internet: www.wtamu.edu

Founded 1910
Academic year: August to May

President: Dr RUSSELL C. LONG
Provost and Vice-President for Academic Affairs: Dr FLAVIUS KILLEBREW

Library of 1,086,936 vols
Number of teachers: 245
Number of students: 6,775

Publication: *The Prairie* (Newspaper).

Texas A & M University System Health Science Center

MS 1361, John B. Connally Building, 301 Tarrow, College Station, TX 77840-7896

Telephone: (979) 458-7200
Fax: (979) 458-7202
E-mail: hsccomm@tamu.edu
Internet: tamushsc.tamu.edu

President: Dr NANCY W. DICKEY
Executive Vice-President: Dr ELVIN E. SMITH

Vice-President for Academic Affairs: Dr WILLIAM H. BINNIE
Vice-President for Research and Graduate Studies: Dr DAVID S. CARLSON
Vice-President of Finance and Administration: Dr BARRY C. NELSON
Vice-President of Governmental Affairs: Dr LAURA R. SMITH
Director of the Medical Sciences Library: MARTHA BEDARD

DEANS

Baylor College of Dentistry: Dr JAMES S. COLE
College of Medicine: Dr CHRISTOPHER C. COLENDA
School of Rural Public Health: Dr CIRO V. SUMAYA
Institute of Biosciences and Technology: Dr RICHARD H. FINNELL (Dir)
Coastal Bend Health Education Center: Dr JUAN F. CASTRO (Dir)

Texas A & M University – Galveston

POB 1675, Galveston, TX 77553-1675

Telephone: (409) 740-4403
Fax: (409) 740-5005
Internet: www.tamug.edu

President: Dr R. BOWEN LOFTIN
Vice-President for Student Affairs and Administration: WILLIAM C. HEARN
Vice-President for Research and Academic Affairs: Dr JAMES M. MCCLOY.

TEXAS CHIROPRACTIC COLLEGE

5912 Spencer Highway, Pasadena, TX 77505-1170

Telephone: (281) 487-1170
Fax: (281) 991-4871
Internet: www.txchiro.edu

Founded 1908

President: Dr RICHARD G. BRASSARD

Number of teachers: 36
Number of students: 517.

TEXAS CHRISTIAN UNIVERSITY

2800 S. University Drive, Fort Worth, TX 76129

Telephone: (817) 257-7000
Fax: (817) 257-7333
E-mail: frogmail@tcu.edu
Internet: www.tcu.edu

Founded 1873
Academic year: September to May

Chancellor: VICTOR BOSCHINI, Jr
Vice-Chancellor for Finance and Business: CHERYL WILSON
Provost and Vice-Chancellor for Academic Affairs: R. NOWELL DONOVAN
Vice-Chancellor for Student Affairs: DONALD B. MILLS
Vice-Chancellor for University Advancement: DONALD WHELAN
Registrar: PATRICK MILLER
Librarian: ROBERT A. SEAL

Library of 2,058,691 vols
Number of teachers: 541
Number of students: 8,632

DEANS

College of Science and Engineering: MICHAEL D. MCCRACKEN
Brite Divinity School: NEWELL WILLIAMS
College of Health and Human Sciences: RHONDA KEEN-PAYNE
M. J. Neeley School of Business: DANIEL G. SHORT
School of Education: SAMUEL M. DEITZ
College of Communication: WILLIAM SLATER
Addran College of Humanities and Social Sciences: MARY L. VOLCANSEK

College of Fine Arts: SCOTT A. SULLIVAN

TEXAS COLLEGE

2404 North Grand Avenue, Tyler, TX 75702
Telephone: (903) 593-8311
E-mail: dmiller@texascollege.edu
Internet: www.texascollege.edu
Founded 1894
Academic year: August to May
President: BILLY C. HAWKINS
Vice-President (Student Affairs): Dr NEVILLE MORGAN
Vice-President (Academic Affairs): Dr JEAN FITTS
Vice-President (Business and Finance): JAMES HARRIS
Number of teachers: 63
Number of students: 740.

TEXAS LUTHERAN UNIVERSITY

Seguin, TX 78155
Telephone: (210) 372-8000
Fax: (210) 372-8096
Internet: www.tlu.edu
Founded 1891
A church-related, co-educational, liberal arts, undergraduate college with programs in business administration, teacher education, computer science, and the health-related fields
President: Dr JON N. MOLINE
Academic Dean: Dr LEONARD G. SCHULZE
Registrar: KRISTIN PLAEHIN
Librarian: PATRICK HSU
Library of 151,402 vols
Number of teachers: 95
Number of students: 1,268.

TEXAS SOUTHERN UNIVERSITY

3100 Cleburne Ave, Houston, TX 77004
Telephone: (713) 313-7011
Fax: (713) 313-1092
Internet: www.tsu.edu
Founded 1947
State control
Academic year: September to August
President: Dr PRISCILLA SLADE
Executive Vice-President: Dr CHARLENE EVANS
Provost/Vice-President for Academic Affairs: Dr BOBBY WILSON
Senior Vice-President for Administration: BRUCE WILSON
Senior Vice-President for Business and Finance: QUINTIN WIGGINS
Senior Vice-President for Enrollment Management and Planning: Dr GAYLA THOMAS
Vice-President for Architectural Engineering and Construction Services: WILLIAM BECKHAM
Registrar: NORMA ROBINSON
Director of Libraries: Dr OBIDIKE KAMAU
Library: Libraries with 729,568 vols
Number of teachers: 509
Number of students: 10,567
Publications: *Ex-Press* (quarterly), *Inside TSU* (monthly), *Urban Notebook* (quarterly)

DEANS

School of Science and Technology: Dr MITCHELL ALLEN
School of Business: Dr JOSEPH BOYD
School of Education: Dr JAY CUMMINGS
School of Law: McKEN CARRINGTON
School of Public Affairs: Dr ANTHONY WOODS
College of Liberal Arts and Behavioral Sciences: Dr MERLINE PITRE
Graduate School: Dr RICHARD PITRE

College of Pharmacy and Health Sciences: Dr BARBARA HAYES

TEXAS STATE UNIVERSITY SYSTEM

Thomas J. Rusk Bldg, 200 East 10th St, Suite 600 Austin, TX 78701-2407
Telephone: (512) 463-1808
Fax: (512) 463-1816
E-mail: chancellor@tsus.edu
Internet: www.tsus.edu
Number of students: 70,000 at nine universities and colleges
Chancellor: CHARLES R. MATTHEWS.

CONSTITUENT UNIVERSITIES

Angelo State University

POB 11007, ASU Station, San Angelo, TX 76909
Telephone: (915) 942-2073
Fax: (915) 942-2038
Internet: www.angelo.edu
Founded 1928
President: Dr E. JAMES HINDMAN
Vice-President for Academic Affairs: Dr RUTH J. PERSON
Vice-President for University Relations and Development: MICHAEL P. RYAN
Vice-President for Fiscal Affairs: ROBERT L. KRUPALA
Director of Admissions: MONIQUE COSSICK
Registrar: ANITA LOSHBOUGH
Librarian: MAURICE FORTIN
Library of 1,247,600 items
Number of teachers: 228 (full-time)
Number of students: 6,234.

Lamar University

POB 10001, Beaumont, TX 77710
Telephone: (409) 880-7011
Fax: (409) 880-8404
Internet: www.lamar.edu
Founded 1923 as South Park Junior College
Chancellor: LAMAR URBANOVSKY
President: Dr JAMES M. SIMMONS
Executive Vice-President for Academic Affairs: Dr STEPHEN DOBLIN
Vice-President for Finance and Operations: MIKE FERGUSON, Jr
Registrar: KEITH CAPPS
Director of Library: LINDA DUGGER
Library of 964,543 vols
Number of teachers: 507
Number of students: 8,235

DEANS

Graduate Studies: Dr JERRY BRADLEY
College of Education: Dr CARL WESTERFIELD
College of Arts and Sciences: Dr BRENDA NICHOLS
College of Business: (vacant)
College of Fine and Applied Arts: Dr RUSS SCHULTZ
College of Engineering: Dr JACK HOPPER

Sam Houston State University

POB 2026, Huntsville, TX 77341
Telephone: (409) 294-1111
E-mail: adm_smm@shsu.edu
Internet: www.shsu.edu
Founded 1879 as Sam Houston Normal Institute
Academic year: August to May
President: JAMES F. GAETNER
Vice-President for Academic Affairs: DAVID E. PAYNE
Vice-President for Finance: JACK PARKER
Vice-President for University Advancement: FRANK HOLMES
Vice-President for Student Services: THELMA DOUGLASS

Director of Admissions: JOEY CHANDLER
Registrar: ROBERT DUNNING
Director of Libraries: ANN HOLDER
Library of 1,379,682 books, 3,556 periodicals, 1,379,682 microforms, 629,489 records and tapes
Number of teachers: 551
Number of students: 13,091
Publications: *Journal of Business Strategies*, *Texas Review* (2 a year), *Crime and Justice International*, *Ed Leadership Review*, *Advancing Women in Leadership*, *The Texas Crime Pole*

DEANS

College of Arts and Sciences: BRIAN CHAPMAN
College of Business Administration: R. DEAN LEWIS
College of Education and Applied Science: GENEVIEVE BROWN
College of Criminal Justice: RICHARD WARD

DIRECTORS OF DEPARTMENTS

Accounting: ROSS QUARLES
Agricultural Sciences and Vocational Education: ROBERT LANE
Art: MARTIN AMOROUS
Biological Sciences: MONTE THIES
Chemistry: RICK WHITE
Consumer Services, Fashion and Design: JANIS WHITE
Curriculum and Instruction: JOHN HUBER
Dance and Drama: JAMES MILLER
Economics and Business Analysis: WILLIAM GREEN
Educational Leadership and Counselling: GENEVIEVE BROWN
English and Foreign Languages: BILL BRIDGES
General Business and Finance: LEROY ASHORN
Geography and Geology: BEN GILLESPIE
Health and Kinesiology: ROBERT CASE
History: JAMES OLSON
Language, Literacy and Special Populations: HOLLIS LOWERY-MOORE
Library Science: ANN HOLDER
Management and Marketing: ROGER ABSHIRE
Mathematical and Information Sciences: JAIMIE HEBERT
Music: ROD CANNON (acting)
Physics: REX ISHAM
Psychology and Philosophy: DONNA M. DESFORGES
Political Science: ROBERT BILES (acting)
Public Communication: J. D. RAGSDALE
Sociology: ALESSANDRO BONANNO
Technology: THOMAS HIGGINS

Sul Ross State University

Alpine, TX 79832
Telephone: (432) 837-8032
Fax: (432) 837-8334
E-mail: rvmorgan@sulross.edu
Internet: www.sulross.edu
Founded 1917
Academic year: September to August
President: Dr R. VIC MORGAN, Jr
Vice-President for Academic Affairs: Dr DAVE COCKRUM
Vice-President for Enrollment Management and Student Services: Dr NADINE F. JENKINS
Librarian: DON DOWDY
Library of 760,700 vols
Number of teachers: 117
Number of students: 3,144

DEANS

Arts and Sciences: (vacant)
Professional Studies: Dr CHET SAMPLE
Agricultural and Natural Resource Sciences: Dr ROB KINUCAN
Rio Grande College: Dr FRANK ABBOTT

ATTACHED COLLEGE

Rio Grande College: 205 Wildcat Dr., Del Rio TX 78840; tel. (830) 703-4832; internet rgc.sulross.edu; Vice-Pres. Dr JOEL E. VELA; 3 campuses located at Del Rio, Eagle Pass and Uvalde.

Texas State University–San Marcos

601 University Drive, JCK 883, San Marcos, TX 78666

Telephone: (512) 245-2386
Fax: (512) 245-8446
Internet: www.txstate.edu

Founded 1899
Academic year: August to May

President: Dr DENISE TRAUTH
Provost and Vice-President for Academic Affairs: Dr PERRY MOORE
Vice-President for Finance and Support Services: BILL NANCE
Vice-President for Information Technology: Dr CARL VAN WYATT
Vice-President for Student Affairs: Dr JOANN SMITH (acting)
Vice-President for University Advancement: T CAY ROWE (acting)
Director for Alumni Affairs: DOROTHY EVANS
Librarian: JOAN HEATH

Library of 1,388,557 vols, 1,873,257 microforms, 8,698 serials, 275,855 audiovisual items, 2,782 electronic books
Number of teachers: 1,288
Number of students: 26,783
Publications: *Electronic Journal of Differential Equations*, *Persona* (student literary journal, annually), *Southwestern American Literature* (2 a year), *The Journal of Texas Music History* (2 a year), *Texas Books in Review* (4 a year)

DEANS

College of Applied Arts: Dr JAIME CHAHIN (acting)
College of Business: Dr DENISE SMART
College of Education: Dr JOHN J. BECK
College of Fine Arts: Dr RICHARD CHEATHAM
College of Health Professions: Dr RUTH WELBORN
College of Liberal Arts: Dr ANN MARIE ELLIS
College of Science: Dr HECTOR E. FLORES (acting)
Graduate College: Dr J. MICHAEL WILLOUGHBY
University College: Dr RONALD C. BROWN

DIRECTORS

Aquarena—The Environmental Learning Center: RON COLEY
Aquifer and Data Research Center: Dr DAVID LONGLEY
Center for Archaeological Studies: Dr BRITT BOUSMAN
Center for Children and Families: Dr KAREN BROWN
Center for Industrial and Environmental Science: Dr REDDY VENUMBAKA
Center of Initiatives in Education: Dr EMILY PAYNE
Center for International Studies: Dr DENNIS J. DUNN
Center for Multicultural and Gender Studies: Dr SANDRA M. MAYO
Center for Safe Communities and Schools: DAVE WILLIAMS
Center for Texas-Mexico Applied Research: Dr DAVID STEA
Center for Texas Music History: Dr GARY HARTMAN
Center for the Study of the Southwest: Dr MARK BUSBY EDWARDS
Gilbert M. Grosvenor Center for Geographic Education: Dr RICHARD G. BOEHM
International Institute for Sustainable Water Resources: Dr WALTER RAST

James and Marilyn Lovell Center for Environmental Geography and Hazards Research: Dr RICHARD W. DIXON
National Centre for School Improvement: Dr STEPHEN GORDON, Dr MARLA MCGHEE
Small Business Development Center: LARRY P. LUCERO
Texas Geographic Information Science Center: Dr BENJAMIN ZHAN
Texas Justice Court Training Centre: ROGER ROUNDTREE
Texas Long Term Care Institute: SANDY RANSOM
Texas Mathworks: Dr MAX WARSHAUER
Walter Richter Institute of Social Work Research: Dr NANCY CHAVKIN
William P. Hobby Center for Public Service: Dr HOWARD R. BALANOFF

Other constituent institutions awarding Associate level degrees include: Lamar Institute of Technology, Lamar State College-Orange and Lamar State College-Port Arthur.

TEXAS TECH UNIVERSITY

Box 42005, Lubbock, TX 79409-2005
Telephone: (806) 742-2121
Internet: www.ttu.edu

Founded 1923

President: DAVID J. SCHMIDLY
Registrar: DON WICKARD
Director of Libraries: E. DALE CLUFF

Library of 1,614,148 vols
Number of teachers: 1,574
Number of students: 24,007

DEANS

College of Agricultural Sciences and Natural Resources: Dr JOHN ABERNATHY
College of Architecture: JAMES WHITE
College of Arts and Sciences: Dr JANE WINER
College of Business Administration: Dr ALLAN McINNIS
College of Education: Dr GREGORY BOWES
College of Engineering: Dr WILLIAM MARCY
College of Human Sciences: Dr LINDA HOOVER
Graduate School: Dr RON ANDERSON
School of Law: FRANK NEWTON

ATTACHED INSTITUTES AND CENTRES

Agricultural Finance Institute: Dir PHILLIP N. JOHNSON.

Insitute for Research in Plant Stress: Dir ROBERT ALDIN.

Pork Industry Institute for Research and Education: Dir JOHN MCGLONE.

Wildlife and Fisheries Management Institute: Dir RON SOSEBEE.

Center for Agricultural Technology Transfer: Dir PAUL VAUGHN.

Center for Applied International Development Studies: Dir GARY S. ELBOW.

Center for Applied Systems Analysis: Dir CLYDE F. MARTIN.

Center for Feed and Industry Research and Education: Dir REED RICHARDSON.

Center for Historic Preservation and Technology: Dir JOE KING.

Center for Petroleum Mathematics: Dir WAYNE FORD.

Center for Forensic Studies: Dir E. ROLAND MENZEL.

Center for Public Service: Dir CHARLES FOX.

Center for the Study of the Vietnam Conflict: Dir JAMES R. RECKNER.

Southwest Center for German Studies: Dir MEREDITH MCCLAIN.

Center of Sports Health and Human Performance: Chair. GIL REAVES.

State Affiliate Census Data Center: Dir EVANS W. CURRY.

Institute for Communications Research: Dir JERRY HUDSON.

Institute for Design and Advanced Technology: Dir A. ERTAS.

Institute for Environmental Sciences: Dir MICHAEL WILLIG.

Institute for Studies in Pragmaticism: Dir KENNETH KETNER.

Center for Professional Development: Dir DAVID ANDERSON.

Small Business Development Center: Dir CRAIG BEAN.

Small Business Institute: Dir ALEX STEWART.

Texas Center for Productivity and Quality of Work Life: Dir BARRY MACY.

Institute for Banking and Financial Studies: Dir STEVE SEARS.

Institute for Management and Leadership Research: Dir ROBERT L. PHILLIPS.

Institute for Marketing Studies: Dir ROY D. HOWELL.

Institute for Studies in Organizational Automation: Dir KATHLEEN HENNESSEY.

Center for Improvement of Teaching Effectiveness: Dir A. L. SMITH.

Center for Excellence in Education: Dir BILL SPARKMAN.

Science and Mathematics Education Center: Dir GERALD SKOOG.

Center for Energy Research: Dir WALT J. OLER.

Center for Hazardous and Toxic Waste Studies: Dir RAGHU NARAYAN.

Water Resources Center: Dir LLOYD V. URBAN.

Center for Applied Research in Industrial Automation and Robotics: Dir WILLIAM KOLARIK.

Wind Engineering Research Center: Dir KISHOR C. MEHTA.

Institute for Disaster Research: Dir JAMES R. MCDONALD.

Institute for Ergonomics Research: Dir M. M. AYOUB.

Institute for Multicomputer Processing and Controls: Dir WILLIAM J. B. OLDHAM.

Murdough Center for Engineering Professionalism: Dir JIMMY SMITH.

Child Development Research Center: Dir CATHY NATHAN.

Home Economics Instructional Curriculum Center: Dir MARILYN WRAGG.

Institute for Multidisciplinary Research on Adolescent and Adult Risk-Taking Behavior: Dir NANCY BELL.

Texas Wine Marketing Research Institute: Dir TIM H. DODD.

Center for Study of Addiction: Dir CARL ANDERSEN.

Leather Research Institute: Dir JINGER EBERSPACHER.

Center for Applied Petrophysical Studies: Dirs GEORGE ASQUITH, MARION ARNOLD.

International Center for Arid and Semiarid Land Studies: Dir KARY MATHIS.

International Center for Textile Research and Development: Dir DEAN ETHRIDGE.

Institute for Child and Family Studies: Dir MARY TOM RILEY.

Institute for the Gifted: Dir MARTHA HISE.

Institute for Biotechnology: Dir DAVID KNAFF.

Institute for Environmental and Human Health: Dir Dr RON KENDALL.

HEALTH SCIENCES CENTRE

Texas Tech University Health Sciences Center

3601 4th St, Lubbock, TX 79430
Telephone: (806) 743-3111
Internet: www.ttuhsc.edu
President: Dr DAVID SMITH

DEANS

School of Medicine: Dr JOEL KUPPERSMITH
School of Nursing: (vacant)
School of Allied Health: (vacant)
School of Pharmacy: ARTHUR NELSON

TEXAS WESLEYAN UNIVERSITY

Fort Worth, TX 76105-1536
Telephone: (817) 531-4444
Fax: (817) 531-4425
E-mail: info@txwesleyan.edu
Internet: www.txwesleyan.edu
Founded 1890
Academic year: September to May
President: HAROLD G. JEFFCOAT
Provost: ALLEN HENDERSON
Vice-Presidents: GARY CUMBIE, PATI ALEXANDER, BILL BLEIBDREY
Registrar: KAHLA VAN TOORN
Librarian: CINDY SWIGGER
Library of 219,053 vols
Number of teachers: 140.

TEXAS WOMAN'S UNIVERSITY

Denton, TX 76204-5619
Telephone: (940) 898-3000
Fax: (940) 898-3198
E-mail: info@twu.edu
Internet: www.twu.edu
Founded 1901
Academic year: August to May
President: Dr ANN STUART
Vice-President for Academic Affairs: Dr LOIS SMITH
Vice-President for Finance and Administration: Dr BRENDA FLOYD
Vice-President for Institutional Advancement (vacant)
Vice-President for Student Life: Dr RICHARD NICHOLAS
Librarian: ELIZABETH SNAPP
Library of 788,271 vols
Number of teachers: 500
Number of students: 8,690.

TRINITY UNIVERSITY

One Trinity Place, San Antonio, TX 78212
Telephone: (210) 999-7011
Fax: (210) 999-7696
E-mail: admissions@trinity.edu
Internet: www.trinity.edu
Founded 1869
Academic year: August to May
President: Dr JOHN R. BRAZIL
Vice-President for Academic Affairs: Dr MICHAEL FISCHER
Dean of Admissions: CHRISTOPHER ELLERTSON
Dean of Students and Director of Residential Life: DAVID TUTTLE
Registrar: ALFRED RODRIGUEZ
Librarian: DIANE GRAVES
Library of 918,000 vols
Number of teachers: 235
Number of students: 2,718
Liberal Arts and Sciences.

UNIVERSITY OF DALLAS

1845 E. Northgate Drive, Irving, TX 75062-4799
Telephone: (214) 721-5000
E-mail: undadmis@acad.udallas.edu
Internet: www.udallas.edu
Founded 1956
President: Mgr MILAM J. JOSEPH (acting)
Vice-President for Administration: ROBERT M. GALECKE
Provost and Dean of the College: Dr GLEN THUROW
Graduate Dean: Dr GLEN THUROW
Registrar: JAN BURK
Librarian: SUE KENDALL (acting)
Library of 259,261 vols
Number of teachers: 188
Number of students: 3,008.

UNIVERSITY OF HOUSTON SYSTEM

4800 Calhoun, Houston, TX 7704
Telephone: (713) 743-8189
Fax: (713) 743-0946
Internet: www.uhsa.uh.edu
Chancellor: JAY GOGUE.

CONSTITUENT INSTITUTIONS

University of Houston

Houston, TX 77204-2018
Telephone: (713) 743-1000
Internet: www.uh.edu
Founded 1927
Academic year: September to August
President: JAY GOGUE
Senior Vice-President (Academic Affairs) and Provost: JERALD STRICKLAND
Vice-President (Administration and Finance): JOHN RUDLEY
Vice-President (Governmental Relations): GROVER CAMPBELL
Vice-President (Information Technology): CHARLES R. SHOMPER
Vice-President (Research): ARTHUR C. VAILAS
Vice-President (Student Affairs): ELWYN C. LEE
Vice-President (University Advancement): ILEANA TREVINO
Dean of the Library: DANA ROOKS
Library of 1,825,282 vols
Number of teachers: 2,923 (1,140 full-time, 1,783 part-time)
Number of students: 35,066
Publications: *Experts Directory*, *UHouston*

DEANS

College of Architecture: JOSEPH L. MASHBURN
C. T. Bauer College of Business Administration: ARTHUR WARGA
College of Education: ROBERT WIMPLEBERG
Conrad N. Hilton College of Hotel and Restaurant Management: JOHN BOWEN
Cullen College of Engineering: RAYMOND FLUMERFELT
Continuing Education: ALICE ROSS
College of Liberal Arts and Social Sciences: JOHN J. ANTEL
U H Law Center: NANCY RAPOPORT
College of Natural Sciences and Mathematics: JOHN BEAR
College of Optometry: EARL L. SMITH
College of Pharmacy: SUNNY OHIA
College of Technology: WILLIAM FITZGIBBON
Honors College: TED L. ESTESS
Graduate School of Social Work: IRA COLBY

ATTACHED INSTITUTIONS

A. A. White Dispute Resolution Institute: Dir (vacant).

Allied Geophysical Laboratories: Dir KURT MARFURT.

CBA Energy Institute: Dir MICHELLE FOSS.

Centre for Entrepreneurship and Innovation: Dir BILL SHERRILL.

Center for Immigration Research: Dirs J. HAGAN, N. RODRIGUEZ.

Center for Public Policy: Dir RICHARD MURRAY.

Center for the Americas: Dir RODOLFO CORTINO.

Composites Engineering and Applications Center: Dir SU SU WANG.

Environmental Institute of Houston: Dir GLENN AUMANN.

Health Law and Policy Institute: Dir MARY ANNE BOBINSKI.

Institute for Beam Particle Dynamics: Dir ROY WEINSTEIN.

Institute for Cardiovascular Studies: Dir BHAGAVAN JANDHYALA.

Institute for Drug Education and Research: Dir DIANA CHOW.

Institute for Energy Studies: Dir MICHELLE FOSS.

Institute for Fluid Dynamics and Turbulence: Dir (vacant) FAZIE HUSSAIN.

Institute for Higher Education Law and Governance: Dir MICHAEL OLIVAS.

Institute for Intellectual Property and Information Law: Dirs JANICKE, JOYCE, NIMMER.

Institute for Molecular Biology: Dir MICHAEL BENEDIK.

Institute for Molecular Design: Dir MONTY PETTITT.

Institute for Regional Forecasting: Dir BARTON SMITH.

Institute for Space Systems Operations: Dir DAVID CRISWELL.

Institute for the Study of Political Economy: Dir STEPHEN CRAIG.

Institute for Theoretical Engineering Sciences: Dir MARTIN GOLUBITSKY.

Institute for Urban Education: Dir ROBERT HOUSTON.

International Law Institute: Dirs SANFORD GAINES, STEPHEN ZAMORA.

Materials Research Science and Engineering Center: Dir ALLAN JACOBSON.

Space Vacuum Epitaxy Center: Dir ALEX IGNATIEV.

Texas Center for Superconductivity: Dir C. W. PAUL CHU.

UH – North Houston Institute: Dir JOEL HAMMETT.

UH – West Houston Institute: Dir KURT CZUPRYN.

UHS at Fort Bend: Dir SHARON BACA.

University Center at The Woodlands: Dir PENNY WESTERFELD.

University Eye Institute: Dir NICK HOLDEMAN.

University of Houston–Clear Lake

2700 Bay Area Blvd, Houston, TX 77058-1098
Telephone: (281) 283-7600
Fax: (281) 283-2010
E-mail: president@cl.uh.edu
Internet: www.uhcl.edu
Founded 1974
Academic year: September to August
President: Dr WILLIAM A. STAPLES
Senior Vice-President and Provost: Dr EDWARD J. HAYES
Vice-President for Administration and Finance: MICHELLE DOTTER
Librarian: KAREN WEILHORSKI

Library of 2,222,020 vols
Number of teachers: 554 (227 full-time, 327 part-time)
Number of students: 7,753

DEANS

School of Business and Public Administration: Dr WILLIAM T. CUMMINGS
School of Education: Dr DENNIS W. SPUCK
School of Human Sciences and Humanities: Dr BRUCE PALMER
School of Natural and Applied Sciences: Dr CHARLES W. MCKAY

University of Houston–Downtown

One Main St, Houston TX 77002
Telephone: (713) 221-8000
Fax: (713) 221-8157
Internet: www.uhd.edu
Founded 1974; adopted present name in 1983
President: Dr MAX CASTILLO
Vice-President for Academic Affairs and Provost: Dr MOLLY R. WOODS
Vice-President for Administration: CHANEY ANDERSON
Executive Assistant to the President and Director of Constituent Relations: IVONNE MONTALBANO
Executive Director of Institutional Advancement: Dr MICHELE SABINO
Dean of Student Affairs (vacant)
Library Director: PAT ENSOR
Library of 230,000 vols
Number of teachers: 528
Number of students: 10,528

DEANS

College of Business: Dr BOBBY BIZZELL
College of Humanities and Social Sciences: Dr MICHAEL DRESSMAN
College of Sciences and Technology: Dr GEORGE PINCUS
University College: Dr CHRIS BIRCHAK

University of Houston–Victoria

3007 N. Ben Wilson, Victoria, TX 77901
Telephone: (877) 970-4848
Fax: (361) 570-4118
E-mail: webmaster@uhv.edu
Internet: www.vic.uh.edu
Founded 1973
President: Dr KAREN HAYNES
Provost and Vice-President for Academic Affairs: Dr DON SMITH
Associate Vice-President of Student Services: RICHARD D. PHILLIPS
Director, Computer Services: JOSEPH S. FERGUSON
Vice-President, Administration and Finance: WAYNE B. BERAN
Executive Director, Institutional Advancement: CAROLE OLIPHANT
Director, Library: Dr JOE F. DAHLSTROM
Library of 170,000 vols
Number of teachers: 57
Number of students: 1,927

CHAIRMEN

Division of Arts and Sciences: Dr DAN JAECKLE
Division of Business Administration: Dr CHARLES BULLOCK
Division of Education: Dr MARY NATIVIDAD

UNIVERSITY OF MARY HARDIN-BAYLOR

Belton, TX 76513
Telephone: (254) 295-8642
Fax: (254) 295-4535
Internet: www.umhb.edu
Founded 1845

President: Dr JERRY G. BAWCOM
Provost and Vice-President for Academic Affairs: Dr GRAHAM HATCHER
Registrar: LILLIAN KROEGER
Director of Admissions: ROBBIN STEEN
Librarian: ROBERT A. STRONG
Library of 145,000 vols
Number of teachers: 126
Number of students: 2,600.

UNIVERSITY OF NORTH TEXAS

POB 311277 Denton, TX 76203-3826
Telephone: (817) 522-7911
Internet: www.unt.edu
Founded 1890
Chancellor and President: Dr ALFRED F. HURLEY
Provost and Vice-President for Academic Affairs: Dr BLAINE A. BROWNELL
Vice-President for Fiscal Affairs: PHILIP C. DIEBEL
Vice-President for External Affairs: WALTER E. PARKER
Vice-President for Administrative Affairs: FREDERICK R. POLE
Vice-President for Development: Dr PETER LANE
Vice-President for Student Affairs: Dr JOE G. STEWART
Vice-President and General Counsel: Dr RICHARD RAFES
Director of Admissions: MARCILLA COLLINS-WORTH
Registrar: JONEEL J. HARRIS
Librarian: Dr B. DONALD GROSE
Library of 2,164,427 vols, 2,190,831 microforms
Number of teachers: 800 full-time, 540 teaching assistants and teaching fellows
Number of students: 25,605

DEANS

Graduate School: Dr ROLLIE SCHAFER
Education: Dr PAUL DIXON
Arts and Sciences: Dr NORA KIZER BELL
Music: Dr DAVID SHRADER
Business Administration: (vacant)
Library Science: (vacant)
Community Service: Dr DANIEL M. JOHNSON
Merchandising and Hospitality Management: Dr SUZANNE LA BRECQUE
School of Visual Arts: Dr D. JACK DAVIS

HEALTH SCIENCES CENTRE

University of North Texas Health Science Center at Fort Worth

3500 Camp Bowie Blvd, Fort Worth, TX 76107
Telephone: (817) 735-2000
Internet: www.hsc.unt.edu
President: RONALD R. BLANCK
Senior Vice-President for Academic Affairs: GREG MCQUEEN
Senior Vice-President: STEVE R. RUSSELL
Vice-President for Governmental Affairs: DANIEL M. JENSEN
Vice-President for Institutional Coordination: GREG UPP
Vice-President for Strategic and Institutional Affairs: ADELA N. GONZALEZ
Vice-President for Advancement: CHERYL GRAY KIMBERLING

UNIVERSITY OF ST THOMAS

3800 Montrose Blvd, Houston, TX 77006
Telephone: (713) 522-7911
Internet: www.stthom.edu
Founded 1947
Private control
Academic year: August to May

President: Fr J. MICHAEL MILLER
Vice-President for Academic Affairs: Dr LEE J. WILLIAMES
Vice-President for Finance: JAMES BOOTH
Vice-President for Information Technology: GARY MCCORMACK
Vice-President for Institutional Advancement: KEN DEDOMINICIS
Vice-President for Strategic Planning, Institutional Research and Evaluation: Dr COLLEEN HESTER
Vice-President for Student Affairs: JACK HANK
Director, Community Services: Fr WILLIAM J. YOUNG
Dean of Admissions: ELSIE BIRON
Registrar: Rev. RICHARD GLOR
Librarian: JAMES PICCININNI
Library of 203,000 vols
Number of teachers: 215
Number of students: 2,696
Publications: *Cauldron* (monthly), *St Thomas Magazine* (2 a year), *UST Insider* (3 a year)

DEANS

School of Arts and Sciences: Dr JEROME KRAMER
School of Theology: Fr LOUIS T. BRUSATTI
Cameron School of Business: Dr YHI-MIN HO
School of Education: Dr RUTH STRUDLER
Special Sessions and Programs: Dr JANICE GORDON-KELTER (Dir)

UNIVERSITY OF TEXAS SYSTEM

601 Colorado St, Austin, TX 78701
Telephone: (512) 499-4201
Internet: www.utsystem.edu
Founded 1883
Chancellor: MARK G. YUDOF
Executive Vice-Chancellor for Academic Affairs: TERESA A. SULLIVAN
Executive Vice-Chancellor for Business Affairs: SCOTT C. KELLEY
Executive Vice-Chancellor for Health Affairs: KENNETH I. SHINE (acting)
Vice-Chancellor for Administration: TONYA MOTEN BROWN
Vice-Chancellor for Community and Business Relations: JOHN DE LA GARZA, Jr
Vice-Chancellor for External Relations: RANDA S. SAFADY
Vice-Chancellor for Federal Relations: WILLIAM H. SHUTE
Vice-Chancellor and General Counsel: BARRY D. BURGDORF
Vice-Chancellor for Governmental Relations and Policy: E. ASHLEY SMITH
Vice-Chancellor for Research and Technology Transfer: ROBERT E. BARNHILL
Counsel and Secretary to the Board of Regents: FRANCIE A. FREDERICK.

CONSTITUENT INSTITUTIONS

University of Texas at Austin

Austin, TX 78712
Telephone: (512) 471-3434
E-mail: utopa@www.utexas.edu
Internet: www.utexas.edu
Founded 1883; formerly University of Texas, Main University
State control
Academic year: September to May (two terms) with two summer sessions
President: LARRY R. FAULKNER
Executive Vice-President and Provost: SHELDON EKLAND-OLSEN
Senior Vice-President: WILLIAM S. LIVINGSTON
Senior Vice-President: SHIRLEY BIRD PERRY

Vice-President and Chief Financial Officer: KEVIN P. HEGARTY
Vice-President for Community and School Relations: JAMES L. HILL
Vice-President for Employee and Campus Services: PATRICIA L. CLUBB
Vice-President for Information Technology: DANIEL A. UPDEGROVE
Vice-President for Institutional Relations and Legal Affairs: PATRICIA C. OHLENDORF
Vice-President for Public Affairs: DONALD A. HALE
Vice-President for Research: JUAN M. SANCHEZ
Vice-President for Resource Development: KEVIN P. HEGARTY
Vice-President for Student Affairs: JAMES W. VICK
Librarian: FRED M. HEATH
Library: see Libraries and Archives
Number of teachers: 2,721
Number of students: 50,377

DEANS

School of Architecture: FREDERICK R. STEINER
McCombs School of Business: GEORGE W. GAU
School of Information: ANDREW P. DILLON
School of Law: WILLIAM C. POWERS, Jr
School of Nursing: DOLORES SANDS
LBJ School of Public Affairs: BOBBY R. INMAN
School of Social Work: BARBARA W. WHITE
College of Communication: RODERICK P. HART
College of Education: MANUEL J. JUSTIZ
College of Engineering: BEN G. STREETMAN
College of Fine Arts: ROBERT S. FREEMAN
College of Liberal Arts: RICHARD W. LARIVIERE
College of Natural Sciences: MARY ANN RANKIN
College of Pharmacy: STEVEN W. LESLIE
Graduate Studies: VICTORIA RODRIGUEZ
Continuing and Extended Education: THOMAS M. HATFIELD

PROFESSORS

School of Architecture:

ALOFSIN, A.
ARUMI, F. N.
ATKINSON, S. D.
BENEDIKT, M. L.
BLACK, J. S.
GARRISON, M. L.
KAHN, T. D.
KWALLEK, N. P.
LEIDING, G.
SPECK, L. W.
SWALLOW, R. P.
WILSON, P. A.

McCombs School of Business:

ALLISON, J. R., Management Science and Information Systems.
ALPERT, M. I., Marketing Administration
ANDERSON, U. L., Accounting
ATIASE, R., Accounting
BAGCHI, U., Management
BALAKRISHNAN, A., Management Science and Information Systems
BARUA, A., Management Science and Information Systems
BROCKETT, P. L., Management Science and Information Systems
BRONIARCZYK, S. M., Marketing Administration
BROWN, K. C., Finance
BUTLER, J. S., Management
COX III, E. P., Marketing Administration
CROSS, F. B., Management Science and Information Systems
CUNNINGHAM, W. H., Marketing Administration
DAMIEN, P., Management Science and Information Systems
DAVIS-BLAKE, A., Management
DEITRICK, J. W., Accounting

DUKERICH, J. M., Management
DYER, J. S., Management Science and Information Systems
FITZSIMMONS, J. A., Management
FREDRICKSON, J. W., Management
FREEMAN, R. N., Accounting
GOLDEN, L. L., Marketing Administration
GRANOF, M. H., Accounting
HENION II, K. E., Marketing Administration
HIRST, D. E., Accounting
HOYER, W. D., Marketing Administration
HUBER, G. P., Management
HUFF, D. L., Marketing Administration
JARVENPAA, S. L., Management Science and Information Systems
JEMISON, D. B., Management
JENNINGS, R. G., Accounting
KACHELMEIER, S. J., Accounting
KINNEY, Jr, W. R., Accounting
KOEHLER, J. J., Management Science and Information Systems
KOONCE, L. L., Accounting
LASDON, L. S., Management Science and Information Systems
LIMBERG, S. T., Accounting
MCALISTER, L. M., Marketing Administration
MCDANIEL, Jr, R. R., Management Science and Information Systems
MAGEE, S. P., Finance
MAHAJAN, V., Marketing Administration
MAY, R. G., Accounting
METTLEN, R. D., Finance
MORRICE, D. J., Management
MURRAY, P. C., Management Science and Information Systems
NEWMAN, D. P., Accounting
PETERSON, R. A., Marketing Administration
PRENTICE, R. A., Management Science and Information Systems
RAO, R. K. S., Finance
ROBINSON, J. R., Accounting
RONN, E. I., Finance
RUEFLI, T. W., Management Science and Information Systems
SAGER, T. W., Management Science and Information Systems
SALBU, S. R., Management Science and Information Systems
SHAW, B. M., Management Science and Information Systems
SHIVELY, T. S., Management Science and Information Systems
SPELLMAN, L. J., Finance
STARKS, L. T., Finance
TITMAN, S., Finance
WESTPHAL, J. D., Management
WHINSTON, A. B., Management Science and Information Systems
YU, G., Management Science and Information Systems

School of Information:

DAVIS, Jr, D. G.
GRACY, II, D. B.
HALLMARK, J.
HARMON, E. G.
IMMROTH, B. F.
LUKENBILL, W. B.
MIKSA, F. L.
ROY, L.

School of Law:

ANDERSON, D. A.
ASCHER, M. L.
BAKER, L. A.
BERMAN, M. N.
BLACK, B. S.
BLAIS, L. E.
BOBBITT, P. C.
CARSON II, L. C.
CHURGIN, M. J.
CLEVELAND, S. H.
COHEN, J. M.
DAWSON, R. O.
DIX, G. E.

DZIENKOWSKI, J. S.
ENGLE, K. L.
FORBATH, W. E.
GERGEN, M. P.
GETMAN, J. G.
GOODE, S. J.
GRAGLIA, L. A.
HANSEN, P. I.
HU, H. T. C.
JOHANSON, S. M.
JOHNSON, C. H.
KLEIN, S. R.
LAYCOCK, H. D.
LEITER, B. R.
LEVINSON, S. V.
MCGARITY, T. O.
MANN, R. J.
MARKESINIS, B. S.
MARKOVITS, I.
MARKOVITS, R. S.
MULLENIX, L. S.
PERONI, R. J.
POWE, Jr, L. A.
RABBAN, D. M.
RAU, A. S.
REESE, R. A.
ROBERTSON, D. W.
ROBERTSON, J. A.
SAGER, L.
SAMPSON, J. J.
SHARLOT, M. M.
SILVER, C. M.
SMITH, E. E.
STEIKER, J. M.
STURLEY, M. F.
TORRES, G.
WAGNER, W. E.
WEINBERG, L.
WELLBORN, O. G.
WESTBROOK, J. L.
WOOLLEY, P.
YOUNG, E. A.

School of Nursing:

GROBE, S. J.
HOUSTON, L. S.
PENTICUFF, J. H.
REW, D. L.
STUIFBERGEN, A. M.
WALKER, L. O.

LBJ School of Public Affairs:

APFEL, K. S.
AUERBACH, R. D.
BOSKE, L. B.
EATON, D. J.
FLAMM, K.
GALBRAITH, J. K.
HAMILTON, D. S.
INMAN, B. R.
RHODES, L.
SCHOTT, R. L.
SPELMAN, W. G.
WARNER, D. C.
WILSON, R. H.

School of Social Work:

CHOI, N.
DINITTO, D. M.
FONG, R.
FRANKLIN, C. G. S.
GREENE, R. R.
LAUDERDALE, M. L.
LEIN, L.
MCROY, R. G.
POOLE, D. L.
RUBIN, A.
SCHWAB, Jr, A. J.
SHORKEY, C. T.
STREETER, C. L.

College of Communication:

ALVES, R. C., Journalism
BERG, C. E., Radio, Television, Film
BRANHAM, L. E., Journalism
BROWNING, L. D., Communication Studies
BRUMMETT, B., Communication Studies
BURNS, N. M., Advertising

CHAMPLIN, C. A., Communication Sciences and Disorders
CHERWITZ, R. A., Communication Studies
CUNNINGHAM, I. C., Advertising
DALY, J. A., Communication Studies
DARLING, D. C., Journalism
DAVIS, B. L., Communication Sciences and Disorders
GILLAM, R. B., Communication Sciences and Disorders
KNAPP, M. L., Communication Studies
LECKENBY, J. D., Advertising
McCOMBS, M. E., Journalism
MARQUARDT, T. P., Communication Sciences and Disorders
MARTIN, F. N., Communication Sciences and Disorders
MAXWELL, M. M., Communication Studies
MORRISON, D. K., Advertising
MURPHY, J. H., Advertising
OLASKY, M. N., Journalism
REESE, S. D., Journalism
RICHARDS, J. I., Advertising
SCHATZ, T. G., Radio-Television-Film
STAIGER, J., Radio-Television-Film
STEKLER, P. J., Radio-Television-Film
STOUT, P. A., Advertising
STRAUBHAAR, J., Radio-Television-Film
STROVER, S. L., Radio-Television-Film
TODD, R. G., Journalism
VANGELISTI, A. L., Communication Studies
WILCOX, G. B., Advertising
WILLIAMS, J. D., Advertising

College of Education:

ABRAHAM, L. D., Curriculum and Instruction
AINSLIE, R. C., Educational Psychology
BARUFALDI, J. P., Curriculum and Instruction
BETHEL, L. J., Curriculum and Instruction
BORICH, G. D., Educational Psychology
BRYANT, D. P., Special Education
CANTU, N. V., Educational Administration
CARLSON, C. I., Educational Psychology
CHALIP, L. II., Kinesiology and Health Education
COYLE, E. F., Kinesiology and Health Education
DAVIS, Jr, O. L., Curriculum and Instruction
DODD, B. G., Educational Psychology
DUNCAN, J. P., Educational Adminstration
EMMER, E. T., Educational Psychology
FALBO, T. L., Educational Psychology
FARRAR, R. P., Kinesiology and Health Education
FIELD, S. L., Curriculum and Instruction
FOLEY, D. E., Curriculum and Instruction
GOTTLIEB, N. H., Kinesiology and Health Education
GUSZAK, F. J., Curriculum and Instruction
HOFFMAN, J. V., Curriculum and Instruction
HOLAHAN, C. K., Kinesiology and Health Education
HORWITZ, E. K., Curriculum and Instruction
IVY, J. L., Kinesiology and Health Education
KAMEEN, M. C., Educational Administration
KEITH, T. Z., Educational Psychology
KOCH, W. R., Educational Psychology
LASHER, W. F., Educational Adminstration
MANASTER, G. J., Educational Psychology
MOORE, W., Educational Administration
ORTIZ, A. A., Special Education
OVANDO, M. N., Educational Administration
PARKER, R. M., Special Education
REIFEL, S., Curriculum and Instruction
RESTA, P. E., Curriculum and Instruction
RICHARDSON, F. C., Educational Psychology
RIETH, H. J., Special Education
ROSER, N. L., Curriculum and Instruction

ROUECHE, Jr, J. E., Educational Administration
SCHALLERT, D. L., Educational Psychology
SCRIBNER, J. D., Educational Administration
SEMRUD-CLIKEMAN, M., Educational Psychology
SIGAFOOS, J., Special Education
SPIRDUSO, W. W., Kinesiology and Health Education
STARK, K. D., Educational Psychology
STARNES, J. W., Kinesiology and Health Education
STEINHARDT, M. A., Kinesiology and Health Education
THOMAS, Jr, M. P., Educational Administration
VALENCIA, R., Educational Psychology
VAUGHN, S., Special Education
WEINSTEIN, C. E., Educational Psychology
WICKER, F. W., Educational Psychology
YATES, J. R., Educational Administration

College of Engineering:

ABRAHAM, J. A., Electrical and Computer Engineering
AGGARWAL, J. K., Electrical and Computer Engineering
ALLEN, D. T., Chemical Engineering
AMBLER, A. P., Electrical and Computer Engineering
ARAPOSTATHIS, A., Electrical and Computer Engineering
BABUSKA, I. M., Aerospace Engineering
BALDICK, R., Electrical and Computer Engineering
BANERJEE, S. K., Electrical and Computer Engineering
BARBER, K. S., Electrical and Computer Engineering
BARD, J. F., Mechanical Engineering
BARNES, J. W., Mechanical Engineering
BARR, R. E., Mechanical Engineering
BEAMAN, Jr, J. J., Mechanical Engineering
BECKER, E. B., Aerospace Engineering
BECKER, M. F., Electrical and Computer Engineering
BENNIGHOF, J. K., Aerospace Engineering
BISHOP, R. H., Aerospace Engineering
BOGARD, D. G., Mechanical Engineering
BONNECAZE, R. T., Chemical Engineering
BOSTICK, Jr, F. X., Electrical and Computer Engineering
BOURELL, D. L., Mechanical Engineering
BOVIK, A. C., Electrical and Computer Engineering
BREEN, J. E., Civil Engineering
BRYANT, M. D., Mechanical Engineering
BUCKMAN, A. B., Electrical and Computer Engineering
CAMPBELL, J. C., Electrical and Computer Engineering
CAREY, G. F., Aerospace Engineering
CHARBENEAU, R. J., Civil Engineering
CHEN, R. T., Electrical and Computer Engineering
COGDELL, J. R., Electrical and Computer Engineering
CORSI, R. L., Civil Engineering
CRAWFORD, M. E., Mechanical Engineering
CRAWFORD, M. M., Mechanical Engineering
CRAWFORD, R. H., Mechanical Engineering
DAWSON, C. N., Aerospace Engineering
DE VECIANA, G. A., Electrical and Computer Engineering
DEMKOWICZ, L. F., Aerospace Engineering
DEPPE, D. G., Electrical and Computer Engineering
DILLER, K. R., Biomedical Engineering
DODABALAPUR, A., Electrical and Computer Engineering
DOLLING, D. S., Aerospace Engineering
DRIGA, M. D., Electrical and Computer Engineering
EDGAR, T. F., Chemical Engineering
EKERDT, J. G., Chemical Engineering

ELLZEY, J. L., Mechanical Engineering
ENGELHARDT, M. D., Civil Engineering
FAHRENTHOLD, E. P., Mechanical Engineering
FLAKE, R. H., Electrical and Computer Engineering
FOWLER, D. W., Civil Engineering
FOWLER, W. T., Aerospace Engineering
FRANK, K. H., Civil Engineering
FREEMAN, B. D., Chemical Engineering
GARG, V. K., Electrical and Computer Engineering
GEORGIOU, G., Chemical Engineering
GHOSH, J., Electrical and Computer Engineering
GIBSON, Jr, G. E., Civil Engineering
GOODENOUGH, J. B., Mechanical Engineering
GRADY, W. M., Electrical and Computer Engineering
GRAY, K. E., Petroleum and Geosystems Engineering
GREEN, P. F., Chemical Engineering
HAAS, C. T., Civil Engineering
HALL, M. J., Mechanical Engineering
HALLOCK, G. A., Electrical and Computer Engineering
HAMILTON, M. F., Mechanical Engineering
HAYES, L. J., Aerospace Engineering
HO, P. S., Mechanical Engineering
HOWELL, J. R., Mechanical Engineering
HUGHES, T. J., Aerospace Engineering
HULL, D. G., Aerospace Engineering
JIRSA, J. O., Civil Engineering
JOHNSTON, K. P., Chemical Engineering
JOSE-YACAMAN, M., Chemical Engineering
KINNAS, S. A., Civil Engineering
KLINGNER, R. E., Civil Engineering
KOEN, B. V., Mechanical Engineering
KWONG, D.-L., Electrical and Computer Engineering
KYRIAKIDES, S., Aerospace Engineering
LAKE, L. W., Petroleum and Geosystems Engineering
LANDSBERGER, S., Mechanical Engineering
LAWLER, D. F., Civil Engineering
LEE, J. C., Electrical and Computer Engineering
LIECHTI, K. M., Aerospace Engineering
LILJESTRAND, H. M., Civil Engineering
LING, H., Electrical and Computer Engineering
LIPOVSKI, G. J., Electrical and Computer Engineering
LLOYD, D. R., Chemical Engineering
McKINNEY, D. C., Civil Engineering
MACHEMEHL, R. B., Civil Engineering
MAIDMENT, D. R., Civil Engineering
MALINA, Jr, J. F., Civil Engineering
MANTHIRAM, A., Mechanical Engineering
MARK, H. M., Aerospace Engineering
MASADA, G. Y., Mechanical Engineering
MATTHEWS, R. D., Mechanical Engineering
MEAR, M. E., Aerospace Engineering
MOON, T. J., Mechanical Engineering
MULLINS, C. B., Chemical Engineering
NEIKIRK, D. P., Electrical and Computer Engineering
NICHOLS, S. P., Mechanical Engineering
O'CONNOR, J. T., Civil Engineering
ODEN, J. T., Aerospace Engineering
PANDY, M. G., Biomedical Engineering
PANTON, R. L., Mechanical Engineering
PATT, Y. N., Electrical and Computer Engineering
PAUL, D. R., Chemical Engineering
PEARCE, J. A., Electrical and Computer Engineering
PEPPAS, N. A., Biomedical Engineering
PERRY, D. E., Electrical and Computer Engineering
PETERS, E. J., Petroleum and Geosystems Engineering
POPE, G. A., Petroleum and Geosystems Engineering

POWERS, Jr, E. J., Electrical and Computer Engineering
QIN, S. Z. J., Chemical Engineering
RALLS, K. M., Mechanical Engineering
RAPPAPORT, T. S., Electrical and Computer Engineering
RAVI-CHANDAR, K. A., Aerospace Engineering
REIBLE, D. D., Civil Engineering
RICHARDS KORTUM, R. R., Biomedical Engineering
ROCHELLE, G. T., Chemical Engineering
RODIN, G. J., Aerospace Engineering
ROSSEN, W. R., Petroleum and Geosystems Engineering
RYLANDER III, H. G., Biomedical Engineering
SANCHEZ, I. C., Chemical Engineering
SANDBERG, I. W., Electrical and Computer Engineering
SCHMIDT, P. S., Mechanical Engineering
SCHUTZ, B. E., Aerospace Engineering
SEPEHRNOORI, K., Petroleum and Geosystems Engineering
SHARMA, M. M., Petroleum and Geosystems Engineering
SORBER, C. A., Civil Engineering
SPEITEL, Jr, G. E., Civil Engineering
STEARMAN, R. O., Aerospace Engineering
STOKOE II, K. H., Civil Engineering
SWARTZLANDER, Jr, E. E., Electrical and Computer Engineering
TAPLEY, B. D., Aerospace Engineering
TASSOULAS, J. L., Civil Engineering
TESAR, D., Mechanical Engineering
VALVANO, J. W., Electrical and Computer Engineering
VANRENSBURG, W. C. J., Petroleum and Geosystems Engineering
VARGHESE, P. L., Aerospace Engineering
VLIET, G. C., Mechanical Engineering
WAGNER, T. J., Electrical and Computer Engineering
WALSER, R. M., Electrical and Computer Engineering
WALTON, C. M., Civil Engineering
WELCH, A. J., Biomedicalr Engineering
WHEELER, M. F., Aerospace Engineering
WILLSON, C. G., Chemical Engineering
WOMACK, B. F., Electrical and Computer Engineering
WOOD, K. L., Mechanical Engineering
WOOD, S. L., Civil Engineering
WRIGHT, S. G., Civil Engineering
YURA, J. A., Civil Engineering

College of Fine Arts:
ALLEN, G. D., Music
ANTOKELETZ, E. M., Music
BALTZER, R. A., Music
BARNITZ, J. E., Art and Art History
BEHAGUE, G. H., Music
BLOOM, M., Theatre and Dance
BOLIN, P. E., Art and Art History
BRICKENS, N. O., Music
BROCKETT, O. G., Theatre and Dance
BROOKS, R. L., Art and Art History
CHANDLER, B. G., Music
CLARKE, J. R., Art and Art History
COLES, T. R., Art and Art History
DALY, S. J., Art and Art History
DEMPSTER, D. J., Theatre and Dance
DESIMONE, R. A., Music
DOLAN, J. S., Theatre and Dance
DORN, F., Theatre and Dance
DUKE, R. A., Music
ERLMANN, V. F., Music
GARRETT, N. B., Music
GLAVAN, J. J., Theatre and Dance
GOODMAN, M. K., Art and Art History
GRANTHAM, D. J., Music
GUERRA, L. A., Music
HALE, K. J., Art and Art History
HELLMER, J. L., Music
HENDERSON, L. D., Art and Art History
HILLEY, M. F., Music

HOLLADAY, J. A., Art and Art History
HOLZMAN, A., Music
ISACKES, R. M., Theatre and Dance
JELLISON, J. A., Music
JENNINGS, C. A., Theatre and Dance
JUNKIN, J. F., Music
LEWIS, W. L., Music
LUCERO, A. L., Theatre and Dance
LUNDBERG, W. A., Art and Art History
MCFARLAND, L. D., Art and Art History
MARCH, H. C., Music
MARIANI, V. A., Art and Art History
MILLER, L. C., Theatre and Dance
MILLIKEN, G., Art and Art History
NEL, A., Music
NEUBERT, B. D., Music
NEUMEYER, D. P., Music
PINKSTON, R. F., Music
PITTEL, H. C., Music
RICHTER, G. A., Music
SASAKI, R. K., Music
SAWYER, M. L., Art and Art History
SCHMIDT, R. N., Theatre and Dance
SHIFF, R. A., Art and Art History
SLAWEK, S. M., Music
SMITH, J. C., Art and Art History
STUART, D. S., Art and Art History
TAYLOR, R. A., Music
TUSA, M. C., Music
ULBRICHT, J. W., Art and Art History
WELCHER, D. E., Music
WILEY, D. C., Music
WIMAN, L. R., Art and Art History
YOUNG, P. C., Music
ZEDER, S. L., Theatre and Dance

College of Liberal Arts:
ABBOUD, P. F., Middle Eastern Studies
ABZUG, R. H., History
ALBRECHT, D. G., Psychology
ALLAIRE, E. B., Philosophy
ANGEL, R. J., Sociology
ANGELELLI, I. A., Philosophy
ARENS, K. M., Germanic Studies
ARMSTRONG, D., Classics
ASHER, N. M., Philosophy
AYRES, J. B., English
BAKER, M.-F. J., French and Italian
BAR-ADON, A., Middle Eastern Studies
BARANY, Z. D., Government
BARNOUW, J., English
BEALER, G., Philosophy
BERNUCCI, L. M., Spanish and Portuguese
BERTELSEN, L., English
BINI, D., French and Italian
BIOW, D. G., French and Italian
BIRDSONG, D. P., French and Italian
BLOCKLEY, M. E., English
BONEVAC, D. A., Philosophy
BRAYBROOKE, D., Government
BRONARS, S. G., Economics
BROW, J. B., Anthropology
BROWN, J. C., History
BROWN, N. D., History
BUCHANAN II, B., Government
BUDZISZEWSKI, J., Government
BUMP, J. F., English
BUSS, A. H., Psychology
BUSS, D. M., Psychology
BUTZER, K. W., Geography
CABLE, T. M., English
CARLSON, C. L., Psychology
CARTER, J. C., Classics
CARTON, E. B., English
CARVER, L. D., English
CAUSEY, R. L., Philosophy
CAUVIN, J.-P. B., French and Italian
CHANG, S.-S., Asian Studies
CHARNEY, D. H., Rhetoric and Composition
COHEN, L. B., Psychology
COOPER, R. W., Economics
CORBAE, P. D., Economics
CREW, D. F., History
CULLINGFORD, E., English
CVETKOVICH, A., English
DACY, D. C., Economics

DAVIES, C. S., Geography
DAWSON, R. L., French and Italian
DEIGH, J., Philosophy
DIEHL, R. L., Psychology
DIETZ, H. A., Government
DOMJAN, M. P., Psychology
DONAHUE, F. E., Germanic Studies
DONALD, S., Economics
DOOLITTLE, W., Geography
DOUGHTY, R. W., Geography
DULLES, J. W. F., American Studies
DUSANSKY, R., Economics
EDLUND-BERRY, I. M., Classics
EDWARDS, D. V., Government
ELLISON, C. G., Sociology
ENELOW, J. M., Government
ENGLAND, N. C., Linguistics
FAIGLEY, L. L., English
FALOLA, O. O., History
FARRELL, J. P., English
FLORES, R. R., Anthropology
FREEMAN, G. P., Government
FRIEDMAN, A. W., English
FRISBIE, W. P., Sociology
FULLERTON, D., Economics
FURMAN, L. J., English
GAGARIN, M., Classics
GALINSKY, G. K., Classics
GALLE, O. R., Sociology
GARRISON, J. D., English
GEISLER III, W. S., Psychology
GERACI, V. J., Economics
GHANOONPARVAR, M., Middle Eastern Studies
GHOSE, Z. A., English
GILDEN, D. L., Psychology
GLADE, W. P., Economics
GLENN, N. D., Sociology
GOETZMANN, W. H., History
GONZALEZ-GERTH, M., Spanish and Portuguese
GONZALEZ-LIMA, F., Psychology
GRAHAM, D. B., English
HAKE, S., Germanic Studies
HAMERMESH, D. S., Economics
HANCOCK, I. F., Linguistics
HANKINSON, R. J., Philosophy
HANSEN, K. G., Asian Studies
HARLOW, B. J., English
HARMS, R. T., Linguistics
HEINZELMAN, K. O., English
HELMREICH, R. L., Psychology
HENDRICKS, K., Economics
HENRY, C. M., Government
HENSEY, F. G., Spanish and Portuguese
HIGGINS, K. M., Philosophy
HIGLEY, J. C., Government
HILFER, A. C., English
HILLMANN, M. C., Middle Eastern Studies
HINICH, M. J., Government
HINOJOSASMITH, R., English
HOBERMAN, J. M., Germanic Studies
HOCHBERG, H. I., Philosophy
HOLAHAN, C. J., Psychology
HOLDEN, G. W., Psychology
HOPKINS, A. G., History
HORN, J. M., Psychology
HUBBARD, T. K., Classics
HUMMER, R. A., Sociology
JACOBSOHN, G. J., Government
KALLET, L., Classics
KANE, R. H., Philosophy
KAPPELMAN, Jr, J. W., Anthropology
KAULBACH, E. N., English
KELLY, W. R., Sociology
KENDRICK, D. A., Economics
KING, R. D., Linguistics
KOLSTI, J. S., Slavic Languages and Literatures
KOONS, R. C., Philosophy
KROLL, J. H., Classics
KRONZ, F. M., Philosophy
KRUPPA, J. E., English
KURTZ, L. R., Sociology
LAMBRECHT, K. P., French and Italian
LAMPHEAR, J. E., History

LANGLOIS, J. H., Psychology
LaSALLE, P. N., English
LEVACK, B. P., History
LIEBOWITZ, H. A., Middle Eastern Studies
LIMON, J. E., English
LINDSTROM, N. E., Spanish and Portuguese
LIPPMANN, J. N., French and Italian
LITVAK, L., Spanish and Portuguese
LOUIS, W. R., History
LUJAN, M. E., Spanish and Portuguese
McFADDEN, D., Psychology
MACKAY, C. H., English
MacNEILAGE, P. F., Psychology
MAGNUSON, J. L., English
MANNERS, I. R., Geography
MARKMAN, A. B., Psychology
MARSHALL, S. E., Sociology
MARTINICH, A. P., Philosophy
MEIER, R. P., Linguistics
MEIKLE, J. L., American Studies
MENCHACA, M., Anthropology
MINAULT, G., History
MIROWSKY, J., Sociology
MONTREUIL, J.-P., French and Italian
MORGAN, M. G., Classics
MOURELATOS, A., Philosophy
MULLIN, J. A., Rhetoric and Composition
NAPIER, S. J., Asian Studies
NETHERCUT, W. R., Classics
NEWTON, A. Z., English
NORMAN, A. L., Economics
OLIVELLE, J. P., Asian Studies
OSHINSKY, D. A., History
PALAIMA, T. G., Classics
PANGLE, T. L., Government
PARKER, D. S., Classics
PELLS, R. H., History
PENNEBAKER, J. W., Psychology
PEREZ, F. L., Geography
PHILLIPS, S. H., Philosophy
POTTER, J. E., Sociology
PRINDLE, D. F., Government
PULLUM, T. W., Sociology
RAMIREZ III, M., Psychology
RAPPAPORT, G. C., Slavic Languages and Literature
REBHORN, Jr, W. A., English
RENWICK, R. D., English
ROBERTS, B. E., Government
ROBERTS, B. R., Sociology
ROSS, C. E., Sociology
ROSSMAN, C. R., English
RUMRICH, J. P., English
RUSZKIEWICZ, J. J., Rhetoric and Composition
SAINSBURY, R. M., Philosophy
SARKAR, S., Philosophy
SCHALLERT, T. J., Psychology
SCHEICK, W. J., English
SEUNG, T. K., Philosophy
SHELMERDINE, C. W., Classics
SHERZER, D. M., French and Italian
SHERZER, J. F., Anthropology
SHUMWAY, N., Spanish and Portuguese
SINGH, D., Psychology
SJOBERG, G. A., Sociology
SLESNICK, D. T., Economics
SMITH, C. S., Linguistics
SOLE, C. A., Spanish and Portuguese
SOLOMON, R. C., Philosophy
STAFFORD, M. C., Sociology
STAHL II, D. O., Economics
STINCHCOMBE, M. B., Economics
STROSS, B. M., Anthropology
SUSSMAN, H. M., Linguistics
SWAFFAR, J. K., Germanic Studies
SWANN, Jr, W. B., Psychology
TELCH, M. J., Psychology
TRIMBLE, J. R., English
TULLY, W. A., History
TWINAM, A., History
TYE, M., Philosophy
TYLER, R. C., History
UMBERSON, D. J., Sociology
VAN OLPHEN, H. H., Asian Studies
WAGNER, R. H., Government

WALKER, J., Rhetoric and Composition
WALKER, J. E., History
WALKER, S. S., Anthropology
WALTERS, S. K., Linguistics
WARD, P., Sociology
WARR, E. M., Sociology
WEINSTOCK, J. M., Germanic Studies
WEVILL, D. A., English
WEYLAND, K. G., Government
WHIGHAM, Jr, F. F., English
WHITBREAD, T. B., English
WHITE, L. M., Classics
WILCZYNSKI, W., Psychology
WILLIAMS, C. L., Sociology
WILSON, P. W., Economics
WILSON, S. M., Anthropology
WINSHIP, M. B., English
WOLITZ, S. L., French and Italian
WOODBURY, A. C., Linguistics
WOODRUFF, P. B., Philosophy
ZIMIC, S., Spanish and Portuguese
ZONN, L. E., Geography

College of Natural Sciences:

ANSLYN, E. V., Chemistry and Biochemistry
ANTONIEWICZ, P. R., Physics
APPLING, D. R., Chemistry and Biochemistry
ARBOGAST, T. J., Mathematics
ARMENDARIZ, E. P., Mathematics
ARTZT, K. J., Molecular Genetics and Microbiology
BAJAJ, C. L., Computer Sciences
BANNER, J. L., Geological Sciences
BARBARA, P. F., Chemistry and Biochemistry
BARD, A. J., Chemistry and Biochemistry
BASH, F. N., Astronomy
BATORY, D. S., Computer Sciences
BAULD, N. L., Chemistry and Biochemistry
BECKNER, W., Mathematics
BENGTSON, R. D., Physics
BENNETT, P. C., Geological Sciences
BERK, H. L., Physics
BICHTELER, K. R., Mathematics
BITTNER, G. D., Neurobiology
BOHM, A. R., Physics
BOSE, H. R., Molecular Genetics and Microbiology
BOYER, R. S., Computer Sciences
BRAND, J. J., Molecular Cell and Development Biology
BRILEY, M. E., Human Ecology
BRODBELT, J. S., Chemistry and Biochemistry
BRONSON, F. H., Integrative Biology
BROWN, Jr, R. M., Molecular Genetics and Microbiology
BROWNE, J. C., Computer Sciences
BULL, J. J., Integrative Biology
BUSKEY, E. J., Marine Science
CAFFARELLI, L. A., Mathematics
CAMPION, A., Chemistry and Biochemistry
CARLSON, W. D., Geological Sciences
CHENEY, E. W., Mathematics
CHIU, C. B., Physics
CLINE, A. K., Computer Sciences
CLOOS, M. P., Geological Sciences
COKER, W. R., Physics
COWLEY, A. H., Chemistry and Biochemistry
CREWS, D. P., Integrative Biology
DANIEL, J. W., Mathematics
DAVIS, R. E., Chemistry and Biochemistry
DE LA LLAVE, R., Mathematics
DE LOZANNE, A. L., Physics
DICUS, D. A., Physics
DINERSTEIN, H. L., Astronomy
DISTLER, J., Physics
DOWNER, M. W., Physics
DRUMMOND, W. E., Physics
DUDLEY, J. P., Molecular Genetics and Microbiology
DUNTON, K. H., Marine Science
DURBIN, J. R., Mathematics

EARHART, C. F., Molecular Genetics and Microbiology
ELLINGTON, A., Chemistry and Biochemistry
EMERSON II, E. A., Computer Sciences
ENGQUIST, B., Mathematics
ERSKINE, J. L., Physics
EVANS II, N. J., Astronomy
FINK, M., Physics
FISCHLER, W., Physics
FISHER, W. L., Geological Sciences
FOWLER, N. L., Integrative Biology
FREED, D. S., Mathematics
FREELAND, J. H., Human Ecology
FREEMAN, G. L., Integrative Biology
FROMMHOLD, L. W., Physics
FUSSELL, D. S., Computer Sciences
GAMBA, I. M., Mathematics
GARDNER, W. S., Marine Science
GENTLE, K. W., Physics
GERTH III, F. E., Mathematics
GILBERT, J. C., Chemistry and Biochemistry
GILBERT, J. E., Mathematics
GILBERT, L. E., Integrative Biology
GLEESON, A. M., Physics
GOMPF, R. E., Mathematics
GORDON, C. M., Mathematics
GOUDA, M. G., Computer Sciences
GRAND, S. P., Geological Sciences
GUY, Jr, W. T., Mathematics
HACKERT, M. L., Chemistry and Biochemistry
HAMRICK, G. C., Mathematics
HARRIS, R. A., Neurobiology
HARSHEY, R. M., Molecular Genetics and Microbiology
HARVEY, P. M., Astronomy
HAZELTINE, R. D., Physics
HEINZEN, D. J., Physics
HEITMANN, R. C., Mathematics
HERRIN, D. L., Molecular Cell and Development Biology
HILLIS, D. M., Integrative Biology
HOFFMANN, G. W., Physics
HOLCOMBE, J. A., Chemistry and Biochemistry
HORTON, Jr, C. W., Physics
HUNT, Jr, W. A., Computer Sciences
HUSTON, A. C., Human Ecology
HUSTON, T. L., Human Ecology
IVERSON, B. L., Chemistry and Biochemistry
JACOBVITZ, D. B., Human Ecology
JAFFE, D. T., Astronomy
JANSEN, R. K., Integrative Biology
JAYARAM, M., Molecular Genetics and Microbiology
JOHNSON, K., Chemistry and Biochemistry
JOHNSTON, D., Neurobiology
JONES, R. A., Chemistry and Biochemistry
KALTHOFF, K. O., Molecular Cell and Development Biology
KAPLUNOVSKY, V., Physics
KEEL, S. M., Mathematics
KETO, J. W., Physics
KIRKPATRICK, M. A., Integrative Biology
KITTO, G. B., Chemistry and Biochemistry
KLEINMAN, L., Physics
KLINE, K., Human Ecology
KOCH, H. A., Mathematics
KOCUREK, G. A., Geological Sciences
KORMENDY, J., Astronomy
KRISCHE, M. J., Chemistry and Biochemistry
KRUG, R. M., Molecular Genetics and Microbiology
KUIPERS, B. J., Computer Sciences
KUMAR, P., Astronomy
KYLE, J. R., Geological Sciences
La CLAIRE II, J. W., Molecular Cell and Development Biology
LACY, J. H., Astronomy
LAGOW, R. J., Chemistry and Biochemistry
LAGOWSKI, J. J., Chemistry and Biochemistry

LAGOWSKI, J. M., Neurobiology
LAM, S. S., Computer Sciences
LAMBOWITZ, A., Molecular Genetics and Microbiology
LANG, K., Physics
LARIMER, J. L., Neurobiology
LAUDE, D. A., Chemistry and Biochemistry
LEVIN, D. A., Integrative Biology
LIFSCHITZ, V., Computer Sciences
LONG, L. E., Geological Sciences
LOOP, R., Human Ecology
LUECKE, J. E., Mathematics
MABRY, T. J., Molecular Cell and Development Biology
McADAM, S. J., Mathematics
McBRIDE, E. F., Geological Sciences
McDEVITT, J. T., Chemistry and Biochemistry
MACDONALD, A. H., Physics
MACDONALD, P. M., Molecular Cell and Development Biology
MAGNUS, P. D., Chemistry and Biochemistry
MARDER, M. P., Physics
MARKERT, J. T., Physics
MARTIN, S. F., Chemistry and Biochemistry
MATZNER, R. A., Physics
MAUSETH, J. D., Integrative Biology
MEYER, R. J., Molecular Genetics and Microbiology
MIIKKULAINEN, R. P., Computer Sciences
MISRA, J., Computer Sciences
MOK, A. K., Computer Sciences
MOLINEUX, I. J., Molecular Genetics and Microbiology
MONTAGNA, P. A., Marine Science
MOONEY, R. J., Computer Sciences
MOORE, C. F., Physics
MOORE II, J. S., Computer Sciences
MORRISON, P. J., Physics
MOSHER, S., Geological Sciences
NAKAMURA, Y., Geological Sciences
NIU, Q., Physics
NOVAK, Jr, G. S., Computer Sciences
OAKES, M. E. L., Physics
ODELL, E. W., Mathematics
PALKA, B. P., Mathematics
PAYNE, S. M., Molecular Genetics and Microbiology
PIANKA, E. R., Integrative Biology
PLAXTON, C. G., Computer Sciences
POLLAK, G. D., Neurobiology
PORTER, B. W., Computer Sciences
RADIN, C. L., Mathematics
RAIZEN, M. G., Physics
RAMACHANDRAN, V., Computer Sciences
REICHL, L. E., Physics
REID, A. W., Mathematics
RICHARDSON, R. H., Integrative Biology
RIGGS II, A. F., Neurobiology
RILEY, P. J., Physics
RITCHIE, J. L., Physics
ROBERTUS, J. D., Chemistry and Biochemistry
ROBINSON, E. L., Astronomy
ROSENTHAL, H. P., Mathematics
ROSSKY, P. J., Chemistry and Biochemistry
ROUX, Jr, S. J., Molecular Cell and Development Biology
ROWE, T. B., Geological Sciences
RYAN, M. J., Integrative Biology
SADUN, L. A., Mathematics
SALTMAN, D. J., Mathematics
SANDERS, B. G., Molecular Genetics and Microbiology
SCALO, J. M., Astronomy
SCHIEVE, W. C., Physics
SCHWITTERS, R. F., Physics
SEN, M. K., Geological Sciences
SESSLER, J. L., Chemistry and Biochemistry
SHANKLAND, S. M., Molecular, Cellular and Developmental Biology
SHAPIRO, P. R., Astronomy
SHARP, Jr, J. M., Geological Sciences
SHIELDS, G. A., Astronomy

SHIH, C.-K., Physics
SIMPSON, B. B., Integrative Biology
SINGER, M. C., Integrative Biology
SITZ, G. O., Physics
SMITH, M. K., Mathematics
SNEDEN, C. A., Astronomy
SOUGDANIDIS, P. E., Mathematics
SPRINKLE, J. T., Geological Sciences
STANTON, J. F., Chemistry and Biochemistry
STARBIRD, M. P., Mathematics
STEEL, R. J., Geological Sciences
SUDARSHAN, G., Physics
SURRA, C. A., Human Ecology
SWIFT, J. B., Physics
SWINNEY, H. L., Physics
SZANISZLO, P. J., Molecular Genetics and Microbiology
TATE, J. T., Mathematics
TATHAM, R. H., Geological Sciences
THOMAS, P., Marine Science
THOMPSON, W. J., Neurobiology
TREISMAN, P. U., Mathematics
TUCKER, P. W., Molecular Genetics and Microbiology
UDAGAWA, T., Physics
UHLENBECK, K., Mathematics
VAALER, J. D., Mathematics
VAN DE GEIJN, R. A., Computer Sciences
VIN, H. M., Computer Sciences
VISHIK, M. M., Mathematics
VOLOCH, J. F., Mathematics
WALKER, J. R., Molecular Genetics and Microbiology
WARNOW, T., Computer Sciences
WEBBER, S. E., Chemistry and Biochemistry
WEINBERG, S., Physics
WHEELER, J. C., Astronomy
WHITE, J. M., Chemistry and Biochemistry
WILLIS, R. A., Human Ecology
WILLS, D., Astronomy
WILSON, C. R., Geological Sciences
WINGET, D. E., Astronomy
WYATT, R. E., Chemistry and Biochemistry
XIN, J., Mathematics
XU, B., Human Ecology
ZAKON, H. H., Neurobiology
ZARIPHOPOULOU, T., Mathematics
ZUCKERMAN, D. I., Computer Sciences

College of Pharmacy:

ABELL, C. W.
BUSSEY, H. I.
COMBS, A. B.
CRISMON, M. L.
DAVIS, P. J.
ERICKSON, C. K.
GONZALES, R. A.
KEHRER, J. P.
KOELLER, J. M.
KUHN, J. G.
LITTLEFIELD, L. C.
LIU, H.-W.
McGINITY, J. W.
PEARLMAN, R.
RASCATI, K. L.
SHEPHERD, M. D.
STAVCHANSKY, S. A.
TALBERT, Jr, R. L.
WHITMAN, C. P.
WILCOX, R. E.

ATTACHED RESEARCH ORGANIZATIONS

Animal Resources Center: Dir JERRY FINEG.

Accessibility Institute: Dir JOHN M. SLATIN.

Applied Research Laboratories: Exec. Dir CLARK PENROD.

Bureau of Economic Geology: Dir SCOTT TINKER.

Center for Agile Technology: Dir DAVID A. BRANT.

Center for Electromechanics: Dir ROBERT HEBNER.

Center for Strategic and Innovative Technologies: Dir Dr STEVE KORNGUTH.

Harry Huntt Ransom Humanities Research Center: Dir THOMAS F. STALEY.

IC² Institute: Dir JOHN SIBLEY BUTLER.

Institute for Advanced Technology: Dir HARRY D. FAIR.

Institute for Computational Engineering and Sciences (ICES): Dir J. TINSLEY ODEN.

National Center for Educational Accountability (NCEA): Exec. Dir MICHAEL HUDSON.

Texas Advanced Computing Center: Dir Dr JOHN R. BOISSEAU.

ATTACHED TO THE RED MCCOMBS SCHOOL OF BUSINESS

Bureau of Business Research: Dir ROBERT A. PETERSON.

C. Aubrey Smith Center for Auditing Education and Research: Dir WILLIAM R. KINNEY.

Center for Business Decision Analysis: Dir TIMOTHY W. RUEFLI.

Center for Business, Technology and Law: Co-Dir SIRKKA JARVENPAA.

Center for International Business Education and Research: Dir DAVID PLATT.

Center for Organizations Research: Dir JANET DUKERICH.

Center for Research in Electronic Commerce: Dir ANDREW WHINSTON.

Center for Risk Management and Insurance: Dir PATRICK L. BROCKETT.

Manufacturing Systems Center: Dir STEVE GILBERT.

ATTACHED TO THE LBJ SCHOOL OF PUBLIC AFFAIRS

Policy Research Institute: Dir ROBERT H. WILSON.

Ray Marshall Center for the Study of Human Resources: Dir CHRISTOPHER T. KING.

ATTACHED TO THE SCHOOL OF SOCIAL WORK

Center for Social Work Research: Dir RUTH G. McROY.

ATTACHED TO THE COLLEGE OF COMMUNICATION

Annette Strauss Institute for Civic Participation: Dir RODERICK P. HART.

ATTACHED TO THE COLLEGE OF ENGINEERING

Advanced Manufacturing Center: Dir JOHN R. HOWELL.

Bureau of Engineering Research: Dir BEN G. STREETMAN.

Center for Advanced Research in Software Engineering: Dir SUZANNE BARBER.

Center for Aeromechanics Research: Dir PHILIP L. VARGHESE.

Center for Biological and Medical Engineering: Dir LISA BRANNON-PEPPAS (Center is also attached to the College of Natural Sciences).

Center for Energy and Environmental Resources: Dir DAVID ALLEN.

Center for Mechanics of Solids, Structures and Materials: Dir STELIOS KYRIAKIDES.

Center for Petroleum and Geosystems Engineering: Dir GARY A. POPE.

Center for Research in Water Resources: Dir DAVID MAIDMENT.

Center for Space Research: Dir BYRON D. TAPLEY.

Center for Transportation Research: Dir RANDY MACHEMEHL.

Computer Engineering Research Center: Dir JACOB A. ABRAHAM.

Construction Industry Institute: Dir Maj.-Gen. HANS VAN WINKLE.

Geotechnical Engineering Center: Dir STEPHEN G. WRIGHT.

Microelectronics Research Center: Dir SANJAY BANERJEE.

Offshore Technology Research Center: Dir SPYROS A. KINNAS.

Phil M. Ferguson Structural Engineering Laboratory: Dir KARL FRANK.

Texas Materials Institute: Dir DONALD R. PAUL.

ATTACHED TO THE COLLEGE OF LIBERAL ARTS

Center for Applied Research in Economics: Dir RICHARD DUSANSKY.

Center for Criminology and Criminal Justice Research: Dir WILLIAM R. KELLY.

Center for Perceptual Systems: Dir WILSON S. GEISLER.

Center for Studies in Texas History: Dir RON C. TYLER.

Institute for Classical Archaeology: Dir JOSEPH C. CARTER.

Institute for the Study of Antiquity and Christian Origins: Dir Dr L. MICHAEL WHITE.

Linguistics Research Center: Dir WINFRED P. LEHMANN.

Population Research Center: Dir ROBERT A. HUMMER.

Teresa Lozano Long Institute of Latin American Studies: Dir NICOLAS SHUMWAY.

Texas Archeological Research Laboratory: Dir DARRELL CREEL.

ATTACHED TO THE COLLEGE OF NATURAL SCIENCES

Artificial Intelligence Laboratory: Dir BRUCE W. PORTER.

Biochemical Institute: Dir MARVIN L. HACKERT.

Brackenridge Field Laboratory: Dir LAWRENCE E. GILBERT.

Center for Behavioral Neuroendocrinology: Dir DAVID CREWS.

Center for Computational Biology and Bioinformatics: Dir DAVID HILLIS.

Center for Learning Memory: Dir DANIEL JOHNSTON.

Center for Materials Chemistry: Dir JOHN M. WHITE.

Center for Nano- and Molecular Science and Technology: Dir PAUL BARBARA.

Center for Nonlinear Dynamics: Dir HARRY L. SWINNEY.

Center for Particle Physics: Dir ROY F. SCHWITTERS.

Center for Relativity: Dir RICHARD A. MATZNER.

Center for Structural Biology: Dir JON ROBERTUS.

Center for Systems and Synthetic Biology: Dir (vacant).

Charles A. Dana Center for Mathematics and Science Education: Dir P. URI TREISMAN.

Culture Collection of Algae: Dir JERRY BRAND.

Environmental Science Institute: Dir JAY BANNER.

Fusion Research Center: Dir KENNETH W. GENTLE.

Ilya Prigogine Center for Studies in Statistical Mechanics and Complex Systems: Dir LINDA REICHL (acting).

Institute for Cellular and Molecular Biology: Dir ALAN LAMBOWITZ.

Institute for Fusion Studies: Dir JAMES VAN DAM.

Institute for Geophysics: Dir PAUL STOFFA.

Institute for Neuroscience: Dir DANIEL JOHNSTON (Institute is also attached to the College of Pharmacy).

Institute for Theoretical Chemistry: Dir PETER ROSSKY.

Laboratory of Electrochemistry: Dir ALLEN J. BARD.

Marine Science Institute: Dir WAYNE S. GARDNER.

McDonald Observatory: Dir DAVID LAMBERT.

Plant Resources Center: Dir BERYL SIMPSON.

Texas Natural Science Center: Dir EDWARD C. THERIOT.

Waggoner Center for Alcohol and Addiction Research: Dir R. ADRON HARRIS.

Weinberg Theory Group: Dir STEVEN WEINBERG.

ATTACHED TO THE COLLEGE OF PHARMACY

Center for Molecular and Cellular Toxicology: Dir JAMES P. KEHRER.

Drug Dynamics Institute: Dir JAMES W. McGINITY.

University of Texas at Arlington

POB 19125, Arlington, TX 76019

Telephone: (817) 272-2101

E-mail: public.affairs@uta.edu

Internet: www.uta.edu

Founded 1895 Arlington College, reorganized as a component of the University of Texas 1965

President: Dr ROBERT E. WITT

Provost: Dr GEORGE C. WRIGHT

Senior Vice-President for Finance and Administration: M. DAN WILLIAMS

Vice-President for Undergraduate Academic and Student Affairs: Dr MARY RIDGWAY

Vice-President for Student Enrollment Services: SHIRLEY BINDER

Vice-President for Development: ANNE ABBE

Librarian: THOMAS WILDING

Library of 1,000,000 vols

Number of teachers: 997

Number of students: 21,200

DEANS

Liberal Arts: Dr RUTH GROSS (acting)

Science: Dr VERNE COX (acting)

Business: Dr DAN WORRELL (acting)

Engineering: Dr RON BAILEY

Science: Dr NEAL SMATRESK

Graduate School: Dr DALE ANDERSON

School of Social Work: Dr SANTOS HERNANDEZ

Architecture: EDWARD BAUM

Nursing: Dr ELIZABETH POSTER

School of Urban and Public Affairs: Dr RICHARD L. COLE

Center for Professional Teacher Education: Dr JEANNE GERLACH

University of Texas at Brownsville and Texas Southernmost College

80 Fort Brown, Brownsville, TX 78520

Telephone: (956) 5448200

Fax: (956) 5448832

E-mail: admissions@utb.edu

Internet: www.utb.edu

Founded 1991 as partnership between University of Texas at Brownsville (f. 1973) and Texas Southernmost College (f. 1926)

President: Dr JULIET V. GARCÍA

Provost and Vice-President (Academic Affairs): Dr JOSÉ G. MARTÍN

Vice-President (Business Affairs): ROSEMARY MARTÍNEZ

Vice-President (Administration and Partnership Affairs): Dr JOHN RONNAU

Vice-President (Student Affairs): Dr HILDA SILVA

Vice-President (Institutional Advancement): Dr WILLIAM STRONG

Vice-President (External Affairs): Dr TONY ZAVALETA

Registrar: AL BARREDA

Library Director: DOUGLAS FERRIER

Library of 170,000 vols

Number of teachers: 357

Number of students: 9,974

DEANS

College of Liberal Arts: Dr FARHAT IFTEKHAR-UDDIN

College of Science, Mathematics and Technology: Dr DIMITRIOS A. SOTIROPOULOS

School of Business: Dr BETSY BOZE

School of Education: Dr SYLVIA PEÑA

School of Health Sciences: Dr ELDON NELSON

University of Texas at Dallas

800 West Campbell Rd Richardson, TX 75080

Telephone: (972) 883-2111

Fax: (972) 883-2237

E-mail: utdallas@utdallas.edu

Internet: www.utdallas.edu

State control

Language of instruction: English

Founded 1969 formerly Southwest Center for Advanced Studies

Academic year: September to August

President: Dr DAVID DANIEL

Executive Vice-President and Provost: Dr B. HOBSON WILDENTHAL

Vice-President for Business Affairs (vacant)

Vice-President for Research and Economic Development: Dr. DA HSUAN FENG

Vice-President for Student Affairs: Dr DARRELENE RACHAVONG

Associate Vice-President, Budget: MITZI MONEY

Director of Enrollment Services (vacant)

Director of Admissions (vacant)

Registrar: KAREN JARRELL

Director of Libraries: Dr LARRY D. SALL

Library of 1,123,848 vols, serial backfiles, and other paper materials

Number of teachers: 696

Number of students: 14,480

Publications: *Issues in Science and Technology* (quarterly), *Political Research Quarterly*, *Public Administration Review* (6 a year), *Translation Review* (3 a year)

DEANS

School of Arts and Humanities: Dr DENNIS M. KRATZ

School of Behavioural and Brain Sciences: Dr BERT MOORE

Erik Jonsson School of Engineering and Computer Science: Dr ROBERT HELMS

School of General Studies: Dr GEORGE W. FAIR

School of Management: Dr HASAN PIRKUL

School of Natural Sciences and Mathematics:
Dr JOHN FERRARIS
School of Social Sciences: Dr BRIAN BERRY
Graduate Studies: Dr AUSTIN CUNNINGHAM
Undergraduate Studies: Dr J. MICHAEL COLE-
MAN

PROGRAMME HEADS

(Graduate Programmes except where indicated)

Accounting and Information Management:
Dr WILLIAM CREADY
Audiology: Dr ROSS ROESER
Chemistry: Dr JOHN FERRARIS
Cognition and Neuroscience: Dr RICHARD
GOLDEN
Communication Sciences and Disorders: Dr
ROBERT D. STILLMAN
Computer Science: Dr D. T. HUYNH
Economics: Dr BARRY SELDON
Electrical Engineering: Dr GERALD BURNHAM
Humanities: Dr W. JACKSON RUSHING
Geosciences: Dr JOHN FERGUSON
Human Development and Early Childhood
Disorders: Dr MARGARET OWEN
Interdisciplinary Studies: Dr GEORGE FAIR
Management Sciences: Dr FRANK BASS
Mathematical Sciences: Dr M. ALI HOOSHYAR
Molecular and Cell Biology: Dr DONALD GRAY
Physics: Dr XINCHOU LOU
Psychological Sciences: Dr DUANE BUHRME-
STER
Public Policy and Political Economy: Dr
RICHARD SCOTCH
Science/Mathematics Education: Dr CYNTHIA
E. LEDBETTER

DIRECTORS

International Business Center: (vacant)
Center for Continuing Education: (vacant)
Center for International Accounting Devel-
opment: Dr ADOLPH ENTHOVEN
Center for Lithospheric Studies: Dr GEORGE
MCMECHAN
Center for Quantum Electronics: Dr CARL
COLLINS
William B. Hanson Center for Space
Sciences: Dr RODERICK HEELIS
Center for Translation Studies: Dr RAINER
SCHULTE
Morris Hite Center for Product Development
and Marketing Science: Dr FRANK BASS
Centre for System Communications and
Signal Processing: Dr LOUIS R. HUNT
Teacher Education Certification Officer: ANN
SHOFFSTALL
Photonic Technology and Engineering Cen-
ter: Dr CYRUS D. CANTRELL
Center for Applied Biology: Dr LEE BULLA
Teacher Development Center: Dr SCHERRY
JOHNSON
Center for Communications and Learning:
Dr GEORGE FAIR
Bruton Center for Development Studies: Dr
PAUL JARGOWSKY
Cybersecurity and Emergency Preparedness
Institute: Dr E. DOUGLAS HARRIS
Institute for Interactive Arts and Engineer-
ing: Dr THOMAS LINEHAN
Center for Advanced Telecommunications
Systems and Services: Dr IMRICH CHLAM-
TAC
Center for US–Mexico Studies: Dr RODOLFO
HERNANDEZ GUERRERO
Embedded Software Center: Dr FAROKH B.
BASTANI
Callier Center for Communication Disorders
Center for Integrated Circuits and Systems:
Dr PORAS BALSARA
NanoTech Institute: Dr RAY BAUGHMAN
Sickle Cell Disease Research Center: Dr
BETTY PACE
Center for Applications for Specific Systems
and Software Engineering: Dr FAROKH B.
BASTANI

PROFESSORS

ABDI, H.
AIKEN, C.
ALI, A.
AMMANN, L.
ARGYROS, A.
ASSMANN, P.
BALKUS, K.
BALSARA, P.
BAMBACH, C.
BARTLETT, J.
BASS, R.
BASTANI, F.
BAUGHMAN, R.
BERRY, B.
BHATTACHARYA, J.
BLANCHARD, A.
BOWER, T.
BRETTELL, R.
BRIGGS, R.
BUHRMESTER, D.
BULLA, L.
BUTTS, T.
CALDWELL, R.
CANTRELL, C.
CHAMPAGNE, A.
CHANDRASEKARAN, R.
CHANEY, R.
CHANNELL, D.
CHAPMAN, S.
CLARKE, H.
COLLINS, C.
CONSTANTINESCU, T.
CURCHACK, F.
DAY, T.
DESS, G.
DOWLING, W.
DRAPER, R.
DUMAS, L.
EDMUNDS, R.
ELLIOTT, E.
ENTHOVEN, A.
FAIR, G.
FARAGO, A.
FENYVES, E.
FERRARIS, J.
FONSEKA, J.
FORD, D.
FRENSLEY, W.
GADDIS, P.
GLOSSER, R.
GNADE, B.
GOLDEN, R.
GOODMAN, S.
GRAY, D.
GUPTA, G.
HAMBLY, G.
HARPHAM, E.
HEELIS, R.
HELMS, C.
HICKS, D.
HOFFMAN, J.
HOOSHYAR, M.
HULSE, R.
HUNT, L.
HUYNH, D.
IZEN, J.
JACOB, V.
JERGER, S.
KEHTARNAVAZ, N.
KEMPF-LEONARD, K.
KIASALEH, K.
KIEL, L.
KONSTANS, C.
KRATZ, D.
LEAF, M.
LEE, G.
LIEBOWITZ, S.
LINEHAN, T.
LOIZOU, P.
LOU, X.
MACDIARMID, A.
MACFARLANE, D.
MAJUMDAR, S.
MALOBERTI, F.

MANTON, W.
MCMECHAN, G.
MELTON, L.
MOLDOVAN, D.
MOLLER, A.
MOOKERJEE, V.
NADIN, M.
NIU, S.
NTAFOS, S.
OBER, R.
O'TOOLE, A.
OVERZET, L.
OWEN, M.
OZSVATH, Z.
OZSVATH, I.
PERVIN, W.
PESSAGNO, E.
PRAGER, K.
RABE, S.
RADHAKRISHNAN, S.
RAGHAVACHARI, B.
RAO, R.
REDMAN, T.
REITZER, L.
REYNOLDS, R.
RICCIO, T.
RINDLER, W.
RODRIGUEZ, R.
ROESER, R.
SANTROCK, J.
SARKAR, S.
SCHULTE, R.
SCOTCH, R.
SELDON, B.
SERFLING, R.
SETHI, S.
SHA, H.
SHERRY, A.
SRISKANDARAJAH, C.
STECKE, K.
STERN, R.
STEWART, M.
STILLMAN, R.
SUDBOROUGH, I.
TAMIL, L.
THURAISINGHAM, B.
TINSLEY, B.
TOBEY, E.
TRACY, P.
TRUEMPER, K.
TURI, J.
TURNER, F.
ULATOWSKA, H.
VAN KLEECK, A.
VIJVERBERG, W.
WALLACE, R.
WATSON, D.
WIORKOWSKI, J.
ZAKHIDOV, A.
ZHENG, S.
ZHOU, D.

ATTACHED INSTITUTE

**Callier Center for Communication Dis-
orders:** 1966 Inwood Rd, Dallas, TX 75235;
Dir Dr ROSS ROESER.

University of Texas at El Paso

El Paso, TX 79968-0500
Telephone: (915) 747-5000
E-mail: uc@utep.edu
Internet: www.utep.edu

Founded 1913 as Texas School of Mines and
Metallurgy; name changed to Texas Western College 1949; current name adopted
1967

President: Dr DIANA NATALICIO
Vice-President for Academic Affairs: Dr
STEPHEN RITER
Vice-President for Finance and Administra-
tion: JUAN SANDOVAL
Dean of Students: Dr WILLIAM SCHAFER
Director of Admissions: IRMA RUBIO
Librarian: PATRICIA A. PHILLIPS

Library: see Libraries
Number of teachers: 923
Number of students: 16,220

Publications: *Southwest Journal of Business and Economics* (occasional), *Nova* (monthly (September to May)), *Southwestern Studies* (occasional), *The Prospector* (2 a week), *Horizons, Shangri-La*

DEANS

Education: Dr ARTURO PACHECO
Engineering: Dr ANDREW H. SWIFT
Liberal Arts: Dr HOWARD DAUDISTEL
Sciences: Dr THOMAS E. BRADY
Business Administration: Dr CHARLES CRESPY
Graduate School: Dr CHARLES AMBLER
Nursing: Dr JOHN CONWAY

University of Texas Pan American

Edinburg, TX 78539

Telephone: (956) 381-2100
Fax: (956) 381-2150
E-mail: info@panam.edu
Internet: www.panam.edu

Founded 1927 as Edinburg College; became Edinburg Junior College 1933, Edinburg Regional College 1948, Pan American College 1952, Pan American University 1971; present name 1989

Academic year: September to August

President: Dr MIGUEL A. NEVÁREZ
Director of Admissions: DAVID ZUNIGA
Director of Financial Aid: MICHELLE ALVARADO
Director of Library: LAWRENCE CAYLOR

Library of 536,204 vols
Number of teachers: 601
Number of students: 14,399.

University of Texas of the Permian Basin

Odessa, TX 79762

Telephone: (915) 552-2000
Internet: www.utpb.edu

Founded 1969

President: CHARLES A. SORBER

Library of 763,000 vols
Number of students: 2,217

DEANS

College of Arts and Sciences: Dr JAMES OLSON
School of Education: Dr PETE IENATSCH
School of Business: Dr GARY KLEIN

University of Texas at San Antonio

6900 N Loop 1604W, San Antonio, TX 782490619

Telephone: (210) 4584011
Fax: (210) 4584117
E-mail: prospects@utsa.edu
Internet: www.utsa.edu

Founded 1969

President: Dr RICARDO ROMO
Provost and Vice-President (Academic Affairs): Dr GUY H. BAILEY
Vice-President (Student Affairs): Dr ROSALIE AMBROSINO
Vice-President (Business Affairs): DAVID R. LARSON
Vice-President (Administration) and Interim Vice-President (University Advancement): GERARD H. BARLOCO
Vice-President (University Advancement) (vacant)
Vice-President (Extended Services): Dr JUDE VALDEZ
Dean of Libraries: Dr MICHAEL KELLY

Number of teachers: 389
Number of students: 18,606 (15,795 undergraduate, 2,811 graduate)

DEANS

College of Business: Dr BRUCE BUBLITZ
College of Education and Human Development: Dr BLANDINA CARDENAS
College of Engineering: Dr ZORICA PANTIC-TANNER
College of Liberal and Fine Arts: Dr DANIEL J. GELO
College of Public Policy: Dr JESSE T. ZAPATA
College of Sciences: Dr WILLIAM SCOUTEN
School of Architecture: JULIUS M. GRIBOU

University of Texas at Tyler

3900 University Blvd, Tyler, TX 75799

Telephone: (903) 5667000
Fax: (903) 5667068
E-mail: info@mail.uttyl.edu
Internet: www.uttyler.edu

Founded 1971 as Tyler State College; present name 1979

Academic year: August to May

President: Dr RODNEY H. MABRY
Provost and Vice-President (Academic Affairs): Dr RICHARD OSBURN
Vice-President (Student Affairs and External Relations): Dr DALE LUNSFORD
Vice-President (University Advancement): NANCY LAMAR
Vice-President (Business Affairs): Dr JIM FERGUSON
Registrar: NINA ROGERS
Library Director: JEANNE PYLE

Library of 215,000 vols
Number of teachers: 267 incl. 180 full-time instructional
Number of students: 4,760 (3,593 undergraduate, 1,167 graduate)

DEANS

College of Arts and Sciences: Dr DONNA DICKERSON
College of Business and Technology: Dr JIM TARTER
College of Education and Psychology: Dr WILLIAM GEIGER
College of Engineering and Computer Science: Dr TROY HENSON
College of Nursing and Health Sciences: Dr LINDA KLOTZ

University of Texas Southwestern Medical Center at Dallas

5323 Harry Hines Blvd, Dallas, TX 75235

Telephone: (214) 648-3111
Fax: (214) 648-8690
Internet: www0.utsouthwestern.edu

Founded 1949; formerly Southwestern Medical School founded 1943

President: KERN WILDENTHAL
Executive Vice-President for Academic Affairs: WILLIAM B. NEAVES
Executive Vice-President for Business Affairs: PETER H. FITZGERALD
Executive Vice-President for Clinical Affairs: WILLIS C. MADDREY
Dean, Southwestern Medical School: ROBERT J. ALPERN
Dean, Graduate School of Biomedical Sciences: JOHN P. PERKINS
Dean, School of Allied Health Sciences: H. GORDON GREEN
Associate Dean for Student Affairs: BARBARA WALLER
Associate Dean for Academic Affairs: Dr JAMES GRIFFIN
Associate Vice-President of Student Services: J. WESLEY NORRED
Librarian: MARTY ADAMSON

Number of teachers: 1,149
Number of students: 800 medical, 499 graduate, 397 allied health

Publications: *Southwestern Magazine* (annually), *Newsletter* (monthly).

University of Texas Medical Branch at Galveston

301 University Blvd, Galveston, TX 77555-0144

Telephone: (409) 772-2618
Fax: (409) 772-6216
E-mail: public.affairs@utmb.edu
Internet: www.utmb.edu

Founded 1891; formerly Medical Branch, Galveston

President: THOMAS N. JAMES
Executive Vice-President for Administration and Business Affairs: E. J. PEDERSON
Director of Library: EMIL FREY

Number of teachers: 873
Number of students: 1,692

DEANS

Medicine: GEORGE T. BRYAN
Graduate School of Biomedical Sciences: K. LEMONE YIELDING
School of Allied Health Sciences: JOHN G. BRUHN
School of Nursing: MARY V. FENTON

University of Texas Health Science Center at Houston, School of Public Health

POB 20186, Houston, TX 77225

Telephone: (713) 500-9050
Fax: (713) 500-9020
E-mail: sphdean@uth.tmc.edu
Internet: www.sph.uth.tmc.edu

Founded 1967

Academic year: August

President: Dr JAMES T. WILLERSON
Dean: Dr GUY S. PARCEL

Number of teachers: 155
Number of students: 900.

University of Texas Health Science Center at San Antonio

7703 Floyd Curl Drive, San Antonio, TX 78284

Telephone: (210) 567-7000
Internet: www.uthscsa.edu

Founded 1959 as South Texas Medical School, a part of The University of Texas System, name changed to University of Texas Medical School at San Antonio 1967, present name 1972

President: Dr JOHN P. HOWE, III
Executive Vice-President for Administration and Business Affairs: ROBERT B. PRICE
Vice-President for University Relations: JUDY P. WOLF
Vice-President for Academic Services: Dr JOHN A. THOMAS
Executive Assistant to the President: MARY G. ETTLINGER
President and Chief Executive Officer, University Health System: JOHN A. GUEST
Director of Student Services (vacant)

Library of 192,576 vols

DEANS

Medical School: Dr JAMES J. YOUNG
Dental School: KENNETH L. KALKWARF
Graduate School of Biomedical Sciences: Dr SANFORD A. MILLER
School of Allied Health Sciences: Dr JAMES G. VAN STRATEN
School of Nursing: Dr ROBIN D. FROMAN

University of Texas M. D. Anderson Cancer Center

1515 Holcombe Blvd, Houston, TX 77030

Telephone: (713) 7926161
Internet: www.mdanderson.org

Founded 1941

Academic year: August to July

President: Dr JOHN MENDELSOHN
Executive Vice-President and Chief Operating Officer: Dr DAVID L. CALLENDER
Executive Vice-President and Chief Academic Officer: Dr MARGARET L. KRIPKE
Executive Vice-President: LEON J. LEACH
Dean of School of Health Sciences: Dr MICHAEL J. AHEARN
Executive Director of Library: KATHY HOFFMAN
Library of 19,611
Number of teachers: 900

DIRECTORS

Clinical Laboratory Science (Medical Technology): KAREN MCCLURE
Cytogenetic Technology: VICKI L HOPWOOD
Cytotechnology: CHRISTINA M. ALAPAT
Histotechnology: HAZEL V. DALTON
Medical Dosimetry: MELISSA JANE CHAPMAN
Radiation Therapy: SHAUN T. CALDWELL

UNIVERSITY OF THE INCARNATE WORD

4301 Broadway, San Antonio, TX 78209-6397
Telephone: (210) 829-6000
Fax: (210) 829-6096
E-mail: admis@universe.uiwtx.edu
Internet: www.uiw.edu
Founded 1881
Academic year: August to June
President: Dr LOUIS J. AGNESE, Jr
Provost: Dr TERRY L. DICIANNA
Vice-President of Administration: Dr DAVID JURENOVICH
Registrar: Dr BOBBYE G. FRY
Director of Admissions: ANDREA CYTERSKI
Dean of Library Services: MENDELL MORGAN, Jr
Library of 190,000 vols
Number of teachers: 341
Number of students: 4,264
Publication: *Journal of Hispanic Higher Education* (4 a year).

WAYLAND BAPTIST UNIVERSITY

Plainview, TX 79072
Telephone: (806) 291-1000
Fax: (806) 291-1960
Internet: www.wbu.edu
Founded 1906, chartered 1908
Academic year: June to May
President: Dr PAUL ARMES
Executive Vice-President: Dr BILL HARDAGE
Vice-President for Academic Services: Dr GLENN SAUL
Vice-President for Enrollment Management: Dr CLAUDE LUSK
Vice-President for Institutional Advancement: BETTY DONALDSON
Chief Financial Officer: JIM SMITH
Registrar: STAN DEMERRITT
Librarian: Dr POLLY LACKEY
Library of 117,287 vols (Plainview campus only)
Number of teachers: 66 (Plainview campus only)
Number of students: 1,067 (Plainview campus only)
Publications: *The Traveler* (yearbook, annually), *Footprints* (every 2 weeks).

WILEY COLLEGE

Marshall, TX 75670
Telephone: (903) 927-3300
Fax: (903) 938-8100
Internet: www.wileyc.edu
Founded 1873
Academic year: August to May

President: Dr HAYWOOD L. STRICKLAND
Executive Vice-President: Dr GLENDA F. CARTER
Vice-President (Academic Affairs): Dr MARION ELBERT
Vice-President for Student Affairs: Dr JOSEPH L. MORALE
Librarian: FRANK FRANCIS
Library of 85,000 vols
Number of teachers: 45
Number of students: 552

DIVISION CHAIRS

Chair of Natural and Computational Sciences: Dr OBADIAH NJUE
Chair of Education: Dr WILLIAM A. BROWN
Chair of Social and Behavioural Sciences: Dr LLOYD THOMPSON
Chair of Humanities: Dr SOLOMON MASENDA

UTAH

BRIGHAM YOUNG UNIVERSITY

Provo, UT 84602
Telephone: (801) 378-4636
E-mail: admissions@byu.edu
Internet: www.byu.edu
Founded 1875 by Pres. Brigham Young of the Church of Jesus Christ of Latter-day Saints
Academic year: August to April
Pres.: CECIL O. SAMUELSON
Vice-Pres. for Academic Affairs: JOHN S. TANNER
Chief Financial Officer and Vice-Pres. for Admin.: BRIAN K. EVANS
Vice-Pres. for Student Life: JANET S. SCHARMAN
Vice-Pres. for Advancement: K. FRED SKOUSEN
Gen. Counsel: THOMAS B. GRIFFITH
Dean of Admissions and Records: ERLEND D. PETERSON
Univ. Librarian: RANDY J. OLSEN
Library of 3,570,930 vols, pamphlets and bulletins
Number of teachers: 1,857 (1,517 full-time, 340 part-time)
Number of students: 39,577

DEANS

School of Law: H. REESE HANSEN
College of Biology and Agriculture: R. KENT CROOKSTON
School of Management: NED C. HILL
School of Education: ROBERT S. PATTERSON
College of Family, Home and Social Sciences: DAVID B. MAGLEBY
College of Fine Arts and Communications: K. NEWELL DAYLEY
College of Humanities: VAN C. GESSEL
College of Eng. and Technology: DOUGLAS M. CHABRIES
College of Nursing: ELAINE MARSHALL
College of Physical and Mathematical Sciences: EARL M. WOOLLEY
College of Health and Human Performance: ROBERT CONLEE
Honors and General Education: GEORGE S. TATE
Graduate Studies: BONNIE BRINTON
Religious Education: ANDREW C. SKINNER
Continuing Education: RICHARD C. EDDY

ITT TECHNICAL INSTITUTE

920 West LeVoy Dr., Murray, UT 84123
Telephone: (801) 263-3313
Fax: (801) 263-3497
Internet: www.itt-tech.edu
Exec. Sec.: NORMA JEAN SEGER.

UNIVERSITY OF UTAH

201 President's Circle, Salt Lake City, UT 84112-9009
Telephone: (801) 581-7200
Fax: (801) 581-3007
Internet: www.utah.edu
Founded 1850 as Univ. of Deseret; present name 1892
Academic year: August to May
Pres.: MICHAEL K. YOUNG
Sr Vice-Pres. for Academic Affairs: DAVID W. PERSHING
Sr Vice-Pres. for Health Sciences: A. LORRIS BETZ
Vice-Pres. for Research: RAYMOND F. GESTELAND
Vice-Pres. for Admin. Services: ARNOLD B. COMBE
Vice-Pres. for Institutional Advancement: FRED C. ESPLIN
Vice-Pres. for Human Resources: LORETTA HARPER
Vice-Pres. for Student Affairs: BARBARA H. SNYDER
Exec. Asst to the Pres.: LIZ MCCOY
Gen. Counsel: JOHN K. MORRIS
Registrar: RALPH O. BOREN
Dir of Library: JOYCE L. OGBURN
Number of teachers: 2,750
Number of students: 28,369
Publications: *Hinckley Journal of Politics*, *Journal of Land Resources and Environmental Law*, *Journal of Law and Family Studies*, *Political Research Quarterly*, *Quarterly West* (creative-writing journal), *Tanner Lectures on Human Values* (cumulative volume of transcripts), *Undergraduate Research Abstracts*, *Utah Foreign Language Abstracts*, *Utah Law Review* (quarterly), *Western Humanities* (quarterly)

DEANS

Architecture: BRENDA C. SCHEER
Business: JACK BRITTAIN
Education: DAVID J. SPERRY
Eng.: RICHARD B. BROWN
Fine Arts: PHYLLIS A. HASKELL
Health: JAMES E. GRAVES
Humanities: ROBERT NEWMAN
Law: SCOTT M. MATHESON, Jr
Medicine: A. LORRIS BETZ
Mines and Earth Sciences: FRANCIS H. BROWN
Nursing: MAUREEN R. KEEFE
Pharmacy: JOHN W. MAUGER
Science: PETER J. STANG
Social and Behavioral Science: STEVEN OTT
Social Work: JANNAH MATHER
Graduate School: DAVID S. CHAPMAN
Continuing Education: RICHARD B. SIMPSON (Assoc. Dean)

CHAIRMEN OF DEPARTMENTS

Business (Kendall Garff Bldg, 1645 East Campus Centre Dr., Salt Lake City, UT 84112; tel. (801) 581-7347; fax (801) 581-7214; e-mail dean@business.utah.edu; internet www.business.utah.edu):

Accounting: R. DAVID PLUMLEE
Finance: URI LOEWENSTEIN
Management: STEVEN B. TALLMAN
Marketing: BILL MOORE

Education (Milton Bennion Hall, 1705 East Campus Center Dr., Salt Lake City, UT 84112; tel. (801) 581-8221; fax (801) 581-5223; e-mail sperry@ed.utah.edu; internet www.gse.utah.edu):

Education, Culture and Society: HARVEY KANTOR
Education, Leadership and Policy: GARY CROW
Educational Psychology: BOB HILL

Special Education: MICHAEL HARDMAN
Teaching and Learning: LYNNE R. SCHRUM

Engineering (Kennecott Research Center, 1515 Mineral Sq., Salt Lake City, UT 84112; tel. (801) 581-6912; fax (801) 581-8692; e-mail stringfellow@coe.utah.edu):

Bioengineering: VLADIMIR HLADY
Chemical Eng.: PHIL SMITH
Civil and Environmental Eng.: LAWRENCE REAVELEY
School of Computing: CHRIS JOHNSON
EGI: RAY LEVY
Electrical and Computer Eng.: MARC BODSON
Materials Science and Eng.: ANIL VIRKAR
Mechanical Eng.: JOSEPH C. KLEWICKI

Fine Arts (Art Bldg, 375 South 1530E, Rm 250, Salt Lake City, UT 84112; tel. (801) 581-6764; fax (801) 585-3066; e-mail phyllis.haskell@finearts.utah.edu; internet www.finearts.utah.edu):

Art and Art History: ELIZABETH PETERSON
Ballet: CAROL IWASAKI
Film Studies: BILL SISKA
Modern Dance: DONNA WHITE
Music: ROBERT WALZEL
Theatre: DAVID DYNAK

Health (Hyper-North, 250 South 1850E, Salt Lake City, UT 84112; tel. (801) 581-8537; fax (801) 581-5580; e-mail cheri.curtis@health.utah.edu; internet www.health.utah.edu):

Communication Disorders: BRUCE L. SMITH
Exercise and Sport Science: PATRICIA A. EISEMAN
Foods and Nutrition: WAYNE ASKEW
Health Promotion and Education: LES CHATELAIN
Occupational Therapy: JOANNE WRIGHT
Parks, Recreation and Tourism: GARY ELLIS
Physical Therapy: SCOTT WARD

Humanities (LNCO, 255 South Central Campus Dr., Rm 2100, Salt Lake City, UT 84112; tel. (801) 581-6214; fax (801) 585-5190; e-mail robert.newman@hum.utah.edu; internet www.hum.utah.edu):

Communication: ANN DARLING
English: STUART CULVER
History: ERIC HINDERAKER
Languages and Literature: MOSHIRA EID
Linguistics: MARIANNA DI PAOLO
Middle East Centre: IBRAHIM KARAWAN
Philosophy: LESLIE FRANCIS
Tanner Humanities Centre: VINCENT CHENG
Writing Programme: THOMAS HUCKIN (Interim Dir.)

Medicine (Moran Eye Center, 50 North Medical Dr., Moran 5th Fl., Salt Lake City, UT 84112; tel. (801) 581-5619; fax (801) 585-3109; e-mail lorris.betz@hsc.utah.edu; internet www.med.utah.edu/som):

Anaesthesiology: MICHAEL CAHALAN
Biochemistry: DANA CARROLL
Dermatology: JOHN ZONE
Family and Preventive Medicine: MICHAEL MAGILL
Human Genetics: MARK F. LEPPERT, MARIO CAPECCHI
Huntsman Cancer Institute: STEVEN PRESCOTT
Internal Medicine: JOHN R. HOIDAL
Medical Informatics: REED M. GARDNER
Neurobiology and Anatomy: TOM PARKS
Neurology: JOHN E. GREENLEE
Neurosurgery: WILLIAM T. COULDWELL
Obstetrics and Gynaecology: ELI Y. ADASHI
Oneological Sciences: BARBARA J. GRAVES
Ophthalmology: R. J. OLSON
Orthopaedics: HAROLD K. DUNN
Pathology: CARL KJELDSBERG
Paediatrics: EDWARD B. CLARK

Pharmacy and Toxicology: WILLIAM R. CROWLEY
Physical Medicine and Rehabilitation Division: PHILIP R. BRYANT
Physiology: SALVADOR FIDONE (acting)
Psychiatry: B. I. GROSSER
Radiation Oncology: DENNIS C. SHRIEVE
Radiology: EDWIN A. STEVENS
Surgery: SEAN MULVIHILL

Mines and Earth Sciences (Browning Bldg, 135 South 1460 E., Rm 209, Salt Lake City, UT 84112; tel. (801) 581-8767; fax (801) 581-5560; e-mail fbrown@mines.utah.edu; internet www.mines.utah.edu):

Geology and Geophysics: MARJORIE CHAN
Metallurgical Eng.: JAN MILLER
Meteorology: EDWARD J. ZIPSER
Mining Eng.: M. K. McCARTER
Seismograph Stations: WALTER J. ARABASZ
UEES: TERRANCE CHATWIN

Pharmacy (Skaggs Pharmacy Bldg, 30 S. 1990 E., Salt Lake City, UT 84112; tel. (801) 581-3402; fax (801) 581-3716; e-mail jmauger@deans.pharm.utah.edu; internet www.pharmacy.utah.edu):

Medicinal Chemistry: CHRIS IRELAND
Pharmaceutics and Pharmaceutical Chemistry: JINDRICH KOPECEK
Pharmacology and Toxicology: WILLIAM R. CROWLEY
Pharmacy Practice: DIANE BRIXNER

Science (James Talmage Bldg, 1430 E. President's Circle, Salt Lake City, UT 84112; tel. (801) 581-6958; fax (801) 585-3169; e-mail stang@chemistry.utah.edu; internet www.science.utah.edu):

Biology: DAVID WOLSTENHOLME
Chemistry: PETER C. ARMENTROUT
Mathematics: GRAEME MILTON
Physics: PIERRE SOKOLSKY

Social and Behavioural Science (Orson Spencer Hall, 260 S. Central Campus Dr., Salt Lake City, UT 84112; tel. (801) 581-8620; fax (801) 585-5081; e-mail jsott@cppa.utah.edu; internet www.csbs.utah.edu):

Aerospace Studies: TIMOTHY MARTIN
Anthropology: JAMES F. O'CONNELL
Economics: KORKUK ERTURK
Family and Consumer Studies: CATHLEEN ZICK
Geography: HARVEY MILLER
Military Science: Maj. EDWIN FREDERICK, III
Naval Science: Capt. TERRY C. WALSTROM
Political Science: RONALD HREBENAR
Psychology: FRANCES J. FRIEDERICH
Sociology: MICHAEL TIMBERLAKE

UTAH STATE UNIVERSITY

Office of the President, 1400 Old Main Hill, Logan, UT 84322-1400

Telephone: (435) 797-1000
Fax: (435) 797-1173
E-mail: prm@usu.edu
Internet: www.usu.edu

Founded 1888
Academic year: August to May

Pres.: STAN L. ALBRECHT
Exec. Vice-Pres. and Provost: RAYMOND T. COWARD
Vice-Pres. for Business and Finance: W. GLENN FORD
Vice-Pres. for Extension and Agriculture: NOELLE E. COCKETT
Vice-Pres. for Information Technology: M. K. JEPPESEN
Vice-Pres. for Research: BRENT C. MILLER
Vice-Pres. for Student Services: GARY A. CHAMBERS
Vice-Pres. for Univ. Advancement: DAVID DRIGGS

Number of teachers: 873

Number of students: 23,474

Publications: Outlook (6 a year), Outreach (monthly), Utah Science (quarterly), Western Historical Quarterly, Western American Literary Journal (quarterly)

DEANS

School of Graduate Studies: (vacant)
College of Agriculture: NOELLE E. COCKETT
College of Business: CARYN L. BECK-DUDLEY
College of Education: CAROL STRONG
College of Eng.: H. SCOTT HINTON
College of Humanities, Arts and Social Sciences: GARY H. KIGER
College of Natural Resources: FRANK E. BUSBY
College of Science: DONALD W. FIESINGER
Continuing Education: JACK M. PAYNE

UTAH VALLEY STATE COLLEGE

800 West University Parkway, Orem, UT 84058

Telephone: (801) 222-8000
Fax: (801) 226-5207
E-mail: info@uvsc.edu
Internet: www.uvsc.edu
Pres.: Dr WILLIAM Λ. SEDERBURG.

WEBER STATE UNIVERSITY

3850 University Circle, Ogden, UT 84408

Telephone: (801) 626-6000
Fax: (801) 626-7922
E-mail: mediarelations@weber.edu
Internet: www.weber.edu

Founded 1889
Academic year: August to August

Pres.: F. ANN MILNER
Provost: MICHAEL B. VAUGHAN
Vice-Pres. for Admin. Services: NORM TARBOX
Vice-Pres. for Student Affairs: Dr JAN WINNIFORD
Registrar: Dr WINSLOW L. HURST
Dir of Library: JOAN G. HUBBARD
Library of 580,000 vols
Number of teachers: 442
Number of students: 14,000

Publications: Vista (2 a year), Legacy (2 a year), U-News (monthly), Metaphor (annual), Weber Studies (quarterly)

Courses in arts and humanities, science, applied science and technology, business and econ., education, social and behavioural science and the health professions.

WESTMINSTER COLLEGE

1840 South 1300 East St, Salt Lake City, UT 84105

Telephone: (801) 484-7651
Fax: (801) 466-6916
E-mail: admissions@wcslc.edu
Internet: www.wcslc.edu

Founded 1875

Pres.: Dr MICHAEL S. BASSIS
Vice-Pres. for Information Technology: Dr SHERYL PHILLIPS
Exec. Vice-Pres. and Treas.: STEPHEN MORGAN
Vice-Pres. for Institutional Advancement: NANCY MICHAEKO
Vice-Pres. for Student Devt and Enrollment Planning: PHIL ALLETTO
Vice-Pres. for Academic Affairs and Dean of the Faculty: Dr STEPHEN R. BAAR
Dean of Students: MARK FERNE
Librarian: DAVID HALES

Library of 84,000 vols
Number of teachers: 216
Number of students: 2,140

DEANS

School of Arts and Sciences: Dr MARY JANE CHASE
School of Business: Dr JAMES SIEDELAMN
School of Education: Dr JANET DYNAK
School of Nursing and Health Sciences: (vacant)

VERMONT

BENNINGTON COLLEGE

Bennington, VT 05201
Telephone: (802) 442-5401
Fax: (802) 442-6164
E-mail: admissions@bennington.edu
Internet: www.bennington.edu

Chartered 1925

President: ELIZABETH COLEMAN
Dean of Admissions and the First Year: ELENA BACHRACH
Director of Financial Aid: MEG WOOLMINGTON
Dean of the College: ROBERT WALDMAN
Vice-President for Finance and Administration: LAWRENCE LEE
Director of Development: DAVID REES
Director of Student Affairs: DONNA BOURASSA
Librarian: ROBERT WALDMAN

Library of 108,000 vols
Number of teachers: 70
Number of students: 400

Publications: *Bennington, Silo, Ben Belitt Chapbooks in Literature.*

BURLINGTON COLLEGE

95 North Ave, Burlington, VT 05401
Telephone: (802) 862-9616
Fax: (802) 660-4331
E-mail: admissions@burlcol.edu
Internet: www.burlingtoncollege.edu

President: ROBERT RICE (acting)
Registrar: MIRA SHEA
Director of Administration: KELLY CIRCE
Director of Development: JACK V. AUSTIN
Director of Human Resources: JOANNE COWARD
Director of Finance: BARBARA DENGLER
Director of Special Programs: PETE SHEAR
Director of Admissions: CATHLEEN SULLIVAN
Director of Library and Information Services: TERESA R. FAUST

CHAIRS OF DEPARTMENTS

Humanities: ANNA BLACKMER
Psychology: ABBY GELFER
Transpersonal Psychology: DAVID JOY
Cinema Studies: BARRY SNYDER

CASTLETON STATE COLLEGE

Castleton, VT 05735
Telephone: (802) 468-5611
Fax: (802) 468-5237
E-mail: info@castleton.edu
Internet: www.csc.vsc.edu

Founded 1787

Liberal arts, career education
Academic year: August to May

President: DAVID S. WOLK
Academic Dean: Dr JOSEPH T. MARK
Director of Admissions: MAURICE OUIMET, Jr
Director of Development: SAM CHANDLER
Dean of Administration: WILLIAM ALLEN
Dean of Students: GREGORY STONE
Dean of Enrollment: WILLIAM ALLEN
Registrar: LORI PATTEN
Director of the Library: SANDRA DULING

Library of 179,326 vols
Number of teachers: 86
Number of students: 2,000.

CHAMPLAIN COLLEGE

163 South Willard Street, Burlington, VT 05401
Telephone: (802) 860-2700
Fax: (802) 862-2772
E-mail: admission@champlain.edu
Internet: www.champlain.edu

Number of teachers: 112
Number of students: 1,568.

COLLEGE OF ST JOSEPH

71 Clement Rd, Rutland, VT 05701
Telephone: (802) 773-5900
E-mail: info@csj.edu
Internet: www.csj.edu

President: FRANK G. MIGLORIE
Academic Dean: GARY M. LAWLER

CHAIRS OF DEPARTMENTS

Arts and Sciences: DONALD E. HARPSTER
Business: BILL W. GODAIR
Education: ROBERTA KAPI REITH
Psychology: CRAIG W. KNAPP

GODDARD COLLEGE

Plainfield, VT 05667
Telephone: (802) 454-8311
Fax: (802) 454-8017
E-mail: admissions@goddard.edu
Internet: www.goddard.edu

Founded 1938

President: MARK SCHULMAN
Registrar: HERVENA MARTIN
Librarian: CLARA BRUNS

Library of 72,000 vols
Number of teachers: 24 full-time
Number of teachers: 8 part-time
Number of students: 500.

GREEN MOUNTAIN COLLEGE

One College Circle, Poultney, VT 05764
Telephone: (802) 287-8000
Fax: (802) 287-8099
Internet: www.greenmtn.edu

Founded 1834 as Troy Conference Academy
Private control
Academic year: September to May

President: JOHN F. BRENNAN
Provost: WILLIAM THROPP
Vice-President for Finance and Administration: JOSEPH MANNING
Dean of Enrollment: JOEL WINCOWSKI
Director of Communications: STEPHEN DIEHL
Director of Library Information and Learning Support: PAUL MILLETTE

Number of teachers: 45
Number of students: 650

DEANS

Division of Humanities, Arts and Natural Sciences: MICHAEL BLUST
Division of Social Sciences: JOAN MULLIGAN

JOHNSON STATE COLLEGE

Johnson, VT 05656
Telephone: (802) 635-2356
Fax: (802) 635-9745
Internet: www.jsc.vsc.edu

Founded 1828

President: Dr ROBERT HAHN
Academic Dean: Dr VINCENT CROCKENBERG
Director of Graduate Programs (vacant)
Registrar: JOHN LORD
Librarian: JOE FARARA

Library of 84,000 vols
Number of teachers: 68 full-time
Number of teachers: 50 part-time

Number of students: 1,672

DIVISION CHAIRMEN

Humanities: GERALD ANDERSON
Mathematics: CHARLES EYLER
Education: ALICE WHITING
Fine and Performing Arts: RUSSELL LONGTIN
Behavioral Sciences: DAVID FINK
Environmental and Health Sciences: PETER KRAMER
English and Writing: ANDREA PERHAM
Business and Economics: EUGENIE WILLIAMS

LYNDON STATE COLLEGE

Lyndonville, VT 05851
Telephone: (802) 626-6200
Fax: (802) 626-9770
Internet: www.lyndonstate.edu

College of the liberal arts and professional programs

Founded 1911

President: Dr CAROL A. MOORE
Dean of Administration: WAYNE T. HAMILTON
Dean of Academic and Student Affairs: MICHAEL FISHBEIN
Director of Admissions: MICHELLE McCAFFREY
Librarian: GARET NELSON

Library of 102,520 vols, 588 periodicals
Number of teachers: 63 (full-time)
Number of students: 1,129.

MARLBORO COLLEGE

Marlboro, VT 05344
Telephone: (802) 257-4333
Fax: (802) 257-4154
E-mail: admissions@marlboro.edu
Internet: www.marlboro.edu

Founded 1946

President: PAUL J. LeBLANC
Dean of Faculty: JOHN HAYES
Dean of Students: AMY GRILLO ANGELL
Admissions Director: KATE HALLAS
Librarian: MOLLY BRENNAN

Library of 60,000 vols
Number of teachers: 36
Number of students: 275.

MIDDLEBURY COLLEGE

Middlebury, VT 05753
Telephone: (802) 443-5000
E-mail: mpaine@middlebury.edu
Internet: www.middlebury.edu

Founded 1800

President: JOHN M. McCARDELL, Jr
Executive Vice-President and Provost: RONALD D. LIEBOWITZ
Executive Vice-President for Facilities Planning: DAVID W. GINEVAN
Vice-President for Administration and Treasurer: F. ROBERT HUTH
Dean of Student Affairs: ANN CRAIG HANSON

Library of 852,000 vols
Number of teachers: 281
Number of students: 2,225

Publication: *New England Review* (4 a year).

NORWICH UNIVERSITY

Northfield, VT 05663
Telephone: (802) 485-2000
Fax: (802) 485-2580
Internet: www.norwich.edu

Founded 1819

President: RICHARD W. SCHNEIDER
Provost and Dean of Faculty: JOSEPH BYRNE (acting)
Senior Vice-President: RICHARD S. HANSEN
Commandant of Cadets: CRAIG LIND

Vice-President and Dean of Vermont College: JACKSON KYTLE
Dean of Admissions: FRANK GRIFFIS
Head Librarian: PAUL HELLER
Library of 260,000 vols and microfilms; military history collection
Number of teachers: 142
Number of students: 2,619.

SAINT MICHAEL'S COLLEGE

One Winooski Park, Colchester, VT 05439
Telephone: (802) 654-2000
Fax: (802) 654-2297
E-mail: admission@smcvt.edu
Internet: www.smcvt.edu

Founded 1904
Academic year: August to May

President: Dr MARC A. VAN DER HEYDEN
Provost and Vice-President Academic Affairs: Dr JANET W. SHEERAN
Vice-President for Admission and Enrollment Management: JERRY FLANAGAN
Vice-President Finance: NEAL ROBINSON
Vice-President Institutional Advancement: ANNE W. HANSEN
Vice-President Student Life: MICHAEL SAMARA
Dean of the College: Dr JEFFREY TRUMBOWER
Registrar: JOHN D. SHEEHEY
Librarian: JOANNE SCHNEIDER
Library of 369,000 units
Number of teachers: 144 full-time
Number of students: 1,900 full-time under-graduates
Publication: The Onion River Review (annually).

SCHOOL FOR INTERNATIONAL TRAINING

Kipling Rd, POB 676, Brattleboro, VT 05302-0676
Telephone: (802) 258-3500
Fax: (802) 258-3248
E-mail: info@sit.edu
Internet: www.sit.edu

President: JAMES A. CRAMER.

SOUTHERN VERMONT COLLEGE

982 Mansion Drive, Bennington, VT 05201-6002
Telephone: (802) 442-5427
Fax: (802) 447-4695
E-mail: info@svc.edu
Internet: www.svc.edu

Founded 1926
Academic year: September to August

President: BARBARA P. SIRVIS
Academic Dean: REBECCA M. DiLIDDO
Dean of Students: SIGRID SOLOMON
Registrar: ADAM EMERSON
Director of Library: SARAH SANFILIPPO
Number of teachers: 40
Number of students: 500

CHAIRS OF DIVISIONS

Business: BOB CONSALVO
Humanities: LINDA SINKIEWICH
Nursing: HOLLY MADISON
Science and Technology: CAROL TUNNEY
Social Sciences: DAVID ROSENTHAL

UNIVERSITY OF VERMONT

Burlington, VT 05405
Telephone: (802) 656-3131
Internet: www.uvm.edu

Founded 1791
State control
Academic year: September to May

Pres.: DANIEL M. FOGEL
Provost: A. JOHN BRAMLEY
Registrar: KEITH P. WILLIAMS
Admissions Dir: DONALD M. HONEMAN
Librarian: MARA R. SAULE
Library of 2,508,000 vols
Number of teachers: 1,185
Number of students: 10,940

DEANS

College of Agriculture and Life Sciences: RACHEL K. JOHNSON
College of Arts and Sciences: JANE E. KNO-DELL
College of Education and Social Services: JILL M. TARULE
College of Eng. and Mathematics: DOMENICO GRASSO
College of Medicine: JOHN N. EVANS
College of Nursing and Health Sciences: BETTY A. RAMBUR
School of Business Admin.: ROCKI-LEE DeWITT
School of the Environment and Natural Resources: DONALD H. DeHAYES
Graduate Studies: FRANCES E. CARR

VERMONT LAW SCHOOL

POB 96, Chelsea St, South Royalton, VT 05068
Internet: www.vermontlaw.edu

President: L. KINVIN WROTH
Vice-President for Finance and Administration: ROBERT A. FOOSE
Vice-President for Institutional Advancement: DEE ROBINSON
Director of Academic Procedures and Registrar: NINA L. THOMAS
Director of Development: SHANNON FLYNN
Director of Human Resources: DIANE GLEW
Director of Foundation and Corporate Relations: MICHAEL HEALY
Director of Media Relations: PETER LEE MILLER
Director of J. D. Internships and Judicial Externships: JENNIFER SOBEL.

VERMONT TECHNICAL COLLEGE

POB 500, Randolph Center, VT 05061-0500
Telephone: (802) 728-1000
Fax: (802) 728-1597
E-mail: admissions@vtc.edu
Internet: www.vtc.edu

President: ALLAN RODGERS.

VIRGINIA

AVERETT UNIVERSITY

420 West Main St, Danville, VA 24541
Telephone: (434) 791-5600
E-mail: admit@averett.edu
Internet: www.averett.edu

President: RICHARD A. PFAU.

BAPTIST THEOLOGICAL SEMINARY AT RICHMOND

3400 Brook Rd, Richmond, VA 23227
Telephone: (804) 355-8135
Fax: (804) 355-8182
Internet: www.btsr.edu

Pres.: TOM GRAVES.

BLUEFIELD COLLEGE

Main Campus, 3000 College Drive, Bluefield, VA 24605
Telephone: (276) 326-3682
Fax: (276) 326-4288
E-mail: bluefield@bluefield.edu

Internet: www.bluefield.edu
President: DANIEL G. MacMILLAN.

BRIDGEWATER COLLEGE

Bridgewater, VA 22812
Telephone: (540) 828-8000
Fax: (540) 828-5481
E-mail: admissions@bridgewater.edu
Internet: www.bridgewater.edu

Founded 1880
Liberal arts college
Academic year: August to May

President: Dr PHILLIP C. STONE
Executive Assistant to the President: ROY W. FERGUSON, Jr
Dean of the College: ART HESSLER
Librarian: DONNA S. BIBLE
Library of 184,160 vols
Number of teachers: 126 (96 full-time, 30 part-time)
Number of students: 1,500
Publication: The Philomathean (annually).

CHRISTENDOM COLLEGE

134 Christendom Drive, Front Royal, VA 22630
Telephone: (540) 636-2900
Fax: (540) 636-1655
E-mail: info@christendom.edu
Internet: www.christendom.edu

President: Dr TIMOTHY T. O'DONNELL
Head of Academic Affairs: JONATHAN J. REYES
Registrar: WALTER JANARO.

CHRISTOPHER NEWPORT UNIVERSITY

1 University Place, Newport News, VA 23606
Telephone: (757) 594-7000
Fax: (757) 594-7333
E-mail: admit@cnu.edu
Internet: www.cnu.edu

President: PAUL S. TRIBLE.

COLLEGE OF WILLIAM AND MARY IN VIRGINIA

Williamsburg, VA 23187-8795
Telephone: (757) 253-4000
Internet: www.wm.edu

Founded 1693
Academic year: September to May

President: DENE R. NICHOL
Provost: P. GEOFFREY FEISS
Vice-President for Finance: SAMUEL E. JONES
Vice-President for Development: DENNIS CROSS
Vice-President for Administration: ANNA K. MARTIN
Vice-President for Student Affairs: SAMUEL SADLER
Vice-President for Public Relations: STEWART GAMAGE
Registrar: CAROLINE BOGGS
Librarian: CONNIE K. McCARTHY
Library: Libraries with 2,128,645 vols
Number of teachers: 736 (576 full-time, 160 part-time)
Number of students: 7,575
Publications: The William and Mary Quarterly, Law Review, Business Review, Environmental Law and Policy Review

DEANS

Faculty of Arts and Sciences: CARL STRIK-WERDA
School of Business Administration: LAWRENCE PULLEY
School of Education: VIRGINIA McLAUGHLIN

William and Mary School of Law: W. TAYLOR REVELEY III
School of Marine Science: L. DONELSON WRIGHT
Research and Graduate Studies: DAVID FINIFTER

EASTERN MENNONITE UNIVERSITY

Harrisonburg, VA 22802-2462
Telephone: (540) 432-4000
Fax: (540) 432-4444
Internet: www.emu.edu

Founded 1917

Liberal arts college affiliated with the Mennonite Church, with programs in 50 subject areas; emphasis on international education
President: Dr JOSEPH L. LAPP
Director of Admissions: ELLEN B. MILLER
Registrar: DAVID A. DETROW
Librarian: BOYD T. REESE
Library of 149,000 vols
Number of teachers: 90
Number of students: 1,408.

EMORY AND HENRY COLLEGE

POB 947, Emory, VA 24327-0947
Telephone: (276) 944-4121
E-mail: ehadmiss@ehc.edu
Internet: www.ehc.edu

Founded 1836

President: Dr THOMAS R. MORRIS.

FERRUM COLLEGE

POB 1000, Ferrum, VA 24088-9001
Telephone: (540) 365-2121
Fax: (540) 365-4266
E-mail: ferrumcollege@mac.com
Internet: www.ferrum.edu

President: Dr JENNIFER L. BRAATEN.

GEORGE MASON UNIVERSITY

4400 University Drive, Fairfax, VA 22030-4444
Telephone: (703) 993-1000
Internet: www.gmu.edu

Founded 1957

President: Dr ALAN G. MERTEN
Senior Vice-President for Finance and Planning: MAURICE W. SCHERRENS
Vice-President for University Life: Dr KAREN ROSENBLUM
Provost: Dr PETER N. STEARNS
Library of 2,846,733 vols
Number of teachers: 1,658 (965 full-time, 693 part-time)
Number of students: 24,897
Publication: *Faculty Bibliography* (annually).

HAMPDEN-SYDNEY COLLEGE

Hampden-Sydney, VA 23943
Telephone: (434) 223-6000
Fax: (434) 223-6346
E-mail: hsapp@hsc.edu
Internet: www.hsc.edu

Founded 1776
Academic year: August to May
President: WALTER M. BORTZ, III
Vice-President for Business Affairs: C. NORMAN KRUEGER
Dean of the Faculty: EARL W. FLECK
Dean of Admissions: ANITA H. GARLAND
Registrar: MARK A. NEWCOMB
Librarian: SHARON I. GOAD
Library of 224,000 vols

Number of teachers: 106
Number of students: 1,082
Men's college of the liberal arts and sciences.

HAMPTON UNIVERSITY

Hampton, VA 23668
Telephone: (804) 727-5000
Fax: (804) 727-5746
Internet: www.hamptonu.edu

Founded 1868

President: Dr WILLIAM R. HARVEY
Executive Vice-President/Provost: Dr DEMETRIUS D. VENABLE
Vice-President for Health: Dr ELNORA D. DANIEL
Vice-President for Business Affairs and Treasurer: LEON SCOTT
Vice-President for Development: LARON J. CLARK
Dean of Students: Dr RODNEY SMITH
Director of Admissions: LEONARD JONES
Registrar: JORSENE COOPER
Library of 331,727 vols
Number of students: 5,305.

HOLLINS UNIVERSITY

POB 9625, Roanoke, VA 24020
Telephone: (540) 362-6401
Fax: (540) 362-6218
E-mail: huadm@hollins.edu
Internet: www.hollins.edu

Founded 1842

Independent liberal arts university with 29 major field of study; undergraduate programmes for women, selected graduate programmes for both men and women
President: NANCY OLIVER GRAY (acting)
Provost: L. WAYNE MARKERT
Dean of Admissions: CELIA McCORMICK
Director of Scholarships and Financial Assistance: REBECCA ECKSTEIN
University Registrar: THOMAS MESNER
University Librarian: JOAN RUELLE
Library of 212,000 vols
Number of teachers: 110 (76 full-time, 35 part-time)
Number of students: 1,057
Publications: *Hollins Magazine* (3 a year), *The Hollins Critic* (4 a year).

JAMES MADISON UNIVERSITY

Harrisonburg, VA 22807
Telephone: (540) 568-6211
Fax: (540) 568-3634
E-mail: got@jmu.edu
Internet: www.jmu.edu

Founded 1908, name changed from Madison College 1977
Academic year: August to May
President: Dr LINWOOD H. ROSE
Executive Vice-President (vacant)
Vice-President for Academic Affairs: Dr DOUGLAS BROW
Vice-President for Student Affairs: Dr MARK WARNER
University Librarian: RALPH ALBERICO
Library of 700,000 vols
Number of teachers: 700 (full-time)
Number of students: 15,000
Colleges of arts and letters, business education and psychology, integrated science and technology, science and mathematics, graduate school.

LIBERTY UNIVERSITY

1971 University Boulevard, Lynchburg, VA 24502
Telephone: (434) 582-2000

Fax: (434) 582-2304
Internet: www.liberty.edu
President: Dr JOHN M. BOREK.

LONGWOOD COLLEGE

Farmville, VA 23909-1899
Telephone: (804) 395-2000
Fax: (804) 395-2635
E-mail: lcadmit@longwood.edu
Internet: www.longwood.edu

Founded 1839 as comprehensive college
Academic year: August to May
President: PATRICIA P. CORMIER
Vice-President for Academic Affairs: NORMAN BREGMAN
Vice-President for Business Affairs: DAVID HARNAGE
Vice-President for Institutional Advancement: BOBBIE BURTON
Vice-President for Student Affairs: PHYLLIS L. MABLE
Director of Public Relations: DENNIS SERCOMBE
Associate Vice-President for Research and Information Systems: RICHARD BRATCHER
Director of Financial Aid: JEFF SCOFIELD
Registrar: ALECIA KNOX
Library of 288,175 vols
Number of teachers: 258 (168 full-time, 90 adjunct)
Number of students: 3,558 (3,145 full-time, 413 part-time)

HEADS OF DEPARTMENTS
Art: HOMER SPRINGER
Business and Economics: BERKWOOD FARMER
Education: DAVID SMITH
English, Philosophy and Foreign Languages: McRAE AMOSS
Health, Physical Education and Recreation: BETTE L. HARRIS
History and Government: WILLIAM HARBOUR
Library Science: CALVIN BOYER
Mathematics and Computer Science: ROBERT WEBBER
Military Science: (vacant)
Music: PAT LUST
Natural Sciences: DAVID BUCKALEW
Education, Special Education and Social Work: FRANK HOWE
Sociology and Anthropology: LEE BIDWELL
Speech and Dramatic Arts: GENE MUTO
Psychology: JENNIFER APPERSON

LYNCHBURG COLLEGE

1501 Lakeside Drive, Lynchburg, VA 24501-3199
Telephone: (804) 544-8100
E-mail: president@lynchburg.edu
Internet: www.lynchburg.edu

Founded 1903

President: Dr CHARLES O. WARREN, Jr
Registrar: JAY WEBB
Vice-President for Enrollment Management: Dr DAVID BEHRS
Dean of the College: Dr JACQUELINE W. ASBURY
Librarian: CHRISTOPHER MILLSON-MARTULA
Library of 243,300 vols
Number of teachers: 130
Number of students: 2,000.

MARY BALDWIN COLLEGE

Staunton, VA 24401
Telephone: (540) 887-7000
Fax: (540) 886-6634
E-mail: CoMPA@mbc.edu
Internet: www.mbc.edu

Founded 1842
Academic year: August to May

President: PAMELA FOX
Dean: JEFFREY BULLER
Registrar: LEWIS D. ASKEGAARD
Librarian: CAROL CREAGER
Library of 228,667 items
Number of teachers: 134
Number of students: 1,718.

MARYMOUNT UNIVERSITY

12807 North Glebe Rd, Arlington, VA 22207-4299

Telephone: (703) 522-5600
Fax: (703) 284-1637
E-mail: admissions@marymount.edu
Internet: www.marymount.edu
President: JAMES E. BUNDSCHUH

DEANS

School of Arts and Humanities: Dr ROSEMARY HUBBARD
School of Business Administration: RONALD P. HUDAK
School of Education and Human Services: MR LESKO
School of Health Professions: THERESA CAPPELLO

NORFOLK STATE UNIVERSITY

700 Park Avenue, Norfolk, VA 23504
Telephone: (757) 823-8600
Fax: (757) 823-2342
Internet: www.nsu.edu
President: Dr MARIE V. McDEMMOND.

OLD DOMINION UNIVERSITY

Norfolk, VA 23529
Telephone: (757) 683-3000
Fax: (757) 683-4505
Internet: www.odu.edu
Founded 1930 as a college
President: ROSEANN RUNTE
Registrar: MARY SWARTZ
Librarian: VIRGINIA S. O'HERRON (acting)
Library of 2,870,692 items
Number of teachers: 632
Number of students: 20,656.

RADFORD UNIVERSITY

Radford, VA 24142
Telephone: (540) 831 5000
Fax: (540) 831-5142
Internet: www.radford.edu
Founded 1910
Academic year: August to May
President: Dr DOUGLAS COVINGTON
Vice-President for Academic Affairs: WARREN P. SELF
Vice-President for Student Affairs: NORLEEN K. POMERANTZ
Vice-President for Business Affairs: DAVID A. BURDETTE
Vice-President for University Advancement: CHARLES A. WOOD
Library of 552,687 vols
Number of teachers: 551 (358 full-time, 193 part-time)
Number of students: 9,142.

RANDOLPH-MACON COLLEGE

POB 5005, Ashland, VA 23005-5505
Telephone: (804) 752-7200
Fax: (804) 752-7231
Internet: www.rmc.edu
Founded 1830
Academic year: September to May
President: Dr ROGER H. MARTIN
Registrar: Dr MARILYN J. GIBBS

Dean of Admissions: JOHN C. CONKRIGHT
Librarian: Dr VIRGINIA E. YOUNG
Library of 182,368 vols
Number of teachers: 88 full-time
Number of students: 1,126.

RANDOLPH-MACON WOMAN'S COLLEGE

Lynchburg, VA 24503-1526
Telephone: (434) 947-8000
Fax: (434) 947-8138
Internet: www.rmwc.edu
Founded 1891
Academic year: August to May
President: KATHLEEN GILL BOWMAN
Vice-President (Academic Affairs): WILLIAM A. COULTER
Vice-President (Development): JAMES C. KUGHN, Jr
Vice-President (Enrollment): CONNIE J. GORES
Vice-President (Finance and Administration): CHRISTOPHER BURNLEY
Vice-President (Student Affairs): SARAH L. SWAGER
Librarian: THEODORE J. HOSTETLER
Library of 150,000 vols
Number of teachers: 96
Number of students: 764

Publications: *Randolph-Macon Alumnae Bulletin* (4 a year), *Hail, Muse!* (annually).

REGENT UNIVERSITY

1000 Regent University Drive, Virginia Beach, VA 23464
Telephone: (757) 226-4127
E-mail: admissions@regent.edu
Internet: www.regent.edu
President: PAT ROBERTSON
Chief Financial Officer: LARRY DANTZLER
Vice-President for Development and Communications: MAUREEN McDONNELL
Vice-President for Student Services: JEFF PITTMAN
Vice-President for Academic Affairs: BARRY RYAN
Vice-President of Information Technology: TRACY STEWART.

ROANOKE COLLEGE

Salem, VA 24153
Telephone: (703) 375-2500
E-mail: admissions@roanoke.edu
Internet: www.roanoke.edu
Founded 1842
President: DAVID M. GRING
Vice-President and Dean: KENNETH R. GARREN
Vice-President for Business Affairs: RICHARD C. HEMBERGER
Vice-President for Resource Development: JUDITH L. NELSON
Vice-President for Student Affairs: McMILLAN JOHNSON
Vice-President for Admissions Services: MICHAEL C. MAXEY
Librarian: STANLEY F. UMBERGER
Library of 170,000 vols
Number of teachers: 150
Number of students: 1,700.

SAINT PAUL'S COLLEGE

115 College Drive, Lawrenceville, VA 23868
Telephone: (434) 848-3111
Internet: www.saintpauls.edu
President: Dr JOHN KENNETH WADDELL
Provost and Vice-President for Academic Affairs: Dr KEATHEN WILSON

Vice-President for Financial Affairs: ANTONIA ROBERTS
Vice-President for Institutional Advancement: PATRICIA BENES
Vice-President for Student Affairs: ROSEMARY LEWIS.

SHENANDOAH UNIVERSITY

1460 University Drive, Winchester, VA 22601
Telephone: (540) 665-4500
Fax: (540) 678-4331
E-mail: pr@su.edu
Internet: www.su.edu
President: Dr JAMES A. DAVIS

DEANS

Conservatory: CHARLOTTE A. COLLINS
Harry F. Byrd School of Business: STAN HARRISON
School of Arts and Sciences: Dr CALVIN ALLEN
Bernard J. Dunn School of Pharmacy: (vacant)
School of Health Professions: (vacant)

SWEET BRIAR COLLEGE

Sweet Briar, VA 24595
Telephone: (804) 381-6100
Fax: (804) 381-6173
E-mail: admissions@sbc.edu
Internet: www.sbc.edu
Liberal arts and sciences college
Founded 1901
Academic year: August to May
President: Dr ELISABETH S. MUHLENFELD
Vice-President for College Relations: IVANA PELNAR-ZAIKO
Dean: Dr GEORGE H. LENZ
Associate Dean of Academic Affairs: Dr ALIX S. INGBER
Dean of Co-Curricular Life: Dr VALDRIE N. WALKER
Director of Alumnae Affairs: LOUISE S. ZINGARO
Director of Admissions: MARGARET WILLIAMS BLOUNT
Registrar: DEBBIE POWELL
Librarian: JOHN JAFFE
Library of 240,000 vols
Number of teachers: 109 (69 full-time, 40 part-time)
Number of students: 710
Publications: *Catalog* (annually), *President's Letter* (3 a year), *Alumnae Magazine* (3 a year), *Admissions Newsletter* (2 a year).

UNION THEOLOGICAL SEMINARY AND PRESBYTERIAN SCHOOL OF CHRISTIAN EDUCATION

1205 Palmyra Ave, Richmond, VA 23227
Telephone: (804) 359-5031
Fax: (804) 254-8060
Internet: www.union-psce.edu
Founded 1914
President: WAYNE G. BOULTON
Registrar: BRENDA C. BARROWS
Librarian: JOHN TROTTI
Library of 260,000 vols
Number of teachers: 14
Number of students: 139.

UNIVERSITY OF MARY WASHINGTON

1301 College Ave, Fredericksburg, VA 22401-5358
Telephone: (540) 654-1000
Fax: (540) 654-1073
Internet: www.umw.edu
Founded 1908

President: Dr WILLIAM M. ANDERSON, Jr
Vice-President for Academic Affairs and Dean of the Faculty: Dr PHILIP L. HALL
Librarian: LEROY S. STROHL, III

Number of teachers: 177
Number of students: 3,700.

UNIVERSITY OF RICHMOND

Richmond, VA 23173
Telephone: (804) 289-8000
E-mail: admissions@richmond.edu
Internet: www.richmond.edu
Chartered as Richmond College 1830; as University of Richmond 1920

President: Dr RICHARD L. MORRILL
Chancellor: E. BRUCE HEILMAN
Vice-President for Business and Finance: L. W. MOELCHERT
Vice-President and Provost: ZEDDIE P. BOWEN
Vice-President for University Relations: H. G. QUIGG
Vice-President for Student Affairs: LEONARD S. GOLDBERG
Registrar: W. VON KLEIN
Librarian (vacant)
Library of 421,000 vols
Number of teachers: 222 full-time

Number of teachers: 179 part-time
Number of students: 3,270 full-time
Number of students: 1,435 part-time

DEANS

Faculty of Arts and Sciences: F. SHELDON WETTACK
Richmond College (Men): R. A. MATEER
Westhampton College (Women): PATRICIA C. HARWOOD
Business Administration: T. L. REUSCHLING
Law: JOSEPH D. HARBAUGH
Graduate: JOHN L. GORDON, Jr
University College, Summer School, Continuing Education: M. C. GRAEBER

UNIVERSITY OF VIRGINIA

Charlottesville, VA 22904-4727
Telephone: (434) 924-0311
Fax: (434) 924-0938
Internet: www.virginia.edu
Founded 1819
Academic year: September to May

President: JOHN T. CASTEEN, III
Provost: GENE D. BLOCK
Executive Vice-President and Chief Operating Officer: LEONARD W. SANDRIDGE, Jr
Registrar: CAROL A. J. STANLEY
Dean of Students: H. E. (PENNY) RUE
Dean of Admissions (Undergraduate): JOHN A. BLACKBURN
Librarian: KARIN WITTENBORG
Library: see Libraries and Archives
Number of teachers: 2,053
Number of students: 23,765

Publications: *Virginia Quarterly Review, Virginia Law Review, Virginia Law Weekly*

DEANS

College and Graduate School of Arts and Sciences: EDWARD L. AYERS
School of Architecture: KAREN VAN LENGEN
School of Education: DAVID W. BRENEMAN
School of Engineering and Applied Science: JAMES AYLOR
Graduate School of Business Administration: ROBERT F. BRUNER
School of Law: JOHN C. JEFFRIES, Jr
School of Medicine: Dr ARTHUR GARSON, Jr
School of Nursing: B. JEANETTE LANCASTER
McIntire School of Commerce: CARL P. ZEITHAML
Continuing and Professional Studies: SONDRA STALLARD

PROFESSORS

School of Arts and Sciences (POB 400772, Charlottesville, VA 22904-4772; tel. (434) 924-3389; fax (434) 924-1317; e-mail grad-a-s@virginia.edu; internet artsandsciences.virginia.edu):

ADLER, P., Biology
ALLEN, S., Asian and Middle Eastern Languages
ALLEN, R., Chemistry
ALLEN, C., Environmental Sciences
ALLEN, J., Psychology
ALLINSON, G., History
ANDERSON, S., Economics
ANDERSON, R., Psychology
ANDERSON, A., Spanish, Italian and Portuguese
ANDREWS, L., Chemistry
ANTONOVICS, J., Biology
ARENTON, M., Physics
ARNOLD, A., French Literature and Linguistics
ARON, M., History
ARRAS, J., Philosophy
AYERS, E., History
BAKER, P., English
BALBUS, S., Astronomy
BALTES, P., Psychology
BARNETT, M., French Literature and Linguistics
BAROLSKY, P., Art
BAUERLE, R., Biology
BEATTIE, A., Creative Writing
BELANGER, T., Arts and Press
BELL, M., Art
BENNETT, B., German Literature
BERLANSTEIN, L., History
BEST, T., German Literature
BLACK, D., Sociology
BLOOM, G., Biology
BLOOMFIELD, L., Physics
BLUMBERG, R., Sociology
BOND, H., History
BOOTH, A., English
BOWERS, M., Biology and Ecology
BRADEN, G., English
BROOKS, P., English
BRUNJES, P., Psychology
BRYANT, G., Biology
BRYANT, R., Chemistry
BURNETT, R., Chemistry
BURTON, E., Economics
BYERS, E., Chemistry
CAFISO, D., Chemistry
CANTOR, P., English
CAPLOW, T., Sociology
CARGILE, J., Philosophy
CASEY, J., Creative Writing
CATES, G., Physics
CEASER, J., Government and Foreign Affairs
CHANG, T., Statistics
CHAPEL, R., Drama
CHASE-LEVENSON, S., English
CHEN, J., History
CHEVALIER, R., Astronomy
CHILDRESS, J., Religious Studies
CHRISTENSEN, B., Biology
CLAY, J., Classics
CLORE, G., Psychology
COHEN, R., English
COLOMB, G., English
CONETTI, S., Physics
CONNOLLY, J., Slavic Languages and Literature
COSBY, B., Environmental Sciences
COX, B., Physics
CRABB, D., Nuclear and Particle Physics
CRADDOCK, L., Chemistry
CRAWFORD, J., Classics
CROSBY, E., History
CROZIER, R., Art
CUSHMAN, S., English
DAMON, F., Anthropology
DASS, D., Art

DAY, D., Nuclear and Particle Physics
DEAVER, B., Physics
DELOACHE, J., Psychology
DEMAS, J., Chemistry
DEVEREUX, D., Philosophy
DILL, R., Psychology
DOBBINS, J., Art
DOLAN, R., Environmental Sciences
DOVE, R., Creative Writing
DRUCKER, J., English
DUGGAN, H., English
DUKES, E., Physics
DUNKL, C., Mathematics
EDMUNDSON, M., English
EISENBERG, D., Creative Writing
ELLENA, J., Chemistry
ELSON, M., Slavic Languages and Literature
ELZINGA, K., Economics
EMERY, R., Psychology
ENGERS, M., Economics
EPPS, T., Economics
FATTON, R., Government and Foreign Affairs
FAULKNER, J., Mathematics
FELDMAN, J., English
FELSKI, R., English
FERREIRA, M., Religious Studies
FINKEL, S., Government and Foreign Affairs
FISHBANE, P., Physics
FOGARTY, G., Religious Studies
FOULDS, G., Chemistry
FOWLER, M., Physics
FRAIMAN, S., English
FREEMAN, J., Psychology
FRICK, J., Drama
FRIESEN, W., Biology
GALLAGHER, G., History
GALLAGHER, T., Physics
GALLOWAY, J., Environmental Sciences
GAMBLE, H., Religious Studies
GARRETT, R., Biology
GARRETT, J., Physics
GEIGER, P., Art
GERLI, E., Spanish, Italian and Portuguese
GERRANS, G., Chemistry
GEYSEN, H., Chemistry
GIES, D., Spanish, Italian and Portuguese
GINESTE, C., Chemistry
GITTLEMAN, J., Biology
GOEDDE, L., Art
GRAINGER, R., Biology
GRISHAM, C., Chemistry
GRONER, P., Religious Studies
HABERLY, D., Spanish, Italian and Portuguese
HANDLER, R., Anthropology
HARMAN, W., Chemistry
HARRISON, A., Chemistry
HAWLEY, J., Astronomy
HAY, J., History
HAYDEN, B., Environmental Sciences
HAYS, S., Sociology
HECHT, S., Chemistry
HERBST, I., Mathematics
HERMAN, M., Environmental Sciences
HESS, G., Physics
HILL, D., Psychology
HIRSH, J., Biology
HOH, L., Drama
HOLT, C., Economics
HOLT, M., History
HOOK, P., Asian and Middle Eastern Languages
HOPKINS, P., Religious Studies
HORNBERGER, G., Environmental Sciences
HOWARD, A., Environmental Sciences
HOWLAND, J., Mathematics
HUECKSTEDT, R., Asian and Middle Eastern Languages
HUMPHREYS, P., Philosophy
HUNG, P., Physics
HUNT, D., Chemistry
HUNTER, J., English
HUNTER, J., Sociology

HYLTON, J., History
IMBRIE, J., Mathematics
INNES, S., History
JAMES, J., Economics
JEAN, L., Music
JEFFERY, E., Chemistry
JOHNSON, W., Economics
JONES, R., Physics
JORDAN, D., Government and Foreign Affairs
JOST, W., English
JUNG, W., German Literature
KAWASAKI, M., Biology
KEENAN, D., Statistics
KEENE, W., Environmental Sciences
KELLER, R., Biology
KETT, J., History
KHARE, R., Anthropology
KINGSTON, P., Sociology
KINNEY, A., Asian and Middle Eastern Languages
KINNEY, J., English
KLOSKO, G., Government and Foreign Affairs
KOLASINSKI, K., Chemistry
KOVACS, P., Classics
KRETSINGER, R., Biology
KRIETE, T., Mathematics
KRUEGER, C., French Literature and Linguistics
KUBOVY, M., Psychology
KUHN, N., Mathematics
KUMAR, J., Sociology
LAGOS, M., Spanish, Italian and Portuguese
LANDERS, J., Chemistry
LANE, A., History
LASIECKA, I., Mathematics
LEFFLER, M., History
LEFFLER, P., History
LEVENSON, M., English
LILLARD, T., Psychology
LINDGREN, R., Nuclear and Particle Physics
LIPSCOMB, G., Environmental Sciences
LOMASKY, L., Philosophy
LOTT, E., English
LOVING, S., Biology
LYNCH, A., Government and Foreign Affairs
LYONS, J., French Literature and Linguistics
MACCLUER, B., Mathematics
MACDONALD, T., Chemistry
MACKO, S., Environmental Sciences
MARLATT, M., Art
MARSH, C., Religious Studies
MARSHALL, J., Chemistry
MARTENS, L., German Literature
MASI, J., Biology and Ecology
MATTHEWS, S., Biology
MAUS, K., English
MCARDLE, J., Psychology
MCCRIMMON, K., Mathematics
MCCURDY, C., History
MCDANIEL, D., Spanish, Italian and Portuguese
MCDONALD, W., German Literature
MCDOWELL, D., English
MCGANN, J., English
MCKINLEY, M., French Literature and Linguistics
MCLAREN, J., Economics
MEGILL, A., History
MEJIA, J., Mathematics
MELLON, D., Biology
MENAKER, M., Biology
MERRICKS, T., Philosophy
METCALF, P., Anthropology
MICHAELS, P., Climatology
MIDELFORT, H., History
MIKALSON, J., Classics
MILANI, F., Asian and Middle Eastern Languages
MILKIS, S., Government and Foreign Affairs
MILLER, J., Classics

MILLER, J., History
MILLIGAN, B., Chemistry
MILLS, D., Economics
MILLS, A., Environmental Sciences
MINEHART, R., Physics
MIRMAN, L., Economics
NELSON, R., English
NELSON, K., Physics
NESSELROADE, J., Psychology
NIMA, T., Religious Studies
NOCK, S., Sociology
NOHRNBERG, J., English
NOLAN, B., English
NORUM, B., Physics
O'BRIEN, D., Government and Foreign Affairs
OCHS, P., Religious Studies
O'CONNELL, R., Astronomy
OLSEN, E., Economics
ONUF, P., History
OPERE, F., Spanish, Italian and Portuguese
ORR, G., Creative Writing
OSHEIM, D., History
PARKER, D., Spanish, Italian and Portuguese
PARSHALL, B., Mathematics
PARSHALL, K., Mathematics
PATE, B., Chemistry
PATTERSON, R., Astronomy
PATTERSON, C., Psychology
PEDDADA, S., Statistics
PERDUE, C., Anthropology
PERIASAMY, A., Biology
PERKOWSKI, J., Slavic Languages and Literature
PERRY, L., Art
PITT, L., Mathematics
PLOG, S., Anthropology
POCANIC, D., Physics
POON, J., Physics
POOSSON, H., Development
POPE, R., Spanish, Italian and Portuguese
PROFFITT, D., Psychology
PU, L., Chemistry
QUANDT, W., Government and Foreign Affairs
RAILTON, S., English
RAMAZANI, R., English
RAMIREZ, D., Mathematics
RAPINCHUK, A., Mathematics
RAY, B., Religious Studies
REPPUCCI, N., Psychology
REYNOLDS, B., Economics
RHOADS, S., Government and Foreign Affairs
RICHARDSON, F., Chemistry
RICKARDS, W., Marine Science
RINI, J., Spanish, Italian and Portuguese
ROBERTS, M., Art
ROGER, P., French Literature and Linguistics
RONDON-ARAMAYO, O., Nuclear and Particle Physics
ROOD, R., Astronomy
ROSS, M., English
ROVNYAK, J., Mathematics
RUVALDS, J., Physics
RYAN, K., Slavic Languages and Literature
SABAT, M., Chemistry
SACHEDINA, A., Religious Studies
SALTHOUSE, T., Psychology
SAPIR, J., Anthropology
SARAZIN, C., Astronomy
SASLAW, W., Astronomy
SAVAGE, J., Government and Foreign Affairs
SAWAIE, M., Asian and Middle Eastern Languages
SCHUKER, S., History
SCHUTTE, A., History
SCHWARTZ, H., Government and Foreign Affairs
SCOTT, L., Mathematics
SENETA, E., Mathematics
SENEVIRATNE, H., Anthropology
SHABANOWITZ, J., Chemistry

SHATIN, J., Music
SHAW, D., Spanish, Italian and Portuguese
SHIFFLETT, T., Physics
SHUGART, H., Environmental Sciences
SIMMONS, A., Philosophy
SKRUTSKIE, M., Astronomy
SMITH, D., Environmental Sciences
SMITH, T., French Literature and Linguistics
SPACKS, P., English
SPEARING, A., English
STAGG, J., History
STERN, S., Economics
STINNETT, B., Economics
STONG, R., Mathematics
STRAWN, S., Art
SUMMERS, J., Art
SUNDBERG, R., Chemistry
TAYLOR, D., Biology
TEKIN, B., Sociology
THACKER, H., Physics
THOMAS, M., History
THOMAS, L., Mathematics
THOMPSON, K., Government and Foreign Affairs
THORNTON, S., Physics
THUAN, T., Astronomy
TILGHMAN, C., Creative Writing
TIMKO, M., Biology
TOLBERT, C., Astronomy
TRADER, S., Music
TRIGGIANI, R., Mathematics
TRINDLE, C., Chemistry
TUCKER, H., English
TURKHEIMER, E., Psychology
UPTON, D., Anthropology
VAN DER MEULEN, L., English
VAN WINCOOP, E., Economics
VORIS, R., German Literature
WAGNER, R., Anthropology
WARD, H., Mathematics
WELLBELOVED-STONE, E., Spanish, Italian and Portuguese
WHITE, S., Government and Foreign Affairs
WHITTLE, D., Astronomy
WIBERG, P., Environmental Sciences
WICKE, J., English
WILBUR, H., Biology
WILKEN, R., Religious Studies
WILLINGHAM, D., Psychology
WILSON, M., Asian and Middle Eastern Languages
WILSON, M., Psychology
WILSON, T., Psychology
WOMACK, B., Government and Foreign Affairs
WOODMAN, A., Classics
WRIGHT, C., Creative Writing
ZIEMAN, J., Environmental Sciences
ZUNZ, O., History

School of Architecture (POB 400122, Charlottesville, VA 22904-4122; tel. (434) 924-3715; fax (434) 982-2678; internet www.virginia.edu/arch):

BEATLEY, T., Planning
BOESCHENSTEIN, W., Architecture
BYRD, W., Landscape
CLARK, W., Architecture
COLLINS, R., Planning
COUTURE, L., Architecture
DRIPPS, R., Architecture
FORD, E., Architecture
LUCY, W., Planning
MONGER, M., Development
MORRISH, W., Architecture
RAINEY, R., Landscape
SPAIN, D., Planning
VAN LENGEN, K., Architecture
WALDMAN, P., Architecture
WILSON, R., History of Architecture

Curry School of Education (POB 400260, Charlottesville, VA 22904-4260; tel. (434) 924-3334; fax (434) 924-0747; e-mail curry@

virginia.edu; internet curry.edschool.virginia .edu):

BANDARRA, T., Continuing and Professional Studies
BREDO, E., Education
BULL, G., Education
BUNKER, L., Human Services
BURBACH, H., Education
BUTLER, A., Education
CALLAHAN, C., Education
CALLAN, H., Continuing and Professional Studies
COHEN, S., Special Education
CONLEY, K., Continuing and Professional Studies
COOK, J., Human Services
CORNELL, D., Human Services
DUKE, D., Education
FAN, X., Education
FLEMING, K., Continuing and Professional Studies
GAESSER, G., Human Services
GANSNEDER, B., Education
GIBBS, A., Education
GILLETTE-MALLARD, K., Continuing and Professional Studies
GUBBINS, M., Continuing and Professional Studies
HALLAHAN, D., Special Education
HOLOD, O., Continuing and Professional Studies
INVERNIZZI, M., Special Education
KAPLAN, V., Continuing and Professional Studies
KELLY, L., Human Services
LANDRUM, T., Special Education
LAWRENCE, E., Human Services
LOPER, A., Human Services
MARSHALL, T., Continuing and Professional Studies
MCNERGNEY, R., Education
MERRYMAN, K., Continuing and Professional Studies
MILLER, M., Education
MONTGOMERY, M., Continuing and Professional Studies
NORDIN, B., Human Services
O'CONNOR, M., Continuing and Professional Studies
ORDORIKA, I., Education
PHILLIPS-MADSON, L., Continuing and Professional Studies
PIANTA, R., Human Services
POWELL, P., Human Services
REEVE, R., Human Services
RICHARDS, H., Education
ROBERSON, S., Continuing and Professional Studies
ROBERTS, S., Education
ROGERS, B., Education
SHERAS, P., Human Services
SHORT, J., Education
SNELL, M., Special Education
STALLARD, S., Continuing and Professional Studies
STERLING, J., Continuing and Professional Studies
STOVALL, J., Human Services
STRANG, H., Education
TOMLINSON, C., Education
WAGONER, J., Education
WEISS, M., Human Services
WELTMAN, A., Human Services
WHITE, S., Continuing and Professional Studies
WILLIS, C., Continuing and Professional Studies
YANG, P., Continuing and Professional Studies

School of Engineering and Applied Science (POB 400246, Charlottesville, VA 22904-4246; tel. (434) 924-3072; fax (434) 924-3555; internet www.seas.virginia.edu):

ALLAIRE, P., Mechanical and Aerospace Engineering

AYLOR, J., Electronic Engineering and Computer Science
BARAGIOLA, R., Mathematical Sciences
BARRETT, L., Mechanical and Aerospace Engineering
BASS, C., Mechanical and Aerospace Engineering
BEAN, J., Electronic Engineering and Computer Science
BEATRICE, J., Electronic Engineering and Computer Science
BROWN, D., Systems and Information Engineering
CAHEN, G., Mathematical Sciences
CARTA, G., Chemical Engineering
COOK, L., Mechanical and Aerospace Engineering
CROWE, T., Electronic Engineering and Computer Science
CUTRIGHT, E., Electronic Engineering and Computer Science
DAVIDSON, J., Computer Science
DAVIS, R., Chemical Engineering
DELONG, T., Electronic Engineering and Computer Science
DEMETSKY, M., Chemical Engineering
DHARMASENA, K., Mathematical Sciences
DITMAR, J., Systems and Information Engineering
DORNING, J., Mathematical Sciences
DUGAN, J., Electronic Engineering and Computer Science
FAULCONER, V., Chemical Engineering
FISHER, S., Mechanical and Aerospace Engineering
FLACK, R., Mechanical and Aerospace Engineering
FORD, R., Chemical Engineering
GAINER, J., Chemical Engineering
GANGLOFF, R., Mathematical Sciences
GARBER, N., Chemical Engineering
GILLIES, G., Mechanical and Aerospace Engineering
GIRAS, T., Electronic Engineering and Computer Science
GRIMSHAW, A., Computer Science
HAIMES, Y., Systems and Information Engineering
HAJ-HARIRI, H., Mechanical and Aerospace Engineering
HARRIOTT, L., Electronic Engineering and Computer Science
HOEL, L., Chemical Engineering
HORGAN, C., Chemical Engineering
HOROWITZ, B., Systems and Information Engineering
HUTCHINSON, T., Systems and Information Engineering
HOWE, J., Mathematical Sciences
HUDSON, J., Chemical Engineering
HULL, R., Mathematical Sciences
HUMPHREY, J., Mechanical and Aerospace Engineering
IWASAKI, T., Mechanical and Aerospace Engineering
JESSER, W., Mathematical Sciences
JOHNSON, B., Electronic Engineering and Computer Science
JOHNSON, R., Mathematical Sciences
JOHNSON, W., Mathematical Sciences
JONES, A., Computer Science
KELLY, R., Mathematical Sciences
KIRWAN, D., Chemical Engineering
KNIGHT, J., Computer Science
KRZYSZTOFOWICZ, R., Systems and Information Engineering
LIEBEHERR, J., Computer Science
LUNG, W., Chemical Engineering
MALONE, S., Electronic Engineering and Computer Science
MARSHALL, P., Electronic Engineering and Computer Science
MASLEN, E., Mechanical and Aerospace Engineering
MCDANIEL, J., Mechanical and Aerospace Engineering

MIKSAD, R., Chemical Engineering
MONFALCONE, M., Electronic Engineering and Computer Science
NEUROCK, M., Chemical Engineering
NGUYEN-TUONG, A., Computer Science
NORRIS, P., Mechanical and Aerospace Engineering
O'CONNELL, J., Chemical Engineering
OLESHKO, V., Mathematical Sciences
OU, Y., Electronic Engineering and Computer Science
PARRISH, P., Mathematical Sciences
PILKEY, W., Mechanical and Aerospace Engineering
PINDERA, M., Chemical Engineering
PREDMORE, S., Systems and Information Engineering
REED, M., Electronic Engineering and Computer Science
REESE, J., Mathematical Sciences
REYNOLDS, P., Computer Science
ROBERTS, W., Mechanical and Aerospace Engineering
ROBINS, G., Computer Science
SCULLY, J., Mathematical Sciences
SHAW, C., Mechanical and Aerospace Engineering
SHIFLET, G., Mathematical Sciences
SILVERSTEIN, S., Electronic Engineering and Computer Science
SKALAK, T., Biomedical Engineering
SOFFA, M., Computer Science
SOFFA, W., Mathematical Sciences
SON, S., Computer Science
STANKOVIC, J., Computer Science
STARKE, E., Mathematical Sciences
THACKER, J., Mechanical and Aerospace Engineering
THOMAS, V., Mathematical Sciences
THOMPSON, S., Mathematical Sciences
TRAIL, J., Mathematical Sciences
VANCE, P., Chemical Engineering
WADLEY, H., Mathematical Sciences
WANNER, A., Systems and Information Engineering
WEAVER, A., Computer Science
WHITE, K., Systems and Information Engineering
WILSDORF, D., Mathematical Sciences
WILSON, S., Electronic Engineering and Computer Science
WOLF, S., Mathematical Sciences
WOOD, H., Mechanical and Aerospace Engineering
WULF, W., Computer Science
ZHU, A., Mathematical Sciences

Darden School (Graduate School of Business Administration) (POB 400321, Charlottesville, VA 22904-4321; tel. (434) 924-3900; fax (434) 924-4859; internet www.darden .edu):

ALLEN, B., Business Administration
ALSTON, S., Business Administration
ANSARI, S., Business Administration
BECKENSTEIN, A., Business Administration
BICKERS, K., Business Administration
BODILY, S., Business Administration
BOURGEOIS, L., Business Administration
BROWNLEE, E., Business Administration
BRUNER, R., Business Administration
CHAPLINSKY, S., Business Administration
CHEN, M., Business Administration
CHESELDINE, C., Business Administration
CLAWSON, J., Business Administration
COLLEY, J., Business Administration
CONROY, R., Business Administration
COOK, D., Business Administration
DAVIS, D., Business Administration
EADES, K., Business Administration
EAKER, M., Business Administration
FARQUHAR, P., Business Administration
FARRIS, P., Business Administration
FREELAND, J., Business Administration
FREEMAN, R., Business Administration
FREY, S., Business Administration

GLYNN, J., Business Administration
HARRIS, R., Business Administration
HASKINS, M., Business Administration
HORNIMAN, A., Business Administration
HUDSON, R., Business Administration
JONES, M., Business Administration
KOZUCH, C., Business Administration
LANDEL, R., Business Administration
LEHMBECK, C., Business Administration
LIEDTKA, J., Business Administration
McCOOL, S., Business Administration
MOORE, M., Business Administration
MOORE, M., Business Administration
MORIARTY, L., Business Administration
PARMAR, B., Business Administration
PARRY, M., Business Administration
PEYTON, M., Business Administration
PFEIFER, P., Business Administration
ROBERTS, D., Business Administration
SHABANOWITZ, G., Business Administration
SIHLER, W., Business Administration
SPEKMAN, R., Business Administration
TEW, A., Business Administration
TRUZY, B., Business Administration
VENKATARAMAN, S., Business Administration
WEBER, R., Business Administration
WEISS, E., Business Administration
WERHANE, P., Business Administration

McIntire School of Commerce (POB 400173, Charlottesville, VA 22904-4173; tel. (434) 924-3257; internet www.commerce.virginia.edu):

AKIN, G.
ATCHISON, M.
AWAD, E.
BATEMAN, T.
BROOME, O.
DE MONG, F.
HATCH, M.
JONES, S.
KEHOE, W.
KEMP, R.
LINDGREN, J.
MALONEY, D.
MATTERA, J.
MICK, D.
NELSON, R.
NETEMEYER, R.
OVERSTREET, G.
PETTIT, J.
SHENKIR, W.
SMITH, D.
TODD, P.
TURNER, A.
WEBB, R.
WHITENER, E.
WILHELM, W.
WILLIAMS, S.
ZEITHAML, C.

School of Law (POB 400405, Charlottesville, VA 22904-4405; tel. (434) 924-7354; fax (434) 924-7536; internet www.law.virginia.edu):

ABRAHAM, K., Law
ARMACOST, B., Law
BALNAVE, R., Law
BEVIER, L., Law
BLASI, V., Law
BONNIE, R., Law
BRADLEY, C., Law
BUCK, D., Law
CANNON, J., Law
COHEN, G., Law
COUGHLIN, A., Law
CUSHMAN, B., Law
DERRICK, C., Law
DOOLEY, M., Law
DUDLEY, E., Law
FORDE-MAZRUI, K., Law
GOETZ, C., Law
HARRISON, J., Law
HINTON, A., Law
HOWARD, A., Law
IBBEKEN, D., Law
JEFFRIES, J., Law

KITCH, E., Law
KLARMAN, M., Law
KORDANA, K., Law
KRAUS, J., Law
LESLIE, D., Law
LILLY, G., Law
LONG, C., Law
LOW, P., Law
MAGILL, M., Law
MAHONEY, J., Law
MAHONEY, P., Law
MARTIN, D., Law
MERRILL, R., Law
MNOOKIN, J., Law
MONAHAN, J., Law
MOORE, J., Law
NELSON, C., Law
O'CONNELL, J., Law
O'NEIL, R., Law
ORTIZ, D., Law
PETERS, R., Law
ROBINSON, G., Law
ROBINSON, M., Law
RUTHERGLEN, G., Law
RYAN, J., Law
SAYLER, R., Law
SCOTT, E., Law
SCOTT, R., Law
SETEAR, J., Law
SINCLAIR, K., Law
STEPHAN, P., Law
TRIANTIS, G., Law
VERKERKE, J., Law
WALKER, W., Law
WALT, S., Law
WHITE, G., Law
WHITE, T., Law
WOOD, K., Law
WOOLHANDLER, N., Law
YIN, G., Law

School of Medicine (POB 800793, Charlottesville, VA 22908-0793; tel. (434) 924-5118; internet www.med.virginia.edu/schools/medschl.html):

ABEL, M., Paediatric Orthopaedics
ALPERN, D., Anaesthesiology
APPREY, M., Psychiatric Medicine
ARKHURST, P., Cell Signalling
ARSURA, E., Medicine
AYERS, C., Medicine
AYERS, S., Prosthetics and Orthotics
BAIRD, J., General Medicine
BALIAN, G., Orthopaedic Research
BANTON, M., Spinal Disease
BARRETT, E., Endocrinology
BARRETT, P., Pharmacology
BARTH, J., Psychiatric Medicine
BATTEN, R., Anaesthesiology
BAUM, V., Anaesthesiology
BECKER, D., General Medicine
BELLER, G., Medicine
BENDER, T., Microbiology
BENNETT, J., Neurology
BERNIER, R., General Medicine
BERTRAM, E., Neurology
BEYER, A., Microbiology
BLACKMAN, J., Paediatrics
BLECK, T., Neurology
BLOEDORN, W., Paediatrics
BLOODGOOD, R., Cell Biology
BOLTON, W., Nephrology
BORISH, L., Allergy Research
BOROWITZ, S., Paediatrics
BOYLE, R., Paediatrics
BRACIALE, T., Pathology
BRANT, W., Thoracoabdominal Radiology
BRAUTIGAN, D., Cell Signalling
BRAYMAN, K., Surgery
BROOKEMAN, J., Radiological Research
BROWN, J., Microbiology
BROWN, G., Psychiatric Medicine
BRUNS, D., Pathology
BUCKMAN, J., Psychiatric Medicine
BURKE, D., Biochemistry and Molecular Genetics

BURNS, J., Microbiology
BYWATERS, S., Pathology
CAMPBELL, M., Microbiology
CANTERBURY, R., Psychiatric Medicine
CAREY, R., Endocrinology
CASTLE, J., Cell Biology
CHERRY, K., Surgery
CHEVALIER, R., Paediatrics
CHIRGWIN, J., Endocrinology
CLARKE, W., Paediatrics
CLAYTON, A., Psychiatric Medicine
COLEMAN, M., Paediatrics
COMINELLI, F., Gastroenterology
CONNELLY, J., General Medicine
CONWAY, B., Ophthalmology
CORWIN, J., Neuroscience
COURTNEY, C., Cardiovascular Disease
COUSAR, J., Pathology
COVERT, L., Psychiatric Medicine
COX, D., Psychiatric Medicine
CRAWFORD, W., Cell Biology
CREUTZ, C., Pharmacology
CRICKENBERGER, T., Surgery
CRISSMAN, H., Orthopaedic Surgery
CROSBY, I., Surgery
DANIEL, T., Surgery
DAY, J., Emergency Medicine
DAY, E., Infectious Diseases
DE LANGE, E., Radiology
DEEDS, L., Developmental Paediatrics
DEREWENDA, Z., Molecular Physics and Biophysics
DESIMONE, D., Cell Biology
DIMARCO, J., Medicine
DONATO, G., Infectious Diseases
DONOWITZ, G., Infectious Diseases
DRAGULEV, B., Microbiology
DULING, B., Molecular Physics and Biophysics
DURBIN, C., Anaesthesiology
DURIEUX, M., Anaesthesiology
DUTTA, A., Biochemistry and Molecular Genetics
DWYER, S., Radiological Research
EGELMAN, E., Biochemistry and Molecular Genetics
ENGELHARD, V., Microbiology
ERNST, P., Gastroenterology
ESTES, P., Psychiatric Medicine
EVANS, W., Endocrinology
EVANS, M., Neurology
FARR, B., Epidemiology
FELDER, R., Pathology
FERGUSON, W., Surgery
FIELDS, H., Surgery
FITCH, P., Neurology
FLAMMIA, A., Surgery
FLICKINGER, C., Cell Biology
FOX, J., Microbiology
FRENCH, J., Microbiology
FRIDAY, V., Paediatrics
FRIEND, R., Genetic and Clinical Research
FRIERSON, H., Pathology
FRYSINGER, R., Multiple Neuralgia
FU, S., Rheumatology
GAL, T., Anaesthesiology
GALAZKA, S., Family Medicine
GARRISON, J., Pharmacology
GASKIN, F., Psychiatric Medicine
GASTON, B., Paediatrics
GAY, S., Radiology
GEAR, A., Biochemistry and Molecular Genetics
GIBSON, R., Medicine
GILES, I., Ophthalmology
GIMPLE, L., Medicine
GOLDBERG, J., Microbiology
GOLDEN, W., Pathology
GREER, K., Dermatology
GRESS, J., Plastic Surgery
GREYSON, C., Psychiatric Medicine
GRIGERA, P., Microbiology
GROSSMAN, L., Paediatrics
GUERRANT, R., Geographic Medicine
GUISE, T., Endocrinology
GUMBINER, B., Cell Biology

GUMM, C., Biomedicine and Ethics
GUTGESELL, H., Paediatrics
GUYENET, P., Pharmacology
HACKETT, J., Molecular Physics and Biophysics
HALEY, E., Neurology
HAMLIN, J., Biochemistry and Molecular Genetics
HAMMARSKJOLD, M., Microbiology
HANDY, D., Orthopaedics
HANEY, S., Radiation Oncology
HANKS, J., Surgery
HARLOW, P., Surgery
HARRIS, D., Endocrinology
HAYDEN, F., Epidemiology
HAYDEN, G., Paediatrics
HAZEN, K., Pathology
HEIMER, L., Neuroscience
HENDLEY, J., Paediatrics
HERNDON, D., Genetic and Clinical Research
HERR, J., Cell Biology
HERRING, P., Radiology
HESS, C., Haemotology and Oncology
HEWLETT, E., Clinical Pharmacy
HEYMANN, P., Paediatrics
HILL, M., Genetics
HILLMAN, B., Radiology
HINTON, B., Cell Biology
HOBBS, W., Psychiatric Medicine
HOLLEY, J., Nephrology
HOLROYD, S., Psychiatric Medicine
HOPKINS, E., General Medicine
HORWITZ, A., Cell Biology
HOSTLER, S., Paediatrics
HOWARDS, S., Urology
HUDSON, W., Family Medicine
HUGHES, S., Infectious Diseases
HURWITZ, S., Orthopaedics
INNES, D., Pathology
JAGGER, J., Infectious Diseases
JANE, J., Paediatrics
JENKINS, P., Anaesthesiology
JENSEN, M., Radiology
JOHNSON, M., Pharmacology
JOHNSON, B., Psychiatric Medicine
JONES, R., Surgery
JU, S., Rheumatology
KACER, M., Family Medicine
KADNER, R., Microbiology
KASSELL, N., Cardiovascular Disease
KATTWINKEL, J., Paediatrics
KAUL, S., Medicine
KERRIGAN, D., Physical Rehabilitation
KIM, Y., Biomedical Engineering
KINNIER, J., Neuroscience
KOENIG, S., Pulmonary Medicine
KONIZER, M., Genetics
KRIIGEL, N., Pathology
KRON, I., Surgery
KURTH, B., Cell Biology
KUTCHAI, H., Molecular Physics and Biophysics
LANG, M., Urology
LANIK, E., Family Medicine
LAURENCIN, C., Sports Medicine
LAWRENCE, J., Pharmacology
LAWS, E., Neuroendocrinology
LAWSON, B., Orthopaedics
LEE, K., Neuroscience
LEY, K., Biomedical Engineering
LINDEN, J., Medicine
LIPPER, M., Neuroradiology
LOCKETT, D., Anaesthesiology
LOGAN, E., Genetic and Clinical Research
LOGIN, I., Neurology
LYNCH, C., Anaesthesiology
LYNCH, K., Pharmacology
MACARA, I., Cell Signalling
MARSHALL, J., Endocrinology
MARTIN, M., Emergency Medicine
MASSARO, T., Paediatrics
MATHERNE, G., Paediatrics
MATSUMOTO, A., Radiology
MATTYSSE, V., Genetic and Clinical Research

MCCALL, A., Endocrinology
MCCUTCHEON, L., Microbiology
MCGEE, N., Radiology
MEACHUM-WHITEHILL, M., General Medicine
MILLER, J., Neurology
MILLER, S., Surgery
MILLS, S., Pathology
MINOR, W., Molecular Physics and Biophysics
MINTZ, P., Pathology
MOORE, C., Emergency Medicine
MOORMAN, J., Medicine
MORGAN, R., Plastic Surgery
MORI, L., Medicine
MUGLER, J., Radiological Research
NADLER, J., Endocrinology
NEWMAN, S., Ophthalmology
NOLAN, S., Surgery
NOWAKOWSKI, B., Pathology
OBRIG, T., Nephrology
OKUSA, M., Nephrology
ORLOVA, A., Biochemistry and Molecular Genetics
OSTEEN, K., Paediatrics
OSWALD, M., Paediatrics
OVERSTREET, S., Neurology
OWENS, G., Molecular Physics and Biophysics
PARKER, W., Neurology
PARSONS, J., Microbiology
PARSONS, S., Microbiology
PATRICK, C., Family Medicine
PATTERSON, J., Pathology
PEARSON, W., Biochemistry and Molecular Genetics
PEARSON, R., Geographic Medicine
PETRI, W., Infectious Diseases
PEURA, D., Gastroenterology
PHILBRICK, J., General Medicine
PHILLIPS, L., Neurology
PHILLIPS, C., Radiology
PLATTS-MILLS, T., Allergy Research
PORTERFIELD, P., Psychiatric Medicine
POWELL, T., Neurology
POWERS, E., Medicine
POWLEY, L., Orthopaedics
PRUETT, T., Surgery
RAVICHANDRAN, K., Microbiology
REBAR, R., Orthopaedics
REED, D., Pathology
REIN, M., Infectious Diseases
REKOSH, D., Microbiology
REMBOLD, C., Medicine
REYNOLDS, D., Biochemistry and Molecular Genetics
RHEUBAN, K., Paediatrics
RICH, G., Anaesthesiology
RICH, T., Radiation Oncology
RISSMAN, E., Biochemistry and Molecular Genetics
RODEHEAVER, G., Plastic Surgery
RODGERS, B., Surgery
ROSE, C., Pulmonary Medicine
ROSS, W., Anaesthesiology
ROSS, M., Haemotology and Oncology
ROWLINGSON, J., Anaesthesiology
ROWSEY, L., Cell Biology
RUST, R., Neurology
SALLER, D., Maternal and Foetal Medicine
SANDO, S., Anaesthesiology
SANTEN, R., Endocrinology
SAREMBOCK, I., Medicine
SAULSBURY, F., Paediatrics
SAVORY, J., Pathology
SCHELD, W., Infectious Diseases
SCHENK, W., Surgery
SCHIRMER, B., Surgery
SCHLAGER, T., Emergency Medicine
SCHORLING, J., General Medicine
SCHWARTZ, M., Microbiology
SEUFFERT, L., Family Medicine
SHAFFER, H., Thoracoabdominal Radiology
SHAFFREY, M., Neuro-Oncology
SHAFFREY, C., Neuro-Oncology

SHAO, Z., Molecular Physics and Biophysics
SHENKER, D., Neurology
SHENTON, P., Cardiovascular Disease
SHIPE, A., Medicine
SHORR, E., Cell Biology
SHUPNIK, M., Endocrinology
SILVERMAN, L., Pathology
SIRAGY, H., Endocrinology
SISK, B., Neurology
SLAWSON, D., Family Medicine
SLINGLUFF, C., Surgery
SLOHODA, P., Paediatrics
SMITH, M., Microbiology
SNOW, T., Pharmacology
SOMLYO, A., Molecular Physics and Biophysics
SPENCER, P., Psychiatric Medicine
SPINNER-CHAMBERS, G., Surgery
SPRADLIN, S., Medicine
STATON, M., Cell Biology
STEERS, W., Urology
STEINER, L., Gamma Knife Surgery
STEVENSON, R., Paediatrics
STOLER, M., Surgical Pathology
STRICKLER, E., Psychiatric Medicine
STURGILL, T., Pharmacology
SURATT, P., Pulmonary Medicine
SUTHERLAND, W., Cell Biology
SUTPHEN, J., Paediatrics
SZABO, G., Molecular Physics and Biophysics
TAMM, L., Molecular Physics and Biophysics
TAPSCOTT, S., Anaesthesiology
TAWNEY, L., Endocrinology
TAYLOR, R., Biochemistry and Molecular Genetics
TEMPLETON, D., Pathology
THEODORESCU, D., Urology
THIELE, M., Surgical Pathology
THOMPSON, A., Pathology
THOMPSON, C., Radiological Research
TIEDEMAN, J., Ophthalmology
TRIBBLE, C., Surgery
TRUWIT, J., Pulmonary Medicine
TUNG, K., Pathology
TURNER, R., Paediatrics
TURNER, T., Urology
TUTTLE, J., Neuroscience
VANCE, M., Endocrinology
VAUGHAN, N., Radiology
WADE, R., Pathology
WARREN, J., Psychiatric Medicine
WATERS, D., Family Medicine
WATSON, D., Radiological Research
WEBER, M., Microbiology
WELLONS, H., General Surgery
WHITE, J., Cell Biology
WHITE, P., Genetics
WHITEHILL, R., Spinal Orthopaedics
WICK, P., Pathology
WILLIAMS, M., General Medicine
WILLIAMS, M., Haemotology and Oncology
WILLIAMSON, B., Nuclear Medicine
WILSON, W., Paediatrics
WISPELWEY, B., Infectious Diseases
WOOTEN, G., Neurology
WRIGHT, C., Pharmacology
YOUNG, R., Diabetes and Hormone Studies

School of Nursing (POB 800782, Charlottesville, VA 22908-0782; tel. (434) 924-0141; e-mail nur-osa@virginia.edu; internet www.nursing.virginia.edu):

HERNDON, M., Nursing
HOLLEN, P., Nursing
JACOX, A., Nursing
KEELING, A., Nursing
LANCASTER, B., Nursing
LYDER, C., Nursing
MERWIN, E., Nursing
PARKER, B., Nursing
QUEEN, G., Nursing
RAPP, J., Nursing
ROVNYAK, V., Nursing

SPENGLER, C., Nursing
TAYLOR, A., Nursing

AFFILIATED COLLEGE

University of Virginia's College at Wise:
Wise, VA 24293; Chancellor STEVEN KAPLAN;
72 teachers; 1,480 students

PROFESSORS

ACHUA, C., Business
BLACKBURN, G., Education and History
CANTRELL, R., Education
COSTA, T., History
DANIEL, V., Chemistry
RICHARDSON, S., Education
ROUSE, D., Philosophy
SCOLNICK, J., Political Science
SHELDON, G., Political Science
SMITH, J., Education and Psychology
TUCKER, M., Chemistry
WHEATLEY, F., Education
WILLS, B., History
YUN, P., Economics
ZYLAWY, R., French

VIRGINIA COMMONWEALTH UNIVERSITY

910 West Franklin St, Richmond, VA 23284
Telephone: (804) 828-0100
E-mail: cipia@vcu.edu
Internet: www.vcu.edu

Founded 1838 as the medical department of Hampden-Sydney College. Richmond Professional Institute and Medical College of Virginia merged in 1968 to form this University

State control

Academic year: August to May

President: Dr EUGENE P. TRANI

Provost and Vice-President for Academic Affairs: RODERICK J. McDAVIS

Vice-President for Finance and Administration: PAUL W. TIMMRECK

Vice-President for Health Sciences and Chief Executive Officer of the VCU Health System: HERMES A. KONTOS

Vice-President for Advancement: PETER L. WYETH

Vice-President for Government and Community Relations: DONALD C. GEHRING

Vice-President for Research: MARSHA R. TORR

Vice-President for University Outreach: SUE A. MESSMER

Library of 1,680,393 vols, 3,007,035 microforms, 0,188 printed journals, 17,441 electronic journals

Number of teachers: 1,660 full-time

Number of students: 25,001

DEANS

College of the Humanities and Sciences: STEPHEN D. GOTTFREDSON

School of the Arts: RICHARD E. TOSCAN

School of Business: MICHAEL SEZNOWITZ

School of Education: RICHARD J. REZBA

School of Social Work: FRANK R. BASKIND

School of Allied Health Professions: CECIL B. DRAIN

School of Dentistry: RONALD J. HUNT

School of Engineering: ROBERT J. MATTAUCH

School of Medicine: HEBER H. NEWSOME, JR.

School of Nursing: NANCY F. LANGSTON

School of Pharmacy: VICTOR A. YANCHICK

School of Graduate Studies: ALBERT T. SNEDEN

VIRGINIA INTERMONT COLLEGE

1013 Moore Street, Bristol, VA 24201
Telephone: (540) 669-6101
Fax: (540) 669-5763
E-mail: vicadmit@vic.edu
Internet: www.vic.edu

Founded 1884
President: Dr STEPHEN G. GREINER.

VIRGINIA MILITARY INSTITUTE

Lexington, VA 24450
Telephone: (540) 464-7207
Internet: www.vmi.edu
Founded 1839
Superintendent: Maj.-Gen. JOSIAH BUNTING III
Dean: Col ALAN F. FARRELL
Business Executive: Col JOHN L. ROWE, Jr
Commandant: Col KEITH D. DICKSON
Treasurer: Lt-Col GARY R. KNICK
Librarian: Lt-Col DONALD H. SAMDAHL, Jr (acting)
Library of 248,000 vols
Number of teachers: 99 full-time; 16 part-time, 26 military
Number of students: 1,300 men and women
Publication: *Catalogue.*

VIRGINIA POLYTECHNIC INSTITUTE AND STATE UNIVERSITY

Blacksburg, VA 24061
Telephone: (703) 231-6000
E-mail: vtadmiss@vt.edu
Internet: www.vt.edu
Founded 1872
State control
Academic year: August to May
President: Dr CHARLES W. STEGER
Provost: MARK G. McNAMEE
Executive Vice-President and Chief Operating Officer: M. E. RIDENOUR
Vice-President, Development: ELIZABETH A. FLANAGAN
Vice-President, Information Technology: EARVING BLYTHE
Vice-President, Student Affairs: LANDRUM CROSS
Director of Admissions: KAREN TORGERSEN
Librarian: EILEEN HITCHINGHAM
Number of teachers: 1,654 full-time
Number of students: 25,912
Publications: *Research Magazine, Virginia Tech Magazine, Virginia Issues and Answers*

DEANS

Agriculture: G. N. BROWN
Architecture: PAUL KNOX
Arts and Sciences: LAY NAM CHANG
Business: R. E. SORENSEN
Engineering: HASSAN AREF
Forestry: G. N. BROWN
Human Resources and Education: JEROME NILES
Graduate: KAREN DePAUW
Veterinary Medicine: P. EYRE
Extension: JOHN DOOLEY
Research: JAMES BLAIR

VIRGINIA STATE UNIVERSITY

Petersburg, VA 23806
Telephone: (804) 524-5000
Fax: (804) 524-6505
E-mail: admiss@vsu.edu
Internet: www.vsu.edu
Founded by State of Virginia as Virginia Normal and Collegiate Institute 1882; opened 1883; name changed to Virginia Normal and Industrial Institute 1902; to Virginia State College for Negroes 1930; to Virginia State College 1946; to Virginia State University 1979
President: EDDIE N. MOORE, Jr
Library of 245,731 vols
Number of teachers: 191

Number of students: 4,007

DEANS

School of Agriculture Sciences and Technology: Dr LORENZA W. LYONS
School of Business: Dr SADIE R. GREGORY
School of Liberal Arts and Education: Dr SAMUEL L. CREIGHTON
School of Continuing Education and Graduate Studies: Dr WAYNE F. VIRAG

VIRGINIA THEOLOGICAL SEMINARY

3737 Seminary Rd, Alexandria, VA 22304
Telephone: (703) 370-6600
Fax: (703) 370-6234
E-mail: admissions@vts.edu
Internet: www.vts.edu
Founded 1823
Dean and President: Very Rev. MARTHA J. HORNE
Vice-President for Academic Affairs: Very Rev. MARTHA J. HORNE
Vice-President for Administration and Finance: MARY LEWIS HIX
Vice-President for Institutional Advancement: EDWIN KING HALL
Librarian: MITZI JARRETT BUDDE.

VIRGINIA UNION UNIVERSITY

1500 North Lombardy St, Richmond, VA 23220
Telephone: (804) 257-5600
Fax: (804) 257-5818
Internet: www.vuu.edu
Founded 1865
Academic year: August to May
President: Dr BERNARD W. FRANKLIN
Vice-President for Academic Affairs: Dr W. WELDON HILL
Vice-President for Financial Affairs: ROBERT BUSCH
Director of University Services: GILBERT L. CARTER
Vice-President for Student Affairs: WILBERT D. TALLEY
Registrar: Mrs JANICE D. BAILEY
Librarian: Dr VONITA W. FOSTER
Library of 162,000 vols
Number of teachers: 102
Number of students: 1,617

DEANS

Sydney Lewis School of Business: Dr PHILIP UMANSKY
School of Arts and Sciences: Dr RAMSEY KLEFF
School of Theology: Dr JOHN W. KINNEY

VIRGINIA WESLEYAN COLLEGE

1584 Wesleyan Drive, Norfolk, VA 23502
Telephone: (757) 455-3200
Fax: (757) 461-5238
Internet: www.vwc.edu
President: WILLIAM T. GREER.

WASHINGTON AND LEE UNIVERSITY

Lexington, VA 24450
Telephone: (540) 463-8400
Internet: www2.wlu.edu
Founded as Augusta Academy 1749, chartered as Liberty Hall Academy 1782, name changed to Washington Academy 1798, to Washington College 1813, and to present name 1871
President: JOHN W. ELROD
Treasurer: LAWRENCE W. BROOMALL
Registrar: D. SCOTT DITTMAN
Librarian: BARBARA J. BROWN

Library: Undergraduate library of 464,000 vols; law library of 350,000 vols
Number of teachers: 197
Number of students: 2,000
Publications: *Shenandoah* (literary quarterly), *Washington and Lee Law Review*, *Journal of Science*, *Political Review*

DEANS

Arts and Sciences: LAURENT BOETSCH
Commerce, Economics and Politics: LARRY C. PEPPERS
Law: BARRY SULLIVAN

WASHINGTON

BASTYR UNIVERSITY

14500 Juanita Dr. NE, Kenmore, WA 98028-4966

Telephone: (425) 823-1300
Fax: (425) 823-6222
E-mail: admissions@bastyr.edu
Internet: www.bastyr.edu
Founded 1978
President: Dr THOMAS SHEPHERD
Number of students: 1,150

Degree programmes in the natural health sciences.

CENTRAL WASHINGTON UNIVERSITY

Ellensburg, WA 98926

Telephone: (509) 963-2111
Internet: www.cwu.edu
Founded 1891
President: JERILYN S. MCINTYRE
Registrar: CAROLYN L. WELLS
Librarian: DAVID KAUFMAN
Provost and Vice-President for Academic Affairs: DAVID SOLTZ
Vice-President for Business Affairs: ABDUL NASSER
Vice-President for Student Affairs and Enrollment Management: CHARLOTTE TULLOS
Vice-President for University Relations: JEN GRAY

Library of 485,417 vols
Number of teachers: 370
Number of students: 7,471 (full-time).

CITY UNIVERSITY

11900 NE First St, Bellevue, WA 98005

Telephone: (425) 637-1010
Fax: (425) 637-9689
E-mail: info@cityu.edu
Internet: www.cityu.edu
Founded 1973 as City College; present name 1982
Private control
Sites in states of Washington and California, and in Canada, Denmark, Germany, Slovakia, Spain and Switzerland
President: Dr W. MICHAEL EASTON
Executive Vice-President for Academic Affairs: Dr FERNANDO LEON GARCIA
Executive Vice-President for Finance and Operations: JAMES R. LADD
Vice-President for Academic and Institutional Assessment: CHRIS J. RIGOS
Vice-President for Admissions and Student Services: MELISSA MECHAM
Vice-President for the Business Office and Controller: MARIETA C. JOHNSON
Vice-President for European Operations: Ing. JAN REBRO
Vice-President for External Relations: Dr WINSTON C. ADDIS

Associate Vice-President for Human Resources: NANCY J. JOHNSTON
Chief Information Officer: GREG FOY
Registrar: MARY R. BELKNAP
Number of teachers: 1,300
Number of students: 6,840 worldwide.

CORNISH COLLEGE OF THE ARTS

710 East Roy Street, Seattle, WA 98102

Telephone: (206) 726-5151
E-mail: admissions@cornish.edu
Internet: www.cornish.edu

President: SERGEI P. TSCHERNISCH
Provost: LOIS HARRIS
Vice-President of Institutional Advancement: JANE EWING

CHAIRS OF DEPARTMENTS

Music: LAURA KAMINSKY
Humanities and Sciences: SHAWN BACHTLER
Performance Production: DAVE TOSTI-LANE
Dance: KATHRYN DANIELS
Visual Art History: AMY BINGAMAN
Theatre: RICHARD E. T. WHITE

EASTERN WASHINGTON UNIVERSITY

Cheney, WA 99004

Telephone: (509) 359-6200
Fax: 359-6946
E-mail: universityre@mail.ewu.edu
Internet: www.ewu.edu
Founded 1882
President: STEPHEN M. JORDAN
Associate Registrar: DEBBIE FOCKLER
Director of Enrollment Management: BRIAN LEVIN-STANKEVICH
Director of Libraries: PATRICIA KELLEY

Library of 483,152 vols
Number of teachers: 365
Number of students: 8,000.

EVERGREEN STATE COLLEGE

2700 Evergreen Parkway Northwest, Olympia, WA 98505

Telephone: (360) 866-6000
E-mail: admissions@evergreen.edu
Internet: www.evergreen.edu
President: JANE L. JERVIS.

GONZAGA UNIVERSITY

Spokane, WA 99258-0001

Telephone: (509) 328-4220
Fax: (509) 484-2818
Internet: www.gonzaga.edu
Founded 1887
Private control
Academic year: September to May, and summer session
Chancellor: Rev. BERNARD J. COUGHLIN
President: Rev. ROBERT SPITZER
Vice-President: Rev. FRANK COSTELLO
Academic Vice-President: Rev. PATRICK FORD
Vice-President for University Relations: MARGOT STANFIELD
Vice-President, Student Life: SUE WEITZ
Vice-President, Finance: CHARLES J. MURPHY
Vice-President, Administration and Planning: HARRY H. SLADICH
Dean of Admissions: PHILLIP BALLINGER
Librarian: EILEEN BELL-GARRISON
Library of 425,000 vols
Number of teachers: 275
Number of students: 5,572
Publications: *Signum* (quarterly), *Gonzaga Bulletin* (weekly), *Charter* (annually), *Reflections* (annually), *Spires* (annually)

DEANS

Arts and Sciences: ROBERT PRUSCH

Law: JOHN E. CLUTE
Engineering: DENNIS HORN
Graduate School: LEONARD DOOHAN
Education: RICHARD WOLFE
Business Administration: CLARENCE BARNES
Dean of Students: SUE WEITZ
Professional Studies: MARY MCFARLAND

HENRY COGSWELL COLLEGE

3002 Colby Avenue, Everett, WA 98201

Telephone: (425) 258-3351
E-mail: information@henrycogswell.edu
Internet: www.henrycogswell.edu

President: RONNIE HUNDLEY

DEANS

Business: Dr JERRY KNUTSON
Digital Arts: KEN ROWE
Engineering and Science: EL-HADI AGGOUNE

HERITAGE UNIVERSITY

3240 Fort Rd, Toppenish, WA 94563

Telephone: (509) 865-8500
Fax: (509) 865-7976
Internet: www.heritage.edu
Founded 1907; university status 2004
Private control; non-profit making
Liberal arts university
President: Dr KATHLEEN ROSS
Vice-President for Academic Affairs: Dr SNEH VEENA
Vice-President for Advancement: MICHAEL P. MOORE
Vice-President for Support Services, and Chief Financial Officer: RICK R. GAGNIER
Dean of Enrollment Management Services: NORBERTO T. ESPINDOLA

Library of 55,000 vols (main campus)
Number of teachers: 45 full-time
Number of teachers: 125 part-time
Number of students: 1,355

DEANS

Arts and Sciences: JAMES FALCO
Education and Psychology: KAREN GARRISON

NORTHWEST COLLEGE

5520 108th Avenue NE, Kirkland, WA 98033

Telephone: (425) 822-8266
E-mail: recpt@ncag.edu
Internet: www.nwcollege.edu
Founded 1907; present name 1982
Liberal arts college
President: DON ARGUE
Senior Vice-President for Academic Affairs: MARSHALL E. FLOWERS
Vice-President for Student Development: CHRISTIAN LINDBECK
Vice-President for College Advancement: DAN NEARY
Vice-President for Administrative Services: DAN SCHIMELFENIG

DEANS

Division of Education: GARY NEWBILL
Division of Humanities: DARREL HOBSON
Division of Natural and Social Sciences: BILL RANDOLPH
School of Nursing: CARL CHRISTENSEN

PACIFIC LUTHERAN UNIVERSITY

Tacoma, WA 98447

Telephone: (206) 531-6900
Fax: (206) 535-8320
Internet: www.plu.edu
Founded 1890
President: LOREN J. ANDERSON
Provost: PAUL T. MENZEL

Dean of Information Resources: CHRIS D. FERGUSON

Library of 363,580 vols
Number of teachers: 250
Number of students: 3,600.

PUGET SOUND CHRISTIAN COLLEGE

7011 226th Place SW, Mountlake Terrace, WA 98043

Telephone: (425) 775-8686
Fax: (425) 775-8688
E-mail: information@pscc.edu
Internet: www.pscc.edu

President: Dr RANDY BRIDGES.

SAINT MARTIN'S COLLEGE

5300 Pacific Ave SE, Lacey, WA 98503

Telephone: (206) 491-4700
Fax: (206) 459-4124
E-mail: information@stmartin.edu
Internet: www.stmartin.edu

Founded 1895
Academic year: September to May

President: Dr DAVID R. SPANGLER
Vice-President for Academic Affairs (vacant)
Vice-President of Finance: MARY SIGMEN
Registrar: MARY LAW
Librarian: DALIA HAGAN

Library of 85,000 vols
Number of teachers: 70
Number of students: 978.

SEATTLE PACIFIC UNIVERSITY

3307 Third Ave West, Seattle, WA 98119

Telephone: (206) 281-2111
Fax: (206) 281-2115
Internet: www.spu.edu

Founded 1891
Academic year: September to June

President: PHILIP W. EATON
Vice-President for Academic Affairs: LES L. STEELE
Vice-President for Business and Planning: DONALD W. MORTENSON
Vice-President for University Advancement: ROBERT D. MCINTOSH
Vice-President for University Relations: MARJORIE R. JOHNSON
Assistant Vice-President and Dean for Enrollment Management: JANET L. WARD
Associate Vice-President and Dean of Student Life: KATHLEEN BRADEN
Director of Student Academic Services and University Registrar: RUTH ADAMS
University Librarian: RAY DOERKSEN

Library of 169,527 vols
Number of teachers: 178
Number of students: 3,615.

SEATTLE UNIVERSITY

Seattle, WA 98122

Telephone: (206) 296-6000
Fax: (206) 296-6200
Internet: www.seattleu.edu

Founded 1891
Academic year: October to July

President: STEPHEN V. SUNDBORG
Provost: Dr JOHN D. ESHELMAN
Vice-President of Planning and Associate Provost: SUSAN SECKER
Assistant Provost for Academic Administration: ROBERT DULLEA
Dean of Admissions: MICHAEL MCKEON
Controller: BINH LE
Librarian: JOHN POPKO

Library of 234,978 vols
Number of teachers: 440

Number of students: 6,337 (3,561 undergraduate, 1,735 postgraduate, 1,041 law)

DEANS

College of Arts and Sciences: Dr WALLACE LOH
Matteo Ricci College: Dr ARTHUR FISHER
School of Business: Dr JOSEPH PHILLIPS
School of Education: Dr SUSAN SCHMITT
School of Science and Engineering: Dr GEORGE SIMMONS
School of Nursing: Dr MARY WALKER
School of Theology and Ministry: Rev. PATRICK HOWELL
School of Law: Dr RUDOLPH HASL

TRINITY LUTHERAN COLLEGE

4221 228th Avenue SE, Issaquah, WA 98029-9299

Telephone: (425) 392-0400
Fax: (425) 392-0404
E-mail: info@tlc.edu
Internet: www.tlc.edu

President: S. TAMM.

UNIVERSITY OF PUGET SOUND

Tacoma, WA 98416

Telephone: (253) 879-3100
Internet: www.ups.edu

Founded 1888
Private control

President: RONALD R. THOMAS
Academic Vice President: KRISTINE M. BARTANEN
Dean of Students (vacant)
Vice-President for Enrollment: GEORGE H. MILLS
Vice-President for Finance (vacant)
Registrar: JOHN FINNEY
Librarian: KAREN FISCHER

Number of teachers: 220
Number of students: 2,600 full-time.

UNIVERSITY OF WASHINGTON

Box 351270, Seattle, WA 98195-1270
Telephone: (206) 543-5630
Fax: (206) 221-4622
E-mail: acadpers@u.washington.edu
Internet: www.washington.edu

Founded 1861

President: MARK EMMERT
Provost: PHYLLIS WISE (acting)
Executive Vice-President: WELDON IHRIG
Vice-President for Computing and Communications: RONALD JOHNSON
Vice-President for Development and Alumni Relations: CONNIE KRAVAS
Vice-President for Human Resources: PATRICIA CARSON
Vice-President for Medical Affairs: PAUL RAMSEY
Vice-President for Minority Affairs: NANCY BARCELO (acting)
Vice-President for Student Affairs: ERNEST MORRIS
Vice-Provost: CHERYL CAMERON (acting)
Vice-Provost for Educational Outreach: DAVID SZATMARY
Vice-Provost for Educational Partnerships: LOUIS FOX
Vice-Provost for Planning and Budgeting: HARLAN PATTERSON
Vice-Provost for Research: CRAIG HOGAN
Vice-Provost for Student Relations: GUS KRAVAS
Vice-Provost for Technology Transfer: JAMES SEVERSON
Director, Federal Relations: BARBARA PERRY
Director, State Relations: RANDY HODGINS
Dean, Undergraduate Education: CHRISTINE INGEBRITSEN (acting)

Director of Libraries: ELIZABETH WILSON
Library: see Libraries
Number of teachers: 3,300 full-time
Number of students: 42,757 (39,136 on Seattle campus)

Publications: *American Journal of Human Genetics, Biochemistry, Journal of Limnology and Oceanography, Modern Language Quarterly, Pacific Northwest Quarterly, Poetry Northwest, Trends in Engineering, Washington Law Review, Journal of Financial and Quantitative Analysis, Papers of Regional Science Association*

DEANS

Business School: J. JIAMBALVO (acting)
Graduate School: S. ORTEGA (acting)
Information School: M. EISENBERG
College of Architecture and Urban Planning: R. MUGERAUER
College of Arts and Sciences: D. HODGE
College of Education: P. WASLEY
College of Engineering: M. SOMA (acting)
College of Forest Resources: B. B. BARE
College of Ocean and Fishery Sciences: A. NOWELL
School of Dentistry: M. SOMERMAN
School of Law: W. H. KNIGHT, Jr
School of Medicine: P. RAMSEY
School of Nursing: N. WOODS
School of Pharmacy: S. NELSON
Evans School of Public Affairs: S. ARCHIBALD
School of Public Health and Community Medicine: P. WAHL
School of Social Work: L. GILCHRIST (acting)
University of Washington, Bothell: S. OLSWANG (Interim Chancellor)
University of Washington, Tacoma: P. SPAKES (Chancellor)

DIRECTORS

Alcoholism and Drug Abuse Institute: H. H. SAMSON
Applied Physics Laboratory: R. C. SPINDEL
Center for Bioengineering: L. HUNTSMAN
Center for Inherited Diseases: A. G. MOTULSKY
Center for Research in Oral Biology: R. C. PAGE
Friday Harbor Laboratories: A. O. D. WILLOWS
Center for Law and Justice: J. G. WEIS
Center for Studies in Demography and Ecology: C. HIRSCHMAN
Institute on Aging: I. B. ABRASS (acting)
Institute for Environmental Studies: C. B. LEOVY
Institute for Marine Studies: E. L. MILES
Quaternary Research Center: S. C. PORTER
Child Development and Mental Retardation Center: M. J. GURALNICK
Fisheries Research Institute: R. C. FRANCIS
Regional Primate Center: D. M. BOWDEN

PROFESSORS

College of Architecture and Urban Planning (Box 355726, Seattle, WA 98195; tel. (206) 543-7679; fax (206) 543-2463; internet www.caup.washington.edu):

BADANES, S. P., Architecture
BLANCO, H. J., Urban Design and Planning
CHING, F. D. K., Architecture
DANIALI, S., Construction Management
FINROW, J. V., Architecture
MILLER, D. E., Architecture
MILLER, D. II., Urban Design and Planning
MUGERAUER, R., Architecture
OCHSNER, J. K., Architecture
PYATOK, M., Architecture
STREATFIELD, D. C., Landscape Architecture
SUTTON, S. E., Architecture
VERNEZ-MOUDON, A., Urban Design and Planning

College of Arts and Sciences (Box 353765, Seattle, WA 98195; tel. (206) 543-5340; fax (206) 543-5462; internet www.artsci.washington.edu):

ADELBERGER, E. G., Physics
ALEXANDER, E., English
ALLEN, C., English
AMMERLAHN, H., German
AMMIRATI, J. F., Biology
ANDERSEN, N. H., Chemistry
ANDERSON, S., Astronomy
BACHMAN, D. M., International Studies
BALDASTY, G. J., Communication
BALICK, B., Astronomy
BARASH, D. P., Psychology
BARDEEN, J. M., Physics
BARLOW, T. E., Women Studies
BARRACK, C. M., German
BARZEL, Y., Economics
BATTISTI, D. S., Atmospheric Science
BEECHER, M. D., Psychology
BEHLER, D. I., German
BEHLMER, G. K., History
BENDICH, A. K., Biology
BENNETT, W. L., Political Science
BERGANTZ, G. W., Earth and Space Sciences
BERGER, P. E., Art
BERNARD, J. W., Music
BERNSTEIN, I. L., Psychology
BERTSCH, G. F., Physics
BESAG, J. E., Statistics
BEYERS, W. B., Geography
BIERDS, L. L., English
BLAKE, K., English
BLAU, H., English
BLIQUEZ, L. J., Classics
BLONDELL, R., Classics
BOARCH-JACOBSEN, M., Comparative Literature
BOERSMA, P. D., Biology
BOLTZ, W., Asian Languages and Literatures
BONJOUR, L. A., Philosophy
BOOKER, J. R., Earth and Space Sciences
BORDEN, W. T., Chemistry
BOULWARE, D. G., Physics
BOURGEOIS, J., Earth and Space Sciences
BOYNTON, P., Physics
BOZARTH, G. S., Music
BRADSHAW, H. D., Biology
BRAME, M. K., Linguistics
BRAVMANN, R. A., Art
BRENOWITZ, E. A., Psychology
BRETHERTON, C. S., Atmospheric Science
BROWN, J. K., German
BROWN, J. M., Earth and Space Sciences
BROWN, M. J., English
BROWNLEE, D. E., Astronomy
BRUCE, N., Economics
BUBE, K. P., Mathematics
BUCK, S. L., Psychology
BULGAC, A., Physics
BURDZY, K., Mathematics
BURKE, J. V., Mathematics
BURNETT, T. H., Physics
BURSTEIN, P., Sociology
BUTLER, J. E., American Ethnic Studies
CALLIS, J. B., Chemistry
CAMPBELL, C. T., Chemistry
CAMPBELL, P. S., Music
CAPORASO, J. A., Political Science
CASTERAS, S. P., Art
CATTOLICO, R. A., Biology
CAUCE, A. M., Psychology
CHALOUPKA, V., Physics
CHAN, K. W., Geography
CHEN, Z., Mathematics
CHENEY, E. S., Earth and Space Sciences
CHIROT, D., International Studies
CIRTAUTAS, I. D., Near Eastern Languages and Literatures
CLATTERBAUGH, K. C., Philosophy
CLAUSEN, M. L., Art
CLAUSS, J. J., Classics

CLOSE, A. E., Anthropology
COBURN, R. C., Philosophy
COHEN, S. M., Philosophy
COLDEWEY, J. C., English
COLLINGWOOD, D., Mathematics
COMAI, L., Biology
COVEY, E., Psychology
COWAN, D. S., Earth and Space Sciences
COX, C. D., Asian Languages and Literatures
CRAMER, J. G., Jr, Physics
CREAGER, K. C., Earth and Space Sciences
CRIMINALE, W. O., Jr, Applied Mathematics
CRUTCHFIELD, R. D., Sociology
CURTIS, E. B., Mathematics
DAHLSTROM, R. A., Drama
DALTON, L. R., Chemistry
DANIEL, T. L., Sociology
DAWSON, G., Psychology
DEL MORAL, R., Biology
DEN NIJS, M. P., Physics
DIAZ, F. L., Psychology
DILLON, G. L., English
DOVICHI, N. J., Chemistry
DROBNY, G. P., Chemistry
DUCHAMP, T. E., Mathematics
DUNN, R. J., English
DURAND, J., Music
DURRAN, D. R., Atmospheric Science
EBREY, P. B., History
ELLINGSON, T. J., Music
ELLIS, J. M., Geography
ELLIS, S. D., Physics
ENGEL, T., Chemistry
EPIOTIS, N., Chemistry
ERICKSON, K. B., Mathematics
EROS, P. S., Music
FAILING, P. A., Art
FAIN, S. C., Physics
FINDLEY, J. M., History
FINE, A. I., Philosophy
FLORES, L. H., American Ethnic Studies
FOLLAND, G. B., Mathematics
FOLSOM, R. C., Speech and Hearing Sciences
FORTSON, E. N., II, Physics
FREY, C. H., English
GAMMON, R. H., Chemistry
GARCIA, A., Physics
GATES, S. N., Drama
GEIST, A. L., Romance Languages and Literatures
GELB, M. H., Chemistry
GHOSE, S., Earth and Space Sciences
GIFFARD, C. A., Communications
GOLDE, H., Computer Science
GOLDSTEIN, A. A., Mathematics
GORE, W. J., Political Science
GOTTMAN, J. M., Psychology
GOUTERMAN, M. P., Chemistry
GRAYSON, D. K., Anthropology
GREENBERG, R., Mathematics
GREENWALD, A. G., Psychology
GREGORY, N. W., Chemistry
GROSSMAN, A. J., Music
GRUNBAUM, B., Mathematics
GUARRERA, F. P., Music
GUEST, A. M., Sociology
GURALNIK, M. J., Psychology and Paediatrics
HALL, B. D., Genetics
HALLET, B., Geological Sciences
HALPERIN, C. S., Botany
HALPERN, I., Physics
HALSEY, G. D., Jr, Chemistry
HALVORSEN, R., Economics
HANEY, J. V., Slavic Languages and Literatures and International Studies
HANKINS, T. L., History
HANLEY, S. B., International Studies
HARMON, D. P., Classics and Comparative Literature
HARRELL, C. S., Anthropology and International Studies
HARTMANN, D., Atmospheric Sciences
HARTWELL, L. H., Genetics

HASKINS, E. F., Botany
HEER, N. L., Near Eastern Languages and Literature
HELLER, E. J., Chemistry and Physics
HELLMANN, D. C., Political Science and School of International Studies
HENLEY, E. M., Physics
HERTLING, G. H., Germanics
HILDEBRAND, G., Art History and Architecture
HIRSCHMAN, C., Sociology
HIXSON, W. J., Art
HOBBS, P. V., Atmospheric Sciences
HODGE, P. W., Astronomy
HOLTON, J. R., Atmospheric Sciences
HOSTETLER, P. S., Drama
HOUZE, R. A., Atmospheric Physics
HU, M., Art
HUEY, R. B., Zoology
HUNN, E. S., Anthropology
HUNT, E. B., Psychology
HUTTON, R. S., Psychology
INGALLS, R. L., Physics
IRVING, R., Mathematics
JACKSON, W. A. D., Geography and School of International Studies
JACOBSON, N., Psychology
JAEGER, C. S., German
JANS, J. P., Mathematics
JOHNSON, C. R., English
JONES, R. C., Art
KAPETANIC, D., Slavic Languages and Literature, and International Studies
KAPLAN, A., Music
KARTIGANER, D. M., English
KENAGY, G. J., Zoology
KEYES, C. F., Anthropology
KEYT, D., Philosophy
KLAUSENBURGER, J., Romance Languages and Literature
KINGSBURY, M., Art History
KNAPP, J. S., Dance
KNECHTGES, D. R., Asian Languages and Literature
KLEE, V. M., Jr, Mathematics
KOBLITZ, N., Mathematics
KOHN, A. J., Zoology
KORG, J., English
KOTTLER, H. W., Art
KOTTWITZ, R., Mathematics
KOWALSKI, B. R., Chemistry
KRUMME, G., Geography
KUHL, P. K., Speech and Hearing
KWIRAM, A. L., Chemistry
LADNER, R. E., Computer Science
LAIRD, C. D., Zoology
LANG, G. E., Communications, Political Science and Sociology
LANG, K., Communications
LARDY, N., International Studies
LAZOWSKA, E., Computer Science
LEGTERS, L. H., School of International Studies
LEOPOLD, E. B., Botany and Forest Resources
LEOVY, C. B., Atmospheric Sciences and Geophysics
LEV, D. S., Political Science
LEVI, M. A., Political Science
LEVY, F. J., History
LEWIS, B., Geophysics and Oceanography
LIND, D. A., Mathematics
LISTER, C. R. B., Geophysics and Oceanography
LOCKARD, J. S., Psychology and Neurosurgery
LOCKWOOD, T. F., English
LOFTUS, E. J., Psychology
LOFTUS, G. R., Psychology
LOPER, R. B., Drama
LORD, J. J., Physics
LUBATTI, H. J., Physics
LUJAN, D., Political Science
LUNDIN, N. K., Art
LUNDQUIST, B. R., Music
LUNNEBORG, C., Psychology and Statistics

MACKAY, P. A., Classics, Comparative Literature and, Near Eastern Language and Civilization
McCALLUM, I. S., Geological Sciences
McCOLL, W. D., Music
McCRACKEN, J. D., English
McCRONE, D. J., Political Science
McDERMOTT, L. C., Physics
McDERMOTT, M. N., Physics
McELROY, C. W., English
McGEE, J. S., Economics
McHUGH, H., English
MARGON, B., Astronomy
MARKS, C. E., Philosophy
MARLATT, G. A., Psychology
MARSHALL, D., Mathematics
MARSHALL, J. C., Art
MARTIN, R. D., Statistics
MATTHEWS, D. R., Political Science
MAYER, J., Geography
MELTZOFF, A., Psychology
MERRILL, R. T., Geophysics and Geological Sciences
MICHAEL, E. A., Mathematics
MICKLESEN, L. R., Slavic Languages and Literature, Linguistics and International Studies
MIGDAL, J. S., International Studies
MILLER, G., Physics
MILLER, R. A., Asian Languages and Literature
MINIFIE, F. D., Speech and Hearing Sciences
MITCHELL, T. R., Management and Organization and Psychology
MODELSKI, G., Political Science
MODIANO, R., English and Comparative Literature
MORRILL, R. L., Geography and Environmental Studies
MORROW, J. A., Mathematics
MOSELEY, S., Art
NAMIOKA, I., Mathematics
NASON, J. D., Anthropology
NELSON, C. R., Economics
NELSON, T. O., Psychology
NEUMAN, D. M., Art
NEWMEYER, F. J., Linguistics
NEWELL, L. L., Anthropology
NOE, J. D., Computer Science
NORMAN, J. G., Chemistry
NORMAN, J. L., Asian Languages and Literatures
NUNKE, R. J., Mathematics
NUTE, P. E., Anthropology
ODELL, G. M., Zoology
O'DOAN, N. D., Music
OLSON, D. J., Political Science
OPPERMAN, H. N., Art
ORIANS, G. H., Zoology and Environmental Studies
OSBORNE, M. S., Mathematics
OTTENBERG, S., Anthropology
PAINE, R. T., Jr, Zoology
PALAIS, J. B., International Studies and History
PALKA, J. M., Zoology
PALMER, J. M., Prosthodontics and Speech and Hearing Sciences
PARKS, G. K., Geophysics
PARKS, R. W., Economics
PASCAL, P., Classics
PEASE, O. A., History
PEMBER, D. R., Communication
PERLMAN, M. D., Statistics
PERRY, E., International Studies
PETERS, P. C., Physics
PHELPS, R. R., Mathematics
PIZZUTO, E., Art
POCKER, Y., Chemistry
PORTER, S. C., Geological Sciences
POTTER, K. H., International Studies and Philosophy
PRINS, D., Speech and Hearing Sciences
PUFF, R. D., Physics
PUNDT, G. H., Art and Architecture

PYKE, R., Mathematics
PYLE, K. B., International Studies and History
RAGOZIN, D., Mathematics
RAHN, J., Music
RAYMOND, C. F., Geophysics
REED, R., Atmospheric Sciences
REHR, J. J., Physics
REID, B. R., Chemistry
REINERT, O., English and Comparative Literature
RENSBERGER, J. M., Geological Sciences
RESHETAR, J. S., Jr, Political Science
RICHMAN, R. J., Philosophy
RIDDIFORD, L. M., Zoology
RIEDEL, E. K., Physics
ROCKAFELLAR, R. T., Mathematics
ROHWER, S. A., Zoology
RORABAUGH, W. J., History
ROSE, N. J., Chemistry
ROSSEL, S. H., Scandinavian Languages and Literatures
ROTHBERG, J. E., Physics
RUBIN, J., Asian Languages and Literatures
RUSS, J., English
RUTHERFOORD, J. P., Physics
RUZICKA, J., Chemistry
SACKETT, G. P., Psychology
SALE, R. H., English
SAPORTA, S., Linguistics and Romance Languages
SARASON, I. G., Psychology
SARASON, L., Mathematics
SAUM, L. O., History
SAX, G., Education
SCHEIDEL, T. M., Speech
SCHEINGOLD, S. A., Political Science
SCHICK, M., Physics
SCHIFFMAN, H. F., Asian Languages and Literatures
SCHMITT, D. R., Sociology
SCHOMAKER, V., Chemistry
SCHUBERT, W. M., Chemistry
SCHUBIGER, G. A., Zoology
SCHURR, J. M., Chemistry
SCHWARTZ, P., Sociology
SCOTT, J. W., American Ethnic Studies, Sociology
SEGAL, J., Mathematics
SHAW, A. C., Computer Science
SHORACK, G. R., Statistics
SHULMAN, R., English
SIKI, B., Music
SILBERBERG, E., Economics
SILBERGELD, J. L., Art
SIMONSON, H. P., English
SIMPSON, J. B., Psychology
SKOWRONEK, F. E., Music
SLUTSKY, L. J., Chemistry
SMITH, C. W., Art
SMITH, J. D., Oceanography, Geophysics and Geological Sciences
SMITH, R. E., Psychology
SMITH, S. W., Geophysics
SMITH, W. O., Music
SNYDER, L., Computer Science
SNYDER, R., Zoology
SPAFFORD, M. C., Art
STADLER, D. R., Genetics
STAMM, K., Communications
STARK, R., Sociology
STARYK, S. S., Music
STEELE, C. M., Psychology
STEENE, B., Scandinavian Languages and Literature and Comparative Literature
STERN, E. A., Physics
STEVICK, R. D., English
STORCH, L., Music
STOUT, E. L., Mathematics
STRATHMANN, R. R., Zoology
STREITBERGER, W., English
STUIVER, M., Geological Sciences
SUGAR, P. F., History and International Studies
SULLIVAN, J. B., Mathematics

SULLIVAN, W., Astronomy
SWINDLER, D. R., Anthropology
TANIMOTO, S. L., Computer Science
TAYLOR, M. J., Political Science
TELLER, D. Y., Psychology and Physiology
THOMAS, C. S., History
THOMAS, M. D., Geography
THOMPSON, E. A., Statistics
THOMPSON, G., Speech and Hearing Sciences
THORNTON, J., Economics
THOULESS, D. J., Physics
TOWNSEND, J. R., International Studies and Political Science
TREADGOLD, D. W., International Studies and History
TRUMAN, J. W., Zoology
TSUKADA, M., Botany
TUFTS, P. D., Music
UHLMANN, G. A., Mathematics
ULLMAN, J. C., History
UNTERSTEINER, N., Atmospheric Sciences and Geophysics
VANDENBOSCH, R., Chemistry
VAN DEN BERGHE, P. L., Sociology
VANDYCK, R. S., Physics
VELIKONJA, J., Geography
VILCHES, O. E., Physics
VOYLES, J. B., Germanics
WAALAND, J. R., Botany
WADDEN, D. J., Art
WAGER, L. W., Sociology
WAGONER, D. R., English
WALLACE, J. M., Atmospheric Sciences
WALLERSTEIN, G., Astronomy
WAN, F. Y., Applied Mathematics
WANG, C. H., Asian Languages and Literature and Comparative Literature
WARASHINA, P. B., Art
WARD, P., Geological Sciences
WARFIELD, R. B., Mathematics
WARNER, G. W., Jr, Mathematics
WATTS, R. O., Chemistry
WEBB, E., International Studies and Comparative Literature
WEIS, J. G., Sociology
WELLNER, J. A., Statistics
WESTWATER, M. J., Mathematics
WHISLER, H. C., Botany
WHITEHILL-WARD, J., Art
WILETS, L., Physics
WILEY, H., Dance
WILLEFORD, W., English and Comparative Literature
WILLIAMS, R. W., Physics
WILLOWS, A. O. D., Zoology
WILSON, W. R., Speech and Hearing Sciences
WINANS, E. V., Anthropology
WINGFIELD, J., Zoology
WITHERSPOON, G., Anthropology
WOODS, S. C., Psychology
YAMAMURA, K., International Studies
YANTIS, P. A., Speech and Hearing Sciences
YOUNG, K. K., Physics
YOUNG, P. R., Computer Science
ZOLLER, W. H., Chemistry

School of Business Administration:
ALBERTS, W. W., Finance, Business Economics and Quantitative Methods
BOURQUE, P. J., Finance, Business Economics and Quantitative Methods
CHIU, J. S. Y., Management Science
D'AMBROSIO, C. A., Finance, Business Economics
DUKES, R. E., Accounting
ETCHESON, W. W., Marketing
FAALAND, B. H., Finance, Business Economics and Quantitative Methods
FROST, P. A., Finance, Business Economics and Quantitative Methods
HALEY, C. W., Finance, Business Economics and Quantitative Methods
HEATH, L. C., Accounting

HENNING, D. A., Management and Organization

HESS, A. C., Finance, Business Economics and Quantitative Methods

HIGGINS, R. C., Finance, Business Economics and Quantitative Methods

INGENE, C., Marketing and International Business

JACOB, N. L., Finance, Business Economics and Quantitative Methods

JIAMBALVO, J., Accounting

JOHANSSON, J. K., Marketing, Transportation, and International Business

JOHNSON, D. W., Finance, Business Economics and Quantitative Methods

KLASTORIN, T., Management Science

KNUDSON, H. R., Management and Organization

LATHAM, G., Management and Organization

MacLACHLAN, D. L., Marketing

MITCHELL, T. R., Management and Organization

MOINPOUR, R., Marketing, Transportation and International Business

MUELLER, G. G., Accounting

NARVER, J. C., Marketing, Transportation and International Business

NEWELL, W. T., Management and Organization, Management Science

NOREEN, E. W., Accounting

PAGE, A. N., Finance, Business Economics and Quantitative Methods

PETERSON, R. B., Finance, Business Economics and Quantitative Methods

RAMANATHAN, K. V., Accounting

ROLEY, V. V., Finance and Business Economics

SAXBERG, B. O., Management and Organization

SCHALL, L. D., Finance, Business Economics and Quantitative Methods

SCOTT, W. G., Management and Organization

SPRATLEN, T. H., Marketing, Transportation and International Business

SUMMER, C. E., Management and Organization

SUNDEM, G. L., Accounting

WHEATLEY, J. J., Marketing, Transportation and International Business

YALCH, R., Marketing

College of Education:

ABBOTT, R. D.
AFFLECK, J. Q.
ANDERSON, R.
ANDREWS, R. L.
BANKS, J. A.
BILLINGSLEY, F. F.
BOLTON, D. L.
BRAMMER, L. M.
BURGESS, C. O.
BUTTERFIELD, E. C.
DOI, J. I.
EDGAR, E. B.
EVANS, E. D.
GOODLAD, J. I.
HARING, N. G.
HUNKINS, F. P.
JENKINS, J. R.
KALTSOUNIS, T.
KERR, D. H.
KERR, S. T.
KLOCKARS, A. J.
LIEBERMAN, A.
LOVITT, T. C.
LOWENBRAUN, S.
MADSEN, D. L.
McCARTIN, R. E.
MORISHIMA, J. K.
NEEL, R. S.
OLSTAD, R. G.
PECKHAM, P. D.
RYCKMAN, D. B.
SAX, G.

SCHILL, W. J.
SEBESTA, S. L.
THOMPSON, M. D.
TOSTBERG, R. E.
WHITE, O.
WINN, W. D.

College of Engineering:

AKSAY, I. A., Materials Science Engineering

ALBRECHT, R. W., Electrical and Nuclear Engineering

ALEXANDER, D. E., Mechanical Engineering

ALEXANDRO, F., Electrical Engineering

ALLAN, G. G., Forest Resources and Chemical Engineering

ANDERSEN, J., Electrical Engineering

ARCHBOLD, T. F., Mining, Metallurgical and Ceramic Engineering

BABB, A. L., Chemical and Nuclear Engineering

BALISE, P. L., Mechanical Engineering

BEREANO, P., Interdepartmental Curricular Programme

BERG, J. C., Chemical Engineering

BOGAN, R. H., Civil Engineering

BOLLARD, R. J. H., Aeronautics and Astronautics

BOWEN, J. R., Chemical Engineering

BRADT, R. C., Mining, Metallurgical and Ceramic Engineering

BROWN, C. B., Civil Engineering

BURGES, S. J., Civil Engineering

CHALUPNIK, J. D., Mechanical Engineering

CHEUNG, P. W., Electrical Engineering and Bioengineering

CHRISTIANSEN, W. H., Aeronautics and Astronautics

CLARK, R. N., Electrical Engineering

COLCORD, J. E., Civil Engineering

CORLETT, R. C., Mechanical Engineering

DALY, C. H., Mechanical Engineering

DAVIS, E. J., Chemical Engineering

DECHER, R., Aeronautics and Astronautics

DEPEW, C. A., Mechanical Engineering

DOW, D. G., Electrical Engineering

ELIAS, Z. M., Civil Engineering

EMERY, A. F., Mechanical Engineering

EVANS, R. J., Civil Engineering

FERGUSON, J. F., Civil Engineering

FINLAYSON, B. A., Chemical Engineering

FISCHBACH, D. B., Materials Science and Engineering

FYFE, I. M., Aeronautics and Astronautics

GARLID, K. L., Chemical and Nuclear Engineering

GESSNER, F., Mechanical Engineering

HARALICK, R. M., Electrical Engineering

HAWKINS, N. M., Civil Engineering

HEIDEGER, W. J., Chemical Engineering

HERTZBERG, A., Aeronautics and Astronautics

HOFFMAN, A. S., Chemical Engineering and Bioengineering

HOLDEN, A., Electrical Engineering

HOLSAPPLE, K. A., Aeronautics and Astronautics

HSU, C.-C., Electrical Engineering

ISHIMARU, A., Electrical Engineering

JOHNSON, D. E., Bioengineering

JOHNSON, D. L., Electrical Engineering

JOPPA, R. G., Aeronautics and Astronautics

JORGENSEN, J. E., Mechanical Engineering

KEVORKIAN, J. K., Aeronautics and Astronautics

KIPPENHAM, C. J., Mechanical Engineering

KOBAYASHI, A. S., Mechanical Engineering

KOSALY, G., Nuclear and Mechanical Engineering

KUROSAKA, M., Aeronautics and Astronautics

LAURITZEN, P. O., Electrical Engineering

LYTLE, D. W., Electrical Engineering

McCORMICK, N. J., Nuclear Engineering

McKEAN, W. T., Chemical Engineering and Forest Resources

MALTE, P. C., Mechanical Engineering

MAR, B. W., Civil Engineering

MARKS, R. J., Electrical Engineering

MATTOCK, A. H., Civil Engineering

MEDITCH, J. S., Electrical Engineering

MONTGOMERY, D. C., Industrial Engineering

MORITZ, W. E., Electrical Engineering

NECE, R. E., Civil Engineering

NIHAN, N. L., Civil Engineering

NOGES, E., Electrical Engineering

PARMETER, R. R., Aeronautics and Astronautics

PEARSON, C. E., Aeronautics and Astronautics, Applied Mathematics

PEDEN, I., Electrical Engineering

PILAT, M. J., Civil Engineering

PINTER, R. E., Electrical Engineering

POLONIS, D. H., Mining, Metallurgical and Ceramic Engineering

PORTER, R. P., Electrical Engineering

PRATT, D. T., Mechanical Engineering

RAO, Y. K., Mining, Metallurgical and Ceramics Engineering

RATNER, B., Bioengineering and Chemical Engineering

RIBE, F. L., Nuclear Engineering

RILEY, J., Mechanical Engineering

ROBKIN, M. A., Nuclear Engineering

ROEDER, C. W., Civil Engineering

RUSSELL, D. A., Aeronautics and Astronautics

SCHNEIDER, J. B., Urban Planning and Civil Engineering

SCOTT, W. D., Mining, Metallurgical and Ceramic Engineering

SEFERIS, J. C., Chemical Engineering

SIGELMANN, R. A., Electrical Engineering

SLEICHER, C. A., Jr, Chemical Engineering

SPINDEL, R. C., Electrical Engineering

STEAR, E. B., Electrical Engineering

STENSEL, H. D., Civil Engineering

STOEBE, T. G., Mining, Metallurgical and Ceramic Engineering

TAGGART, R., Mechanical Engineering

TSANG, L., Electrical Engineering

VAGNERS, J., Aeronautics and Astronautics

VENKATA, S. S., Electrical Engineering

VERESS, S. A., Civil Engineering

VESPER, K. H., Mechanical Engineering and Management and Organization, Marine Studies

VLASES, G. C., Nuclear Engineering

WELCH, E. B., Civil Engineering

WOLAK, J., Mechanical Engineering

WOODRUFF, G. L., Nuclear Engineering

YEE, S. S., Electrical Engineering

ZICK, G. L., Electrical Engineering

College of Ocean and Fishery Science
School of Oceanography:

BANSE, K.
CARPENTER, R.
COACHMAN, L.
CREAGER, H. S.
DELANEY, J.
EMERSON, S.
ERIKSEN, C.
FROST, B. W.
HEATH, G. R.
HEDGES, J.
HERSHMAN, M. J.
JUMARS, P. A.
LEWIS, B.
LISTER, C. R. B.
McMANUS, D. A.
MERRILL, R. T.
MILES, E. L.
MURPHY, S. R.
MURRAY, J.
NOWELL, A. R. M.
RHINES, P. B.
RICHARDS, F. A.
SMITH, J. D.
STERNBERG, R. W.
WELANDER, P.

WINTER, D. R.
WOOSTER, W. S.

School of Fisheries:

BRANNON, E. L.
BROWN, G. W.
CHEW, K. K.
FORD, E. D.
FRANCIS, R. C.
GALLUCCI, V. F.
HALVER, J. D.
HILBORN, R. W.
LANDOLT, M.
LISTON, J.
MATCHES, J. R.
MATHEWS, S. B.
MILLER, B. S.
PIETSCH, T. W.
PIGOTT, G. M.
SCHELL, W. R.
SMITH, L. S.
STICKNEY, R. R.
TAUB, F.
WHITNEY, R. R.

College of Forest Resources:

ADAMS, D. M.
AGEE, J. K.
ALLAN, G. G., Forest Resources and Chemical Engineering
BARE, B. B.
BETHEL, J. S.
BRUBAKER, L. B.
COLE, D. W.
DOWDLE, B.
EDMONDS, R. L.
FIELD, D. R.
FRITSCHEN, L. J.
GARA, R. I.
HATHEWAY, W. H.
HINCKLEY, T. M.
HRUTFIORD, B. F.
LEE, R. G.
MANUWAL, D. A.
OLIVER, C.
PICKFORD, S. G.
SARKANEN, K., Forest Resources and Chemical Engineering
SCHREUDER, G. F.
SHARPE, G. W.
STETTLER, R. F.
THORUD, D. B.
TUKEY, H. B.
UGOLINI, F. C.
WAGGENER, T. R.
WOTT, J. A.

Graduate School of Library and Information Science:

CHISHOLM, M. E., Library and Information Science

Graduate School of Public Affairs:

DENNY, B. C.
KROLL, M., Public Affairs and Political Science
LOCKE, H. G.
LYDEN, F. J.
WILLIAMS, W.
ZERBE, R. O.

School of Dentistry:

AMMONS, W. F., Periodontics
BOLENDER, C. L., Prosthodontics
BRUDVIK, J. S., Prosthodontics
CANFIELD, R. C., Restorative Dentistry
CLAGETT, J. A., Periodontics and Microbiology
CONRAD, D. A., Dental Public Health Sciences and Health Services
DeRONEN, T. A., Dental Public Health Services, Biostatistics
DWORKIN, S. F., Oral Surgery
ENGEL, D., Periodontics
FRANK, R. P., Prosthodontics
GEHRIG, J. D., Oral Surgery
HARRINGTON, G. W., Endodontics
JOHNSON, R. H., Periodontics

KOKICH, V., Orthodontics
LEWIS, T. M., Restorative Dentistry
LITTLE, R. M., Orthodontics
MILGROM, P. M., Dental Public Health Services
MOFFETT, B. C., Orthodontics
MYALL, R. W., Oral Surgery
NATKIN, E., Endodontics
NICHOLLS, J. I., Restorative Dentistry
OMNELL, K.-A., Oral Medicine
PAGE, R. C., Pathology and Periodontics
PALMER, J. M., Speech and Hearing Sciences and Prosthodontics
ROBINOVITCH, M. R., Oral Biology
SHAPIRO, P., Orthodontics
SMITH, D. E., Prosthodontics
TAMARIN, A., Oral Biology
WARNICK, M. E., Restorative Dentistry
WORTHINGTON, P., Oral and Maxillofacial Surgery
YUODELIS, R. A., Restorative Dentistry

School of Law:

ANDERSON, W. R.
ARONSON, R. H.
BURKE, W. T.
CHISUM, D. S.
FITZPATRICK, J. F.
FLETCHER, R. L.
HALEY, J. O.
HARDISTY, J. H.
HAZELTON, P. A.
HENDERSON, D. F.
HJORTH, R. L.
HUME, L. S.
HUSTON, J. C.
JAY, S. M.
JOHNSON, R. W.
JUNKER, J. M.
KUMMERT, R. O.
LOH, W. D.
MORRIS, A.
PECK, C. J.
PRICE, J. R.
PROSTERMAN, R. L.
RODDIS, R. S.
RODGERS, W. H.
ROMBAUER, M.
SMITH, F. W., Jr
STOEBUCK, W. B.
TRAUTMAN, P. A.

School of Medicine:

ABELSON, H. T., Paediatrics
ABRASS, I., Medicine
ADAMSON, J. W., Medicine
ALBERT, R., Medicine
ALMERS, W., Physiology and Biophysics
ALVORD, E. C., Pathology
ANDERSON, M. E., Rehabilitation Medicine and Physiology
ANSELL, J. S., Urology
APPELBAUM, F., Medicine
BARNES, G. W., Urology
BASSINGTHWAIGHTE, J. B., Bioengineering
BEAVO, J., Pharmacology
BECKER, J., Psychiatry, Psychology
BELKNAP, B. H., Medicine
BENEDETTI, T. J., Obstetrics and Gynaecology
BEN-MENACHEM, Y., Radiology
BERGER, A. J., Physiology and Biophysics
BERGMAN, A. B., Paediatrics
BERNSTEIN, I. D., Paediatrics
BIERMAN, E. L., Medicine
BINDER, M., Physiology and Biophysics
BIRD, T., Medicine
BLACKMON, J. R., Medicine
BLAGG, C. R., Medicine
BLEYER, W. A., Paediatrics
BORNSTEIN, P., Medicine and Biochemistry
BOWDEN, D. M., Psychiatry
BREMNER, W. J., Medicine
BRENGELMANN, G., Physiology and Biophysics
BROWN, B. G., Medicine
BRUNZELL, J. D., Medicine

BUCHANAN, T. M., Medicine and Pathobiology
BUCKNER, C. D., Medicine
BUNT-MILAM, A. H., Ophthalmology
BUTLER, J., Medicine
BYERS, P., Medicine and Pathology
CARR, J. E., Psychiatry and Psychology
CARRICO, C. J., Surgery
CATTERALL, W. A., Pharmacology
CHAIT, A., Medicine
CHAMPOUX, J. J., Microbiology
CHAPMAN, C. R., Anaesthesiology and Psychiatry
CHAPMAN, W. H., Urology
CHATRIAN, G. E., Laboratory Medicine and Neurological Surgery
CHEEVER, M. A., Medicine
CHENEY, F. W., Anaesthesiology
CHESNUT, C. H., Radiology and Medicine
CLARREN, S., Paediatrics
COBB, L. A., Medicine
COPASS, M. K., Medicine
COUNTS, G. W., Medicine
COUSER, W. G., Medicine
COREY, L., Laboratory Medicine and Microbiology
COUNTS, G. W., Medicine
CRILL, W. E., Medicine, Physiology and Biophysics
CROAKE, J. S., Psychiatry
CULLEN, B. F., Anaesthesiology
CUMMINGS, C. W., Otolaryngology
DALE, D. C., Medicine
DAVIE, E. W., Biochemistry
DEISHER, R. W., Paediatrics
DELATEUR, B. J., Rehabilitation Medicine
DETTER, J. C., Laboratory Medicine
DETWILER, P., Physiology and Biophysics
DILLARD, D. H., Surgery
DOBIE, R. A., Otolaryngology
DODGE, H. T., Medicine
DODRILL, C. B., Neurological Surgery
DOERR, H. O., Psychiatry and Psychology
DOHNER, C. W., Medicine and Education
DONALDSON, J. A., Otolaryngology
DUNNER, D. L., Psychiatry
EISENBERG, M., Medicine
EMANUEL, I., Epidemiology and International Health and Paediatrics
ENSINCK, J. W., Medicine
ESCHENBACH, D., Obstetrics and Gynaecology
EYRE, D. R., Orthopaedics
FARRELL, D. F., Medicine
FEFER, A., Medicine
FEIGL, E., Physiology and Biophysics
FETZ, E. E., Physiology and Biophysics
FIALKOW, P. J., Medicine and Genetics
FIGGE, D. C., Obstetrics and Gynaecology
FIGLEY, M. M., Radiology
FISCHER, E. H., Biochemistry
FRENCH, J. W., Paediatrics
FUCHS, A., Physiology and Biophysics
FUJIMOTO, W. Y., Medicine
GARTLER, S. M., Medicine, Genetics
GEYMAN, J. P., Family Medicine
GILLILAND, B., Laboratory Medicine and Medicine
GLOMSET, J. A., Medicine and Biochemistry
GODWIN, J. D., Radiology
GOLDMAN, M. L., Radiology
GOODNER, C. J., Medicine
GORDON, A. M., Physiology and Biophysics
GORDON, M., Biochemistry
GRAHAM, C. B., Radiology and Paediatrics
GREENBERG, P., Medicine
GREENE, H. L., Medicine
GREER, B. E., Obstetrics and Gynaecology
GRIFFIN, T. W., Radiation Oncology
GROMAN, N. B., Microbiology
GROUDINE, M., Radiation Oncology
GUNTHEROTH, W. G., Paediatrics
GUY, A., Rehabilitation Medicine and Bioengineering
HAGGITT, R. C., Pathology

HAKOMORI, S., Pathobiology and Microbiology
HALAR, E. M., Rehabilitation Medicine
HANDSFIELD, H. H., Medicine
HANSEN, J. A., Medicine
HANSEN, S., Orthopaedics
HARLEY, J. D., Radiology
HARRIS, A. B., Neurological Surgery
HAUSCHKA, S. D., Biochemistry
HAYDEN, P., Paediatrics
HEIMAN, J., Psychiatry and Behavioural Sciences
HEIMBACH, D. M., Surgery
HELLSTROM, I. E., Microbiology
HELLSTROM, K. E., Pathology
HENDERSON, M., Medicine and Epidemiology
HENDRICKSON, A. E., Ophthalmology and Biological Structure
HERMAN, C. M., Surgery
HILLE, B., Physiology and Biophysics
HILDEBRANDT, J., Physiology and Medicine
HLASTALA, M. P., Physiology and Biophysics and Medicine
HODSON, W. A., Paediatrics
HOLBROOK, K. A., Biological Structure
HOLMES, K. K., Medicine
HORITA, A., Pharmacology
HORNBEIN, T. F., Anaesthesiology, Physiology and Biophysics
HUDSON, L. D., Medicine
HUNTSMAN, L. L., Bioengineering
INUI, T. S., Medicine and Health Services
IVEY, T. D., Surgery
JOHANSEN, K. H., Surgery
JOHNSON, M. H., Psychiatry
JONES, R. F., Surgery
JONSEN, A. R., Medical History and Ethics
JUCHAU, M. R., Pharmacology
KALINA, R. E., Ophthalmology
KEHL, T. H., Physiology, Biophysics and Computer Science
KELLY, W. A., Neurological Surgery
KENNEDY, J. W., Medicine
KENNY, M. A., Laboratory Medicine
KLEBANOFF, S. J., Medicine
KNOPP, R. H., Medicine
KOEHLER, J. K., Biological Structure
KOERKER, D. J., Physiology and Biophysics and Medicine
KRAFT, G. H., Rehabilitation Medicine
KREBS, E. G., Pharmacology and Biochemistry
KROHN, K., Radiology
LABBE, R. F., Laboratory Medicine
LAKSHMINARAYAN, S., Medicine
LANDESMAN, S., Psychiatry
LARAMORE, G., Radiation Oncology
LARSON, E., Medicine
LEHMANN, J. F., Rehabilitation Medicine
LEIN, J. N., Obstetrics and Gynaecology
LEMIRE, R. J., Paediatrics
LIVINGSTON, R. B., Medicine
LOCKARD, J. S., Neurological Surgery
LOEB, L. A., Pathology
LOESER, J. B., Neurological Surgery
LOGERFO, J. P., Medicine and Health Services
LOOP, J. W., Radiology
LUFT, J. H., Biological Structure
MACK, L. A., Radiology
MACKLER, B., Paediatrics
MANNIK, M., Medicine
MARAVILLA, K. R., Radiology and Neurological Surgery
MARCHIORO, T. L., Surgery
MARTIN, G. M., Pathology
MARTIN, J. C., Psychiatry
MATSEN, F. A., Orthopaedics
MAYO, M. E., Urology
MCARTHUR, J. R., Medicine
MCDONALD, G. B., Medicine
MEYERS, J., Medicine
MILLS, R. P., Ophthalmology
MONSEN, E. R., Medicine
MORRIS, D. R., Biochemistry

MOSS, A. A., Radiology
MOTTET, N. K., Pathology and Environmental Health
MOTULSKY, A., Genetics and Medicine
MURPHY, T. M., Anaesthesiology
NEFF, J. M., Paediatrics
NEIMAN, P. E., Medicine
NELP, W. B., Medicine and Radiology
NELSON, J. A., Radiology
NESTER, E. W., Microbiology
NORWOOD, T., Pathology
NOVACK, A. H., Paediatrics
OCHS, H. D., Paediatrics
ODLAND, G. F., Medicine, Biological Structure
OJEMANN, G. A., Neurological Surgery
OMENN, G. S., Medicine and Environmental Health
PAGE, R. C., Pathology and Periodontics
PALMER, J., Medicine
PALMITER, R. D., Biochemistry
PAPAYANNOPOULOU, T., Medicine
PARSON, W. W., Biochemistry
PAULSEN, C. A., Medicine
PETRA, P. H., Obstetrics and Gynaecology and Biochemistry
PHILLIPS, T. J., Family Medicine
PIERSON, D., Medicine
PIOUS, D. A., Paediatrics
PLORDE, J. J., Laboratory Medicine
POLLACK, G. H., Bioengineering
POPE, C. E., Medicine
PORTE, D., Medicine
PRESTON, T. A., Medicine
PRINZ, P., Psychiatry
RAISYS, V., Laboratory Medicine
RASEY, J. S., Radiation Oncology
RASKIND, M. A., Psychiatry
RAUSCH, R. L., Animal Medicine and Pathobiology
REICHENBACH, D. D., Pathology
REICHLER, R. J., Psychiatry
REID, B. R., Biochemistry and Chemistry
RICE, C. L., Surgery
RITCHIE, J. L., Medicine
ROBERTS, T. S., Neurological Surgery
ROBERTSON, W. O., Paediatrics
ROBINSON, N. L., Psychiatry
RODIECK, R. W., Ophthalmology
ROHRMAN, C. A., Radiology
ROOS, B. A., Medicine
ROSENBLATT, R. A., Family Medicine
ROSS, R., Pathology
ROSSE, C., Biological Structure
ROWELL, L. B., Physiology and Biophysics
RUBELL, E. W., Otolaryngology
RUBIN, C. E., Medicine
RUVALCABA, R., Paediatrics
SAARI, J. C., Ophthalmology and Biochemistry
SALE, G., Pathology
SAUNDERS, D. R., Medicine
SCHER, A. M., Physiology and Biophysics
SCHMER, G., Laboratory Medicine
SCHOENKNECHT, F. D., Laboratory Medicine and Microbiology
SCHUFFLER, M., Medicine
SCHWARTZ, S. M., Pathology
SCHWARTZKROIN, P., Neurological Surgery and Physiology, Biophysics
SCHWINDT, P. C., Physiology and Biophysics
SCOTT, C. R., Paediatrics
SCRIBNER, B. H., Medicine
SELLS, C. J., Paediatrics
SHAPIRO, B. M., Biochemistry
SHAW, C., Pathology
SHEPARD, T. H., Paediatrics
SHERRARD, D. J., Medicine
SHERRIS, J. C., Microbiology
SHURTLEFF, D. B., Paediatrics
SILVERSTEIN, F., Medicine
SIMKIN, P. A., Medicine
SINGER, J., Medicine
SLICHTER, S., Medicine
SMITH, A. L., Paediatrics

SMITH, O. A. Jr, Physiology and Biophysics
SNYDER, J. M., Otolaryngology
SOULES, M. R., Obstetrics and Gynaecology
SPADONI, L. R., Obstetrics and Gynaecology
SPENCE, A. M., Medicine
STAHELI, L. T., Orthopaedics
STAHL, W., Medicine, Physiology and Biophysics
STALEY, J. T., Microbiology
STAMATOYANNOPOULOS, G., Medicine
STAMM, W., Medicine
STEINER, R., Obstetrics and Gynaecology, Physiology and Biophysics
STENCHEVER, M. A., Obstetrics and Gynaecology
STEVENSON, J. G., Paediatrics
STIRLING, C. E., Physiology and Biophysics
STOLOV, W. C., Rehabilitation Medicine
STORM, D. R., Pharmacology
STRANDJORD, P. E., Laboratory Medicine
STRANDNESS, D. E., Surgery
STREISSGUTH, A. P., Psychiatry
SUMI, S. M., Medicine and Pathology
SWANSON, P. D., Medicine
TAPPER, D., Surgery
TELLER, D. C., Biochemistry
TELLER, D. Y., Physiology and Psychology
THOMAS, E. D., Medicine
THOMPSON, A. R., Medicine
TOWE, A. L., Physiology and Biophysics
TOWNES, B. D., Psychiatry
TRIER, W. C., Surgery
TRUOG, W. E., Paediatrics
TUCKER, G. J., Psychiatry
TURCK, M., Medicine
VANARSDEL, P. P., Medicine
VANCITTERS, R. L., Physiology and Biophysics, Medicine
VANHOOSIER, G. L., Animal Medicine
VESTAL, R., Medicine
VINCENZI, F. F., Pharmacology
VONTVER, L., Obstetrics and Gynaecology
VRACKO, R., Pathology
WALKER, R. D., Psychiatry and Behavioural Science
WALLACE, J. F., Medicine
WALSH, K. A., Biochemistry
WARD, R. J., Anaesthesiology
WEDGWOOD, R. J., Paediatrics
WESTRUM, L. E., Neurological Surgery and Biological Structure
WEYMULLER, E. A., Otolaryngology
WHITELEY, H. R., Microbiology
WHORTON, J. C., Biomedical History
WIGHT, T., Pathology
WINN, H. R., Neurological Surgery
WINTERSCHEID, L. C., Surgery
WOODRUM, D. E., Paediatrics
WOOTON, P., Radiation Oncology
YOUNG, E. T., Biochemistry
ZAGER, R., Medicine

School of Nursing:

BARNARD, K. E., Parent and Child Nursing
BATEY, M. V., Community Health Care Systems
BENOLIEL, J. Q., Community Health Care Systems
CHRISMAN, N. J., Community Health Care Systems
DE TORNYAY, R., Community Health Care Systems
EYRES, S. J., Parent and Child Nursing
GALLUCCI, B. J., Physiological Nursing
GOERTZEN, I. E., Community Health Care Systems
HORN, B. J., Community Health Care Systems
HEGYVARY, S. T., Community Health Care Systems
KOGAN, H., Psychosocial Nursing
KURAMOTO, A., Physiological Nursing
LEWIS, F. M., Community Health Care Systems
MITCHELL, P. H., Physiological Nursing
OSBORNE, O. H., Psychosocial Nursing

PATRICK, M. I., Physiological Nursing
ROSE, M. H., Parent and Child Nursing
WOLF-WILETS, V. C., Psychosocial Nursing
WOODS, N. A., Physiological Nursing

School of Pharmacy:

BAILLIE, T., Medicinal Chemistry
BRADY, L. R., Medicinal Chemistry
CAMPBELL, W. H., Pharmacy Practice
GIBALDI, M., Pharmaceutics
KRADJAN, W., Pharmacy Practice
LEVY, R. H., Pharmaceutics
NELSON, S. D., Medicinal Chemistry
NELSON, W. L., Medicinal Chemistry
PLEIN, J. B., Pharmacy Practice
TRAGER, W. F., Medicinal Chemistry

School of Social Work:

BRIAR, S.
GOTTLIEB, N. R.
HAWKINS, J. D.
JAFFEE, B.
LEVY, R. L.
PATTI, R. J.
RESNICK, H.
TAKAGI, C. Y.
WHITTAKER, J. K.

School of Public Health and Community Medicine:

BRESLOW, N. E., Biostatistics
BUCHANAN, T. L., Pathobiology and Medicine
CROWLEY, J. J., Biostatistics
DALING, J. R., Epidemiology
DAVIS, K. A., Biostatistics
DAY, R. W., Health Services
DE ROUEN, T., Biostatistics
DIEHR, P. K., Biostatistics
EMANUEL, I., Epidemiology and Paediatrics
FEIGL, P., Biostatistics
FISHER, L. D., Biostatistics
FLEMING, T. R., Biostatistics
FOY, H. M., Epidemiology
GALE, J. I., Epidemiology
GRAYSTON, J. T., Epidemiology
HAKOMORI, S., Pathobiology and Microbiology
HENDERSON, M. M., Epidemiology and Medicine
INUI, T. S., Health Services and Medicine
JACKSON, K. L., Environmental Health
KENNY, G. E., Pathobiology
KOEPSELL, T., Health Services, Epidemiology
KRONMAL, R. A., Biostatistics
KUO, C.-C., Pathobiology
LEE, J. A., Environmental Health
LOGERFO, J. P., Health Services and Medicine
MARTIN, D. C., Biostatistics
MOOLGAVKAR, S. H., Epidemiology
MOTTET, N. K., Environmental Health and Pathology
MURPHY, S. D., Environmental Health
OMENN, G. S., Environmental Health and Medicine
PATRICK, D. L., Health Services
PERINE, P. L., Epidemiology
PERRIN, E. B., Health Services
PETERSON, A. V., Biostatistics
PRENTICE, R. L., Biostatistics
RAUSCH, R. L., Pathobiology
ROBKIN, M. A., Environmental Health and Nuclear Engineering
THOMAS, D. B., Epidemiology
VAN BELLE, G., Biostatistics
WAGNER, E. H., Health Services
WAHL, P. W., Biostatistics
WANG, S., Pathobiology
WEISS, N. S., Epidemiology
WILSON, J. T., Environmental Health
WORTHINGTON-ROBERTS, B., Epidemiology

WALLA WALLA COLLEGE

204 South College Avenue, College Place, WA 99324

Telephone: (509) 527-2615
Fax: (509) 527-2253
Internet: www.wwc.edu

Founded 1892
Academic year: September to June
President (vacant)
Vice-President for Academic Administration: JOHN BRUNT
Vice-President for Admissions and Marketing: VICTOR BROWN
Vice-President for College Advancement: KAREN JOHNSON
Vice-President for Financial Administration: MANFORD SIMCOCK
Vice-President for Student Administration: NELSON THOMAS
Registrar: CAROLYN DENNEY
Director of Libraries: CAROLYN GASKELL

Library of 170,000 vols
Number of teachers: 125
Number of students: 1,650.

WASHINGTON STATE UNIVERSITY

Pullman, WA 99164

Telephone: (509) 335-3564
E-mail: comments@wsu.edu
Internet: www.wsu.edu

Founded 1890 as college; university status 1959
Academic year: August to May
President: V. LANE RAWLINS
Provost: ROBERT BATES
Vice-President for Business Affairs: GREG ROYER
Vice-President for Student Affairs: CHARLENE JAEGER
Vice-President for Information Technology: MARY DOYLE
Vice-President for University Relations: SALLY SAVAGE
Vice-President for University Development: RICHARD FRISCH
Dean of Spokane Campus: ROM MARKIN
Dean of Tri-Cities Campus: LARRY JAMES
Dean of Vancouver Campus: HAROLD DENGERINK
Registrar: DAVID A. GUZMAN
Director, Libraries: VIRGINIA STEEL

Library of 2,044,856 vols
Number of teachers: 1,238
Number of students: 21,073

Publications: *Northwest Science* (4 a year), *Northwest Theatre Review* (annually)

DEANS

College of Agriculture and Home Economics: JAMES J. ZUICHES
College of Economics and Business: LEN JESSUP
College of Education: JUDY MITCHELL
College of Engineering and Architecture: ANJAN BOSE
Graduate School: HOWARD GRIMES
Intercollegiate College of Nursing, Spokane: DOROTHY DETLOR
College of Pharmacy: WILLIAM FASSETT
College of Sciences: MIKE GRISWOLD
College of Veterinary Medicine: WARWICK BAYLY
College of Liberal Arts: BARBARA COUTURE
Honors College: MARY WACK
Extended University Services: MURIEL OAKS

WESTERN WASHINGTON UNIVERSITY

Bellingham, WA 98225

Telephone: (360) 650-3000
E-mail: admit@cc.wwu.edu

Internet: www.wwu.edu

Founded 1893 as Bellingham Normal School, name changed to Western Washington College of Education 1937, finally Western Washington University 1977
Academic year: September to June

President: Dr KAREN W. MORSE
Provost/Vice-President for Academic Affairs: Dr ANDREW BODMAN
Vice-President for Business and Financial Affairs: Dr GEORGE A. PIERCE
Vice-President for Student Affairs: Dr EILEEN V. COUGHLIN
Vice-President for External Affairs: ROBERT EDIE
Librarian: BÉLA FOLTIN, Jr

Library of 1,900,000 vols
Number of teachers: 615
Number of students: 11,708

Publications: *Bellingham Review* (literary, 2 a year), *Journal of Cross-Cultural Psychology* (international, annually), *Journal of Rural Sociology* (annually), *Studies in American Indian Literature* (4 a year), *Northwest Journal of Business and Economics* (annually).

WHITMAN COLLEGE

345 Boyer Ave, Walla Walla, WA 99362

Telephone: (509) 527-5111
E-mail: communication@whitman.edu
Internet: www.whitman.edu

Founded 1859
President: Dr THOMAS CRONIN
Vice-President for Development: STEPHEN BECKER
Dean of Faculty: PATRICK KEEF
Dean of Students: CHARLES CLEVELAND
Registrar: RONALD URBAN
Librarian: HENRY YAPLE

Library of 325,000 vols
Number of teachers: 101 full-time
Number of students: 1,300.

WHITWORTH COLLEGE

300 West Hawthorne Rd, Spokane, WA 99251

Telephone: (509) 777-1000
Fax: (509) 777-3221
Internet: www.whitworth.edu

Founded 1890
Christian liberal arts college in the Reformed tradition

President: Dr WILLIAM P. ROBINSON
Vice-President of Academic Affairs: Dr TAMMY REID
Library Director: Dr HANS BYNAGLE

Library of 165,000 vols
Number of teachers: 267
Number of students: 2,100.

WEST VIRGINIA

ALDERSON-BROADDUS COLLEGE

College Hill Road, Philippi, WV 26416

Telephone: (304) 457-1700
Fax: (304) 457-6239
Internet: www.ab.edu

Founded 1871
Pres.: Dr STEPHEN E. MARKWOOD
Provost and Vice-Pres. for Academic Affairs: Dr DENNIS H. STULL
Dir. of Admissions: KIM N. KLAUS
Dir. of Financial Aid: BRIAN WEINGART
Dir. of Annual Giving and Alumni Relations: JAMIE COOPER
Dir of Dovt: ANNETTE FETTY
Vice-Pres. for Advancement: CARL GITTINGS

Dirr of Communications: NATHAN PRICE
Vice-Pres. for Student Services and Enrollment Management: Dr ALLEN B. WITHERS
Vice-Pres. for Business and Finance: MARSHA DENNISTON
Dir of Information and Research: JULIA AUVIL
Vice-Pres. for Assessment, Planning and Technology: BRUCE BLANKENSHIP
Registrar: SAUDRA HOXIE
Librarian: DAVID E. HOXIE
Library of 110,000 vols
Number of teachers: 66 (51 full-time, 15 part-time)
Number of students: 780

4-Year liberal arts college.

APPALACHIAN BIBLE COLLEGE

POB ABC, Bradley, WV 25818
161 College Dr., Mount Hope, WV 25880
Telephone: (304) 877-6428
Fax: (304) 877-5082
E-mail: abc@abc.edu
Internet: www.abc.edu
Founded 1950
Number of students: 300

Pres.: Dr DANIEL ANDERSON

Ind., non-denominational.

BETHANY COLLEGE

Bethany, WV 26032
Telephone: (304) 829-7000
Fax: (304) 829-7108
Internet: www.bethanywv.edu
Founded 1840
Private control
Academic year: August to May
Pres.: G. T. SMITH
Provost and Dean of Faculty: MICHAEL MIHALYO
Sr Vice-Pres.: JOHN S. CUNNINGHAM
Spec. Counsel to the Pres.: JOSEPH M. KUREY
Exec. Vice-Pres. and Treas.: WILLIAM KIEFER
Exec. Vice-Pres.: PATRICIA MLODZIK
Vice-Pres. for Admission and Institutional Advancement: SVEN DE JONG
Assoc. Vice-Pres. for Student Services: SANDRA NEEL
Provost: KATHLEEN C. GODINA
Librarian: MARY-BESS HALFORD
Library of 275,340 vols
Number of teachers: 78 (56 full-time, 9 part-time)
Number of students: 830

4-Year liberal arts college; depts of Biology, Chemistry, Communication, Econ. and Business, English, Equine Studies, Fine Arts, Fundamental Studies, Gen. Science, History and Political Science, Interdisciplinary Studies, Mathematics and Computer Science, Philosophy, Physical Education and Sports Studies, Physics, Psychology, Religious Studies, Social Science, Teaching and Social Services, World Languages and Cultures.

BLUEFIELD STATE COLLEGE

219 Rock St, Bluefield, WV 24701
Telephone: (304) 327-4000
Fax: (304) 325-7747
E-mail: bscadmit@bluefieldstate.edu
Internet: www.bluefieldstate.edu
Founded 1895
Academic year: August to May
Pres.: ALBERT L. WALKER
Dir of Enrollment Management and Vice-Pres. for Student Affairs: JOHN C. CARDWELL
Vice-Pres. for Financial and Admin. Affairs: SHELIA JOHNSON

Vice-Pres. for Academic Affairs and Provost: DONALD H. SMITH
Dir of Library Services: JOANNA THOMPSON
Library of 75,700 vols
Number of teachers: 90
Number of students: 3,600

4-Year state-supported college; offers liberal arts and professional programmes.

CONCORD COLLEGE

Vermillion St, POB 1000, Athens, WV 24712-1000
Telephone: (304) 384-3115
Fax: (304) 384-9044
E-mail: info@concord.edu
Internet: www.concord.edu
Founded 1872
Academic year: September to May
Pres.: Dr JERRY L. BEASLEY
Vice-Pres. and Academic Dean: Dr DEAN TURNER
Vice-Pres. for Business and Finance: JIM CAMERON
Vice-Pres. for Admissions and Financial Aid: MICHAEL CURRY
Associate Vice-Pres. for Devt: LORETTA YOUNG
Vice-Pres. for Student Affairs and Dean of Student: Dr JOHN DAVID SMITH
Librarian: Dr STEPHEN ROWE
Library of 145,000 vols, 5,000 periodicals
Number of teachers: 95
Number of students: 2,900

4-Year public liberal arts college.

DAVIS AND ELKINS COLLEGE

100 Campus Dr., Elkins, WV 26241
Telephone: (304) 637-1900
Internet: www.davisandelkins.edu
Founded 1904
Academic year: August to May
Pres.: Dr G. THOMAS MANN
Vice-Pres. and Dean of the Faculty: Dr LAURENCE B. MCARTHUR
Vice-Pres. for College Advancement: PATRICIA J. SCHUMANN
Vice-Pres. for Student Life and Dean of Students: DAVID SNEED
Dir of the Library: JACKIE SCHNEIDER
Library of 116,000 vols
Number of students: full-time 635

Liberal arts college; depts of Biology and Environmental Science, Business Admin. and Econ., Chemistry, Education, English, Communications and Foreign Languages, Fine and Performing Arts, Health, Sport and Movement Sciences, History and Political Science, Mathematics, Computer Science and Physics, Nursing, Psychology and Human Services, Sociology and Criminology, Religion and Philosophy.

FAIRMONT STATE UNIVERSITY

1201 Locust Ave, Fairmont, WV 26554
Telephone: (304) 367-4892
Fax: (304) 366-4870
E-mail: admit@fairmontstate.edu
Internet: www.fscwv.edu
Founded 1867
Pres.: Dr DANIEL BRADLEY
Pres., Pierpont Community and Technical College: BLAIR MONTGOMERY
Vice-Pres. for Institutional Advancement: K. JEAN AHWESH
Vice-Pres. for Student Services: MICHAEL BELMEAR
Vice-Pres. and Chief Information Officer: MICHAEL BESTUL
Dir of Communications: SARAH HENSLEY

Vice-Pres. for Research and Graduate Studies: Dr PHILLIP MASON
Provost and Vice-Pres. for Academic Affairs: ANNE L. PATTERSON
Vice-Pres. for Admin. and Fiscal Affairs: ENRICO PORTO
Vice-Pres. for Academic Services and Dir of Retention: Dr MARIA ROSE
Dir of Library Services: THELMA HUTCHINS
Library of 265,000 vols
Number of teachers: 190
Number of students: 7,740

Incl. Pierpont Community and Technical College.

GLENVILLE STATE COLLEGE

200 High St, Glenville, WV 26351
Telephone: (304) 462-7361
E-mail: admissions@glenville.edu
Internet: www.glenville.edu
Founded 1872
Academic year: August to May
Pres.: Dr PETER BARR
Dean of Academic Affairs: Dr KATHY BUTLER
Librarian: GAIL WESTBROOK
Library of 110,000 vols, 483 microforms, 625 hard copy periodical titles, 18 newspaper titles
Number of teachers: 52 full-time, 30 part-time
Number of students: 1,400

Depts of Business, Education, English, Fine Arts, Land Resources, Science and Mathematics, Social Science.

MARSHALL UNIVERSITY

1 John Marshall Dr., Huntington, WV 25755
Telephone: (304) 696-3170
Fax: (304) 696-3135
Internet: www.marshall.edu
Founded 1837
Academic year: August to May
Pres.: Dr STEPHEN J. KOPP
Chief of Staff and Senior Vice-Pres. for Communications: BILL BISSETT
Provost and Senior Vice-Pres. for Academic Affairs: Dr SARAH DENMAN
Associate Vice-Pres. for Academic Affairs: Dr FRANCES HENSLEY
Gen. Counsel and Vice-Pres. for External Affairs: LAYTON COTTRILL
Dean of Libraries: BARBARA WINTERS
Library of 1,411,480 vols, documents, journal suscriptions, microforms and audiovisual items
Number of teachers: 666 full-time
Number of students: 14,000

DEANS

Lewis College of Business: Dr PAUL USELDING
College of Education and Human Services: Dr ROSALYN ANSTINE TEMPLETON
College of Fine Arts: DONALD VAN HORN
College of Information Technology and Engineering: Dr TONY B. SZWILSKI
College of Liberal Arts: Dr CHRISTINA MURPHY
College of Health Professions: Dr SHORTIE MCKINNEHY
College of Science: Dr ANDREW ROGERSON
School of Journalism and Mass Communications: Dr CORLEY DENNISON
Graduate School: Dr LEONARD J. DEUTSCH
School of Extended Education: DON COMBS
Joan C. Edwards School of Medicine: Dr CHARLES H. MCKOWN, JR
Marshall Community and Technical College: JANET AMOS

MOUNTAIN STATE UNIVERSITY

POB 9003, Beckley, WV 25802
Telephone: (304) 929-1300
E-mail: gomsu@mountainstate.edu
Internet: www.mountainstate.edu
Pres.: CHARLES H. POLK
Vice-Pres. and Chief of Staff: CINDY ALEXANDER
Assoc. Vice-Pres. and Dean of PLA: JILL HOPKINS
Vice-Pres. for Legal Affairs: JOHN REED
Vice-Pres. for Finance and Chief Financial Officer: MICHELE SARRETT
Exec. Vice-Pres. and Chief Academic Officer: JAMES G. SILOSKY
Vice-Pres. for Operations: RON WARD
Registrar: REBECCA HALL
Dir of Library and Technology Resources: JUDY ALTIS
Number of teachers: 368 (87 full-time, 281 part-time)
Number of students: 4,422.

OHIO VALLEY UNIVERSITY

1 Campus View Dr., Vienna, WV 26105-8000
Telephone: (304) 865-6000
E-mail: contact@ovc.edu
Internet: www.ovu.edu
Founded 1958
Pres.: Dr JAMES A. JOHNSON
Vice-Pres. for Enrollment: ROB DUDLEY
Exec. Vice-Pres.: STEVE ECKMAN
Sr Vice-Pres. for Academic Affairs and Provost: Dr C. JOY JAMES
Librarian: JOHN FOUST
Library of 34,000 vols, 142 print periodical subscriptions, 60,203 microforms, 6,779 audio visual materials
Number of students: 560.

SALEM UNIVERSITY

223 West Main Street, POB 500, Salem, WV 26426-0500
Telephone: (304) 782-5011
Fax: (304) 782-5395
E-mail: admissions@salemiu.edu
Internet: www.salemiu.edu
Founded 1888
Pres.: Dr RONALD E. OHL
Vice-Pres. for Academic Affairs and Provost: Dr WAYNE H. ENGLAND
Registrar: CYNTHIA J. CALISE
Librarian: Dr PHYLLIS D. FREEDMAN
Library of 200,000 vols
Number of teachers: 55
Number of students: 810.

SHEPHERD UNIVERSITY

POB 3210 Shepherdstown, WV 25443
Telephone: (304) 876-5000
Fax: (304) 876-3101
Internet: www.shepherd.edu
Founded 1871
Academic year: August to May
Pres.: Dr SUZANNE SHIPLEY
Vice-Pres. for Academic Affairs: Dr MARK STERN
Vice-Pres. for Admin. and Finance: ED MAGEE
Vice-Pres. for Advancement: ROBIN ZANOTTI
Librarians: FLOYD MILLER, JEAN ELLIOTT
Library of 196,700 vols
Number of teachers: 292 (115 full-time, 177 part-time)
Number of students: 4,000.

UNIVERSITY OF CHARLESTON

2300 MacCorkle Ave, SE, Charleston, WV 25304
Telephone: (304) 357-4800
Fax: (304) 357-4715
E-mail: admissions@ucwv.edu
Internet: www.ucwv.edu
Founded 1888 as Morris Harvey College, present name 1979
Academic year: August to April
Pres.: Dr EDWIN H. WELCH
Vice-Pres. for Admin. and Finance: CLETA M. HARLESS
Provost and Dean of Faculty: Dr CHARLES STEBBINS
Vice-Pres. for Enrollment and Student Life: BRAD PARRISH
Dir of Library Services: LYNN SHEEHAN
Library of 106,000 vols
Number of teachers: 65 full-time
Number of students: 1,200
Divs of Arts and Sciences, Business, Health Sciences; Center for Pharmacy Education.

WEST LIBERTY STATE COLLEGE

West Liberty, WV 26074
Telephone: (304) 336-5000
Fax: (304) 336-8403
Internet: www.westliberty.edu
Founded 1837
Academic year: August to May
Pres.: Dr JOHN P. McCULLOUGH
Vice-Pres. for Student Affairs and Enrollment Management: J. D. CARPENTER
Acting Provost and Vice-Pres. for Academic Affairs: Dr DONNA J. LUKICH
Registrar: SCOTT A. COOK
Librarian: CHERYL HARSHMAN
Library of 194,711 vols
Number of teachers: 166 (112 full-time, 54 part-time)
Number of students: 2,654.

WEST VIRGINIA SCHOOL OF OSTEOPATHIC MEDICINE

Office of Communications, 400 North Lee St, Lewisburg, WV 24901
Telephone: (304) 647-6238
E-mail: jmanchester@wvsom.edu
Internet: www.wvsom.edu
Pres.: OLEN E. JONES
Vice-Pres. for Academic Affairs and Dean: Dr MICHAEL D. O. ADELMAN
Vice-Pres. for Finance and Facilities: LAWRENCE KELLEY
Library of 17,000 vols, 450 journals, 2,000 multimedia titles
Number of teachers: 49
Number of students: 503.

WEST VIRGINIA STATE UNIVERSITY

POB 1000 Institute, WV 25112
Telephone: (304) 766-3000
E-mail: admissions@wvstateu.edu
Internet: www.wvstateu.edu
Founded 1891 as a land-grant college by West Virginia Legislature
Pres.: Dr HAZO W. CARTER, Jr
Vice-Pres. for Academic Affairs: Dr R. CHARLES BYERS
Vice-Pres. for Admin. Services: Dr CASSANDRA B. WHYTE
Vice-Pres. for Finance: ROBERT PARKER
Vice-Pres. for Planning and Advancement: Dr R. CHARLES BYERS
Vice-Pres. for Student Affairs: BRYCE CASTO
Dir of Library Resources: PATRICK HALL
Library of 200,000 vols, 300 periodical subscriptions

Number of teachers: 137 full-time
Number of teachers: 116 part-time
Number of students: 3,344
Depts of Art, Biology, Business Admin., Chemistry, Communications, Criminal Justice, Econ., Education, English, Health and Human Performance, History, Mathematics, Modern Foreign Languages, Music, Physics, Political Science, Psychology, Social Work, Sociology.

WEST VIRGINIA UNIVERSITY

POB 6201, Morgantown, WV 26506-6201
Telephone: (304) 293-0111
Fax: (304) 293-3080
E-mail: wvuadmissions@arc.wvu.edu
Internet: www.wvu.edu
Founded 1867
Pres.: MICHAEL GARRISON
Provost: Dr GERALD E. LANG
Vice-Pres. for Student Affairs: KENNETH D. GRAY
Vice-Pres. for Health Sciences: Dr ROBERT M. d'ALESSANDRI
Vice-Pres. for Administration and Finance: NARVEL G. WEESE, Jr
Vice-Pres. for Univ. Advancement and Marketing: CHRISTINE MARTIN
Vice-Pres. for Research and Economic Devt: JOHN D. WEETE
Library: see Libraries and Archives
Number of teachers: 1,845
Number of students: 25,255

DEANS

College of Business and Econ.: Dr STEPHEN SEARS
College of Creative Arts: J. BERNARD SCHULTZ
College of Eng. and Mineral Resources: Dr EUGENE V. CILENTO
College of Human Resources and Education: Dr ANNE H. NARDI
College of Law: JOHN W. FISHER, II
David College of Agriculture, Forestry and Consumer Sciences: CAMERON HACKNEY
Eberly College of Arts and Sciences: MARY ELLEN MAZEY
School of Dentistry: Dr LOUISE VESELICKY,
School of Medicine: Dr JOHN E. PRESCOTT
Perley Isaac Reed School of Journalism: MARYANNE REED
Potomac State College: KERRY S. ODELL
School of Physical Education: Dr DANA D. BROOKS

WEST VIRGINIA UNIVERSITY INSTITUTE OF TECHNOLOGY

405 Fayette Pike, Montgomery, WV 25136
Telephone: (304) 442-3071
Fax: (304) 442-3059
E-mail: admissions@wvutech.edu
Internet: www.wvutech.edu
Founded 1895
Pres.: CHARLES E. BAYLESS
Provost and Vice-Pres. for Academic and Student Affairs: Dr GALAN JANEKSELA
Dir of Library: BARBARA CRIST
Library of 160,000 vols, 360,000 microtexts, 3,000 periodical subscriptions
Number of teachers: 167 (102 full-time, 65 part-time)
Number of students: 2,252.

WEST VIRGINIA WESLEYAN COLLEGE

59 College Ave, Buckhannon, WV 26201
Telephone: (304) 473-8000
Fax: (304) 473-8187
Internet: www.wvwc.edu
Founded 1890

Pres.: PAMELA BALCH
Dean of the College: LARRY R. PARSONS
Vice-Pres. for Finance: BARRY R. PRITTS
Vice-Pres. forStudent Affairs and Enrollment Management: JULIA KEEHNER
Vice-Pres. for Information Technology and Chief Information Officer: R. DUWANE SQUIRES
Vice-Pres. for Institutional Advancement: TANYA SHELTON
Dir of Marketing and Communication: ROBERT N. SKINNER, II
Dir of Library: PAULA McGREW
Library of 149,085 vols
Number of teachers: 160 (80 full-time, 80 part-time)
Number of students: 1,366 (undergraduates).

WHEELING JESUIT UNIVERSITY

316 Washington Ave, Wheeling, WV 26003-6295

Telephone: (304) 243-2000
Fax: (304) 243-2243
E-mail: news@wju.edu
Internet: www.wju.edu

Founded 1954
Jesuit Liberal Arts Univ.
Academic year: August to May
Pres.: Rev. JULIO GIULIETTI
Controller: MICHAEL LEO
Vice-Pres. for Institutional Advancement: BRENT BUSH
Dean for Student Devt: CORY KING
Associate Dir of Admissions: BETH LOY
Registrar: CHAD CARTER
Librarian: KELLY MUMMERT (acting)
Library of 139,000 vols
Number of teachers: 97
Number of students: 1,527.

WISCONSIN

ALVERNO COLLEGE

3400 South 43 St, POB 343922, Milwaukee, WI 53234-3922

Telephone: (414) 382-6000
Fax: (414) 382-6354
Internet: www.alverno.edu

Founded 1887
Academic year: August to May
Pres.: Dr MARY MEEHAN
Vice-Pres. for Academic Affairs: KATHLEEN O'BRIEN
Vice-Pres. for Devt: JULIE LANDES
Vice-Pres. for Finance and Management Services: JAMES OPPERMANN
Registrar: PATRICIA HARTMAN
Dir of Library: CAROL BRILL
Library of 82,416 vols, 1,382 periodicals, 287,726 microforms, 15,728 audiovisual items
Number of teachers: 107 full-time
Number of students: 2,480.

BELLIN COLLEGE OF NURSING

725 South Webster Ave, POB 23400, Green Bay, WI 54305-3400

Telephone: (920) 433-3560
Fax: (920) 433-7416
E-mail: admission@bcon.edu
Internet: www.bcon.edu

Founded 1909 as Bellin Hospital School of Nursing, adopted current name in 1988
Pres.: JANE MUHL
Vice-Pres. and Dir of Business: JOSEPH KEEBAUGH
Vice-Pres. for Student Services: JO WOELFEL
Dir of Grants: DALE WHEELOCK
Dir of Admissions: PENELOPE CROGHAN

Dir of Financial Aid: LENA GOODMAN
Registrar: VICKY SCHAULAND
Number of teachers: 19
Number of students: 290.

BELOIT COLLEGE

700 College St, Beloit, WI 53511

Telephone: (608) 363-2000
Fax: (608) 363-2717
E-mail: pubaff@www.beloit.edu
Internet: www.beloit.edu

Founded 1846
Academic year: June to May
Pres.: JOHN E. BURRIS
Vice-Pres. for Academic Affairs and Dean of the College: LYNN FRANKEN
Vice-Pres. for Admin. and Treas.: JOHN M. NICHOLAS
Vice-Pres. for Student Affairs and Dean of Students: WILLIAM J. FLANAGAN
Vice-Pres. for Enrollment Services: NANCY BENEDICT
Registrar: MARY BOROS-KAZAI
Library of 240,000 vols, 1,100 periodical and newspaper titles
Number of teachers: 90
Number of students: 1,200
Publications: *The Round Table* (weekly), *Avatar* (annual), *Beloit Magazine* (3 a year).

CARDINAL STRITCH UNIVERSITY

6801 North Yates Rd, Milwaukee, WI 53217

Telephone: (414) 410-4000
Internet: www.stritch.edu

Founded 1937
Pres.: Sister MARY LEA SCHNEIDER
Exec. Vice-Pres. and Chief Operating Officer: PETER HOLBROOK
Vice-Pres. for Academic Affairs: Dr MARNA BOYLE
Vice-Pres. for Univ. Advancement: MICHAEL BRAUER
Vice-Pres. for Information Technology: LINDA CABOT
Vice-Pres. for Facilities: JACK GLYNN
Vice-Pres. for Student Devt and Dean of Students: CHRISTINE ROBINSON
Vice-Pres. for Public Relations and Communications: LINDA STEINER
Vice-Pres. for Business and Finance: KAREN WALRATH
Library Dir: DAVID WEINBERG-KINSEY
Library: Library with 139,000 vols
Number of teachers: 98
Number of students: 6,900
Ind., Franciscan institution; comprises College of Arts and Sciences, College of Business, College of Education and Leadership and the Ruth S. Coleman College of Learning.

CARROLL COLLEGE

100 North East Ave, Waukesha, WI 53186

Telephone: (414) 547-1211
Fax: (414) 524-7139
E-mail: ccinfo@carroll1.cc.edu
Internet: www.cc.edu

Founded 1846
Pres.: Dr DOUGLAS N. HASTAD
Dean of Students: PATRICK PEYER (acting)
Dir of Library: LELAN McLEMORE
Library of 196,000 vols
Number of teachers: 111 full-time
Number of teachers: 175 part-time
Number of students: 3,292 full-time.

CONCORDIA UNIVERSITY WISCONSIN

12800 North Lake Shore Dr., Mequon, WI 53097

Telephone: (262) 243-5700
Fax: (262) 243-4351
E-mail: admissions@cuw.edu
Internet: www.cuw.edu

Founded 1881
Pres.: Dr PATRICK T. FERRY
Number of students: 5,574
4-Year, Lutheran liberal arts college.

EDGEWOOD COLLEGE

1000 Edgewood College Dr., Madison, WI 53711

Telephone: (608) 663-2294
Fax: (608) 663-3291
Internet: www.edgewood.edu

4-Year liberal arts college; coeducational
Founded 1927
Academic year: September to May
Pres.: Dr DANIEL J. CAREY
Vice-Pres. for Academic Affairs and Academic Dean: MARY KELLY-POWELL
Vice-Pres. for Student Devt and Dean of Students: MAGGIE BALISTRERI-CLARKE
Registrar: ELLEN FEHRING
Dir of Library: SYLVIA CONTRERAS
Library of 93,000 vols
Number of teachers: 159 (72 full-time, 87 part-time)
Number of students: 2,400.

LAKELAND COLLEGE

POB 359, Sheboygan, WI 53082-0359

Telephone: (414) 565-2111
Fax: (414) 565-1206
Internet: www.lakeland.edu

4-Year liberal arts college
Founded 1862
Pres.: Dr STEPHEN A. GOULD
Vice-Pres. for Finance: JOSEPH D. BOTANA, II
Vice-Pres. for Advancement: JAMES C. CAPE
Gen. Counsel and Vice-Pres. for Int. Programs: E. ANTHONY FESSLER
Vice-Pres. for Academic Affairs and Dean of the College: Dr TIMOTHY E. FULOP
Dean of Students and Vice-Pres. for Student Affairs: SANDRA GIBBONS-VOLLBRECHT
Vice-Pres. for Enrollment Management: ALLAN D. MITCHLER
Librarian: ANN PENKE
Library of 70,000 vols
Number of teachers: 41
Number of students: 954.

LAWRENCE UNIVERSITY

POB 599, Appleton, WI 54912
115 South Drew St, Appleton, WI 54911

Telephone: (920) 832-7000
Internet: www.lawrence.edu

Private college of the liberal arts and sciences with conservatory of music
Founded 1847
Academic year: September to June
Pres.: JILL BECK
Exec. Vice-Pres.: GREGORY A. VOLK
Provost and Dean of the Faculty: DAVID BURROWS
Library Dir: PETE GILBERT
Library of 367,000 vols
Number of teachers: 125 full-time
Number of students: 1,405.

MARANATHA BAPTIST BIBLE COLLEGE

745 West Main St, Watertown, WI 53094

Telephone: (920) 261-9300
Fax: (920) 261-9109
E-mail: webmaster@mbbc.edu
Internet: www.mbbc.edu

Founded 1968
Academic year: September to May

Pres.: Dr CHUCK PHELPS
Vice-Pres. for Academic Affairs: JOHN BROCK
Vice-Pres. for Institutional Advancement: JIM HARRISON
Vice-Pres. for Business Affairs: MARK STEVENS
Dean of Students: DOUG RICHARDS
Registrar: DAVID HERSHBERGER

Number of teachers: 40
Number of students: 862.

MARIAN COLLEGE OF FOND DU LAC

45 South National Ave, Fond du Lac, WI 54935

Telephone: (920) 923-7600
Fax: (920) 923-7154
E-mail: admissions@mariancollege.edu
Internet: www.mariancollege.edu

Catholic liberal arts college

Founded 1936
Academic year: August to May

Pres.: Dr JOSEFINA CASTILLO BALTODANO
Vice-Pres. of Student Life: WILLIAM McGEE
Academic Dean: SHERYL AYALA
Dir of Admissions: ERIC PETERSON
Librarian: MARY ELLEN GORMICAN

Library of 92,000 vols
Number of teachers: 88 full-time, 3 part-time
Number of students: 1,226 full-time.

MARQUETTE UNIVERSITY

POB 1881, Milwaukee, WI 53201-1881

Telephone: (414) 288-7250
Fax: (414) 288-7197
Internet: www.marquette.edu
Private control (Jesuit)

Founded 1881 as Marquette College; chartered as univ. in 1907

Pres.: Rev. ROBERT A. WILD
Provost: MADELINE WAKE
Sr Vice-Pres.: GREG KLIEBHAN
Vice-Pres. for Public Affairs: RANA H. ALTENBURG
Vice-Pres. and Gen. Counsel: CYNTHIA M. BAUER
Vice-Pres. for Marketing and Communication: TRICIA GERAGHTY
Vice-Pres. for Finance: JOHN C. LAMB
Vice-Pres. for Student Affairs: Rev. ANDREW J. THON
Vice-Pres. for Admin.: ARTHUR F. SCHEUBER
Vice-Pres. for Univ. Advancement: JULIE TOLAN
Dean of Univ. Library: JANICE SIMMONS-WELBURN

Library of 1,500,000 vols
Number of teachers: 1,057
Number of students: 10,892

DEANS AND DIRECTORS

College of Arts and Sciences: Dr MICHAEL A. McKINNEY
College of Business Admin. and Graduate School of Management: Dr DAVID L. SHROCK
College of Communication: Dr JOHN J. PAULY
School of Dentistry: Dr WILLIAM K. LOBB
School of Education: Dr WILLIAM A. HENK
School of Eng.: Dr STANLEY V. JASKOLSKI
College of Health Sciences: Dr JACK C. BROOKS

Law School: JOSEPH D. KEARNEY
College of Nursing: Dr LEA T. ACORD
College of Professional Studies: Dr ROBERT J. DEAHL

MEDICAL COLLEGE OF WISCONSIN

8701 Watertown Plank Rd, Milwaukee, WI 53226

Telephone: (414) 456-8296
Fax: (414) 456-6550
Internet: www.mcw.edu

Founded 1893

Pres. and CEO: T. MICHAEL BOLGER
Dean and Exec. Vice-Pres.: MICHAEL J. DUNN

Number of teachers: 900 faculty physicians
Number of students: 1,365.

MILWAUKEE INSTITUTE OF ART AND DESIGN

273 East Erie St, Milwaukee, WI 53202

Telephone: (414) 276-7889
Fax: (414) 291-8077
E-mail: miadadm@miad.edu
Internet: www.miad.edu

Provost: DAVID MARTIN (acting).

MILWAUKEE SCHOOL OF ENGINEERING

1025 North Broadway, Milwaukee, WI 53202-3109

Telephone: (414) 277-7300
Internet: www.msoe.edu

Pres.: HERMANN VIETS
Vice-Pres. of Academics: Dr ROGER FRANKOWSKI
Vice-Pres. of Devt: FRANK HABIB
Vice-Pres. of Finance and Chief Financial Officer: ARMUND JANTO
Vice-Pres. for Student Life and Dean of Students: PATRICK J. COFFEY
Dir of the Library: GARY SHIMEK.

MOUNT MARY COLLEGE

2900 North Menomonee River Parkway, Milwaukee, WI 53222

Telephone: (414) 258-4810
Internet: www.mtmary.edu

Catholic women's college

Founded 1913

Pres.: Dr LINDA TIMM
Library Dir.: VOLKER H. KRIEGISCH

Library of 111,000 vols
Number of teachers: 144
Number of students: 1,700.

NASHOTAH HOUSE

2777 Mission Rd, Nashotah, WI 53058

Telephone: (262) 646-6500
E-mail: nashotah@nashotah.edu
Internet: www.nashotah.edu

Seminary of the Episcopal Church in the Anglican Communion of Churches

Founded 1842

Dean and Pres.: Very Rev. ROBERT S. MUNDAY
Associate Dean for Academic Affairs: Rev. Canon Dr J. DOUGLAS McGLYNN
Assoc. Dean for Admin. and Devt: Rev. Dr TIMOTHY J. JOHNSON
Registrar and Dir of Admissions: Dr CAROL KLUKAS
Dir of Library: DAVID SHERWOOD
Publication: *The Missioner*.

NORTHLAND COLLEGE

1411 Ellis Ave, Ashland, WI 54806

Telephone: (715) 682-1699
Fax: (715) 682-1308
E-mail: admit@northland.edu
Internet: www.northland.edu

Founded 1892

Pres.: KAREN I. HALBERSLEBEN
Dean of Admission: JASON TURLEY
Exec. Dir, Sigurd Olson Environmental Institute: THERESA BEIRL

Library of 72,000 vols
Number of teachers: 45 full-time
Number of students: 700

Publications: *Eco-Vision* (annual), *Northland College Annual Report and Honor Roll* (annual), *Northland College Magazine* (2 a year), *The Drifts* (online).

RIPON COLLEGE

POB 248, Ripon, WI 54971

Telephone: (920) 748-8115
E-mail: adminfo@ripon.edu
Internet: www.ripon.edu

4-Year private liberal arts and sciences college

Founded 1851

Pres.: Rev. Dr DAVID C. JOYCE
Vice Pres. and Dean of Faculty: GERALD SEAMAN
Vice-Pres. and Dean of Students: CHRISTOPHER M. OGLE
Vice-Pres. for Advancement: LINDA J. CARTER
Vice-Pres. and Dean of Admission and Financial Aid: STEVE SCHUETZ
Vice-Pres. for Finance: MARY DeREGNIER
Chair. of Library Dept: VALERIE VIERS

Library of 150,000 vols
Number of teachers: 75
Number of students: 750.

SACRED HEART SCHOOL OF THEOLOGY

7335 South Highway 100, POB 429, Hales Corners, WI 53130-0429

Telephone: (414) 425-8300
Internet: www.shst.edu

Founded 1929
Roman Catholic seminary
Academic year: September to June
Library of 100,000 vols, 450 periodicals

Pres.-Rector: Very Rev. JAMES BRACKIN
Vice Rector: Rev. RAÚL GÓMEZ
Vice-Pres. for Finance: SALLY A. OMITO
Academic Dean: FR THOMAS KNOEBEL
Dir of Spiritual Formation: FR MARTIN BARNUM
Dir of Pastoral Education: FR ROBERT SCHIAVONE
Registrar: ROSE M. STINEFAST
Chief Librarian: KATHY HARTY

Number of teachers: 35.

ST FRANCIS SEMINARY

3257 South Lake Dr., St Francis, WI 53235

Telephone: (414) 747-6400
E-mail: mkarr@sfs.edu
Internet: www.sfs.edu

Founded 1845

Rector: Rev. DONALD J. HYING
Dirs of Library: MARY CARIAN, KATHY FRYMARK

Library of 80,000 vols.

ST NORBERT COLLEGE

100 Grant St, De Pere, WI 54115

Telephone: (920) 403-3557

Fax: (920) 403-4010
Internet: www.snc.edu
Catholic liberal arts college
Founded 1898
Pres.: WILLIAM J. HYNES
Dean of the College and Academic Vice-Pres.:
MICHAEL MARSDEN
Vice-Pres. for College Advancement: MARK
W. JONES
Registrar: RICHARD GUILD
Dir of Library: FELICE E. MACIEJEWSKI
Library of 175,000 vols
Number of teachers: 115 full-time
Number of teachers: 25 part-time
Number of students: 1,987
Publication: *The Chronicle* (online).

SILVER LAKE COLLEGE

2406 South Alverno Rd, Manitowoc, WI
54220-9319
Telephone: (920) 684-6691
Fax: (920) 684-7082
Internet: www.sl.edu
Founded 1935
Academic year: August to May
Pres.: Dr GEORGE ARNOLD
Academic Dean: Dr GEORGE GRINDE
Registrar: Sister JANICE STINGLE
Librarian: Sister RITA ROSE STAHL
Library of 59,691 vols
Number of teachers: 88 (42 full-time, 46 part-
time)
Number of students: 900
Publications: *SLC Update* (weekly), *New
Directions* (quarterly), *Silver Reflections*
(annual)
Depts of Art, English and World Languages,
Mathematics and Computer Sciences,
Music, Natural Science, Nursing, Religious
Studies and Philosophy, Social Science and
History.

UNIVERSITY OF WISCONSIN SYSTEM

1220 Linden Dr., 1720 Van Hise Hall,
Madison, WI 53706-1559
Telephone: (608) 262-2321
Fax: (608) 262-3985
Internet: www.wisconsin.edu
Founded 1848; in 1971 the Univ. of Wiscon-
sin System merged with the Wisconsin
State Univs system; there are 13 instns
offering 4-year courses (constituent univs),
and 2 other instns offering 2-year courses
(other constituent institutions)
Pres.: KEVIN P. REILLY
Exec. Sr Vice-Pres.: DON MASH
Sr Vice-Pres. for Academic Affairs: REBECCA
MARTIN
Vice-Pres. for Finance: DEBORAH A. DURCAN
Gen. Counsel: PATRICIA BRADY
Assoc. Vice-Pres. for Budget and Planning:
FREDA HARRIS
Assoc. Vice-Pres. for Human Resources: ALAN
CRIST
Number of students: 160,000 (26 campuses).

CONSTITUENT UNIVERSITIES

UNIVERSITY OF WISCONSIN–EAU CLAIRE

105 Garfield Ave, POB 4004, Eau Claire, WI
54702-4004
Telephone: (715) 836-2637
Fax: (715) 836-2902
Internet: www.uwec.edu
Founded 1916
Academic year: September to May
Chancellor: BRIAN LEVIN-STANKEVICH

Provost and Vice-Chancellor for Academic
Affairs: STEVEN TALLANT
Vice-Chancellor for Business and Student
Services: ANDREW SOLL
Assoc. Vice-Chancellor for Academic Affairs:
ANDREW PHILLIPS
Assoc. Vice-Chancellor for Student Devt and
Diversity: KIMBERLY BARRETT
Registrar: SUE MOORE
Librarian: ROBERT ROSE
Library of 574,000 vols
Number of teachers: 700
Number of students: 10,500

DEANS

College of Arts and Sciences: DONALD CHRIS-
TIAN
College of Business: V. THOMAS DOCK
College of Education and Human Sciences:
KATHERINE A. RHOADES
College of Nursing and Health Sciences: Dr
L. ELAINE WENDT

UNIVERSITY OF WISCONSIN–GREEN BAY

2420 Nicolet Dr., Green Bay, WI 54311-7001
Telephone: (920) 465-2000
Fax: (920) 465-2032
E-mail: uwgb@uwgb.edu
Internet: www.uwgb.edu
Founded 1965
Academic year: September to May
Chancellor: Dr BRUCE SHEPARD
Provost and Vice-Chancellor and Academic
Affairs: Dr SUE K. HAMMERSMITH
Vice-Chancellor for Planning and Budget: Dr
DEAN RODEHEAVER
Vice-Chancellor for Business and Finance:
THOMAS D. MAKI
Library Dir: LEANNE HANSEN
Library: 1m. bibliographic items
Number of teachers: 300
Number of students: 5,300
Liberal arts, performing arts and profes-
sional programmes.

UNIVERSITY OF WISCONSIN–LA CROSSE

1725 State St, La Crosse, WI 54601
Telephone: (608) 785-8000
Fax: (608) 785-8809
Internet: www.uwlax.edu
Founded 1909
Chancellor: JOE GOW
Interim Provost and Vice-Chancellor for
Academic Affairs: Dr BILL COLCLOUGH
Vice-Chancellor for Admin. and Finance: Dr
BILL COLCLOUGH
Dean of Student Devt and Academic Ser-
vices: Dr PAULA M. KNUDSON
Chair. of Library Dept: PAUL BECK
Library of 691,282 vols
Number of teachers: 443
Number of students: 8,992.

UNIVERSITY OF WISCONSIN–MADISON

Madison, WI 53706
Telephone: (608) 263-2400
Fax: (608) 262-8333
Internet: www.wisc.edu
Founded 1848
Academic year: September to May
Chancellor: JOHN D. WILEY
Provost and Vice-Chancellor for Academic
Affairs: PETER SPEAR
Vice-Chancellor for Admin.: DARRELL BAZ-
ZELL
Registrar: JOANNE BERG
Dir of Admissions: ROBERT SELTZER
Sec. of the Faculty: DAVID MUSOLF
Dir, Gen. Library System: KENNETH FRAZIER

Library: see Libraries
Number of teachers: 2,200
Number of students: 41,000

DEANS

College of Agriculture and Life Sciences:
MOLLY JAHN
School of Business: MICHAEL M. KNETTER
School of Education: (vacant)
College of Letters and Science: GARY SANDE-
FUR
School of Human Ecology: ROBIN DOUTHITT
School of Library and Information Studies:
ROBIN DOUTHITT
School of Medicine and Public Health: Dr
ROBERT GOLDEN
School of Nursing: KATHARYN A. MAY
School of Pharmacy: JEANETTE ROBERTS
School of Veterinary Medicine: Dr DARYL D.
BUSS

PROFESSORS

Some Professors serve in more than one
College or School

College of Agricultural and Life Sciences (116
Agricultural Hall, 1450 Linden Dr., Madison,
WI 53704; tel. (608) 262-3003; fax (608) 265-
5905; e-mail asa@cals.wisc.edu; internet
www.cals.wisc.edu):

ALANEN, A. R., Landscape Architecture
ALBRECHT, K. A., Agronomy
ALBRECHT, R. M., Animal Science
AMASINO, R. M., Biochemistry
ANDERSON, P., Genetics
ANDREWS, J. H., Plant Pathology
ARMENTANO, L. E., Dairy Science
ATKINSON, R. L., Nutritional Sciences,
Medicine
ATTIE, A. D., Biochemistry
BALKE, N. E., Agronomy
BARHAM, B. L., Program on Agricultural
Technology Studies
BISHOP, J. R., Food Science
BISHOP, R. C., Agricultural and Applied
Econ.
BLAND, W. L., Soil Science
BLATTNER, F. R., Genetics
BLEAM, W. F., Soil Science
BOCKHEIM, J. G., Soil Science
BOERBOOM, C. M., Agronomy
BOHNHOFF, D. R., Biological Systems Eng.
BROMLEY, D. W., Agricultural and Applied
Econ.
BROWN, M. R., Life Sciences Communica-
tion
BUEGE, D. R., Animal Science
BUNDY, L. G., Soil Science
BUONGIORNO, J., Forest Ecology and Man-
agement
BUTTEL, F. H., Rural Sociology
CAMPBELL, G. R., Agricultural and Applied
Econ.
CARROLL, S. B., Genetics
CARTER, M. R., Agricultural and Applied
Econ.
CHAMBLISS, G. H., Bacteriology
CHENOWETH, R. E., Urban and Regional
Planning
CLAGETT-DAME, M., Biochemistry
CLAYTON, M. K., Statistics
CLELAND, W. W., Biochemistry
COLLINS, J. L., Rural Sociology
COLLINS, J. L., Women's Studies Program
COMBS, D. K., Dairy Science
CONVERSE, J. C., Biological Systems Eng.
COOK, M. E., Animal Science
COORS, J. G., Agronomy
COX, M. M., Biochemistry
COX, T. L., Agricultural and Applied Econ.
COXHEAD, I. A., Agricultural and Applied
Econ.
CRAIG, E. A., Biochemistry
CRAVEN, S. R., Wildlife Ecology
CRENSHAW, T. D., Animal Science
DAMODARAN, S., Food Science

DELLER, S. C., Agricultural and Applied Econ.
DELUCA, H. F., Biochemistry
DOEBLEY, J., Genetics
DOLL, J. D., Agronomy
DONOHUE, T. J., Bacteriology
DOWNS, D. M., Bacteriology
DUKE, S. H., Agronomy
EIDE, D. J., Nutritional Sciences
ENGELS, W. R., Genetics
ESCALANTE, J. C., Bacteriology
ETZEL, M. R., Food Science
FIELD, D. R., Forest Ecology and Management
FILUTOWICZ, M. S., Bacteriology
FIRST, N. L., Animal Science
FOX, B. G., Biochemistry
FOX, B. G., Enzyme Institute
FREY, P. A., Biochemistry
FRIESEN, P. D., Biochemistry
FRIESEN, P. D., Institute for Molecular Virology
GANETZKY, B. S., Genetics
GERMAN, T. L., Entomology
GIANOLA, D., Animal Science
GILBERT, J. C., Rural Sociology
GOLDMAN, I. L., Horticulture
GOODMAN, R. M., Plant Pathology
GOODMAN, W. G., Entomology
GOURSE, R. L., Bacteriology
GOWER, S. T., Forest Ecology and Management
GRAU, C. R., Plant Pathology
GREASER, M. L., Animal Science
GREEN, G. P., Rural Sociology
GRUMMER, R. R., Dairy Science
GUNASEKARAN, S., Biological Systems Eng.
GUNTHER, A. C., Life Sciences Communication
GURIES, R. P., Forest Ecology and Management
HANDELSMAN, J., Plant Pathology
HARRINGTON, J. A., Landscape Architecture
HARRIS, P. E., Agricultural and Applied Econ.
HARTEL, R. W., Food Science
HAYES, C. E., Biochemistry
HELMKE, P. A., Soil Science
HICKEY, W. J., Soil Science
HITCHON, J. C., Life Sciences Communication
HOLDEN, H. M., Biochemistry
HOLMES, B. J., Biological Systems Eng.
HOWELL, E. A., Landscape Architecture
INGHAM, S. C., Food Science
INMAN, R. B., Biochemistry
INMAN, R. B., Institute for Molecular Virology
JEANNE, R. L., Entomology
JESSE, E. V., Agricultural and Applied Econ.
JIANG, J., Horticulture
JOHNSON, E. A., Food Microbiology and Toxicology
JOHNSON, M. B., Agricultural and Applied Econ.
JONES, B. L., Agricultural Database for Decision Support
KAEPPLER, S. M., Agronomy
KAMMEL, D. W., Biological Systems Eng.
KARASOV, W. H., Wildlife Ecology
KASPAR, C. W., Food Microbiology and Toxicology
KELLER, N. P., Food Microbiology and Toxicology
KELLER, N. P., Plant Pathology
KIMBLE, J. E., Biochemistry
KIRKPATRICK, B. W., Animal Science
KLOPPENBURG, J. R., Rural Sociology
KRUGER, E. L., Forest Ecology and Management
KUNG, C., Genetics
KUNG, C., Molecular Biology
KUNG, K.-J. S., Soil Science
KUSSOW, W. R., Soil Science

LAGRO, Jr, J. A., Urban and Regional Planning
LANDICK, R. C., Bacteriology
LAUER, J. G., Agronomy
LAUGHON, A. S., Genetics
LINDROTH, R. L., Entomology
LINDSAY, R. C., Food Science
LORIMER, C. G., Forest Ecology and Management
LOWERY, B., Soil Science
MACGUIDWIN, A. E., Plant Pathology
MADISON, F. W., Soil Science
MAHR, D. L., Entomology
MANSFIELD, J. M., Bacteriology
MARKLEY, J. L., Biochemistry
MARTIN, T. F. J., Biochemistry
MASSON, P. H., Genetics
MCCLAIN, W. H., Bacteriology
MCCOWN, B. H., Horticulture
MENON, A. K., Biochemistry
MLADENOFF, D. J., Forest Ecology and Management, Statistics
NELSON, D. L., Biochemistry
NEY, D. M., Nutritional Sciences
NIENHUIS, J., Horticulture
NITZKE, S. A., Nutritional Sciences
NORBACK, J. P., Food Science
NORDHEIM, E. V., Statistics
NORMAN, J. M., Soil Science
NOWAK, P., Soil and Water Conservation
NTAMBI, J. M., Biochemistry
NTAMBI, J. M., Nutritional Sciences
OSBORN, T. C., Agronomy
PALMENBERG, A. C., Biochemistry
PALTA, J. P., Horticulture
PARIZA, M. W., Food Microbiology and Toxicology
PARKIN, K. L., Food Science
PARRISH, J. J., Animal Science
PASKEWITZ, S. M., Entomology
PETERSON, J. O., Environmental Resources Center
PHILLIPS, Jr, G. N., Biochemistry
PIKE, J. W., Biochemistry
PINGREE, S., Life Sciences Communication
POSNER, J. L., Agronomy
RAFFA, K. F., Entomology
RAINES, R. T., Biochemistry
RAYMENT, I., Biochemistry
RAYMENT, I., Enzyme Institute
REED, G. H., Biochemistry
REINEMANN, D. J., Biological Systems Eng.
REZNIKOFF, W. S., Biochemistry
ROBERTS, G. P., Bacteriology
ROPER, T. R., Horticulture
ROUSE, D. I., Plant Pathology
RUTLEDGE, J. J., Animal Science
SCHAEFER, D. M., Animal Science
SCHOELLER, D. A., Nutritional Sciences
SCHULER, R. T., Biological Systems Eng.
SHAVER, R. D., Dairy Science
SHEFFIELD, L. G., Dairy Science
SHINNERS, K. J., Biological Systems Eng.
SHOOK, G. E., Dairy Science
SMITH, S. M., Nutritional Sciences
STANOSZ, G. R., Plant Pathology
STEELE, J. L., Food Science
STEVENSON, W. R., Plant Pathology
STIER, J. C., Forest Ecology and Management
STIMART, D. P., Horticulture
STOLTENBERG, D. E., Agronomy
SUNDE, R. A., Nutritional Sciences
SUSSMAN, M. R., Biochemistry
TEMPLE, S. A., Wildlife Ecology
THOMAS, D. L., Animal Science
TIGGES, L. M., Rural Sociology
TRACY, W. F., Agronomy
TYLER, E. J., Small-scale Waste
TYLER, E. J., Soil Science
UNDERSANDER, D. J., Agronomy
VIERSTRA, R. D., Genetics
VOSS, P. R., Rural Sociology
WALSH, P. W., Biological Systems Eng.
WENDORFF, W. J., Food Science
WENTWORTH, B. C., Animal Science

WICKENS, M. P., Biochemistry
WILTBANK, M. C., Dairy Science
WONG, A. C., Food Microbiology and Toxicology
WYMAN, J. A., Entomology
YOUNG, D. K., Entomology

College of Engineering (2640 Engineering Hall, 1415 Engineering Dr., Madison, WI 53706; tel. (608) 262-3484; internet www .engr.wisc.edu):
ABBOTT, N. L., Chemical Eng.
ADAMS, T. M., Civil and Environmental Eng.
ANDERSON, D. T., Electrical and Computer Eng.
ANDERSON, M. A., Civil and Environmental Eng.
ARMSTRONG, D. E., Civil and Environmental Eng.
BABCOCK, S. E., Materials Science and Eng.
BANK, L., Civil and Environmental Eng.
BARMISH, B. R., Electrical and Computer Eng.
BENSON, C. H., Civil and Environmental Eng.
BIER, V. M., Industrial Eng.
BISOGNANO, J. J., Synchrotron Radiation Center
BLANCHARD, J. P., Eng. Physics
BOOSKE, J. H., Electrical and Computer Eng.
BOSSCHER, P. J., Civil and Environmental Eng.
BOTEZ, D., Electrical and Computer Eng.
BUCKLEW, J. A., Electrical and Computer Eng.
CARAYON, P., Industrial Eng.
CERRINA, F., Electrical and Computer Eng.
CHANG, Y. A., Materials Science and Eng.
CORRADINI, M. L., Eng. Physics
CRAMER, S. M., Civil and Environmental Eng.
DAVIS, J. L., Eng. Outreach Technical Japanese
DAVIS, J. L., Technical Communications
DEMARCO, C., Electrical and Computer Eng.
DEPABLO, J. J., Chemical Eng.
DEVRIES, M. F., Mechanical Eng.
DOBSON, I., Electrical and Computer Eng.
DRUGAN, W. J., Eng. Physics
DUFFIE, N. A., Mechanical Eng.
DUMESIC, J. A., Chemical Eng.
EDIL, T. B., Civil and Environmental Eng.
ENGELSTAD, R. L., Mechanical Eng.
EOM, C.-B., Materials Science and Eng.
FARRELL, P. V., Mechanical Eng.
FONCK, R. J., Eng. Physics
FOSTER, D. E., Mechanical Eng.
FRONCZAK, F. J., Mechanical Eng.
GIACOMIN, A. J., Mechanical Eng.
GRAHAM, M. D., Chemical Eng.
HAIMSON, B. C., Materials Science and Eng.
HANNA, A. S., Civil and Environmental Eng.
HELLSTROM, E. E., Materials Science and Eng.
HENDERSON, D. L., Eng. Physics
HERSHKOWITZ, N., Eng. Physics
HILL, Jr, C. G., Chemical Eng.
HITCHON, W. N., Electrical and Computer Eng.
HOOPES, J. A., Civil and Environmental Eng.
HU, Y. H., Electrical and Computer Eng.
JAHNS, T., Electrical and Computer Eng.
KAMMER, D. C., Eng. Physics
KLEIN, S. A., Mechanical Eng.
KOU, S., Materials Science and Eng.
KUECH, T. F., Chemical Eng.
LAGALLY, M. G., Materials Science and Eng.
LAKES, R. C., Eng. Physics

LARBALESTIER, D. C., Materials Science and Eng.
LIPO, T. A., Electrical and Computer Eng.
LORENZ, R. D., Mechanical Eng.
LOVELL, E. G., Mechanical Eng.
LUMELSKY, V. J., Mechanical Eng.
MARTIN, J. K., Mechanical Eng.
McCAUGHAN, L., Electrical and Computer Eng.
MOSES, G. A., Eng. Physics
MOSKWA, J. J., Mechanical Eng.
MURPHY, R. M., Chemical Eng.
OLEARY, P. R., Eng. Professional Devt
OSSWALD, T. A., Mechanical Eng.
PARK, J. K., Civil and Environmental Eng.
PEREPEZKO, J. H., Materials Science and Eng.
PLESHA, M. E., Eng. Physics
POTTER, K. W., Civil and Environmental Eng.
RADWIN, R. G., Biomedical Eng.
RAMANATHAN, P., Electrical and Computer Eng.
RAWLINGS, J. B., Chemical Eng.
REITZ, R. D., Mechanical Eng.
ROBINSON, S. M., Industrial Eng.
ROWLANDS, R. E., Mechanical Eng.
RUSSELL, J. S., Civil and Environmental Eng.
RUTLAND, C. J., Mechanical Eng.
SALUJA, K. K., Electrical and Computer Eng.
SCHARER, J. E., Electrical and Computer Eng.
SETHARES, W. A., Electrical and Computer Eng.
SHAPIRO, V., Mechanical Eng.
SHI, L., Industrial Eng.
SHOHET, J. L., Electrical and Computer Eng.
SMITH, J. E., Electrical and Computer Eng.
SMITH, M. J., Industrial Eng.
STEUDEL, H. J., Industrial Eng.
SURI, R., Industrial Eng.
SURI, R., Manufacturing Systems Eng.
TOMPKINS, W. J., Biomedical Eng.
UICKER, Jr, J. J., Mechanical Eng.
VANDERHEIDEN, G. C., Industrial Eng.
VANDERWEIDE, D. W., Electrical and Computer Eng.
VAN VEEN, B. D., Electrical and Computer Eng.
VEERAMANI, D., Industrial Eng.
VONDEROHE, A. P., Civil and Environmental Eng.
WENDT, A. E., Electrical and Computer Eng.
YIN, J., Chemical Eng.
ZIMMERMANN, D. R., Industrial Eng.

College of Letters and Science (500 Lincoln Dr., Room B12, Madison, WI 53706; tel. (608) 262-2644; fax (608) 262-5093; internet www.ls.wisc.edu):

ABRAMSON, L. Y., Psychology
ACKERMAN, S. A., Space Science and Eng. Center
ADELL, S. A., Afro-American Studies
ADEM, A., Mathematics
ADLER, H., German
AHERN, P. R., Mathematics
ALBUQUERQUE, S. J., Spanish and Portuguese
ALEY, J. E., School of Music
ALIBALI, M. W., Psychology
ALLEN, T. F., Botany
ANDERSON, L. A., School of Music
ANDERSON, M. P., Geology and Geophysics
ANDREONI, J., Econ.
ANGENENT, S. B., Mathematics
ARCHDEACON, T. J., History
ASSADI, A. H., Mathematics
ATIS, S. G., Languages and Cultures of Asia
BACH, C. E., Computer Sciences
BAHR, J. M., Geology and Geophysics

BAKER, T. B., Gen. Internal Medicine
BALANTEKIN, A. B., Physics
BARGER, V. D., Physics
BARTLEY, L. L., School of Music
BATES, D. M., Statistics
BAUGHMAN, J. L., Journalism and Mass Communication
BAUM, D. A., Botany
BECK, A., Mathematics
BECKER, D. E., School of Music
BEISSINGER, M., Political Science
BENDER, T. K., English
BENKART, G. M., Mathematics
BERG, W. J., French and Italian
BERGHAHN, K. L., German
BERNARD-DONALS, M. F., English
BERNAULT, F., History
BERNSTEIN, S. D., English
BERRIDGE, C. W., Psychology
BERRY, P. E., Botany
BETHEA, D. M., Slavic Languages
BICKNER, R. J., Languages and Cultures of Asia
BILBIJA, K., Spanish and Portuguese
BLAIR, S. S., Zoology
BLANCO, A., Spanish and Portuguese
BLEECKER, A. B., Botany
BLESS, D. M., Communicative Disorders
BLUM, D. L., Journalism and Mass Communication
BOLOTIN, S. V., Mathematics
BORN, S. M., Urban and Regional Planning
BOSTON, N., Mathematics
BOWIE, K. A., Anthropology
BOYDSTON, J., History
BOYETTE, P. J., Theatre and Drama
BRANDT, D. L., English
BRANTLY, S. C., Scandinavian Studies
BRENNER, R. F., Hebrew and Semitic Studies
BRIGHOUSE, M. H., Philosophy
BROCK, W. A., Econ.
BROWER, A. M., Social Work
BROWN, P. E., Geology and Geophysics
BRUALDI, R. A., Mathematics
BRUCH, L. W., Physics
BUCCINI, S., French and Italian
BUENGER, B. C., Art History
BÜHNEMANN, G., Languages and Cultures of Asia
BUNKER, S. G., Sociology
BUNN, H. T., Anthropology
BURKE, S. D., Chemistry
BURSTYN, J. N., Chemistry
BURT, J. E., Geography
BUSBY, K. R., French and Italian
BYERS, C. W., Geology and Geophysics
CAI, J.-Y., Computer Sciences
CALDERON, J. F., School of Music
CAMIC, C., Sociology
CANCIAN, M., Institute for Research on Poverty
CANON, D. T., Political Science
CARD, C. F., Philosophy
CARLSMITH, D. L., Physics
CARPENTER, S. R., Zoology
CARROLL, A. R., Geology and Geophysics
CARROLL, N., Philosophy
CASEY, C. P., Chemistry
CASPI, A., Psychology
CASSINELLI, J. P., Astronomy
CASTRONOVO, R., English
CAULKINS, J. H., French and Italian
CHAPPELL, R. J., Biostatistics and Medical Informatics
CHAVEZ, M. M. T., German
CHE, Y.-K., Econ.
CHENG, T. F., East Asian Languages and Literature
CHIAL, M. R., Communicative Disorders
CHINN, M. D., Econ.
CHISHOLM, S. L., School of Music
CHUBUKOV, A. V., Physics
CHURCHWELL, E. B., Astronomy
COE, C. L., Psychology
COHEN, C. L., History

COHEN, L. K., Comparative Literature
COLEMAN, J. J., Political Science
COOK, S. C., School of Music
COOPER, Jr, J. M., History
COPPERSMITH, S. N., Physics
CORFIS, I. A., Spanish and Portuguese
CORN, R. M., Chemistry
CORTEZ, E. M., Library and Information Studies
COURTENAY, W. J., History
COWELL, D. C., African Languages and Literature
COX, D. P., Physics
CRAVENS, T. D., French and Italian
CRIM, Jr, F. F., Chemistry
CRONON, W., History
CROOK, D., School of Music
CURTIN, M. J., Communication Arts
CUTTER, R. J., East Asian Languages and Literature
D'ACCI, J., Communication Arts
DAHL, L. F., Chemistry
DANNEMILLER, J. L., Psychology
DAVIDSON, R. J., Psychology
DAVIS, R., School of Music
DE STASIO, G., Physics
DEBAISIEUX, M. M., French and Italian
DELAMATER, J. D., Sociology
DEMBSKI, S., School of Music
DEMETS, D. C., Geology and Geophysics
DENECKERE, R. J., Econ.
DESAN, S. M., History
DESAUTELS, E. J., Computer Sciences
DEVINE, P. G., Psychology
DeWITT, D. J., Computer Sciences
DICKEY, L. W., History
DICKEY, R. W., Mathematics
DILL, C. W., School of Music
DOANE, A. N., English
DODSON, S. I., Zoology
DOKSUM, K. A., Statistics
DOLININ, A. A., Slavic Languages
DONNELLY, Jr, J. S., History
DORN, D. L., Theatre and Drama
DOWNS, D. A., Political Science
DRAINE, B., English
DRECHSEL, R. E., Journalism and Mass Communication
DRESANG, D. L., Political Science
DREWAL, H. J., Art History
DuBOIS, T. A., Scandinavian Studies
DUBROW, H., English
DUNLAVY, C. A., History
DUNWOODY, S. L., Journalism and Mass Communication
DURAND, B., Physics
DURLAUF, S. N., Econ.
DYER, C. R., Computer Sciences
EARP, L. M., School of Music
EDIGER, M. D., Chemistry
EELLS, E. T., Philosophy
ELDER, J. W., Languages and Cultures of Asia
ELLIS, A. B., Chemistry
ELLIS WEISMER, S., Communicative Disorders
ENC, M., Linguistics
ENGEL, C. M., Econ.
ERWIN, A. R., Physics
ESSIG, L., Theatre and Drama
FAIR, J. E., Journalism and Mass Communication
FERNANDEZ, D. E., Botany
FERREE, M. M., Sociology
FERRIS, M. C., Computer Sciences
FILIPOWICZ, H., Slavic Languages
FINK, M. D., School of Music
FISCHER, C. N., Computer Sciences
FITZPATRICK, M. A., Communication Arts
FOLEY, J. A., Sustainability and Global Environment
FORD, C. E., English
FORSTER, M. R., Philosophy
FOWLER, C. G., Communicative Disorders
FOX, M. V., Hebrew and Semitic Studies
FRANKLIN, C. H., Political Science

FRIEDLAND, L. A., Journalism and Mass Communication
FRIEDMAN, E., Political Science
FRIEDMAN, S. S., English
FUJIMURA, J., Sociology
FULMER, M. K., School of Music
GALLAGHER III, J. S., Astronomy
GAMORAN, A., Center for Education Research
GEARY, D. H., Geology and Geophysics
GEIGER, G. L., Art History
GELLMAN, S. H., Chemistry
GEORGE, K. M., Anthropology
GERNSBACHER, M. A., Psychology
GIVNISH, T. J., Botany
GLENBERG, A. M., Psychology
GOLDSMITH, H. H., Psychology
GOLDSTEIN, K. M., Political Science
GOODKIN, R. E., French and Italian
GOODMAN, J. R., Computer Sciences
GORSKI, P. S., Sociology
GOTTLIEB, P. L., Philosophy
GRAHAM, L. K., Botany
GREENBERG, J., Social Work
GREIVE, T. D., School of Music
GRIFFEATH, D. S., Mathematics
GROSS, S. D., German
GUERIN GONZALES, C., Chicano Studies
HAEBERLI, W., Physics
HALZEN, F. I., Physics
HAMERS, R. J., Chemistry
HAN, T., Physics
HANSEN, B. E., Econ.
HARACKIEWICZ, J. M., Psychology
HARDIN, J. D., Zoology
HARRIS, R. A., Spanish and Portuguese
HAUSER, R. M., Sociology
HAUSMAN, D., Philosophy
HAWKINS, R. P., Journalism and Mass Communication
HENDEL, I. E., Econ.
HILDNER, D. J., Spanish and Portuguese
HILL, D. D., School of Music
HILL, M. D., Computer Sciences
HILL, R. J., English
HILMES, M., Communication Arts
HILTS, V. L, History of Science
HIMPSEL, F. J., Physics
HINDEN, M. C., English
HITCHMAN, M. H., Atmospheric and Oceanic Sciences
HOESSEL, J. G., Astronomy
HORWITZ, S. B., Computer Sciences
HOWELL, R. B., German
HUBER, D. L., Physics
HUDDLESTON, J. R., Urban and Regional Planning
HUNT, L. H., Philosophy
HUNTER, L., African Languages and Literature
HUTCHINSON, S. E., Anthropology
HUTCHINSON, S., Spanish and Portuguese
HUTCHISON, J. C., Art History
HYDE, J. S., Women's Studies Research Center
HYER, B., School of Music
IONEL, E.-N., Mathematics
ISAACS, I. M., Mathematics
IVES, A. R., Zoology
JACOBS, H. M., Urban and Regional Planning
JACOBS, L., Communication Arts
JAMES, C. J., German
JAMES, S. M., Afro-American Studies
JENISON, R. L., Psychology
JENSEN, J. L., School of Music
JIN, S., Mathematics
JOHNSON, A. A., Mathematics
JOHNSON, C. M., Geology and Geophysics
JOHNSON, R. A., Statistics
JOYNT, R. J., Physics
KAISER, N. A., German
KAISER, N. A., Women's Studies Program
KAISER, R. J., Geography
KARP, P. D., School of Music
KAUTSKY, C. C., School of Music

KEENE, N., Communication Arts
KELLER, L., English
KELLEY, T. M., English
KENNAN, J. F., Econ.
KENOYER, J. M., Anthropology
KENT, R. D., Waisman Center for Mentally Retarded People and Human Devt
KEPLEY, V. I., Communication Arts
KERCHEVAL, J. L., English
KHAZANOV, A., Anthropology
KIESSLING, L. L., Biochemistry
KIRSCH, J. A. W., Zoology
KITCHELL, J. F., Zoology
KLEINHENZ, C., French and Italian
KLUENDER, K. R., Psychology
KLUGE, C. L., German
KNOWLES, R. A. J., English
KNOX, J. C., Geography
KNUTSON, L. D., Physics
KOSHAR, R. J., History
KOSOROK, M. R., Biostatistics and Medical Informatics
KRAVETZ, D., Social Work
KRITZER, H. M., Political Science
KUELBS, J. D., Mathematics
KUNEN, K., Mathematics
KURTZ, T. G., Mathematics
KURTZ, T. G., Statistics
LANDIS, C. R., Chemistry
LANGER, U. G., French and Italian
LAWLER, J. E., Physics
LAYOUN, M. N., Comparative Literature
LEARY, J. P., Folklore
LECKRONE, M. E., School of Music
LEE, J. B., History
LEMPP, S., Mathematics
LEPOWSKY, M. A., Anthropology
LEZRA, J., English
LI, Y., Linguistics
LIN, C. C., Physics
LINDSTROM, D. L., History
LIU, Z.-U., Atmospheric and Oceanic Sciences
LIVNY, M., Computer Sciences
LOEWENSTEIN, D. A., English
LOH, W.-Y., Statistics
LONGINOVIC, T., Slavic Languages
LOUDEN, M. L., German
LUCAS, S. E., Communication Arts
LUNDIN, A. H., Library and Information Studies
LUTFI, R. A., Communicative Disorders
MACAULAY, M. A., Linguistics
MACDONALD, M. C., Psychology
MACKEN, M. A., Linguistics
MAGNAN, S. S., French and Italian
MALLON, F. E., History
MANION, M., Political Science
MANOOGIAN, V. I., School of Music
MANUELLI, R. E., Econ.
MARCOUILLER, D. W., Urban and Regional Planning
MARLER, C. A., Psychology
MARQUEZ, B., Political Science
MARTIN, J. E., Atmospheric and Oceanic Sciences
MATHIEU, R. D., Astronomy
MAYER, K. R., Political Science
MAYNARD, D. W., Sociology
MAZZAOUI, M. F., History
McCAMMON, D., Physics
McCLINTOCK, A. P., English
McCLURE, L. K., Integrated Liberal Studies
McCOY, A. W., History
McDONALD, D. M., History
McGLOIN, N. H., East Asian Languages and Literature
McKAY, N. Y., Afro-American Studies
McKAY, N. Y., English
McKEOWN, J. C., Classics
McLEOD, D. M., Journalism and Mass Communication
McMAHON, R. J., Chemistry
MEMON, M. U., Languages and Cultures of Asia

MENOCAL, N. G., Art History
MEYER, D. R., Social Work
MEYER, R. R., Computer Sciences
MICKELSON, D. M., Geology and Geophysics
MIERNOWSKI, J., French and Italian
MILEWSKI, P. A., Mathematics
MILLER, A. W., Mathematics
MILLER, B. P., Computer Sciences
MILLER, J. F., Communicative Disorders
MITMAN, G. A., History of Science
MOFFITT, T. E., Psychology
MOORE, C. F., Psychology
MOORE, J. W., Chemistry
MOORE, M. L., English
MORAHG, G., Hebrew and Semitic Studies
MORGAN, D. O., Institute for Humanities Research
MORSE, R. M., Physics
MORTENSEN, C. D., Communication Arts
MURPHY, J. J., Communication Arts
MURRAY, J. K., Art History
NADLER, S. M., Philosophy
NARAYAN, K., Anthropology
NATHANSON, G. M., Chemistry
NAUGHTON, J. F., Computer Sciences
NELSEN, S. F., Chemistry
NEWLANDS, C., Classics
NEWMAN, J. P., Psychology
NICHOLS, D. A., Lafollette School of Public Affairs
NIENHAUSER, W. H., East Asian Languages and Literature
NILES, J. D., English
NILES, J. D., Institute for Humanities Research
NIXON, R. D., English
NORDSIECK, K. H., Astronomy
NYSTRAND, P. M., English
OGELMAN, H. B., Physics
OH, Y.-G., Mathematics
OHNUKI-TIERNEY, E., Anthropology
OLANIYAN, T., African Languages and Literature
OLIVER, P. E., Sociology
OLSSON, M. G., Physics
ONELLION, M. F., Physics
ONO, K., Mathematics
ORLIK, P. P., Mathematics
OSTERGREN, R. C., Geography
PALLONI, A., Sociology
PAN, Z., Communication Arts
PASSMAN, D. S., Mathematics
PAWLEY, J. B., Zoology
PAYNE, L. A., Political Science
PAYNE, S. G., History
PECK, J. A., Geography
PERRY, D., School of Music
PETTY, G. W., Atmospheric and Oceanic Sciences
PHILLIPS, Q. E., Art History
PILIAVIN, J. A., Sociology
PLUMMER, B. G., Afro-American Studies
PODESTA, G. A., Spanish and Portuguese
PONDROM, C. N., English
PONDROM, L. G., Physics
PORTER, W. P., Zoology
POWELL, B. B., Classics
PRAGER, S. C., Physics
PREPOST, R., Physics
PRICE, T. D., Anthropology
RABINOWITZ, P. H., Mathematics
RADANO, R. M., School of Music
RAFFERTY, E. M., Languages and Cultures of Asia
RAM, A., Mathematics
RAMAKRISHNAN, R., Computer Sciences
RAND, N. T., French and Italian
RAO, V. N., Languages and Cultures of Asia
REAMES, S. L., English
RECORD, Jr, M. T., Biochemistry
REEDER, D. D., Physics
REICH, H. J., Chemistry
REPS, T. W., Computer Sciences
RESCHOVSKY, A. M., Lafollette School of Public Affairs

REYNOLDS, A. J., Waisman Center for Mentally Retarded People and Human Devt
REYNOLDS, R. J., Astronomy
RICHARDSON, N. R., Political Science
RICHARDSON, W. W., Music
RIFKIN, B., Slavic Languages
RILEY, P. T., Political Science
RISLEY, W. R., Spanish and Portuguese
ROBBIN, J. W., Mathematics
ROBBINS, L. S., Library and Information Studies
ROBERTS, M. L., History
ROESLER, F. L., Physics
RON, A., Computer Sciences
ROSAY, J.-P., Mathematics
ROSENMEYER, P., Classics
ROTHSTEIN, E., English
RUAN, Y., Mathematics
RZCHOWSKI, M. S., Physics
SACK, R. D., Geography
SAIZ, P., Comparative Literature
SALMONS, J. C., German
SALOMON, F. L., Anthropology
SAMUELSON, L. W., Econ.
SAPIRO, V., Academic Affairs
SAVAGE, B. D., Astronomy
SCARANO, F. A., History
SCHAEFFER, N. C., Sociology
SCHAFFER, J. W., School of Music
SCHAMILOGLU, U., Languages and Cultures of Asia
SCHATZBERG, M. G., Political Science
SCHAUB, T. H., English
SCHEUB, H. E., African Languages and Literature
SCHEUFELE, D. A., Journalism and Mass Communication
SCHLEICHER, A. Y., African Languages and Literature
SCHOLZ, J. K., Econ.
SCHULTZ, S. K., History
SCHWARTZ, D. C., Chemistry
SEEGER, A., Mathematics
SEIDENBERG, M. S., Psychology
SEIDMAN, G. W., Sociology
SCHAFER, B. E., Political Science
SCHAFER-LANDAU, R. S., Philosophy
SHAH, D. V., Journalism and Mass Communication
SHAH, H. G., Journalism and Mass Communication
SHAKHASHIRI, B. Z., Chemistry
SHANK, M. H., History of Science
SHAO, J., Statistics
SCHAPIRO, L. A., Philosophy
SHARKEY, T. D., Botany
SHARPLESS, J. B., History
SHAVLIK, J. W., Computer Sciences
SHCHEGLOV, Y. K., Slavic Languages
SIBERT, E. L., Chemistry
SIDELLE, A. G., Philosophy
SILBERMAN, M. D., German
SIMO, J. A., Geology and Geophysics
SKINNER, J. L., Chemistry
SKLOOT, R., Theatre and Drama
SLEMROD, M., Mathematics
SMITH, J. R., School of Music
SMITH, LESLIE M., Mathematics
SMITH, LLOYD M., Chemistry
SMITH, W. H., Physics
SNOWDON, C. T., Psychology
SOBER, E. R., Philosophy
SOHI, G. S., Computer Sciences
SOLL, A. I., Philosophy
SOLOMON, M. H., Computer Sciences
SOMMERVILLE, J. P., History
SORKIN, D. J., Institute for Humanities Research
SPALDING, E. P., Botany
SPARKE, L. S., Astronomy
SPROTT, J. C., Physics
STAIGER, R. W., Econ.
STAMPE, D. W., Philosophy
STEAKLEY, J. D., German
STEELE, J. A., English

STERN, S. J., History
STEUDEL, K. L., Zoology
STEVENS, J. D, School of Music
STOWE, J. C., School of Music
STRETTON, A. O., Zoology
STRIER, K. B., Anthropology
STRIKWERDA, J. C., Computer Sciences
SUCHMAN, M. C., Sociology
SUTTON, R. A., School of Music
SWACK, J. R., School of Music
SWEENEY, S. R., Theatre and Drama
SYTSMA, K. J., Botany
TAYLOR, M. S., Econ.
TEMPRANO, J. C., Spanish and Portuguese
TERRY, P. W., Physics
TERWILLIGER, P. M., Mathematics
TESFAGIORGIS, F. H. W., Afro-American Studies
THIMMIG, L. L., School of Music
THOMSON, E. J., Sociology
THORNTON, M. C., Afro-American Studies
THURBER, C. H., Geology and Geophysics
TIMBIE, P. T., Physics
TREICHEL, P. M., Chemistry
TRIPOLI, A., Political Science
TRIPP, G. J., Atmospheric and Oceanic Sciences
TSUI, K.-W., Statistics
TURNER, M. G., Zoology
TZAVARAS, A., Mathematics
UHLENBROCK, D., Mathematics
VALLEY, J. W., Geology and Geophysics
VAN DEBURG, W. L., Afro-American Studies
VANDENHEUVEL, M. J., Theatre and Drama
VARDI, U., School of Music
VAUGHN, S. L., Journalism and Mass Communication
VERNON, M. K., Computer Sciences
WAHBA, G. G., Statistics
WAINGER, S., Mathematics
WALEFFE, F., Mathematics
WALKER, J. R., Econ.
WALKER, T. G., Physics
WALLACE, R. W., English
WALLER, D. M., Botany
WANDEL, L. P., History
WANDEL, L. P., Institute for Humanities Research
WANG, P.-K., Atmospheric and Oceanic Sciences
WARDROP, R. L., Statistics
WEIMER, D., Political Science
WEINBROT, H. D., English
WEINHOLD, F. A., Chemistry
WEISMER, G. G., Communicative Disorders
WEISMER, G. G., Waisman Center for Mentally Retarded People and Human Devt
WEISSHAAR, J. C., Chemistry
WELBOURNE, T. G., School of Music
WERNER, C., Afro-American Studies
WEST, K. D., Econ.
WHITEHEAD, N. L., Anthropology
WHITLOCK, Jr, H. W., Chemistry
WILSON, F. D., Sociology
WILSON, G. K., Political Science
WILSON, R. L., Mathematics
WINICHAKUL, T., History
WINK, A., History
WINOKUR, M. J., Physics
WINSPUR, S., French and Italian
WITTE, J. F., Political Science
WOFFORD, S., English
WOLF, K., Scandinavian Studies
WOOD, D. A., Computer Sciences
WOODS, R. C., Chemistry
WORCESTER, N. A., Women's Studies Program
WRIGHT, E. O., Sociology
WRIGHT, J. C., Chemistry
WRIGHT, S. J., Computer Science
WU, S. L. Y., Physics
YANDELL, K. E., Philosophy
YETHIRAJ, A., Chemistry
YOUNG, J. A., Atmospheric and Oceanic Sciences

YOUNG, R. F., English
ZAMORA, M. M., Spanish and Portuguese
ZEDLER, J. B., Arboretum: Tours
ZEDLER, J. B., Botany
ZEITLIN, J., Lafollette School of Public Affairs
ZEITLIN, J., Sociology
ZEPPENFELD, D., Physics
ZIMMERER, K. S., Geography
ZIMMERMAN, H. E., Chemistry
ZUENGLER, J, English
ZWEIBEL, E. G., Physics

School of Business (2265 Grainger Hall, 975 University Ave, Madison, WI 53706; tel. (608) 262-0471; fax (608) 265-6041; e-mail busundergrads@bus.wisc.edu; internet www .bus.wisc.edu):

ALDAG, R. J., School of Business
ANDERSON, D. R., School of Business
ANTONIONI, D. T., School of Business
BROWN, D. P., School of Business
BROWNE, M. J., School of Business
COVALESKI, M. A., School of Business
DAVIS, J. S., School of Business
DUNHAM, R. B., School of Business
EICHENSEHER, J. W., School of Business
FREES, E. W., ASchool of Business
GERHART, B. A., School of Business
HARMATUCK, D. J., School of Business
HAUSCH, D. B., School of Business
HEIDE, J. B., School of Business
HODDER, J. E., School of Business
JOHANNES, J. M., School of Business
KRAINER, R. E., School of Business
MALPEZZI, S., School of Business
MARIEN, E. J., School of Business
MILLER, R. B., School of Business
MINER, A. S., School of Business
MORRIS, J. G., School of Business
NAIR, R. D., School of Business
NEVIN, J. R., School of Business
PETER, J. P., School of Business
RIDDIOUGH, T. J., School of Business
RITTENBERG, L. E., School of Business
SCHMIT, J. T., School of Business
SHILLING, J. D., Real Estate
STEVENSON, R. E., School of Business
THOMPSON, J. C., Marketing
VANDELL, K. D., School of Business
WEMMERLÖV, U., School of Business
WEYGANDT, J. J., School of Business
WILD, J. J., School of Business

School of Education (Dean's Office, 123 Education, 1000 Bascom Hall, Madison, WI 53706; tel. (608) 262-1763; fax (608) 265-3284; e-mail easinfo@education.wisc.edu; internet www.education.wisc.edu):

ABBEDUTO, L. J., Educational Psychology
APPLE, M. W., Curriculum and Instruction
BECKER, D. H., Art
BERVEN, N. L., Rehabilitation Psychology and Spec. Education
BLOCH, M., Curriculum and Instruction
BRECKENRIDGE, B. M., Art
BREDESON, P. V., Gen.
BROWN, B. B., Educational Psychology
CABRERA, A. F., Gen.
CAPPER, C. A., Gen.
CHAN, F., Rehabilitation Psychology and Spec. Education
COLEMAN, H. L. K., Counselling Psychology
CONRAD, C. F., Gen.
DAMER, J. F., Art
DERRY, S. J., Educational Psychology
ENRIGHT, R. D., Educational Psychology
ESCALANTE, J. A., Art
FENNELL, P., Art
FENSTER, F., Art
FEREN, S. F., Art
FULTZ, M., Educational Policy Studies
GEE, J. P., Curriculum and Instruction
GETTINGER, M., Educational Psychology
GLORIA, A. M., Counselling Psychology
GOMEZ, M. L., Curriculum and Instruction
GRANT, C. A., Curriculum and Instruction

GRAUE, M. E., Center for Education Research
HANLEY-MAXWELL, C. D., Rehabilitation Psychology and Spec. Education
HAYES, E. R., Curriculum and Instruction
HEWSON, P. W., Curriculum and Instruction
JI, L.-L., Kinesiology
KALISH, C. W., Educational Psychology
KAZAMIAS, A. M., Educational Policy Studies
KETCHUM, C. G., Art
KNOX, A. B., Gen.
KOYKKAR, J. N., Dance
KOZA, J. E., Curriculum and Instruction
KRATOCHWILL, T. R., Educational Psychology
KRATOCHWILL, T. R., Center for Education Research
LADSON-BILLINGS, G. J., Curriculum and Instruction
LEE, S. J., Educational Policy Studies
LI, C.-P., Dance
LOCKWOOD, A. L., Curriculum and Instruction
LOESER, T., Art
LONG, R. L., Art
LOWE, T. T., Art
LYNCH, R. T., Rehabilitation Psychology and Spec. Education
MARSCHALEK, D. G., Art
MELROSE, C. A., Dance
METZ, M. H., Educational Policy Studies
MORGAN, W. P., Kinesiology
MYERS, F. J., Art
ODDEN, A. R., Center for Education Research
OLNECK, M. R., Educational Policy Studies
PEKARSKY, D. N., Educational Policy Studies
PETERSON, K. D., Gen.
PHELPS, L. A., Center on Education and Work
PHELPS, L. A., Gen.
POPKEWITZ, T. S., Curriculum and Instruction
PRICE, G. G., Curriculum and Instruction
PYLANT, C. S., Art
QUINTANA, S. M., Counselling Psychology
REESE, W. J., Educational Policy Studies
RIEBEN, J. R., Art
SCHEER, J. M., Art
SCHNEIDER, M. L., Kinesiology
SCHRAG, F. K., Educational Policy Studies
SERLIN, R. C., Educational Psychology
STEWART, J. II., Curriculum and Instruction
STREIBEL, M. J., Curriculum and Instruction
SUBKOVIAK, M. J., Educational Psychology
TARVER, S. G., Rehabilitation Psychology and Spec. Education
TOCHON, F. V., Curriculum and Instruction
VANDELI, D. L., Educational Psychology
WAMPOLD, B. E., Counselling Psychology
ZEICHNER, K. M., Curriculum and Instruction

School of Human Ecology (1300 Linden Dr., Madison, WI 53706; tel. (608) 262-2608; fax (608) 265-4969; internet www.sohe.wisc .edu):

APPLE, R. D., Consumer Science
AQUILINO, W. S., Human Devt and Family Studies
BOGENSCHNEIDER, K. P., Human Devt and Family Studies
BOYD, V. T., Environment, Textiles and Design
DOHR, J. H., Environment, Textiles and Design
DONG, W., Environment, Textiles and Design
GOEBEL, K. P., Consumer Science
GORDON, B., Environment, Textiles and Design

HOLDEN, K. C., Lafollette School of Public Affairs
HOYT, A. A., Consumer Science
HUNT, M. E., Environment, Textiles and Design
JASPER, C. R., Consumer Science
MARKS, N. F., Human Devt and Family Studies
RILEY, D. A., Human Devt and Family Studies
ROSSING, B. E., Interdisciplinary Studies
SARMADI, M., Environment, Textiles and Design
SHEEHAN, D., Environment, Textiles and Design
SMALL, S. A., Human Devt and Family Studies
WAY, W. L., Gen.
ZEPEDA, L., Consumer Science

School of Nursing (600 Highland Ave, H6/ 150, Madison, WI 53792; tel. (608) 263-5155; fax (608) 263-5323; e-mail clangsdo@facstaff .wisc.edu; internet www.son.wisc.edu):

BAUMANN, L. J.
BOWERS, B. J.
BRENNAN, P.
BROWN, R. L.
DIEKELMANN, N. L.
DIEMER, G. A.
ESSER-ANDERSON, J. J.
GALAROWICZ, L. R. B.
KIRCHHOFF, K.
LASKY, P. A.
LITTLEFIELD, V. M.
MAY, K. A.
McCARTHY, D. O.
McCUBBIN, M. A.
OWEN, B. D.
RATHER, M. L.
RIESCH, S.
WARD, S. E.
WELLS, T.

School of Pharmacy (Renn & Bohm Hall, 777 Highland Ave, Madison, WI 53705; tel. (608) 262-1416; fax (608) 262-3397; internet www .pharmacy.wisc.edu):

DEMUTH, J. E., Pharmacy Outreach
HANSON, A. L., Pharmacy Outreach
HEIDEMAN, W., Pharmacy
HORNEMANN, U., Pharmacy
KRELING, D. H., Pharmacy
MELLON, W. S., Pharmacy
NORTHROP, D. B., Pharmacy
PETERSON, R. E., Pharmacy
RICH, D. H., Pharmacy
ROBINSON, J. R., Pharmacy
RUDY, T. A., Pharmacy
SCARBOROUGH, J., Pharmacy
SHEN, B., Pharmacy
THORSON, J. S., Pharmacy

School of Veterinary Medicine (2015 Linden Dr., Madison, WI 53706; tel. (608) 263-6716; internet www.vetmed.wisc.edu):

AIKEN, J. M.
BEHAN, M., Comparative Biosciences
BJORLING, D. E., Surgical Sciences
BOSU, W. T., Medical Sciences
CAREY, H. V., Comparative Biosciences
CHRISTENSEN, B. M.
COLLINS, M.
CZUPRYNSKI, C. J
DUBIELZIG, R. R.
DUNCAN, I. D., Medical Sciences
ELFARRA, A. A., Comparative Biosciences
GINTHER, O. J.
HELLEKANT, G.
KAWAOKA, Y.
MacWILLIAMS, P. S.
MANLEY, P. A., Surgical Sciences
MARKEL, M. D., Medical Sciences
McGUIRK, S. M., Medical Sciences
MESSING, A.
MILETIC, V., Comparative Biosciences
MITCHELL, G. S., Comparative Biosciences

MURPHY, C. J., Surgical Sciences
OAKS, J. A., Comparative Biosciences
OLSEN, C. W.
SCHULER, L. A., Comparative Biosciences
SCHULTZ, R. D.
SPLITTER, G. A.
WILSMAN, N. J., Comparative Biosciences
YOSHINO, T. P.

Law School (975 Bascom Hall, Madison, WI 53706; tel. (608) 262-2240; fax (608) 262-5485; e-mail deansoffice@law.wisc.edu; internet www.law.wisc.edu):

ALTHOUSE, A.
BRITO, T. L.
CARSTENSEN, P. C.
CHARO, R. A.
CHURCH, W. L.
CLAUSS, C. A.
DICKEY, W. J.
ERLANGER, H. S.
GREENE, L. S.
IRISH, C. R.
KAPLAN, L. V.
KIDWELL, J. A.
KLUG, H. J.
KOMESAR, N. K.
LARSON, J. E.
MACAULAY, S.
McEVOY, A. F.
MERTZ, E. E.
MORAN, B. I.
NOURSE, V. F.
PALAY, T. M.
SCHACTER, J. S.
SCHULTZ, D. E.
SHAFFER, G. C.
SMITH, D. G.
SMITH, M. E.
THOMPSON, C. F.
TRUBEK, D. M.

Medical School (1300 University Ave, Madison, WI 53706; tel. (608) 263-4900; fax (608) 262-2327; internet www.med.wisc.edu):

ABBOTT, D. H., Primate Research Center
ABBS, J. H., Neurology
ALBANESE, M. A., Population Health Sciences
ALBERT, D. M., Ophthalmology and Visual Sciences
ALLEN-HOFFMANN, B. L., Anatomic Pathology
ANDERSON, R. A., Pharmacology
ANDERSON, W. H., History of Medicine
BACH-Y-RITA, P., Rehabilitation Medicine
BANGS, J. D., Medical Microbiology
BENCA, R. M., Psychiatry
BENTZ, M. L., Dental and Plastic Surgery
BERSU, E. T., Anatomy
BERTICS, P. J., Biomolecular Chemistry
BIANCO, J. A., Nuclear Medicine
BIRD, I. M., Obstetrics and Gynaecology
BRADFIELD, C. A., Oncology
BRANDT, C. R., Ophthalmology and Visual Sciences
BRESNICK, E. H., Pharmacology
BROOKS, B. R., Neurology
BROW, D. A., Biomolecular Chemistry
BRUSKEWITZ, R. C., Urology
BURGESS, R. R., Oncology
CARNES, M. L., Geriatrics and Adult Devt
CHIU, S.-Y., Physiology
COMPTON, T., Oncology
CORONADO, R., Physiology
CRAIG, W. A., Infectious Disease
CRUICKSHANKS, K. J., Ophthalmology and Visual Sciences
DAHL, J. L., Pharmacology
DAHLBERG, J. E., Biomolecular Chemistry
DALESSANDRO, A., Transplant Research and Devt
DEJESUS, O. T., Medical Physics
DELUCA, Jr, P. M., Medical Physics
DEMETS, D. L., Biostatistics and Medical Informatics
DEMPSEY, J. A., Population Health Sciences

DEMPSEY, R. J., Neurological Surgery
DENNISTON, C., Genetics
DESMET, A. A., Diagnostic
DIAMOND, R. J., Psychiatry
DOVE, Sr, W. F., Oncology
DREZNER, M. K., Endocrinology
DRINKWATER, N. R., Oncology
EHRMEYER, S. L., Clinical Laboratory Science Program
EPSTEIN, M. L., Anatomy
ERVASTI, J. M., Physiology
FAHL, W. E., Oncology
FALLON, J. F., Anatomy
FETTIPLACE, R., Physiology
FILLINGAME, R. H., Biomolecular Chemistry
FIORE, M. C., Gen. Internal Medicine
FLEMING, J. O., Neurology
FLEMING, M. F., Research Grants
FOLTS, J. D., Cardiology
FORD, C. N., Otolaryngology
FOST, N. C., Paediatrics
FREY, J. J., Family Medicine
FRYBACK, D. G., Population Health Sciences
GENTRY, L. R., Diagnostic
GERN, J. E., Paediatrics
GJERDE, C. L., Education Research and Devt
GLASSROTH, J. L., Medicine
GOLOS, T. G., Obstetrics and Gynaecology
GOULD, M. N., Oncology
GRAZIANO, F. M., Rheumatology
GREENSPAN, D. S., Anatomic Pathology
GREER, F. R., Paediatrics
GRIEP, A. E., Anatomy
GRIST, T. M., Diagnostic
GURMAN, A. S., Psychiatry
GUSTAFSON, J. P., Psychiatry
HABERLY, L. B., Anatomy
HACKNEY, C. M., Anatomy
HALL, T. J., Medical Physics
HARMS, B. A., Gen. Surgery
HART, M. N., Anatomic Pathology
HARTING, J. K., Anatomy
HAUGHTON, V. M, Diagnostic
HERMANN, B. P., Neurology
HOFFMANN, F. M., Oncology
HOLDEN, J. E., Medical Physics
JACKSON, M. B., Physiology
JANUARY, C. T., Cardiology
JARJOUR, N. N., Pulmonary Medicine
JEFCOATE, C. R., Pharmacology
KAHAN, L., Biomolecular Chemistry
KALAYOGLU, M., Transplant Research and Devt
KALIL, K., Anatomy
KALIL, R. E., Center for Neuroscience
KALIN, N. H., Psychiatry
KANAREK, M. S., Population Health Sciences
KAUFMAN, P. L., Ophthalmology and Visual Sciences
KEENE, J. S., Orthopaedics
KELLEY, A. E., Psychiatry
KILEY, P. J., Biomolecular Medicine
KIM, K.-M., Biostatistics and Medical Informatics
KLEIN, B. E. K., Ophthalmology and Visual Sciences
KLEIN, B. S., Paediatrics
KLEIN, M. H., Psychiatry
KLEIN, R., Ophthalmology and Visual Sciences
KLIEWER, M. A., Diagnostic
KNECHTLE, M. J., Transplant Research and Devt
KUDSK, K. A., Gen. Surgery
KUHLMAN, J. E., Diagnostic
LALLEY, P. M., Physiology
LAMBERT, P. F., Oncology
LAUBE, D. W., Obstetrics and Gynaecology
LEAVITT, J. W., History of Medicine
LEAVITT, L. A., Paediatrics
LEMANSKE, R. F., Paediatrics
LINZER, M., Gen. Internal Medicine

LIPTON, P., Physiology
LOEB, D. D., Oncology
LONGLEY, B. J., Dept of Dermatology
LOVE, R. R., Clinical Oncology
LUCEY, M. R., Gastroenterology
MACDONALD, M. J., Paediatrics
MACK, E. A., Gen. Surgery
MACKIE, T. R., Medical Physics
MAGNESS, R. R., Obstetrics and Gynaecology
MAKI, D. G., Infectious Disease
MAKIELSKI, J. C., Cardiology
MALKOVSKY, M., Medical Microbiology
MALTER, J. S., Anatomic Pathology
MARES, J. A., Ophthalmology and Visual Sciences
MARSHALL, J. R., Psychiatry
MCBRIDE, P. E., Cardiology
MEHTA, M. P., Human Oncology
MEISNER, L. F., Population Health Sciences
MERTZ, J. E., Oncology
MEYER, K. C., Pulmonary Medicine
MISTRETTA, C. A., Medical Physics
MONTERO, V. M., Physiology
MOSHER, D. F., Haematology
MOSS, R. L., Physiology
MUKHTAR, H., Dept of Dermatology
MULLAHY, J., Population Health Sciences
NICKLES, R. J., Medical Physics
NIEDERHUBER, J. E., Comprehensive Cancer Center
NIETO, F. J., Population Health Sciences
NUMBERS, R. L., History of Medicine
OBERLEY, T. D., Anatomic PathologyMedicine
OERTEL, D., Physiology
OLIVE, D. L., Obstetrics and Gynaecology
PALIWAL, B. R., Human Oncology
PALTA, M., Population Health Sciences
PAULI, R. M., Genetics
PAULNOCK, D. M., Medical Microbiology
PEARCE, R. A., Anaesthesiology
PROCTOR, R. A., Infectious Disease
PROCTOR, R. A., Medical Microbiology
RAPRAEGER, A. C., Anatomic Pathology
REMINGTON, P. L., Population Health Sciences
RHODE, W. S., Physiology
RIKKERS, L., Dept of Surgery
ROBBINS, J., Gastroenterology
ROBINS, H. I., Clinical Oncology
ROSS, J., Oncology
RUOHO, A. E., Pharmacology
RUTECKI, P. A., Neurology
SANDOR, M., Anatomic Pathology
SCHILLER, J. H., Clinical Oncology
SCHULTZ, E., Anatomy
SKATRUD, J. B., Pulmonary Medicine
SKOCHELAK, S. E., Family Medicine
SOBKOWICZ, H. M., Neurology
SOLLINGER, H. W., Transplant Research and Devt
SONDEL, P. M., Paediatrics
SONZOGNI, W. C., Environmental Health Admin.
STAFSTROM, C. E., Neurology
STARLING, J. R., Gen. Surgery
STEELE, T. H., Nephrology
SUGDEN, W. M., Oncology
SUTULA, T. P., Neurology
SVENDSEN, C. N., Anatomy
TERASAWA-GRILLEY, E. I., Primate Research Center
THOMSON, J. A., Anatomy
TONONI, G., Psychiatry
TURNIPSEED, W. D., Gen. Surgery
TURSKI, P. A., Diagnostic
UEHLING, D. T., Urology
VALDIVIA, H. H., Physiology
VANDERBY, Jr, R., Orthopaedics
VERMA, A. K., Human Oncology
WAKAI, R. T., Medical Physics
WALKER, J. W., Physiology
WATKINS, D. I., Anatomic Pathology
WEIDANZ, W. P., Medical Microbiology

WEINDRUCH, R. H., Geriatics and Adult Devt
WEISBLUM, B., Pharmacology
WELCH, R. A., Medical Microbiology
WESTGARD, J. O., Anatomic Pathology
WHITE, J. G., Molecular Biology
WOLFE, B. L., Population Health Sciences
WOLFF, J. A., Paediatrics
WOOD, G. S., Dept of Dermatology
YIN, T. C. T., Physiology
YOUNG, J. A. T., Oncology
YOUNG, T. B., Population Health Sciences
ZAGZEBSKI, J. A., Medical Physics
ZDEBLICK, T. A., Orthopaedics
ZISKIND-CONHAIM, L., Physiology

Division of Continuing Studies (tel. (608) 262-1156; fax (608) 265-4555; e-mail info@dcs.wisc.edu; internet www.dcs.wisc.edu):

AUERBACH, E. K., Liberal Studies and the Arts
CAMPBELL, J. A., Professional Devt and Applied Studies
COOK, M. J., Liberal Studies and the Arts
KESSEL, R., Professional Devt and Applied Studies
NELSON, L. J., Liberal Studies and the Arts
ORTON, B. M., Professional Devt and Applied Studies
PADDOCK, S. C., Professional Devt and Applied Studies
SCHULENBURG, J. A., Liberal Studies and the Arts
WILLIAMS, R. T., Professional Devt and Applied Studies

Institute for Environmental Studies (Science Hall, 550 North Park St, Madison, WI 53706; tel. (608) 263-1796; internet www.ies.wisc.edu):

ADAMS, M. S., Botany
ALANEN, A. R., Landscape Architecture
ALBRECHT, K. A., Agronomy
ALLEN, T. F., Botany, Integrated Liberal Studies
ALVARADO, F. L., Electrical and Computer Eng.
ANDERSON, D. R., Business
ANDERSON, M. P., Geology and Geophysics
ANDREN, A. W., Civil and Environmental Eng.
ANDREWS, J. H., Plant Pathology
ARMSTRONG, D. E., Civil and Environmental Eng.
BAHR, J. M., Geology and Geophysics, Geological Eng.
BARROWS, R. L., Agricultural and Applied Econ.
BAYLIS, J. R., Zoology
BERRY, P. E., Botany
BISHOP, R. C., Agricultural and Applied Econ.
BLEAM, W. F., Soil Science
BOCKHEIM, J. G., Soil Science
BORN, S. M., Urban and Regional Planning
BRETHERTON, F. P., Atmospheric and Oceanic Sciences
BRINKMANN, W. A. R., Geography
BROWN, M. R., Agricultural Journalism
BUBENZER, G. D., Biological Systems Eng.
BUONGIORNO, J., Forest Ecology and Management
BUTTEL, F. H., Rural Sociology
CAMPBELL, G. R., Agricultural and Applied Econ.
CARD, C. F., Philosophy, Women's Studies
CARPENTER, S. R., Zoology
CHENOWETH, R. E., Urban and Regional Planning
COLLINS, J. L., Sociology, Women's Studies
COMPTON, J. L., Forest Ecology and Management
CONVERSE, J. C., Biological Systems Eng.
CORRADINI, M. L., Eng. Physics, Mechanical Eng.
CRONON, W., History, Geography
DEWITT, C. B., Environmental Studies

DODSON, S., Zoology
DUNWOODY, S. L., Journalism and Mass Communication
ELDER, J. W., Sociology, Languages and Cultures of Asia
FELSTEHAUSEN, H. H., Urban and Regional Planning
FELTSKOG, E. N., English
FIELD, D. R., Forest Ecology and Management, Rural Sociology
FREUDENBURG, W. R., Rural Sociology
FRIEDMAN, E., Political Science
GIVNISH, T. J., Botany
GOODMAN, R. M., Plant Pathology
GRAHAM, L. K., Botany
GURIES, R. P., Forest Ecology and Management
HAMERS, R. J., Chemistry
HARRINGTON, J. A., Landscape Architecture
HAVEMAN, R. H., Econ.
HEBERLEIN, T. A., Rural Sociology
HILL, R. J., English, American Indian Studies
HOOPES, J. A., Civil and Environmental Eng.
HOWELL, E. A., Landscape Architecture
HUDDLESTON, J. R., Urban and Regional Planning
IRISH, C. R., Law
JACOBS, H. M., Urban and Regional Planning
JEANNE, R. L., Entomology
JEFFRIES, T. W., Bacteriology
JOERES, E. F., Civil and Environmental Eng.
KANAREK, M. S., Preventive Medicine
KARASOV, W. H., Wildlife Ecology, Zoology
KITCHELL, J. F., Zoology
KNOX, J. C., Geography
KOEGEL, R. C., Biological Systems Eng., Mechanical Eng.
KULCINSKI, G. L., Eng. Physics
KUTZBACH, J. E., Atmospheric and Oceanic Sciences
LEPOWSKY, M., Anthropology, Women's Studies
LILLESAND, T. M., Forest Ecology and Management, Civil and Environmental Eng.
LINDROTH, R. L., Entomology
LONG, W. F., Electrical and Computer Eng.
LOWERY, B., Soil Science
MADISON, F. W., Soil Science
MARIEN, E. J., Business
McCOWN, B. H., Horticulture
McEVOY, A. F., Law, History
McSWEENEY, K., Soil Science
MICKELSON, D. M., Geology and Geophysics
MITCHELL, J. W., Mechanical Eng.
MOERMOND, T. C., Zoology
NIEMANN, JR, B. J., Urban and Regional Planning
NORMAN, J. M., Soil Science, Atmospheric and Oceanic Sciences
NOWAK, P., Rural Sociology
O'KEEFE, G. J., Life Sciences Communication
O'LEARY, P. R., Biological Systems Eng.
PALLONI, A., Sociology
PINGREE, S., Life Sciences Communication, Human Ecology
PORTER, W. P., Zoology
POSNER, J. L., Agronomy
POTTER, K. W., Civil and Environmental Eng.
RAY, R. O., Forest Ecology and Management
REED, J. D., Animal Sciences, Dairy Science
RICHARDSON, N. R., Political Science
RUTLEDGE, J. J., Animal Sciences, Genetics
SCARPACE, F. L., Civil and Environmental Eng.
SCHMIT, J. T., Business
SCHULER, R. T., Biological Systems Eng.
SNOWDON, C. T., Psychology, Zoology

SONZOGNI, W. C., Civil and Environmental Eng.
STEVENSON, R. E., Business
STEVENSON, W. R., Plant Pathology
STEWART, J. H., Curriculum and Instruction
STIER, J. C., Forest Ecology and Management
STRAUB, R. J., Biological Systems Eng.
STRIER, K. B., Anthropology, Zoology
TAYLOR, M. S., Econ.
TEMPLE, S. A., Wildlife Ecology
TISHLER, W. H., Landscape Architecture
TRIPLETT, E. W., Agronomy
VALE, T. R., Geography
VANDELL, K. D., Business
VENTURA, S. J., Soil Science
VONDEROHE, A. P., Civil and Environmental Eng.
WALLER, D. M., Botany
WANG, P. K., Atmospheric and Oceanic Sciences
YANDELL, B. S., Statistics, Horticulture
YUILL, T. M., Animal Health and Biomedical Sciences, Pathobiological Sciences, Wildlife Ecology
ZEDLER, J. B., Botany, Arboretum
ZEDLER, P. H., Arboretum
ZIMMERER, K. S., Geography

UNIVERSITY OF WISCONSIN—MILWAUKEE

POB 413, Milwaukee, WI 53201-0413

Telephone: (414) 229-1122

Internet: www4.uwm.edu

Founded 1885

Academic year: September to May

Chancellor: CARLOS E. SANTIAGO
Provost and Vice-Chancellor for Academic Affairs: RITA CHENG
Vice-Chancellor for Finance and Admin. Affairs: SHERWOOD G. WILSON
Secretary of the University: RANDALL J. RYDER

Number of teachers: 1,381 (817 full-time, 564 part-time)
Number of students: 28,356

DEANS

Graduate School: WILLIAM REED RAYBURN
College of Letters and Science: G. RICHARD MEADOWS
School of Architecture and Urban Planning: ROBERT C. GREENSTREET
School of Education: ALFONZO THURMAN
College of Eng. and Applied Science: Dr RONALD PEREZ
School of Social Welfare: Dr STAN STOJKOVIC
School of Business: Dr V. KANTI PRASAD
College of Nursing: SALLY LUNDEEN
School of Information Studies: Dr JOHANNES BRITZ
School of Continuing Education: MARK KRUEGER
School of the Arts: ROBERT BUCKER
College of Health Sciences: RANDALL LAMBRECHT

CHAIRS OF DEPARTMENT

College of Letters and Science (POB 413, Milwaukee, WI 53201; tel. (414) 229-4654; fax (414) 229-6827; internet www.uwm.edu/letsci):

Africology: BARTHOLEMEW ARMAH
Anthropology: JOSEPH PATRICK GRAY
Art History: BARRY WIND
Biological Sciences: JAMES COGGINS
Chemistry: DENNIS BENNETT
Communication: RENEE MEYERS
Econ.: WILLIAM HOLAHAN
English: JAMES SAPPENFIELD
Foreign Languages and Linguistics: GARRY DAVIS

French, Italian and Comparative Literature: RACHEL SKALITZKY
Geography: MICHAEL DAY
Geosciences: NORMAN LASCA
History: Prof. JEFFREY MERRICK
Mass Communication: Prof. DAVID PRITCHARD
Mathematical Sciences: KAREN BRUCKS
Philosophy: MICHAEL LISTON
Physics: MARIJA GAJDARDZISKA-JOSIFOV
Political Science: Prof. MARCUS ETHRIDGE
Psychology: Prof. RAYMOND FLEMING
Sociology: STACEY OLIKER
Spanish and Portuguese: Prof. JULIO RODRIGUEZ-LUIS

School of Education (POB 413, Milwaukee, WI 53201; tel. (414) 229-4725; internet www.uwm.edu/SOE):

Admin. Leadership: Prof. LARRY MARTIN
Educational Policy and Community Studies: IAN HARRIS
Curriculum and Instruction: Prof. LINDA POST
Educational Psychology: Prof. DOUG MICKELSON
Exceptional Education: ALISON FORD

School of Architecture and Urban Planning (POB 413, Milwaukee, WI 53201; tel. (414) 229-4014; fax (414) 229-6976; internet www.uwm.edu/SARUP):

Architecture: DONALD HANLON
Urban Planning: NANCY FRANK

College of Engineering and Applied Science (3200 North Cramer St, Milwaukee, WI 53211; tel. (414) 229-4768; fax (414) 229-6958; internet www.uwm.edu/CEAS):

Civil Eng. and Mechanics: FATTAH SHAIKH
Electrical Eng.: Prof. DEVENDRA MISRA
Computer Science: Prof. K. VAIRAVAN
Industrial and Manufacturing Eng.: MINNIE PATEL
Materials Eng.: HUGO LOPEZ
Mechanical Eng.: RYOICHI AMANO

School of Allied Health Professions (POB 413, Milwaukee, WI 53201; tel. (414) 229-5981; fax (414) 906-3920; internet www.uwm.edu/SAHP):

Health Sciences: MARY K. MADSEN
Human Kinetics: CYNTHIA HASBROOK
Communication Sciences and Disorders: MARYLOU GELFER

School of Fine Arts (POB 413, Milwaukee, WI 53201; tel. (414) 229-4762; fax (414) 229-6154; internet www.uwm.edu/SOA):

Art: LESLIE VANSEN
Film: ROB YEO
Music: SCOTT EMMONS
Theatre and Dance: LEROY STONER

School of Nursing (POB 413, Milwaukee, WI 53201; tel. (414) 229-4801; fax (414) 229-6474; internet www.umw.edu/Dept/Nursing):

Foundations of Nursing: BETH ROGERS
Health Maintenance: EILEN SHEIL
Health Restoration: MARY WIERENGA

UNIVERSITY OF WISCONSIN—OSHKOSH

800 Algoma Blvd, Oshkosh, WI 54901

Telephone: (920) 424-1234
Fax: (920) 424-7317
Internet: www.uwosh.edu

Founded 1871

Chancellor: RICHARD H. WELLS
Provost and Vice-Chancellor for Academic Affairs: Dr LANE EARNS
Vice-Chancellor for Student Affairs: PETRA ROTA
Dean of Students: Dr JAMES M. CHITWOOD
Dir of Library: PATRICK WILKINSON

Library of 1,140,000 vols

Number of teachers: 535
Number of students: 10,619

DEANS

College of Education and Human Services:
Dr FREDERICK YEO
College of Business Administration: Dr E.
ALAN HARTMAN
College of Letters and Science: JOHN KOKER
College of Nursing: ROSEMARY SMITH

UNIVERSITY OF WISCONSIN—
PARKSIDE

Box 2000, 900 Wood Rd, Kenosha, WI 53141-
2000

Telephone: (262) 595-2345
Internet: www.uwp.edu

Founded 1968
Academic year: September to May

Chancellor: JOHN P. KEATING
Provost: GERALD GREENFIELD
Registrar: RHONDA HOLLAND
Library Dir: VANAJA MENON

Library of 395,000 vols
Number of students: 5,000.

UNIVERSITY OF WISCONSIN—
PLATTEVILLE

1 University Plaza, Platteville, WI 53818

Telephone: (608) 342-1491
Fax: (608) 342-1232
E-mail: web@uwplatt.edu
Internet: www.uwplatt.edu

Founded 1866

Chancellor: DAVID J. MARKEE
Provost and Vice-Chancellor: CAROL SUE
BUTTS
Assoc. Vice-Chancellor: DAVID VAN BUREN
Asst Chancellor for Admin. Services: JIM
MUELLER
Asst Chancellor for Student Affairs: MICK
VIREY
Assoc. Vice-Chancellor for Information Ser-
vices: JOHN KROGMAN

Library of 195,000 vols
Number of teachers: 270
Number of students: 5,100

DEANS

College of Eng., Mathematics and Science:
RICHARD SHULTZ
College of Business, Industry, Life Science
and Agriculture: DUANE MERLIN FORD
College of Liberal Arts and Education: MITTIE
NIMOCKS

UNIVERSITY OF WISCONSIN—RIVER
FALLS

410 South Third Street, River Falls, WI
54022

Telephone: (715) 425-3911
Fax: (715) 425-4487
Internet: www.uwrf.edu

Founded 1874
State control
Academic year: August to May

Chancellor: Dr DON BETZ
Provost and Vice-Chancellor for Academic
Affairs: Dr CHARLES D. HURT
Vice-Chancellor for Administration and
Finance: MARY L. HALADA

Library of 260,000 vols
Number of teachers: 222
Number of students: 6,000

DEANS

College of Agriculture, Food and Environ-
mental Sciences: DALE GALLENBERG
College of Arts and Sciences: TERRY BROWN
College of Business and Econ.: BARBARA
NEMECEK

College of Education and Professional Stu-
dies: CONNIE FOSTER
Outreach and Graduate Studies: Dr DOUG
JOHNSON

UNIVERSITY OF WISCONSIN—
STEVENS POINT

2100 Main St, Stevens Point, WI 54481

Telephone: (715) 346-0123
Fax: (715) 346-2561
Internet: www.uwsp.edu

Founded 1894
Academic year: September to May

Chancellor: LINDA BUNNELL
Provost and Vice-Chancellor: VIRGINIA HELM
Vice-Chancellor for Business Affairs: GREG
DIEMER
Vice-Chancellor for Business Affairs: BOB
TOMLINSON

Library: 1,925,000 items
Number of teachers: 400
Number of students: 8,800

Publication: *Issues in Writing* (2 a year).

UNIVERSITY OF WISCONSIN—STOUT

Menomonie, WI 54751

Telephone: (715) 232-1122
Fax: (715) 232-1667
Internet: www.uwstout.edu

Founded 1891
State control
Academic year: September to May

Chancellor: Dr CHARLES W. SORENSON
Provost and Vice-Chancellor for Academic
and Student Affairs: JULIE FURST-BOWE
Dir, Library Learning Center: PAUL ROBERTS

Library of 221,392 vols
Number of teachers: 389
Number of students: 7,702

Publication: *Stoutonia* (2 a week)

DEANS

College of Arts and Sciences: Dr JOHN E.
MURPHY
College of Technology, Eng. and Manage-
ment: Dr ROBERT MEYER
College of Human Devt: Dr JOHN WESOLEK
School of Education: Dr MARY HOPKINS-BEST

UNIVERSITY OF WISCONSIN—
SUPERIOR

POB 2000, Superior, WI 54880-4500

Telephone: (715) 394-8101
E-mail: relations@uwsuper.edu
Internet: www.uwsuper.edu

Founded 1893

Chancellor: JULIUS E. ERLENBACH
Registrar: BARB ERICKSON
Librarian: FELIX UNAEZE

Library of 240,000 vols
Number of teachers: 135
Number of students: 2,800.

UNIVERSITY OF WISCONSIN—
WHITEWATER

800 West Main St, Whitewater, WI 53190-
1790

Telephone: (262) 472-1918
Fax: (262) 472-1518
Internet: www.uww.edu

Founded 1868
Academic year: August to May

Chancellor: MARTHA SAUNDERS
Provost and Vice-Chancellor for Academic
Affairs: JOHN HEYER
Vice-Chancellor for |Admin. Affairs: JAMES
W. FREER

Library of 1,970,600 vols
Number of teachers: 331
Number of students: 10,502.

OTHER CONSTITUENT INSTITUTIONS

UNIVERSITY OF WISCONSIN
COLLEGES

780 Regent St, POB 8680, Madison, WI
53708-8680

Telephone: (608) 262-1783
Internet: www.uwc.edu

Chancellor: Dr DAVID WILSON

2-Year courses
Number of students: 12,261

Colleges at Barron County, Baraboo/Sauk
County, Manitowoc, Marathon County,
Marshfield/Wood County, Marinette, Fox
Valley, Fond du Lac, Richland, Rock
County, Sheboygan, Washington County,
Waukesha.

UNIVERSITY OF WISCONSIN
EXTENSION

Madison, WI 53706
Internet: www.uwex.edu

Chancellor: Dr DAVID WILSON
Provost and Vice-Chancellor: MARV VAN
KEKERIX.

VITERBO UNIVERSITY

900 Viterbo Dr., La Crosse, WI 54601

Telephone: (608) 796-3000
E-mail: communication@viterbo.edu
Internet: www.viterbo.edu

Founded 1890
Academic year: August to May
Roman Catholic (Franciscan) liberal arts
college

Pres.: Dr RICK ARTMAN
Vice-Pres. for Academic Affairs: JACK HAVER-
TAPE
Vice-Pres. for Student Devt: DIANE BRIMMER
Vice-Pres. for Admin. and Finance: TODD
ERICSON
Vice-Pres. for Institutional Advancement:
GARY KLEIN
Vice-Pres. for Admission: ROLAND NELSON
Vice-Pres. for Mission and Ministry: Father
TOM O'NEILL
Vice-Pres. for Communications and Market-
ing: PATRICK KERRIGAN
Library Dir: RITA MAGNO

Library of 90,000 vols
Number of teachers: 176 (92 full-time, 84
part-time)
Number of students: 4,311

Schools of Adult Learning, Business, Education, Fine Arts, Letters and Sciences,
Nursing.

WYOMING

UNIVERSITY OF WYOMING

1000 East University Ave, Laramie, WY
82071

Telephone: (307) 766-1121
Internet: www.uwyo.edu

Founded 1886
Academic year: September to May

Pres.: THOMAS BUCHANAN
Vice-Pres. for Academic Affairs: MYRON
ALLEN
Assoc. Vice-Pres. for Academic Affairs and
Dean of the Outreach School: MAGGI
MURDOCK
Vice-Pres. for Student Affairs: SARA AXELSON
Vice-Pres. for Admin.: PHILL HARRIS
Vice-Pres. for Research: WILLIAM GERN

Vice-Pres. for Institutional Advancement: BEN BLALOCK
Vice-Pres. for Govt, Community and Legal Affairs: RICK MILLER
Vice-Pres. for Information Technology: ROBERT AYLWARD
Athletics Dir for Intercollegiate Athletics: TOM BURMAN

Library of 1,274,830 vols
Number of teachers: 685

Number of students: 13,000

Colleges of Agriculture, Arts and Sciences, Business, Education, Eng., Health Sciences and Law; incl. Helga Otto Haub School of Environment and Natural Resources, Graduate School and Outreach School

DEANS

College of Agriculture: FRANK GALEY

College of Arts and Sciences: B. OLIVER WALTER
College of Business: BRENT HATHAWAY
College of Education: PATRICIA MCCLURG
College of Eng.: GUS PLUMB
College of Health Sciences: ROBERT O. KELLEY
College of Law: JERRY PARKINSON
Graduate School: DON ROTH
Outreach School: MAGGI MURDOCK

GUAM

Learned Society

BIBLIOGRAPHY, LIBRARY SCIENCE AND MUSEOLOGY

Guam Library Association: POB 22515 GMF, Barrigada, GU 96921; tel. 475-4753; fax 477-9777; e-mail cmatson@guamcc.net; internet www.uog.edu/rfk/gla.html; Pres. CHRISTINE B. MATSON.

Library

Hagåtña

Guam Public Library System: Guam Public Library, 254 Martyr St, Hagåtña, GU 96910; tel. 475-4753; fax 477-9777; e-mail gpls.cat@mail.gov.gu; br. libraries in Agat (tel. 475-4767) and Dededo (tel. 632-5503); local govt document depository; Dir CHRISTINE N. M. WATSON.

Museum

Hagåtña

Guam Museum: Faninadahen Kosas Guahan, POB 2950, Hagåtña, GU 96932; tel. 475-4228; fax 475-6727; internet www.guam.net/gov/museum; Dir TONY PALOMO.

University

UNIVERSITY OF GUAM

UOG Station, Mangilao, GU 96923

Telephone: 735-2990
Fax: 734-2296
E-mail: admitme@uog9.uog.edu
Internet: www.uog.edu

Founded 1952; formerly the College of Guam
Academic year: August to May

Pres.: Dr HAROLD L. ALLEN, Jr
Senior Vice-President (Academic and Student Affairs): Dr HELEN J. D. WHIPPY
Vice-President (Administration and Finance): DAVID M. O'BRIEN
Vice-President (University and Community Engagement): Dr JEFF D. T. BARCINAS

Registrar: DEBORAH D. LEON GUERRERO

Library of 1,050,000 items
Number of teachers: 211
Number of students: 2,923

Publications: *Isla* (2 a year), *Micronesian Educator* (annually), *Micronesica* (2 a year), *Storyboard: A Journal of Pacific Imagery*

DEANS

College of Agriculture: Dr LEE S. YUDIN (acting)
College of Business and Public Administration: Dr ANITA B. WILLIAMS
College of Education: Dr MARILYN C. SALAS
College of Liberal Arts and Social Sciences: Dr MARY L. SPENCER (acting)
College of Natural and Applied Sciences: Dr LEE S. YUDIN (acting)
College of Nursing and Health Sciences: Dr MAUREEN M. FOCHTMAN
College of Professional Studies: Dr SHEYING CHEN (acting)
Enrollment Management and Student Services: Dr JULIE ULLOA
Graduate School: Dr JOYCE M. CAMACHO
Learning Resources: Dr CHRISTINE SCOTT-SMITH (acting)

PUERTO RICO

Learned Societies

GENERAL

Ateneo de Ponce: Apdo de Correos 1923, Ponce; f. 1956; Pres. Lic. HILDA CHAVIER; Sec. VICENTE RUIZ.

Ateneo Puertorriqueño: Apdo 902118, San Juan, PR 00902-1180; tel. 721-3877; fax 725-3873; e-mail ateneopr@caribe.net; internet www.ateneopr.com; f. 1876; literature, theatre, arts and sciences; 600 mems; library of 20,000 vols; art gallery; Pres. Lic. EDUARDO MORALES COLL; Dir Prof. ROBERTO RAMOS PEREA; publ. *Revista* (2 a year).

BIBLIOGRAPHY, LIBRARY SCIENCE AND MUSEOLOGY

Sociedad de Bibliotecarios de Puerto Rico: Apdo 22898, San Juan, PR 00931-2898; tel. 764-0000 ext. 5229; fax 763-4611; e-mail mzavala@rrpac.upr.clu.edu; internet www.geocities.com/sociedadsbpr; f. 1961; 280 mems; Pres. JOESFINA GÓMEZ DE HILLYER; Sec. MARÍA DE LOS ANGELES ZAVALA-COLÓN; publs *Informa* (4 a year), *Acceso: revista puertorriqueña de bibliotecología y documentación* (annually).

FINE AND PERFORMING ARTS

Sociedad Mayagüezana Pro Bellas Artes: POB 5004, Mayagüez, PR 00709; f.

1977; 300 mems; ballet, opera, concerts, lectures, symphonies, art and sculpture exhibitions; Pres. Dr LUIS E. BACÓ RODRÍGUEZ.

HISTORY, GEOGRAPHY AND ARCHAEOLOGY

Academia Puertorriqueña de la Historia: Apdo 1447, San Juan; f. 1932; 40 mems; Pres. LUIS E. GONZÁLEZ VALES; publ. *Boletín.*

LANGUAGE AND LITERATURE

Academia Puertorriqueña de la Lengua Española (Puerto Rican Academy): Apdo 4008G, San Juan, PR 00936; tel. 721-6070;

fax 781-6111; e-mail malaret@coqui.net; internet www.acaple.org; f. 1955; corresp. of the Real Academia Española (Madrid); 28 mems; Dir Dr José Luis Vega; Sec. Dr María Vaquero de Ramírez; publ. *Boletín* (quarterly).

PEN Club de Puerto Rico: Calle San Sebastián 270, San Juan, PR 00901; f. 1966; 40 mems; Sec. Ernesto Juan Fonfrías.

Research Institutes
GENERAL
Instituto de Cultura Puertorriqueña: Apdo 4184, San Juan, PR 00902; f. 1955; studies and preserves Puerto Rican historical and cultural patrimony and promotes study of Puerto Rican culture; Dir Dr José Luis Vega.

AGRICULTURE, FISHERIES AND VETERINARY SCIENCE
Institute of Tropical Forestry: USDA Forest Service, Southern Forest Experiment Station, Call Box 25000, Rio Piedras, PR 00928-2500; f. 1939; research in timber management, tropical ecosystem, plantation forestry, wildlife management, watershed management and global change research; co-operative assistance to State and private forest landowners, timber processors; co-operative research with universities and US and foreign governmental agencies; trains foreign forestry students in co-operation with FAO and USAID; library of 15,000 vols; Dir Dr Ariel E. Lugo.

Tropical Agriculture Research Station: POB 70, Mayagüez, PR 00681; tel. 831-3435; fax 831-3386; attached to Agricultural Research Service of United States Department of Agriculture; Dir Dr Antonio Soto-mayor-Ríos.

NATURAL SCIENCES
Biological Sciences
Institute for Tropical Ecosystem Studies: GPO Box 363682, San Juan, PR 00936; tel. 767-0350; fax 758-0815; f. 1957 as PR Nuclear Center; operated by the University of Puerto Rico; research, and development of tropical terrestrial ecological studies; graduate-level research and training centre in basic ecological principles primarily for minorities; Dir Dr Jess K. Zimmerman; publ. *Long-Term Ecological Research Newsletter*.

Physical Sciences
Arecibo Observatory: HC-3 POB 53995 Arecibo, PR 00617; tel. 878-2612; fax 878-1861; f. 1960; world's largest radio/radar telescope, for use by scientists from all over the world; 1,000-ft diameter fixed spherical reflector with movable feeds; for use in the radar study of planets and the properties of the earth's upper atmosphere and reception of natural radio emissions from celestial objects including pulsars and quasars; reflector surface upgraded to work at higher frequencies; library of 2,300 vols, 845 periodicals; National Astronomy and Ionosphere Centre is operated by Cornell University under a co-operative agreement with the National Science Foundation; Dir of Operations Dr Sixto Gonzales.

Libraries and Archives
Mayagüez
University of Puerto Rico, Mayagüez Campus, General Library: POB 9022, Mayagüez, PR 00681; tel. 834-0788; fax 265-5483; e-mail library@rumlib.uprm.edu; internet www.uprm.edu/library; f. 1911; 250,000 vols; Dir Prof. Irma N. Ramírez Avilés; publs *List of Publications on Agriculture and Related Sciences* (monthly), *Bibliorum* (quarterly), *Conoce Tu Biblioteca* (annually), *Serials Holdings in the Mayagüez Library* (every 2 years).

Ponce
Ponce Public Library: Apdo Postal 7477, Ponce, PR 00732; premises at: Calle Reina, Esquina Fogos, Ponce, 00731; f. 1942; 9,516 mems; 20,000 vols; Librarian M. Madera.

Pontifical Catholic University of Puerto Rico, Encarnación Valdés Library: Ponce, PR 00731; tel. 841-2000 ext. 1801; fax 284-0235; internet www.pucpr.edu; f. 1948; 269,000 vols, 46,000 periodicals, 4,600 microfilms, 2,600 CDs; special collections: Puerto Rican materials, Murga Collection; Dir Esther Irizarry Vázquez.

Pontifical Catholic University of Puerto Rico Law Library: 2250 Avda Las Américas, Suite 544, Ponce, PR 00717-0777; tel. 841-2000, ext. 1850; fax 841-5354; e-mail bib_derecho@email.pucpr.edu; f. 1961; 210,470 vols; special collections: US and United Nations documents, Puerto Rico; Dir Noelia Padua; publ. *Revista de Derecho Puertorriqueño* (quarterly).

San Juan
Archivo General de Puerto Rico: Instituto de Cultura Puertorriqueña, Apdo 9024184, San Juan, PR 00902-4184; tel. 722-2113; fax 722-9097; f. 1955; 55,000 cubic ft of records; Dir José A. Flores-Rivera (acting).

Biblioteca Madre María Teresa Guevara (Universidad del Sagrado Corazón): Apdo 12383, San Juan, PR 00914-12383; tel. 728-1515 ext. 4353; fax 268-8868; f. 1935; 130,000 vols, 1,375 periodicals; Librarian Sonia Díaz-Latorre; publs *Delflinea* (Library News, 3 a year), *Lista de Publicaciones Periódicas* (annually).

Caribbean and Latin American Studies Library: POB 21927, San Juan, PR 00931-1927; tel. 764-0000, ext. 3319; fax 763-5685; e-mail afiguer@upracd.upr.clu.edu; f. 1946 in Trinidad; moved to Puerto Rico 1961; specializes in humanities and social sciences in Latin America and the Caribbean; 50,000 vols; special collection of Caribbean Commission documents; Librarian Prof. Almaluces Figueroa.

Carnegie Public Library: e-mail maryjeanhaver@yahoo.com 7 Avda Ponce de León, San Juan, PR 00901-2010; tel. 722-4753; fax 725-0261; f. 1916; 50,000 vols; Dir Mary Jean Haver.

Commonwealth of Puerto Rico, Department of Justice Library: POB 9020192, San Juan, PR 00902-0192; tel. 724-6869; fax 721-3977; e-mail jdeleon@justicia.gobierno.pr; internet www.justicemail.com; f. 1950; law library of 75,000 vols; Dir of the Law Library Johanna de León; publs *Opiniones del Secretario de Justicia de Puerto Rico*, *Informe Anual del Secretario de Justicia de Puerto Rico*, *Anuario Estadístico*.

Attached library:

Supreme Court of Puerto Rico Library: Ponce de León Ave, Stop 8, Apdo 2392, San Juan, PR 00903; tel. 723-3863; f. 1953; law library with special

collections of Puerto Rican law, common law, Spanish and French civil law; 75,243 vols; Librarian (vacant); publ. *Nuevas Adquisiciones* (monthly).

Public Library Services, Department of Education: POB 759, San Juan, PR 00919; 1,500,000 vols; Dir Maria Lugo.

University of Puerto Rico Law Library: POB 23310, University Station, San Juan 00931-3310; tel. 763-7199; fax 764-2660; e-mail motero@upracd.upr.clu.edu; f. 1913; 382,000 vols; Caribbean Basin legal collection, judicial archives; Dir Lcda María M. Otero; publ. *Lista Selectiva de Nuevas Adquisiciones*.

University of Puerto Rico Library System, Río Piedras Campus: Box 23302, San Juan, PR 00931-3302; tel. 764-0000, ext. 3296; fax 763-5685; f. 1903; main library and eleven departmental libraries; 4,092,000 vols; Librarian Jorge Encarnación Torres; publs *Lumbre* (every 2 months), *Perspectiva* (2 a year), *Boletines de Divulgación* (irregular), *Biblionotas* (monthly), *Servicio de Alerta* (irregular), *Entorno* (2 a year), *Al Día* (4 a year).

Museums and Art Galleries
Ponce
Museo de Arte de Ponce: c/o The Luis A. Ferré Foundation Inc, Apdo 9027, Ponce, PR 00732; tel. 848-0505; fax 841-7309; e-mail map@museoarteponce.org; internet www.museoarteponce.org; f. 1956; European, American and Hispanic American paintings and sculptures; library of 7,000 vols; CEO Agustín Arteaga (acting).

San Germán
Museo de Arte Religioso: Apdo 1160, San Germán, PR 00683; Located at: Iglesia Porta Coeli, Calle Ramas Esq. Dr Veves, San Germán; tel. 892-5845; 17th c. church of Porta Coeli, constructed as a chapel for convent of Dominican Friars in San Germán; restored and converted into museum of religious art; Administrator Guido Barletta.

San Juan
Casa del Libro: Calle del Cristo 255, San Juan, PR 00901; tel. 723-0354; f. 1955; library-museum devoted to the art and history of the book; 5,000 vols; Dir María Teresa Arrarás de Colón.

Museo de Bellas Artes: Calle Cristo 253, Old San Juan; f. 1967 by the Institute of Culture; exhibition of paintings and sculptures by Puerto Rican artists from 18th century.

Museo de Historia Militar y Naval: Fuerte San Jerónimo, Puerta de Tierra, San Juan; historical castle converted into museum of military history; collection of weapons, flags and uniforms; run by the Museums and Parks dept of Inst. de Cultura Puertorriqueña.

Universities
BAYAMÓN CENTRAL UNIVERSITY
POB 1725, Bayamón, PR 00960-1725

Telephone: 786-3030

Fax: 740-2200

Internet: www.ucb.edu.pr
Founded 1961
Private control
Language of instruction: Spanish
Academic year: August to May, and long-vacation courses

President: P. BENITO REYES RIVERA
Academic Dean: Dra MARITZA ORTIZ
Registrar: VICTOR COLÓN-RODRÍGUEZ
Librarian: Prof. WANDA OCASIO

Library of 51,011 vols
Number of teachers: 57 (full-time)
Number of students: 3,228

Publications: *President's Letter* (quarterly), *Cruz Ansata* (annually), *Familia y Escuela* (monthly)

DEANS

Business Administration: NYDIA COLÓN
Education: Dra NITZA MARQUEZ
Humanities: Dra PURA ECHANDI
Natural Sciences: Dra PADILLA

INTER-AMERICAN UNIVERSITY OF PUERTO RICO

POB 363255, San Juan, PR 00936-3255
Telephone: 766-1912
Internet: www.inter.edu
Founded 1912
Private control
Languages of instruction: Spanish, English
Academic year: August to May (two semesters)

President: MANUEL T. FERNÓS
Chief of Staff: TOMÁS M. JIMÉNEZ

Number of teachers: 2,548
Number of students: 39,000

Publications: *Interamericana Newspaper*, *Homines*.

CONSTITUENT CAMPUSES

Aguadilla Campus: Apdo 20000, Aguadilla, PR 00605-2000; tel. 891-0925; Chancellor Dr JUAN A. APONTE; Dean of Studies Dr ELIE E. AGÉSILAS; Registrar MIRIAM MARCIAL; Dir of the Information Centre JUAN LÓPEZ BAIRÓN.

Arecibo Campus: Apdo 4050, Arecibo, PR 00614-4050; tel. 878-5475; Chancellor Dra JEAN MARIE GONZÁLEZ; Dean of Studies Dra KAREN WOOLWOCK; Registrar CARMEN RODRÍGUEZ; Dir of the Information Centre SARA ABREU.

Barranquitas Campus: Apdo 517, Barranquitas, PR 00794; tel. 857-3600; Chancellor Dr IRENE FERNÁNDEZ; Dean of Studies Dr JUAN A. NEGRÓN BERRÍOS; Registrar MARIBEL DÍAZ PEÑA; Dir of the Information Centre MARIBEL LÓPEZ.

Bayamón Campus: Carretera 830 (Suite 500), Bayamón, PR 00957; tel. 279-1912; Chancellor Prof. MARILINA WAYLAND; Dean of Studies Dr OMAR CUETO; Registrar EDDIE AYALA; Dir of the Information Centre EDUARDO ORTIZ.

Fajardo Campus: Apdo 70003, Fajardo, PR 00738-7003; tel. 863-2390; Chancellor Dr ISMAEL SUÁREZ; Dean of Studies Dr FRANCISCO J. MALDONADO; Registrar ABIGAIL RIVERA; Dir of the Information Centre ANGIE COLÓN.

Guayama Campus: Apdo 10004, Guayama, PR 00785; tel. 864-2222; Chancellor Dr CARLOS COLÓN; Dean of Studies Dr ANGELA DE JESÚS ALICEA; Registrar LUIS A. SOTO RIVERA; Dir of the Information Centre ANGEL R. RIVERA RODRÍGUEZ.

Metropolitan Campus: Apdo 191293, San Juan, PR 00936-1293; tel. 250-1912; Chan-

cellor (vacant); Dean of Studies MIGDALIA TEXIDOR; Registrar LISSETTE RIVERA; Dir of the Information System JAIRO PULIDO.

Ponce Campus: Carr. 1, Bo. Sabanetas, Mercedita, Ponce, PR 00715; tel. 284-1912; Chancellor Dr VILMA COLÓN; Dean of Studies Dr BERNADETTE FELICIANO; Registrar MARÍA DEL CARMEN PÉREZ; Dir of the Information Centre Dra SHARON CLAMPITT.

San Germán Campus: Apdo 5100, San Germán, PR 00683; tel. 264-1912; Chancellor Prof. AGNES MOJICA; Dean of Studies Dr NYVIA ALVARADO; Dir of the Information Centre Prof. DORIS ASCENCIO.

School of Law: Apdo 70351, San Juan, PR 00936-8351; tel. 571-1912; Dean LUIS MARIANO NEGRÓN PORTILLO; Dean of Studies Prof. ANDRÉS L. CARDÓNA; Registrar MARÍA DE L. RIVERA; Dir of the Information Centre HÉCTOR R. SÁNCHEZ.

School of Optometry: Apdo 191049, San Juan, PR 00919-1049; tel. 765-1915; Dean Dr HÉCTOR SANTIAGO; Dean of Academic Affairs Dr ANDRÉS PAGÁN; Dir of the Information Centre ROSA M. ROSARIO.

UNIVERSITY OF PUERTO RICO

POB 364984, San Juan, PR 00936-4984
Telephone: 250-0000
Fax: 759-6917
Internet: www.upr.clu.edu
Founded 1903
State control
Languages of instruction: Spanish, English
Academic year: August to May

President: Dr JORGE L. SÁNCHEZ (acting)
Director, Academic Affairs: MANUEL GÓMEZ
Director, Budget: BASILIO RIVERA (acting)
Director, Finance: NAZEERAH ELMADAH (acting)
Director, Financial Aid: HERNÁN VAZQUEZ-TELL
Director, Information Systems: SANDRA SANTOS (acting)
Director, Planning and Development: IRVING JIMÉNEZ (acting)
Director, Public Relations (vacant)

Number of teachers: 5,076
Number of students: 69,567

Publications: *La Torre*, *RIE* (quarterly).

CONSTITUENT CAMPUSES

Mayagüez Campus: POB 5000, College Station, Mayagüez, PR 00709-5000; tel. 832-4040; fax 834-3031; f. 1911; 1,075 teachers; 12,414 students; Chancellor PABLO RODRÍGUEZ (acting); Registrar BRISEIDA MELÉNDEZ-MARRERO; Librarian ISABEL TARDI

DEANS

Agricultural Sciences: ERNESTO O. RIQUELME (acting)
Arts and Sciences: RENÉ VIETA
Engineering: RAMÓN E. VÁZQUEZ

Medical Sciences Campus: POB 365067, San Juan, PR 00936-5067; tel. 758-2525; fax 754-0474; f. 1926; 762 teachers; 3,255 students; Chancellor JOSÉ R. CARLO (acting); Registrar ELIZABETH SÁNCHEZ; Librarian FRANCISCA CORRADA

DEANS

Biosocial Sciences and Graduate School of Public Health: ANTONIO SILVA
Dentistry: FERNANDO HADDOCK
Health Related Professions: ESTELA ESTAPÉ
Medicine: FRANCISCO M. JOGLAR
Nursing: MARIA E. ROSA (acting)
Pharmacy: ILIA OQUENDO JIMÉNEZ

Río Piedras Campus: POB 23300, UPR Station, San Juan, PR 00931-3300; tel. 764-0000; fax 764-8799; f. 1903; 1,444 teachers; 21,539 students; Chancellor GEORGE V. HILLYER; Registrar JUAN M. APONTE; Librarian RAMÓN BUDET

DEANS

Architecture: JOHN B. HERTZ
Business Administration: JORGE AYALA-CRUZ
Education: MARÍA A. IRIZARRY
General Studies: MARCOS A. LÓPEZ
Humanities: JOSÉ L. VEGA
Law: EFRÉN RIVERA
Natural Sciences: BRAD WEINER
Social Sciences: IDA DE JESÚS

CONSTITUENT COLLEGES

Cayey University College: Antonio R. Barceló Ave, Cayey, PR 00736; tel. 738-2161; fax 738-8039; f. 1967; 224 teachers; 3,758 students; Chancellor RAFAEL RIVERA-LEHMAN; Registrar ANGEL L. MATOS.

Humacao University College: CUH Station, Humacao, PR 00792; tel. 850-0000; fax 852-4638; f. 1962; 340 teachers; 4,294 students; Chancellor ENRIQUE ALVARADO (acting); Registrar JORGE ACEVEDO.

REGIONAL COLLEGES

University of Puerto Rico at Aguadilla: POB 250160, Ramey, Aguadilla, PR 00604-0160; tel. 890-2681; fax 891-3455; f. 1972; 167 teachers; 3,218 students; Chancellor JUANA SEGARRA DE JARAMILLO; Registrar NILDA GÓMEZ.

University of Puerto Rico at Arecibo: POB 4010, Arecibo, PR 00613-4010; tel. 878-2831; fax 880-2245; f. 1967; 270 teachers; 4,617 students; Chancellor JOSEFA GARCÍA FIRPI; Registrar NEREIDA GONZÁLEZ.

University of Puerto Rico at Bayamón: Bayamón, PR 00959-1919; tel. 786-2885; fax 798-1595; f. 1971; 300 teachers; 5,875 students; Chancellor CARMEN A. RIVERA; Registrar WANDA RIVERA.

University of Puerto Rico at Carolina: POB 4800, Carolina, PR 00984-4800; tel. 257-0000; fax 750-7940; f. 1974; 200 teachers; 4,198 students; Chancellor VÍCTOR PÉREZ-ROQUE; Registrar GLORIA ROSARIO.

University of Puerto Rico at Ponce: POB 7186, Ponce, PR 00732; tel. 844-8181; fax 840-8679; f. 1970; 204 teachers; 4,150 students; Chancellor IRMA RODRÍGUEZ-VEGA; Registrar AIDA HERNÁNDEZ.

University of Puerto Rico at Utuado: POB 2500, Utuado, PR 00761; tel. 894-2828; fax 894-2824; f. 1979; 90 teachers; 1,620 students; Chancellor CATALINA SOTO-MERCADO; Registrar SILMA MALDONADO.

UNIVERSITY OF THE SACRED HEART

POB 12383, San Juan, PR 00914-0383
Telephone: 728-1515
Fax: 728-1692
Internet: www.usc.clu.edu
Founded 1935
Private control
Language of instruction: Spanish

President: Dr JOSÉ JAIME RIVERA
Dean of Academic and Student Affairs: Dr CÉSAR REY
Dean of Administration: LOURDES BERTRÁN
Librarian: MARÍA DE LOS A. GARÍN

Number of teachers: 151 (full-time), 225 (part-time)
Number of students: 4,943

DIRECTORS
Department of Business Administration: Prof. YEZMIN HERNÁNDEZ
Department of Communications: Prof. MARÍA T. MARTÍNEZ
Department of Continuing Education: ELVIA ÁGOSTO
Department of Education: Prof. FERNANDO PIERAS

Department of Humanities: Prof. IRMA HERNÁNDEZ
Department of Natural Sciences: Dr CARMEN PADIAL
Department of Social Sciences: Lic. ROSA RAQUEL RUIZ
Evening Programs: NOEMÍ TORRES

College

Conservatory of Music of Puerto Rico: 350 Calle Rafael Lamar, San Juan, PR 00918; tel. 751-0160; fax 758-8268; e-mail rectoria@cmpr.gobierno.pr; internet www .cmpr.edu; f. 1959; library: library of 35,000 items; 140 teachers; 1,600 students; Chancellor MARIA DEL CARMEN GIL.

UNITED STATES VIRGIN ISLANDS

Museums and Art Galleries

St Thomas

American Caribbean Museum: 32 Raadets Gade, St Thomas; tel. 714-5150; e-mail Museum@St-Thomas.com; internet www .st-thomas.com/museum/; history of the Virgin Islands since 15th c.

Virgin Islands Museum: Waterfront, Charlotte Amalie, St Thomas; tel. 776-4566; housed within Fort Christian, the oldest standing structure in St Thomas; period furniture, military hardware.

University

UNIVERSITY OF THE VIRGIN ISLANDS

2 John Brewer's Bay, St Thomas, VI 00802-9990

Telephone: 693-1150
E-mail: pr@uvi.edu
Internet: www.uvi.edu
Founded 1962
Branch campus at St Croix
President: Dr ORVILLE KEAN
Vice-President for Academic Affairs: Dr DENIS PAUL
Vice-President for Business and Financial Affairs: MALCOLM C. KIRWAN
Vice-President for Institutional Advancement: Dr GWEN-MARIE MOOLENAAR

Vice-President for Research and Public Service: Dr LaVERNE RAGSTER
Vice-President for Student Affairs: Dr RONALD HARRIGAN
Director of Admissions: Dr JUDITH EDWIN
Director of Libraries: JENNIFER JACKSON
Library: St Croix Campus: 53,000 vols, 167 periodicals; St Thomas campus: 80,500 vols, 690 periodicals, 590,000 microforms, 20,000 other items, 15,000 US govt docs
Number of teachers: 270
Number of students: 2,610 (1,212 full-time, 1,498 part-time)
Publications: *The Caribbean Writer* (annually), *Graduate Bulletin* (annually), *UVI Magazine* (annually)
Four-year liberal arts college with Divisions of Business Administration, Education, Humanities, Nursing, Science and Mathematics, and Social Sciences.

URUGUAY

The Higher Education System

Institutions of higher education date from after Uruguay's independence from Spain in 1825, the oldest being Universidad de la República, which was founded in 1849. The next oldest institution is Universidad del Trabajo de Uruguay, which was founded in 1878. All education, including university tuition, is provided free of charge. Higher education is provided by public universities (universidades públicas), private universities (universidades privadas), university institutes (institutos universitarios), public non-university higher institutions (institutos terciarios no universitario públicos) and private non-university higher institutions (institutos terciarios no universitario privados). There were six public universities in 2003 with 72,100 students. In 2006 there were 4 private universities, 11 university institutes (private), 12 public non-university institutes and 5 private non-university institutes.

The main requirement for admission to higher education is the main secondary school award, the Bachillerato Diversificado, with specialization depending on the degree applied for. Intermediate degrees (carreras intermedios) last two-and-a-half to three years and often culminate with the award of a professional title; students may then graduate to full undergraduate degrees. Undergraduate degrees (carreras de grado) usually last four years and lead to the award of Título de Licenciado in the subject studied. Professional degrees, such as Licenciado en Enfermería (nursing), Licenciado en Nutrición (nutrition) and Licenciado en Psicología (psychology) last upwards of five years. Medical degrees last eight years and students receive the title Doctor en Medicina. The first postgraduate degree is the especialización (specialist course), a course lasting one year which leads to the titles Título de Especialista or the Título de Diplomado. The Masters (Título de Maestría) is a two-year programme of study; students are required to submit a thesis in the second year to complete the degree. Finally, the highest level of postgraduate studies is at doctoral level, where students work for three years to achieve the Doctorate (Doctorado).

The Consejo de Educación Técnico y Professional—Universidad de Trabajo is responsible for providing post-secondary technical and vocational education (however, despite what its name might suggest, it does not offer degree-level qualifications). The primary qualification awarded at this level is the Título Técnico in the subject studied.

Uruguay is a Mercosur state and therefore participates in the El Mecanismo Experimental de Acreditación de Carreras del Mercosur, which has so far accredited programmes in agronomy, medicine and engineering. However, Uruguay is the only member of Mercosur that does not have a national accreditation or quality assurance agency.

Learned Societies

AGRICULTURE, FISHERIES AND VETERINARY SCIENCE

Asociación Rural del Uruguay (Rural Association): Avda Uruguay 864, Montevideo; tel. (2) 902-04-84; fax (2) 902-04-89; e-mail presidencia@aru.org.uy; internet www.aru.org.uy; f. 1871; 3,000 mems; library of 3,000 vols; Pres. Dr FERNANDO ALFONSO; publ. *Revista* (monthly).

ARCHITECTURE AND TOWN PLANNING

Sociedad de Arquitectos del Uruguay (Society of Architects): Gonzalo Ramírez 2030, 11200 Montevideo; tel. (2) 419-34-63; e-mail sau@sau.org.uy; internet www.sau.org.uy; f. 1914; 2,000 mems; library of 2,000 vols; Pres. Arq. JOSÉ OLIVER; Exec. Sec. Arq. GRICELDA BARRIOS; publ. *Boletín de Arquitectura* (6 a year).

BIBLIOGRAPHY, LIBRARY SCIENCE AND MUSEOLOGY

Agrupación Bibliotecológica del Uruguay (Library Association): Cerro Largo 1666, 11200 Montevideo; tel. (2) 400-57-40; f. 1960; activities include library science, archives, documentation, bibliography, history and numismatics; 238 mems; Pres. LUIS ALBERTO MUSSO; publs *Bibliografía uruguaya sobre Brasil*, *Aportes para la historia de la bibliotecología en el Uruguay*, *Bibliografía y documentación en el Uruguay*, *Bibliografía bibliográfica y bibliotecología*, *Bibliografía básica de la historia de la República Oriental del Uruguay*, *Legislación Uruguaya sobre Brasil*, *Bibliografía Uruguaya sobre Historia Argentina*, *Bibliografía de Luis Alberto Musso*, *De Libros y Lectores*, *Anales del Senado del Uruguay–Cronología* (2nd edition), *Colonización canaria en la Banda Oriental*, *Archivos del Uruguay*, *El Río de la Plata en el Archivo de Indias*, *Uruguay, Brasil y sus Medallas*, *Indice Suplemento Diario 'El Día'*, *Documentalistas Uruguayos*, *Indice de la Revista Jurídica 'Los Debates'*, *Indice de la Revista Jurídica 'La Revista Nueva'*.

Asociación de Bibliotecólogos del Uruguay (Uruguayan Library Association): Eduardo V. Haedo 2255, 11200 Montevideo; tel. (2) 409-99-89; fax (2) 409-99-89; e-mail abu@adinet.com.uy; f. 1978; 300 mems; Pres. Lic. ALICIA OCASO FERREIRA; publ. *Panel de Notilxius*.

HISTORY, GEOGRAPHY AND ARCHAEOLOGY

Instituto Histórico y Geográfico del Uruguay: Convención 1366, 3° piso, Montevideo; f. 1843; 40 academicians; Pres. Prof. EDMUNDO M. NARANCIO; publ. *Revista*.

Sociedad de Amigos de Arqueología (Archaeological Society): Buenos Aires 652, Casilla 399, Montevideo; f. 1926; 70 mems; 16 foreign mems; publ. *Revista*.

LANGUAGE AND LITERATURE

Academia Nacional de Letras (National Academy of Literature): Ituzaingó 1255, 11000 Montevideo; tel. (2) 915-23-74; fax (2) 016-74-60; f. 1946; 10 mems; Pres. ANTONIO CRAVOTTO; Sec. CARLOS JONES GAYE; publs *Boletín*, *Ensayos Literarios*.

Alliance Française: Avda 18 de julio 1772, Casilla 326, 11200 Montevideo; tel. (2) 408-60-12; fax (2) 401-14-70; e-mail info@alliancefrancaise.edu.uy; internet www.alliancefrancaise.edu.uy; f. 1923; offers courses and exams in French language and culture and promotes cultural exchange with France; attached teaching centres in Artigas, Florida, Melo, Mercedes, Nueva Palmira, Paysandú, Rocha, Salto, San Carlos, San José, Tacuerembó and Trinidad.

Goethe-Institut: Canelones 1524, 11200 Montevideo; tel. (2) 410-58-13; fax (2) 410-44-32; e-mail info@montevideo.goethe.org; internet www.goethe.de/montevideo; offers courses and exams in German language and culture and promotes cultural exchange with Germany; library of 8,000 vols, 23 periodicals; Dir MIKKO FRITZE.

MEDICINE

Academia Nacional de Medicina del Uruguay: 18 de Julio 2175, 5° piso, Montevideo; tel. (2) 408-41-03; fax (2) 401-60-58; e-mail academiamed@adinet.com.uy; f. 1976; 26 mems; Dir Dr ROBERTO DE BELLIS; publ. *Boletín* (annually).

Asociación Odontológica Uruguaya (Odontological Association): Avda Durazno 937-39, Montevideo; tel. and fax (2) 900-15-72; e-mail aou@adinet.com.uy; internet www.aou.org.uy; f. 1946; 3,000 mems; comprises 8 depts and 6 sections; museum; library of 6,000 vols; Pres. Dr ALVARO RODA; Sec. Dra VIVIANA MISURRACO; publs *Odontología Uruguaya* (2 a year), *Boletín Informativo* (monthly).

Sociedad de Cirugía del Uruguay (Surgical Society): CC 10972, Montevideo; tel. (2) 402-68-20; fax (2) 403-05-32; e-mail scu@cirugia-uy.com; internet cirugia-uy.com; f. 1920; 403 mems; library of 3,400 vols; Pres. Dr ALBERTO PIÑEYRO; Sec.-Gen. Dr AUGUSTO MÜLLER; publ. *Cirugía del Uruguay* (4 a year).

Sociedad de Radiología e Imagenología del Uruguay: Julio César 1460 bis, Montevideo; tel. and fax (2) 481-17-14; e-mail sriu@adinet.com.uy; internet www.sriu.org .uy; f. 1923; scientific activity linked to the Médicos Imagenólogos; holds conferences and seminars; 150 mems; Pres. Dr IVONNE MARTINEZ; Sec. Dr LUIS DIBARBOURE; publ. *Revista de Imagenología del Uruguay*.

Has attached:

Gremial Uruguaya de Médicos Radiólogos: Montevideo; f. 1972; 70 mems; Pres. Dr ERNESTO H. CIBILS.

Sociedad Uruguaya de Historia de la Medicina: Casilla de Correo 157, Montevideo; tel. (2) 401-47-01; fax (2) 409-16-03; e-mail histmed@fmed.edu.uy; f. 1971; research on history of medicine and allied sciences; 80 mems; Pres. Prof. Dr FERNANDO MAÑÉ GARZÓN; Sec. Dr JUAN I. GIL; publ. *Sesiones de la Sociedad Uruguaya* (annually).

Sociedad Uruguaya de Pediatría (Paediatrics Society): Centro Hospitalario Pereira Rossell, Bulevar Artigas 1550, Montevideo; tel. (2) 709-18-01; fax (2) 708-52-13; e-mail pedsoc@adinet.com.uy; internet www.sup .org.uy; f. 1915; 500 mems, affiliated to the Asociación Latino Americana de Pediatría; library of 3,500 vols, 6,500 periodicals; Pres. Dr ÁLVARO GALIANA; Sec. Dr DANIEL BORBONET; publ. *Archivos de Pediatría del Uruguay* (quarterly).

NATURAL SCIENCES
Biological Sciences

Sociedad Malacológica del Uruguay (Malacological Society): Casilla 1401, 11000 Montevideo; e-mail smu@adinet.com.uy; internet moluscos.net/smu; f. 1957; 210 mems; Pres. JORGE BROGGI; Sec. JUAN CARLOS ZAFFARONI; publ. *Comunicaciones* (2 a year).

Sociedad Zoológica del Uruguay: Casilla 1073P, Igua 4225 (Piso 9), A la Sur, CP 11400, Montevideo; tel. (2) 525-86-18; fax (2) 525-86-17; e-mail szu@fcien.edu.uy; internet www.inetwork.com.uy/szu; f. 1961; 200 mems; Pres. Prof. MIGUEL A. KLAPPENBACH; publ. *Boletín* (annually).

TECHNOLOGY

Academia Nacional de Ingeniería: Cuareim 1492, Montevideo; tel. (2) 901-17-62; fax (2) 900-89-51; e-mail cutinella@redfacil.com .uy; internet www.artech.com.uy/aniu; f. 1965; 40 full mems; Pres. Ing. ALVARO CUTINELLA; Sec. Ing. EDISON GARCÍA REGUEIRO.

Asociación de Ingenieros del Uruguay (Association of Uruguayan Engineers): Cuareim 1492, Montevideo; tel. (2) 901-17-62; fax (2) 900-89-51; e-mail asocing@adinet.com.uy; internet www.aiu.org.uy; f. 1905; 1,400 mems, also hon. and corresp. abroad; Pres. Ing. EDUARDO ALVAREZ MAZZA; Sec. Ing. CARLOS MALCUORI; affiliated to the Unión Panamericana de Asociaciones de Ingenieros; library of 2,000 vols; publ. *Revista de Ingeniería*.

Research Institutes
GENERAL

Dirección Nacional de Ciencia, Tecnología y Innovación (DINACYT):; tel. (2)901-42-85; fax (2) 902-48-70; e-mail info@dinacyt .gub.uy; internet www.dinacyt.gub.uy; f. 1961 to encourage research in all branches of knowledge, especially scientific, technological and innovation policies; fmrly Consejo Nacional de Investigaciones Científicas y Técnicas (CONICYT); 14 council mems; library of 7,000 vols, 275 periodicals; Gen. Dir Dr AMILCAR DAVYT; publs *Boletín electrónico* (weekly), *Claro Que Se Puede* (irregular), *El Proceso de Innovación en la Industria Uruguaya* (every 2 years), *Indicadores de Ciencia y Tecnología* (irregular).

UNESCO Office Montevideo and Regional Office for Science in Latin America and the Caribbean: Casilla de correo 859, Montevideo; Edificio del MERCOSUR (ex Parque Hotel), Calle Dr Luis Piera 1992 (2° piso), 11200 Montevideo; tel. (2) 413-20-75; fax (2) 413-20-94; e-mail montevideo@unesco .org.uy; internet www.unesco.org.uy; f. 1949; designated Cluster Office for Argentina, Brazil, Paraguay, Uruguay; co-ordinates Unesco's programmes in the region, particularly: basic sciences, environmental and water sciences, science, technology and society, earth sciences and natural hazards, marine sciences, information and communication, education; culture and world heritage; Dir JORGE GRANDI.

AGRICULTURE, FISHERIES AND VETERINARY SCIENCE

Instituto Nacional de Investigación Agropecuaria (National Agricultural Research Institute): Andes 1365, Piso 12 CP, 11100 Montevideo; tel. (2) 902-05-50; fax (2) 902-36-33; e-mail bib_le@inia.org.uy; internet www.inia.org.uy; f. 1914; library of 12,000 vols, 1,000 periodicals; Dir MARIO ALLEGRI; publs *Serie Técnica*, *Boletín de Divulgación*, *Serie Actividades de Difusión*, *Hojas de Divulgación*.

Instituto Nacional de Pesca (National Fishery Institute): Constituyente 1497, 11200 Montevideo; tel. 48-31-80; fax 41-32-16; f. 1975; 196 staff; library of 1,200 vols; Dir Gen. JUAN JOSÉ FERNANDEZ PARES.

ECONOMICS, LAW AND POLITICS

Centro de Estadísticas Nacionales y Comercio Internacional del Uruguay (CENCI Uruguay): Juncal 1327D, Piso 16, Oficina 1603, Montevideo; tel. (2) 915-29-30; fax (2) 915-45-78; e-mail cenci@cenci.com.uy; internet www.cenci.com.uy; f. 1956 to provide economic and statistical information on all American countries; to operate computer programmes handling the import tariffs on commodities; library of 900 vols; Dir KENNETH BRUNNER; publs *Anuario estadístico sobre el intercambio comercial* (annually), *Boletines: Noticias Latinoamericanas*, *Dictámenes de Clasificación Arancelaria – MERCOSUR*, *Estudios del Mercado*, *Industrias por sectores de actividad*, *Manual práctico Aduanero* (monthly), *Manual práctico del Contribuyente* (monthly), *Manual práctico del Exportador* (monthly), *Manual práctico del Importador* (monthly), *Régimen de Origen–ALADI y MERCOSUR*.

Instituto Nacional de Estadística (Statistical Office): Río Negro 1520, Montevideo; tel. (2) 903-28-78; fax (2) 903-28-81; e-mail difusion@ine.gub.uy; internet www.ine.gub .uy; f. 1829; library of 4,000 vols; Dir-Gen. ORUAL ANDINA; publs *Síntesis Estadística*, *Boletín Trimestral* (4 a year), *Encuesta Continua de Hogares*, *Anuario Estadístico*.

HISTORY, GEOGRAPHY AND ARCHAEOLOGY

Servicio Geográfico Militar (Military Geographical Institute): Avda 8 de Octubre 3255, 11600 Montevideo; tel. (2) 487-18-10; fax (2) 487-08-68; e-mail sgm@iau.gub.uy; f. 1913; geodesy, photogrammetry, geophysics and cartography; library of 3,500 vols; Dir Col ARTIGAS P. BACCI; publs *Boletín*, scale aeronautic and aerial maps.

MEDICINE

Instituto de Endocrinología 'Profesor Dr Juan C. Mussio Fournier' (Institute of Endocrinology): Hospital Pasteur, Calle Larravide 74, Montevideo; f. 1937; under Ministry of Health; Dir Prof. Dr ALFREDO NAVARRO; publ. *Archivos*.

Instituto de Oncología: Avda 8 de Octubre 3265, Montevideo; f. 1960; Dir Prof. Dr ALFONSO FRANGELLA.

Liga Uruguaya contra la Tuberculosis (Anti-Tuberculosis League): Magallanes 1320, 11200 Montevideo; tel. (2) 408-35-70; fax (2) 400-55-75; e-mail ligatub@adinet.com .uy; f. 1902; specializes in combating tuberculosis in children and the elderly; library of 3,000 vols; Pres. MÁXIMO A. SAAVEDRA; Sec. NORVAL SILVERA DE LEÓN.

NATURAL SCIENCES
Biological Sciences

Instituto de Investigaciones Biológicas Clemente Estable: Avda Italia 3318, 11600 Montevideo; tel. (2) 487-16-16; fax (2) 487-55-48; e-mail root@iibce.edu.uy; internet www .iibce.edu.uy; f. 1927; 12 divisions, 3 depts; biological research; library of 12,000 vols.

Physical Sciences

Dirección Nacional de Meteorología del Uruguay (National Meteorological Directorate): Javier Barrios Amorín 1488, Casilla de Correo 64, 11200 Montevideo; tel. (2) 400-56-55; fax (2) 409-73-91; e-mail dnm25255@ adinet.com.uy; internet www.meteorologia .com.uy; f. 1895; library of 6,000 vols, 13,800 documents; Dir RAUL MICHELINI; publs *Boletín Agrometeorológico*, *Anuario Climatológico*, *Notas Técnicas*, *Boletín Pluviométrico*.

Observatorio Astronómico de Montevideo (Montevideo Astronomical Observatory): Casilla de Correo 867, 11000 Montevideo; tel. (2) 48-58-25; f. 1928; library of 5,000 vols; Dir Prof. LUIS HERMIDA.

RELIGION, SOCIOLOGY AND ANTHROPOLOGY

Instituto Interamericano del Niño (Inter-American Children's Institute): Avda 8 de Octubre 2904, 11600 Montevideo; tel. (2) 487-21-50; fax (2) 487-32-42; e-mail iin@oas .org; internet www.iin.oea.org; f. 1927; specialized organization of the OAS; library: specialized library of 50,000 vols, open to the public; computerized information centre; Pres. CARMEN BERGÉS DE AMARO; Dir-Gen. ALEJANDRO BONASSO; publ. *Boletín*.

TECHNOLOGY

Dirección Nacional de Minería y Geología: Calle Hervidero 2861, CP 11800, Montevideo; tel. (2) 209-31-96; fax (2) 209-49-05; e-mail secretaria@dinamige.miem.gub.uy; internet www.dinamige.gub.uy; f. 1912; 100 mems; library of 3,000 vols; Dir Ing. LUIS FERRARI; publ. *Industria Extractiva del Uruguay* (annually).

Dirección Nacional de Tecnología Nuclear: Mercedes 1041, 11100 Montevideo; tel. (2) 900-69-19; fax (2) 902-16-19; e-mail dntndes@adinet.com.uy; f. 1955 as Comisión Nacional de Energía Atómica; controls activities involving the use of radioactive materials or equipment producing ionizing radiation; prepares technical and safety rules for activities involving nuclear technology; liaises with national and international institutions on procedural aspects of nuclear technology; library of 3,500 vols; collection of microfiches; Dir ROSARIO ODINO; publs *Revista* (annually), *Memoria* (annually).

Instituto Uruguayo de Normas Técnicas (Uruguayan Standards Institution): Plaza Independencia 812, (2°piso), Montevideo; tel. (2) 901-20-48; fax (2) 902-16-81; e-mail unit-iso@unit.org.uy; internet www.unit.org.uy; f. 1939; standardization, certification, information on standards, training in high-level management; library of 250,000 vols; Dir Eng. PABLO BENIA; publ. *UNIT Standards*.

Libraries and Archives

Florida

Biblioteca Pública Municipal: Barreiro 420, CP 94000 Florida; tel. (35) 2-21-20; f. 1889; 42,000 vols; Dir SONIA MERCADAL.

Montevideo

Archivo General de la Nación (National Archives): Calle Convención 1474, Montevideo; tel. (2) 900-72-32; fax (2) 908-13-30; e-mail agn@adinet.com.uy; internet www.mec.gub.uy/agn; f. 1926; 14,000 vols; Dir ABELARDO MANUAL GARCIA VIERA; publ. *Revista*.

Biblioteca Central y Publicaciones del Consejo de Educación Secundaria: Eduardo Acevedo 1427, Montevideo; tel. (2) 408-42-73; fax (2) 408-12-52; e-mail biblos@adinet.com.uy; f. 1885; secondary and higher education; 105,000 vols; collection of rare books.

Biblioteca del Museo Histórico Nacional (Library of the National Historical Museum): Rincón 437, C.P. 11.000, Montevideo; f. 1940; 150,000 vols, 4,000 vols of MSS; specialization in the history of America and history of art; iconography, engravings, maps, numismatics; the entire library and Uruguayan collections of Dr Pablo Blanco Acevedo; Dir ELISA SILVA CAZET.

Biblioteca del Palacio Legislativo: Avda Libertador Brigadier Gral Lavelleja y Avda Gral Flores, Montevideo; f. 1929; legal deposit library in conjunction with National Library; 322,000 vols; specializes in jurisprudence; Dir LUIS H. BOIONS POMBO; publs *Bibliografía Uruguaya*, *Boletín Bibliográfico* (monthly).

Biblioteca Municipal 'Dr Francisco Albero Schinca': 8 de Octubre 4210, Montevideo; tel. (2) 508-81-52, f. 1920; 14,000 vols; Dir GRACIELA NAVARRO.

Biblioteca Municipal 'Dr Joaquín de Salterain': Solis 1456 y 25 de Mayo, Montevideo; tel. (2) 915-62-82; 36,000 vols; includes a slide library; Librarian GRACIELA FERNÁNDEZ RIBEIRO.

Biblioteca Nacional del Uruguay (National Library): 18 de Julio 1790, CC 452, Montevideo; tel. (2) 408-50-30; fax (2) 409-69-02; e-mail bibna@adinet.com.uy; f. 1816; 900,000 vols, 20,000 periodicals; comprises reference service, copyright office, legal deposit, Uruguayan and special materials, restoration of printed works, National Information System project, cultural extension; Dir-Gen. RAÚL RICARDO VALLARINO; publ. *Revista de la Biblioteca Nacional*.

Has attached:

    Centro Nacional de Documentación Científica, Técnica y Económica: 18 de Julio 1790, CC 452, Montevideo; tel. (2) 408-41-72; fax (2) 409-69-02; f. 1953; part of National Library; Dir ELENA CASTRO.

Biblioteca Pedagógica Central (Pedagogic Library): Plaza Cagancha 1175, Montevideo; f. 1889; 117,630 vols; Dir ANAIR MARTINOL; publs *Información Bibliográfica*

(2 a year), *Temas, Traducciones, Bibliografía Uruguaya sobre Educación*.

Museums and Art Galleries

Montevideo

Museo de Descubrimiento: Zabala y Piedras, Montevideo; evokes the journeys of Cristobal Colon, the meeting of the two worlds; maps, dioramas and photographs.

Museo Histórico Nacional (National Historical Museum): Casa Rivera, Calle Rincón 437, 11000 Montevideo; tel. (2) 915-10-51; fax (2) 915-68-63; e-mail mhistoricnac@mixmail.com; f. 1900; sectional collections of local Indian cultures (prehistoric, colonial epoch, development and political history of the country); portraits, relics, arms, documents, coins, medals, etc., relating to the Wars of Independence, British invasion, early revolutions, etc.; Dir Prof. ENRIQUE MENA SAGARRA; publ. *Revista Histórica*.

Museo Municipal de Bellas Artes: Avda Millán 4015, Montevideo; tel. (2) 336-22-48; fax (2) 336-71-34; e-mail museoblanes@correo.imm.gub.uy; f. 1928; paintings, drawings, wood-carvings, sculptures; Dir MARIO C. TEMPONE.

Museo Nacional de Bellas Artes (National Museum of Fine Arts): Tomás Giribaldi 2283, Parque Rodó, Montevideo; f. 1911; 4,217 paintings, engravings, drawings, sculptures, ceramics; Dir ANGEL KALENBERG.

Museo Nacional de Historia Natural y Antropología (National Museum of Natural History and Anthropology): Casilla 399, 11000 Montevideo; tel. (2) 916-09-08; fax (2) 917-02-13; e-mail mnhn@internet.com.uy; internet www.mec.gub.uy/natura; f. 1837 as National Museum; zoology, botany, palaeontology, archaeology, ethnography, history of natural sciences; library of 250,000 vols; Dir ALVARO MONES; publs *Anales* (irregular), *Comunicaciones Zoológicas* (irregular), *Comunicaciones Botánicas* (irregular), *Comunicaciones Antropológicas* (irregular), *Comunicaciones Paleontológicas* (irregular), *Publicación Extra* (irregular).

Museo Pedagógico (Pedagogic Museum): Plaza Cagancha 1175, Montevideo; f. 1888; Dir Sra NILDA BARBAGELATA DE RITTER; publ. *Boletín* (weekly).

Museo y Archivo Histórico Municipal: Palacio del Cabildo, Calle Juan Carlos Gómez 1362, Montevideo; tel. and fax 915-96-85; e-mail museocabildo@correo.imm.gub.uy; f. 1915; permanent exhibition of the history of Montevideo from 1726; furniture, icons, paintings, jewellery and maps; library of 9,000 vols; Hon. Dir JORGE R. DELUCCHI; publ. *Anales*.

Museo y Jardin Botánico de Montevideo: Avda 19 de Abril 1181, Montevideo; tel. (2) 336-40-05; fax (2) 336-64-88; e-mail botanico@adinet.com.uy; f. 1902; Dir Ing. Agr. PABLO B. ROSS.

Museo Zoológico 'Dámaso Antonio Larrañaga': Rambla República de Chile 4215, Montevideo; tel. (2) 622-02-58; f. 1956; instruction on national and exotic fauna; library of 2,000 specialized vols; 2,000 species of fauna and molluscs, etc.; Dir JUAN PABLO CUELLO.

San José de Mayo

Museo de Bellas Artes Departamental de San José: Calle Dr Julián Becerro de Bengoa 493, 80000 San José de Mayo; tel. 3642; paintings, drawings, sculptures, ceramics; f. 1947; school of art; library of 3,000

vols; Dir CÉSAR BERNESCONI; publ. *Notimuseo* (monthly).

Tacuarembó

Museo del Indio y del Gaucho: Calle 25 de Mayo 315, Tacuarembó; affiliated to the Museo Histórico de Montevideo; large collection representing ancient native crafts, weapons and other implements of the aboriginal Indians and gauchos; Founder and Dir WASHINGTON ESCOBAR.

Universities

UNIVERSIDAD CATÓLICA DEL URUGUAY

Avda 8 de Octubre 2738, 11600 Montevideo

Telephone: (2) 487-27-17

Fax: (2) 480-81-24

E-mail: relinter@ucu.edu.uy

Internet: www.ucu.edu.uy

Founded 1985

Private control

Academic year: March to November

Chancellor: Mons. NICOLÁS COTUGNO

Vice-Chancellor: Fr JOSÉ LUIS MOSCA

Rector: Fr ANTONIO OCAÑA

Vice-Presidents: Dr PABLO DA SILVEIRA (Academic), Cr. AUGUSTO BAYLEY (Administrative), Ing. JOHN MILES (Development), Fr MARCELO COPPETTI (University Environment)

Librarian: Mag. ALBERTO GONZÁLEZ

Number of teachers: 607

Number of students: 5,000

Publications: *Cuadernos de Negocios Internacionales e Integración, Prisma, Relaciones Laborales en el Uruguay, Revista de Derecho, Revista FCE (Facultad de Ciencias Empresariales), Revista Lazos, Revista Págines del Area Educación*

DEANS

Faculty of Business Administration: Ec. ROBERTO HORTA

Faculty of Dentistry: Dr WALTER LIEBER

Faculty of Engineering and Technology. Ing. OMAR PAGANINI

Faculty of Human Sciences: A. S. CECILIA ZAFFARONI

Faculty of Law: Dr MARTÍN RISSO

Faculty of Psychology: Psic. PABLO GELSI

Postgraduate Centre: Dr PABLO LANDONI (Dir)

ATTACHED INSTITUTES

Department of Communication: Dir Dr LUCIANO ÁLVAREZ.

Department of Education: Dir Dra ADRIANA ARISTIMUÑO.

Department of Mathematics: Dir Mag. EDUARDO LACUÉS.

Department of Philosophy: Dir Dr PABLO DA SILVEIRA.

Department of Social Sciences: Dir Mag. CARLOS FIGUEIRA.

School of Nursing: Dir Lic. TERESA DELGADO.

Institute of Bioethics: Dir Dr OMAR FRANÇA.

Institute of History: Dir Dra SUSANA MONREAL.

UNIVERSIDAD DE LA REPÚBLICA

Avda 18 de Julio 1968 (2° piso), 11200 Montevideo

Telephone: (2) 408-49-01

Fax: (2) 408-03-03

E-mail: secretar@oce.edu.uy

Internet: www.rau.edu.uy/universidad
Founded 1849
State control
Language of instruction: Spanish
Academic year: March to December

Rector: Ing. RAFAEL GUARGA
Vice-Rector: MIGUEL GALMÉS

Libraries with 1,000,000 vols

Number of teachers: 4,982
Number of students: 59,436

Publication: Publications: faculty bulletins

DEANS

Faculty of Agronomy: Ing. Agr. GONZALO GONZÁLEZ
Faculty of Architecture: Arq. RUBEN OTERO
Faculty of Chemistry: Dr ALBERTO NIETO
Faculty of Dentistry: Prof. Dr ALVARO MAGLIA
Faculty of Economics: Cr. MIGUEL GALMÉS
Faculty of Engineering: Ing. MARÍA SIMÓN
Faculty of Humanities: Prof. ADOLFO ELIZAINCÍN
Faculty of Law: Esc. TERESA GNAZZO
Faculty of Medicine: Prof. Dr ANA MARÍA FERRARI
Faculty of Psychology: Prof. VICTOR GIORGI

Faculty of Science: Dr RICARDO EHRLICH
Faculty of Social Sciences: Dr LUIS BÉRTOLA
Faculty of Veterinary Medicine: Prof. Dr GASTÓN CASAUX

DIRECTORS

School of Fine Arts: Prof. FERNANDO ODRIOZOLA
School of Librarianship and Related Sciences: Lic. MARÍA GLADYS CERETTA (see Escuela Universitaria de Bibliotecología y Ciencias Afines 'Ing. Federico E. Capurro')
School of Music: Prof. ANTONIO MASTROGIOVANNI
Institute of Social Sciences: Prof. ALFREDO ERRANDONEA
Research and Postgraduate Centre: Cr. RAÚL TRAJTEMBERG

Colleges

Escuela Universitaria de Bibliotecología y Ciencias Afines 'Ing. Federico E. Capurro': Emilio Frugoni 1427, 11200 Montevideo; tel. (2) 400-58-10; fax (2) 400-58-10; e-mail eubca@adinet.com.uy; f. 1945; attached to Univ. de la República; 4-year courses in library and information science, 3-year courses in archive studies; library: 13,150 books and monographs, 200 periodicals; 50 teachers; 500 students; Dir Lic. MARÍA GLADYS CERETTA; publ. *Informatio* (annually).

Instituto Superior de Electrotecnía, Electrónica y Computación: Calle Joaquín Requena 1931, Montevideo; tel. 492520; f. 1922; electrical engineering, electronics and computing; library: 6,000 vols; 300 teachers; Dir Ing. AMÉRICO HARTMANN.

Universidad del Trabajo del Uruguay: Calle San Salvador 1674, Montevideo; e-mail web.utu@anep.edu.uy; internet www.utu.edu.uy; f. 1878; offers 220 different courses at 81 colleges in agriculture, handicrafts, industry and commerce; lower- and intermediate-level education and training; 4,500 full-time teachers; 50,000 students; Dir Dr FANNY ARON NÚÑEZ; publs *UTU Visión*, *Anales*.

UZBEKISTAN

The Higher Education System

Institutions of higher education predate Uzbekistan (formerly Uzbek SSR)'s independence from the USSR in 1991, the oldest being the Uzbek National University, Tashkent State Medical Institute and Tashkent Institute of Irrigation and Melioration, which were all founded in 1920. In 1997 major reforms of the education system at all levels commenced under the National Programme for Personnel Training (NPPT). Reforms specific to the higher education sector include the re-modelling of the degree system, particularly the abolition of the old-style Soviet-era degrees and introduction of two-tier Bachelors and Masters degrees; institutional restructuring; strengthening of links between universities and industries; and improvements to part-time and distance education programmes. Higher education is mostly the responsibility of the Ministry of Higher and Specialized Secondary Education although other Ministries administer the relevant specialist schools. In 2004 higher education was provided in 63 institutes with a total enrolment of 263,600 students.

The main requirements for admission to higher education are the certificate for completion of secondary education and results achieved in the national university entrance examination (Kirish Imtakhoni), which is administered by the State Testing Centre (Devlet Test Markazi). The old-style Soviet degree system consisted primarily of a single five-year Specialist Diploma followed by doctoral-level studies. Since the implementation of the NPPT students are required to gain both the Bachelors and Masters degrees before pursuing doctoral studies. The Bachelors degree (Bakalavr Diplomi) lasts four years divided into two phases of two years each. In the first phase students undertake a general programme of study before, in the second phase, focusing on a 'major' subject. The Bachelors is a first degree, which may last longer in other (usually professional) fields of study, such as medicine, dentistry and veterinary medicine (upwards of six years). Graduates who have been awarded the Bachelors are eligible for the Masters (Magistr Diplomi), which is a two-year course, often in the same subject as the undergraduate degree. At the doctoral level, the Soviet distinction between the titles of Candidate of Science and Doctor of Science has been retained, albeit under their Uzbek names of, respectively, Fanlari Nomzodi and Fanlari Doctori. The Candidate of Science is a three-year period of study consisting of independent research leading to the submission of a thesis. Students intending to a career in research or academia then work towards the title of Doctor of Science, which is awarded after an unspecified period of study and research.

Post-secondary technical and vocational education takes the form of two- to four-year courses in 260 areas of specialization, resulting in the award of the Diploma of Post Secondary Vocational Education (O'rta Maxsus Ta'lim To'g'risidagi Diplom). The Monitoring Department of the Ministry of Higher and Specialized Secondary Education is responsible for accreditation and quality assurance at the tertiary level, standards for which are defined by the Ministry.

Learned Societies

GENERAL

UNESCO Office Tashkent: 70000 Tashkent, Ul. Amir Temur 95; tel. (71) 120-71-16; fax (71) 132-13-82; e-mail tashkent@unesco .org; Dir BARRY LANE.

Uzbek Academy of Sciences: 700047 Tashkent, Acad. Yahyo Gulomov 70; tel. (71) 133-68-47; fax (71) 133-49-01; e-mail academy@uzsci.net; internet www.academy .uz; f. 1943; divisions of Technical Sciences (Chair. Dr S. LUTPULLAEV), Natural Sciences (Chair. Prof. T. F. ARIPOV), Humanities (Chair. Prof. T. MIRZAEV); 156 mems (71 ordinary, 85 corresp.); regional branches and attached research institutes: see Research Institutes; library: see Libraries and Archives; Pres. Prof. BEKHZOD YULDASHEV; Sec.-Gen. Dr SHUKRAT EHGAMBERDIYEV; publs Doklady (Reports), Uzbeksky Biologichesky Zhurnal (Uzbek Biological Journal), Uzbekskii Khimicheskii Zhurnal (Uzbek Chemical Journal), Uzbekskii Zhurnal—Problemy Mekhaniki (Uzbek Journal—Problems of Mechanics), Uzbekskii Zhurnal—Problemy Informatiki i Energetiki (Uzbek Journal—Problems of Informatics and Energetics), Uzbekskii Matematicheskii Zhurnal (Uzbek Journal of Mathematics), Uzbekskii Fizicheskii Zhurnal (Uzbek Journal of Physics), Obshchestvennye Nauki v Uzbekistane (Social Sciences in Uzbekistan), Uzbeksky Yazik i Literatura (Uzbek Language and Literature), Uzbek Geological Journal, Science and Life.

LANGUAGE AND LITERATURE

Alliance Française: 703004 Samarkand, Ul. Baraka 26; tel. and fax (66) 33-66-27; offers courses and exams in French language and culture and promotes cultural exchange with France.

British Council: 700031 Tashkent, University of World Languages Bldg, Ul. Kounaev 11; tel. (71) 120-67-52; fax (71) 120-63-71; e-mail bc-tashkent@britishcouncil.uz; internet www.britishcouncil.org/uzbekistan; offers courses and exams in English language and British culture and promotes cultural exchange with the UK; library of 5,000 vols; Dir NEVILLE McBAIN.

Goethe-Institut: 700031 Tashkent, Ul. Kunayev ko'chasi 11; tel. (71) 152-70-23; fax (71) 152-70-24; e-mail il-taschkent@goethe .uz; internet www.goethe.de/oe/tas/deindex .htm; offers courses and exams in German language and culture and promotes cultural exchange with Germany; Dir DR CHRISTIANE GÜNTHER.

Research Institutes

GENERAL

Bukhara Scientific Centre: 705009 Bukhara, Naqshbandi 153; tel. (65) 225-02-41; fax (65) 225-42-30; e-mail alexz@uzpak .uz; attached to Uzbek Acad. of Sciences; Dir I. SAFAROV.

Karakalpak Branch of the Uzbek Academy of Sciences: 742000 Nukus, Pr. Berdah 41; tel. (61) 217-15-59; fax (61) 217-72-28; e-mail udasa@uzpak.uz; Chair. T. ESHCHANOV.

Khorezm Academy of Mamun: 741400 Khiva, Markaz-1; tel. and fax (62) 375-51-43; e-mail mamun@dri.uz; attached to Uzbek Acad. of Sciences; Dir A. SADULLAYEV.

Research Institute of Regional Problems: 703000 Samarkand, Temur Malik 3; tel. (662) 33-19-94; fax (662) 31-00-39; e-mail samacdem@online.ru; attached to Uzbek Acad. of Sciences; Dir B. KHUJAYOROV.

Samarkand Branch of the Uzbek Academy of Sciences: 703000 Samarkand, Temur Malik 3; tel. (662) 33-39-50; fax (662) 31-00-39; e-mail samacdem@online.ru; Chair. T. SHIRINOV.

AGRICULTURE, FISHERIES AND VETERINARY SCIENCE

Institute of Soil Research and Agrochemistry: 700109 Tashkent, Ul. Kamarniso 3; tel. (71) 246-09-50; fax (71) 246-02-63; Dir D. S. SATTAROV.

Research Institute of Karakul Sheep Breeding and Ecology of Deserts: 700300 Samarkand, Ul. Mirzo Ulugbek 47; tel. (662) 33-32-79; fax (662) 33-34-81; e-mail ecokar@rol.uz; f. 1930; 100 mems; library of 56,000 vols; Dir Dr SURATBEK YUNUSOVICH YUSUPOV; publ. Collection of Contributions Concerning Karakul Sheep Breeding and Arid Fodder Production (every 2 years).

ECONOMICS, LAW AND POLITICS

Abu Raihan Beruni Institute of Oriental Studies: 700170 Tashkent, Ul. Abdullaeva 81; tel. (71) 162-54-61; fax (71) 162-52-77; e-mail beruni@globalnet.uz; f. 1943; attached to Uzbek Acad. of Sciences; research activity in the sphere of medieval oriental manuscripts, and in the field of medieval and modern history of Central Asia; Dir B. A. ABDUKHALIMOV; publ. Sharqshunoslik (annually).

Institute of Economics: 700060 Tashkent, Ul. Borovskogo 5; tel. and fax (71) 133-14-78; e-mail econ@uzsci.net; f. 1943; attached to Uzbek Acad. of Sciences; Dir O. KHIKMATOV.

Muminov, I., Institute of Philosophy and Law: 700170 Tashkent, Ul. Muminova 9; tel. (71) 162-38-87; e-mail tashphil@uzsci.net; attached to Uzbek Acad. of Sciences; Dir A. M. JALALOV.

EDUCATION

Scientific and Training Centre 'Fanum': 700170 Tashkent, Ul. Muminova 9; tel. (71) 162-93-31; e-mail fanum@uzsci.net; attached to Uzbek Acad. of. Sciences; Dir N. Y. TURAYEV.

HISTORY, GEOGRAPHY AND ARCHAEOLOGY

Institute of Archaeology: 703051 Samarkand, Ul. Abdullaeva 3; tel. (662) 32-15-13; fax (662) 31-12-90; e-mail archaeo@online.ru; f. 1970; attached to Uzbek Acad. of Sciences; Dir T. SHIRINOV.

Institute of History: Ul. Muminova 9, 700170 Tashkent; tel. (71) 162-38-73; fax (71) 162-93-51; e-mail tarih@uzsci.net; internet www.history.uzsci.net; f. 1943; attached to Uzbek Acad. of Sciences; Dir DILOROM AGZAMOVNA ALIMOVA; publ. *Uzbekiston Tarihi* (4 a year).

Institute of History, Archaeology and Ethnography: 742000 Nukus, Amir Temur 179A; tel. (61) 224-05-98; fax (61) 217-72-28; e-mail vyagodin@online.ru; attached to Uzbek Acad. of Sciences; Dir V. YAGODIN.

LANGUAGE AND LITERATURE

Institute of Language and Literature: 742000 Nukus, Amir Temur 199A; tel. (61) 217-21-61; attached to Uzbek Acad. of Sciences; Dir S. BAHADIROVA.

Navoi Institute of Language and Literature: 700170 Tashkent, Ul. Muminova 9; tel. (71) 162-42-64; attached to Uzbek Acad. of Sciences; Dir T. M. MIRZAEV.

MEDICINE

Institute for Dermatology and Venereology: 700109 Tashkent, Farabi 3; tel. (71) 246-08-07; f. 1932; attached to Min. of Health; library of 14,000 vols; Dir Prof. V. A. AKOVBAYAN; publ. *Pathogenesis and Therapy for Skin and Venereal Diseases* (annually).

Institute of Haematology and Blood Transfusion: 700059 Tashkent, Druzhba Narodov 42; tel. (71) 279-79-35; fax (71) 279-95-26.

Institute of Immunology: 700060 Tashkent, Ya. Gulamov 74; tel. (71) 133-08-05; fax (71) 133-08-55; e-mail immuno@uzsci.net; attached to Uzbek Acad. of Sciences; Dir R. RUZIBAKIYEV.

Institute of Vaccines and Sera: 700084 Tashkent, Abdurashidov 37; tel. (71) 243-79-53; fax (71) 234-77-22; Dir B. A. SHEVCHENKO.

Isaev, L.M., Research Institute of Medical Parasitology: 703005 Samarkand, Isaeva 38; tel. (662) 37-42-42; f. 1923; library of 45,000 vols; Dir SH. A. RAZAKOV; publ. *Current Problems of Medical Parasitology* (annually).

Research Institute of Cardiology: 700052 Tashkent, Ul. Murtazaeva 4; tel. (71) 136-08-16; e-mail cardio@dostlink.net; f. 1976; Dir Prof. RAVSHANBEK KURBANOV.

Research Institute of Clinical and Experimental Medicine: 742000 Nukus, Ul. M. Gorkogo 185; tel. (612) 24-50-41.

Research Institute of Epidemiology, Microbiology and Infectious Diseases: 700133 Tashkent, Reshetova 2; tel. (71) 243-36-05; e-mail shamasir@epid.silk.ord; f. 1961; Dir SH. SH. SHAVAKHABOV.

Uzbek Institute of Rehabilitation and Physiotherapy (Semashko Institute): 700084 Tashkent, Khurshida 4; tel. (71) 234-55-00; fax (71) 235-30-63; f. 1919; physiotherapy in cardiology, arthropology, neurology and pulmonology, oriental medicine, phytotherapy; library of 16,210 vols; Dir Prof. KARIM U. ULDASHEV; publ. *Collection of Scientific Works* (annually).

Uzbek Orthopaedics and Traumatology Research Institute: 700047 Tashkent, Musakhanov 78; tel. (71) 133-10-30; f. 1946; library of 28,000 vols; Dir Prof. T. UNGBAYEV; publ. *Works of the Institute* (annually).

NATURAL SCIENCES

General

Institute for Natural Sciences: 742000 Nukus, Pr. Berdah 41; tel. (612) 17-18-03; fax (612) 17-72-82; attached to Uzbek Acad. of Sciences; Dir E. SEYTMURATOV.

Biological Sciences

Institute of Biochemistry: 700143 Tashkent, Ul. Abdullaeva 56; tel. (71) 162-25-66; fax (71) 162-24-41; e-mail saatov@uzsci.net; attached to Uzbek Acad. of Sciences; Dir T. S. SAATOV.

Institute of Bioecology: 742000 Nukus, Pr. Berdah 1; tel. (612) 17-17-13; fax (612) 17-72-28; e-mail ecol@online.ru; attached to Uzbek Acad. of Sciences; Dir A. BAKHIYEV.

Institute of Botany: 700143 Tashkent, Ul. Khodzhaeva 32; tel. (71) 162-70-65; fax (71) 162-79-38; e-mail botany@uzsci.net; attached to Uzbek Acad. of Sciences; Dir Prof. Dr OZODBEK A. ASHURMETOV.

Institute of the Chemistry of Plant Substances: 700170 Tashkent, Ul. Abdullaeva 77; tel. (71) 162-59-13; fax (71) 162-73-48; e-mail icps@uzsci.net; attached to Uzbek Acad. of Sciences; Dir KHUSNUTDIN SHAKHIDOYATOV.

Institute of Genetics and Plant Experimental Biology: 702151 Tashkent, Kibray Dist., Yukori-Yuz; tel. (71) 264-23-90; fax (71) 264-22-30; e-mail inst@gen.org.uz; attached to Uzbek Acad. of Sciences; Dir A. ABDUKARIMOV.

Institute of Microbiology: 700128 Tashkent, Pr. Abdulla Kadiri 7B; tel. (71) 144-25-19; fax (71) 144-25-82; e-mail imbasru@uzsci.net; f. 1965; attached to Uzbek Acad. of Sciences; Dir K. DAVRANOV; publ. *Uzbeksky Biologichesky Zhurnal.*

Institute of Physiology and Biophysics: 700095 Tashkent, Ul. A. Niyazova 1; tel. (71) 246-95-17; fax (71) 246-92-54; e-mail pusman@uzsci.net; f. 1975; attached to Uzbek Acad. of Sciences; Dir Prof. P. B. USMANOV.

Institute of Zoology: 700095 Tashkent, Ul. A. Niyazova 1; tel. (71) 246-07-18; fax (71) 120-67-91; e-mail uzzool@uzsci.net; f. 1950; attached to Uzbek Acad. of Sciences; Dir J. AZIMOV.

Sodiqov, A., Institute of Bio-organic Chemistry: 700143 Tashkent, Ul. Abdullaeva 83; tel. (71) 162-70-62; fax (71) 162-70-71; e-mail ibchem@uzsci.net; f. 1977; attached to Uzbek Acad. of Sciences; Dir SH. I. SALIKHOV.

Mathematical Sciences

Romanovsky, V. I., Institute of Mathematics: 700125 Tashkent, Akademgorodok, F. Khodjaev ul. 29; tel. (71) 162-56-94; fax (71) 162-73-57; e-mail mathinst@mail.ru; f. 1943; attached to Uzbek Acad. of Sciences; 40 mems; Dir Prof. SHAVKAT AYUPOV; publ. *Uzbek Mathematical Journal* (4 a year).

Physical Sciences

Abdullaev, Kh. M., Institute of Geology and Geophysics: 700017 Tashkent, N. Khodjibaeva 49; tel. (71) 162-65-16; fax (71) 162-63-81; e-mail igg@uzsci.net; f. 1939; attached to Uzbek Acad. of Sciences; Dir S. T. KHUSANOV; publ. *Geology and Mineral Resources* (6 a year).

Heat Physics Department of the Uzbek Academy of Sciences: 700135 Tashkent; tel. (71) 276-44-57; fax (71) 276-26-68; e-mail saidov@uzsci.net; f. 1977; Dir P. KHABIBULLAYEV.

Institute of General and Inorganic Chemistry: 700170 Tashkent, Ul. Kh. Abdullaeva 77A; tel. (71) 162-56-60; fax (71) 162-79-90; e-mail igic@uzsci.net; internet www.igic.uzsci.net; f. 1933; attached to Uzbek Acad. of Sciences; research into colloidal, inorganic, electro- and petroleum chemistry; library of 50,000 vols; Dir Prof. ZAKIRJAN SALIMOV; publs *Reports of Uzbekistan Academy of Sciences–Joint Academic Institutes Journal* (6 a year), *Uzbekistan Journal of Chemistry* (6 a year).

Institute of Mineral Resources: 700060 Tashkent, Ul. T. Shevchenko 11-A; tel. (712) 56-13-49; fax (71) 120-68-12; e-mail mineral@cu.uz; internet www.geology.uz; f. 1957; Dir B. A. ISAKHODJAYEV; publ. *Geology and Mineral Resources* (6 a year).

Institute of Nuclear Physics: 702132 Tashkent, Ulugbek; tel. and fax (71) 264-25-90; e-mail yuldashev@iae.tashkent.su; f. 1956; attached to Uzbek Acad. of Sciences; Dir B. S. YULDASHEV.

Institute of Seismology: 700128 Tashkent, Ul. Zulfiyakhonim 3; tel. (71) 241-51-70; fax (71) 241-53-14; e-mail seismo@uzsci.net; f. 1966; attached to Uzbek Acad. of Sciences; library of 43,000 vols; Dir Prof. K. N. ABDULLABEKOV; publ. *Uzbek Geological Journal* (6 a year).

Institute of the Chemistry and Physics of Polymers: 700128 Tashkent, Ul. A. Kadiri 7B; tel. (71) 241-70-80; fax (71) 244-26-61; e-mail carbon@uzsci.net; attached to Uzbek Acad. of Sciences; Dir S. SH. RASHIDOVA.

Physical-Technical Institute: 700084 Tashkent, G. Mavlyanov 2B; tel. (71) 133-12-71; fax (71) 235-42-91; e-mail lutp@physic.uzsci.net; attached to Uzbek Acad. of Sciences; Dir S. LUTPULLAYEV; publ. *Applied Solar Engineering.*

Ulugh Beg Astronomical Institute: 700052 Tashkent, Astronomicheskaya ul. 33; tel. (71) 235-81-02; fax (71) 136-00-37; e-mail admin@astrin.uzsci.net; internet www.astrin.uzsci.net; attached to Uzbek Acad. of Sciences; Dir SH. A. EHGAMBERDIEV.

RELIGION, SOCIOLOGY AND ANTHROPOLOGY

Institute for Socio-Economic Problems of the Aral Sea Region: 742000 Nukus, Amir Temur 179A; tel. (612) 24-22-09; fax (612) 17-72-28; e-mail udasa@uzpak.uz; attached to Uzbek Acad. of Sciences; Dir N. AIMBETOV.

TECHNOLOGY

Arifov Institute of Electronics: 700125 Tashkent, F. Khodjaev 33; tel. (71) 162-79-40; fax (71) 162-87-67; e-mail ariel@uzsci.net; f. 1967; attached to Uzbek Acad. of Sciences; Dir U. KH. RASULEV.

Institute of Cybernetics: 700125 Tashkent, Ul. Khodzhaeva 34; tel. (71) 162-72-47; fax (71) 162-73-21; e-mail shavkat@cyber

.uzsci.net; f. 1966; attached to Uzbek Acad. of Sciences; library of 100,000 vols; Dir F. SHAVKAT; publs *Problemy Informatiki i Energetiki* (6 a year), *Voprosy Kibernetiki* (3 a year), *Voprosy Vychislitelnoi i Prikladnoi Matematiki* (3 a year), *Algoritmy* (3 a year), *Voprosy Modelirovaniya i Informatizatsii Ekonomiki* (3 a year).

Institute of Hydrogeology and Engineering Geology: 700041 Tashkent, Ul .N. Khodjibaev 64; tel. (71) 162-47-01; fax (71) 162-47-63; e-mail hydrouz@rambler.ru; f. 1960; research into hydrogeology, petroleum, geoecology, landslides and remote-sensing; library of 18,000 vols; Dir Dr NARIMAN G. MAVLYANOV; publs *Geology and Mineral Resources* (2 a year), *Hydrogeology and Engineering Geology Problems in Uzbekistan* (annually).

Institute of Materials Science: 700084 Tashkent, Mavlyanov 2B; tel. (71) 133-12-71; fax (71) 235-42-91; e-mail jabbar@uzsci.net; attached to Uzbek Acad. of Sciences; Dir A. ABDURAKHMANOV.

Institute of Mechanics and Seismic Stability of Structures: 700125 Tashkent, Akademia Shaharchasi, F Hodjaev 31; tel. (71) 162-72-97; fax (71) 162-71-52; e-mail instmech@uzsci.net; f. 1959; attached to Uzbek Acad. of Sciences; Dir A. A. RIZAEV; publs *Problems of Mechanics* (6 a year), *Architecture and Construction*.

Institute of Power Engineering and Automation: 700143 Tashkent, Akademgorodok; tel. (71) 162-05-22; fax (71) 162-09-19; e-mail ipea@uzsci.net; f. 1941; attached to Uzbek Acad. of Sciences; Dir R. A. ZAKHIDOV.

Institute of Water Problems: 700187 Tashkent, Ul. Khodjaeva 25 A; tel. and fax (71) 169-12-70; e-mail root@pwater.tashkent.su; f. 1992; attached to Uzbek Acad. of Sciences; Dir ERNAZAR J. MAKHMUDOV.

Scientific and Production Association 'Akademasbob': 700143 Tashkent, Akademia Shaharchasi; tel. (71) 162-72-73; fax (712) 65-42-50; e-mail bahramov@online.ru; f. 1962; attached to Uzbek Acad. of Sciences; design of scientific instruments and equipment for agriculture, medicine and industry; Dir-Gen. S. A. DAKHRAMOV.

Scientific Production Centre 'Modern Information Technologies': 700143 Tashkent, Ul. Khodzhaeva 34; tel. (71) 162-72-47; fax (71) 162-73-12; e-mail shavkat@cyber.uzsci.net; attached to Uzbek Acad. of Sciences; Dir O. NABIYEV.

Uzbek Research Institute of Sericulture: 702044 Jar-Arik, Tashkent Viloyat, Zangyata; f. 1927; attached to Min. of Agriculture and Water; Dir SH. YULDASHEV; publ. *Silk*.

UzLITIneftgaz (Uzbekistan Research and Design Institute of the Gas and Oil Industry): 700029 Tashkent, Ul. T. Shevchenko 2; tel. (71) 256-74-17; fax (71) 256-66-48; Dir U. S. NAZAROV; publ. *Uzbek Journal of Oil and Gas* (4 a year).

Libraries and Archives
Samarkand
Samarkand State University Central Library: 702004 Samarkand, Pl. Navoi 15; tel. (662) 35-19-38; fax (662) 35-64-90; e-mail soleev@samuni.silk.org; 1,632,000 vols; spec. collns incl. ancient oriental literature; Dir R. KHOLMURODOV.

Tashkent
Alisher Navoi National Library of Uzbekistan: 700078 Tashkent, Mustakillik maydoni 5; tel. (71) 139-16-58; fax (71) 133-09-08; e-mail navoi@physic.uzsci.net; f. 1870, incorporates Republican Library for Science and Technology since 2002; 10,000,000 vols; Dir ZUHRIDDIN ISAMIDDINOV.

Central State Archive of Uzbekistan: 700043 Tashkent, Ul. Chilonzara 2; tel. (712) 77-10-92; Dir IRKIN A. ABDULLAEV.

Foundation Library of the Uzbek Academy of Sciences: 700170 Tashkent, Ul. Muminova 13; tel. (71) 162-74-56; fax (71) 162-74-58; e-mail acadlib@acadlib.uzsci.net; f. 1934; Uzbek Academy of Sciences library system includes 31 other research institute libraries; 3,000,000 vols; Dir B. N. KADIROV.

Uzbek National University Libraries: 700095 Tashkent, Vozgorodok, Universitatskaya 95; 18 brs; 350,000 vols, 45,000 journals, 2,600 govt docs, 4,000 maps; Dir L. S. YUGAI.

Museums and Art Galleries
Nukus
Botanical Garden: 742004 Nukus, Ul. Chimbay; tel. (612) 22-30-47; fax (612) 17-72-28; attached to Uzbek Acad. of Sciences; Dir T. OTENOV.

Karakalpak Art Museum: 742000 Karakalpakstan, Nukus, Pr. Doslyk 127; tel. (612) 22-25-73; fax (612) 22-25-56; e-mail museum@online.ru; internet savitskymuseum.freenet.uz; f. 1966 by the archaeologist and ethnographer Igor Savitsky; archaeology of ancient Khorezym, Karakalpak folk art, Russian avant-garde art 1910–1935; library of 9,450 vols; Dir M. BABANAZAROVA.

Karakalpak Historical Museum: Nukus, Ul. Rakhmatova 3; illustrates the part played by the Uzbek people in the October Socialist Revolution, the Civil War and the Second World War.

Samarkand
Samarkand State United Historical-Architectural and Art Museum Preserve: 703000 Samarkand, Registan ul. 1; tel. (66) 35-38-96; f. 1982; comprises nine museums in Samarkand city and viloyat, containing more than 182,000 exhibits in total.

Tashkent
Museum of Uzbek History: 700000 Tashkent, Ul. Sharaf Rashidov 3; tel. (71) 139-10-83, f. 1992 by merger of the Museum of the History of the People of Uzbekistan and the Lenin Central Museums; more than 300,000 exhibits; Dir G. R. RASHIDOV.

Navoi, A. State Museum of Literature: 700011 Tashkent, Ul. Navoi 69; tel. (71) 142-02-75; fax (71) 144-00-61; e-mail a_navoi@yahoo.com; internet www.navoimuseum.uz; f. 1991; attached to Uzbek Acad. of Sciences; collects, investigates, maintains and displays the history of Uzbek literature, incl. manuscripts, documents, pictures, archives and photographic materials; Dir Prof. SAIDBEK KHASANOV.

Oibek, M. T., Historical Museum of Uzbekistan: 700047 Tashkent, Ul. Sh. Rashidova 3; tel. (71) 139-10-83; fax (71) 139-44-25; attached to Uzbek Acad. of Sciences; Dir K. INOYATOV.

State Museum of Timurid History: 700000 Tashkent, Amir Temur 1; tel. and fax (71) 132-02-13; e-mail temurid@uzsci.net; attached to Uzbek Acad. of Sciences; Dir N. KHABIBULLAYEV.

Uzbek State Museum of Art: 700060 Tashkent, Movarounnakhr 16; tel. (71) 136-74-36; fax (71) 136-77-40; f. 1918; library of 22,700 vols; Dir D. S. RUSIBAYEV.

Universities
ACADEMY OF STATE AND SOCIAL CONSTRUCTION
700029 Tashkent, Uzbekistana 45
Telephone: (71) 245-69-51
Founded 1995
State control
Languages of instruction: Uzbek, Russian
Rector: ALISHER AZIZHOJAYEV.

ANDIZHAN STATE UNIVERSITY
710000 Andizhan, Namangan 129
Telephone: (742) 25-05-09
Fax: (742) 22-18-63
E-mail: asu2001@rambler.ru
Founded 1931
State control
Languages of instruction: Uzbek, Russian
Academic year: September to June
Rector: SIROJIDDIN ZAYNOBBIDINOV
Vice-Rector: TOLIB MADUMAROV
Library of 320,314 vols
Number of teachers: 434
Number of students: 5,021

DEANS
Faculty of Biology: ALIJON DADAMIRZAYEV
Faculty of Chemistry: MIRAHMAD KHOJIMATOV
Faculty of History: ZOKIR KUTIBOYEV
Faculty of Mathematics: ABDUVAHOB MILADJONOV
Faculty of Philology: DILMUROD QURONOV
Faculty of Physical Training: NOIB YULDASHEV
Faculty of Physics: ABDULQAHOR ORTIQOV
Faculty of Physical Education: DEHQONBOY MAMATISAQOV
Faculty of Teacher Training: MUHTOR VOHIDOV

BUKHARA STATE UNIVERSITY
705018 Bukhara, Muhammad Ikbol kuch. 11
Telephone: (65) 223-23-14
Fax: (65) 223-12-54
E-mail: bukhsu-monitor@mail.ru
Internet: www.bukhsu.uzsci.net
Founded 1930
State control
Academic year: September to June
Rector: K. M. MUQIMOV
Vice-Rector: O. M. EYRIYEV
Number of teachers: 361
Number of students: 5,577
Publications: *University Review* (monthly), *Marifat Nuri* (monthly)
Faculties of Agriculture, Biology and Chemistry, Economics, Education, Foreign Philosophy, Graphic Arts, History and Geography, Physics and Mathematics, Sociology and Uzbek-Tajik Philology.

FERGHANA STATE UNIVERSITY
712000 Ferghana, Usmanhojayev 19
Telephone: (732) 24-28-71
Fax: (732) 24-35-32
E-mail: fdu@fdu.vodiy.uz
Founded 1991
State control
Languages of instruction: Uzbek, Russian
Rector: AHMADJON URINOV
Vice-Rector: MADAMIN AKHMEDOV
Library of 757,461 vols
Number of teachers: 459
Number of students: 5,639

HEADS OF DEPARTMENTS
Economics: ZAKIR TADJIBAYEV
Education and Culture: ABDURAHMOB NIZO-
MOV
Foreign Philology: NEMAT SOBIROV
Law: MIRZAMAHMAD JIYANOV
Mathematics: KHURSANALI KOSIMOV
Natural Sciences: VALIJON MAHMUDOV
Physical Education: ODIL NAZIROV
Physics and Engineering: MUHAMMAD
NABIYEV
Social and Human Sciences: KHASAN RAHMA-
TULLAYEV
Uzbek Philology: SIDDIQ MUMINOV

GULISTAN STATE UNIVERSITY

707000 Gulistan, Microraion 4
Telephone: (672) 25-45-72
Fax: (672) 25-02-72
E-mail: gdu@intal.uz
Founded 1966
State control
Languages of instruction: Uzbek, Russian
Rector: AZIMJON P. RARPIYEV
Library of 195,000 vols
Faculties of Economics and Engineering,
Education, Foreign Languages, History and
Uzbek Philology, Kazakh Philology, Natural
Sciences, Physics and Mathematics.

KARAKALPAK STATE UNIVERSITY

742012 Nukus, Ch. Abidov 1
Telephone: (612) 23-60-47
Fax: (612) 23-60-78
E-mail: korun@korun.silk.org
Founded 1979
State control
Rector: Prof. K. ATENIYAZOV
Number of students: 7,000
Faculties of Agriculture, Chemistry, Con-
struction, Engineering, Economics, Law and
History, Natural Sciences, Philology, Physics
and Mathematics.

KARSHI STATE UNIVERSITY

730003 Karshi, Kuchabog 17
Telephone: (752) 25-77-63
Fax: (752) 21-13-12
Internet: qardu.uzpak.uz
Founded 1956
State control
Languages of instruction: Uzbek, Russian
Rector: NAZAR H. HAKIMOV
Library of 10,000 vols
Faculties of Correspondence Studies, Eco-
nomics, Education, History and Psychology,
Mathematics, Natural Sciences, Physical
Education and Sports, Physics and Technol-
ogy, Uzbek Philology.

NAMANGAN STATE UNIVERSITY

716019 Namangan, Uychi 316
Telephone: (692) 26-55-01
Fax: (692) 26-61-07
E-mail: nomsu@silk.org
Founded 1942
State control
Languages of instruction: Uzbek, Russian
Academic year: September to June
Rector: TURSUNBOY FAYZULLAYEV
Library of 500,000 vols
Number of teachers: 313
Number of students: 4,050

DEANS
Faculty of Art and Drawing: BOTIRSHER
JABBOROV

Faculty of Biology and Chemistry: YOL-
DOSHALI TOSHMATOV
Faculty of Education: MUNOJATHON MIRAB-
DULLAYEVA
Faculty of Geography and Economics:
MUHAMMADSOLI MUMINOV
Faculty of Graduate Studies: SHAVKAT
ABDULLAYEV
Faculty of History: RUZIMAT JURAYEV
Faculty of Law: YULDOSHALI RHIMOV
Faculty of Mathematics: SOBIRJON ALIHANOV
Faculty of Physical Education and Sport:
SOBITHON AZIZOV
Faculty of Physics and Labour Education:
TOSHKINBOY UMARALIYEV
Faculty of Uzbek Philology: TOHIRJON RAH-
MONOV
Faculty of World Languages: SAIDUMOR SAI-
DALIYEV

SAMARKAND STATE UNIVERSITY

703004 Samarkand, bul. Universiteti 15
Telephone: (662) 33-54-83
Fax: (662) 33-27-24
E-mail: safarovsh@rambler.ru
Internet: www.samdu.uz
Founded 1927
State control
Languages of instruction: Uzbek, Russian,
Tajik
Academic year: September to June
Rector: Dr T. SH. SHIRINOV
Vice-Rector: Prof. Dr M. K. MHIDDINOV
Number of teachers: 800
Number of students: 13,000
Publication: *Samarkand Davlat Universiteti*
(weekly)
Faculties of History, Geography, Foreign
Languages, Mathematics, Applied Mathe-
matics, Physics, Chemistry, Biology, Uzbek,
Tajik and Russian Philology, Law, Econom-
ics, Sociology, Management, Physical Train-
ing, Musical Education, Pre-school and
Primary Education.

TASHKENT ISLAMIC UNIVERSITY

700006 Tashkent, Abdullah Qodiriy 11
Telephone: (71) 139-52-15
Fax: (71) 139-82-15
Founded 1999
State control
Languages of instruction: Uzbek, Arabic
Academic year: September to June
Rector: HAMIDULLA KAROMATOV
Vice-Rector: ABDULHAY ABDULLAYEV
Number of students: 100
Faculties of Islamic history and Natural
Sciences.

TASHKENT NIZAMI STATE PEDAGOGICAL UNIVERSITY

700100 Tashkent, Yusuf Has Hajib 103
Telephone: (71) 254-92-02
Fax: (71) 254-92-17
E-mail: tdpu@albatros.uz
Founded 1935
State control
Languages of instruction: Uzbek, Russian
Languages of instruction: Kazakh, Korean
Languages of instruction: German, English
Academic year: September to June
Rector: BAHRAM G. KADIROV
Number of teachers: 932
Number of students: 10,380
Faculties:

DEANS
Faculty of Applied Physiologists Training:
FAZLIDDIN KHAYDAROV

Faculty of Drawing and Applied Art: BOTOR
BOYMETOV
Faculty of Foreign Languages: QURBON SHOD-
MONOV
Faculty of Handicrafts Education: NARZULLA
MUSLIMOV
Faculty of History: SAMAD TORAYEV
Faculty of Military Physical Training: ILHOM
IKROMOV
Faculty of Music: HAMIDULLA NURMATOV
Faculty of Natural Sciences: FARIDA MURHA-
MIDOVA
Faculty of Pedagogics and Defectology:
MAMAD KHAYDAROV
Faculty of Physics and Mathematics: ERKIN
SAYDAMATOV
Faculty of Russian and Korean Philology:
RUSTAM KOBILOV
Faculty of Teaching Skills Enhancement:
NURIDDIN DOSANOV
Faculty of Uzbek and Kazakh Language and
Literature: IBROHIM YULDASHEV

TERMIZ STATE UNIVERSITY

732011 Termiz, F. Hodjayev 43
Telephone: (762) 23-19-08
Fax: (762) 24-25-36
Founded 1992
State control
Languages of instruction: Uzbek, Russian
Rector: SAYFULLO T. TURSUNOV
Library of 183,000
Number of students: 47,000
Faculties of Chemistry, Economics, Educa-
tion, Education and Psychology, Finance and
Management, Foreign Languages, History,
Industrial Education, Natural Sciences and
Geography, Physical Education, Physics and
Mathematics, Russian Philology, Technology
and Engineering, Training of Specialists and
Retraining.

URGENCH AL-KHARAZMI STATE UNIVERSITY

740013 Urgench, H. Alimjan 14
Telephone: (622) 26-61-66
Fax: (622) 26-35-44
E-mail: ayus@khorsu.silk.org
Internet: urdu.freenet.uz
Founded 1992
State control
Languages of instruction: Uzbek, Russian
Rector: AZIMBAY S. SAGDULLAYEV
Number of students: 34,000
Faculties of Economics, Engineering and
Technology, Natural Sciences, Physics and
Mathematics, Uzbek Philology and History,
World Languages.

UZBEK NATIONAL UNIVERSITY

70014 Tashkent, Vozgorodok, Universitets-
kaya 95
Telephone: (71) 246-02-24
Fax: (71) 144-73-12
E-mail: oms@tsu.silk.org
Internet: www.nuu.uz
Founded 1920
State control
Rector: Dr T. N. DALIMOV
Vice-Rector: R. MURAZAYEVA
Library Director: L. S. YUGAI
Number of teachers: 1,480
Number of students: 19,300
Faculties of History, Uzbek Philology, Rus-
sian Philology, Romance and Germanic phi-
lology, Oriental Studies, Journalism,
Philosophy and Economics, Law, Mathe-
matics, Applied Mathematics, Physics,

Chemistry, Biology and Soil Science, Geology and Geography.

Other Higher Educational Institutes

Academy of Arts of Uzbekistan: 700029 Tashkent, Pr. Sharif Rashidov 40; tel. (71) 256-50-47; fax (71) 256-50-46; e-mail acart@umid.uz; internet www.arts-academy.uz; f. 1997 by merger of existing instns; 190 teachers; 900 students; Rector TURSUNALI KUZIYEV.

Andizhan Cotton Institute: 711520 Andizhan, Selo Kuigan-Yar, Andizhan raion; tel. (742) 24-54-34.

Andizhan State Medical Institute: 710000 Andizhan, Atabekova 1; tel. (742) 37-93-53; fax (742) 22-19-41; e-mail agmi@online.ru; internet www.andmi.uz; library: 105,000 vols; Rector Prof. MAMAZAIR A. KHUJAMBERDIEV.

Andizhan State Pedagogical Institute of Languages: 710011 Andizhan, Ul. Babur 5; tel. (742) 24-75-15; fax (742) 24-75-26; e-mail adtpi@online.ru; f. 1966; faculties: Russian language and literature, foreign languages (English, German, French); Rector RASHID G. BARATOV; publ. *Scientific Proceedings*.

Bukhara State Medical Institute: 705018 Bukhara, Ul. Navoi 1; tel. (65) 223-00-50; fax (65) 223-49-43; e-mail buhme@rambler.ru; internet www.buhmi.uz; f. 1990; library: 90,000 vols; 240 teachers; 1,728 students; Rector Prof. RAKHMAT M. AKHMEDOV.

Bukhara Technological Institute of Food and Light Industry: 705017 Bukhara, K. Murtazoev 15; tel. (65) 223-61-97; fax (65) 223-78-84; e-mail javlonbek@intal.uz; f. 1976; faculties: oil and gas, mechanical engineering, light industry, professional education, food technology, business and management; 320 teachers; 4,800 students; Rector Prof. Dr MUHSIN T. HODJIEV.

Ferghana Polytechnic Institute: 712022 Ferghana, Ferganskaya ul. 86; tel. (732) 22-13-50; fax (732) 22-13-33; e-mail monitoring@farpi.uz; internet www.farpi.uz; f. 1967; faculties: chemical technology, power, mechanics, construction, economics; device building centre; library: 290,000 vols; 234 teachers; 3,239 students; Rector RASUL J. TOJIYEV; publ. *Scientific-Technical Journal* (4 a year).

Samarkand Agricultural Institute: 703003 Samarkand, M. Ulugbek 77; tel. (662) 34-33-20; fax (662) 34-07-86; e-mail samsi@uzpak.uz; f. 1929; faculties: agronomics, agro-engineering, animal husbandry, economics and accounting, Karakul (sheep-breeding), veterinary science, zootechnics; library: 533,777 vols; 274 teachers; 3,500 students (2,000 full-time, 1,500 correspondence); Rector Prof. Dr ABDI-KADIR ERGASHEV.

Samarkand Co-operative Institute: 703000 Samarkand, A. Temur 9; tel. (662) 33-38-72; fax (662) 31-12-53; e-mail samki@intal.uz; f. 1931; faculties: engineering technology, trade economics, trade, accounting; library: 205,718 vols; 210 teachers; 7,000 students; Rector AKBARALI N. JABRIYEV.

Samarkand State Architectural and Civil Engineering Institute: 703047 Samarkand, Lolazor 70; tel. (662) 37-15-93; fax (662) 31-04-52; e-mail unesco_aliance@rambler.ru; f. 1966; depts: architecture, economics, building, building technology, engineering, professional education, building engineering and ecology, machine construction and land cadastre; library: 400,000 vols;

266 teachers; 2,000 students; Rector SOBIR M. BOBOEV.

Samarkand State Institute of Foreign Languages: 703004 Samarkand, Akhunbabaev 93; tel. (662) 33-78-43; fax (662) 35-66-19; e-mail samdchti@online.ru; internet sifl.50megs.com; f. 1994; library: 91,000 vols; 225 teachers; 2,165 students (1,387 undergraduate, 778 postgraduate); Rector Prof. M. SH. MAMATOV.

Samarkand State Medical Institute: 703000 Samarkand, Ul. Amir Temur 18,; tel. and fax (662) 33-54-21; e-mail info@sammi.samuni.silk.org; internet www.sammi.da.ru; f. 1930; faculties of general practice and paediatrics; library: 330,000 vols; Rector B. U. SOBIROV.

Tashkent Abu Reihan Beruni State Technical University: 700095 Tashkent, Universitetskaya 2; tel. (71) 246-46-00; fax (71) 229-48-96; e-mail intdep@online.ru; internet www.tstu.re.uz; f. 1929; faculties: oil and gas, electronics, automation and computer hardware, power engineering, mechanical engineering and machine building, mining and geology, humanities; 2,000 teachers; 20,000 students; Rector KAKHRAMON R. ALLAYEV.

Tashkent Automobile and Road Construction Institute: 700060 Tashkent, Mavoraunnakhr 20A; tel. (71) 133-08-27; fax (71) 132-14-80; e-mail tayi.admin@mail.ru; f. 1972; faculties: road building machinery, roads, road transport, road transport management, engineering economics; br. in Termez; Rector S. M. KADIROV.

Tashkent Institute of Architecture and Construction: 700011 Tashkent, Navoi 13; tel. (71) 241-15-01; fax (71) 241-80-00; e-mail ismoil_i@mail.ru; internet www.tasi.uzsci.net; 200 teachers; 2,400 students; Rector BAKHTIYAR A. ASKAROV.

Tashkent Institute of Finance: 700084 Tashkent, Asomova 7; tel. (71) 234-55-37; fax (71) 235-77-04; e-mail tfi@online.ru; 4,200 students; Rector M. SHARIFKHOJAYEV.

Tashkent Institute of Irrigation and Melioration: 700000 Tashkent, Ul Qari-Niyazova 39; tel. (71) 137-46-68; fax (71) 133-14-39; e-mail tiiame@freenet.uz; internet www.tiiame.uzsci.net; f. 1920; faculties: hydromelioration, agricultural mechanization, electrical energetic of agriculture and water management, land management, economics, management and marketing, education science, natural resources management, irrigation and land improvement of hydromeliorative works, magistracy; library: 864,000 vols; 484 teachers; 5,371 students; Rector Prof. T. S. HUDOYBERDIYEV; Vice-Rector UKTAM PARDAYEVICH UMURZAKOV.

Tashkent Institute of Railway Transport Engineers: 700167 Tashkent, Adilkhodjayeva 1; tel. (71) 191-14-40; fax (71) 191-10-73; f. 1931; faculties: engineering, automation, telemechanics and communication, traffic management, industrial and civil construction, construction, economics; f. 1931; library: 500,000 vols; 400 teachers; 12,000 students; Rector ANVAR E. ODILKHUJAYEV.

Tashkent Institute of Textile and Light Industry: 700100 Tashkent, Shokhyahon 5; tel. (71) 253-06-06; fax (71) 253-36-17; e-mail titlp@buzton.com; f. 1932; faculties: cotton technology, mechanical technology, technology for light industry, engineering economics, chemical technology; library: 644,000 vols; 242 teachers; 2,214 students; Rector Prof. KH. ALIMOVA.

Tashkent Law Institute: 700047 Tashkent, Sayilgokh 3; tel. (71) 133-41-09; fax (71)

133-37-46; e-mail interlaw1@uzsci.net; Rector M. KH. RUSTAMBAYEV.

Tashkent Paediatric Medical Institute: 700140 Tashkent, Obidova 223; tel. (71) 162-28-71; fax (71) 162-33-14; e-mail tpmi@uzsci.net; Rector ANVAR V. ALIMOV.

Tashkent Pharmaceutical Institute: 700015 Tashkent, Ul. Oibek 45; tel. (71) 256-37-38; fax (71) 256-45-04; e-mail pharmi@bcc.com.uz; internet www.pharmi.re.uz; f. 1937; library: 423,420 vols; 212 teachers; 1,323 students; Dir Dr A. N. YUNUSKHOJAYEV.

Tashkent State Agrarian University: 700140 Tashkent, Kibray District, Universitetskaya 5; tel. and fax (71) 263-76-00; e-mail gulumov@atabah.silk.org; f. 1930; depts: agrochemistry and soil science, agronomy, fruit and vegetable growing, viticulture, plant protection, silkworm breeding, economics and management, forestry, accounting; library: 196,000 vols; 320 teachers; 7,200 students; Rector H. C. H. BURIYEV.

Tashkent State Conservatoire: 700000 Tashkent, Ul. Pushkina 31; tel. (71) 133-52-74; fax (71) 133-10-35; f. 1936; piano, orchestral, Uzbek folk instruments, singing, choral conducting, composition, musicology, sound production; library: 243,000 vols; 288 teachers; 548 students; Rector R. Y. YUNUSOV.

Tashkent State Institute of Culture: 700164 Tashkent, Yalangach 127A; tel. and fax (71) 162-03-23; e-mail bbdjuraev@yahoo.com; librarianship, educational and cultural work; br. in Namangan.; Rector AZIZ A. TURAYEV.

Tashkent State Medical Institute: 700048 Tashkent, Ul. Khamza 103; tel. (71) 267-63-05; fax (71) 233-62-26; e-mail tashmi@mail.ru; f. 1920; trains general practitioners and stomatologists; library: 600,000 vols; 450 teachers; 3,000 students; Rector Prof. T. A. DAMINOV.

Tashkent State University of Economics: 700003 Tashkent, Uzbekistanskaya 49; tel. (71) 132-64-21; fax (71) 139-41-23; e-mail info@tsue.uz; internet www.tsue.uz; f. 1931; faculties: economic planning, agricultural economics, trade economics, financial economics, accounting, economic cybernetics; library: 300,000 vols; 600 teachers; 11,000 students; br. in Andizhan; Rector Prof. RAIMJON KH. ALIMOV.

Tashkent University of Information Technology: 700084 Tashkent, Ul. Amir Temur 108; tel. (71) 138-04-20, fax (71) 105-10-40; e-mail teic@uzpak.uz; f. 1955; faculties: radio communication, television and broadcasting, special communication, economics, telecommunication transmission systems, telecommunication networks and switching systems; library: 500,000 vols; 271 teachers; 3,100 students; Rector Prof. Dr S. S. KASIMOV.

University of World Economics and Diplomacy: 700045 Tashkent, Buyuk Ipak Yuli 54; tel. (71) 267-67-69; fax (71) 267-09-13; e-mail uwed@list.ru; internet www.uwed.uz; f. 1992; 350 teachers; 1,200 students; First Vice-Rector Dr A. FAYZULLAEV.

Uzbek State World Languages University: 700015 Tashkent, Ul. Sobir Yusupov 21A, Block G9A; tel. (71) 275-77-95; fax (71) 275-55-57; internet uswlu.freenet.uz; f. 1992 by merger of Tashkent State Pedagogical Institute of Foreign Languages and Republican Russian Language and Literature Pedagogic Institute; faculties of English, German, Spanish, Romance, Russian, translation, international journalism; Rector GAYRAT B. SHOUMAROV.

VANUATU

The Higher Education System

Higher education in Vanuatu is limited, the only institution being a campus of the University of the South Pacific. Gross enrolment at tertiary level was just 5% in 2005.

Learned Societies

BIBLIOGRAPHY, LIBRARY SCIENCE AND MUSEOLOGY

Pacific Islands Museum Association (PIMA): Cultural Centre, Port Vila; tel. (678) 23197; fax (678) 26590; internet www.pacificislandsmuseum.org; regional, multilingual, multicultural, non-profit org. to preserve, celebrate and nurture the heritage of the peoples of the Pacific Islands; Dir FAUSTINA REHUHER.

Vanuatu Library Association: Port Vila; tel. (678) 22888; fax (678) 24494; internet www.vanuatu.usp.ac.fj/library/vla/homepage.htm; to develop and improve library services in Vanuatu; support and encourage devt of libraries archives and associated professions; Pres. FLORA DIXON; Sec. PAULINE KALO.

Research Institute

NATURAL SCIENCES

Biological Sciences

Environment Unit: Pompidou Complex, Port Vila; e-mail environ@vanuatu.com.vu; internet www.biodiversity.com.vu; govt agency; programmes for devt, conservation and management of natural resources; Dir ERNEST BANI.

Libraries and Archives

Port Vila

National Library: Nat. Museum Bldg, Port Vila; tel. (678) 22129; fax (678) 26590; e-mail nasonal.laebri@vanuatuculture.org; internet www.vanuatuculture.org; 2 spec. collns, Pacific and Vanuatu in English, French and Bislama; linguistics section on the 113 vernacular languages; anthropological and archaeological materials, art and arts references, autobiographical records and biographies, large section of works on the languages of Vanuatu, mission histories, oral traditions, cultural, historical and political records; Librarians ANNE NAUPA, JUNE NORMAN.

National Photo, Film and Sound Archive: POB 184, Port Vila; tel. (678) 23197; fax (678) 26590; internet www.vanuatuculture.org; to preserve information about custom, culture and tradition; 3,000 hours of footage (8mm films, Video 8 and VHS ½-inch video) and photographs of oral traditions and rituals.

Port Vila Public Library: Cultural Centre, Port Vila; tel. (678) 23837; fax (678) 27837; internet www.vanuatuculture.org; f. 1960; only public library in Vanuatu; Librarian NAOMI ANIEL.

Museum

Port Vila

Vanuatu Cultural Centre and National Museum (Vanuatu Kaljoral Senta): POB 184, Port Vila; tel. (678) 23197; fax (678) 26590; e-mail vks@vanuatu.com.vu; internet www.vanuatuculture.org; f. 1960 as Port Vila Library; Museum opened in 1995; incl. Malakula Cultural Centre in Lakatoro; houses Vanuatu Cultural and Historic Sites Survey (VCHSS), Young People's Project; Women's Cultural Project; collns of traditional artefacts (masks, slit gongs, outrigger canoes), daily screenings of cultural documentaries; Dir RALPH REGENVANU.

University

UNIVERSITY OF THE SOUTH PACIFIC, EMALUS CAMPUS

POB 9072, Port Vila

Telephone: (678) 22748
Fax: (678) 22633
E-mail: ngwele_a@vanuatu.usp.ac.fj
Internet: www.vanuatu.usp.ac.fj
School of Law, Pacific Languages Unit, Early Childhood Education
Dir: JOHN LYNCH
Librarian: MARGARET AUSTRAI-KAILO.

VATICAN CITY

The Higher Education System

The State of the Vatican City is situated entirely within the Italian capital, Rome. In 1929 the Lateran Treaty was concluded between the Italian Government and the Holy See (a term designating the papacy, i.e. the office of the Pope, and thus the central governing body of the Roman Catholic Church).

Higher education principally consists of Pontifical universities and institutes offering training for the priesthood and conducting research relating to the Roman Catholic Church, the oldest being the Pontificia Gregoriana Universitas, which was founded in 1553. The majority of institutions are located in Rome outside the boundaries of the Vatican City itself.

Learned Societies

GENERAL

Pontificia Accademia di S. Tommaso d'Aquino (Pontifical Academy of St Thomas Aquinas): 00120 Vatican City; tel. 06-69881441; fax 06-69885218; f. 1879; 50 mems; theological, philosophical and juridico-economic sections; Pres. P. EDWARD KACZYŃSKI; Sec. HE Mgr MARCELO SÁNCHEZ SORONDO; publ. *Doctor Communis* (irregular).

ECONOMICS, LAW AND POLITICS

Pontificia Academia Scientiarum Socialium (Pontifical Academy of Social Sciences): Casina Pio IV, 00120 Vatican City; tel. 06-69881441; fax 06-69885218; e-mail social .sciences@acdscience.va; internet www .vatican.va/roman_curia/pontifical_academ ies/acdscience/index.htm; f. 1994; social, economic, political and juridical sciences; 33 mems; Pres. Prof. MARY ANN GLENDON; Chancellor Prof. HE Msgr MARCELO SÁNCHEZ SORONDO; publs *Acta*, *Miscellanea*.

FINE AND PERFORMING ARTS

Pontificia Insigne Accademia di Belle Arti e Lettere dei Virtuosi al Pantheon: Palazzo della Cancelleria Apostolica, Piazza della Cancelleria 1, 00186 Rome, Italy; tel. 06-69885275; f. 1542; 90 mems; Pres. Dott. VITALIANO TIBERIA; Sec. Prof. ERNESTO LAMAGNA; publ. *Annali* (annually).

HISTORY, GEOGRAPHY AND ARCHAEOLOGY

Pontificia Accademia Romana di Archeologia (Pontifical Roman Academy of Archaeology): Palazzo della Cancelleria Apostolica, 00186 Rome, Italy; f. 1810; 108 mems; Pres. LETIZIA PANI ERMINI; Sec. VINCENZO FIOCCHI NICOLAI; publs *Memorie, Rendiconti*.

NATURAL SCIENCES

General

Pontificia Academia Scientiarum (Pontifical Academy of Sciences, The): Casina Pio IV, 00120 Vatican City; tel. 06-69883451; fax 06-69885218; e-mail academy.sciences@ acdscience.va; internet www.vatican.va/ roman_curia/pontifical_academies/ acdscience; f. 1603; aims to promote the advance of the mathematical, physical and natural sciences and the study of related epistemological problems; 80 mems; Pres. Prof. NICOLA CABIBBO; Chancellor Prof. Msgr MARCELO SÁNCHEZ SORONDO; publs *Acta, Commentarii, Documenta, Scripta Varia*.

RELIGION, SOCIOLOGY AND ANTHROPOLOGY

Collegium Cultorum Martyrum: Via Napoleone III 1, 00185 Rome, Italy; f. 1879; *c.* 750 mems; Master Mgr EMANUELE CLARIZIO; Sec. LUIGI CIOTTI.

Pontificia Academia Mariana Internationalis (Pontifical International Marian Academy): Via Merulana 124, 00185 Rome, Italy; premises in Vatican City; tel. 06-70373235; fax 06-70373234; e-mail academiamariana@libero.it; f. 1946, Pontifical since 1959; studies on Our Lady; 75 mems; 155 corresp. mems; 134 hon. mems; Pres. VINCENZO BATTAGLIA; Sec. STEFANO CECCHIN; publ. publs Scientific collections.

Pontificia Accademia dell'Immacolata (Academy of the Immaculate Conception): Via del Serafico 1, 00142 Rome, Italy; f. 1835; 15 mems; promotes Marian studies and culture, especially the doctrine of the Immaculate Conception in the fields of theology, literature and art; Pres. Cardinal ANDREA M. DESKUR; Sec. and Archivist Fr LORENZO DI FONZO.

Pontificia Accademia di Teologia: Piazza S. Giovanni in Laterano 4, 00120 Vatican City; tel. 06-69895513; e-mail path@pul.it; f. 1718; 7 emeritus mems; 39 ordinary mems, 25 normally resident in Rome, 36 in the rest of Italy and 108 in other countries; 196 corresp. mems; Pres. MARCELLO BORDONI; Sec. Prof. PIERO CODA; publ. *PATH* (termly).

Research Institute

NATURAL SCIENCES

Physical Sciences

Vatican Observatory: 00120 Vatican City; tel. 06-69885266; f. 1889; carries out research into dark matter and energy in the cosmos, the acceleration of the universe, quasars, globular clusters; library of 33,000 vols; Dir Fr JOSÉ GABRIEL FUNES; publ. *Newsletter* (2 a year).

Attached centre:

Vatican Observatory Research Group (VORG): see entry for Mount Graham International Observatory in USA chapter.

Libraries and Archives

Vatican City

Archivio Segreto Vaticano (Papal Archives): 00120 Vatican City; f. 1611; attached school: see Schools; Prefect SERGIO PAGANO; publs *Collectanea Archivi Vaticani, Varia*.

Biblioteca Apostolica Vaticana (Vatican Library): 00120 Vatican City; tel. 06-69883301; fax 06-69884795; e-mail bav@ vatlib.it; internet bav.vatican.va/it/ v_home_bav/home_bav.shtml; f. 1451 as a public library by Pope Nicholas V, and provided with staff and a structure by Sixtus IV in 1475; at the present time it contains some 75,000 MSS, 80,000 archival files, 100,000 engravings, 8,000 incunabula, and 1,000,000 other vols; among famous collections which have helped to build up the Library are those of the Dukes of Urbino (1657), of Queen Christina of Sweden (1690), of the Florentine Marquis Capponi (1745), of Barberini (1902), of Chigi (1923), and the Borghese collection, which included many items housed in the Papal Library at Avignon; the Sistine Chapel collection is of the greatest importance to historians of music; among the many rare and precious MSS in the Library are a 4th c. Greek Bible, Vergils from the 4th–6th c., a 4th–5th c. palimpsest of Cicero's *Republic*, autographs of St Thomas Aquinas, Tasso, Petrarch, Boccaccio, Poliziano, Michelangelo, and Luther; houses numismatic colln; attached museums: see Museums and Art Galleries; attached school: see Schools; Protector Cardinal JEAN-LOUIS TAURAN; Prefect Prof. Don RAFFAELE FARINA.

Museums and Art Galleries

Vatican City

Vatican Museums and Galleries: 00120 Vatican City; tel. 06-69883333; fax 06-69885061; internet mv.vatican.va/ StartNew_EN.html; Dir-Gen. Dr FRANCESCO BURANELLI; Administrator Dr FRANCESCO RICCARDI; Sec. Dr EDITH CICERCHIA; publs *Bollettino dei Monumenti, Musei e Gallerie Pontificie*.

Constituent museums:

Collezione d'Arte Religiosa Moderna (Collection of Modern Religious Art): 00120 Vatican City; f. 1973 by Pope Paul VI; paintings, sculptures and drawings offered to the Pope by over 200 artists and donors; Curator Dott. MARIO FERRAZZA.

Padiglione delle Carrozze (Carriage Pavilion): 00120 Vatican City; f. 1973 by Pope Paul VI; in the Vatican gardens, containing carriages, berlins and the first cars used by the Popes; Dir Asst Mons. PIETRO AMATO.

Museo Chiaramonti e Braccio Nuovo (Chiaramonti Museum and 'New Side'): 00120 Vatican City; f. by Pope Pius VII at the beginning of the 19th century, to house the many new findings excavated in that period; exhibits include the statues of the Nile, of Demosthenes and of the Augustus 'of Prima Porta'; Curator Dott. PAOLO LIVERANI.

Museo Gregoriano Egizio (Gregorian Egyptian Museum): 00120 Vatican City; internet mv.vatican.va/3_EN/pages/MEZ/ MEZ_Main.html; f. 1839 by Pope Gregory XVI; contains artefacts from Ancient Egypt; 9 exhibition rooms dating from 2600 BC to 8th century AD incl. hieroglyphic stelae and statues, finds from Ancient Mesopotamia and Syria–Palestine, Hellenistic and Roman Egypt; Curator Dr ALESSIA AMENTA.

Museo Gregoriano Etrusco (Gregorian Etruscan Museum): 00120 Vatican City; internet mv.vatican.va/3_EN/pages/MGE/ MGE_Main.html; f. by Pope Gregory XVI in 1837; contains objects from the Tomba Regolini Galassi of Cerveteri, the Mars of Todi, bronzes, terracottas and jewellery, and Greek vases from Etruscan tombs; Curator Dott. MAURIZIO SANNIBALE.

Museo Gregoriano Profano (Gregorian Museum of Profane Art): 00120 Vatican City; f. by Gregory XVI in 1844 and housed in the Lateran Palace; transferred from fmr site in the Vatican and opened to the public in 1970; Roman sculptures from the Pontifical States; portrait-statue of Sophocles, the Marsyas of the Myronian group of Athena and Marsyas, the Flavian reliefs from the Palace of the Apostolic Chancery; Curator Dott. PAOLO LIVERANI.

Museo Missionario Etnologico (Ethnological Missionary Museum): 00120 Vatican City; internet mv.vatican.va/3_EN/ pages/MET/MET_Main.html; f. by Pius XI in 1926 and housed in the Lateran Palace; transferred from fmr site in the Vatican and opened to the public in 1973; ethnographical collns from all over the world; Curator Rev. ROBERTO ZAGNOLI.

Museo Pio Clementino (Museum of Popes Clement XIV and Pius VI): 00120 Vatican City; f. by Pope Clement XIV (1769–74), and enlarged by his successor, Pius VI (1775–1799); exhibits include the Apollo of Belvedere, Roman copies of the Apoxyomenos by Lysippus, of the Meleager by Skopas and of the Apollo Sauroktonous by Praxiteles; the original Vatican Colln was begun with the Apollo—already in possession of Pope Julius II when he was still a Cardinal, at the end of the 15th century—and the Laocoon Group, found in 1506; Curator Dott. PAOLO LIVERANI.

Museo Pio Cristiano (Christian Museum): 00120 Vatican City; tel. 06-69881349; fax 06-69885061; e-mail ap.musei@scv.va; f. by Pius IX in 1854 and housed in the Lateran Palace; transferred from fmr site in the Vatican and opened to the public in 1970; large colln of sarcophagi; Latin and Greek inscriptions from Christian cemeteries and basilicas; the Good Shepherd; inscriptions from Jewish catacombs; Curator Dr UMBERTO UTRO.

Pinacoteca Vaticana (Vatican Picture Gallery): 00120 Vatican City; internet mv.vatican.va/3_EN/pages/PIN/PIN_Main.html; inaugurated by Pope Pius XI in 1932; incl. paintings by Giotto, Fra Angelico, Raphael, Leonardo da Vinci, Titian and Caravaggio, and the Raphael Tapestries; Curator Dott. ARNOLD NESSELRATH.

Vatican Palaces: 00120 Vatican City; Nicoline Chapel decorated by Beato Angelico (1448–1450); Sistine Chapel restructured by Sixtus IV (1477–1483): frescoes by Perugino, Botticelli, Cosimo Rosselli, Ghirlandaio, Luca Signorelli, Michelangelo; Borgia Apartment: decorated by Pinturic-

chio and his workshop; Chapel of Urban VIII (1631–1635); Raphael Stanze and loggias decorated by Raphael and his assistants; Gallery of Maps (1580–83), Gallery of Tapestries, etc.; Curator Dott. ARNOLD NESSELRATH.

Universities

PONTIFICIA UNIVERSITAS GREGORIANA
(Pontifical Gregorian University)

Piazza della Pilotta 4, 00187 Rome, Italy

Telephone: 06-67011

Fax: 06-67015413

E-mail: segreteria@unigre.it

Internet: www.unigre.it

Founded by St Ignatius Loyola and St Francis Borgia, and constituted by Pope Julius III in 1553; confirmed and established by Pope Gregory XIII in 1582

The central university for ecclesiastical studies is under the direction of the Jesuit Order; Pontificium Institutum Biblicum and Pontificium Institutum Orientalium Studiorum are autonomous colleges associated with the University.

Languages of instruction: Italian, English

Languages of instruction: German, French

Languages of instruction: Spanish, Portuguese

Academic year: October to June (two terms)

Grand Chancellor: H. Em. Card. ZENON GROCHOLEWSKI

Vice-Grand Chancellor: Rev. PETER-HANS KOLVENBACH

Rector Magnificus: Rev. GIANFRANCO GHIRLANDA

Vice-Rector: Rev. FRANCISCO J. EGAÑA

Academic Vice-Rector: Rev. SERGIO BASTIANEL

Administrative Vice-Rector: Rev. VITALE SAVIO

Secretary-General: LUIGI ALLENA

Librarian: Dr MARTA GIORGI DEBANNE

Library of 900,000 vols

Number of teachers: 423

Number of students: 2,949

Publications: *Acta Nuntiaturae Gallicae, Analecta Gregoriana, Archivum Historiae Pontificiae, Documenta Missionalia, Gregorianum, Inculturation, Miscellanea Historiae Pontificiae, Periodica de re morali canonica liturgica, Saggi ISR, Studia Missionalia, Studia Socialia, Tesi Gregoriana*

DEANS AND DIRECTORS

Faculty of Canon Law: M. HILBERT
Faculty of Ecclesiastical History: M. INGLOT
Faculty of Missionary Work: A. WOLANIN
Faculty of Philosophy: K. FLANNERY
Faculty of Social Sciences: J. JELENIC
Faculty of Theology: L. LADARIA
Institute of Psychology: T. HEALY
Institute of Religious Sciences: S. BARLONE
Institute of Spirituality: M. SZENTMÁRTONI
Cultural Heritage of the Church: J. JANSSEN
Interdisciplinary Centre on Social Communication: J. SRAMPICKAL

PROFESSORS

Faculty of Church History (tel. 06-67015410; e-mail inglot@unigre.it):

BENITEZ, J. M., Modern Church History
DE LASALA CLAVER, F., History of the Roman Curia
GUTIERREZ, A., Church History of Latin America
INGLOT, M., History of the Roman Curia
JANSSENS, J., Christian Archaeology – Historical Methodology
MEZZADRI, L., Modern Church History

PFEIFFER, H., Christian Art

Faculty of Law (tel. 06-67015123; e-mail hilbert@unigre.it):

ASTIGUETA, D., Text of Canon Law
CONN, J., Text of Canon Law
GHIRLANDA, G., Canon Law and Theology of Church Law
HILBERT, M., Text of Canon Law
KOWAL, J., Canon Law and Sacraments
SUGAWARA, Y., Text of Canon Law

Faculty of Missiology Work (tel. 06-67015240; e-mail wolanin@unigre.it):

FARAHIAN, E., Missionary Biblical Theology
FUSS, M., Buddhism
SHELKE, C., Comparative Study of Religions
WOLANIN, A., Mission Dogmatics

Faculty of Philosophy (tel. and fax 06-67015441; e-mail filosofia@unigre.it):

BABOLIN, S., Aesthetics and Philosophy of Human Culture
CARUANA, L., Philosophy of Science and Nature
DI MAIO, A., Medieval Philosophy
FLANNERY, K., Greek Philosophy
GILBERT, P., Metaphysics
GORCZYCA, J., Ethics
LECLERC, M., History of Modern Philosophy
LUCAS LUCAS, R., Philosophical Anthropology
NKERAMIHIGO, T., Philosophy of Theology
PANGALLO, M., History of Medieval Philosophy

Faculty of Social Sciences (tel. 06-67015316; e-mail scienzesoc@unigre.it):

BAUGH, L., Film and Television Language
JELENIC, J., Social Sciences
SCARVAGLIERI, G., General Religious Sociology

Faculty of Theology (tel. and fax 06-67015262; e-mail teologia@unigre.it):

ATTARD, M., Moral Theology
BASTIANEL, S., Moral Theology
CALDUCH BENAGES, N., Old Testament Exegesis
CHAPPIN, M., Church History
CONROY, C., Old Testament Exegesis
COSTACURTA, B., Exegesis
FARRUGIA, M., Dogmatic Theology
GALLAGHER, M. P., Fundamental Theology
GRILLI, M., New Testament Exegesis
HENN, W., Dogmatic Theology
LADÁRIA, L., Dogmatic Theology
MEYNET, R., New Testament Exegesis
MILLÁS, J. M., Dogmatic Theology
PASTOR, F., Dogmatic Theology
PECKLERS, K., Liturgy
SCHMITZ, P., Moral Theology
TANNER, N., Patristic Theology
VITALI, D., Dogmatic Theology

Institute of Psychology (tel. 06-67015299; e-mail psicologia@unigre.it):

HEALY, T., Psychology and Statistics
IMODA, F., Psychology
KIELY, B., Psychopathology
VERSALDI, G., Psychology and Psychotherapy

Institute of Spirituality (tel. 06-67015532; e-mail szentmartoni@unigre.it):

COSTA, M., Spiritual Theology
GARCÍA MATEO, R., Spiritual Theology
SECONDIN, B., Pastoral Theology
SZENTMÁRTONI, M., Pastoral Psychology

Institute of Religious Sciences (tel. and fax 06-67015405; e-mail segrsr@unigre.it):

BARLONE, S., Fundamental Theology
FINAMORE, R., Education
SALATIELLO, G., Anthropology

Cultural Heritage of the Church (tel. 06-67015114; e-mail segrbcc@unigre.it):

JANSSENS, J., Church History

PFEIFFER, H., Art History
Interdisciplinary Centre on Social Communication (tel. 06-67015393; fax 06-67015124; e-mail comunicazione@unigre.it):

BABOLIN, S., Symbology
BAUGH, L., Film and Television Language

AFFILIATED INSTITUTES

Filozofsko-Teološki Institut Družbe Isusove: Jordanovac 110, 41001 Zagreb, Croatia; Dir M. STEINER.

Istituto di Filosofia 'Aloisianum': Via Donatello 24, 35123 Padua, Italy; Dir S. BONGIOVANNI.

Institut de Philosophie St Pierre Canisius: Kimwenza, BP 3724, Kinshasa-Gombe, Democratic Republic of the Congo; Rector R. DE HAES; Sec. E. STIENNON.

Instituto Superior de Direito Canônico do Brasil: Rua Benjamin Constant 23, 20241 Rio de Janeiro, Brazil; Dir L. MADERO LOPEZ.

Istituto Superiore per i Formatori: Seminario Vescovile, c/o Almo Collegio Capranica 98, 00186 Rome, Italy; Dir A. RAVAGLIOLI.

Istituto Superiore di Scienze Religiose 'Giuseppe Toniolo': Via S. Benedetto da Norcia 2, 65127 Pescara, Italy; Pres. G. CILLI.

Jesuit School of Philosophy and Theology 'Arrupe College': POB MP320, Mount Pleasant, Harare, Zimbabwe; Pres. A. L. SHIRIMA.

Pontificio Istituto 'Regina Mundi': Lungotevere Tor di Nona 7, 00186 Rome, Italy; Rector C. MCGOVERN.

Priesterseminar Redemptoris Mater des Erzbistum Berlin: Fortunaallee 29, 12683 Berlin, Germany; Rector S. LATINI.

PONTIFICIA UNIVERSITAS LATERANENSIS
(Pontifical Lateran University)

Piazza S. Giovanni in Laterano 4, 00120 Vatican City
Telephone: 06-69886401
Fax: 06-69886508
E-mail: info@pul.it
Internet: www.pul.it
Founded 1773
Language of instruction: Italian
Academic year: October to June

Grand Chancellor: H. E. Card. CAMILLO RUINI
Rector: H. E. Bishop RINO FISICHELLA
General Secretary and Registrar: Rev. Fr GRAHAM BELL
Chief Bursar: Rev. Fr PAOLO NICOLINI

Library of 700,000 vols
Number of teachers: 210
Number of students: 4,000

Publications: *Anthropotes* (Anthropology, Marriage and Family, 2 a year), *Apollinaris* (Questions in Canon and Comparative Law, 2 a year), *Aquinas* (Philosophy, 4 a year), *Centro Vaticano II* (Vatican Council II and its Interpretation, annually), *Civitas et Iustitiae* (Civil and International Law, 2 a year), *Lateranum* (Theology, 4 a year), *Nuntium* (Cultural Journal, 43 a year), *Storia et Documenta Historiae et Iuris* (Roman Law, annually)

DEANS

Faculty of Canon Law: Rev. Prof. MANUEL ARROBA CONDE
Faculty of Civil Law: Rev. Prof. GAETANO DE SIMONE
Faculty of Philosophy: Rev. Prof. ANTONIO LIVI
Faculty of Theology: Rev. Prof. NICOLA CIOLA

INCORPORATED INSTITUTES

Istituto Patristico 'Augustinianum': Via Paolo VI 25, 00193 Rome, Italy; Pres. Rev. Fr ROBERT DODARO.

Istituto Superiore di Teologia Morale 'Accademia Alfonsiana': Via Merulana 31, 00185 Rome, Italy; Pres. Very Rev. Fr SABATINO MAJORANO.

Istituto di Teologia della Vita Consacrata 'Claretianum': Largo Lorenzo Mossa 4, 00165 Rome, Italy; Pres. Rev. Fr SANTIAGO M. GONZALEZ SILVA.

AGGREGATED INSTITUTES

Instituto Diocesano de Estudios Canónicos: C/ Corona 34, 46003 Valencia, Spain; Pres. Mgr IGNACIO PÉREZ DE HEREDIA Y VALLÉ.

Instituto di Direito Canônico 'Pe. Dr Giuseppe Beinto Pegoraro': Av. Nazaré 993, Ipiranga, 04263-100 São Paulo, Brazil; Dir Mgr MARTIN SEGÚ GIRONA.

Institut Supérieur pour l'Enseignement du Droit 'Université La Sagesse' de Beyrouth: POB 50-501, Furn El Chebbak, Baada 1011 2050, Lebanon; teaching of law; Pres. Mgr JOSEPH MERHEJ.

Istituto Teologico di Assisi: Piazza S. Francesco 2, 06082 Assisi Santuario, Italy; Pres. Rev. Mgr VITTORIO PERI.

Istituto Teologico Marchigiano: Via Monte Dago 87, 60131 Ancona, Italy; Pres. Mgr AGOSTINO GASPERONI.

AFFILIATED INSTITUTES

Istituto Filosofico della Facoltà di Teologia di Lugano: Via Buffi 13, CP 4663, 6904 Lugano, Switzerland; Rector Prof. LIBERO GEROSA.

Istituto Teologico Abruzzese-Molisano di Chieti: Via Nicoletto Vernia 1, 66100 Chieti, Italy; Prefect of Studies Fr LUIGI GENTILE.

Istituto Teologico 'S. Giovanni Crisostomo' del Seminario di S. Pietroburgo: Vysshaya Dukhovnaya Seminariya 'Maria-Tsaritsa Apostolov', Ul. 1 aya Krasnoarmeiskaya 11, 198005 St Petersburg, Russia; Prefect of Studies (vacant) Fr JOSÉ MARÍA VEGAS.

Istituto Teologico San Giuseppe del Seminario di Vilnius: Juozapo Kunigu Seminarija, Kalvariju 325, 2021 Vilnius, Latvia; Prefect of Studies Fr HANS FRIEDRICH FISCHER.

Istituto Teologico del Seminario di Denver: St John Vianney Theological Seminary, 1300 South Steele St, Denver, CO 80210-2599, USA; Prefect of Studies Dr ANTHONY LILLES.

Istituto Teologico del Seminario di Guadalajara: Seminario Mayor, Santo Domingo 1120, Col. Chapalita, 45040 Guadalajara, Jal., Mexico; Prefect of Studies Prof. FRANCISCO GARCÍA VELARDE.

Istituto Teologico del Seminario di Györ: Gyori Hittudományi Főiskola, Káptalandomb 7, 9021 Györ, Hungary; Prefect of Studies Fr ISTVÁN BOGNÁR.

Istituto Teologico del Seminario di Kamyanets - Podilskyi 'Seminarium Maius S. Spiritus': Provulok O. Wanagsa 14, 32000 Gorodok, Khmelnystka obl., Ukraine; Prefect of Studies Fr JERZY.

Istituto Teologico del Seminario di Montréal: Institut de formation théologique, 2065 rue Sherbrooke Ouest, Montréal, QB H3H 1G6, Canada; Dir Fr CHRISTIAN LÉPINE.

Istituto Teologico del Seminario di Riga: Katolu Teologijas Augstskola, Katolu iela 16, 1003 Riga, Latvia; Prefect of Studies Fr PAULS KLAVINS.

Istituto Teologico del Seminario Roermond: Grootseminarie Rolduc, Heyendallaan 82, 6464 EP Kerkrade, Netherlands; Rector Mgr JOHANNES VRIES.

Istituto Teologico 'Willibrordhuis' della Diocesi di Haarlem: Willibrordhuis, Bekslaan 11, 2114 CB Vogelenzang, Netherlands; Prefect of Studies Fr J. MANUEL TERCERO SIMÓN.

Institutul Teologic Romano-Catolic: Str. Văscăuteanu 6, 700462 Iaşi, Romania; Prefect of Studies Fr STEFAN LUPU.

Institutul Teologic Romano-Catolic Universitar: Str. Bibliotecii 3, 510009 Alba Iulia, Romania; Prefect of Studies Fr GÉZA TÓFALVI.

Oratory of St Philip Neri: 1372 King St, West Toronto, ON MGK 1H3, Canada; Prefect of Studies Rev. DEREK CROSS.

Studio Filosofico del Seminario di Montreal: Institut de Formation Théologique de Montréal, 2065 rue Sherbrooke Ouest, Montréal, QC H3H 1G6, Canada; Dir of Studies Fr CHRISTIAN LÉPINE.

Studio Filosofico del Seminario Patriarcale Latino di Gerusalemme: Seminaire Patriarchal Latin, POB 14152, Jerusalem, Israel; Rector Fr MAROUN LAHMAN.

Studio Teologico di Curitiba 'Studium Theologicum': CP 153, 80001-970 Curitiba, PR, Brazil; Located at: Av. Presidente Getúlio Vargas 1193, 80250-180 Curitiba, PR, Brazil, Dir Fr VALDINEI DE JESUS RIBEIRO.

Studio Teologico del Seminario di Gerusalemme: Séminaire Patriarcal Latin, POB 14152, Jerusalem, Israel; Rector Fr MAROUN LAHHAM.

Studio Teologico 'S. Zeno': Via Seminario 8, 37129 Verona, Italy; Dir Fr AUGUSTO BARBI.

INSTITUTES WITHIN THE PREMISES

Pontifical John Paul II Institute for Studies on Marriage and Family: Pres. H. E. Bishop RINO FISICHELLA.

Pontificium Institutum Pastorale: Piazza S. Giovanni in Laterano 4, 00184 Rome, Italy; Pres. Rev. Prof. DENIS BIJU-DUVAL.

PONTIFICIA UNIVERSITÀ DELLA SANTA CROCE
(Pontifical University of the Holy Cross)

Piazza di Sant'Apollinare 49, 00186 Rome, Italy
Telephone: 06-681641
Fax: 06-68164400
E-mail: santacroce@pusc.it
Internet: www.pusc.it
Founded 1985; university status 1998
Private control (Opus Dei)

Chancellor: Rev. Bishop JAVIER ECHEVARRÍA
Vice-Chancellor: Mgr Prof. FERNANDO OCÁRIZ
Rector: Rev. Prof. MARIANO FAZIO
Vice-Rector: Rev. Prof. HÉCTOR FRANCESCHI
General Secretary: Rev. ALFONSO MONROY
Director of Academic Affairs: Rev. Prof. PHILIP GOYRET
Director of Development: Dott. PABLO RODRÍGUEZ
Librarian: Dott. JUAN DIEGO RAMÍREZ

Number of teachers: 237 teachers (125 teachers and 33 visiting teachers in the 4 schools; 29 teachers and 50 visiting teachers in the Higher Institute for Religious Studies)
Number of students: 1,465 students (925 students in the 4 schools; 540 students in the Higher Institute for Religious Studies)
Publications: *Rivista Internazionale Quadrimestrale di Diritto Canonico*, *Rivista Inter-*

nazionale Semestrale di Filosofia, Rivista Semestrale di Teologia

HEADS OF SCHOOLS

School of Canon Law: Rev. Prof. EDUARDO BAURA
School of Institutional Social Communication: Prof. NORBERTO GONZÁLEZ GAITANO
School of Philosophy: Rev. Prof. LUIS ROMERA
School of Theology: Rev. Prof. PAUL O'CALLAGHAN
Higher Institute for Religious Studies: Rev. Prof. MARCO PORTA

PONTIFICIA UNIVERSITÀ SAN TOMMASO D'AQUINO
(St Thomas Aquinas Pontifical University)

Largo Angelicum 1, 00184 Rome, Italy

Telephone: 06-67021

Fax: 06-6790407

E-mail: segreteria@pust.urbe.it

Internet: www.angelicum.org

Founded College founded 1580; became University 1909; present title conferred 1963

Languages of instruction: Italian, English

Academic year: October to June

Grand Chancellor: Rev. CARLOS AZPIROZ COSTA
Rector Magnificus: Rev. FRANCESCO COMPAGNONI
Administrator: Rev. DANIELE CARA
Secretary-General (Registrar): Rev. MARCO REALI
Librarian: Rev. MIGUEL ITZA

Library of 200,000 vols

Number of teachers: 111

Number of students: 1,500

Publications: *Angelicum, Istituto S. Tommaso: Studi, Oikonomia* (ethics and social sciences, 3 a year), *Rassegna di Letteratura Tomistica, Studia Univ. S. Thomae In Urbe*

DEANS

Faculty of Canon Law: Rev. F. RAMOS
Faculty of Philosophy: Rev. C. MOREROD
Faculty of Social Sciences: Rev. Sr H. ALFORD
Faculty of Theology: Rev. M. SALVATI

DIRECTORS

Institute of St Thomas: Prof. MARGHERITA MARIA ROSSI
Institute of Spirituality: Rev. JOSEPH PAN THAN THANH
'Mater Ecclesiae' Institute: Rev. M. SALVATI

PONTIFICIA UNIVERSITAS URBANIANA
(Pontifical Urbanian University)

Via Urbano VIII 16, 00165 Rome, Italy

Telephone: 06-69889611

Fax: 06-69881871

E-mail: segreteria@urbaniana.edu

Internet: www.urbaniana.edu

Founded 1627 by Pope Urban VIII

Language of instruction: Italian

Academic year: October to June

Chancellor: Cardinal CRESCENZIO SEPE
Vice-Chancellor (vacant)
Rector Magnificus: Rev. Mgr AMBROGIO SPREAFICO
Vice-Rector: Rev. Mgr GUIDO MAZZOTTA
Secretary-General: Rev. P. GIOVANNI MARCONCINI
Librarian: Rev. Fr MAREK ROSTKOWSKI

Number of teachers: 158 (incl. 40 full-time)

Number of students: 1,659

Publications: *Annales, Bibliografia Missionaria, Euntes Docete, Urbaniana*

DEANS

Faculty of Canon Law: Rev. Prof. VELASIO DE PAOLIS
Faculty of Missiology: Rev. Prof. GIUSEPPE CAVALLOTTO
Faculty of Philosophy: Rev. Prof. GUIDO MAZZOTTA
Faculty of Theology: Rev. Prof. FRANCESCO CICCIMARRA

PROFESSORS

Faculty of Canon Law:

D'AURIA, A., General Norms
DE PAOLIS, V., Matrimony and Canon Law
SABBARESE, L., Matrimony and Canon Law
SALACHAS, D., Oriental Canon Law
SASTRE SANTOS, E., History of Canon Law

Faculty of Missiology:

BARREDA, J., Ecumenism
CAVALLOTTO, G., Catechesis
COLZANI, G., Missionary Systematic Theology
DINH DUC, D., Missiography
DOTOLO, C., History and Phenomenology of Religions
GIGLIONI, P., Liturgical Spirituality
KAROTEMPREL, S., Theology of Mission
ODASSO, G., Theology of Religions
TREVISIOL, A., History of Missions

Faculty of Philosophy:

CONTAT, A., Logic, Philosophy of Knowledge
MAZZOTTA, G., Metaphysics
MICCOLI, P., Modern and Contemporary History
MURA, G., Hermeneutics
ONAH, I. G., Methodology, Anthropology
VENDEMIATI, A., General Ethics

Faculty of Theology:

BIGUZZI, G., New Testament Exegesis
CICCIMARRA, F., Canon Law
COLOMBO, G., Moral Theology
DEIANA, G., Biblical Languages and Scriptures
EGBULEFU, J., Sacramental Theology
GONZALEZ FERNANDEZ, F., Church History
ILUNGA MUYA, J., Fundamental Theology
NOCE, C., Patrology
PIRC, J., Ecclesiology
RIZZI, G., Old Testament Exegesis
SCHMID, E., Moral Theology
SPADA, D., Dogmatic Theology
SPREAFICO, A., Old Testament Exegesis
ZUCCARO, C., Special Moral Theology

DIRECTORS

Department of Languages: Rev. GIOVANNI DEIANA
Department of Social Communication: CLAUDIO PIGHIN
Affiliated Institutes: Rev. P. GIUSEPPE IULIANO
Institute for Missionary Catechesis and Spirituality: Rev. LUCIANO MEDDI
Institute for the Study of Atheism: Rev. Prof. GODFREY I. ONAH
Chinese Study Centre: Rev. PAUL PANG

UNIVERSITÀ PONTIFICIA SALESIANA
(Salesian Pontifical University)

Piazza Ateneo Salesiano 1, 00139 Rome, Italy

Telephone: 06-872901

Fax: 06-87290222

E-mail: segreteria@ups.urbe.it

Internet: www.unisal.it

Founded 1940; university status granted by Pope Paul VI 1973

Language of instruction: Italian

Academic year: October to June (2 semesters)

Chancellor: Very Rev. PASCUAL CHÁVEZ VILLANUEVA
Rector: Very Rev. MARIO TOSO
Vice-Rectors: Very Rev. CARLO NANNI, Very Rev. RICCARDO TONELLI
Administrator: Very Rev. ROQUE CELLA
Secretary-General: Very Rev. JAROSŁAW ROCHOWIAK
Librarian: Very Rev. JUAN PICCA

Library of 750,000 vols

Number of teachers: 210

Number of students: 2,625

Publications: *Orientamenti Pedagogici* (6 a year), *Salesianum* (4 a year)

DEANS

Faculty of Canon Law: Very Rev. SABINO ARDITO
Faculty of Education: Prof. NATALE ZANNI
Faculty of Letters (Christian and Classics): Very Rev. BIAGIO AMATA
Faculty of Philosophy: Very Rev. SCARIA THURUTHIYIL
Faculty of Social Communication Sciences: Very Rev. TADEUSZ LEWICKI
Faculty of Theology: Very Rev. GEORGIO ZEVINI
Department of Youth Pastoral Theology and Catechetics: Very Rev. RICCARDO TONELLI
Postgraduate School of Clinical Psychology: Very Rev. PIO SCILLIGO

PROFESSORS

Faculty of Canon Law (tel. 06-87290639; fax 06-87290258; e-mail fdc@ups.urbe.it):

ARDITO, S., Text of Canon Law
GRAULICH, M., Foundation and History of Canon Law

Faculty of Education (tel. 06-87290426; fax 06-87290656; e-mail fse@ups.urbe.it):

ARTO, A., Developmental Psychology
BAJZEK, J., Sociology of Religion
CASELLA, F., History of Pedagogy
COMOGLIO, M., Didactics
DE SOUZA, C., Anthropology and Catechesis
MACARIO, L., Pedagogical Developmental Methodology
MALIZIA, G., Sociology and School Politics
MION, R., Sociology of Family and Youth
MORANTE, G., Methodology of Catechetics
NANNI, C., Philosophy of Education
ORLANDO, V., Social Pedagogy
PELLEREY, M., General Didactics
TRENTI, Z., Pastoral and Catechesis
VALLABARAJ, J., Catechesis
ZANNI, N., Didactics

Faculty of Letters (Christian and Classics) (tel. 06-87290304; fax 06-87290641; e-mail lettere@ups.urbe.it):

AMATA, B., Greek and Latin Patristics
BRACCHI, R., History of the Greek and Latin Languages
DAL COVOLO, E., Ancient Christian Greek Literature

Faculty of Philosophy (tel. 06-87290491; fax 06-87290640; e-mail filosofia@ups.urbe.it):

ABBÀ, G., Ethics
ALESSI, A., Metaphysics
CHENIS, C., Philosophy
MANTOVANI, M., Metaphysics
MARIN, M., History of Philosophy
PALUMBIERI, S., Anthropology
THURUTHIYIL, S., History of Philosophy
TOSO, M., Social and Political Philosophy

Faculty of Social Communication Sciences (tel. 06-87290331; fax 06-87290536; e-mail fsc@ups.urbe.it; internet fscs.ups.urbe.it):

COSTA, G., Journalism
LEVER, F., Theory and Technics of Television/Mass Media and Catechesis
LEWICKI, T., Theory and Technics of Theatre

Faculty of Theology (tel. 06-87290297; fax 06-87290556; e-mail teologia@ups.urbe.it):

ANTHONY, F. V.., Pastoral Theology
BERGAMELLI, F., Patrology
BOZZOLO, A., Dogmatics
BUZZETTI, C., New Testament Literature
CARLOTTI, P., Moral Theology
CASTELLANO, A., Dogmatics
CAVIGLIA, G., Fundamental Theology
CIMOSA, M., Old Testament
COFFELE, G., Fundamental Theology
ESCUDERO, A., Dogmatics
FRIGATO, S., Moral Theology
GALLO, L., Dogmatics
MARITANO, M., Ancient Church History and Patrology
MERLO, P., Moral Theology
MOSETTO, F., New Testament
PERRENCHIO, F., New Testament
PICCA, J., New Testament
SEMERARO, C., Contemporary Church History
SODI, M., Liturgy
STRUS, A., Old Testament
TONELLI, R., Pastoral Theology
VICENT, R., Old Testament
VINCENT, A. F., Pastoral Theology
WIRTH, M., Spirituality
ZEVINI, G., New Testament

ATTACHED RESEARCH INSTITUTES

Historical Institute of Canon Law.
Institute of Catechetics.
Institute of Didactics.
Institute of Dogmatic Theology.
Institute of Pastoral Theology.
Institute of Pedagogic Methodology.
Institute of Psychology.
Institute of Sociology of Education.
Institute of Spirituality.
Institute of Theory and History of Education.
Observatory on Youth.
Psychopedagogical Research Centre.
Studies on Don Bosco Centre.

ATTACHED INSTITUTES

Centre Saint-Augustin: Villa contiguë au Village S.O.S., BP 15222, Dakar, Senegal; Dean Very Rev. BONAVENTURA PEDEMONTE.

Département de Philosophie de l'Université Catholique de l'Afrique Centrale: BP 11628, Yaoundé, Cameroon; Dean Rev GABRIEL NDINGA.

Departamento de Filosofía del Instituto de Teología para Religiosos: 3a Avda con 6a Transversal (H. B. Pinto), Apdo 68865 Altamira, Caracas 1062-A, Venezuela; Dean Rev. PABLO PERON.

Don Bosco International Institute: Via Caboto 27, 10129 Turin, Italy; section of Roman Faculty of Theology; Vice-Dean Very Rev. SABINO FRIGATO.

Institut de Philosophie 'Saint-Joseph-Mukasa': Nkol-Bisson, BP 1859, Yaoundé, Cameroon; Dean Rev. ELIE DELPLACE.

Institut de Théologie 'S. François de Sales': BP 882, Lubumbashi, Democratic Republic of the Congo; Dean Very Rev. JEAN-LUC VANDE KERKHOVE.

Instituto Salesiano de Estudios Teológicos 'Cristo Buen Pastor': Hipólito Yrigoyen 3951, 1208 Buenos Aires, Argentina; Dir Very Rev. ROBERTO CASTELLO.

Instituto 'Santo Tomás de Aquino': Rua Itutinga 300, 30535-640 Belo Horizonte, MG, Brazil; Dean Prof. MARIA HELENA MORRA.

Institut Superior de Cièncias Religioses 'Don Bosco': Avda Card. Vidal i Barraquer 1, 08035 Barcelona, Spain; Dean Very Rev. MIGUEL A. CALAVIA CALAVIA.

Instituto Superior de Communication Social: Yapeyú 197, 1202 Buenos Aires, Argentina; Dean Very Rev. JOSÉ ELLERO.

Instituto Superior de Pastoral Catequetica de Chile: Miguel Claro 337, Santiago, Chile; Dean Very Rev. ENRIQUE GARCIA AHUMADA.

Instituto de Teología para Religiosos–ITER: 3a Avda con 6a Transversal (H. B. Pinto), Apdo 68865 Altamira, Caracas 1062-A, Venezuela; Dean Very Rev. PABLO PERON.

Instituto Universitario Salesiano 'Padre Ojeda': Avda El Liceo, Apdo 43, Los Teques, 1201-A Venezuela; Dean Very Rev. RAÚL BIORD CASTILLO.

Philosophische-Theologische Hochschule der Salesianer: Don Bosco-Str. 1, 83671 Benediktbeuern, Germany; Rector Very Rev. KARL BOPP.

Salesian House Philosophical Studies, Nave: Centro di Studi 'Paolo VI', Via S. Giovanni Bosco 1, 25075 Nave, Italy; Dean Prof. PAOLO ZINI.

Salesian House Philosophical Studies, Santiago: Avda Lo Cañas 3636, Casilla 53, La Florida, Santiago, Chile; Dean Very Rev. SEPÚLVEDA ANGEL MERCADO.

Salesian House Philosophical Studies, Yercaud: The Retreat, Yercaud 636601, India; Dean Very Rev. SUSAI AMALRAJ.

Salesian House Theological Studies, Bangalore: Kristu Jyoti College, Krishnarajapuram, Bangalore 560036, India; Dean Very Rev. DOMINIC VELIATH.

Salesian House Theological Studies, Barcelona: Avda Card. Vidal i Barraquer 1, 08035 Barcelona, Spain; Dean Very Rev. MIGUEL A. CALAVIA CALAVIA.

Salesian House Theological Studies 'D. Bosco': Ronda D. Bosco 5, 28044 Madrid, Spain; Dean Very Rev. EUGENIO ALBURQUERQUE.

Salesian House Theological Studies, Guadalajara: Tonalá 344, Ap. p. 66, Tlaquepaque, 45500 Guadalajara, Mexico; Dean Very Rev. JAVIER RUIZ GONZÁLEZ.

Salesian House Theological Studies, Guatemala: 20 Avda 13 45, Zona 11, Guatemala City, Guatemala 01011, CA; Dean Very Rev. MARIO FIANDRI.

Salesian House Theological Studies, Jerusalem: St Paul, 26 Shmuel Hanagid St, POB 7336, 91072 Jerusalem, Israel; Dean Very Rev. FRANCESCO MOSETTO.

Salesian House Theological Studies, Manila: POB 8206, CPO 1700, Parañaque City, Metro. Manila, Philippines; Dean Very Rev. RENATO DE GUZMAN.

Salesian House Theological Studies, Meghalaya: Sacred Heart Theological College, Mawlai, Shillong 793008, Meghalaya, India; Dean Very Rev. JAMES POONTHURUTHIL.

Salesian House Theological Studies, Messina: Via del Pozzo 43, CP 28, 98121 Messina, Italy; Dean Very Rev. GIUSEPPE RUTA.

Salesian House Theological Studies, São Paulo: Rua Pio XI 1100 (Lapa), 05060-001 São Paulo, Brazil; Dean Very Rev. RONALDO ZACHARIAS.

Salesian Institute of Philosophy: Divya Daan, College Rd, Nasik 422005, India; Dean Very Rev. ASHLEY MIRANDA.

Colleges

ATHENAEUM PONTIFICIUM REGINA APOSTOLORUM

Via degli Aldobrandeschi 190, 00163 Rome, Italy
Telephone: 06-66527800
Fax: 06-66527814
E-mail: segreteria@upra.org
Internet: www.upra.org
Founded 1993
Rector: Fr PAOLO SCARAFONI
Secretary-General: Fr LUCA MARIA GALLIZIA

DEANS

Faculty of Bioethics: Fr GONZALO MIRANDA
Faculty of Philosophy: Fr MICHAEL RYAN
Faculty of Theology: Fr THOMAS WILLIAMS

PONTIFICIA FACOLTÀ DI SCIENZE DELL'EDUCAZIONE 'AUXILIUM'

Via Cremolino 141, 00166 Rome, Italy
Telephone: 06-6157201
Fax: 06-61564640
E-mail: auxilium@pcn.net
Internet: www.pfse-auxilium.org
Founded 1954
Academic year: October to July
Grand Chancellor: Rev. PASCUAL CHAVEZ
President: BIANCA TORAZZA
Secretary: M. GIOVANNA CERUTI
Number of teachers: 60
Number of students: 350
Publication: *Rivista di Scienze dell' Educazione* (3 a year).

PONTIFICIA FACOLTÀ TEOLOGICA DI S. BONAVENTURA

Via del Serafico 1, 00142 Rome, Italy
Telephone: 06-51503206
Fax: 06-5192067
E-mail: seraphicum1@ofmconv.org
Internet: www.bon.ofmconv.org
Founded 1587, re-founded 1905
Grand Chancellor: Most Rev. AGOSTINO GARDIN
President: Rev. Fr GIOVANNI IAMMARRONE
Vice-President: Rev. Fr MAURIZIO WSZOLEK
Secretary: Rev. Fr JULIAN ZAMBANINI
Librarian: Rev. Fr BONAVENTURA DANZA
Library of 210,000 vols
Number of teachers: 41
Number of students: 130
Publication: *Miscellanea Francescana* (quarterly).

PONTIFICIA FACOLTÀ TEOLOGICA 'MARIANUM'

Viale Trenta Aprile 6, 00153 Rome, Italy
Telephone: 06-58391601
Fax: 06-5880292
E-mail: marianum@marianum.it
Internet: www.marianum.it
Founded 1950
Academic year: October to July
Grand Chancellor: Rev. Fr ANGEL M. RUIZ GORNICA
President: Rev. Fr SILVANO M. MAGGIANI
Secretary: Sister ORNELLA DI ANGELO
Library of 109,000 vols on Mariological studies
Number of teachers: 55
Number of students: 318
Publication: *Marianum* (2 a year).

PONTIFICIA FACOLTÀ TEOLOGICA TERESIANUM

Piazza San Pancrazio 5A, 00152 Rome, Italy
Telephone: 06-58540248
Fax: 06-58540243
E-mail: segreteria@teresianum.org
Internet: www.teresianum.org
Founded 1935
Academic year: October to June
Grand Chancellor: Most Rev. Fr LUIS AROS-
TEGUI GAMBOA
President: Fr VIRGILIO PASQUETTO
Secretary-General: Fr ADRIAN ATTARD
Librarian: Fr ARTURO BELTRAN
Library of 500,000 vols (open to the public)
Number of teachers: 51
Number of students: 450
Publications: *Bibliographia Internationalis
Spiritualitatis*, *Studia Theologica*, *Teresia-
num* (specialist review, 2 a year).

ATTACHED INSTITUTE

Pontificio Istituto di Spiritualità: f. 1957;
30 teachers; 300 students; centre for bibliographical research in field of spiritual theology; Moderator Fr BENITO GOYA.

PONTIFICIO ATENEO S. ANSELMO

Piazza Cavalieri di Malta 5, 00153 Rome,
Italy
Telephone: 06-5791401
Fax: 06-5791402
E-mail: segreteria@santanselmo.org
Internet: www.santanselmo.org
Founded 1687
Language of instruction: Italian
Academic year: October to June
Grand Chancellor: Most Rev. Fr NOTKER
WOLF
Rector Magnificus: Rev. Fr MARK SHERIDAN
Registrar: Rev. Fr STEFANO VISINTIN
Librarian: Rev. Fr JAMES LEACHMAN
Treasurer: Rev. Fr GERARDO GAREGNANI
Library of 131,000 vols
Number of teachers: 78
Number of students: 423
Publications: *Corpus Consuetudinum Mon-
asticarum*, *Ecclesia Orans* (Liturgical Inst.
Review), *Rerum Ecclesiasticarum Docu-
menta* (Critical Editions of Liturgical
Texts), *Studia Anselmiana*

DEANS

Faculty of Philosophy: Rev. Mons. ANICETO
MOLINARO
Faculty of Theology: Rev. Fr DANIEL HOMBER-
GEN
Pontifical Liturgical Institute: Rev. Fr JUAN
JAVIER FLORES ARCAS

PONTIFICIO ATENEO ANTONIA

Via Merulana 124, 00185 Rome, Italy
Telephone: 06-70373502
Fax: 06-70373604
E-mail: segreteriapaa@ofm.org
Internet: www.antonianum.ofm.org
Founded 1933
Franciscan International University
Grand Chancellor: Most Rev. J. RODRÍGUEZ
CARBALLO
Rector Magnificus: Rev. Fr JOHANNES B.
FREYER
Vice-Rector (vacant)
Secretary-General: Rev. Fr JORGE HORTA
Librarian: Rev. Fr MARCELLO SARDELLI
Library of 500,000 vols
Number of professors: 145
Publication: *Antonianum*

DEANS

Faculty of Biblical Science and Archaeology:
Rev. Fr GIOVANNI C. BOTTINI
Faculty of Canon Law: Rev. Fr PRIAMO ETZI
Faculty of Philosophy: Rev. Fr STÉPHANE
OPPES
Faculty of Theology: Rev. Fr VINCENZO
BATTAGLIA

DIRECTORS

Higher School of Medieval and Franciscan
Studies: Rev. Fr A. CACCIOTTI
Higher Institute of Religious Studies: Sr M.
MELONE
Institute of Ecumenical Studies: Rev. Fr R.
GIRALDO
Institute of Spirituality: Rev. Fr P. MARTI-
NELLI

PONTIFICIO ISTITUTO DI ARCHEOLOGIA CRISTIANA

Via Napoleone III 1, 00185 Rome, Italy
Telephone: 06-4465574
Fax: 06-4469197
E-mail: piac@piac.it
Internet: www.piac.it
Founded 1925 by Pope Pius XI
Academic year: November to May
Grand Chancellor: Bishop ZENON GROCHO-
LEWSKI
Rector: Prof. DANILO MAZZOLENI
Secretary: R. P. Dr SALVATORE BURRAFATO
Librarian and Prefect of Collections: Dr
GIORGIO NESTORI
Library of 60,000 vols
Number of teachers: 8
Number of students: 80
Publications: *Inscriptiones Christianae Urbis
Romae*, *Monumenti di Antichità Cristiana*,
Rivista di Archeologia Cristiana, *Roma
Sotterranea Cristiana*, *Studi di Antichità
Cristiana*, *Sussidi allo Studio delle Antic-
hità Cristiane*

PROFESSORS

BISCONTI, F., Christian Iconography
DATTRINO, L., Patristics
FIOCCHI NICOLAI, V., Christian Cemeteries
and Topography of Ancient Rome
GUIDOBALDI, F., Ancient Sacred Architecture
HEID, S., Hagiography and Liturgy of the
Early Church
MAZZOLENI, D., Classical and Christian Epi-
graphy
PERGOLA, PH., 'Orbis Christianus' and Clas-
sical Topography
RAMIERI, A. M., Art History
SPERA, L., Christian Topography of Rome

PONTIFICIUM INSTITUTUM BIBLICUM

Via della Pilotta 25, 00187 Rome, Italy
Telephone: 06-695266179
Fax: 06-695266211
E-mail: pibsegr@biblico.it
Internet: www.biblico.it
Founded 1909 by Pope Pius X for scriptural
studies; Faculty of Ancient Oriental Stu-
dies added 1932; Pontifical Biblical Insti-
tute of Jerusalem founded 1927 (branch of
Roman Institute)
Associated with the Pontifical Gregorian
University (see above)
Academic year: October to June
Rector: Rev. STEPHEN PISANO
Secretary: CARLO VALENTINO
Librarian: Rev. J. DUGAN
Number of teachers: 40

Number of students: 310
Publications: *Acta Pont. Inst. Biblici*
(annually), *Analecta Biblica*, *Analecta
Orientalia*, *Biblica* (4 a year), *Biblica et
Orientalia*, *Elenchus of Biblica* (annually),
Orientalia (4 a year), *Studia Pohl*, *Sub-
sidia Biblica*

DEANS

Faculty of Ancient Oriental Studies: Rev. K.
STOCK
Faculty of Biblical Studies: Rev. J.-N. ALETTI

PROFESSORS

Faculty of Ancient Oriental Studies:
ALTHANN, R., Languages and Literature of
Ancient Israel
GIANTO, A., Semitic Philology and Linguis-
tics
MAYER, W., Accadian Language and Lit-
erature
MORRISON, C., Syriac and Targumic-Ara-
maic Languages
Faculty of Biblical Studies:
ALETTI, J.-N., New Testament Exegesis
BARBIERO, G., Old Testament Exegesis
BOVATI, P., Old Testament Exegesis
LUZARRAGA, J., New Testament Exegesis
NEUDECKER, R., Rabbinic Literature
O'TOOLE, R. F., New Testament Exegesis
PISANO, S., Textual Criticism
SIEVERS, J., History and Literature of the
Intertestamental Period
SIMIAN-YOFRE, H., Old Testament Exegesis
SKA, J. L., Old Testament Exegesis

PONTIFICIO ISTITUTO DI MUSICA SACRA

Via di Torre Rossa 21, 00165 Rome, Italy
Telephone: 06-6638792
Fax: 06-6622453
E-mail: pims@musica-sacra.va
Internet: www.vatican.va
Founded 1911 by Pope Pius X
Academic year: October to June
Grand Chancellor: HE Rev. ma Mgr ZENON
GROCHOLEWSKI
President: Mgr VALENTINO MISERACHS GRAU
Secretary: GIUSEPPE MORETTI
Librarian: ANTONIO ADDAMIANO
Library of 40,000 vols
Number of teachers: 18
Number of students: 100
Publication: *Calendar* (annually).

PONTIFICIO ISTITUTO ORIENTALE
(Pontifical Oriental Institute)

Piazza Santa Maria Maggiore 7, 00185
Rome, Italy
Telephone: 06-4474170
Fax: 06-4465576
E-mail: piosgr@pio.urbe.it
Internet: www.pio.urbe.it
Founded 1917 by Pope Benedict XV for the
benefit of Eastern and Western scholars
both Catholic and non-Catholic, interested
in Oriental ecclesiastical questions
Associated with the Pontifical Gregorian
University (see above)
Rector: Rev. Prof. HÉCTOR VALL VILARDELL
Secretary: MAURIZIO DOMENICUCCI
Librarian: Rev. FRANÇOIS GICK
Library of 171,000 vols
Number of teachers: 71
Number of students: 350
Publications: *Anaphorae Orientales*, *Kano-
nika*, *Orientalia Christiana Analecta*,
Orientalia Christiana Periodica

DEANS

Faculty of Oriental Canon Law: Rev. CYRIL VASIL
Faculty of Oriental Ecclesiastical Studies: Rev. EDWARD FERRUGIA

PROFESSORS

ARRANZ, L. M., Oriental Liturgy
CECCARELLI MOROLLI, D., Oriental Canon Law
FARRUGIA, E., Oriental Theology
GARGANO, G., Oriental Patrology
GIRAUDO, C., Liturgy and Dogmatic Theology
LUISIER, P., Coptic Patrology and Language
NEDUNGATT, G., Oriental Canon Law
RUGGERI, V., Byzantine History and Archaeology
SENYK, S., Ukrainian Church History
SIMON, C., Slavic History
TAFT, R., Byzantine Liturgy
VALL VILARDELL, H., Ecumenism
VASIL, C., Oriental Canon Law

YOUSSIF, P., Syriac Patrology
ŽUŽEK, I., Oriental Canon Law

PONTIFICIO ISTITUTO DI STUDI ARABI E D'ISLAMISTICA

Viale di Trastevere 89, 00153 Rome, Italy
Telephone: 06-58392611
Fax: 06-5882595
E-mail: info@pisai.org
Founded 1949
Academic year: October to June

Director: Fr JUSTO LACUNZA BALDA
Librarian: Fr GIAN BATTISTA MAFFI

Library of 25,000 vols
Number of teachers: 10
Number of students: 45

Publications: *Encounter* (Documents for Christian-Muslim Understanding, 10 a year), *Etudes Arabes* (annually), *Islamochristiana* (annually).

Schools

Scuola Vaticana di Biblioteconomia (Vatican School of Library Services): 00120 Vatican City; tel. 06-69879526; fax 06-69879525; e-mail scuola@vatlib.it; internet www-urbs.vatlib.it/scuola; f. 1934; attached to Vatican Apostolic Library; 6 teachers; 48 students a year; Dir Prof. Don RAFFAELE FARINA.

Scuola Vaticana di Paleografia, Diplomatica e Archivistica (Vatican School of Paleography, Diplomacy and Archive Science): 00120 Vatican City; tel. 06-69883595; fax 06-69881377; e-mail asv@asv.va; attached to Papal Archives; Dir SERGIO PAGANO; publ. *Littera Antiqua*.

VENEZUELA

The Higher Education System

Institutions of higher education predate Venezuela's independence from Spain in 1830, the oldest being Universidad Central de Venezuela, which was founded in 1721. The next oldest institution is Universidad de los Andes, which was founded in 1785 (current status 1810). The Ministry of Higher Education has supreme authority over higher education, which consists of public and private universities, polytechnic institutes and an 'open' university (for distance-learning and continuing education). In 2003/04 there were 48 universities with 626,837 students.

The main requirement for admission to higher education is the Bachillerato, the secondary school certificate. The undergraduate degree is the Licenciado, which lasts four to five years. (Alternatively, a professional title may be awarded.)

Following the award of the Licenciado, graduates may study for a further year for the award of the Especialización, which indicates specialization in a particular area or subject. Alternatively, graduates study for two years after the Licenciado for the Masters (Maestría) degree, which culminates with the submission of a thesis. Finally, the highest university degree is the Doctorado, a research-based degree lasting three years following the award of either the Maestría or Especializacion.

Post-secondary technical and vocational education is offered by technological institutes (institutos universitarios de tecnología) and university colleges (colegios universitarios) but the qualifications are regarded as sub-degree level. The main qualification is the Técnico Superior, a three-year course comprising mostly of practical study.

Learned Societies

GENERAL

Academia Venezolana (Academy of Venezuela): Bolsa a San Francisco, Caracas 1010; tel. (212) 481-87-16; f. 1883; corresp. of the Real Academia Española (Madrid); 24 mems; library: see Libraries and Archives; Dir LUIS PASTORI; Sec. LUIS BELTRAN GUERRERO; publs *Boletín* (quarterly), *Clásicos Venezolanos*.

ARCHITECTURE AND TOWN PLANNING

Asociación de Agrimensores de Venezuela (Surveyors' Association): c/o Colegio de Ingenieros de Venezuela, Apdo 2006, Bosque Los Caobos, Caracas 1010; Pres. Agm. GERMÁN AÑEZ OTERO; Sec. Agm. RAFAEL ELSTER NODA.

Colegio de Arquitectos de Venezuela (Venezuela Architects' Association): Avda Colegio de Arquitectos, Urb. La Urbina, Sector Norte, Prolongación Antigua Carretera Petare-Guarenas, Caracas 1070; tel. 2418007; f. 1945 as Sociedad Venezolana de Arquitectos; 3,600 mems; Pres. Arq. ITALO BALBI; Sec. Arq. HENRY SAAD; publ. *Revista del CAV*.

BIBLIOGRAPHY, LIBRARY SCIENCE AND MUSEOLOGY

Colegio de Bibliotecólogos y Archivólogos de Venezuela (Venezuelan Librarians' and Archivists' Association): Parroquia Altagracia, Avda Panteón, Foro Libertador, Biblioteca Nacional, Cuerpo 2, S1, Caracas; tel. (212) 564-12-03; fax (212) 564-12-03; e-mail cbiarchiv@hotmail.com; internet personales.com/venezuela/caracas/cbav; f. 1989; 419 mems; Pres. Lic. ELSI JIMENEZ DE DÍAZ; Vice-Pres. Lic. FLOR MARINA LUNA; publs *AB Te Informa* (4 a year), *CBActualidad* (irregular).

ECONOMICS, LAW AND POLITICS

Academia de Ciencias Políticas y Sociales (Academy of Political and Social Sciences): Palacio de las Academias, Bolsa a San Francisco, Caracas 1010; tel. (212) 481-60-35; fax (212) 483-26-74; e-mail acienpol@cantv.net; internet www.acienpol.com; f. 1917; 33 mems; Pres. Dr JOSÉ MÉLICH ORSINI; Sec. Dr GONZALO PÉREZ LUCIANI; publ. *Boletín*.

Colegio de Abogados del Distrito Capital (Lawyers' Association): Edificio Colegio de Abogados, Avda Paez, Apdo 347, El Paraíso, Caracas 1021; tel. (212) 451-5754; fax (212) 451-4754; e-mail secretaria@justicia.net; internet www.colegio-abogados.org.ve; f. 1788; 2,000 mems; Pres. Abog. RAFAEL VELOZ GARCIA; Sec. Abog. ROSAURA SÁNCHEZ; publ. *Revista*.

EDUCATION

Consejo Nacional de Universidades (National University Council): Avda Urdaneta, Edif Bco Italo, 4° piso, Caracas; f. 1946; consists of staff and student representatives of all universities and representatives from the Ministry of Finance and the Science Council; library of 2,000 vols; Pres. THE MINISTER OF EDUCATION; Perm. Sec. ALBERTO DRAYER B.; publ. *Boletín Informativo* (quarterly).

Grupo Universitario Latinoamericano de Estudio para la Reforma y el Perfeccionamiento de la Educación (GULERPE) (Latin American University Group for Reform and Improvement in Education): Residencias Araucaria, Apdo 43, Santa Fe Sur, Caracas 1080-150; Located at: Piso 4, Avda Santa Fe Sur, Santa Fe, Caracas 1080-150; tel. (212) 9799263; fax (212) 9799263; e-mail elizacaldera@cautv.net; internet www.universitas2000.usb.ve; f. 1965; higher education, research, and educational policy, administration and planning; 150 mems; Pres. Dra ELIZABETH Y. DE CALDERA; Exec. Sec. Prof. FELIPE BEZARA; publ. *Universitas 2000* (in single or double editions, 4 a year).

FINE AND PERFORMING ARTS

Asociación Venezolana Amigos del Arte Colonial (Venezuelan Association of Friends of Colonial Art): Museo de Arte Colonial, Quinta de 'Anauco', Avda Panteón, San Bernardino, Caracas 1011; tel. and fax (212) 5518517; e-mail artecolonialanauco@cantv.net; internet www.quintadeanauco.org.ve; f. 1942; preservation and collection of period furniture, paintings, architectural forms, music, silver, sculpture, glass, bronze, iron, textiles, ceramics, porcelain from the 16th–18th c.; Pres. JUAN CARLOS SOSA; Dir CARLOS F. DUARTE; publ. *Revista*.

Consejo Nacional de la Cultura (CONAC) (National Cultural Council): Torre Norte, Pisos 12–16, Centro Simón Bolívar, Apdo 50995, Caracas; tel. (212) 483-49-80; e-mail directorgeneral@conac.gov.ve; internet www.conac.gov.ve; f. 1990 for the planning, promotion, dissemination and formation of human resources in the fields of music, theatre, dancing, plastic arts, literature, libraries, historic and artistic resources, museums, cinema and folklore; Pres. Dr FRANCISCO SESTO NOVAS; Dir-Gen. SILVIA DÍAZ ALVARADO; Sec. GUSTAVO ARNSTEIN; publs *Revista Nacional de Cultura* (quarterly), *Revista 'IMAGEN'* (monthly), *Revista de Cine 'ENCUADRE'* (quarterly).

Attached foundation:

Fundación de Etnomusicología y Folklore del CONAC (Foundation for Ethnomusicology and Folklore): Apdo 81015, Caracas 1080; f. 1990; consists of: Instituto Nacional de Folklore (INAF, f. 1950), Instituto Interamericano de Etnomusicología y Folklore (INIDEF, f. 1970), Museo Nacional de Folklore (f. 1971), Centro Interamericano de Etnomusicología y Folklore (CIDEF, f. 1973) for the OAS Regional Development Programme; aims to preserve and protect the American cultural heritage; annual courses in ethnomusicology, folklore, handicrafts, ethnohistory, anthropolinguistic studies; PRA/OAS scholarships; archive of ethnomusic, slides and photographs; library: specialized library of 2,700 vols, 308 periodicals; Dir Dra ISABEL ARETZ; publ. *Anuario FUNDEF*.

Instituto Zuliano de la Cultura 'Andrés E. Blanco': Gobernación del Estado Zulia, Academia de Bellas Artes 'Neptali Rincón', Maracaibo; f. 1972; administers all the cultural institutes in the state; Dir CARMEN DELGADO PEÑA; Administrator DOMINGO GUZMÁN RAMOS.

HISTORY, GEOGRAPHY AND ARCHAEOLOGY

Academia de Historia del Zulia: Centro de Bellas Artes de Maracaibo, 67-217, Avda 3–F, Maracaibo, Estado Zulia; f. 1940; 12 mems; Pres. ABRAHÁN BELLOSO; Sec.-Gen. ANICETO RAMÍREZ Y ASTIER; Librarian JOSÉ A. BUTRÓN OLIVARES; publ. *Boletín*.

Academia Nacional de la Historia (National Academy of History): Palacio de las Academias, Bolsa a San Francisco, Caracas 1010; tel. (212) 482-67-20; fax (212) 482-67-20; e-mail anhistoria@cantv.net; internet www.acadnachistoria.org; f. 1888; library: see Libraries and Archives; Dir RAFAEL FERNÁNDEZ HERES; Sec. MARIANELA PONCE; publs *Boletín*, *Memorias*.

Centro de Historia del Táchira (Historical Centre): Carrera 4, No 13-68, San Cristóbal; f. 1942; Dir Mons. RAÚL MÉNDEZ-MONCADA; Sec. Lic. HORACIO MORENO; publ. *Boletín*.

Centro de Historia Larense (Lara Historical Centre): Casa Colonial, Calle 22, diagonal a Plaza Lara, Apdo 406, Barquisimeto, Distrito Iribarren; f. 1941; 12 mems; library: c. 1,000 vols; publ. *Boletín*.

Centro Histórico Sucrense (Historical Centre): Cumaná; f. 1945; 24 national and 14 foreign corresp. mems; Dir R. P. Fray CAYETANO DE CARROCERA; Sec.-Gen. Br. ALBERTO SANABRIA; publ. *Boletín*.

Junta Nacional Protectora y Conservadora del Patrimonio Histórico y Artístico de la Nación (Commission for the Protection and Preservation of the Historical and Artistic Heritage of the Nation): Palacio de Miraflores, Avda Urdaneta, Caracas; there is a subsidiary office in each State; authorizes exploration and excavation of sites; mems are nominated by the Government for five-year terms, and may be re-elected; Dir Dr RAFAEL ARMANDO ROJAS.

Sociedad Bolivariana de Venezuela (Bolivar Society): Esquina de San Jacinto, Caracas; tel. 545-72-71; to promote by all available media the knowledge of Simón Bolívar's life and works, as well as his political, cultural and social ideas and publishes about 15,000 volumes of historical works per year; 300 mems; library of 6,000 vols; Pres. Gral CANDIDO PEREZ MENDEZ; Sec. Gral ADOLFO ROMERO LUENGO; publ. *Revista*.

LANGUAGE AND LITERATURE

Alliance Française: Avdo Mohedano 1–2, Transversal La Castellana, Apdo 61000, Caracas 1060; tel. (212) 264-4611; fax (212) 267-3470; e-mail dgaf@telcel.net.ve; internet www.afcaracas.org; offers courses and exams in French language and culture and promotes cultural exchange with France; attached teaching centres in Barquisimeto, Maracaibo, Mérida, Nueva Esparta, Porlamar and Valencia.

British Council: Torre Credicard, Piso 3, Avda Principal de El Bosque, Chacaíto, Caracas; tel. (212) 952-9965; fax (212) 952-9691; e-mail bc-venezuela@britishcouncil.org.ve; internet www.britishcouncil.org.ve; teaching centre; offers courses and exams in English language and British culture and promotes cultural exchange with the UK; Dir BARBARA WICKHAM.

Goethe-Institut: Avda Juan Germán Roscio, cruce con Avda Jorge Washington, Qta. 'Asociación Cultural Humboldt', San Bernardino, Apdo 60501, Caracas 1060; tel. (212) 552-6445; fax (212) 552-5621; e-mail sekr@caracas.goethe.de; internet www.goethe.de/hn/car; offers courses and exams in German language and culture and promotes cultural exchange with Germany; library of 4,000 vols; Dir Dr ULRICH GMÜNDER.

MEDICINE

Academia de Medicina del Zulia: Apdo 1725, Maracaibo, Zulia 4001A; tel. (61) 42-34-42; fax (61) 42-34-42; f. 1927; 150 mems; library of 950 vols; Pres. Dr GILBERTO OLIVARES; Sec. Dr JOSÉ A. COLINA-CHOURIO; publ. *Revista*.

Academia Nacional de Medicina (National Academy of Medicine): Bolsa a San Francisco, Apdo 804, Caracas 1010; tel. 42-18-68; f. 1904; 40 mems; 50 nat. corresp. mems; 30 foreign corresp. mems; library: see Libraries and Archives; Pres. Dr AUGUSTO LEÓN C.; Sec. Dr JULIAN MORALES R.; publ. *Gaceta Médica de Caracas* (quarterly).

Colegio de Farmacéuticos del Distrito Federal y Estado Miranda (Association of Pharmacists): Urbanización Las Mercedes, Caracas 1060; deals with all aspects of the pharmaceutical industry; 1,200 mems; library of 600 vols; Pres. Dr PEDRO RODRÍGUEZ MURILLO; Sec. Dra ESTHER VALERA DE PÉREZ B.; Librarian Dra CARMEN ELENA GARCIA; publ. *Revista 'Colfar'*.

Colegio de Médicos del Distrito Metropolitano de Caracas (Doctors' Association): Plaza de Bellas Artes, Avda Bellas Artes, Los Chaguaramos, Caracas; tel. (212) 979-98-46; fax (212) 979-29-86; e-mail presidencia@cmdmc.com.ve; internet www.cmdmc.com.ve; f. 1942; 2,800 mems; Pres. Dr FERNANDO JOSE BIANCO COLMENARES; Sec. Dra TAHIRI MARIÑEZ; publ. *Acta Médica Venezolana*.

Colegio de Médicos del Estado Miranda (Doctors' Association): Avda El Golf, Qta La Setentiseis, El Bosque, Caracas; f. 1944; 3,100 mems; professional and scientific association; Pres. Dr HERNÁN VÁSQUEZ RIGUAL; Gen. Sec. Dr RUBEN HERNÁNDEZ SERRANO; publ. *Cuadernos Medicos*.

Instituto J. I. Baldó: El Algodonal, Antimano, Caracas, f. 1937; lung diseases; Pres. Dr MANUEL ADRIANZA.

Sociedad de Obstetricia y Ginecología de Venezuela (Society of Obstetrics and Gynaecology): Maternidad Concepción Palacios, Avda San Martín, Apdo 20081, Caracas 1020-A; tel. 4510895; fax 4510895; e-mail sogvz@cantv.net; internet www.sogvzla.org; f. 1940; 1,200 mems; Pres. Dra LEONOR ZAPATA; publ. *Revista de Obstetricia y Ginecología de Venezuela* (4 a year).

Sociedad Venezolana de Anestesiología (Society of Anaesthesiology): Colegio de Médicos, Apdo 40 217, Caracas; Pres. OSCAR LOYNAZ-REVERÓN.

Sociedad Venezolana de Cardiología (Society of Cardiology): Oficina B-1, Piso 2, Torre Colegio de Médicos, Avda José María Vargas, Urb. Santa Fe Norte, Caracas 1080; e-mail vc@cantv.net; 196 mems; Pres. Dr JOSÉ ANTONIO CANDADO R.; Sec.-Gen. Dr GUILLERMO VILLORIA.

Sociedad Venezolana de Cirugía (Society of Surgery): Torre del Colegio, 15°, Oficina A, Avda José María Vargas, Urb. Santa Fé, Caracas 1080; f. 1945; Pres. Dr AUGUSTO DIEZ; Sec.-Gen. Dr ISMAEL J. SALAS M..

Sociedad Venezolana de Cirugía Ortopédica y Traumatología (Society of Orthopaedics and Traumatological Surgery): Colegio de Médicos del DF, Plaza Las Tres Gracias, Los Chaguaramos, Caracas; f. 1949; 197 mems; Pres. Dr ALBERTO J. JACIR S.; publ. *Boletín de Ortopedia y Traumatología* (quarterly).

Sociedad Venezolana de Dermatología (Society of Dermatology): Colegios de Médicos del DF, 2° piso, Caracas; Pres. Dr ANTONIO JOSÉ RONDÓN LUGO.

Sociedad Venezolana de Gastroenterología (Venezuelan Society of Gastroenterology): Apdo 81245, Prados del Este, Caracas 1050-A; tel. 9799380; fax 9799380; f. 1945; 606 mems; Pres. Dr CARLOS E. PARADISI; Sec. Dr PASCUAL CANDIA; publ. *GEN* (quarterly).

Sociedad Venezolana de Hematología (Society of Haematology): Avda José María Vargas, Edif. Torre del Colegio, Piso 2, Local E–2 Urb. Santa Fé Norte, Caracas 1080; tel. (212) 9795664; f. 1959; library of 527 vols, 14 periodicals; Pres. Dr CARLOS GOLDSTEIN.

Sociedad Venezolana de Historia de la Medicina (History of Medicine Society): Palacio de las Academias, Bolsa a San Francisco, Caracas 1010; tel. (212) 824834361; fax (212) 4614889; e-mail migongue@yahoo.com; f. 1944; 75 mems; Pres. Dr MIGUEL GONZÁLEZ GUERRA; publ. *Revista* (2 a year).

Sociedad Venezolana de Medicina Interna (Society of Internal Medicine): Hospital Universitaria, Ciudad Universitaria, Caracas; Pres. Dr ADOLFO STAROSTA.

Sociedad Venezolana de Oftalmología (Society of Ophthalmology): Avda Principal de Los Ruices, Centro Empresarial Los Ruices (Piso 05, Oficina 507), Caracas; tel. (2) 2398127; fax (2) 2394384; e-mail svo@reacciun.ve; internet www.svo.org.ve; f. 1953; 600 mems; Pres. Dra SILVIA SALINAS; Sec.-Gen. Dr ROSEADO CASTELLANOS; publ. *Revista Oftalmológica Venezolana* (quarterly).

Sociedad Venezolana de Otorinolaringología (Society of Oto-Rhino-Laryngology): Avda Cajigal, San Bernardino, Caracas 1011; Pres. Dr FRANÇOIS CONDE JAHN; Sec. Dr GERMÁN TOVAR BUSTAMANTE; publ. *Acta Venezolana de ORL* (annually).

Sociedad Venezolana de Psiquiatría (Society of Psychiatry): Apdo 3380, Caracas 1010A; tel. (212) 731-20-24; fax (212) 731-20-24; f. 1942; 600 mems; library of 1,650 vols; Pres. Dr MANUEL MATUTE; Sec.-Gen. Dr EDGAR BELFORT; publ. *Archivos Venezolanos de Psiquiatría y Neurología* (2 a year).

Sociedad Venezolana de Puericultura y Pediatría (Society of Puericulture and Paediatrics): Avda Libertador, Edif. La Linea, 9° piso, Ofc. 93A, Caracas 1050; Pres. Dr XAVIER MUGARRA T.

Sociedad Venezolana de Radiología (Society of Radiology): Policlínica Méndez Gimón, Avda Andrés Bello, Caracas; Pres. Dr SEBASTIÁN NUÑEZ MIER Y TERÁN.

NATURAL SCIENCES
General

Academia de Ciencias Físicas, Matemáticas y Naturales (Academy of Physical, Mathematical and Natural Sciences): Bolsa a San Francisco, Avda Universidad, Apdo 1421, Caracas 1010; tel. (212) 482-29-54; fax (212) 484-66-11; e-mail acfiman@cantv.net; internet www.acfiman.org.ve; f. 1917; 80 (30 ordinary, 20 Venezuelan corresp., 30 foreign corresp.); Pres. Dr LUIS MANUEL CARBONELL; Sec. JOSÉ M. CARRILLO; publ. *Boletín* (4 a year).

Asociación Venezolana para el Avance de la Ciencia (ASOVAC) (Venezuelan Association for the Advancement of Science): Edificio Fundavac–Asovac, Calle Neverí, Colinas de Bello Monte, Caracas; internet www.asovac.org.ve; f. 1950; 3,000 mems; President FRANCISCO EMIRO DURÁN; Sec.-Gen. YOLANDA SEVILLA; publ. *Acta Científica Venezolana* (every 2 months).

Fundación La Salle de Ciencias Naturales (La Salle Foundation of Natural Sciences): Edificio Fundación La Salle, Avda Boyacá, Apdo 1930, Caracas 1010A; tel. 709-58-11; fax 793-74-93; e-mail info@fundacionlasalle.org.ve; internet www.fundacionlasalle.org.ve; f. 1957; oceanography, anthropology, limnology, aquaculture, agronomy, mining and forestry; runs stations for marine, agricultural and hydrobiological research, the *Instituto Universitario de Tec-*

nología del Mar on the island of Margarita, *Instituto de Tecnología Agropecuaria* at San Carlos and at Boconó, *Instituto de Tecnología Industrial* at San Félix, *Instituto Universitario de Technología* at Tumeremo and *Instituto Universitario de Technología Amazonas* in Amazonas State; library: library (see under Libraries); 1,300 mems; Pres. Hno. GINÉS; Exec. Vice-Pres. (vacant); publs *Antropológica* (review, 4 a year), *Memoria* (oceanography and natural science studies, 2 a year), *Natura* (3 a year).

Biological Sciences

Sociedad de Ciencias Naturales 'La Salle' ('La Salle' Society of Natural Sciences): Edificio Fundación La Salle, Avda Boyacá, Apdo 1930, Caracas 1010A; tel. (212) 21-76-53; fax (212) 22-48-12; f. 1940; 504 mems; 17 hon., 42 national and 30 foreign corresps, 500 associates; comprises three depts: Botany, Zoology and Publications; the Museum contains more than 100,000 exhibits; Dir Lic. JESÚS HOYOS; Pres. Dr LUIS RIVAS L.; Sec. Dr CARLOS ACEVEDO; publs *Memoria* (2 a year), *Natura* (quarterly).

Sociedad Venezolana de Ciencias Naturales (Venezuelan Society of Natural Sciences): Calle Arichuna y Cumaco, El Marqués, Apdo 1521, Caracas 1010A; tel. (212) 21-76-53; fax (212) 22-48-12; f. 1931; 1,100 mems; library of 12,000 vols, 400 periodicals; annual exhibitions, lectures, films on nature conservation; department of speleology for study and exploration of caves throughout the country; biological station for research on flora and fauna, soil science and crop studies, ecology of neo-tropical savannas; dept for education on environmental protection; depts for the study of tropical orchids, bromeliads and astronomy; studies in environmental pollution; Pres. R. AVELEDO HOSTOS; Gen. Sec. Dr RICARDO MUÑOZ TÉBAR; publs *Boletín de la SVCN*, *Boletín Informativo*.

Physical Sciences

Sociedad Venezolana de Geólogos (Venezuelan Geological Society): Apdo 17493, Parque Central, Caracas, 1015-A; Located at: Avda A, Quinta Mercedes 13-10, Urbanización, La Carlota, Caracas; tel. (212) 234-40-85; fax (212) 234-07-16; e-mail svg@mailser.reacciun.ve; internet www.socvengeo.org; f. 1955; 1,050 mems; Pres. DANIEL LOUREIRO; Sec. FRANCISCO BARRIOS; publs *Geologia de Venezuela*, *Boletín* (3 a year).

TECHNOLOGY

Asociación Venezolana de Ingeniería Sanitaria y Ambiental (Sanitary and Environmental Engineering Association): c/o Colegio de Ingenieros de Venezuela, Apdo 2006, Caracas 1010; Pres. Ing. OCTAVIO JELAMBI.

Colegio de Ingenieros de Venezuela (Engineers' Association): Apdo 2006, Bosque Los Caobos, Caracas 101; f. 1861; 7,000 mems; library of 4,000 vols; Pres. DARÍO BRILLEMBOURG; Sec. JULIO URBINA; publ. *Boletín* (monthly).

Sociedad Venezolana de Ingeniería Hidráulica (Society of Hydraulic Engineering): c/o Colegio de Ingenieros de Venezuela, Apdo 2006, Caracas; f. 1960; Pres. FEDERICO LOVERA.

Sociedad Venezolana de Ingenieros Agrónomos (Society of Agricultural Engineers): c/o Colegio de Ingenieros de Venezuela, Apdo 2006, Caracas; f. 1944; Pres. Ing. Agr. HUMBERTO FONTANA.

Sociedad Venezolana de Ingenieros Civiles (Society of Civil Engineers): c/o Colegio de Ingenieros de Venezuela, Apdo

2006, Caracas; Pres. MANUEL FERNANDO MEJÍAS.

Sociedad Venezolana de Ingenieros de Petróleo (Society of Petroleum Engineers): c/o Colegio de Ingenieros de Venezuela, Apdo 2006, Caracas; Pres. RUBÉN A. CARLO.

Sociedad Venezolana de Ingenieros Forestales (Society of Forestry Engineers): c/o Colegio de Ingenieros de Venezuela, Apdo 2006, Caracas; tel. 5713122, ext. 167; f. 1960; 1,122 mems; library of 8,000 vols; Pres. RAFAEL VILORIA; Sec. LOURDES ALTUVE; publ. *Revista Forestal* (quarterly).

Sociedad Venezolana de Ingenieros Químicos (Society of Chemical Engineers): c/o Colegio de Ingenieros de Venezuela; Apdo 2006, Caracas; f. 1958 to promote the chemical engineering profession and exchange information with similar orgs in Venezuela and abroad; 1,000 mems; Exec. Dir YOLANDA DE OSORIO; publ. *Boletín* (quarterly).

Research Institutes
GENERAL

Consejo Nacional de Investigaciones Científicas y Tecnológicas (CONICIT) (National Council for Scientific and Technological Research): Apdo 70617, Los Ruices, Caracas; fax 2398677; f. 1967 for the promotion of scientific and technological research, and for co-ordinating the activities of organizations involved in the science and technology sector, and of organizations of the national executive; Pres. Dr IGNACIO AVALOS GUTIERREZ; Vice-Pres. Dr MICHAEL SUAREZ F.

Instituto Venezolano de Investigaciones Científicas (IVIC) (Venezuelan Scientific Research Institute): Apdo 21827, Caracas 1020 A; tel. (212) 504-1122; fax (212) 504-1428; e-mail webmaster@ivic.ve; internet www.ivic.ve; f. 1959; research in biology, medicine, chemistry, physics, mathematics and technology, atomic research, archaeology, anthropology, sociology of science; postgraduate studies; library: see Libraries and Archives; Dir MAXIMO GARCIO SUCRE.

AGRICULTURE, FISHERIES AND VETERINARY SCIENCE

Centro Nacional de Investigaciones Agropecuarias (Agricultural Research Centre): Avda Casanova Godoy, Maracay 2103, Estado Aragua; tel. (243) 2453075; fax (243) 2454320; internet www.ceniap.gov.ve; f. 1937; attached to the Instituto Nacional de Investigaciones Agricolas de Venezuela; Dir Dra SUSMIRA GODOY; publs *Agronomía tropical*, *Zootecnia Tropical*, *Veterinaria Tropical*.

Estación Experimental Tachira: Bramón, Rubio, Edo Táchira; tel. (76) 66783; f. 1953; agricultural research; library of 1,100 vols; Dir JOSÉ ROSARIO MANRIQUE; publ. *Annual Report*.

Instituto Agrario Nacional (Agrarian Institute): Quinta Barrancas, Avda San Carlos, Vista Alegre, Caracas 102; f. 1949; concerned with agrarian reform activities; Pres. ANTONIO MERCHAN; publ. *Memoria y Cuenta*.

Instituto de Investigaciones Veterinarias (Veterinary Research Institute): Apdo 70, Maracay, Estado Aragua; f. 1940; small specialized library; 55 mems; Dir Dr CLAUDIO FUENMAYOR F.

Instituto Nacional de Investigaciones Agrícolas de Venezuela (National Institute for Agricultural Research): Via El Limon, Maracay, Estado Aragua; fax (243) 2836978; e-mail ger_inia@impsat.com.ve;

internet www.inia.gov.ve; f. 1961 as Fondo Nacional de Investigaciones Agropecuarias, 2000 re-named; centres and experimental stations: Amazonas, Anzoátegui, Apure, Barinas, CENIAP, Delta Amacuro, Falcón, Guárico, Lara, Mérida, Miranda, Monagas, Portuguesa, Sucre, Táchira, Trujillo, Yaracuy, Zulia; Pres. PRUDENCIO CHACÓN; Gen.-Man. ALICIA LEÓN.

ARCHITECTURE AND TOWN PLANNING

Dirección General de Desarrollo Urbanistico del Ministerio del Desarrollo Urbano (Bureau of Urban Development of the Ministry of Urban Development): Edificio Banco de Venezuela, 5° piso, Caracas; f. 1946; 350 mems; library of 20,000 vols; Dir Arq. DANIEL BARREIRO DELGADO.

ECONOMICS, LAW AND POLITICS

Centro de Estudios del Desarrollo (Centre for Development Studies): POB 47604, Caracas 1041A; tel. (212) 753-34-75; fax (212) 751-26-91; e-mail cendes@reaccium.ve; internet www.rect.ucv.ve/cendes; f. 1961; centre for research and graduate studies on problems relating to economic, social, educational, regional, political, ecological, environmental and scientific-technological development of Venezuela and Latin America; library of 36,000 vols specializing in development problems and planning; Dir SONIA NOGUEIRA DE BARRIOS; publs *Cuadernos del CENDES* (3 a year), *CENDES Newsletter* (3 a year).

Instituto Iberoamericano de Derecho Agrario y Reforma Agraria: Facultad de Ciencias Jurídicas y Políticas, Universidad de los Andes, Mérida; tel. (275) 402646; fax (275) 402644; f. 1973; 12 mem. countries; training and research in agrarian law, agricultural economics, rural sociology; postgraduate courses; library of 4,000 vols; Pres. RAMÓN VICENTE CASANOVA; publ. *Revista de Derecho Agrario y Reforma Agraria*.

Oficina Central de Estadística e Informática (Central Office of Statistics and Informatics): Apdo 4593, Caracas 1010; tel. (212) 782-11-33; e-mail ocei@platino.gov.ve; internet www.ocei.gov.ve; f. 1978; Dir Dr GUSTAVO MÉNDEZ; publs *Anuario Estadístico de Venezuela*, *Anuario del Comercio Exterior de Venezuela*.

EDUCATION

Instituto Latinoamericano de Investigaciones Científicas en Educación a Distancia (Latin American Institute of Scientific Research on Distance Education): Calle California, Qta. Las Churrucas, Apdo 69680, Las Mercedes 1060A, Caracas; f. 1980; research, teaching and planning in distance and open education; library of 8,000 vols; Pres. MIGUEL A. ESCOTET; publ. *ILICED Newsletter* (quarterly).

HISTORY, GEOGRAPHY AND ARCHAEOLOGY

Centro de Historia del Estado Carabobo: Valencia, Edo de Carabobo; f. 1979 to conduct research into national and regional history, preserve and improve regional archives, conserve monuments, encourage and publicize celebrations of national historic events, and establish cultural relations with similar Venezuelan and foreign organizations; 24 mems; Pres. Lic. LUIS CUBILLÁN; Sec. Dr MARCO TULIO MÉRIDA; publ. *Boletín*.

Instituto de Geografía y Conservación de Recursos Naturales (Institute of Geography and Conservation of Natural Resources): Vía Chorros de Milla, Mérida; tel. (275) 401603; fax (275) 401603; e-mail regeoven@forest.ula.ve; f. 1959; library of 20,236 vols and 44,555 periodicals; research in theoretical geography, applied geography and geographical techniques; committees for research and teaching technical co-ordination; documentation and information; Dir Prof. RICARDO PONTE R.; publs *Revista Geográfica Venezolana* (2 a year), *Cuadernos Geográficos* (irregular).

Ministerio del Ambiente y de los Recursos Naturales Renovables, Servicio Autónomo del Geografía y Cartografía Nacional: Avda Este 6, Esquina de Camejo, Edificio Camejo (Piso 2-220), Centro Simón Bolívar, Caracas; tel. (212) 482-22-18; fax (212) 542-03-74; e-mail sagecan@marnr.gov.ve; f. 1935; Dir-Gen. Lic. ALICIA MOREAU D.

MEDICINE

Instituto de Medicina Experimental (Institute of Experimental Medicine): POB 50.587, Sabana Grande, Ciudad Universitaria, Caracas 1051; tel. 693-18-62; fax 693-12-60; f. 1940; research in biochemistry, pharmacology, physiology, neurology, general and applied pathology; 130 staff; library of 30,176 vols, 4,100 periodicals; Dir Dra ITALA LIPPO DE BECEMBERG; Librarian Lic. TRINA YANES DE RAMÍREZ; publ. *Boletín Informativo Sistema Nacional de Documentación e Información Biomédica*; (see also under the Universidad Central de Venezuela).

Instituto Nacional de Nutrición (Institute of Nutrition): Apdo 2049, Caracas; f. 1949; library of 10,000 vols; Dir Dr LUIS BERMÚDEZ CHAURIO; publ. *Archivos Latinoamericanos de Nutrición*.

NATURAL SCIENCES
General

Estación de Investigaciones Marinas (EDIMAR): Apdo 144, Porlamar, Punta de Piedras, Isla de Margarita, Edo Nueva Esparta; tel. (295) 239-8051; fax (295) 239-8051; e-mail marllano@edimar.org; internet www.edimar.org; affiliated to the Fundación La Salle de Ciencias Naturales (see under Learned Societies); f. 1958; fisheries, marine biology, oceanography, marine geology, aquaculture, marine food processing; library: library 'H. Ginés' of 18,000 vols, 1,200 periodicals; Dir Dr MARTÍN LLANO GARCÍA; publ. *Memoria de la Sociedad La Salle de Ciencias Naturales*.

Biological Sciences

Estación Biológica de los Llanos (Biological Station): Calabozo, Estado Guárico; f. 1961; library of 3,200 vols; Dirs F. TAMAYO, R. A. HOSTOS, L. ARISTEGUIETA.

Fundación Instituto Botánico de Venezuela (Botanical Institute): Apdo 2156, Jardín Botánico de Caracas, Avda Salvador Allende, Caracas 1010A; tel. (212) 605-39-83; fax (212) 662-90-81; e-mail anibalcastillo@cantv.net; internet www.ucv.ve/fibv.htm; f. 1991; library of 14,000 vols, 1,300 periodicals; Pres. Dr ANÍBAL CASTILLO SUÁREZ; publs *Acta Botanica Venezuelica* (2 a year), *Flora de Venezuela*.

Physical Sciences

Dirección de Geología del Ministerio de Energía y Minas (Department of Geology of the Ministry of Energy and Mines): Torre Oeste, 4° piso, Parque Central, Caracas 1010; f. 1936; conducts national geological surveys, and research in geotechnics, marine geology and mineralogy; library of 120,000 vols; Dir SIMÓN E. RODRIGUEZ; publs *Boletín de Geología* (2 a year), *Cuadernos Geológicos* (3 a year), *Boletín Informativo del Centro de Análisis de Información Geológica-Minera*

(CAIGEOMIN) (2 a year), research bulletins, statistical and other data (annually).

Estación Meteorológica (Meteorological Station): Ciudad Bolívar; f. 1940; undertakes meteorological research and hydrographical surveys of the River Orinoco and its tributaries; Dir E. SIFONTES; numerous publications on meteorology and climatology of Venezuela.

Observatorio Naval 'Juan Manuel Cagigal' (Juan Manuel Cagigal Naval Observatory): Apdo 6745, La Planicie, 23 Enero, Caracas; tel. (212) 481-22-66; fax (212) 483-58-78; e-mail dhn@truevision.net; f. 1888; astronomy, meteorology, oceanography, hydrography, planetarium; Dir GREGORIO PÉREZ MORENO; publs *Boletín Meteorologico* (monthly and annually), *Boletín Avisos a los Navegantes*, *Almanaque Astronómico Venezolano*, *Boletín Climatológico Anual*.

RELIGION, SOCIOLOGY AND ANTHROPOLOGY

Fundación 'Lisandro Alvarado': Apdo 4518, Maracay 2101A, Estado Aragua; tel. (43) 453420; f. 1965; archaeological and historical research; museums of history and anthropology, specialized library (in preparation); brs in Valencia (museums of art, history, anthropology, historical archives) and Puerto Cabello (museum of art and history); 40 mems; Pres. Dra ADELAIDA DE DÍAZ UNGRÍA; Dir HENRIQUETA PEÑALVER GÓMEZ.

Instituto Caribe de Antropología y Sociología: Apdo 1930, Caracas 1010A; tel. 782-8711 ext. 226; department of the Fundación La Salle de Ciencias Naturales (see under Learned Societies); f. 1962; anthropological research and development programmes among Indian populations of Venezuela; 6 mems; library of 3,000 vols; Dir WERNER WILBERT; publ. *Antropológica* (2 a year).

TECHNOLOGY

Dirección de Minas del Ministerio de Minas e Hidrocarburos (Department of Mining of the Ministry of Mines and Hydrocarbons): Torre Norte, 20° piso, Caracas 101; f. 1936; Dir BRÍGIDO R. NATERA.

PDUSA-INTEVEP, Centro de Investigación y Apoyo Tecnológico: Apdo 76343, Caracas 1070A; tel. (212) 908-6111; fax (212) 908-6447; f. 1974; research and development branch of Petróleos de Venezuela, concerned with hydrocarbons and petrochemicals; Information Centre of 30,000 publs, 1,600 periodicals, connected to int. online systems; Pres. FRANCISCO PRADAS; publ. *Visión Tecnológica* (2 a year).

Libraries and Archives
Barquisimeto

Biblioteca Pública 'Pio Tamayo' (Public Library): Calle 26, entre Carreras 20 y 21, Barquisimeto; f. 1911; 21,943 vols; Librarian GERMÁN HURTADO REYES.

Biblioteca Técnica Científica Centralizada 'Froilan Alvarez Yepez' (Central Scientific and Technical Library): Apdo 254, Barquisimeto; fax 544394; f. 1966; specializes in social sciences, economic development and technology; 50,000 vols, 800 periodicals; Librarian Lic. CECILIA VEGA F.; publ. *Indice Bibliográfico de los estudios de FUDECO*.

Caracas

Archivo de Música Colonial Venezolano (Archives of Colonial Music): Escuela Superior de Música, Veroes a Santa Capilla, Caracas; Librarian GARCÍA LAZO.

Archivo General de la Nación (National Archives): Santa Capilla a Carmelitas, Caracas; f. 1910; sections: La Colonia (1498–1810), La Revolución (1810–21), La Gran Colombia (1821–30), La República (1830 to present day); comprises Seminario de Investigación Archivística and courses on palaeography; Dir Dr MARIO BRICEÑO PEROZO; publs *Biblioteca Venezolana de Historia* (2 a year), *Boletín* (2 a year).

Biblioteca Central de la Universidad Católica 'Andrés Bello' (Central Library of the 'Andrés Bello' Catholic University): Urb. Montalbán, La Vega, Apdo 29068, Caracas; f. 1953; 111,558 vols; Librarian Lic. EMILIO PÍRIZ PÉREZ; publ. *Montalbán*.

Biblioteca Central de la Universidad Central de Venezuela (Central University Library): Ciudad Universitaria, Los Chaguaramos, Caracas; tel. (212) 662-84-27; f. 1850; sections on social science, the humanities, pure science and technology; official publications; reference section; 280,000 vols; 3,500 periodicals; Dir Prof. MANUEL RODRIGUEZ CAMPOS.

Biblioteca Central del Ministerio de Agricultura y Cría (Library of the Ministry of Agriculture): Avda Lecuna, Parque Central, Torre Este, 1° piso, Caracas; f. 1936; 70,000 vols; Librarian TUSNELDA CRESPO PIETRI.

Biblioteca Central del Ministerio del Trabajo (Library of the Ministry of Labour): Centro Simón Bolívar, Edificio Sur, 5° piso, Caracas; f. 1988; 3,200 vols; Librarian MARCELA GARCÍA JORDAN; publ. *Boletín Legislativo*.

Biblioteca Central 'Juan Pablo Pérez Alfonzo' (Library of the Ministry of Energy and Mines): Avda Lecuna, Torre Oeste, 2° piso, Parque Central, Caracas; tel. (212) 507-52-06; fax (212) 575-43-86; f. 1950; specializes in mines, petroleum, gas, geology, refinement, petrochemicals; 20,000 vols; Librarian Lic. SILVIA PERNIA C.; publs *Boletín de Geología, Memoria y Cuenta del Ministerio de Energía y Minas, Petróleo y otros Datos Estadísticos, Anuario Estadísticos Mineros, Carta Semanal, Compendia Estadística del Sector Eléctrico*.

Biblioteca de la Academia Nacional de la Historia (Library of the National Academy of History): Palacio de las Academias, Avda Universidad, Bolsa a San Francisco, Caracas; tel. (212) 482-38-49; fax (212) 482-67-20; f. 1888; 120,000 vols; Dir Dr RAFAEL FERNÁNDEZ HERES; publ. *Boletín de la Academia Nacional de la Historia*.

Biblioteca de la Academia Nacional de Medicina (Library of the National Academy of Medicine): Palacio de las Academias, Bolsa a San Francisco, Apdo 804, Caracas 1010; tel. (212) 481-89-39; f. 1893; 4,000 vols; Librarian Dr TULIO BRICEÑO MAAZ; publ. *Gaceta Médica de Caracas*.

Biblioteca de la Academia Venezolana (Library of the Academy of Venezuela): Palacio de las Academias, Bolsa a San Francisco, Caracas 1010; f. 1883; 25,000 vols; special collections: Venezuelan classics, dictionaries, Ayacucho collection, 'El Coyo Ilustrado'; Librarian MARIO TORREALBA LOSSI.

Biblioteca de la Corte Suprema de Justicia (Law Courts Library): Esquina de la Bolsa, Caracas; f. 1942; 4,500 vols; Dir Br FERNANDO ARAUJO M.

Biblioteca del Congreso (Congress Library): Plaza del Capitolio, Caracas; f. 1915; 9,000 vols; Librarian LOURDES GARCÍA.

Biblioteca del Ministerio de Fomento (Library of the Ministry of Development):

Centro Simón Bolívar, Edificio Sur, 5° piso, Oficina 535, Caracas; f. 1953; 6,000 vols; Librarian ROSARIO BARNOLA.

Biblioteca del Ministerio de Obras Públicas (Library of the Ministry of Public Works): Centro Simón Bolívar, Edificio Camejo, Mezzanina, Caracas; f. 1948; 4,312 vols; Dir CARLOS A. ARREAZA F.

Biblioteca del Ministerio de Relaciones Exteriores (Library of the Ministry of Foreign Affairs): Caracas; 5,000 vols; specializes in international law; Librarian ALICIA CURIEL.

Biblioteca del Ministerio de Relaciones Interiores (Library of the Ministry of the Interior): Esquina de Carmelitas, 2° piso, Caracas; 3,585 vols; Librarian Dr RUIZ LANDER.

Biblioteca del Ministerio de Sanidad y Asistencia Social (Library of the Ministry of Health): C/o Ministerio de Salud y Desarrollo Social, Parque Central, Torre Oeste Piso 30-41 Distrito Federal, Caracas; f. 1936; 9,411 vols; Librarian ESPERANZA REYES BAENA; publs *Revista Venezolana de Sanidad y Asistencia Social, Memorias del MSAS.*

Biblioteca 'Dr M. A. Sánchez Carvajal' de la Sociedad de Obstetricia y Ginecología de Venezuela (Dr M. A. Sánchez Carvajal Library of the Society for Obstetrics and Gynaecology of Venezuela): Maternidad Concepción Palacios, Avda San Martín, Apdo 20081, Caracas 1020A; tel. and fax (212) 451-08-95; e-mail sogvzla@cantv.net; internet www.sogvzla.org; f. 1940; 8,500 vols, 113 periodicals, also MSS and medical history collection; Librarian Dra FANNY FLEITAS.

Biblioteca 'Ernesto Peltzer' del Banco Central de Venezuela: Torre Financiera, 16° piso, Esq. de Santa Capilla, Avda Urdaneta, Apdo 2017, Caracas 1010; tel. (212) 801-51-11; fax (212) 861-00-48; f. 1940; economics and finance; 96,891 vols, 1,000 periodicals; Dir SILVIO CASTELLANOS.

Biblioteca Fundación La Salle de Ciencias Naturales (Library of the 'La Salle' Foundation for Natural Sciences): Avda Boyacá, Cota Mil., Edif. Fundación La Salle, Apdo 1930, Caracas 1010A; tel. (212) 793-42-55; fax (212) 793-74-93; f. 1942; 100,000 vols; special collection: cultural anthropology, local languages, Venezuelan Indians, zoology, botany, natural resources contamination; Librarian MIREYA VILORIA.

Biblioteca 'Marcel Roche' del Instituto Venezolano de Investigaciones Científicas (Library of the Venezuelan Institute for Scientific Research): Altos de Pipe, Km 11, Carretera Panamericana, Apdo 21827, Caracas 1020A; tel. (212) 504-15-15; fax (212) 504-14-23; e-mail xjayaro@ivic.ivic.ve; internet www.zeus.ivic.ve/biblioteca/; f. 1959; 500,000 vols, 5,817 periodicals; Dir Dr EGIDIO ROMANO; Librarian XIOMARA JAYARO Y.

Biblioteca Nacional de Venezuela (National Library of Venezuela): Parroquia Altagracia, Final Avda Panteón, Esquina Fe a Remedios, Caracas 1010; tel. (212) 505-92-54; fax (212) 505-91-75; internet www.bibliotecanacional.bib.ve; f. 1883; 6,500,000 books, newspapers, MSS and audiovisual items, 2,500,000 records on database; Dir SAÉL IBÁNEZ; publ. *Revista Bibliotecas Públicas* (4 a year).

Biblioteca Pública 'Mariano Picón Salas' (Public Library): Parque Arístides Rojas, Avda Andrés Bello, Caracas; f. 1965; 23,689 vols; Dir Lic. ROMULO NAVEA SOTO.

Cumaná

Biblioteca General de la Universidad de Oriente (General Library of the Universidad de Oriente): Apdo 245, Cerro Colorado, Cumaná; 154,000 vols; Librarian Lic. ROSA GONZÁLEZ DE LÓPEZ.

Maracaibo

Biblioteca de la Universidad del Zulia: Apdo de Correos 526, Maracaibo; f. 1946; 19,000 vols; Librarian Lic. EGLA ORTEGA.

Biblioteca Pública del Estado Zulia: Maracaibo; administered by the Instituto Zuliano de la Cultura (*q.v.*); Dir FERNANDO GUERRERO MATHEUS.

Maracay

Biblioteca Central del Centro Nacional de Investigaciones Agropecuarias (Library of the National Agricultural Research Centre): Apdo A4653, Maracay 2101, Edo Aragua; tel. 452491; fax 454320; f. 1937; 200,000 vols; Library Assistant NANCY GARCÉS DE HERNÁNDEZ.

Mérida

Servicios Bibliotecarios Universidad de los Andes (Los Andes University Library Services): Edificio Administrativo de la Universidad de los Andes, 2° piso, Mérida 5101; tel. (275) 402731; fax (275) 402507; f. 1889; *c.* 250,000 vols, 7,817 periodical titles; reference books for all subjects taught in the University; small collection of 16th- and 17th-century books; Co-ordinator Lic. MARÍA E. CHÁVEZ DE BURGOS.

Trujillo

Biblioteca '24 de Julio' (Public Library): Trujillo; f. 1930; 12,000 vols; Librarian ITALA BRICEÑO RUMBOS.

Valencia

Biblioteca Central de la Universidad de Carabobo: Valencia; 11,000 vols; Librarian ANTONIETA PINTO DE KATZ.

Museums and Art Galleries

Caracas

Casa Natal del Libertador Simón Bolívar (Simón Bolívar's Birthplace): San Jacinto a Traposos, Caracas; tel. (212) 541-25-63; murals by Tito Salas depicting the life of Bolívar and events of the Independence Movement; Curator JOSEFINA DE SANDOVAL.

Colección Ornitológica Phelps (Phelps Ornithological Collection): c/o Robin Restall, POB 025304, Miami, FL 33102-5304, USA; Located at: Blvd Sabana Grande, Edif. Gran Sabana, 3° piso, Apdo 2009, Caracas, 1001A; tel. (212) 719-238; fax (212) 762-5921; f. 1938; library of 10,000 vols; Pres. KATHLEEN PHELPS; Curator M. LENTINO R.

Fundación Museo de Ciencias: Avda Mexico, Plaza de los Museos, Parque Los Caobos, Apdo Postal 5883, Caracas 1010; tel. (212) 577-50-94; fax (212) 571-12-65; e-mail mciencia@reacciun.ve; internet www.museo-de-ciencias.org; f. 1875 as Museo Nacional, subsequently Museo de Ciencias Naturales; archaeology, palaeontology, geology, zoology, anthropology, entomology, ethnology; library of 2,100 vols; Pres. Ing. SERGIO ANTILLANO ARMAS.

Galería de Arte Nacional: Plaza de los Museos, Los Caobos, Apdo 6729, Caracas 1010; tel. (212) 578-18-18; fax (212) 578-16-61; e-mail fgan@infoline.wtfe.com; internet www.wtfe.com/gan; f. 1976; Venezuelan visual art from pre-Hispanic time to the present; Pres. CLEMENTINA VAAMONDE B.; Exec. Dir RAFAEL SANTANA.

Museo Bolivariano (Bolívar Museum): San Jacinto a Traposos, Caracas; f. 1911 and inaugurated in present building 1960; contains 1,546 exhibits; mementos, portraits, personal relics and historical paintings of Simón Bolívar and his fellow-workers in the Independence Movement; library of 1,200 vols; Dir FLOR ZAMBRANO DE GENTILE.

Museo de Arte Colonial (Museum of Colonial Art): Quinta de Anauco, Avda Panteón, San Bernardino, Caracas 1011; tel. (212) 551-86-50; fax (212) 551-85-17; e-mail artecolonialanauco@cantv.net; internet www.quintadeanauco.org.ve; f. 1942; painting, sculpture, decorative arts; library; under the supervision of the Asociación Venezolana de Amigos del Arte Colonial (*q.v.*); Dir CARLOS F. DUARTE.

Museo de Arte Contemporáneo de Caracas Sofía Imber (Sofía Imber Museum of Contemporary Art in Caracas): Zona Cultural, Parque Central, Apdo 17093, Caracas 1010; tel. (212) 577-00-75; fax (212) 577-18-83; e-mail info@maccsi.org.ve; internet www.maccsi.org.ve; f. 1973; incl. works by Picasso, Braque, Chagall, Bacon, Matisse, Kandinsky and Miró; Dir RITA SALVESTRINI.

Museo de Bellas Artes de Caracas (Museum of Fine Arts): Plaza Morelos, Parque Los Caobos, Caracas 105; tel. (212) 578-21-97; fax (212) 571-01-69; e-mail fmba@reacciun.ve; internet www.museodebellasartes.org; f. 1917; paintings and sculpture by national and foreign artists; library of 6,000 vols; Dir MARÍA ELENA RAMOS.

Ciudad Bolívar

Museo 'Talavera': Casa San Isidro, Ciudad Bolívar; f. 1940; pre-Columbian and Colonial period exhibits, religious art, natural science, numismatics; Dir Dr J. GABRIEL MACHADO; publ. *Museo Talavera.*

El Tocuyo

Museo Colonial (Historical Museum): El Tocuyo; f. 1945.

Maracaibo

Museo Histórico 'General Rafel Urdaneta' (Museum of Military History): 7A-70, Calle 91A, Maracaibo; f. 1936; Dir Prof. J. C. BORGES ROSALES.

Trujillo

Museo 'Cristóbal Mendoza' (Historical Museum): Trujillo.

Universities

UNIVERSIDAD NACIONAL ABIERTA (Open University)

Apdo 2096, Caracas 1010A

Telephone: (212) 574-1322

Fax: (212) 574-4075

E-mail: mromero@reacciun.ve

Internet: www.una.edu.ve

Founded 1977 on the 'open university' principle, using modern methods of communication and educational technology. One national centre in Caracas and 20 regional centres

State control

Language of instruction: Spanish

Academic year: October to July

Rector: Dra MARUJA ROMERO YÉPEZ (acting)

Academic Vice-Rector: Dr MANUEL CASTRO PEREIRA

Administrative Vice-Rector: Dr JOSÉ RAMÓN ORTIZ (acting)

Secretary: Prof. ROSE MARY DIAZ DEL VALLE

Librarian: Lic. CARMEN IBARRA

Number of teachers: 831
Number of students: 61,648
Publications: *Informe de Investigaciones Educativas, Una Documenta*

COURSE CO-ORDINATORS

Academic Areas and Courses: Prof. MARÍA J. BERMÚDEZ
Academic Co-ordinator: Dr MANUEL CASTRO PEREIRA
Academic Evaluation: Prof. ISALIV MATHEUS
Accountancy: Prof. FRANCISCO EGAÑEZ
Administration: Dr PEDRO RUIZ
Administration and Accountancy: Dr PEDRO RUIZ
Education: Dra ERICKA NAVEDA
General Studies: Dra MARÍA CLARA SALAS
Industrial Engineering: Prof. MARTHA URBINA
Mathematics: Prof. SERGIO RIVAS
Planning and Evaluation: Dra ARLETTE URGELLES
Regional and Local Centres: Prof. MIRIAM PÉREZ
Student Services: Prof. OMAIRA CORDERO
Systems Engineering: Prof. JUDIT CARVALLO
University Extension: Prof. TERESITA PÉREZ DE MAZA

LOCAL CENTRES

Anzoátegui: Dir Prof. LUIS RIVAS.
Apure: Dir Prof. JOSÉ GREGORIO FIGUEROA.
Aragua: Dir Prof. NELSON GUARDIA.
Barinas: Dir Prof. RAMÓN CHACÓN.
Bolívar: Dir Prof. ELMES PÉREZ.
Carabobo: Dir Prof. LUCILA CABRICES.
Cojedes: Dir (vacant).
Falcón: Dir Prof. NOÉ JIMENEZ.
Guárico: Dir Prof. DUNIA SISO.
Lara: Dir Prof. MILAGROS BARTOLOMÉ.
Mérida: Dir Prof. NAPOLEÓN SÁNCHEZ.
Metropolitano: Dir Prof. OSCAR ODÓN.
Monagas: Dir Prof. LUIS BALBAS.
Nueva Esparta: Dir Prof. AQUILES ROJAS.
Portuguesa: Dir Prof. NANCY CONTRERAS.
Sucre: Dir Prof. FREDDY PÉREZ.
Táchira: Dir MARÍA LOURDES RINCÓN.
Trujillo: Dir Prof. EVELYN HACKETT.
Yaracuy: Dir Prof. JORGE MILLA.
Zulia: Dir Prof. ANA YSOLINA SOTO.
T. F. Delta Amacuro: Dir Prof. JUANA LUGO.

UNIVERSIDAD DE CARABOBO

Avda Bolívar 125-39, Apdo Postal 129, Valencia 2001
Telephone: (41) 215-044
Internet: www.uc.edu.ve
Founded 1852
State control
Academic year: September to February, March to July
Rector: Dr GUSTAVO HIDALGO-VITALE
Academic Vice-Rector: Dr ELIS MERCADO MATUTE
Administrative Vice-Rector: Ing. JOSÉ BOTELLO WILSON
Secretary: Dr RUBÉN BALLESTEROS
Librarian: ANTONIETA PINTO DE KATZ
Library: see Libraries and Archives
Number of teachers: 2,585
Number of students: 44,654
Publications: *Boletín Universitario, Utopia y Praxis*

DEANS

Faculty of Economics and Social Sciences: Econ. LIONEL AGUDO
Faculty of Education: Lic. CARLOS HERRERA

Faculty of Engineering: Ing. GIOVANNI NANI
Faculty of Health Sciences: Dr CLAUDIO ROMANO
Faculty of Law: Ab. ELOY RUTMAN CISNEROS
Postgraduate Studies: Dr ALEJANDRO SUE MACHADO

UNIVERSIDAD CATÓLICA 'ANDRÉS BELLO'

Urb. Montalbán, La Vega, Apdo 1020, Caracas 1020
Telephone: (212) 407-4444
Fax: (212) 407-4349
E-mail: webmaster@ucab.edu.ve
Internet: www.ucab.edu.ve
Founded 1953
Private control (Society of Jesus)
Academic year: October to July
Campuses in San Cristóbal, Táchira
Chancellor: Rev. Fr PEDRO NICOLÁS BERMÚDEZ
Vice-Chancellor: Rev. Fr JESUS MARÍA ORBEGOZO EGUIGUREN
Rector: Rev. Fr LUIS UGALDE
Academic Vice-Rector: Dra MIRIAM LÓPEZ DE VALDIVIESO
Administrative Vice-Rector: Ing. LORENZO CALDENTEY LUQUE
Dean of Student Development: Dr RUBÉN ANGEL PEÑALVER GODINES
Secretary-General: Rev. Fr GUSTAVO SUCRE
Librarian: Lic. EMILIO PÍRIZ PÉREZ
Library: see Libraries and Archives
Number of teachers: 1,225
Number of students: 14,131
Publications: *Analogías del Comportamiento, Cuadernos Venezolanos de Filosofía, Encuentro EAC y Cuadernos UCAB-Educación, Espacios, Pensamiento Agustiniano, Revista de la Facultad de Derecho, Revista Montalbán, Revista de Relaciones Industriales y Laborales, Revista Tekhne de la Facultad de Ingeniería, Temas de Comunicación Social, Temas de Coyuntura*

DEANS

Faculty of Engineering: Ing. RAFAEL HERNÁNDEZ SÁNCHEZ-OCAÑA
Faculty of Humanities and Education: Dra SILVANA CAMPAGNARO
Faculty of Law: Dr JESÚS MARÍA CASAL
Faculty of Social and Economic Sciences: Dr EDUARDO OTIZ
Faculty of Theology: Rev. Fr GIAN PAOLO PERÓN

DIRECTORS

School of Business Administration and Accounting: Lic. FREDDY MARTÍN
School of Civil Engineering: Ing. JOSÉ OCHOA ITURBE
School of Economics: Econ. MARÍA ISABEL MARTÍNEZ ABAL
School of Education: Dra MARÍA ELENA FEBRES-CORDERO BRICEÑO
School of Engineering: Ing. MILAGROS BOSCHETTI
School of Industrial Engineering: Ing. VICENTE NAPOLITANO CASTALDO
School of Informatics: Ing. SUSANA GARCÍA MARTÍNEZ
School of Law: Abga AURA JANESKY LEHMANN
School of Letters: Lic. MARÍA DE LOS ÁNGELES PEÑA
School of Philosophy: Lic. JESÚS HERNÁEZ
School of Psychology: Dr GUSTAVO PEÑA
School of Social Sciences: Lic. INGRID OCHOA DE PÉREZ
School of Teleommunications Engineering: Ing. MAYRA NARVÁEZ
School of Theology: Rev. Fr RAFAEL SERRANO
Institute of Economic and Social Research: Lic. LUIS PEDRO ESPAÑA NAVARRO

Institute of Historical Research: Dr ELÍAS PINO ITURRIETA
Centre of Advice and Human Development: Lic. ALCIRA TEXEIRA DE CERRADA
Centre of Behavioural Studies: Dra SILVANA CAMPAGNARO
Centre of Communication Research: Lic. ERCILIA VÁSQUEZ
Centre of Engineering Research: Ing. LOURDES ORTIZ
Centre of Human Rights: Abga LIGIA BOLÍVAR
Centre of Legal Research: Dra. MARÍA GRACIA MORAIS DIAZ
Centre of Philosophical Studies: Dra SILVANA CAMPAGNARO
Centre of Religious Studies: Dra SILVANA CAMPAGNARO
Engineering Laboratories: Ing. FRANCISCO MORERA

UNIVERSIDAD CATÓLICA DEL TÁCHIRA

Calle 14 con Carrera 14, Apdo 306, San Cristóbal 5001, Edo Táchira
Telephone: (76) 430-510
Fax: (76) 446-183
E-mail: biucat@funtha.gov.ve
Internet: www.ucat.edu.ve
Founded 1982
Rector: JOSÉ DEL REY FAJARDO
Vice-Rector: ASTRID RICO DE MÉNDEZ
Chief Administrative Officer: FÉLIDA ROA DE ROA
Librarian: EMILIO J. URBINA MENDOZA
Number of teachers: 336
Number of students: 5,000
Publications: *Paramillo* (annually), *Revista Tachirense de Derecho* (annually), *Siglo XXI* (annually), *Tributum* (annually)

DEANS

Faculty of Economics and Social Sciences: MARINÉS SÁNCHEZ
Faculty of Humanities and Education: EDUARDO FAJARDO RUEDA
Faculty of Law and Political Science: JESÚS ALBERTO LABRADOR SUÁREZ
Faculty of Religion: EDUARDO FAJARDO RUEDA

HEADS OF DEPARTMENTS

Faculty of Economics and Social Sciences:

Accounting: NEYDO ALBORNOZ
Administration: IVI SÁNCHEZ
Economics and Complementary Disciplines: MARIELA CONTRERAS
Legislation and Basic Support: ABDA HERIKA MORA
Mathematics and Statistics: MARTIN GÁRATE

Faculty of Humanities and Education:

Biological Sciences: MERCEDES ESCALANTE LABRADOR
Computer Science: BERNARDO CONTRERAS
Professional Practice: VICTOR OMAÑA

Faculty of Law and Political Science:

Basic and Complementary Disciplines: FANNY RUBIO CALDERA
Practical Work: LAURA OMAÑA ECARRI
Private Law: FÉLIDA ROA DE ROA
Public Law: JOSÉ LUIS VILLEGAS MORENO
Tutorials and Research: CHRYSA CHIMARAS MAURY

UNIVERSIDAD CENTRAL DE VENEZUELA

Apdo Postal 1050, Ciudad Universitaria, Los Chaguaramos, Caracas 1051
Telephone: (212) 605-4050
Fax: (212) 605-4086
Internet: www.ucv.ve
Founded 1721

State control
Language of instruction: Spanish
Academic year: January to December

Rector: GIUSEPPE GIANNETTO
Academic Vice-Rector: ERNESTO GONZÁLEZ
Administrative Vice-Rector: MANUEL MARIÑA
Registrar: Dr ANTONIO DEL NOGAL
General Co-ordinator: JEANETTE BLANCO DE MÉNDEZ
Secretary: ELIZABETH MARVAL
Librarian: Dr EUDIS BORRA

Number of teachers: 6,987
Number of students: 45,000

Publications: *Acta Odontologica, Akademos* (2 a year), *Aula Magna, Boletín del Archivo Histórico, Boletín de Lingüística, Correo Ucevista, Gaceta Universitaria, Revista Alcance 57* (organic soil science, 2 a year), *Revista del Centro de Información y Documentación* (6 a year), *Revista Escuela de Metalurgia, Revista de la Facultad de Agronomía* (2 a year), *Revista de la Facultad de Ciencias Jurídicas y Políticas* (4 a year), *Revista de la Facultad de Ciencias Veterinarias, Revista de la Facultad de Farmacia* (4 a year), *Revista de la Facultad de Ingeniería* (6 a year), *Revista de la Facultad de Medicina, Revista Latinoamericana de Estudios Avanzados, Revista Tecnología y Construcción* (3 a year), *Revista Tharsis, Revista Urbana* (town planning, 2 a year), *Revista Venezolana de Economía y Ciencias Sociales, Revista Venezolana de Estudios Internacionales*

DEANS

Faculty of Agriculture: FRANKLÍN CHACÍN LUGO
Faculty of Architecture and Town Planning: ABNER COLMENARES
Faculty of Dentistry: CECILIA GARCÍA AROCHA
Faculty of Economic and Social Sciences: VÍCTOR RAGO
Faculty of Engineering: RAFAEL ROCA
Faculty of Humanities and Education: BENJAMÍN SÁNCHEZ
Faculty of Law and Political Science: PEDRO GUEVARA
Faculty of Medicine: MIGUEL REQUENA
Faculty of Pharmacy: ORLANDO VIZCARRONDO
Faculty of Science: MASSIMO CANESTRARI
Faculty of Veterinary Science: RAFAEL INFANTES

UNIVERSIDAD CENTRO-OCCIDENTAL 'LISANDRO ALVARADO'

Apdo 400, Barquisimeto, Lara

Telephone: (251) 259-1061
Fax: (251) 259-1064
Internet: www.ucla.edu.ve

Founded 1963 as Experimental Centre of Higher Education; university status 1968
State control
Language of instruction: Spanish
Academic year: January to December

Rector: Dr RICARDO GARCÍA DE LONGORIA
Academic Vice-Rector: Dra GADRA SÁNCHEZ DE PÉREZ
Administrative Vice-Rector: Dr GUÉDEZ CORTEZ
Secretary-General: Dr RICARDO GÁSPERI MAGO
Librarian: Lic. MORELLA BARRANCOS

Number of teachers: 930
Number of students: 9,665

Publications: *Boletín Científico, Boletín Informativo, El Veterinario* (monthly), *Escuela de Administración, Escuela de Agronomía, Memoria y Cuenta* (annually), *Tarea Común* (quarterly)

DEANS

Faculty of Administration and Accountancy: Lic. CÉSAR MORENO
Faculty of Agronomy: Ing. JOSÉ PASTOR GUTIÉRREZ
Faculty of Civil Engineering: Ing. HERMES ESPINOZA
Faculty of Medicine: Dr RÉGULO CARPIO
Faculty of Sciences: Dr JOSÉ BETHELMY
Faculty of Veterinary Medicine: Dr RAMÓN SALCEDO

ATTACHED INSTITUTES

Consejo Asesor de Investigación y Servicios (Advisory Council on Research and Services): assessment and consultation on the planning of research; Pres. Dr FRANCISCO MONTES DE OCA.

Instituto de la Uva (Institute for Research on Grapes): research on grape cultivation and advisory service to wine growers; Dir MARIA LUISA DE PIRE.

UNIVERSIDAD DE LOS ANDES

Avda 3, Independencia, Edif. Rectorado, Mérida 5101

Telephone: (275) 240-1111
Fax: (275) 240-1998
E-mail: dsia@ula.ve
Internet: www.ula.ve

Founded 1785 as the Real Colegio Seminario de San Buenaventura de Mérida, became University 1810

Campuses at Trujillo and Táchira
State control
Language of instruction: Spanish
Academic year: January to December

Rector: GENRY VARGAS
Academic Vice-Rector: MANUEL HERNÁNDEZ
Administrative Vice-Rector: JULIO FLORES MENESINI
Secretary: GLADYS BECERRA DEPABLOS
Registrar (vacant)
Librarian: NILZA GONZÁLEZ DE GUTIÉRREZ

Library: see Libraries and Archives
Number of teachers: 2,947
Number of students: 34,294

DEANS

Faculty of Architecture: Arq. INÉS BENAVIDES
Faculty of Economic and Social Sciences: MANUEL ARANGUREN
Faculty of Engineering: Ing. RUBÉN AÑEZ
Faculty of Forestry: Prof. CERES BOADA
Faculty of Humanities and Education: FRANCISCO GAVIDIA
Faculty of Law and Political Science: ANDREY GROMIKO URDANETA
Faculty of Medicine: Dr JOSÉ FREYTEZ O'CALLAGHAN
Faculty of Odontology: Dr PATRICIO JARPA
Faculty of Pharmacy: Dr ALFREDO CARABOT CUERVO
Faculty of Sciences: CARLOS ALVAREZ
Rafael Rangel Campus: Dr CONRADO DABOÍN VÁSQUEZ
Táchira Campus: Dr RAMÓN GONZÁLEZ E.

UNIVERSIDAD METROPOLITANA

Apdo 76819, Caracas 1070

Telephone: (212) 242-2958
Fax: (212) 242-5450
E-mail: cvicentini@unimet.edu.ve
Internet: www.unimet.edu.ve

Founded 1970
Private control
Language of instruction: Spanish
Academic year: October to September

President: Ing. HERNAN ANZOLA
Rector: Ing. JOSÉ IGNACIO MORENO LEÓN

Academic Vice-Rector: Ing. JOSÉ ROBERTO BELLO
Administrative Vice-Rector: Ing. ANTINIO IZSAK
Registrar: Prof. MARÍA DE LOURDES ACEDO DE SUCRE
Librarian: Dr ELEIDA GARCÍA

Number of teachers: 438
Number of students: 4,670

Publications: *Anales de la Universidad Metropolitana* (2 a year), *Revista UNIMET* (monthly)

DEANS

Arts and Sciences: Prof. JAVIER RÍOS
Economics and Social Sciences: Prof. JOSÉ ANGEL VELÁZQUEZ
Engineering: Ing. MARIA BLANCA FERNÁNDEZ

HEADS OF DEPARTMENTS

Arts and Sciences:
School of Education: Dr SONIA P. DE LINARES
School of Mathematics: Prof. SILVIA VILLEGAS
School of Modern Languages: Prof. CLARA GONZÁLEZ
Department of Chemistry: Prof. FERNANDO ARMAS
Department of Development: Prof. COLUMBA D. DE MATA
Department of Educational Models: Prof. RENATA CURCI
Department of English: NANCY GUTIERREZ
Department of Humanities: Prof. JORGE PORTILLA
Department of Initial Area: Prof. MARY CARMEN LOMBAO
Department of Pedagogy: Dr NATALIA CASTAÑÓN
Department of Physics: Prof. CARMEN SAINZ
Department of Programming and Educational Technology: Prof. ELVIRA NARAS

Economics and Social Sciences:
School of Accounting: Prof. PEDRO CHARLITAS
School of Banking and Finance: Prof. EDUARDO FAGRE
School of Law: Dr GILBERTO MARVEZ
School of Management: Prof. MARIO EUGÜI

Engineering:
School of Chemical Engineering: Prof. ALICIA DIENNES
School of Civil Engineering: Prof. CRISTINA MALDONADO
School of Electrical Engineering: Prof. REBECA LANDEAU
School of Mechanical Engineering: Prof. ALICIA DIENNES
School of Production Engineering: (vacant)
School of Systems Engineering: Prof. REBECA LANDEAU

School of Graduate Studies:
Corporate Management: Prof. ALBERTO SILVA
Engineering Management: Prof. JOSÉ RAMÓN SOLANO
Finance: Dr TOMÁS EGUREN
Integrated Communications: (vacant)
Real Estate Management: Prof. ALEJANDRO MARTUCCI

UNIVERSIDAD NACIONAL EXPERIMENTAL FRANCISCO DE MIRANDA

Calle Norte, Edif. Universitario, Coro, Estado Falcón 4101

Telephone: (293) 430-2100
Fax: (293) 302-132
Internet: www.unefm.edu.ve

Founded 1977

Academic year: January to December (2 semesters)

Chancellor: SIMON ALBERTO CONSALVI

Rector: Dr PEDRO BORREGALES P.

Academic Vice-Rector: Dr OSCAR ABREU

Administrative Vice-Rector: Dr JULIO LÓPEZ P.

Administrator: Lic. CESAR VELÁSQUEZ

Librarian: Lic. NIDYA PETIT DE MOTTA

Number of teachers: 350
Number of students: 3,000

Publications: *Boletín* (weekly), *Cultura Falconiana* (quarterly), *Gaceta Universitaria* (quarterly)

DEANS

Faculty of Civil and Industrial Engineering: Ing. ORANGEL NUÑEZ

Faculty of Medicine: Dr ROBERTO GRAND L.

Faculty of Veterinary Medicine and Agriculture: Dr DIOGENES RODRÍGUEZ

UNIVERSIDAD NACIONAL EXPERIMENTAL DE GUAYANA

Avda Las Américas, Edificio General de Seguros, Puerto Ordaz, Estado Bolívar

Telephone: (286) 923-2423

Fax: (286) 922-5673

E-mail: secretaria@uneg.edu.ve

Internet: www.uneg.edu.ve

Founded 1982

State control

Rector: JOSÉ TARAZONA

Vice-Rector (Academic): Dr LUIS ALEXIS VELÁSQUEZ

Vice-Rector (Administration): Dra MARÍA ELENA LATUFF

Secretary-General: Dra MYRIAN ARLENY ZAMBRANO DE GUERRERO

Publications: *Copérnico*, *Gaceta Universitaria* (annually), *Kaleidoscopio* (quarterly)

Departments of Education, Humanities and Arts, Man and the Environment, Management and Science and Technology.

UNIVERSIDAD 'ROMULO GALLEGOS'

102A San Juan de los Morros, Estado Guárico 2301A

Telephone: (46) 310-831

Fax: (46) 312-670

Internet: www.urg.edu.ve

Founded 1977

State control

Language of instruction: Spanish

Academic year: March to December (2 semesters)

President and Rector: Ing. GIOVANNI NANI R.

Academic Vice-Rector: Ing. ENRIQUE MUJICA ALVÁREZ

Administrative Vice-Rector: Lic. GHENRY J. NAVARRO U.

Librarian: Lic. RHAIZA MARQUEZ

Number of teachers: 367

Number of students: 5,306

Publication: *Horizontes Universitarios*

DEANS

Faculty of Economics: Lic. CARLOS HERRERA

Faculty of Education: Lic. CECILIA REQUENA R.

Faculty of Engineering: Ing. NELSON MARTE

Faculty of Health: Dra MARTHA CANTAVELLA

Faculty of Odontology: Dr OMAR SCOVINO

Faculty of Veterinary Medicine: Méd. Vet. SALVADOR DE J. PÉREZ ALEMÁN

Continuing Education: Lic. YOLANDA VILLASMIL

Postgraduate Studies: Lic. GLADYS MORENO V.

Research and Extension: Prof. GEOMAIRA MONTENEGRO

ATTACHED INSTITUTES

Centre for Legal Studies: Dir Abog. GLADYS BOYER.

Centre for Minimal Intervention in Farming: Dir Prof. RAFAEL SÁNCHEZ.

Centre for the Study of Grain: Dir Prof. ANGEL DAVID RIVILLO.

UNIVERSIDAD NACIONAL EXPERIMENTAL DE LOS LLANOS OCCIDENTALES 'EZEQUIEL ZAMORA'

Apdo Postal 19, Barinas 5201

Telephone: (73) 41-201

Fax: (73) 41-858

Internet: www.unellez.edu.ve

Founded 1975

Language of instruction: Spanish

Academic year: January to December (2 semesters)

Experimental government-sponsored institute of higher education, serving the Los Llanos Occidentales region, and the States of Apure, Barinas, Cojedes and Portuguesa

Rector: Dr RICARDO J. CASTRO ALVAREZ

Vice-Rector: Dr JOSÉ ALFREDO GUERRERO SOSA

Secretary: Dr LUIS A. SUÁREZ CORDERO

Librarian: Dra MIGDALIA DE LARA

Number of teachers: 600

Number of students: 8,000

Publications: *Biollania*, *Revista UNELLEZ de Ciencia y Tecnología*

Courses in agriculture and mechanization, economics, social development, regional planning, human ecology.

UNIVERSIDAD NACIONAL EXPERIMENTAL MARÍTIMA DEL CARIBE

Calle El Ejército, Catia la Mar, Vargas, Caracas

Telephone: (212) 351-0834

Fax: (212) 351-0834

E-mail: unem@umc.edu.ve

Internet: www.umc.edu.ve

Founded 2000

State control

Rector: MIGUEL LÓPEZ

Vice-Rector (Academic): REYNALDO MONTES DE OCA

Vice-Rector (Administration): MANUEL PÉREZ ALVAREZ.

UNIVERSIDAD NACIONAL EXPERIMENTAL POLITECNICA 'ANTONIO JOSÉ DE SUCRE'

Apdo Postal 539, Barquisimeto, Edo Lara

Telephone: (251) 420-133

Fax: (251) 413-880

Internet: www.unellez.edu.ve

Founded 1962

Private control

Rector: Dr IVÁN OLAIZOLA D'ALESSANDRO

Vice-Rector (Secretarial): Dr RAMÓN VIELMA

Regional Vice-Rectors: Ing. AMAEL CASTELLANO (Barquisimeto campus): Ing. ILDELFONSO MEJÍA ZAMBRANO (Caracas campus): Ing. LUIS CÁRDENAS CASTILLO (Puerto Ordaz campus)

Academic Administrative Co-ordinator: Ing. EDUARDO CABRÉ TRUJILLO

Co-ordinator: Lic. XIOMARA DE BARRA

Library of 19,200 vols, 9,000 periodicals

Number of teachers: 900

Number of students: 10,000

Publications: *Avance Universitario* (2 a year), *Boletín Bibliográfico de Publicaciones Recibidas* (2 a year), *Información General de la Universidad* (annually)

Faculties of Mechanical Engineering, Electrical Engineering, Electronic Engineering, Systems, Metallurgy, Chemistry and Industrial Engineering.

UNIVERSIDAD NACIONAL EXPERIMENTAL RAFAEL MARÍA BARALT

Avda El Rosario, Parroquia Carmen Herrera, Cabimas, Estado Zulia

Telephone: (264) 241-5306

E-mail: rectorado@unermb.edu.ve

Internet: www.unermb.edu.ve

Founded 1982

State control

Rector: Dr VICTOR HUGO MERIÑO CÓRDOBA

Vice-Rector (Academic): BOLÍVAR SÁENZ TRAÑA

Vice-Rector (Administration): AÍDA CÓRTES DE VERBEL

Secretary-General: ODA GONZÁLEZ RINCÓN.

UNIVERSIDAD NACIONAL EXPERIMENTAL SIMÓN RODRÍGUEZ

Calle 1, Zona Industrial Urb. Palo Verde, Caracas

Telephone: 251-3684

Internet: www.unesr.edu.ve

Founded 1974

Regional centres in 13 towns

President: Dr GUSTAVO GONZÁLEZ ERASO

Rector: Dr MANUEL MARIÑAS

Academic Vice-Rector: JUDITH SOSA DE VÁZQUEZ

Administrative Vice-Rector: ASDRÚBAL LOZANO FERNÁNDEZ

Secretary: MARÍA SILVA VIVANCO

Number of teachers: 387

Number of students: 12,859

Publications: *Gaceta Universitaria* (4 a year), *Memoria y Cuenta de la Universidad* (annually), *Revista de Cultura* (4 a year)

Faculties of Administration, Education and Food Technology.

UNIVERSIDAD NACIONAL EXPERIMENTAL DEL TÁCHIRA

Apdo 436, Avda Universidad, Paramillo, San Cristóbal, Táchira

Telephone: (276) 353-0422

Fax: (276) 353-2896

E-mail: rectorad@unet.edu.ve

Internet: www.unet.edu.ve

Founded 1974

State control

Language of instruction: Spanish

Academic year: February to December

Rector: Lic. JOSÉ VICENTE SÁNCHEZ FRANK

Academic Vice-Rector: Ing. CARLOS CHACÓN LABRADOR

Administrative Vice-Rector: Ing. MARTÍN PAZ

Secretary: Arq. OSCAR MEDINA HERNÁNDEZ

Dean of Extension: Ing. SALVADOR GALEANO

Dean of Graduate Studies: Ing. JESÚS WILFREDO BOLÍVAR

Dean of Research: Ing. RAÚL CASANOVA

Dean of Teaching: Ing. JOSÉ BECERRA

Dean of Undergraduate Studies: Ing. LUIS VERGARA

Librarian: Ing. ERLAND MARTÍNEZ

Number of teachers: 530

Number of students: 10,500 (6,000 undergraduate, 1,500 propaedeutic, 3,000 graduate)

Publications: *Aleph sub cero*, *Boletín*, *Boletín Estadístico*, *Gaceta*, *Revista Científica UNET*, *Vocero Universitario*

HEADS OF DEPARTMENTS

Agricultural Engineering: (vacant)
Animal Production Engineering: Ing. ARMANDO GARCÍA B.
Architecture: Arq. FREDDY SILVA
Biochemistry: Lic. MIREYA CASTILLO
Computer Science: Lic. ALEXANDER CONTRERAS
Earth and Environment: Ing. JOSÉ ROA
Educational Development: Lic. JOSEFINA BALBO
Electronic Engineering: Ing. ARMANDO BOLCOÑO
Industrial Engineering: Ing. LÍA ZAMBRANO
Laboratories and Projects: Ing. REINALDO AGUILERA
Mathematics and Physics: Lic. RAÚL
Mechanical Engineering: Ing. MILEXA PEÑA DE VARGAS
Social Sciences: Lic. JOHN RAMÍREZ

UNIVERSIDAD NACIONAL EXPERIMENTAL DEL YARACUY

Zona Industrial Agustín Rivero, Edificio Fundación CIEPE, San Felipe, Estado Yaracuy
Telephone: (254) 232-2441
Fax: (254) 232-1351
E-mail: rectorado@uney.edu.ve
Internet: www.uney.edu.ve
Founded 1999
State control

Rector: Dr FREDDY CASTILLO CASTELLANOS
Vice-Rector: Ing. JOSÉ LUIS NAJUL SALDIVIA
Secretary-General: Ing. RAMÓN G. SÁNCHEZ SIVIRA

Courses in food science and sport.

UNIVERSIDAD DE ORIENTE

Edificio Rectorado, Apdo 094, Cumaná, Estado Sucre
Telephone: (93) 23366
Internet: www.udo.edu.ve
Founded 1958
State control
Academic year: February to December

Rector: Dr ANDRÉS PASTRANA VÁSQUEZ
Academic Vice-Rector: Dr OSWALDO BETANCOURT
Administrative Vice-Rector: Dr DIOGENES FIGUEROA LUGO
Secretary-General: Dr CESAR A. BOADA SALAZAR

Library: see Libraries and Archives
Number of teachers: 1,382
Number of students: 23,084

Publications: *Boletín del Instituto Oceanográfico, Catálogo de la UDO* (annually), *Directorio del Personal Docente e Investigación* (annually), *Lagena, Oriente Agropecuario, Oriente Universitario* (monthly bulletin), *La UDO Investiga.*

CONSTITUENT CAMPUSES

Universidad de Oriente, Nucleo Anzoátegui

Apdo postal 4327, Puerto La Cruz, Anzoátegui
Telephone: 663827
Internet: www.anz.udo.edu.ve
Founded 1965
Dean: Prof. MANUEL LÓPEZ FARÍAS
Number of teachers: 418
Number of students: 9,000

HEADS OF SCHOOLS

Administrative Sciences: Prof. JUAN D. GUAICAIN
Basic Courses: Prof. PEDRO JIMÉNEZ

Engineering and Applied Science: Prof. RUBÉN AULAR

ATTACHED INSTITUTES

Centro de Desarrollo Tecnológico: Dir Prof. RENÉ P. CABRERA.
Centro de Investigación Tecnológica Oriente: Dir Dr CLEMENTE VALLENILLA.

Universidad de Oriente, Nucleo Bolívar

La Sabanita, Ciudad Bolívar
Internet: www.bolivar.udo.edu.ve
Dean: Dr ARTURO RAUL LARA ROJAS

DIRECTORS

Basic Courses: Prof. MARGOTH SISO DE SAN MARTIN
Geology and Mines: Prof. OSCAR GARCÍA CACHAZO
Medicine: Prof. VICTOR ESPINOZA LEÓN

ATTACHED INSTITUTES

Centre for Biomedical Research: Dir Dr OTTO SÁNCHEZ.
Geosciences Centre: Dir Prof. MANUEL FUNES ARIZA.

Universidad de Oriente, Nucleo de Monagas

Avda Universidad, Maturín, Edo Monagas
Internet: www.monagas.udo.edu.ve
Founded 1961
Dean: Dr JOSÉ JIMÉNEZ TIAMO
Academic Co-ordinator: Ing. LUIS ARISMENDI
Administrative Co-ordinator: Ing. MARCIAL VIÑAS DE LA HOZ
Librarian: Lic. RAMÓN JOSÉ NÚÑEZ
Publication: *Oriente Agropecuario* (2 a year)

HEADS OF SCHOOLS

Basic Courses: Prof. JOSÉ VICENTE ANDÉRICO
School of Agricultural Engineering: NILDA ALCORCES DE GUERRA
School of Animal Husbandry: (vacant)
Programme of Administrative Science: Prof. ARNALDO ROJAS
Programme of Human Resources: Prof. LUIS MÁRQUEZ

ATTACHED INSTITUTE

Instituto de Investigaciones Agropecuarias: Dir Dr TOMÁS RODRÍGUEZ.

Universidad de Oriente, Nucleo Nueva Esparta

Apdo Postal 147, Guatamare, Nueva Esparta
Telephone: (95) 610131
Fax: (95) 610131
Internet: www.ne.udo.edu.ve
Founded 1958
State control
Dean: Ing. CASTO GONZÁLEZ M.
Academic Co-ordinator: Prof. JOSÉ G. MARCANO
Administrative Co-ordinator: Ing. LUIS MARCANO

HEADS OF SCHOOLS

Applied Ocean Sciences: Prof. JOSÉ LUIS FUENTES
Basic Courses: Prof. ESTEBAN OBANDO
Hotel and Tourism: Prof. JOSÉ M. VELÁSQUEZ

ATTACHED INSTITUTE

Instituto de Investigaciones Científicas: Dir Prof. DOMINGO GONZÁLEZ.

Universidad de Oriente, Nucleo de Sucre

Cumaná
Internet: www.sucre.udo.edu.ve

Dean: Prof. FRANCIA PADILLA DE KORCHOFF

HEADS OF SCHOOLS

Administration and Accountancy: Prof. JOSÉ ANTONIO ARISTIMUÑO
Basic Courses: Prof. FORTUNATO MALAN
Humanities and Education: Prof. EZEQUIEL SALAZAR
Sciences: Prof. ELSIE ROMERO DE BELLORIN
Social Sciences: Prof. MARÍA ELENA ZAJÍA

ATTACHED INSTITUTES

Centro de Microscopía Electrónica: Dir Prof. SUSAN TAI DE DÍAZ.
Centro de Sismología: Dir Prof. JUAN DE MARTÍN MARFIL.
Centro de Tecnología Educativa: Dir Lic. MARY PLAZAS DE N.
Instituto Oceanográfico: Dir Prof. ANIBAL VELEZ..

UNIVERSIDAD PEDAGÓGICA EXPERIMENTAL LIBERTADOR

Avda Sucre, Parque del Oeste, Catia, 1030 Caracas
Telephone: (212) 864-7511
Fax: (212) 864-7977
Internet: www.upel.edu.ve
Founded 1983
State control
Academic year: September to July

Rector: Prof. ÁNGEL ARÍSTIDES HERNÁNDEZ ABREU
Vice-Rector (Extension): Prof. LUIS MARÍN
Vice-Rector (Research and Postgraduate Studies): Prof. MAXIMILIANO BEZADA
Vice-Rector (Teaching): Prof. JESÚS RODRÍGUEZ
Secretary: Prof. FRANCIA CELIS.

CONSTITUENT INSTITUTES

Institutio Pedagógico de Barquisimeto

Avda Los Horcones con Calle 64, Barquisimeto, Estado Lara
Telephone: (251) 442-5333
Fax: (251) 423-887
E-mail: r.valera@ipb.upel.edu.ve
Internet: www.ipb.upel.edu.ve
Director: RAFAEL VALERA.

Instituto Pedagógico de Caracas

Avda Páez, El Paraíso, Caracas 1020
Telephone: (212) 461-6121
Fax: (212) 462-2760
E-mail: webmaster@ipc.upel.edu.ve
Internet: www.ipc.upel.edu.ve
Founded 1936 as Instituto Pedagógico Nacional; present status 1987
Academic year: May to February (two semesters)

Director: Prof. CRISTIAN SÁNCHEZ
Sub-Director (Extension): Prof. ÁNGEL FLORES
Sub-Director (Research and Postgraduate Studies): Prof. SILVANA MESSORI DE NEGRETE
Sub-Director (Teaching): Prof. HEAGDLINE ARIAS
Librarian: Lic. MELVIS PIRE

Publications: *Candidus Infantil* (quarterly), *Lingvo & Internacia Komunikado, Revista de Investigación, Tiempo y Espacio*

HEADS OF DEPARTMENTS

Art: Prof. ALEJANDRO VÁSQUEZ
Biology and Chemistry: Prof. JUAN ACOSTA BOOL
Castilian, Literature and Latin: Prof. LUIS FLORES GIRALDO
Earth Sciences: Prof. ANA TERESA ISTÚRIZ

Educational Technology: Prof. MARÍA TERESA MATO

Geography and History: Prof. MARÍA ELENA HURTADO

Mathematics and Physics: Prof. ANA MARÍA ALBERO

Modern Languages: Prof. INGRID ORIHUELA DE GONZÁLEZ

Pedagogy: Prof. ZORELYS LEÓN

Physical Education: Prof. HERNÁN HERNÁNDEZ

Special Education: Prof. BEATRIZ LUQUE

Teaching Practice: Prof. MARÍA VICTORIA MANTILLA

Instituto de Mejoramiento Profesional del Magisterio

Avda Rómulo Gallegos, Segunda Transversal de Montecristo, Caracas 1071

Telephone: (212) 234-6640
Fax: (212) 234-6608
E-mail: pontivero@impm.upel.edu.ve
Internet: www.impm.upel.edu.ve.

Instituto Pedagógico de Maturín

Carretera Sur, Maturín 6263, Estado Monagas

Telephone: (291) 641-6863
Fax: (291) 641-7750
E-mail: carzolay@ipm.upel.edu.ve
Internet: www.ipm.upcl.cdu.vc

Dir: COSME ALZOLAY.

Instituto Pedagógico de Miranda

Calle 6, Edificio Papeca Modulo 2, Urbanización La Urbina, Caracas 1070

Telephone: (212) 461-6472
Fax: (212) 462-2760
E-mail: nbarreto@ipmjmsm.upel.edu.ve
Internet: www.ipmjmsm.upel.edu.ve

Dir: NANCY BARRETO.

Instituto Pedagógico Rural 'El Mácaro'

Carretera Nacional Maracay/Turmero, Maracay 2115, Estado Aragua

Telephone: (244) 631-294
Fax: (244) 61-380
E-mail: aperales@iprm.upel.edu.ve
Internet: www.iprm.upel.edu.ve

Dir: AURA DÍAZ DE PERALES.

Instituto Pedagógico Rural 'Gervasio Rubio'

Final Avda Dr 'Manuel Pulido Méndez', Vía Bramón, Rubio, Estado Táchira

Telephone: (276) 762-1746
Fax: (276) 762-4041
E-mail: fespinel@iprgr.upel.edu.ve
Internet: www.iprgr.upel.edu.ve

Dir: FRANCISCO ESPINEL.

UNIVERSIDAD SIMÓN BOLÍVAR

Carretera Hoyo de la Puerta, Valle de Sartenejas Baruta Estado Miranda

Telephone: (212) 906-3111
Fax: (212) 962-1615
Internet: www.usb.ve

Founded 1970
State control
Language of instruction: Spanish
Academic year: September to July

Rector: Ing. PEDRO ASO
Academic Vice-Rector: Dr OSMAR ISSA
Administrative Vice-Rector: Ing. JUAN LEON
General Secretary: Dr PEDRO MARÍA ASO
Librarian: Dra ROSARIO GASSOL DE HOROWITZ

Number of teachers: 850
Number of students: 10,000

Publications: *Argos, Atlántida, Perfiles*

DEANS

General Studies: JUAN CARLOS RODRÍGUEZ
Postgraduate Studies: CARLOS PÉREZ
Professional Studies: RAUL GONCALVES
Research: BENJAMÍN SCHARIFKER

DIVISION DIRECTORS

Biological Sciences: DAISY PÉREZ DE ACOSTA
Humanities and Social Sciences: ANA MARÍA RAJKAY
Physics and Mathematics: ROBERTO RÉQUIZ
Technological Studies (Núcleo Universitario del Litoral): ENRIQUE LÓPEZ CONTRERAS

RESEARCH INSTITUTES

Instituto de Altos Estudios de América Latina: Dir MIGUEL ANGEL BURELLI RIVAS.

Instituto de Estudios Regionales y Urbanos: Dir NELSON GEIGEL LOPE-BELLO.

Instituto de Investigaciones Históricas 'Bolivarium': Dir JUAN MANUEL MORALES.

Instituto de Recursos Naturales Renovables: Dir HAYMARA ALVAREZ.

Instituto de Tecnologías Ciencias Marinas: Dir DAVID BONE.

UNIVERSIDAD DEL ZULIA

Apdo de Correos 526, Maracaibo 4011, Estado Zulia

Telephone: (261) 517-697
Fax: (261) 512-525
Internet: www.luz.ve

Founded 1891, closed 1904, reopened 1946
State control
Academic year: September to July

Rector: Dr ANGEL LOMBARDI LOMBARDI
Academic Vice-Rector: Lic. ANTONIO CASTEJÓN
Administrative Vice-Rector: Econ. NEURO VILLALOBOS
Secretary: Ing. ANGEL LARREAL
Librarian: Lic. EGLA ORTEGA

Library: see Libraries and Archives
Number of teachers: 3,652
Number of students: 47,590

Publications: *Gaceta* (quarterly), *Memoria y Cuenta de LUZ* (annually), *Publicaciones de la Unidad de Estadísticas*

DEANS

Faculty of Agriculture: Prof. ALONSO FERNÁNDEZ
Faculty of Architecture: Prof. IGNACIO DE OTEIZA
Faculty of Dentistry: Prof. EXEQUIADES PAZ A.
Faculty of Economic and Social Sciences: Prof. JULIANA FERRER
Faculty of Engineering: Prof. NELSON MOLERO
Faculty of Experimental Sciences: Prof. TERESITA ALVAREZ DE FERNANDEZ
Faculty of Humanities and Education: Prof. NERÍO VÍLCHEZ
Faculty of Law: Dr HERMANN PETZOLD PERNÍA
Faculty of Medicine: Dr RAFAEL MARTÍNEZ
Faculty of Veterinary Sciences: Prof. GUSTAVO SOTO

ATTACHED RESEARCH INSTITUTES

Centro de Documentación e Investigación Pedagógica (Centre for Educational Documentation and Research): Dir Prof. VIRGINIA PIRELA.

Centro de Estadísticas e Investigación de Operaciones (Centre for Statistics and Operations Research): Dir Econ. IGOR GARCÍA.

Centro de Estudios de la Empresa (Centre for Business Studies): Dir Lic. JESÚS DANIEL BORGES.

Centro de Estudios Filosóficos (Centre for Philosophical Studies): Dir Dr ANGEL BUSTILLOS.

Centro de Estudios Históricos (Centre for Historical Studies): Dir Dr RUTILIO ORTEGA.

Centro de Estudios Literarios (Centre for Literary Studies): Dir Prof. LUIS OQUENDO.

Centro Experimental de Producción Animal (Experimental Centre for Animal Production): Dir Dr WILLIAM ISEA

Centro Experimental de Estudios Latinoamericanos (Experimental Centre for Latin American Studies): Dir Dr GASTÓN PARRA LUZARDO.

Centro de Investigaciones Biológicas (Centre for Biological Research): Dir Prof. JOAQUIN LEÓN.

Centro de Investigaciones y Estudios Laborales y Disciplinas Afines (Centre for Research on Labour and Related Disciplines): Dir Dr LUIS EDUARDO DÍAZ.

Instituto de Cálculo Aplicado (Institute of Applied Calculus): Dir Ing. CARLOS MORALES.

Instituto Criminología del Derecho (Institute for Criminology): Dir FRANCISCO DELGADO.

Instituto de Filosofía del Derecho (Institute of Legal Philosophy): Dir Dra BRIGITTE BERNARD.

Instituto de Investigaciones Agronómicas (Institute of Agricultural Research): Dir Ing. ISIDRO MELÉNDEZ.

Instituto de Investigaciones de Arquitectura y Sistemas Ambientales (Institute of Research on Architecture and Environmental Systems): Dir Arq. EDGARDO IBAÑEZ.

Instituto de Investigaciones Biológicas (Biological Research Institute): basic and applied research in biology and experimental medicine; Dir Dra CONSUELO VALERO.

Instituto de Investigaciones Clínicas (Institute of Clinical Research): Dir Dr HUMBERTO MARTINEZ.

Instituto de Investigaciones de la Facultad de Ciencias Económicas y Sociales (Institute of Economic Research): Dir Econ. JOSE MORENO.

Instituto de Investigaciones Petroleras (Centre for Petroleum Research): Dir Ing. RENATO ACOSTA.

Instituto de Medicina del Trabajo e Higiene Industrial (Institute of Industrial Medicine and Hygiene): Dir Dra NORA VARGAS DE PINEDA.

Unidad Co-ordinadora de Proyectos Conjuntos (Co-ordinating Unit for Related Projects): research on inter-relation between social sciences, agriculture and veterinary science in rural development; Dir Econ. JOSÉ E. FUENTES.

Unidad de Genética Médica (Unit for Medical Genetics): Dir Dra LENNIE PINEDA DE DELVILLAR.

Polytechnic Institute

INSTITUTO UNIVERSITARIO POLITÉCNICO 'LUIS CABALLERO MEJÍAS'

Apdo 20955, San Martin, Caracas 1020A

Telephone: (212) 498-917

Founded 1974

Director: Ing. RAFAEL DUQUE SALINAS
Deputy Director (Academic): Ing. IDELFONSO MEJÍAS
Deputy Director (Administrative): Lic. RAMÓN PELLES

Librarian: Lic. MYRIAM LÓPEZ ACOSTA
Number of teachers: 216
Number of students: 2,017

HEADS OF DEPARTMENTS

Basic Sciences: Lic. FRANKLIN PIRELA
Foundation Courses: Lic. LIADA RONDON DE MOSQUERA
General Courses: Lic. RAFAEL RENÉ RAMIREZ
Industrial Engineering: Lic. OSWALDO GUILLERMO
Mechanical Engineering: Lic. CALÓGERO SALVO
Professional Studies: Lic. PEDRO LECUE
Systems Engineering: Lic. PEDRO LECUE

College

Instituto de Estudios Superiores de Administración (IESA) (Institute for Advanced Studies in Administration): Edificio IESA, Avda IESA, San Bernardino, Caracas 1010; tel. (212) 552-20-55; e-mail relinsti@iesa.edu.ve; internet www.iesa.edu.ve; f. 1965; private non-profit business school; President RAMÓN PIÑANGO.

Schools of Art and Music

Centro de Bellas Artes (Center for Fine Arts): Apdo 10015, Bella Vista, Maracaibo; tel. (61) 912950; fax (61) 920195; f. 1954 to promote cultural activities; theatre, two art galleries, school of ballet and modern dance, Maracaibo Contemporary Dance Troupe, Maracaibo Symphony Orchestra, National Youth Theatre, Goajiro Indian workshop, *Colegio Bellas Artes*, library; Dir OSCAR D'EMPAIRE.

Conservatorio de Música 'José Luis Paz': Edif. Secretaría de Cultura, 3° piso, Avda 2, Maracaibo; tel. (261) 223868; Dir Prof. OSCAR FACCIO.

Escuela de Artes Visuales 'Cristóbal Rojas' (Cristóbal Rojas School of Visual Arts): Esquina Ño Pastor, frente a la Plaza Parque Carabobo, La Candelaria, Caracas 1010; tel. (14) 9117294; f. 1936; Dir EMELY HERNÁNDEZ DE VILLAROEL.

Escuela Superior de Arte 'Neptali Rincón': Centro Vocacional Dr O. Hernández, Avda El Milagro Diagonal al Hospital Central, Maracaibo; tel. (261) 223868; f. 1957; courses in painting, sculpture, ceramics, etc.; 12 teachers; 300 students; Dir Prof. ANIBAL LARES M.

Escuela Superior de Música 'José Angel Lamas' (Lamas High School of Music): Veroes a Santa Capilla, Caracas; f. 1887; Dir VICENTE EMILIO SOJO.

Fundación Teresa Carreño: Teatro Teresa Carreño, Final Paseo Colón, Caracas; tel. (212) 5749122; e-mail webmaster@teatroteresacarreno.com; internet www.teatroteresacarreno.com; f. 1983; concerts, opera, ballet, master classes and courses for opera singers; Dir-Gen. BEATRICE RANGEL MANTILLA.

VIET NAM

The Higher Education System

Institutions of higher education predate Viet Nam's partition in 1954 (it was reunified as the Socialist Republic of Viet Nam in 1976), the oldest being Hanoi University of Medicine, which was founded in 1902 when Viet Nam was under French colonial rule. Over 30 institutions were founded during the period of partition (1954–76), including major universities in Hanoi and Ho Chi Minh City (formerly Saigon). In 1989 Viet Nam's first private college since 1954 was opened in Hanoi; Thang Long College was to cater for university students. The Ministry of Education and Training is responsible for higher education, although institutions of health education and military or security training come under the appropriate Ministries. In 2003/04 there were 187 universities and colleges of higher education, with a total enrolment of 993,900 students.

Since academic year 2003/04 a national university entrance examination has been the determining factor in university admissions. Students sit examinations in one of four subject streams, depending on the course of study for which the student has applied. A College Diploma or Associate degree (Tot nghiep dai hoc) is a three-year course that can be upgraded to a Bachelors degree after one year. The Bachelors degree (Bang tot nghiep dai hoc) is the main undergraduate qualifications and often lasts four years, although degrees in veterinary medicine (five years) and medicine (six years) are longer in duration. Graduates who have been awarded the Bachelors degree are eligible to sit the entrance examination for admission to the Masters degree (Thac si), a two-year taught or research-based course. The Doctorate (Tien si) is open to students who hold either the Bachelors or the Masters degree and admission is again based on competitive examination. However, students with Bachelors must study for four to five years to gain the Doctorate (and usually earn a Masters 'in passing') while students with the Masters are awarded the Doctorate after two or three years. Technical and vocational education at the post-secondary level is offered by universities through professional programmes of study (see above).

The Division of Quality Accreditation was established in 2002 to administer accreditation of institutions and quality assurance.

Learned Societies

GENERAL

UNESCO Office Hanoi: 23 Cao Ba Quat, Hanoi; tel. (4) 7470275; fax (4) 7470274; e-mail registry@unesco.org; internet www.un.org.vn; Dir ROSAMARIA DURAND.

Viet Nam Union of Literary and Arts Associations: 51 Tran Hung Dao St, Hanoi; tel (4) 8682608; fax (4) 9437431; f. 1957; 10 mem.orgs (assocs of writers, cinematographers, fine arts, composers and musicologists, theatre artists, photographers, folklorists, dancers, architects, and minority writers and artists), with a total of 10,000 mems; Pres. NGUYEN DINH THI; Sec.-Gen. THANH TO NGOC; publ. *Dien dan van nghe Viet nam* (Forum of Vietnamese Literature and Arts, 4 a year).

Viet Nam Union of Science and Technology Associations: 53 Nguyen Du St, Hanoi; tel. 56781; e-mail vanphonglhh@vnn.vn; internet www.vusta.org.vn; f. 1983; 51 mem. socs.; Pres. Prof. VU TUYEN HOANG.

AGRICULTURE, FISHERIES AND VETERINARY SCIENCE

Gardeners' Association: Nguyen Cong Tru St, Hanoi; f. 1985; Sec.-Gen. NGHIEM XUAN YEM.

Vietnam Forestry Association: 114 Hoang Quoc Viet St, Cau Giay District, Hanoi; tel. (4) 7541311; Pres. NGUYEN NGOC LUNG; Sec.-Gen. NGO DUC MINH.

ARCHITECTURE AND TOWN PLANNING

Builders' Association: 34 Hang Chuoi St, Hanoi; Sec.-Gen. LE QUANG BAU.

ECONOMICS, LAW AND POLITICS

Economics Association: 27 Tran Xuan Soan St, Hanoi.

Law Association: Nguyen Thuong Hien, Hanoi; tel. 57149; Sec.-Gen. PHAN ANH.

HISTORY, GEOGRAPHY AND ARCHAEOLOGY

Vietnamese Association of Historians: 25 Tong Dan St, Hanoi; tel. (4) 8256588; Pres. PHAN HUY LE; Sec.-Gen. DUONG TRUNG QUOC.

LANGUAGE AND LITERATURE

British Council: 40 Cat Linh St, Dong Da Dsitrict, Hanoi; tel. (4) 8436780; fax (4) 8434962; e-mail bchanoi@britishcouncil.org.vn; internet www.britishcouncil.org/vietnam; f. 1993; teaching centre; offers courses and exams in English language and British culture and promotes cultural exchange with the UK; attached teaching centre in Ho Chi Minh City; Dir KEITH DAVIES; Training Centre Man. TIM HOOD.

Goethe-Institut: Nguyen Thai Hoc Str. 56–58, Ba Dinh District, Hanoi; tel. (4) 7342251; fax (4) 7342254; e-mail gihanoi-il@fpt.vn; internet www.goethe.de/so/han/deindex.htm; offers courses and exams in German language and culture and promotes cultural exchange with Germany; Dir FRANZ XAVER AUGUSTIN.

MEDICINE

Traditional Medicine Association of Viet Nam: 19 Tong Dan St, Hanoi; tel. (4) 8253006; Pres. NGUYEN XUAN HUONG.

Vietnam General Association of Medicine and Pharmacy: 68 Ba Trieu St, Hanoi; tel. 52323; f. 1955; 21 mem. socs; Pres. DANG DUC TRACH; Sec.-Gen. TRAN HUU THANG.

NATURAL SCIENCES

Biological Sciences

Vietnam Association of Biological Science Societies: Biological Experiment Centre, Ha Noi Pedagogical Institute, Hanoi; tel. (4) 8347654; Pres. VU TUYEN HOANG; Sec.-Gen. NGUYEN LAN HUNG.

Mathematical Sciences

Vietnam Mathematical Society: 46 Lieu Giai St, Hanoi; tel. (4) 8682414; President DO LONG VAN; Sec.-Gen. TONG DINH QUY.

Physical Sciences

Geological Society of Viet Nam: 6 Pham Ngu Lao, Hanoi; tel. (4) 8260752; fax (4) 8260752; e-mail thanh_ngt_2000@yahoo.com; f. 1983; 5,000 mems; Sec.-Gen. NGUYEN TIEN THANH.

Viet Nam Physical Society: P104-46 Nguyen Van Ngoc St, Hanoi; tel. (4) 8349209; fax (4) 8349050; Pres. PHAN HONG KHOI.

TECHNOLOGY

Mining Association: 54 Hai Ba Trung, Hanoi; Sec.-Gen. TRAN ANH VINH.

Vietnam Foundry and Metallurgical Association: 54 Hai Ba Trung St, Hanoi; tel. (4) 8262052; Pres. PHAN TU PHUNG.

Vietnamese Association of Mechanics: Building K10A-P407 Bach Khoa, Hanoi; tel. (4) 8693402; Pres. NGUYEN VAN DAO; Sec.-Gen. DO SANH.

Research Institutes

GENERAL

Institute of Culture: O Cho Dua, Hanoi; tel. 56415; f. 1971; 50 staff; study of Vietnamese culture in all its aspects and relations with other countries; library of 5,000 vols; Dir Prof. LE ANH TRA; Sec. Dr LAM TO LOC; publ. *Culture Research Information.*

AGRICULTURE, FISHERIES AND VETERINARY SCIENCE

Animal Husbandry Research Institute: Chem, Tu Liem, Hanoi; tel. 43971; f. 1969; research on domestic animals; extension service; Dir Dr LE VIET LY; publ. *Scientific and Technical Journal on Animal Husbandry.*

Centre for Applied Research in Agricultural Engineering: 10A, Tran Nhat Duat St, 1st Dist, Ho Chi Minh City; tel. (8) 8442947; fax (8) 8438842; f. 1976; 100 mems; library of 3,000 vols; Head of Administration PHAM VAN TAN; publ. *Agricultural Engineering* (annually).

Centre for Research on Inland Aquatic Products: Tien Son District, Ha Bac Province; f. 1975.

Dalat Centre for Scientific Research: 116 Xo Viet Nghe Tinh St, Da Lat, Lam Dong Province; tel. 2078; f. 1978; development and reproduction of animals, cow and buffalo embryo transplantation, cryobiology, chemistry of natural substances, introduction and acclimatization of plants; 18 scientists; Dir Dr NGUYEN DANG KHOI.

Food Crops Research Institute: Lien Hong, Gia Loc, Hai Duong Province; tel. (320) 716463; fax (320) 716385; e-mail vcltctp@fpt.vn; f. 1968; research on varietal and technological improvement of rice, root and tuber crops, legumes, vegetables and fruit-tree crops; library of 1,950 vols, 170 journals; Dir Dr NGUYEN, TAN HINH (acting); publ. *Research Bulletin of Food Crops* (every 2–3 years).

Forest Science Institute of Vietnam (FSIV): Chem, Tu Liem District, Hanoi; tel. (4) 8389031; fax (4) 8389722; e-mail vkhln@vista.gov.vn; f. 1988; Dir-Gen. Prof. Dr TRIEU VAN HUNG; publ. *Vietnam Forestry Review* (quarterly).

Institute of Agricultural Science of Southern Vietnam: 121 Nguyen Binh Khiem St, 1st District, Ho Chi Minh City; tel. (8) 8291746; fax (8) 8297650; f. 1981; research on pedology, crop sciences and animal sciences; library of 10,000 vols; collection of insects; Dir Prof. PHAM VAN BIEN; publ. *Annual Report of Research Results*.

Institute of Agro-Chemistry and Pedology: Tu Liem District, Hanoi; f. 1968.

Institute of Forestry: Tu Liem District, Hanoi; f. 1974.

Institute of Fruit-tree and Industrial Crop Research: Phong Chau, Vinh Phu Province; f. 1969.

Institute of Veterinary Research: Dong Da Precinct, Hanoi; f. 1968.

National Institute of Plant Protection: POB Chem, Tu Liem District, Hanoi; tel. 344723; fax (4) 8363563; e-mail nipp.vietnam@bdvn.vnmail.vnd.net; f. 1968; plant protection research and development with emphasis on biological and genetic control, integrated pest management of food and vegetable and specific tropical crops; library of 700 vols; Dir Dr NGUYEN VAN TUAT; publ. *Plant Protection Bulletin* (every 2 months).

Research Institute of Marine Fisheries: 170 Le Lai St, 35000 Haiphong 84; tel. (31) 767335; fax (31) 836812; e-mail nthong@rimf.org.vn; f. 1961; study, training and research in fisheries biology, stock assessment, brackish water aquaculture, mariculture, oceanography, technology of fishing and processing; library of 12,000 vols; Dir Prof. Dr DO VAN KHUONG; publs *Aquaculture, Aquaculture Research, Aquaculture International, Infofish International, World Fishing, Journal of Fish Disease, Aquaculture Asia*.

Rubber Research Institute of Viet Nam: 177 Hai Ba Trung St, Ho Chi Minh City; tel. (8) 294139; fax (8) 298599; e-mail rriv@hcm.vnn.vn; f. 1975; library of 3,000 vols; Gen. Dir MAI VAN SON.

Viet Nam Institute of Agricultural Engineering: Phuong Mai, Dong Da, Hanoi; tel. (4) 8523187; fax (4) 8521131; f. 1968; research machinery for agricultural production and food processing; library of 3,000 vols; Dir Prof. Dr PHAM VAN LANG; publ. *Agricultural and Food Industries* (monthly, in Vietnamese with a summary in English).

Viet Nam Institute of Agricultural Science and Technology: Thanh Tri District, Hanoi; f. 1978; Dir Prof. DAO THE TUAN.

ECONOMICS, LAW AND POLITICS

Institute of Economic Management: 68 Phan Dinh Phung St, Hanoi; tel. 256254; fax 256795; f. 1978.

Institute of Economics: 27 Tran Xuan Soan St, Hanoi; tel. (4) 9721633; fax (4) 8261632; e-mail nam@ie-ncss.ac.vn; internet www.varenet.ac.vn/ie; f. 1960; library of 16,000 vols; Dir DO HOAI NAM; publs *Nghien Cuu Kinh Te* (Economic Studies Review, monthly in Vietnamese), *Viet Nam's Socio-Economic Development* (4 a year).

Institute of Finance: 8 Phan Huy Chu St, Hanoi; tel. 58111-301, 279; f. 1961.

Institute of International Relations: Lang Thuong, Dong Da, Hanoi; tel. (4) 8343543; fax (4) 8343543; f. 1959; library of 25,000 vols; publ. *International Studies* (6 a year in Vietnamese, 2 a year in English).

Institute of Labour Science and Social Affairs: 2 Dinh Le St, Hanoi; tel. 269733; fax 254728; f. 1978; labour relations, working conditions, wages and living standards, levels of skill, social security; Dir Dr DO MINH CUONG.

Institute of Law: 27 Tran Xuan Soan St, Hanoi; tel. 54774-49; f. 1960.

Institute of Planning Research: 6 Hoang Dieu St, Hanoi; tel. 58171; f. 1975.

Institute of Social Sciences: 49 Nguyen Thi Minh Khai St, District 1, Ho Chi Minh City; tel. (8) 8223995; fax (8) 8223735; e-mail mdstd@hcm.vnn.vn; f. 1978; Dir Dr NGUYEN THE NGHIA; publ. *Journal of Social Sciences* (6 a year).

Institute of Statistical Science and Economic Information: 66 Hoang Dieu St, Hanoi; tel. 58171; f.1976; 27 staff; library of 2,600 foreign books, 1,100 Vietnamese; special collections in field of statistics; Dir NGUYEN XUAN TUONG (acting); publs *Bulletin of Statistical Science*, Selection of Information Dissemination Periodicals.

Research Institute of Trade: 46 Ngo Quyen St, Hoan Kiem District, Hanoi; tel. (4) 8262720; fax (4) 8248279; f. 1995 following merger of Research Institute for Foreign Economic Relations and Institute of Economic and Technological Research on Trade.

EDUCATION

Institute of Higher and Secondary Vocational Education Research: Dai Co Viet St, Hanoi; tel. 57944, 56943; f. 1977.

National Institute for Educational Science: 101 Tran Hung Dao St, Hanoi; tel. (4) 8256978; fax (4) 8221521; e-mail dinhphuong@bdvn.vnmail.vnd.net; f. 1961; library of 40,000 vols; Dir Assoc. Prof. Dr TRAN KIEU; publ. *Information on Educational Sciences* (6 a year).

Vietnam Sports Science Institute: 141 Nguyen Thai Hoc St, Ba Dinh, Hanoi; tel. (4) 7330286; e-mail vkh-tt@fpt.vn; f. 1979; 5,000 mems; library of 10,000 vols on sports science; publ. *Bulletin* (16 a year).

FINE AND PERFORMING ARTS

Institute of Stage Arts: O Cho Dua, Hanoi; tel. 56415; f. 1978.

Vietnamese Institute for Musicology: 32 Nguyen Thai Hoc St, Ba Dinh District, Hanoi; tel. (4) 8457368; fax (4) 8434953; e-mail musicology@hn.vnn.vn; f. 1976; research in the national heritage of music, song, dance; Dir Prof. NGUYEN PHUC LINH; publ. *Bulletin* (in English and Vietnamese, 3 a year).

HISTORY, GEOGRAPHY AND ARCHAEOLOGY

Institute of Archaeology: 61 Phan Chu Trinh St, Hanoi; tel. 53203; f. 1960.

Institute of History: 38 Hang Chuoi St, Hanoi; tel. 53200; f. 1960.

Vietnam Research Institute of Land Administration: Hoang Quoc Viet St, Cau Giay, Hanoi; tel. (4) 7561154; fax (4) 7540186; e-mail vgcr@hn.vnn.vn; internet www.virila.ac.vn; f. 1994; attached to Min. of Natural Resources and Environment; scientific research and technological development in geodesy, cartography, and land administration; dependent centres: GIS and databases, geodynamics, spatial images and aerial photography; 240 staff; Dir Dr NGUYEN DUNG TIEN.

LANGUAGE AND LITERATURE

Institute of Linguistics: 36 Hang Chuoi St, Hanoi; tel. (4) 9710968; fax (4) 9712247; e-mail lytoanthang@yahoo.com; f. 1968; library of 12,000 vols; Dir Dr LY TOAN CHANG; publ. *Ngon Ngu* (quarterly).

Institute of Literary Studies: 20 Ly Thai To St, Hanoi; tel. (4) 8253548; fax (4) 8250385; f. 1959; library of 150,000 vols; Dir Prof. Dr. PHAN TRONG THUONG; publ. *Tap chi Nghien cuu Van hoc* (Literary Studies Review, monthly).

Institute of Research on Chinese and Demotic Characters: 26 Ly Thuong Kiet St, Hanoi; tel. 57795; f. 1970.

MEDICINE

Central Institute of Ophthalmology: 38 Tran Nhan Tong, Hanoi; tel. 53967; f. 1957.

High Plateaux (Tay Nguyen) Institute of Hygiene and Epidemiology: Buon Ma Thuoc, Dac Lac Province; f. 1976.

Ho Chi Minh City Institute of Hygiene and Epidemiology: 167 Nguyen Thi Minh Khai St, Ho Chi Minh City; tel. 40909, 90352; f. 1977.

Ho Chi Minh City Institute of Hygiene and Public Health: 159 Hung Phu St, District 8, Ho Chi Minh City; tel. (8) 8559503; fax (8) 8563164; e-mail vienvsytcc@hcm.vnn.vn; f. 1977; Dir Prof. LE THE THU.

Ho Chi Minh City Institute of National Medicine: 273 Nam Ky Khoi St, Ho Chi Minh City; tel. 45954, 41308; f. 1975.

Institute for the Protection of the Mother and Newborn Child: 43 Trang Thi St, 08-4 Hanoi; tel. (4) 8252161; fax (4) 8254638; e-mail ipmn@hn.vnn.vn; f. 1966; obstetrics, gynaecology, care of the newborn child and family planning, in-vitro fertilization; library of 5,000 vols; Dir Dr NGUYEN DUC VY; publs *Nôi san San Phu Khoa* (internal journal of obstetrics and gynaecology, annually), *Tông kêt công trinh nghiên cúu khoa hoc* (review of scientific studies, annually).

Institute of Child Care: Bach Mai, Hanoi; f. 1969.

Institute of Malariology, Entomology and Parasitology: Tu Liem District, Hanoi; tel. 54847; f. 1957.

Institute of Materia Medica: 3B Quang Trung St, Hanoi; tel. 52644; fax (4) 254357; f. 1961; multidisciplinary research on pharmaceutical materials, mainly medicinal plants; postgraduate training; library of 6,000 vols; Dir Prof. NGUYEN GIA CHAN; publ. *Materia Medica Bulletin* (quarterly).

Institute of Odonto-Maxillo-Facial Research: Hanoi.

Institute of Vaccine and Serum Production Research: 9 Phan Thanh Gian St, Nha Trang; also 18 Le Hong Phong St, Da Lat; f. 1979.

National Institute of Drug Quality Control: 48 Hai Ba Trung St, Hanoi; tel. (4) 8255341; fax (4) 8256911; e-mail quyvkn@hn .vnn.vn; f. 1971; Dir Prof. Dr TRINH VAN QUY; publ. *Drug Quality Control Newsletter* (4 a year).

National Institute of Hygiene and Epidemiology: 1 Yersin St, 10000 Hanoi; tel. (4) 8213241; fax (4) 8210853; e-mail nihe@ netnam.org.vn; f. 1924; epidemiology of communicable diseases, vaccine development; library of 12,000 vols; Dir Prof. HOANG THUY LONG; publ. *Tap Chi Ve Sinh Phong Dich* (Journal, in Vietnamese with abstract in English, quarterly).

National Institute of Nutrition: 48 Tang Bat Ho St, Hanoi; tel. (4) 9717090; fax (4) 9717885; e-mail nin@netnam.org.vn; f. 1980; depts of basic nutrition, community nutrition, applied nutrition, clinical nutrition, food science, food safety, dietetics, experiment workshop, library; Dir Prof. HÀ HUY KHÔI; publ. nutrition newsletter (quarterly).

National Institute of Occupational and Environmental Health Research: IB pho Yec Xanh, Hanoi; tel. (4) 9713649; fax (4) 8212894; e-mail letrung@hn.vnn.vn; Dir Prof. Dr LE VAN TRUNG.

National Institute of Otorhinolaryngology: Bachmai Hospital Centre, Hanoi; tel. 254706; fax 253525; f. 1969; 200 staff; library of 1,000 vols; Dir Prof. LUONG SY CAN; publs *Noi San Tai Mui Hong* (annually), *Thong Tin Tai Mui Hong* (annually).

National Institute of Traditional Medicine: The National Hospital of Traditional Medicine, 29 Nguyen Binh Khiem, Hanoi 04; tel. 9432442; fax 8229353; e-mail yhcotruyen@hn.vnn.vn; internet www .natiotradimedhos.org.vn; f. 1957; traditional medicine; library of 19,343 vols, special collection of books on Chinese medicine and medicine in Viet Nam since 15th c.; Dir Prof. DI CHU QUOC TRUONG; publ. *Journal of Research in Vietnamese Traditional Medicine and Pharmacy* (quarterly).

National Institute of Tuberculosis and Respiratory Diseases: 120 Hoang Hoa Tham St, Hanoi; tel. (4) 8326249; fax (4) 8326162; f. 1957; research on tuberculosis, lung cancer, chronic bronchitis, asthma, occupational lung diseases; operates two national programmes: National Tuberculosis Control Programme, Acute Respiratory Infections in Children; library of 10,000 vols; Dir Prof. N. V. CO; publ. *Lao và bênh phôi* (4 a year).

Nha Trang Institute of Hygiene and Epidemiology: 10 Tran Phu St, Nha Trang, Phu Khanh Province; tel. 20405, 20410; f. 1976.

NATURAL SCIENCES
General

National Centre for Scientific Research of Viet Nam, Ho Chi Minh City Branch: 1 Mac Dinh Chi St, Ho Chi Minh City; tel. 95814; f. 1975; fundamental and applied research in biology, chemistry, physics,

mathematics, geoscience; Pres. Prof. Dr HO SI THOANG; Sec. Prof. Dr NGUYEN VAN TRONG.

Biological Sciences

Institute of Biology: Nghia Do, Tu Liem District, Hanoi; tel. 58333-551; f. 1975; biochemistry and molecular biology of nitrogen fixation; plant genetics; Dir Prof. LE XUAN TU; publs *Annual Scientific Reports*, *Journal of Biology*.

Mathematical Sciences

Institute of Mathematics: POB 631, Bo Ho, 10000 Hanoi; tel. (4) 7563474; fax (4) 7564303; e-mail vientruong@thevinh.ncst.ac .vn; internet www.math.ac.vn; f. 1969; operations research, optimal control theory, dynamic systems, probability and mathematical statistics, discrete mathematics, functional analysis, numerical analysis, partial differential equations, methods of mathematical physics, algebra, geometry and topology; library of 12,000 vols, 350 periodicals; Dir Prof. HA HUY KHOAI; publ. *Acta Mathematica Vietnamica* (3 a year).

Physical Sciences

Institute of Chemistry, National Centre for Natural Science and Technology of Viet Nam: Hoang Quoc Viet Rd, Cau Giay District, Hanoi; tel. (4) 7564312; fax (4) 8361283; e-mail tvs@ich.ncst.ac.vn; f. 1978; basic and applied research and engineering in organic, inorganic, physicochemical and analytical chemistry; chemistry of natural poducts and polymers; library of 5,420 vols; Dir Prof. Dr TRAN VAN SUNG; publs *Tap chí Hóa hoc* (Journal of Chemistry, 4 a year), *Collection of Selected Scientific Works* (annually).

Institute of Earth Science: Tu Liem District, Hanoi; tel. 58331-372; f. 1967.

Institute of Meteorology and Hydrology: Lang Trung, Dong Da, Hanoi; tel. (4) 8359540; fax (4) 8355993; e-mail vienkttv@ hn.vnn.vn; f. 1977; Dir Dr TRAN DUY BINH.

Institute of Oceanography: 01 Cau Da, Nha Trang, Khanh Hoa Province; tel (58) 590036; fax (58) 590034; e-mail haiduong@ dng.vnn.vn; internet www.vnio.org; f. 1923; library of 60,000 vols; incorporates National Oceanographic Museum and Aquarium; Dir Dr NGUYEN TAC AN; publs *Collection of Marine Research Works* (annually), *Journal of Marine Science and Technology* (4 a year).

Institute of Physics: Tu Liem District, Hanoi; tel. 52129; f. 1969.

Vietnam Institute of Geosciences and Mineral Resources: Ministry of Natural Resources and Environment, Thanh Xuan, Hanoi; tel. (4) 8547335; fax (4) 8542125; e-mail van@vigmr.vn; f. 1976; Dir Assoc. Prof. NGUYEN XUAN KHIEN; publ. *Geology and Mineral Resources* (irreg.).

PHILOSOPHY AND PSYCHOLOGY

Institute of Philosophy: 59 Lang Ha St, Ba Dinh District, Hanoi; tel. (4) 5143338; fax (4) 5141935; e-mail ducphilosophy@yahoo.com; f. 1962; library of 50,000 vols; Dir Prof. PHAM VAN DUC; publ. *Philosophy* (monthly).

RELIGION, SOCIOLOGY AND ANTHROPOLOGY

Institute of Ethnology: 27 Tran Xuan Soan St, Hanoi; tel. 54771; f. 1968; research in cultural history and social structure of the nationalities in Viet Nam and Southeast Asia; 62 staff; library of 10,000 vols; Dir BE VIET DANG; publ. *Ethnographical Studies* (quarterly).

TECHNOLOGY

Broadcast Research and Application Center: 171 Ly Chinh Thang St, Dist. 3, Ho Chi Minh City; tel. (8) 8298427; fax (8) 8293487; f. 1978; 150 staff; library of 3,000 vols; Dir Prof. NGUYEN KIM SACH.

Food Industries Research Institute: Km. 8 Nguyen Trai Rd, Dong Da, Hanoi; tel. (4) 8584554; fax (4) 8584554; f. 1967; microbiology, biotechnology, food processing, quality control of food; Dir Prof. Dr NGO THI MAI.

Hydraulic Engineering Consultants Corporation No. 1: 95/2 Chùa Bôc, Dong Da, Hanoi; tel. (4) 8534162; fax (4) 5632169; e-mail hec1@hn.vnn.vn; f. 1956; library of 9,000 vols; Dir-Gen. HOANG MINH DZUNG; publ. *Hydraulic Engineering* (annually).

Institute for Building Science and Technology: Tran Cung St, Nghia Tan Ward, Cau Giay District, Hanoi; tel. (4) 7544196; fax (4) 8361197; e-mail ibsthoa@netnam.org .vn; internet www.ibst.org.vn; f. 1963; geotechnical and foundation engineering, geodesy and engineering surveying, structural engineering, concrete and concrete technology, structural testing, environmental engineering, construction chemistry, corrosive research and structural protection, construction technology, water supply and drainage technology, fire safety for houses and engineering works; 370 mems; library of 22,000 vols; Dir Assoc. Prof. Dr CAO DUY TIEN; publ. *Building Science and Technology Journal* (quarterly).

Institute for Standardization in Construction: 303 Doi Can St, Hanoi; tel. 343689; f. 1979; library of 5,000 vols; Dir Dr PHAM KINH CUONG; publs *Vietnamese Standards* (TCVN), *National Typification Design in Construction*.

Institute for Tropical Technology: 18 Hoang Quoc Viet, Cau Giay, Hanoi; tel. (4) 8360376; fax (4) 7564696; e-mail hien-vktnd@hn.vnn.vn; f. 1980; corrosion testing and metal protection, concrete protection, testing of non-metallic materials, their resistance to tropical climates and lifetime prediction, development of new materials, new coatings (organic and inorganic), tropicproofing of electrical and electronic equipment; small library; Dir Dr LE XUAN HIEN.

Institute of Building Materials: 25B Cat Linh St, Hanoi; tel. 52521; f. 1975.

Institute of Cybernetics and Computing Technology: Tu Liem District, Hanoi; f. 1976.

Institute of Electronics, Informatics and Automation: 156 A. Quan Thanh St, Hanoi; tel. (4) 8454855; fax (4) 8231842; e-mail nxquynh@vielin.ac.vn; f. 1985 as Viet Nam Institute of Research and Development in Electronics; research and application of new technologies, techniques and products concerned with electronics, informatics and automation; centers and laboratories: Information Technology Center, High-Tech Center, Quality Measurement Center, Automatic Control Center, Information Technology Support Center, Special Laboratory of PLC, Hydrodynamics and Automation, Robotics Laboratory, High Quality Printed Circuit Laboratory; 81 researchers and employees; Dir Prof. Dr NGUYEN XUAN QUYNH.

Branch office:

Branch Institute of Electronics, Informatics and Automation: 138 To Thien Thanh St, 10th District, Ho Chi Minh City; tel. (8) 8652126; fax (8) 8652126; juridical basics.

Institute of Energy: Ton That Tung St, Khuong Thuong, Dong Da, Hanoi; tel. (4) 8523741; fax (4) 8523311; f. 1988; research, programs and projects concerning energy development in Viet Nam; departments: science and technology; nuclear, thermal power and the environment; electrical design; computers; electrical power systems development; energy demand forecasting and management; energy economics; high voltage electrical techniques; Gia Sang Research Station for the Protection of Electrical Lines from Lightning; hydropower; electrical network planning; biogas energy; rural energy planning and fuel; solar and wind energy; basic construction projects; production; 193 staff; Dir Dr TRAN QUOC CUONG.

Institute of Farm Machinery Research: Thanh Xuan, Hanoi; tel. 544429; fax (34) 26677; f. 1970; research, machinery design; library of 5,500 vols; Dir NGUYEN VAN HOI.

Institute of Industrial Chemistry: 2 Pham Ngu Lao St, Hoan Kiem District, Hanoi; tel. (4) 8253930; fax (4) 8257383; e-mail vienhoacn@hn.vnn.vn; internet www .vinachem.com.vn/english/CompanyDetail .asp?ComID=43; f. 1959; Dir Prof. Dr MAI NGOC CHUC.

Institute of Machinery and Industrial Instruments: 34 Lang Ha St, Dong Da District, Hanoi; tel. 344565; fax 344975; f. 1973; library of 10,000 vols; Dir Dr TRAN VIET HUNG.

Institute of Mechanics: 264 Doi Can St, Ba Dinh, Hanoi; tel. (4) 8325541; fax (4) 8333039; f. 1979; basic and applied research in the fields of fluids, deformable solids and vibration mechanics; library of 14,182 vols; Dir Prof. NGUYEN TIEN KHIEM; publ. *Journal of Mechanics* (quarterly).

Institute of Motor Transport: 28 Tran Hung Dao St, Hanoi; tel. 56064; f. 1978.

Institute of Paper and Cellulose Research: Viet Tri, Vinh Phu Province; f. 1970.

Institute of Research on Mining Technology: Phuong Liet, Thanh Xuan, Hanoi; tel. (4) 8642024; fax (4) 8641564; e-mail ttthan@hn.vnn.vn; f. 1979; research on underground and opencast mining, mine development and construction, excavating and tunnelling, environmental mine safety, ventilation, electro-mechanization, transport, coal preparation and processing; library of 9,000 vols; Dir Dr PHUNG MANH DAC; publs *Mining Technology Information* (6 a year), *Works Collection* (every 5 years), *Mining Management* (monthly).

National Food Industries Research Institute (FIRI): Km. 8 Nguyen Trai Rd, Thanh Xuan, Dong Da, Hanoi; tel. 244318; f. 1967; carries out research in biotechnology, food processing technology using local raw materials, and other areas connected with food; Dir Prof. Dr NGO THI MAI.

National Institute for Urban and Rural Planning: 37 Le Dai Hanh St, Hanoi; tel. (4) 9760691; fax (4) 9764339; f. 1956, current name 1990; research and establishment of construction planning projects, and environmental and landscape organisation in the territorial regions, urban and rural settlements; 8 research, design and planning divisions, 4 administrative divisions; centers: Center for Research on Urban and Rural Environmental Planning, Center for Rural Planning and Development, Center for Urban and Rural Planning in the Middle Regions; 290 staff; Dir Prof. Dr LE HONG KE.

National Research Institute for Mechanical Engineering: Thang Long St, Caugiay, Hanoi; tel. (4) 8344225; fax (4) 8347883; f. 1962 as the Institute of Mechanical Design and Manufacture; 4 professional depts: economic planning, scientific management, finance, administration and personnel;

research depts: dynamics, mechanical design, hydro-mechanical and hydro-electrical heavy mechanics, technology, 'cold' welding; 265 staff; Dir Prof. Dr HAN DUC KIM.

National Research Institute of Mining and Metallurgy: 30B Doan Thi Diem St, Hanoi; tel. (4) 8233775; fax (4) 8456983; e-mail vimluki@netnam.org.vn; f. 1967; library of 10,000 vols; Dir NGUYEN ANH.

Research Institute of Posts and Telecommunications (RIPT): Nghia Tan, Tu Liem, Hanoi; tel. 344254; fax 345485; Dir Prof. Dr NGUYEN CANH TUAN; publ. *Ket Qua Nghien Cuu Khoa Hoc* (annually).

Scientific and Technological Institute for Communications and Transport: 2 Lang Thuong, Cau Giay, Dong Da, Hanoi; tel. 343404; fax 343403; f. 1956; Dir Asst Prof. Dr NGUYEN VAN LAP.

Shipbuilding Science and Technology Institute–SHIPSCITECH: 80b Tran Hung Dao St, Hanoi; tel. (4) 8257070; fax (4) 8258672; f. 1983; development and application of new technologies in shipbuilding, design, building and modernisation of marine facilities, consultancy services, training of staff and development of standards; units and facilities: professional design department, Centre for Research and Testing of Models, pilot production workshops, testing tank; Dir Dr NGO CAN (acting).

Textile Research Institute: 478 Minhkhai St, Hanoi; tel. (4) 8624025; fax (4) 8622867; e-mail viendetmay@hn.vnn.vn; f. 1969; research in material technology, machinery for spinning, weaving and finishing; inspection of quality of material and finished products, fashion design; library of 3,500 vols; Dir Dr NGUYEN VAN THONG; publs *Textiles Magazine* (6 a year), *Textile Research Journal* (annually).

Viet Nam Atomic Energy Commission: 59 Ly Thuong Kiet St, Hanoi; tel. (4) 8256479; fax (4) 8266133; e-mail hg.vaec@ hn.vn.vnn; internet www.vaec.gov.vn; f. 1979; nuclear science and technology; Chair. TRAN HUU PHAT; publ. *Nuclear Science and Technology*.

Viet Nam Institute of Water Conservation: 299 Tayson St, Dong Da District, Hanoi; tel. (4) 8522086; fax (4) 8536290; f. 1959; units: Centre for Termite Prevention, Centre for Irrigation, Centre for Water Treatment and Environmental research, Centre for Research in River and Marine Dynamics, Centre for Hydraulic Research, Centre for Structures and Materials, Centre for Small-scale Hydroelectric Research, Geotechnics Division, Hydraulic Research Division, Irrigation Systems Management Division, Pump Research Division; 236 staff; Dir Dr NGUYEN TUAN ANH.

Libraries and Archives

Hanoi

Central Institute for Medical Science Information: 13–15 Lê Thánh Tông, Hanoi; tel. (4) 8264040; fax (4) 8242668; e-mail vttyh@hn.vnn.vn; f. 1979 to succeed fmr Central Library for Medical Sciences; attached to Ministry of Health; 50,000 vols; Dir Eng. NGUYEN TUAN KHOA; publs *Vietnam Medical Information* (quarterly, in English), *Bibliography of Vietnamese Medical Literature* (annually, in Vietnamese).

Central Institute of Scientific and Technical Information: 39 Tran Dung Dao St, Hanoi; tel. 52731; f. 1972.

Central Library for Science and Technology: 24–26 Lý Thuồng Kiết, Hanoi; tel.

263491; fax 263127; f. 1960; attached to the National Centre for Scientific and Technological Information and Documentation; 230,000 vols, 4,500 periodicals; Dir VU VAN SON.

Institute of Social Sciences Information–National Social Sciences Library: 26 Lý Thuồng Kiết, Hanoi; tel. and fax (4) 8253074; f. 1975 by amalgamation of Dept. of Social Sciences Information and Central Social Sciences Library; attached to Viet Nam Academy of Social Sciences; 1,000,000 vols; Dir Ho SI QUY; publs *Review of Social Sciences Information* (monthly), *Bibliography of Social Sciences* (annually).

National Library of Viet Nam: 31 Tràng Thi, 10000 Hanoi; tel. (4) 8253040; fax (4) 8253357; e-mail ptkhang@nlv.gov.vn; f. 1917; attached to Ministry of Culture and Information; 1,200,000 vols, 8,000 periodical titles; Dir PHAM THE KHANG; publs *National Bibliography* (monthly and annually), *Information on Culture and Arts*, *Library and Bibliographical Work* (4 a year), *Library Magazine* (4 a year).

Ho Chi Minh City

General Sciences Library of Ho Chi Minh City: 69 Ly Tu Trong, District 1, Ho Chi Minh City; tel. (8) 8225055; fax (8) 8299318; e-mail gsl.hcmc@hcm.vnn.vn; internet www.gslhcm.org.vn; f. 1976; attached to Service of Culture and Information of Ho Chi Minh City; 700,000 vols, 4,500 periodical titles, databases; Dir NGUYEN THI BAC.

Social Sciences Library: 34 Ly-Tú-Trong, Ho Chi Minh City; tel. (8) 8296744; fax (8) 223735; f. 1975; the collections of the fmr Archaeological Research Institute have been added to the library; provides facilities for research in philosophy, sociology, literature, linguistics, archaeology, ethnology, history, economics, law; 145,000 vols; Dir TRAN MINH DUC.

Museums and Art Galleries

Haiphong

Haiphong Museum: Haiphong; f. 1959; local history.

Hanoi

Ho Chi Minh Museum: Hanoi; tel. 58261; f. 1977; study of the President's life and work; Dir HA HUY GIAP.

People's Army Museum: Dien Bien Phu St, Hanoi; f. 1959; Dir LE CHIEU.

Viet Nam Fine Arts Museum: 66 Nguyên Thái Hoc St, Hanoi; tel. (4) 8233084; fax (4) 7341427; e-mail binhtruong451@hn.vnn.vn; f. 1966; preservation and presentation of national cultural heritage; research on ancient and modern fine arts, ceramics, handicrafts, folk arts; exhibitions of foreign art; library of 1,100 vols; Dir TRUONG QUOC BINH.

Viet Nam History Museum: 1 Trang Tien, Hanoi; tel. (4) 853518; fax (4) 8252853; f. 1958; research and conservation, history of Viet Nam from palaeolithic period to 1945; Dir Dr PHAM QUOC QUÂN; publ. *Bulletin* (annually).

Viet Nam Revolution Museum: 25 Tong Dan St, Hanoi; tel. (4) 8254323; f. 1959; study of revolutionary history of Viet Nam; library of 21,000 vols and historical documents, 17,900 documentary photographs; Dir Prof. Dr PHAM MAI HUNG.

Ho Chi Minh City

Ho Chi Minh City Museum: Botanical Gardens, Ho Chi Minh City; f. 1977; two sections: one devoted to the revolution, the other to ancient arts.

Hue

Hue Museum: Hue; tel. (54) 523759; fax (54) 526083; e-mail hue-mcc@dng.vnn.vn; history of the old capital; incorporates Hue Monuments Conservation Centre; Dir THAI CONG NGUYEN.

Thai Nguyen

Museum of the Cultures of Ethnic Groups in Viet Nam: Doi Can Rd, Thai Nguyen 84, Thai Nguyen province; tel. (280) 855781; fax (280) 752940; e-mail Baotangvh@hn.vnn.vn; f. 1960; conserves and publicises the cultural heritage of Viet Nam's ethnic groups; Dir HA THI NU.

Vinh

Nghe-Tinh Museum: Vinh, Nghe Tinh Province; study of the Nghe-Tinh 'Soviet' Uprising, 1930-31.

Universities

CANTHO UNIVERSITY

3/2 Street, Cantho City, Cantho Province
Telephone: (71) 838237
Fax: (71) 838474
E-mail: ductri@ctu.edu.vn
Internet: www.ctu.edu.vn
Founded 1966
State control
Academic year: September to July
Rector: TRAN THUONG TUAN
Vice-Rectors: CHAU VAN LUC, Dr LE QUANG MINH
Library of 30,000 vols
Number of teachers: 752
Number of students: 14,000
Publications: annual scientific and technology reports.

DEANS

School of Agriculture: Prof. TRAN THUONG TUAN
School of Economics and Business Administration: NGUYEN TAN NHAN
School of Education: Dr LE PHUOC LOC
College of Information Technology: VO VAN CHIN
School of Law: Dr NGUYEN NGOC DIEN
School of Medicine, Dentistry and Pharmacy: PHAM HUNG LUC
School of Sciences: NGUYEN XUAN TRANH
School of Technology: LE QUANG MINH

ATTACHED INSTITUTES

Biotechnology Research and Development Centre: Dir Prof. TRAN PHUOC DUONG.
Foreign Languages Centre: Dir LE THI TUYET MAI.
Mekong Delta Farming System Research and Development Centre: Dir Prof. VO TONG XUAN.
Renewable Energy Centre: Dir LE HOANG VIET.
Science and Information Centre: Dir DANG DUC TRI.
Shrimp-Artemia Research and Development Centre: Dir TRUONG TRONG NGHIA.

UNIVERSITY OF DALAT

01 Phu Dong Thien, Vuong, Dalat
Telephone: (63) 822246

Fax: (63) 823380
E-mail: dluirdep@hcm.vnn.vn
Internet: www.dalatunifoundation.com
Founded 1958
State control
Academic year: September to June
Rector: NGUYEN HUU DUC
Vice-Rectors: NGUYEN VAN TONG, LÊ BA DUNG, NGUYEN DINH HAO
Number of students: 10,000
Faculties: mathematics, information technology, physics, chemistry, biology, agronomy, environmental studies, business administration, law, philology, history, oriental studies, foreign languages, tourism, social work and community development, teacher training, graduate studies
Publication: *Scientific Journal* (annually).

UNIVERSITY OF DANANG

41 Le Duan St, Da Nang
Telephone: (511) 822041
Fax: (511) 823683
E-mail: relint@dng.vnn.vn
Internet: www.ud.edu.vn
Founded 1994
State control
Library of 25,000 vols, 250 periodicals
Number of teachers: 889
Number of students: 35,000
President: Prof. Dr PHAN QUANG XUNG
Vice-Presidents: Dr LE THE GIOI, Prof. Dr BUI VAN GA

DIRECTORS

College of Economics and Business Administration: Dr VO XUAN TIEN
College of Education: NGUYEN KHAC SINH
College of Technology: Prof. Dr PHAM PHU LY
School of Technology: DANG VAN SON

DUY TAN UNIVERSITY

184 Nguyen Van Linh St, Thank Khe District, Danang City
Telephone: (511) 650403
Fax: (511) 650443
E-mail: duytandn@dtu.edu.vn
Internet: www.dtu.edu.vn
Founded 1994
President: LE CONG CO
Faculties of Accountancy and Finance, Business, Engineering, Languages and Technology.

UNIVERSITY OF FISHERIES

2 Nguyen Dinh Chieu, Nhatrang City, Khan Hoa Province
Telephone: (58) 831149
Fax: (58) 831147
E-mail: dhtsnt@dng.vnn.vn
Founded 1959
Rector: Assoc. Prof. Dr QUAC DINH LIEN
Vice-Rectors: Assoc. Prof. Dr TRAN THI LUYEN, Dr THAI VAN NGAN, VU VAN THUNG
Library of 18,000 vols, 500 periodicals
Number of teachers: 300
Number of students: 7,000
Publications: *Fisheries Journal* (4 a year), *Journal of Science and Technology* (4 a year)
Faculties of Basic Sciences, Marine Mechanics, Navigation and Marine Exploitation, Aquaculture, Marine Products Processing and Fishery Economics.

FOREIGN TRADE UNIVERSITY

91 Chua Lang St, Lng Thuong, Dong Da, Hanoi
Telephone: (4) 8345359
Fax: (4) 8343605
Internet: www.ftu.edu.vn
Founded 1960
Rector: NGUYEN THI MO
Vice-Rectors: Prof. Dr HOANG VAN CHAU, Prof. Dr NGUYEN PHUC KHANH, Prof. Dr HOANG NGOC THIET
Number of teachers: 193
Number of students: 10,720
Publication: *External Economics Review* (quarterly)

DEANS

Faculty of Business Administration: Dr BU NGOC SON
Faculty of Business English: Dr NGUYEN DUC HOAT
Faculty of Basic and Fundamental Studies: Prof. Dr LE THANH CUONG
Faculty of Foreign Trade Economics: Dr VU SY TUAN
Faculty of In-Service Training: NGUYEN THI MO
Faculty of Marxism and Leninism Studies: Dr DOAN VAN KHAI
Faculty of Postgraduate Studies: Prof. Dr VU CHI LOC

HAIPHONG UNIVERSITY OF MEDICINE

213 Tran Quoc Toan (Lach Tray), Ngo Quyen, Haiphong
Telephone: (31) 731907
Fax: (31) 731224
Rector: HUU CHINH NGUYEN.

HANOI AGRICULTURAL UNIVERSITY

Trau Quy, Gia Lam, Hanoi
Telephone: (4) 276906
Fax: (4) 276554
E-mail: webmaster@hau1.edu.vn
Internet: www.hau1.edu.vn
Founded 1956
Academic year: August to June
Number of teachers: 490
Number of students: 3,250
Rector: VIET TUNG NGUYEN
Faculties of Agronomy and Agricultural Resources Environment Management, Animal Husbandry and Veterinary Medicine, Economics and Rural Development, Farm Engineering and Rural Electricity, Land Resources and Environment, Post-Harvest Technology and Food Processing, Postgraduate Studies and Technical Teachers Training; Institute of Agricultural Biology; Experimental and Demonstration Station, Viet Nam Agricultural College Training, Research and Development Center, Center for Sustainable Agriculture Research and Development, Professional Dogs Research Center, Botanical Garden and Germplasm Conservation, Center for Agricultural Research and Environmental Studies (CARES) and Cadastral Center.

HANOI LAW UNIVERSITY

Duong Lang, Hanoi
Telephone: (4) 4243226
Founded 1979
Rector: LE MINH TAM
Faculties of Administrative and State Law, Economic Law, International Law, Justice, Part-time Learning and Postgraduate Training.

HANOI NATIONAL ECONOMICS UNIVERSITY

207 Duong Giai Phong, Quan Hai Ba Trung, Hanoi 04

Telephone: (4) 8692120
Fax: (4) 8695992
E-mail: HTQTNEU@hu.vun.vn
Internet: www.neu.edu.vn

Founded 1956
Languages of instruction: French, English
Number of teachers: 1,000
Number of students: 32,000

Publication: *Economics and Development Review* (monthly)

Faculties of Accountancy and Auditing, Agricultural Economics, Banking and Finance, Industrial Economics, Labour Economics, Planning and Statistics.

HANOI NATIONAL OPEN UNIVERSITY

Nha B-101 Phuong Bach Khoa, Quan Hai Ba Trung, Hanoi

Telephone: (4) 694822
Fax: (4) 691587

Founded 1990, university status since 1993
Language of instruction: Vietnamese
Academic year: August to June

Number of teachers: 470
Number of students: 19,000

Faculties of Biological Technology, Education and Training, Foreign Languages, Industrial Design, Information Systems, Law, Management Training, Telecommunication Technology; Multimedia Centre; Research Centre of Distance Education.

HANOI UNIVERSITY OF ARCHITECTURE

Km 10, Nguyen Trai Rd, Thanh Xuan, Hanoi
Telephone: (4) 8544346
Fax: (4) 8541616
E-mail: pth@hn.vnn.vn
Internet: www.hau.edu.vn

Founded 1969

Rector: TRONG HAN TRAN

Faculties of Architecture, Civil Engineering, Postgraduate Study, Urban Infrastructure, Environment and Urban Planning; Institute of Tropical Architecture; Centres of Applied Informatics, Foreign Languages, Information and Library Studies and Urban Management.

HANOI UNIVERSITY OF CIVIL ENGINEERING

55 Giai Phong Rd, Hanoi
Telephone: (4) 8691302
Fax: (4) 8691684
E-mail: dngoaidhxd@hn.vnn.vn
Internet: www.dhxd.edu.vn

Founded 1956, university status since 1966
Language of instruction: Vietnamese
Academic year: August to June

Number of teachers: 700
Number of students: 14,000

Publication: *Science-Technology*

Rector: LE NINH NGUYEN

Faculties of Architecture, Civil and Industrial Engineering, Construction Engineering, Environmental Engineering, Highway and Bridge Construction, Hydraulic Engineering, Industrial Economics, Information Technology, Mechanical Engineering and Postgraduate Studies; Institute of Offshore Engineering; Centre for Continuing Education.

HANOI UNIVERSITY OF CULTURE

103 De La Thanh, Hanoi
Telephone: (4) 4255486
Founded 1977
Faculty of Cultural Studies.

HANOI UNIVERSITY OF EDUCATION

136 Duong Xuan Thuy, Quan Hoa Cau Giay, Tu Liem, Hanoi
Telephone: (4) 7683423
Fax: (4) 8340721
Internet: www.dhsphn.edu.vn

Founded 1967

Faculties of Foreign Languages Education and Teacher Training.

HANOI UNIVERSITY OF FINANCE AND ACCOUNTANCY

Dong Ngac, Me Linh, Hanoi
Telephone: (4) 8362161
Founded 1963
Faculties of Accountancy and Finance.

HANOI UNIVERSITY OF FINE ARTS

42 Yet kien, Hanoi
Telephone: (4) 4257598
Fax: (4) 8226418
E-mail: dhmythuathn@hn.vnn.vn
Founded 1957.

HANOI UNIVERSITY OF FOREIGN STUDIES

Km 9, Nguyen Trai St, Thanh Xuan, Hanoi
Telephone: (4) 8544338
Fax: (4) 8544550
E-mail: hufs@netnam.vn
Internet: www.hufs.edu.vn

Founded 1959

Departments of Accountancy, Business, Commerce, Economics, Human Resource Management, International Studies, Languages and Tourism.

HANOI UNIVERSITY OF FOREIGN TRADE

Lang Thuong St, Dong Da, Hanoi
Telephone: (4) 4243349
E-mail: ftuedcom@fpt.vn

Founded 1965

Rector: Prof Dr THI MO NGUYEN
Vice-Rectors: Prof. Dr NGUYEN HONG DAM, HOANG NGOC THIET

Faculties of International Business, Business Administration and Commercial English.

HANOI UNIVERSITY OF INDUSTRIAL FINE ARTS

O Cho Dua, Dong Da, Hanoi
Telephone: (4) 4257264
Founded 1965
Department of Industrial Art.

HANOI UNIVERSITY OF MEDICINE

1 Ton That Tung St, Dong Da, Hanoi
Telephone: (4) 8523798
Fax: (4) 8525115
E-mail: daihocyhn@hn.vnn.vn
Internet: www.hmu.edu.vn

Founded 1902

Rector: Prof. TON THAT BACH
Vice-Rectors: DO HAN (Finance and Equipment Supply), PHAM NHAT AN (Postgraduate Training), DO DOAN LOI (Science and Techniques Management), Assoc. Prof. DAO VAN LONG (Undergraduate Training)

HEADS OF FACULTIES AND SCHOOLS

Faculty of Maxilo-Odontolgy: Prof. Dr TRAN XUAN THUONG
Faculty of Public Health: Prof.Dr DAO NGOC PHONG
Faculty of Traditional Medicine: Assoc. Prof. Dr PHAM VAN TRINH
Department of Anaesthetics: DO NGOC LAM
Department of Anatomo-Pathology: Prof. Dr NGUYEN VUONG
Department of Anatomy: NGUYEN TRAN QUYNH
Department of Biology: Assoc. Prof. Dr TRAN THI THANH
Department of Cardiology: Prof. Dr NGUYEN LAN VIET
Department of Chemistry and Biochemistry: Assoc. Prof. Dr PHAN AN
Department of Clinical Allergo-Immunology: Assoc. Prof. Dr NGUYEN NANG AN
Department of Embryo-Histology: Prof. Dr TRINH BINH
Department of Foreign Languages: VUONG THU MINH
Department of Forensic Medicine: Prof. Dr TRAN VAN LIEU
Department of Haematology: Prof. Dr DO TRUNG PHAN
Department of Imagery Diagnoses: Dr NGUYEN DUY HUE
Department of Immuno-Physio-Pathology: Assoc. Prof. Dr VAN DINH HOA
Department of Infectious Diseases: Prof. Dr LE DANG HA
Department of Intensive Care: Assoc. Prof. Dr NGUYEN THI DU
Department of Internal Medicine: Prof. Dr NGUYEN KHANH TRACH
Department of Mathematics: Dr DANG DUC HAU
Department of Medical Education: Prof. Dr PHAM THI MINH DUC
Department of Medical Physics: Assoc. Prof. Dr NGUYEN VAN THIEN
Department of Microbiology: Assoc. Prof. Dr LE HUY CHINH
Department if Military Medicine: DO THIEU Y
Department of Neurology: Assoc. Prof. Dr LE QUANG CUONG
Department of Nuclear Medicine: Assoc. Prof. Dr PHAN SY AN
Department of Nursing: HOANG GIA
Department of Obstetrics and Gynaecology: Assoc. Prof. Dr NGUYEN DUC VY
Department of Oncology: Assoc. Prof. Dr NGUYEN BA DUC
Department of Ophtalmology: Assoc. Prof. Dr TON KIM THANH
Department of Oto-Rhino-Laryngology: Assoc. Prof. PHAM KHANH HOA
Department of Paediatrics: Assoc. Prof. Dr LE NAM TRA
Department of Parasitology: Assoc. Prof. Dr PHAM VAN THAN
Department of Pharmacology: Prof. Dr DAO VAN THAN
Department of Philosophy: Assoc. Prof. Dr TRAN VAN THUY
Department of Physiology: Prof. Dr PHAM THI MINH DUC
Department of Plastic Surgery: Assoc. Prof. Dr NGUYEN BAC HUNG
Department of Psychiatry: Assoc. Prof. Dr NGUYEN VIET THIEM
Department of Rehabilitation: Assoc. Prof. Dr NGUYEN XUAN NGHIEN
Department of Sport and Gymnastics: HUANG THE THUONG
Department of Surgery: Assoc. Prof. HA VAN QUET
Department of Surgical Technique: TRAN XUAN VINH

Department of Tuberculosis and Respiratory Diseases: Assoc. Prof. Dr NGUYEN VIET CO
Department of Venero-Dermatology: Assoc. Prof. PHAM VAN PHIEN

ATTACHED RESEARCH INSTITUTES

Centre for Bronchial Asthma Research: Dir Prof. Dr NGUYEN NANG AN.

Centre for Clinical Epidemiology: Prof. Dr DUONG DIEN THIEN.

Centre Laboratory: Dir LE VAN PHUNG.

Centre for Medical Informatic Technology: Dir TRINH VAN TUAN.

Centre for Population, Family Planning and Reproductive Health: Dir Prof. TON THAT BACH.

Centre for Population and Family Training Health: Dir Prof. Dr LE VAN KHANG.

Centre for Training Research on Bone Diseases: Dir TRAN NGOC AN.

Centre for Training and Research on HIV/AIDS: Dir Prof. TON THAT BACH.

Community Health Research Unit: Dir TON THAT BACH.

HANOI UNIVERSITY OF MINING AND GEOLOGY

Dong Ngac Commune, Tu Liem District, Hanoi

Telephone: (4) 8389633
Fax: (4) 8389633
E-mail: didn@hn.vnn.vn
Internet: www.humg.edu.vn

Founded 1966

Rector: BUI HOC
Vice-Rectors: Assoc. Prof. Dr TRAN XUAN HA, Assoc. Prof. Dr TRAN DINH KIEN, Dr HOANG BA NANG, Assoc. Prof. Dr TRAN DINH KIEN

Library of 100,000 vols, 900 periodicals
Number of students: 5,338

DEANS

Faculty of Economics and Business Management: Assoc. Prof. NHAM VAN TOAN
Faculty of General Education: Dr HUANG BA NANG
Faculty of Geology: Assoc. Prof. Dr DANG VAN BAT
Faculty of Information Technology: Assoc. Prof. Dr NGUYEN TRUONG XUAN
Faculty of Marxism-Leninism and Ho Chi Minh Ideology: Dr TRAN DINH THAO
Faculty of Mining: Dr NGUYEN PHU VU
Faculty of National Defence Education: Lt Eng. DO KIM CHIEN
Faculty of Oil and Gas: Assoc. Prof. Dr MAI THANH TAN
Faculty of Surveying: Prof. Dr PHAM HOANG LAN
Department of Graduate and Post-Graduate Training: Assoc. Prof. Dr NHU VAN BACH
Department of Science and Technology: Assoc. Prof. Dr NGUYEN QUANG PHICH

HANOI UNIVERSITY OF TECHNOLOGY

1 Dai Co Viet Rd, Hanoi

Telephone: (4) 8696099
Fax: (4) 8692006
E-mail: qhqt@mail.hut.edu.vn
Internet: www.hut.edu.vn

Founded 1956
Language of instruction: Vietnamese
Academic year: August to July

Rector: QUOC THANG TRAN
Vice-Rectors: Prof. Dr CONG HOA LE
Chief Administrative Officer: DUONG VAN NGHI
Librarian: GIAN HUU CAN

Library of 700,000 vols
Number of teachers: 1,500
Number of students: 35,650

Publication: *Sciences et Techniques* (quarterly)

DEANS

Applied Mathematics: Dr NGUYEN CANH LUONG
Chemical Technology: Dr VU DAO THANG
Economics and Management: Dr TRAN VAN BINH
Electronics and Telecommunications: Dr PHAM MINH VIET
Energy: Prof. LE VAN DOANH (Head of Department)
Engineering Education: Prof. NGUYEN HOA TOAN
Foreign Languages: DO VAN MOC
General Chemistry: LE CONG HOA
Hydraulic Machinery and Automation: NGUYEN PHU VINH
Industrial Management: NGUYEN MINH DUE
Information Technology: Prof. NGUYEN THUC HAI
Mechanical Engineering: Prof. TANG HUY
Metallurgy and Materials Technology: Prof. DO MINH NGHIEP
Physical Education: LE VAN LINH
Social Sciences: Prof. NGO MINH KHANG
Textile Engineering: Dr TRAN MINH NAM

RESEARCH CENTRES AND INSTITUTES

Centre for International Co-operation in the Training and Transfer of Technology: Dir Prof. PHAM DUC GIA.

Centre for Research and Development of High Technology: Dir Prof. NGUYEN CONG HIEN.

Computer Centre: Dir Prof. PHAN TANG DA.

Corrosion and Protection Research Centre: Dir Prof. PHAN LUONG CAM.

Inorganic Materials Centre: Dir Prof. LA VAN BINH.

Institute of Engineering Physics: Dir Prof. DO TRAN CAT.

Institute of Environmental Science and Technology: Dir Prof. Dr TRAN VAN NHAN.

Japanese Language Centre: Dirs DOAN XUAN HUONG, ONISHI KAZUHIKO.

Materials Science Centre: Dir Prof. DO MINH NGHIEP.

Network Communication Centre: Dir Prof. PHAM MINH HA.

Polymer Centre: Dir Prof. TRAN VINH DIEU.

Polytechnology Co. Ltd. Dir NGUYEN LUYEN.

Precise Machinery Centre: Dir NGUYEN NGOC UYEN.

Renewable Energy Centre: Dir Dr DANG DINH THONG.

Vietnamese–German Centre for Science and Technology Exchange: Dir Prof. MAI XUAN KY.

HANOI WATER RESOURCES UNIVERSITY

175 Tay Son Sy, Dong Da Hanoi

Telephone: (4) 8522201
Fax: (4) 8534198
E-mail: wru@fpt.vn
Internet: www.hwru.edu.vn

Founded 1959

Rectors: Assoc. Prof. Dr DO VAN HUA, Prof. Dr LE KIM TRUYEN
Vice-Rectors: Prof. Dr DAO XUAN HOC, Assoc. Prof. Dr PHAM NGOC QUY
Chief Librarian: Dr NGUYEN HUU THAI

Number of teachers: 520
Number of students: 6,930

DEANS

Faculty of Hydraulic Construction: Assoc. Dr NGUYEN VAN MAO
Faculty of Hydraulic Machinery and Equipment: Dr NGUYEN DANG CUONG
Faculty of Hydrology and Environment: Assoc. Prof. Dr DO TAT TUC
Faculty of Hydrology Power: Assoc. Prof. Dr HO SY DU
Faculty of Information Technology: Prof. Dr NGUYEN VAN LE
Faculty of In-Service Training: TRAN NGU PHUC
Faculty of Planning and Management of Water Resources Systems: Dr PHAM NGOC HAI
Faculty of Postgraduate Studies: Assoc. Prof. Dr DUONG VAN TIEN
Faculty of Water Resources Economics: Dr NGUYEN XUAN PHU
Department of Foreign Languages: LE VAN KHANG (Head)
Department of Marxist-Leninist Philosophy and Sociology: Dr NGUYEN QUOC LUAT (Head)
Department of Military and Physical Education: Sr Lt-Col NGUYEN SY HOI (Head)

ATTACHED RESEARCH INSTITUTES

Centre for Applied Hydrology and Environment Engineering: Dir Prof. Dr NGO DINH TUAN.

Centre of Applied Informatics: Dir Prof. Dr NGUYEN VAN LE.

Centre for Hydraulic Machinery and Technology: Dir Eng. NGUYEN DINH TAN.

Centre for Water Resources Research and Engineering Applications: Dir Prof. Dr NGO TRI VIENG.

DH2 Centre: Dir Eng. DUONG VAN BUOM.

Foreign Language Centre: Dir LE VAN KHANG.

HO CHI MINH CITY OPEN UNIVERSITY

97 Vo Van Tan, District 3, Ho Chi Minh City

Telephone: (8) 9300983
Fax: (8) 9300085
E-mail: international@ou.edu.vn
Internet: www.ou.edu.vn

Founded 1990, university status since 1993
Language of instruction: Vietnamese
Academic year: September to July

Rector: Assoc. Prof. Dr LE BAO DONG
Vice-Rector: Dr NGUYEN THUAN

Library of 12,000
Number of teachers: 530
Number of students: 14,000

Faculties of Economics and Business Administration, Computer Science, Foreign Languages, Biotechnology, Engineering and Technology, South-East Asian Studies and Sociology; Centres of Distance Training, Professional Accounting, Applied Computer Science, Foreign Languages and Overseas Studies.

HO CHI MINH CITY UNIVERSITY OF ARCHITECTURE

196 rue Pasteur, Q. 3, Ho Chi Minh City

Telephone: (8) 22748
Fax: (8) 8244678
Internet: www.hcmuarc.edu.vn

Founded 1976

Rector: NHU TAN HOANG.

HO CHI MINH CITY UNIVERSITY OF ECONOMICS

59C, Nguyen Dinh Chieu, District 3, Ho Chi Minh City

Telephone: (8) 895299
Fax: (8) 8241186
E-mail: tchc@hcmueco.edu.vn
Internet: www.ueh.edu.vn

Founded 1976
Languages of instruction: Vietnamese, English, French
Academic year: September to July

Rector: TUYEN NGUYEN THAN

Number of teachers: 1,350
Number of students: 49,660

Library of 40,000 vols

Publication: *Economic Development Review* (monthly)

Faculties of Accounting and Auditing, Business Administration, Business Law, Commerce and Tourism, Corporate Finance and Monetary Affairs, Development Economics, Political Economics, Public Finance and Statistics, Econometrics and Informatics.

HO CHI MINH CITY UNIVERSITY OF EDUCATION

280 An Duong Vuong, Ho Chi Minh City
Telephone: (8) 8391080
Fax: (8) 8398946
Internet: www.hcmupeda.edu.vn
Founded 1976
Rector: MANH NHI BUI
Faculties of Education and Teacher Training.

HO CHI MINH CITY UNIVERSITY OF FINE ARTS

5 Phan Dang Luu, Ho Chi Minh City
Telephone: (8) 8412691
Fax: (8) 8412695
E-mail: thongtinmythuat@hcm.fpt.vn
Founded 1913
Director: Prof. NGUYEN HUY LONG
Number of teachers: 58
Number of students: 700
Publication: *Fine Arts Information*
Courses taught include Painting, Sculpture, Graphic Arts and Graphic Design; Departments of Applied Arts, Basic Knowledge, Fine Arts Pedagogy, Fine Arts Critique, Fine Art Higher Education.

HO CHI MINH CITY UNIVERSITY OF FOREIGN LANGUAGES AND INFORMATION TECHNOLOGY

155 Su Van Hanh St (Extension), Ward 13, District 10, Ho Chi Minh City
Telephone: (8) 8629233
Fax: (8) 8650991
E-mail: htcuoc@hcm.vnn.vn
Internet: www.huflit.vnn.vn
Founded 1994
President: HUYNH THE CUOC
Number of teachers: 100
Number of students: 1,200
Schools of Foreign Languages, Computer Sciences and Eastern Cultures and Languages.

HO CHI MINH CITY UNIVERSITY OF LAW

2–4 Nguyen tat Thanh Q.4, Ho Chi Minh City
Telephone: (8) 8259703
Fax: (8) 8260567
E-mail: daotaodhl@hcm.vnn.vn
Internet: www.hcmulaw.edu.vn
Founded 1996
Rector: VAN LUYEN NGUYEN
Faculties of Administrative and State Law, Business Law, Civil Law, Criminal Law, International Law, Part-time Training and Postgraduate Training.

HO CHI MINH CITY UNIVERSITY OF MEDICINE AND PHARMACY

217 Hong Bang, Q. 5, Ho Chi Minh City
Telephone: (8) 8558411
Fax: (8) 8552304
E-mail: info@yds.edu.vn
Internet: www.yds.edu.vn
Founded 1947 as Saigon University of Medicine and Pharmacy, present name since 1976
Rector: DINH HOI NGUYEN
Number of teachers: 982
Number of students: 7,966
Library of 30,000 vols, 700 periodicals
Publication: *Journal of Medicine of Ho Chi Minh City* (quarterly)
Faculties of Fundamental Sciences, Medicine, Odonto-Stomatology, Traditional Medicine, Pharmacy, Nursing-Medical Techniques and Public Health; University Medical Center; Advanced Medical Technology Center; Bio-medical Laboratory; Pharma.Technology Center, Medical Skill-slab Unit.

HO CHI MINH CITY UNIVERSITY OF PERFORMING ARTS AND CINEMA

125 Cong Quynh St, Q1, Ho Chi Minh City
Founded 1995
Cinema, pantomime and mime, radio and television, theatre and theatre design.

HO CHI MINH CITY UNIVERSITY OF TRANSPORT

2 D3 St, Binh Thanh District M, Ho Chi Minh City
E-mail: hcmut@hcm.vnn.vn
Internet: www.hcmutrans.edu.vn
Founded 1962 as part of Vietnam Maritime University; independent status since 2001
Rector: CANH VINH TRAN
Vice-Rectors: VAN THU NGUYEN, HUU KHUONG NGUYEN
Number of teachers: 298
Number of students: 8,062
Faculties of Navigation, Marine Engineering, Naval Architecture and Floating Construction, Marine Electrical and Electronic Engineering, Construction, Information Technology, Mechanics and Transport Economics; departments of Basic Education, Political Reasoning Education, Foreign Languages, In-Service Training and Postgraduate Studies; Merchant Marine Training Centre; Training Centre of Transport Vocation; Centre of Foreign Languages and Information Technology.

HONG DUC UNIVERSITY

307 Le Lai Rd, Dong Son Ward, Than Hoa City
Telephone: (37) 852-222
Fax: (37) 850-475
E-mail: hongduc-th@hn.vnn.vn
Internet: www.hdu.edu.vn
Founded 1977 by amalgamation of 3 colleges

HEADS OF DEPARTMENTS
Faculty of Agriculture and Forestry: Dr LE HUU CAN
Faculty of Economics and Business Administration: Dr NGUYEN HUU DIEN
Faculty of Medicine: NGUYEN THI TRUONG
Faculty of Natural Science: Dr DUONG DINH HOAN
Faculty of Nursery Teacher Training: NGUYEN THI TRUONG
Faculty of Primary Teacher Training: Dr NGUYEN DINH MAI
Faculty of Social Science: Dr NGUYEN VAN TRUONG
Faculty of Technology: Dr NGUYEN MANH AN
Department of Foreign Languages: PHAM VAN CHU

HUE UNIVERSITY

3 Lê Loi, Hue City, Thua Thien Huê
Telephone: (54) 825866
E-mail: dhhue@hueuni.edu.vn
Internet: www.hueuni.edu.vn
Founded 1957
Language of instruction: Vietnamese
Academic year: November to July
Rector: VIEN THO NGUYEN
Library of 30,000
Number of teachers: 1,316
Number of students: 16,181 full-time, 19,387 part-time
Colleges of Sciences, Pedagogy, Medicine, Agriculture and Forestry, Economics and Arts.

HUE UNIVERSITY OF AGRICULTURE AND FORESTRY

24 Phung Hung, Huê
Telephone: (54) 822535
Fax: (54) 824923
E-mail: huaf@dng.vnn.vn
Founded 1967
Language of instruction: Vietnamese
Academic year: September to July
Rector: Prof. Dr TRAN VAN MINH
Vice-Rector: Dr HOANG MANH QUAN
Library of 200,000
Number of teachers: 210
Number of students: 2,800

DEANS
Faculty of Agricultural Engineering and Post-Harvest Technology: DINH HUNG
Faculty of Agronomy: Dr NGUYEN MINH HIEU
Faculty of Animal Sciences: Dr LE DUC NGOAN
Faculty of Forestry: DUONG VIET TINH
Department of Sciences and International Relations: LE VAN AN (Director)
Central Research and Development in Agro-Forestry Technology: Dr NGUYEN MINH HIEU (Director)
Centre for Rural Development: Dr HOANG MANH QUAN (Director)

NONG LAM UNIVERSITY

Khu Pho 6, Linh Trung Ward, Thu Duc District, Ho Chi Minh City
Telephone: (8) 8960711
Fax: (8) 8960713
E-mail: bctuyen@hcm.vnn.vn
Internet: www.hcmuaf.edu.vn
Founded 1955, as University of Forestry and Agriculture
Language of instruction: Vietnamese
Academic year: September to July
Rector: Dr BUI CACH TUYEN
Library of 60,000
Number of teachers: 400

Number of students: 11,000

Publication: *University Journal of Agricultural Sciences and Technology* (quarterly)

Faculties of Faculties of Agronomy, Animal Science and Veterinary Medicine, Forestry, Engineering, Fishery, Economics, Food Science and Technology, Science, Foreign Languages, Environmental Technology and Information Technology; Experimental Research and Technology Transfer Centre; Foreign Language Centre; Computer Centre; Environmental Technology and Management Centre; Chemical and Biological Analysis and Experiment Centre; Biotechnological Research Centre; Fruit and Vegetable Processing Research Centre; Centre for Research and Application of Cadastral Science and Technology; Wood Science and Technology Research Centre; Industrial Crops Centre; Agricultural Energy and Machinery Research Centre; Continuing Education and Placement Service Centre; Veterinary Clinic.

RMIT INTERNATIONAL UNIVERSITY VIET NAM

21 Pham Ngoc Thach Street, District 3, Ho Chi Minh City

Telephone: (8) 8224992

Fax: (8) 8225039

E-mail: enquiries@rmit.edu.vn

Internet: www.rmit.edu.vn

Founded 2001 by RMIT University, Australia

Academic year: February to January

President: MICHAEL MANN

Vice-President: Prof. ROBERT SNOW

Campus Development Manager: SUZANNE ARDAGH

Director of Teaching and Learning: ROBERTA ABELL

Academic Registrar: TRISH CHAPMAN

Number of teachers: 70

Number of students: 800

Undergraduate programmes: university preparation, BSc (information technology for business, information technology and multimedia, applied science in software engineering, commerce); Postgraduate programmes: MEd Leadership, MBA and Management, Graduate Diploma in Tertiary Teaching and Learning; English programmes; CELTA courses.

UNIVERSITY OF TECHNICAL EDUCATION

1 Vo van Ngan St, Thu Duc, Ho Chi Minh City

Telephone: (8) 8968641

Fax: (8) 8964922

Founded 1962 as Ho Chi Minh City Pedagogical University of Technology; became College of Technical Teacher Training 1996; present name and status 2002

State control

Academic year: September to May

Rector: Assoc. Prof. Dr PHUNG RAN

Vice-Rectors: Assoc. Prof. Dr THAI BA CAN, NGUYEN VAN THUC

Director of Office for Personnel and Administration: NGUYEN VAN MINH

Librarian: DOAN BICH NGOC

Library of 220,000 vols

Number of teachers: 250

Number of students: 6,500

Publication: *Tap san Su Pham Ky Thuat* (quarterly)

DEANS

Department of Automotive Engineering: Dr DO VAN DUNG

Department of Electrical and Electronic Engineering: NGUYEN TRONG THANG

Department of Fundamental Technology: DANG THANH TAN

Department of Home Economics: TRAN THI THEU

Department of Mechanical Engineering: Dr NGUYEN TIEN DUNG

Department of Printing Engineering: NGUYEN VAN QUYEN

Department of Technical Education: NGUYEN THI LAN

Centre for Computer Science: BUI HUY QUYNH

Centre for Foreign Languages: TRAN HUU LICH

Vietnamese–German Centre: Dr DO DUC TUY

UNIVERSITY OF TECHNOLOGY OF DANANG

37 Ngu Hanh St, District 3, Quant Nam, Da Nang City

Telephone: (51) 36139

Fax: (51) 36255

Faculties of Engineering and Technology.

THAI NGUYEN UNIVERSITY

Luong Ngoc Quyen St, Tan Thinh Ward, Thai Nguyen

Telephone: (280) 751681

Fax: (280) 852665

E-mail: khhtqt@hn.vnn.vn

Founded 1994

State control

Academic year: September to June

Pres.: LE CAO THANG

Number of teachers: 1,400

Number of students: 39,000, of which 23,000 full-time

Faculties of Agriculture, Industrial Technology, Medicine, General Education and Teacher Training.

THAI NGUYEN UNIVERSITY OF FORESTRY AND AGRICULTURE

Thinhdan Commune, Thai Nguyen City, Thai Nguyen

Telephone: (280) 855564

Fax: (280) 852921

E-mail: tuaf@hn.vnn.vn

Founded 1970

Rector: TU QUANG HIEN

Number of teachers: 168

Number of students: 6,000

Faculties of Agricultural Economics, Agricultural Technology, Pedagogy, Agronomy, Animal Husbandry and Veterinary Science, Forestry, Graduate Studies and Land Management; Agro-forestry Research and Development Centre for Northern mountainous regions of Viet Nam; Centre for mountainous natural resources and environment; experimental farm.

UNIVERSITY OF THAI NGUYEN BUONMATHUOT

Km 4, Route 14, Buonmathuot, Dak Lak Province

Telephone: (280) 52290

Founded 1977

President: LE CAO TANG

Faculties of Agricultural Sciences, Forestry, Fundamental Sciences and Medical

Sciences; Centres of Applied Computer Science, Forestry and Agriculture.

VAN LANG UNIVERSITY

45 Nguyen Khac Nhu, Q.1, Ho Chi Minh City

Telephone: (8) 8399838

Fax: (8) 8324716

E-mail: dhdlvanlang@vol.vnn.vn

Internet: www.dhdlvanlang.edu.vn

Rector: DUNG NGUYEN

Faculty of Foreign Languages.

VIET NAM FORESTRY UNIVERSITY

Thi Tran Xuan Mai, Chuong My, Ha Tay

Telephone: (34) 840441

Fax: (34) 840540

E-mail: vfuhtqt@hn.vnn.vn

Internet: www.vfu.edu.vn

Founded 1964

Academic year: August to June

Rector: NGUYEN DINH TU

Number of teachers: 257

Number of students: 5,000

Faculties of Silviculture, Forest Resources and Environmental Management, Economics and Business Management, Faculty of Forest Products Technology, Industry for Rural Development, Humanities and Social Sciences, Post-graduation Studies; Secondary School for Ethnic Minority Pupils, Centre for Applied Research on Biotechnology and Social Forestry Training Centre

Publications: *Forest Science and Technology Newsletter* (quarterly), *Scientific Research Periodical* (quarterly).

VIET NAM MARITIME UNIVERSITY

484 Lachtray St, Ngo Quyen District, Haiphong City

Telephone: (31) 829109

Fax: (31) 735282

E-mail: vimaru@hn.vnn.vn

Internet: www.vimaru.edu.vn

Founded 1956

Academic year: August to May

Rector: Dr DANG VAN UY

Vice-Rectors: Prof. Dr PHAM VAN CUONG, Dr LUONG CONG NIIO, Prof. Dr PHAM TIEN TINH

Librarian: TRAN THI YEN

Number of teachers: 800

Number of students: 15,000

Publication: *Newsletter of Science and Technology*

DEANS

Faculty of Information Technology: LE QUOC DINH

Faculty of Marine Electrical and Electronic Engineering: PHAM NGOC TIEP

Faculty of Marine Engineering: NGUYEN DAI AN

Faculty of Navigation: DINH XUAN MANH

Faculty of Sea-Transport Economics: PHAM VAN CUONG

Faculty of Shipbuilding: NGUYEN VINH PHAT

Faculty of Waterway Construction: NGUYEN VAN NGOC

Department of Postgraduate Studies: LE VIET LUONG

HEADS OF DEPARTMENTS

Department of Basic Safety Training: TRINH DINH BICH

Department of Chemistry: NGUYEN CONG THOA

Department of Descriptive Geometry and Technical Drawing: VU QUYET THANG

Department of Foreign Languages: NGUYEN THI HUONG
Department of Mathematics: HOANG VAN HUNG
Department of Mechanics: NGUYEN VAN PHONG
Department of Philosophy: LE THI HIEN
Department of Physical Education: TRAN DUC LUAN
Department of Physics: NGUYEN DANG HA
Division of Strength of Materials: DO THI NHUNG

VIETNAM NATIONAL UNIVERSITY, HANOI

144 Xuan Thuy Rd, Cau Giay, Hanoi
Telephone: (4) 8332015
Fax: (4) 7680429
E-mail: vandao@vnu.ac.vn
Internet: www.vnu.edu.vn

Founded 1993 by amalgamation of University of Hanoi and other instns of higher education in Hanoi
State control
Academic year: September to July

Rector: Prof. Dr DAO TRONG THI
Vice-Rector: Prof. NGUYEN DUC CHINH
Librarian: NGUYEN HUY CHUONG
Library of 800,000 vols, 3,000 periodicals
Number of teachers: 1,320
Number of students: 22,761
Publication: *Tap Chí Khoa Hoc* (Scientific Journal)

Faculties of General Education, Science, Social Sciences and Humanities, Teacher Training and Foreign Languages; Colleges of Foreign Languages, Science, Social Sciences and Humanities; School of Business; Institute of Information Technology Training; Centres of Biotechnology, Co-operation in Mechanics Training, Education Quality Assurance and Research Development, Natural Resources Management and Environmental Studies, Systems Development, Teachers of Political Theory, Vietnamese and Intercultural Studies and Women's Studies; Research Centres in Applied Microbiology and Asian Studies.

VIETNAM NATIONAL UNIVERSITY, HO CHI MINH CITY

3, Cong-Truong Quoc Te, Ho Chi Minh City
Telephone: (8) 8230494
Fax: (8) 8258627
Internet: www.vnuhcm.edu.vn
Founded 1954, present structure since 1995
President: NGUYEN TAN PHAT.

CONSTITUENT UNIVERSITIES

UNIVERSITY OF NATURAL SCIENCES

227 Nguyen Van Cu, District 5, Ho Chi Minh City
Telephone: (8) 8353193
Fax: (8) 8350096
Internet: www.hcmuns.edu.vn
Founded as a division of the Indochina College of Sciences, Hanoi 1942, became Faculty of Sciences of University of Saigon 1956; part of Ho Chi Minh University 1977; current status since 1996
Rector: Assoc. Prof. Dr DUONG AI PHUONG
Vice Rectors: Assoc. Prof. Dr PHAM DINH HUNG, NGUYEN THANH HUONG, Assoc. Prof. Dr DONG THI BICH THUY
Library Director: NGUYEN MINH HIEP
Library of 50,000 vols, 392 periodicals

DEANS
Faculty of Biology: Assoc. Prof. Dr TRAN LINH THUOC
Faculty of Chemistry: Assoc. Prof. Dr HA THUC HUY
Faculty of Environmental Science: Assoc. Prof. Dr LE MANH TAN
Faculty of Geology: TRAN PHU HUNG
Faculty of Information Technology: Dr DUONG ANH DUC
Faculty of Mathematics and Informatics: Dr TO ANH DUNG
Faculty of Physics: Dr DAV VAN LIET
Department of Foreign Languages: NGUYEN HOANG TUAN (Head)
Department of Material Science: Prof. Dr LE KHAC BINH (Head)
Department of Physical Education: NGUYEN VAN HUNG

ATTACHED RESEARCH INSTITUTES

Applied Chemistry Centre: Dir Dr LE VIET TIEN.

Bioscience and Biotechnology Centre: Dir Assoc. Prof. TRAN LINH THUOC.

Centre for Geological Research and Application: Dir NGUYEN PHAT MINH.

Centre for Plant Breeding Research and Development: Dir KIEU NGOC AN.

Centre for Scientific and Technical Creativity: Dir Assoc. Prof. PHAN DUNG.

Computer Science Centre: Dir Assoc. Prof. Dr DONG THI BICH THUY.

Electronics and Computer Centre: Dir Assoc. Prof. Dr NGUYEN HUU PHUONG.

Environment and Sustainable Development Centre: Dir Assoc. Prof. Dr VU CHI HIEU.

Foreign Language Centre: Dir Associate Prof. Dr PHAM DINH HUNG.

Material Science Centre: Dir Assoc. Prof. Dr TRAN TUAN.

UNIVERSITY OF SOCIAL SCIENCES AND HUMANITIES

10–12 Dinh Tien Hoang St, Ho Chi Minh City
E-mail: nckhhtqt@hcmc.netnam.vn
Internet: www.hcmussh.edu.vn
Founded 1996
Language of instruction: Vietnamese
Academic year: October to June
Rector: VAN LE NGO
Librarian: Dr BUI LOAN THUY
Library of 87,784 vols, 375 periodicals
Faculties of Philosophy, Literature, Linguistics and Journalism, Oriental Studies, History, English Linguistics and Literature, Russian Linguistics and Literature, French Linguistics and Literature, Chinese Linguistics and Literature, German Linguistics and Literature, Geography, Sociology and Viet Nam Studies and Vietnamese for Foreigners; Sections of Culture Studies, Anthropology and Physical Education; Vietnamese and South-East Asian Research Centre; Centre for Research in Social Development and Poverty Reduction; Centre for Foreign Languages; Centre for Overseas Studies; Centre for Informatics Technology.

UNIVERSITY OF TECHNOLOGY

268 Ly Thuong Kiet St, District 10, Ho Chi Minh City
Telephone: (8) 8654087
Fax: (8) 8653823
Internet: www.hcmut.edu.vn
Rector: TUOI PHAN THI
Faculties of Chemical Technology, Civil Engineering, Electrical and Electronic Engineering, Environmental Management, Geology and Petroleum, Industrial Management, Information Technology, Mechanical Engineering and Transportation Engineering.

VIETNAM UNIVERSITY OF COMMERCE

Mai Dich, Cau Giay, Hanoi
Telephone: (4) 7643219
Fax: (4) 7643228
E-mail: dhtm@vcu.edu.vn
Internet: www.vcu.edu.vn
Founded 1965
Rector: Prof. Dr PHAM VU LUAN
Vice-Rectors: NGUYEN THIEN DAT, Assoc. Prof. Dr TRAN THI DUNG, Assoc. Prof. Dr NGUYEN BACH KHOA
Library Director: VU THI HUE
Library of 100,000 vols
Number of teachers: 267
Number of students: 7,600

DEANS
Faculty of Business Administration: VU THUY DUONG
Faculty of Economics: Dr THAN DANH PHUC
Faculty of Finance and Accounting: Dr DO MINH THANH
Faculty of Hospitality and Tourism: Dr BUI XUAN NHAN
Faculty of International Trade: Dr NGUYEN VAN THANH
Faculty of Part-Time Training: Assoc. Prof. Dr NGUYEN THI MINH NGUYET
Faculty of Post-Graduate Training: Dr NGUYEN VAN MINH
Faculty of Trading Business: Dr DO THI NGOC
Section of Environment Economics: NGUYEN QUOC TIEN (Head)
Section of Foreign Languages: NGUYEN DUC CHAU (Head)
Section of the History of Vietnam's Communist Party and Socialism: NGO XUAN DAU (Head)
Section of Mathematics: Dr HOANG VAN LAM (Head)
Section of Philosophy: Dr PHUONG KY SON (Head)
Section of Physical and Military Training: NGUYEN VAN KHANH (Head)
Section of Political Economy: Dr DINH THI THUY (Head)

ATTACHED RESEARCH INSTITUTES

Centre for Research and Development of Foodstuffs: Dir LAI KIM GIANG.

Centre for Researching French (CEDIMES): Dir Prof. Dr PHAM VU LUAN.

Research and Development Centre of Trading Technology: Dir NGUYEN HUU KHOA.

VINH UNIVERSITY

182 Le Duan St, Vinh
Telephone: (38) 855452
Fax: (38) 855269
E-mail: lprvvinh@hn.vnn.vn
Rector: NGUYEN DINH HUAN
Vice-Rectors: NGUYEN NGOC HOI, TRAN NGOC GIAO
Number of students: 10,000.

Colleges

ART AND SOCIAL ARTS AND CONSERVATOIRES

College of Law: Thuong Tin, Ha Son Binh Province.

College of Stage Arts and Cinematography: 33 Hong Hoa Tham St, Hanoi.

Conservatoire of Hanoi: O Cho Dua, Hanoi.

Conservatoire of Ho Chi Minh City: 112 Nguyen Du St, District 1, Ho Chi Minh City; tel. (8) 225841; fax (8) 220916; f. 1956; theory, composition, conducting, singing, national and orchestral instruments, electric instruments; 136 teachers; 758 students; Dir Prof. HOANG COONG.

Hanoi Cultural Workers College: O Cho Dua, Hanoi; there are 4 faculties.

Viet Nam College of Fine Arts: Yet Kieu St, Hanoi; there are 3 faculties.

ECONOMICS AND PLANNING

Academy of Finance: 7 Ly Thuong Kiet St, Hoan Kiem District, Hanoi; tel. (4) 9331853; fax (4) 9331865; e-mail hvtc@hn.vnn.vn; internet www.hvtc.edu.vn; f. 2001; faculties of accounting, banking and insurance, business administration, continuing education, corporate finance, customs taxation, economic information systems, foundation studies, international finance, Marx-Lenin-Ho Chi Minh ideology, postgraduate training, public finance; institutes of financial science, and for market and price research; library: 157,000 vols (16,500 titles), 162 current periodicals, 2,100 other publications; 350 teachers; 13,274 students; Dir-Gen. CHI NGO THE; publs *Finance and Accounting Research* (monthly), *Financial Bulletin* (2 a month), *International Economics and Finance News* (weekly), *Market Bulletin* (online, daily), *Market and Price Bulletin* (in English, weekly), *Monography* (5 a year), *News for Leaders* (2 a month), *Scientific Research* (10 a year).

College of Commerce: Tu Liem District, Hanoi; there are 5 faculties.

Hanoi College of Economics and Planning: Nam Bo St, Hanoi; there are 12 faculties.

Ho Chi Minh City College of Finance and Accountancy: College Library, 279 Nguyen Tri Phuong Street, District 10, Ho Chi Minh City; tel. (848) 855-0783; there are 3 faculties.

MEDICINE, PHYSICAL EDUCATION AND SPORTS

College of Physical Training and Sports: Tu Son District, Bac Ninh Province; tel. (241) 831609; fax (241) 832550; f. 1959; there are 6 faculties; 215 teachers; 2,500 students; Dir Prof. Dr TRAN DUC DUNG.

Hanoi College of Pharmacy: 13 Le Thanh Tong St, Hanoi; tel. 54539; f. 1961; 160 teachers; 780 students; library: 20,000 vols; Dean Prof. Dr NGUYEN THANH DO.

Hanoi Medical School: Ton That Tung St, Dong Da, Hanoi; tel. (4) 8524752; fax (4) 8525115; f. 1902; graduate and postgraduate courses; 926 staff; library: 50,000 vols; Dir Prof. TON THAT BACH.

Thai Binh College of Pharmacy: Thai Binh, Thai Binh Province; there are 33 faculties.

TECHNICAL AND INDUSTRIAL

College of Water Conservancy: Dong Da Precinct, Hanoi; there are 6 faculties.

Geology and Mining College: Tu Liem District, Hanoi; there are 8 faculties.

Hanoi College of Architecture: Kilometre No. 7, Hanoi-Ha Dong Highway; there are 4 faculties.

Industrial Decorative Arts College: O Cho Dua, Hanoi; f. 1965; there are 5 faculties.

Posts and Telecommunications Training Centre No. 1: Km M.10, Hadong Rd, Ha Tay, Hanoi; tel. (4) 8544256; fax (34) 825523; f. 1953; library: 7,000 vols; Dir Dr NGUYEN KIM LAN.

Road and Rail Transport College: Tu Liem District, Hanoi; there are 5 faculties.

YEMEN

The Higher Education System

Institutions of higher education predate Yemen's formation from a merger of the Yemen Arab Republic (YAR) and the People's Democratic Republic of Yemen (PDRY) in 1990, the oldest being San'a University, which was founded in 1970. In 1975 the University of Aden was founded and these remained the principal institutions of higher education until the 1990s. In 2003/04 some 184,072 students were enrolled at seven state-controlled institutions of higher education. The most recent legislation pertaining to higher education is the Universities, Colleges and Institutions of Higher Education Law (No. 14, 2005).

The general secondary education certificate (thanawiya) is the principal requirement for admission to both public and private higher education. In 2001 the pass-mark in the thanawiya for entry to all undergraduate degrees was set at 70%; additionally, applicants to popular programmes such as engineering or medicine may have to sit a university entrance examination and attend a personal interview. Universities offer two-year, sub-degree Diplomas in professional and technical fields from which can progress onto advanced degree programmes. Bachelors degrees must last at least four years, and students are required to accumulate a minimum of 132 'credits' for graduation. (The Bachelors of Medicine is a six-year programme of study.)

Traditionally, Yemeni graduate students travelled abroad to study for postgraduate degrees, however in recent years Yemeni institutions have begun awarding postgraduate degrees (although the range is still quite limited). The first postgraduate qualification is the postgraduate Diploma, which is a one-year course that is also regarded as a preparatory course for the Masters degree, which lasts two years. Finally, although Doctorates are now being offered by universities on an 'in-house' basis there is no uniform system for their award.

Post-secondary technical and vocational education is offered by a range of different professional and vocational institutes and is divided into Regular (or General), Parallel and Further (or Continuing) Education and Training. The Certificate in Technical Education is awarded after a two-year course at technical institutes and is open to students with the thanawiya or Certificate of Vocational Training. US-style 'community' colleges have been established and they specialize in three-year Diploma courses, admission to which requires the thanawiya.

Learned Society

LANGUAGE AND LITERATURE

British Council: 3rd Fl., Administrative Tower, San'a Trade Centre, Algiers St, POB 2157, San'a; tel. (1) 448356; fax (1) 448360; e-mail britishcouncil@ye.britishcouncil.org; internet irww.britishcouncil.org/yemen; offers courses and exams in English language and British culture and promotes cultural exchange with the UK; Asst Dir, Resources AZIZ AL-BAAR.

Libraries and Archives

Aden

Miswat Library: Aden; previously called Lake Library; administered by Aden Municipality; 30,000 vols, in English, Arabic and Urdu.

Teachers' Club Library: Aden; over 2,000 vols.

Travelling Library: Aden; ancillary to Miswat Library; administered by Aden Municipality; 9,500 vols, in English and Arabic.

San'a

Library of the Great Mosque of San'a: San'a; f. 1925; the collection of 10,000 MSS and printed vols is not at present accessible to the public; Librarian ZAID BIN ALI ENAN.

Universities

UNIVERSITY OF ADEN

POB 6312, Khormaksar, Aden
Telephone: (2) 234428
Fax: (2) 234426
E-mail: adenuniversity@y.net.ye
Internet: www.adenuniversity.edu.ye
Founded 1975

State control
Languages of instruction: Arabic, English
Academic year: September to June

Rector: Prof. Dr ABDUL WAHAB RAWEH
Vice-Rector for Academic Affairs: Assoc. Prof. Dr SAEED ABDO GABALI
Vice-Rector for Scientific Research and Post-graduate Studies: Assoc. Prof. Dr AHMED ALI AL-HAMDANI
Vice-Rector for Students' Affairs: Asst Prof. Dr NASSER A. NASSER
Secretary-General: Assoc. Prof. Dr AHMED SALEH MUNASSER

Number of teachers: 1,482
Number of students: 22,761

Publications: *Al-Tawassul* (2 a year), *Al-Yemen* (2 a year), *Journal of Natural and Applied Sciences* (2 a year), *Journal of Social Sciences and Humanities* (2 a year), *Saba* (2 a year), *Theses, Summaries and Abstracts* (annually), *Yemen Engineer* (3 a year), *Yemeni Journal for Agricultural Research* (2 a year)

DEANS

Faculty of Administration: Assoc. Prof. FUAD RASHED ABDO
Faculty of Agricultural Sciences: Assoc. Prof. Dr ABBAS BAWAZIR
Faculty of Arts: Assoc. Prof. Dr SULAIMAN FARAJ BIN AZOON
Faculty of Economics: Prof. Dr MOHAMED A WARET
Faculty of Education (Aden): Asst Prof. Dr YACOOB A. KASSEM
Faculty of Education (Dalea): Asst Prof. Dr MOHD S. OBADI
Faculty of Education (Loder): Asst Prof. Dr SALEH A AL BORKANI
Faculty of Education (Radfan): Asst Prof. Dr ABDULLA MOHAMMED
Faculty of Education (Sabr): Assoc. Prof. Dr ALI QASEM AKLAN
Faculty of Education (Shabwa): Assoc. Prof. Dr NASER SALEH HABTOOR
Faculty of Education (Tur Al-Baha): Asst Prof. Dr HAMID ABDUL MAGEED QUBATI
Faculty of Education (Yafai): Assoc. Prof. Dr ABDUL RAHMAN AL-WALI
Faculty of Education (Zingibar): Assoc. Prof. Dr MOHAMMED A. HOSEEN
Faculty of Engineering: Assoc. Prof. Dr ABDUL WALI HADI
Faculty of Law: Assoc. Prof. Dr SAAD M. SAAD
Faculty of Medicine: Assoc. Prof. Dr ABDULLA SAEED. HATAB
Faculty of Oil and Minerals: Asst Prof. Dr KHALED ALI. AL SHAMSI

ATTACHED INSTITUTES

Centre for British, American and Translation Studies: Dir Assoc. Prof. SALEM ABDULAZIZ.

Centre for Environmental Studies and Sciences: Dir Prof. Dr HUSSEIN A. ALKAFF.

Centre for Health Care: Dir Asst Prof. Dr MOHD S. BERRAYA.

Centre for Science and Technology: Dir Prof. Dr ABDULLA AIDAH BAHASHWAN.

Computer Centre: Dir Assoc. Prof. Dr MOHAMMED FADLE ABDULLA.

Continuing Education Centre: Dir Asst Prof. Dr SALEM ALI ALBANI.

Language Institute: Dir Asst Prof. Dr MUHAMMAD SALIH.

University Consultancy Centre: Dir Asst Prof. Dr ABUBAKER MOHAMMED BA-RAHEEM.

Women's Research and Training Centre: Dir Dr RUKHSANA M. ISMAIL.

Yemeni Research and Study Centre: Dir Prof. Dr JAFFER DHFARI.

UNIVERSITY OF DHAMAR

POB 87246, Dhamar
Telephone: (6) 509554
Fax: (6) 509556
Faculty of Engineering.

HADHRAMOUT UNIVERSITY OF SCIENCE AND TECHNOLOGY

POB 50511, Mukalla
Telephone: (5) 303535
Fax: (5) 303513
E-mail: hadhramoutuniv@y.net.ye
Internet: www.hust.edu.ye
Founded 1993
Vice-Rector: SALEM AWAD RAMODHA.

HODEIDAH UNIVERSITY

POB 3114, Hodeidah
Telephone: (3) 222703
Fax: (3) 222703
E-mail: info@hoduniv.edu.ye
Internet: www.hoduniv.edu.ye
State control
Rector: QASSIM M. BERIHE
Faculties of Education, Management Systems and Marine Sciences.

IBB UNIVERSITY

POB 70270, Ibb
Telephone: (4) 408069
Fax: (4) 408068
E-mail: ibbunv@y.net.ye
Internet: www.ibbunv.com.ye
Founded 1996
State control
Rector: Prof. Dr AHMED M. SHUQ'A ALDEEN
Faculties of Agriculture and Veterinary Science, Arts, Dentistry, Economics and Management, Education, Engineering and Architecture and Science; Centres for Agricultural and Environmental Consultancy, Educational Technology and Engineering Consultancy.

SAN'A UNIVERSITY

POB 1247, San'a
Telephone: (1) 250555
Fax: (1) 200564
Internet: www.su.edu.ye
Founded 1970
State control; financial support from Kuwait
Languages of instruction: Arabic, English
Academic year: October to June
President: NASSER AL-AULAQI
Number of teachers: 332
Number of students: 10,715
Publication: Publications: Faculty research journals

DEANS

Faculty of Agriculture: Dr NASSER AULAQI (acting)
Faculty of Arts: Dr AHMED AL SAYDI
Faculty of Commerce and Economics: Dr NASSER AULAQI
Faculty of Education: Dr MOHAMED AL KHADER
Faculty of Engineering: Dr AWAD SALEH
Faculty of Law and Sharia: Dr ABDUL MUNIM AL BADRAWI
Faculty of Medicine and Health Sciences: Dr ABDALLAH AL-HURAYBI

Faculty of Science: Dr ALI AL SHUKAI

TAIZ UNIVERSITY

POB 6803, Taiz
Telephone: (4) 221378
Fax: (4) 221381
Founded 1995
State control
President: HOSEIN AL-ERYANI
Number of teachers: 269
Number of students: 30,250
Publication: Taiz University Research Journal (annually)

DEANS

Faculty of Administration: MOHAMMAD ALKAHTANI
Faculty of Arts: THABET BEDARI
Faculty of Education: ABAS SOSWAH
Faculty of Engineering: FISAL IBRAHEEM
Faculty of Law: KAEED TARBOSH
Faculty of Medicine: FAUD ALKHLI
Faculty of Science: ABDULRAHMAN ALZOBIRI

College

Kulliat Asshari'a Wa Alqanun (Faculty of Islamic Law): San'a; f. 1970.

ZAMBIA

The Higher Education System

Institutions of higher education predate the independence of the Republic of Zambia (formerly Northern Rhodesia) from the United Kingdom in 1964, the oldest being Zambia College of Agriculture, which was founded in 1947. In 1965 the University of Zambia was founded and it remained the only university-level institution until the foundation of Copperbelt University in 1987. In 1999/2000 there were an estimated 24,553 students enrolled in tertiary education, which is administered by the Ministry of Education.

The standard administrative structure consists of the Chancellor, Vice-Chancellor, Registrar, Bursar, University Council, Senate, Boards of Studies, Deans and Heads of Department. The Chancellor is appointed by the Head of State while the Vice-Chancellors are appointed by the Minister of Education, who also appoints the University Council. The Registrar and Bursar are appointed by the University Council. Other than the State, the main source of university funding is students' tuition fees.

Students are required to obtain five credit-level passes on the Zambian School Certificate (Grade 12) for admission to university. The Bachelors is the main undergraduate degree and is generally four years in duration, except for degrees in agriculture, architecture, engineering (five years), veterinary science (six years) and medicine (seven years). The postgraduate Masters degree is open to students who have been awarded the Bachelors and is a two- to four-year programme of study. The PhD is the highest university degree in Zambia but is only available in a limited number of subjects; it requires four years of study.

The Ministry of Science, Technology and Vocational Training is responsible for providing post-secondary vocational and technical education. Within the Ministry, the Department of Technical Education and Vocational Training administers 11 institutions and 90 technical courses. The principal qualifications are (in ascending order) the Craft Certificate, Certificate, Advanced Certificate and Diploma.

Learned Societies

BIBLIOGRAPHY, LIBRARY SCIENCE AND MUSEOLOGY

Zambia Library Association: POB 38636, Lusaka 10101; internet www.zla.co.zm; Chair. BENSON NJOBVU; Hon. Sec. MUTINTA NABUYANDA; publs *Journal* (quarterly), *Newsletter* (every 2 months).

LANGUAGE AND LITERATURE

Alliance Française: Plot 22725, Alick Nkhata Ave, Longacres, POB 30948, 10101 Lusaka; tel. (1) 253467; fax (1) 254735; e-mail afl@microlink.zm; offers courses and exams in French language and culture and promotes cultural exchange with France; attached teaching centres in Kabwe, Kitwe, Livingstone and Ndola.

British Council: Heroes Place, Cairo Rd, POB 34571, Lusaka; tel. (1) 223602; fax (1) 224122; e-mail info@britishcouncil.org.zm; internet www.britishcouncil.org/zambia; offers courses and exams in English language and British culture and promotes cultural exchange with the UK; Dir JOHN MITCHELL.

MEDICINE

Zambia Medical Association: POB RW 148, Lusaka; Chair. Dr S. SIKANETA; Sec. Dr D. LEVITT; publ. *Medical Journal of Zambia* (every 2 months).

NATURAL SCIENCES

Biological Sciences

Wildlife Conservation Society of Zambia: POB 30255, Lusaka; tel. and fax (1) 254226; e-mail wcsz@zamnet.zm; f. 1953; wildlife and natural resource conservation, environmental education; 2,000 mems; Pres. G. R. KAYUKWA; Exec. Dir M. SICHILONGO; publs *Kobus* (monthly), *Chongololo Chipembele for Schools*, *Teacher's Guide* (both every 2 months).

TECHNOLOGY

Engineering Institution of Zambia: POB 34730, Lusaka; f. 1955; 2,600 mems; Pres. G. K. CHIBUYE; Vice-Pres. Dr K. AKAPELWA; publ. *Journal* (quarterly).

Research Institutes

GENERAL

National Institute for Scientific and Industrial Research: POB 310158, International Airport Rd, 15302 Lusaka; tel. (1) 281081; fax (1) 283533; e-mail nisiris@zamnet.zm; internet www.nisir.org.zm; f. 1967; statutory body to conduct scientific and industrial research and to collect and disseminate scientific information; incorporates Livestock and Pest Research Centre, Tree Improvement Research Centre, Radioisotopes Research Unit, Food Technology Research Unit, Water Resources Research Unit, Building and Industrial Minerals Research Unit, Information Services Unit, Technical Services Unit and Material Testing Unit; library of 9,200 vols, 100 periodicals; Chair. the MINISTER OF SCIENCE, TECHNOLOGY AND VOCATIONAL TRAINING; Exec. Dir Dr MWANANYANDA MBIKUSITA LEWANIKA; publs *Zambia Journal of Science and Technology* (irreg.), *Zambia Science Abstracts* (annually), *Annual Report*, *Sci-Tech Newsletter* (4 a year).

AGRICULTURE, FISHERIES AND VETERINARY SCIENCE

Central Fisheries Research Institute: POB 350100, Chilanga; tel. (1) 278597; fax (1) 278173; e-mail piscator@zamnet.zm; f. 1965; hydrobiological research directed towards increasing fish production, co-management research directed towards sustainable fisheries management, fish-stock assessment, social and economic studies in fishing regions; library of 4,700 vols; Deputy Dir C. K. KAPASA; Chief Fisheries Research Officer P. NGALANDE; publs *Fisheries Statistics*, *Annual Report*, *Project Reports* (occasional).

Central Veterinary Research Station: POB 33980, Lusaka; tel. (1) 233444; e-mail cvri@zamnet.zm; f. 1926; directed by the Ministry of Lands and Agriculture; general veterinary diagnosis and research; Principal Veterinary Research Officer Dr S. H. KABILIKA.

Division of Forest Products Research: POB 20388, Kitwe; tel. (2) 227088; f. 1963; controls research into wood utilization, timber properties preservation, engineering, forest products and wood composite studies; Chief Officer S. M. MUTEMWA; publs *Bulletin*, *Records* (irregular).

Division of Forest Research: POB 22099, Kitwe; tel. (2) 220456; fax (2) 224110; f. 1956; ecological and botanical studies; soil and site assessment investigations; silvicultural research, exotic plantations and indigenous forests and woodlands; mensurational studies of plantation growth; tree breeding and selection; agroforestry and fuelwood projects; forest pathology and entomology; seed collection, processing, testing and low-temperature storage; staff of 24; library of 7,800 vols, 150 periodicals and 100 serials; Chief Forest Research Officer F. M. MALAYA; publs *Research Notes*, *Research Pamphlets*, *Research Bulletins*, *Research Newsletter*.

International Red Locust Control Organisation for Central and Southern Africa: POB 240252, Ndola; tel. (2) 651251; fax (2) 650117; e-mail locust@zamnet.zm; f. 1970; to prevent plagues of red locust by controlling incipient outbreaks, to assist mem. countries in the management of army worm and grain-eating birds and to carry out research and training; member countries: Kenya, Malawi, Mozambique, Tanzania, Zambia, Zimbabwe; library of 3,000 vols, 35 periodicals; Dir A. D. GADABU; publs *Annual Report*, *Quarterly Reports*, *Scientific Papers*.

Mount Makulu Agricultural Research Station: Private Bag 7, Chilanga; tel. (1) 278008; e-mail genetics@zamnet.zm; f. 1952; Headquarters of Department of Research and Specialist Services, Ministry of Agriculture, Food and Fisheries, and 11 regional and specialist research stations; research on soils, soil classification, vegetation types and land classification; agronomy; chemistry; ecology; entomology; pasture research; phytosanitary services; plant breeding; plant pathology; Seeds Control and Certification Institute; stored products entomology; cotton entomology; main crops under investigation: maize, groundnuts, cotton, tobacco, pastures and pasture legumes, beans, wheat, sorghum, soyabeans; library of 30,000 vols, 20,000 reports, 15,000 reprints; Principal Agricultural Research Officer BERNADETTE LUBOZUYA; publs *Accessions List* (every 2 months), *Annual Report*, *Production Farming in Zambia* (monthly), *Reprints of Articles by Staff Members*, *Research Branch Memoranda* (occasional).

ECONOMICS, LAW AND POLITICS

Pan-African Institute for Development, East and Southern Africa: POB 80448, Kabwe; tel. (5) 223651; fax (5) 223451; e-mail paidesa@zamnet.zm; f. 1979; training, research, surveys, follow-up action; library of 8,000 vols; Dir Dr LUTHER BANGA; publ. *Current Contents: Development Studies* (4 a year).

MEDICINE

National Food and Nutrition Commission: POB 32669, 10101 Lusaka; tel. (1) 227803; fax (1) 221426; e-mail nfnc@zamnet .zm; f. 1967; statutory body to improve the nutritional status of the people of Zambia; 98 mems; Chair. CRESTA KALUBA; Exec. Dir PRISCILLA N. LIKWASI.

Occupational Health Safety and Research Bureau: Independence Ave, POB 20205, Kitwe; tel. (2) 228977; fax (2) 222823; e-mail ohmb@zamnet.zm; internet www.geocities.com/ohsrb; f. 1950; research on pneumoconiosis and related chest diseases, assessment and advice on control of hazardous conditions in industrial workplaces; library of 300 vols; Dir Dr C. M. MUSOWE.

Tropical Diseases Research Centre: POB 71769, Ndola; tel. (2) 621860; fax (2) 612837; e-mail tdrc@zamtel.zm; internet www.tdrc .org.zm; f. 1976; research in communicable diseases, support for disease control and primary health care programmes; trains Zambian scientists in the field of bio-medical research, serves as international research and training centre; epidemiological research, clinical trials, research in malaria, schistosomiasis, trypanosomiasis, diarrhoeal diseases, etc.; 28 researchers, 76 support staff; library of 2,200 vols, 219 periodicals; Dir Dr EMMANUEL KAFWEMBE; publs *Annual Report*, *Tropical Diseases Research Centre Newsletter*.

NATURAL SCIENCES
Physical Sciences

Geological Survey of Zambia (Ministry of Mines and Minerals Development): POB 50135, Lusaka; tel. (1) 250174; fax (1) 250174; e-mail gsd@zamnet.zm; f. 1951; statutory depository for all mining and prospecting records and reports; responsible for geological mapping, economic mineral investigations, assisting the public on mineral matters, and advising the Ministry on all mineral and geological matters; library of 89,346 vols; Dir D. MULELA; publs *Annual Report*, *Records*, *Bulletins*, *Memoirs*, *Reports*, *Occasional Papers*, *Economic Reports*, *Annotated Bibliography and Index of the Geology of Zambia*, and maps.

Libraries and Archives
Kitwe

Hammarskjöld Memorial Library: POB 21493, Kitwe; tel. (2) 211488; fax (2) 211001; e-mail daglib@zamnet.zm; internet www .mindolo.org/dml; f. 1963; 26,000 vols; collection of films, filmstrips, slides, microfiche, videotapes, tape-recordings on local history; rare book collection on the history of central Africa; specializes in social sciences; research library and archives of the Mindolo Ecumenical Foundation; Librarian DUNSTAN CHIKONKA.

Kitwe Public Library: POB 20070, Kaunda Sq., Kitwe; tel. 213685; f. 1954; 33,000 vols; one branch library; publ. *Annual Report*.

Lusaka

Lusaka City Libraries: POB 31304, Katondo Rd, Lusaka; tel. (1) 227282; f. 1943; 3 br. libraries and a mobile library; 145,000 vols, 200 periodicals, 320 maps; Librarian J. C. NKOLE; publs *Annual Report*, *Library Bulletin* (quarterly).

National Archives of Zambia: POB 50010, Lusaka; tel. (1) 254081; fax (1) 254080; e-mail naz@zamnet.zm; f. 1947; covers national literature from 1890 to the present day in the forms of national archives, historical MSS, microfilms, cartographic, philatelic, currency, pictorial and printed publication collections; 18,000 linear metres of records; depository and reference library of 17,000 vols and 11,000 periodicals; the National Archives Library is a reference and legal deposit library for all printed publications published in Zambia; Dir CRISPIN HAMOOYA; Senior Archivist T. M. SUUYA; Senior Librarian H. K. NYENDWA; publs *Annual National Bibliography*, *Annual Reports*, *Calendars of District Note Books, vols I and IV*, *Information About the National Archives of Zambia*, *List of Periodicals, vols I and II*.

Zambia Library Service: POB 50092, Haile Selassie Ave, Lusaka; tel. (1) 254993; fax (1) 252510; e-mail zamlibs@zamnet.zm; f. 1962; 6 regional libraries, 18 branch libraries and a central library of 500,000 vols; aims to provide a countrywide free public library service; Chief Librarian ETHEL N. TEMBO; publ. *Zambia Library Service Newsletter* (irregular).

Ndola

Ndola Public Library: POB 70388, Independence Way, Ndola; tel. (2) 617173; f. 1934; 90,000 vols, 140 periodicals; public library services in Lusaka serving Ndola City Council Community; central library, four brs, two prison library centres; centre for American Circulating Library from American Cultural Center; Librarian Dr K. MUMBA CHISAKA; publ. *Copperbelt Library Bulletin* (irregular).

Museums and Art Galleries
Livingstone

Livingstone Museum: Mosi-oa-Tunya Rd, POB 60498, Livingstone; tel. (3) 324429; fax (3) 323566; e-mail livmus@zamnet.zm; f. 1934; ethnology of the peoples of Zambia; prehistory, history and natural history of Zambia; autograph, letters and relics of David Livingstone; library of 20,000 vols, 200 periodicals, including special collection of 2,000 vols on prehistory, history, ethnography and Africana; supporting depts of taxidermy, conservation and education; Dir V. K. KATANEKWA; publs *Zambia Museum Journal*, *The Livingstone Museum Newsletter*.

Mbala

Moto Moto Museum: POB 420230, Mbala; tel. (4) 450098; fax (4) 450098; e-mail motomoto@zamnet.zm; f. 1974; research in ethnography, pre-history and history; educational and exhibition programmes; library of 4,500 vols; Dir FLEXON M. MIZINGA; publs *Zambia Museums Journal* (irregular), *Annual Report*, *Newsletter* (irregular).

Ndola

Copperbelt Museum: 911 Buteko Ave, POB 71444, Ndola; tel. (2) 613591; fax (2) 617450; e-mail cbmus@zamnet.zm; f. 1962; collection, conservation, preservation, documentation and exhibit of geological and historical items, ethnography and natural history; Dir STANFORD MUDENDA SIACHOONO.

Universities
COPPERBELT UNIVERSITY

POB 21692, Kitwe
Telephone: (2) 225155
Fax: (2) 222218
E-mail: registrar@cbu.ac.zm
Internet: www.cbu.edu.zm

Founded 1979 as Ndola Campus of University of Zambia; independent university status 1987
State Control
Language of instruction: English
Academic year: March to December (3 terms)
Chancellor: Prof. MUYUNDA MWANALUSHI
Vice-Chancellor: Prof. MICHAEL MUSONDA
Deputy Vice-Chancellor: Dr ERNEST M. BEELE
Registrar: ALLAN M. ILLUNGA
Librarian: C. B. M. LUNGU
Number of teachers: 211
Number of students: 3,197
Publication: *Journal of Business* (4 a year)

DEANS
School of Built Environment: G. C. NGOMA
School of Business: Dr S. CHAMA
School of Natural Resources: EMMANUEL CHUNDA
School of Technology: Dr I. S. SINGH

HEADS OF DEPARTMENTS
School of Built Environment (tel. (2) 225086; e-mail deansbe@cbu.ac.zm):

   Architecture: BERNARD MABO
   Building Science: JABSI SIMUDII
   Civil Engineering and Construction: Eng. DANFORD BANDA
   Land Economy: AKAKANDELWA NALUMINO
   Urban and Regional Planning: J. A. OKRA

School of Business (tel. (2) 227946; fax (2) 228346; e-mail deansb@cbu.ac.zm):

   Accounting and Finance: P. A. N. MUSOKWA
   Business Administration: A. MULAMBYA
   Postgraduate Programme: Dr T. K. TAYLOR
   Production Management: FLOYD BANDA

School of Natural Resources (tel. (2) 227946; e-mail forestry@cbu.ac.zm):

   Fisheries: (vacant)
   Forest Resource Management: FELIX NJOVU
   Wildlife Management: (vacant): FABIAN MALAMBO
   Wood Science and Technology: FABIAN MALAMBO

School of Technology (tel. (2) 228212; fax (2) 228212; e-mail deanst@cbu.ac.zm):

   Chemical Engineering: J. J. KANYMEBO
   Computer Science: Dr H. M. LIBATI
   Electrical Engineering: J. BANGILI

Mining: B. L. CHULU

ATTACHED INSTITUTES

Centre for Lifelong Education: Dir Col (rtd) LLOYD MWILA.

Institute of Environmental Management: Dir M. NABUYANDA.

UNIVERSITY OF ZAMBIA

POB 32379, Lusaka
Telephone: (1) 291777
Fax: (1) 253952
E-mail: registrar@admin.unza.zm
Internet: www.unza.zm
Founded 1965
State control
Language of instruction: English
Academic year: November to September

Chancellor: Dr JACOB M. MWANZA
Vice-Chancellor: Prof. ROBERT SERPELL
Deputy Vice-Chancellor: Prof. GEOFFREY LUNGWANGWA
Registrar: STEPHEN NDHLOVU
Librarian: Dr H. MWACALIMBA

Number of teachers: 535
Number of students: 3,464

Publications: *African Social Research, Journal of Humanities, Journal of Medicine, Journal of Sciences and Technology, Zambia Law Journal, Zambian Papers, Zango*

DEANS

Agricultural Sciences: Prof. V. R. N. CHINENE
Distance Education: Prof. R. SIACIWENA (Dir)
Education: Prof. D. MWANSA (acting)
Engineering: Dr S. B. KANYANGA
Humanities and Social Sciences: Dr J. D. CHILESHE
Law: Dr F. NGANDU
Medicine: Prof. MUNKONGE
Mines: Dr F. TEMBO
Natural Sciences: Dr L. E. MUMBA
Research and Graduate Studies: Prof. G. LUNGWANGWA (Dir)
Veterinary Medicine: Prof. K. L. SAMUI

HEADS OF DEPARTMENTS

Agricultural Sciences (e-mail deanagric@agric.unza.zm):

Agricultural Economics and Extension Education: Dr T. KALINDA
Animal Sciences: Dr E. S. K. YAMBAYAMBA
Crop Science: Dr M. S. MWALA
Soil Science: Prof. I. O. LUNGU

Education (e-mail deanedu@edu.unza.zm):

Adult Education and Extension Studies: W. CHAKANIKA
Educational Administration and Policy Studies: H. J. MSANGO

Educational Psychology, Sociology and Special Education: Dr S. K. NGANDU
In-Service Education and Advisory Science Education: Dr C. P. CHISHIMBA
Library and Information Studies: S. ZULU
Language and Social Sciences Education: G. TAMBULUKANI
Mathematics and Science Education: C. HAMBOKOMA

Engineering (e-mail deaneng@eng.unza.zm):

Agricultural Engineering: Dr N. J. KWENDAKWEMA
Civil Engineering: Dr M. N. MULENGA
Electrical and Electronic Engineering: L. D. NYIRENDA
Mechanical Engineering: Dr A. N. NG'ANDU
Surveying: Dr P. NSOMBO

Humanities and Social Sciences (e-mail deanhss@hss.unza.zm):

Development Studies: M. LIPALITE
Economics: Dr C. N. MWIKISA
Gender Studies: Dr M. C. MILIMO
History: F. E. MULENGA
Literature and Languages: Dr J. K. SIKULUMBA
Philosophy: Prof. C. DILLON-MALONE
Political and Administrative Studies: Dr L. C. W. KAELA
Psychology: D. SIAKALIMA
Social Development Studies: Dr M. LEMBA

Medicine (e-mail deanmed@medicine.unza.zm):

Anatomy: Dr E. B. KAFUMUKACHE
Community Medicine: Dr S. SIZIYA (acting)
Internal Medicine: Dr P. MATONDO
Medical Education: Dr S. S. BANDA
Obstetrics and Gynaecology: Dr C. KASEBA
Paediatrics and Child Health: Prof. G. J. BHAT
Pathology and Microbiology: Dr T. KAILE
Physiological Sciences: Prof. A. K. MANAKOV
Post-Basic Nursing: E. LAMBWE
Psychiatry: Prof. A. HAWORTH
Surgery: Assoc. Prof. K. ERZINGATSIAN

Mines (e-mail dean@mines.unza.zm):

Geology: Dr C. W. NKHUWA
Metallurgy and Mineral Processing: Dr L. K. WITIKA
Mining Engineering: Dr S. KAMBANI

Natural Sciences (e-mail dean@natsci.unza.zm):

Biological Sciences: Dr D. M. WACHINGA
Chemistry: Dr S. F. BANDA
Geography: Dr G. P. A. BANDA
Mathematics and Statistics: J. LUSWILI
Physics: Dr H. V. MWEENE

Veterinary Medicine (e-mail dean@vet.unza.zm):

Biomedical Sciences: Dr J. N. SIULAPWA

Clinical Studies: Dr I. K. PHIRI (acting)
Disease Control: Dr A. NAMBOTA
Paraclinical Studies: Dr H. CHITAMBO

ATTACHED INSTITUTES

Centre for Creative Arts: Dir Dr M. MAPOPA.

Computer Centre: Dir J. S. MUNSAKA.

Institute for Economic and Social Research: Dir Assoc. Prof. O. SAASA.

Colleges

Evelyn Hone College of Applied Arts and Commerce: POB 30029, Lusaka; tel. (1) 235344; fax (1) 225127; e-mail ehcbs@zamnet.zm; f. 1963; library: 14,000 vols; 145 teachers; 3,000 students (1,600 full-time, 1,400 part-time); Principal MICHAEL TANDEO; Librarian SEBASTIAN NGWIRA.

National Institute of Public Administration: POB 31990, 10101 Lusaka; tel. (1) 228802; fax (1) 227213; e-mail nipa@zamnet.zm; f. 1963; trains government administrators and accounting personnel for central and local government; offers training and consultancy in the private sector in the management, secretarial work, purchasing and supplies, and law and information technology; library: 28,000 vols; 50 teachers; 1,316 students; Exec. Dir. Dr M. C. BWALYA; Registrar PAUL SIMUKOKO; Librarian N. MTANGA; publ. *NIPA Newsletter* (every 2 weeks).

Natural Resources Development College: POB 310099, Lusaka; tel. (1) 284639; fax (1) 281941; f. 1964; 3-year diploma courses in agriculture, agricultural education and engineering, nutrition, fisheries, water engineering; library: 32,000 vols; 48 teachers; 430 students; Principal T. F. F. MALUZA; Librarian M. M. MISENGO.

Northern Technical College: POB 250093, Ndola; tel. (2) 680141; fax (2) 680423; e-mail nortec@zamnet.zm; f. 1960; automotive, electrical, heavy duty and mechanical engineering, business studies and communication skills, refrigeration and air-conditioning; library: 20,000 vols; 96 teachers (68 full-time, 28 part-time); 1,300 students (800 full-time, 500 part-time); Principal (vacant); Administration Man. (vacant); Librarian NABOMBE PUMULO.

Zambia College of Agriculture: POB 660053, Monze; f. 1947; 2-year certificate course; 42 staff; library: 3,000 vols; 240 students; Principal D. H. MCCLEERY.

ZIMBABWE

The Higher Education System

Institutions of higher education predate the independence of Zimbabwe (formerly Southern Rhodesia) from the United Kingdom in 1980, the oldest being Esigodini Agricultural Institute, which was founded in 1921. the oldest university-level institution is the University of Zimbabwe (formerly the University College of Rhodesia), which was founded in 1955 (present status since 1970 and present name since 1980). In 1998 some 11,451 students were attending universities, while 36,830 students were enrolled at institutions of higher education.

The Head of State is the Chancellor of the public universities while their day-to-day administration is overseen by a Vice-Chancellor. Both public and private universities are governed by University Councils.

Two grade 'E' passes at GCE A-level is the minimum requirement for admission to undergraduate studies; however, the strength of competition has effectively raised the bar for admission to grade 'C' in at least three subjects. Admission is also granted to applicants who hold the National Diploma. The principal undergraduate degree is the Bachelors, which may be classified either 'General' or 'Honours' (the distinction lies in the content of the course and not its length). On average, the Bachelors lasts three to four years, but in some subjects the period of study is longer, such as the Bachelors of Medicine and Bachelors of Surgery (both five years). Masters degrees are the first postgraduate-level qualifications, and vary in length from one to two years; they are usually a composite of coursework and research for dissertation, but the MPhil is a purely research degree. The main doctoral-level degree is the DPhil, which is three to four years in duration.

In 1990 the Government initiated wide-ranging reforms of technical and vocational education owing to the failure of the secondary and higher education sectors to match the expectations of both students and employers. Colleges, polytechnics and technical colleges, universities and university colleges all offer vocational training combining class-work and workplace experience. Vocational training centres were first established in 1998 to provide for a Government initiative known as the Skills Training programme. The principal technical and vocational awards are as follows: National Certificate, National Diploma and Higher National Diploma.

Learned Societies

GENERAL

UNESCO Office Harare: POB HG 435, Highlands, Harare; Located at: 8 Kenilworth Rd, Newlands, Harare; tel. (4) 332222; fax (4) 332344; e-mail hiv-aids@unesco.co.zw; internet www.zimaids.co.zw/hae; designated Cluster Office for Botswana, Malawi, Mozambique, Zambia and Zimbabwe; Dir KO-CHIH TUNG.

AGRICULTURE, FISHERIES AND VETERINARY SCIENCE

Crop Science Society of Zimbabwe: POB UA 409, Union Ave, Harare; f. 1970; 200 mems.

Zimbabwe Agricultural Society: POB 442, Harare; tel. (4) 705641; fax (4) 705644; f. 1895; 3,500 mems; Gen. Man. J. R. PEAROD.

Zimbabwe Veterinary Association: POB 8397, Causeway, Harare; tel. (4) 303574; fax (4) 307349; e-mail zva@gonzo.icon.co.zw; f. 1920; 175 mems; Pres. Dr G. GELDART; publ. *Zimbabwe Veterinary Journal* (2 a year).

BIBLIOGRAPHY, LIBRARY SCIENCE AND MUSEOLOGY

Zimbabwe Library Association: POB 3133, Harare; tel. (4) 792641; fax (4) 703050; f. 1959; 254 mems; Chair. DRIDEN KUNAKA; Sec. ALBERT MASHEKA; publ. *Zimbabwe Librarian*.

EDUCATION

Zimbabwe National Association for Distance and Open Learning: POB 2713, Harare; fax (4) 737640; e-mail college@speciss.co.zw; internet www.saide.org.za/worldbank/countries/zimbabwe/zinadol.htm; f. 1997; Chair. NARAN KALA; Sec. EVISON MUTI.

HISTORY, GEOGRAPHY AND ARCHAEOLOGY

Geographical Association of Zimbabwe: c/o Dept of Geography and Environmental Science, University of Zimbabwe, Box MP167, Mount Pleasant, Harare; tel. (4) 303211; fax (4) 883264; e-mail cumming@arts.uz.ac.zw; f. 1967; 500 mems; Chair. T. ZINYANDU; Sec. A. CHIKANDA; publs *Geographical Journal of Zimbabwe* (annually), *Geographical Education Magazine* (2 a year).

Prehistory Society of Zimbabwe: POB 876, Harare; tel. (4) 300516; f. 1958; promotion of the study of early history, pre-history and archaeology in Africa, with particular reference to Zimbabwe; 100 mems; library of 1,000 vols; Chair. (vacant); publ. *Zimbabwean Prehistory* (every 2 years).

LANGUAGE AND LITERATURE

Alliance Française: 328 Herbert Chitepo Ave, POB 2515, Harare; tel. (4) 704795; fax (4) 704801; e-mail afharare@telco.co.zw; offers courses and exams in French language and culture and promotes cultural exchange with France; attached teaching centre in Bulawayo.

British Council: Corner House, Samora Michel Ave, POB 664, Harare; tel. (4) 775313; fax (4) 756661; e-mail general.enquiries@britishcouncil.org.zw; internet www.britishcouncil.org.zw; offers courses and exams in English language and British culture and promotes cultural exchange with the UK; attached office in Bulawayo; Regional Dir, Central Africa DAVID MARTIN; Dir Operations, Zimbabwe RAJIV BENDRE.

Zimbabwe Writers Union: Gloag High School, POB 61, Turk Mine; Pres. CONT MHLANGA; Sec.-Gen. PATHISA NYATHI.

MEDICINE

Pharmaceutical Society of Zimbabwe: POB 1476, Harare; tel. (4) 706967; fax (4) 706967; Pres. G. N. MAHLANGY; Sec. Dr F. CHINYANGANYA.

Zimbabwe Dental Association: 113 Sam Nujoma St, POB 2236, Harare; tel. (4) 791201; fax (4) 791259; e-mail musiyaw@netconnect.co.zw; f. 1939; affiliated to World Dental Federation; Dir Dr WEBSTER MUSIYA.

Zimbabwe Medical Association: POB 3671, Harare; tel. (4) 720731; Pres. B. G. MAUCHAZA; Sec. E. VUSHE.

NATURAL SCIENCES

General

Zimbabwe Scientific Association: POB CY124, The Causeway, Harare; fax (4) 335143; e-mail husseiny@ecoweb.co.zw; f. 1899; 380 mems; Pres. Dr L. MHLANGA; Sec. Dr J. HUSSEIN; publs *Transactions* (annually), *Zimbabwe Science News* (2 a year).

Biological Sciences

Birdlife Zimbabwe: POB RV100, Runiville, Harare; tel. (4) 481496; fax (4) 490208; e-mail birds@zol.co.zw; internet site.mweb.co.zw/birdlife; f. 1948; 650 mems; Dir CLARE DAVIES; publs *Honeyguide* (2 a year), *Babbler* (every 2 months).

Botanical Society of Zimbabwe: POB 461, Harare; tel. (4) 735163; f. 1934; Hon. Sec. J. R. JAMES.

Kirk Biological Society: Dept of Biological Sciences, University of Zimbabwe, POB MP167, Mount Pleasant, Harare; tel. (4) 303211; fax (4) 333407; e-mail jmugodo@yahoo.com; f. 1969; botany, zoology, ecology, microbiology; Chair. JAMES MUGODO.

Lowveld Natural History Branch, Wildlife and Environment Zimbabwe: POB 81, Chiredzi; f. 1968; promotion of conservation and natural history education; 186 mems; Chair. G. DABBS; Sec. S. DE ROBILLARD; publs *Newsletter* (monthly), *The Hartebeest* (annually).

Wildlife & Environment Zimbabwe: Mukuvisi Environment Centre, POB HG 996, Highlands, Harare; tel. (4) 747648; fax (4) 747174; e-mail zimwild@ecoweb.co.zw; internet www.zimwild.org; f. 1927; all aspects of wildlife conservation and environmental awareness; 2,500 mems; Pres. JERRY GOTORA; Programme Man. Dr WILLIE K. NDUKU; publ. *Zimbabwe Wildlife* (4 a year).

Physical Sciences

Geological Society of Zimbabwe: POB CY1719, Causeway, Harare; e-mail hjelsma@geology.uz.zw; internet www .mining.co.zw/GSZ.htm; f. 1981; 320 mems; Chair. M. L. VINYU; Sec. H. A. JELSMA.

Mennell Society: Dept of Geology, University of Zimbabwe, POB MP167, Mount Pleasant, Harare; f. 1964; to promote the understanding of earth sciences through lectures, films, field trips; 40 mems; Pres. H. MUNYANYIWA; Chair W. MOYCE; publ. *Detritus*.

TECHNOLOGY

Institution of Materials, Minerals and Mining (Zimbabwe Section): POB MP 791, Mount Pleasant, Harare; e-mail kirmir@zol.co.zw; f. 1931; Chair. J. L. NIXON; Hon. Sec. M. R. RICHARDSON.

Survey Institute of Zimbabwe: POB 3869, Harare; f. 1967; 80 mems; voluntary asscn of surveyors in the fields of land, engineering, topographical and mine surveying; Pres. S. Z. ZHOU; Hon. Sec. J. BIRKETT.

Zimbabwe Institution of Engineers: POB 660, Harare; tel. (4) 746821; fax (4) 746652; e-mail zie@zarnet.ac.zw; internet www.zie .org.zw; f. 1944; 2,568 mems; Pres. Eng. DANIEL MACKENZIE NCUBE; Deputy Pres. Eng. D. Z. MAREYA; publs *Proceedings* (2 a year), *Zimbabwe Engineer* (monthly).

Research Institutes

GENERAL

Research Council of Zimbabwe: POB CY 294, Causeway, Harare; tel. (4) 727562; fax (4) 726860; e-mail secretariat@zarnet.ac.zw; internet www.rcz.ac.zw; f. 1964, reconstituted 1984; advisory body to the Government on general scientific policy and official channel for exchange of national and international scientific and technical information; Chair. Dr F. P. GUDJANGA; Sec. S. MUZITE; publs *Directory of Organizations concerned with Scientific Research and Services in Zimbabwe* (every 2 years), *Zimbabwe Research Index* (annually), *Symposium Proceedings* (every 2 years).

AGRICULTURE, FISHERIES AND VETERINARY SCIENCE

Agricultural Research Council of Zimbabwe: POB CY 594, Causeway, Harare; internet www.arc.org.zw; f. 1970; advises on agricultural research policy and programmes in Zimbabwe; administers regional research institutes and stations through the Department of Research and Specialist Services (Dir Dr N. R. GATA); Chair. Prof. M. RUKUNI; publs *Annual Report*, *Zimbabwe Agricultural Journal* (6 a year), *Zimbabwe Journal of Agricultural Research* (2 a year), *Kirkia – Journal of Botany of Zimbabwe* (annually).

Research institutes and stations:

Agronomy Research Institute: POB CY 550, Causeway, Harare; tel. (4) 704531; fax (4) 728317; e-mail dhikwa@africaonline.co .zw; f. 1975; research into crop agronomy, crop ecology and crop production; Head D. HIKWA; publ. *Annual Report*.

Biometrics Bureau: POB 594, Causeway, Harare; tel. (4) 704531; f. 1967; undertakes applied biometrical research, provides professional advice on experimental design, statistical problems and computer services for research workers; Head F. ZINYANDU (acting).

Chemistry and Soil Research Institute: POB CY 550, Causeway, Harare; tel. (4) 704531; fax (4) 728317; f. 1905; research and advisory work on soils and agricultural chemistry; registration and regulation of fertilizers and foodstuffs; crop nutrition, chemistry, pedology, soil physics and soil productivity research sections; Head C. F. MUSHAMBI.

Coffee Research Station: POB 61, Chipinge; tel. (27) 2400; fax (27) 2951; f. 1964; research into all aspects of coffee management, growth, pest and disease control; tea research projects; Officer-in-Charge D. KUTYWAYO; publ. *Annual Report*.

Cotton Research Institute: Private Bag 765, Kadoma; tel. (68) 23994; fax (68) 23996; e-mail zimcott@africaonline.co.zw; f. 1925; all aspects of cotton agronomy, breeding, pest and disease research; Head L. T. GONO (acting); publ. *Annual Report*.

Crop Breeding Institute: POB CY 550, Causeway, Harare; tel. (4) 704531; fax (4) 728317; f. 1948; responsible for breeding programmes on maize, soya beans, groundnuts, wheat, barley, potatoes, sunflowers, cowpen, bambara, groundnut and foodbean; Head Dr A. MASHIRIGWANI; publ. *Annual Report*.

Farming Systems Research Unit: POB 550, Causeway, Harare; f. 1983; responsible for adapting, developing and testing on farms improved crop and livestock production technologies and systems, and a model for farm systems research acceptable to the Department of Research and Specialist Services and suitable for wide-scale application in Zimbabwe; Team Leader B. MOMBESHORA.

Grasslands Research Station: Private Bag 3701, Marondera; tel. (79) 23526; fax (79) 23198; f. 1930; research on pasture, animal and crop production for the high-rainfall sandveld area; selection and testing of Rhizobium strains and commercial production of legume inoculants; Head G. MANYAN.

Henderson Research Station: Private Bag 2004, Mazowe; tel. (75) 2281; fax (75) 2284; f. 1948; pasture work on the introduction and screening of grasses and legumes for suitability as fertilized pastures; research in ruminant nutrition; herbicide and weed control research; Head Mr SCHAKEREDZA (acting); publ. *Annual Report*.

Horticultural Research Centre: Grasslands Research Station, POB 810, Marondera; tel. (79) 24122; fax (79) 23198; f. 1975; responsible for all aspects of horticultural research; Officer-in-Charge N. NENGUWO.

Lowveld Research Station: POB 97, Chiredzi; tel. (31) 2397; f. 1967; research in irrigation agronomy in South-Eastern Lowveld; sub-tropical horticulture and vegetable crops; Head Dr P. NYAMUDEZA.

Matopos Research Station: Private Bag K5137, Bulawayo; tel. (83) 8212; fax (83) 8289; f. 1903; research in veld management, ecology of regional soil types, bush encroachment, cattle breeding, and beef production; Head Dr S. MAYO.

Makoholi Experiment Station: Private Bag 9182, Masvingo; f. 1962; research into problems of animal and crop production for sandveld and medium rainfall districts of Zimbabwe; crop agronomy, cattle production (indigenous breeds) and natural grazing management; Head I. CHIGAMBA.

Nyanga Experimental Station: POB 2061, Nyanga; fax (31) 2739; f. 1911; Pome fruit research; Officer-in-Charge N. NAUBE.

Plant Protection Research Institute: POB CY 550, Causeway, Harare; tel. (4) 704531; fax (4) 728317; e-mail plantpro@ ecoweb.co.zw; f. 1964; research and advisory work on plant pests and diseases; biological control, entomology, pathology and nematology sections; Head Dr S. Z. SITHOLE; publ. *Annual Report*.

Agricultural Research Trust: POB MP 81, Mount Pleasant, Harare; tel. (4) 860413; fax (4) 860416; e-mail artfarm@mweb.co.zw; internet www.artfarm.co.zw; f. 1980; research into cereals, grains, oilseed and horticultural crops and the provision of research field sites for crop breeders, agronomists and the crop chemical industry; Dir NICK BROOKE; publs *Summer Report* (annually), *Winter Report* (annually).

Department of Veterinary Services; Tsetse Control Branch: POB CY52, Causeway, Harare; tel. (4) 707381; fax (4) 722684; e-mail wshereni@rhcp.org.zw; under the Ministry of Lands and Agriculture; f. 1909; for the control of the tsetse fly population and the investigation of methods of control; laboratory at Harare and research station in the Zambezi Valley; Chief Research Officer W. SHERENI.

Attached laboratory:

Central Veterinary Laboratory: POB CY551, Causeway, Harare; tel. (4) 705885; fax (4) 707952; e-mail vetlabs@africaonline .co.zw; f. 1906; diagnostic centre and research institute for animal diseases; 35 mems; library of 1,500 vols; Head of Veterinary Diagnostics and Research Branch Dr P. V. HAKAYA.

Forestry Commission: POB HG 139, Highlands, Harare; tel. (4) 498439; fax (4) 497070; f. 1954; state forest authority, responsible for formulating forest policy in Zimbabwe; engaged in large-scale plantation operations; research and advisory services, forestry extension and wildlife utilization..

Attached centre:

Forest Research Centre: POB HG 595, Highlands, Harare; tel. (4) 498816; fax (4) 497070; conducts research into many aspects of forestry, principally high-yielding plantations, with special emphasis on tree genetics and the production of progressively improved pine and eucalypt seed, wood quality, general plantation management and fertilizer research; screening of multi-purpose tree species for use in fuelwood plantations and social forestry.; Deputy Gen. Man. Dr DANAZU MAHUWIRA; publ. *Format* (4 a year).

Tobacco Research Board: POB 1909, Harare; tel. (4) 575289; fax (4) 575288; e-mail tobres@kutsaga.co.zw; f. 1950; conducts research into all types of tobacco, agronomy, breeding, engineering and pest control; operates three research stations; board mems, appointed by the Minister of Agriculture, represent growers, buyers, and Ministry of Agriculture; library of 12,000 vols, 250 periodicals; Chair. Dr R. M. MUPAWOSE; Dir A. J. MASUKA; publ. *Annual Report and Accounts*.

ECONOMICS, LAW AND POLITICS

Central Statistical Office: POB CY342, Causeway, Harare; tel. (4) 703971; fax (4) 728529; f. 1927; co-ordinated statistical service for the Government; staff of 400; Dir L. MACHIROVI.

Institute of Development Studies: University of Zimbabwe, POB MP 167, Harare;

tel. (4) 333341; fax (4) 333345; f. 1982 to undertake policy-oriented research, consultancy and training; three research departments: agrarian and labour studies, economics and technology studies and international relations and social development studies; poverty reduction forum; library of 17,500 vols, 24,000 documents; Dir Dr DONALD P. CHIMANIKIRE.

MEDICINE

Public Health Laboratory: Box CY 430, Causeway, Harare; tel. and fax (4) 720746; e-mail maxhove@yahoo.com; f. 1909; Dir Dr M. G. M. HOVE; Pathologist Dr D. MADZIWA; Chief Medical Technologists Dr O. MAYO, L. ZAWAIRA.

NATURAL SCIENCES

Physical Sciences

Geological Survey of Zimbabwe: POB CY 210, Causeway, Harare; tel. (4) 726342; fax (4) 739601; e-mail zimgeosv@africaonline.co .zw; internet www.geosurvey.co.zw; f. 1910; geological mapping and survey of mineral resources; library of 1,400 vols, 800 symposia, 11,900 periodicals, 2,600 technical files; museum displaying Zimbabwean geology and economic minerals; Dir W. MAGALELA; publs Annals, Bulletins, Mineral Resources Series (irregular), short reports and maps.

Meteorological Service: POB BE 150, Belvedere, Harare; tel. (4) 778173; fax (4) 778161; e-mail tor@weather.utande.co.zw; internet weather.utande.co.zw; f. 1897; part of the Ministry of Transport and Communications; Dir RUNGANO P. KARIMANZIRA; publs Monthly Meteorological Summaries, Rainfall Handbook Supplements, Climate Handbook Supplements, Agromet Bulletin (October–March), daily weather reports and forecasts, weekly rainfall maps during rainy season November–March.

Affiliated institute:

Goetz Observatory: POB AC 65, Ascot, Bulawayo; tel. (9) 66197; fax (9) 77811; e-mail goetz@harare.iafrica.com; also seismology; publs Seismological Bulletin, Agricultural Meteorological Bulletin (monthly).

TECHNOLOGY

Department of Metallurgy: Ministry of Mines, POB 1375, Causeway, Harare; tel. (4) 726629; fax (4) 793065; f. 1962; 88 staff; library of 280 vols; conducts investigations on methods of economic extraction from precious, base-metal and non-metallic ores and industrial minerals evaluation, also on physical metallurgy, e.g. non-destructive testing, impact testing, etc.; Dir T. I. NYATSANGA; publ. Testwork Reports.

Standards Association of Zimbabwe: POB 2259, Harare; tel. (4) 885511; fax (4) 882020; e-mail info@saz.org.zw; internet www.saz.org.zw; f. 1957; laboratory facilities for testing raw materials and manufactured goods and operates certification mark schemes; prepares and publishes Zimbabwean national standards; provides an information service on standards and a WTO/Technical Barriers to Trade enquiry point on standards and conformity assessment; provides training on standards; Chair. E. JINDA; Dir-Gen. M. P. MUTASA; publs Annual Report, Fulcrum (official bulletin), Catalogue of Zimbabwe Standards.

Libraries and Archives

Bulawayo

Bulawayo Public Library: 100 Fort St, Bulawayo; tel. (9) 60965; fax (9) 60966; e-mail bpl@graffiti.net; internet www .angelfire.com/ky/bpl; f. 1896; reference, lending, junior library; mobile library; postal service to rural readers; braille collection; African and Zimbabwe collections; Zimbabwe map collection; legal deposit library for Zimbabwe; video and audio cassette collns; 16,000 mems; 100,000 vols; Librarian and Sec. ROBIN WILLIAM DOUST; publ. Triennial Report.

National Library and Documentation Service National Free Library of Zimbabwe: POB 1773, Bulawayo; tel. (9) 62359; fax (9) 77662; f. 1943 as national lending library for educational, scientific and technical books; national centre for inter-library loans; maintains National Union Catalogue; 100,000 vols; Librarian H. R. NCUBE.

Harare

Harare City Library: POB 1087, Harare; tel. (4) 751834; e-mail hararecitylibrary@ yahoo.com; f. 1902; 100,000 vols; Librarian and Sec. TRYMORE SIMANGO.

Library of Parliament: POB CY 298, Causeway, Harare; tel. (4) 700181 ext. 2131; fax (4) 795548; f. 1923; 115,000 vols; wide range of parliamentary and government documents obtained from Zimbabwe Parliament and from several Commonwealth countries; general collection specializing in political science, history, political biography, economics, sociology, public administration and management, education, foreign relations; separate law collection, separate archival and reference collection and Zimbabweana; Librarian N. MASAWI.

National Archives of Zimbabwe: Private Bag 7729, Causeway, Harare; tel. (4) 792741; fax (4) 792398; e-mail archives@zim.gov.zw; f. 1935 as the Government Archives of Southern Rhodesia; Dir. I. MURAMBIWA; incorp. archives of Northern Rhodesia and Nyasaland and designated the Central African Archives 1947; became National Archives of Rhodesia and Nyasaland 1958–63; reverted January 1964 to Rhodesian Government and responsibility for Northern Rhodesia and Nyasaland archives ceased; also serves Zimbabwean municipalities and some parastatal bodies and holds archives of Federation of Rhodesia and Nyasaland, comprises sections of Records Management, Research (Public Archives, Historical Manuscripts), Library (nat. historical reference colln, incl. photographic and map collns; legal deposit, depository for UNESCO publications) and Technical (Reprographic Unit, Conservation Unit, Oral History, Automation, Audio-Visual Archives Unit); exhibition gallery; four provincial records centres; Dir. I. MURAMBIWA; publs Oppenheimer Series, Bibliographical Series, Zimbabwe National Bibliography (annually), Guide to the Public Archives of Rhodesia, Vol. 1, 1890–1923, Guide to the Historical Manuscripts in the National Archives, Report of the Director (annually), Current Periodicals, Directory of Libraries.

University of Zimbabwe Library: POB MP45, Mount Pleasant, Harare; tel. (4) 303211; fax (4) 335383; e-mail infocentre@ uzlib.uz.ac.zw; internet www.uz.ac.zw/ library; f. 1956; 500,000 vols; 5,250 periodicals; Medical library; Mpilo Hospital library; Law library; Education library; Institute of Development Studies Library; Lake Kariba Research Station library; Map library; Veterinary library; Africana (Zimbabweana) col-

lection; collection of African languages; U.Z. Theses Collection; Librarian Dr B. MBAMBO; publ. Newsletter (monthly).

Zimbabwe National Library and Documentation Service: POB 758, Harare; tel. (4) 774943; f. 1972; co-ordinates all libraries in govt depts, colleges of education, agriculture and technology, public libraries; combined stock (100 libraries): 1,000,000 vols; Dir S. R. DUBE; publs Directory of Zimbabwean Libraries, Government Library Service Newsletter.

Mutare

City of Mutare Public Libraries: POB 48, Mutare; tel. (20) 63412; fax (20) 67785; e-mail dmandowo@mutare.mweb.co.zw; f. 1902; incorporates Sakubva Public Library (f. 1972, 27,000 vols), Dangamvura Public Library (f. 1988, 18,000 vols), Turner Memorial Library (f. 1902, 40,000 vols), Chikanga Public Library (f. 2004, 5,000 vols); Head of Library Services D. MANDOWO.

Museums and Art Galleries

Bulawayo

Natural History Museum of Zimbabwe: Leopold Takawira Ave and Park Rd, POB 240, Bulawayo; tel. (9) 230046; fax (9) 234019; e-mail natmuse@acacia.samara.co .zw; f. 1901; geological, palaeontological, entomological and zoological; study collections and exhibits covering Ethiopian region, with special reference to southern Africa; historical, ethnographical and prehistorical exhibits appertaining to Zimbabwe and adjacent regions; Dir A. KUMIRAI; Curator of Mammals F. P. D. COTTERILL; Curator of Entomology R. SITHOLE; Curator of Arachnology M. FITZPATRICK; Curator of Ornithology A. MSIMANGA; Curator of Herpetology R. L. CHIDAVAENZI; Curator of Palaeontology D. MUNYIKWA; Curator of Ichthyology P. MAKONI; publs Arnoldia (Zimbabwe), Syntarsus.

Gweru

Military Museum of Zimbabwe: Lobengula Ave, POB 1300, Gweru; tel. (54) 22816; fax (54) 20321; e-mail museum@harare .iafrica.com; f. 1972; history of Zimbabwe Midlands and military history of Zimbabwe; Dir T. TSOMONDO.

Harare

National Gallery of Zimbabwe: 20 Julius Nyerere Way, POB CY 848, Causeway, Harare; tel. (4) 704666; fax (4) 704668; e-mail ngallery@harare.iafrica.com; f. 1957; national collection of sculpture, paintings, drawings, prints, ceramics and artefacts by Zimbabwean and other Southern African artists; also includes European works of art dating from 16th century, and traditional and contemporary African art; regular exhibition programme; education programme; BAT studio for emerging young artists; library of 6,500 vols; Dir Prof. GEORGE P. KAHARI; publ. Annual Report.

National Herbarium and Botanic Garden: POB A889, Avondale, Harare; tel. (4) 744170; fax (4) 708938; internet www .nationalherbarium.co.zw; f. 1909; attached to Department of Agricultural Research and Extension (AREX); maintains a comprehensive collection of 500,000 specimens, provides an identification service for workers in agriculture and related fields and contributes to knowledge of the flora of South-Central Africa; taxonomic and ecological research, and research on medicinal and poisonous plants; library of 544 vols; Head NOZIPO NOBANDA; publ. *Kirkia* (annually).

Zimbabwe Museum of Human Sciences: Civic Centre, POB CY33, Causeway, Harare; tel. (4) 751797; fax (4) 774207; e-mail nmmz@ pci.co.zw; internet www.zimheritage.co.zw/ site/nr_museum.htm; f. 1902; zoological, ethnographical, archaeological and historical exhibits, study collections of archaeological, ethnographical material, rock art appertaining to Zimbabwe and adjacent areas; Dir T. MASONA; publs *Zimbabwea, Cookeia.*

Masvingo

Great Zimbabwe National Monument: PB 1060, Masvingo; tel. (39) 62080; fax (39) 63310; e-mail greatzim@mweb.co.zw; internet www.zimheritage.co.zw; ruins of medieval dry stone buildings representing the Zimbabwe culture; history and development of Great Zimbabwe shown in site museum; world heritage site; Dir E. MATENGA.

Mutare

Mutare Museum: Aerodrome Rd, POB 920, Mutare; tel. (20) 63672; fax (20) 61100; e-mail mutarmus@ecoweb.co.zw; internet www .zimheritage.co.zw; f. 1959; archaeological, zoological and historical exhibits, appertaining to the Eastern Districts in particular; national collection of road transport and firearms; aviary with 200 birds of 24 species; Dir TRAUDE ALLISON ROGERS.

Universities

BINDURA UNIVERSITY OF SCIENCE EDUCATION

Private Bag 1020, Bindura, Mashonaland Central

Telephone: (71) 7531
Fax: (71) 7534
E-mail: info@mailhost.buse.ac.zw
Internet: www.buse.ac.zw

Founded 1996 as part of University of Zimbabwe; university status 2000
State Control
Language of instruction: English
Rector: SABA ABEL TSWANA
Registrar: ELIOT P. DZARAMBA
Librarian: A. MHALANGA

Library of 12,073 vols, 22 periodicals
Number of teachers: 79
Number of students: 1,016

DEANS

Faculty of Agriculture and Environmental Science: J. F. MUPANGWA
Faculty of Science Education: A. ZENGAYA

HEADS OF DEPARTMENTS

Agriculture: J. F. MUPANGWA
Biological Sciences: P. P. CHIBATAMOTO
Chemistry: T. NGARIVHUME
Computer Science: S. VIRIRI
Education: A. ZENGEYA
Environmental Sciences: K. A. T. KATSVANGA
Geography: E. CHIMBAMBO
Mathematics: R. BAPPOO
Physics: C. KUFAZVINEI

MIDLANDS STATE UNIVERSITY

Private Bag 9055, Gweru
Telephone: (54) 60409
Fax: (54) 60311
E-mail: registrar@msu.ac.zw
Internet: www.msu.ac.zw
Founded 1999 by Act of Parliament
State Control

Academic year: March to December
Vice-Chancellor: Prof. NGWABI BHEBE
Pro-Vice-Chancellor: Prof. RUNGANO J. ZVOBGO
Registrar: G. T. GUNIRA
Library of 50,850 vols
Number of teachers: 229
Number of students: 8,979
Publications: *The Dyke* (social sciences, quarterly), *Southern African Journal of Science and Agriculture and Technology* (quarterly)

DEANS

Faculty of Arts: Prof. CAROLINE HARFORD
Faculty of Commerce: KATAZO C. MBETU
Faculty of Education: Dr O. P. NDAWI
Faculty of Natural Resources Management and Agriculture: FRANCIS MUGABE
Faculty of Science: A. CHAWANDA
Faculty of Social Sciences: C. N. GWATIDZO

NATIONAL UNIVERSITY OF SCIENCE AND TECHNOLOGY

POB AC 939, Ascot, Bulawayo
Telephone: (9) 282842
Fax: (9) 289057
E-mail: mtkariwo@nust.ac.zw
Internet: www.nust.ac.zw
Founded 1990
State control
Language of instruction: English
Academic year: August to May
Chancellor: Pres. R. G. MUGABE
Vice-Chancellor (vacant)
Pro Vice-Chancellor: Prof. L. R. NDLOVU
Registrar: M. T. KARIWO
Librarian: K. MATSIKA

Number of teachers: 150 full-time
Number of students: 2,800
Publication: *University Year Book*

DEANS

Faculty of Applied Sciences: Dr. M. M. BHALA
Faculty of Architecture and Quantity Surveying: Prof. S. IK-UMENNE
Faculty of Commerce: R. TADU
Faculty of Communication and Information Sciencw: Prof. S. M. MADE
Faculty of Industrial Technology: Dr P. K. KUIPA

Departments of Accounting, Applied Biology, Applied Chemistry, Applied Mathematics, Applied Physics, Architecture, Banking, Business Management, Chemical Engineering, Computer Science, Civil and Water Engineering, Electronic Engineering, Finance, Industrial and Manufacturing Engineering, Insurance and Actuarial Science, Textile Technology, Business School, Quantity Surveying, Environmental Science and Health, Journalism and Media Studies, Technical Teacher Education, Sports Science and Coaching, and Library, Information Science and Archives; Centre for Continuing Education, Forestry Resources and Wildlife Management; Medical School

PROFESSORS

Faculty of Applied Sciences:
  GHOLAP, A. V.
  MUNDY, P.J.
  READ, J. S.
Faculty of Architecture and Quantity Surveying:
  HYLAND, A. D. C.
Faculty of Communication and Information Science:
  MADE, S. M.

UNIVERSITY OF ZIMBABWE

POB MP167, Mount Pleasant, Harare
Telephone: (4) 303211
Fax: (4) 333407
Internet: www.uz.ac.zw
Founded 1955 as University College of Rhodesia; became University of Rhodesia in 1970, and University of Zimbabwe in 1980.
Language of instruction: English
Academic year: August to June
Chancellor: HE The President of the Republic of Zimbabwe
Vice-Chancellor: Prof. LEVI NYAGURA
Registrar: SERGEANT CHEVO
Librarian: B. MBAMBO

Number of teachers: 834
Number of students: 8,784
Publications: *Central African Journal of Medicine* (monthly), *Journal of Applied Science in Southern Africa* (2 a year), *UZ-News, Zambezia* (2 a year)

DEANS

Faculty of Agriculture: Dr C. MUTISI
Faculty of Arts: (vacant)
Faculty of Commerce: J. T. CHIKONDO
Faculty of Education: Dr C. DYANDA
Faculty of Engineering: D. J. SIMBI
Faculty of Law: E. MAGADE (acting)
Faculty of Medicine: Dr W. B. MUJAJI
Faculty of Science: Dr T. G. ZENGENI
Faculty of Social Studies: (vacant)
Faculty of Veterinary Science: Dr S. MUKAR-ATIRWA

CHAIRMEN OF DEPARTMENTS

Agriculture (tel. and fax (4) 333880; e-mail mutisi@agric.uz.ac.zw):
  Agricultural Economics and Extension: Dr L. RUGUBE
  Animal Science: Dr I. D. T. MPOFU
  Crop Science: Dr A. B. MASHINGAIDZE
  Soil Science and Agricultural Engineering: Dr M. WUTA

Arts (tel. (4) 333529; fax (4) 308296; e-mail dean@arts.uz.az.zw):
  African Languages and Literature: S. HADEBE
  Economic History: Dr J. P. MTISI
  English: Dr M. MLAMBO
  Geography: Dr L. ZANAMWE
  History: Dr K. MANUNGO
  Linguistics: W. B. GWETE
  Modern Languages: T. T. GWANZURA
  Religious Studies, Classics and Philosophy: J. KURASHA (acting)
  Theatre Arts: O. SEDA

Commerce (tel. (4) 334054; fax (4) 333674; e-mail dean@commerce.uz.ac.zw):
  Accountancy: J. MUSAKANYA
  Business Studies: J. MUSHIPE (acting)

Education (tel. and fax (4) 303291; e-mail dean@education.uz.ac.zw):
  Adult Education: F. N. B. MASHAYAMOMBE
  Centre for Educational Technology: Dr J. P. RWAMBIWA
  Curriculum and Arts Education: P. MAVHUNGA
  Educational Administration: R. D. MAKONI
  Educational Foundations: H. M. RINASHE
  Science and Mathematics Education: T. CHINAKA
  Teacher Education: Dr O. SHUMBA
  Technical Education: S. GWERU

Engineering (fax (4) 303280; e-mail dsimbi@ eng.uz.ac.zw):
  Civil Engineering: Dr A. SALAHUDDIN
  Electrical Engineering: Dr E. T. KAPUYA
  Mechanical Engineering: Dr W. NYEMBA
  Metallurgy: E. MAGOMBEDZE

Mining Engineering: Dr F. KARONGA (acting)

Surveying: C. MATYUKIRA

Law (tel. and fax (4) 304008; e-mail emagade04@yahoo.co.uk):

Private Law: S. KANYANGARARA
Procedural Law: T. MATYSKAZ (acting)
Public Law: Dr L. MADHUKU

Medicine (POB A178, Avondale, Harare; tel. (4) 708127; fax (4) 705155; e-mail wmujaji@medsch.uz.ac.zw):

Anaesthetics: Dr S. SHUMBAIRERWA
Anatomy: Prof. L. LEVY
Chemical Pathology: Prof. Z. A. R. GOMO
Clinical Pharmacology: Prof. C. F. B. NHACHI
Community Medicine: Prof. G. WOELK
Haematology: A. MANDISODZA
Histopathology: Dr R. MAKUNIKE
Immunology: Dr L. ZIJENAH
Institute of Continuing Health Education: C. A. SAMKANGE
Medical Laboratory Technology: Prof. L. GWANZURA
Medical Microbiology: Prof. S. R. MOYO
Medicine: Prof. J. G. HAKIM
Nursing Science: Dr K. G. MAPANGA (acting)
Obstetrics and Gynaecology: Dr M. CHIRENJE
Paediatrics and Child Health: Dr I. E. PAZVAKAVAMBWA
Pharmacy: Dr C. C. MAPONGA
Physiology: J. CHIFAMBA
Psychiatry: Dr S. NHIWATIWA
Rehabilitation: O. MADZIVIRE
Surgery and Radiology: A. C. HARID

Science (fax (4) 307130; e-mail zengeni@science.uz.ac.zw):

Biochemistry: Dr M. MUCHUWETI
Biological Science: Dr A. MABVENI
Chemistry: Dr L. R. M. NHAMO
Computing Science: D. MUSIYANDAKA (acting)
Geology: N. MATURA
IMR: S. KAHWAI
Mathematics: Prof. A. R. G. STEWART
Physics: Dr M. MATHUTHU
Statistics: J. MAFODYA
Food, Nutrition and Family Science: Dr T. H. GADAGA

Social Studies (fax (4) 333674; e-mail dean@social.uz.ac.zw):

Centre for Applied Social Science: Dr P. MUGABE
Centre for Population Studies: J. KEMBO
Economics: Dr I. MATSHE
Political and Administrative Studies: E. MASUNUNGURE
Psychology: T. MUROMO
Rural and Urban Planning: G. MANIKAI

Sociology: Dr F. MAPHOSA

Veterinary Science (tel. (4) 333683; fax (4) 333683; e-mail vetscience@esanef.zw):

Clinical Veterinary Studies: Dr M. T. TIVAPASI
Paraclinical Veterinary Studies: Dr R. L. MADEKUROZVA
Preclinical Veterinary Studies: Dr S. RUZIWA

ATTACHED INSTITUTES

Computer Centre: Dir Dr G. T. HAPANYENGWI.

Development Technology Centre: Dir T. RUKUNI.

Human Resources Research Centre: Dir (vacant) Prof. F. ZINDI.

Institute of Developmental Studies: Dir Dr P. CHIMANIKIRE (acting).

Institute of Water and Sanitation: Dir Dr P. TAYLOR.

University Lake Kariba Research Station: Dir J. CHIMBARI.

University Teaching and Learning Centre: Dir Dr V. NYAWARANDA.

ZIMBABWE OPEN UNIVERSITY

POB MP 1119, Mt Pleasant, Harare

Telephone: (4) 333452
Fax: (4) 303151
E-mail: kdzvimbo@icon.co.zw

Founded 1999
State control
Language of instruction: English
Chancellor: The President of the Republic of Zimbabwe
Vice-Chancellor: Prof. K. P. DZVIMBO
Registrar: R. E. MHASVI
Librarian: L. MAENZANISE
Library of 16,214 books, 16 periodicals
Number of teachers: 78 full-time
Number of students: 13,877 (13,443 undergraduate, 434 postgraduate)

DEANS

Faculty of Education and the Humanities: Prof. M. IZUAGIE
Faculty of Science and the Social Sciences: Dr R. CHIMEDZA
Faculty of Commerce and Law: C. J. MUROMBEDZI

Colleges

Bulawayo Polytechnic: Park Rd, 12th Ave, POB 1392, Bulawayo; tel. (9) 63181; f. 1927; tertiary education in technical, commercial, scientific, design and catering fields; library: 37,170 vols; 210 full-time, 150 part-time teachers; 5,448 students; Principal A. MWADIWA.

Chibero College of Agriculture: Private Bag 901, Norton; tel. (62) 2238; f. 1960; 2-year national diploma in agriculture; library: 6,000 vols; 15 teachers; 120 students; Principal M. E. NYAMANGARA; publ. *Agricultural Education.*

Esigodini Agricultural Institute: Private Bag 5808, Esigodini; tel. (88) 297; fax (88) 296; f. 1921; 18 teachers; 120 students; Principal DAVID THEMBA MGUNI.

Gwebi College of Agriculture: Private Bag 376B, Harare; tel. (4) 304515; fax (4) 333850; e-mail gwebiagric@gta.gov.zw; f. 1950; 3-year diploma in agriculture, 15-month higher national diploma in horticulture; library: 2,300 vols; 15 teachers; 120 students; Principal W. MATIZHA.

Harare Polytechnic: POB CY 407, Causeway, Harare; tel. (4) 752311; fax (4) 720955; f. 1927; full-time and sandwich courses for technicians and craftsmen; courses in printing and adult education; full-time and part-time courses in library and information science, computer studies, civil construction, mechanical engineering, mass communication, business studies, science and technology, automotive engineering, secretarial studies; library: 68,000 vols; 500 teachers (incl. part-time); 9,000 students; Principal S. RAZA.

Kushinga-Phikelela National Farmer Training Centre: Private Bag 3705, Marondera; tel. (79) 24329; fax (79) 23916; e-mail kushinga@africaonline.co.zw; f. 1982; 3-year certificate courses in commercial farming; short courses in animal production, crop production, farm machinery and farm and agri-business; library: 3,100 vols; 13 teachers; 120 students; Principal B. NLEYA.

Mlezu Institute of Agriculture: POB 8062, Kwekwe; f. 1982; 2-year course; Principal J. K. D. MARIPFONDE (acting).

School of Social Work: University of Zimbabwe, Private Bag 66022, Kopje, Harare; tel. (4) 752965; fax (4) 751903; e-mail sswprinc@samara.co.zw; f. 1964; first degrees, certificate, Master's degree and diploma courses; library: 19,870 vols; 13 teachers; 250 students; Dir Prof. E. KASEKE.

Zimbabwe College of Music: Box 66352, Kopje, Harare; tel. and fax (4) 749077; e-mail zcmlib@zol.co.zw; f. 1948; library: 3,000 vols, 35 teachers; 500 students; Chair. BEN ZULU; Dir CHRISTOPHER TIMBE; Registrar FRIDAY MBIRIMI; Librarian PRISCILLA CHIDOHWE.

INDEX OF INSTITUTIONS

Academie van Beeldende Kunsten Rotterdam, 1498

Academie van Bouwkunst, Amsterdam, 1498

Academie van Bouwkunst, Arnhem, 1498

Academie van Bouwkunst, Maastricht, 1498

Academie van Bouwkunst Rotterdam, 1498

Académie Vétérinaire de France, 705

Academie voor Architectuur en Stedebouw, Tilburg, 1498

Academie voor Beeldende Kunst en Vormgeving, HVG, Groningen, 1498

Academy of Agricultural Science, Pyongyang, 1318

Academy of Agricultural Sciences, Ulan Bator, 1449

Academy of Anthropology, Ulan Bator, 1449

Academy of Architecture, Mumbai, 1040

Academy of Art, Architecture and Design, 626

Academy of Art University, San Francisco, 2342

Academy of Arts, Giza, 666

Academy of Arts of Uzbekistan, 2751

Academy of Astrology, Ulan Bator, 1449

Academy of Athens Library, 912

Academy of Cinematic Art, Ulan Bator, 1449

Academy of Family Physicians of Malaysia, 1393

Academy of Finance, Hanoi, 2781

Academy of Fine Arts Vienna, 170

Academy of Fisheries, Pyongyang, 1318

Academy of Forestry, Pyongyang, 1318

Academy of Health Management, Ulan Bator, 1449

Academy of Information Sciences, Ulan Bator, 1449

Academy of Korean Studies, Pundang, 1322

Academy of Learned Societies for the Social Sciences, London, 2125

Academy of Legal Sciences of Ukraine, 2098

Academy of Light Industry Science, Pyongyang, 1318

Academy of Management, Ulan Bator, 1453

Academy of Management under the President of the Kyrgyz Republic, 1357

Academy of Medical Sciences, London, 2135

Academy of Medical Sciences of Ukraine, 2099

Academy of Medical Sciences, Pyongyang, 1318

Academy of Medical Sciences, Ulan Bator, 1449

Academy of Medicine, Singapore, 1836

Academy of Medicine, Toronto, 325

Academy of Music, Curaçao, 1499

Academy of Natural Sciences of Philadelphia, 2294

Academy of Natural Sciences, Ulan Bator, 1449

Academy of Nomadic Culture and Civilization, Ulan Bator, 1449

Academy of Pedagogical Sciences of Ukraine, 2098

Academy of Political Science, New York, 2287

Academy of Public Administration of the President of the Republic of Belarus, 213

Academy of Railway Sciences, Pyongyang, 1318

Academy of Sanskrit Research, Melkote, 975

Academy of Sciences for the Developing World, 66

Academy of Sciences Library, Pyongyang, 1320

Academy of Sciences of Afghanistan, 73

Academy of Sciences of Albania, Tiranë, 75

Academy of Sciences of Moldova, 1444

Academy of Sciences of Turkmenistan, 2091

Academy of Sciences, Pyongyang, 1318

Academy of Scientific Research and Technology, Cairo, 658

Academy of Social Sciences Library, Pyongyang, 1320

Academy of Social Sciences, Moscow, 1793

Academy of Social Sciences, Pyongyang, 1318

Academy of State and Law, Ulan Bator, 1449

Academy of State and Social Construction, Tashkent, 2749

Academy of the Arabic Language, Cairo, 657

Academy of the Hebrew Language, Jerusalem, 1093

Academy of the Ministry of Internal Affairs, 213

Academy of the Social Sciences in Australia, 117

Academy of Zoology, Agra, 971

Acadia University, Wolfville, 335

Accademia Albertina di Belle Arti, Turin, 1167

Accademia Archeologica Italiana, Rome, 1122

Accademia Carrara di Belle Arti–Museo, Bergamo, 1138

Accademia dei Georgofili, Florence, 1120

Accademia della Crusca, Florence, 1122

Accademia delle Scienze dell'Istituto di Bologna, 1119

Accademia delle Scienze di Ferrara, 1119

Accademia delle Scienze di Torino, 1119

Accademia delle Scienzi Mediche di Palermo, 1123

Accademia di Agricoltura di Torino, 1120

Accademia di Belle Arti di Bologna, 1167

Accademia di Belle Arti di Firenze, 1167

Accademia di Belle Arti di Lecce, 1167

Accademia di Belle Arti di Milano, Milan, 1167

Accademia di Belle Arti di Napoli, 1167

Accademia di Belle Arti di Palermo, 1167

Accademia di Belle Arti di Perugia, Perugia, 1167

Accademia di Belle Arti di Ravenna, 1167

Accademia di Belle Arti di Roma, 1167

Accademia di Belle Arti di Venezia, 1167

Accademia di Belle Arti e Liceo Artistico, Carrara, 1167

Accademia di Danimarca, Rome, 1129

Accademia di Francia, Rome, 1121

Accademia di Medicina di Torino, 1123

Accademia Etrusca, 1119

Accademia Filarmonica Romana, 1167

Accademia Gioenia di Catania, 1120

Accademia Italiana di Economia Aziendale, 1121

Accademia Italiana di Scienze Forestali, 1120

Accademia Ligure di Scienze e Lettere, 1120

Accademia Medica di Roma, 1123

Accademia Musicale Chigiana, 1167

Accademia Nazionale dei Lincei, Rome, 1120

Accademia Nazionale delle Scienze, detta dei XL, Rome, 1124

Accademia Nazionale di Agricoltura, Bologna, 1120

Accademia Nazionale di Arte Drammatica 'Silvio d'Amico', Rome, 1167

Accademia Nazionale di Danza, Rome, 1167

Accademia Nazionale di San Luca, 1120

Accademia Nazionale di Santa Cecilia, Rome, 1120

Accademia Nazionale Virgiliana di Scienze, Lettere e Arti, 1120

Accademia Petrarca di Lettere, Arti e Scienze, Arezzo, 1120

Accademia Pugliese delle Scienze, 1120

Accademia Raffaello, 1121

Accademia Roveretana degli Agiati, 1120

Accademia Tedesca, Rome, 1129

Accademia Tiberina, 1120

Accademia Toscana di Scienze e Lettere 'La Colombaria', 1120

Accounting Machine Building Research Institute, Moscow, 1745

Accra Central Library, 905

Accra Polytechnic, 907

Accra Technical Training Centre, 907

Acharya N. G. Ranga Agricultural University, 983

Acharya Narendra Dev Pustakalaya, 981

Acoustical Society of America, 2296

Acoustical Society of China, 428

Acropolis Museum, Athens, 912

Acuario Nacional de Cuba, 600

ACUM Ltd. (Society of Authors, Composers and Music Publishers in Israel), 1093

Adam Mickiewicz University in Poznań, 1648

Adamawa State University, 1536

Adams National Historical Park, 2322

Adams State College of Colorado, 2379

Adamson University, 1604

Adamson University Library, 1603

Adana Bölge Müzesi, 2060

Addis Ababa University, 677

Addis Ababa University Libraries, 677

Adelhausermuseum, Freiburg im Breisgau, 815

Adelphi University, Garden City, 2570

Adler Museum of Medicine, Johannesburg, 1869

Adler Planetarium, Chicago, 2320

Adler School of Professional Psychology, Chicago, 2424

Administracion Nacional de Laboratorios e Institutos de Salud 'Carlos G. Malbran', Buenos Aires, 93

Administrative Bibliotek, Copenhagen, 632

Administrative Staff College of India, 1039

Admiral Makarov State Maritime Academy, St Petersburg, 1795

Adnan Malki Museum, Damascus, 2022

Adnan Menderes Üniversitesi, Aydin, 2061

Adrian College, 2504

Adult Education Association of Guyana, 930

Adult Learning Australia Quest, 116

Advanced Centre for Treatment, Research and Education in Cancer (ACTREC), Mumbai, 976

Advanced Science and Technology Institute, Manila, 1602

Advisory Centre for Education (ACE) Ltd, London, 2129

Adyar Library and Research Centre, 980

Adygea Agricultural Research Institute, 1730

Adyghe State University, Maykop, 1762

AECL Research, Chalk River Laboratories, 329

AECL Research, Whiteshell Laboratories, 329

Aegean University, 2070

Aeronautical Society of India, 972

Aeronautical Society of South Africa (AeSSA), 1865

Aerospace Medical Association, Alexandria, 2291

Afanasev, V. A., Research Institute of Fur-Bearing Animals and Rabbits, Moscow, 1731

Afdeling Biologisch Rijksuniversiteit Groningen, Haren, 1480

Afet İşleri Genel Müdürlüğü Deprem Araştırma Dairesi, Ankara, 2059

Afghanistan Research and Evaluation Unit (AREU), Kabul, 73

AFI Conservatory, 2342

Africa Institute of South Africa, 1865

Africa Nazarene University, Nairobi, 1312

Africa Rice Center (WARDA), 41

African Academy of Sciences, 66

African and Mauritius Council on Higher Education, 50

African Association for the Advancement of Science and Technology, 66

African Association of Science EditorsAfrican Association of Science Editors, 66

African Centre for Applied Research and Training in Social Development (ACARTSOD), Tripoli, 1373

African Medical and Research Foundation, 61

African Network of Scientific and Technological Institutions (ANSTI), Nairobi, 1310

African Oil Chemists' Society, 66

African Organization for Cartography and Remote Sensing, 66

African Regional Centre for Technology, Dakar, 1813

African Society, Cairo, 657

African Studies Association, New Brunswick, 2298

African Studies Association of the United Kingdom, 2141

African Training and Research Centre in Administration for Development, 47

African Virtual University, Nairobi, 1312

Africana Museum, Monrovia, 1370

AFRO Health Sciences Library and Documentation Centre, 582

AFW Wirtschaftsakademie Bad Harzburg GmbH, 788

Afyon Kocatepe Üniversitesi, 2062

Aga Khan University, 1570

Agder Musikkonservatorium, 1560

Agence de la Francophonie, Paris, 705

Agence Universitaire de la Francophonie, 50

Agencia Española de Co-operación International, 1886

Agencia Nacional de Evaluación de la Calidad y Acreditación, Madrid, 1886

Agencija za Statistiku Bosne i Hercegovine, 246

Agfa Foto-Historama, Cologne, 813

AGH University of Science and Technology, 1657

Agnes Scott College, 2413

Agraren Universitet Plovdiv, 304

Agrarian Institute, Moscow, 1731

Agrarian Society, Valletta, 1407

Agrarsoziale Gesellschaft eV (ASG), Göttingen, 787

AgResearch, 1503

Agri-Horticultural Society of India, 968

Agri-Horticultural Society of Madras, 968

Agricultural Association of China, Taipei, 552

Agricultural Chemical Research Institute, Pyongyang, 1318

Agricultural Department Library, Zanzibar, 2028

Agricultural Economics Research Institute, Giza, 658

Agricultural Economics Research Institute, Ulan Bator, 1449

Agricultural Economics Society, Uckfield, 2125

Agricultural Engineering Research Institute, Giza, 658

Agricultural Extension and Rural Development Research Institute, Giza, 658

Agricultural Institute of Canada, 324

Agricultural Institute, Shumen, 299

Agricultural Irrigation Research Institute, Onchon County, 1318

Agricultural Mechanization Research Institute, Pyongyang, 1318

Agricultural Museum, Cairo, 661

Agricultural Museum, Damascus, 2022

Agricultural Research and Extension Trust, Lilongwe, 1391

Agricultural Research Centre Library, Tripoli, 1372

Agricultural Research Centre, Ministry of Agriculture, Cairo, 658

Agricultural Research Centre, Ras Al Khaimah, 2120

Agricultural Research Corporation Central Library, Wad Medani, 1961

Agricultural Research Corporation, Wad Medani, 1960

Agricultural Research Council of Zimbabwe, 2788

Agricultural Research Council, Pretoria, 1865

Agricultural Research Institute, Baku, 184

Agricultural Research Institute for the Central Areas of the Non-Black Soil (Nechernozem) Zone, 1731

Agricultural Research Institute, Khovd, 1449

Agricultural Research Institute (Mlingano), 2027

Agricultural Research Institute of Northern Ireland, 2273

Agricultural Research Institute of Rwanda–Ruhande Station, 1799

Agricultural Research Institute, Washington, 2300

Agricultural Research Organization, Bet-Dagan, 1094

Agricultural Research Trust, Harare, 2788

Agricultural Science Information Center, Taipei, 554

Agricultural Society of Kenya, 1310

Agricultural Society of Trinidad and Tobago, 2051

Agricultural Technology Science, Technology and Production Corporation, Ulan Bator, 1451

Agricultural University of Iceland, 965

Agricultural University of Tiranë, 78

Agriculture and Water Resources Research Centre, Baghdad, 1074

Agriculture and Water Resources Research Centre, Fudhailiyah, 1074

Agrimetrics Institute, Pretoria, 1865

Agro-Economic Research Centre, Santiniketan, 974

Agronomy Research Institute, Harare, 2788

Agronomy Society of New Zealand, 1501

Agrophysical Research Institute, St Petersburg, 1731

Agroscope FAL Reckenholz: Station Fédérale de Recherches en Ecologie et Agriculture, Zürich, 2000

Agroscope FAT Tänikon: Recherches d'Economie d'Entreprise et de Génie rural, 2000

Agroscope FAW: Recherches en Arboriculture, Viticulture et Horticulture de Wädenswil, 2000

Agroscope Liebefeld-Posieux, Bern, 2000

Agroscope RAC Changins: Station Fédérale de Recherches Agronomique, Nyon, 2000

Agrotechnology and Food Innovations, Wageningen, 1478

Agrupación Bibliotecológica del Uruguay, 2743

Ägyptisches Museum und Papyrussammlung, Berlin, 812

Ahmadu Bello University, Zaria, 1523

Ahmed Al-Farsi Library (College of Health Sciences), Manama, 189

Ahmedabad Textile Industry's Research Association, 979

Ahsan Manzil Museum, Dhaka, 193

Ahsanullah University of Science and Technology, 193

Ahwaz Jondishapour University of Medical Sciences, 1062

Aichi Gakuin University, 1269

Aichi Prefectural University, Aichi, 1187

Aichi University, 1269

Aigantighe Art Gallery, 1506

Ain Shams University, Cairo, 661

Air Force Institute of Technology, Wright-Patterson Air Force Base, 2617

Air University, Islamabad, 1571

Aircraft Building Society, Moscow, 1730

Aitkhozhin, M. A., Institute of Molecular Biology and Biochemistry, Almaty, 1304

Ajia Seikei Gakkai, 1172

Ajman University of Science and Technology (Aust), 2120

Ajou University, 1323

Akademi Seni Karawitan Indonesia Padang Panjang, 1059

Akademi Seni Tari Indonesia, 1059

Akademi Teknologi Kulit, Yogyakarta, 1043

Akademia e Arteve, Tiranë, 78

Akademia Ekonomiczna im. Karola Adamieckiego w Katowicach, 1670

Akademia Ekonomiczna im. Oskara Langego we Wrocławiu, 1670

Akademia Ekonomiczna w Krakowie, 1670

Akademia Ekonomiczna w Poznaniu, 1670

Akademia Górniczo-hutnicza Im. Stanisława Staszica w Krakowie, 1657

Akademia Inżynierska w Polsce, 1625

Akademia Medyczna im. Karola Marcinkowskiego w Poznaniu, 1671

Akademia Medyczna im. Ludwika Rydygiera w Bydgoszczy, 1670

Akademia Medyczna w Białymstoku, 1670

Akademia Medyczna w Gdańsku, 1670

Akademia Medyczna w Łodzi, 1671

Akademia Medyczna w Lublinie, 1671

Akademia Medyczna w Warszawie, 1671

Akademia Medyczna we Wrocławiu, 1671

Akademia Morska w Gdyni, 1671

Akademia Muzyczna im. Feliksa Nowowiejskiego w Bydgoszczy, 1671

Akademia Muzyczna im. Fryderyka Chopina w Warszawie, 1672

Akademia Muzyczna im. Ignacego Jana Paderewskiego w Poznaniu, 1672

Akademia Muzyczna im. Karola Lipińskiego we Wrocławiu, 1672

Akademia Muzyczna im. Karola Szymanowskiego w Katowicach, 1672

Akademia Muzyczna im. Stanisława Moniuszki w Gdańsku, 1671

Akademia Muzyczna w Krakowie, 1672

Akademia Muzyczna w Łodzi, 1672

Akademia Rolnicza im. Augusta Cieszkowskiego, 1670

Akademia Rolnicza im. Hugona Kołłątaja w Krakowie, 1670

Akademia Rolnicza w Lublinie, 1670

Akademia Rolnicza w Szczecinie, 1670

Akademia Rolnicza we Wrocławiu, 1670

Akademia Sztuk Pięknych im. Jana Matejki w Krakowie, 1672

Akademia Sztuk Pięknych im. Władysława Strzemińskiego w Łodzi, 1672

Akademia Sztuk Pięknych w Gdańsku, 1672

Akademia Sztuk Pięknych w Poznaniu, 1672

Akademia Sztuk Pięknych w Warszawie, 1672

Akademia Sztuk Pięknych we Wrocławiu, 1672

Akademia Teatralna im. Al. Zelwerowicza w Warszawie, 1672

Akademia Techniczno-Rolnicza im. J. J. Śniadeckich w Bydgoszczy, 1670

Akademie der Bildenden Künste in Nürnberg, 900

Akademie der Bildenden Künste, Munich, 900

Akademie der Bildenden Künste Wien, 170

Akademie der Künste, Berlin, 786

Akademie der Wissenschaften in Göttingen, 786

Akademie der Wissenschaften und der Literatur Mainz, 786

Akademie für Fremdsprachen, Berlin, 901

Akademie für Raumforschung und Landesplanung, Hannover, 796

Akademie věd České republiky (AV ČR), 607

Akademiebibliothek der Berlin-Brandenburgischen Akademie der Wissenschaften, Berlin, 803

Akademiet for de Tekniske Videnskaber, Lyngby, 630

Akademija Nauka i Umjetnosti BiH, 245

Akademija za Muzikalno i Tanzovo Izkustvo, Plovdiv, 312

Akademin för Tekniska Vetenskaper r.y., Espoo, 684

Akademisk Arkitektforening, 628

Akadimia Athinon, 909

Akanu Ibiam Federal Polytechnic, Unwana, 1540

Akdeniz Üniversitesi, 2062

Akhmedsafin, U. M., Institute of Hydrogeology and Hydrophysics, Almaty, 1305

Akhundov, M. F., State Library of Azerbaijan, 185

AKI Akademie voor Beeldende Kunst en Vormgeving, Enschede, 1498

Akita Prefectural Library, 1183

Akkreditierungs-, Certifizierungs- und Qualitätssicherungs-Instituts (ACQUIN), Bonn, 785

Akkreditierungsagentur für Studiengänge im Bereich Heilpädagogik, Pflege, Gesundheit und Soziale Arbeit eV (AHPGS), Freiburg, 785

Akkreditierungsrat, Bonn, 785

Aklan State University, Aklan, 1605

Akmola Agricultural Research Institute, 1303

Akron-Summit County Public Library, 2315

Aktau Sh. Yesenov University, 1306

Aktobe K. Zhubanov State University, 1306

Aktobe State Medical Institute, 1308

Al-Ain Museum, 2120

Al Al-Bayt University, Mafraq, 1300

Al-Aqsa University, Gaza, 1115

Al-arab Medical University, 1372

Al-Awqaf Central Library, Baghdad, 1075

Al-Azhar University, Cairo, 662

Al-Azhar University, Gaza, 1116

Al-Azhar University Library, 660

Al-Baath University, Homs, 2022

Al-Balqa' Applied University, Salt, 1300

Al-farabi Kazakh National University, 1306

Al-Farabi Kazakh State University Central Library, 1305

Al-Fashir University, El Fashir, 1961

Al-Fateh University for Medical Sciences, Tripoli, Libya, 1373

Al-Fateh University, Tripoli, 1373

Al-Gawhara Palace Museum, Cairo, 661

Al-Husn Polytechnic, 1302

Al-Imam Al-a'dham College, Baghdad, 1078

Al-Imam al-Ouzai University, 1365

Al Maktabah Al Wataniah, Aleppo, 2021

Al-Mustansiriya University, Baghdad, 1076

Al-Mustansiriya University Library, Baghdad, 1075

Al-Nahrain University, 1076

Al-Neelain University, Khartoum, 1961

Al-Quds Open University, East Jerusalem, 1118

Al-Quds University, Jerusalem, 1118

Al-Tahadi University, Sirt, 1373

Al Zahiriah, Damascus, 2021

Al-Zahra University, Tehran, 1062

Al-zaiem Al-azhari University, 1961

Alabama Agricultural and Mechanical University, 2328

Alabama Museum of Natural History, University of Alabama, 2317

Alabama State University, 2328

Alagappa University, 984

Ålands konstmuseum, 703

Ålands kulturstiftelse, 703

Ålands museum, 703

Ålands Sjöfartsmuseum, 703

Alapítvány Érc- és Ásványbányászati Múzeum, Rudabánya, 947

Alaska Bible College, 2332

Alaska Pacific University, 2332

Alaska State Library, 2308

Alaska State Museum, 2318

Albanian National Culture Museum, Tiranë, 77

Albany College of Pharmacy, 2571

Albany Law School, 2571

Albany Medical College, 2571

Albany Museum, Grahamstown, 1869

Albany State University, 2413

Albert-ludwigs-universität Freiburg, 849

Alberta College of Art and Design, 405

Alberta Research Council Inc., 327

Albertson College of Idaho, 2423

Albertus Magnus College, 2383

Albertus-Magnus-Institut, 792

Albion College, 2504

Ålborg Historiske Museum, 633

Albrecht-Dürer-Haus, Nuremberg, 819

Albright College, 2643

Albright-Knox Art Gallery, 2324

Albright, William Foxwell, Institute of Archaeological Research in Jerusalem, 1094

Alcázar de Diego Colón, 647

Alcorn State University, 2541

Alderney Maritime Trust, 2278

Alderney Society, 2278

Alderson-broaddus College, 2725

Aleksander Xhuvani University of Elbasan, 77

Alele Museum, Library and National Archives, Majuro, 1410

Alemaya University, Dire Dawa, 677

Aleppo National Museum, 2022

Alexander Center for Applied Population Biology, 2321

Alexander Dubček University in Trenčín, 1849

Alexandria Institute of Oceanography and Fisheries, 659

Alexandria Medical Association, 658

Alexandria Municipal Library, 660

Alexandria University, 661

Alexandria University Central Library, 660

Alexandrov, N. N., Research Institute of Oncology and Medical Radiology, 207

Alfred P. Sloan Foundation, New York, 2282

Alfred University, 2571

Alfred-Wegener-Institut für Polar- und Meeresforschung, 800

Algemene Nederlandse Vereniging voor Wijsbegeerte, 1477

Algonquin Radio Observatory, 329

Alice Holt Research Station, Farnham, 2146

Alice Lloyd College, Pippa Passes, 2461

Aligarh Muslim University, 985

Alipore Observatory and Meteorological Office, Kolkata, 978

Alisher Navoi National Library of Uzbekistan, 2749

All India Association for Educational Research, 969

All India Council for Technical Education, New Delhi, 967

All-India Fine Arts and Crafts Society, 969

All India Institute of Hygiene and Public Health, 1039

All-India Institute of Medical Sciences, New Delhi, 1030

All-India Ophthalmological Society, 970

All-India Oriental Conference, 975

All Pakistan Educational Conference Library, 1568

All-Russia Antibiotics Research Institute, 1736

All-Russia Electrotechnical Institute (VEI), 1745

All-Russia Geological Oil Research Institute (VNIGNI), Moscow, 1742

All-Russia Horticulture Institute for Breeding, Agrotechnology and Nursery, 1731

All-Russia Institute of Plant Protection, 1731

All-Russia Legumes and Pulse Crops Research Institute, 1731

All-Russia Logachev Scientific Research Institute of Exploration Geophysics (VIRG-Rudgeofizika), St Petersburg, 1745

All-Russia Maize Research Institute, 1731

All-Russia Meat Research Institute, 1731

All-Russia Oil Geological Prospecting Institute, 1745

All-Russia Patent Technical Library, 1752

All-Russia Potato Research Institute, 1731

All-Russia Poultry Research and Technology Institute, 1731

All-Russia Railway Transport Research Institute, Moscow, 1745

All-Russia Rapeseed Research and Technological Institute, 1731

All-Russia Research and Design Institute for Atomic Power Station Equipment, 1745

All-Russia Research and Design Institute for Problems of the Development of Oil and Gas Resources on the Continental Shelf, 1745

All-Russia Research and Design Institute of Electroceramics, 1746

All-Russia Research and Design Institute of Metallurgical Engineering, 1746

All-Russia Research and Design Institute of the Oil-Refining and Petrochemical Industry, 1746

All-Russia Research and Design Institute of the Statistical Information System, 1733

All-Russia Research and Technological Institute for Chemical Land Reclamation, 1731

All-Russia Research and Technological Institute for Chemicalization in Agriculture, 1731

All-Russia Research and Technological Institute for Mechanization in Livestock Raising, 1731

All-Russia Research and Technological Institute for Organic Fertilizers, 1731

All-Russia Research, Design and Technological Institute of Lighting Technology, 1746

All-Russia Research Institute for Agricultural Biotechnology, 1731

All-Russia Research Institute for Agricultural Economics and Standards and Norms, 1731

All-Russia Research Institute for Beef Cattle Breeding and Production, 1731

All-Russia Research Institute for Biological Control, 1731

All-Russia Research Institute for Cybernetics in the Agro-industrial Complex, 1731

All-Russia Research Institute for Economics, Labour and Management in Agriculture, 1731

All-Russia Research Institute for Electrification in Agriculture, 1731

All-Russia Research Institute for Farm Animal Genetics and Breeding, 1731

All-Russia Research Institute for Flowers and Tropical Crops, 1731

All-Russia Research Institute for Horse Breeding, 1731

All-Russia Research Institute for Irrigated Arable Farming, 1731

All-Russia Research Institute for Irrigated Horticulture and Vegetable Crops Production, 1731

All-Russia Research Institute for Mechanization in Agriculture, 1731

All-Russia Research Institute for Nature Conservation, 1740

All-Russia Research Institute for Nuclear Power Plant Operation, 1746

All-Russia Research Institute for Oil Refining JSC, 1746

All-Russia Research Institute for Sheep and Goat Breeding, 1731

All-Russia Research Institute for the Agricultural Use of Reclaimed and Improved Land, 1731

All-Russia Research Institute for the Biosynthesis of Protein Substances, 1731

All-Russia Research Institute for the Canned and Vegetable Dry Products Industry, 1746

All-Russia Research Institute for the Dairy Industry, 1746

All-Russia Research Institute for the Geology and Mineral Resources of the World's Oceans, St Petersburg, 1742

All-Russia Research Institute for the Protection of Metals from Corrosion, 1746

All-Russia Research Institute for the Refrigeration Industry, 1746

All-Russia Research Institute for Vegetable Breeding and Seed Production, 1731

All-Russia Research Institute for Veterinary Sanitation, Hygiene and Ecology, 1731

All-Russia Research Institute of Agricultural Microbiology, 1731

All-Russia Research Institute of Animal Husbandry, 1731

All-Russia Research Institute of Applied Microbiology, 1740

All-Russia Research Institute of Arable Farming and Soil Erosion Control, 1731

All-Russia Research Institute of Chemical Technology, 1742

All-Russia Research Institute of Economic Problems in Development of Science and Technology, 1733

All-Russia Research Institute of Economics in Agriculture, 1731

All-Russia Research Institute of Electrical Insulating Materials and Foiled Dielectrics, 1746

All-Russia Research Institute of Electromechanics (VNIIEM), 1746

All-Russia Research Institute of Especially Pure Biopreparations, 1740

All-Russia Research Institute of Exploration Geophysics, 1746

All-Russia Research Institute of Eye Diseases, 1736

All-Russia Research Institute of Fibre-Optic Systems of Communication and Data Processing, 1746

All-Russia Research Institute of Food Biotechnology, 1746

All-Russia Research Institute of Fuel and Energy Problems (VNIIKTEP), 1746

All-Russia Research Institute of Geological, Geophysical and Geochemical Systems (VNIIgeosystem), 1742

All-Russia Research Institute of Helium Technology, 1746

All-Russia Research Institute of Hydrolysis, 1742

All-Russia Research Institute of Information, Technological and Economic Research on the Agro-Industrial Complex, 1731

All-Russia Research Institute of Marine Fisheries and Oceanography, 1732

All-Russia Research Institute of Medicinal and Aromatic Plants, 1732

All-Russia Research Institute of Mineral Resources and the Use of the Subsurface, 1746

All-Russia Research Institute of Natural Gases and Gas Technology, 1742

All-Russia Research Institute of Optical and Physical Measurements, 1742

All-Russia Research Institute of Organic Synthesis (VNIIOS), 1746

All-Russia Research Institute of Pharmaceutical Plants, 1736

All-Russia Research Institute of Physical-Technical and Radiotechnical Measurements, 1742

All-Russia Research Institute of Phytopathology, 1732

All-Russia Research Institute of Plant Quarantine, 1732

All-Russia Research Institute of Pond Fishery, 1732

All-Russia Research Institute of Problems of Computer Technology and Information Science, 1746

All-Russia Research Institute of Radiotechnology, 1746

All-Russia Research Institute of Refractory Metals and Hard Alloys, 1746

All-Russia Research Institute of Restoration, 1733

All-Russia Research Institute of Starch Products, 1746

All-Russia Research Institute of Television and Radio Broadcasting JSC, 1746

All-Russia Research Institute of the Cable Industry, 1746

All-Russia Research Institute of the Technology of Blood Substitutes and Hormonal Preparations, 1736

All-Russia Research Institute of Tobacco, Makhorka and Tobacco Products, 1732

All-Russia Research Institute of Trunk Pipeline Construction, 1746

All-Russia Rice Research Institute, Belozernoe, 1732

All-Russia Scientific and Research Institute of Patent Information (VNIIPI), 1752

All-Russia Scientific Research Institute for Exploration Methods and Engineering, St Petersburg, 1746

All-Russia Scientific Research Institute of Aviation Materials (VIAM), Moscow, 1746

All-Russia Scientific Research Institute of Fats, 1746

All-Russia Scientific Research Institute of Mineral Resources, 1742

All-Russia Scientific Research Institute of Natural and Synthetic Diamonds and Tools, 1746

All-Russia Scientific Research Institute of Technical Physics and Automation, Moscow, 1746

All-Russia Vegetable Production Research Institute, 1732

All-Russia Veterinary Research Institute for Poultry Diseases, 1732

All-Russia 'znanie' Society, Moscow, 1728

All-Russian Distance Institute of Finance and Economics, 1795

All-Russian Extra-Mural Agricultural Institute, 1795

All-Russian Geological Library, St Petersburg, 1753

All Souls College, Oxford, 2250

Allahabad Agricultural Institute, Allahabad, 1034

Allahabad Mathematical Society, 971

Allahabad Public Library, 980

Allama I. I. Kazi Library (University of Sindh), 1568

Allama Iqbal Open University, 1571

Allama Iqbal Open University Central Library, Islamabad, 1568

Allameh Tabataba'i University, 1063

Allard Pierson Museum Amsterdam, 1483

Állattenyésztési és Takarmányozási Kutatóintézet, Herceghalom, 939

Allegheny College, Meadville, 2643

Allen College, Waterloo, Iowa, 2452

Allen County Public Library, 2311

Allen University, Columbia, South Carolina, Columbia, South Carolina, 2672

Allergen State Unitary Enterprise, Stavropol, 1736

Allgemeine Bibliotheken der Gesellschaft für das Gute und Gemeinnützige, Basel, 2001

Alliance Française, Abu Dhabi, 2120

Alliance Française, Accra, 904

Alliance Française, Addis Ababa, 676

Alliance Française, Agadez, Niger, 1516

Alliance Française, Andorra, 85

Alliance Française, Antananarivo, 1388

Alliance Française, Asmara, 671

Alliance Française, Asunción, 1587

Alliance Française, Bandung, 1041

Alliance Française, Bangkok, 2032

Alliance Française, Bangui, 407

Alliance Française, Banjul, 779

Alliance Française, Basel, Basel, 1998

Alliance Française, Beijing, 427

Alliance Française, Bethlehem, 1115

Alliance Française, Bishkek, 1356

Alliance Française, Bitola, 1386

Alliance Française, Bogatá, 562

Alliance Française, Bratislava, 1841

Alliance Française, Brunei, 296

Alliance Française, Brussels, 217

Alliance Française, Bucharest, 1692

Alliance Française, Buenos Aires, 90

Alliance Française, Canberra, 118

Alliance Française, Caracas, 2761

Alliance Française, Castries, 1802

Alliance Française, Chisinau, 1444

Alliance Française, Coimbra, 1675

Alliance Française, Colombo, 1953

Alliance Française, Copenhagen, 629

Alliance Française, Dakar, 1812

Alliance Française, Dar es Salaam, 2027

Alliance Française de Paris, 705

Alliance Française, Dhaka, 191

Alliance Française, Djibouti, 644

Alliance Française, Dublin, 1081

Alliance Française, El Jadida, 1457

Alliance Française, El Obeid, 1960

Alliance Française, Freetown, 1834

Alliance Française, Gaborone, 250

Alliance Française, Georgetown, 930

Alliance Française, Guatemala City, 925

Alliance Française, Harare, 2787

Alliance Française, Havana, 598

Alliance Française, Hong Kong, 545

Alliance Française, Islamabad, 1564

Alliance Française, Johannesburg, 1863

Alliance Française, Kampala, 2094

Alliance Française, Kathmandu, 1472

Alliance Française, Kiev, 2099

Alliance Française, Kingston, Jamaica, 1168

Alliance Française, Kingstown, 1803

Alliance Française, Kinshasa, 579

Alliance Française, Kuala Lumpur, 1393

Alliance Française, La Paz, 239

Alliance Française, Lagos, 1519

Alliance Française, Lima, 1590

Alliance Française, Limassol, 604

Alliance Française, London, 2133

Alliance Française, Luanda, 86

Alliance Française, Lusaka, 2784

Alliance Française, Macao, 551

Alliance Française, Madrid, 1889

Alliance Française, Managua, 1513

Alliance Française, Manama, 189

Alliance Française, Manila, 1601

Alliance Française, Maseru, 1369

Alliance Française, Mbabane, 1966

Alliance Française, Mindelo, Cape Verde, 406

Alliance Française, Monrovia, 1370

Alliance Française, Monte Carlo, 1448

Alliance Française, Montevideo, 2743

Alliance Française, Nairobi, 1310

Alliance Française, Nassau, 188

Alliance Française, New Delhi, 969

Alliance Française, Ngaoundéré, 319

Alliance Française, Nouakchott, 1411

Alliance Française, Osaka, 1174

Alliance Française, Oslo, 1544

Alliance Française, Ottawa, 325

Alliance Française, Panamá, 1582

Alliance Française, Paramaribo, 1965

Alliance Française, Plovdiv, 298

Alliance Française, Port Gentil, Gabon, 777

Alliance Française, Port Louis, Mauritius, 1412

Alliance Française, Port Moresby, 1585

Alliance Française, Port Saïd, 658

Alliance Française, Port-au-Prince, 932

Alliance Française, Port-of-Spain, 2051

Alliance Française, Prague, 608

Alliance Française, Quito, 650

Alliance Française, Riga, 1361

Alliance Française, Rio de Janeiro, 254

Alliance Française, Rome, 1122

Alliance Française, Roseau, 645
Alliance Française, St John's, 88
Alliance Française, St Kitts and Nevis, 1801
Alliance Française, St Michael, Barbados, 204
Alliance Française, St Petersburg, 1728
Alliance Française, Samarkand, 2747
Alliance Française, San José, Costa Rica, 584
Alliance Française, San Marino, 1805
Alliance Française, San Salvador, 667
Alliance Française, Santiago, Chile, 411
Alliance Française, Santo Domingo, 646
Alliance Française, São Tomé e Principe, 1806
Alliance Française, Seoul, 1322
Alliance Française, Singapore, 1836
Alliance Française, Stockholm, 1970
Alliance Française, Suva, 679
Alliance Française, Szeged, 937
Alliance Française, Tallinn, 672
Alliance Française, Tegucigalpa, 934
Alliance Française, Tirana, 75
Alliance Française, Utrecht, 1476
Alliance Française, Victoria, Seychelles, 1833
Alliance Française, Vilnius, 1376
Alliance Française, Warsaw, 1622
Alliance Française, Washington, DC, 2291
Alliance Française, Wellington, 1501
Alliance Française, Yamoussoukro, 589
Alliance Française, Yerevan, 112
Alliance Française, Zagreb, 592
Alliance Française–Alianza Francesa México, Mexico City, 1415
Alliance of Literary Societies, Havant, 2133
Alliant International University, 2342
Alma College, 2504
Almaty Abai State University, 1306
Almaty Institute of Power Engineering and Telecommunication, 1308
Almaty Kurmangazy State Conservatoire, 1308
Almaty State Theatrical and Cinema Institute, 1308
Almaty Technological University, 1306
Almedalsbiblioteket, 1974
Alšova jihočeska galerie, 613
Altai Experimental Farm, 1732
Altai State Agrarian University, 1760
Altai State Institute of Culture, 1797
Altai State Medical University, 1779
Altai State Technical University, 1781
Altai State University, 1762
Altai State University Library, 1751
Alte Nationalgalerie, Berlin, 812
Alterra, Research Instituut voor de Groene Ruimte, 1478
Altes Schloss, Giessen, 815
Altonaer Museum in Hamburg/ Norddeutsches Landesmuseum, 816
Alupe Leprosy and Other Skin Diseases Research Centre, 1311
Alupka State Palace and Park Preserve, 2104
Alushta Literary Memorial Museum of S. M. Sergeev-Tsensky, 2104
Alvernia College, Reading, Pennsylvania, 2643
Alverno College, Milwaukee, 2728
Amalienborgmuseet, 634
Amasya Müzesi, 2060
Amateur Society of Basque Language and Culture, Tbilisi, 780
Amathole Museum, 1870
Ambrose Alli University, 1536
AMDEL, Australia, 124
American Academy in Rome, 1129
American Academy of Allergy, Asthma and Immunology, 2291
American Academy of Arts and Letters, 2283
American Academy of Arts and Sciences, 2283
American Academy of Family Physicians, 2291
American Academy of Ophthalmology, 2291
American Academy of Otolaryngology– Head and Neck Surgery, 2291
American Academy of Pediatrics, 2291

American Academy of Periodontology, 2291
American Academy of Political and Social Science, 2287
American Academy of Religion, 2298
American Accounting Association, 2287
American Anthropological Association, 2298
American Antiquarian Society, 2289
American Arbitration Association, 2287
American Association for Cancer Research, Inc., 2302
American Association for Higher Education, 2282
American Association for State and Local History, 2289
American Association for the Advancement of Science, 2294
American Association of Anatomists, 2292
American Association of Collegiate Registrars and Admissions Officers, Washington, 2282
American Association of Community Colleges, Washington, 2282
American Association of Immunologists, 2292
American Association of Law Libraries, 2286
American Association of Museums, 2286
American Association of Petroleum Geologists, 2296
American Association of State Colleges and Universities, 2282
American Association of University Professors, 2282
American Astronomical Society, 2296
American Baptist College, 2677
American Baptist Seminary of the West, 2342
American Bar Association, 2287
American Cancer Society Inc., 2292
American Caribbean Museum, St Thomas, 2742
American Catholic Historical Association, 2289
American Center of PEN, 2291
American Ceramic Society, 2299
American Classical League, 2291
American College, Bryn Mawr, 2643
American College of Chest Physicians, 61
American College of Greece, 923
American College of Obstetricians and Gynecologists, 2292
American College of Physicians, 2292
American College of Rheumatism, 2292
American College of Surgeons, 2292
American Comparative Literature Association, 2291
American Conservatory Theater, 2343
American Council for the Arts, 2288
American Council of Engineering Companies, 2299
American Council of Learned Societies, 2283
American Council on Education, 2282
American Counseling Association, 2298
American Crystallographic Association, 2296
American Dairy Science Association, Washington, 2285
American Dental Association, 2292
American Dialect Society, 2291
American Dietetic Association, 2292
American Economic Association, 2287
American Educational Research Association, 2301
American Federation for Medical Research, 2302
American Federation of Arts, 2289
American Federation of Teachers, Washington, 2282
American Finance Association, 2287
American Folklore Society, 2298
American Forests, 2285
American Genetic Association, 2295
American Geographical Society Collection of the University of Wisconsin–Milwaukee Library, 2317
American Geological Institute, 2296
American Geophysical Union, 2296

American Geriatrics Society, Inc., 2292
American Graduate School of International Relations and Diplomacy, Paris, 770
American Gynecological and Obstetrical Society, 2292
American Heart Association, 2292
American Historical Association, 2289
American Hospital Association, 2292
American Indian College, 2332
American Institute of Aeronautics and Astronautics, 2299
American Institute of Architects, 2285
American Institute of Biological Sciences, 2295
American Institute of Chemical Engineers, 2299
American Institute of Chemists, 2296
American Institute of Mining, Metallurgical and Petroleum Engineers, Inc., 2299
American Institute of Physics, 2296
American Institute of the History of Pharmacy, 2292
American Institutes for Research, 2306
American InterContinental University, 2413
American International College, Springfield, 2479
American International School of Medicine, Georgetown, 931
American International University Bangladesh, 193
American Irish Historical Society, 2289
American Iron and Steel Institute, 2299
American Jewish Historical Society, 2289
American Judicature Society, 2287
American Laryngological, Rhinological and Otological Society, Inc. (Triological Society), 2292
American Law Institute, 2287
American Law Institute-American Bar Association Committee on Continuing Professional Education, 2287
American Library Association, 2286
American Library in Paris, 724
American Lung Association, 2292
American Malacological Society, 2295
American Mathematical Society, 2296
American Medical Association, 2292
American Medical Association. James S. Todd Memorial Library, 2310
American Medical Technologists, 2292
American Meteorological Society, 2296
American Microscopical Society, 2297
American Museum in Britain, 2169
American Museum of Natural History, 2324
American Museum of Natural History Library, 2314
American Museum of Science and Energy, 2327
American Musicological Society, 2289
American National Standards Institute, 2299
American Neurological Association, 2292
American Nuclear Society, 2297
American Numismatic Society, 2289
American Occupational Therapy Association, Inc., 2292
American Optometric Association, Inc., 2292
American Oriental Society, 2298
American Ornithologists' Union, 2295
American Peace Society, 2287
American Pediatric Society, 2292
American Pharmacists Association, 2297
American Philological Association, 2291
American Philosophical Association, 2297
American Philosophical Society, 2283
American Philosophical Society Library, 2316
American Physical Society, 2297
American Physical Therapy Association, 2292
American Physiological Society, 2292
American Phytopathological Society, 2295
American Planning Association, 2286

American Political Science Association, 2287
American Psychiatric Association, 2292
American Psychological Association, 2297
American Public Health Association, 2292
American Research Center in Egypt (ARCE), 2306
American Roentgen Ray Society, Reston, 2293
American School of Classical Studies at Athens, 922
American Schools of Oriental Research, 2306
American Society for Aesthetics, 2289
American Society for Biochemistry and Molecular Biology, 2297
American Society for Clinical Laboratory Science, 2293
American Society for Clinical Pathology, 2293
American Society for Eighteenth-Century Studies, 2289
American Society for Engineering Education, 2299
American Society for Ethnohistory, 2298
American Society for Horticultural Science, 2285
American Society for Information Science and Technology (ASIST), 2286
American Society for Investigative Pathology, Inc., 2293
American Society for Microbiology, 2293
American Society for Nutritional Sciences, 2293
American Society for Pharmacology and Experimental Therapeutics, Inc., 2293
American Society for Photobiology, 2295
American Society for Photogrammetry and Remote Sensing, 2299
American Society for Political and Legal Philosophy, 2287
American Society for Psychical Research, Inc., 2306
American Society for Public Administration, 2287
American Society for Theatre Research, 2289
American Society of Agricultural Engineers, 2285
American Society of Agronomy, 2285
American Society of Animal Science, 2285
American Society of Church History, 2289
American Society of Civil Engineers, 2299
American Society of Clinical Hypnosis, 2293
American Society of Composers, Authors and Publishers (ASCAP), 2289
American Society of Heating, Refrigerating and Air-Conditioning Engineers, Inc., 2299
American Society of Human Genetics, 2295
American Society of Ichthyologists and Herpetologists, 2295
American Society of International Law, 2287
American Society of Limnology and Oceanography, 2294
American Society of Mammalogists, 2295
American Society of Mechanical Engineers, 2299
American Society of Naturalists, 2295
American Society of Naval Engineers, Inc., 2299
American Society of Parasitologists, 2295
American Society of Tropical Medicine and Hygiene, 2293
American Sociological Association, 2298
American Speech-Language-Hearing Association, 2293
American Statistical Association, 2287
American Surgical Association, 2293

American Swedish Historical Museum, 2326

American Theological Library Association, 2286

American University in Cairo, 662

American University in Cairo Library, 660

American University Museum, Ras Beirut, 1365

American University of Beirut, 1365

American University of Beirut Libraries, 1365

American University of Paris, 768

American University of Rome, 1164

American University, Washington, 2397

American Urological Association, Inc., 2293

American Veterinary Medical Association, 2285

American Vocational Association, Inc., 2282

American Welding Society, 2299

Amerikanski Universitet v Bulgaria, 304

Ames Research Center, Moffet Field, 2307

Amgueddfa Cymru – National Museum Wales, 2170

Amgueddfa Cymru – National MuseumWales Library, 2156

Amherst College, 2479

Amics de la Cultura, Escaldes-Engordany, 85

Amics dels Museus de Catalunya, Barcelona, 1888

Amirkabir University of Technology, Tehran, 1063

Amman University College for Applied Engineering, 1302

Amoud University, 1861

Amravati University, 985

Amrita Vishwa Vidyapeetham, Coimbatore, 1034

Amstelkring Museum, Amsterdam, 1483

Amsterdams Historisch Museum, 1483

Amur Complex Research Institute, 1742

Amur State University, 1762

Amurin Työläismuseokortteli, 687

AMVC—Letterenhuis, Antwerp, 220

An-najah National University, 1117

Anadolu Medeniyetleri Müzesi, 2060

Anadolu Üniversitesi, 2062

Anatolian University, 2062

Anatomical Society of Great Britain and Ireland, 2135

Anatomische Gesellschaft, Lübeck, 789

Ancient House Museum, Thetford, 2177

Ancient Iran Cultural Society, Tehran, 1060

Ancient Monuments Society, London, 2131

Ancient Orient Museum, Tokyo, 1186

Anderson College, 2672

Anderson Museum, Cairo, 661

Anderson Park Art Gallery (Inc.), 1505

Anderson University, 2442

Andhra Pradesh State Museum, 982

Andhra University, 985

Andizhan Cotton Institute, 2751

Andizhan State Medical Institute, 2751

Andizhan State Pedagogical Institute of Languages, 2751

Andizhan State University, 2749

Andong National University, 1323

Andover Newton Theological School, 2479

Andreev Acoustics Institute, Michigan, 1742

Andreev, N., House Museum, Orel, 1757

Andrews University, Michigan, 2504

Andronikashvili Institute of Physics, Tbilisi, 781

Angeles University Foundation, Angeles City, Philippines, 1605

Anglia Polytechnic University Library, 2156

Anglia Ruskin University, 2180

Angus L. Macdonald Library, Antigonish, 331

Anhaltische Landesbücherei Dessau, 805

Anhui Provincial Library, 435

Anhui University, 437

Animal Health Research Centre, Entebbe, 2094

Animal Health Research Institute, Dokki, 658

Animal Health Trust, Kentford, 2145

Animal Husbandry Research Institute, Comilla, 192

Animal Husbandry Research Institute, Hanoi, 2771

Animal Improvement Institute, Irene, 1865

Animal Nutrition and Animal Products Institute, Irene, 1865

Animal Production Corporation, Research Division, Khartoum, 1960

Animal Production Research Institute, Dokki, 658

Animal Reproduction Research Institute, Giza, 659

Animal Research Institute, Achimota, 905

Animal Science Research Institute, Tehran, 1060

Anjuman-i-Islam Islamic Research Association, Mumbai, 979

Anjuman-i-Islam Urdu Research Institute, 975

Anjuman Taraqqi-e-Urdu Pakistan, 1564

Ankara Nükleer Araştırma ve Eğitim Merkezi, 2059

Ankara Üniversitesi, 2063

Ankara Üniversitesi, Kütüphane ve Dokümantasyon Daire Başkanlığı, 2059

Anna Freud Centre, London, 2151

Anna Maria College, Paxton, 2479

Anna University, Chennai, 985

Annamalai University, 986

Annonciade, Musée de St-Tropez, 732

Anokhin, P. K., Institute of Normal Physiology, Moscow, 1736

Anotati Scholi Kalon Technon, 914

Ansto Training, Menai, 159

Antalya Müzesi, 2060

Antalya Tekelioğlu İl Halk Kütüphanesi, 2059

Antenne IRD de Bouaké, Paris, 720

Anthropological Research Institute, Tehran, 1061

Anthropological Society of Mumbai, 971

Anthropological Survey of India, 979

Anthropologische Gesellschaft in Wien, 163

Antigua and Barbuda International Institute of Technology (ABIIT), St Johns, 88

Antigua and Barbuda National Archives, St John's, 88

Antigua State College, St Johns, 88

Antikenmuseum Basel und Sammlung Ludwig, 2003

Antikensammlung, Pergamonmuseum und Altes Museum, Berlin, 812

Antikvarisk-topografiska arkivet, Stockholm, 1973

Antioch University, Yellow Springs, 2617

Antiquarian and Numismatic Society of Montreal (Château Ramezay Museum), 325

Antiquarische Gesellschaft in Zürich, 1997

Antiquarium Nazionale di Boscoreale, 1141

Antiquities Service Library, Khartoum, 1960

Anıtkabir Atatürk Müzesi, 2060

Anton de Kom Universiteit Van Suriname, 1965

Anton de Kom University of Suriname, 1965

Anuchin, D. N., Anthropological Institute and Museum, 1755

Anuradhapura Folk Museum, 1955

Aomori University of Health and Welfare, Aomori, 1264

Aosdána, Dublin, 1081

Aoyama Gakuin University, 1269

Apartheid Museum, Johannesburg, 1869

Apollonia Museum, Marsa Soussa, 1372

Apothecaries of London, Worshipful Society of, 2135

Appalachian Bible College, 2726

Appalachian State University, 2601

Applied Economics Research Centre, Karachi, 1565

Applied Interdisciplinary Development Research Institute, Youth Entrepreneurship Development Organisation (YEDO), Chennai, 979

Applied Linguistics Institute, Beijing, 431

Applied Science Research Institute, Kyoto, 1182

AQAS eV, Bonn, 786

Aquaproiect, SA, Bucharest, 1693

Aquazoo Löbbecke Museum, 814

Aquinas College, Grand Rapids, 2504

Aquinas College, Nashville, 2677

Aquinas College of Higher Studies, Colombo, 1959

Aquinas Institute of Theology, 2544

Aquinas University, Legazpi City, 1605

Aquincum Múzeum, 944

Arab Academy for Science and Technology and Maritime Transport, Alexandria, 666

Arab Bureau of Education for the Gulf States, Riyadh, 50

Arab Center for the Study of Arid Zones and Dry Lands (ACSAD), Damascus, 2021

Arab Centre for Arabization, Translation, Authorship and Publication, Damascus, 2021

Arab Conservatory of Music, Aleppo, 2023

Arab Gulf States Information and Documentation Center, Baghdad, 1075

Arab League Information Centre (Library), Cairo, 660

Arab Library, Boutilimit, 1411

Arab Library, Chinguetti, 1411

Arab Library, Kaédi, 1411

Arab Library, Oualata, 1411

Arab Library, Tidjikja, 1411

Arab Literacy and Adult Education Organization (ARLO), Baghdad, 1074

Arab Petroleum Training Institute, 56

Arab Planning Institute, Kuwait, 1354

Arab Regional Branch of the International Council on Archives (ARBICA), Riyadh, 1807

Arabian Gulf University, 190

Arabic Language Academy of Damascus, 2021

Arabization Center for Medical Science, Safat, 1354

Aral Scientific and Research Institute of Agroecology and Agriculture, Kyzylorda, 1303

Arany János Múzeum, 947

Araştırma Dairesi Başkanlığı (Demiryollar, Limanlar ve Hava Meydanları İnşaatı Genel Müdürlüğünün), Ankara, 2059

Arbeia Roman Fort, 2176

Arbeitsgemeinschaft der Spezialbibliotheken eV, Jülich, 787

Arbeitsgemeinschaft Deutscher Wirtschaftswissenschaftlicher Forschungsinstitut eV, 797

Arbeitsgemeinschaft Historischer Kommissionen und Landesgeschichtlicher Institute, Marburg/Lahn, 788

Arbeitsgemeinschaft Industrieller Forschungsvereinigungen 'Otto von Guericke' eV (AiF), 802

Arbeitsgemeinschaft Sozialwissenschaftlicher Institute eV, Bonn, 801

Arbeitsstelle Friedensforschung Bonn, 798

Arbeitsstelle für Osterreichische Literatur und Kultur Robert-Musil-Forschung, 799

Arbil Museum, 1075

Arbuzov, A. E., Institute of Organic and Physical Chemistry, Kazan, 1742

ARC Infruitec-Nietvoorbij, Stellenbosch, 1865

Arcadia University, 2644

Archaeological Institute of America, 2289

Archaeological Institute, Sofia, 300

Archaeological Library, Taxila, 1569

Archaeological Museum, Bodh Gaya, 982

Archaeological Museum, Corfu, 913

Archaeological Museum, Delphi, 913

Archaeological Museum, Durrës, 77

Archaeological Museum, Fier, 77

Archaeological Museum, Guntur, 982

Archaeological Museum, Harappa, 1569

Archaeological Museum, Heraklion, 913

Archaeological Museum in Corinth, 913

Archaeological Museum, Moenjodaro, 1570

Archaeological Museum, Nalanda, 983

Archaeological Museum of Canea, 913

Archaeological Museum of Thessaloniki, 913

Archaeological Museum, Olympia, 913

Archaeological Museum Red Fort Delhi, 982

Archaeological Museum, Rethymnon, 913

Archaeological Museum, Rhodes, 913

Archaeological Museum, Taxila, 1570

Archaeological, Natural History, Epigraphy, Prehistory and Ethnography Museums, Tripoli, 1372

Archaeological (Rockefeller) Museum, Jerusalem, 1097

Archaeological Society of Sri Lanka, 1953

Archaeological Survey Department of Sri Lanka, 1954

Archaeological Survey of India, 975

Archaeologiki Hetairia, Athens, 909

Archaeology Institute, Beijing, 430

Archäologie Schweiz, 1997

Archäologische Staatssammlung München, Munich, 818

Archäologisches Landesmuseum, Konstanz, 817

Archäologisches Landesmuseum, Schleswig, 819

Archäologisches Landesmuseum und Landesamt für Bodendenkmalpflege Mecklenburg-Vorpommern, 819

Archäologisches Museum Carnuntinum, 169

Archäologisches Museum, Frankfurt am Main, 815

Archdiocesan Archives, Mechelen, 221

Archdiocesan Museum of Manila, Manila, 1604

Archeological Institute, Addis Ababa, 676

Archeologický ústav AV ČR, Brno, 609

Archeologický ústav AV ČR, Praha, 610

Archéologie Suisse/Archeologia Svizzera, 1997

Archief en Stadsbibliotheek, Mechelen, 221

Architectural Association (Inc.), London, 2126

Architectural Association of Ireland, 1081

Architectural Society of China, 427

Architecture and Building Foundation, Prague, 609

Archiv AV ČR, Prague, 612

Archiv, Bibliothek und Sammlungen der Gesellschaft der Musikfreunde in Wien, 167

Archiv der Hansestadt Lübeck, 808

Archiv der sozialen Demokratie (Friedrich-Ebert-Stiftung), Bonn, 804

Archiv der Universität Wien, 167

Archiv des Stiftes Schotten, 167

Archiv für Schweizerische Kunstgeschichte, Basel, 2001

Archival Museum, Peshawar, 1569

Archive and Library of Ashkenaz House, 1096

Archive of Art and Design, London, 2162

Archives d'Etat, Geneva, 2001

Archives de Côte d'Ivoire, 589

Archives de France, 724

Associazione Italiana Nucleare, 1124
Associazione Nazionale dei Musei Italiani, 1121
Associazione Pedagogica Italiana, 1121
Associazione Termotecnica Italiana, 1125
Associazone Professionale Svizzera della Psicologia Applicata, 1999
Assumption College, Worcester, 2479
Assumption University, Bangkok, 2033
Astan-i-Quds Razavi Museums, 1062
Astana State Medical Academy, 1308
ASTED (Association pour l'avancement des sciences et des techniques de la documentation) Inc., Montréal, 324
ASTM International, West Conshohocken, Pennsylvania, 2300
Aston University, 2181
Aston University Library and Information Services, 2153
Astrakhan State B. M. Kustodiev Gallery, 1754
Astrakhan State Conservatoire, 1797
Astrakhan State Medical Academy, 1794
Astrakhan State Technical University, 1781
Astronomical and Geodesical Society, Moscow, 1730
Astronomical Association of Indonesia, 1041
Astronomical Institute, Tatranská Lomnica, 1843
Astronomical Institute, Utrecht, 1480
Astronomical Observatory, Kolkata, 978
Astronomical Observatory of St Xavier's College, Kolkata, 978
Astronomical Observatory of the University of the Punjab, 1567
Astronomical Observatory, Ulan Bator, 1450
Astronomical Society of Australia, 121
Astronomical Society of Bermuda, 2277
Astronomical Society of India, 971
Astronomical Society of South Australia (Inc.), 121
Astronomical Society of Southern Africa, 1864
Astronomical Society of Tasmania Inc., 121
Astronomical Society of Victoria Inc., 121
Astronomický ústav AV ČR, Ondřejov, 611
Astronomisch-Physikalisches Kabinett, Kassel, 816
Astronomische Gesellschaft, Jena, 791
Astronomisches Institut der Universität Würzburg, 800
Astronomisches Rechen-Institut, Heidelberg, 800
Astronomisk Selskab, Copenhagen, 630
Astronomska Opservatorija u Beogradu, 1816
Astronomy Technology Centre, Edinburgh, 2151
Astrophysikalisches Institut und Universitäts-Sternwarte, Jena, 800
Asutosh Museum of Indian Art, 982
Atatürk Kitaplığı, 2060
Atatürk Museum, Konya, 2061
Atatürk Üniversitesi, 2064
Atcharian Institute of Linguistics, Yerevan, 113
Ateneo Art Gallery, Quezon City, 1604
Ateneo Científico, Literario y Artístico de Madrid, Madrid, 1888
Ateneo Científico, Literario y Artístico, Minorca, 1888
Ateneo de Davao University, 1605
Ateneo de La Habana, 598
Ateneo de Manila University, 1605
Ateneo de Manila University Rizal Library, 1603
Ateneo de Medicina de Sucre, 239
Ateneo de Ponce, 2739
Ateneo Nacional de Ciencias y Artes de México, 1416
Ateneo Puertorriqueño, 2739
Ateneo Veracruzano, 1415
Ateneu Barcelonès, 1888
'Atenisi Institute, Nuku'alofa, 2050
Athabasca University, Edmonton, 336
Athenaeum of Ohio, 2617

Athenaeum Pontificium Regina Apostolorum, 2757
Athens Center of Ekistics, 911
Athens State University, 2328
Athens University of Economics and Business Library, 912
Athlone Institute of Technology, 1090
Atkinson Art Gallery, Southport, 2178
Atlanta Christian College, 2414
Atlanta-Fulton Public Library, 2310
Atlantic Council of the United States, 2287
Atlantic Union College, Lancaster, Massachusetts, 2480
Atılım Üniversitesi, 2065
Atoll Research Activities, Tarawa, 1317
Atomic Energy Centre, Dhaka, 192
Atomic Energy Council, Taipei, 553
Atomic Energy Medical Centre (AEMC), Karachi, 1567
Atomic Energy Minerals Centre (AEMC), Lahore, 1567
Atomic Energy Minerals Centre Library, Lahore, 1569
Atomic Energy of Canada, Ltd (AECL), 329
Atomic Energy Research Establishment, Dhaka, 192
Atominstitut der Österreichischen Universitäten, 165
Atyrau H. Dosmuhamedov State University, 1306
Atyrau Scientific and Research Institute of Agriculture, 1303
Auburn University, 2328
Auckland Art Gallery Toi o Tāmaki, 1505
Auckland City Libraries, 1504
Auckland Medical Research Foundation, 1503
Auckland Museum, 1505
Auckland University of Technology, 1507
Auezov, M. O., Institute of Literature and Arts, Almaty, 1304
Augsburg College, Minneapolis, 2526
Augusta State University, 2414
Augustana College, Rock Island, 2425
Augustana College, Sioux Falls, 2675
Augustana Hochschule, Neuendettelsau, 902
Augustana University College, Alberta, 337
Augustinermuseum, Freiburg im Breisgau, 815
Aurora University, 2425
Auschwitz-Birkenau Memorial and Museum in Oświęcim, 1638
Austin College, 2687
Austin Peay State University, 2677
Austin Presbyterian Theological Seminary, 2688
Austin Public Library, 2317
Australasian and Pacific Society for Eighteenth-Century Studies, 119
Australasian Association of Clinical Biochemists, 119
Australasian Association of Philosophy, 121
Australasian Ceramic Society, 121
Australasian Chapter of Sexual Health Medicine, 119
Australasian College of Dermatologists, 119
Australasian College of Physical Scientists and Engineers in Medicine, 121
Australasian Institute of Mining and Metallurgy, 121
Australasian Political Studies Association, 117
Australia Council for the Arts, 118
Australian Academy of Science, 120
Australian Academy of Technological Sciences and Engineering, 121
Australian Academy of the Humanities, 117
Australian Acoustical Society, 121
Australian and New Zealand Association for Medieval and Early Modern Studies, 118
Australian and New Zealand Association for the Advancement of Science (ANZAAS), 120

Australian Association of Neurologists, 119
Australian Bar Association, 117
Australian Bureau of Statistics, 123
Australian Catholic University, 128
Australian College of Educators, 118
Australian Conservation Foundation, 120
Australian Council for Educational Research Ltd, 122
Australian Council of National Trusts, 117
Australian Dental Association, 119
Australian Film, Television and Radio School, 159
Australian Graduate School of Management, 145
Australian Institute of Aboriginal and Torres Strait Islander Studies, 124
Australian Institute of Agricultural Science and Technology, 117
Australian Institute of Archaeology, 124
Australian Institute of Credit Management, St Leonards, 117
Australian Institute of Criminology, 124
Australian Institute of Criminology, J. V. Barry Library, 124
Australian Institute of Energy, 121
Australian Institute of Food Science and Technology, Inc., 121
Australian Institute of Holistic Medicine, 119
Australian Institute of International Affairs, 117
Australian Institute of Management, 117
Australian Institute of Marine Science, 123
Australian Institute of Nuclear Science and Engineering, 121
Australian Institute of Physics, 121
Australian Institute of Quantity Surveyors, 117
Australian Library and Information Association, 117
Australian Maritime College, 159
Australian Mathematical Society, 121
Australian Medical Association, 119
Australian Museum, 126
Australian National Botanic Gardens, 123
Australian National Maritime Museum, 126
Australian National University, 128
Australian National University Library, 124
Australian Nuclear Science and Technology Organisation (ANSTO), 123
Australian Numismatic Society, 118
Australian Physiological Society, 119
Australian Physiotherapy Association, 119
Australian Property Institute, 117
Australian Psychological Society, 121
Australian Qualifications Framework Advisory Board (AQFAB), Carlton, 116
Australian Radiation Protection and Nuclear Safety Agency, 122
Australian Research Council, 116, 122
Australian Robotics and Automation Association Inc., 121
Australian Society for Fish Biology, 120
Australian Society for Limnology, 120
Australian Society for Medical Research, 122
Australian Society for Microbiology Inc., 120
Australian Society for Parasitology, 120
Australian Society of Authors Ltd, 119
Australian Society of Clinical Hypnotherapists, 119
Australian Sociological Association, 121
Australian Veterinary Association, 117
Australian Vice-Chancellors' Committee, 117
Australian War Memorial, 126
Austria Esperantista Federacio, 162
Auswärtiges Amt, Referat Bibliothek und Informationsvermittlung, Bonn, 803

Authority for the Protection and Management of Angkor and the Region of Siem Reap (APSARA), 317
Automotive Research Association of India, 979
Autonomous University of Baja California Sur, 1425
Avadh University, 987
Ave Maria College, Ypsilanti, 2504
Ave Maria School of Law, Ann Arbor, 2504
Avele College, Apia, 1804
Avele College Library, Apia, 1804
Averett University, 2709
Avila College, Kansas City, Missouri, 2544
Avinashilingam Institute for Home Science and Higher Education for Women, Coimbatore, 1034
Avokatska Komora Bosne i Hercegovine, 245
Awadhesh Pratap Singh University, 987
Awasa Agriculture Research Centre, Awasa, 676
Awkaf Supreme Council Library, Jerusalem, 1096
Ayal Bihari Vajpayee Indian Institute of Information Technology and Management, Gwalior, 1034
Ayala Museum, Makati City, 1603
Ayasofya (Saint Sophia) Museum, Istanbul, 2061
Aydın Müzesi, 2060
Ayuthaya Agricultural College, 2046
Azabu University, 1270
Azerbaijan Agricultural Institute, 187
Azerbaijan Architecture and Construction University, 186
Azerbaijan Energy Research Institute, 185
Azerbaijan Institute of Orthopaedics and Traumatology, 185
Azerbaijan Institute of Tuberculosis and Pulmonology, 185
Azerbaijan Medical Association, 185
Azerbaijan Medical University, 186
Azerbaijan National Academy of Sciences, 184
Azerbaijan National Aerospace Agency, 185
Azerbaijan Petroleum Machinery Research and Design Institute (Azinmash), 185
Azerbaijan Research Institute of Haematology and Blood Transfusion, 185
Azerbaijan Research Institute of Ophthalmology, 185
Azerbaijan Scientific and Technical Library, 185
Azerbaijan Scientific Gas Research and Projects Institute, Baku, 185
Azerbaijan State Academy for Physical Training and Sports, 187
Azerbaijan State Economic University, 186
Azerbaijan State Marine Academy, 187
Azerbaijan State Museum of Art, 185
Azerbaijan State Oil Academy, 187
Azerbaijan State Pedagogical University 'Nasreddin Tusi', 186
Azerbaijan State University of Culture and Fine Arts, 186
Azerbaijan State University of Languages, 186
Azerbaijan Technical University, 186
Azerbaijan Technological University, 187
Azov-Black Sea Institute of Agricultural Mechanization, 1795
Azusa Pacific University, 2343

B

B. M. Institute of Mental Health, Ahmedabad, 976
Baba Farid University of Health Sciences, Faridkot, 987
Babasaheb Bhimrao Ambedkar University, Lucknow, 987
Babcock University, Ikeja, 1539
Babraham Institute, Cambridge, 2145
Babson College, Wellesley, 2480

British Council, Moscow, 1728
British Council, Muscat, 1561
British Council, Nairobi, 1310
British Council, New Delhi, 969
British Council, Nicosia, 604
British Council, Oslo, 1544
British Council, Ottawa, 325
British Council, Paris, 708
British Council, Port-of-Spain, 2051
British Council, Prague, 608
British Council, Pretoria, 1863
British Council, Rabat, 1457
British Council, Riga, 1361
British Council, Riyadh, 1807
British Council, Rome, 1123
British Council, Sana'a, 2782
British Council, Santiago, Chile, 411
British Council, Sarajevo, 245
British Council, Seoul, 1322
British Council, Seychelles, 1833
British Council, Singapore, 1836
British Council, Skopje, 1386
British Council, Sofia, 298
British Council, Stockholm, 1970
British Council, Sydney, 119
British Council, Ta' Xbiex, 1407
British Council, Taipei, 552
British Council, Tajikistan, 2024
British Council, Tallinn, 672
British Council, Tashkent, 2747
British Council, Tbilsi, 780
British Council, Tehran, 1060
British Council, Tel Aviv, 1093
British Council, Tirana, 75
British Council, Tokyo, 1174
British Council, Tripoli, 1372
British Council, Tunis, 2053
British Council, Vienna, 162
British Council, Vilnius, 1376
British Council, Warsaw, 1622
British Council, Washington, DC, 2291
British Council, Wellington, 1502
British Council, Windhoek, 1469
British Council, Yangon, 1465
British Council, Yaoundé, 319
British Council, Yerevan, 112
British Council, Zagreb, 592
British Cryoengineering Society, 2140
British Dental Association, 2135
British Dietetic Association, 2135
British Ecological Society, 2138
British Educational Communications
  and Technology Agency (Becta),
  2123
British Educational Management and
  Administration Society, 2129
British Empire and Commonwealth
  Museum, 2170
British Film Institute, 2129
British Film Institute (BFI), National
  Film and Television Archive and
  National Library, London, 2159
British Geological Survey, 2150
British Geological Survey Library, 2158
British Geological Survey London
  Information Office, 2160
British Geriatrics Society, 2135
British Horological Institute, 2140
British Institute at Ankara, 2058
British Institute in Eastern Africa,
  Nairobi, 1311
British Institute of Florence, 1129
British Institute of International and
  Comparative Law, 2127
British Institute of Persian Studies,
  Tehran, 1060
British Institute of Professional
  Photography, Ware, 2130
British Institute of Radiology, 2135
British Interplanetary Society, 2140
British Library, 2160
British Library, Chandigarh, 980
British Library, Ljubljana, 1857
British Library of Political and
  Economic Science, 2160
British Library, Thiruvananthapuram,
  981
British Lichen Society, 2138
British Masonry Society, 2142
British Medical Association, 2135
British Medical Association Library,
  2160
British Museum, 2174
British Mycological Society, 2138

British Nuclear Energy Society, 2140
British Numismatic Society, 2131
British Nutrition Foundation, 2135
British Ornithologists' Union, 2138
British Orthodontic Society, 2135
British Orthopaedic Association, 2135
British Pharmacological Society, 2135
British Postal Museum and Archive,
  London, 2174
British Psycho-Analytical Society, 2135
British Psychological Society, 2141
British Records Association, 2131
British School at Athens, 922
British School at Rome, 1130
British School of Archaeology in Iraq,
  1075
British Society for Middle Eastern
  Studies, 2141
British Society for Plant Pathology,
  2138
British Society for Research on Ageing,
  2135
British Society for Rheumatology, 2135
British Society for the History of
  Mathematics, 2139
British Society for the History of
  Science, 2137
British Society of Aesthetics, 2141
British Society of Animal Science, 2125
British Society of Gastroenterology,
  2135
British Society of Painters, Ilkley, 2130
British Society of Rheology, 2142
British Society of Soil Science, 2125
British Sociological Association, 2141
British Textile Technology Group
  (BTTG), 2152
British Trust for Ornithology, 2138
British Veterinary Association, 2125
British Watercolour Society, 2130
Brlić House (Ivana Brlić-Mažuranić
  Memorial), Slavonski Brod, 594
Brno University of Technology, 624
Broadcast Research and Application
  Center, Ho Chi Minh City, 2773
Brock University, St Catharines,
  Ontario, 340
Bromley Public Libraries, 2160
Brontë Society, Haworth, 2134
Brookhaven National Laboratory, Long
  Island, 2307
Brookings Institution, Washington,
  2301
Brooklands Museum, Weybridge, 2179
Brooklyn Botanic Garden, 2324
Brooklyn Children's Museum, 2324
Brooklyn College, New York, 2572
Brooklyn Historical Society, 2290
Brooklyn Law School, 2571
Brooklyn Museum of Art, 2324
Brooklyn Public Library, 2314
Brooks Institute of Photography, Santa
  Barbara, 2343
Broward County Division of Libraries,
  2310
Brown University Library, Providence,
  2316
Brown University, Providence, 2671
Brücke-Museum, Berlin, 811
Brüder Grimm-Museum Kassel, 816
Bruggemuseum–Archeologie, Bruges,
  222
Bruggemuseum–Gruuthuse, 222
Brunei Agricultural Research Centre,
  Department of Agriculture, Brunei,
  296
Brunei History Centre, 296
Brunei Museum, 296
Brunel University, 2187
Bryansk State Agricultural Academy,
  1792
Bryansk State Museum of Soviet Fine
  Arts, 1755
Bryansk State Technical University,
  1781
Bryansk State University, 1763
Bryansk Technological Institute, 1796
Bryant College, Smithfield, Rhode
  Island, 2671
Bryn Athyn College of the New Church,
  2644
Bryn Mawr College, 2644
BSI Group (British Standards
  Institution), 2142

Bu-Ali Sina University, Hamadan, 1063
Büchereien Wien, 168
Buckinghamshire Chilterns University
  College, High Wycombe, 2270
Buckinghamshire County Library, 2153
Bucknell University, Lewisburg, 2644
Budapest Főváros Levéltára, 942
Budapest University of Technology and
  Economics, 949
Budapesti Corvinus Egyetem, 948
Budapesti Corvinus Egyetem Entz
  Ferenc Könyvtár és Levéltár,
  Budapest, 942
Budapesti Corvinus Egyetem Központi
  Könyvtár, 942
Budapesti Gazdasági Főiskola
  Kereskedelmi, Vendéglátóipari és
  Idegenforgalmi Főiskolai Kar,
  Budapest, 962
Budapesti Műszaki És
  Gazdaságtudományi Egyetem, 949
Budapesti Műszaki és
  Gazdaságtudományi Egyetem
  Országos Műszaki Információs
  Központ és Könyvtár (BME
  OMIKK), 942
Budapesti Műszaki Főiskola, 962
Budapesti Tanárképző Intézet, 953
Budapesti Történeti Múzeum, 944
Budavári Mátyás-templom
  Egyházmüvészeti Gyüjteménye,
  Budapest, 944
Buddhist Academy of Ceylon, 1954
Buddhist Association, Phnom-Penh, 317
Buddhist Research Centre, Bangkok,
  2032
Budnikov, P. P., All-Russia Research
  Institute of Construction Materials
  and Structures, Moscow, 1746
Buena Vista University, Storm Lake,
  2453
Buffalo and Erie County Public Library,
  2314
Buffalo City Municipal Library Service,
  1867
Buffalo Museum of Science, 2324
Buffalo Nations Museum, Banff, 333
Buffalo Society of Natural Sciences,
  2294
Builders' Association, Hanoi, 2771
Building and Road Research Institute,
  Kumasi, 905
Building Institute, Ulan Bator, 1450
Building Research Board, Washington,
  2307
Building Research Centre, Jadiriya,
  1074
Building Research Establishment Ltd,
  Watford, 2152
Building Research Institute, Tsukuba,
  1182
Bukhara Scientific Centre, 2747
Bukhara State Medical Institute, 2751
Bukhara State University, 2749
Bukhara Technological Institute of Food
  and Light Industry, 2751
Bukkyo University, 1270
Bukovinian State Medical University,
  Chernivtsi, 2111
Bukura Agricultural College, 1316
Bulacan State University, Malolos, 1606
Bulawayo Polytechnic, 2791
Bulawayo Public Library, Bulawayo,
  2789
Bulgarian Academy of Sciences, 298
Bulgarian Association of Criminology,
  298
Bulgarian Association of International
  Law, 298
Bulgarian Astronautical Society, 299
Bulgarian Botanical Society, 299
Bulgarian Geographical Society, 298
Bulgarian Geological Society, 299
Bulgarian Pedagogical Society, 299
Bulgarian Philologists' Society, 298
Bulgarian Philosophical Association,
  299
Bulgarian Society of Natural History,
  299
Bulgarian Society of Neurosciences, 299
Bulgarian Society of Parasitology, 299
Bulgarian Society of Sports Medicine
  and Kinesitherapy, Sofia, 299
Bulgarian Sociological Association, 299

Bulgarian Translators' Union, 298
Buma Bibliotheek, Leeuwarden, 1482
Búnadarskólinn á Hólum i Hjaltadal,
  966
Bund-Länder-Kommission für
  Bildungsplanung und
  Forschungsförderung, Bonn, 785
Bund Schweizer Architekten (BSA),
  1996
Bunda College of Agriculture, 1392
Bundelkhand University, 990
Bundesamt für Meteorologie und
  Klimatologie (MeteoSchweiz), 1999
Bundesamt für Seeschiffahrt und
  Hydrographie, Hamburg, 800
Bundesamt und Forschungszentrum für
  Landwirtschaft, Wien, 164
Bundesamt und Forschungszentrum für
  Wald, Vienna, 164
Bundesamts für Bauwesen und
  Raumordnung, Wissenschaftliche
  Bibliothek, Bad Godesberg, 804
Bundesanstalt für Agrarwirtschaft,
  Vienna, 164
Bundesanstalt für Alpenländische
  Landwirtschaft, Gumpenstein, 164
Bundesanstalt für Geowissenschaften
  und Rohstoffe (BGR), Hanover, 800
Bundesanstalt für Materialforschung
  und -prüfung, Berlin, 802
Bundesarchiv, Koblenz, 807
Bundesdenkmalamt, Vienna, 161
Bundesforschungsanstalt für
  Ernährung und Lebensmittel,
  Karlsruhe, 802
Bundesforschungsanstalt für Fischerei,
  Hamburg, 796
Bundesforschungsanstalt für
  Landwirtschaft (FAL),
  Braunschweig, 796
Bundesinstitut für
  Bevölkerungsforschung,
  Wiesbaden, 801
Bundesstaatliche Paedagogische
  Bibliothek beim Landesschulrat für
  Niederösterreich, 168
Bündner Kunstmuseum, Chur, 2003
Buniatian, H., Institute of
  Biochemistry, 113
Bunin Museum, Orel, 1757
Bunkyo University, Tokyo, 1188
Burapha University, Muang Chonburi,
  2034
Burden Neurological Institute, Bristol,
  2148
Burdenko Neurosurgical Institute,
  Moscow, 1736
Bureau Canadien de l'Education
  Internationale, 323
Bureau de Recherches et de
  Participations Minières (BRPM),
  Rabat, 1458
Bureau de Recherches Géologiques et
  Minières (BRGM), Abidjan, 589
Bureau de Recherches Géologiques et
  Minières (BRGM), Antananarivo,
  1389
Bureau de Recherches Géologiques et
  Minières (BRGM), Dakar, 1813
Bureau de Recherches Géologiques et
  Minières (BRGM), Jeddah, 1807
Bureau de Recherches Géologiques et
  Minières (BRGM), Kinshasa, 579
Bureau de Recherches Géologiques et
  Minières (BRGM), Libreville, 777
Bureau de Recherches Géologiques et
  Minières (BRGM), Niamey, 1516
Bureau de Recherches Géologiques et
  Minières (BRGM), Orléans, 720
Bureau de Recherches Géologiques et
  Minières (BRGM), Ouagadougou,
  314
Bureau des Longitudes, Paris, 720
Bureau for Nature Conservation,
  Zagreb, 593
Bureau International des Poids et
  Mesures, 69
Bureau National d'Ethnologie, Port-au-
  Prince, 932
Bureau of Indian Standards (BIS), 980
Bureau of Plant Industry, Manila, 1602
Bureau of the Census Library,
  Washington, 2309

Bureau of University and Higher Education, Minorities Education, Book Promotion and Copyrights, Ministry of Human Resources Development, New Delhi, 967

Burenie Scientific and Production Co., Krasnodar, 1746

Burg Giebichenstein Hochschule für Kunst und Design Halle, 902

Burgas Prof. Assen Zlatarov University, 305

Burgaski Svoboden Universitet, 305

Burgenländische Landesbibliothek, 167

Burgenländisches Landesarchiv, 167

Burgenländisches Landesmuseum, 169

Burgerbibliothek Bern, 2001

Burlington College, 2708

Burns Cottage and Museum, Ayr, 2169

Burrell Collection, Glasgow, 2171

Bursa Arkeoloji Müzesi, 2060

Bursa Türk ve Islâm Eserleri Müzesi, 2061

Buryat State Agricultural Academy, 1792

Buryat State University, Ulan-Ude, 1763

Busra Museum, 2022

Butler University, 2443

Butsuri Tansa Gakkai, Tokyo, 1177

Bvumbwe Agricultural Research Station, 1391

Býarbókasavnid, Tórshavn, 642

Bydgoskie Towarzystwo Naukowe, 1620

Byggecentrum, Hoersholm, 630

Byrd Polar Research Center, Columbus, 2305

Byurakan Astrophysical Observatory, 113

Byzantine and Christian Museum, Athens, 913

C

C. & O. Vogt-Institut für Hirnforschung, Universität Düsseldorf, 799

C. G. Jung Institute Zürich, 2019

Ca' Rezzonico, Venice, 1144

CAB International (CABI), 41

Cabinet des Estampes, Geneva, 2003

Cabinet Office Library, Kampala, 2095

Cabinet War Rooms, London, 2175

Cabrini College, Radnor, Pennsylvania, 2644

Caerphilly Libraries, 2167

Çağ Üniversitesi, Yenice/Mercin, 2067

Cagayan de Oro City Public Library, 1603

Cagayan State University, 1606

CAIJ – Montréal, 332

Cairo Geological Museum, 661

Cairo Museum of Hygiene, 661

Cairo Odontological Society, 658

Cairo Polytechnic Institute, 666

Cairo University, 663

Cairo University Library, 660

Calcutta Mathematical Society, 971

Caldwell College, 2561

Calgary Public Library, 329

Calico Museum of Textiles, Ahmedabad, 982

California Academy of Sciences, 2294

California Baptist University, 2343

California College of the Arts, 2344

California Historical Society, 2290

California Institute of Integral Studies, 2344

California Institute of Technology, 2344

California Institute of the Arts, 2345

California Library Association, 2286

California Lutheran University, 2345

California Maritime Academy, 2345

California Pacific Medical Center Research Institute, 2302

California Palace of the Legion of Honor, 2318

California Polytechnic State University, 2346

California School Library Association, 2286

California State Library, 2308

California State Polytechnic University, Pomona, 2346

California State University, Bakersfield, 2346

California State University, Chico, 2346

California State University, Dominguez Hills, 2346

California State University, East Bay, 2347

California State University, Fresno, 2346

California State University, Fullerton, 2347

California State University, Long Beach, 2347

California State University, Los Angeles, 2347

California State University, Monterey Bay, 2347

California State University, Northridge, 2347

California State University, Sacramento, 2347

California State University, San Bernardino, 2348

California State University, San Marcos, 2348

California State University, Stanislaus, 2348

California State University System, 2346

California University of Pennsylvania, Pennsylvania, 2652

California Western School of Law, 2348

Calumet College of St Joseph, Whiting, Indiana, 2443

Calvary Bible College and Theological Seminary, Kansas City, 2544

Calvin College, Grand Rapids, 2505

Calvin Theological Seminary, Grand Rapids, 2505

Cama, K. R., Oriental Institute, Mumbai, 976

Cámara de Comercio y Producción de Santo Domingo, Centro de Información y Documentación Comercial, Santo Domingo, 646

Cambodia Development Resource Institute (CDRI), 317

Cambodian Institute for Co-operation and Peace, 317

Cambodian Institute of Human Rights, 317

Cambodian Society of Agriculture, 317

Camborne School of Mines, University of Exeter, 2273

Cambrian Archaeological Association, 2131

Cambridge Bibliographical Society, 2127

Cambridge College, 2482

Cambridge Philosophical Society, 2137

Cambridge University Botanic Garden, 2150

Cambridge University Institute of Astronomy, 2151

Cambridge University Library, 2154

Cambridgeshire Libraries and Information Service, 2155

Camden Leisure and Community Services (Libraries, Arts and Tourism), 2160

Campaign to Protect Rural England (CPRE), 2126

Campbell University, Buie's Creek, 2601

Campbellsville College, 2462

Campion College, Regina, 381

Campion Hall, Oxford, 2250

Campo Agrícola Experimental Río Bravo, 1417

Campo de Santana, Rio de Janeiro, 257

Canada Centre for Inland Waters, 329

Canada Council for the Arts, 324

Canada Institute for Scientific and Technical Information (CISTI), 331

Canada Science and Technology Museum Corporation, Ottawa, 334

Canadian Academy of Engineering, 327

Canadian Aeronautics and Space Institute, 327

Canadian Agriculture Library, Ottawa, 331

Canadian Association for Anatomy, Neurobiology and Cell Biology, 325

Canadian Association for Distance Education, Ottawa, 323

Canadian Association of African Studies, 327

Canadian Association of Geographers, 325

Canadian Association of Latin American and Caribbean Studies, 327

Canadian Association of Law Libraries, 324

Canadian Association of Optometrists, 325

Canadian Association of Physicists, 326

Canadian Authors Association, 325

Canadian Bar Association, 324

Canadian Bureau for International Education, Ottawa, 323

Canadian Centre for Architecture, 334

Canadian Council for International Co-operation, 324

Canadian Council of Professional Engineers, 327

Canadian Dental Association, 325

Canadian Economics Association, 324

Canadian Education and Training Accreditation Commission (CETAC), Toronto, 323

Canadian Education Association, 324

Canadian Electricity Association, 327

Canadian Federation for the Humanities and Social Sciences, 329

Canadian Film Institute, 325

Canadian Forest Service, 328

Canadian Forestry Association, 324

Canadian Historical Association, 325

Canadian Institute of Chartered Accountants, 324

Canadian Institute of International Affairs, 324

Canadian Institute of Mining, Metallurgy and Petroleum, 327

Canadian Institutes of Health Research, 328

Canadian Library Association, 324

Canadian Linguistic Association, 325

Canadian Lung Association, 326

Canadian Mathematical Society, 326

Canadian Medical Association, 326

Canadian Meteorological and Oceanographic Society, 327

Canadian Museum of Civilization, 335

Canadian Museum of Nature, 334

Canadian Museums Association, 324

Canadian Music Centre, 325

Canadian Paediatric Society, 326

Canadian Pharmacists Association, 326

Canadian Philosophical Association, 327

Canadian Physiological Society, 326

Canadian Phytopathological Society, 326

Canadian Political Science Association, 324

Canadian Postal Archives, 331

Canadian Psychiatric Association, 326

Canadian Psychological Association, 327

Canadian Public Health Association, 326

Canadian Society for Cellular and Molecular Biology, 326

Canadian Society for Immunology, 326

Canadian Society for Nutritional Sciences, 326

Canadian Society for the Study of Education, 324

Canadian Society of Animal Science, 324

Canadian Society of Biblical Studies, 327

Canadian Society of Biochemistry, Molecular and Cellular Biology, 327

Canadian Society of Landscape Architects, 324

Canadian Society of Microbiologists, 326

Canadian Society of Petroleum Geologists, 327

Canadian Veterinary Medical Association, 324

Çanakkale Onsekiz Mart Üniversitesi, 2067

Cancer Care Ontario, 328

Cancer Institute and Hospital, Beijing, 431

Cancer Institute, Japanese Foundation for Cancer Research, 1180

Cancer Research Institute, Bratislava, 1843

Cancer Research Institute, Karachi, 1566

Cancer Research UK, 2148

Cancer Research UK Beatson Laboratories, 2148

Cancer Society of Finland, 683

Canisius College, Buffalo, 2571

Çankaya Üniversitesi, 2068

Canning House Library, London, 2160

Canning Research Institute, Plovdiv, 299

Canterbury and York Society, 2131

Canterbury Cathedral Archives and Library, 2155

Canterbury Christ Church University, 2193

Canterbury Medical Research Foundation, 1503

Canterbury Museum, Christchurch, 1505

Cantho University, 2775

CAP Art Center and President Osmeña Memorabilia, Cebu City, 1603

Cape Breton University, Sydney, 344

Cape Coast Castle Museum, 906

Cape Peninsula University of Technology, 1870

Cape Town City Libraries, 1867

Capital Library, Beijing, 434

Capital Normal University, Beijing, 445

Capital University, Columbus, 2618

Capital University of Medical Sciences, Beijing, 446

Capitol College, 2471

Capitolo Colombiano de las Federaciones Latinoamericanas de Asociaciones de Cancer, 562

Cappella Brancacci, 1139

Cappella degli Scrovegni, Padua, 1142

Cardiff Central Library and County Library Headquarters, 2156

Cardiff County Libraries, 2156

Cardiff University, Cardiff, 2193

Cardiff University Library Service, 2156

Cardinal Stefan Wyszyński University in Warsaw, 1654

Cardinal Stritch University, 2728

Cardiological Research Centre, Moscow, 1736

Cardiovascular Diseases Institute, Beijing, 431

Carey Hall and Carey Theological College, Vancouver, 340

Caribbean Agricultural Research and Development Institute (CARDI), 2051

Caribbean and Latin American Studies Library, San Juan, 2740

Caribbean Conservation Association, St Michael, 204

Caribbean Food and Nutrition Institute (CFNI), Kingston, 1168

Caribbean Law Institute Centre, 205

Caribbean Network of Educational Innovation for Development (CARNEID), 50

Caribbean Regional Council for Adult Education, 51

Carl Nielsen Museet, 634

Carl V. Ossietzky Universität Oldenburg, 885

Carleton College, 2526

Carleton University, 344

Carleton University Library, 331

Carlow College, 2644

Carlsberg Laboratorium, 630

Carlyle's House, Chelsea, 2174

CARMABI Foundation, 1499

Carmarthenshire County Library, 2156

Carmarthenshire County Museum, 2170

Carnegie Corporation of New York, 2288

Carnegie Endowment for International Peace, Washington, 2288

Carnegie Institution of Washington, 2303

Carnegie Library, Curepipe, 1412

Carnegie Library of Pittsburgh, 2316
Carnegie Mellon University, 2644
Carnegie Public Library, San Juan, 2740
Carnegie Science Center, 2326
Carré d'Art Bibliothèque, Nîmes, 724
Carrie Bow Marine Field Station – Caribbean Coral Reef Ecosystems (CCRE), 236
Carroll College, Helena, 2553
Carroll College, Waukesha, 2728
Carson-newman College, 2677
Carter Observatory, Wellington, 1503
Casa de Cervantes, Valladolid, 1901
Casa de la Cultura de la Costa, Bogotá, 561
Casa de la Cultura Ecuatoriana 'Benjamín Carrión', Quito, 650
Casa de la Independencia, Asunción, 1588
Casa de La Libertad, Sucre, 240
Casa de las Américas, Havana, 598
Casa de Velázquez, 1887
Casa del Libro, San Juan, 2740
Casa di Carlo Goldoni, Venice, 1145
Casa dos Patudos—Museu de Alpiarça, Alpiarça, 1679
Casa-Fuerte de Ponce de León, 647
Casa Gorordo Museum, Cebu City, 1603
Casa-Museo 'Jorge Eliécer Gaitán', Bogotá, 564
Casa Museo Quinta de Bolívar, Bogotá, 564
Casa Museu Teixeira Lopes, Vila Nova de Gaia, 1682
Casa Natal del Libertador Simón Bolívar, Caracas, 2764
Casa Pairal, Musée Catalan des Arts et Traditions Populaires, Perpignan, 732
Casa Taller José Clemente Orozco, 1420
Case Western Reserve University, 2618
Case Western Reserve University Library, 2315
Caspian Research Institute for Arid Arable Farming, Astrakhan, 1732
Castello D'Albertis, Genoa, 1140
Castello del Buonconsiglio–Monumenti e Collezioni Provinciali, Trento, 1144
Castello di San Giusto e Civico Museo del Castello, Lapidario Tergestino, Trieste, 1144
Castillo de la Real Fuerza de la Havana, 601
Castleton State College, 2708
Catalyst—Science Discovery Centre, Widnes, 2179
Catawba College, 2601
Catholic Library Association, Pittsfield, 2286
Catholic Record Society, London, 2131
Catholic Theological Union, Chicago, 2425
Catholic University of America, 2397
Catholic University of Brussels, 225
Catholic University of Chile, 420
Catholic University of Eastern Africa, 1312
Catholic University of Korea, 1323
Catholic University of Leuven, 228
Catholic University of Louvain, 229
Catholic University of Taegu-Hyosung, 1324
Catholic University of the Sacred Heart, 1164
Cato Manor Heritage Centre, Durban, 1869
Cavite State University, Indang, 1607
Cawthron Institute, Nelson, 1503
Cayey University College, 2741
Cazenovia College, 2571
Cebu City Public Library, 1603
Cebu Doctors' University College of Medicine, 1619
Cebu Normal University, Cebu City, 1607
Cedar Crest College, 2647
Cedarville University, 2621
Cédias—Musée Social, Paris, 726
Celal Bayer Üniversitesi, 2068
Cement och Betong Institutet, Stockholm, 1972
Cenacolo Triestino, 1121

CENRADERU—IRCT, Mahajanga, 1388
Centenary College, Hackettstown, 2561
Centenary College of Louisiana, 2465
Centennial University, 2090
Center for Advanced Study in the Behavioral Sciences, Stanford, 2306
Center for Art and Public Life, 2344
Center for Comparative and International Studies (CIS) Zürich, 2000
Center for Creative Photography, Tucson, 2289
Center for Economic Research, Bishkek, 1356
Center for Finance Research, 1297
Center for International Forestry Research (CIFOR), Sindangbarang, 41
Center for International Study, 2588
Center for Jewish History, New York, 2314
Center for Professional Legal Education and Research, 1297
Center for Quality Assurance in International Education, Alexandria, 2282
Center for Reformation Research, St Louis, 2301
Center for Social Development, Phnom-Penh, 317
Center for Strategic and International Studies (CSIS), 2301
Center for Teaching Excellence, 2588
Center for the Study of Aging and Human Development, Durham, NC, 2293
Center for the Study of Democratic Institutions, Los Angeles, 2301
Center of Experimental Seismology, Central Station, Chişinău, 1445
Center of Medical Genetics, Yerevan, 113
Center of Traumatology, Orthopaedics, Burns and Radiology, 113
Centraal Bureau voor de Statistiek, Voorburg, 1479
Centraal Bureau voor Genealogie, the Hague, 1476
Centraal Museum Utrecht, 1486
Centraalbureau voor Schimmelcultures, Utrecht, 1480
Central A. A. Bakhrushin State Theatrical Museum, 1755
Central Academy of Arts and Design, Beijing, 447
Central Academy of Fine Arts, Beijing, 448
Central Aerological Observatory, Moscow, 1742
Central Agricultural Library, Sofia, 302
Central Agricultural University, Imphal, 993
Central Agriculture Research Institute, Suakoko, 1370
Central American Technical Institute, Santa Tecla, 669
Central Applications Office, Galway, 1080
Central Archaeological Library, New Delhi, 980
Central Archives for the History of the Jewish People, Jerusalem, 1096
Central Archives of China, 434
Central Arid Zone Research Institute, Jodhpur, 974
Central Asian Plague Prevention Research Institute, Almaty, 1304
Central Automobile and Automobile Engine Scientific Research Institute, Moscow, 1746
Central Baptist College, 2340
Central Bible College, Springfield, 2544
Central Biomedical Library, Yangon, 1465
Central Boiler and Turbine Institute, St Petersburg, 1746
Central Botanical Garden, Ashgabat, 2091
Central Botanical Garden, Minsk, 208
Central Botanical Gardens, Tbilisi, 781
Central Building Research Institute, Roorkee, 972
Central Catholic Library, Dublin, 1083

Central China Normal University, 448
Central China Teachers' University Library, 436
Central Christian College of the Bible, Moberly, 2545
Central College of Commerce, Glasgow, 2272
Central College, Pella, 2453
Central Connecticut State University, 2383
Central Conservatory of Music, Beijing, 450
Central Cotton Research Institute, Multan, 1565
Central Cotton Research Institute, Nawabshah, 1565
Central Council of Physical Recreation, London, 2136
Central Design and Research Institute of the Standard and Experimental Design of Livestock Units for the Production of Milk, Beef and Pork, Moscow, 1746
Central Diesels Research and Development Institute, St Petersburg, 1746
Central Documentation and Library of the Ministry of Information, Jakarta, 1044
Central Drug Research Institute, Lucknow, 972
Central Economics and Mathematics Institute, Moscow, 1733
Central Economics Research Institute, Moscow, 1733
Central Electrochemical Research Institute, Karaikudi, 972
Central Electronics Engineering Research Institute, Pilani, 972
Central Electronics Research Institute, Moscow, 1746
Central European University, 950
Central Fisheries Research Institute, Chilanga, 2784
Central Food Technological Research Institute, Mysore, 972
Central Forest Library, Peshawar, 1569
Central Fuel Research Institute, Dhanbad, 972
Central Geological Survey, Taipei, 553
Central Glass and Ceramic Research Institute, Kolkata, 972
Central Health Laboratories, Cairo, 659
Central Hindi Directorate, New Delhi, 969
Central Inland Capture Fisheries Research Institute, Barrackpore, 974
Central Institute for Leprosy Research, Jakarta, 1043
Central Institute for Medical Science Information, Hanoi, 2774
Central Institute for Research on Cotton Technology, Mumbai, 980
Central Institute of Advanced Qualification of Teachers, Dushanbe, 2025
Central Institute of Aviation Engines, Moscow, 1746
Central Institute of English and Foreign Languages, Hyderabad, 1034
Central Institute of Experimental Analysis, Pyongsong, 1319
Central Institute of Fisheries Education, Mumbai, 1035
Central Institute of Higher Tibetan Studies, Varanasi, 1035
Central Institute of Indian Languages, Mysore, 1039
Central Institute of Medicinal and Aromatic Plants, Lucknow, 972
Central Institute of Ophthalmology, Hanoi, 2772
Central Institute of Scientific and Technical Information, Hanoi, 2774
Central Institute of Technology, Upper Hutt, 1511
Central Institute of Traumatology and Orthopaedics, Moscow, 1736
Central Jalma Institute for Leprosy, Agra, 976
Central Kazakhstan Scientific and Research Institute of Agriculture, 1303

Central Laboratory for Agricultural Pesticides, Giza, 659
Central Laboratory for Food and Feed, Giza, 659
Central Laboratory for Statistical Design and Analysis, Giza, 659
Central Laboratory of Applied Physics, Plovdiv, 302
Central Laboratory of Electrochemical Power Sources, Sofia, 301
Central Laboratory of General Ecology, Sofia, 301
Central Laboratory of Geodesy, Sofia, 301
Central Laboratory of Mechatronics and Instrumentation, Sofia, 302
Central Laboratory of Mineralogy and Crystallography, Sofia, 302
Central Laboratory of Molecular Biology, Preparatory Office, Taipei, 553
Central Laboratory of Optical Storage and the Processing of Information, Sofia, 301
Central Laboratory of Photoprocesses, Sofia, 301
Central Laboratory of Physico-Chemical Mechanics, Sofia, 302
Central Laboratory of Seismic Mechanics and Earthquake Engineering, Sofia, 302
Central Laboratory of Socio-Economic Measurements, Moscow, 1733
Central Laboratory of Solar Energy and New Energy Sources, Sofia, 301
Central Leather Research Institute, Chennai, 972
Central Leprosy Teaching and Research Institute, Chingalpattu, 976
Central Library and Documentation Centre of Shahid Beheshti University, 1061
Central Library and Documentation Centre of Tehran University, 1061
Central Library, Bahawalpur, 1568
Central Library, Baroda, 980
Central Library for Science and Technology, Hanoi, 2774
Central Library for the Blind, Moscow, 1752
Central Library of Rochester and Monroe County, 2314
Central Library of St Lucia, 1802
Central Library of Sofia, 302
Central Library of the Academy of Medical Sciences, Moscow, 1752
Central Library of the Agricultural Research Centre, Giza, 660
Central Library of the Azerbaijan Academy of Sciences, 185
Central Library of the Bulgarian Academy of Sciences, Sofia, 303
Central Library of the European Commission, Brussels, 220
Central Library of the former Kazakh Academy of Sciences, 1305
Central Library of the Georgian Academy of Sciences, 782
Central Library of the National Academy of Sciences of the Kyrgyz Republic, 1357
Central Library of Trinidad and Tobago, 2051
Central Luzon State University, 1607
Central Marine Research and Design Institute Ltd (CNIIMF), St Petersburg, 1746
Central Mechanical Engineering Research Institute, Durgapur, 972
Central Medical Library, Bowshar, 1561
Central Medical Library, Lagos, 1522
Central Medical Library, Sofia, 303
Central Medical Veterinary Research Institute, Sofia, 299
Central Metallurgical Research and Development Institute, Cairo, 660
Central Methodist University, Fayette, 2545
Central Michigan University, 2505
Central Mindanao University, 1607
Central Mining Research Institute, Dhanbad, 973
Central Missouri State University, 2545
Central Museum, Nagpur, 983

Centre de Recherches Océanographiques et des Pêches (CROP), Algiers, 80

Centre de Recherches sur les Ressources Biologiques Terrestres (CRBT), Algiers, 80

Centre de Recherches Zootechniques de Dahra-Djoloff, 1812

Centre de Recherches Zootechniques de Kolda, 1812

Centre de Sélection Bovine de Songa, 1799

Centre de Trobada de les Cultures Pirenenques, Andorra la Vella, 85

Centre des Archives Contemporaines, Fontainebleau, 725

Centre des Archives d'Outre-Mer, Aix-en-Provence, 725

Centre des Archives du Monde du Travail, Roubaix, 725

Centre des Monuments Nationaux (Monum), Paris, 730

Centre des Sciences Humaines, Abidjan, 589

Centre du Riz pour l'Afrique (ADRAO), 41

Centre Européen d'Education Permanente (CEDEP), Fontainebleau, 769

Centre Européen de Recherches sur les Congrégations et Ordres Religieux (CERCOR), Saint-Etienne, 722

Centre Européen pour l'Enseignement Supérieur (CEPES), Bucharest, 54

Centre for Adult Education (CAE), Melbourne, 117

Centre for Agricultural Research in Suriname, 1965

Centre for Allergy Research and Environmental Health, London, 2232

Centre for Applied Microbiology and Research, Salisbury, 2148

Centre for Applied Research in Agricultural Engineering, Ho Chi Minh City, 2772

Centre for Arab Unity Studies, Beirut, 1364

Centre for Architectural Studies, Sofia, 300

Centre for Asia Minor Studies, Athens, 911

Centre for Asian Documentation, Kolkata, 981

Centre for Atmospheric Science, Cambridge, 2150

Centre for Aviation and Aerospace, Hsinchu, 554

Centre for Basic Research, Kampala, 2094

Centre for Biochemicals Technology, Delhi, 973

Centre for Biomedical Engineering, Sofia, 301

Centre for Cellular and Molecular Biology, Hyderabad, 973

Centre for Defence Studies, London, 2224

Centre for Democracy and Development, London and Abuja, 47

Centre for Development Information, Colombo, 1954

Centre for Documentation and Information, Chinese Academy of Social Sciences, Beijing, 434

Centre for Documentation and Research, Abu Dhabi, 2120

Centre for Dungan Studies, Bishkek, 1357

Centre for Ecological-Noosphere Studies, Yerevan, 113

Centre for Ecology and Hydrology, Crowmarsh Gifford, 2150

Centre for Educational and Psychological Research, Baghdad, 1075

Centre for European Policy Studies (CEPS), Brussels, 219

Centre for European Studies, Sofia, 303

Centre for Gender and Development Studies, 205

Centre for Global Economic, Social, Technological Research in Agriculture and Agroindustry, 1426

Centre for Health Improvement and Leadership in Lincoln (CHILL), 2217

Centre for Industrial Safety and Health Technology, Hsinchu, 554

Centre for Industrial Technology Information Services, Moratuwa, 1955

Centre for International Services, 205

Centre for Management Development, 205

Centre for Management Development, Ikeja, 1520

Centre for Manx Studies, University of Liverpool, Douglas, 2279

Centre for Measurement Standards, Hsinchu, 554

Centre for Mechanisms of Human Toxicity, Leicester, 2148

Centre for Medical Education (CME), Dhaka, 192

Centre for National Culture, Accra, 904

Centre for North-East Asian Studies, Ulan Bator, 1450

Centre for Nuclear Medicine (CENUM), Lahore, 1567

Centre for Pathology and Pathobiology, Chişinău, 1445

Centre for Peace and Conflict Research of the University of Groningen, 1479

Centre for Philosophical Research, Sarajevo, 246

Centre for Pollution Control Technology, Hsinchu, 554

Centre for Population Biology, Ascot, 2150

Centre for Pre-School Education, Moscow, 1734

Centre for Regional Co-operation for Adult Education in Latin America and the Caribbean, 1414

Centre for Research in Islamic Education, Mecca, 1807

Centre for Research on Inland Aquatic Products, Tien Son District, 2772

Centre for Scientific and Technical Information and Documentation, Tiranë, 77

Centre for Scientific and Technical Information (at the National Centre for Agricultural Science), Sofia, 303

Centre for Scientific Information in the Social Sciences, Chişinău, 1445

Centre for Social Pedagogics, Moscow, 1734

Centre for Social Research, Bishkek, 1357

Centre for Socio-Economic Documentation and Publications, Tehran, 1061

Centre for South Asian Studies, Lahore, 1565

Centre for Strategic and International Studies, Jakarta, 1042

Centre for Studies and Research in International Law and International Relations, the Hague, 58

Centre for the Chemistry of Drugs—All-Russia Chemical and Pharmaceutical Research Institute, Moscow, 1736

Centre for the Environment, Fisheries and Aquaculture Science (CEFAS), Lowestoft, 2146

Centre for the Preservation of Historical Documentary Collections, Moscow, 1752

Centre for the Preservation of the Reserve Collection, Yalutorovsk, 1754

Centre for the Study of International Relations, Stockholm, 1969

Centre for the Study of Marketing Problems, Chişinău, 1445

Centre for the Study of Nationality Problems, Moscow, 1733

Centre Français de Droit Comparé, Paris, 763

Centre Historique des Archives Nationales, Paris, 725

Centre IFREMER de Brest, 721

Centre IFREMER de Nantes, 721

Centre IFREMER de Toulon, 721

Centre IFREMER Océanologique du Pacifique, 721

Centre International d'Etudes Monétaires et Bancaires, 48

Centre International d'Etudes Pédagogiques de Sèvres, 719

Centre International d'Etudes Romanes, Tournus, 707

Centre International de Formation de l'OIT, 47

Centre International de Hautes Etudes Agronomiques Méditerranéennes, 42

Centre International de la Tapisserie Ancienne et Moderne, 44

Centre International de Recherche en Aménagement Linguistique, 329

Centre International de Recherche sur le Cancer, 62

Centre International de Recherches Médicales de Franceville, 777

Centre International des Civilisations Bantu, 47

Centre International du Film pour l'Enfance et la Jeunesse, 44

Centre International pour la Formation et les Echanges en Géosciences (CIFEG), Orléans, 721

Centre Interuniversitaire de Mécanique (UNIMECA), 734

Centre IRD de Bondy, 720

Centre IRD de Bretagne, 720

Centre Ivoirien de Recherches et d'Etudes Juridiques, 589

Centre Mondial de la Paix, des Libertés et des Droits de l'Homme, Verdun, 733

Centre National d'Astronomie, d'Astrophysique et de Géophysique (CNAAG), Algiers, 79

Centre National d'Education, Yaoundé, 320

Centre National d'Etudes Agronomiques des Régions Chaudes, Montpellier, 763

Centre National d'Etudes et de Recherches pour l'Aménagement du Territoire (CNERAT), Algiers, 79

Centre National d'Etudes Spatiales (CNES), Paris, 722

Centre National d'Hydrométéorologie, Bujumbura, 316

Centre National de Documentation et de Recherche en Pédagogie (CNDRP), Algiers, 79

Centre National de Documentation et de Recherche Scientifique (CNDRS), 578

Centre National de Documentation, Rabat, 1458

Centre National de Documentation Scientifique et Technique (CNDST), Dakar, 1813

Centre National de la Recherche Scientifique (CNRS), Paris, 711

Centre National de la Recherche Scientifique et Technologique, Bamako, 1405

Centre National de la Recherche Scientifique et Technologique (CENAREST), Libreville, 777

Centre National de la Recherche Scientifique et Technologique, Ouagadougou, 314

Centre National de l'Informatique, Tunis, 2054

Centre National de Littérature, Mersch, 1383

Centre National de Recherche Agronomique (CNRA), Côte d'Ivoire, 589

Centre National de Recherche Appliquée au Développement Rural (CENRADERU), Antananarivo, 1388

Centre National de Recherche sur les Zones Arides (CNRZA), Algiers, 79

Centre National de Recherches Agronomiques (CNRA), Bambey, 1812

Centre National de Recherches de Logique, Louvain-la-Neuve, 219

Centre National de Recherches et d'Application des Géosciences (CRAG), Algiers, 79

Centre National de Recherches Fruitières, Bamako, 1405

Centre National de Recherches Météorologiques, Toulouse, 721

Centre National de Recherches Préhistoriques Anthropologiques et Historiques, Algiers, 80

Centre National de Recherches Zootechniques, Bamako, 1405

Centre National de Traduction et de Terminologie Arabe (CNTTA), Algiers, 79

Centre National des Archives, Ouagadougou, 314

Centre National du Livre, Paris, 708

Centre National du Microfilm, St-Gilles-du-Gard, 725

Centre National pour la Recherche Scientifique et Technique, Rabat, 1458

Centre Océanologique du Pacifique, Taravao, 772

Centre of Documentation and Studies on Ancient Egypt, Cairo, 660

Centre of Excellence in Marine Biology, Karachi, 1566

Centre of International and European Economic Law, Thessaloniki, 910

Centre of Natural Sciences, Kabul, 73

Centre of Physiotherapy and Rehabilitation, Sofia, 301

Centre of Planning and Economic Research, Athens, 910

Centre of Seismology and Geomagnetism, Ulan Bator, 1450

Centre pour le Développement de l'Horticulture (CDH), Dakar, 1812

Centre pour l'Etude des Problèmes du Monde Musulman Contemporain, Brussels, 218

Centre Régional Africain de Technologie, 1813

Centre Régional de Recherche et de Documentation pour le Développement Culturel (CREDEC), Dakar, 1813

Centre Régional de Recherche et de Documentation sur les Traditions Orales et pour le Développement des Langues Africaines (CERDOTOLA), Yaoundé, 320

Centre Régional de Recherche Sud-Bénin, 237

Centre Saint-Augustin, Dakar, 2757

Centre Scientifique de Monaco, 1448

Centre Social et Éducatif, Bujumbura, 316

Centre Technique Forestier Tropical, Antananarivo, 1388

Centre Technique Forestier Tropical, Section Gabon, 777

Centre Territorial de Recherche et de Documentation Pédagogiques de Nouvelle-Calédonie, Nouméa, 774

Centre Universitaire d'Education et de Formation des Adultes (CUEFA), Saint-Martin-d'Hères, 762

Centre Universitaire de Recherches, d'Etudes et de Réalisations (CURER), Constantine, 80

Centres de Recherche Rizicole, Kankan, 1405

Centro Agronómico Tropical de Investigación y Enseñanza (CATIE), Turrialba, 584

Centro Amazónico de Antropología y Aplicación Práctica (CAAAP), Lima, 1591

Centro Aquicola do Rio Ave, Vila do Conde, 1677

Centro Argentino de Datos Oceanográficos (CEADO), 93

Centro Argentino de Espeleología, 92

Centro Argentino de Etnología Americana (CAEA), 93

Centro Argentino de Información Científica y Tecnológica (CAICYT), 96

Centro Argentino de Ingenieros, 92

Centro Argentino de Primates (CAPRIM), 93

Cotton Research Institute, Giza, 659
Cotton Research Institute, Kadoma, 2788
Council for Agricultural Science and Technology, Ames, 2285
Council for British Archaeology, 2131
Council for British Research in the Levant, Amman, 1299
Council for Cultural Co-operation, Strasbourg, 51
Council for Education in World Citizenship, London, 2129
Council for Environmental Education, Reading, 2137
Council for European Studies, New York, 2288
Council for Geoscience, Pretoria, 1866
Council for Higher Education Accreditation, Washington, 2281
Council for Higher Education, Jerusalem, 1093
Council for International Congresses of Entomology, 66
Council for International Organizations of Medical Sciences (CIOMS), 59
Council for Quality Assurance in General and Further Education and Training, Pretoria, 1862
Council for Scientific and Industrial Research (CSIR), Accra, 905
Council for Scientific and Industrial Research (CSIR) Information Services, Pretoria, 1868
Council for Scientific and Industrial Research (CSIR), Pretoria, 1865
Council for the Care of Churches, London, 2126
Council for the Central Laboratory of the Research Councils, Chilton, 2151
Council for the Curriculum, Examinations and Assessment, Belfast, 2123
Council for the Study of Productive Forces of Ukraine, 2100
Council of Academies of Engineering and Technological Sciences (CAETS), 56
Council of Agriculture (COA), Taipei, 553
Council of British Geography, 2131
Council of Ministers of Education, Canada/Conseil des Ministres de l'éducation (Canada) (CMEC), Toronto, 323
Council of Scientific and Industrial Research, New Delhi, 972
Council of State Governments, Lexington, 2288
Council on Foreign Relations, Inc., New York, 2288
Council on Higher Education, Pretoria, 1862
Council on International Educational Exchange, Portland, 2283
Council on Library and Information Resources, Washington, 2287
Counterpart International, Inc., Washington, 2301
Courtauld Institute Gallery, 2174
Courtauld Institute of Art, 2219
Couven-Museum, Aachen, 811
Covenant Theological Seminary, St Louis, 2545
Covenant University, Ogun State, 1539
Coventry Libraries and Information Services, 2156
Coventry University, 2197
CPA Grand Sud-Ouest, 770
CPA Lyon, 770
CPA Madrid, 770
CPA Méditerranée, 770
CPA Nord, 770
CPA Paris, 770
Cracow University of Technology, 1660
Crafts Council, London, 2143
Crafts Museum, New Delhi, 982
Cranbrook Academy of Art, 2505
Cranbrook Institute of Science, 2294
Cranfield University, 2197
Crawford College of Art and Design, 1090
Círculo de Bellas Artes, La Paz, 239

Creative New Zealand (Arts Council of New Zealand Toi Aotearoa), 1501
Creighton University, 2554
Crichton College, 2677
Crimean State Agrarian University, Simferopol, 2106
Crimean State Medical University 'S. I. Georgievsky', Simferopol, 2111
Criswell College, 2688
Critchlow Labour College, Georgetown, 931
Crnogorska akademija nauka i umjetnosti (CANU), 1455
Croatian Geographic Society, 592
Croatian Medical Association, 592
Croatian Pharmaceutical Society, 592
Cromer Museum, 2177
Crop Breeding Institute, Harare, 2788
Crop Cultivation Research Institute, Pyongyang, 1318
Crop Improvement Society of India, 968
Crop Science Research Institute, Sunchon, 1318
Crop Science Society of China, 426
Crop Science Society of the Philippines, 1601
Crop Science Society of Zimbabwe, 2787
Crops Research Institute, Kumasi, 905
Crossroads College, 2527
Crown College, 2527
Croydon Public Libraries, 2160
Crypta Balbi, 1143
Csiki Székely Múzeum, 1702
CSIRO–Australia Telescope National Facility, 123
CSL Ltd, Parkville, 122
Csontváry Múzeum, 947
Çukurova Üniversitesi, 2068
Culinary Institute of America, 2585
Cultural Center of the Philippines Museum, Pasay City, 1604
Culver-stockton College, 2545
Cumberland University, 2677
Cumbria County Library, 2156
Cuming Museum (Borough of Southwark), 2174
Curaçao Museum, 1499
Currier Museum of Art, 2324
Curry College, 2483
Curtin University of Technology, 131
Curtin University of Technology Library and Information Service, 126
Curtis Institute of Music, 2647
Cuttington University College, Monrovia, 1371
CWI – Centrum voor Wiskunde en Informatica, Amsterdam, 1480
Cyprus American Archaeological Research Institute, Nicosia, 605
Cyprus College, 606
Cyprus College of Art, 606
Cyprus Folk Art Museum, Nicosia, 605
Cyprus Forestry College, 606
Cyprus Geographical Association, 604
Cyprus Historical Museum and Archives, 605
Cyprus International Institute of Management, 606
Cyprus Library, Nicosia, 605
Cyprus Medieval Museum, 605
Cyprus Museum, 605
Cyprus Museum Library, 605
Cyprus Research Centre, 604
Cyprus Turkish National Library, Nicosia, 605
Cyrene Museum, 1372
Cyril and Methodius Research Centre, Sofia, 300
Czech Centre of International PEN, 608
Czech Technical University in Prague, 615
Czech University of Agriculture, Prague, 616
Częstochowa University of Technology, 1658

D

D-Day Museum and Overlord Embroidery, 2178
'D. Serikbaev' East Kazakhstan State Technical University, 1308

D'Youville College, 2585
Dachverband Wissenschaftlicher Gesellschaften der Agrar-, Forst-, Ernährungs-, Veterinär- und Umweltforschung eV, Frankfurt, 787
Daebul University, 1328
Daegu National University of Education, 1328
Daegu University, 1328
Daemen College, 2585
Dagestan Agricultural Research Institute, 1732
Dagestan Medical Research Centre, Makhachkala, 1736
Dagestan Museum of Fine Arts, 1755
Dagestan State Agricultural Academy, 1792
Dagestan State Medical Academy, 1794
Dagestan State Technical University, Makhachkala, 1782
Dagestan State University, 1764
Dagestan State University Library, 1752
Dagon University, 1466
Daheshite Museum and Library, Beirut, 1365
Daido Institute of Technology, Nagoya, 1264
Daigaku Kijun Kyokai, Tokyo, 1171
Daigoji Reihokan, 1185
Dairy and Meat Technology Institute, Kyiv, 2099
Dairy Industry Association of Australia Inc., 117
Dairy Research Institute, Vidin, 299
Daito Bunka University, 1271
DAI–Verband Deutscher Architekten- und Ingenieurvereine eV, 787
Dakota State University, 2676
Dakota Wesleyan University, 2676
Dakshina Bharat Hindi Prachar Sabha, Chennai, 1031
Dalat Centre for Scientific Research, 2772
Dalhousie University, 346
Dalhousie University Libraries, 331
Dalian City Library, 435
Dalian Institute of Chemical Physics, 432
Dalian Maritime University, 462
Dalian University of Technology (Dut), 462
Dallas Baptist University, 2688
Dallas Christian College, 2688
Dallas Historical Society, 2290
Dallas Museum of Art, 2327
Dallas Public Library, 2317
Dallas Theological Seminary, 2688
Damanhour Municipal Library, 661
Damat İbrahim Paşa Library, 2060
Damjanich János Múzeum, 948
Dana College, 2554
Dance Museum, Stockholm, 1074
Danchi-Nogaku Kenkyu-Kai, 1171
Daniel Webster College, 2557
Dankook University, 1328
Danmarks Biblioteksforening, 628
Danmarks Biblioteksskole, 640
Danmarks Biblioteksskole Aalborg, 640
Danmarks Biblioteksskoles Bibliotek, 632
Danmarks Designskole, Copenhagen, 640
Danmarks Evalueringsinstitut (EVA), Copenhagen, 628
Danmarks Farmaceutisk Universitet, 636
Danmarks Farmaceutiske Bibliotek, Københavns Universitet, 632
Danmarks Farmaceutiske Selskab, 629
Danmarks Fiskeriundersøgelser, 631
Danmarks Forskningsbiblioteksforening, 628
Danmarks Forskningspolitiske Råd, Copenhagen, 630
Danmarks Jordbrugs Forsknings, Tjele, 630
Danmarks Jurist- og Økonomforbund, 628
Danmarks Kunstbibliotek, Copenhagen, 632
Danmarks Meteorologiske Institut, 631
Danmarks Miljøundersøgelser, 636

Danmarks Miljøundersøgelser, Afdeling for Arktisk Miljø, 642
Danmarks Naturfredningsforening, 629
Danmarks og Grønlands Geologiske Undersøgelse, 631
Danmarks Paedagogiske Bibliotek, 632
Danmarks Pædagogiske Universitetsskole, 636
Danmarks Statistik, 631
Danmarks Statistiks Bibliotek og Information, 632
Danmarks Tekniske Museum, 634
Danmarks Tekniske Universitet, 636
Danmarks Tekniske Videncenter (DTV), 632
Danmarks Veterinaer- og Jordbrugsbibliotek, 632
Dansk Biblioteks Center AS, Ballerup, 628
Dansk Billedhuggersamfund, 628
Dansk Botanisk Forening, 629
Dansk Byplanlaboratorium, 628
Dansk Center for Internationale Studier og Menneskerettigheder, Copenhagen, 631
Dansk Farmaceutforening, 629
Dansk Forfatterforening, 629
Dansk Fysisk Selskab, 630
Dansk Geologisk Forening, 630
Dansk Husflidsselskab, 630
Dansk Institut for Internationale Studier (DIIS), 631
Dansk Komponistforening, 628
Dansk Korforening, 628
Dansk Landbrugsmuseum, Auning, 633
Dansk Medicinsk Selskab, 629
Dansk Naturhistorisk Forening, 629
Dansk Ornithologisk Forening, 630
Dansk Polarcenter, 642
Dansk Psykolog Forening, 630
Dansk Selskab for Europaforskning, 628
Dansk Selskab for Oldtids- og Middelalderforskning, 629
Dansk Skovforening, 628
Dansk Tandlægeforening, 629
Dansk Veterinærhistorisk Samfund, 628
Danske Bibelselskab, 630
Danske Filminstitut – Museum og Cinematek, Copenhagen, 633
Danske Historiske Forening, 629
Danske Komité for Historikernes Internationale Samarbejde, 631
Danske Kunsthåndværkeres, 628
Danske Sprog- og Litteraturselskab, 629
Danube University Krems/University of Continuing Education, 171
Danzan Ravjaa Museum, Dornogobi, 1451
Daqing Petroleum Institute, 462
Dar al-Kutub al-Wataniah, Homs, 2021
Dar es Salaam Institute of Technology, 2031
Daresbury Laboratory, 2151
Darjavna Muzikalna Akademija 'Prof. Pančo Vladigerov', 312
Darkhan Higher School, 1453
Darlington Libraries, 2156
Dartmouth College, 2557
Darwin College, Cambridge, 2192
Daugavpils University, Daugavpils, 1362
Davao City Library, 1603
Davao Museum, Davao City, 1603
Davee Center for Epidemiology and Endocrinology, 2321
Davenport University, 2505
David Davies Memorial Institute of International Studies, London, 2128
David Dunlap Observatory of the University of Toronto, 329
David Lubin Memorial Library, Food and Agriculture Organization (FAO) of the United Nations, Rome, 1137
David Rotlevi National Mediation Institute of the Israel Bar, 1092
Davidson College, 2601
Davis and Elkins College, 2726
Davis College, 2585
Davitashvili, L. Sh., Institute of Palaeobiology, 781

Ecole Supérieure d'Art Clermont Communauté, Clermont-Ferrand, 772

Ecole Supérieure d'Economie, d'Art et de Communication – Groupe E.A.C., Paris, 769

Ecole Supérieure d'Electricité, Gif sur Yvette, 771

Ecole Supérieure d'Informatique, Montreuil, 771

Ecole Supérieure d'Ingénieurs des Techniques de l'Industrie, Nancy, 762

Ecole Supérieure d'Ingénieurs en Electrotechnique et Electronique, Noisy-le-Grand, 771

Ecole Supérieure d'Ingénieurs en Systèmes Industriels Avancés Rhône-Alpes (ESISAR), 761

Ecole Supérieure d'Ingénieurs et de Techniciens pour l'Agriculture, Val de Reuil, 769

Ecole Supérieure d'Optique et Institut d'Optique, Orsay, 771

Ecole Supérieure de Chimie Organique et Minérale, Cergy, 767

Ecole Supérieure de Commerce d'Alger, 84

Ecole Supérieure de Commerce de Lille, 769

Ecole Supérieure de Commerce de Montpellier, 769

Ecole Supérieure de Commerce de Pau, 769

Ecole Supérieure de Commerce du Burundi, 316

Ecole Supérieure de Fonderie, Paris, 771

Ecole Supérieure de Journalisme, Paris, 770

Ecole Supérieure de l'Agro-Alimentaire, Casablanca, 1462

Ecole Supérieure de Management et l'Entreprise (ESPEME), Lille, 768

École Supérieure de Microbiologie et Sécurité Alimentaire de Brest (ESMISAB), 739

Ecole Supérieure de Physique et de Chimie Industrielles de la Ville de Paris, 767

Ecole Supérieure de Traducteurs, Interprètes, et de Cadres du Commerce Extérieur (ESTICE), Lille, 767

Ecole Supérieure des Beaux-Arts, Algiers, 84

Ecole Supérieure des Beaux-Arts, Geneva, 2020

Ecole Supérieure des Industries du Caoutchouc, Vitry-sur-Seine, 771

Ecole Supérieure des Industries du Vêtement, Paris, 771

Ecole Supérieure des Industries Textiles d'Epinal, 771

Ecole Supérieure des Sciences Commerciales d'Angers, Angers, 768

Ecole Supérieure des Sciences Economiques et Commerciales (ESSEC Business School – Paris), Cergy-Pontoise, 769

Ecole Supérieure des Techniques Aéronautiques et de Construction Automobile, Levallois-Perret, 771

Ecole Supérieure des Techniques Industrielles et des Textiles (ESTIT), Villeneuve d'Ascq, 767

Ecole Supérieure du Bois, Nantes, 771

Ecole Supérieure du Soudage et de ses Applications, Roissy, 771

Ecole Supérieure Interafricaine de l'Electricité, Bingerville, 591

Ecole Supérieure Polytechnique, Dakar, 1814

Ecole Supérieure Privée d'Application des Sciences (ESPAS), Lille, 768

Ecole Technique Supérieure de Chimie de l'Ouest, Angers, 768

Ecole Technique Supérieure du Laboratoire, Paris, 771

Ecole Territoriale d'Agriculture, Grimari, 408

Ecological Society of America, 2295

Ecological Society of Australia Inc., 120

Ecological Society of China, 428

Ecological Society of Nigeria, 1519

Ecomusée d'Alsace, 733

Ecomusée de Marie Galante, 773

Econometric Society, Evanston, 47

Economic and Social Research Council, Swindon, 2151

Economic and Social Research Institute, Dublin, 1083

Economic History Association, Lawrence, 2288

Economic History Society, Glasgow, 2131

Economic Research Council, London, 2147

Economic Research Institute of the Ministry of the Economy, Minsk, 207

Economic Research Unit, Colombo, 1954

Economic Society of Australia, 117

Economic Society of Ghana, 904

Economic Society of South Africa, 1863

Economics and Business Education Association, Hassocks, 2128

Economics Association, Hanoi, 2771

Economics Institute, Beijing, 430

Economics Society, Moscow, 1728

Economisch-Historische Bibliotheek Amsterdam, 1481

Economische Hogeschool Sint-aloysius, 233

Economists' Society of Serbia, 1815

ECORYS Nederland BV, 1479

Ecumenical Patriarchate Library, Istanbul, 2060

Eden Theological Seminary, St Louis, 2546

Edgehill Theological College, Belfast, 2276

Edgewood College, 2728

EDHEC Nice, 767

Edinboro University of Pennsylvania, 2653

Edinburgh Bibliographical Society, 2127

Edinburgh City Libraries and Information Services, 2157

Edinburgh City Museums and Art Galleries, 2171

Edinburgh College of Art, 2271

Edinburgh University Library, Museums and Galleries, 2157

Edison Electric Institute, 2300

Edith Cowan University, 133

Edk/ides, 1995

Edmonton Art Gallery, 333

Edmonton Public Library, 330

Edo State Library Board, Benin City, 1521

Edogawa University, 1264

Education and Training Inspectorate, Bangor, 2123

Education Commission of the States, Denver, 2283

Education International (EI), 51

Education Network Association, 51

Educational Documentation Centre, Khartoum, 1960

Educational Documentation Library, Baghdad, 1075

Educational Documentation Library, Manama, 189

Educational Institute of Scotland, 2123

Educational Library, Jeddah, 1807

Educational Science Museum, Safat, 1354

Educator Training Support Centre, Riga, 1361

Eduskunnan Kirjasto, Helsinki, 685

Edward Waters College, 2407

Efes Müzesi Müdürlüğü, 2061

Efremov, D. V., Institute of Electrophysical Apparatus, St Petersburg, 1747

EGE Üniversitesi, Izmir, 2070

Egerton University, 1313

EGID Bordeaux, 737

Egry József Emlékmúzeum, 944

Egypt Exploration Society, London, 2132

Egyptian Association for Library and Information Science, 657

Egyptian Association for Mental Health, 658

Egyptian Association for Psychological Studies, 658

Egyptian Atomic Energy Authority, 660

Egyptian Botanical Society, 658

Egyptian Geographical Society, 658

Egyptian Holding Company for Biological Products and Vaccines, 659

Egyptian Library, Cairo, 660

Egyptian Medical Association, 658

Egyptian National Authority for Remote Sensing and Space Sciences, 659

Egyptian National Library, 660

Egyptian (National) Museum, 661

Egyptian National Railways Museum, 661

Egyptian Orthopaedic Association, 658

Egyptian Petroleum Research Institute, 660

Egyptian Society of Dairy Science, 657

Egyptian Society of Engineers, 658

Egyptian Society of International Law, 657

Egyptian Society of Parasitology, 658

Egyptian Society of Political Economy, Statistics and Legislation, 657

Ehime University, 1191

Eidgenössische Anstalt für Wasserversorgung, Abwasserreinigung und Gewässerschutz (EAWAG), Dübendorf, 2019

Eidgenössische Forschungsanstalt für Wald, Schnee und Landschaft (WSL), Birmensdorf, 2019

Eidgenössische Materialprüfungs- und Forschungsanstalt (EMPA), Dübendorf, 2019

Eidgenössische Parlaments- und Zentralbibliothek, Bern, 2001

Eidgenössische Technische Hochschule Zürich, 2017

Eidgenössisches Institut für Schnee- und Lawinenforschung (SLF), Davos Dorf, 2001

Eindhoven University of Technology, 1489

Eisenkunstgussmuseum Büdelsdorf, Schleswig, 819

Ekaterinburg Institute of Restorative Surgery, Traumatology and Orthopaedics, 1736

Ekaterinburg Picture Gallery, 1755

Ekaterinburg Region Institute of Dermatology and Venereal Diseases, 1736

Ekaterinburg State Theatrical Institute, 1797

Ekaterinburg Viral Infections Research Institute, 1736

Ekonomická Univerzita V Bratislave, 1845

Ekonomický ústav, Bratislava, 1842

Ekonomiska Forskningsinstitutet vid Handelshögskolan i Stockholm, 1990

Ekonomiska Samfundet i Finland, 682

Ekonomski Institut na Univerzitetet 'Sveti Kiril i Metodij', Skopje, 1386

Ekonomski Institut Sarajevo, 246

Ekonomski Institut Tuzla, 246

El-Dalang University, El-Dalang, 1961

El-Djazairia el-Mossilia, Algiers, 79

El-Gadarif University, El-Gadarif, 1961

El-Imam El-Mahdi University, Kosti, 1961

Eläinmuseo/Zoologiska Museet, Helsinki, 687

Elam School of Fine Arts, Auckland, 1512

Elbasan Public Library, 77

Elda Vaccari Collection of Multicultural Studies, 124

Eldoret Polytechnic, 1316

Electoral Reform Society, 2128

Electric Power Research Centre, Tehran, 1061

Electrochemical Society of India, 971

Electrochemical Society, Pennington, 2297

Electronic Control Machines Research Institute, Moscow, 1747

Electronic Equipment and Machine Studies Science, Technology and

Production Corporation, Ulan Bator, 1451

Electronics and Computer Research Centre, Jadiriya, 1074

Electronics and Telecommunications Research Institute (ETRI), Daejeon, 1322

Electronics Research and Service Organization, Hsinchu, 554

Elektroteknisk Forening, Odense, 630

Elets State University 'I. A. Bunin', 1765

Eliashvili Institute of Control Systems, Tbilisi, 782

Elinkeinoelämän Tutkimuslaitos, ETLA, Helsinki, 685

Eliyava Institute of Bacteriophage, Microbiology and Virology, Tbilisi, 781

Elizabeth City State University, 2605

Elizabeth University of Music, Hiroshima, 1297

Elizabethan House Museum, Great Yarmouth, 2177

Elizabethtown College, 2648

Elliniki Epitropi Atomikis Energhias, Athens, 910

Elliniki Mathimatiki Eteria, Athens, 910

Elliniko Anoikto Panepistimio, Patra, 916

Elmhurst College, 2427

Elmira College, 2585

Elms College, 2483

Elon University, 2605

EM Lyon, 769

Embry-Riddle Aeronautical University, 2407

Embry-Riddle Aeronautical University – Worldwide, 2408

Emerson College, 2483

Emirates Institute for Banking and Financial Studies, 2121

Emmanuel College, Boston, 2483

Emmanuel College, Cambridge, 2192

Emmanuel College, Franklin Springs, 2415

Emmanuel College Library, Cambridge, 2154

Emmanuel College, Toronto, 395

Emmaus Bible College, 2454

Emory and Henry College, 2710

Emory University, 2415

Emporia State University, 2459

Empresa Brasileira de Pesquisa Agropecuária (EMBRAPA), 255

Endocrinology Research Centre, Moscow, 1736

Energiagazdálkodási Tudományos Egyesület, Budapest, 938

Energiewirtschaftliches Institut an der Universität zu Köln, 797

Energy and Resources Laboratories, Hsinchu, 554

Energy Institute, London, 2143

Energy Systems Institute, Irkutsk, 1747

Enfield Libraries, 2160

Engei Gakkai, 1171

Engelhardt Institute of Molecular Biology, Moscow, 1740

Engineering and Physical Sciences Research Council, Swindon, 2149

Engineering Centre 'Plazmoteg', 208

Engineering Council UK, London, 2143

Engineering Institute of Canada, 327

Engineering Institution of Zambia, 2784

Engineering Research Institute, Tokyo, 1182

English Academy of Southern Africa, 1864

English Association, 2134

English Association Sydney Inc., 119

English Centre of International PEN, 2134

English Folk Dance and Song Society, 2130

English Place-Name Society, 2132

English Speaking Board, 2134

English Speaking Union of Sri Lanka, 1953

English-Speaking Union (of the Commonwealth), London, 2125

English-Speaking Union of the United States, 2284

Ethnographical Museum, Khartoum, 1961
Ethnographical Museum, Khentii, 1451
Ethnographical Museum, Plovdiv, 303
Ethnologisches Museum, Berlin, 812
Etisalat College of Engineering, Sharjah, 2121
Etnografisch Museum, Antwerp, 221
Etnografiska Museet, Stockholm, 1974
Etnografski muzej Split, 594
Etnografski muzej u Beogradu, Belgrade, 1817
Etnografski muzej, Zagreb, 594
Etnologický ústav AV ČR, 611
Eton College Library, 2157
Etruria Industrial Museum, Stoke on Trent, 2178
Etz Hayim, General Talmud, Torah and Grand Teshivah, Jerusalem, 1114
Eugene Bible College, 2638
Eugenides Foundation Library, Athens, 912
Euler, L., International Institute of Mathematics, 1741
Euphrates University, 2072
Eureka College, 2427
EuroArab Management School (EAMS), Granada, 1951
Europa Nostra, 43
Europa-universität Viadrina, 848
Europäische Bibliotheken für Theologie, 45
Europäische Gesellschaft für Ingenieur-Ausbildung, 56
European Academy of Anaesthesiology, 61
European Association for Health Information and Libraries, 45
European Association for Population Studies, 47
European Association for the Education of Adults, 51
European Association of Distance Teaching Universities, 51
European Atomic Energy Community (Euratom), 67
European Business School London, 2272
European Business School, Oestrich-Winkel, 901
European Centre for Medium-Range Weather Forecasts, 67
European Centre for Social Welfare Policy and Research, 47
European Confederation of Agriculture, 42
European Cultural Foundation, 43
European Distance and E-Learning Network (EDEN), 52
European Documentation and Information System for Education (EUDISED), 52
European Economic Association, 47
European Federation of Internal Medicine, 61
European Festivals Association, 65
European Foundation for Management Development (EFMD), 47
European Geosciences Union, 67
European Institute of Education and Social Policy, 52
European Institute of Environmental Medicine, 67
European Institute of Public Administration, Maastricht, 1497
European Institute of Technology, Paris, 771
European Molecular Biology Laboratory, 67
European Molecular Biology Organization (EMBO), 67
European Movement, 2128
European Organisation for Civil Aviation Equipment (EUROCAE), 56
European Organization for Nuclear Research (CERN), 67
European Physical Society, 67
European Science Foundation, 67
European Society of Cardiology, 61
European Southern Observatory (ESO), Santiago, 413
European Southern Observatory, Garching, 67

European Space Agency, 67
European Theological Libraries, 45
European University Association, 50
European University Institute, Florence, 1164
European University of Lefke, 606
Euskal Herriko Unibertsitatea, 1932
Euskaltzaindia, Bayonne, 705
Evangel University of the Assemblies of God, Springfield, 2546
Evangelical School of Theology, Myerstown, 2648
Evangélikus Hittudományi Egyetem, 961
Evangelische Akademie Wien, 163
Evangelischer Presseverband für Bayern eV, Munich, 808
Evelyn Hone College of Applied Arts and Commerce, Lusaka, 2786
Evergreen State College, 2718
EVTEK-ammattikorkeakoulu (Espoon-Vantaan teknillinen ammattikorkeakoulu), 701
Ewell Sale Stewart Library of the Academy of Natural Sciences, Philadelphia, 2316
Ewha Woman's University Library, 1323
Ewha Women's University, 1330
Ewing Memorial Library, Lahore, 1569
Excelsior College, 2585
Exeter Cathedral Library, 2157
Exeter College Library, Oxford, 2166
Exeter College, Oxford, 2250
Experimental and Research Centre for Leather, Ulan Bator, 1451
Experimental and Research Centre for Wool, Ulan Bator, 1451
Experimental Factory for Analytical Instrumentation, St Petersburg, 1747
Experimental Factory for Scientific Instrumentation, Chernogolovka, 1747
Experimental Psychology Society, Bristol, 2141
Experimental Research Institute of Metal-Cutting Machine Tools, Moscow, 1747
Exposition Permanente du Débarquement, Arromanches, 728

F

Fabian Society, London, 2128
Fachakkreditierungsagentur für Studiengänge der Ingenieurwissenschaften, der Informatik, der Naturwissenschaften und der Mathematik eV (ASIIN), Duesseldorf, 786
Fachgebiet Wasserwirtschaft und Hydroinformatik, 793
Fachhochschul-Studiengang Bauingenieurwesen-Baumanagement, 182
Fachhochschul-Studiengang Burgenland, Eisenstadt, 182
Fachhochschul-Studiengang Oberösterreich, Graz, 182
Fachhochschul-Studiengang Salzburg, 182
Fachhochschul-Studiengänge bfi Wien, 182
Fachhochschul-Studiengänge Campus Wien, 182
Fachhochschul-Studiengänge der Wiener Neustadt, 182
Fachhochschul-Studiengänge Kufstein, 182
Fachhochschul-Studiengänge St Pölten, 182
Fachhochschul-Studiengänge Technikum Joanneum, Graz, 182
Fachhochschul-Studiengänge WIFI Steiermark, Graz, 182
Fachhochschule IMC Krems, 182
Fachhochschule Technikum Kärnten, 182
Fachhochschule Technikum Wien, 183
Fachhochschule Vorarlberg, 183
Fachleute Geomatik Schweiz, 2000

Faculdade de Belas Artes de São Paulo, 295
Faculdade de Ciências de Barretos, 295
Faculdade de Ciências Econômicas do Sul de Minas, 294
Faculdade de Ciências Econômicas e Administrativas de Santo André, 294
Faculdade de Ciências Econômicas e Administrativas de Taubaté, 294
Faculdade de Ciências Médicas de Pernambuco, 294
Faculdade de Ciências Políticas e Econômicas de Cruz Alta, 294
Faculdade de Direito Cândido Mendes, Rio de Janeiro, 294
Faculdade de Direito da Guiné-Bissau, 929
Faculdade de Direito de Caruarú, 294
Faculdade de Direito de São Bernardo do Campo, 294
Faculdade de Direito de Sorocaba, 294
Faculdade de Engenharia de Barretos, 295
Faculdade de Filosofia, Ciências e Letras de Ouro Fino, 294
Faculdade de Informática de Lins, 295
Faculdade de Medicina do Triângulo Mineiro, 294
Faculdade de Música Mãe de Deus, Londrina, 295
Faculdade de Odontologia de Lins, 294
Faculdade de Odontologia de Pernambuco, 294
Faculdade de Odontologia do Triângulo Mineiro, 294
Faculdade de Odontologia, Universidade de Passo Fundo, 294
Faculdade Estadual de Ciências Econômicas de Apucarana, 294
Faculdade Santa Marcelina – (FASM), Perdizes, 295
Faculdades Integradas de São José dos Campos, 294
Faculdades Integradas Hebraico Brasileira Renascença, 293
Faculdades Oswaldo Cruz, 293
Faculdades Salesianas – Unidade de Ensino de Lorens, 295
Facultad de Teología, Granada, 1910
Facultad Latinoamericana de Ciencias Sociales (FLACSO), Santiago, 425
Faculté de Médecine, de Pharmacie et d'Odonto-Stomatologie, Bamako, 1406
Faculté des Lettres et Sciences Sociales, Brest, 770
Faculté des Sciences Juridiques et Economiques, Bamako, 1406
Faculté Libre de Théologie Protestante de Paris, 770
Faculté Polytechnique de Mons, 230
Faculté Universitaire de Théologie Protestante de Bruxelles, 230
Faculté Universitaire des Sciences Agronomiques de Gembloux, 230
Facultés Universitaires Catholiques de Mons, 230
Facultés Universitaires Notre-Dame de la Paix, Namur, 231
Facultés Universitaires Saint-Louis, Brussels, 232
Faculty of Actuaries, Edinburgh, 2128
Faculty of Advocates, Edinburgh, 2128
Faculty of Hygiene and Environmental Studies, Khartoum, 1964
Faculty of Royal Designers for Industry, London, 2143
Failaka Island Archaeological Museum, 1354
Failaka Island Ethnographic Museum, 1354
Faipari Tudományos Egyesület, Budapest, 938
Fairfax County Public Library, 2317
Fairfield University, 2383
Fairleigh Dickinson University, 2562
Fairmont State University, 2726
Faisalabad Government College University, Faisalabad, 1573
Faith Baptist Bible College and Theological Seminary, 2454
Fakir Mohan University, Balasore, 997

Fakultätsbibliothek für Rechtswissenschaften, Vienna, 168
Falkirk Council Library Services, 2158
Falmouth College of Arts, 2271
Family History Library of the Church of Jesus Christ of Latter-day Saints, Salt Lake City, 2317
Family History Society, Peel, 2279
Fan S. Noli University, 77
Far East State Agrarian University, 1761
Far Eastern Institute of Geology, Vladivostok, 1742
Far Eastern Institute of Trade, Vladivostok, 1796
Far Eastern Research Institute of Mineral Raw Materials, Khabarovsk, 1747
Far-Eastern State Academy of Arts, Vladivostok, 1797
Far Eastern State Marine Reserve, Vladivostok, 1760
Far-Eastern State Maritime Academy, Vladivostok, 1795
Far Eastern State Technical Fisheries University, Vladivostok, 1782
Far Eastern State Technical University, Vladivostok, 1782
Far Eastern State Transport University, Khabarovsk, 1782
Far Eastern State University Central Library, Vladivostok, 1754
Far Eastern State University, Vladivostok, 1765
Far Eastern University Library, Manila, 1603
Far Eastern University, Manila, 1609
Faraday Centre, Napier, 1505
Farmaceutsko Društvo na Makedonija, 1386
Farmakologický ústav AV ČR, 610
Farming Systems Research Unit, Harare, 2788
Fashion and Textile Museum, London, 2174
Fatih Üniversitesi, 2072
Fatima Jinnah Women University, Rawalpindi, 1573
Faulkner University, 2329
Fauna and Flora International, Cambridge, 2138
Fayetteville State University, 2605
Fazl-i-Omar Research Institute, 1566
FDI World Dental Federation, 59
Federação Brasileira de Associações de Bibliotecários (FEBAB), 253
Federação de Escolas Superiores, Belo Horizonte, 294
Federación Argentina de Asociaciones de Anestesiología, 91
Federación de Instituciones Mexicanas Particulares de Educación Superior, México, 1414
Federación Española de Religiosos de Enseñanza (FERE), 1891
Federación Internacional de Mujeres de Negocios y Profesionales, 48
Federación Lanera Argentina, 92
Federación Médica Colombiana, 562
Federación Médica Ecuatoriana, Quito, 650
Federación Médica Peruana, Lima, 1591
Federación Mexicana de Ginecología y Obstetricia, 1416
Federación Mundial de Sociedades de Anestesiólogos, 65
Federacja Stowarzyszeń Naukowo-Technicznych–Naczelna Organizacja Techniczna (FSNT-NOT), Warsaw, 1625
Federal Agency for Education, Moscow, 1727
Federal Archival Service of Russia, 1752
Federal Bar Association, Washington, 2288
Federal Bureau for Medical and Social Expertise, Moscow, 1737
Federal Bureau of Statistics, Islamabad, 1566
Federal College of Agriculture, Akure, 1542
Federal College of Agriculture, Ibadan, 1542

Fondazione Giangiacomo Feltrinelli, 1129

Fondazione Guglielmo Marconi, 1132

Fondazione Internazionale Premio E. Balzan – 'Premio', Milan, 1125

Fondazione Luigi Villa, Milan, 1123

Fondazione Marco Besso, Rome, 1125

Fondazione Romano nel Cenacolo di Santo Spirito, 1139

Fondazione Rui, Rome, 1119

Fondazione Scientifica Querini-Stampalia, Venice, 1138

Fondo Nacional de las Artes, Buenos Aires, 90

Fonds National Suisse de la Recherche Scientifique, 1996

Fonds zur Förderung der wissenschaftlichen Forschung, Vienna, 165

Fontbonne University, 2546

Food and Agriculture Organization of the United Nations, 40

Food and Nutrition Research Institute, Manila, 1602

Food Crops Research Institute, Gialoc, 2772

Food Industries Research Institute, Hanoi, 2773

Food Research Institute, Accra, 905

Food Technology Research Institute, Giza, 659

Forage Institute, Pleven, 299

Ford Green Hall, Stoke on Trent, 2178

Fordham University, 2585

Foreign and Commonwealth Office Library, London, 2160

Foreign Literature Institute, Beijing, 431

Foreign Policy Association, Inc., New York, 2288

Foreign Trade University, Hanoi, 2775

Foreningen af Mejerilledere og Funktionærer, Odense, 628

Föreningen Svenska Tonsättare, 1969

Foreningen til norske Fortidsminnesmerkers Bevaring, 1544

Forest and Forest Products Research Institute, Ibaraki, 1179

Forest Economics Research Institute, Beijing, 430

Forest Information Network for Latin America and the Caribbean (RIFALC), 97

Forest Products Research and Development Division, Bangkok, 2032

Forest Products Research and Development Institute (FPRDI), Laguna, 1602

Forest Products Society, Madison, 2300

Forest Research Centre, Harare, 2788

Forest Research, Farnham, 2146

Forest Research Institute, Dehra Dun, 1035

Forest Research Institute Malaysia (FRIM), Kuala Lumpur, 1394

Forest Research Institute of Malawi, 1391

Forest Research Institute, Petrozavodsk, 1732

Forest Research Institute, Sofia, 299

Forest Research Institute, Yezin, 1465

Forest Research, Rotorua, 1503

Forest Resource and Insect Research Institute, Kunming, 430

Forest Science Institute of Vietnam (FSIV), Hanoi, 2772

Forestry and Beekeeping Division, Dar es Salaam, 2027

Forestry and Wood Processing Industry Institute, Ulan Bator, 1451

Forestry Association of Nigeria, 1518

Forestry Commission, Harare, 2788

Forestry Department Library, Kampala, 2095

Forestry Research Centre, Khartoum, 1960

Forestry Research Institute, Beijing, 430

Forestry Research Institute of Ghana, 905

Forestry Research Institute of Nigeria (FRIN), 1519

Forestry Research Institute of Nigeria Library, 1521

Føroya Forngripafelag, 641

Føroya Fornminnissavn, Tórshavn, 642

Føroya Landsbókasavn, 642

Føroya Landsskjalasavn, 642

Føroya Náttúrugripasavn, Tórshavn, 642

Føroya Verkfrøðingafelag, 641

Forrester Gallery, Oamaru, 1505

Forschungsgesellschaft für Agrarpolitik und Agrarsoziologie, Bonn, 796

Forschungsgesellschaft Wiener Stadtarchäologie, Vienna, 165

Forschungsgruppe für Anthropologie und Religionsgeschichte eV, Altenberge, 801

Forschungsinstitut Edelmetalle und Metallchemie, Schwäbisch Gmünd, 802

Forschungsinstitut für Wärmeschutz eV München, 802

Forschungsinstitut und Naturmuseum Senckenberg, 800

Forschungsstelle für Allgemeine und Textile Marktwirtschaft an der Universität Münster, 797

Forschungsstelle Potsdam des Alfred-Wegener-Instituts für Polar und Meeresforschung, 800

Forschungszentrum Borstel–zentrum für Medizin und Biowissenschaften, 800

Forschungszentrum Jülich GmbH, 801

Forschungszentrum Karlsruhe GmbH, 801

Forskningscenter Risø, 631

Forskningsråd for Kultur og Kommunikation, Copenhagen, 630

Forskningsråd for Samfund og Erhverv, Copenhagen, 630

Forskningsråd for Sundhed og Sygdom, Copenhagen, 630

Forskningsråd for Teknologi og Produktion, Copenhagen, 630

Forskningsrådet for Natur og Univers, Copenhagen, 630

Forskningsrådet Formas, Stockholm, 1971

Forsøgsstationen 'Upernaviarsuk', 642

Forsvarsmuseet, Oslo, 1547

Fort Anne National Historic Site and Museum, 334

Fort Beauséjour – Fort Cumberland National Historic Site of Canada, 333

Fort Charlotte, Kingstown, 1803

Fort Fleur d'Epée, 773

Fort Hays State University, 2459

Fort Jesus Museum, Mombasa, 1312

Fort Lewis College, 2380

Fort Museum, Chennai, 982

Fort Valley State University, 2418

Fort Worth Public Library, 2317

Fortaleza de San Felipe, 647

Fortress of Louisbourg National Historic Site, 334

Főszékesegyházi Könyvtár, Esztergom, 943

Foundation Center, New York City, 2282

Foundation for International Business Administration Accreditation (FIBAA), Bonn, 786

Foundation for International Scientific Co-ordination, 67

Foundation for Research and Technology–Hellas, 919

Foundation for Science and Technology, 2138

Foundation for Technical Institutes, Baghdad, 1079

Foundation Library of the Uzbek Academy of Sciences, 2749

Foundation of the Hellenic World, Athens, 911

Foundation University, 1609

Founder's Library, St George's University, 924

Foundling Museum, London, 2174

Fourah Bay College Library, 1834

Fővárosi Képtár, Budapest, 944

Fővárosi Szabó Ervin Könyvtár, Budapest, 942

Fox Chase Cancer Center, Philadelphia, 2302

FPInnovations – Forintek Division, 329

Framingham State College, 2484

France Telecom R & D, Issy les Moulineaux, 722

Francis A. Countway Library of Medicine, 2312

Francis Bacon Society Inc., 2134

Francis Marion University, 2674

Franciscan School of Theology, 2350

Franciscan University of Steubenville, 2623

Franjevački Samostan Fojnica, Biblioteka, 247

Franjevački Samostan Kraljeva Sutjeska, Biblioteka, 247

Franjevački Samostan Kreševo, Biblioteka, 247

Fränkische Geographische Gesellschaft, 789

Franklin and Marshall College, 2648

Franklin College, Franklin, 2443

Franklin College Switzerland, 2020

Franklin D. Roosevelt Presidential Library, 2314

Franklin Institute, Philadelphia, 2294

Franklin Institute Science Museum, 2326

Franklin Pierce College, Rindge, 2560

Franklin Pierce Law Center, Concord, 2560

Franklin University, 2623

Frans Halsmuseum, Haarlem, 1484

Frantsevich, I. N., Institute of Problems of Materials Science, Kyiv, 2103

Fraser-Hickson Institute, Montréal, 332

Fraser Valley Regional Library, 330

Frashëri Brothers Museum, Përmet, 77

Fraunhofer-Informationszentrum Raum und Bau (IRB), Stuttgart, 810

Fraunhofer-Institut für Bauphysik, Stuttgart, 801

Fraunhofer-Institut für Verfahrenstechnik und Verpackung, 802

Frederiksberg Bibliotek, 632

Fredrikstad Museum, 1547

Free Library of Philadelphia, 2316

Free State Library and Information Services, 1866

Free University, Amsterdam, 1494

Free University of Bozen/Bolzano, 1164

Free Will Baptist Bible College, 2678

Freed-Hardeman University, 2678

Freer Gallery of Art, 2319

Freie Universität Berlin, 827

Freies Deutsches Hochstift, Frankfurter Goethe-Museum (Goethe-Haus), 815

French University of Armenia, 114

Freshwater Biological Association, Ambleside, 2139

Freshwater Fisheries Research Centre, Malacca, 1394

Freshwater Fisheries Research Institute, Plovdiv, 299

Fresno Pacific University, 2350

Freud Museum, London, 2174

Frick Collection, 2325

Friedrich-alexander-universität Erlangen-nürnberg, 844

Friedrich Christian Flick Collection, Berlin, 812

Friedrich-Miescher-Laboratorium für biologische Arbeitsgruppen in der Max-Planck-Gesellschaft, Tübingen, 794

Friedrich-schiller-universität Jena, 863

Friedrichswerdersche Kirche, Berlin, 812

Friends Historical Society, London, 2132

Friends of the National Libraries, London, 2127

Friends University, Wichita, 2459

Fries Museum, 1485

Frihedsmuseet, 633

Frilandsmuseet, 633

Fritz-Haber-Institut der Max-Planck-Gesellschaft, Berlin, 794

Frobenius-Institut an der Johann Wolfgang Goethe-Universität, 798

Froebel College of Education, 1086

Frostburg State University, 2478

Fruit Cultivation Research Institute, Sukchon County, 1318

Fruit-Growing Research Institute, Plovdiv, 299

Fryske Akademy, 1478

Fu-Jen Catholic University, Taipei, 556

Fu Ssu-Nien Library, Institute of History and Philology, Taipei, 554

Fudan University, 464

Fudan University Library, 436

Fuji Women's University, Hokkaido, 1264

Fujian Agricultural and Forestry University, 464

Fujian Institute of Research on the Structure of Matter, 431

Fujian Medical University, 465

Fujian Normal University, 465

Fujian Provincial Library, 435

Fujisawa Foundation, 1181

Fujita Health University, Aichi-Ken, 1264

Fukada Geological Institute, Tokyo, 1181

Fukui University, 1191

Fukui University of Technology, Fukui, 1265

Fukuoka Institute of Technology, Fukuoka, 1265

Fukuoka University, 1272

Fukushima Medical University, 1265

Fukushima University, 1191

Fukuyama University, Hiroshima, 1191

Fuller Theological Seminary, 2350

Fundação Armando Alvares Penteado, São Paulo, 295

Fundação Carlos Chagas, São Paulo, 253

Fundação Casa de Rui Barbosa, 260

Fundação de Desenvolvimento de Pessoal (FUNDESP), 253

Fundação Ezequiel Dias, 257

Fundação Faculdade Federal de Ciências Médicas de Porto Alegre, 294

Fundação Getúlio Vargas, Rio de Janeiro, 253

Fundação Instituto Brasileiro de Geografia e Estatística, 256

Fundação Instituto Brasileiro de Geografia e Estatística – Centro de Documentação e Disseminação de Informações, Divisão de Biblioteca e Acervos Especiais, 260

Fundação Joaquim Nabuco, Recife, 258

Fundação Oswaldo Cruz, 256

Fundação para a Ciência e a Tecnologia, Lisbon, 1675

Fundação Santista, São Paulo, 252

Fundação Universidade de Pernambuco, 281

Fundação Universidade Federal de Mato Grosso do Sul, 275

Fundação Universidade Federal de Rondônia, 285

Fundação Valeparaibana de Ensino, 294

Fundació Catalana per a la Recerca, 1894

Fundación Charles Darwin para las Islas Galápagos, 66

Fundación de Etnomusicología y Folklore del CONAC, Caracas, 2760

Fundación Galileo Galilei, Brena Baja, 1895

Fundación Instituto Botánico de Venezuela, 2763

Fundación Juan March, Madrid, 1886

Fundación la Salle de Ciencias Naturales, Caracas, 2761

Fundación Lázaro Galdiano, 1899

Fundación 'Lisandro Alvarado', Maracay, 2763

Fundación Miguel Lillo, San Miguel de Tucumán, 95

Fundación Museo de Ciencias, Caracas, 2764

Fundación Omar Dengo, San José, 585

Fundación Ortega y Gasset, 1888

Fundación para el Fomento de la Lectura—(FUNDALECTURA), 561

Fundación Teresa Carreño, 2770

Fundación Universidad Central, Bogotá, 572

George Washington University, 2398
Georgetown College, 2462
Georgetown University, 2403
Georgi Dimitrov National Museum, Sofia, 304
Georgia College and State University, Milledgeville, 2418
Georgia Institute of Technology, 2418
Georgia Southern University, 2419
Georgia Southwestern State University, 2419
Georgia State University, 2419
Georgian Academy of Physical Education, Tbilisi, 782
Georgian Academy of Sciences, 780
Georgian Bio-Medico-Technical Society, 780
Georgian Botanical Society, 780
Georgian Court University, 2562
Georgian Geographical Society, 780
Georgian Geological Society, 780
Georgian History Society, 780
Georgian National Speleological Society, 780
Georgian Neuroscience Association, Tbilisi, 780
Georgian Philosophy Society, 780
Georgian S. Rustaveli State Institute of Theatre and Cinematography, 784
Georgian Scientific Research Institute of Industrial Hygiene and Occupational Diseases, 781
Georgian Society of Biochemists, 780
Georgian Society of Geneticists and Selectionists, 780
Georgian Society of Parasitologists, 780
Georgian Society of Patho-Anatomists, 780
Georgian Society of Psychologists, 780
Georgian State Academy of Animal Husbandry and Veterinary Medicine, Tbilisi, 783
Georgian State Agrarian University, 784
Georgian State Art Museum, 782
Georgian State Institute of Subtropical Agriculture, 784
Georgian State Museum of Oriental Art, 782
Georgian Technical University, 783
Geoscience Australia (GA), Canberra, 123
Gépipari és Automatizálási Műszaki Főiskola, Kecskemét, 962
Gépipari Tudományos Egyesület (GTE), Budapest, 938
Germa Museum, 1372
German Historical Institute, London, 2147
Germanisches Nationalmuseum, Nuremberg, 819
Gerontological Society of America, 2293
Gerontology and Geriatrics Society, Kiev, 2099
Gesamtverein der Deutschen Geschichts- und Altertumsvereine, 789
Geschichtsverein für Kärnten, 161
Gesellschaft der Ärzte in Wien, 162
Gesellschaft der Chirurgen in Wien, 162
Gesellschaft der Musikfreunde in Wien, 161
Gesellschaft Deutscher Chemiker, 792
Gesellschaft Deutscher Naturforscher und Ärzte eV, 790
Gesellschaft für Angewandte Mathematik und Mechanik, Dresden, 791
Gesellschaft für Anthropologie, Bremen, 792
Gesellschaft für Antike Philosophie eV (GANPH), 792
Gesellschaft für Biochemie und Molekularbiologie, Tutzing, 791
Gesellschaft für deutsche Sprache eV, Wiesbaden, 789
Gesellschaft für Deutsche Sprache und Literatur in Zürich, 1998
Gesellschaft für Deutschlandforschung eV, Berlin, 798
Gesellschaft für die Geschichte des Protestantismus in Österreich, 164
Gesellschaft für Erdkunde zu Berlin, 789

Gesellschaft für Geistesgeschichte eV, Potsdam, 792
Gesellschaft für Hopfenforschung, 796
Gesellschaft für Informatik eV, Bonn, 793
Gesellschaft für Klassische Philologie in Innsbruck, 162
Gesellschaft für Landeskunde von Oberösterreich, 160
Gesellschaft für Musikforschung, Kassel, 798
Gesellschaft für Naturkunde in Württemberg, 791
Gesellschaft für Öffentliche Wirtschaft, Berlin, 788
Gesellschaft für Operations Research eV (GOR), Bochum, 791
Gesellschaft für Pädagogik und Information eV, Paderborn, 798
Gesellschaft für Rechtsvergleichung, Freiburg, 788
Gesellschaft für Schweizerische Kunstgeschichte, 1997
Gesellschaft für Schwerionenforschung (GSI), mbH, Darmstadt, 802
Gesellschaft für Sozial- und Wirtschaftsgeschichte, Bamberg, 788
Gesellschaft für vergleichende Kunstforschung, Vienna, 164
Gesellschaft für Wissenschaftliche Gerichts- und Rechtpsychologie (GWG), 792
Gesellschaft Österreichischer Chemiker, 163
Gesellschaft Schweizerischer Maler, Bildhauer und Architekten, 1997
Gesellschaft Schweizerischer Tierärzte, 1996
Gesellschaft Sozialwissenschaftlicher Infrastruktureinrichtungen eV, Mannheim, 801
Gesellschaft zur Förderung Pädagogischer Forschung eV, Frankfurt, 798
Gesellschaft zur Förderung Slawistischer Studien, Vienna, 162
Getty Conservation Institute, 2301
Getty, J. Paul, Museum, Los Angeles, 2318
Getty Research Institute, 2300
Getty Villa, Malibu, 2318
Gettysburg College, 2648
Gezira Research Station Library, 1961
GfK-Nürnberg, Gesellschaft für Konsum-, Markt- und Absatzforschung eV, 797
Ghana Academy of Arts and Sciences, 904
Ghana Association of Writers, 904
Ghana Bar Association, 904
Ghana Geographical Association, 904
Ghana Institute of Architects, 904
Ghana Institute of Management and Public Administration, 907
Ghana Institution of Engineers, 905
Ghana Library Association, 904
Ghana Library Board, 905
Ghana Meteorological Services Department, 905
Ghana National Museum, 906
Ghana Science Association, 905
Ghana Sociological Association, 905
Ghazni Museum, 73
Ghent University, 226
Gibbes Museum of Art, 2327
Gibraltar Garrison Library, 2278
Gibraltar Government Archives, 2278
Gibraltar Museum, 2278
Gibraltar Ornithological and Natural History Society, 2278
Gidan Makama Museum, 1522
Gifu Pharmaceutical University, 1265
Gifu University, 1192
Gilbert White's House and Garden and the Oates Museum, 2178
Gipsformerei, Berlin, 812
Giri, V. V., Labour Institute, Noida, 979
Girton College, Cambridge, 2192
Girton College Library, 2154
Gjirokastër Public Library, 77
Gladstone Pottery Museum, Stoke on Trent, 2178

Glasbenonarodopisni Inštitut ZRC SAZU, 1856
Glasgow Caledonian University, 2208
Glasgow Caledonian University Library, 2158
Glasgow City Libraries and Archives, 2158
Glasgow Metropolitan College, 2273
Glasgow Museums, 2171
Glasgow School of Art, 2271
Glenbow Library and Archives, 330
Glenbow Museum, Calgary, 333
Glenn Research Center, Cleveland, Ohio, 2307
Glenville State College, 2726
'Glinka, M. I.', State Central Museum of Musical Culture, 1756
Gloucester Folk Museum, 2172
Gloucestershire County Library, Arts and Museums Service, 2158
Główna Biblioteka Lekarska, Warsaw, 1636
Główna Biblioteka Pracy i Zabezpieczenia Społecznego, Warsaw, 1636
Główny Instytut Górnictwa, Katowice, 1632
Glyptothèque HAZU, Zagreb, 594
GNS Science, Lower Hutt, 1503
Goa University, 998
Göcseji Falumúzeum, 948
Göcseji Múzeum, 948
Goddard College, 2708
Goddard Institute for Space Studies, 2305
Goddard Space Flight Center, Greenbelt, Maryland, 2307
Goethe-Gedenkstätte (im Inspektorhaus des Botanischen Gartens), Jena, 816
Goethe-Gesellschaft in Weimar eV, 786
Goethe-Informationszentrum, Pyongyang, 1318
Goethe-Institut, Abidjan, 589
Goethe-Institut, Addis Ababa, 676
Goethe-Institut, Almaty, 1303
Goethe Institut, Amman, 1299
Goethe-Institut, Amsterdam, 1476
Goethe-Institut, Ankara, 2057
Goethe-Institut, Athens, 909
Goethe-Institut, Bangkok, 2032
Goethe-Institut, Beijing, 427
Goethe-Institut, Beirut, 1364
Goethe-Institut, Belgrade, 1815
Goethe-Institut, Bogatá, 562
Goethe-Institut, Bratislava, 1841
Goethe-Institut, Brussels, 217
Goethe-Institut, Bucharest, 1692
Goethe-Institut, Budapest, 937
Goethe-Institut, Buenos Aires, 90
Goethe-Institut, Cairo, 658
Goethe-Institut, Caracas, 2761
Goethe-Institut, Chişinău, 1444
Goethe-Institut, Colombo, 1953
Goethe-Institut, Copenhagen, 629
Goethe-Institut, Dakar, 1812
Goethe-Institut, Damascus, 2021
Goethe-Institut, Dhaka, 191
Goethe-Institut, Dublin, 1082
Goethe-Institut, Ghana, 905
Goethe-Institut, Hanoi, 2771
Goethe-Institut, Helsinki, 683
Goethe-Institut, Hong Kong, 545
Goethe-Institut, Jakarta, 1041
Goethe-Institut, Jerusalem, 1093
Goethe-Institut, Johannesburg, 1864
Goethe-Institut, Kabul, 73
Goethe-Institut, Karachi, 1564
Goethe-Institut, Kiev, 2099
Goethe-Institut, Kuala Lumpur, 1393
Goethe-Institut, La Paz, 239
Goethe-Institut, Lagos, 1519
Goethe-Institut, Lima, 1590
Goethe-Institut, Lisbon, 1675
Goethe-Institut, Ljubljana, 1855
Goethe-Institut, Lomé, 2048
Goethe-Institut, London, 2134
Goethe-Institut, Madrid, 1889
Goethe-Institut, Manilla, 1601
Goethe-Institut, México, 1415
Goethe-Institut, Minsk, 206
Goethe-Institut, Montevideo, 2743
Goethe-Institut, Montréal, 325
Goethe-Institut, Munich, 786

Goethe-Institut, Nairobi, 1311
Goethe-Institut, New York, 2291
Goethe-Institut, Oslo, 1544
Goethe-Institut, Paris, 708
Goethe-Institut, Prague, 608
Goethe-Institut, Rabat, 1457
Goethe-Institut, Riga, 1361
Goethe-Institut, Rome, 1123
Goethe-Institut, Santiago, Chile, 411
Goethe-Institut, São Paulo, 254
Goethe-Institut, Sarajevo, 246
Goethe-Institut, Seoul, 1322
Goethe-Institut, Singapore, 1836
Goethe-Institut, Sofia, 298
Goethe-Institut, Stockholm, 1970
Goethe-Institut, Sydney, 119
Goethe-Institut, Tallinn, 672
Goethe-Institut, Tashkent, 2747
Goethe-Institut, Tbilissi, 780
Goethe-Institut, Tokyo, 1174
Goethe-Institut, Tunis, 2053
Goethe-Institut, Vilnius, 1376
Goethe-Institut, Warsaw, 1622
Goethe-Institut, Yaoundé, 319
Goethe-Institut, Zagreb, 592
Goethe-Zentrum/Namibisch-Deutsche Stiftung für kulturelle Zusammenarbeit, Windhoek, 1469
Goetz Observatory, Bulawayo, 2789
Gogol, N. V., House-Museum and Gogol Study Centre, Moscow, 1756
Gokhale Institute of Politics and Economics, Pune, 1035
Golden Gate Baptist Theological Seminary, 2350
Golden Gate University, 2350
Goldey-Beacom College, 2395
Goldsmiths College, 2220
Golestan Palace Museum, 1062
Gomal University, 1573
Gomal University Central Library, 1568
Gomel Oblast Universal Library 'V. I. Lenin', 209
Gomel State Medical University, 212
Gomel State Technical University 'P. Sukhoi', 212
Gomel State University 'F. Skorina', 212
Gonville and Caius College, Cambridge, 2192
Gonville and Caius College Library, 2154
Gonzaga University, 2718
Gordion Museum, Ankara, 2061
Gordon College, 2484
Gordon-Conwell Theological Seminary, 2484
Gori State University, 783
Gorky, A. M., Archives, Moscow, 1752
Gorky, A. M., Institute of World Literature, Moscow, 1735
Gorky, A. M., Memorial Museum, Moscow, 1756
Gorky, A. M., Museum, Moscow, 1756
Gorno-Altaisk State University, 1766
Görres-Gesellschaft zur Pflege der Wissenschaft, 790
Gorsium Szabadtéri Múzeum, 948
Gorsky State Agricultural University, 1761
Goshen College, 2443
Göteborgs Konstmuseum, 1974
Göteborgs Naturhistoriska Museet, 1974
Göteborgs Sjöfartsmuseum, Göteborg, 1974
Göteborgs stads kulturförvaltning, 1974
Göteborgs stadsbibliotek, 1972
Göteborgs Stadsmuseum, 1974
Göteborgs Universitet, 1975
Göteborgs universitetsbibliotek, 1972
Gothenburg University, 1975
Gotoh Museum, 1187
Gottfried-Wilhelm-Leibniz-Gesellschaft eV, 792
Gottlieb Duttweiler Institute for Economic and Social Studies, 1996
Goucher College, 2471
Government Archives and Records Service, Seoul, 1323
Government Chemist Department, Kampala, 2095
Government College of Technology, Karachi, 1576

Houghton College, 2586
Hounslow Library Network, 2161
House of Commons Library, 2161
House of Lords Library, 2161
House of Representatives Library, Washington, 2309
Houston Baptist University, 2689
Houston Public Library, 2317
Howard Payne University, 2689
Howard University, 2405
Howon University, 1332
Hristo Botev National Museum, Kalofer, 303
Hrvatska Akademija Znanosti i Umjetnosti, 592
Hrvatski državni arhiv, 594
Hrvatski muzej naivne umjetnosti, 594
Hrvatski pedagoško-književni zbor, 592
Hrvatski povijesni muzej, Zagreb, 594
Hrvatski prirodoslovni muzej, 594
Hrvatski restauratorski zavod, Zagreb, 593
Hrvatski školski muzej, Zagreb, 595
Hrvatsko Knjižničarsko Društvo, 592
Hrvatsko Kulturno Društvo Napredak, Sarajevo, 245
Hrvatsko Muzejsko Društvo, 592
Hrvatsko Numizmatičko Društvo, 592
Hrvatsko Prirodoslovno Društvo, 592
Huachiew Chalermprakiet University, 2036
Huaqiao University, 475
Huazhong Agricultural University, 476
Huazhong University of Science and Technology, 476
Hubei Provincial Library, 436
Hubei University, 476
Hubert Kariuki Memorial University, Dar es Salaam, 2029
Hue Museum, 2775
Hue University of Agriculture and Forestry, Huê, 2778
Hue University, Thua Thien Huê, 2778
Hughes Hall, Cambridge, 2192
Huguenot Memorial Museum and Monument, Franschhoek, 1869
Huguenot Society of Great Britain and Ireland, 2132
Hull York Medical School, 2273
Hult International Business School, 2491
Humacao University College, 2741
HUMAK (Hakutoimistoon), Kiviranta, 702
Human Sciences Research Council, Centre for Library and Information Services, Pretoria, 1868
Human Sciences Research Council (HSRC), Pretoria, 1866
Humanistisk-samhällsvetenskapliga, Stockholm, 1971
Humboldt Gesellschaft für Wissenschaft, Kunst und Bildung eV, 788
Humboldt State University, Arcata, 2351
Humboldt-universität zu Berlin, 827
Humid Forest Ecoregional Center, Yaoundé, 319
Hunan Agricultural University, 477
Hunan Medical University, 477
Hunan Normal University, 478
Hunan Provincial Library, 435
Hunan University, 477
Hungarian Association for Geo-Information (HUNAGI), 938
Hungarian Dance Academy, 954
Hungarian PEN Centre, 937
Hungarian University of Craft and Design, 953
Hunter College, 2572
Hunterian Art Gallery, Glasgow, 2172
Hunterian Museum and Art Gallery, Glasgow, 2172
Hunterian Museum at the Royal College of Surgeons, London, 2174
Huntingdon College, 2329
Huntington College, 2444
Huntington Library, Art Collections and Botanical Gardens, (Art Collection), 2318
Huntington Library, Art Collections and Botanical Gardens, Library, 2308

Huntington Medical Research Institutes, 2302
Huntington Museum of Art, 2328
Huntington University, Sudbury, 350
Huntsman Marine Science Centre, 328
Huron University, 2676
Huron University College, London, Ont., 401
Hus-Museum, Konstanz, 817
Huseyn Javid Memorial Flat–Museum, Baku, 185
Husitské Muzeum, Tábor, 615
Husson College, 2469
Huston-tillotson University, 2689
Hutt Valley Polytechnic, 1511
Hwa Kang Museum, Taipei, 554
HWP – Hamburger Universität für Wirtschaft und Politik, 901
Hyderabad Educational Conference, 969
Hydraulic Engineering Consultants Corporation No. 1, Hanoi, 2773
Hydraulics Research Institute, Delta Barrage, 660
Hydrobiological Society, Moscow, 1730
Hydrobiologický ústav AV ČR, 610
Hydrocarbon Development Institute of Pakistan, 1567
Hydrochemical Institute, Rostov on Don, 1747
Hypogée des Dunes, Poitiers, 732

I

Ibaraki University, 1203
Ibb University, 2783
Ibero-Amerikanisches Institut Preussischer Kulturbesitz, Berlin, 803
IBFD International Tax Academy, 58
Ibn Hayyan Information House, Baghdad, 1075
Ibn Khaldun Center for Development Studies, 660
Ibragimov, G., Institute of Language, Literature and Art, Kazan, 1735
ICDDR,B: Centre for Health and Population Research, 192
Iceland Academy of Arts, 965
Iceland University of Education, 965
Icelandic College of Engineering and Technology, 965
ICHCA International Ltd, 56
Idaho State University, 2424
Idntæknistofnun Íslands, Reykjavík, 964
IDP Education Australia Ltd, 118
Idrottshögskolan, Stockholm, 1991
IEFSI L'Ingénieur – Manager (Institut d'Economie, d'Entreprise et de Formation Sociale pour Ingénieurs), Lille, 767
ifo-Institut für Wirtschaftsforschung, Munich, 797
IFP Research AB, Mölndal, 1972
Iga-ryu Ninja Museum, 1187
Igbinedion University, Benin City, 1539
Ikatan Dokter Indonesia, 1041
Ikomasan Tenmon Kyokai, 1177
Ikonen-Museum, Recklinghausen, 819
Ikonomikon Panepistimion Athinon, 918
Il Colosseo, 1143
Il Halk Kütüphanesi, Balıkesir, 2060
Ilia Chavchavadze State University, Tbilisi, 783
Iliff School of Theology, 2380
Illinois College, 2428
Illinois College of Optometry, 2428
Illinois Institute of Technology, 2428
Illinois State Library, 2310
Illinois State Museum, 2321
Illinois State Museum at Springfield, 2321
Illinois State University, 2428
Illinois Wesleyan University, 2428
Illuminating Engineering Society of North America, 2300
Il·lustre Col·legi d'Advocats de Barcelona, 1888
Ilmatieteen laitos/Meteorologiska institutet, Helsinki, 685
Image Processing Systems Institute, Samara, 1747

Immaculata University, 2649
Immigration Museum, Melbourne, 127
Imo State Library Board, 1522
Imo State University, Enugu, 1537
Imomec, 232
Imperial College London, 2220
Imperial College of London Libraries, 2161
Imperial Household Agency Library, Tokyo, 1184
Imperial War Museum Duxford, Cambridge, 2174
Imperial War Museum, London, 2174
Imperial War Museum North, Manchester, 2175
In-Service Training Institute, Peradeniya, 1959
INAF – Osservatorio Astronomico di Trieste, 1131
Inclusion International, 62
Incorporated Association of Organists, Northfield, 2130
Incorporated Society of Musicians, London, 2130
Independence Museum, Vlorë, 77
Independent International University of Social Studies in Rome, 1166
Independent Schools Inspectorate, London, 2124
Independent University, Bangladesh, 200
India International Centre, New Delhi, 968
India International Photographic Council, 969
India Meteorological Department, 978
India Society of Engineers, 972
Indian Academy of International Law and Diplomacy, 1039
Indian Academy of Sciences, 970
Indian Adult Education Association, 967
Indian Agricultural Research Institute, 1035
Indian Agricultural Statistics Research Institute, 974
Indian Anthropological Association, 971
Indian Association for the Cultivation of Science, 971
Indian Association for the Cultivation of Science (IACS), Kolkata, 977
Indian Association of Biological Sciences, 971
Indian Association of Geohydrologists, 972
Indian Association of Parasitologists, 970
Indian Association of Special Libraries and Information Centres (IASLIC), 968
Indian Association of Systematic Zoologists, 977
Indian Biophysical Society, 971
Indian Botanical Society, 971
Indian Brain Research Association, 976
Indian Bureau of Mines, 978
Indian Cancer Society, 970
Indian Ceramic Society, 972
Indian Chemical Society, 971
Indian Council for Cultural Relations, 968
Indian Council of Agricultural Research (ICAR), 974
Indian Council of Forestry Research and Education, 974
Indian Council of Historical Research, 975
Indian Council of Medical Research, 976
Indian Council of Social Science Research, 979
Indian Council of World Affairs, 969
Indian Council of World Affairs Library, 981
Indian Dairy Association, 968
Indian Economic Association, 969
Indian Institute of Advanced Study, Shimla, 975
Indian Institute of Architects, 968
Indian Institute of Astrophysics, 978
Indian Institute of Chemical Biology, 973
Indian Institute of Chemical Technology, Hyderabad, 973
Indian Institute of Foreign Trade, New Delhi, 1035

Indian Institute of Geomagnetism, 978
Indian Institute of Information Technology, Allahabad, 1035
Indian Institute of Management, Ahmedabad, 1039
Indian Institute of Management, Bangalore, 1039
Indian Institute of Management, Indore, 1039
Indian Institute of Management, Kolkata, 1039
Indian Institute of Management, Kozhikode, 1039
Indian Institute of Management, Lucknow, 1039
Indian Institute of Metals, 972
Indian Institute of Petroleum, 973
Indian Institute of Public Administration, 975
Indian Institute of Science, 1035
Indian Institute of Technology, Bombay, 1031
Indian Institute of Technology Central Library, 980
Indian Institute of Technology, Delhi, New Delhi, 1031
Indian Institute of Technology, Guwahati, 1031
Indian Institute of Technology, Kanpur, 1032
Indian Institute of Technology, Kharagpur, 1032
Indian Institute of Technology, Madras, 1032
Indian Institute of Technology, Roorkee, 1032
Indian Institute of World Culture, 968
Indian Lac Research Institute, 980
Indian Law Institute, 969
Indian Library Association, 968
Indian Mathematical Society, 971
Indian Medical Association, 970
Indian Museum, Kolkata, 983
Indian National Academy of Engineering, 972
Indian National Science Academy, 971
Indian Pharmaceutical Association, 970
Indian Phytopathological Society, 971
Indian Plywood Industries Research and Training Institute, 974
Indian Psychometric and Educational Research Association, 975
Indian Public Health Association, 970
Indian Rubber Manufacturers Research Association, 980
Indian School of Mines, 1036
Indian Science Congress Association, 971
Indian Society for Afro-Asian Studies, 972
Indian Society for Medical Statistics, 970
Indian Society of Agricultural Economics, 968
Indian Society of Anaesthetists, 970
Indian Society of Genetics and Plant Breeding, 971
Indian Society of Mechanical Engineers (ISME), 972
Indian Society of Oriental Art (Calcutta), 969
Indian Society of Soil Science, 968
Indian Space Research Organization (ISRO), 978
Indian Statistical Institute, Kolkata, 1032
Indian Veterinary Research Institute, Izatnagar, 974, 1036
Indiana Institute of Technology, 2444
Indiana State Library, 2311
Indiana State Museum, 2321
Indiana State University, 2444
Indiana University, 2444
Indiana University — Purdue University at Fort Wayne, 2446
Indiana University — Purdue University at Indianapolis, 2446
Indiana University at Kokomo, 2446
Indiana University at South Bend, 2446
Indiana University East, 2446
Indiana University Libraries, 2311
Indiana University Northwest, 2446
Indiana University of Pennsylvania, 2653

Institute for Soil, Climate and Water, Pretoria, 1865

Institute for Sorption and Endoecology Problems, Kiev, 2101

Institute for Standardization in Construction, Hanoi, 2773

Institute for State and Law, Minsk, 207

Institute for Superhard Materials, Kiev, 2103

Institute for Superplasticity Problems in Metals, Ufa, 1742

Institute for Systems Analysis, Moscow, 1747

Institute for Technology and the Storage of Agricultural Products, Bet-Dagan, 1094

Institute for the Application of Remote Sensing Information, Changsha, 432

Institute for the Bulgarian Language, Sofia, 300

Institute for the Complex Utilization of Natural Resources (ICUNR), Osh, 1357

Institute for the Control of Foot and Mouth Disease and Dangerous Infections, Sliven, 299

Institute for the History of Science and Technology – St Petersburg Branch, 1740

Institute for the Mechanization of Agriculture, 207

Institute for the Occupational Training of Youth, Moscow, 1734

Institute for the Philosophy of Science and Peace, Zagreb, 593

Institute for the Preparation of Serums and Vaccines, Mogadishu, 1861

Institute for the Protection of the Mother and Baby, Khabarovsk, 1737

Institute for the Protection of the Mother and Newborn Child, Hanoi, 2772

Institute for the Study of Mankind in Africa, Johannesburg, 1866

Institute for the Study of the Americas, London, 2233

Institute for Trade Studies and Research, Tehran, 1061

Institute for Tropical Ecosystem Studies, San Juan, 2740

Institute for Tropical Technology, Hanoi, 2773

Institute for Water and Environmental Problems, Barnaul, 1741

Institute Nacional de Estudos e Pesquisas Educacionais Anício Teixeira (INEP), Brasilia, 252

Institute of Acoustics, Beijing, 432

Institute of Acoustics, St Albans, 2140

Institute of Actuaries, London, 2128

Institute of Administration, Baghdad, 1079

Institute of Administration, Karkh (Baghdad), 1079

Institute of Advanced Business Studies (IESE), Barcelona, 1930

Institute of Advanced Legal Studies Library, London, 2161

Institute of Advanced Legal Studies, London, 2232

Institute of Advanced Studies in Education, Sardarshahr, 1036

Institute of Aesthetic Studies, Colombo, 1959

Institute of African Studies, Freetown, 1834

Institute of Agricultural Architecture, Ulan Bator, 1450

Institute of Agricultural Economics, Kiev, 2099

Institute of Agricultural Economics, Minsk, 207

Institute of Agricultural Economics, Sofia, 299

Institute of Agricultural Engineering, Bet-Dagan, 1094

Institute of Agricultural Meteorology, Beijing, 430

Institute of Agricultural Radiology, 207

Institute of Agricultural Research and Training (IART), Ibadan, 1519

Institute of Agricultural Science of Southern Vietnam, 2772

Institute of Agriculture, Chabani, 2099

Institute of Agriculture, Kabul, 74

Institute of Agro-Chemistry and Pedology, Hanoi, 2772

Institute of American Studies, Beijing, 430

Institute of Analytical Chemistry, Hamhung, 1319

Institute of Analytical Instrumentation, St Petersburg, 1747

Institute of Animal Biochemistry and Genetics, Ivanka pri Dunaji, 1843

Institute of Animal Husbandry and Veterinary Science Library, Pyinmana, 1465

Institute of Animal Physiology, Košice, 1843

Institute of Animal Production, 207

Institute of Animal Science, Bet-Dagan, 1094

Institute of Animal Science, Kostinbrod, 299

Institute of Applied Arts, Baghdad, 1079

Institute of Applied Astronomy, St Petersburg, 1742

Institute of Applied Ecology, Shenyang, 431

Institute of Applied Manpower Research, New Delhi, 979

Institute of Applied Mathematics and Mechanics, Donetsk, 2103

Institute of Applied Mathematics, Beijing, 432

Institute of Applied Mathematics, Vladivostok, 1747

Institute of Applied Mechanics, Moscow, 1747

Institute of Applied Optics, Mogilev, 208

Institute of Applied Physics, Chişinău, 1445

Institute of Applied Physics, Minsk, 208

Institute of Applied Physics, Nizhnii Novgorod, 1742

Institute of Applied Problems in Physics, Yerevan, 113

Institute of Aquaculture, 910

Institute of Arab Music, Alexandria, 657

Institute of Arab Music, Cairo, 657

Institute of Arab Research and Studies, Cairo, 659

Institute of Arabic and Religious Study, Kabul, 74

Institute of Arable Farming, 207

Institute of Archaeology and Ancient History, Chişinău, 1445

Institute of Archaeology and Ethnography, Baku, 184

Institute of Archaeology and Ethnography, Yerevan, 112

Institute of Archaeology and Museum Studies, Jos, 1520

Institute of Archaeology, Hanoi, 2772

Institute of Archaeology, Kyiv, 2100

Institute of Archaeology, Moscow, 1735

Institute of Archaeology, Nitra, 1843

Institute of Archaeology, Pyongyang, 1318

Institute of Archaeology, Samarkand, 2748

Institute of Archaeology, Ulan Bator, 1450

Institute of Architecture and Art, Baku, 184

Institute of Architecture and Building Engineering, Pyongyang, 1318

Institute of Architecture and Town Planning, Ulan Bator, 1450

Institute of Armament Technology, Pune, 1036

Institute of Art, Folklore Studies and Ethnography 'M. T. Rylsky', Kyiv, 2103

Institute of Art History, Bratislava, 1842

Institute of Art Studies, Sofia, 300

Institute of Arts, Ethnography and Folklore, Minsk, 208

Institute of Astrology, Ulan Bator, 1451

Institute of Astronomy, Moscow, 1742

Institute of Astronomy of the University of Latvia, 1362

Institute of Astrophysics, Dushanbe, 2024

Institute of Atmospheric Optics, Tomsk, 1742

Institute of Atmospheric Physics, Beijing, 432

Institute of Atmospheric Physics, Moscow, 1742

Institute of Atmospheric Sounding, Beijing, 432

Institute of Atomic and Molecular Sciences, Preparatory Office, Taipei, 553

Institute of Automatics, Bishkek, 1357

Institute of Automation and Control Processes, Vladivostok, 1747

Institute of Automation and Electrometry, Novosibirsk, 1747

Institute of Automation, Beijing, 434

Institute of Balkan Studies, Sofia, 300

Institute of Bankers in South Africa, 1863

Institute of Basic Medical Sciences, Beijing, 431

Institute of Beekeeping, P. I. Prokopovych, Kyiv, 2099

Institute of Bio-organic Chemistry and Petrochemistry, Kyiv, 2102

Institute of Bio-organic Chemistry, Minsk, 208

Institute of Bio-organic Chemistry, Novosibirsk, 1740

Institute of Biochemistry, Grodno, 208

Institute of Biochemistry, Novosibirsk, 1737

Institute of Biochemistry, Tashkent, 2748

Institute of Biochemistry, Vilnius, 1377

Institute of Biodiversity Conservation and Research, Addis Ababa, 677

Institute of Bioecology, Nukus, 2748

Institute of Biological Chemistry, Taipei, 553

Institute of Biological Instrumentation, Moscow, 1747

Institute of Biological Problems of the North, Magadan, 1740

Institute of Biological Research and Biotechnology, Athens, 910

Institute of Biology and Soil Science, Vladivostok, 1740

Institute of Biology and Soil Studies, Bishkek, 1356

Institute of Biology, Hanoi, 2773

Institute of Biology, London, 2139

Institute of Biology, Novosibirsk, 1740

Institute of Biology of Southern Seas, Sevastopol, 2101

Institute of Biology, Petrozavodsk, 1740

Institute of Biology, Salaspils, 1361

Institute of Biology, Syktyvkar, 1740

Institute of Biology, Ufa, 1740

Institute of Biology, Ulan Bator, 1450

Institute of Biology, Ulan-Ude, 1740

Institute of Biology, Yakutsk, 1740

Institute of Biomedical Chemistry, Moscow, 1737

Institute of Biomedical Engineering, 1296

Institute of Biomedical Problems, Moscow, 1737

Institute of Biomedical Research and Therapy, Moscow, 1737

Institute of Biomedical Science, London, 2136

Institute of Biomedical Sciences, Preparatory Office, Taipei, 553

Institute of Biophysics and Cell Engineering, Minsk, 208

Institute of Biophysics, Krasnoyarsk, 1740

Institute of Biophysics, Moscow, 1740

Institute of Biophysics, Beijing, 431

Institute of Biophysics, Sofia, 301

Institute of Biotechnology, Bishkek, 1356

Institute of Biotechnology, Vilnius, 1377

Institute of Botany, Ama-Ata, 1304

Institute of Botany, Ashgabat, 2091

Institute of Botany, Baku, 185

Institute of Botany, Beijing, 431

Institute of Botany, Bratislava, 1843

Institute of Botany, Dushanbe, 2024

Institute of Botany 'M. G. Kholodny', Kyiv, 2101

Institute of Botany, Pyongyang, 1319

Institute of Botany, Sofia, 301

Institute of Botany, Taipei, 553

Institute of Botany, Tashkent, 2748

Institute of Botany, Ulan Bator, 1450

Institute of Botany, Vilnius, 1377

Institute of Botany, Yerevan, 113

Institute of Brain and Blood Vessels, Isezaki, 1181

Institute of Buddhist Studies, Ulan Bator, 1451

Institute of Building Materials, Hanoi, 2773

Institute of Business, St Augustine, 2052

Institute of Business Studies, Moscow, 1796

Institute of Cancer Biology, Copenhagen, 631

Institute of Cancer Research, London, 2233

Institute of Cardiology, Tomsk, 1739

Institute of Cardiovascular Surgery, M. Amosov, Kiev, 2100

Institute of Catalysis, Sofia, 301

Institute of Cattle and Sheep Breeding, Stara Zagora, 300

Institute of Cell Biophysics, Moscow, 1740

Institute of Cellular Biology and Genetic Engineering, Kiev, 2101

Institute of Cereals, Dnipropetrovsk, 2099

Institute of Chartered Accountants in England and Wales, 2128

Institute of Chartered Accountants in Ireland, 1081

Institute of Chartered Accountants of India, 969

Institute of Chartered Accountants of Scotland, 2128

Institute of Chartered Foresters, Edinburgh, 2125

Institute of Chartered Secretaries and Administrators, London, 2128

Institute of Chemical Engineering, Hamhung, 1319

Institute of Chemical Engineering, Sofia, 302

Institute of Chemical Kinetics and Combustion, Novosibirsk, 1742

Institute of Chemical Physics, Chernogolovka, 1742

Institute of Chemical Physics, Yerevan, 113

Institute of Chemical Problems, Baku, 185

Institute of Chemical Technology, Prague, 624

Institute of Chemistry and Chemical Technology, Bishkek, 1357

Institute of Chemistry and Chemical Technology, Krasnoyarsk, 1747

Institute of Chemistry and Chemical Technology, Ulan Bator, 1450

Institute of Chemistry, Ashgabat, 2091

Institute of Chemistry, Beijing, 432

Institute of Chemistry, Bratislava, 1843

Institute of Chemistry, Chişinău, 1445

Institute of Chemistry, National Centre for Natural Science and Technology of Viet Nam, Hanoi, 2773

Institute of Chemistry of Ireland, 1082

Institute of Chemistry of New Materials, Minsk, 208

Institute of Chemistry, Taipei, 554

Institute of Chemistry, Vilnius, 1377

Institute of Chemistry, Vladivostok, 1742

Institute of Chemotherapy, Ichikawa, 1181

Institute of Child Care, Hanoi, 2772

Institute of Child Health, Kolkata, 976

Institute of Child Health, London, 2232

Institute of Classical Studies, London, 2233

Institute of Climatology, Beijing, 432

Institute of Clinical and Experimental Lymphology, Novosibirsk, 1737

Institute of Clinical and Preventive Cardiology, Tyumen, 1737

Institute of Clinical Endocrinology, Moscow, 1736

Institute of Clinical Genetics, Moscow, 1738

Institute of Clinical Immunology, Novosibirsk, 1737

Institute of Clinical Radiology, Kyiv, 2100

Institute of Coal and Coal Chemistry, Kemerovo, 1743

Institute of Coal Chemistry, Taiyuan, 434

Institute of Colloid Chemistry and Water Chemistry 'A. V. Dumansky', Kyiv, 2102

Institute of Commonwealth Studies, London, 2233

Institute of Community Studies, London, 2141

Institute of Computational Technologies, Novosibirsk, 1748

Institute of Computer and Communication Systems, Sofia, 302

Institute of Computer Science and Technology Library, Yangon, 1466

Institute of Computer Science and Technology, Yangon, 1467

Institute of Computer Technology, Beijing, 434

Institute of Computer Technology Problems, Yaroslavl, 1749

Institute of Computer Technology, Shenyang, 434

Institute of Construction and Architecture, Bratislava, 1842

Institute of Constructional Mechanization, Pyongyang, 1319

Institute of Contemporary Arts, London, 2130

Institute of Contemporary British History, London, 2147

Institute of Contemporary History—Wiener Library, 2161

Institute of Continuous Media Mechanics, Perm, 1748

Institute of Control and Systems Research, Sofia, 302

Institute of Control Sciences, Automation and Telemechanics, Moscow, 1748

Institute of Corrosion, Leighton Buzzard, 2143

Institute of Cosmophysical Research and Aeronomy im. Yu. G. Shafer, Yakutsk, 1743

Institute of Cost and Management Accountants of Pakistan, 1563

Institute of Culture and Arts, Vilnius, 1376

Institute of Culture, Hanoi, 2771

Institute of Cybernetics and Computing Technology, Hanoi, 2773

Institute of Cybernetics, Baku, 185

Institute of Cybernetics, Tallinn, 673

Institute of Cybernetics, Tashkent, 2748

Institute of Cybernetics, Tbilisi, 782

Institute of Cybernetics 'V. M. Hlushkov', Kyiv, 2103

Institute of Cytology and Genetics, Novosibirsk, 1740

Institute of Cytology, St Petersburg, 1740

Institute of Deep Oil and Gas Deposits, Baku, 185

Institute of Demography and Sociological Studies, Tbilisi, 782

Institute of Demography, Sofia, 300

Institute of Dental Medicine, Yangon, 1467

Institute of Dental Research, Sydney, 122

Institute of Dermatology and Venereology, Kharkiv, 2100

Institute of Deserts, Flora and Fauna, Ashgabat, 2091

Institute of Development Management, Gaborone, 251

Institute of Development Studies, Brighton, 2264

Institute of Development Studies, Harare, 2788

Institute of Developmental Biology, Beijing, 431

Institute of Developmental Physiology, Moscow, 1734

Institute of Diabetes, Moscow, 1736

Institute of Earth Science, Hanoi, 2773

Institute of Earth Sciences, Taipei, 554

Institute of Earthquake Engineering and Seismology, Dushanbe, 2024

Institute of East European, Russian and Central Asian Studies, Beijing, 430

Institute of Ecology of Vilnius University, Vilnius, 1377

Institute of Ecology, Tallinn, 673

Institute of Economic Affairs, London, 2129

Institute of Economic and International Problems of the Assimilation of the Ocean, Vladivostok, 1740

Institute of Economic and Social Problems of the North, Syktyvkar, 1734

Institute of Economic Growth, Delhi, 979

Institute of Economic Management, Hanoi, 2772

Institute of Economic Problems, Apatity, 1734

Institute of Economic Research, Chişinău, 1445

Institute of Economic Research, Khabarovsk, 1734

Institute of Economics, Almaty, 1304

Institute of Economics, Ashgabat, 2091

Institute of Economics, Baku, 184

Institute of Economics, Dushanbe, 2024

Institute of Economics, Ekaterinburg, 1734

Institute of Economics, Hanoi, 2772

Institute of Economics, Kyiv, 2100

Institute of Economics Library, Yangon, 1466

Institute of Economics, Moscow, 1734

Institute of Economics of the National Academy of Sciences of Belarus, Minsk, 207

Institute of Economics, Riga, 1361

Institute of Economics, Sofia, 300

Institute of Economics, Taipei, 553

Institute of Economics, Tashkent, 2748

Institute of Economics, Ulan Bator, 1450

Institute of Economics, Vilnius, 1376

Institute of Economics, Yangon, 1467

Institute of Economics, Yerevan, 112

Institute of Education Library, Yangon, 1466

Institute of Education, London, 2222

Institute of Education, Yangon, 1467

Institute of Electrical and Electronics Engineers, Inc., New York, 2300

Institute of Electrical Engineering, Bratislava, 1844

Institute of Electricity, Pyongsong, 1319

Institute of Electrodynamics, Kyiv, 2103

Institute of Electronic Measurement 'Kvarz', Nizhny Novgorod, 1748

Institute of Electronics 'Acad. Emil Djakov', Sofia, 302

Institute of Electronics and Computer Science, Riga, 1362

Institute of Electronics, Beijing, 434

Institute of Electronics, Informatics and Automation, Hanoi, 2773

Institute of Electronics, Minsk, 208

Institute of Electrophysics, Ekaterinburg, 1743

Institute of Employment Studies, Brighton, 2264

Institute of Energetics Problems, Minsk, 208

Institute of Energy Economics, Japan, 1182

Institute of Energy, Hanoi, 2773

Institute of Energy Problems of Chemical Physics, Moscow, 1743

Institute of Energy Research, Moscow, 1748

Institute of Engineering Cybernetics, Minsk, 208

Institute of Engineering Geology and Hydrogeology, Tbilisi, 782

Institute of Engineering Mechanics 'A. M. Pidhorny', Kharkiv, 2103

Institute of Engineering Mechanics, Harbin, 434

Institute of Engineering Science, Ekaterinburg, 1748

Institute of Engineering Thermophysics, Beijing, 434

Institute of Engineering Thermophysics, Kyiv, 2103

Institute of English Studies, London, 2233

Institute of Environmental Protection, Pyongyang, 1319

Institute of Environmental Science and Research Ltd (ESR), Porirua, 1503

Institute of Epidemiology and Infectious Diseases 'L. V. Gromashevsky', Kyiv, 2100

Institute of Epidemiology and Microbiology, Irkutsk, 1736

Institute of Epidemiology and Microbiology, Vladivostok, 1737

Institute of Epidemiology, Disease Control and Research (IEDCR), Dhaka, 192

Institute of Ethiopian Studies, Addis Ababa, 677

Institute of Ethiopian Studies Library, Addis Ababa, 677

Institute of Ethnic Classics, Pyongyang, 1319

Institute of Ethnic Literature, Beijing, 431

Institute of Ethnography and Folklore, Chişinău, 1445

Institute of Ethnology and Folklore Research, Zagreb, 593

Institute of Ethnology, Bratislava, 1844

Institute of Ethnology, Hanoi, 2773

Institute of Ethnology, Taipei, 554

Institute of Europe, Moscow, 1734

Institute of European and American Studies, Taipei, 554

Institute of European Studies, Beijing, 430

Institute of Experimental and Clinical Medicine, University of Latvia, Riga, 1361

Institute of Experimental Biology, Almaty, 1304

Institute of Experimental Biology, Harku, 673

Institute of Experimental Botany 'V. Kuprevich', Minsk, 208

Institute of Experimental Cardiology, Moscow, 1736

Institute of Experimental Endocrinology, Bratislava, 1843

Institute of Experimental Endocrinology, Moscow, 1736

Institute of Experimental Medicine, St Petersburg, 1737

Institute of Experimental Meteorology, Obninsk, 1743

Institute of Experimental Mineralogy, Moscow, 1743

Institute of Experimental Morphology and Anthropology, Sofia, 301

Institute of Experimental Pathology and Parasitology, Sofia, 301

Institute of Experimental Pharmacology, Bratislava, 1843

Institute of Experimental Physics, Košice, 1843

Institute of Experimental Phytopathology and Entomology, Ivanka pri Dunaji, 1843

Institute of Experimental Psychology, Bratislava, 1844

Institute of Experimental Veterinary Medicine 'S. N. Wyshelesski', 207

Institute of Eye Diseases, Moscow, 1737

Institute of Far Eastern Studies, Moscow, 1734

Institute of Farm Machinery Research, Hanoi, 2774

Institute of Ferrous Metals, Nampo, 1319

Institute of Field and Garden Crops, Bet-Dagan, 1094

Institute of Finance, Hanoi, 2772

Institute of Finance Management, Dar es Salaam, 2031

Institute of Financial Services, Canterbury, 2129

Institute of Fine Organic Chemistry, Yerevan, 113

Institute of Fisheries, Minsk, 207

Institute of Fisheries, Varna, 300

Institute of Folklore, Sofia, 302

Institute of Food Science and Technology, Dhaka, 192

Institute of Food Science and Technology, London, 2143

Institute of Food Substances, Moscow, 1740

Institute of Food Technologists, Chicago, 2300

Institute of Foreign Economic Research, Moscow, 1734

Institute of Forest and Walnut Studies, Bishkek, 1356

Institute of Forest Ecology, Zvolen, 1843

Institute of Forest Research, Uspenskoe, 1732

Institute of Forestry and Hunting, Ulan Bator, 1449

Institute of Forestry, Ekaterinburg, 1732

Institute of Forestry, Gomel, 207

Institute of Forestry, Hanoi, 2772

Institute of Forestry, Pyinmana, 1467

Institute of Freshwater Fishery Biology, Cairo, 659

Institute of Fruit Cultivation, 207

Institute of Fruit Growing, Kyustendil, 300

Institute of Fruit-tree and Industrial Crop Research, Phong Chau, 2772

Institute of Fuel Research and Development, Dhaka, 192

Institute of Fuel, Songrim, 1319

Institute of Gastroentorology, Dushanbe, 2024

Institute of General and Inorganic Chemistry, Minsk, 208

Institute of General and Inorganic Chemistry, Sofia, 301

Institute of General and Inorganic Chemistry, Tashkent, 2748

Institute of General and Inorganic Chemistry 'V. I. Vernadsky', Kyiv, 2102

Institute of General and Inorganic Chemistry, Yerevan, 113

Institute of General Genetics and Cytology, Almaty, 1304

Institute of General Pathology and Pathological Physiology, Moscow, 1737

Institute of Genetic Resources, Baku, 184

Institute of Genetics and Cytology, Minsk, 208

Institute of Genetics and Developmental Biology, Beijing, 431

Institute of Genetics and Plant Experimental Biology, Tashkent, 2748

Institute of Genetics, Chişinău, 1445

Institute of Genetics, Pyongyang, 1319

Institute of Genetics, Sofia, 301

Institute of Geochemistry and Geophysics, Minsk, 208

Institute of Geochemistry, Guiyang, 432

Institute of Geochemistry, Irkutsk, 1743

Institute of Geochemistry, Mineralogy and Ore Formation, Kyiv, 2102

Institute of Geoecology, Ulan Bator, 1450

Institute of Geography, Almaty, 1304

Institute of Geography, Baku, 184

Institute of Geography, Beijing, 431

Institute of Geography, Bratislava, 1843

Institute of Geography, Chişinău, 1445

Institute of Geography, Irkutsk, 1735

Institute of Geography, Moscow, 1735

Institute of Geography, Pyongyang, 1318

Institute of Geography, Sofia, 300

Institute of Geography, Ulan Bator, 1450

Institute of Geological Sciences, Kyiv, 2102

Institute of Geology and Geochemistry of Combustible Minerals, Lviv, 2102

Institute of Geology and Geography, Vilnius, 1376

Institute of Geology and Mineral Enrichment, Ulan Bator, 1450

Institute of Geology and Precambrian Geochronology, St Petersburg, 1743
Institute of Geology, Apatity, 1743
Institute of Geology, Ashgabat, 2091
Institute of Geology, Baku, 185
Institute of Geology, Beijing, 432
Institute of Geology, Bishkek, 1357
Institute of Geology, Bratislava, 1843
Institute of Geology, Dushanbe, 2024
Institute of Geology, Makhachkala, 1743
Institute of Geology, Moscow, 1743
Institute of Geology, Petrozavodsk, 1743
Institute of Geology, Pyongsong, 1319
Institute of Geology, Syktyvkar, 1743
Institute of Geology, Tallinn, 673
Institute of Geology, Ufa, 1743
Institute of Geology, Yakutsk, 1743
Institute of Geology, Yerevan, 113
Institute of Geomechanics, Beijing, 432
Institute of Geomechanics, Moscow, 1743
Institute of Geophysics and Engineering Seismology, Gjumry, 113
Institute of Geophysics and Geology, Chişinău, 1445
Institute of Geophysics, Beijing, 432
Institute of Geophysics, Bratislava, 1844
Institute of Geophysics, Ekaterinburg, 1743
Institute of Geophysics, Kyiv, 2102
Institute of Geophysics, Sofia, 301
Institute of Geophysics, Tbilisi, 781
Institute of Geotechnical Mechanics, Dnipropetrovsk, 2103
Institute of Geotechnics, Košice, 1844
Institute of Geotectonics, Changsha, 432
Institute of Germanic and Romance Studies, London, 2233
Institute of Gerontology, Kyiv, 2100
Institute of Global Climate and Ecology, Moscow, 1740
Institute of Grains and Feed Industry, Kostinbrod, 300
Institute of Greek and Roman Antiquity, Athens, 910
Institute of Haematology and Blood Transfusion, Tashkent, 2748
Institute of Health Sciences, Ruwi, 1562
Institute of Heraldic and Genealogical Studies, Canterbury, 2132
Institute of High-Altitude Physiology and Experimental Pathology of High Rocks, Bishkek, 1357
Institute of High Current Electronics, Tomsk, 1748
Institute of High Energy Physics, Beijing, 432
Institute of High-Energy Physics, Protvino, 1743
Institute of High-Pressure Physics, 1631
Institute of High-Pressure Physics, Troitsk, 1743
Institute of High-Temperature Electrochemistry, Ekaterinburg, 1743
Institute of High-Temperature Physics, Moscow, 1743
Institute of Higher and Secondary Vocational Education Research, Hanoi, 2772
Institute of Higher Education, Moscow, 1734
Institute of Higher Nervous Activity and Neurophysiology, Moscow, 1740
Institute of Himalayan Bioresources Technology, Palampur, 973
Institute of Historical Research Library, London, 2161
Institute of Historical Research, London, 2233
Institute of Historical Studies, Bratislava, 1843
Institute of History and Archaeology, Ekaterinburg, 1735
Institute of History and Philology, Taipei, 553
Institute of History, Archaeology and Ethnography, Nukus, 2748
Institute of History, Baku, 184
Institute of History, Bishkek, 1356

Institute of History, Chişinău, 1445
Institute of History, Hanoi, 2772
Institute of History, Language and Literature, Ufa, 1735
Institute of History, Minsk, 207
Institute of History of Latvia, Riga, 1361
Institute of History, Philology and Philosophy, Novosibirsk, 1735
Institute of History, Pyongyang, 1318
Institute of History, Sofia, 300
Institute of History, Tallinn, 673
Institute of History, Tashkent, 2748
Institute of History, Ulan Bator, 1450
Institute of History, Yerevan, 113
Institute of Horticulture, Bet-Dagan, 1094
Institute of Human and Animal Physiology, Almaty, 1304
Institute of Human Genetics, Moscow, 1738
Institute of Human Morphology, Moscow, 1737
Institute of Hydraulic Engineering, Pyongyang, 1319
Institute of Hydraulics and Hydrology, Chingleput, 980
Institute of Hydrobiology, Kiev, 2101
Institute of Hydrobiology, Wuhan, 431
Institute of Hydrodynamics, Novosibirsk, 1743
Institute of Hydrogeology and Engineering Geology, Tashkent, 2749
Institute of Hydrogeology and Engineering Geology, Zhengding, 434
Institute of Hydrology, Bratislava, 1844
Institute of Hydromechanics, Kyiv, 2103
Institute of Hydrometeorology, Tbilisi, 782
Institute of Hydroponics Problems, Yerevan, 112
Institute of Hygiene, Epidemiology and Microbiology, Ulan Bator, 1450
Institute of Hygiene, Vilnius, 1377
Institute of Immunology, Lyubuchany, 1737
Institute of Immunology, Moscow, 1737
Institute of Immunology, Tashkent, 2748
Institute of Immunology, Vilnius, 1377
Institute of Industrial Biology, Pyongsong, 1319
Institute of Industrial Chemistry, Hanoi, 2774
Institute of Industrial Economics, Bergen, 1545
Institute of Industrial Economics, Donetsk, 2100
Institute of Industrial Electronic Engineering, Karachi, 1566
Institute of Industrial Engineers, Norcross, 2300
Institute of Industrial Medicine and Human Ecology, Angarsk, 1736
Institute of Influenza, St Petersburg, 1737
Institute of Informatics and Control Problems, Almaty, 1305
Institute of Informatics and Mathematical Modelling of Technological Processes, Apatity, 1749
Institute of Informatics, Bratislava, 1844
Institute of Informatics Problems of the Russian Academy of Sciences (IPIRAN), Moscow, 1748
Institute of Information Science and Automation, St Petersburg, 1748
Institute of Information Science, Taipei, 554
Institute of Information Technology, Baku, 185
Institute of Information Technology, Sofia, 302
Institute of Information Transmission Problems, Moscow, 1748
Institute of Inland Waters, 910
Institute of Inorganic Chemistry and Electrical Chemistry, Tbilisi, 782
Institute of Inorganic Chemistry, Bratislava, 1844

Institute of Inorganic Chemistry, Hamhung, 1319
Institute of Inorganic Chemistry, Salaspils, 1362
Institute of Internal Medicine, Novosibirsk, 1737
Institute of International Affairs, Pyongyang, 1318
Institute of International and Social Studies, Tallinn, 673
Institute of International Education, New York, 2283, 2288
Institute of International Law, Founex, 58
Institute of International Politics and Economics, Belgrade, 1816
Institute of International Public Law and International Relations, Thessaloniki, 910
Institute of International Relations, Hanoi, 2772
Institute of International Relations, St Augustine, 2052
Institute of International Studies, Ulan Bator, 1450
Institute of Introduction and Plant Genetic Resources, Sadovo, 300
Institute of Islamic Culture, Lahore, 1564
Institute of Islamic Studies, Male', 1404
Institute of Ismaili Studies, 2151
Institute of Jamaica, 1168
Institute of Juche Literature, Pyongyang, 1319
Institute of Karst Geology, Guilin, 433
Institute of Kiswahili Research, Dar es Salaam, 2028
Institute of Laboratory Animal Science, Beijing, 431
Institute of Labour Science and Social Affairs, Hanoi, 2772
Institute of Land Reclamation and Grass Management, 207
Institute of Landscape Ecology, Bratislava, 1843
Institute of Language and Literature, Nukus, 2748
Institute of Language, Literature and Arts, Makhachkala, 1735
Institute of Language, Literature and History, Syktyvkar, 1735
Institute of Languages and Literature, Kabul, 73
Institute of Laser and Information Technology, Shatura, 1748
Institute of Laser Research, 1773
Institute of Laser Technology, Sofia, 302
Institute of Latin American Studies, Beijing, 430
Institute of Law, Hanoi, 2772
Institute of Law, Pyongyang, 1318
Institute of Leather Technology, Dhaka, 203
Institute of Legal Studies, Sofia, 300
Institute of Limnology, Irkutsk, 1740
Institute of Limnology, St Petersburg, 1740
Institute of Linguistic Research, St Petersburg, 1735
Institute of Linguistics, Beijing, 431
Institute of Linguistics, Bishkek, 1356
Institute of Linguistics, Chişinău, 1445
Institute of Linguistics, Hanoi, 2772
Institute of Linguistics, Literature and History, Petrozavodsk, 1735
Institute of Linguistics, Moscow, 1735
Institute of Linguistics 'O. O. Potebni', Kyiv, 2100
Institute of Linguistics, Pyongyang, 1319
Institute of Linguistics 'Ya. Kolas', Minsk, 207
Institute of Literary Studies, Hanoi, 2772
Institute of Literature and Folklore, Chişinău, 1445
Institute of Literature, Folklore and Art, Riga, 1361
Institute of Literature, Minsk, 207
Institute of Literature 'Shevchenko, T. G.', Kyiv, 2100
Institute of Lithuanian History, Vilnius, 1377

Institute of Lithuanian Language, Vilnius, 1377
Institute of Lithuanian Literature and Folklore, Vilnius, 1377
Institute of Low-Temperature Physics and Engineering 'B. I. Verkin', Kharkiv, 2103
Institute of Machine Mechanics and Reliability, Minsk, 209
Institute of Machine Mechanics, Tbilisi, 782
Institute of Machinery and Industrial Instruments, Hanoi, 2774
Institute of Machinery Research, Bishkek, 1357
Institute of Macro-Molecular Compounds, St Petersburg, 1743
Institute of Macromolecular Chemistry, Hamhung, 1319
Institute of Malariology, Entomology and Parasitology, Hanoi, 2772
Institute of Management and Technology, Enugu, 1541
Institute of Management Development, Ulan Bator, 1450
Institute of Management Services, Enfield, 2143
Institute of Manuscripts, Baku, 184
Institute of Manuscripts, Dushanbe, 2024
Institute of Marine Biological Resources, 910
Institute of Marine Biology and Oceanography, Freetown, 1834
Institute of Marine Biology, Petropavlovsk-Kamchatskii, 1740
Institute of Marine Biology, Vladivostok, 1740
Institute of Marine Biology/Genetics, 910
Institute of Marine Engineering, Science and Technology (IMarEST), London, 2143
Institute of Marine Geology and Geophysics, Yuzhno-Sakhalinsk, 1743
Institute of Market Studies, Ulan Bator, 1450
Institute of Materia Medica, Hanoi, 2773
Institute of Materials and Machine Mechanics, Bratislava, 1844
Institute of Materials, Minerals and Mining, London, 2143
Institute of Materials Research, Košice, 1844
Institute of Materials Science, Tashkent, 2749
Institute of Mathematical Sciences, Chennai, 977
Institute of Mathematical Statistics, Hayward, 68
Institute of Mathematics, Almaty, 1305
Institute of Mathematics and Computer Science, Chişinău, 1445
Institute of Mathematics and Informatics, Sofia, 301
Institute of Mathematics and Informatics, Vilnius, 1377
Institute of Mathematics and its Applications, Southend, 2139
Institute of Mathematics and Mechanics, Ashgabat, 2091
Institute of Mathematics and Mechanics, Baku, 185
Institute of Mathematics and Mechanics, Ekaterinburg, 1748
Institute of Mathematics, Beijing, 432
Institute of Mathematics, Bishkek, 1356
Institute of Mathematics, Bratislava, 1843
Institute of Mathematics, Dushanbe, 2024
Institute of Mathematics, Hanoi, 2773
Institute of Mathematics, Kyiv, 2102
Institute of Mathematics, Minsk, 208
Institute of Mathematics, Novosibirsk, 1742
Institute of Mathematics, Pyongsong, 1319
Institute of Mathematics, Taipei, 553
Institute of Mathematics, Ufa, 1742
Institute of Mathematics, Ulan Bator, 1450

Institute of Plant Physiology and Genetics, Kyiv, 2101

Institute of Plant Physiology, Chişinău, 1445

Institute of Plant Physiology, Pyongyang, 1319

Institute of Plant Protection, Bet-Dagan, 1094

Institute of Plant Protection, Kyiv, 2099

Institute of Plant Protection, Minsk, 207

Institute of Plastic Surgery, Beijing, 431

Institute of Political Science, Bratislava, 1842

Institute of Political Science, Tbilisi, 781

Institute of Polymer Materials, Sumgait, 185

Institute of Polymer Mechanics, Riga, 1362

Institute of Polymer Research, Bratislava, 1844

Institute of Polymers, Sofia, 302

Institute of Population and Labour Economics, Beijing, 433

Institute of Power Engineering and Automation, Tashkent, 2749

Institute of Power Engineering and Microelectronics, Jalal-Abad, 1357

Institute of Power Engineering, Chişinău, 1445

Institute of Primate Research, Nairobi, 1311

Institute of Problems in Cybernetics, Moscow, 1748

Institute of Problems in Informatics and Automation, Yerevan, 113

Institute of Problems in the Complex Utilization of Mineral Resources, Moscow, 1748

Institute of Problems in the Safe Development of Nuclear Energy, Moscow, 1748

Institute of Problems of Assimilation of the North, Tyumen, 1734

Institute of Problems of Marine Technology, Vladivostok, 1748

Institute of Problems of Mechanics, Moscow, 1748

Institute of Problems of the Geology and Extraction of Oil and Gas, Moscow, 1743

Institute of Problems of the Industrial Ecology of the North (INEP KSC), Apatity, 1741

Institute of Problems of the Market-place, Moscow, 1734

Institute of Process Engineering, Beijing, 433

Institute of Programmable Systems, Pereslavl-Zalesskii, 1748

Institute of Protein Research, Moscow, 1741

Institute of Psychology, Beijing, 433

Institute of Psychology, Moscow, 1745

Institute of Psychology, Sofia, 302

Institute of Public Administration Library, Riyadh, 1808

Institute of Public Administration, Riyadh, 1811

Institute of Public Administration, Ruwi, 1562

Institute of Public Affairs, Jolimont, 118

Institute of Public and Environmental Health Studies, 1961

Institute of Public Health, Kabul, 73

Institute of Public Health, Tokyo, 1181

Institute of Public Health, Ulan Bator, 1450

Institute of Pulmonology and Phthisiology, Minsk, 207

Institute of Pulse Research and Engineering, Mykolayiv, 2103

Institute of Pure Metals, Hamhung, 1319

Institute of Quarrying, Nottingham, 2143

Institute of Race Relations, London, 2142

Institute of Radiation Physical-Chemical Problems, Minsk, 209

Institute of Radiation Problems, Baku, 185

Institute of Radio Astronomy, Kharkiv, 2102

Institute of Radio Engineering and Electronics, Moscow, 1748

Institute of Radiobiology, Minsk, 208

Institute of Radioecological Problems, Minsk, 209

Institute of Radiology and Interventional Diagnostics, Tbilisi, 781

Institute of Radiophysics and Electronics, Ashtarak, 113

Institute of Radiophysics and Electronics 'O. Ya. Usikov', Kharkiv, 2103

Institute of Radiophysics and Electronics, University of Calcutta, 1039

Institute of Radiotherapy and Nuclear Medicine (IRNUM), Peshawar, 1567

Institute of Refrigeration, Carshalton, 2143

Institute of Regional Pathology and Pathological Morphology, Novosibirsk, 1737

Institute of Regional Systems Research, Birobidzhan, 1748

Institute of Remote Sensing Methods for Geology (VNIIKAM), St Petersburg, 1748

Institute of Research and Innovation, Japan, 1182

Institute of Research in the Humanities, Yakutsk, 1735

Institute of Research on Chinese and Demotic Characters, Hanoi, 2772

Institute of Research on Mining Technology, Hanoi, 2774

Institute of Rheumatology, Moscow, 1737

Institute of Rock and Mineral Analysis, Beijing, 433

Institute of Rocks, Physics and Mechanics, Bishkek, 1357

Institute of Russian History, Moscow, 1735

Institute of Russian Literature (Pushkin House), St Petersburg, 1735

Institute of Science Technology, Lichfield, 2143

Institute of Scientific and Technical Communicators, St Neots, 2144

Institute of Scientific and Technical Development, Ulan Bator, 1450

Institute of Scientific and Technical Information, Moscow, 1752

Institute of Scientific and Technical Information of China (ISTIC), 434

Institute of Scientific and Technological Information on Forestry, Beijing, 434

Institute of Secondary Education, Moscow, 1734

Institute of Secondary Specialized Education, Kazan, 1734

Institute of Seismology, Almaty, 1305

Institute of Seismology, Bishkek, 1357

Institute of Seismology, Tashkent, 2748

Institute of Semiconductor Physics, Kiev, 2102

Institute of Semiconductor Physics, Novosibirsk, 1743

Institute of Semiconductor Physics, Vilnius, 1377

Institute of Semiconductors, Beijing, 434

Institute of Silicate Engineering, Sijong-Gu, 1319

Institute of Sindhology Library, Jamshoro, 1568

Institute of Sindhology, Sindh, 1567

Institute of Single Crystals, Kharkiv, 2102

Institute of Sinhala Culture, Colombo, 1953

Institute of Slavonic Studies, Moscow, 1735

Institute of Slovak Literature, Bratislava, 1843

Institute of Social Sciences, Ho Chi Minh City, 2772

Institute of Social Sciences Information–National Social Sciences Library, Hanoi, 2774

Institute of Social Sciences, Kabul, 73

Institute of Social Sciences, Košice, 1844

Institute of Social Sciences, Osh, 1357

Institute of Social Sciences, Ulan-Ude, 1734

Institute of Social Studies, the Hague, 1497

Institute of Socio-Economic Problems of the Development of the Agroindustrial Complex, Saratov, 1734

Institute of Socio-Political Research, Moscow, 1734

Institute of Sociology, Bratislava, 1844

Institute of Sociology, Kyiv, 2103

Institute of Sociology, Minsk, 208

Institute of Sociology, Moscow, 1745

Institute of Sociology, Sofia, 302

Institute of Soil Research and Agrochemistry, Tashkent, 2747

Institute of Soil Science and Agrochemistry, Baku, 184

Institute of Soil Science and Agrochemistry, Novosibirsk, 1732

Institute of Soil Science, Nanjing, 430

Institute of Soils and Water, Bet-Dagan, 1094

Institute of Solid State and Semiconductor Physics, Minsk, 208

Institute of Solid State Chemistry and Mechanochemistry, Novosibirsk, 1748

Institute of Solid State Chemistry, Ekaterinburg, 1743

Institute of Solid State Physics, Moscow, 1743

Institute of Solution Chemistry, Ivanovo, 1743

Institute of Southeast Asian Studies, Singapore, 1837

Institute of Soya Bean Growing, Pavlikeni, 300

Institute of Space Physics, Beijing, 433

Institute of Space Physics Research and the Diffusion of Radio Waves, Paratunka, 1743

Institute of Space Research, Almaty, 1305

Institute of Space Research, Moscow, 1743

Institute of Space Research, Sofia, 302

Institute of Spectroscopy, Moscow, 1743

Institute of Stage Arts, Hanoi, 2772

Institute of State and Law, Almaty, 1304

Institute of State and Law, Bratislava, 1842

Institute of State and Law, Moscow, 1734

Institute of State and Law, Tbilisi, 781

Institute of State and Law 'V. M. Koretsky', Kyiv, 2100

Institute of Statistical Mathematics, Tokyo, 1181

Institute of Statistical Science and Economic Information, Hanoi, 2772

Institute of Statistical Science, Taipei, 553

Institute of Strategic Studies, Islamabad, 1566

Institute of Strategic Studies, Ulan Bator, 1450

Institute of Strength Physics and Materials Science, Tomsk, 1744

Institute of Structural Macrokinetics and Materials Science, Chernogolovka, 1744

Institute of Surface Chemistry, Kyiv, 2102

Institute of Surgery and Transplantology, Kyiv, 2101

Institute of Surgery, Irkutsk, 1736

Institute of Synoptic and Dynamic Meteorology, Beijing, 433

Institute of Synthetic Polymer Materials, Moscow, 1748

Institute of Systemic Archaeology, 1704

Institute of Systems Science, Beijing, 434

Institute of Teaching and Learning Resources, Moscow, 1734

Institute of Technical Acoustics, Vitebsk, 209

Institute of Technical Chemistry, Perm, 1748

Institute of Technical Education (ITE), Singapore, 1837

Institute of Technology, Baghdad, 1079

Institute of Technology Blanchardstown, 1090

Institute of Technology Carlow, 1090

Institute of Technology of Metals, Mogilev, 209

Institute of Technology Sligo, 1091

Institute of Technology Tallaght, Dublin, 1091

Institute of Technology Tralee, 1091

Institute of Technology, Yangon, 999, 1467

Institute of Tectonics and Geophysics, Khabarovsk, 1744

Institute of Terrestrial Magnetism, the Ionosphere and Radio Wave Propagation, Troitsk, 1744

Institute of Textile Technology, Charlottesville, 2307

Institute of the Arts, Yerevan, 112

Institute of the Automation of Design, Moscow, 1748

Institute of the Biochemistry and Physiology of Micro-organisms, Moscow, 1741

Institute of the Biochemistry and Physiology of Plants and Micro-organisms, Saratov, 1741

Institute of the Biology and Immunology of the Reproduction and Development of Organisms, Sofia, 301

Institute of the Biology of Inland Waters, Borok, 1741

Institute of the Biosphere, Dzhalal-Abad, 1357

Institute of the Brain, Moscow, 1737

Institute of the Chemistry and Physics of Polymers, Tashkent, 2748

Institute of the Chemistry and Technology of Rare Elements and Mineral Raw Materials, Apatity, 1744

Institute of the Chemistry of High-Purity Substances, Nizhny Novgorod, 1744

Institute of the Chemistry of Plant Substances, Tashkent, 2748

Institute of the Corrosion and Protection of Metals, Shenyang, 433

Institute of the Earth's Crust, Irkutsk, 1744

Institute of the Ecology and Genetics of Micro-organisms, Perm, 1741

Institute of the Ecology of Natural Complexes, Tomsk, 1741

Institute of the Ecology of the Volga Basin, 1741

Institute of the Economics and Organization of Industrial Production, Novosibirsk, 1748

Institute of the Economics of the Comprehensive Assimilation of the Natural Resources of the North, Yakutsk, 1734

Institute of the Estonian Language, Tallinn, 673

Institute of the Geology and Exploitation of Fossil Fuels, Moscow, 1749

Institute of the Geology of Ore Deposits, Petrography, Mineralogy and Geochemistry, Moscow, 1744

Institute of the History and Theory of Art, Chişinău, 1445

Institute of the History, Archaeology and Ethnography of the Peoples of the Far East, Vladivostok, 1735

Institute of the History of Material Culture, St Petersburg, 1735

Institute of the History of Natural Sciences, Beijing, 431

Institute of the History of Science and Technology, Moscow, 1740

Institute of the Ionosphere, Almaty, 1305

Institute of the Ionosphere, Kharkiv, 2102

Institute of the Mineralogy, Geochemistry and Crystal Chemistry of Rare Elements, Moscow, 1744

Institute of the Molecular Pathology and Biochemistry of Ecology, Novosibirsk, 1737

Institute of the Physiology and Pathology of Breathing, Blagoveshchensk, 1737

Institute of the Problems of Cryobiology and Cryomedicine of the National Academy of Sciences of Ukraine, Kharkiv, 2101

Institute of the Sugar Industry and Bioproducts, Gorna Orjahovica, 300

Institute of Theatre and Film (Kabinet divadla a filmu SAV), Bratislava, 1843

Institute of Theoretical and Applied Mathematics, Almaty, 1305

Institute of Theoretical and Applied Mechanics, Novosibirsk, 1749

Institute of Theoretical and Experimental Biophysics, Pushchino, 1741

Institute of Theoretical and Experimental Physics, Moscow, 1744

Institute of Theoretical and Physical Chemistry, Athens, 910

Institute of Theoretical Astronomy, St Petersburg, 1744

Institute of Theoretical Pedagogics and International Research in Education, Moscow, 1734

Institute of Theoretical Physics and Astronomy, Vilnius, 1377

Institute of Theoretical Physics, Beijing, 433

Institute of Thermal Engineering, Pyongsong, 1319

Institute of Thermal Physics, Ekaterinburg, 1744

Institute of Thermophysics, Novosibirsk, 1744

Institute of Thracian Studies 'Prof. Alexnder Fol', Sofia, 300

Institute of Tideland Construction, Pyongyang, 1320

Institute of Trade and Economics, Pyongyang, 1318

Institute of Trade Machinery, Moscow, 1749

Institute of Traditional Medicine, Ulan Bator, 1450

Institute of Translation and Interpreting, London, 2134

Institute of Traumatology and Orthopaedics, Irkutsk, 1736

Institute of Tropical and Subtropical Crops, Nelspruit, 1865

Institute of Tropical Forestry, Rio Piedras, 2740

Institute of Turkology Library, Istanbul, 2000

Institute of Upland Stockbreeding and Agriculture, Trojan, 300

Institute of USA and Canada Studies, Moscow, 1734

Institute of Vaccine and Serum Production Research, Nha Trang, 2773

Institute of Vaccines and Sera, Tashkent, 2748

Institute of Vegetable Crops, 207

Institute of Vertebrate Palaeontology and Palaeo-Anthropology, Beijing, 431

Institute of Veterinary Research, Hanoi, 2772

Institute of Veterinary Research of the Ukrainian Academy of Agricultural Sciences, Kyiv, 2099

Institute of Veterinary Research, Ulan Bator, 1449

Institute of Viral Preparations, Moscow, 1737

Institute of Virology, Bratislava, 1843

Institute of Viticulture and Oenology, Pleven, 300

Institute of Vocational Education, St Petersburg, 1735

Institute of Volcanology and Seismology, Petropavlovsk-Kamchatskii, 1744

Institute of Water and Ecological Problems, Khabarovsk, 1741

Institute of Water Management and Engineering Ecology, Tbilisi, 780

Institute of Water Problems and Hydropower, Bishkek, 1357

Institute of Water Problems, Moscow, 1744

Institute of Water Problems of the North, Petrozavodsk, 1744

Institute of Water Problems, Sofia, 300

Institute of Water Problems, Tashkent, 2749

Institute of Weather Modification, Beijing, 433

Institute of Welding, Nampo, 1320

Institute of West Asian and African Studies, Beijing, 430

Institute of Wheat and Sunflower 'Dobroudja', 300

Institute of Wood Chemistry, Riga, 1361

Institute of World Economics and International Relations, Moscow, 1734

Institute of World Economy and International Relations, Kyiv, 2100

Institute of World History, Moscow, 1735

Institute of World Literature, Bratislava, 1843

Institute of World Religions, Beijing, 433

Institute of Zoology, Almaty, 1305

Institute of Zoology and Botany, Tartu, 673

Institute of Zoology, Ashgabat, 2091

Institute of Zoology, Baku, 185

Institute of Zoology, Beijing, 431

Institute of Zoology, Bratislava, 1843

Institute of Zoology, Chişinău, 1445

Institute of Zoology 'I. I. Schmalhausen', Kyiv, 2101

Institute of Zoology, London, 2150

Institute of Zoology, Minsk, 208

Institute of Zoology, Pyongyang, 1319

Institute of Zoology, Sofia, 301

Institute of Zoology, Taipei, 553

Institute of Zoology, Tashkent, 2748

Institute of Zoology, Tbilisi, 781

Institute of Zoology, Yerevan, 113

Institute Museum of Genocide, Yerevan, 112

Institutes for Applied Research, Ben-Gurion University of the Negev, 1095

Institutes of Technology and Polytechnics of New Zealand, Wellington, 1500

Institutet för Internationellt Företagande, Stockholm, 1990

Institutet för Näringslivsforskning, Stockholm, 1971

Instituti i Arkeologjisë, Tiranë, 76

Instituti i Duhanit, Cërrik, 75

Instituti i Energjetikës, Tiranë, 76

Instituti i Fizikës Bërthamore, Tiranë, 76

Instituti i Gjuhësisë dhe i Letërsisë, Tiranë, 76

Instituti i Hidrometeorologjisë, Tiranë, 76

Instituti i Historisë, Tiranë, 76

Instituti i Informatikës dhe i Matematikës së Aplikuar, Tiranë, 76

Instituti i Kërkimeve Biologjike, Tiranë, 76

Instituti i Kërkimeve Bujqësore Lushnje, 75

Instituti i Kërkimeve Pyjore dhe Kullotave, Tiranë, 75

Instituti i Kërkimeve të Foragjere, Fushë-Krujë, 75

Instituti i Kërkimeve të Pemëve Frutore dhe Vreshtave, Tiranë, 75

Instituti i Kerkimeve të Ushqimit, Tiranë, 76

Instituti i Kërkimeve të Zooteknisë, Tiranë, 76

Instituti i Kërkimeve Veterinare, Tiranë, 75

Instituti i Kerkimit te Bimeve te Arave, Stacioni Eksperimental, Korçe, 75

Instituti i Kulturës Popullore, Tiranë, 76

Instituti i Mbrojtjes Bimeve, Durrës, 75

Instituti i Misrit dhe Orizit, Shkodër, 75

Instituti i Mjekësisë Popullore, Tiranë, 76

Instituti i Monumenteve të Kulturës, Tiranë, 76

Instituti i Perimeve dhe i Patates, Tiranë, 75

Instituti i Shëndetit Publik, Tiranë, 76

Instituti i Sizmologjise, Tiranë, 76

Instituti i Studimeve dhe i Projektimeve Gjeologjike të Naftës e të Gazit, Fier, 76

Instituti i Studimeve dhe i Projektimeve të Hidrocentraleve, Tiranë, 76

Instituti i Studimeve dhe i Projektimeve të Metalurgjise, Elbasan, 76

Instituti i Studimeve dhe i Projektimeve të Minierave, Tiranë, 76

Instituti i Studimeve dhe i Projektimeve të Teknologjisë Kimike, Tiranë, 76

Instituti i Studimeve dhe i Projektimeve të Teknologjisë Mekanike, Tiranë, 76

Instituti i Studimeve dhe i Projektimeve të Veprave të Kullimit dhe Ujitjes, Tiranë, 75

Instituti i Studimeve dhe i Projektimeve Teknologjike të Mineraleve, Tiranë, 76

Instituti i Studimeve dhe i Projektimeve Teknologjike të Naftës e të Gazit, Tiranë, 76

Instituti i Studimeve dhe i Teknologjisë Ndërtimit, Tiranë, 76

Instituti i Studimeve dhe Projektimeve Mekanike, Tiranë, 76

Instituti i Studimeve dhe Projektimeve të Gjeologjise, Tiranë, 76

Instituti i Studimeve e Projektimeve Urbanistikë, Tiranë, 76

Instituti i Studimeve Pedagogjike, Tiranë, 76

Instituti i Studimeve të Marrëdhënievc Ndërkombëtare, Tiranë, 76

Instituti i Studimit të Tokave, Tiranë, 76

Instituti i Ullirit dhe i Agrumeve, Vlorë, 76

Institution of Agricultural Engineers, Bedford, 2125

Institution of Certificated Mechanical and Electrical Engineers, South Africa, 1865

Institution of Chemical Engineers, Rugby, 2144

Institution of Civil Engineers, London, 2144

Institution of Civil Engineers (Republic of Ireland Division), 1082

Institution of Electrical and Electronics Engineers Pakistan, 1565

Institution of Electrical Engineers Ireland Branch, 1082

Institution of Electronics and Telecommunication Engineers (IETE), New Delhi, 972

Institution of Electronics, Spital, 2144

Institution of Engineering and Technology Library and Archives, London, 2161

Institution of Engineering and Technology, London, 2144

Institution of Engineering Designers, Westbury, 2144

Institution of Engineers and Shipbuilders in Scotland, 2144

Institution of Engineers, Australia, 121

Institution of Engineers, Bangladesh, 192

Institution of Engineers (India), 972

Institution of Engineers of Ireland, 1082

Institution of Engineers of Kenya, 1311

Institution of Engineers (Pakistan), 1565

Institution of Engineers, Sri Lanka, 1954

Institution of Environmental Sciences, Bourne, 2138

Institution of Fire Engineers, Leicester, 2144

Institution of Gas Engineers and Managers, London, 2144

Institution of Highways and Transportation, London, 2144

Institution of Incorporated Engineers (IIE), London, 2144

Institution of Lighting Engineers, Rugby, 2144

Institution of Materials, Minerals and Mining (Zimbabwe Section), 2788

Institution of Mechanical Engineers, London, 2144

Institution of Nuclear Engineers, London, 2144

Institution of Professional Engineers New Zealand, 1502

Institution of Structural Engineers, London, 2144

Institution of Surveyors, Australia, 122

Instituto Açoriano de Cultura, 1674

Instituto 'Adolfo Lutz', São Paulo, 257

Instituto Agrario Argentino de Cultura Rural, 92

Instituto Agrario Nacional, Caracas, 2762

Instituto Agrícola Metodista 'El Vergel', 425

Instituto Agronômico, Campinas, 256

Instituto Antártico Argentino, 93

Instituto Antártico Chileno, 413

Instituto Argentino de Investigaciónes de las Zonas Aridas (IADIZA), 94

Instituto Argentino de Nivologia, Glaciología y Ciencias Ambientales (IANIGLA), 94

Instituto Argentino de Normalización (IRAM), 95

Instituto Argentino de Oceanografía (IADO), 94

Instituto Argentino de Radioastronomía (IAR), 94

Instituto Arqueológico, Histórico e Geográfico Pernambucano, 253

Instituto Aula de 'Mediterráneo', 1890

Instituto Azucarero Dominicano, 646

Instituto 'Benjamin Constant', Urca, 257

Instituto Biológico, São Paulo, 257

Instituto Boliviano de Ciencia y Tecnología Nuclear, 240

Instituto Boliviano del Petróleo (IBP), 240

Instituto Bonaerense de Numismática y Antigüedades, 90

Instituto Brasileiro de Economia, 253

Instituto Brasileiro de Educação, Ciência e Cultura (IBECC), Rio de Janeiro, 252

Instituto Brasileiro de Estudos e Pesquisas de Gastroenterologia (IBEPEGE), 257

Instituto Brasileiro de Informação em Ciência e Tecnologia (IBICT), 259

Instituto Brasileiro de Petróleo, 258

Instituto Brasileiro do Meio Ambiente e dos Recursos Naturais Renováveis (IBAMA), 256

Instituto Butantan, 257

Instituto Cajal, 1005

Instituto Camões, Lisbon, 1674

Instituto Caribe de Antropología y Sociología, Caracas, 2763

Instituto Caro y Cuervo, Bogotá, 562

Instituto Cartográfico Militar de las Fuerzas Armadas, Santo Domingo, 646

Instituto Centroamericano de Administración de Empresas (INCAE), Alajuela, 587

Instituto Centroamericano de Administración de Empresas (INCAE), Managua, 1515

Instituto Centroamericano de Administración Pública (ICAP), San José, 584, 588

Instituto Centroamericano de Investigación y Tecnología Industrial (ICAITI), Guatemala City, 926

Instituto Cervantes, Algiers, 79

Instituto Cervantes, Amman, 1299

Instituto Cervantes, Athens, 909

Instituto Cervantes, Beirut, 1364

Instituto Cervantes, Berlin, 789

Instituto Cervantes, Brussels, 217

Instituto Cervantes, Bucharest, 1692

Instituto Cervantes, Budapest, 937

Instituto Cervantes, Cairo, 658

Instituto Cervantes, Damascus, 2021
Instituto Cervantes, Dublin, 1082
Instituto Cervantes, Istanbul, 2057
Instituto Cervantes, Lisbon, 1675
Instituto Cervantes, London, 2134
Instituto Cervantes, Madrid, 1887
Instituto Cervantes, Manila, 1601
Instituto Cervantes, Moscow, 1728
Instituto Cervantes, New York, 2291
Instituto Cervantes, Paris, 708
Instituto Cervantes, Rabat, 1457
Instituto Cervantes, Rio de Janeiro, 254
Instituto Cervantes, Rome, 1123
Instituto Cervantes, Stockholm, 1970
Instituto Cervantes, Tel Aviv, 1093
Instituto Cervantes, Tunis, 2053
Instituto Cervantes, Utrecht, 1476
Instituto Cervantes, Vienna, 162
Instituto Cervantes, Warsaw, 1622
Instituto Colombiano Agropecuario, 563
Instituto Colombiano de Antropología e Historia, 563
Instituto Colombiano de Crédito Educativo y Estudios Técnicos en el Exterior (ICETEX), 561
Instituto Colombiano de Geología y Minería (INGEOMINAS), Bogotá, 563
Instituto Colombiano de Normas Técnicas y Certificación (ICONTEC), 563
Instituto Colombiano del Petróleo, 563
Instituto Colombiano para el Desarrollo de la Ciencia y la Tecnología 'Francisco José de Caldas' (Colciencias), 563
Instituto Colombiano para el Fomento de la Educación Superior, 563
Instituto Conmemorativo Gorgas de Estudios de la Salud, Panamá, 1582
Instituto Costarricense de Investigación y Enseñanza en Nutrición y Salud (INCIENSA), 585
Instituto Cubano de Investigaciones de los Derivados de la Caña de Azúcar (ICIDCA), 599
Instituto Cubano de Investigaciones Mineras y Metalúrgicas, 599
Instituto Cultural de Macau, 551
Instituto de Administración, Bayamo, 599
Instituto de Algodão de Moçambique, 1463
Instituto de Altos Estudos, Lisbon, 1675
Instituto de Antropología e Historia, Guatemala City, 925
Instituto de Arte Peruano 'José Sabogal', 1590
Instituto de Astrofísica de Canarias (IAC), 1895
Instituto de Astronomía, México, 1418
Instituto de Astronomía y Geodesia, Madrid, 1895
Instituto de Bibliografía del Ministerio de Educación de la Provincia de Buenos Aires, 92
Instituto de Biología Andina, Lima, 1592
Instituto de Biología y Medicina Experimental, Buenos Aires, 93
Instituto de Botánica 'C. Spegazzini', Buenos Aires, 95
Instituto de Botánica 'Darwinion', 95
Instituto de Botánica del Nordeste (IBONE), Corrientes, 94
Instituto de Botánica, São Paulo, 257
Instituto de Cancerología 'Cupertino Arteaga', 240
Instituto de Chile, 410
Instituto de Cibernética, Matemática y Física (ICIMAF), Havana, 599
Instituto de Ciencias Naturales, Bogotá, 563
Instituto de Ciencias Nucleares, Quito, 651
Instituto de Ciencias Nucleares y Energías Alternativas, Bogotá, 563
Instituto de Coimbra, 1674
Instituto de Cooperación con el Mundo Arabe, Mediterráneo y Países en Desarrollo, Madrid, 1886
Instituto de Cooperación Iberoamericana, Madrid, 1887

Instituto de Cultura Alimentaria Birchner-Benner, 1591
Instituto de Cultura Dominicana, 646
Instituto de Cultura Puertorriqueña, 2740
Instituto de Desarrollo Económico y Social, Buenos Aires, 93
Instituto de Desarrollo Tecnológico para la Industria Química (INTEC), Santa Fé, 94
Instituto de Ecología, AC, Xalapa, 1418
Instituto de Ecología y Sistemática, Havana, 599
Instituto de Economia Agrícola, São Paulo, 256
Instituto de Edafología Agrícola, Buenos Aires, 92
Instituto de Empresa, Madrid, 1951
Instituto de Endocrinología 'Profesor Dr Juan C. Mussio Fournier', 2744
Instituto de Engenharia Nuclear (IEN), Rio de Janeiro, 258
Instituto de Enseñanza Superior del Ejército Buenos Aires, 110
Instituto de España, 1887
Instituto de Estudios Etnológicos, Lima, 1591
Instituto de Estudios Fiscales, Madrid, 1894
Instituto de Estudios Islámicos, Lima, 1591
Instituto de Estudios Norteamericanos, Barcelona, 1887
Instituto de Estudios Superiores de Administración (IESA), Caracas, 2770
Instituto de Estudios Superiores en Ciencia y Tecnología del Mar, Veracruz, 1442
Instituto de Filosofía, Havana, 600
Instituto de Filosofía, Madrid, 1895
Instituto de Fomento Pesquero, Valparaíso, 412
Instituto de Geocronología y Geología Isotópica (INGEIS), Buenos Aires, 94
Instituto de Geofísica y Astronomía, Havana, 599
Instituto de Geografía Tropical, Havana, 599
Instituto de Geografía y Conservación de Recursos Naturales, Mérida, 2762
Instituto de Historia y Cultura Naval, Madrid, 1889
Instituto de Información Científica Tecnológica (IDICT), Havana, 600
Instituto de Ingenieros de Chile, 412
Instituto de Ingenieros de Minas de Chile, 412
Instituto de Investigação Agronómica, Huambo, 86
Instituto de Investigação Científica 'Bento da Rocha Cabral', 1677
Instituto de Investigação Científica Tropical, Lisbon, 1675
Instituto de Investigação das Pescas e do Mar, Lisbon, 1677
Instituto de Investigação Veterinária, Lubango, 86
Instituto de Investigación Agropecuaria de Panamá, Panama City, 1582
Instituto de Investigación de Productos Naturales, de Análisis y de Síntesis Orgánica (IPNAYS), Santa Fé, 94
Instituto de Investigación Médica 'Mercedes y Martín Ferreyra' (INIMEC), 94
Instituto de Investigaciones Agropecuarias 'Jorge Dimitrov', 599
Instituto de Investigaciones Agropecuarias, Santiago, 412
Instituto de Investigaciones Alérgicas 'Dr Luis E. Betetta', San Miguel, 1591
Instituto de Investigaciones Arqueológicas y Museo 'R.P. Gustavo le Paige, S.J.', 413
Instituto de Investigaciones Avícolas, Havana, 599
Instituto de Investigaciones Bibliográficas, México, 1417
Instituto de Investigaciones Biológicas Clemente Estable, 2744

Instituto de Investigaciones Bioquímicas (INIBIBB), Bahía Blanca, 94
Instituto de Investigaciones de Sanidad Vegetal, Havana, 599
Instituto de Investigaciones Eléctricas, Cuernavaca, 1419
Instituto de Investigaciónes en Catálisis y Petroquímica (INCAPE), Santa Fé, 94
Instituto de Investigaciones en Riego y Drenaje, Havana, 599
Instituto de Investigaciones en Viandas Tropicales, Santo Domingo, 599
Instituto de Investigaciones Estadísticas, Havana, 599
Instituto de Investigaciones Estadísticas (INIE), Tucumán, 94
Instituto de Investigaciones Farmacológicas (ININFA), Buenos Aires, 94
Instituto de Investigaciones Forestales, Havana, 599
Instituto de Investigaciones Fundamentales en Agricultura Tropical 'Alejandro de Humboldt', 599
Instituto de Investigaciones Geohistóricas (IIGHI), Resistencia, 94
Instituto de Investigaciones Marinas de Punta de Betín 'José Benito Vives de Andreis' (INVEMAR), 563
Instituto de Investigaciones Médicas 'Alfredo Lanari', Buenos Aires, 93
Instituto de Investigaciones para el Desarrollo de la Salud, Quito, 650
Instituto de Investigaciones para la Mecanización Agropecuaria, Capdevila, 599
Instituto de Investigaciones Porcinas, Bauta, 599
Instituto de Investigaciones Veterinarias, Maracay, 2762
Instituto de Investigaciones y Ensayes de Materiales (IDIEM) Universidad de Chile, 413
Instituto de la Ingeniería de España, 1891
Instituto de la Patagonia, Punta Arenas, 418
Instituto de Letras e Artes, Pelotas, 295
Instituto de Lexicología e Lexicografía da Língua Portuguesa, Lisbon, 1677
Instituto de Limnología Dr Raul A. Ringuelet (ILPLA), 94
Instituto de Literatura y Lingüística, Havana, 599
Instituto de Matemática (INMABB), Bahía Blanca, 94
Instituto de Matemáticas, México, 1418
Instituto de Mecánica Aplicada (IMA), Bahía Blanca, 94
Instituto de Mecánica Aplicada y Estructuras, Santa Fé, 95
Instituto de Medicina Experimental, Caracas, 2763
Instituto de Medicina Experimental del Servicio Nacional de Salud, Santiago, 413
Instituto de Medicina Molecular, Lisbon, 1677
Instituto de Mejoramiento Profesional del Magisterio, 2769
Instituto de Meteorología, Havana, 600
Instituto de Meteorologia, Lisbon, 1677
Instituto de Neurobiología (IDNEU), Buenos Aires, 94
Instituto de Numismática y Antigüedades del Paraguay, Asunción, 1587
Instituto de Nutrición de Centro América y Panamá (INCAP), Guatemala City, 925
Instituto de Oceanología, Havana, 599
Instituto de Oncología, Montevideo, 2744
Instituto de Pesquisas do Jardim Botânico do Rio de Janeiro, 257
Instituto de Pesquisas Energéticas e Nucleares (IPEN), São Paulo, 258
Instituto de Pesquisas Tecnológicas do Estado de São Paulo S.A. (IPT), 258

Instituto de Planeamiento Regional y Urbano (IPRU), Buenos Aires, 92
Instituto de Radioproteção e Dosimetria (IRD), Rio de Janeiro, 258
Instituto de Relaciones Europeo-Latinoamericanas (IRELA), Madrid, 1894
Instituto de Salud Pública de Chile, 413
Instituto de Saúde, São Paulo, 257
Instituto de Sociología Boliviana (ISBO), 240
Instituto de Suelos y Agroquímica, Havana, 599
Instituto de Superación Educacional (ISE), Havana, 599
Instituto de Tecnología do Paraná, 258
Instituto de Teología para Religiosos–ITER, Caracas, 2757
Instituto de Valencia de Don Juan, 1899
Instituto de Zootecnia, Nova Odessa, 256
Instituto del Mar del Perú (IMARPE), 1591
Instituto del Patrimonio Histórico, Madrid, 1895
Instituto do Ceará, 253
Instituto dos Advogados Brasileiros, 253
Instituto dos Arquivos Nacionais, Torre do Tombo, Lisbon, 1679
Instituto Ecuatoriano de Antropología y Geografía, Quito, 651
Instituto Ecuatoriano de Ciencias Naturales, Quito, 651
Instituto Egipcio de Estudios Islámicos, Madrid, 1887
Instituto Español de Enseñanza Secundaria 'Severo Ochoa', 1462
Instituto Español de Hematología y Hemoterapia, 1895
Instituto Español de Oceanografía, 1895
Instituto Evandro Chagas (MS-Fundação Nacional de Saúde), Belém, 257
Instituto Experimental de Educación Primaria No. 1, Lima, 1591
Instituto Florestal (Estado de São Paulo), 256
Instituto Forestal, Santiago, 412
Instituto Formación Profesional 'Islas Filipinas', Madrid, 1952
Instituto Genealógico Brasileiro, 253
Instituto Geofísico del Perú, 1592
Instituto Geográfico 'Agustín Codazzi', Bogotá, 563
Instituto Geográfico e Histórico da Bahia, 253
Instituto Geográfico e Histórico do Amazonas (IGHA), 253
Instituto Geográfico Militar, Asunción, 1587
Instituto Geográfico Militar, Buenos Aires, 93
Instituto Geográfico Militar, La Paz, 240
Instituto Geográfico Militar, Quito, 650
Instituto Geográfico Militar, Santiago, 411
Instituto Geográfico Nacional (IGN), Tegucigalpa, 934
Instituto Geográfico Nacional 'Ing. Alfredo Obiols Gómez', Guatemala City, 925
Instituto Geográfico Nacional, Lima, 1590
Instituto Geográfico Nacional, Madrid, 1889
Instituto Geográfico Nacional, San José, 585
Instituto Geográfico Português, 1674
Instituto Geológico, Minero y Metalúrgico, Lima, 1592
Instituto Geológico, São Paulo, 253
Instituto Gregoriano de Lisboa, 1674
Instituto Hidrográfico, Lisbon, 1677
Instituto Histórico da Ilha Terceira, 1674
Instituto Histórico de Alagoas, 253
Instituto Histórico e Geográfico Brasileiro, 253
Instituto Histórico e Geográfico de Goiás, 253
Instituto Histórico e Geográfico de Santa Catarina, 253
Instituto Histórico e Geográfico de São Paulo, 253

Instituto Tecnológico de Ciudad Madero, 1441
Instituto Tecnológico de Costa Rica, 587
Instituto Tecnológico de Durango, 1441
Instituto Tecnológico de Electrónica 'Fernando Aguado Rico', 600
Instituto Tecnológico de la Caña de Azúcar 'Carlos M. de Cespedes', 599
Instituto Tecnológico de Mérida, 1441
Instituto Tecnológico de Morelia, 1442
Instituto Tecnológico de Oaxaca, 1442
Instituto Tecnológico de Orizaba, 1442
Instituto Tecnológico de Querétaro, 1442
Instituto Tecnológico de Saltillo, 1442
Instituto Tecnológico de Santo Domingo, 649
Instituto Tecnológico de Sonora, 1442
Instituto Tecnológico del Mar, Veracruz, 1418
Instituto Tecnológico do Estado de Pernambuco (ITEP), 258
Instituto Tecnológico e Científico 'Roberto Rios' (INTEC), 295
Instituto Tecnológico Geominero de España, 1895
Instituto Tecnológico y de Estudios Superiores de Monterrey, 1440
Instituto Tecnológico y de Estudios Superiores de Occidente, AC, Tlaquepaque, 1441
Instituto Torcuato di Tella, 92
Instituto Universitario Aeronáutico, Córdoba, 110
Instituto Universitario de la Policía Federal Argentina, Buenos Aires, 111
Instituto Universitário de Pesquisas do Rio de Janeiro, 294
Instituto Universitario de Seguridad Marítima, Buenos Aires, 111
Instituto Universitario Nacional del Arte, Buenos Aires, 111
Instituto Universitario Naval, Buenos Aires, 111
Instituto Universitario Ortega y Gasset, 1894
Instituto Universitario Politécnico 'Luis Caballero Mejías', Caracas, 2769
Instituto Universitario Salesiano 'Padre Ojeda', Los Teques, 2757
Instituto Uruguayo de Normas Técnicas, 2745
Instituto Venezolano de Investigaciones Científicas (IVIC), 2762
Instituto Vizcardo de Estudios Históricos, Miraflores, 1590
Instituto Zuliano de la Cultura 'Andrés E. Blanco', 2760
Instituts du Ministère de l'Enseignement Supérieur, Yaoundé, 319
Instituts für niederrheinische Kulturgeschichte und Regionalenwicklung, 841
Institutt for energiteknikk, Kjeller, 1545
Instituttet for sammenlignende kulturforskning, Oslo, 1545
Institutul Astronomic, Bucharest, 1696
Institutul Biblic și de Misiune al Bisericii Ortodoxe Române, 1693
Institutul Cultural Român, 1692
Institutul de Arheologie, Bucharest, 1695
Institutul de Arheologie, Iași, 1695
Institutul de Arheologie și Istoria Artei, Cluj-Napoca, 1695
Institutul de Arhitectură 'Ion Mincu', Bucharest, 1726
Institutul de Biochimie, Bucharest, 1696
Institutul de Biologie, Bucharest, 1696
Institutul de Biologie și Nutriție Animală Balotești, Balotești, 1693
Institutul de Biologie și Patologie Celulară 'Nicolae Simionescu', 1696
Institutul de Cercetare a Calității Vieții, Bucharest, 1697
Institutul de Cercetare-Dezvoltare pentru Apicultură, Bucharest, 1693
Institutul de Cercetare-Dezvoltare pentru Cartof si Sfeclă de Zahar, Brașov, 1693

Institutul de Cercetare-Dezvoltare pentru Cultura și Industrializarea Sfeclei de Zahăr și Substanțelor Dulci, Fundulea, 1693
Institutul de Cercetare Dezvoltare pentru Pomicultura, Pitești-Mărăcineni, 1694
Institutul de Cercetare și Dezvoltare pentru Bovine, Balotești, 1693
Institutul de Cercetare și Dezvoltare pentru Valorificarea Produselor Horticole, Bucharest, 1693
Institutul de Cercetare și Inginerie Tehnologică pentru Irigații și Drenaje, Băneasa, 1693
Institutul de Cercetare și Producție pentru Creșterea Ovinelor și Caprinelor, Constanța Palas, 1694
Institutul de Cercetare și Producție pentru Creșterea Păsărilor și Animalelor Mici, Balotești, 1694
Institutul de Cercetare și Producție pentru Cultura Pajiștilor, Brașov, 1694
Institutul de Cercetare și Proiectare Delta Dunării, Tulcea, 1696
Institutul de Cercetări Biologice Cluj-Napoca, 1696
Institutul de Cercetări Biologice Iași, 1696
Institutul de Cercetări Chimice, Bucharest, 1696
Institutul de Cercetări-Dezvoltare pentru Pedologie, Agrochimie și Protectia Mediului, Bucharest, 1694
Institutul de Cercetări Eco-Muzeale Tulcea, 1696
Institutul de Cercetări Economice 'Gheorghe Zane', 1694
Institutul de Cercetări Juridice, Bucharest, 1694
Institutul de Cercetări pentru Cereale și Plante Tehnice, Fundulea, 1694
Institutul de Cercetări pentru Ingineria Mediului, Bucharest, 1694
Institutul de Cercetări pentru Legumicultură și Floricultură, Vidra, 1694
Institutul de Cercetări pentru Viticultură și Vinificație, Valea Călugărească, 1694
Institutul de Cercetări și Amenajări Silvice, Bucharest, 1694
Institutul de Cercetări Socio-Umane 'C. S. Nicolaescu-Plopsor', Craiova, 1697
Institutul de Cercetări Socio-Umane, Sibiu, 1697
Institutul de Cercetări Socio-Umane, Timișoara, 1697
Institutul de Cercetări Socio-Umane, Tîrgu Mureș, 1697
Institutul de Chimie Alimentară, Bucharest, 1694
Institutul de Chimie Fizică, Bucharest, 1696
Institutul de Chimie Macromoleculară 'Petru Poni', 1696
Institutul de Chimie Organică 'Costin D. Nenițescu', Bucharest, 1696
Institutul de Chimie Timișoara, 1696
Institutul de Economie a Industriei, Bucharest, 1694
Institutul de Economie Agrară, Bucharest, 1694
Institutul de Economie Mondială, Bucharest, 1694
Institutul de Economie Națională, Bucharest, 1694
Institutul de Endocrinologie 'C.I. Parhon', Bucharest, 1695
Institutul de Etnografie și Folclor 'Constantin Brăiloiu', Bucharest, 1697
Institutul de Filologie Română 'Al. Philippide', 1696
Institutul de Filosofie și Psihologie 'C. Rădulescu-Motru', Bucharest, 1697
Institutul de Finanțe, Prețuri și Probleme Valutare 'Victor Slavescu', Bucharest, 1695
Institutul de Fizică Atomică 'Horia Hulubei', Bucharest, 1696

Institutul de Fiziologie Normală și Patologică 'D. Danielopolu', Bucharest, 1695
Institutul de Geodinamică 'Sabba S. Ștefănescu', Bucharest, 1696
Institutul de Geografie, Bucharest, 1695
Institutul de Informatică Teoretică, Iași, 1697
Institutul de Istoria Artei 'George Oprescu', Bucharest, 1695
Institutul de Istorie 'A. D. Xenopol', Iași, 1695
Institutul de Istorie 'Nicolae Iorga', Bucharest, 1695
Institutul de Istorie și Teorie Literară 'G. Călinescu', Bucharest, 1695
Institutul de Lingvistica 'Iorgu Iordan–Al. Rosetti', 1695
Institutul de Matematică 'Octav Mayer', Iași, 1696
Institutul de Matematică 'Simion Stoilow', Bucharest, 1696
Institutul de Mecanica Solidelor, Bucharest, 1697
Institutul de Medicină Internă 'Nicolae Gh. Lupu', Bucharest, 1695
Institutul de Neurologie și Psihiatrie, Bucharest, 1695
Institutul de Patologie și Genetică Medicală 'V. Babeș', 1695
Institutul de Prognoză Economică, Bucharest, 1695
Institutul de Psihologie, Bucharest, 1697
Institutul de Relații Internaționale din Moldova, 1447
Institutul de Sănătate Publică, București, 1695
Institutul de Sănătate Publică, Iași, 1695
Institutul de Sănătate Publică 'Prof. Dr Iuliu Moldovan', Cluj-Napoca, 1695
Institutul de Sănătate Publică 'Prof. Dr Leonida Georgescu', Timișoara, 1696
Institutul de Sociologie, Bucharest, 1697
Institutul de Speologie 'Emil Racoviță', 1696
Institutul de Statistică Matematică și Matematică Aplicată, Bucharest, 1696
Institutul de Științe Politice și Relații Internaționale, Bucharest, 1697
Institutul de Științe Socio-Umane, Iași, 1697
Institutul de Virusologie 'ștefan S. Nicolau' (IVN), Bucharest, 1696
Institutul Geologic al României, Bucharest, 1696
Institutul Național de Cercetare-Dezvoltare 'Dr I. Cantacuzino', Bucharest, 1696
Institutul Național de Cercetare-Dezvoltare pentru Fizică Tehnică – IFT Iași, 1697
Institutul Național de Cercetare-Dezvoltare pentru Protecția Mediului (ICIM București), Bucharest, 1697
Institutul Național de Cercetări Economice, Bucharest, 1695
Institutul Național de Educație Fizică și Sport, Chișinău, 1447
Institutul Național de Informare și Documentare, Bucharest, 1697
Institutul Național de Medicină Legală 'Mina Minovici', 1696
Institutul Național de Medicină Veterinară Pasteur, Bucharest, 1694
Institutul Național de Meteorologie și Hidrologie, Bucharest, 1697
Institutul Național de Metrologie, Bucharest, 1697
Institutul Oncologic, Bucharest, 1696
Institutul pentru Controlul de Stat al Medicamentului și Cercetări Farmaceutice 'Petre Ionescu-Stoian', Bucharest, 1696
Institutul Român de Cercetări Marine, 1694
Institutum Romanum Finlandiae, Rome, 1130

Instituut voor Milieu en Agritechniek (IMAG-DLO), Wageningen, 1481
Instituut voor Plantenziektenkundig Onderzoek (IPO–DLO), Wageningen, 1480
Instrument Society of America, 2300
Instytut Agrofizyki im. Bohdana Dobrzańskiego PAN, 1626
Instytut Archeologii i Etnologii PAN, 1628
Instytut Automatyki Systemów Energetycznych, Wrocław, 1632
Instytut Badań Edukacyjnych, Warsaw, 1628
Instytut Badań Literackich PAN, 1629
Instytut Badań Systemowych PAN, 1632
Instytut Badawczy Dróg i Mostów, Warsaw, 1632
Instytut Badawczy Leśnictwa, Warsaw, 1626
Instytut Biochemii i Biofizyki PAN, 1630
Instytut Biocybernetyki i Inżynierii Biomedycznej PAN, Warsaw, 1629
Instytut Biologii Doświadczalnej im M. Nenckiego, 1630
Instytut Biopolimerów i Włókien Chemicznych, Łódź, 1634
Instytut Biotechnologii Przemysłu Rolno-Spożywczego, Warsaw, 1626
Instytut Botaniki im. Władysława Szafera PAN, 1630
Instytut Budownictwa, Mechanizacji i Elektryfikacji Rolnictwa, Warsaw, 1626
Instytut Budownictwa Wodnego PAN, 1632
Instytut Celulozowo-Papierniczy, Warsaw, 1626
Instytut-Centrum Badań Molekularnych i Makromolekularnych PAN, 1631
Instytut Chemii Bioorganicznej PAN, 1630
Instytut Chemii Fizycznej PAN, 1631
Instytut Chemii i Techniki Jądrowej, Warsaw, 1632
Instytut Chemii Nieorganicznej, Gliwice, 1632
Instytut Chemii Organicznej PAN, 1631
Instytut Chemii Przemysłowej, Warsaw, 1632
Instytut Dendrologii PAN, 1630
Instytut Ekonomiki Rolnictwa i Gospodarki Żywnościowej, Warsaw, 1626
Instytut Ekspertyz Sądowych, Cracow, 1627
Instytut Elektrotechniki, Warsaw, 1632
Instytut Energetyki, Warsaw, 1633
Instytut Energii Atomowej, Otwock-Świerk, 1633
Instytut Farmaceutyczny, Warsaw, 1629
Instytut Farmakologii PAN, 1629
Instytut Filozofii i Socjologii PAN, 1632
Instytut Finansów, Warsaw, 1627
Instytut Fizjologii i Żywienia Zwierząt im. Jana Kielanowskiego PAN, 1626
Instytut Fizjologii Roślin im. Franciszka Górskiego PAN, 1626
Instytut Fizyki Jądrowej im. Henryka Niewodniczańskiego, 1631
Instytut Fizyki Molekularnej PAN, 1631
Instytut Fizyki PAN, 1631
Instytut Fizyki Plazmy i Laserowej Mikrosyntezy im. Sylwestra Kaliskiego, 1631
Instytut Funkcjonowania Gospodarki Narodowej, Warsaw, 1627
Instytut Genetyki Człowieka PAN, 1629
Instytut Genetyki i Hodowli Zwierząt PAN, 1626
Instytut Genetyki Roślin PAN, 1626
Instytut Geodezji i Kartografii, Warsaw, 1628
Instytut Geofizyki PAN, 1631
Instytut Geografii i Przestrzennego Zagospodarowania im. S. Leszczyckiego PAN, 1628
Instytut Gospodarki Mieszkaniowej, Filtrowa, 1627

International Centre for Advanced Mediterranean Agronomic Studies, 42

International Centre for Agricultural Education (CIEA), 52

International Centre for Ancient and Modern Tapestry, 44

International Centre for Brewing and Distilling, Edinburgh, 2210

International Centre for Classical Research, Athens, 911

International Centre for Environmental Biology, Tallinn, 673

International Centre for Ethnic Studies, 48

International Centre for Integrated Mountain Development (ICIMOD), Kathmandu, 1472

International Centre for Island Technology, Stromness, 2210

International Centre for Mathematical Sciences, Edinburgh, 2210

International Centre for Pashtu Studies Kabul, 73

International Centre for Science and High Technology (ICS), 56

International Centre for Scientific and Technical Information, Moscow, 1752

International Centre for the Study of the Preservation and Restoration of Cultural Property (ICCROM), 44

International Centre for Tropical Agriculture, 41

International Centre of Films for Children and Young People, 44

International Centre of Insect Physiology and Ecology, 69

International Christian University Library, Tokyo, 1184

International Christian University, Tokyo, 1274

International College of Surgeons, 60

International Commission for Food Industries, 42

International Commission for Optics (ICO), 69

International Commission for the History of Representative and Parliamentary Institutions, 48

International Commission for the Scientific Exploration of the Mediterranean Sea, 69

International Commission of Agricultural Engineering, 42, 55

International Commission of Jurists, 58

International Commission on Glass (ICG), 55

International Commission on Illumination, 56

International Commission on Irrigation and Drainage, 55

International Commission on Large Dams, 55

International Commission on Occupational Health, 63

International Commission on Zoological Nomenclature, 69

International Committee for Social Science Information and Documentation, 46

International Committee for the History of Art, 37

International Committee of Historical Sciences, 37

International Committee of Military Medicine, 61

International Committee on Veterinary Gross Anatomical Nomenclature (ICVGAN), 42

International Communication Association, Austin, 2300

International Community of Writers' Unions, Moscow, 1729

International Comparative Literature Association, 44

International Confederation for Thermal Analysis and Calorimetry (ICTAC), 69

International Confederation of Societies of Authors and Composers, 58

International Congress of African Studies, 38

International Congress on Animal Reproduction, 42

International Congress on Fracture (ICF), 55

International Congress on Tropical Medicine and Malaria, 61

International Council for Adult Education, 52

International Council for Film, Television and Audiovisual Communication, 44

International Council for Open and Distance Education, 52

International Council for Philosophy and Humanistic Studies (ICPHS), 37

International Council for Research and Innovation in Building and Construction, 56

International Council for Scientific and Technical Information, 56

International Council for the Exploration of the Sea (ICES), 69

International Council for Traditional Music, 65

International Council of Graphic Design Associations (ICOGRADA), 44

International Council of Museums, Andorran National Committee, 85

International Council of Museums (ICOM), 44

International Council of Nurses (ICN), 60

International Council of Scientific Unions (ICSU), 35

International Council on Alcohol and Addictions, 61

International Council on Archives, 46

International Council on Large Electric Systems, 56

International Council on Monuments and Sites (ICOMOS), 44

International Council on Social Welfare, 48

International Crops Research Institute for the Semi-Arid Tropics (ICRISAT), 41

International Cystic Fibrosis Association, 63

International Dairy Federation, 42

International Development Law Organization, 59

International Development Research Centre, Ottawa, 328

International Diabetes Federation, 60

International Earth Rotation and Reference Systems Service (IERS), 70

International Economic Association, 38

International Education Association of South Africa, Durban, 1862

International Electrotechnical Commission, 56

International Epidemiological Association, 63

International Federation for Cell Biology, 70

International Federation for European Law, 59

International Federation for Information Processing, 57

International Federation for Medical and Biological Engineering, 63

International Federation for Modern Languages and Literatures, 38

International Federation for Theatre Research, 44

International Federation of Agricultural Producers, 43

International Federation of Anatomists, 63

International Federation of Automatic Control (IFAC), 55

International Federation of Automotive Engineering Societies, 57

International Federation of Business and Professional Women (BPW International), 48

International Federation of Catholic Universities, 52

International Federation of Clinical Chemistry and Laboratory Medicine, 61

International Federation of Clinical Neurophysiology, 60

International Federation of Film Archives, 46

International Federation of Gynaecology and Obstetrics, 63

International Federation of Library Associations and Institutions (IFLA), 46

International Federation of Medical Students' Associations, 61

International Federation of Musicians, 65

International Federation of Operational Research Societies (IFORS), 57

International Federation of Ophthalmological Societies, 63

International Federation of Oto-Rhino-Laryngological Societies, 60

International Federation of Philosophical Societies, 38

International Federation of Physical Education, 63

International Federation of Robotics, 57

International Federation of Social Science Organizations, 39

International Federation of Societies for Microscopy, 70

International Federation of Surgical Colleges, 60

International Federation of Teachers of French, 52

International Federation of the Societies of Classical Studies, 38

International Federation of University Women, 52

International Federation of Workers' Education Associations, 53

International Fiscal Association, 48

International Food Information Service, 70

International Food Policy Research Institute, 41

International Foundation of the High-Altitude Research Stations, Jungfraujoch and Gornergrat, 70

International Gas Union, 55

International Genetics Federation, 70

International Geographical Union (IGU), 35

International Geological Congress, 70

International Glaciological Society, 70

International Hospital Federation, 63

International Hydrographic Organization, 70

International Institute for Applied Systems Analysis (IIASA), 70

International Institute for Asian Studies, Leiden, 1479

International Institute for Conservation of Historic and Artistic Works, 44

International Institute for Geo-Information Science and Earth Observation (ITC), Enschede, 1497

International Institute for Labour Studies, 46

International Institute for Land Reclamation and Improvement (Alterra–ILRI), Wageningen, 1478

International Institute for Ligurian Studies, 48

International Institute for Population Sciences, Mumbai, 1036

International Institute for Strategic Studies, London, 2147

International Institute for the Unification of Private Law, 59

International Institute of Administrative Sciences, 39

International Institute of Communications, 57

International Institute of Earthquake Prediction Theory and Mathematical Geophysics, Moscow, 1744

International Institute of Histadrut, Tel-Aviv, 1114

International Institute of Information Technology, Hyderabad, 1036

International Institute of Islamic Thought and Civilization (ISTAC), Kuala Lumpur, 1396

International Institute of Philosophy (IIP), 48

International Institute of Refrigeration, 57

International Institute of Seismology and Earthquake Engineering, 70

International Institute of Sociology, 48

International Institute of Space Law (IISL), 59

International Institute of Tropical Agriculture, 41

International Institute of Welding, 55

International Institute on Ageing, 63

International Iron and Steel Institute (IISI), 57

International Islamic University Central Library, Islamabad, 1568

International Islamic University, Islamabad, 1574

International Islamic University Malaysia, 1396

International Juridical Institute, 59

International Labour Office Library, Geneva, 2002

International Labour Organisation (ILO), 46

International Law Association, 39

International Law Association, Danish Branch, 628

International Law Association, Finnish Branch, 682

International Law Association, Swedish Branch, 1969

International League Against Epilepsy, 63

International Leprosy Association, 60

International Literary and Artistic Association, 45

International Livestock Research Institute, 41

International Maize and Wheat Improvement Center, 41

International Maritime Committee, 59

International Marketing Institute, Chestnut Hill, 2301

International Mathematical Union (IMU), 35

International Measurement Confederation (IMEKO), 55

International Medical and Technological University, Dar es Salaam, 2029

International Mineralogical Association (IMA), 70

International Monetary Fund Institute, 48

International Montessori Society, 2288

International Museum and Library—Akum, 320

International Music and Media Centre, 65

International Music Council (IMC), 65

International Musicological Society, 38

International Navigation Association, 55

International Numismatic Commission, 45

International Organization Against Trachoma, 63

International Organization for Biological Control of Noxious Animals and Plants (IOBC), 43

International Organization for Standardization, 57

International Organization of Legal Metrology, 70

International Ornithological Congress, 70

International Palaeontological Association, 70

International Peace Academy, 48

International Peace Research Association, 39

International Peace Research Institute, Oslo (PRIO), 1545

International Pediatric Association, 60

International PEN (A World Association of Writers), 45

International PEN Club, French-speaking Branch, Kraainem, 217

International PEN Club, PEN-Centre Belgium, 217

International Phonetic Association (IPA), 53

International Political Science Association (IPSA), 39

Islamic Educational, Scientific and Cultural Organization (ISESCO), 53
Islamic Library, Male', 1404
Islamic Museum, Tripoli, 1372
Islamic Research and Training Institute, Jeddah, 1807
Islamic Research Foundation, Astan Quds Razavi, Mashhad, 1061
Islamic Research Institute, Islamabad, 1567
Islamic University at Medina, 1808
Islamic University, Baghdad, 1077
Islamic University in Uganda, 2095
Islamic University, Kushtia, 200
Islamic University Library, Medina, 1808
Islamic University of Gaza, 1116
Islamic University of Imam Muhammad ibn Saud, Riyadh, 1808
Islamic University of Indonesia, 1055
Islamic University of Indonesia in Cirebon, 1055
Islamic University of North Sumatra, 1056
Islamic University of Riau, 1056
Islamic University of Technology, Gazipur, 200
Islamic World Academy of Sciences (IAS), Amman, 40
Isle of Anglesey County Library, 2159
Isle of Man College, 2279
Isle of Man International Business School, 2279
Isle of Man Natural History and Antiquarian Society, 2279
Isle of Wight Council Library Services, 2165
Íslenzka fornleifafélag, 964
Íslenzka náttúrufrædifélag, 964
Islington Libraries, 2161
ISM Chicago Gallery, 2321
Ismail Rahimtulla Trust Library, 1312
ISMCM-CESTI Paris, St Ouen, 767
ISOMATIC Labs Ltd, Sofia, 302
Israel Academy of Sciences and Humanities, 1092
Israel Antiquities Authority, 1093
Israel Antiquities Authority Archives Branch, 1096
Israel Atomic Energy Commission, Tel-Aviv, 1095
Israel Bar, 1092
Israel Bible Museum, Safad, 1098
Israel Ceramic and Silicate Institute, 1095
Israel Chemical Society, 1094
Israel Exploration Society, 1094
Israel Fiber Institute, Jerusalem, 1096
Israel Geographical Association, 1093
Israel Geological Society, 1094
Israel Gerontological Society, 1093
Israel Institute for Biological Research, 1095
Israel Institute of Metals, 1096
Israel Institute of Plastics, 1096
Israel Librarians' Association, 1092
Israel Mathematical Union, 1093
Israel Medical Association, 1093
Israel Meteorological Service, 1095
Israel Museum, 1097
Israel Music Institute, 1093
Israel Oceanographic and Limnological Research, 1095
Israel Oriental Society, 1094
Israel Painters and Sculptors Association, 1093
Israel Physical Society, 1094
Israel Political Science Association, 1092
Israel Prehistoric Society, 1093
Israel Psychological Association, 1094
Israel Society of Aeronautics and Astronautics, 1094
Israel Society of Biochemistry and Molecular Biology, 1093
Israel Society of Internal Medicine, 1093
Israel Society of Libraries and Information Centers (ASMI), 1092
Israel State Archives, 1096
Israel Wine Institute, Rehovot, 1096
Israeli Center for Libraries, Jerusalem, 1092
Issyk-Kul State University 'K. Tynystanov', 1357

Istanbul Arkeoloji Müzeleri, 2061
İstanbul Bilgi Üniversitesi, 2078
Istanbul Deniz Müzesi, 2061
İstanbul Kültür Üniversitesi, 2079
Istanbul Policy Centre, 2087
Istanbul Resim ve Heykel Müzesi, 2061
İstanbul Teknik Üniversitesi, 2079
Istanbul Teknik Üniversitesi Kütüphane ve Dokümantasyon Daire, 2060
İstanbul Üniversitesi, 2078
Istanbul Üniversitesi Deniz Bilimleri ve İşletmeciliği Enstitüsü, 2059
Istanbul University Library and Documentation Centre, 2060
ISTD: Centre for Crime and Justice Studies, London, 2151
Istituti Culturali ed Artistici, Forlì, 1140
Istituto Affari Internazionali, Rome, 1129
Istituto Agronomico per l'Oltremare, Florence, 1121
Istituto Centrale per il Catalogo Unico delle Biblioteche Italiane e per le Informazioni Bibliografiche, Rome, 1137
Istituto Centrale per il Restauro, Rome, 1129
Istituto Centrale per la Patologia del Libro, Rome, 1121
Istituto dei Materiali per l'Elettronica ed il Magnetismo, 1126
Istituto dei Sistemi Complessi (Sperimentale), 1126
Istituto di Analisi dei Sistemi ed Informatica 'Antonio Ruberti', 1128
Istituto di Astrofisica Spaziale e Fisica Cosmica, 1125
Istituto di Biochimica delle Proteine, 1127
Istituto di Biofisica, 1127
Istituto di Bioimmagini e Fisiologia Molecolare, 1127
Istituto di Biologia Agro-ambientale e Forestale, 1127
Istituto di Biologia Cellulare, 1127
Istituto di Biologia e Biotecnologia Agraria, 1127
Istituto di Biologia e Patologia Molecolari, 1127
Istituto di Biomedicina e di Immunologia Molecolare 'Alberto Monroy', 1127
Istituto di Biomembrane e Bioenergetica, 1127
Istituto di Biometeorologia, 1127
Istituto di Biostrutture e Bioimmagini, 1127
Istituto di Calcolo e Reti ad Alte Prestazioni, 1128
Istituto di Chimica Biomolecolare, 1127
Istituto di Chimica dei Composti Organo Metallici, 1125
Istituto di Chimica del Riconoscimento Molecolare, 1127
Istituto di Chimica e Tecnologia dei Polimeri, 1125
Istituto di Chimica Inorganica e delle Superfici, 1125
Istituto di Cibernetica 'Edoardo Caianiello', 1125
Istituto di Cristallografia, 1125
Istituto di Diritto Romano e dei Diritti dell'Oriente Mediterraneo, Rome, 1121
Istituto di Elettronica e di Ingegneria dell'Informazione e delle Telecomunicazioni, 1128
Istituto di Filosofia 'Aloisianum', 2755
Istituto di Fisica Applicata 'Nello Carrara', 1126
Istituto di Fisica del Plasma 'Piero Caldirola', 1126
Istituto di Fisica dello Spazio Interplanetario, 1126
Istituto di Fisiologia Clinica, 1127
Istituto di Fotonica e Nanotecnologie, 1126
Istituto di Genetica delle Popolazioni, 1127
Istituto di Genetica e Biofisica 'Adriano Buzzati Traverso', 1127
Istituto di Genetica Molecolare, 1127

Istituto di Genetica Vegetale, 1127
Istituto di Geologia Ambientale e Geoingegneria, 1126
Istituto di Geoscienze e Georisorse, 1126
Istituto di Informatica e Telematica, 1128
Istituto di Ingegneria Biomedica, 1128
Istituto di Linguistica Computazionale, 1127
Istituto di Matematica Applicata e Tecnologie Informatiche, 1126
Istituto di Metodologie Chimiche, 1126
Istituto di Metodologie Inorganiche e dei Plasmi, 1126
Istituto di Metodologie per l'Analisi Ambientale, 1126
Istituto di Metrologia 'Gustavo Colonnetti', 1128
Istituto di Neurobiologia e Medicina Molecolare, 1127
Istituto di Neurogenetica e Neurofarmacologia, 1128
Istituto di Neuroscienze, 1128
Istituto di Norvegia in Roma di Archeologia e Storia dell'Arte, 1130
Istituto di Radioastronomia, 1126
Istituto di Ricerca per la Protezione Idrogeologica, 1126
Istituto di Ricerca sui Sistemi Giudiziari, 1127
Istituto di Ricerca sulle Acque, 1126
Istituto di Ricerca sull'Impresa e lo Sviluppo, 1127
Istituto di Ricerche Farmacologiche 'Mario Negri', 1130
Istituto di Ricerche sulla Combustione, 1128
Istituto di Ricerche sulla Popolazione e le Politiche Sociali, 1127
Istituto di Ricerche sulle Attività Terziarie, 1127
Istituto di Scienza dell'Alimentazione, 1128
Istituto di Scienza e Tecnologia dei Materiali Ceramici, 1128
Istituto di Scienza e Tecnologie dell'Informazione 'Alessandro Faedo', 1128
Istituto di Scienze dell'Atmosfera e del Clima, 1126
Istituto di Scienze delle Produzioni Alimentari, 1128
Istituto di Scienze e Tecnologie della Cognizione, 1128
Istituto di Scienze e Tecnologie Molecolari, 1126
Istituto di Scienze Marine, 1126
Istituto di Scienze Neurologiche, 1128
Istituto di Storia dell'Arte di Firenze, 1122
Istituto di Storia dell'Europa Mediterranea, 1127
Istituto di Struttura della Materia, 1126
Istituto di Studi Europei 'Alcide de Gasperi', Rome, 1129
Istituto di Studi Filosofici 'Enrico Castelli', Rome, 1132
Istituto di Studi Giuridici Internazionali, 1127
Istituto di Studi Nucleari per l'Agricoltura (ISNA), Rome, 1125
Istituto di Studi sui Sistemi Intelligenti per l'Automazione, 1128
Istituto di Studi sui Sistemi Regionali Federali e sulle Autonomie 'Massimo Severo Giannini', 1127
Istituto di Studi sulle Civiltà dell'Egeo e del Vicino Oriente, 1127
Istituto di Studi sulle Civiltà Italiche e del Mediterraneo Antico, 1127
Istituto di Studi sulle Società del Mediterraneo, 1127
Istituto di Tecnologie Avanzate per l'Energia 'Nicola Giordano', 1128
Istituto di Tecnologie Biomediche, 1128
Istituto di Tecnologie Industriali e Automazione, 1128
Istituto di Teoria e Tecniche dell'Informazione Giuridica, 1127
Istituto di Virologia Vegetale, 1128
Istituto e Museo di Storia della Scienza, Florence, 1139
Istituto Elettrotecnico Nazionale 'Galileo Ferraris', Turin, 1132

Istituto Ellenico di Studi Bizantini e Postbizantini di Venezia, 1130
Istituto Gas Ionizzati, 1128
Istituto Gemmologico Italiano, 1131
Istituto Geografico Militare, Florence, 1122
Istituto Idrografico della Marina, Genoa, 1131
Istituto Internazionale di Studi Liguri, 48
Istituto Internazionale per la Ricerca Teatrale, Venice, 1129
Istituto Italiano del Marchio di Qualità (IMQ), 1125
Istituto Italiano della Saldatura, 1125
Istituto Italiano di Antropologia, 1132
Istituto Italiano di Numismatica, 1122
Istituto Italiano di Paleontologia Umana, 1122
Istituto Italiano di Speleologia, 1131
Istituto Italiano di Studi Germanici, 1130
Istituto Italiano di Studi Legislativi, 1129
Istituto Italiano per gli Studi Storici, 1130
Istituto Italiano per la Storia Antica, 1122
Istituto Italiano per la Storia della Musica, 1122
Istituto Italiano per l'Africa e l'Oriente (IsIAO), 1132
Istituto Italo-Latino Americano, 49
Istituto Lombardo Accademia di Scienze e Lettere, 1120
Istituto Luigi Sturzo, Rome, 1132
Istituto Motori, 1128
Istituto Nazionale di Alta Matematica Francesco Severi, Rome, 1131
Istituto Nazionale di Archeologia e Storia dell'Arte, Rome, 1122
Istituto Nazionale di Architettura (IN-ARCH), Rome, 1121
Istituto Nazionale di Astrofisica, Rome, 1131
Istituto Nazionale di Fisica Nucleare (INFN), Frascati, 1131
Istituto Nazionale di Geofisica e Vulcanologia, Rome, 1131
Istituto Nazionale di Oceanografia e di Geofisico Sperimentale, Trieste, 1131
Istituto Nazionale di Ottica Applicata (INOA), 1128
Istituto Nazionale di Ricerca per gli Alimenti e la Nutrizione, Rome, 1131
Istituto Nazionale di Statistica, Rome, 1129
Istituto Nazionale di Studi Etruschi ed Italici, Florence, 1122
Istituto Nazionale di Studi Romani, Rome, 1130
Istituto Nazionale di Studi sul Rinascimento, Florence, 1130
Istituto Nazionale di Studi Verdiani, Parma, 1122
Istituto Nazionale di Urbanistica (INU), Rome, 1121
Istituto Nazionale per la Grafica, Rome, 1142
Istituto Nazionale per la Ricerca sul Cancro, Genoa, 1131
Istituto Nazionale per la Valutazione del Sistema dell'Istruzione, Frascati, 1119
Istituto Nazionale per Studi ed Esperienze di Architettura Navale, Rome, 1132
Istituto Opera del Vocabolario Italiano, 1127
Istituto Papirologico 'Girolamo Vitelli', 1130
Istituto per gli Studi di Politica Internazionale, Milan, 1129
Istituto per i Beni Archeologici e Monumentali, 1126
Istituto per i Materiali Compositi e Biomedici, 1126
Istituto per i Processi Chimico-Fisici, 1126
Istituto per i Sistemi Agricoli e Forestali del Mediterraneo, 1128

Jimma University, 678
Jinan University, 482
Jingu Bunko, 1183
Jingu Chokokan, 1185
Jingu Nogyokan, 1185
Jinju National University, 1333
Jinnah Postgraduate Medical Centre, 1580
Jishoji (Ginkakuji), 1185
Jiwaji University, 1004
Joachim Jungius-Gesellschaft der Wissenschaften eV, 790
Jôchi University, 1292
Jodrell Bank Observatory, 2151
Joe Alon Centre for Regional and Folklore Studies, 1095
Joensuun kaupunginkirjasto–Pohjois-Karjalan maakuntakirjasto, 686
Joensuun Yliopisto, 691
Joensuun yliopiston kirjasto, 686
Jõgeva Plant Breeding Institute, 672
Johann Strauss-Gesellschaft Wien, 161
Johann Wolfgang Goethe-universität Frankfurt, 846
Johannes Gutenberg-universität Mainz, 877
Johannes Kepler Universität Linz, 172
Johannesburg Art Gallery, 1869
John A. Hartford Foundation, Inc., New York, 2294
John and Mable Ringling Museum of Art, 2320
John Brown University, 2340
John Cabot University, Rome, 1164
John Carroll University, 2623
John Carter Brown Library, 2316
John Crerar Library of the University of Chicago, 2311
John F. Kennedy Space Center, Cape Canaveral, 2307
John F. Kennedy University, 2351
John G. Shedd Aquarium, 2321
John Jay College of Criminal Justice, 2572
John Mackintosh Hall Library, 2278
John Marshall Law School, Chicago, 2428
John Paul II Catholic University of Lublin, 1645
John Paul II Library, National University of Ireland, Maynooth, 1084
John Rylands University Library, University of Manchester, 2164
John Snow College, Stockton, 2200
John W. Graham Library, University of Trinity College, 331
John Wesley College, 2605
Johns Hopkins University, 2472
Johns Hopkins University Libraries, 2312
Johnson and Wales University, 2671
Johnson Bible College, 2678
Johnson C. Smith University, 2606
Johnson State College, 2708
Joho Kagaku Gijutsu Kyokai, 1172
Joint Institute for Nuclear Research, Dubna, 1744
Joint Russian-Vietnamese Tropical Research and Testing Centre, 1749
Jöklarannsóknafélag Íslands, 964
Jomo Kenyatta University of Agriculture and Technology, 1313
Jones College, 2410
Jönköpings stadsbibliotek, 1972
Jordan Archaeological Museum, 1300
Jordan Historical Museum of the Twenty, 334
Jordan Institute of Public Administration, Amman, 1302
Jordan Library Association, 1299
Jordan Schnitzer Museum of Art, 2326
Jordan Statistical Training Centre, 1302
Jordan University of Science and Technology (Just), 1301
Jordbrugsakademikernes Forbund, Klampenborg, 628
Jordbrugsvidenskabelige Fakultet, 636
Jorge B. Vargas Museum and Filipiniana Research Center, Quezon City, 1604
Jorvik–The Viking City, 2179
Jósa András Múzeum, 947

Josef-Haubrich-Kunsthalle, 813
Joseph Conrad Society, 2134
Josephine Butler College, Stockton, 2200
Josip Juraj Strossmayer University of Osijek, 595
Journalism Institute, Beijing, 431
JTI – Institutet för jordbruks- och miljöteknik, Uppsala, 1971
Jubilee Library, Brighton, 2154
Jüdisches Museum Rendsburg, Schleswig, 819
Judson College, 2429
Jugoslovenski Bibliografsko-Informacijski Institut, 1816
Juilliard School, 2587
Jungfraujoch and Gornergrat Scientific Stations, 2000
Juniata College, 2649
Junta de Historia Eclesiástica Argentina, 90
Junta Nacional Protectora y Conservadora del Patrimonio Histórico y Artístico de la Nación, Caracas, 2761
Jura-Museum, 818
Jurists' Association of Yugoslavia, 1815
Justice Policy Research Centre, 146
Justus-Liebig-Universität Gießen, 850
Jysk Arkaeologisk Selskab, Højbjerg, 629
Jysk Selskab for Historie, Århus, 629
Jyske Musikkonservatorium, Århus, 641
Jyväskylän ammattikorkeakoulu, 702
Jyväskylän Yliopisto, 692
Jyväskylän Yliopiston Kirjasto, 686

K

K. N. Toosi University of Technology, Tehran, 1067
Kabarda-Balkar Art Museum, 1757
Kabardino-Balkar Land Improvement Institute, 1795
Kabardino-Balkar State University Library, 1753
Kabardino-Balkarian State University, 1766
Kabinet Grafike, Zagreb, 595
Kabinet pro klasická studia FLÚ AV ČR, 610
Kabul Art School, 74
Kabul Medical University, 74
Kabul Museum, 74
Kabul University, 74
Kabul University Library, 73
Kabushikikaisha Mitsubishi Sogo Kenkyusho, 1180
Kachchh University, Kachchh, 1004
Kadir Has Üniversitesi, 2080
Kaduna Polytechnic, 1541
Kaduna State Library Board, 1522
Kaesong City Library, 1320
Kaesong Historical Library, 1320
Kafkas Üniversitesi, 2080
Kagaku-Gijutsu Shinko Kiko (JST), 1172
Kagawa University, 1204
Kagoshima Prefectural Library, 1183
Kagoshima University, 1204
Kahn, W., Institute of Theoretical Psychiatry and Neuroscience, 1479
Kahramanmaraş Sütçü İmam Üniversitesi, 2080
Kaiserliche Hofburg, Innsbruck, 169
Kaiyoo Kisho Gakkai, 1177
Kajaanin ammattikorkeakoulu, Kajaani, 702
Kakatiya University, 1004
Kalaallit Atuakkiortut, Nuuk, 642
Kalakshetra Foundation, Chennai, 1040
Kalamazoo College, 2506
Kalinga Institute of Industrial Technology, Bhubaneshwar, 1036
Kaliningrad State Technical University, 1783
Kaliningrad State University 'Immanuel Kant', 1766
Kaliningrad State University Library, 1752
Kalmar Stadsbibliotek, 1972
Kalmyk State University, 1767

Kalmyk State University Library, 1751
Kaluga Museum of Art, 1755
Kalyani University, 1004
Kamakura Kokuhokan, 1185
Kamarupa Anusandhana Samiti, 975
Kamchatka State Fishing Fleet Academy, 1795
Kameshwara Singh Darbhanga Sanskrit University, 1005
Kamizsai Dorottya Múzeum, 947
Kampala University, 2095
Kamra tal-Periti Malta, Gzira, 1407
Kamuzu College of Nursing, 1392
Kamyanets-Podilsk Institute of Agriculture, 2118
Kamyanets-Podilsky State Historical Museum-Preserve, 2105
Kanagawa Prefectural Kanazawa Bunko Museum, 1187
Kanagawa Prefectural Library, 1185
Kanagawa University, Yokohama, 1204
Kanazawa City Library, 1183
Kanazawa College of Art, 1297
Kanazawa Municipal Izumino Library, 1183
Kanazawa University, 1205
Kandahar Museum, 74
Kandahar University, Kandahar, 74
Kandy National Museum, 1955
Kangnam University, 1333
Kangnung National University, 1333
Kangweon National University, 1333
Kangwon Provincial Library, 1320
Kannada University Hampi, Hospet, 1005
Kannur University, Kannur, 1005
Kano State Library Board, 1522
Kano State Polytechnic, 1541
Kano State University of Technology, Wudil, 1537
Kansai University, 1275
Kansai University Library, 1183
Kansai Zosen Kyokai, 1172
Kansallisarkisto, Helsinki, 686
Kansantaloudellinen Yhdistys, Helsinki, 682
Kansas City Art Institute, 2546
Kansas City Museum, 2323
Kansas City Public Library, 2313
Kansas City University of Medicine and Biosciences, Kansas City, 2546
Kansas State Historical Society, 2311
Kansas State University, 2459
Kansas State University Libraries, 2311
Kansas Wesleyan University, 2459
Kantonalni Zavod a Zaštitut Kulturni-Historisjkog i Prirodnog Naslijedja Sarajevo, 246
Kantonalni-županijski Arhiv Travnik, 247
Kantons- und Universitätsbibliothek, Fribourg, 2001
Kantonsbibliothek Vadiana St Gallen, 2002
Kaohsiung Medical University, 560
Kaohsiung Museum of Fine Arts, 554
Kapitza, P. L., Institute of Physical Problems, Moscow, 1744
Kaposvári Egyetem, 953
Karachi Institute of Nuclear Power and Engineering (KINPOE), 1567
Karachi Institute of Radiotherapy and Nuclear Medicine (KIRAN), 1567
Karachi Theosophical Society, 1565
Karadeniz Teknik Üniversitesi, 2080
Karaev, A. I., Institute of Physiology, Baku, 184
Karaganda E. A. Buketov State University, 1307
Karaganda Kazpotrebsoyuz University of Economics, 1308
Karaganda Metallurgical Institute, 1308
Karaganda State Medical Academy, 1308
Karaganda State Technical University, 1309
Karaganda State University Library, 1305
Karakalpak Art Museum, 2749
Karakalpak Branch of the Uzbek Academy of Sciences, Nukus, 2747
Karakalpak Historical Museum, 2749
Karakalpak State University, 2750

Karakuram International University, Gilgit, 1575
Karelian Museum of Fine Arts, 1758
Karelian State Regional Museum, 1758
Kargin, V. A., Polymer Research Institute, 1749
Karl-franzens-universität Graz, 173
Karlovarské muzeum, 614
Karlstads Universitet, 1978
Karnatak Historical Research Society, 975
Karnatak University, 1006
Karnataka Government Secretariat Library, 980
Karnataka State Open University, Mysore, 1005
Karnataka State Women University, Bijapur, 1006
Kärntner Landesarchiv, 167
Kärntner Landeskonservatorium, 183
Károli Gáspár Református Egyetem, 961
Karolinska Institutet, 1990
Karolinska Institutet, Universitetsbiblioteket, 1973
Karpinsky, A. P., All-Russia Geological Research Institute, St Petersburg, 1744
Karpov Institute of Physical Chemistry, Moscow, 1744
Karshi State University, 2750
Kartografiska Sällskapet, Gävle, 1970
Karunya Institute of Technology and Sciences, Coimbatore, 1036
Kasetsart University, 2037
Kasetsart University, Main Library, 2033
Kasinthula Agricultural Research Station, 1391
Kassala University, Kassala, 1962
Kastélymúzeum, Fertőd, 946
Kasteyev Kazakh State Art Museum, 1306
Kasugataisha Homotsuden, 1186
Kasvimuseo/Botaniska Museet, Helsinki, 687
Kasvinsuojeluseura r.y., Helsinki, 683
Kasvintuotannon tutkimus, Jokioinen, 684
Katharinenkirche, Lübeck, 817
Käthe-Kollwitz-Museum, 812
Kathmandu University, Kathmandu, 1472
Katholieke Theologische Universiteit Te Utrecht, 1496
Katholieke Universiteit Brussel, 225
Katholieke Universiteit Leuven, 228
Katholische Universität Eichstätt-Ingolstadt, Düsseldorf, 843
Katholischer Akademischer Ausländer-Dienst, Bonn, 786
Katolícka Univerzita v Ružomberku, 1846
Katolicki Uniwersytet Lubelski Jana Pawła II, 1645
Katona József Múzeum, 946
Kaunas Botanical Garden, 1377
Kauno Medicinos Universitetas, 1378
Kauno Technologijos Universitetas, 1378
Kavak ve Hızlı Gelişen Tür Orman Ağaçları Araştırma Müdürlüğü, Izmit, 2058
Kavetsky, R. E., Institute of Experimental Pathology, Oncology and Radiobiology, Kyiv, 2101
Kavilkulguru Kalidas Sanskrit Vishwavidyalaya, Ramtek, 1006
Kawanda Agricultural Research Institute, Kampala, 2094
Kaya University, 1333
Kazakh Ablai Khan University of International Relations and World Languages, 1309
Kazakh Humanitarian Law University, 1307
Kazakh K. I. Satbayev National Technical University, 1307
Kazakh Leading Academy of Architecture and Civil Engineering, 1309
Kazakh Research Technological Institute for Operation and

L

La Fondation du Roi Abdul Aziz pour les Etudes Islamiques et les Sciences Humaines, Casablanca, 1458
La France Latine, Paris, 708
La Roche College, 2649
La Salle University, 2649
La Sierra University, 2352
La Trobe University, 136
La Trobe University Library, 125
Laboratoire Central de Recherches Vétérinaires, Maisons-Alfort, 719
Laboratoire d'Astronomie de l'Université des Sciences et Techniques de Lille-Flandres-Artois, 721
Laboratoire d'Enzymologie Moléculaire (LEM), 720
Laboratoire d'Ingénierie des Macromolécules (LIM), 720
Laboratoire de Biophysique Moléculaire (LBM), 720
Laboratoire de Biotechnologie de l'Environnement, Narbonne, 722
Laboratoire de Cristallographie et Cristallogenèse des Protéines (LCCP), 720
Laboratoire de Cristallographie Macromoléculaire (LCM), 720
Laboratoire de Dynamique Moléculaire (LDM), 720
Laboratoire de Microscopie Electronique Structurale (LMES), 720
Laboratoire de Recherches Vétérinaires et Zootechniques de Farcha, N'Djamena, 409
Laboratoire de Résonance Magnétique Nucléaire (LRMN), 720
Laboratoire de Spectrométrie de Masse des Protéines (LSMP), 720
Laboratoire Départemental d'Hygiène de la Martinique, 774
Laboratoire des Protéines du Cytosquelette (LPC), 720
Laboratoire des Protéines Membranaires (LPM), 720
Laboratoire Médical, Bujumbura, 316
Laboratoire Public d'Essais et d'Etudes, Casablanca, 1458
Laboratoire Vétérinaire de Niamey, 1516
Laboratoř anorganických materiálů, Prague, 611
Laboratori Nazionali di Frascati dell' INFN, Rome, 1131
Laboratorio Arte Alameda, 1420
Laboratório de Análises, Rio de Janeiro, 257
Laboratorio de S. Mamede de Infesta, S. Mamede de Infesta, 1678
Laboratório Nacional de Engenharia Civil, Lisbon, 1678
Laboratorium Kesehatan Daerah, Medan, 1043
Laboratorium Kesehatan Pusat Lembaga Eijkman, Jakarta, 1043
Laboratory Institute of Merchandising, New York, 2587
Laboratory of Experimental Biological Models, Svetlye Gory, 1738
Laboratory of Experimental Biomedical Models, Tomsk, 1739
Laboratory of Hygiene and Prophylaxis, Mogadishu, 1861
Laboratory of Polar Medicine, Norilsk, 1738
Laczkó Dezső Múzeum, 948
Ladha Meghji Indian Public Library, Mwanza, 2028
Ladoke Akintola University of Technology, 1537
Lady Lever Art Gallery, 2173
Lady Margaret Hall, Oxford, 2250
Lafayette College, 2649
Lagos City Libraries, 1522
Lagos State Polytechnic, 1541
Lagos State University, 1538
LaGrange College, 2419
Lahden ammattikorkeakoulu, 702
Lahore College for Women University, Lahore, 1575
Lahore Fort Museum, 1569

Lahore Museum, 1569
Lahore University of Management Sciences, 1575
Lahore Zoological Gardens, Lahore, 1570
Laing Art Gallery, Newcastle upon Tyne, 2177
Lake Chad Research Institute (LCRI), Maiduguri, 1519
Lake Erie College, 2624
Lake Forest College, 2429
Lake Forest Graduate School of Management, 2429
Lake Superior State University, 2507
Lakehead University, 349
Lakeland College, 2728
Lakshmibai National Institute of Physical Education, Gwalior, 1036
Lalit Kala Akademi, 969
Lalit Narayan Mithila University, 1008
Lamar University, 2694
Lambeth Library Service, 2161
Lambeth Palace Library, 2161
Lambuth University, 2678
Lamont-Doherty Earth Observatory of Columbia University, 2305
Lamu Museum, 1312
Lancashire County Library, 2167
Lancaster Bible College, 2649
Land Use Research Institute, Kyiv, 2100
Landau, L. D., Institute of Theoretical Physics, Moscow, 1744
Landbouw-Economisch Instituut, the Hague, 1479
Landbouwproefstation, Paramaribo, 1965
Landbunaðarháskóli Íslands, 965
Landcare Research New Zealand Ltd, 1503
Lander University, 2674
Landesamt für Archäologie mit Landesmuseum für Vorgeschichte, Dresden, 813
Landesamt für Denkmalpflege und Archäologie Sachsen-Anhalt (Landesmuseum für Vorgeschichte), 816
Landesarchiv Baden-Württemberg– Abteilung Staatsarchiv Sigmaringen, 810
Landesarchiv Baden-Württemberg— Generallandesarchiv Karlsruhe, 807
Landesarchiv Berlin, 803
Landesarchiv Nordrhein-Westfalen, 805
Landesarchiv Nordrhein-Westfalen-Staats- und Personenstandarchiv Detmold, 805
Landesarchiv Nordrhein-Westfalen, Staatsarchiv Münster, 809
Landesarchiv Saarbrücken, 809
Landesarchiv Schleswig-Holstein, 809
Landesarchiv, Speyer, 810
Landesbibliothek, Coburg, 804
Landesbibliothek Mecklenburg-Vorpommern, Schwerin, 809
Landesbibliothek, Oldenburg, 809
Landeshauptarchiv, Koblenz, 807
Landeshauptarchiv Sachsen-Anhalt, Magdeburg, 808
Landeskirchliches Archiv Nürnberg der Evangelisch-Lutherischen Kirche in Bayern, 809
Landesmuseum für Kärnten, 169
Landesmuseum für Kunst und Kulturgeschichte, Schleswig, 819
Landesmuseum Kärnten, Kärntner Botanikzentrum, 169
Landesmuseum Mainz, 817
Landessternwarte auf dem Königstuhl bei Heidelberg, 801
Landesumweltamt Nordrhein Westfalen, 802
Landsarkivet for Fyn, Odense, 633
Landsarkivet for Nørrejylland, Viborg, 633
Landsarkivet i Lund, 1973
Landsbókasafn Íslands-Háskólabókasafn, Reykjavík, 964
Landscape Institute, London, 2126
Landslaget for Lokalhistorie, Dragvoll, 1544
Lane College, 2678

Langley Research Center, Hampton, Virginia, 2307
Langston University, 2634
Language and Literature Bureau Library, Bandar Seri Begawan, 296
Language Institute, Sarajevo, 246
Language Teaching Institute, Doha, 1690
Lankaran State University, 187
Lanzhou Institute of Physics, 433
Lanzhou University, 483
Lao Buddhist Fellowship, Vientiane, 1360
Lapin Yliopisto, 694
Lappeenrannan Teknillinen Korkeakoulu, 694
Lappeenranta University of Technology, 694
Lärarhögskolan i Stockholm, 1990
Larenstein University of Professional Education, 1497
Large Binocular Telescope Observatory (LBTO), 2305
Larkana Institute of Nuclear Medicine and Radiotherapy (LINAR), 1567
Lasell College, 2491
L'Atelier, Alexandria, 657
Latin America Institute, Moscow, 1734
Latin American Association of Analysis and Behavioural Modification, 61
Latin American Association of Linguistics and Philology, 43
Latin American Information and Documentation Network for Education (REDUC), 412
Latin American Institute for Educational Communication, 53
Latinamerika-institutet i Stockholm, 1971
Latvia University of Agriculture, 1363
Latvian Academic Library, 1362
Latvian Academy of Arts, 1363
Latvian Academy of Music, 1363
Latvian Academy of Sciences, 1361
Latvian Institute of Organic Synthesis, 1362
Latvian Language Institute, Riga, 1361
Latvian Museum of Natural History, 1362
Latvian Open-Air Ethnographical Museum, 1362
Laurea ammattikorkeakoulu, Vantaa, 702
Laurentian Forestry Centre, Ste-Foy, 328
Laurentian University of Sudbury, 349
Law Association, Hanoi, 2771
Law Association of Trinidad and Tobago, 2051
Law Council of Australia, 118
Law Institute, Beijing, 430
Law Library, Colombo, 1955
Law Library of Ireland, Dublin, 1083
Law Society Library, London, 2161
Law Society, London, 2129
Law Society of Ireland, 1081
Law Society of Kenya, 1310
Law Society of New South Wales, 118
Lawrence Technological University, 2507
Lawrence University, 2728
Le Bibliophile, Cap Haïtien, 932
Le Moyne College, 2587
Le Moyne-Owen College, 2678
Learning and Skills Council (LSC), Coventry, 2123
Lebanese American University, 1366
Lebanese Center for Policy Studies, Beirut, 1364
Lebanese Library Association, 1364
Lebanon Valley College, 2650
Lebedev, P. N., Physics Institute, Moscow, 1744
Lebedev, S. A., Institute of Precision Mechanics and Computing Technology, Moscow, 1749
Lebedev, S. V., All-Russia Synthetic Rubber Research Institute, 1749
Lee University, 2678
Leeds City Art Gallery, 2173
Leeds Library and Information Services, 2159
Leeds Metropolitan University, 2216
Leeds Museums and Galleries, 2173

Leeds Philosophical and Literary Society Ltd, 2141
Leeds University Library, 2159
Lees-McRae College, 2606
Leeszaal Faculteit Landbouwkundige en Toegepaste Biologische Wetenschappen, Ghent, 221
Legislative Library, Fredericton, 330
Legislative Library of Manitoba, 330
Legislative Library, Victoria, 330
Legislature Library, Edmonton, 330
Lehigh University, 2650
Lehman College, New York, 2572
Lehr- und Forschungsgebiet Internationale Wirtschaftsbeziehungen, 802
Leib'sches Haus, Giessen, 815
Leicester City Libraries, 2159
Leicestershire Library Services, 2159
Leicestershire Museums, 2173
Leiden University, 1487
Leksikografski Zavod 'Miroslav Krleža', 593
Lembaga Administrasi Negara, Jakarta, 1043
Lembaga Ilmu Pengetahuan Indonesia, 1041
Lembaga Malaria, Jakarta, 1043
Lembaga Pers dan Pendapat Umum, Jakarta, 1043
Lembaga Research dan Pengujian Materiil Angkatan Darat, Bandung, 1044
Leningrad State University 'A. S. Pushkin', St Petersburg, 1768
Lenoir-rhyne College, 2606
Lentos Kunstmuseum Linz, 169
Leo Baeck Institute, Inc., New York, 2302
Leo Baeck Institute Jerusalem, 1095
Leo Bradley Library, 236
Leo Tolstoy Museum and Estate, 1760
Leopold Museum, 170
Leprosy Research Centre, Tokyo, 1181
Leptis Magna Museum, 1372
Lermontov State Museum 'Tarkhany', 1755
Les Arts Décoratifs, Paris, 730
Les Naturalistes Parisiens, 710
Leskov, N. S., House Museum, Orel, 1757
Lesley University, 2491
Lesotehničeski University, Sofia, 306
Lesotho Agricultural College, 1369
Lesotho Library Association, 1369
Lesotho National Archives, 1369
Lesotho National Library Service, Maseru, 1369
Lessius Hogeschool, Antwerp, 234
Lester E. Fisher Center for the Study and Conservation of Apes, 2321
Letecké muzeum Kbely, 614
LeTourneau University, 2689
Letterkenny Institute of Technology, 1091
Lewis and Clark College, 2638
Lewis-Clark State College, 2424
Lewis University, 2429
Lewisham Library Service, 2161
Lexington Theological Seminary, 2463
Leyte Institute of Technology, 1619
Leyte Normal University, Tacloban City, 1609
Leyte State University, Baybay, 1609
Liaoning Normal University, 484
Liaoning Provincial Library, 436
Liaoning Technical University, 484
Liaoning University, 483
Liaquat Hall Library, 1569
Liaquat Memorial Library, 1569
Liaquat University of Mcdical and Health Sciences, Jamshoro, 1575
Libera Università di Bolzano, 1164
Libera Università di Lingue e Comunicazione Iulm, Milan, 1166
Libera Università Internazionale degli Studi Sociali Guido Carli in Roma, 1166
Libera Università Maria Ss. Assunta, 1166
Liberia Arts and Crafts Association, 1370
Liberian Information Service Library, 1370

Lubelskie Towarzystwo Naukowe, 1621
Lucian Blaga University of Sibiu, 1711
Lüderitz Museum, 1469
Ľudovít Štúr Institute of Linguistics, 1843
Ludwig Boltzmann Institut für Festkörperphysik, 165
Ludwig Forum für Internationale Kunst, 811
Ludwig-maximilians-universität München, 881
Lugansk Agricultural Institute, 2118
Luhansk State Medical University, 2112
Luigj Gurakuqi University of Shkodër, 77
Lukianenko, P. P., Krasnodar Agricultural Research Institute, 1732
Luleå Stadsbiblioteket, 1973
Luleå Tekniska Universitet, 1979
Luleå University of Technology, 1979
Lunar and Planetary Institute, Houston, 2305
Lunds Matematiska Sällskap, 1970
Lunds Universitet, 1980
Lunyangwa Agricultural Research Station, 1391
Luonnontieteellinen Keskusmuseo/Naturhistoriska Centralmuseet, Helsinki, 687
Lusaka City Libraries, 2785
Luther College, Decorah, 2456
Luther College, Regina, 381
Luther Seminary, 2527
Lutheran School of Theology at Chicago, 2430
Lutheran Theological Seminary at Gettysburg, 2651
Lutheran Theological Seminary at Philadelphia, 2651
Lutheran Theological Southern Seminary, Columbia, 2674
Lutherhaus, Reformationsgeschichtliches Museum, Wittenberg, 820
Lutherische Theologische Hochschule Oberursel, 902
Luton Libraries, 2164
Lviv Academy of Arts, 2119
Lviv Academy of Veterinary Medicine, 2117
Lviv Commercial Academy, 2118
Lviv Historical Museum, 2105
Lviv Ivan Franko State University Library, 2104
Lviv National Medical University 'Danylo Halytskiy', 2112
'Lviv Polytechnic' National University, 2115
Lviv Scientific Library of the National Academy of Sciences of Ukraine 'V. Stefanyk', 2104
Lviv Scientific Research Institute of Hereditary Pathology, 2101
Lviv State Agrarian University, 2106
Lviv State Picture Gallery, 2105
Lycée privé commercial 'De la Salle', Lille, 768
Lycée privé Notre-Dame de Grâce, Maubeuge, 768
Lycée privé Saint-Joseph, Saint-Martin-lez-Boulogne, 768
Lycée Technique, Bujumbura, 316
Lycée Technologique OZANAM, Lille, 768
Lyceum Museum, Pushkin, 1759
Lyceum of the Philippines, 1619
Lycoming College, 2651
Lynchburg College, 2710
Lyndon B. Johnson Space Center, Houston, 2307
Lyndon State College, 2708
Lynn Museum, 2177
Lynn University, 2410
Lyon College, 2340
'Lyuben Karavelov' Regional Library, Ruse, 302

M

Maa-ja elintarviketalouden tutkimuskeskus, Jokioinen, 684

Maanmittaustieteiden seura r.y., Helsinki, 684
Maastricht School of Management (Msm), 1497
Maatalousteknologian tutkimus, Vihti, 685
Maatschappij 'Arti et Amicitiae', Amsterdam, 1475
Maatschappij der Nederlandse Letterkunde, Leiden, 1476
Maatschappij tot Bevordering der Toonkunst, Amsterdam, 1476
Ma'ayan Baruch Prehistory Museum of the Huleh Valley, 1098
Macalester College, 2527
Macaulay Institute, 2146
Macedonian Museum of Contemporary Art of Thessaloniki, 913
MacKenzie Art Gallery, Regina, 335
Macleay Museum, 126
Macmurray College, 2430
Macquarie University, 137
Macquarie University Library, 124
Madan Puraskar Pustakalaya, Lalitpur, 1472
Maden Tetkik ve Arama Genel Müdürlüğü Kütüphanesi, Ankara, 2059
Maden Tetkik ve Arama Genel Müdürlüğü (MTA), Ankara, 2059
Madhya Pradesh Bhoj (Open) University, Bhopal, 1009
Madonna University, 2507
Madras Institute of Development Studies, 975
Madras Literary Society, 969
Madras Literary Society Library, 980
Madrasat Ahl Al Hadith Library, Mecca, 1808
Madrasat Ahl Al Hadith, Mecca, 1811
Madurai-kamaraj University, 1009
Mae Fah Luang University, 2039
Maejo University, 2039
Magadh University, 1009
Magarach Institute of the Vine and Wine, Yalta, 2100
Magdalen College Library, Oxford, 2166
Magdalen College, Oxford, 2250
Magdalene College, Cambridge, 2192
Magdalene College Old Library, 2155
Magdeburger Museen, 817
Maghreb Studies Association, London, 2142
Magnitogorsk State Technical University 'G. I. Nosov', 1784
Magnitogorsk State University, 1768
Magnolia Bible College, 2542
Magtymguly Institute of Literature, Ashgabat, 2091
Magtymguly Turkmen State University, 2091
Magtymguly Turkmen State University Library, 2091
Magway Degree College, 1467
Magway University Library, 1465
Magwe University, 1466
Magyar Agrártudományi Egyesület, 936
Magyar Állami Eötvös Loránd Geofizikai Intézet, 941
Magyar Asztronautikai Társaság, 938
Magyar Bélyegmúzeum, 945
Magyar Biofizikai Társaság, 937
Magyar Biokémiai Egyesület, 937
Magyar Biológiai Társaság, 937
Magyar Biomassza Társaság, 937
Magyar Elektrotechnikai Egyesület, 938
Magyar Élelmezésipari Tudományos Egyesület (MÉTE), 936
Magyar Építészeti Múzeum, 945
Magyar Filozófiai Társaság, 938
Magyar Földmérési, Térképészeti és Távérzékelési Társaság, Budapest, 937
Magyar Földrajzi Társaság, 937
Magyar Geofizikusok Egyesülete, 938
Magyar Gyógyszerészeti Társaság, 937
Magyar Hidrológiai Társaság, 938
Magyar Iparjogvédelmi és Szerzői Jogi Egyesület, 938
Magyar Iparművészeti Egyetem, 953
Magyar Irodalomtörténeti Társaság, 937
Magyar Írók Könyvtára, 942

Magyar Írószövetség, 937
Magyar Karszt- és Barlangkutató Társulat, 938
Magyar Kémikusok Egyesülete, 938
Magyar Képzőművészeti Főiskola, Budapest, 954
Magyar Kereskedelmi és Vendéglátóipari Múzeum, 945
Magyar Könyvtárosok Egyesülete, 936
Magyar Környezetvédelmi és Vízügyi Múzeum, 946
Magyar Levéltárosok Egyesülete, 937
Magyar Meteorológiai Társaság, 938
Magyar Mezőgazdasági Múzeum, 945
Magyar Művelődési Intézet, Budapest, 937
Magyar Naiv Művészek Múzeuma, 946
Magyar Nemzeti Galéria, 945
Magyar Nemzeti Galéria Könyvtára, 942
Magyar Nemzeti Múzeum, 945
Magyar Nemzeti Múzeum Régészeti Könyvtára, 942
Magyar Nemzeti Múzeum Vértesszőllősi Bemutatóhelye, 948
Magyar Néprajzi Társaság, 938
Magyar Nyelvtudományi Társaság, 937
Magyar Olajipari Múzeum, 948
Magyar Országos Levéltár, 942
Magyar Orvostársaságok és Egyesületek Szövetsége (MOTESZ), 937
Magyar Pszichológiai Társaság, 938
Magyar Régészeti és Művészettörténeti Társulat, 937
Magyar Rovartani Társaság, 937
Magyar Sportmúzeum, Budapest, 945
Magyar Szociológiai Társaság, 938
Magyar Táncművészeti Főiskola, 954
Magyar Tejgazdasági Kísérleti Intézet, 939
Magyar Természettudományi Múzeum, 945
Magyar Történelmi Társulat, 937
Magyar Tudományos Akadémia, 936
Magyar Tudományos Akadémia Állatorvos-tudományi Kutatóintézete, 939
Magyar Tudományos Akadémia Atommagkutató Intézete, 941
Magyar Tudományos Akadémia Balatoni Limnológiai Kutatóintézete, 940
Magyar Tudományos Akadémia Csillagászati Kutatóintézete, 941
Magyar Tudományos Akadémia Csillagászati Kutatóintézetének Napfizikai Obszervatóriuma, 941
Magyar Tudományos Akadémia Filozófiai Kutatóintézete, 941
Magyar Tudományos Akadémia Földrajztudományi Kutató Intézet Könyvtára, 942
Magyar Tudományos Akadémia Földrajztudományi Kutatóintézete, 940
Magyar Tudományos Akadémia Geodéziai és Geofizikai Kutató Intézete, 941
Magyar Tudományos Akadémia Irodalomtudományi Intézete, 940
Magyar Tudományos Akadémia Jogtudományi Intézete, 939
Magyar Tudományos Akadémia, Kémiai Kutatóközpont, 941
Magyar Tudományos Akadémia Kémiai Kutatóközpont Izotóp- és Felületkémiai Intézet, 941
Magyar Tudományos Akadémia, KFKI Anyagtudományi Kutató Intézet, 941
Magyar Tudományos Akadémia, KFKI Atomenergia Kutató Intézet, 941
Magyar Tudományos Akadémia, KFKI Mérés- és Számítástechnikai Kutató Intézet, 941
Magyar Tudományos Akadémia Könyvtára, 942
Magyar Tudományos Akadémia Közgazdaságtudományi Kutatóközpont, 939
Magyar Tudományos Akadémia Kísérleti Orvostudományi Kutatóintézete, 940

Magyar Tudományos Akadémia Mezőgazdasági Kutatóintézete, 939
Magyar Tudományos Akadémia Műszaki Kémiai Kutató Intézet, 941
Magyar Tudományos Akadémia Művészettörténeti Kutatóintézet, 940
Magyar Tudományos Akadémia Néprajzi Kutatóintézete, 941
Magyar Tudományos Akadémia Növényvédelmi Kutatóintézete, 939
Magyar Tudományos Akadémia Nyelvtudományi Intézete, 940
Magyar Tudományos Akadémia Ökológiai és Botanikai Kutatóintézete, 940
Magyar Tudományos Akadémia Politikai Tudományok Intézete, Budapest, 939
Magyar Tudományos Akadémia Pszichológiai Kutatóintézet, 941
Magyar Tudományos Akadémia Régészeti Intézete, 940
Magyar Tudományos Akadémia Regionális Kutatások Központja, 940
Magyar Tudományos Akadémia Rényi Alfréd Matematikai Kutatóintézet, 941
Magyar Tudományos Akadémia Számítástechnikai és Automatizálási Kutató Intézete, 942
Magyar Tudományos Akadémia Szegedi Biológiai Központja, 940
Magyar Tudományos Akadémia Szociológiai Kutatóintézet, 941
Magyar Tudományos Akadémia Talajtani és Agrokémiai Kutató Intézete, 939
Magyar Tudományos Akadémia Történettudományi Intézete, 940
Magyar Tudományos Akadémia Világgazdasági Kutató Intézete, 939
Magyar Tudományos Akadémia Zenetudományi Intézete, 940
Magyar Ujságírók Országos Szövetsége, 937
Magyar Vegyészeti Múzeum, 948
Magyar Zenei Tanács, 937
Magyar Zeneművészeti Társaság, 937
Magyar Zsidó Múzeum és Levéltár, 945
Magyarhoni Földtani Társulat, 938
Maha Bodhi Society of Sri Lanka, 1954
Mahanakorn University of Technology, 2039, 2046
Maharaja Sawai Man Singh II Museum, 982
Maharaja Sayajirao University of Baroda, 1010
Maharana Pratap University of Agriculture and Technology, Udaipur, 1011
Maharashtra Animal and Fishery Sciences University, Nagpur, 1011
Maharashtra University of Health Sciences, Nashik, 1011
Maharishi Mahesh Yogi Vedic Vishwavidyalaya, Jabalpur, 1011
Maharishi University of Management, 2456
Maharshi Dayanand Saraswati University, 1011
Maharshi Dayanand University, Rohtak, 1011
Mahasarakham University, 2040
Mahatama Gandhi Antarrashtriya Hindi Vishwavidyalaya, Wardha, 1011
Mahatma Gandhi Chitrakoot Gramodaya University, Chitrakoot, 1011
Mahatma Gandhi Institute, Moka, 1413
Mahatma Gandhi Kashi Vidyapeeth, Varanasi, 1012
Mahatma Gandhi University, 1012
Mahatma Phule Krishi Vidyapeeth, 1012
Mahendra Sanskrit University, 1473
Mahidol University, 2040
Maimana Museum, 74
Main Astronomical Observatory, Kyiv, 2102
Main Astronomical Observatory, St Petersburg, 1744

Modern Churchpeople's Union, 2142

Modern Humanitarian University, Khujand, 2025

Modern Humanities Research Association, Bath, 2148

Modern Language Association of America, 2291

Modern Magyar Képtár I, 947

Modern Magyar Képtár II, 947

Moderna galerija, Ljubljana, 1857

Moderna Galerija, Zagreb, 595

Moderna Museet, Stockholm, 1975

Mody Institute of Technology and Science, Lakshmangarh, 1037

Moesgård Museum, Højbjerg, 634

Mogilev Oblast Library 'V. I. Lenin', 209

Mogilev State Foodstuffs University, 213

Mogilev State University 'A. A. Kuleshov', 213

Mohan Lal Sukhadia University, 1013

Mohyla míru, Prace u Brna, 614

Moi University, 1314

Mokpo National Maritime University, 1342

Mokpo National University, 1343

Mokwon University, 1343

Moldovan Sociological Association, 1444

Moldovan State University Library, 1446

Molloy College, 2588

Mombasa Polytechnic, 1316

Mommsen-Gesellschaft, 789

Momoyama Gakuin University (St Andrew's University), Osaka, 1282

Mon State Museum, Mawlamyine, 1466

Monash University, 139

Monash University Library, 125

Monasterio de la Encarnación, Madrid, 1900

Monasterio de las Descalzas Reales, Madrid, 1900

Monasterio de las Huelgas, 1900

Monasterio de San Lorenzo de El Escorial, 1900

Monasterio de Santa Clara, 1900

Monasterio Valle de Los Caídos, 1900

Mondragon Unibertsitatea, 1925

'Mongol' Higher School, 1454

Mongolian Academy of Sciences, 1449

Mongolian Agricultural University, 1452

Mongolian Business Institute, 1454

Mongolian Civil Engineers' Association, 1449

Mongolian Development Research Centre, 1450

Mongolian Muslims' Society, Ulan Bator, 1449

Mongolian National Gallery of Modern Art, Ulan Bator, 1451

Mongolian National Higher School, Ulan Bator, 1454

Mongolian National Mining Association, Ulan Bator, 1449

Mongolian National Water Association, Ulan Bator, 1449

Mongolian State Education University, 1452

Mongolian University of Arts and Culture, Ulan Bator, 1452

Mongolian University of Science and Technology, 1453

Monkwearmouth Station Museum, 2177

Monmouth College, 2431

Monmouth University, West Long Branch, 2562

Monmouthshire Libraries and Information Service, 2156

'Monos' Higher School of Medicine, Ulan Bator, 1454

Montana Historical Society Museum, 2323

Montana State University, 2553

Montana State University – Billings, 2553

Montana State University—Northern, 2553

Montana Tech of the University of Montana, 2553

Montanuniversität Leoben, 175

Montclair Art Museum, 2324

Montclair State University, 2562

Montenegrin PEN Centre, 1455

Monterey Institute of International Studies, 2353

Montréal Biodôme, 335

Montreal Diocesan Theological College, Montréal, 357

Montreal Museum of Fine Arts, Montreal, 335

Montreat College, 2606

Montserrat College of Art, Massachusetts, 2497

Monumenta Germaniae Historica, Munich, 789

Monumental Brass Society, Stratford St Mary, 2132

Monywa University, 1467

Moody Bible Institute, 2431

Moore College of Art and Design, 2652

Moorepark Research and Development Division (Teagasc), 1082

Moorland-Spingarn Research Center, 2309

Móra Ferenc Múzeum, 947

Moralogy Kenkyusho, 1178

Moravian College, 2652

Moravská galerie v Brně, 613

Moravská zemská knihovna, Brno, 612

Moravské zemské muzeum, 613

Moravskoslezská vědecká knihovna v Ostravě, 612

Mordovian N. P. Ogarev State University Library, 1754

Mordovian Republic S. D. Erzi Museum of Fine Arts, 1759

Mordovian State University, 1768

Moredun Research Institute, 2147

Morehead Planetarium and Science Center, 2325

Morehead State University, 2463

Morehouse College, 2420

Morehouse School of Medicine, 2420

Morgan Library, 2314

Morgan State University, 2476

Mori Art Museum, 1187

Morningside College, 2456

Morris Brown College, 2420

Morris College, 2674

Morski Instytut Rybacki, Gdynia, 1627

Mosad Harav Kook, 1115

Moscow Agricultural Academy 'K. A. Timiryazev', 1792

Moscow Architectural Institute, 1795

Moscow Arts Theatre Museum, 1756

Moscow Aviation Institute (State Technical University), 1784

Moscow Choreographic Institute, 1797

Moscow Engineering Physics Institute (State University), 1784

Moscow G. N. Gabrichevskii Institute of Epidemiology and Microbiology, 1738

Moscow Helmholtz Research Institute of Eye Diseases, 1738

Moscow Higher School of Industrial Art, 1797

Moscow House of Scientists, 1730

Moscow Institute of Economics, Statistics and Informatics, 1796

Moscow Institute of Electronic Technology (Technical University), 1784

Moscow Institute of Municipal Economy and Construction, 1795

Moscow Institute of Physics and Technology (State University), 1784

Moscow Institute of Printing, 1796

Moscow Literary Institute of the Union of Writers 'M. Gorky', 1797

Moscow Municipal Research First Aid Institute, 1738

Moscow Power Engineering Institute (Technical University), 1784

Moscow Radiotechnical Institute, 1744

Moscow Research Institute of Psychiatry, 1738

Moscow Scientific-Industrial Association 'Spektr', 1749

Moscow Society of Naturalists, 1730

Moscow State Academy of Applied Biotechnology, 1794

Moscow State Academy of Fine Chemical Technology 'M. V. Lomonosov', 1784

Moscow State Academy of Food Industry, 1794

Moscow State Academy of Instrumentation and Informatics, 1794

Moscow State Academy of Light Industry, 1793

Moscow State Academy of Veterinary Medicine and Biotechnology 'K. I. Skryabin', 1792

Moscow State Academy of Water Transport, 1795

Moscow State Agro-Engineering University, V. P. Goryachkin, 1761

Moscow State Art Institute 'V. I. Surikov', 1797

Moscow State Automobile and Road Technical University, 1784

Moscow State Conservatoire 'P. I. Tchaikovsky', 1797

Moscow State Food Institute, 1796

Moscow State Forestry University, 1784

Moscow State Geological Prospecting Academy, 1794

Moscow State Industrial University, 1784

Moscow State Institute of Culture, 1797

Moscow State Institute of Electronics and Mathematics (Technical University), 1785

Moscow State Institute of International Relations, 1796

Moscow State Institute of Radio Technology, Electronics and Automation (Technical University), 1785

Moscow State Linguistics University, 1780

Moscow State Medical-Stomatological University, 1779

Moscow State Mining University, 1785

Moscow State Regional University, Moscow, 1769

Moscow State Technical University 'mami', 1785

Moscow State Technical University 'N. E. Bauman', 1785

Moscow State Technical University of Civil Aviation, 1785

Moscow State Technological University, Stankin, 1785

Moscow State Textile University, 1785

Moscow State University 'M. V. Lomonsov', 1769

Moscow State University Museum of Zoology, 1756

Moscow State University of Civil Engineering, 1785

Moscow State University of Engineering Ecology, 1785

Moscow State University of Environmental Engineering, 1785

Moscow State University of Geodesy and Cartography, 1786

Moscow State University of Land Management, 1761

Moscow State University of Railway Engineering, 1786

Moscow State University Scientific Library, 1752

Moscow Technical University of Communication and Informatics, 1786

Moscow Technological Institute, 1796

Moscow University of Consumer Co-operatives, 1769

Moshi University College of Co-operative and Business Studies, Moshi, 2031

Moshood Abiola Polytechnic, Abeokuta, 1542

Moss Landing Marine Laboratories, 2304

Mosul Museum, 1075

Mote Marine Laboratory, Inc., 2304

Mother Teresa Women's University, 1013

Moto Moto Museum, Mbala, 2785

Mount Allison University, 371

Mount Allison University Libraries and Archives, Sackville, 330

Mount Graham International Observatory, 2339

Mount Graham International Observatory (MGIO), Safford, 2305

Mount Holyoke College, 2497

Mount Ida College, 2497

Mount John University Observatory, 1504

Mount Makulu Agricultural Research Station, 2784

Mount Marty College, 2676

Mount Mary College, 2729

Mount Mercy College, 2456

Mount Olive College, 2606

Mount Saint Mary College, Newburgh, 2588

Mount Saint Mary's University, Emmitsburg, 2476

Mount Saint Vincent University, 371

Mount St Mary's College, Los Angeles, 2353

Mount Stromlo and Siding Spring Observatories, 123

Mount Union College, 2624

Mount Vernon Nazarene University, 2624

Mountain Taiga Station, Gornotaezhnoe, 1740

Mozarteum, Salzburg, 169

Mozarts Wohnhaus, Salzburg, 169

Mozgássérültek Pető András Nevelőképző és Nevelőintézete, Budapest, 940

Mpisi Cattle Breeding Experimental Station, 1966

MRC Anatomical Neuropharmacology Unit, Oxford, 2148

MRC Biomedical Nuclear Magnetic Resonance Centre, London, 2148

MRC Biostatistics Unit, Cambridge, 2148

MRC Cambridge Centre for Brain Repair, 2148

MRC Centre, Cambridge, 2148

MRC Centre for Protein Engineering, Cambridge, 2148

MRC Centre for Synaptic Plasticity, Bristol, 2148

MRC Centre, London, 2148

MRC Centre, Oxford, 2148

MRC Clinical Sciences Centre, London, 2148

MRC Clinical Trials Units, London, 2148

MRC Cognition and Brain Sciences Unit, Cambridge, 2148

MRC Dunn Human Nutrition Unit, Cambridge, 2148

MRC Epidemiology Resource Centre, Southampton, 2148

MRC Functional Genetics Unit, 2149

MRC Harwell (Mammalian Genetics Unit), 2149

MRC Harwell (Mouse Genome Centre), 2149

MRC Harwell (Radiation and Genome Stability Unit), 2149

MRC Health Services Research Collaboration, Bristol, 2149

MRC Human Genetics Unit, Edinburgh, 2149

MRC Human Immunology Unit, Oxford, 2149

MRC Human Reproductive Sciences Unit, Edinburgh, 2149

MRC Immunochemistry Unit, Oxford, 2149

MRC Institute of Hearing Research, Nottingham, 2149

MRC Interdisciplinary Research Centre for Cognitive Neuroscience, Oxford, 2149

MRC Interdisciplinary Research Centre in Cell Biology, London, 2149

MRC Laboratories, the Gambia, 2149

MRC Laboratory of Molecular Biology, Cambridge, 2149

MRC Molecular Haematology Unit, Oxford, 2149

MRC Muscle and Cell Motility Unit, London, 2149

MRC Prion Unit, London, 2149

MRC Protein Phosphorylation Unit, Dundee, 2149

MRC Resource Centre for Human Nutrition Research, Cambridge, 2149

MRC Social and Public Health Sciences Unit, Glasgow, 2149

N

National Institute of Education, Minsk, 207

National Institute of Education, Samtse, 238

National Institute of Educational Planning and Administration, New Delhi, 1039

National Institute of Environmental Health Sciences, Bethesda, 2303

National Institute of Fashion Technology, New Delhi, 1039

National Institute of Fruit Tree Science, Ibaraki, 1179

National Institute of General Medical Sciences, Bethesda, 2303

National Institute of Genetics, Mishima, 1181

National Institute of Health and Family Welfare (NIHFW), New Delhi, 1039

National Institute of Health and Nutrition, Tokyo, 1181

National Institute of Health Sciences, Tokyo, 1181

National Institute of Historical and Cultural Research, Islamabad, 1566

National Institute of Hydrology, Roorkee, 980

National Institute of Hygiene and Epidemiology, Hanoi, 2773

National Institute of Industrial Health, Kawasaki, 1181

National Institute of Infectious Diseases, Tokyo, 1181

National Institute of Japanese Literature Library, Tokyo, 1184

National Institute of Livestock and Grassland Science, Tsukuba, 1179

National Institute of Medicine, Ulan Bator, 1450

National Institute of Mental Health and Neurosciences, Bangalore, 1037

National Institute of Mental Health, National Centre of Neurology and Psychiatry, Ichikawa, 1181

National Institute of Mental Health (NIMH), 2303

National Institute of Meteorology and Hydrology, Sofia, 302

National Institute of Neurological Disorders and Stroke, Bethesda, 2303

National Institute of Nursing Research, Bethesda, 2303

National Institute of Nutrition, Hanoi, 2773

National Institute of Nutrition, Hyderabad, 977

National Institute of Occupational and Environmental Health Research, Hanoi, 2773

National Institute of Oceanography, Panaji, 973

National Institute of Otorhinolaryngology, Hanoi, 2773

National Institute of Pharmaceutical Education and Research, Mohali, 1033

National Institute of Pharmaceutical Research and Development (NIPRD), Idu, 1521

National Institute of Plant Protection, Hanoi, 2772

National Institute of Population and Social Security Research, Tokyo, 1180

National Institute of Public Administration, Lahore, 1566

National Institute of Public Administration, Lusaka, 2786

National Institute of Public Health, Phnom-Penh, 317

National Institute of Rock Mechanics, Kolar Gold Fields, 978

National Institute of Rural Development, Rajendranagar, 979

National Institute of Science Communication and Information Resources, 981

National Institute of Science, Technology and Development Studies, New Delhi, 973

National Institute of Sericultural and Entomological Science, Tsukuba, 1179

National Institute of Social Sciences, New York, 2298

National Institute of Standards and Technology, Gaithersburg, 2307

National Institute of Standards and Technology Research Library, Gaithersburg, 2312

National Institute of Technology, Calicut, 1037

National Institute of Technology, Durgapur, 1037

National Institute of Technology, Hamirpur, 1037

National Institute of Technology, Jamshedpur, 1037

National Institute of Technology, Karnataka, Srinivasnagar, 1037

National Institute of Technology, Kurukshetra, 1037

National Institute of Technology, Rourkela, 1037

National Institute of Technology, Silchar, 1037

National Institute of Technology, Srinagar, 1037

National Institute of Technology, Tiruchirapalli, Tiruchirappalli, 1037

National Institute of Technology, Warangal, 1037

National Institute of Traditional Medicine, Hanoi, 2773

National Institute of Tuberculosis and Respiratory Diseases, Hanoi, 2773

National Institute of Vegetable and Tea Science, Shizuoka, 1179

National Institute of Water & Atmospheric Research Ltd–NIWA, Auckland, 1504

National Institute on Aging, Bethesda, 2302

National Institute on Alcohol Abuse and Alcoholism (NIAAA), 2302

National Institute on Deafness and Other Communication Disorders, Bethesda, 2303

National Institute on Drug Abuse (NIDA), 2303

National Institutes of Health, Bethesda, 2302

National Institutes of Health Library, Bethesda, 2312

National Kaohsiung University of Applied Sciences, 560

National Kyiv-Pechersk Lavra Museum, 2105

National Language Authority, Islamabad, 1564

National Law Institute University, Bhopal, 1016

National Law School of India University, 1037

National Law University, Jodhpur, 1016

National Library, Abu Dhabi, 2120

National Library, Amman, 1300

National Library and Archives, Bairiki, 1317

National Library and Archives, Funafuti, 2093

National Library and Archives of Ethiopia, 677

National Library and Archives of Iran, 1062

National Library and Documentation Centre, 1955

National Library and Documentation Service National Free Library of Zimbabwe, 2789

National Library, Baghdad, 1075

National Library Board, Singapore, 1837

National Library, Doha, 1689

National Library for the Blind, Stockport, 2168

National Library, Georgetown, 930

National Library, Kolkata, 981

National Library, Male', 1404

National Library of Armenia, 114

National Library of Australia, 124

National Library of Bangladesh, 192

National Library of Bashkortostan, 1754

National Library of Belarus, Minsk, 209

National Library of Bhutan, 238

National Library of Cambodia, 317

National Library of China, 434

National Library of Education, Washington, 2310

National Library of Engineering Sciences, Lahore, 1569

National Library of Estonia, 673

National Library of Georgia, 782

National Library of Greece, 912

National Library of Ingushetia, 1752

National Library of Ireland, 1083

National Library of Izmir, 2060

National Library of Jamaica, 1169

National Library of Korea, Seoul, 1323

National Library of Kuwait, Safat, 1354

National Library of Latvia, 1362

National Library of Libya, Benghazi, 1372

National Library of Malaysia, 1395

National Library of Malta, 1407

National Library of Medicine, Bethesda, 2312

National Library of Namibia, 1469

National Library of New Zealand, Te Puna Matauranga o Aotearoa, 1504

National Library of Nigeria, 1522

National Library of Pakistan, 1568

National Library of Russia, St Petersburg, 1754

National Library of Scotland, Edinburgh, 2157

National Library of Scotland Map Library, 2157

National Library of Somalia, 1861

National Library of Thailand, 2033

National Library of the Kyrgyz Republic, 1357

National Library of the Philippines, Manila, 1603

National Library of the Republic of Kazakhstan, 1305

National Library of the Republic of Moldova, 1446

National Library of Turkmenistan, 2091

National Library of Uganda, Kampala, 2095

National Library of Viet Nam, 2774

National Library of Wales, 2153

National Library, Port Vila, 2752

National Library, Riyadh, 1808

National Library Service, Waigani, 1585

National Library, Tiranë, 77

National Library, Yangon, 1466

National Maritime Museum, Alexandria, 661

National Maritime Museum, Greenwich, 2175

National Maritime Museum, Haifa, 1097

National Media Museum, Bradford, 2169

National Medical and Technical Scientific Society, Moscow, 1729

National Medical University 'O. Bohomolets', 2112

National Mental Health Association, Alexandria, 2294

National Metallurgical Academy of Ukraine, 2118

National Metallurgical Laboratory, Jamshedpur, 973

National Meteorological Library and Archive, Bracknell, 2158

National Mining University of Ukraine, 2115

National Motor Museum, Beaulieu, 2169

National Museum and Art Gallery of Trinidad & Tobago, 2052

National Museum at Ruwi, Muscat, 1561

National Museum, Bairiki, 1317

National Museum Bangkok, Bangkok, 2033

National Museum, Benin, 1522

National Museum, Bloemfontein, 1868

National Museum Cardiff, 2170

National Museum (Cultural), Colombo, 1955

National Museum, Damascus, 2022

National Museum in Lviv 'Andrey Sheptytsky', 2105

National Museum Institute of History of Art, Conservation and Museology, New Delhi, 1037

National Museum, Jos, 1522

National Museum, Kaduna, 1522

National Museum, Lagos, 1522

National Museum, Male', 1404

National Museum, Monrovia, 1370

National Museum, Monuments and Art Gallery, Gaborone, 250

National Museum (Natural History), Colombo, 1955

National Museum of African Art, Smithsonian Institution, Washington, 2319

National Museum of American History, Washington, 2319

National Museum of American Illustration, 2327

National Museum of Archaeology, Tiranë, 77

National Museum of Architecture, Veliko Tarnovo, 304

National Museum of Art and Archaeology, Yangon, 1466

National Museum of Arts, Phnom-Penh, 318

National Museum of Australia, 126

National Museum of Bhutan, 238

National Museum of China, Beijing, 436

National Museum of Contemporary Art (EMST), Athens, 913

National Museum of Contemporary Art, Seoul, 1323

National Museum of Ecclesiastical History and Archaeology, Sofia, 304

National Museum of Eritrea, 671

National Museum of Ethiopia, Addis Ababa, 677

National Museum of Ethnology, Osaka, 1186

National Museum of Fine Arts of Moldova, 1446

National Museum of History, Sofia, 304

National Museum of History, Taipei, 554

National Museum of India, 982

National Museum of Ireland, 1084

National Museum of Korea, Seoul, 1323

National Museum of Literature, Sofia, 304

National Museum of Lithuania, 1377

National Museum of Malaysia, 1395

National Museum of Medieval Art, Korçë, 77

National Museum of Military History, Sofia, 304

National Museum of Modern Art, Baghdad, 1075

National Museum of Modern Art, Kyoto, 1186

National Museum of Modern Art, Tokyo, 1187

National Museum of Mongolian History, Ulan Bator, 1451

National Museum of Namibia, 1469

National Museum of Natural History, New Delhi, 982

National Museum of Natural History, Washington, 2320

National Museum of Nepal, 1472

National Museum of Pakistan, 1569

National Museum of the American Indian, Smithsonian Institution, New York, 2325

National Museum of the History and Culture of Belarus, Minsk, 209

National Museum of the History of Ukraine, 2105

National Museum of the Philippines, 1604

National Museum of the Republic of Tatarstan, 1755

National Museum of the United States Air Force, 2326

National Museum of Turkmenistan, 2091

National Museum of Western Art, Tokyo, 1187

National Museum of Wildlife Art, 2328

National Museum, Oron, 1522

National Museum, Riyadh, 1808

National Museum, Victoria, Seychelles, 1833

National Museums Liverpool, 2173

National Museums Northern Ireland, Belfast, 2274

National Museums of Kenya, 1312

National Museums of Scotland, 2171

National Museums of Scotland Library, 2157

National Museums of Tanzania, 2028

National Natural History Museum, Sofia, 304

National Nuclear Centre, Kurchatov, 1305

National Nutrition Institute, Cairo, 659

National Observatory of Athens, 911

National Oceanic and Atmospheric Administration, Environmental Data and Information Service, Environmental Science Information Center, Library and Information Services Division, Silver Spring, 2309

National Oceanography Centre, 2150

National Oncological Centre, Sofia, 301

National Open University of Nigeria, Abuja, 1531

National Open University, Taipei, 557

National Ophthalmological Society, Moscow, 1729

National Organization for Drug Control and Research, Giza, 659

National Palace Museum, Taipei, 555

National Parliamentary Library of Ukraine, 2104

National Pedagogical University 'M. Drahomanov', 2113

National Pharmaceutical Society, Moscow, 1729

National Photo, Film and Sound Archive, Port Vila, 2752

National Physical Laboratory, Jerusalem, 1096

National Physical Laboratory, New Delhi, 973

National Physical Laboratory, Teddington, 2152

National Pingtung University of Science and Technology, 558

National Polytechnic School, 652

National Polytechnical Museum, Sofia, 304

National Portrait Gallery, London, 2175

National Portrait Gallery, Washington, 2320

National Preserve of Tauric Chersonesos, 2105

National Productivity Council, New Delhi, 975

National Public Health Laboratory Services (Medical Department), Nairobi, 1311

National Pushkin Museum, St Petersburg, 1759

National Qualifications Authority of Ireland, Dublin, 1080

National Radio Astronomy Observatory, Charlottesville, 2305

National Rail Museum, New Delhi, 982

National Railway Museum, York, 2179

National Records Office, Khartoum, 1960

National Renewable Energy Laboratory, Golden, 2307

National Research and Development Foundation, Castries, 1802

National Research Centre of Radiation Medicine, Kyiv, 2101

National Research Council Canada, Ottawa, 323

National Research Council of Canada, 327

National Research Council of the Philippines, 1602

National Research Council, Washington, 2284

National Research Institute, Boroko, 1585

National Research Institute for Chemical Technology (NARICT), Basawa, 1521

National Research Institute for Earth Science and Disaster Prevention (NIED), Ibaraki, 1182

National Research Institute for Mechanical Engineering, Hanoi, 2774

National Research Institute of Astronomy and Geophysics, Cairo, 660

National Research Institute of Brewing, Tokyo, 1182

National Research Institute of Mining and Metallurgy, Hanoi, 2774

National Research Laboratory for Conservation of Cultural Property, Lucknow, 975

National Roman Legion Museum, Caerleon, 2170

National Root Crops Research Institute (NRCRI), Umuahia, 1520

National School of Anthropology and History, 1441

National School of Drama, New Delhi, 1040

National School of Librarianship and Archives, 1441

National Science and Technology Museum, Dhaka, 193

National Science Council, Taipei, 553

National Science Foundation, Colombo, 1954

National Science Museum, Seoul, 1323

National Science Resources Center, Washington, 2301

National Science Teachers Association, Arlington, 2294

National Scientific and Technical Information Centre, Safat, 1354

National Scientific Medical Society of Anatomists, Histologists and Embryologists, Moscow, 1729

National Scientific Medical Society of Endocrinologists, Moscow, 1729

National Scientific Medical Society of Haemotologists and Transfusiologists, Moscow, 1729

National Scientific Medical Society of Hygienists, Moscow, 1729

National Scientific Medical Society of Infectionists, Moscow, 1729

National Scientific Medical Society of Nephrologists, Moscow, 1729

National Scientific Medical Society of Neuropathologists and Psychiatrists, Moscow, 1729

National Scientific Medical Society of Obstetricians and Gynaecologists, Moscow, 1729

National Scientific Medical Society of Oto-Rhino-Laryngologists, Moscow, 1729

National Scientific Medical Society of Paediatricians, Moscow, 1729

National Scientific Medical Society of Phthisiologists, Moscow, 1729

National Scientific Medical Society of Physical Therapists and Health-Resort Physicians, Moscow, 1729

National Scientific Medical Society of Physicians-Analysts, Moscow, 1729

National Scientific Medical Society of Physicians in Curative Physical Culture and Sports Medicine, Moscow, 1729

National Scientific Medical Society of Roentgenologists and Radiologists, Moscow, 1729

National Scientific Medical Society of Stomatologists, Moscow, 1729

National Scientific Medical Society of Surgeons, Moscow, 1729

National Scientific Medical Society of the History of Medicine, Moscow, 1729

National Scientific Medical Society of Therapists, Moscow, 1729

National Scientific Medical Society of Toxicologists, St Petersburg, 1729

National Scientific Medical Society of Traumatic Surgeons and Orthopaedists, Moscow, 1729

National Scientific Medical Society of Urological Surgeons, Moscow, 1729

National Scientific Medical Society of Venereologists and Dermatologists, Moscow, 1729

National Sculpture Society, New York, 2289

National Shipbuilding University 'Admiral Makarov', Kyiv, 2115

National Slate Museum, Llauberis, 2170

National Social Science Documentation Centre, New Delhi, 981

National Social Welfare Training Institute, Dar es Salaam, 2031

National Society (Church of England) for Promoting Religious Education, 2142

National Society for Clean Air and Environmental Protection, Brighton, 2144

National Society for Education in Art and Design, Corsham, 2124

National Society for the Study of Education, Chicago, 2283

National Society of Professional Engineers, Alexandria, 2300

National Solar Observatory, 2305

National Space Centre, Leicester, 2173

National Sugar Institute, Kanpur, 974

National Taiwan Arts Education Center, 553

National Taiwan College of Arts, 560

National Taiwan Museum, 555

National Taiwan Normal University, 558

National Taiwan Ocean University, 558

National Taiwan Science Education Center, 555

National Taiwan University, 558

National Taiwan University of Science and Technology, 559

National Taras Shevchenko Museum, Kyiv, 2105

National Technical University of Athens, 916

National Technical University of Athens Library, 912

National Textile University, Faisalabad, 1576

National Theatre Conservatory, Denver, 2381

National Transport University, Kyiv, 2116

National Trust for Historic Preservation in the United States, 2286

National Trust for Places of Historic Interest or Natural Beauty, London, 2126

National Trust for Scotland, 2126

National Trust Museum, St George's, 2278

National Tsing Hua University, Hsinchu, 559

National Tuberculosis Institute, Bangalore, 977

National Union of Architects of Ukraine, 2098

National Union of Cinematographers of Ukraine, 2098

National University, Gazipur, 201

National University, La Jolla, 2353

National University, Manila, 1611

National University of Food Technologies, Kyiv, 2116

National University of Health Sciences, Lombard, 2431

National University of Ireland, 1086

National University of Ireland, Galway, 1087

National University of Ireland, Galway, James Hardiman Library, 1084

National University of Ireland, Maynooth, 1088

National University of Kyiv-Mohyla Academy, 2109

National University of Laos, 1360

National University of Laos Central Library, 1360

National University of Lesotho, 1369

National University of Lviv 'Ivan Franko', 2109

National University of Malaysia, 1396

National University of Modern Languages, Islamabad, 1576

National University of Mongolia, 1452

National University of Pharmacy, Kharkiv, 2112

National University of Physical Education and Sports of Ukraine, 2112

National University of Samoa, 1804

National University of Science and Technology, Bulawayo, 2790

National University of Science and Technology, Rawalpindi, 1576

National University of Singapore, 1838

National University of Singapore Libraries, 1837

National University of Timor Lorosa'e Library, Dili, 2047

National University of Water Management and Natural Resources, Rivne, 2116

National Veterinary Research Centre (MUGUGA), Kikuyu, 1311

National Veterinary Research Institute (NVRI), Vom, 1520

National Vision Research Institute of Australia, 122

National War College Library, Taipei, 554

National War Museum of Scotland, 2171

National Water Research Institute, Burlington, Ontario, 329

National Waterfront Museum, Swansea, 2170

National Wildlife Federation, Vienna, VA, 2295

National Wine and Spirituous Beverages Research Institute, Sofia, 300

National Wool Museum, Llaudysul, 2170

National Writers' Union of Ukraine, 2098

National Zoological Gardens of South Africa, Pretoria, 1866

Nationale Plantentuin van België, 219

Nationalekonomisk Forening, Copenhagen, 628

Nationalekonomiska Föreningen, Stockholm, 1969

Nationalhistoriske Museum paa Frederiksborg Slot, Hillerød, 634

Nationalities Studies Institute, Beijing, 433

National–Louis University, Chicago, 2431

Nationalmuseet, Copenhagen, 633

Nationalmuseum, Stockholm, 1975

Nationalökonomische Gesellschaft, Vienna, 160

Natishvili, A. N., Institute of Experimental Morphology, 781

Native American Educational Services, 2431

NATO Library, Public Diplomacy Division, Brussels, 221

Natsagdorj Central Public Library, Ulan Bator, 1451

Natsagdorj Museum, 1451

Náttúrufrædistofnun Íslands, Reykjavík, 964

Natural Environment Research Council (NERC), Swindon, 2149

Natural Freezing and Food Technology Institute, Ulan Bator, 1451

Natural History Museum, Ankara, 2060

Natural History Museum, Library and Information Services, London, 2162

Natural History Museum, London, 2175

Natural History Museum, Obafemi Awolowo University, 1522

Natural History Museum of Los Angeles County, 2318

Natural History Museum of the University of Basrah, 1075

Natural History Museum of Zimbabwe, Bulawayo, 2789

Natural History Museum, Ulan Bator, 1451

Natural History Museum, University of Kansas, 2321

Natural Resources Canada, Headquarters Library, 331

Natural Resources Development College, Lusaka, 2786

Natural Resources Institute, Chatham Maritime, 2152

P

Population Association of America, Inc., 2298
Population Association of New Zealand, 1501
Population Council, New York, 2298
Porcelán Múzeum, Herend, 946
Porin kaupunginkirjasto–Satakunnan maakuntakirjasto, 687
Port and Harbour Research Institute, Yokosuka, 1183
Port Erin Marine Laboratory, 2279
Port Louis Museum, 1413
Port Natal Maritime Museum, Durban, 1869
Port Vila Public Library, Port Vila, 2752
Porte de Hal, 223
Portland State University, 2639
Portsmouth City Libraries, 2167
Portsmouth City Museum and Records Office, 2178
Porzellansammlung, Dresden, 814
Posavski muzej, Brežice, 1857
Post University, 2384
Postamúzeum, Budapest, 945
Postgraduate Institute of Medical Education and Research, Chandigarh, 1033
Postmuseum des Fürstentums Liechtenstein, 1375
Poštovní muzeum, Prague, 615
Posts and Telecommunications Institute, Tripoli, 1374
Posts and Telecommunications Training Centre No. 1, Hanoi, 2781
Potapenko, Ya. I., All-Russia Research Institute for Viticulture and Winemaking, 1732
Potteries Museum and Art Gallery, Stoke on Trent, 2178
Potti Sreeramulu Telugu University, Hyderabad, 1020
Poultry Science Association Inc., Savoy, 2285
Poultry Science Research Institute, Pyongyang, 1318
Povolzhsky Research Institute for the Economics and Development of the Agro-industrial Complex, 1732
Power and Electrical Power Engineering Society, St Petersburg, 1730
Power Institute, Ulan Bator, 1451
Powys Library and Archive Service, 2159
Poznań University of Technology, 1663
Poznańskie Towarzystwo Przyjaciół Nauk, 1621
Prairie View A & M University, 2693
Pratap Centre of Philosophy, 979
Pratt Institute, 2595
Pražská konzervatoř, 626
Precarpathian National University 'Vasyl Stefanyk', 2110
Prehistoric Society, London, 2132
Prehistory Society of Zimbabwe, 2787
Presbyterian College, Clinton, 2675
Presbyterian College, Montréal, 357
Presbyterian Historical Society, Philadelphia, 2290
Prescott College, 2333
Presentation College, 2676
Prešovská Univerzita, 1846
Press Society, Moscow, 1729
Pretoria Art Museum (Municipal Art Gallery), 1870
Priaulx Library, St Peter Port, 2279
Pricing Research Institute, Moscow, 1734
Priesterseminar Redemptoris Mater des Erzbistum Berlin, Rome, 2755
Primary Industries and Resources South Australia, 123
Primary Industries Ministerial Council, Canberra, 117
Primorsky State Agricultural Academy, 1792
Prince Albert Historical Museum, 335
Prince Consort's Library, 2153
Prince Edward Island Provincial Library, 332
Prince Leopold Institute for Tropical Medicine, 234
Prince of Songkla University, 2041

Princess Grace Irish Library, Monaco, 1448
Princess Sumaya University College for Technology, Amman, 1302
Princessehof Leeuwarden, Nationaal Keramiekmuseum, 1485
Princeton Theological Seminary, 2563
Princeton University, 2563
Princeton University Libraries, 2314
Principia College, 2432
Prinz-Albert-Gesellschaft eV, 787
Prirodnjacki muzej, Podgorica, 1455
Prirodnjački muzej u Beogradu, 1817
Prirodonaučen muzej na Makedonija, 1387
Prirodoslovni muzej, Rijeka, 594
Prirodoslovni muzej Slovenije, Ljubljana, 1857
Prirodoslovni muzej, Split, 594
Prirodoslovno Društvo Slovenije, 1855
Private Higher School of Oriental Philosophy and History, Ulan Bator, 1454
Pro Helvetia, 1997
Process Research ORTECH Corporation, 328
Prodomus SA – Institut de Studii şi Proiectare pentru Construcţii Civile, 1694
Proed SA – Institut de Studii şi Proiectare pentru Lucrări Tehnico-Edilitare, 1694
Prognostického ústavu, Bratislava, 1842
'Prognoz' Institute of Socio-Political Studies, Ulan Bator, 1450
Projects Development Institute (PRODA), Enugu, 1521
Provand's Lordship, glasgow, 2172
Providence College, 2671
Providence Public Library, 2316
Provincial Archives of Alberta, 330
Provincial Archives of New Brunswick, 330
Provincial Museum of Alberta, 333
Provincial Resource Library, St John's, 331
Provinsjale Biblioteek fan Fryslân, Leeuwarden, 1482
Přírodovědecké muzeum, Prague, 614
Pryanishnikov, D. N., All-Russia Research Institute of Fertilizers and Agropedology, 1732
Prydniprovska State Academy of Civil Engineering and Architecture, Dnipropetrovsk, 2118
Przemysłowy Instytut Automatyki i Pomiarów, Warsaw, 1634
Przemysłowy Instytut Elektroniki, Warsaw, 1634
Przemysłowy Instytut Maszyn Budowlanych, Kobyłka, 1634
Przemysłowy Instytut Maszyn Rolniczych, Poznań, 1634
Przemysłowy Instytut Motoryzacji, Warsaw, 1634
Przemysłowy Instytut Telekomunikacji, Warsaw, 1634
Psychological and Educational Research Centre, Jadiriya, 1074
Psychological Institute, Moscow, 1735
Psychological Society of Ireland, 1082
Psychologický ústav AV ČR, 611
Psychometric Society, Champaign, 2298
Psychotechnisches Institut, 166
Ptolemais Museum, 1372
Public Archives and Records Office, Charlottetown, 332
Public Archives of Sierra Leone, 1834
Public Health Laboratory, Harare, 2789
Public Health Laboratory Service, London, 2149
Public Library, Ankara, 2059
Public Library, Benghazi, 1372
Public Library, Bridgetown, 204
Public Library InterLINK, Burnaby, 330
Public Library, Kabul, 73
Public Library, Konya, 2060
Public Library of Charlotte and Mecklenburg County, 2315
Public Library of Cincinnati and Hamilton County, 2315
Public Library of Latakia, 2021

Public Library, Ramallah, 1115
Public Library Services, Department of Education, San Juan, 2740
Public Library, Shumen, 302
Public Record Office of Northern Ireland, 2274
Public Record Office of Victoria, 125
Public Records and Archives Administration Department, Accra, 905
Public Records Office, Nassau, 188
Public Records Office of Hong Kong, 546
Puget Sound Christian College, 2719
Pukyong National University, 1343
Pulp and Paper Research Institute, Jaykaypur, 980
Pulp and Paper Research Institute of Canada (Paprican), 329
Punjab Agricultural University, 1021
Punjab Bureau of Education, Lahore, 1564
Punjab Engineering College, Chandigarh, 1037
Punjab Institute of Nuclear Medicine (PINUM), 1567
Punjab Public Library, Lahore, 1569
Punjab Technical University, Jalandhar, 1021
Punjab Veterinary Research Institute, 1565
Punjabi University, 1021
Purbanchal University, 1473
Purdue University, 2448
Purdue University Libraries, 2311
Purdue University North Central, 2449
Purple Mountain Observatory, 433
Pusan National University, 1343
Pusan National University Library, 1322
Pusan National University Museum, 1323
Pusan National University of Education, 1343
Pusan University of Foreign Studies, 1343
Pusan Women's College, 1344
Pusat Bahasa. Departemen Pendidikan Nasional, Jakarta, 1043
Pusat Dokumentasi dan Informasi Ilmiah – Lembaga Ilmu Pengetahuan Indonesia (PDII-LIPI), Jakarta, 1044
Pusat Dokumentasi Melayu (Dewan Bahasa dan Pustaka), 1395
Pusat Penelitian Arkeologi, Jakarta, 1043
Pusat Penelitian dan Pengembangan Biologi, Bogor, 1043
Pusat Penelitian dan Pengembangan Geologi, Bandung, 1043
Pusat Penelitian dan Pengembangan Hortikultura, Jakarta, 1042
Pusat Penelitian dan Pengembangan Pelayanan dan Technologi Kesehatan, Surabaya, 1043
Pusat Penelitian dan Pengembangan Peternakan, Bogor, 1042
Pusat Penelitian dan Pengembangan Sumber Daga Air, Bandung, 1044
Pusat Penelitian dan Pengembangan Tanaman Pangan, Bogor, 1042
Pusat Penelitian Kelapa Sawit, Medan, 1042
Pusat Penelitian Oseanografi, Jakarta, 1043
Pusat Penelitian Perkebunan Gula Indonesia, Pasuruan, 1042
Pusat Penelitian Tanah dan Agroklimat, Bogor, 1042
Pusat Perpustakaan Angkatan Darat, Bandung, 1044
Pusat Perpustakaan Pertanian dan Komunikasi Penelitian, Bogor, 1044
Pushchino Scientific Centre, 1740
Pushkin Apartment Museum, St Petersburg, 1759
Pushkin Country House Museum, Pushkin, 1759
Pustovoit, V. S., All-Russia Research Institute of Oil Crops, 1732
Putra University, Malaysia, 1399
Pyatigorsk Pharmaceutical Institute, 1796

Pyatigorsk State Linguistic University, 1781
Pyongyang Astronomical Observatory, 1319
Pyongyang Scientific Library, 1320
Pyongyang University of Agriculture, 1320
Pyongyang University of Medicine, 1320
Pyrethrum Board of Kenya, Nakuru, 1311

Q

Qatar National Museum, 1689
Qendra e Enciklopedisë Shqiptare, Tiranë, 76
Qendra e Kërkimeve Gjeografike, Tiranë, 76
Qendra e Kerkimeve Hidraulike, Tiranë, 77
Qendra e Studimeve të Artit, Tiranë, 76
QinetiQ, Farnborough, 2152
Qinghai Institute of Salt Lakes, 431
Qinghai Nationalities College, 503
Qinghai Provincial Library, 436
Qom Museum, 1062
Quaid-e-awam University of Engineering, Sciences and Technology, Nawabshah, 1578
Quaid-e-Azam Library, Lahore, 1569
Quaid-i-Azam Academy, 1563
Quaid-i-Azam Birthplace, Reading Room, Museum and Library, 1569
Quaid-i-azam University, 1578
Quaid-i-Azam University Dr Raziuddin Siddiqi Memorial Library, 1568
Qualifications and Curriculum Authority (QCA), London, 2123
Quality Assurance Agency for Higher Education, Gloucester, 2124
Quality Improvement Agency, Coventry, 2124
Quantitative and Technical Economics Institute, Beijing, 430
Quanzhou Museum for Overseas Communications History, 437
Queen Elizabeth II Library, St John's, 331
Queen Margaret University College, Edinburgh, 2270
Queen Mary, University of London, 2226
Queen Mary, University of London, Library, 2162
Queen Victoria Museum and Art Gallery, Launceston, 127
Queens Borough Public Library, 2315
Queens' College, Cambridge, 2192
Queens College, Flushing, 2572
Queen's College Library, Oxford, 2166
Queens' College Old Library, Cambridge, 2155
Queen's College, The, Oxford, 2250
Queen's Theological College, Kingston, 380
Queen's University at Kingston, 378
Queen's University Belfast, 2274
Queen's University Library, Belfast, 2274
Queen's University Library, Kingston, Ont., 332
Queen's University Museums, Kingston, 334
Queens University of Charlotte, Charlotte, 2607
Queensland Art Gallery, 126
Queensland Department of Natural Resourcesand Water, 123
Queensland Herbarium, 126
Queensland Institute of Medical Research, 122
Queensland Museum, 127
Queensland Parliamentary Library, 125
Queensland University of Technology, 149
Queensland University of Technology Library, 125
Quekett Microscopical Club, 2140
Qufu Normal University, 503
Quincy University, 2432
Quinnipiac University, 2384
Qurm Museum, 1561

R

Raad voor Cultuur, Den Haag, 1475
Rabindra Bharati University, 1021
Rabindra Bhavan Art Gallery, 982
Rabindra-Bhavana, 983
Raccolta d'Arte Contemporanea 'Alberto della Ragione', 1139
Raccolta Manzù, Ardea, 1143
Raccolte Frugone in Villa Grimaldi, 1140
Raccolte Storiche del Comune di Milano, Biblioteca e Archivio, 1134
Raccolte Storiche del Comune di Milano, Museo del Risorgimento, 1141
Rada Główna Szkolnictwa Wyższego, Warsaw, 1620
Rada vědeckých společností České republiky, Prague, 607
Rada vedeckých spoločností, Bratislava, 1842
Radboud Universiteit Nijmegen, 1488
Rådet för högre utbildning, Stockholm, 1968
Radford University, 2711
Radiation Medicine Institute, Tianjin, 431
Radiation Research Society, Oak Brook, 2303
Radio and Television Higher School, Ulan Bator, 1454
Radio Society of Great Britain, 2145
Radiological Society of North America, Inc., 2294
Radiophysics Research Institute, Nizhny Novgorod, 1745
Radnička biblioteka 'Božidar Adžija' Zagreb, 594
Railway College, Ulan Bator, 1454
Railway Technical Research Institute, Tokyo, 1183
Rainis Museum of the History of Literature and Arts, 1362
Rajably Scientific Research Institute of Horticulture and Sub-Tropical Plants, Guba, 184
Rajamangala Institute of Technology, Bangkok Technical Campus, 2046
Rajamangala Institute of Technology, Khon Kaen Campus, 2046
Rajamangola Institute of Technology, Surin Campus, 2046
Rajarata University of Sri Lanka, 1958
Rajasthan Agricultural University, Bikaner, 1022
Rajasthan Ayurveda University, Jodhpur, 1022
Rajasthan Sanskrit University, Jaipur, 1022
Rajendra Agricultural University, 1022
Rajiv Gandhi Proudyogiki Vishwavidyalaya, Bhopal, 1022
Rajiv Gandhi University of Health Sciences, Karnataka, Bangalore, 1022
Rajputana Museum, Ajmer, 982
Rajshahi University Library, 192
Rajshahi University of Engineering and Technology, Rajshahi, 203
Rakenteiden Mekaniikan Seura, Espoo, 684
Rakhine State Museum, Sitture, 1466
Rákóczi Múzeum, 947
Ralph J. Bunche Library of the Department of State, Washington, 2310
Raman Research Institute, Bangalore, 977
Ramapo College of New Jersey, 2566
Ramkhamhaeng University, 2042
Ramon Magsaysay Technological University, Zambales, 1615
Ranchi University, 1022
RAND Corporation, Santa Monica, 2300
Randolph-macon College, 2711
Randolph-macon Woman's College, 2711
Range and Forage Institute, Pretoria, 1865
Rangsit University, 2043
Rani Durgavati University, 1022
Rannsóknarráð Íslands, Reykjavík, 964
Rannsóknastofa Háskólans, Reykjavík, 964

Rannsóknastofnun byggingaidnadarins, Reykjavík, 964
Rannsóknastofnun fiskidnadarins, Reykjavík, 964
Rannsóknastofnun landbúnadarins, Reykjavík, 964
Rare-earth Information Center (RIC), Ames, 2305
Rashtriya Sanskrit Sansthana, New Delhi, 1037
Rashtriya Sanskrit Vidyapeetha, Tirupati, 1037
Rat der Eidgenössischen Technischen Hochschulen/Conseil des Ecoles polytechniques fédérales, Zürich, 1995
Ráth György Múzeum, Budapest, 944
Rathausbücherei der Landeshauptstadt Stuttgart, 810
Rathenau Instituut, 1478
Rationalisierungs-Kuratorium der Deutschen Wirtschaft eV (RKW), 793
Ratnapura National Museum, 1955
Rautenstrauch-Joest-Museum, 813
Ravensbourne College of Design and Communication, 2271
Raw Materials Research and Development Council (RMRDC), Onikan, 1521
Rawalpindi Government College of Technology, 1580
Ray Society, London, 2139
Razi University, 1068
Razi Vaccine and Serum Research Institute, 1061
Razmadze, A., Mathematical Institute, Tbilisi, 781
Reading Borough Libraries, 2167
Reading University Library, 2167
Real Academia de Bellas Artes de la Purísima Concepción, Valladolid, 1889
Real Academia de Bellas Artes de San Fernando, 1887
Real Academia de Bellas Artes de San Telmo, 1889
Real Academia de Bellas Artes de Santa Isabel de Hungría, 1889
Real Academia de Bellas Artes y Ciencias Históricas de Toledo, 1887
Real Academia de Ciencias, Bellas Letras y Nobles Artes de Córdoba, 1887
Real Academia de Ciencias Exactas, Físicas, Químicas y Naturales de Zaragoza, Zaragoza, 1890
Real Academia de Ciencias Exactas, Físicas y Naturales, Madrid, 1887
Real Academia de Ciencias Morales y Políticas, Madrid, 1887
Real Academia de Ciencias Veterinarias, 1888
Real Academia de Ciencias y Artes de Barcelona, 1887
Real Academia de Doctores, Madrid, 1887
Real Academia de Jurisprudencia y Legislación, Madrid, 1887
Real Academia de la Historia, Madrid, 1887
Real Academia de la Lengua Vasca, Bilbao, 1889
Real Academia de Medicina y Cirugía de Palma de Mallorca, 1890
Real Academia de Nobles y Bellas Artes de San Luis, Zaragoza, 1889
Real Academia Española, 1887
Real Academia Gallega, 1887
Real Academia Hispano-Americana, Cádiz, 1888
Real Academia Nacional de Farmacia, Madrid, 1887
Real Academia Nacional de Medicina, Madrid, 1887
Real Academia Sevillana de Buenas Letras, 1890
Real Biblioteca del Monasterio de San Lorenzo de El Escorial, 1897
Real Biblioteca, Madrid, 1897
Real Colegio de San Clemente de los Españoles, Bologna, 1130
Real Colegio Universitario 'Escorial-María Cristina', Madrid, 1951

Real Conservatorio Profesional de Música 'Manuel de Falla', Cádiz, 1952
Real Conservatorio Superior de Música de Madrid, 1952
Real Escuela Superior de Arte Dramático, Madrid, 1952
Real Instituto Arqueológico de Portugal, 1674
Real Instituto de Estudios Asturianos, Oviedo, 1891
Real Instituto y Observatorio de la Armada, Cádiz, 1895
Real Jardín Botánico, Madrid, 1900
Real Sociedad Bascongada de los Amigos del País, 1891
Real Sociedad Económica de Amigos del País de Tenerife, 1888
Real Sociedad Española de Física, 1890
Real Sociedad Española de Historia Natural, 1890
Real Sociedad Española de Química, 1890
Real Sociedad Fotográfica, 1889
Real Sociedad Geográfica, Madrid, 1889
Real Sociedad Matemática Española, 1890
Real Sociedade Arqueológica Lusitana, 1674
Reale Istituto Neerlandese a Roma, 1130
Rectoren College, Utrecht, 1474
Rectors' Conference of Thailand, 2032
Red Sea University, Port Sudan, 1963
Redeemer University College, Ancaster, 380
Redpath Museum, 335
Reed College, 2639
Reed Research Institute, Haeju, 1318
Reformed Bible College, 2513
Reformed Theological Seminary, Jackson, 2543
Regent College, Vancouver, 340
Regent University, 2711
Regents Business School London, 2272
Regent's Park College, Oxford, 2250
Regeringskansliet Utrikesdepartementets Bibliotek, Stockholm, 1973
Regina Public Library, 332
Regionaal Archief, Alkmaar, 1481
Regional Burgas Museum, Burgas, 303
Regional Centre for Adult Education (ASFEC), Menoufia, 666
Regional Library, Burgas, 302
Regional Library, Stara Zagora, 303
Regional Museum of Archaeology, Plovdiv, 304
Regional Museum of History, Dobrich, 303
Regional Museum of History, Haskovo, 303
Regional Museum of History, Lovech, 303
Regional Museum of History, Montana, 303
Regional Museum of History, Pazardzhik, 303
Regional Museum of History, Pernik, 303
Regional Museum of History, Pleven, 303
Regional Museum of History, Plovdiv, 304
Regional Museum of History, Ruse, 304
Regional Museum of History, Shumen, 304
Regional Museum of History, Stara Zagora, 304
Regional Museum of History, Varna, 304
Regional Museum of History, Veliko Tarnovo, 304
Regional Museum of History, Vidin, 304
Regional Museum of History, Vratsa, 304
Regional Research Laboratory, Bhopal, 974
Regional Research Laboratory, Bhubaneswar, 973
Regional Research Laboratory, Jammu-Tawi, 973
Regional Research Laboratory, Jorhat, 973

Regional Research Laboratory, Trivandrum, 974
Regional Studies Association, Seaford, 2132
Regional Training Centre, Doha, 1690
Regional Veterinary Institute, Plovdiv, 300
Regional Veterinary Institute, Veliko Tarnovo, 300
Regional Veterinary Research Institute and Centre, Stara Zagora, 300
Regionální muzeum v Kolíně, 614
Regionální muzeum v Teplicích, 615
Regionalni Historijski Arhiv Tuzla, 247
Regionalni Muzej Doboj, 247
Regionalni zavod za zaštitu spomenika kulture, Split, 593
Regis College, Toronto, 395
Regis College, Weston, 2498
Regis University, 2381
Reguly Antal Historic Library, 943
Rehabilitation International— International Society for Rehabilitation of the Disabled, 61
Reial Acadèmia Catalana de Belles Arts de Sant Jordi, 1889
Reial Acadèmia de Bones Lletres, Barcelona, 1890
Reial Societat Arqueològica Tarraconense, 1889
Reims Management School, 770
Reinhardt College, 2421
Reiss-Engelhorn-Museen Mannheim, 818
Rektorkollegiet, Copenhagen, 627
Religious Research Association, Washington, 2298
Rembrandthuis Museum, Amsterdam, 1483
Remeis-Sternwarte, Bamberg, 801
Remote Sensing and Photogrammetry Society, Nottingham, 2145
Renaissance College, 373
Renaissance Society of America, 2290
Renewable Energy Science, Technology and Production Corporation, Ulan Bator, 1451
Renfrewshire Libraries, 2167
Rengeoin (Sanjusangendo), 1186
Renison College, Waterloo, 398
Renmin University of China, 503
Renmin University of China Library, 435
Rensselaer at Hartford, 2384
Rensselaer Polytechnic Institute, 2596
Representative Church Body Library, Dublin, 1083
Republic Engineering-Technical Centre for the Restoration and Strengthening of Components of Machines and Mechanisms, Tomsk, 1749
Republic Polytechnic, Singapore, 1840
Republican Institute of Advanced Teachers' Studies, Dushanbe, 2025
Republican Library for Science and Technology of Belarus, 209
Republican Scientific and Engineering Centre for Environmental Remote Sensing 'Ecomir', Minsk, 209
Republican Scientific and Technical Library of Tajikistan, 2025
Republican Scientific Medical Library, 209
Republican Scientific Practical Centre of Hygiene, Minsk, 207
Republički Zavod za Statistiku Republike Srpske, 247
Republički zavod za zaštitu spomenika kulture, Belgrade, 1816
Republički zavod za zaštitu spomenika kulture, Cetinje, 1455
Research and Design Institute for Oil Engineering, Baku, 185
Research and Design Institute for the Mechanical Processing of Minerals, St Petersburg, 1749
Research and Design Institute of Artificial Fibres, Mytishchi, 1749
Research and Design Institute of Autogenous Engineering, Moscow, 1749
Research and Design Institute of Basic Chemistry, Kharkiv, 2102

Research and Design Institute of Chemical Engineering, Moscow, 1749

Research and Design Institute of Construction Materials 'BelNIIS', 207

Research and Design Institute of Management Information Technology, Moscow, 1749

Research and Design Institute of Metallurgical Engineering, Moscow, 1749

Research and Design Institute of Polymer Construction Materials, Moscow, 1749

Research and Design Institute of the Bearings Industry, Moscow, 1749

Research and Design Institute of Woodworking Machinery, Moscow, 1749

Research and Design Technological Institute of Heavy Engineering, Ekaterinburg, 1749

Research and Development Institute of Molecular Biology and Medicine, Bishkek, 1356

Research and Development Institute of the Merchant Marine of Ukraine, 2103

Research and Documents Section, Doha, 1689

Research and Experimental Design Institute of Machinery for the Food Industry, Moscow, 1749

Research and Production Centre of Biotechnology, Ulan Bator, 1450

Research and Production Institute of Biological Preparations and Blood, Ulan Bator, 1450

Research and Teaching Clinical and Experimental Centre of Traumatology and Orthopaedics, Tbilisi, 781

Research and Technological Institute for Agricultural Biotechnology, Saratov, 1732

Research and Technological Institute of Livestock Raising, Tausamaly, 1304

Research and Training Centre for Problems of Human Activity, Moscow, 1745

Research Centre for Aesthetic Education, Moscow, 1735

Research Centre for Astronomy and Geophysics, Ulan Bator, 1450

Research Centre for Atomic Energy, Pyongyang, 1319

Research Centre for Environmental Sciences, Beijing, 432

Research Centre for Epidemiology, Virology and Medical Parasitology, Yerevan, 113

Research Centre for Fundamental Problems of Computer Technology and Control Systems, Moscow, 1749

Research Centre for Islamic History, Art and Culture (IRCICA), Istanbul, 2058

Research Centre for Mauritius Flora and Fauna, 1412

Research Centre for Medical Genetics, Moscow, 1738

Research Centre for Modern Greek Dialectics, Athens, 911

Research Centre for Molecular Diagnostics and Therapy, Moscow, 1738

Research Centre for Obstetrics, Gynaecology and Perinatology, 1738

Research Centre for Radiation Medicine, Kiev, 2101

Research Centre for Scientific Terms and Neologisms, Athens, 911

Research Centre for Space Probes, Moscow, 1749

Research Centre for the Study of Properties of Surfaces and Vacuums, Moscow, 1745

Research Centre for the Teaching of Russian, Moscow, 1735

Research Centre of Electronics and Automation, Pyongsong, 1320

Research Centre of Medical Radiology, Obninsk, 1738

Research Centre of Mental Health, Moscow, 1738

Research Centre of Obstetrics, Gynaecology and Perinatology, Moscow, 1738

Research Centre of Pure and Applied Mathematics (RCPAM), 911

Research Centre of Surgery, Moscow, 1738

Research Council of Zimbabwe, 2788

Research, Design and Technological Institute of Electrothermic Equipment, Moscow, 1749

Research Design-Technological Institute for Coal Machinery, Moscow, 1750

Research Designs and Standards Organization, Lucknow, 980

Research Institute for Animal Nutrition, Ermolovo, 1732

Research Institute for Biological Plant Protection, Chişinău, 1445

Research Institute for Breeding and Diversity in Horticulture, Zhilina, 1732

Research Institute for Complex Problems of Hygiene and Occupational Diseases, Novokuznetsk, 1738

Research Institute for Evaluation of the Working Capacity of Disabled People, Minsk, 208

Research Institute for Food Concentrates and Food Technologies and Special Food Technology, Moscow, 1750

Research Institute for Human Settlements and United Nations Regional Centre for Research on Human Settlements, Bandung, 1042

Research Institute for Instrumentation, Moscow, 1750

Research Institute for Irrigation, Drainage and Hydraulic Engineering, Sofia, 300

Research Institute for Land Policy, Ulan Bator, 1450

Research Institute for Maize and Sorghum, Pașcani, 1445

Research Institute for Monitoring Land and Ecosystems, Moscow, 1741

Research Institute for Plant Protection, Rakhat, 1304

Research Institute for Production Development, Kyoto, 1183

Research Institute for Roses, Aromatic and Medicinal Plants, Kazanlak, 300

Research Institute for Systems Research, Moscow, 1750

Research Institute for the Bakery and Confectionery Industry, Moscow, 1750

Research Institute for the Beer, Soft Drinks and Wine Industry, Moscow, 1750

Research Institute for the Biological Testing of Chemical Compounds, Kupavna, 1741

Research Institute for the Cultivation of Medicinal Herbs, Sariwon, 1319

Research Institute for the Genetics and Selection of Industrial Micro-organisms, Moscow, 1741

Research Institute for the Organization, Management and Economics of the Oil and Gas Industry, Moscow, 1750

Research Institute for the Processing of Casing Head Gas, Krasnodar, 1750

Research Institute for the Strengthening of the Legal System and Law and Order, Moscow, 1734

Research Institute for Tropical Medicine, Cairo, 659

Research Institute of Abrasives and Grinding, St Petersburg, 1750

Research Institute of Agricultural Engineering, Moscow, 1750

Research Institute of Agricultural Forest Reclamation, Volgograd, 1732

Research Institute of Animal Husbandry 'J. Sambuu', Ulan Bator, 1449

Research Institute of Antibiotics, Sunchon, 1319

Research Institute of Applied Automated Systems, Moscow, 1750

Research Institute of Atomic Reactors, Dimitrovgrad, 1750

Research Institute of Automated Systems in Construction, Kyiv, 2100

Research Institute of Automobile Electronics and Electrical Equipment, Moscow, 1750

Research Institute of Automobile Industry Technology, Moscow, 1750

Research Institute of Biomedicine, Pyongyang, 1319

Research Institute of Building Ceramics, Moscow, 1750

Research Institute of Carcinogenesis, Moscow, 1736

Research Institute of Cardiology, Minsk, 208

Research Institute of Cardiology, Tashkent, 2748

Research Institute of Chemical Fibres and Composite Materials, St Petersburg, 1750

Research Institute of Chemical Means of Plant Protection, Moscow, 1732

Research Institute of Chemical Reagents and Ultrapure Chemical Substances, Moscow, 1750

Research Institute of Chemicals for Polymer Materials, Tambov, 1750

Research Institute of Child Nutrition, Pyongyang, 1319

Research Institute of Children's Infections, St Petersburg, 1738

Research Institute of Clinical and Experimental Medicine, Nukus, 2748

Research Institute of Clinical and Experimental Surgery, Almaty, 1304

Research Institute of Construction and Road Machinery, Moscow, 1750

Research Institute of Construction Physics, Moscow, 1750

Research Institute of Criminalistics and Forensic Expertise, Minsk, 207

Research Institute of Culture and Arts, Ulan Bator, 1450

Research Institute of Current Sources, Moscow, 1750

Research Institute of Drilling Technology, Moscow, 1750

Research Institute of Earthmoving Machinery, St Petersburg, 1750

Research Institute of Economic Studies, Ulan Bator, 1450

Research Institute of Elastic Materials and Products, Moscow, 1750

Research Institute of Electrical Engineering, St Petersburg, 1750

Research Institute of Electro-welding Technology, St Petersburg, 1750

Research Institute of Electromeasuring Equipment, St Petersburg, 1750

Research Institute of Endocrinology, Pyongyang, 1319

Research Institute of Epidemiology and Microbiology, Minsk, 208

Research Institute of Epidemiology and Microbiology, Nizhnii Novgorod, 1738

Research Institute of Epidemiology, Microbiology and Infectious Diseases, Tashkent, 2748

Research Institute of Experimental Physics, Arzamas, 1745

Research Institute of Experimental Therapy and Tumour Diagnosis, Moscow, 1736

Research Institute of Experimental Therapy, Hamhung, 1319

Research Institute of Farm Animal Physiology, Biochemistry and Nutrition, Borovsk, 1732

Research Institute of Film Art, Moscow, 1735

Research Institute of Food Biotechnology, Moscow, 1741

Research Institute of Forensic Medicine, Moscow, 1738

Research Institute of Forensic Sciences and Criminology, Sofia, 300

Research Institute of Forestry and Agroforestry Reclamation, Shchuchinsk, 1304

Research Institute of Foundations and Underground Structures, Moscow, 1733

Research Institute of Foundry Machinery and the Technology and Automation of Foundry Production, Moscow, 1750

Research Institute of Gas Use in the Economy and Underground Storage of Oil, Oil Products and Liquefied Gases, Moscow, 1750

Research Institute of Gastroenterology, Baku, 185

Research Institute of Geophysical Research on Exploration Wells, Oktyabrsky, 1745

Research Institute of Geophysical Shock Waves, Ramenskoe, 1745

Research Institute of Gold and Rare Metals, Magadan, 1745

Research Institute of Haematology and Intensive Therapy, Moscow, 1738

Research Institute of Hydrogeology and Engineering Geology (VSEGINGEO), Zelenyi, 1750

Research Institute of Hygiene, Pyongyang, 1319

Research Institute of Infectious and Parasitic Diseases, Sofia, 301

Research Institute of Instrumentation Technology, Moscow, 1750

Research Institute of Karakul Sheep Breeding and Ecology of Deserts, Samarkand, 2747

Research Institute of Laser Medicine, Moscow, 1738

Research Institute of Light Alloys, Moscow, 1750

Research Institute of Light and Textile Machinery, Moscow, 1750

Research Institute of Marine Fisheries, Haiphong, 2772

Research Institute of Medical Instruments, Pyongyang, 1320

Research Institute of Medical Primatology, Sochi-Adler, 1738

Research Institute of Medical Rehabilitation and Natural Therapeutic Factors, Baku, 185

Research Institute of Microbiology, Pyongsong, 1319

Research Institute of Natural Drugs, Hamhung, 1319

Research Institute of Neurology, Neurosurgery and Physiotherapy, Minsk, 208

Research Institute of Non-infectious Animal Diseases, Istrinsky raion, 1733

Research Institute of Occupational Safety under the auspices of the Independent Russian Trade Unions, 1738

Research Institute of Oncology, Pyongyang, 1319

Research Institute of Organizational Technology, Moscow, 1750

Research Institute of Paediatrics, Obstetrics and Gynaecology, Kyiv, 2101

Research Institute of Pastoral Animal Husbandry in the Gobi Region, 1450

Research Institute of Pediatric Oncology, Moscow, 1736

Research Institute of Pharmacology, Pyongyang, 1319

Research Institute of Photoelectronics, Baku, 185

Research Institute of Physical Methods of Treatment and Medical Climatology 'I. M. Sechenov', Yalta, 2101

Research Institute of Planning and Normatives, Moscow, 1734

Research Institute of Plant Protection, Ulan Bator, 1450

Socialforskningsinstituttet, Copenhagen, 631
Socialstyrelsen, Stockholm, 1970
Sociedad Agronómica de Chile, 410
Sociedad Agronómica Mexicana, 1414
Sociedad Argentina de Antropología, 92
Sociedad Argentina de Autores y Compositores de Música (SADAIC), 90
Sociedad Argentina de Biología, 91
Sociedad Argentina de Ciencias Fisiológicas, 91
Sociedad Argentina de Ciencias Neurológicas, Psiquiátricas y Neuroquirúrgicas, 91
Sociedad Argentina de Dermatología, 91
Sociedad Argentina de Endocrinología y Metabolismo, 91
Sociedad Argentina de Estudios Geográficos, 90
Sociedad Argentina de Farmacología y Terapéutica, 91
Sociedad Argentina de Fisiología Vegetal, 91
Sociedad Argentina de Gastroenterología, 91
Sociedad Argentina de Gerontología y Geriatría, 91
Sociedad Argentina de Hematología, 91
Sociedad Argentina de Investigación Clínica, 91
Sociedad Argentina de Oftalmología, 91
Sociedad Argentina de Patología, 91
Sociedad Argentina de Pediatría, 91
Sociedad Argentina de Psicología, 92
Sociedad Argentina de Sociología, 92
Sociedad Astronómica de México, AC, 1416
Sociedad Bolivariana de Colombia, 561
Sociedad Bolivariana de Venezuela, 2761
Sociedad Botánica de México, AC, 1416
Sociedad Central de Arquitectos, Buenos Aires, 89
Sociedad Chilena de Cancerología, 411
Sociedad Chilena de Cardiología y Cirugía Cardiovascular, 411
Sociedad Chilena de Dermatología y Venereología, 411
Sociedad Chilena de Endocrinología y Metabolismo, 411
Sociedad Chilena de Enfermedades Respiratorias, 411
Sociedad Chilena de Entomología, 411
Sociedad Chilena de Fotogrametría y Percepción Remota, 412
Sociedad Chilena de Física, 412
Sociedad Chilena de Gastroenterología, 411
Sociedad Chilena de Historia y Geografía, 411
Sociedad Chilena de Inmunología, 411
Sociedad Chilena de Lingüística, 411
Sociedad Chilena de Neurocirugía, 411
Sociedad Chilena de Obstetricia y Ginecología, 411
Sociedad Chilena de Oftalmología, 411
Sociedad Chilena de Ortopedia y Traumatología, 411
Sociedad Chilena de Pediatría, 411
Sociedad Chilena de Producción Animal, 410
Sociedad Chilena de Química, 412
Sociedad Chilena de Reumatología, 411
Sociedad Chilena de Tecnología en Alimentos, 412
Sociedad Científica Argentina, 91
Sociedad Científica Chilena 'Claudio Gay', 411
Sociedad Colombiana de Biología, 562
Sociedad Colombiana de Cardiología, 562
Sociedad Colombiana de Ciencias Químicas, 562
Sociedad Colombiana de Cirugía Ortopédica y Traumatología, 562
Sociedad Colombiana de Economistas, 561
Sociedad Colombiana de Ingenieros, 562
Sociedad Colombiana de Matemáticas, 562
Sociedad Colombiana de Obstetricia y Ginecología, 562
Sociedad Colombiana de Patología, 562

Sociedad Colombiana de Pediatría, 562
Sociedad Colombiana de Radiología, 562
Sociedad Cubana de Historia de la Medicina, 598
Sociedad Cubana de Ingenieros, 598
Sociedad Cubana de Radiología, 598
Sociedad de Agricultores de Colombia, 561
Sociedad de Amigos de Arqueología, Montevideo, 2743
Sociedad de Arquitectos del Uruguay, 2743
Sociedad de Bibliotecarios de Puerto Rico, 2739
Sociedad de Biología de Chile, 411
Sociedad de Bioquímica de Concepción, 412
Sociedad de Bioquímica y Biología Molecular de Chile, 412
Sociedad de Ciencias 'Aranzadi' Zientzi Elkartea, 1890
Sociedad de Ciencias, Letras y Artes 'El Museo Canario', 1889
Sociedad de Ciencias Naturales 'La Salle', Caracas, 2762
Sociedad de Cirugía de Buenos Aires, 91
Sociedad de Cirugía del Uruguay, 2743
Sociedad de Estudios Geográficos e Históricos, Santa Cruz de la Sierra, 239
Sociedad de Farmacología de Chile, 411
Sociedad de Genética de Chile, 411
Sociedad de Ginecología y Obstetricia de El Salvador, 667
Sociedad de Ingenieros del Perú, 1591
Sociedad de Matemática de Chile, 412
Sociedad de Neurología, Psiquiatría y Neurocirugía de Chile, 411
Sociedad de Obstetricia y Ginecología de Venezuela, 2761
Sociedad de Oftalmología Nicaragüense, 1513
Sociedad de Pediatría de Cochabamba, 239
Sociedad de Pediatría de Madrid y Castilla la Mancha, 1890
Sociedad de Pediatría y Puericultura del Paraguay, Asunción, 1587
Sociedad de Psicología Médica, Psicoanálisis y Medicina Psicosomática, Buenos Aires, 91
Sociedad de Radiología e Imagenología del Uruguay, 2744
Sociedad de Vida Silvestre de Chile, 412
Sociedad Dominicana de Bibliófilos Inc., 646
Sociedad Entomológica Argentina (SEA), 91
Sociedad Entomológica del Perú, 1591
Sociedad Española de Astronomía, 1890
Sociedad Española de Cerámica y Vidrio, 1891
Sociedad Española de Etología, 1890
Sociedad Española de Patología Digestiva y de la Nutrición, Madrid, 1890
Sociedad Española de Radiología Médica, 1890
Sociedad Forestal Mexicana, 1414
Sociedad General de Autores de la Argentina (Argentores), 90
Sociedad General de Autores y Editores, Madrid, 1890
Sociedad Geográfica de Colombia, 561
Sociedad Geográfica de La Paz, 239
Sociedad Geográfica de Lima, 1590
Sociedad Geográfica y de Historia 'Potosí', 239
Sociedad Geográfica y de Historia 'Sucre', 239
Sociedad Geológica de Chile, 412
Sociedad Geológica de España, 1891
Sociedad Geológica del Perú, 1591
Sociedad Geológica Mexicana, AC, 1416
Sociedad Malacológica del Uruguay, 2744
Sociedad Matemática Mexicana, 1416
Sociedad Mayagüezana Pro Bellas Artes, 2739
Sociedad Médica de Concepción, 411
Sociedad Médica de Santiago, 411
Sociedad Médica de Valparaíso, 411
Sociedad Mexicana de Antropología, 1417

Sociedad Mexicana de Biología, 1416
Sociedad Mexicana de Cardiología, 1416
Sociedad Mexicana de Entomología, 1416
Sociedad Mexicana de Estudios Psico-Pedagógicos, 1417
Sociedad Mexicana de Fitogenética, 1416
Sociedad Mexicana de Fitopatología, AC, 1416
Sociedad Mexicana de Geografía y Estadística, 1415
Sociedad Mexicana de Historia de la Ciencia y la Tecnología, 1415
Sociedad Mexicana de Historia Natural, 1416
Sociedad Mexicana de Ingeniería Sísmica, AC, 1417
Sociedad Mexicana de Micología, 1416
Sociedad Mexicana de Nutrición y Endocrinología, AC, 1416
Sociedad Mexicana de Parasitología, AC, 1416
Sociedad Mexicana de Pediatría, 1416
Sociedad Mexicana de Salud Pública, 1416
Sociedad Nacional de Agricultura, Santiago, 410
Sociedad Nacional de Minería, Santiago, 412
Sociedad Nicaragüense de Psiquiatría y Psicología, 1513
Sociedad Odontológica de Concepción, 411
Sociedad Peruana de Espeleología, 1591
Sociedad Peruana de Tisiología y Enfermedades Respiratorias, 1591
Sociedad Pro-Arte Musical, Guatemala City, 925
Sociedad Química de México, 1416
Sociedad Química del Perú, 1591
Sociedad Rural Argentina, 89
Sociedad Rural Boliviana, 239
Sociedad Uruguaya de Historia de la Medicina, 2744
Sociedad Uruguaya de Pediatría, 2744
Sociedad Venezolana de Anestesiología, 2761
Sociedad Venezolana de Cardiología, 2761
Sociedad Venezolana de Ciencias Naturales, 2762
Sociedad Venezolana de Cirugía, 2761
Sociedad Venezolana de Cirugía Ortopédica y Traumatología, 2761
Sociedad Venezolana de Dermatología, 2761
Sociedad Venezolana de Gastroenterología, 2761
Sociedad Venezolana de Geólogos, 2762
Sociedad Venezolana de Hematología, 2761
Sociedad Venezolana de Historia de la Medicina, 2761
Sociedad Venezolana de Ingeniería Hidráulica, 2762
Sociedad Venezolana de Ingenieros Agrónomos, 2762
Sociedad Venezolana de Ingenieros Civiles, 2762
Sociedad Venezolana de Ingenieros de Petróleo, 2762
Sociedad Venezolana de Ingenieros Forestales, 2762
Sociedad Venezolana de Ingenieros Químicos, 2762
Sociedad Venezolana de Medicina Interna, 2761
Sociedad Venezolana de Oftalmología, 2761
Sociedad Venezolana de Otorinolaringología, 2761
Sociedad Venezolana de Psiquiatría, 2761
Sociedad Venezolana de Puericultura y Pediatría, 2761
Sociedad Venezolana de Radiología, 2761
Sociedad Zoológica del Uruguay, 2744
Sociedade Afonso Chaves, 1677
Sociedade Anatómica Portuguesa, 1675
Sociedade Brasileira de Autores (SBAT), 254

Sociedade Brasileira de Cartografia (SBC), 254
Sociedade Brasileira de Dermatologia, 254
Sociedade Brasileira de Entomologia, 255
Sociedade Brasileira de Filosofia, 255
Sociedade Brasileira de Geografia, 254
Sociedade Brasileira para o Progresso da Ciência, 255
Sociedade Broteriana, Coimbra, 1675
Sociedade Científica da Universidade Católica Portuguesa, 1674
Sociedade de Geografia de Lisboa, 1675
Sociedade de Medicina de Alagoas, 255
Sociedade de Pediatria de Bahia, 255
Sociedade Geológica de Portugal, 1675
Sociedade Hebraico Brasileira Renascença, 255
Sociedade Martins Sarmento, 1675
Sociedade Nacional de Agricultura, Rio de Janeiro, 253
Sociedade Nacional de Belas Artes, Lisbon, 1674
Sociedade Portuguesa de Antropologia e Etnologia, 1675
Sociedade Portuguesa de Autores, 1675
Sociedade Portuguesa de Ciências Naturais, 1675
Sociedade Portuguesa de Ciências Veterinárias, 1674
Sociedade Portuguesa de Patologia Animal, 1674
Sociedade Portuguesa de Química, 1675
Sociedade Portuguesa de Reprodução Animal, 1674
Sociedade Portuguesa Veterinária de Anatomia Comparativa, 1674
Sociedade Portuguesa Veterinária de Estudos Sociológicos, 1674
Società Adriatica di Scienze, Trieste, 1124
Società Astronomica Italiana, 1124
Società Botanica Italiana Onlus, 1124
Società Chimica Italiana, 1124
Società d'Incoraggiamento d'Arti e Mestieri, Milan, 1122
Società Dante Alighieri, Rome, 1123
Società Dantesca Italiana, 1122
Società di Letture e Conversazioni Scientifiche, Genoa, 1120
Società di Minerva, Trieste, 1122
Società di Studi Geografici, Florence, 1122
Società Entomologica Italiana, 1124
Società Europea di Cultura, 43
Società Filologica Romana, 1123
Società Filosofica Italiana, 1124
Società Geografica Italiana, 1122
Società Geologica Italiana, 1124
Società Italiana degli Autori ed Editori (SIAE), 1123
Società Italiana degli Economisti, 1121
Società Italiana delle Scienze Veterinarie, 1121
Società Italiana di Anestesiologia e Rianimazione, 1123
Società Italiana di Antropologia e Etnologia, 1125
Società Italiana di Biochimica Clinica e Biologia Molecolare Clinica, 1124
Società Italiana di Biochimica e Biologia Molecolare, 1124
Società Italiana di Cancerologia, 1123
Società Italiana di Chirurgia, 1123
Società Italiana di Ecologia (SItE), 1124
Società Italiana di Economia Agraria, 1121
Società Italiana di Economia, Demografia e Statistica, 1121
Società Italiana di Farmacologia, 1123
Società Italiana di Filosofia Giuridica e Politica, 1121
Società Italiana di Fisica, 1124
Società Italiana di Ginecologia ed Ostetricia, 1123
Società Italiana di Medicina Interna, 1123
Società Italiana di Medicina Legale e delle Assicurazioni, 1123
Società Italiana di Microbiologia, 1124
Società Italiana di Musicologia, 1122
Società Italiana di Odontostomatologia e Chirurgia Maxillo-Facciale, 1123

Société Nationale de Protection de la Nature, Paris, 710

Société Nationale de Recherches et d'Exploitation des Ressources Minières de Mali (SONAREM), Service de Documentation, 1405

Société Nationale des Antiquaires de France, 708

Société Nationale des Beaux-Arts, Paris, 707

Société Nationale Française de Gastro-Entérologie, 710

Société Odontologique de Paris (SOP), 710

Société Paléontologique Suisse (SPS), 1999

Société Philosophique de Louvain, 218

Société pour la Protection des Paysages, et de l'Esthétique de la France, 706

Société pour le Développement Minier de la Côte d'Ivoire (SODEMI), 589

Société Royale Belge d'Anthropologie et de Préhistoire, 218

Société Royale Belge d'Astronomie, de Météorologie et de Physique du Globe, 218

Société Royale Belge d'Entomologie, 218

Société Royale Belge de Géographie, 217

Société Royale Belge des Electriciens, 218

Société Royale Belge des Ingénieurs et des Industriels, 218

Société Royale d'Archéologie de Bruxelles, 217

Société Royale d'Astronomie d'Anvers, 218

Société Royale d'Economie Politique de Belgique, 216

Société Royale de Botanique de Belgique, 218

Société Royale de Chimie, Brussels, 218

Société Royale de Numismatique de Belgique, 217

Société Royale des Beaux-Arts, Brussels, 216

Société Royale des Sciences de Liège, 218

Société Royale Zoologique de Belgique, 218

Société Scientifique d'Hygiène Alimentaire, Paris, 710

Société Scientifique de Bruxelles, 218

Société Suisse d'Astrophysique et d'Astronomie, 2001

Société Suisse d'Etudes Africaines, 1999

Société Suisse d'Histoire, 1998

Société Suisse d'Histoire de la Médecine et des Sciences Naturelles, 1998

Société Suisse d'Orthopédie, 1998

Société Suisse de Chirurgie, 1998

Société Suisse de Droit International, 1997

Société Suisse de Linguistique, 1998

Société Suisse de Médecine Interne, 1998

Société Suisse de Médecine Thermale et Climatique, 1998

Société Suisse de Numismatique, 1998

Société Suisse de Philosophie, 1999

Société Suisse de Physique, 1999

Société Suisse de Psychologie, 1999

Société Suisse de Sociologie, 1999

Société Suisse de Statistique et d'Economie Politique, 1996

Société Suisse de Théologie, 1999

Société Suisse des Beaux-Arts, 1997

Société Suisse des Bibliophiles, 1996

Société Suisse des Ingénieurs et des Architectes, 1996

Société Suisse des Pharmaciens, 1999

Société Suisse des Traditions Populaires, 1999

Société Vaudoise d'Histoire et d'Archéologie, 1998

Société Vaudoise des Sciences Naturelles, 1999

Société Vétérinaire Pratique de France, 705

Société Zoologique de France, 710

Societies for the Promotion of Hellenic and Roman Studies Joint Library, London, 2163

Society for Applied Anthropology, Oklahoma City, 2298

Society for Army Historical Research, London, 2133

Society for Coptic Archaeology, Cairo, 658

Society for Developmental Biology, Bethesda, 2295

Society for Economic Botany, Columbia, 2295

Society for Endocrinology, Bristol, 2137

Society for Ethnomusicology, Inc., Bloomington, 2289

Society for Experimental Biology and Medicine, New York, 2296

Society for General Microbiology, Reading, 2139

Society for Industrial and Applied Mathematics Society, Philadelphia, 2296

Society for International Development, 49

Society for Medicine and Law in Israel, 1093

Society for Medieval Archaeology, Shrewsbury, 2133

Society for Mining, Metallurgy and Exploration, Inc., Littleton, 2299

Society for Nautical Research, London, 2133

Society for Pediatric Research, the Woodlands, 2303

Society for Post-Medieval Archaeology Ltd, London, 2133

Society for Renaissance Studies, London, 2133

Society for Research into Higher Education Ltd, London, 2147

Society for Sedimentary Geology (SEPM), Tulsa, 2297

Society for South Asian Studies, London, 2142

Society for the History of Technology, Auburn, 2300

Society for the Preservation of Muslim Heritage, Karachi, 1565

Society for the Promotion of Hellenic Studies, London, 2134

Society for the Promotion of Roman Studies, London, 2134

Society for the Protection of Ancient Buildings, London, 2126

Society for the Protection of Nature in Israel, 1093

Society for the Scientific Study of Religion Inc., W. Lafayette, 2299

Society for the Study of Evolution, Lawrence, 2299

Society for the Study of Medieval Languages and Literature, Oxford, 2135

Society for Theatre Research, London, 2131

Society for Underwater Technology, London, 2145

Society of Actuaries, Schaumburg, 2288

Society of Aesthetes and Art and Literary Critics, Sofia, 298

Society of American Archivists, 2287

Society of American Foresters, 2285

Society of American Historians, 2290

Society of Antiquaries Library, London, 2163

Society of Antiquaries of London, 2133

Society of Antiquaries of Scotland, 2133

Society of Architectural Historians, Chicago, 2286

Society of Architectural Illustration, Stroud, 2131

Society of Archivists, Taunton, 2133

Society of Arts, Literature and Welfare, Chittagong, 191

Society of Australian Genealogists, 118

Society of Authors, London, 2135

Society of Automotive Engineers, Inc., Warrendale, 2300

Society of Automotive Engineers of China, 430

Society of Biblical Literature, Decatur, 2291

Society of Biological Chemists, India, 971

Society of Botanists of Moldova, 1444

Society of British Neurological Surgeons, 2137

Society of Bulgarian Psychologists, 299

Society of Cardiology, Moscow, 1730

Society of Chartered Surveyors, Dublin, 1081

Society of Chemical Industry (Canadian Section), 327

Society of College, National and University Libraries (SCONUL), London, 2127

Society of Composers, Authors and Music Publishers of Canada (SOCAN), 325

Society of Consulting Marine Engineers and Ship Surveyors, London, 2145

Society of Dairy Technology, Long Hanborough, 2126

Society of Designer Craftsmen, London, 2145

Society of Dyers and Colourists, Bradford, 2145

Society of Economic Geologists, Lakewood, 2297

Society of Engineers, Colchester, 2145

Society of Genealogists, London, 2133

Society of Geneticists of Moldova, 1444

Society of Glass Technology, Sheffield, 2145

Society of Helminthologists, Moscow, 1730

Society of Hydrobiologists and Ichthyologists, 1444

Society of Irish Foresters, 1081

Society of Jurists of Slovenia, 1855

Society of Liberian Authors, 1370

Society of Light Industry, Moscow, 1730

Society of Malawi, 1391

Society of Manufacturing Engineers, Dearborn, 2300

Society of Mathematicians of Serbia, 1815

Society of Medical Jurisprudence, New York, 2294

Society of Miniaturists, Ilkley, 2130

Society of Mongolian Surgeons, 1449

Society of Municipal Engineers of Israel, 1094

Society of Naval Architects and Marine Engineers, Jersey City, 2300

Society of Non-Ferrous Metallurgy, Moscow, 1730

Society of Occupational Medicine, London, 2137

Society of Operations Engineers, London, 2145

Society of Ornithologists, Moscow, 1730

Society of Petroleum Engineers, Richardson, 2299

Society of Plant Physiology and Biochemistry of Moldova, 1444

Society of Protozoologists, St Petersburg, 1730

Society of Psychologists, Moscow, 1730

Society of Rheology, Woodbury, 2300

Society of Scribes and Illuminators, London, 2131

Society of South African Geographers, 1863

Society of the Food Industry, Moscow, 1730

Society of the Instrument Manufacturing Industry and Metrologists, Moscow, 1730

Society of the Timber and Forestry Industry, Moscow, 1728

Society of Vertebrate Paleontology, Chicago, 2296

Society of Wildlife Artists, London, 2130

Socio-Economic Research Institute, Kolkata, 975

Sociological Association of Ukraine, 2099

Sociologický ústav AV ČR, 611

Sociology Institute, Beijing, 433

Södertörns Högskola, 1990

Sodiqov, A., Institute of Bio-organic Chemistry, Tashkent, 2748

Sofia Museum of History, 304

Sofiiski Universitet 'sveti Kliment Ohridsky', 308

Sogang University, 1345

Sogo Kenkyu Kaihatsu Kiko, 1179

Sögufélagið, Reykjavík, 964

Soil and Water Research Institute, Giza, 659

Soil Research Institute, Kumasi, 905

Soil Resources Agency, Sofia, 298

Soil Science Research Institute, Pyongyang, 1318

Soil Science Society, Moscow, 1728

Soil Science Society of America, 2285

Soil Science Society of China, 426

Sojourner-Douglass College, 2477

Sojuz na društvata na arhivskite rabotnici na Makedonija, 1385

Sojuz na Društvata na Istoričarite na Republika Makedonija, 1386

Sojuz na Društvata na Matematičarite na Makedonija, 1386

Sojuz na Društvata na Veterinarnite Lekari i Tehničari na Makedonija, 1385

Sojuz na Društvata za Makedonski Jazik i Literatura, Skopje, 1386

Sojuz na Ekonomistite na Makedonija, 1385

Sojuz na Inženeri i Tehničari na Makedonija, 1386

Sojuz na Inženeri i Tehničari po Sumarstvo i Industrija za Prerabotka na Drvo na Makedonija, 1385

Sojuz na Kompozitorite na Makedonija, 1385

Sojuz na Združenijata na Pravnicite na Makedonija, 1385

Soka University, 1292

Sokhumi Botanical Garden, 782

Sokoine National Agricultural Library, Morogoro, 2028

Sokoine University of Agriculture, 2030

Solar Energy Research Centre, Jadiriya, 1074

Solar Terrestrial Influences Laboratory, Sofia, 302

Solomon Islands College of Higher Education, 1860

Solomon Islands National Archives, 1860

Solomon Islands National Library, 1860

Solomon Islands National Museum and Cultural Centre, 1860

Somali Institute of Public Administration Library, 1861

Somali National Museum, 1861

Somali National University, 1861

Somerset County Library, 2154

Somerville College, Oxford, 2250

Somogy Megyei Múzeumok Igazgatósága, Kaposvár, 946

Somogyi-könyvtár, Szeged, 944

Sonnenobservatorium Kanzelhöhe der Universität Graz, 165

Sonoma State University, 2358

Soochow University, 519

Soochow University, Taipei, 559

Sookmyung Women's University, 1347

Soongsil University, 1347

Sophia (Jôchi) University Library, 1184

Sophia University, 1292

Sophie Davis School of Biomedical Education, New York, 2572

Soprintendenza alla Galleria Nazionale d'Arte Moderna e Contemporanea, Rome, 1143

Soprintendenza Archeologica di Pompei, 1141

Soprintendenza Archeologica di Roma, 1143

Soprintendenza per i Beni Archeologici della Liguria, Genoa, 1140

Soproni Múzeum, 947

Soreq Nuclear Research Centre, 1095

SORIN Biomedica SpA, Saluggia, 1132

Sota-arkisto, Helsinki, 686

Sourasky Central Library, Tel-Aviv University, 1097

Sous-Direction de l'Archéologie, Paris, 720

South African Academy of Science and Arts, 1863

South African Archaeological Society, 1863

South African Astronomical Observatory, Sutherland, 1866

South African Brain Research Institute, 1866

South African Bureau of Standards, Pretoria, 1866

South African Chemical Institute, 1864

South African Institute of Agricultural Engineers, 1865
South African Institute of Architects, 1863
South African Institute of Assayers and Analysts, 1865
South African Institute of Electrical Engineers, 1865
South African Institute of International Affairs, 1863
South African Institute of Mining and Metallurgy, 1865
South African Institute of Physics, 1864
South African Institute of Race Relations, 1864
South African Institution of Civil Engineering (SAICE), 1865
South African Institution of Mechanical Engineering, 1865
South African Library, 1867
South African Medical Association, 1864
South African Medical Research Council, Tygerberg, 1866
South African National Association for the Visual Arts (SANAVA), 1863
South African National Biodiversity Institute, Claremont, 1864
South African PEN Centre, 1864
South African Pharmacology Society, 1864
South African Society for Animal Science, 1863
South African Society for Microbiology, 1864
South African Society of Biochemistry and Molecular Biology, 1864
South African Society of Dairy Technology, 1863
South African Society of Obstetricians and Gynaecologists, 1864
South African Universities' Vice-Chancellors' Association, 1862
South Australian Museum, 127
South Carolina State Museum, 2327
South Carolina State University, 2675
South China Agricultural University, 520
South China Institute of Botany, 432
South China Normal University, 520
South China Sea Institute of Oceanology, Guangzhou, 431
South China Teachers' University Library, 435
South China University of Technology, 521
South Dakota Art Museum, 2327
South Dakota School of Mines and Technology, 2676
South Dakota State University, 2677
South-East Agricultural Research Institute, Saratov, 1733
South-East Asia University, 2044
South-Eastern Education and Library Board, Ballynahinch, 2274
South Eastern University of Sri Lanka, 1959
South Gujarat University, 1024
South Hamgyong Provincial Library, 1320
South Hwanghae Provincial Library, 1320
South India Society of Painters, 969
South Kazakhstan Scientific and Research Institute of Agriculture, 1304
South Kazakhstan Technical University, 1309
South London Gallery, 2176
South Pyongan Provincial Library, 1320
South Russia State Technical University (Novocherkassk Polytechnic Institute), 1790
South Shields Museum and Art Gallery, 2177
South Texas College of Law, 2691
South Ural State University, 1774
South Urals Agricultural Research Institute, 1733
South Valley University, Kena, 664
South Wales Institute of Engineers, 2145
South Western University of Finance and Economics, 521
Southampton City Art Gallery, 2178

Southampton City Libraries, 2168
Southampton Solent University, Southampton, 2259
Southeast Asian Ministers of Education Organization (SEAMEO), 54
Southeast Asian Ministers of Education Organization (SEAMEO) Regional Language Centre (RELC), Singapore, 1840
Southeast Missouri State University, 2550
Southeast University, Nanjing, 522
Southeastern Baptist College, 2543
Southeastern Baptist Theological Seminary, Wake Forest, 2607
Southeastern Bible College, 2330
Southeastern Louisiana University., 2468
Southeastern Oklahoma State University, 2636
Southeastern University of the Assemblies of God, 2411
Southeastern University, Washington, 2405
Southend on Sea Borough Council Education and Libraries Department, 2168
Southern Adventist University, 2679
Southern Africa Association for the Advancement of Science, 1864
Southern African Institute of Forestry, 1863
Southern African Museums Association, 1863
Southern African Society of Aquatic Scientists, 1864
Southern African Wildlife Management Association, 1864
Southern Arkansas University, 2341
Southern Association of Colleges and Schools: Commission on Colleges, Decatur, 2282
Southern Baptist Theological Seminary, 2464
Southern California Academy of Sciences, 2294
Southern California College of Optometry, 2358
Southern California University of Health Sciences, 2358
Southern Christian University, 2330
Southern College of Optometry, 2680
Southern Connecticut State University, 2385
Southern Cross University, 151
Southern Education and Library Board Library Service, Armagh, 2273
Southern Illinois University Carbondale, 2434
Southern Illinois University Edwardsville, 2434
Southern Kazakhstan Auezv Humanities University, 1308
Southern Kazakhstan Medical Academy, 1308
Southern Methodist University, 2691
Southern Nazarene University, 2636
Southern New England School of Law, 2499
Southern New Hampshire University, 2560
Southern Newfoundland Seamen's Museum, 333
Southern Oregon University, 2639
Southern Polytechnic State University, 2421
Southern Research Institute, Birmingham, AL, 2304
Southern Technical Institute, Songkla, 2046
Southern Turkmen Multidisciplinary Archaeological Expedition, Ashgabat, 2091
Southern University at New Orleans, 2467
Southern University at Shreveport, 2467
Southern University of Chile, 421
Southern University System, Baton Rouge, 2467
Southern Vermont College, 2709
Southern Wesleyan University, 2675
Southern Yangtze University, 522

Southland Museum and Art Gallery, 1505
Southsea Castle, 2178
Southwark Libraries, 2164
Southwest Agricultural University, 523
Southwest Baptist University, Missouri, 2550
Southwest China Normal University, 523
Southwest Foundation for Biomedical Research, San Antonio, 2303
Southwest Jiaotong University, 524
Southwest Minnesota State University, Marshall, 2529
Southwest Petroleum Institute, 525
Southwest Research Institute, San Antonio, 2307
Southwest University of Political Science and Law, 526
Southwestern Adventist University, 2691
Southwestern Assemblies of God University, 2691
Southwestern Baptist Theological Seminary, 2691
Southwestern Christian College, Terrell, 2692
Southwestern Christian University, 2636
Southwestern College, Phoenix, 2333
Southwestern College, Santa Fe, 2568
Southwestern College, Winfield, 2460
Southwestern Institute of Physics, Chengdu, 433
Southwestern Oklahoma State University, 2636
Southwestern University, Cebu City, 1617
Southwestern University, Georgetown, 2692
Southwestern University Museum, Cebu City, 1603
Southwestern University School of Law, Los Angeles, 2358
Sovrintendenza Tal-Patrimonju Kulturali, Valletta, 1407
Sozialwissenschaftliche Bibliothek der Kammer für Arbeiter und Angestellte für Wien, 168
Space Activities Commission, Tokyo, 1182
Space Research Centre, Jadiriya, 1074
Spalding University, 2464
Special Astrophysical Observatory, Nizhny Arkhyz, 1745
Special Design Bureau for Applied Geophysics, Novosibirsk, 1751
Special Design Bureau for Automation of Marine Research, Yuzhno-Sakhalinsk, 1751
Special Design Bureau for High Capacity Electronics, Tomsk, 1751
Special Design Bureau for Hydroimpulse Technology, Novosibirsk, 1751
Special Design Bureau for Microelectronics and Computer Technology, Yaroslavl, 1749
Special Design Bureau for Scientific Instruments, Novosibirsk, 1751
Special Design-Technological Bureau for Special Electronics and Analytical Instrumentation, Novosibirsk, 1751
Special Design-Technological Bureau 'Nauka', 1751
Special Experimental Design Technological Institute, Gjumry, 113
Special Libraries Association, Washington, 2287
Specola Solare Ticinese, 2001
Spectroscopy Society of Canada, 327
Speelgoedmuseum Deventer, 1484
Spektroskopická společnost J. Marca Marci, Prague, 609
Spelman College, 2421
Spencer Museum of Art, University of Kansas, 2321
Spertus Institute of Jewish Studies, 2434
SPNM–Promoting New Music, London, 2131

Společná laboratoř chemie pevných látek AV ČR a Univerzity Pardubice, 611
Společnost pro dějiny věd a techniky, Prague, 608
Společnost pro estetiku, Prague, 608
Spoločnosť učiteľov nemeckého jazyka a germanistov Slovenska (SUNG), Bratislava, 1842
Spolok architektov Slovenska, 1841
Spolok slovenských spisovateľov, 1842
Sports Museum, Thessaloniki, 914
Spring Arbor University, 2514
Spring Hill College, 2330
Springfield College, 2499
Springfield Library, 2313
Sproul Observatory, 2306
Squire Law Library, Cambridge, 2155
Sree Chitra Tirunal Institute for Medical Sciences and Technology, Thiruvananthapuram, 1034
Sree Sankaracharya University of Sanskrit, Kalady, 1024
Sri Aurobindo Centre, New Delhi, 979
Sri Chandrasekharenda Saraswathi Viswa Mahavidyalaya, Enathur, 1038
Sri Chitra Art Gallery, Gallery of Asian Paintings, 983
SRI International, Menlo Park, 2307
Sri Krishnadevaraya University, 1025
Sri Lanka Association for the Advancement of Science, 1953
Sri Lanka Law College, 1959
Sri Lanka Library Association, 1953
Sri Lanka Medical Association, 1953
Sri Lanka Technical College, 1959
Sri Lanka Water Resources Board, 1954
Sri Padmavathi Mahila Visvavidyalayam, Tirupati, 1025
Sri Pratap Singh Museum, 983
Sri Rallabandi Subbarao Government Museum, 983
Sri Ramachandra Medical College and Research Institute, Chennai, 1038
Sri Sathya Sai Institute of Higher Learning, Andhra, 1038
Sri Varalakshmi Academies of Fine Arts, Mysore, 1040
Sri Venkateswara University, 1025
Sri Venkateswara University Oriental Research Institute, 976
Srinakharinwirot University, 2044
Srinakharinwirot University Library, 2033
Sripatum University, 2044
Srpska Akademija Nauka i Umetnosti, 1815
Srpska književna zadruga, 1815
Srpsko Prosvjetno Kulturno Drustvo 'Prosvjeta' Sarajevo, 245
Staatliche Akademie der Bildenden Künste, Karlsruhe, 901
Staatliche Akademie der Bildenden Künste, Stuttgart, 901
Staatliche Antikensammlungen und Glyptothek, Munich, 818
Staatliche Bibliothek, Passau, 809
Staatliche Bibliothek Regensburg, 809
Staatliche Ethnographische Sammlungen Sachsen, 817
Staatliche Ethnographische Sammlungen Sachsen, Dresden, 814
Staatliche Graphische Sammlung München, Munich, 818
Staatliche Hochschule für Bildende Künste–Städelschule, Frankfurt, 901
Staatliche Hochschule für Musik Karlsruhe, 902
Staatliche Hochschule für Musik und Darstellende Kunst Heidelberg-Mannheim, 902
Staatliche Hochschule für Musik und Darstellende Kunst, Stuttgart, 902
Staatliche Kunsthalle, Baden-Baden, 811
Staatliche Kunsthalle, Karlsruhe, 816
Staatliche Kunstsammlungen Dresden, 814
Staatliche Materialprüfungsanstalt Darmstadt–Fachgebiet und Institut für Werkstoffkunde, 802

V

Virsaladze Institute of Medical Parasitology and Tropical Medicine, 781

Vishnevsky, A. V., Institute of Surgery, Moscow, 1740

Vishveshvaranand Vedic Research Institute, 976

Vishveshvaranand Vishva Bandhu Institute of Sanskrit and Indological Studies, 976

Viski Károly Múzeum, 946

Viðskiptaháskólinn á Bifröst, Borganes, 965

Visš Medicinski Institut Plovdiv, Plovdiv, 313

Visual Arts Ontario, 325

Visva-bharati, 1029

Visvesvaraya Industrial and Technological Museum, 982

Visvesvaraya National Institute of Technology, Nagpur, 1038

Visveswaraiah Technological University, Belgaum, 1030

Vitebsk Oblast Library 'V. I. Lenin', 209

Vitebsk State Academy of Veterinary Medicine, 214

Vitebsk State Medical University, 213

Vitebsk State Technological University, 213

Vitebsk State University 'P. M. Masherov', 213

Vitenskapsmuseet, Norges Teknisk-Naturvitenskapelige Universitet, 1548

Viterbo University, 2738

Vitterhetsakademiens Bibliotek, Stockholm, 1974

Vitus Bering Center for Videregående Uddannelse, 641

Vizon SciTech Inc, 328

Vlaamse hogescholenraad (VLHORA), Brussels, 215

Vlaamse Interuniversitaire Raad (VLIR), Brussels, 215

Vlaamse Museumvereniging, 216

Vladimir State University, 1777

Vladivostok State Medical University, 1780

Vladivostok State University of Economics, 1777

Vlerick Leuven Gent Management School, 234

Vniichimprojekt Institute, Kyiv, 2104

'VNIPIenergoprom' Association JSC, Moscow, 1751

Vocational Training Centre, Ruwi, 1562

Voeikov, A. I., Main Geophysical Observatory, 1745

Vojenské historické múzeum, 1845

Vojenské technické muzeum, Prague, 614

Vojni Muzej, Belgrade, 1817

Volga Region State Academy of Telecommunications and Informatics, 1795

Volga State Academy of Water Transport, 1795

Volgograd Academy of Public Administration, 1793

Volgograd Plague Prevention Research Institute, 1740

Volgograd State Agricultural Academy, 1793

Volgograd State Medical University, 1780

Volgograd State Museum and Panorama of the Battle of Stalingrad, 1760

Volgograd State Pedagogical University, 1781

Volgograd State Technical University, 1791

Volgograd State University, 1777

Volgograd State University of Architecture and Civil Engineering, 1791

Volkenrechtelijk Instituut, Utrecht, 1475

Völkerkundemuseum Herrnhut, 817

Völkerkundesammlung, Lübeck, 817

Volkskunde Museum Schleswig, Schleswig, 819

Volkskundemuseum, Antwerp, 222

Vologda Historical, Architectural and Artistic Museum Reserve, 1760

Vologda Picture Gallery, 1760

Vologda State Dairy Academy 'N. V. Vereschagin', 1793

Vologda State Technical University, 1791

Vologdin, V. P., Research Institute of High-Frequency Currents, St Petersburg, 1751

Von Karman Institute for Fluid Dynamics, Rhode-St-Genese, 220

Voorhees College, 2675

Vorarlberger Landesarchiv, 166

Vorarlberger Landesbibliothek, 167

Vorarlberger Landesmuseum, 169

Vorderasiatisches Museum, Berlin, 812

Voronezh Art Museum, 1760

Voronezh Region Radiological and Oncological Institute, 1740

Voronezh State Academy of Forestry Engineering, 1793

Voronezh State Agrarian University, K. D. Glinka, 1762

Voronezh State Institute of Fine Arts, 1797

Voronezh State Medical Academy 'N. N. Burdenko', 1794

Voronezh State Pedagogical University, 1781

Voronezh State Technical University, 1791

Voronezh State Technological Academy, 1795

Voronezh State University, 1777

Voronezh State University of Architecture and Civil Engineering, 1792

Vorres Museum of Greek Art, Paiania, 913

Vrije Universiteit, Amsterdam, 1494

Vrije Universiteit Brussel, Universiteitsbibliotheek, 221

Vísindafélag Íslendinga, 964

VTT Technical Research Centre of Finland, Espoo, 685

Vúje Trnava Inc., 1844

VUTS Liberec a.s., 612

Vyatka State Agricultural Academy, 1793

Vyatka State Technical University, 1791

Východočeské muzeum v Pardubicich, 614

Východoslovenské múzeum, 1845

Vysoká Škola Báňská – Technická Univerzita Ostrava, 623

Vysoká Škola Chemicko-technologická V Praze, 624

Vysoká Škola Ekonomická V Praze, Prague, 624

Vysoká Škola Uměleckoprůmyslová, Prague, 626

Vysoké Učení Technické V Brně, 624

Vytautas the Great War Museum, 1377

Vytauto Didžiojo Universitetas, 1381

Výzkumný ústav geodetický, topografický a kartografický (VÚGTK), Zdiby, 610

Vízgazdálkodási Tudományos Kutató Rt. (VITUKI), Budapest, 939

W

Wabash College, 2452

Wadden Sea Station, List/Sylt, 800

Wadham College Library, Oxford, 2166

Wadham College, Oxford, 2250

Wadsworth Atheneum Museum of Art, 2319

Wageningen Universiteit, 1494

Wagner College, 2600

Wagner Genootschap Nederland, Amsterdam, 1476

Waikato Institute of Technology, 1511

Waitangi Treaty Grounds, 1506

Wakayama Medical University, 1268

Wakayama University, 1262

Wake Forest University, 2613

Wakefield Metropolitan District Council Access and Culture–Libraries and Museums, 2178

Walailak University, 2046

Walker Art Center, 2323

Walker Art Gallery, 2174

Walla Walla College, 2725

Wallace Collection, 2176

Wallenfels'sches Haus, Giessen, 815

Wallraf-Richartz-Museum, 813

Walsh College of Accountancy and Business Administration, 2522

Walsh University, 2633

Walter and Eliza Hall Institute of Medical Research, 122

Walter Anderson Museum of Art, 2323

Walter Sisulu University for Technology and Science, Eastern Cape, 1872

Walters Art Museum, 2322

Waltham Forest Public Libraries, 2164

Wandsworth Public Libraries, 2164

Wapiti Regional Library, 333

War Museum, Cairo, 661

Warburg Institute Library, 2164

Warburg Institute, London, 2233

Warner and Swasey Observatory, 2306

Warner Pacific College, 2643

Warner Southern College, 2413

Warren Wilson College, 2615

Warrington Borough Libraries, 2168

Warsaw Agricultural University, 1669

Warsaw University of Technology, 1666

Warszawskie Towarzystwo Muzyczne im. Stanisława Moniuszki, 1622

Wartburg College, 2458

Wartburg Theological Seminary, 2458

Warwickshire Library and Information Service, 2168

Waseda Daigaku Tsubouchi Hakase Kinen Engeki Hakubutsukan, 1187

Waseda Institute for Advanced Study, 1297

Waseda Institute for Sport Sciences, 1297

Waseda University Library, 1184

Waseda University, Tokyo, 1297

Washington & Jefferson College, 2670

Washington and Lee University, 2717

Washington Bible College/Capital Bible Seminary, Maryland, 2479

Washington College, Chestertown, 2479

Washington State History Museum, 2327

Washington State Library, 2317

Washington State University, 2725

Washington Theological Union, 2406

Washington University in Saint Louis, 2552

Wat Sisaket, Vientiane, 1360

Water Policy Research Institute, Ulan Bator, 1451

Water Research Foundation of Australia, 124

Water Research Institute, Accra, 905

Water Transport Society, Moscow, 1730

Waterford City Council Central Library, 1084

Waterford County Library Headquarters, 1084

Waterford Institute of Technology, 1091

Waterloo Historical Society, Kitchener, 325

Wattis Institute for Contemporary Arts, 2344

Wayamba University of Sri Lanka, Kutiyapitiya, 1959

Wayland Baptist University, 2706

Wayne State College, 2556

Wayne State University, 2522

Wayne State University Libraries, 2313

Waynesburg College, 2670

Weald and Downland Open Air Museum, 2178

Webb Institute, 2600

Webber International University, 2413

Weber-Museum, Dresden, 814

Weber State University, 2707

Webster University, 2552

WEINSTADTMuseum, Krems, 169

Weitz Center for Development Studies, Rehovot, 1094

Weizmann Archives, Rehovot, 1097

Weizmann Institute of Science, 1113

Weizmann Institute of Science Libraries, 1097

Wellcome Library, 2164

Wellesley College, 2503

Wellington Medical Research Foundation, 1503

Wellington Public Library, 1505

Wells College, 2600

Wells, H. G., Society, Bottesford, 2135

Welsh Academy, The, 2133

Welsh Institute of Rural Studies, 2271

Weltverband der Anaesthesisten-Gesellschaften, 65

Wenner-Gren Foundation for Anthropological Research, Inc., 2307

Wenner-Gren Stiftelserna, Stockholm, 1970

Wentworth Institute of Technology, 2503

Wereldmuseum Rotterdam, 1485

Wesley College, Belize City, 236

Wesley College, Dover, 2397

Wesley College, Florence, Mississippi, 2544

Wesley Historical Society, 2133

Wesley Theological Seminary, 2406

Wesleyan College, Macon, 2422

Wesleyan University, Middletown, 2389

Wessex Institute of Technology, 2273

West Africa Computer Science Institute, Accra, 908

West African Association of Agricultural Economics, Ibadan, 1518

West African Examinations Council, Accra, 904

West African Health Organisation (WAHO), 64

West African Science Association, Legon, 905

West Bengal University of Animal and Fishery Sciences, Kolkata, 1030

West Bengal University of Technology, Kolkata, 1030

West Berkshire Libraries, 2165

West Chester University of Pennsylvania, 2654

West China Centre of Medical Sciences, 533

West Coast Historical Museum, Hokitika, 1505

West Liberty State College, 2727

West Sussex County Council Library Service, 2156

West Texas A & M University, 2693

West Virginia School of Osteopathic Medicine, 2727

West Virginia State Museum and Cultural Center, 2328

West Virginia State University, 2727

West Virginia University, 2727

West Virginia University Institute of Technology, 2727

West Virginia University Libraries, 2317

West Virginia Wesleyan College, 2727

West Visayas State University, Iloilo City, 1618

Western Association of Schools and Colleges: Accrediting Commission for Senior Colleges and Universities, Alameda, 2282

Western Australian Museum, 127

Western Cape Education Library and Information Service (EDULIS), 1867

Western Cape Provincial Library Service, 1867

Western Carolina University, 2616

Western Connecticut State University, 2389

Western Education and Library Board, Omagh, 2274

Western Illinois University, 2442

Western International University, 2339

Western Kazakhstan State University, 1309

Western Kentucky University, 2465

Western Michigan University, 2526

Western Mindanao State University, 1618

Western New England College, 2503

Western New Mexico University, 2570

Western Oregon University, 2643

Western Regional Library, Lautoka, 679

Western Regional Library, Sekondi, 906

Western Reserve Historical Society, 2290

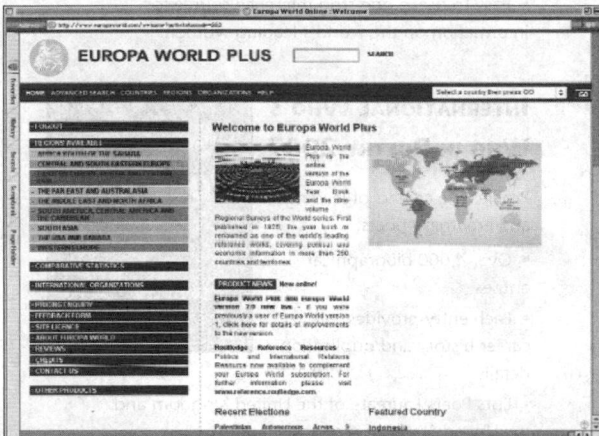
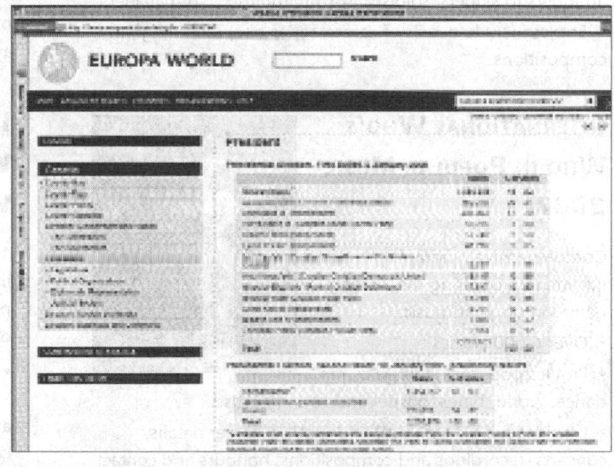

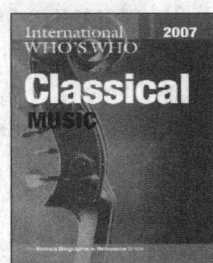

Routledge
Taylor & Francis Group

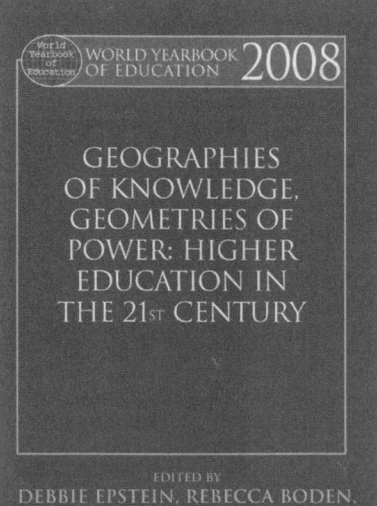

WORLD YEARBOOK OF EDUCATION 2008:

GEOGRAPHIES OF KNOWLEDGE, GEOMETRIES OF POWER: HIGHER EDUCATION IN THE 21ST CENTURY

January 2008—Hardback—352pp
ISBN: 978-0-415-96378-7

About the Editors:
Debbie Epstein is a Professor in the School of Social Sciences at Cardiff University, UK
Rebecca Boden is a Professor of Critical Management at the University of Wales Institute, UK
Rosemary Deem is a Professor of Education at University of Bristol's Graduate School of Education and the Research Director for the Faculty of Social Sciences and Law, UK
Fazal Rizvi is a Professor in the Educational Policy Studies Department at the University of Illinois at Urbana-Champaign, USA
Susan Wright is a Professor of Educational Anthropology at the Danish School of Education, University of Århus, Denmark

This volume examines higher education in globalised conditions through a focus on the spatial, historic and economic relations of power in which it is embedded. Distinct geometries of power are emerging as the knowledge production capability of universities is increasingly globalized. Changes in the organisation and practices of higher education tend to travel from the 'West to the rest'. Thus distinctive geographies of knowledge are being produced, intersected by geometries of power and raising questions about the recognition, production, control and usage of university-produced knowledge in different regions of the world.

The 2008 volume is interdisciplinary in its approach, drawing on scholarship from accounting, finance and human geography as well as from the field of education. Transnational influences examined include UNESCO and OECD, GATS and the effects of digital technologies. Contrasting contexts include Central and Eastern Europe, Finland, China and India and England. With its emphasis on the interrelationship of knowledge and power, and its attention to emergent spatial inequalities, Geographies of Knowledge, Geometries of Power: Higher Education in the 21st Century provides a rich and compelling resource for understanding emergent practices and relations of knowledge production and exchange in global higher education.

Table of Contents: